Microsoft®

MICROSOFT® .NET FRAMEWORK 1.1 CLASS LIBRARY REFERENCE

VOLUME 7a: SYSTEM.WINDOWS.FORMS

Microsoft® .net™

PUBLISHED BY
Microsoft Press
A Division of Microsoft Corporation
One Microsoft Way
Redmond, Washington 98052-6399

Library of Congress Cataloging-in-Publication Data pending.

Printed and bound in the United States of America.

1 2 3 4 5 6 7 8 9 QWT 8 7 6 5 4 3

Distributed in Canada by H.B. Fenn and Company Ltd.

A CIP catalogue record for this book is available from the British Library.

Microsoft Press books are available through booksellers and distributors worldwide. For further information about international editions, contact your local Microsoft Corporation office or contact Microsoft Press International directly at fax (425) 936-7329. Visit our Web site at www.microsoft.com/mspress. Send comments to *mspinput@microsoft.com.*

For Microsoft:
Acquisitions Editor: Juliana Aldous Atkinson
Project Editor: Dick Brown

For mediaService, Siegen, Germany:
Project Manager: Gerhard Alfes

SubAssy Part No. X09-56601
Body Part No. X08-98408

Contents

Document Conventions

The following table shows the typographic conventions used in this book.

Convention	Description	Example
Monospace	Indicates source code, code examples, input to the command line, application output, code lines embedded in text, and variables and code elements.	`Public Class`
Bold	Indicates most predefined programming elements, including namespaces, classes, delegates, objects, interfaces, methods, functions, macros, structures, constructors, properties, events, enumerations, fields, operators, statements, directives, data types, keywords, exceptions, non-HTML attributes, and configuration t ags, as well as registry keys, subkeys, and values. Also indicates the following HTML elements: attributes, directives, keywords, values, and headers. In addition, indicates required user input, including command-line options, that must be entered exactly as shown.	**Path** class **Resolve** method
Italic	Indicates placeholders, most often method or function parameters and HTML placeholders; these placeholders represent information that must be supplied by the implementation or the user. For command-line input, indicates parameter values.	*context* parameter
Capital letters	Indicates the names of keys and key sequences.	ENTER CTRL+R
Plus sign	Indicates a combination of keys. For example, ALT+F1 means to h old down the ALT key while pressing the F1 key.	ALT+F1
↲	The "rundown" is a line-continuation character this book uses in code samples for Visual Basic, C#, C++, and JScript. It indicates that a code statement is too long to fit on one line in the book, and so has been continued on the next line. All code samples are available in the .NET Framework 1.1 online documentation, which is also included in the Visual Studio .NET 2003 Help.	`string strSource ="We will ↲` `search on this string";`

System.Windows.Forms Namespace

The **System.Windows.Forms** namespace contains classes for creating Windows-based applications that take full advantage of the rich user interface features available in the Microsoft Windows operating system.

The classes in this namespace can be grouped into the following categories:

- **Control, User Control, and Form.** Most classes within the **System.Windows.Forms** namespace derive from the **Control** class. The **Control** class provides the base functionality for all controls that are displayed on a **Form**. The **Form** class represents a window within an application. This includes dialog boxes, modeless windows, and Multiple Document Interface (MDI) client and parent windows. To create a custom control that is a composite of other controls, use the **UserControl** class.
- **Controls.** The **System.Windows.Forms** namespace provides a variety of control classes that allow you to create rich user interfaces. Some controls are designed for data entry within the application, such as **TextBox** and **ComboBox** controls. Other controls display application data, such as **Label** and **ListView**. The namespace also provides controls for invoking commands within the application, such as **Button** and **ToolBar**. In addition, the **PropertyGrid** control can be used to create your own Windows Forms designer that displays the designer-visible properties of the controls.
- **Components**. In addition to controls, the **System.Windows.Forms** namespace provides other classes that do not derive from the Control class but still provide visual features to a Windows-based application. Some classes, such as **ToolTip** and **ErrorProvider**, extend the capabilities or provide information to the user. Other classes, such as **Menu**, **MenuItem**, and **ContextMenu**, provide the ability display menus to the user to invoke commands within an application. The **Help** and **HelpProvider** classes enable you to display help information to the user of your applications.
- **Common Dialog Boxes**. Windows provides a number of common dialog boxes that can be used to give your application a consistent user interface when performing tasks such as opening and saving files, manipulating the font or text color, or printing. The **OpenFileDialog** and **SaveFileDialog** classes provide the functionality to display a dialog box that allows the user to browse to and enter the name of a file to open or save. The **FontDialog** class displays a dialog box to change elements of the **Font** object used by your application. The **PageSetupDialog**, **PrintPreviewDialog**, and **PrintDialog** classes display dialog boxes that allow the user to control aspects of printing documents. For more information on printing from a Windows-based application, see the **System.Drawing.Printing** namespace. In addition to the common dialog boxes, the **System.Windows.Forms** namespace provides the **MessageBox** class for displaying a message box that can display and retrieve data from the user.

There are a number of classes within the **System.Windows.Forms** namespace that provide support to the classes mentioned in the preceding summary. Example of the supporting classes are enumerations, event argument classes, and delegates used by events within controls and components.

Note To make your Windows Forms application support Windows XP visual styles, be sure to set the **FlatStyle** property of your controls to **FlatStyle.System** and include a manifest with your executable. A manifest is an XML file that is included either as a resource within your application executable or as a seperate file that resides in the same directory as the executable file. For an example of a manifest, see the Example section for the **FlatStyle** enumeration. For more information about using the visual styles available in Windows XP, see the Using Windows XP Visual Styles in the User Interface Design and Development section of the MSDN Library.

AccessibleEvents Enumeration

Specifies events that are reported by accessible applications.

[Visual Basic]
```
<Serializable>
Public Enum AccessibleEvents
```
[C#]
```
[Serializable]
public enum AccessibleEvents
```
[C++]
```
[Serializable]
__value public enum AccessibleEvents
```
[JScript]
```
public
   Serializable
enum AccessibleEvents
```

Remarks

The operating system and accessibility server applications generate accessibility events in response to changes in the user interface.

This enumeration is used by **AccessibleObject** and **Control**.

For additional information on the accessibility application, search for "Microsoft Active Accessibility" in the MSDN Library.

Members

Member name	Description
AcceleratorChange	An object's **KeyboardShortcut** property changed. Server applications send the event for their accessible objects.
Create	An object was created. The operating system sends the event for the following user interface elements: caret, header control, list view control, tab control, toolbar control, tree view control, and window object. Server applications send this event for their accessible objects. Servers must send this event for all an object's child objects before sending the event for the parent object. Servers must ensure that all child objects are fully created and ready to accept calls from clients when the parent object sends the event.

Member name	Description
DefaultActionChange	An object's **DefaultAction** property changed. The system sends this event for dialog boxes. Server applications send this event for their accessible objects. Therefore, server applications do not need to send this event for the child objects. Hidden objects have a state of **AccessibleStates.Invisible**, and shown objects do not. Events of type **AccessibleEvents.Hide** indicate that a state of **Accessible-States.Invisible** has been set. Therefore, servers do not need to send the **AccessibleEvents.StateChange** event in this case.
DescriptionChange	An object's **Description** property changed. Server applications send this event for their accessible objects.
Destroy	An object was destroyed. The system sends this event for the following user interface elements: caret, header control, list view control, tab control, toolbar control, tree view control, and window object. Server applications send this event for their accessible objects. This event may or may not be sent for child objects. However, clients can assume that all the children of an object have been destroyed when the parent object sends this event.
Focus	An object has received the keyboard focus. The system sends this event for the following user interface elements: list view control, menu bar, shortcut menu, switch window, tab control, tree view control, and window object. Server applications send this event for their accessible objects.
HelpChange	An object's **Help** property changed. Server applications send this event for their accessible objects.
Hide	An object is hidden. The system sends the event for the following user interface elements: caret and cursor. Server applications send the event for their accessible objects. When the event is generated for a parent object, all child objects have already been hidden. Therefore, server applications do not need to send the event for the child objects. The system does not send the event consistently.

Member name	Description
LocationChange	An object has changed location, shape, or size. The system sends this event for the following user interface elements: caret and window object. Server applications send this event for their accessible objects. This event is generated in response to the top-level object within the object hierarchy that has changed, not for any children it might contain. For example, if the user resizes a window, the system sends this notification for the window, but not for the menu bar, title bar, scroll bars, or other objects that have also changed. The system does not send this event for every non-floating child window when the parent moves. However, if an application explicitly resizes child windows as a result of being resized, the system sends multiple events for the resized children. If an object's **State** property is set to **Accessible-States.Floating**, servers should send a location change event whenever the object changes location. If an object does not have this state, servers should raise this event when the object moves relative to its parent.
NameChange	An object's **Name** property changed. The system sends this event for the following user interface elements: check box, cursor, list view control, push button, radio button, status bar control, tree view control, and window object. Server applications send this event for their accessible objects.
ParentChange	An object has a new parent object. Server applications send this event for their accessible objects.
Reorder	A container object has added, removed, or reordered its children. The system sends this event for the following user interface elements: header control, list view control, toolbar control, and window object. Server applications send this event as appropriate for their accessible objects. This event is also sent by a parent window when the z order for the child windows changes.
Selection	An accessible object within a container object has been selected. This event signals a single selection. Either a child has been selected in a container that previously did not contain any selected children, or the selection has changed from one child to another.

Member name	Description
SelectionAdd	An item within a container object was added to the selection. The system sends this event for the following user interface elements: list box, list view control, and tree view control. Server applications send this event for their accessible objects. This event signals that a child has been added to an existing selection.
SelectionRemove	An item within a container object was removed from the selection. The system sends this event for the following user interface elements: list box, list view control, and tree view control. Server applications send this event for their accessible objects. This event signals that a child has been removed from an existing selection.
SelectionWithin	Numerous selection changes occurred within a container object. The system sends this event for list boxes. Server applications send this event for their accessible objects. This event can be sent when the selected items within a control have changed substantially. This event informs the client that many selection changes have occurred. This is preferable to sending several **SelectionAdd** or **SelectionRemove** events.
Show	A hidden object is being shown. The system sends this event for the following user interface elements: caret, cursor, and window object. Server applications send this event for their accessible objects. Clients can assume that, when this event is sent by a parent object, all child objects have already been displayed. Therefore, server applications do not need to send this event for the child objects.
StateChange	An object's state has changed. The system sends the event for the following user interface elements: check box, combo box, header control, push button, radio button, scroll bar, toolbar control, tree view control, up-down control, and window object. Server applications send the event for their accessible objects. For example, a state change can occur when a button object has been pressed or released, or when an object is being enabled or disabled. The system does not send the event consistently.
SystemAlert	An alert was generated. Server applications send this event whenever an important user interface change has occurred that a user might need to know about. The system does not send the event consistently for dialog box objects.

Member name	Description
SystemCaptureEnd	A window has lost mouse capture. The system sends the event; servers never send this event.
SystemCaptureStart	A window is being moved or resized. The system sends the event; servers never send this event.
SystemContextHelpEnd	A window exited context-sensitive Help mode. The system does not send the event consistently.
SystemContextHelpStart	A window entered context-sensitive Help mode. The system does not send the event consistently.
SystemDialogEnd	A dialog box was closed. The system does not send the event for standard dialog boxes. Servers send this event for custom dialog boxes. The system does not send the event consistently.
SystemDialogStart	A dialog box was displayed. The system sends the event for standard dialog boxes. Servers send this event for custom dialog boxes. The system does not send the event consistently.
SystemDragDropEnd	An application is about to exit drag-and-drop mode. Applications that support drag-and-drop operations must send this event; the system does not.
SystemDragDropStart	An application is about to enter drag-and-drop mode. Applications that support drag-and-drop operations must send this event; the system does not.
SystemForeground	The foreground window changed. The system sends this event even if the foreground window is changed to another window in the same thread. Server applications never send this event.
SystemMenuEnd	A menu from the menu bar was closed. The system sends this event for standard menus. Servers send this event for custom menus.
SystemMenuPopupEnd	A shortcut menu was closed. The system sends this event for standard menus. Servers send this event for custom menus. When a shortcut menu is closed, the client receives this message followed almost immediately by the **SystemMenuEnd** event. The system does not send the event consistently.
SystemMenuPopupStart	A shortcut menu was displayed. The system sends this event for standard menus. Servers send this event for custom menus. The system does not send the event consistently.
SystemMenuStart	A menu item on the menu bar was selected. The system sends this event for standard menus. Servers send this event for custom menus. The system might raise more than one **MenuStart** event that might or might not have a corresponding **MenuEnd** event.

Member name	Description
SystemMinimizeEnd	A window object was minimized or maximized. The system sends the event; servers never send this event.
SystemMinimizeStart	A window object is about to be minimized or maximized. The system sends the event; servers never send this event.
SystemMoveSizeEnd	The movement or resizing of a window is finished. The system sends the event; servers never send this event.
SystemMoveSizeStart	A window is being moved or resized. The system sends the event; servers never send this event.
SystemScrollingEnd	Scrolling has ended on a scroll bar. The system sends this event for scroll bars attached to a window and for standard scroll bar controls. Servers send this event for custom scroll bars.
SystemScrollingStart	Scrolling has started on a scroll bar. The system sends the event for scroll bars attached to a window and for standard scroll bar controls. Servers send this event for custom scroll bars.
SystemSound	A sound was played. The system sends this event when a system sound, such as for menus, is played, even if no sound is audible. This might be caused by lack of a sound file or sound card. Servers send this event if a custom user interface element generates a sound.
SystemSwitchEnd	The user released ALT+TAB. The system sends the **SwitchEnd** event; servers never send this event. If only one application is running when the user presses ALT+TAB, the system sends the **SwitchEnd** event without a corresponding **SwitchStart** event.
SystemSwitchStart	The user pressed ALT+TAB, which activates the switch window. If only one application is running when the user presses ALT+TAB, the system raises the **SwitchEnd** event without a corresponding **SwitchStart** event.
ValueChange	An object's **Value** property changed. The system raises the **ValueChange** event for the following user interface elements: edit control, header control, hot key control, progress bar control, scroll bar, slider control, and up-down control. Server applications send this event for their accessible objects.

Example

[Visual Basic, C#, C++] The following example demonstrates the creation of an accessibility-aware chart control, using the **AccessibleObject** and **Control.ControlAccessibleObject** classes to expose accessible information. The control plots two curves along with a legend. The `ChartControlAccessibleObject` class, which derives from **ControlAccessibleObject**, is used in the **CreateAccessibilityInstance** method to provide custom accessible information for the chart control. Since the chart legend is not an actual **Control**-based control, but instead is drawn by the chart control, it does not any built-in accessible information. Because of this, the `ChartControlAccessibleObject` class overrides the **GetChild** method to return the `CurveLegendAccessibleObject` that represents accessible information for each part of the legend. When an accessible-aware application uses this control, the control can provide the necessary accessible information.

[Visual Basic, C#, C++] This code excerpt demonstrates using the **AccessibleEvents** enumeration with the **AccessibilityNotifyClients** method. See the **AccessibleObject** class overview for the complete code example.

[Visual Basic]

```
' Gets or sets the location for the curve legend.
Public Property Location() As Point
    Get
        Return m_location
    End Get
    Set
        m_location = value
        chart.Invalidate()

        ' Notifies the chart of the location change. This is used for
        ' the accessibility information.
AccessibleEvents.LocationChange
        ' tells the chart the reason for the notification.
        chart.ExposeAccessibilityNotifyClients
 (AccessibleEvents.LocationChange, _
                CType(AccessibilityObject,
CurveLegendAccessibleObject).ID)
    End Set
End Property

' Gets or sets the Name for the curve legend.
Public Property Name() As String
    Get
        Return m_name
    End Get
    Set
        If m_name <> value Then
            m_name = value
            chart.Invalidate()

            ' Notifies the chart of the name change. This is used for
            ' the accessibility information.
AccessibleEvents.NameChange
            ' tells the chart the reason for the notification.

chart.ExposeAccessibilityNotifyClients(AccessibleEvents.NameChange, _
                CType(AccessibilityObject,
CurveLegendAccessibleObject).ID)
        End If
    End Set
End Property

' Gets or sets the Selected state for the curve legend.
Public Property Selected() As Boolean
    Get
        Return m_selected
    End Get
    Set
        If m_selected <> value Then
            m_selected = value
            chart.Invalidate()

            ' Notifies the chart of the selection value change.
This is used for
            ' the accessibility information. The AccessibleEvents
value varies
            ' on whether the selection is true
(AccessibleEvents.SelectionAdd) or
```

```
            ' false (AccessibleEvents.SelectionRemove).
            If m_selected Then

chart.ExposeAccessibilityNotifyClients(AccessibleEvents.SelectionAdd, _
                        CType(AccessibilityObject,                    ↵
CurveLegendAccessibleObject).ID)
            Else
                chart.ExposeAccessibilityNotifyClients                ↵
 (AccessibleEvents.SelectionRemove, _
                        CType(AccessibilityObject,                    ↵
CurveLegendAccessibleObject).ID)
            End If
        End If
    End Set
End Property
```

[C#]

```
// Gets or sets the location for the curve legend.
public Point Location
{
    get {
        return location;
    }
    set {
        location = value;
        chart.Invalidate();

        // Notifies the chart of the location change. This is used for
        // the accessibility information.                              ↵
AccessibleEvents.LocationChange
        // tells the chart the reason for the notification.


chart.AccessibilityNotifyClients(AccessibleEvents.LocationChange,
            ((CurveLegendAccessibleObject)AccessibilityObject).ID);
    }
}

// Gets or sets the Name for the curve legend.
public string Name
{
    get {
        return name;
    }
    set {
        if (name != value)
        {
            name = value;
            chart.Invalidate();

            // Notifies the chart of the name change. This is used for
            // the accessibility information.                          ↵
AccessibleEvents.NameChange
            // tells the chart the reason for the notification.

           chart.AccessibilityNotifyClients(AccessibleEvents.NameChange,
                ((CurveLegendAccessibleObject)AccessibilityObject).ID);
        }
    }
}

// Gets or sets the Selected state for the curve legend.
public bool Selected
{
    get {
        return selected;
    }
    set {
        if (selected != value)
        {
            selected = value;
            chart.Invalidate();

            // Notifies the chart of the selection value change.       ↵
 This is used for
            // the accessibility information. The                      ↵
AccessibleEvents value depends upon
            // if the selection is true                                ↵
 (AccessibleEvents.SelectionAdd) or
            // false (AccessibleEvents.SelectionRemove).
            chart.AccessibilityNotifyClients(
                selected ? AccessibleEvents.SelectionAdd :             ↵
AccessibleEvents.SelectionRemove,
                ((CurveLegendAccessibleObject)AccessibilityObject).ID);
        }
    }
}
```

[C++]

```
// Gets or sets the location for the curve legend.
   public:
__property Point get_Location() {
   return location;
}
__property void set_Location(Point value) {
   location = value;
   chart->Invalidate();

   // Notifies the chart of the location change. This is used for
   // the accessibility information. AccessibleEvents::LocationChange
   // tells the chart the reason for the notification.

   chart->AccessibilityNotifyClients(AccessibleEvents::LocationChange,
      (dynamic_cast<CurveLegendAccessibleObject*>(AccessibilityObject))-
>ID);
}

// Gets or sets the Name for the curve legend.
   public:
__property String* get_Name() {
   return name;
}
__property void set_Name(String* value) {
   if (name != value) {
      name = value;
      chart->Invalidate();

      // Notifies the chart of the name change. This is used for
      // the accessibility information. AccessibleEvents::NameChange
      // tells the chart the reason for the notification.

      chart->AccessibilityNotifyClients(AccessibleEvents::NameChange,

(dynamic_cast<CurveLegendAccessibleObject*>(AccessibilityObject))->ID);
   }
}

// Gets or sets the Selected state for the curve legend.
   public:
__property bool get_Selected() {
   return selected;
}
__property void set_Selected(bool value) {
   if (selected != value) {
      selected = value;
      chart->Invalidate();

      // Notifies the chart of the selection value change. This         ↵
 is used for
      // the accessibility information. The AccessibleEvents            ↵
 value depends upon
      // if the selection is true (AccessibleEvents::SelectionAdd) or
      // false (AccessibleEvents::SelectionRemove).
      chart->AccessibilityNotifyClients(selected ?                      ↵
AccessibleEvents::SelectionAdd : AccessibleEvents::SelectionRemove,

(dynamic_cast<CurveLegendAccessibleObject*>(AccessibilityObject))->ID);
   }
}
```

Requirements

Namespace: System.Windows.Forms

Platforms: Windows 98, Windows NT 4.0, Windows Millennium Edition, Windows 2000, Windows XP Home Edition, Windows XP Professional, Windows Server 2003 family

Assembly: System.Windows.Forms (in System.Windows.Forms.dll)

AccessibleNavigation Enumeration

Specifies values for navigating among accessible objects.

```
[Visual Basic]
<Serializable>
Public Enum AccessibleNavigation
[C#]
[Serializable]
public enum AccessibleNavigation
[C++]
[Serializable]
__value public enum AccessibleNavigation
[JScript]
public
   Serializable
enum AccessibleNavigation
```

Remarks

Accessible navigation directions are either spatial (up, down, left, and right) or logical (first child, last child, next, and previous). Logical directions are used when clients navigate from one user interface element to another within the same container.

AccessibleObject uses this enumeration.

For additional information on the accessibility application, search for the "Microsoft Active Accessibility" topic in the MSDN library.

Members

Member name	Description
Down	Navigation to a sibling object located below the starting object.
FirstChild	Navigation to the first child of the object.
LastChild	Navigation to the last child of the object.
Left	Navigation to the sibling object located to the left of the starting object.
Next	Navigation to the next logical object, typically from a sibling object to the starting object.
Previous	Navigation to the previous logical object, typically from a sibling object to the starting object.
Right	Navigation to the sibling object located to the right of the starting object.
Up	Navigation to a sibling object located above the starting object.

Example

[Visual Basic, C#, C++] The following example demonstrates the creation of an accessibility-aware chart control, using the **Accessible-Object** and **Control.ControlAccessibleObject** classes to expose accessible information. The control plots two curves along with a legend. The `ChartControlAccessibleObject` class, which derives from **ControlAccessibleObject**, is used in the **CreateAccessibility-Instance** method to provide custom accessible information for the chart control. Since the chart legend is not an actual **Control**-based control, but instead is drawn by the chart control, it does not any built-in accessible information. Because of this, the `ChartControl-AccessibleObject` class overrides the **GetChild** method to return the `CurveLegendAccessibleObject` that represents accessible information for each part of the legend. When an accessible-aware application uses this control, the control can provide the necessary accessible information.

[Visual Basic, C#, C++] This code excerpt demonstrates using the **AccessibleNavigation** enumeration with the **Navigate** method. See the **AccessibleObject** class overview for the complete code example.

[Visual Basic]
```
' Inner Class ChartControlAccessibleObject represents
 accessible information
' associated with the ChartControl.
' The ChartControlAccessibleObject is returned in the '
 ChartControl.CreateAccessibilityInstance override.
Public Class ChartControlAccessibleObject
    Inherits Control.ControlAccessibleObject

    Private chartControl As ChartControl

    Public Sub New(ctrl As ChartControl)
        MyBase.New(ctrl)
        chartControl = ctrl
    End Sub 'New

    ' Get the role for the Chart. This is used by
accessibility programs.
    Public Overrides ReadOnly Property Role() As AccessibleRole
        Get
            Return System.Windows.Forms.AccessibleRole.Chart
        End Get
    End Property

    ' Get the state for the Chart. This is used by
accessibility programs.
    Public Overrides ReadOnly Property State() As AccessibleStates
        Get
            Return AccessibleStates.ReadOnly
        End Get
    End Property

    ' The CurveLegend objects are "child" controls in terms
of accessibility so
    ' return the number of ChartLengend objects.
    Public Overrides Function GetChildCount() As Integer
        Return chartControl.Legends.Length
    End Function

    ' Get the Accessibility object of the child CurveLegend
identified by index.
    Public Overrides Function GetChild(index As Integer) As
AccessibleObject
        If index >= 0 And index < chartControl.Legends.Length Then
            Return chartControl.Legends(index).AccessibilityObject
        End If
        Return Nothing
    End Function

    ' Helper function that is used by the CurveLegend's
accessibility object
    ' to navigate between sibiling controls. Specifically,
this function is used in
    ' the CurveLegend.CurveLegendAccessibleObject.Navigate function.
    Friend Function NavigateFromChild(child As
CurveLegend.CurveLegendAccessibleObject, _
                                    navdir As
AccessibleNavigation) As AccessibleObject
        Select Case navdir
            Case AccessibleNavigation.Down, AccessibleNavigation.Next
                    Return GetChild(child.ID + 1)

            Case AccessibleNavigation.Up, AccessibleNavigation.Previous
                    Return GetChild(child.ID - 1)
        End Select
        Return Nothing
    End Function
```

```
    ' Helper function that is used by the CurveLegend's ↵
accessibility object
    ' to select a specific CurveLegend control. Specifically, ↵
this function is used
    ' in the CurveLegend.CurveLegendAccessibleObject.Select function.
    Friend Sub SelectChild(child As ↵
CurveLegend.CurveLegendAccessibleObject, selection As ↵
AccessibleSelection)
        Dim childID As Integer = child.ID

        ' Determine which selection action should occur, based on the
        ' AccessibleSelection value.
        If (selection And AccessibleSelection.TakeSelection) <> 0 Then
            Dim i As Integer
            For i = 0 To chartControl.Legends.Length - 1
                If i = childID Then
                    chartControl.Legends(i).Selected = True
                Else
                    chartControl.Legends(i).Selected = False
                End If
            Next i

            ' AccessibleSelection.AddSelection means that the ↵
CurveLegend will be selected.
            If (selection And AccessibleSelection.AddSelection) ↵
<> 0 Then
                chartControl.Legends(childID).Selected = True
            End If

            ' AccessibleSelection.AddSelection means that the ↵
CurveLegend will be unselected.
            If (selection And ↵
AccessibleSelection.RemoveSelection) <> 0 Then
                chartControl.Legends(childID).Selected = False
            End If
        End If
    End Sub 'SelectChild
End Class 'ChartControlAccessibleObject
```

[C#]

```
// Inner class ChartControlAccessibleObject represents ↵
accessible information associated with the ChartControl.
// The ChartControlAccessibleObject is returned in the ↵
ChartControl.CreateAccessibilityInstance override.
public class ChartControlAccessibleObject : ControlAccessibleObject
{
    ChartControl chartControl;

    public ChartControlAccessibleObject(ChartControl ctrl) : base(ctrl)
    {
        chartControl = ctrl;
    }

    // Gets the role for the Chart. This is used by ↵
 accessibility programs.
    public override AccessibleRole Role
    {
        get {
            return AccessibleRole.Chart;
        }
    }

    // Gets the state for the Chart. This is used by ↵
accessibility programs.
    public override AccessibleStates State
    {
        get {
            return AccessibleStates.ReadOnly;
        }
    }

    // The CurveLegend objects are "child" controls in ↵
terms of accessibility so
    // return the number of ChartLengend objects.
    public override int GetChildCount()
    {
        return chartControl.Legends.Length;
    }

    // Gets the Accessibility object of the child ↵
CurveLegend identified by index.
    public override AccessibleObject GetChild(int index)
    {
        if (index >= 0 && index < chartControl.Legends.Length) {
            return chartControl.Legends[index].AccessibilityObject;
        }
        return null;
    }

    // Helper function that is used by the CurveLegend's ↵
accessibility object
    // to navigate between sibiling controls. Specifically, ↵
 this function is used in
    // the CurveLegend.CurveLegendAccessibleObject.Navigate function.
    internal AccessibleObject
NavigateFromChild(CurveLegend.CurveLegendAccessibleObject child,
                                AccessibleNavigation navdir)
    {
        switch(navdir) {
            case AccessibleNavigation.Down:
            case AccessibleNavigation.Next:
                return GetChild(child.ID + 1);

            case AccessibleNavigation.Up:
            case AccessibleNavigation.Previous:
                return GetChild(child.ID - 1);
        }
        return null;
    }

    // Helper function that is used by the CurveLegend's ↵
 accessibility object
    // to select a specific CurveLegend control. Specifically, ↵
 this function is used
    // in the CurveLegend.CurveLegendAccessibleObject.Select function.
    internal void SelectChild ↵
(CurveLegend.CurveLegendAccessibleObject child, ↵
 AccessibleSelection selection)
    {
        int childID = child.ID;

        // Determine which selection action should occur, based on the
        // AccessibleSelection value.
        if ((selection & AccessibleSelection.TakeSelection) != 0) {
            for(int i = 0; i < chartControl.Legends.Length; i++) {
                if (i == childID) {
                    chartControl.Legends[i].Selected = true;
                } else {
                    chartControl.Legends[i].Selected = false;
                }
            }

            // AccessibleSelection.AddSelection means that the ↵
CurveLegend will be selected.
            if ((selection & AccessibleSelection.AddSelection) != 0) {
                chartControl.Legends[childID].Selected = true;
            }

            // AccessibleSelection.AddSelection means that the ↵
CurveLegend will be unselected.
            if ((selection & ↵
AccessibleSelection.RemoveSelection) != 0) {
                chartControl.Legends[childID].Selected = false;
            }
        }
    }
}
```

[C++]

```
// Inner class ChartControlAccessibleObject represents
accessible information associated with the ChartControl.
// The ChartControlAccessibleObject is returned in the
ChartControl::CreateAccessibilityInstance .
public:
__gc class ChartControlAccessibleObject : public
ControlAccessibleObject {
   ChartControl* chartControl;

public:
   ChartControlAccessibleObject(ChartControl* ctrl) :
ControlAccessibleObject (ctrl) {
      chartControl = ctrl;
   }

   // Gets the role for the Chart. This is used by
accessibility programs.
public:
   __property System::Windows::Forms::AccessibleRole get_Role() {
      return AccessibleRole::Chart;
   }

   // Gets the state for the Chart. This is used by
accessibility programs.
public:
   __property AccessibleStates get_State() {
      return AccessibleStates::ReadOnly;
   }

   // The CurveLegend objects are S"child" controls in
 terms of accessibility so
   // return the number of ChartLengend objects.
public:
   int GetChildCount() {
      return chartControl->Legends->Length;
   }

   // Gets the Accessibility Object* of the child
CurveLegend identified by index.
public:
   AccessibleObject* GetChild(int index) {
      if (index >= 0 && index < chartControl->Legends->Length) {
         return chartControl->Legends[index]->AccessibilityObject;
      }
      return 0;
   }

   // Helper function that is used by the CurveLegend's
accessibility Object*
   // to navigate between sibiling controls. Specifically, this
function is used in
   // the CurveLegend::CurveLegendAccessibleObject.Navigate function.
public private:
   AccessibleObject*
NavigateFromChild(CurveLegend::CurveLegendAccessibleObject* child,
      AccessibleNavigation navdir) {
         switch(navdir) {
                case AccessibleNavigation::Down:
                case AccessibleNavigation::Next:
                   return GetChild(child->ID + 1);

                case AccessibleNavigation::Up:
                case AccessibleNavigation::Previous:
                   return GetChild(child->ID - 1);
         }
         return 0;
      }

      // Helper function that is used by the CurveLegend's
 accessibility Object*
      // to select a specific CurveLegend control. Specifically,
 this function is used
      // in the CurveLegend::CurveLegendAccessibleObject.Select
 function.
public private:
   void SelectChild(CurveLegend::CurveLegendAccessibleObject*
 child, AccessibleSelection selection) {
      int childID = child->ID;

      // Determine which selection action should occur, based on the
      // AccessibleSelection value.
      if ((selection & AccessibleSelection::TakeSelection) != 0) {
         for (int i = 0; i < chartControl->Legends->Length; i++) {
            if (i == childID) {
               chartControl->Legends[i]->Selected = true;
            } else {
               chartControl->Legends[i]->Selected = false;
            }
         }

         // AccessibleSelection->AddSelection means that the
CurveLegend will be selected.
         if ((selection & AccessibleSelection::AddSelection) != 0) {
            chartControl->Legends[childID]->Selected = true;
         }

         // AccessibleSelection->AddSelection means that the
CurveLegend will be unselected.
         if ((selection & AccessibleSelection::RemoveSelection) != 0) {
            chartControl->Legends[childID]->Selected = false;
         }
      }
   }
}; // class ChartControlAccessibleObject
```

Requirements

Namespace: System.Windows.Forms

Platforms: Windows 98, Windows NT 4.0, Windows Millennium Edition, Windows 2000, Windows XP Home Edition, Windows XP Professional, Windows Server 2003 family

Assembly: System.Windows.Forms (in System.Windows.Forms.dll)

AccessibleObject Class

Provides information that accessibility applications use to adjust an application's UI for users with impairments.

System.Object
  System.MarshalByRefObject
    System.Windows.Forms.AccessibleObject
      System.Windows.Forms.Control.ControlAccessibleObject
      System.Windows.Forms.Design.ControlDesigner.ControlDesignerAccessibleObject

[Visual Basic]
```
<ComVisible(True)>
Public Class AccessibleObject
   Inherits MarshalByRefObject
   Implements IReflect, IAccessible
```
[C#]
```
[ComVisible(true)]
public class AccessibleObject : MarshalByRefObject, IReflect,
   IAccessible
```
[C++]
```
[ComVisible(true)]
public __gc class AccessibleObject : public MarshalByRefObject,
   IReflect, IAccessible
```
[JScript]
```
public
   ComVisible(true)
class AccessibleObject extends MarshalByRefObject implements
   IReflect, IAccessible
```

Thread Safety

Any public static (**Shared** in Visual Basic) members of this type are safe for multithreaded operations. Any instance members are not guaranteed to be thread safe.

Remarks

Accessibility applications can adjust features of the application to improve usability for users with disabilities.

For users who are visually impaired, you can adjust software and operating system features to comply with their needs. For example, you can enlarge text and images and render them with a contrast. In addition, you can accommodate color-blindness with the appropriate use of colors. For users who are severely visually impaired, computers are accessible with screen review aids that translate on-screen text to speech or to a dynamic, refreshable, Braille display.

For users who are hard of hearing, you can design programs that use visual cues, such as a flashing toolbar; or you can display spoken messages as text. For example, when turned on, the **SoundSentry** feature, an accessibility option in Control Panel, provides a visual warning whenever the system makes an alarm sound.

For users with motion disabilities, you can design controls that refine or eliminate keyboard and mouse use, thereby improving computer accessibility. Control Panel offers assistance. For example, one alternative is to use the numeric keypad instead of the mouse for navigation. Another option, called **StickyKeys**, enables users who cannot hold down two or more keys at a time (such as CTRL+P) to get the same result by typing one key at a time.

For users with cognitive and language disabilities, you can design software programs to better accommodate their needs. For example, using conspicuous or cued sequencing, uncomplicated displays, fewer words, and a reading level targeted to elementary school standards can benefit these users.

For users with seizure disorders, you can design software programs to eliminate seizure provoking patterns.

For an overview on accessibility, including additional information on accessibility applications, see the documentation for Microsoft Accessibility in the MSDN library or at the Microsoft Web site.

Notes to Inheritors: When you inherit from this class, you can override all the members.

Note To use the **AccessibleObject**, you must add a reference to the **Accessibility** assembly installed with the .NET Framework.

Example

[Visual Basic, C#, C++] The following example demonstrates the creation of an accessibility-aware chart control, using the **AccessibleObject** and **Control.ControlAccessibleObject** classes to expose accessible information. The control plots two curves along with a legend. The `ChartControlAccessibleObject` class, which derives from **ControlAccessibleObject**, is used in the **CreateAccessibilityInstance** method to provide custom accessible information for the chart control. Since the chart legend is not an actual **Control**-based control, but instead is drawn by the chart control, it does not any built-in accessible information. Because of this, the `ChartControlAccessibleObject` class overrides the **GetChild** method to return the `CurveLegendAccessibleObject` that represents accessible information for each part of the legend. When an accessible-aware application uses this control, the control can provide the necessary accessible information.

[Visual Basic]
```
Option Explicit

Imports System
Imports System.Drawing
Imports System.Windows.Forms

Namespace ChartControlNameSpace

    Public Class Form1
        Inherits System.Windows.Forms.Form

        ' Test out the Chart Control.
        Private chart1 As ChartControl

        <System.STAThread()> _
        Public Shared Sub Main()
            System.Windows.Forms.Application.Run(New Form1())
        End Sub 'Main

        Public Sub New()
            ' Create a chart control and add it to the form.
            Me.chart1 = New ChartControl()
            Me.ClientSize = New System.Drawing.Size(920, 566)

            Me.chart1.Location = New System.Drawing.Point(47, 16)
            Me.chart1.Size = New System.Drawing.Size(600, 400)

            Me.Controls.Add(Me.chart1)
        End Sub
    End Class

    ' Declares a chart control that demonstrates Accessibility
in Windows Forms.
    Public Class ChartControl
        Inherits System.Windows.Forms.UserControl

        Private legend1 As CurveLegend
        Private legend2 As CurveLegend
```

```
        Public Sub New()
            ' The ChartControl draws the chart in the OnPaint override.
            SetStyle(ControlStyles.ResizeRedraw, True)
            SetStyle(ControlStyles.DoubleBuffer, True)
            SetStyle(ControlStyles.AllPaintingInWmPaint, True)

            Me.BackColor = System.Drawing.Color.White
            Me.Name = "ChartControl"

            ' The CurveLengend is not Control-based, it just
            ' represent the parts of the legend.
            legend1 = New CurveLegend(Me, "A")
            legend1.Location = New Point(20, 30)
            legend2 = New CurveLegend(Me, "B")
            legend2.Location = New Point(20, 50)
        End Sub 'New

        ' Overridden to return the custom AccessibleObject
        ' for the entire chart.
        Protected Overrides Function                                    ↵
CreateAccessibilityInstance() As AccessibleObject
            Return New ChartControlAccessibleObject(Me)
        End Function

        Protected Overrides Sub OnPaint(e As PaintEventArgs)
            ' The ChartControl draws the chart in the OnPaint override.
            MyBase.OnPaint(e)

            Dim bounds As Rectangle = Me.ClientRectangle
            Dim border As Integer = 5

            ' Draw the legends first.
            Dim format As New StringFormat()
            format.Alignment = StringAlignment.Center
            format.LineAlignment = StringAlignment.Center

            If Not (legend1 Is Nothing) Then
                If legend1.Selected Then
                    e.Graphics.FillRectangle(New                        ↵
SolidBrush(Color.Blue), legend1.Bounds)
                Else
                    e.Graphics.DrawRectangle(Pens.Blue, legend1.Bounds)
                End If
                e.Graphics.DrawString(legend1.Name, Me.Font,           ↵
Brushes.Black, RectangleF.op_Implicit(legend1.Bounds), format)
            End If
            If Not (legend2 Is Nothing) Then
                If legend2.Selected Then
                    e.Graphics.FillRectangle(New SolidBrush            ↵
 (Color.Red), legend2.Bounds)
                Else
                    e.Graphics.DrawRectangle(Pens.Red, legend2.Bounds)
                End If
                e.Graphics.DrawString(legend2.Name, Me.Font,           ↵
Brushes.Black, RectangleF.op_Implicit(legend2.Bounds), format)
            End If

            ' Chart out the actual curves that represent data          ↵
 in the Chart.
            bounds.Inflate(-border, -border)
            Dim curve1() As Point = {New Point(bounds.Left,            ↵
bounds.Bottom), _
                                     New Point(bounds.Left +           ↵
bounds.Width / 3, bounds.Top + bounds.Height / 5), _
                                     New Point(bounds.Right -          ↵
bounds.Width / 3,(bounds.Top + bounds.Bottom) / 2), _
                                     New Point(bounds.Right,           ↵
bounds.Top)}

            Dim curve2() As Point = {New Point(bounds.Left,            ↵
bounds.Bottom - bounds.Height / 3), _
                                     New Point(bounds.Left +           ↵
bounds.Width / 3, bounds.Top + bounds.Height / 5), _
                                     New Point(bounds.Right -          ↵
bounds.Width / 3,(bounds.Top + bounds.Bottom) / 2), _
                                     New Point(bounds.Right,           ↵
bounds.Top + bounds.Height / 2)}

            ' Draw the actual curve only if it is selected.
            If legend1.Selected Then
                e.Graphics.DrawCurve(Pens.Blue, curve1)
            End If
            If legend2.Selected Then
                e.Graphics.DrawCurve(Pens.Red, curve2)
            End If
            e.Graphics.DrawRectangle(Pens.Blue, bounds)
        End Sub 'OnPaint

        ' Handle the QueryAccessibilityHelp event.
        Private Sub ChartControl_QueryAccessibilityHelp(sender         ↵
 As Object, _
                            e As
System.Windows.Forms.QueryAccessibilityHelpEventArgs) Handles          ↵
MyBase.QueryAccessibilityHelp
            e.HelpString = "Displays chart data"
        End Sub

        ' Handle the Click event for the chart.
        ' Toggle the selection of whatever legend was clicked.
        Private Sub ChartControl_Click(sender As Object, e As          ↵
System.EventArgs) Handles MyBase.Click

            Dim pt As Point = Me.PointToClient(Control.MousePosition)
            If legend1.Bounds.Contains(pt) Then
                legend1.Selected = Not legend1.Selected
            Else
                If legend2.Bounds.Contains(pt) Then
                    legend2.Selected = Not legend2.Selected
                End If
            End If
        End Sub 'ChartControl_Click

        ' Get an array of the CurveLengends used in the Chart.
        Public ReadOnly Property Legends() As CurveLegend()
            Get
                Return New CurveLegend() {legend1, legend2}
            End Get
        End Property

        Protected Sub ExposeAccessibilityNotifyClients(ByVal           ↵
accEvent As AccessibleEvents, ByVal childID As Integer)
            AccessibilityNotifyClients(accEvent, childID)
        End Sub

        ' Inner Class ChartControlAccessibleObject represents          ↵
accessible information
        ' associated with the ChartControl.
        ' The ChartControlAccessibleObject is returned in the  '       ↵
 ChartControl.CreateAccessibilityInstance override.
        Public Class ChartControlAccessibleObject
            Inherits Control.ControlAccessibleObject

            Private chartControl As ChartControl

            Public Sub New(ctrl As ChartControl)
                MyBase.New(ctrl)
                chartControl = ctrl
            End Sub 'New

            ' Get the role for the Chart. This is used by              ↵
accessibility programs.
            Public Overrides ReadOnly Property Role() As AccessibleRole
                Get
                    Return System.Windows.Forms.AccessibleRole.Chart
                End Get
            End Property

            ' Get the state for the Chart. This is used by             ↵
accessibility programs.
            Public Overrides ReadOnly Property State() As              ↵
```

```
AccessibleStates
                Get
                    Return AccessibleStates.ReadOnly
                End Get
            End Property

            ' The CurveLegend objects are "child" controls in         ↵
terms of accessibility so
            ' return the number of ChartLengend objects.
            Public Overrides Function GetChildCount() As Integer
                Return chartControl.Legends.Length
            End Function

            ' Get the Accessibility object of the child               ↵
CurveLegend idetified by index.
            Public Overrides Function GetChild(index As Integer)      ↵
As AccessibleObject
                If index >= 0 And index <                             ↵
chartControl.Legends.Length Then
                    Return chartControl.Legends(index).AccessibilityObject
                End If
                Return Nothing
            End Function

            ' Helper function that is used by the CurveLegend's       ↵
accessibility object
            ' to navigate between sibiling controls.                  ↵
Specifically, this function is used in
            ' the                                                     ↵
CurveLegend.CurveLegendAccessibleObject.Navigate function.
            Friend Function NavigateFromChild(child As                ↵
CurveLegend.CurveLegendAccessibleObject, _
                                               navdir As              ↵
AccessibleNavigation) As AccessibleObject
                Select Case navdir
                    Case AccessibleNavigation.Down,                   ↵
AccessibleNavigation.Next
                            Return GetChild(child.ID + 1)

                    Case AccessibleNavigation.Up,                     ↵
AccessibleNavigation.Previous
                            Return GetChild(child.ID - 1)
                End Select
                Return Nothing
            End Function

            ' Helper function that is used by the                     ↵
CurveLegend's accessibility object
            ' to select a specific CurveLegend control.               ↵
Specifically, this function is used
            ' in the                                                  ↵
CurveLegend.CurveLegendAccessibleObject.Select function.
            Friend Sub SelectChild(child As                           ↵
CurveLegend.CurveLegendAccessibleObject, selection As                 ↵
AccessibleSelection)
                Dim childID As Integer = child.ID

                ' Determine which selection action should             ↵
occur, based on the
                ' AccessibleSelection value.
                If (selection And                                     ↵
 AccessibleSelection.TakeSelection) <> 0 Then
                    Dim i As Integer
                    For i = 0 To chartControl.Legends.Length - 1
                        If i = childID Then
                            chartControl.Legends(i).Selected = True
                        Else
                            chartControl.Legends(i).Selected = False
                        End If
                    Next i

                    ' AccessibleSelection.AddSelection means          ↵
that the CurveLegend will be selected.
                    If (selection And                                 ↵
AccessibleSelection.AddSelection) <> 0 Then
                        chartControl.Legends(childID).Selected = True
                    End If

                    ' AccessibleSelection.AddSelection means          ↵
that the CurveLegend will be unselected.
                    If (selection And AccessibleSelection.RemoveSelection)
<> 0 Then
                        chartControl.Legends(childID).Selected = False
                    End If
                End If
            End Sub 'SelectChild
        End Class 'ChartControlAccessibleObject

        ' Inner Class that represents a legend for a curve            ↵
 in the chart.
        Public Class CurveLegend
            Private m_name As String
            Private chart As ChartControl
            Private accObj As CurveLegendAccessibleObject
            Private m_selected As Boolean = True
            Private m_location As Point

            Public Sub New(chart As ChartControl, name As String)
                Me.chart = chart
                Me.m_name = name
            End Sub 'New

            ' Gets the accessibility object for the curve legend.
            Public ReadOnly Property AccessibilityObject() As         ↵
AccessibleObject
                Get
                    If accObj Is Nothing Then
                        accObj = New CurveLegendAccessibleObject(Me)
                    End If
                    Return accObj
                End Get
            End Property

            ' Gets the bounds for the curve legend.
            Public ReadOnly Property Bounds() As Rectangle
                Get
                    Return New Rectangle(Location, Size)
                End Get
            End Property

            ' Gets or sets the location for the curve legend.
            Public Property Location() As Point
                Get
                    Return m_location
                End Get
                Set
                    m_location = value
                    chart.Invalidate()

                    ' Notifies the chart of the location change.      ↵
 This is used for
                    ' the accessibility information.                  ↵
AccessibleEvents.LocationChange
                    ' tells the chart the reason for the notification.
                    chart.ExposeAccessibilityNotifyClients            ↵
 (AccessibleEvents.LocationChange, _
                            CType(AccessibilityObject,                ↵
CurveLegendAccessibleObject).ID)
                End Set
            End Property

            ' Gets or sets the Name for the curve legend.
            Public Property Name() As String
                Get
                    Return m_name
                End Get
                Set
                    If m_name <> value Then
                        m_name = value
                        chart.Invalidate()
```

```
                    ' Notifies the chart of the name change.        ↵
This is used for
                    ' the accessibility information.                ↵
AccessibleEvents.NameChange
                    ' tells the chart the reason for the            ↵
notification.

chart.ExposeAccessibilityNotifyClients(AccessibleEvents.NameChange, _
                                CType(AccessibilityObject,          ↵
CurveLegendAccessibleObject).ID)
                End If
            End Set
        End Property

        ' Gets or sets the Selected state for the curve legend.
        Public Property Selected() As Boolean
            Get
                Return m_selected
            End Get
            Set
                If m_selected <> value Then
                    m_selected = value
                    chart.Invalidate()

                    ' Notifies the chart of the selection           ↵
value change. This is used for
                    ' the accessibility information. The            ↵
AccessibleEvents value varies
                    ' on whether the selection is true              ↵
 (AccessibleEvents.SelectionAdd) or
                    ' false (AccessibleEvents.SelectionRemove).
                    If m_selected Then

chart.ExposeAccessibilityNotifyClients(AccessibleEvents.SelectionAdd, _
                                    CType(AccessibilityObject,      ↵
CurveLegendAccessibleObject).ID)
                    Else
                        chart.ExposeAccessibilityNotifyClients      ↵
 (AccessibleEvents.SelectionRemove, _
                                    CType(AccessibilityObject,      ↵
CurveLegendAccessibleObject).ID)
                    End If
                End If
            End Set
        End Property

        ' Gets the Size for the curve legend.
        Public ReadOnly Property Size() As Size
            Get
                Dim legendHeight As Integer = chart.Font.Height + 4
                Dim g As Graphics = chart.CreateGraphics()
                Dim legendWidth As Integer =                        ↵
CInt(g.MeasureString(Name, chart.Font).Width) + 4

                Return New Size(legendWidth, legendHeight)
            End Get
        End Property

        ' Inner class CurveLegendAccessibleObject                   ↵
 represents accessible information
        ' associated with the CurveLegend object.
        Public Class CurveLegendAccessibleObject
            Inherits AccessibleObject

            Private curveLegend As CurveLegend

            Public Sub New(curveLegend As CurveLegend)
                Me.curveLegend = curveLegend
            End Sub 'New

            ' Private property that helps get the                   ↵
reference to the parent ChartControl.
            Private ReadOnly Property ChartControl() As             ↵
ChartControlAccessibleObject
                Get
                    Return CType(Parent,                            ↵
ChartControlAccessibleObject)
                End Get
            End Property

            ' Friend helper function that returns the ID            ↵
 for this CurveLegend.
            Friend ReadOnly Property ID() As Integer
                Get
                    Dim i As Integer
                    For i = 0 To (ChartControl.GetChildCount()) - 1
                        If ChartControl.GetChild(i) Is Me Then
                            Return i
                        End If
                    Next i
                    Return - 1
                End Get
            End Property

            ' Gets the Bounds for the CurveLegend. This is          ↵
used by accessibility programs.
            Public Overrides ReadOnly Property Bounds() As          ↵
Rectangle
                Get
                    ' The bounds is in screen coordinates.
                    Dim loc As Point = curveLegend.Location
                    Return New
Rectangle(curveLegend.chart.PointToScreen(loc), curveLegend.Size)
                End Get
            End Property

            ' Gets or sets the Name for the CurveLegend.            ↵
This is used by accessibility programs.
            Public Overrides Property Name() As String
                Get
                    Return curveLegend.Name
                End Get
                Set
                    curveLegend.Name = value
                End Set
            End Property

            ' Gets the Curve Legend Parent's Accessible object.
            ' This is used by accessibility programs.
            Public Overrides ReadOnly Property Parent() As          ↵
AccessibleObject
                Get
                    Return curveLegend.chart.AccessibilityObject
                End Get
            End Property

            ' Gets the role for the CurveLegend. This is used       ↵
 by accessibility programs.
            Public Overrides ReadOnly Property Role() As            ↵
AccessibleRole
                Get
                    Return                                          ↵
System.Windows.Forms.AccessibleRole.StaticText
                End Get
            End Property

            ' Gets the state based on the selection for the         ↵
CurveLegend.
            ' This is used by accessibility programs.
            Public Overrides ReadOnly Property State() As           ↵
AccessibleStates
                Get
                    Dim stateTemp As AccessibleStates =             ↵
AccessibleStates.Selectable
                    If curveLegend.Selected Then
                        stateTemp = stateTemp Or                    ↵
AccessibleStates.Selected
                    End If
                    Return stateTemp
                End Get
            End Property
```

```
                ' Navigates through siblings of this                    ↵
CurveLegend. This is used by accessibility programs.
                Public Overrides Function Navigate(navdir As            ↵
AccessibleNavigation) As AccessibleObject
                    ' Use the Friend NavigateFromChild helper           ↵
function that exists
                    ' on ChartControlAccessibleObject.
                    Return ChartControl.NavigateFromChild(Me, navdir)
                End Function

                ' Selects or unselects this CurveLegend. This           ↵
is used by accessibility programs.
                Public Overrides Sub [Select](selection As              ↵
AccessibleSelection)

                    ' Use the internal SelectChild helper               ↵
 function that exists
                    ' on ChartControlAccessibleObject.
                    ChartControl.SelectChild(Me, selection)
                End Sub

            End Class 'CurveLegendAccessibleObject

        End Class 'CurveLegend

    End Class 'ChartControl

End Namespace 'ChartControlNameSpace
```

[C#]

```
using System;
using System.Drawing;
using System.Windows.Forms;

namespace ChartControl
{
    public class Form1 : System.Windows.Forms.Form
    {
        // Test out the Chart Control.
        private ChartControl chart1;

        [STAThread]
        static void Main()
        {
            Application.Run(new Form1());
        }

        public Form1() {
            // Create a chart control and add it to the form.
            this.chart1 = new ChartControl();
            this.ClientSize = new System.Drawing.Size(920, 566);

            this.chart1.Location = new System.Drawing.Point(47, 16);
            this.chart1.Size = new System.Drawing.Size(600, 400);

            this.Controls.Add(this.chart1);
        }
    }

    // Declare a chart control that demonstrates accessibility     ↵
 in Windows Forms.
    public class ChartControl : System.Windows.Forms.UserControl
    {
        private CurveLegend legend1;
        private CurveLegend legend2;

        public ChartControl()
        {
            // The ChartControl draws the chart in the OnPaint      ↵
override.
            SetStyle(ControlStyles.ResizeRedraw, true);
            SetStyle(ControlStyles.DoubleBuffer, true);
            SetStyle(ControlStyles.AllPaintingInWmPaint, true);

            this.BackColor = System.Drawing.Color.White;
            this.Name = "ChartControl";

            this.Click += new                                       ↵
System.EventHandler(this.ChartControl_Click);
            this.QueryAccessibilityHelp +=
                new                                                 ↵
System.Windows.Forms.QueryAccessibilityHelpEventHandler(
                                                                    ↵
this.ChartControl_QueryAccessibilityHelp);

            // The CurveLengend is not Control-based, it just
            // represents the parts of the legend.
            legend1 = new CurveLegend(this, "A");
            legend1.Location = new Point(20, 30);
            legend2 = new CurveLegend(this, "B");
            legend2.Location = new Point(20, 50);
        }

        // Overridden to return the custom AccessibleObject
        // for the entire chart.
        protected override AccessibleObject                         ↵
CreateAccessibilityInstance()
        {
            return new ChartControlAccessibleObject(this);
        }

        protected override void OnPaint(PaintEventArgs e)
        {
            // The ChartControl draws the chart in                  ↵
the OnPaint override.
            base.OnPaint(e);

            Rectangle bounds = this.ClientRectangle;
            int border = 5;

            // Draws the legends first.
            StringFormat format = new StringFormat();
            format.Alignment = StringAlignment.Center;
            format.LineAlignment = StringAlignment.Center;

            if (legend1 != null) {
                if (legend1.Selected) {
                    e.Graphics.FillRectangle(new                    ↵
SolidBrush(Color.Blue), legend1.Bounds);
                } else {
                    e.Graphics.DrawRectangle(Pens.Blue,             ↵
legend1.Bounds);
                }

                e.Graphics.DrawString(legend1.Name,                 ↵
 this.Font, Brushes.Black, legend1.Bounds, format);
            }
            if (legend2 != null) {
                if (legend2.Selected) {
                    e.Graphics.FillRectangle                        ↵
 (new SolidBrush(Color.Red), legend2.Bounds);
                } else {
                    e.Graphics.DrawRectangle(Pens.Red, legend2.Bounds);
                }
                e.Graphics.DrawString(legend2.Name, this.Font,      ↵
Brushes.Black, legend2.Bounds, format);
            }

            // Charts out the actual curves that represent data     ↵
in the Chart.
            bounds.Inflate(-border, -border);
            Point[] curve1 = new Point[] {new Point(bounds.Left,    ↵
bounds.Bottom),
                            new Point(bounds.Left + bounds.Width    ↵
/ 3, bounds.Top + bounds.Height / 5),
                            new Point(bounds.Right -                ↵
bounds.Width / 3, (bounds.Top + bounds.Bottom) / 2),
                            new Point(bounds.Right, bounds.Top)};
```

```
            Point[] curve2 = new Point[] {new Point                    ↵
 (bounds.Left, bounds.Bottom - bounds.Height / 3),
                             new Point(bounds.Left +                   ↵
bounds.Width / 3, bounds.Top + bounds.Height / 5),
                             new Point(bounds.Right -                  ↵
bounds.Width / 3, (bounds.Top + bounds.Bottom) / 2),
                             new Point(bounds.Right, bounds.Top +      ↵
bounds.Height / 2)};

            // Draws the actual curve only if it is selected.
            if (legend1.Selected) e.Graphics.DrawCurve                 ↵
 (Pens.Blue, curve1);
            if (legend2.Selected) e.Graphics.DrawCurve                 ↵
 (Pens.Red, curve2);

            e.Graphics.DrawRectangle(Pens.Blue, bounds);
        }

        // Handles the QueryAccessibilityHelp event.
        private void ChartControl_QueryAccessibilityHelp(object sender,
                                                                       ↵
System.Windows.Forms.QueryAccessibilityHelpEventArgs e)
        {
            e.HelpString = "Displays chart data";
        }

        // Handles the Click event for the chart.
        // Toggles the selection of whatever legend was clicked on
        private void ChartControl_Click(object sender,                 ↵
System.EventArgs e)
        {
            Point pt = this.PointToClient(Control.MousePosition);
            if (legend1.Bounds.Contains(pt)) {
                legend1.Selected = !legend1.Selected;

            } else if (legend2.Bounds.Contains(pt)) {
                legend2.Selected = !legend2.Selected;
            }
        }

        // Gets an array of CurveLengends used in the Chart.
        public CurveLegend[] Legends
        {
            get {
                return new CurveLegend[] { legend1, legend2 };
            }
        }

        // Inner class ChartControlAccessibleObject                    ↵
 represents accessible information associated with the ChartControl.
        // The ChartControlAccessibleObject is returned                ↵
 in the ChartControl.CreateAccessibilityInstance override.
        public class ChartControlAccessibleObject :                    ↵
ControlAccessibleObject
        {
            ChartControl chartControl;

            public ChartControlAccessibleObject(ChartControl           ↵
ctrl) : base(ctrl)
            {
                chartControl = ctrl;
            }

            // Gets the role for the Chart. This is used by            ↵
accessibility programs.
            public override AccessibleRole Role
            {
                get {
                    return AccessibleRole.Chart;
                }
            }

            // Gets the state for the Chart. This is used by           ↵
accessibility programs.
            public override AccessibleStates State
            {
                get {
                    return AccessibleStates.ReadOnly;
                }
            }

            // The CurveLegend objects are "child" controls            ↵
in terms of accessibility so
            // return the number of ChartLengend objects.
            public override int GetChildCount()
            {
                return chartControl.Legends.Length;
            }

            // Gets the Accessibility object of the child              ↵
CurveLegend idetified by index.
            public override AccessibleObject GetChild(int index)
            {
                if (index >= 0 && index <                              ↵
chartControl.Legends.Length) {
                    return
chartControl.Legends[index].AccessibilityObject;
                }
                return null;
            }

            // Helper function that is used by the                     ↵
 CurveLegend's accessibility object
            // to navigate between sibiling controls.                  ↵
 Specifically, this function is used in
            // the                                                     ↵
CurveLegend.CurveLegendAccessibleObject.Navigate function.
            internal AccessibleObject                                  ↵
NavigateFromChild(CurveLegend.CurveLegendAccessibleObject child,
                AccessibleNavigation navdir)
            {
                switch(navdir) {
                    case AccessibleNavigation.Down:
                    case AccessibleNavigation.Next:
                        return GetChild(child.ID + 1);

                    case AccessibleNavigation.Up:
                    case AccessibleNavigation.Previous:
                        return GetChild(child.ID - 1);
                }
                return null;
            }

            // Helper function that is used by the                     ↵
 CurveLegend's accessibility object
            // to select a specific CurveLegend control.               ↵
 Specifically, this function is used
            // in the                                                  ↵
CurveLegend.CurveLegendAccessibleObject.Select function.
            internal void                                              ↵
SelectChild(CurveLegend.CurveLegendAccessibleObject child,             ↵
AccessibleSelection selection)
            {
                int childID = child.ID;

                // Determine which selection action                    ↵
should occur, based on the
                // AccessibleSelection value.
                if ((selection &                                       ↵
AccessibleSelection.TakeSelection) != 0) {
                    for(int i = 0; i <                                 ↵
chartControl.Legends.Length; i++) {
                        if (i == childID) {
                          chartControl.Legends[i].Selected = true;
                        } else {
                            chartControl.Legends[i].Selected = false;
                        }
                    }
```

```
                    // AccessibleSelection.AddSelection means                ↵
that the CurveLegend will be selected.
                    if ((selection &                                          ↵
 AccessibleSelection.AddSelection) != 0) {
                chartControl.Legends[childID].Selected = true;
                    }

                    // AccessibleSelection.AddSelection means                ↵
that the CurveLegend will be unselected.
                    if ((selection &                                          ↵
AccessibleSelection.RemoveSelection) != 0) {
                        chartControl.Legends[childID].Selected = false;
                    }
                }
            }
        }

        // Inner Class that represents a legend for a curve                  ↵
 in the chart.
        public class CurveLegend
        {
            private string name;
            private ChartControl chart;
            private CurveLegendAccessibleObject accObj;
            private bool selected = true;
            private Point location;

            public CurveLegend(ChartControl chart, string name)
            {
                this.chart = chart;
                this.name = name;
            }

            // Gets the accessibility object for the curve legend.
            public AccessibleObject AccessibilityObject
            {
                get {
                    if (accObj == null) {
                        accObj = new CurveLegendAccessibleObject(this);
                    }
                    return accObj;
                }
            }

            // Gets the bounds for the curve legend.
            public Rectangle Bounds
            {
                get {
                    return new Rectangle(Location, Size);
                }
            }

            // Gets or sets the location for the curve legend.
            public Point Location
            {
                get {
                    return location;
                }
                set {
                    location = value;
                    chart.Invalidate();

                    // Notifies the chart of the location                     ↵
change. This is used for
                    // the accessibility information.                         ↵
AccessibleEvents.LocationChange
                    // tells the chart the reason for the notification.

                                                                              ↵
chart.AccessibilityNotifyClients(AccessibleEvents.LocationChange,
                                                                              ↵
 ((CurveLegendAccessibleObject)AccessibilityObject).ID);
                }
            }

            // Gets or sets the Name for the curve legend.
            public string Name
            {
                get {
                    return name;
                }
                set {
                    if (name != value)
                    {
                        name = value;
                        chart.Invalidate();

                        // Notifies the chart of the name                     ↵
change. This is used for
                        // the accessibility information.                     ↵
AccessibleEvents.NameChange
                        // tells the chart the reason for                     ↵
 the notification.

                                                                              ↵
chart.AccessibilityNotifyClients(AccessibleEvents.NameChange,
                                                                              ↵
 ((CurveLegendAccessibleObject)AccessibilityObject).ID);
                    }
                }
            }

            // Gets or sets the Selected state for the curve legend.
            public bool Selected
            {
                get {
                    return selected;
                }
                set {
                    if (selected != value)
                    {
                        selected = value;
                        chart.Invalidate();

                        // Notifies the chart of the selection                ↵
value change. This is used for
                        // the accessibility information. The                 ↵
AccessibleEvents value depends upon
                        // if the selection is true                           ↵
 (AccessibleEvents.SelectionAdd) or
                        // false (AccessibleEvents.SelectionRemove).
                        chart.AccessibilityNotifyClients(
                            selected ?                                        ↵
AccessibleEvents.SelectionAdd : AccessibleEvents.SelectionRemove,
                                                                              ↵
 ((CurveLegendAccessibleObject)AccessibilityObject).ID);
                    }
                }
            }

            // Gets the Size for the curve legend.
            public Size Size
            {
                get {
                    int legendHeight = chart.Font.Height + 4;
                    Graphics g = chart.CreateGraphics();
                    int legendWidth =                                         ↵
 (int)g.MeasureString(Name, chart.Font).Width + 4;

                    return new Size(legendWidth, legendHeight);
                }
            }

            // Inner class CurveLegendAccessibleObject                        ↵
represents accessible information
            // associated with the CurveLegend object.
            public class CurveLegendAccessibleObject : AccessibleObject
            {
                private CurveLegend curveLegend;
```

```
            public CurveLegendAccessibleObject(CurveLegend          ↵
curveLegend) : base()
            {
                this.curveLegend = curveLegend;
            }

            // Private property that helps get the                  ↵
reference to the parent ChartControl.
            private ChartControlAccessibleObject ChartControl
            {
                get {
                    return Parent as ChartControlAccessibleObject;
                }
            }

            // Internal helper function that returns the            ↵
ID for this CurveLegend.
            internal int ID
            {
                get {
                    for(int i = 0; i <                              ↵
ChartControl.GetChildCount(); i++) {
                        if (ChartControl.GetChild(i) == this) {
                            return i;
                        }
                    }
                    return -1;
                }
            }

            // Gets the Bounds for the CurveLegend. This            ↵
 is used by accessibility programs.
            public override Rectangle Bounds
            {
                get {
                    // The bounds is in screen coordinates.
                    Point loc = curveLegend.Location;
                    return new                                      ↵
Rectangle(curveLegend.chart.PointToScreen(loc), curveLegend.Size);
                }
            }

            // Gets or sets the Name for the CurveLegend.           ↵
 This is used by accessibility programs.
            public override string Name
            {
                get {
                    return curveLegend.Name;
                }
                set {
                    curveLegend.Name = value;
                }
            }

            // Gets the Curve Legend Parent's Accessible object.
            // This is used by accessibility programs.
            public override AccessibleObject Parent
            {
                get {
                    return curveLegend.chart.AccessibilityObject;
                }
            }

            // Gets the role for the CurveLegend. This is           ↵
 used by accessibility programs.
            public override AccessibleRole Role
            {
                get {
                    return AccessibleRole.StaticText;
                }
            }

            // Gets the state based on the selection for            ↵
 the CurveLegend.
            // This is used by accessibility programs.
            public override AccessibleStates State
            {
                get {
                    AccessibleStates state =                        ↵
AccessibleStates.Selectable;
                    if (curveLegend.Selected)
                    {
                        state |= AccessibleStates.Selected;
                    }
                    return state;
                }
            }

            // Navigates through siblings of this                   ↵
CurveLegend. This is used by accessibility programs.
            public override AccessibleObject                        ↵
Navigate(AccessibleNavigation navdir)
            {
                // Uses the internal NavigateFromChild              ↵
 helper function that exists
                // on ChartControlAccessibleObject.
                return ChartControl.NavigateFromChild(this,         ↵
navdir);
            }

            // Selects or unselects this CurveLegend. This          ↵
is used by accessibility programs.
            public override void Select(AccessibleSelection         ↵
selection)
            {
                // Uses the internal SelectChild helper             ↵
function that exists
                // on ChartControlAccessibleObject.
                ChartControl.SelectChild(this, selection);
            }
        }
    }
}
```

[C++]

```
#using <mscorlib.dll>
#using <Accessibility.dll>
#using <System.dll>
#using <System.Windows.Forms.dll>
#using <System.Drawing.dll>

using namespace System;
using namespace System::Drawing;
using namespace System::Windows::Forms;

namespace ChartControl {

   // Declare a chart control that demonstrates accessibility      ↵
in Windows Forms.
public __gc class ChartControl : public
System::Windows::Forms::UserControl {
public:
   __gc class ChartControlAccessibleObject; // forward declaration

   // Inner Class that represents a legend for a curve in the chart.
public:
   __gc class CurveLegend {

      // Inner class CurveLegendAccessibleObject represents         ↵
 accessible information
      // associated with the CurveLegend Object*.
   public:
      __gc class CurveLegendAccessibleObject : public               ↵
AccessibleObject {
      private:
         CurveLegend*  curveLegend;

      public:
         CurveLegendAccessibleObject(CurveLegend*                   ↵
```

```
curveLegend) : AccessibleObject() {
            this->curveLegend = curveLegend;
         }

         // Private property that helps get the reference to        ↵
 the parent ChartControl.
      private:
         __property ChartControlAccessibleObject* get_ChartControl() {
            return dynamic_cast<ChartControlAccessibleObject*>(Parent);
         }

         // Internal helper function that returns the ID for        ↵
 this CurveLegend.
      public private:
         __property int get_ID() {
            for (int i = 0; i < ChartControl->GetChildCount(); i++) {
               if (ChartControl->GetChild(i) == this) {
                  return i;
               }
            }
            return -1;
         }

         // Gets the Bounds for the CurveLegend. This is        ↵
used by accessibility programs.
      public:
         __property Rectangle get_Bounds() {
            // The bounds is in screen coordinates.
            Point loc = curveLegend->Location;
            return Rectangle(curveLegend->chart->        ↵
PointToScreen(loc), curveLegend->Size);
         }

         // Gets or sets the Name for the CurveLegend. This        ↵
is used by accessibility programs.
      public:
         __property String* get_Name() {
            return curveLegend->Name;
         }
         __property void set_Name(String* value) {
            curveLegend->Name = value;
         }

         // Gets the Curve Legend Parent's Accessible Object*.
         // This is used by accessibility programs.
      public:
         __property AccessibleObject* get_Parent() {
            return curveLegend->chart->AccessibilityObject;
         }

         // Gets the role for the CurveLegend. This is used        ↵
by accessibility programs.
      public:
         __property System::Windows::Forms::AccessibleRole get_Role() {
            return AccessibleRole::StaticText;
         }

         // Gets the state based on the selection for the CurveLegend.
         // This is used by accessibility programs.
      public:
         __property AccessibleStates get_State() {
            AccessibleStates state = AccessibleStates::Selectable;
            if (curveLegend->Selected) {
               state = static_cast<AccessibleStates>( state |        ↵
AccessibleStates::Selected );
            }
            return state;
         }

         // Navigates through siblings of this CurveLegend. This        ↵
 is used by accessibility programs.
      public:
         AccessibleObject* Navigate(AccessibleNavigation navdir) {
            // Uses the internal NavigateFromChild helper        ↵
 function that exists
            // on ChartControlAccessibleObject.
            return ChartControl->NavigateFromChild(this, navdir);
         }

         // Selects or unselects this CurveLegend. This is        ↵
used by accessibility programs.
      public:
         void Select(AccessibleSelection selection) {
            // Uses the internal SelectChild helper function        ↵
 that exists
            // on ChartControlAccessibleObject.
            ChartControl->SelectChild(this, selection);
         }
      }; // class CurveLgendAccessibleObject

   private:
      String*  name;
   private:
      ChartControl*  chart;
   private:
      CurveLegendAccessibleObject*  accObj;
   private:
      bool  selected;
   private:
      Point  location;

   public:
      CurveLegend(ChartControl* chart, String* name) {
         this->chart = chart;
         this->name = name;
         selected = true;
      }

      // Gets the accessibility Object* for the curve legend.
   public:
      __property AccessibleObject* get_AccessibilityObject() {
         if (accObj == 0) {
            accObj = new CurveLegendAccessibleObject(this);
         }
         return accObj;
      }

      // Gets the bounds for the curve legend.
   public:
      __property Rectangle get_Bounds() {
         return Rectangle(Location, Size);
      }

      // Gets or sets the location for the curve legend.
   public:
      __property Point get_Location() {
         return location;
      }
      __property void set_Location(Point value) {
         location = value;
         chart->Invalidate();

         // Notifies the chart of the location change. This is used for
         // the accessibility information.        ↵
AccessibleEvents::LocationChange
         // tells the chart the reason for the notification.

         chart-        ↵
>AccessibilityNotifyClients(AccessibleEvents::LocationChange,

(dynamic_cast<CurveLegendAccessibleObject*>(AccessibilityObject))->ID);
      }

      // Gets or sets the Name for the curve legend.
   public:
      __property String* get_Name() {
         return name;
      }
      __property void set_Name(String* value) {
         if (name != value) {
```

```
         name = value;
         chart->Invalidate();

         // Notifies the chart of the name change. This is used for
         // the accessibility information.                            ↵
AccessibleEvents::NameChange
         // tells the chart the reason for the notification.

         chart-                                                       ↵
>AccessibilityNotifyClients(AccessibleEvents::NameChange,

(dynamic_cast<CurveLegendAccessibleObject*>(AccessibilityObject))->ID);
      }
   }

   // Gets or sets the Selected state for the curve legend.
  public:
   __property bool get_Selected() {
      return selected;
   }
   __property void set_Selected(bool value) {
      if (selected != value) {
         selected = value;
         chart->Invalidate();

         // Notifies the chart of the selection value                 ↵
 change. This is used for
         // the accessibility information. The                        ↵
AccessibleEvents value depends upon
         // if the selection is true                                  ↵
 (AccessibleEvents::SelectionAdd) or
         // false (AccessibleEvents::SelectionRemove).
         chart->AccessibilityNotifyClients(selected ?                 ↵
AccessibleEvents::SelectionAdd : AccessibleEvents::SelectionRemove,

(dynamic_cast<CurveLegendAccessibleObject*>(AccessibilityObject))->ID);
      }
   }

   // Gets the Size for the curve legend.
  public:
   __property System::Drawing::Size get_Size() {
      int legendHeight = chart->Font->Height + 4;
      Graphics* g = chart->CreateGraphics();
      int legendWidth = (int)g->MeasureString(Name, chart-            ↵
>Font).Width + 4;

      return System::Drawing::Size(legendWidth, legendHeight);
   }

  }; // class CurveLegend

private:
   CurveLegend*  legend1;
private:
   CurveLegend*  legend2;

public:
   ChartControl() {
      // The ChartControl draws the chart in the OnPaint .
      SetStyle(ControlStyles::ResizeRedraw, true);
      SetStyle(ControlStyles::DoubleBuffer, true);
      SetStyle(ControlStyles::AllPaintingInWmPaint, true);

      this->BackColor = System::Drawing::Color::White;
      this->Name = S"ChartControl";

      this->Click += new System::EventHandler(this,                    ↵
ChartControl_Click);
      this->QueryAccessibilityHelp += new                              ↵
System::Windows::Forms::QueryAccessibilityHelpEventHandler
 (this, ChartControl_QueryAccessibilityHelp);

      // The CurveLengend is not Control-based, it just
      // represents the parts of the legend.
      legend1 = new CurveLegend(this, S"A");
      legend1->Location = Point(20, 30);
      legend2 = new CurveLegend(this, S"B");
      legend2->Location = Point(20, 50);
   }

   // Overridden to return the custom AccessibleObject
   // for the entire chart.
protected:
   AccessibleObject* CreateAccessibilityInstance() {
      return new ChartControlAccessibleObject(this);
   }

protected:
   void OnPaint(PaintEventArgs* e) {
      // The ChartControl draws the chart in the OnPaint .
      System::Windows::Forms::UserControl::OnPaint(e);

      Rectangle bounds = this->ClientRectangle;
      int border = 5;

      // Draws the legends first.
      StringFormat* format = new StringFormat();
      format->Alignment = StringAlignment::Center;
      format->LineAlignment = StringAlignment::Center;

      if (legend1 != 0) {
         if (legend1->Selected) {
            e->Graphics->FillRectangle(new SolidBrush                  ↵
 (Color::Blue), legend1->Bounds);
         } else {
            e->Graphics->DrawRectangle(Pens::Blue, legend1->Bounds);
         }

         e->Graphics->DrawString(legend1->Name, this->Font,            ↵
Brushes::Black, RectangleF::op_Implicit(legend1->Bounds), format);
      }
      if (legend2 != 0) {
         if (legend2->Selected) {
            e->Graphics->FillRectangle(new SolidBrush                  ↵
 (Color::Red), legend2->Bounds);
         } else {
            e->Graphics->DrawRectangle(Pens::Red, legend2->Bounds);
         }
         e->Graphics->DrawString(legend2->Name, this->Font,            ↵
Brushes::Black, RectangleF::op_Implicit(legend2->Bounds), format);
      }

      // Charts [Out] the* actual curves that represent                ↵
data in the Chart.
      bounds.Inflate(-border, -border);
      Point temp1[] = {        Point(bounds.Left, bounds.Bottom),
         Point(bounds.Left + bounds.Width / 3, bounds.Top +            ↵
bounds.Height / 5),
         Point(bounds.Right - bounds.Width / 3, (bounds.Top            ↵
+ bounds.Bottom) / 2),
         Point(bounds.Right, bounds.Top)};
      Point curve1[] = temp1;

      Point temp2[] = {        Point(bounds.Left,                      ↵
bounds.Bottom - bounds.Height / 3),
         Point(bounds.Left + bounds.Width / 3, bounds.Top +            ↵
bounds.Height / 5),
         Point(bounds.Right - bounds.Width / 3, (bounds.Top +          ↵
bounds.Bottom) / 2),
         Point(bounds.Right, bounds.Top + bounds.Height / 2)};
      Point curve2[] = temp2;

      // Draws the actual curve only if it is selected.
      if (legend1->Selected) e->Graphics->DrawCurve(Pens::Blue,        ↵
 curve1);
      if (legend2->Selected) e->Graphics->DrawCurve(Pens::Red, curve2);

      e->Graphics->DrawRectangle(Pens::Blue, bounds);
   }
```

```
   // Handles the QueryAccessibilityHelp event.
private:
   void ChartControl_QueryAccessibilityHelp(Object* sender,
      System::Windows::Forms::QueryAccessibilityHelpEventArgs* e) {
         e->HelpString = S"Displays chart data";
      }

      // Handles the Click event for the chart.
      // Toggles the selection of whatever legend was clicked on
private:
   void ChartControl_Click(Object* sender, System::EventArgs* e) {
      Point pt = this->PointToClient(Control::MousePosition);
      if (legend1->Bounds.Contains(pt)) {
         legend1->Selected = !legend1->Selected;

      } else if (legend2->Bounds.Contains(pt)) {
         legend2->Selected = !legend2->Selected;
      }
   }

   // Gets an array of CurveLengends used in the Chart.
public:
   __property CurveLegend* get_Legends()[] {
      CurveLegend* temp3[] = { legend1, legend2 };
      return temp3;
   }

   // Inner class ChartControlAccessibleObject represents accessible information associated with the ChartControl.
   // The ChartControlAccessibleObject is returned in the ChartControl::CreateAccessibilityInstance .
public:
   __gc class ChartControlAccessibleObject : public ControlAccessibleObject {
      ChartControl* chartControl;

   public:
      ChartControlAccessibleObject(ChartControl* ctrl) : ControlAccessibleObject (ctrl) {
         chartControl = ctrl;
      }

      // Gets the role for the Chart. This is used by accessibility programs.
   public:
      __property System::Windows::Forms::AccessibleRole get_Role() {
         return AccessibleRole::Chart;
      }

      // Gets the state for the Chart. This is used by accessibility programs.
   public:
      __property AccessibleStates get_State() {
         return AccessibleStates::ReadOnly;
      }

      // The CurveLegend objects are S"child" controls in terms of accessibility so
      // return the number of ChartLengend objects.
   public:
      int GetChildCount() {
         return chartControl->Legends->Length;
      }

      // Gets the Accessibility Object* of the child CurveLegend idetified by index.
   public:
      AccessibleObject* GetChild(int index) {
         if (index >= 0 && index < chartControl->Legends->Length) {
            return chartControl->Legends[index]->AccessibilityObject;
         }
         return 0;
      }
```

```
      // Helper function that is used by the CurveLegend's accessibility Object*
      // to navigate between sibiling controls. Specifically, this function is used in
      // the CurveLegend::CurveLegendAccessibleObject.Navigate function.
   public private:
      AccessibleObject* NavigateFromChild(CurveLegend::CurveLegendAccessibleObject* child,
         AccessibleNavigation navdir) {
            switch(navdir) {
                  case AccessibleNavigation::Down:
                  case AccessibleNavigation::Next:
                     return GetChild(child->ID + 1);

                  case AccessibleNavigation::Up:
                  case AccessibleNavigation::Previous:
                     return GetChild(child->ID - 1);
            }
            return 0;
         }

         // Helper function that is used by the CurveLegend's accessibility Object*
         // to select a specific CurveLegend control. Specifically, this function is used
         // in the CurveLegend::CurveLegendAccessibleObject.Select function.
   public private:
      void SelectChild(CurveLegend::CurveLegendAccessibleObject* child, AccessibleSelection selection) {
         int childID = child->ID;

         // Determine which selection action should occur, based on the
         // AccessibleSelection value.
         if ((selection & AccessibleSelection::TakeSelection) != 0) {
            for (int i = 0; i < chartControl->Legends->Length; i++) {
               if (i == childID) {
                  chartControl->Legends[i]->Selected = true;
               } else {
                  chartControl->Legends[i]->Selected = false;
               }
            }

            // AccessibleSelection->AddSelection means that the CurveLegend will be selected.
            if ((selection & AccessibleSelection::AddSelection) != 0) {
               chartControl->Legends[childID]->Selected = true;
            }

            // AccessibleSelection->AddSelection means that the CurveLegend will be unselected.
            if ((selection & AccessibleSelection::RemoveSelection) != 0) {
               chartControl->Legends[childID]->Selected = false;
            }
         }
      }
   }; // class ChartControlAccessibleObject

}; // class ChartControl

public __gc class Form1 : public System::Windows::Forms::Form {
   // Test out the Chart Control.
private:
   ChartControl*  chart1;

public:
   Form1() {
      // Create a chart control and add it to the form.
      this->chart1 = new ChartControl();
      this->ClientSize = System::Drawing::Size(920, 566);
      this->chart1->Location = System::Drawing::Point(47, 16);
      this->chart1->Size = System::Drawing::Size(600, 400);
```

```
      this->Controls->Add(this->chart1);
   }
}; // class Form1
}
[STAThread]
int main() {
   Application::Run(new ChartControl::Form1());
}
```

Requirements

Namespace: **System.Windows.Forms**

Platforms: Windows 98, Windows NT 4.0, Windows Millennium Edition, Windows 2000, Windows XP Home Edition, Windows XP Professional, Windows Server 2003 family

Assembly: System.Windows.Forms (in System.Windows.Forms.dll)

AccessibleObject Constructor

Initializes a new instance of the **AccessibleObject** class.

[Visual Basic]
```
Public Sub New()
```
[C#]
```
public AccessibleObject();
```
[C++]
```
public: AccessibleObject();
```
[JScript]
```
public function AccessibleObject();
```

Remarks

Typically, when you use this method to create an accessible object, you are providing your own implementations of the properties and methods of the class to provide functionality specific to your application.

Requirements

Platforms: Windows 98, Windows NT 4.0, Windows Millennium Edition, Windows 2000, Windows XP Home Edition, Windows XP Professional, Windows Server 2003 family

AccessibleObject.Bounds Property

Gets the location and size of the accessible object.

[Visual Basic]
```
Public Overridable ReadOnly Property Bounds As Rectangle
```
[C#]
```
public virtual Rectangle Bounds {get;}
```
[C++]
```
public: __property virtual Rectangle get_Bounds();
```
[JScript]
```
public function get Bounds() : Rectangle;
```

Property Value

A **Rectangle** that represents the bounds of the accessible object.

Exceptions

Exception Type	Condition
COMException	The bounds of control cannot be retrieved.

Remarks

The **Bounds** property retrieves the object's bounding rectangle in screen coordinates. If the object has a nonrectangular shape, then this property represents the smallest rectangle that completely encompasses the entire object region. Therefore, for nonrectangular objects such as list view items, the coordinates of the object's bounding rectangle can fail, if tested, by calling the **HitTest** method, because **HitTest** determines the object's boundaries on a pixel-by-pixel basis.

Notes to Inheritors: The default implementation returns the accessible object's bounding rectangle if the object wraps a system control; otherwise, it returns **Rectangle.Empty**. All visible accessible objects must support this method. Sound objects do not support this method.

Example

See related example in the **System.Windows.Forms.AccessibleObject** class topic.

Requirements

Platforms: Windows 98, Windows NT 4.0, Windows Millennium Edition, Windows 2000, Windows XP Home Edition, Windows XP Professional, Windows Server 2003 family

AccessibleObject.DefaultAction Property

Gets a string that describes the default action of the object. Not all objects have a default action.

[Visual Basic]
```
Public Overridable ReadOnly Property DefaultAction As String
```
[C#]
```
public virtual string DefaultAction {get;}
```
[C++]
```
public: __property virtual String* get_DefaultAction();
```
[JScript]
```
public function get DefaultAction() : String;
```

Property Value

A description of the default action for an object, or a null reference (**Nothing** in Visual Basic) if this object has no default action.

Exceptions

Exception Type	Condition
COMException	The default action for the control cannot be retrieved.

Remarks

The string describes the action that is performed on an object, not what the object does as a result. That is, a toolbar button that prints a document has a default action of "Press" rather than "Prints the current document." Do not confuse an object's default action with its value.

Notes to Inheritors: The default implementation returns the accessible object's default action if the object wraps a system control that has a default action; otherwise, it returns a null reference (**Nothing** in Visual Basic). Only controls that perform actions should support this method. Not all objects have default actions, and some objects might have a default action that is related to its **Value** property, such as in the following examples: A selected check box has a default action of "Uncheck" and a value of "Checked." A cleared check box has a default action of "Check" and a value of "Unchecked." A button labeled "Print" has a default action of "Press," with no value. A static text control or an edit control that shows "Printer" has no default action, but would have a value of "Printer." An object's **DefaultAction** property should be a verb or a short verb phrase.

Requirements

Platforms: Windows 98, Windows NT 4.0, Windows Millennium Edition, Windows 2000, Windows XP Home Edition, Windows XP Professional, Windows Server 2003 family

AccessibleObject.Description Property

Gets a string that describes the visual appearance of the specified object. Not all objects have a description.

```
[Visual Basic]
Public Overridable ReadOnly Property Description As String
[C#]
public virtual string Description {get;}
[C++]
public: __property virtual String* get_Description();
[JScript]
public function get Description() : String;
```

Property Value

A description of the object's visual appearance to the user, or a null reference (**Nothing** in Visual Basic) if the object does not have a description.

Exceptions

Exception Type	Condition
COMException	The description for the control cannot be retrieved.

Remarks

This property describes the object's visual appearance to the user.

Notes to Inheritors: The default implementation returns the accessible object's description if the object wraps a system control; otherwise, it returns a null reference (**Nothing** in Visual Basic). The description is typically used to provide greater context for low-vision or blind users. It can also be used for context searching or other applications. Servers need to support the **Description** property if the description is not obvious, or if it is redundant based on the object's **Name**, **Role**, **State**, and **Value** properties. For example, a button with "OK" does not need additional information, but a button that shows a picture of a cactus would. The **Name**, **Role**, and perhaps **Help** properties for the cactus button describe its purpose, but the **Description** property conveys information that is less tangible, like "A button that shows a picture of a cactus".

Requirements

Platforms: Windows 98, Windows NT 4.0, Windows Millennium Edition, Windows 2000, Windows XP Home Edition, Windows XP Professional, Windows Server 2003 family

AccessibleObject.Help Property

Gets a description of what the object does or how the object is used.

```
[Visual Basic]
Public Overridable ReadOnly Property Help As String
[C#]
public virtual string Help {get;}
[C++]
public: __property virtual String* get_Help();
[JScript]
public function get Help() : String;
```

Property Value

A **String** that contains the description of what the object does or how the object is used. Returns a null reference (**Nothing** in Visual Basic) if no help is defined.

Exceptions

Exception Type	Condition
COMException	The help string for the control cannot be retrieved.

Remarks

Notes to Inheritors: Not all objects need to support this property. Typically, this property contains ToolTip style information that is used either to describe what the object does or how to use it. For example, the **Help** property for a toolbar button that shows a printer might be "Prints the current document." The text for the **Help** property does not have to be unique within the user interface. Servers do not need to support the **Help** property if other properties provide sufficient information about the object's purpose and what actions the object might perform.

Requirements

Platforms: Windows 98, Windows NT 4.0, Windows Millennium Edition, Windows 2000, Windows XP Home Edition, Windows XP Professional, Windows Server 2003 family

AccessibleObject.KeyboardShortcut Property

Gets the shortcut key or access key for the accessible object.

```
[Visual Basic]
Public Overridable ReadOnly Property KeyboardShortcut As String
[C#]
public virtual string KeyboardShortcut {get;}
[C++]
public: __property virtual String* get_KeyboardShortcut();
[JScript]
public function get KeyboardShortcut() : String;
```

Property Value

The shortcut key or access key for the accessible object, or a null reference (**Nothing** in Visual Basic) if there is no shortcut key associated with the object.

Exceptions

Exception Type	Condition
COMException	The shortcut for the control cannot be retrieved.

Remarks

An access key, also known as a mnemonic, is an underlined character in the text of a menu, menu item, label of a button, or some other control. For example, a user can display a menu by pressing the ALT key while also pressing the indicated underlined key, such as ALT+F, to open the **File** menu. To use the access key of a menu item, the menu containing the item must be active. Controls such as toolbar buttons and menu items often have an associated shortcut key. A menu item can have both an access key and a shortcut key associated with it. If the value of the **KeyboardShortcut** property is a single character, you can assume it is an access key.

Notes to Inheritors: All objects that have a shortcut key or access key should support this property.

Requirements

Platforms: Windows 98, Windows NT 4.0, Windows Millennium Edition, Windows 2000, Windows XP Home Edition, Windows XP Professional, Windows Server 2003 family

AccessibleObject.Name Property

Gets or sets the object name.

[Visual Basic]
```
Public Overridable Property Name As String
```
[C#]
```
public virtual string Name {get; set;}
```
[C++]
```
public: __property virtual String* get_Name();
public: __property virtual void set_Name(String*);
```
[JScript]
```
public function get Name() : String;
public function set Name(String);
```

Property Value

The object name, or a null reference (**Nothing** in Visual Basic) if the property has not been set.

Exceptions

Exception Type	Condition
COMException	The name of the control cannot be retrieved or set.

Remarks

The **Name** property is a string used by clients to identify, find, or announce an object for the user. To access the name of a child object, you must first call **GetChild** with the index of the child whose name you are retrieving.

Notes to Inheritors: All objects should support this property. An object's name should be intuitive so that users understand the object's meaning or purpose. Also, ensure that the **Name** property is unique relative to any sibling objects in the parent. Navigation within tables presents especially difficult problems for some users. Therefore, server developers should make table cell names as descriptive as possible. For example, you might create a cell name by combining the names of the row and column it occupies, such as "A1." However, it is generally better to use more descriptive names, such as "Karin, February." Many objects, such as icons, menus, check boxes, combo boxes, and other controls, have labels that are displayed to users. Any label displayed to users should be used for the object's **Name** property. For more information, see the **Name** Property.

If you are using menu or button text for the **Name** property, strip out the ampersands (&) that mark the keyboard access keys.

Example

See related example in the **System.Windows.Forms.AccessibleObject** class topic.

Requirements

Platforms: Windows 98, Windows NT 4.0, Windows Millennium Edition, Windows 2000, Windows XP Home Edition, Windows XP Professional, Windows Server 2003 family

AccessibleObject.Parent Property

Gets the parent of an accessible object.

[Visual Basic]
```
Public Overridable ReadOnly Property Parent As AccessibleObject
```
[C#]
```
public virtual AccessibleObject Parent {get;}
```
[C++]
```
public: __property virtual AccessibleObject* get_Parent();
```
[JScript]
```
public function get Parent() : AccessibleObject;
```

Property Value

An **AccessibleObject** that represents the parent of an accessible object, or a null reference (**Nothing** in Visual Basic) if there is no parent object.

Remarks

Notes to Inheritors: All objects should support this property.

Example

See related example in the **System.Windows.Forms.AccessibleObject** class topic.

Requirements

Platforms: Windows 98, Windows NT 4.0, Windows Millennium Edition, Windows 2000, Windows XP Home Edition, Windows XP Professional, Windows Server 2003 family

AccessibleObject.Role Property

Gets the role of this accessible object.

[Visual Basic]
```
Public Overridable ReadOnly Property Role As AccessibleRole
```
[C#]
```
public virtual AccessibleRole Role {get;}
```
[C++]
```
public: __property virtual AccessibleRole get_Role();
```
[JScript]
```
public function get Role() : AccessibleRole;
```

Property Value

One of the **AccessibleRole** values, or **AccessibleRole.None** if no role has been specified.

Remarks

The role of the object helps describe the function of the object.

Notes to Inheritors: All objects should support this property.

Example

See related example in the **System.Windows.Forms.AccessibleObject** class topic.

Requirements

Platforms: Windows 98, Windows NT 4.0, Windows Millennium Edition, Windows 2000, Windows XP Home Edition, Windows XP Professional, Windows Server 2003 family

AccessibleObject.State Property

Gets the state of this accessible object.

[Visual Basic]
```
Public Overridable ReadOnly Property State As AccessibleStates
```
[C#]
```
public virtual AccessibleStates State {get;}
```
[C++]
```
public: __property virtual AccessibleStates get_State();
```
[JScript]
```
public function get State() : AccessibleStates;
```

Property Value

One of the **AccessibleStates** values, or **AccessibleStates.None**, if no state has been set.

Remarks

Notes to Inheritors: All objects should support this property.

Example

See related example in the **System.Windows.Forms.AccessibleObject** class topic.

Requirements

Platforms: Windows 98, Windows NT 4.0, Windows Millennium Edition, Windows 2000, Windows XP Home Edition, Windows XP Professional, Windows Server 2003 family

AccessibleObject.Value Property

Gets or sets the value of an accessible object.

[Visual Basic]
```
Public Overridable Property Value As String
```
[C#]
```
public virtual string Value {get; set;}
```
[C++]
```
public: __property virtual String* get_Value();
public: __property virtual void set_Value(String*);
```
[JScript]
```
public function get Value() : String;
public function set Value(String);
```

Property Value

The value of an accessible object, or a null reference (**Nothing** in Visual Basic) if the object has no value set.

Exceptions

Exception Type	Condition
COMException	The value cannot be set or retrieved.

Remarks

Typically, the **Value** property represents visual information contained by the object. Not all objects support the **Value** property.

In most cases, the **Value** property is used to tell the client about what visual information an object contains. For example, the value for an edit control is the text it contains, but a menu item has no value.

The **Value** property can provide hierarchical information in cases such as a tree view control. Although the parent object in the tree view control does not provide information in the **Value** property, each item within the control has a zero-based value that represents its level within the hierarchy. Top-level items have a value of zero, second-level items have a value of one, and so on.

Note The values returned from scroll bar and trackbar accessible objects indicate percentages, so they are integers between 0 and 100, inclusive.

Requirements

Platforms: Windows 98, Windows NT 4.0, Windows Millennium Edition, Windows 2000, Windows XP Home Edition, Windows XP Professional, Windows Server 2003 family

AccessibleObject.DoDefaultAction Method

Performs the default action associated with this accessible object.

[Visual Basic]
```
Public Overridable Sub DoDefaultAction()
```
[C#]
```
public virtual void DoDefaultAction();
```
[C++]
```
public: virtual void DoDefaultAction();
```
[JScript]
```
public function DoDefaultAction();
```

Exceptions

Exception Type	Condition
COMException	The default action for the control cannot be performed.

Remarks

Clients can retrieve the object's default action by inspecting an object's **DefaultAction** property. A client can use automation (if supported) instead of **DoDefaultAction** to perform an object's default action. However, **DoDefaultAction** provides an easy way to perform an object's most commonly used action.

Notes to Inheritors: The default action performed by system-provided user interface elements depends on the keyboard state. That is, if a modifier key such as SHIFT, ALT, or CTRL is down (either by a user action or programmatically) when **DoDefaultAction** is called, the default action might not be the same as when those keys are not down. Not all objects have a default action.

Requirements

Platforms: Windows 98, Windows NT 4.0, Windows Millennium Edition, Windows 2000, Windows XP Home Edition, Windows XP Professional, Windows Server 2003 family

AccessibleObject.GetChild Method

Retrieves the accessible child corresponding to the specified index.

[Visual Basic]
```
Public Overridable Function GetChild( _
   ByVal index As Integer _
) As AccessibleObject
```
[C#]
```
public virtual AccessibleObject GetChild(
   int index
);
```
[C++]
```
public: virtual AccessibleObject* GetChild(
   int index
);
```

```
[JScript]
public function GetChild(
   index : int
) : AccessibleObject;
```

Parameters

index

The zero-based index of the accessible child.

Return Value

An **AccessibleObject** that represents the accessible child corresponding to the specified index.

Remarks

Notes to Inheritors: All accessible objects must support this property. If the method is not overridden, it returns a null reference (**Nothing** in Visual Basic). Override this method when an accessible object needs to provide custom accessible children. If the index is invalid, then this method should return a null reference (**Nothing**). When you override this method, you must also override **GetChildCount**.

Example

See related example in the **System.Windows.Forms.AccessibleObject** class topic.

Requirements

Platforms: Windows 98, Windows NT 4.0, Windows Millennium Edition, Windows 2000, Windows XP Home Edition, Windows XP Professional, Windows Server 2003 family

AccessibleObject.GetChildCount Method

Retrieves the number of children belonging to an accessible object.

```
[Visual Basic]
Public Overridable Function GetChildCount() As Integer
[C#]
public virtual int GetChildCount();
[C++]
public: virtual int GetChildCount();
[JScript]
public function GetChildCount() : int;
```

Return Value

The number of children belonging to an accessible object.

Remarks

Notes to Inheritors: All objects must support this property. The default implementation returns -1. Override this method when an accessible object needs to provide custom accessible children. When you override this method, you must also override **GetChild**.

Example

See related example in the **System.Windows.Forms.AccessibleObject** class topic.

Requirements

Platforms: Windows 98, Windows NT 4.0, Windows Millennium Edition, Windows 2000, Windows XP Home Edition, Windows XP Professional, Windows Server 2003 family

AccessibleObject.GetFocused Method

Retrieves the object that has the keyboard focus.

```
[Visual Basic]
Public Overridable Function GetFocused() As AccessibleObject
[C#]
public virtual AccessibleObject GetFocused();
[C++]
public: virtual AccessibleObject* GetFocused();
[JScript]
public function GetFocused() : AccessibleObject;
```

Return Value

An **AccessibleObject** that specifies the currently focused child. This method returns the calling object if the object itself is focused. Returns a null reference (**Nothing** in Visual Basic) if no object has focus.

Exceptions

Exception Type	Condition
COMException	The control cannot be retrieved.

Remarks

The concept of keyboard focus is related to that of an active window. An active window is the foreground window in which the user is working. The object with the keyboard focus is either the active window or a child object of the active window.

Only one object or item within a container can have the focus at any one time. The object with the keyboard focus is not necessarily the selected object.

Notes to Inheritors: All objects that can receive the keyboard focus must support this property.

Requirements

Platforms: Windows 98, Windows NT 4.0, Windows Millennium Edition, Windows 2000, Windows XP Home Edition, Windows XP Professional, Windows Server 2003 family

AccessibleObject.GetHelpTopic Method

Gets an identifier for a Help topic identifier and the path to the Help file associated with this accessible object.

```
[Visual Basic]
Public Overridable Function GetHelpTopic( _
   <Out()> ByRef fileName As String _
) As Integer
[C#]
public virtual int GetHelpTopic(
   out string fileName
);
[C++]
public: virtual int GetHelpTopic(
   [
   Out
] String** fileName
);
[JScript]
public function GetHelpTopic(
   fileName : String
) : int;
```

Parameters

fileName

On return, this property contains the path to the Help file associated with this accessible object.

Return Value

An identifier for a Help topic, or -1 if there is no Help topic. On return, the *fileName* parameter contains the path to the Help file associated with this accessible object.

Exceptions

Exception Type	Condition
COMException	The Help topic for the control cannot be retrieved.

Remarks

To display help for the **AccessibleObject** using the Windows Help system, you can pass the file name and topic ID to the appropriate **Help.ShowHelp** method of **Help**.

Notes to Inheritors: Not all objects need to support this property.

Requirements

Platforms: Windows 98, Windows NT 4.0, Windows Millennium Edition, Windows 2000, Windows XP Home Edition, Windows XP Professional, Windows Server 2003 family

AccessibleObject.GetSelected Method

Retrieves the currently selected child.

```
[Visual Basic]
Public Overridable Function GetSelected() As AccessibleObject
[C#]
public virtual AccessibleObject GetSelected();
[C++]
public: virtual AccessibleObject* GetSelected();
[JScript]
public function GetSelected() : AccessibleObject;
```

Return Value

An **AccessibleObject** that represents the currently selected child. This method returns the calling object if the object itself is selected. Returns a null reference (**Nothing** in Visual Basic) if is no child is currently selected and the object itself does not have focus.

Exceptions

Exception Type	Condition
COMException	The selected child cannot be retrieved.

Remarks

Notes to Inheritors: All objects that can be selected should support this property.

Requirements

Platforms: Windows 98, Windows NT 4.0, Windows Millennium Edition, Windows 2000, Windows XP Home Edition, Windows XP Professional, Windows Server 2003 family

AccessibleObject.HitTest Method

Retrieves the child object at the specified screen coordinates.

```
[Visual Basic]
Public Overridable Function HitTest( _
   ByVal x As Integer, _
   ByVal y As Integer _
) As AccessibleObject
[C#]
public virtual AccessibleObject HitTest(
   int x,
   int y
);
[C++]
public: virtual AccessibleObject* HitTest(
   int x,
   int y
);
[JScript]
public function HitTest(
   x : int,
   y : int
) : AccessibleObject;
```

Parameters

x

The horizontal screen coordinate.

y

The vertical screen coordinate.

Return Value

An **AccessibleObject** that represents the child object at the given screen coordinates. This method returns the calling object if the object itself is at the location specified. Returns a null reference (**Nothing** in Visual Basic) if no object is at the tested location.

Exceptions

Exception Type	Condition
COMException	The control cannot be hit tested.

Remarks

For nonrectangular objects such as list view items, the coordinates of the object's bounding rectangle retrieved by **Bounds** can fail if tested with **HitTest**, because **HitTest** determines the object's boundaries on a pixel-by-pixel basis.

Notes to Inheritors: All visual objects must support this method; sound objects do not support it.

Requirements

Platforms: Windows 98, Windows NT 4.0, Windows Millennium Edition, Windows 2000, Windows XP Home Edition, Windows XP Professional, Windows Server 2003 family

AccessibleObject.IAccessible.accDoDefault-Action Method

This member supports the .NET Framework infrastructure and is not intended to be used directly from your code.

```
[Visual Basic]
Private Sub accDoDefaultAction( _
   ByVal childID As Object _
) Implements IAccessible.accDoDefaultAction
```

```
[C#]
void IAccessible.accDoDefaultAction(
   object childID
);
[C++]
private: void IAccessible::accDoDefaultAction(
   Object* childID
);
[JScript]
private function IAccessible.accDoDefaultAction(
   childID : Object
);
```

AccessibleObject.IAccessible.accHitTest Method

This member supports the .NET Framework infrastructure and is not intended to be used directly from your code.

```
[Visual Basic]
Private Function accHitTest( _
   ByVal xLeft As Integer, _
   ByVal yTop As Integer _
) As Object Implements IAccessible.accHitTest
[C#]
object IAccessible.accHitTest(
   int xLeft,
   int yTop
);
[C++]
private: Object* IAccessible::accHitTest(
   int xLeft,
   int yTop
);
[JScript]
private function IAccessible.accHitTest(
   xLeft : int,
   yTop : int
) : Object;
```

AccessibleObject.IAccessible.accLocation Method

This member supports the .NET Framework infrastructure and is not intended to be used directly from your code.

```
[Visual Basic]
Private Sub accLocation( _
   <Out()> ByRef pxLeft As Integer, _
   <Out()> ByRef pyTop As Integer, _
   <Out()> ByRef pcxWidth As Integer, _
   <Out()> ByRef pcyHeight As Integer, _
   ByVal childID As Object _
) Implements IAccessible.accLocation
[C#]
void IAccessible.accLocation(
   out int pxLeft,
   out int pyTop,
   out int pcxWidth,
   out int pcyHeight,
   object childID
);
[C++]
private: void IAccessible::accLocation(
   [
   Out
] int* pxLeft,
   [
   Out
] int* pyTop,
   [
   Out
] int* pcxWidth,
   [
   Out
] int* pcyHeight,
   Object* childID
);
[JScript]
private function IAccessible.accLocation(
   pxLeft : int,
   pyTop : int,
   pcxWidth : int,
   pcyHeight : int,
   childID : Object
);
```

AccessibleObject.IAccessible.accNavigate Method

This member supports the .NET Framework infrastructure and is not intended to be used directly from your code.

```
[Visual Basic]
Private Function accNavigate( _
   ByVal navDir As Integer, _
   ByVal childID As Object _
) As Object Implements IAccessible.accNavigate
[C#]
object IAccessible.accNavigate(
   int navDir,
   object childID
);
[C++]
private: Object* IAccessible::accNavigate(
   int navDir,
   Object* childID
);
[JScript]
private function IAccessible.accNavigate(
   navDir : int,
   childID : Object
) : Object;
```

AccessibleObject.IAccessible.accSelect Method

This member supports the .NET Framework infrastructure and is not intended to be used directly from your code.

```
[Visual Basic]
Private Sub accSelect( _
   ByVal flagsSelect As Integer, _
   ByVal childID As Object _
) Implements IAccessible.accSelect
```

```
[C#]
void IAccessible.accSelect(
   int flagsSelect,
   object childID
);
[C++]
private: void IAccessible::accSelect(
   int flagsSelect,
   Object* childID
);
[JScript]
private function IAccessible.accSelect(
   flagsSelect : int,
   childID : Object
);
```

AccessibleObject.IAccessible.get_accChild Method

This member supports the .NET Framework infrastructure and is not intended to be used directly from your code.

```
[Visual Basic]
Private Function get_accChild( _
   ByVal childID As Object _
) As Object Implements IAccessible.get_accChild
[C#]
object IAccessible.get_accChild(
   object childID
);
[C++]
private: Object* IAccessible::get_accChild(
   Object* childID
);
[JScript]
private function IAccessible.get_accChild(
   childID : Object
) : Object;
```

AccessibleObject.IAccessible.get_accDefault-Action Method

This member supports the .NET Framework infrastructure and is not intended to be used directly from your code.

```
[Visual Basic]
Private Function get_accDefaultAction( _
   ByVal childID As Object _
) As String Implements IAccessible.get_accDefaultAction
[C#]
string IAccessible.get_accDefaultAction(
   object childID
);
[C++]
private: String* IAccessible::get_accDefaultAction(
   Object* childID
);
[JScript]
private function IAccessible.get_accDefaultAction(
   childID : Object
) : String;
```

AccessibleObject.IAccessible.get_acc-Description Method

This member supports the .NET Framework infrastructure and is not intended to be used directly from your code.

```
[Visual Basic]
Private Function get_accDescription( _
   ByVal childID As Object _
) As String Implements IAccessible.get_accDescription
[C#]
string IAccessible.get_accDescription(
   object childID
);
[C++]
private: String* IAccessible::get_accDescription(
   Object* childID
);
[JScript]
private function IAccessible.get_accDescription(
   childID : Object
) : String;
```

AccessibleObject.IAccessible.get_accHelp Method

This member supports the .NET Framework infrastructure and is not intended to be used directly from your code.

```
[Visual Basic]
Private Function get_accHelp( _
   ByVal childID As Object _
) As String Implements IAccessible.get_accHelp
[C#]
string IAccessible.get_accHelp(
   object childID
);
[C++]
private: String* IAccessible::get_accHelp(
   Object* childID
);
[JScript]
private function IAccessible.get_accHelp(
   childID : Object
) : String;
```

AccessibleObject.IAccessible.get_accHelp-Topic Method

This member supports the .NET Framework infrastructure and is not intended to be used directly from your code.

```
[Visual Basic]
Private Function get_accHelpTopic( _
   <Out()> ByRef pszHelpFile As String, _
   ByVal childID As Object _
) As Integer Implements IAccessible.get_accHelpTopic
[C#]
int IAccessible.get_accHelpTopic(
   out string pszHelpFile,
   object childID
);
```

```
[C++]
private: int IAccessible::get_accHelpTopic(
   [
   Out
] String** pszHelpFile,
   Object* childID
);
[JScript]
private function IAccessible.get_accHelpTopic(
   pszHelpFile : String,
   childID : Object
) : int;
```

AccessibleObject.IAccessible.get_accKeyboard-Shortcut Method

This member supports the .NET Framework infrastructure and is not intended to be used directly from your code.

```
[Visual Basic]
Private Function get_accKeyboardShortcut( _
   ByVal childID As Object _
) As String Implements IAccessible.get_accKeyboardShortcut
[C#]
string IAccessible.get_accKeyboardShortcut(
   object childID
);
[C++]
private: String* IAccessible::get_accKeyboardShortcut(
   Object* childID
);
[JScript]
private function IAccessible.get_accKeyboardShortcut(
   childID : Object
) : String;
```

AccessibleObject.IAccessible.get_accName Method

This member supports the .NET Framework infrastructure and is not intended to be used directly from your code.

```
[Visual Basic]
Private Function get_accName( _
   ByVal childID As Object _
) As String Implements IAccessible.get_accName
[C#]
string IAccessible.get_accName(
   object childID
);
[C++]
private: String* IAccessible::get_accName(
   Object* childID
);
[JScript]
private function IAccessible.get_accName(
   childID : Object
) : String;
```

AccessibleObject.IAccessible.get_accRole Method

This member supports the .NET Framework infrastructure and is not intended to be used directly from your code.

```
[Visual Basic]
Private Function get_accRole( _
   ByVal childID As Object _
) As Object Implements IAccessible.get_accRole
[C#]
object IAccessible.get_accRole(
   object childID
);
[C++]
private: Object* IAccessible::get_accRole(
   Object* childID
);
[JScript]
private function IAccessible.get_accRole(
   childID : Object
) : Object;
```

AccessibleObject.IAccessible.get_accState Method

This member supports the .NET Framework infrastructure and is not intended to be used directly from your code.

```
[Visual Basic]
Private Function get_accState( _
   ByVal childID As Object _
) As Object Implements IAccessible.get_accState
[C#]
object IAccessible.get_accState(
   object childID
);
[C++]
private: Object* IAccessible::get_accState(
   Object* childID
);
[JScript]
private function IAccessible.get_accState(
   childID : Object
) : Object;
```

AccessibleObject.IAccessible.get_accValue Method

This member supports the .NET Framework infrastructure and is not intended to be used directly from your code.

```
[Visual Basic]
Private Function get_accValue( _
   ByVal childID As Object _
) As String Implements IAccessible.get_accValue
[C#]
string IAccessible.get_accValue(
   object childID
);
[C++]
private: String* IAccessible::get_accValue(
   Object* childID
);
```

```
[JScript]
private function IAccessible.get_accValue(
   childID : Object
) : String;
```

AccessibleObject.IAccessible.set_accName Method

This member supports the .NET Framework infrastructure and is not intended to be used directly from your code.

```
[Visual Basic]
Private Sub set_accName( _
   ByVal childID As Object, _
   ByVal newName As String _
) Implements IAccessible.set_accName
[C#]
void IAccessible.set_accName(
   object childID,
   string newName
);
[C++]
private: void IAccessible::set_accName(
   Object* childID,
   String* newName
);
[JScript]
private function IAccessible.set_accName(
   childID : Object,
   newName : String
);
```

AccessibleObject.IAccessible.set_accValue Method

This member supports the .NET Framework infrastructure and is not intended to be used directly from your code.

```
[Visual Basic]
Private Sub set_accValue( _
   ByVal childID As Object, _
   ByVal newValue As String _
) Implements IAccessible.set_accValue
[C#]
void IAccessible.set_accValue(
   object childID,
   string newValue
);
[C++]
private: void IAccessible::set_accValue(
   Object* childID,
   String* newValue
);
[JScript]
private function IAccessible.set_accValue(
   childID : Object,
   newValue : String
);
```

AccessibleObject.IReflect.GetField Method

This member supports the .NET Framework infrastructure and is not intended to be used directly from your code.

```
[Visual Basic]
Private Function GetField( _
   ByVal name As String, _
   ByVal bindingAttr As BindingFlags _
) As FieldInfo Implements IReflect.GetField
[C#]
FieldInfo IReflect.GetField(
   string name,
   BindingFlags bindingAttr
);
[C++]
private: FieldInfo* IReflect::GetField(
   String* name,
   BindingFlags bindingAttr
);
[JScript]
private function IReflect.GetField(
   name : String,
   bindingAttr : BindingFlags
) : FieldInfo;
```

AccessibleObject.IReflect.GetFields Method

This member supports the .NET Framework infrastructure and is not intended to be used directly from your code.

```
[Visual Basic]
Private Function GetFields( _
   ByVal bindingAttr As BindingFlags _
) As FieldInfo() Implements IReflect.GetFields
[C#]
FieldInfo[] IReflect.GetFields(
   BindingFlags bindingAttr
);
[C++]
private: FieldInfo* IReflect::GetFields(
   BindingFlags bindingAttr
) [];
[JScript]
private function IReflect.GetFields(
   bindingAttr : BindingFlags
) : FieldInfo[];
```

AccessibleObject.IReflect.GetMember Method

This member supports the .NET Framework infrastructure and is not intended to be used directly from your code.

```
[Visual Basic]
Private Function GetMember( _
   ByVal name As String, _
   ByVal bindingAttr As BindingFlags _
) As MemberInfo() Implements IReflect.GetMember
[C#]
MemberInfo[] IReflect.GetMember(
   string name,
   BindingFlags bindingAttr
);
```

```
[C++]
private: MemberInfo* IReflect::GetMember(
   String* name,
   BindingFlags bindingAttr
) [];
[JScript]
private function IReflect.GetMember(
   name : String,
   bindingAttr : BindingFlags
) : MemberInfo[];
```

AccessibleObject.IReflect.GetMembers Method

This member supports the .NET Framework infrastructure and is not intended to be used directly from your code.

```
[Visual Basic]
Private Function GetMembers( _
   ByVal bindingAttr As BindingFlags _
) As MemberInfo() Implements IReflect.GetMembers
[C#]
MemberInfo[] IReflect.GetMembers(
   BindingFlags bindingAttr
);
[C++]
private: MemberInfo* IReflect::GetMembers(
   BindingFlags bindingAttr
) [];
[JScript]
private function IReflect.GetMembers(
   bindingAttr : BindingFlags
) : MemberInfo[];
```

AccessibleObject.IReflect.GetMethod Method

This member supports the .NET Framework infrastructure and is not intended to be used directly from your code.

Overload List

This member supports the .NET Framework infrastructure and is not intended to be used directly from your code.

[Visual Basic] **Overloads Private Function GetMethod(String, BindingFlags) As MethodInfo Implements IReflect.GetMethod**

[C#] **MethodInfo IReflect.GetMethod(string, BindingFlags);**

[C++] **private: MethodInfo* IReflect::GetMethod(String*, BindingFlags);**

[JScript] **private function IReflect.GetMethod(String, BindingFlags) : MethodInfo;**

This member supports the .NET Framework infrastructure and is not intended to be used directly from your code.

[Visual Basic] **Overloads Private Function GetMethod(String, BindingFlags, Binder, Type(), ParameterModifier()) As MethodInfo Implements IReflect.GetMethod**

[C#] **MethodInfo IReflect.GetMethod(string, BindingFlags, Binder, Type[], ParameterModifier[]);**

[C++] **private: MethodInfo* IReflect::GetMethod(String*, BindingFlags, Binder*, Type[], ParameterModifier[]);**

[JScript] **private function IReflect.GetMethod(String, BindingFlags, Binder, Type[], ParameterModifier[]) : MethodInfo;**

AccessibleObject.IReflect.GetMethod Method (String, BindingFlags)

This member supports the .NET Framework infrastructure and is not intended to be used directly from your code.

```
[Visual Basic]
Private Function GetMethod( _
   ByVal name As String, _
   ByVal bindingAttr As BindingFlags _
) As MethodInfo Implements IReflect.GetMethod
[C#]
MethodInfo IReflect.GetMethod(
   string name,
   BindingFlags bindingAttr
);
[C++]
private: MethodInfo* IReflect::GetMethod(
   String* name,
   BindingFlags bindingAttr
);
[JScript]
private function IReflect.GetMethod(
   name : String,
   bindingAttr : BindingFlags
) : MethodInfo;
```

AccessibleObject.IReflect.GetMethod Method (String, BindingFlags, Binder, Type[], ParameterModifier[])

This member supports the .NET Framework infrastructure and is not intended to be used directly from your code.

```
[Visual Basic]
Private Function GetMethod( _
   ByVal name As String, _
   ByVal bindingAttr As BindingFlags, _
   ByVal binder As Binder, _
   ByVal types() As Type, _
   ByVal modifiers() As ParameterModifier _
) As MethodInfo Implements IReflect.GetMethod
[C#]
MethodInfo IReflect.GetMethod(
   string name,
   BindingFlags bindingAttr,
   Binder binder,
   Type[] types,
   ParameterModifier[] modifiers
);
[C++]
private: MethodInfo* IReflect::GetMethod(
   String* name,
   BindingFlags bindingAttr,
   Binder* binder,
   Type* types[],
   ParameterModifier modifiers[]
);
[JScript]
private function IReflect.GetMethod(
   name : String,
   bindingAttr : BindingFlags,
   binder : Binder,
   types : Type[],
   modifiers : ParameterModifier[]
) : MethodInfo;
```

AccessibleObject.IReflect.GetMethods Method

This member supports the .NET Framework infrastructure and is not intended to be used directly from your code.

[Visual Basic]
```
Private Function GetMethods( _
   ByVal bindingAttr As BindingFlags _
) As MethodInfo() Implements IReflect.GetMethods
```
[C#]
```
MethodInfo[] IReflect.GetMethods(
   BindingFlags bindingAttr
);
```
[C++]
```
private: MethodInfo* IReflect::GetMethods(
   BindingFlags bindingAttr
) [];
```
[JScript]
```
private function IReflect.GetMethods(
   bindingAttr : BindingFlags
) : MethodInfo[];
```

AccessibleObject.IReflect.GetProperties Method

This member supports the .NET Framework infrastructure and is not intended to be used directly from your code.

[Visual Basic]
```
Private Function GetProperties( _
   ByVal bindingAttr As BindingFlags _
) As PropertyInfo() Implements IReflect.GetProperties
```
[C#]
```
PropertyInfo[] IReflect.GetProperties(
   BindingFlags bindingAttr
);
```
[C++]
```
private: PropertyInfo* IReflect::GetProperties(
   BindingFlags bindingAttr
) [];
```
[JScript]
```
private function IReflect.GetProperties(
   bindingAttr : BindingFlags
) : PropertyInfo[];
```

AccessibleObject.IReflect.GetProperty Method

This member supports the .NET Framework infrastructure and is not intended to be used directly from your code.

Overload List

This member supports the .NET Framework infrastructure and is not intended to be used directly from your code.

[Visual Basic] **Overloads Private Function GetProperty(String, BindingFlags) As PropertyInfo Implements IReflect.GetProperty**

[C#] **PropertyInfo IReflect.GetProperty(string, BindingFlags);**

[C++] **private: PropertyInfo* IReflect::GetProperty(String*, BindingFlags);**

[JScript] **private function IReflect.GetProperty(String, BindingFlags) : PropertyInfo;**

This member supports the .NET Framework infrastructure and is not intended to be used directly from your code.

[Visual Basic] **Overloads Private Function GetProperty(String, BindingFlags, Binder, Type, Type(), ParameterModifier()) As PropertyInfo Implements IReflect.GetProperty**

[C#] **PropertyInfo IReflect.GetProperty(string, BindingFlags, Binder, Type, Type[], ParameterModifier[]);**

[C++] **private: PropertyInfo* IReflect::GetProperty(String*, BindingFlags, Binder*, Type*, Type[], ParameterModifier[]);**

[JScript] **private function IReflect.GetProperty(String, BindingFlags, Binder, Type, Type[], ParameterModifier[]) : PropertyInfo;**

AccessibleObject.IReflect.GetProperty Method (String, BindingFlags)

This member supports the .NET Framework infrastructure and is not intended to be used directly from your code.

[Visual Basic]
```
Private Function GetProperty( _
   ByVal name As String, _
   ByVal bindingAttr As BindingFlags _
) As PropertyInfo Implements IReflect.GetProperty
```
[C#]
```
PropertyInfo IReflect.GetProperty(
   string name,
   BindingFlags bindingAttr
);
```
[C++]
```
private: PropertyInfo* IReflect::GetProperty(
   String* name,
   BindingFlags bindingAttr
);
```
[JScript]
```
private function IReflect.GetProperty(
   name : String,
   bindingAttr : BindingFlags
) : PropertyInfo;
```

AccessibleObject.IReflect.GetProperty Method (String, BindingFlags, Binder, Type, Type[], ParameterModifier[])

This member supports the .NET Framework infrastructure and is not intended to be used directly from your code.

[Visual Basic]
```
Private Function GetProperty( _
   ByVal name As String, _
   ByVal bindingAttr As BindingFlags, _
   ByVal binder As Binder, _
   ByVal returnType As Type, _
   ByVal types() As Type, _
   ByVal modifiers() As ParameterModifier _
) As PropertyInfo Implements IReflect.GetProperty
```
[C#]
```
PropertyInfo IReflect.GetProperty(
   string name,
   BindingFlags bindingAttr,
   Binder binder,
   Type returnType,
   Type[] types,
   ParameterModifier[] modifiers
);
```

[C++]
```
private: PropertyInfo* IReflect::GetProperty(
   String* name,
   BindingFlags bindingAttr,
   Binder* binder,
   Type* returnType,
   Type* types[],
   ParameterModifier modifiers[]
);
```
[JScript]
```
private function IReflect.GetProperty(
   name : String,
   bindingAttr : BindingFlags,
   binder : Binder,
   returnType : Type,
   types : Type[],
   modifiers : ParameterModifier[]
) : PropertyInfo;
```

AccessibleObject.IReflect.InvokeMember Method

This member supports the .NET Framework infrastructure and is not intended to be used directly from your code.

[Visual Basic]
```
Private Function InvokeMember( _
   ByVal name As String, _
   ByVal invokeAttr As BindingFlags, _
   ByVal binder As Binder, _
   ByVal target As Object, _
   ByVal args() As Object, _
   ByVal modifiers() As ParameterModifier, _
   ByVal culture As CultureInfo, _
   ByVal namedParameters() As String _
) As Object Implements IReflect.InvokeMember
```
[C#]
```
object IReflect.InvokeMember(
   string name,
   BindingFlags invokeAttr,
   Binder binder,
   object target,
   object[] args,
   ParameterModifier[] modifiers,
   CultureInfo culture,
   string[] namedParameters
);
```
[C++]
```
private: Object* IReflect::InvokeMember(
   String* name,
   BindingFlags invokeAttr,
   Binder* binder,
   Object* target,
   Object* args __gc[],
   ParameterModifier modifiers[],
   CultureInfo* culture,
   String* namedParameters __gc[]
);
```
[JScript]
```
private function IReflect.InvokeMember(
   name : String,
   invokeAttr : BindingFlags,
   binder : Binder,
   target : Object,
   args : Object[],
   modifiers : ParameterModifier[],
   culture : CultureInfo,
   namedParameters : String[]
) : Object;
```

AccessibleObject.Navigate Method

Navigates to another accessible object.

[Visual Basic]
```
Public Overridable Function Navigate( _
   ByVal navdir As AccessibleNavigation _
) As AccessibleObject
```
[C#]
```
public virtual AccessibleObject Navigate(
   AccessibleNavigation navdir
);
```
[C++]
```
public: virtual AccessibleObject* Navigate(
   AccessibleNavigation navdir
);
```
[JScript]
```
public function Navigate(
   navdir : AccessibleNavigation
) : AccessibleObject;
```

Parameters

navdir

One of the **AccessibleNavigation** values.

Return Value

An **AccessibleObject** that represents one of the **AccessibleNavigation** values.

Exceptions

Exception Type	Condition
COMException	The navigation attempt fails.

Remarks

Navigation, both spatial and logical, is always restricted to the user interface elements within a container. With spatial navigation, clients can navigate only to a sibling of the starting object. Depending on the navigational flag used with logical navigation, clients can navigate to either a child or to a sibling of the starting object. This method does not change the selection or focus. To change the focus or to select an object, use **Select**. The **Navigate** method retrieves only user interface elements that have a defined screen location.

Notes to Inheritors: All visual objects must support this method. If an object has the state **AccessibleStates.Invisible**, navigation to this hidden object might fail. Some system-defined interface elements such as menus, menu items, and pop-up menus allow navigation to objects that are not visible. However, other system-defined user interface elements do not support this. If possible, servers should support navigation to objects that are not visible, but this support is not required and clients should not expect it.

Example

See related example in the **System.Windows.Forms.AccessibleObject** class topic.

Requirements

Platforms: Windows 98, Windows NT 4.0, Windows Millennium Edition, Windows 2000, Windows XP Home Edition, Windows XP Professional, Windows Server 2003 family

AccessibleObject.Select Method

Modifies the selection or moves the keyboard focus of the accessible object.

```
[Visual Basic]
Public Overridable Sub Select( _
   ByVal flags As AccessibleSelection _
)
[C#]
public virtual void Select(
   AccessibleSelection flags
);
[C++]
public: virtual void Select(
   AccessibleSelection flags
);
[JScript]
public function Select(
   flags : AccessibleSelection
);
```

Parameters

flags

One of the **AccessibleSelection** values.

Exceptions

Exception Type	Condition
COMException	The selection cannot be performed.

Remarks

Applications can use this method to perform complex selection operations.

The following describes which **AccessibleSelection** values to specify when calling **Select** to perform complex selection operations.

Operation	Flag Combination
To simulate a click	**AccessibleSelection.TakeFocus OR AccessibleSelection.TakeSelection**
To select a target item by simulating CTRL + click	**AccessibleSelection.TakeFocus OR AccessibleSelection.AddSelection**
To cancel selection of a target item by simulating CTRL + click	**AccessibleSelection.TakeFocus OR AccessibleSelection.RemoveSelection**
To simulate SHIFT + click	**AccessibleSelection.TakeFocus OR AccessibleSelection.ExtendSelection**
To select a range of objects and put focus on the last object	Specify **AccessibleSelection.TakeFocus** on the starting object to set the selection anchor. Then call **Select** again and specify **AccessibleSelection.TakeFocus OR AccessibleSelection.ExtendSelection** on the last object.
To deselect all objects	Specify **AccessibleSelection.TakeSelection** on any object. This flag deselects all selected objects except the one just selected. Then call **Select** again and specify **AccessibleSelection.RemoveSelection** on the same object.

Notes to Inheritors: All objects that can be selected or receive the keyboard focus must support this method.

Example

See related example in the **System.Windows.Forms.AccessibleObject** class topic.

Requirements

Platforms: Windows 98, Windows NT 4.0, Windows Millennium Edition, Windows 2000, Windows XP Home Edition, Windows XP Professional, Windows Server 2003 family

AccessibleObject.UseStdAccessibleObjects Method

This member supports the .NET Framework infrastructure and is not intended to be used directly from your code.

Overload List

This member supports the .NET Framework infrastructure and is not intended to be used directly from your code.

[Visual Basic] **Overloads Protected Sub UseStdAccessibleObjects(IntPtr)**

[C#] **protected void UseStdAccessibleObjects(IntPtr);**

[C++] **protected: void UseStdAccessibleObjects(IntPtr);**

[JScript] **protected function UseStdAccessibleObjects(IntPtr);**

This member supports the .NET Framework infrastructure and is not intended to be used directly from your code.

[Visual Basic] **Overloads Protected Sub UseStdAccessibleObjects(IntPtr, Integer)**

[C#] **protected void UseStdAccessibleObjects(IntPtr, int);**

[C++] **protected: void UseStdAccessibleObjects(IntPtr, int);**

[JScript] **protected function UseStdAccessibleObjects(IntPtr, int);**

AccessibleObject.UseStdAccessibleObjects Method (IntPtr)

This member supports the .NET Framework infrastructure and is not intended to be used directly from your code.

```
[Visual Basic]
Overloads Protected Sub UseStdAccessibleObjects( _
   ByVal handle As IntPtr _
)
```

[C#]
```
protected void UseStdAccessibleObjects(
   IntPtr handle
);
```
[C++]
```
protected: void UseStdAccessibleObjects(
   IntPtr handle
);
```
[JScript]
```
protected function UseStdAccessibleObjects(
   handle : IntPtr
);
```

AccessibleObject.UseStdAccessibleObjects Method (IntPtr, Int32)

This member supports the .NET Framework infrastructure and is not intended to be used directly from your code.

[Visual Basic]
```
Overloads Protected Sub UseStdAccessibleObjects( _
   ByVal handle As IntPtr, _
   ByVal objid As Integer _
)
```
[C#]
```
protected void UseStdAccessibleObjects(
   IntPtr handle,
   int objid
);
```
[C++]
```
protected: void UseStdAccessibleObjects(
   IntPtr handle,
   int objid
);
```
[JScript]
```
protected function UseStdAccessibleObjects(
   handle : IntPtr,
   objid : int
);
```

AccessibleRole Enumeration

Specifies values representing possible roles for an accessible object.

[Visual Basic]
```
<Serializable>
Public Enum AccessibleRole
```
[C#]
```
[Serializable]
public enum AccessibleRole
```
[C++]
```
[Serializable]
__value public enum AccessibleRole
```
[JScript]
```
public
   Serializable
enum AccessibleRole
```

Remarks

The role of the object describes the function of the object and is used by accessibility applications.

This enumeration is used by **AccessibleObject** and **Control.AccessibleRole**

For additional information on the accessibility application, search for "Microsoft Active Accessibility" in the Microsoft Developer Network (MSDN) library.

Members

Member name	Description
Alert	An alert or condition that you can notify a user about. Use this role only for objects that embody an alert but are not associated with another user interface element, such as a message box, graphic, text, or sound.
Animation	An animation control, which contains content that is changing over time, such as a control that displays a series of bitmap frames, like a filmstrip. Animation controls are usually displayed when files are being copied, or when some other time-consuming task is being performed.
Application	The main window for an application.
Border	A window border. The entire border is represented by a single object, rather than by separate objects for each side.
ButtonDropDown	A button that drops down a list of items.
ButtonDropDownGrid	A button that drops down a grid.
ButtonMenu	A button that drops down a menu.
Caret	A caret, which is a flashing line, block, or bitmap that marks the location of the insertion point in a window's client area.
Cell	A cell within a table.
Character	A cartoon-like graphic object, such as Microsoft Office Assistant, which is typically displayed to provide help to users of an application.
Chart	A graphical image used to represent data.
CheckButton	A check box control, which is an option that can be turned on or off independent of other options.
Client	A window's user area.
Clock	A control that displays the time.
Column	A column of cells within a table.
ColumnHeader	A column header, which provides a visual label for a column in a table.
ComboBox	A combo box, which is an edit control with an associated list box that provides a set of predefined choices.
Cursor	A mouse pointer.
Default	A system-provided role.
Diagram	A graphical image used to diagram data.
Dial	A dial or knob. This can also be a read-only object, like a speedometer.
Dialog	A dialog box or message box.
Document	A document window, which is always contained within an application window. This role applies only to multiple-document interface (MDI) windows and refers to an object that contains the MDI title bar.
DropList	A drop-down list box. This control shows one item and allows the user to display and select another from a list of alternative choices.
Equation	A mathematical equation.
Graphic	A picture.
Grip	A special mouse pointer, which allows a user to manipulate user interface elements such as a window. For example, a user can click and drag a sizing grip in the lower-right corner of a window to resize it.
Grouping	The objects grouped in a logical manner. There can be a parent-child relationship between the grouping object and the objects it contains.
HelpBalloon	A Help display in the form of a ToolTip or Help balloon, which contains buttons and labels that users can click to open custom Help topics.
HotkeyField	A hot-key field that allows the user to enter a combination or sequence of keystrokes to be used as a hot key, which enables users to perform an action quickly. A hot-key control displays the keystrokes entered by the user and ensures that the user selects a valid key combination.
Indicator	An indicator, such as a pointer graphic, that points to the current item.
Link	A link, which is a connection between a source document and a destination document. This object might look like text or a graphic, but it acts like a button.

Member name	Description
List	A list box, which allows the user to select one or more items.
ListItem	An item in a list box or the list portion of a combo box, drop-down list box, or drop-down combo box.
MenuBar	A menu bar, usually beneath the title bar of a window, from which users can select menus.
MenuItem	A menu item, which is an entry in a menu that a user can choose to carry out a command, select an option, or display another menu. Functionally, a menu item can be equivalent to a push button, radio button, check box, or menu.
MenuPopup	A menu, which presents a list of options from which the user can make a selection to perform an action. All menu types must have this role, including drop-down menus that are displayed by selection from a menu bar, and shortcut menus that are displayed when the right mouse button is clicked.
None	No role.
Outline	An outline or tree structure, such as a tree view control, which displays a hierarchical list and usually allows the user to expand and collapse branches.
OutlineItem	An item in an outline or tree structure.
PageTab	A property page that allows a user to view the attributes for a page, such as the page's title, whether it is a home page, or whether the page has been modified. Normally, the only child of this control is a grouped object that contains the contents of the associated page.
PageTabList	A container of page tab controls.
Pane	A separate area in a frame, a split document window, or a rectangular area of the status bar that can be used to display information. Users can navigate between panes and within the contents of the current pane, but cannot navigate between items in different panes. Thus, panes represent a level of grouping lower than frame windows or documents, but above individual controls. Typically, the user navigates between panes by pressing TAB, F6, or CTRL+TAB, depending on the context.
ProgressBar	A progress bar, which indicates the progress of a lengthy operation by displaying colored lines inside a horizontal rectangle. The length of the lines in relation to the length of the rectangle corresponds to the percentage of the operation that is complete. This control does not take user input.

Member name	Description
PropertyPage	A property page, which is a dialog box that controls the appearance and the behavior of an object, such as a file or resource. A property page's appearance differs according to its purpose.
PushButton	A push button control, which is a small rectangular control that a user can turn on or off. A push button, also known as a command button, has a raised appearance in its default off state and a sunken appearance when it is turned on.
RadioButton	An option button, also known as a radio button. All objects sharing a single parent that have this attribute are assumed to be part of a single mutually exclusive group. You can use grouped objects to divide option buttons into separate groups when necessary.
Row	A row of cells within a table.
RowHeader	A row header, which provides a visual label for a table row.
ScrollBar	A vertical or horizontal scroll bar, which can be either part of the client area or used in a control.
Separator	A space divided visually into two regions, such as a separator menu item or a separator dividing split panes within a window.
Slider	A control, sometimes called a trackbar, that allows a user to adjust a setting in given increments between minimum and maximum values by moving a slider. The volume controls in the Windows operating system are slider controls.
Sound	A system sound, which is associated with various system events.
SpinButton	A spin box, also known as an up-down control, which contains a pair of arrow buttons. A user clicks the arrow buttons with a mouse to increment or decrement a value. A spin button control is most often used with a companion control, called a buddy window, where the current value is displayed.
StaticText	The read-only text, such as in a label, for other controls or instructions in a dialog box. Static text cannot be modified or selected.
StatusBar	A status bar, which is an area typically at the bottom of an application window that displays information about the current operation, state of the application, or selected object. The status bar can have multiple fields that display different kinds of information, such as an explanation of the currently selected menu command in the status bar.

Member name	Description
Table	A table containing rows and columns of cells and, optionally, row headers and column headers.
Text	The selectable text that can be editable or read-only.
TitleBar	A title or caption bar for a window.
ToolBar	A toolbar, which is a grouping of controls that provide easy access to frequently used features.
ToolTip	A tool tip, which is a small rectangular pop-up window that displays a brief description of the purpose of a button.
WhiteSpace	A blank space between other objects.
Window	A window frame, which usually contains child objects such as a title bar, client, and other objects typically contained in a window.

Requirements

Namespace: System.Windows.Forms

Platforms: Windows 98, Windows NT 4.0, Windows Millennium Edition, Windows 2000, Windows XP Home Edition, Windows XP Professional, Windows Server 2003 family

Assembly: System.Windows.Forms (in System.Windows.Forms.dll)

AccessibleSelection Enumeration

Specifies how an accessible object is selected or receives focus.

This enumeration has a **FlagsAttribute** attribute that allows a bitwise combination of its member values.

[Visual Basic]
```
<Flags>
<Serializable>
Public Enum AccessibleSelection
```
[C#]
```
[Flags]
[Serializable]
public enum AccessibleSelection
```
[C++]
```
[Flags]
[Serializable]
__value public enum AccessibleSelection
```
[JScript]
```
public
   Flags
   Serializable
enum AccessibleSelection
```

Remarks

A focused object is the one object that receives keyboard input. The object with the keyboard focus is either the active window or a child object of the active window. A selected object is marked to participate in some type of group operation.

This enumeration is used by **AccessibleObject.Select**.

For additional information on the accessibility application, search for "Microsoft Active Accessibility" in the Microsoft Developer Network (MSDN) library.

Members

Member name	Description	Value
AddSelection	Adds the object to the selection.	8
ExtendSelection	Selects all objects between the anchor and the selected object.	4
None	The selection or focus of an object is unchanged.	0
RemoveSelection	Removes the object from the selection.	16
TakeFocus	Assigns focus to an object and makes it the anchor, which is the starting point for the selection. Can be combined with **TakeSelection**, **ExtendSelection**, **AddSelection**, or **RemoveSelection**.	1
TakeSelection	Selects the object and deselects all other objects in the container.	2

Requirements

Namespace: System.Windows.Forms

Platforms: Windows 98, Windows NT 4.0, Windows Millennium Edition, Windows 2000, Windows XP Home Edition, Windows XP Professional, Windows Server 2003 family

Assembly: System.Windows.Forms (in System.Windows.Forms.dll)

AccessibleStates Enumeration

Specifies values representing possible states for an accessible object.

This enumeration has a **FlagsAttribute** attribute that allows a bitwise combination of its member values.

[Visual Basic]
```
<Flags>
<Serializable>
Public Enum AccessibleStates
```
[C#]
```
[Flags]
[Serializable]
public enum AccessibleStates
```
[C++]
```
[Flags]
[Serializable]
__value public enum AccessibleStates
```
[JScript]
```
public
   Flags
   Serializable
enum AccessibleStates
```

Remarks

An accessible object can be associated with one or more of these states.

For additional information on the accessibility application, search for "Microsoft Active Accessibility" in the Microsoft Developer Network (MSDN) library.

Members

Member name	Description	Value
AlertHigh	The important information that should be conveyed to the user immediately. For example, a battery level indicator reaching a critical low level would transition to this state, in which case, a blind access utility would announce this information immediately to the user, and a screen magnification program would scroll the screen so that the battery indicator is in view. This state is also appropriate for any prompt or operation that must be completed before the user can continue.	268435456
AlertLow	The low-priority information that might not be important to the user.	67108864
AlertMedium	The important information that does not need to be conveyed to the user immediately. For example, when a battery level indicator is starting to reach a low level, it could generate a medium-level alert. Blind access utilities could then generate a sound to let the user know that important information is available, without actually interrupting the user's work. Users can then query the alert information at their leisure.	134217728
Animated	The object that rapidly or constantly changes appearance. Graphics that are occasionally animated, but not always, should be defined as **Graphic OR Animated**. This state should not be used to indicate that the object's location is changing.	16384
Busy	A control that cannot accept input in its current condition.	2048
Checked	An object with a selected check box.	16
Collapsed	The hidden children of the object that are items in an outline or tree structure.	1024
Default	The default button or menu item.	256
Expanded	The displayed children of the object that are items in an outline or tree structure.	512
ExtSelectable	The altered selection such that all objects between the selection anchor, which is the object with the keyboard focus, and this object take on the anchor object's selection state. If the anchor object is not selected, the objects are removed from the selection. If the anchor object is selected, the selection is extended to include this object and all objects in between. You can set the selection state by combining this with **AccessibleSelection.AddSelection** or **AccessibleSelection.RemoveSelection**. This state does not change the focus or the selection anchor unless it is combined with **AccessibleSelection.TakeFocus**.	33554432

Member name	Description	Value
Floating	The object that is not fixed to the boundary of its parent object and that does not move automatically along with the parent.	4096
Focusable	The object on the active window that can receive keyboard focus.	1048576
Focused	An object with the keyboard focus.	4
HotTracked	The object hot-tracked by the mouse, meaning its appearance is highlighted to indicate the mouse pointer is located over it.	128
Indeterminate	A three-state check box or toolbar button whose state is indeterminate. The check box is neither checked nor unchecked, and it is in the third or mixed state.	32
Invisible	An object without a visible user interface.	32768
Linked	A linked object that has not been previously selected.	4194304
Marqueed	An object with scrolling or moving text or graphics.	8192
Mixed	A three-state check box or toolbar button whose state is indeterminate. The check box is neither checked nor unchecked, and it is in the third or mixed state.	32
Moveable	A movable object.	262144
MultiSelectable	An object that accepts multiple selected items.	16777216
None	No state.	0
Offscreen	No on-screen representation. A sound or alert object would have this state, or a hidden window that is never made visible.	65536
Pressed	A pressed object.	8
Protected	A password-protected edit control.	536870912
ReadOnly	A read-only object.	64
Selectable	An object that can accept selection.	2097152
Selected	A selected object.	2
SelfVoicing	The object or child can use text-to-speech (TTS) to describe itself. A speech-based accessibility aid should not announce information when an object with this state has the focus, because the object automatically announces information about itself.	524288
Sizeable	A sizable object.	131072
Traversed	A linked object that has previously been selected.	8388608
Unavailable	An unavailable object.	1
Valid	A valid object.	1073741823

Requirements

Namespace: System.Windows.Forms

Platforms: Windows 98, Windows NT 4.0, Windows Millennium Edition, Windows 2000, Windows XP Home Edition, Windows XP Professional, Windows Server 2003 family

Assembly: System.Windows.Forms (in System.Windows.Forms.dll)

AmbientProperties Class

Provides ambient property values to top-level controls.

System.Object
  System.Windows.Forms.AmbientProperties

```
[Visual Basic]
NotInheritable Public Class AmbientProperties
[C#]
public sealed class AmbientProperties
[C++]
public __gc __sealed class AmbientProperties
[JScript]
public class AmbientProperties
```

Thread Safety

Any public static (**Shared** in Visual Basic) members of this type are safe for multithreaded operations. Any instance members are not guaranteed to be thread safe.

Remarks

An ambient property is a property on a control that, if not set, is retrieved from the parent control. If the control does not have a parent and the property is not set, the control tries to find the value of the ambient property through the **Site** property. If the control is not sited, the site does not support ambient properties, or the property is not set on the **AmbientProperties** object, the **Control** uses its own default values. Some objects derived from the **Control** class might set the property even if you do not. For example, the **Form** class always sets the **ForeColor** and **BackColor** properties.

Requirements

Namespace: System.Windows.Forms

Platforms: Windows 98, Windows NT 4.0, Windows Millennium Edition, Windows 2000, Windows XP Home Edition, Windows XP Professional, Windows Server 2003 family

Assembly: System.Windows.Forms (in System.Windows.Forms.dll)

AmbientProperties Constructor

Initializes a new instance of the **AmbientProperties** class.

```
[Visual Basic]
Public Sub New()
[C#]
public AmbientProperties();
[C++]
public: AmbientProperties();
[JScript]
public function AmbientProperties();
```

Remarks

The default constructor initializes any fields to their default values.

Requirements

Platforms: Windows 98, Windows NT 4.0, Windows Millennium Edition, Windows 2000, Windows XP Home Edition, Windows XP Professional, Windows Server 2003 family

AmbientProperties.BackColor Property

Gets or sets the ambient background color of an object.

```
[Visual Basic]
Public Property BackColor As Color
[C#]
public Color BackColor {get; set;}
[C++]
public: __property Color get_BackColor();
public: __property void set_BackColor(Color);
[JScript]
public function get BackColor() : Color;
public function set BackColor(Color);
```

Property Value

A **Color** value that represents the background color of an object.

Remarks

If there is no ambient background color, the value of the **BackColor** property is set to **Color.Empty**.

Requirements

Platforms: Windows 98, Windows NT 4.0, Windows Millennium Edition, Windows 2000, Windows XP Home Edition, Windows XP Professional, Windows Server 2003 family

AmbientProperties.Cursor Property

Gets or sets the ambient cursor of an object.

```
[Visual Basic]
Public Property Cursor As Cursor
[C#]
public Cursor Cursor {get; set;}
[C++]
public: __property Cursor* get_Cursor();
public: __property void set_Cursor(Cursor*);
[JScript]
public function get Cursor() : Cursor;
public function set Cursor(Cursor);
```

Property Value

A **Cursor** that represents the cursor of an object.

Remarks

If there is no ambient cursor, the value of the **Cursor** property is a null reference (**Nothing** in Visual Basic).

Requirements

Platforms: Windows 98, Windows NT 4.0, Windows Millennium Edition, Windows 2000, Windows XP Home Edition, Windows XP Professional, Windows Server 2003 family

AmbientProperties.Font Property

Gets or sets the ambient font of an object.

[Visual Basic]
```
Public Property Font As Font
```
[C#]
```
public Font Font {get; set;}
```
[C++]
```
public: __property Font* get_Font();
public: __property void set_Font(Font*);
```
[JScript]
```
public function get Font() : Font;
public function set Font(Font);
```

Property Value

A **Font** that represents the font used when displaying text within an object.

Remarks

If there is no ambient font, the value of the **Font** property is a null reference (**Nothing** in Visual Basic).

Requirements

Platforms: Windows 98, Windows NT 4.0, Windows Millennium Edition, Windows 2000, Windows XP Home Edition, Windows XP Professional, Windows Server 2003 family

AmbientProperties.ForeColor Property

Gets or sets the ambient foreground color of an object.

[Visual Basic]
```
Public Property ForeColor As Color
```
[C#]
```
public Color ForeColor {get; set;}
```
[C++]
```
public: __property Color get_ForeColor();
public: __property void set_ForeColor(Color);
```
[JScript]
```
public function get ForeColor() : Color;
public function set ForeColor(Color);
```

Property Value

A **Color** value that represents the foreground color of an object.

Remarks

If there is no ambient foreground color, the value of the **ForeColor** property is set to **Color.Empty**.

Requirements

Platforms: Windows 98, Windows NT 4.0, Windows Millennium Edition, Windows 2000, Windows XP Home Edition, Windows XP Professional, Windows Server 2003 family

AnchorStyles Enumeration

Specifies how a control anchors to the edges of its container.

This enumeration has a **FlagsAttribute** attribute that allows a bitwise combination of its member values.

[Visual Basic]
```
<Flags>
<Serializable>
Public Enum AnchorStyles
```
[C#]
```
[Flags]
[Serializable]
public enum AnchorStyles
```
[C++]
```
[Flags]
[Serializable]
__value public enum AnchorStyles
```
[JScript]
```
public
   Flags
   Serializable
enum AnchorStyles
```

Remarks

When a control is anchored to an edge of its container, the distance between the control and the specified edge remains constant when the container resizes. For example, if a control is anchored to the right edge of its container, the distance between the right edge of the control and the right edge of the container remains constant when the container resizes. A control can be anchored to any combination of control edges. If the control is anchored to opposite edges of its container (for example, to the top and bottom), it resizes when the container resizes. If a control has its **Anchor** property set to **AnchorStyles.None**, the control moves half of the distance that the container of the control is resized. For example, if a **Button** has its **Anchor** property set to **AnchorStyles.None** and the **Form** that the control is located on is resized by 20 pixels in either direction, the button will be moved 10 pixels in both directions.

Members

Member name	Description	Value
Bottom	The control is anchored to the bottom edge of its container.	2
Left	The control is anchored to the left edge of its container.	4
None	The control is not anchored to any edges of its container.	0
Right	The control is anchored to the right edge of its container.	8
Top	The control is anchored to the top edge of its container.	1

Requirements

Namespace: System.Windows.Forms

Platforms: Windows 98, Windows NT 4.0, Windows Millennium Edition, Windows 2000, Windows XP Home Edition, Windows XP Professional, Windows Server 2003 family

Assembly: System.Windows.Forms (in System.Windows.Forms.dll)

Appearance Enumeration

Specifies the appearance of a control.

[Visual Basic]

```
<Serializable>
<ComVisible(True)>
Public Enum Appearance
```

[C#]

```
[Serializable]
[ComVisible(true)]
public enum Appearance
```

[C++]

```
[Serializable]
[ComVisible(true)]
__value public enum Appearance
```

[JScript]

```
public
   Serializable
   ComVisible(true)
enum Appearance
```

Remarks

Use the members of this enumeration in controls that provide the **Appearance** property to set its value.

Members

Member name	Description
Button	The appearance of a Windows button.
Normal	The default appearance defined by the control class.

Requirements

Namespace: System.Windows.Forms

Platforms: Windows 98, Windows NT 4.0, Windows Millennium Edition, Windows 2000, Windows XP Home Edition, Windows XP Professional, Windows Server 2003 family

Assembly: System.Windows.Forms (in System.Windows.Forms.dll)

Application Class

Provides static (**Shared** in Visual Basic) methods and properties to manage an application, such as methods to start and stop an application, to process Windows messages, and properties to get information about an application. This class cannot be inherited.

System.Object
  System.Windows.Forms.Application

[Visual Basic]
```
NotInheritable Public Class Application
```
[C#]
```
public sealed class Application
```
[C++]
```
public __gc __sealed class Application
```
[JScript]
```
public class Application
```

Thread Safety

Any public static (**Shared** in Visual Basic) members of this type are safe for multithreaded operations. Any instance members are not guaranteed to be thread safe.

Remarks

The **Application** class has methods to start and stop applications and threads, and to process Windows messages. Call **Run** to start an application message loop on the current thread and, optionally, to make a form visible. Call **Exit** or **ExitThread** to stop a message loop. Call **DoEvents** to process messages while your program is in a loop. Call **AddMessageFilter** to add a message filter to the application message pump to monitor Windows messages. An **IMessageFilter** lets you stop an event from being raised or perform special operations before invoking an event handler.

This class has **CurrentCulture** and **CurrentInputLanguage** properties to get or set culture information for the current thread.

You cannot create an instance of this class.

Example

[Visual Basic, C#, C++] The following example lists numbers in a list box on a form. Each time you click `button1`, the application adds another number to the list.

[Visual Basic, C#, C++] The `Main` method calls **Run** to start the application, which creates the form, `listBox1` and `button1`. When the user clicks `button1`, the `button1_Click` method adds numbers one to three to the list box, and displays a **MessageBox**. If the user clicks **No** on the **MessageBox**, the `button1_Click` method adds another number to the list. If the user clicks **Yes**, the application calls **Exit** to process all remaining messages in the queue and then to quit.

[Visual Basic, C#, C++] The example assumes that `listBox1` and `button1` have been created and placed on a form.

[Visual Basic]
```
<STAThread()> _
Shared Sub Main()
   ' Starts the application.
   Application.Run(New Form1())
End Sub

Public Sub button1_Click(sender as object, e as System.EventArgs)
   ' Populates a list box with three numbers.
   Dim i As Integer = 3
   Dim j As Integer
   For j = 1 To i - 1
      listBox1.Items.Add(j)
   Next

   ' Determines whether the user wants to exit the application.
   ' If not, add another number to the list box.
   While (MessageBox.Show("Exit application?", "", ↵
MessageBoxButtons.YesNo) = DialogResult.No)
      ' Increments the counter and adds the number to the list box.
      i = i + 1
      listBox1.Items.Add(i)
   End While

   ' The user wants to exit the application. Close everything down.
   Application.Exit()
End Sub
```

[C#]
```
public static void Main(string[] args) {
    // Starts the application.
    Application.Run(new Form1());
 }

 protected void button1_Click(object sender, System.EventArgs e) {
    // Populates a list box with three numbers.
    int i = 3;
    for(int j=1; j<=i; j++) {
       listBox1.Items.Add(j);
    }

    /* Checks to see whether the user wants to exit the application.
     * If not, adds another number to the list box. */
    while (MessageBox.Show("Exit application?", "", ↵
MessageBoxButtons.YesNo) ==
       DialogResult.No) {
       // Increment the counter and add the number to the list box.
       i++;
       listBox1.Items.Add(i);
    }

    // The user wants to exit the application. Close everything down.
    Application.Exit();
 }
```

[C++]
```
void main() {
    // Starts the application.
    Application::Run(new Form1());
}

void Form1::button1_Click( Object* sender, EventArgs* e) {
    // Populates a list box with three numbers.
    int i = 3;
    for(int j=1; j<=i; j++) {
       listBox1->Items->Add( __box(j) );
    }

    // Checks to see whether the user wants to exit the application.
    // If not, adds another number to the list box.
    while (MessageBox::Show(S"Exit application?", S"", ↵
MessageBoxButtons::YesNo) ==
       DialogResult::No) {
       // Increment the counter and add the number to the list box.
       i++;
       listBox1->Items->Add( __box(i) );
    }

    // The user wants to exit the application. Close everything down.
    Application::Exit();
}
```

Requirements

Namespace: System.Windows.Forms

Platforms: Windows 98, Windows NT 4.0, Windows Millennium Edition, Windows 2000, Windows XP Home Edition, Windows XP Professional, Windows Server 2003 family, .NET Compact Framework - Windows CE .NET

Assembly: System.Windows.Forms (in System.Windows.Forms.dll)

Application.AllowQuit Property

Gets a value indicating whether the caller can quit this application.

[Visual Basic]
```
Public Shared ReadOnly Property AllowQuit As Boolean
```
[C#]
```
public static bool AllowQuit {get;}
```
[C++]
```
public: __property static bool get_AllowQuit();
```
[JScript]
```
public static function get AllowQuit() : Boolean;
```

Property Value

true if the caller can quit this application; otherwise, **false**.

Remarks

This property returns **false** if it is called from a **Control** being hosted within a Web browser. Thus, the **Control** cannot quit the **Application**.

Requirements

Platforms: Windows 98, Windows NT 4.0, Windows Millennium Edition, Windows 2000, Windows XP Home Edition, Windows XP Professional, Windows Server 2003 family

Application.CommonAppDataPath Property

Gets the path for the application data that is shared among all users.

[Visual Basic]
```
Public Shared ReadOnly Property CommonAppDataPath As String
```
[C#]
```
public static string CommonAppDataPath {get;}
```
[C++]
```
public: __property static String* get_CommonAppDataPath();
```
[JScript]
```
public static function get CommonAppDataPath() : String;
```

Property Value

The path for the application data that is shared among all users.

Remarks

If a path does not exist, one is created in the following format:

Base Path\ **CompanyName**\ **ProductName**\ **ProductVersion**

A typical Base Path, as identified in the path above, is C:\Documents and Settings\ *username*\Application Data.

Requirements

Platforms: Windows 98, Windows NT 4.0, Windows Millennium Edition, Windows 2000, Windows XP Home Edition, Windows XP Professional, Windows Server 2003 family

Application.CommonAppDataRegistry Property

Gets the registry key for the application data that is shared among all users.

[Visual Basic]
```
Public Shared ReadOnly Property CommonAppDataRegistry As _
   RegistryKey
```
[C#]
```
public static RegistryKey CommonAppDataRegistry {get;}
```
[C++]
```
public: __property static RegistryKey* get_CommonAppDataRegistry();
```
[JScript]
```
public static function get CommonAppDataRegistry() : RegistryKey;
```

Property Value

A **RegistryKey** representing the registry key of the application data that is shared among all users.

Remarks

If the key does not exist, it is created in the following format:

LocalMachine\Software\ **CompanyName**\ **ProductName**\ **ProductVersion**

Requirements

Platforms: Windows 98, Windows NT 4.0, Windows Millennium Edition, Windows 2000, Windows XP Home Edition, Windows XP Professional, Windows Server 2003 family

Application.CompanyName Property

Gets the company name associated with the application.

[Visual Basic]
```
Public Shared ReadOnly Property CompanyName As String
```
[C#]
```
public static string CompanyName {get;}
```
[C++]
```
public: __property static String* get_CompanyName();
```
[JScript]
```
public static function get CompanyName() : String;
```

Property Value

The company name.

Example

[Visual Basic, C#, C++] The following example gets this property and displays its value in a text box. The example assumes that `textBox1` has been placed on a form.

[Visual Basic]
```
Private Sub PrintCompanyName()
   textBox1.Text = "The company name is: " & _
      Application.CompanyName
End Sub
```

[C#]
```
private void PrintCompanyName() {
    textBox1.Text = "The company name is: " + Application.CompanyName;
 }
```

[C++]
```
private:
   void PrintCompanyName() {
      textBox1->Text = S"The company name is: {0}",                    ↵
Application::CompanyName;
   }
```

Requirements

Platforms: Windows 98, Windows NT 4.0, Windows Millennium Edition, Windows 2000, Windows XP Home Edition, Windows XP Professional, Windows Server 2003 family

Application.CurrentCulture Property

Gets or sets the culture information for the current thread.

[Visual Basic]
```
Public Shared Property CurrentCulture As CultureInfo
```
[C#]
```
public static CultureInfo CurrentCulture {get; set;}
```
[C++]
```
public: __property static CultureInfo* get_CurrentCulture();
public: __property static void set_CurrentCulture(CultureInfo*);
```
[JScript]
```
public static function get CurrentCulture() : CultureInfo;
public static function set CurrentCulture(CultureInfo);
```

Property Value

A **CultureInfo** representing the culture information for the current thread.

Example

[Visual Basic, C#, C++] The following example gets this property and displays its value in a text box. The example assumes that `textBox1` has been placed on a form.

[Visual Basic]
```
Private Sub PrintCurrentCulture()
   textBox1.Text = "The current culture is: " & _
      Application.CurrentCulture.EnglishName
End Sub
```

[C#]
```
private void PrintCurrentCulture() {
    textBox1.Text = "The current culture is: " +
       Application.CurrentCulture.EnglishName;
 }
```

[C++]
```
private:
   void PrintCurrentCulture() {
      textBox1->Text = S"The current culture is: {0}", ↵
Application::CurrentCulture->EnglishName;
   }
```

Requirements

Platforms: Windows 98, Windows NT 4.0, Windows Millennium Edition, Windows 2000, Windows XP Home Edition, Windows XP Professional, Windows Server 2003 family

.NET Framework Security:

- **UIPermission** for all windows to set this property. Associated enumeration: **UIPermissionWindow.AllWindows**

Application.CurrentInputLanguage Property

Gets or sets the current input language for the current thread.

[Visual Basic]
```
Public Shared Property CurrentInputLanguage As InputLanguage
```
[C#]
```
public static InputLanguage CurrentInputLanguage {get; set;}
```
[C++]
```
public: __property static InputLanguage* get_CurrentInputLanguage();
public: __property static void
set_CurrentInputLanguage(InputLanguage*);
```
[JScript]
```
public static function get CurrentInputLanguage() : InputLanguage;
public static function set CurrentInputLanguage(InputLanguage);
```

Property Value

An **InputLanguage** representing the current input language for the current thread.

Example

[Visual Basic, C#, C++] The following example gets this property and displays its value in a text box. The example assumes that `textBox1` has been placed on a form.

[Visual Basic]
```
Private Sub PrintCurrentInputLanguage()
   textBox1.Text = "The current input language is: " & _
      Application.CurrentInputLanguage.Culture.EnglishName
End Sub
```

[C#]
```
private void PrintCurrentInputLanguage() {
    textBox1.Text = "The current input language is: " +
       Application.CurrentInputLanguage.Culture.EnglishName;
 }
```

[C++]
```
private:
   void PrintCurrentInputLanguage() {
      textBox1->Text = S"The current input language is: {0}", ↵
Application::CurrentInputLanguage->Culture->EnglishName;
   }
```

Requirements

Platforms: Windows 98, Windows NT 4.0, Windows Millennium Edition, Windows 2000, Windows XP Home Edition, Windows XP Professional, Windows Server 2003 family

.NET Framework Security:

- **SecurityPermission** for the immediate caller to call unmanaged code. Associated enumeration: **SecurityPermissionFlag.UnmanagedCode**

Application.ExecutablePath Property

Gets the path for the executable file that started the application, including the executable name.

[Visual Basic]
```
Public Shared ReadOnly Property ExecutablePath As String
```
[C#]
```
public static string ExecutablePath {get;}
```
[C++]
```
public: __property static String* get_ExecutablePath();
```
[JScript]
```
public static function get ExecutablePath() : String;
```

Property Value

The path and executable name for the executable file that started the application.

Requirements

Platforms: Windows 98, Windows NT 4.0, Windows Millennium Edition, Windows 2000, Windows XP Home Edition, Windows XP Professional, Windows Server 2003 family

.NET Framework Security:

- **FileIOPermission** for getting the path. Associated enumeration: **FileIOPermissionAccess.PathDiscovery**

Application.LocalUserAppDataPath Property

Gets the path for the application data of a local, non-roaming user.

[Visual Basic]
```
Public Shared ReadOnly Property LocalUserAppDataPath As String
```
[C#]
```
public static string LocalUserAppDataPath {get;}
```
[C++]
```
public: __property static String* get_LocalUserAppDataPath();
```
[JScript]
```
public static function get LocalUserAppDataPath() : String;
```

Property Value

The path for the application data of a local, non-roaming user.

Remarks

A local user is one whose user profile is stored on the system on which the user logged on. If a path does not exist, one is created in the following format:

Base Path\ **CompanyName**\ **ProductName**\ **ProductVersion**

A typical Base Path, as identified in the path above, is C:\Documents and Settings\ *username*\Local Settings\Application Data.

Example

See related example in the **Systems.Windows.Forms.Application** class topic.

Requirements

Platforms: Windows 98, Windows NT 4.0, Windows Millennium Edition, Windows 2000, Windows XP Home Edition, Windows XP Professional, Windows Server 2003 family

Application.MessageLoop Property

Gets a value indicating whether a message loop exists on this thread.

[Visual Basic]
```
Public Shared ReadOnly Property MessageLoop As Boolean
```
[C#]
```
public static bool MessageLoop {get;}
```
[C++]
```
public: __property static bool get_MessageLoop();
```
[JScript]
```
public static function get MessageLoop() : Boolean;
```

Property Value

true if a message loop exists; otherwise, **false**.

Requirements

Platforms: Windows 98, Windows NT 4.0, Windows Millennium Edition, Windows 2000, Windows XP Home Edition, Windows XP Professional, Windows Server 2003 family

Application.ProductName Property

Gets the product name associated with this application.

[Visual Basic]
```
Public Shared ReadOnly Property ProductName As String
```
[C#]
```
public static string ProductName {get;}
```
[C++]
```
public: __property static String* get_ProductName();
```
[JScript]
```
public static function get ProductName() : String;
```

Property Value

The product name.

Example

[Visual Basic, C#, C++] The following example gets this property and displays its value in a text box. The example assumes that `textBox1` has been placed on a form.

[Visual Basic]
```
Private Sub PrintProductName()
   textBox1.Text = "The product name is: " & _
      Application.ProductName
End Sub
```

[C#]
```
private void PrintProductName() {
    textBox1.Text = "The product name is: " +
       Application.ProductName;
 }
```

[C++]
```
private:
   void PrintProductName() {
      textBox1->Text = S"The product name is: {0}",                ↵
Application::ProductName;
   }
```

Requirements

Platforms: Windows 98, Windows NT 4.0, Windows Millennium Edition, Windows 2000, Windows XP Home Edition, Windows XP Professional, Windows Server 2003 family

Application.ProductVersion Property

Gets the product version associated with this application.

[Visual Basic]
```
Public Shared ReadOnly Property ProductVersion As String
```
[C#]
```
public static string ProductVersion {get;}
```
[C++]
```
public: __property static String* get_ProductVersion();
```
[JScript]
```
public static function get ProductVersion() : String;
```

Property Value

The product version.

Remarks

Typically, a version number displays as "major number.minor number.build number.private part number".

Example

[Visual Basic, C#, C++] The following example gets this property and displays its value in a text box. The example assumes that `textBox1` has been placed on a form.

[Visual Basic]
```
Private Sub PrintProductVersion()
   textBox1.Text = "The product version is: " & _
      Application.ProductVersion
End Sub
```

[C#]
```
private void PrintProductVersion() {
    textBox1.Text = "The product version is: " +
       Application.ProductVersion;
 }
```

[C++]
```
private:
   void PrintProductVersion() {
      textBox1->Text = S"The product version is: {0}",
Application::ProductVersion;
   }
```

Requirements

Platforms: Windows 98, Windows NT 4.0, Windows Millennium Edition, Windows 2000, Windows XP Home Edition, Windows XP Professional, Windows Server 2003 family

Application.SafeTopLevelCaptionFormat Property

Gets or sets the format string to apply to top-level window captions when they are displayed with a warning banner.

[Visual Basic]
```
Public Shared Property SafeTopLevelCaptionFormat As String
```
[C#]
```
public static string SafeTopLevelCaptionFormat {get; set;}
```
[C++]
```
public: __property static String* get_SafeTopLevelCaptionFormat();
public: __property static void set_SafeTopLevelCaptionFormat(String*);
```
[JScript]
```
public static function get SafeTopLevelCaptionFormat() : String;
public static function set SafeTopLevelCaptionFormat(String);
```

Property Value

The format string to apply to top-level window captions.

Requirements

Platforms: Windows 98, Windows NT 4.0, Windows Millennium Edition, Windows 2000, Windows XP Home Edition, Windows XP Professional, Windows Server 2003 family

.NET Framework Security:

- **UIPermission** for all windows to set this property. Associated enumeration: **UIPermissionWindow.AllWindows**

Application.StartupPath Property

Gets the path for the executable file that started the application, not including the executable name.

[Visual Basic]
```
Public Shared ReadOnly Property StartupPath As String
```
[C#]
```
public static string StartupPath {get;}
```
[C++]
```
public: __property static String* get_StartupPath();
```
[JScript]
```
public static function get StartupPath() : String;
```

Property Value

The path for the executable file that started the application.

Example

[Visual Basic, C#, C++] The following example gets this property and displays its value in a text box. The example assumes that `textBox1` has been placed on a form.

[Visual Basic]
```
Private Sub PrintStartupPath()
   textBox1.Text = "The path for the executable file that " & _
      "started the application is: " & _
      Application.StartupPath
End Sub
```

[C#]
```
private void PrintStartupPath() {
    textBox1.Text = "The path for the executable file that " +
       "started the application is: " +
       Application.StartupPath;
 }
```

[C++]
```
private:
   void PrintStartupPath() {
      textBox1->Text =
         String::Concat(S"The path for the executable file that
 started the application is: {0}", Application::StartupPath);
   }
```

Requirements

Platforms: Windows 98, Windows NT 4.0, Windows Millennium Edition, Windows 2000, Windows XP Home Edition, Windows XP Professional, Windows Server 2003 family

.NET Framework Security:

- **FileIOPermission** for getting the path. Associated enumeration: **FileIOPermissionAccess.PathDiscovery**

Application.UserAppDataPath Property

Gets the path for the application data of a user.

[Visual Basic]
```
Public Shared ReadOnly Property UserAppDataPath As String
```
[C#]
```
public static string UserAppDataPath {get;}
```
[C++]
```
public: __property static String* get_UserAppDataPath();
```
[JScript]
```
public static function get UserAppDataPath() : String;
```

Property Value

The path for the application data of a user.

Remarks

If a path does not exist, one is created in the following format:

Base Path\ **CompanyName**\ **ProductName**\ **ProductVersion**

Data stored in this path is part of user profile that is enabled for roaming. A roaming user works on more than one computer in a network. The user profile for a roaming user is kept on a server on the network and is loaded onto a system when the user logs on. For a user profile to be considered for roaming, the operating system must support roaming profiles and it must be enabled.

A typical Base Path, as identified in the path above, is C:\Documents and Settings\ *username*\Application Data.

Example

See related example in the **Systems.Windows.Forms.Application** class topic.

Requirements

Platforms: Windows 98, Windows NT 4.0, Windows Millennium Edition, Windows 2000, Windows XP Home Edition, Windows XP Professional, Windows Server 2003 family

Application.UserAppDataRegistry Property

Gets the registry key for the application data of a user.

```
[Visual Basic]
Public Shared ReadOnly Property UserAppDataRegistry As RegistryKey
[C#]
public static RegistryKey UserAppDataRegistry {get;}
[C++]
public: __property static RegistryKey* get_UserAppDataRegistry();
[JScript]
public static function get UserAppDataRegistry() : RegistryKey;
```

Property Value

A **RegistryKey** representing the registry key for the application data specific to the user.

Remarks

If the key does not exist, it is created in the following format:

CurrentUser\Software\ **CompanyName\ ProductName\ ProductVersion**

Data stored in this key is part of user profile that is enabled for roaming. A roaming user works on more than one computer in a network. The user profile for a roaming user is kept on a server on the network and is loaded onto a system when the user logs on. For a user profile to be considered for roaming, the operating system must support roaming profiles and it must be enabled.

Requirements

Platforms: Windows 98, Windows NT 4.0, Windows Millennium Edition, Windows 2000, Windows XP Home Edition, Windows XP Professional, Windows Server 2003 family

Application.AddMessageFilter Method

Adds a message filter to monitor Windows messages as they are routed to their destinations.

```
[Visual Basic]
Public Shared Sub AddMessageFilter( _
   ByVal value As IMessageFilter _
)
[C#]
public static void AddMessageFilter(
   IMessageFilter value
);
[C++]
public: static void AddMessageFilter(
   IMessageFilter* value
);
[JScript]
public static function AddMessageFilter(
   value : IMessageFilter
);
```

Parameters

value

The implementation of the **IMessageFilter** interface you want to install.

Remarks

Use a message filter to prevent specific events from being raised or to perform special operations for an event before it is passed to an event handler. Message filters are unique to a specific thread.

To prevent a message from being dispatched, the *value* parameter instance that you pass to this method must override the **PreFilterMessage** method with the code to handle the message. The method must return **false**.

> **CAUTION** Adding message filters to the message pump for an application can degrade performance.

Example

See related example in the **Systems.Windows.Forms.Application** class topic.

Requirements

Platforms: Windows 98, Windows NT 4.0, Windows Millennium Edition, Windows 2000, Windows XP Home Edition, Windows XP Professional, Windows Server 2003 family

.NET Framework Security:

- **SecurityPermission** for the immediate caller to call unmanaged code. Associated enumeration: **SecurityPermissionFlag.UnmanagedCode**

Application.DoEvents Method

Processes all Windows messages currently in the message queue.

```
[Visual Basic]
Public Shared Sub DoEvents()
[C#]
public static void DoEvents();
[C++]
public: static void DoEvents();
[JScript]
public static function DoEvents();
```

Remarks

When you run a Windows Form, it creates the new form, which then waits for events to handle. Each time the form handles an event, it processes all the code associated with that event. All other events wait in the queue. While your code handles the event, your application does not respond. For example, the window does not repaint if another window is dragged on top.

If you call **DoEvents** in your code, your application can handle the other events. For example, if you have a form that adds data to a **ListBox** and add **DoEvents** to your code, your form repaints when another window is dragged over it. If you remove **DoEvents** from your code, your form will not repaint until the click event handler of the button is finished executing.

Typically, you use this method in a loop to process messages.

> **CAUTION** Calling this method can cause code to be re-entered if a message raises an event.

Requirements

Platforms: Windows 98, Windows NT 4.0, Windows Millennium Edition, Windows 2000, Windows XP Home Edition, Windows XP Professional, Windows Server 2003 family, .NET Compact Framework - Windows CE .NET

Application.EnableVisualStyles Method

Note: This namespace, class, or member is supported only in version 1.1 of the .NET Framework.

Enables Windows XP visual styles for the application.

```
[Visual Basic]
Public Shared Sub EnableVisualStyles()
[C#]
public static void EnableVisualStyles();
[C++]
public: static void EnableVisualStyles();
[JScript]
public static function EnableVisualStyles();
```

Remarks

This method enables Windows XP visual styles for the application. Controls will draw with visual styles if the control and the operating system supports it. To have an effect, **EnableVisualStyles** must be called before creating any controls in the application; typically, **EnableVisualStyles** is the first line in the **Main** function. A separate manifest is not required to enable visual styles when calling **EnableVisualStyles**.

Be sure to set the **FlatStyle** property to the **FlatStyle.System** value for the controls that support the **FlatStyle** property.

> **Note** This call will have no effect for controls in the browser.

XP Platform Note: Visual styles are only supported on Windows XP Home Edition, Windows XP Professional, and the Windows .NET Server family.

Example

See related example in the **Systems.Windows.Forms.Application** class topic.

Requirements

Platforms: Windows 98, Windows NT 4.0, Windows Millennium Edition, Windows 2000, Windows XP Home Edition, Windows XP Professional, Windows Server 2003 family

Application.Exit Method

Informs all message pumps that they must terminate, and then closes all application windows after the messages have been processed.

```
[Visual Basic]
Public Shared Sub Exit()
[C#]
public static void Exit();
[C++]
public: static void Exit();
[JScript]
public static function Exit();
```

Remarks

This method stops all running message loops on all threads and closes all windows of the application. This method does not force the application to exit. The **Exit** method is typically called from within a message loop, and forces **Run** to return. To exit a message loop for the current thread only, call **ExitThread**.

> **CAUTION** The **Form.Closed** and **Form.Closing** events are not raised when the **Application.Exit** method is called to exit your application. If you have validation code in either of these events that must be executed, you should call the **Form.Close** method for each open form individually before calling the **Exit** method.

Example

See related example in the **Systems.Windows.Forms.Application** class topic.

Requirements

Platforms: Windows 98, Windows NT 4.0, Windows Millennium Edition, Windows 2000, Windows XP Home Edition, Windows XP Professional, Windows Server 2003 family, .NET Compact Framework - Windows CE .NET

.NET Framework Security:

- **SecurityPermission** for the immediate caller to call unmanaged code. Associated enumeration: **SecurityPermissionFlag.UnmanagedCode**

Application.ExitThread Method

Exits the message loop on the current thread and closes all windows on the thread.

```
[Visual Basic]
Public Shared Sub ExitThread()
[C#]
public static void ExitThread();
[C++]
public: static void ExitThread();
[JScript]
public static function ExitThread();
```

Remarks

Use this method to exit the message loop of the current thread. This method causes the call to **Run** for the current thread to return. To exit the entire application, call **Exit**.

Requirements

Platforms: Windows 98, Windows NT 4.0, Windows Millennium Edition, Windows 2000, Windows XP Home Edition, Windows XP Professional, Windows Server 2003 family

.NET Framework Security:

- **SecurityPermission** for the immediate caller to call unmanaged code. Associated enumeration: **SecurityPermissionFlag.UnmanagedCode**

Application.OleRequired Method

Initializes OLE on the current thread.

```
[Visual Basic]
Public Shared Function OleRequired() As ApartmentState
[C#]
public static ApartmentState OleRequired();
[C++]
public: static ApartmentState OleRequired();
[JScript]
public static function OleRequired() : ApartmentState;
```

Return Value

One of the **ApartmentState** values.

Remarks

Call this method before calling any **Microsoft.Win32** method that requires OLE. **OleRequired** first checks to see if OLE has been initialized on the current thread. If not, it initializes the thread for OLE.

Note Unless a thread calls OLE methods directly, you do not need to call this method.

Requirements

Platforms: Windows 98, Windows NT 4.0, Windows Millennium Edition, Windows 2000, Windows XP Home Edition, Windows XP Professional, Windows Server 2003 family

Application.OnThreadException Method

Raises the **ThreadException** event.

```
[Visual Basic]
Public Shared Sub OnThreadException( _
   ByVal t As Exception _
)
[C#]
public static void OnThreadException(
   Exception t
);
[C++]
public: static void OnThreadException(
   Exception* t
);
[JScript]
public static function OnThreadException(
   t : Exception
);
```

Parameters

t

An **Exception** that represents the exception that was thrown.

Remarks

This event enables an application to handle an exception intelligently. A window procedure calls this event when it receives a thread exception. Attach your event handlers to this event.

Raising an event invokes the event handler through a delegate.

Notes to Inheritors: When overriding **OnThreadException** in a derived class, be sure to call the **OnThreadException** method of the base class.

Example

See related example in the **Systems.Windows.Forms.Application** class topic.

Requirements

Platforms: Windows 98, Windows NT 4.0, Windows Millennium Edition, Windows 2000, Windows XP Home Edition, Windows XP Professional, Windows Server 2003 family

Application.RemoveMessageFilter Method

Removes a message filter from the message pump of the application.

```
[Visual Basic]
Public Shared Sub RemoveMessageFilter( _
   ByVal value As IMessageFilter _
)
[C#]
public static void RemoveMessageFilter(
   IMessageFilter value
);
[C++]
public: static void RemoveMessageFilter(
   IMessageFilter* value
);
[JScript]
public static function RemoveMessageFilter(
   value : IMessageFilter
);
```

Parameters

value

The implementation of the **IMessageFilter** to remove from the application.

Remarks

You can remove a message filter when you no longer want to capture Windows messages before they are dispatched.

Example

See related example in the **Systems.Windows.Forms.Application** class topic.

Requirements

Platforms: Windows 98, Windows NT 4.0, Windows Millennium Edition, Windows 2000, Windows XP Home Edition, Windows XP Professional, Windows Server 2003 family

Application.Run Method

Begins running a standard application message loop on the current thread.

Overload List

Begins running a standard application message loop on the current thread, without a form.

[Visual Basic] **Overloads Public Shared Sub Run()**

[C#] **public static void Run();**

[C++] **public: static void Run();**

[JScript] **public static function Run();**

Begins running a standard application message loop on the current thread, with an **ApplicationContext**.

[Visual Basic] **Overloads Public Shared Sub Run(ApplicationContext)**

[C#] **public static void Run(ApplicationContext);**

[C++] **public: static void Run(ApplicationContext*);**

[JScript] **public static function Run(ApplicationContext);**

Begins running a standard application message loop on the current thread, and makes the specified form visible.

Supported by the .NET Compact Framework.

[Visual Basic] **Overloads Public Shared Sub Run(Form)**

[C#] **public static void Run(Form);**

[C++] **public: static void Run(Form*);**

[JScript] **public static function Run(Form);**

Example

See related example in the **Systems.Windows.Forms.Application** class topic.

Application.Run Method ()

Begins running a standard application message loop on the current thread, without a form.

```
[Visual Basic]
Overloads Public Shared Sub Run()
[C#]
public static void Run();
[C++]
public: static void Run();
[JScript]
public static function Run();
```

Exceptions

Exception Type	Condition
InvalidOperation-Exception	A main message loop is already running on this thread.

Remarks

The message loop runs until **Exit** or **ExitThread** is called.

Requirements

Platforms: Windows 98, Windows NT 4.0, Windows Millennium Edition, Windows 2000, Windows XP Home Edition, Windows XP Professional, Windows Server 2003 family

Application.Run Method (ApplicationContext)

Begins running a standard application message loop on the current thread, with an **ApplicationContext**.

```
[Visual Basic]
Overloads Public Shared Sub Run( _
   ByVal context As ApplicationContext _
)
[C#]
public static void Run(
   ApplicationContext context
);
[C++]
public: static void Run(
   ApplicationContext* context
);
[JScript]
public static function Run(
   context : ApplicationContext
);
```

Parameters

context

An **ApplicationContext** in which the application is run.

Exceptions

Exception Type	Condition
InvalidOperation-Exception	A main message loop is already running on this thread.

Remarks

The message loop runs until **Exit** or **ExitThread** is called or the **ThreadExit** event is raised on the context object.

Example

See related example in the **Systems.Windows.Forms.Application** class topic.

Requirements

Platforms: Windows 98, Windows NT 4.0, Windows Millennium Edition, Windows 2000, Windows XP Home Edition, Windows XP Professional, Windows Server 2003 family

Application.Run Method (Form)

Begins running a standard application message loop on the current thread, and makes the specified form visible.

```
[Visual Basic]
Overloads Public Shared Sub Run( _
   ByVal mainForm As Form _
)
[C#]
public static void Run(
   Form mainForm
);
[C++]
public: static void Run(
   Form* mainForm
);
[JScript]
public static function Run(
   mainForm : Form
);
```

Parameters

mainForm

A **Form** that represents the form to make visible.

Exceptions

Exception Type	Condition
InvalidOperation-Exception	A main message loop is already running on the current thread.

Remarks

Typically, the main function of an application calls this method and passes to it the main window of the application.

This method adds an event handler to the *mainForm* parameter for the **Closed** event. The event handler calls **ExitThread** to clean up the application.

> **Note** The **Dispose** method of the **Form** class will be called prior to the return of this method.

Example

See related example in the **Systems.Windows.Forms.Application** class topic.

Requirements

Platforms: Windows 98, Windows NT 4.0,
Windows Millennium Edition, Windows 2000,
Windows XP Home Edition, Windows XP Professional,
Windows Server 2003 family,
.NET Compact Framework - Windows CE .NET

Application.ApplicationExit Event

Occurs when the application is about to shut down.

```
[Visual Basic]
Public Shared Event ApplicationExit As EventHandler
[C#]
public static event EventHandler ApplicationExit;
[C++]
public: static __event EventHandler* ApplicationExit;
```

[JScript] In JScript, you can handle the events defined by a class, but you cannot define your own.

Event Data

The event handler receives an argument of type **EventArgs**.

Remarks

You must attach the event handlers to the **Exit** event to perform unhandled, required tasks before the application stops running. You can close files opened by this application, or dispose of objects that garbage collection did not reclaim.

Example

See related example in the **Systems.Windows.Forms.Application** class topic.

Requirements

Platforms: Windows 98, Windows NT 4.0,
Windows Millennium Edition, Windows 2000,
Windows XP Home Edition, Windows XP Professional,
Windows Server 2003 family

Application.Idle Event

Occurs when the application finishes processing and is about to enter the idle state.

```
[Visual Basic]
Public Shared Event Idle As EventHandler
[C#]
public static event EventHandler Idle;
[C++]
public: static __event EventHandler* Idle;
```

[JScript] In JScript, you can handle the events defined by a class, but you cannot define your own.

Event Data

The event handler receives an argument of type **EventArgs**.

Remarks

If you have tasks that you must perform before the thread becomes idle, attach them to this event.

Requirements

Platforms: Windows 98, Windows NT 4.0,
Windows Millennium Edition, Windows 2000,
Windows XP Home Edition, Windows XP Professional,
Windows Server 2003 family

Application.ThreadException Event

Occurs when an untrapped thread exception is thrown.

```
[Visual Basic]
Public Shared Event ThreadException As ThreadExceptionEventHandler
[C#]
public static event ThreadExceptionEventHandler ThreadException;
[C++]
public: static __event ThreadExceptionEventHandler*
   ThreadException;
```

[JScript] In JScript, you can handle the events defined by a class, but you cannot define your own.

Event Data

The event handler receives an argument of type **ThreadExceptionEventArgs** containing data related to this event. The following **ThreadExceptionEventArgs** property provides information specific to this event.

Property	Description
Exception	Gets the **Exception** that occurred.

Remarks

This event enables an application to handle an exception intelligently when it receives a thread exception from a window procedure. Attach your event handlers to the **ThreadException** event to deal with the exception. An appropriate event handler does not terminate the thread, and allow your application to continue executing.

Example

See related example in the **Systems.Windows.Forms.Application** class topic.

Requirements

Platforms: Windows 98, Windows NT 4.0,
Windows Millennium Edition, Windows 2000,
Windows XP Home Edition, Windows XP Professional,
Windows Server 2003 family

.NET Framework Security:

- **SecurityPermission** for the immediate caller to call unmanaged code when adding a handler to this event. Associated enumeration: **SecurityPermissionFlag.UnmanagedCode**

Application.ThreadExit Event

Occurs when a thread is about to shut down. When the main thread for an application is about to be shut down, this event is raised first, followed by an **ApplicationExit** event.

[Visual Basic]
```
Public Shared Event ThreadExit As EventHandler
```
[C#]
```
public static event EventHandler ThreadExit;
```
[C++]
```
public: static __event EventHandler* ThreadExit;
```

[JScript] In JScript, you can handle the events defined by a class, but you cannot define your own.

Event Data

The event handler receives an argument of type **EventArgs**.

Remarks

You must attach the event handlers to the **ThreadExit** event to perform any unhandled, required tasks before the thread stops running. Close files opened by this thread, or dispose of objects that the garbage collector did not reclaim.

Requirements

Platforms: Windows 98, Windows NT 4.0, Windows Millennium Edition, Windows 2000, Windows XP Home Edition, Windows XP Professional, Windows Server 2003 family

ApplicationContext Class

Specifies the contextual information about an application thread.

System.Object
  System.Windows.Forms.ApplicationContext

```
[Visual Basic]
Public Class ApplicationContext
[C#]
public class ApplicationContext
[C++]
public __gc class ApplicationContext
[JScript]
public class ApplicationContext
```

Thread Safety

Any public static (**Shared** in Visual Basic) members of this type are safe for multithreaded operations. Any instance members are not guaranteed to be thread safe.

Remarks

You can use the **ApplicationContext** class to redefine the circumstances that cause a message loop to exit. By default, the **ApplicationContext** listens to the **Closed** event on the application's main **Form**, then exits the thread's message loop.

Example

See related example in the **Systems.Windows.Forms.Application** class topic.

Requirements

Platforms: Windows 98, Windows NT 4.0, Windows Millennium Edition, Windows 2000, Windows XP Home Edition, Windows XP Professional, Windows Server 2003 family

ApplicationContext Constructor

Initializes a new instance of the **ApplicationContext** class.

Overload List

Initializes a new instance of the **ApplicationContext** class with no context.

[Visual Basic] **Public Sub New()**

[C#] **public ApplicationContext();**

[C++] **public: ApplicationContext();**

[JScript] **public function ApplicationContext();**

Initializes a new instance of the **ApplicationContext** class with the specified **Form**.

[Visual Basic] **Public Sub New(Form)**

[C#] **public ApplicationContext(Form);**

[C++] **public: ApplicationContext(Form*);**

[JScript] **public function ApplicationContext(Form);**

ApplicationContext Constructor ()

Initializes a new instance of the **ApplicationContext** class with no context.

```
[Visual Basic]
Public Sub New()
[C#]
public ApplicationContext();
[C++]
public: ApplicationContext();
[JScript]
public function ApplicationContext();
```

Requirements

Platforms: Windows 98, Windows NT 4.0, Windows Millennium Edition, Windows 2000, Windows XP Home Edition, Windows XP Professional, Windows Server 2003 family

ApplicationContext Constructor (Form)

Initializes a new instance of the **ApplicationContext** class with the specified **Form**.

```
[Visual Basic]
Public Sub New( _
   ByVal mainForm As Form _
)
[C#]
public ApplicationContext(
   Form mainForm
);
[C++]
public: ApplicationContext(
   Form* mainForm
);
[JScript]
public function ApplicationContext(
   mainForm : Form
);
```

Parameters

mainForm
   The main **Form** of the application to use for context.

Remarks

If **OnMainFormClosed** is not overridden, the message loop of the thread terminates when **MainForm** is closed.

Requirements

Platforms: Windows 98, Windows NT 4.0, Windows Millennium Edition, Windows 2000, Windows XP Home Edition, Windows XP Professional, Windows Server 2003 family

ApplicationContext.MainForm Property

Gets or sets the **Form** to use as context.

```
[Visual Basic]
Public Property MainForm As Form
[C#]
public Form MainForm {get; set;}
[C++]
public: __property Form* get_MainForm();
public: __property void set_MainForm(Form*);
[JScript]
public function get MainForm() : Form;
public function set MainForm(Form);
```

Property Value

The **Form** to use as context.

Remarks

This property determines the main **Form** for this context. This property can change at any time. If **OnMainFormClosed** is not overridden, the message loop of the thread terminates when the *mainForm* parameter closes.

Requirements

Platforms: Windows 98, Windows NT 4.0, Windows Millennium Edition, Windows 2000, Windows XP Home Edition, Windows XP Professional, Windows Server 2003 family

ApplicationContext.Dispose Method

Releases the resources used by the **ApplicationContext**.

Overload List

Releases all resources used by the **ApplicationContext**.

[Visual Basic] **Overloads Public Sub Dispose()**

[C#] **public void Dispose();**

[C++] **public: void Dispose();**

[JScript] **public function Dispose();**

Releases the unmanaged resources used by the **ApplicationContext** and optionally releases the managed resources.

[Visual Basic] **Overloads Protected Overridable Sub Dispose(Boolean)**

[C#] **protected virtual void Dispose(bool);**

[C++] **protected: virtual void Dispose(bool);**

[JScript] **protected function Dispose(Boolean);**

ApplicationContext.Dispose Method ()

Releases all resources used by the **ApplicationContext**.

[Visual Basic]
```
Overloads Public Sub Dispose()
```
[C#]
```
public void Dispose();
```
[C++]
```
public: void Dispose();
```
[JScript]
```
public function Dispose();
```

Remarks

Calling **Dispose** allows the resources used by the **ApplicationContext**. to be reallocated for other purposes.

Requirements

Platforms: Windows 98, Windows NT 4.0, Windows Millennium Edition, Windows 2000, Windows XP Home Edition, Windows XP Professional, Windows Server 2003 family

ApplicationContext.Dispose Method (Boolean)

Releases the unmanaged resources used by the **ApplicationContext** and optionally releases the managed resources.

[Visual Basic]
```
Overloads Protected Overridable Sub Dispose( _
   ByVal disposing As Boolean _
)
```
[C#]
```
protected virtual void Dispose(
   bool disposing
);
```
[C++]
```
protected: virtual void Dispose(
   bool disposing
);
```
[JScript]
```
protected function Dispose(
   disposing : Boolean
);
```

Parameters

disposing

true to release both managed and unmanaged resources; **false** to release only unmanaged resources.

Remarks

This method is called by the public **Dispose()** method and the **Finalize** method. **Dispose()** invokes the protected **Dispose(Boolean)** method with the *disposing* parameter set to **true**. **Finalize** invokes **Dispose** with *disposing* set to **false**.

When the *disposing* parameter is **true**, this method releases all resources held by any managed objects that this **ApplicationContext** references. This method invokes the **Dispose()** method of each referenced object.

Notes to Inheritors: **Dispose** can be called multiple times by other objects. When overriding **Dispose(Boolean)**, be careful not to reference objects that have been previously disposed of in an earlier call to **Dispose**.

Requirements

Platforms: Windows 98, Windows NT 4.0, Windows Millennium Edition, Windows 2000, Windows XP Home Edition, Windows XP Professional, Windows Server 2003 family

ApplicationContext.ExitThread Method

Terminates the message loop of the thread.

[Visual Basic]
```
Public Sub ExitThread()
```
[C#]
```
public void ExitThread();
```
[C++]
```
public: void ExitThread();
```
[JScript]
```
public function ExitThread();
```

Remarks

This method calls **ExitThreadCore**.

> **Note** **ExitThread** and **ExitThreadCore** do not actually cause the thread to terminate. These methods raise the **ThreadExit** event to which the **Application** object listens. The **Application** object then terminates the thread.

Example

See related example in the **Systems.Windows.Forms.Application** class topic.

Requirements

Platforms: Windows 98, Windows NT 4.0, Windows Millennium Edition, Windows 2000, Windows XP Home Edition, Windows XP Professional, Windows Server 2003 family

ApplicationContext.ExitThreadCore Method

Terminates the message loop of the thread.

[Visual Basic]
```
Protected Overridable Sub ExitThreadCore()
```
[C#]
```
protected virtual void ExitThreadCore();
```
[C++]
```
protected: virtual void ExitThreadCore();
```
[JScript]
```
protected function ExitThreadCore();
```

Remarks

This method is called from **ExitThread**.

> **Note** **ExitThread** and **ExitThreadCore** do not actually cause the thread to terminate. These methods raise the **ThreadExit** event to which the **Application** object listens. The **Application** object then terminates the thread.

Requirements

Platforms: Windows 98, Windows NT 4.0, Windows Millennium Edition, Windows 2000, Windows XP Home Edition, Windows XP Professional, Windows Server 2003 family

ApplicationContext.Finalize Method

Attempts to free resources and perform other cleanup operations before the application context is reclaimed by garbage collection.

[C#] In C#, finalizers are expressed using destructor syntax.

[C++] In C++, finalizers are expressed using destructor syntax.

[Visual Basic]
```
Overrides Protected Sub Finalize()
```
[C#]
```
~ApplicationContext();
```
[C++]
```
~ApplicationContext();
```
[JScript]
```
protected override function Finalize();
```

Remarks

This method overrides **Object.Finalize** and cleans up resources by calling **Dispose(false)**. Override **Dispose(Boolean)** to customize the cleanup.

Application code should not call this method; an object's **Finalize** method is automatically invoked during garbage collection, unless finalization by the garbage collector has been disabled by a call to the **GC.SuppressFinalize** method.

Requirements

Platforms: Windows 98, Windows NT 4.0, Windows Millennium Edition, Windows 2000, Windows XP Home Edition, Windows XP Professional, Windows Server 2003 family

ApplicationContext.OnMainFormClosed Method

Calls **ExitThreadCore**, which raises the **ThreadExit** event.

[Visual Basic]
```
Protected Overridable Sub OnMainFormClosed( _
   ByVal sender As Object, _
   ByVal e As EventArgs _
)
```
[C#]
```
protected virtual void OnMainFormClosed(
   object sender,
   EventArgs e
);
```
[C++]
```
protected: virtual void OnMainFormClosed(
   Object* sender,
   EventArgs* e
);
```
[JScript]
```
protected function OnMainFormClosed(
   sender : Object,
   e : EventArgs
);
```

Parameters

sender
: The object that raised the event.

e
: The **EventArgs** that contains the event data.

Remarks

The default implementation of this method calls **ExitThreadCore**.

Requirements

Platforms: Windows 98, Windows NT 4.0, Windows Millennium Edition, Windows 2000, Windows XP Home Edition, Windows XP Professional, Windows Server 2003 family

ApplicationContext.ThreadExit Event

Occurs when the message loop of the thread should be terminated, by calling **ExitThread**.

[Visual Basic]
```
Public Event ThreadExit As EventHandler
```
[C#]
```
public event EventHandler ThreadExit;
```
[C++]
```
public: __event EventHandler* ThreadExit;
```

[JScript] In JScript, you can handle the events defined by a class, but you cannot define your own.

Event Data

The event handler receives an argument of type **EventArgs**.

Requirements

Platforms: Windows 98, Windows NT 4.0, Windows Millennium Edition, Windows 2000, Windows XP Home Edition, Windows XP Professional, Windows Server 2003 family

ArrangeDirection Enumeration

Specifies the direction in which the system arranges minimized windows.

[Visual Basic]
```
<Serializable>
<ComVisible(True)>
Public Enum ArrangeDirection
```
[C#]
```
[Serializable]
[ComVisible(true)]
public enum ArrangeDirection
```
[C++]
```
[Serializable]
[ComVisible(true)]
__value public enum ArrangeDirection
```
[JScript]
```
public
   Serializable
   ComVisible(true)
enum ArrangeDirection
```

Remarks

This enumeration is used by the **ArrangeDirection** property of the **SystemInformation** class.

Members

Member name	Description
Down	Arranged vertically, from top to bottom. Valid with **TopLeft** and **TopRight ArrangeStartingPosition** enumeration values.
Left	Arranged horizontally, from left to right. Valid with **BottomRight** and **TopRight ArrangeStartingPosition** enumeration values.
Right	Arranged horizontally, from right to left. Valid with **BottomLeft** and **TopLeft ArrangeStartingPosition** enumeration values.
Up	Arranged vertically, from bottom to top. Valid with **BottomLeft** and **TopRight ArrangeStartingPosition** enumeration values.

Requirements

Namespace: System.Windows.Forms

Platforms: Windows 98, Windows NT 4.0, Windows Millennium Edition, Windows 2000, Windows XP Home Edition, Windows XP Professional, Windows Server 2003 family

Assembly: System.Windows.Forms (in System.Windows.Forms.dll)

ArrangeStartingPosition Enumeration

Specifies the starting position that the system uses to arrange minimized windows.

[Visual Basic]
```
<Serializable>
Public Enum ArrangeStartingPosition
```
[C#]
```
[Serializable]
public enum ArrangeStartingPosition
```
[C++]
```
[Serializable]
__value public enum ArrangeStartingPosition
```
[JScript]
```
public
   Serializable
enum ArrangeStartingPosition
```

Remarks

This enumeration is used by the **ArrangeStartingPosition** property of the **SystemInformation** class.

Members

Member name	Description
BottomLeft	Starts at the lower-left corner of the screen, which is the default position.
BottomRight	Starts at the lower-right corner of the screen.
Hide	Hides minimized windows by moving them off the visible area of the screen.
TopLeft	Starts at the upper-left corner of the screen.
TopRight	Starts at the upper-right corner of the screen.

Requirements

Namespace: System.Windows.Forms

Platforms: Windows 98, Windows NT 4.0, Windows Millennium Edition, Windows 2000, Windows XP Home Edition, Windows XP Professional, Windows Server 2003 family

Assembly: System.Windows.Forms (in System.Windows.Forms.dll)

AxHost Class

Wraps ActiveX controls and exposes them as fully featured Windows Forms controls.

System.Object
  System.MarshalByRefObject
    System.ComponentModel.Component
      System.Windows.Forms.Control
        System.Windows.Forms.AxHost

```
[Visual Basic]
MustInherit Public Class AxHost
   Inherits Control
   Implements ISupportInitialize, ICustomTypeDescriptor
[C#]
public abstract class AxHost : Control, ISupportInitialize,
   ICustomTypeDescriptor
[C++]
public __gc __abstract class AxHost : public Control,
   ISupportInitialize, ICustomTypeDescriptor
[JScript]
public abstract class AxHost extends Control implements
   ISupportInitialize, ICustomTypeDescriptor
```

Thread Safety

Any public static (**Shared** in Visual Basic) members of this type are safe for multithreaded operations. Any instance members are not guaranteed to be thread safe.

Remarks

You typically do not use the **AxHost** class directly. You can use the **Windows Forms ActiveX Control Importer (AxImp.exe)** to generate the wrappers that extend **AxHost**.

The ActiveX Control Importer generates a class that is derived from the **AxHost** class, and compiles it into a library file (DLL) that can be added as a reference to your application. Alternatively, you can use the /source switch with the ActiveX Control Importer and a C# file is generated for your **AxHost** derived class. You can then make changes to the code and recompile it into a library file.

> **Note** If the name of a member of the ActiveX control matches a name defined in the .NET Framework, then the ActiveX Control Importer will prefix the member name with "Ctl" when it creates the **AxHost** derived class. For example, if your ActiveX control has a member named "Layout", it is renamed "CtlLayout" in the **AxHost** derived class because the **Layout** event is defined within the .NET Framework.

Most of the common properties of the **AxHost** class are only valid and used if the underlying ActiveX control exposes those properties. A few examples of the common properties are **BackColor**, **Cursor**, **Font**, and **Text**.

> **Note** If you are using Visual Studio .NET as your Windows Forms design environment, you can make an ActiveX control available to your application by adding the ActiveX control to your Toolbox. To accomplish this, right-click the Toolbox, select Customize Toolbox, then browse to the ActiveX control's .ocx file. For more information, see "Adding ActiveX Controls to Windows Forms" in the Visual Studio .NET documentation.

Requirements

Namespace: System.Windows.Forms

Platforms: Windows 98, Windows NT 4.0, Windows Millennium Edition, Windows 2000, Windows XP Home Edition, Windows XP Professional, Windows Server 2003 family

Assembly: System.Windows.Forms (in System.Windows.Forms.dll)

AxHost Constructor

This member supports the .NET Framework infrastructure and is not intended to be used directly from your code.

Overload List

This member supports the .NET Framework infrastructure and is not intended to be used directly from your code.

[Visual Basic] **Protected Sub New(String)**

[C#] **protected AxHost(string);**

[C++] **protected: AxHost(String*);**

[JScript] **protected function AxHost(String);**

This member supports the .NET Framework infrastructure and is not intended to be used directly from your code.

[Visual Basic] **Protected Sub New(String, Integer)**

[C#] **protected AxHost(string, int);**

[C++] **protected: AxHost(String*, int);**

[JScript] **protected function AxHost(String, int);**

AxHost Constructor (String)

This member supports the .NET Framework infrastructure and is not intended to be used directly from your code.

```
[Visual Basic]
Protected Sub New( _
   ByVal clsid As String _
)
[C#]
protected AxHost(
   string clsid
);
[C++]
protected: AxHost(
   String* clsid
);
[JScript]
protected function AxHost(
   clsid : String
);
```

AxHost Constructor (String, Int32)

This member supports the .NET Framework infrastructure and is not intended to be used directly from your code.

```
[Visual Basic]
Protected Sub New( _
   ByVal clsid As String, _
   ByVal flags As Integer _
)
```

```
[C#]
protected AxHost(
   string clsid,
   int flags
);
[C++]
protected: AxHost(
   String* clsid,
   int flags
);
[JScript]
protected function AxHost(
   clsid : String,
   flags : int
);
```

AxHost.BackColor Property

This member overrides **Control.BackColor**.

```
[Visual Basic]
Overrides Public Property BackColor As Color
[C#]
public override Color BackColor {get; set;}
[C++]
public: __property Color get_BackColor();
public: __property void set_BackColor(Color);
[JScript]
public override function get BackColor() : Color;
public override function set BackColor(Color);
```

Requirements

Platforms: Windows 98, Windows NT 4.0, Windows Millennium Edition, Windows 2000, Windows XP Home Edition, Windows XP Professional, Windows Server 2003 family

AxHost.BackgroundImage Property

This member overrides **Control.BackgroundImage**.

```
[Visual Basic]
Overrides Public Property BackgroundImage As Image
[C#]
public override Image BackgroundImage {get; set;}
[C++]
public: __property Image* get_BackgroundImage();
public: __property void set_BackgroundImage(Image*);
[JScript]
public override function get BackgroundImage() : Image;
public override function set BackgroundImage(Image);
```

Requirements

Platforms: Windows 98, Windows NT 4.0, Windows Millennium Edition, Windows 2000, Windows XP Home Edition, Windows XP Professional, Windows Server 2003 family

AxHost.ContainingControl Property

Gets or sets the control containing the ActiveX control.

```
[Visual Basic]
Public Property ContainingControl As ContainerControl
[C#]
public ContainerControl ContainingControl {get; set;}
[C++]
public: __property ContainerControl* get_ContainingControl();
public: __property void set_ContainingControl(ContainerControl*);
[JScript]
public function get ContainingControl() : ContainerControl;
public function set ContainingControl(ContainerControl);
```

Property Value

A **ContainerControl** that represents the control containing the ActiveX control.

Remarks

The **ContainingControl** property value can be different from the **Parent** property. The **ContainerControl** represented by this property is the ActiveX control's logical container. For example, if an ActiveX control is hosted in a **GroupBox** control, and the **GroupBox** is contained on a **Form**, then the **ContainingControl** property value of the ActiveX control is the **Form**, and the **Parent** property value is the **GroupBox** control.

Requirements

Platforms: Windows 98, Windows NT 4.0, Windows Millennium Edition, Windows 2000, Windows XP Home Edition, Windows XP Professional, Windows Server 2003 family

.NET Framework Security:

- **UIPermission** for all windows to get this property value. Associated enumeration: **UIPermissionWindow.AllWindows**

AxHost.ContextMenu Property

This member overrides **Control.ContextMenu**.

```
[Visual Basic]
Overrides Public Property ContextMenu As ContextMenu
[C#]
public override ContextMenu ContextMenu {get; set;}
[C++]
public: __property ContextMenu* get_ContextMenu();
public: __property void set_ContextMenu(ContextMenu*);
[JScript]
public override function get ContextMenu() : ContextMenu;
public override function set ContextMenu(ContextMenu);
```

Requirements

Platforms: Windows 98, Windows NT 4.0, Windows Millennium Edition, Windows 2000, Windows XP Home Edition, Windows XP Professional, Windows Server 2003 family

AxHost.CreateParams Property

This member overrides **Control.CreateParams**.

```
[Visual Basic]
Overrides Protected ReadOnly Property CreateParams As CreateParams
[C#]
protected override CreateParams CreateParams {get;}
[C++]
protected: __property CreateParams* get_CreateParams();
[JScript]
protected override function get CreateParams() : CreateParams;
```

Requirements

Platforms: Windows 98, Windows NT 4.0, Windows Millennium Edition, Windows 2000, Windows XP Home Edition, Windows XP Professional, Windows Server 2003 family

AxHost.Cursor Property

This member overrides **Control.Cursor**.

```
[Visual Basic]
Overrides Public Property Cursor As Cursor
[C#]
public override Cursor Cursor {get; set;}
[C++]
public: __property Cursor* get_Cursor();
public: __property void set_Cursor(Cursor*);
[JScript]
public override function get Cursor() : Cursor;
public override function set Cursor(Cursor);
```

Requirements

Platforms: Windows 98, Windows NT 4.0, Windows Millennium Edition, Windows 2000, Windows XP Home Edition, Windows XP Professional, Windows Server 2003 family

AxHost.DefaultSize Property

This member overrides **Control.DefaultSize**.

```
[Visual Basic]
Overrides Protected ReadOnly Property DefaultSize As Size
[C#]
protected override Size DefaultSize {get;}
[C++]
protected: __property Size get_DefaultSize();
[JScript]
protected override function get DefaultSize() : Size;
```

Requirements

Platforms: Windows 98, Windows NT 4.0, Windows Millennium Edition, Windows 2000, Windows XP Home Edition, Windows XP Professional, Windows Server 2003 family

AxHost.EditMode Property

This member supports the .NET Framework infrastructure and is not intended to be used directly from your code.

```
[Visual Basic]
Public ReadOnly Property EditMode As Boolean
[C#]
public bool EditMode {get;}
[C++]
public: __property bool get_EditMode();
[JScript]
public function get EditMode() : Boolean;
```

AxHost.Enabled Property

Gets or sets a value indicating whether the ActiveX control is in an enabled state.

```
[Visual Basic]
Public Overridable Property Enabled As Boolean
[C#]
public virtual bool Enabled {get; set;}
[C++]
public: __property virtual bool get_Enabled();
public: __property virtual void set_Enabled(bool);
[JScript]
public function get Enabled() : Boolean;
public function set Enabled(Boolean);
```

Property Value

true if the ActiveX control is in an enabled state; otherwise, **false**.

Remarks

Notes to Inheritors: When overriding the **Enabled** property in a derived class, use the base class's **Enabled** property to extend the base implementation. Otherwise, you must provide all the implementation. You are not required to override both the **get** and **set** accessors of the **Enabled** property; you can override only one if needed.

Requirements

Platforms: Windows 98, Windows NT 4.0, Windows Millennium Edition, Windows 2000, Windows XP Home Edition, Windows XP Professional, Windows Server 2003 family

AxHost.Font Property

This member overrides **Control.Font**.

```
[Visual Basic]
Overrides Public Property Font As Font
[C#]
public override Font Font {get; set;}
[C++]
public: __property Font* get_Font();
public: __property void set_Font(Font*);
[JScript]
public override function get Font() : Font;
public override function set Font(Font);
```

Requirements

Platforms: Windows 98, Windows NT 4.0, Windows Millennium Edition, Windows 2000, Windows XP Home Edition, Windows XP Professional, Windows Server 2003 family

AxHost.ForeColor Property

This member overrides **Control.ForeColor**.

```
[Visual Basic]
Overrides Public Property ForeColor As Color
[C#]
public override Color ForeColor {get; set;}
[C++]
public: __property Color get_ForeColor();
public: __property void set_ForeColor(Color);
```

```
[JScript]
public override function get ForeColor() : Color;
public override function set ForeColor(Color);
```

Requirements

Platforms: Windows 98, Windows NT 4.0, Windows Millennium Edition, Windows 2000, Windows XP Home Edition, Windows XP Professional, Windows Server 2003 family

AxHost.HasAboutBox Property

Gets a value indicating whether the ActiveX control has an About dialog box.

```
[Visual Basic]
Public ReadOnly Property HasAboutBox As Boolean
[C#]
public bool HasAboutBox {get;}
[C++]
public: __property bool get_HasAboutBox();
[JScript]
public function get HasAboutBox() : Boolean;
```

Property Value

true if the ActiveX control has an About dialog box; otherwise, **false**.

Remarks

The About dialog box typically displays version and copyright information about the ActiveX control.

Requirements

Platforms: Windows 98, Windows NT 4.0, Windows Millennium Edition, Windows 2000, Windows XP Home Edition, Windows XP Professional, Windows Server 2003 family

AxHost.OcxState Property

Gets or sets the persisted state of the ActiveX control.

```
[Visual Basic]
Public Property OcxState As AxHost.State
[C#]
public AxHost.State OcxState {get; set;}
[C++]
public: __property AxHost.State* get_OcxState();
public: __property void set_OcxState(AxHost.State*);
[JScript]
public function get OcxState() : AxHost.State;
public function set OcxState(AxHost.State);
```

Property Value

An **AxHost.State** that represents the persisted state of the ActiveX control.

Exceptions

Exception Type	Condition
Exception	The ActiveX control is already loaded.

Remarks

The value of the **OcxState** property is used after the control is created but before it is shown. The persisted state of the underlying ActiveX control is returned in the **AxHost.State**.

Requirements

Platforms: Windows 98, Windows NT 4.0, Windows Millennium Edition, Windows 2000, Windows XP Home Edition, Windows XP Professional, Windows Server 2003 family

AxHost.RightToLeft Property

Gets or sets a Boolean value indicating whether ActiveX control's elements are aligned to support locales using right-to-left fonts.

```
[Visual Basic]
Public Overridable Property RightToLeft As Boolean
[C#]
public virtual bool RightToLeft {get; set;}
[C++]
public: __property virtual bool get_RightToLeft();
public: __property virtual void set_RightToLeft(bool);
[JScript]
public function get RightToLeft() : Boolean;
public function set RightToLeft(Boolean);
```

Property Value

true if the ActiveX control's elements are aligned to support locales using right-to-left fonts; otherwise, **false**.

Remarks

As implemented in the **AxHost** class, the **RightToLeft** property always returns **true**.

The **RightToLeft** property is used for international applications where the language is written from right to left, such as Hebrew or Arabic. When this property is set to **true**, control elements that include text are displayed from right to left.

Notes to Inheritors: When overriding the **RightToLeft** property in a derived class, use the base class's **RightToLeft** property to extend the base implementation. Otherwise, you must provide all the implementation. You are not required to override both the **get** and **set** accessors of the **RightToLeft** property; you can override only one if needed.

Requirements

Platforms: Windows 98, Windows NT 4.0, Windows Millennium Edition, Windows 2000, Windows XP Home Edition, Windows XP Professional, Windows Server 2003 family

AxHost.Site Property

This member overrides **Control.Site**.

```
[Visual Basic]
Property Site As ISite  Implements IComponent.Site
[C#]
ISite Site {set;}
[C++]
public: __property void set_Site(ISite*);
[JScript]
public override function set Site(ISite);
```

Requirements

Platforms: Windows 98, Windows NT 4.0, Windows Millennium Edition, Windows 2000, Windows XP Home Edition, Windows XP Professional, Windows Server 2003 family

AxHost.Text Property

This member overrides **Control.Text**.

```
[Visual Basic]
Overrides Public Property Text As String
[C#]
public override string Text {get; set;}
[C++]
public: __property String* get_Text();
public: __property void set_Text(String*);
[JScript]
public override function get Text() : String;
public override function set Text(String);
```

Requirements

Platforms: Windows 98, Windows NT 4.0, Windows Millennium Edition, Windows 2000, Windows XP Home Edition, Windows XP Professional, Windows Server 2003 family

AxHost.AttachInterfaces Method

When overridden in a derived class, attaches interfaces to the underlying ActiveX control.

```
[Visual Basic]
Protected Overridable Sub AttachInterfaces()
[C#]
protected virtual void AttachInterfaces();
[C++]
protected: virtual void AttachInterfaces();
[JScript]
protected function AttachInterfaces();
```

Remarks

Notes to Inheritors: Classes that extend **AxHost** should override this method. Within an overridden version of this method, the extending class should call **GetOcx** to retrieve its own interface. In most cases, the **GetOcx** method should not be called before this method is called.

Requirements

Platforms: Windows 98, Windows NT 4.0, Windows Millennium Edition, Windows 2000, Windows XP Home Edition, Windows XP Professional, Windows Server 2003 family

AxHost.BeginInit Method

Begins the initialization of the ActiveX control.

```
[Visual Basic]
Public Overridable Sub BeginInit() Implements _
   ISupportInitialize.BeginInit
[C#]
public virtual void BeginInit();
[C++]
public: virtual void BeginInit();
[JScript]
public function BeginInit();
```

Implements

ISupportInitialize.BeginInit

Remarks

Design environments typically use this method to start the initialization of a component that is used on a form or used by another component. The **EndInit** method ends the initialization. Using the **BeginInit** and **EndInit** methods prevents the control from being used before it is fully initialized. The initialization occurs at run time.

Requirements

Platforms: Windows 98, Windows NT 4.0, Windows Millennium Edition, Windows 2000, Windows XP Home Edition, Windows XP Professional, Windows Server 2003 family

AxHost.CreateHandle Method

This member overrides **Control.CreateHandle**.

```
[Visual Basic]
Overrides Protected Sub CreateHandle()
[C#]
protected override void CreateHandle();
[C++]
protected: void CreateHandle();
[JScript]
protected override function CreateHandle();
```

Requirements

Platforms: Windows 98, Windows NT 4.0, Windows Millennium Edition, Windows 2000, Windows XP Home Edition, Windows XP Professional, Windows Server 2003 family

AxHost.CreateSink Method

This member supports the .NET Framework infrastructure and is not intended to be used directly from your code.

```
[Visual Basic]
Protected Overridable Sub CreateSink()
[C#]
protected virtual void CreateSink();
[C++]
protected: virtual void CreateSink();
[JScript]
protected function CreateSink();
```

AxHost.DestroyHandle Method

This member overrides **Control.DestroyHandle**.

```
[Visual Basic]
Overrides Protected Sub DestroyHandle()
[C#]
protected override void DestroyHandle();
[C++]
protected: void DestroyHandle();
[JScript]
protected override function DestroyHandle();
```

Requirements

Platforms: Windows 98, Windows NT 4.0, Windows Millennium Edition, Windows 2000, Windows XP Home Edition, Windows XP Professional, Windows Server 2003 family

AxHost.DetachSink Method

This member supports the .NET Framework infrastructure and is not intended to be used directly from your code.

```
[Visual Basic]
Protected Overridable Sub DetachSink()
[C#]
protected virtual void DetachSink();
[C++]
protected: virtual void DetachSink();
[JScript]
protected function DetachSink();
```

AxHost.Dispose Method

Overload List

This member supports the .NET Framework infrastructure and is not intended to be used directly from your code.

[Visual Basic] **Overloads Overrides Protected Sub Dispose(Boolean)**

[C#] **protected override void Dispose(bool);**

[C++] **protected: void Dispose(bool);**

[JScript] **protected override function Dispose(Boolean);**

Inherited from **Component**.

[Visual Basic] **Overloads Public Overridable Sub Dispose() Implements IDisposable.Dispose**

[C#] **public virtual void Dispose();**

[C++] **public: virtual void Dispose();**

[JScript] **public function Dispose();**

AxHost.Dispose Method (Boolean)

This member overrides **Control.Dispose**.

```
[Visual Basic]
Overrides Overloads Protected Sub Dispose( _
   ByVal disposing As Boolean _
)
[C#]
protected override void Dispose(
   bool disposing
);
[C++]
protected: void Dispose(
   bool disposing
);
[JScript]
protected override function Dispose(
   disposing : Boolean
);
```

Requirements

Platforms: Windows 98, Windows NT 4.0, Windows Millennium Edition, Windows 2000, Windows XP Home Edition, Windows XP Professional, Windows Server 2003 family

AxHost.DoVerb Method

This member supports the .NET Framework infrastructure and is not intended to be used directly from your code.

```
[Visual Basic]
Public Sub DoVerb( _
   ByVal verb As Integer _
)
[C#]
public void DoVerb(
   int verb
);
[C++]
public: void DoVerb(
   int verb
);
[JScript]
public function DoVerb(
   verb : int
);
```

AxHost.EndInit Method

Ends the initialization of an ActiveX control.

```
[Visual Basic]
Public Overridable Sub EndInit() Implements _
   ISupportInitialize.EndInit
[C#]
public virtual void EndInit();
[C++]
public: virtual void EndInit();
[JScript]
public function EndInit();
```

Implements

ISupportInitialize.EndInit

Remarks

Design environments typically use this method to finish the initialization of a component that is used on a form or used by another component. The **EndInit** method ends the initialization. Using the **BeginInit** and **EndInit** methods prevents the control from being used before it is fully initialized. The initialization occurs at run time.

Requirements

Platforms: Windows 98, Windows NT 4.0, Windows Millennium Edition, Windows 2000, Windows XP Home Edition, Windows XP Professional, Windows Server 2003 family

AxHost.GetColorFromOleColor Method

This member supports the .NET Framework infrastructure and is not intended to be used directly from your code.

```
[Visual Basic]
<CLSCompliant(False)>
Protected Shared Function GetColorFromOleColor( _
   ByVal color As UInt32 _
) As Color
```

[C#]
```
[CLSCompliant(false)]
protected static Color GetColorFromOleColor(
   uint color
);
```
[C++]
```
[CLSCompliant(false)]
protected: static Color GetColorFromOleColor(
   unsigned int color
);
```
[JScript]
```
protected
   CLSCompliant(false)
static function GetColorFromOleColor(
   color : UInt32
) : Color;
```

AxHost.GetFontFromIFont Method

This member supports the .NET Framework infrastructure and is not intended to be used directly from your code.

[Visual Basic]
```
Protected Shared Function GetFontFromIFont( _
   ByVal font As Object _
) As Font
```
[C#]
```
protected static Font GetFontFromIFont(
   object font
);
```
[C++]
```
protected: static Font* GetFontFromIFont(
   Object* font
);
```
[JScript]
```
protected static function GetFontFromIFont(
   font : Object
) : Font;
```

AxHost.GetFontFromIFontDisp Method

This member supports the .NET Framework infrastructure and is not intended to be used directly from your code.

[Visual Basic]
```
Protected Shared Function GetFontFromIFontDisp( _
   ByVal font As Object _
) As Font
```
[C#]
```
protected static Font GetFontFromIFontDisp(
   object font
);
```
[C++]
```
protected: static Font* GetFontFromIFontDisp(
   Object* font
);
```
[JScript]
```
protected static function GetFontFromIFontDisp(
   font : Object
) : Font;
```

AxHost.GetIFontDispFromFont Method

This member supports the .NET Framework infrastructure and is not intended to be used directly from your code.

[Visual Basic]
```
Protected Shared Function GetIFontDispFromFont( _
   ByVal font As Font _
) As Object
```
[C#]
```
protected static object GetIFontDispFromFont(
   Font font
);
```
[C++]
```
protected: static Object* GetIFontDispFromFont(
   Font* font
);
```
[JScript]
```
protected static function GetIFontDispFromFont(
   font : Font
) : Object;
```

AxHost.GetIFontFromFont Method

This member supports the .NET Framework infrastructure and is not intended to be used directly from your code.

[Visual Basic]
```
Protected Shared Function GetIFontFromFont( _
   ByVal font As Font _
) As Object
```
[C#]
```
protected static object GetIFontFromFont(
   Font font
);
```
[C++]
```
protected: static Object* GetIFontFromFont(
   Font* font
);
```
[JScript]
```
protected static function GetIFontFromFont(
   font : Font
) : Object;
```

AxHost.GetIPictureDispFromPicture Method

This member supports the .NET Framework infrastructure and is not intended to be used directly from your code.

[Visual Basic]
```
Protected Shared Function GetIPictureDispFromPicture( _
   ByVal image As Image _
) As Object
```
[C#]
```
protected static object GetIPictureDispFromPicture(
   Image image
);
```
[C++]
```
protected: static Object* GetIPictureDispFromPicture(
   Image* image
);
```
[JScript]
```
protected static function GetIPictureDispFromPicture(
   image : Image
) : Object;
```

AxHost.GetIPictureFromCursor Method

This member supports the .NET Framework infrastructure and is not intended to be used directly from your code.

```
[Visual Basic]
Protected Shared Function GetIPictureFromCursor( _
   ByVal cursor As Cursor _
) As Object
[C#]
protected static object GetIPictureFromCursor(
   Cursor cursor
);
[C++]
protected: static Object* GetIPictureFromCursor(
   Cursor* cursor
);
[JScript]
protected static function GetIPictureFromCursor(
   cursor : Cursor
) : Object;
```

AxHost.GetIPictureFromPicture Method

This member supports the .NET Framework infrastructure and is not intended to be used directly from your code.

```
[Visual Basic]
Protected Shared Function GetIPictureFromPicture( _
   ByVal image As Image _
) As Object
[C#]
protected static object GetIPictureFromPicture(
   Image image
);
[C++]
protected: static Object* GetIPictureFromPicture(
   Image* image
);
[JScript]
protected static function GetIPictureFromPicture(
   image : Image
) : Object;
```

AxHost.GetOADateFromTime Method

This member supports the .NET Framework infrastructure and is not intended to be used directly from your code.

```
[Visual Basic]
Protected Shared Function GetOADateFromTime( _
   ByVal time As DateTime _
) As Double
[C#]
protected static double GetOADateFromTime(
   DateTime time
);
[C++]
protected: static double GetOADateFromTime(
   DateTime time
);
[JScript]
protected static function GetOADateFromTime(
   time : DateTime
) : double;
```

AxHost.GetOcx Method

Retrieves a reference to the underlying ActiveX control.

```
[Visual Basic]
Public Function GetOcx() As Object
[C#]
public object GetOcx();
[C++]
public: Object* GetOcx();
[JScript]
public function GetOcx() : Object;
```

Return Value

An object that represents the ActiveX control.

Requirements

Platforms: Windows 98, Windows NT 4.0, Windows Millennium Edition, Windows 2000, Windows XP Home Edition, Windows XP Professional, Windows Server 2003 family

AxHost.GetOleColorFromColor Method

This member supports the .NET Framework infrastructure and is not intended to be used directly from your code.

```
[Visual Basic]
<CLSCompliant(False)>
Protected Shared Function GetOleColorFromColor( _
   ByVal color As Color _
) As UInt32
[C#]
[CLSCompliant(false)]
protected static uint GetOleColorFromColor(
   Color color
);
[C++]
[CLSCompliant(false)]
protected: static unsigned int GetOleColorFromColor(
   Color color
);
[JScript]
protected
   CLSCompliant(false)
static function GetOleColorFromColor(
   color : Color
) : UInt32;
```

AxHost.GetPictureFromIPicture Method

This member supports the .NET Framework infrastructure and is not intended to be used directly from your code.

```
[Visual Basic]
Protected Shared Function GetPictureFromIPicture( _
   ByVal picture As Object _
) As Image
[C#]
protected static Image GetPictureFromIPicture(
   object picture
);
```

[C++]
```
protected: static Image* GetPictureFromIPicture(
   Object* picture
);
```
[JScript]
```
protected static function GetPictureFromIPicture(
   picture : Object
) : Image;
```

AxHost.GetPictureFromIPictureDisp Method

This member supports the .NET Framework infrastructure and is not intended to be used directly from your code.

[Visual Basic]
```
Protected Shared Function GetPictureFromIPictureDisp( _
   ByVal picture As Object _
) As Image
```
[C#]
```
protected static Image GetPictureFromIPictureDisp(
   object picture
);
```
[C++]
```
protected: static Image* GetPictureFromIPictureDisp(
   Object* picture
);
```
[JScript]
```
protected static function GetPictureFromIPictureDisp(
   picture : Object
) : Image;
```

AxHost.GetTimeFromOADate Method

This member supports the .NET Framework infrastructure and is not intended to be used directly from your code.

[Visual Basic]
```
Protected Shared Function GetTimeFromOADate( _
   ByVal date As Double _
) As DateTime
```
[C#]
```
protected static DateTime GetTimeFromOADate(
   double date
);
```
[C++]
```
protected: static DateTime GetTimeFromOADate(
   double date
);
```
[JScript]
```
protected static function GetTimeFromOADate(
   date : double
) : DateTime;
```

AxHost.HasPropertyPages Method

Determines if the ActiveX control has a property page.

[Visual Basic]
```
Public Function HasPropertyPages() As Boolean
```
[C#]
```
public bool HasPropertyPages();
```
[C++]
```
public: bool HasPropertyPages();
```
[JScript]
```
public function HasPropertyPages() : Boolean;
```

Return Value

true if the ActiveX control has a property page; otherwise, **false**.

Remarks

Property pages allow an ActiveX control user to view and change ActiveX control properties. These properties are accessed by invoking a control properties dialog box, which contains one or more property pages that provide a customized, graphical interface for viewing and editing the control properties.

Requirements

Platforms: Windows 98, Windows NT 4.0, Windows Millennium Edition, Windows 2000, Windows XP Home Edition, Windows XP Professional, Windows Server 2003 family

AxHost.ICustomTypeDescriptor.GetAttributes Method

This member supports the .NET Framework infrastructure and is not intended to be used directly from your code.

[Visual Basic]
```
Private Function GetAttributes() As AttributeCollection Implements _
   ICustomTypeDescriptor.GetAttributes
```
[C#]
```
AttributeCollection ICustomTypeDescriptor.GetAttributes();
```
[C++]
```
private: AttributeCollection*
   ICustomTypeDescriptor::GetAttributes();
```
[JScript]
```
private function ICustomTypeDescriptor.GetAttributes() :
   AttributeCollection;
```

AxHost.ICustomTypeDescriptor.GetClassName Method

This member supports the .NET Framework infrastructure and is not intended to be used directly from your code.

[Visual Basic]
```
Private Function GetClassName() As String Implements _
   ICustomTypeDescriptor.GetClassName
```
[C#]
```
string ICustomTypeDescriptor.GetClassName();
```
[C++]
```
private: String* ICustomTypeDescriptor::GetClassName();
```
[JScript]
```
private function ICustomTypeDescriptor.GetClassName() : String;
```

AxHost.ICustomTypeDescriptor.GetComponent-Name Method

This member supports the .NET Framework infrastructure and is not intended to be used directly from your code.

[Visual Basic]
```
Private Function GetComponentName() As String Implements _
   ICustomTypeDescriptor.GetComponentName
```
[C#]
```
string ICustomTypeDescriptor.GetComponentName();
```

[C++]
```
private: String* ICustomTypeDescriptor::GetComponentName();
```
[JScript]
```
private function ICustomTypeDescriptor.GetComponentName() : String;
```

AxHost.ICustomTypeDescriptor.GetConverter Method

This member supports the .NET Framework infrastructure and is not intended to be used directly from your code.

[Visual Basic]
```
Private Function GetConverter() As TypeConverter Implements _
   ICustomTypeDescriptor.GetConverter
```
[C#]
```
TypeConverter ICustomTypeDescriptor.GetConverter();
```
[C++]
```
private: TypeConverter* ICustomTypeDescriptor::GetConverter();
```
[JScript]
```
private function ICustomTypeDescriptor.GetConverter() :
   TypeConverter;
```

AxHost.ICustomTypeDescriptor.GetDefaultEvent Method

This member supports the .NET Framework infrastructure and is not intended to be used directly from your code.

[Visual Basic]
```
Private Function GetDefaultEvent() As EventDescriptor Implements _
   ICustomTypeDescriptor.GetDefaultEvent
```
[C#]
```
EventDescriptor ICustomTypeDescriptor.GetDefaultEvent();
```
[C++]
```
private: EventDescriptor* ICustomTypeDescriptor::GetDefaultEvent();
```
[JScript]
```
private function ICustomTypeDescriptor.GetDefaultEvent() :
   EventDescriptor;
```

AxHost.ICustomTypeDescriptor.GetDefault-Property Method

This member supports the .NET Framework infrastructure and is not intended to be used directly from your code.

[Visual Basic]
```
Private Function GetDefaultProperty() As PropertyDescriptor _
   Implements ICustomTypeDescriptor.GetDefaultProperty
```
[C#]
```
PropertyDescriptor ICustomTypeDescriptor.GetDefaultProperty();
```
[C++]
```
private: PropertyDescriptor*
   ICustomTypeDescriptor::GetDefaultProperty();
```
[JScript]
```
private function ICustomTypeDescriptor.GetDefaultProperty() :
   PropertyDescriptor;
```

AxHost.ICustomTypeDescriptor.GetEditor Method

This member supports the .NET Framework infrastructure and is not intended to be used directly from your code.

[Visual Basic]
```
Private Function GetEditor( _
   ByVal editorBaseType As Type _
) As Object Implements ICustomTypeDescriptor.GetEditor
```
[C#]
```
object ICustomTypeDescriptor.GetEditor(
   Type editorBaseType
);
```
[C++]
```
private: Object* ICustomTypeDescriptor::GetEditor(
   Type* editorBaseType
);
```
[JScript]
```
private function ICustomTypeDescriptor.GetEditor(
   editorBaseType : Type
) : Object;
```

AxHost.ICustomTypeDescriptor.GetEvents Method

This member supports the .NET Framework infrastructure and is not intended to be used directly from your code.

Overload List

This member supports the .NET Framework infrastructure and is not intended to be used directly from your code.

[Visual Basic] **Overloads Private Function GetEvents() As EventDescriptorCollection Implements ICustomType-Descriptor.GetEvents**

[C#] **EventDescriptorCollection ICustomType-Descriptor.GetEvents();**

[C++] **private: EventDescriptorCollection* ICustomType-Descriptor::GetEvents();**

[JScript] **private function ICustomType-Descriptor.GetEvents() : EventDescriptorCollection;**

This member supports the .NET Framework infrastructure and is not intended to be used directly from your code.

[Visual Basic] **Overloads Private Function GetEvents(Attribute()) As EventDescriptorCollection Implements ICustomTypeDescriptor.GetEvents**

[C#] **EventDescriptorCollection ICustomType-Descriptor.GetEvents(Attribute[]);**

[C++] **private: EventDescriptorCollection* ICustomType-Descriptor::GetEvents(Attribute*[]);**

[JScript] **private function ICustomTypeDescriptor.Get-Events(Attribute[]) : EventDescriptorCollection;**

AxHost.ICustomTypeDescriptor.GetEvents Method ()

This member supports the .NET Framework infrastructure and is not intended to be used directly from your code.

[Visual Basic]
```
Private Function GetEvents() As EventDescriptorCollection Implements _
   ICustomTypeDescriptor.GetEvents
```
[C#]
```
EventDescriptorCollection ICustomTypeDescriptor.GetEvents();
```

```
[C++]
private: EventDescriptorCollection*
   ICustomTypeDescriptor::GetEvents();
[JScript]
private function ICustomTypeDescriptor.GetEvents() :
   EventDescriptorCollection;
```

AxHost.ICustomTypeDescriptor.GetEvents Method (Attribute[])

This member supports the .NET Framework infrastructure and is not intended to be used directly from your code.

```
[Visual Basic]
Private Function GetEvents( _
   ByVal attributes() As Attribute _
) As EventDescriptorCollection Implements
ICustomTypeDescriptor.GetEvents
[C#]
EventDescriptorCollection ICustomTypeDescriptor.GetEvents(
   Attribute[] attributes
);
[C++]
private: EventDescriptorCollection* ICustomTypeDescriptor::GetEvents(
   Attribute* attributes[]
);
[JScript]
private function ICustomTypeDescriptor.GetEvents(
   attributes : Attribute[]
) : EventDescriptorCollection;
```

AxHost.ICustomTypeDescriptor.GetProperties Method

This member supports the .NET Framework infrastructure and is not intended to be used directly from your code.

Overload List

This member supports the .NET Framework infrastructure and is not intended to be used directly from your code.

[Visual Basic] **Overloads Private Function GetProperties() As PropertyDescriptorCollection Implements ICustomType-Descriptor.GetProperties**

[C#] **PropertyDescriptorCollection ICustomType-Descriptor.GetProperties();**

[C++] **private: PropertyDescriptorCollection* ICustomType-Descriptor::GetProperties();**

[JScript] **private function ICustomTypeDescriptor.Get-Properties() : PropertyDescriptorCollection;**

This member supports the .NET Framework infrastructure and is not intended to be used directly from your code.

[Visual Basic] **Overloads Private Function GetProper-ties(Attribute()) As PropertyDescriptorCollection Implements ICustomTypeDescriptor.GetProperties**

[C#] **PropertyDescriptorCollection ICustomType-Descriptor.GetProperties(Attribute[]);**

[C++] **private: PropertyDescriptorCollection* ICustomType-Descriptor::GetProperties(Attribute*[]);**

[JScript] **private function ICustomTypeDescriptor.Get-Properties(Attribute[]) : PropertyDescriptorCollection;**

AxHost.ICustomTypeDescriptor.GetProperties Method ()

This member supports the .NET Framework infrastructure and is not intended to be used directly from your code.

```
[Visual Basic]
Private Function GetProperties() As PropertyDescriptorCollection _
   Implements ICustomTypeDescriptor.GetProperties
[C#]
PropertyDescriptorCollection ICustomTypeDescriptor.GetProperties();
[C++]
private: PropertyDescriptorCollection*
   ICustomTypeDescriptor::GetProperties();
[JScript]
private function ICustomTypeDescriptor.GetProperties() :
   PropertyDescriptorCollection;
```

AxHost.ICustomTypeDescriptor.GetProperties Method (Attribute[])

This member supports the .NET Framework infrastructure and is not intended to be used directly from your code.

```
[Visual Basic]
Private Function GetProperties( _
   ByVal attributes() As Attribute _
) As PropertyDescriptorCollection Implements
ICustomTypeDescriptor.GetProperties
[C#]
PropertyDescriptorCollection ICustomTypeDescriptor.GetProperties(
   Attribute[] attributes
);
[C++]
private: PropertyDescriptorCollection*
ICustomTypeDescriptor::GetProperties(
   Attribute* attributes[]
);
[JScript]
private function ICustomTypeDescriptor.GetProperties(
   attributes : Attribute[]
) : PropertyDescriptorCollection;
```

AxHost.ICustomTypeDescriptor.GetProperty-Owner Method

This member supports the .NET Framework infrastructure and is not intended to be used directly from your code.

```
[Visual Basic]
Private Function GetPropertyOwner( _
   ByVal pd As PropertyDescriptor _
) As Object Implements ICustomTypeDescriptor.GetPropertyOwner
[C#]
object ICustomTypeDescriptor.GetPropertyOwner(
   PropertyDescriptor pd
);
[C++]
private: Object* ICustomTypeDescriptor::GetPropertyOwner(
   PropertyDescriptor* pd
);
[JScript]
private function ICustomTypeDescriptor.GetPropertyOwner(
   pd : PropertyDescriptor
) : Object;
```

AxHost.InvokeEditMode Method

This member supports the .NET Framework infrastructure and is not intended to be used directly from your code.

[Visual Basic]
```
Public Sub InvokeEditMode()
```
[C#]
```
public void InvokeEditMode();
```
[C++]
```
public: void InvokeEditMode();
```
[JScript]
```
public function InvokeEditMode();
```

AxHost.IsInputChar Method

Determines if a character is an input character that the ActiveX control recognizes.

[Visual Basic]
```
Overrides Protected Function IsInputChar( _
   ByVal charCode As Char _
) As Boolean
```
[C#]
```
protected override bool IsInputChar(
   char charCode
);
```
[C++]
```
protected: bool IsInputChar(
   __wchar_t charCode
);
```
[JScript]
```
protected override function IsInputChar(
   charCode : Char
) : Boolean;
```

Parameters

charCode

The character to test.

Return Value

true if the character should be sent directly to the ActiveX control and not preprocessed; otherwise, **false**.

Remarks

The **IsInputChar** method is called during window message preprocessing to determine whether the given input character should be preprocessed or sent directly to the ActiveX control. The preprocessing of a character includes checking whether the character is a mnemonic of another control.

As implemented in the **AxHost** class, the **IsInputChar** method always returns **true**, so the specified character is sent directly to the ActiveX control.

Requirements

Platforms: Windows 98, Windows NT 4.0, Windows Millennium Edition, Windows 2000, Windows XP Home Edition, Windows XP Professional, Windows Server 2003 family

.NET Framework Security:

- **UIPermission** for all windows for inheriting classes to call this method. Associated enumeration: **UIPermissionWindow.AllWindows**

AxHost.MakeDirty Method

This member supports the .NET Framework infrastructure and is not intended to be used directly from your code.

[Visual Basic]
```
Public Sub MakeDirty()
```
[C#]
```
public void MakeDirty();
```
[C++]
```
public: void MakeDirty();
```
[JScript]
```
public function MakeDirty();
```

AxHost.OnBackColorChanged Method

This member overrides **Control.OnBackColorChanged**.

[Visual Basic]
```
Overrides Protected Sub OnBackColorChanged( _
   ByVal e As EventArgs _
)
```
[C#]
```
protected override void OnBackColorChanged(
   EventArgs e
);
```
[C++]
```
protected: void OnBackColorChanged(
   EventArgs* e
);
```
[JScript]
```
protected override function OnBackColorChanged(
   e : EventArgs
);
```

Requirements

Platforms: Windows 98, Windows NT 4.0, Windows Millennium Edition, Windows 2000, Windows XP Home Edition, Windows XP Professional, Windows Server 2003 family

AxHost.OnFontChanged Method

This member overrides **Control.OnFontChanged**.

[Visual Basic]
```
Overrides Protected Sub OnFontChanged( _
   ByVal e As EventArgs _
)
```
[C#]
```
protected override void OnFontChanged(
   EventArgs e
);
```
[C++]
```
protected: void OnFontChanged(
   EventArgs* e
);
```
[JScript]
```
protected override function OnFontChanged(
   e : EventArgs
);
```

Requirements

Platforms: Windows 98, Windows NT 4.0, Windows Millennium Edition, Windows 2000, Windows XP Home Edition, Windows XP Professional, Windows Server 2003 family

AxHost.OnForeColorChanged Method

This member overrides **Control.OnForeColorChanged**.

```
[Visual Basic]
Overrides Protected Sub OnForeColorChanged( _
   ByVal e As EventArgs _
)
[C#]
protected override void OnForeColorChanged(
   EventArgs e
);
[C++]
protected: void OnForeColorChanged(
   EventArgs* e
);
[JScript]
protected override function OnForeColorChanged(
   e : EventArgs
);
```

Requirements

Platforms: Windows 98, Windows NT 4.0, Windows Millennium Edition, Windows 2000, Windows XP Home Edition, Windows XP Professional, Windows Server 2003 family

AxHost.OnHandleCreated Method

This member overrides **Control.OnHandleCreated**.

```
[Visual Basic]
Overrides Protected Sub OnHandleCreated( _
   ByVal e As EventArgs _
)
[C#]
protected override void OnHandleCreated(
   EventArgs e
);
[C++]
protected: void OnHandleCreated(
   EventArgs* e
);
[JScript]
protected override function OnHandleCreated(
   e : EventArgs
);
```

Requirements

Platforms: Windows 98, Windows NT 4.0, Windows Millennium Edition, Windows 2000, Windows XP Home Edition, Windows XP Professional, Windows Server 2003 family

AxHost.OnInPlaceActive Method

This member supports the .NET Framework infrastructure and is not intended to be used directly from your code.

```
[Visual Basic]
Protected Overridable Sub OnInPlaceActive()
[C#]
protected virtual void OnInPlaceActive();
[C++]
protected: virtual void OnInPlaceActive();
[JScript]
protected function OnInPlaceActive();
```

AxHost.OnLostFocus Method

This member overrides **Control.OnLostFocus**.

```
[Visual Basic]
Overrides Protected Sub OnLostFocus( _
   ByVal e As EventArgs _
)
[C#]
protected override void OnLostFocus(
   EventArgs e
);
[C++]
protected: void OnLostFocus(
   EventArgs* e
);
[JScript]
protected override function OnLostFocus(
   e : EventArgs
);
```

Requirements

Platforms: Windows 98, Windows NT 4.0, Windows Millennium Edition, Windows 2000, Windows XP Home Edition, Windows XP Professional, Windows Server 2003 family

AxHost.PreProcessMessage Method

This member overrides **Control.PreProcessMessage**.

```
[Visual Basic]
Overrides Public Function PreProcessMessage( _
   ByRef msg As Message _
) As Boolean
[C#]
public override bool PreProcessMessage(
   ref Message msg
);
[C++]
public: bool PreProcessMessage(
   Message* msg
);
[JScript]
public override function PreProcessMessage(
   msg : Message
) : Boolean;
```

Requirements

Platforms: Windows 98, Windows NT 4.0, Windows Millennium Edition, Windows 2000, Windows XP Home Edition, Windows XP Professional, Windows Server 2003 family

AxHost.ProcessDialogKey Method

This member overrides **Control.ProcessDialogKey**.

```
[Visual Basic]
Overrides Protected Function ProcessDialogKey( _
   ByVal keyData As Keys _
) As Boolean
[C#]
protected override bool ProcessDialogKey(
   Keys keyData
);
[C++]
protected: bool ProcessDialogKey(
   Keys keyData
);
[JScript]
protected override function ProcessDialogKey(
   keyData : Keys
) : Boolean;
```

Requirements

Platforms: Windows 98, Windows NT 4.0, Windows Millennium Edition, Windows 2000, Windows XP Home Edition, Windows XP Professional, Windows Server 2003 family

AxHost.ProcessMnemonic Method

This member overrides **Control.ProcessMnemonic**.

```
[Visual Basic]
Overrides Protected Function ProcessMnemonic( _
   ByVal charCode As Char _
) As Boolean
[C#]
protected override bool ProcessMnemonic(
   char charCode
);
[C++]
protected: bool ProcessMnemonic(
   __wchar_t charCode
);
[JScript]
protected override function ProcessMnemonic(
   charCode : Char
) : Boolean;
```

Requirements

Platforms: Windows 98, Windows NT 4.0, Windows Millennium Edition, Windows 2000, Windows XP Home Edition, Windows XP Professional, Windows Server 2003 family

AxHost.PropsValid Method

This member supports the .NET Framework infrastructure and is not intended to be used directly from your code.

```
[Visual Basic]
Protected Function PropsValid() As Boolean
[C#]
protected bool PropsValid();
[C++]
protected: bool PropsValid();
[JScript]
protected function PropsValid() : Boolean;
```

AxHost.RaiseOnMouseDown Method

This member supports the .NET Framework infrastructure and is not intended to be used directly from your code.

Overload List

This member supports the .NET Framework infrastructure and is not intended to be used directly from your code.

[Visual Basic] **Overloads Protected Sub RaiseOnMouseDown(Short, Short, Integer, Integer)**

[C#] **protected void RaiseOnMouseDown(short, short, int, int);**

[C++] **protected: void RaiseOnMouseDown(short, short, int, int);**

[JScript] **protected function RaiseOnMouseDown(Int16, Int16, int, int);**

This member supports the .NET Framework infrastructure and is not intended to be used directly from your code.

[Visual Basic] **Overloads Protected Sub RaiseOnMouseDown(Short, Short, Single, Single)**

[C#] **protected void RaiseOnMouseDown(short, short, float, float);**

[C++] **protected: void RaiseOnMouseDown(short, short, float, float);**

[JScript] **protected function RaiseOnMouseDown(Int16, Int16, float, float);**

This member supports the .NET Framework infrastructure and is not intended to be used directly from your code.

[Visual Basic] **Overloads Protected Sub RaiseOnMouseDown(Object, Object, Object, Object)**

[C#] **protected void RaiseOnMouseDown(object, object, object, object);**

[C++] **protected: void RaiseOnMouseDown(Object*, Object*, Object*, Object*);**

[JScript] **protected function RaiseOnMouseDown(Object, Object, Object, Object);**

AxHost.RaiseOnMouseDown Method (Int16, Int16, Int32, Int32)

This member supports the .NET Framework infrastructure and is not intended to be used directly from your code.

```
[Visual Basic]
Overloads Protected Sub RaiseOnMouseDown( _
   ByVal button As Short, _
   ByVal shift As Short, _
   ByVal x As Integer, _
   ByVal y As Integer _
)
```

```
[C#]
protected void RaiseOnMouseDown(
   short button,
   short shift,
   int x,
   int y
);
[C++]
protected: void RaiseOnMouseDown(
   short button,
   short shift,
   int x,
   int y
);
[JScript]
protected function RaiseOnMouseDown(
   button : Int16,
   shift : Int16,
   x : int,
   y : int
);
```

AxHost.RaiseOnMouseDown Method (Int16, Int16, Single, Single)

This member supports the .NET Framework infrastructure and is not intended to be used directly from your code.

```
[Visual Basic]
Overloads Protected Sub RaiseOnMouseDown( _
   ByVal button As Short, _
   ByVal shift As Short, _
   ByVal x As Single, _
   ByVal y As Single _
)
[C#]
protected void RaiseOnMouseDown(
   short button,
   short shift,
   float x,
   float y
);
[C++]
protected: void RaiseOnMouseDown(
   short button,
   short shift,
   float x,
   float y
);
[JScript]
protected function RaiseOnMouseDown(
   button : Int16,
   shift : Int16,
   x : float,
   y : float
);
```

AxHost.RaiseOnMouseDown Method (Object, Object, Object, Object)

This member supports the .NET Framework infrastructure and is not intended to be used directly from your code.

```
[Visual Basic]
Overloads Protected Sub RaiseOnMouseDown( _
   ByVal o1 As Object, _
   ByVal o2 As Object, _
   ByVal o3 As Object, _
   ByVal o4 As Object _
)
[C#]
protected void RaiseOnMouseDown(
   object o1,
   object o2,
   object o3,
   object o4
);
[C++]
protected: void RaiseOnMouseDown(
   Object* o1,
   Object* o2,
   Object* o3,
   Object* o4
);
[JScript]
protected function RaiseOnMouseDown(
   o1 : Object,
   o2 : Object,
   o3 : Object,
   o4 : Object
);
```

AxHost.RaiseOnMouseMove Method

This member supports the .NET Framework infrastructure and is not intended to be used directly from your code.

Overload List

This member supports the .NET Framework infrastructure and is not intended to be used directly from your code.

[Visual Basic] **Overloads Protected Sub RaiseOnMouseMove(Short, Short, Integer, Integer)**

[C#] **protected void RaiseOnMouseMove(short, short, int, int);**

[C++] **protected: void RaiseOnMouseMove(short, short, int, int);**

[JScript] **protected function RaiseOnMouseMove(Int16, Int16, int, int);**

This member supports the .NET Framework infrastructure and is not intended to be used directly from your code.

[Visual Basic] **Overloads Protected Sub RaiseOnMouseMove(Short, Short, Single, Single)**

[C#] **protected void RaiseOnMouseMove(short, short, float, float);**

[C++] **protected: void RaiseOnMouseMove(short, short, float, float);**

[JScript] **protected function RaiseOnMouseMove(Int16, Int16, float, float);**

This member supports the .NET Framework infrastructure and is not intended to be used directly from your code.

[Visual Basic] **Overloads Protected Sub RaiseOnMouseMove(Object, Object, Object, Object)**

[C#] **protected void RaiseOnMouseMove(object, object, object, object);**

[C++] **protected: void RaiseOnMouseMove(Object*, Object*, Object*, Object*);**

[JScript] **protected function RaiseOnMouseMove(Object, Object, Object, Object);**

AxHost.RaiseOnMouseMove Method (Int16, Int16, Int32, Int32)

This member supports the .NET Framework infrastructure and is not intended to be used directly from your code.

```
[Visual Basic]
Overloads Protected Sub RaiseOnMouseMove( _
   ByVal button As Short, _
   ByVal shift As Short, _
   ByVal x As Integer, _
   ByVal y As Integer _
)
[C#]
protected void RaiseOnMouseMove(
   short button,
   short shift,
   int x,
   int y
);
[C++]
protected: void RaiseOnMouseMove(
   short button,
   short shift,
   int x,
   int y
);
[JScript]
protected function RaiseOnMouseMove(
   button : Int16,
   shift : Int16,
   x : int,
   y : int
);
```

AxHost.RaiseOnMouseMove Method (Int16, Int16, Single, Single)

This member supports the .NET Framework infrastructure and is not intended to be used directly from your code.

```
[Visual Basic]
Overloads Protected Sub RaiseOnMouseMove( _
   ByVal button As Short, _
   ByVal shift As Short, _
   ByVal x As Single, _
   ByVal y As Single _
)
[C#]
protected void RaiseOnMouseMove(
   short button,
   short shift,
   float x,
   float y
);
[C++]
protected: void RaiseOnMouseMove(
   short button,
   short shift,
   float x,
   float y
);
[JScript]
protected function RaiseOnMouseMove(
   button : Int16,
   shift : Int16,
   x : float,
   y : float
);
```

AxHost.RaiseOnMouseMove Method (Object, Object, Object, Object)

This member supports the .NET Framework infrastructure and is not intended to be used directly from your code.

```
[Visual Basic]
Overloads Protected Sub RaiseOnMouseMove( _
   ByVal o1 As Object, _
   ByVal o2 As Object, _
   ByVal o3 As Object, _
   ByVal o4 As Object _
)
[C#]
protected void RaiseOnMouseMove(
   object o1,
   object o2,
   object o3,
   object o4
);
[C++]
protected: void RaiseOnMouseMove(
   Object* o1,
   Object* o2,
   Object* o3,
   Object* o4
);
[JScript]
protected function RaiseOnMouseMove(
   o1 : Object,
   o2 : Object,
   o3 : Object,
   o4 : Object
);
```

AxHost.RaiseOnMouseUp Method

This member supports the .NET Framework infrastructure and is not intended to be used directly from your code.

Overload List

This member supports the .NET Framework infrastructure and is not intended to be used directly from your code.

[Visual Basic] **Overloads Protected Sub RaiseOnMouseUp(Short, Short, Integer, Integer)**

[C#] **protected void RaiseOnMouseUp(short, short, int, int);**

[C++] **protected: void RaiseOnMouseUp(short, short, int, int);**

[JScript] **protected function RaiseOnMouseUp(Int16, Int16, int, int);**

This member supports the .NET Framework infrastructure and is not intended to be used directly from your code.

[Visual Basic] **Overloads Protected Sub RaiseOnMouseUp(Short, Short, Single, Single)**

[C#] **protected void RaiseOnMouseUp(short, short, float, float);**

[C++] **protected: void RaiseOnMouseUp(short, short, float, float);**

[JScript] **protected function RaiseOnMouseUp(Int16, Int16, float, float);**

This member supports the .NET Framework infrastructure and is not intended to be used directly from your code.

[Visual Basic] **Overloads Protected Sub RaiseOnMouseUp(Object, Object, Object, Object)**

[C#] **protected void RaiseOnMouseUp(object, object, object, object);**

[C++] **protected: void RaiseOnMouseUp(Object*, Object*, Object*, Object*);**

[JScript] **protected function RaiseOnMouseUp(Object, Object, Object, Object);**

AxHost.RaiseOnMouseUp Method (Int16, Int16, Int32, Int32)

This member supports the .NET Framework infrastructure and is not intended to be used directly from your code.

[Visual Basic]
```
Overloads Protected Sub RaiseOnMouseUp( _
   ByVal button As Short, _
   ByVal shift As Short, _
   ByVal x As Integer, _
   ByVal y As Integer _
)
```
[C#]
```
protected void RaiseOnMouseUp(
   short button,
   short shift,
   int x,
   int y
);
```
[C++]
```
protected: void RaiseOnMouseUp(
   short button,
   short shift,
   int x,
   int y
);
```
[JScript]
```
protected function RaiseOnMouseUp(
   button : Int16,
   shift : Int16,
   x : int,
   y : int
);
```

AxHost.RaiseOnMouseUp Method (Int16, Int16, Single, Single)

This member supports the .NET Framework infrastructure and is not intended to be used directly from your code.

[Visual Basic]
```
Overloads Protected Sub RaiseOnMouseUp( _
   ByVal button As Short, _
   ByVal shift As Short, _
   ByVal x As Single, _
   ByVal y As Single _
)
```
[C#]
```
protected void RaiseOnMouseUp(
   short button,
   short shift,
   float x,
   float y
);
```
[C++]
```
protected: void RaiseOnMouseUp(
   short button,
   short shift,
   float x,
   float y
);
```
[JScript]
```
protected function RaiseOnMouseUp(
   button : Int16,
   shift : Int16,
   x : float,
   y : float
);
```

AxHost.RaiseOnMouseUp Method (Object, Object, Object, Object)

This member supports the .NET Framework infrastructure and is not intended to be used directly from your code.

[Visual Basic]
```
Overloads Protected Sub RaiseOnMouseUp( _
   ByVal o1 As Object, _
   ByVal o2 As Object, _
   ByVal o3 As Object, _
   ByVal o4 As Object _
)
```
[C#]
```
protected void RaiseOnMouseUp(
   object o1,
   object o2,
   object o3,
   object o4
);
```

```
[C++]
protected: void RaiseOnMouseUp(
   Object* o1,
   Object* o2,
   Object* o3,
   Object* o4
);
[JScript]
protected function RaiseOnMouseUp(
   o1 : Object,
   o2 : Object,
   o3 : Object,
   o4 : Object
);
```

AxHost.SetAboutBoxDelegate Method

Calls the **ShowAboutBox** method to display the ActiveX control's About dialog box.

```
[Visual Basic]
Protected Sub SetAboutBoxDelegate( _
   ByVal d As AxHost.AboutBoxDelegate _
)
[C#]
protected void SetAboutBoxDelegate(
   AxHost.AboutBoxDelegate d
);
[C++]
protected: void SetAboutBoxDelegate(
   AxHost.AboutBoxDelegate* d
);
[JScript]
protected function SetAboutBoxDelegate(
   d : AxHost.AboutBoxDelegate
);
```

Parameters

d

The **AxHost.AboutBoxDelegate** to call.

Remarks

The **SetAboutBoxDelegate** method also allows derived classes to handle the **ShowAboutBox** method without attaching a delegate. This is the preferred technique for handling the **ShowAboutBox** method in a derived class.

Notes to Inheritors: When overriding **SetAboutBoxDelegate** in a derived class, be sure to call the base class's **SetAboutBoxDelegate** method so that registered delegates receive the **ShowAboutBox** method.

Requirements

Platforms: Windows 98, Windows NT 4.0, Windows Millennium Edition, Windows 2000, Windows XP Home Edition, Windows XP Professional, Windows Server 2003 family

AxHost.SetBoundsCore Method

This member overrides **Control.SetBoundsCore**.

```
[Visual Basic]
Overrides Protected Sub SetBoundsCore( _
   ByVal x As Integer, _
   ByVal y As Integer, _
   ByVal width As Integer, _
   ByVal height As Integer, _
   ByVal specified As BoundsSpecified _
)
[C#]
protected override void SetBoundsCore(
   int x,
   int y,
   int width,
   int height,
   BoundsSpecified specified
);
[C++]
protected: void SetBoundsCore(
   int x,
   int y,
   int width,
   int height,
   BoundsSpecified specified
);
[JScript]
protected override function SetBoundsCore(
   x : int,
   y : int,
   width : int,
   height : int,
   specified : BoundsSpecified
);
```

Requirements

Platforms: Windows 98, Windows NT 4.0, Windows Millennium Edition, Windows 2000, Windows XP Home Edition, Windows XP Professional, Windows Server 2003 family

AxHost.SetVisibleCore Method

This member overrides **Control.SetVisibleCore**.

```
[Visual Basic]
Overrides Protected Sub SetVisibleCore( _
   ByVal value As Boolean _
)
[C#]
protected override void SetVisibleCore(
   bool value
);
[C++]
protected: void SetVisibleCore(
   bool value
);
[JScript]
protected override function SetVisibleCore(
   value : Boolean
);
```

Requirements

Platforms: Windows 98, Windows NT 4.0, Windows Millennium Edition, Windows 2000, Windows XP Home Edition, Windows XP Professional, Windows Server 2003 family

AxHost.ShowAboutBox Method

Displays the ActiveX control's About dialog box.

```
[Visual Basic]
Public Sub ShowAboutBox()
[C#]
public void ShowAboutBox();
[C++]
public: void ShowAboutBox();
[JScript]
public function ShowAboutBox();
```

Remarks

If **HasAboutBox** is **false**, no About dialog box is displayed.

Requirements

Platforms: Windows 98, Windows NT 4.0, Windows Millennium Edition, Windows 2000, Windows XP Home Edition, Windows XP Professional, Windows Server 2003 family

AxHost.ShowPropertyPages Method

Displays the property pages associated with the ActiveX control.

Overload List

Displays the property pages associated with the ActiveX control.

[Visual Basic] **Overloads Public Sub ShowPropertyPages()**

[C#] **public void ShowPropertyPages();**

[C++] **public: void ShowPropertyPages();**

[JScript] **public function ShowPropertyPages();**

Displays the property pages associated with the ActiveX control assigned to the specified parent control.

[Visual Basic] **Overloads Public Sub ShowPropertyPages(Control)**

[C#] **public void ShowPropertyPages(Control);**

[C++] **public: void ShowPropertyPages(Control*);**

[JScript] **public function ShowPropertyPages(Control);**

AxHost.ShowPropertyPages Method ()

Displays the property pages associated with the ActiveX control.

```
[Visual Basic]
Overloads Public Sub ShowPropertyPages()
[C#]
public void ShowPropertyPages();
[C++]
public: void ShowPropertyPages();
[JScript]
public function ShowPropertyPages();
```

Remarks

If **HasPropertyPages** is **false**, no property pages are displayed.

Property pages allow an ActiveX control user to view and change ActiveX control properties. These properties are accessed by invoking a control properties dialog box, which contains one or more property pages that provide a customized, graphical interface for viewing and editing the control properties.

Requirements

Platforms: Windows 98, Windows NT 4.0, Windows Millennium Edition, Windows 2000, Windows XP Home Edition, Windows XP Professional, Windows Server 2003 family

AxHost.ShowPropertyPages Method (Control)

Displays the property pages associated with the ActiveX control assigned to the specified parent control.

```
[Visual Basic]
Overloads Public Sub ShowPropertyPages( _
   ByVal control As Control _
)
[C#]
public void ShowPropertyPages(
   Control control
);
[C++]
public: void ShowPropertyPages(
   Control* control
);
[JScript]
public function ShowPropertyPages(
   control : Control
);
```

Parameters

control

The parent **Control** of the ActiveX control.

Remarks

If **HasPropertyPages** is **false**, no property pages are displayed.

Property pages allow an ActiveX control user to view and change ActiveX control properties. These properties are accessed by invoking a control properties dialog box, which contains one or more property pages that provide a customized, graphical interface for viewing and editing the control properties.

Requirements

Platforms: Windows 98, Windows NT 4.0, Windows Millennium Edition, Windows 2000, Windows XP Home Edition, Windows XP Professional, Windows Server 2003 family

AxHost.WndProc Method

This member overrides **Control.WndProc**.

```
[Visual Basic]
Overrides Protected Sub WndProc( _
   ByRef m As Message _
)
[C#]
protected override void WndProc(
   ref Message m
);
[C++]
protected: void WndProc(
   Message* m
);
```

```
[JScript]
protected override function WndProc(
   m : Message
);
```

Requirements

Platforms: Windows 98, Windows NT 4.0, Windows Millennium Edition, Windows 2000, Windows XP Home Edition, Windows XP Professional, Windows Server 2003 family

AxHost.BackColorChanged Event

The **BackColorChanged** event is not supported by the **AxHost** class.

```
[Visual Basic]
Public Shadows Event BackColorChanged As EventHandler
[C#]
public new event EventHandler BackColorChanged;
[C++]
public: __event EventHandler* BackColorChanged;
```

[JScript] In JScript, you can handle the events defined by a class, but you cannot define your own.

Event Data

The event handler receives an argument of type **EventArgs**.

Remarks

If you attempt to add or remove a handler for the **BackColor-Changed** event, a **NotSupportedException** is thrown. The events derived from the **Control** class are not supported by the **AxHost** class. The events exposed by the ActiveX control when the **AxHost** wrapper is created are the events that should be used.

Requirements

Platforms: Windows 98, Windows NT 4.0, Windows Millennium Edition, Windows 2000, Windows XP Home Edition, Windows XP Professional, Windows Server 2003 family

AxHost.BackgroundImageChanged Event

The **BackgroundImageChanged** event is not supported by the **AxHost** class.

```
[Visual Basic]
Public Shadows Event BackgroundImageChanged As EventHandler
[C#]
public new event EventHandler BackgroundImageChanged;
[C++]
public: __event EventHandler* BackgroundImageChanged;
```

[JScript] In JScript, you can handle the events defined by a class, but you cannot define your own.

Event Data

The event handler receives an argument of type **EventArgs**.

Remarks

If you attempt to add or remove a handler for the **Background-ImageChanged** event, a **NotSupportedException** is thrown. The events derived from the **Control** class are not supported by the **AxHost** class. The events exposed by the ActiveX control when the **AxHost** wrapper is created are the events that should be used.

Requirements

Platforms: Windows 98, Windows NT 4.0, Windows Millennium Edition, Windows 2000, Windows XP Home Edition, Windows XP Professional, Windows Server 2003 family

AxHost.BindingContextChanged Event

The **BindingContextChanged** event is not supported by the **AxHost** class.

```
[Visual Basic]
Public Shadows Event BindingContextChanged As EventHandler
[C#]
public new event EventHandler BindingContextChanged;
[C++]
public: __event EventHandler* BindingContextChanged;
```

[JScript] In JScript, you can handle the events defined by a class, but you cannot define your own.

Event Data

The event handler receives an argument of type **EventArgs**.

Remarks

If you attempt to add or remove a handler for the **BindingContext-Changed** event, a **NotSupportedException** is thrown. The events derived from the **Control** class are not supported by the **AxHost** class. The events exposed by the ActiveX control when the **AxHost** wrapper is created are the events that should be used.

Requirements

Platforms: Windows 98, Windows NT 4.0, Windows Millennium Edition, Windows 2000, Windows XP Home Edition, Windows XP Professional, Windows Server 2003 family

AxHost.ChangeUICues Event

The **ChangeUICues** event is not supported by the **AxHost** class.

```
[Visual Basic]
Public Shadows Event ChangeUICues As UICuesEventHandler
[C#]
public new event UICuesEventHandler ChangeUICues;
[C++]
public: __event UICuesEventHandler* ChangeUICues;
```

[JScript] In JScript, you can handle the events defined by a class, but you cannot define your own.

Event Data

The event handler receives an argument of type **UICuesEventArgs** containing data related to this event. The following **UICuesEvent-Args** properties provide information specific to this event.

Property	Description
Changed	Gets the bitwise combination of the **UICues** values.
Change-Focus	Gets a value indicating whether the state of the focus cues has changed.
Change-Keyboard	Gets a value indicating whether the state of the keyboard cues has changed.
ShowFocus	Gets a value indicating whether focus rectangles are shown after the change.
Show-Keyboard	Gets a value indicating whether keyboard cues are underlined after the change.

Remarks

If you attempt to add or remove a handler for the **ChangeUICues** event, a **NotSupportedException** is thrown. The events derived from the **Control** class are not supported by the **AxHost** class. The events exposed by the ActiveX control when the **AxHost** wrapper is created are the events that should be used.

Requirements

Platforms: Windows 98, Windows NT 4.0, Windows Millennium Edition, Windows 2000, Windows XP Home Edition, Windows XP Professional, Windows Server 2003 family

AxHost.Click Event

The **Click** event is not supported by the **AxHost** class.

[Visual Basic]
```
Public Shadows Event Click As EventHandler
```
[C#]
```
public new event EventHandler Click;
```
[C++]
```
public: __event EventHandler* Click;
```

[JScript] In JScript, you can handle the events defined by a class, but you cannot define your own.

Event Data

The event handler receives an argument of type **EventArgs**.

Remarks

If you attempt to add or remove a handler for the **Click** event, a **NotSupportedException** is thrown. The events derived from the **Control** class are not supported by the **AxHost** class. The events exposed by the ActiveX control when the **AxHost** wrapper is created are the events that should be used.

Requirements

Platforms: Windows 98, Windows NT 4.0, Windows Millennium Edition, Windows 2000, Windows XP Home Edition, Windows XP Professional, Windows Server 2003 family

AxHost.ContextMenuChanged Event

The **ContextMenuChanged** event is not supported by the **AxHost** class.

[Visual Basic]
```
Public Shadows Event ContextMenuChanged As EventHandler
```
[C#]
```
public new event EventHandler ContextMenuChanged;
```
[C++]
```
public: __event EventHandler* ContextMenuChanged;
```

[JScript] In JScript, you can handle the events defined by a class, but you cannot define your own.

Event Data

The event handler receives an argument of type **EventArgs**.

Remarks

If you attempt to add or remove a handler for the **ContextMenuChanged** event, a **NotSupportedException** is thrown. The events derived from the **Control** class are not supported by the **AxHost** class. The events exposed by the ActiveX control when the **AxHost** wrapper is created are the events that should be used.

Requirements

Platforms: Windows 98, Windows NT 4.0, Windows Millennium Edition, Windows 2000, Windows XP Home Edition, Windows XP Professional, Windows Server 2003 family

AxHost.CursorChanged Event

The **CursorChanged** event is not supported by the **AxHost** class.

[Visual Basic]
```
Public Shadows Event CursorChanged As EventHandler
```
[C#]
```
public new event EventHandler CursorChanged;
```
[C++]
```
public: __event EventHandler* CursorChanged;
```

[JScript] In JScript, you can handle the events defined by a class, but you cannot define your own.

Event Data

The event handler receives an argument of type **EventArgs**.

Remarks

If you attempt to add or remove a handler for the **CursorChanged** event, a **NotSupportedException** is thrown. The events derived from the **Control** class are not supported by the **AxHost** class. The events exposed by the ActiveX control when the **AxHost** wrapper is created are the events that should be used.

Requirements

Platforms: Windows 98, Windows NT 4.0, Windows Millennium Edition, Windows 2000, Windows XP Home Edition, Windows XP Professional, Windows Server 2003 family

AxHost.DoubleClick Event

The **DoubleClick** event is not supported by the **AxHost** class.

[Visual Basic]
```
Public Shadows Event DoubleClick As EventHandler
```
[C#]
```
public new event EventHandler DoubleClick;
```
[C++]
```
public: __event EventHandler* DoubleClick;
```

[JScript] In JScript, you can handle the events defined by a class, but you cannot define your own.

Event Data

The event handler receives an argument of type **EventArgs**.

Remarks

If you attempt to add or remove a handler for the **DoubleClick** event, a **NotSupportedException** is thrown. The events derived from the **Control** class are not supported by the **AxHost** class. The events exposed by the ActiveX control when the **AxHost** wrapper is created are the events that should be used.

Requirements

Platforms: Windows 98, Windows NT 4.0, Windows Millennium Edition, Windows 2000, Windows XP Home Edition, Windows XP Professional, Windows Server 2003 family

AxHost.DragDrop Event

The **DragDrop** event is not supported by the **AxHost** class.

[Visual Basic]
```
Public Shadows Event DragDrop As DragEventHandler
```
[C#]
```
public new event DragEventHandler DragDrop;
```
[C++]
```
public: __event DragEventHandler* DragDrop;
```

[JScript] In JScript, you can handle the events defined by a class, but you cannot define your own.

Event Data

The event handler receives an argument of type **DragEventArgs** containing data related to this event. The following **DragEventArgs** properties provide information specific to this event.

Property	Description
AllowedEffect	Gets which drag-and-drop operations are allowed by the originator (or source) of the drag event.
Data	Gets the **IDataObject** that contains the data associated with this event.
Effect	Gets or sets the target drop effect in a drag-and-drop operation.
KeyState	Gets the current state of the SHIFT, CTRL, and ALT keys, as well as the state of the mouse buttons.
X	Gets the x-coordinate of the mouse pointer, in screen coordinates.
Y	Gets the y-coordinate of the mouse pointer, in screen coordinates.

Remarks

If you attempt to add or remove a handler for the **DragDrop** event, a **NotSupportedException** is thrown. The events derived from the **Control** class are not supported by the **AxHost** class. The events exposed by the ActiveX control when the **AxHost** wrapper is created are the events that should be used.

Requirements

Platforms: Windows 98, Windows NT 4.0, Windows Millennium Edition, Windows 2000, Windows XP Home Edition, Windows XP Professional, Windows Server 2003 family

AxHost.DragEnter Event

The **DragEnter** event is not supported by the **AxHost** class.

[Visual Basic]
```
Public Shadows Event DragEnter As DragEventHandler
```
[C#]
```
public new event DragEventHandler DragEnter;
```
[C++]
```
public: __event DragEventHandler* DragEnter;
```

[JScript] In JScript, you can handle the events defined by a class, but you cannot define your own.

Event Data

The event handler receives an argument of type **DragEventArgs** containing data related to this event. The following **DragEventArgs** properties provide information specific to this event.

Property	Description
AllowedEffect	Gets which drag-and-drop operations are allowed by the originator (or source) of the drag event.
Data	Gets the **IDataObject** that contains the data associated with this event.
Effect	Gets or sets the target drop effect in a drag-and-drop operation.
KeyState	Gets the current state of the SHIFT, CTRL, and ALT keys, as well as the state of the mouse buttons.
X	Gets the x-coordinate of the mouse pointer, in screen coordinates.
Y	Gets the y-coordinate of the mouse pointer, in screen coordinates.

Remarks

If you attempt to add or remove a handler for the **DragEnter** event, a **NotSupportedException** is thrown. The events derived from the **Control** class are not supported by the **AxHost** class. The events exposed by the ActiveX control when the **AxHost** wrapper is created are the events that should be used.

Requirements

Platforms: Windows 98, Windows NT 4.0, Windows Millennium Edition, Windows 2000, Windows XP Home Edition, Windows XP Professional, Windows Server 2003 family

AxHost.DragLeave Event

The **DragLeave** event is not supported by the **AxHost** class.

[Visual Basic]
```
Public Shadows Event DragLeave As EventHandler
```
[C#]
```
public new event EventHandler DragLeave;
```
[C++]
```
public: __event EventHandler* DragLeave;
```

[JScript] In JScript, you can handle the events defined by a class, but you cannot define your own.

Event Data

The event handler receives an argument of type **EventArgs**.

Remarks

If you attempt to add or remove a handler for the **DragLeave** event, a **NotSupportedException** is thrown. The events derived from the **Control** class are not supported by the **AxHost** class. The events exposed by the ActiveX control when the **AxHost** wrapper is created are the events that should be used.

Requirements

Platforms: Windows 98, Windows NT 4.0, Windows Millennium Edition, Windows 2000, Windows XP Home Edition, Windows XP Professional, Windows Server 2003 family

AxHost.DragOver Event

The **DragOver** event is not supported by the **AxHost** class.

[Visual Basic]
```
Public Shadows Event DragOver As DragEventHandler
```
[C#]
```
public new event DragEventHandler DragOver;
```
[C++]
```
public: __event DragEventHandler* DragOver;
```

[JScript] In JScript, you can handle the events defined by a class, but you cannot define your own.

Event Data

The event handler receives an argument of type **DragEventArgs** containing data related to this event. The following **DragEventArgs** properties provide information specific to this event.

Property	Description
AllowedEffect	Gets which drag-and-drop operations are allowed by the originator (or source) of the drag event.
Data	Gets the **IDataObject** that contains the data associated with this event.
Effect	Gets or sets the target drop effect in a drag-and-drop operation.
KeyState	Gets the current state of the SHIFT, CTRL, and ALT keys, as well as the state of the mouse buttons.
X	Gets the x-coordinate of the mouse pointer, in screen coordinates.
Y	Gets the y-coordinate of the mouse pointer, in screen coordinates.

Remarks

If you attempt to add or remove a handler for the **DragOver** event, a **NotSupportedException** is thrown. The events derived from the **Control** class are not supported by the **AxHost** class. The events exposed by the ActiveX control when the **AxHost** wrapper is created are the events that should be used.

Requirements

Platforms: Windows 98, Windows NT 4.0, Windows Millennium Edition, Windows 2000, Windows XP Home Edition, Windows XP Professional, Windows Server 2003 family

AxHost.EnabledChanged Event

The **EnabledChanged** event is not supported by the **AxHost** class.

[Visual Basic]
```
Public Shadows Event EnabledChanged As EventHandler
```
[C#]
```
public new event EventHandler EnabledChanged;
```
[C++]
```
public: __event EventHandler* EnabledChanged;
```

[JScript] In JScript, you can handle the events defined by a class, but you cannot define your own.

Event Data

The event handler receives an argument of type **EventArgs**.

Remarks

If you attempt to add or remove a handler for the **EnabledChanged** event, a **NotSupportedException** is thrown. The events derived from the **Control** class are not supported by the **AxHost** class. The events exposed by the ActiveX control when the **AxHost** wrapper is created are the events that should be used.

Requirements

Platforms: Windows 98, Windows NT 4.0, Windows Millennium Edition, Windows 2000, Windows XP Home Edition, Windows XP Professional, Windows Server 2003 family

AxHost.FontChanged Event

The **FontChanged** event is not supported by the **AxHost** class.

[Visual Basic]
```
Public Shadows Event FontChanged As EventHandler
```
[C#]
```
public new event EventHandler FontChanged;
```
[C++]
```
public: __event EventHandler* FontChanged;
```

[JScript] In JScript, you can handle the events defined by a class, but you cannot define your own.

Event Data

The event handler receives an argument of type **EventArgs**.

Remarks

If you attempt to add or remove a handler for the **FontChanged** event, a **NotSupportedException** is thrown. The events derived from the **Control** class are not supported by the **AxHost** class. The events exposed by the ActiveX control when the **AxHost** wrapper is created are the events that should be used.

Requirements

Platforms: Windows 98, Windows NT 4.0, Windows Millennium Edition, Windows 2000, Windows XP Home Edition, Windows XP Professional, Windows Server 2003 family

AxHost.ForeColorChanged Event

The **ForeColorChanged** event is not supported by the **AxHost** class.

[Visual Basic]
```
Public Shadows Event ForeColorChanged As EventHandler
```
[C#]
```
public new event EventHandler ForeColorChanged;
```
[C++]
```
public: __event EventHandler* ForeColorChanged;
```

[JScript] In JScript, you can handle the events defined by a class, but you cannot define your own.

Event Data

The event handler receives an argument of type **EventArgs**.

Remarks

If you attempt to add or remove a handler for the **ForeColorChanged** event, a **NotSupportedException** is thrown. The events derived from the **Control** class are not supported by the **AxHost** class. The events exposed by the ActiveX control when the **AxHost** wrapper is created are the events that should be used.

Requirements

Platforms: Windows 98, Windows NT 4.0, Windows Millennium Edition, Windows 2000, Windows XP Home Edition, Windows XP Professional, Windows Server 2003 family

AxHost.GiveFeedback Event

The **GiveFeedback** event is not supported by the **AxHost** class.

[Visual Basic]
```
Public Shadows Event GiveFeedback As GiveFeedbackEventHandler
```
[C#]
```
public new event GiveFeedbackEventHandler GiveFeedback;
```
[C++]
```
public: __event GiveFeedbackEventHandler* GiveFeedback;
```

[JScript] In JScript, you can handle the events defined by a class, but you cannot define your own.

Event Data

The event handler receives an argument of type **GiveFeedbackEventArgs** containing data related to this event. The following **GiveFeedbackEventArgs** properties provide information specific to this event.

Property	Description
Effect	Gets the drag-and-drop operation feedback that is displayed.
UseDefaultCursors	Gets or sets whether drag operation should use the default cursors that are associated with drag-drop effects.

Remarks

If you attempt to add or remove a handler for the **GiveFeedback** event, a **NotSupportedException** is thrown. The events derived from the **Control** class are not supported by the **AxHost** class. The events exposed by the ActiveX control when the **AxHost** wrapper is created are the events that should be used.

Requirements

Platforms: Windows 98, Windows NT 4.0, Windows Millennium Edition, Windows 2000, Windows XP Home Edition, Windows XP Professional, Windows Server 2003 family

AxHost.HelpRequested Event

The **HelpRequested** event is not supported by the **AxHost** class.

[Visual Basic]
```
Public Shadows Event HelpRequested As HelpEventHandler
```
[C#]
```
public new event HelpEventHandler HelpRequested;
```
[C++]
```
public: __event HelpEventHandler* HelpRequested;
```

[JScript] In JScript, you can handle the events defined by a class, but you cannot define your own.

Event Data

The event handler receives an argument of type **HelpEventArgs** containing data related to this event. The following **HelpEventArgs** properties provide information specific to this event.

Property	Description
Handled	Gets or sets a value indicating whether the help event was handled.
MousePos	Gets the screen coordinates of the mouse pointer.

Remarks

If you attempt to add or remove a handler for the **HelpRequested** event, a **NotSupportedException** is thrown. The events derived from the **Control** class are not supported by the **AxHost** class. The events exposed by the ActiveX control when the **AxHost** wrapper is created are the events that should be used.

Requirements

Platforms: Windows 98, Windows NT 4.0, Windows Millennium Edition, Windows 2000, Windows XP Home Edition, Windows XP Professional, Windows Server 2003 family

AxHost.ImeModeChanged Event

The **ImeModeChanged** event is not supported by the **AxHost** class.

[Visual Basic]
```
Public Shadows Event ImeModeChanged As EventHandler
```
[C#]
```
public new event EventHandler ImeModeChanged;
```
[C++]
```
public: __event EventHandler* ImeModeChanged;
```

[JScript] In JScript, you can handle the events defined by a class, but you cannot define your own.

Event Data

The event handler receives an argument of type **EventArgs**.

Remarks

If you attempt to add or remove a handler for the **ImeModeChanged** event, a **NotSupportedException** is thrown. The events derived from the **Control** class are not supported by the **AxHost** class. The events exposed by the ActiveX control when the **AxHost** wrapper is created are the events that should be used.

Requirements

Platforms: Windows 98, Windows NT 4.0, Windows Millennium Edition, Windows 2000, Windows XP Home Edition, Windows XP Professional, Windows Server 2003 family

AxHost.KeyDown Event

The **KeyDown** event is not supported by the **AxHost** class.

[Visual Basic]
```
Public Shadows Event KeyDown As KeyEventHandler
```
[C#]
```
public new event KeyEventHandler KeyDown;
```
[C++]
```
public: __event KeyEventHandler* KeyDown;
```

[JScript] In JScript, you can handle the events defined by a class, but you cannot define your own.

Event Data

The event handler receives an argument of type **KeyEventArgs** containing data related to this event. The following **KeyEventArgs** properties provide information specific to this event.

Property	Description
Alt	Gets a value indicating whether the ALT key was pressed.
Control	Gets a value indicating whether the CTRL key was pressed.
Handled	Gets or sets a value indicating whether the event was handled.
KeyCode	Gets the keyboard code for a **KeyDown** or **KeyUp** event.
KeyData	Gets the key data for a **KeyDown** or **KeyUp** event.
KeyValue	Gets the keyboard value for a **KeyDown** or **KeyUp** event.
Modifiers	Gets the modifier flags for a **KeyDown** or **KeyUp** event. This indicates which combination of modifier keys (CTRL, SHIFT, and ALT) were pressed.
Shift	Gets a value indicating whether the SHIFT key was pressed.

Remarks

If you attempt to add or remove a handler for the **KeyDown** event, a **NotSupportedException** is thrown. The events derived from the **Control** class are not supported by the **AxHost** class. The events exposed by the ActiveX control when the **AxHost** wrapper is created are the events that should be used.

Requirements

Platforms: Windows 98, Windows NT 4.0, Windows Millennium Edition, Windows 2000, Windows XP Home Edition, Windows XP Professional, Windows Server 2003 family

AxHost.KeyPress Event

The **KeyPress** event is not supported by the **AxHost** class.

```
[Visual Basic]
Public Shadows Event KeyPress As KeyPressEventHandler
[C#]
public new event KeyPressEventHandler KeyPress;
[C++]
public: __event KeyPressEventHandler* KeyPress;
```

[JScript] In JScript, you can handle the events defined by a class, but you cannot define your own.

Event Data

The event handler receives an argument of type **KeyPressEventArgs** containing data related to this event. The following **KeyPressEventArgs** properties provide information specific to this event.

Property	Description
Handled	Gets or sets a value indicating whether the **KeyPress** event was handled.
KeyChar	Gets the character corresponding to the key pressed.

Remarks

If you attempt to add or remove a handler for the **KeyPress** event, a **NotSupportedException** is thrown. The events derived from the **Control** class are not supported by the **AxHost** class. The events exposed by the ActiveX control when the **AxHost** wrapper is created are the events that should be used.

Requirements

Platforms: Windows 98, Windows NT 4.0, Windows Millennium Edition, Windows 2000, Windows XP Home Edition, Windows XP Professional, Windows Server 2003 family

AxHost.KeyUp Event

The **KeyUp** event is not supported by the **AxHost** class.

```
[Visual Basic]
Public Shadows Event KeyUp As KeyEventHandler
[C#]
public new event KeyEventHandler KeyUp;
[C++]
public: __event KeyEventHandler* KeyUp;
```

[JScript] In JScript, you can handle the events defined by a class, but you cannot define your own.

Event Data

The event handler receives an argument of type **KeyEventArgs** containing data related to this event. The following **KeyEventArgs** properties provide information specific to this event.

Property	Description
Alt	Gets a value indicating whether the ALT key was pressed.
Control	Gets a value indicating whether the CTRL key was pressed.
Handled	Gets or sets a value indicating whether the event was handled.
KeyCode	Gets the keyboard code for a **KeyDown** or **KeyUp** event.
KeyData	Gets the key data for a **KeyDown** or **KeyUp** event.
KeyValue	Gets the keyboard value for a **KeyDown** or **KeyUp** event.
Modifiers	Gets the modifier flags for a **KeyDown** or **KeyUp** event. This indicates which combination of modifier keys (CTRL, SHIFT, and ALT) were pressed.
Shift	Gets a value indicating whether the SHIFT key was pressed.

Remarks

If you attempt to add or remove a handler for the **KeyUp** event, a **NotSupportedException** is thrown. The events derived from the **Control** class are not supported by the **AxHost** class. The events exposed by the ActiveX control when the **AxHost** wrapper is created are the events that should be used.

Requirements

Platforms: Windows 98, Windows NT 4.0, Windows Millennium Edition, Windows 2000, Windows XP Home Edition, Windows XP Professional, Windows Server 2003 family

AxHost.Layout Event

The **Layout** event is not supported by the **AxHost** class.

[Visual Basic]
```
Public Shadows Event Layout As LayoutEventHandler
```
[C#]
```
public new event LayoutEventHandler Layout;
```
[C++]
```
public: __event LayoutEventHandler* Layout;
```

[JScript] In JScript, you can handle the events defined by a class, but you cannot define your own.

Event Data

The event handler receives an argument of type **LayoutEventArgs** containing data related to this event. The following **LayoutEventArgs** properties provide information specific to this event.

Property	Description
AffectedControl	Gets the child control affected by the change.
AffectedProperty	Gets the property affected by the change.

Remarks

If you attempt to add or remove a handler for the **Layout** event, a **NotSupportedException** is thrown. The events derived from the **Control** class are not supported by the **AxHost** class. The events exposed by the ActiveX control when the **AxHost** wrapper is created are the events that should be used.

Requirements

Platforms: Windows 98, Windows NT 4.0, Windows Millennium Edition, Windows 2000, Windows XP Home Edition, Windows XP Professional, Windows Server 2003 family

AxHost.MouseDown Event

The **MouseDown** event is not supported by the **AxHost** class.

[Visual Basic]
```
Public Shadows Event MouseDown As MouseEventHandler
```
[C#]
```
public new event MouseEventHandler MouseDown;
```
[C++]
```
public: __event MouseEventHandler* MouseDown;
```

[JScript] In JScript, you can handle the events defined by a class, but you cannot define your own.

Event Data

The event handler receives an argument of type **MouseEventArgs** containing data related to this event. The following **MouseEventArgs** properties provide information specific to this event.

Property	Description
Button	Gets which mouse button was pressed.
Clicks	Gets the number of times the mouse button was pressed and released.
Delta	Gets a signed count of the number of detents the mouse wheel has rotated. A detent is one notch of the mouse wheel.
X	Gets the x-coordinate of the mouse.
Y	Gets the y-coordinate of the mouse.

Remarks

If you attempt to add or remove a handler for the **MouseDown** event, a **NotSupportedException** is thrown. The events derived from the **Control** class are not supported by the **AxHost** class. The events exposed by the ActiveX control when the **AxHost** wrapper is created are the events that should be used.

Requirements

Platforms: Windows 98, Windows NT 4.0, Windows Millennium Edition, Windows 2000, Windows XP Home Edition, Windows XP Professional, Windows Server 2003 family

AxHost.MouseEnter Event

The **MouseEnter** event is not supported by the **AxHost** class.

[Visual Basic]
```
Public Shadows Event MouseEnter As EventHandler
```
[C#]
```
public new event EventHandler MouseEnter;
```
[C++]
```
public: __event EventHandler* MouseEnter;
```

[JScript] In JScript, you can handle the events defined by a class, but you cannot define your own.

Event Data

The event handler receives an argument of type **EventArgs**.

Remarks

If you attempt to add or remove a handler for the **MouseEnter** event, a **NotSupportedException** is thrown. The events derived from the **Control** class are not supported by the **AxHost** class. The events exposed by the ActiveX control when the **AxHost** wrapper is created are the events that should be used.

Requirements

Platforms: Windows 98, Windows NT 4.0, Windows Millennium Edition, Windows 2000, Windows XP Home Edition, Windows XP Professional, Windows Server 2003 family

AxHost.MouseHover Event

The **MouseHover** event is not supported by the **AxHost** class.

[Visual Basic]
```
Public Shadows Event MouseHover As EventHandler
```
[C#]
```
public new event EventHandler MouseHover;
```
[C++]
```
public: __event EventHandler* MouseHover;
```

[JScript] In JScript, you can handle the events defined by a class, but you cannot define your own.

Event Data

The event handler receives an argument of type **EventArgs**.

Remarks

If you attempt to add or remove a handler for the **MouseHover** event, a **NotSupportedException** is thrown. The events derived from the **Control** class are not supported by the **AxHost** class. The events exposed by the ActiveX control when the **AxHost** wrapper is created are the events that should be used.

Requirements

Platforms: Windows 98, Windows NT 4.0, Windows Millennium Edition, Windows 2000, Windows XP Home Edition, Windows XP Professional, Windows Server 2003 family

AxHost.MouseLeave Event

The **MouseLeave** event is not supported by the **AxHost** class.

```
[Visual Basic]
Public Shadows Event MouseLeave As EventHandler
[C#]
public new event EventHandler MouseLeave;
[C++]
public: __event EventHandler* MouseLeave;
```

[JScript] In JScript, you can handle the events defined by a class, but you cannot define your own.

Event Data

The event handler receives an argument of type **EventArgs**.

Remarks

If you attempt to add or remove a handler for the **MouseLeave** event, a **NotSupportedException** is thrown. The events derived from the **Control** class are not supported by the **AxHost** class. The events exposed by the ActiveX control when the **AxHost** wrapper is created are the events that should be used.

Requirements

Platforms: Windows 98, Windows NT 4.0, Windows Millennium Edition, Windows 2000, Windows XP Home Edition, Windows XP Professional, Windows Server 2003 family

AxHost.MouseMove Event

The **MouseMove** event is not supported by the **AxHost** class.

```
[Visual Basic]
Public Shadows Event MouseMove As MouseEventHandler
[C#]
public new event MouseEventHandler MouseMove;
[C++]
public: __event MouseEventHandler* MouseMove;
```

[JScript] In JScript, you can handle the events defined by a class, but you cannot define your own.

Event Data

The event handler receives an argument of type **MouseEventArgs** containing data related to this event. The following **MouseEventArgs** properties provide information specific to this event.

Property	Description
Button	Gets which mouse button was pressed.
Clicks	Gets the number of times the mouse button was pressed and released.
Delta	Gets a signed count of the number of detents the mouse wheel has rotated. A detent is one notch of the mouse wheel.
X	Gets the x-coordinate of the mouse.
Y	Gets the y-coordinate of the mouse.

Remarks

If you attempt to add or remove a handler for the **MouseMove** event, a **NotSupportedException** is thrown. The events derived from the **Control** class are not supported by the **AxHost** class. The events exposed by the ActiveX control when the **AxHost** wrapper is created are the events that should be used.

Requirements

Platforms: Windows 98, Windows NT 4.0, Windows Millennium Edition, Windows 2000, Windows XP Home Edition, Windows XP Professional, Windows Server 2003 family

AxHost.MouseUp Event

The **MouseUp** event is not supported by the **AxHost** class.

```
[Visual Basic]
Public Shadows Event MouseUp As MouseEventHandler
[C#]
public new event MouseEventHandler MouseUp;
[C++]
public: __event MouseEventHandler* MouseUp;
```

[JScript] In JScript, you can handle the events defined by a class, but you cannot define your own.

Event Data

The event handler receives an argument of type **MouseEventArgs** containing data related to this event. The following **MouseEventArgs** properties provide information specific to this event.

Property	Description
Button	Gets which mouse button was pressed.
Clicks	Gets the number of times the mouse button was pressed and released.
Delta	Gets a signed count of the number of detents the mouse wheel has rotated. A detent is one notch of the mouse wheel.
X	Gets the x-coordinate of the mouse.
Y	Gets the y-coordinate of the mouse.

Remarks

If you attempt to add or remove a handler for the **MouseUp** event, a **NotSupportedException** is thrown. The events derived from the **Control** class are not supported by the **AxHost** class. The events exposed by the ActiveX control when the **AxHost** wrapper is created are the events that should be used.

Requirements

Platforms: Windows 98, Windows NT 4.0, Windows Millennium Edition, Windows 2000, Windows XP Home Edition, Windows XP Professional, Windows Server 2003 family

AxHost.MouseWheel Event

The **MouseWheel** event is not supported by the **AxHost** class.

```
[Visual Basic]
Public Shadows Event MouseWheel As MouseEventHandler
[C#]
public new event MouseEventHandler MouseWheel;
[C++]
public: __event MouseEventHandler* MouseWheel;
```

[JScript] In JScript, you can handle the events defined by a class, but you cannot define your own.

Event Data

The event handler receives an argument of type **MouseEventArgs** containing data related to this event. The following **MouseEventArgs** properties provide information specific to this event.

Property	Description
Button	Gets which mouse button was pressed.
Clicks	Gets the number of times the mouse button was pressed and released.
Delta	Gets a signed count of the number of detents the mouse wheel has rotated. A detent is one notch of the mouse wheel.
X	Gets the x-coordinate of the mouse.
Y	Gets the y-coordinate of the mouse.

Remarks

If you attempt to add or remove a handler for the **MouseWheel** event, a **NotSupportedException** is thrown. The events derived from the **Control** class are not supported by the **AxHost** class. The events exposed by the ActiveX control when the **AxHost** wrapper is created are the events that should be used.

Requirements

Platforms: Windows 98, Windows NT 4.0, Windows Millennium Edition, Windows 2000, Windows XP Home Edition, Windows XP Professional, Windows Server 2003 family

AxHost.Paint Event

The **Paint** event is not supported by the **AxHost** class.

```
[Visual Basic]
Public Shadows Event Paint As PaintEventHandler
[C#]
public new event PaintEventHandler Paint;
[C++]
public: __event PaintEventHandler* Paint;
```

[JScript] In JScript, you can handle the events defined by a class, but you cannot define your own.

Event Data

The event handler receives an argument of type **PaintEventArgs** containing data related to this event. The following **PaintEventArgs** properties provide information specific to this event.

Property	Description
ClipRectangle	Gets the rectangle in which to paint.
Graphics	Gets the graphics used to paint.

Remarks

If you attempt to add or remove a handler for the **Paint** event, a **NotSupportedException** is thrown. The events derived from the **Control** class are not supported by the **AxHost** class. The events exposed by the ActiveX control when the **AxHost** wrapper is created are the events that should be used.

Requirements

Platforms: Windows 98, Windows NT 4.0, Windows Millennium Edition, Windows 2000, Windows XP Home Edition, Windows XP Professional, Windows Server 2003 family

AxHost.QueryAccessibilityHelp Event

The **QueryAccessibilityHelp** event is not supported by the **AxHost** class.

```
[Visual Basic]
Public Shadows Event QueryAccessibilityHelp As _
   QueryAccessibilityHelpEventHandler
[C#]
public new event QueryAccessibilityHelpEventHandler
   QueryAccessibilityHelp;
[C++]
public: __event QueryAccessibilityHelpEventHandler*
   QueryAccessibilityHelp;
```

[JScript] In JScript, you can handle the events defined by a class, but you cannot define your own.

Event Data

The event handler receives an argument of type **QueryAccessibilityHelpEventArgs** containing data related to this event. The following **QueryAccessibilityHelpEventArgs** properties provide information specific to this event.

Property	Description
HelpKeyword	Gets or sets the Help keyword for the specified control.
HelpNamespace	Gets or sets a value specifying the name of the Help file.
HelpString	Gets or sets the string defining what Help to get for the **AccessibleObject**.

Remarks

If you attempt to add or remove a handler for the **QueryAccessibilityHelp** event, a **NotSupportedException** is thrown. The events derived from the **Control** class are not supported by the **AxHost** class. The events exposed by the ActiveX control when the **AxHost** wrapper is created are the events that should be used.

Requirements

Platforms: Windows 98, Windows NT 4.0, Windows Millennium Edition, Windows 2000, Windows XP Home Edition, Windows XP Professional, Windows Server 2003 family

AxHost.QueryContinueDrag Event

The **QueryContinueDrag** event is not supported by the **AxHost** class.

```
[Visual Basic]
Public Shadows Event QueryContinueDrag As _
   QueryContinueDragEventHandler
[C#]
public new event QueryContinueDragEventHandler QueryContinueDrag;
[C++]
public: __event QueryContinueDragEventHandler* QueryContinueDrag;
```

[JScript] In JScript, you can handle the events defined by a class, but you cannot define your own.

Event Data

The event handler receives an argument of type **QueryContinueDragEventArgs** containing data related to this event. The following **QueryContinueDragEventArgs** properties provide information specific to this event.

Property	Description
Action	Gets or sets the status of a drag-and-drop operation.
EscapePressed	Gets whether the user pressed the ESC key.
KeyState	Gets the current state of the SHIFT, CTRL, and ALT keys.

Remarks

If you attempt to add or remove a handler for the **QueryContinueDrag** event, a **NotSupportedException** is thrown. The events derived from the **Control** class are not supported by the **AxHost** class. The events exposed by the ActiveX control when the **AxHost** wrapper is created are the events that should be used.

Requirements

Platforms: Windows 98, Windows NT 4.0, Windows Millennium Edition, Windows 2000, Windows XP Home Edition, Windows XP Professional, Windows Server 2003 family

AxHost.RightToLeftChanged Event

The **RightToLeftChanged** event is not supported by the **AxHost** class.

```
[Visual Basic]
Public Shadows Event RightToLeftChanged As EventHandler
[C#]
public new event EventHandler RightToLeftChanged;
[C++]
public: __event EventHandler* RightToLeftChanged;
```

[JScript] In JScript, you can handle the events defined by a class, but you cannot define your own.

Event Data

The event handler receives an argument of type **EventArgs**.

Remarks

If you attempt to add or remove a handler for the **RightToLeftChanged** event, a **NotSupportedException** is thrown. The events derived from the **Control** class are not supported by the **AxHost** class. The events exposed by the ActiveX control when the **AxHost** wrapper is created are the events that should be used.

Requirements

Platforms: Windows 98, Windows NT 4.0, Windows Millennium Edition, Windows 2000, Windows XP Home Edition, Windows XP Professional, Windows Server 2003 family

AxHost.StyleChanged Event

The **StyleChanged** event is not supported by the **AxHost** class.

```
[Visual Basic]
Public Shadows Event StyleChanged As EventHandler
[C#]
public new event EventHandler StyleChanged;
[C++]
public: __event EventHandler* StyleChanged;
```

[JScript] In JScript, you can handle the events defined by a class, but you cannot define your own.

Event Data

The event handler receives an argument of type **EventArgs**.

Remarks

If you attempt to add or remove a handler for the **StyleChanged** event, a **NotSupportedException** is thrown. The events derived from the **Control** class are not supported by the **AxHost** class. The events exposed by the ActiveX control when the **AxHost** wrapper is created are the events that should be used.

Requirements

Platforms: Windows 98, Windows NT 4.0, Windows Millennium Edition, Windows 2000, Windows XP Home Edition, Windows XP Professional, Windows Server 2003 family

AxHost.TabIndexChanged Event

The **TabIndexChanged** event is not supported by the **AxHost** class.

[Visual Basic]
```
Public Shadows Event TabIndexChanged As EventHandler
```
[C#]
```
public new event EventHandler TabIndexChanged;
```
[C++]
```
public: __event EventHandler* TabIndexChanged;
```

[JScript] In JScript, you can handle the events defined by a class, but you cannot define your own.

Event Data

The event handler receives an argument of type **EventArgs**.

Remarks

If you attempt to add or remove a handler for the **TabIndexChanged** event, a **NotSupportedException** is thrown. The events derived from the **Control** class are not supported by the **AxHost** class. The events exposed by the ActiveX control when the **AxHost** wrapper is created are the events that should be used.

Requirements

Platforms: Windows 98, Windows NT 4.0, Windows Millennium Edition, Windows 2000, Windows XP Home Edition, Windows XP Professional, Windows Server 2003 family

AxHost.TabStopChanged Event

The **TabStopChanged** event is not supported by the **AxHost** class.

[Visual Basic]
```
Public Shadows Event TabStopChanged As EventHandler
```
[C#]
```
public new event EventHandler TabStopChanged;
```
[C++]
```
public: __event EventHandler* TabStopChanged;
```

[JScript] In JScript, you can handle the events defined by a class, but you cannot define your own.

Event Data

The event handler receives an argument of type **EventArgs**.

Remarks

If you attempt to add or remove a handler for the **TabStopChanged** event, a **NotSupportedException** is thrown. The events derived from the **Control** class are not supported by the **AxHost** class. The events exposed by the ActiveX control when the **AxHost** wrapper is created are the events that should be used.

Requirements

Platforms: Windows 98, Windows NT 4.0, Windows Millennium Edition, Windows 2000, Windows XP Home Edition, Windows XP Professional, Windows Server 2003 family

AxHost.TextChanged Event

The **TextChanged** event is not supported by the **AxHost** class.

[Visual Basic]
```
Public Shadows Event TextChanged As EventHandler
```
[C#]
```
public new event EventHandler TextChanged;
```
[C++]
```
public: __event EventHandler* TextChanged;
```

[JScript] In JScript, you can handle the events defined by a class, but you cannot define your own.

Event Data

The event handler receives an argument of type **EventArgs**.

Remarks

If you attempt to add or remove a handler for the **TextChanged** event, a **NotSupportedException** is thrown. The events derived from the **Control** class are not supported by the **AxHost** class. The events exposed by the ActiveX control when the **AxHost** wrapper is created are the events that should be used.

Requirements

Platforms: Windows 98, Windows NT 4.0, Windows Millennium Edition, Windows 2000, Windows XP Home Edition, Windows XP Professional, Windows Server 2003 family

AxHost.AboutBoxDelegate Delegate

Represents the method that will display an ActiveX control's About dialog box.

[Visual Basic]
```
<Serializable>
Protected Delegate Sub AxHost.AboutBoxDelegate()
```
[C#]
```
[Serializable]
protected delegate void AxHost.AboutBoxDelegate();
```
[C++]
```
[Serializable]
protected __gc __delegate void AxHost.AboutBoxDelegate();
```

[JScript] In JScript, you can use the delegates in the .NET Framework, but you cannot define your own.

Parameters [Visual Basic, C#, C++]

The declaration of your callback method must have the same parameters as the **AxHost.AboutBoxDelegate** delegate declaration.

Remarks

The **AxHost.AboutBoxDelegate** provides you the ability to be notified when the ActiveX control's About box is going to be displayed. Code added to the delegate method is executed before the About box is displayed.

When you create an **AxHost.AboutBoxDelegate** delegate, you identify the method that will handle the display of an ActiveX control's About dialog box if it has one. To associate the method with your handler, add an instance of the delegate to the method. The handler is called whenever the method is called, unless you remove the delegate.

Requirements

Namespace: System.Windows.Forms

Platforms: Windows 98, Windows NT 4.0, Windows Millennium Edition, Windows 2000, Windows XP Home Edition, Windows XP Professional, Windows Server 2003 family

Assembly: System.Windows.Forms (in System.Windows.Forms.dll)

AxHost.ActiveXInvokeKind Enumeration

Specifies the type of member that referenced the ActiveX control while it was in an invalid state.

```
[Visual Basic]
<Serializable>
Public Enum AxHost.ActiveXInvokeKind
[C#]
[Serializable]
public enum AxHost.ActiveXInvokeKind
[C++]
[Serializable]
__value public enum AxHost.ActiveXInvokeKind
[JScript]
public
   Serializable
enum AxHost.ActiveXInvokeKind
```

Members

Member name	Description
MethodInvoke	A method referenced the ActiveX control.
PropertyGet	The get accessor of a property referenced the ActiveX control.
PropertySet	The set accessor of a property referenced the ActiveX control.

Example

The **AxHost.ActiveXInvokeKind** enumeration is used by the **AxHost.InvalidActiveXStateException** exception to specify the type of member that referenced the ActiveX control while it was an invalid state.

Requirements

Namespace: System.Windows.Forms

Platforms: Windows 98, Windows NT 4.0, Windows Millennium Edition, Windows 2000, Windows XP Home Edition, Windows XP Professional, Windows Server 2003 family

Assembly: System.Windows.Forms (in System.Windows.Forms.dll)

AxHost.AxComponentEditor Class

This type supports the .NET Framework infrastructure and is not intended to be used directly from your code.

```
[Visual Basic]
Public Class AxHost.AxComponentEditor
   Inherits WindowsFormsComponentEditor
[C#]
public class AxHost.AxComponentEditor : WindowsFormsComponentEditor
[C++]
public __gc class AxHost.AxComponentEditor : public
   WindowsFormsComponentEditor
[JScript]
public class AxHost.AxComponentEditor extends
   WindowsFormsComponentEditor
```

AxHost.AxComponentEditor Constructor

This member supports the .NET Framework infrastructure and is not intended to be used directly from your code.

```
[Visual Basic]
Public Sub New()
[C#]
public AxHost.AxComponentEditor();
[C++]
public: AxComponentEditor();
[JScript]
public function AxHost.AxComponentEditor();
```

AxHost.AxComponentEditor.EditComponent Method

This member supports the .NET Framework infrastructure and is not intended to be used directly from your code.

Overload List

This member overrides **WindowsFormsComponentEditor.EditComponent**.

[Visual Basic] **Overloads Overrides Public Function EditComponent(ITypeDescriptorContext, Object, IWin32Window) As Boolean**

[C#] **public override bool EditComponent(IType-DescriptorContext, object, IWin32Window);**

[C++] **public: bool EditComponent(IType-DescriptorContext*, Object*, IWin32Window*);**

[JScript] **public override function EditComponent(IType-DescriptorContext, Object, IWin32Window) : Boolean;**

This member supports the .NET Framework infrastructure and is not intended to be used directly from your code.

[Visual Basic] **Overloads Public Function Edit-Component(Object) As Boolean**

[C#] **public bool EditComponent(object);**

[C++] **public: bool EditComponent(Object*);**

[JScript] **public function EditComponent(Object) : Boolean;**

This member supports the .NET Framework infrastructure and is not intended to be used directly from your code.

[Visual Basic] **Overloads Public Overridable Function EditComponent(ITypeDescriptorContext, Object) As Boolean**

[C#] **public virtual bool EditComponent(IType-DescriptorContext, object);**

[C++] **public: virtual bool EditComponent(IType-DescriptorContext*, Object*);**

[JScript] **public function EditComponent(ITypeDescriptor-Context, Object) : Boolean;**

This member supports the .NET Framework infrastructure and is not intended to be used directly from your code.

[Visual Basic] **Overloads Public Function EditComponent(Object, IWin32Window) As Boolean**

[C#] **public bool EditComponent(object, IWin32Window);**

[C++] **public: bool EditComponent(Object*, IWin32-Window*);**

[JScript] **public function EditComponent(Object, IWin32-Window) : Boolean;**

AxHost.AxComponentEditor.EditComponent Method (ITypeDescriptorContext, Object, IWin32Window)

This member overrides **WindowsFormsComponent-Editor.EditComponent**.

```
[Visual Basic]
Overrides Overloads Public Function EditComponent( _
   ByVal context As ITypeDescriptorContext, _
   ByVal obj As Object, _
   ByVal parent As IWin32Window _
) As Boolean
[C#]
public override bool EditComponent(
   ITypeDescriptorContext context,
   object obj,
   IWin32Window parent
);
[C++]
public: bool EditComponent(
   ITypeDescriptorContext* context,
   Object* obj,
   IWin32Window* parent
);
[JScript]
public override function EditComponent(
   context : ITypeDescriptorContext,
   obj : Object,
   parent : IWin32Window
) : Boolean;
```

Requirements

Platforms: Windows 98, Windows NT 4.0, Windows Millennium Edition, Windows 2000, Windows XP Home Edition, Windows XP Professional, Windows Server 2003 family

AxHost.ClsidAttribute Class

This type supports the .NET Framework infrastructure and is not intended to be used directly from your code.

[Visual Basic]
```
<AttributeUsage(AttributeTargets.Class)>
NotInheritable Public Class AxHost.ClsidAttribute
   Inherits Attribute
```
[C#]
```
[AttributeUsage(AttributeTargets.Class)]
public sealed class AxHost.ClsidAttribute : Attribute
```
[C++]
```
[AttributeUsage(AttributeTargets::Class)]
public __gc __sealed class AxHost.ClsidAttribute : public
   Attribute
```
[JScript]
```
public
   AttributeUsage(AttributeTargets.Class)
class AxHost.ClsidAttribute extends Attribute
```

AxHost.ClsidAttribute Constructor

This member supports the .NET Framework infrastructure and is not intended to be used directly from your code.

[Visual Basic]
```
Public Sub New( _
   ByVal clsid As String _
)
```
[C#]
```
public AxHost.ClsidAttribute(
   string clsid
);
```
[C++]
```
public: ClsidAttribute(
   String* clsid
);
```
[JScript]
```
public function AxHost.ClsidAttribute(
   clsid : String
);
```

AxHost.ClsidAttribute.Value Property

This member supports the .NET Framework infrastructure and is not intended to be used directly from your code.

[Visual Basic]
```
Public ReadOnly Property Value As String
```
[C#]
```
public string Value {get;}
```
[C++]
```
public: __property String* get_Value();
```
[JScript]
```
public function get Value() : String;
```

AxHost.ConnectionPointCookie Class

This type supports the .NET Framework infrastructure and is not intended to be used directly from your code.

```
[Visual Basic]
<ComVisible(False)>
Public Class AxHost.ConnectionPointCookie
[C#]
[ComVisible(false)]
public class AxHost.ConnectionPointCookie
[C++]
[ComVisible(false)]
public __gc class AxHost.ConnectionPointCookie
[JScript]
public
   ComVisible(false)
class AxHost.ConnectionPointCookie
```

AxHost.ConnectionPointCookie Constructor

This member supports the .NET Framework infrastructure and is not intended to be used directly from your code.

```
[Visual Basic]
Public Sub New( _
   ByVal source As Object, _
   ByVal sink As Object, _
   ByVal eventInterface As Type _
)
[C#]
public AxHost.ConnectionPointCookie(
   object source,
   object sink,
   Type eventInterface
);
[C++]
public: ConnectionPointCookie(
   Object* source,
   Object* sink,
   Type* eventInterface
);
[JScript]
public function AxHost.ConnectionPointCookie(
   source : Object,
   sink : Object,
   eventInterface : Type
);
```

AxHost.ConnectionPointCookie.Disconnect Method

This member supports the .NET Framework infrastructure and is not intended to be used directly from your code.

```
[Visual Basic]
Public Sub Disconnect()
[C#]
public void Disconnect();
[C++]
public: void Disconnect();
[JScript]
public function Disconnect();
```

AxHost.ConnectionPointCookie.Finalize Method

This member overrides **Object.Finalize**.

```
[Visual Basic]
Overrides Protected Sub Finalize()
[C#]
~ConnectionPointCookie();
[C++]
~ConnectionPointCookie();
[JScript]
protected override function Finalize();
```

Requirements

Platforms: Windows 98, Windows NT 4.0, Windows Millennium Edition, Windows 2000, Windows XP Home Edition, Windows XP Professional, Windows Server 2003 family

AxHost.InvalidActiveXState-Exception Class

The exception that is thrown when the ActiveX control is referenced while in an invalid state.

For a list of all members of this type, see **AxHost.InvalidActiveX-StateException Members**.

System.Object
  System.Exception
    System.Windows.Forms.AxHost.InvalidActiveXState-Exception

```
[Visual Basic]
Public Class AxHost.InvalidActiveXStateException
   Inherits Exception
[C#]
public class AxHost.InvalidActiveXStateException : Exception
[C++]
public __gc class AxHost.InvalidActiveXStateException : public
   Exception
[JScript]
public class AxHost.InvalidActiveXStateException extends Exception
```

Thread Safety

Any public static (**Shared** in Visual Basic) members of this type are safe for multithreaded operations. Any instance members are not guaranteed to be thread safe.

Remarks

The public properties and methods of an ActiveX control can only be referenced after the ActiveX control has been instantiated and initialized completely; otherwise the **AxHost.InvalidActiveXState-Exception** exception is thrown. The **AxHost.InvalidActiveXState-Exception** exception class contains the name of the member that made the reference and the member type. The member type is one of the **AxHost.ActiveXInvokeKind** enumerated values.

Requirements

Namespace: System.Windows.Forms

Platforms: Windows 98, Windows NT 4.0, Windows Millennium Edition, Windows 2000, Windows XP Home Edition, Windows XP Professional, Windows Server 2003 family

Assembly: System.Windows.Forms (in System.Windows.Forms.dll)

AxHost.InvalidActiveXStateException Constructor

Initializes a new instance of the **AxHost.InvalidActiveXState-Exception** class.

```
[Visual Basic]
Public Sub New( _
   ByVal name As String, _
   ByVal kind As AxHost.ActiveXInvokeKind _
)
[C#]
public AxHost.InvalidActiveXStateException(
   string name,
   AxHost.ActiveXInvokeKind kind
);
[C++]
public: InvalidActiveXStateException(
   String* name,
   AxHost.ActiveXInvokeKind kind
);
[JScript]
public function AxHost.InvalidActiveXStateException(
   name : String,
   kind : AxHost.ActiveXInvokeKind
);
```

Parameters

name
  The name of the member that referenced the ActiveX control while it was in an invalid state.

kind
  One of the **AxHost.ActiveXInvokeKind** values.

Requirements

Platforms: Windows 98, Windows NT 4.0, Windows Millennium Edition, Windows 2000, Windows XP Home Edition, Windows XP Professional, Windows Server 2003 family

AxHost.InvalidActiveXStateException.ToString Method

This member overrides **Exception.ToString**.

```
[Visual Basic]
Overrides Public Function ToString() As String
[C#]
public override string ToString();
[C++]
public: String* ToString();
[JScript]
public override function ToString() : String;
```

Requirements

Platforms: Windows 98, Windows NT 4.0, Windows Millennium Edition, Windows 2000, Windows XP Home Edition, Windows XP Professional, Windows Server 2003 family

AxHost.State Class

Encapsulates the persisted state of an ActiveX control.

For a list of all members of this type, see **AxHost.State Members**.

System.Object
  System.Windows.Forms.AxHost.State

```
[Visual Basic]
<Serializable>
Public Class AxHost.State
   Implements ISerializable
[C#]
[Serializable]
public class AxHost.State : ISerializable
[C++]
[Serializable]
public __gc class AxHost.State : public ISerializable
[JScript]
public
   Serializable
class AxHost.State implements ISerializable
```

Thread Safety

Any public static (**Shared** in Visual Basic) members of this type are safe for multithreaded operations. Any instance members are not guaranteed to be thread safe.

Remarks

The **AxHost.State** can be retrieved using the **AxHost.OcxState** property, or by reading the control's state from a data stream.

For more information, see the documentation for **IPersistStream** and **IPersistPropertyBag** in the MSDN library. **IPersistStream** can be found in the interface reference section of the COM SDK documentation, and **IPersistPropertyBag** can be found in the COM Fundamentals interface reference section of the COM SDK documentation.

Requirements

Namespace: System.Windows.Forms

Platforms: Windows 98, Windows NT 4.0, Windows Millennium Edition, Windows 2000, Windows XP Home Edition, Windows XP Professional, Windows Server 2003 family

Assembly: System.Windows.Forms (in System.Windows.Forms.dll)

AxHost.State Constructor

This member supports the .NET Framework infrastructure and is not intended to be used directly from your code.

```
[Visual Basic]
Public Sub New( _
   ByVal ms As Stream, _
   ByVal storageType As Integer, _
   ByVal manualUpdate As Boolean, _
   ByVal licKey As String _
)
[C#]
public AxHost.State(
   Stream ms,
   int storageType,
   bool manualUpdate,
   string licKey
);
[C++]
public: State(
   Stream* ms,
   int storageType,
   bool manualUpdate,
   String* licKey
);
[JScript]
public function AxHost.State(
   ms : Stream,
   storageType : int,
   manualUpdate : Boolean,
   licKey : String
);
```

AxHost.State.ISerializable.GetObjectData Method

This member supports the .NET Framework infrastructure and is not intended to be used directly from your code.

```
[Visual Basic]
Private Sub GetObjectData( _
   ByVal si As SerializationInfo, _
   ByVal context As StreamingContext _
) Implements ISerializable.GetObjectData
[C#]
void ISerializable.GetObjectData(
   SerializationInfo si,
   StreamingContext context
);
[C++]
private: void ISerializable::GetObjectData(
   SerializationInfo* si,
   StreamingContext context
);
[JScript]
private function ISerializable.GetObjectData(
   si : SerializationInfo,
   context : StreamingContext
);
```

AxHost.StateConverter Class

This type supports the .NET Framework infrastructure and is not intended to be used directly from your code.

[Visual Basic]
```
Public Class AxHost.StateConverter
   Inherits TypeConverter
```
[C#]
```
public class AxHost.StateConverter : TypeConverter
```
[C++]
```
public __gc class AxHost.StateConverter : public TypeConverter
```
[JScript]
```
public class AxHost.StateConverter extends TypeConverter
```

AxHost.StateConverter Constructor

This member supports the .NET Framework infrastructure and is not intended to be used directly from your code.

[Visual Basic]
```
Public Sub New()
```
[C#]
```
public AxHost.StateConverter();
```
[C++]
```
public: StateConverter();
```
[JScript]
```
public function AxHost.StateConverter();
```

AxHost.StateConverter.CanConvertFrom Method

This member supports the .NET Framework infrastructure and is not intended to be used directly from your code.

Overload List

This member overrides **TypeConverter.CanConvertFrom**.

[Visual Basic] **Overloads Overrides Public Function CanConvertFrom(ITypeDescriptorContext, Type) As Boolean**

[C#] **public override bool CanConvertFrom(ITypeDescriptorContext, Type);**

[C++] **public: bool CanConvertFrom(ITypeDescriptorContext*, Type*);**

[JScript] **public override function CanConvertFrom(ITypeDescriptorContext, Type) : Boolean;**

This member supports the .NET Framework infrastructure and is not intended to be used directly from your code.

[Visual Basic] **Overloads Public Function CanConvertFrom(Type) As Boolean**

[C#] **public bool CanConvertFrom(Type);**

[C++] **public: bool CanConvertFrom(Type*);**

[JScript] **public function CanConvertFrom(Type) : Boolean;**

AxHost.StateConverter.CanConvertFrom Method (ITypeDescriptorContext, Type)

This member overrides **TypeConverter.CanConvertFrom**.

[Visual Basic]
```
Overrides Overloads Public Function CanConvertFrom( _
   ByVal context As ITypeDescriptorContext, _
   ByVal sourceType As Type _
) As Boolean
```
[C#]
```
public override bool CanConvertFrom(
   ITypeDescriptorContext context,
   Type sourceType
);
```
[C++]
```
public: bool CanConvertFrom(
   ITypeDescriptorContext* context,
   Type* sourceType
);
```
[JScript]
```
public override function CanConvertFrom(
   context : ITypeDescriptorContext,
   sourceType : Type
) : Boolean;
```

Requirements

Platforms: Windows 98, Windows NT 4.0, Windows Millennium Edition, Windows 2000, Windows XP Home Edition, Windows XP Professional, Windows Server 2003 family

AxHost.StateConverter.CanConvertTo Method

This member supports the .NET Framework infrastructure and is not intended to be used directly from your code.

Overload List

This member overrides **TypeConverter.CanConvertTo**.

[Visual Basic] **Overloads Overrides Public Function CanConvertTo(ITypeDescriptorContext, Type) As Boolean**

[C#] **public override bool CanConvertTo(ITypeDescriptorContext, Type);**

[C++] **public: bool CanConvertTo(ITypeDescriptorContext*, Type*);**

[JScript] **public override function CanConvertTo(ITypeDescriptorContext, Type) : Boolean;**

This member supports the .NET Framework infrastructure and is not intended to be used directly from your code.

[Visual Basic] **Overloads Public Function CanConvertTo(Type) As Boolean**

[C#] **public bool CanConvertTo(Type);**

[C++] **public: bool CanConvertTo(Type*);**

[JScript] **public function CanConvertTo(Type) : Boolean;**

AxHost.StateConverter.CanConvertTo Method (ITypeDescriptorContext, Type)

This member overrides **TypeConverter.CanConvertTo**.

```
[Visual Basic]
Overrides Overloads Public Function CanConvertTo( _
   ByVal context As ITypeDescriptorContext, _
   ByVal destinationType As Type _
) As Boolean
[C#]
public override bool CanConvertTo(
   ITypeDescriptorContext context,
   Type destinationType
);
[C++]
public: bool CanConvertTo(
   ITypeDescriptorContext* context,
   Type* destinationType
);
[JScript]
public override function CanConvertTo(
   context : ITypeDescriptorContext,
   destinationType : Type
) : Boolean;
```

Requirements

Platforms: Windows 98, Windows NT 4.0, Windows Millennium Edition, Windows 2000, Windows XP Home Edition, Windows XP Professional, Windows Server 2003 family

AxHost.StateConverter.ConvertFrom Method

This member supports the .NET Framework infrastructure and is not intended to be used directly from your code.

Overload List

This member overrides **TypeConverter.ConvertFrom**.

[Visual Basic] **Overloads Overrides Public Function ConvertFrom(ITypeDescriptorContext, CultureInfo, Object) As Object**

[C#] **public override object ConvertFrom(ITypeDescriptorContext, CultureInfo, object);**

[C++] **public: Object* ConvertFrom(ITypeDescriptorContext*, CultureInfo*, Object*);**

[JScript] **public override function ConvertFrom(ITypeDescriptorContext, CultureInfo, Object) : Object;**

This member supports the .NET Framework infrastructure and is not intended to be used directly from your code.

[Visual Basic] **Overloads Public Function ConvertFrom(Object) As Object**

[C#] **public object ConvertFrom(object);**

[C++] **public: Object* ConvertFrom(Object*);**

[JScript] **public function ConvertFrom(Object) : Object;**

AxHost.StateConverter.ConvertFrom Method (ITypeDescriptorContext, CultureInfo, Object)

This member overrides **TypeConverter.ConvertFrom**.

```
[Visual Basic]
Overrides Overloads Public Function ConvertFrom( _
   ByVal context As ITypeDescriptorContext, _
   ByVal culture As CultureInfo, _
   ByVal value As Object _
) As Object
[C#]
public override object ConvertFrom(
   ITypeDescriptorContext context,
   CultureInfo culture,
   object value
);
[C++]
public: Object* ConvertFrom(
   ITypeDescriptorContext* context,
   CultureInfo* culture,
   Object* value
);
[JScript]
public override function ConvertFrom(
   context : ITypeDescriptorContext,
   culture : CultureInfo,
   value : Object
) : Object;
```

Requirements

Platforms: Windows 98, Windows NT 4.0, Windows Millennium Edition, Windows 2000, Windows XP Home Edition, Windows XP Professional, Windows Server 2003 family

AxHost.StateConverter.ConvertTo Method

This member supports the .NET Framework infrastructure and is not intended to be used directly from your code.

Overload List

This member overrides **TypeConverter.ConvertTo**.

[Visual Basic] **Overloads Overrides Public Function ConvertTo(ITypeDescriptorContext, CultureInfo, Object, Type) As Object**

[C#] **public override object ConvertTo(ITypeDescriptorContext, CultureInfo, object, Type);**

[C++] **public: Object* ConvertTo(ITypeDescriptorContext*, CultureInfo*, Object*, Type*);**

[JScript] **public override function ConvertTo(ITypeDescriptorContext, CultureInfo, Object, Type) : Object;**

This member supports the .NET Framework infrastructure and is not intended to be used directly from your code.

[Visual Basic] **Overloads Public Function ConvertTo(Object, Type) As Object**

[C#] **public object ConvertTo(object, Type);**

[C++] **public: Object* ConvertTo(Object*, Type*);**

[JScript] **public function ConvertTo(Object, Type) : Object;**

AxHost.StateConverter.ConvertTo Method (ITypeDescriptorContext, CultureInfo, Object, Type)

This member overrides **TypeConverter.ConvertTo**.

[Visual Basic]
```
Overrides Overloads Public Function ConvertTo( _
   ByVal context As ITypeDescriptorContext, _
   ByVal culture As CultureInfo, _
   ByVal value As Object, _
   ByVal destinationType As Type _
) As Object
```
[C#]
```
public override object ConvertTo(
   ITypeDescriptorContext context,
   CultureInfo culture,
   object value,
   Type destinationType
);
```
[C++]
```
public: Object* ConvertTo(
   ITypeDescriptorContext* context,
   CultureInfo* culture,
   Object* value,
   Type* destinationType
);
```
[JScript]
```
public override function ConvertTo(
   context : ITypeDescriptorContext,
   culture : CultureInfo,
   value : Object,
   destinationType : Type
) : Object;
```

Requirements

Platforms: Windows 98, Windows NT 4.0, Windows Millennium Edition, Windows 2000, Windows XP Home Edition, Windows XP Professional, Windows Server 2003 family

AxHost.TypeLibraryTimeStampAttribute Class

This type supports the .NET Framework infrastructure and is not intended to be used directly from your code.

```
[Visual Basic]
<AttributeUsage(AttributeTargets.Assembly)>
NotInheritable Public Class AxHost.TypeLibraryTimeStampAttribute
   Inherits Attribute
[C#]
[AttributeUsage(AttributeTargets.Assembly)]
public sealed class AxHost.TypeLibraryTimeStampAttribute :
   Attribute
[C++]
[AttributeUsage(AttributeTargets::Assembly)]
public __gc __sealed class AxHost.TypeLibraryTimeStampAttribute :
   public Attribute
[JScript]
public
   AttributeUsage(AttributeTargets.Assembly)
class AxHost.TypeLibraryTimeStampAttribute extends Attribute
```

AxHost.TypeLibraryTimeStampAttribute Constructor

This member supports the .NET Framework infrastructure and is not intended to be used directly from your code.

```
[Visual Basic]
Public Sub New( _
   ByVal timestamp As String _
)
[C#]
public AxHost.TypeLibraryTimeStampAttribute(
   string timestamp
);
[C++]
public: TypeLibraryTimeStampAttribute(
   String* timestamp
);
[JScript]
public function AxHost.TypeLibraryTimeStampAttribute(
   timestamp : String
);
```

AxHost.TypeLibraryTimeStampAttribute.Value Property

This member supports the .NET Framework infrastructure and is not intended to be used directly from your code.

```
[Visual Basic]
Public ReadOnly Property Value As DateTime
[C#]
public DateTime Value {get;}
[C++]
public: __property DateTime get_Value();
[JScript]
public function get Value() : DateTime;
```

BaseCollection Class

Provides the base functionality for creating data-related collections in the **System.Windows.Forms** namespace.

System.Object
  System.MarshalByRefObject
    System.Windows.Forms.BaseCollection
      System.Windows.Forms.BindingsCollection
      System.Windows.Forms.GridColumnStylesCollection
      System.Windows.Forms.GridTableStylesCollection

```
[Visual Basic]
Public Class BaseCollection
   Inherits MarshalByRefObject
   Implements ICollection, IEnumerable
[C#]
public class BaseCollection : MarshalByRefObject, ICollection,
   IEnumerable
[C++]
public __gc class BaseCollection : public MarshalByRefObject,
   ICollection, IEnumerable
[JScript]
public class BaseCollection extends MarshalByRefObject implements
   ICollection, IEnumerable
```

Thread Safety

Any public static (**Shared** in Visual Basic) members of this type are safe for multithreaded operations. Any instance members are not guaranteed to be thread safe.

Remarks

The **BaseCollection** class is not intended for use by application developers. Application developers should use **CollectionBase** instead.

The **BaseCollection** class implements the **ICollection** interface.

Classes that derive from the **BaseCollection** class include:

- **BindingsCollection**
- **GridColumnStylesCollection**
- **GridTableStylesCollection**

Requirements

Namespace: System.Windows.Forms

Platforms: Windows 98, Windows NT 4.0, Windows Millennium Edition, Windows 2000, Windows XP Home Edition, Windows XP Professional, Windows Server 2003 family, .NET Compact Framework - Windows CE .NET

Assembly: System.Windows.Forms (in System.Windows.Forms.dll)

BaseCollection Constructor

Initializes a new instance of the **BaseCollection** class.

```
[Visual Basic]
Public Sub New()
[C#]
public BaseCollection();
[C++]
public: BaseCollection();
[JScript]
public function BaseCollection();
```

Remarks

The default constructor initializes any fields to their default values.

Requirements

Platforms: Windows 98, Windows NT 4.0, Windows Millennium Edition, Windows 2000, Windows XP Home Edition, Windows XP Professional, Windows Server 2003 family, .NET Compact Framework - Windows CE .NET

BaseCollection.Count Property

Gets the total number of elements in the collection.

```
[Visual Basic]
Public Overridable ReadOnly Property Count As Integer  Implements _
   ICollection.Count
[C#]
public virtual int Count {get;}
[C++]
public: __property virtual int get_Count();
[JScript]
public function get Count() : int;
```

Property Value

The total number of elements in the collection.

Implements

ICollection.Count

Requirements

Platforms: Windows 98, Windows NT 4.0, Windows Millennium Edition, Windows 2000, Windows XP Home Edition, Windows XP Professional, Windows Server 2003 family, .NET Compact Framework - Windows CE .NET

BaseCollection.IsReadOnly Property

Gets a value indicating whether the collection is read-only.

```
[Visual Basic]
Public ReadOnly Property IsReadOnly As Boolean
[C#]
public bool IsReadOnly {get;}
[C++]
public: __property bool get_IsReadOnly();
[JScript]
public function get IsReadOnly() : Boolean;
```

Property Value

This property is always **false**.

Remarks

The collections which derive from the **BaseCollection** class are always writable, which is why this property always returns **false**.

Requirements

Platforms: Windows 98, Windows NT 4.0, Windows Millennium Edition, Windows 2000, Windows XP Home Edition, Windows XP Professional, Windows Server 2003 family, .NET Compact Framework - Windows CE .NET

BaseCollection.IsSynchronized Property

Gets a value indicating whether access to the **ICollection** is synchronized.

```
[Visual Basic]
Public Overridable ReadOnly Property IsSynchronized As Boolean _
   Implements ICollection.IsSynchronized
[C#]
public virtual bool IsSynchronized {get;}
[C++]
public: __property virtual bool get_IsSynchronized();
[JScript]
public function get IsSynchronized() : Boolean;
```

Property Value

This property always returns **false**.

Implements

ICollection.IsSynchronized

Remarks

If a collection is thread safe, the **IsSynchronized** property returns **true**, and the programmer does not have to do anything to keep the collection safe.

If, as is the case with the **BaseCollection**, the **IsSynchronized** property returns **false**, then the **SyncRoot** property returns an object that can be used with the C# **lock** keyword. Use the static **Enter** and **Exit** methods of the **Monitor** class to manually lock and unlock the synchronization object.

Requirements

Platforms: Windows 98, Windows NT 4.0,
Windows Millennium Edition, Windows 2000,
Windows XP Home Edition, Windows XP Professional,
Windows Server 2003 family,
.NET Compact Framework - Windows CE .NET

BaseCollection.List Property

Gets the list of elements contained in the **BaseCollection** instance.

```
[Visual Basic]
Protected Overridable ReadOnly Property List As ArrayList
[C#]
protected virtual ArrayList List {get;}
[C++]
protected: __property virtual ArrayList* get_List();
[JScript]
protected function get List() : ArrayList;
```

Property Value

An **ArrayList** containing the elements of the collection. This property returns a null reference (**Nothing** in Visual Basic) unless overridden in a derived class.

Requirements

Platforms: Windows 98, Windows NT 4.0,
Windows Millennium Edition, Windows 2000,
Windows XP Home Edition, Windows XP Professional,
Windows Server 2003 family,
.NET Compact Framework - Windows CE .NET

BaseCollection.SyncRoot Property

Gets an object that can be used to synchronize access to the **BaseCollection**.

```
[Visual Basic]
Public Overridable ReadOnly Property SyncRoot As Object  Implements _
   ICollection.SyncRoot
[C#]
public virtual object SyncRoot {get;}
[C++]
public: __property virtual Object* get_SyncRoot();
[JScript]
public function get SyncRoot() : Object;
```

Property Value

An object that can be used to synchronize the **BaseCollection**.

Implements

ICollection.SyncRoot

Remarks

If, as is the case with the **BaseCollection**, the **IsSynchronized** property returns **false**, then the **SyncRoot** property returns an object that can be used with the C# **lock** keyword.

Requirements

Platforms: Windows 98, Windows NT 4.0,
Windows Millennium Edition, Windows 2000,
Windows XP Home Edition, Windows XP Professional,
Windows Server 2003 family,
.NET Compact Framework - Windows CE .NET

BaseCollection.CopyTo Method

Copies all the elements of the current one-dimensional **Array** to the specified one-dimensional **Array** starting at the specified destination **Array** index.

```
[Visual Basic]
Public Overridable Sub CopyTo( _
   ByVal ar As Array, _
   ByVal index As Integer _
) Implements ICollection.CopyTo
[C#]
public virtual void CopyTo(
   Array ar,
   int index
);
[C++]
public: virtual void CopyTo(
   Array* ar,
   int index
);
[JScript]
public function CopyTo(
   ar : Array,
   index : int
);
```

Parameters

ar
: The one-dimensional **Array** that is the destination of the elements copied from the current Array.

index
: The zero-based relative index in *ar* at which copying begins.

Implements

ICollection.CopyTo

Requirements

Platforms: Windows 98, Windows NT 4.0,
Windows Millennium Edition, Windows 2000,
Windows XP Home Edition, Windows XP Professional,
Windows Server 2003 family,
.NET Compact Framework - Windows CE .NET

BaseCollection.GetEnumerator Method

Gets the object that allows iterating through the members of the collection.

[Visual Basic]
```
Public Overridable Function GetEnumerator() As IEnumerator _
   Implements IEnumerable.GetEnumerator
```
[C#]
```
public virtual IEnumerator GetEnumerator();
```
[C++]
```
public: virtual IEnumerator* GetEnumerator();
```
[JScript]
```
public function GetEnumerator() : IEnumerator;
```

Return Value

An object that implements the **IEnumerator** interface.

Implements

IEnumerable.GetEnumerator

Requirements

Platforms: Windows 98, Windows NT 4.0,
Windows Millennium Edition, Windows 2000,
Windows XP Home Edition, Windows XP Professional,
Windows Server 2003 family,
.NET Compact Framework - Windows CE .NET

Binding Class

Represents the simple binding between the property value of an object and the property value of a control.

System.Object
  System.Windows.Forms.Binding

[Visual Basic]
```
Public Class Binding
```
[C#]
```
public class Binding
```
[C++]
```
public __gc class Binding
```
[JScript]
```
public class Binding
```

Thread Safety

Any public static (**Shared** in Visual Basic) members of this type are safe for multithreaded operations. Any instance members are not guaranteed to be thread safe.

Remarks

Use the **Binding** class to create and maintain a simple binding between the property of a control and either the property of an object, or the property of the current object in a list of objects.

As an example of the first case, you can bind the **Text** property of a **TextBox** control to the FirstName property of a Customer object. As an example of the second case, you can bind the **Text** property of a **TextBox** control to the FirstName property of a **DataTable** containing customers.

The **Binding** class also enables you to format values for display through the **Format** event and to retrieve formatted values through the **Parse** event.

When constructing a **Binding** instance with the **Binding** contructor, you must specify three items: the name of the control property to bind to, the data source, and the navigation path that resolves to a list or property in the data source. The navigation path is also used to create the object's **BindingMemberInfo**.

First, you must specify name of the control property you want to bind the data to. For example, to display data in a **TextBox** control, specify the **Text** property. Second, you can specify an instance of any of the following classes as the data source:

Description	Example
Any class that implements **IBindingList** or **ITypedList**. These include: **DataSet**, **DataTable**, **DataView**, or **DataViewManager**.	A C# example: `DataSet ds = new DataSet("myDataSet");`

Any class that implements **IList** to create an indexed collection of objects. The collection must be created and filled before creating the **Binding** object. The objects in the list must all be of the same type; otherwise an exception will be thrown.	A C# example:
	`ArrayList ar1 = new ArrayList;`
	`Customer1 cust1 = new Customer("Louis");`
	`ar1.Add(cust1);`

Strongly typed **IList** of strongly typed objects	A C# example: `Customer [] custList = new Customer[3];`

Third, you must specify the navigation path, which can be an empty string (""), a single property name, or a period-delimited hierarchy of names. If you set the navigation path to an empty string, the **ToString** method will be called on the underlying data source object.

If the data source is a **DataTable**, which can contain multiple **DataColumn** objects, the navigation path must be used to resolve to a specific column.

> **Note** When the data source is a **DataSet**, **DataViewManager**, or **DataTable**, you are actually binding to a **DataView**. Consequently, the bound rows are actually **DataRowView** objects.

A period-delimited navigation path is required when the data source is set to an object that contains multiple **DataTable** objects (such as a **DataSet** or **DataViewManager**). You can also use a period-delimited navigation path when you bind to an object whose properties return references to other objects (such as a class with properties that return other class objects). For example, the following navigation paths all describe valid data fields:

- "Size.Height"
- "Suppliers.CompanyName"
- "Regions.regionsToCustomers.CustomerFirstName"
- "Regions.regionsToCustomers.customersToOrders.ordersToDetails .Quantity"

Each member of the path can return either a property that resolves to a single value(such as an integer), or a list of values (such as an array of strings). Although each member in the path can be a list or property, the final member must resolve to a property. Each member builds on the previous member: "Size.Height" resolves to the **Height** for the current **Size**; "Regions.regionsToCustomers.Customer-FirstName" resolves to the first name for the current customer, where the customer is one of the customers for the current region.

A **DataRelation** returns a list of values by linking one **DataTable** to a second **DataTable** in a **DataSet**. If the **DataSet** contains **Data-Relation** objects, you can specify the data member as a **TableName** followed by a **RelationName**, and then a **ColumnName**. For example, if the **DataTable** named "Suppliers" contains a **Data-Relation** named "suppliers2products", the data member could be "Suppliers.suppliers2products.ProductName".

The data source can consist of a set of related classes. For example, imagine a set of classes that catalogs solar systems. The class named System contains a property named Stars that returns a collection of star objects. Each Star object has Name and Mass properties, as well as a Planets property that returns a collection of Planet objects. In this system, each planet also has Mass and Name properties. Each Planet object further has a Moons property that returns a collection of Moon objects, each of which also has Name and Mass properties. If you specify a System object as the data source, you can specify any of the following as the data member:

- "Stars.Name"
- "Stars.Mass"
- "Stars.Planets.Name"
- "Stars.Planets.Mass"
- "Stars.Planets.Moons.Name"
- "Stars.Planets.Moons.Mass"

Controls that can be simple-bound feature a collection of **Binding** objects in a **ControlBindingsCollection**, which you can access through the control's **DataBindings** property. You add a **Binding** object to the collection by calling the **Add** method, thereby binding a property of the control to a property of an object (or to a property of the current object in a list).

You can simple-bind to any object that derives from the **System.Windows.Forms.Control** class, for example, the following Windows controls:

- **Button**
- **CheckBox**
- **CheckedListBox**
- **ComboBox**
- **DateTimePicker**
- **DomainUpDown**
- **GroupBox**
- **HScrollBar**
- **Label**
- **LinkLabel**
- **ListBox**
- **ListView**
- **MonthCalendar**
- **NumericUpDown**
- **PictureBox**
- **ProgressBar**
- **RadioButton**
- **RichTextBox**
- **ScrollBar**
- **StatusBar**
- **TextBox**
- **TreeView**
- **VScrollBar**

Note Only the **SelectedValue** property of the **ComboBox**, **CheckedListBox**, and **ListBox** control is simple bound.

The **BindingManagerBase** class is an abstract class that manages all the **Binding** objects for a particular data source and data member. Classes that derive from **BindingManagerBase** are the **CurrencyManager** and the **PropertyManager** classes. How a **Binding** is managed depends on whether the **Binding** is a list binding or a property binding. For example, if it is a list binding, you can use the **BindingManagerBase** object to specify a **Position** in the list; the **Position**, therefore, determines which item (out of all items in the list) is actually bound to a control. To return the appropriate **BindingManagerBase**, use the **BindingContext**.

To add a new row to a set of controls bound to the same **DataSource**, use the **AddNew** method of the **BindingManagerBase** class. Use the **Item** property of the **BindingContext** class to return the appropriate **CurrencyManager**. To escape the addition of the new row, use the **CancelCurrentEdit** method.

Example

The following example creates a Windows Form with several controls that demonstrate simple data binding. The example creates a **DataSet** with two tables named **Customers** and **Orders**, and a **DataRelation** named **custToOrders**. Four controls (a **DateTimePicker** and three **TextBox** controls) are data bound to columns in the tables. For each control, the example creates and adds a **Binding** to the control through the **DataBindings** property. The example returns a **BindingManagerBase** object for each table through the form's **BindingContext** object. Four **Button** controls increment or decrement the **Position** property on the **BindingManagerBase** objects.

[Visual Basic]

```
Imports System
Imports System.ComponentModel
Imports System.Data
Imports System.Drawing
Imports System.Globalization
Imports System.Windows.Forms

Public Class Form1
   Inherits Form

   Private components As Container
   Private button1 As Button
   Private button2 As Button
   Private button3 As Button
   Private button4 As Button
   Private text1 As TextBox
   Private text2 As TextBox
   Private text3 As TextBox

   Private bmCustomers As BindingManagerBase
   Private bmOrders As BindingManagerBase
   Private ds As DataSet
   Private DateTimePicker1 As DateTimePicker

   Public Sub New
      ' Required for Windows Form Designer support.
      InitializeComponent
      ' Call SetUp to bind the controls.
      SetUp
   End Sub

   Protected Overloads Overrides Sub Dispose(ByVal disposing As ↵
Boolean)
      If disposing Then
         If Not (components Is Nothing) Then
            components.Dispose()
         End If
      End If
      MyBase.Dispose(disposing)
   End Sub

   Private Sub InitializeComponent
      ' Create the form and its controls.
      With Me
         .components = New Container
         .button1 = New Button
         .button2 = New Button
         .button3 = New Button
         .button4 = New Button
         .text1 = New TextBox
         .text2 = New TextBox
         .text3 = New TextBox

         .DateTimePicker1 = New DateTimePicker

         .AutoScaleBaseSize = New Size(5, 13)
         .Text = "Binding Sample"
         .ClientSize = New Size(450, 200)

         With .button1
            .Location = New Point(24, 16)
            .Size = New Size(64, 24)
            .Text = "<"
            AddHandler button1.click, AddressOf button1_Click
         End With
```

```
        With .button2
            .Location = New Point(90, 16)
            .Size = New Size(64, 24)
            .Text = ">"
            AddHandler button2.click, AddressOf button2_Click
        End With

        With .button3
            .Location = New Point(90, 100)
            .Size = New Size(64, 24)
            .Text = ">"
            AddHandler button3.click, AddressOf button3_Click
        End With

        With .button4
            .Location = New Point(150, 100)
            .Size = New Size(64, 24)
            .Text = ">"
            AddHandler button4.click, AddressOf button4_Click
        End With

        With .text1
            .Location = New Point(24, 50)
            .Size = New Size(150, 24)
        End With

        With .text2
            .Location = New Point(190, 50)
            .Size = New Size(150, 24)
        End With

        With .text3
            .Location = New Point(290, 150)
            .Size = New Size(150, 24)
        End With

           With .DateTimePicker1
              .Location = New Point(90, 150)
              .Size = New Size(200, 800)
           End With

           With .Controls
           .Add(button1)
           .Add(button2)
           .Add(button3)
           .Add(button4)
           .Add(text1)
           .Add(text2)
           .Add(text3)
           .Add(DateTimePicker1)
           End With
     End With
  End Sub

  Public Shared Sub Main
     Application.Run(new Form1)
  End Sub

  Private Sub SetUp
     ' Create a DataSet with two tables and one relation.
     MakeDataSet
     BindControls
  End Sub

  Private Sub BindControls
     ' Create two Binding objects for the first two TextBox
     ' controls. The data-bound property for both controls
     ' is the Text property.  The data source is a DataSet
     ' (ds). The data member is the
     ' TableName.ColumnName" string.

     text1.DataBindings.Add(New _
        Binding("Text", ds, "customers.custName"))
     text2.DataBindings.Add(New _
        Binding("Text", ds, "customers.custID"))
     ' Bind the DateTimePicker control by adding a new Binding.
     ' The data member of the DateTimePicker is a
     ' TableName.RelationName.ColumnName string
     DateTimePicker1.DataBindings.Add(New _
        Binding("Value", ds, "customers.CustToOrders.OrderDate"))
     ' Add event delegates for the Parse and Format events to a
     ' new Binding object, and add the object to the third
     ' TextBox control's BindingsCollection. The delegates
     ' must be added before adding the Binding to the
     ' collection; otherwise, no formatting occurs until
     ' the Current object of the BindingManagerBase for
     ' the data source changes.
     Dim b As Binding = New _
        Binding("Text", ds, "customers.custToOrders.OrderAmount")
     AddHandler b.Parse, AddressOf CurrencyStringToDecimal
     AddHandler b.Format, AddressOf DecimalToCurrencyString
     text3.DataBindings.Add(b)

        ' Get the BindingManagerBase for the Customers table.
        bmCustomers = Me.BindingContext(ds, "Customers")

        ' Get the BindingManagerBase for the Orders table using the
        ' RelationName.
        bmOrders = Me.BindingContext(ds, "customers.CustToOrders")
  End Sub

  Private Sub DecimalToCurrencyString(sender As Object, ↵
cevent As ConvertEventArgs)
     ' This method is the Format event handler. Whenever the
     ' control displays a new value, the value is converted from
     ' its native Decimal type to a string. The ToString method
     ' then formats the value as a Currency, by using the
     ' formatting character "c".

     ' The application can only convert to string type.

     If Not cevent.DesiredType Is GetType(String) Then
        Exit Sub
     End If

     cevent.Value = CType(cevent.Value, decimal).ToString("c")
  End Sub

  Private Sub CurrencyStringToDecimal(sender As Object, ↵
cevent As ConvertEventArgs)
     ' This method is the Parse event handler. The Parse event
     ' occurs whenever the displayed value changes. The static
     ' ToDecimal method of the Convert class converts the
     ' value back to its native Decimal type.

     ' Can only convert to decimal type.
     If Not cevent.DesiredType Is GetType(decimal) Then
        Exit Sub
     End If

     cevent.Value = Decimal.Parse(cevent.Value.ToString, _
     NumberStyles.Currency, nothing)

     ' To see that no precision is lost, print the unformatted
     ' value. For example, changing a value to "10.0001"
     ' causes the control to display "10.00", but the
     ' unformatted value remains "10.0001".
     Console.WriteLine(cevent.Value)
  End Sub

  Protected Sub button1_Click(sender As Object, e As System.EventArgs)
     ' Go to the previous item in the Customer list.
     bmCustomers.Position -= 1
  End Sub

  Protected Sub button2_Click(sender As Object, e As System.EventArgs)
     ' Go to the next item in the Customer list.
     bmCustomers.Position += 1
  End Sub
```

```
    Protected Sub button3_Click(sender As Object, e As System.EventArgs)
       ' Go to the previous item in the Order list.
       bmOrders.Position -= 1
    End Sub

    Protected Sub button4_Click(sender As Object, e As System.EventArgs)
       ' Go to the next item in the Orders list.
       bmOrders.Position += 1
    End Sub

    ' Creates a DataSet with two tables and populates it.
    Private Sub MakeDataSet
       ' Create a DataSet.
       ds = New DataSet("myDataSet")

       ' Creates two DataTables.
       Dim tCust As DataTable = New DataTable("Customers")
       Dim tOrders As DataTable = New DataTable("Orders")

       ' Create two columns, and add them to the first table.
       Dim cCustID As DataColumn = New DataColumn("CustID", _
       System.Type.GetType("System.Int32"))
       Dim cCustName As DataColumn = New DataColumn("CustName")
       tCust.Columns.Add(cCustID)
       tCust.Columns.Add(cCustName)

       ' Create three columns, and add them to the second table.
       Dim cID As DataColumn = _
          New DataColumn("CustID", System.Type.GetType("System.Int32"))
       Dim cOrderDate As DataColumn = _
          New DataColumn("orderDate",
System.Type.GetType("System.DateTime"))
       Dim cOrderAmount As DataColumn = _
          New DataColumn("OrderAmount",
System.Type.GetType("System.Decimal"))
       tOrders.Columns.Add(cOrderAmount)
       tOrders.Columns.Add(cID)
       tOrders.Columns.Add(cOrderDate)

       ' Add the tables to the DataSet.
       ds.Tables.Add(tCust)
       ds.Tables.Add(tOrders)

       ' Create a DataRelation, and add it to the DataSet.
       Dim dr As DataRelation = New _
          DataRelation("custToOrders", cCustID, cID)
       ds.Relations.Add(dr)

       ' Populate the tables. For each customer and orders,
       ' create two DataRow variables.
       Dim newRow1 As DataRow
       Dim newRow2 As DataRow

          ' Create three customers in the Customers Table.
          Dim i As Integer
          For i = 1 to 3
             newRow1 = tCust.NewRow
             newRow1("custID") = i
             ' Adds the row to the Customers table.
             tCust.Rows.Add(newRow1)
          Next

          ' Give each customer a distinct name.
          tCust.Rows(0)("custName") = "Alpha"
          tCust.Rows(1)("custName") = "Beta"
          tCust.Rows(2)("custName") = "Omega"

          ' For each customer, create five rows in the Orders table.
          Dim j As Integer
          For i = 1 to 3
          For j = 1 to 5
             newRow2 = tOrders.NewRow
             newRow2("CustID") = i
             newRow2("orderDate") = New DateTime(2001, i, j * 2)
             newRow2("OrderAmount") = i * 10 + j * .1
             ' Add the row to the Orders table.
             tOrders.Rows.Add(newRow2)
          Next
          Next
    End Sub
End Class
```

[C#]

```
using System;
using System.Data;
using System.Drawing;
using System.Globalization;
using System.Windows.Forms;

public class Form1 : System.Windows.Forms.Form
{
   private System.ComponentModel.Container components;
   private Button button1;
   private Button button2;
   private Button button3;
   private Button button4;
   private TextBox text1;
   private TextBox text2;
   private TextBox text3;

   private BindingManagerBase bmCustomers;
   private BindingManagerBase bmOrders;
   private DataSet ds;
   private DateTimePicker DateTimePicker1;

   public Form1()
   {
      // Required for Windows Form Designer support.
      InitializeComponent();
      // Call SetUp to bind the controls.
      SetUp();
   }

   private void InitializeComponent()
   {
      // Create the form and its controls.
      this.components = new System.ComponentModel.Container();
      this.button1 = new System.Windows.Forms.Button();
      this.button2 = new System.Windows.Forms.Button();
      this.button3 = new System.Windows.Forms.Button();
      this.button4 = new System.Windows.Forms.Button();

      this.text1= new System.Windows.Forms.TextBox();
      this.text2= new System.Windows.Forms.TextBox();
      this.text3= new System.Windows.Forms.TextBox();

      this.DateTimePicker1 = new DateTimePicker();

      this.AutoScaleBaseSize = new System.Drawing.Size(5, 13);
      this.Text = "Binding Sample";
      this.ClientSize = new System.Drawing.Size(450, 200);

      button1.Location = new System.Drawing.Point(24, 16);
      button1.Size = new System.Drawing.Size(64, 24);
      button1.Text = "<";
      button1.Click+=new System.EventHandler(button1_Click);

      button2.Location = new System.Drawing.Point(90, 16);
      button2.Size = new System.Drawing.Size(64, 24);
      button2.Text = ">";
      button2.Click+=new System.EventHandler(button2_Click);

      button3.Location = new System.Drawing.Point(90, 100);
      button3.Size = new System.Drawing.Size(64, 24);
      button3.Text = "<";
      button3.Click+=new System.EventHandler(button3_Click);

      button4.Location = new System.Drawing.Point(150, 100);
      button4.Size = new System.Drawing.Size(64, 24);
```

```
      button4.Text = ">";
      button4.Click+=new System.EventHandler(button4_Click);

      text1.Location = new System.Drawing.Point(24, 50);
      text1.Size = new System.Drawing.Size(150, 24);

      text2.Location = new System.Drawing.Point(190, 50);
      text2.Size = new System.Drawing.Size(150, 24);

      text3.Location = new System.Drawing.Point(290, 150);
      text3.Size = new System.Drawing.Size(150, 24);

      DateTimePicker1.Location = new System.Drawing.Point(90, 150);
      DateTimePicker1.Size = new System.Drawing.Size(200, 800);

      this.Controls.Add(button1);
      this.Controls.Add(button2);
      this.Controls.Add(button3);
      this.Controls.Add(button4);
      this.Controls.Add(text1);
      this.Controls.Add(text2);
      this.Controls.Add(text3);
      this.Controls.Add(DateTimePicker1);
   }

   protected override void Dispose( bool disposing ){
      if( disposing ){
         if (components != null){
            components.Dispose();}
      }
      base.Dispose( disposing );
   }
   public static void Main()
   {
      Application.Run(new Form1());
   }

   private void SetUp()
   {
      // Create a DataSet with two tables and one relation.
      MakeDataSet();
      BindControls();
   }

   protected void BindControls()
   {
      /* Create two Binding objects for the first two TextBox
         controls. The data-bound property for both controls
         is the Text property. The data source is a DataSet
         (ds). The data member is the
         "TableName.ColumnName" string. */
      text1.DataBindings.Add(new Binding
      ("Text", ds, "customers.custName"));
      text2.DataBindings.Add(new Binding
      ("Text", ds, "customers.custID"));

      /* Bind the DateTimePicker control by adding a new Binding.
         The data member of the DateTimePicker is a
         TableName.RelationName.ColumnName string. */
      DateTimePicker1.DataBindings.Add(new
      Binding("Value", ds, "customers.CustToOrders.OrderDate"));

      /* Add event delegates for the Parse and Format events to a
         new Binding object, and add the object to the third
         TextBox control's BindingsCollection. The delegates
         must be added before adding the Binding to the
         collection; otherwise, no formatting occurs until
         the Current object of the BindingManagerBase for
         the data source changes. */
         Binding b = new Binding
         ("Text", ds, "customers.custToOrders.OrderAmount");
      b.Parse+=new ConvertEventHandler(CurrencyStringToDecimal);
      b.Format+=new ConvertEventHandler(DecimalToCurrencyString);
      text3.DataBindings.Add(b);

      // Get the BindingManagerBase for the Customers table.
      bmCustomers = this.BindingContext [ds, "Customers"];

      /* Get the BindingManagerBase for the Orders table using the
         RelationName. */
      bmOrders = this.BindingContext[ds, "customers.CustToOrders"];
   }

   private void DecimalToCurrencyString(object sender, ↵
ConvertEventArgs cevent)
   {
      /* This method is the Format event handler. Whenever the
         control displays a new value, the value is converted from
         its native Decimal type to a string. The ToString method
         then formats the value as a Currency, by using the
         formatting character "c". */

      // The application can only convert to string type.
      if(cevent.DesiredType != typeof(string)) return;

      cevent.Value = ((decimal) cevent.Value).ToString("c");
   }

   private void CurrencyStringToDecimal(object sender, ↵
ConvertEventArgs cevent)
   {
      /* This method is the Parse event handler. The Parse event
         occurs whenever the displayed value changes. The static
         ToDecimal method of the Convert class converts the
         value back to its native Decimal type. */

      // Can only convert to decimal type.
      if(cevent.DesiredType != typeof(decimal)) return;

      cevent.Value = Decimal.Parse(cevent.Value.ToString(),
          NumberStyles.Currency, null);

      /* To see that no precision is lost, print the unformatted
         value. For example, changing a value to "10.0001"
         causes the control to display "10.00", but the
         unformatted value remains "10.0001". */
      Console.WriteLine(cevent.Value);
   }

   protected void button1_Click(object sender, System.EventArgs e)
   {
      // Go to the previous item in the Customer list.
      bmCustomers.Position -= 1;
   }

   protected void button2_Click(object sender, System.EventArgs e)
   {
      // Go to the next item in the Customer list.
      bmCustomers.Position += 1;
   }

   protected void button3_Click(object sender, System.EventArgs e)
   {
      // Go to the previous item in the Orders list.
      bmOrders.Position-=1;
   }

   protected void button4_Click(object sender, System.EventArgs e)
   {
      // Go to the next item in the Orders list.
      bmOrders.Position+=1;
   }

   // Create a DataSet with two tables and populate it.
   private void MakeDataSet()
   {
      // Create a DataSet.
      ds = new DataSet("myDataSet");
```

```
      // Create two DataTables.
      DataTable tCust = new DataTable("Customers");
      DataTable tOrders = new DataTable("Orders");

      // Create two columns, and add them to the first table.
      DataColumn cCustID = new DataColumn("CustID", typeof(int));
      DataColumn cCustName = new DataColumn("CustName");
      tCust.Columns.Add(cCustID);
      tCust.Columns.Add(cCustName);

      // Create three columns, and add them to the second table.
      DataColumn cID =
         new DataColumn("CustID", typeof(int));
      DataColumn cOrderDate =
         new DataColumn("orderDate",typeof(DateTime));
      DataColumn cOrderAmount =
         new DataColumn("OrderAmount", typeof(decimal));
      tOrders.Columns.Add(cOrderAmount);
      tOrders.Columns.Add(cID);
      tOrders.Columns.Add(cOrderDate);

      // Add the tables to the DataSet.
      ds.Tables.Add(tCust);
      ds.Tables.Add(tOrders);

      // Create a DataRelation, and add it to the DataSet.
      DataRelation dr = new DataRelation
      ("custToOrders", cCustID , cID);
      ds.Relations.Add(dr);

      /* Populate the tables. For each customer and order,
         create two DataRow variables. */
      DataRow newRow1;
      DataRow newRow2;

      // Create three customers in the Customers Table.
      for(int i = 1; i < 4; i++)
      {
         newRow1 = tCust.NewRow();
         newRow1["custID"] = i;
         // Add the row to the Customers table.
         tCust.Rows.Add(newRow1);
      }
      // Give each customer a distinct name.
      tCust.Rows[0]["custName"] = "Alpha";
      tCust.Rows[1]["custName"] = "Beta";
      tCust.Rows[2]["custName"] = "Omega";

      // For each customer, create five rows in the Orders table.
      for(int i = 1; i < 4; i++)
      {
         for(int j = 1; j < 6; j++)
         {
            newRow2 = tOrders.NewRow();
            newRow2["CustID"]= i;
            newRow2["orderDate"]= new DateTime(2001, i, j * 2);
            newRow2["OrderAmount"] = i * 10 + j  * .1;
            // Add the row to the Orders table.
            tOrders.Rows.Add(newRow2);
         }
      }
   }
}
```

[JScript]

```
import System;
import System.Data;
import System.Drawing;
import System.Globalization;
import System.Windows.Forms;

public class Form1 extends System.Windows.Forms.Form
{
   private var components : System.ComponentModel.Container;
   private var button1 : Button;
   private var button2 : Button;
   private var button3 : Button;
   private var button4 : Button;
   private var text1 : TextBox;
   private var text2 : TextBox;
   private var text3 : TextBox;

   private var bmCustomers : BindingManagerBase;
   private var bmOrders : BindingManagerBase;
   private var ds : DataSet;
   private var DateTimePicker1 : DateTimePicker;

   public function Form1()
   {
      // Required for Windows Form Designer support.
      InitializeComponent();
      // Call SetUp to bind the controls.
      SetUp();
   }

   private function InitializeComponent()
   {
      // Create the form and its controls.
      this.components = new System.ComponentModel.Container();
      this.button1 = new System.Windows.Forms.Button();
      this.button2 = new System.Windows.Forms.Button();
      this.button3 = new System.Windows.Forms.Button();
      this.button4 = new System.Windows.Forms.Button();

      this.text1= new System.Windows.Forms.TextBox();
      this.text2= new System.Windows.Forms.TextBox();
      this.text3= new System.Windows.Forms.TextBox();

      this.DateTimePicker1 = new DateTimePicker();

      this.AutoScaleBaseSize = new System.Drawing.Size(5, 13);
      this.Text = "Binding Sample";
      this.ClientSize = new System.Drawing.Size(450, 200);

      button1.Location = new System.Drawing.Point(24, 16);
      button1.Size = new System.Drawing.Size(64, 24);
      button1.Text = "<";
      button1.add_Click(button1_Click);

      button2.Location = new System.Drawing.Point(90, 16);
      button2.Size = new System.Drawing.Size(64, 24);
      button2.Text = ">";
      button2.add_Click(button2_Click);

      button3.Location = new System.Drawing.Point(90, 100);
      button3.Size = new System.Drawing.Size(64, 24);
      button3.Text = "<";
      button3.add_Click(button3_Click);

      button4.Location = new System.Drawing.Point(150, 100);
      button4.Size = new System.Drawing.Size(64, 24);
      button4.Text = ">";
      button4.add_Click(button4_Click);

      text1.Location = new System.Drawing.Point(24, 50);
      text1.Size = new System.Drawing.Size(150, 24);

      text2.Location = new System.Drawing.Point(190, 50);
      text2.Size = new System.Drawing.Size(150, 24);

      text3.Location = new System.Drawing.Point(290, 150);
      text3.Size = new System.Drawing.Size(150, 24);

      DateTimePicker1.Location = new System.Drawing.Point(90, 150);
      DateTimePicker1.Size = new System.Drawing.Size(200, 800);

      this.Controls.Add(button1);
      this.Controls.Add(button2);
      this.Controls.Add(button3);
      this.Controls.Add(button4);
      this.Controls.Add(text1);
      this.Controls.Add(text2);
      this.Controls.Add(text3);
```

```
      this.Controls.Add(DateTimePicker1);
   }

   protected override function Dispose(disposing : boolean){
      if( disposing ){
         if (components != null){
            components.Dispose();}
      }
      super.Dispose( disposing );
   }

   public static function Main()
   {
      Application.Run(new Form1());
   }

   private function SetUp()
   {
      // Create a DataSet with two tables and one relation.
      MakeDataSet();
      BindControls();
   }

   protected function BindControls()
   {
      /* Create two Binding objects for the first two TextBox
         controls. The data-bound property for both controls
         is the Text property. The data source is a DataSet
         (ds). The data member is the
         "TableName.ColumnName" string. */
      text1.DataBindings.Add(new Binding
      ("Text", ds, "customers.custName"));
      text2.DataBindings.Add(new Binding
      ("Text", ds, "customers.custID"));

      /* Bind the DateTimePicker control by adding a new Binding.
         The data member of the DateTimePicker is a
         TableName.RelationName.ColumnName string. */
      DateTimePicker1.DataBindings.Add(new
      Binding("Value", ds, "customers.CustToOrders.OrderDate"));

      /* Add event delegates for the Parse and Format events to a
         new Binding object, and add the object to the third
         TextBox control's BindingsCollection. The delegates
         must be added before adding the Binding to the
         collection; otherwise, no formatting occurs until
         the Current object of the BindingManagerBase for
         the data source changes. */
      var b : Binding = new Binding
         ("Text", ds, "customers.custToOrders.OrderAmount");
      b.add_Parse(CurrencyStringToDecimal);
      b.add_Format(DecimalToCurrencyString);
      text3.DataBindings.Add(b);

      // Get the BindingManagerBase for the Customers table.
      bmCustomers = this.BindingContext [ds, "Customers"];

      /* Get the BindingManagerBase for the Orders table using the
         RelationName. */
      bmOrders = this.BindingContext[ds, "customers.CustToOrders"];
   }

   private function DecimalToCurrencyString(sender, cevent : ↵
ConvertEventArgs)
   {
      /* This method is the Format event handler. Whenever the
         control displays a new value, the value is converted from
         its native Decimal type to a string. The ToString method
         then formats the value as a Currency, by using the
         formatting character "c". */

      // The application can only convert to string type.
      if(cevent.DesiredType != String.GetType()) return;

      cevent.Value = (Decimal(cevent.Value)).ToString("c");
   }

   private function CurrencyStringToDecimal(sender, cevent : ↵
ConvertEventArgs)
   {
      /* This method is the Parse event handler. The Parse event
         occurs whenever the displayed value changes. The static
         ToDecimal method of the Convert class converts the
         value back to its native Decimal type. */

      // Can only convert to Decimal type.
      if(cevent.DesiredType != Decimal.GetType()) return;

      cevent.Value = Decimal.Parse(cevent.Value.ToString(),
          NumberStyles.Currency, null);

      /* To see that no precision is lost, print the unformatted
         value. For example, changing a value to "10.0001"
         causes the control to display "10.00", but the
         unformatted value remains "10.0001". */
      Console.WriteLine(cevent.Value);
   }

   protected function button1_Click(sender, e : System.EventArgs)
   {
      // Go to the previous item in the Customer list.
      bmCustomers.Position -= 1;
   }

   protected function button2_Click(sender, e : System.EventArgs)
   {
      // Go to the next item in the Customer list.
      bmCustomers.Position += 1;
   }

   protected function button3_Click(sender, e : System.EventArgs)
   {
      // Go to the previous item in the Orders list.
      bmOrders.Position-=1;
   }

   protected function button4_Click(sender, e : System.EventArgs)
   {
      // Go to the next item in the Orders list.
      bmOrders.Position+=1;
   }

   // Create a DataSet with two tables and populate it.
   private function MakeDataSet()
   {
      // Create a DataSet.
      ds = new DataSet("myDataSet");

      // Create two DataTables.
      var tCust : DataTable = new DataTable("Customers");
      var tOrders : DataTable= new DataTable("Orders");

      // Create two columns, and add them to the first table.
      var cCustID : DataColumn = new DataColumn("CustID", Int32);
      var cCustName : DataColumn = new DataColumn("CustName");
      tCust.Columns.Add(cCustID);
      tCust.Columns.Add(cCustName);

      // Create three columns, and add them to the second table.
      var cID : DataColumn  =
         new DataColumn("CustID", Int32);
      var cOrderDate : DataColumn  =
         new DataColumn("orderDate", DateTime);
      var cOrderAmount : DataColumn =
         new DataColumn("OrderAmount", Decimal);
      tOrders.Columns.Add(cOrderAmount);
      tOrders.Columns.Add(cID);
      tOrders.Columns.Add(cOrderDate);

      // Add the tables to the DataSet.
      ds.Tables.Add(tCust);
      ds.Tables.Add(tOrders);

      // Create a DataRelation, and add it to the DataSet.
      var dr : DataRelation = new DataRelation
```

```
    ("custToOrders", cCustID , cID);
    ds.Relations.Add(dr);

    /* Populate the tables. For each customer and order,
       create two DataRow variables. */
    var newRow1 : DataRow;
    var newRow2 : DataRow;

    // Create three customers in the Customers Table.
    for(var i : int = 1; i < 4; i++)
    {
       newRow1 = tCust.NewRow();
       newRow1["custID"] = i;
       // Add the row to the Customers table.
       tCust.Rows.Add(newRow1);
    }
    // Give each customer a distinct name.
    tCust.Rows[0]["custName"] = "Alpha";
    tCust.Rows[1]["custName"] = "Beta";
    tCust.Rows[2]["custName"] = "Omega";

    // For each customer, create five rows in the Orders table.
    for(var j : int = 1; j < 4; j++)
    {
       for(var k : int = 1; k < 6; k++)
       {
          newRow2 = tOrders.NewRow();
          newRow2["CustID"]= j;
          newRow2["orderDate"]= new DateTime(2001, j, k * 2);
          newRow2["OrderAmount"] = j * 10 + k  * .1;
          // Add the row to the Orders table.
          tOrders.Rows.Add(newRow2);
       }
    }
  }
}
```

Requirements

Namespace: System.Windows.Forms

Platforms: Windows 98, Windows NT 4.0,
Windows Millennium Edition, Windows 2000,
Windows XP Home Edition, Windows XP Professional,
Windows Server 2003 family,
.NET Compact Framework - Windows CE .NET

Assembly: System.Windows.Forms (in System.Windows.Forms.dll)

Binding Constructor

Initializes a new instance of the **Binding** class that simple-binds the specified control property to the specified data member of the specified data source.

```
[Visual Basic]
Public Sub New( _
   ByVal propertyName As String, _
   ByVal dataSource As Object, _
   ByVal dataMember As String _
)
[C#]
public Binding(
   string propertyName,
   object dataSource,
   string dataMember
);
[C++]
public: Binding(
   String* propertyName,
   Object* dataSource,
   String* dataMember
);
[JScript]
public function Binding(
   propertyName : String,
   dataSource : Object,
   dataMember : String
);
```

Parameters

propertyName
The name of the control property to bind.

dataSource
An **Object** that represents the data source.

dataMember
The property or list to bind to.

Exceptions

Exception Type	Condition
Exception	The *propertyName* is neither a valid property of a control nor an empty string ("").

Remarks

You can specify an instance of any of the following classes for the data source:

- **DataSet**
- **DataTable**
- **DataView**
- **DataViewManager**
- Any class that implements the **IList** interface.
- Any class.

See the **Binding** class for more information about creating the *dataMember* string.

Example

See related example in the **System.Windows.Forms.Binding** class topic.

Requirements

Platforms: Windows 98, Windows NT 4.0,
Windows Millennium Edition, Windows 2000,
Windows XP Home Edition, Windows XP Professional,
Windows Server 2003 family,
.NET Compact Framework - Windows CE .NET

Binding.BindingManagerBase Property

Gets this binding's **BindingManagerBase**.

```
[Visual Basic]
Public ReadOnly Property BindingManagerBase As BindingManagerBase
[C#]
public BindingManagerBase BindingManagerBase {get;}
[C++]
public: __property BindingManagerBase* get_BindingManagerBase();
[JScript]
public function get BindingManagerBase() : BindingManagerBase;
```

Property Value

The **BindingManagerBase** that manages this **Binding**.

Remarks

Use the **BindingManagerBase** to iterate through a data-bound list by incrementing or decrementing the **Position** property. The **BindingManagerBase** class is abstract. The **CurrencyManager** class, which manages data-bound lists, inherits from the **BindingManagerBase** class.

Example

See related example in the **System.Windows.Forms.Binding** class topic.

Requirements

Platforms: Windows 98, Windows NT 4.0,
Windows Millennium Edition, Windows 2000,
Windows XP Home Edition, Windows XP Professional,
Windows Server 2003 family,
.NET Compact Framework - Windows CE .NET

Binding.BindingMemberInfo Property

Gets an object that contains information about this binding based on the *dataMember* parameter in the **Binding** constructor.

```
[Visual Basic]
Public ReadOnly Property BindingMemberInfo As BindingMemberInfo
[C#]
public BindingMemberInfo BindingMemberInfo {get;}
[C++]
public: __property BindingMemberInfo get_BindingMemberInfo();
[JScript]
public function get BindingMemberInfo() : BindingMemberInfo;
```

Property Value

A **BindingMemberInfo** that contains information about this **Binding**.

Remarks

The **BindingMemberInfo** is created from the *dataMember* string passed to the **Binding** constructor.

Example

See related example in the **System.Windows.Forms.Binding** class topic.

Requirements

Platforms: Windows 98, Windows NT 4.0,
Windows Millennium Edition, Windows 2000,
Windows XP Home Edition, Windows XP Professional,
Windows Server 2003 family,
.NET Compact Framework - Windows CE .NET

Binding.Control Property

Gets the control that the binding belongs to.

```
[Visual Basic]
Public ReadOnly Property Control As Control
[C#]
public Control Control {get;}
[C++]
public: __property Control* get_Control();
[JScript]
public function get Control() : Control;
```

Property Value

The **Control** that the binding belongs to.

Example

See related example in the **System.Windows.Forms.Binding** class topic.

Requirements

Platforms: Windows 98, Windows NT 4.0,
Windows Millennium Edition, Windows 2000,
Windows XP Home Edition, Windows XP Professional,
Windows Server 2003 family,
.NET Compact Framework - Windows CE .NET

Binding.DataSource Property

Gets the data source for this binding.

```
[Visual Basic]
Public ReadOnly Property DataSource As Object
[C#]
public object DataSource {get;}
[C++]
public: __property Object* get_DataSource();
[JScript]
public function get DataSource() : Object;
```

Property Value

An **Object** that represents the data source.

Remarks

Possible data sources include:

- **DataSet**
- **DataTable**
- **DataView**
- **DataViewManager**
- Any object that implements the **IList** interface.
- Any object.

Example

See related example in the **System.Windows.Forms.Binding** class topic.

Requirements

Platforms: Windows 98, Windows NT 4.0,
Windows Millennium Edition, Windows 2000,
Windows XP Home Edition, Windows XP Professional,
Windows Server 2003 family,
.NET Compact Framework - Windows CE .NET

Binding.IsBinding Property

Gets a value indicating whether the binding is active.

```
[Visual Basic]
Public ReadOnly Property IsBinding As Boolean
[C#]
public bool IsBinding {get;}
[C++]
public: __property bool get_IsBinding();
[JScript]
public function get IsBinding() : Boolean;
```

Property Value

true, if the binding is active; otherwise, **false**.

Remarks

A binding is active when it meets these conditions: all its properties are set, the user did not call **ResumeBinding** or **SuspendBinding** on the **BindingManagerBase** that the **Binding** belongs to, and the control to which the **Binding** belongs has been created.

Example

See related example in the **System.Windows.Forms.Binding** class topic.

Requirements

Platforms: Windows 98, Windows NT 4.0, Windows Millennium Edition, Windows 2000, Windows XP Home Edition, Windows XP Professional, Windows Server 2003 family, .NET Compact Framework - Windows CE .NET

Binding.PropertyName Property

Gets or sets the name of the control's data-bound property.

```
[Visual Basic]
Public ReadOnly Property PropertyName As String
[C#]
public string PropertyName {get;}
[C++]
public: __property String* get_PropertyName();
[JScript]
public function get PropertyName() : String;
```

Property Value

The name of a control property to bind to.

Remarks

Use the **PropertyName** to specify the control property that you want to bind to a list in a data source. Most commonly, you bind a display property such as the **Text** property of a **TextBox** control. However, because you can bind any property of a control, you can programmatically create controls at run time using data from a database.

Example

See related example in the **System.Windows.Forms.Binding** class topic.

Requirements

Platforms: Windows 98, Windows NT 4.0, Windows Millennium Edition, Windows 2000, Windows XP Home Edition, Windows XP Professional, Windows Server 2003 family, .NET Compact Framework - Windows CE .NET

Binding.OnFormat Method

Raises the **Format** event.

```
[Visual Basic]
Protected Overridable Sub OnFormat( _
   ByVal cevent As ConvertEventArgs _
)
[C#]
protected virtual void OnFormat(
   ConvertEventArgs cevent
);
[C++]
protected: virtual void OnFormat(
   ConvertEventArgs* cevent
);
[JScript]
protected function OnFormat(
   cevent : ConvertEventArgs
);
```

Parameters

cevent
A **ConvertEventArgs** that contains the event data.

Remarks

Raising an event invokes the event handler through a delegate. For more information, see **Raising an Event**.

The **OnFormat** method also allows derived classes to handle the event without attaching a delegate. This is the preferred technique for handling the event in a derived class.

Notes to Inheritors: When overriding **OnFormat** in a derived class, be sure to call the base class's **OnFormat** method so that registered delegates receive the event.

Requirements

Platforms: Windows 98, Windows NT 4.0, Windows Millennium Edition, Windows 2000, Windows XP Home Edition, Windows XP Professional, Windows Server 2003 family, .NET Compact Framework - Windows CE .NET

Binding.OnParse Method

Raises the **Parse** event.

```
[Visual Basic]
Protected Overridable Sub OnParse( _
   ByVal cevent As ConvertEventArgs _
)
[C#]
protected virtual void OnParse(
   ConvertEventArgs cevent
);
[C++]
protected: virtual void OnParse(
   ConvertEventArgs* cevent
);
[JScript]
protected function OnParse(
   cevent : ConvertEventArgs
);
```

Parameters

cevent
A **ConvertEventArgs** that contains the event data.

Remarks

Raising an event invokes the event handler through a delegate.

The **OnParse** method also allows derived classes to handle the event without attaching a delegate. This is the preferred technique for handling the event in a derived class.

Notes to Inheritors: When overriding **OnParse** in a derived class, be sure to call the base class's **OnParse** method so that registered delegates receive the event.

Requirements

Platforms: Windows 98, Windows NT 4.0,
Windows Millennium Edition, Windows 2000,
Windows XP Home Edition, Windows XP Professional,
Windows Server 2003 family,
.NET Compact Framework - Windows CE .NET

Binding.Format Event

Occurs when the property of a control is bound to a data value.

[Visual Basic]
```
Public Event Format As ConvertEventHandler
```
[C#]
```
public event ConvertEventHandler Format;
```
[C++]
```
public: __event ConvertEventHandler* Format;
```

[JScript] In JScript, you can handle the events defined by a class, but you cannot define your own.

Event Data

The event handler receives an argument of type **ConvertEventArgs** containing data related to this event. The following **ConvertEventArgs** properties provide information specific to this event.

Property	Description
DesiredType	Gets the data type of the desired value.
Value	Gets or sets the value of the **ConvertEventArgs** object.

Remarks

The **Format** event occurs both when data is pushed from the data source into the control, and when the data is pulled from the control into the data source. When the data is pushed from the data source into the control, the **Binding** will use the **Format** event to put the formatted data into the control. When the data is pushed from the control into the data source, the **Binding** will first parse the data using the **Parse** event, then format the data and push the it into the control.

The **Format** and **Parse** events allow you to create custom formats for displaying data. For example, if the data in a table is of type **Decimal**, you can display the data in the local currency format by setting the **Value** property of the **ConvertEventArgs** object to the formatted value in the **Format** event. You must consequently unformat the displayed value in the **Parse** event.

The **Format** event occurs whenever the **Current** value of the **BindingManagerBase** changes, which includes:

- The first time the property is bound.
- Any time the **Position** changes.
- Whenever the data-bound list is sorted or filtered, which is accomplished when a **DataView** supplies the list.

The **Format** event also occurs after the **Parse** event. For example, when a control loses focus, its contents are parsed. Immediately afterwards, as new data is pushed into the control, the **Format** event occurs allowing the new contents to be formatted.

Example

See related example in the **System.Windows.Forms.Binding** class topic.

Requirements

Platforms: Windows 98, Windows NT 4.0,
Windows Millennium Edition, Windows 2000,
Windows XP Home Edition, Windows XP Professional,
Windows Server 2003 family

Binding.Parse Event

Occurs when the value of a data-bound control changes.

[Visual Basic]
```
Public Event Parse As ConvertEventHandler
```
[C#]
```
public event ConvertEventHandler Parse;
```
[C++]
```
public: __event ConvertEventHandler* Parse;
```

[JScript] In JScript, you can handle the events defined by a class, but you cannot define your own.

Event Data

The event handler receives an argument of type **ConvertEventArgs** containing data related to this event. The following **ConvertEventArgs** properties provide information specific to this event.

Property	Description
DesiredType	Gets the data type of the desired value.
Value	Gets or sets the value of the **ConvertEventArgs** object.

Remarks

The **Format** and **Parse** events allow you to create custom formats for displaying data. For example, if the data in a table is of type **Decimal**, you can display the data in the local currency format by setting the **Value** property of the **ConvertEventArgs** object to the formatted value in the **Format** event. You must consequently unformat the displayed value in the **Parse** event.

The **Parse** event occurs under the following conditions:

- after the **Validated** event of the **Control** object occurs.
- when the **EndCurrentEdit** method of the **BindingManagerBase** is called.
- when the **Current** object of the **BindingManagerBase** changes (in other words, when the **Position** changes).

For more information about handling events, see **Consuming Events**.

Example

See related example in the **System.Windows.Forms.Binding** class topic.

Requirements

Platforms: Windows 98, Windows NT 4.0,
Windows Millennium Edition, Windows 2000,
Windows XP Home Edition, Windows XP Professional,
Windows Server 2003 family

BindingContext Class

Manages the collection of **BindingManagerBase** objects for any object that inherits from the **Control** class.

System.Object
  System.Windows.Forms.BindingContext

```
[Visual Basic]
Public Class BindingContext
   Implements ICollection, IEnumerable
[C#]
public class BindingContext : ICollection, IEnumerable
[C++]
public __gc class BindingContext : public ICollection, IEnumerable
[JScript]
public class BindingContext implements ICollection, IEnumerable
```

Thread Safety

Any public static (**Shared** in Visual Basic) members of this type are safe for multithreaded operations. Any instance members are not guaranteed to be thread safe.

Remarks

Each object that inherits from the **Control** class can have a single **BindingContext** object. That **BindingContext** manages the **BindingManagerBase** objects for that control and any contained controls. Use the **BindingContext** to create or return the **BindingManagerBase** for a data source used by the contained data-bound controls. Most commonly, you use the **Form** class's **BindingContext** to return **BindingManagerBase** objects for the data-bound controls on the form. If you use a container control, such as a **GroupBox**, **Panel**, or **TabControl**, to contain data-bound controls, you can create a **BindingContext** for just that container control and its controls. This allows each part of your form to be managed by its own **BindingManagerBase** object. See the **BindingContext** constructor for more details on creating multiple **BindingManagerBase** objects for the same data source.

To return a particular **BindingManagerBase** object, you must pass one of the following parameters to the **Item** property:

- Just the data source, if the desired **BindingManagerBase** does not require a navigation path. For example, if the **Binding-ManagerBase** manages a set of **Binding** objects that use an **ArrayList** or **DataTable** as the **DataSource**, no navigation path is required. (See below for more information about creating a navigation path.)
- The data source and navigation path. A navigation path (set to the **Item** property's *dataMember* parameter) is required when the **BindingManagerBase** manages a set of **Binding** objects for which the data source contains multiple objects. For example, a **DataSet** can contain several **DataTable** objects linked by **DataRelation** objects. In such a case, the navigation path is required to enable the **BindingContext** to return the correct **BindingManagerBase**.

See the **Binding** class for a list of possible data sources.

Because the **BindingManagerBase** class is abstract, the **Type** of the returned object is either a **CurrencyManager** or a **Property-Manager**. If the data source is an object that can return only a single property (instead of a list of objects), the **Type** will be a **Property-Manager**. For example, if you specify a **TextBox** as the data source, a **PropertyManager** will be returned. On the other hand, if the data source is an object that implements **IList** or **IBindingList**, a **CurrencyManager** will be returned.

If the desired **BindingManagerBase** manages a list, the navigation path must also end with a list. For example, the C# code below binds a **TextBox** control to the order date in a table of orders by adding new **Binding** object to the **ControlBindingsCollection**. The navigation path includes the **TableName**, the **RelationName**, and the **ColumnName**. The second line uses the **BindingContext** to return a **BindingManagerBase**-- retrieved by passing the **TableName** and **RelationName** (which resolves to a list) to the **Item** property.

```
/* Create a new Binding object and add to the ↵
ControlBindingsColllection.
The navigation path (Customers.custOrders.OrderDate) used to
create a Binding ends with a property. */
textBox1.DataBindings.Add
("Text", dataSet1, "Customers.custToOrders.OrderDate");
/* The navigation path (Customers.custToOrders) used to
return the BindingManagerBase ends with a list. */
BindingManagerBase bmOrders =
this.BindingContext[dataSet1, "Customers.custToOrders"];
```

When returning a **BindingManagerBase**, you should use the same data source as the **Binding** and modify only the navigation path. The following C# code seems to return the same **BindingManagerBase**, but the results are different:

```
BindingManagerBase bmCustomers = this.BindingContext
[myDataSet, "Customers"];
// This returns a different BindingManagerBase:
BindingManagerBase bmOther = this.BindingContext
[myDataSet.Tables[Customers], ""];
// This line returns true.
Console.WriteLine(bmCustomers != bmOther);
```

For each object passed to the **BindingContext**, a different **Binding-ManagerBase** object is returned. In the example above, the objects passed to the **Item** property are different, and therefore the **BindingManagerBase** returned for each object is different.

> **Note** When using the **Item** property, the **BindingContext** will create a new **BindingManagerBase** if one does not already exist. This can lead to some confusion, as the returned object may not manage the list (or any list) that you intend. To prevent returning an invalid **BindingManagerBase**, use the **Contains** method to determine if the desired **BindingManagerBase** already exists.

Example

See related example in the **System.Windows.Forms.Binding** class topic.

Requirements

Namespace: System.Windows.Forms

Platforms: Windows 98, Windows NT 4.0, Windows Millennium Edition, Windows 2000, Windows XP Home Edition, Windows XP Professional, Windows Server 2003 family, .NET Compact Framework - Windows CE .NET

Assembly: System.Windows.Forms (in System.Windows.Forms.dll)

BindingContext Constructor

Initializes a new instance of the **BindingContext** class.

```
[Visual Basic]
Public Sub New()
[C#]
public BindingContext();
```

```
[C++]
public: BindingContext();
[JScript]
public function BindingContext();
```

Remarks

Create a new **BindingContext** and set it to the **BindingContext** property of an object that inherits from **Control** when you want to have multiple **BindingManagerBase** instances for the same data source.

For example, if you have two **BindingManagerBase** objects (from two different **BindingContext** objects), you can set the **Position** properties of each **BindingManagerBase** to different values causing each set of data-bound controls will display different values from the same data source.

Example

See related example in the **System.Windows.Forms.Binding** class topic.

Requirements

Platforms: Windows 98, Windows NT 4.0,
Windows Millennium Edition, Windows 2000,
Windows XP Home Edition, Windows XP Professional,
Windows Server 2003 family,
.NET Compact Framework - Windows CE .NET

BindingContext.IsReadOnly Property

This member supports the .NET Framework infrastructure and is not intended to be used directly from your code.

```
[Visual Basic]
Public ReadOnly Property IsReadOnly As Boolean
[C#]
public bool IsReadOnly {get;}
[C++]
public: __property bool get_IsReadOnly();
[JScript]
public function get IsReadOnly() : Boolean;
```

BindingContext.Item Property

Gets a **BindingManagerBase**.

[C#] In C#, this property is the indexer for the **BindingContext** class.

Overload List

Gets the **BindingManagerBase** that is associated with the specified data source.

[Visual Basic] **Overloads Public Default ReadOnly Property Item(Object) As BindingManagerBase**

[C#] **public BindingManagerBase this[object] {get;}**

[C++] **public: __property BindingManagerBase* get_Item(Object*);**

[JScript] **BindingContext.Item (Object)**

Gets a **BindingManagerBase** that is associated with the specified data source and data member.

[Visual Basic] **Overloads Public Default ReadOnly Property Item(Object, String) As BindingManagerBase**

[C#] **public BindingManagerBase this[object, string] {get;}**

[C++] **public: __property BindingManagerBase* get_Item(Object*, String*);**

[JScript] **BindingContext.Item (Object, String)**

Example

See related example in the **System.Windows.Forms.Binding** class topic.

BindingContext.Item Property (Object)

Gets the **BindingManagerBase** that is associated with the specified data source.

[C#] In C#, this property is the indexer for the **BindingContext** class.

```
[Visual Basic]
Overloads Public Default ReadOnly Property Item( _
   ByVal dataSource As Object _
) As BindingManagerBase
[C#]
public BindingManagerBase this[
   object dataSource
] {get;}
[C++]
public: __property BindingManagerBase* get_Item(
   Object* dataSource
);
[JScript]
returnValue = BindingContextObject.Item(dataSource);
-or-
returnValue = BindingContextObject(dataSource);
```

[JScript] In JScript, you can use the default indexed properties defined by a type, but you cannot explicitly define your own. However, specifying the **expando** attribute on a class automatically provides a default indexed property whose type is **Object** and whose index type is **String**.

Arguments [JScript]

dataSource

The data source associated with a particular **BindingManagerBase**.

Parameters [Visual Basic, C#, C++]

dataSource

The data source associated with a particular **BindingManagerBase**.

Property Value

A **BindingManagerBase** for the specified data source.

Remarks

Use this overload if the **BindingManagerBase** you want does not require a navigation path. For example, if the **BindingManagerBase** manages a set of **Binding** objects that use an **ArrayList** or **DataTable** as the **DataSource**, no navigation path is required.

> **Note** The **Item** property will always return a **BindingManagerBase**, and never return a null reference (**Nothing** in Visual Basic).

See the **Binding** class for a list of possible data sources and for details on creating bindings between controls and data sources.

Example

See related example in the **System.Windows.Forms.Binding** class topic.

Requirements

Platforms: Windows 98, Windows NT 4.0, Windows Millennium Edition, Windows 2000, Windows XP Home Edition, Windows XP Professional, Windows Server 2003 family

BindingContext.Item Property (Object, String)

Gets a **BindingManagerBase** that is associated with the specified data source and data member.

[C#] In C#, this property is the indexer for the **BindingContext** class.

```
[Visual Basic]
Overloads Public Default ReadOnly Property Item( _
   ByVal dataSource As Object, _
   ByVal dataMember As String _
) As BindingManagerBase
[C#]
public BindingManagerBase this[
   object dataSource,
   string dataMember
] {get;}
[C++]
public: __property BindingManagerBase* get_Item(
   Object* dataSource,
   String* dataMember
);
[JScript]
returnValue = BindingContextObject.Item(dataSource, dataMember);
-or-
returnValue = BindingContextObject(dataSource, dataMember);
```

[JScript] In JScript, you can use the default indexed properties defined by a type, but you cannot explicitly define your own. However, specifying the **expando** attribute on a class automatically provides a default indexed property whose type is **Object** and whose index type is **String**.

Arguments [JScript]

dataSource

The data source associated with a particular **BindingManagerBase**.

dataMember

A navigation path containing the information that resolves to a specific **BindingManagerBase**.

Parameters [Visual Basic, C#, C++]

dataSource

The data source associated with a particular **BindingManagerBase**.

dataMember

A navigation path containing the information that resolves to a specific **BindingManagerBase**.

Property Value

The **BindingManagerBase** for the specified data source and data member.

Exceptions

Exception Type	Condition
Exception	A child list can't be created for the specified *dataMember*.

Remarks

Use this overload when the **BindingManagerBase** manages a set of **Binding** objects for which the data source contains multiple objects. For example, a **DataSet** can contain several **DataTable** objects linked by **DataRelation** objects. In such a case, the navigation path is required to enable the **BindingContext** to return the correct **BindingManagerBase**.

> **Note** The **Item** property will always return a **BindingManagerBase**, and never return a null reference (**Nothing** in Visual Basic).

See the **Binding** class for a list of possible data sources and for details on creating bindings between controls and data sources.

If the desired **BindingManagerBase** manages a list, the navigation path must also end with a list. For example, the C# code below binds a **TextBox** control to the order date in a table of orders. The navigation path includes the **TableName**, the **RelationName**, and the **ColumnName**. However, the **BindingManagerBase** must be retrieved using only the **TableName** and **RelationName** (which resolves to a list).

```
// The navigation path for a Binding ends with a property.
textBox1.DataBindings.Add
("Text", dataSet1, "Customers.custToOrders.OrderDate");
// The navigation path for the BindingManagerBase ends with a list.
BindingManagerBase bmOrders = this.BindingContext
[dataSet1, "Customers.custToOrders"];
```

When returning a **BindingManagerBase**, you should use the same data source as the **Binding** and modify only the navigation path.Use the **Contains** method to determine if the desired **BindingManagerBase** already exists.

Example

See related example in the **System.Windows.Forms.Binding** class topic.

Requirements

Platforms: Windows 98, Windows NT 4.0, Windows Millennium Edition, Windows 2000, Windows XP Home Edition, Windows XP Professional, Windows Server 2003 family

BindingContext.System.Collections.ICollection.Count Property

Note: This namespace, class, or member is supported only in version 1.1 of the .NET Framework.

This member supports the .NET Framework infrastructure and is not intended to be used directly from your code.

```
[Visual Basic]
Private ReadOnly Property Count As Integer Implements _
   ICollection.Count
[C#]
int ICollection.Count {get;}
```

```
[C++]
private: __property int
   System::Collections::ICollection::get_Count();
[JScript]
private function get ICollection.Count() : int;
```

BindingContext.System.Collections.ICollection.IsSynchronized Property

Note: This namespace, class, or member is supported only in version 1.1 of the .NET Framework.

This member supports the .NET Framework infrastructure and is not intended to be used directly from your code.

```
[Visual Basic]
Private ReadOnly Property IsSynchronized As Boolean Implements _
   ICollection.IsSynchronized
[C#]
bool ICollection.IsSynchronized {get;}
[C++]
private: __property bool
   System::Collections::ICollection::get_IsSynchronized();
[JScript]
private function get ICollection.IsSynchronized() : Boolean;
```

BindingContext.System.Collections.ICollection.SyncRoot Property

Note: This namespace, class, or member is supported only in version 1.1 of the .NET Framework.

This member supports the .NET Framework infrastructure and is not intended to be used directly from your code.

```
[Visual Basic]
Private ReadOnly Property SyncRoot As Object Implements _
   ICollection.SyncRoot
[C#]
object ICollection.SyncRoot {get;}
[C++]
private: __property Object*
   System::Collections::ICollection::get_SyncRoot();
[JScript]
private function get ICollection.SyncRoot() : Object;
```

BindingContext.Add Method

Adds the **BindingManagerBase** associated with a specific data source to the collection.

```
[Visual Basic]
Protected Friend Sub Add( _
   ByVal dataSource As Object, _
   ByVal listManager As BindingManagerBase _
)
[C#]
protected internal void Add(
   object dataSource,
   BindingManagerBase listManager
);
[C++]
protected public: void Add(
   Object* dataSource,
   BindingManagerBase* listManager
);
[JScript]
protected internal function Add(
   dataSource : Object,
   listManager : BindingManagerBase
);
```

Parameters

dataSource

The **Object** associated with the **BindingManagerBase**.

listManager

The **BindingManagerBase** to add.

Requirements

Platforms: Windows 98, Windows NT 4.0, Windows Millennium Edition, Windows 2000, Windows XP Home Edition, Windows XP Professional, Windows Server 2003 family

BindingContext.AddCore Method

This member supports the .NET Framework infrastructure and is not intended to be used directly from your code.

```
[Visual Basic]
Protected Overridable Sub AddCore( _
   ByVal dataSource As Object, _
   ByVal listManager As BindingManagerBase _
)
[C#]
protected virtual void AddCore(
   object dataSource,
   BindingManagerBase listManager
);
[C++]
protected: virtual void AddCore(
   Object* dataSource,
   BindingManagerBase* listManager
);
[JScript]
protected function AddCore(
   dataSource : Object,
   listManager : BindingManagerBase
);
```

BindingContext.Clear Method

Clears the collection of any **BindingManagerBase** objects.

```
[Visual Basic]
Protected Friend Sub Clear()
[C#]
protected internal void Clear();
[C++]
protected public: void Clear();
[JScript]
protected internal function Clear();
```

Requirements

Platforms: Windows 98, Windows NT 4.0, Windows Millennium Edition, Windows 2000, Windows XP Home Edition, Windows XP Professional, Windows Server 2003 family

BindingContext.ClearCore Method

This member supports the .NET Framework infrastructure and is not intended to be used directly from your code.

```
[Visual Basic]
Protected Overridable Sub ClearCore()
[C#]
protected virtual void ClearCore();
[C++]
protected: virtual void ClearCore();
[JScript]
protected function ClearCore();
```

BindingContext.Contains Method

Gets a value indicating whether the **BindingContext** contains the specified **BindingManagerBase**.

Overload List

Gets a value indicating whether the **BindingContext** contains the **BindingManagerBase** associated with the specified data source.

Supported by the .NET Compact Framework.

[Visual Basic] **Overloads Public Function Contains(Object) As Boolean**

[C#] **public bool Contains(object);**

[C++] **public: bool Contains(Object*);**

[JScript] **public function Contains(Object) : Boolean;**

Gets a value indicating whether the **BindingContext** contains the **BindingManagerBase** associated with the specified data source and data member.

Supported by the .NET Compact Framework.

[Visual Basic] **Overloads Public Function Contains(Object, String) As Boolean**

[C#] **public bool Contains(object, string);**

[C++] **public: bool Contains(Object*, String*);**

[JScript] **public function Contains(Object, String) : Boolean;**

Example

See related example in the **System.Windows.Forms.Binding** class topic.

BindingContext.Contains Method (Object)

Gets a value indicating whether the **BindingContext** contains the **BindingManagerBase** associated with the specified data source.

```
[Visual Basic]
Overloads Public Function Contains( _
   ByVal dataSource As Object _
) As Boolean
[C#]
public bool Contains(
   object dataSource
);
[C++]
public: bool Contains(
   Object* dataSource
);
[JScript]
public function Contains(
   dataSource : Object
) : Boolean;
```

Parameters

dataSource
An **Object** that represents the data source.

Return Value

true, if the **BindingContext** contains the specified **BindingManagerBase**; otherwise, **false**.

Remarks

See the **Binding** class for a list of possible data sources and details on creating bindings between controls and data sources.

See the **Item** property for details on returning a **BindingManagerBase** object using only a data source.

Example

See related example in the **System.Windows.Forms.Binding** class topic.

Requirements

Platforms: Windows 98, Windows NT 4.0, Windows Millennium Edition, Windows 2000, Windows XP Home Edition, Windows XP Professional, Windows Server 2003 family, .NET Compact Framework - Windows CE .NET

BindingContext.Contains Method (Object, String)

Gets a value indicating whether the **BindingContext** contains the **BindingManagerBase** associated with the specified data source and data member.

```
[Visual Basic]
Overloads Public Function Contains( _
   ByVal dataSource As Object, _
   ByVal dataMember As String _
) As Boolean
[C#]
public bool Contains(
   object dataSource,
   string dataMember
);
[C++]
public: bool Contains(
   Object* dataSource,
   String* dataMember
);
[JScript]
public function Contains(
   dataSource : Object,
   dataMember : String
) : Boolean;
```

Parameters

dataSource
An **Object** that represents the data source.

dataMember
The information needed to resolve to a specific **BindingManagerBase**.

Return Value

true if the **BindingContext** contains the specified **BindingManagerBase**; otherwise, **false**.

Remarks

See the **Binding** class for a list of possible data sources and for details on creating bindings between controls and data sources.

See the **Item** property for details on returning a **BindingManagerBase** object using a data source and data member.

Example

See related example in the **System.Windows.Forms.Binding** class topic.

Requirements

Platforms: Windows 98, Windows NT 4.0,
Windows Millennium Edition, Windows 2000,
Windows XP Home Edition, Windows XP Professional,
Windows Server 2003 family,
.NET Compact Framework - Windows CE .NET

BindingContext.ICollection.CopyTo Method

This member supports the .NET Framework infrastructure and is not intended to be used directly from your code.

```
[Visual Basic]
Private Sub CopyTo( _
   ByVal ar As Array, _
   ByVal index As Integer _
) Implements ICollection.CopyTo
[C#]
void ICollection.CopyTo(
   Array ar,
   int index
);
[C++]
private: void ICollection::CopyTo(
   Array* ar,
   int index
);
[JScript]
private function ICollection.CopyTo(
   ar : Array,
   index : int
);
```

BindingContext.IEnumerable.GetEnumerator Method

This member supports the .NET Framework infrastructure and is not intended to be used directly from your code.

```
[Visual Basic]
Private Function GetEnumerator() As IEnumerator Implements _
   IEnumerable.GetEnumerator
[C#]
IEnumerator IEnumerable.GetEnumerator();
[C++]
private: IEnumerator* IEnumerable::GetEnumerator();
[JScript]
private function IEnumerable.GetEnumerator() : IEnumerator;
```

BindingContext.OnCollectionChanged Method

This member supports the .NET Framework infrastructure and is not intended to be used directly from your code.

```
[Visual Basic]
Protected Overridable Sub OnCollectionChanged( _
   ByVal ccevent As CollectionChangeEventArgs _
)
[C#]
protected virtual void OnCollectionChanged(
   CollectionChangeEventArgs ccevent
);
[C++]
protected: virtual void OnCollectionChanged(
   CollectionChangeEventArgs* ccevent
);
[JScript]
protected function OnCollectionChanged(
   ccevent : CollectionChangeEventArgs
);
```

BindingContext.Remove Method

Deletes the **BindingManagerBase** associated with the specified data source.

```
[Visual Basic]
Protected Friend Sub Remove( _
   ByVal dataSource As Object _
)
[C#]
protected internal void Remove(
   object dataSource
);
[C++]
protected public: void Remove(
   Object* dataSource
);
[JScript]
protected internal function Remove(
   dataSource : Object
);
```

Parameters

dataSource
The data source associated with the **BindingManagerBase** to remove.

Requirements

Platforms: Windows 98, Windows NT 4.0,
Windows Millennium Edition, Windows 2000,
Windows XP Home Edition, Windows XP Professional,
Windows Server 2003 family

BindingContext.RemoveCore Method

This member supports the .NET Framework infrastructure and is not intended to be used directly from your code.

[Visual Basic]
```
Protected Overridable Sub RemoveCore( _
   ByVal dataSource As Object _
)
```
[C#]
```
protected virtual void RemoveCore(
   object dataSource
);
```
[C++]
```
protected: virtual void RemoveCore(
   Object* dataSource
);
```
[JScript]
```
protected function RemoveCore(
   dataSource : Object
);
```

BindingContext.CollectionChanged Event

This member supports the .NET Framework infrastructure and is not intended to be used directly from your code.

[Visual Basic]
```
Public Event CollectionChanged As CollectionChangeEventHandler
```
[C#]
```
public event CollectionChangeEventHandler CollectionChanged;
```
[C++]
```
public: __event CollectionChangeEventHandler* CollectionChanged;
```

[JScript] In JScript, you can handle the events defined by a class, but you cannot define your own.

BindingManagerBase Class

Manages all **Binding** objects that are bound to the same data source and data member. This class is abstract.

System.Object
  System.Windows.Forms.BindingManagerBase
    System.Windows.Forms.CurrencyManager
    System.Windows.Forms.PropertyManager

```
[Visual Basic]
MustInherit Public Class BindingManagerBase
[C#]
public abstract class BindingManagerBase
[C++]
public __gc __abstract class BindingManagerBase
[JScript]
public abstract class BindingManagerBase
```

Thread Safety

Any public static (**Shared** in Visual Basic) members of this type are safe for multithreaded operations. Any instance members are not guaranteed to be thread safe.

Remarks

The **BindingManagerBase** enables the synchronization of data-bound controls on a Windows form that are bound to the same data source. (To simple-bind a control to a data source, add a **Binding** object to the control's **ControlBindingsCollection**, which is accessed through the **DataBindings** property). For example, suppose that a form contains two **TextBox** controls that are bound to the same data source but to different columns (The data source might be a **DataTable** that contains customer names, while the columns might contain the first name and last names). The two controls must be synchronized in order to display the correct first and last names together for the same customer. The **CurrencyManager**, which inherits from the **BindingManagerBase** class, accomplishes this synchronization by maintaining a pointer to the current item for the list. The **TextBox** controls are bound to the current item so they display the information for the same row. When the current item changes, the **CurrencyManager** notifies all the bound controls so that they can refresh their data. Furthermore, you can set the **Position** property to specify the row in the **DataTable** that the controls are point to. To determine how many rows exist in the list, use the **Count** property.

The **CurrencyManager** is necessary because data sources do not necessarily maintain a current-item pointer. For instance, arrays and **ArrayList** objects can be data sources, but they do not have a property that returns the current item. To get the current item, use the **Current** property.

The **PropertyManager** also inherits from the **BindingManager-Base**, and it is used to maintain the current property of an object, rather than the property of a current object in a list. For this reason, trying to set the **Position** or **Count** property for a **PropertyManager** has no effect.

To create a **BindingManagerBase** object, use the **BindingContext** class--which returns either a **CurrencyManager** or a **Property-Manager**, depending on the data source being managed.

Notes to Inheritors: When you inherit from **BindingManagerBase**, you must override the following members: **AddNew**, **Count**, **CancelCurrentEdit**, **Current**, **EndCurrentEdit**, **GetItemProperties**, **OnCurrentChanged**, **Position**, **RemoveAt**, **ResumeBinding**, **SuspendBinding**, and **UpdateIsBinding**.

Example

See related example in the **System.Windows.Forms.Binding** class topic.

Requirements

Namespace: System.Windows.Forms

Platforms: Windows 98, Windows NT 4.0, Windows Millennium Edition, Windows 2000, Windows XP Home Edition, Windows XP Professional, Windows Server 2003 family, .NET Compact Framework - Windows CE .NET

Assembly: System.Windows.Forms (in System.Windows.Forms.dll)

BindingManagerBase Constructor

Initializes a new instance of the **BindingManagerBase** class.

```
[Visual Basic]
Public Sub New()
[C#]
public BindingManagerBase();
[C++]
public: BindingManagerBase();
[JScript]
public function BindingManagerBase();
```

Requirements

Platforms: Windows 98, Windows NT 4.0, Windows Millennium Edition, Windows 2000, Windows XP Home Edition, Windows XP Professional, Windows Server 2003 family, .NET Compact Framework - Windows CE .NET

BindingManagerBase.onCurrentChanged-Handler Field

Specifies the event handler for the **CurrentChanged** event.

```
[Visual Basic]
Protected onCurrentChangedHandler As EventHandler
[C#]
protected EventHandler onCurrentChangedHandler;
[C++]
protected: EventHandler* onCurrentChangedHandler;
[JScript]
protected var onCurrentChangedHandler : EventHandler;
```

Requirements

Platforms: Windows 98, Windows NT 4.0, Windows Millennium Edition, Windows 2000, Windows XP Home Edition, Windows XP Professional, Windows Server 2003 family, .NET Compact Framework - Windows CE .NET

BindingManagerBase.onPositionChanged-Handler Field

Specifies the event handler for the **PositionChanged** event.

```
[Visual Basic]
Protected onPositionChangedHandler As EventHandler
```

```
[C#]
protected EventHandler onPositionChangedHandler;
[C++]
protected: EventHandler* onPositionChangedHandler;
[JScript]
protected var onPositionChangedHandler : EventHandler;
```

Requirements

Platforms: Windows 98, Windows NT 4.0, Windows Millennium Edition, Windows 2000, Windows XP Home Edition, Windows XP Professional, Windows Server 2003 family, .NET Compact Framework - Windows CE .NET

BindingManagerBase.Bindings Property

Gets the collection of bindings being managed.

```
[Visual Basic]
Public ReadOnly Property Bindings As BindingsCollection
[C#]
public BindingsCollection Bindings {get;}
[C++]
public: __property BindingsCollection* get_Bindings();
[JScript]
public function get Bindings() : BindingsCollection;
```

Property Value

A **BindingsCollection** that contains the **Binding** objects managed by this **BindingManagerBase**.

Example

See related example in the **System.Windows.Forms.Binding** class topic.

Requirements

Platforms: Windows 98, Windows NT 4.0, Windows Millennium Edition, Windows 2000, Windows XP Home Edition, Windows XP Professional, Windows Server 2003 family, .NET Compact Framework - Windows CE .NET

BindingManagerBase.Count Property

When overridden in a derived class, gets the number of rows managed by the **BindingManagerBase**.

```
[Visual Basic]
Public MustOverride ReadOnly Property Count As Integer
[C#]
public abstract int Count {get;}
[C++]
public: __property virtual int get_Count() = 0;
[JScript]
public abstract function get Count() : int;
```

Property Value

The number of rows managed by the **BindingManagerBase**.

Remarks

Use the **Count** property to determine the last item in the list of rows maintained by the **BindingManagerBase**. To go to the last item, set the **Position** property to the **Count** property value minus one.

Example

See related example in the **System.Windows.Forms.Binding** class topic.

Requirements

Platforms: Windows 98, Windows NT 4.0, Windows Millennium Edition, Windows 2000, Windows XP Home Edition, Windows XP Professional, Windows Server 2003 family, .NET Compact Framework - Windows CE .NET

BindingManagerBase.Current Property

When overridden in a derived class, gets the current object.

```
[Visual Basic]
Public MustOverride ReadOnly Property Current As Object
[C#]
public abstract object Current {get;}
[C++]
public: __property virtual Object* get_Current() = 0;
[JScript]
public abstract function get Current() : Object;
```

Property Value

An **Object** that represents the current object.

Remarks

The **Current** object contains the value of the current item in the data source. To use the value of the current item, you must cast the item to the **Type** of the object contained by the **DataSource**. For example, a **DataTable** contains **DataRowView** objects. To determine the type of the current object, use the **GetType** and **ToString** methods.

> **Note** When the **DataSource** is a **DataSet**, **DataViewManager**, or **DataTable**, you are actually binding to a **DataView**. Consequently, each **Current** object is a **DataRowView** object.

Example

See related example in the **System.Windows.Forms.Binding** class topic.

Requirements

Platforms: Windows 98, Windows NT 4.0, Windows Millennium Edition, Windows 2000, Windows XP Home Edition, Windows XP Professional, Windows Server 2003 family, .NET Compact Framework - Windows CE .NET

BindingManagerBase.Position Property

When overridden in a derived class, gets or sets the position in the underlying list that controls bound to this data source point to.

```
[Visual Basic]
Public MustOverride Property Position As Integer
[C#]
public abstract int Position {get; set;}
[C++]
public: __property virtual int get_Position() = 0;
public: __property virtual void set_Position(int) = 0;
```

[JScript]
```
public abstract function get Position() : int;
public abstract function set Position(int);
```

Property Value

A zero-based index that specifies a position in the underlying list.

Remarks

Use the **Position** to iterate through the underlying list maintained by the **BindingManagerBase**. To go to the first item, set the **Position** to zero. To go to the end of the list, set the **Position** to the value of the **Count** property minus one.

The **PositionChanged** event occurs when the **Position** property value changes.

Example

See related example in the **System.Windows.Forms.Binding** class topic.

Requirements

Platforms: Windows 98, Windows NT 4.0,
Windows Millennium Edition, Windows 2000,
Windows XP Home Edition, Windows XP Professional,
Windows Server 2003 family,
.NET Compact Framework - Windows CE .NET

BindingManagerBase.AddNew Method

When overridden in a derived class, adds a new item to the underlying list.

[Visual Basic]
```
Public MustOverride Sub AddNew()
```
[C#]
```
public abstract void AddNew();
```
[C++]
```
public: virtual void AddNew() = 0;
```
[JScript]
```
public abstract function AddNew();
```

Requirements

Platforms: Windows 98, Windows NT 4.0,
Windows Millennium Edition, Windows 2000,
Windows XP Home Edition, Windows XP Professional,
Windows Server 2003 family,
.NET Compact Framework - Windows CE .NET

BindingManagerBase.CancelCurrentEdit Method

When overridden in a derived class, cancels the current edit.

[Visual Basic]
```
Public MustOverride Sub CancelCurrentEdit()
```
[C#]
```
public abstract void CancelCurrentEdit();
```
[C++]
```
public: virtual void CancelCurrentEdit() = 0;
```
[JScript]
```
public abstract function CancelCurrentEdit();
```

Remarks

This method is supported only if the data source implements the **IEditableObject** interface. If the object does not implement the **IEditableObject** interface, changes made to the data will not be discarded.

Calling the **CancelCurrentEdit** method causes the **Format** event to occur.

Example

See related example in the **System.Windows.Forms.Binding** class topic.

Requirements

Platforms: Windows 98, Windows NT 4.0,
Windows Millennium Edition, Windows 2000,
Windows XP Home Edition, Windows XP Professional,
Windows Server 2003 family,
.NET Compact Framework - Windows CE .NET

BindingManagerBase.EndCurrentEdit Method

When overridden in a derived class, ends the current edit.

[Visual Basic]
```
Public MustOverride Sub EndCurrentEdit()
```
[C#]
```
public abstract void EndCurrentEdit();
```
[C++]
```
public: virtual void EndCurrentEdit() = 0;
```
[JScript]
```
public abstract function EndCurrentEdit();
```

Remarks

This method is supported only if the data source implements the **IEditableObject** interface. In that case, changes will be saved. If the object does not implement the **IEditableObject** interface, changes made to the data will not be saved.

Example

See related example in the **System.Windows.Forms.Binding** class topic.

Requirements

Platforms: Windows 98, Windows NT 4.0,
Windows Millennium Edition, Windows 2000,
Windows XP Home Edition, Windows XP Professional,
Windows Server 2003 family,
.NET Compact Framework - Windows CE .NET

BindingManagerBase.GetItemProperties Method

Get or sets the list of property descriptors for the data source.

Overload List

When overridden in a derived class, gets the collection of property descriptors for the binding.

Supported by the .NET Compact Framework.

[Visual Basic] **Overloads Public MustOverride Function GetItemProperties() As PropertyDescriptorCollection**

[C#] **public abstract PropertyDescriptorCollection GetItemProperties();**

[C++] **public: virtual PropertyDescriptorCollection* GetItemProperties() = 0;**

[JScript] **public abstract function GetItemProperties() : PropertyDescriptorCollection;**

Gets the collection of property descriptors for the binding using the specified **ArrayList**.

[Visual Basic] **Overloads Protected Friend Overridable Function GetItemProperties(ArrayList, ArrayList) As PropertyDescriptorCollection**

[C#] **protected internal virtual PropertyDescriptorCollection GetItemProperties(ArrayList, ArrayList);**

[C++] **protected public: virtual PropertyDescriptor-Collection* GetItemProperties(ArrayList*, ArrayList*);**

[JScript] **protected internal function GetItem-Properties(ArrayList, ArrayList) : PropertyDescriptor-Collection;**

Gets the list of properties of the items managed by this **BindingManagerBase**.

Supported by the .NET Compact Framework.

[Visual Basic] **Overloads Protected Overridable Function GetItemProperties(Type, Integer, ArrayList, ArrayList) As PropertyDescriptorCollection**

[C#] **protected virtual PropertyDescriptorCollection GetItemProperties(Type, int, ArrayList, ArrayList);**

[C++] **protected: virtual PropertyDescriptorCollection* GetItemProperties(Type*, int, ArrayList*, ArrayList*);**

[JScript] **protected function GetItemProperties(Type, int, ArrayList, ArrayList) : PropertyDescriptorCollection;**

Example

See related example in the **System.Windows.Forms.Binding** class topic.

BindingManagerBase.GetItemProperties Method ()

When overridden in a derived class, gets the collection of property descriptors for the binding.

[Visual Basic]
```
Overloads Public MustOverride Function GetItemProperties() As _
   PropertyDescriptorCollection
```
[C#]
```
public abstract PropertyDescriptorCollection GetItemProperties();
```
[C++]
```
public: virtual PropertyDescriptorCollection* GetItemProperties() =
   0;
```
[JScript]
```
public abstract function GetItemProperties() :
   PropertyDescriptorCollection;
```

Return Value

A **PropertyDescriptorCollection** that represents the property descriptors for the binding.

Example

See related example in the **System.Windows.Forms.Binding** class topic.

Requirements

Platforms: Windows 98, Windows NT 4.0, Windows Millennium Edition, Windows 2000, Windows XP Home Edition, Windows XP Professional, Windows Server 2003 family, .NET Compact Framework - Windows CE .NET

BindingManagerBase.GetItemProperties Method (ArrayList, ArrayList)

Gets the collection of property descriptors for the binding using the specified **ArrayList**.

[Visual Basic]
```
Overloads Protected Friend Overridable Function GetItemProperties( _
   _
   ByVal dataSources As ArrayList, _
   ByVal listAccessors As ArrayList _
) As PropertyDescriptorCollection
```
[C#]
```
protected internal virtual PropertyDescriptorCollection
GetItemProperties(
   ArrayList dataSources,
   ArrayList listAccessors
);
```
[C++]
```
protected public: virtual PropertyDescriptorCollection*
GetItemProperties(
   ArrayList* dataSources,
   ArrayList* listAccessors
);
```
[JScript]
```
protected internal function GetItemProperties(
   dataSources : ArrayList,
   listAccessors : ArrayList
) : PropertyDescriptorCollection;
```

Parameters

dataSources
: An **ArrayList** containing the data sources.

listAccessors
: An **ArrayList** containing the table's bound properties.

Return Value

A **PropertyDescriptorCollection** that represents the property descriptors for the binding.

Remarks

This method is used by developers creating data-bound controls.

Requirements

Platforms: Windows 98, Windows NT 4.0, Windows Millennium Edition, Windows 2000, Windows XP Home Edition, Windows XP Professional, Windows Server 2003 family

BindingManagerBase.GetItemProperties Method (Type, Int32, ArrayList, ArrayList)

Gets the list of properties of the items managed by this **BindingManagerBase**.

[Visual Basic]
```
Overloads Protected Overridable Function GetItemProperties( _
   ByVal listType As Type, _
   ByVal offset As Integer, _
   ByVal dataSources As ArrayList, _
   ByVal listAccessors As ArrayList _
) As PropertyDescriptorCollection
```

[C#]
```
protected virtual PropertyDescriptorCollection GetItemProperties(
   Type listType,
   int offset,
   ArrayList dataSources,
   ArrayList listAccessors
);
```
[C++]
```
protected: virtual PropertyDescriptorCollection* GetItemProperties(
   Type* listType,
   int offset,
   ArrayList* dataSources,
   ArrayList* listAccessors
);
```
[JScript]
```
protected function GetItemProperties(
   listType : Type,
   offset : int,
   dataSources : ArrayList,
   listAccessors : ArrayList
) : PropertyDescriptorCollection;
```

Parameters

listType

The **Type** of the bound list.

offset

A counter used to recursively call the method.

dataSources

An **ArrayList** containing the data sources.

listAccessors

An **ArrayList** containing the table's bound properties.

Return Value

A **PropertyDescriptorCollection** that represents the property descriptors for the binding.

Remarks

This overload is used by developers creating data-bound controls.

Example

See related example in the **System.Windows.Forms.Binding** class topic.

Requirements

Platforms: Windows 98, Windows NT 4.0,
Windows Millennium Edition, Windows 2000,
Windows XP Home Edition, Windows XP Professional,
Windows Server 2003 family,
.NET Compact Framework - Windows CE .NET

BindingManagerBase.GetListName Method

When overridden in a derived class, gets the name of the list supplying the data for the binding.

[Visual Basic]
```
Protected Friend MustOverride Function GetListName( _
   ByVal listAccessors As ArrayList _
) As String
```
[C#]
```
protected internal abstract string GetListName(
   ArrayList listAccessors
);
```
[C++]
```
protected public: virtual String* GetListName(
   ArrayList* listAccessors
) = 0;
```
[JScript]
```
protected internal abstract function GetListName(
   listAccessors : ArrayList
) : String;
```

Parameters

listAccessors

An **ArrayList** containing the table's bound properties.

Return Value

The name of the list supplying the data for the binding.

Requirements

Platforms: Windows 98, Windows NT 4.0,
Windows Millennium Edition, Windows 2000,
Windows XP Home Edition, Windows XP Professional,
Windows Server 2003 family

BindingManagerBase.OnCurrentChanged Method

When overridden in a derived class, raises the **CurrentChanged** event.

[Visual Basic]
```
Protected Friend MustOverride Sub OnCurrentChanged( _
   ByVal e As EventArgs _
)
```
[C#]
```
protected internal abstract void OnCurrentChanged(
   EventArgs e
);
```
[C++]
```
protected public: virtual void OnCurrentChanged(
   EventArgs* e
) = 0;
```
[JScript]
```
protected internal abstract function OnCurrentChanged(
   e : EventArgs
);
```

Parameters

e

The **EventArgs** that contains the event data.

Remarks

Raising an event invokes the event handler through a delegate.

The **OnCurrentChanged** method also allows derived classes to handle the event without attaching a delegate. This is the preferred technique for handling the event in a derived class.

Notes to Inheritors: When overriding **OnCurrentChanged** in a derived class, be sure to call the base class's **OnCurrentChanged** method so that registered delegates receive the event.

Requirements

Platforms: Windows 98, Windows NT 4.0,
Windows Millennium Edition, Windows 2000,
Windows XP Home Edition, Windows XP Professional,
Windows Server 2003 family

BindingManagerBase.PullData Method

Pulls data from the data-bound control into the data source.

```
[Visual Basic]
Protected Sub PullData()
[C#]
protected void PullData();
[C++]
protected: void PullData();
[JScript]
protected function PullData();
```

Requirements

Platforms: Windows 98, Windows NT 4.0, Windows Millennium Edition, Windows 2000, Windows XP Home Edition, Windows XP Professional, Windows Server 2003 family, .NET Compact Framework - Windows CE .NET

BindingManagerBase.PushData Method

Pushes data from the data source into the data-bound control.

```
[Visual Basic]
Protected Sub PushData()
[C#]
protected void PushData();
[C++]
protected: void PushData();
[JScript]
protected function PushData();
```

Requirements

Platforms: Windows 98, Windows NT 4.0, Windows Millennium Edition, Windows 2000, Windows XP Home Edition, Windows XP Professional, Windows Server 2003 family, .NET Compact Framework - Windows CE .NET

BindingManagerBase.RemoveAt Method

When overridden in a derived class, deletes the row at the specified index from the underlying list.

```
[Visual Basic]
Public MustOverride Sub RemoveAt( _
   ByVal index As Integer _
)
[C#]
public abstract void RemoveAt(
   int index
);
[C++]
public: virtual void RemoveAt(
   int index
) = 0;
[JScript]
public abstract function RemoveAt(
   index : int
);
```

Parameters

index
The index of the row to delete.

Exceptions

Exception Type	Condition
IndexOutOfRange-Exception	There is no row at the specified *index*.

Remarks

The **RemoveAt** method relies on the underlying data source to determine how the method behaves. (See the **Binding** class for a list of supported data sources). For classes that implement **IList**, **IBindingList**, **ITypedList**, as well as strongly typed classes that implement **IList**, the **RemoveAt** method actually deletes the row in the underlying list instead of removing it.

If the underlying list implements the **IBindingList** interface, the **AllowRemove** property must return **true**. If the underlying list implements the **IList** interface, the **IsFixedSize** property must return **false**.

Example

See related example in the **System.Windows.Forms.Binding** class topic.

Requirements

Platforms: Windows 98, Windows NT 4.0, Windows Millennium Edition, Windows 2000, Windows XP Home Edition, Windows XP Professional, Windows Server 2003 family, .NET Compact Framework - Windows CE .NET

BindingManagerBase.ResumeBinding Method

When overridden in a derived class, resumes data binding.

```
[Visual Basic]
Public MustOverride Sub ResumeBinding()
[C#]
public abstract void ResumeBinding();
[C++]
public: virtual void ResumeBinding() = 0;
[JScript]
public abstract function ResumeBinding();
```

Remarks

SuspendBinding and **ResumeBinding** are two methods that allow the temporary suspension and resumption of data binding. You would typically suspend data binding if the user must be allowed to make several edits to data fields before validation occurs. For example, if one field must be changed in accordance with a second, but where validating the first field would cause the second field to be in error.

Example

See related example in the **System.Windows.Forms.Binding** class topic.

Requirements

Platforms: Windows 98, Windows NT 4.0, Windows Millennium Edition, Windows 2000, Windows XP Home Edition, Windows XP Professional, Windows Server 2003 family

BindingManagerBase.SuspendBinding Method

When overridden in a derived class, suspends data binding.

[Visual Basic]
```
Public MustOverride Sub SuspendBinding()
```
[C#]
```
public abstract void SuspendBinding();
```
[C++]
```
public: virtual void SuspendBinding() = 0;
```
[JScript]
```
public abstract function SuspendBinding();
```

Remarks

SuspendBinding and **ResumeBinding** are two methods that allow the temporary suspension and resumption of data binding. You would typically suspend data binding if the user must be allowed to make several edits to data fields before validation occurs. For example, if one field must be changed in accordance with a second, but where validating the first field would cause the second field to be in error.

Example

See related example in the **System.Windows.Forms.Binding** class topic.

Requirements

Platforms: Windows 98, Windows NT 4.0,
Windows Millennium Edition, Windows 2000,
Windows XP Home Edition, Windows XP Professional,
Windows Server 2003 family

BindingManagerBase.UpdateIsBinding Method

When overridden in a derived class, updates the binding.

[Visual Basic]
```
Protected MustOverride Sub UpdateIsBinding()
```
[C#]
```
protected abstract void UpdateIsBinding();
```
[C++]
```
protected: virtual void UpdateIsBinding() = 0;
```
[JScript]
```
protected abstract function UpdateIsBinding();
```

Requirements

Platforms: Windows 98, Windows NT 4.0,
Windows Millennium Edition, Windows 2000,
Windows XP Home Edition, Windows XP Professional,
Windows Server 2003 family,
.NET Compact Framework - Windows CE .NET

BindingManagerBase.CurrentChanged Event

Occurs when the bound value changes.

[Visual Basic]
```
Public Event CurrentChanged As EventHandler
```
[C#]
```
public event EventHandler CurrentChanged;
```
[C++]
```
public: __event EventHandler* CurrentChanged;
```

[JScript] In JScript, you can handle the events defined by a class, but you cannot define your own.

Event Data

The event handler receives an argument of type **EventArgs**.

Example

See related example in the **System.Windows.Forms.Binding** class topic.

Requirements

Platforms: Windows 98, Windows NT 4.0,
Windows Millennium Edition, Windows 2000,
Windows XP Home Edition, Windows XP Professional,
Windows Server 2003 family

BindingManagerBase.PositionChanged Event

Occurs when the **Position** has changed.

[Visual Basic]
```
Public Event PositionChanged As EventHandler
```
[C#]
```
public event EventHandler PositionChanged;
```
[C++]
```
public: __event EventHandler* PositionChanged;
```

[JScript] In JScript, you can handle the events defined by a class, but you cannot define your own.

Event Data

The event handler receives an argument of type **EventArgs**.

Example

See related example in the **System.Windows.Forms.Binding** class topic.

Requirements

Platforms: Windows 98, Windows NT 4.0,
Windows Millennium Edition, Windows 2000,
Windows XP Home Edition, Windows XP Professional,
Windows Server 2003 family

BindingMemberInfo Structure

Contains information that enables a **Binding** to resolve a data binding to either the property of an object or the property of the current object in a list of objects.

System.Object
  System.ValueType
    System.Windows.Forms.BindingMemberInfo

```
[Visual Basic]
Public Structure BindingMemberInfo
[C#]
public struct BindingMemberInfo
[C++]
public __value struct BindingMemberInfo
```

[JScript] In JScript, you can use the structures in the .NET Framework, but you cannot define your own.

Thread Safety

Any public static (**Shared** in Visual Basic) members of this type are safe for multithreaded operations. Any instance members are not guaranteed to be thread safe.

Remarks

The **BindingMemberInfo** is returned by the **BindingMemberInfo** property of the **Binding** class.

The **BindingMemberInfo** is created from the string passed to the **Binding** constructor.

Example

See related example in the **System.Windows.Forms.Binding** class topic.

Requirements

Namespace: System.Windows.Forms

Platforms: Windows 98, Windows NT 4.0, Windows Millennium Edition, Windows 2000, Windows XP Home Edition, Windows XP Professional, Windows Server 2003 family, .NET Compact Framework - Windows CE .NET

Assembly: System.Windows.Forms (in System.Windows.Forms.dll)

BindingMemberInfo Constructor

Initializes a new instance of the **BindingMemberInfo** class.

```
[Visual Basic]
Public Sub New( _
   ByVal dataMember As String _
)
[C#]
public BindingMemberInfo(
   string dataMember
);
[C++]
public: BindingMemberInfo(
   String* dataMember
);
[JScript]
public function BindingMemberInfo(
   dataMember : String
);
```

Parameters

dataMember
: A navigation path that resolves to either the property of an object or the property of the current object in a list of objects.

Remarks

A **BindingMemberInfo** object is created automatically when you call the **Binding** constructor with a control-property name, data source, and navigation path. The *dataMember* parameter contains the **BindingMember** string.

Requirements

Platforms: Windows 98, Windows NT 4.0, Windows Millennium Edition, Windows 2000, Windows XP Home Edition, Windows XP Professional, Windows Server 2003 family, .NET Compact Framework - Windows CE .NET

BindingMemberInfo.BindingField Property

Gets the data-bound object's property name.

```
[Visual Basic]
Public ReadOnly Property BindingField As String
[C#]
public string BindingField {get;}
[C++]
public: __property String* get_BindingField();
[JScript]
public function get BindingField() : String;
```

Property Value

The data-bound object's property name.

Remarks

The **BindingField** is the last item found in the navigation path returned by the **BindingMember** property. For example, if the navigation path is "Customers.custToOrders.OrderDate", the **BindingField** returns "OrderDate" which names the data-bound property of the data source.

Example

See related example in the **System.Windows.Forms.Binding** class topic.

Requirements

Platforms: Windows 98, Windows NT 4.0, Windows Millennium Edition, Windows 2000, Windows XP Home Edition, Windows XP Professional, Windows Server 2003 family, .NET Compact Framework - Windows CE .NET

BindingMemberInfo.BindingMember Property

Gets the information that is used to specify the data-bound object's property name.

```
[Visual Basic]
Public ReadOnly Property BindingMember As String
[C#]
public string BindingMember {get;}
[C++]
public: __property String* get_BindingMember();
[JScript]
public function get BindingMember() : String;
```

Property Value

An empty string (""), a single property name, or a hierarchy of period-delimited property names that resolves to the final data-bound object's property name.

Remarks

A **BindingMemberInfo** object is created automatically when you call the **Binding** constructor with a control-property name, data source, and navigation path. The *dataMember* parameter contains the **BindingMember** string.

Example

See related example in the **System.Windows.Forms.Binding** class topic.

Requirements

Platforms: Windows 98, Windows NT 4.0,
Windows Millennium Edition, Windows 2000,
Windows XP Home Edition, Windows XP Professional,
Windows Server 2003 family,
.NET Compact Framework - Windows CE .NET

BindingMemberInfo.BindingPath Property

Gets the property name, or the period-delimited hierarchy of property names, that precedes the data-bound object's property name.

```
[Visual Basic]
Public ReadOnly Property BindingPath As String
[C#]
public string BindingPath {get;}
[C++]
public: __property String* get_BindingPath();
[JScript]
public function get BindingPath() : String;
```

Property Value

The property name, or the period-delimited hierarchy of property names, that precedes the data-bound object property name.

Example

See related example in the **System.Windows.Forms.Binding** class topic.

Requirements

Platforms: Windows 98, Windows NT 4.0,
Windows Millennium Edition, Windows 2000,
Windows XP Home Edition, Windows XP Professional,
Windows Server 2003 family,
.NET Compact Framework - Windows CE .NET

BindingMemberInfo.Equals Method

This member overrides **ValueType.Equals**.

```
[Visual Basic]
Overrides Public Function Equals( _
   ByVal otherObject As Object _
) As Boolean
[C#]
public override bool Equals(
   object otherObject
);
[C++]
public: bool Equals(
   Object* otherObject
);
[JScript]
public override function Equals(
   otherObject : Object
) : Boolean;
```

Requirements

Platforms: Windows 98, Windows NT 4.0,
Windows Millennium Edition, Windows 2000,
Windows XP Home Edition, Windows XP Professional,
Windows Server 2003 family,
.NET Compact Framework - Windows CE .NET

BindingMemberInfo.GetHashCode Method

This member overrides **ValueType.GetHashCode**.

```
[Visual Basic]
Overrides Public Function GetHashCode() As Integer
[C#]
public override int GetHashCode();
[C++]
public: int GetHashCode();
[JScript]
public override function GetHashCode() : int;
```

Requirements

Platforms: Windows 98, Windows NT 4.0,
Windows Millennium Edition, Windows 2000,
Windows XP Home Edition, Windows XP Professional,
Windows Server 2003 family,
.NET Compact Framework - Windows CE .NET

BindingsCollection Class

Represents a collection of **Binding** objects for a control.

System.Object
  System.MarshalByRefObject
    System.Windows.Forms.BaseCollection
      System.Windows.Forms.BindingsCollection
        System.Windows.Forms.ControlBindingsCollection

[Visual Basic]
```
Public Class BindingsCollection
   Inherits BaseCollection
```
[C#]
```
public class BindingsCollection : BaseCollection
```
[C++]
```
public __gc class BindingsCollection : public BaseCollection
```
[JScript]
```
public class BindingsCollection extends BaseCollection
```

Thread Safety

Any public static (**Shared** in Visual Basic) members of this type are safe for multithreaded operations. Any instance members are not guaranteed to be thread safe.

Remarks

Simple data binding is accomplished by adding **Binding** objects to a **BindingsCollection**. Any object that inherits from the **Control** class can access the **BindingsCollection** through the **DataBindings** property. For a list of Windows controls that support data binding, see the **Binding** class.

Example

See related example in the **System.Windows.Forms.Binding** class topic.

Requirements

Namespace: System.Windows.Forms

Platforms: Windows 98, Windows NT 4.0, Windows Millennium Edition, Windows 2000, Windows XP Home Edition, Windows XP Professional, Windows Server 2003 family, .NET Compact Framework - Windows CE .NET

Assembly: System.Windows.Forms (in System.Windows.Forms.dll)

BindingsCollection.Count Property

This member overrides **BaseCollection.Count**.

[Visual Basic]
```
Overrides Public ReadOnly Property Count As Integer  Implements _
   ICollection.Count
```
[C#]
```
public override int Count {get;}
```
[C++]
```
public: __property int get_Count();
```
[JScript]
```
public override function get Count() : int;
```

Requirements

Platforms: Windows 98, Windows NT 4.0, Windows Millennium Edition, Windows 2000, Windows XP Home Edition, Windows XP Professional, Windows Server 2003 family, .NET Compact Framework - Windows CE .NET

BindingsCollection.Item Property

Gets the **Binding** at the specified index.

[C#] In C#, this property is the indexer for the **BindingsCollection** class.

[Visual Basic]
```
Public Default ReadOnly Property Item( _
   ByVal index As Integer _
) As Binding
```
[C#]
```
public Binding this[
   int index
] {get;}
```
[C++]
```
public: __property Binding* get_Item(
   int index
);
```
[JScript]
```
returnValue = BindingsCollectionObject.Item(index);
-or-
returnValue = BindingsCollectionObject(index);
```

[JScript] In JScript, you can use the default indexed properties defined by a type, but you cannot explicitly define your own. However, specifying the **expando** attribute on a class automatically provides a default indexed property whose type is **Object** and whose index type is **String**.

Arguments [JScript]

index
  The index of the **Binding** to find.

Parameters [Visual Basic, C#, C++]

index
  The index of the **Binding** to find.

Property Value

The **Binding** at the specified index.

Exceptions

Exception Type	Condition
IndexOutOfRange-Exception	The collection doesn't contain an item at the specified index.

Example

See related example in the **System.Windows.Forms.Binding** class topic.

Requirements

Platforms: Windows 98, Windows NT 4.0, Windows Millennium Edition, Windows 2000, Windows XP Home Edition, Windows XP Professional, Windows Server 2003 family

BindingsCollection.List Property

This member overrides **BaseCollection.List**.

[Visual Basic]
```
Overrides Protected ReadOnly Property List As ArrayList
```
[C#]
```
protected override ArrayList List {get;}
```
[C++]
```
protected: __property ArrayList* get_List();
```

```
[JScript]
protected override function get List() : ArrayList;
```

Requirements

Platforms: Windows 98, Windows NT 4.0, Windows Millennium Edition, Windows 2000, Windows XP Home Edition, Windows XP Professional, Windows Server 2003 family, .NET Compact Framework - Windows CE .NET

BindingsCollection.Add Method

Adds the specified binding to the collection.

```
[Visual Basic]
Protected Friend Sub Add( _
   ByVal binding As Binding _
)
[C#]
protected internal void Add(
   Binding binding
);
[C++]
protected public: void Add(
   Binding* binding
);
[JScript]
protected internal function Add(
   binding : Binding
);
```

Parameters

binding

The **Binding** to add to the collection.

Requirements

Platforms: Windows 98, Windows NT 4.0, Windows Millennium Edition, Windows 2000, Windows XP Home Edition, Windows XP Professional, Windows Server 2003 family

BindingsCollection.AddCore Method

This member supports the .NET Framework infrastructure and is not intended to be used directly from your code.

```
[Visual Basic]
Protected Overridable Sub AddCore( _
   ByVal dataBinding As Binding _
)
[C#]
protected virtual void AddCore(
   Binding dataBinding
);
[C++]
protected: virtual void AddCore(
   Binding* dataBinding
);
[JScript]
protected function AddCore(
   dataBinding : Binding
);
```

BindingsCollection.Clear Method

Clears the collection of binding objects.

```
[Visual Basic]
Protected Friend Sub Clear()
[C#]
protected internal void Clear();
[C++]
protected public: void Clear();
[JScript]
protected internal function Clear();
```

Remarks

The **CollectionChanged** event occurs when you invoke the **Clear** method.

Requirements

Platforms: Windows 98, Windows NT 4.0, Windows Millennium Edition, Windows 2000, Windows XP Home Edition, Windows XP Professional, Windows Server 2003 family

BindingsCollection.ClearCore Method

This member supports the .NET Framework infrastructure and is not intended to be used directly from your code.

```
[Visual Basic]
Protected Overridable Sub ClearCore()
[C#]
protected virtual void ClearCore();
[C++]
protected: virtual void ClearCore();
[JScript]
protected function ClearCore();
```

BindingsCollection.OnCollectionChanged Method

Raises the **CollectionChanged** event.

```
[Visual Basic]
Protected Overridable Sub OnCollectionChanged( _
   ByVal ccevent As CollectionChangeEventArgs _
)
[C#]
protected virtual void OnCollectionChanged(
   CollectionChangeEventArgs ccevent
);
[C++]
protected: virtual void OnCollectionChanged(
   CollectionChangeEventArgs* ccevent
);
[JScript]
protected function OnCollectionChanged(
   ccevent : CollectionChangeEventArgs
);
```

Parameters

ccevent

A **CollectionChangeEventArgs** that contains the event data.

Remarks

Raising an event invokes the event handler through a delegate.

The **OnCollectionChanged** method also allows derived classes to handle the event without attaching a delegate. This is the preferred technique for handling the event in a derived class.

Notes to Inheritors: When overriding **OnCollectionChanged** in a derived class, be sure to call the base class's **OnCollectionChanged** method so that registered delegates receive the event.

Requirements

Platforms: Windows 98, Windows NT 4.0, Windows Millennium Edition, Windows 2000, Windows XP Home Edition, Windows XP Professional, Windows Server 2003 family, .NET Compact Framework - Windows CE .NET

BindingsCollection.Remove Method

Deletes the specified binding from the collection.

```
[Visual Basic]
Protected Friend Sub Remove( _
   ByVal binding As Binding _
)
[C#]
protected internal void Remove(
   Binding binding
);
[C++]
protected public: void Remove(
   Binding* binding
);
[JScript]
protected internal function Remove(
   binding : Binding
);
```

Parameters

binding
The Binding to remove from the collection.

Requirements

Platforms: Windows 98, Windows NT 4.0, Windows Millennium Edition, Windows 2000, Windows XP Home Edition, Windows XP Professional, Windows Server 2003 family

BindingsCollection.RemoveAt Method

Deletes the binding from the collection at the specified index.

```
[Visual Basic]
Protected Friend Sub RemoveAt( _
   ByVal index As Integer _
)
[C#]
protected internal void RemoveAt(
   int index
);
[C++]
protected public: void RemoveAt(
   int index
);
[JScript]
protected internal function RemoveAt(
   index : int
);
```

Parameters

index
The index of the **Binding** to remove.

Requirements

Platforms: Windows 98, Windows NT 4.0, Windows Millennium Edition, Windows 2000, Windows XP Home Edition, Windows XP Professional, Windows Server 2003 family

BindingsCollection.RemoveCore Method

This member supports the .NET Framework infrastructure and is not intended to be used directly from your code.

```
[Visual Basic]
Protected Overridable Sub RemoveCore( _
   ByVal dataBinding As Binding _
)
[C#]
protected virtual void RemoveCore(
   Binding dataBinding
);
[C++]
protected: virtual void RemoveCore(
   Binding* dataBinding
);
[JScript]
protected function RemoveCore(
   dataBinding : Binding
);
```

BindingsCollection.ShouldSerializeMyAll Method

Gets a value that indicates whether the collection should be serialized.

```
[Visual Basic]
Protected Friend Function ShouldSerializeMyAll() As Boolean
[C#]
protected internal bool ShouldSerializeMyAll();
[C++]
protected public: bool ShouldSerializeMyAll();
[JScript]
protected internal function ShouldSerializeMyAll() : Boolean;
```

Return Value

true if the collection count is greater than zero; otherwise, **false**.

Requirements

Platforms: Windows 98, Windows NT 4.0, Windows Millennium Edition, Windows 2000, Windows XP Home Edition, Windows XP Professional, Windows Server 2003 family

BindingsCollection.CollectionChanged Event

Occurs when the collection has changed.

[Visual Basic]
```
Public Event CollectionChanged As CollectionChangeEventHandler
```
[C#]
```
public event CollectionChangeEventHandler CollectionChanged;
```
[C++]
```
public: __event CollectionChangeEventHandler* CollectionChanged;
```

[JScript] In JScript, you can handle the events defined by a class, but you cannot define your own.

Event Data

The event handler receives an argument of type **CollectionChangeEventArgs** containing data related to this event. The following **CollectionChangeEventArgs** properties provide information specific to this event.

Property	Description
Action	Gets an action that specifies how the collection changed.
Element	Gets the instance of the collection with the change.

Remarks

For more information about handling events, see **Consuming Events**.

Example

See related example in the **System.Windows.Forms.Binding** class topic.

Requirements

Platforms: Windows 98, Windows NT 4.0,
Windows Millennium Edition, Windows 2000,
Windows XP Home Edition, Windows XP Professional,
Windows Server 2003 family

BootMode Enumeration

Specifies the mode the computer was started in.

[Visual Basic]
```
<Serializable>
Public Enum BootMode
```
[C#]
```
[Serializable]
public enum BootMode
```
[C++]
```
[Serializable]
__value public enum BootMode
```
[JScript]
```
public
   Serializable
enum BootMode
```

Remarks

This enumeration is used by the **BootMode** property in the **SystemInformation** class.

FailSafe is also called safe mode.

Members

Member name	Description
FailSafe	The computer was started by using only the basic files and drivers.
FailSafeWithNetwork	The computer was started by using the basic files, drivers, and services necessary to start networking.
Normal	The computer was started in standard mode.

Requirements

Namespace: System.Windows.Forms

Platforms: Windows 98, Windows NT 4.0, Windows Millennium Edition, Windows 2000, Windows XP Home Edition, Windows XP Professional, Windows Server 2003 family

Assembly: System.Windows.Forms (in System.Windows.Forms.dll)

Border3DSide Enumeration

Specifies the sides of a rectangle to apply a three-dimensional border to.

This enumeration has a **FlagsAttribute** attribute that allows a bitwise combination of its member values.

[Visual Basic]
```
<Flags>
<Serializable>
<ComVisible(True)>
Public Enum Border3DSide
```
[C#]
```
[Flags]
[Serializable]
[ComVisible(true)]
public enum Border3DSide
```
[C++]
```
[Flags]
[Serializable]
[ComVisible(true)]
__value public enum Border3DSide
```
[JScript]
```
public
   Flags
   Serializable
   ComVisible(true)
enum Border3DSide
```

Remarks

Use the members of this enumeration with the **DrawBorder3D** method of the **ControlPaint** class.

Members

Member name	Description	Value
All	A three-dimensional border on all four sides of the rectangle. The middle of the rectangle is filled with the color defined for three-dimensional controls.	2063
Bottom	A three-dimensional border on the bottom side of the rectangle.	8
Left	A three-dimensional border on the left edge of the rectangle.	1
Middle	The interior of the rectangle is filled with the color defined for three-dimensional controls instead of the background color for the form.	2048
Right	A three-dimensional border on the right side of the rectangle.	4
Top	A three-dimensional border on the top edge of the rectangle.	2

Requirements

Namespace: System.Windows.Forms

Platforms: Windows 98, Windows NT 4.0, Windows Millennium Edition, Windows 2000, Windows XP Home Edition, Windows XP Professional, Windows Server 2003 family

Assembly: System.Windows.Forms (in System.Windows.Forms.dll)

Border3DStyle Enumeration

Specifies the style of a three-dimensional border.

[Visual Basic]
```
<Serializable>
<ComVisible(True)>
Public Enum Border3DStyle
```
[C#]
```
[Serializable]
[ComVisible(true)]
public enum Border3DStyle
```
[C++]
```
[Serializable]
[ComVisible(true)]
__value public enum Border3DStyle
```
[JScript]
```
public
   Serializable
   ComVisible(true)
enum Border3DStyle
```

Remarks

Use the members of this enumeration when calling the **DrawBorder3D** method of the **ControlPaint** class.

Members

Member name	Description
Adjust	The border is drawn outside the specified rectangle, preserving the dimensions of the rectangle for drawing.
Bump	The inner and outer edges of the border have a raised appearance.
Etched	The inner and outer edges of the border have an etched appearance.
Flat	The border has no three-dimensional effects.
Raised	The border has raised inner and outer edges.
RaisedInner	The border has a raised inner edge and no outer edge.
RaisedOuter	The border has a raised outer edge and no inner edge.
Sunken	The border has sunken inner and outer edges.
SunkenInner	The border has a sunken inner edge and no outer edge.
SunkenOuter	The border has a sunken outer edge and no inner edge.

Requirements

Namespace: System.Windows.Forms

Platforms: Windows 98, Windows NT 4.0, Windows Millennium Edition, Windows 2000, Windows XP Home Edition, Windows XP Professional, Windows Server 2003 family

Assembly: System.Windows.Forms (in System.Windows.Forms.dll)

BorderStyle Enumeration

Specifies the border style for a control.

[Visual Basic]
```
<Serializable>
<ComVisible(True)>
Public Enum BorderStyle
```
[C#]
```
[Serializable]
[ComVisible(true)]
public enum BorderStyle
```
[C++]
```
[Serializable]
[ComVisible(true)]
__value public enum BorderStyle
```
[JScript]
```
public
   Serializable
   ComVisible(true)
enum BorderStyle
```

Remarks

Use the members of this enumeration to set the border style for controls that have a changeable border.

Members

Member name	Description
Fixed3D Supported by the .NET Compact Framework.	A three-dimensional border.
FixedSingle Supported by the .NET Compact Framework.	A single-line border.
None Supported by the .NET Compact Framework.	No border.

Requirements

Namespace: System.Windows.Forms

Platforms: Windows 98, Windows NT 4.0, Windows Millennium Edition, Windows 2000, Windows XP Home Edition, Windows XP Professional, Windows Server 2003 family, .NET Compact Framework - Windows CE .NET

Assembly: System.Windows.Forms (in System.Windows.Forms.dll)

BoundsSpecified Enumeration

Specifies the bounds of the control to use when defining a control's size and position.

This enumeration has a **FlagsAttribute** attribute that allows a bitwise combination of its member values.

[Visual Basic]
```
<Flags>
<Serializable>
Public Enum BoundsSpecified
```
[C#]
```
[Flags]
[Serializable]
public enum BoundsSpecified
```
[C++]
```
[Flags]
[Serializable]
__value public enum BoundsSpecified
```
[JScript]
```
public
   Flags
   Serializable
enum BoundsSpecified
```

Remarks

Use the members of this enumeration when calling the **SetBoundsCore** and **SetBounds** methods of the **Control** class.

Members

Member name	Description	Value
All	Both **Location** and **Size** property values are defined.	15
Height	The height of the control is defined.	8
Location	Both **X** and **Y** coordinates of the control are defined.	3
None	No bounds are specified.	0
Size	Both **Width** and **Height** property values of the control are defined.	12
Width	The width of the control is defined.	4
X	The left edge of the control is defined.	1
Y	The top edge of the control is defined.	2

Example

[Visual Basic]
```
    Private Sub MyForm_Layout(ByVal sender As Object, _
        ByVal e As System.Windows.Forms.LayoutEventArgs)        ↵
Handles MyBase.Layout

        ' Center the Form on the user's screen everytime it     ↵
requires a Layout.
        Me.SetBounds                                             ↵
 ((System.Windows.Forms.Screen.GetBounds(Me).Width / 2) -       ↵
 (Me.Width / 2), _
            (System.Windows.Forms.Screen.GetBounds(Me).Height   ↵
 / 2) - (Me.Height / 2), _
            Me.Width, Me.Height,                                 ↵
System.Windows.Forms.BoundsSpecified.Location)
    End Sub
```

[C#]
```
private void MyForm_Layout(object sender,                      ↵
System.Windows.Forms.LayoutEventArgs e)
{
    // Center the Form on the user's screen everytime it       ↵
requires a Layout.
   this.SetBounds((Screen.GetBounds(this).Width/2) - (this.Width/2),
       (Screen.GetBounds(this).Height/2) - (this.Height/2),
       this.Width, this.Height, BoundsSpecified.Location);
}
```

[C++]
```
private:
    void MyForm_Layout(Object* sender,                          ↵
System::Windows::Forms::LayoutEventArgs* e) {
        // Center the Form on the user's screen everytime       ↵
it requires a Layout.
        this->SetBounds((Screen::GetBounds(this).Width/2) -     ↵
 (this->Width/2),
            (Screen::GetBounds(this).Height/2) - (this->Height/2),
            this->Width, this->Height, BoundsSpecified::Location);
    }
```

Requirements

Namespace: System.Windows.Forms

Platforms: Windows 98, Windows NT 4.0, Windows Millennium Edition, Windows 2000, Windows XP Home Edition, Windows XP Professional, Windows Server 2003 family

Assembly: System.Windows.Forms (in System.Windows.Forms.dll)

Button Class

Represents a Windows button control.

System.Object
  System.MarshalByRefObject
    System.ComponentModel.Component
      System.Windows.Forms.Control
        System.Windows.Forms.ButtonBase
          System.Windows.Forms.Button

[Visual Basic]
```
Public Class Button
   Inherits ButtonBase
   Implements IButtonControl
```
[C#]
```
public class Button : ButtonBase, IButtonControl
```
[C++]
```
public __gc class Button : public ButtonBase, IButtonControl
```
[JScript]
```
public class Button extends ButtonBase implements IButtonControl
```

Thread Safety

Any public static (**Shared** in Visual Basic) members of this type are safe for multithreaded operations. Any instance members are not guaranteed to be thread safe.

Remarks

A **Button** can be clicked by using the mouse, ENTER key, or SPACEBAR if the button has focus.

Set the **AcceptButton** or **CancelButton** property of a **Form** to allow users to click a button by pressing the ENTER or ESC keys even if the button does not have focus. This gives the form the behavior of a dialog box.

When you display a form using the **ShowDialog** method, you can use the **DialogResult** property of a button to specify the return value of **ShowDialog**.

You can change the button's appearance. For example, to make it appear flat for a Web look, set the **FlatStyle** property to **FlatStyle.Flat**. The **FlatStyle** property can also be set to **FlatStyle.Popup**, which appears flat until the mouse pointer passes over the button; then the button takes on the standard Windows button appearance.

> **Note** If the control that has focus accepts and processes the ENTER key press, the **Button** does not process it. For example, if a multiline **TextBox** or another button has focus, that control processes the ENTER key press instead of the accept button.

Example

The following example creates a **Button**, sets its **DialogResult** property to **DialogResult.OK**, and adds it to a **Form**.

[Visual Basic]
```
Private Sub InitializeMyButton()
    ' Create and initialize a Button.
    Dim button1 As New Button()

    ' Set the button to return a value of OK when clicked.
    button1.DialogResult = DialogResult.OK

    ' Add the button to the form.
    Controls.Add(button1)
End Sub 'InitializeMyButton
```

[C#]
```
private void InitializeMyButton()
 {
    // Create and initialize a Button.
    Button button1 = new Button();

    // Set the button to return a value of OK when clicked.
    button1.DialogResult = DialogResult.OK;

    // Add the button to the form.
    Controls.Add(button1);
 }
```

[C++]
```
private:
    void InitializeMyButton() {
        // Create and initialize a Button.
        Button __gc *button1 = new Button();

        // Set the button to return a value of OK when clicked.
        button1->DialogResult = DialogResult::OK;

        // Add the button to the form.
        Controls->Add(button1);
    };
```

[JScript]
```
private function InitializeMyButton()
 {
    // Create and initialize a Button.
    var button1 : Button = new Button();

    // Set the button to return a value of OK when clicked.
    button1.DialogResult = System.Windows.Forms.DialogResult.OK;

    // Add the button to the form.
    Controls.Add(button1);
 }
```

Requirements

Namespace: System.Windows.Forms

Platforms: Windows 98, Windows NT 4.0, Windows Millennium Edition, Windows 2000, Windows XP Home Edition, Windows XP Professional, Windows Server 2003 family, .NET Compact Framework - Windows CE .NET

Assembly: System.Windows.Forms (in System.Windows.Forms.dll)

Button Constructor

Initializes a new instance of the **Button** class.

[Visual Basic]
```
Public Sub New()
```
[C#]
```
public Button();
```
[C++]
```
public: Button();
```
[JScript]
```
public function Button();
```

Remarks

By default the **Button** displays no caption. To specify the caption text, set the **Text** property.

Example

See related example in the **System.Windows.Forms.Button** class topic.

Requirements

Platforms: Windows 98, Windows NT 4.0,
Windows Millennium Edition, Windows 2000,
Windows XP Home Edition, Windows XP Professional,
Windows Server 2003 family,
.NET Compact Framework - Windows CE .NET

Button.CreateParams Property

This member overrides **Control.CreateParams**.

[Visual Basic]
```
Overrides Protected ReadOnly Property CreateParams As CreateParams
```
[C#]
```
protected override CreateParams CreateParams {get;}
```
[C++]
```
protected: __property CreateParams* get_CreateParams();
```
[JScript]
```
protected override function get CreateParams() : CreateParams;
```

Requirements

Platforms: Windows 98, Windows NT 4.0,
Windows Millennium Edition, Windows 2000,
Windows XP Home Edition, Windows XP Professional,
Windows Server 2003 family

Button.DialogResult Property

Gets or sets a value that is returned to the parent form when the button is clicked.

[Visual Basic]
```
Public Overridable Property DialogResult As DialogResult _
   Implements IButtonControl.DialogResult
```
[C#]
```
public virtual DialogResult DialogResult {get; set;}
```
[C++]
```
public: __property virtual DialogResult get_DialogResult();
public: __property virtual void set_DialogResult(DialogResult);
```
[JScript]
```
public function get DialogResult() : DialogResult;
public function set DialogResult(DialogResult);
```

Property Value

One of the **DialogResult** values. The default value is **None**.

Implements

IButtonControl.DialogResult

Exceptions

Exception Type	Condition
InvalidEnumArgument-Exception	The value assigned is not one of the **DialogResult** values.

Remarks

If the value of this property is set to anything other than **Dialog-Result.None**, and if the parent form was displayed through the **ShowDialog** method, clicking the button closes the parent form without your having to hook up any events. The form's **DialogResult** property is then set to the **DialogResult** of the button when the button is clicked.

For example, to create a "Yes/No/Cancel" dialog, simply add three buttons and set their **DialogResult** properties to **DialogResult.Yes**, **DialogResult.No**, and **DialogResult.Cancel**.

Example

See related example in the **System.Windows.Forms.Button** class topic.

Requirements

Platforms: Windows 98, Windows NT 4.0,
Windows Millennium Edition, Windows 2000,
Windows XP Home Edition, Windows XP Professional,
Windows Server 2003 family,
.NET Compact Framework - Windows CE .NET

Button.NotifyDefault Method

Notifies the **Button** whether it is the default button so that it can adjust its appearance accordingly.

[Visual Basic]
```
Public Overridable Sub NotifyDefault( _
   ByVal value As Boolean _
) Implements IButtonControl.NotifyDefault
```
[C#]
```
public virtual void NotifyDefault(
   bool value
);
```
[C++]
```
public: virtual void NotifyDefault(
   bool value
);
```
[JScript]
```
public function NotifyDefault(
   value : Boolean
);
```

Parameters

value
: **true** if the button is to have the appearance of the default button; otherwise, **false**.

Implements

IButtonControl.NotifyDefault

Remarks

This method is called by the parent form to notify the **Button** that it should be set as the default button and to allow it to adjust its appearance accordingly. Typically, a button that is the default button for a form has a thicker border than other buttons on the form.

Calling the **NotifyDefault** method only draws the button as a default button; it does not change its behavior. To make the button behave like a default button, it must be assigned to the **AcceptButton** property of the **Form**.

Notes to Inheritors: When overriding **NotifyDefault** in a derived class, be sure to call the base class's **NotifyDefault** method.

Requirements

Platforms: Windows 98, Windows NT 4.0,
Windows Millennium Edition, Windows 2000,
Windows XP Home Edition, Windows XP Professional,
Windows Server 2003 family

Button.OnClick Method

This member overrides **Control.OnClick**.

```
[Visual Basic]
Overrides Protected Sub OnClick( _
   ByVal e As EventArgs _
)
[C#]
protected override void OnClick(
   EventArgs e
);
[C++]
protected: void OnClick(
   EventArgs* e
);
[JScript]
protected override function OnClick(
   e : EventArgs
);
```

Requirements

Platforms: Windows 98, Windows NT 4.0, Windows Millennium Edition, Windows 2000, Windows XP Home Edition, Windows XP Professional, Windows Server 2003 family, .NET Compact Framework - Windows CE .NET

Button.OnMouseUp Method

This member overrides **Control.OnMouseUp**.

```
[Visual Basic]
Overrides Protected Sub OnMouseUp( _
   ByVal mevent As MouseEventArgs _
)
[C#]
protected override void OnMouseUp(
   MouseEventArgs mevent
);
[C++]
protected: void OnMouseUp(
   MouseEventArgs* mevent
);
[JScript]
protected override function OnMouseUp(
   mevent : MouseEventArgs
);
```

Requirements

Platforms: Windows 98, Windows NT 4.0, Windows Millennium Edition, Windows 2000, Windows XP Home Edition, Windows XP Professional, Windows Server 2003 family, .NET Compact Framework - Windows CE .NET

Button.PerformClick Method

Generates a **Click** event for a button.

```
[Visual Basic]
Public Overridable Sub PerformClick() Implements _
   IButtonControl.PerformClick
[C#]
public virtual void PerformClick();
[C++]
public: virtual void PerformClick();
[JScript]
public function PerformClick();
```

Implements

IButtonControl.PerformClick

Remarks

This method can be called to raise the **Click** event.

Example

See related example in the **System.Windows.Forms.Button** class topic.

Requirements

Platforms: Windows 98, Windows NT 4.0, Windows Millennium Edition, Windows 2000, Windows XP Home Edition, Windows XP Professional, Windows Server 2003 family

Button.ProcessMnemonic Method

This member overrides **Control.ProcessMnemonic**.

```
[Visual Basic]
Overrides Protected Function ProcessMnemonic( _
   ByVal charCode As Char _
) As Boolean
[C#]
protected override bool ProcessMnemonic(
   char charCode
);
[C++]
protected: bool ProcessMnemonic(
   __wchar_t charCode
);
[JScript]
protected override function ProcessMnemonic(
   charCode : Char
) : Boolean;
```

Requirements

Platforms: Windows 98, Windows NT 4.0, Windows Millennium Edition, Windows 2000, Windows XP Home Edition, Windows XP Professional, Windows Server 2003 family

Button.ToString Method

This member overrides **Object.ToString**.

```
[Visual Basic]
Overrides Public Function ToString() As String
[C#]
public override string ToString();
[C++]
public: String* ToString();
[JScript]
public override function ToString() : String;
```

Requirements

Platforms: Windows 98, Windows NT 4.0, Windows Millennium Edition, Windows 2000, Windows XP Home Edition, Windows XP Professional, Windows Server 2003 family, .NET Compact Framework - Windows CE .NET

Button.WndProc Method

This member overrides **Control.WndProc**.

[Visual Basic]
```
Overrides Protected Sub WndProc( _
   ByRef m As Message _
)
```
[C#]
```
protected override void WndProc(
   ref Message m
);
```
[C++]
```
protected: void WndProc(
   Message* m
);
```
[JScript]
```
protected override function WndProc(
   m : Message
);
```

Requirements

Platforms: Windows 98, Windows NT 4.0, Windows Millennium Edition, Windows 2000, Windows XP Home Edition, Windows XP Professional, Windows Server 2003 family

Button.DoubleClick Event

This member supports the .NET Framework infrastructure and is not intended to be used directly from your code.

[Visual Basic]
```
Public Shadows Event DoubleClick As EventHandler
```
[C#]
```
public new event EventHandler DoubleClick;
```
[C++]
```
public: __event EventHandler* DoubleClick;
```

[JScript] In JScript, you can handle the events defined by a class, but you cannot define your own.

ButtonBase Class

Implements the basic functionality common to button controls.

System.Object
  System.MarshalByRefObject
    System.ComponentModel.Component
      System.Windows.Forms.Control
        System.Windows.Forms.ButtonBase
          System.Windows.Forms.Button
          System.Windows.Forms.CheckBox
          System.Windows.Forms.RadioButton

```
[Visual Basic]
MustInherit Public Class ButtonBase
   Inherits Control
[C#]
public abstract class ButtonBase : Control
[C++]
public __gc __abstract class ButtonBase : public Control
[JScript]
public abstract class ButtonBase extends Control
```

Thread Safety

Any public static (**Shared** in Visual Basic) members of this type are safe for multithreaded operations. Any instance members are not guaranteed to be thread safe.

Remarks

You do not typically inherit from **ButtonBase**. To create your own button class, inherit from the **Button**, **CheckBox**, or **RadioButton** class.

To have the derived button control display an image, set the **Image** property or the **ImageList** and **ImageIndex** properties. The image can be aligned on the button control by setting the **ImageAlign** property. Likewise, to align the **Text** displayed on the button control, set the **TextAlign** property.

The **FlatStyle** property determines the style and appearance of the control. If the **FlatStyle** property is set to **FlatStyle.System**, the user's operating system determines the appearance of the control.

Requirements

Namespace: System.Windows.Forms

Platforms: Windows 98, Windows NT 4.0, Windows Millennium Edition, Windows 2000, Windows XP Home Edition, Windows XP Professional, Windows Server 2003 family, .NET Compact Framework - Windows CE .NET

Assembly: System.Windows.Forms (in System.Windows.Forms.dll)

ButtonBase Constructor

Initializes a new instance of the **ButtonBase** class.

```
[Visual Basic]
Protected Sub New()
[C#]
protected ButtonBase();
[C++]
protected: ButtonBase();
[JScript]
protected function ButtonBase();
```

Requirements

Platforms: Windows 98, Windows NT 4.0, Windows Millennium Edition, Windows 2000, Windows XP Home Edition, Windows XP Professional, Windows Server 2003 family

ButtonBase.CreateParams Property

This member overrides **Control.CreateParams**.

```
[Visual Basic]
Overrides Protected ReadOnly Property CreateParams As CreateParams
[C#]
protected override CreateParams CreateParams {get;}
[C++]
protected: __property CreateParams* get_CreateParams();
[JScript]
protected override function get CreateParams() : CreateParams;
```

Requirements

Platforms: Windows 98, Windows NT 4.0, Windows Millennium Edition, Windows 2000, Windows XP Home Edition, Windows XP Professional, Windows Server 2003 family

ButtonBase.DefaultImeMode Property

Gets the default Input Method Editor (IME) mode supported by this control.

```
[Visual Basic]
Overrides Protected ReadOnly Property DefaultImeMode As ImeMode
[C#]
protected override ImeMode DefaultImeMode {get;}
[C++]
protected: __property ImeMode get_DefaultImeMode();
[JScript]
protected override function get DefaultImeMode() : ImeMode;
```

Property Value

One of the **ImeMode** values.

Remarks

As implemented in the **ButtonBase** class, this property always returns the **ImeMode.Disable** value.

Requirements

Platforms: Windows 98, Windows NT 4.0, Windows Millennium Edition, Windows 2000, Windows XP Home Edition, Windows XP Professional, Windows Server 2003 family

ButtonBase.DefaultSize Property

This member overrides **Control.DefaultSize**.

```
[Visual Basic]
Overrides Protected ReadOnly Property DefaultSize As Size
[C#]
protected override Size DefaultSize {get;}
[C++]
protected: __property Size get_DefaultSize();
[JScript]
protected override function get DefaultSize() : Size;
```

Requirements

Platforms: Windows 98, Windows NT 4.0, Windows Millennium Edition, Windows 2000, Windows XP Home Edition, Windows XP Professional, Windows Server 2003 family

ButtonBase.FlatStyle Property

Gets or sets the flat style appearance of the button control.

[Visual Basic]
```
Public Property FlatStyle As FlatStyle
```
[C#]
```
public FlatStyle FlatStyle {get; set;}
```
[C++]
```
public: __property FlatStyle get_FlatStyle();
public: __property void set_FlatStyle(FlatStyle);
```
[JScript]
```
public function get FlatStyle() : FlatStyle;
public function set FlatStyle(FlatStyle);
```

Property Value

One of the **FlatStyle** values. The default value is **Standard**.

Exceptions

Exception Type	Condition
InvalidEnumArgument-Exception	The value assigned is not one of the **FlatStyle** values.

Remarks

When the **FlatStyle** property of the **RadioButton** and **CheckBox** classes is set to **FlatStyle.System**, the control is drawn by the user's operating system and the check alignment is based upon the **CheckAlign** and **TextAlign** property values. The **CheckAlign** property value is not changed, but the appearance of the control can be affected. The check box is horizontally aligned with either the left or right edge of the control (a left or center alignment appears left aligned, right remains unchanged), and vertically aligned the same as the descriptive text. For example, if you have a **CheckBox** control with a **CheckAlign** property value of **ContentAlignment.MiddleCenter** and a **TextAlign** property value of **ContentAlignment.TopRight**, and the **FlatStyle** property value is set to **System**, the check box alignment will appear to be **ContentAlignment.TopLeft** while the text alignment remains unchanged.

Note If the **FlatStyle** property is set to **FlatStyle.System**, any images assigned to the **Image** property are not displayed.

Example

The following example uses the derived class, **Button** and sets some of its common properties. The result will be a flat button with text on the left and an image on the right. This code assumes you have a bitmap image named `MyBitMap.bmp` stored in the `C:\Graphics` directory, and a reference to the **System.Drawing** namespace is included.

[Visual Basic]
```
Private Sub SetMyButtonProperties()
    ' Assign an image to the button.
    button1.Image = Image.FromFile("C:\Graphics\MyBitmap.bmp")
    ' Align the image and text on the button.
    button1.ImageAlign = ContentAlignment.MiddleRight
    button1.TextAlign = ContentAlignment.MiddleLeft
    ' Give the button a flat appearance.
    button1.FlatStyle = FlatStyle.Flat
End Sub 'SetMyButtonProperties
```

[C#]
```
private void SetMyButtonProperties()
 {
    // Assign an image to the button.
    button1.Image = Image.FromFile("C:\\Graphics\\MyBitmap.bmp");
    // Align the image and text on the button.
    button1.ImageAlign = ContentAlignment.MiddleRight;
    button1.TextAlign = ContentAlignment.MiddleLeft;
    // Give the button a flat appearance.
    button1.FlatStyle = FlatStyle.Flat;
 }
```

[C++]
```
private:
    void SetMyButtonProperties() {
    // Assign an image to the button.
    button1->Image = Image::FromFile(S"C:\\Graphics\\MyBitmap.bmp");
    // Align the image and text on the button.
    button1->ImageAlign = ContentAlignment::MiddleRight;
    button1->TextAlign = ContentAlignment::MiddleLeft;
    // Give the button a flat appearance.
    button1->FlatStyle = FlatStyle::Flat;
    }
```

[JScript]
```
private function SetMyButtonProperties()
 {
    // Assign an image to the button.
    button1.Image = Image.FromFile("C:\\Graphics\\MyBitmap.bmp");
    // Align the image and text on the button.
    button1.ImageAlign = ContentAlignment.MiddleRight;
    button1.TextAlign = ContentAlignment.MiddleLeft;
    // Give the button a flat appearance.
    button1.FlatStyle = FlatStyle.Flat;
 }
```

Requirements

Platforms: Windows 98, Windows NT 4.0, Windows Millennium Edition, Windows 2000, Windows XP Home Edition, Windows XP Professional, Windows Server 2003 family

ButtonBase.Image Property

Gets or sets the image that is displayed on a button control.

[Visual Basic]
```
Public Property Image As Image
```
[C#]
```
public Image Image {get; set;}
```
[C++]
```
public: __property Image* get_Image();
public: __property void set_Image(Image*);
```
[JScript]
```
public function get Image() : Image;
public function set Image(Image);
```

Property Value

The **Image** displayed on the button control. The default value is a null reference (**Nothing** in Visual Basic).

Remarks

When the **Image** property is set, the **ImageList** property will be set to a null reference (**Nothing** in Visual Basic), and the **ImageIndex** property will be set to its default, -1.

Example

The following example uses the derived class, **Button** and sets some of its common properties. The result will be a flat button with text on the left and an image on the right. This code assumes you have a bitmap image named `MyBitMap.bmp` stored in the `C:\Graphics` directory, and a reference to the **System.Drawing** namespace is included.

[Visual Basic]
```
Private Sub SetMyButtonProperties()
    ' Assign an image to the button.
    button1.Image = Image.FromFile("C:\Graphics\MyBitmap.bmp")
    ' Align the image and text on the button.
    button1.ImageAlign = ContentAlignment.MiddleRight
    button1.TextAlign = ContentAlignment.MiddleLeft
    ' Give the button a flat appearance.
    button1.FlatStyle = FlatStyle.Flat
End Sub 'SetMyButtonProperties
```

[C#]
```
private void SetMyButtonProperties()
 {
    // Assign an image to the button.
    button1.Image = Image.FromFile("C:\\Graphics\\MyBitmap.bmp");
    // Align the image and text on the button.
    button1.ImageAlign = ContentAlignment.MiddleRight;
    button1.TextAlign = ContentAlignment.MiddleLeft;
    // Give the button a flat appearance.
    button1.FlatStyle = FlatStyle.Flat;
 }
```

[C++]
```
private:
    void SetMyButtonProperties() {
    // Assign an image to the button.
    button1->Image = Image::FromFile(S"C:\\Graphics\\MyBitmap.bmp");
    // Align the image and text on the button.
    button1->ImageAlign = ContentAlignment::MiddleRight;
    button1->TextAlign = ContentAlignment::MiddleLeft;
    // Give the button a flat appearance.
    button1->FlatStyle = FlatStyle::Flat;
    }
```

[JScript]
```
private function SetMyButtonProperties()
 {
    // Assign an image to the button.
    button1.Image = Image.FromFile("C:\\Graphics\\MyBitmap.bmp");
    // Align the image and text on the button.
    button1.ImageAlign = ContentAlignment.MiddleRight;
    button1.TextAlign = ContentAlignment.MiddleLeft;
    // Give the button a flat appearance.
    button1.FlatStyle = FlatStyle.Flat;
 }
```

Requirements

Platforms: Windows 98, Windows NT 4.0, Windows Millennium Edition, Windows 2000, Windows XP Home Edition, Windows XP Professional, Windows Server 2003 family

ButtonBase.ImageAlign Property

Gets or sets the alignment of the image on the button control.

[Visual Basic]
```
Public Property ImageAlign As ContentAlignment
```
[C#]
```
public ContentAlignment ImageAlign {get; set;}
```
[C++]
```
public: __property ContentAlignment get_ImageAlign();
public: __property void set_ImageAlign(ContentAlignment);
```
[JScript]
```
public function get ImageAlign() : ContentAlignment;
public function set ImageAlign(ContentAlignment);
```

Property Value

One of the **ContentAlignment** values. The default value is **MiddleCenter**.

Exceptions

Exception Type	Condition
InvalidEnumArgumentException	The value assigned is not one of the **ContentAlignment** values.

Example

The following example uses the derived class, **Button** and sets some of its common properties. The result will be a flat button with text on the left and an image on the right. This code assumes you have a bitmap image named `MyBitMap.bmp` stored in the `C:\Graphics` directory, and a reference to the **System.Drawing** namespace is included.

[Visual Basic]
```
Private Sub SetMyButtonProperties()
    ' Assign an image to the button.
    button1.Image = Image.FromFile("C:\Graphics\MyBitmap.bmp")
    ' Align the image and text on the button.
    button1.ImageAlign = ContentAlignment.MiddleRight
    button1.TextAlign = ContentAlignment.MiddleLeft
    ' Give the button a flat appearance.
    button1.FlatStyle = FlatStyle.Flat
End Sub 'SetMyButtonProperties
```

[C#]
```
private void SetMyButtonProperties()
 {
    // Assign an image to the button.
    button1.Image = Image.FromFile("C:\\Graphics\\MyBitmap.bmp");
    // Align the image and text on the button.
    button1.ImageAlign = ContentAlignment.MiddleRight;
    button1.TextAlign = ContentAlignment.MiddleLeft;
    // Give the button a flat appearance.
    button1.FlatStyle = FlatStyle.Flat;
 }
```

[C++]
```
private:
    void SetMyButtonProperties() {
    // Assign an image to the button.
    button1->Image = Image::FromFile(S"C:\\Graphics\\MyBitmap.bmp");
    // Align the image and text on the button.
    button1->ImageAlign = ContentAlignment::MiddleRight;
    button1->TextAlign = ContentAlignment::MiddleLeft;
    // Give the button a flat appearance.
    button1->FlatStyle = FlatStyle::Flat;
    }
```

[JScript]
```
private function SetMyButtonProperties()
 {
    // Assign an image to the button.
    button1.Image = Image.FromFile("C:\\Graphics\\MyBitmap.bmp");
    // Align the image and text on the button.
    button1.ImageAlign = ContentAlignment.MiddleRight;
    button1.TextAlign = ContentAlignment.MiddleLeft;
    // Give the button a flat appearance.
    button1.FlatStyle = FlatStyle.Flat;
 }
```

Requirements

Platforms: Windows 98, Windows NT 4.0, Windows Millennium Edition, Windows 2000, Windows XP Home Edition, Windows XP Professional, Windows Server 2003 family

ButtonBase.ImageIndex Property

Gets or sets the image list index value of the image displayed on the button control.

```
[Visual Basic]
Public Property ImageIndex As Integer
[C#]
public int ImageIndex {get; set;}
[C++]
public: __property int get_ImageIndex();
public: __property void set_ImageIndex(int);
[JScript]
public function get ImageIndex() : int;
public function set ImageIndex(int);
```

Property Value

A zero-based index, which represents the image position in an **ImageList**. The default is -1.

Exceptions

Exception Type	Condition
ArgumentException	The assigned value is less than the lower bounds of the **ImageIndex**.

Remarks

When the **ImageIndex** or **ImageList** properties are set, the **Image** property is set to its default value, a null reference (**Nothing** in Visual Basic).

Note If the **ImageList** property value is changed to a null reference (**Nothing**), the **ImageIndex** property returns its default value, -1. However, the assigned **ImageIndex** value is retained internally and used when another **ImageList** object is assigned to the **ImageList** property. If the new **ImageList** assigned to the **ImageList** property has an **ImageCollection.Count** property value that is less than or equal to the value assigned to the **ImageIndex** property minus one (to account for the collection being a zero-based index), the **ImageIndex** property value is adjusted to one less than the **Count** property value. For example, consider a button control whose **ImageList** has three images and whose **ImageIndex** property is set to 2. If a new **ImageList** that has only two images is assigned to the button, the **ImageIndex** value changes to 1.

Example

The following example uses the derived class, **Button** and sets the **ImageList** and **ImageIndex** properties. This code assumes an **ImageList** has been created and a minimum of one **Image** has been assigned to it. This code assumes you have a bitmap image named `MyBitMap.bmp` stored in the `C:\Graphics` directory.

[Visual Basic]
```
Private Sub AddMyImage()
    ' Assign an image to the ImageList.
    ImageList1.Images.Add(Image.FromFile("C:\Graphics\MyBitmap.bmp"))
    ' Assign the ImageList to the button control.
    button1.ImageList = ImageList1
    ' Select the image from the ImageList (using the ImageIndex ↵
property).
    button1.ImageIndex = 0
End Sub 'AddMyImage
```

[C#]
```
private void AddMyImage()
{
    // Assign an image to the ImageList.                              ↵
ImageList1.Images.Add(Image.FromFile("C:\\Graphics\\MyBitmap.bmp"));
    // Assign the ImageList to the button control.
    button1.ImageList = ImageList1;
    // Select the image from the ImageList (using the ImageIndex      ↵
property).
    button1.ImageIndex = 0;
}
```

[C++]
```
private:
    void AddMyImage() {
    // Assign an image to the imageList.
    imageList1->Images-                                               ↵
>Add(Image::FromFile(S"C:\\Graphics\\MyBitmap.bmp"));
    // Assign the imageList to the button control.
    button1->ImageList = imageList1;
    // Select the image from the ImageList (using the                 ↵
ImageIndex property).
    button1->ImageIndex = 0;
    }
```

[JScript]
```
private function AddMyImage()
{
    // Assign an image to the ImageList.
    ImageList1 = new ImageList;
    ImageList1.Images.Add(Image.FromFile("C:\\Graphics\\MyBitmap.bmp"));
    // Assign the ImageList to the button control.
    button1.ImageList = ImageList1;
    // Select the image from the ImageList (using the                 ↵
ImageIndex property).
    button1.ImageIndex = 0;
}
```

Requirements

Platforms: Windows 98, Windows NT 4.0, Windows Millennium Edition, Windows 2000, Windows XP Home Edition, Windows XP Professional, Windows Server 2003 family

ButtonBase.ImageList Property

Gets or sets the **ImageList** that contains the **Image** displayed on a button control.

```
[Visual Basic]
Public Property ImageList As ImageList
[C#]
public ImageList ImageList {get; set;}
[C++]
public: __property ImageList* get_ImageList();
public: __property void set_ImageList(ImageList*);
[JScript]
public function get ImageList() : ImageList;
public function set ImageList(ImageList);
```

Property Value

An **ImageList**. The default value is a null reference (**Nothing** in Visual Basic).

Remarks

When the **ImageList** or **ImageIndex** property is set, the **Image** property is set a null reference (**Nothing** in Visual Basic), which is its default value.

Note If the **ImageList** property value is changed to a null reference (**Nothing**), the **ImageIndex** property returns its default value, -1. However, the assigned **ImageIndex** value is retained internally and used when another **ImageList** is assigned to the **ImageList** property. If the new **ImageList** assigned to the **ImageList** property has an **ImageCollection.Count** property value that is less than or equal to the value assigned to the **ImageIndex** property minus one (because the collection is a zero-based index), the **ImageIndex** property value is adjusted to one less than the **Count** property value. For example, consider a button control whose **ImageList** has three images and whose **ImageIndex** property is set to 2. If a new **ImageList** that has only two images is assigned to the button, the **ImageIndex** value changes to 1.

Example

The following example uses the derived class, **Button** and sets the **ImageList** and **ImageIndex** properties. This code assumes an **ImageList** has been created and a minimum of one **Image** has been assigned to it. This code assumes you have a bitmap image named `MyBitMap.bmp` stored in the `C:\Graphics` directory.

[Visual Basic]
```
Private Sub AddMyImage()
    ' Assign an image to the ImageList.
    ImageList1.Images.Add(Image.FromFile("C:\Graphics\MyBitmap.bmp"))
    ' Assign the ImageList to the button control.
    button1.ImageList = ImageList1
    ' Select the image from the ImageList (using the ↵
ImageIndex property).
    button1.ImageIndex = 0
End Sub 'AddMyImage
```

[C#]
```
private void AddMyImage()
 {
    // Assign an image to the ImageList.
    ImageList1.Images.Add(Image.FromFile("C:\\Graphics\\MyBitmap.bmp"));
    // Assign the ImageList to the button control.
    button1.ImageList = ImageList1;
    // Select the image from the ImageList (using the ImageIndex ↵
property).
    button1.ImageIndex = 0;
 }
```

[C++]
```
private:
    void AddMyImage() {
    // Assign an image to the imageList.
    imageList1->Images- ↵
>Add(Image::FromFile(S"C:\\Graphics\\MyBitmap.bmp"));
    // Assign the imageList to the button control.
    button1->ImageList = imageList1;
    // Select the image from the ImageList (using the ↵
 ImageIndex property).
    button1->ImageIndex = 0;
    }
```

[JScript]
```
private function AddMyImage()
 {
    // Assign an image to the ImageList.
    ImageList1 = new ImageList;
    ImageList1.Images.Add(Image.FromFile("C:\\Graphics\\MyBitmap.bmp"));
    // Assign the ImageList to the button control.
    button1.ImageList = ImageList1;
    // Select the image from the ImageList (using the ↵
ImageIndex property).
    button1.ImageIndex = 0;
 }
```

Requirements

Platforms: Windows 98, Windows NT 4.0, Windows Millennium Edition, Windows 2000, Windows XP Home Edition, Windows XP Professional, Windows Server 2003 family

ButtonBase.ImeMode Property

Gets or sets the Input Method Editor (IME) mode supported by this control.

[Visual Basic]
```
Public Shadows Property ImeMode As ImeMode
```
[C#]
```
public new ImeMode ImeMode {get; set;}
```
[C++]
```
public: __property ImeMode get_ImeMode();
public: __property void set_ImeMode(ImeMode);
```
[JScript]
```
public hide function get ImeMode() : ImeMode;
public hide function set ImeMode(ImeMode);
```

Property Value

One of the **ImeMode** values.

Requirements

Platforms: Windows 98, Windows NT 4.0, Windows Millennium Edition, Windows 2000, Windows XP Home Edition, Windows XP Professional, Windows Server 2003 family

ButtonBase.IsDefault Property

Gets or sets a value indicating whether the button control is the default button.

[Visual Basic]
```
Protected Property IsDefault As Boolean
```
[C#]
```
protected bool IsDefault {get; set;}
```
[C++]
```
protected: __property bool get_IsDefault();
protected: __property void set_IsDefault(bool);
```
[JScript]
```
protected function get IsDefault() : Boolean;
protected function set IsDefault(Boolean);
```

Property Value

true if the button control is the default button; otherwise, **false**.

Remarks

When the **IsDefault** property is set to **true**, the button is the default button for the **Form**. This means that the button is clicked when the ENTER key is pressed if no other button or any other control that captures the ENTER key has focus.

To specify the default button of a form, set the **AcceptButton** property of the form to the desired button.

Requirements

Platforms: Windows 98, Windows NT 4.0, Windows Millennium Edition, Windows 2000, Windows XP Home Edition, Windows XP Professional, Windows Server 2003 family

ButtonBase.TextAlign Property

Gets or sets the alignment of the text on the button control.

```
[Visual Basic]
Public Overridable Property TextAlign As ContentAlignment
[C#]
public virtual ContentAlignment TextAlign {get; set;}
[C++]
public: __property virtual ContentAlignment get_TextAlign();
public: __property virtual void set_TextAlign(ContentAlignment);
[JScript]
public function get TextAlign() : ContentAlignment;
public function set TextAlign(ContentAlignment);
```

Property Value

One of the **ContentAlignment** values. The default is **MiddleCenter**.

Exceptions

Exception Type	Condition
InvalidEnumArgument-Exception	The value assigned is not one of the **ContentAlignment** values.

Example

The following example uses the derived class, **Button** and sets some of its common properties. The result will be a flat button with text on the left and an image on the right. This code assumes you have a bitmap image named `MyBitMap.bmp` stored in the `C:\Graphics` directory, and a reference to the **System.Drawing** namespace is included.

```
[Visual Basic]
Private Sub SetMyButtonProperties()
    ' Assign an image to the button.
    button1.Image = Image.FromFile("C:\Graphics\MyBitmap.bmp")
    ' Align the image and text on the button.
    button1.ImageAlign = ContentAlignment.MiddleRight
    button1.TextAlign = ContentAlignment.MiddleLeft
    ' Give the button a flat appearance.
    button1.FlatStyle = FlatStyle.Flat
End Sub 'SetMyButtonProperties
```

```
[C#]
private void SetMyButtonProperties()
 {
    // Assign an image to the button.
    button1.Image = Image.FromFile("C:\\Graphics\\MyBitmap.bmp");
    // Align the image and text on the button.
    button1.ImageAlign = ContentAlignment.MiddleRight;
    button1.TextAlign = ContentAlignment.MiddleLeft;
    // Give the button a flat appearance.
    button1.FlatStyle = FlatStyle.Flat;
 }
```

```
[C++]
private:
    void SetMyButtonProperties() {
    // Assign an image to the button.
    button1->Image = Image::FromFile(S"C:\\Graphics\\MyBitmap.bmp");
    // Align the image and text on the button.
    button1->ImageAlign = ContentAlignment::MiddleRight;
    button1->TextAlign = ContentAlignment::MiddleLeft;
    // Give the button a flat appearance.
    button1->FlatStyle = FlatStyle::Flat;
    }
```

```
[JScript]
private function SetMyButtonProperties()
 {
    // Assign an image to the button.
    button1.Image = Image.FromFile("C:\\Graphics\\MyBitmap.bmp");
    // Align the image and text on the button.
    button1.ImageAlign = ContentAlignment.MiddleRight;
    button1.TextAlign = ContentAlignment.MiddleLeft;
    // Give the button a flat appearance.
    button1.FlatStyle = FlatStyle.Flat;
 }
```

Requirements

Platforms: Windows 98, Windows NT 4.0, Windows Millennium Edition, Windows 2000, Windows XP Home Edition, Windows XP Professional, Windows Server 2003 family

ButtonBase.CreateAccessibilityInstance Method

This member overrides **Control.CreateAccessibilityInstance**.

```
[Visual Basic]
Overrides Protected Function CreateAccessibilityInstance() As _
   AccessibleObject
[C#]
protected override AccessibleObject CreateAccessibilityInstance();
[C++]
protected: AccessibleObject* CreateAccessibilityInstance();
[JScript]
protected override function CreateAccessibilityInstance() :
   AccessibleObject;
```

Requirements

Platforms: Windows 98, Windows NT 4.0, Windows Millennium Edition, Windows 2000, Windows XP Home Edition, Windows XP Professional, Windows Server 2003 family

ButtonBase.Dispose Method

Overload List

This member supports the .NET Framework infrastructure and is not intended to be used directly from your code.

Supported by the .NET Compact Framework.

[Visual Basic] **Overloads Overrides Protected Sub Dispose(Boolean)**

[C#] **protected override void Dispose(bool);**

[C++] **protected: void Dispose(bool);**

[JScript] **protected override function Dispose(Boolean);**

Inherited from **Component**.

Supported by the .NET Compact Framework.

[Visual Basic] **Overloads Public Overridable Sub Dispose() Implements IDisposable.Dispose**

[C#] **public virtual void Dispose();**

[C++] **public: virtual void Dispose();**

[JScript] **public function Dispose();**

ButtonBase.Dispose Method (Boolean)

This member overrides **Control.Dispose**.

[Visual Basic]
```
Overrides Overloads Protected Sub Dispose( _
   ByVal disposing As Boolean _
)
```
[C#]
```
protected override void Dispose(
   bool disposing
);
```
[C++]
```
protected: void Dispose(
   bool disposing
);
```
[JScript]
```
protected override function Dispose(
   disposing : Boolean
);
```

Requirements

Platforms: Windows 98, Windows NT 4.0, Windows Millennium Edition, Windows 2000, Windows XP Home Edition, Windows XP Professional, Windows Server 2003 family, .NET Compact Framework - Windows CE .NET

ButtonBase.OnEnabledChanged Method

This member overrides **Control.OnEnabledChanged**.

[Visual Basic]
```
Overrides Protected Sub OnEnabledChanged( _
   ByVal e As EventArgs _
)
```
[C#]
```
protected override void OnEnabledChanged(
   EventArgs e
);
```
[C++]
```
protected: void OnEnabledChanged(
   EventArgs* e
);
```
[JScript]
```
protected override function OnEnabledChanged(
   e : EventArgs
);
```

Requirements

Platforms: Windows 98, Windows NT 4.0, Windows Millennium Edition, Windows 2000, Windows XP Home Edition, Windows XP Professional, Windows Server 2003 family, .NET Compact Framework - Windows CE .NET

ButtonBase.OnGotFocus Method

This member overrides **Control.OnGotFocus**.

[Visual Basic]
```
Overrides Protected Sub OnGotFocus( _
   ByVal e As EventArgs _
)
```
[C#]
```
protected override void OnGotFocus(
   EventArgs e
);
```
[C++]
```
protected: void OnGotFocus(
   EventArgs* e
);
```
[JScript]
```
protected override function OnGotFocus(
   e : EventArgs
);
```

Requirements

Platforms: Windows 98, Windows NT 4.0, Windows Millennium Edition, Windows 2000, Windows XP Home Edition, Windows XP Professional, Windows Server 2003 family, .NET Compact Framework - Windows CE .NET

ButtonBase.OnKeyDown Method

This member overrides **Control.OnKeyDown**.

[Visual Basic]
```
Overrides Protected Sub OnKeyDown( _
   ByVal kevent As KeyEventArgs _
)
```
[C#]
```
protected override void OnKeyDown(
   KeyEventArgs kevent
);
```
[C++]
```
protected: void OnKeyDown(
   KeyEventArgs* kevent
);
```
[JScript]
```
protected override function OnKeyDown(
   kevent : KeyEventArgs
);
```

Requirements

Platforms: Windows 98, Windows NT 4.0, Windows Millennium Edition, Windows 2000, Windows XP Home Edition, Windows XP Professional, Windows Server 2003 family, .NET Compact Framework - Windows CE .NET

ButtonBase.OnKeyUp Method

This member overrides **Control.OnKeyUp**.

[Visual Basic]
```
Overrides Protected Sub OnKeyUp( _
   ByVal kevent As KeyEventArgs _
)
```
[C#]
```
protected override void OnKeyUp(
   KeyEventArgs kevent
);
```
[C++]
```
protected: void OnKeyUp(
   KeyEventArgs* kevent
);
```

```
[JScript]
protected override function OnKeyUp(
   kevent : KeyEventArgs
);
```

Requirements

Platforms: Windows 98, Windows NT 4.0, Windows Millennium Edition, Windows 2000, Windows XP Home Edition, Windows XP Professional, Windows Server 2003 family, .NET Compact Framework - Windows CE .NET

ButtonBase.OnLostFocus Method

This member overrides **Control.OnLostFocus**.

```
[Visual Basic]
Overrides Protected Sub OnLostFocus( _
   ByVal e As EventArgs _
)
[C#]
protected override void OnLostFocus(
   EventArgs e
);
[C++]
protected: void OnLostFocus(
   EventArgs* e
);
[JScript]
protected override function OnLostFocus(
   e : EventArgs
);
```

Requirements

Platforms: Windows 98, Windows NT 4.0, Windows Millennium Edition, Windows 2000, Windows XP Home Edition, Windows XP Professional, Windows Server 2003 family, .NET Compact Framework - Windows CE .NET

ButtonBase.OnMouseDown Method

This member overrides **Control.OnMouseDown**.

```
[Visual Basic]
Overrides Protected Sub OnMouseDown( _
   ByVal mevent As MouseEventArgs _
)
[C#]
protected override void OnMouseDown(
   MouseEventArgs mevent
);
[C++]
protected: void OnMouseDown(
   MouseEventArgs* mevent
);
[JScript]
protected override function OnMouseDown(
   mevent : MouseEventArgs
);
```

Requirements

Platforms: Windows 98, Windows NT 4.0, Windows Millennium Edition, Windows 2000, Windows XP Home Edition, Windows XP Professional, Windows Server 2003 family, .NET Compact Framework - Windows CE .NET

ButtonBase.OnMouseEnter Method

This member overrides **Control.OnMouseEnter**.

```
[Visual Basic]
Overrides Protected Sub OnMouseEnter( _
   ByVal eventargs As EventArgs _
)
[C#]
protected override void OnMouseEnter(
   EventArgs eventargs
);
[C++]
protected: void OnMouseEnter(
   EventArgs* eventargs
);
[JScript]
protected override function OnMouseEnter(
   eventargs : EventArgs
);
```

Requirements

Platforms: Windows 98, Windows NT 4.0, Windows Millennium Edition, Windows 2000, Windows XP Home Edition, Windows XP Professional, Windows Server 2003 family

ButtonBase.OnMouseLeave Method

This member overrides **Control.OnMouseLeave**.

```
[Visual Basic]
Overrides Protected Sub OnMouseLeave( _
   ByVal eventargs As EventArgs _
)
[C#]
protected override void OnMouseLeave(
   EventArgs eventargs
);
[C++]
protected: void OnMouseLeave(
   EventArgs* eventargs
);
[JScript]
protected override function OnMouseLeave(
   eventargs : EventArgs
);
```

Requirements

Platforms: Windows 98, Windows NT 4.0, Windows Millennium Edition, Windows 2000, Windows XP Home Edition, Windows XP Professional, Windows Server 2003 family

ButtonBase.OnMouseMove Method

This member overrides **Control.OnMouseMove**.

```
[Visual Basic]
Overrides Protected Sub OnMouseMove( _
   ByVal mevent As MouseEventArgs _
)
[C#]
protected override void OnMouseMove(
   MouseEventArgs mevent
);
[C++]
protected: void OnMouseMove(
   MouseEventArgs* mevent
);
[JScript]
protected override function OnMouseMove(
   mevent : MouseEventArgs
);
```

Requirements

Platforms: Windows 98, Windows NT 4.0, Windows Millennium Edition, Windows 2000, Windows XP Home Edition, Windows XP Professional, Windows Server 2003 family, .NET Compact Framework - Windows CE .NET

ButtonBase.OnMouseUp Method

This member overrides **Control.OnMouseUp**.

```
[Visual Basic]
Overrides Protected Sub OnMouseUp( _
   ByVal mevent As MouseEventArgs _
)
[C#]
protected override void OnMouseUp(
   MouseEventArgs mevent
);
[C++]
protected: void OnMouseUp(
   MouseEventArgs* mevent
);
[JScript]
protected override function OnMouseUp(
   mevent : MouseEventArgs
);
```

Requirements

Platforms: Windows 98, Windows NT 4.0, Windows Millennium Edition, Windows 2000, Windows XP Home Edition, Windows XP Professional, Windows Server 2003 family, .NET Compact Framework - Windows CE .NET

ButtonBase.OnPaint Method

This member overrides **Control.OnPaint**.

```
[Visual Basic]
Overrides Protected Sub OnPaint( _
   ByVal pevent As PaintEventArgs _
)
[C#]
protected override void OnPaint(
   PaintEventArgs pevent
);
[C++]
protected: void OnPaint(
   PaintEventArgs* pevent
);
[JScript]
protected override function OnPaint(
   pevent : PaintEventArgs
);
```

Requirements

Platforms: Windows 98, Windows NT 4.0, Windows Millennium Edition, Windows 2000, Windows XP Home Edition, Windows XP Professional, Windows Server 2003 family, .NET Compact Framework - Windows CE .NET

ButtonBase.OnParentChanged Method

This member overrides **Control.OnParentChanged**.

```
[Visual Basic]
Overrides Protected Sub OnParentChanged( _
   ByVal e As EventArgs _
)
[C#]
protected override void OnParentChanged(
   EventArgs e
);
[C++]
protected: void OnParentChanged(
   EventArgs* e
);
[JScript]
protected override function OnParentChanged(
   e : EventArgs
);
```

Requirements

Platforms: Windows 98, Windows NT 4.0, Windows Millennium Edition, Windows 2000, Windows XP Home Edition, Windows XP Professional, Windows Server 2003 family, .NET Compact Framework - Windows CE .NET

ButtonBase.OnTextChanged Method

This member overrides **Control.OnTextChanged**.

```
[Visual Basic]
Overrides Protected Sub OnTextChanged( _
   ByVal e As EventArgs _
)
[C#]
protected override void OnTextChanged(
   EventArgs e
);
[C++]
protected: void OnTextChanged(
   EventArgs* e
);
```

[JScript]
```
protected override function OnTextChanged(
   e : EventArgs
);
```

Requirements

Platforms: Windows 98, Windows NT 4.0, Windows Millennium Edition, Windows 2000, Windows XP Home Edition, Windows XP Professional, Windows Server 2003 family, .NET Compact Framework - Windows CE .NET

ButtonBase.OnVisibleChanged Method

This member overrides **Control.OnVisibleChanged**.

[Visual Basic]
```
Overrides Protected Sub OnVisibleChanged( _
   ByVal e As EventArgs _
)
```
[C#]
```
protected override void OnVisibleChanged(
   EventArgs e
);
```
[C++]
```
protected: void OnVisibleChanged(
   EventArgs* e
);
```
[JScript]
```
protected override function OnVisibleChanged(
   e : EventArgs
);
```

Requirements

Platforms: Windows 98, Windows NT 4.0, Windows Millennium Edition, Windows 2000, Windows XP Home Edition, Windows XP Professional, Windows Server 2003 family

ButtonBase.ResetFlagsandPaint Method

This member supports the .NET Framework infrastructure and is not intended to be used directly from your code.

[Visual Basic]
```
Protected Sub ResetFlagsandPaint()
```
[C#]
```
protected void ResetFlagsandPaint();
```
[C++]
```
protected: void ResetFlagsandPaint();
```
[JScript]
```
protected function ResetFlagsandPaint();
```

ButtonBase.WndProc Method

This member overrides **Control.WndProc**.

[Visual Basic]
```
Overrides Protected Sub WndProc( _
   ByRef m As Message _
)
```
[C#]
```
protected override void WndProc(
   ref Message m
);
```
[C++]
```
protected: void WndProc(
   Message* m
);
```
[JScript]
```
protected override function WndProc(
   m : Message
);
```

Requirements

Platforms: Windows 98, Windows NT 4.0, Windows Millennium Edition, Windows 2000, Windows XP Home Edition, Windows XP Professional, Windows Server 2003 family

ButtonBase.ImeModeChanged Event

This member supports the .NET Framework infrastructure and is not intended to be used directly from your code.

[Visual Basic]
```
Public Shadows Event ImeModeChanged As EventHandler
```
[C#]
```
public new event EventHandler ImeModeChanged;
```
[C++]
```
public: __event EventHandler* ImeModeChanged;
```

[JScript] In JScript, you can handle the events defined by a class, but you cannot define your own.

ButtonBase.ButtonBase-AccessibleObject Class

This type supports the .NET Framework infrastructure and is not intended to be used directly from your code.

```
[Visual Basic]
<ComVisible(True)>
Public Class ButtonBase.ButtonBaseAccessibleObject
   Inherits Control.ControlAccessibleObject
[C#]
[ComVisible(true)]
public class ButtonBase.ButtonBaseAccessibleObject :
   Control.ControlAccessibleObject
[C++]
[ComVisible(true)]
public __gc class ButtonBase.ButtonBaseAccessibleObject : public
   Control.ControlAccessibleObject
[JScript]
public
   ComVisible(true)
class ButtonBase.ButtonBaseAccessibleObject extends
   Control.ControlAccessibleObject
```

ButtonBase.ButtonBaseAccessible-Object Constructor

This member supports the .NET Framework infrastructure and is not intended to be used directly from your code.

```
[Visual Basic]
Public Sub New( _
   ByVal owner As Control _
)
[C#]
public ButtonBase.ButtonBaseAccessibleObject(
   Control owner
);
[C++]
public: ButtonBaseAccessibleObject(
   Control* owner
);
[JScript]
public function ButtonBase.ButtonBaseAccessibleObject(
   owner : Control
);
```

ButtonBase.ButtonBaseAccessible-Object.DoDefaultAction Method

This member overrides **AccessibleObject.DoDefaultAction**.

```
[Visual Basic]
Overrides Public Sub DoDefaultAction()
[C#]
public override void DoDefaultAction();
[C++]
public: void DoDefaultAction();
[JScript]
public override function DoDefaultAction();
```

Requirements

Platforms: Windows 98, Windows NT 4.0, Windows Millennium Edition, Windows 2000, Windows XP Home Edition, Windows XP Professional, Windows Server 2003 family

ButtonBorderStyle Enumeration

Specifies the border style for a button control.

[Visual Basic]

```
<Serializable>
Public Enum ButtonBorderStyle
```

[C#]

```
[Serializable]
public enum ButtonBorderStyle
```

[C++]

```
[Serializable]
__value public enum ButtonBorderStyle
```

[JScript]

```
public
   Serializable
enum ButtonBorderStyle
```

Remarks

This enumeration is used by **ControlPaint.DrawBorder**.

DrawBorder updates the display of the button when controls are initially drawn or refreshed.

Members

Member name	Description
Dashed	A dashed border.
Dotted	A dotted-line border.
Inset	A sunken border.
None	No border.
Outset	A raised border.
Solid	A solid border.

Requirements

Namespace: System.Windows.Forms

Platforms: Windows 98, Windows NT 4.0, Windows Millennium Edition, Windows 2000, Windows XP Home Edition, Windows XP Professional, Windows Server 2003 family

Assembly: System.Windows.Forms (in System.Windows.Forms.dll)

ButtonState Enumeration

Specifies the appearance of a button.

This enumeration has a **FlagsAttribute** attribute that allows a bitwise combination of its member values.

[Visual Basic]
```
<Flags>
<Serializable>
Public Enum ButtonState
```
[C#]
```
[Flags]
[Serializable]
public enum ButtonState
```
[C++]
```
[Flags]
[Serializable]
__value public enum ButtonState
```
[JScript]
```
public
   Flags
   Serializable
enum ButtonState
```

Remarks

This enumeration represents the different states of a button. The default state is **Normal**.

Members

Member name	Description	Value
All	All flags except **Normal** are set.	18176
Checked	The button has a checked or latched appearance. Use this appearance to show that a toggle button has been pressed.	1024
Flat	The button has a flat, two-dimensional appearance.	16384
Inactive	The button is inactive (grayed).	256
Normal	The button has its normal appearance (three-dimensional).	0
Pushed	The button appears pressed.	512

Example

[Visual Basic, C#, C++] In this example, you use the **ButtonState** enumeration as a parameter to the method **DrawButton** to specify the state of `button1`. To run the example, create two buttons, `button1` and `button2`. Then replace the `button2_Click` method with the example code. Click `button2` to redraw `button1` and change its state to **Flat**.

[Visual Basic]
```
Private Sub button2_Click(sender As Object, e As System.EventArgs)
    ' Draws a flat button on button1.

ControlPaint.DrawButton(System.Drawing.Graphics.FromHwnd(button1.Handle)
, 0, 0, button1.Width, button1.Height, ButtonState.Flat)
End Sub 'button2_Click
```

[C#]
```
private void button2_Click(object sender, System.EventArgs e)
{
    // Draws a flat button on button1.
    ControlPaint.DrawButton(
    System.Drawing.Graphics.FromHwnd                                   ↵
(button1.Handle),0,0,button1.Width,button1.Height,
            ButtonState.Flat);
}
```

[C++]
```
private:
    void button2_Click(Object* sender, System::EventArgs* e) {
        // Draws a flat button on button1.
        ControlPaint::DrawButton(System::Drawing::Graphics::FromHwnd ↵
 (button1->Handle),
            0, 0, button1->Width, button1->Height,                   ↵
ButtonState::Flat);
    }
```

Requirements

Namespace: System.Windows.Forms

Platforms: Windows 98, Windows NT 4.0, Windows Millennium Edition, Windows 2000, Windows XP Home Edition, Windows XP Professional, Windows Server 2003 family

Assembly: System.Windows.Forms (in System.Windows.Forms.dll)

CaptionButton Enumeration

Specifies the type of caption button to display.

[Visual Basic]
```
<Serializable>
Public Enum CaptionButton
```
[C#]
```
[Serializable]
public enum CaptionButton
```
[C++]
```
[Serializable]
__value public enum CaptionButton
```
[JScript]
```
public
   Serializable
enum CaptionButton
```

Remarks

This enumeration is used by **ControlPaint.DrawCaptionButton**.

Caption buttons are the system buttons usually found on the rightmost side of a form's title bar.

Members

Member name	Description
Close	A Close button.
Help	A Help button.
Maximize	A Maximize button.
Minimize	A Minimize button.
Restore	A Restore button.

Requirements

Namespace: System.Windows.Forms

Platforms: Windows 98, Windows NT 4.0, Windows Millennium Edition, Windows 2000, Windows XP Home Edition, Windows XP Professional, Windows Server 2003 family

Assembly: System.Windows.Forms (in System.Windows.Forms.dll)

CharacterCasing Enumeration

Specifies the case of characters in a **TextBox** control.

[Visual Basic]
```
<Serializable>
Public Enum CharacterCasing
```
[C#]
```
[Serializable]
public enum CharacterCasing
```
[C++]
```
[Serializable]
__value public enum CharacterCasing
```
[JScript]
```
public
   Serializable
enum CharacterCasing
```

Remarks

Use the members of this enumeration to set the value of the **CharacterCasing** property of the **TextBox** control.

Members

Member name	Description
Lower	Converts all characters to lowercase.
Normal	The case of characters is left unchanged.
Upper	Converts all characters to uppercase.

Example

[Visual Basic, C#, JScript] The following example creates a **TextBox** control that is used to accept a password. This example uses the **CharacterCasing** property to change all characters typed to uppercase and the **MaxLength** property to restrict the password length to eight characters. This example also uses the **TextAlign** property to center the password in the **TextBox** control.

[Visual Basic]
```
Public Sub CreateMyPasswordTextBox()
    ' Create an instance of the TextBox control.
    Dim textBox1 As New TextBox()
    ' Set the maximum length of text in the control to eight.
    textBox1.MaxLength = 8
    ' Assign the asterisk to be the password character.
    textBox1.PasswordChar = "*"c
    ' Change all text entered to be lowercase.
    textBox1.CharacterCasing = CharacterCasing.Upper
    ' Align the text in the center of the TextBox control.
    textBox1.TextAlign = HorizontalAlignment.Center
End Sub
```

[C#]
```
public void CreateMyPasswordTextBox()
 {
    // Create an instance of the TextBox control.
    TextBox textBox1 = new TextBox();
    // Set the maximum length of text in the control to eight.
    textBox1.MaxLength = 8;
    // Assign the asterisk to be the password character.
    textBox1.PasswordChar = '*';
    // Change all text entered to be lowercase.
    textBox1.CharacterCasing = CharacterCasing.Upper;
    // Align the text in the center of the TextBox control.
    textBox1.TextAlign = HorizontalAlignment.Center;
 }
```

[JScript]
```
public function CreateMyPasswordTextBox()
 {
    // Create an instance of the TextBox control.
    textBox1 = new TextBox();
    // Set the maximum length of text in the control to eight.
    textBox1.MaxLength = 8;
    // Assign the asterisk to be the password character.
    textBox1.PasswordChar = '*';
    // Change all text entered to be lowercase.
    textBox1.CharacterCasing = CharacterCasing.Upper;
    // Align the text in the center of the TextBox control.
    textBox1.TextAlign = HorizontalAlignment.Center;
 }
```

Requirements

Namespace: System.Windows.Forms

Platforms: Windows 98, Windows NT 4.0, Windows Millennium Edition, Windows 2000, Windows XP Home Edition, Windows XP Professional, Windows Server 2003 family

Assembly: System.Windows.Forms (in System.Windows.Forms.dll)

CheckBox Class

Represents a Windows check box.

System.Object
  System.MarshalByRefObject
    System.ComponentModel.Component
      System.Windows.Forms.Control
        System.Windows.Forms.ButtonBase
          System.Windows.Forms.CheckBox

[Visual Basic]
```
Public Class CheckBox
   Inherits ButtonBase
```
[C#]
```
public class CheckBox : ButtonBase
```
[C++]
```
public __gc class CheckBox : public ButtonBase
```
[JScript]
```
public class CheckBox extends ButtonBase
```

Thread Safety

Any public static (**Shared** in Visual Basic) members of this type are safe for multithreaded operations. Any instance members are not guaranteed to be thread safe.

Remarks

Use a **CheckBox** to give the user an option, such as true/false or yes/no. The check box control can display an image or text or both.

CheckBox and **RadioButton** controls have a similar function: they allow the user to choose from a list of options. **CheckBox** controls let the user pick a combination of options. In contrast, **RadioButton** controls allow a user to choose from mutually exclusive options.

The **Appearance** property determines whether the check box appears as a typical check box or as a button.

The **ThreeState** property determines whether the control supports two or three states. Use the **Checked** property to get or set the value of a two-state check box control and use the **CheckState** property to get or set the value of a three-state check box control.

> **Note** If the **ThreeState** property is set to **true**, the **Checked** property will return **true** for either a checked or indeterminate state.

The **FlatStyle** property determines the style and appearance of the control. If the **FlatStyle** property is set to **FlatStyle.System**, the user's operating system determines the appearance of the control.

> **Note** When the **FlatStyle** property is set to **FlatStyle.System**, the **CheckAlign** property is ignored and the control is displayed using the **ContentAlignment.MiddleLeft** or **ContentAlignment.MiddleRight** alignment. If the **CheckAlign** property is set to one of the right alignments, the control is displayed using the **ContentAlignment.MiddleRight** alignment; otherwise, it is displayed using the **ContentAlignment.MiddleLeft** alignment.

The following describes an indeterminate state: You have a check box that determines if the selected text in a **RichTextBox** is bold. When you select text you can click the check box to bold the selection. Likewise, when you select some text, the check box displays whether the selected text is bold. If your selected text contains text that is bold and normal, the check box will have an indeterminate state.

Example

[Visual Basic, C#, JScript] The following example creates and initializes a **CheckBox**, gives it the appearance of a toggle button, sets **AutoCheck** to **false**, and adds it to a **Form**.

[Visual Basic]
```
Public Sub InstantiateMyCheckBox()
    ' Create and initialize a CheckBox.
    Dim checkBox1 As New CheckBox()

    ' Make the check box control appear as a toggle button.
    checkBox1.Appearance = Appearance.Button

    ' Turn off the update of the display on the click of the control.
    checkBox1.AutoCheck = False

    ' Add the check box control to the form.
    Controls.Add(checkBox1)
End Sub 'InstantiateMyCheckBox
```

[C#]
```
public void InstantiateMyCheckBox()
 {
    // Create and initialize a CheckBox.
    CheckBox checkBox1 = new CheckBox();

    // Make the check box control appear as a toggle button.
    checkBox1.Appearance = Appearance.Button;

    // Turn off the update of the display on the click of the control.
    checkBox1.AutoCheck = false;

    // Add the check box control to the form.
    Controls.Add(checkBox1);
 }
```

[JScript]
```
public function InstantiateMyCheckBox()
 {
    // Create and initialize a CheckBox.
    var checkBox1 : CheckBox = new CheckBox();

    // Make the check box control appear as a toggle button.
    checkBox1.Appearance = Appearance.Button;

    // Turn off the update of the display on the click of the control.
    checkBox1.AutoCheck = false;

    // Add the check box control to the form.
    Controls.Add(checkBox1);
 }
```

Requirements

Namespace: System.Windows.Forms

Platforms: Windows 98, Windows NT 4.0, Windows Millennium Edition, Windows 2000, Windows XP Home Edition, Windows XP Professional, Windows Server 2003 family, .NET Compact Framework - Windows CE .NET

Assembly: System.Windows.Forms (in System.Windows.Forms.dll)

CheckBox Constructor

Initializes a new instance of the **CheckBox** class.

[Visual Basic]
```
Public Sub New()
```
[C#]
```
public CheckBox();
```

[C++]
```
public: CheckBox();
```
[JScript]
```
public function CheckBox();
```

Remarks

By default, when a new **CheckBox** is instantiated, **AutoCheck** is set to **true**, **Checked** is set to **false**, and **Appearance** is set to **Normal**.

Example

[Visual Basic, C#, JScript] The following example creates and initializes a **CheckBox**, gives it the appearance of a toggle button, sets **AutoCheck** to **false**, and adds it to a **Form**.

[Visual Basic]
```
Public Sub InstantiateMyCheckBox()
    ' Create and initialize a CheckBox.
    Dim checkBox1 As New CheckBox()

    ' Make the check box control appear as a toggle button.
    checkBox1.Appearance = Appearance.Button

    ' Turn off the update of the display on the click of the control.
    checkBox1.AutoCheck = False

    ' Add the check box control to the form.
    Controls.Add(checkBox1)
End Sub 'InstantiateMyCheckBox
```

[C#]
```
public void InstantiateMyCheckBox()
 {
    // Create and initialize a CheckBox.
    CheckBox checkBox1 = new CheckBox();

    // Make the check box control appear as a toggle button.
    checkBox1.Appearance = Appearance.Button;

    // Turn off the update of the display on the click of the control.
    checkBox1.AutoCheck = false;

    // Add the check box control to the form.
    Controls.Add(checkBox1);
 }
```

[JScript]
```
public function InstantiateMyCheckBox()
 {
    // Create and initialize a CheckBox.
    var checkBox1 : CheckBox = new CheckBox();

    // Make the check box control appear as a toggle button.
    checkBox1.Appearance = Appearance.Button;

    // Turn off the update of the display on the click of the control.
    checkBox1.AutoCheck = false;

    // Add the check box control to the form.
    Controls.Add(checkBox1);
 }
```

Requirements

Platforms: Windows 98, Windows NT 4.0, Windows Millennium Edition, Windows 2000, Windows XP Home Edition, Windows XP Professional, Windows Server 2003 family, .NET Compact Framework - Windows CE .NET

CheckBox.Appearance Property

Gets or sets the value that determines the appearance of a check box control.

[Visual Basic]
```
Public Property Appearance As Appearance
```
[C#]
```
public Appearance Appearance {get; set;}
```
[C++]
```
public: __property Appearance get_Appearance();
public: __property void set_Appearance(Appearance);
```
[JScript]
```
public function get Appearance() : Appearance;
public function set Appearance(Appearance);
```

Property Value

One of the **Appearance** values. The default value is **Normal**.

Exceptions

Exception Type	Condition
InvalidEnumArgument-Exception	The value assigned is not one of the **Appearance** values.

Remarks

If **Appearance** value is set to **Appearance.Normal**, the check box has a typical appearance. If the value is set to **Button**, the check box appears like a toggle button, which can be toggled to an up or down state.

Example

[Visual Basic, C#, JScript] The following example creates and initializes a **CheckBox**, gives it the appearance of a toggle button, sets **AutoCheck** to **false**, and adds it to a **Form**.

[Visual Basic]
```
Public Sub InstantiateMyCheckBox()
    ' Create and initialize a CheckBox.
    Dim checkBox1 As New CheckBox()

    ' Make the check box control appear as a toggle button.
    checkBox1.Appearance = Appearance.Button

    ' Turn off the update of the display on the click of the control.
    checkBox1.AutoCheck = False

    ' Add the check box control to the form.
    Controls.Add(checkBox1)
End Sub 'InstantiateMyCheckBox
```

[C#]
```
public void InstantiateMyCheckBox()
 {
    // Create and initialize a CheckBox.
    CheckBox checkBox1 = new CheckBox();

    // Make the check box control appear as a toggle button.
    checkBox1.Appearance = Appearance.Button;

    // Turn off the update of the display on the click of the control.
    checkBox1.AutoCheck = false;

    // Add the check box control to the form.
    Controls.Add(checkBox1);
 }
```

[JScript]
```
public function InstantiateMyCheckBox()
 {
```

```
    // Create and initialize a CheckBox.
    var checkBox1 : CheckBox = new CheckBox();

    // Make the check box control appear as a toggle button.
    checkBox1.Appearance = Appearance.Button;

    // Turn off the update of the display on the click of the control.
    checkBox1.AutoCheck = false;

    // Add the check box control to the form.
    Controls.Add(checkBox1);
}
```

Requirements

Platforms: Windows 98, Windows NT 4.0, Windows Millennium Edition, Windows 2000, Windows XP Home Edition, Windows XP Professional, Windows Server 2003 family

CheckBox.AutoCheck Property

Gets or set a value indicating whether the **Checked** or **CheckState** values and the check box's appearance are automatically changed when the check box is clicked.

[Visual Basic]
```
Public Property AutoCheck As Boolean
```
[C#]
```
public bool AutoCheck {get; set;}
```
[C++]
```
public: __property bool get_AutoCheck();
public: __property void set_AutoCheck(bool);
```
[JScript]
```
public function get AutoCheck() : Boolean;
public function set AutoCheck(Boolean);
```

Property Value

true if the **Checked** value or **CheckState** value and the appearance of the control are automatically changed on the **Click** event; otherwise, **false**. The default value is **true**.

Remarks

If **AutoCheck** is set to false, you will need to add code to update the **Checked** or **CheckState** values in the **Click** event handler.

Example

[Visual Basic, C#, JScript] The following example creates and initializes a **CheckBox**, gives it the appearance of a toggle button, sets **AutoCheck** to **false**, and adds it to a **Form**.

[Visual Basic]
```
Public Sub InstantiateMyCheckBox()
    ' Create and initialize a CheckBox.
    Dim checkBox1 As New CheckBox()

    ' Make the check box control appear as a toggle button.
    checkBox1.Appearance = Appearance.Button

    ' Turn off the update of the display on the click of the control.
    checkBox1.AutoCheck = False

    ' Add the check box control to the form.
    Controls.Add(checkBox1)
End Sub 'InstantiateMyCheckBox
```

[C#]
```
public void InstantiateMyCheckBox()
{
    // Create and initialize a CheckBox.
    CheckBox checkBox1 = new CheckBox();

    // Make the check box control appear as a toggle button.
    checkBox1.Appearance = Appearance.Button;

    // Turn off the update of the display on the click of the control.
    checkBox1.AutoCheck = false;

    // Add the check box control to the form.
    Controls.Add(checkBox1);
}
```

[JScript]
```
public function InstantiateMyCheckBox()
{
    // Create and initialize a CheckBox.
    var checkBox1 : CheckBox = new CheckBox();

    // Make the check box control appear as a toggle button.
    checkBox1.Appearance = Appearance.Button;

    // Turn off the update of the display on the click of the control.
    checkBox1.AutoCheck = false;

    // Add the check box control to the form.
    Controls.Add(checkBox1);
}
```

Requirements

Platforms: Windows 98, Windows NT 4.0, Windows Millennium Edition, Windows 2000, Windows XP Home Edition, Windows XP Professional, Windows Server 2003 family, .NET Compact Framework - Windows CE .NET

CheckBox.CheckAlign Property

Gets or sets the horizontal and vertical alignment of a check box on a check box control.

[Visual Basic]
```
Public Property CheckAlign As ContentAlignment
```
[C#]
```
public ContentAlignment CheckAlign {get; set;}
```
[C++]
```
public: __property ContentAlignment get_CheckAlign();
public: __property void set_CheckAlign(ContentAlignment);
```
[JScript]
```
public function get CheckAlign() : ContentAlignment;
public function set CheckAlign(ContentAlignment);
```

Property Value

One of the **ContentAlignment** values. The default value is **MiddleLeft**.

Exceptions

Exception Type	Condition
InvalidEnumArgument-Exception	The value assigned is not one of the **ContentAlignment** enumeration values.

Example

[Visual Basic, C#, JScript] The following code example displays the values of three properties in a label. The **ThreeState** property alternates between **true** and **false** with alternating clicks of the button and the **CheckAlign** alternates between **MiddleRight** and **MiddleLeft**. This example shows how the property values change as the **ThreeState** property changes and the button is checked. This code assumes that a **CheckBox**, **Label** and **Button** have all been instantiated on a form and that the label is large enough to display three lines of text, as well as a reference to the **System.Drawing** namespace. This code should be called in the **Click** event handler of the button.

[Visual Basic]
```
Private Sub AdjustMyCheckBoxProperties()
    ' Concatenate the property values together on three lines.
    label1.Text = "ThreeState: " &                                    ↵
checkBox1.ThreeState.ToString() & ControlChars.Cr & _
        "Checked: " & checkBox1.Checked.ToString() &                  ↵
ControlChars.Cr & _
        "CheckState: " & checkBox1.CheckState.ToString()

    ' Change the ThreeState and CheckAlign properties on every        ↵
 other click.
    If Not checkBox1.ThreeState Then
        checkBox1.ThreeState = True
        checkBox1.CheckAlign = ContentAlignment.MiddleRight
    Else
        checkBox1.ThreeState = False
        checkBox1.CheckAlign = ContentAlignment.MiddleLeft
    End If
End Sub 'AdjustMyCheckBoxProperties
```

[C#]
```
private void AdjustMyCheckBoxProperties()
 {
    // Concatenate the property values together on three lines.
    label1.Text = "ThreeState: " +                                    ↵
checkBox1.ThreeState.ToString() + "\n" +
                  "Checked: " + checkBox1.Checked.ToString() + "\n" +
                  "CheckState: " + checkBox1.CheckState.ToString();

    // Change the ThreeState and CheckAlign properties on              ↵
 every other click.
    if (!checkBox1.ThreeState)
    {
       checkBox1.ThreeState = true;
       checkBox1.CheckAlign = ContentAlignment.MiddleRight;
    }
    else
    {
       checkBox1.ThreeState = false;
       checkBox1.CheckAlign = ContentAlignment.MiddleLeft;
    }
 }
```

[JScript]
```
private function AdjustMyCheckBoxProperties()
 {
    // Concatenate the property values together on three lines.
    label1.Text = "ThreeState: " +                                    ↵
checkBox1.ThreeState.ToString() + "\n" +
                  "Checked: " + checkBox1.Checked.ToString() + "\n" +
                  "CheckState: " + checkBox1.CheckState.ToString();

    // Change the ThreeState and CheckAlign properties on every        ↵
 other click.
    if (!checkBox1.ThreeState)
    {
       checkBox1.ThreeState = true;
       checkBox1.CheckAlign = ContentAlignment.MiddleRight;
    }
    else
    {
       checkBox1.ThreeState = false;
       checkBox1.CheckAlign = ContentAlignment.MiddleLeft;
    }
 }
```

Requirements

Platforms: Windows 98, Windows NT 4.0, Windows Millennium Edition, Windows 2000, Windows XP Home Edition, Windows XP Professional, Windows Server 2003 family

CheckBox.Checked Property

Gets or set a value indicating whether the check box is in the checked state.

[Visual Basic]
```
Public Property Checked As Boolean
```
[C#]
```
public bool Checked {get; set;}
```
[C++]
```
public: __property bool get_Checked();
public: __property void set_Checked(bool);
```
[JScript]
```
public function get Checked() : Boolean;
public function set Checked(Boolean);
```

Property Value

true if the check box is in the checked state; otherwise, **false**. The default value is **false**.

> **Note** If the **ThreeState** property is set to **true**, the **Checked** property will return **true** for either a **Checked** or **Indeterminate CheckState**.

Remarks

When the value is **true**, the check box portion of the control displays a check mark. If the **Appearance** property is set to **Button**, the control will appear sunken when **Checked** is **true** and raised like a standard button when **false**.

Example

See related example in the **System.Windows.Forms.CheckBox.Align** property topic.

Requirements

Platforms: Windows 98, Windows NT 4.0, Windows Millennium Edition, Windows 2000, Windows XP Home Edition, Windows XP Professional, Windows Server 2003 family, .NET Compact Framework - Windows CE .NET

CheckBox.CheckState Property

Gets or sets the state of the check box.

[Visual Basic]
```
Public Property CheckState As CheckState
```
[C#]
```
public CheckState CheckState {get; set;}
```
[C++]
```
public: __property CheckState get_CheckState();
public: __property void set_CheckState(CheckState);
```
[JScript]
```
public function get CheckState() : CheckState;
public function set CheckState(CheckState);
```

Property Value

One of the **CheckState** enumeration values. The default value is **Unchecked**.

Exceptions

Exception Type	Condition
InvalidEnumArgument-Exception	The value assigned is not one of the **CheckState** enumeration values.

Remarks

If the **ThreeState** property is set to **false**, the **CheckState** property value can only be set to **CheckState.Indeterminate** in code and not by user interaction.

The following table describes the appearance of the check box control in its different states for the **Appearance.Normal** and **Appearance.Button** style control **Appearance**.

CheckState	Appearance.Normal	Appearance.Button
Checked	The check box displays a check mark.	The control appears sunken.
Unchecked	The check box is empty.	The control appears raised.
Indeterminate	The check box displays a check mark and is shaded.	The control appears flat.

Example

See related example in the **System.Windows.Forms.Check-Box.Align** property topic.

Requirements

Platforms: Windows 98, Windows NT 4.0, Windows Millennium Edition, Windows 2000, Windows XP Home Edition, Windows XP Professional, Windows Server 2003 family, .NET Compact Framework - Windows CE .NET

CheckBox.CreateParams Property

This member overrides **Control.CreateParams**.

```
[Visual Basic]
Overrides Protected ReadOnly Property CreateParams As CreateParams
[C#]
protected override CreateParams CreateParams {get;}
[C++]
protected: __property CreateParams* get_CreateParams();
[JScript]
protected override function get CreateParams() : CreateParams;
```

Requirements

Platforms: Windows 98, Windows NT 4.0, Windows Millennium Edition, Windows 2000, Windows XP Home Edition, Windows XP Professional, Windows Server 2003 family

CheckBox.DefaultSize Property

This member overrides **Control.DefaultSize**.

```
[Visual Basic]
Overrides Protected ReadOnly Property DefaultSize As Size
[C#]
protected override Size DefaultSize {get;}
[C++]
protected: __property Size get_DefaultSize();
[JScript]
protected override function get DefaultSize() : Size;
```

Requirements

Platforms: Windows 98, Windows NT 4.0, Windows Millennium Edition, Windows 2000, Windows XP Home Edition, Windows XP Professional, Windows Server 2003 family

CheckBox.TextAlign Property

This member overrides **ButtonBase.TextAlign**.

```
[Visual Basic]
Overrides Public Property TextAlign As ContentAlignment
[C#]
public override ContentAlignment TextAlign {get; set;}
[C++]
public: __property ContentAlignment get_TextAlign();
public: __property void set_TextAlign(ContentAlignment);
[JScript]
public override function get TextAlign() : ContentAlignment;
public override function set TextAlign(ContentAlignment);
```

Requirements

Platforms: Windows 98, Windows NT 4.0, Windows Millennium Edition, Windows 2000, Windows XP Home Edition, Windows XP Professional, Windows Server 2003 family

CheckBox.ThreeState Property

Gets or sets a value indicating whether the check box will allow three check states rather than two.

```
[Visual Basic]
Public Property ThreeState As Boolean
[C#]
public bool ThreeState {get; set;}
[C++]
public: __property bool get_ThreeState();
public: __property void set_ThreeState(bool);
[JScript]
public function get ThreeState() : Boolean;
public function set ThreeState(Boolean);
```

Property Value

true if the **CheckBox** is able to display three check states; otherwise, **false**. The default value is **false**.

Remarks

If the **ThreeState** property is set to **false**, the **CheckState** property value can only be set to **CheckState.Indeterminate** in code and not by user interaction.

Example

See related example in the **System.Windows.Forms.Check-Box.Align** property topic.

Requirements

Platforms: Windows 98, Windows NT 4.0, Windows Millennium Edition, Windows 2000, Windows XP Home Edition, Windows XP Professional, Windows Server 2003 family, .NET Compact Framework - Windows CE .NET

CheckBox.CreateAccessibilityInstance Method

This member overrides **Control.CreateAccessibilityInstance**.

```
[Visual Basic]
Overrides Protected Function CreateAccessibilityInstance() As _
   AccessibleObject
[C#]
protected override AccessibleObject CreateAccessibilityInstance();
[C++]
protected: AccessibleObject* CreateAccessibilityInstance();
[JScript]
protected override function CreateAccessibilityInstance() :
   AccessibleObject;
```

Requirements

Platforms: Windows 98, Windows NT 4.0, Windows Millennium Edition, Windows 2000, Windows XP Home Edition, Windows XP Professional, Windows Server 2003 family

CheckBox.OnAppearanceChanged Method

Raises the **AppearanceChanged** event.

```
[Visual Basic]
Protected Overridable Sub OnAppearanceChanged( _
   ByVal e As EventArgs _
)
[C#]
protected virtual void OnAppearanceChanged(
   EventArgs e
);
[C++]
protected: virtual void OnAppearanceChanged(
   EventArgs* e
);
[JScript]
protected function OnAppearanceChanged(
   e : EventArgs
);
```

Parameters

e

An **EventArgs** that contains the event data.

Remarks

Raising an event invokes the event handler through a delegate.

The **OnAppearanceChanged** method also allows derived classes to handle the event without attaching a delegate. This is the preferred technique for handling the event in a derived class.

Notes to Inheritors: When overriding **OnAppearanceChanged** in a derived class, be sure to call the base class's **OnAppearance-Changed** method so that registered delegates receive the event.

Requirements

Platforms: Windows 98, Windows NT 4.0, Windows Millennium Edition, Windows 2000, Windows XP Home Edition, Windows XP Professional, Windows Server 2003 family

CheckBox.OnCheckedChanged Method

Raises the **CheckedChanged** event.

```
[Visual Basic]
Protected Overridable Sub OnCheckedChanged( _
   ByVal e As EventArgs _
)
[C#]
protected virtual void OnCheckedChanged(
   EventArgs e
);
[C++]
protected: virtual void OnCheckedChanged(
   EventArgs* e
);
[JScript]
protected function OnCheckedChanged(
   e : EventArgs
);
```

Parameters

e

An **EventArgs** that contains the event data.

Remarks

Raising an event invokes the event handler through a delegate. For more information, see **Raising an Event**.

The **OnCheckedChanged** method also allows derived classes to handle the event without attaching a delegate. This is the preferred technique for handling the event in a derived class.

Notes to Inheritors: When overriding **OnCheckedChanged** in a derived class, be sure to call the base class's **OnCheckedChanged** method so that registered delegates receive the event.

Requirements

Platforms: Windows 98, Windows NT 4.0, Windows Millennium Edition, Windows 2000, Windows XP Home Edition, Windows XP Professional, Windows Server 2003 family

CheckBox.OnCheckStateChanged Method

Raises the **CheckStateChanged** event.

```
[Visual Basic]
Protected Overridable Sub OnCheckStateChanged( _
   ByVal e As EventArgs _
)
[C#]
protected virtual void OnCheckStateChanged(
   EventArgs e
);
[C++]
protected: virtual void OnCheckStateChanged(
   EventArgs* e
);
```

```
[JScript]
protected function OnCheckStateChanged(
   e : EventArgs
);
```

Parameters

e

An **EventArgs** that contains the event data.

Remarks

Raising an event invokes the event handler through a delegate.

The **OnCheckStateChanged** method also allows derived classes to handle the event without attaching a delegate. This is the preferred technique for handling the event in a derived class.

Notes to Inheritors: When overriding **OnCheckStateChanged** in a derived class, be sure to call the base class's **OnCheckStateChanged** method so that registered delegates receive the event.

Requirements

Platforms: Windows 98, Windows NT 4.0, Windows Millennium Edition, Windows 2000, Windows XP Home Edition, Windows XP Professional, Windows Server 2003 family, .NET Compact Framework - Windows CE .NET

CheckBox.OnClick Method

This member overrides **Control.OnClick**.

```
[Visual Basic]
Overrides Protected Sub OnClick( _
   ByVal e As EventArgs _
)
[C#]
protected override void OnClick(
   EventArgs e
);
[C++]
protected: void OnClick(
   EventArgs* e
);
[JScript]
protected override function OnClick(
   e : EventArgs
);
```

Requirements

Platforms: Windows 98, Windows NT 4.0, Windows Millennium Edition, Windows 2000, Windows XP Home Edition, Windows XP Professional, Windows Server 2003 family, .NET Compact Framework - Windows CE .NET

CheckBox.OnHandleCreated Method

This member overrides **Control.OnHandleCreated**.

```
[Visual Basic]
Overrides Protected Sub OnHandleCreated( _
   ByVal e As EventArgs _
)
[C#]
protected override void OnHandleCreated(
   EventArgs e
);
[C++]
protected: void OnHandleCreated(
   EventArgs* e
);
[JScript]
protected override function OnHandleCreated(
   e : EventArgs
);
```

Requirements

Platforms: Windows 98, Windows NT 4.0, Windows Millennium Edition, Windows 2000, Windows XP Home Edition, Windows XP Professional, Windows Server 2003 family

CheckBox.OnMouseUp Method

This member overrides **Control.OnMouseUp**.

```
[Visual Basic]
Overrides Protected Sub OnMouseUp( _
   ByVal mevent As MouseEventArgs _
)
[C#]
protected override void OnMouseUp(
   MouseEventArgs mevent
);
[C++]
protected: void OnMouseUp(
   MouseEventArgs* mevent
);
[JScript]
protected override function OnMouseUp(
   mevent : MouseEventArgs
);
```

Requirements

Platforms: Windows 98, Windows NT 4.0, Windows Millennium Edition, Windows 2000, Windows XP Home Edition, Windows XP Professional, Windows Server 2003 family, .NET Compact Framework - Windows CE .NET

CheckBox.ProcessMnemonic Method

This member overrides **Control.ProcessMnemonic**.

```
[Visual Basic]
Overrides Protected Function ProcessMnemonic( _
   ByVal charCode As Char _
) As Boolean
[C#]
protected override bool ProcessMnemonic(
   char charCode
);
[C++]
protected: bool ProcessMnemonic(
   __wchar_t charCode
);
```

[JScript]
```
protected override function ProcessMnemonic(
   charCode : Char
) : Boolean;
```

Requirements

Platforms: Windows 98, Windows NT 4.0, Windows Millennium Edition, Windows 2000, Windows XP Home Edition, Windows XP Professional, Windows Server 2003 family

CheckBox.ToString Method

This member overrides **Object.ToString**.

[Visual Basic]
```
Overrides Public Function ToString() As String
```
[C#]
```
public override string ToString();
```
[C++]
```
public: String* ToString();
```
[JScript]
```
public override function ToString() : String;
```

Requirements

Platforms: Windows 98, Windows NT 4.0, Windows Millennium Edition, Windows 2000, Windows XP Home Edition, Windows XP Professional, Windows Server 2003 family, .NET Compact Framework - Windows CE .NET

CheckBox.AppearanceChanged Event

Occurs when the value of the **Appearance** property changes.

[Visual Basic]
```
Public Event AppearanceChanged As EventHandler
```
[C#]
```
public event EventHandler AppearanceChanged;
```
[C++]
```
public: __event EventHandler* AppearanceChanged;
```

[JScript] In JScript, you can handle the events defined by a class, but you cannot define your own.

Event Data

The event handler receives an argument of type **EventArgs**.

Requirements

Platforms: Windows 98, Windows NT 4.0, Windows Millennium Edition, Windows 2000, Windows XP Home Edition, Windows XP Professional, Windows Server 2003 family

CheckBox.CheckedChanged Event

Occurs when the value of the **Checked** property changes.

[Visual Basic]
```
Public Event CheckedChanged As EventHandler
```
[C#]
```
public event EventHandler CheckedChanged;
```
[C++]
```
public: __event EventHandler* CheckedChanged;
```

[JScript] In JScript, you can handle the events defined by a class, but you cannot define your own.

Event Data

The event handler receives an argument of type **EventArgs**.

Requirements

Platforms: Windows 98, Windows NT 4.0, Windows Millennium Edition, Windows 2000, Windows XP Home Edition, Windows XP Professional, Windows Server 2003 family

CheckBox.CheckStateChanged Event

Occurs when the value of the **CheckState** property changes.

[Visual Basic]
```
Public Event CheckStateChanged As EventHandler
```
[C#]
```
public event EventHandler CheckStateChanged;
```
[C++]
```
public: __event EventHandler* CheckStateChanged;
```

[JScript] In JScript, you can handle the events defined by a class, but you cannot define your own.

Event Data

The event handler receives an argument of type **EventArgs**.

Requirements

Platforms: Windows 98, Windows NT 4.0, Windows Millennium Edition, Windows 2000, Windows XP Home Edition, Windows XP Professional, Windows Server 2003 family

CheckBox.DoubleClick Event

This member supports the .NET Framework infrastructure and is not intended to be used directly from your code.

[Visual Basic]
```
Public Shadows Event DoubleClick As EventHandler
```
[C#]
```
public new event EventHandler DoubleClick;
```
[C++]
```
public: __event EventHandler* DoubleClick;
```

[JScript] In JScript, you can handle the events defined by a class, but you cannot define your own.

CheckBox.CheckBox-AccessibleObject Class

This type supports the .NET Framework infrastructure and is not intended to be used directly from your code.

```
[Visual Basic]
<ComVisible(True)>
Public Class CheckBox.CheckBoxAccessibleObject
   Inherits ButtonBase.ButtonBaseAccessibleObject
[C#]
[ComVisible(true)]
public class CheckBox.CheckBoxAccessibleObject :
   ButtonBase.ButtonBaseAccessibleObject
[C++]
[ComVisible(true)]
public __gc class CheckBox.CheckBoxAccessibleObject : public
   ButtonBase.ButtonBaseAccessibleObject
[JScript]
public
   ComVisible(true)
class CheckBox.CheckBoxAccessibleObject extends
   ButtonBase.ButtonBaseAccessibleObject
```

Requirements

Platforms: Windows 98, Windows NT 4.0, Windows Millennium Edition, Windows 2000, Windows XP Home Edition, Windows XP Professional, Windows Server 2003 family

CheckBox.CheckBoxAccessibleObject Constructor

This member supports the .NET Framework infrastructure and is not intended to be used directly from your code.

```
[Visual Basic]
Public Sub New( _
   ByVal owner As Control _
)
[C#]
public CheckBox.CheckBoxAccessibleObject(
   Control owner
);
[C++]
public: CheckBoxAccessibleObject(
   Control* owner
);
[JScript]
public function CheckBox.CheckBoxAccessibleObject(
   owner : Control
);
```

CheckBox.CheckBoxAccessibleObject.DefaultAction Property

This member overrides **AccessibleObject.DefaultAction**.

```
[Visual Basic]
Overrides Public ReadOnly Property DefaultAction As String
[C#]
public override string DefaultAction {get;}
[C++]
public: __property String* get_DefaultAction();
[JScript]
public override function get DefaultAction() : String;
```

CheckBox.CheckBoxAccessibleObject.Role Property

This member overrides **AccessibleObject.Role**.

```
[Visual Basic]
Overrides Public ReadOnly Property Role As AccessibleRole
[C#]
public override AccessibleRole Role {get;}
[C++]
public: __property AccessibleRole get_Role();
[JScript]
public override function get Role() : AccessibleRole;
```

Requirements

Platforms: Windows 98, Windows NT 4.0, Windows Millennium Edition, Windows 2000, Windows XP Home Edition, Windows XP Professional, Windows Server 2003 family

CheckBox.CheckBoxAccessibleObject.State Property

This member overrides **AccessibleObject.State**.

```
[Visual Basic]
Overrides Public ReadOnly Property State As AccessibleStates
[C#]
public override AccessibleStates State {get;}
[C++]
public: __property AccessibleStates get_State();
[JScript]
public override function get State() : AccessibleStates;
```

Requirements

Platforms: Windows 98, Windows NT 4.0, Windows Millennium Edition, Windows 2000, Windows XP Home Edition, Windows XP Professional, Windows Server 2003 family

CheckedListBox Class

Displays a **ListBox** in which a check box is displayed to the left of each item.

System.Object
  System.MarshalByRefObject
    System.ComponentModel.Component
      System.Windows.Forms.Control
        System.Windows.Forms.ListControl
          System.Windows.Forms.ListBox
            System.Windows.Forms.CheckedListBox

[Visual Basic]
```
Public Class CheckedListBox
   Inherits ListBox
```
[C#]
```
public class CheckedListBox : ListBox
```
[C++]
```
public __gc class CheckedListBox : public ListBox
```
[JScript]
```
public class CheckedListBox extends ListBox
```

Thread Safety

Any public static (**Shared** in Visual Basic) members of this type are safe for multithreaded operations. Any instance members are not guaranteed to be thread safe.

Remarks

This control presents a list of items that the user can navigate by using the keyboard or the scrollbar on the right side of the control. The user can place a check mark by one or more items and the checked items can be navigated with the **CheckedListBox.CheckedItemCollection** and **CheckedListBox.CheckedIndexCollection**.

To add objects to the list at run time, assign an array of object references with the **AddRange** method. The list then displays the default string value for each object. You can add individual items to the list with the **Add** method.

The **CheckedListBox** object supports three states through the **CheckState** enumeration: **Checked**, **Indeterminate**, and **Unchecked**. You must set the state of **Indeterminate** in the code because the user interface for a **CheckedListBox** does not provide a mechanism to do so.

If **UseTabStops** is **true**, the **CheckedListBox** will recognize and expand tab characters in an item's text, creating columns. However, the tab stops are present and cannot be changed.

The **CheckedListBox** class supports the following three indexed collections:

Collection	Encapsulating Class
All items contained in the **CheckedListBox** control.	**CheckedListBox.ObjectCollection**
Checked items (including items in an indeterminate state), which is a subset of the items contained in the **CheckedListBox** control.	**CheckedListBox.CheckedItemCollection**
Checked indexes, which is a subset of the indexes into the items collection. These indexes specify items in a checked or indeterminate state.	**CheckedListBox.CheckedIndexCollection**

The following three tables are examples of the three indexed collections that the **CheckedListBox** class supports.

The first table provides an example of the indexed collection of items in the control (all items contained in the control).

Index	Item	Check State
0	Object 1	**Unchecked**
1	Object 2	**Checked**
2	Object 3	**Unchecked**
3	Object 4	**Indeterminate**
4	Object 5	**Checked**

The second table provides an example of the indexed collection of the checked items.

Index	Item
0	Object 2
1	Object 4
2	Object 5

The third table provides an example of the indexed collection of indexes of checked items.

Index	Index of Item
0	1
1	3
2	4

Example

[Visual Basic, C#] The following example illustrates how you can use the methods, properties, and collections of a **CheckedListBox**. This is a complete sample ready to run once you have copied it to your project. You can check and uncheck items, use the text box to add items and once you have clicked the save button, clear the checked items.

[Visual Basic]
```
Option Explicit
Option Strict

Imports System
Imports System.Drawing
Imports System.Collections
Imports System.ComponentModel
Imports System.Windows.Forms
Imports System.Data
Imports System.IO

Namespace WindowsApplication1
    Public Class Form1
        Inherits System.Windows.Forms.Form
        Private WithEvents checkedListBox1 As ↵
System.Windows.Forms.CheckedListBox
        Private WithEvents textBox1 As System.Windows.Forms.TextBox
        Private WithEvents button1 As System.Windows.Forms.Button
        Private WithEvents button2 As System.Windows.Forms.Button
        Private WithEvents listBox1 As System.Windows.Forms.ListBox
        Private WithEvents button3 As System.Windows.Forms.Button
        Private components As System.ComponentModel.Container

        Public Sub New()
            InitializeComponent()

            ' Sets up the initial objects in the CheckedListBox.
            Dim myFruit As String() = {"Apples", "Oranges", "Tomato"}
            checkedListBox1.Items.AddRange(myFruit)
```

```
        ' Changes the selection mode from double-click to          ↵
single click.
        checkedListBox1.CheckOnClick = True
    End Sub 'New

    Protected Overloads Overrides Sub Dispose(ByVal disposing     ↵
 As Boolean)
        If disposing Then
            If Not (components Is Nothing) Then
                components.Dispose()
            End If
        End If
        MyBase.Dispose(disposing)
    End Sub

    Private Sub InitializeComponent()
        Me.components = New System.ComponentModel.Container()
        Me.textBox1 = New System.Windows.Forms.TextBox()
        Me.checkedListBox1 = New                                   ↵
System.Windows.Forms.CheckedListBox()
        Me.listBox1 = New System.Windows.Forms.ListBox()
        Me.button1 = New System.Windows.Forms.Button()
        Me.button2 = New System.Windows.Forms.Button()
        Me.button3 = New System.Windows.Forms.Button()
        Me.textBox1.Location = New System.Drawing.Point(144, 64)
        Me.textBox1.Size = New System.Drawing.Size(128, 20)
        Me.textBox1.TabIndex = 1
        Me.checkedListBox1.Location =                              ↵
 New System.Drawing.Point(16, 64)
        Me.checkedListBox1.Size = New System.Drawing.Size(120, 184)
        Me.checkedListBox1.TabIndex = 0
        Me.listBox1.Location = New System.Drawing.Point(408, 64)
        Me.listBox1.Size = New System.Drawing.Size(128, 186)
        Me.listBox1.TabIndex = 3
        Me.button1.Enabled = False
        Me.button1.Location = New System.Drawing.Point(144, 104)
        Me.button1.Size = New System.Drawing.Size(104, 32)
        Me.button1.TabIndex = 2
        Me.button1.Text = "Add Fruit"
        Me.button2.Enabled = False
        Me.button2.Location = New System.Drawing.Point(288, 64)
        Me.button2.Size = New System.Drawing.Size(104, 32)
        Me.button2.TabIndex = 2
        Me.button2.Text = "Show Order"
        Me.button3.Enabled = False
        Me.button3.Location = New System.Drawing.Point(288, 104)
        Me.button3.Size = New System.Drawing.Size(104, 32)
        Me.button3.TabIndex = 2
        Me.button3.Text = "Save Order"
        Me.AutoScaleBaseSize = New System.Drawing.Size(5, 13)
        Me.ClientSize = New System.Drawing.Size(563, 273)
        Me.Controls.AddRange(New System.Windows.Forms.Control()   ↵
{Me.listBox1, Me.button3, Me.button2, Me.button1,
Me.textBox1, Me.checkedListBox1})
        Me.Text = "Fruit Order"
    End Sub 'InitializeComponent

    <STAThread()> _
    Public Shared Sub Main()
        Application.Run(New Form1())
    End Sub 'Main

    ' Adds the string if the text box has data in it.
    Private Sub button1_Click(sender As Object, _
            e As System.EventArgs) Handles button1.Click
        If textBox1.Text <> "" Then
            If checkedListBox1.CheckedItems.Contains               ↵
 (textBox1.Text) = False Then
                checkedListBox1.Items.Add(textBox1.Text,           ↵
CheckState.Checked)
            End If
            textBox1.Text = ""
        End If
    End Sub 'button1_Click

    ' Activates or deactivates the Add button.
    Private Sub textBox1_TextChanged(sender As Object, _
            e As System.EventArgs) Handles textBox1.TextChanged
        If textBox1.Text = "" Then
            button1.Enabled = False
        Else
            button1.Enabled = True
        End If
    End Sub 'textBox1_TextChanged

    ' Moves the checked items from the CheckedListBox              ↵
to the listBox.
    Private Sub button2_Click(sender As Object, _
            e As System.EventArgs) Handles button2.Click
        listBox1.Items.Clear()
        button3.Enabled = False
        Dim i As Integer
        For i = 0 To checkedListBox1.CheckedItems.Count - 1
            listBox1.Items.Add(checkedListBox1.CheckedItems(i))
        Next i
        If listBox1.Items.Count > 0 Then
            button3.Enabled = True
        End If
    End Sub 'button2_Click

    ' Activates the move button if there are checked items.
    Private Sub checkedListBox1_ItemCheck(sender As Object, _
            e As ItemCheckEventArgs) Handles                       ↵
checkedListBox1.ItemCheck
        If e.NewValue = CheckState.Unchecked Then
            If checkedListBox1.CheckedItems.Count = 1 Then
                button2.Enabled = False
            End If
        Else
            button2.Enabled = True
        End If
    End Sub 'checkedListBox1_ItemCheck

    ' Saves the items to a file.
    Private Sub button3_Click(sender As Object, _
            e As System.EventArgs) Handles button3.Click
        ' Insert code to save a file.
        listBox1.Items.Clear()
        Dim myEnumerator As IEnumerator
        myEnumerator =                                             ↵
checkedListBox1.CheckedIndices.GetEnumerator()
        Dim y As Integer
        While myEnumerator.MoveNext() <> False
            y = CInt(myEnumerator.Current)
            checkedListBox1.SetItemChecked(y, False)
        End While
        button3.Enabled = False
    End Sub 'button3_Click
  End Class 'Form1
End Namespace 'WindowsApplication1
```

[C#]

```
namespace WindowsApplication1
{
   using System;
   using System.Drawing;
   using System.Collections;
   using System.ComponentModel;
   using System.Windows.Forms;
   using System.Data;
   using System.IO ;

   public class Form1 : System.Windows.Forms.Form
   {
      private System.Windows.Forms.CheckedListBox checkedListBox1;
      private System.Windows.Forms.TextBox textBox1;
      private System.Windows.Forms.Button button1;
      private System.Windows.Forms.Button button2;
      private System.Windows.Forms.ListBox listBox1;
```

```
      private System.Windows.Forms.Button button3;
        private System.ComponentModel.Container components;

      public Form1()
      {
            InitializeComponent();

         // Sets up the initial objects in the CheckedListBox.
            string[] myFruit = {"Apples", "Oranges","Tomato"};
         checkedListBox1.Items.AddRange(myFruit);

            // Changes the selection mode from double-click to          ↵
 single click.
         checkedListBox1.CheckOnClick = true;
      }

      protected override void Dispose( bool disposing )
      {
        if( disposing )
        {
            if (components != null)
            {
              components.Dispose();
            }
        }
        base.Dispose( disposing );
      }

      private void InitializeComponent()
      {
         this.components = new System.ComponentModel.Container();
         this.textBox1 = new System.Windows.Forms.TextBox();
         this.checkedListBox1 = new                                     ↵
System.Windows.Forms.CheckedListBox();
         this.listBox1 = new System.Windows.Forms.ListBox();
         this.button1 = new System.Windows.Forms.Button();
         this.button2 = new System.Windows.Forms.Button();
         this.button3 = new System.Windows.Forms.Button();
         this.textBox1.Location = new System.Drawing.Point(144, 64);
         this.textBox1.Size = new System.Drawing.Size(128, 20);
         this.textBox1.TabIndex = 1;
         this.textBox1.TextChanged += new                               ↵
System.EventHandler(this.textBox1_TextChanged);
         this.checkedListBox1.Location = new System.Drawing.Point       ↵
 (16, 64);
         this.checkedListBox1.Size = new System.Drawing.Size(120, 184);
         this.checkedListBox1.TabIndex = 0;
         this.checkedListBox1.ItemCheck += new                          ↵
System.Windows.Forms.ItemCheckEventHandler                              ↵
 (this.checkedListBox1_ItemCheck);
         this.listBox1.Location = new System.Drawing.Point(408, 64);
         this.listBox1.Size = new System.Drawing.Size(128, 186);
         this.listBox1.TabIndex = 3;
         this.button1.Enabled = false;
         this.button1.Location = new System.Drawing.Point(144, 104);
         this.button1.Size = new System.Drawing.Size(104, 32);
         this.button1.TabIndex = 2;
         this.button1.Text = "Add Fruit";
         this.button1.Click += new                                      ↵
System.EventHandler(this.button1_Click);
         this.button2.Enabled = false;
         this.button2.Location = new System.Drawing.Point(288, 64);
         this.button2.Size = new System.Drawing.Size(104, 32);
         this.button2.TabIndex = 2;
         this.button2.Text = "Show Order";
         this.button2.Click += new                                      ↵
System.EventHandler(this.button2_Click);
         this.button3.Enabled = false;
         this.button3.Location = new System.Drawing.Point(288, 104);
         this.button3.Size = new System.Drawing.Size(104, 32);
         this.button3.TabIndex = 2;
         this.button3.Text = "Save Order";
         this.button3.Click += new                                      ↵
System.EventHandler(this.button3_Click);
         this.AutoScaleBaseSize = new System.Drawing.Size(5, 13);
```

```
         this.ClientSize = new System.Drawing.Size(563, 273);
         this.Controls.AddRange(new                                     ↵
System.Windows.Forms.Control[] {this.listBox1,
                                                   this.button3,
                                                   this.button2,
                                                   this.button1,
                                                   this.textBox1,

this.checkedListBox1});
         this.Text = "Fruit Order";
      }

      [STAThread]
      public static void Main(string[] args)
      {
         Application.Run(new Form1());
      }

      // Adds the string if the text box has data in it.
      private void button1_Click(object sender, System.EventArgs e)
      {
         if(textBox1.Text != "")
         {
            if(checkedListBox1.CheckedItems.Contains                    ↵
 (textBox1.Text)== false)

checkedListBox1.Items.Add(textBox1.Text,CheckState.Checked);
            textBox1.Text = "";
         }

      }
      // Activates or deactivates the Add button.
      private void textBox1_TextChanged(object sender,                  ↵
System.EventArgs e)
      {
         if (textBox1.Text == "")
         {
            button1.Enabled = false;
         }
         else
         {
            button1.Enabled = true;
         }

       }

      // Moves the checked items from the CheckedListBox                ↵
to the listBox.
      private void button2_Click(object sender, System.EventArgs e)
      {
         listBox1.Items.Clear();
         button3.Enabled=false;
         for (int i=0; i< checkedListBox1.CheckedItems.Count;i++)
         {
            listBox1.Items.Add(checkedListBox1.CheckedItems[i]);
         }
         if (listBox1.Items.Count>0)
            button3.Enabled=true;

      }
        // Activates the move button if there are checked items.
      private void checkedListBox1_ItemCheck(object sender,             ↵
ItemCheckEventArgs e)
      {
         if(e.NewValue==CheckState.Unchecked)
         {
            if(checkedListBox1.CheckedItems.Count==1)
            {
               button2.Enabled = false;
            }
         }
         else
         {
            button2.Enabled = true;
         }
      }
```

```
      // Saves the items to a file.
      private void button3_Click(object sender, System.EventArgs e)
      {
         // Insert code to save a file.
         listBox1.Items.Clear();
         IEnumerator myEnumerator;
         myEnumerator = checkedListBox1.CheckedIndices.GetEnumerator();
         int y;
         while (myEnumerator.MoveNext() != false)
         {
            y =(int) myEnumerator.Current;
            checkedListBox1.SetItemChecked(y, false);
         }
         button3.Enabled = false ;
      }
   }
}
```

Requirements

Namespace: System.Windows.Forms

Platforms: Windows 98, Windows NT 4.0, Windows Millennium Edition, Windows 2000, Windows XP Home Edition, Windows XP Professional, Windows Server 2003 family

Assembly: System.Windows.Forms (in System.Windows.Forms.dll)

CheckedListBox Constructor

Initializes a new instance of the **CheckedListBox** class.

[Visual Basic]
```
Public Sub New()
```
[C#]
```
public CheckedListBox();
```
[C++]
```
public: CheckedListBox();
```
[JScript]
```
public function CheckedListBox();
```

Remarks

By default, **CheckedListBox** uses **SetStyle** and **ResizeRedraw** to specify that the control is redrawn when resized.

Requirements

Platforms: Windows 98, Windows NT 4.0, Windows Millennium Edition, Windows 2000, Windows XP Home Edition, Windows XP Professional, Windows Server 2003 family

CheckedListBox.CheckedIndices Property

Collection of checked indexes in this **CheckedListBox**.

[Visual Basic]
```
Public ReadOnly Property CheckedIndices As _
   CheckedListBox.CheckedIndexCollection
```
[C#]
```
public CheckedListBox.CheckedIndexCollection CheckedIndices {get;}
```
[C++]
```
public: __property CheckedListBox.CheckedIndexCollection*
   get_CheckedIndices();
```
[JScript]
```
public function get CheckedIndices() :
   CheckedListBox.CheckedIndexCollection;
```

Property Value

The **CheckedListBox.CheckedIndexCollection** collection for the **CheckedListBox**.

Remarks

The collection of checked indexes is a subset of the indexes into the collection of all items in the **CheckedListBox** control. These indexes specify items in a checked or indeterminate state.

Example

See related example in the **System.Windows.Forms.CheckedListBox** class topic.

Requirements

Platforms: Windows 98, Windows NT 4.0, Windows Millennium Edition, Windows 2000, Windows XP Home Edition, Windows XP Professional, Windows Server 2003 family

CheckedListBox.CheckedItems Property

Collection of checked items in this **CheckedListBox**.

[Visual Basic]
```
Public ReadOnly Property CheckedItems As _
   CheckedListBox.CheckedItemCollection
```
[C#]
```
public CheckedListBox.CheckedItemCollection CheckedItems {get;}
```
[C++]
```
public: __property CheckedListBox.CheckedItemCollection*
   get_CheckedItems();
```
[JScript]
```
public function get CheckedItems() :
   CheckedListBox.CheckedItemCollection;
```

Property Value

The **CheckedListBox.CheckedItemCollection** collection for the **CheckedListBox**.

Remarks

The collection is a subset of the objects in the **Items** collection, representing only those items that are in a state of **CheckState.Checked** or **CheckState.Indeterminate**. The indexes in this collection are in ascending order.

Example

See related example in the **System.Windows.Forms.CheckedListBox** class topic.

Requirements

Platforms: Windows 98, Windows NT 4.0, Windows Millennium Edition, Windows 2000, Windows XP Home Edition, Windows XP Professional, Windows Server 2003 family

CheckedListBox.CheckOnClick Property

Gets or sets a value indicating whether the check box should be toggled when an item is selected.

[Visual Basic]
```
Public Property CheckOnClick As Boolean
```
[C#]
```
public bool CheckOnClick {get; set;}
```

[C++]
```
public: __property bool get_CheckOnClick();
public: __property void set_CheckOnClick(bool);
```
[JScript]
```
public function get CheckOnClick() : Boolean;
public function set CheckOnClick(Boolean);
```

Property Value

true if the check mark is applied immediately; otherwise, **false**. The default is **false**.

Remarks

CheckOnClick indicates whether the check box should be toggled whenever an item is selected. The default behavior is to change the selection on the first click, and then have the user click again to apply the check mark. In some instances, however, you might prefer have the item checked as soon as it is clicked.

Requirements

Platforms: Windows 98, Windows NT 4.0,
Windows Millennium Edition, Windows 2000,
Windows XP Home Edition, Windows XP Professional,
Windows Server 2003 family

CheckedListBox.CreateParams Property

This member overrides **Control.CreateParams**.

[Visual Basic]
```
Overrides Protected ReadOnly Property CreateParams As CreateParams
```
[C#]
```
protected override CreateParams CreateParams {get;}
```
[C++]
```
protected: __property CreateParams* get_CreateParams();
```
[JScript]
```
protected override function get CreateParams() : CreateParams;
```

Requirements

Platforms: Windows 98, Windows NT 4.0,
Windows Millennium Edition, Windows 2000,
Windows XP Home Edition, Windows XP Professional,
Windows Server 2003 family

CheckedListBox.DataSource Property

This member supports the .NET Framework infrastructure and is not intended to be used directly from your code.

[Visual Basic]
```
Public Shadows Property DataSource As Object
```
[C#]
```
public new object DataSource {get; set;}
```
[C++]
```
public: __property Object* get_DataSource();
public: __property void set_DataSource(Object*);
```
[JScript]
```
public hide function get DataSource() : Object;
public hide function set DataSource(Object);
```

CheckedListBox.DisplayMember Property

This member supports the .NET Framework infrastructure and is not intended to be used directly from your code.

[Visual Basic]
```
Public Shadows Property DisplayMember As String
```
[C#]
```
public new string DisplayMember {get; set;}
```
[C++]
```
public: __property String* get_DisplayMember();
public: __property void set_DisplayMember(String*);
```
[JScript]
```
public hide function get DisplayMember() : String;
public hide function set DisplayMember(String);
```

CheckedListBox.DrawMode Property

This member overrides **ListBox.DrawMode**.

[Visual Basic]
```
Overrides Public Property DrawMode As DrawMode
```
[C#]
```
public override DrawMode DrawMode {get; set;}
```
[C++]
```
public: __property DrawMode get_DrawMode();
public: __property void set_DrawMode(DrawMode);
```
[JScript]
```
public override function get DrawMode() : DrawMode;
public override function set DrawMode(DrawMode);
```

Requirements

Platforms: Windows 98, Windows NT 4.0,
Windows Millennium Edition, Windows 2000,
Windows XP Home Edition, Windows XP Professional,
Windows Server 2003 family

CheckedListBox.ItemHeight Property

This member overrides **ListBox.ItemHeight**.

[Visual Basic]
```
Overrides Public Property ItemHeight As Integer
```
[C#]
```
public override int ItemHeight {get; set;}
```
[C++]
```
public: __property int get_ItemHeight();
public: __property void set_ItemHeight(int);
```
[JScript]
```
public override function get ItemHeight() : int;
public override function set ItemHeight(int);
```

Requirements

Platforms: Windows 98, Windows NT 4.0,
Windows Millennium Edition, Windows 2000,
Windows XP Home Edition, Windows XP Professional,
Windows Server 2003 family

CheckedListBox.Items Property

Gets the collection of items in this **CheckedListBox**.

```
[Visual Basic]
Public Shadows ReadOnly Property Items As _
   CheckedListBox.ObjectCollection
[C#]
public new CheckedListBox.ObjectCollection Items {get;}
[C++]
public: __property CheckedListBox.ObjectCollection* get_Items();
[JScript]
public hide function get Items() : CheckedListBox.ObjectCollection;
```

Property Value

The **CheckedListBox.ObjectCollection** collection representing the items in the **CheckedListBox**.

Remarks

The **Items** property enables you to obtain a reference to the list of items that are currently stored in a **CheckedListBox** control. With this reference, you can add items, remove items, and obtain a count of the items in the collection. For more information on the tasks that can be performed with the item collection, see the **CheckedListBox.ObjectCollection** class reference topics.

Example

See related example in the **System.Windows.Forms.CheckedListBox** class topic.

Requirements

Platforms: Windows 98, Windows NT 4.0, Windows Millennium Edition, Windows 2000, Windows XP Home Edition, Windows XP Professional, Windows Server 2003 family

CheckedListBox.SelectionMode Property

Gets or sets a value specifying the selection mode.

```
[Visual Basic]
Overrides Public Property SelectionMode As SelectionMode
[C#]
public override SelectionMode SelectionMode {get; set;}
[C++]
public: __property SelectionMode get_SelectionMode();
public: __property void set_SelectionMode(SelectionMode);
[JScript]
public override function get SelectionMode() : SelectionMode;
public override function set SelectionMode(SelectionMode);
```

Property Value

Either **SelectionMode.One** or **SelectionMode.None**.

Exceptions

Exception Type	Condition
ArgumentException	An attempt was made to assign a value that is not **SelectionMode.One** or **SelectionMode.None**.

Remarks

For **CheckedListBox** objects, multiple selection is not supported. You can set the mode to one item or no items.

Requirements

Platforms: Windows 98, Windows NT 4.0, Windows Millennium Edition, Windows 2000, Windows XP Home Edition, Windows XP Professional, Windows Server 2003 family

CheckedListBox.ThreeDCheckBoxes Property

Gets or sets a value indicating whether the check boxes display as **Flat** or **Normal** in appearance.

```
[Visual Basic]
Public Property ThreeDCheckBoxes As Boolean
[C#]
public bool ThreeDCheckBoxes {get; set;}
[C++]
public: __property bool get_ThreeDCheckBoxes();
public: __property void set_ThreeDCheckBoxes(bool);
[JScript]
public function get ThreeDCheckBoxes() : Boolean;
public function set ThreeDCheckBoxes(Boolean);
```

Property Value

true if the check box has a flat appearance; otherwise, **false**. The default is **true**.

Requirements

Platforms: Windows 98, Windows NT 4.0, Windows Millennium Edition, Windows 2000, Windows XP Home Edition, Windows XP Professional, Windows Server 2003 family

CheckedListBox.ValueMember Property

This member supports the .NET Framework infrastructure and is not intended to be used directly from your code.

```
[Visual Basic]
Public Shadows Property ValueMember As String
[C#]
public new string ValueMember {get; set;}
[C++]
public: __property String* get_ValueMember();
public: __property void set_ValueMember(String*);
[JScript]
public hide function get ValueMember() : String;
public hide function set ValueMember(String);
```

CheckedListBox.CreateAccessibilityInstance Method

This member overrides **Control.CreateAccessibilityInstance**.

```
[Visual Basic]
Overrides Protected Function CreateAccessibilityInstance() As _
   AccessibleObject
[C#]
protected override AccessibleObject CreateAccessibilityInstance();
[C++]
protected: AccessibleObject* CreateAccessibilityInstance();
[JScript]
protected override function CreateAccessibilityInstance() :
   AccessibleObject;
```

Requirements

Platforms: Windows 98, Windows NT 4.0, Windows Millennium Edition, Windows 2000, Windows XP Home Edition, Windows XP Professional, Windows Server 2003 family

CheckedListBox.CreateItemCollection Method

This member overrides **ListBox.CreateItemCollection**.

```
[Visual Basic]
Overrides Protected Function CreateItemCollection() As _
   ObjectCollection
[C#]
protected override ObjectCollection CreateItemCollection();
[C++]
protected: ObjectCollection* CreateItemCollection();
[JScript]
protected override function CreateItemCollection() :
   ObjectCollection;
```

Requirements

Platforms: Windows 98, Windows NT 4.0, Windows Millennium Edition, Windows 2000, Windows XP Home Edition, Windows XP Professional, Windows Server 2003 family

CheckedListBox.GetItemChecked Method

Returns a value indicating whether the specified item is checked.

```
[Visual Basic]
Public Function GetItemChecked( _
   ByVal index As Integer _
) As Boolean
[C#]
public bool GetItemChecked(
   int index
);
[C++]
public: bool GetItemChecked(
   int index
);
[JScript]
public function GetItemChecked(
   index : int
) : Boolean;
```

Parameters

index

The index of the item.

Return Value

true if the item is checked; otherwise, **false**.

Exceptions

Exception Type	Condition
ArgumentException	The *index* specified is less than zero. -or- The *index* specified is greater than or equal to the count of items in the list.

Remarks

GetItemChecked returns **true** if the item is **Checked** or **Indeterminate .** To determine the specific state the item is in, use the **GetItemCheckState** method.

Requirements

Platforms: Windows 98, Windows NT 4.0, Windows Millennium Edition, Windows 2000, Windows XP Home Edition, Windows XP Professional, Windows Server 2003 family

CheckedListBox.GetItemCheckState Method

Returns a value indicating the check state of the current item.

```
[Visual Basic]
Public Function GetItemCheckState( _
   ByVal index As Integer _
) As CheckState
[C#]
public CheckState GetItemCheckState(
   int index
);
[C++]
public: CheckState GetItemCheckState(
   int index
);
[JScript]
public function GetItemCheckState(
   index : int
) : CheckState;
```

Parameters

index

The index of the item to get the checked value of.

Return Value

One of the **CheckState** values.

Exceptions

Exception Type	Condition
ArgumentException	The *index* specified is less than zero. -or- The *index* specified is greater than or equal to the count of items in the list.

Remarks

The **GetItemCheckState** method provides the ability to get the **CheckState** value of an item, given the index. If you never set the check state of an item to **Indeterminate**, then use the **GetItem-Checked** method.

Example

See related example in the **System.Windows.Forms.Checked-ListBox** class topic.

Requirements

Platforms: Windows 98, Windows NT 4.0, Windows Millennium Edition, Windows 2000, Windows XP Home Edition, Windows XP Professional, Windows Server 2003 family

CheckedListBox.OnBackColorChanged Method

This member overrides **Control.OnBackColorChanged**.

```
[Visual Basic]
Overrides Protected Sub OnBackColorChanged( _
   ByVal e As EventArgs _
)
[C#]
protected override void OnBackColorChanged(
   EventArgs e
);
[C++]
protected: void OnBackColorChanged(
   EventArgs* e
);
[JScript]
protected override function OnBackColorChanged(
   e : EventArgs
);
```

Requirements

Platforms: Windows 98, Windows NT 4.0, Windows Millennium Edition, Windows 2000, Windows XP Home Edition, Windows XP Professional, Windows Server 2003 family

CheckedListBox.OnClick Method

This member overrides **Control.OnClick**.

```
[Visual Basic]
Overrides Protected Sub OnClick( _
   ByVal e As EventArgs _
)
[C#]
protected override void OnClick(
   EventArgs e
);
[C++]
protected: void OnClick(
   EventArgs* e
);
[JScript]
protected override function OnClick(
   e : EventArgs
);
```

Requirements

Platforms: Windows 98, Windows NT 4.0, Windows Millennium Edition, Windows 2000, Windows XP Home Edition, Windows XP Professional, Windows Server 2003 family

CheckedListBox.OnDrawItem Method

This member overrides **ListBox.OnDrawItem**.

```
[Visual Basic]
Overrides Protected Sub OnDrawItem( _
   ByVal e As DrawItemEventArgs _
)
[C#]
protected override void OnDrawItem(
   DrawItemEventArgs e
);
[C++]
protected: void OnDrawItem(
   DrawItemEventArgs* e
);
[JScript]
protected override function OnDrawItem(
   e : DrawItemEventArgs
);
```

Requirements

Platforms: Windows 98, Windows NT 4.0, Windows Millennium Edition, Windows 2000, Windows XP Home Edition, Windows XP Professional, Windows Server 2003 family

CheckedListBox.OnFontChanged Method

This member overrides **Control.OnFontChanged**.

```
[Visual Basic]
Overrides Protected Sub OnFontChanged( _
   ByVal e As EventArgs _
)
[C#]
protected override void OnFontChanged(
   EventArgs e
);
[C++]
protected: void OnFontChanged(
   EventArgs* e
);
[JScript]
protected override function OnFontChanged(
   e : EventArgs
);
```

Requirements

Platforms: Windows 98, Windows NT 4.0, Windows Millennium Edition, Windows 2000, Windows XP Home Edition, Windows XP Professional, Windows Server 2003 family

CheckedListBox.OnHandleCreated Method

This member overrides **Control.OnHandleCreated**.

```
[Visual Basic]
Overrides Protected Sub OnHandleCreated( _
   ByVal e As EventArgs _
)
[C#]
protected override void OnHandleCreated(
   EventArgs e
);
[C++]
protected: void OnHandleCreated(
   EventArgs* e
);
```

[JScript]
```
protected override function OnHandleCreated(
   e : EventArgs
);
```

Requirements

Platforms: Windows 98, Windows NT 4.0, Windows Millennium Edition, Windows 2000, Windows XP Home Edition, Windows XP Professional, Windows Server 2003 family

CheckedListBox.OnItemCheck Method

This member supports the .NET Framework infrastructure and is not intended to be used directly from your code.

[Visual Basic]
```
Protected Overridable Sub OnItemCheck( _
   ByVal ice As ItemCheckEventArgs _
)
```
[C#]
```
protected virtual void OnItemCheck(
   ItemCheckEventArgs ice
);
```
[C++]
```
protected: virtual void OnItemCheck(
   ItemCheckEventArgs* ice
);
```
[JScript]
```
protected function OnItemCheck(
   ice : ItemCheckEventArgs
);
```

CheckedListBox.OnKeyPress Method

This member overrides **Control.OnKeyPress**.

[Visual Basic]
```
Overrides Protected Sub OnKeyPress( _
   ByVal e As KeyPressEventArgs _
)
```
[C#]
```
protected override void OnKeyPress(
   KeyPressEventArgs e
);
```
[C++]
```
protected: void OnKeyPress(
   KeyPressEventArgs* e
);
```
[JScript]
```
protected override function OnKeyPress(
   e : KeyPressEventArgs
);
```

Requirements

Platforms: Windows 98, Windows NT 4.0, Windows Millennium Edition, Windows 2000, Windows XP Home Edition, Windows XP Professional, Windows Server 2003 family

CheckedListBox.OnMeasureItem Method

This member overrides **ListBox.OnMeasureItem**.

[Visual Basic]
```
Overrides Protected Sub OnMeasureItem( _
   ByVal e As MeasureItemEventArgs _
)
```
[C#]
```
protected override void OnMeasureItem(
   MeasureItemEventArgs e
);
```
[C++]
```
protected: void OnMeasureItem(
   MeasureItemEventArgs* e
);
```
[JScript]
```
protected override function OnMeasureItem(
   e : MeasureItemEventArgs
);
```

Requirements

Platforms: Windows 98, Windows NT 4.0, Windows Millennium Edition, Windows 2000, Windows XP Home Edition, Windows XP Professional, Windows Server 2003 family

CheckedListBox.OnSelectedIndexChanged Method

Raises the **SelectedIndexChanged** event.

[Visual Basic]
```
Overrides Protected Sub OnSelectedIndexChanged( _
   ByVal e As EventArgs _
)
```
[C#]
```
protected override void OnSelectedIndexChanged(
   EventArgs e
);
```
[C++]
```
protected: void OnSelectedIndexChanged(
   EventArgs* e
);
```
[JScript]
```
protected override function OnSelectedIndexChanged(
   e : EventArgs
);
```

Parameters

e

An **EventArgs** that contains the event data.

Remarks

Raising an event invokes the event handler through a delegate. For more information, see **Raising an Event**.

The **OnSelectedIndexChanged** method also allows derived classes to handle the event without attaching a delegate. This is the preferred technique for handling the event in a derived class.

Notes to Inheritors: When overriding **OnSelectedIndexChanged** in a derived class, be sure to call the base class's **OnSelectedIndexChanged** method so that registered delegates receive the event.

Requirements

Platforms: Windows 98, Windows NT 4.0, Windows Millennium Edition, Windows 2000, Windows XP Home Edition, Windows XP Professional, Windows Server 2003 family

CheckedListBox.SetItemChecked Method

Sets the item at the specified index to **CheckState.Checked**.

[Visual Basic]
```
Public Sub SetItemChecked( _
   ByVal index As Integer, _
   ByVal value As Boolean _
)
```
[C#]
```
public void SetItemChecked(
   int index,
   bool value
);
```
[C++]
```
public: void SetItemChecked(
   int index,
   bool value
);
```
[JScript]
```
public function SetItemChecked(
   index : int,
   value : Boolean
);
```

Parameters

index
The index of the item to set the check state for.

value
true to set the item as checked; otherwise, **false**.

Exceptions

Exception Type	Condition
ArgumentException	The index specified is less than zero. -or- The index is greater than the count of items in the list.

Remarks

When a value of **true** is passed, this method sets the checked value of the item to **Checked**. A value of **false** will set the item to **Unchecked**.

Example

See related example in the **System.Windows.Forms.Checked-ListBox** class topic.

Requirements

Platforms: Windows 98, Windows NT 4.0, Windows Millennium Edition, Windows 2000, Windows XP Home Edition, Windows XP Professional, Windows Server 2003 family

CheckedListBox.SetItemCheckState Method

Sets the check state of the item at the specified index.

[Visual Basic]
```
Public Sub SetItemCheckState( _
   ByVal index As Integer, _
   ByVal value As CheckState _
)
```
[C#]
```
public void SetItemCheckState(
   int index,
   CheckState value
);
```
[C++]
```
public: void SetItemCheckState(
   int index,
   CheckState value
);
```
[JScript]
```
public function SetItemCheckState(
   index : int,
   value : CheckState
);
```

Parameters

index
The index of the item to set the state for.

value
One of the **CheckState** values.

Exceptions

Exception Type	Condition
ArgumentException	The *index* specified is less than zero. -or- The *index* is greater than or equal to the count of items in the list.
InvalidEnumArgument-Exception	The *value* is not one of the **CheckState** values.

Remarks

The **SetItemCheckState** method raises the **ItemCheck** event.

Items set to **CheckState.Indeterminate** appear with a check mark in the check box, but the box is grayed to indicate the indeterminate status of the checked item.

Example

See related example in the **System.Windows.Forms.Checked-ListBox** class topic.

Requirements

Platforms: Windows 98, Windows NT 4.0, Windows Millennium Edition, Windows 2000, Windows XP Home Edition, Windows XP Professional, Windows Server 2003 family

CheckedListBox.WmReflectCommand Method

This member supports the .NET Framework infrastructure and is not intended to be used directly from your code.

```
[Visual Basic]
Overrides Protected Sub WmReflectCommand( _
   ByRef m As Message _
)
[C#]
protected override void WmReflectCommand(
   ref Message m
);
[C++]
protected: void WmReflectCommand(
   Message* m
);
[JScript]
protected override function WmReflectCommand(
   m : Message
);
```

CheckedListBox.WndProc Method

This member overrides **Control.WndProc**.

```
[Visual Basic]
Overrides Protected Sub WndProc( _
   ByRef m As Message _
)
[C#]
protected override void WndProc(
   ref Message m
);
[C++]
protected: void WndProc(
   Message* m
);
[JScript]
protected override function WndProc(
   m : Message
);
```

Requirements

Platforms: Windows 98, Windows NT 4.0, Windows Millennium Edition, Windows 2000, Windows XP Home Edition, Windows XP Professional, Windows Server 2003 family

CheckedListBox.Click Event

This member supports the .NET Framework infrastructure and is not intended to be used directly from your code.

```
[Visual Basic]
Public Shadows Event Click As EventHandler
[C#]
public new event EventHandler Click;
[C++]
public: __event EventHandler* Click;
```

[JScript] In JScript, you can handle the events defined by a class, but you cannot define your own.

CheckedListBox.DataSourceChanged Event

This member supports the .NET Framework infrastructure and is not intended to be used directly from your code.

```
[Visual Basic]
Public Shadows Event DataSourceChanged As EventHandler
[C#]
public new event EventHandler DataSourceChanged;
[C++]
public: __event EventHandler* DataSourceChanged;
```

[JScript] In JScript, you can handle the events defined by a class, but you cannot define your own.

CheckedListBox.DisplayMemberChanged Event

This member supports the .NET Framework infrastructure and is not intended to be used directly from your code.

```
[Visual Basic]
Public Shadows Event DisplayMemberChanged As EventHandler
[C#]
public new event EventHandler DisplayMemberChanged;
[C++]
public: __event EventHandler* DisplayMemberChanged;
```

[JScript] In JScript, you can handle the events defined by a class, but you cannot define your own.

CheckedListBox.DrawItem Event

This member supports the .NET Framework infrastructure and is not intended to be used directly from your code.

```
[Visual Basic]
Public Shadows Event DrawItem As DrawItemEventHandler
[C#]
public new event DrawItemEventHandler DrawItem;
[C++]
public: __event DrawItemEventHandler* DrawItem;
```

[JScript] In JScript, you can handle the events defined by a class, but you cannot define your own.

CheckedListBox.ItemCheck Event

Occurs when the checked state of an item changes.

```
[Visual Basic]
Public Event ItemCheck As ItemCheckEventHandler
[C#]
public event ItemCheckEventHandler ItemCheck;
[C++]
public: __event ItemCheckEventHandler* ItemCheck;
```

[JScript] In JScript, you can handle the events defined by a class, but you cannot define your own.

Event Data

The event handler receives an argument of type **ItemCheckEventArgs** containing data related to this event. The following **ItemCheckEventArgs** properties provide information specific to this event.

Property	Description
CurrentValue	Gets a value indicating the current state of the item's check box.
Index	Gets the zero-based index of the item to change.
NewValue	Gets or sets a value indicating whether to set the check box for the item to be checked, unchecked, or indeterminate.

Requirements

Platforms: Windows 98, Windows NT 4.0, Windows Millennium Edition, Windows 2000, Windows XP Home Edition, Windows XP Professional, Windows Server 2003 family

CheckedListBox.MeasureItem Event

This member supports the .NET Framework infrastructure and is not intended to be used directly from your code.

[Visual Basic]
```
Public Shadows Event MeasureItem As MeasureItemEventHandler
```
[C#]
```
public new event MeasureItemEventHandler MeasureItem;
```
[C++]
```
public: __event MeasureItemEventHandler* MeasureItem;
```

[JScript] In JScript, you can handle the events defined by a class, but you cannot define your own.

CheckedListBox.ValueMemberChanged Event

This member supports the .NET Framework infrastructure and is not intended to be used directly from your code.

[Visual Basic]
```
Public Shadows Event ValueMemberChanged As EventHandler
```
[C#]
```
public new event EventHandler ValueMemberChanged;
```
[C++]
```
public: __event EventHandler* ValueMemberChanged;
```

[JScript] In JScript, you can handle the events defined by a class, but you cannot define your own.

CheckedListBox.CheckedIndexCollection Class

Encapsulates the collection of indexes of checked items (including items in an indeterminate state) in a **CheckedListBox**.

System.Object
  System.Windows.Forms.CheckedListBox.CheckedIndexCollection

[Visual Basic]
```
Public Class CheckedListBox.CheckedIndexCollection
   Implements IList, ICollection, IEnumerable
```
[C#]
```
public class CheckedListBox.CheckedIndexCollection : IList,
   ICollection, IEnumerable
```
[C++]
```
public __gc class CheckedListBox.CheckedIndexCollection : public
   IList, ICollection, IEnumerable
```
[JScript]
```
public class CheckedListBox.CheckedIndexCollection implements
   IList, ICollection, IEnumerable
```

Thread Safety

Any public static (**Shared** in Visual Basic) members of this type are safe for multithreaded operations. Any instance members are not guaranteed to be thread safe.

Remarks

The checked indexes collection is a subset of the indexes into the collection of all items in the **CheckedListBox** control. These indexes specify items in a checked or indeterminate state.

The following table is an example of the indexed collection of items in the control (all items contained in the control).

Index	Item	Check State
0	object 1	**Unchecked**
1	object 2	**Checked**
2	object 3	**Unchecked**
3	object 4	**Indeterminate**
4	object 5	**Checked**

Based on the previous example, the following table shows the indexed collection of indexes of checked items.

Index	Index of Item
0	1
1	3
2	4

The **CheckedListBox** class has two members that allow you to access the stored indexes, the **Item** property and the **IndexOf** method.

Based on the previous example, a call to the **Item** property with a parameter value of 1 returns a value of 3. A call to **IndexOf** with a parameter of 3 returns a value of 1.

Example

See related example in the **System.Windows.Forms.CheckedListBox** class topic.

Requirements

Namespace: System.Windows.Forms

Platforms: Windows 98, Windows NT 4.0, Windows Millennium Edition, Windows 2000, Windows XP Home Edition, Windows XP Professional, Windows Server 2003 family

Assembly: System.Windows.Forms (in System.Windows.Forms.dll)

CheckedListBox.CheckedIndexCollection.Count Property

Gets the number of checked items.

[Visual Basic]
```
Public Overridable ReadOnly Property Count As Integer  Implements _
   ICollection.Count
```
[C#]
```
public virtual int Count {get;}
```
[C++]
```
public: __property virtual int get_Count();
```
[JScript]
```
public function get Count() : int;
```

Property Value

The number of indexes in the collection.

Implements

ICollection.Count

Requirements

Platforms: Windows 98, Windows NT 4.0, Windows Millennium Edition, Windows 2000, Windows XP Home Edition, Windows XP Professional, Windows Server 2003 family

CheckedListBox.CheckedIndexCollection.IsReadOnly Property

Gets a value indicating whether the collection is read-only.

[Visual Basic]
```
Public Overridable ReadOnly Property IsReadOnly As Boolean  _
   Implements IList.IsReadOnly
```
[C#]
```
public virtual bool IsReadOnly {get;}
```
[C++]
```
public: __property virtual bool get_IsReadOnly();
```
[JScript]
```
public function get IsReadOnly() : Boolean;
```

Property Value

Always **true**.

Implements

IList.IsReadOnly

Requirements

Platforms: Windows 98, Windows NT 4.0, Windows Millennium Edition, Windows 2000, Windows XP Home Edition, Windows XP Professional, Windows Server 2003 family

CheckedListBox.CheckedIndexCollection.Item Property

Gets the index of a checked item in the **CheckedListBox** control.

[C#] In C#, this property is the indexer for the **CheckedListBox.CheckedIndexCollection** class.

```
[Visual Basic]
Public Default ReadOnly Property Item( _
   ByVal index As Integer _
) As Integer
[C#]
public int this[
   int index
] {get;}
[C++]
public: __property int get_Item(
   int index
);
[JScript]
returnValue = CheckedIndexCollectionObject.Item(index);
-or-
returnValue = CheckedIndexCollectionObject(index);
```

[JScript] In JScript, you can use the default indexed properties defined by a type, but you cannot explicitly define your own. However, specifying the **expando** attribute on a class automatically provides a default indexed property whose type is **Object** and whose index type is **String**.

Arguments [JScript]

index

An index into the checked indexes collection. This index specifies the index of the checked item you want to retrieve.

Parameters [Visual Basic, C#, C++]

index

An index into the checked indexes collection. This index specifies the index of the checked item you want to retrieve.

Property Value

The index of the checked item. For more information, see the examples in the **CheckedListBox.CheckedIndexCollection** class overview.

Exceptions

Exception Type	Condition
ArgumentException	The *index* is less than zero. -or- The *index* is not in the collection.

Remarks

The *index* parameter is an index into the checked indexes collection. The return value is the corresponding indexed value, which is the index of the checked item in the items collection.

Requirements

Platforms: Windows 98, Windows NT 4.0, Windows Millennium Edition, Windows 2000, Windows XP Home Edition, Windows XP Professional, Windows Server 2003 family

CheckedListBox.CheckedIndexCollection.Contains Method

Determines whether the specified index is located in the collection.

```
[Visual Basic]
Public Function Contains( _
   ByVal index As Integer _
) As Boolean
[C#]
public bool Contains(
   int index
);
[C++]
public: bool Contains(
   int index
);
[JScript]
public function Contains(
   index : int
) : Boolean;
```

Parameters

index

The index to locate in the collection.

Return Value

true if the specified index from the **CheckedListBox.ObjectCollection** is an item in this collection; otherwise, **false**.

Remarks

You can use this method to determine whether an index from the **Items** collection is in the **CheckedIndices** collection.

Requirements

Platforms: Windows 98, Windows NT 4.0, Windows Millennium Edition, Windows 2000, Windows XP Home Edition, Windows XP Professional, Windows Server 2003 family

CheckedListBox.CheckedIndexCollection.CopyTo Method

Copies the entire collection into an existing array at a specified location within the array.

```
[Visual Basic]
Public Overridable Sub CopyTo( _
   ByVal dest As Array, _
   ByVal index As Integer _
) Implements ICollection.CopyTo
[C#]
public virtual void CopyTo(
   Array dest,
   int index
);
[C++]
public: virtual void CopyTo(
   Array* dest,
   int index
);
[JScript]
public function CopyTo(
   dest : Array,
   index : int
);
```

Parameters

dest

The destination array.

index

The zero-based relative index in *dest* at which copying begins.

Implements

ICollection.CopyTo

Exceptions

Exception Type	Condition
ArgumentNullException	*array* is a null reference (**Nothing** in Visual Basic).
RankException	*array* is multidimensional.
ArgumentOutOfRangeException	*index* is less than zero.
ArgumentException	*index* is equal to or greater than the length of array. -or- The number of elements in the source **Array** is greater than the available space from index to the end of the destination **Array**.
ArrayTypeMismatchException	The type of the source **Array** cannot be cast automatically to the type of the destination **Array**.

Remarks

You can use this method to combine the selected indexes from multiple collections into a single array.

Requirements

Platforms: Windows 98, Windows NT 4.0, Windows Millennium Edition, Windows 2000, Windows XP Home Edition, Windows XP Professional, Windows Server 2003 family

CheckedListBox.CheckedIndexCollection.GetEnumerator Method

Returns an enumerator that can be used to iterate through the **CheckedIndices** collection.

```
[Visual Basic]
Public Overridable Function GetEnumerator() As IEnumerator _
   Implements IEnumerable.GetEnumerator
[C#]
public virtual IEnumerator GetEnumerator();
[C++]
public: virtual IEnumerator* GetEnumerator();
[JScript]
public function GetEnumerator() : IEnumerator;
```

Return Value

An **IEnumerator** for navigating through the list.

Implements

IEnumerable.GetEnumerator

Requirements

Platforms: Windows 98, Windows NT 4.0, Windows Millennium Edition, Windows 2000, Windows XP Home Edition, Windows XP Professional, Windows Server 2003 family

CheckedListBox.CheckedIndexCollection.IList.Add Method

This member supports the .NET Framework infrastructure and is not intended to be used directly from your code.

```
[Visual Basic]
Private Function Add( _
   ByVal value As Object _
) As Integer Implements IList.Add
[C#]
int IList.Add(
   object value
);
[C++]
private: int IList::Add(
   Object* value
);
[JScript]
private function IList.Add(
   value : Object
) : int;
```

CheckedListBox.CheckedIndexCollection.IList.Clear Method

This member supports the .NET Framework infrastructure and is not intended to be used directly from your code.

```
[Visual Basic]
Private Sub Clear() Implements IList.Clear
[C#]
void IList.Clear();
[C++]
private: void IList::Clear();
[JScript]
private function IList.Clear();
```

CheckedListBox.CheckedIndexCollection.IList.Contains Method

This member supports the .NET Framework infrastructure and is not intended to be used directly from your code.

```
[Visual Basic]
Private Function Contains( _
   ByVal index As Object _
) As Boolean Implements IList.Contains
[C#]
bool IList.Contains(
   object index
);
[C++]
private: bool IList::Contains(
   Object* index
);
[JScript]
private function IList.Contains(
   index : Object
) : Boolean;
```

CheckedListBox.CheckedIndexCollection.IList.IndexOf Method

This member supports the .NET Framework infrastructure and is not intended to be used directly from your code.

```
[Visual Basic]
Private Function IndexOf( _
   ByVal index As Object _
) As Integer Implements IList.IndexOf
[C#]
int IList.IndexOf(
   object index
);
[C++]
private: int IList::IndexOf(
   Object* index
);
[JScript]
private function IList.IndexOf(
   index : Object
) : int;
```

CheckedListBox.CheckedIndexCollection.IList.Insert Method

This member supports the .NET Framework infrastructure and is not intended to be used directly from your code.

```
[Visual Basic]
Private Sub Insert( _
   ByVal index As Integer, _
   ByVal value As Object _
) Implements IList.Insert
[C#]
void IList.Insert(
   int index,
   object value
);
[C++]
private: void IList::Insert(
   int index,
   Object* value
);
[JScript]
private function IList.Insert(
   index : int,
   value : Object
);
```

CheckedListBox.CheckedIndexCollection.IList.Remove Method

This member supports the .NET Framework infrastructure and is not intended to be used directly from your code.

```
[Visual Basic]
Private Sub Remove( _
   ByVal value As Object _
) Implements IList.Remove
[C#]
void IList.Remove(
   object value
);
[C++]
private: void IList::Remove(
   Object* value
);
[JScript]
private function IList.Remove(
   value : Object
);
```

CheckedListBox.CheckedIndexCollection.IList.RemoveAt Method

This member supports the .NET Framework infrastructure and is not intended to be used directly from your code.

```
[Visual Basic]
Private Sub RemoveAt( _
   ByVal index As Integer _
) Implements IList.RemoveAt
[C#]
void IList.RemoveAt(
   int index
);
[C++]
private: void IList::RemoveAt(
   int index
);
[JScript]
private function IList.RemoveAt(
   index : int
);
```

CheckedListBox.CheckedIndexCollection.IndexOf Method

Returns an index into the collection of checked indexes.

```
[Visual Basic]
Public Function IndexOf( _
   ByVal index As Integer _
) As Integer
[C#]
public int IndexOf(
   int index
);
[C++]
public: int IndexOf(
   int index
);
[JScript]
public function IndexOf(
   index : int
) : int;
```

Parameters

index
The index of the checked item.

Return Value

The index that specifies the index of the checked item or -1 if the *index* parameter is not in the checked indexes collection. For more information, see the examples in the **CheckedListBox.CheckedIndexCollection** class overview.

Remarks

The *index* parameter is the index of a checked item in the items collection. The return value is the corresponding index into the checked indexes collection.

Requirements

Platforms: Windows 98, Windows NT 4.0,
Windows Millennium Edition, Windows 2000,
Windows XP Home Edition, Windows XP Professional,
Windows Server 2003 family

CheckedListBox.CheckedItemCollection Class

Encapsulates the collection of checked items (including items in an indeterminate state) in a **CheckedListBox** control.

System.Object
System.Windows.Forms.CheckedListBox.CheckedItemCollection

[Visual Basic]
```
Public Class CheckedListBox.CheckedItemCollection
   Implements IList, ICollection, IEnumerable
```
[C#]
```
public class CheckedListBox.CheckedItemCollection : IList,
   ICollection, IEnumerable
```
[C++]
```
public __gc class CheckedListBox.CheckedItemCollection : public
   IList, ICollection, IEnumerable
```
[JScript]
```
public class CheckedListBox.CheckedItemCollection implements IList,
   ICollection, IEnumerable
```

Thread Safety

Any public static (**Shared** in Visual Basic) members of this type are safe for multithreaded operations. Any instance members are not guaranteed to be thread safe.

Remarks

The checked items collection is a subset of all items in the **CheckedListBox** control; it contains only those items that are in a checked or indeterminate state.

The following table is an example of the indexed collection of items in the control (all items contained in the control).

Index	Item	Check State
0	object 1	**Unchecked**
1	object 2	**Checked**
2	object 3	**Unchecked**
3	object 4	**Indeterminate**
4	object 5	**Checked**

Based on the previous example, the following table shows the indexed collection of the checked items.

Index	Item
0	object 2
1	object 4
2	object 5

The **CheckedListBox** class has two members that allow you to access the stored indexes, the **Item** property and the **IndexOf** method.

Based on the previous example, a call to the **Item** property with a parameter value of 1 returns object 4. A call to **IndexOf** with a parameter of object 4 returns a value of 1.

Example

See related example in the **System.Windows.Forms.CheckedListBox** class topic.

Requirements

Namespace: System.Windows.Forms

Platforms: Windows 98, Windows NT 4.0, Windows Millennium Edition, Windows 2000, Windows XP Home Edition, Windows XP Professional, Windows Server 2003 family

Assembly: System.Windows.Forms (in System.Windows.Forms.dll)

CheckedListBox.CheckedItemCollection.Count Property

Gets the number of items in the collection.

[Visual Basic]
```
Public Overridable ReadOnly Property Count As Integer Implements _
   ICollection.Count
```
[C#]
```
public virtual int Count {get;}
```
[C++]
```
public: __property virtual int get_Count();
```
[JScript]
```
public function get Count() : int;
```

Property Value

The number of items in the collection.

Implements

ICollection.Count

Requirements

Platforms: Windows 98, Windows NT 4.0, Windows Millennium Edition, Windows 2000, Windows XP Home Edition, Windows XP Professional, Windows Server 2003 family

CheckedListBox.CheckedItemCollection.IsReadOnly Property

Gets a value indicating if the collection is read-only.

[Visual Basic]
```
Public Overridable ReadOnly Property IsReadOnly As Boolean _
   Implements IList.IsReadOnly
```
[C#]
```
public virtual bool IsReadOnly {get;}
```
[C++]
```
public: __property virtual bool get_IsReadOnly();
```
[JScript]
```
public function get IsReadOnly() : Boolean;
```

Property Value

Always **true**.

Implements

IList.IsReadOnly

Requirements

Platforms: Windows 98, Windows NT 4.0, Windows Millennium Edition, Windows 2000, Windows XP Home Edition, Windows XP Professional, Windows Server 2003 family

CheckedListBox.CheckedItemCollection.Item Property

Gets an object in the checked items collection.

[C#] In C#, this property is the indexer for the **CheckedListBox.CheckedItemCollection** class.

```
[Visual Basic]
Public Overridable Default Property Item( _
   ByVal index As Integer _
) As Object  Implements IList.Item
[C#]
public virtual object this[
   int index
] {get; set;}
[C++]
public: __property virtual Object* get_Item(
   int index
);
public: __property virtual void set_Item(
   int index,
   Object*
);
[JScript]
returnValue = CheckedItemCollectionObject.Item(index);
CheckedItemCollectionObject.Item(index) = returnValue;
-or-
returnValue = CheckedItemCollectionObject(index);
CheckedItemCollectionObject(index) = returnValue;
```

[JScript] In JScript, you can use the default indexed properties defined by a type, but you cannot explicitly define your own. However, specifying the **expando** attribute on a class automatically provides a default indexed property whose type is **Object** and whose index type is **String**.

Arguments [JScript]

index

An index into the collection of checked items. This collection index corresponds to the index of the checked item.

Parameters [Visual Basic, C#, C++]

index

An index into the collection of checked items. This collection index corresponds to the index of the checked item.

Property Value

The object at the specified index. For more information, see the examples in the **CheckedListBox.CheckedItemCollection** class overview.

Implements

IList.Item

Exceptions

Exception Type	Condition
NotSupportedException	You tried to set the object.

Remarks

The **CheckedItems** collection is a subset of the objects in the **Items** collection, representing only items that are checked. This collection is ordered in ascending order.

Requirements

Platforms: Windows 98, Windows NT 4.0, Windows Millennium Edition, Windows 2000, Windows XP Home Edition, Windows XP Professional, Windows Server 2003 family

CheckedListBox.CheckedItemCollection.Contains Method

Determines whether the specified item is located in the collection.

```
[Visual Basic]
Public Overridable Function Contains( _
   ByVal item As Object _
) As Boolean Implements IList.Contains
[C#]
public virtual bool Contains(
   object item
);
[C++]
public: virtual bool Contains(
   Object* item
);
[JScript]
public function Contains(
   item : Object
) : Boolean;
```

Parameters

item

An object from the items collection.

Return Value

true if item is in the collection; otherwise, **false**.

Implements

IList.Contains

Remarks

This method determines if an object from the **Items** collection is in the **CheckedItems** collection.

Requirements

Platforms: Windows 98, Windows NT 4.0, Windows Millennium Edition, Windows 2000, Windows XP Home Edition, Windows XP Professional, Windows Server 2003 family

CheckedListBox.CheckedItemCollection.CopyTo Method

Copies the entire collection into an existing array at a specified location within the array.

```
[Visual Basic]
Public Overridable Sub CopyTo( _
   ByVal dest As Array, _
   ByVal index As Integer _
) Implements ICollection.CopyTo
[C#]
public virtual void CopyTo(
   Array dest,
   int index
);
```

```
[C++]
public: virtual void CopyTo(
   Array* dest,
   int index
);
[JScript]
public function CopyTo(
   dest : Array,
   index : int
);
```

Parameters

dest
The destination array.

index
The zero-based relative index in *dest* at which copying begins.

Implements

ICollection.CopyTo

Exceptions

Exception Type	Condition
ArgumentNull-Exception	*array* is a null reference (**Nothing** in Visual Basic).
RankException	*array* is multidimensional.
ArgumentOutOfRange-Exception	*index* is less than zero.
ArgumentException	*index* is equal to or greater than the length of array. -or- The number of elements in the source **Array** is greater than the available space from index to the end of the destination **Array**.
ArrayTypeMismatch-Exception	The type of the source **Array** cannot be cast automatically to the type of the destination **Array**.

Remarks

You can use this method to combine the selected indexes from multiple collections into a single array.

Requirements

Platforms: Windows 98, Windows NT 4.0, Windows Millennium Edition, Windows 2000, Windows XP Home Edition, Windows XP Professional, Windows Server 2003 family

CheckedListBox.CheckedItemCollection.GetEnumerator Method

Returns an enumerator that can be used to iterate through the **CheckedItems** collection.

```
[Visual Basic]
Public Overridable Function GetEnumerator() As IEnumerator _
   Implements IEnumerable.GetEnumerator
[C#]
public virtual IEnumerator GetEnumerator();
[C++]
public: virtual IEnumerator* GetEnumerator();
[JScript]
public function GetEnumerator() : IEnumerator;
```

Return Value

An **IEnumerator** for navigating through the list.

Implements

IEnumerable.GetEnumerator

Requirements

Platforms: Windows 98, Windows NT 4.0, Windows Millennium Edition, Windows 2000, Windows XP Home Edition, Windows XP Professional, Windows Server 2003 family

CheckedListBox.CheckedItemCollection.IList.Add Method

This member supports the .NET Framework infrastructure and is not intended to be used directly from your code.

```
[Visual Basic]
Private Function Add( _
   ByVal value As Object _
) As Integer Implements IList.Add
[C#]
int IList.Add(
   object value
);
[C++]
private: int IList::Add(
   Object* value
);
[JScript]
private function IList.Add(
   value : Object
) : int;
```

CheckedListBox.CheckedItemCollection.IList.Clear Method

This member supports the .NET Framework infrastructure and is not intended to be used directly from your code.

```
[Visual Basic]
Private Sub Clear() Implements IList.Clear
[C#]
void IList.Clear();
[C++]
private: void IList::Clear();
[JScript]
private function IList.Clear();
```

CheckedListBox.CheckedItemCollection.IList.Insert Method

This member supports the .NET Framework infrastructure and is not intended to be used directly from your code.

```
[Visual Basic]
Private Sub Insert( _
   ByVal index As Integer, _
   ByVal value As Object _
) Implements IList.Insert
```

[C#]
```
void IList.Insert(
   int index,
   object value
);
```
[C++]
```
private: void IList::Insert(
   int index,
   Object* value
);
```
[JScript]
```
private function IList.Insert(
   index : int,
   value : Object
);
```

CheckedListBox.CheckedItemCollection.IList.Remove Method

This member supports the .NET Framework infrastructure and is not intended to be used directly from your code.

[Visual Basic]
```
Private Sub Remove( _
   ByVal value As Object _
) Implements IList.Remove
```
[C#]
```
void IList.Remove(
   object value
);
```
[C++]
```
private: void IList::Remove(
   Object* value
);
```
[JScript]
```
private function IList.Remove(
   value : Object
);
```

CheckedListBox.CheckedItemCollection.IList.RemoveAt Method

This member supports the .NET Framework infrastructure and is not intended to be used directly from your code.

[Visual Basic]
```
Private Sub RemoveAt( _
   ByVal index As Integer _
) Implements IList.RemoveAt
```
[C#]
```
void IList.RemoveAt(
   int index
);
```
[C++]
```
private: void IList::RemoveAt(
   int index
);
```
[JScript]
```
private function IList.RemoveAt(
   index : int
);
```

CheckedListBox.CheckedItemCollection.IndexOf Method

Returns an index into the collection of checked items.

[Visual Basic]
```
Public Overridable Function IndexOf( _
   ByVal item As Object _
) As Integer Implements IList.IndexOf
```
[C#]
```
public virtual int IndexOf(
   object item
);
```
[C++]
```
public: virtual int IndexOf(
   Object* item
);
```
[JScript]
```
public function IndexOf(
   item : Object
) : int;
```

Parameters

item

The object whose index you want to retrieve. This object must belong to the checked items collection.

Return Value

The index of the object in the checked item collection or -1 if the object is not in the collection. For more information, see the examples in the **CheckedListBox.CheckedItemCollection** class overview.

Implements

IList.IndexOf

Remarks

The **CheckedItems** collection is a subset of the objects in the **Items** collection, representing only items that are checked. This collection is ordered in ascending order.

Requirements

Platforms: Windows 98, Windows NT 4.0, Windows Millennium Edition, Windows 2000, Windows XP Home Edition, Windows XP Professional, Windows Server 2003 family

CheckedListBox.ObjectCollection Class

Represents the collection of items in a **CheckedListBox**.

System.Object
  System.Windows.Forms.ListBox.ObjectCollection
    System.Windows.Forms.CheckedListBox.ObjectCollection

```
[Visual Basic]
Public Class CheckedListBox.ObjectCollection
   Inherits ListBox.ObjectCollection
[C#]
public class CheckedListBox.ObjectCollection :
   ListBox.ObjectCollection
[C++]
public __gc class CheckedListBox.ObjectCollection : public
   ListBox.ObjectCollection
[JScript]
public class CheckedListBox.ObjectCollection extends
   ListBox.ObjectCollection
```

Thread Safety

Any public static (**Shared** in Visual Basic) members of this type are safe for multithreaded operations. Any instance members are not guaranteed to be thread safe.

Remarks

The collection is accessed from the parent control, **CheckedListBox**, by the **Items** property. To create a collection of objects to display in the **CheckedListBox** control, you can add or remove the items individually by using the **Add** and **Remove** methods.

Example

See related example in the **System.Windows.Forms.CheckedListBox** class topic.

Requirements

Namespace: System.Windows.Forms

Platforms: Windows 98, Windows NT 4.0, Windows Millennium Edition, Windows 2000, Windows XP Home Edition, Windows XP Professional, Windows Server 2003 family

Assembly: System.Windows.Forms (in System.Windows.Forms.dll)

CheckedListBox.ObjectCollection Constructor

Initializes a new instance of the **System.Windows.Forms.CheckedListBox.ObjectCollection** class.

```
[Visual Basic]
Public Sub New( _
   ByVal owner As CheckedListBox _
)
[C#]
public CheckedListBox.ObjectCollection(
   CheckedListBox owner
);
[C++]
public: ObjectCollection(
   CheckedListBox* owner
);
[JScript]
public function CheckedListBox.ObjectCollection(
   owner : CheckedListBox
);
```

Parameters

owner
  The **CheckedListBox** that owns the collection.

Requirements

Platforms: Windows 98, Windows NT 4.0, Windows Millennium Edition, Windows 2000, Windows XP Home Edition, Windows XP Professional, Windows Server 2003 family

CheckedListBox.ObjectCollection.Add Method

Adds an item to the list of items for a **CheckedListBox**.

Overload List

Adds an item to the list of items for a **CheckedListBox**, specifying the object to add and whether it is checked.

[Visual Basic] **Overloads Public Function Add(Object, Boolean) As Integer**

[C#] **public int Add(object, bool);**

[C++] **public: int Add(Object*, bool);**

[JScript] **public function Add(Object, Boolean) : int;**

Adds an item to the list of items for a **CheckedListBox**, specifying the object to add and the initial checked value.

[Visual Basic] **Overloads Public Function Add(Object, CheckState) As Integer**

[C#] **public int Add(object, CheckState);**

[C++] **public: int Add(Object*, CheckState);**

[JScript] **public function Add(Object, CheckState) : int;**

Inherited from **ListBox.ObjectCollection**.

[Visual Basic] **Overloads Public Function Add(Object) As Integer**

[C#] **public int Add(object);**

[C++] **public: int Add(Object*);**

[JScript] **public function Add(Object) : int;**

CheckedListBox.ObjectCollection.Add Method (Object, Boolean)

Adds an item to the list of items for a **CheckedListBox**, specifying the object to add and whether it is checked.

```
[Visual Basic]
Overloads Public Function Add( _
   ByVal item As Object, _
   ByVal isChecked As Boolean _
) As Integer
[C#]
public int Add(
   object item,
   bool isChecked
);
```

```
[C++]
public: int Add(
   Object* item,
   bool isChecked
);
[JScript]
public function Add(
   item : Object,
   isChecked : Boolean
) : int;
```

Parameters

item

An object representing the item to add to the collection.

isChecked

true to check the item; otherwise, **false**.

Return Value

The index of the newly added item.

Remarks

This method adds an item to the list. For a list, the item is added to the end of the existing list of items. For a sorted checked list box, the item is inserted into the list according to its sorted position. A **SystemException** occurs if there is insufficient space available to store the new item.

Requirements

Platforms: Windows 98, Windows NT 4.0, Windows Millennium Edition, Windows 2000, Windows XP Home Edition, Windows XP Professional, Windows Server 2003 family

CheckedListBox.ObjectCollection.Add Method (Object, CheckState)

Adds an item to the list of items for a **CheckedListBox**, specifying the object to add and the initial checked value.

```
[Visual Basic]
Overloads Public Function Add( _
   ByVal item As Object, _
   ByVal check As CheckState _
) As Integer
[C#]
public int Add(
   object item,
   CheckState check
);
[C++]
public: int Add(
   Object* item,
   CheckState check
);
[JScript]
public function Add(
   item : Object,
   check : CheckState
) : int;
```

Parameters

item

An object representing the item to add to the collection.

check

The initial **CheckState** for the checked portion of the item.

Return Value

The index of the newly added item.

Exceptions

Exception Type	Condition
InvalidEnumArgument-Exception	The *check* parameter is not one of the valid **CheckState** values.

Remarks

This method adds an item to the checked list box. For an unsorted checked list box, the item is added to the end of the existing list of items. For a sorted checked list box, the item is inserted into the list according to its sorted position. A **SystemException** occurs if there is insufficient space available to store the new item.

Requirements

Platforms: Windows 98, Windows NT 4.0, Windows Millennium Edition, Windows 2000, Windows XP Home Edition, Windows XP Professional, Windows Server 2003 family

CheckState Enumeration

Specifies the state of a control, such as a check box, that can be checked, unchecked, or set to an indeterminate state.

[Visual Basic]
```
<Serializable>
Public Enum CheckState
```
[C#]
```
[Serializable]
public enum CheckState
```
[C++]
```
[Serializable]
__value public enum CheckState
```
[JScript]
```
public
   Serializable
enum CheckState
```

Remarks

Multiple methods in **CheckBox**, **CheckedListBox**, and **ItemCheckEventArgs** use this enumeration.

Note Use an indeterminately checked control when you do not want to set a default value.

Members

Member name	Description
Checked Supported by the .NET Compact Framework.	The control is checked.
Indeterminate Supported by the .NET Compact Framework.	The control is indeterminate. An indeterminate control generally has a shaded appearance.
Unchecked Supported by the .NET Compact Framework.	The control is unchecked.

Example

[Visual Basic]
```
Option Explicit
Option Strict

Imports System
Imports System.Drawing
Imports System.Collections
Imports System.ComponentModel
Imports System.Windows.Forms
Imports System.Data
Imports System.IO

Namespace WindowsApplication1
    Public Class Form1
        Inherits System.Windows.Forms.Form
        Private WithEvents checkedListBox1 As ↵
System.Windows.Forms.CheckedListBox
        Private WithEvents textBox1 As System.Windows.Forms.TextBox
        Private WithEvents button1 As System.Windows.Forms.Button
        Private WithEvents button2 As System.Windows.Forms.Button
        Private WithEvents listBox1 As System.Windows.Forms.ListBox
        Private WithEvents button3 As System.Windows.Forms.Button
        Private components As System.ComponentModel.Container

        Public Sub New()
            InitializeComponent()

            ' Sets up the initial objects in the CheckedListBox.
            Dim myFruit As String() = {"Apples", "Oranges", "Tomato"}
            checkedListBox1.Items.AddRange(myFruit)

            ' Changes the selection mode from double-click to ↵
single click.
            checkedListBox1.CheckOnClick = True
        End Sub 'New

        Protected Overloads Overrides Sub Dispose(ByVal ↵
disposing As Boolean)
            If disposing Then
                If Not (components Is Nothing) Then
                    components.Dispose()
                End If
            End If
            MyBase.Dispose(disposing)
        End Sub

        Private Sub InitializeComponent()
            Me.components = New System.ComponentModel.Container()
            Me.textBox1 = New System.Windows.Forms.TextBox()
            Me.checkedListBox1 = New ↵
System.Windows.Forms.CheckedListBox()
            Me.listBox1 = New System.Windows.Forms.ListBox()
            Me.button1 = New System.Windows.Forms.Button()
            Me.button2 = New System.Windows.Forms.Button()
            Me.button3 = New System.Windows.Forms.Button()
            Me.textBox1.Location = New System.Drawing.Point(144, 64)
            Me.textBox1.Size = New System.Drawing.Size(128, 20)
            Me.textBox1.TabIndex = 1
            Me.checkedListBox1.Location = New ↵
System.Drawing.Point(16, 64)
            Me.checkedListBox1.Size = New ↵
System.Drawing.Size(120, 184)
            Me.checkedListBox1.TabIndex = 0
            Me.listBox1.Location = New System.Drawing.Point(408, 64)
            Me.listBox1.Size = New System.Drawing.Size(128, 186)
            Me.listBox1.TabIndex = 3
            Me.button1.Enabled = False
            Me.button1.Location = New System.Drawing.Point(144, 104)
            Me.button1.Size = New System.Drawing.Size(104, 32)
            Me.button1.TabIndex = 2
            Me.button1.Text = "Add Fruit"
            Me.button2.Enabled = False
            Me.button2.Location = New System.Drawing.Point(288, 64)
            Me.button2.Size = New System.Drawing.Size(104, 32)
            Me.button2.TabIndex = 2
            Me.button2.Text = "Show Order"
            Me.button3.Enabled = False
            Me.button3.Location = New System.Drawing.Point(288, 104)
            Me.button3.Size = New System.Drawing.Size(104, 32)
            Me.button3.TabIndex = 2
            Me.button3.Text = "Save Order"
            Me.AutoScaleBaseSize = New System.Drawing.Size(5, 13)
            Me.ClientSize = New System.Drawing.Size(563, 273)
            Me.Controls.AddRange(New ↵
System.Windows.Forms.Control() {Me.listBox1, Me.button3, ↵
Me.button2, Me.button1, Me.textBox1, Me.checkedListBox1})
            Me.Text = "Fruit Order"
        End Sub 'InitializeComponent

        <STAThread()> _
        Public Shared Sub Main()
            Application.Run(New Form1())
        End Sub 'Main

        ' Adds the string if the text box has data in it.
        Private Sub button1_Click(sender As Object, _
                e As System.EventArgs) Handles button1.Click
            If textBox1.Text <> "" Then
                If checkedListBox1.CheckedItems.Contains ↵
(textBox1.Text) = False Then
                    checkedListBox1.Items.Add(textBox1.Text, ↵
CheckState.Checked)
```

```
                End If
                textBox1.Text = ""
            End If
        End Sub 'button1_Click

        ' Activates or deactivates the Add button.
        Private Sub textBox1_TextChanged(sender As Object, _
                e As System.EventArgs) Handles textBox1.TextChanged
            If textBox1.Text = "" Then
                button1.Enabled = False
            Else
                button1.Enabled = True
            End If
        End Sub 'textBox1_TextChanged

        ' Moves the checked items from the CheckedListBox ↵
to the listBox.
        Private Sub button2_Click(sender As Object, _
                e As System.EventArgs) Handles button2.Click
            listBox1.Items.Clear()
            button3.Enabled = False
            Dim i As Integer
            For i = 0 To checkedListBox1.CheckedItems.Count - 1
                listBox1.Items.Add(checkedListBox1.CheckedItems(i))
            Next i
            If listBox1.Items.Count > 0 Then
                button3.Enabled = True
            End If
        End Sub 'button2_Click

        ' Activates the move button if there are checked items.
        Private Sub checkedListBox1_ItemCheck(sender As Object, _
                e As ItemCheckEventArgs) Handles ↵
checkedListBox1.ItemCheck
            If e.NewValue = CheckState.Unchecked Then
                If checkedListBox1.CheckedItems.Count = 1 Then
                    button2.Enabled = False
                End If
            Else
                button2.Enabled = True
            End If
        End Sub 'checkedListBox1_ItemCheck

        ' Saves the items to a file.
        Private Sub button3_Click(sender As Object, _
                e As System.EventArgs) Handles button3.Click
            ' Insert code to save a file.
            listBox1.Items.Clear()
            Dim myEnumerator As IEnumerator
            myEnumerator = ↵
checkedListBox1.CheckedIndices.GetEnumerator()
            Dim y As Integer
            While myEnumerator.MoveNext() <> False
                y = CInt(myEnumerator.Current)
                checkedListBox1.SetItemChecked(y, False)
            End While
            button3.Enabled = False
        End Sub 'button3_Click
    End Class 'Form1
End Namespace 'WindowsApplication1
```

[C#]

```
namespace WindowsApplication1
{
   using System;
   using System.Drawing;
   using System.Collections;
   using System.ComponentModel;
   using System.Windows.Forms;
   using System.Data;
   using System.IO ;

   public class Form1 : System.Windows.Forms.Form
   {
      private System.Windows.Forms.CheckedListBox checkedListBox1;
      private System.Windows.Forms.TextBox textBox1;
      private System.Windows.Forms.Button button1;
      private System.Windows.Forms.Button button2;
      private System.Windows.Forms.ListBox listBox1;
      private System.Windows.Forms.Button button3;
        private System.ComponentModel.Container components;

      public Form1()
      {
            InitializeComponent();

         // Sets up the initial objects in the CheckedListBox.
            string[] myFruit = {"Apples", "Oranges","Tomato"};
         checkedListBox1.Items.AddRange(myFruit);

            // Changes the selection mode from double-click ↵
   to single click.
         checkedListBox1.CheckOnClick = true;
      }

      protected override void Dispose( bool disposing )
      {
        if( disposing )
        {
            if (components != null)
            {
              components.Dispose();
            }
        }
        base.Dispose( disposing );
      }

      private void InitializeComponent()
      {
           this.components = new System.ComponentModel.Container();
           this.textBox1 = new System.Windows.Forms.TextBox();
           this.checkedListBox1 = new ↵
System.Windows.Forms.CheckedListBox();
           this.listBox1 = new System.Windows.Forms.ListBox();
           this.button1 = new System.Windows.Forms.Button();
           this.button2 = new System.Windows.Forms.Button();
           this.button3 = new System.Windows.Forms.Button();
           this.textBox1.Location = new System.Drawing.Point(144, 64);
           this.textBox1.Size = new System.Drawing.Size(128, 20);
           this.textBox1.TabIndex = 1;
           this.textBox1.TextChanged += new ↵
System.EventHandler(this.textBox1_TextChanged);
           this.checkedListBox1.Location = new ↵
 System.Drawing.Point(16, 64);
           this.checkedListBox1.Size = new System.Drawing.Size(120, 184);
           this.checkedListBox1.TabIndex = 0;
           this.checkedListBox1.ItemCheck += new ↵
System.Windows.Forms.ItemCheckEventHandler ↵
 (this.checkedListBox1_ItemCheck);
           this.listBox1.Location = new System.Drawing.Point(408, 64);
           this.listBox1.Size = new System.Drawing.Size(128, 186);
           this.listBox1.TabIndex = 3;
           this.button1.Enabled = false;
           this.button1.Location = new System.Drawing.Point(144, 104);
           this.button1.Size = new System.Drawing.Size(104, 32);
           this.button1.TabIndex = 2;
           this.button1.Text = "Add Fruit";
           this.button1.Click += new
System.EventHandler(this.button1_Click);
           this.button2.Enabled = false;
           this.button2.Location = new System.Drawing.Point(288, 64);
           this.button2.Size = new System.Drawing.Size(104, 32);
           this.button2.TabIndex = 2;
           this.button2.Text = "Show Order";
           this.button2.Click += new ↵
System.EventHandler(this.button2_Click);
           this.button3.Enabled = false;
           this.button3.Location = new System.Drawing.Point(288, 104);
           this.button3.Size = new System.Drawing.Size(104, 32);
           this.button3.TabIndex = 2;
```

```
        this.button3.Text = "Save Order";
        this.button3.Click += new                                    ↵
System.EventHandler(this.button3_Click);
        this.AutoScaleBaseSize = new System.Drawing.Size(5, 13);
        this.ClientSize = new System.Drawing.Size(563, 273);
        this.Controls.AddRange(new System.Windows.Forms.Control[]
{this.listBox1,
                                                this.button3,
                                                this.button2,
                                                this.button1,
                                                this.textBox1,
                                          this.checkedListBox1});
        this.Text = "Fruit Order";
     }

     [STAThread]
     public static void Main(string[] args)
     {
        Application.Run(new Form1());
     }

     // Adds the string if the text box has data in it.
     private void button1_Click(object sender, System.EventArgs e)
     {
        if(textBox1.Text != "")
        {
           if                                                         ↵
 (checkedListBox1.CheckedItems.Contains(textBox1.Text)== false)

checkedListBox1.Items.Add(textBox1.Text,CheckState.Checked);
           textBox1.Text = "";
        }

     }
     // Activates or deactivates the Add button.
     private void textBox1_TextChanged(object sender,                 ↵
 System.EventArgs e)
     {
        if (textBox1.Text == "")
        {
           button1.Enabled = false;
        }
        else
        {
           button1.Enabled = true;
        }

     }

     // Moves the checked items from the CheckedListBox                ↵
 to the listBox.
     private void button2_Click(object sender, System.EventArgs e)
     {
        listBox1.Items.Clear();
        button3.Enabled=false;
        for (int i=0; i< checkedListBox1.CheckedItems.Count;i++)
        {
           listBox1.Items.Add(checkedListBox1.CheckedItems[i]);
        }
        if (listBox1.Items.Count>0)
           button3.Enabled=true;

     }
      // Activates the move button if there are checked items.
     private void checkedListBox1_ItemCheck(object sender,             ↵
 ItemCheckEventArgs e)
     {
        if(e.NewValue==CheckState.Unchecked)
        {
           if(checkedListBox1.CheckedItems.Count==1)
           {
              button2.Enabled = false;
           }
        }
        else
        {
           button2.Enabled = true;
        }
     }

      // Saves the items to a file.
     private void button3_Click(object sender, System.EventArgs e)
     {
        // Insert code to save a file.
        listBox1.Items.Clear();
        IEnumerator myEnumerator;
        myEnumerator = checkedListBox1.CheckedIndices.GetEnumerator();
        int y;
        while (myEnumerator.MoveNext() != false)
        {
           y =(int) myEnumerator.Current;
           checkedListBox1.SetItemChecked(y, false);
        }
        button3.Enabled = false ;
     }
   }
}
```

Requirements

Namespace: System.Windows.Forms

Platforms: Windows 98, Windows NT 4.0, Windows Millennium Edition, Windows 2000, Windows XP Home Edition, Windows XP Professional, Windows Server 2003 family, .NET Compact Framework - Windows CE .NET

Assembly: System.Windows.Forms (in System.Windows.Forms.dll)

Clipboard Class

Provides methods to place data on and retrieve data from the system clipboard. This class cannot be inherited.

For a list of all members of this type, see **Clipboard Members**.

System.Object
  System.Windows.Forms.Clipboard

[Visual Basic]
```
NotInheritable Public Class Clipboard
```
[C#]
```
public sealed class Clipboard
```
[C++]
```
public __gc __sealed class Clipboard
```
[JScript]
```
public class Clipboard
```

Thread Safety

Any public static (**Shared** in Visual Basic) members of this type are safe for multithreaded operations. Any instance members are not guaranteed to be thread safe.

Remarks

For a list of predefined formats to use with the **Clipboard** class, see the **DataFormats** class.

Call **SetDataObject** to put data on the clipboard. To place a persistent copy of the data on the clipboard, set the *copy* parameter to **true**.

Note Place data on the clipboard in multiple formats to maximize the possibility that a target application, whose format requirements you might not know, can successfully retrieve the data.

Call **GetDataObject** to retrieve data from the clipboard. The data is returned as an object that implements the **IDataObject** interface. Use the methods specified by **IDataObject** and fields in **DataFormats** to extract the data from the object. If you do not know the format of the data you retrieved, call the **GetFormats** method of the **IDataObject** interface to get a list of all formats that data is stored in. Then call the **GetData** method of the **IDataObject** interface, and specify a format that your application can use.

Note All Windows applications share the system clipboard, so the contents are subject to change when you switch to another application.

Note A class must be serializable for it to be put on the clipboard.

Example

[Visual Basic, C#, JScript] The following example uses **Clipboard** methods to place data on and retrieve it from the system clipboard. This code assumes `button1`, `button2`, `textBox1`, and `textBox2` have been created and placed on the form.

[Visual Basic, C#, JScript] The `button1_Click` method calls **SetDataObject** to take selected text from the text box and place it on the system clipboard.

[Visual Basic, C#, JScript] The `button2_Click` method calls **GetDataObject** to retrieve data from the system clipboard. The code uses **IDataObject** and **DataFormats** to extract the data returned and displays the data in `textBox2`.

[Visual Basic]
```
Private Sub button1_Click(sender As Object, e As System.EventArgs)
    ' Takes the selected text from a text box and puts it                ↵
 on the clipboard.
    If textBox1.SelectedText <> "" Then
        Clipboard.SetDataObject(textBox1.SelectedText)
    Else
        textBox2.Text = "No text selected in textBox1"
    End If
End Sub 'button1_Click

Private Sub button2_Click(sender As Object, e As System.EventArgs)
    ' Declares an IDataObject to hold the data returned from             ↵
 the clipboard.
    ' Retrieves the data from the clipboard.
    Dim iData As IDataObject = Clipboard.GetDataObject()

    ' Determines whether the data is in a format you can use.
    If iData.GetDataPresent(DataFormats.Text) Then
        ' Yes it is, so display it in a text box.
        textBox2.Text = CType(iData.GetData(DataFormats.Text), String)
    Else
        ' No it is not.
        textBox2.Text = "Could not retrieve data off the clipboard."
    End If
End Sub 'button2_Click
```

[C#]
```
private void button1_Click(object sender, System.EventArgs e) {
    // Takes the selected text from a text box and puts it               ↵
on the clipboard.
    if(textBox1.SelectedText != "")
       Clipboard.SetDataObject(textBox1.SelectedText);
    else
       textBox2.Text = "No text selected in textBox1";
 }

 private void button2_Click(object sender, System.EventArgs e) {
    // Declares an IDataObject to hold the data returned                 ↵
from the clipboard.
    // Retrieves the data from the clipboard.
    IDataObject iData = Clipboard.GetDataObject();

    // Determines whether the data is in a format you can use.
    if(iData.GetDataPresent(DataFormats.Text)) {
       // Yes it is, so display it in a text box.
       textBox2.Text = (String)iData.GetData(DataFormats.Text);
    }
    else {
       // No it is not.
       textBox2.Text = "Could not retrieve data off the clipboard.";
    }
 }
```

[JScript]
```
private function button1_Click(sender : Object, e : System.EventArgs) {
    //Take the selected text from a text box and put it on               ↵
the clipboard.
    if(textBox1.SelectedText != "")
       Clipboard.SetDataObject(textBox1.SelectedText);
    else
       textBox2.Text = "No text selected in textBox1";
 }

 private function button2_Click(sender : Object, e :                     ↵
System.EventArgs) {
    //Declare an IDataObject to hold the data returned from              ↵
the clipboard.
    //Then retrieve the data from the clipboard.
    var iData : IDataObject = Clipboard.GetDataObject();

    //Determine whether the data is in a format you can use.
    if(iData.GetDataPresent(DataFormats.Text)) {
       //Yes it is, so display it in a text box.
       textBox2.Text = String(iData.GetData(DataFormats.Text));
```

```
    }
    else {
       //No it is not.
       textBox2.Text = "Could not retrieve data off the clipboard.";
    }
}
```

Requirements

Namespace: System.Windows.Forms

Platforms: Windows 98, Windows NT 4.0, Windows Millennium Edition, Windows 2000, Windows XP Home Edition, Windows XP Professional, Windows Server 2003 family

Assembly: System.Windows.Forms (in System.Windows.Forms.dll)

Clipboard.GetDataObject Method

Retrieves the data that is currently on the system clipboard.

```
[Visual Basic]
Public Shared Function GetDataObject() As IDataObject
[C#]
public static IDataObject GetDataObject();
[C++]
public: static IDataObject* GetDataObject();
[JScript]
public static function GetDataObject() : IDataObject;
```

Return Value

An **IDataObject** that represents the data currently on the clipboard, or a null reference (**Nothing** in Visual Basic) if there is no data on the clipboard.

Exceptions

Exception Type	Condition
ExternalException	Data could not be retrieved from the clipboard.
ThreadStateException	The **ApartmentState** property of the application is not set to **ApartmentState.STA**.

Remarks

Because the data type of the object returned from the clipboard can vary, this method returns the data in an **IDataObject**. Then you can use methods of the **IDataObject** interface to extract the data in its proper data type.

Example

See related example in the **System.Windows.Forms.Clipboard** class topic.

Requirements

Platforms: Windows 98, Windows NT 4.0, Windows Millennium Edition, Windows 2000, Windows XP Home Edition, Windows XP Professional, Windows Server 2003 family

.NET Framework Security:

- **UIPermission** for access to the system clipboard. Associated enumeration: **UIPermissionClipboard.AllClipboard**

Clipboard.SetDataObject Method

Places data on the system clipboard.

Overload List

Places nonpersistent data on the system clipboard.

[Visual Basic] **Overloads Public Shared Sub SetDataObject(Object)**

[C#] **public static void SetDataObject(object);**

[C++] **public: static void SetDataObject(Object*);**

[JScript] **public static function SetDataObject(Object);**

Places data on the system clipboard and specifies whether the data should remain on the clipboard after the application exits.

[Visual Basic] **Overloads Public Shared Sub SetDataObject(Object, Boolean)**

[C#] **public static void SetDataObject(object, bool);**

[C++] **public: static void SetDataObject(Object*, bool);**

[JScript] **public static function SetDataObject(Object, Boolean);**

Example

See related example in the **System.Windows.Forms.Clipboard** class topic.

Clipboard.SetDataObject Method (Object)

Places nonpersistent data on the system clipboard.

```
[Visual Basic]
Overloads Public Shared Sub SetDataObject( _
   ByVal data As Object _
)
[C#]
public static void SetDataObject(
   object data
);
[C++]
public: static void SetDataObject(
   Object* data
);
[JScript]
public static function SetDataObject(
   data : Object
);
```

Parameters

data

The data to place on the clipboard.

Exceptions

Exception Type	Condition
ExternalException	Data could not be placed on the clipboard.
ThreadStateException	The **ApartmentState** property of the application is not set to **ApartmentState.STA**.
ArgumentNull-Exception	The value of *data* is a null reference (**Nothing** in Visual Basic).

Remarks

Data will be deleted from system clipboard when the application exits.

> **Note** A class must be serializable for it to be put on the clipboard. See **Serializing Objects** for more information on serialization.

Example

See related example in the **System.Windows.Forms.Clipboard** class topic.

Requirements

Platforms: Windows 98, Windows NT 4.0, Windows Millennium Edition, Windows 2000, Windows XP Home Edition, Windows XP Professional, Windows Server 2003 family

.NET Framework Security:

- **UIPermission** for access to the system clipboard. Associated enumeration: **UIPermissionClipboard.AllClipboard**

Clipboard.SetDataObject Method (Object, Boolean)

Places data on the system clipboard and specifies whether the data should remain on the clipboard after the application exits.

```
[Visual Basic]
Overloads Public Shared Sub SetDataObject( _
   ByVal data As Object, _
   ByVal copy As Boolean _
)
[C#]
public static void SetDataObject(
   object data,
   bool copy
);
[C++]
public: static void SetDataObject(
   Object* data,
   bool copy
);
[JScript]
public static function SetDataObject(
   data : Object,
   copy : Boolean
);
```

Parameters

data

The data to place on the clipboard.

copy

true if you want data to remain on the clipboard after this application exits; otherwise, **false**.

Exceptions

Exception Type	Condition
ExternalException	Data could not be placed on the clipboard.
ThreadStateException	The **ApartmentState** property of the application is not set to **ApartmentState.STA**.
ArgumentNull-Exception	The value of *data* is a null reference (**Nothing** in Visual Basic).

Remarks

If the *copy* parameter is **false**, the data will be deleted from system clipboard when the application exits.

> **Note** A class must be serializable for it to be put on the clipboard.

Example

See related example in the **System.Windows.Forms.Clipboard** class topic.

Requirements

Platforms: Windows 98, Windows NT 4.0, Windows Millennium Edition, Windows 2000, Windows XP Home Edition, Windows XP Professional, Windows Server 2003 family

.NET Framework Security:

- **UIPermission** for access to the system clipboard. Associated enumeration: **UIPermissionClipboard.AllClipboard**

ColorDepth Enumeration

Specifies the number of colors used to display an image in an **ImageList** control.

[Visual Basic]
```
<Serializable>
Public Enum ColorDepth
```
[C#]
```
[Serializable]
public enum ColorDepth
```
[C++]
```
[Serializable]
__value public enum ColorDepth
```
[JScript]
```
public
   Serializable
enum ColorDepth
```

Remarks

This enumeration is used by the **ColorDepth** property of the **ImageList** class.

Members

Member name	Description
Depth16Bit	A 16-bit image.
Depth24Bit	A 24-bit image.
Depth32Bit	A 32-bit image.
Depth4Bit	A 4-bit image.
Depth8Bit	An 8-bit image.

Requirements

Namespace: System.Windows.Forms

Platforms: Windows 98, Windows NT 4.0, Windows Millennium Edition, Windows 2000, Windows XP Home Edition, Windows XP Professional, Windows Server 2003 family

Assembly: System.Windows.Forms (in System.Windows.Forms.dll)

ColorDialog Class

Represents a common dialog box that displays available colors along with controls that allow the user to define custom colors.

System.Object
  System.MarshalByRefObject
    System.ComponentModel.Component
      System.Windows.Forms.CommonDialog
        System.Windows.Forms.ColorDialog

[Visual Basic]
```
Public Class ColorDialog
   Inherits CommonDialog
```
[C#]
```
public class ColorDialog : CommonDialog
```
[C++]
```
public __gc class ColorDialog : public CommonDialog
```
[JScript]
```
public class ColorDialog extends CommonDialog
```

Thread Safety

Any public static (**Shared** in Visual Basic) members of this type are safe for multithreaded operations. Any instance members are not guaranteed to be thread safe.

Remarks

The inherited member **ShowDialog** must be invoked to create this specific common dialog box. **HookProc** can be overridden to implement specific dialog box hook functionality. Use **Color** to retrieve the color selected by the user.

When you create an instance of **ColorDialog**, some of the read/write properties are set to initial values. For a list of these values, see the **ColorDialog** constructor.

Example

[Visual Basic, C#] The following example illustrates the creation of new **ColorDialog**. This example assumes that the method is called from within an existing form, that has a **TextBox** and **Button** placed on it.

[Visual Basic]
```
Protected Sub button1_Click(sender As Object, e As System.EventArgs)
    Dim MyDialog As New ColorDialog()
    ' Keeps the user from selecting a custom color.
    MyDialog.AllowFullOpen = False
    ' Allows the user to get help. (The default is false.)
    MyDialog.ShowHelp = True
    ' Sets the initial color select to the current text color,
    MyDialog.Color = textBox1.ForeColor

    ' Update the text box color if the user clicks OK
    If (MyDialog.ShowDialog() = DialogResult.OK) Then
        textBox1.ForeColor =  MyDialog.Color
    End If

End Sub 'button1_Click
```

[C#]
```
protected void button1_Click(object sender, System.EventArgs e)
 {
    ColorDialog MyDialog = new ColorDialog();
    // Keeps the user from selecting a custom color.
    MyDialog.AllowFullOpen = false ;
    // Allows the user to get help. (The default is false.)
    MyDialog.ShowHelp = true ;
    // Sets the initial color select to the current text color.
    MyDialog.Color = textBox1.ForeColor ;

    // Update the text box color if the user clicks OK
    if (MyDialog.ShowDialog() == DialogResult.OK)
        textBox1.ForeColor =  MyDialog.Color;
 }
```

Requirements

Namespace: System.Windows.Forms

Platforms: Windows 98, Windows NT 4.0, Windows Millennium Edition, Windows 2000, Windows XP Home Edition, Windows XP Professional, Windows Server 2003 family

Assembly: System.Windows.Forms (in System.Windows.Forms.dll)

ColorDialog Constructor

Initializes a new instance of the **ColorDialog** class.

[Visual Basic]
```
Public Sub New()
```
[C#]
```
public ColorDialog();
```
[C++]
```
public: ColorDialog();
```
[JScript]
```
public function ColorDialog();
```

Remarks

When you create an instance of **ColorDialog**, the following read/write properties are set to initial values.

Property	Initial Value
AllowFullOpen	**true**
AnyColor	**false**
Color	**Color.Black**
CustomColors	A null reference (**Nothing** in Visual Basic)
FullOpen	**false**
ShowHelp	**false**
SolidColorOnly	**false**

You can change the value for any of these properties through a separate call to the property.

Requirements

Platforms: Windows 98, Windows NT 4.0, Windows Millennium Edition, Windows 2000, Windows XP Home Edition, Windows XP Professional, Windows Server 2003 family

ColorDialog.AllowFullOpen Property

Gets or sets a value indicating whether the user can use the dialog box to define custom colors.

[Visual Basic]
```
Public Overridable Property AllowFullOpen As Boolean
```
[C#]
```
public virtual bool AllowFullOpen {get; set;}
```
[C++]
```
public: __property virtual bool get_AllowFullOpen();
public: __property virtual void set_AllowFullOpen(bool);
```

```
[JScript]
public function get AllowFullOpen() : Boolean;
public function set AllowFullOpen(Boolean);
```

Property Value

true if the user can define custom colors; otherwise, **false**. The default is **true**.

Remarks

When set to **false**, the associated button in the dialog box is disabled and the user cannot access the custom colors control in the dialog box.

Example

[Visual Basic, C#] The following example illustrates the creation of new **ColorDialog**. This example assumes that the method is called from within an existing form, that has a **TextBox** and **Button** placed on it.

[Visual Basic]

```
Protected Sub button1_Click(sender As Object, e As System.EventArgs)
    Dim MyDialog As New ColorDialog()
    ' Keeps the user from selecting a custom color.
    MyDialog.AllowFullOpen = False
    ' Allows the user to get help. (The default is false.)
    MyDialog.ShowHelp = True
    ' Sets the initial color select to the current text color,
    MyDialog.Color = textBox1.ForeColor

    ' Update the text box color if the user clicks OK
    If (MyDialog.ShowDialog() = DialogResult.OK) Then
        textBox1.ForeColor = MyDialog.Color
    End If

End Sub 'button1_Click
```

[C#]

```
protected void button1_Click(object sender, System.EventArgs e)
 {
    ColorDialog MyDialog = new ColorDialog();
    // Keeps the user from selecting a custom color.
    MyDialog.AllowFullOpen = false ;
    // Allows the user to get help. (The default is false.)
    MyDialog.ShowHelp = true ;
    // Sets the initial color select to the current text color.
    MyDialog.Color = textBox1.ForeColor ;

    // Update the text box color if the user clicks OK
    if (MyDialog.ShowDialog() == DialogResult.OK)
        textBox1.ForeColor = MyDialog.Color;
 }
```

Requirements

Platforms: Windows 98, Windows NT 4.0, Windows Millennium Edition, Windows 2000, Windows XP Home Edition, Windows XP Professional, Windows Server 2003 family

ColorDialog.AnyColor Property

Gets or sets a value indicating whether the dialog box displays all available colors in the set of basic colors.

```
[Visual Basic]
Public Overridable Property AnyColor As Boolean
[C#]
public virtual bool AnyColor {get; set;}
[C++]
public: __property virtual bool get_AnyColor();
public: __property virtual void set_AnyColor(bool);
[JScript]
public function get AnyColor() : Boolean;
public function set AnyColor(Boolean);
```

Property Value

true if the dialog box displays all available colors in the set of basic colors; otherwise, **false**. The default value is **false**.

Requirements

Platforms: Windows 98, Windows NT 4.0, Windows Millennium Edition, Windows 2000, Windows XP Home Edition, Windows XP Professional, Windows Server 2003 family

ColorDialog.Color Property

Gets or sets the color selected by the user.

```
[Visual Basic]
Public Property Color As Color
[C#]
public Color Color {get; set;}
[C++]
public: __property Color get_Color();
public: __property void set_Color(Color);
[JScript]
public function get Color() : Color;
public function set Color(Color);
```

Property Value

The color selected by the user. If a color is not selected, the default value is black.

Remarks

The color selected by the user in the dialog box at run time, as defined in **Color** structure.

Example

[Visual Basic, C#] The following example illustrates the creation of new **ColorDialog**. This example assumes that the method is called from within an existing form, that has a **TextBox** and **Button** placed on it.

[Visual Basic]

```
Protected Sub button1_Click(sender As Object, e As System.EventArgs)
    Dim MyDialog As New ColorDialog()
    ' Keeps the user from selecting a custom color.
    MyDialog.AllowFullOpen = False
    ' Allows the user to get help. (The default is false.)
    MyDialog.ShowHelp = True
    ' Sets the initial color select to the current text color,
    MyDialog.Color = textBox1.ForeColor

    ' Update the text box color if the user clicks OK
    If (MyDialog.ShowDialog() = DialogResult.OK) Then
        textBox1.ForeColor = MyDialog.Color
    End If

End Sub 'button1_Click
```

[C#]

```
protected void button1_Click(object sender, System.EventArgs e)
 {
    ColorDialog MyDialog = new ColorDialog();
    // Keeps the user from selecting a custom color.
    MyDialog.AllowFullOpen = false ;
    // Allows the user to get help. (The default is false.)
    MyDialog.ShowHelp = true ;
```

```
    // Sets the initial color select to the current text color.
    MyDialog.Color = textBox1.ForeColor ;

    // Update the text box color if the user clicks OK
    if (MyDialog.ShowDialog() == DialogResult.OK)
        textBox1.ForeColor =  MyDialog.Color;
}
```

Requirements

Platforms: Windows 98, Windows NT 4.0, Windows Millennium Edition, Windows 2000, Windows XP Home Edition, Windows XP Professional, Windows Server 2003 family

ColorDialog.CustomColors Property

Gets or sets the set of custom colors shown in the dialog box.

[Visual Basic]
```
Public Property CustomColors As Integer ()
```
[C#]
```
public int[] CustomColors {get; set;}
```
[C++]
```
public: __property int get_CustomColors();
public: __property void set_CustomColors(int __gc[]);
```
[JScript]
```
public function get CustomColors() : int[];
public function set CustomColors(int[]);
```

Property Value

A set of custom colors shown by the dialog box. The default value is a null reference (**Nothing** in Visual Basic).

Remarks

Users can create their own set of custom colors. These colors are contained in an **Int32** composed of the ARGB component (alpha, red, green, and blue) values necessary to create the color. For more information on the structure of this data, see **Color**.

Custom colors can only be defined if **AllowFullOpen** is set to **true**.

Example

[Visual Basic, C#, C++] The following example shows how to add an array of type **Int32** representing custom colors to **CustomColors**. This example assumes that the code is run from within a **Form**.

[Visual Basic]
```
Dim MyDialog = New ColorDialog()
' Allows the user to select or edit a custom color.
MyDialog.AllowFullOpen = True
' Assigns an array of custom colors to the CustomColors property.
MyDialog.CustomColors = New Integer() {6916092, 15195440,                ↵
 16107657, 1836924, _
   3758726, 12566463, 7526079, 7405793, 6945974, 241502,                 ↵
2296476, 5130294, _
   3102017, 7324121, 14993507, 11730944}

' Allows the user to get help. (The default is false.)
MyDialog.ShowHelp = True
' Sets the initial color select to the current text color,
' so that if the user cancels out, the original color is restored.
MyDialog.Color = Me.BackColor
MyDialog.ShowDialog()
Me.BackColor = MyDialog.Color
```

[C#]
```
System.Windows.Forms.ColorDialog MyDialog = new ColorDialog();
// Allows the user to select or edit a custom color.
MyDialog.AllowFullOpen = true ;
// Assigns an array of custom colors to the CustomColors property
MyDialog.CustomColors = new int[]{6916092, 15195440, 16107657, 1836924,
   3758726, 12566463, 7526079, 7405793, 6945974, 241502,                ↵
2296476, 5130294,
   3102017, 7324121, 14993507, 11730944,};

// Allows the user to get help. (The default is false.)
MyDialog.ShowHelp = true ;
// Sets the initial color select to the current text color,
// so that if the user cancels out, the original color is restored.
MyDialog.Color = this.BackColor;
MyDialog.ShowDialog();
this.BackColor =  MyDialog.Color;
```

[C++]
```
System::Windows::Forms::ColorDialog* MyDialog = new ColorDialog();
// Allows the user to select or edit a custom color.
MyDialog->AllowFullOpen = true ;
// Assigns an array of custom colors to the CustomColors property

int temp0 __gc[] = {6916092, 15195440, 16107657, 1836924,
   3758726, 12566463, 7526079, 7405793, 6945974, 241502,                ↵
2296476, 5130294,
   3102017, 7324121, 14993507, 11730944,};

MyDialog->CustomColors = temp0;

// Allows the user to get help. (The default is false.)
MyDialog->ShowHelp = true ;
// Sets the initial color select to the current text color,
// so that if the user cancels out, the original color is restored.
MyDialog->Color = this->BackColor;
MyDialog->ShowDialog();
this->BackColor =  MyDialog->Color;
```

Requirements

Platforms: Windows 98, Windows NT 4.0, Windows Millennium Edition, Windows 2000, Windows XP Home Edition, Windows XP Professional, Windows Server 2003 family

ColorDialog.FullOpen Property

Gets or sets a value indicating whether the controls used to create custom colors are visible when the dialog box is opened

[Visual Basic]
```
Public Overridable Property FullOpen As Boolean
```
[C#]
```
public virtual bool FullOpen {get; set;}
```
[C++]
```
public: __property virtual bool get_FullOpen();
public: __property virtual void set_FullOpen(bool);
```
[JScript]
```
public function get FullOpen() : Boolean;
public function set FullOpen(Boolean);
```

Property Value

true if the custom color controls are available when the dialog box is opened; otherwise, **false**. The default value is **false**.

Remarks

By default, the custom color controls are not visible when the dialog box is first opened. You must click the **Custom Colors** button to display them.

> **Note** If **AllowFullOpen** is **false**, then **FullOpen** has no effect.

Requirements

Platforms: Windows 98, Windows NT 4.0, Windows Millennium Edition, Windows 2000, Windows XP Home Edition, Windows XP Professional, Windows Server 2003 family

ColorDialog.Instance Property

This member supports the .NET Framework infrastructure and is not intended to be used directly from your code.

[Visual Basic]
```
Protected Overridable ReadOnly Property Instance As IntPtr
```
[C#]
```
protected virtual IntPtr Instance {get;}
```
[C++]
```
protected: __property virtual IntPtr get_Instance();
```
[JScript]
```
protected function get Instance() : IntPtr;
```

ColorDialog.Options Property

This member supports the .NET Framework infrastructure and is not intended to be used directly from your code.

[Visual Basic]
```
Protected Overridable ReadOnly Property Options As Integer
```
[C#]
```
protected virtual int Options {get;}
```
[C++]
```
protected: __property virtual int get_Options();
```
[JScript]
```
protected function get Options() : int;
```

ColorDialog.ShowHelp Property

Gets or sets a value indicating whether a Help button appears in the color dialog box.

[Visual Basic]
```
Public Overridable Property ShowHelp As Boolean
```
[C#]
```
public virtual bool ShowHelp {get; set;}
```
[C++]
```
public: __property virtual bool get_ShowHelp();
public: __property virtual void set_ShowHelp(bool);
```
[JScript]
```
public function get ShowHelp() : Boolean;
public function set ShowHelp(Boolean);
```

Property Value

true if the Help button is shown in the dialog box; otherwise, **false**. The default value is **false**.

Example

[Visual Basic, C#] The following example illustrates the creation of new **ColorDialog**. This example assumes that the method is called from within an existing form, that has a **TextBox** and **Button** placed on it.

[Visual Basic]
```
Protected Sub button1_Click(sender As Object, e As System.EventArgs)
    Dim MyDialog As New ColorDialog()
    ' Keeps the user from selecting a custom color.
    MyDialog.AllowFullOpen = False
    ' Allows the user to get help. (The default is false.)
    MyDialog.ShowHelp = True
    ' Sets the initial color select to the current text color,
    MyDialog.Color = textBox1.ForeColor

    ' Update the text box color if the user clicks OK
    If (MyDialog.ShowDialog() = DialogResult.OK) Then
        textBox1.ForeColor =  MyDialog.Color
    End If

End Sub 'button1_Click
```

[C#]
```
protected void button1_Click(object sender, System.EventArgs e)
 {
    ColorDialog MyDialog = new ColorDialog();
    // Keeps the user from selecting a custom color.
    MyDialog.AllowFullOpen = false ;
    // Allows the user to get help. (The default is false.)
    MyDialog.ShowHelp = true ;
    // Sets the initial color select to the current text color.
    MyDialog.Color = textBox1.ForeColor ;

    // Update the text box color if the user clicks OK
    if (MyDialog.ShowDialog() == DialogResult.OK)
        textBox1.ForeColor =  MyDialog.Color;
 }
```

Requirements

Platforms: Windows 98, Windows NT 4.0, Windows Millennium Edition, Windows 2000, Windows XP Home Edition, Windows XP Professional, Windows Server 2003 family

ColorDialog.SolidColorOnly Property

Gets or sets a value indicating whether the dialog box will restrict users to selecting solid colors only.

[Visual Basic]
```
Public Overridable Property SolidColorOnly As Boolean
```
[C#]
```
public virtual bool SolidColorOnly {get; set;}
```
[C++]
```
public: __property virtual bool get_SolidColorOnly();
public: __property virtual void set_SolidColorOnly(bool);
```
[JScript]
```
public function get SolidColorOnly() : Boolean;
public function set SolidColorOnly(Boolean);
```

Property Value

true if users can select only solid colors; otherwise, **false.** The default value is **false**.

Remarks

This property is applicable to systems with 256 or fewer colors. On these types of systems, some colors are composites of others.

Requirements

Platforms: Windows 98, Windows NT 4.0, Windows Millennium Edition, Windows 2000, Windows XP Home Edition, Windows XP Professional, Windows Server 2003 family

ColorDialog.Reset Method

Resets all options to their default values, the last selected color to black, and the custom colors to their default values.

```
[Visual Basic]
Overrides Public Sub Reset()
[C#]
public override void Reset();
[C++]
public: void Reset();
[JScript]
public override function Reset();
```

Requirements

Platforms: Windows 98, Windows NT 4.0, Windows Millennium Edition, Windows 2000, Windows XP Home Edition, Windows XP Professional, Windows Server 2003 family

ColorDialog.RunDialog Method

This member overrides **CommonDialog.RunDialog**.

```
[Visual Basic]
Overrides Protected Function RunDialog( _
   ByVal hwndOwner As IntPtr _
) As Boolean
[C#]
protected override bool RunDialog(
   IntPtr hwndOwner
);
[C++]
protected: bool RunDialog(
   IntPtr hwndOwner
);
[JScript]
protected override function RunDialog(
   hwndOwner : IntPtr
) : Boolean;
```

Requirements

Platforms: Windows 98, Windows NT 4.0, Windows Millennium Edition, Windows 2000, Windows XP Home Edition, Windows XP Professional, Windows Server 2003 family

ColorDialog.ToString Method

This member overrides **Object.ToString**.

```
[Visual Basic]
Overrides Public Function ToString() As String
[C#]
public override string ToString();
[C++]
public: String* ToString();
[JScript]
public override function ToString() : String;
```

Requirements

Platforms: Windows 98, Windows NT 4.0, Windows Millennium Edition, Windows 2000, Windows XP Home Edition, Windows XP Professional, Windows Server 2003 family

ColumnClickEventArgs Class

Provides data for the **ColumnClick** event.

System.Object
 System.EventArgs
  System.Windows.Forms.ColumnClickEventArgs

```
[Visual Basic]
Public Class ColumnClickEventArgs
   Inherits EventArgs
[C#]
public class ColumnClickEventArgs : EventArgs
[C++]
public __gc class ColumnClickEventArgs : public EventArgs
[JScript]
public class ColumnClickEventArgs extends EventArgs
```

Thread Safety

Any public static (**Shared** in Visual Basic) members of this type are safe for multithreaded operations. Any instance members are not guaranteed to be thread safe.

Remarks

The **ColumnClickEventArgs** class provides the zero-based index within the **ListView.ColumnHeaderCollection** class of the column that is clicked in the **ListView** control. You can use this information in an event handler for the **ColumnClick** event to determine which column is being clicked to perform tasks on the data within the column.

Requirements

Namespace: System.Windows.Forms

Platforms: Windows 98, Windows NT 4.0, Windows Millennium Edition, Windows 2000, Windows XP Home Edition, Windows XP Professional, Windows Server 2003 family, .NET Compact Framework - Windows CE .NET

Assembly: System.Windows.Forms (in System.Windows.Forms.dll)

ColumnClickEventArgs Constructor

Initializes a new instance of the **ColumnClickEventArgs** class.

```
[Visual Basic]
Public Sub New( _
   ByVal column As Integer _
)
[C#]
public ColumnClickEventArgs(
   int column
);
[C++]
public: ColumnClickEventArgs(
   int column
);
[JScript]
public function ColumnClickEventArgs(
   column : int
);
```

Parameters

column

The zero-based index of the column that is clicked.

Requirements

Platforms: Windows 98, Windows NT 4.0, Windows Millennium Edition, Windows 2000, Windows XP Home Edition, Windows XP Professional, Windows Server 2003 family, .NET Compact Framework - Windows CE .NET

ColumnClickEventArgs.Column Property

Gets the zero-based index of the column that is clicked.

```
[Visual Basic]
Public ReadOnly Property Column As Integer
[C#]
public int Column {get;}
[C++]
public: __property int get_Column();
[JScript]
public function get Column() : int;
```

Property Value

The zero-based index within the **ListView.ColumnHeader-Collection** of the column that is clicked.

Remarks

You can use the information provided by this property in an event handler for the **ColumnClick** event to determine which column is being clicked to perform tasks on the data within the column.

Requirements

Platforms: Windows 98, Windows NT 4.0, Windows Millennium Edition, Windows 2000, Windows XP Home Edition, Windows XP Professional, Windows Server 2003 family, .NET Compact Framework - Windows CE .NET

ColumnClickEventHandler Delegate

Represents the method that will handle the **ColumnClick** event of a **ListView**.

[Visual Basic]
```
<Serializable>
Public Delegate Sub ColumnClickEventHandler( _
   ByVal sender As Object, _
   ByVal e As ColumnClickEventArgs _
)
```
[C#]
```
[Serializable]
public delegate void ColumnClickEventHandler(
   object sender,
   ColumnClickEventArgs e
);
```
[C++]
```
[Serializable]
public __gc __delegate void ColumnClickEventHandler(
   Object* sender,
   ColumnClickEventArgs* e
);
```

[JScript] In JScript, you can use the delegates in the .NET Framework, but you cannot define your own.

Parameters [Visual Basic, C#, C++]

The declaration of your event handler must have the same parameters as the **ColumnClickEventHandler** delegate declaration.

sender

The source of the event.

e

A **ColumnClickEventArgs** that contains the event data.

Remarks

When you create a **ColumnClickEventHandler** delegate, you identify the method that will handle the event. To associate the event with your event handler, add an instance of the delegate to the event. The event handler is called whenever the event occurs, unless you remove the delegate.

Requirements

Namespace: System.Windows.Forms

Platforms: Windows 98, Windows NT 4.0, Windows Millennium Edition, Windows 2000, Windows XP Home Edition, Windows XP Professional, Windows Server 2003 family, .NET Compact Framework - Windows CE .NET

Assembly: System.Windows.Forms (in System.Windows.Forms.dll)

ColumnHeader Class

Displays a single column header in a **ListView** control.

System.Object
  System.MarshalByRefObject
    System.ComponentModel.Component
      System.Windows.Forms.ColumnHeader

```
[Visual Basic]
Public Class ColumnHeader
   Inherits Component
   Implements ICloneable
[C#]
public class ColumnHeader : Component, ICloneable
[C++]
public __gc class ColumnHeader : public Component, ICloneable
[JScript]
public class ColumnHeader extends Component implements ICloneable
```

Thread Safety

Any public static (**Shared** in Visual Basic) members of this type are safe for multithreaded operations. Any instance members are not guaranteed to be thread safe.

Remarks

A column header is an item in a **ListView** control that contains heading text. **ColumnHeader** objects can be added to a **ListView** using the **Add** method of the **ListView.ColumnHeaderCollection** class. To add a group of columns to a **ListView**, you can use the **AddRange** method of the **ListView.ColumnHeaderCollection** class. You can use the **Index** property of the **ColumnHeader** class to determine where the **ColumnHeader** is located in the **ListView.ColumnHeaderCollection**.

ColumnHeader provides the **Text** and **TextAlign** properties to set the text displayed in the control and the alignment of the text in the column header. To determine whether a **ColumnHeader** is associated with a **ListView** control, you can reference the **ListView** property. If you want to copy a **ColumnHeader** for use in another **ListView** control, you can use the **Clone** method.

Requirements

Namespace: System.Windows.Forms

Platforms: Windows 98, Windows NT 4.0, Windows Millennium Edition, Windows 2000, Windows XP Home Edition, Windows XP Professional, Windows Server 2003 family, .NET Compact Framework - Windows CE .NET

Assembly: System.Windows.Forms (in System.Windows.Forms.dll)

ColumnHeader Constructor

Initializes a new instance of the **ColumnHeader** class.

```
[Visual Basic]
Public Sub New()
[C#]
public ColumnHeader();
[C++]
public: ColumnHeader();
[JScript]
public function ColumnHeader();
```

Requirements

Platforms: Windows 98, Windows NT 4.0, Windows Millennium Edition, Windows 2000, Windows XP Home Edition, Windows XP Professional, Windows Server 2003 family, .NET Compact Framework - Windows CE .NET

ColumnHeader.Index Property

Gets the location with the **ListView** control's **ListView.ColumnHeaderCollection** of this column.

```
[Visual Basic]
Public ReadOnly Property Index As Integer
[C#]
public int Index {get;}
[C++]
public: __property int get_Index();
[JScript]
public function get Index() : int;
```

Property Value

The zero-based index of the column header within the **ListView.ColumnHeaderCollection** of the **ListView** control it is contained in.

Remarks

The value of this property does not necessarily correspond to the current visual position of the column header within the **ListView**. This can be due to the user reordering the column headers at run time (when the **AllowColumnReorder** property is set to **true**). If the **ColumnHeader** is not contained within a **ListView** control this property returns a value of -1.

Requirements

Platforms: Windows 98, Windows NT 4.0, Windows Millennium Edition, Windows 2000, Windows XP Home Edition, Windows XP Professional, Windows Server 2003 family

ColumnHeader.ListView Property

Gets the **ListView** control the **ColumnHeader** is located in.

```
[Visual Basic]
Public ReadOnly Property ListView As ListView
[C#]
public ListView ListView {get;}
[C++]
public: __property ListView* get_ListView();
[JScript]
public function get ListView() : ListView;
```

Property Value

A **ListView** control that represents the control that contains the **ColumnHeader**.

Remarks

You can use this property to determine which **ListView** control a specific **ColumnHeader** object is associated with.

Requirements

Platforms: Windows 98, Windows NT 4.0, Windows Millennium Edition, Windows 2000, Windows XP Home Edition, Windows XP Professional, Windows Server 2003 family

ColumnHeader.Text Property

Gets or sets the text displayed in the column header.

[Visual Basic]
```
Public Property Text As String
```
[C#]
```
public string Text {get; set;}
```
[C++]
```
public: __property String* get_Text();
public: __property void set_Text(String*);
```
[JScript]
```
public function get Text() : String;
public function set Text(String);
```

Property Value

The text displayed in the column header.

Requirements

Platforms: Windows 98, Windows NT 4.0, Windows Millennium Edition, Windows 2000, Windows XP Home Edition, Windows XP Professional, Windows Server 2003 family, .NET Compact Framework - Windows CE .NET

ColumnHeader.TextAlign Property

Gets or sets the horizontal alignment of the text displayed in the **ColumnHeader**.

[Visual Basic]
```
Public Property TextAlign As HorizontalAlignment
```
[C#]
```
public HorizontalAlignment TextAlign {get; set;}
```
[C++]
```
public: __property HorizontalAlignment get_TextAlign();
public: __property void set_TextAlign(HorizontalAlignment);
```
[JScript]
```
public function get TextAlign() : HorizontalAlignment;
public function set TextAlign(HorizontalAlignment);
```

Property Value

One of the **HorizontalAlignment** values. The default is **HorizontalAlignment.Left**.

Remarks

You can use this property to provide different text alignment settings for the text displayed in each **ColumnHeader**. For example, you might want to align the first **ColumnHeader** in a **ListView** control to the left while keeping the rest of the fields center or right aligned.

Requirements

Platforms: Windows 98, Windows NT 4.0, Windows Millennium Edition, Windows 2000, Windows XP Home Edition, Windows XP Professional, Windows Server 2003 family, .NET Compact Framework - Windows CE .NET

ColumnHeader.Width Property

Gets or sets the width of the column.

[Visual Basic]
```
Public Property Width As Integer
```
[C#]
```
public int Width {get; set;}
```
[C++]
```
public: __property int get_Width();
public: __property void set_Width(int);
```
[JScript]
```
public function get Width() : int;
public function set Width(int);
```

Property Value

The width of the column, in pixels.

Remarks

This property enables you to set the **Width** of the **ColumnHeader**. The **ColumnHeader** can be set to adjust at run time to the column contents or heading. To adjust the width of the longest item in the column, set the **Width** property to -1. To autosize to the width of the column heading, set the **Width** property to -2.

Requirements

Platforms: Windows 98, Windows NT 4.0, Windows Millennium Edition, Windows 2000, Windows XP Home Edition, Windows XP Professional, Windows Server 2003 family, .NET Compact Framework - Windows CE .NET

ColumnHeader.Clone Method

Creates an identical copy of the current **ColumnHeader** that is not attached to any list view control.

[Visual Basic]
```
Public Overridable Function Clone() As Object Implements _
   ICloneable.Clone
```
[C#]
```
public virtual object Clone();
```
[C++]
```
public: virtual Object* Clone();
```
[JScript]
```
public function Clone() : Object;
```

Return Value

An object representing a copy of this **ColumnHeader** object.

Implements

ICloneable.Clone

Remarks

You can use this method to copy existing **ColumnHeader** objects from an existing **ListView** control for use in other **ListView** controls.

Requirements

Platforms: Windows 98, Windows NT 4.0, Windows Millennium Edition, Windows 2000, Windows XP Home Edition, Windows XP Professional, Windows Server 2003 family

ColumnHeader.Dispose Method

Overload List

This member supports the .NET Framework infrastructure and is not intended to be used directly from your code.

Supported by the .NET Compact Framework.

[Visual Basic] **Overloads Overrides Protected Sub Dispose(Boolean)**

[C#] **protected override void Dispose(bool);**

[C++] **protected: void Dispose(bool);**

[JScript] **protected override function Dispose(Boolean);**

Inherited from **Component**.

[Visual Basic] **Overloads Public Overridable Sub Dispose() Implements IDisposable.Dispose**

[C#] **public virtual void Dispose();**

[C++] **public: virtual void Dispose();**

[JScript] **public function Dispose();**

ColumnHeader.Dispose Method (Boolean)

This member overrides **Component.Dispose**.

```
[Visual Basic]
Overrides Overloads Protected Sub Dispose( _
   ByVal disposing As Boolean _
)
[C#]
protected override void Dispose(
   bool disposing
);
[C++]
protected: void Dispose(
   bool disposing
);
[JScript]
protected override function Dispose(
   disposing : Boolean
);
```

Requirements

Platforms: Windows 98, Windows NT 4.0, Windows Millennium Edition, Windows 2000, Windows XP Home Edition, Windows XP Professional, Windows Server 2003 family, .NET Compact Framework - Windows CE .NET

ColumnHeader.ToString Method

This member overrides **Object.ToString**.

```
[Visual Basic]
Overrides Public Function ToString() As String
[C#]
public override string ToString();
[C++]
public: String* ToString();
[JScript]
public override function ToString() : String;
```

Requirements

Platforms: Windows 98, Windows NT 4.0, Windows Millennium Edition, Windows 2000, Windows XP Home Edition, Windows XP Professional, Windows Server 2003 family, .NET Compact Framework - Windows CE .NET

ColumnHeaderStyle Enumeration

Specifies the styles of the column headers in a **ListView** control.

[Visual Basic]
```
<Serializable>
Public Enum ColumnHeaderStyle
```
[C#]
```
[Serializable]
public enum ColumnHeaderStyle
```
[C++]
```
[Serializable]
__value public enum ColumnHeaderStyle
```
[JScript]
```
public
   Serializable
enum ColumnHeaderStyle
```

Remarks

Use the members of this enumeration to set the value of the **HeaderStyle** property of the **ListView** control.

Members

Member name	Description
Clickable Supported by the .NET Compact Framework.	The column headers function like buttons and can carry out an action, such as sorting, when clicked.
Nonclickable Supported by the .NET Compact Framework.	The column headers do not respond to the click of a mouse.
None Supported by the .NET Compact Framework.	The column header is not displayed in report view.

Requirements

Namespace: System.Windows.Forms

Platforms: Windows 98, Windows NT 4.0, Windows Millennium Edition, Windows 2000, Windows XP Home Edition, Windows XP Professional, Windows Server 2003 family, .NET Compact Framework - Windows CE .NET

Assembly: System.Windows.Forms (in System.Windows.Forms.dll)

ComboBox Class

Represents a Windows combo box control.

System.Object
  System.MarshalByRefObject
    System.ComponentModel.Component
      System.Windows.Forms.Control
        System.Windows.Forms.ListControl
          System.Windows.Forms.ComboBox

[Visual Basic]
```
Public Class ComboBox
   Inherits ListControl
```
[C#]
```
public class ComboBox : ListControl
```
[C++]
```
public __gc class ComboBox : public ListControl
```
[JScript]
```
public class ComboBox extends ListControl
```

Thread Safety

Any public static (**Shared** in Visual Basic) members of this type are safe for multithreaded operations. Any instance members are not guaranteed to be thread safe.

Remarks

A **ComboBox** displays an editing field combined with a **ListBox**, allowing the user to select from the list or to enter new text. The default behaviour of **ComboBox** displays an edit field with a hidden drop-down list. The **DropDownStyle** property determines the style of combo box to display. You can enter a value that allows for a simple drop-down, where the list always displays, a drop-down list box, where the text portion is not editable and you must select an arrow to view the drop-down list box, or the default drop-down list box, where the text portion is editable and the user must press the arrow key to view the list. To always display a list that the user cannot edit, use a **ListBox** control.

To add objects to the list at run time, assign an array of object references with the **AddRange** method. The list then displays the default string value for each object. You can add individual objects with the **Add** method.

In addition to display and selection functionality, the **ComboBox** also provides features that enable you to efficiently add items to the **ComboBox** and to find text within the items of the list. The **BeginUpdate** and **EndUpdate** methods enable you to add a large number of items to the **ComboBox** without the control being repainted each time an item is added to the list. The **FindString** and **FindStringExact** methods enable you to search for an item in the list that contains a specific search string.

You can use these properties to manage the currently selected item in the list, the **Text** property to specify the string displayed in the editing field, the **SelectedIndex** property to get or set the current item, and the **SelectedItem** property to get or set a reference to the object.

Example

[Visual Basic, C#, C++] The following example is a complete application illustrating how you can use the **Add** method to add items to a **ComboBox**, the **FindString** method to find items in a **ComboBox**, and the **BeginUpdate** and **EndUpdate** methods to add a large number items to a **ComboBox** in an efficient manner.

[Visual Basic]
```
Imports System
Imports System.Windows.Forms

Namespace ComboBoxSampleNamespace

    Public Class ComboBoxSample
        Inherits System.Windows.Forms.Form

        Private addButton As System.Windows.Forms.Button
        Private textBox2 As System.Windows.Forms.TextBox
        Private addGrandButton As System.Windows.Forms.Button
        Private comboBox1 As System.Windows.Forms.ComboBox
        Private showSelectedButton As System.Windows.Forms.Button
        Private textBox1 As System.Windows.Forms.TextBox
        Private findButton As System.Windows.Forms.Button
        Private label1 As System.Windows.Forms.Label

        Public Sub New()
            MyBase.New()
            Me.InitializeComponent()
        End Sub

        <System.STAThreadAttribute()> Public Shared Sub Main()
            System.Windows.Forms.Application.Run(New ComboBoxSample())
        End Sub

        Private Sub InitializeComponent()
            Me.addButton = New System.Windows.Forms.Button()
            Me.textBox2 = New System.Windows.Forms.TextBox()
            Me.addGrandButton = New System.Windows.Forms.Button()
            Me.comboBox1 = New System.Windows.Forms.ComboBox()
            Me.showSelectedButton = New System.Windows.Forms.Button()
            Me.textBox1 = New System.Windows.Forms.TextBox()
            Me.findButton = New System.Windows.Forms.Button()
            Me.label1 = New System.Windows.Forms.Label()
            Me.addButton.Location = New System.Drawing.Point(248, 32)
            Me.addButton.Size = New System.Drawing.Size(40, 24)
            Me.addButton.TabIndex = 1
            Me.addButton.Text = "Add"
            AddHandler Me.addButton.Click, AddressOf Me.addButton_Click
            Me.textBox2.Location = New System.Drawing.Point(8, 64)
            Me.textBox2.Size = New System.Drawing.Size(232, 20)
            Me.textBox2.TabIndex = 6
            Me.textBox2.Text = ""
            Me.addGrandButton.Location = New System.Drawing.Point      ↵
(8, 96)
            Me.addGrandButton.Size = New System.Drawing.Size(280, 23)
            Me.addGrandButton.TabIndex = 2
            Me.addGrandButton.Text = "Add 1,000 Items"
            AddHandler Me.addGrandButton.Click, AddressOf      ↵
Me.addGrandButton_Click
            Me.comboBox1.Anchor =      ↵
((System.Windows.Forms.AnchorStyles.Bottom Or      ↵
System.Windows.Forms.AnchorStyles.Left) _
                        Or System.Windows.Forms.AnchorStyles.Right)
            Me.comboBox1.DropDownWidth = 280
            Me.comboBox1.Items.AddRange(New Object() {"Item 1",      ↵
"Item 2", "Item 3", "Item 4", "Item 5"})
            Me.comboBox1.Location = New System.Drawing.Point(8, 248)
            Me.comboBox1.Size = New System.Drawing.Size(280, 21)
            Me.comboBox1.TabIndex = 7
            Me.showSelectedButton.Location = New      ↵
System.Drawing.Point(8, 128)
            Me.showSelectedButton.Size = New      ↵
System.Drawing.Size(280, 24)
            Me.showSelectedButton.TabIndex = 4
            Me.showSelectedButton.Text = "What Item is Selected?"
            AddHandler Me.showSelectedButton.Click, AddressOf      ↵
Me.showSelectedButton_Click
            Me.textBox1.Location = New System.Drawing.Point(8, 32)
            Me.textBox1.Size = New System.Drawing.Size(232, 20)
            Me.textBox1.TabIndex = 5
            Me.textBox1.Text = ""
            Me.findButton.Location = New System.Drawing.Point(248, 64)
```

```
            Me.findButton.Size = New System.Drawing.Size(40, 24)
            Me.findButton.TabIndex = 3
            Me.findButton.Text = "Find"
            AddHandler Me.findButton.Click, AddressOf ↵
Me.findButton_Click
            Me.label1.Location = New System.Drawing.Point(8, 224)
            Me.label1.Size = New System.Drawing.Size(144, 23)
            Me.label1.TabIndex = 0
            Me.label1.Text = "Test ComboBox"
            Me.AutoScaleBaseSize = New System.Drawing.Size(5, 13)
            Me.ClientSize = New System.Drawing.Size(292, 273)
            Me.Controls.AddRange(New ↵
System.Windows.Forms.Control() {Me.comboBox1, ↵
 Me.textBox2, Me.textBox1, Me.showSelectedButton, ↵
Me.findButton, Me.addGrandButton, Me.addButton, Me.label1})
            Me.Text = "ComboBox Sample"
        End Sub

        Private Sub addButton_Click(ByVal sender As Object, ↵
 ByVal e As System.EventArgs)
            comboBox1.Items.Add(textBox1.Text)
        End Sub

        Private Sub findButton_Click(ByVal sender As Object, ↵
ByVal e As System.EventArgs)
            Dim index As Integer
            index = comboBox1.FindString(textBox2.Text)
            comboBox1.SelectedIndex = index
        End Sub

        Private Sub addGrandButton_Click(ByVal sender As Object, ↵
 ByVal e As System.EventArgs)
            comboBox1.BeginUpdate()
            Dim I As Integer
            For I = 0 To 1000
                comboBox1.Items.Add("Item 1" + i.ToString())
            Next
            comboBox1.EndUpdate()
        End Sub

        Private Sub showSelectedButton_Click(ByVal sender As ↵
Object, ByVal e As System.EventArgs)
            Dim selectedIndex As Integer
            selectedIndex = comboBox1.SelectedIndex
            Dim selectedItem As Object
            selectedItem = comboBox1.SelectedItem

            MessageBox.Show("Selected Item Text: " & ↵
selectedItem.ToString() & Microsoft.VisualBasic.Constants.vbCrLf & _
                            "Index: " & selectedIndex.ToString())
        End Sub
    End Class
End Namespace
```

[C#]

```
using System;
using System.Windows.Forms;

namespace Win32Form1Namespace {

    public class Win32Form1 : System.Windows.Forms.Form {
        private System.Windows.Forms.Button addButton;
        private System.Windows.Forms.TextBox textBox2;
        private System.Windows.Forms.Button addGrandButton;
        private System.Windows.Forms.ComboBox comboBox1;
        private System.Windows.Forms.Button showSelectedButton;
        private System.Windows.Forms.TextBox textBox1;
        private System.Windows.Forms.Button findButton;
        private System.Windows.Forms.Label label1;

        public Win32Form1() {
            this.InitializeComponent();
        }

        [System.STAThreadAttribute()]
        public static void Main() {
            System.Windows.Forms.Application.Run(new Win32Form1());
        }

        private void InitializeComponent() {
            this.addButton = new System.Windows.Forms.Button();
            this.textBox2 = new System.Windows.Forms.TextBox();
            this.addGrandButton = new System.Windows.Forms.Button();
            this.comboBox1 = new System.Windows.Forms.ComboBox();
            this.showSelectedButton = new ↵
System.Windows.Forms.Button();
            this.textBox1 = new System.Windows.Forms.TextBox();
            this.findButton = new System.Windows.Forms.Button();
            this.label1 = new System.Windows.Forms.Label();
            this.addButton.Location = new System.Drawing.Point(248, 32);
            this.addButton.Size = new System.Drawing.Size(40, 24);
            this.addButton.TabIndex = 1;
            this.addButton.Text = "Add";
            this.addButton.Click += new ↵
System.EventHandler(this.addButton_Click);
            this.textBox2.Location = new System.Drawing.Point(8, 64);
            this.textBox2.Size = new System.Drawing.Size(232, 20);
            this.textBox2.TabIndex = 6;
            this.textBox2.Text = "";
            this.addGrandButton.Location = new ↵
System.Drawing.Point(8, 96);
            this.addGrandButton.Size = new ↵
System.Drawing.Size(280, 23);
            this.addGrandButton.TabIndex = 2;
            this.addGrandButton.Text = "Add 1,000 Items";
            this.addGrandButton.Click += new ↵
System.EventHandler(this.addGrandButton_Click);
            this.comboBox1.Anchor = ↵
 ((System.Windows.Forms.AnchorStyles.Bottom | ↵
System.Windows.Forms.AnchorStyles.Left)
                        | System.Windows.Forms.AnchorStyles.Right);
            this.comboBox1.DropDownWidth = 280;
            this.comboBox1.Items.AddRange(new object[] {"Item 1",
                        "Item 2",
                        "Item 3",
                        "Item 4",
                        "Item 5"});
            this.comboBox1.Location = new System.Drawing.Point(8, 248);
            this.comboBox1.Size = new System.Drawing.Size(280, 21);
            this.comboBox1.TabIndex = 7;
            this.showSelectedButton.Location = new ↵
System.Drawing.Point(8, 128);
            this.showSelectedButton.Size = new ↵
System.Drawing.Size(280, 24);
            this.showSelectedButton.TabIndex = 4;
            this.showSelectedButton.Text = "What Item is Selected?";
            this.showSelectedButton.Click += new ↵
System.EventHandler(this.showSelectedButton_Click);
            this.textBox1.Location = new System.Drawing.Point(8, 32);
            this.textBox1.Size = new System.Drawing.Size(232, 20);
            this.textBox1.TabIndex = 5;
            this.textBox1.Text = "";
            this.findButton.Location = new ↵
System.Drawing.Point(248, 64);
            this.findButton.Size = new System.Drawing.Size(40, 24);
            this.findButton.TabIndex = 3;
            this.findButton.Text = "Find";
            this.findButton.Click += new ↵
System.EventHandler(this.findButton_Click);
            this.label1.Location = new System.Drawing.Point(8, 224);
            this.label1.Size = new System.Drawing.Size(144, 23);
            this.label1.TabIndex = 0;
            this.label1.Text = "Test ComboBox";
            this.AutoScaleBaseSize = new System.Drawing.Size(5, 13);
            this.ClientSize = new System.Drawing.Size(292, 273);
            this.Controls.AddRange ↵
 (new System.Windows.Forms.Control[] {this.comboBox1,
                        this.textBox2,
                        this.textBox1,
```

```
                    this.showSelectedButton,
                    this.findButton,
                    this.addGrandButton,
                    this.addButton,
                    this.label1});
            this.Text = "ComboBox Sample";
        }

        private void addButton_Click(object sender,                    ↵
System.EventArgs e) {
            comboBox1.Items.Add(textBox1.Text);
        }

        private void addGrandButton_Click(object sender,               ↵
System.EventArgs e) {
            comboBox1.BeginUpdate();
            for (int i = 0; i < 1000; i++) {
                comboBox1.Items.Add("Item 1" + i.ToString());
            }
            comboBox1.EndUpdate();
        }

        private void findButton_Click(object sender,                   ↵
System.EventArgs e) {
            int index = comboBox1.FindString(textBox2.Text);
            comboBox1.SelectedIndex = index;
        }

        private void showSelectedButton_Click(object                   ↵
sender, System.EventArgs e) {
            int selectedIndex = comboBox1.SelectedIndex;
            Object selectedItem = comboBox1.SelectedItem;

            MessageBox.Show("Selected Item Text: " +                   ↵
selectedItem.ToString() + "\n" +
                            "Index: " + selectedIndex.ToString());
        }
    }
}
```

[C++]

```
using namespace System;
using namespace System::Windows::Forms;

namespace Win32Form1Namespace {

public __gc class Win32Form1 : public System::Windows::Forms::Form {

private:
    System::Windows::Forms::Button* addButton;
    System::Windows::Forms::TextBox* textBox2;
    System::Windows::Forms::Button* addGrandButton;
    System::Windows::Forms::ComboBox* comboBox1;
    System::Windows::Forms::Button* showSelectedButton;
    System::Windows::Forms::TextBox* textBox1;
    System::Windows::Forms::Button* findButton;
    System::Windows::Forms::Label* label1;

public:
    Win32Form1() {
        this->InitializeComponent();
    }

private:
    void InitializeComponent() {
        this->addButton = new System::Windows::Forms::Button();
        this->textBox2 = new System::Windows::Forms::TextBox();
        this->addGrandButton = new System::Windows::Forms::Button();
        this->comboBox1 = new System::Windows::Forms::ComboBox();
        this->showSelectedButton = new                                 ↵
System::Windows::Forms::Button();
        this->textBox1 = new System::Windows::Forms::TextBox();
        this->findButton = new System::Windows::Forms::Button();
        this->label1 = new System::Windows::Forms::Label();
        this->addButton->Location = System::Drawing::Point(248, 32);
        this->addButton->Size = System::Drawing::Size(40, 24);
        this->addButton->TabIndex = 1;
        this->addButton->Text = S"Add";
        this->addButton->Click += new                                  ↵
System::EventHandler(this, addButton_Click);
        this->textBox2->Location = System::Drawing::Point(8, 64);
        this->textBox2->Size = System::Drawing::Size(232, 20);
        this->textBox2->TabIndex = 6;
        this->textBox2->Text = S"";
        this->addGrandButton->Location = System::Drawing::Point(8, 96);
        this->addGrandButton->Size = System::Drawing::Size(280, 23);
        this->addGrandButton->TabIndex = 2;
        this->addGrandButton->Text = S"Add 1, 000 Items";
        this->addGrandButton->Click += new                             ↵
System::EventHandler(this, addGrandButton_Click);
        this->comboBox1->Anchor =                                      ↵
static_cast<System::Windows::Forms::AnchorStyles>(
            (System::Windows::Forms::AnchorStyles:                     ↵
:Bottom | System::Windows::Forms::AnchorStyles::Left)
            | System::Windows::Forms::AnchorStyles::Right);
        this->comboBox1->DropDownWidth = 280;
        Object* objectArray[] = {S"Item 1",
            S"Item 2",
            S"Item 3",
            S"Item 4",
            S"Item 5"};
        this->comboBox1->Items->AddRange(objectArray);
        this->comboBox1->Location = System::Drawing::Point(8, 248);
        this->comboBox1->Size = System::Drawing::Size(280, 21);
        this->comboBox1->TabIndex = 7;
        this->showSelectedButton->Location =                           ↵
System::Drawing::Point(8, 128);
        this->showSelectedButton->Size =                               ↵
System::Drawing::Size(280, 24);
        this->showSelectedButton->TabIndex = 4;
        this->showSelectedButton->Text = S"What Item is Selected?";
        this->showSelectedButton->Click += new                         ↵
System::EventHandler(this, showSelectedButton_Click);
        this->textBox1->Location = System::Drawing::Point(8, 32);
        this->textBox1->Size = System::Drawing::Size(232, 20);
        this->textBox1->TabIndex = 5;
        this->textBox1->Text = S"";
        this->findButton->Location = System::Drawing::Point(248, 64);
        this->findButton->Size = System::Drawing::Size(40, 24);
        this->findButton->TabIndex = 3;
        this->findButton->Text = S"Find";
        this->findButton->Click += new System::EventHandler            ↵
 (this, findButton_Click);
        this->label1->Location = System::Drawing::Point(8, 224);
        this->label1->Size = System::Drawing::Size(144, 23);
        this->label1->TabIndex = 0;
        this->label1->Text = S"Test ComboBox";
        this->AutoScaleBaseSize = System::Drawing::Size(5, 13);
        this->ClientSize = System::Drawing::Size(292, 273);
        System::Windows::Forms::Control* controlsArray[] =             ↵
 {this->comboBox1,
            this->textBox2,
            this->textBox1,
            this->showSelectedButton,
            this->findButton,
            this->addGrandButton,
            this->addButton,
            this->label1};
        this->Controls->AddRange(controlsArray);
        this->Text = S"ComboBox Sample";
    }

    void addButton_Click(Object* sender, System::EventArgs* e) {
        comboBox1->Items->Add(textBox1->Text);
    }

    void addGrandButton_Click(Object* sender, System::EventArgs* e) {
        comboBox1->BeginUpdate();
        for (int i = 0; i < 1000; i++) {
            comboBox1->Items->Add(String::Concat(S"Item 1 ",           ↵
```

```
i.ToString()));
        }
        comboBox1->EndUpdate();
    }

    void findButton_Click(Object* sender, System::EventArgs* e) {
        int index = comboBox1->FindString(textBox2->Text);
        comboBox1->SelectedIndex = index;
    }

    void showSelectedButton_Click(Object* sender,                    ↵
System::EventArgs* e) {
        int selectedIndex = comboBox1->SelectedIndex;
        Object* selectedItem = comboBox1->SelectedItem;

        MessageBox::Show(String::Concat(S"Selected                   ↵
Item Text: ", selectedItem->ToString(),
            S"\n Index: ", selectedIndex.ToString()));
    }
};

}
[System::STAThreadAttribute]
int main() {
    System::Windows::Forms::Application::Run(new                     ↵
Win32Form1Namespace::Win32Form1());
}
```

Requirements

Namespace: System.Windows.Forms

Platforms: Windows 98, Windows NT 4.0,
Windows Millennium Edition, Windows 2000,
Windows XP Home Edition, Windows XP Professional,
Windows Server 2003 family,
.NET Compact Framework - Windows CE .NET

Assembly: System.Windows.Forms (in System.Windows.Forms.dll)

ComboBox Constructor

Initializes a new instance of the **ComboBox** class.

[Visual Basic]
```
Public Sub New()
```
[C#]
```
public ComboBox();
```
[C++]
```
public: ComboBox();
```
[JScript]
```
public function ComboBox();
```

Requirements

Platforms: Windows 98, Windows NT 4.0,
Windows Millennium Edition, Windows 2000,
Windows XP Home Edition, Windows XP Professional,
Windows Server 2003 family,
.NET Compact Framework - Windows CE .NET

ComboBox.BackColor Property

This member overrides **Control.BackColor**.

[Visual Basic]
```
Overrides Public Property BackColor As Color
```
[C#]
```
public override Color BackColor {get; set;}
```
[C++]
```
public: __property Color get_BackColor();
public: __property void set_BackColor(Color);
```
[JScript]
```
public override function get BackColor() : Color;
public override function set BackColor(Color);
```

Requirements

Platforms: Windows 98, Windows NT 4.0,
Windows Millennium Edition, Windows 2000,
Windows XP Home Edition, Windows XP Professional,
Windows Server 2003 family

ComboBox.BackgroundImage Property

This member overrides **Control.BackgroundImage**.

[Visual Basic]
```
Overrides Public Property BackgroundImage As Image
```
[C#]
```
public override Image BackgroundImage {get; set;}
```
[C++]
```
public: __property Image* get_BackgroundImage();
public: __property void set_BackgroundImage(Image*);
```
[JScript]
```
public override function get BackgroundImage() : Image;
public override function set BackgroundImage(Image);
```

Requirements

Platforms: Windows 98, Windows NT 4.0,
Windows Millennium Edition, Windows 2000,
Windows XP Home Edition, Windows XP Professional,
Windows Server 2003 family

ComboBox.CreateParams Property

This member overrides **Control.CreateParams**.

[Visual Basic]
```
Overrides Protected ReadOnly Property CreateParams As CreateParams
```
[C#]
```
protected override CreateParams CreateParams {get;}
```
[C++]
```
protected: __property CreateParams* get_CreateParams();
```
[JScript]
```
protected override function get CreateParams() : CreateParams;
```

Requirements

Platforms: Windows 98, Windows NT 4.0,
Windows Millennium Edition, Windows 2000,
Windows XP Home Edition, Windows XP Professional,
Windows Server 2003 family

ComboBox.DefaultSize Property

This member overrides **Control.DefaultSize**.

[Visual Basic]
```
Overrides Protected ReadOnly Property DefaultSize As Size
```
[C#]
```
protected override Size DefaultSize {get;}
```
[C++]
```
protected: __property Size get_DefaultSize();
```
[JScript]
```
protected override function get DefaultSize() : Size;
```

Requirements

Platforms: Windows 98, Windows NT 4.0, Windows Millennium Edition, Windows 2000, Windows XP Home Edition, Windows XP Professional, Windows Server 2003 family

ComboBox.DrawMode Property

Gets or sets a value indicating whether your code or the operating system will handle drawing of elements in the list.

```
[Visual Basic]
Public Property DrawMode As DrawMode
[C#]
public DrawMode DrawMode {get; set;}
[C++]
public: __property DrawMode get_DrawMode();
public: __property void set_DrawMode(DrawMode);
[JScript]
public function get DrawMode() : DrawMode;
public function set DrawMode(DrawMode);
```

Property Value

One of the **DrawMode** enumeration values. The default is **DrawMode.Normal**.

Exceptions

Exception Type	Condition
InvalidEnumArgumentException	The value is not a valid **DrawMode** enumeration value.

Requirements

Platforms: Windows 98, Windows NT 4.0, Windows Millennium Edition, Windows 2000, Windows XP Home Edition, Windows XP Professional, Windows Server 2003 family

ComboBox.DropDownStyle Property

Gets or sets a value specifying the style of the combo box.

```
[Visual Basic]
Public Property DropDownStyle As ComboBoxStyle
[C#]
public ComboBoxStyle DropDownStyle {get; set;}
[C++]
public: __property ComboBoxStyle get_DropDownStyle();
public: __property void set_DropDownStyle(ComboBoxStyle);
[JScript]
public function get DropDownStyle() : ComboBoxStyle;
public function set DropDownStyle(ComboBoxStyle);
```

Property Value

One of the **ComboBoxStyle** values. The default is **ComboBoxStyle.DropDown**.

Exceptions

Exception Type	Condition
InvalidEnumArgumentException	The assigned value is not one of the **ComboBoxStyle** values.

Remarks

The **DropDownStyle** property controls the interface that is presented to the user. You can enter a value that allows for a simple drop-down list box, where the list always displays, a drop-down list box, where the text portion is not editable and you must select an arrow to view the drop-down, or the default drop-down list box, where the text portion is editable and the user must press the arrow key to view the list. To always display a list that the user cannot edit, use a **ListBox** control.

Requirements

Platforms: Windows 98, Windows NT 4.0, Windows Millennium Edition, Windows 2000, Windows XP Home Edition, Windows XP Professional, Windows Server 2003 family, .NET Compact Framework - Windows CE .NET

ComboBox.DropDownWidth Property

Gets or sets the width of the of the drop-down portion of a combo box.

```
[Visual Basic]
Public Property DropDownWidth As Integer
[C#]
public int DropDownWidth {get; set;}
[C++]
public: __property int get_DropDownWidth();
public: __property void set_DropDownWidth(int);
[JScript]
public function get DropDownWidth() : int;
public function set DropDownWidth(int);
```

Property Value

The width, in pixels, of the drop-down box.

Exceptions

Exception Type	Condition
ArgumentException	The specified value is less than one.

Remarks

If a value has not been set for the **DropDownWidth**, this property returns the **Width** of the combo box.

Note The width of the drop-down cannot be smaller than the **ComboBox** width.

Requirements

Platforms: Windows 98, Windows NT 4.0, Windows Millennium Edition, Windows 2000, Windows XP Home Edition, Windows XP Professional, Windows Server 2003 family

ComboBox.DroppedDown Property

Gets or sets a value indicating whether the combo box is displaying its drop-down portion.

```
[Visual Basic]
Public Property DroppedDown As Boolean
[C#]
public bool DroppedDown {get; set;}
```

```
[C++]
public: __property bool get_DroppedDown();
public: __property void set_DroppedDown(bool);
[JScript]
public function get DroppedDown() : Boolean;
public function set DroppedDown(Boolean);
```

Property Value

true if the drop-down portion is displayed; otherwise, **false**. The default is false.

Requirements

Platforms: Windows 98, Windows NT 4.0, Windows Millennium Edition, Windows 2000, Windows XP Home Edition, Windows XP Professional, Windows Server 2003 family

ComboBox.Focused Property

This member overrides **Control.Focused**.

```
[Visual Basic]
Overrides Public ReadOnly Property Focused As Boolean
[C#]
public override bool Focused {get;}
[C++]
public: __property bool get_Focused();
[JScript]
public override function get Focused() : Boolean;
```

Requirements

Platforms: Windows 98, Windows NT 4.0, Windows Millennium Edition, Windows 2000, Windows XP Home Edition, Windows XP Professional, Windows Server 2003 family, .NET Compact Framework - Windows CE .NET

ComboBox.ForeColor Property

This member overrides **Control.ForeColor**.

```
[Visual Basic]
Overrides Public Property ForeColor As Color
[C#]
public override Color ForeColor {get; set;}
[C++]
public: __property Color get_ForeColor();
public: __property void set_ForeColor(Color);
[JScript]
public override function get ForeColor() : Color;
public override function set ForeColor(Color);
```

Requirements

Platforms: Windows 98, Windows NT 4.0, Windows Millennium Edition, Windows 2000, Windows XP Home Edition, Windows XP Professional, Windows Server 2003 family

ComboBox.IntegralHeight Property

Gets or sets a value indicating whether the control should resize to avoid showing partial items.

```
[Visual Basic]
Public Property IntegralHeight As Boolean
[C#]
public bool IntegralHeight {get; set;}
[C++]
public: __property bool get_IntegralHeight();
public: __property void set_IntegralHeight(bool);
[JScript]
public function get IntegralHeight() : Boolean;
public function set IntegralHeight(Boolean);
```

Property Value

true if the list portion can contain only complete items; otherwise, **false**. The default is **true**.

Remarks

When this property is set to **true**, the control automatically resizes to ensure that an item is not partially displayed. If you want to maintain the original size of the **ComboBox** based on the space requirements of your form, set this property to **false**. If the **ComboBox** does not contain any items, this property has no effect.

> **Note** If the **DrawMode** property is set to **DrawMode.OwnerDrawVariable**, this property has no effect.

Requirements

Platforms: Windows 98, Windows NT 4.0, Windows Millennium Edition, Windows 2000, Windows XP Home Edition, Windows XP Professional, Windows Server 2003 family

ComboBox.ItemHeight Property

Gets or sets the height of an item in the combo box.

```
[Visual Basic]
Public Property ItemHeight As Integer
[C#]
public int ItemHeight {get; set;}
[C++]
public: __property int get_ItemHeight();
public: __property void set_ItemHeight(int);
[JScript]
public function get ItemHeight() : int;
public function set ItemHeight(int);
```

Property Value

The height, in pixels, of an item in the combo box.

Exceptions

Exception Type	Condition
ArgumentException	The item height value is less than zero.

Remarks

When the **DrawMode** property is set to **DrawMode.OwnerDrawFixed**, all items have the same height. When the **DrawMode** property is set to **DrawMode.OwnerDrawVariable**, the **ItemHeight** property specifies the height of each item added to the **ComboBox**. Because each item in an owner-drawn list can have a different height, you can use the **GetItemHeight** method to get the height of a specific item in the **ComboBox**. If you use the **ItemHeight** property on a **ComboBox** with items of variable height, this property returns the height of the first item in the control.

Requirements

Platforms: Windows 98, Windows NT 4.0, Windows Millennium Edition, Windows 2000, Windows XP Home Edition, Windows XP Professional, Windows Server 2003 family

ComboBox.Items Property

Gets an object representing the collection of the items contained in this **ComboBox**.

```
[Visual Basic]
Public ReadOnly Property Items As ComboBox.ObjectCollection
[C#]
public ComboBox.ObjectCollection Items {get;}
[C++]
public: __property ComboBox.ObjectCollection* get_Items();
[JScript]
public function get Items() : ComboBox.ObjectCollection;
```

Property Value

A **System.Windows.Forms.ComboBox.ObjectCollection** representing the items in the **ComboBox**.

Remarks

This property enables you to obtain a reference to the list of items that are currently stored in the **ComboBox**. With this reference, you can add items, remove items, and obtain a count of the items in the collection. For more information on the tasks that can be performed with the item collection, see the **System.Windows.Forms.ComboBox.ObjectCollection** class reference topics.

Example

```
[Visual Basic]
Private Sub addButton_Click(ByVal sender As Object, ByVal e ↵
As System.EventArgs)
    comboBox1.Items.Add(textBox1.Text)
End Sub

[C#]
private void addButton_Click(object sender, System.EventArgs e) {
   comboBox1.Items.Add(textBox1.Text);
}

[C++]
private:
    void addButton_Click(Object* sender, System::EventArgs* e) {
        comboBox1->Items->Add(textBox1->Text);
    }
```

Requirements

Platforms: Windows 98, Windows NT 4.0, Windows Millennium Edition, Windows 2000, Windows XP Home Edition, Windows XP Professional, Windows Server 2003 family, .NET Compact Framework - Windows CE .NET

ComboBox.MaxDropDownItems Property

Gets or sets the maximum number of items to be shown in the drop-down portion of the **ComboBox**.

```
[Visual Basic]
Public Property MaxDropDownItems As Integer
[C#]
public int MaxDropDownItems {get; set;}
[C++]
public: __property int get_MaxDropDownItems();
public: __property void set_MaxDropDownItems(int);
[JScript]
public function get MaxDropDownItems() : int;
public function set MaxDropDownItems(int);
```

Property Value

The maximum number of items of in the drop-down portion. The minimum for this property is 1 and the maximum is 100.

Exceptions

Exception Type	Condition
ArgumentException	The maxium number is set less than one or greater than 100.

Requirements

Platforms: Windows 98, Windows NT 4.0, Windows Millennium Edition, Windows 2000, Windows XP Home Edition, Windows XP Professional, Windows Server 2003 family

ComboBox.MaxLength Property

Gets or sets the maximum number of characters allowed in the editable portion of a combo box.

```
[Visual Basic]
Public Property MaxLength As Integer
[C#]
public int MaxLength {get; set;}
[C++]
public: __property int get_MaxLength();
public: __property void set_MaxLength(int);
[JScript]
public function get MaxLength() : int;
public function set MaxLength(int);
```

Property Value

The maximum number of characters the user can enter. Values of less than zero are reset to zero.

Requirements

Platforms: Windows 98, Windows NT 4.0, Windows Millennium Edition, Windows 2000, Windows XP Home Edition, Windows XP Professional, Windows Server 2003 family

ComboBox.PreferredHeight Property

Gets the preferred height of the **ComboBox**.

```
[Visual Basic]
Public ReadOnly Property PreferredHeight As Integer
[C#]
public int PreferredHeight {get;}
[C++]
public: __property int get_PreferredHeight();
[JScript]
public function get PreferredHeight() : int;
```

Property Value

The preferred height, in pixels, of the item area of the combo box.

Remarks

The preferred height is a value based on the font height and an adjustment for the border.

Requirements

Platforms: Windows 98, Windows NT 4.0, Windows Millennium Edition, Windows 2000, Windows XP Home Edition, Windows XP Professional, Windows Server 2003 family

ComboBox.SelectedIndex Property

Gets or sets the index specifying the currently selected item.

[Visual Basic]
```
Overrides Public Property SelectedIndex As Integer
```
[C#]
```
public override int SelectedIndex {get; set;}
```
[C++]
```
public: __property int get_SelectedIndex();
public: __property void set_SelectedIndex(int);
```
[JScript]
```
public override function get SelectedIndex() : int;
public override function set SelectedIndex(int);
```

Property Value

A zero-based index of the currently selected item. A value of negative one (-1) is returned if no item is selected.

Exceptions

Exception Type	Condition
ArgumentOutOfRange-Exception	The specified index is less than or equal to -2. -or- The specified index is greater than or equal to the number of items in the combo box.

Remarks

This property indicates the zero-based index of the currently selected item in the combo box list. Setting a new index raises the **SelectedIndexChanged** event.

Note To deselect the currently selected item, set the **SelectedIndex** to -1.

Example

[Visual Basic, C#, C++] The following example illustrates the usage of the **FindString** method and **SelectedIndex** property. The example is part of a runnable code sample in the **ComboBox** class overview.

[Visual Basic]
```
Private Sub findButton_Click(ByVal sender As Object, ByVal e ↵
As System.EventArgs)
    Dim index As Integer
    index = comboBox1.FindString(textBox2.Text)
    comboBox1.SelectedIndex = index
End Sub
```

[C#]
```
private void findButton_Click(object sender, System.EventArgs e) {
    int index = comboBox1.FindString(textBox2.Text);
    comboBox1.SelectedIndex = index;
}
```

[C++]
```
private:
    void findButton_Click(Object* sender, System::EventArgs* e) {
        int index = comboBox1->FindString(textBox2->Text);
        comboBox1->SelectedIndex = index;
    }
```

Requirements

Platforms: Windows 98, Windows NT 4.0, Windows Millennium Edition, Windows 2000, Windows XP Home Edition, Windows XP Professional, Windows Server 2003 family, .NET Compact Framework - Windows CE .NET

ComboBox.SelectedItem Property

Gets or sets currently selected item in the **ComboBox**.

[Visual Basic]
```
Public Property SelectedItem As Object
```
[C#]
```
public object SelectedItem {get; set;}
```
[C++]
```
public: __property Object* get_SelectedItem();
public: __property void set_SelectedItem(Object*);
```
[JScript]
```
public function get SelectedItem() : Object;
public function set SelectedItem(Object);
```

Property Value

The object that is the currently selected item or a null reference (**Nothing** in Visual Basic) if there is no currently selected item.

Remarks

When you set the **SelectedItem** property to an object, the **ComboBox** attempts to make that object the currently selected one in the list. If the object is found in the list, it is displayed in the edit portion of the **ComboBox** and the **SelectedIndex** property is set to the corresponding index. If the object does not exist in the list the **SelectedIndex** property is left at its current value.

Example

[Visual Basic, C#, C++] The following example illustrates the usage of the **SelectedIndex** and the **SelectedItem** properties. The example is part of a runnable code sample in the **ComboBox** class overview.

[Visual Basic]
```
Private Sub showSelectedButton_Click(ByVal sender As Object, ↵
 ByVal e As System.EventArgs)
    Dim selectedIndex As Integer
    selectedIndex = comboBox1.SelectedIndex
    Dim selectedItem As Object
    selectedItem = comboBox1.SelectedItem

    MessageBox.Show("Selected Item Text: " & ↵
selectedItem.ToString() & Microsoft.VisualBasic.Constants.vbCrLf & _
                    "Index: " & selectedIndex.ToString())
End Sub
```

[C#]
```
private void showSelectedButton_Click(object sender, ↵
System.EventArgs e) {
    int selectedIndex = comboBox1.SelectedIndex;
    Object selectedItem = comboBox1.SelectedItem;

    MessageBox.Show("Selected Item Text: " + ↵
selectedItem.ToString() + "\n" +
                    "Index: " + selectedIndex.ToString());
}
```

```
[C++]
private:
    void showSelectedButton_Click(Object* sender, ↵
System::EventArgs* e) {
        int selectedIndex = comboBox1->SelectedIndex;
        Object* selectedItem = comboBox1->SelectedItem;

        MessageBox::Show(String::Concat(S"Selected Item Text: ",
            selectedItem->ToString(), S"\n Index: ", ↵
selectedIndex.ToString()));
    }
```

Requirements

Platforms: Windows 98, Windows NT 4.0,
Windows Millennium Edition, Windows 2000,
Windows XP Home Edition, Windows XP Professional,
Windows Server 2003 family,
.NET Compact Framework - Windows CE .NET

ComboBox.SelectedText Property

Gets or sets the text that is selected in the editable portion of a **ComboBox**.

```
[Visual Basic]
Public Property SelectedText As String
[C#]
public string SelectedText {get; set;}
[C++]
public: __property String* get_SelectedText();
public: __property void set_SelectedText(String*);
[JScript]
public function get SelectedText() : String;
public function set SelectedText(String);
```

Property Value

A string that represents the currently selected text in the combo box. If **DropDownStyle** is set to **ComboBoxStyle.DropDownList**, the return is an empty string ("").

Remarks

You can assign text to this property to change the text currently selected in the combo box. If no text is currently selected in the combo box, this property returns a zero-length string.

Requirements

Platforms: Windows 98, Windows NT 4.0,
Windows Millennium Edition, Windows 2000,
Windows XP Home Edition, Windows XP Professional,
Windows Server 2003 family

ComboBox.SelectionLength Property

Gets or sets the number of characters selected in the editable portion of the combo box.

```
[Visual Basic]
Public Property SelectionLength As Integer
[C#]
public int SelectionLength {get; set;}
[C++]
public: __property int get_SelectionLength();
public: __property void set_SelectionLength(int);
[JScript]
public function get SelectionLength() : int;
public function set SelectionLength(int);
```

Property Value

The number of characters selected in the combo box.

Exceptions

Exception Type	Condition
ArgumentException	The value was less than zero.

Remarks

You can use this property to determine whether any characters are currently selected in the combo box control before performing operations on the selected text. When the value of the **SelectionLength** property is set to a value that is larger than the number of characters within the text of the control, the value of the **SelectionLength** property is set to the entire length of text within the control minus the value of the **SelectionStart** property (if any value is specified for the **SelectionStart** property).

Requirements

Platforms: Windows 98, Windows NT 4.0,
Windows Millennium Edition, Windows 2000,
Windows XP Home Edition, Windows XP Professional,
Windows Server 2003 family

ComboBox.SelectionStart Property

Gets or sets the starting index of text selected in the combo box.

```
[Visual Basic]
Public Property SelectionStart As Integer
[C#]
public int SelectionStart {get; set;}
[C++]
public: __property int get_SelectionStart();
public: __property void set_SelectionStart(int);
[JScript]
public function get SelectionStart() : int;
public function set SelectionStart(int);
```

Property Value

The zero-based index of the first character in the string of the current text selection.

Exceptions

Exception Type	Condition
ArgumentException	The value is less than zero.

Remarks

If no text is selected in the control, this property indicates the insertion point for new text. If you set this property to a location beyond the length of the text in the control, the selection start position is placed after the last character. When text is selected in the text box control, changing this property can release the value of the **SelectionLength** property. If the remaining text in the control after the position indicated by the **SelectionStart** property is less than the value of the **SelectionLength** property, the value of the **SelectionLength** property is automatically decreased. The value of the **SelectionStart** property never causes an increase in the **SelectionLength** property.

Requirements

Platforms: Windows 98, Windows NT 4.0,
Windows Millennium Edition, Windows 2000,
Windows XP Home Edition, Windows XP Professional,
Windows Server 2003 family

ComboBox.Sorted Property

Gets or sets a value indicating whether the items in the combo box are sorted.

```
[Visual Basic]
Public Property Sorted As Boolean
[C#]
public bool Sorted {get; set;}
[C++]
public: __property bool get_Sorted();
public: __property void set_Sorted(bool);
[JScript]
public function get Sorted() : Boolean;
public function set Sorted(Boolean);
```

Property Value

true if the combo box is sorted; otherwise, **false**. The default is **false**.

Exceptions

Exception Type	Condition
ArgumentException	An attempt was made to sort a **ComboBox** that is attached to a data source.

Remarks

This property specifies whether the **ComboBox** sorts exisitng entries and add new entries to the appropriate sorted position in the list. You can use this property to automatically sort items in a **ComboBox**. As items are added to a sorted **ComboBox**, the items are moved to the appropriate location in the sorted list. When you set the property to **false,** new items are added to the end of the existing list. The sort is case-insensitive and in alphabetically ascending order.

Requirements

Platforms: Windows 98, Windows NT 4.0,
Windows Millennium Edition, Windows 2000,
Windows XP Home Edition, Windows XP Professional,
Windows Server 2003 family

ComboBox.Text Property

Gets or sets the text associated with this control.

```
[Visual Basic]
Overrides Public Property Text As String
[C#]
public override string Text {get; set;}
[C++]
public: __property String* get_Text();
public: __property void set_Text(String*);
[JScript]
public override function get Text() : String;
public override function set Text(String);
```

Property Value

The text associated with this control.

Remarks

When setting the **Text** property, a null reference (**Nothing** in Visual Basic) or an empty string("") sets the **SelectedIndex** to -1.

Requirements

Platforms: Windows 98, Windows NT 4.0,
Windows Millennium Edition, Windows 2000,
Windows XP Home Edition, Windows XP Professional,
Windows Server 2003 family,
.NET Compact Framework - Windows CE .NET

ComboBox.AddItemsCore Method

Adds the specified items to the combo box.

```
[Visual Basic]
Protected Overridable Sub AddItemsCore( _
   ByVal value() As Object _
)
[C#]
protected virtual void AddItemsCore(
   object[] value
);
[C++]
protected: virtual void AddItemsCore(
   Object* value __gc[]
);
[JScript]
protected function AddItemsCore(
   value : Object[]
);
```

Parameters

value

An array of **Object** to append to the **ComboBox**.

Exceptions

Exception Type	Condition
ArgumentNull-Exception	The value was a null reference (**Nothing** in Visual Basic).

Remarks

The **AddItemsCore** method allows derived classes to provide special behaviour when adding items.

Notes to Inheritors: When overriding **AddItemsCore** in a derived class, be sure to call the base class's **AddItemsCore** method.

Requirements

Platforms: Windows 98, Windows NT 4.0,
Windows Millennium Edition, Windows 2000,
Windows XP Home Edition, Windows XP Professional,
Windows Server 2003 family

ComboBox.BeginUpdate Method

Maintains performance when items are added to the **ComboBox** one at a time.

```
[Visual Basic]
Public Sub BeginUpdate()
[C#]
public void BeginUpdate();
[C++]
public: void BeginUpdate();
[JScript]
public function BeginUpdate();
```

Remarks

This method prevents the control from painting until the **EndUpdate** method is called.

The preferred way to add items to the **ComboBox** is to use the **AddRange** method of the **ComboBox.ObjectCollection** class (through the **Items** property of the **ComboBox**). This enables you to add an array of items to the list at one time. However, if you want to add items one at a time using the **Add** method of the **ComboBox.ObjectCollection** class, you can use the **BeginUpdate** method to prevent the control from repainting the **ComboBox** each time an item is added to the list. Once you have completed the task of adding items to the list, call the **EndUpdate** method to enable the **ComboBox** to repaint. This way of adding items can prevent flicker during the drawing of the **ComboBox** when a large number of items are being added to the list.

Example

[Visual Basic, C#, C++] The following example illustrates the usage of the **BeginUpdate** and **EndUpdate** methods. The example is part of a runnable code sample in the **ComboBox** class overview.

[Visual Basic]
```
Private Sub addGrandButton_Click(ByVal sender As Object, ByVal e
As System.EventArgs)
    comboBox1.BeginUpdate()
    Dim I As Integer
    For I = 0 To 1000
        comboBox1.Items.Add("New Item " + i.ToString())
    Next
    comboBox1.EndUpdate()
End Sub
```

[C#]
```
private void addGrandButton_Click(object sender, System.EventArgs e) {
    comboBox1.BeginUpdate();
    for (int i = 0; i < 1000; i++) {
        comboBox1.Items.Add("New Item " + i.ToString());
    }
    comboBox1.EndUpdate();
}
```

[C++]
```
private:
    void addGrandButton_Click(Object* sender, System::EventArgs* e) {
        comboBox1->BeginUpdate();
        for (int i = 0; i < 1000; i++) {
            comboBox1->Items->Add(String::Concat(S"New Item ",
i.ToString()));
        }
        comboBox1->EndUpdate();
    }
```

Requirements

Platforms: Windows 98, Windows NT 4.0, Windows Millennium Edition, Windows 2000, Windows XP Home Edition, Windows XP Professional, Windows Server 2003 family

ComboBox.Dispose Method

Overload List

This member supports the .NET Framework infrastructure and is not intended to be used directly from your code.

Supported by the .NET Compact Framework.

[Visual Basic] **Overloads Overrides Protected Sub Dispose(Boolean)**

[C#] **protected override void Dispose(bool);**

[C++] **protected: void Dispose(bool);**

[JScript] **protected override function Dispose(Boolean);**

Inherited from **Component**.

Supported by the .NET Compact Framework.

[Visual Basic] **Overloads Public Overridable Sub Dispose() Implements IDisposable.Dispose**

[C#] **public virtual void Dispose();**

[C++] **public: virtual void Dispose();**

[JScript] **public function Dispose();**

ComboBox.Dispose Method (Boolean)

This member overrides **Control.Dispose**.

[Visual Basic]
```
Overrides Overloads Protected Sub Dispose( _
   ByVal disposing As Boolean _
)
```
[C#]
```
protected override void Dispose(
   bool disposing
);
```
[C++]
```
protected: void Dispose(
   bool disposing
);
```
[JScript]
```
protected override function Dispose(
   disposing : Boolean
);
```

Requirements

Platforms: Windows 98, Windows NT 4.0, Windows Millennium Edition, Windows 2000, Windows XP Home Edition, Windows XP Professional, Windows Server 2003 family, .NET Compact Framework - Windows CE .NET

ComboBox.EndUpdate Method

Resumes painting the **ComboBox** control after painting is suspended by the **BeginUpdate** method.

[Visual Basic]
```
Public Sub EndUpdate()
```
[C#]
```
public void EndUpdate();
```
[C++]
```
public: void EndUpdate();
```
[JScript]
```
public function EndUpdate();
```

Remarks

The preferred way to add items to the **ComboBox** is to use the **AddRange** method of the **ComboBox.ObjectCollection** class (through the **Items** property of the **ComboBox**). This enables you to add an array of items to the list at one time. However, if you want to add items one at a time using the **Add** method of the **ComboBox.ObjectCollection** class, you can use the **BeginUpdate** method to prevent the control from repainting the **ComboBox** each time an item is added to the list. Once you have completed the task of adding items to the list, call the **EndUpdate** method to enable the **ComboBox** to repaint. This way of adding items can prevent flickered drawing of the **ComboBox** when a large number of items are being added to the list.

Example

[Visual Basic, C#, C++] The following example illustrates the usage of the **BeginUpdate** and **EndUpdate** methods. The example is part of a runnable code sample in the **ComboBox** class overview.

[Visual Basic]
```
Private Sub addGrandButton_Click(ByVal sender As Object, ByVal e ↵
As System.EventArgs)
    comboBox1.BeginUpdate()
    Dim I As Integer
    For I = 0 To 1000
        comboBox1.Items.Add("New Item " + i.ToString())
    Next
    comboBox1.EndUpdate()
End Sub
```

[C#]
```
private void addGrandButton_Click(object sender, System.EventArgs e) {
    comboBox1.BeginUpdate();
    for (int i = 0; i < 1000; i++) {
        comboBox1.Items.Add("New Item " + i.ToString());
    }
    comboBox1.EndUpdate();
}
```

[C++]
```
private:
    void addGrandButton_Click(Object* sender, System::EventArgs* e) {
        comboBox1->BeginUpdate();
        for (int i = 0; i < 1000; i++) {
            comboBox1->Items->Add(String::Concat(S"New Item ", ↵
i.ToString()));
        }
        comboBox1->EndUpdate();
    }
```

Requirements

Platforms: Windows 98, Windows NT 4.0, Windows Millennium Edition, Windows 2000, Windows XP Home Edition, Windows XP Professional, Windows Server 2003 family

ComboBox.FindString Method

Finds the first item in the **ComboBox** that starts with the specified string.

Overload List

Finds the first item in the combo box that starts with the specified string.

[Visual Basic] **Overloads Public Function FindString(String) As Integer**

[C#] **public int FindString(string);**

[C++] **public: int FindString(String*);**

[JScript] **public function FindString(String) : int;**

Finds the first item after the given index which starts with the given string. The search is not case sensitive.

[Visual Basic] **Overloads Public Function FindString(String, Integer) As Integer**

[C#] **public int FindString(string, int);**

[C++] **public: int FindString(String*, int);**

[JScript] **public function FindString(String, int) : int;**

Example

[Visual Basic, C#, C++] The following example illustrates the usage of the **FindString** method and **SelectedIndex** property. The example is part of a runnable code sample in the **ComboBox** class overview.

> [Visual Basic, C#, C++] **Note** This example shows how to use one of the overloaded versions of **FindString**. For other examples that might be available, see the individual overload topics.

[Visual Basic]
```
Private Sub findButton_Click(ByVal sender As Object, ByVal ↵
 e As System.EventArgs)
    Dim index As Integer
    index = comboBox1.FindString(textBox2.Text)
    comboBox1.SelectedIndex = index
End Sub
```

[C#]
```
private void findButton_Click(object sender, System.EventArgs e) {
    int index = comboBox1.FindString(textBox2.Text);
    comboBox1.SelectedIndex = index;
}
```

[C++]
```
private:
    void findButton_Click(Object* sender, System::EventArgs* e) {
        int index = comboBox1->FindString(textBox2->Text);
        comboBox1->SelectedIndex = index;
    }
```

ComboBox.FindString Method (String)

Finds the first item in the combo box that starts with the specified string.

[Visual Basic]
```
Overloads Public Function FindString( _
   ByVal s As String _
) As Integer
```
[C#]
```
public int FindString(
   string s
);
```
[C++]
```
public: int FindString(
   String* s
);
```
[JScript]
```
public function FindString(
   s : String
) : int;
```

Parameters

s

The **String** to search for.

Return Value

The zero-based index of the first item found; returns -1 if no match is found.

Remarks

The search performed by this method is not case-sensitive. The *s* parameter is a substring to compare against the text associated with the items in the combo box list. The search performs a partial match starting from the beginning of the text, and returning the first item in the list that matches the specified substring. You can then perform tasks, such as removing the item that contains the search text using the **Remove** method or changeing the item's text. Once you have found the specified text, if you want to search for other instances of the text in the **ComboBox**, you must use the version of the **FindString** method that provides a parameter for specifying a starting index within the **ComboBox**. If you want to perform a search for an exact word match instead of a partial match, use the **FindStringExact** method.

Example

[Visual Basic, C#, C++] The following example illustrates the usage of the **FindString** method and **SelectedIndex** property. The example is part of a runnable code sample in the **ComboBox** class overview.

[Visual Basic]
```
Private Sub findButton_Click(ByVal sender As Object, ByVal
 e As System.EventArgs)
    Dim index As Integer
    index = comboBox1.FindString(textBox2.Text)
    comboBox1.SelectedIndex = index
End Sub
```

[C#]
```
private void findButton_Click(object sender, System.EventArgs e) {
    int index = comboBox1.FindString(textBox2.Text);
    comboBox1.SelectedIndex = index;
}
```

[C++]
```
private:
    void findButton_Click(Object* sender, System::EventArgs* e) {
        int index = comboBox1->FindString(textBox2->Text);
        comboBox1->SelectedIndex = index;
    }
```

Requirements

Platforms: Windows 98, Windows NT 4.0, Windows Millennium Edition, Windows 2000, Windows XP Home Edition, Windows XP Professional, Windows Server 2003 family

ComboBox.FindString Method (String, Int32)

Finds the first item after the given index which starts with the given string. The search is not case sensitive.

[Visual Basic]
```
Overloads Public Function FindString( _
   ByVal s As String, _
   ByVal startIndex As Integer _
) As Integer
```
[C#]
```
public int FindString(
   string s,
   int startIndex
);
```
[C++]
```
public: int FindString(
   String* s,
   int startIndex
);
```
[JScript]
```
public function FindString(
   s : String,
   startIndex : int
) : int;
```

Parameters

s

The **String** to search for.

startIndex

The zero-based index of the item before the first item to be searched. Set to -1 to search from the beginning of the control.

Return Value

The zero-based index of the first item found; returns -1 if no match is found.

Exceptions

Exception Type	Condition
ArgumentOutOfRange-Exception	The *startIndex* is less than -1. -or- The *startIndex* is greater than the last index in the collection.

Remarks

The search performed by this method is not case-sensitive. The *s* parameter is a substring to compare against the text associated with the items in the combo box list. The search performs a partial match starting from the beginning of the text, returning the first item in the list that matches the specified substring. You can then perform tasks, such as removing the item that contains the search text using the **Remove** method or changing the item's text. This method is typically used after a call has been made using the version of this method that does not specify a starting index. Once an initial item has been found in the list, this method is typically used to find further instances of the search text by specifying the index position in the *startIndex* parameter of the item after the first found instance of the search text. If you want to perform a search for an exact word match instead of a partial match, use the **FindStringExact** method.

Requirements

Platforms: Windows 98, Windows NT 4.0, Windows Millennium Edition, Windows 2000, Windows XP Home Edition, Windows XP Professional, Windows Server 2003 family

ComboBox.FindStringExact Method

Finds the item that exactly matches the specified string.

Overload List

Finds the first item in the combo box that matches the specified string.

[Visual Basic] **Overloads Public Function FindStringExact(String) As Integer**

[C#] **public int FindStringExact(string);**

[C++] **public: int FindStringExact(String*);**

[JScript] **public function FindStringExact(String) : int;**

Finds the first item after the specified index that matches the specified string.

[Visual Basic] **Overloads Public Function FindStringExact(String, Integer) As Integer**

[C#] **public int FindStringExact(string, int);**

[C++] **public: int FindStringExact(String*, int);**

[JScript] **public function FindStringExact(String, int) : int;**

ComboBox.FindStringExact Method (String)

Finds the first item in the combo box that matches the specified string.

[Visual Basic]
```
Overloads Public Function FindStringExact( _
   ByVal s As String _
) As Integer
```
[C#]
```
public int FindStringExact(
   string s
);
```
[C++]
```
public: int FindStringExact(
   String* s
);
```
[JScript]
```
public function FindStringExact(
   s : String
) : int;
```

Parameters

s
: The **String** to search for.

Return Value

The zero-based index of the first item found; returns -1 if no match is found.

Remarks

The search performed by this method is not case-sensitive. The *s* parameter is a string to compare against the text associated with the items in the combo box list. The search looks for a match starting from the beginning of the text, returning the first item in the list that matches the specified substring. You can then perform tasks, such as removing the item that contains the search text using the **Remove** method or changing the item's text. Once you have found the specified text, if you want to search for other instances of the text in the **ComboBox**, you must use the version of the **FindStringExact** method that provides a parameter for specifying a starting index within the **ComboBox**. If you want to perform partial word search instead of an exact word match, use the **FindString** method.

Requirements

Platforms: Windows 98, Windows NT 4.0, Windows Millennium Edition, Windows 2000, Windows XP Home Edition, Windows XP Professional, Windows Server 2003 family

ComboBox.FindStringExact Method (String, Int32)

Finds the first item after the specified index that matches the specified string.

[Visual Basic]
```
Overloads Public Function FindStringExact( _
   ByVal s As String, _
   ByVal startIndex As Integer _
) As Integer
```
[C#]
```
public int FindStringExact(
   string s,
   int startIndex
);
```
[C++]
```
public: int FindStringExact(
   String* s,
   int startIndex
);
```
[JScript]
```
public function FindStringExact(
   s : String,
   startIndex : int
) : int;
```

Parameters

s
: The **String** to search for.

startIndex
: The zero-based index of the item before the first item to be searched. Set to -1 to search from the beginning of the control.

Return Value

The zero-based index of the first item found; returns -1 if no match is found.

Exceptions

Exception Type	Condition
ArgumentOutOfRange-Exception	The *startIndex* is less than -1. -or- The *startIndex* is greater than the last index in the collection.

Remarks

The search performed by this method is not case-sensitive. The *s* parameter is a string to compare against the text associated with the items in the combo box list. The search looks for a match starting from the beginning of the text, returning the first item in the list that matches the specified substring. You can then perform tasks, such as removing the item that contains the search text using the **Remove** method or changing the item's text. This method is typically used after a call has been made using the version of this method that does not specify a starting index. Once an intial item has been found in the list, this method is typically used to find further instances of the search text by specifying the index position in the *startIndex* parameter of the item after the first found instance of the search text. If you want to perform partial word search instead of an exact word match, use the **FindString** method.

Requirements

Platforms: Windows 98, Windows NT 4.0, Windows Millennium Edition, Windows 2000, Windows XP Home Edition, Windows XP Professional, Windows Server 2003 family

ComboBox.GetItemHeight Method

Returns the height of an item in the **ComboBox**.

[Visual Basic]
```
Public Function GetItemHeight( _
   ByVal index As Integer _
) As Integer
```
[C#]
```
public int GetItemHeight(
   int index
);
```

```
[C++]
public: int GetItemHeight(
   int index
);
[JScript]
public function GetItemHeight(
   index : int
) : int;
```

Parameters

index

The index of the item to return the height of.

Return Value

The height, in pixels, of the item at the specified index.

Exceptions

Exception Type	Condition
ArgumentOutOfRange-Exception	The *index* is less than zero. -or- The *index* is greater than count of items in the list.

Remarks

If the **DrawMode** property is not set to **DrawMode.Owner-DrawVariable**, the value of the *index* parameter is ignored because all items in a standard **ComboBox** are the same size. You can use this property when you are using an owner-drawn **ComboBox** to determine the size of any item within the **ComboBox**.

For more information on specifying the height for items in an owner-drawn list, see **MeasureItem** event.

Requirements

Platforms: Windows 98, Windows NT 4.0, Windows Millennium Edition, Windows 2000, Windows XP Home Edition, Windows XP Professional, Windows Server 2003 family

ComboBox.IsInputKey Method

This member overrides **Control.IsInputKey**.

```
[Visual Basic]
Overrides Protected Function IsInputKey( _
   ByVal keyData As Keys _
) As Boolean
[C#]
protected override bool IsInputKey(
   Keys keyData
);
[C++]
protected: bool IsInputKey(
   Keys keyData
);
[JScript]
protected override function IsInputKey(
   keyData : Keys
) : Boolean;
```

Requirements

Platforms: Windows 98, Windows NT 4.0, Windows Millennium Edition, Windows 2000, Windows XP Home Edition, Windows XP Professional, Windows Server 2003 family

ComboBox.OnBackColorChanged Method

This member overrides **Control.OnBackColorChanged**.

```
[Visual Basic]
Overrides Protected Sub OnBackColorChanged( _
   ByVal e As EventArgs _
)
[C#]
protected override void OnBackColorChanged(
   EventArgs e
);
[C++]
protected: void OnBackColorChanged(
   EventArgs* e
);
[JScript]
protected override function OnBackColorChanged(
   e : EventArgs
);
```

Requirements

Platforms: Windows 98, Windows NT 4.0, Windows Millennium Edition, Windows 2000, Windows XP Home Edition, Windows XP Professional, Windows Server 2003 family

ComboBox.OnDataSourceChanged Method

This member overrides **ListControl.OnDataSourceChanged**.

```
[Visual Basic]
Overrides Protected Sub OnDataSourceChanged( _
   ByVal e As EventArgs _
)
[C#]
protected override void OnDataSourceChanged(
   EventArgs e
);
[C++]
protected: void OnDataSourceChanged(
   EventArgs* e
);
[JScript]
protected override function OnDataSourceChanged(
   e : EventArgs
);
```

Requirements

Platforms: Windows 98, Windows NT 4.0, Windows Millennium Edition, Windows 2000, Windows XP Home Edition, Windows XP Professional, Windows Server 2003 family, .NET Compact Framework - Windows CE .NET

ComboBox.OnDisplayMemberChanged Method

This member overrides **ListControl.OnDisplayMemberChanged**.

```
[Visual Basic]
Overrides Protected Sub OnDisplayMemberChanged( _
   ByVal e As EventArgs _
)
[C#]
protected override void OnDisplayMemberChanged(
   EventArgs e
);
[C++]
protected: void OnDisplayMemberChanged(
   EventArgs* e
);
[JScript]
protected override function OnDisplayMemberChanged(
   e : EventArgs
);
```

Requirements

Platforms: Windows 98, Windows NT 4.0, Windows Millennium Edition, Windows 2000, Windows XP Home Edition, Windows XP Professional, Windows Server 2003 family, .NET Compact Framework - Windows CE .NET

ComboBox.OnDrawItem Method

Raises the **DrawItem** event.

```
[Visual Basic]
Protected Overridable Sub OnDrawItem( _
   ByVal e As DrawItemEventArgs _
)
[C#]
protected virtual void OnDrawItem(
   DrawItemEventArgs e
);
[C++]
protected: virtual void OnDrawItem(
   DrawItemEventArgs* e
);
[JScript]
protected function OnDrawItem(
   e : DrawItemEventArgs
);
```

Parameters

e

A **DrawItemEventArgs** that contains the event data.

Remarks

This method is called each time an owner-drawn **ComboBox** item needs to be drawn and after **OnMeasureItem** is called.

Raising an event invokes the event handler through a delegate.

The **OnDrawItem** method also allows derived classes to handle the event without attaching a delegate. This is the preferred technique for handling the event in a derived class.

Notes to Inheritors: When overriding **OnDrawItem** in a derived class, be sure to call the base class's **OnDrawItem** method so that registered delegates receive the event.

Requirements

Platforms: Windows 98, Windows NT 4.0, Windows Millennium Edition, Windows 2000, Windows XP Home Edition, Windows XP Professional, Windows Server 2003 family

ComboBox.OnDropDown Method

Raises the **DropDown** event.

```
[Visual Basic]
Protected Overridable Sub OnDropDown( _
   ByVal e As EventArgs _
)
[C#]
protected virtual void OnDropDown(
   EventArgs e
);
[C++]
protected: virtual void OnDropDown(
   EventArgs* e
);
[JScript]
protected function OnDropDown(
   e : EventArgs
);
```

Parameters

e

An **EventArgs** that contains the event data.

Remarks

This event is raised each time the drop-down is displayed.

Raising an event invokes the event handler through a delegate.

The **OnDropDown** method also allows derived classes to handle the event without attaching a delegate. This is the preferred technique for handling the event in a derived class.

Notes to Inheritors: When overriding **OnDropDown** in a derived class, be sure to call the base class's **OnDropDown** method so that registered delegates receive the event.

Requirements

Platforms: Windows 98, Windows NT 4.0, Windows Millennium Edition, Windows 2000, Windows XP Home Edition, Windows XP Professional, Windows Server 2003 family

ComboBox.OnDropDownStyleChanged Method

Raises the **DropDownStyleChanged** event.

```
[Visual Basic]
Protected Overridable Sub OnDropDownStyleChanged( _
   ByVal e As EventArgs _
)
[C#]
protected virtual void OnDropDownStyleChanged(
   EventArgs e
);
[C++]
protected: virtual void OnDropDownStyleChanged(
   EventArgs* e
);
```

```
[JScript]
protected function OnDropDownStyleChanged(
   e : EventArgs
);
```

Parameters

e

An **EventArgs** that contains the event data.

Remarks

This event is raised when you set **DropDownStyle** to a new value.

Raising an event invokes the event handler through a delegate. For more information, see **Raising an Event**.

The **OnDropDownStyleChanged** method also allows derived classes to handle the event without attaching a delegate. This is the preferred technique for handling the event in a derived class.

Notes to Inheritors: When overriding **OnDropDownStyle-Changed** in a derived class, be sure to call the base class's **OnDrop-DownStyleChanged** method so that registered delegates receive the event.

Requirements

Platforms: Windows 98, Windows NT 4.0, Windows Millennium Edition, Windows 2000, Windows XP Home Edition, Windows XP Professional, Windows Server 2003 family

ComboBox.OnFontChanged Method

This member overrides **Control.OnFontChanged**.

```
[Visual Basic]
Overrides Protected Sub OnFontChanged( _
   ByVal e As EventArgs _
)
[C#]
protected override void OnFontChanged(
   EventArgs e
);
[C++]
protected: void OnFontChanged(
   EventArgs* e
);
[JScript]
protected override function OnFontChanged(
   e : EventArgs
);
```

Requirements

Platforms: Windows 98, Windows NT 4.0, Windows Millennium Edition, Windows 2000, Windows XP Home Edition, Windows XP Professional, Windows Server 2003 family

ComboBox.OnForeColorChanged Method

This member overrides **Control.OnForeColorChanged**.

```
[Visual Basic]
Overrides Protected Sub OnForeColorChanged( _
   ByVal e As EventArgs _
)
[C#]
protected override void OnForeColorChanged(
   EventArgs e
);
[C++]
protected: void OnForeColorChanged(
   EventArgs* e
);
[JScript]
protected override function OnForeColorChanged(
   e : EventArgs
);
```

Requirements

Platforms: Windows 98, Windows NT 4.0, Windows Millennium Edition, Windows 2000, Windows XP Home Edition, Windows XP Professional, Windows Server 2003 family

ComboBox.OnHandleCreated Method

This member overrides **Control.OnHandleCreated**.

```
[Visual Basic]
Overrides Protected Sub OnHandleCreated( _
   ByVal e As EventArgs _
)
[C#]
protected override void OnHandleCreated(
   EventArgs e
);
[C++]
protected: void OnHandleCreated(
   EventArgs* e
);
[JScript]
protected override function OnHandleCreated(
   e : EventArgs
);
```

Requirements

Platforms: Windows 98, Windows NT 4.0, Windows Millennium Edition, Windows 2000, Windows XP Home Edition, Windows XP Professional, Windows Server 2003 family

ComboBox.OnHandleDestroyed Method

This member overrides **Control.OnHandleDestroyed**.

```
[Visual Basic]
Overrides Protected Sub OnHandleDestroyed( _
   ByVal e As EventArgs _
)
[C#]
protected override void OnHandleDestroyed(
   EventArgs e
);
[C++]
protected: void OnHandleDestroyed(
   EventArgs* e
);
```

```
[JScript]
protected override function OnHandleDestroyed(
   e : EventArgs
);
```

Requirements

Platforms: Windows 98, Windows NT 4.0, Windows Millennium Edition, Windows 2000, Windows XP Home Edition, Windows XP Professional, Windows Server 2003 family

ComboBox.OnKeyPress Method

This member overrides **Control.OnKeyPress.**

```
[Visual Basic]
Overrides Protected Sub OnKeyPress( _
   ByVal e As KeyPressEventArgs _
)
[C#]
protected override void OnKeyPress(
   KeyPressEventArgs e
);
[C++]
protected: void OnKeyPress(
   KeyPressEventArgs* e
);
[JScript]
protected override function OnKeyPress(
   e : KeyPressEventArgs
);
```

Requirements

Platforms: Windows 98, Windows NT 4.0, Windows Millennium Edition, Windows 2000, Windows XP Home Edition, Windows XP Professional, Windows Server 2003 family, .NET Compact Framework - Windows CE .NET

ComboBox.OnMeasureItem Method

Raises the **MeasureItem** event.

```
[Visual Basic]
Protected Overridable Sub OnMeasureItem( _
   ByVal e As MeasureItemEventArgs _
)
[C#]
protected virtual void OnMeasureItem(
   MeasureItemEventArgs e
);
[C++]
protected: virtual void OnMeasureItem(
   MeasureItemEventArgs* e
);
[JScript]
protected function OnMeasureItem(
   e : MeasureItemEventArgs
);
```

Parameters

e

The **MeasureItemEventArgs** that was raised.

Remarks

This method is called each time an owner-drawn **ComboBox** item needs to be drawn and before **OnDrawItem** is called. For more information, see **MeasureItem**.

Raising an event invokes the event handler through a delegate. For more information, see **Raising an Event**.

The **OnMeasureItem** method also allows derived classes to handle the event without attaching a delegate. This is the preferred technique for handling the event in a derived class.

Notes to Inheritors: When overriding **OnMeasureItem** in a derived class, be sure to call the base class's **OnMeasureItem** method so that registered delegates receive the event.

Requirements

Platforms: Windows 98, Windows NT 4.0, Windows Millennium Edition, Windows 2000, Windows XP Home Edition, Windows XP Professional, Windows Server 2003 family

ComboBox.OnParentBackColorChanged Method

This member overrides **Control.OnParentBackColorChanged.**

```
[Visual Basic]
Overrides Protected Sub OnParentBackColorChanged( _
   ByVal e As EventArgs _
)
[C#]
protected override void OnParentBackColorChanged(
   EventArgs e
);
[C++]
protected: void OnParentBackColorChanged(
   EventArgs* e
);
[JScript]
protected override function OnParentBackColorChanged(
   e : EventArgs
);
```

Requirements

Platforms: Windows 98, Windows NT 4.0, Windows Millennium Edition, Windows 2000, Windows XP Home Edition, Windows XP Professional, Windows Server 2003 family

ComboBox.OnResize Method

This member overrides **Control.OnResize.**

```
[Visual Basic]
Overrides Protected Sub OnResize( _
   ByVal e As EventArgs _
)
[C#]
protected override void OnResize(
   EventArgs e
);
[C++]
protected: void OnResize(
   EventArgs* e
);
```

```
[JScript]
protected override function OnResize(
   e : EventArgs
);
```

Requirements

Platforms: Windows 98, Windows NT 4.0, Windows Millennium Edition, Windows 2000, Windows XP Home Edition, Windows XP Professional, Windows Server 2003 family, .NET Compact Framework - Windows CE .NET

ComboBox.OnSelectedIndexChanged Method

This member overrides **ListControl.OnSelectedIndexChanged**.

```
[Visual Basic]
Overrides Protected Sub OnSelectedIndexChanged( _
   ByVal e As EventArgs _
)
[C#]
protected override void OnSelectedIndexChanged(
   EventArgs e
);
[C++]
protected: void OnSelectedIndexChanged(
   EventArgs* e
);
[JScript]
protected override function OnSelectedIndexChanged(
   e : EventArgs
);
```

Requirements

Platforms: Windows 98, Windows NT 4.0, Windows Millennium Edition, Windows 2000, Windows XP Home Edition, Windows XP Professional, Windows Server 2003 family, .NET Compact Framework - Windows CE .NET

ComboBox.OnSelectedItemChanged Method

This member supports the .NET Framework infrastructure and is not intended to be used directly from your code.

```
[Visual Basic]
Protected Overridable Sub OnSelectedItemChanged( _
   ByVal e As EventArgs _
)
[C#]
protected virtual void OnSelectedItemChanged(
   EventArgs e
);
[C++]
protected: virtual void OnSelectedItemChanged(
   EventArgs* e
);
[JScript]
protected function OnSelectedItemChanged(
   e : EventArgs
);
```

ComboBox.OnSelectedValueChanged Method

This member overrides **ListControl.OnSelectedValueChanged**.

```
[Visual Basic]
Overrides Protected Sub OnSelectedValueChanged( _
   ByVal e As EventArgs _
)
[C#]
protected override void OnSelectedValueChanged(
   EventArgs e
);
[C++]
protected: void OnSelectedValueChanged(
   EventArgs* e
);
[JScript]
protected override function OnSelectedValueChanged(
   e : EventArgs
);
```

Requirements

Platforms: Windows 98, Windows NT 4.0, Windows Millennium Edition, Windows 2000, Windows XP Home Edition, Windows XP Professional, Windows Server 2003 family, .NET Compact Framework - Windows CE .NET

ComboBox.OnSelectionChangeCommitted Method

Raises the **SelectionChangeCommitted** event.

```
[Visual Basic]
Protected Overridable Sub OnSelectionChangeCommitted( _
   ByVal e As EventArgs _
)
[C#]
protected virtual void OnSelectionChangeCommitted(
   EventArgs e
);
[C++]
protected: virtual void OnSelectionChangeCommitted(
   EventArgs* e
);
[JScript]
protected function OnSelectionChangeCommitted(
   e : EventArgs
);
```

Parameters

e

An **EventArgs** that contains the event data.

Remarks

This event is raised when a new item is selected and that change to that item is completed. This event is also raised when you set **SelectedIndex**.

Raising an event invokes the event handler through a delegate.

The **OnSelectionChangeCommitted** method also allows derived classes to handle the event without attaching a delegate. This is the preferred technique for handling the event in a derived class.

Notes to Inheritors: When overriding **OnSelectionChangeCommitted** in a derived class, be sure to call the base class's **OnSelectionChangeCommitted** method so that registered delegates receive the event.

Requirements

Platforms: Windows 98, Windows NT 4.0, Windows Millennium Edition, Windows 2000, Windows XP Home Edition, Windows XP Professional, Windows Server 2003 family

ComboBox.RefreshItem Method

This member overrides **ListControl.RefreshItem**.

[Visual Basic]
```
Overrides Protected Sub RefreshItem( _
   ByVal index As Integer _
)
```
[C#]
```
protected override void RefreshItem(
   int index
);
```
[C++]
```
protected: void RefreshItem(
   int index
);
```
[JScript]
```
protected override function RefreshItem(
   index : int
);
```

Requirements

Platforms: Windows 98, Windows NT 4.0, Windows Millennium Edition, Windows 2000, Windows XP Home Edition, Windows XP Professional, Windows Server 2003 family

ComboBox.Select Method

Selects a range of text.

Overload List

Selects a range of text in the editable portion of the **ComboBox**.

[Visual Basic] **Overloads Public Sub Select(Integer, Integer)**

[C#] **public void Select(int, int);**

[C++] **public: void Select(int, int);**

[JScript] **public function Select(int, int);**

Inherited from **Control**.

[Visual Basic] **Overloads Public Sub Select()**

[C#] **public void Select();**

[C++] **public: void Select();**

[JScript] **public function Select();**

Inherited from **Control**.

[Visual Basic] **Overloads Protected Overridable Sub Select(Boolean, Boolean)**

[C#] **protected virtual void Select(bool, bool);**

[C++] **protected: virtual void Select(bool, bool);**

[JScript] **protected function Select(Boolean, Boolean);**

ComboBox.Select Method (Int32, Int32)

Selects a range of text in the editable portion of the **ComboBox**.

[Visual Basic]
```
Overloads Public Sub Select( _
   ByVal start As Integer, _
   ByVal length As Integer _
)
```
[C#]
```
public void Select(
   int start,
   int length
);
```
[C++]
```
public: void Select(
   int start,
   int length
);
```
[JScript]
```
public function Select(
   start : int,
   length : int
);
```

Parameters

start

The position of the first character in the current text selection within the text box.

length

The number of characters to select.

Exceptions

Exception Type	Condition
ArgumentException	The *start* is less than zero. -or- The *length* is less than zero.

Remarks

If you want to set the start position to the first character in the control's text, set the *start* parameter to zero. You can use this method to select a substring of text, such as when searching through the text of the control and replacing information.

Requirements

Platforms: Windows 98, Windows NT 4.0, Windows Millennium Edition, Windows 2000, Windows XP Home Edition, Windows XP Professional, Windows Server 2003 family

ComboBox.SelectAll Method

Selects all the text in the editable portion of the **ComboBox**.

[Visual Basic]
```
Public Sub SelectAll()
```
[C#]
```
public void SelectAll();
```
[C++]
```
public: void SelectAll();
```
[JScript]
```
public function SelectAll();
```

Requirements

Platforms: Windows 98, Windows NT 4.0, Windows Millennium Edition, Windows 2000, Windows XP Home Edition, Windows XP Professional, Windows Server 2003 family

ComboBox.SetBoundsCore Method

This member overrides **Control.SetBoundsCore**.

```
[Visual Basic]
Overrides Protected Sub SetBoundsCore( _
   ByVal x As Integer, _
   ByVal y As Integer, _
   ByVal width As Integer, _
   ByVal height As Integer, _
   ByVal specified As BoundsSpecified _
)
[C#]
protected override void SetBoundsCore(
   int x,
   int y,
   int width,
   int height,
   BoundsSpecified specified
);
[C++]
protected: void SetBoundsCore(
   int x,
   int y,
   int width,
   int height,
   BoundsSpecified specified
);
[JScript]
protected override function SetBoundsCore(
   x : int,
   y : int,
   width : int,
   height : int,
   specified : BoundsSpecified
);
```

Requirements

Platforms: Windows 98, Windows NT 4.0, Windows Millennium Edition, Windows 2000, Windows XP Home Edition, Windows XP Professional, Windows Server 2003 family

ComboBox.SetItemCore Method

This member supports the .NET Framework infrastructure and is not intended to be used directly from your code.

```
[Visual Basic]
Overrides Protected Sub SetItemCore( _
   ByVal index As Integer, _
   ByVal value As Object _
)
[C#]
protected override void SetItemCore(
   int index,
   object value
);
[C++]
protected: void SetItemCore(
   int index,
   Object* value
);
[JScript]
protected override function SetItemCore(
   index : int,
   value : Object
);
```

ComboBox.SetItemsCore Method

This member supports the .NET Framework infrastructure and is not intended to be used directly from your code.

```
[Visual Basic]
Overrides Protected Sub SetItemsCore( _
   ByVal value As IList _
)
[C#]
protected override void SetItemsCore(
   IList value
);
[C++]
protected: void SetItemsCore(
   IList* value
);
[JScript]
protected override function SetItemsCore(
   value : IList
);
```

ComboBox.ToString Method

This member overrides **Object.ToString**.

```
[Visual Basic]
Overrides Public Function ToString() As String
[C#]
public override string ToString();
[C++]
public: String* ToString();
[JScript]
public override function ToString() : String;
```

Requirements

Platforms: Windows 98, Windows NT 4.0, Windows Millennium Edition, Windows 2000, Windows XP Home Edition, Windows XP Professional, Windows Server 2003 family, .NET Compact Framework - Windows CE .NET

ComboBox.WndProc Method

This member overrides **Control.WndProc**.

```
[Visual Basic]
Overrides Protected Sub WndProc( _
   ByRef m As Message _
)
[C#]
protected override void WndProc(
   ref Message m
);
```

```
[C++]
protected: void WndProc(
   Message* m
);
[JScript]
protected override function WndProc(
   m : Message
);
```

Requirements

Platforms: Windows 98, Windows NT 4.0,
Windows Millennium Edition, Windows 2000,
Windows XP Home Edition, Windows XP Professional,
Windows Server 2003 family

ComboBox.BackgroundImageChanged Event

This member supports the .NET Framework infrastructure and is not intended to be used directly from your code.

```
[Visual Basic]
Public Shadows Event BackgroundImageChanged As EventHandler
[C#]
public new event EventHandler BackgroundImageChanged;
[C++]
public: __event EventHandler* BackgroundImageChanged;
```

[JScript] In JScript, you can handle the events defined by a class, but you cannot define your own.

ComboBox.DrawItem Event

Occurs when a visual aspect of an owner-drawn **ComboBox** changes.

```
[Visual Basic]
Public Event DrawItem As DrawItemEventHandler
[C#]
public event DrawItemEventHandler DrawItem;
[C++]
public: __event DrawItemEventHandler* DrawItem;
```

[JScript] In JScript, you can handle the events defined by a class, but you cannot define your own.

Event Data

The event handler receives an argument of type **DrawItemEventArgs** containing data related to this event. The following **DrawItemEventArgs** properties provide information specific to this event.

Property	Description
BackColor	Gets the background color of the item that is being drawn.
Bounds	Gets the rectangle that represents the bounds of the item that is being drawn.
Font	Gets the font assigned to the item being drawn.
ForeColor	Gets the foreground color of the of the item being drawn.
Graphics	Gets the graphics surface to draw the item on.
Index	Gets the index value of the item that is being drawn.
State	Gets the state of the item being drawn.

Remarks

This event is used by an owner-drawn **ComboBox**. You can use this event to perform the tasks needed to draw items in the **ComboBox**. If you have a variable sized item (when the **DrawMode** property set to **DrawMode.OwnerDrawVariable**), before drawing an item, the **MeasureItem** event is raised. You can create an event handler for the **MeasureItem** event to specify the size for the item that you are going to draw in your event handler for the **DrawItem** event.

Requirements

Platforms: Windows 98, Windows NT 4.0,
Windows Millennium Edition, Windows 2000,
Windows XP Home Edition, Windows XP Professional,
Windows Server 2003 family

ComboBox.DropDown Event

Occurs when the drop-down portion of a **ComboBox** is shown.

```
[Visual Basic]
Public Event DropDown As EventHandler
[C#]
public event EventHandler DropDown;
[C++]
public: __event EventHandler* DropDown;
```

[JScript] In JScript, you can handle the events defined by a class, but you cannot define your own.

Event Data

The event handler receives an argument of type **EventArgs**.

Requirements

Platforms: Windows 98, Windows NT 4.0,
Windows Millennium Edition, Windows 2000,
Windows XP Home Edition, Windows XP Professional,
Windows Server 2003 family

ComboBox.DropDownStyleChanged Event

Occurs when the **DropDownStyle** property has changed.

```
[Visual Basic]
Public Event DropDownStyleChanged As EventHandler
[C#]
public event EventHandler DropDownStyleChanged;
[C++]
public: __event EventHandler* DropDownStyleChanged;
```

[JScript] In JScript, you can handle the events defined by a class, but you cannot define your own.

Event Data

The event handler receives an argument of type **EventArgs**.

Requirements

Platforms: Windows 98, Windows NT 4.0,
Windows Millennium Edition, Windows 2000,
Windows XP Home Edition, Windows XP Professional,
Windows Server 2003 family

ComboBox.MeasureItem Event

Occurs each time an owner-drawn **ComboBox** item needs to be drawn and when the sizes of the list items are determined.

```
[Visual Basic]
Public Event MeasureItem As MeasureItemEventHandler
[C#]
public event MeasureItemEventHandler MeasureItem;
[C++]
public: __event MeasureItemEventHandler* MeasureItem;
```

[JScript] In JScript, you can handle the events defined by a class, but you cannot define your own.

Event Data

The event handler receives an argument of type **MeasureItemEventArgs** containing data related to this event. The following **MeasureItemEventArgs** properties provide information specific to this event.

Property	Description
Graphics	Gets the **Graphics** object to measure against.
Index	Gets or sets the index of the item for which the height and width is needed.
ItemHeight	Gets or sets the height of the item specified by the **Index**.
ItemWidth	Gets or sets the width of the item specified by the **Index**.

Remarks

You can create an event handler for this event to specify the size an item is made before it is drawn in the **DrawItem** event.

Requirements

Platforms: Windows 98, Windows NT 4.0, Windows Millennium Edition, Windows 2000, Windows XP Home Edition, Windows XP Professional, Windows Server 2003 family

ComboBox.Paint Event

This member supports the .NET Framework infrastructure and is not intended to be used directly from your code.

```
[Visual Basic]
Public Shadows Event Paint As PaintEventHandler
[C#]
public new event PaintEventHandler Paint;
[C++]
public: __event PaintEventHandler* Paint;
```

[JScript] In JScript, you can handle the events defined by a class, but you cannot define your own.

ComboBox.SelectedIndexChanged Event

Occurs when the **SelectedIndex** property has changed.

```
[Visual Basic]
Public Event SelectedIndexChanged As EventHandler
[C#]
public event EventHandler SelectedIndexChanged;
[C++]
public: __event EventHandler* SelectedIndexChanged;
```

[JScript] In JScript, you can handle the events defined by a class, but you cannot define your own.

Event Data

The event handler receives an argument of type **EventArgs**.

Remarks

You can create an event handler for this event to determine when the selected index in the **ComboBox** has been changed. This can be useful when you need to display information in other controls based on the current selection in the **ComboBox**. You can use the event handler for this event to load the information in the other controls.

Requirements

Platforms: Windows 98, Windows NT 4.0, Windows Millennium Edition, Windows 2000, Windows XP Home Edition, Windows XP Professional, Windows Server 2003 family

ComboBox.SelectionChangeCommitted Event

Occurs when the selected item has changed and that change is committed.

```
[Visual Basic]
Public Event SelectionChangeCommitted As EventHandler
[C#]
public event EventHandler SelectionChangeCommitted;
[C++]
public: __event EventHandler* SelectionChangeCommitted;
```

[JScript] In JScript, you can handle the events defined by a class, but you cannot define your own.

Event Data

The event handler receives an argument of type **EventArgs**.

Remarks

You can create a **SelectionChangeCommitted** event handler to provide special handling for the **ComboBox** when the user changes the selected item in the list.

Requirements

Platforms: Windows 98, Windows NT 4.0, Windows Millennium Edition, Windows 2000, Windows XP Home Edition, Windows XP Professional, Windows Server 2003 family

ComboBox.ChildAccessibleObject Class

This type supports the .NET Framework infrastructure and is not intended to be used directly from your code.

[Visual Basic]
```
<ComVisible(True)>
Public Class ComboBox.ChildAccessibleObject
   Inherits AccessibleObject
```
[C#]
```
[ComVisible(true)]
public class ComboBox.ChildAccessibleObject : AccessibleObject
```
[C++]
```
[ComVisible(true)]
public __gc class ComboBox.ChildAccessibleObject : public
   AccessibleObject
```
[JScript]
```
public
   ComVisible(true)
class ComboBox.ChildAccessibleObject extends
   AccessibleObject
```

ComboBox.ChildAccessibleObject Constructor

This member supports the .NET Framework infrastructure and is not intended to be used directly from your code.

[Visual Basic]
```
Public Sub New( _
   ByVal owner As ComboBox, _
   ByVal handle As IntPtr _
)
```
[C#]
```
public ComboBox.ChildAccessibleObject(
   ComboBox owner,
   IntPtr handle
);
```
[C++]
```
public: ChildAccessibleObject(
   ComboBox* owner,
   IntPtr handle
);
```
[JScript]
```
public function ComboBox.ChildAccessibleObject(
   owner : ComboBox,
   handle : IntPtr
);
```

ComboBox.ChildAccessibleObject.Name Property

This member supports the .NET Framework infrastructure and is not intended to be used directly from your code.

[Visual Basic]
```
Overrides Public ReadOnly Property Name As String
```
[C#]
```
public override string Name {get;}
```
[C++]
```
public: __property String* get_Name();
```
[JScript]
```
public override function get Name() : String;
```

ComboBox.ObjectCollection Class

Represents the collection of items in a **ComboBox**.

System.Object
System.Windows.Forms.ComboBox.ObjectCollection

```
[Visual Basic]
Public Class ComboBox.ObjectCollection
   Implements IList, ICollection, IEnumerable
[C#]
public class ComboBox.ObjectCollection : IList, ICollection,
   IEnumerable
[C++]
public __gc class ComboBox.ObjectCollection : public IList,
   ICollection, IEnumerable
[JScript]
public class ComboBox.ObjectCollection implements IList,
   ICollection, IEnumerable
```

Thread Safety

Any public static (**Shared** in Visual Basic) members of this type are safe for multithreaded operations. Any instance members are not guaranteed to be thread safe.

Remarks

The **System.Windows.Forms.ComboBox.ObjectCollection** class encapsulates the items in the **ComboBox**. The object collection of a combo box can be used to manage many types of objects, including strings, images, and custom business objects.

You can add items to the collection in several ways. The **Add** method adds one object to the collection. To add a number of objects to the collection, it is best to create an array of items and assign with the **AddRange** method. To insert an object at a specific location within the collection, you can use the **Insert** method. To remove items at a known index in the collection you can use either the **Remove** method or the **RemoveAt** method. The **ComboBox** method removes all the items from the collection.

In addition to methods and properties for adding and removing items, the **System.Windows.Forms.ComboBox.ObjectCollection** also provides methods to find items within the collection. The **Contains** method enables you to determine if an object is a member of the collection. Once you know that the item is located within the collection, you can use the **IndexOf** method to determine where the item is located within the collection.

Requirements

Namespace: System.Windows.Forms

Platforms: Windows 98, Windows NT 4.0, Windows Millennium Edition, Windows 2000, Windows XP Home Edition, Windows XP Professional, Windows Server 2003 family, .NET Compact Framework - Windows CE .NET

Assembly: System.Windows.Forms (in System.Windows.Forms.dll)

ComboBox.ObjectCollection Constructor

Initializes a new instance of **System.Windows.Forms.ComboBox.ObjectCollection**.

```
[Visual Basic]
Public Sub New( _
   ByVal owner As ComboBox _
)
[C#]
public ComboBox.ObjectCollection(
   ComboBox owner
);
[C++]
public: ObjectCollection(
   ComboBox* owner
);
[JScript]
public function ComboBox.ObjectCollection(
   owner : ComboBox
);
```

Parameters

owner
The **ComboBox** that owns this object collection.

Remarks

An instance of this class cannot be created without associating it with a **ComboBox** control.

Requirements

Platforms: Windows 98, Windows NT 4.0, Windows Millennium Edition, Windows 2000, Windows XP Home Edition, Windows XP Professional, Windows Server 2003 family

ComboBox.ObjectCollection.Count Property

Gets the number of items in the collection.

```
[Visual Basic]
Public Overridable ReadOnly Property Count As Integer  Implements _
   ICollection.Count
[C#]
public virtual int Count {get;}
[C++]
public: __property virtual int get_Count();
[JScript]
public function get Count() : int;
```

Property Value

The number of items in the collection.

Implements

ICollection.Count

Remarks

This property enables you to determine the number of items in the **ComboBox**. You can use this value when looping through the values of the collection.

Requirements

Platforms: Windows 98, Windows NT 4.0, Windows Millennium Edition, Windows 2000, Windows XP Home Edition, Windows XP Professional, Windows Server 2003 family, .NET Compact Framework - Windows CE .NET

ComboBox.ObjectCollection.IsReadOnly Property

Gets a value indicating whether this collection can be modified.

```
[Visual Basic]
Public Overridable ReadOnly Property IsReadOnly As Boolean _
   Implements IList.IsReadOnly
[C#]
public virtual bool IsReadOnly {get;}
[C++]
public: __property virtual bool get_IsReadOnly();
[JScript]
public function get IsReadOnly() : Boolean;
```

Property Value

Always **false**.

Implements

IList.IsReadOnly

Requirements

Platforms: Windows 98, Windows NT 4.0, Windows Millennium Edition, Windows 2000, Windows XP Home Edition, Windows XP Professional, Windows Server 2003 family, .NET Compact Framework - Windows CE .NET

ComboBox.ObjectCollection.Item Property

Retrieves the item at the specified index within the collection.

[C#] In C#, this property is the indexer for the **ComboBox.ObjectCollection** class.

```
[Visual Basic]
Public Overridable Default Property Item( _
   ByVal index As Integer _
) As Object  Implements IList.Item
[C#]
public virtual object this[
   int index
] {get; set;}
[C++]
public: __property virtual Object* get_Item(
   int index
);
public: __property virtual void set_Item(
   int index,
   Object*
);
[JScript]
returnValue = ObjectCollectionObject.Item(index);
ObjectCollectionObject.Item(index) = returnValue;
-or-
returnValue = ObjectCollectionObject(index);
ObjectCollectionObject(index) = returnValue;
```

[JScript] In JScript, you can use the default indexed properties defined by a type, but you cannot explicitly define your own. However, specifying the **expando** attribute on a class automatically provides a default indexed property whose type is **Object** and whose index type is **String**.

Arguments [JScript]

index

The index of the item in the collection to retrieve.

Parameters [Visual Basic, C#, C++]

index

The index of the item in the collection to retrieve.

Property Value

An object representing the item located at the specified index within the collection.

Implements

IList.Item

Exceptions

Exception Type	Condition
ArgumentOutOfRange-Exception	The index was less than zero. -or- The *index* was greater than the count of items in the collection.

Remarks

You can use this method to obtain the item at the specified location within the collection. You can use **IndexOf** to find the location of an item, or you can use the index return from the **Add** method.

Requirements

Platforms: Windows 98, Windows NT 4.0, Windows Millennium Edition, Windows 2000, Windows XP Home Edition, Windows XP Professional, Windows Server 2003 family

ComboBox.ObjectCollection.System.Collections.ICollection.IsSynchronized Property

Note: This namespace, class, or member is supported only in version 1.1 of the .NET Framework.

This member supports the .NET Framework infrastructure and is not intended to be used directly from your code.

```
[Visual Basic]
Private ReadOnly Property IsSynchronized As Boolean Implements _
   ICollection.IsSynchronized
[C#]
bool ICollection.IsSynchronized {get;}
[C++]
private: __property bool
   System::Collections::ICollection::get_IsSynchronized();
[JScript]
private function get ICollection.IsSynchronized() : Boolean;
```

ComboBox.ObjectCollection.System.Collections.ICollection.SyncRoot Property

Note: This namespace, class, or member is supported only in version 1.1 of the .NET Framework.

This member supports the .NET Framework infrastructure and is not intended to be used directly from your code.

```
[Visual Basic]
Private ReadOnly Property SyncRoot As Object Implements _
   ICollection.SyncRoot
[C#]
object ICollection.SyncRoot {get;}
[C++]
private: __property Object*
   System::Collections::ICollection::get_SyncRoot();
[JScript]
private function get ICollection.SyncRoot() : Object;
```

ComboBox.ObjectCollection.System.Collections.IList.IsFixedSize Property

Note: This namespace, class, or member is supported only in version 1.1 of the .NET Framework.

This member supports the .NET Framework infrastructure and is not intended to be used directly from your code.

```
[Visual Basic]
Private ReadOnly Property IsFixedSize As Boolean Implements _
   IList.IsFixedSize
[C#]
bool IList.IsFixedSize {get;}
[C++]
private: __property bool
   System::Collections::IList::get_IsFixedSize();
[JScript]
private function get IList.IsFixedSize() : Boolean;
```

ComboBox.ObjectCollection.Add Method

Adds an item to the list of items for a **ComboBox**.

```
[Visual Basic]
Public Function Add( _
   ByVal item As Object _
) As Integer
[C#]
public int Add(
   object item
);
[C++]
public: int Add(
   Object* item
);
[JScript]
public function Add(
   item : Object
) : int;
```

Parameters

item

An object representing the item to add to the collection.

Return Value

The zero-based index of the item in the collection.

Exceptions

Exception Type	Condition
ArgumentNull-Exception	The *item* parameter was a null reference (**Nothing** in Visual Basic).

Remarks

This method adds an item to the combo box. If the **Sorted** property of the **ComboBox** is set to **true**, the item is inserted into the list alphabetically. Otherwise, the item is inserted at the end of the list.

A visual representation of the item is displayed in the combo box. This content representation is specified by the **DisplayMember** property. If the **DisplayMember** property is a null reference (**Nothing** in Visual Basic), the item's **ToString** method is called to obtain the string that is displayed in the combo box; otherwise, the property of the stored object as specified by the **DisplayMember** property is displayed. A **SystemException** occurs if there is insufficient space available to store the new item. To add a set of items to the combo box it is best to use the **AddRange** method. If you choose to use the **Add** method to add a number of items to the combo box, use the **BeginUpdate** method to suspend repainting during your add and the **EndUpdate** method to resume repainting. You can use the **Insert** method to specify the location in the list where an item is added. When an object is added to the collection, the **ComboBox** calls the object's **ToString** method to obtain the string to display in the list.

Requirements

Platforms: Windows 98, Windows NT 4.0, Windows Millennium Edition, Windows 2000, Windows XP Home Edition, Windows XP Professional, Windows Server 2003 family, .NET Compact Framework - Windows CE .NET

ComboBox.ObjectCollection.AddRange Method

Adds an array of items to the list of items for a **ComboBox**.

```
[Visual Basic]
Public Sub AddRange( _
   ByVal items() As Object _
)
[C#]
public void AddRange(
   object[] items
);
[C++]
public: void AddRange(
   Object* items __gc[]
);
[JScript]
public function AddRange(
   items : Object[]
);
```

Parameters

items

An array of objects to add to the list.

Exceptions

Exception Type	Condition
ArgumentNull-Exception	An item in the *items* parameter was a null reference (**Nothing** in Visual Basic).

Remarks

If the **Sorted** property of the **ComboBox** is set to true, the items are inserted into the list alphabetically. Otherwise, the items are inserted in the order they occur within the array. This method is typically passed an array of **String** objects, but an array of any type of object can be passed to this method. When an object is added to the collection, the method calls the object's **ToString** method to obtain the string to display in the list. When using this method to add items to the collection, you do not need to call the **BeginUpdate** and **EndUpdate** methods to optimize performance.

Requirements

Platforms: Windows 98, Windows NT 4.0,
Windows Millennium Edition, Windows 2000,
Windows XP Home Edition, Windows XP Professional,
Windows Server 2003 family

ComboBox.ObjectCollection.Clear Method

Removes all items from the **ComboBox**.

```
[Visual Basic]
Public Overridable Sub Clear() Implements IList.Clear
[C#]
public virtual void Clear();
[C++]
public: virtual void Clear();
[JScript]
public function Clear();
```

Implements

IList.Clear

Remarks

When you remove items from the list, all information about the deleted items is lost. To remove a single item from the **ComboBox**, use the **Remove** or **RemoveAt** method.

Requirements

Platforms: Windows 98, Windows NT 4.0,
Windows Millennium Edition, Windows 2000,
Windows XP Home Edition, Windows XP Professional,
Windows Server 2003 family,
.NET Compact Framework - Windows CE .NET

ComboBox.ObjectCollection.Contains Method

Determines if the specified item is located within the collection.

```
[Visual Basic]
Public Overridable Function Contains( _
   ByVal value As Object _
) As Boolean Implements IList.Contains
[C#]
public virtual bool Contains(
   object value
);
[C++]
public: virtual bool Contains(
   Object* value
);
[JScript]
public function Contains(
   value : Object
) : Boolean;
```

Parameters

value

An object representing the item to locate in the collection.

Return Value

true if the item is located within the collection; otherwise, **false**.

Implements

IList.Contains

Remarks

The **Contains** method enables you to determine if an object is a member of the collection. Once you know that the item is located within the collection, you can use the **IndexOf** method to determine where the item is located within the collection.

Requirements

Platforms: Windows 98, Windows NT 4.0,
Windows Millennium Edition, Windows 2000,
Windows XP Home Edition, Windows XP Professional,
Windows Server 2003 family,
.NET Compact Framework - Windows CE .NET

ComboBox.ObjectCollection.CopyTo Method

Copies the entire collection into an existing array of objects at a specified location within the array.

```
[Visual Basic]
Public Sub CopyTo( _
   ByVal dest() As Object, _
   ByVal arrayIndex As Integer _
)
[C#]
public void CopyTo(
   object[] dest,
   int arrayIndex
);
[C++]
public: void CopyTo(
   Object* dest __gc[],
   int arrayIndex
);
[JScript]
public function CopyTo(
   dest : Object[],
   arrayIndex : int
);
```

Parameters

dest

The object array to copy the collection to.

arrayIndex

The location in the destination array to copy the collection to.

Remarks

You can use this method to combine the items from multiple collections into a single array. You can then use this array to populate the contents of another **ComboBox** control using the **AddRange** method of the **ComboBox.ObjectCollection** class.

Requirements

Platforms: Windows 98, Windows NT 4.0,
Windows Millennium Edition, Windows 2000,
Windows XP Home Edition, Windows XP Professional,
Windows Server 2003 family

ComboBox.ObjectCollection.GetEnumerator Method

Returns an enumerator that can be used to iterate through the item collection.

```
[Visual Basic]
Public Overridable Function GetEnumerator() As IEnumerator _
   Implements IEnumerable.GetEnumerator
[C#]
public virtual IEnumerator GetEnumerator();
[C++]
public: virtual IEnumerator* GetEnumerator();
[JScript]
public function GetEnumerator() : IEnumerator;
```

Return Value

An **IEnumerator** object that represents the item collection.

Implements

IEnumerable.GetEnumerator

Requirements

Platforms: Windows 98, Windows NT 4.0, Windows Millennium Edition, Windows 2000, Windows XP Home Edition, Windows XP Professional, Windows Server 2003 family, .NET Compact Framework - Windows CE .NET

ComboBox.ObjectCollection.ICollection.CopyTo Method

This member supports the .NET Framework infrastructure and is not intended to be used directly from your code.

```
[Visual Basic]
Private Sub CopyTo( _
   ByVal dest As Array, _
   ByVal index As Integer _
) Implements ICollection.CopyTo
[C#]
void ICollection.CopyTo(
   Array dest,
   int index
);
[C++]
private: void ICollection::CopyTo(
   Array* dest,
   int index
);
[JScript]
private function ICollection.CopyTo(
   dest : Array,
   index : int
);
```

ComboBox.ObjectCollection.IList.Add Method

This member supports the .NET Framework infrastructure and is not intended to be used directly from your code.

```
[Visual Basic]
Private Function Add( _
   ByVal item As Object _
) As Integer Implements IList.Add
[C#]
int IList.Add(
   object item
);
[C++]
private: int IList::Add(
   Object* item
);
[JScript]
private function IList.Add(
   item : Object
) : int;
```

ComboBox.ObjectCollection.IndexOf Method

Retrieves the index within the collection of the specified item.

```
[Visual Basic]
Public Overridable Function IndexOf( _
   ByVal value As Object _
) As Integer Implements IList.IndexOf
[C#]
public virtual int IndexOf(
   object value
);
[C++]
public: virtual int IndexOf(
   Object* value
);
[JScript]
public function IndexOf(
   value : Object
) : int;
```

Parameters

value
An object representing the item to locate in the collection.

Return Value

The zero-based index where the item is located within the collection; otherwise, -1.

Implements

IList.IndexOf

Exceptions

Exception Type	Condition
ArgumentNull-Exception	The *value* parameter was a null reference (**Nothing** in Visual Basic).

Remarks

The **IndexOf** method enables you to determine where an item is located within the collection. To determine if an item is located within the collection before calling this method, use the **Contains** method.

Requirements

Platforms: Windows 98, Windows NT 4.0, Windows Millennium Edition, Windows 2000, Windows XP Home Edition, Windows XP Professional, Windows Server 2003 family, .NET Compact Framework - Windows CE .NET

ComboBox.ObjectCollection.Insert Method

Inserts an item into the collection at the specified index.

```
[Visual Basic]
Public Overridable Sub Insert( _
   ByVal index As Integer, _
   ByVal item As Object _
) Implements IList.Insert
[C#]
public virtual void Insert(
   int index,
   object item
);
[C++]
public: virtual void Insert(
   int index,
   Object* item
);
[JScript]
public function Insert(
   index : int,
   item : Object
);
```

Parameters

index

The zero-based index location where the item is inserted.

item

An object representing the item to insert.

Return Value

The zero-based index of the newly added item.

Implements

IList.Insert

Exceptions

Exception Type	Condition
ArgumentNull-Exception	The *item* was a null reference (**Nothing** in Visual Basic).
ArgumentOutOfRange-Exception	The *index* was less than zero. -or- The *index* was greater than the count of items in the collection.

Remarks

If the **sorted** property of the **ComboBox** is true, the *index* parameter is ignored. When an object is added to the collection, the **ComboBox** calls the object's **ToString** method is to obtain the string to display in the list.

Requirements

Platforms: Windows 98, Windows NT 4.0, Windows Millennium Edition, Windows 2000, Windows XP Home Edition, Windows XP Professional, Windows Server 2003 family, .NET Compact Framework - Windows CE .NET

ComboBox.ObjectCollection.Remove Method

Removes the specified item from the **ComboBox**.

```
[Visual Basic]
Public Overridable Sub Remove( _
   ByVal value As Object _
) Implements IList.Remove
[C#]
public virtual void Remove(
   object value
);
[C++]
public: virtual void Remove(
   Object* value
);
[JScript]
public function Remove(
   value : Object
);
```

Parameters

value

The **Object** to remove from the list.

Implements

IList.Remove

Exceptions

Exception Type	Condition
ArgumentOutOfRange-Exception	The *value* parameter was less than zero. -or- The *value* parameter was greater than or equal to the count of items in the collection.

Requirements

Platforms: Windows 98, Windows NT 4.0, Windows Millennium Edition, Windows 2000, Windows XP Home Edition, Windows XP Professional, Windows Server 2003 family, .NET Compact Framework - Windows CE .NET

ComboBox.ObjectCollection.RemoveAt Method

Removes an item from the **ComboBox** at the specified index.

```
[Visual Basic]
Public Overridable Sub RemoveAt( _
   ByVal index As Integer _
) Implements IList.RemoveAt
[C#]
public virtual void RemoveAt(
   int index
);
[C++]
public: virtual void RemoveAt(
   int index
);
[JScript]
public function RemoveAt(
   index : int
);
```

Parameters

index

The index of the item to remove.

Implements

IList.RemoveAt

Exceptions

Exception Type	Condition
ArgumentOutOfRange-Exception	The *value* parameter was less than zero. -or- The *value* parameter was greater than or equal to the count of items in the collection.

Requirements

Platforms: Windows 98, Windows NT 4.0, Windows Millennium Edition, Windows 2000, Windows XP Home Edition, Windows XP Professional, Windows Server 2003 family, .NET Compact Framework - Windows CE .NET

ComboBoxStyle Enumeration

Specifies the **ComboBox** style.

[Visual Basic]
```
<Serializable>
Public Enum ComboBoxStyle
```
[C#]
```
[Serializable]
public enum ComboBoxStyle
```
[C++]
```
[Serializable]
__value public enum ComboBoxStyle
```
[JScript]
```
public
   Serializable
enum ComboBoxStyle
```

Remarks

The **DropDownStyle** property determines whether the user can enter a new value in the text portion, and whether the list portion is always displayed.

Members

Member name	Description
DropDown	The text portion is editable. The user must click the arrow button to display the list portion.
DropDownList Supported by the .NET Compact Framework.	The user cannot directly edit the text portion. The user must click the arrow button to display the list portion.
Simple	The text portion is editable. The list portion is always visible.

Requirements

Namespace: System.Windows.Forms

Platforms: Windows 98, Windows NT 4.0, Windows Millennium Edition, Windows 2000, Windows XP Home Edition, Windows XP Professional, Windows Server 2003 family, .NET Compact Framework - Windows CE .NET

Assembly: System.Windows.Forms (in System.Windows.Forms.dll)

CommonDialog Class

Specifies the base class used for displaying dialog boxes on the screen.

System.Object
  System.MarshalByRefObject
    System.ComponentModel.Component
      System.Windows.Forms.CommonDialog
        Derived classes

[Visual Basic]
```
MustInherit Public Class CommonDialog
   Inherits Component
```
[C#]
```
public abstract class CommonDialog : Component
```
[C++]
```
public __gc __abstract class CommonDialog : public Component
```
[JScript]
```
public abstract class CommonDialog extends Component
```

Thread Safety

Any public static (**Shared** in Visual Basic) members of this type are safe for multithreaded operations. Any instance members are not guaranteed to be thread safe.

Remarks

Inheritied classes are required to implement **RunDialog** by invoking **ShowDialog** to create a specific common dialog box. Inherited classes can optionally override **HookProc** to implement specific dialog box hook functionality.

Example

[Visual Basic, C#] The following example uses the **ColorDialog** implementation of **CommonDialog** and illustrates creating and showing a dialog box. This example assumes that the method is called from within an existing form, that has a **TextBox** and **Button** placed on it.

[Visual Basic]
```
Protected Sub button1_Click(sender As Object, e As System.EventArgs)
    Dim MyDialog As New ColorDialog()
    ' Keeps the user from selecting a custom color.
    MyDialog.AllowFullOpen = False
    ' Allows the user to get help. (The default is false.)
    MyDialog.ShowHelp = True
    ' Sets the initial color select to the current text color,
    MyDialog.Color = textBox1.ForeColor

    ' Update the text box color if the user clicks OK
    If (MyDialog.ShowDialog() = DialogResult.OK) Then
        textBox1.ForeColor =  MyDialog.Color
    End If

End Sub 'button1_Click
```

[C#]
```
protected void button1_Click(object sender, System.EventArgs e)
 {
    ColorDialog MyDialog = new ColorDialog();
    // Keeps the user from selecting a custom color.
    MyDialog.AllowFullOpen = false ;
    // Allows the user to get help. (The default is false.)
    MyDialog.ShowHelp = true ;
    // Sets the initial color select to the current text color.
    MyDialog.Color = textBox1.ForeColor ;

    // Update the text box color if the user clicks OK
    if (MyDialog.ShowDialog() == DialogResult.OK)
        textBox1.ForeColor =  MyDialog.Color;
 }
```

Requirements

Namespace: System.Windows.Forms

Platforms: Windows 98, Windows NT 4.0, Windows Millennium Edition, Windows 2000, Windows XP Home Edition, Windows XP Professional, Windows Server 2003 family, .NET Compact Framework - Windows CE .NET

Assembly: System.Windows.Forms (in System.Windows.Forms.dll)

CommonDialog Constructor

Initializes a new instance of the **CommonDialog** class.

[Visual Basic]
```
Public Sub New()
```
[C#]
```
public CommonDialog();
```
[C++]
```
public: CommonDialog();
```
[JScript]
```
public function CommonDialog();
```

Requirements

Platforms: Windows 98, Windows NT 4.0, Windows Millennium Edition, Windows 2000, Windows XP Home Edition, Windows XP Professional, Windows Server 2003 family, .NET Compact Framework - Windows CE .NET

CommonDialog.HookProc Method

Defines the common dialog box hook procedure that is overridden to add specific functionality to a common dialog box.

[Visual Basic]
```
Protected Overridable Function HookProc( _
   ByVal hWnd As IntPtr, _
   ByVal msg As Integer, _
   ByVal wparam As IntPtr, _
   ByVal lparam As IntPtr _
) As IntPtr
```
[C#]
```
protected virtual IntPtr HookProc(
   IntPtr hWnd,
   int msg,
   IntPtr wparam,
   IntPtr lparam
);
```
[C++]
```
protected: virtual IntPtr HookProc(
   IntPtr hWnd,
   int msg,
   IntPtr wparam,
   IntPtr lparam
);
```
[JScript]
```
protected function HookProc(
   hWnd : IntPtr,
   msg : int,
   wparam : IntPtr,
   lparam : IntPtr
) : IntPtr;
```

Parameters

hWnd
The handle to the dialog box window.

msg
The message being received.

wparam
Additional information about the message.

lparam
Additional information about the message.

Return Value

A zero value if the default dialog box procedure processes the message; a nonzero value if the default dialog box procedure ignores the message.

Remarks

A hook procedure is a mechanism by which a function can intercept events before they reach an application. When you override the **HookProc** method for a **CommonDialog** class, the operating system invokes your override of the function to post operating system messages to the window.

By default, the hook procedure centers the dialog box on the screen in response to a WM_INITDIALOG message.

Notes to Inheritors: Inheriting classes can override this method to add specific functionality to a common dialog box. When overriding **HookProc** in a derived class, be sure to call the base class's **HookProc** method.

Example

[Visual Basic, C#, C++] The following example demonstrates how to override the **HookProc** method. The example consists of a class that inherits the **CommonDialog** class. In the class's **HookProc** override, the example evaluates the method's *msg* parameter against constant values for particular Windows messages. If the *msg* parameter equals the specified constant, the example writes trace output identifying the Windows message that was passed to the **HookProc** method. This example assumes that the class in which the **HookProc** method is declared inherits the **CommonDialog** class.

[Visual Basic]
```
' Defines the constants for Windows messages.

Const WM_SETFOCUS = &H7
Const WM_INITDIALOG = &H110
Const WM_LBUTTONDOWN = &H201
Const WM_RBUTTONDOWN = &H204
Const WM_MOVE = &H3
<System.Security.Permissions.PermissionSetAttribute ↵
(System.Security.Permissions.SecurityAction.Demand, ↵
 Name:="FullTrust")> _
Protected Overrides Function HookProc(ByVal hWnd As IntPtr, ↵
ByVal msg As Integer, ByVal wParam As IntPtr, ByVal lParam ↵
 As IntPtr) As IntPtr

    ' Evaluates the message parameter to determine the user action.

    Select Case msg

        Case WM_INITDIALOG
            System.Diagnostics.Trace.Write("The WM_INITDIALOG ↵
message was received.")
        Case WM_SETFOCUS
            System.Diagnostics.Trace.Write("The WM_SETFOCUS ↵
message was received.")
        Case WM_LBUTTONDOWN
            System.Diagnostics.Trace.Write("The WM_LBUTTONDOWN message
was received.")
        Case WM_RBUTTONDOWN
            System.Diagnostics.Trace.Write("The WM_RBUTTONDOWN ↵
message was received.")
        Case WM_MOVE
            System.Diagnostics.Trace.Write("The WM_MOVE message ↵
 was received.")

    End Select

    ' Always call the base class hook procedure.

    Return MyBase.HookProc(hWnd, msg, wParam, lParam)

End Function
```

[C#]
```
// Defines the constants for Windows messages.

const int WM_SETFOCUS = 0x0007;
const int WM_INITDIALOG = 0x0110;
const int WM_LBUTTONDOWN = 0x0201;
const int WM_RBUTTONDOWN = 0x0204;
const int WM_MOVE = 0x0003;

// Overrides the base class hook procedure...
[System.Security.Permissions.PermissionSet ↵
 (System.Security.Permissions.SecurityAction.Demand, Name="FullTrust")]
protected override IntPtr HookProc(IntPtr hWnd, int msg, ↵
 IntPtr wParam, IntPtr lParam)
{

    // Evaluates the message parameter to determine the user action.

    switch(msg)
    {

        case WM_INITDIALOG:
            System.Diagnostics.Trace.Write("The WM_INITDIALOG ↵
message was received.");
            break;
        case WM_SETFOCUS:
            System.Diagnostics.Trace.Write("The WM_SETFOCUS ↵
message was received.");
            break;
        case WM_LBUTTONDOWN:
            System.Diagnostics.Trace.Write("The WM_LBUTTONDOWN ↵
message was received.");
            break;
        case WM_RBUTTONDOWN:
            System.Diagnostics.Trace.Write("The WM_RBUTTONDOWN ↵
message was received.");
            break;
        case WM_MOVE:
            System.Diagnostics.Trace.Write("The WM_MOVE message ↵
was received.");
            break;

    }

    // Always call the base class hook procedure.

    return base.HookProc(hWnd, msg, wParam, lParam);

}
```

[C++]
```
    // Defines the constants for Windows messages.
    const static int WM_SETFOCUS = 0x0007;
    const static int WM_INITDIALOG = 0x0110;
    const static int WM_LBUTTONDOWN = 0x0201;
    const static int WM_RBUTTONDOWN = 0x0204;
    const static int WM_MOVE = 0x0003;
```

```
protected:
    // Overrides the base class hook procedure...
    [System::Security::Permissions::PermissionSet                    ↵
 (System::Security::Permissions::SecurityAction::Demand,             ↵
Name="FullTrust")]
    IntPtr HookProc(IntPtr hWnd, int msg, IntPtr wParam,             ↵
IntPtr lParam) {

        // Evaluates the message parameter to determine the user    ↵
action.
        switch(msg) {

        case WM_INITDIALOG:
            System::Diagnostics::Trace::Write(S"The                  ↵
WM_INITDIALOG message was received.");
            break;
        case WM_SETFOCUS:
            System::Diagnostics::Trace::Write(S"The WM_SETFOCUS      ↵
message was received.");
            break;
        case WM_LBUTTONDOWN:
            System::Diagnostics::Trace::Write(S"The                  ↵
WM_LBUTTONDOWN message was received.");
            break;
        case WM_RBUTTONDOWN:
            System::Diagnostics::Trace::Write(S"The                  ↵
WM_RBUTTONDOWN message was received.");
            break;
        case WM_MOVE:
            System::Diagnostics::Trace::Write(S"The WM_MOVE          ↵
message was received.");
            break;

        }

        // Always call the base class hook procedure.
        return FontDialog::HookProc(hWnd, msg, wParam, lParam);
    }
```

Requirements

Platforms: Windows 98, Windows NT 4.0, Windows Millennium Edition, Windows 2000, Windows XP Home Edition, Windows XP Professional, Windows Server 2003 family

.NET Framework Security:

- **SecurityPermission** for inheriting classes to call unmanaged code. Associated enumeration: **SecurityPermissionFlag.UnmanagedCode**
- **SecurityPermission** for the immediate caller to call unmanaged code. Associated enumeration: **SecurityPermissionFlag.UnmanagedCode**

CommonDialog.OnHelpRequest Method

Raises the **HelpRequest** event.

```
[Visual Basic]
Protected Overridable Sub OnHelpRequest( _
   ByVal e As EventArgs _
)
[C#]
protected virtual void OnHelpRequest(
   EventArgs e
);
[C++]
protected: virtual void OnHelpRequest(
   EventArgs* e
);
[JScript]
protected function OnHelpRequest(
   e : EventArgs
);
```

Parameters

e

An **HelpEventArgs** that provides the event data.

Remarks

This method is invoked when the Help button is clicked. Inheriting classes can override this method to handle the event.

Requirements

Platforms: Windows 98, Windows NT 4.0, Windows Millennium Edition, Windows 2000, Windows XP Home Edition, Windows XP Professional, Windows Server 2003 family

CommonDialog.OwnerWndProc Method

Defines the owner window procedure that is overridden to add specific functionality to a common dialog box.

```
[Visual Basic]
Protected Overridable Function OwnerWndProc( _
   ByVal hWnd As IntPtr, _
   ByVal msg As Integer, _
   ByVal wparam As IntPtr, _
   ByVal lparam As IntPtr _
) As IntPtr
[C#]
protected virtual IntPtr OwnerWndProc(
   IntPtr hWnd,
   int msg,
   IntPtr wparam,
   IntPtr lparam
);
[C++]
protected: virtual IntPtr OwnerWndProc(
   IntPtr hWnd,
   int msg,
   IntPtr wparam,
   IntPtr lparam
);
[JScript]
protected function OwnerWndProc(
   hWnd : IntPtr,
   msg : int,
   wparam : IntPtr,
   lparam : IntPtr
) : IntPtr;
```

Parameters

hWnd

The window handle of the message to send.

msg

The Win32 message to send.

wparam

The *wparam* to send with the message.

lparam

The *lparam* to send with the message.

Return Value

The result of the message processing, which is dependent on the message sent.

Remarks

Control is transferred here when messages are sent to the owner window of the common dialog box. Inheriting classes can override this method to add specific functionality to a common dialog box.

Requirements

Platforms: Windows 98, Windows NT 4.0, Windows Millennium Edition, Windows 2000, Windows XP Home Edition, Windows XP Professional, Windows Server 2003 family

.NET Framework Security:

- **SecurityPermission** for inheriting classes to call unmanaged code. Associated enumeration: **SecurityPermissionFlag.UnmanagedCode**
- **SecurityPermission** for the immediate caller to call unmanaged code. Associated enumeration: **SecurityPermissionFlag.UnmanagedCode**

CommonDialog.Reset Method

When overridden in a derived class, resets the properties of a common dialog box to their default values.

```
[Visual Basic]
Public MustOverride Sub Reset()
[C#]
public abstract void Reset();
[C++]
public: virtual void Reset() = 0;
[JScript]
public abstract function Reset();
```

Remarks

Notes to Inheritors: Inheriting classes can override this method to reset their properties.

Requirements

Platforms: Windows 98, Windows NT 4.0, Windows Millennium Edition, Windows 2000, Windows XP Home Edition, Windows XP Professional, Windows Server 2003 family

.NET Framework Security:

- **SecurityPermission** for unmanaged code to call this method. Associated enumeration: **UnmanagedCode**

CommonDialog.RunDialog Method

When overridden in a derived class, specifies a common dialog box.

```
[Visual Basic]
Protected MustOverride Function RunDialog( _
   ByVal hwndOwner As IntPtr _
) As Boolean
[C#]
protected abstract bool RunDialog(
   IntPtr hwndOwner
);
[C++]
protected: virtual bool RunDialog(
   IntPtr hwndOwner
) = 0;
[JScript]
protected abstract function RunDialog(
   hwndOwner : IntPtr
) : Boolean;
```

Parameters

hwndOwner

A value that represents the window handle of the owner window for the common dialog box.

Return Value

true if the dialog box was successfully run; otherwise, **false**.

Remarks

This method is invoked when the user of a common dialog box calls **ShowDialog**, and it must be overridden by inherited classes of **CommonDialog** to implement a specific common dialog box. An implementation of this method should store the *hwndOwner* parameter in the common dialog box structure's **hwndOwner** field.

Requirements

Platforms: Windows 98, Windows NT 4.0, Windows Millennium Edition, Windows 2000, Windows XP Home Edition, Windows XP Professional, Windows Server 2003 family

.NET Framework Security:

- **SecurityPermission** for unmanaged code to call this method. Associated enumeration: **UnmanagedCode**

CommonDialog.ShowDialog Method

Runs a common dialog box.

Overload List

Runs a common dialog box with a default owner.

Supported by the .NET Compact Framework.

[Visual Basic] **Overloads Public Function ShowDialog() As DialogResult**

[C#] **public DialogResult ShowDialog();**

[C++] **public: DialogResult ShowDialog();**

[JScript] **public function ShowDialog() : DialogResult;**

Runs a common dialog box with the specified owner.

[Visual Basic] **Overloads Public Function ShowDialog(IWin32Window) As DialogResult**

[C#] **public DialogResult ShowDialog(IWin32Window);**

[C++] **public: DialogResult ShowDialog(IWin32Window*);**

[JScript] **public function ShowDialog(IWin32Window) : DialogResult;**

Example

[Visual Basic, C#] The following example uses the **ColorDialog** implementation of **CommonDialog** and illustrates creating and showing a dialog box. This example assumes that the method is called from within an existing form, that has a **TextBox** and **Button** placed on it.

[Visual Basic, C#] **Note** This example shows how to use one of the overloaded versions of **ShowDialog**. For other examples that might be available, see the individual overload topics.

[Visual Basic]
```
Protected Sub button1_Click(sender As Object, e As System.EventArgs)
    Dim MyDialog As New ColorDialog()
    ' Keeps the user from selecting a custom color.
    MyDialog.AllowFullOpen = False
    ' Allows the user to get help. (The default is false.)
    MyDialog.ShowHelp = True
    ' Sets the initial color select to the current text color,
    MyDialog.Color = textBox1.ForeColor

    ' Update the text box color if the user clicks OK
    If (MyDialog.ShowDialog() = DialogResult.OK) Then
        textBox1.ForeColor =  MyDialog.Color
    End If

End Sub 'button1_Click
```

[C#]
```
protected void button1_Click(object sender, System.EventArgs e)
 {
    ColorDialog MyDialog = new ColorDialog();
    // Keeps the user from selecting a custom color.
    MyDialog.AllowFullOpen = false ;
    // Allows the user to get help. (The default is false.)
    MyDialog.ShowHelp = true ;
    // Sets the initial color select to the current text color.
    MyDialog.Color = textBox1.ForeColor ;

    // Update the text box color if the user clicks OK
    if (MyDialog.ShowDialog() == DialogResult.OK)
        textBox1.ForeColor =  MyDialog.Color;
 }
```

CommonDialog.ShowDialog Method ()

Runs a common dialog box with a default owner.

[Visual Basic]
```
Overloads Public Function ShowDialog() As DialogResult
```
[C#]
```
public DialogResult ShowDialog();
```
[C++]
```
public: DialogResult ShowDialog();
```
[JScript]
```
public function ShowDialog() : DialogResult;
```

Return Value

DialogResult.OK if the user clicks **OK** in the dialog box; otherwise, **DialogResult.Cancel** .

Remarks

This method implements **RunDialog**.

Example

[Visual Basic, C#] The following example uses the **ColorDialog** implementation of **CommonDialog** and illustrates creating and showing a dialog box. This example assumes that the method is called from within an existing form, that has a **TextBox** and **Button** placed on it.

[Visual Basic]
```
Protected Sub button1_Click(sender As Object, e As System.EventArgs)
    Dim MyDialog As New ColorDialog()
    ' Keeps the user from selecting a custom color.
    MyDialog.AllowFullOpen = False
    ' Allows the user to get help. (The default is false.)
    MyDialog.ShowHelp = True
    ' Sets the initial color select to the current text color,
    MyDialog.Color = textBox1.ForeColor

    ' Update the text box color if the user clicks OK
    If (MyDialog.ShowDialog() = DialogResult.OK) Then
        textBox1.ForeColor =  MyDialog.Color
    End If

End Sub 'button1_Click
```

[C#]
```
protected void button1_Click(object sender, System.EventArgs e)
 {
    ColorDialog MyDialog = new ColorDialog();
    // Keeps the user from selecting a custom color.
    MyDialog.AllowFullOpen = false ;
    // Allows the user to get help. (The default is false.)
    MyDialog.ShowHelp = true ;
    // Sets the initial color select to the current text color.
    MyDialog.Color = textBox1.ForeColor ;

    // Update the text box color if the user clicks OK
    if (MyDialog.ShowDialog() == DialogResult.OK)
        textBox1.ForeColor =  MyDialog.Color;
 }
```

Requirements

Platforms: Windows 98, Windows NT 4.0, Windows Millennium Edition, Windows 2000, Windows XP Home Edition, Windows XP Professional, Windows Server 2003 family, .NET Compact Framework - Windows CE .NET

.NET Framework Security:

- **PrintingPermission** to print from a **PrintDialog**. Associated enumeration: **PrintingPermissionLevel.SafePrinting**
- **UIPermission** for safe subwindows to call this method. Associated enumeration: **UIPermissionWindow.SafeSubWindows**

CommonDialog.ShowDialog Method (IWin32Window)

Runs a common dialog box with the specified owner.

[Visual Basic]
```
Overloads Public Function ShowDialog( _
   ByVal owner As IWin32Window _
) As DialogResult
```
[C#]
```
public DialogResult ShowDialog(
   IWin32Window owner
);
```
[C++]
```
public: DialogResult ShowDialog(
   IWin32Window* owner
);
```
[JScript]
```
public function ShowDialog(
   owner : IWin32Window
) : DialogResult;
```

Parameters

owner

Any object that implements **IWin32Window** that represents the top-level window that will own the modal dialog box.

Return Value

DialogResult.OK if the user clicks **OK** in the dialog box; otherwise, **DialogResult.Cancel** .

Remarks

This version of the **ShowDialog** method allows you to specify a specific form or control that will own the dialog box that is shown. If you use the version of this method that has no parameters, the dialog box being shown would be owned automatically by the currently active window of your application.

Requirements

Platforms: Windows 98, Windows NT 4.0,
Windows Millennium Edition, Windows 2000,
Windows XP Home Edition, Windows XP Professional,
Windows Server 2003 family

.NET Framework Security:

- **PrintingPermission** to print from a **PrintDialog**. Associated enumeration: **PrintingPermissionLevel.SafePrinting**
- **UIPermission** for safe subwindows to call this method. Associated enumeration: **UIPermissionWindow.SafeSubWindows**

CommonDialog.HelpRequest Event

Occurs when the user clicks the Help button on a common dialog box.

[Visual Basic]
```
Public Event HelpRequest As EventHandler
```
[C#]
```
public event EventHandler HelpRequest;
```
[C++]
```
public: __event EventHandler* HelpRequest;
```

[JScript] In JScript, you can handle the events defined by a class, but you cannot define your own.

Event Data

The event handler receives an argument of type **EventArgs**.

Requirements

Platforms: Windows 98, Windows NT 4.0,
Windows Millennium Edition, Windows 2000,
Windows XP Home Edition, Windows XP Professional,
Windows Server 2003 family

ContainerControl Class

Provides focus management functionality for controls that can function as a container for other controls.

System.Object
System.MarshalByRefObject
System.ComponentModel.Component
System.Windows.Forms.Control
System.Windows.Forms.ScrollableControl
System.Windows.Forms.ContainerControl
System.Windows.Forms.Form
System.Windows.Forms.PropertyGrid
System.Windows.Forms.UpDownBase
System.Windows.Forms.UserControl

[Visual Basic]
```
Public Class ContainerControl
   Inherits ScrollableControl
   Implements IContainerControl
```
[C#]
```
public class ContainerControl : ScrollableControl,
   IContainerControl
```
[C++]
```
public __gc class ContainerControl : public ScrollableControl,
   IContainerControl
```
[JScript]
```
public class ContainerControl extends ScrollableControl implements
   IContainerControl
```

Thread Safety

Any public static (**Shared** in Visual Basic) members of this type are safe for multithreaded operations. Any instance members are not guaranteed to be thread safe.

Remarks

A **ContainerControl** represents a control that can function as a container for other controls and provides focus management. Controls that inherit from this class can track the active control they contain, even when the focus moves somewhere within a different container.

ContainerControl objects provide a logical boundary for contained controls. The container control can capture the TAB key press and move focus to the next control in the collection.

> **Note** The container control does not receive focus; the focus is always set to the first child control in the collection of contained controls.

You do not typically inherit directly from this class. **Form**, **UserControl**, and **UpDownBase** classes inherit from **ContainerControl**.

Example

[Visual Basic, C#, C++] The following example inherits from the **ScrollableControl** class and implements the **IContainerControl** interface. Implementation is added to the **ActiveControl** property and the **ActivateControl** method.

[Visual Basic]
```
Imports System
Imports System.Windows.Forms
Imports System.Drawing

   Public Class MyContainerControl
      Inherits ScrollableControl
      Implements IContainerControl

      Private myActiveControl As Control

      Public Sub New()
         ' Make the container control Blue so it can be ↵
distinguished on the form.
         Me.BackColor = Color.Blue

         ' Make the container scrollable.
         Me.AutoScroll = True
      End Sub

      ' Add implementation to the ↵
IContainerControl.ActiveControl property.
      Public Property ActiveControl() As Control ↵
Implements IContainerControl.ActiveControl
         Get
            Return Me.myActiveControl
         End Get

         Set
            ' Make sure the control is a member of the ↵
ControlCollection.
            If Me.Controls.Contains(value) Then
               Me.myActiveControl = value
            End If
         End Set
      End Property

      ' Add implementation to the ↵
IContainerControl.ActivateControl(Control) method.
      public Function ActivateControl(active As Control) As ↵
Boolean Implements IContainerControl.ActivateControl
         If Me.Controls.Contains(active) Then
            ' Select the control and scroll the control into ↵
view if needed.
            active.Select()
            Me.ScrollControlIntoView(active)
            Me.myActiveControl = active
            Return True
         End If
         Return False
      End Function

   End Class
```

[C#]
```
using System;
using System.Windows.Forms;
using System.Drawing;

   public class MyContainer : ScrollableControl, IContainerControl
   {
      private Control activeControl;
      public MyContainer()
      {
         // Make the container control Blue so it can be ↵
distinguished on the form.
         this.BackColor = Color.Blue;

         // Make the container scrollable.
         this.AutoScroll = true;
      }

      // Add implementation to the ↵
IContainerControl.ActiveControl property.
      public Control ActiveControl
      {
         get
         {
            return activeControl;
         }

         set
         {
            // Make sure the control is a member of ↵
the ControlCollection.
```

```
            if(this.Controls.Contains(value))
            {
                activeControl = value;
            }
        }
    }

    // Add implementations to the
IContainerControl.ActivateControl(Control) method.
    public bool ActivateControl(Control active)
    {
        if(this.Controls.Contains(active))
        {
            // Select the control and scroll the control
 into view if needed.
            active.Select();
            this.ScrollControlIntoView(active);
            this.activeControl = active;
            return true;
        }
        return false;
    }
}
```

[C++]

```
using namespace System;
using namespace System::Windows::Forms;
using namespace System::Drawing;

    public __gc class MyContainer : public ScrollableControl,
 public IContainerControl {
    private:
        Control*  activeControl;

    public:
        MyContainer() {
            // Make the container control Blue so it can be
distinguished on the form.
            this->BackColor = Color::Blue;

            // Make the container scrollable.
            this->AutoScroll = true;
        }

        // Add implementation to the
IContainerControl*.ActiveControl property.
        __property Control* get_ActiveControl() {
            return activeControl;
        }

        __property void set_ActiveControl(Control* value) {
            // Make sure the control is a member of the
ControlCollection.
            if (this->Controls->Contains(value)) {
                activeControl = value;
            }
        }

        // Add implementations to the
IContainerControl*.ActivateControl(Control) method.
        bool ActivateControl(Control* active) {
            if (this->Controls->Contains(active)) {
                // Select the control and scroll the control
into view if needed.
                active->Select();
                this->ScrollControlIntoView(active);
                this->activeControl = active;
                return true;
            }
            return false;
        }
    };
```

Requirements

Namespace: System.Windows.Forms

Platforms: Windows 98, Windows NT 4.0, Windows Millennium Edition, Windows 2000, Windows XP Home Edition, Windows XP Professional, Windows Server 2003 family, .NET Compact Framework - Windows CE .NET

Assembly: System.Windows.Forms (in System.Windows.Forms.dll)

ContainerControl Constructor

Initializes a new instance of the **ContainerControl** class.

[Visual Basic]
```
Public Sub New()
```
[C#]
```
public ContainerControl();
```
[C++]
```
public: ContainerControl();
```
[JScript]
```
public function ContainerControl();
```

Example

See related example in the **System.Windows.Forms.ContainerControl** class topic.

Requirements

Platforms: Windows 98, Windows NT 4.0, Windows Millennium Edition, Windows 2000, Windows XP Home Edition, Windows XP Professional, Windows Server 2003 family, .NET Compact Framework - Windows CE .NET

ContainerControl.ActiveControl Property

Gets or sets the active control on the container control.

[Visual Basic]
```
Public Overridable Property ActiveControl As Control  Implements _
   IContainerControl.ActiveControl
```
[C#]
```
public virtual Control ActiveControl {get; set;}
```
[C++]
```
public: __property virtual Control* get_ActiveControl();
public: __property virtual void set_ActiveControl(Control*);
```
[JScript]
```
public function get ActiveControl() : Control;
public function set ActiveControl(Control);
```

Property Value

The **Control** that is currently active on the **ContainerControl**.

Implements

IContainerControl.ActiveControl

Exceptions

Exception Type	Condition
ArgumentException	The **Control** assigned could not be activated.

Remarks

This property activates or retrieves the active control on the container control.

Example

See related example in the **System.Windows.Forms.Container-Control** class topic.

Requirements

Platforms: Windows 98, Windows NT 4.0, Windows Millennium Edition, Windows 2000, Windows XP Home Edition, Windows XP Professional, Windows Server 2003 family

ContainerControl.BindingContext Property

This member overrides **Control.BindingContext**.

```
[Visual Basic]
Overrides Public Property BindingContext As BindingContext
[C#]
public override BindingContext BindingContext {get; set;}
[C++]
public: __property BindingContext* get_BindingContext();
public: __property void set_BindingContext(BindingContext*);
[JScript]
public override function get BindingContext() : BindingContext;
public override function set BindingContext(BindingContext);
```

Requirements

Platforms: Windows 98, Windows NT 4.0, Windows Millennium Edition, Windows 2000, Windows XP Home Edition, Windows XP Professional, Windows Server 2003 family, .NET Compact Framework - Windows CE .NET

ContainerControl.CreateParams Property

This member overrides **Control.CreateParams**.

```
[Visual Basic]
Overrides Protected ReadOnly Property CreateParams As CreateParams
[C#]
protected override CreateParams CreateParams {get;}
[C++]
protected: __property CreateParams* get_CreateParams();
[JScript]
protected override function get CreateParams() : CreateParams;
```

Requirements

Platforms: Windows 98, Windows NT 4.0, Windows Millennium Edition, Windows 2000, Windows XP Home Edition, Windows XP Professional, Windows Server 2003 family

ContainerControl.ParentForm Property

Gets the form that the container control is assigned to.

```
[Visual Basic]
Public ReadOnly Property ParentForm As Form
[C#]
public Form ParentForm {get;}
[C++]
public: __property Form* get_ParentForm();
[JScript]
public function get ParentForm() : Form;
```

Property Value

The **Form** that the container control is assigned to.

Example

See related example in the **System.Windows.Forms.Container-Control** class topic.

Requirements

Platforms: Windows 98, Windows NT 4.0, Windows Millennium Edition, Windows 2000, Windows XP Home Edition, Windows XP Professional, Windows Server 2003 family

.NET Framework Security:

- **UIPermission** for all windows to get this property value. Associated enumeration: **UIPermissionWindow.AllWindows**

ContainerControl.AdjustFormScrollbars Method

This member supports the .NET Framework infrastructure and is not intended to be used directly from your code.

```
[Visual Basic]
Overrides Protected Sub AdjustFormScrollbars( _
   ByVal displayScrollbars As Boolean _
)
[C#]
protected override void AdjustFormScrollbars(
   bool displayScrollbars
);
[C++]
protected: void AdjustFormScrollbars(
   bool displayScrollbars
);
[JScript]
protected override function AdjustFormScrollbars(
   displayScrollbars : Boolean
);
```

ContainerControl.Dispose Method

Overload List

This member supports the .NET Framework infrastructure and is not intended to be used directly from your code.

Supported by the .NET Compact Framework.

[Visual Basic] **Overloads Overrides Protected Sub Dispose(Boolean)**

[C#] **protected override void Dispose(bool);**

[C++] **protected: void Dispose(bool);**

[JScript] **protected override function Dispose(Boolean);**

Inherited from **Component**.

Supported by the .NET Compact Framework.

[Visual Basic] **Overloads Public Overridable Sub Dispose() Implements IDisposable.Dispose**

[C#] **public virtual void Dispose();**

[C++] **public: virtual void Dispose();**

[JScript] **public function Dispose();**

ContainerControl.Dispose Method (Boolean)

This member overrides **Control.Dispose**.

```
[Visual Basic]
Overrides Overloads Protected Sub Dispose( _
   ByVal disposing As Boolean _
)
[C#]
protected override void Dispose(
   bool disposing
);
[C++]
protected: void Dispose(
   bool disposing
);
[JScript]
protected override function Dispose(
   disposing : Boolean
);
```

Requirements

Platforms: Windows 98, Windows NT 4.0, Windows Millennium Edition, Windows 2000, Windows XP Home Edition, Windows XP Professional, Windows Server 2003 family, .NET Compact Framework - Windows CE .NET

ContainerControl.IContainerControl.ActivateControl Method

This member supports the .NET Framework infrastructure and is not intended to be used directly from your code.

```
[Visual Basic]
Private Function ActivateControl( _
   ByVal control As Control _
) As Boolean Implements IContainerControl.ActivateControl
[C#]
bool IContainerControl.ActivateControl(
   Control control
);
[C++]
private: bool IContainerControl::ActivateControl(
   Control* control
);
[JScript]
private function IContainerControl.ActivateControl(
   control : Control
) : Boolean;
```

ContainerControl.OnControlRemoved Method

This member overrides **Control.OnControlRemoved**.

```
[Visual Basic]
Overrides Protected Sub OnControlRemoved( _
   ByVal e As ControlEventArgs _
)
[C#]
protected override void OnControlRemoved(
   ControlEventArgs e
);
[C++]
protected: void OnControlRemoved(
   ControlEventArgs* e
);
[JScript]
protected override function OnControlRemoved(
   e : ControlEventArgs
);
```

Requirements

Platforms: Windows 98, Windows NT 4.0, Windows Millennium Edition, Windows 2000, Windows XP Home Edition, Windows XP Professional, Windows Server 2003 family

ContainerControl.OnCreateControl Method

This member overrides **Control.OnCreateControl**.

```
[Visual Basic]
Overrides Protected Sub OnCreateControl()
[C#]
protected override void OnCreateControl();
[C++]
protected: void OnCreateControl();
[JScript]
protected override function OnCreateControl();
```

Requirements

Platforms: Windows 98, Windows NT 4.0, Windows Millennium Edition, Windows 2000, Windows XP Home Edition, Windows XP Professional, Windows Server 2003 family

ContainerControl.ProcessDialogChar Method

This member overrides **Control.ProcessDialogChar**.

```
[Visual Basic]
Overrides Protected Function ProcessDialogChar( _
   ByVal charCode As Char _
) As Boolean
[C#]
protected override bool ProcessDialogChar(
   char charCode
);
[C++]
protected: bool ProcessDialogChar(
   __wchar_t charCode
);
[JScript]
protected override function ProcessDialogChar(
   charCode : Char
) : Boolean;
```

Requirements

Platforms: Windows 98, Windows NT 4.0, Windows Millennium Edition, Windows 2000, Windows XP Home Edition, Windows XP Professional, Windows Server 2003 family

ContainerControl.ProcessDialogKey Method

This member overrides **Control.ProcessDialogKey**.

```
[Visual Basic]
Overrides Protected Function ProcessDialogKey( _
   ByVal keyData As Keys _
) As Boolean
[C#]
protected override bool ProcessDialogKey(
   Keys keyData
);
[C++]
protected: bool ProcessDialogKey(
   Keys keyData
);
[JScript]
protected override function ProcessDialogKey(
   keyData : Keys
) : Boolean;
```

Requirements

Platforms: Windows 98, Windows NT 4.0, Windows Millennium Edition, Windows 2000, Windows XP Home Edition, Windows XP Professional, Windows Server 2003 family

ContainerControl.ProcessMnemonic Method

This member overrides **Control.ProcessMnemonic**.

```
[Visual Basic]
Overrides Protected Function ProcessMnemonic( _
   ByVal charCode As Char _
) As Boolean
[C#]
protected override bool ProcessMnemonic(
   char charCode
);
[C++]
protected: bool ProcessMnemonic(
   __wchar_t charCode
);
[JScript]
protected override function ProcessMnemonic(
   charCode : Char
) : Boolean;
```

Requirements

Platforms: Windows 98, Windows NT 4.0, Windows Millennium Edition, Windows 2000, Windows XP Home Edition, Windows XP Professional, Windows Server 2003 family

ContainerControl.ProcessTabKey Method

Selects the next available control and makes it the active control.

```
[Visual Basic]
Protected Overridable Function ProcessTabKey( _
   ByVal forward As Boolean _
) As Boolean
[C#]
protected virtual bool ProcessTabKey(
   bool forward
);
[C++]
protected: virtual bool ProcessTabKey(
   bool forward
);
[JScript]
protected function ProcessTabKey(
   forward : Boolean
) : Boolean;
```

Parameters

forward

true to cycle forward through the controls in the **Container-Control**; otherwise, **false**.

Return Value

true if a control is selected; otherwise, **false**.

Remarks

A control with its **TabStop** property set to **false** cannot be selected, so the next available control will be selected.

Requirements

Platforms: Windows 98, Windows NT 4.0, Windows Millennium Edition, Windows 2000, Windows XP Home Edition, Windows XP Professional, Windows Server 2003 family

ContainerControl.Select Method

Overload List

This member supports the .NET Framework infrastructure and is not intended to be used directly from your code.

[Visual Basic] **Overloads Overrides Protected Sub Select(Boolean, Boolean)**

[C#] **protected override void Select(bool, bool);**

[C++] **protected: void Select(bool, bool);**

[JScript] **protected override function Select(Boolean, Boolean);**

Inherited from **Control**.

[Visual Basic] **Overloads Public Sub Select()**

[C#] **public void Select();**

[C++] **public: void Select();**

[JScript] **public function Select();**

ContainerControl.Select Method (Boolean, Boolean)

This member overrides **Control.Select**.

```
[Visual Basic]
Overrides Overloads Protected Sub Select( _
   ByVal directed As Boolean, _
   ByVal forward As Boolean _
)
[C#]
protected override void Select(
   bool directed,
   bool forward
);
[C++]
protected: void Select(
   bool directed,
   bool forward
);
```

[JScript]
```
protected override function Select(
   directed : Boolean,
   forward : Boolean
);
```

Requirements

Platforms: Windows 98, Windows NT 4.0, Windows Millennium Edition, Windows 2000, Windows XP Home Edition, Windows XP Professional, Windows Server 2003 family

ContainerControl.UpdateDefaultButton Method

This member supports the .NET Framework infrastructure and is not intended to be used directly from your code.

[Visual Basic]
```
Protected Overridable Sub UpdateDefaultButton()
```
[C#]
```
protected virtual void UpdateDefaultButton();
```
[C++]
```
protected: virtual void UpdateDefaultButton();
```
[JScript]
```
protected function UpdateDefaultButton();
```

ContainerControl.Validate Method

Validates the last invalidated control and its ancestors up through, but not including, the current control.

[Visual Basic]
```
Public Function Validate() As Boolean
```
[C#]
```
public bool Validate();
```
[C++]
```
public: bool Validate();
```
[JScript]
```
public function Validate() : Boolean;
```

Return Value

true if validation is successful; otherwise, **false**.

Requirements

Platforms: Windows 98, Windows NT 4.0, Windows Millennium Edition, Windows 2000, Windows XP Home Edition, Windows XP Professional, Windows Server 2003 family

ContainerControl.WndProc Method

This member overrides **Control.WndProc**.

[Visual Basic]
```
Overrides Protected Sub WndProc( _
   ByRef m As Message _
)
```
[C#]
```
protected override void WndProc(
   ref Message m
);
```
[C++]
```
protected: void WndProc(
   Message* m
);
```
[JScript]
```
protected override function WndProc(
   m : Message
);
```

Requirements

Platforms: Windows 98, Windows NT 4.0, Windows Millennium Edition, Windows 2000, Windows XP Home Edition, Windows XP Professional, Windows Server 2003 family

ContentsResizedEventArgs Class

Provides data for the **ContentsResized** event.

System.Object
  System.EventArgs
    System.Windows.Forms.ContentsResizedEventArgs

[Visual Basic]
```
Public Class ContentsResizedEventArgs
   Inherits EventArgs
```
[C#]
```
public class ContentsResizedEventArgs : EventArgs
```
[C++]
```
public __gc class ContentsResizedEventArgs : public EventArgs
```
[JScript]
```
public class ContentsResizedEventArgs extends EventArgs
```

Thread Safety

Any public static (**Shared** in Visual Basic) members of this type are safe for multithreaded operations. Any instance members are not guaranteed to be thread safe.

Remarks

This event is raised when the bounding rectangle necessary to accept new text changes. If the text within the control spans multiple lines, the requested rectangle will always be the width of the control. You can handle this event in your control to implement auto-resizing for multiline **RichTextBox** controls. The **ContentsResizedEventArgs** identifies the requested size of the **RichTextBox**.

Requirements

Namespace: System.Windows.Forms

Platforms: Windows 98, Windows NT 4.0, Windows Millennium Edition, Windows 2000, Windows XP Home Edition, Windows XP Professional, Windows Server 2003 family

Assembly: System.Windows.Forms (in System.Windows.Forms.dll)

ContentsResizedEventArgs Constructor

Initializes a new instance of the **ContentsResizedEventArgs** class.

[Visual Basic]
```
Public Sub New( _
   ByVal newRectangle As Rectangle _
)
```
[C#]
```
public ContentsResizedEventArgs(
   Rectangle newRectangle
);
```
[C++]
```
public: ContentsResizedEventArgs(
   Rectangle newRectangle
);
```
[JScript]
```
public function ContentsResizedEventArgs(
   newRectangle : Rectangle
);
```

Parameters

newRectangle
  A **Rectangle** that specifies the requested dimensions of the **RichTextBox** control.

Requirements

Platforms: Windows 98, Windows NT 4.0, Windows Millennium Edition, Windows 2000, Windows XP Home Edition, Windows XP Professional, Windows Server 2003 family

ContentsResizedEventArgs.NewRectangle Property

Represents the requested size of the **RichTextBox** control.

[Visual Basic]
```
Public ReadOnly Property NewRectangle As Rectangle
```
[C#]
```
public Rectangle NewRectangle {get;}
```
[C++]
```
public: __property Rectangle get_NewRectangle();
```
[JScript]
```
public function get NewRectangle() : Rectangle;
```

Property Value

A **Rectangle** that represents the requested size of the **RichTextBox** control.

Remarks

When text is entered into the **RichTextBox** control, the **RichTextBox** control determines the proper size of the control in order to display all of the contents of the control. You can use the **NewRectangle** property in an event handler for the **ContentsResized** event of the **RichTextBox** control to properly size the control to display all of the control's contents.

Requirements

Platforms: Windows 98, Windows NT 4.0, Windows Millennium Edition, Windows 2000, Windows XP Home Edition, Windows XP Professional, Windows Server 2003 family

ContentsResizedEventHandler Delegate

Represents the method that will handle the **ContentsResized** event of a **RichTextBox**.

[Visual Basic]

```
<Serializable>
Public Delegate Sub ContentsResizedEventHandler( _
   ByVal sender As Object, _
   ByVal e As ContentsResizedEventArgs _
)
```

[C#]

```
[Serializable]
public delegate void ContentsResizedEventHandler(
   object sender,
   ContentsResizedEventArgs e
);
```

[C++]

```
[Serializable]
public __gc __delegate void ContentsResizedEventHandler(
   Object* sender,
   ContentsResizedEventArgs* e
);
```

[JScript] In JScript, you can use the delegates in the .NET Framework, but you cannot define your own.

Parameters [Visual Basic, C#, C++]

The declaration of your event handler must have the same parameters as the **ContentsResizedEventHandler** delegate declaration.

Remarks

When you create a **ContentsResizedEventArgs** delegate, you identify the method that will handle the event. To associate the event with your event handler, add an instance of the delegate to the event. The event handler is called whenever the event occurs, unless you remove the delegate.

Requirements

Namespace: System.Windows.Forms

Platforms: Windows 98, Windows NT 4.0, Windows Millennium Edition, Windows 2000, Windows XP Home Edition, Windows XP Professional, Windows Server 2003 family

Assembly: System.Windows.Forms (in System.Windows.Forms.dll)

ContextMenu Class

Represents a shortcut menu.

System.Object
  System.MarshalByRefObject
    System.ComponentModel.Component
      System.Windows.Forms.Menu
        System.Windows.Forms.ContextMenu

[Visual Basic]
```
Public Class ContextMenu
   Inherits Menu
```
[C#]
```
public class ContextMenu : Menu
```
[C++]
```
public __gc class ContextMenu : public Menu
```
[JScript]
```
public class ContextMenu extends Menu
```

Thread Safety

Any public static (**Shared** in Visual Basic) members of this type are safe for multithreaded operations. Any instance members are not guaranteed to be thread safe.

Remarks

The **ContextMenu** class represents shortcut menus that can be displayed when the user clicks the right mouse button over a control or area of the form. Shortcut menus are typically used to combine different menu items from a **MainMenu** of a form that are useful for the user given the context of the application. For example, you can use a shortcut menu assigned to a **TextBox** control to provide menu items for changing the font of the text, finding text within the control, or Clipboard features for copying and pasting text. You can also display new **MenuItem** objects in a shortcut menu that are not located within a **MainMenu** to provide situation specific commands that are not appropriate for the **MainMenu** to display.

Typically, a shortcut menu is displayed when a user clicks the right mouse button over a control or the form itself. Visible controls and **Form** have a **ContextMenu** property that binds the **ContextMenu** class to the control that displays the shortcut menu. More than one control can use a **ContextMenu**. You can use the **SourceControl** property to determine which control last displayed the shortcut menu in order to perform tasks specific to the control or to modify the shortcut menu displayed for the control.

You might want to know when the shortcut menu is being displayed in order to set check marks, disable items, and perform other menu tasks before the menu is displayed to the user. You can handle the **Popup** event to determine when the shortcut menu is being displayed.

> **Note** In order to reuse **MenuItem** objects that are displayed in a **MainMenu** for use in a **ContextMenu**, you must create a copy of the menu using the **CloneMenu** method of the **MenuItem** class. You can also merge menu items and their submenu items into a single **MenuItem** object using the **MergeMenu** method of the **MenuItem** class.

.NET Compact Framework - Windows CE .NET Platform Note: On the Pocket PC, avoid using shortcut menus on secondary forms because they remain displayed after you destroy their parent forms.

Example

[Visual Basic, C#] The following example creates an event handler for the **Popup** event of the **ContextMenu**. The code in the event handler determines which of two controls a **PictureBox** named `pictureBox1` and a **TextBox** named `textBox1` is the control displaying the shortcut menu. Depending on which control caused the **ContextMenu** to display its shortcut menu, the control adds the appropriate **MenuItem** objects to the **ContextMenu**. This example assumes that you have an instance of the **ContextMenu** class, named `contextMenu1`, defined within the form. This example also assumes that you have a **TextBox** and **PictureBox** added to a form and that the **ContextMenu** property of these controls is set to `contextMenu1`.

[Visual Basic]
```
Protected Sub MyPopupEventHandler(sender As System.Object, e ↵
 As System.EventArgs)
    ' Define the MenuItem objects to display for the TextBox.
    Dim menuItem1 As New MenuItem("&Copy")
    Dim menuItem2 As New MenuItem("&Find and Replace")
    ' Define the MenuItem object to display for the PictureBox.
    Dim menuItem3 As New MenuItem("C&hange Picture")

    ' Clear all previously added MenuItems.
    contextMenu1.MenuItems.Clear()

    If contextMenu1.SourceControl Is textBox1 Then
        ' Add MenuItems to display for the TextBox.
        contextMenu1.MenuItems.Add(menuItem1)
        contextMenu1.MenuItems.Add(menuItem2)
    ElseIf contextMenu1.SourceControl Is pictureBox1 Then
        ' Add the MenuItem to display for the PictureBox.
        contextMenu1.MenuItems.Add(menuItem3)
    End If
End Sub 'MyPopupEventHandler '
```

[C#]
```
protected void MyPopupEventHandler(System.Object sender, ↵
System.EventArgs e)
 {
    // Define the MenuItem objects to display for the TextBox.
    MenuItem menuItem1 = new MenuItem("&Copy");
    MenuItem menuItem2 = new MenuItem("&Find and Replace");
    // Define the MenuItem object to display for the PictureBox.
    MenuItem menuItem3 = new MenuItem("C&hange Picture");

    // Clear all previously added MenuItems.
    contextMenu1.MenuItems.Clear();

    if(contextMenu1.SourceControl == textBox1)
    {
       // Add MenuItems to display for the TextBox.
       contextMenu1.MenuItems.Add(menuItem1);
       contextMenu1.MenuItems.Add(menuItem2);
    }
    else if(contextMenu1.SourceControl == pictureBox1)
    {
       // Add the MenuItem to display for the PictureBox.
       contextMenu1.MenuItems.Add(menuItem3);
    }
 }
```

Requirements

Namespace: System.Windows.Forms

Platforms: Windows 98, Windows NT 4.0, Windows Millennium Edition, Windows 2000, Windows XP Home Edition, Windows XP Professional, Windows Server 2003 family, .NET Compact Framework - Windows CE .NET

Assembly: System.Windows.Forms (in System.Windows.Forms.dll)

ContextMenu Constructor

Initializes a new instance of the **ContextMenu** class.

Overload List

Initializes a new instance of the **ContextMenu** class with no menu items specified.

Supported by the .NET Compact Framework.

[Visual Basic] **Public Sub New()**

[C#] **public ContextMenu();**

[C++] **public: ContextMenu();**

[JScript] **public function ContextMenu();**

Initializes a new instance of the **ContextMenu** class with a specified set of **MenuItem** objects.

[Visual Basic] **Public Sub New(MenuItem())**

[C#] **public ContextMenu(MenuItem[]);**

[C++] **public: ContextMenu(MenuItem*[]);**

[JScript] **public function ContextMenu(MenuItem[]);**

ContextMenu Constructor ()

Initializes a new instance of the **ContextMenu** class with no menu items specified.

```
[Visual Basic]
Public Sub New()
[C#]
public ContextMenu();
[C++]
public: ContextMenu();
[JScript]
public function ContextMenu();
```

Remarks

Once you have used this version of the constructor, you can add menu items to the **ContextMenu** by using the **Add** method of the **Menu.MenuItemCollection** class. You can access the **Menu.MenuItemCollection** through the **MenuItems** property.

Requirements

Platforms: Windows 98, Windows NT 4.0, Windows Millennium Edition, Windows 2000, Windows XP Home Edition, Windows XP Professional, Windows Server 2003 family, .NET Compact Framework - Windows CE .NET

ContextMenu Constructor (MenuItem[])

Initializes a new instance of the **ContextMenu** class with a specified set of **MenuItem** objects.

```
[Visual Basic]
Public Sub New( _
   ByVal menuItems() As MenuItem _
)
[C#]
public ContextMenu(
   MenuItem[] menuItems
);
[C++]
public: ContextMenu(
   MenuItem* menuItems[]
);
[JScript]
public function ContextMenu(
   menuItems : MenuItem[]
);
```

Parameters

menuItems

An array of **MenuItem** objects that represent the menu items to add to the shortcut menu.

Remarks

You can use this version of the constructor to create a **ContextMenu** that has its menu items specified at the time it is created. Once you have used this version of the constructor, you can add additional menu items to the **ContextMenu** by using the **Add** method of the **Menu.MenuItemCollection** class. You can access the **Menu.MenuItemCollection** through the **MenuItems** property.

Requirements

Platforms: Windows 98, Windows NT 4.0, Windows Millennium Edition, Windows 2000, Windows XP Home Edition, Windows XP Professional, Windows Server 2003 family

ContextMenu.RightToLeft Property

Gets or sets a value indicating whether text displayed by the control is displayed from right to left.

```
[Visual Basic]
Public Overridable Property RightToLeft As RightToLeft
[C#]
public virtual RightToLeft RightToLeft {get; set;}
[C++]
public: __property virtual RightToLeft get_RightToLeft();
public: __property virtual void set_RightToLeft(RightToLeft);
[JScript]
public function get RightToLeft() : RightToLeft;
public function set RightToLeft(RightToLeft);
```

Property Value

One of the **RightToLeft** values.

Exceptions

Exception Type	Condition
InvalidEnumArgumentException	The value assigned to the property is not a valid member of the **RightToLeft** enumeration.

Remarks

This property allows your menus to support languages that are written from right to left. When this property is set to **RightToLeft.Yes**, the menu item text is displayed from right to left instead of the default left to right method.

Note For more information about how enabling right-to-left alignment effects Windows Forms controls, see the **RightToLeft** property.

Requirements

Platforms: Windows 98, Windows NT 4.0, Windows Millennium Edition, Windows 2000, Windows XP Home Edition, Windows XP Professional, Windows Server 2003 family

ContextMenu.SourceControl Property

Gets the control that is displaying the shortcut menu.

```
[Visual Basic]
Public ReadOnly Property SourceControl As Control
[C#]
public Control SourceControl {get;}
[C++]
public: __property Control* get_SourceControl();
[JScript]
public function get SourceControl() : Control;
```

Property Value

A **Control** that represents the control that is displaying the shortcut menu. If no control has displayed the shortcut menu, the property returns a null reference (**Nothing** in Visual Basic).

Remarks

This property enables you to determine which control currently displays the shortcut menu defined in the **ContextMenu**. If the shortcut menu is not currently displayed, you can use this property to determine which control last displayed the shortcut menu. You can use this property in the **Popup** event to ensure that the control displays the proper menu items. You can also use this property to pass a reference to the control to a method that performs the tasks associated with a menu command displayed in the shortcut menu. Since the **Form** class inherits from **Control**, you can also use this property if the **ContextMenu** is associated with a form.

Example

[Visual Basic, C#] The following example creates an event handler for the **Popup** event of the **ContextMenu**. The code in the event handler determines which of two controls a **PictureBox** named `pictureBox1` and a **TextBox** named `textBox1` is the control displaying the shortcut menu. Depending on which control caused the **ContextMenu** to display its shortcut menu, the control adds the appropriate **MenuItem** objects to the **ContextMenu**. This example assumes that you have an instance of the **ContextMenu** class, named `contextMenu1`, defined within the form. This example also assumes that you have a **TextBox** and **PictureBox** added to a form and that the **ContextMenu** property of these controls is set to `contextMenu1`.

```
[Visual Basic]
Protected Sub MyPopupEventHandler(sender As System.Object, e As System.EventArgs)
    ' Define the MenuItem objects to display for the TextBox.
    Dim menuItem1 As New MenuItem("&Copy")
    Dim menuItem2 As New MenuItem("&Find and Replace")
    ' Define the MenuItem object to display for the PictureBox.
    Dim menuItem3 As New MenuItem("C&hange Picture")

    ' Clear all previously added MenuItems.
    contextMenu1.MenuItems.Clear()

    If contextMenu1.SourceControl Is textBox1 Then
        ' Add MenuItems to display for the TextBox.
        contextMenu1.MenuItems.Add(menuItem1)
        contextMenu1.MenuItems.Add(menuItem2)
    ElseIf contextMenu1.SourceControl Is pictureBox1 Then
        ' Add the MenuItem to display for the PictureBox.
        contextMenu1.MenuItems.Add(menuItem3)
    End If
End Sub 'MyPopupEventHandler '

[C#]
protected void MyPopupEventHandler(System.Object sender, System.EventArgs e)
{
   // Define the MenuItem objects to display for the TextBox.
   MenuItem menuItem1 = new MenuItem("&Copy");
   MenuItem menuItem2 = new MenuItem("&Find and Replace");
   // Define the MenuItem object to display for the PictureBox.
   MenuItem menuItem3 = new MenuItem("C&hange Picture");

   // Clear all previously added MenuItems.
   contextMenu1.MenuItems.Clear();

   if(contextMenu1.SourceControl == textBox1)
   {
      // Add MenuItems to display for the TextBox.
      contextMenu1.MenuItems.Add(menuItem1);
      contextMenu1.MenuItems.Add(menuItem2);
   }
   else if(contextMenu1.SourceControl == pictureBox1)
   {
      // Add the MenuItem to display for the PictureBox.
      contextMenu1.MenuItems.Add(menuItem3);
   }
}
```

Requirements

Platforms: Windows 98, Windows NT 4.0, Windows Millennium Edition, Windows 2000, Windows XP Home Edition, Windows XP Professional, Windows Server 2003 family

ContextMenu.OnPopup Method

This member supports the .NET Framework infrastructure and is not intended to be used directly from your code.

```
[Visual Basic]
Protected Friend Overridable Sub OnPopup( _
   ByVal e As EventArgs _
)
[C#]
protected internal virtual void OnPopup(
   EventArgs e
);
[C++]
protected public: virtual void OnPopup(
   EventArgs* e
);
[JScript]
protected internal function OnPopup(
   e : EventArgs
);
```

ContextMenu.Show Method

Displays the shortcut menu at the specified position.

```
[Visual Basic]
Public Sub Show( _
   ByVal control As Control, _
   ByVal pos As Point _
)
[C#]
public void Show(
   Control control,
   Point pos
);
```

```
[C++]
public: void Show(
   Control* control,
   Point pos
);
[JScript]
public function Show(
   control : Control,
   pos : Point
);
```

Parameters

control

A **Control** object that specifies the control with which this shortcut menu is associated.

pos

A **Point** object that specifies the coordinates at which to display the menu. These coordinates are specified relative to the client coordinates of the control specified in the *control* parameter.

Remarks

Typically, a **ContextMenu** is displayed when the user clicks the right mouse button on a control or area of the form that the **ContextMenu** is bound to. You can use this method to manually display the shortcut menu at a specific location and bind it with a specific control. This method does not return until the menu is dismissed.

Requirements

Platforms: Windows 98, Windows NT 4.0, Windows Millennium Edition, Windows 2000, Windows XP Home Edition, Windows XP Professional, Windows Server 2003 family, .NET Compact Framework - Windows CE .NET

ContextMenu.Popup Event

Occurs before the shortcut menu is displayed.

```
[Visual Basic]
Public Event Popup As EventHandler
[C#]
public event EventHandler Popup;
[C++]
public: __event EventHandler* Popup;
```

[JScript] In JScript, you can handle the events defined by a class, but you cannot define your own.

Event Data

The event handler receives an argument of type **EventArgs**.

Remarks

You can use this event to initialize the **MenuItem** objects before they are displayed. For example, if you use a **ContextMenu** for three **TextBox** controls and you want to disable certain menu items in the **ContextMenu** depending on which **TextBox** is displaying the shortcut menu, you can create an event handler for this event. You could use the **SourceControl** property to determine which **TextBox** is about to display the **ContextMenu** and disable the appropriate **MenuItem** objects.

For more information about handling events, see **Consuming Events**.

Example

[Visual Basic, C#] The following example creates an event handler for the **Popup** event of the **ContextMenu**. The code in the event handler determines which of two controls a **PictureBox** named `pictureBox1` and a **TextBox** named `textBox1` is the control displaying the shortcut menu. Depending on which control caused the **ContextMenu** to display its shortcut menu, the control adds the appropriate **MenuItem** objects to the **ContextMenu**. This example assumes that you have an instance of the **ContextMenu** class, named `contextMenu1`, defined within the form. This example also assumes that you have a **TextBox** and **PictureBox** added to a form and that the **ContextMenu** property of these controls is set to `contextMenu1`.

```
[Visual Basic]
Protected Sub MyPopupEventHandler(sender As System.Object, e As ↵
System.EventArgs)
    ' Define the MenuItem objects to display for the TextBox.
    Dim menuItem1 As New MenuItem("&Copy")
    Dim menuItem2 As New MenuItem("&Find and Replace")
    ' Define the MenuItem object to display for the PictureBox.
    Dim menuItem3 As New MenuItem("C&hange Picture")

    ' Clear all previously added MenuItems.
    contextMenu1.MenuItems.Clear()

    If contextMenu1.SourceControl Is textBox1 Then
        ' Add MenuItems to display for the TextBox.
        contextMenu1.MenuItems.Add(menuItem1)
        contextMenu1.MenuItems.Add(menuItem2)
    ElseIf contextMenu1.SourceControl Is pictureBox1 Then
        ' Add the MenuItem to display for the PictureBox.
        contextMenu1.MenuItems.Add(menuItem3)
    End If
End Sub 'MyPopupEventHandler '
```

```
[C#]
protected void MyPopupEventHandler(System.Object sender, ↵
System.EventArgs e)
 {
    // Define the MenuItem objects to display for the TextBox.
    MenuItem menuItem1 = new MenuItem("&Copy");
    MenuItem menuItem2 = new MenuItem("&Find and Replace");
    // Define the MenuItem object to display for the PictureBox.
    MenuItem menuItem3 = new MenuItem("C&hange Picture");

    // Clear all previously added MenuItems.
    contextMenu1.MenuItems.Clear();

    if(contextMenu1.SourceControl == textBox1)
    {
       // Add MenuItems to display for the TextBox.
       contextMenu1.MenuItems.Add(menuItem1);
       contextMenu1.MenuItems.Add(menuItem2);
    }
    else if(contextMenu1.SourceControl == pictureBox1)
    {
       // Add the MenuItem to display for the PictureBox.
       contextMenu1.MenuItems.Add(menuItem3);
    }
 }
```

Requirements

Platforms: Windows 98, Windows NT 4.0, Windows Millennium Edition, Windows 2000, Windows XP Home Edition, Windows XP Professional, Windows Server 2003 family

Control Class

Defines the base class for controls, which are components with visual representation.

System.Object
 System.MarshalByRefObject
  System.ComponentModel.Component
   System.Windows.Forms.Control
    Derived classes

[Visual Basic]
```
Public Class Control
   Inherits Component
   Implements ISynchronizeInvoke, IWin32Window
```
[C#]
```
public class Control : Component, ISynchronizeInvoke, IWin32Window
```
[C++]
```
public __gc class Control : public Component, ISynchronizeInvoke,
   IWin32Window
```
[JScript]
```
public class Control extends Component implements
   ISynchronizeInvoke, IWin32Window
```

Thread Safety

Only the following members are safe for multithreaded operations: **BeginInvoke**, **EndInvoke**, **Invoke**, **InvokeRequired**, and **CreateGraphics**.

Remarks

To create your own control class, inherit from the **UserControl**, **Control** classes, or from the other Windows Forms provided controls.

The **Control** class implements very basic functionality required by classes that display information to the user. It handles user input through the keyboard and pointing devices. It handles message routing and security. It defines the bounds of a control (its position and size), although it does not implement painting. It provides a window handle (hWnd).

Windows Forms controls use ambient properties so child controls can appear like their surrounding environment. An ambient property is a control property that, if not set, is retrieved from the parent control. If the control does not have a **Parent** and the property is not set, the control tries to determine the value of the ambient property through the **Site** property. If the control is not sited, if the site does not support ambient properties, or if the property is not set on the **AmbientProperties** object, the control uses its own default values. Typically, an ambient property represents a characteristic of a control, such as **BackColor**, that is communicated to a child control. For example, a **Button** will have the same **BackColor** as its parent **Form** by default. Ambient properties provided by the **Control** class include: **Cursor**, **Font**, **BackColor**, **ForeColor**, and **RightToLeft**.

> **Note** To make your Windows Forms application support Windows XP visual styles, be sure to set the **FlatStyle** property to **FlatStyle.System** and include a manifest with your executable. A manifest is an XML file that is included either as a resource within your application executable or as a separate file that resides in the same directory as the executable file. For an example of a manifest, see the Example section of the **FlatStyle** enumeration. For more information about using the visual styles available in Windows XP, see Using Windows XP Visual Styles in the Windows Development section of the MSDN Library.

Windows Forms has accessibility support built in, and provides information about your application that allows it to work with accessibility client applications such as screen enlarger and reviewer utilities, voice input utilities, on-screen keyboards, alternative input devices, and keyboard enhancement utilities. There are instances when you will want to provide additional information to accessibility client applications. There are two ways of providing this additional information. You can set the **AccessibleName**, **AccessibleDescription**, **AccessibleDefaultActionDescription**, and **AccessibleRole** property values, which will be reported to accessibility client applications. This method is typically used to provide limited accessibility information for existing controls. Alternatively, you can write your own class deriving from the **AccessibleObject** or **Control.ControlAccessibleObject** classes, providing as much accessibility information as needed.

> **Note** In order to maintain better performance, you should not set the size of a control in its constructor. The preferred method is to override the **DefaultSize** property.

The majority of the controls in the **System.Windows.Forms** namespace use the underlying Windows Common Control as a base to build upon. For more information about the Windows Common Controls, see the General Introduction to the Common Controls topic in the Windows Common Controls section of the Platform SDK documentation in the MSDN Library.

Requirements

Namespace: System.Windows.Forms

Platforms: Windows 98, Windows NT 4.0, Windows Millennium Edition, Windows 2000, Windows XP Home Edition, Windows XP Professional, Windows Server 2003 family, .NET Compact Framework - Windows CE .NET

Assembly: System.Windows.Forms (in System.Windows.Forms.dll)

Control Constructor

Initializes a new instance of the **Control** class.

Overload List

Initializes a new instance of the **Control** class with default settings.

Supported by the .NET Compact Framework.

[Visual Basic] **Public Sub New()**

[C#] **public Control();**

[C++] **public: Control();**

[JScript] **public function Control();**

Initializes a new instance of the **Control** class with specific text.

[Visual Basic] **Public Sub New(String)**

[C#] **public Control(string);**

[C++] **public: Control(String*);**

[JScript] **public function Control(String);**

Initializes a new instance of the **Control** class as a child control, with specific text.

[Visual Basic] **Public Sub New(Control, String)**

[C#] **public Control(Control, string);**

[C++] **public: Control(Control*, String*);**

[JScript] **public function Control(Control, String);**

Initializes a new instance of the **Control** class with specific text, size, and location.

[Visual Basic] **Public Sub New(String, Integer, Integer, Integer, Integer)**

[C#] **public Control(string, int, int, int, int);**

[C++] **public: Control(String*, int, int, int, int);**

[JScript] **public function Control(String, int, int, int, int);**

Initializes a new instance of the **Control** class as a child control, with specific text, size, and location.

[Visual Basic] **Public Sub New(Control, String, Integer, Integer, Integer, Integer)**

[C#] **public Control(Control, string, int, int, int, int);**

[C++] **public: Control(Control*, String*, int, int, int, int);**

[JScript] **public function Control(Control, String, int, int, int, int);**

Control Constructor ()

Initializes a new instance of the **Control** class with default settings.

```
[Visual Basic]
Public Sub New()
[C#]
public Control();
[C++]
public: Control();
[JScript]
public function Control();
```

Remarks

The **Control** class is the base class for all controls used in a Windows Forms application. Because this class is not typically used to create an instance of the class, this constructor is typically not called directly but is instead called by a derived class.

Requirements

Platforms: Windows 98, Windows NT 4.0, Windows Millennium Edition, Windows 2000, Windows XP Home Edition, Windows XP Professional, Windows Server 2003 family, .NET Compact Framework - Windows CE .NET

Control Constructor (String)

Initializes a new instance of the **Control** class with specific text.

```
[Visual Basic]
Public Sub New( _
   ByVal text As String _
)
[C#]
public Control(
   string text
);
[C++]
public: Control(
   String* text
);
[JScript]
public function Control(
   text : String
);
```

Parameters

text

The text displayed by the control.

Remarks

The **Control** class is the base class for all controls used in a Windows Forms application. Because this class is not typically used to create an instance of the class, this constructor is typically not called directly but is instead called by a derived class.

This version of the **ctor** constructor sets the initial **Text** property value to the *text* parameter value.

Requirements

Platforms: Windows 98, Windows NT 4.0, Windows Millennium Edition, Windows 2000, Windows XP Home Edition, Windows XP Professional, Windows Server 2003 family

Control Constructor (Control, String)

Initializes a new instance of the **Control** class as a child control, with specific text.

```
[Visual Basic]
Public Sub New( _
   ByVal parent As Control, _
   ByVal text As String _
)
[C#]
public Control(
   Control parent,
   string text
);
[C++]
public: Control(
   Control* parent,
   String* text
);
[JScript]
public function Control(
   parent : Control,
   text : String
);
```

Parameters

parent

The **Control** to be the parent of the control.

text

The text displayed by the control.

Remarks

The **Control** class is the base class for all controls used in a Windows Forms application. Because this class is not typically used to create an instance of the class, this constructor is typically not called directly but is instead called by a derived class.This version of the **ctor** constructor sets the initial **Text** property value to the *text* parameter value. The constructor also adds the control to the parent control's **Control.ControlCollection**.

Requirements

Platforms: Windows 98, Windows NT 4.0, Windows Millennium Edition, Windows 2000, Windows XP Home Edition, Windows XP Professional, Windows Server 2003 family

Control Constructor (String, Int32, Int32, Int32, Int32)

Initializes a new instance of the **Control** class with specific text, size, and location.

[Visual Basic]
```
Public Sub New( _
   ByVal text As String, _
   ByVal left As Integer, _
   ByVal top As Integer, _
   ByVal width As Integer, _
   ByVal height As Integer _
)
```
[C#]
```
public Control(
   string text,
   int left,
   int top,
   int width,
   int height
);
```
[C++]
```
public: Control(
   String* text,
   int left,
   int top,
   int width,
   int height
);
```
[JScript]
```
public function Control(
   text : String,
   left : int,
   top : int,
   width : int,
   height : int
);
```

Parameters

text
: The text displayed by the control.

left
: The **X** position of the control, in pixels, from the left edge of the control's container. The value is assigned to the **Left** property.

top
: The **Y** position of the control, in pixels, from the top edge of the control's container. The value is assigned to the **Top** property.

width
: The width of the control, in pixels. The value is assigned to the **Width** property.

height
: The height of the control, in pixels. The value is assigned to the **Height** property.

Remarks

The **Control** class is the base class for all controls used in a Windows Forms application. Because this class is not typically used to create an instance of the class, this constructor is typically not called directly but is instead called by a derived class.

This version of the **ctor** constructor sets the initial **Text** property value to the *text* parameter value. The initial **Size** and **Location** of the control are determined by the *left*, *top*, *width* and *height* parameter values.

Note In order to maintain better performance, you should not set the size of a control in its constructor. The preferred method is to override the **DefaultSize** property.

Requirements

Platforms: Windows 98, Windows NT 4.0, Windows Millennium Edition, Windows 2000, Windows XP Home Edition, Windows XP Professional, Windows Server 2003 family

Control Constructor (Control, String, Int32, Int32, Int32, Int32)

Initializes a new instance of the **Control** class as a child control, with specific text, size, and location.

[Visual Basic]
```
Public Sub New( _
   ByVal parent As Control, _
   ByVal text As String, _
   ByVal left As Integer, _
   ByVal top As Integer, _
   ByVal width As Integer, _
   ByVal height As Integer _
)
```
[C#]
```
public Control(
   Control parent,
   string text,
   int left,
   int top,
   int width,
   int height
);
```
[C++]
```
public: Control(
   Control* parent,
   String* text,
   int left,
   int top,
   int width,
   int height
);
```
[JScript]
```
public function Control(
   parent : Control,
   text : String,
   left : int,
   top : int,
   width : int,
   height : int
);
```

Parameters

parent
: The **Control** to be the parent of the control.

text
: The text displayed by the control.

left
: The **X** position of the control, in pixels, from the left edge of the control's container. The value is assigned to the **Left** property.

top
The **Y** position of the control, in pixels, from the top edge of the control's container. The value is assigned to the **Top** property.

width
The width of the control, in pixels. The value is assigned to the **Width** property.

height
The height of the control, in pixels. The value is assigned to the **Height** property.

Remarks

The **Control** class is the base class for all controls used in a Windows Forms application. Because this class is not typically used to create an instance of the class, this constructor is typically not called directly but is instead called by a derived class.

This version of the **ctor** constructor sets the initial **Text** property value to the *text* parameter value. The constructor also adds the control to the parent control's **Control.ControlCollection**. The initial **Size** and **Location** of the control are determined by the *left*, *top*, *width* and *height* parameter values.

> **Note** In order to maintain better performance, you should not set the size of a control in its constructor. The preferred method is to override the **DefaultSize** property.

Requirements

Platforms: Windows 98, Windows NT 4.0,
Windows Millennium Edition, Windows 2000,
Windows XP Home Edition, Windows XP Professional,
Windows Server 2003 family

Control.AccessibilityObject Property

Gets the **AccessibleObject** assigned to the control.

```
[Visual Basic]
Public ReadOnly Property AccessibilityObject As AccessibleObject
[C#]
public AccessibleObject AccessibilityObject {get;}
[C++]
public: __property AccessibleObject* get_AccessibilityObject();
[JScript]
public function get AccessibilityObject() : AccessibleObject;
```

Property Value

The **AccessibleObject** assigned to the control.

Remarks

To control the instance returned from this method, override the **CreateAccessibilityInstance** method.

If no **AccessibleObject** is currently assigned to the control, a new instance of one is created.

> **Note** To get or set the **AccessibilityObject** property, you must add a reference to the **Accessibility** assembly installed with the .NET Framework.

For more information about accessible objects, see the Active Accessibility section of the MSDN Library.

Requirements

Platforms: Windows 98, Windows NT 4.0,
Windows Millennium Edition, Windows 2000,
Windows XP Home Edition, Windows XP Professional,
Windows Server 2003 family

Control.AccessibleDefaultActionDescription Property

Gets or sets the default action description of the control for use by accessibility client applications.

```
[Visual Basic]
Public Property AccessibleDefaultActionDescription As String
[C#]
public string AccessibleDefaultActionDescription {get; set;}
[C++]
public: __property String* get_AccessibleDefaultActionDescription();
public: __property void
set_AccessibleDefaultActionDescription(String*);
[JScript]
public function get AccessibleDefaultActionDescription() : String;
public function set AccessibleDefaultActionDescription(String);
```

Property Value

The default action description of the control for use by accessibility client applications.

Remarks

An object's **AccessibleDefaultActionDescription** property describes the object's primary method of manipulation from the user's viewpoint. This property should be a verb or a short verb phrase.

> **Note** Not all objects have default actions, and some objects might have a default action that is related to its **AccessibleObject.Value** property, such as in the following examples:

- A selected check box has a default action of "Uncheck" and a value of "Checked."
- A cleared check box has a default action of "Check" and a value of "Unchecked."
- A button labeled "Print" has a default action of "Press," with no value.
- A label or a text box control that shows "Printer" has no default action, but would have a value of "Printer."

For more information about properties of accessible objects, see the Content of Descriptive Properties topic in the Active Accessibility section of the MSDN Library.

Requirements

Platforms: Windows 98, Windows NT 4.0,
Windows Millennium Edition, Windows 2000,
Windows XP Home Edition, Windows XP Professional,
Windows Server 2003 family

Control.AccessibleDescription Property

Gets or sets the description of the control used by accessibility client applications.

```
[Visual Basic]
Public Property AccessibleDescription As String
[C#]
public string AccessibleDescription {get; set;}
[C++]
public: __property String* get_AccessibleDescription();
public: __property void set_AccessibleDescription(String*);
[JScript]
public function get AccessibleDescription() : String;
public function set AccessibleDescription(String);
```

Property Value

The description of the control used by accessibility client applications. The default is a null reference (**Nothing** in Visual Basic).

Remarks

An object's **AccessibleDescription** property provides a textual description about an object's visual appearance. The description is primarily used to provide greater context for low-vision or blind users, but can also be used for context searching or other applications.

The **AccessibleDescription** property is needed if the description is not obvious, or if it is redundant based on the object's **AccessibleName**, **AccessibleRole**, **State**, and **Value** properties. For example, a button with "OK" would not need additional information, but a button that shows a picture of a cactus would. The **AccessibleName**, and **AccessibleRole** (and perhaps **Help**) properties for the cactus button would describe its purpose, but the **AccessibleDescription** property would convey information that is less tangible, such as "A button that shows a picture of a cactus."

For more information about properties of accessible objects, see the Content of Descriptive Properties topic in the Active Accessibility section of the MSDN Library.

Example

[Visual Basic, C#, C++] The following example creates an instance of a **CheckBox** derived class, `MyCheckBox`, assigns it an **Image** to its **Image** property and sets the **AccessibleName** and **AccessibleDescription** properties since the **Text** property is a null reference (**Nothing** in Visual Basic). This example assumes you have a **Form** named `MyForm`.

[Visual Basic]
```
Public Sub New()
   ' Create a 'MyCheckBox' control and
   ' display an image on it.
   Dim myCheckBox As New MyCustomControls.MyCheckBox()
   myCheckBox.Location = New Point(5, 5)
   myCheckBox.Image = Image.FromFile( _
     Application.CommonAppDataPath + "\Preview.jpg")

   ' Set the AccessibleName property
   ' since there is no Text displayed.
   myCheckBox.AccessibleName = "Preview"

   ' Set the AccessibleDescription text.
   myCheckBox.AccessibleDescription = _
     "A toggle button used to show the document preview."
   Me.Controls.Add(myCheckBox)
End Sub
```

[C#]
```
public MyForm()
{
   // Create a 'MyCheckBox' control and
   // display an image on it.
   MyCustomControls.MyCheckBox myCheckBox =
      new MyCustomControls.MyCheckBox();
   myCheckBox.Location = new Point(5,5);
   myCheckBox.Image = Image.FromFile(
     Application.CommonAppDataPath + "\\Preview.jpg");

   // Set the AccessibleName property
   // since there is no Text displayed.
   myCheckBox.AccessibleName = "Preview";
   myCheckBox.AccessibleDescription =
     "A toggle button used to show the document preview.";
   this.Controls.Add(myCheckBox);
}
```

[C++]
```
public:
   MyForm() {
      // Create a 'MyCheckBox' control and
      // display an image on it.
      MyCustomControls::MyCheckBox* myCheckBox = new ↵
MyCustomControls::MyCheckBox();
      myCheckBox->Location =  Point(5, 5);
      myCheckBox->Image = ↵
Image::FromFile(String::Concat ↵
 (Application::CommonAppDataPath, S"\\Preview.jpg"));

      // Set the AccessibleName property
      // since there is no Text displayed.
      myCheckBox->AccessibleName = S"Preview";
      myCheckBox->AccessibleDescription =
         S"A toggle button used to show the document preview.";
      this->Controls->Add(myCheckBox);
   }
```

Requirements

Platforms: Windows 98, Windows NT 4.0, Windows Millennium Edition, Windows 2000, Windows XP Home Edition, Windows XP Professional, Windows Server 2003 family

Control.AccessibleName Property

Gets or sets the name of the control used by accessibility client applications.

[Visual Basic]
```
Public Property AccessibleName As String
```
[C#]
```
public string AccessibleName {get; set;}
```
[C++]
```
public: __property String* get_AccessibleName();
public: __property void set_AccessibleName(String*);
```
[JScript]
```
public function get AccessibleName() : String;
public function set AccessibleName(String);
```

Property Value

The name of the control used by accessibility client applications. The default is a null reference (**Nothing** in Visual Basic).

Remarks

The **AccessibleName** property is a label that briefly describes and identifies the object within its container, such as the text in a **Button**, the name of a **MenuItem**, or a label displayed next to a **TextBox** control.

For more information about properties of accessible objects, see the Content of Descriptive Properties topic in the Active Accessibility section of the MSDN Library.

Example

See related example in the **System.Windows.Forms.Control.AccessibleDescription** property topic.

Requirements

Platforms: Windows 98, Windows NT 4.0, Windows Millennium Edition, Windows 2000, Windows XP Home Edition, Windows XP Professional, Windows Server 2003 family

Control.AccessibleRole Property

Gets or sets the accessible role of the control

[Visual Basic]
```
Public Property AccessibleRole As AccessibleRole
```
[C#]
```
public AccessibleRole AccessibleRole {get; set;}
```
[C++]
```
public: __property AccessibleRole get_AccessibleRole();
public: __property void set_AccessibleRole(AccessibleRole);
```
[JScript]
```
public function get AccessibleRole() : AccessibleRole;
public function set AccessibleRole(AccessibleRole);
```

Property Value

The **AccessibleRole** of the control. The default is **Default**.

Exceptions

Exception Type	Condition
InvalidEnumArgumentException	The value assigned is not one of the **AccessibleRole** values.

Remarks

The **AccessibleRole** property describes what kind of user interface element an object is. If the control's role cannot be determined, the **AccessibleRole** property is set to **AccessibleRole.Default**.

For more information about properties of accessible objects, see the Content of Descriptive Properties topic in the Active Accessibility section of the MSDN Library.

Requirements

Platforms: Windows 98, Windows NT 4.0, Windows Millennium Edition, Windows 2000, Windows XP Home Edition, Windows XP Professional, Windows Server 2003 family

Control.AllowDrop Property

Gets or sets a value indicating whether the control can accept data that the user drags onto it.

[Visual Basic]
```
Public Overridable Property AllowDrop As Boolean
```
[C#]
```
public virtual bool AllowDrop {get; set;}
```
[C++]
```
public: __property virtual bool get_AllowDrop();
public: __property virtual void set_AllowDrop(bool);
```
[JScript]
```
public function get AllowDrop() : Boolean;
public function set AllowDrop(Boolean);
```

Property Value

true if drag-and-drop operations are allowed in the control; otherwise, **false**. The default is **false**.

Remarks

Notes to Inheritors: When overriding the **AllowDrop** property in a derived class, use the base class's **AllowDrop** property to extend the base implementation. Otherwise, you must provide all the implementation. You are not required to override both the **get** and **set** accessors of the **AllowDrop** property; you can override only one if needed.

Example

[Visual Basic, C#, C++] The following example enables the user to drag an image or image file onto the form, and have it be displayed at the point on it is dropped. The **OnPaint** method is overridden to repaint the image each time the form is painted; otherwise the image would only persist until the next repainting. The **DragEnter** event-handling method determines the type of data being dragged into the form and provides the appropriate feedback. The **DragDrop** event-handling method displays the image on the form, if an **Image** can be created from the data. Because the **DragEventArgs.X** and **DragEventArgs.Y** values are screen coordinates, the example uses the **PointToClient** method to convert them to client coordinates.

[Visual Basic]
```
Private picture As Image
Private pictureLocation As Point

Public Sub New()
   ' Enable drag-and-drop operations.
   Me.AllowDrop = True
End Sub

Protected Overrides Sub OnPaint(ByVal e As PaintEventArgs)
   MyBase.OnPaint(e)

   ' If there is an image and it has a location,
   ' paint it when the Form is repainted.
   If Not (Me.picture Is Nothing) And _
     Not (Me.pictureLocation.Equals(Point.Empty)) Then
      e.Graphics.DrawImage(Me.picture, Me.pictureLocation)
   End If
End Sub

Private Sub Form1_DragDrop(ByVal sender As Object, _
  ByVal e As DragEventArgs) Handles MyBase.DragDrop
   ' Handle FileDrop data.
   If e.Data.GetDataPresent(DataFormats.FileDrop) Then
      ' Assign the file names to a string array, in
      ' case the user has selected multiple files.
      Dim files As String() =                                    ↵
CType(e.Data.GetData(DataFormats.FileDrop), String())
      Try
         ' Assign the first image to the 'picture' variable.
         Me.picture = Image.FromFile(files(0))
         ' Set the picture location equal to the drop point.
         Me.pictureLocation = Me.PointToClient(New Point(e.X, e.Y))
      Catch ex As Exception
         MessageBox.Show(ex.Message)
         Return
      End Try
   End If

   ' Handle Bitmap data.
   If e.Data.GetDataPresent(DataFormats.Bitmap) Then
      Try
         ' Create an Image and assign it to the picture variable.
         Me.picture = CType(e.Data.GetData(DataFormats.Bitmap), Image)
         ' Set the picture location equal to the drop point.
         Me.pictureLocation = Me.PointToClient(New Point(e.X, e.Y))
      Catch ex As Exception
         MessageBox.Show(ex.Message)
         Return
      End Try
   End If

   ' Force the form to be redrawn with the image.
   Me.Invalidate()
End Sub

Private Sub Form1_DragEnter(ByVal sender As Object, _
  ByVal e As DragEventArgs) Handles MyBase.DragEnter
   ' If the data is a file or a bitmap, display the copy cursor.
```

```
   If e.Data.GetDataPresent(DataFormats.Bitmap) _
      Or e.Data.GetDataPresent(DataFormats.FileDrop) Then
      e.Effect = DragDropEffects.Copy
   Else
      e.Effect = DragDropEffects.None
   End If
End Sub
```

[C#]

```
private Image picture;
private Point pictureLocation;

public Form1()
{
   // Enable drag-and-drop operations and
   // add handlers for DragEnter and DragDrop.
   this.AllowDrop = true;
   this.DragDrop += new DragEventHandler(this.Form1_DragDrop);
   this.DragEnter += new DragEventHandler(this.Form1_DragEnter);
}

protected override void OnPaint(PaintEventArgs e)
{
   // If there is an image and it has a location,
   // paint it when the Form is repainted.
   base.OnPaint(e);
   if(this.picture != null && this.pictureLocation != Point.Empty)
   {
      e.Graphics.DrawImage(this.picture, this.pictureLocation);
   }
}

private void Form1_DragDrop(object sender, DragEventArgs e)
{
   // Handle FileDrop data.
   if(e.Data.GetDataPresent(DataFormats.FileDrop) )
   {
      // Assign the file names to a string array, in
      // case the user has selected multiple files.
      string[] files = (string[])e.Data.GetData(DataFormats.FileDrop);
      try
      {
         // Assign the first image to the picture variable.
         this.picture = Image.FromFile(files[0]);
         // Set the picture location equal to the drop point.
         this.pictureLocation = this.PointToClient(new Point ↵
 (e.X, e.Y) );
      }
      catch(Exception ex)
      {
         MessageBox.Show(ex.Message);
         return;
      }
   }

   // Handle Bitmap data.
   if(e.Data.GetDataPresent(DataFormats.Bitmap) )
   {
      try
      {
         // Create an Image and assign it to the picture variable.
         this.picture = (Image)e.Data.GetData(DataFormats.Bitmap);
         // Set the picture location equal to the drop point.
         this.pictureLocation = this.PointToClient(new Point ↵
 (e.X, e.Y) );
      }
      catch(Exception ex)
      {
         MessageBox.Show(ex.Message);
         return;
      }
   }
   // Force the form to be redrawn with the image.
   this.Invalidate();
}

private void Form1_DragEnter(object sender, DragEventArgs e)
{
   // If the data is a file or a bitmap, display the copy cursor.
   if (e.Data.GetDataPresent(DataFormats.Bitmap) ||
      e.Data.GetDataPresent(DataFormats.FileDrop) )
   {
      e.Effect = DragDropEffects.Copy;
   }
   else
   {
      e.Effect = DragDropEffects.None;
   }
}
```

[C++]

```
private:
   Image*  picture;
   Point  pictureLocation;

public:
   Form1() {
      // Enable drag-and-drop operations and
      // add handlers for DragEnter and DragDrop.
      this->AllowDrop = true;
      this->DragDrop += new DragEventHandler(this, Form1_DragDrop);
      this->DragEnter += new DragEventHandler(this, Form1_DragEnter);
   }

protected:
   void OnPaint(PaintEventArgs* e) {
      // If there is an image and it has a location,
      // paint it when the Form is repainted.
      Form::OnPaint(e);
      if (this->picture != 0 && this->pictureLocation ↵
 != Point::Empty) {
         e->Graphics->DrawImage(this->picture, this->pictureLocation);
      }
   }

private:
   void Form1_DragDrop(Object* sender, DragEventArgs* e) {
      // Handle FileDrop data.
      if (e->Data->GetDataPresent(DataFormats::FileDrop)) {
         // Assign the file names to a String* array, in
         // case the user has selected multiple files.
         String* files[] = (String*[])e->Data- ↵
>GetData(DataFormats::FileDrop);
         try {
            // Assign the first image to the picture variable.
            this->picture = Image::FromFile(files[0]);
            // Set the picture location equal to the drop point.
            this->pictureLocation = this->PointToClient( ↵
Point(e->X, e->Y));
         } catch (Exception* ex) {
            MessageBox::Show(ex->Message);
            return;
         }
      }

      // Handle Bitmap data.
      if (e->Data->GetDataPresent(DataFormats::Bitmap)) {
         try {
            // Create an Image and assign it to the picture variable.
            this->picture = dynamic_cast<Image*>(e->Data- ↵
>GetData(DataFormats::Bitmap));
            // Set the picture location equal to the drop point.
            this->pictureLocation = this->PointToClient( ↵
Point(e->X, e->Y));
         } catch (Exception* ex) {
            MessageBox::Show(ex->Message);
            return;
         }
      }
      // Force the form to be redrawn with the image.
```

```
      this->Invalidate();
   }

   void Form1_DragEnter(Object* sender, DragEventArgs* e) {
      // If the data is a file or a bitmap, display the copy cursor.
      if (e->Data->GetDataPresent(DataFormats::Bitmap) ||
         e->Data->GetDataPresent(DataFormats::FileDrop)) {
            e->Effect = DragDropEffects::Copy;
         } else {
            e->Effect = DragDropEffects::None;
         }
   }
```

Requirements

Platforms: Windows 98, Windows NT 4.0, Windows Millennium Edition, Windows 2000, Windows XP Home Edition, Windows XP Professional, Windows Server 2003 family

.NET Framework Security:

- **UIPermission** for unrestricted Clipboard access to set this property to **true**. Associated enumeration: **UIPermission-Clipboard.AllClipboard**

Control.Anchor Property

Gets or sets which edges of the control are anchored to the edges of its container.

[Visual Basic]
```
Public Overridable Property Anchor As AnchorStyles
```
[C#]
```
public virtual AnchorStyles Anchor {get; set;}
```
[C++]
```
public: __property virtual AnchorStyles get_Anchor();
public: __property virtual void set_Anchor(AnchorStyles);
```
[JScript]
```
public function get Anchor() : AnchorStyles;
public function set Anchor(AnchorStyles);
```

Property Value

A bitwise combination of the **AnchorStyles** values. The default is **Top** and **Left**.

Remarks

A control can be anchored to one or more edges of its parent container. Anchoring a control to its parent ensures that the anchored edges remain in the same position relative to the edges of the parent container when the parent container is resized. For example, if you have a **Form** with a **Button** whose **Anchor** property value is set to **AnchorStyles.Top** and **AnchorStyles.Bottom**, the **Button** is stretched to maintain the anchored distance to the top and bottom edges of the **Form** as the **Height** of the **Form** is increased.

Notes to Inheritors: When overriding the **Anchor** property in a derived class, use the base class's **Anchor** property to extend the base implementation. Otherwise, you must provide all the implementation. You are not required to override both the **get** and **set** accessors of the **Anchor** property; you can override only one if needed.

Example

[Visual Basic, C#, C++] The following example adds a **Button** to a form and sets some of its common properties. The example anchors the button to the bottom-right corner of the form so it keeps its relative position as the form is resized. Next it sets the **Background-Image** and resizes the button to the same size as the **Image**. The example then sets the **TabStop** to **true** and sets the **TabIndex** property. Lastly, it adds an event handler to handle the **Click** event of the button. This example assumes you have an **ImageList** named `imageList1`.

[Visual Basic]
```
' Add a button to a form and set some of its common properties.
Private Sub AddMyButton()
   ' Create a button and add it to the form.
   Dim button1 As New Button()

   ' Anchor the button to the bottom right corner of the form
   button1.Anchor = AnchorStyles.Bottom Or AnchorStyles.Right

   ' Assign a background image.
   button1.BackgroundImage = imageList1.Images(0)

   ' Make the button the same size as the image.
   button1.Size = button1.BackgroundImage.Size

   ' Set the button's TabIndex and TabStop properties.
   button1.TabIndex = 1
   button1.TabStop = True

   ' Add a delegate to handle the Click event.
   AddHandler button1.Click, AddressOf Me.button1_Click

   ' Add the button to the form.
   Me.Controls.Add(button1)
End Sub
```

[C#]
```
// Add a button to a form and set some of its common properties.
private void AddMyButton()
{
   // Create a button and add it to the form.
   Button button1 = new Button();

   // Anchor the button to the bottom right corner of the form
   button1.Anchor = (AnchorStyles.Bottom | AnchorStyles.Right);

   // Assign a background image.
   button1.BackgroundImage = imageList1.Images[0];

   // Make the button the same size as the image.
   button1.Size = button1.BackgroundImage.Size;

   // Set the button's TabIndex and TabStop properties.
   button1.TabIndex = 1;
   button1.TabStop = true;

   // Add a delegate to handle the Click event.
   button1.Click += new System.EventHandler(this.button1_Click);

   // Add the button to the form.
   this.Controls.Add(button1);
}
```

[C++]
```
// Add a button to a form and set some of its common properties.
private:
void AddMyButton() {
   // Create a button and add it to the form.
   Button* button1 = new Button();

   // Anchor the button to the bottom right corner of the form
   button1->Anchor = static_cast<AnchorStyles>
 (AnchorStyles::Bottom | AnchorStyles::Right);

   // Assign a background image.
   button1->BackgroundImage = imageList1->Images->Item[0];

   // Make the button the same size as the image.
   button1->Size = button1->BackgroundImage->Size;
```

```
   // Set the button's TabIndex and TabStop properties.
   button1->TabIndex = 1;
   button1->TabStop = true;

   // Add a delegate to handle the Click event.
   button1->Click += new System::EventHandler(this, button1_Click);

   // Add the button to the form.
   this->Controls->Add(button1);
}
```

Requirements

Platforms: Windows 98, Windows NT 4.0, Windows Millennium Edition, Windows 2000, Windows XP Home Edition, Windows XP Professional, Windows Server 2003 family

Control.BackColor Property

Gets or sets the background color for the control.

[Visual Basic]
```
Public Overridable Property BackColor As Color
```
[C#]
```
public virtual Color BackColor {get; set;}
```
[C++]
```
public: __property virtual Color get_BackColor();
public: __property virtual void set_BackColor(Color);
```
[JScript]
```
public function get BackColor() : Color;
public function set BackColor(Color);
```

Property Value

A **Color** that represents the background color of the control. The default is the value of the **DefaultBackColor** property.

Remarks

The **BackColor** property does not support transparent colors unless the **ControlStyles.SupportsTransparentBackColor** style bit is set to **true**.

The **BackColor** property is an ambient property. An ambient property is a control property that, if not set, is retrieved from the parent control. For example, a **Button** will have the same **BackColor** as its parent **Form** by default. For more information about ambient properties, see the **AmbientProperties** class or the **Control** class overview.

Notes to Inheritors: When overriding the **BackColor** property in a derived class, use the base class's **BackColor** property to extend the base implementation. Otherwise, you must provide all the implementation. You are not required to override both the **get** and **set** accessors of the **BackColor** property; you can override only one if needed.

Example

[Visual Basic, C#, C++] The following example sets the **BackColor** and **ForeColor** of the controls to the default system colors. The code recursively calls itself if the control has any child controls. This code example assumes you have a **Form** with at least one child control; however, a child container control, like a **Panel** or **GroupBox**, with its own child control(s) would better demonstrate the recursion.

[Visual Basic]
```
' Reset all the controls to the user's default Control color.
Private Sub ResetAllControlsBackColor(control As Control)
   control.BackColor = SystemColors.Control
   control.ForeColor = SystemColors.ControlText
   If Me.HasChildren Then
      ' Recursively call this method for each child control.
      Dim childControl As Control
      For Each childControl In  control.Controls
         ResetAllControlsBackColor(childControl)
      Next childControl
   End If
End Sub
```

[C#]
```
// Reset all the controls to the user's default Control color.
private void ResetAllControlsBackColor(Control control)
{
   control.BackColor = SystemColors.Control;
   control.ForeColor = SystemColors.ControlText;
   if(this.HasChildren)
   {
      // Recursively call this method for each child control.
      foreach(Control childControl in control.Controls)
      {
         ResetAllControlsBackColor(childControl);
      }
   }
}
```

[C++]
```
// Reset all the controls to the user's default Control color.
private:
void ResetAllControlsBackColor(Control* control) {
   control->BackColor = SystemColors::Control;
   control->ForeColor = SystemColors::ControlText;
   if (this->HasChildren) {
      // Recursively call this method for each child control.
      IEnumerator* myEnum = control->Controls->GetEnumerator();
      while (myEnum->MoveNext()) {
         Control* childControl = __try_cast<Control*>(myEnum->Current);
         ResetAllControlsBackColor(childControl);
      }
   }
}
```

Requirements

Platforms: Windows 98, Windows NT 4.0, Windows Millennium Edition, Windows 2000, Windows XP Home Edition, Windows XP Professional, Windows Server 2003 family, .NET Compact Framework - Windows CE .NET

Control.BackgroundImage Property

Gets or sets the background image displayed in the control.

[Visual Basic]
```
Public Overridable Property BackgroundImage As Image
```
[C#]
```
public virtual Image BackgroundImage {get; set;}
```
[C++]
```
public: __property virtual Image* get_BackgroundImage();
public: __property virtual void set_BackgroundImage(Image*);
```
[JScript]
```
public function get BackgroundImage() : Image;
public function set BackgroundImage(Image);
```

Property Value

An **Image** that represents the image to display in the background of the control.

Remarks

> **Note** Images with translucent or transparent colors are not supported by Windows Forms controls as background images.

Notes to Inheritors: When overriding the **BackgroundImage** property in a derived class, use the base class's **BackgroundImage** property to extend the base implementation. Otherwise, you must provide all the implementation. You are not required to override both the **get** and **set** accessors of the **BackgroundImage** property; you can override only one if needed.

Example

[Visual Basic, C#, C++] The following example adds a **Button** to a form and sets some of its common properties. The example anchors the button to the bottom-right corner of the form so it keeps its relative position as the form is resized. Next it sets the **BackgroundImage** and resizes the button to the same size as the **Image**. The example then sets the **TabStop** to **true** and sets the **TabIndex** property. Lastly, it adds an event handler to handle the **Click** event of the button. This example assumes you have an **ImageList** named `imageList1`.

[Visual Basic]

```
' Add a button to a form and set some of its common properties.
Private Sub AddMyButton()
   ' Create a button and add it to the form.
   Dim button1 As New Button()

   ' Anchor the button to the bottom right corner of the form
   button1.Anchor = AnchorStyles.Bottom Or AnchorStyles.Right

   ' Assign a background image.
   button1.BackgroundImage = imageList1.Images(0)

   ' Make the button the same size as the image.
   button1.Size = button1.BackgroundImage.Size

   ' Set the button's TabIndex and TabStop properties.
   button1.TabIndex = 1
   button1.TabStop = True

   ' Add a delegate to handle the Click event.
   AddHandler button1.Click, AddressOf Me.button1_Click

   ' Add the button to the form.
   Me.Controls.Add(button1)
End Sub
```

[C#]

```
// Add a button to a form and set some of its common properties.
private void AddMyButton()
{
   // Create a button and add it to the form.
   Button button1 = new Button();

   // Anchor the button to the bottom right corner of the form
   button1.Anchor = (AnchorStyles.Bottom | AnchorStyles.Right);

   // Assign a background image.
   button1.BackgroundImage = imageList1.Images[0];

   // Make the button the same size as the image.
   button1.Size = button1.BackgroundImage.Size;

   // Set the button's TabIndex and TabStop properties.
   button1.TabIndex = 1;
   button1.TabStop = true;

   // Add a delegate to handle the Click event.
   button1.Click += new System.EventHandler(this.button1_Click);

   // Add the button to the form.
   this.Controls.Add(button1);
}
```

[C++]

```
// Add a button to a form and set some of its common properties.
private:
void AddMyButton() {
   // Create a button and add it to the form.
   Button* button1 = new Button();

   // Anchor the button to the bottom right corner of the form
   button1->Anchor = static_cast<AnchorStyles>                          ↵
 (AnchorStyles::Bottom | AnchorStyles::Right);

   // Assign a background image.
   button1->BackgroundImage = imageList1->Images->Item[0];

   // Make the button the same size as the image.
   button1->Size = button1->BackgroundImage->Size;

   // Set the button's TabIndex and TabStop properties.
   button1->TabIndex = 1;
   button1->TabStop = true;

   // Add a delegate to handle the Click event.
   button1->Click += new System::EventHandler(this, button1_Click);

   // Add the button to the form.
   this->Controls->Add(button1);
}
```

Requirements

Platforms: Windows 98, Windows NT 4.0, Windows Millennium Edition, Windows 2000, Windows XP Home Edition, Windows XP Professional, Windows Server 2003 family

Control.BindingContext Property

Gets or sets the **BindingContext** for the control.

[Visual Basic]

```
Public Overridable Property BindingContext As BindingContext
```

[C#]

```
public virtual BindingContext BindingContext {get; set;}
```

[C++]

```
public: __property virtual BindingContext* get_BindingContext();
public: __property virtual void set_BindingContext(BindingContext*);
```

[JScript]

```
public function get BindingContext() : BindingContext;
public function set BindingContext(BindingContext);
```

Property Value

A **BindingContext** for the control.

Remarks

The **BindingContext** object of a **Control** is used to return a single **BindingManagerBase** object for all data-bound controls contained by the **Control**. The **BindingManagerBase** object keeps all controls that are bound to the same data source synchronized. For example, setting the **Position** property of the **BindingManagerBase** specifies the item in the underlying list that all data-bound controls point to.

For more information about creating a new **BindingContext** and assigning it to the **BindingContext** property, see the **BindingContext**.

Notes to Inheritors: When overriding the **BindingContext** property in a derived class, use the base class's **BindingContext** property to extend the base implementation. Otherwise, you must provide all the implementation. You are not required to override both the **get** and **set** accessors of the **BindingContext** property; you can override only one if needed.

Example

[Visual Basic, C#, C++] The following example creates four **Binding** objects to bind five controls, a **DateTimePicker** and four **TextBox** controls, to several data sources. The **BindingContext** is then used to get the **BindingManagerBase** for each data source.

[Visual Basic]
```
Protected Sub BindControls()

   ' Create two Binding objects for the first two TextBox
   '   controls. The data-bound property for both controls
   '   is the Text property. The data source is a DataSet
   '   (ds). The data member is the string
   '   "TableName.ColumnName".
   text1.DataBindings.Add(New Binding _
      ("Text", ds, "customers.custName"))
   text2.DataBindings.Add(New Binding _
      ("Text", ds, "customers.custID"))

   ' Bind the DateTimePicker control by adding a new Binding.
   '   The data member of the DateTimePicker is a
   '   TableName.RelationName.ColumnName string.
   DateTimePicker1.DataBindings.Add(New Binding _
      ("Value", ds, "customers.CustToOrders.OrderDate"))

   ' Add event delegates for the Parse and Format events to a
   '   new Binding object, and add the object to the third
   '   TextBox control's BindingsCollection. The delegates
   '   must be added before adding the Binding to the
   '   collection; otherwise, no formatting occurs until
   '   the Current object of the BindingManagerBase for
   '   the data source changes.
   Dim b As Binding = New Binding _
      ("Text", ds, "customers.custToOrders.OrderAmount")
   AddHandler b.Parse,  New ConvertEventHandler(AddressOf           ↵
CurrencyStringToDecimal)
   AddHandler b.Format, New ConvertEventHandler(AddressOf           ↵
DecimalToCurrencyString)
   text3.DataBindings.Add(b)

   ' Get the BindingManagerBase for the Customers table.
   bmCustomers = Me.BindingContext(ds, "Customers")

   ' Get the BindingManagerBase for the Orders table using the
   '   RelationName.
   bmOrders = Me.BindingContext(ds, "customers.CustToOrders")

   ' Bind the fourth TextBox control's Text property to the
   ' third control's Text property.
   text4.DataBindings.Add("Text", text3, "Text")

End Sub
```

[C#]
```
protected void BindControls()
{
   /* Create two Binding objects for the first two TextBox
      controls. The data-bound property for both controls
      is the Text property. The data source is a DataSet
      (ds). The data member is a navigation path in the form:
      "TableName.ColumnName". */
   text1.DataBindings.Add(new Binding
   ("Text", ds, "customers.custName"));
   text2.DataBindings.Add(new Binding
   ("Text", ds, "customers.custID"));

   /* Bind the DateTimePicker control by adding a new Binding.
      The data member of the DateTimePicker is a navigation path:
      TableName.RelationName.ColumnName string. */
   DateTimePicker1.DataBindings.Add(new
   Binding("Value", ds, "customers.CustToOrders.OrderDate"));

   /* Add event delegates for the Parse and Format events to a
      new Binding object, and add the object to the third
      TextBox control's BindingsCollection. The delegates
      must be added before adding the Binding to the
      collection; otherwise, no formatting occurs until
      the Current object of the BindingManagerBase for
      the data source changes. */
      Binding b = new Binding
      ("Text", ds, "customers.custToOrders.OrderAmount");
   b.Parse+=new ConvertEventHandler(CurrencyStringToDecimal);
   b.Format+=new ConvertEventHandler(DecimalToCurrencyString);
   text3.DataBindings.Add(b);

   // Get the BindingManagerBase for the Customers table.
   bmCustomers = this.BindingContext [ds, "Customers"];

   /* Get the BindingManagerBase for the Orders table using the
      RelationName. */
   bmOrders = this.BindingContext[ds, "customers.CustToOrders"];

   /* Bind the fourth TextBox control's Text property to the
   third control's Text property. */
   text4.DataBindings.Add("Text", text3, "Text");
}
```

[C++]
```
void BindControls() {
/* Create two Binding objects for the first two TextBox
  controls. The data-bound property for both controls
  is the Text property. The data source is a DataSet
  (ds). The data member is a navigation path in the form:
  "TableName.ColumnName". */
    text1->DataBindings->Add(new Binding(S"Text", ds,           ↵
S"customers.custName"));
    text2->DataBindings->Add(new Binding(S"Text", ds,           ↵
S"customers.custID"));

    /* Bind the DateTimePicker control by adding a new Binding.
  The data member of the DateTimePicker is a navigation path:
  TableName.RelationName.ColumnName string. */
    DateTimePicker1->DataBindings->Add(new Binding(S"Value",    ↵
ds, S"customers.CustToOrders.OrderDate"));

    /* Add event delegates for the Parse and Format events to a
  new Binding object, and add the object to the third
  TextBox control's BindingsCollection. The delegates
  must be added before adding the Binding to the
  collection; otherwise, no formatting occurs until
  the Current object of the BindingManagerBase for
  the data source changes. */
    Binding __gc *b = new Binding (S"Text", ds,                 ↵
S"customers.custToOrders.OrderAmount");
    b->Parse += new ConvertEventHandler(this,                   ↵
&Form1::CurrencyStringToDecimal);
    b->Format += new ConvertEventHandler(this,                  ↵
&Form1::DecimalToCurrencyString);
    text3->DataBindings->Add(b);

    // Get the BindingManagerBase for the Customers table.
    bmCustomers = this->BindingContext->Item[ds, S"Customers"];

    /* Get the BindingManagerBase for the Orders table using the
  RelationName. */
    bmOrders = this->BindingContext->get_Item(ds,               ↵
S"customers.CustToOrders");

    /* Bind the fourth TextBox control's Text property to the
    third control's Text property. */
    text4->DataBindings->Add(S"Text", text3, S"Text");
};
```

Requirements

Platforms: Windows 98, Windows NT 4.0, Windows Millennium Edition, Windows 2000, Windows XP Home Edition, Windows XP Professional, Windows Server 2003 family, .NET Compact Framework - Windows CE .NET

Control.Bottom Property

Gets the distance between the bottom edge of the control and the top edge of its container's client area.

[Visual Basic]
```
Public ReadOnly Property Bottom As Integer
```
[C#]
```
public int Bottom {get;}
```
[C++]
```
public: __property int get_Bottom();
```
[JScript]
```
public function get Bottom() : int;
```

Property Value

The bottom coordinate, in pixels.

Remarks

The value of this property is equal to the sum of the **Top** property value, and the **Height** property value.

The **Bottom** property is a read-only property. You can manipulate this property value by changing the value of the **Top** or **Height** properties or calling the **SetBounds**, **SetBoundsCore**, **UpdateBounds**, or **SetClientSizeCore** methods.

Example

[Visual Basic]
```
' This example demonstrates how to use the KeyUp event with ↵
the Help class to display
' pop-up style help to the user of the application. When the ↵
user presses F1, the Help
' class displays a pop-up window, similar to a ToolTip, near ↵
the control. This example assumes
' that a TextBox control, named textBox1, has been added to ↵
the form and its KeyUp
' event has been contected to this event handling method.
Private Sub textBox1_KeyUp(ByVal sender As Object, ByVal e As ↵
 System.Windows.Forms.KeyEventArgs) Handles textBox1.KeyUp
    ' Determine whether the key entered is the F1 key. Display ↵
help if it is.
    If e.KeyCode = Keys.F1 Then
        ' Display a pop-up help topic to assist the user.
        Help.ShowPopup(textBox1, "Enter your first name", New ↵
Point(textBox1.Right, Me.textBox1.Bottom))
    End If
End Sub 'textBox1_KeyUp
```

[C#]
```
// This example demonstrates how to use the KeyUp event with ↵
the Help class to display
// pop-up style help to the user of the application. When the ↵
 user presses F1, the Help
// class displays a pop-up window, similar to a ToolTip, near ↵
the control. This example assumes
// that a TextBox control, named textBox1, has been added to ↵
the form and its KeyUp
// event has been contected to this event handling method.
private void textBox1_KeyUp(object sender, ↵
System.Windows.Forms.KeyEventArgs e)
{
    // Determine whether the key entered is the F1 key. Display ↵
 help if it is.
    if(e.KeyCode == Keys.F1)
    {
        // Display a pop-up help topic to assist the user.
        Help.ShowPopup(textBox1, "Enter your first name", new ↵
Point(textBox1.Right, this.textBox1.Bottom));
    }
}
```

Requirements

Platforms: Windows 98, Windows NT 4.0, Windows Millennium Edition, Windows 2000, Windows XP Home Edition, Windows XP Professional, Windows Server 2003 family, .NET Compact Framework - Windows CE .NET

Control.Bounds Property

Gets or sets the size and location of the control including its nonclient elements.

[Visual Basic]
```
Public Property Bounds As Rectangle
```
[C#]
```
public Rectangle Bounds {get; set;}
```
[C++]
```
public: __property Rectangle get_Bounds();
public: __property void set_Bounds(Rectangle);
```
[JScript]
```
public function get Bounds() : Rectangle;
public function set Bounds(Rectangle);
```

Property Value

A **Rectangle** that represents the size and location of the control including its nonclient elements.

Remarks

The bounds of the control includes the nonclient elements such as scroll bars, borders, title bars, and menus. The **SetBoundsCore** method is called to set the **Bounds** property. The **Bounds** property is not always changed through its **set** method so you should override the **SetBoundsCore** method to ensure that your code is executed when the **Bounds** property is set.

Example

[Visual Basic, C#, C++] The following example creates three **Button** controls on a form and sets their size and location by using the various size-related and location-related properties. This example assumes you have a **Form** that has a width and height of at least 300 pixels.

[Visual Basic]
```
' Create three buttons and place them on a form using
' several size and location related properties.
Private Sub AddOKCancelButtons()
   ' Set the button size and location using
      ' the Size and Location properties.
   Dim buttonOK As New Button()
   buttonOK.Location = New Point(136, 248)
   buttonOK.Size = New Size(75, 25)
   ' Set the Text property and make the
   ' button the form's default button.
   buttonOK.Text = "&OK"
   Me.AcceptButton = buttonOK

   ' Set the button size and location using the Top,
   ' Left, Width, and Height properties.
   Dim buttonCancel As New Button()
   buttonCancel.Top = buttonOK.Top
   buttonCancel.Left = buttonOK.Right + 5
   buttonCancel.Width = buttonOK.Width
   buttonCancel.Height = buttonOK.Height
   ' Set the Text property and make the
   ' button the form's cancel button.
   buttonCancel.Text = "&Cancel"
   Me.CancelButton = buttonCancel
```

```
   ' Set the button size and location using
   ' the Bounds property.
   Dim buttonHelp As New Button()
   buttonHelp.Bounds = New Rectangle(10, 10, 75, 25)
   ' Set the Text property of the button.
   buttonHelp.Text = "&Help"

   ' Add the buttons to the form.
   Me.Controls.AddRange(New Control() {buttonOK, buttonCancel, ↵
buttonHelp})
End Sub
```

[C#]
```
// Create three buttons and place them on a form using
// several size and location related properties.
private void AddOKCancelButtons()
{
   // Set the button size and location using
   // the Size and Location properties.
   Button buttonOK = new Button();
   buttonOK.Location = new Point(136,248);
   buttonOK.Size = new Size(75,25);
   // Set the Text property and make the
   // button the form's default button.
   buttonOK.Text = "&OK";
   this.AcceptButton = buttonOK;

   // Set the button size and location using the Top,
   // Left, Width, and Height properties.
   Button buttonCancel = new Button();
   buttonCancel.Top = buttonOK.Top;
   buttonCancel.Left = buttonOK.Right + 5;
   buttonCancel.Width = buttonOK.Width;
   buttonCancel.Height = buttonOK.Height;
   // Set the Text property and make the
   // button the form's cancel button.
   buttonCancel.Text = "&Cancel";
   this.CancelButton = buttonCancel;

   // Set the button size and location using
   // the Bounds property.
   Button buttonHelp = new Button();
   buttonHelp.Bounds = new Rectangle(10,10, 75, 25);
   // Set the Text property of the button.
   buttonHelp.Text = "&Help";

   // Add the buttons to the form.
   this.Controls.AddRange(new Control[] {buttonOK, buttonCancel, ↵
buttonHelp} );
}
```

[C++]
```
// Create three buttons and place them on a form using
// several size and location related properties.
void AddOKCancelButtons() {
   // Set the button size and location using
   // the Size and Location properties.
   Button* buttonOK = new Button();
   buttonOK->Location =  Point(136, 248);
   buttonOK->Size =  System::Drawing::Size(75, 25);
   // Set the Text property and make the
   // button the form's default button.
   buttonOK->Text = S"&OK";
   this->AcceptButton = buttonOK;

   // Set the button size and location using the Top,
   // Left, Width, and Height properties.
   Button* buttonCancel = new Button();
   buttonCancel->Top = buttonOK->Top;
   buttonCancel->Left = buttonOK->Right + 5;
   buttonCancel->Width = buttonOK->Width;
   buttonCancel->Height = buttonOK->Height;
   // Set the Text property and make the
   // button the form's cancel button.
   buttonCancel->Text = S"&Cancel";
   this->CancelButton = buttonCancel;

   // Set the button size and location using
   // the Bounds property.
   Button* buttonHelp = new Button();
   buttonHelp->Bounds =  Rectangle(10, 10, 75, 25);
   // Set the Text property of the button.
   buttonHelp->Text = S"&Help";

   // Add the buttons to the form.

   Control* temp1 [] = {buttonOK, buttonCancel, buttonHelp};
   this->Controls->AddRange(temp1);
}
```

Requirements

Platforms: Windows 98, Windows NT 4.0, Windows Millennium Edition, Windows 2000, Windows XP Home Edition, Windows XP Professional, Windows Server 2003 family, .NET Compact Framework - Windows CE .NET

Control.CanFocus Property

Gets a value indicating whether the control can receive focus.

[Visual Basic]
```
Public ReadOnly Property CanFocus As Boolean
```
[C#]
```
public bool CanFocus {get;}
```
[C++]
```
public: __property bool get_CanFocus();
```
[JScript]
```
public function get CanFocus() : Boolean;
```

Property Value

true if the control can receive focus; otherwise, **false**.

Remarks

In order for a control to receive input focus, the control must have a handle assigned to it, and the **Visible** and **Enabled** properties must both be set to **true**.

Example

[Visual Basic, C#, C++] The following example sets focus to the specified **Control**, if it can receive focus.

[Visual Basic]
```
Public Sub ControlSetFocus(control As Control)
   ' Set focus to the control, if it can receive focus.
   If control.CanFocus Then
      control.Focus()
   End If
End Sub
```

[C#]
```
public void ControlSetFocus(Control control)
{
   // Set focus to the control, if it can receive focus.
   if(control.CanFocus)
   {
      control.Focus();
   }
}
```

[C++]
```
public:
   void ControlSetFocus(Control* control) {
      // Set focus to the control, if it can receive focus.
      if (control->CanFocus) {
         control->Focus();
      }
   }
```

Requirements

Platforms: Windows 98, Windows NT 4.0, Windows Millennium Edition, Windows 2000, Windows XP Home Edition, Windows XP Professional, Windows Server 2003 family

Control.CanSelect Property

Gets a value indicating whether the control can be selected.

[Visual Basic]
```
Public ReadOnly Property CanSelect As Boolean
```
[C#]
```
public bool CanSelect {get;}
```
[C++]
```
public: __property bool get_CanSelect();
```
[JScript]
```
public function get CanSelect() : Boolean;
```

Property Value

true if the control can be selected; otherwise, **false**.

Remarks

This property returns **true** if the control has **ControlStyles.Selectable** set to **true**, is contained in another control, and all its parent controls are both visible and enabled.

The Windows Forms controls in the following list are not selectable and will return a value of **false** for the **CanSelect** property. Controls derived from these controls are also not selectable.

- **Panel**
- **GroupBox**
- **PictureBox**
- **ProgressBar**
- **Splitter**
- **Label**
- **LinkLabel** (when there is no link present in the control)

Example

[Visual Basic, C#, C++] The following example selects the specified **Control**, if it is selectable.

[Visual Basic]
```
Public Sub ControlSelect(control As Control)
   ' Select the control, if it can be selected.
   If control.CanSelect Then
      control.Select()
   End If
End Sub
```

[C#]
```
public void ControlSelect(Control control)
{
   // Select the control, if it can be selected.
   if(control.CanSelect)
   {
      control.Select();
   }
}
```

[C++]
```
public:
   void ControlSelect(Control* control) {
      // Select the control, if it can be selected.
      if (control->CanSelect) {
         control->Select();
      }
   }
```

Requirements

Platforms: Windows 98, Windows NT 4.0, Windows Millennium Edition, Windows 2000, Windows XP Home Edition, Windows XP Professional, Windows Server 2003 family

Control.Capture Property

Gets or sets a value indicating whether the control has captured the mouse.

[Visual Basic]
```
Public Property Capture As Boolean
```
[C#]
```
public bool Capture {get; set;}
```
[C++]
```
public: __property bool get_Capture();
public: __property void set_Capture(bool);
```
[JScript]
```
public function get Capture() : Boolean;
public function set Capture(Boolean);
```

Property Value

true if the control has captured the mouse; otherwise, **false**.

Remarks

When a control has captured the mouse, it receives mouse input whether or not the cursor is within its borders. The mouse is typically only captured during drag operations.

Only the foreground window can capture the mouse. When a background window attempts to do so, the window receives messages only for mouse events that occur when the mouse cursor is within the visible portion of the window. Also, even if the foreground window has captured the mouse, the user can still click another window, bringing it to the foreground.

When the mouse is captured, shortcut keys do not work.

Requirements

Platforms: Windows 98, Windows NT 4.0, Windows Millennium Edition, Windows 2000, Windows XP Home Edition, Windows XP Professional, Windows Server 2003 family, .NET Compact Framework - Windows CE .NET

.NET Framework Security:

- **UIPermission** for all windows to set this property value. Associated enumeration: **UIPermissionWindow.AllWindows**

Control.CausesValidation Property

Gets or sets a value indicating whether the control causes validation to be performed on any controls that require validation when it receives focus.

[Visual Basic]
```
Public Property CausesValidation As Boolean
```
[C#]
```
public bool CausesValidation {get; set;}
```
[C++]
```
public: __property bool get_CausesValidation();
public: __property void set_CausesValidation(bool);
```
[JScript]
```
public function get CausesValidation() : Boolean;
public function set CausesValidation(Boolean);
```

Property Value

true if the control causes validation to be performed on any controls requiring validation when it receives focus; otherwise, **false**. The default is **true**.

Remarks

If the **CausesValidation** property is set to **false**, the **Validating** and **Validated** events are suppressed.

The **CausesValidation** property value is typically set to **false** for controls such as a Help button.

Requirements

Platforms: Windows 98, Windows NT 4.0, Windows Millennium Edition, Windows 2000, Windows XP Home Edition, Windows XP Professional, Windows Server 2003 family

Control.ClientRectangle Property

Gets the rectangle that represents the client area of the control.

```
[Visual Basic]
Public ReadOnly Property ClientRectangle As Rectangle
[C#]
public Rectangle ClientRectangle {get;}
[C++]
public: __property Rectangle get_ClientRectangle();
[JScript]
public function get ClientRectangle() : Rectangle;
```

Property Value

A **Rectangle** that represents the client area of the control.

Remarks

The client area of a control is the bounds of the control, minus the nonclient elements such as scroll bars, borders, title bars, and menus.

Because client coordinates are relative to the upper-left corner of the client area of the control, the coordinates of the upper-left corner of the rectangle returned by this property are (0,0). You can use this property to obtain the size and coordinates of the client area of the control for tasks such as drawing on the surface of the control.

Example

[Visual Basic, C#] The following example enables auto-scrolling for a form, resizes the form, and ensures that a button remains visible after the form is resized. This example assumes that you have a **Form** with a **Button** named `button2` on it.

```
[Visual Basic]
Private Sub ResizeForm()
   ' Enable auto-scrolling for the form.
   Me.AutoScroll = True

   ' Resize the form.
   Dim r As Rectangle = Me.ClientRectangle
   ' Subtract 100 pixels from each side of the Rectangle.
   r.Inflate(- 100, - 100)
   Me.Bounds = Me.RectangleToScreen(r)

   ' Make sure button2 is visible.
   Me.ScrollControlIntoView(button2)
End Sub
```

```
[C#]
private void ResizeForm()
{
   // Enable auto-scrolling for the form.
   this.AutoScroll = true;

   // Resize the form.
   Rectangle r = this.ClientRectangle;
   // Subtract 100 pixels from each side of the Rectangle.
   r.Inflate(-100, -100);
   this.Bounds = this.RectangleToScreen(r);

   // Make sure button2 is visible.
   this.ScrollControlIntoView(button2);
}
```

Requirements

Platforms: Windows 98, Windows NT 4.0, Windows Millennium Edition, Windows 2000, Windows XP Home Edition, Windows XP Professional, Windows Server 2003 family, .NET Compact Framework - Windows CE .NET

Control.ClientSize Property

Gets or sets the height and width of the client area of the control.

```
[Visual Basic]
Public Property ClientSize As Size
[C#]
public Size ClientSize {get; set;}
[C++]
public: __property Size get_ClientSize();
public: __property void set_ClientSize(Size);
[JScript]
public function get ClientSize() : Size;
public function set ClientSize(Size);
```

Property Value

A **Size** that represents the dimensions of the client area of the control.

Remarks

The client area of a control is the bounds of the control, minus the nonclient elements such as scroll bars, borders, title bars, and menus. The **SetClientSizeCore** method is called to set the **ClientSize** property. The **ClientSize** property is not always changed through its **set** method so you should override the **SetClientSizeCore** method to ensure that your code is executed when the **ClientSize** property is set.

The **Size.Width** and **Size.Height** properties represent the width and height of the client area of the control. You can use this property to obtain the size of the client area of the control for tasks such as drawing on the surface of the control.

Example

[Visual Basic, C#] The following example resizes the specified control so the control will accommodate its formatted text. The formatted text is the **Text** property with the control's assigned **Font** applied to the text. The `AutoSizeControl` method in this example also has a `textPadding` parameter that represents the padding to apply to all edges of the control. To make the padding appear equal, align the text with the **ContentAlignment.MiddleCenter** value, if your control supports it.

[Visual Basic]
```
Private Sub AutoSizeControl(control As Control, textPadding As Integer)
   ' Create a Graphics object for the Control.
   Dim g As Graphics = control.CreateGraphics()

   ' Get the Size needed to accommodate the formatted Text.
   Dim preferredSize As Size = g.MeasureString( _
     control.Text, control.Font).ToSize()

   ' Pad the text and resize the control.
   control.ClientSize = New Size( _
     preferredSize.Width + textPadding * 2, _
     preferredSize.Height + textPadding * 2)

   ' Clean up the Graphics object.
   g.Dispose()
End Sub
```

[C#]
```
private void AutoSizeControl(Control control, int textPadding)
{
   // Create a Graphics object for the Control.
   Graphics g = control.CreateGraphics();

   // Get the Size needed to accommodate the formatted Text.
   Size preferredSize = g.MeasureString(
      control.Text, control.Font).ToSize();

   // Pad the text and resize the control.
   control.ClientSize = new Size(
      preferredSize.Width + (textPadding * 2),
      preferredSize.Height+(textPadding * 2) );

   // Clean up the Graphics object.
   g.Dispose();
}
```

Requirements

Platforms: Windows 98, Windows NT 4.0, Windows Millennium Edition, Windows 2000, Windows XP Home Edition, Windows XP Professional, Windows Server 2003 family, .NET Compact Framework - Windows CE .NET

Control.CompanyName Property

Gets the name of the company or creator of the application containing the control.

[Visual Basic]
```
Public ReadOnly Property CompanyName As String
```
[C#]
```
public string CompanyName {get;}
```
[C++]
```
public: __property String* get_CompanyName();
```
[JScript]
```
public function get CompanyName() : String;
```

Property Value

The company name or creator of the application containing the control.

Remarks

The **CompanyName** property is a read-only property. In order to change the value of this property, set the **Company** property value of the **AssemblyCompanyAttribute**. The following line of C# code sets the **CompanyName** property.

[C#]
```
[assembly: AssemblyCompany("Microsoft")]
```

Note It is strongly recommended that you provide the company name, product name, and product version. Providing this information enables the use of Windows Forms features such as **Application.UserAppDataPath** that make it easier to write applications that comply with the "Certified for Windows" program. For more information on the Certified for Windows program, see http://msdn.microsoft.com/certification.

Example

[Visual Basic, C#, C++] The following example displays information about the application in a **Label** contained by a **Form**. This code assumes the **CompanyName**, **ProductName** and **ProductVersion** have been set.

[Visual Basic]
```
Private Sub AboutDialog_Load(sender As Object, e As EventArgs)        ↵
 Handles MyBase.Load
    ' Display the application information in the label.
   Me.labelVersionInfo.Text = _
      Me.CompanyName + "  " + _
      Me.ProductName + "  Version: " + _
      Me.ProductVersion
   End Sub
```

[C#]
```
private void AboutDialog_Load(object sender, EventArgs e)
{
   // Display the application information in the label.
   this.labelVersionInfo.Text =
      this.CompanyName + "  " +
      this.ProductName + "  Version: " +
      this.ProductVersion;
}
```

[C++]
```
void AboutDialog_Load(Object* sender, EventArgs* e) {
   // Display the application information in the label.
   this->labelVersionInfo->Text =
      String::Format( "{0} {1} Version: {2}", this->CompanyName,        ↵
 this->ProductName, this->ProductVersion );
}
```

Requirements

Platforms: Windows 98, Windows NT 4.0, Windows Millennium Edition, Windows 2000, Windows XP Home Edition, Windows XP Professional, Windows Server 2003 family

Control.ContainsFocus Property

Gets a value indicating whether the control, or one of its child controls, currently has the input focus.

[Visual Basic]
```
Public ReadOnly Property ContainsFocus As Boolean
```
[C#]
```
public bool ContainsFocus {get;}
```
[C++]
```
public: __property bool get_ContainsFocus();
```
[JScript]
```
public function get ContainsFocus() : Boolean;
```

Property Value

true if the control or one of its child controls currently has the input focus; otherwise, **false**.

Remarks

You can use this property to determine whether a control or any of the controls contained within it has the input focus. To determine whether the control has focus, regardless of whether any of its child controls have focus, use the **Focused** property. To give a control the input focus, use the **Focus** or **Select** methods.

Requirements

Platforms: Windows 98, Windows NT 4.0, Windows Millennium Edition, Windows 2000, Windows XP Home Edition, Windows XP Professional, Windows Server 2003 family

Control.ContextMenu Property

Gets or sets the shortcut menu associated with the control.

[Visual Basic]
```
Public Overridable Property ContextMenu As ContextMenu
```
[C#]
```
public virtual ContextMenu ContextMenu {get; set;}
```
[C++]
```
public: __property virtual ContextMenu* get_ContextMenu();
public: __property virtual void set_ContextMenu(ContextMenu*);
```
[JScript]
```
public function get ContextMenu() : ContextMenu;
public function set ContextMenu(ContextMenu);
```

Property Value

A **ContextMenu** that represents the shortcut menu associated with the control.

Remarks

A shortcut menu is also known as a context menu. Shortcut menus are used to give context-specific menu options to users when they right-click on the control.

Notes to Inheritors: When overriding the **ContextMenu** property in a derived class, use the base class's **ContextMenu** property to extend the base implementation. Otherwise, you must provide all the implementation. You are not required to override both the **get** and **set** accessors of the **ContextMenu** property; you can override only one if needed.

Example

[Visual Basic, C#, C++] The following example displays the **ContextMenu** assigned to a **TreeView** when the right mouse button is clicked and released. This code assumes you have a **Form** with a **TreeView** on it. It is also assumed that the **TreeView** has a **ContextMenu** assigned to its **ContextMenu** property.

[Visual Basic]
```
Private Sub treeView1_MouseUp(sender As Object, _
  e As MouseEventArgs) Handles treeView1.MouseUp
    ' If the right mouse button was clicked and released,
    ' display the context menu assigned to the TreeView.
    If e.Button = MouseButtons.Right Then
       treeView1.ContextMenu.Show(treeView1, New Point(e.X, e.Y))
    End If
End Sub
```

[C#]
```
private void treeView1_MouseUp(object sender, MouseEventArgs e)
{
   // If the right mouse button was clicked and released,
   // display the context menu assigned to the TreeView.
   if(e.Button == MouseButtons.Right)
   {
      treeView1.ContextMenu.Show(treeView1, new Point(e.X, e.Y) );
   }
}
```

[C++]
```
private:
   void treeView1_MouseUp(Object* sender, MouseEventArgs* e) {
      // If the right mouse button was clicked and released,
      // display the context menu assigned to the TreeView.
      if (e->Button == MouseButtons::Right) {
         treeView1->ContextMenu->Show(treeView1, Point(e->X, e->Y));
      }
   }
```

Requirements

Platforms: Windows 98, Windows NT 4.0, Windows Millennium Edition, Windows 2000, Windows XP Home Edition, Windows XP Professional, Windows Server 2003 family, .NET Compact Framework - Windows CE .NET

Control.Controls Property

Gets the collection of controls contained within the control.

[Visual Basic]
```
Public ReadOnly Property Controls As Control.ControlCollection
```
[C#]
```
public Control.ControlCollection Controls {get;}
```
[C++]
```
public: __property Control.ControlCollection* get_Controls();
```
[JScript]
```
public function get Controls() : Control.ControlCollection;
```

Property Value

A **Control.ControlCollection** representing the collection of controls contained within the control.

Remarks

A **Control** can act as a parent to a collection of controls. For example, when several controls are added to a **Form**, each of the controls is a member of the **Control.ControlCollection** object assigned to the **Controls** property of the form, which is derived from the **Control** class.

You can manipulate the controls in the **Control.ControlCollection** object assigned to the **Controls** property by using the methods available in the **Control.ControlCollection** class.

When adding several controls to a parent control, it is recommended that you call the **SuspendLayout** method before initializing the controls to be added. After adding the controls to the parent control, call the **ResumeLayout** method. Doing so will increase the performance of applications with many controls.

Example

[Visual Basic, C#, C++] The following example removes a **Control** from the **Control.ControlCollection** of the derived class **Panel** if it is a member of the collection. The example assumes you have created a **Panel**, a **Button**, and at least one **RadioButton** control on a **Form**. The **RadioButton** control(s) are added to the **Panel** control, and the **Panel** control added to the **Form**. When the button is clicked, the radio button named `radioButton2` is removed from the **Control.ControlCollection**.

[Visual Basic]
```
' Remove the RadioButton control if it exists.
Private Sub RemoveButton_Click(ByVal sender As System.Object, _
    ByVal e As System.EventArgs) Handles RemoveButton.Click
    If Panel1.Controls.Contains(RadioAddRangeButton) Then
        Panel1.Controls.Remove(RadioAddRangeButton)
    End If
End Sub
```

[C#]
```
// Remove the RadioButton control if it exists.
private void removeButton_Click(object sender, System.EventArgs e)
{
   if(panel1.Controls.Contains(removeButton))
   {
      panel1.Controls.Remove(removeButton);
   }
}
```

[C++]
```
// Remove the RadioButton control if it exists.
private:
void removeButton_Click(Object* sender, System::EventArgs* e) {
    if (panel1->Controls->Contains(removeButton)) {
        panel1->Controls->Remove(removeButton);
    }
}
```

Requirements

Platforms: Windows 98, Windows NT 4.0, Windows Millennium Edition, Windows 2000, Windows XP Home Edition, Windows XP Professional, Windows Server 2003 family, .NET Compact Framework - Windows CE .NET

Control.Created Property

Gets a value indicating whether the control has been created.

[Visual Basic]
```
Public ReadOnly Property Created As Boolean
```
[C#]
```
public bool Created {get;}
```
[C++]
```
public: __property bool get_Created();
```
[JScript]
```
public function get Created() : Boolean;
```

Property Value

true if the control has been created; otherwise, **false**.

Remarks

The **Created** property returns **true** if the **Control** was successfully created even though the control's handle might not have been created or recreated yet.

Requirements

Platforms: Windows 98, Windows NT 4.0, Windows Millennium Edition, Windows 2000, Windows XP Home Edition, Windows XP Professional, Windows Server 2003 family

Control.CreateParams Property

Gets the required creation parameters when the control handle is created.

[Visual Basic]
```
Protected Overridable ReadOnly Property CreateParams As _
   CreateParams
```
[C#]
```
protected virtual CreateParams CreateParams {get;}
```
[C++]
```
protected: __property virtual CreateParams* get_CreateParams();
```
[JScript]
```
protected function get CreateParams() : CreateParams;
```

Property Value

A **CreateParams** object that contains the required creation parameters when the handle to the control is created.

Remarks

The **CreateParams** property should not be overridden and used to adjust the properties of your derived control. Properties such as the **CreateParams.Caption**, **CreateParams.Width**, and **CreateParams.Height** should be set by the corresponding properties in your control such as **Control.Text**, **Control.Width** and **Control.Height**. The **CreateParams** object should only be extended when you are wrapping a standard Windows control class or to set styles not provided by the Windows Forms namespace. For more information about creating control parameters, see the **CreateWindow** and **CreateWindowEx** functions and the **CREATESTRUCT** structure documentation in the Windows Platform SDK reference located in the MSDN Library.

Notes to Inheritors: When overriding the **CreateParams** property in a derived class, use the base class's **CreateParams** property to extend the base implementation. Otherwise, you must provide all the implementation.

Requirements

Platforms: Windows 98, Windows NT 4.0, Windows Millennium Edition, Windows 2000, Windows XP Home Edition, Windows XP Professional, Windows Server 2003 family

.NET Framework Security:

- **SecurityPermission** for inheriting classes to call unmanaged code when getting the property value. Associated enumeration: **SecurityPermissionFlag.UnmanagedCode**
- **SecurityPermission** for the immediate caller to call unmanaged code when getting the property value. Associated enumeration: **SecurityPermissionFlag.UnmanagedCode**

Control.Cursor Property

Gets or sets the cursor that is displayed when the mouse pointer is over the control.

[Visual Basic]
```
Public Overridable Property Cursor As Cursor
```
[C#]
```
public virtual Cursor Cursor {get; set;}
```
[C++]
```
public: __property virtual Cursor* get_Cursor();
public: __property virtual void set_Cursor(Cursor*);
```
[JScript]
```
public function get Cursor() : Cursor;
public function set Cursor(Cursor);
```

Property Value

A **Cursor** object that represents the cursor to display when the mouse pointer is over the control.

Remarks

Assign a **Cursor** to the **Cursor** property of the control to change the cursor displayed when the mouse pointer is over the control. To temporarily change the mouse cursor for all controls on your application set the **Cursor.Current** property. Typically you would set the **Cursor.Current** property to a wait cursor when populating a **ComboBox** or saving or loading a file.

The **Cursor** property is an ambient property. An ambient property is a control property that, if not set, is retrieved from the parent control. For example, a **Button** will have the same **BackColor** as its parent **Form** by default. For more information about ambient properties, see the **AmbientProperties** class or the **Control** class overview.

Notes to Inheritors: When overriding the **Cursor** property in a derived class, use the base class's **Cursor** property to extend the base implementation. Otherwise, you must provide all the implementation. You are not required to override both the **get** and **set** methods of the **Cursor** property; you can override only one if needed.

Example

[Visual Basic, C#, C++] The following example fills a **ComboBox** with the user's available logical drives. The example also sets the combo box's **Cursor** property so the **Cursors.Hand** cursor is displayed when the mouse pointer is over the drop-down button. This code assumes you have a **Form** with a **ComboBox** on it.

[Visual Basic]
```
Private Sub Form1_Load(sender As Object, _
  e As EventArgs) Handles MyBase.Load
   ' Display the hand cursor when the mouse pointer
   ' is over the combo box drop-down button.
   comboBox1.Cursor = Cursors.Hand

   ' Fill the combo box with all the logical
   ' drives available to the user.
   Try
      Dim logicalDrive As String
      For Each logicalDrive In  Environment.GetLogicalDrives()
         comboBox1.Items.Add(logicalDrive)
      Next logicalDrive
   Catch ex As Exception
      MessageBox.Show(ex.Message)
   End Try
End Sub
```

[C#]
```
private void Form1_Load(object sender, EventArgs e)
{
   // Display the hand cursor when the mouse pointer
   // is over the combo box drop-down button.
   comboBox1.Cursor = Cursors.Hand;

   // Fill the combo box with all the logical
   // drives available to the user.
   try
   {
      foreach(string logicalDrive in Environment.GetLogicalDrives() )
      {
         comboBox1.Items.Add(logicalDrive);
      }
   }
   catch(Exception ex)
   {
      MessageBox.Show(ex.Message);
   }
}
```

[C++]
```
private:
   void Form1_Load(Object* sender, EventArgs* e) {
      // Display the hand cursor when the mouse pointer
      // is over the combo box drop-down button.
      comboBox1->Cursor = Cursors::Hand;

      // Fill the combo box with all the logical
      // drives available to the user.
      try {
         IEnumerator* myEnum =                                          ↵
Environment::GetLogicalDrives()->GetEnumerator();
         while (myEnum->MoveNext()) {
            String* logicalDrive = __try_cast<String*>                  ↵
(myEnum->Current);

            comboBox1->Items->Add(logicalDrive);
         }
      } catch (Exception* ex) {
         MessageBox::Show(ex->Message);
      }
   }
```

Requirements

Platforms: Windows 98, Windows NT 4.0, Windows Millennium Edition, Windows 2000, Windows XP Home Edition, Windows XP Professional, Windows Server 2003 family

.NET Framework Security:

- **UIPermission** for safe subwindows to set this property value. Associated enumeration: **UIPermissionWindow.SafeSubWindows**

Control.DataBindings Property

Gets the data bindings for the control.

[Visual Basic]
```
Public ReadOnly Property DataBindings As ControlBindingsCollection
```
[C#]
```
public ControlBindingsCollection DataBindings {get;}
```
[C++]
```
public: __property ControlBindingsCollection* get_DataBindings();
```
[JScript]
```
public function get DataBindings() : ControlBindingsCollection;
```

Property Value

A **ControlBindingsCollection** that contains the **Binding** objects for the control.

Remarks

Use the **DataBindings** property to access the **ControlBindingsCollection**. By adding **Binding** objects to the collection, you can bind any property of a control to the property of an object.

Example

[Visual Basic, C#, JScript] The following example adds **Binding** objects to the **ControlBindingsCollection** of five controls: four **TextBox** controls and a **DateTimePicker** control. The **ControlBindingsCollection** is accessed through the **DataBindings** property of the **Control** class.

[Visual Basic]
```
Protected Sub BindControls()
    ' Create two Binding objects for the first two TextBox
    ' controls. The data-bound property for both controls
    ' is the Text property. The data source is a DataSet
    ' (ds). The data member is specified by a navigation
```

```
    ' path in the form : TableName.ColumnName.
    textBox1.DataBindings.Add _
       (New Binding("Text", ds, "customers.custName"))
    textBox2.DataBindings.Add _
       (New Binding("Text", ds, "customers.custID"))

    ' Bind the DateTimePicker control by adding a new Binding.
    ' The data member of the DateTimePicker is specified by a
    ' navigation path in the form: TableName.RelationName.ColumnName.
    DateTimePicker1.DataBindings.Add _
       (New Binding("Value", ds, "customers.CustToOrders.OrderDate"))

    ' Create a new Binding using the DataSet and a
    ' navigation path(TableName.RelationName.ColumnName).
    ' Add event delegates for the Parse and Format events to
    ' the Binding object, and add the object to the third
    ' TextBox control's BindingsCollection. The delegates
    ' must be added before adding the Binding to the
    ' collection; otherwise, no formatting occurs until
    ' the Current object of the BindingManagerBase for
    ' the data source changes.
    Dim b As New Binding("Text", ds,                              ↵
"customers.custToOrders.OrderAmount")
    AddHandler b.Parse, AddressOf CurrencyStringToDecimal
    AddHandler b.Format, AddressOf DecimalToCurrencyString
    textBox3.DataBindings.Add(b)

    ' Bind the fourth TextBox to the Value of the
    ' DateTimePicker control. This demonstrates how one control
    ' can be bound to another.
    textBox4.DataBindings.Add("Text", DateTimePicker1, "Value")
    Dim bmText As BindingManagerBase =                            ↵
Me.BindingContext(DateTimePicker1)

    ' Print the Type of the BindingManagerBase, which is
    ' a PropertyManager because the data source
    ' returns only a single property value.
    Console.WriteLine(bmText.GetType().ToString())
    ' Print the count of managed objects, which is 1.
    Console.WriteLine(bmText.Count)

    ' Get the BindingManagerBase for the Customers table.
    bmCustomers = Me.BindingContext(ds, "Customers")
    ' Print the Type and count of the BindingManagerBase.
    ' Because the data source inherits from IBindingList,
    ' it is a RelatedCurrencyManager (derived from CurrencyManager).
    Console.WriteLine(bmCustomers.GetType().ToString())
    Console.WriteLine(bmCustomers.Count)

    ' Get the BindingManagerBase for the Orders of the current
    ' customer using a navigation path: TableName.RelationName.
    bmOrders = Me.BindingContext(ds, "customers.CustToOrders")
End Sub
```

[C#]

```
protected void BindControls()
{
   /* Create two Binding objects for the first two TextBox
   controls. The data-bound property for both controls
   is the Text property. The data source is a DataSet
   (ds). The data member is specified by a navigation
   path in the form : TableName.ColumnName. */
   textBox1.DataBindings.Add(new Binding
   ("Text", ds, "customers.custName"));
   textBox2.DataBindings.Add(new Binding
   ("Text", ds, "customers.custID"));

   /* Bind the DateTimePicker control by adding a new Binding.
   The data member of the DateTimePicker is specified by a
   navigation path in the form: TableName.RelationName.ColumnName. */
   DateTimePicker1.DataBindings.Add(new
   Binding("Value", ds, "customers.CustToOrders.OrderDate"));

   /* Create a new Binding using the DataSet and a
   navigation path(TableName.RelationName.ColumnName).
   Add event delegates for the Parse and Format events to
   the Binding object, and add the object to the third
   TextBox control's BindingsCollection. The delegates
   must be added before adding the Binding to the
   collection; otherwise, no formatting occurs until
   the Current object of the BindingManagerBase for
   the data source changes. */
   Binding b = new Binding
   ("Text", ds, "customers.custToOrders.OrderAmount");
   b.Parse += new ConvertEventHandler(CurrencyStringToDecimal);
   b.Format += new ConvertEventHandler(DecimalToCurrencyString);
   textBox3.DataBindings.Add(b);

   /*Bind the fourth TextBox to the Value of the
   DateTimePicker control. This demonstrates how one control
   can be bound to another.*/
   textBox4.DataBindings.Add("Text", DateTimePicker1,"Value");
   BindingManagerBase bmText = this.BindingContext[
   DateTimePicker1];

   /* Print the Type of the BindingManagerBase, which is
   a PropertyManager because the data source
   returns only a single property value. */
   Console.WriteLine(bmText.GetType().ToString());
   // Print the count of managed objects, which is 1.
   Console.WriteLine(bmText.Count);

   // Get the BindingManagerBase for the Customers table.
   bmCustomers = this.BindingContext [ds, "Customers"];
   /* Print the Type and count of the BindingManagerBase.
   Because the data source inherits from IBindingList,
   it is a RelatedCurrencyManager (derived from CurrencyManager). */
   Console.WriteLine(bmCustomers.GetType().ToString());
   Console.WriteLine(bmCustomers.Count);

   /* Get the BindingManagerBase for the Orders of the current
   customer using a navigation path: TableName.RelationName. */
   bmOrders = this.BindingContext[ds, "customers.CustToOrders"];
}
```

[JScript]

```
protected function BindControls()
{
   /* Create two Binding objects for the first two TextBox
   controls. The data-bound property for both controls
   is the Text property. The data source is a DataSet
   (ds). The data member is specified by a navigation
   path in the form : TableName.ColumnName. */
   textBox1.DataBindings.Add(new Binding
   ("Text", ds, "customers.custName"));
   textBox2.DataBindings.Add(new Binding
   ("Text", ds, "customers.custID"));

   /* Bind the DateTimePicker control by adding a new Binding.
   The data member of the DateTimePicker is specified by a
   navigation path in the form: TableName.RelationName.ColumnName. */
   DateTimePicker1.DataBindings.Add(new
   Binding("Value", ds, "customers.CustToOrders.OrderDate"));

   /* Create a new Binding import the DataSet and a
   navigation path(TableName.RelationName.ColumnName).
   Add event delegates for the Parse and Format events to
   the Binding object, and add the object to the third
   TextBox control's BindingsCollection. The delegates
   must be added before adding the Binding to the
   collection; otherwise, no formatting occurs until
   the Current object of the BindingManagerBase for
   the data source changes. */
   var b : Binding = new Binding
   ("Text", ds, "customers.custToOrders.OrderAmount");
   b.add_Parse(CurrencyStringToDecimal);
   b.add_Format(DecimalToCurrencyString);
   textBox3.DataBindings.Add(b);
```

```
    /*Bind the fourth TextBox to the Value of the
    DateTimePicker control. This demonstrates how one control
    can be bound to another.*/
    textBox4.DataBindings.Add("Text", DateTimePicker1,"Value");
    var bmText : BindingManagerBase = this.BindingContext[
    DateTimePicker1];

    /* Print the Type of the BindingManagerBase, which is
    a PropertyManager because the data source
    returns only a single property value. */
    Console.WriteLine(bmText.GetType().ToString());
    // Print the count of managed objects, which is 1.
    Console.WriteLine(bmText.Count);

    // Get the BindingManagerBase for the Customers table.
    bmCustomers = this.BindingContext [ds, "Customers"];
    /* Print the Type and count of the BindingManagerBase.
    Because the data source inherits from IBindingList,
    it is a RelatedCurrencyManager (derived from CurrencyManager). */
    Console.WriteLine(bmCustomers.GetType().ToString());
    Console.WriteLine(bmCustomers.Count);

    /* Get the BindingManagerBase for the Orders of the current
    customer import a navigation path: TableName.RelationName. */
    bmOrders = this.BindingContext[ds, "customers.CustToOrders"];
}
```

Requirements

Platforms: Windows 98, Windows NT 4.0, Windows Millennium Edition, Windows 2000, Windows XP Home Edition, Windows XP Professional, Windows Server 2003 family, .NET Compact Framework - Windows CE .NET

Control.DefaultBackColor Property

Gets the default background color of the control.

[Visual Basic]
```
Public Shared ReadOnly Property DefaultBackColor As Color
```
[C#]
```
public static Color DefaultBackColor {get;}
```
[C++]
```
public: __property static Color get_DefaultBackColor();
```
[JScript]
```
public static function get DefaultBackColor() : Color;
```

Property Value

The default background **Color** of the control. The default is **SystemColors.Control**.

Remarks

This is the default **BackColor** property value of a generic top-level control. Derived classes can have different defaults.

Requirements

Platforms: Windows 98, Windows NT 4.0, Windows Millennium Edition, Windows 2000, Windows XP Home Edition, Windows XP Professional, Windows Server 2003 family

Control.DefaultFont Property

Gets the default font of the control.

[Visual Basic]
```
Public Shared ReadOnly Property DefaultFont As Font
```
[C#]
```
public static Font DefaultFont {get;}
```
[C++]
```
public: __property static Font* get_DefaultFont();
```
[JScript]
```
public static function get DefaultFont() : Font;
```

Property Value

The default **Font** of the control. The default value is the **FontFamily.GenericSansSerif** font currently in use by the user's operating system.

Exceptions

Exception Type	Condition
ArgumentException	The default font or the regional alternative fonts are not installed on the client computer.

Remarks

If no **FontFamily.GenericSansSerif** fonts are installed on the user's computer, the DEFAULT_GUI_FONT is used. The DEFAULT_-GUI_FONT is the default font used by user interface objects such as menus and dialog boxes.

If no font has been explicitly set for the control, this property returns the font for the parent control. If no font has been explicitly set for the control or its parent control, this property returns the default graphical user interface (GUI) font

Derived classes can have a different default font.

Requirements

Platforms: Windows 98, Windows NT 4.0, Windows Millennium Edition, Windows 2000, Windows XP Home Edition, Windows XP Professional, Windows Server 2003 family

Control.DefaultForeColor Property

Gets the default foreground color of the control.

[Visual Basic]
```
Public Shared ReadOnly Property DefaultForeColor As Color
```
[C#]
```
public static Color DefaultForeColor {get;}
```
[C++]
```
public: __property static Color get_DefaultForeColor();
```
[JScript]
```
public static function get DefaultForeColor() : Color;
```

Property Value

The default foreground **Color** of the control. The default is **SystemColors.ControlText**.

Remarks

This is the default **ForeColor** property value of a nonparented control. Derived classes can have different defaults.

Requirements

Platforms: Windows 98, Windows NT 4.0, Windows Millennium Edition, Windows 2000, Windows XP Home Edition, Windows XP Professional, Windows Server 2003 family

Control.DefaultImeMode Property

Gets the default Input Method Editor (IME) mode supported by the control.

[Visual Basic]
```
Protected Overridable ReadOnly Property DefaultImeMode As ImeMode
```
[C#]
```
protected virtual ImeMode DefaultImeMode {get;}
```
[C++]
```
protected: __property virtual ImeMode get_DefaultImeMode();
```
[JScript]
```
protected function get DefaultImeMode() : ImeMode;
```

Property Value

One of the **ImeMode** values.

Remarks

An input method editor (IME) is a program that allows users to enter complex characters and symbols, such as Japanese Kanji characters, by using a standard keyboard.

As implemented in the **Control** class, this property always returns the **ImeMode.Inherit** value. The **Inherit** value specifies that the IME mode is inherited from the parent control.

Notes to Inheritors: When overriding the **DefaultImeMode** property in a derived class, use the base class's **DefaultImeMode** property to extend the base implementation. Otherwise, you must provide all the implementation.

Example

[Visual Basic, C#, C++] The following example overrides the **DefaultImeMode** property to turn off the Input Method Editor.

[Visual Basic]
```
Protected Overrides ReadOnly Property DefaultImeMode() As ImeMode
   Get
      ' Disable the IME mode for the control.
      Return ImeMode.Off
   End Get
End Property
```

[C#]
```
protected override ImeMode DefaultImeMode
{
   get
   {
      // Disable the IME mode for the control.
      return ImeMode.Off;
   }
}
```

[C++]
```
protected:
   __property System::Windows::Forms::ImeMode get_DefaultImeMode() {

      // Disable the IME mode for the control.
      return ImeMode::Off;

   }
```

Requirements

Platforms: Windows 98, Windows NT 4.0, Windows Millennium Edition, Windows 2000, Windows XP Home Edition, Windows XP Professional, Windows Server 2003 family

Control.DefaultSize Property

Gets the default size of the control.

[Visual Basic]
```
Protected Overridable ReadOnly Property DefaultSize As Size
```
[C#]
```
protected virtual Size DefaultSize {get;}
```
[C++]
```
protected: __property virtual Size get_DefaultSize();
```
[JScript]
```
protected function get DefaultSize() : Size;
```

Property Value

The default **Size** of the control.

Remarks

The **DefaultSize** property represents the **Size** of the control when it is initially created. You can adjust the size of the control by setting its **Size** property value.

> **Note** In order to maintain better performance, you should not set the **Size** of a control in its constructor. The preferred method is to override the **DefaultSize** property.

Notes to Inheritors: When overriding the **DefaultSize** property in a derived class, it is preferable return a **Size** object with the desired dimensions rather than overriding all the implementation.

Example

[Visual Basic, C#, C++] The following example overrides the **DefaultSize** property, and makes the default size of the form 500 pixels square.

[Visual Basic]
```
Protected Overrides ReadOnly Property DefaultSize() As Size
   Get
      ' Set the default size of
      ' the form to 500 pixels square.
      Return New Size(500, 500)
   End Get
End Property
```

[C#]
```
protected override Size DefaultSize
{
   get
   {
      // Set the default size of
      // the form to 500 pixels square.
      return new Size(500,500);
   }
}
```

[C++]
```
protected:
   __property System::Drawing::Size get_DefaultSize() {

      // Set the default size of
      // the form to 500 pixels square.
      return System::Drawing::Size(500, 500);

   }
```

Requirements

Platforms: Windows 98, Windows NT 4.0, Windows Millennium Edition, Windows 2000, Windows XP Home Edition, Windows XP Professional, Windows Server 2003 family

Control.DisplayRectangle Property

Gets the rectangle that represents the display area of the control.

[Visual Basic]
```
Public Overridable ReadOnly Property DisplayRectangle As Rectangle
```
[C#]
```
public virtual Rectangle DisplayRectangle {get;}
```
[C++]
```
public: __property virtual Rectangle get_DisplayRectangle();
```
[JScript]
```
public function get DisplayRectangle() : Rectangle;
```

Property Value

A **Rectangle** that represents the display area of the control.

Remarks

The **DisplayRectangle** property returns the client rectangle of the display area of the control. For the base control class, this is equal to the client rectangle. However, inheriting controls might want to change this if their client area differs from their display area. The display rectangle is the smallest **Rectangle** that encloses a control and is used to lay out controls.

Notes to Inheritors: When overriding the **DisplayRectangle** property in a derived class, use the base class's **DisplayRectangle** property to extend the base implementation. Alternatively, you must provide all the implementation.

Requirements

Platforms: Windows 98, Windows NT 4.0, Windows Millennium Edition, Windows 2000, Windows XP Home Edition, Windows XP Professional, Windows Server 2003 family

Control.Disposing Property

Gets a value indicating whether the control is in the process of being disposed of.

[Visual Basic]
```
Public ReadOnly Property Disposing As Boolean
```
[C#]
```
public bool Disposing {get;}
```
[C++]
```
public: __property bool get_Disposing();
```
[JScript]
```
public function get Disposing() : Boolean;
```

Property Value

true if the control is in the process of being disposed of; otherwise, **false**.

Remarks

When this property returns **true**, the control is in the process of being disposed of. After the control is disposed of, it can no longer be referenced as a valid Windows control. Even though the instance of a control is disposed of, it is still maintained in memory until it is removed from memory through garbage collection. When a control is disposed of, you can not call its **RecreateHandle** method.

Requirements

Platforms: Windows 98, Windows NT 4.0, Windows Millennium Edition, Windows 2000, Windows XP Home Edition, Windows XP Professional, Windows Server 2003 family

Control.Dock Property

Gets or sets which edge of the parent container a control is docked to.

[Visual Basic]
```
Public Overridable Property Dock As DockStyle
```
[C#]
```
public virtual DockStyle Dock {get; set;}
```
[C++]
```
public: __property virtual DockStyle get_Dock();
public: __property virtual void set_Dock(DockStyle);
```
[JScript]
```
public function get Dock() : DockStyle;
public function set Dock(DockStyle);
```

Property Value

One of the **DockStyle** values. The default is **None**.

Exceptions

Exception Type	Condition
InvalidEnumArgument-Exception	The value assigned is not one of the **DockStyle** values.

Remarks

A control can be docked to one edge of its parent container or can be docked to all edges and fill the parent container. For example, if you set this property to **DockStyle.Left**, the left edge of the control will be docked to the left edge of its parent control. Additionally, the docked edge of the control is resized to match that of its container control. Controls are docked in order of their z-order.

Notes to Inheritors: When overriding the **Dock** property in a derived class, use the base class's **Dock** property to extend the base implementation. Otherwise, you must provide all the implementation. You are not required to override both the **get** and **set** methods of the **Dock** property; you can override only one if needed.

Example

[Visual Basic, C#, C++] The following example creates a **GroupBox** and sets some of its common properties. The example creates a **TextBox** and sets its **Location** within the group box. Next, it sets the **Text** property of the group box, and docks the group box to the top of the form. Lastly, it disables the group box by setting the **Enabled** property to **false**, which causes all controls contained within the group box to be disabled.

[Visual Basic]
```
' Add a GroupBox to a form and set some of its common properties.
Private Sub AddMyGroupBox()
   ' Create a GroupBox and add a TextBox to it.
   Dim groupBox1 As New GroupBox()
   Dim textBox1 As New TextBox()
   textBox1.Location = New Point(15, 15)
   groupBox1.Controls.Add(textBox1)

   ' Set the Text and Dock properties of the GroupBox.
   groupBox1.Text = "MyGroupBox"
   groupBox1.Dock = DockStyle.Top
```

```
    ' Disable the GroupBox (which disables all its child controls)
    groupBox1.Enabled = False

    ' Add the Groupbox to the form.
    Me.Controls.Add(groupBox1)
End Sub
```

[C#]
```
// Add a GroupBox to a form and set some of its common properties.
private void AddMyGroupBox()
{
    // Create a GroupBox and add a TextBox to it.
    GroupBox groupBox1 = new GroupBox();
    TextBox textBox1 = new TextBox();
    textBox1.Location = new Point(15, 15);
    groupBox1.Controls.Add(textBox1);

    // Set the Text and Dock properties of the GroupBox.
    groupBox1.Text = "MyGroupBox";
    groupBox1.Dock = DockStyle.Top;

    // Disable the GroupBox (which disables all its child controls)
    groupBox1.Enabled = false;

    // Add the Groupbox to the form.
    this.Controls.Add(groupBox1);
}
```

[C++]
```
// Add a GroupBox to a form and set some of its common properties.
private:
void AddMyGroupBox() {
    // Create a GroupBox and add a TextBox to it.
    GroupBox* groupBox1 = new GroupBox();
    TextBox* textBox1 = new TextBox();
    textBox1->Location =  Point(15, 15);
    groupBox1->Controls->Add(textBox1);

    // Set the Text and Dock properties of the GroupBox.
    groupBox1->Text = S"MyGroupBox";
    groupBox1->Dock = DockStyle::Top;

    // Disable the GroupBox (which disables all its child controls)
    groupBox1->Enabled = false;

    // Add the Groupbox to the form.
    this->Controls->Add(groupBox1);
}
```

Requirements

Platforms: Windows 98, Windows NT 4.0, Windows Millennium Edition, Windows 2000, Windows XP Home Edition, Windows XP Professional, Windows Server 2003 family

Control.Enabled Property

Gets or sets a value indicating whether the control can respond to user interaction.

[Visual Basic]
```
Public Property Enabled As Boolean
```
[C#]
```
public bool Enabled {get; set;}
```
[C++]
```
public: __property bool get_Enabled();
public: __property void set_Enabled(bool);
```
[JScript]
```
public function get Enabled() : Boolean;
public function set Enabled(Boolean);
```

Property Value

true if the control can respond to user interaction; otherwise, **false**. The default is **true**.

Remarks

The **Enabled** property allows controls to be enabled or disabled at run time. For example, you can disable controls that do not apply to the current state of the application. You can also disable a control to restrict its use. For example, a button can be disabled to prevent the user from clicking it. If a control is disabled, it cannot be selected.

When a container control has its enabled property set to **false**, all its contained controls are disabled, as well. For example, if the user clicks on any of the controls contained in a disabled **GroupBox** control, no events are raised.

> **Note** When a scrollable control is disabled, the scroll bars are also disabled. For example, a disabled multiline textbox is unable to scroll to display all the lines of text.

Example

[Visual Basic, C#, C++] The following example creates a **GroupBox** and sets some of its common properties. The example creates a **TextBox** and sets its **Location** within the group box. Next, it sets the **Text** property of the group box, and docks the group box to the top of the form. Lastly, it disables the group box by setting the **Enabled** property to **false**, which causes all controls contained within the group box to be disabled.

[Visual Basic]
```
' Add a GroupBox to a form and set some of its common properties.
Private Sub AddMyGroupBox()
    ' Create a GroupBox and add a TextBox to it.
    Dim groupBox1 As New GroupBox()
    Dim textBox1 As New TextBox()
    textBox1.Location = New Point(15, 15)
    groupBox1.Controls.Add(textBox1)

    ' Set the Text and Dock properties of the GroupBox.
    groupBox1.Text = "MyGroupBox"
    groupBox1.Dock = DockStyle.Top

    ' Disable the GroupBox (which disables all its child controls)
    groupBox1.Enabled = False

    ' Add the Groupbox to the form.
    Me.Controls.Add(groupBox1)
End Sub
```

[C#]
```
// Add a GroupBox to a form and set some of its common properties.
private void AddMyGroupBox()
{
    // Create a GroupBox and add a TextBox to it.
    GroupBox groupBox1 = new GroupBox();
    TextBox textBox1 = new TextBox();
    textBox1.Location = new Point(15, 15);
    groupBox1.Controls.Add(textBox1);

    // Set the Text and Dock properties of the GroupBox.
    groupBox1.Text = "MyGroupBox";
    groupBox1.Dock = DockStyle.Top;

    // Disable the GroupBox (which disables all its child controls)
    groupBox1.Enabled = false;

    // Add the Groupbox to the form.
    this.Controls.Add(groupBox1);
}
```

[C++]
```
// Add a GroupBox to a form and set some of its common properties.
private:
void AddMyGroupBox() {
   // Create a GroupBox and add a TextBox to it.
   GroupBox* groupBox1 = new GroupBox();
   TextBox* textBox1 = new TextBox();
   textBox1->Location =  Point(15, 15);
   groupBox1->Controls->Add(textBox1);

   // Set the Text and Dock properties of the GroupBox.
   groupBox1->Text = S"MyGroupBox";
   groupBox1->Dock = DockStyle::Top;

   // Disable the GroupBox (which disables all its child controls)
   groupBox1->Enabled = false;

   // Add the Groupbox to the form.
   this->Controls->Add(groupBox1);
}
```

Requirements

Platforms: Windows 98, Windows NT 4.0, Windows Millennium Edition, Windows 2000, Windows XP Home Edition, Windows XP Professional, Windows Server 2003 family, .NET Compact Framework - Windows CE .NET

Control.Focused Property

Gets a value indicating whether the control has input focus.

[Visual Basic]
```
Public Overridable ReadOnly Property Focused As Boolean
```
[C#]
```
public virtual bool Focused {get;}
```
[C++]
```
public: __property virtual bool get_Focused();
```
[JScript]
```
public function get Focused() : Boolean;
```

Property Value

true if the control has focus; otherwise, **false**.

Remarks

Notes to Inheritors: When overriding the **Focused** property in a derived class, use the base class's **Focused** property to extend the base implementation. Otherwise, you must provide all the implementation.

Example

[Visual Basic, C#, C++] The following example disables a MenuItem if a TextBox does not have focus. This example assumes you have a **Form** with a **TextBox** named `textBox1` and two **MenuItem** objects named `menuItemEdit` and `menuItemEditInsertCustomerInfo`.

[Visual Basic]
```
Private Sub menuItemEdit_Popup(sender As Object, _
  e As EventArgs) Handles menuItemEdit.Popup
    ' Disable the menu item if the text box does not have focus.
    Me.menuItemEditInsertCustomerInfo.Enabled = Me.textBox1.Focused
End Sub
```

[C#]
```
private void menuItemEdit_Popup(object sender, EventArgs e)
{
   // Disable the menu item if the text box does not have focus.
   this.menuItemEditInsertCustomerInfo.Enabled = this.textBox1.Focused;
}
```

[C++]
```
private:
    void menuItemEdit_Popup(Object* /*sender*/, EventArgs* /*e*/) {
        // Disable the menu item if the text box does not have focus.
        this->menuItemEditInsertCustomerInfo->Enabled = ↵
this->textBox1->Focused;
    }
```

Requirements

Platforms: Windows 98, Windows NT 4.0, Windows Millennium Edition, Windows 2000, Windows XP Home Edition, Windows XP Professional, Windows Server 2003 family, .NET Compact Framework - Windows CE .NET

Control.Font Property

Gets or sets the font of the text displayed by the control.

[Visual Basic]
```
Public Overridable Property Font As Font
```
[C#]
```
public virtual Font Font {get; set;}
```
[C++]
```
public: __property virtual Font* get_Font();
public: __property virtual void set_Font(Font*);
```
[JScript]
```
public function get Font() : Font;
public function set Font(Font);
```

Property Value

The **Font** object to apply to the text displayed by the control. The default is the value of the **DefaultFont** property.

Remarks

The **Font** property is an ambient property. An ambient property is a control property that, if not set, is retrieved from the parent control. For example, a **Button** will have the same **BackColor** as its parent **Form** by default. For more information about ambient properties, see the **AmbientProperties** class or the **Control** class overview.

Because the **Font** object is immutable (meaning that you cannot adjust any of it's properties), you can only assign the **Font** property a new **Font** object. However, you can base the new font on the existing font.

[Visual Basic, C#] The following is an example of how to adjust the existing font to make it bold:

[C#]
```
myControl.Font = new Font(myControl.Font,
   myControl.Font.Style | FontStyle.Bold);
```

[Visual Basic]

```
MyControl.Font = New Font(MyControl.Font, _
   MyControl.Font.Style Or FontStyle.Bold)
```

Notes to Inheritors: When overriding the **Font** property in a derived class, use the base class's **Font** property to extend the base implementation. Otherwise, you must provide all the implementation. You are not required to override both the **get** and **set** accessors of the **Font** property; you can override only one if needed.

Example

[Visual Basic, C#, C++] The following example displays a **FontDialog** to the user and changes the **Font** of a **DateTimePicker** control. This example assumes you have a **Form** with **Button** and a **DateTimePicker** on it.

[Visual Basic]
```
Private Sub myButton_Click(sender As Object, e As EventArgs)
   Dim myFontDialog As FontDialog
   myFontDialog = New FontDialog()

   If myFontDialog.ShowDialog() = DialogResult.OK Then
      ' Set the control's font.
      myDateTimePicker.Font = myFontDialog.Font
   End If
End Sub
```

[C#]
```
private void myButton_Click(object sender, EventArgs e)
{
   FontDialog myFontDialog = new FontDialog();
   if(myFontDialog.ShowDialog() == DialogResult.OK)
   {
      // Set the control's font.
      myDateTimePicker.Font = myFontDialog.Font;
   }
}
```

[C++]
```
private:
    void myButton_Click(Object* sender, EventArgs* e) {
        FontDialog* myFontDialog = new FontDialog();
        if (myFontDialog->ShowDialog() == DialogResult::OK) {
            // Set the control's font.
            myDateTimePicker->Font = myFontDialog->Font;
        }
    }
```

Requirements

Platforms: Windows 98, Windows NT 4.0, Windows Millennium Edition, Windows 2000, Windows XP Home Edition, Windows XP Professional, Windows Server 2003 family, .NET Compact Framework - Windows CE .NET

Control.FontHeight Property

Gets or sets the height of the font of the control.

[Visual Basic]
```
Protected Property FontHeight As Integer
```
[C#]
```
protected int FontHeight {get; set;}
```
[C++]
```
protected: __property int get_FontHeight();
protected: __property void set_FontHeight(int);
```
[JScript]
```
protected function get FontHeight() : int;
protected function set FontHeight(int);
```

Property Value

The height of the **Font** of the control in pixels.

Remarks

Note The **FontHeight** property should not be set to any value other than the control's **Font.Height** value, or -1. Setting **FontHeight** to -1 has the effect of clearing the cached height value, and the value is recalculated the next time the property is referenced.

Requirements

Platforms: Windows 98, Windows NT 4.0, Windows Millennium Edition, Windows 2000, Windows XP Home Edition, Windows XP Professional, Windows Server 2003 family

Control.ForeColor Property

Gets or sets the foreground color of the control.

[Visual Basic]
```
Public Overridable Property ForeColor As Color
```
[C#]
```
public virtual Color ForeColor {get; set;}
```
[C++]
```
public: __property virtual Color get_ForeColor();
public: __property virtual void set_ForeColor(Color);
```
[JScript]
```
public function get ForeColor() : Color;
public function set ForeColor(Color);
```

Property Value

The foreground **Color** of the control. The default is the value of the **DefaultForeColor** property.

Remarks

The **ForeColor** property is an ambient property. An ambient property is a control property that, if not set, is retrieved from the parent control. For example, a **Button** will have the same **BackColor** as its parent **Form** by default. For more information about ambient properties, see the **AmbientProperties** class or the **Control** class overview.

Notes to Inheritors: When overriding the **ForeColor** property in a derived class, use the base class's **ForeColor** property to extend the base implementation. Otherwise, you must provide all the implementation. You are not required to override both the **get** and **set** accessors of the **ForeColor** property; you can override only one if needed.

Example

[Visual Basic, C#, C++] The following example sets the **BackColor** and **ForeColor** of the controls to the default system colors. The code recursively calls itself if the control has any child controls. This code example assumes you have a **Form** with at least one child control; however, a child container control, like a **Panel** or **GroupBox**, with its own child control(s) would better demonstrate the recursion.

[Visual Basic]
```
' Reset all the controls to the user's default Control color.
Private Sub ResetAllControlsBackColor(control As Control)
   control.BackColor = SystemColors.Control
   control.ForeColor = SystemColors.ControlText
   If Me.HasChildren Then
      ' Recursively call this method for each child control.
      Dim childControl As Control
      For Each childControl In  control.Controls
         ResetAllControlsBackColor(childControl)
      Next childControl
   End If
End Sub
```

[C#]
```
// Reset all the controls to the user's default Control color.
private void ResetAllControlsBackColor(Control control)
{
   control.BackColor = SystemColors.Control;
   control.ForeColor = SystemColors.ControlText;
   if(this.HasChildren)
   {
      // Recursively call this method for each child control.
      foreach(Control childControl in control.Controls)
      {
         ResetAllControlsBackColor(childControl);
      }
   }
}
```

[C++]
```
// Reset all the controls to the user's default Control color.
private:
void ResetAllControlsBackColor(Control* control) {
   control->BackColor = SystemColors::Control;
   control->ForeColor = SystemColors::ControlText;
   if (this->HasChildren) {
      // Recursively call this method for each child control.
      IEnumerator* myEnum = control->Controls->GetEnumerator();
      while (myEnum->MoveNext()) {
         Control* childControl = __try_cast<Control*>(myEnum->Current);
         ResetAllControlsBackColor(childControl);
      }
   }
}
```

Requirements

Platforms: Windows 98, Windows NT 4.0, Windows Millennium Edition, Windows 2000, Windows XP Home Edition, Windows XP Professional, Windows Server 2003 family, .NET Compact Framework - Windows CE .NET

Control.Handle Property

Gets the window handle that the control is bound to.

[Visual Basic]
```
Public Overridable ReadOnly Property Handle As IntPtr  Implements _
   IWin32Window.Handle
```
[C#]
```
public virtual IntPtr Handle {get;}
```
[C++]
```
public: __property virtual IntPtr get_Handle();
```
[JScript]
```
public function get Handle() : IntPtr;
```

Property Value

An **IntPtr** that contains the window handle (HWND) of the control.

Implements

IWin32Window.Handle

Remarks

The value of the **Handle** property is a Windows HWND. If the handle has not yet been created, referencing this property will force the handle to be created.

Requirements

Platforms: Windows 98, Windows NT 4.0, Windows Millennium Edition, Windows 2000, Windows XP Home Edition, Windows XP Professional, Windows Server 2003 family

Control.HasChildren Property

Gets a value indicating whether the control contains one or more child controls.

[Visual Basic]
```
Public ReadOnly Property HasChildren As Boolean
```
[C#]
```
public bool HasChildren {get;}
```
[C++]
```
public: __property bool get_HasChildren();
```
[JScript]
```
public function get HasChildren() : Boolean;
```

Property Value

true if the control contains one or more child controls; otherwise, **false**.

Remarks

If the **Controls** collection has a **Count** greater than zero, the **HasChildren** property will return **true**. Accessing the **HasChildren** property does not force the creation of a **Control.ControlCollection** if the control has no children, so referencing this property can provide a performance benefit when walking a tree of controls.

Example

[Visual Basic, C#, C++] The following example sets the **BackColor** and **ForeColor** of the controls to the default system colors. The code recursively calls itself if the control has any child controls. This code example assumes you have a **Form** with at least one child control; however, a child container control, like a **Panel** or **GroupBox**, with its own child control(s) would better demonstrate the recursion.

[Visual Basic]
```
' Reset all the controls to the user's default Control color.
Private Sub ResetAllControlsBackColor(control As Control)
   control.BackColor = SystemColors.Control
   control.ForeColor = SystemColors.ControlText
   If Me.HasChildren Then
      ' Recursively call this method for each child control.
      Dim childControl As Control
      For Each childControl In  control.Controls
         ResetAllControlsBackColor(childControl)
      Next childControl
   End If
End Sub
```

[C#]
```
// Reset all the controls to the user's default Control color.
private void ResetAllControlsBackColor(Control control)
{
   control.BackColor = SystemColors.Control;
   control.ForeColor = SystemColors.ControlText;
   if(this.HasChildren)
   {
      // Recursively call this method for each child control.
      foreach(Control childControl in control.Controls)
      {
         ResetAllControlsBackColor(childControl);
      }
   }
}
```

[C++]
```
// Reset all the controls to the user's default Control color.
private:
void ResetAllControlsBackColor(Control* control) {
   control->BackColor = SystemColors::Control;
   control->ForeColor = SystemColors::ControlText;
   if (this->HasChildren) {
      // Recursively call this method for each child control.
      IEnumerator* myEnum = control->Controls->GetEnumerator();
      while (myEnum->MoveNext()) {
         Control* childControl = __try_cast<Control*>(myEnum->Current);
         ResetAllControlsBackColor(childControl);
      }
   }
}
```

Requirements

Platforms: Windows 98, Windows NT 4.0, Windows Millennium Edition, Windows 2000, Windows XP Home Edition, Windows XP Professional, Windows Server 2003 family

Control.Height Property

Gets or sets the height of the control.

[Visual Basic]
```
Public Property Height As Integer
```
[C#]
```
public int Height {get; set;}
```
[C++]
```
public: __property int get_Height();
public: __property void set_Height(int);
```
[JScript]
```
public function get Height() : int;
public function set Height(int);
```

Property Value

The height of the control in pixels.

Remarks

Changes made to the **Height** and **Top** property values cause the **Bottom** property value of the control to change.

> **Note** The minimum height for the derived control **Splitter** is one pixel. The default height for the **Splitter** control is three pixels. Setting the height of the **Splitter** control to a value less than one will reset the property value to the default height.

Example

[Visual Basic, C#, C++] The following example creates three **Button** controls on a form and sets their size and location by using the various size-related and location-related properties. This example assumes you have a **Form** that has a width and height of at least 300 pixels.

[Visual Basic]
```
' Create three buttons and place them on a form using
' several size and location related properties.
Private Sub AddOKCancelButtons()
    ' Set the button size and location using
    ' the Size and Location properties.
    Dim buttonOK As New Button()
    buttonOK.Location = New Point(136, 248)
    buttonOK.Size = New Size(75, 25)
    ' Set the Text property and make the
    ' button the form's default button.
    buttonOK.Text = "&OK"
    Me.AcceptButton = buttonOK

    ' Set the button size and location using the Top,
    ' Left, Width, and Height properties.
    Dim buttonCancel As New Button()
    buttonCancel.Top = buttonOK.Top
    buttonCancel.Left = buttonOK.Right + 5
    buttonCancel.Width = buttonOK.Width
    buttonCancel.Height = buttonOK.Height
    ' Set the Text property and make the
    ' button the form's cancel button.
    buttonCancel.Text = "&Cancel"
    Me.CancelButton = buttonCancel

    ' Set the button size and location using
    ' the Bounds property.
    Dim buttonHelp As New Button()
    buttonHelp.Bounds = New Rectangle(10, 10, 75, 25)
    ' Set the Text property of the button.
    buttonHelp.Text = "&Help"

    ' Add the buttons to the form.
    Me.Controls.AddRange(New Control() {buttonOK, buttonCancel, ↵
buttonHelp})
End Sub
```

[C#]
```
// Create three buttons and place them on a form using
// several size and location related properties.
private void AddOKCancelButtons()
{
    // Set the button size and location using
    // the Size and Location properties.
    Button buttonOK = new Button();
    buttonOK.Location = new Point(136,248);
    buttonOK.Size = new Size(75,25);
    // Set the Text property and make the
    // button the form's default button.
    buttonOK.Text = "&OK";
    this.AcceptButton = buttonOK;

    // Set the button size and location using the Top,
    // Left, Width, and Height properties.
    Button buttonCancel = new Button();
    buttonCancel.Top = buttonOK.Top;
    buttonCancel.Left = buttonOK.Right + 5;
    buttonCancel.Width = buttonOK.Width;
    buttonCancel.Height = buttonOK.Height;
    // Set the Text property and make the
    // button the form's cancel button.
    buttonCancel.Text = "&Cancel";
    this.CancelButton = buttonCancel;

    // Set the button size and location using
    // the Bounds property.
    Button buttonHelp = new Button();
    buttonHelp.Bounds = new Rectangle(10,10, 75, 25);
    // Set the Text property of the button.
    buttonHelp.Text = "&Help";

    // Add the buttons to the form.
    this.Controls.AddRange(new Control[] {buttonOK, buttonCancel, ↵
buttonHelp} );
}
```

[C++]
```
// Create three buttons and place them on a form using
// several size and location related properties.
void AddOKCancelButtons() {
    // Set the button size and location using
    // the Size and Location properties.
    Button* buttonOK = new Button();
    buttonOK->Location =  Point(136, 248);
    buttonOK->Size =  System::Drawing::Size(75, 25);
    // Set the Text property and make the
    // button the form's default button.
    buttonOK->Text = S"&OK";
    this->AcceptButton = buttonOK;

    // Set the button size and location using the Top,
    // Left, Width, and Height properties.
    Button* buttonCancel = new Button();
    buttonCancel->Top = buttonOK->Top;
    buttonCancel->Left = buttonOK->Right + 5;
    buttonCancel->Width = buttonOK->Width;
    buttonCancel->Height = buttonOK->Height;
    // Set the Text property and make the
    // button the form's cancel button.
    buttonCancel->Text = S"&Cancel";
    this->CancelButton = buttonCancel;

    // Set the button size and location using
    // the Bounds property.
    Button* buttonHelp = new Button();
    buttonHelp->Bounds =  Rectangle(10, 10, 75, 25);
    // Set the Text property of the button.
    buttonHelp->Text = S"&Help";

    // Add the buttons to the form.

    Control* temp1 [] = {buttonOK, buttonCancel, buttonHelp};
    this->Controls->AddRange(temp1);
}
```

Requirements

Platforms: Windows 98, Windows NT 4.0, Windows Millennium Edition, Windows 2000, Windows XP Home Edition, Windows XP Professional, Windows Server 2003 family, .NET Compact Framework - Windows CE .NET

Control.ImeMode Property

Gets or sets the Input Method Editor (IME) mode of the control.

```
[Visual Basic]
Public Property ImeMode As ImeMode
[C#]
public ImeMode ImeMode {get; set;}
[C++]
public: __property ImeMode get_ImeMode();
public: __property void set_ImeMode(ImeMode);
[JScript]
public function get ImeMode() : ImeMode;
public function set ImeMode(ImeMode);
```

Property Value

One of the **ImeMode** values. The default is **Inherit**.

Exceptions

Exception Type	Condition
InvalidEnumArgumentException	The assigned value is not one of the **ImeMode** enumeration values.

Remarks

An input method editor (IME) is a program that allows users to enter complex characters and symbols, such as Japanese Kanji characters, using a standard keyboard. The **ImeMode** property is typically set to **ImeMode.Off** for a **TextBox** control that is intended to only enter numeric values. The **ImeMode** property value is set to **ImeMode.NoControl** for the **Form** class.

Requirements

Platforms: Windows 98, Windows NT 4.0, Windows Millennium Edition, Windows 2000, Windows XP Home Edition, Windows XP Professional, Windows Server 2003 family

Control.InvokeRequired Property

Gets a value indicating whether the caller must call an invoke method when making method calls to the control because the caller is on a different thread than the one the control was created on.

```
[Visual Basic]
Public Overridable ReadOnly Property InvokeRequired As Boolean _
   Implements ISynchronizeInvoke.InvokeRequired
[C#]
public virtual bool InvokeRequired {get;}
[C++]
public: __property virtual bool get_InvokeRequired();
[JScript]
public function get InvokeRequired() : Boolean;
```

Property Value

true if the control's **Handle** was created on a different thread than the calling thread (indicating that you must make calls to the control through an invoke method); otherwise, **false**.

Implements

ISynchronizeInvoke.InvokeRequired

Remarks

Controls in Windows Forms are bound to a specific thread and are not thread safe. Therefore, if you are calling a control's method from a different thread, you must use one of the control's invoke methods to marshal the call to the proper thread. This property can be used to determine if you must call an invoke method, which can be useful if you do not know what thread owns a control. There are four methods on a control that are safe to call from any thread: **Invoke**, **BeginInvoke**, **EndInvoke** and **CreateGraphics**. For all other method calls, you should use one of these invoke methods when calling from a different thread.

Requirements

Platforms: Windows 98, Windows NT 4.0, Windows Millennium Edition, Windows 2000, Windows XP Home Edition, Windows XP Professional, Windows Server 2003 family

Control.IsAccessible Property

Gets or sets a value indicating whether the control is visible to accessibility applications.

```
[Visual Basic]
Public Property IsAccessible As Boolean
[C#]
public bool IsAccessible {get; set;}
[C++]
public: __property bool get_IsAccessible();
public: __property void set_IsAccessible(bool);
[JScript]
public function get IsAccessible() : Boolean;
public function set IsAccessible(Boolean);
```

Property Value

true if the control is visible to accessibility applications; otherwise, **false**.

Requirements

Platforms: Windows 98, Windows NT 4.0, Windows Millennium Edition, Windows 2000, Windows XP Home Edition, Windows XP Professional, Windows Server 2003 family

Control.IsDisposed Property

Gets a value indicating whether the control has been disposed of.

```
[Visual Basic]
Public ReadOnly Property IsDisposed As Boolean
[C#]
public bool IsDisposed {get;}
[C++]
public: __property bool get_IsDisposed();
[JScript]
public function get IsDisposed() : Boolean;
```

Property Value

true if the control has been disposed of; otherwise, **false**.

Remarks

When this property returns **true**, the control is disposed of and can no longer be referenced as a valid Windows control. Even though the instance of a control is disposed of, it is still maintained in memory until it is removed from memory through garbage collection. When a control is disposed, you can not call its **RecreateHandle** method.

Requirements

Platforms: Windows 98, Windows NT 4.0, Windows Millennium Edition, Windows 2000, Windows XP Home Edition, Windows XP Professional, Windows Server 2003 family

Control.IsHandleCreated Property

Gets a value indicating whether the control has a handle associated with it.

[Visual Basic]
```
Public ReadOnly Property IsHandleCreated As Boolean
```
[C#]
```
public bool IsHandleCreated {get;}
```
[C++]
```
public: __property bool get_IsHandleCreated();
```
[JScript]
```
public function get IsHandleCreated() : Boolean;
```

Property Value

true if a handle has been assigned to the control; otherwise, **false**.

Requirements

Platforms: Windows 98, Windows NT 4.0, Windows Millennium Edition, Windows 2000, Windows XP Home Edition, Windows XP Professional, Windows Server 2003 family

Control.Left Property

Gets or sets the x-coordinate of a control's left edge in pixels.

[Visual Basic]
```
Public Property Left As Integer
```
[C#]
```
public int Left {get; set;}
```
[C++]
```
public: __property int get_Left();
public: __property void set_Left(int);
```
[JScript]
```
public function get Left() : int;
public function set Left(int);
```

Property Value

The x-coordinate of a control's left edge in pixels.

Remarks

The **Left** property value is equivalent to the **Point.X** property of the **Location** property value of the control.

Changes made to the **Width** and **Left** property values cause the **Right** property value of the control to change.

Example

[Visual Basic, C#, C++] The following example creates three **Button** controls on a form and sets their size and location by using the various size-related and location-related properties. This example assumes you have a **Form** that has a width and height of at least 300 pixels.

[Visual Basic]
```
' Create three buttons and place them on a form using
' several size and location related properties.
Private Sub AddOKCancelButtons()
    ' Set the button size and location using
       ' the Size and Location properties.
   Dim buttonOK As New Button()
   buttonOK.Location = New Point(136, 248)
   buttonOK.Size = New Size(75, 25)
   ' Set the Text property and make the
   ' button the form's default button.
   buttonOK.Text = "&OK"
   Me.AcceptButton = buttonOK

   ' Set the button size and location using the Top,
   ' Left, Width, and Height properties.
   Dim buttonCancel As New Button()
   buttonCancel.Top = buttonOK.Top
   buttonCancel.Left = buttonOK.Right + 5
   buttonCancel.Width = buttonOK.Width
   buttonCancel.Height = buttonOK.Height
   ' Set the Text property and make the
   ' button the form's cancel button.
   buttonCancel.Text = "&Cancel"
   Me.CancelButton = buttonCancel

   ' Set the button size and location using
   ' the Bounds property.
   Dim buttonHelp As New Button()
   buttonHelp.Bounds = New Rectangle(10, 10, 75, 25)
   ' Set the Text property of the button.
   buttonHelp.Text = "&Help"

   ' Add the buttons to the form.
   Me.Controls.AddRange(New Control() {buttonOK, buttonCancel, ↵
buttonHelp})
End Sub
```

[C#]
```
// Create three buttons and place them on a form using
// several size and location related properties.
private void AddOKCancelButtons()
{
   // Set the button size and location using
   // the Size and Location properties.
   Button buttonOK = new Button();
   buttonOK.Location = new Point(136,248);
   buttonOK.Size = new Size(75,25);
   // Set the Text property and make the
   // button the form's default button.
   buttonOK.Text = "&OK";
   this.AcceptButton = buttonOK;

   // Set the button size and location using the Top,
   // Left, Width, and Height properties.
   Button buttonCancel = new Button();
   buttonCancel.Top = buttonOK.Top;
   buttonCancel.Left = buttonOK.Right + 5;
   buttonCancel.Width = buttonOK.Width;
   buttonCancel.Height = buttonOK.Height;
   // Set the Text property and make the
   // button the form's cancel button.
   buttonCancel.Text = "&Cancel";
   this.CancelButton = buttonCancel;

   // Set the button size and location using
   // the Bounds property.
```

```
    Button buttonHelp = new Button();
    buttonHelp.Bounds = new Rectangle(10,10, 75, 25);
    // Set the Text property of the button.
    buttonHelp.Text = "&Help";

    // Add the buttons to the form.
    this.Controls.AddRange(new Control[] {buttonOK, buttonCancel,
buttonHelp} );
}
```

[C++]

```
// Create three buttons and place them on a form using
// several size and location related properties.
void AddOKCancelButtons() {
    // Set the button size and location using
    // the Size and Location properties.
    Button* buttonOK = new Button();
    buttonOK->Location =  Point(136, 248);
    buttonOK->Size =  System::Drawing::Size(75, 25);
    // Set the Text property and make the
    // button the form's default button.
    buttonOK->Text = S"&OK";
    this->AcceptButton = buttonOK;

    // Set the button size and location using the Top,
    // Left, Width, and Height properties.
    Button* buttonCancel = new Button();
    buttonCancel->Top = buttonOK->Top;
    buttonCancel->Left = buttonOK->Right + 5;
    buttonCancel->Width = buttonOK->Width;
    buttonCancel->Height = buttonOK->Height;
    // Set the Text property and make the
    // button the form's cancel button.
    buttonCancel->Text = S"&Cancel";
    this->CancelButton = buttonCancel;

    // Set the button size and location using
    // the Bounds property.
    Button* buttonHelp = new Button();
    buttonHelp->Bounds =  Rectangle(10, 10, 75, 25);
    // Set the Text property of the button.
    buttonHelp->Text = S"&Help";

    // Add the buttons to the form.

    Control* temp1 [] = {buttonOK, buttonCancel, buttonHelp};
    this->Controls->AddRange(temp1);
}
```

Requirements

Platforms: Windows 98, Windows NT 4.0, Windows Millennium Edition, Windows 2000, Windows XP Home Edition, Windows XP Professional, Windows Server 2003 family, .NET Compact Framework - Windows CE .NET

Control.Location Property

Gets or sets the coordinates of the upper-left corner of the control relative to the upper-left corner of its container.

[Visual Basic]

```
Public Property Location As Point
```

[C#]

```
public Point Location {get; set;}
```

[C++]

```
public: __property Point get_Location();
public: __property void set_Location(Point);
```

[JScript]

```
public function get Location() : Point;
public function set Location(Point);
```

Property Value

The **Point** that represents the upper-left corner of the control relative to the upper-left corner of its container.

Remarks

Because the **Point** class is a value type (**Structure** in Visual Basic, **struct** in C#), it is returned by value, meaning accessing the property returns a copy of the upper-left point of the control. So, adjusting the **X** or **Y** properties of the **Point** object returned from this property will not affect the **Left**, **Right**, **Top**, or **Bottom** property values of the control. To adjust these properties set each property value individually, or set the **Location** property with a new **Point** object.

If the **Control** is a **Form**, the **Location** property value represents the upper-left corner of the **Form** in screen coordinates.

Example

[Visual Basic, C#, C++] The following example creates a **GroupBox** and sets some of its common properties. The example creates a **TextBox** and sets its **Location** within the group box. Next, it sets the **Text** property of the group box, and docks the group box to the top of the form. Lastly, it disables the group box by setting the **Enabled** property to **false**, which causes all controls contained within the group box to be disabled.

[Visual Basic]

```
' Add a GroupBox to a form and set some of its common properties.
Private Sub AddMyGroupBox()
    ' Create a GroupBox and add a TextBox to it.
    Dim groupBox1 As New GroupBox()
    Dim textBox1 As New TextBox()
    textBox1.Location = New Point(15, 15)
    groupBox1.Controls.Add(textBox1)

    ' Set the Text and Dock properties of the GroupBox.
    groupBox1.Text = "MyGroupBox"
    groupBox1.Dock = DockStyle.Top

    ' Disable the GroupBox (which disables all its child controls)
    groupBox1.Enabled = False

    ' Add the Groupbox to the form.
    Me.Controls.Add(groupBox1)
End Sub
```

[C#]

```
// Add a GroupBox to a form and set some of its common properties.
private void AddMyGroupBox()
{
    // Create a GroupBox and add a TextBox to it.
    GroupBox groupBox1 = new GroupBox();
    TextBox textBox1 = new TextBox();
    textBox1.Location = new Point(15, 15);
    groupBox1.Controls.Add(textBox1);

    // Set the Text and Dock properties of the GroupBox.
    groupBox1.Text = "MyGroupBox";
    groupBox1.Dock = DockStyle.Top;

    // Disable the GroupBox (which disables all its child controls)
    groupBox1.Enabled = false;

    // Add the Groupbox to the form.
    this.Controls.Add(groupBox1);
}
```

[C++]

```
// Add a GroupBox to a form and set some of its common properties.
private:
void AddMyGroupBox() {
    // Create a GroupBox and add a TextBox to it.
    GroupBox* groupBox1 = new GroupBox();
```

```
    TextBox* textBox1 = new TextBox();
    textBox1->Location =  Point(15, 15);
    groupBox1->Controls->Add(textBox1);

    // Set the Text and Dock properties of the GroupBox.
    groupBox1->Text = S"MyGroupBox";
    groupBox1->Dock = DockStyle::Top;

    // Disable the GroupBox (which disables all its child controls)
    groupBox1->Enabled = false;

    // Add the Groupbox to the form.
    this->Controls->Add(groupBox1);
}
```

Requirements

Platforms: Windows 98, Windows NT 4.0, Windows Millennium Edition, Windows 2000, Windows XP Home Edition, Windows XP Professional, Windows Server 2003 family, .NET Compact Framework - Windows CE .NET

Control.ModifierKeys Property

Gets a value indicating which of the modifier keys (SHIFT, CTRL, and ALT) is in a pressed state.

[Visual Basic]
```
Public Shared ReadOnly Property ModifierKeys As Keys
```
[C#]
```
public static Keys ModifierKeys {get;}
```
[C++]
```
public: __property static Keys get_ModifierKeys();
```
[JScript]
```
public static function get ModifierKeys() : Keys;
```

Property Value

A bitwise combination of the **Keys** values. The default is **None**.

Example

[Visual Basic, C#, C++] The following example hides a button when the CTRL key is pressed while the button is clicked. This example assumes you have a **Button** named `button1` on a **Form**.

[Visual Basic]
```
Private Sub button1_Click(sender As Object, _
  e As EventArgs) Handles button1.Click
   ' If the CTRL key is pressed when the
   ' control is clicked, hide the control.
   If Control.ModifierKeys = Keys.Control Then
      CType(sender, Control).Hide()
   End If
End Sub
```

[C#]
```
private void button1_Click(object sender, System.EventArgs e)
{
   /* If the CTRL key is pressed when the
      * control is clicked, hide the control. */
   if(Control.ModifierKeys == Keys.Control)
   {
      ((Control)sender).Hide();
   }
}
```

[C++]
```
private:
    void button1_Click(Object* sender, System::EventArgs* /*e*/) {
        /* If the CTRL key is pressed when the
         * control is clicked, hide the control. */
        if (Control::ModifierKeys == Keys::Control) {
            (dynamic_cast<Control*>(sender))->Hide();
        }
    }
```

Requirements

Platforms: Windows 98, Windows NT 4.0, Windows Millennium Edition, Windows 2000, Windows XP Home Edition, Windows XP Professional, Windows Server 2003 family

Control.MouseButtons Property

Gets a value indicating which of the mouse buttons is in a pressed state.

[Visual Basic]
```
Public Shared ReadOnly Property MouseButtons As MouseButtons
```
[C#]
```
public static MouseButtons MouseButtons {get;}
```
[C++]
```
public: __property static MouseButtons get_MouseButtons();
```
[JScript]
```
public static function get MouseButtons() : MouseButtons;
```

Property Value

A bitwise combination of the **MouseButtons** enumeration values. The default is **None**.

Requirements

Platforms: Windows 98, Windows NT 4.0, Windows Millennium Edition, Windows 2000, Windows XP Home Edition, Windows XP Professional, Windows Server 2003 family, .NET Compact Framework - Windows CE .NET

Control.MousePosition Property

Gets the position of the mouse cursor in screen coordinates.

[Visual Basic]
```
Public Shared ReadOnly Property MousePosition As Point
```
[C#]
```
public static Point MousePosition {get;}
```
[C++]
```
public: __property static Point get_MousePosition();
```
[JScript]
```
public static function get MousePosition() : Point;
```

Property Value

A **Point** that contains the coordinates of the mouse cursor relative to the upper-left corner of the screen.

Remarks

The **MousePosition** property returns a **Point** that represents the mouse cursor position at the time the property was referenced.

Example

[Visual Basic, C#, C++] The following example puts a **TreeNode** label into an editble state when the user presses ALT-E while the mouse cursor is over the tree node. After the user is done editing the label, the labels cannot be edited again until the ALT-E key combination is pressed again. This example assumes you have a **TreeView** on a **Form**. The tree view should also have at least one **TreeNode** in its **Nodes** collection.

[Visual Basic]
```
Private Sub treeView1_KeyDown(sender As Object, _
  e As KeyEventArgs) Handles treeView1.KeyDown
    ' If the 'Alt' and 'E' keys are pressed,
    ' allow the user to edit the TreeNode label.
    If e.Alt And e.KeyCode = Keys.E Then
       treeView1.LabelEdit = True
       ' If there is a TreeNode under the mose cursor, begin editing.
       Dim editNode As TreeNode = treeView1.GetNodeAt( _
         treeView1.PointToClient(Control.MousePosition))
       If Not (editNode Is Nothing) Then
          editNode.BeginEdit()
       End If
    End If
End Sub

Private Sub treeView1_AfterLabelEdit(sender As Object, _
  e As NodeLabelEditEventArgs) Handles treeView1.AfterLabelEdit
    ' Disable the ability to edit the TreeNode labels.
    treeView1.LabelEdit = False
End Sub
```

[C#]
```
private void treeView1_KeyDown(object sender, KeyEventArgs e)
{
   /* If the 'Alt' and 'E' keys are pressed,
      * allow the user to edit the TreeNode label. */
   if(e.Alt && e.KeyCode == Keys.E)

   {
      treeView1.LabelEdit = true;
      // If there is a TreeNode under the mose cursor, begin editing.
      TreeNode editNode = treeView1.GetNodeAt(
         treeView1.PointToClient(Control.MousePosition));
      if(editNode != null)
      {
         editNode.BeginEdit();
      }
   }
}

private void treeView1_AfterLabelEdit(object sender,                    ↵
NodeLabelEditEventArgs e)
{
   // Disable the ability to edit the TreeNode labels.
   treeView1.LabelEdit = false;
}
```

[C++]
```
private:
    void treeView1_KeyDown(Object* /*sender*/, KeyEventArgs* e) {
        /* If the 'Alt' and 'E' keys are pressed,
         * allow the user to edit the TreeNode label. */
        if (e->Alt && e->KeyCode == Keys::E) {
            treeView1->LabelEdit = true;
            // If there is a TreeNode under the mose cursor,          ↵
begin editing.
            TreeNode* editNode = treeView1->GetNodeAt(
                treeView1->PointToClient(Control::MousePosition));
            if (editNode != 0) {
                editNode->BeginEdit();
            }
        }
    }

    void treeView1_AfterLabelEdit(Object* /*sender*/,                  ↵
NodeLabelEditEventArgs* /*e*/) {
        // Disable the ability to edit the TreeNode labels.
        treeView1->LabelEdit = false;
    }
```

Requirements

Platforms: Windows 98, Windows NT 4.0, Windows Millennium Edition, Windows 2000, Windows XP Home Edition, Windows XP Professional, Windows Server 2003 family, .NET Compact Framework - Windows CE .NET

Control.Name Property

Gets or sets the name of the control.

[Visual Basic]
```
Public Property Name As String
```
[C#]
```
public string Name {get; set;}
```
[C++]
```
public: __property String* get_Name();
public: __property void set_Name(String*);
```
[JScript]
```
public function get Name() : String;
public function set Name(String);
```

Property Value

The name of the control. The default is an empty string ("").

Remarks

The **Name** property can be used at run time to evaluate the object by name rather than type and programmatic name. Because the **Name** property returns a **String** type, it can be evaluated in case-style logic statements (**Select** statement in Visual Basic, **switch** statement in C# and C++).

Example

[Visual Basic]
```
' This example demonstrates the use of the ControlAdded and
' ControlRemoved events. This example assumes that two Button controls
' are added to the form and connected to the addControl_Click and
' removeControl_Click event handling methods.
Private Sub Form1_Load(ByVal sender As Object, ByVal e As              ↵
System.EventArgs) Handles MyBase.Load
    ' Connect the ControlRemoved and ControlAdded event handlers       ↵
to the event handling methods.
    ' ControlRemoved and ControlAdded are not available at design time.
    AddHandler Me.ControlRemoved, AddressOf Me.Control_Removed
    AddHandler Me.ControlAdded, AddressOf Me.Control_Added
End Sub 'Form1_Load

Private Sub Control_Added(ByVal sender As Object, ByVal e As           ↵
System.Windows.Forms.ControlEventArgs)
    MessageBox.Show(("The control named " + e.Control.Name + "        ↵
 has been added to the form."))
End Sub

Private Sub Control_Removed(ByVal sender As Object, ByVal e As         ↵
System.Windows.Forms.ControlEventArgs)
    MessageBox.Show(("The control named " + e.Control.Name + "        ↵
has been removed from the form."))
End Sub

' Click event handler for a Button control. Adds a TextBox to the form.
Private Sub addControl_Click(ByVal sender As Object, ByVal e As        ↵
System.EventArgs) Handles button1.Click
    ' Create a new TextBox control and add it to the form.
    Dim textBox1 As New TextBox()
    textBox1.Size = New Size(100, 10)
    textBox1.Location = New Point(10, 10)
    ' Name the control in order to remove it later.
    ' The name must be specified if a control is added at run time.
    textBox1.Name = "textBox1"
```

```
    ' Add the control to the form's control collection.
    Me.Controls.Add(textBox1)
End Sub

' Click event handler for a Button control.
' Removes the previously added TextBox from the form.
Private Sub removeControl_Click(ByVal sender As Object, ByVal ↵
 e As System.EventArgs) Handles button2.Click
    ' Loop through all controls in the form's control collection.
    Dim tempCtrl As Control
    For Each tempCtrl In Me.Controls
        ' Determine whether the control is textBox1,
        ' and if it is, remove it.
        If tempCtrl.Name = "textBox1" Then
            Me.Controls.Remove(tempCtrl)
        End If
    Next tempCtrl
End Sub
```

[C#]

```
// This example demonstrates the use of the ControlAdded and
// ControlRemoved events. This example assumes that two Button controls
// are added to the form and connected to the addControl_Click and
// removeControl_Click event handling methods.
private void Form1_Load(object sender, System.EventArgs e)
{
    // Connect the ControlRemoved and ControlAdded event handlers
    // to the event handling methods.
    // ControlRemoved and ControlAdded are not available at ↵
design time.
    this.ControlRemoved += new ↵
System.Windows.Forms.ControlEventHandler(this.Control_Removed);
    this.ControlAdded += new ↵
System.Windows.Forms.ControlEventHandler(this.Control_Added);
}

private void Control_Added(object sender, ↵
System.Windows.Forms.ControlEventArgs e)
{
    MessageBox.Show("The control named " + e.Control.Name + " ↵
has been added to the form.");
}

private void Control_Removed(object sender, ↵
System.Windows.Forms.ControlEventArgs e)
{
    MessageBox.Show("The control named " + e.Control.Name + " ↵
has been removed from the form.");
}

// Click event handler for a Button control. Adds a TextBox to ↵
 the form.
private void addControl_Click(object sender, System.EventArgs e)
{
    // Create a new TextBox control and add it to the form.
    TextBox textBox1 = new TextBox();
    textBox1.Size = new Size(100,10);
    textBox1.Location = new Point(10,10);
    // Name the control in order to remove it later. The name ↵
must be specified
    // if a control is added at run time.
    textBox1.Name = "textBox1";

    // Add the control to the form's control collection.
    this.Controls.Add(textBox1);
}

// Click event handler for a Button control.
// Removes the previously added TextBox from the form.
private void removeControl_Click(object sender, System.EventArgs e)
{
    // Loop through all controls in the form's control collection.
    foreach (Control tempCtrl in this.Controls)
    {
        // Determine whether the control is textBox1,
        // and if it is, remove it.
        if (tempCtrl.Name == "textBox1")
        {
            this.Controls.Remove(tempCtrl);
        }
    }
}
```

Requirements

Platforms: Windows 98, Windows NT 4.0, Windows Millennium Edition, Windows 2000, Windows XP Home Edition, Windows XP Professional, Windows Server 2003 family

Control.Parent Property

Gets or sets the parent container of the control.

[Visual Basic]

```
Public Property Parent As Control
```

[C#]

```
public Control Parent {get; set;}
```

[C++]

```
public: __property Control* get_Parent();
public: __property void set_Parent(Control*);
```

[JScript]

```
public function get Parent() : Control;
public function set Parent(Control);
```

Property Value

A **Control** object that represents the parent or container control of the control.

Remarks

Setting the **Parent** property value to a null reference (**Nothing** in Visual Basic) removes the control from the **Control.ControlCollection** of its current parent control.

Example

[Visual Basic]

```
' This example uses the Parent property and the Find method of ↵
 Control to set
' properties on the parent control of a Button and its Form. The ↵
example assumes
' that a Button control named button1 is located within a ↵
GroupBox control. The
' example also assumes that the Click event of the Button control ↵
 is connected to
' the event handling method defined in the example.
Private Sub button1_Click(sender As Object, e As ↵
System.EventArgs) Handles button1.Click
   ' Get the control the Button control is located in. In this ↵
case a GroupBox.
   Dim control As Control = button1.Parent
   ' Set the text and backcolor of the parent control.
   control.Text = "My Groupbox"
   control.BackColor = Color.Blue
   ' Get the form that the Button control is contained within.
   Dim myForm As Form = button1.FindForm()
   ' Set the text and color of the form containing the Button.
   myForm.Text = "The Form of My Control"
   myForm.BackColor = Color.Red
End Sub
```

[C#]

```
// This example uses the Parent property and the Find method ↵
of Control to set
// properties on the parent control of a Button and its Form. ↵
The example assumes
// that a Button control named button1 is located within a ↵
```

```
GroupBox control. The
// example also assumes that the Click event of the Button ↵
 control is connected to
// the event handling method defined in the example.
private void button1_Click(object sender, System.EventArgs e)
{
   // Get the control the Button control is located in. In this ↵
 case a GroupBox.
   Control control = button1.Parent;
   // Set the text and backcolor of the parent control.
   control.Text = "My Groupbox";
   control.BackColor = Color.Blue;
   // Get the form that the Button control is contained within.
   Form myForm = button1.FindForm();
   // Set the text and color of the form containing the Button.
   myForm.Text = "The Form of My Control";
   myForm.BackColor = Color.Red;
}
```

Requirements

Platforms: Windows 98, Windows NT 4.0, Windows Millennium Edition, Windows 2000, Windows XP Home Edition, Windows XP Professional, Windows Server 2003 family, .NET Compact Framework - Windows CE .NET

.NET Framework Security:

- **UIPermission** for all windows to get this property value. Associated enumeration: **UIPermissionWindow.AllWindows**

Control.ProductName Property

Gets the product name of the assembly containing the control.

[Visual Basic]
```
Public ReadOnly Property ProductName As String
```
[C#]
```
public string ProductName {get;}
```
[C++]
```
public: __property String* get_ProductName();
```
[JScript]
```
public function get ProductName() : String;
```

Property Value

The product name of the assembly containing the control.

Remarks

The **ProductName** property is a read-only property. In order to change the value of this property, set the **Product** property value of the **AssemblyProductAttribute**. The following line of C# code sets the **ProductName** property.

```
[assembly: AssemblyProduct("MyApplication")]
```

> **Note** It is strongly recommended that you provide the company name, product name, and product version. Providing this information enables the use of Windows Forms features such as **Application.UserAppDataPath** that make it easier to write applications that comply with the "Certified for Windows" program. For more information on the Certified for Windows program, see http://msdn.microsoft.com/certification.

Example

[Visual Basic, C#, C++] The following example displays information about the application in a **Label** contained by a **Form**. This code assumes the **CompanyName**, **ProductName** and **ProductVersion** have been set.

[Visual Basic]
```
Private Sub AboutDialog_Load(sender As Object, e As EventArgs) ↵
Handles MyBase.Load
   ' Display the application information in the label.
   Me.labelVersionInfo.Text = _
      Me.CompanyName + "  " + _
      Me.ProductName + "  Version: " + _
      Me.ProductVersion
   End Sub
```

[C#]
```
private void AboutDialog_Load(object sender, EventArgs e)
{
   // Display the application information in the label.
   this.labelVersionInfo.Text =
      this.CompanyName + "  " +
      this.ProductName + "  Version: " +
      this.ProductVersion;
}
```

[C++]
```
void AboutDialog_Load(Object* sender, EventArgs* e) {
   // Display the application information in the label.
   this->labelVersionInfo->Text =
      String::Format( "{0} {1} Version: {2}", this->CompanyName, ↵
this->ProductName, this->ProductVersion );
}
```

Requirements

Platforms: Windows 98, Windows NT 4.0, Windows Millennium Edition, Windows 2000, Windows XP Home Edition, Windows XP Professional, Windows Server 2003 family

Control.ProductVersion Property

Gets the version of the assembly containing the control.

[Visual Basic]
```
Public ReadOnly Property ProductVersion As String
```
[C#]
```
public string ProductVersion {get;}
```
[C++]
```
public: __property String* get_ProductVersion();
```
[JScript]
```
public function get ProductVersion() : String;
```

Property Value

The file version of the assembly containing the control.

Remarks

The **ProductVersion** property is a read-only property. In order to change the value of this property, set the **Version** property value of the **AssemblyVersionAttribute**. The following line of C# code sets the **ProductVersion** property.

```
[assembly: AssemblyVersion("1.0.1")]
```

> **Note** It is strongly recommended that you provide the company name, product name, and product version. Providing this information enables the use of Windows Forms features such as **Application.UserAppDataPath** that make it easier to write applications that comply with the "Certified for Windows" program. For more information on the Certified for Windows program, see http://msdn.microsoft.com/certification.

Example

[Visual Basic, C#, C++] The following example displays information about the application in a **Label** contained by a **Form**. This code assumes the **CompanyName**, **ProductName** and **ProductVersion** have been set.

[Visual Basic]
```
Private Sub AboutDialog_Load(sender As Object, e As EventArgs) ↵
Handles MyBase.Load
   ' Display the application information in the label.
   Me.labelVersionInfo.Text = _
      Me.CompanyName + "  " + _
      Me.ProductName + "  Version: " + _
      Me.ProductVersion
   End Sub
```

[C#]
```
private void AboutDialog_Load(object sender, EventArgs e)
{
   // Display the application information in the label.
   this.labelVersionInfo.Text =
      this.CompanyName + "  " +
      this.ProductName + "  Version: " +
      this.ProductVersion;
}
```

[C++]
```
void AboutDialog_Load(Object* sender, EventArgs* e) {
   // Display the application information in the label.
   this->labelVersionInfo->Text =
      String::Format( "{0} {1} Version: {2}", this-> ↵
CompanyName, this->ProductName, this->ProductVersion );
}
```

Requirements

Platforms: Windows 98, Windows NT 4.0, Windows Millennium Edition, Windows 2000, Windows XP Home Edition, Windows XP Professional, Windows Server 2003 family

Control.RecreatingHandle Property

Gets a value indicating whether the control is currently re-creating its handle.

[Visual Basic]
```
Public ReadOnly Property RecreatingHandle As Boolean
```
[C#]
```
public bool RecreatingHandle {get;}
```
[C++]
```
public: __property bool get_RecreatingHandle();
```
[JScript]
```
public function get RecreatingHandle() : Boolean;
```

Property Value

true if the control is currently re-creating its handle; otherwise, **false**.

Requirements

Platforms: Windows 98, Windows NT 4.0, Windows Millennium Edition, Windows 2000, Windows XP Home Edition, Windows XP Professional, Windows Server 2003 family

Control.Region Property

Gets or sets the window region associated with the control.

[Visual Basic]
```
Public Property Region As Region
```
[C#]
```
public Region Region {get; set;}
```
[C++]
```
public: __property Region* get_Region();
public: __property void set_Region(Region*);
```
[JScript]
```
public function get Region() : Region;
public function set Region(Region);
```

Property Value

The window **Region** associated with the control.

Remarks

The window region is a collection of pixels within the window where the operating system permits drawing. The operating system does not display any portion of a window that lies outside of the window region. The coordinates of a control's region are relative to the upper-left corner of the control, not the client area of the control.

> **Note** The collection of pixels contained with the region can be noncontiguous.

Requirements

Platforms: Windows 98, Windows NT 4.0, Windows Millennium Edition, Windows 2000, Windows XP Home Edition, Windows XP Professional, Windows Server 2003 family

.NET Framework Security:

- **UIPermission** for all windows to set this property value. Associated enumeration: **UIPermissionWindow.AllWindows**

Control.RenderRightToLeft Property

This member supports the .NET Framework infrastructure and is not intended to be used directly from your code.

[Visual Basic]
```
Protected ReadOnly Property RenderRightToLeft As Boolean
```
[C#]
```
protected bool RenderRightToLeft {get;}
```
[C++]
```
protected: __property bool get_RenderRightToLeft();
```
[JScript]
```
protected function get RenderRightToLeft() : Boolean;
```

Control.ResizeRedraw Property

Gets or sets a value indicating whether the control redraws itself when resized.

[Visual Basic]
```
Protected Property ResizeRedraw As Boolean
```
[C#]
```
protected bool ResizeRedraw {get; set;}
```
[C++]
```
protected: __property bool get_ResizeRedraw();
protected: __property void set_ResizeRedraw(bool);
```

[JScript]
```
protected function get ResizeRedraw() : Boolean;
protected function set ResizeRedraw(Boolean);
```

Property Value

true if the control redraws itself when resized; otherwise, **false**.

Remarks

The **ResizeRedraw** property value is equivalent to the return value of the **GetStyle** method when passing in the **ControlStyles.ResizeRedraw** value as a parameter.

Requirements

Platforms: Windows 98, Windows NT 4.0, Windows Millennium Edition, Windows 2000, Windows XP Home Edition, Windows XP Professional, Windows Server 2003 family

Control.Right Property

Gets the distance between the right edge of the control and the left edge of its container.

[Visual Basic]
```
Public ReadOnly Property Right As Integer
```
[C#]
```
public int Right {get;}
```
[C++]
```
public: __property int get_Right();
```
[JScript]
```
public function get Right() : int;
```

Property Value

The distance between the right edge of the control and the left edge of its container.

Remarks

The value of the **Right** property is equal to the sum of the **Left** property value and the **Width** property value.

The **Right** property is read-only. You can change this property value indirectly by changing the value of the **Left** or **Width** properties or calling the **SetBounds**, **SetBoundsCore**, **UpdateBounds**, or **SetClientSizeCore** methods.

Example

[Visual Basic, C#, C++] The following example creates three **Button** controls on a form and sets their size and location by using the various size-related and location-related properties. This example assumes you have a **Form** that has a width and height of at least 300 pixels.

[Visual Basic]
```
' Create three buttons and place them on a form using
' several size and location related properties.
Private Sub AddOKCancelButtons()
   ' Set the button size and location using
     ' the Size and Location properties.
   Dim buttonOK As New Button()
   buttonOK.Location = New Point(136, 248)
   buttonOK.Size = New Size(75, 25)
   ' Set the Text property and make the
   ' button the form's default button.
   buttonOK.Text = "&OK"
   Me.AcceptButton = buttonOK

   ' Set the button size and location using the Top,
   ' Left, Width, and Height properties.
   Dim buttonCancel As New Button()
   buttonCancel.Top = buttonOK.Top
   buttonCancel.Left = buttonOK.Right + 5
   buttonCancel.Width = buttonOK.Width
   buttonCancel.Height = buttonOK.Height
   ' Set the Text property and make the
   ' button the form's cancel button.
   buttonCancel.Text = "&Cancel"
   Me.CancelButton = buttonCancel

   ' Set the button size and location using
   ' the Bounds property.
   Dim buttonHelp As New Button()
   buttonHelp.Bounds = New Rectangle(10, 10, 75, 25)
   ' Set the Text property of the button.
   buttonHelp.Text = "&Help"

   ' Add the buttons to the form.
   Me.Controls.AddRange(New Control() {buttonOK, buttonCancel, ↵
buttonHelp})
End Sub
```

[C#]
```
// Create three buttons and place them on a form using
// several size and location related properties.
private void AddOKCancelButtons()
{
   // Set the button size and location using
   // the Size and Location properties.
   Button buttonOK = new Button();
   buttonOK.Location = new Point(136,248);
   buttonOK.Size = new Size(75,25);
   // Set the Text property and make the
   // button the form's default button.
   buttonOK.Text = "&OK";
   this.AcceptButton = buttonOK;

   // Set the button size and location using the Top,
   // Left, Width, and Height properties.
   Button buttonCancel = new Button();
   buttonCancel.Top = buttonOK.Top;
   buttonCancel.Left = buttonOK.Right + 5;
   buttonCancel.Width = buttonOK.Width;
   buttonCancel.Height = buttonOK.Height;
   // Set the Text property and make the
   // button the form's cancel button.
   buttonCancel.Text = "&Cancel";
   this.CancelButton = buttonCancel;

   // Set the button size and location using
   // the Bounds property.
   Button buttonHelp = new Button();
   buttonHelp.Bounds = new Rectangle(10,10, 75, 25);
   // Set the Text property of the button.
   buttonHelp.Text = "&Help";

   // Add the buttons to the form.
   this.Controls.AddRange(new Control[] {buttonOK, buttonCancel, ↵
buttonHelp} );
}
```

[C++]
```
// Create three buttons and place them on a form using
// several size and location related properties.
void AddOKCancelButtons() {
   // Set the button size and location using
   // the Size and Location properties.
   Button* buttonOK = new Button();
   buttonOK->Location =  Point(136, 248);
   buttonOK->Size =  System::Drawing::Size(75, 25);
   // Set the Text property and make the
   // button the form's default button.
   buttonOK->Text = S"&OK";
   this->AcceptButton = buttonOK;

   // Set the button size and location using the Top,
   // Left, Width, and Height properties.
```

```
    Button* buttonCancel = new Button();
    buttonCancel->Top = buttonOK->Top;
    buttonCancel->Left = buttonOK->Right + 5;
    buttonCancel->Width = buttonOK->Width;
    buttonCancel->Height = buttonOK->Height;
    // Set the Text property and make the
    // button the form's cancel button.
    buttonCancel->Text = S"&Cancel";
    this->CancelButton = buttonCancel;

    // Set the button size and location using
    // the Bounds property.
    Button* buttonHelp = new Button();
    buttonHelp->Bounds =  Rectangle(10, 10, 75, 25);
    // Set the Text property of the button.
    buttonHelp->Text = S"&Help";

    // Add the buttons to the form.

    Control* temp1 [] = {buttonOK, buttonCancel, buttonHelp};
    this->Controls->AddRange(temp1);
}
```

[Visual Basic]

```
' This example demonstrates how to use the KeyUp event with the ↵
 Help class to display
' pop-up style help to the user of the application. When the ↵
user presses F1, the Help
' class displays a pop-up window, similar to a ToolTip, near ↵
the control. This example assumes
' that a TextBox control, named textBox1, has been added to the ↵
 form and its KeyUp
' event has been contected to this event handling method.
Private Sub textBox1_KeyUp(ByVal sender As Object, ByVal e As ↵
System.Windows.Forms.KeyEventArgs) Handles textBox1.KeyUp
    ' Determine whether the key entered is the F1 key. Display ↵
help if it is.
    If e.KeyCode = Keys.F1 Then
        ' Display a pop-up help topic to assist the user.
        Help.ShowPopup(textBox1, "Enter your first name", New ↵
Point(textBox1.Right, Me.textBox1.Bottom))
    End If
End Sub 'textBox1_KeyUp
```

[C#]

```
// This example demonstrates how to use the KeyUp event with ↵
the Help class to display
// pop-up style help to the user of the application. When the ↵
 user presses F1, the Help
// class displays a pop-up window, similar to a ToolTip, near ↵
the control. This example assumes
// that a TextBox control, named textBox1, has been added to ↵
the form and its KeyUp
// event has been contected to this event handling method.
private void textBox1_KeyUp(object sender, ↵
System.Windows.Forms.KeyEventArgs e)
{
    // Determine whether the key entered is the F1 key. Display ↵
 help if it is.
    if(e.KeyCode == Keys.F1)
    {
        // Display a pop-up help topic to assist the user.
        Help.ShowPopup(textBox1, "Enter your first name", new ↵
Point(textBox1.Right, this.textBox1.Bottom));
    }
}
```

Requirements

Platforms: Windows 98, Windows NT 4.0, Windows Millennium Edition, Windows 2000, Windows XP Home Edition, Windows XP Professional, Windows Server 2003 family, .NET Compact Framework - Windows CE .NET

Control.RightToLeft Property

Gets or sets a value indicating whether control's elements are aligned to support locales using right-to-left fonts.

[Visual Basic]

```
Public Overridable Property RightToLeft As RightToLeft
```

[C#]

```
public virtual RightToLeft RightToLeft {get; set;}
```

[C++]

```
public: __property virtual RightToLeft get_RightToLeft();
public: __property virtual void set_RightToLeft(RightToLeft);
```

[JScript]

```
public function get RightToLeft() : RightToLeft;
public function set RightToLeft(RightToLeft);
```

Property Value

One of the **RightToLeft** values. The default is **Inherit**.

Exceptions

Exception Type	Condition
InvalidEnumArgument-Exception	The assigned value is not one of the **RightToLeft** values.

Remarks

The **RightToLeft** property is an ambient property. An ambient property is a control property that, if not set, is retrieved from the parent control. For example, a **Button** will have the same **Back-Color** as its parent **Form** by default. For more information about ambient properties, see the **AmbientProperties** class or the **Control** class overview.

The **RightToLeft** property is used for international applications where the language is written from right to left, such as Hebrew or Arabic. When this property is set to **RightToLeft.Yes**, control elements that include text are displayed from right to left.

If the control is a top-level control, the user's operating system is queried to determine if the control needs to enable right-to-left support.

The following are a few examples of how control elements are affected by the **RightToLeft** property value of **RightToLeft.Yes**:

- Vertical scroll bars are displayed on the left side rather than right side of scrollable controls (for example, **Form**, **Panel**, multiline **TextBox**, and **RichTextBox**).
- Horizontal scroll bars start with the scroll box (thumb) right-aligned.
- The check box element alignment, controlled by the **CheckAlign** property, is reversed for **CheckBox** and **RadioButton** controls.
- Text displayed in the title bar of a **Form** is right-aligned. The icon and control box retain their left and right alignment respectively.
- Items in list box, combo box, and up-down controls are right aligned.
- Up and down buttons are left-aligned on **NumericUpDown** and **DomainUpDown** controls.
- Menus (**MainMenu**, **MenuItem**, and **ContextMenu**) are displayed right-aligned.
- The alignment of toolbar buttons on a **ToolBar** control or the alignment of text on a **ToolBarButton** is not affected by the **RightToLeft** property.
- **AxHost** supports right-to-left alignment; however, the effect on an ActiveX control depends on the extent to which the control author implemented support for right-to-left display.

Note When the **RightToLeft** property value is set to **RightToLeft.Yes**, the horizontal alignment of the control's elements are reversed, yet the elements' alignment values are unchanged. For example, in a **TextBox** control with the **TextAlign** property value of **HorizontalAlignment.Left**, text is displayed right-aligned, but the property value remains **HorizontalAlignment.Left**. However, if the **RightToLeft** property value is set to **RightToLeft.Yes** while the **TextAlign** property is set to **HorizontalAlignment.Right**, the text is displayed left-aligned.

Notes to Inheritors: When overriding the **RightToLeft** property in a derived class, use the base class's **RightToLeft** property to extend the base implementation. Otherwise, you must provide all the implementation. You are not required to override both the **get** and **set** accessors of the **RightToLeft** property; you can override only one if needed.

Requirements

Platforms: Windows 98, Windows NT 4.0, Windows Millennium Edition, Windows 2000, Windows XP Home Edition, Windows XP Professional, Windows Server 2003 family

Control.ShowFocusCues Property

Gets a value indicating whether the control should display focus rectangles.

```
[Visual Basic]
Protected Overridable ReadOnly Property ShowFocusCues As Boolean
[C#]
protected virtual bool ShowFocusCues {get;}
[C++]
protected: __property virtual bool get_ShowFocusCues();
[JScript]
protected function get ShowFocusCues() : Boolean;
```

Property Value

true if the control should display focus rectangles; otherwise, **false**.

Remarks

For more information on this feature, see the **WM_CHANGEUISTATE**, **WM_QUERYUISTATE**, and **WM_UPDATEUISTATE** topics located in the Windows Platform SDK in the MSDN Library.

Notes to Inheritors: When overriding the **ShowFocusCues** property in a derived class, use the base class's **ShowFocusCues** property to extend the base implementation. Otherwise, you must provide all the implementation.

Windows 2000, Windows Server 2003 family Platform Note: Setting the **ShowFocusCues** property to **true** causes controls to conform to the Windows 2000 behavior that hides focus cues until the user performs a keyboard action.

Requirements

Platforms: Windows 98, Windows NT 4.0, Windows Millennium Edition, Windows 2000, Windows XP Home Edition, Windows XP Professional, Windows Server 2003 family

Control.ShowKeyboardCues Property

Gets a value indicating whether the control should display keyboard shortcuts.

```
[Visual Basic]
Protected ReadOnly Property ShowKeyboardCues As Boolean
[C#]
protected bool ShowKeyboardCues {get;}
[C++]
protected: __property bool get_ShowKeyboardCues();
[JScript]
protected function get ShowKeyboardCues() : Boolean;
```

Property Value

true if the user the control should display keyboard shortcuts; otherwise, **false**.

Remarks

For more information on this feature, see the **WM_CHANGEUISTATE**, **WM_QUERYUISTATE**, and **WM_UPDATEUISTATE** topics located in the Windows Platform SDK in the MSDN Library.

Windows 2000, Windows Server 2003 family Platform Note: Setting the **ShowKeyboardCues** property to **true** causes controls to conform to the Windows 2000 behavior that hides keyboard cues until the user performs a keyboard action.

Requirements

Platforms: Windows 98, Windows NT 4.0, Windows Millennium Edition, Windows 2000, Windows XP Home Edition, Windows XP Professional, Windows Server 2003 family

Control.Site Property

Gets or sets the site of the control.

```
[Visual Basic]
Overrides Public Property Site As ISite  Implements IComponent.Site
[C#]
public override ISite Site {get; set;}
[C++]
public: __property ISite* get_Site();
public: __property void set_Site(ISite*);
[JScript]
public override function get Site() : ISite;
public override function set Site(ISite);
```

Property Value

The **ISite** associated with the **Control**, if any.

Implements

IComponent.Site

Requirements

Platforms: Windows 98, Windows NT 4.0, Windows Millennium Edition, Windows 2000, Windows XP Home Edition, Windows XP Professional, Windows Server 2003 family

Control.Size Property

Gets or sets the height and width of the control.

[Visual Basic]
```
Public Property Size As Size
```
[C#]
```
public Size Size {get; set;}
```
[C++]
```
public: __property Size get_Size();
public: __property void set_Size(Size);
```
[JScript]
```
public function get Size() : Size;
public function set Size(Size);
```

Property Value

The **Size** object that represents the height and width of the control in pixels.

Remarks

Because the **Size** class is a value type (**Structure** in Visual Basic, **struct** in C#), it is returned by value, meaning accessing the property returns a copy of the size of the control. So, adjusting the **Width** or **Height** properties of the **Size** object returned from this property will not affect the **Width** or **Height** of the control. To adjust the **Width** or **Height** of the control, you must set the control's **Width** or **Height** property, or set the **Size** property with a new **Size** object.

> **Note** In order to maintain better performance, you should not set the **Size** of a control in its constructor. The preferred method is to override the **DefaultSize** property.

Example

[Visual Basic, C#, C++] The following example adds a **Button** to a form and sets some of its common properties. The example anchors the button to the bottom-right corner of the form so it keeps its relative position as the form is resized. Next it sets the **BackgroundImage** and resizes the button to the same size as the **Image**. The example then sets the **TabStop** to **true** and sets the **TabIndex** property. Lastly, it adds an event handler to handle the **Click** event of the button. This example assumes you have an **ImageList** named `imageList1`.

[Visual Basic]
```
' Add a button to a form and set some of its common properties.
Private Sub AddMyButton()
   ' Create a button and add it to the form.
   Dim button1 As New Button()

   ' Anchor the button to the bottom right corner of the form
   button1.Anchor = AnchorStyles.Bottom Or AnchorStyles.Right

   ' Assign a background image.
   button1.BackgroundImage = imageList1.Images(0)

   ' Make the button the same size as the image.
   button1.Size = button1.BackgroundImage.Size

   ' Set the button's TabIndex and TabStop properties.
   button1.TabIndex = 1
   button1.TabStop = True

   ' Add a delegate to handle the Click event.
   AddHandler button1.Click, AddressOf Me.button1_Click

   ' Add the button to the form.
   Me.Controls.Add(button1)
End Sub
```

[C#]
```
// Add a button to a form and set some of its common properties.
private void AddMyButton()
{
   // Create a button and add it to the form.
   Button button1 = new Button();

   // Anchor the button to the bottom right corner of the form
   button1.Anchor = (AnchorStyles.Bottom | AnchorStyles.Right);

   // Assign a background image.
   button1.BackgroundImage = imageList1.Images[0];

   // Make the button the same size as the image.
   button1.Size = button1.BackgroundImage.Size;

   // Set the button's TabIndex and TabStop properties.
   button1.TabIndex = 1;
   button1.TabStop = true;

   // Add a delegate to handle the Click event.
   button1.Click += new System.EventHandler(this.button1_Click);

   // Add the button to the form.
   this.Controls.Add(button1);
}
```

[C++]
```
// Add a button to a form and set some of its common properties.
private:
void AddMyButton() {
   // Create a button and add it to the form.
   Button* button1 = new Button();

   // Anchor the button to the bottom right corner of the form
   button1->Anchor = static_cast<AnchorStyles>
(AnchorStyles::Bottom | AnchorStyles::Right);

   // Assign a background image.
   button1->BackgroundImage = imageList1->Images->Item[0];

   // Make the button the same size as the image.
   button1->Size = button1->BackgroundImage->Size;

   // Set the button's TabIndex and TabStop properties.
   button1->TabIndex = 1;
   button1->TabStop = true;

   // Add a delegate to handle the Click event.
   button1->Click += new System::EventHandler(this, button1_Click);

   // Add the button to the form.
   this->Controls->Add(button1);
}
```

Requirements

Platforms: Windows 98, Windows NT 4.0, Windows Millennium Edition, Windows 2000, Windows XP Home Edition, Windows XP Professional, Windows Server 2003 family, .NET Compact Framework - Windows CE .NET

Control.TabIndex Property

Gets or sets the tab order of the control within its container.

[Visual Basic]
```
Public Property TabIndex As Integer
```
[C#]
```
public int TabIndex {get; set;}
```
[C++]
```
public: __property int get_TabIndex();
public: __property void set_TabIndex(int);
```

```
[JScript]
public function get TabIndex() : int;
public function set TabIndex(int);
```

Property Value

The index value of the control within the set of controls within its container that are included in the tab order.

Remarks

A tab index can consist of any valid integer greater than or equal to zero, lower numbers being earlier in the tab order. If more than one control on the same parent control has the same tab index, the z-order of the controls determines the order to cycle through the controls.

For a control to be included in the tab order, its **TabStop** property must be set to **true**.

Example

[Visual Basic, C#, C++] The following example adds a **Button** to a form and sets some of its common properties. The example anchors the button to the bottom-right corner of the form so it keeps its relative position as the form is resized. Next it sets the **BackgroundImage** and resizes the button to the same size as the **Image**. The example then sets the **TabStop** to **true** and sets the **TabIndex** property. Lastly, it adds an event handler to handle the **Click** event of the button. This example assumes you have an **ImageList** named `imageList1`.

[Visual Basic]

```
' Add a button to a form and set some of its common properties.
Private Sub AddMyButton()
   ' Create a button and add it to the form.
   Dim button1 As New Button()

   ' Anchor the button to the bottom right corner of the form
   button1.Anchor = AnchorStyles.Bottom Or AnchorStyles.Right

   ' Assign a background image.
   button1.BackgroundImage = imageList1.Images(0)

   ' Make the button the same size as the image.
   button1.Size = button1.BackgroundImage.Size

   ' Set the button's TabIndex and TabStop properties.
   button1.TabIndex = 1
   button1.TabStop = True

   ' Add a delegate to handle the Click event.
   AddHandler button1.Click, AddressOf Me.button1_Click

   ' Add the button to the form.
   Me.Controls.Add(button1)
End Sub
```

[C#]

```
// Add a button to a form and set some of its common properties.
private void AddMyButton()
{
   // Create a button and add it to the form.
   Button button1 = new Button();

   // Anchor the button to the bottom right corner of the form
   button1.Anchor = (AnchorStyles.Bottom | AnchorStyles.Right);

   // Assign a background image.
   button1.BackgroundImage = imageList1.Images[0];

   // Make the button the same size as the image.
   button1.Size = button1.BackgroundImage.Size;

   // Set the button's TabIndex and TabStop properties.
   button1.TabIndex = 1;
   button1.TabStop = true;

   // Add a delegate to handle the Click event.
   button1.Click += new System.EventHandler(this.button1_Click);

   // Add the button to the form.
   this.Controls.Add(button1);
}
```

[C++]

```
// Add a button to a form and set some of its common properties.
private:
void AddMyButton() {
   // Create a button and add it to the form.
   Button* button1 = new Button();

   // Anchor the button to the bottom right corner of the form
   button1->Anchor = static_cast<AnchorStyles>                    ↵
 (AnchorStyles::Bottom | AnchorStyles::Right);

   // Assign a background image.
   button1->BackgroundImage = imageList1->Images->Item[0];

   // Make the button the same size as the image.
   button1->Size = button1->BackgroundImage->Size;

   // Set the button's TabIndex and TabStop properties.
   button1->TabIndex = 1;
   button1->TabStop = true;

   // Add a delegate to handle the Click event.
   button1->Click += new System::EventHandler(this, button1_Click);

   // Add the button to the form.
   this->Controls->Add(button1);
}
```

Requirements

Platforms: Windows 98, Windows NT 4.0, Windows Millennium Edition, Windows 2000, Windows XP Home Edition, Windows XP Professional, Windows Server 2003 family

Control.TabStop Property

Gets or sets a value indicating whether the user can give the focus to this control using the TAB key.

```
[Visual Basic]
Public Property TabStop As Boolean
[C#]
public bool TabStop {get; set;}
[C++]
public: __property bool get_TabStop();
public: __property void set_TabStop(bool);
[JScript]
public function get TabStop() : Boolean;
public function set TabStop(Boolean);
```

Property Value

true if the user can give the focus to the control using the TAB key; otherwise, **false**. The default is **true**.

Remarks

When the user presses the TAB key, the input focus is set to the next control in the tab order. Controls with the **TabStop** property value of **false** are not included in the collection of controls in the tab order. The tab order can be manipulated by setting the control's **TabIndex** property value.

Example

[Visual Basic, C#, C++] The following example adds a **Button** to a form and sets some of its common properties. The example anchors the button to the bottom-right corner of the form so it keeps its relative position as the form is resized. Next it sets the **BackgroundImage** and resizes the button to the same size as the **Image**. The example then sets the **TabStop** to **true** and sets the **TabIndex** property. Lastly, it adds an event handler to handle the **Click** event of the button. This example assumes you have an **ImageList** named `imageList1`.

[Visual Basic]
```
' Add a button to a form and set some of its common properties.
Private Sub AddMyButton()
   ' Create a button and add it to the form.
   Dim button1 As New Button()

   ' Anchor the button to the bottom right corner of the form
   button1.Anchor = AnchorStyles.Bottom Or AnchorStyles.Right

   ' Assign a background image.
   button1.BackgroundImage = imageList1.Images(0)

   ' Make the button the same size as the image.
   button1.Size = button1.BackgroundImage.Size

   ' Set the button's TabIndex and TabStop properties.
   button1.TabIndex = 1
   button1.TabStop = True

   ' Add a delegate to handle the Click event.
   AddHandler button1.Click, AddressOf Me.button1_Click

   ' Add the button to the form.
   Me.Controls.Add(button1)
End Sub
```

[C#]
```
// Add a button to a form and set some of its common properties.
private void AddMyButton()
{
   // Create a button and add it to the form.
   Button button1 = new Button();

   // Anchor the button to the bottom right corner of the form
   button1.Anchor = (AnchorStyles.Bottom | AnchorStyles.Right);

   // Assign a background image.
   button1.BackgroundImage = imageList1.Images[0];

   // Make the button the same size as the image.
   button1.Size = button1.BackgroundImage.Size;

   // Set the button's TabIndex and TabStop properties.
   button1.TabIndex = 1;
   button1.TabStop = true;

   // Add a delegate to handle the Click event.
   button1.Click += new System.EventHandler(this.button1_Click);

   // Add the button to the form.
   this.Controls.Add(button1);
}
```

[C++]
```
// Add a button to a form and set some of its common properties.
private:
void AddMyButton() {
   // Create a button and add it to the form.
   Button* button1 = new Button();

   // Anchor the button to the bottom right corner of the form
   button1->Anchor = static_cast<AnchorStyles>
 (AnchorStyles::Bottom | AnchorStyles::Right);

   // Assign a background image.
   button1->BackgroundImage = imageList1->Images->Item[0];

   // Make the button the same size as the image.
   button1->Size = button1->BackgroundImage->Size;

   // Set the button's TabIndex and TabStop properties.
   button1->TabIndex = 1;
   button1->TabStop = true;

   // Add a delegate to handle the Click event.
   button1->Click += new System::EventHandler(this, button1_Click);

   // Add the button to the form.
   this->Controls->Add(button1);
}
```

Requirements

Platforms: Windows 98, Windows NT 4.0, Windows Millennium Edition, Windows 2000, Windows XP Home Edition, Windows XP Professional, Windows Server 2003 family

Control.Tag Property

Gets or sets the object that contains data about the control.

[Visual Basic]
```
Public Property Tag As Object
```
[C#]
```
public object Tag {get; set;}
```
[C++]
```
public: __property Object* get_Tag();
public: __property void set_Tag(Object*);
```
[JScript]
```
public function get Tag() : Object;
public function set Tag(Object);
```

Property Value

An **Object** that contains data about the control. The default is a null reference (**Nothing** in Visual Basic).

Remarks

Any type derived from the **Object** class can be assigned to this property. If the **Tag** property is set through the Windows Forms designer, only text can be assigned.

A common use for the **Tag** property is to store data that is closely associated with the control. For example, if you have a control that displays information about a customer you, might store a **DataSet** that contains the customer's order history in that control's **Tag** property so the data can be accessed quickly.

Example

[Visual Basic, C#, C++] The following example displays a form and stores a `Customer` object in its **Tag** property. This example assumes you have defined a class that derives from **Form** named `CustomerForm` and that you have defined a `Customer` object.

[Visual Basic]
```
Private Sub buttonNewCustomer_Click(sender As Object, _
  e As EventArgs) Handles buttonNewCustomer.Click
    ' Create a new customer form and assign a new
    ' Customer object to the Tag property.
   Dim customerForm As New CustomerForm()
   customerForm.Tag = New Customer()
   customerForm.Show()
End Sub
```

[C#]
```
private void buttonNewCustomer_Click(object sender, EventArgs e)
{
   /* Create a new customer form and assign a new
    * Customer object to the Tag property. */
   CustomerForm customerForm = new CustomerForm();
   customerForm.Tag = new Customer();
   customerForm.Show();
}
```

[C++]
```
private:
   void buttonNewCustomer_Click(Object* /*sender*/,                    ↵
EventArgs* /*e*/) {
      /* Create a new customer form and assign a new
       * Customer object to the Tag property. */
      CustomerForm* customerForm = new CustomerForm();
      customerForm->Tag = new Customer();
      customerForm->Show();
   }
```

Requirements

Platforms: Windows 98, Windows NT 4.0, Windows Millennium Edition, Windows 2000, Windows XP Home Edition, Windows XP Professional, Windows Server 2003 family

Control.Text Property

Gets or sets the text associated with this control.

[Visual Basic]
```
Public Overridable Property Text As String
```
[C#]
```
public virtual string Text {get; set;}
```
[C++]
```
public: __property virtual String* get_Text();
public: __property virtual void set_Text(String*);
```
[JScript]
```
public function get Text() : String;
public function set Text(String);
```

Property Value

The text associated with this control.

Remarks

The **Text** property of the control is used differently by each derived class. For example the **Text** property of a **Form** is displayed in the title bar at the top of the form, is fairly small in character count, and usually displays the application or document name. However, the **Text** property of a **RichTextBox** can be large and can include numerous nonvisual characters used to format the text. For example, the text displayed in a **RichTextBox** can be formatted by adjusting the **Font** properties, or by the addition of spaces or tab characters to align the text.

Notes to Inheritors: When overriding the **Text** property in a derived class, use the base class's **Text** property to extend the base implementation. Otherwise, you must provide all the implementation. You are not required to override both the **get** and **set** accessors of the **Text** property; you can override only one if needed.

Example

[Visual Basic, C#, C++] The following example creates a **GroupBox** and sets some of its common properties. The example creates a **TextBox** and sets its **Location** within the group box. Next, it sets the **Text** property of the group box, and docks the group box to the top of the form. Lastly, it disables the group box by setting the **Enabled** property to **false**, which causes all controls contained within the group box to be disabled.

[Visual Basic]
```
' Add a GroupBox to a form and set some of its common properties.
Private Sub AddMyGroupBox()
   ' Create a GroupBox and add a TextBox to it.
   Dim groupBox1 As New GroupBox()
   Dim textBox1 As New TextBox()
   textBox1.Location = New Point(15, 15)
   groupBox1.Controls.Add(textBox1)

   ' Set the Text and Dock properties of the GroupBox.
   groupBox1.Text = "MyGroupBox"
   groupBox1.Dock = DockStyle.Top

   ' Disable the GroupBox (which disables all its child controls)
   groupBox1.Enabled = False

   ' Add the Groupbox to the form.
   Me.Controls.Add(groupBox1)
End Sub
```

[C#]
```
// Add a GroupBox to a form and set some of its common properties.
private void AddMyGroupBox()
{
   // Create a GroupBox and add a TextBox to it.
   GroupBox groupBox1 = new GroupBox();
   TextBox textBox1 = new TextBox();
   textBox1.Location = new Point(15, 15);
   groupBox1.Controls.Add(textBox1);

   // Set the Text and Dock properties of the GroupBox.
   groupBox1.Text = "MyGroupBox";
   groupBox1.Dock = DockStyle.Top;

   // Disable the GroupBox (which disables all its child controls)
   groupBox1.Enabled = false;

   // Add the Groupbox to the form.
   this.Controls.Add(groupBox1);
}
```

[C++]
```
// Add a GroupBox to a form and set some of its common properties.
private:
void AddMyGroupBox() {
   // Create a GroupBox and add a TextBox to it.
   GroupBox* groupBox1 = new GroupBox();
   TextBox* textBox1 = new TextBox();
   textBox1->Location =  Point(15, 15);
   groupBox1->Controls->Add(textBox1);

   // Set the Text and Dock properties of the GroupBox.
   groupBox1->Text = S"MyGroupBox";
   groupBox1->Dock = DockStyle::Top;

   // Disable the GroupBox (which disables all its child controls)
   groupBox1->Enabled = false;

   // Add the Groupbox to the form.
   this->Controls->Add(groupBox1);
}
```

Requirements

Platforms: Windows 98, Windows NT 4.0, Windows Millennium Edition, Windows 2000, Windows XP Home Edition, Windows XP Professional, Windows Server 2003 family, .NET Compact Framework - Windows CE .NET

Control.Top Property

Gets or sets the y-coordinate of the control's top edge in pixels.

[Visual Basic]
```
Public Property Top As Integer
```
[C#]
```
public int Top {get; set;}
```
[C++]
```
public: __property int get_Top();
public: __property void set_Top(int);
```
[JScript]
```
public function get Top() : int;
public function set Top(int);
```

Property Value

The y-coordinate of the control's top edge in pixels.

Remarks

The **Top** property value is equivalent to the **Point.Y** property of the **Location** property value of the control.

Changes made to the **Height** and **Top** property values cause the **Bottom** property value of the control to change.

Example

[Visual Basic, C#, C++] The following example creates three **Button** controls on a form and sets their size and location by using the various size-related and location-related properties. This example assumes you have a **Form** that has a width and height of at least 300 pixels.

[Visual Basic]
```
' Create three buttons and place them on a form using
' several size and location related properties.
Private Sub AddOKCancelButtons()
   ' Set the button size and location using
      ' the Size and Location properties.
   Dim buttonOK As New Button()
   buttonOK.Location = New Point(136, 248)
   buttonOK.Size = New Size(75, 25)
   ' Set the Text property and make the
   ' button the form's default button.
   buttonOK.Text = "&OK"
   Me.AcceptButton = buttonOK

   ' Set the button size and location using the Top,
   ' Left, Width, and Height properties.
   Dim buttonCancel As New Button()
   buttonCancel.Top = buttonOK.Top
   buttonCancel.Left = buttonOK.Right + 5
   buttonCancel.Width = buttonOK.Width
   buttonCancel.Height = buttonOK.Height
   ' Set the Text property and make the
   ' button the form's cancel button.
   buttonCancel.Text = "&Cancel"
   Me.CancelButton = buttonCancel

   ' Set the button size and location using
   ' the Bounds property.
   Dim buttonHelp As New Button()
   buttonHelp.Bounds = New Rectangle(10, 10, 75, 25)
   ' Set the Text property of the button.
   buttonHelp.Text = "&Help"

   ' Add the buttons to the form.
   Me.Controls.AddRange(New Control() {buttonOK, buttonCancel, ↵
buttonHelp})
End Sub
```

[C#]
```
// Create three buttons and place them on a form using
// several size and location related properties.
private void AddOKCancelButtons()
{
   // Set the button size and location using
   // the Size and Location properties.
   Button buttonOK = new Button();
   buttonOK.Location = new Point(136,248);
   buttonOK.Size = new Size(75,25);
   // Set the Text property and make the
   // button the form's default button.
   buttonOK.Text = "&OK";
   this.AcceptButton = buttonOK;

   // Set the button size and location using the Top,
   // Left, Width, and Height properties.
   Button buttonCancel = new Button();
   buttonCancel.Top = buttonOK.Top;
   buttonCancel.Left = buttonOK.Right + 5;
   buttonCancel.Width = buttonOK.Width;
   buttonCancel.Height = buttonOK.Height;
   // Set the Text property and make the
   // button the form's cancel button.
   buttonCancel.Text = "&Cancel";
   this.CancelButton = buttonCancel;

   // Set the button size and location using
   // the Bounds property.
   Button buttonHelp = new Button();
   buttonHelp.Bounds = new Rectangle(10,10, 75, 25);
   // Set the Text property of the button.
   buttonHelp.Text = "&Help";

   // Add the buttons to the form.
   this.Controls.AddRange(new Control[] {buttonOK, buttonCancel, ↵
buttonHelp} );
}
```

[C++]
```
// Create three buttons and place them on a form using
// several size and location related properties.
void AddOKCancelButtons() {
   // Set the button size and location using
   // the Size and Location properties.
   Button* buttonOK = new Button();
   buttonOK->Location =  Point(136, 248);
   buttonOK->Size =  System::Drawing::Size(75, 25);
   // Set the Text property and make the
   // button the form's default button.
   buttonOK->Text = S"&OK";
   this->AcceptButton = buttonOK;

   // Set the button size and location using the Top,
   // Left, Width, and Height properties.
   Button* buttonCancel = new Button();
   buttonCancel->Top = buttonOK->Top;
   buttonCancel->Left = buttonOK->Right + 5;
   buttonCancel->Width = buttonOK->Width;
   buttonCancel->Height = buttonOK->Height;
   // Set the Text property and make the
   // button the form's cancel button.
   buttonCancel->Text = S"&Cancel";
   this->CancelButton = buttonCancel;

   // Set the button size and location using
   // the Bounds property.
   Button* buttonHelp = new Button();
   buttonHelp->Bounds =  Rectangle(10, 10, 75, 25);
   // Set the Text property of the button.
   buttonHelp->Text = S"&Help";

   // Add the buttons to the form.

   Control* temp1 [] = {buttonOK, buttonCancel, buttonHelp};
   this->Controls->AddRange(temp1);
}
```

Requirements

Platforms: Windows 98, Windows NT 4.0, Windows Millennium Edition, Windows 2000, Windows XP Home Edition, Windows XP Professional, Windows Server 2003 family, .NET Compact Framework - Windows CE .NET

Control.TopLevelControl Property

Gets the parent control that is not parented by another Windows Forms control. Typically, this is the outermost **Form** that the control is contained in.

[Visual Basic]
```
Public ReadOnly Property TopLevelControl As Control
```
[C#]
```
public Control TopLevelControl {get;}
```
[C++]
```
public: __property Control* get_TopLevelControl();
```
[JScript]
```
public function get TopLevelControl() : Control;
```

Property Value

The **Control** that represents the top-level control that contains the current control.

Remarks

The top-level control is defined as the parent control that is not parented by another Windows Forms control. Typically, this is the outermost **Form** that the control is contained in. For example, if the control is contained on an MDI child **Form**, then the top-level control is the Multiple Document Interface (MDI) parent **Form**.

Requirements

Platforms: Windows 98, Windows NT 4.0, Windows Millennium Edition, Windows 2000, Windows XP Home Edition, Windows XP Professional, Windows Server 2003 family, .NET Compact Framework - Windows CE .NET

.NET Framework Security:

- **UIPermission** for all windows to get this property value. Associated enumeration: **UIPermissionWindow.AllWindows**

Control.Visible Property

Gets or sets a value indicating whether the control is displayed.

[Visual Basic]
```
Public Property Visible As Boolean
```
[C#]
```
public bool Visible {get; set;}
```
[C++]
```
public: __property bool get_Visible();
public: __property void set_Visible(bool);
```
[JScript]
```
public function get Visible() : Boolean;
public function set Visible(Boolean);
```

Property Value

true if the control is displayed; otherwise, **false**. The default is **true**.

Example

[Visual Basic, C#, JScript] The following example uses the derived classes **VScrollBar** and **HScrollBar** and sets their **Visible** property values, based on the size of an **Image** being displayed in a **PictureBox** control. This example assumes that a **PictureBox** has been created on a form and that **HScrollBar** and **VScrollBar** controls have been created on the **PictureBox**. This code should be called when the image is loaded into the picture box and by the **Resize** event of the form.

[Visual Basic]
```
Public Sub DisplayScrollBars()
    ' Display or hide the scroll bars based upon
    ' whether the image is larger than the PictureBox.
    If pictureBox1.Width > pictureBox1.Image.Width Then
        hScrollBar1.Visible = False
    Else
        hScrollBar1.Visible = True
    End If

    If pictureBox1.Height > pictureBox1.Image.Height Then
        vScrollBar1.Visible = False
    Else
        vScrollBar1.Visible = True
    End If
End Sub 'DisplayScrollBars
```

[C#]
```
public void DisplayScrollBars()
 {
    // Display or hide the scroll bars based upon
    // whether the image is larger than the PictureBox.
    if (pictureBox1.Width > pictureBox1.Image.Width)
    {
       hScrollBar1.Visible = false;
    }
    else
    {
       hScrollBar1.Visible = true;
    }

    if (pictureBox1.Height > pictureBox1.Image.Height)
    {
       vScrollBar1.Visible = false;
    }
    else
    {
       vScrollBar1.Visible = true;
    }
 }
```

[JScript]
```
public function DisplayScrollBars()
 {
    // Display or hide the scroll bars based upon
    // whether the image is larger than the PictureBox.
    if (pictureBox1.Width > pictureBox1.Image.Width)
    {
       hScrollBar1.Visible = false;
    }
    else
    {
       hScrollBar1.Visible = true;
    }

    if (pictureBox1.Height > pictureBox1.Image.Height)
    {
       vScrollBar1.Visible = false;
    }
    else
    {
       vScrollBar1.Visible = true;
    }
 }
```

Requirements

Platforms: Windows 98, Windows NT 4.0, Windows Millennium Edition, Windows 2000, Windows XP Home Edition, Windows XP Professional, Windows Server 2003 family, .NET Compact Framework - Windows CE .NET

Control.Width Property

Gets or sets the width of the control.

[Visual Basic]
```
Public Property Width As Integer
```
[C#]
```
public int Width {get; set;}
```
[C++]
```
public: __property int get_Width();
public: __property void set_Width(int);
```
[JScript]
```
public function get Width() : int;
public function set Width(int);
```

Property Value

The width of the control in pixels.

Remarks

Changes made to the **Width** and **Left** property values cause the **Right** property value of the control to change.

Example

[Visual Basic, C#, C++] The following example creates three **Button** controls on a form and sets their size and location by using the various size-related and location-related properties. This example assumes you have a **Form** that has a width and height of at least 300 pixels.

[Visual Basic]
```
' Create three buttons and place them on a form using
' several size and location related properties.
Private Sub AddOKCancelButtons()
    ' Set the button size and location using
      ' the Size and Location properties.
    Dim buttonOK As New Button()
    buttonOK.Location = New Point(136, 248)
    buttonOK.Size = New Size(75, 25)
    ' Set the Text property and make the
    ' button the form's default button.
    buttonOK.Text = "&OK"
    Me.AcceptButton = buttonOK

    ' Set the button size and location using the Top,
    ' Left, Width, and Height properties.
    Dim buttonCancel As New Button()
    buttonCancel.Top = buttonOK.Top
    buttonCancel.Left = buttonOK.Right + 5
    buttonCancel.Width = buttonOK.Width
    buttonCancel.Height = buttonOK.Height
    ' Set the Text property and make the
    ' button the form's cancel button.
    buttonCancel.Text = "&Cancel"
    Me.CancelButton = buttonCancel

    ' Set the button size and location using
    ' the Bounds property.
    Dim buttonHelp As New Button()
    buttonHelp.Bounds = New Rectangle(10, 10, 75, 25)
    ' Set the Text property of the button.
    buttonHelp.Text = "&Help"

    ' Add the buttons to the form.
    Me.Controls.AddRange(New Control() {buttonOK, buttonCancel, ↵
buttonHelp})
End Sub
```

[C#]
```
// Create three buttons and place them on a form using
// several size and location related properties.
private void AddOKCancelButtons()
{
    // Set the button size and location using
    // the Size and Location properties.
    Button buttonOK = new Button();
    buttonOK.Location = new Point(136,248);
    buttonOK.Size = new Size(75,25);
    // Set the Text property and make the
    // button the form's default button.
    buttonOK.Text = "&OK";
    this.AcceptButton = buttonOK;

    // Set the button size and location using the Top,
    // Left, Width, and Height properties.
    Button buttonCancel = new Button();
    buttonCancel.Top = buttonOK.Top;
    buttonCancel.Left = buttonOK.Right + 5;
    buttonCancel.Width = buttonOK.Width;
    buttonCancel.Height = buttonOK.Height;
    // Set the Text property and make the
    // button the form's cancel button.
    buttonCancel.Text = "&Cancel";
    this.CancelButton = buttonCancel;

    // Set the button size and location using
    // the Bounds property.
    Button buttonHelp = new Button();
    buttonHelp.Bounds = new Rectangle(10,10, 75, 25);
    // Set the Text property of the button.
    buttonHelp.Text = "&Help";

    // Add the buttons to the form.
    this.Controls.AddRange(new Control[] {buttonOK, buttonCancel, ↵
buttonHelp} );
}
```

[C++]
```
// Create three buttons and place them on a form using
// several size and location related properties.
void AddOKCancelButtons() {
    // Set the button size and location using
    // the Size and Location properties.
    Button* buttonOK = new Button();
    buttonOK->Location =  Point(136, 248);
    buttonOK->Size =  System::Drawing::Size(75, 25);
    // Set the Text property and make the
    // button the form's default button.
    buttonOK->Text = S"&OK";
    this->AcceptButton = buttonOK;

    // Set the button size and location using the Top,
    // Left, Width, and Height properties.
    Button* buttonCancel = new Button();
    buttonCancel->Top = buttonOK->Top;
    buttonCancel->Left = buttonOK->Right + 5;
    buttonCancel->Width = buttonOK->Width;
    buttonCancel->Height = buttonOK->Height;
    // Set the Text property and make the
    // button the form's cancel button.
    buttonCancel->Text = S"&Cancel";
    this->CancelButton = buttonCancel;

    // Set the button size and location using
    // the Bounds property.
    Button* buttonHelp = new Button();
    buttonHelp->Bounds =  Rectangle(10, 10, 75, 25);
```

```
    // Set the Text property of the button.
    buttonHelp->Text = S"&Help";

    // Add the buttons to the form.

    Control* templ [] = {buttonOK, buttonCancel, buttonHelp};
    this->Controls->AddRange(templ);
}
```

Requirements

Platforms: Windows 98, Windows NT 4.0, Windows Millennium Edition, Windows 2000, Windows XP Home Edition, Windows XP Professional, Windows Server 2003 family, .NET Compact Framework - Windows CE .NET

Control.WindowTarget Property

This member supports the .NET Framework infrastructure and is not intended to be used directly from your code.

```
[Visual Basic]
Public Property WindowTarget As IWindowTarget
[C#]
public IWindowTarget WindowTarget {get; set;}
[C++]
public: __property IWindowTarget* get_WindowTarget();
public: __property void set_WindowTarget(IWindowTarget*);
[JScript]
public function get WindowTarget() : IWindowTarget;
public function set WindowTarget(IWindowTarget);
```

Control.AccessibilityNotifyClients Method

Notifies the accessibility client applications of the specified **AccessibleEvents** for the specified child control.

```
[Visual Basic]
Protected Sub AccessibilityNotifyClients( _
   ByVal accEvent As AccessibleEvents, _
   ByVal childID As Integer _
)
[C#]
protected void AccessibilityNotifyClients(
   AccessibleEvents accEvent,
   int childID
);
[C++]
protected: void AccessibilityNotifyClients(
   AccessibleEvents accEvent,
   int childID
);
[JScript]
protected function AccessibilityNotifyClients(
   accEvent : AccessibleEvents,
   childID : int
);
```

Parameters

accEvent
The **AccessibleEvents** object to notify the accessibility client applications of.

childID
The child **Control** to notify of the accessible event.

Remarks

You must call the **ControlAccessibleObject.NotifyClients** method for each **AccessibleEvents** object the accessibility client applications are to be notified of. The **NotifyClients** method is typically called when a property is set or from within an event handler. For example, you might call the **NotifyClients** method and pass in **AccessibleEvents.Hide** from within the event handler for the **Control.VisibleChanged** event.

Example

[Visual Basic, C#, C++] The following example demonstrates the creation of an accessibility-aware chart control, using the **AccessibleObject** and **Control.ControlAccessibleObject** classes to expose accessible information. The control plots two curves along with a legend. The `ChartControlAccessibleObject` class, which derives from **ControlAccessibleObject**, is used in the **CreateAccessibilityInstance** method to provide custom accessible information for the chart control. Since the chart legend is not an actual **Control**-based control, but instead is drawn by the chart control, it does not any built-in accessible information. Because of this, the `ChartControlAccessibleObject` class overrides the **GetChild** method to return the `CurveLegendAccessibleObject` that represents accessible information for each part of the legend. When an accessible-aware application uses this control, the control can provide the necessary accessible information.

[Visual Basic, C#, C++] This code excerpt demonstrates calling the **AccessibilityNotifyClients** method. See the **AccessibleObject** class overview for the complete code example.

```
[Visual Basic]
' Gets or sets the location for the curve legend.
Public Property Location() As Point
    Get
        Return m_location
    End Get
    Set
        m_location = value
        chart.Invalidate()

        ' Notifies the chart of the location change. This is used for
        ' the accessibility information.                                ↵
AccessibleEvents.LocationChange
        ' tells the chart the reason for the notification.
        chart.ExposeAccessibilityNotifyClients                          ↵
(AccessibleEvents.LocationChange, _
                CType(AccessibilityObject,                              ↵
CurveLegendAccessibleObject).ID)
    End Set
End Property

' Gets or sets the Name for the curve legend.
Public Property Name() As String
    Get
        Return m_name
    End Get
    Set
        If m_name <> value Then
            m_name = value
            chart.Invalidate()

            ' Notifies the chart of the name change. This is used for
            ' the accessibility information.                            ↵
AccessibleEvents.NameChange
            ' tells the chart the reason for the notification.

chart.ExposeAccessibilityNotifyClients(AccessibleEvents.NameChange, _
                    CType(AccessibilityObject,                          ↵
CurveLegendAccessibleObject).ID)
        End If
    End Set
End Property
```

```
' Gets or sets the Selected state for the curve legend.
Public Property Selected() As Boolean
    Get
        Return m_selected
    End Get
    Set
        If m_selected <> value Then
            m_selected = value
            chart.Invalidate()

            ' Notifies the chart of the selection value change.        ↵
 This is used for
            ' the accessibility information. The AccessibleEvents      ↵
 value varies
            ' on whether the selection is true                          ↵
 (AccessibleEvents.SelectionAdd) or
            ' false (AccessibleEvents.SelectionRemove).
            If m_selected Then

chart.ExposeAccessibilityNotifyClients(AccessibleEvents.SelectionAdd, _
                        CType(AccessibilityObject,                       ↵
CurveLegendAccessibleObject).ID)
            Else
                chart.ExposeAccessibilityNotifyClients                   ↵
 (AccessibleEvents.SelectionRemove, _
                        CType(AccessibilityObject,                       ↵
CurveLegendAccessibleObject).ID)
            End If
        End If
    End Set
End Property
```

[C#]

```
// Gets or sets the location for the curve legend.
public Point Location
{
    get {
        return location;
    }
    set {
        location = value;
        chart.Invalidate();

        // Notifies the chart of the location change. This is used for
        // the accessibility information.                               ↵
AccessibleEvents.LocationChange
        // tells the chart the reason for the notification.


chart.AccessibilityNotifyClients(AccessibleEvents.LocationChange,
            ((CurveLegendAccessibleObject)AccessibilityObject).ID);
    }
}

// Gets or sets the Name for the curve legend.
public string Name
{
    get {
        return name;
    }
    set {
        if (name != value)
        {
            name = value;
            chart.Invalidate();

            // Notifies the chart of the name change. This is used for
            // the accessibility information.                           ↵
AccessibleEvents.NameChange
            // tells the chart the reason for the notification.

            chart.AccessibilityNotifyClients(AccessibleEvents.NameChange,
                ((CurveLegendAccessibleObject)AccessibilityObject).ID);
        }
    }
}

// Gets or sets the Selected state for the curve legend.
public bool Selected
{
    get {
        return selected;
    }
    set {
        if (selected != value)
        {
            selected = value;
            chart.Invalidate();

            // Notifies the chart of the selection value change.        ↵
This is used for
            // the accessibility information. The                       ↵
AccessibleEvents value depends upon
            // if the selection is true                                 ↵
 (AccessibleEvents.SelectionAdd) or
            // false (AccessibleEvents.SelectionRemove).
            chart.AccessibilityNotifyClients(
                selected ? AccessibleEvents.SelectionAdd :              ↵
AccessibleEvents.SelectionRemove,
                ((CurveLegendAccessibleObject)AccessibilityObject).ID);
        }
    }
}
```

[C++]

```
// Gets or sets the location for the curve legend.
   public:
__property Point get_Location() {
   return location;
}
__property void set_Location(Point value) {
   location = value;
   chart->Invalidate();

   // Notifies the chart of the location change. This is used for
   // the accessibility information. AccessibleEvents::LocationChange
   // tells the chart the reason for the notification.

   chart->AccessibilityNotifyClients(AccessibleEvents::LocationChange,
      (dynamic_cast<CurveLegendAccessibleObject*>(AccessibilityObject))-
>ID);
}

// Gets or sets the Name for the curve legend.
   public:
__property String* get_Name() {
   return name;
}
__property void set_Name(String* value) {
   if (name != value) {
      name = value;
      chart->Invalidate();

      // Notifies the chart of the name change. This is used for
      // the accessibility information. AccessibleEvents::NameChange
      // tells the chart the reason for the notification.

      chart->AccessibilityNotifyClients(AccessibleEvents::NameChange,

(dynamic_cast<CurveLegendAccessibleObject*>(AccessibilityObject))->ID);
   }
}

// Gets or sets the Selected state for the curve legend.
   public:
__property bool get_Selected() {
   return selected;
}
__property void set_Selected(bool value) {
   if (selected != value) {
      selected = value;
      chart->Invalidate();
```

```
      // Notifies the chart of the selection value change.       ↵
This is used for
      // the accessibility information. The AccessibleEvents     ↵
value depends upon
      // if the selection is true (AccessibleEvents::SelectionAdd) or
      // false (AccessibleEvents::SelectionRemove).
      chart->AccessibilityNotifyClients(selected ?
AccessibleEvents::SelectionAdd : AccessibleEvents::SelectionRemove,

(dynamic_cast<CurveLegendAccessibleObject*>(AccessibilityObject))->ID);
   }
}
```

Requirements

Platforms: Windows 98, Windows NT 4.0, Windows Millennium Edition, Windows 2000, Windows XP Home Edition, Windows XP Professional, Windows Server 2003 family

Control.BeginInvoke Method

Executes a delegate asynchronously on the thread that the control's underlying handle was created on.

Overload List

Executes the specified delegate asynchronously on the thread that the control's underlying handle was created on.

[Visual Basic] **Overloads Public Function BeginInvoke(Delegate) As IAsyncResult**

[C#] **public IAsyncResult BeginInvoke(Delegate);**

[C++] **public: IAsyncResult* BeginInvoke(Delegate*);**

[JScript] **public function BeginInvoke(Delegate) : IAsyncResult;**

Executes the specified delegate asynchronously with the specified arguments, on the thread that the control's underlying handle was created on.

[Visual Basic] **Overloads Public Overridable Function BeginInvoke(Delegate, Object()) As IAsyncResult Implements ISynchronizeInvoke.BeginInvoke**

[C#] **public virtual IAsyncResult BeginInvoke(Delegate, object[]);**

[C++] **public: virtual IAsyncResult* BeginInvoke(Delegate*, Object[]);**

[JScript] **public function BeginInvoke(Delegate, Object[]) : IAsyncResult;**

Control.BeginInvoke Method (Delegate)

Executes the specified delegate asynchronously on the thread that the control's underlying handle was created on.

[Visual Basic]
```
Overloads Public Function BeginInvoke( _
   ByVal method As Delegate _
) As IAsyncResult
```
[C#]
```
public IAsyncResult BeginInvoke(
   Delegate method
);
```
[C++]
```
public: IAsyncResult* BeginInvoke(
   Delegate* method
);
```
[JScript]
```
public function BeginInvoke(
   method : Delegate
) : IAsyncResult;
```

Parameters

method
A delegate to a method that takes no parameters.

Return Value

An **IAsyncResult** object that represents the result of the **BeginInvoke** operation.

Remarks

The delegate is called asynchronously, and this method returns immediately. You can call this method from any thread, even the thread that owns the control's handle. If the control's handle does not exist yet, this method searches up the control's parent chain until it finds a control or form that does have a window handle. If no appropriate handle can be found, **BeginInvoke** will throw an exception. Exceptions within the delegate method are considered untrapped and will be sent to the application's untrapped exception handler.

> **Note** The **BeginInvoke** method calls the specified delegate back on a different thread pool thread. You should not block a thread pool thread for any length of time.

> **Note** There are four methods on a control that are safe to call from any thread: **Invoke**, **BeginInvoke**, **EndInvoke**, and **CreateGraphics**. For all other method calls, you should use one of the invoke methods to marshal the call to the control's thread.

Requirements

Platforms: Windows 98, Windows NT 4.0, Windows Millennium Edition, Windows 2000, Windows XP Home Edition, Windows XP Professional, Windows Server 2003 family

Control.BeginInvoke Method (Delegate, Object[])

Executes the specified delegate asynchronously with the specified arguments, on the thread that the control's underlying handle was created on.

[Visual Basic]
```
Overloads Public Overridable Function BeginInvoke( _
   ByVal method As Delegate, _
   ByVal args() As Object _
) As IAsyncResult Implements ISynchronizeInvoke.BeginInvoke
```
[C#]
```
public virtual IAsyncResult BeginInvoke(
   Delegate method,
   object[] args
);
```
[C++]
```
public: virtual IAsyncResult* BeginInvoke(
   Delegate* method,
   Object* args __gc[]
);
```
[JScript]
```
public function BeginInvoke(
   method : Delegate,
   args : Object[]
) : IAsyncResult;
```

Parameters

method

A delegate to a method that takes parameters of the same number and type that are contained in the *args* parameter.

args

An array of objects to pass as arguments to the given method. This can be null if no arguments are needed.

Return Value

An **IAsyncResult** object that represents the result of the **BeginInvoke** operation.

Implements

ISynchronizeInvoke.BeginInvoke

Remarks

The delegate is called asynchronously, and this method returns immediately. You can call this method from any thread, even the thread that owns the control's handle. If the control's handle does not exist yet, this method searches up the control's parent chain until it finds a control or form that does have a window handle. If no appropriate handle can be found, **BeginInvoke** will throw an exception. Exceptions within the delegate method are considered untrapped and will be sent to the application's untrapped exception handler.

> **Note** The **BeginInvoke** method calls the specified delegate back on a different thread pool thread. You should not block a thread pool thread for any length of time.

> **Note** There are four methods on a control that are safe to call from any thread: **Invoke**, **BeginInvoke**, **EndInvoke**, and **CreateGraphics**. For all other method calls, you should use one of the invoke methods to marshal the call to the control's thread.

Requirements

Platforms: Windows 98, Windows NT 4.0, Windows Millennium Edition, Windows 2000, Windows XP Home Edition, Windows XP Professional, Windows Server 2003 family

Control.BringToFront Method

Brings the control to the front of the z-order.

```
[Visual Basic]
Public Sub BringToFront()
[C#]
public void BringToFront();
[C++]
public: void BringToFront();
[JScript]
public function BringToFront();
```

Remarks

The control is moved to the front of the z-order. If the control is a child of another control, the child control is moved to the front of the z-order. **BringToFront** does not make a control a top-level control.

Example

[Visual Basic, C#, C++] The following example ensures that a **Label** is visible by calling its **BringToFront** method. This example assumes you have a **Form** with a **Panel** named `panel1`, and a **Label** named `label1`.

```
[Visual Basic]
Private Sub MakeLabelVisible()
   ' If the panel contains label1, bring it
   ' to the front to make sure it is visible.
   If panel1.Contains(label1) Then
      label1.BringToFront()
   End If
End Sub
```

```
[C#]
private void MakeLabelVisible()
{
   /* If the panel contains label1, bring it
   * to the front to make sure it is visible. */
   if(panel1.Contains(label1))
   {
      label1.BringToFront();
   }
}
```

```
[C++]
private:
    void MakeLabelVisible() {
        /* If the panel contains label1, bring it
         * to the front to make sure it is visible. */
        if (panel1->Contains(label1)) {
            label1->BringToFront();
        }
    }
```

Requirements

Platforms: Windows 98, Windows NT 4.0, Windows Millennium Edition, Windows 2000, Windows XP Home Edition, Windows XP Professional, Windows Server 2003 family, .NET Compact Framework - Windows CE .NET

Control.Contains Method

Retrieves a value indicating whether the specified control is a child of the control.

```
[Visual Basic]
Public Function Contains( _
   ByVal ctl As Control _
) As Boolean
[C#]
public bool Contains(
   Control ctl
);
[C++]
public: bool Contains(
   Control* ctl
);
[JScript]
public function Contains(
   ctl : Control
) : Boolean;
```

Parameters

ctl

The **Control** to evaluate.

Return Value

true if the specified control is a child of the control; otherwise, **false**.

Example

[Visual Basic, C#, C++] The following example ensures that a **Label** is visible by calling its **BringToFront** method. This example assumes you have a **Form** with a **Panel** named `panel1`, and a **Label** named `label1`.

[Visual Basic]
```
Private Sub MakeLabelVisible()
   ' If the panel contains label1, bring it
   ' to the front to make sure it is visible.
   If panel1.Contains(label1) Then
      label1.BringToFront()
   End If
End Sub
```

[C#]
```
private void MakeLabelVisible()
{
   /* If the panel contains label1, bring it
   * to the front to make sure it is visible. */
   if(panel1.Contains(label1))
   {
      label1.BringToFront();
   }
}
```

[C++]
```
private:
    void MakeLabelVisible() {
        /* If the panel contains label1, bring it
         * to the front to make sure it is visible. */
        if (panel1->Contains(label1)) {
            label1->BringToFront();
        }
    }
```

[JScript] No example is available for JScript. To view a Visual Basic, C#, or C++ example, click the Language Filter button <IMG SRC="filter1a.gif" ALT="Language Filter" BORDER=0> in the upper-left corner of the page.

Requirements

Platforms: Windows 98, Windows NT 4.0, Windows Millennium Edition, Windows 2000, Windows XP Home Edition, Windows XP Professional, Windows Server 2003 family

Control.CreateAccessibilityInstance Method

Creates a new accessibility object for the control.

[Visual Basic]
```
Protected Overridable Function CreateAccessibilityInstance() As _
   AccessibleObject
```
[C#]
```
protected virtual AccessibleObject CreateAccessibilityInstance();
```
[C++]
```
protected: virtual AccessibleObject* CreateAccessibilityInstance();
```
[JScript]
```
protected function CreateAccessibilityInstance() : AccessibleObject;
```

Return Value

A new **AccessibleObject** for the control.

Remarks

If you do not explicitly call the **CreateAccessibilityInstance** method, it will be called when the **AccessibilityObject** property is referenced.

> **Note** To get or set the **AccessibilityObject** property, you must add a reference to the **Accessibility** assembly installed with the .NET Framework.

Notes to Inheritors: When overriding **CreateAccessibility-Instance** in a derived class, you should not call the base class's **CreateAccessibilityInstance** method.

Example

[Visual Basic, C#, C++] The following example demonstrates the creation of an accessibility-aware chart control, using the **AccessibleObject** and **Control.ControlAccessibleObject** classes to expose accessible information. The control plots two curves along with a legend. The `ChartControlAccessibleObject` class, which derives from **ControlAccessibleObject**, is used in the **CreateAccessibility-Instance** method to provide custom accessible information for the chart control. Since the chart legend is not an actual **Control**-based control, but instead is drawn by the chart control, it does not any built-in accessible information. Because of this, the `ChartControl-AccessibleObject` class overrides the **GetChild** method to return the `CurveLegendAccessibleObject` that represents accessible information for each part of the legend. When an accessible-aware application uses this control, the control can provide the necessary accessible information.

[Visual Basic, C#, C++] This code excerpt demonstrates overriding the **CreateAccessibilityInstance** method. See the **AccessibleObject** class overview for the complete code example.

[Visual Basic]
```
' Overridden to return the custom AccessibleObject
' for the entire chart.
Protected Overrides Function CreateAccessibilityInstance() As
AccessibleObject
    Return New ChartControlAccessibleObject(Me)
End Function
```

[C#]
```
// Overridden to return the custom AccessibleObject
// for the entire chart.
protected override AccessibleObject CreateAccessibilityInstance()
{
    return new ChartControlAccessibleObject(this);
}
```

[C++]
```
// Overridden to return the custom AccessibleObject
// for the entire chart.
protected:
AccessibleObject* CreateAccessibilityInstance() {
   return new ChartControlAccessibleObject(this);
}
```

Requirements

Platforms: Windows 98, Windows NT 4.0, Windows Millennium Edition, Windows 2000, Windows XP Home Edition, Windows XP Professional, Windows Server 2003 family

Control.CreateControl Method

Forces the creation of the control, including the creation of the handle and any child controls.

[Visual Basic]
```
Public Sub CreateControl()
```
[C#]
```
public void CreateControl();
```

```
[C++]
public: void CreateControl();
[JScript]
public function CreateControl();
```

Remarks

The **CreateControl** method forces a handle to be created for the control and its child controls. This method is used when you need a handle immediately for manipulation of the control or its children; simply calling a control's constructor does not create the **Handle**.

Requirements

Platforms: Windows 98, Windows NT 4.0,
Windows Millennium Edition, Windows 2000,
Windows XP Home Edition, Windows XP Professional,
Windows Server 2003 family

Control.CreateControlsInstance Method

Creates a new instance of the control collection for the control.

```
[Visual Basic]
Protected Overridable Function CreateControlsInstance() As _
   ControlCollection
[C#]
protected virtual ControlCollection CreateControlsInstance();
[C++]
protected: virtual ControlCollection* CreateControlsInstance();
[JScript]
protected function CreateControlsInstance() : ControlCollection;
```

Return Value

A new instance of **Control.ControlCollection** assigned to the control.

Remarks

Notes to Inheritors: The base class version of this method should not be called by a derived class.

Requirements

Platforms: Windows 98, Windows NT 4.0,
Windows Millennium Edition, Windows 2000,
Windows XP Home Edition, Windows XP Professional,
Windows Server 2003 family

Control.CreateGraphics Method

Creates the **Graphics** object for the control.

```
[Visual Basic]
Public Function CreateGraphics() As Graphics
[C#]
public Graphics CreateGraphics();
[C++]
public: Graphics* CreateGraphics();
[JScript]
public function CreateGraphics() : Graphics;
```

Return Value

The **Graphics** object for the control.

Remarks

The returned **Graphics** object must be disposed through a call to its **Dispose** method when it is no longer needed. The **Graphics** object is only valid for the duration of the current window's message.

> **Note** There are four methods on a control that are safe to call from any thread: **Invoke**, **BeginInvoke**, **EndInvoke**, and **CreateGraphics**. For all other method calls, you should use one of the invoke methods to marshal the call to the control's thread.

Example

[Visual Basic, C#] The following example resizes the specified control so the control will accommodate its formatted text. The formatted text is the **Text** property with the control's assigned **Font** applied to the text. The `AutoSizeControl` method in this example also has a `textPadding` parameter that represents the padding to apply to all edges of the control. To make the padding appear equal, align the text with the **ContentAlignment.MiddleCenter** value, if your control supports it.

```
[Visual Basic]
Private Sub AutoSizeControl(control As Control, textPadding As Integer)
   ' Create a Graphics object for the Control.
   Dim g As Graphics = control.CreateGraphics()

   ' Get the Size needed to accommodate the formatted Text.
   Dim preferredSize As Size = g.MeasureString( _
     control.Text, control.Font).ToSize()

   ' Pad the text and resize the control.
   control.ClientSize = New Size( _
     preferredSize.Width + textPadding * 2, _
     preferredSize.Height + textPadding * 2)

   ' Clean up the Graphics object.
   g.Dispose()
End Sub
```

```
[C#]
private void AutoSizeControl(Control control, int textPadding)
{
   // Create a Graphics object for the Control.
   Graphics g = control.CreateGraphics();

   // Get the Size needed to accommodate the formatted Text.
   Size preferredSize = g.MeasureString(
      control.Text, control.Font).ToSize();

   // Pad the text and resize the control.
   control.ClientSize = new Size(
      preferredSize.Width + (textPadding * 2),
      preferredSize.Height+(textPadding * 2) );

   // Clean up the Graphics object.
   g.Dispose();
}
```

Requirements

Platforms: Windows 98, Windows NT 4.0,
Windows Millennium Edition, Windows 2000,
Windows XP Home Edition, Windows XP Professional,
Windows Server 2003 family,
.NET Compact Framework - Windows CE .NET

.NET Framework Security:

- **UIPermission** for safe subwindows to call this method. Associated enumeration: **UIPermissionWindow.SafeSubWindows**

Control.CreateHandle Method

Creates a handle for the control.

[Visual Basic]
```
Protected Overridable Sub CreateHandle()
```
[C#]
```
protected virtual void CreateHandle();
```
[C++]
```
protected: virtual void CreateHandle();
```
[JScript]
```
protected function CreateHandle();
```

Exceptions

Exception Type	Condition
ObjectDisposed-Exception	The object is in a disposed state.

Remarks

You typically should not call the **CreateHandle** method directly. The preferred method is to call the **CreateControl** method, which forces a handle to be created for the control and its child controls when the control is created.

Notes to Inheritors: When overriding **CreateHandle** in a derived class, be sure to call the base class's **CreateHandle** method to ensure that the handle is created.

Requirements

Platforms: Windows 98, Windows NT 4.0, Windows Millennium Edition, Windows 2000, Windows XP Home Edition, Windows XP Professional, Windows Server 2003 family

.NET Framework Security:

- **UIPermission** for all windows for inheriting classes to call this method. Associated enumeration: **UIPermissionWindow.AllWindows**

Control.DefWndProc Method

Sends the specified message to the default window procedure.

[Visual Basic]
```
Protected Overridable Sub DefWndProc( _
   ByRef m As Message _
)
```
[C#]
```
protected virtual void DefWndProc(
   ref Message m
);
```
[C++]
```
protected: virtual void DefWndProc(
   Message* m
);
```
[JScript]
```
protected function DefWndProc(
   m : Message
);
```

Parameters

m

The Windows **Message** to process.

Remarks

For more information about processing Windows messages, see the **WindowProc** function documentation in the Windows Platform SDK reference located in the MSDN Library.

Requirements

Platforms: Windows 98, Windows NT 4.0, Windows Millennium Edition, Windows 2000, Windows XP Home Edition, Windows XP Professional, Windows Server 2003 family

.NET Framework Security:

- **SecurityPermission** for inheriting classes to call unmanaged code. Associated enumeration: **SecurityPermissionFlag.UnmanagedCode**
- **SecurityPermission** for the immediate caller to call unmanaged code. Associated enumeration: **SecurityPermissionFlag.UnmanagedCode**

Control.DestroyHandle Method

Destroys the handle associated with the control.

[Visual Basic]
```
Protected Overridable Sub DestroyHandle()
```
[C#]
```
protected virtual void DestroyHandle();
```
[C++]
```
protected: virtual void DestroyHandle();
```
[JScript]
```
protected function DestroyHandle();
```

Remarks

Notes to Inheritors: When overriding **DestroyHandle** in a derived class, be sure to call the base class's **DestroyHandle** method to ensure that the handle is destroyed.

Requirements

Platforms: Windows 98, Windows NT 4.0, Windows Millennium Edition, Windows 2000, Windows XP Home Edition, Windows XP Professional, Windows Server 2003 family

.NET Framework Security:

- **SecurityPermission** for inheriting classes to call unmanaged code. Associated enumeration: **SecurityPermissionFlag.UnmanagedCode**
- **SecurityPermission** for the immediate caller to call unmanaged code. Associated enumeration: **SecurityPermissionFlag.UnmanagedCode**

Control.Dispose Method

Releases all resources used by the **Control**.

Overload List

Releases the unmanaged resources used by the **Control** and optionally releases the managed resources.

Supported by the .NET Compact Framework.

[Visual Basic] **Overloads Overrides Protected Sub Dispose(Boolean)**

[C#] **protected override void Dispose(bool);**

[C++] **protected: void Dispose(bool);**

[JScript] **protected override function Dispose(Boolean);**

Inherited from **Component**.

Supported by the .NET Compact Framework.

[Visual Basic] **Overloads Public Overridable Sub Dispose() Implements IDisposable.Dispose**

[C#] **public virtual void Dispose();**

[C++] **public: virtual void Dispose();**

[JScript] **public function Dispose();**

Control.Dispose Method (Boolean)

Releases the unmanaged resources used by the **Control** and optionally releases the managed resources.

```
[Visual Basic]
Overrides Overloads Protected Sub Dispose( _
   ByVal disposing As Boolean _
)
[C#]
protected override void Dispose(
   bool disposing
);
[C++]
protected: void Dispose(
   bool disposing
);
[JScript]
protected override function Dispose(
   disposing : Boolean
);
```

Parameters

disposing

true to release both managed and unmanaged resources; **false** to release only unmanaged resources.

Remarks

This method is called by the public **Dispose()** method and the **Finalize** method. **Dispose()** invokes the protected **Dispose(Boolean)** method with the *disposing* parameter set to **true**. **Finalize** invokes **Dispose** with *disposing* set to **false**.

When the *disposing* parameter is **true**, this method releases all resources held by any managed objects that this **Control** references. This method invokes the **Dispose()** method of each referenced object.

Notes to Inheritors: **Dispose** can be called multiple times by other objects. When overriding **Dispose(Boolean)**, be careful not to reference objects that have been previously disposed of in an earlier call to **Dispose**.

Requirements

Platforms: Windows 98, Windows NT 4.0, Windows Millennium Edition, Windows 2000, Windows XP Home Edition, Windows XP Professional, Windows Server 2003 family, .NET Compact Framework - Windows CE .NET

Control.DoDragDrop Method

Begins a drag-and-drop operation.

```
[Visual Basic]
Public Function DoDragDrop( _
   ByVal data As Object, _
   ByVal allowedEffects As DragDropEffects _
) As DragDropEffects
[C#]
public DragDropEffects DoDragDrop(
   object data,
   DragDropEffects allowedEffects
);
[C++]
public: DragDropEffects DoDragDrop(
   Object* data,
   DragDropEffects allowedEffects
);
[JScript]
public function DoDragDrop(
   data : Object,
   allowedEffects : DragDropEffects
) : DragDropEffects;
```

Parameters

data

The data to drag.

allowedEffects

One of the **DragDropEffects** values.

Return Value

A value from the **DragDropEffects** enumeration that represents the final effect that was performed during the drag-and-drop operation.

Remarks

The *allowedEffects* parameter determines which drag operations can occur. If the drag operation needs to interoperate with applications in another process, data should either be a base managed class (**String**, **Bitmap**, or **Metafile**), or an object that implements **ISerializable** or **IDataObject**.

The following describes how and when events related to drag-and-drop operations are raised.

The **DoDragDrop** method determines the control under the current cursor location. It then checks to see if the control is a valid drop target.

If the control is a valid drop target, the **GiveFeedback** event is raised with the drag-and-drop effect specified. For a list of drag-and-drop effects, see the **DragDropEffects** enumeration.

Changes in the mouse cursor position, keyboard state, and mouse button state are tracked.

- If the user moves out of a window, the **DragLeave** event is raised.
- If the mouse enters another control, the **DragEnter** for that control is raised.
- If the mouse moves but stays within the same control, the **DragOver** event is raised.

If there is a change in the keyboard or mouse button state, the **QueryContinueDrag** event is raised and determines whether to continue the drag, to drop the data, or to cancel the operation based on the value of the **Action** property of the event's **QueryContinueDragEventArgs**.

- If the value is **DragAction.Continue**, the **DragOver** event is raised to continue the operation and the **GiveFeedback** event is raised with the new effect so appropriate visual feedback can be set. For a list of valid drop effects, see the **DragDropEffects** enumeration.

> **Note** The **DragOver** and **GiveFeedback** events are paired so that as the mouse moves across the drop target, the user is given the most up-to-date feedback on the mouse's position.

If the value is **DragAction.Drop**, the drop effect value is returned to the source, so the source application can perform the appropriate operation on the source data; for example, cut the data if the operation was a move.

If the value is **DragAction.Cancel**, the **DragLeave** event is raised.

Example

[Visual Basic, C#, C++] The following example demonstrates a drag-and-drop operation between two **ListBox** controls. The example calls the **DoDragDrop** method when the drag action starts. The drag action starts if the mouse has moved more than **SystemInformation.DragSize** from the mouse location during the **MouseDown** event. The **IndexFromPoint** method is used to determine the index of the item to drag during the **MouseDown** event.

[Visual Basic, C#, C++] The example also demonstrates using custom cursors for the drag-and-drop operation. The example assumes that two cursor files, `3dwarro.cur` and `3dwno.cur`, exist in the application directory, for the custom drag and no-drop cursors, respectively. The custom cursors will be used if the `UseCustomCursorsCheck` **CheckBox** is checked. The custom cursors are set in the **GiveFeedback** event handler.

[Visual Basic, C#, C++] The keyboard state is evaluated in the **DragOver** event handler for the right **ListBox**, to determine what the drag operation will be based upon state of the SHIFT, CTRL, ALT, or CTRL+ALT keys. The location in the **ListBox** where the drop would occur is also determined during the **DragOver** event. If the data to drop is not a **String**, then the **DragEventArgs.Effect** is set to **DragDropEffects.None**. Finally, the status of the drop is displayed in the `DropLocationLabel` **Label**.

[Visual Basic, C#, C++] The data to drop for the right **ListBox** is determined in the **DragDrop** event handler and the **String** value is added at the appropriate place in the **ListBox**. If the drag operation moves outside the bounds of the form, then the drag-and-drop operation is canceled in the **QueryContinueDrag** event handler.

[Visual Basic]

```
Imports System
Imports System.Drawing
Imports System.Windows.Forms

Public NotInheritable Class Form1
    Inherits System.Windows.Forms.Form

    Friend WithEvents ListDragSource As System.Windows.Forms.ListBox
    Friend WithEvents ListDragTarget As System.Windows.Forms.ListBox
    Friend WithEvents UseCustomCursorsCheck As ↵
System.Windows.Forms.CheckBox
    Friend WithEvents DropLocationLabel As System.Windows.Forms.Label

    Private indexOfItemUnderMouseToDrag As Integer
    Private indexOfItemUnderMouseToDrop As Integer

    Private dragBoxFromMouseDown As Rectangle
    Private screenOffset as Point

    Private MyNoDropCursor As Cursor
    Private MyNormalCursor As Cursor

    <System.STAThread()> _
    Public Shared Sub Main()
        System.Windows.Forms.Application.Run(New Form1())
    End Sub 'Main

    Public Sub New()
        MyBase.New()

        Me.ListDragSource = New System.Windows.Forms.ListBox()
        Me.ListDragTarget = New System.Windows.Forms.ListBox()
        Me.UseCustomCursorsCheck = New System.Windows.Forms.CheckBox()
        Me.DropLocationLabel = New System.Windows.Forms.Label()

        Me.SuspendLayout()

        ' ListDragSource
        Me.ListDragSource.Items.AddRange(New Object() {"one", ↵
"two", "three", "four", _
                                    "five", "six", "seven", "eight", _
                                        "nine", "ten"})
        Me.ListDragSource.Location = New System.Drawing.Point(10, 17)
        Me.ListDragSource.Size = New System.Drawing.Size(120, 225)

        ' ListDragTarget
        Me.ListDragTarget.AllowDrop = True
        Me.ListDragTarget.Location = New System.Drawing.Point(154, 17)
        Me.ListDragTarget.Size = New System.Drawing.Size(120, 225)

        ' UseCustomCursorsCheck
        Me.UseCustomCursorsCheck.Location = New ↵
System.Drawing.Point(10, 243)
        Me.UseCustomCursorsCheck.Size = ↵
New System.Drawing.Size(137, 24)
        Me.UseCustomCursorsCheck.Text = "Use Custom Cursors"

        ' DropLocationLabel
        Me.DropLocationLabel.Location = ↵
New System.Drawing.Point(154, 245)
        Me.DropLocationLabel.Size = New System.Drawing.Size(137, 24)
        Me.DropLocationLabel.Text = "None"

        ' Form1
        Me.AutoScaleBaseSize = New System.Drawing.Size(5, 13)
        Me.ClientSize = New System.Drawing.Size(292, 270)
        Me.Controls.AddRange(New ↵
System.Windows.Forms.Control() {Me.ListDragSource, _
                Me.ListDragTarget, Me.UseCustomCursorsCheck, _
                                            Me.DropLocationLabel})

        Me.Text = "Drag and Drop Example"
        Me.ResumeLayout(False)
    End Sub

    Private Sub ListDragSource_MouseDown(ByVal ↵
sender As Object, ByVal e As MouseEventArgs) Handles ↵
ListDragSource.MouseDown

        ' Get the index of the item the mouse is below.
        indexOfItemUnderMouseToDrag = ↵
ListDragSource.IndexFromPoint(e.X, e.Y)

        If (indexOfItemUnderMouseToDrag <> ListBox.NoMatches) Then

            ' Remember the point where the mouse down occurred. ↵
The DragSize indicates
            ' the size that the mouse can move before a drag ↵
 event should be started.
            Dim dragSize As Size = SystemInformation.DragSize

            ' Create a rectangle using the DragSize, with the ↵
 mouse position being
            ' at the center of the rectangle.
            dragBoxFromMouseDown = New Rectangle ↵
 (New Point(e.X - (dragSize.Width / 2), _
                            e.Y - (dragSize.Height / 2)), dragSize)
        Else
            ' Reset the rectangle if the mouse is not over ↵
 an item in the ListBox.
            dragBoxFromMouseDown = Rectangle.Empty
        End If

    End Sub
```

```
    Private Sub ListDragSource_MouseUp(ByVal sender As ↵
Object, ByVal e As MouseEventArgs) Handles ListDragSource.MouseUp

        ' Reset the drag rectangle when the mouse button is raised.
        dragBoxFromMouseDown = Rectangle.Empty
    End Sub

    Private Sub ListDragSource_MouseMove(ByVal sender As ↵
Object, ByVal e As MouseEventArgs) Handles ListDragSource.MouseMove

        If ((e.Button And MouseButtons.Left) = MouseButtons.Left) Then

            ' If the mouse moves outside the rectangle, start the drag.
            If (Rectangle.op_Inequality(dragBoxFromMouseDown, ↵
Rectangle.Empty) And _
                Not dragBoxFromMouseDown.Contains(e.X, e.Y)) Then

                ' Creates custom cursors for the ↵
drag-and-drop operation.
                Try
                    MyNormalCursor = New Cursor("3dwarro.cur")
                    MyNoDropCursor = New Cursor("3dwno.cur")

                Catch
                    ' An error occurred while attempting to ↵
load the cursors so use
                    ' standard cursors.
                    UseCustomCursorsCheck.Checked = False
                Finally
                    ' The screenOffset is used to account ↵
for any desktop bands
                    ' that may be at the top or left side of ↵
the screen when
                    ' determining when to cancel the drag ↵
drop operation.
                    screenOffset = ↵
SystemInformation.WorkingArea.Location

                    ' Proceed with the drag and drop, passing ↵
in the list item.
                    Dim dropEffect As DragDropEffects = ↵
ListDragSource.DoDragDrop(ListDragSource.Items ↵
(indexOfItemUnderMouseToDrag), _
                        DragDropEffects.All Or DragDropEffects.Link)

          ' If the drag operation was a move then remove the item.
                    If (dropEffect = DragDropEffects.Move) Then
ListDragSource.Items.RemoveAt(indexOfItemUnderMouseToDrag)

         ' Select the previous item in the list as long as ↵
the list has an item.
                        If (indexOfItemUnderMouseToDrag > 0) Then
                            ListDragSource.SelectedIndex = ↵
indexOfItemUnderMouseToDrag - 1

                        ElseIf (ListDragSource.Items.Count > 0) Then
                            ' Selects the first item.
                            ListDragSource.SelectedIndex = 0
                        End If
                    End If

                    ' Dispose the cursors since they are ↵
no longer needed.
                    If (Not MyNormalCursor Is Nothing) Then _
                        MyNormalCursor.Dispose()

                    If (Not MyNoDropCursor Is Nothing) Then _
                        MyNoDropCursor.Dispose()
                End Try

            End If
        End If
    End Sub
    Private Sub ListDragSource_GiveFeedback(ByVal sender As ↵
Object, ByVal e As GiveFeedbackEventArgs) Handles ↵
ListDragSource.GiveFeedback

        ' Use custom cursors if the check box is checked.
        If (UseCustomCursorsCheck.Checked) Then

            ' Set the custom cursor based upon the effect.
            e.UseDefaultCursors = False
            If ((e.Effect And DragDropEffects.Move) = ↵
DragDropEffects.Move) Then
                Cursor.Current = MyNormalCursor
            Else
                Cursor.Current = MyNoDropCursor
            End If
        End If

    End Sub

    Private Sub ListDragTarget_DragOver(ByVal sender As Object, ↵
ByVal e As DragEventArgs) Handles ListDragTarget.DragOver
        ' Determine whether string data exists in the drop data. ↵
If not, then
        ' the drop effect reflects that the drop cannot occur.
        If Not (e.Data.GetDataPresent(GetType(System.String))) Then

            e.Effect = DragDropEffects.None
            DropLocationLabel.Text = "None - no string data."
            Return
        End If

        ' Set the effect based upon the KeyState.
        If ((e.KeyState And (8 + 32)) = (8 + 32) And _
            (e.AllowedEffect And DragDropEffects.Link) = ↵
DragDropEffects.Link) Then
            ' KeyState 8 + 32 = CTL + ALT

            ' Link drag and drop effect.
            e.Effect = DragDropEffects.Link

        ElseIf ((e.KeyState And 32) = 32 And _
            (e.AllowedEffect And DragDropEffects.Link) = ↵
DragDropEffects.Link) Then

            ' ALT KeyState for link.
            e.Effect = DragDropEffects.Link

        ElseIf ((e.KeyState And 4) = 4 And _
            (e.AllowedEffect And DragDropEffects.Move) = ↵
DragDropEffects.Move) Then

            ' SHIFT KeyState for move.
            e.Effect = DragDropEffects.Move

        ElseIf ((e.KeyState And 8) = 8 And _
            (e.AllowedEffect And DragDropEffects.Copy) = ↵
DragDropEffects.Copy) Then

            ' CTL KeyState for copy.
            e.Effect = DragDropEffects.Copy

        ElseIf ((e.AllowedEffect And DragDropEffects.Move) = ↵
DragDropEffects.Move) Then

            ' By default, the drop action should be move, if allowed.
            e.Effect = DragDropEffects.Move

        Else
            e.Effect = DragDropEffects.None
        End If

        ' Gets the index of the item the mouse is below.

        ' The mouse locations are relative to the screen, so ↵
they must be
        ' converted to client coordinates.
```

```
        indexOfItemUnderMouseToDrop = _
            ListDragTarget.IndexFromPoint(ListDragTarget.PointToClient ↵
(New Point(e.X, e.Y)))

        ' Updates the label text.
        If (indexOfItemUnderMouseToDrop <> ListBox.NoMatches) Then

            DropLocationLabel.Text = "Drops before item #"             ↵
& (indexOfItemUnderMouseToDrop + 1)
        Else
            DropLocationLabel.Text = "Drops at the end."
        End If

    End Sub

    Private Sub ListDragTarget_DragDrop(ByVal sender As Object,        ↵
ByVal e As DragEventArgs) Handles ListDragTarget.DragDrop
        ' Ensures that the list item index is contained in the data.

        If (e.Data.GetDataPresent(GetType(System.String))) Then

            Dim item As Object =                                       ↵
CType(e.Data.GetData(GetType(System.String)), System.Object)

            ' Perform drag and drop, depending upon the effect.
            If (e.Effect = DragDropEffects.Copy Or _
                e.Effect = DragDropEffects.Move) Then

                ' Insert the item.
                If (indexOfItemUnderMouseToDrop <>                     ↵
ListBox.NoMatches) Then

ListDragTarget.Items.Insert(indexOfItemUnderMouseToDrop, item)
                Else
                    ListDragTarget.Items.Add(item)

                End If
            End If
            ' Reset the label text.
            DropLocationLabel.Text = "None"
        End If
    End Sub
    Private Sub ListDragSource_QueryContinueDrag(ByVal                 ↵
sender As Object, ByVal e As QueryContinueDragEventArgs)               ↵
Handles ListDragSource.QueryContinueDrag
        ' Cancel the drag if the mouse moves off the form.
        Dim lb as ListBox = CType(sender, System.Windows.Forms.ListBox)

        If Not (lb is nothing) Then

            Dim f as Form = lb.FindForm()

            ' Cancel the drag if the mouse moves off the form.         ↵
 The screenOffset
            ' takes into account any desktop bands that may be         ↵
 at the top or left
            ' side of the screen.
            If (((Control.MousePosition.X - screenOffset.X) <          ↵
f.DesktopBounds.Left) Or _
                ((Control.MousePosition.X - screenOffset.X) >          ↵
f.DesktopBounds.Right) Or _
                ((Control.MousePosition.Y - screenOffset.Y) <          ↵
f.DesktopBounds.Top) Or _
                ((Control.MousePosition.Y - screenOffset.Y) >          ↵
f.DesktopBounds.Bottom)) Then

                e.Action = DragAction.Cancel
            End If
        End if
    End Sub
    Private Sub ListDragTarget_DragEnter(ByVal sender As Object,       ↵
 ByVal e As DragEventArgs) Handles ListDragTarget.DragEnter

        ' Reset the label text.
        DropLocationLabel.Text = "None"
    End Sub
    Private Sub ListDragTarget_DragLeave(ByVal sender As Object,       ↵
ByVal e As System.EventArgs) Handles ListDragTarget.DragLeave

        ' Reset the label text.
        DropLocationLabel.Text = "None"
    End Sub
End Class
```

[C#]

```
using System;
using System.Drawing;
using System.Windows.Forms;

namespace Snip_DragNDrop
{
    public class Form1 : System.Windows.Forms.Form
    {
        private System.Windows.Forms.ListBox ListDragSource;
        private System.Windows.Forms.ListBox ListDragTarget;
        private System.Windows.Forms.CheckBox UseCustomCursorsCheck;
        private System.Windows.Forms.Label DropLocationLabel;

        private int indexOfItemUnderMouseToDrag;
        private int indexOfItemUnderMouseToDrop;

        private Rectangle dragBoxFromMouseDown;
        private Point screenOffset;

        private Cursor MyNoDropCursor;
        private Cursor MyNormalCursor;

        /// The main entry point for the application.
        [STAThread]
        static void Main()
        {
            Application.Run(new Form1());
        }

        public Form1()
        {
            this.ListDragSource = new System.Windows.Forms.ListBox();
            this.ListDragTarget = new System.Windows.Forms.ListBox();
            this.UseCustomCursorsCheck = new                           ↵
System.Windows.Forms.CheckBox();
            this.DropLocationLabel = new System.Windows.Forms.Label();

            this.SuspendLayout();

            // ListDragSource
            this.ListDragSource.Items.AddRange(new object[]            ↵
{"one", "two", "three", "four",
                                "five", "six", "seven", "eight",
                                "nine", "ten"});
          this.ListDragSource.Location = new System.Drawing.Point(10, 17);
            this.ListDragSource.Size = new System.Drawing.Size(120, 225);
            this.ListDragSource.MouseDown += new                       ↵
System.Windows.Forms.MouseEventHandler(this.ListDragSource_MouseDown);
            this.ListDragSource.QueryContinueDrag += new               ↵
System.Windows.Forms.QueryContinueDragEventHandler                     ↵
 (this.ListDragSource_QueryContinueDrag);
            this.ListDragSource.MouseUp += new                         ↵
System.Windows.Forms.MouseEventHandler(this.ListDragSource_MouseUp);
            this.ListDragSource.MouseMove += new                       ↵
System.Windows.Forms.MouseEventHandler(this.ListDragSource_MouseMove);
            this.ListDragSource.GiveFeedback += new                    ↵
System.Windows.Forms.GiveFeedbackEventHandler(this.ListDragSource_GiveFe
edback);

            // ListDragTarget
            this.ListDragTarget.AllowDrop = true;
            this.ListDragTarget.Location = new                         ↵
System.Drawing.Point(154, 17);
            this.ListDragTarget.Size = new                             ↵
System.Drawing.Size(120, 225);
```

```
            this.ListDragTarget.DragOver += new                        ↵
System.Windows.Forms.DragEventHandler(this.ListDragTarget_DragOver);
            this.ListDragTarget.DragDrop += new                        ↵
System.Windows.Forms.DragEventHandler(this.ListDragTarget_DragDrop);
            this.ListDragTarget.DragEnter += new                       ↵
System.Windows.Forms.DragEventHandler(this.ListDragTarget_DragEnter);
            this.ListDragTarget.DragLeave += new                       ↵
System.EventHandler(this.ListDragTarget_DragLeave);

            // UseCustomCursorsCheck
            this.UseCustomCursorsCheck.Location = new                  ↵
System.Drawing.Point(10, 243);
            this.UseCustomCursorsCheck.Size = new                      ↵
System.Drawing.Size(137, 24);
            this.UseCustomCursorsCheck.Text = "Use Custom Cursors";

            // DropLocationLabel
            this.DropLocationLabel.Location = new                      ↵
System.Drawing.Point(154, 245);
            this.DropLocationLabel.Size = new                          ↵
 System.Drawing.Size(137, 24);
            this.DropLocationLabel.Text = "None";

            // Form1
            this.AutoScaleBaseSize = new System.Drawing.Size(5, 13);
            this.ClientSize = new System.Drawing.Size(292, 270);
            this.Controls.AddRange(new                                 ↵
System.Windows.Forms.Control[] {this.ListDragSource,
         this.ListDragTarget, this.UseCustomCursorsCheck,
              this.DropLocationLabel});
            this.Text = "Drag and Drop Example";

            this.ResumeLayout(false);

        }

        private void ListDragSource_MouseDown                          ↵
 (object sender, System.Windows.Forms.MouseEventArgs e)
        {
            // Get the index of the item the mouse is below.
            indexOfItemUnderMouseToDrag =                              ↵
ListDragSource.IndexFromPoint(e.X, e.Y);

            if (indexOfItemUnderMouseToDrag != ListBox.NoMatches) {

                // Remember the point where the mouse                  ↵
 down occurred. The DragSize indicates
                // the size that the mouse can move                    ↵
before a drag event should be started.
                Size dragSize = SystemInformation.DragSize;

                // Create a rectangle using the DragSize,              ↵
with the mouse position being
                // at the center of the rectangle.
                dragBoxFromMouseDown = new Rectangle(new               ↵
 Point(e.X - (dragSize.Width /2),
                  e.Y - (dragSize.Height /2)), dragSize);
            } else
                // Reset the rectangle if the mouse is not             ↵
over an item in the ListBox.
                dragBoxFromMouseDown = Rectangle.Empty;

        }

        private void ListDragSource_MouseUp(object sender,             ↵
System.Windows.Forms.MouseEventArgs e) {
            // Reset the drag rectangle when the mouse button          ↵
is raised.
            dragBoxFromMouseDown = Rectangle.Empty;
        }

        private void ListDragSource_MouseMove(object sender,           ↵
System.Windows.Forms.MouseEventArgs e)
        {
            if ((e.Button & MouseButtons.Left) == MouseButtons.Left) {

                // If the mouse moves outside the rectangle,           ↵
start the drag.
                if (dragBoxFromMouseDown != Rectangle.Empty &&
                    !dragBoxFromMouseDown.Contains(e.X, e.Y)) {

                    // Create custom cursors for the drag-and-         ↵
drop operation.
                    try {
                        MyNormalCursor = new Cursor("3dwarro.cur");
                        MyNoDropCursor = new Cursor("3dwno.cur");

                    } catch {
                        // An error occurred while attempting to       ↵
 load the cursors, so use
                        // standard cursors.
                        UseCustomCursorsCheck.Checked = false;
                    }finally {

                        // The screenOffset is used to account         ↵
for any desktop bands
                        // that may be at the top or left side         ↵
of the screen when
                        // determining when to cancel the drag         ↵
 drop operation.
                        screenOffset =                                 ↵
SystemInformation.WorkingArea.Location;

                        // Proceed with the drag and drop,             ↵
passing in the list item.
                        DragDropEffects dropEffect =                   ↵
ListDragSource.DoDragDrop(ListDragSource.Items                         ↵
 [indexOfItemUnderMouseToDrag], DragDropEffects.All |                  ↵
DragDropEffects.Link);

// If the drag operation was a move then remove the item.
                if (dropEffect == DragDropEffects.Move) {
 ListDragSource.Items.RemoveAt(indexOfItemUnderMouseToDrag);

 // Selects the previous item in the list as long as the               ↵
 list has an item.
                            if (indexOfItemUnderMouseToDrag > 0)
       ListDragSource.SelectedIndex = indexOfItemUnderMouseToDrag -1;

                            else if (ListDragSource.Items.Count > 0)
                                // Selects the first item.
                                ListDragSource.SelectedIndex =0;
                        }

 // Dispose of the cursors since they are no longer needed.
                        if (MyNormalCursor != null)
                            MyNormalCursor.Dispose();

                        if (MyNoDropCursor != null)
                            MyNoDropCursor.Dispose();
                    }
                }
            }
        }
        private void ListDragSource_GiveFeedback                       ↵
 (object sender, System.Windows.Forms.GiveFeedbackEventArgs e)
        {
            // Use custom cursors if the check box is checked.
            if (UseCustomCursorsCheck.Checked) {

                // Sets the custom cursor based upon the effect.
                e.UseDefaultCursors = false;
                if ((e.Effect & DragDropEffects.Move) ==               ↵
DragDropEffects.Move)
                    Cursor.Current = MyNormalCursor;
                else
                    Cursor.Current = MyNoDropCursor;
            }
```

```
        }
        private void ListDragTarget_DragOver(object sender,        ↵
System.Windows.Forms.DragEventArgs e)
        {

            // Determine whether string data exists in the drop        ↵
 data. If not, then
            // the drop effect reflects that the drop cannot occur.
            if (!e.Data.GetDataPresent(typeof(System.String))) {

                e.Effect = DragDropEffects.None;
                DropLocationLabel.Text = "None - no string data.";
                return;
            }

            // Set the effect based upon the KeyState.
            if ((e.KeyState & (8+32)) == (8+32) &&
                (e.AllowedEffect & DragDropEffects.Link) ==        ↵
DragDropEffects.Link) {
                // KeyState 8 + 32 = CTL + ALT

                // Link drag and drop effect.
                e.Effect = DragDropEffects.Link;

            } else if ((e.KeyState & 32) == 32 &&
                (e.AllowedEffect & DragDropEffects.Link) ==        ↵
DragDropEffects.Link) {

                // ALT KeyState for link.
                e.Effect = DragDropEffects.Link;

            } else if ((e.KeyState & 4) == 4 &&
                (e.AllowedEffect & DragDropEffects.Move) ==        ↵
DragDropEffects.Move) {

                // SHIFT KeyState for move.
                e.Effect = DragDropEffects.Move;

            } else if ((e.KeyState & 8) == 8 &&
                (e.AllowedEffect & DragDropEffects.Copy) ==        ↵
DragDropEffects.Copy) {

                // CTL KeyState for copy.
                e.Effect = DragDropEffects.Copy;

            } else if ((e.AllowedEffect & DragDropEffects.Move)        ↵
== DragDropEffects.Move)  {

                // By default, the drop action should be move,        ↵
 if allowed.
                e.Effect = DragDropEffects.Move;

            } else
                e.Effect = DragDropEffects.None;

            // Get the index of the item the mouse is below.

            // The mouse locations are relative to the screen,        ↵
 so they must be
            // converted to client coordinates.

            indexOfItemUnderMouseToDrop =

ListDragTarget.IndexFromPoint(ListDragTarget.PointToClient(new        ↵
Point(e.X, e.Y)));

            // Updates the label text.
            if (indexOfItemUnderMouseToDrop != ListBox.NoMatches){

                DropLocationLabel.Text = "Drops before item        ↵
 #" + (indexOfItemUnderMouseToDrop + 1);
            } else
                DropLocationLabel.Text = "Drops at the end.";
        }
        private void ListDragTarget_DragDrop(object sender,        ↵
System.Windows.Forms.DragEventArgs e)
        {
            // Ensure that the list item index is contained in        ↵
the data.
            if (e.Data.GetDataPresent(typeof(System.String))) {

                Object item =        ↵
 (object)e.Data.GetData(typeof(System.String));

                // Perform drag and drop, depending upon the effect.
                if (e.Effect == DragDropEffects.Copy ||
                    e.Effect == DragDropEffects.Move) {

                    // Insert the item.
                    if (indexOfItemUnderMouseToDrop !=        ↵
ListBox.NoMatches)

ListDragTarget.Items.Insert(indexOfItemUnderMouseToDrop, item);
                    else
                        ListDragTarget.Items.Add(item);

                }
            }
            // Reset the label text.
            DropLocationLabel.Text = "None";
        }
        private void ListDragSource_QueryContinueDrag        ↵
 (object sender, System.Windows.Forms.QueryContinueDragEventArgs e) {
            // Cancel the drag if the mouse moves off the form.
            ListBox lb = sender as ListBox;

            if (lb != null) {

                Form f = lb.FindForm();

                // Cancel the drag if the mouse moves off the        ↵
 form. The screenOffset
                // takes into account any desktop bands that        ↵
 may be at the top or left
                // side of the screen.
                if (((Control.MousePosition.X -        ↵
screenOffset.X) < f.DesktopBounds.Left) ||
                    ((Control.MousePosition.X -        ↵
screenOffset.X) > f.DesktopBounds.Right) ||
                    ((Control.MousePosition.Y -        ↵
screenOffset.Y) < f.DesktopBounds.Top) ||
                    ((Control.MousePosition.Y -        ↵
screenOffset.Y) > f.DesktopBounds.Bottom)) {

                    e.Action = DragAction.Cancel;
                }
            }
        }
        private void ListDragTarget_DragEnter(object        ↵
 sender, System.Windows.Forms.DragEventArgs e) {
            // Reset the label text.
            DropLocationLabel.Text = "None";
        }
        private void ListDragTarget_DragLeave(object sender,        ↵
 System.EventArgs e) {
            // Reset the label text.
            DropLocationLabel.Text = "None";
        }
    }
}
```

[C++]

```
using namespace System;
using namespace System::Drawing;
using namespace System::Windows::Forms;

namespace Snip_DragNDrop {
public __gc class Form1 : public System::Windows::Forms::Form {
```

```
private:
    System::Windows::Forms::ListBox*  ListDragSource;
    System::Windows::Forms::ListBox*  ListDragTarget;
    System::Windows::Forms::CheckBox*  UseCustomCursorsCheck;
    System::Windows::Forms::Label*  DropLocationLabel;
    Int32  indexOfItemUnderMouseToDrag;
    Int32  indexOfItemUnderMouseToDrop;
    Rectangle  dragBoxFromMouseDown;
    Point  screenOffset;
    System::Windows::Forms::Cursor*  MyNoDropCursor;
    System::Windows::Forms::Cursor*  MyNormalCursor;

public:
    Form1() {
        this->ListDragSource = new System::Windows::Forms::ListBox();
        this->ListDragTarget = new System::Windows::Forms::ListBox();
        this->UseCustomCursorsCheck = new                                ↵
System::Windows::Forms::CheckBox();
        this->DropLocationLabel = new System::Windows::Forms::Label();

        this->SuspendLayout();

        // ListDragSource
Object* temp0 [] = {
S"five", S"six", S"seven", S"eight",
S"nine", S"ten"};
        this->ListDragSource->Items->AddRange(temp0
);
        this->ListDragSource->Location =                                 ↵
System::Drawing::Point(10, 17);
        this->ListDragSource->Size = System::Drawing::Size(120, 225);
        this->ListDragSource->MouseDown += new                           ↵
System::Windows::Forms::MouseEventHandler(this,                          ↵
ListDragSource_MouseDown);
        this->ListDragSource->QueryContinueDrag += new                   ↵
 System::Windows::Forms::QueryContinueDragEventHandler(this,             ↵
ListDragSource_QueryContinueDrag);
        this->ListDragSource->MouseUp += new                             ↵
System::Windows::Forms::MouseEventHandler(this,                          ↵
ListDragSource_MouseUp);
        this->ListDragSource->MouseMove += new                           ↵
System::Windows::Forms::MouseEventHandler(this,                          ↵
ListDragSource_MouseMove);
        this->ListDragSource->GiveFeedback += new                        ↵
System::Windows::Forms::GiveFeedbackEventHandler(this,                   ↵
ListDragSource_GiveFeedback);

        // ListDragTarget
        this->ListDragTarget->AllowDrop = true;
        this->ListDragTarget->Location = System::Drawing::Point          ↵
 (154, 17);
        this->ListDragTarget->Size = System::Drawing::Size(120, 225);
        this->ListDragTarget->DragOver += new                            ↵
System::Windows::Forms::DragEventHandler(this,                           ↵
ListDragTarget_DragOver);
        this->ListDragTarget->DragDrop += new                            ↵
System::Windows::Forms::DragEventHandler(this,                           ↵
ListDragTarget_DragDrop);
        this->ListDragTarget->DragEnter += new                           ↵
System::Windows::Forms::DragEventHandler(this,                           ↵
ListDragTarget_DragEnter);
        this->ListDragTarget->DragLeave += new                           ↵
System::EventHandler(this, ListDragTarget_DragLeave);

        // UseCustomCursorsCheck
this->UseCustomCursorsCheck->Location =                                  ↵
 System::Drawing::Point(10, 243);
        this->UseCustomCursorsCheck->Size =                              ↵
 System::Drawing::Size(137, 24);
        this->UseCustomCursorsCheck->Text =                              ↵
 S"Use Custom Cursors";

        // DropLocationLabel
 this->DropLocationLabel->Location = System::Drawing::Point(154, 245);
        this->DropLocationLabel->Size = System::Drawing::Size(137, 24);
        this->DropLocationLabel->Text = S"None";

        // Form1
 this->AutoScaleBaseSize = System::Drawing::Size(5, 13);
        this->ClientSize = System::Drawing::Size(292, 270);
System::Windows::Forms::Control* formControls[]                          ↵
= {this->ListDragSource,
          this->ListDragTarget, this->UseCustomCursorsCheck,
          this->DropLocationLabel};
        this->Controls->AddRange(formControls);
        this->Text = S"Drag and Drop Example";

        this->ResumeLayout(false);

    }

private:
    void ListDragSource_MouseDown(Object* /*sender*/,                    ↵
System::Windows::Forms::MouseEventArgs* e) {
        // Get the index of the item the mouse is below.
        indexOfItemUnderMouseToDrag = this->ListDragSource-              ↵
>IndexFromPoint(e->X, e->Y);

        if (indexOfItemUnderMouseToDrag != ListBox::NoMatches) {

            // Remember the point where the mouse down                   ↵
 occurred. The DragSize indicates
            // the size that the mouse can move before a                 ↵
drag event should be started.
            System::Drawing::Size dragSize =                             ↵
SystemInformation::DragSize;

            // Create a rectangle using the DragSize, with               ↵
the mouse position being
            // at the center of the rectangle.
            dragBoxFromMouseDown = Rectangle(Point(e->X -                ↵
 (dragSize.Width /2),
                e->Y - (dragSize.Height /2)), dragSize);
        } else
            // Reset the rectangle if the mouse is not over an           ↵
 item in the ListBox.
            dragBoxFromMouseDown = Rectangle::Empty;

    }

    void ListDragSource_MouseUp(Object* /*sender*/,                      ↵
System::Windows::Forms::MouseEventArgs* /*e*/) {
        // Reset the drag rectangle when the mouse button is raised.
        dragBoxFromMouseDown = Rectangle::Empty;
    }

private:
    void ListDragSource_MouseMove(Object* /*sender*/,                    ↵
System::Windows::Forms::MouseEventArgs* e) {

        if ((e->Button & MouseButtons::Left) == MouseButtons::Left) {

            // If the mouse moves outside the rectangle, start           ↵
 the drag.
            if (dragBoxFromMouseDown != Rectangle::Empty &&
                !dragBoxFromMouseDown.Contains(e->X, e->Y)) {

                    // Create custom cursors for the                     ↵
drag-and-drop operation.
                    try {
                        MyNormalCursor = new                             ↵
System::Windows::Forms::Cursor(S"3dwarro.cur");
                        MyNoDropCursor = new
System::Windows::Forms::Cursor(S"3dwno.cur");

                    } catch (Exception*) {
                        // An error occurred while attempting            ↵
 to load the cursors, so use
                        // standard cursors.
```

```
                    this->UseCustomCursorsCheck->Checked = false;
                }__finally {

                    // The screenOffset is used to account                ↵
for any desktop bands
                    // that may be at the top or left side                ↵
of the screen when
                    // determining when to cancel the drag                ↵
 drop operation.
                    screenOffset =                                        ↵
SystemInformation::WorkingArea.Location;

                    // Proceed with the drag and drop,                    ↵
passing in the list item.
                    DragDropEffects dropEffect = this-                    ↵
>ListDragSource->DoDragDrop(
                        ListDragSource->Items-                            ↵
>Item[indexOfItemUnderMouseToDrag],

static_cast<DragDropEffects>(DragDropEffects::All |                       ↵
DragDropEffects::Link));

                    // If the drag operation was a move then              ↵
 remove the item.
                    if (dropEffect == DragDropEffects::Move) {
                        ListDragSource->Items-                            ↵
>RemoveAt(indexOfItemUnderMouseToDrag);

                        // Selects the previous item in the               ↵
 list as long as the list has an item.
                        if (indexOfItemUnderMouseToDrag > 0)
                            ListDragSource->SelectedIndex                 ↵
= indexOfItemUnderMouseToDrag -1;

                        else if (ListDragSource->Items->Count > 0)
                            // Selects the first item.
                            ListDragSource->SelectedIndex =0;
                    }

                    // Dispose of the cursors since they                  ↵
are no longer needed.
                    if (MyNormalCursor != 0)
                        MyNormalCursor->Dispose();

                    if (MyNoDropCursor != 0)
                        MyNoDropCursor->Dispose();
                }
            }
        }
    }
private:
    void ListDragSource_GiveFeedback(Object* /*sender*/,
        System::Windows::Forms::GiveFeedbackEventArgs* e) {

        // Use custom cursors if the check box is checked.
        if (UseCustomCursorsCheck->Checked) {

            // Sets the custom cursor based upon the effect.
            e->UseDefaultCursors = false;
            if ((e->Effect & DragDropEffects::Move) ==                    ↵
DragDropEffects::Move)
                Cursor::Current = MyNormalCursor;
            else
                Cursor::Current = MyNoDropCursor;
        }

    }
private:
    void ListDragTarget_DragOver(Object* /*sender*/,
        System::Windows::Forms::DragEventArgs* e) {

        // Determine whether String* data exists in the                   ↵
 drop data. If not, then
        // the drop effect reflects that the drop cannot occur.
        if (!e->Data->GetDataPresent(__typeof(System::String))) {

            e->Effect = DragDropEffects::None;
            DropLocationLabel->Text = S"None - no String* data.";
            return;
        }

        // Set the effect based upon the KeyState.
        if ((e->KeyState & (8+32)) == (8+32) &&
            (e->AllowedEffect & DragDropEffects::Link) ==                 ↵
DragDropEffects::Link) {
            // KeyState 8 + 32 = CTL + ALT

            // Link drag and drop effect.
            e->Effect = DragDropEffects::Link;

        } else if ((e->KeyState & 32) == 32 &&
            (e->AllowedEffect &                                           ↵
DragDropEffects::Link) == DragDropEffects::Link) {

                // ALT KeyState for link.
                e->Effect = DragDropEffects::Link;

            } else if ((e->KeyState & 4) == 4 &&
                (e->AllowedEffect & DragDropEffects::Move) ==
                DragDropEffects::Move) {
                    // SHIFT KeyState for move.
                    e->Effect = DragDropEffects::Move;

                } else if ((e->KeyState & 8) == 8 &&
                    (e->AllowedEffect & DragDropEffects::Copy) ==
                    DragDropEffects::Copy) {
                        // CTL KeyState for copy.
                        e->Effect = DragDropEffects::Copy;

                    } else if ((e->AllowedEffect &                        ↵
DragDropEffects::Move) ==
                        DragDropEffects::Move) {
                        // By default, the drop action                    ↵
 should be move, if allowed.
                        e->Effect = DragDropEffects::Move;

                    } else
                        e->Effect = DragDropEffects::None;

                    // Get the index of the item the                      ↵
 mouse is below.

                    // The mouse locations are relative                   ↵
 to the screen, so they must be
                    // converted to client coordinates.

                    indexOfItemUnderMouseToDrop =
                        ListDragTarget->IndexFromPoint(
                        ListDragTarget->PointToClient                     ↵
 (Point(e->X, e->Y)));

                    // Updates the label text.
                    if (indexOfItemUnderMouseToDrop !=                    ↵
ListBox::NoMatches) {

                        DropLocationLabel->Text =
                            String::Concat(S"Drops before item # ",
                            __box(                                        ↵
 (indexOfItemUnderMouseToDrop + 1)));
                    } else
                        DropLocationLabel->Text =                         ↵
 S"Drops at the end.";

    }
private:
    void ListDragTarget_DragDrop(Object* /*sender*/,
        System::Windows::Forms::DragEventArgs* e) {
        // Ensure that the list item index is contained in the data.
        if (e->Data->GetDataPresent(__typeof(System::String))) {
            Object* item = dynamic_cast<Object*>(
                e->Data->GetData(__typeof(System::String)));
```

```
            // Perform drag and drop, depending upon the effect.
            if (e->Effect == DragDropEffects::Copy ||
                e->Effect == DragDropEffects::Move) {

                // Insert the item.
                if (indexOfItemUnderMouseToDrop !=                    ↵
ListBox::NoMatches)
                    ListDragTarget->Items->Insert(
                    indexOfItemUnderMouseToDrop, item);
                else
                    ListDragTarget->Items->Add(item);

            }
        }
        // Reset the label text.
        DropLocationLabel->Text = S"None";
    }
private:
    void ListDragSource_QueryContinueDrag(Object* sender,
        System::Windows::Forms::QueryContinueDragEventArgs* e) {
        // Cancel the drag if the mouse moves off the form.
        ListBox* lb = dynamic_cast<ListBox*>(sender);

        if (lb != 0) {

            Form* f = lb->FindForm();

            // Cancel the drag if the mouse moves off the             ↵
form. The screenOffset
            // takes into account any desktop bands that may          ↵
 be at the top or left
            // side of the screen.
            if (((Control::MousePosition.X - screenOffset.X)          ↵
 < f->DesktopBounds.Left) ||
                ((Control::MousePosition.X - screenOffset.X)          ↵
 > f->DesktopBounds.Right) ||
                ((Control::MousePosition.Y - screenOffset.Y)          ↵
 < f->DesktopBounds.Top) ||
                ((Control::MousePosition.Y - screenOffset.Y)          ↵
 > f->DesktopBounds.Bottom)) {

                e->Action = DragAction::Cancel;
            }
        }
    }
private:
    void ListDragTarget_DragEnter(Object* /*sender*/,                 ↵
System::Windows::Forms::DragEventArgs* /*e*/) {
        // Reset the label text.
        DropLocationLabel->Text = S"None";
    }
private:
    void ListDragTarget_DragLeave(Object* /*sender*/,                 ↵
System::EventArgs* /*e*/) {
        // Reset the label text.
        DropLocationLabel->Text = S"None";
    }
};
}

/// The main entry point for the application.
[STAThread]
int main() {
    Application::Run(new Snip_DragNDrop::Form1());
}
```

[Visual Basic, C#, C++] The following example shows how to use the **DragDropEffects** enumeration to specify how data should be transferred between the controls involved in a drag-and-drop operation. This example assumes that your form includes a **RichTextBox** control and a **Label** control and that the **Label** control is populated with a list of valid file names. When the user drags a file name onto the **RichTextBox** control, the control's **DragEnter** event is raised. Within the event handler, the **DragEventArgs** object's **Effect** property is initialized to **DragDropEffects** to indicate that the data referenced by the file path should be copied to the **RichTextBox** control.

[Visual Basic]

```
Private Sub Form1_Load(ByVal sender As System.Object, ByVal e         ↵
As System.EventArgs) Handles MyBase.Load
   ' Sets the AllowDrop property so that data can be dragged          ↵
onto the control.
   RichTextBox1.AllowDrop = True

   ' Add code here to populate the ListBox1 with paths to text files.

End Sub

Private Sub RichTextBox1_DragEnter(ByVal sender As Object, ByVal      ↵
 e As System.Windows.Forms.DragEventArgs) Handles                     ↵
RichTextBox1.DragEnter
   ' If the data is text, copy the data to the RichTextBox control.
   If (e.Data.GetDataPresent("Text")) Then
      e.Effect = DragDropEffects.Copy
   End If
End Sub

Private Overloads Sub RichTextBox1_DragDrop(ByVal sender              ↵
As Object, ByVal e As System.Windows.Forms.DragEventArgs)             ↵
 Handles RichTextBox1.DragDrop
   ' Loads the file into the control.
   RichTextBox1.LoadFile(e.Data.GetData("Text"),                      ↵
System.Windows.Forms.RichTextBoxStreamType.RichText)
End Sub

Private Sub ListBox1_MouseDown(ByVal sender As Object,                ↵
 ByVal e As System.Windows.Forms.MouseEventArgs) Handles              ↵
ListBox1.MouseDown
   Dim Lb As ListBox
   Dim Pt As New Point(e.X, e.Y)
   Dim Index As Integer

   ' Determines which item was selected.
   Lb = sender
   Index = Lb.IndexFromPoint(Pt)

   ' Starts a drag-and-drop operation with that item.
   If Index >= 0 Then
      Lb.DoDragDrop(Lb.Items(Index), DragDropEffects.Link)
   End If
End Sub
```

[C#]

```
private void Form1_Load(object sender, EventArgs e)
{
   // Sets the AllowDrop property so that data can be dragged         ↵
 onto the control.
   richTextBox1.AllowDrop = true;

   // Add code here to populate the ListBox1 with paths to text files.

}

private void listBox1_MouseDown(object sender,                        ↵
System.Windows.Forms.MouseEventArgs e)
{
   // Determines which item was selected.
   ListBox lb =( (ListBox)sender);
   Point pt = new Point(e.X,e.Y);
   int index = lb.IndexFromPoint(pt);

   // Starts a drag-and-drop operation with that item.
   if(index>=0)
   {
      lb.DoDragDrop(lb.Items[index].ToString(), DragDropEffects.Link);
   }
}
```

```
private void richTextBox1_DragEnter(object sender, DragEventArgs e)
{
   // If the data is text, copy the data to the RichTextBox control.
   if(e.Data.GetDataPresent("Text"))
      e.Effect = DragDropEffects.Copy;
}

private void richTextBox1_DragDrop(object sender, DragEventArgs e)
{
   // Loads the file into the control.
   richTextBox1.LoadFile((String)e.Data.GetData("Text"),                ↵
System.Windows.Forms.RichTextBoxStreamType.RichText);
}
```

[C++]

```
private:
    void Form1_Load(Object* /*sender*/, EventArgs* /*e*/) {
        // Sets the AllowDrop property so that data can be                ↵
dragged onto the control.
        richTextBox1->AllowDrop = true;

        // Add code here to populate the ListBox1 with paths              ↵
 to text files.
    }

    void listBox1_MouseDown(Object* sender,                               ↵
System::Windows::Forms::MouseEventArgs* e) {
        // Determines which item was selected.
        ListBox* lb =(dynamic_cast<ListBox*>(sender));
        Point pt = Point(e->X, e->Y);
        int index = lb->IndexFromPoint(pt);

        // Starts a drag-and-drop operation with that item.
        if (index>=0) {
            lb->DoDragDrop(lb->Items->Item[index],                        ↵
DragDropEffects::Link);
        }
    }

    void richTextBox1_DragEnter(Object* /*sender*/, DragEventArgs* e) {
        // If the data is text, copy the data to the                      ↵
RichTextBox control.
        if (e->Data->GetDataPresent(S"Text"))
            e->Effect = DragDropEffects::Copy;
    }

    void richTextBox1_DragDrop(Object* /*sender*/, DragEventArgs* e) {
        // Loads the file into the control.
        richTextBox1->LoadFile(dynamic_cast<String*>(e->Data-             ↵
>GetData(S"Text")),
            System::Windows::Forms::RichTextBoxStreamType::RichText);
    }
```

Requirements

Platforms: Windows 98, Windows NT 4.0, Windows Millennium Edition, Windows 2000, Windows XP Home Edition, Windows XP Professional, Windows Server 2003 family

Control.EndInvoke Method

Retrieves the return value of the asynchronous operation represented by the **IAsyncResult** object passed.

[Visual Basic]

```
Public Overridable Function EndInvoke( _
   ByVal asyncResult As IAsyncResult _
) As Object Implements ISynchronizeInvoke.EndInvoke
```

[C#]

```
public virtual object EndInvoke(
   IAsyncResult asyncResult
);
```

[C++]

```
public: virtual Object* EndInvoke(
   IAsyncResult* asyncResult
);
```

[JScript]

```
public function EndInvoke(
   asyncResult : IAsyncResult
) : Object;
```

Parameters

asyncResult

The **IAsyncResult** object that represents a specific invoke asynchronous operation, returned when calling **BeginInvoke**.

Return Value

The **Object** generated by the asynchronous operation.

Implements

ISynchronizeInvoke.EndInvoke

Exceptions

Exception Type	Condition
ArgumentNull-Exception	The *asyncResult* parameter value is a null reference (**Nothing** in Visual Basic).
ArgumentException	The *asyncResult* object was not created by a preceding call of the **BeginInvoke** method from the same control.

Remarks

If the asynchronous operation has not been completed, this function will block until the result is available.

Note There are four methods on a control that are safe to call from any thread: **Invoke**, **BeginInvoke**, **EndInvoke**, and **CreateGraphics**. For all other method calls, you should use one of the invoke methods to marshal the call to the control's thread.

Requirements

Platforms: Windows 98, Windows NT 4.0, Windows Millennium Edition, Windows 2000, Windows XP Home Edition, Windows XP Professional, Windows Server 2003 family

Control.FindForm Method

Retrieves the form that the control is on.

[Visual Basic]

```
Public Function FindForm() As Form
```

[C#]

```
public Form FindForm();
```

[C++]

```
public: Form* FindForm();
```

[JScript]

```
public function FindForm() : Form;
```

Return Value

The **Form** that the control is on.

Remarks

The control's **Parent** property value might not be the same as the **Form** returned by **FindForm** method. For example, if a **RadioButton** control is contained within a **GroupBox** control, and the **GroupBox** is on a **Form**, the **RadioButton** control's **Parent** is the **GroupBox** and the **GroupBox** control's **Parent** is the **Form**.

Example

[Visual Basic]
```
' This example uses the Parent property and the Find method ↵
of Control to set
' properties on the parent control of a Button and its Form. ↵
 The example assumes
' that a Button control named button1 is located within a ↵
GroupBox control. The
' example also assumes that the Click event of the Button ↵
control is connected to
' the event handling method defined in the example.
Private Sub button1_Click(sender As Object, e ↵
As System.EventArgs) Handles button1.Click
   ' Get the control the Button control is located in. ↵
In this case a GroupBox.
   Dim control As Control = button1.Parent
   ' Set the text and backcolor of the parent control.
   control.Text = "My Groupbox"
   control.BackColor = Color.Blue
   ' Get the form that the Button control is contained within.
   Dim myForm As Form = button1.FindForm()
   ' Set the text and color of the form containing the Button.
   myForm.Text = "The Form of My Control"
   myForm.BackColor = Color.Red
End Sub
```

[C#]
```
// This example uses the Parent property and the Find method ↵
of Control to set
// properties on the parent control of a Button and its Form. ↵
 The example assumes
// that a Button control named button1 is located within a ↵
GroupBox control. The
// example also assumes that the Click event of the Button ↵
control is connected to
// the event handling method defined in the example.
private void button1_Click(object sender, System.EventArgs e)
{
   // Get the control the Button control is located in. In ↵
this case a GroupBox.
   Control control = button1.Parent;
   // Set the text and backcolor of the parent control.
   control.Text = "My Groupbox";
   control.BackColor = Color.Blue;
   // Get the form that the Button control is contained within.
   Form myForm = button1.FindForm();
   // Set the text and color of the form containing the Button.
   myForm.Text = "The Form of My Control";
   myForm.BackColor = Color.Red;
}
```

Requirements

Platforms: Windows 98, Windows NT 4.0, Windows Millennium Edition, Windows 2000, Windows XP Home Edition, Windows XP Professional, Windows Server 2003 family

.NET Framework Security:

- **UIPermission** for all windows to call this method. Associated enumeration: **UIPermissionWindow.AllWindows**

Control.Focus Method

Sets input focus to the control.

[Visual Basic]
```
Public Function Focus() As Boolean
```
[C#]
```
public bool Focus();
```
[C++]
```
public: bool Focus();
```
[JScript]
```
public function Focus() : Boolean;
```

Return Value

true if the input focus request was successful; otherwise, **false**.

Remarks

The **Focus** method returns **true** if the control successfully received input focus. The control can have the input focus while not displaying any visual cues of having the focus. This behavior is primarily observed by the nonselectable controls listed below, or any controls derived from them.

A control can be selected and receive input focus if all the following are **true**: its **ControlStyles.Selectable** style bit is set to **true**, it is contained in another control, and all its parent controls are both visible and enabled.

The Windows Forms controls in the following list are not selectable. Controls derived from these controls are also not selectable.

- **Panel**
- **GroupBox**
- **PictureBox**
- **ProgressBar**
- **Splitter**
- **Label**
- **LinkLabel** (when there is no link present in the control)

Example

[Visual Basic, C#, C++] The following example sets focus to the specified **Control**, if it can receive focus.

[Visual Basic]
```
Public Sub ControlSetFocus(control As Control)
   ' Set focus to the control, if it can receive focus.
   If control.CanFocus Then
      control.Focus()
   End If
End Sub
```

[C#]
```
public void ControlSetFocus(Control control)
{
   // Set focus to the control, if it can receive focus.
   if(control.CanFocus)
   {
      control.Focus();
   }
}
```

[C++]
```
public:
   void ControlSetFocus(Control* control) {
      // Set focus to the control, if it can receive focus.
      if (control->CanFocus) {
         control->Focus();
      }
   }
```

Requirements

Platforms: Windows 98, Windows NT 4.0,
Windows Millennium Edition, Windows 2000,
Windows XP Home Edition, Windows XP Professional,
Windows Server 2003 family,
.NET Compact Framework - Windows CE .NET

.NET Framework Security:

- **UIPermission** for all windows to call this method. Associated enumeration: **UIPermissionWindow.AllWindows**

Control.FromChildHandle Method

Retrieves the control that contains the specified handle.

```
[Visual Basic]
Public Shared Function FromChildHandle( _
   ByVal handle As IntPtr _
) As Control
[C#]
public static Control FromChildHandle(
   IntPtr handle
);
[C++]
public: static Control* FromChildHandle(
   IntPtr handle
);
[JScript]
public static function FromChildHandle(
   handle : IntPtr
) : Control;
```

Parameters

handle
The window handle (HWND) to search for.

Return Value

The **Control** that represents the control associated with the specified handle; returns a null reference (**Nothing** in Visual Basic) if no control with the specified handle is found.

Remarks

This method searches up the window handle parent chain until it finds a handle that is associated with a control. This method is more reliable than the **FromHandle** method, because it correctly returns controls that own more than one handle.

Requirements

Platforms: Windows 98, Windows NT 4.0,
Windows Millennium Edition, Windows 2000,
Windows XP Home Edition, Windows XP Professional,
Windows Server 2003 family

.NET Framework Security:

- **UIPermission** for all windows to call this method. Associated enumeration: **UIPermissionWindow.AllWindows**

Control.FromHandle Method

Returns the control that is currently associated with the specified handle.

```
[Visual Basic]
Public Shared Function FromHandle( _
   ByVal handle As IntPtr _
) As Control
[C#]
public static Control FromHandle(
   IntPtr handle
);
[C++]
public: static Control* FromHandle(
   IntPtr handle
);
[JScript]
public static function FromHandle(
   handle : IntPtr
) : Control;
```

Parameters

handle
The window handle (HWND) to search for.

Return Value

A **Control** that represents the control associated with the specified handle; returns a null reference (**Nothing** in Visual Basic) if no control with the specified handle is found.

Remarks

Use the **FromChildHandle** method if you need to return controls that own more than one handle.

Requirements

Platforms: Windows 98, Windows NT 4.0,
Windows Millennium Edition, Windows 2000,
Windows XP Home Edition, Windows XP Professional,
Windows Server 2003 family

.NET Framework Security:

- **UIPermission** for all windows to call this method. Associated enumeration: **UIPermissionWindow.AllWindows**

Control.GetChildAtPoint Method

Retrieves the child control that is located at the specified coordinates.

```
[Visual Basic]
Public Function GetChildAtPoint( _
   ByVal pt As Point _
) As Control
[C#]
public Control GetChildAtPoint(
   Point pt
);
[C++]
public: Control* GetChildAtPoint(
   Point pt
);
[JScript]
public function GetChildAtPoint(
   pt : Point
) : Control;
```

Parameters

pt
A **Point** that contains the coordinates where you want to look for a control. Coordinates are expressed relative to the upper-left corner of the control's client area.

Return Value

A **Control** that represents the control that is located at the specified point.

Remarks

If there is no child control at the specified point, the **GetChild-AtPoint** method returns a null reference (**Nothing** in Visual Basic).

Requirements

Platforms: Windows 98, Windows NT 4.0, Windows Millennium Edition, Windows 2000, Windows XP Home Edition, Windows XP Professional, Windows Server 2003 family

.NET Framework Security:

- **UIPermission** for all windows to call this method if the control returned is not a child of the control. Associated enumeration: **UIPermissionWindow.AllWindows**

Control.GetContainerControl Method

Returns the next **ContainerControl** up the control's chain of parent controls.

```
[Visual Basic]
Public Function GetContainerControl() As IContainerControl
[C#]
public IContainerControl GetContainerControl();
[C++]
public: IContainerControl* GetContainerControl();
[JScript]
public function GetContainerControl() : IContainerControl;
```

Return Value

An **IContainerControl** object, that represents the parent of the **Control**.

Requirements

Platforms: Windows 98, Windows NT 4.0, Windows Millennium Edition, Windows 2000, Windows XP Home Edition, Windows XP Professional, Windows Server 2003 family

.NET Framework Security:

- **UIPermission** for all windows to call this method. Associated enumeration: **UIPermissionWindow.AllWindows**

Control.GetNextControl Method

Retrieves the next control forward or back in the tab order of child controls.

```
[Visual Basic]
Public Function GetNextControl( _
   ByVal ctl As Control, _
   ByVal forward As Boolean _
) As Control
[C#]
public Control GetNextControl(
   Control ctl,
   bool forward
);
[C++]
public: Control* GetNextControl(
   Control* ctl,
   bool forward
);
[JScript]
public function GetNextControl(
   ctl : Control,
   forward : Boolean
) : Control;
```

Parameters

ctl

The **Control** to start the search with.

forward

true to search forward in the tab order; **false** to search backward.

Return Value

The next **Control** in the tab order.

Requirements

Platforms: Windows 98, Windows NT 4.0, Windows Millennium Edition, Windows 2000, Windows XP Home Edition, Windows XP Professional, Windows Server 2003 family

Control.GetStyle Method

Retrieves the value of the specified control style bit for the control.

```
[Visual Basic]
Protected Function GetStyle( _
   ByVal flag As ControlStyles _
) As Boolean
[C#]
protected bool GetStyle(
   ControlStyles flag
);
[C++]
protected: bool GetStyle(
   ControlStyles flag
);
[JScript]
protected function GetStyle(
   flag : ControlStyles
) : Boolean;
```

Parameters

flag

The **ControlStyles** bit to return the value from.

Return Value

true if the specified control style bit is set to **true**; otherwise, **false**.

Remarks

Control style bit flags are used to categorize supported behavior. A control can enable a style by calling the **SetStyle** method and passing in the appropriate **ControlStyles** bit and the Boolean value to set the bit to. To determine the value assigned to a specified **ControlStyles** bit, use the **GetStyle** method and pass in the **ControlStyles** member to evaluate.

Example

[Visual Basic, C#, C++] The following example returns the value of the double-buffering related style bits for a **Form**. This example returns **true** only if all the style bits are set to **true**.

[Visual Basic]
```
Public Function DoubleBufferingEnabled() As Boolean
   ' Get the value of the double-buffering style bits.
   Return Me.GetStyle((ControlStyles.DoubleBuffer _
     Or ControlStyles.UserPaint _
     Or ControlStyles.AllPaintingInWmPaint))
End Function
```

[C#]
```
public bool DoubleBufferingEnabled()
{
   // Get the value of the double-buffering style bits.
   return this.GetStyle(ControlStyles.DoubleBuffer |
      ControlStyles.UserPaint |
      ControlStyles.AllPaintingInWmPaint);
}
```

[C++]
```
public:
   bool DoubleBufferingEnabled() {
      // Get the value of the double-buffering style bits.
      return this-
>GetStyle(static_cast<ControlStyles>(ControlStyles::DoubleBuffer |
         ControlStyles::UserPaint |
         ControlStyles::AllPaintingInWmPaint));
   }
```

Requirements

Platforms: Windows 98, Windows NT 4.0, Windows Millennium Edition, Windows 2000, Windows XP Home Edition, Windows XP Professional, Windows Server 2003 family

Control.GetTopLevel Method

Determines if the control is a top-level control.

[Visual Basic]
```
Protected Function GetTopLevel() As Boolean
```
[C#]
```
protected bool GetTopLevel();
```
[C++]
```
protected: bool GetTopLevel();
```
[JScript]
```
protected function GetTopLevel() : Boolean;
```

Return Value

true if the control is a top-level control; otherwise, **false**.

Requirements

Platforms: Windows 98, Windows NT 4.0, Windows Millennium Edition, Windows 2000, Windows XP Home Edition, Windows XP Professional, Windows Server 2003 family

Control.Hide Method

Conceals the control from the user.

[Visual Basic]
```
Public Sub Hide()
```
[C#]
```
public void Hide();
```
[C++]
```
public: void Hide();
```
[JScript]
```
public function Hide();
```

Remarks

Hiding the control is equivalent to setting the **Visible** property to **false**. After the **Hide** method is called, the **Visible** property returns a value of **false** until the **Show** method is called.

Example

[Visual Basic, C#, C++] The following example hides a button when the CTRL key is pressed while the button is clicked. This example assumes you have a **Button** named `button1` on a **Form**.

[Visual Basic]
```
Private Sub button1_Click(sender As Object, _
  e As EventArgs) Handles button1.Click
   ' If the CTRL key is pressed when the
   ' control is clicked, hide the control.
   If Control.ModifierKeys = Keys.Control Then
      CType(sender, Control).Hide()
   End If
End Sub
```

[C#]
```
private void button1_Click(object sender, System.EventArgs e)
{
   /* If the CTRL key is pressed when the
    * control is clicked, hide the control. */
   if(Control.ModifierKeys == Keys.Control)
   {
      ((Control)sender).Hide();
   }
}
```

[C++]
```
private:
    void button1_Click(Object* sender, System::EventArgs* /*e*/) {
        /* If the CTRL key is pressed when the
         * control is clicked, hide the control. */
        if (Control::ModifierKeys == Keys::Control) {
            (dynamic_cast<Control*>(sender))->Hide();
        }
    }
```

Requirements

Platforms: Windows 98, Windows NT 4.0, Windows Millennium Edition, Windows 2000, Windows XP Home Edition, Windows XP Professional, Windows Server 2003 family, .NET Compact Framework - Windows CE .NET

Control.InitLayout Method

Called after the control has been added to another container.

[Visual Basic]
```
Protected Overridable Sub InitLayout()
```
[C#]
```
protected virtual void InitLayout();
```
[C++]
```
protected: virtual void InitLayout();
```
[JScript]
```
protected function InitLayout();
```

Remarks

The **InitLayout** method is called immediately after adding a control to a container. The **InitLayout** method allows a control to initialize its layout state based upon its container. For example, you would typically apply anchoring and docking to the control in the **InitLayout** method.

Notes to Inheritors: When overriding **InitLayout** in a derived class, be sure to call the base class's **InitLayout** method so that the control is displayed correctly.

Requirements

Platforms: Windows 98, Windows NT 4.0, Windows Millennium Edition, Windows 2000, Windows XP Home Edition, Windows XP Professional, Windows Server 2003 family

Control.Invalidate Method

Invalidates a specific region of the control and causes a paint message to be sent to the control.

Overload List

Invalidates a specific region of the control and causes a paint message to be sent to the control.

Supported by the .NET Compact Framework.

[Visual Basic] **Overloads Public Sub Invalidate()**

[C#] **public void Invalidate();**

[C++] **public: void Invalidate();**

[JScript] **public function Invalidate();**

Invalidates a specific region of the control and causes a paint message to be sent to the control. Optionally, invalidates the child controls assigned to the control.

[Visual Basic] **Overloads Public Sub Invalidate(Boolean)**

[C#] **public void Invalidate(bool);**

[C++] **public: void Invalidate(bool);**

[JScript] **public function Invalidate(Boolean);**

Invalidates the specified region of the control (adds it to the control's update region, which is the area that will be repainted at the next paint operation), and causes a paint message to be sent to the control.

Supported by the .NET Compact Framework.

[Visual Basic] **Overloads Public Sub Invalidate(Rectangle)**

[C#] **public void Invalidate(Rectangle);**

[C++] **public: void Invalidate(Rectangle);**

[JScript] **public function Invalidate(Rectangle);**

Invalidates the specified region of the control (adds it to the control's update region, which is the area that will be repainted at the next paint operation), and causes a paint message to be sent to the control.

[Visual Basic] **Overloads Public Sub Invalidate(Region)**

[C#] **public void Invalidate(Region);**

[C++] **public: void Invalidate(Region*);**

[JScript] **public function Invalidate(Region);**

Invalidates the specified region of the control (adds it to the control's update region, which is the area that will be repainted at the next paint operation), and causes a paint message to be sent to the control. Optionally, invalidates the child controls assigned to the control.

[Visual Basic] **Overloads Public Sub Invalidate(Rectangle, Boolean)**

[C#] **public void Invalidate(Rectangle, bool);**

[C++] **public: void Invalidate(Rectangle, bool);**

[JScript] **public function Invalidate(Rectangle, Boolean);**

Invalidates the specified region of the control (adds it to the control's update region, which is the area that will be repainted at the next paint operation), and causes a paint message to be sent to the control. Optionally, invalidates the child controls assigned to the control.

[Visual Basic] **Overloads Public Sub Invalidate(Region, Boolean)**

[C#] **public void Invalidate(Region, bool);**

[C++] **public: void Invalidate(Region*, bool);**

[JScript] **public function Invalidate(Region, Boolean);**

Example

[Visual Basic, C#, C++] The following example enables the user to drag an image or image file onto the form, and have it be displayed at the point on it is dropped. The **OnPaint** method is overridden to repaint the image each time the form is painted; otherwise the image would only persist until the next repainting. The **DragEnter** event-handling method determines the type of data being dragged into the form and provides the appropriate feedback. The **DragDrop** event-handling method displays the image on the form, if an **Image** can be created from the data. Because the **DragEventArgs.X** and **DragEventArgs.Y** values are screen coordinates, the example uses the **PointToClient** method to convert them to client coordinates.

> [Visual Basic, C#, C++] **Note** This example shows how to use one of the overloaded versions of **Invalidate**. For other examples that might be available, see the individual overload topics.

[Visual Basic]

```
Private picture As Image
Private pictureLocation As Point

Public Sub New()
   ' Enable drag-and-drop operations.
   Me.AllowDrop = True
End Sub

Protected Overrides Sub OnPaint(ByVal e As PaintEventArgs)
   MyBase.OnPaint(e)

   ' If there is an image and it has a location,
   ' paint it when the Form is repainted.
   If Not (Me.picture Is Nothing) And _
     Not (Me.pictureLocation.Equals(Point.Empty)) Then
      e.Graphics.DrawImage(Me.picture, Me.pictureLocation)
   End If
End Sub

Private Sub Form1_DragDrop(ByVal sender As Object, _
  ByVal e As DragEventArgs) Handles MyBase.DragDrop
   ' Handle FileDrop data.
   If e.Data.GetDataPresent(DataFormats.FileDrop) Then
      ' Assign the file names to a string array, in
      ' case the user has selected multiple files.
      Dim files As String() =                                    ↵
CType(e.Data.GetData(DataFormats.FileDrop), String())
      Try
         ' Assign the first image to the 'picture' variable.
         Me.picture = Image.FromFile(files(0))
         ' Set the picture location equal to the drop point.
         Me.pictureLocation = Me.PointToClient(New Point(e.X, e.Y))
      Catch ex As Exception
         MessageBox.Show(ex.Message)
         Return
      End Try
   End If

   ' Handle Bitmap data.
   If e.Data.GetDataPresent(DataFormats.Bitmap) Then
      Try
```

```
        ' Create an Image and assign it to the picture variable.
        Me.picture = CType(e.Data.GetData(DataFormats.Bitmap), Image)
        ' Set the picture location equal to the drop point.
        Me.pictureLocation = Me.PointToClient(New Point(e.X, e.Y))
     Catch ex As Exception
        MessageBox.Show(ex.Message)
        Return
     End Try
  End If

  ' Force the form to be redrawn with the image.
  Me.Invalidate()
End Sub

Private Sub Form1_DragEnter(ByVal sender As Object, _
  ByVal e As DragEventArgs) Handles MyBase.DragEnter
  ' If the data is a file or a bitmap, display the copy cursor.
  If e.Data.GetDataPresent(DataFormats.Bitmap) _
     Or e.Data.GetDataPresent(DataFormats.FileDrop) Then
     e.Effect = DragDropEffects.Copy
  Else
     e.Effect = DragDropEffects.None
  End If
End Sub
```

[C#]

```
private Image picture;
private Point pictureLocation;

public Form1()
{
   // Enable drag-and-drop operations and
   // add handlers for DragEnter and DragDrop.
   this.AllowDrop = true;
   this.DragDrop += new DragEventHandler(this.Form1_DragDrop);
   this.DragEnter += new DragEventHandler(this.Form1_DragEnter);
}

protected override void OnPaint(PaintEventArgs e)
{
   // If there is an image and it has a location,
   // paint it when the Form is repainted.
   base.OnPaint(e);
   if(this.picture != null && this.pictureLocation != Point.Empty)
   {
      e.Graphics.DrawImage(this.picture, this.pictureLocation);
   }
}

private void Form1_DragDrop(object sender, DragEventArgs e)
{
   // Handle FileDrop data.
   if(e.Data.GetDataPresent(DataFormats.FileDrop) )
   {
      // Assign the file names to a string array, in
      // case the user has selected multiple files.
      string[] files = (string[])e.Data.GetData(DataFormats.FileDrop);
      try
      {
         // Assign the first image to the picture variable.
         this.picture = Image.FromFile(files[0]);
         // Set the picture location equal to the drop point.
         this.pictureLocation = this.PointToClient(new Point        ↲
 (e.X, e.Y) );
      }
      catch(Exception ex)
      {
         MessageBox.Show(ex.Message);
         return;
      }
   }

   // Handle Bitmap data.
   if(e.Data.GetDataPresent(DataFormats.Bitmap) )
   {
      try
      {
         // Create an Image and assign it to the picture variable.
         this.picture = (Image)e.Data.GetData(DataFormats.Bitmap);
         // Set the picture location equal to the drop point.
         this.pictureLocation = this.PointToClient(new Point        ↲
 (e.X, e.Y) );
      }
      catch(Exception ex)
      {
         MessageBox.Show(ex.Message);
         return;
      }
   }
   // Force the form to be redrawn with the image.
   this.Invalidate();
}

private void Form1_DragEnter(object sender, DragEventArgs e)
{
   // If the data is a file or a bitmap, display the copy cursor.
   if (e.Data.GetDataPresent(DataFormats.Bitmap) ||
      e.Data.GetDataPresent(DataFormats.FileDrop) )
   {
      e.Effect = DragDropEffects.Copy;
   }
   else
   {
      e.Effect = DragDropEffects.None;
   }
}
```

[C++]

```
private:
   Image*  picture;
   Point  pictureLocation;

public:
   Form1() {
      // Enable drag-and-drop operations and
      // add handlers for DragEnter and DragDrop.
      this->AllowDrop = true;
      this->DragDrop += new DragEventHandler(this, Form1_DragDrop);
      this->DragEnter += new DragEventHandler(this, Form1_DragEnter);
   }

protected:
   void OnPaint(PaintEventArgs* e) {
      // If there is an image and it has a location,
      // paint it when the Form is repainted.
      Form::OnPaint(e);
      if (this->picture != 0 && this->pictureLocation !=        ↲
Point::Empty) {
         e->Graphics->DrawImage(this->picture, this->pictureLocation);
      }
   }

private:
   void Form1_DragDrop(Object* sender, DragEventArgs* e) {
      // Handle FileDrop data.
      if (e->Data->GetDataPresent(DataFormats::FileDrop)) {
         // Assign the file names to a String* array, in
         // case the user has selected multiple files.
         String* files[] = (String*[])e->Data-
>GetData(DataFormats::FileDrop);
         try {
            // Assign the first image to the picture variable.
            this->picture = Image::FromFile(files[0]);
            // Set the picture location equal to the drop point.
            this->pictureLocation = this->PointToClient(        ↲
Point(e->X, e->Y));
         } catch (Exception* ex) {
            MessageBox::Show(ex->Message);
            return;
         }
      }
```

```
      // Handle Bitmap data.
      if (e->Data->GetDataPresent(DataFormats::Bitmap)) {
         try {
            // Create an Image and assign it to the picture variable.
            this->picture = dynamic_cast<Image*>(e->Data-           ↵
>GetData(DataFormats::Bitmap));
            // Set the picture location equal to the drop point.
            this->pictureLocation = this->PointToClient(            ↵
Point(e->X, e->Y));
         } catch (Exception* ex) {
            MessageBox::Show(ex->Message);
            return;
         }
      }
      // Force the form to be redrawn with the image.
      this->Invalidate();
   }

   void Form1_DragEnter(Object* sender, DragEventArgs* e) {
      // If the data is a file or a bitmap, display the copy cursor.
      if (e->Data->GetDataPresent(DataFormats::Bitmap) ||
         e->Data->GetDataPresent(DataFormats::FileDrop)) {
            e->Effect = DragDropEffects::Copy;
         } else {
            e->Effect = DragDropEffects::None;
         }
   }
```

Control.Invalidate Method ()

Invalidates a specific region of the control and causes a paint message to be sent to the control.

[Visual Basic]
```
Overloads Public Sub Invalidate()
```
[C#]
```
public void Invalidate();
```
[C++]
```
public: void Invalidate();
```
[JScript]
```
public function Invalidate();
```

Remarks

Calling the **Invalidate** method does not force a synchronous paint; to force a synchronous paint, call the **Update** method after calling the **Invalidate** method. When this method is called with no parameters, the entire client area is added to the update region.

Example

[Visual Basic, C#, C++] The following example enables the user to drag an image or image file onto the form, and have it be displayed at the point on it is dropped. The **OnPaint** method is overridden to repaint the image each time the form is painted; otherwise the image would only persist until the next repainting. The **DragEnter** event-handling method determines the type of data being dragged into the form and provides the appropriate feedback. The **DragDrop** event-handling method displays the image on the form, if an **Image** can be created from the data. Because the **DragEventArgs.X** and **DragEventArgs.Y** values are screen coordinates, the example uses the **PointToClient** method to convert them to client coordinates.

[Visual Basic]
```
Private picture As Image
Private pictureLocation As Point

Public Sub New()
   ' Enable drag-and-drop operations.
   Me.AllowDrop = True
End Sub

Protected Overrides Sub OnPaint(ByVal e As PaintEventArgs)
   MyBase.OnPaint(e)

   ' If there is an image and it has a location,
   ' paint it when the Form is repainted.
   If Not (Me.picture Is Nothing) And _
     Not (Me.pictureLocation.Equals(Point.Empty)) Then
      e.Graphics.DrawImage(Me.picture, Me.pictureLocation)
   End If
End Sub

Private Sub Form1_DragDrop(ByVal sender As Object, _
  ByVal e As DragEventArgs) Handles MyBase.DragDrop
   ' Handle FileDrop data.
   If e.Data.GetDataPresent(DataFormats.FileDrop) Then
      ' Assign the file names to a string array, in
      ' case the user has selected multiple files.
      Dim files As String() = CType(e.Data.GetData(DataFormats.FileDrop),
String())
      Try
         ' Assign the first image to the 'picture' variable.
         Me.picture = Image.FromFile(files(0))
         ' Set the picture location equal to the drop point.
         Me.pictureLocation = Me.PointToClient(New Point(e.X, e.Y))
      Catch ex As Exception
         MessageBox.Show(ex.Message)
         Return
      End Try
   End If

   ' Handle Bitmap data.
   If e.Data.GetDataPresent(DataFormats.Bitmap) Then
      Try
         ' Create an Image and assign it to the picture variable.
         Me.picture = CType(e.Data.GetData(DataFormats.Bitmap), Image)
         ' Set the picture location equal to the drop point.
         Me.pictureLocation = Me.PointToClient(New Point(e.X, e.Y))
      Catch ex As Exception
         MessageBox.Show(ex.Message)
         Return
      End Try
   End If

   ' Force the form to be redrawn with the image.
   Me.Invalidate()
End Sub

Private Sub Form1_DragEnter(ByVal sender As Object, _
  ByVal e As DragEventArgs) Handles MyBase.DragEnter
   ' If the data is a file or a bitmap, display the copy cursor.
   If e.Data.GetDataPresent(DataFormats.Bitmap) _
      Or e.Data.GetDataPresent(DataFormats.FileDrop) Then
      e.Effect = DragDropEffects.Copy
   Else
      e.Effect = DragDropEffects.None
   End If
End Sub
```

[C#]
```
private Image picture;
private Point pictureLocation;

public Form1()
{
   // Enable drag-and-drop operations and
   // add handlers for DragEnter and DragDrop.
   this.AllowDrop = true;
   this.DragDrop += new DragEventHandler(this.Form1_DragDrop);
   this.DragEnter += new DragEventHandler(this.Form1_DragEnter);
}

protected override void OnPaint(PaintEventArgs e)
{
   // If there is an image and it has a location,
   // paint it when the Form is repainted.
```

```
    base.OnPaint(e);
    if(this.picture != null && this.pictureLocation != Point.Empty)
    {
        e.Graphics.DrawImage(this.picture, this.pictureLocation);
    }
}

private void Form1_DragDrop(object sender, DragEventArgs e)
{
    // Handle FileDrop data.
    if(e.Data.GetDataPresent(DataFormats.FileDrop) )
    {
        // Assign the file names to a string array, in
        // case the user has selected multiple files.
        string[] files = (string[])e.Data.GetData(DataFormats.FileDrop);
        try
        {
            // Assign the first image to the picture variable.
            this.picture = Image.FromFile(files[0]);
            // Set the picture location equal to the drop point.
            this.pictureLocation = this.PointToClient(new Point ↵
 (e.X, e.Y) );
        }
        catch(Exception ex)
        {
            MessageBox.Show(ex.Message);
            return;
        }
    }

    // Handle Bitmap data.
    if(e.Data.GetDataPresent(DataFormats.Bitmap) )
    {
        try
        {
            // Create an Image and assign it to the picture variable.
            this.picture = (Image)e.Data.GetData(DataFormats.Bitmap);
            // Set the picture location equal to the drop point.
            this.pictureLocation = this.PointToClient(new Point ↵
 (e.X, e.Y) );
        }
        catch(Exception ex)
        {
            MessageBox.Show(ex.Message);
            return;
        }
    }
    // Force the form to be redrawn with the image.
    this.Invalidate();
}

private void Form1_DragEnter(object sender, DragEventArgs e)
{
    // If the data is a file or a bitmap, display the copy cursor.
    if (e.Data.GetDataPresent(DataFormats.Bitmap) ||
        e.Data.GetDataPresent(DataFormats.FileDrop) )
    {
        e.Effect = DragDropEffects.Copy;
    }
    else
    {
        e.Effect = DragDropEffects.None;
    }
}
```

[C++]

```
private:
    Image* picture;
    Point  pictureLocation;

public:
    Form1() {
        // Enable drag-and-drop operations and
        // add handlers for DragEnter and DragDrop.
        this->AllowDrop = true;
        this->DragDrop += new DragEventHandler(this, Form1_DragDrop);
        this->DragEnter += new DragEventHandler(this, Form1_DragEnter);
    }

protected:
    void OnPaint(PaintEventArgs* e) {
        // If there is an image and it has a location,
        // paint it when the Form is repainted.
        Form::OnPaint(e);
        if (this->picture != 0 && this->pictureLocation != ↵
Point::Empty) {
            e->Graphics->DrawImage(this->picture, this->pictureLocation);
        }
    }

private:
    void Form1_DragDrop(Object* sender, DragEventArgs* e) {
        // Handle FileDrop data.
        if (e->Data->GetDataPresent(DataFormats::FileDrop)) {
            // Assign the file names to a String* array, in
            // case the user has selected multiple files.
            String* files[] = (String*[])e->Data- ↵
>GetData(DataFormats::FileDrop);
            try {
                // Assign the first image to the picture variable.
                this->picture = Image::FromFile(files[0]);
                // Set the picture location equal to the drop point.
                this->pictureLocation = this->PointToClient( Point ↵
 (e->X, e->Y));
            } catch (Exception* ex) {
                MessageBox::Show(ex->Message);
                return;
            }
        }

        // Handle Bitmap data.
        if (e->Data->GetDataPresent(DataFormats::Bitmap)) {
            try {
                // Create an Image and assign it to the picture variable.
                this->picture = dynamic_cast<Image*>(e->Data- ↵
>GetData(DataFormats::Bitmap));
                // Set the picture location equal to the drop point.
                this->pictureLocation = this->PointToClient( Point ↵
 (e->X, e->Y));
            } catch (Exception* ex) {
                MessageBox::Show(ex->Message);
                return;
            }
        }
        // Force the form to be redrawn with the image.
        this->Invalidate();
    }

    void Form1_DragEnter(Object* sender, DragEventArgs* e) {
        // If the data is a file or a bitmap, display the copy cursor.
        if (e->Data->GetDataPresent(DataFormats::Bitmap) ||
            e->Data->GetDataPresent(DataFormats::FileDrop)) {
            e->Effect = DragDropEffects::Copy;
        } else {
            e->Effect = DragDropEffects::None;
        }
    }
```

Requirements

Platforms: Windows 98, Windows NT 4.0, Windows Millennium Edition, Windows 2000, Windows XP Home Edition, Windows XP Professional, Windows Server 2003 family, .NET Compact Framework - Windows CE .NET

Control.Invalidate Method (Boolean)

Invalidates a specific region of the control and causes a paint message to be sent to the control. Optionally, invalidates the child controls assigned to the control.

[Visual Basic]
```
Overloads Public Sub Invalidate( _
   ByVal invalidateChildren As Boolean _
)
```
[C#]
```
public void Invalidate(
   bool invalidateChildren
);
```
[C++]
```
public: void Invalidate(
   bool invalidateChildren
);
```
[JScript]
```
public function Invalidate(
   invalidateChildren : Boolean
);
```

Parameters

invalidateChildren

true to invalidate the control's child controls; otherwise, **false**.

Remarks

Calling the **Invalidate** method does not force a synchronous paint; to force a synchronous paint, call the **Update** method after calling the **Invalidate** method. When this method is called with no parameters, the entire client area is added to the update region.

Requirements

Platforms: Windows 98, Windows NT 4.0, Windows Millennium Edition, Windows 2000, Windows XP Home Edition, Windows XP Professional, Windows Server 2003 family

Control.Invalidate Method (Rectangle)

Invalidates the specified region of the control (adds it to the control's update region, which is the area that will be repainted at the next paint operation), and causes a paint message to be sent to the control.

[Visual Basic]
```
Overloads Public Sub Invalidate( _
   ByVal rc As Rectangle _
)
```
[C#]
```
public void Invalidate(
   Rectangle rc
);
```
[C++]
```
public: void Invalidate(
   Rectangle rc
);
```
[JScript]
```
public function Invalidate(
   rc : Rectangle
);
```

Parameters

rc

A **Rectangle** object that represents the region to invalidate.

Remarks

Calling the **Invalidate** method does not force a synchronous paint; to force a synchronous paint, call the **Update** method after calling the **Invalidate** method. When this method is called with no parameters, the entire client area is added to the update region.

Requirements

Platforms: Windows 98, Windows NT 4.0, Windows Millennium Edition, Windows 2000, Windows XP Home Edition, Windows XP Professional, Windows Server 2003 family, .NET Compact Framework - Windows CE .NET

Control.Invalidate Method (Region)

Invalidates the specified region of the control (adds it to the control's update region, which is the area that will be repainted at the next paint operation), and causes a paint message to be sent to the control.

[Visual Basic]
```
Overloads Public Sub Invalidate( _
   ByVal region As Region _
)
```
[C#]
```
public void Invalidate(
   Region region
);
```
[C++]
```
public: void Invalidate(
   Region* region
);
```
[JScript]
```
public function Invalidate(
   region : Region
);
```

Parameters

region

The **Region** to invalidate.

Remarks

Calling the **Invalidate** method does not force a synchronous paint; to force a synchronous paint, call the **Update** method after calling the **Invalidate** method. When this method is called with no parameters, the entire client area is added to the update region.

Requirements

Platforms: Windows 98, Windows NT 4.0, Windows Millennium Edition, Windows 2000, Windows XP Home Edition, Windows XP Professional, Windows Server 2003 family

Control.Invalidate Method (Rectangle, Boolean)

Invalidates the specified region of the control (adds it to the control's update region, which is the area that will be repainted at the next paint operation), and causes a paint message to be sent to the control. Optionally, invalidates the child controls assigned to the control.

[Visual Basic]
```
Overloads Public Sub Invalidate( _
   ByVal rc As Rectangle, _
   ByVal invalidateChildren As Boolean _
)
```

```
[C#]
public void Invalidate(
   Rectangle rc,
   bool invalidateChildren
);
[C++]
public: void Invalidate(
   Rectangle rc,
   bool invalidateChildren
);
[JScript]
public function Invalidate(
   rc : Rectangle,
   invalidateChildren : Boolean
);
```

Parameters

rc
A **Rectangle** object that represents the region to invalidate.

invalidateChildren
true to invalidate the control's child controls; otherwise, **false**.

Remarks

Calling the **Invalidate** method does not force a synchronous paint; to force a synchronous paint, call the **Update** method after calling the **Invalidate** method. When this method is called with no parameters, the entire client area is added to the update region.

Requirements

Platforms: Windows 98, Windows NT 4.0, Windows Millennium Edition, Windows 2000, Windows XP Home Edition, Windows XP Professional, Windows Server 2003 family

Control.Invalidate Method (Region, Boolean)

Invalidates the specified region of the control (adds it to the control's update region, which is the area that will be repainted at the next paint operation), and causes a paint message to be sent to the control. Optionally, invalidates the child controls assigned to the control.

```
[Visual Basic]
Overloads Public Sub Invalidate( _
   ByVal region As Region, _
   ByVal invalidateChildren As Boolean _
)
[C#]
public void Invalidate(
   Region region,
   bool invalidateChildren
);
[C++]
public: void Invalidate(
   Region* region,
   bool invalidateChildren
);
[JScript]
public function Invalidate(
   region : Region,
   invalidateChildren : Boolean
);
```

Parameters

region
The **Region** to invalidate.

invalidateChildren
true to invalidate the control's child controls; otherwise, **false**.

Remarks

Calling the **Invalidate** method does not force a synchronous paint; to force a synchronous paint, call the **Update** method after calling the **Invalidate** method. When this method is called with no parameters, the entire client area is added to the update region.

Requirements

Platforms: Windows 98, Windows NT 4.0, Windows Millennium Edition, Windows 2000, Windows XP Home Edition, Windows XP Professional, Windows Server 2003 family

Control.Invoke Method

Executes a delegate on the thread that owns the control's underlying window handle.

Overload List

Executes the specified delegate on the thread that owns the control's underlying window handle.

Supported by the .NET Compact Framework.

[Visual Basic] **Overloads Public Function Invoke(Delegate) As Object**

[C#] **public object Invoke(Delegate);**

[C++] **public: Object* Invoke(Delegate*);**

[JScript] **public function Invoke(Delegate) : Object;**

Executes the specified delegate, on the thread that owns the control's underlying window handle, with the specified list of arguments.

[Visual Basic] **Overloads Public Overridable Function Invoke(Delegate, Object()) As Object Implements ISynchronizeInvoke.Invoke**

[C#] **public virtual object Invoke(Delegate, object[]);**

[C++] **public: virtual Object* Invoke(Delegate*, Object[]);**

[JScript] **public function Invoke(Delegate, Object[]) : Object;**

Control.Invoke Method (Delegate)

Executes the specified delegate on the thread that owns the control's underlying window handle.

```
[Visual Basic]
Overloads Public Function Invoke( _
   ByVal method As Delegate _
) As Object
[C#]
public object Invoke(
   Delegate method
);
[C++]
public: Object* Invoke(
   Delegate* method
);
[JScript]
public function Invoke(
   method : Delegate
) : Object;
```

Parameters

method

A delegate that contains a method to be called in the control's thread context.

Return Value

The return value from the delegate being invoked, or a null reference (**Nothing** in Visual Basic) if the delegate has no return value.

Remarks

If the control's handle does not exist yet, this method searches up the control's parent chain until it finds a control or form that does have a window handle. If no appropriate handle can be found, the **Invoke** method will throw an exception. Exceptions that are raised during the call will be propagated back to the caller.

> **Note** There are four methods on a control that are safe to call from any thread: **Invoke**, **BeginInvoke**, **EndInvoke**, and **CreateGraphics**. For all other method calls, you should use one of the invoke methods to marshal the call to the control's thread.

The delegate can be an instance of **EventHandler**, in which case the sender parameter will contain this control, and the event parameter will contain **EventArgs.Empty**. The delegate can also be an instance of **MethodInvoker**, or any other delegate that takes a void parameter list. A call to an **EventHandler** or **MethodInvoker** delegate will be faster than a call to another type of delegate.

Requirements

Platforms: Windows 98, Windows NT 4.0,
Windows Millennium Edition, Windows 2000,
Windows XP Home Edition, Windows XP Professional,
Windows Server 2003 family,
.NET Compact Framework - Windows CE .NET

Control.Invoke Method (Delegate, Object[])

Executes the specified delegate, on the thread that owns the control's underlying window handle, with the specified list of arguments.

```
[Visual Basic]
Overloads Public Overridable Function Invoke( _
   ByVal method As Delegate, _
   ByVal args() As Object _
) As Object Implements ISynchronizeInvoke.Invoke
[C#]
public virtual object Invoke(
   Delegate method,
   object[] args
);
[C++]
public: virtual Object* Invoke(
   Delegate* method,
   Object* args __gc[]
);
[JScript]
public function Invoke(
   method : Delegate,
   args : Object[]
) : Object;
```

Parameters

method

A delegate to a method that takes parameters of the same number and type that are contained in the *args* parameter.

args

An array of objects to pass as arguments to the specified method. This parameter can be a null reference (**Nothing** in Visual Basic) if the method takes no arguments.

Return Value

An **Object** that contains the return value from the delegate being invoked, or a null reference (**Nothing** in Visual Basic) if the delegate has no return value.

Implements

ISynchronizeInvoke.Invoke

Remarks

If the control's handle does not exist yet, this method searches up the control's parent chain until it finds a control or form that does have a window handle. If no appropriate handle can be found, the **Invoke** method will throw an exception. Exceptions that are raised during the call will be propagated back to the caller.

> **Note** There are four methods on a control that are safe to call from any thread: **Invoke**, **BeginInvoke**, **EndInvoke**, and **CreateGraphics**. For all other method calls, you should use one of the invoke methods to marshal the call to the control's thread.

The delegate can be an instance of **EventHandler**, in which case the sender parameter will contain this control, and the event parameter will contain **EventArgs.Empty**. The delegate can also be an instance of **MethodInvoker**, or any other delegate that takes a void parameter list. A call to an **EventHandler** or **MethodInvoker** delegate will be faster than a call to another type of delegate.

Requirements

Platforms: Windows 98, Windows NT 4.0,
Windows Millennium Edition, Windows 2000,
Windows XP Home Edition, Windows XP Professional,
Windows Server 2003 family

Control.InvokeGotFocus Method

Raises the **GotFocus** event for the specified control.

```
[Visual Basic]
Protected Sub InvokeGotFocus( _
   ByVal toInvoke As Control, _
   ByVal e As EventArgs _
)
[C#]
protected void InvokeGotFocus(
   Control toInvoke,
   EventArgs e
);
[C++]
protected: void InvokeGotFocus(
   Control* toInvoke,
   EventArgs* e
);
[JScript]
protected function InvokeGotFocus(
   toInvoke : Control,
   e : EventArgs
);
```

Parameters

toInvoke

The **Control** to assign the event to.

e

An **EventArgs** that contains the event data.

Requirements

Platforms: Windows 98, Windows NT 4.0, Windows Millennium Edition, Windows 2000, Windows XP Home Edition, Windows XP Professional, Windows Server 2003 family

Control.InvokeLostFocus Method

Raises the **LostFocus** event for the specified control.

```
[Visual Basic]
Protected Sub InvokeLostFocus( _
   ByVal toInvoke As Control, _
   ByVal e As EventArgs _
)
[C#]
protected void InvokeLostFocus(
   Control toInvoke,
   EventArgs e
);
[C++]
protected: void InvokeLostFocus(
   Control* toInvoke,
   EventArgs* e
);
[JScript]
protected function InvokeLostFocus(
   toInvoke : Control,
   e : EventArgs
);
```

Parameters

toInvoke

The **Control** to assign the event to.

e

An **EventArgs** that contains the event data.

Requirements

Platforms: Windows 98, Windows NT 4.0, Windows Millennium Edition, Windows 2000, Windows XP Home Edition, Windows XP Professional, Windows Server 2003 family

Control.InvokeOnClick Method

Raises the **Click** event for the specified control.

```
[Visual Basic]
Protected Sub InvokeOnClick( _
   ByVal toInvoke As Control, _
   ByVal e As EventArgs _
)
[C#]
protected void InvokeOnClick(
   Control toInvoke,
   EventArgs e
);
[C++]
protected: void InvokeOnClick(
   Control* toInvoke,
   EventArgs* e
);
[JScript]
protected function InvokeOnClick(
   toInvoke : Control,
   e : EventArgs
);
```

Parameters

toInvoke

The **Control** to assign the **Click** event to.

e

An **EventArgs** that contains the event data.

Requirements

Platforms: Windows 98, Windows NT 4.0, Windows Millennium Edition, Windows 2000, Windows XP Home Edition, Windows XP Professional, Windows Server 2003 family

Control.InvokePaint Method

Raises the **Paint** event for the specified control.

```
[Visual Basic]
Protected Sub InvokePaint( _
   ByVal c As Control, _
   ByVal e As PaintEventArgs _
)
[C#]
protected void InvokePaint(
   Control c,
   PaintEventArgs e
);
[C++]
protected: void InvokePaint(
   Control* c,
   PaintEventArgs* e
);
[JScript]
protected function InvokePaint(
   c : Control,
   e : PaintEventArgs
);
```

Parameters

c

The **Control** to assign the **Paint** event to.

e

An **PaintEventArgs** that contains the event data.

Requirements

Platforms: Windows 98, Windows NT 4.0, Windows Millennium Edition, Windows 2000, Windows XP Home Edition, Windows XP Professional, Windows Server 2003 family

Control.InvokePaintBackground Method

Raises the **PaintBackground** event for the specified control.

[Visual Basic]
```
Protected Sub InvokePaintBackground( _
   ByVal c As Control, _
   ByVal e As PaintEventArgs _
)
```
[C#]
```
protected void InvokePaintBackground(
   Control c,
   PaintEventArgs e
);
```
[C++]
```
protected: void InvokePaintBackground(
   Control* c,
   PaintEventArgs* e
);
```
[JScript]
```
protected function InvokePaintBackground(
   c : Control,
   e : PaintEventArgs
);
```

Parameters

c

The **Control** to assign the **Paint** event to.

e

An **PaintEventArgs** that contains the event data.

Requirements

Platforms: Windows 98, Windows NT 4.0, Windows Millennium Edition, Windows 2000, Windows XP Home Edition, Windows XP Professional, Windows Server 2003 family

Control.IsInputChar Method

Determines if a character is an input character that the control recognizes.

[Visual Basic]
```
Protected Overridable Function IsInputChar( _
   ByVal charCode As Char _
) As Boolean
```
[C#]
```
protected virtual bool IsInputChar(
   char charCode
);
```
[C++]
```
protected: virtual bool IsInputChar(
   __wchar_t charCode
);
```
[JScript]
```
protected function IsInputChar(
   charCode : Char
) : Boolean;
```

Parameters

charCode

The character to test.

Return Value

true if the character should be sent directly to the control and not preprocessed; otherwise, **false**.

Remarks

This method is called during window message preprocessing to determine whether the given input character should be preprocessed or sent directly to the control. If the **IsInputChar** method returns **true**, the specified character is sent directly to the control. However, if the method returns **false**, the character is preprocessed and only sent to the control if it is not consumed by the preprocessing phase. The preprocessing of a character includes checking whether the character is a mnemonic of another control.

Requirements

Platforms: Windows 98, Windows NT 4.0, Windows Millennium Edition, Windows 2000, Windows XP Home Edition, Windows XP Professional, Windows Server 2003 family

.NET Framework Security:

- **UIPermission** for all windows for inheriting classes to call this method. Associated enumeration: **UIPermissionWindow.AllWindows**

Control.IsInputKey Method

Determines whether the specified key is a regular input key or a special key that requires preprocessing.

[Visual Basic]
```
Protected Overridable Function IsInputKey( _
   ByVal keyData As Keys _
) As Boolean
```
[C#]
```
protected virtual bool IsInputKey(
   Keys keyData
);
```
[C++]
```
protected: virtual bool IsInputKey(
   Keys keyData
);
```
[JScript]
```
protected function IsInputKey(
   keyData : Keys
) : Boolean;
```

Parameters

keyData

One of the **Keys** values.

Return Value

true if the specified key is a regular input key; otherwise, **false**.

Remarks

Call the **IsInputChar** method during window-message preprocessing to determine whether the specified key is a regular input key that should be sent directly to the control or a special key (such as PAGE UP, PAGE DOWN, ENTER, ESC, TAB, or arrow keys) that should preprocessed. In the latter case, the key is sent to the control only if it is not consumed by the preprocessing phase.

Requirements

Platforms: Windows 98, Windows NT 4.0, Windows Millennium Edition, Windows 2000, Windows XP Home Edition, Windows XP Professional, Windows Server 2003 family

.NET Framework Security:

- **UIPermission** for all windows for inheriting classes to call this method. Associated enumeration: **UIPermissionWindow.AllWindows**

Control.IsMnemonic Method

Determines if the specified character is the mnemonic character assigned to the control in the specified string.

```
[Visual Basic]
Public Shared Function IsMnemonic( _
   ByVal charCode As Char, _
   ByVal text As String _
) As Boolean
[C#]
public static bool IsMnemonic(
   char charCode,
   string text
);
[C++]
public: static bool IsMnemonic(
   __wchar_t charCode,
   String* text
);
[JScript]
public static function IsMnemonic(
   charCode : Char,
   text : String
) : Boolean;
```

Parameters

charCode
The character to test.

text
The string to search.

Return Value

true if the *charCode* character is the mnemonic character assigned to the control; otherwise, **false**.

Remarks

The mnemonic character is the character immediately following the first instance of "&" in a **String**.

Requirements

Platforms: Windows 98, Windows NT 4.0, Windows Millennium Edition, Windows 2000, Windows XP Home Edition, Windows XP Professional, Windows Server 2003 family

.NET Framework Security:

- **UIPermission** for all windows for inheriting classes to call this method. Associated enumeration: **UIPermissionWindow.AllWindows**

Control.NotifyInvalidate Method

This member supports the .NET Framework infrastructure and is not intended to be used directly from your code.

```
[Visual Basic]
Protected Overridable Sub NotifyInvalidate( _
   ByVal invalidatedArea As Rectangle _
)
[C#]
protected virtual void NotifyInvalidate(
   Rectangle invalidatedArea
);
[C++]
protected: virtual void NotifyInvalidate(
   Rectangle invalidatedArea
);
[JScript]
protected function NotifyInvalidate(
   invalidatedArea : Rectangle
);
```

Control.OnBackColorChanged Method

Raises the **BackColorChanged** event.

```
[Visual Basic]
Protected Overridable Sub OnBackColorChanged( _
   ByVal e As EventArgs _
)
[C#]
protected virtual void OnBackColorChanged(
   EventArgs e
);
[C++]
protected: virtual void OnBackColorChanged(
   EventArgs* e
);
[JScript]
protected function OnBackColorChanged(
   e : EventArgs
);
```

Parameters

e
An **EventArgs** that contains the event data.

Remarks

Raising an event invokes the event handler through a delegate.

The **OnBackColorChanged** method also allows derived classes to handle the event without attaching a delegate. This is the preferred technique for handling the event in a derived class.

Notes to Inheritors: When overriding **OnBackColorChanged** in a derived class, be sure to call the base class's **OnBackColorChanged** method so that registered delegates receive the event.

Example

[Visual Basic, C#, C++] The example below is an event-raising method that is executed when the **Text** property value changes. The **Control** class has several methods with the name pattern **On** PropertyName **Changed** that raise the corresponding PropertyName **Changed** event when the PropertyName value changes(PropertyName represents the name of the corresponding property).

[Visual Basic, C#, C++] The following example changes the **ForeColor** of a **TextBox** derived class displaying currency data. The example converts the text to a decimal number and changes the **ForeColor** to **Color.Red** if the number is negative and to **Color.Black** if the number is positive. This example assumes you have a class that derives from the **TextBox** class.

[Visual Basic]
```
Protected Overrides Sub OnTextChanged(e As System.EventArgs)
   Try
      ' Convert the text to a Double and determine
      ' if it is a negative number.
      If Double.Parse(Me.Text) < 0 Then
         ' If the number is negative, display it in Red.
         Me.ForeColor = Color.Red
      Else
         ' If the number is not negative, display it in Black.
         Me.ForeColor = Color.Black
      End If
   Catch
      ' If there is an error, display the
      ' text using the system colors.
      Me.ForeColor = SystemColors.ControlText
   End Try

   MyBase.OnTextChanged(e)
End Sub
```

[C#]
```
protected override void OnTextChanged(System.EventArgs e)
{
   try
   {
      // Convert the text to a Double and determine
      // if it is a negative number.
      if(double.Parse(this.Text) < 0)
      {
         // If the number is negative, display it in Red.
         this.ForeColor = Color.Red;
      }
      else
      {
         // If the number is not negative, display it in Black.
         this.ForeColor = Color.Black;
      }
   }
   catch
   {
      // If there is an error, display the
      // text using the system colors.
      this.ForeColor = SystemColors.ControlText;
   }

   base.OnTextChanged(e);
}
```

[C++]
```
protected:
   void OnTextChanged(System::EventArgs* e) {
      try {
         // Convert the text to a Double and determine
         // if it is a negative number.
         if (Double::Parse(this->Text) < 0) {
            // If the number is negative, display it in Red.
            this->ForeColor = Color::Red;
         } else {
            // If the number is not negative, display it in Black.
            this->ForeColor = Color::Black;
         }
      } catch (Exception*) {
         // If there is an error, display the
         // text using the system colors.
         this->ForeColor = SystemColors::ControlText;
      }

      TextBox::OnTextChanged(e);
   }
```

Requirements

Platforms: Windows 98, Windows NT 4.0, Windows Millennium Edition, Windows 2000, Windows XP Home Edition, Windows XP Professional, Windows Server 2003 family

Control.OnBackgroundImageChanged Method

Raises the **BackgroundImageChanged** event.

[Visual Basic]
```
Protected Overridable Sub OnBackgroundImageChanged( _
   ByVal e As EventArgs _
)
```
[C#]
```
protected virtual void OnBackgroundImageChanged(
   EventArgs e
);
```
[C++]
```
protected: virtual void OnBackgroundImageChanged(
   EventArgs* e
);
```
[JScript]
```
protected function OnBackgroundImageChanged(
   e : EventArgs
);
```

Parameters

e

An **EventArgs** that contains the event data.

Remarks

Raising an event invokes the event handler through a delegate. For more information, see **Raising an Event**.

The **OnBackgroundImageChanged** method also allows derived classes to handle the event without attaching a delegate. This is the preferred technique for handling the event in a derived class.

Notes to Inheritors: When overriding **OnBackgroundImageChanged** in a derived class, be sure to call the base class's **OnBackgroundImageChanged** method so that registered delegates receive the event.

Example

[Visual Basic, C#, C++] The example below is an event-raising method that is executed when the **Text** property value changes. The **Control** class has several methods with the name pattern **On** PropertyName **Changed** that raise the corresponding PropertyName **Changed** event when the PropertyName value changes(PropertyName represents the name of the corresponding property).

[Visual Basic, C#, C++] The following example changes the **ForeColor** of a **TextBox** derived class displaying currency data. The example converts the text to a decimal number and changes the **ForeColor** to **Color.Red** if the number is negative and to **Color.Black** if the number is positive. This example assumes you have a class that derives from the **TextBox** class.

[Visual Basic]
```
Protected Overrides Sub OnTextChanged(e As System.EventArgs)
   Try
      ' Convert the text to a Double and determine
      ' if it is a negative number.
      If Double.Parse(Me.Text) < 0 Then
         ' If the number is negative, display it in Red.
         Me.ForeColor = Color.Red
      Else
         ' If the number is not negative, display it in Black.
         Me.ForeColor = Color.Black
      End If
   Catch
      ' If there is an error, display the
      ' text using the system colors.
```

```
    Me.ForeColor = SystemColors.ControlText
  End Try

  MyBase.OnTextChanged(e)
End Sub
```

[C#]
```
protected override void OnTextChanged(System.EventArgs e)
{
   try
   {
      // Convert the text to a Double and determine
      // if it is a negative number.
      if(double.Parse(this.Text) < 0)
      {
         // If the number is negative, display it in Red.
         this.ForeColor = Color.Red;
      }
      else
      {
         // If the number is not negative, display it in Black.
         this.ForeColor = Color.Black;
      }
   }
   catch
   {
      // If there is an error, display the
      // text using the system colors.
      this.ForeColor = SystemColors.ControlText;
   }

   base.OnTextChanged(e);
}
```

[C++]
```
protected:
   void OnTextChanged(System::EventArgs* e) {
      try {
         // Convert the text to a Double and determine
         // if it is a negative number.
         if (Double::Parse(this->Text) < 0) {
            // If the number is negative, display it in Red.
            this->ForeColor = Color::Red;
         } else {
            // If the number is not negative, display it in Black.
            this->ForeColor = Color::Black;
         }
      } catch (Exception*) {
         // If there is an error, display the
         // text using the system colors.
         this->ForeColor = SystemColors::ControlText;
      }

      TextBox::OnTextChanged(e);
   }
```

Requirements

Platforms: Windows 98, Windows NT 4.0, Windows Millennium Edition, Windows 2000, Windows XP Home Edition, Windows XP Professional, Windows Server 2003 family

Control.OnBindingContextChanged Method

Raises the **BindingContextChanged** event.

[Visual Basic]
```
Protected Overridable Sub OnBindingContextChanged( _
   ByVal e As EventArgs _
)
```
[C#]
```
protected virtual void OnBindingContextChanged(
   EventArgs e
);
```
[C++]
```
protected: virtual void OnBindingContextChanged(
   EventArgs* e
);
```
[JScript]
```
protected function OnBindingContextChanged(
   e : EventArgs
);
```

Parameters

e

An **EventArgs** that contains the event data.

Remarks

Raising an event invokes the event handler through a delegate.

The **OnBindingContextChanged** method also allows derived classes to handle the event without attaching a delegate. This is the preferred technique for handling the event in a derived class.

Notes to Inheritors: When overriding **OnBindingContextChanged** in a derived class, be sure to call the base class's **OnBindingContextChanged** method so that registered delegates receive the event.

Example

[Visual Basic, C#, C++] The example below is an event-raising method that is executed when the **Text** property value changes. The **Control** class has several methods with the name pattern **On <PropertyName> Changed** that raise the corresponding event when the property value changes. You can create an event-raising method similar to the following example to raise the appropriate event when the the corresponding property value changes.

[Visual Basic, C#, C++] The following example changes the **ForeColor** of a **TextBox** derived class displaying currency data. The example converts the text to a decimal number and changes the **ForeColor** to **Color.Red** if the number is negative and to **Color.Black** if the number is positive. This example assumes you have a class that derives from the **TextBox** class.

[Visual Basic]
```
Protected Overrides Sub OnTextChanged(e As System.EventArgs)
   Try
      ' Convert the text to a Double and determine
      ' if it is a negative number.
      If Double.Parse(Me.Text) < 0 Then
         ' If the number is negative, display it in Red.
         Me.ForeColor = Color.Red
      Else
         ' If the number is not negative, display it in Black.
         Me.ForeColor = Color.Black
      End If
   Catch
      ' If there is an error, display the
      ' text using the system colors.
      Me.ForeColor = SystemColors.ControlText
   End Try

   MyBase.OnTextChanged(e)
End Sub
```

[C#]
```
protected override void OnTextChanged(System.EventArgs e)
{
   try
   {
      // Convert the text to a Double and determine
      // if it is a negative number.
      if(double.Parse(this.Text) < 0)
```

```
      {
         // If the number is negative, display it in Red.
         this.ForeColor = Color.Red;
      }
      else
      {
         // If the number is not negative, display it in Black.
         this.ForeColor = Color.Black;
      }
   }
   catch
   {
      // If there is an error, display the
      // text using the system colors.
      this.ForeColor = SystemColors.ControlText;
   }

   base.OnTextChanged(e);
}
```

[C++]

```
protected:
   void OnTextChanged(System::EventArgs* e) {
      try {
         // Convert the text to a Double and determine
         // if it is a negative number.
         if (Double::Parse(this->Text) < 0) {
            // If the number is negative, display it in Red.
            this->ForeColor = Color::Red;
         } else {
            // If the number is not negative, display it in Black.
            this->ForeColor = Color::Black;
         }
      } catch (Exception*) {
         // If there is an error, display the
         // text using the system colors.
         this->ForeColor = SystemColors::ControlText;
      }

      TextBox::OnTextChanged(e);
   }
```

Requirements

Platforms: Windows 98, Windows NT 4.0, Windows Millennium Edition, Windows 2000, Windows XP Home Edition, Windows XP Professional, Windows Server 2003 family, .NET Compact Framework - Windows CE .NET

Control.OnCausesValidationChanged Method

Raises the **CausesValidationChanged** event.

[Visual Basic]

```
Protected Overridable Sub OnCausesValidationChanged( _
   ByVal e As EventArgs _
)
```

[C#]

```
protected virtual void OnCausesValidationChanged(
   EventArgs e
);
```

[C++]

```
protected: virtual void OnCausesValidationChanged(
   EventArgs* e
);
```

[JScript]

```
protected function OnCausesValidationChanged(
   e : EventArgs
);
```

Parameters

e

An **EventArgs** that contains the event data.

Remarks

Raising an event invokes the event handler through a delegate. For more information, see **Raising an Event**.

The **OnCausesValidationChanged** method also allows derived classes to handle the event without attaching a delegate. This is the preferred technique for handling the event in a derived class.

Notes to Inheritors: When overriding **OnCausesValidation-Changed** in a derived class, be sure to call the base class's **OnCausesValidationChanged** method so that registered delegates receive the event.

Example

[Visual Basic, C#, C++] The example below is an event-raising method that is executed when the **Text** property value changes. The **Control** class has several methods with the name pattern **On** PropertyName **Changed** that raise the corresponding PropertyName **Changed** event when the PropertyName value changes(Property-Name represents the name of the corresponding property).

[Visual Basic, C#, C++] The following example changes the **ForeColor** of a **TextBox** derived class displaying currency data. The example converts the text to a decimal number and changes the **ForeColor** to **Color.Red** if the number is negative and to **Color.Black** if the number is positive. This example assumes you have a class that derives from the **TextBox** class.

[Visual Basic]

```
Protected Overrides Sub OnTextChanged(e As System.EventArgs)
   Try
      ' Convert the text to a Double and determine
      ' if it is a negative number.
      If Double.Parse(Me.Text) < 0 Then
         ' If the number is negative, display it in Red.
         Me.ForeColor = Color.Red
      Else
         ' If the number is not negative, display it in Black.
         Me.ForeColor = Color.Black
      End If
   Catch
      ' If there is an error, display the
      ' text using the system colors.
      Me.ForeColor = SystemColors.ControlText
   End Try

   MyBase.OnTextChanged(e)
End Sub
```

[C#]

```
protected override void OnTextChanged(System.EventArgs e)
{
   try
   {
      // Convert the text to a Double and determine
      // if it is a negative number.
      if(double.Parse(this.Text) < 0)
      {
         // If the number is negative, display it in Red.
         this.ForeColor = Color.Red;
      }
      else
      {
         // If the number is not negative, display it in Black.
         this.ForeColor = Color.Black;
      }
   }
```

```
catch
{
   // If there is an error, display the
   // text using the system colors.
   this.ForeColor = SystemColors.ControlText;
}

base.OnTextChanged(e);
}
```

[C++]

```
protected:
   void OnTextChanged(System::EventArgs* e) {
      try {
         // Convert the text to a Double and determine
         // if it is a negative number.
         if (Double::Parse(this->Text) < 0) {
            // If the number is negative, display it in Red.
            this->ForeColor = Color::Red;
         } else {
            // If the number is not negative, display it in Black.
            this->ForeColor = Color::Black;
         }
      } catch (Exception*) {
         // If there is an error, display the
         // text using the system colors.
         this->ForeColor = SystemColors::ControlText;
      }

      TextBox::OnTextChanged(e);
   }
```

Requirements

Platforms: Windows 98, Windows NT 4.0, Windows Millennium Edition, Windows 2000, Windows XP Home Edition, Windows XP Professional, Windows Server 2003 family

Control.OnChangeUICues Method

Raises the **ChangeUICues** event.

[Visual Basic]

```
Protected Overridable Sub OnChangeUICues( _
   ByVal e As UICuesEventArgs _
)
```

[C#]

```
protected virtual void OnChangeUICues(
   UICuesEventArgs e
);
```

[C++]

```
protected: virtual void OnChangeUICues(
   UICuesEventArgs* e
);
```

[JScript]

```
protected function OnChangeUICues(
   e : UICuesEventArgs
);
```

Parameters

e

A **UICuesEventArgs** that contains the event data.

Remarks

Raising an event invokes the event handler through a delegate.

The **OnChangeUICues** method also allows derived classes to handle the event without attaching a delegate. This is the preferred technique for handling the event in a derived class.

Notes to Inheritors: When overriding **OnChangeUICues** in a derived class, be sure to call the base class's **OnChangeUICues** method so that registered delegates receive the event.

Requirements

Platforms: Windows 98, Windows NT 4.0, Windows Millennium Edition, Windows 2000, Windows XP Home Edition, Windows XP Professional, Windows Server 2003 family

Control.OnClick Method

Raises the **Click** event.

[Visual Basic]

```
Protected Overridable Sub OnClick( _
   ByVal e As EventArgs _
)
```

[C#]

```
protected virtual void OnClick(
   EventArgs e
);
```

[C++]

```
protected: virtual void OnClick(
   EventArgs* e
);
```

[JScript]

```
protected function OnClick(
   e : EventArgs
);
```

Parameters

e

An **EventArgs** that contains the event data.

Remarks

Raising an event invokes the event handler through a delegate.

The **OnClick** method also allows derived classes to handle the event without attaching a delegate. This is the preferred technique for handling the event in a derived class.

Notes to Inheritors: When overriding **OnClick** in a derived class, be sure to call the base class's **OnClick** method so that registered delegates receive the event.

Example

[Visual Basic]

```
' This example uses the Parent property and the Find method of ↵
 Control to set
' properties on the parent control of a Button and its Form. ↵
The example assumes
' that a Button control named button1 is located within a ↵
GroupBox control. The
' example also assumes that the Click event of the Button ↵
control is connected to
' the event handling method defined in the example.
Private Sub button1_Click(sender As Object, e As ↵
System.EventArgs) Handles button1.Click
   ' Get the control the Button control is located in. In this ↵
 case a GroupBox.
   Dim control As Control = button1.Parent
   ' Set the text and backcolor of the parent control.
   control.Text = "My Groupbox"
   control.BackColor = Color.Blue
   ' Get the form that the Button control is contained within.
   Dim myForm As Form = button1.FindForm()
   ' Set the text and color of the form containing the Button.
```

```
    myForm.Text = "The Form of My Control"
    myForm.BackColor = Color.Red
End Sub
```

[C#]

```
// This example uses the Parent property and the Find method ↵
of Control to set
// properties on the parent control of a Button and its Form. ↵
 The example assumes
// that a Button control named button1 is located within a ↵
 GroupBox control. The
// example also assumes that the Click event of the Button ↵
control is connected to
// the event handling method defined in the example.
private void button1_Click(object sender, System.EventArgs e)
{
    // Get the control the Button control is located in. In this ↵
 case a GroupBox.
    Control control = button1.Parent;
    // Set the text and backcolor of the parent control.
    control.Text = "My Groupbox";
    control.BackColor = Color.Blue;
    // Get the form that the Button control is contained within.
    Form myForm = button1.FindForm();
    // Set the text and color of the form containing the Button.
    myForm.Text = "The Form of My Control";
    myForm.BackColor = Color.Red;
}
```

Requirements

Platforms: Windows 98, Windows NT 4.0, Windows Millennium Edition, Windows 2000, Windows XP Home Edition, Windows XP Professional, Windows Server 2003 family, .NET Compact Framework - Windows CE .NET

Control.OnContextMenuChanged Method

Raises the **ContextMenuChanged** event.

[Visual Basic]

```
Protected Overridable Sub OnContextMenuChanged( _
   ByVal e As EventArgs _
)
```

[C#]

```
protected virtual void OnContextMenuChanged(
   EventArgs e
);
```

[C++]

```
protected: virtual void OnContextMenuChanged(
   EventArgs* e
);
```

[JScript]

```
protected function OnContextMenuChanged(
   e : EventArgs
);
```

Parameters

e

An **EventArgs** that contains the event data.

Remarks

Raising an event invokes the event handler through a delegate.

The **OnContextMenuChanged** method also allows derived classes to handle the event without attaching a delegate. This is the preferred technique for handling the event in a derived class.

Notes to Inheritors: When overriding **OnContextMenuChanged** in a derived class, be sure to call the base class's **OnContextMenu-Changed** method so that registered delegates receive the event.

Example

[Visual Basic, C#, C++] The example below is an event-raising method that is executed when the **Text** property value changes. The **Control** class has several methods with the name pattern **On** PropertyName **Changed** that raise the corresponding PropertyName **Changed** event when the PropertyName value changes(Property-Name represents the name of the corresponding property).

[Visual Basic, C#, C++] The following example changes the **ForeColor** of a **TextBox** derived class displaying currency data. The example converts the text to a decimal number and changes the **ForeColor** to **Color.Red** if the number is negative and to **Color.Black** if the number is positive. This example assumes you have a class that derives from the **TextBox** class.

[Visual Basic]

```
Protected Overrides Sub OnTextChanged(e As System.EventArgs)
   Try
      ' Convert the text to a Double and determine
      ' if it is a negative number.
      If Double.Parse(Me.Text) < 0 Then
         ' If the number is negative, display it in Red.
         Me.ForeColor = Color.Red
      Else
         ' If the number is not negative, display it in Black.
         Me.ForeColor = Color.Black
      End If
   Catch
      ' If there is an error, display the
      ' text using the system colors.
      Me.ForeColor = SystemColors.ControlText
   End Try

   MyBase.OnTextChanged(e)
End Sub
```

[C#]

```
protected override void OnTextChanged(System.EventArgs e)
{
   try
   {
      // Convert the text to a Double and determine
      // if it is a negative number.
      if(double.Parse(this.Text) < 0)
      {
         // If the number is negative, display it in Red.
         this.ForeColor = Color.Red;
      }
      else
      {
         // If the number is not negative, display it in Black.
         this.ForeColor = Color.Black;
      }
   }
   catch
   {
      // If there is an error, display the
      // text using the system colors.
      this.ForeColor = SystemColors.ControlText;
   }

   base.OnTextChanged(e);
}
```

[C++]

```
protected:
   void OnTextChanged(System::EventArgs* e) {
      try {
         // Convert the text to a Double and determine
         // if it is a negative number.
         if (Double::Parse(this->Text) < 0) {
```

```
        // If the number is negative, display it in Red.
        this->ForeColor = Color::Red;
      } else {
        // If the number is not negative, display it in Black.
        this->ForeColor = Color::Black;
      }
    } catch (Exception*) {
      // If there is an error, display the
      // text using the system colors.
      this->ForeColor = SystemColors::ControlText;
    }

    TextBox::OnTextChanged(e);
  }
```

Requirements

Platforms: Windows 98, Windows NT 4.0, Windows Millennium Edition, Windows 2000, Windows XP Home Edition, Windows XP Professional, Windows Server 2003 family

Control.OnControlAdded Method

Raises the **ControlAdded** event.

[Visual Basic]
```
Protected Overridable Sub OnControlAdded( _
   ByVal e As ControlEventArgs _
)
```
[C#]
```
protected virtual void OnControlAdded(
   ControlEventArgs e
);
```
[C++]
```
protected: virtual void OnControlAdded(
   ControlEventArgs* e
);
```
[JScript]
```
protected function OnControlAdded(
   e : ControlEventArgs
);
```

Parameters

e

A **ControlEventArgs** that contains the event data.

Remarks

Called when a child control is added to the control.

Raising an event invokes the event handler through a delegate.

The **OnControlAdded** method also allows derived classes to handle the event without attaching a delegate. This is the preferred technique for handling the event in a derived class.

Notes to Inheritors: When overriding **OnControlAdded** in a derived class, be sure to call the base class's **OnControlAdded** method so that registered delegates receive the event.

Example

[Visual Basic]
```
' This example demonstrates the use of the ControlAdded and
' ControlRemoved events. This example assumes that two Button controls
' are added to the form and connected to the addControl_Click and
' removeControl_Click event handling methods.
Private Sub Form1_Load(ByVal sender As Object, ByVal e As ┘
System.EventArgs) Handles MyBase.Load
    ' Connect the ControlRemoved and ControlAdded event handlers ┘
to the event handling methods.
    ' ControlRemoved and ControlAdded are not available at design time.
    AddHandler Me.ControlRemoved, AddressOf Me.Control_Removed
    AddHandler Me.ControlAdded, AddressOf Me.Control_Added
End Sub 'Form1_Load

Private Sub Control_Added(ByVal sender As Object, ByVal e As ┘
System.Windows.Forms.ControlEventArgs)
    MessageBox.Show(("The control named " + e.Control.Name + " ┘
has been added to the form."))
End Sub

Private Sub Control_Removed(ByVal sender As Object, ByVal e As ┘
System.Windows.Forms.ControlEventArgs)
    MessageBox.Show(("The control named " + e.Control.Name + " ┘
has been removed from the form."))
End Sub

' Click event handler for a Button control. Adds a TextBox to the form.
Private Sub addControl_Click(ByVal sender As Object, ByVal e As ┘
System.EventArgs) Handles button1.Click
    ' Create a new TextBox control and add it to the form.
    Dim textBox1 As New TextBox()
    textBox1.Size = New Size(100, 10)
    textBox1.Location = New Point(10, 10)
    ' Name the control in order to remove it later.
    ' The name must be specified if a control is added at run time.
    textBox1.Name = "textBox1"

    ' Add the control to the form's control collection.
    Me.Controls.Add(textBox1)
End Sub

' Click event handler for a Button control.
' Removes the previously added TextBox from the form.
Private Sub removeControl_Click(ByVal sender As Object, ByVal ┘
 e As System.EventArgs) Handles button2.Click
    ' Loop through all controls in the form's control collection.
    Dim tempCtrl As Control
    For Each tempCtrl In Me.Controls
        ' Determine whether the control is textBox1,
        ' and if it is, remove it.
        If tempCtrl.Name = "textBox1" Then
            Me.Controls.Remove(tempCtrl)
        End If
    Next tempCtrl
End Sub
```

[C#]
```
// This example demonstrates the use of the ControlAdded and
// ControlRemoved events. This example assumes that two Button controls
// are added to the form and connected to the addControl_Click and
// removeControl_Click event handling methods.
private void Form1_Load(object sender, System.EventArgs e)
{
    // Connect the ControlRemoved and ControlAdded event handlers
    // to the event handling methods.
    // ControlRemoved and ControlAdded are not available at ┘
 design time.
    this.ControlRemoved += new ┘
System.Windows.Forms.ControlEventHandler(this.Control_Removed);
    this.ControlAdded += new ┘
System.Windows.Forms.ControlEventHandler(this.Control_Added);
}

private void Control_Added(object sender, ┘
System.Windows.Forms.ControlEventArgs e)
{
    MessageBox.Show("The control named " + e.Control.Name + " ┘
 has been added to the form.");
}

private void Control_Removed(object sender, ┘
System.Windows.Forms.ControlEventArgs e)
{
    MessageBox.Show("The control named " + e.Control.Name + " ┘
 has been removed from the form.");
}
```

```
// Click event handler for a Button control. Adds a TextBox to
 the form.
private void addControl_Click(object sender, System.EventArgs e)
{
    // Create a new TextBox control and add it to the form.
    TextBox textBox1 = new TextBox();
    textBox1.Size = new Size(100,10);
    textBox1.Location = new Point(10,10);
    // Name the control in order to remove it later. The name
must be specified
    // if a control is added at run time.
    textBox1.Name = "textBox1";

    // Add the control to the form's control collection.
    this.Controls.Add(textBox1);
}

// Click event handler for a Button control.
// Removes the previously added TextBox from the form.
private void removeControl_Click(object sender, System.EventArgs e)
{
    // Loop through all controls in the form's control collection.
    foreach (Control tempCtrl in this.Controls)
    {
        // Determine whether the control is textBox1,
        // and if it is, remove it.
        if (tempCtrl.Name == "textBox1")
        {
            this.Controls.Remove(tempCtrl);
        }
    }
}
```

Requirements

Platforms: Windows 98, Windows NT 4.0, Windows Millennium Edition, Windows 2000, Windows XP Home Edition, Windows XP Professional, Windows Server 2003 family

Control.OnControlRemoved Method

Raises the **ControlRemoved** event.

[Visual Basic]
```
Protected Overridable Sub OnControlRemoved( _
   ByVal e As ControlEventArgs _
)
```
[C#]
```
protected virtual void OnControlRemoved(
   ControlEventArgs e
);
```
[C++]
```
protected: virtual void OnControlRemoved(
   ControlEventArgs* e
);
```
[JScript]
```
protected function OnControlRemoved(
   e : ControlEventArgs
);
```

Parameters

e

A **ControlEventArgs** that contains the event data.

Remarks

Called when a child control is removed from the control.

Raising an event invokes the event handler through a delegate.

The **OnControlRemoved** method also allows derived classes to handle the event without attaching a delegate. This is the preferred technique for handling the event in a derived class.

Notes to Inheritors: When overriding **OnControlRemoved** in a derived class, be sure to call the base class's **OnControlRemoved** method so that registered delegates receive the event.

Example

See related example in the **System.Windows.Forms.Control.OnControlAdded** method topic.

Requirements

Platforms: Windows 98, Windows NT 4.0, Windows Millennium Edition, Windows 2000, Windows XP Home Edition, Windows XP Professional, Windows Server 2003 family

Control.OnCreateControl Method

Raises the **CreateControl** event.

[Visual Basic]
```
Protected Overridable Sub OnCreateControl()
```
[C#]
```
protected virtual void OnCreateControl();
```
[C++]
```
protected: virtual void OnCreateControl();
```
[JScript]
```
protected function OnCreateControl();
```

Remarks

The **OnCreateControl** method is called when the control is first created.

The **OnCreateControl** method also allows derived classes to handle the event without attaching a delegate. This is the preferred technique for handling the event in a derived class.

Notes to Inheritors: When overriding **OnCreateControl** in a derived class, be sure to call the base class's **OnCreateControl** method so that registered delegates receive the event.

Requirements

Platforms: Windows 98, Windows NT 4.0, Windows Millennium Edition, Windows 2000, Windows XP Home Edition, Windows XP Professional, Windows Server 2003 family

Control.OnCursorChanged Method

Raises the **CursorChanged** event.

[Visual Basic]
```
Protected Overridable Sub OnCursorChanged( _
   ByVal e As EventArgs _
)
```
[C#]
```
protected virtual void OnCursorChanged(
   EventArgs e
);
```
[C++]
```
protected: virtual void OnCursorChanged(
   EventArgs* e
);
```
[JScript]
```
protected function OnCursorChanged(
   e : EventArgs
);
```

Parameters

e

An **EventArgs** that contains the event data.

Remarks

Raising an event invokes the event handler through a delegate.

The **OnCursorChanged** method also allows derived classes to handle the event without attaching a delegate. This is the preferred technique for handling the event in a derived class.

Notes to Inheritors: When overriding **OnCursorChanged** in a derived class, be sure to call the base class's **OnCursorChanged** method so that registered delegates receive the event.

Example

[Visual Basic, C#, C++] The example below is an event-raising method that is executed when the **Text** property value changes. The **Control** class has several methods with the name pattern **On** PropertyName **Changed** that raise the corresponding PropertyName **Changed** event when the PropertyName value changes(PropertyName represents the name of the corresponding property).

[Visual Basic, C#, C++] The following example changes the **ForeColor** of a **TextBox** derived class displaying currency data. The example converts the text to a decimal number and changes the **ForeColor** to **Color.Red** if the number is negative and to **Color.Black** if the number is positive. This example assumes you have a class that derives from the **TextBox** class.

[Visual Basic]
```
Protected Overrides Sub OnTextChanged(e As System.EventArgs)
   Try
      ' Convert the text to a Double and determine
      ' if it is a negative number.
      If Double.Parse(Me.Text) < 0 Then
         ' If the number is negative, display it in Red.
         Me.ForeColor = Color.Red
      Else
         ' If the number is not negative, display it in Black.
         Me.ForeColor = Color.Black
      End If
   Catch
      ' If there is an error, display the
      ' text using the system colors.
      Me.ForeColor = SystemColors.ControlText
   End Try

   MyBase.OnTextChanged(e)
End Sub
```

[C#]
```
protected override void OnTextChanged(System.EventArgs e)
{
   try
   {
      // Convert the text to a Double and determine
      // if it is a negative number.
      if(double.Parse(this.Text) < 0)
      {
         // If the number is negative, display it in Red.
         this.ForeColor = Color.Red;
      }
      else
      {
         // If the number is not negative, display it in Black.
         this.ForeColor = Color.Black;
      }
   }
   catch
   {
      // If there is an error, display the
      // text using the system colors.
      this.ForeColor = SystemColors.ControlText;
   }

   base.OnTextChanged(e);
}
```

[C++]
```
protected:
   void OnTextChanged(System::EventArgs* e) {
      try {
         // Convert the text to a Double and determine
         // if it is a negative number.
         if (Double::Parse(this->Text) < 0) {
            // If the number is negative, display it in Red.
            this->ForeColor = Color::Red;
         } else {
            // If the number is not negative, display it in Black.
            this->ForeColor = Color::Black;
         }
      } catch (Exception*) {
         // If there is an error, display the
         // text using the system colors.
         this->ForeColor = SystemColors::ControlText;
      }

      TextBox::OnTextChanged(e);
   }
```

Requirements

Platforms: Windows 98, Windows NT 4.0, Windows Millennium Edition, Windows 2000, Windows XP Home Edition, Windows XP Professional, Windows Server 2003 family

Control.OnDockChanged Method

Raises the **DockChanged** event.

[Visual Basic]
```
Protected Overridable Sub OnDockChanged( _
   ByVal e As EventArgs _
)
```
[C#]
```
protected virtual void OnDockChanged(
   EventArgs e
);
```
[C++]
```
protected: virtual void OnDockChanged(
   EventArgs* e
);
```
[JScript]
```
protected function OnDockChanged(
   e : EventArgs
);
```

Parameters

e

An **EventArgs** that contains the event data.

Remarks

Raising an event invokes the event handler through a delegate.

The **OnDockChanged** method also allows derived classes to handle the event without attaching a delegate. This is the preferred technique for handling the event in a derived class.

Notes to Inheritors: When overriding **OnDockChanged** in a derived class, be sure to call the base class's **OnDockChanged** method so that registered delegates receive the event.

Example

[Visual Basic, C#, C++] The example below is an event-raising method that is executed when the **Text** property value changes. The **Control** class has several methods with the name pattern **On** PropertyName **Changed** that raise the corresponding PropertyName **Changed** event when the PropertyName value changes(PropertyName represents the name of the corresponding property).

[Visual Basic, C#, C++] The following example changes the **ForeColor** of a **TextBox** derived class displaying currency data. The example converts the text to a decimal number and changes the **ForeColor** to **Color.Red** if the number is negative and to **Color.Black** if the number is positive. This example assumes you have a class that derives from the **TextBox** class.

[Visual Basic]
```
Protected Overrides Sub OnTextChanged(e As System.EventArgs)
   Try
      ' Convert the text to a Double and determine
      ' if it is a negative number.
      If Double.Parse(Me.Text) < 0 Then
         ' If the number is negative, display it in Red.
         Me.ForeColor = Color.Red
      Else
         ' If the number is not negative, display it in Black.
         Me.ForeColor = Color.Black
      End If
   Catch
      ' If there is an error, display the
      ' text using the system colors.
      Me.ForeColor = SystemColors.ControlText
   End Try

   MyBase.OnTextChanged(e)
End Sub
```

[C#]
```
protected override void OnTextChanged(System.EventArgs e)
{
   try
   {
      // Convert the text to a Double and determine
      // if it is a negative number.
      if(double.Parse(this.Text) < 0)
      {
         // If the number is negative, display it in Red.
         this.ForeColor = Color.Red;
      }
      else
      {
         // If the number is not negative, display it in Black.
         this.ForeColor = Color.Black;
      }
   }
   catch
   {
      // If there is an error, display the
      // text using the system colors.
      this.ForeColor = SystemColors.ControlText;
   }

   base.OnTextChanged(e);
}
```

[C++]
```
protected:
   void OnTextChanged(System::EventArgs* e) {
      try {
         // Convert the text to a Double and determine
         // if it is a negative number.
         if (Double::Parse(this->Text) < 0) {
            // If the number is negative, display it in Red.
            this->ForeColor = Color::Red;
         } else {
            // If the number is not negative, display it in Black.
            this->ForeColor = Color::Black;
         }
      } catch (Exception*) {
         // If there is an error, display the
         // text using the system colors.
         this->ForeColor = SystemColors::ControlText;
      }

      TextBox::OnTextChanged(e);
   }
```

Requirements

Platforms: Windows 98, Windows NT 4.0, Windows Millennium Edition, Windows 2000, Windows XP Home Edition, Windows XP Professional, Windows Server 2003 family

Control.OnDoubleClick Method

Raises the **DoubleClick** event.

[Visual Basic]
```
Protected Overridable Sub OnDoubleClick( _
   ByVal e As EventArgs _
)
```
[C#]
```
protected virtual void OnDoubleClick(
   EventArgs e
);
```
[C++]
```
protected: virtual void OnDoubleClick(
   EventArgs* e
);
```
[JScript]
```
protected function OnDoubleClick(
   e : EventArgs
);
```

Parameters

e

An **EventArgs** that contains the event data.

Remarks

Raising an event invokes the event handler through a delegate.

The **OnDoubleClick** method also allows derived classes to handle the event without attaching a delegate. This is the preferred technique for handling the event in a derived class.

Notes to Inheritors: When overriding **OnDoubleClick** in a derived class, be sure to call the base class's **OnDoubleClick** method so that registered delegates receive the event.

Example

[Visual Basic]
```
' This example uses the DoubleClick event of a ListBox to      ↵
load text files
' listed in the ListBox into a TextBox control. This example
' assumes that the ListBox, named listBox1, contains a list     ↵
 of valid file
' names with path and that this event handling method
' is connected to the DoublClick event of a ListBox control     ↵
 named listBox1.
' This example requires code access permission to access files.
Private Sub listBox1_DoubleClick(ByVal sender As Object,        ↵
 ByVal e As System.EventArgs) Handles listBox1.DoubleClick
```

```
    ' Get the name of the file to open from the ListBox.
    Dim file As [String] = listBox1.SelectedItem.ToString()

    Try
        ' Determine if the file exists before loading.
        If System.IO.File.Exists(file) Then
            ' Open the file and use a TextReader to read the ↵
contents into the TextBox.
            Dim myFile As New ↵
System.IO.FileInfo(listBox1.SelectedItem.ToString())
            Dim myData As System.IO.TextReader = myFile.OpenText()

            textBox1.Text = myData.ReadToEnd()
            myData.Close()
        End If
        ' Exception is thrown by the OpenText method of the ↵
FileInfo class.
    Catch
        MessageBox.Show("The file you specified does not exist.")
        ' Exception is thrown by the ReadToEnd method of the ↵
TextReader class.
    Catch
     MessageBox.Show("There was a problem loading the file ↵
into the TextBox. Ensure that the file is a valid text file.")
    End Try
End Sub
```

[C#]

```
// This example uses the DoubleClick event of a ListBox to ↵
load text files
// listed in the ListBox into a TextBox control. This example
// assumes that the ListBox, named listBox1, contains a list ↵
of valid file
// names with path and that this event handling method
// is connected to the DoublClick event of a ListBox control ↵
 named listBox1.
// This example requires code access permission to access files.
private void listBox1_DoubleClick(object sender, System.EventArgs e)
{
    // Get the name of the file to open from the ListBox.
    String file = listBox1.SelectedItem.ToString();

    try
    {
        // Determine if the file exists before loading.
        if (System.IO.File.Exists(file))
        {
            // Open the file and use a TextReader to read the ↵
contents into the TextBox.
            System.IO.FileInfo myFile = new ↵
System.IO.FileInfo(listBox1.SelectedItem.ToString());
            System.IO.TextReader myData = myFile.OpenText();;

            textBox1.Text = myData.ReadToEnd();
            myData.Close();
        }
    }
        // Exception is thrown by the OpenText method of the ↵
FileInfo class.
    catch(System.IO.FileNotFoundException)
    {
        MessageBox.Show("The file you specified does not exist.");
    }
        // Exception is thrown by the ReadToEnd method of the ↵
TextReader class.
    catch(System.IO.IOException)
    {
        MessageBox.Show("There was a problem loading the file ↵
into the TextBox. Ensure that the file is a valid text file.");
    }
}
```

Requirements

Platforms: Windows 98, Windows NT 4.0, Windows Millennium Edition, Windows 2000, Windows XP Home Edition, Windows XP Professional, Windows Server 2003 family

Control.OnDragDrop Method

Raises the **DragDrop** event.

[Visual Basic]

```
Protected Overridable Sub OnDragDrop( _
   ByVal drgevent As DragEventArgs _
)
```

[C#]

```
protected virtual void OnDragDrop(
   DragEventArgs drgevent
);
```

[C++]

```
protected: virtual void OnDragDrop(
   DragEventArgs* drgevent
);
```

[JScript]

```
protected function OnDragDrop(
   drgevent : DragEventArgs
);
```

Parameters

drgevent

A **DragEventArgs** that contains the event data.

Remarks

Raising an event invokes the event handler through a delegate.

The **OnDragDrop** method also allows derived classes to handle the event without attaching a delegate. This is the preferred technique for handling the event in a derived class.

Notes to Inheritors: When overriding **OnDragDrop** in a derived class, be sure to call the base class's **OnDragDrop** method so that registered delegates receive the event.

Requirements

Platforms: Windows 98, Windows NT 4.0, Windows Millennium Edition, Windows 2000, Windows XP Home Edition, Windows XP Professional, Windows Server 2003 family

Control.OnDragEnter Method

Raises the **DragEnter** event.

[Visual Basic]

```
Protected Overridable Sub OnDragEnter( _
   ByVal drgevent As DragEventArgs _
)
```

[C#]

```
protected virtual void OnDragEnter(
   DragEventArgs drgevent
);
```

[C++]

```
protected: virtual void OnDragEnter(
   DragEventArgs* drgevent
);
```

[JScript]

```
protected function OnDragEnter(
   drgevent : DragEventArgs
);
```

Parameters

drgevent

A **DragEventArgs** that contains the event data.

Remarks

Raising an event invokes the event handler through a delegate.

The **OnDragEnter** method also allows derived classes to handle the event without attaching a delegate. This is the preferred technique for handling the event in a derived class.

Notes to Inheritors: When overriding **OnDragEnter** in a derived class, be sure to call the base class's **OnDragEnter** method so that registered delegates receive the event.

Requirements

Platforms: Windows 98, Windows NT 4.0,
Windows Millennium Edition, Windows 2000,
Windows XP Home Edition, Windows XP Professional,
Windows Server 2003 family

Control.OnDragLeave Method

Raises the **DragLeave** event.

```
[Visual Basic]
Protected Overridable Sub OnDragLeave( _
   ByVal e As EventArgs _
)
[C#]
protected virtual void OnDragLeave(
   EventArgs e
);
[C++]
protected: virtual void OnDragLeave(
   EventArgs* e
);
[JScript]
protected function OnDragLeave(
   e : EventArgs
);
```

Parameters

e

An **EventArgs** that contains the event data.

Remarks

Raising an event invokes the event handler through a delegate.

The **OnDragLeave** method also allows derived classes to handle the event without attaching a delegate. This is the preferred technique for handling the event in a derived class.

Notes to Inheritors: When overriding **OnDragLeave** in a derived class, be sure to call the base class's **OnDragLeave** method so that registered delegates receive the event.

Requirements

Platforms: Windows 98, Windows NT 4.0,
Windows Millennium Edition, Windows 2000,
Windows XP Home Edition, Windows XP Professional,
Windows Server 2003 family

Control.OnDragOver Method

Raises the **DragOver** event.

```
[Visual Basic]
Protected Overridable Sub OnDragOver( _
   ByVal drgevent As DragEventArgs _
)
[C#]
protected virtual void OnDragOver(
   DragEventArgs drgevent
);
[C++]
protected: virtual void OnDragOver(
   DragEventArgs* drgevent
);
[JScript]
protected function OnDragOver(
   drgevent : DragEventArgs
);
```

Parameters

drgevent

A **DragEventArgs** that contains the event data.

Remarks

Raising an event invokes the event handler through a delegate.

The **OnDragOver** method also allows derived classes to handle the event without attaching a delegate. This is the preferred technique for handling the event in a derived class.

Notes to Inheritors: When overriding **OnDragOver** in a derived class, be sure to call the base class's **OnDragOver** method so that registered delegates receive the event.

Requirements

Platforms: Windows 98, Windows NT 4.0,
Windows Millennium Edition, Windows 2000,
Windows XP Home Edition, Windows XP Professional,
Windows Server 2003 family

Control.OnEnabledChanged Method

Raises the **EnabledChanged** event.

```
[Visual Basic]
Protected Overridable Sub OnEnabledChanged( _
   ByVal e As EventArgs _
)
[C#]
protected virtual void OnEnabledChanged(
   EventArgs e
);
[C++]
protected: virtual void OnEnabledChanged(
   EventArgs* e
);
[JScript]
protected function OnEnabledChanged(
   e : EventArgs
);
```

Parameters

e

An **EventArgs** that contains the event data.

Remarks

Raising an event invokes the event handler through a delegate.

The **OnEnabledChanged** method also allows derived classes to handle the event without attaching a delegate. This is the preferred technique for handling the event in a derived class.

Notes to Inheritors: When overriding **OnEnabledChanged** in a derived class, be sure to call the base class's **OnEnabledChanged** method so that registered delegates receive the event.

Example

[Visual Basic, C#, C++] The example below is an event-raising method that is executed when the **Text** property value changes. The **Control** class has several methods with the name pattern **On** PropertyName **Changed** that raise the corresponding PropertyName **Changed** event when the PropertyName value changes(PropertyName represents the name of the corresponding property).

[Visual Basic, C#, C++] The following example changes the **ForeColor** of a **TextBox** derived class displaying currency data. The example converts the text to a decimal number and changes the **ForeColor** to **Color.Red** if the number is negative and to **Color.Black** if the number is positive. This example assumes you have a class that derives from the **TextBox** class.

[Visual Basic]

```
Protected Overrides Sub OnTextChanged(e As System.EventArgs)
   Try
      ' Convert the text to a Double and determine
      ' if it is a negative number.
      If Double.Parse(Me.Text) < 0 Then
         ' If the number is negative, display it in Red.
         Me.ForeColor = Color.Red
      Else
         ' If the number is not negative, display it in Black.
         Me.ForeColor = Color.Black
      End If
   Catch
      ' If there is an error, display the
      ' text using the system colors.
      Me.ForeColor = SystemColors.ControlText
   End Try

   MyBase.OnTextChanged(e)
End Sub
```

[C#]

```
protected override void OnTextChanged(System.EventArgs e)
{
   try
   {
      // Convert the text to a Double and determine
      // if it is a negative number.
      if(double.Parse(this.Text) < 0)
      {
         // If the number is negative, display it in Red.
         this.ForeColor = Color.Red;
      }
      else
      {
         // If the number is not negative, display it in Black.
         this.ForeColor = Color.Black;
      }
   }
   catch
   {
      // If there is an error, display the
      // text using the system colors.
      this.ForeColor = SystemColors.ControlText;
   }

   base.OnTextChanged(e);
}
```

[C++]

```
protected:
   void OnTextChanged(System::EventArgs* e) {
      try {
         // Convert the text to a Double and determine
         // if it is a negative number.
         if (Double::Parse(this->Text) < 0) {
            // If the number is negative, display it in Red.
            this->ForeColor = Color::Red;
         } else {
            // If the number is not negative, display it in Black.
            this->ForeColor = Color::Black;
         }
      } catch (Exception*) {
         // If there is an error, display the
         // text using the system colors.
         this->ForeColor = SystemColors::ControlText;
      }

      TextBox::OnTextChanged(e);
   }
```

Requirements

Platforms: Windows 98, Windows NT 4.0, Windows Millennium Edition, Windows 2000, Windows XP Home Edition, Windows XP Professional, Windows Server 2003 family, .NET Compact Framework - Windows CE .NET

Control.OnEnter Method

Raises the **Enter** event.

[Visual Basic]

```
Protected Overridable Sub OnEnter( _
   ByVal e As EventArgs _
)
```

[C#]

```
protected virtual void OnEnter(
   EventArgs e
);
```

[C++]

```
protected: virtual void OnEnter(
   EventArgs* e
);
```

[JScript]

```
protected function OnEnter(
   e : EventArgs
);
```

Parameters

e

An **EventArgs** that contains the event data.

Remarks

Raising an event invokes the event handler through a delegate.

The **OnEnter** method also allows derived classes to handle the event without attaching a delegate. This is the preferred technique for handling the event in a derived class.

Notes to Inheritors: When overriding **OnEnter** in a derived class, be sure to call the base class's **OnEnter** method so that registered delegates receive the event.

Requirements

Platforms: Windows 98, Windows NT 4.0, Windows Millennium Edition, Windows 2000, Windows XP Home Edition, Windows XP Professional, Windows Server 2003 family

Control.OnFontChanged Method

Raises the **FontChanged** event.

```
[Visual Basic]
Protected Overridable Sub OnFontChanged( _
   ByVal e As EventArgs _
)
[C#]
protected virtual void OnFontChanged(
   EventArgs e
);
[C++]
protected: virtual void OnFontChanged(
   EventArgs* e
);
[JScript]
protected function OnFontChanged(
   e : EventArgs
);
```

Parameters

e

An **EventArgs** that contains the event data.

Remarks

Raising an event invokes the event handler through a delegate.

The **OnFontChanged** method also allows derived classes to handle the event without attaching a delegate. This is the preferred technique for handling the event in a derived class.

Notes to Inheritors: When overriding **OnFontChanged** in a derived class, be sure to call the base class's **OnFontChanged** method so that registered delegates receive the event.

Example

[Visual Basic, C#, C++] The example below is an event-raising method that is executed when the **Text** property value changes. The **Control** class has several methods with the name pattern **On** PropertyName **Changed** that raise the corresponding PropertyName **Changed** event when the PropertyName value changes(PropertyName represents the name of the corresponding property).

[Visual Basic, C#, C++] The following example changes the **ForeColor** of a **TextBox** derived class displaying currency data. The example converts the text to a decimal number and changes the **ForeColor** to **Color.Red** if the number is negative and to **Color.Black** if the number is positive. This example assumes you have a class that derives from the **TextBox** class.

```
[Visual Basic]
Protected Overrides Sub OnTextChanged(e As System.EventArgs)
   Try
      ' Convert the text to a Double and determine
      ' if it is a negative number.
      If Double.Parse(Me.Text) < 0 Then
         ' If the number is negative, display it in Red.
         Me.ForeColor = Color.Red
      Else
         ' If the number is not negative, display it in Black.
         Me.ForeColor = Color.Black
      End If
   Catch
      ' If there is an error, display the
      ' text using the system colors.
      Me.ForeColor = SystemColors.ControlText
   End Try

   MyBase.OnTextChanged(e)
End Sub
```

```
[C#]
protected override void OnTextChanged(System.EventArgs e)
{
   try
   {
      // Convert the text to a Double and determine
      // if it is a negative number.
      if(double.Parse(this.Text) < 0)
      {
         // If the number is negative, display it in Red.
         this.ForeColor = Color.Red;
      }
      else
      {
         // If the number is not negative, display it in Black.
         this.ForeColor = Color.Black;
      }
   }
   catch
   {
      // If there is an error, display the
      // text using the system colors.
      this.ForeColor = SystemColors.ControlText;
   }

   base.OnTextChanged(e);
}
```

```
[C++]
protected:
   void OnTextChanged(System::EventArgs* e) {
      try {
         // Convert the text to a Double and determine
         // if it is a negative number.
         if (Double::Parse(this->Text) < 0) {
            // If the number is negative, display it in Red.
            this->ForeColor = Color::Red;
         } else {
            // If the number is not negative, display it in Black.
            this->ForeColor = Color::Black;
         }
      } catch (Exception*) {
         // If there is an error, display the
         // text using the system colors.
         this->ForeColor = SystemColors::ControlText;
      }

      TextBox::OnTextChanged(e);
   }
```

Requirements

Platforms: Windows 98, Windows NT 4.0, Windows Millennium Edition, Windows 2000, Windows XP Home Edition, Windows XP Professional, Windows Server 2003 family

Control.OnForeColorChanged Method

Raises the **ForeColorChanged** event.

```
[Visual Basic]
Protected Overridable Sub OnForeColorChanged( _
   ByVal e As EventArgs _
)
[C#]
protected virtual void OnForeColorChanged(
   EventArgs e
);
[C++]
protected: virtual void OnForeColorChanged(
   EventArgs* e
);
```

```
[JScript]
protected function OnForeColorChanged(
   e : EventArgs
);
```

Parameters

e

An **EventArgs** that contains the event data.

Remarks

Raising an event invokes the event handler through a delegate.

The **OnForeColorChanged** method also allows derived classes to handle the event without attaching a delegate. This is the preferred technique for handling the event in a derived class.

Notes to Inheritors: When overriding **OnForeColorChanged** in a derived class, be sure to call the base class's **OnForeColorChanged** method so that registered delegates receive the event.

Example

[Visual Basic, C#, C++] The example below is an event-raising method that is executed when the **Text** property value changes. The **Control** class has several methods with the name pattern **On** PropertyName **Changed** that raise the corresponding PropertyName **Changed** event when the PropertyName value changes(PropertyName represents the name of the corresponding property).

[Visual Basic, C#, C++] The following example changes the **ForeColor** of a **TextBox** derived class displaying currency data. The example converts the text to a decimal number and changes the **ForeColor** to **Color.Red** if the number is negative and to **Color.Black** if the number is positive. This example assumes you have a class that derives from the **TextBox** class.

```
[Visual Basic]
Protected Overrides Sub OnTextChanged(e As System.EventArgs)
   Try
      ' Convert the text to a Double and determine
      ' if it is a negative number.
      If Double.Parse(Me.Text) < 0 Then
         ' If the number is negative, display it in Red.
         Me.ForeColor = Color.Red
      Else
         ' If the number is not negative, display it in Black.
         Me.ForeColor = Color.Black
      End If
   Catch
      ' If there is an error, display the
      ' text using the system colors.
      Me.ForeColor = SystemColors.ControlText
   End Try

   MyBase.OnTextChanged(e)
End Sub
```

```
[C#]
protected override void OnTextChanged(System.EventArgs e)
{
   try
   {
      // Convert the text to a Double and determine
      // if it is a negative number.
      if(double.Parse(this.Text) < 0)
      {
         // If the number is negative, display it in Red.
         this.ForeColor = Color.Red;
      }
      else
      {
         // If the number is not negative, display it in Black.
         this.ForeColor = Color.Black;
      }
   }
   catch
   {
      // If there is an error, display the
      // text using the system colors.
      this.ForeColor = SystemColors.ControlText;
   }

   base.OnTextChanged(e);
}
```

```
[C++]
protected:
   void OnTextChanged(System::EventArgs* e) {
      try {
         // Convert the text to a Double and determine
         // if it is a negative number.
         if (Double::Parse(this->Text) < 0) {
            // If the number is negative, display it in Red.
            this->ForeColor = Color::Red;
         } else {
            // If the number is not negative, display it in Black.
            this->ForeColor = Color::Black;
         }
      } catch (Exception*) {
         // If there is an error, display the
         // text using the system colors.
         this->ForeColor = SystemColors::ControlText;
      }

      TextBox::OnTextChanged(e);
   }
```

Requirements

Platforms: Windows 98, Windows NT 4.0, Windows Millennium Edition, Windows 2000, Windows XP Home Edition, Windows XP Professional, Windows Server 2003 family

Control.OnGiveFeedback Method

Raises the **GiveFeedback** event.

```
[Visual Basic]
Protected Overridable Sub OnGiveFeedback( _
   ByVal gfbevent As GiveFeedbackEventArgs _
)
[C#]
protected virtual void OnGiveFeedback(
   GiveFeedbackEventArgs gfbevent
);
[C++]
protected: virtual void OnGiveFeedback(
   GiveFeedbackEventArgs* gfbevent
);
[JScript]
protected function OnGiveFeedback(
   gfbevent : GiveFeedbackEventArgs
);
```

Parameters

gfbevent

A **GiveFeedbackEventArgs** that contains the event data.

Remarks

Raising an event invokes the event handler through a delegate.

The **OnGiveFeedback** method also allows derived classes to handle the event without attaching a delegate. This is the preferred technique for handling the event in a derived class.

Notes to Inheritors: When overriding **OnGiveFeedback** in a derived class, be sure to call the base class's **OnGiveFeedback** method so that registered delegates receive the event.

Requirements

Platforms: Windows 98, Windows NT 4.0, Windows Millennium Edition, Windows 2000, Windows XP Home Edition, Windows XP Professional, Windows Server 2003 family

Control.OnGotFocus Method

Raises the **GotFocus** event.

```
[Visual Basic]
Protected Overridable Sub OnGotFocus( _
   ByVal e As EventArgs _
)
[C#]
protected virtual void OnGotFocus(
   EventArgs e
);
[C++]
protected: virtual void OnGotFocus(
   EventArgs* e
);
[JScript]
protected function OnGotFocus(
   e : EventArgs
);
```

Parameters

e

An **EventArgs** that contains the event data.

Remarks

Raising an event invokes the event handler through a delegate.

The **OnGotFocus** method also allows derived classes to handle the event without attaching a delegate. This is the preferred technique for handling the event in a derived class.

Notes to Inheritors: When overriding **OnGotFocus** in a derived class, be sure to call the base class's **OnGotFocus** method so that registered delegates receive the event.

Requirements

Platforms: Windows 98, Windows NT 4.0, Windows Millennium Edition, Windows 2000, Windows XP Home Edition, Windows XP Professional, Windows Server 2003 family, .NET Compact Framework - Windows CE .NET

Control.OnHandleCreated Method

Raises the **HandleCreated** event.

```
[Visual Basic]
Protected Overridable Sub OnHandleCreated( _
   ByVal e As EventArgs _
)
[C#]
protected virtual void OnHandleCreated(
   EventArgs e
);
[C++]
protected: virtual void OnHandleCreated(
   EventArgs* e
);
[JScript]
protected function OnHandleCreated(
   e : EventArgs
);
```

Parameters

e

An **EventArgs** that contains the event data.

Remarks

Raising an event invokes the event handler through a delegate.

The **OnHandleCreated** method also allows derived classes to handle the event without attaching a delegate. This is the preferred technique for handling the event in a derived class.

Notes to Inheritors: When overriding **OnHandleCreated** in a derived class, be sure to call the base class's **OnHandleCreated** method so that registered delegates receive the event.

Requirements

Platforms: Windows 98, Windows NT 4.0, Windows Millennium Edition, Windows 2000, Windows XP Home Edition, Windows XP Professional, Windows Server 2003 family

Control.OnHandleDestroyed Method

Raises the **HandleDestroyed** event.

```
[Visual Basic]
Protected Overridable Sub OnHandleDestroyed( _
   ByVal e As EventArgs _
)
[C#]
protected virtual void OnHandleDestroyed(
   EventArgs e
);
[C++]
protected: virtual void OnHandleDestroyed(
   EventArgs* e
);
[JScript]
protected function OnHandleDestroyed(
   e : EventArgs
);
```

Parameters

e

An **EventArgs** that contains the event data.

Remarks

Raising an event invokes the event handler through a delegate.

The **OnHandleDestroyed** method also allows derived classes to handle the event without attaching a delegate. This is the preferred technique for handling the event in a derived class.

Notes to Inheritors: When overriding **OnHandleDestroyed** in a derived class, be sure to call the base class's **OnHandleDestroyed** method so that registered delegates receive the event.

Requirements

Platforms: Windows 98, Windows NT 4.0, Windows Millennium Edition, Windows 2000, Windows XP Home Edition, Windows XP Professional, Windows Server 2003 family

Control.OnHelpRequested Method

Raises the **HelpRequested** event.

```
[Visual Basic]
Protected Overridable Sub OnHelpRequested( _
   ByVal hevent As HelpEventArgs _
)
[C#]
protected virtual void OnHelpRequested(
   HelpEventArgs hevent
);
[C++]
protected: virtual void OnHelpRequested(
   HelpEventArgs* hevent
);
[JScript]
protected function OnHelpRequested(
   hevent : HelpEventArgs
);
```

Parameters

hevent

A **HelpEventArgs** that contains the event data.

Remarks

Raising an event invokes the event handler through a delegate.

The **OnHelpRequested** method also allows derived classes to handle the event without attaching a delegate. This is the preferred technique for handling the event in a derived class.

Notes to Inheritors: When overriding **OnHelpRequested** in a derived class, be sure to call the base class's **OnHelpRequested** method so that registered delegates receive the event.

Requirements

Platforms: Windows 98, Windows NT 4.0, Windows Millennium Edition, Windows 2000, Windows XP Home Edition, Windows XP Professional, Windows Server 2003 family

Control.OnImeModeChanged Method

Raises the **ImeModeChanged** event.

```
[Visual Basic]
Protected Overridable Sub OnImeModeChanged( _
   ByVal e As EventArgs _
)
[C#]
protected virtual void OnImeModeChanged(
   EventArgs e
);
[C++]
protected: virtual void OnImeModeChanged(
   EventArgs* e
);
[JScript]
protected function OnImeModeChanged(
   e : EventArgs
);
```

Parameters

e

An **EventArgs** that contains the event data.

Remarks

Raising an event invokes the event handler through a delegate.

The **OnImeModeChanged** method also allows derived classes to handle the event without attaching a delegate. This is the preferred technique for handling the event in a derived class.

Notes to Inheritors: When overriding **OnImeModeChanged** in a derived class, be sure to call the base class's **OnImeModeChanged** method so that registered delegates receive the event.

Example

[Visual Basic, C#, C++] The example below is an event-raising method that is executed when the **Text** property value changes. The **Control** class has several methods with the name pattern **On** PropertyName **Changed** that raise the corresponding PropertyName **Changed** event when the PropertyName value changes(PropertyName represents the name of the corresponding property).

[Visual Basic, C#, C++] The following example changes the **ForeColor** of a **TextBox** derived class displaying currency data. The example converts the text to a decimal number and changes the **ForeColor** to **Color.Red** if the number is negative and to **Color.Black** if the number is positive. This example assumes you have a class that derives from the **TextBox** class.

```
[Visual Basic]
Protected Overrides Sub OnTextChanged(e As System.EventArgs)
   Try
      ' Convert the text to a Double and determine
      ' if it is a negative number.
      If Double.Parse(Me.Text) < 0 Then
         ' If the number is negative, display it in Red.
         Me.ForeColor = Color.Red
      Else
         ' If the number is not negative, display it in Black.
         Me.ForeColor = Color.Black
      End If
   Catch
      ' If there is an error, display the
      ' text using the system colors.
      Me.ForeColor = SystemColors.ControlText
   End Try

   MyBase.OnTextChanged(e)
End Sub
```

```
[C#]
protected override void OnTextChanged(System.EventArgs e)
{
   try
   {
      // Convert the text to a Double and determine
      // if it is a negative number.
      if(double.Parse(this.Text) < 0)
      {
         // If the number is negative, display it in Red.
         this.ForeColor = Color.Red;
      }
      else
```

```
      {
         // If the number is not negative, display it in Black.
         this.ForeColor = Color.Black;
      }
   }
   catch
   {
      // If there is an error, display the
      // text using the system colors.
      this.ForeColor = SystemColors.ControlText;
   }

   base.OnTextChanged(e);
}
```

[C++]

```
protected:
   void OnTextChanged(System::EventArgs* e) {
      try {
         // Convert the text to a Double and determine
         // if it is a negative number.
         if (Double::Parse(this->Text) < 0) {
            // If the number is negative, display it in Red.
            this->ForeColor = Color::Red;
         } else {
            // If the number is not negative, display it in Black.
            this->ForeColor = Color::Black;
         }
      } catch (Exception*) {
         // If there is an error, display the
         // text using the system colors.
         this->ForeColor = SystemColors::ControlText;
      }

      TextBox::OnTextChanged(e);
   }
```

Requirements

Platforms: Windows 98, Windows NT 4.0,
Windows Millennium Edition, Windows 2000,
Windows XP Home Edition, Windows XP Professional,
Windows Server 2003 family

Control.OnInvalidated Method

Raises the **Invalidated** event.

[Visual Basic]

```
Protected Overridable Sub OnInvalidated( _
   ByVal e As InvalidateEventArgs _
)
```

[C#]

```
protected virtual void OnInvalidated(
   InvalidateEventArgs e
);
```

[C++]

```
protected: virtual void OnInvalidated(
   InvalidateEventArgs* e
);
```

[JScript]

```
protected function OnInvalidated(
   e : InvalidateEventArgs
);
```

Parameters

e

An **InvalidateEventArgs** that contains the event data.

Remarks

Raising an event invokes the event handler through a delegate.

The **OnInvalidated** method also allows derived classes to handle the event without attaching a delegate. This is the preferred technique for handling the event in a derived class.

Notes to Inheritors: When overriding **OnInvalidated** in a derived class, be sure to call the base class's **OnInvalidated** method so that registered delegates receive the event.

Requirements

Platforms: Windows 98, Windows NT 4.0,
Windows Millennium Edition, Windows 2000,
Windows XP Home Edition, Windows XP Professional,
Windows Server 2003 family

Control.OnKeyDown Method

Raises the **KeyDown** event.

[Visual Basic]

```
Protected Overridable Sub OnKeyDown( _
   ByVal e As KeyEventArgs _
)
```

[C#]

```
protected virtual void OnKeyDown(
   KeyEventArgs e
);
```

[C++]

```
protected: virtual void OnKeyDown(
   KeyEventArgs* e
);
```

[JScript]

```
protected function OnKeyDown(
   e : KeyEventArgs
);
```

Parameters

e

A **KeyEventArgs** that contains the event data.

Remarks

Raising an event invokes the event handler through a delegate.

The **OnKeyDown** method also allows derived classes to handle the event without attaching a delegate. This is the preferred technique for handling the event in a derived class.

Notes to Inheritors: When overriding **OnKeyDown** in a derived class, be sure to call the base class's **OnKeyDown** method so that registered delegates receive the event.

Requirements

Platforms: Windows 98, Windows NT 4.0,
Windows Millennium Edition, Windows 2000,
Windows XP Home Edition, Windows XP Professional,
Windows Server 2003 family,
.NET Compact Framework - Windows CE .NET

Control.OnKeyPress Method

Raises the **KeyPress** event.

[Visual Basic]

```
Protected Overridable Sub OnKeyPress( _
   ByVal e As KeyPressEventArgs _
)
```

[C#]
```
protected virtual void OnKeyPress(
   KeyPressEventArgs e
);
```
[C++]
```
protected: virtual void OnKeyPress(
   KeyPressEventArgs* e
);
```
[JScript]
```
protected function OnKeyPress(
   e : KeyPressEventArgs
);
```

Parameters

e

A **KeyPressEventArgs** that contains the event data.

Remarks

Raising an event invokes the event handler through a delegate.

The **OnKeyPress** method also allows derived classes to handle the event without attaching a delegate. This is the preferred technique for handling the event in a derived class.

Notes to Inheritors: When overriding **OnKeyPress** in a derived class, be sure to call the base class's **OnKeyPress** method so that registered delegates receive the event.

Requirements

Platforms: Windows 98, Windows NT 4.0, Windows Millennium Edition, Windows 2000, Windows XP Home Edition, Windows XP Professional, Windows Server 2003 family, .NET Compact Framework - Windows CE .NET

Control.OnKeyUp Method

Raises the **KeyUp** event.

[Visual Basic]
```
Protected Overridable Sub OnKeyUp( _
   ByVal e As KeyEventArgs _
)
```
[C#]
```
protected virtual void OnKeyUp(
   KeyEventArgs e
);
```
[C++]
```
protected: virtual void OnKeyUp(
   KeyEventArgs* e
);
```
[JScript]
```
protected function OnKeyUp(
   e : KeyEventArgs
);
```

Parameters

e

A **KeyEventArgs** that contains the event data.

Remarks

Raising an event invokes the event handler through a delegate.

The **OnKeyUp** method also allows derived classes to handle the event without attaching a delegate. This is the preferred technique for handling the event in a derived class.

Notes to Inheritors: When overriding **OnKeyUp** in a derived class, be sure to call the base class's **OnKeyUp** method so that registered delegates receive the event.

Example

[Visual Basic]
```
' This example demonstrates how to use the KeyUp event with ↵
the Help class to display
' pop-up style help to the user of the application. When the ↵
user presses F1, the Help
' class displays a pop-up window, similar to a ToolTip, near ↵
the control. This example assumes
' that a TextBox control, named textBox1, has been added to ↵
the form and its KeyUp
' event has been contected to this event handling method.
Private Sub textBox1_KeyUp(ByVal sender As Object, ByVal e As ↵
System.Windows.Forms.KeyEventArgs) Handles textBox1.KeyUp
    ' Determine whether the key entered is the F1 key. Display ↵
 help if it is.
    If e.KeyCode = Keys.F1 Then
        ' Display a pop-up help topic to assist the user.
        Help.ShowPopup(textBox1, "Enter your first name", New ↵
Point(textBox1.Right, Me.textBox1.Bottom))
    End If
End Sub 'textBox1_KeyUp
```

[C#]
```
// This example demonstrates how to use the KeyUp event with ↵
the Help class to display
// pop-up style help to the user of the application. When the ↵
user presses F1, the Help
// class displays a pop-up window, similar to a ToolTip, near ↵
the control. This example assumes
// that a TextBox control, named textBox1, has been added to ↵
the form and its KeyUp
// event has been contected to this event handling method.
private void textBox1_KeyUp(object sender,
System.Windows.Forms.KeyEventArgs e)
{
    // Determine whether the key entered is the F1 key. Display ↵
help if it is.
    if(e.KeyCode == Keys.F1)
    {
        // Display a pop-up help topic to assist the user.
        Help.ShowPopup(textBox1, "Enter your first name", new ↵
Point(textBox1.Right, this.textBox1.Bottom));
    }
}
```

Requirements

Platforms: Windows 98, Windows NT 4.0, Windows Millennium Edition, Windows 2000, Windows XP Home Edition, Windows XP Professional, Windows Server 2003 family, .NET Compact Framework - Windows CE .NET

Control.OnLayout Method

Raises the **Layout** event.

[Visual Basic]
```
Protected Overridable Sub OnLayout( _
   ByVal levent As LayoutEventArgs _
)
```
[C#]
```
protected virtual void OnLayout(
   LayoutEventArgs levent
);
```

```
[C++]
protected: virtual void OnLayout(
   LayoutEventArgs* levent
);
[JScript]
protected function OnLayout(
   levent : LayoutEventArgs
);
```

Parameters

levent

A **LayoutEventArgs** that contains the event data.

Remarks

Raising an event invokes the event handler through a delegate.

The **OnLayout** method also allows derived classes to handle the event without attaching a delegate. This is the preferred technique for handling the event in a derived class.

Notes to Inheritors: When overriding **OnLayout** in a derived class, be sure to call the base class's **OnLayout** method so that registered delegates receive the event and for normal docking and anchoring functions to work. Derived classes should override this method to do any custom layout logic.

Requirements

Platforms: Windows 98, Windows NT 4.0, Windows Millennium Edition, Windows 2000, Windows XP Home Edition, Windows XP Professional, Windows Server 2003 family

Control.OnLeave Method

Raises the **Leave** event.

```
[Visual Basic]
Protected Overridable Sub OnLeave( _
   ByVal e As EventArgs _
)
[C#]
protected virtual void OnLeave(
   EventArgs e
);
[C++]
protected: virtual void OnLeave(
   EventArgs* e
);
[JScript]
protected function OnLeave(
   e : EventArgs
);
```

Parameters

e

An **EventArgs** that contains the event data.

Remarks

Raising an event invokes the event handler through a delegate.

The **OnLeave** method also allows derived classes to handle the event without attaching a delegate. This is the preferred technique for handling the event in a derived class.

Notes to Inheritors: When overriding **OnLeave** in a derived class, be sure to call the base class's **OnLeave** method so that registered delegates receive the event.

Requirements

Platforms: Windows 98, Windows NT 4.0, Windows Millennium Edition, Windows 2000, Windows XP Home Edition, Windows XP Professional, Windows Server 2003 family

Control.OnLocationChanged Method

Raises the **LocationChanged** event.

```
[Visual Basic]
Protected Overridable Sub OnLocationChanged( _
   ByVal e As EventArgs _
)
[C#]
protected virtual void OnLocationChanged(
   EventArgs e
);
[C++]
protected: virtual void OnLocationChanged(
   EventArgs* e
);
[JScript]
protected function OnLocationChanged(
   e : EventArgs
);
```

Parameters

e

An **EventArgs** that contains the event data.

Remarks

Raising an event invokes the event handler through a delegate.

The **OnLocationChanged** method also allows derived classes to handle the event without attaching a delegate. This is the preferred technique for handling the event in a derived class.

Notes to Inheritors: When overriding **OnLocationChanged** in a derived class, be sure to call the base class's **OnLocationChanged** method so that registered delegates receive the event.

Example

[Visual Basic, C#, C++] The example below is an event-raising method that is executed when the **Text** property value changes. The **Control** class has several methods with the name pattern **On** PropertyName **Changed** that raise the corresponding PropertyName **Changed** event when the PropertyName value changes(PropertyName represents the name of the corresponding property).

[Visual Basic, C#, C++] The following example changes the **ForeColor** of a **TextBox** derived class displaying currency data. The example converts the text to a decimal number and changes the **ForeColor** to **Color.Red** if the number is negative and to **Color.Black** if the number is positive. This example assumes you have a class that derives from the **TextBox** class.

```
[Visual Basic]
Protected Overrides Sub OnTextChanged(e As System.EventArgs)
   Try
      ' Convert the text to a Double and determine
      ' if it is a negative number.
      If Double.Parse(Me.Text) < 0 Then
         ' If the number is negative, display it in Red.
         Me.ForeColor = Color.Red
      Else
         ' If the number is not negative, display it in Black.
         Me.ForeColor = Color.Black
```

```
      End If
   Catch
      ' If there is an error, display the
      ' text using the system colors.
      Me.ForeColor = SystemColors.ControlText
   End Try

   MyBase.OnTextChanged(e)
End Sub
```

[C#]
```
protected override void OnTextChanged(System.EventArgs e)
{
   try
   {
      // Convert the text to a Double and determine
      // if it is a negative number.
      if(double.Parse(this.Text) < 0)
      {
         // If the number is negative, display it in Red.
         this.ForeColor = Color.Red;
      }
      else
      {
         // If the number is not negative, display it in Black.
         this.ForeColor = Color.Black;
      }
   }
   catch
   {
      // If there is an error, display the
      // text using the system colors.
      this.ForeColor = SystemColors.ControlText;
   }

   base.OnTextChanged(e);
}
```

[C++]
```
protected:
   void OnTextChanged(System::EventArgs* e) {
      try {
         // Convert the text to a Double and determine
         // if it is a negative number.
         if (Double::Parse(this->Text) < 0) {
            // If the number is negative, display it in Red.
            this->ForeColor = Color::Red;
         } else {
            // If the number is not negative, display it in Black.
            this->ForeColor = Color::Black;
         }
      } catch (Exception*) {
         // If there is an error, display the
         // text using the system colors.
         this->ForeColor = SystemColors::ControlText;
      }

      TextBox::OnTextChanged(e);
   }
```

Requirements

Platforms: Windows 98, Windows NT 4.0, Windows Millennium Edition, Windows 2000, Windows XP Home Edition, Windows XP Professional, Windows Server 2003 family

Control.OnLostFocus Method

Raises the **LostFocus** event.

[Visual Basic]
```
Protected Overridable Sub OnLostFocus( _
   ByVal e As EventArgs _
)
```
[C#]
```
protected virtual void OnLostFocus(
   EventArgs e
);
```
[C++]
```
protected: virtual void OnLostFocus(
   EventArgs* e
);
```
[JScript]
```
protected function OnLostFocus(
   e : EventArgs
);
```

Parameters

e

An **EventArgs** that contains the event data.

Remarks

Raising an event invokes the event handler through a delegate.

The **OnLostFocus** method also allows derived classes to handle the event without attaching a delegate. This is the preferred technique for handling the event in a derived class.

Notes to Inheritors: When overriding **OnLostFocus** in a derived class, be sure to call the base class's **OnLostFocus** method so that registered delegates receive the event.

Requirements

Platforms: Windows 98, Windows NT 4.0, Windows Millennium Edition, Windows 2000, Windows XP Home Edition, Windows XP Professional, Windows Server 2003 family, .NET Compact Framework - Windows CE .NET

Control.OnMouseDown Method

Raises the **MouseDown** event.

[Visual Basic]
```
Protected Overridable Sub OnMouseDown( _
   ByVal e As MouseEventArgs _
)
```
[C#]
```
protected virtual void OnMouseDown(
   MouseEventArgs e
);
```
[C++]
```
protected: virtual void OnMouseDown(
   MouseEventArgs* e
);
```
[JScript]
```
protected function OnMouseDown(
   e : MouseEventArgs
);
```

Parameters

e

A **MouseEventArgs** that contains the event data.

Remarks

Raising an event invokes the event handler through a delegate.

The **OnMouseDown** method also allows derived classes to handle the event without attaching a delegate. This is the preferred technique for handling the event in a derived class.

Notes to Inheritors: When overriding **OnMouseDown** in a derived class, be sure to call the base class's **OnMouseDown** method so that registered delegates receive the event.

Requirements

Platforms: Windows 98, Windows NT 4.0,
Windows Millennium Edition, Windows 2000,
Windows XP Home Edition, Windows XP Professional,
Windows Server 2003 family,
.NET Compact Framework - Windows CE .NET

Control.OnMouseEnter Method

Raises the **MouseEnter** event.

```
[Visual Basic]
Protected Overridable Sub OnMouseEnter( _
   ByVal e As EventArgs _
)
[C#]
protected virtual void OnMouseEnter(
   EventArgs e
);
[C++]
protected: virtual void OnMouseEnter(
   EventArgs* e
);
[JScript]
protected function OnMouseEnter(
   e : EventArgs
);
```

Parameters

e

An **EventArgs** that contains the event data.

Remarks

Raising an event invokes the event handler through a delegate.

The **OnMouseEnter** method also allows derived classes to handle the event without attaching a delegate. This is the preferred technique for handling the event in a derived class.

Notes to Inheritors: When overriding **OnMouseEnter** in a derived class, be sure to call the base class's **OnMouseEnter** method so that registered delegates receive the event.

Requirements

Platforms: Windows 98, Windows NT 4.0,
Windows Millennium Edition, Windows 2000,
Windows XP Home Edition, Windows XP Professional,
Windows Server 2003 family

Control.OnMouseHover Method

Raises the **MouseHover** event.

```
[Visual Basic]
Protected Overridable Sub OnMouseHover( _
   ByVal e As EventArgs _
)
[C#]
protected virtual void OnMouseHover(
   EventArgs e
);
[C++]
protected: virtual void OnMouseHover(
   EventArgs* e
);
[JScript]
protected function OnMouseHover(
   e : EventArgs
);
```

Parameters

e

An **EventArgs** that contains the event data.

Remarks

Raising an event invokes the event handler through a delegate.

The **OnMouseHover** method also allows derived classes to handle the event without attaching a delegate. This is the preferred technique for handling the event in a derived class.

Notes to Inheritors: When overriding **OnMouseHover** in a derived class, be sure to call the base class's **OnMouseHover** method so that registered delegates receive the event.

Requirements

Platforms: Windows 98, Windows NT 4.0,
Windows Millennium Edition, Windows 2000,
Windows XP Home Edition, Windows XP Professional,
Windows Server 2003 family

Control.OnMouseLeave Method

Raises the **MouseLeave** event.

```
[Visual Basic]
Protected Overridable Sub OnMouseLeave( _
   ByVal e As EventArgs _
)
[C#]
protected virtual void OnMouseLeave(
   EventArgs e
);
[C++]
protected: virtual void OnMouseLeave(
   EventArgs* e
);
[JScript]
protected function OnMouseLeave(
   e : EventArgs
);
```

Parameters

e

An **EventArgs** that contains the event data.

Remarks

Raising an event invokes the event handler through a delegate.

The **OnMouseLeave** method also allows derived classes to handle the event without attaching a delegate. This is the preferred technique for handling the event in a derived class.

Notes to Inheritors: When overriding **OnMouseLeave** in a derived class, be sure to call the base class's **OnMouseLeave** method so that registered delegates receive the event.

Requirements

Platforms: Windows 98, Windows NT 4.0, Windows Millennium Edition, Windows 2000, Windows XP Home Edition, Windows XP Professional, Windows Server 2003 family

Control.OnMouseMove Method

Raises the **MouseMove** event.

```
[Visual Basic]
Protected Overridable Sub OnMouseMove( _
   ByVal e As MouseEventArgs _
)
[C#]
protected virtual void OnMouseMove(
   MouseEventArgs e
);
[C++]
protected: virtual void OnMouseMove(
   MouseEventArgs* e
);
[JScript]
protected function OnMouseMove(
   e : MouseEventArgs
);
```

Parameters

e

A **MouseEventArgs** that contains the event data.

Remarks

Raising an event invokes the event handler through a delegate.

The **OnMouseMove** method also allows derived classes to handle the event without attaching a delegate. This is the preferred technique for handling the event in a derived class.

Notes to Inheritors: When overriding **OnMouseMove** in a derived class, be sure to call the base class's **OnMouseMove** method so that registered delegates receive the event.

Requirements

Platforms: Windows 98, Windows NT 4.0, Windows Millennium Edition, Windows 2000, Windows XP Home Edition, Windows XP Professional, Windows Server 2003 family, .NET Compact Framework - Windows CE .NET

Control.OnMouseUp Method

Raises the **MouseUp** event.

```
[Visual Basic]
Protected Overridable Sub OnMouseUp( _
   ByVal e As MouseEventArgs _
)
[C#]
protected virtual void OnMouseUp(
   MouseEventArgs e
);
[C++]
protected: virtual void OnMouseUp(
   MouseEventArgs* e
);
[JScript]
protected function OnMouseUp(
   e : MouseEventArgs
);
```

Parameters

e

A **MouseEventArgs** that contains the event data.

Remarks

Raising an event invokes the event handler through a delegate.

The **OnMouseUp** method also allows derived classes to handle the event without attaching a delegate. This is the preferred technique for handling the event in a derived class.

Notes to Inheritors: When overriding **OnMouseUp** in a derived class, be sure to call the base class's **OnMouseUp** method so that registered delegates receive the event.

Requirements

Platforms: Windows 98, Windows NT 4.0, Windows Millennium Edition, Windows 2000, Windows XP Home Edition, Windows XP Professional, Windows Server 2003 family, .NET Compact Framework - Windows CE .NET

Control.OnMouseWheel Method

Raises the **MouseWheel** event.

```
[Visual Basic]
Protected Overridable Sub OnMouseWheel( _
   ByVal e As MouseEventArgs _
)
[C#]
protected virtual void OnMouseWheel(
   MouseEventArgs e
);
[C++]
protected: virtual void OnMouseWheel(
   MouseEventArgs* e
);
[JScript]
protected function OnMouseWheel(
   e : MouseEventArgs
);
```

Parameters

e

A **MouseEventArgs** that contains the event data.

Remarks

Raising an event invokes the event handler through a delegate.

The **OnMouseWheel** method also allows derived classes to handle the event without attaching a delegate. This is the preferred technique for handling the event in a derived class.

Notes to Inheritors: When overriding **OnMouseWheel** in a derived class, be sure to call the base class's **OnMouseWheel** method so that registered delegates receive the event.

Requirements

Platforms: Windows 98, Windows NT 4.0, Windows Millennium Edition, Windows 2000, Windows XP Home Edition, Windows XP Professional, Windows Server 2003 family

Control.OnMove Method

Raises the **Move** event.

[Visual Basic]
```
Protected Overridable Sub OnMove( _
   ByVal e As EventArgs _
)
```
[C#]
```
protected virtual void OnMove(
   EventArgs e
);
```
[C++]
```
protected: virtual void OnMove(
   EventArgs* e
);
```
[JScript]
```
protected function OnMove(
   e : EventArgs
);
```

Parameters

e

An **EventArgs** that contains the event data.

Remarks

Raising an event invokes the event handler through a delegate.

The **OnMove** method also allows derived classes to handle the event without attaching a delegate. This is the preferred technique for handling the event in a derived class.

Notes to Inheritors: When overriding **OnMove** in a derived class, be sure to call the base class's **OnMove** method so that registered delegates receive the event.

Requirements

Platforms: Windows 98, Windows NT 4.0, Windows Millennium Edition, Windows 2000, Windows XP Home Edition, Windows XP Professional, Windows Server 2003 family

Control.OnNotifyMessage Method

Notifies the control of Windows messages.

[Visual Basic]
```
Protected Overridable Sub OnNotifyMessage( _
   ByVal m As Message _
)
```
[C#]
```
protected virtual void OnNotifyMessage(
   Message m
);
```
[C++]
```
protected: virtual void OnNotifyMessage(
   Message m
);
```
[JScript]
```
protected function OnNotifyMessage(
   m : Message
);
```

Parameters

m

A **Message** that represents the Windows message.

Remarks

The **OnNotifyMessage** method is called if the control's **ControlStyles.EnableNotifyMessage** style bit is set. The **EnableNotifyMessage** style allows the control to be notified when the **WndProc** method receives a Windows message. This method allows semi-trusted controls to listen for Windows messages without allowing them to modify the message.

Notes to Inheritors: When overriding **OnNotifyMessage** in a derived class, calling the base class's **OnNotifyMessage** method is not necessary because there is no initial implementation.

Requirements

Platforms: Windows 98, Windows NT 4.0, Windows Millennium Edition, Windows 2000, Windows XP Home Edition, Windows XP Professional, Windows Server 2003 family

Control.OnPaint Method

Raises the **Paint** event.

[Visual Basic]
```
Protected Overridable Sub OnPaint( _
   ByVal e As PaintEventArgs _
)
```
[C#]
```
protected virtual void OnPaint(
   PaintEventArgs e
);
```
[C++]
```
protected: virtual void OnPaint(
   PaintEventArgs* e
);
```
[JScript]
```
protected function OnPaint(
   e : PaintEventArgs
);
```

Parameters

e

A **PaintEventArgs** that contains the event data.

Remarks

Raising an event invokes the event handler through a delegate.

The **OnPaint** method also allows derived classes to handle the event without attaching a delegate. This is the preferred technique for handling the event in a derived class.

Notes to Inheritors: When overriding **OnPaint** in a derived class, be sure to call the base class's **OnPaint** method so that registered delegates receive the event.

Example

[Visual Basic, C#, C++] The following example enables the user to drag an image or image file onto the form, and have it be displayed at the point on it is dropped. The **OnPaint** method is overridden to repaint the image each time the form is painted; otherwise the image would only persist until the next repainting. The **DragEnter** event-handling method determines the type of data being dragged into the form and provides the appropriate feedback. The **DragDrop** event-handling method displays the image on the form, if an **Image** can be created from the data. Because the **DragEventArgs.X** and **DragEventArgs.Y** values are screen coordinates, the example uses the **PointToClient** method to convert them to client coordinates.

[Visual Basic]

```
Private picture As Image
Private pictureLocation As Point

Public Sub New()
   ' Enable drag-and-drop operations.
   Me.AllowDrop = True
End Sub

Protected Overrides Sub OnPaint(ByVal e As PaintEventArgs)
   MyBase.OnPaint(e)

   ' If there is an image and it has a location,
   ' paint it when the Form is repainted.
   If Not (Me.picture Is Nothing) And _
     Not (Me.pictureLocation.Equals(Point.Empty)) Then
      e.Graphics.DrawImage(Me.picture, Me.pictureLocation)
   End If
End Sub

Private Sub Form1_DragDrop(ByVal sender As Object, _
  ByVal e As DragEventArgs) Handles MyBase.DragDrop
   ' Handle FileDrop data.
   If e.Data.GetDataPresent(DataFormats.FileDrop) Then
      ' Assign the file names to a string array, in
      ' case the user has selected multiple files.
      Dim files As String() = ↵
CType(e.Data.GetData(DataFormats.FileDrop), String())
      Try
         ' Assign the first image to the 'picture' variable.
         Me.picture = Image.FromFile(files(0))
         ' Set the picture location equal to the drop point.
         Me.pictureLocation = Me.PointToClient(New Point(e.X, e.Y))
      Catch ex As Exception
         MessageBox.Show(ex.Message)
         Return
      End Try
   End If

   ' Handle Bitmap data.
   If e.Data.GetDataPresent(DataFormats.Bitmap) Then
      Try
         ' Create an Image and assign it to the picture variable.
         Me.picture = CType(e.Data.GetData(DataFormats.Bitmap), Image)
         ' Set the picture location equal to the drop point.
         Me.pictureLocation = Me.PointToClient(New Point(e.X, e.Y))
      Catch ex As Exception
         MessageBox.Show(ex.Message)
         Return
      End Try
   End If

   ' Force the form to be redrawn with the image.
   Me.Invalidate()
End Sub

Private Sub Form1_DragEnter(ByVal sender As Object, _
  ByVal e As DragEventArgs) Handles MyBase.DragEnter
   ' If the data is a file or a bitmap, display the copy cursor.
   If e.Data.GetDataPresent(DataFormats.Bitmap) _
      Or e.Data.GetDataPresent(DataFormats.FileDrop) Then
      e.Effect = DragDropEffects.Copy
   Else
      e.Effect = DragDropEffects.None
   End If
End Sub
```

[C#]

```
private Image picture;
private Point pictureLocation;

public Form1()
{
   // Enable drag-and-drop operations and
   // add handlers for DragEnter and DragDrop.
   this.AllowDrop = true;
   this.DragDrop += new DragEventHandler(this.Form1_DragDrop);
   this.DragEnter += new DragEventHandler(this.Form1_DragEnter);
}

protected override void OnPaint(PaintEventArgs e)
{
   // If there is an image and it has a location,
   // paint it when the Form is repainted.
   base.OnPaint(e);
   if(this.picture != null && this.pictureLocation != Point.Empty)
   {
      e.Graphics.DrawImage(this.picture, this.pictureLocation);
   }
}

private void Form1_DragDrop(object sender, DragEventArgs e)
{
   // Handle FileDrop data.
   if(e.Data.GetDataPresent(DataFormats.FileDrop) )
   {
      // Assign the file names to a string array, in
      // case the user has selected multiple files.
      string[] files = (string[])e.Data.GetData(DataFormats.FileDrop);
      try
      {
         // Assign the first image to the picture variable.
         this.picture = Image.FromFile(files[0]);
         // Set the picture location equal to the drop point.
         this.pictureLocation = this.PointToClient(new Point ↵
 (e.X, e.Y) );
      }
      catch(Exception ex)
      {
         MessageBox.Show(ex.Message);
         return;
      }
   }

   // Handle Bitmap data.
   if(e.Data.GetDataPresent(DataFormats.Bitmap) )
   {
      try
      {
         // Create an Image and assign it to the picture variable.
         this.picture = (Image)e.Data.GetData(DataFormats.Bitmap);
         // Set the picture location equal to the drop point.
         this.pictureLocation = this.PointToClient(new Point ↵
 (e.X, e.Y) );
      }
      catch(Exception ex)
      {
         MessageBox.Show(ex.Message);
         return;
      }
   }
   // Force the form to be redrawn with the image.
   this.Invalidate();
}

private void Form1_DragEnter(object sender, DragEventArgs e)
{
   // If the data is a file or a bitmap, display the copy cursor.
   if (e.Data.GetDataPresent(DataFormats.Bitmap) ||
      e.Data.GetDataPresent(DataFormats.FileDrop) )
   {
      e.Effect = DragDropEffects.Copy;
   }
   else
   {
      e.Effect = DragDropEffects.None;
   }
}
```

[C++]

```
private:
   Image* picture;
   Point  pictureLocation;

public:
   Form1() {
      // Enable drag-and-drop operations and
      // add handlers for DragEnter and DragDrop.
      this->AllowDrop = true;
      this->DragDrop += new DragEventHandler(this, Form1_DragDrop);
      this->DragEnter += new DragEventHandler(this, Form1_DragEnter);
   }

protected:
   void OnPaint(PaintEventArgs* e) {
      // If there is an image and it has a location,
      // paint it when the Form is repainted.
      Form::OnPaint(e);
      if (this->picture != 0 && this->pictureLocation !=                    ↵
Point::Empty) {
         e->Graphics->DrawImage(this->picture, this->pictureLocation);
      }
   }

private:
   void Form1_DragDrop(Object* sender, DragEventArgs* e) {
      // Handle FileDrop data.
      if (e->Data->GetDataPresent(DataFormats::FileDrop)) {
         // Assign the file names to a String* array, in
         // case the user has selected multiple files.
         String* files[] = (String*[])e->Data-                              ↵
>GetData(DataFormats::FileDrop);
         try {
            // Assign the first image to the picture variable.
            this->picture = Image::FromFile(files[0]);
            // Set the picture location equal to the drop point.
            this->pictureLocation = this->PointToClient                     ↵
 ( Point(e->X, e->Y));
         } catch (Exception* ex) {
            MessageBox::Show(ex->Message);
            return;
         }
      }

      // Handle Bitmap data.
      if (e->Data->GetDataPresent(DataFormats::Bitmap)) {
         try {
            // Create an Image and assign it to the picture variable.
            this->picture = dynamic_cast<Image*>(e->Data-                   ↵
>GetData(DataFormats::Bitmap));
            // Set the picture location equal to the drop point.
            this->pictureLocation = this->PointToClient(                    ↵
Point(e->X, e->Y));
         } catch (Exception* ex) {
            MessageBox::Show(ex->Message);
            return;
         }
      }
      // Force the form to be redrawn with the image.
      this->Invalidate();
   }

   void Form1_DragEnter(Object* sender, DragEventArgs* e) {
      // If the data is a file or a bitmap, display the copy cursor.
      if (e->Data->GetDataPresent(DataFormats::Bitmap) ||
         e->Data->GetDataPresent(DataFormats::FileDrop)) {
            e->Effect = DragDropEffects::Copy;
         } else {
            e->Effect = DragDropEffects::None;
         }
   }
```

[Visual Basic]

```
' This example creates a PictureBox control on the form and              ↵
 draws to it.
' This example assumes that the Form_Load event handling                 ↵
method is connected
' to the Load event of the form.
Private pictureBox1 As New PictureBox()

Private Sub Form1_Load(ByVal sender As Object, ByVal e As                ↵
System.EventArgs) Handles MyBase.Load
    ' Dock the PictureBox to the form and set its background to white.
    pictureBox1.Dock = DockStyle.Fill
    pictureBox1.BackColor = Color.White
    ' Connect the Paint event of the PictureBox to the event             ↵
 handling method.
    AddHandler pictureBox1.Paint, AddressOf Me.pictureBox1_Paint

    ' Add the PictureBox control to the Form.
    Me.Controls.Add(pictureBox1)
End Sub 'Form1_Load

Private Sub pictureBox1_Paint(ByVal sender As Object, ByVal e As         ↵
System.Windows.Forms.PaintEventArgs)
    ' Create a local version of the graphics object for the PictureBox.
    Dim g As Graphics = e.Graphics

    ' Draw a string on the PictureBox.
    g.DrawString("This is a diagonal line drawn on the control", _
        New Font("Arial", 10), Brushes.Red, New PointF(30.0F, 30.0F))
    ' Draw a line in the PictureBox.
    g.DrawLine(System.Drawing.Pens.Red, pictureBox1.Left, _
        pictureBox1.Top, pictureBox1.Right, pictureBox1.Bottom)
End Sub 'pictureBox1_Paint
```

[C#]

```
// This example creates a PictureBox control on the form and             ↵
 draws to it.
// This example assumes that the Form_Load event handling method is
// connected to the Load event of the form.

private PictureBox pictureBox1 = new PictureBox();
private void Form1_Load(object sender, System.EventArgs e)
{
    // Dock the PictureBox to the form and set its background to white.
    pictureBox1.Dock = DockStyle.Fill;
    pictureBox1.BackColor = Color.White;
    // Connect the Paint event of the PictureBox to the event            ↵
handling method.
    pictureBox1.Paint += new                                             ↵
System.Windows.Forms.PaintEventHandler(this.pictureBox1_Paint);

    // Add the PictureBox control to the Form.
    this.Controls.Add(pictureBox1);
}

private void pictureBox1_Paint(object sender,                            ↵
System.Windows.Forms.PaintEventArgs e)
{
    // Create a local version of the graphics object for                 ↵
the PictureBox.
    Graphics g = e.Graphics;

    // Draw a string on the PictureBox.
    g.DrawString("This is a diagonal line drawn on the control",
        new Font("Arial",10), System.Drawing.Brushes.Blue, new           ↵
Point(30,30));
    // Draw a line in the PictureBox.
    g.DrawLine(System.Drawing.Pens.Red, pictureBox1.Left,                ↵
pictureBox1.Top,
        pictureBox1.Right, pictureBox1.Bottom);
}
```

Requirements

Platforms: Windows 98, Windows NT 4.0, Windows Millennium Edition, Windows 2000, Windows XP Home Edition, Windows XP Professional, Windows Server 2003 family, .NET Compact Framework - Windows CE .NET

Control.OnPaintBackground Method

Paints the background of the control.

[Visual Basic]
```
Protected Overridable Sub OnPaintBackground( _
   ByVal pevent As PaintEventArgs _
)
```
[C#]
```
protected virtual void OnPaintBackground(
   PaintEventArgs pevent
);
```
[C++]
```
protected: virtual void OnPaintBackground(
   PaintEventArgs* pevent
);
```
[JScript]
```
protected function OnPaintBackground(
   pevent : PaintEventArgs
);
```

Parameters

pevent

A **PaintEventArgs** that contains information about the control to paint.

Remarks

The **OnPaintBackground** method allows derived classes to handle the event without attaching a delegate. This is the preferred technique for handling the event in a derived class.

Notes to Inheritors: Inheriting classes should override this method to handle the erase background request from windows. When overriding **OnPaintBackground** in a derived class it is not necessary to call the base class's **OnPaintBackground** method.

Requirements

Platforms: Windows 98, Windows NT 4.0,
Windows Millennium Edition, Windows 2000,
Windows XP Home Edition, Windows XP Professional,
Windows Server 2003 family,
.NET Compact Framework - Windows CE .NET

Control.OnParentBackColorChanged Method

Raises the **BackColorChanged** event when the **BackColor** property value of the control's container changes.

[Visual Basic]
```
Protected Overridable Sub OnParentBackColorChanged( _
   ByVal e As EventArgs _
)
```
[C#]
```
protected virtual void OnParentBackColorChanged(
   EventArgs e
);
```
[C++]
```
protected: virtual void OnParentBackColorChanged(
   EventArgs* e
);
```
[JScript]
```
protected function OnParentBackColorChanged(
   e : EventArgs
);
```

Parameters

e

An **EventArgs** that contains the event data.

Remarks

Raising an event invokes the event handler through a delegate.

The **OnParentBackColorChanged** method also allows derived classes to handle the event without attaching a delegate. This is the preferred technique for handling the event in a derived class.

Notes to Inheritors: When overriding **OnParentBackColorChanged** in a derived class, be sure to call the base class's **OnParentBackColorChanged** method so that registered delegates receive the event.

Example

[Visual Basic, C#, C++] The example below is an event-raising method that is executed when the **Text** property value changes. The **Control** class has several methods with the name pattern **On**PropertyName **Changed** that raise the corresponding PropertyName **Changed** event when the PropertyName value changes(PropertyName represents the name of the corresponding property).

[Visual Basic, C#, C++] The following example changes the **ForeColor** of a **TextBox** derived class displaying currency data. The example converts the text to a decimal number and changes the **ForeColor** to **Color.Red** if the number is negative and to **Color.Black** if the number is positive. This example assumes you have a class that derives from the **TextBox** class.

[Visual Basic]
```
Protected Overrides Sub OnTextChanged(e As System.EventArgs)
   Try
      ' Convert the text to a Double and determine
      ' if it is a negative number.
      If Double.Parse(Me.Text) < 0 Then
         ' If the number is negative, display it in Red.
         Me.ForeColor = Color.Red
      Else
         ' If the number is not negative, display it in Black.
         Me.ForeColor = Color.Black
      End If
   Catch
      ' If there is an error, display the
      ' text using the system colors.
      Me.ForeColor = SystemColors.ControlText
   End Try

   MyBase.OnTextChanged(e)
End Sub
```

[C#]
```
protected override void OnTextChanged(System.EventArgs e)
{
   try
   {
      // Convert the text to a Double and determine
      // if it is a negative number.
      if(double.Parse(this.Text) < 0)
      {
         // If the number is negative, display it in Red.
         this.ForeColor = Color.Red;
      }
      else
      {
         // If the number is not negative, display it in Black.
         this.ForeColor = Color.Black;
      }
   }
   catch
   {
      // If there is an error, display the
```

```
         // text using the system colors.
         this.ForeColor = SystemColors.ControlText;
      }

      base.OnTextChanged(e);
   }
```

[C++]

```
protected:
   void OnTextChanged(System::EventArgs* e) {
      try {
         // Convert the text to a Double and determine
         // if it is a negative number.
         if (Double::Parse(this->Text) < 0) {
            // If the number is negative, display it in Red.
            this->ForeColor = Color::Red;
         } else {
            // If the number is not negative, display it in Black.
            this->ForeColor = Color::Black;
         }
      } catch (Exception*) {
         // If there is an error, display the
         // text using the system colors.
         this->ForeColor = SystemColors::ControlText;
      }

      TextBox::OnTextChanged(e);
   }
```

Requirements

Platforms: Windows 98, Windows NT 4.0, Windows Millennium Edition, Windows 2000, Windows XP Home Edition, Windows XP Professional, Windows Server 2003 family

Control.OnParentBackgroundImageChanged Method

Raises the **BackgroundImageChanged** event when the **BackgroundImage** property value of the control's container changes.

[Visual Basic]

```
Protected Overridable Sub OnParentBackgroundImageChanged( _
   ByVal e As EventArgs _
)
```

[C#]

```
protected virtual void OnParentBackgroundImageChanged(
   EventArgs e
);
```

[C++]

```
protected: virtual void OnParentBackgroundImageChanged(
   EventArgs* e
);
```

[JScript]

```
protected function OnParentBackgroundImageChanged(
   e : EventArgs
);
```

Parameters

e

An **EventArgs** that contains the event data.

Remarks

Raising an event invokes the event handler through a delegate.

The **OnParentBackgroundImageChanged** method also allows derived classes to handle the event without attaching a delegate. This is the preferred technique for handling the event in a derived class.

Notes to Inheritors: When overriding **OnParentBackgroundImageChanged** in a derived class, be sure to call the base class's **OnParentBackgroundImageChanged** method so that registered delegates receive the event.

Example

[Visual Basic, C#, C++] The example below is an event-raising method that is executed when the **Text** property value changes. The **Control** class has several methods with the name pattern **On** PropertyName **Changed** that raise the corresponding PropertyName **Changed** event when the PropertyName value changes(PropertyName represents the name of the corresponding property).

[Visual Basic, C#, C++] The following example changes the **ForeColor** of a **TextBox** derived class displaying currency data. The example converts the text to a decimal number and changes the **ForeColor** to **Color.Red** if the number is negative and to **Color.Black** if the number is positive. This example assumes you have a class that derives from the **TextBox** class.

[Visual Basic]

```
Protected Overrides Sub OnTextChanged(e As System.EventArgs)
   Try
      ' Convert the text to a Double and determine
      ' if it is a negative number.
      If Double.Parse(Me.Text) < 0 Then
         ' If the number is negative, display it in Red.
         Me.ForeColor = Color.Red
      Else
         ' If the number is not negative, display it in Black.
         Me.ForeColor = Color.Black
      End If
   Catch
      ' If there is an error, display the
      ' text using the system colors.
      Me.ForeColor = SystemColors.ControlText
   End Try

   MyBase.OnTextChanged(e)
End Sub
```

[C#]

```
protected override void OnTextChanged(System.EventArgs e)
{
   try
   {
      // Convert the text to a Double and determine
      // if it is a negative number.
      if(double.Parse(this.Text) < 0)
      {
         // If the number is negative, display it in Red.
         this.ForeColor = Color.Red;
      }
      else
      {
         // If the number is not negative, display it in Black.
         this.ForeColor = Color.Black;
      }
   }
   catch
   {
      // If there is an error, display the
      // text using the system colors.
      this.ForeColor = SystemColors.ControlText;
   }

   base.OnTextChanged(e);
}
```

[C++]

```
protected:
   void OnTextChanged(System::EventArgs* e) {
      try {
```

```
      // Convert the text to a Double and determine
      // if it is a negative number.
      if (Double::Parse(this->Text) < 0) {
         // If the number is negative, display it in Red.
         this->ForeColor = Color::Red;
      } else {
         // If the number is not negative, display it in Black.
         this->ForeColor = Color::Black;
      }
   } catch (Exception*) {
      // If there is an error, display the
      // text using the system colors.
      this->ForeColor = SystemColors::ControlText;
   }

   TextBox::OnTextChanged(e);
}
```

Requirements

Platforms: Windows 98, Windows NT 4.0, Windows Millennium Edition, Windows 2000, Windows XP Home Edition, Windows XP Professional, Windows Server 2003 family

Control.OnParentBindingContextChanged Method

Raises the **BindingContextChanged** event when the **BindingContext** property value of the control's container changes.

[Visual Basic]
```
Protected Overridable Sub OnParentBindingContextChanged( _
   ByVal e As EventArgs _
)
```
[C#]
```
protected virtual void OnParentBindingContextChanged(
   EventArgs e
);
```
[C++]
```
protected: virtual void OnParentBindingContextChanged(
   EventArgs* e
);
```
[JScript]
```
protected function OnParentBindingContextChanged(
   e : EventArgs
);
```

Parameters

e

An **EventArgs** that contains the event data.

Remarks

Raising an event invokes the event handler through a delegate.

The **OnParentBindingContextChanged** method also allows derived classes to handle the event without attaching a delegate. This is the preferred technique for handling the event in a derived class.

Notes to Inheritors: When overriding **OnParentBindingContextChanged** in a derived class, be sure to call the base class's **OnParentBindingContextChanged** method so that registered delegates receive the event.

Example

[Visual Basic, C#, C++] The example below is an event-raising method that is executed when the **Text** property value changes. The **Control** class has several methods with the name pattern **On**PropertyName **Changed** that raise the corresponding PropertyName **Changed** event when the PropertyName value changes(PropertyName represents the name of the corresponding property).

[Visual Basic, C#, C++] The following example changes the **ForeColor** of a **TextBox** derived class displaying currency data. The example converts the text to a decimal number and changes the **ForeColor** to **Color.Red** if the number is negative and to **Color.Black** if the number is positive. This example assumes you have a class that derives from the **TextBox** class.

[Visual Basic]
```
Protected Overrides Sub OnTextChanged(e As System.EventArgs)
   Try
      ' Convert the text to a Double and determine
      ' if it is a negative number.
      If Double.Parse(Me.Text) < 0 Then
         ' If the number is negative, display it in Red.
         Me.ForeColor = Color.Red
      Else
         ' If the number is not negative, display it in Black.
         Me.ForeColor = Color.Black
      End If
   Catch
      ' If there is an error, display the
      ' text using the system colors.
      Me.ForeColor = SystemColors.ControlText
   End Try

   MyBase.OnTextChanged(e)
End Sub
```

[C#]
```
protected override void OnTextChanged(System.EventArgs e)
{
   try
   {
      // Convert the text to a Double and determine
      // if it is a negative number.
      if(double.Parse(this.Text) < 0)
      {
         // If the number is negative, display it in Red.
         this.ForeColor = Color.Red;
      }
      else
      {
         // If the number is not negative, display it in Black.
         this.ForeColor = Color.Black;
      }
   }
   catch
   {
      // If there is an error, display the
      // text using the system colors.
      this.ForeColor = SystemColors.ControlText;
   }

   base.OnTextChanged(e);
}
```

[C++]
```
protected:
   void OnTextChanged(System::EventArgs* e) {
      try {
         // Convert the text to a Double and determine
         // if it is a negative number.
         if (Double::Parse(this->Text) < 0) {
            // If the number is negative, display it in Red.
            this->ForeColor = Color::Red;
         } else {
            // If the number is not negative, display it in Black.
            this->ForeColor = Color::Black;
         }
      } catch (Exception*) {
```

```
            // If there is an error, display the
            // text using the system colors.
            this->ForeColor = SystemColors::ControlText;
        }

        TextBox::OnTextChanged(e);
    }
```

Requirements

Platforms: Windows 98, Windows NT 4.0, Windows Millennium Edition, Windows 2000, Windows XP Home Edition, Windows XP Professional, Windows Server 2003 family

Control.OnParentChanged Method

Raises the **ParentChanged** event.

[Visual Basic]
```
Protected Overridable Sub OnParentChanged( _
   ByVal e As EventArgs _
)
```
[C#]
```
protected virtual void OnParentChanged(
   EventArgs e
);
```
[C++]
```
protected: virtual void OnParentChanged(
   EventArgs* e
);
```
[JScript]
```
protected function OnParentChanged(
   e : EventArgs
);
```

Parameters

e

An **EventArgs** that contains the event data.

Remarks

Raising an event invokes the event handler through a delegate.

The **OnParentChanged** method also allows derived classes to handle the event without attaching a delegate. This is the preferred technique for handling the event in a derived class.

Notes to Inheritors: When overriding **OnParentChanged** in a derived class, be sure to call the base class's **OnParentChanged** method so that registered delegates receive the event.

Example

[Visual Basic, C#, C++] The example below is an event-raising method that is executed when the **Text** property value changes. The **Control** class has several methods with the name pattern **On** PropertyName **Changed** that raise the corresponding PropertyName **Changed** event when the PropertyName value changes(Property-Name represents the name of the corresponding property).

[Visual Basic, C#, C++] The following example changes the **ForeColor** of a **TextBox** derived class displaying currency data. The example converts the text to a decimal number and changes the **ForeColor** to **Color.Red** if the number is negative and to **Color.Black** if the number is positive. This example assumes you have a class that derives from the **TextBox** class.

[Visual Basic]
```
Protected Overrides Sub OnTextChanged(e As System.EventArgs)
   Try
      ' Convert the text to a Double and determine
      ' if it is a negative number.
      If Double.Parse(Me.Text) < 0 Then
         ' If the number is negative, display it in Red.
         Me.ForeColor = Color.Red
      Else
         ' If the number is not negative, display it in Black.
         Me.ForeColor = Color.Black
      End If
   Catch
      ' If there is an error, display the
      ' text using the system colors.
      Me.ForeColor = SystemColors.ControlText
   End Try

   MyBase.OnTextChanged(e)
End Sub
```

[C#]
```
protected override void OnTextChanged(System.EventArgs e)
{
   try
   {
      // Convert the text to a Double and determine
      // if it is a negative number.
      if(double.Parse(this.Text) < 0)
      {
         // If the number is negative, display it in Red.
         this.ForeColor = Color.Red;
      }
      else
      {
         // If the number is not negative, display it in Black.
         this.ForeColor = Color.Black;
      }
   }
   catch
   {
      // If there is an error, display the
      // text using the system colors.
      this.ForeColor = SystemColors.ControlText;
   }

   base.OnTextChanged(e);
}
```

[C++]
```
protected:
   void OnTextChanged(System::EventArgs* e) {
      try {
         // Convert the text to a Double and determine
         // if it is a negative number.
         if (Double::Parse(this->Text) < 0) {
            // If the number is negative, display it in Red.
            this->ForeColor = Color::Red;
         } else {
            // If the number is not negative, display it in Black.
            this->ForeColor = Color::Black;
         }
      } catch (Exception*) {
         // If there is an error, display the
         // text using the system colors.
         this->ForeColor = SystemColors::ControlText;
      }

      TextBox::OnTextChanged(e);
   }
```

Requirements

Platforms: Windows 98, Windows NT 4.0, Windows Millennium Edition, Windows 2000, Windows XP Home Edition, Windows XP Professional, Windows Server 2003 family, .NET Compact Framework - Windows CE .NET

Control.OnParentEnabledChanged Method

Raises the **EnabledChanged** event when the **Enabled** property value of the control's container changes.

[Visual Basic]
```
Protected Overridable Sub OnParentEnabledChanged( _
   ByVal e As EventArgs _
)
```
[C#]
```
protected virtual void OnParentEnabledChanged(
   EventArgs e
);
```
[C++]
```
protected: virtual void OnParentEnabledChanged(
   EventArgs* e
);
```
[JScript]
```
protected function OnParentEnabledChanged(
   e : EventArgs
);
```

Parameters

e

An **EventArgs** that contains the event data.

Remarks

Raising an event invokes the event handler through a delegate.

The **OnParentEnabledChanged** method also allows derived classes to handle the event without attaching a delegate. This is the preferred technique for handling the event in a derived class.

Notes to Inheritors: When overriding **OnParentEnabledChanged** in a derived class, be sure to call the base class's **OnParentEnabledChanged** method so that registered delegates receive the event.

Example

[Visual Basic, C#, C++] The example below is an event-raising method that is executed when the **Text** property value changes. The **Control** class has several methods with the name pattern **On** PropertyName **Changed** that raise the corresponding PropertyName **Changed** event when the PropertyName value changes(PropertyName represents the name of the corresponding property).

[Visual Basic, C#, C++] The following example changes the **ForeColor** of a **TextBox** derived class displaying currency data. The example converts the text to a decimal number and changes the **ForeColor** to **Color.Red** if the number is negative and to **Color.Black** if the number is positive. This example assumes you have a class that derives from the **TextBox** class.

[Visual Basic]
```
Protected Overrides Sub OnTextChanged(e As System.EventArgs)
   Try
      ' Convert the text to a Double and determine
      ' if it is a negative number.
      If Double.Parse(Me.Text) < 0 Then
         ' If the number is negative, display it in Red.
         Me.ForeColor = Color.Red
      Else
         ' If the number is not negative, display it in Black.
         Me.ForeColor = Color.Black
      End If
   Catch
      ' If there is an error, display the
      ' text using the system colors.
      Me.ForeColor = SystemColors.ControlText
   End Try

   MyBase.OnTextChanged(e)
End Sub
```

[C#]
```
protected override void OnTextChanged(System.EventArgs e)
{
   try
   {
      // Convert the text to a Double and determine
      // if it is a negative number.
      if(double.Parse(this.Text) < 0)
      {
         // If the number is negative, display it in Red.
         this.ForeColor = Color.Red;
      }
      else
      {
         // If the number is not negative, display it in Black.
         this.ForeColor = Color.Black;
      }
   }
   catch
   {
      // If there is an error, display the
      // text using the system colors.
      this.ForeColor = SystemColors.ControlText;
   }

   base.OnTextChanged(e);
}
```

[C++]
```
protected:
   void OnTextChanged(System::EventArgs* e) {
      try {
         // Convert the text to a Double and determine
         // if it is a negative number.
         if (Double::Parse(this->Text) < 0) {
            // If the number is negative, display it in Red.
            this->ForeColor = Color::Red;
         } else {
            // If the number is not negative, display it in Black.
            this->ForeColor = Color::Black;
         }
      } catch (Exception*) {
         // If there is an error, display the
         // text using the system colors.
         this->ForeColor = SystemColors::ControlText;
      }

      TextBox::OnTextChanged(e);
   }
```

Requirements

Platforms: Windows 98, Windows NT 4.0, Windows Millennium Edition, Windows 2000, Windows XP Home Edition, Windows XP Professional, Windows Server 2003 family

Control.OnParentFontChanged Method

Raises the **FontChanged** event when the **Font** property value of the control's container changes.

[Visual Basic]
```
Protected Overridable Sub OnParentFontChanged( _
   ByVal e As EventArgs _
)
```
[C#]
```
protected virtual void OnParentFontChanged(
   EventArgs e
);
```

[C++]
```
protected: virtual void OnParentFontChanged(
   EventArgs* e
);
```
[JScript]
```
protected function OnParentFontChanged(
   e : EventArgs
);
```

Parameters

e

An **EventArgs** that contains the event data.

Remarks

Raising an event invokes the event handler through a delegate.

The **OnParentFontChanged** method also allows derived classes to handle the event without attaching a delegate. This is the preferred technique for handling the event in a derived class.

Notes to Inheritors: When overriding **OnParentFontChanged** in a derived class, be sure to call the base class's **OnParentFont-Changed** method so that registered delegates receive the event.

Example

[Visual Basic, C#, C++] The example below is an event-raising method that is executed when the **Text** property value changes. The **Control** class has several methods with the name pattern **On** PropertyName **Changed** that raise the corresponding PropertyName **Changed** event when the PropertyName value changes(Property-Name represents the name of the corresponding property).

[Visual Basic, C#, C++] The following example changes the **ForeColor** of a **TextBox** derived class displaying currency data. The example converts the text to a decimal number and changes the **ForeColor** to **Color.Red** if the number is negative and to **Color.Black** if the number is positive. This example assumes you have a class that derives from the **TextBox** class.

[Visual Basic]
```
Protected Overrides Sub OnTextChanged(e As System.EventArgs)
   Try
      ' Convert the text to a Double and determine
      ' if it is a negative number.
      If Double.Parse(Me.Text) < 0 Then
         ' If the number is negative, display it in Red.
         Me.ForeColor = Color.Red
      Else
         ' If the number is not negative, display it in Black.
         Me.ForeColor = Color.Black
      End If
   Catch
      ' If there is an error, display the
      ' text using the system colors.
      Me.ForeColor = SystemColors.ControlText
   End Try

   MyBase.OnTextChanged(e)
End Sub
```

[C#]
```
protected override void OnTextChanged(System.EventArgs e)
{
   try
   {
      // Convert the text to a Double and determine
      // if it is a negative number.
      if(double.Parse(this.Text) < 0)
      {
         // If the number is negative, display it in Red.
         this.ForeColor = Color.Red;
      }
      else
      {
         // If the number is not negative, display it in Black.
         this.ForeColor = Color.Black;
      }
   }
   catch
   {
      // If there is an error, display the
      // text using the system colors.
      this.ForeColor = SystemColors.ControlText;
   }

   base.OnTextChanged(e);
}
```

[C++]
```
protected:
   void OnTextChanged(System::EventArgs* e) {
      try {
         // Convert the text to a Double and determine
         // if it is a negative number.
         if (Double::Parse(this->Text) < 0) {
            // If the number is negative, display it in Red.
            this->ForeColor = Color::Red;
         } else {
            // If the number is not negative, display it in Black.
            this->ForeColor = Color::Black;
         }
      } catch (Exception*) {
         // If there is an error, display the
         // text using the system colors.
         this->ForeColor = SystemColors::ControlText;
      }

      TextBox::OnTextChanged(e);
   }
```

Requirements

Platforms: Windows 98, Windows NT 4.0, Windows Millennium Edition, Windows 2000, Windows XP Home Edition, Windows XP Professional, Windows Server 2003 family

Control.OnParentForeColorChanged Method

Raises the **ForeColorChanged** event when the **ForeColor** property value of the control's container changes.

[Visual Basic]
```
Protected Overridable Sub OnParentForeColorChanged( _
   ByVal e As EventArgs _
)
```
[C#]
```
protected virtual void OnParentForeColorChanged(
   EventArgs e
);
```
[C++]
```
protected: virtual void OnParentForeColorChanged(
   EventArgs* e
);
```
[JScript]
```
protected function OnParentForeColorChanged(
   e : EventArgs
);
```

Parameters

e

An **EventArgs** that contains the event data.

Remarks

Raising an event invokes the event handler through a delegate.

The **OnParentForeColorChanged** method also allows derived classes to handle the event without attaching a delegate. This is the preferred technique for handling the event in a derived class.

Notes to Inheritors: When overriding **OnParentForeColorChanged** in a derived class, be sure to call the base class's **OnParentForeColorChanged** method so that registered delegates receive the event.

Example

[Visual Basic, C#, C++] The example below is an event-raising method that is executed when the **Text** property value changes. The **Control** class has several methods with the name pattern **On** PropertyName **Changed** that raise the corresponding PropertyName **Changed** event when the PropertyName value changes(PropertyName represents the name of the corresponding property).

[Visual Basic, C#, C++] The following example changes the **ForeColor** of a **TextBox** derived class displaying currency data. The example converts the text to a decimal number and changes the **ForeColor** to **Color.Red** if the number is negative and to **Color.Black** if the number is positive. This example assumes you have a class that derives from the **TextBox** class.

[Visual Basic]
```
Protected Overrides Sub OnTextChanged(e As System.EventArgs)
   Try
      ' Convert the text to a Double and determine
      ' if it is a negative number.
      If Double.Parse(Me.Text) < 0 Then
         ' If the number is negative, display it in Red.
         Me.ForeColor = Color.Red
      Else
         ' If the number is not negative, display it in Black.
         Me.ForeColor = Color.Black
      End If
   Catch
      ' If there is an error, display the
      ' text using the system colors.
      Me.ForeColor = SystemColors.ControlText
   End Try

   MyBase.OnTextChanged(e)
End Sub
```

[C#]
```
protected override void OnTextChanged(System.EventArgs e)
{
   try
   {
      // Convert the text to a Double and determine
      // if it is a negative number.
      if(double.Parse(this.Text) < 0)
      {
         // If the number is negative, display it in Red.
         this.ForeColor = Color.Red;
      }
      else
      {
         // If the number is not negative, display it in Black.
         this.ForeColor = Color.Black;
      }
   }
   catch
   {
      // If there is an error, display the
      // text using the system colors.
      this.ForeColor = SystemColors.ControlText;
   }

   base.OnTextChanged(e);
}
```

[C++]
```
protected:
   void OnTextChanged(System::EventArgs* e) {
      try {
         // Convert the text to a Double and determine
         // if it is a negative number.
         if (Double::Parse(this->Text) < 0) {
            // If the number is negative, display it in Red.
            this->ForeColor = Color::Red;
         } else {
            // If the number is not negative, display it in Black.
            this->ForeColor = Color::Black;
         }
      } catch (Exception*) {
         // If there is an error, display the
         // text using the system colors.
         this->ForeColor = SystemColors::ControlText;
      }

      TextBox::OnTextChanged(e);
   }
```

Requirements

Platforms: Windows 98, Windows NT 4.0, Windows Millennium Edition, Windows 2000, Windows XP Home Edition, Windows XP Professional, Windows Server 2003 family

Control.OnParentRightToLeftChanged Method

Raises the **RightToLeftChanged** event when the **RightToLeft** property value of the control's container changes.

[Visual Basic]
```
Protected Overridable Sub OnParentRightToLeftChanged( _
   ByVal e As EventArgs _
)
```
[C#]
```
protected virtual void OnParentRightToLeftChanged(
   EventArgs e
);
```
[C++]
```
protected: virtual void OnParentRightToLeftChanged(
   EventArgs* e
);
```
[JScript]
```
protected function OnParentRightToLeftChanged(
   e : EventArgs
);
```

Parameters

e

An **EventArgs** that contains the event data.

Remarks

Raising an event invokes the event handler through a delegate.

The **OnParentRightToLeftChanged** method also allows derived classes to handle the event without attaching a delegate. This is the preferred technique for handling the event in a derived class.

Notes to Inheritors: When overriding **OnParentRightToLeftChanged** in a derived class, be sure to call the base class's **OnParentRightToLeftChanged** method so that registered delegates receive the event.

Example

[Visual Basic, C#, C++] The example below is an event-raising method that is executed when the **Text** property value changes. The **Control** class has several methods with the name pattern **On** PropertyName **Changed** that raise the corresponding PropertyName **Changed** event when the PropertyName value changes(PropertyName represents the name of the corresponding property).

[Visual Basic, C#, C++] The following example changes the **ForeColor** of a **TextBox** derived class displaying currency data. The example converts the text to a decimal number and changes the **ForeColor** to **Color.Red** if the number is negative and to **Color.Black** if the number is positive. This example assumes you have a class that derives from the **TextBox** class.

[Visual Basic]
```
Protected Overrides Sub OnTextChanged(e As System.EventArgs)
   Try
      ' Convert the text to a Double and determine
      ' if it is a negative number.
      If Double.Parse(Me.Text) < 0 Then
         ' If the number is negative, display it in Red.
         Me.ForeColor = Color.Red
      Else
         ' If the number is not negative, display it in Black.
         Me.ForeColor = Color.Black
      End If
   Catch
      ' If there is an error, display the
      ' text using the system colors.
      Me.ForeColor = SystemColors.ControlText
   End Try

   MyBase.OnTextChanged(e)
End Sub
```

[C#]
```
protected override void OnTextChanged(System.EventArgs e)
{
   try
   {
      // Convert the text to a Double and determine
      // if it is a negative number.
      if(double.Parse(this.Text) < 0)
      {
         // If the number is negative, display it in Red.
         this.ForeColor = Color.Red;
      }
      else
      {
         // If the number is not negative, display it in Black.
         this.ForeColor = Color.Black;
      }
   }
   catch
   {
      // If there is an error, display the
      // text using the system colors.
      this.ForeColor = SystemColors.ControlText;
   }

   base.OnTextChanged(e);
}
```

[C++]
```
protected:
   void OnTextChanged(System::EventArgs* e) {
      try {
         // Convert the text to a Double and determine
         // if it is a negative number.
         if (Double::Parse(this->Text) < 0) {
            // If the number is negative, display it in Red.
            this->ForeColor = Color::Red;
         } else {
            // If the number is not negative, display it in Black.
            this->ForeColor = Color::Black;
         }
      } catch (Exception*) {
         // If there is an error, display the
         // text using the system colors.
         this->ForeColor = SystemColors::ControlText;
      }

      TextBox::OnTextChanged(e);
   }
```

Requirements

Platforms: Windows 98, Windows NT 4.0, Windows Millennium Edition, Windows 2000, Windows XP Home Edition, Windows XP Professional, Windows Server 2003 family

Control.OnParentVisibleChanged Method

Raises the **VisibleChanged** event when the **Visible** property value of the control's container changes.

[Visual Basic]
```
Protected Overridable Sub OnParentVisibleChanged( _
   ByVal e As EventArgs _
)
```
[C#]
```
protected virtual void OnParentVisibleChanged(
   EventArgs e
);
```
[C++]
```
protected: virtual void OnParentVisibleChanged(
   EventArgs* e
);
```
[JScript]
```
protected function OnParentVisibleChanged(
   e : EventArgs
);
```

Parameters

e

An **EventArgs** that contains the event data.

Remarks

Raising an event invokes the event handler through a delegate.

The **OnParentVisibleChanged** method also allows derived classes to handle the event without attaching a delegate. This is the preferred technique for handling the event in a derived class.

Notes to Inheritors: When overriding **OnParentVisibleChanged** in a derived class, be sure to call the base class's **OnParentVisibleChanged** method so that registered delegates receive the event.

Example

[Visual Basic, C#, C++] The example below is an event-raising method that is executed when the **Text** property value changes. The **Control** class has several methods with the name pattern **On** PropertyName **Changed** that raise the corresponding PropertyName **Changed** event when the PropertyName value changes(PropertyName represents the name of the corresponding property).

[Visual Basic, C#, C++] The following example changes the **ForeColor** of a **TextBox** derived class displaying currency data. The example converts the text to a decimal number and changes the

ForeColor to **Color.Red** if the number is negative and to **Color.Black** if the number is positive. This example assumes you have a class that derives from the **TextBox** class.

[Visual Basic]
```
Protected Overrides Sub OnTextChanged(e As System.EventArgs)
   Try
      ' Convert the text to a Double and determine
      ' if it is a negative number.
      If Double.Parse(Me.Text) < 0 Then
         ' If the number is negative, display it in Red.
         Me.ForeColor = Color.Red
      Else
         ' If the number is not negative, display it in Black.
         Me.ForeColor = Color.Black
      End If
   Catch
      ' If there is an error, display the
      ' text using the system colors.
      Me.ForeColor = SystemColors.ControlText
   End Try

   MyBase.OnTextChanged(e)
End Sub
```

[C#]
```
protected override void OnTextChanged(System.EventArgs e)
{
   try
   {
      // Convert the text to a Double and determine
      // if it is a negative number.
      if(double.Parse(this.Text) < 0)
      {
         // If the number is negative, display it in Red.
         this.ForeColor = Color.Red;
      }
      else
      {
         // If the number is not negative, display it in Black.
         this.ForeColor = Color.Black;
      }
   }
   catch
   {
      // If there is an error, display the
      // text using the system colors.
      this.ForeColor = SystemColors.ControlText;
   }

   base.OnTextChanged(e);
}
```

[C++]
```
protected:
   void OnTextChanged(System::EventArgs* e) {
      try {
         // Convert the text to a Double and determine
         // if it is a negative number.
         if (Double::Parse(this->Text) < 0) {
            // If the number is negative, display it in Red.
            this->ForeColor = Color::Red;
         } else {
            // If the number is not negative, display it in Black.
            this->ForeColor = Color::Black;
         }
      } catch (Exception*) {
         // If there is an error, display the
         // text using the system colors.
         this->ForeColor = SystemColors::ControlText;
      }

      TextBox::OnTextChanged(e);
   }
```

Requirements

Platforms: Windows 98, Windows NT 4.0, Windows Millennium Edition, Windows 2000, Windows XP Home Edition, Windows XP Professional, Windows Server 2003 family

Control.OnQueryContinueDrag Method

Raises the **QueryContinueDrag** event.

[Visual Basic]
```
Protected Overridable Sub OnQueryContinueDrag( _
   ByVal qcdevent As QueryContinueDragEventArgs _
)
```
[C#]
```
protected virtual void OnQueryContinueDrag(
   QueryContinueDragEventArgs qcdevent
);
```
[C++]
```
protected: virtual void OnQueryContinueDrag(
   QueryContinueDragEventArgs* qcdevent
);
```
[JScript]
```
protected function OnQueryContinueDrag(
   qcdevent : QueryContinueDragEventArgs
);
```

Parameters

qcdevent

A **QueryContinueDragEventArgs** that contains the event data.

Remarks

After dragging has begun, this method is called repeatedly by the .NET Framework until the drag operation is either canceled or completed.

> **Note** Override this method if you want to change the point at which dragging is canceled or at which a drop occurs.

Raising an event invokes the event handler through a delegate.

The **OnQueryContinueDrag** method also allows derived classes to handle the event without attaching a delegate. This is the preferred technique for handling the event in a derived class.

Notes to Inheritors: When overriding **OnQueryContinueDrag** in a derived class, be sure to call the base class's **OnQueryContinueDrag** method so that registered delegates receive the event.

Requirements

Platforms: Windows 98, Windows NT 4.0, Windows Millennium Edition, Windows 2000, Windows XP Home Edition, Windows XP Professional, Windows Server 2003 family

Control.OnResize Method

Raises the **Resize** event.

[Visual Basic]
```
Protected Overridable Sub OnResize( _
   ByVal e As EventArgs _
)
```
[C#]
```
protected virtual void OnResize(
   EventArgs e
);
```

[C++]
```
protected: virtual void OnResize(
   EventArgs* e
);
```
[JScript]
```
protected function OnResize(
   e : EventArgs
);
```

Parameters

e

An **EventArgs** that contains the event data.

Remarks

Raising an event invokes the event handler through a delegate.

The **OnResize** method also allows derived classes to handle the event without attaching a delegate. This is the preferred technique for handling the event in a derived class.

Notes to Inheritors: When overriding **OnResize** in a derived class, be sure to call the base class's **OnResize** method so that registered delegates receive the event. The **OnResize** method can be called during construction, so if you override **OnResize** it can be called before the control constructor is called.

Requirements

Platforms: Windows 98, Windows NT 4.0, Windows Millennium Edition, Windows 2000, Windows XP Home Edition, Windows XP Professional, Windows Server 2003 family, .NET Compact Framework - Windows CE .NET

Control.OnRightToLeftChanged Method

Raises the **RightToLeftChanged** event.

[Visual Basic]
```
Protected Overridable Sub OnRightToLeftChanged( _
   ByVal e As EventArgs _
)
```
[C#]
```
protected virtual void OnRightToLeftChanged(
   EventArgs e
);
```
[C++]
```
protected: virtual void OnRightToLeftChanged(
   EventArgs* e
);
```
[JScript]
```
protected function OnRightToLeftChanged(
   e : EventArgs
);
```

Parameters

e

An **EventArgs** that contains the event data.

Remarks

Raising an event invokes the event handler through a delegate.

The **OnRightToLeftChanged** method also allows derived classes to handle the event without attaching a delegate. This is the preferred technique for handling the event in a derived class.

Notes to Inheritors: When overriding **OnRightToLeftChanged** in a derived class, be sure to call the base class's **OnRightToLeftChanged** method so that registered delegates receive the event.

Example

[Visual Basic, C#, C++] The example below is an event-raising method that is executed when the **Text** property value changes. The **Control** class has several methods with the name pattern **On**PropertyName **Changed** that raise the corresponding PropertyName **Changed** event when the PropertyName value changes(PropertyName represents the name of the corresponding property).

[Visual Basic, C#, C++] The following example changes the **ForeColor** of a **TextBox** derived class displaying currency data. The example converts the text to a decimal number and changes the **ForeColor** to **Color.Red** if the number is negative and to **Color.Black** if the number is positive. This example assumes you have a class that derives from the **TextBox** class.

[Visual Basic]
```
Protected Overrides Sub OnTextChanged(e As System.EventArgs)
   Try
      ' Convert the text to a Double and determine
      ' if it is a negative number.
      If Double.Parse(Me.Text) < 0 Then
         ' If the number is negative, display it in Red.
         Me.ForeColor = Color.Red
      Else
         ' If the number is not negative, display it in Black.
         Me.ForeColor = Color.Black
      End If
   Catch
      ' If there is an error, display the
      ' text using the system colors.
      Me.ForeColor = SystemColors.ControlText
   End Try

   MyBase.OnTextChanged(e)
End Sub
```

[C#]
```
protected override void OnTextChanged(System.EventArgs e)
{
   try
   {
      // Convert the text to a Double and determine
      // if it is a negative number.
      if(double.Parse(this.Text) < 0)
      {
         // If the number is negative, display it in Red.
         this.ForeColor = Color.Red;
      }
      else
      {
         // If the number is not negative, display it in Black.
         this.ForeColor = Color.Black;
      }
   }
   catch
   {
      // If there is an error, display the
      // text using the system colors.
      this.ForeColor = SystemColors.ControlText;
   }

   base.OnTextChanged(e);
}
```

[C++]
```
protected:
   void OnTextChanged(System::EventArgs* e) {
      try {
         // Convert the text to a Double and determine
         // if it is a negative number.
         if (Double::Parse(this->Text) < 0) {
```

```
            // If the number is negative, display it in Red.
            this->ForeColor = Color::Red;
         } else {
            // If the number is not negative, display it in Black.
            this->ForeColor = Color::Black;
         }
      } catch (Exception*) {
         // If there is an error, display the
         // text using the system colors.
         this->ForeColor = SystemColors::ControlText;
      }

      TextBox::OnTextChanged(e);
   }
```

Requirements

Platforms: Windows 98, Windows NT 4.0, Windows Millennium Edition, Windows 2000, Windows XP Home Edition, Windows XP Professional, Windows Server 2003 family

Control.OnSizeChanged Method

Raises the **SizeChanged** event.

[Visual Basic]
```
Protected Overridable Sub OnSizeChanged( _
   ByVal e As EventArgs _
)
```
[C#]
```
protected virtual void OnSizeChanged(
   EventArgs e
);
```
[C++]
```
protected: virtual void OnSizeChanged(
   EventArgs* e
);
```
[JScript]
```
protected function OnSizeChanged(
   e : EventArgs
);
```

Parameters

e

An **EventArgs** that contains the event data.

Remarks

Raising an event invokes the event handler through a delegate.

The **OnSizeChanged** method also allows derived classes to handle the event without attaching a delegate. This is the preferred technique for handling the event in a derived class.

Notes to Inheritors: When overriding **OnSizeChanged** in a derived class, be sure to call the base class's **OnSizeChanged** method so that registered delegates receive the event.

Example

[Visual Basic, C#, C++] The example below is an event-raising method that is executed when the **Text** property value changes. The **Control** class has several methods with the name pattern **On** PropertyName **Changed** that raise the corresponding PropertyName **Changed** event when the PropertyName value changes(PropertyName represents the name of the corresponding property).

[Visual Basic, C#, C++] The following example changes the **ForeColor** of a **TextBox** derived class displaying currency data. The example converts the text to a decimal number and changes the **ForeColor** to **Color.Red** if the number is negative and to **Color.Black** if the number is positive. This example assumes you have a class that derives from the **TextBox** class.

[Visual Basic]
```
Protected Overrides Sub OnTextChanged(e As System.EventArgs)
   Try
      ' Convert the text to a Double and determine
      ' if it is a negative number.
      If Double.Parse(Me.Text) < 0 Then
         ' If the number is negative, display it in Red.
         Me.ForeColor = Color.Red
      Else
         ' If the number is not negative, display it in Black.
         Me.ForeColor = Color.Black
      End If
   Catch
      ' If there is an error, display the
      ' text using the system colors.
      Me.ForeColor = SystemColors.ControlText
   End Try

   MyBase.OnTextChanged(e)
End Sub
```

[C#]
```
protected override void OnTextChanged(System.EventArgs e)
{
   try
   {
      // Convert the text to a Double and determine
      // if it is a negative number.
      if(double.Parse(this.Text) < 0)
      {
         // If the number is negative, display it in Red.
         this.ForeColor = Color.Red;
      }
      else
      {
         // If the number is not negative, display it in Black.
         this.ForeColor = Color.Black;
      }
   }
   catch
   {
      // If there is an error, display the
      // text using the system colors.
      this.ForeColor = SystemColors.ControlText;
   }

   base.OnTextChanged(e);
}
```

[C++]
```
protected:
   void OnTextChanged(System::EventArgs* e) {
      try {
         // Convert the text to a Double and determine
         // if it is a negative number.
         if (Double::Parse(this->Text) < 0) {
            // If the number is negative, display it in Red.
            this->ForeColor = Color::Red;
         } else {
            // If the number is not negative, display it in Black.
            this->ForeColor = Color::Black;
         }
      } catch (Exception*) {
         // If there is an error, display the
         // text using the system colors.
         this->ForeColor = SystemColors::ControlText;
      }

      TextBox::OnTextChanged(e);
   }
```

Requirements

Platforms: Windows 98, Windows NT 4.0, Windows Millennium Edition, Windows 2000, Windows XP Home Edition, Windows XP Professional, Windows Server 2003 family

Control.OnStyleChanged Method

Raises the **StyleChanged** event.

```
[Visual Basic]
Protected Overridable Sub OnStyleChanged( _
   ByVal e As EventArgs _
)
[C#]
protected virtual void OnStyleChanged(
   EventArgs e
);
[C++]
protected: virtual void OnStyleChanged(
   EventArgs* e
);
[JScript]
protected function OnStyleChanged(
   e : EventArgs
);
```

Parameters

e

An **EventArgs** that contains the event data.

Remarks

Raising an event invokes the event handler through a delegate.

The **OnStyleChanged** method also allows derived classes to handle the event without attaching a delegate. This is the preferred technique for handling the event in a derived class.

Notes to Inheritors: When overriding **OnStyleChanged** in a derived class, be sure to call the base class's **OnStyleChanged** method so that registered delegates receive the event.

Requirements

Platforms: Windows 98, Windows NT 4.0, Windows Millennium Edition, Windows 2000, Windows XP Home Edition, Windows XP Professional, Windows Server 2003 family

Control.OnSystemColorsChanged Method

Raises the **SystemColorsChanged** event.

```
[Visual Basic]
Protected Overridable Sub OnSystemColorsChanged( _
   ByVal e As EventArgs _
)
[C#]
protected virtual void OnSystemColorsChanged(
   EventArgs e
);
[C++]
protected: virtual void OnSystemColorsChanged(
   EventArgs* e
);
[JScript]
protected function OnSystemColorsChanged(
   e : EventArgs
);
```

Parameters

e

An **EventArgs** that contains the event data.

Remarks

Raising an event invokes the event handler through a delegate.

The **OnSystemColorsChanged** method also allows derived classes to handle the event without attaching a delegate. This is the preferred technique for handling the event in a derived class.

Notes to Inheritors: When overriding **OnSystemColorsChanged** in a derived class, be sure to call the base class's **OnSystemColors-Changed** method so that registered delegates receive the event.

Requirements

Platforms: Windows 98, Windows NT 4.0, Windows Millennium Edition, Windows 2000, Windows XP Home Edition, Windows XP Professional, Windows Server 2003 family

Control.OnTabIndexChanged Method

Raises the **TabIndexChanged** event.

```
[Visual Basic]
Protected Overridable Sub OnTabIndexChanged( _
   ByVal e As EventArgs _
)
[C#]
protected virtual void OnTabIndexChanged(
   EventArgs e
);
[C++]
protected: virtual void OnTabIndexChanged(
   EventArgs* e
);
[JScript]
protected function OnTabIndexChanged(
   e : EventArgs
);
```

Parameters

e

An **EventArgs** that contains the event data.

Remarks

Raising an event invokes the event handler through a delegate.

The **OnTabIndexChanged** method also allows derived classes to handle the event without attaching a delegate. This is the preferred technique for handling the event in a derived class.

Notes to Inheritors: When overriding **OnTabIndexChanged** in a derived class, be sure to call the base class's **OnTabIndexChanged** method so that registered delegates receive the event.

Example

[Visual Basic, C#, C++] The example below is an event-raising method that is executed when the **Text** property value changes. The **Control** class has several methods with the name pattern **On** PropertyName **Changed** that raise the corresponding PropertyName

Changed event when the PropertyName value changes(Property-Name represents the name of the corresponding property).

[Visual Basic, C#, C++] The following example changes the **ForeColor** of a **TextBox** derived class displaying currency data. The example converts the text to a decimal number and changes the **ForeColor** to **Color.Red** if the number is negative and to **Color.Black** if the number is positive. This example assumes you have a class that derives from the **TextBox** class.

[Visual Basic]
```
Protected Overrides Sub OnTextChanged(e As System.EventArgs)
   Try
      ' Convert the text to a Double and determine
      ' if it is a negative number.
      If Double.Parse(Me.Text) < 0 Then
         ' If the number is negative, display it in Red.
         Me.ForeColor = Color.Red
      Else
         ' If the number is not negative, display it in Black.
         Me.ForeColor = Color.Black
      End If
   Catch
      ' If there is an error, display the
      ' text using the system colors.
      Me.ForeColor = SystemColors.ControlText
   End Try

   MyBase.OnTextChanged(e)
End Sub
```

[C#]
```
protected override void OnTextChanged(System.EventArgs e)
{
   try
   {
      // Convert the text to a Double and determine
      // if it is a negative number.
      if(double.Parse(this.Text) < 0)
      {
         // If the number is negative, display it in Red.
         this.ForeColor = Color.Red;
      }
      else
      {
         // If the number is not negative, display it in Black.
         this.ForeColor = Color.Black;
      }
   }
   catch
   {
      // If there is an error, display the
      // text using the system colors.
      this.ForeColor = SystemColors.ControlText;
   }

   base.OnTextChanged(e);
}
```

[C++]
```
protected:
   void OnTextChanged(System::EventArgs* e) {
      try {
         // Convert the text to a Double and determine
         // if it is a negative number.
         if (Double::Parse(this->Text) < 0) {
            // If the number is negative, display it in Red.
            this->ForeColor = Color::Red;
         } else {
            // If the number is not negative, display it in Black.
            this->ForeColor = Color::Black;
         }
      } catch (Exception*) {
         // If there is an error, display the
         // text using the system colors.
         this->ForeColor = SystemColors::ControlText;
      }

      TextBox::OnTextChanged(e);
   }
```

Requirements

Platforms: Windows 98, Windows NT 4.0, Windows Millennium Edition, Windows 2000, Windows XP Home Edition, Windows XP Professional, Windows Server 2003 family

Control.OnTabStopChanged Method

Raises the **TabStopChanged** event.

[Visual Basic]
```
Protected Overridable Sub OnTabStopChanged( _
   ByVal e As EventArgs _
)
```
[C#]
```
protected virtual void OnTabStopChanged(
   EventArgs e
);
```
[C++]
```
protected: virtual void OnTabStopChanged(
   EventArgs* e
);
```
[JScript]
```
protected function OnTabStopChanged(
   e : EventArgs
);
```

Parameters

e

An **EventArgs** that contains the event data.

Remarks

Raising an event invokes the event handler through a delegate.

The **OnTabStopChanged** method also allows derived classes to handle the event without attaching a delegate. This is the preferred technique for handling the event in a derived class.

Notes to Inheritors: When overriding **OnTabStopChanged** in a derived class, be sure to call the base class's **OnTabStopChanged** method so that registered delegates receive the event.

Example

[Visual Basic, C#, C++] The example below is an event-raising method that is executed when the **Text** property value changes. The **Control** class has several methods with the name pattern **On** PropertyName **Changed** that raise the corresponding PropertyName **Changed** event when the PropertyName value changes(Property-Name represents the name of the corresponding property).

[Visual Basic, C#, C++] The following example changes the **ForeColor** of a **TextBox** derived class displaying currency data. The example converts the text to a decimal number and changes the **ForeColor** to **Color.Red** if the number is negative and to **Color.Black** if the number is positive. This example assumes you have a class that derives from the **TextBox** class.

[Visual Basic]
```
Protected Overrides Sub OnTextChanged(e As System.EventArgs)
   Try
      ' Convert the text to a Double and determine
      ' if it is a negative number.
```

```
        If Double.Parse(Me.Text) < 0 Then
            ' If the number is negative, display it in Red.
            Me.ForeColor = Color.Red
        Else
            ' If the number is not negative, display it in Black.
            Me.ForeColor = Color.Black
        End If
    Catch
        ' If there is an error, display the
        ' text using the system colors.
        Me.ForeColor = SystemColors.ControlText
    End Try

    MyBase.OnTextChanged(e)
End Sub
```

[C#]

```
protected override void OnTextChanged(System.EventArgs e)
{
   try
   {
      // Convert the text to a Double and determine
      // if it is a negative number.
      if(double.Parse(this.Text) < 0)
      {
         // If the number is negative, display it in Red.
         this.ForeColor = Color.Red;
      }
      else
      {
         // If the number is not negative, display it in Black.
         this.ForeColor = Color.Black;
      }
   }
   catch
   {
      // If there is an error, display the
      // text using the system colors.
      this.ForeColor = SystemColors.ControlText;
   }

   base.OnTextChanged(e);
}
```

[C++]

```
protected:
   void OnTextChanged(System::EventArgs* e) {
      try {
         // Convert the text to a Double and determine
         // if it is a negative number.
         if (Double::Parse(this->Text) < 0) {
            // If the number is negative, display it in Red.
            this->ForeColor = Color::Red;
         } else {
            // If the number is not negative, display it in Black.
            this->ForeColor = Color::Black;
         }
      } catch (Exception*) {
         // If there is an error, display the
         // text using the system colors.
         this->ForeColor = SystemColors::ControlText;
      }

      TextBox::OnTextChanged(e);
   }
```

Requirements

Platforms: Windows 98, Windows NT 4.0, Windows Millennium Edition, Windows 2000, Windows XP Home Edition, Windows XP Professional, Windows Server 2003 family

Control.OnTextChanged Method

Raises the **TextChanged** event.

[Visual Basic]

```
Protected Overridable Sub OnTextChanged( _
   ByVal e As EventArgs _
)
```

[C#]

```
protected virtual void OnTextChanged(
   EventArgs e
);
```

[C++]

```
protected: virtual void OnTextChanged(
   EventArgs* e
);
```

[JScript]

```
protected function OnTextChanged(
   e : EventArgs
);
```

Parameters

e

An **EventArgs** that contains the event data.

Remarks

Raising an event invokes the event handler through a delegate.

The **OnTextChanged** method also allows derived classes to handle the event without attaching a delegate. This is the preferred technique for handling the event in a derived class.

Notes to Inheritors: When overriding **OnTextChanged** in a derived class, be sure to call the base class's **OnTextChanged** method so that registered delegates receive the event.

Example

[Visual Basic, C#, C++] The following example changes the **ForeColor** of a **TextBox** derived class displaying currency data. The example converts the text to a decimal number and changes the **ForeColor** to **Color.Red** if the number is negative and to **Color.Black** if the number is positive. This example assumes you have a class that derives from the **TextBox** class.

[Visual Basic]

```
Protected Overrides Sub OnTextChanged(e As System.EventArgs)
    Try
        ' Convert the text to a Double and determine
        ' if it is a negative number.
        If Double.Parse(Me.Text) < 0 Then
            ' If the number is negative, display it in Red.
            Me.ForeColor = Color.Red
        Else
            ' If the number is not negative, display it in Black.
            Me.ForeColor = Color.Black
        End If
    Catch
        ' If there is an error, display the
        ' text using the system colors.
        Me.ForeColor = SystemColors.ControlText
    End Try

    MyBase.OnTextChanged(e)
End Sub
```

[C#]

```
protected override void OnTextChanged(System.EventArgs e)
{
   try
   {
      // Convert the text to a Double and determine
```

```
      // if it is a negative number.
      if(double.Parse(this.Text) < 0)
      {
         // If the number is negative, display it in Red.
         this.ForeColor = Color.Red;
      }
      else
      {
         // If the number is not negative, display it in Black.
         this.ForeColor = Color.Black;
      }
   }
   catch
   {
      // If there is an error, display the
      // text using the system colors.
      this.ForeColor = SystemColors.ControlText;
   }

   base.OnTextChanged(e);
}
```

[C++]

```
protected:
   void OnTextChanged(System::EventArgs* e) {
      try {
         // Convert the text to a Double and determine
         // if it is a negative number.
         if (Double::Parse(this->Text) < 0) {
            // If the number is negative, display it in Red.
            this->ForeColor = Color::Red;
         } else {
            // If the number is not negative, display it in Black.
            this->ForeColor = Color::Black;
         }
      } catch (Exception*) {
         // If there is an error, display the
         // text using the system colors.
         this->ForeColor = SystemColors::ControlText;
      }

      TextBox::OnTextChanged(e);
   }
```

Requirements

Platforms: Windows 98, Windows NT 4.0,
Windows Millennium Edition, Windows 2000,
Windows XP Home Edition, Windows XP Professional,
Windows Server 2003 family,
.NET Compact Framework - Windows CE .NET

Control.OnValidated Method

Raises the **Validated** event.

[Visual Basic]

```
Protected Overridable Sub OnValidated( _
   ByVal e As EventArgs _
)
```

[C#]

```
protected virtual void OnValidated(
   EventArgs e
);
```

[C++]

```
protected: virtual void OnValidated(
   EventArgs* e
);
```

[JScript]

```
protected function OnValidated(
   e : EventArgs
);
```

Parameters

e

An **EventArgs** that contains the event data.

Remarks

Raising an event invokes the event handler through a delegate.

The **OnValidated** method also allows derived classes to handle the event without attaching a delegate. This is the preferred technique for handling the event in a derived class.

Notes to Inheritors: When overriding **OnValidated** in a derived class, be sure to call the base class's **OnValidated** method so that registered delegates receive the event.

Requirements

Platforms: Windows 98, Windows NT 4.0,
Windows Millennium Edition, Windows 2000,
Windows XP Home Edition, Windows XP Professional,
Windows Server 2003 family

Control.OnValidating Method

Raises the **Validating** event.

[Visual Basic]

```
Protected Overridable Sub OnValidating( _
   ByVal e As CancelEventArgs _
)
```

[C#]

```
protected virtual void OnValidating(
   CancelEventArgs e
);
```

[C++]

```
protected: virtual void OnValidating(
   CancelEventArgs* e
);
```

[JScript]

```
protected function OnValidating(
   e : CancelEventArgs
);
```

Parameters

e

A **CancelEventArgs** that contains the event data.

Remarks

Raising an event invokes the event handler through a delegate.

The **OnValidating** method also allows derived classes to handle the event without attaching a delegate. This is the preferred technique for handling the event in a derived class.

Notes to Inheritors: When overriding **OnValidating** in a derived class, be sure to call the base class's **OnValidating** method so that registered delegates receive the event.

Requirements

Platforms: Windows 98, Windows NT 4.0,
Windows Millennium Edition, Windows 2000,
Windows XP Home Edition, Windows XP Professional,
Windows Server 2003 family

Control.OnVisibleChanged Method

Raises the **VisibleChanged** event.

[Visual Basic]
```
Protected Overridable Sub OnVisibleChanged( _
   ByVal e As EventArgs _
)
```
[C#]
```
protected virtual void OnVisibleChanged(
   EventArgs e
);
```
[C++]
```
protected: virtual void OnVisibleChanged(
   EventArgs* e
);
```
[JScript]
```
protected function OnVisibleChanged(
   e : EventArgs
);
```

Parameters

e

An **EventArgs** that contains the event data.

Remarks

Raising an event invokes the event handler through a delegate.

The **OnVisibleChanged** method also allows derived classes to handle the event without attaching a delegate. This is the preferred technique for handling the event in a derived class.

Notes to Inheritors: When overriding **OnVisibleChanged** in a derived class, be sure to call the base class's **OnVisibleChanged** method so that registered delegates receive the event.

Example

[Visual Basic, C#, C++] The example below is an event-raising method that is executed when the **Text** property value changes. The **Control** class has several methods with the name pattern **On** PropertyName **Changed** that raise the corresponding PropertyName **Changed** event when the PropertyName value changes(Property-Name represents the name of the corresponding property).

[Visual Basic, C#, C++] The following example changes the **ForeColor** of a **TextBox** derived class displaying currency data. The example converts the text to a decimal number and changes the **ForeColor** to **Color.Red** if the number is negative and to **Color.Black** if the number is positive. This example assumes you have a class that derives from the **TextBox** class.

[Visual Basic]
```
Protected Overrides Sub OnTextChanged(e As System.EventArgs)
   Try
      ' Convert the text to a Double and determine
      ' if it is a negative number.
      If Double.Parse(Me.Text) < 0 Then
         ' If the number is negative, display it in Red.
         Me.ForeColor = Color.Red
      Else
         ' If the number is not negative, display it in Black.
         Me.ForeColor = Color.Black
      End If
   Catch
      ' If there is an error, display the
      ' text using the system colors.
      Me.ForeColor = SystemColors.ControlText
   End Try

   MyBase.OnTextChanged(e)
End Sub
```

[C#]
```
protected override void OnTextChanged(System.EventArgs e)
{
   try
   {
      // Convert the text to a Double and determine
      // if it is a negative number.
      if(double.Parse(this.Text) < 0)
      {
         // If the number is negative, display it in Red.
         this.ForeColor = Color.Red;
      }
      else
      {
         // If the number is not negative, display it in Black.
         this.ForeColor = Color.Black;
      }
   }
   catch
   {
      // If there is an error, display the
      // text using the system colors.
      this.ForeColor = SystemColors.ControlText;
   }

   base.OnTextChanged(e);
}
```

[C++]
```
protected:
   void OnTextChanged(System::EventArgs* e) {
      try {
         // Convert the text to a Double and determine
         // if it is a negative number.
         if (Double::Parse(this->Text) < 0) {
            // If the number is negative, display it in Red.
            this->ForeColor = Color::Red;
         } else {
            // If the number is not negative, display it in Black.
            this->ForeColor = Color::Black;
         }
      } catch (Exception*) {
         // If there is an error, display the
         // text using the system colors.
         this->ForeColor = SystemColors::ControlText;
      }

      TextBox::OnTextChanged(e);
   }
```

Requirements

Platforms: Windows 98, Windows NT 4.0, Windows Millennium Edition, Windows 2000, Windows XP Home Edition, Windows XP Professional, Windows Server 2003 family

Control.PerformLayout Method

Forces the control to apply layout logic to child controls.

Overload List

Forces the control to apply layout logic to all its child controls.

[Visual Basic] **Overloads Public Sub PerformLayout()**

[C#] **public void PerformLayout();**

[C++] **public: void PerformLayout();**

[JScript] **public function PerformLayout();**

Forces the control to apply layout logic to all its child controls.

[Visual Basic] **Overloads Public Sub PerformLayout(Control, String)**

[C#] **public void PerformLayout(Control, string);**

[C++] **public: void PerformLayout(Control*, String*);**

[JScript] **public function PerformLayout(Control, String);**

Control.PerformLayout Method ()

Forces the control to apply layout logic to all its child controls.

```
[Visual Basic]
Overloads Public Sub PerformLayout()
[C#]
public void PerformLayout();
[C++]
public: void PerformLayout();
[JScript]
public function PerformLayout();
```

Remarks

If the **SuspendLayout** method was called before calling the **PerformLayout** method, the **Layout** event is suppressed.

The **AffectedControl** and **AffectedProperty** properties of the **LayoutEventArgs** object created are set to a null reference (**Nothing** in Visual Basic) if no values were provided when the **PerformLayout** method was called.

Requirements

Platforms: Windows 98, Windows NT 4.0, Windows Millennium Edition, Windows 2000, Windows XP Home Edition, Windows XP Professional, Windows Server 2003 family

Control.PerformLayout Method (Control, String)

Forces the control to apply layout logic to all its child controls.

```
[Visual Basic]
Overloads Public Sub PerformLayout( _
   ByVal affectedControl As Control, _
   ByVal affectedProperty As String _
)
[C#]
public void PerformLayout(
   Control affectedControl,
   string affectedProperty
);
[C++]
public: void PerformLayout(
   Control* affectedControl,
   String* affectedProperty
);
[JScript]
public function PerformLayout(
   affectedControl : Control,
   affectedProperty : String
);
```

Parameters

affectedControl
A **Control** that represents the most recently changed control.

affectedProperty
The name of the most recently changed property on the control.

Remarks

If the **SuspendLayout** method was called before calling the **PerformLayout** method, the **Layout** event is suppressed.

The *affectedControl* and *affectedProperty* parameters can both be set to a null reference (**Nothing** in Visual Basic). Doing so causes the **AffectedControl** and **AffectedProperty** properties of the **LayoutEventArgs** object created to be set to a null reference (**Nothing**).

Requirements

Platforms: Windows 98, Windows NT 4.0, Windows Millennium Edition, Windows 2000, Windows XP Home Edition, Windows XP Professional, Windows Server 2003 family

Control.PointToClient Method

Computes the location of the specified screen point into client coordinates.

```
[Visual Basic]
Public Function PointToClient( _
   ByVal p As Point _
) As Point
[C#]
public Point PointToClient(
   Point p
);
[C++]
public: Point PointToClient(
   Point p
);
[JScript]
public function PointToClient(
   p : Point
) : Point;
```

Parameters

p
The screen coordinate **Point** to convert.

Return Value

A **Point** that represents the converted **Point**, *p*, in client coordinates.

Example

[Visual Basic, C#, C++] The following example enables the user to drag an image or image file onto the form, and have it be displayed at the point on it is dropped. The **OnPaint** method is overridden to repaint the image each time the form is painted; otherwise the image would only persist until the next repainting. The **DragEnter** event-handling method determines the type of data being dragged into the form and provides the appropriate feedback. The **DragDrop** event-handling method displays the image on the form, if an **Image** can be created from the data. Because the **DragEventArgs.X** and **DragEventArgs.Y** values are screen coordinates, the example uses the **PointToClient** method to convert them to client coordinates.

```
[Visual Basic]
Private picture As Image
Private pictureLocation As Point

Public Sub New()
   ' Enable drag-and-drop operations.
   Me.AllowDrop = True
End Sub
```

```
Protected Overrides Sub OnPaint(ByVal e As PaintEventArgs)
   MyBase.OnPaint(e)

   ' If there is an image and it has a location,
   ' paint it when the Form is repainted.
   If Not (Me.picture Is Nothing) And _
     Not (Me.pictureLocation.Equals(Point.Empty)) Then
      e.Graphics.DrawImage(Me.picture, Me.pictureLocation)
   End If
End Sub

Private Sub Form1_DragDrop(ByVal sender As Object, _
  ByVal e As DragEventArgs) Handles MyBase.DragDrop
   ' Handle FileDrop data.
   If e.Data.GetDataPresent(DataFormats.FileDrop) Then
      ' Assign the file names to a string array, in
      ' case the user has selected multiple files.
      Dim files As String() =                                              ┘
CType(e.Data.GetData(DataFormats.FileDrop), String())
      Try
         ' Assign the first image to the 'picture' variable.
         Me.picture = Image.FromFile(files(0))
         ' Set the picture location equal to the drop point.
         Me.pictureLocation = Me.PointToClient(New Point(e.X, e.Y))
      Catch ex As Exception
         MessageBox.Show(ex.Message)
         Return
      End Try
   End If

   ' Handle Bitmap data.
   If e.Data.GetDataPresent(DataFormats.Bitmap) Then
      Try
         ' Create an Image and assign it to the picture variable.
         Me.picture = CType(e.Data.GetData(DataFormats.Bitmap), Image)
         ' Set the picture location equal to the drop point.
         Me.pictureLocation = Me.PointToClient(New Point(e.X, e.Y))
      Catch ex As Exception
         MessageBox.Show(ex.Message)
         Return
      End Try
   End If

   ' Force the form to be redrawn with the image.
   Me.Invalidate()
End Sub

Private Sub Form1_DragEnter(ByVal sender As Object, _
  ByVal e As DragEventArgs) Handles MyBase.DragEnter
   ' If the data is a file or a bitmap, display the copy cursor.
   If e.Data.GetDataPresent(DataFormats.Bitmap) _
      Or e.Data.GetDataPresent(DataFormats.FileDrop) Then
      e.Effect = DragDropEffects.Copy
   Else
      e.Effect = DragDropEffects.None
   End If
End Sub
```

[C#]

```
private Image picture;
private Point pictureLocation;

public Form1()
{
   // Enable drag-and-drop operations and
   // add handlers for DragEnter and DragDrop.
   this.AllowDrop = true;
   this.DragDrop += new DragEventHandler(this.Form1_DragDrop);
   this.DragEnter += new DragEventHandler(this.Form1_DragEnter);
}

protected override void OnPaint(PaintEventArgs e)
{
   // If there is an image and it has a location,
   // paint it when the Form is repainted.
   base.OnPaint(e);
   if(this.picture != null && this.pictureLocation != Point.Empty)
   {
      e.Graphics.DrawImage(this.picture, this.pictureLocation);
   }
}

private void Form1_DragDrop(object sender, DragEventArgs e)
{
   // Handle FileDrop data.
   if(e.Data.GetDataPresent(DataFormats.FileDrop) )
   {
      // Assign the file names to a string array, in
      // case the user has selected multiple files.
      string[] files = (string[])e.Data.GetData(DataFormats.FileDrop);
      try
      {
         // Assign the first image to the picture variable.
         this.picture = Image.FromFile(files[0]);
         // Set the picture location equal to the drop point.
         this.pictureLocation = this.PointToClient(new Point               ┘
(e.X, e.Y) );
      }
      catch(Exception ex)
      {
         MessageBox.Show(ex.Message);
         return;
      }
   }

   // Handle Bitmap data.
   if(e.Data.GetDataPresent(DataFormats.Bitmap) )
   {
      try
      {
         // Create an Image and assign it to the picture variable.
         this.picture = (Image)e.Data.GetData(DataFormats.Bitmap);
         // Set the picture location equal to the drop point.
         this.pictureLocation = this.PointToClient(new Point               ┘
(e.X, e.Y) );
      }
      catch(Exception ex)
      {
         MessageBox.Show(ex.Message);
         return;
      }
   }
   // Force the form to be redrawn with the image.
   this.Invalidate();
}

private void Form1_DragEnter(object sender, DragEventArgs e)
{
   // If the data is a file or a bitmap, display the copy cursor.
   if (e.Data.GetDataPresent(DataFormats.Bitmap) ||
      e.Data.GetDataPresent(DataFormats.FileDrop) )
   {
      e.Effect = DragDropEffects.Copy;
   }
   else
   {
      e.Effect = DragDropEffects.None;
   }
}
```

[C++]

```
private:
   Image* picture;
   Point pictureLocation;

public:
   Form1() {
      // Enable drag-and-drop operations and
      // add handlers for DragEnter and DragDrop.
      this->AllowDrop = true;
```

```
      this->DragDrop += new DragEventHandler(this, Form1_DragDrop);
      this->DragEnter += new DragEventHandler(this, Form1_DragEnter);
   }

protected:
   void OnPaint(PaintEventArgs* e) {
      // If there is an image and it has a location,
      // paint it when the Form is repainted.
      Form::OnPaint(e);
      if (this->picture != 0 && this->pictureLocation !=          ↵
Point::Empty) {
         e->Graphics->DrawImage(this->picture, this->pictureLocation);
      }
   }

private:
   void Form1_DragDrop(Object* sender, DragEventArgs* e) {
      // Handle FileDrop data.
      if (e->Data->GetDataPresent(DataFormats::FileDrop)) {
         // Assign the file names to a String* array, in
         // case the user has selected multiple files.
         String* files[] = (String*[])e->Data-
>GetData(DataFormats::FileDrop);
         try {
            // Assign the first image to the picture variable.
            this->picture = Image::FromFile(files[0]);
            // Set the picture location equal to the drop point.
            this->pictureLocation = this->PointToClient            ↵
 ( Point(e->X, e->Y));
         } catch (Exception* ex) {
            MessageBox::Show(ex->Message);
            return;
         }
      }

      // Handle Bitmap data.
      if (e->Data->GetDataPresent(DataFormats::Bitmap)) {
         try {
            // Create an Image and assign it to the picture variable.
            this->picture = dynamic_cast<Image*>(e->Data-         ↵
>GetData(DataFormats::Bitmap));
            // Set the picture location equal to the drop point.
            this->pictureLocation = this->PointToClient( Point    ↵
 (e->X, e->Y));
         } catch (Exception* ex) {
            MessageBox::Show(ex->Message);
            return;
         }
      }
      // Force the form to be redrawn with the image.
      this->Invalidate();
   }

   void Form1_DragEnter(Object* sender, DragEventArgs* e) {
      // If the data is a file or a bitmap, display the copy cursor.
      if (e->Data->GetDataPresent(DataFormats::Bitmap) ||
         e->Data->GetDataPresent(DataFormats::FileDrop)) {
            e->Effect = DragDropEffects::Copy;
         } else {
            e->Effect = DragDropEffects::None;
         }
   }
```

Requirements

Platforms: Windows 98, Windows NT 4.0,
Windows Millennium Edition, Windows 2000,
Windows XP Home Edition, Windows XP Professional,
Windows Server 2003 family,
.NET Compact Framework - Windows CE .NET

Control.PointToScreen Method

Computes the location of the specified client point into screen coordinates.

```
[Visual Basic]
Public Function PointToScreen( _
   ByVal p As Point _
) As Point
[C#]
public Point PointToScreen(
   Point p
);
[C++]
public: Point PointToScreen(
   Point p
);
[JScript]
public function PointToScreen(
   p : Point
) : Point;
```

Parameters

p
: The client coordinate **Point** to convert.

Return Value

A **Point** that represents the converted **Point**, *p*, in screen coordinates.

Requirements

Platforms: Windows 98, Windows NT 4.0,
Windows Millennium Edition, Windows 2000,
Windows XP Home Edition, Windows XP Professional,
Windows Server 2003 family,
.NET Compact Framework - Windows CE .NET

Control.PreProcessMessage Method

Preprocesses input messages within the message loop before they are dispatched.

```
[Visual Basic]
Public Overridable Function PreProcessMessage( _
   ByRef msg As Message _
) As Boolean
[C#]
public virtual bool PreProcessMessage(
   ref Message msg
);
[C++]
public: virtual bool PreProcessMessage(
   Message* msg
);
[JScript]
public function PreProcessMessage(
   msg : Message
) : Boolean;
```

Parameters

msg
: A **Message**, passed by reference, that represents the message to process.

Return Value

true if the message was processed by the control; otherwise, **false**.

Remarks

This method is only called when the control is hosted in a Windows Forms application or as an ActiveX control.

Requirements

Platforms: Windows 98, Windows NT 4.0, Windows Millennium Edition, Windows 2000, Windows XP Home Edition, Windows XP Professional, Windows Server 2003 family

.NET Framework Security:

- **UIPermission** for all windows for inheriting classes to call this method. Associated enumeration: **UIPermissionWindow.AllWindows**
- **UIPermission** for all windows for the immediate caller to call this method. Associated enumeration: **UIPermissionWindow.AllWindows**

Control.ProcessCmdKey Method

Processes a command key.

[Visual Basic]
```
Protected Overridable Function ProcessCmdKey( _
   ByRef msg As Message, _
   ByVal keyData As Keys _
) As Boolean
```
[C#]
```
protected virtual bool ProcessCmdKey(
   ref Message msg,
   Keys keyData
);
```
[C++]
```
protected: virtual bool ProcessCmdKey(
   Message* msg,
   Keys keyData
);
```
[JScript]
```
protected function ProcessCmdKey(
   msg : Message,
   keyData : Keys
) : Boolean;
```

Parameters

msg

A **Message**, passed by reference, that represents the window message to process.

keyData

One of the **Keys** values that represents the key to process.

Return Value

true if the character was processed by the control; otherwise, **false**.

Remarks

This method is called during message preprocessing to handle command keys. Command keys are keys that always take precedence over regular input keys. Examples of command keys include accelerators and menu shortcuts. The method must return **true** to indicate that it has processed the command key, or **false** to indicate that the key is not a command key. This method is only called when the control is hosted in a Windows Forms application or as an ActiveX control.

The **ProcessCmdKey** method first determines whether the control has a **ContextMenu**, and if so, allows the **ContextMenu** process the command key. If the command key is not a menu shortcut and the control has a parent, the key is passed to the parent's **ProcessCmdKey** method. The net effect is that command keys are "bubbled" up the control hierarchy. In addition to the key the user pressed, the key data also indicates which, if any, modifier keys were pressed at the same time as the key. Modifier keys include the SHIFT, CTRL, and ALT keys.

Notes to Inheritors: When overriding the **ProcessCmdKey** method in a derived class, a control should return **true** to indicate that it has processed the key. For keys that are not processed by the control, the result of calling the base class's **ProcessCmdKey** method should be returned. Controls will seldom, if ever, need to override this method.

Requirements

Platforms: Windows 98, Windows NT 4.0, Windows Millennium Edition, Windows 2000, Windows XP Home Edition, Windows XP Professional, Windows Server 2003 family

.NET Framework Security:

- **UIPermission** for all windows for inheriting classes to call this method. Associated enumeration: **UIPermissionWindow.AllWindows**

Control.ProcessDialogChar Method

Processes a dialog character.

[Visual Basic]
```
Protected Overridable Function ProcessDialogChar( _
   ByVal charCode As Char _
) As Boolean
```
[C#]
```
protected virtual bool ProcessDialogChar(
   char charCode
);
```
[C++]
```
protected: virtual bool ProcessDialogChar(
   __wchar_t charCode
);
```
[JScript]
```
protected function ProcessDialogChar(
   charCode : Char
) : Boolean;
```

Parameters

charCode

The character to process.

Return Value

true if the character was processed by the control; otherwise, **false**.

Remarks

This method is called during message preprocessing to handle dialog characters, such as control mnemonics. This method is called only if the **IsInputChar** method indicates that the control is not processing the character. The **ProcessDialogChar** method simply sends the character to the parent's **ProcessDialogChar** method, or returns **false** if the control has no parent. The **Form** class overrides this method to perform actual processing of dialog characters. This method is only called when the control is hosted in a Windows Forms application or as an ActiveX control.

Notes to Inheritors: When overriding the **ProcessDialogChar** method in a derived class, a control should return **true** to indicate that it has processed the character. For characters that are not processed by the control, the result of calling the base class's **ProcessDialogChar** method should be returned. Controls will seldom, if ever, need to override this method.

Requirements

Platforms: Windows 98, Windows NT 4.0, Windows Millennium Edition, Windows 2000, Windows XP Home Edition, Windows XP Professional, Windows Server 2003 family

.NET Framework Security:

- **UIPermission** for all windows for inheriting classes to call this method. Associated enumeration: **UIPermissionWindow.AllWindows**

Control.ProcessDialogKey Method

Processes a dialog key.

[Visual Basic]
```
Protected Overridable Function ProcessDialogKey( _
   ByVal keyData As Keys _
) As Boolean
```
[C#]
```
protected virtual bool ProcessDialogKey(
   Keys keyData
);
```
[C++]
```
protected: virtual bool ProcessDialogKey(
   Keys keyData
);
```
[JScript]
```
protected function ProcessDialogKey(
   keyData : Keys
) : Boolean;
```

Parameters

keyData
One of the **Keys** values that represents the key to process.

Return Value

true if the key was processed by the control; otherwise, **false**.

Remarks

This method is called during message preprocessing to handle dialog characters, such as TAB, RETURN, ESCAPE, and arrow keys. This method is called only if the **IsInputKey** method indicates that the control is not processing the key. The **ProcessDialogKey** simply sends the character to the parent's **ProcessDialogKey** method, or returns **false** if the control has no parent. The **Form** class overrides this method to perform actual processing of dialog keys. This method is only called when the control is hosted in a Windows Forms application or as an ActiveX control.

Notes to Inheritors: When overriding the **ProcessDialogKey** method in a derived class, a control should return **true** to indicate that it has processed the key. For keys that are not processed by the control, the result of calling the base class's **ProcessDialogChar** method should be returned. Controls will seldom, if ever, need to override this method.

Requirements

Platforms: Windows 98, Windows NT 4.0, Windows Millennium Edition, Windows 2000, Windows XP Home Edition, Windows XP Professional, Windows Server 2003 family

.NET Framework Security:

- **UIPermission** for all windows for inheriting classes to call this method. Associated enumeration: **UIPermissionWindow.AllWindows**

Control.ProcessKeyEventArgs Method

Processes a key message and generates the appropriate control events.

[Visual Basic]
```
Protected Overridable Function ProcessKeyEventArgs( _
   ByRef m As Message _
) As Boolean
```
[C#]
```
protected virtual bool ProcessKeyEventArgs(
   ref Message m
);
```
[C++]
```
protected: virtual bool ProcessKeyEventArgs(
   Message* m
);
```
[JScript]
```
protected function ProcessKeyEventArgs(
   m : Message
) : Boolean;
```

Parameters

m
A **Message**, passed by reference, that represents the window message to process.

Return Value

true if the message was processed by the control; otherwise, **false**.

Remarks

This method is called when a control receives a keyboard message. The method is responsible for generating the appropriate key events for the message by calling the **OnKeyPress**, **OnKeyDown**, or **OnKeyUp** methods. The *m* parameter contains the window message that must be processed. Possible values for the **Message.Msg** property are WM_CHAR, WM_KEYDOWN, WM_SYSKEY-DOWN, WM_KEYUP, WM_SYSKEYUP, and WM_IMECHAR.

Notes to Inheritors: When overriding the **ProcessKeyEventArgs** method in a derived class, a control should return **true** to indicate that it has processed the key. For keys that are not processed by the control, the result of calling the base class's **ProcessKeyEventArgs** method should be returned. Controls will seldom, if ever, need to override this method.

Requirements

Platforms: Windows 98, Windows NT 4.0, Windows Millennium Edition, Windows 2000, Windows XP Home Edition, Windows XP Professional, Windows Server 2003 family

.NET Framework Security:

- **UIPermission** for all windows for inheriting classes to call this method. Associated enumeration: **UIPermissionWindow.AllWindows**

Control.ProcessKeyMessage Method

Processes a keyboard message.

```
[Visual Basic]
Protected Friend Overridable Function ProcessKeyMessage( _
   ByRef m As Message _
) As Boolean
[C#]
protected internal virtual bool ProcessKeyMessage(
   ref Message m
);
[C++]
protected public: virtual bool ProcessKeyMessage(
   Message* m
);
[JScript]
protected internal function ProcessKeyMessage(
   m : Message
) : Boolean;
```

Parameters

m

A **Message**, passed by reference, that represents the window message to process.

Return Value

true if the message was processed by the control; otherwise, **false**.

Remarks

This method is called when a control receives a keyboard message. The method first determines whether the control has a parent; if so, it calls the parent's **ProcessKeyMessage** method. If the parent's **ProcessKeyMessage** method does not process the message then the **ProcessKeyEventArgs** method is called to generate the appropriate keyboard events. The *m* parameter contains the window message that must be processed. Possible values for the **Message.Msg** property are WM_CHAR, WM_KEYDOWN, WM_SYSKEY-DOWN, WM_KEYUP, and WM_SYSKEYUP.

Notes to Inheritors: When overriding the **ProcessKeyMessage** method, a control should return **true** to indicate that it has processed the key. For keys that are not processed by the control, the result of the base class's **ProcessKeyEventArgs** should be returned. Controls will seldom, if ever, need to override this method.

Requirements

Platforms: Windows 98, Windows NT 4.0, Windows Millennium Edition, Windows 2000, Windows XP Home Edition, Windows XP Professional, Windows Server 2003 family

.NET Framework Security:

- **UIPermission** for all windows for inheriting classes to call this method. Associated enumeration: **UIPermissionWindow.AllWindows**

Control.ProcessKeyPreview Method

Previews a keyboard message.

```
[Visual Basic]
Protected Overridable Function ProcessKeyPreview( _
   ByRef m As Message _
) As Boolean
[C#]
protected virtual bool ProcessKeyPreview(
   ref Message m
);
[C++]
protected: virtual bool ProcessKeyPreview(
   Message* m
);
[JScript]
protected function ProcessKeyPreview(
   m : Message
) : Boolean;
```

Parameters

m

A **Message**, passed by reference, that represents the window message to process.

Return Value

true if the message was processed by the control; otherwise, **false**.

Remarks

This method is called by a child control when the child control receives a keyboard message. The child control calls this method before generating any keyboard events for the message. If this method returns **true**, the child control considers the message processed and does not generate any keyboard events. The *m* parameter contains the window message to preview. Possible values for the **Message.Msg** property are WM_CHAR, WM_KEYDOWN, WM_SYSKEYDOWN, WM_KEYUP, and WM_SYSKEYUP. The **ProcessKeyPreview** method simply sends the character to the parent's **ProcessKeyPreview** method, or returns **false** if the control has no parent. The **Form** class overrides this method to perform actual processing of dialog keys.

Notes to Inheritors: When overriding the **ProcessKeyPreview** method in a derived class, a control should return **true** to indicate that it has processed the key. For keys that are not processed by the control, the result of calling the base class's **ProcessKeyEventArgs** method should be returned.

Requirements

Platforms: Windows 98, Windows NT 4.0, Windows Millennium Edition, Windows 2000, Windows XP Home Edition, Windows XP Professional, Windows Server 2003 family

.NET Framework Security:

- **UIPermission** for all windows for inheriting classes to call this method. Associated enumeration: **UIPermissionWindow.AllWindows**

Control.ProcessMnemonic Method

Processes a mnemonic character.

```
[Visual Basic]
Protected Overridable Function ProcessMnemonic( _
   ByVal charCode As Char _
) As Boolean
[C#]
protected virtual bool ProcessMnemonic(
   char charCode
);
```

```
[C++]
protected: virtual bool ProcessMnemonic(
   __wchar_t charCode
);
[JScript]
protected function ProcessMnemonic(
   charCode : Char
) : Boolean;
```

Parameters

charCode
The character to process.

Return Value

true if the character was processed as a mnemonic by the control; otherwise, **false**.

Remarks

This method is called to give a control the opportunity to process a mnemonic character. The method should determine whether the control is in a state to process mnemonics and if whether the given character represents a mnemonic. If so, the method should perform the action associated with the mnemonic and return **true**. If not, the method should return **false**. Implementations of this method often use the **IsMnemonic** method to determine whether the given character matches a mnemonic in the control's text.

For example:

```
[C#]
if (CanSelect && IsMnemonic(charCode, MyControl.Text) {
      // Perform action associated with mnemonic.
      }
```

This default implementation of the **ProcessMnemonic** method simply returns **false** to indicate that the control has no mnemonic.

Requirements

Platforms: Windows 98, Windows NT 4.0, Windows Millennium Edition, Windows 2000, Windows XP Home Edition, Windows XP Professional, Windows Server 2003 family

.NET Framework Security:

- **UIPermission** for all windows for inheriting classes to call this method. Associated enumeration: **UIPermissionWindow.AllWindows**

Control.RaiseDragEvent Method

This member supports the .NET Framework infrastructure and is not intended to be used directly from your code.

```
[Visual Basic]
Protected Sub RaiseDragEvent( _
   ByVal key As Object, _
   ByVal e As DragEventArgs _
)
[C#]
protected void RaiseDragEvent(
   object key,
   DragEventArgs e
);
[C++]
protected: void RaiseDragEvent(
   Object* key,
   DragEventArgs* e
);
[JScript]
protected function RaiseDragEvent(
   key : Object,
   e : DragEventArgs
);
```

Control.RaiseKeyEvent Method

This member supports the .NET Framework infrastructure and is not intended to be used directly from your code.

```
[Visual Basic]
Protected Sub RaiseKeyEvent( _
   ByVal key As Object, _
   ByVal e As KeyEventArgs _
)
[C#]
protected void RaiseKeyEvent(
   object key,
   KeyEventArgs e
);
[C++]
protected: void RaiseKeyEvent(
   Object* key,
   KeyEventArgs* e
);
[JScript]
protected function RaiseKeyEvent(
   key : Object,
   e : KeyEventArgs
);
```

Control.RaiseMouseEvent Method

This member supports the .NET Framework infrastructure and is not intended to be used directly from your code.

```
[Visual Basic]
Protected Sub RaiseMouseEvent( _
   ByVal key As Object, _
   ByVal e As MouseEventArgs _
)
[C#]
protected void RaiseMouseEvent(
   object key,
   MouseEventArgs e
);
[C++]
protected: void RaiseMouseEvent(
   Object* key,
   MouseEventArgs* e
);
[JScript]
protected function RaiseMouseEvent(
   key : Object,
   e : MouseEventArgs
);
```

Control.RaisePaintEvent Method

This member supports the .NET Framework infrastructure and is not intended to be used directly from your code.

```
[Visual Basic]
Protected Sub RaisePaintEvent( _
   ByVal key As Object, _
   ByVal e As PaintEventArgs _
)
[C#]
protected void RaisePaintEvent(
   object key,
   PaintEventArgs e
);
[C++]
protected: void RaisePaintEvent(
   Object* key,
   PaintEventArgs* e
);
[JScript]
protected function RaisePaintEvent(
   key : Object,
   e : PaintEventArgs
);
```

Control.RecreateHandle Method

Forces the re-creation of the handle for the control.

```
[Visual Basic]
Protected Sub RecreateHandle()
[C#]
protected void RecreateHandle();
[C++]
protected: void RecreateHandle();
[JScript]
protected function RecreateHandle();
```

Requirements

Platforms: Windows 98, Windows NT 4.0,
Windows Millennium Edition, Windows 2000,
Windows XP Home Edition, Windows XP Professional,
Windows Server 2003 family

Control.RectangleToClient Method

Computes the size and location of the specified screen rectangle in client coordinates.

```
[Visual Basic]
Public Function RectangleToClient( _
   ByVal r As Rectangle _
) As Rectangle
[C#]
public Rectangle RectangleToClient(
   Rectangle r
);
[C++]
public: Rectangle RectangleToClient(
   Rectangle r
);
[JScript]
public function RectangleToClient(
   r : Rectangle
) : Rectangle;
```

Parameters

r

The screen coordinate **Rectangle** to convert.

Return Value

A **Rectangle** that represents the converted **Rectangle**, *r*, in client coordinates.

Requirements

Platforms: Windows 98, Windows NT 4.0,
Windows Millennium Edition, Windows 2000,
Windows XP Home Edition, Windows XP Professional,
Windows Server 2003 family,
.NET Compact Framework - Windows CE .NET

Control.RectangleToScreen Method

Computes the size and location of the specified client rectangle in screen coordinates.

```
[Visual Basic]
Public Function RectangleToScreen( _
   ByVal r As Rectangle _
) As Rectangle
[C#]
public Rectangle RectangleToScreen(
   Rectangle r
);
[C++]
public: Rectangle RectangleToScreen(
   Rectangle r
);
[JScript]
public function RectangleToScreen(
   r : Rectangle
) : Rectangle;
```

Parameters

r

The screen coordinate **Rectangle** object to convert.

Return Value

A **Rectangle** that represents the converted **Rectangle**, *p*, in screen coordinates.

Requirements

Platforms: Windows 98, Windows NT 4.0,
Windows Millennium Edition, Windows 2000,
Windows XP Home Edition, Windows XP Professional,
Windows Server 2003 family,
.NET Compact Framework - Windows CE .NET

Control.ReflectMessage Method

Reflects the specified message to the control that is bound to the specified handle.

[Visual Basic]
```
Protected Shared Function ReflectMessage( _
   ByVal hWnd As IntPtr, _
   ByRef m As Message _
) As Boolean
```
[C#]
```
protected static bool ReflectMessage(
   IntPtr hWnd,
   ref Message m
);
```
[C++]
```
protected: static bool ReflectMessage(
   IntPtr hWnd,
   Message* m
);
```
[JScript]
```
protected static function ReflectMessage(
   hWnd : IntPtr,
   m : Message
) : Boolean;
```

Parameters

hWnd
: An **IntPtr** representing the handle of the control to reflect the message to.

m
: A **Message** representing the Windows message to reflect.

Return Value

true if the message was reflected; otherwise, **false**.

Remarks

The **ReflectMessage** method is an infrastructure method and typically should not be called from your code.

If the *hWnd* parameter does not represent a valid control, the **ReflectMessage** method returns **false**.

Because Windows messages are returned to the top-level window, the **ReflectMessage** method is used to propagate the return message to the control that sent the message. For more information about Windows messages, see the General Introduction to the Common Controls topic in the Platform SDK documentation of the MSDN Library.

Requirements

Platforms: Windows 98, Windows NT 4.0, Windows Millennium Edition, Windows 2000, Windows XP Home Edition, Windows XP Professional, Windows Server 2003 family

.NET Framework Security:

- **UIPermission** for all windows to call this method. Associated enumeration: **UIPermissionWindow.AllWindows**

Control.Refresh Method

Forces the control to invalidate its client area and immediately redraw itself and any child controls.

[Visual Basic]
```
Public Overridable Sub Refresh()
```
[C#]
```
public virtual void Refresh();
```
[C++]
```
public: virtual void Refresh();
```
[JScript]
```
public function Refresh();
```

Remarks

Notes to Inheritors: When overriding **Refresh** in a derived class, be sure to call the base class's **Refresh** method so the control and its child controls are invalidated and redrawn.

Requirements

Platforms: Windows 98, Windows NT 4.0, Windows Millennium Edition, Windows 2000, Windows XP Home Edition, Windows XP Professional, Windows Server 2003 family, .NET Compact Framework - Windows CE .NET

Control.ResetBackColor Method

Resets the **BackColor** property to its default value.

[Visual Basic]
```
Public Overridable Sub ResetBackColor()
```
[C#]
```
public virtual void ResetBackColor();
```
[C++]
```
public: virtual void ResetBackColor();
```
[JScript]
```
public function ResetBackColor();
```

Remarks

You typically use this method if you are either creating a designer for the **Control** or creating your own control incorporating the **Control**.

Requirements

Platforms: Windows 98, Windows NT 4.0, Windows Millennium Edition, Windows 2000, Windows XP Home Edition, Windows XP Professional, Windows Server 2003 family

Control.ResetBindings Method

Resets the **DataBindings** property to its default value.

[Visual Basic]
```
Public Sub ResetBindings()
```
[C#]
```
public void ResetBindings();
```
[C++]
```
public: void ResetBindings();
```
[JScript]
```
public function ResetBindings();
```

Remarks

You typically use this method if you are either creating a designer for the **Control** or creating your own control incorporating the **Control**.

Requirements

Platforms: Windows 98, Windows NT 4.0, Windows Millennium Edition, Windows 2000, Windows XP Home Edition, Windows XP Professional, Windows Server 2003 family

Control.ResetCursor Method

Resets the **Cursor** property to its default value.

[Visual Basic]
```
Public Overridable Sub ResetCursor()
```
[C#]
```
public virtual void ResetCursor();
```
[C++]
```
public: virtual void ResetCursor();
```
[JScript]
```
public function ResetCursor();
```

Remarks

You typically use this method if you are either creating a designer for the **Control** or creating your own control incorporating the **Control**.

Requirements

Platforms: Windows 98, Windows NT 4.0, Windows Millennium Edition, Windows 2000, Windows XP Home Edition, Windows XP Professional, Windows Server 2003 family

Control.ResetFont Method

Resets the **Font** property to its default value.

[Visual Basic]
```
Public Overridable Sub ResetFont()
```
[C#]
```
public virtual void ResetFont();
```
[C++]
```
public: virtual void ResetFont();
```
[JScript]
```
public function ResetFont();
```

Remarks

You typically use this method if you are either creating a designer for the **Control** or creating your own control incorporating the **Control**.

Requirements

Platforms: Windows 98, Windows NT 4.0, Windows Millennium Edition, Windows 2000, Windows XP Home Edition, Windows XP Professional, Windows Server 2003 family

Control.ResetForeColor Method

Resets the **ForeColor** property to its default value.

[Visual Basic]
```
Public Overridable Sub ResetForeColor()
```
[C#]
```
public virtual void ResetForeColor();
```
[C++]
```
public: virtual void ResetForeColor();
```
[JScript]
```
public function ResetForeColor();
```

Remarks

You typically use this method if you are either creating a designer for the **Control** or creating your own control incorporating the **Control**.

Requirements

Platforms: Windows 98, Windows NT 4.0, Windows Millennium Edition, Windows 2000, Windows XP Home Edition, Windows XP Professional, Windows Server 2003 family

Control.ResetImeMode Method

Resets the **ImeMode** property to its default value.

[Visual Basic]
```
Public Sub ResetImeMode()
```
[C#]
```
public void ResetImeMode();
```
[C++]
```
public: void ResetImeMode();
```
[JScript]
```
public function ResetImeMode();
```

Remarks

You typically use this method if you are either creating a designer for the **Control** or creating your own control incorporating the **Control**.

Requirements

Platforms: Windows 98, Windows NT 4.0, Windows Millennium Edition, Windows 2000, Windows XP Home Edition, Windows XP Professional, Windows Server 2003 family

Control.ResetMouseEventArgs Method

This member supports the .NET Framework infrastructure and is not intended to be used directly from your code.

[Visual Basic]
```
Protected Sub ResetMouseEventArgs()
```
[C#]
```
protected void ResetMouseEventArgs();
```
[C++]
```
protected: void ResetMouseEventArgs();
```
[JScript]
```
protected function ResetMouseEventArgs();
```

Control.ResetRightToLeft Method

Resets the **RightToLeft** property to its default value.

[Visual Basic]
```
Public Overridable Sub ResetRightToLeft()
```
[C#]
```
public virtual void ResetRightToLeft();
```
[C++]
```
public: virtual void ResetRightToLeft();
```
[JScript]
```
public function ResetRightToLeft();
```

Remarks

You typically use this method if you are either creating a designer for the **Control** or creating your own control incorporating the **Control**.

Requirements

Platforms: Windows 98, Windows NT 4.0, Windows Millennium Edition, Windows 2000, Windows XP Home Edition, Windows XP Professional, Windows Server 2003 family

Control.ResetText Method

Resets the **Text** property to its default value.

[Visual Basic]
```
Public Overridable Sub ResetText()
```
[C#]
```
public virtual void ResetText();
```
[C++]
```
public: virtual void ResetText();
```
[JScript]
```
public function ResetText();
```

Remarks

You typically use this method if you are either creating a designer for the **Control** or creating your own control incorporating the **Control**.

Requirements

Platforms: Windows 98, Windows NT 4.0, Windows Millennium Edition, Windows 2000, Windows XP Home Edition, Windows XP Professional, Windows Server 2003 family

Control.ResumeLayout Method

Resumes normal layout logic.

Overload List

Resumes normal layout logic.

[Visual Basic] **Overloads Public Sub ResumeLayout()**

[C#] **public void ResumeLayout();**

[C++] **public: void ResumeLayout();**

[JScript] **public function ResumeLayout();**

Resumes normal layout logic. Optionally forces an immediate layout of pending layout requests.

[Visual Basic] **Overloads Public Sub ResumeLayout(Boolean)**

[C#] **public void ResumeLayout(bool);**

[C++] **public: void ResumeLayout(bool);**

[JScript] **public function ResumeLayout(Boolean);**

Example

[Visual Basic, C#, C++] The following example adds two buttons to a form. The example transactions the addition of the buttons by using the **SuspendLayout** and **ResumeLayout** methods.

> [Visual Basic, C#, C++] **Note** This example shows how to use one of the overloaded versions of **ResumeLayout**. For other examples that might be available, see the individual overload topics.

[Visual Basic]
```
Private Sub AddButtons()
   ' Suspend the form layout and add two buttons.
   Me.SuspendLayout()
   Dim buttonOK As New Button()
   buttonOK.Location = New Point(10, 10)
   buttonOK.Size = New Size(75, 25)
   buttonOK.Text = "OK"

   Dim buttonCancel As New Button()
   buttonCancel.Location = New Point(90, 10)
   buttonCancel.Size = New Size(75, 25)
   buttonCancel.Text = "Cancel"

   Me.Controls.AddRange(New Control() {buttonOK, buttonCancel})
   Me.ResumeLayout()
End Sub
```

[C#]
```
private void AddButtons()
{
   // Suspend the form layout and add two buttons.
   this.SuspendLayout();
   Button buttonOK = new Button();
   buttonOK.Location = new Point(10, 10);
   buttonOK.Size = new Size(75, 25);
   buttonOK.Text = "OK";

   Button buttonCancel = new Button();
   buttonCancel.Location = new Point(90, 10);
   buttonCancel.Size = new Size(75, 25);
   buttonCancel.Text = "Cancel";

   this.Controls.AddRange(new Control[]{buttonOK, buttonCancel});
   this.ResumeLayout();
}
```

[C++]
```
private:
    void AddButtons() {
        // Suspend the form layout and add two buttons.
        this->SuspendLayout();
        Button* buttonOK = new Button();
        buttonOK->Location =  Point(10, 10);
        buttonOK->Size =  System::Drawing::Size(75, 25);
        buttonOK->Text = S"OK";

        Button* buttonCancel = new Button();
        buttonCancel->Location =  Point(90, 10);
        buttonCancel->Size =  System::Drawing::Size(75, 25);
        buttonCancel->Text = S"Cancel";
        Control* temp5 [] = {buttonOK, buttonCancel};
        this->Controls->AddRange(temp5);
        this->ResumeLayout();
    }
```

Control.ResumeLayout Method ()

Resumes normal layout logic.

[Visual Basic]
```
Overloads Public Sub ResumeLayout()
```
[C#]
```
public void ResumeLayout();
```
[C++]
```
public: void ResumeLayout();
```
[JScript]
```
public function ResumeLayout();
```

Remarks

Calling the **ResumeLayout** method forces an immediate layout if there are any pending layout requests.

The **SuspendLayout** and **ResumeLayout** methods are used in tandem to suppress multiple **Layout** events while you adjust multiple attributes of the control. For example, you would typically call the **SuspendLayout** method, then set the **Size**, **Location**,

Anchor, or **Dock** properties of the control, and then call the **ResumeLayout** method to allow the changes to take effect.

Example

[Visual Basic, C#, C++] The following example adds two buttons to a form. The example transactions the addition of the buttons by using the **SuspendLayout** and **ResumeLayout** methods.

[Visual Basic]
```
Private Sub AddButtons()
   ' Suspend the form layout and add two buttons.
   Me.SuspendLayout()
   Dim buttonOK As New Button()
   buttonOK.Location = New Point(10, 10)
   buttonOK.Size = New Size(75, 25)
   buttonOK.Text = "OK"

   Dim buttonCancel As New Button()
   buttonCancel.Location = New Point(90, 10)
   buttonCancel.Size = New Size(75, 25)
   buttonCancel.Text = "Cancel"

   Me.Controls.AddRange(New Control() {buttonOK, buttonCancel})
   Me.ResumeLayout()
End Sub
```

[C#]
```
private void AddButtons()
{
   // Suspend the form layout and add two buttons.
   this.SuspendLayout();
   Button buttonOK = new Button();
   buttonOK.Location = new Point(10, 10);
   buttonOK.Size = new Size(75, 25);
   buttonOK.Text = "OK";

   Button buttonCancel = new Button();
   buttonCancel.Location = new Point(90, 10);
   buttonCancel.Size = new Size(75, 25);
   buttonCancel.Text = "Cancel";

   this.Controls.AddRange(new Control[]{buttonOK, buttonCancel});
   this.ResumeLayout();
}
```

[C++]
```
private:
    void AddButtons() {
        // Suspend the form layout and add two buttons.
        this->SuspendLayout();
        Button* buttonOK = new Button();
        buttonOK->Location =  Point(10, 10);
        buttonOK->Size =  System::Drawing::Size(75, 25);
        buttonOK->Text = S"OK";

        Button* buttonCancel = new Button();
        buttonCancel->Location =  Point(90, 10);
        buttonCancel->Size =  System::Drawing::Size(75, 25);
        buttonCancel->Text = S"Cancel";
        Control* temp5 [] = {buttonOK, buttonCancel};
        this->Controls->AddRange(temp5);
        this->ResumeLayout();
    }
```

Requirements

Platforms: Windows 98, Windows NT 4.0, Windows Millennium Edition, Windows 2000, Windows XP Home Edition, Windows XP Professional, Windows Server 2003 family

Control.ResumeLayout Method (Boolean)

Resumes normal layout logic. Optionally forces an immediate layout of pending layout requests.

[Visual Basic]
```
Overloads Public Sub ResumeLayout( _
   ByVal performLayout As Boolean _
)
```
[C#]
```
public void ResumeLayout(
   bool performLayout
);
```
[C++]
```
public: void ResumeLayout(
   bool performLayout
);
```
[JScript]
```
public function ResumeLayout(
   performLayout : Boolean
);
```

Parameters

performLayout
: **true** to execute pending layout requests; otherwise, **false**.

Remarks

Calling the **ResumeLayout** method forces an immediate layout if there are any pending layout requests. When the *performLayout* parameter is set to **true**, an immediate layout occurs if there are any pending layout requests.

The **SuspendLayout** and **ResumeLayout** methods are used in tandem to suppress multiple **Layout** events while you adjust multiple attributes of the control. For example, you would typically call the **SuspendLayout** method, then set the **Size**, **Location**, **Anchor**, or **Dock** properties of the control, and then call the **ResumeLayout** method to allow the changes to take effect.

Requirements

Platforms: Windows 98, Windows NT 4.0, Windows Millennium Edition, Windows 2000, Windows XP Home Edition, Windows XP Professional, Windows Server 2003 family

Control.RtlTranslateAlignment Method

Converts the current alignment to the appropriate alignment to support right-to-left text.

Overload List

Converts the specified **ContentAlignment** to the appropriate **ContentAlignment** to support right-to-left text.

[Visual Basic] **Overloads Protected Function RtlTranslateAlignment(ContentAlignment) As ContentAlignment**

[C#] **protected ContentAlignment RtlTranslateAlignment(ContentAlignment);**

[C++] **protected: ContentAlignment RtlTranslateAlignment(ContentAlignment);**

[JScript] **protected function RtlTranslateAlignment(ContentAlignment) : ContentAlignment;**

Converts the specified **HorizontalAlignment** to the appropriate **HorizontalAlignment** to support right-to-left text.

[Visual Basic] **Overloads Protected Function RtlTranslateAlignment(HorizontalAlignment) As HorizontalAlignment**

[C#] **protected HorizontalAlignment RtlTranslate-Alignment(HorizontalAlignment);**

[C++] **protected: HorizontalAlignment RtlTranslate-Alignment(HorizontalAlignment);**

[JScript] **protected function RtlTranslate-Alignment(HorizontalAlignment) : HorizontalAlignment;**

Converts the specified **LeftRightAlignment** to the appropriate **LeftRightAlignment** to support right-to-left text.

[Visual Basic] **Overloads Protected Function RtlTranslate-Alignment(LeftRightAlignment) As LeftRightAlignment**

[C#] **protected LeftRightAlignment RtlTranslate-Alignment(LeftRightAlignment);**

[C++] **protected: LeftRightAlignment RtlTranslate-Alignment(LeftRightAlignment);**

[JScript] **protected function RtlTranslate-Alignment(LeftRightAlignment) : LeftRightAlignment;**

Control.RtlTranslateAlignment Method (ContentAlignment)

Converts the specified **ContentAlignment** to the appropriate **ContentAlignment** to support right-to-left text.

```
[Visual Basic]
Overloads Protected Function RtlTranslateAlignment( _
   ByVal align As ContentAlignment _
) As ContentAlignment
[C#]
protected ContentAlignment RtlTranslateAlignment(
   ContentAlignment align
);
[C++]
protected: ContentAlignment RtlTranslateAlignment(
   ContentAlignment align
);
[JScript]
protected function RtlTranslateAlignment(
   align : ContentAlignment
) : ContentAlignment;
```

Parameters

align

One of the **ContentAlignment** values.

Return Value

One of the **ContentAlignment** values.

Remarks

If the **RightToLeft** property is set to **RightToLeft.No**, the return value is equal to the *align* parameter passed in.

Requirements

Platforms: Windows 98, Windows NT 4.0, Windows Millennium Edition, Windows 2000, Windows XP Home Edition, Windows XP Professional, Windows Server 2003 family

Control.RtlTranslateAlignment Method (HorizontalAlignment)

Converts the specified **HorizontalAlignment** to the appropriate **HorizontalAlignment** to support right-to-left text.

```
[Visual Basic]
Overloads Protected Function RtlTranslateAlignment( _
   ByVal align As HorizontalAlignment _
) As HorizontalAlignment
[C#]
protected HorizontalAlignment RtlTranslateAlignment(
   HorizontalAlignment align
);
[C++]
protected: HorizontalAlignment RtlTranslateAlignment(
   HorizontalAlignment align
);
[JScript]
protected function RtlTranslateAlignment(
   align : HorizontalAlignment
) : HorizontalAlignment;
```

Parameters

align

One of the **HorizontalAlignment** values.

Return Value

One of the **HorizontalAlignment** values.

Remarks

If the **RightToLeft** property is set to **RightToLeft.No**, the return value is equal to the *align* parameter passed in.

Requirements

Platforms: Windows 98, Windows NT 4.0, Windows Millennium Edition, Windows 2000, Windows XP Home Edition, Windows XP Professional, Windows Server 2003 family

Control.RtlTranslateAlignment Method (LeftRightAlignment)

Converts the specified **LeftRightAlignment** to the appropriate **LeftRightAlignment** to support right-to-left text.

```
[Visual Basic]
Overloads Protected Function RtlTranslateAlignment( _
   ByVal align As LeftRightAlignment _
) As LeftRightAlignment
[C#]
protected LeftRightAlignment RtlTranslateAlignment(
   LeftRightAlignment align
);
[C++]
protected: LeftRightAlignment RtlTranslateAlignment(
   LeftRightAlignment align
);
[JScript]
protected function RtlTranslateAlignment(
   align : LeftRightAlignment
) : LeftRightAlignment;
```

Parameters

align

One of the **LeftRightAlignment** values.

Return Value

One of the **LeftRightAlignment** values.

Remarks

If the **RightToLeft** property is set to **RightToLeft.No**, the return value is equal to the *align* parameter passed in.

Requirements

Platforms: Windows 98, Windows NT 4.0, Windows Millennium Edition, Windows 2000, Windows XP Home Edition, Windows XP Professional, Windows Server 2003 family

Control.RtlTranslateContent Method

Converts the specified **ContentAlignment** to the appropriate **ContentAlignment** to support right-to-left text.

```
[Visual Basic]
Protected Function RtlTranslateContent( _
   ByVal align As ContentAlignment _
) As ContentAlignment
[C#]
protected ContentAlignment RtlTranslateContent(
   ContentAlignment align
);
[C++]
protected: ContentAlignment RtlTranslateContent(
   ContentAlignment align
);
[JScript]
protected function RtlTranslateContent(
   align : ContentAlignment
) : ContentAlignment;
```

Parameters

align

One of the **ContentAlignment** values.

Return Value

One of the **ContentAlignment** values.

Remarks

If the **RightToLeft** property is set to **RightToLeft.No**, the return value is equal to the *align* parameter passed in.

Requirements

Platforms: Windows 98, Windows NT 4.0, Windows Millennium Edition, Windows 2000, Windows XP Home Edition, Windows XP Professional, Windows Server 2003 family

Control.RtlTranslateHorizontal Method

Converts the specified **HorizontalAlignment** to the appropriate **HorizontalAlignment** to support right-to-left text.

```
[Visual Basic]
Protected Function RtlTranslateHorizontal( _
   ByVal align As HorizontalAlignment _
) As HorizontalAlignment
[C#]
protected HorizontalAlignment RtlTranslateHorizontal(
   HorizontalAlignment align
);
[C++]
protected: HorizontalAlignment RtlTranslateHorizontal(
   HorizontalAlignment align
);
[JScript]
protected function RtlTranslateHorizontal(
   align : HorizontalAlignment
) : HorizontalAlignment;
```

Parameters

align

One of the **HorizontalAlignment** values.

Return Value

One of the **HorizontalAlignment** values.

Remarks

If the **RightToLeft** property is set to **RightToLeft.No**, the return value is equal to the *align* parameter passed in.

Requirements

Platforms: Windows 98, Windows NT 4.0, Windows Millennium Edition, Windows 2000, Windows XP Home Edition, Windows XP Professional, Windows Server 2003 family

Control.RtlTranslateLeftRight Method

Converts the specified **LeftRightAlignment** to the appropriate **LeftRightAlignment** to support right-to-left text.

```
[Visual Basic]
Protected Function RtlTranslateLeftRight( _
   ByVal align As LeftRightAlignment _
) As LeftRightAlignment
[C#]
protected LeftRightAlignment RtlTranslateLeftRight(
   LeftRightAlignment align
);
[C++]
protected: LeftRightAlignment RtlTranslateLeftRight(
   LeftRightAlignment align
);
[JScript]
protected function RtlTranslateLeftRight(
   align : LeftRightAlignment
) : LeftRightAlignment;
```

Parameters

align

One of the **LeftRightAlignment** values.

Return Value

One of the **LeftRightAlignment** values.

Remarks

If the **RightToLeft** property is set to **RightToLeft.No**, the return value is equal to the *align* parameter passed in.

Requirements

Platforms: Windows 98, Windows NT 4.0,
Windows Millennium Edition, Windows 2000,
Windows XP Home Edition, Windows XP Professional,
Windows Server 2003 family

Control.Scale Method

Scales the control and any child controls.

Overload List

Scales the control and any child controls to the specified ratio.

[Visual Basic] **Overloads Public Sub Scale(Single)**

[C#] **public void Scale(float);**

[C++] **public: void Scale(float);**

[JScript] **public function Scale(float);**

Scales the control and any child controls by the specified horizontal and vertical ratios.

[Visual Basic] **Overloads Public Sub Scale(Single, Single)**

[C#] **public void Scale(float, float);**

[C++] **public: void Scale(float, float);**

[JScript] **public function Scale(float, float);**

Example

The following example resizes the child controls of a **Form** using the **Scale** method. This example scales the height of each control to 1.5 times its current size while the current width of each control is maintained.

Control.Scale Method (Single)

Scales the control and any child controls to the specified ratio.

```
[Visual Basic]
Overloads Public Sub Scale( _
   ByVal ratio As Single _
)
[C#]
public void Scale(
   float ratio
);
[C++]
public: void Scale(
   float ratio
);
[JScript]
public function Scale(
   ratio : float
);
```

Parameters

ratio
The ratio by which to scale the control horizontally and vertically.

Remarks

This version of the **Scale** method uses the *ratio* parameter value to scale both the height and width of the control. To scale the height and width of the control independantly, use the version of the **Scale** method that takes two parameters.

The **ScaleCore** method is called by the **Scale** methods to scale the control. You should override the **ScaleCore** method to ensure that your code is executed when either of the **Scale** methods is called.

Example

The following example resizes the child controls of a **Form** using the **Scale** method. This example scales the height and width of each control to 1.5 times its current size.

Requirements

Platforms: Windows 98, Windows NT 4.0,
Windows Millennium Edition, Windows 2000,
Windows XP Home Edition, Windows XP Professional,
Windows Server 2003 family

Control.Scale Method (Single, Single)

Scales the control and any child controls by the specified horizontal and vertical ratios.

```
[Visual Basic]
Overloads Public Sub Scale( _
   ByVal dx As Single, _
   ByVal dy As Single _
)
[C#]
public void Scale(
   float dx,
   float dy
);
[C++]
public: void Scale(
   float dx,
   float dy
);
[JScript]
public function Scale(
   dx : float,
   dy : float
);
```

Parameters

dx
The ratio by which to scale the control horizontally.

dy
The ratio by which to scale the control vertically.

Remarks

This version of the **Scale** method uses the *dx* and *dy* parameter values to scale the height and width of the control independently. To keep the height and width of the control in proportion to their current size, use the version of the **Scale** method that takes one parameter.

The **ScaleCore** method is called by the **Scale** methods to scale the control. You should override the **ScaleCore** method to ensure that your code is executed when either of the **Scale** methods is called.

Example

The following example resizes the child controls of a **Form** using the **Scale** method. This example scales the height of each control to 1.5 times its current size while the current width of each control is maintained.

Requirements

Platforms: Windows 98, Windows NT 4.0,
Windows Millennium Edition, Windows 2000,
Windows XP Home Edition, Windows XP Professional,
Windows Server 2003 family

Control.ScaleCore Method

Performs the work of scaling the entire control and any child controls.

[Visual Basic]
```
Protected Overridable Sub ScaleCore( _
   ByVal dx As Single, _
   ByVal dy As Single _
)
```
[C#]
```
protected virtual void ScaleCore(
   float dx,
   float dy
);
```
[C++]
```
protected: virtual void ScaleCore(
   float dx,
   float dy
);
```
[JScript]
```
protected function ScaleCore(
   dx : float,
   dy : float
);
```

Parameters

dx

The ratio by which to scale the control horizontally.

dy

The ratio by which to scale the control vertically.

Remarks

This **ScaleCore** method uses the *dx* and *dy* parameter values to scale both the height and width of the control independantly. To keep the height and width of the control in proportion to their current size, use the same value for the *dx* and *dy* parameters, or call the version of the **Scale** method that takes one parameter.

You would typically override this method to change the scaling behavior of the control.

Notes to Inheritors: When overriding **ScaleCore** in a derived class, be sure to call the base class's **ScaleCore** method so that the control is resized properly.

Example

[Visual Basic, C#, C++] The following example overrides the **ScaleCore** method to ensure that the derived control and its child controls are scaled. This example assumes you have a class that is either directly or indirectly derived from the **Control** class.

[Visual Basic]
```
Protected Overrides Sub ScaleCore(dx As Single, dy As Single)
   ' Scale all child controls.
   Me.SuspendLayout()

   Dim myClientSize As Size = Me.ClientSize
   myClientSize.Height = CInt(myClientSize.Height * dx)
   myClientSize.Width = CInt(myClientSize.Width * dy)

   ' Scale the child controls because
   ' MyBase.ScaleCore was not called.
   Dim childControl As Control
   For Each childControl In  Me.Controls
      childControl.Scale(dx, dy)
   Next childControl
   Me.ResumeLayout()

   Me.ClientSize = myClientSize
End Sub
```

[C#]
```
protected override void ScaleCore(float dx, float dy)
{
   // Scale all child controls.
   this.SuspendLayout();

   Size myClientSize = this.ClientSize;
   myClientSize.Height = (int)(myClientSize.Height * dx);
   myClientSize.Width = (int)(myClientSize.Width * dy);

   /* Scale the child controls because
    * base.ScaleCore was not called. */
   foreach(Control childControl in this.Controls)
   {
      childControl.Scale(dx, dy);
   }
   this.ResumeLayout();

   this.ClientSize = myClientSize;
}
```

[C++]
```
protected:
   void ScaleCore(float dx, float dy) {
      // Scale all child controls.
      this->SuspendLayout();

      System::Drawing::Size myClientSize = this->ClientSize;
      myClientSize.Height = (int)(myClientSize.Height * dx);
      myClientSize.Width = (int)(myClientSize.Width * dy);

      /* Scale the child controls because
      * UserControl::ScaleCore was not called. */
      System::Collections::IEnumerator* myEnum = this->
Controls->GetEnumerator();
      while (myEnum->MoveNext()) {
         Control* childControl = __try_cast<Control*>(myEnum->Current);

         childControl->Scale(dx, dy);
      }
      this->ResumeLayout();

      this->ClientSize = myClientSize;
   }
```

Requirements

Platforms: Windows 98, Windows NT 4.0, Windows Millennium Edition, Windows 2000, Windows XP Home Edition, Windows XP Professional, Windows Server 2003 family

Control.Select Method

Activates a control.

Overload List

Activates the control.

[Visual Basic] **Overloads Public Sub Select()**

[C#] **public void Select();**

[C++] **public: void Select();**

[JScript] **public function Select();**

Activates a child control. Optionally specifies the direction in the tab order to select the control from.

[Visual Basic] **Overloads Protected Overridable Sub Select(Boolean, Boolean)**

[C#] **protected virtual void Select(bool, bool);**

[C++] **protected: virtual void Select(bool, bool);**

[JScript] **protected function Select(Boolean, Boolean);**

Example

[Visual Basic, C#, C++] The following example selects the specified **Control**, if it is selectable.

> [Visual Basic, C#, C++] **Note** This example shows how to use one of the overloaded versions of **Select**. For other examples that might be available, see the individual overload topics.

[Visual Basic]
```
Public Sub ControlSelect(control As Control)
   ' Select the control, if it can be selected.
   If control.CanSelect Then
      control.Select()
   End If
End Sub
```

[C#]
```
public void ControlSelect(Control control)
{
   // Select the control, if it can be selected.
   if(control.CanSelect)
   {
      control.Select();
   }
}
```

[C++]
```
public:
   void ControlSelect(Control* control) {
      // Select the control, if it can be selected.
      if (control->CanSelect) {
         control->Select();
      }
   }
```

Control.Select Method ()

Activates the control.

[Visual Basic]
```
Overloads Public Sub Select()
```
[C#]
```
public void Select();
```
[C++]
```
public: void Select();
```
[JScript]
```
public function Select();
```

Remarks

The **Select** method activates the control if the control's **ControlStyles.Selectable** style bit is set to **true**, it is contained in another control, and all its parent controls are both visible and enabled.

The Windows Forms controls in the following list are not selectable. Controls derived from controls in the list will also not be selectable.

- **Label**
- **Panel**
- **GroupBox**
- **PictureBox**
- **ProgressBar**
- **Splitter**
- **LinkLabel** (when there is no link present in the control)

Example

[Visual Basic, C#, C++] The following example selects the specified **Control**, if it is selectable.

[Visual Basic]
```
Public Sub ControlSelect(control As Control)
   ' Select the control, if it can be selected.
   If control.CanSelect Then
      control.Select()
   End If
End Sub
```

[C#]
```
public void ControlSelect(Control control)
{
   // Select the control, if it can be selected.
   if(control.CanSelect)
   {
      control.Select();
   }
}
```

[C++]
```
public:
   void ControlSelect(Control* control) {
      // Select the control, if it can be selected.
      if (control->CanSelect) {
         control->Select();
      }
   }
```

Requirements

Platforms: Windows 98, Windows NT 4.0, Windows Millennium Edition, Windows 2000, Windows XP Home Edition, Windows XP Professional, Windows Server 2003 family

Control.Select Method (Boolean, Boolean)

Activates a child control. Optionally specifies the direction in the tab order to select the control from.

[Visual Basic]
```
Overloads Protected Overridable Sub Select( _
   ByVal directed As Boolean, _
   ByVal forward As Boolean _
)
```
[C#]
```
protected virtual void Select(
   bool directed,
   bool forward
);
```
[C++]
```
protected: virtual void Select(
   bool directed,
   bool forward
);
```
[JScript]
```
protected function Select(
   directed : Boolean,
   forward : Boolean
);
```

Parameters

directed
: **true** to specify the direction of the control to select; otherwise, **false**.

forward
: **true** to move forward in the tab order; **false** to move backward in the tab order.

Remarks

The *directed* and *forward* parameters are used by container-style controls. When the *directed* parameter is set to **true**, the *forward* parameter is evaluated to determine which control to select. When *forward* is set to **true**, the next control in the tab order is selected; when **false**, the previous control in the tab order is selected.

The **Select** method activates the control if the control's **ControlStyles.Selectable** style bit set to **true**, it is contained in another control, and all its parent controls are both visible and enabled.

The Windows Forms controls in the following list are not selectable. Controls derived from controls in the list will also not be selectable.

- **Label**
- **Panel**
- **GroupBox**
- **PictureBox**
- **ProgressBar**
- **Splitter**
- **LinkLabel** (when there is no link present in the control)

Requirements

Platforms: Windows 98, Windows NT 4.0, Windows Millennium Edition, Windows 2000, Windows XP Home Edition, Windows XP Professional, Windows Server 2003 family

Control.SelectNextControl Method

Activates the next control.

[Visual Basic]
```
Public Function SelectNextControl( _
   ByVal ctl As Control, _
   ByVal forward As Boolean, _
   ByVal tabStopOnly As Boolean, _
   ByVal nested As Boolean, _
   ByVal wrap As Boolean _
) As Boolean
```
[C#]
```
public bool SelectNextControl(
   Control ctl,
   bool forward,
   bool tabStopOnly,
   bool nested,
   bool wrap
);
```
[C++]
```
public: bool SelectNextControl(
   Control* ctl,
   bool forward,
   bool tabStopOnly,
   bool nested,
   bool wrap
);
```
[JScript]
```
public function SelectNextControl(
   ctl : Control,
   forward : Boolean,
   tabStopOnly : Boolean,
   nested : Boolean,
   wrap : Boolean
) : Boolean;
```

Parameters

ctl
: The **Control** at which to start the search.

forward
: **true** to move forward in the tab order; **false** to move backward in the tab order.

tabStopOnly
: **true** to ignore the controls with the **TabStop** property set to **false**; otherwise, **false**.

nested
: **true** to include nested (children of child controls) child controls; otherwise, **false**.

wrap
: **true** to continue searching from the first control in the tab order after the last control has been reached; otherwise, **false**.

Return Value

true if a control was activated; otherwise, **false**.

Remarks

The **SelectNextControl** method activates the next control in the tab order if the control's **ControlStyles.Selectable** style bit set to **true**, it is contained in another control, and all its parent controls are both visible and enabled.

The Windows Forms controls in the following list are not selectable. Controls derived from controls in the list will also not be selectable.

- **Label**
- **Panel**
- **GroupBox**
- **PictureBox**
- **ProgressBar**
- **Splitter**
- **LinkLabel** (when there is no link present in the control)

Requirements

Platforms: Windows 98, Windows NT 4.0, Windows Millennium Edition, Windows 2000, Windows XP Home Edition, Windows XP Professional, Windows Server 2003 family

Control.SendToBack Method

Sends the control to the back of the z-order.

[Visual Basic]
```
Public Sub SendToBack()
```
[C#]
```
public void SendToBack();
```
[C++]
```
public: void SendToBack();
```
[JScript]
```
public function SendToBack();
```

Remarks

The control is moved to the back of the z-order. If the control is a child of another control, the child control is moved to the back of the z-order.

Requirements

Platforms: Windows 98, Windows NT 4.0, Windows Millennium Edition, Windows 2000, Windows XP Home Edition, Windows XP Professional, Windows Server 2003 family, .NET Compact Framework - Windows CE .NET

Control.SetBounds Method

Sets the bounds of the control.

Overload List

Sets the bounds of the control to the specified location and size.

[Visual Basic] **Overloads Public Sub SetBounds(Integer, Integer, Integer, Integer)**

[C#] **public void SetBounds(int, int, int, int);**

[C++] **public: void SetBounds(int, int, int, int);**

[JScript] **public function SetBounds(int, int, int, int);**

Sets the specified bounds of the control to the specified location and size.

[Visual Basic] **Overloads Public Sub SetBounds(Integer, Integer, Integer, BoundsSpecified)**

[C#] **public void SetBounds(int, int, int, int, BoundsSpecified);**

[C++] **public: void SetBounds(int, int, int, int, BoundsSpecified);**

[JScript] **public function SetBounds(int, int, int, int, BoundsSpecified);**

Example

[Visual Basic, C#, C++] The following example centers a **Form** on the screen in the **Layout** event. This will keep the form centered as the user resizes it. This example assumes you have created a **Form** control.

> [Visual Basic, C#, C++] **Note** This example shows how to use one of the overloaded versions of **SetBounds**. For other examples that might be available, see the individual overload topics.

[Visual Basic]
```
    Private Sub MyForm_Layout(ByVal sender As Object, _
        ByVal e As System.Windows.Forms.LayoutEventArgs)                ↵
Handles MyBase.Layout

        ' Center the Form on the user's screen everytime it             ↵
 requires a Layout.
        Me.SetBounds((                                                   ↵
System.Windows.Forms.Screen.GetBounds(Me).Width / 2) -                  ↵
 (Me.Width / 2), _
            (System.Windows.Forms.Screen.GetBounds(Me).Height           ↵
 / 2) - (Me.Height / 2), _
            Me.Width, Me.Height,                                        ↵
System.Windows.Forms.BoundsSpecified.Location)
    End Sub
```

[C#]
```
private void MyForm_Layout(object sender,                               ↵
System.Windows.Forms.LayoutEventArgs e)
{
   // Center the Form on the user's screen everytime it                 ↵
requires a Layout.
   this.SetBounds((Screen.GetBounds(this).Width/2) - (this.Width/2),
       (Screen.GetBounds(this).Height/2) - (this.Height/2),
       this.Width, this.Height, BoundsSpecified.Location);
}
```

[C++]
```
private:
    void MyForm_Layout(Object* sender,                                  ↵
System::Windows::Forms::LayoutEventArgs* e) {
        // Center the Form on the user's screen everytime               ↵
it requires a Layout.
        this->SetBounds((Screen::GetBounds(this).Width/2) -             ↵
 (this->Width/2),
            (Screen::GetBounds(this).Height/2) - (this->Height/2),
            this->Width, this->Height, BoundsSpecified::Location);
    }
```

Control.SetBounds Method (Int32, Int32, Int32, Int32)

Sets the bounds of the control to the specified location and size.

[Visual Basic]
```
Overloads Public Sub SetBounds( _
   ByVal x As Integer, _
   ByVal y As Integer, _
   ByVal width As Integer, _
   ByVal height As Integer _
)
```
[C#]
```
public void SetBounds(
   int x,
   int y,
   int width,
   int height
);
```
[C++]
```
public: void SetBounds(
   int x,
   int y,
   int width,
   int height
);
```
[JScript]
```
public function SetBounds(
   x : int,
   y : int,
   width : int,
   height : int
);
```

Parameters

x
The new **Left** property value of the control.

y
The new **Right** property value of the control.

width
The new **Width** property value of the control.

height
The new **Height** property value of the control.

Requirements

Platforms: Windows 98, Windows NT 4.0, Windows Millennium Edition, Windows 2000, Windows XP Home Edition, Windows XP Professional, Windows Server 2003 family

Control.SetBounds Method (Int32, Int32, Int32, Int32, BoundsSpecified)

Sets the specified bounds of the control to the specified location and size.

[Visual Basic]
```
Overloads Public Sub SetBounds( _
   ByVal x As Integer, _
   ByVal y As Integer, _
   ByVal width As Integer, _
   ByVal height As Integer, _
   ByVal specified As BoundsSpecified _
)
```

```
[C#]
public void SetBounds(
   int x,
   int y,
   int width,
   int height,
   BoundsSpecified specified
);
[C++]
public: void SetBounds(
   int x,
   int y,
   int width,
   int height,
   BoundsSpecified specified
);
[JScript]
public function SetBounds(
   x : int,
   y : int,
   width : int,
   height : int,
   specified : BoundsSpecified
);
```

Parameters

x
: The new **Left** property value of the control.

y
: The new **Right** property value of the control.

width
: The new **Width** property value of the control.

height
: The new **Height** property value of the control.

specified
: A bitwise combination of the **BoundsSpecified** values. For any parameter not specified, the current value will be used.

Example

[Visual Basic, C#, C++] The following example centers a **Form** on the screen in the **Layout** event. This will keep the form centered as the user resizes it. This example assumes you have created a **Form** control.

[Visual Basic]

```
    Private Sub MyForm_Layout(ByVal sender As Object, _
        ByVal e As System.Windows.Forms.LayoutEventArgs)                 ↵
Handles MyBase.Layout

        ' Center the Form on the user's screen everytime                 ↵
it requires a Layout.
        Me.SetBounds((System.Windows.Forms.Screen.GetBounds(Me)          ↵
.Width / 2) - (Me.Width / 2), _
            (System.Windows.Forms.Screen.GetBounds(Me).Height            ↵
 / 2) - (Me.Height / 2), _
            Me.Width, Me.Height,                                         ↵
System.Windows.Forms.BoundsSpecified.Location)
    End Sub
```

[C#]

```
private void MyForm_Layout(object sender,                                ↵
System.Windows.Forms.LayoutEventArgs e)
{
   // Center the Form on the user's screen everytime it                  ↵
requires a Layout.
   this.SetBounds((Screen.GetBounds(this).Width/2) - (this.Width/2),
       (Screen.GetBounds(this).Height/2) - (this.Height/2),
       this.Width, this.Height, BoundsSpecified.Location);
}
```

[C++]

```
private:
    void MyForm_Layout(Object* sender,                                   ↵
System::Windows::Forms::LayoutEventArgs* e) {
        // Center the Form on the user's screen everytime               ↵
it requires a Layout.
        this->SetBounds((Screen::GetBounds(this).Width/2)               ↵
 - (this->Width/2),
            (Screen::GetBounds(this).Height/2) - (this->Height/2),
            this->Width, this->Height, BoundsSpecified::Location);
    }
```

Requirements

Platforms: Windows 98, Windows NT 4.0, Windows Millennium Edition, Windows 2000, Windows XP Home Edition, Windows XP Professional, Windows Server 2003 family

Control.SetBoundsCore Method

Performs the work of setting the specified bounds of this control.

```
[Visual Basic]
Protected Overridable Sub SetBoundsCore( _
   ByVal x As Integer, _
   ByVal y As Integer, _
   ByVal width As Integer, _
   ByVal height As Integer, _
   ByVal specified As BoundsSpecified _
)
[C#]
protected virtual void SetBoundsCore(
   int x,
   int y,
   int width,
   int height,
   BoundsSpecified specified
);
[C++]
protected: virtual void SetBoundsCore(
   int x,
   int y,
   int width,
   int height,
   BoundsSpecified specified
);
[JScript]
protected function SetBoundsCore(
   x : int,
   y : int,
   width : int,
   height : int,
   specified : BoundsSpecified
);
```

Parameters

x
: The new **Left** property value of the control.

y
: The new **Right** property value of the control.

width

The new **Width** property value of the control.

height

The new **Height** property value of the control.

specified

A bitwise combination of the **BoundsSpecified** values.

Remarks

Typically, the parameters that correspond to the bounds not included in the *specified* parameter are passed in with their current values. For example, the **Height**, **Width**, or the **X** or **Y** properties of the **Location** property can be passed in with a reference to the current instance of the control. However all values passed in are honored and applied to the control.

The *boundsSpecified* parameter represents the elements of the controls **Bounds** changed by your application. For example, if you change the **Size** of the control, the *boundsSpecified* parameter value is **BoundsSpecified.Size**. However, if the **Size** is adjusted in response to the **Dock** property being set, the *boundsSpecified* parameter value is **BoundsSpecified.None**.

Notes to Inheritors: When overriding **SetBoundsCore** in a derived class, be sure to call the base class's **SetBoundsCore** method to force the bounds of the control to change. Derived classes can add size restrictions to the **SetBoundsCore** method.

Example

[Visual Basic, C#, C++] The following example overrides the **Set-BoundsCore** method to ensure that the control remains a fixed size. This example assumes you have a class that is either directly or indirectly derived from the **Control** class.

[Visual Basic]
```
Protected Overrides Sub SetBoundsCore(x As Integer, _
  y As Integer, width As Integer, _
  height As Integer, specified As BoundsSpecified)
    ' Set a fixed height and width for the control.
    MyBase.SetBoundsCore(x, y, 150, 75, specified)
End Sub
```

[C#]
```
protected override void SetBoundsCore(int x, int y,
   int width, int height, BoundsSpecified specified)
{
   // Set a fixed height and width for the control.
   base.SetBoundsCore(x, y, 150, 75, specified);
}
```

[C++]
```
protected:
   void SetBoundsCore(int x, int y,
      int width, int height, BoundsSpecified specified) {
         // Set a fixed height and width for the control.
         UserControl::SetBoundsCore(x, y, 150, 75, specified);
      }
```

Requirements

Platforms: Windows 98, Windows NT 4.0, Windows Millennium Edition, Windows 2000, Windows XP Home Edition, Windows XP Professional, Windows Server 2003 family

Control.SetClientSizeCore Method

Sets the size of the client area of the control.

[Visual Basic]
```
Protected Overridable Sub SetClientSizeCore( _
   ByVal x As Integer, _
   ByVal y As Integer _
)
```
[C#]
```
protected virtual void SetClientSizeCore(
   int x,
   int y
);
```
[C++]
```
protected: virtual void SetClientSizeCore(
   int x,
   int y
);
```
[JScript]
```
protected function SetClientSizeCore(
   x : int,
   y : int
);
```

Parameters

x

The client area width, in pixels.

y

The client area height, in pixels.

Remarks

The client area starts at the (0, 0) location and extends to the (*x*, *y*) location.

Typically, you do not set the **ClientSize** of the control.

Notes to Inheritors: When overriding **SetClientSizeCore** in a derived class, be sure to call the base class's **SetClientSizeCore** method so that the **ClientSize** property is adjusted.

For more information about drawing on controls, see **Rendering a Windows Forms Control**.

Example

[Visual Basic, C#, C++] The following example overrides the **Set-ClientSizeCore** method to ensure that the control remains square. This example assumes you have a class that is either directly or indirectly derived from the **Control** class.

[Visual Basic]
```
Protected Overrides Sub SetClientSizeCore(x As Integer, y As Integer)
   ' Keep the client size square.
   If x > y Then
      MyBase.SetClientSizeCore(x, x)
   Else
      MyBase.SetClientSizeCore(y, y)
   End If
End Sub
```

[C#]
```
protected override void SetClientSizeCore(int x, int y)
{
   // Keep the client size square.
   if(x > y)
   {
      base.SetClientSizeCore(x, x);
   }
   else
   {
```

```
        base.SetClientSizeCore(y, y);
    }
}
```

[C++]
```
protected:
    void SetClientSizeCore(int x, int y) {
        // Keep the client size square.
        if (x > y) {
            UserControl::SetClientSizeCore(x, x);
        } else {
            UserControl::SetClientSizeCore(y, y);
        }
    }
```

Requirements

Platforms: Windows 98, Windows NT 4.0,
Windows Millennium Edition, Windows 2000,
Windows XP Home Edition, Windows XP Professional,
Windows Server 2003 family

Control.SetStyle Method

Sets the specified style bit to the specified value.

[Visual Basic]
```
Protected Sub SetStyle( _
    ByVal flag As ControlStyles, _
    ByVal value As Boolean _
)
```
[C#]
```
protected void SetStyle(
    ControlStyles flag,
    bool value
);
```
[C++]
```
protected: void SetStyle(
    ControlStyles flag,
    bool value
);
```
[JScript]
```
protected function SetStyle(
    flag : ControlStyles,
    value : Boolean
);
```

Parameters

flag
The **ControlStyles** bit to set.

value
true to apply the specified style to the control; otherwise, **false**.

Remarks

Control style bit flags are used to categorize supported behavior. A control can enable a style by calling the **SetStyle** method and passing in the appropriate **ControlStyles** bit (or bits) and the Boolean value to set the bit(s) to. To determine the value assigned to a specified **ControlStyles** bit, use the **GetStyle** method and pass in the **ControlStyles** member to evaluate.

CAUTION Setting the control style bits can substantially change the behavior of the control. Review the **ControlStyles** enumeration documentation to understand the effects of changing the control style bits before calling the **SetStyle** method.

Example

[Visual Basic, C#, C++] The following example enables double-buffering on a **Form** and updates the styles to reflect the changes.

[Visual Basic]
```
Public Sub EnableDoubleBuffering()
    ' Set the value of the double-buffering style bits to true.
    Me.SetStyle(ControlStyles.DoubleBuffer _
      Or ControlStyles.UserPaint _
      Or ControlStyles.AllPaintingInWmPaint, _
      True)
    Me.UpdateStyles()
End Sub
```

[C#]
```
public void EnableDoubleBuffering()
{
    // Set the value of the double-buffering style bits to true.
    this.SetStyle(ControlStyles.DoubleBuffer |
        ControlStyles.UserPaint |
        ControlStyles.AllPaintingInWmPaint,
        true);
    this.UpdateStyles();
}
```

[C++]
```
public:
    void EnableDoubleBuffering() {
        // Set the value of the double-buffering style bits to true.
        this-
>SetStyle(static_cast<ControlStyles>(ControlStyles::DoubleBuffer |
            ControlStyles::UserPaint |
            ControlStyles::AllPaintingInWmPaint),
            true);
        this->UpdateStyles();
    }
```

Requirements

Platforms: Windows 98, Windows NT 4.0,
Windows Millennium Edition, Windows 2000,
Windows XP Home Edition, Windows XP Professional,
Windows Server 2003 family

Control.SetTopLevel Method

Sets the control as the top-level control.

[Visual Basic]
```
Protected Sub SetTopLevel( _
    ByVal value As Boolean _
)
```
[C#]
```
protected void SetTopLevel(
    bool value
);
```
[C++]
```
protected: void SetTopLevel(
    bool value
);
```
[JScript]
```
protected function SetTopLevel(
    value : Boolean
);
```

Parameters

value
true to set the control as the top-level control; otherwise, **false**.

Exceptions

Exception Type	Condition
InvalidOperation-Exception	The *value* parameter is set to **true** and the control is an ActiveX control.
Exception	The **GetTopLevel** return value is not equal to the *value* parameter and the **Parent** property is not a null reference (**Nothing** in Visual Basic).

Remarks

If you call the **SetTopLevel** method of a **Form** and pass in a value of **false**, the form will not be visible until you call **SetTopLevel** again, passing in a value of **true**.

Requirements

Platforms: Windows 98, Windows NT 4.0, Windows Millennium Edition, Windows 2000, Windows XP Home Edition, Windows XP Professional, Windows Server 2003 family

.NET Framework Security:

- **UIPermission** to set the control as a top-level control if it is of type **Form**. This permission is only demanded if the *value* parameter is **true** and the control is not an ActiveX control. Associated enumeration: **UIPermissionWindow.SafeTopLevelWindows**
- **UIPermission** to set the control as a top-level control if it is of any type other than **Form**. This permission is only demanded if the *value* parameter is **true** and the control is not an ActiveX control. Associated enumeration: **UIPermissionWindow.AllWindows**

Control.SetVisibleCore Method

Sets the control to the specified visible state.

```
[Visual Basic]
Protected Overridable Sub SetVisibleCore( _
   ByVal value As Boolean _
)
[C#]
protected virtual void SetVisibleCore(
   bool value
);
[C++]
protected: virtual void SetVisibleCore(
   bool value
);
[JScript]
protected function SetVisibleCore(
   value : Boolean
);
```

Parameters

value

true to make the control visible; otherwise, **false**.

Remarks

You would typically override this method to change the visibility behavior of the control.

Notes to Inheritors: When overriding **SetVisibleCore** in a derived class, be sure to call the base class's **SetVisibleCore** method to force the visibility of the control to change.

Requirements

Platforms: Windows 98, Windows NT 4.0, Windows Millennium Edition, Windows 2000, Windows XP Home Edition, Windows XP Professional, Windows Server 2003 family

Control.Show Method

Displays the control to the user.

```
[Visual Basic]
Public Sub Show()
[C#]
public void Show();
[C++]
public: void Show();
[JScript]
public function Show();
```

Remarks

Showing the control is equivalent to setting the **Visible** property to **true**. After the **Show** method is called, the **Visible** property returns a value of **true** until the **Hide** method is called.

Example

[Visual Basic, C#, C++] The following example displays an about dialog box and temporarily draws a blue square on it's surface. This example assumes you have defined a class that derives from **Form** named `AboutDialog`.

```
[Visual Basic]
Private Sub menuItemHelpAbout_Click(sender As Object, _
  e As EventArgs) Handles menuItemHelpAbout.Click
   ' Create and display a modless about dialog box.
   Dim about As New AboutDialog()
   about.Show()

   ' Draw a blue square on the form.
   ' NOTE: This is not a persistent object, it will no longer be
   ' visible after the next call to OnPaint. To make it persistent,
   ' override the OnPaint method and draw the square there
   Dim g As Graphics = about.CreateGraphics()
   g.FillRectangle(Brushes.Blue, 10, 10, 50, 50)
End Sub
```

```
[C#]
private void menuItemHelpAbout_Click(object sender, EventArgs e)
{
   // Create and display a modless about dialog box.
   AboutDialog about = new AboutDialog();
   about.Show();

   // Draw a blue square on the form.
   /* NOTE: This is not a persistent object, it will no longer be
    * visible after the next call to OnPaint. To make it persistent,
    * override the OnPaint method and draw the square there */
   Graphics g = about.CreateGraphics();
   g.FillRectangle(Brushes.Blue, 10, 10, 50, 50);
}
```

```
[C++]
private:
    void menuItemHelpAbout_Click(Object* /*sender*/,
 EventArgs* /*e*/) {
       // Create and display a modless about dialog box.
       AboutDialog* about = new AboutDialog();
       about->Show();

       // Draw a blue square on the form.
       /* NOTE: This is not a persistent object, it will no longer be
```

```
        * visible after the next call to OnPaint. To make it
persistent,
        *  the OnPaint method and draw the square there */
        Graphics* g = about->CreateGraphics();
        g->FillRectangle(Brushes::Blue, 10, 10, 50, 50);
    }
```

Requirements

Platforms: Windows 98, Windows NT 4.0, Windows Millennium Edition, Windows 2000, Windows XP Home Edition, Windows XP Professional, Windows Server 2003 family, .NET Compact Framework - Windows CE .NET

Control.SuspendLayout Method

Temporarily suspends the layout logic for the control.

[Visual Basic]
```
Public Sub SuspendLayout()
```
[C#]
```
public void SuspendLayout();
```
[C++]
```
public: void SuspendLayout();
```
[JScript]
```
public function SuspendLayout();
```

Remarks

The layout logic of the control is suspended until the **ResumeLayout** method is called.

The **SuspendLayout** and **ResumeLayout** methods are used in tandem to suppress multiple **Layout** events while you adjust multiple attributes of the control. For example, you would typically call the **SuspendLayout** method, then set the **Size**, **Location**, **Anchor**, or **Dock** properties of the control, and then call the **ResumeLayout** method to allow the changes to take effect.

Example

[Visual Basic, C#, C++] The following example adds two buttons to a form. The example transactions the addition of the buttons by using the **SuspendLayout** and **ResumeLayout** methods.

[Visual Basic]
```
Private Sub AddButtons()
    ' Suspend the form layout and add two buttons.
    Me.SuspendLayout()
    Dim buttonOK As New Button()
    buttonOK.Location = New Point(10, 10)
    buttonOK.Size = New Size(75, 25)
    buttonOK.Text = "OK"

    Dim buttonCancel As New Button()
    buttonCancel.Location = New Point(90, 10)
    buttonCancel.Size = New Size(75, 25)
    buttonCancel.Text = "Cancel"

    Me.Controls.AddRange(New Control() {buttonOK, buttonCancel})
    Me.ResumeLayout()
End Sub
```

[C#]
```
private void AddButtons()
{
    // Suspend the form layout and add two buttons.
    this.SuspendLayout();
    Button buttonOK = new Button();
    buttonOK.Location = new Point(10, 10);
    buttonOK.Size = new Size(75, 25);
    buttonOK.Text = "OK";

    Button buttonCancel = new Button();
    buttonCancel.Location = new Point(90, 10);
    buttonCancel.Size = new Size(75, 25);
    buttonCancel.Text = "Cancel";

    this.Controls.AddRange(new Control[]{buttonOK, buttonCancel});
    this.ResumeLayout();
}
```

[C++]
```
private:
    void AddButtons() {
        // Suspend the form layout and add two buttons.
        this->SuspendLayout();
        Button* buttonOK = new Button();
        buttonOK->Location =  Point(10, 10);
        buttonOK->Size =  System::Drawing::Size(75, 25);
        buttonOK->Text = S"OK";

        Button* buttonCancel = new Button();
        buttonCancel->Location =  Point(90, 10);
        buttonCancel->Size =  System::Drawing::Size(75, 25);
        buttonCancel->Text = S"Cancel";
        Control* temp5 [] = {buttonOK, buttonCancel};
        this->Controls->AddRange(temp5);
        this->ResumeLayout();
    }
```

Requirements

Platforms: Windows 98, Windows NT 4.0, Windows Millennium Edition, Windows 2000, Windows XP Home Edition, Windows XP Professional, Windows Server 2003 family

Control.Update Method

Causes the control to redraw the invalidated regions within its client area.

[Visual Basic]
```
Public Sub Update()
```
[C#]
```
public void Update();
```
[C++]
```
public: void Update();
```
[JScript]
```
public function Update();
```

Remarks

Executes any pending requests for painting.

For more information, see the **WM_PAINT** topic of the Painting and Drawing section of the Platform SDK documentation in the MSDN Library.

Requirements

Platforms: Windows 98, Windows NT 4.0, Windows Millennium Edition, Windows 2000, Windows XP Home Edition, Windows XP Professional, Windows Server 2003 family, .NET Compact Framework - Windows CE .NET

Control.UpdateBounds Method

Updates the bounds of the control.

Overload List

Updates the bounds of the control with the current size and location.

[Visual Basic] **Overloads Protected Sub UpdateBounds()**

[C#] **protected void UpdateBounds();**

[C++] **protected: void UpdateBounds();**

[JScript] **protected function UpdateBounds();**

Updates the bounds of the control with the specified size and location.

[Visual Basic] **Overloads Protected Sub Update-Bounds(Integer, Integer, Integer, Integer)**

[C#] **protected void UpdateBounds(int, int, int, int);**

[C++] **protected: void UpdateBounds(int, int, int, int);**

[JScript] **protected function UpdateBounds(int, int, int, int);**

Updates the bounds of the control with the specified size, location, and client size.

[Visual Basic] **Overloads Protected Sub Update-Bounds(Integer, Integer, Integer, Integer, Integer, Integer)**

[C#] **protected void UpdateBounds(int, int, int, int, int, int);**

[C++] **protected: void UpdateBounds(int, int, int, int, int, int);**

[JScript] **protected function UpdateBounds(int, int, int, int, int, int);**

Control.UpdateBounds Method ()

Updates the bounds of the control with the current size and location.

[Visual Basic]
```
Overloads Protected Sub UpdateBounds()
```
[C#]
```
protected void UpdateBounds();
```
[C++]
```
protected: void UpdateBounds();
```
[JScript]
```
protected function UpdateBounds();
```

Remarks

If the new **Size** of the control is different from the previous **Size**, the **SizeChanged** event is raised. Likewise, if the **Location** of the control changes, the **LocationChanged** event is raised.

Requirements

Platforms: Windows 98, Windows NT 4.0, Windows Millennium Edition, Windows 2000, Windows XP Home Edition, Windows XP Professional, Windows Server 2003 family

Control.UpdateBounds Method (Int32, Int32, Int32, Int32)

Updates the bounds of the control with the specified size and location.

[Visual Basic]
```
Overloads Protected Sub UpdateBounds( _
   ByVal x As Integer, _
   ByVal y As Integer, _
   ByVal width As Integer, _
   ByVal height As Integer _
)
```
[C#]
```
protected void UpdateBounds(
   int x,
   int y,
   int width,
   int height
);
```
[C++]
```
protected: void UpdateBounds(
   int x,
   int y,
   int width,
   int height
);
```
[JScript]
```
protected function UpdateBounds(
   x : int,
   y : int,
   width : int,
   height : int
);
```

Parameters

x
: The **X** coordinate of the control.

y
: The **Y** coordinate of the control.

width
: The **Width** of the control.

height
: The **Height** of the control.

Remarks

If the new **Size** of the control if different from the previous **Size**, the **SizeChanged** event is raised. Likewise, is the **Location** of the control changes, the **LocationChanged** event is raised.

Requirements

Platforms: Windows 98, Windows NT 4.0, Windows Millennium Edition, Windows 2000, Windows XP Home Edition, Windows XP Professional, Windows Server 2003 family

Control.UpdateBounds Method (Int32, Int32, Int32, Int32, Int32, Int32)

Updates the bounds of the control with the specified size, location, and client size.

[Visual Basic]
```
Overloads Protected Sub UpdateBounds( _
   ByVal x As Integer, _
   ByVal y As Integer, _
   ByVal width As Integer, _
   ByVal height As Integer, _
   ByVal clientWidth As Integer, _
   ByVal clientHeight As Integer _
)
```

[C#]
```
protected void UpdateBounds(
   int x,
   int y,
   int width,
   int height,
   int clientWidth,
   int clientHeight
);
```
[C++]
```
protected: void UpdateBounds(
   int x,
   int y,
   int width,
   int height,
   int clientWidth,
   int clientHeight
);
```
[JScript]
```
protected function UpdateBounds(
   x : int,
   y : int,
   width : int,
   height : int,
   clientWidth : int,
   clientHeight : int
);
```

Parameters

x
  The **X** coordinate of the control.

y
  The **Y** coordinate of the control.

width
  The **Width** of the control.

height
  The **Height** of the control.

clientWidth
  The client **Width** of the control.

clientHeight
  The client **Height** of the control.

Remarks

If the new **Size** of the control is different from the previous **Size**, the **SizeChanged** event is raised. Likewise, if the **Location** of the control changes, the **LocationChanged** event is raised.

Requirements

Platforms: Windows 98, Windows NT 4.0, Windows Millennium Edition, Windows 2000, Windows XP Home Edition, Windows XP Professional, Windows Server 2003 family

Control.UpdateStyles Method

Forces the assigned styles to be reapplied to the control.

[Visual Basic]
```
Protected Sub UpdateStyles()
```
[C#]
```
protected void UpdateStyles();
```
[C++]
```
protected: void UpdateStyles();
```
[JScript]
```
protected function UpdateStyles();
```

Remarks

This method calls the **CreateParams** method to get the styles to apply. The styles assigned to the **Style** and **ExStyle** properties of the **CreateParams** object assigned to the control's **CreateParams** property are reapplied. The control is repainted to reflect the style changes if necessary.

The **UpdateStyles** method has no effect if the **IsHandleCreated** property value is **false**.

Example

[Visual Basic, C#, C++] The following example enables double-buffering on a **Form** and updates the styles to reflect the changes.

[Visual Basic]
```
Public Sub EnableDoubleBuffering()
   ' Set the value of the double-buffering style bits to true.
   Me.SetStyle(ControlStyles.DoubleBuffer _
     Or ControlStyles.UserPaint _
     Or ControlStyles.AllPaintingInWmPaint, _
     True)
   Me.UpdateStyles()
End Sub
```

[C#]
```
public void EnableDoubleBuffering()
{
   // Set the value of the double-buffering style bits to true.
   this.SetStyle(ControlStyles.DoubleBuffer |
      ControlStyles.UserPaint |
      ControlStyles.AllPaintingInWmPaint,
      true);
   this.UpdateStyles();
}
```

[C++]
```
public:
   void EnableDoubleBuffering() {
      // Set the value of the double-buffering style bits to true.
      this-
>SetStyle(static_cast<ControlStyles>(ControlStyles::DoubleBuffer |
         ControlStyles::UserPaint |
         ControlStyles::AllPaintingInWmPaint),
         true);
      this->UpdateStyles();
   }
```

Requirements

Platforms: Windows 98, Windows NT 4.0, Windows Millennium Edition, Windows 2000, Windows XP Home Edition, Windows XP Professional, Windows Server 2003 family

Control.UpdateZOrder Method

Updates the control in its parent's z-order.

[Visual Basic]
```
Protected Sub UpdateZOrder()
```
[C#]
```
protected void UpdateZOrder();
```
[C++]
```
protected: void UpdateZOrder();
```
[JScript]
```
protected function UpdateZOrder();
```

Remarks

The **UpdateZOrder** method updates the position of the control in its parent control's z-order. For example, if this control is a newly created control that was added to a **Control.ControlCollection**, the z-order is updated with the new control added to the back.

Requirements

Platforms: Windows 98, Windows NT 4.0, Windows Millennium Edition, Windows 2000, Windows XP Home Edition, Windows XP Professional, Windows Server 2003 family

Control.WndProc Method

Processes Windows messages.

[Visual Basic]

```
Protected Overridable Sub WndProc( _
   ByRef m As Message _
)
```

[C#]

```
protected virtual void WndProc(
   ref Message m
);
```

[C++]

```
protected: virtual void WndProc(
   Message* m
);
```

[JScript]

```
protected function WndProc(
   m : Message
);
```

Parameters

m

The Windows **Message** to process.

Remarks

All messages are sent to the **WndProc** method after getting filtered through the **PreProcessMessage** method.

The **WndProc** method corresponds exactly to the Windows **WindowProc** function. For more information about processing Windows messages, see the **WindowProc** function documentation in the Windows Platform SDK reference located in the MSDN Library.

Notes to Inheritors: Inheriting controls should call the base class's **WndProc** method to process any messages that they do not handle.

Example

[Visual Basic, C#, C++] The following example demonstrates overriding the **WndProc** method to handle operating system messages identified in the **Message** structure. The WM_ACTIVATEAPP operating system message is handled in this example to know when another application is becoming active. Refer to the Platform SDK documentation reference located in the MSDN Library to understand the available **Message.Msg**, **Message.LParam**, and **Message.WParam** values. Actual constant values can be found in the windows.h header file included in the Platform SDK (Core SDK section) download, which is also available on MSDN.

[Visual Basic]

```
Imports System
Imports System.Drawing
Imports System.Windows.Forms

Namespace csTempWindowsApplication1

    Public Class Form1
        Inherits System.Windows.Forms.Form

        ' Constant value was found in the "windows.h" header file.
        Private Const WM_ACTIVATEAPP As Integer = &H1C
        Private appActive As Boolean = True

        <STAThread()> _
        Shared Sub Main()
            Application.Run(New Form1())
        End Sub 'Main

        Public Sub New()
            MyBase.New()

            Me.Size = New System.Drawing.Size(300, 300)
            Me.Text = "Form1"
            Me.Font = New System.Drawing.Font("Microsoft
Sans Serif", 18.0!, System.Drawing.FontStyle.Bold,
System.Drawing.GraphicsUnit.Point, CType(0, Byte))
        End Sub

        Protected Overrides Sub OnPaint(ByVal e As PaintEventArgs)

            ' Paint a string in different styles depending
 on whether the
            ' application is active.
            If (appActive) Then
                e.Graphics.FillRectangle
 (SystemBrushes.ActiveCaption, 20, 20, 260, 50)
                e.Graphics.DrawString
 ("Application is active", Me.Font,
SystemBrushes.ActiveCaptionText, 20, 20)
            Else
                e.Graphics.FillRectangle
 (SystemBrushes.InactiveCaption, 20, 20, 260, 50)
                e.Graphics.DrawString
 ("Application is Inactive", Me.Font,
SystemBrushes.ActiveCaptionText, 20, 20)
            End If
        End Sub
    <System.Security.Permissions.PermissionSetAttribute
 (System.Security.Permissions.SecurityAction.Demand,
Name:="FullTrust")> _
        Protected Overrides Sub WndProc(ByRef m As Message)
            ' Listen for operating system messages
            Select Case (m.Msg)
                ' The WM_ACTIVATEAPP message occurs
 when the application
                ' becomes the active application or becomes inactive.
            Case WM_ACTIVATEAPP

                    ' The WParam value identifies what is occurring.
                    appActive = (m.WParam.ToInt32() <> 0)

                    ' Invalidate to get new text painted.
                    Me.Invalidate()

            End Select
            MyBase.WndProc(m)
        End Sub
    End Class
End Namespace
```

[C#]

```
using System;
using System.Drawing;
using System.Windows.Forms;
```

```
namespace csTempWindowsApplication1
{
    public class Form1 : System.Windows.Forms.Form
    {
        // Constant value was found in the "windows.h" header file.
        private const int WM_ACTIVATEAPP = 0x001C;
        private bool appActive = true;

        [STAThread]
        static void Main()
        {
            Application.Run(new Form1());
        }

        public Form1()
        {
            this.Size = new System.Drawing.Size(300,300);
            this.Text = "Form1";
            this.Font = new System.Drawing.Font                         ↵
 ("Microsoft Sans Serif", 18F,                                          ↵
System.Drawing.FontStyle.Bold,                                          ↵
System.Drawing.GraphicsUnit.Point, ((System.Byte)(0)));
        }

        protected override void OnPaint(PaintEventArgs e)
        {
            // Paint a string in different styles depending            ↵
 on whether the
            // application is active.
            if (appActive)
            {

e.Graphics.FillRectangle(SystemBrushes.ActiveCaption,20,20,260,50);
                e.Graphics.DrawString("Application                      ↵
 is active", this.Font, SystemBrushes.ActiveCaptionText, 20,20);
            }
            else
            {

e.Graphics.FillRectangle(SystemBrushes.InactiveCaption,20,20,260,50);
                e.Graphics.DrawString("Application is                   ↵
Inactive", this.Font, SystemBrushes.ActiveCaptionText, 20,20);
            }
        }

    [System.Security.Permissions.PermissionSet                          ↵
 (System.Security.Permissions.SecurityAction.Demand, Name="FullTrust")]
        protected override void WndProc(ref Message m)
        {
            // Listen for operating system messages.
            switch (m.Msg)
            {
                // The WM_ACTIVATEAPP message occurs                    ↵
when the application
                // becomes the active application or becomes inactive.
                case WM_ACTIVATEAPP:

                    // The WParam value identifies what is occurring.
                    appActive = (((int)m.WParam != 0));

                    // Invalidate to get new text painted.
                    this.Invalidate();

                    break;
            }
            base.WndProc(ref m);
        }
    }
}
```

[C++]

```
using namespace System;
using namespace System::Drawing;
using namespace System::Windows::Forms;

namespace csTempWindowsApplication1 {
public __gc class Form1 : public System::Windows::Forms::Form {
private:
    // Constant value was found in the S"windows.h" header file.
    const static Int32 WM_ACTIVATEAPP = 0x001C;

    Boolean appActive;

public:
    Form1() {
        appActive = true;
        this->Size = System::Drawing::Size(300, 300);
        this->Text = S"Form1";
        this->Font = new System::Drawing::Font(S"Microsoft Sans Serif",
            18.0F, System::Drawing::FontStyle::Bold,
            System::Drawing::GraphicsUnit::Point, ((System::Byte)(0)));
    }

protected:
    void OnPaint(PaintEventArgs* e) {
        // Paint a String* in different styles depending on whether the
        // application is active.
        if (appActive) {
            e->Graphics->FillRectangle(SystemBrushes::ActiveCaption,
                20, 20, 260, 50);
            e->Graphics->DrawString(S"Application is active",
                this->Font, SystemBrushes::ActiveCaptionText, 20, 20);
        } else {
            e->Graphics->FillRectangle(SystemBrushes::InactiveCaption,
                20, 20, 260, 50);
            e->Graphics->DrawString(S"Application is Inactive",
                this->Font, SystemBrushes::ActiveCaptionText, 20, 20);
        }
    }

    [System::Security::Permissions::PermissionSet                       ↵
 (System::Security::Permissions::SecurityAction::Demand,                ↵
Name="FullTrust")]
    void WndProc(Message* m) {
        // Listen for operating system messages.
        switch (m->Msg) {
            // The WM_ACTIVATEAPP message occurs when the application
            // becomes the active application or becomes inactive.
                case WM_ACTIVATEAPP:

                    // The WParam value identifies what is occurring.
                    appActive = (((int)m->WParam != 0));

                    // Invalidate to get new text painted.
                    this->Invalidate();

                    break;
        }
        Form::WndProc(m);
    }
};
}

[STAThread]
int main() {
    Application::Run(new csTempWindowsApplication1::Form1());
}
```

Requirements

Platforms: Windows 98, Windows NT 4.0, Windows Millennium Edition, Windows 2000, Windows XP Home Edition, Windows XP Professional, Windows Server 2003 family

.NET Framework Security:

- **SecurityPermission** for inheriting classes to call unmanaged code. Associated enumeration: **SecurityPermissionFlag.UnmanagedCode**
- **SecurityPermission** for the immediate caller to call unmanaged code. Associated enumeration: **SecurityPermissionFlag.UnmanagedCode**

Control.BackColorChanged Event

Occurs when the value of the **BackColor** property changes.

[Visual Basic]
```
Public Event BackColorChanged As EventHandler
```
[C#]
```
public event EventHandler BackColorChanged;
```
[C++]
```
public: __event EventHandler* BackColorChanged;
```

[JScript] In JScript, you can handle the events defined by a class, but you cannot define your own.

Event Data

The event handler receives an argument of type **EventArgs**.

Remarks

This event is raised if the **BackColor** property is changed by either a programmatic modification or user interaction.

Example

[Visual Basic, C#, C++] The example below is an event handling method that is executed when the **Text** property value changes. The **Control** class has several methods with the name pattern Property-Name **Changed** that are raised when the corresponding Property-Name value changes(PropertyName represents the name of the corresponding property).

[Visual Basic, C#, C++] The following example changes the **ForeColor** of a **TextBox** displaying currency data. The example converts the text to a decimal number and changes the **ForeColor** to **Color.Red** if the number is negative and to **Color.Black** if the number is positive. This example assumes you have a **Form** that contains a **TextBox**.

[Visual Basic]
```
Private Sub currencyTextBox_TextChanged(sender As Object, _
  e As EventArgs) Handles currencyTextBox.TextChanged
    Try
        ' Convert the text to a Double and determine if it is a ↵
negative number.
        If Double.Parse(currencyTextBox.Text) < 0 Then
            ' If the number is negative, display it in Red.
            currencyTextBox.ForeColor = Color.Red
        Else
            ' If the number is not negative, display it in Black.
            currencyTextBox.ForeColor = Color.Black
        End If
    Catch
        ' If there is an error, display the text using the system colors.
        currencyTextBox.ForeColor = SystemColors.ControlText
    End Try
End Sub
```

[C#]
```
private void currencyTextBox_TextChanged(object sender, EventArgs e)
{
    try
    {
        // Convert the text to a Double and determine if it is a ↵
negative number.
        if(double.Parse(currencyTextBox.Text) < 0)
        {
            // If the number is negative, display it in Red.
            currencyTextBox.ForeColor = Color.Red;
        }
        else
        {
            // If the number is not negative, display it in Black.
            currencyTextBox.ForeColor = Color.Black;
        }
    }
    catch
    {
        // If there is an error, display the text using the ↵
system colors.
        currencyTextBox.ForeColor = SystemColors.ControlText;
    }
}
```

[C++]
```
private:
    void currencyTextBox_TextChanged(Object* /*sender*/, ↵
 EventArgs* /*e*/) {
        try {
            // Convert the text to a Double and determine if it ↵
is a negative number.
            if (Double::Parse(currencyTextBox->Text) < 0) {
                // If the number is negative, display it in Red.
                currencyTextBox->ForeColor = Color::Red;
            } else {
                // If the number is not negative, display it in Black.
                currencyTextBox->ForeColor = Color::Black;
            }
        } catch (Exception*) {
            // If there is an error, display the text using the ↵
 system colors.
            currencyTextBox->ForeColor = SystemColors::ControlText;
        }
    }
```

Requirements

Platforms: Windows 98, Windows NT 4.0, Windows Millennium Edition, Windows 2000, Windows XP Home Edition, Windows XP Professional, Windows Server 2003 family

Control.BackgroundImageChanged Event

Occurs when the value of the **BackgroundImage** property changes.

[Visual Basic]
```
Public Event BackgroundImageChanged As EventHandler
```
[C#]
```
public event EventHandler BackgroundImageChanged;
```
[C++]
```
public: __event EventHandler* BackgroundImageChanged;
```

[JScript] In JScript, you can handle the events defined by a class, but you cannot define your own.

Event Data

The event handler receives an argument of type **EventArgs**.

Remarks

This event is raised if the **BackgroundImage** property is changed by either a programmatic modification or user interaction.

Example

[Visual Basic, C#, C++] The example below is an event handling method that is executed when the **Text** property value changes. The **Control** class has several methods with the name pattern Property-Name **Changed** that are raised when the corresponding Property-Name value changes(PropertyName represents the name of the corresponding property).

[Visual Basic, C#, C++] The following example changes the **ForeColor** of a **TextBox** displaying currency data. The example converts the text to a decimal number and changes the **ForeColor** to **Color.Red** if the number is negative and to **Color.Black** if the number is positive. This example assumes you have a **Form** that contains a **TextBox**.

[Visual Basic]
```
Private Sub currencyTextBox_TextChanged(sender As Object, _
  e As EventArgs) Handles currencyTextBox.TextChanged
    Try
        ' Convert the text to a Double and determine if it is a ↵
negative number.
        If Double.Parse(currencyTextBox.Text) < 0 Then
            ' If the number is negative, display it in Red.
            currencyTextBox.ForeColor = Color.Red
        Else
            ' If the number is not negative, display it in Black.
            currencyTextBox.ForeColor = Color.Black
        End If
    Catch
        ' If there is an error, display the text using the system colors.
        currencyTextBox.ForeColor = SystemColors.ControlText
    End Try
End Sub
```

[C#]
```
private void currencyTextBox_TextChanged(object sender, EventArgs e)
{
   try
   {
      // Convert the text to a Double and determine if it is a ↵
negative number.
      if(double.Parse(currencyTextBox.Text) < 0)
      {
         // If the number is negative, display it in Red.
         currencyTextBox.ForeColor = Color.Red;
      }
      else
      {
         // If the number is not negative, display it in Black.
         currencyTextBox.ForeColor = Color.Black;
      }
   }
   catch
   {
      // If there is an error, display the text using the ↵
system colors.
      currencyTextBox.ForeColor = SystemColors.ControlText;
   }
}
```

[C++]
```
private:
    void currencyTextBox_TextChanged(Object* /*sender*/, ↵
 EventArgs* /*e*/) {
        try {
            // Convert the text to a Double and determine if ↵
it is a negative number.
            if (Double::Parse(currencyTextBox->Text) < 0) {
                // If the number is negative, display it in Red.
                currencyTextBox->ForeColor = Color::Red;
            } else {
                // If the number is not negative, display it in Black.
                currencyTextBox->ForeColor = Color::Black;
            }
        } catch (Exception*) {
            // If there is an error, display the text using ↵
the system colors.
            currencyTextBox->ForeColor = SystemColors::ControlText;
        }
    }
```

Requirements

Platforms: Windows 98, Windows NT 4.0, Windows Millennium Edition, Windows 2000, Windows XP Home Edition, Windows XP Professional, Windows Server 2003 family

Control.BindingContextChanged Event

Occurs when the value of the **BindingContext** property changes.

[Visual Basic]
```
Public Event BindingContextChanged As EventHandler
```
[C#]
```
public event EventHandler BindingContextChanged;
```
[C++]
```
public: __event EventHandler* BindingContextChanged;
```

[JScript] In JScript, you can handle the events defined by a class, but you cannot define your own.

Event Data

The event handler receives an argument of type **EventArgs**.

Remarks

To add a new **BindingContext** to the **Control** through the **BindingContext** property, see the **BindingContext** constructor.

This event is raised if the **BindingContext** property is changed is changed by either a programmatic modification or user interaction.

Example

[Visual Basic, C#, JScript] The following example adds an **EventHandler** delegate to the **BindingContextChanged** event of a **TextBox** control.

[Visual Basic]
```
Private Sub AddEventHandler()
    AddHandler textBox1.BindingContextChanged, _
       AddressOf BindingContext_Changed
End Sub

Private Sub BindingContext_Changed(sender As Object, e As EventArgs)
    Console.WriteLine("BindingContext changed")
End Sub
```

[C#]
```
private void AddEventHandler()
{
   textBox1.BindingContextChanged += new ↵
EventHandler(BindingContext_Changed);
}

private void BindingContext_Changed(object sender, EventArgs e)
{
   Console.WriteLine("BindingContext changed");
}
```

[JScript]
```
private function AddEventHandler()
{
   textBox1.add_BindingContextChanged(BindingContext_Changed);
}

private function BindingContext_Changed(sender : Object, e : EventArgs)
{
   Console.WriteLine("BindingContext changed");
}
```

Requirements

Platforms: Windows 98, Windows NT 4.0, Windows Millennium Edition, Windows 2000, Windows XP Home Edition, Windows XP Professional, Windows Server 2003 family

Control.CausesValidationChanged Event

Occurs when the value of the **CausesValidation** property changes.

[Visual Basic]
```
Public Event CausesValidationChanged As EventHandler
```
[C#]
```
public event EventHandler CausesValidationChanged;
```
[C++]
```
public: __event EventHandler* CausesValidationChanged;
```

[JScript] In JScript, you can handle the events defined by a class, but you cannot define your own.

Event Data

The event handler receives an argument of type **EventArgs**.

Remarks

This event is raised if the **CausesValidation** property is changed by either a programmatic modification or user interaction.

Example

[Visual Basic, C#, C++] The example below is an event handling method that is executed when the **Text** property value changes. The **Control** class has several methods with the name pattern Property-Name **Changed** that are raised when the corresponding Property-Name value changes(PropertyName represents the name of the corresponding property).

[Visual Basic, C#, C++] The following example changes the **ForeColor** of a **TextBox** displaying currency data. The example converts the text to a decimal number and changes the **ForeColor** to **Color.Red** if the number is negative and to **Color.Black** if the number is positive. This example assumes you have a **Form** that contains a **TextBox**.

[Visual Basic]
```
Private Sub currencyTextBox_TextChanged(sender As Object, _
  e As EventArgs) Handles currencyTextBox.TextChanged
    Try
        ' Convert the text to a Double and determine if it
is a negative number.
        If Double.Parse(currencyTextBox.Text) < 0 Then
            ' If the number is negative, display it in Red.
            currencyTextBox.ForeColor = Color.Red
        Else
            ' If the number is not negative, display it in Black.
            currencyTextBox.ForeColor = Color.Black
        End If
    Catch
        ' If there is an error, display the text using the system colors.
        currencyTextBox.ForeColor = SystemColors.ControlText
    End Try
End Sub
```

[C#]
```
private void currencyTextBox_TextChanged(object sender, EventArgs e)
{
    try
    {
        // Convert the text to a Double and determine if it
 is a negative number.
        if(double.Parse(currencyTextBox.Text) < 0)
        {
            // If the number is negative, display it in Red.
            currencyTextBox.ForeColor = Color.Red;
        }
        else
        {
            // If the number is not negative, display it in Black.
            currencyTextBox.ForeColor = Color.Black;
        }
    }
    catch
    {
        // If there is an error, display the text using the
system colors.
        currencyTextBox.ForeColor = SystemColors.ControlText;
    }
}
```

[C++]
```
private:
    void currencyTextBox_TextChanged(Object* /*sender*/,
EventArgs* /*e*/) {
        try {
            // Convert the text to a Double and determine
 if it is a negative number.
            if (Double::Parse(currencyTextBox->Text) < 0) {
                // If the number is negative, display it in Red.
                currencyTextBox->ForeColor = Color::Red;
            } else {
                // If the number is not negative, display it in Black.
                currencyTextBox->ForeColor = Color::Black;
            }
        } catch (Exception*) {
            // If there is an error, display the text using
the system colors.
            currencyTextBox->ForeColor = SystemColors::ControlText;
        }
    }
```

Requirements

Platforms: Windows 98, Windows NT 4.0, Windows Millennium Edition, Windows 2000, Windows XP Home Edition, Windows XP Professional, Windows Server 2003 family

Control.ChangeUICues Event

Occurs when the focus or keyboard user interface (UI) cues change.

[Visual Basic]
```
Public Event ChangeUICues As UICuesEventHandler
```
[C#]
```
public event UICuesEventHandler ChangeUICues;
```
[C++]
```
public: __event UICuesEventHandler* ChangeUICues;
```

[JScript] In JScript, you can handle the events defined by a class, but you cannot define your own.

Event Data

The event handler receives an argument of type **UICuesEventArgs** containing data related to this event. The following **UICuesEventArgs** properties provide information specific to this event.

Property	Description
Changed	Gets the bitwise combination of the **UICues** values.
ChangeFocus	Gets a value indicating whether the state of the focus cues has changed.
ChangeKeyboard	Gets a value indicating whether the state of the keyboard cues has changed.
ShowFocus	Gets a value indicating whether focus rectangles are shown after the change.
ShowKeyboard	Gets a value indicating whether keyboard cues are underlined after the change.

Requirements

Platforms: Windows 98, Windows NT 4.0, Windows Millennium Edition, Windows 2000, Windows XP Home Edition, Windows XP Professional, Windows Server 2003 family

Control.Click Event

Occurs when the control is clicked.

```
[Visual Basic]
Public Event Click As EventHandler
[C#]
public event EventHandler Click;
[C++]
public: __event EventHandler* Click;
```

[JScript] In JScript, you can handle the events defined by a class, but you cannot define your own.

Event Data

The event handler receives an argument of type **EventArgs**.

Remarks

The **Click** event passes an **EventArgs** object to its event handler, so it only indicates that a click has occurred. If you need more specific mouse information (button, number of clicks, wheel rotation, or location), use the **MouseDown** and **MouseUp** events which pass a **MouseEventArgs** object to the event handler.

A double-click is determined by the mouse settings of the user's operating system. The user can set the time between clicks of a mouse button that should be considered a double-click rather than two clicks. The **Click** event is raised every time a control is double-clicked. For example, if you have an event-handling methods for the **Click** and **DoubleClick** events of a **Form**, the **Click** and **DoubleClick** events are raised when the form is double-clicked and both methods are called. If a control is double-clicked and that control does not support the **DoubleClick** event, the **Click** event might be raised twice.

The **ControlStyles.StandardClick** style bit must be set to **true** for this event to be raised.

Notes to Inheritors: Inheriting from a standard Windows Forms control and changing the **StandardClick** or **StandardDoubleClick** bit values to **true** can cause unexpected behavior or have no effect at all if the control does not support the **Click** or **DoubleClick** events.

Example

[Visual Basic]

```
' This example uses the Parent property and the Find method ↵
of Control to set
' properties on the parent control of a Button and its Form. ↵
The example assumes
' that a Button control named button1 is located within a ↵
GroupBox control. The
' example also assumes that the Click event of the Button ↵
control is connected to
' the event handling method defined in the example.
Private Sub button1_Click(sender As Object, e As ↵
System.EventArgs) Handles button1.Click
   ' Get the control the Button control is located in. In ↵
this case a GroupBox.
   Dim control As Control = button1.Parent
   ' Set the text and backcolor of the parent control.
   control.Text = "My Groupbox"
   control.BackColor = Color.Blue
   ' Get the form that the Button control is contained within.
   Dim myForm As Form = button1.FindForm()
   ' Set the text and color of the form containing the Button.
   myForm.Text = "The Form of My Control"
   myForm.BackColor = Color.Red
End Sub
```

[C#]

```
// This example uses the Parent property and the Find method ↵
of Control to set
// properties on the parent control of a Button and its Form. ↵
The example assumes
// that a Button control named button1 is located within a ↵
GroupBox control. The
// example also assumes that the Click event of the Button ↵
control is connected to
// the event handling method defined in the example.
private void button1_Click(object sender, System.EventArgs e)
{
   // Get the control the Button control is located in. In this ↵
case a GroupBox.
   Control control = button1.Parent;
   // Set the text and backcolor of the parent control.
   control.Text = "My Groupbox";
   control.BackColor = Color.Blue;
   // Get the form that the Button control is contained within.
   Form myForm = button1.FindForm();
   // Set the text and color of the form containing the Button.
   myForm.Text = "The Form of My Control";
   myForm.BackColor = Color.Red;
}
```

Requirements

Platforms: Windows 98, Windows NT 4.0, Windows Millennium Edition, Windows 2000, Windows XP Home Edition, Windows XP Professional, Windows Server 2003 family

Control.ContextMenuChanged Event

Occurs when the value of the **ContextMenu** property changes.

```
[Visual Basic]
Public Event ContextMenuChanged As EventHandler
[C#]
public event EventHandler ContextMenuChanged;
[C++]
public: __event EventHandler* ContextMenuChanged;
```

[JScript] In JScript, you can handle the events defined by a class, but you cannot define your own.

Event Data

The event handler receives an argument of type **EventArgs**.

Remarks

This event is raised if the **ContextMenu** property is changed by either a programmatic modification or user interaction.

Example

[Visual Basic, C#, C++] The example below is an event handling method that is executed when the **Text** property value changes. The **Control** class has several methods with the name pattern PropertyName **Changed** that are raised when the corresponding PropertyName value changes(PropertyName represents the name of the corresponding property).

[Visual Basic, C#, C++] The following example changes the **ForeColor** of a **TextBox** displaying currency data. The example converts the text to a decimal number and changes the **ForeColor** to **Color.Red** if the number is negative and to **Color.Black** if the number is positive. This example assumes you have a **Form** that contains a **TextBox**.

[Visual Basic]
```
Private Sub currencyTextBox_TextChanged(sender As Object, _
  e As EventArgs) Handles currencyTextBox.TextChanged
   Try
      ' Convert the text to a Double and determine if it is a
 negative number.
      If Double.Parse(currencyTextBox.Text) < 0 Then
         ' If the number is negative, display it in Red.
         currencyTextBox.ForeColor = Color.Red
      Else
         ' If the number is not negative, display it in Black.
         currencyTextBox.ForeColor = Color.Black
      End If
   Catch
      ' If there is an error, display the text using the system colors.
      currencyTextBox.ForeColor = SystemColors.ControlText
   End Try
End Sub
```

[C#]
```
private void currencyTextBox_TextChanged(object sender, EventArgs e)
{
   try
   {
      // Convert the text to a Double and determine if it is
a negative number.
      if(double.Parse(currencyTextBox.Text) < 0)
      {
         // If the number is negative, display it in Red.
         currencyTextBox.ForeColor = Color.Red;
      }
      else
      {
         // If the number is not negative, display it in Black.
         currencyTextBox.ForeColor = Color.Black;
      }
   }
   catch
   {
      // If there is an error, display the text using
 the system colors.
      currencyTextBox.ForeColor = SystemColors.ControlText;
   }
}
```

[C++]
```
private:
    void currencyTextBox_TextChanged(Object* /*sender*/,
 EventArgs* /*e*/) {
        try {
            // Convert the text to a Double and determine
 if it is a negative number.
            if (Double::Parse(currencyTextBox->Text) < 0) {
                // If the number is negative, display it in Red.
                currencyTextBox->ForeColor = Color::Red;
            } else {
                // If the number is not negative, display it in Black.
                currencyTextBox->ForeColor = Color::Black;
            }
        } catch (Exception*) {
            // If there is an error, display the text using
 the system colors.
            currencyTextBox->ForeColor = SystemColors::ControlText;
        }
    }
```

Requirements

Platforms: Windows 98, Windows NT 4.0, Windows Millennium Edition, Windows 2000, Windows XP Home Edition, Windows XP Professional, Windows Server 2003 family

Control.ControlAdded Event

Occurs when a new control is added to the **Control.ControlCollection**.

[Visual Basic]
```
Public Event ControlAdded As ControlEventHandler
```
[C#]
```
public event ControlEventHandler ControlAdded;
```
[C++]
```
public: __event ControlEventHandler* ControlAdded;
```

[JScript] In JScript, you can handle the events defined by a class, but you cannot define your own.

Event Data

The event handler receives an argument of type **ControlEventArgs** containing data related to this event. The following **ControlEventArgs** property provides information specific to this event.

Property	Description
Control	Gets the control object used by this event.

Remarks

Example

[Visual Basic]
```
' This example demonstrates the use of the ControlAdded and
' ControlRemoved events. This example assumes that two Button controls
' are added to the form and connected to the addControl_Click and
' removeControl_Click event handling methods.
Private Sub Form1_Load(ByVal sender As Object, ByVal e As
System.EventArgs) Handles MyBase.Load
    ' Connect the ControlRemoved and ControlAdded event handlers
 to the event handling methods.
    ' ControlRemoved and ControlAdded are not available at design time.
    AddHandler Me.ControlRemoved, AddressOf Me.Control_Removed
    AddHandler Me.ControlAdded, AddressOf Me.Control_Added
End Sub 'Form1_Load

Private Sub Control_Added(ByVal sender As Object, ByVal e As
System.Windows.Forms.ControlEventArgs)
    MessageBox.Show(("The control named " + e.Control.Name + "
 has been added to the form."))
End Sub

Private Sub Control_Removed(ByVal sender As Object, ByVal e As
System.Windows.Forms.ControlEventArgs)
    MessageBox.Show(("The control named " + e.Control.Name + "
has been removed from the form."))
End Sub

' Click event handler for a Button control. Adds a TextBox to the form.
Private Sub addControl_Click(ByVal sender As Object, ByVal e As
System.EventArgs) Handles button1.Click
    ' Create a new TextBox control and add it to the form.
    Dim textBox1 As New TextBox()
    textBox1.Size = New Size(100, 10)
    textBox1.Location = New Point(10, 10)
    ' Name the control in order to remove it later.
    ' The name must be specified if a control is added at run time.
    textBox1.Name = "textBox1"

    ' Add the control to the form's control collection.
    Me.Controls.Add(textBox1)
End Sub

' Click event handler for a Button control.
' Removes the previously added TextBox from the form.
Private Sub removeControl_Click(ByVal sender As Object,
 ByVal e As System.EventArgs) Handles button2.Click
    ' Loop through all controls in the form's control collection.
```

```
    Dim tempCtrl As Control
    For Each tempCtrl In Me.Controls
        ' Determine whether the control is textBox1,
        ' and if it is, remove it.
        If tempCtrl.Name = "textBox1" Then
            Me.Controls.Remove(tempCtrl)
        End If
    Next tempCtrl
End Sub
```

[C#]

```
// This example demonstrates the use of the ControlAdded and
// ControlRemoved events. This example assumes that two Button controls
// are added to the form and connected to the addControl_Click and
// removeControl_Click event handling methods.
private void Form1_Load(object sender, System.EventArgs e)
{
    // Connect the ControlRemoved and ControlAdded event handlers
    // to the event handling methods.
    // ControlRemoved and ControlAdded are not available at ↲
 design time.
    this.ControlRemoved += new ↲
System.Windows.Forms.ControlEventHandler(this.Control_Removed);
    this.ControlAdded += new ↲
System.Windows.Forms.ControlEventHandler(this.Control_Added);
}

private void Control_Added(object sender, ↲
System.Windows.Forms.ControlEventArgs e)
{
    MessageBox.Show("The control named " + e.Control.Name + ↲
 " has been added to the form.");
}

private void Control_Removed(object sender, ↲
System.Windows.Forms.ControlEventArgs e)
{
    MessageBox.Show("The control named " + e.Control.Name + ↲
" has been removed from the form.");
}

// Click event handler for a Button control. Adds a TextBox ↲
 to the form.
private void addControl_Click(object sender, System.EventArgs e)
{
    // Create a new TextBox control and add it to the form.
    TextBox textBox1 = new TextBox();
    textBox1.Size = new Size(100,10);
    textBox1.Location = new Point(10,10);
    // Name the control in order to remove it later. The name ↲
must be specified
    // if a control is added at run time.
    textBox1.Name = "textBox1";

    // Add the control to the form's control collection.
    this.Controls.Add(textBox1);
}

// Click event handler for a Button control.
// Removes the previously added TextBox from the form.
private void removeControl_Click(object sender, System.EventArgs e)
{
    // Loop through all controls in the form's control collection.
    foreach (Control tempCtrl in this.Controls)
    {
        // Determine whether the control is textBox1,
        // and if it is, remove it.
        if (tempCtrl.Name == "textBox1")
        {
            this.Controls.Remove(tempCtrl);
        }
    }
}
```

Requirements

Platforms: Windows 98, Windows NT 4.0, Windows Millennium Edition, Windows 2000, Windows XP Home Edition, Windows XP Professional, Windows Server 2003 family

Control.ControlRemoved Event

Occurs when a control is removed from the **Control.ControlCollection**.

[Visual Basic]

```
Public Event ControlRemoved As ControlEventHandler
```

[C#]

```
public event ControlEventHandler ControlRemoved;
```

[C++]

```
public: __event ControlEventHandler* ControlRemoved;
```

[JScript] In JScript, you can handle the events defined by a class, but you cannot define your own.

Event Data

The event handler receives an argument of type **ControlEventArgs** containing data related to this event. The following **ControlEventArgs** property provides information specific to this event.

Property	Description
Control	Gets the control object used by this event.

Remarks

Example

[Visual Basic]

```
' This example demonstrates the use of the ControlAdded and
' ControlRemoved events. This example assumes that two Button controls
' are added to the form and connected to the addControl_Click and
' removeControl_Click event handling methods.
Private Sub Form1_Load(ByVal sender As Object, ByVal e As ↲
System.EventArgs) Handles MyBase.Load
    ' Connect the ControlRemoved and ControlAdded event handlers ↲
to the event handling methods.
    ' ControlRemoved and ControlAdded are not available at design time.
    AddHandler Me.ControlRemoved, AddressOf Me.Control_Removed
    AddHandler Me.ControlAdded, AddressOf Me.Control_Added
End Sub 'Form1_Load

Private Sub Control_Added(ByVal sender As Object, ByVal e As ↲
System.Windows.Forms.ControlEventArgs)
    MessageBox.Show(("The control named " + e.Control.Name + ↲
 " has been added to the form."))
End Sub

Private Sub Control_Removed(ByVal sender As Object, ByVal e As ↲
System.Windows.Forms.ControlEventArgs)
    MessageBox.Show(("The control named " + e.Control.Name + " ↲
 has been removed from the form."))
End Sub

' Click event handler for a Button control. Adds a TextBox to the form.
Private Sub addControl_Click(ByVal sender As Object, ByVal e As ↲
System.EventArgs) Handles button1.Click
    ' Create a new TextBox control and add it to the form.
    Dim textBox1 As New TextBox()
    textBox1.Size = New Size(100, 10)
    textBox1.Location = New Point(10, 10)
    ' Name the control in order to remove it later.
    ' The name must be specified if a control is added at run time.
    textBox1.Name = "textBox1"
```

```
    ' Add the control to the form's control collection.
    Me.Controls.Add(textBox1)
End Sub

' Click event handler for a Button control.
' Removes the previously added TextBox from the form.
Private Sub removeControl_Click(ByVal sender As Object, ByVal ↵
 e As System.EventArgs) Handles button2.Click
    ' Loop through all controls in the form's control collection.
    Dim tempCtrl As Control
    For Each tempCtrl In Me.Controls
        ' Determine whether the control is textBox1,
        ' and if it is, remove it.
        If tempCtrl.Name = "textBox1" Then
            Me.Controls.Remove(tempCtrl)
        End If
    Next tempCtrl
End Sub
```

[C#]

```
// This example demonstrates the use of the ControlAdded and
// ControlRemoved events. This example assumes that two Button controls
// are added to the form and connected to the addControl_Click and
// removeControl_Click event handling methods.
private void Form1_Load(object sender, System.EventArgs e)
{
    // Connect the ControlRemoved and ControlAdded event handlers
    // to the event handling methods.
    // ControlRemoved and ControlAdded are not available at ↵
design time.
    this.ControlRemoved += new ↵
System.Windows.Forms.ControlEventHandler(this.Control_Removed);
    this.ControlAdded += new ↵
System.Windows.Forms.ControlEventHandler(this.Control_Added);
}

private void Control_Added(object sender, ↵
System.Windows.Forms.ControlEventArgs e)
{
    MessageBox.Show("The control named " + e.Control.Name + " ↵
 has been added to the form.");
}

private void Control_Removed(object sender, ↵
System.Windows.Forms.ControlEventArgs e)
{
    MessageBox.Show("The control named " + e.Control.Name + ↵
" has been removed from the form.");
}

// Click event handler for a Button control. Adds a TextBox ↵
 to the form.
private void addControl_Click(object sender, System.EventArgs e)
{
    // Create a new TextBox control and add it to the form.
    TextBox textBox1 = new TextBox();
    textBox1.Size = new Size(100,10);
    textBox1.Location = new Point(10,10);
    // Name the control in order to remove it later. The name ↵
 must be specified
    // if a control is added at run time.
    textBox1.Name = "textBox1";

    // Add the control to the form's control collection.
    this.Controls.Add(textBox1);
}

// Click event handler for a Button control.
// Removes the previously added TextBox from the form.
private void removeControl_Click(object sender, System.EventArgs e)
{
    // Loop through all controls in the form's control collection.
    foreach (Control tempCtrl in this.Controls)
    {
        // Determine whether the control is textBox1,
        // and if it is, remove it.
        if (tempCtrl.Name == "textBox1")
        {
            this.Controls.Remove(tempCtrl);
        }
    }
}
```

Requirements

Platforms: Windows 98, Windows NT 4.0, Windows Millennium Edition, Windows 2000, Windows XP Home Edition, Windows XP Professional, Windows Server 2003 family

Control.CursorChanged Event

Occurs when the value of the **Cursor** property changes.

[Visual Basic]
```
Public Event CursorChanged As EventHandler
```
[C#]
```
public event EventHandler CursorChanged;
```
[C++]
```
public: __event EventHandler* CursorChanged;
```

[JScript] In JScript, you can handle the events defined by a class, but you cannot define your own.

Event Data

The event handler receives an argument of type **EventArgs**.

Remarks

This event is raised if the **Cursor** property is changed by either a programmatic modification or user interaction.

Example

[Visual Basic, C#, C++] The following example demonstrates changing the mouse cursor using the **Control.Cursor** property, the **Cursor** class, and the **Cursors** class. The example creates a form that contains a **ComboBox** control, a **Panel** control, and a **ListView** control. The **ComboBox** contains all cursors provided by the **Cursors** class. When the user selects a mouse cursor in the **ComboBox**, the **Control.Cursor** property is set to the selected cursor, which updates the cursor for the **Panel**. The **ListView** is updated every time the **Control.CursorChanged** event occurs.

[Visual Basic]
```
Imports System
Imports System.Drawing
Imports System.Windows.Forms

Namespace Snippet

    ' Summary description for Form1.
    Public NotInheritable Class Form1
        Inherits System.Windows.Forms.Form

        Friend WithEvents cursorSelectionComboBox As ↵
System.Windows.Forms.ComboBox
        Friend WithEvents testPanel As System.Windows.Forms.Panel

        Private label1 As System.Windows.Forms.Label
        Private label2 As System.Windows.Forms.Label
        Private cursorEventViewer As System.Windows.Forms.ListView
        Private label3 As System.Windows.Forms.Label

        <System.STAThread()> _
        Public Shared Sub Main()
            System.Windows.Forms.Application.Run(New Form1)
        End Sub 'Main
```

```
        Public Sub New()

            Me.cursorSelectionComboBox = New ↵
System.Windows.Forms.ComboBox
            Me.testPanel = New System.Windows.Forms.Panel
            Me.label1 = New System.Windows.Forms.Label
            Me.label2 = New System.Windows.Forms.Label
            Me.cursorEventViewer = New System.Windows.Forms.ListView
            Me.label3 = New System.Windows.Forms.Label

            ' Select Cursor Label
            Me.label2.Location = New System.Drawing.Point(24, 16)
            Me.label2.Size = New System.Drawing.Size(80, 16)
            Me.label2.Text = "Select cursor:"          '

            ' Cursor Testing Panel Label
            Me.label1.Location = New System.Drawing.Point(24, 80)
            Me.label1.Size = New System.Drawing.Size(144, 23)
            Me.label1.Text = "Cursor testing panel:"

            ' Cursor Changed Events Label
            Me.label3.Location = New System.Drawing.Point(184, 16)
            Me.label3.Size = New System.Drawing.Size(128, 16)
            Me.label3.Text = "Cursor changed events:"

            ' Cursor Selection ComboBox
            Me.cursorSelectionComboBox.Location = New ↵
System.Drawing.Point(24, 40)
            Me.cursorSelectionComboBox.Size = New ↵
System.Drawing.Size(152, 21)
            Me.cursorSelectionComboBox.TabIndex = 0

            ' Cursor Test Panel
            Me.testPanel.BackColor = ↵
System.Drawing.SystemColors.ControlDark
            Me.testPanel.Location = New System.Drawing.Point(24, 104)
            Me.testPanel.Size = New System.Drawing.Size(152, 160)

            ' Cursor Event ListView
            Me.cursorEventViewer.Location = New ↵
System.Drawing.Point(184, 40)
            Me.cursorEventViewer.Size = New ↵
System.Drawing.Size(256, 224)
            Me.cursorEventViewer.TabIndex = 4
            Me.cursorEventViewer.View = System.Windows.Forms.View.List

            ' Set up how the form should be displayed and ↵
 add the controls to the form.
            Me.ClientSize = New System.Drawing.Size(456, 286)
            Me.Controls.AddRange(New ↵
System.Windows.Forms.Control() {Me.label3, _
                    Me.cursorEventViewer, Me.label2, Me.label1, _
                            Me.testPanel, Me.cursorSelectionComboBox})

            Me.Text = "Cursors Example"

            ' Add all the cursor types to the combobox.
            Dim cursor As Cursor
            For Each cursor In CursorList()
                cursorSelectionComboBox.Items.Add(cursor)
            Next cursor
        End Sub 'New

        Private Function CursorList() As Cursor()
            ' Make an array of all the types of cursors in ↵
 Windows Forms.
            return New Cursor() {Cursors.AppStarting, ↵
Cursors.Arrow, Cursors.Cross, _
                                Cursors.Default, ↵
Cursors.Hand, Cursors.Help, _
                                Cursors.HSplit, ↵
Cursors.IBeam, Cursors.No, _
                                Cursors.NoMove2D, ↵
 Cursors.NoMoveHoriz, Cursors.NoMoveVert, _
                                Cursors.PanEast, ↵
Cursors.PanNE, Cursors.PanNorth, _
                                Cursors.PanNW, ↵
Cursors.PanSE, Cursors.PanSouth, _
                                Cursors.PanSW, ↵
Cursors.PanWest, Cursors.SizeAll, _
                                Cursors.SizeNESW, ↵
Cursors.SizeNS, Cursors.SizeNWSE, _
                                Cursors.SizeWE, ↵
Cursors.UpArrow, Cursors.VSplit, Cursors.WaitCursor}
        End Function

        Private Sub cursorSelectionComboBox_SelectedIndexChanged ↵
 (ByVal sender As Object, ByVal e As System.EventArgs) Handles ↵
cursorSelectionComboBox.SelectedIndexChanged
            ' Set the cursor in the test panel to be the ↵
selected cursor style.
            testPanel.Cursor = ↵
CType(cursorSelectionComboBox.SelectedItem, Cursor)

        End Sub

        Private Sub testPanel_CursorChanged(ByVal ↵
sender As Object, ByVal e As System.EventArgs) Handles ↵
testPanel.CursorChanged
            ' Build up a string containing the type of ↵
object sending the event, and the event.
            Dim cursorEvent As String = String.Format ↵
 ("[{0}]: {1}", sender.GetType().ToString(), "Cursor changed")

            ' Records this event in the list view.
            Me.cursorEventViewer.Items.Add(cursorEvent)

        End Sub

    End Class 'Form1
End Namespace 'Snippet
```

[C#]

```
using System;
using System.Drawing;
using System.Windows.Forms;

namespace Snippet
{
    public class Form1 : System.Windows.Forms.Form
    {
        private System.Windows.Forms.ComboBox cursorSelectionComboBox;

        private System.Windows.Forms.Panel testPanel;
        private System.Windows.Forms.Label label1;
        private System.Windows.Forms.Label label2;
        private System.Windows.Forms.ListView cursorEventViewer;
        private System.Windows.Forms.Label label3;

        [STAThread]
        static void Main()
        {
            Application.Run(new Form1());
        }

        public Form1()
        {
            this.cursorSelectionComboBox = new ↵
System.Windows.Forms.ComboBox();
            this.testPanel = new System.Windows.Forms.Panel();
            this.label1 = new System.Windows.Forms.Label();
            this.label2 = new System.Windows.Forms.Label();
            this.cursorEventViewer = new ↵
System.Windows.Forms.ListView();
            this.label3 = new System.Windows.Forms.Label();

            // Select Cursor Label
            this.label2.Location = new System.Drawing.Point(24, 16);
            this.label2.Size = new System.Drawing.Size(80, 16);
            this.label2.Text = "Select cursor:";
```

```
        // Cursor Testing Panel Label
        this.label1.Location = new System.Drawing.Point(24, 80);
        this.label1.Size = new System.Drawing.Size(144, 23);
        this.label1.Text = "Cursor testing panel:";

        // Cursor Changed Events Label
        this.label3.Location = new System.Drawing.Point(184, 16);
        this.label3.Size = new System.Drawing.Size(128, 16);
        this.label3.Text = "Cursor changed events:";

        // Cursor Selection ComboBox
        this.cursorSelectionComboBox.Location = new                ↵
System.Drawing.Point(24, 40);
        this.cursorSelectionComboBox.Size = new                    ↵
System.Drawing.Size(152, 21);
        this.cursorSelectionComboBox.TabIndex = 0;
        this.cursorSelectionComboBox.SelectedIndexChanged +=
            new                                                    ↵
System.EventHandler(this.cursorSelectionComboBox_SelectedIndexChanged);

        // Cursor Test Panel
        this.testPanel.BackColor =                                 ↵
System.Drawing.SystemColors.ControlDark;
        this.testPanel.Location = new System.Drawing.Point         ↵
 (24, 104);
        this.testPanel.Size = new System.Drawing.Size(152, 160);
        this.testPanel.CursorChanged += new                        ↵
System.EventHandler(this.testPanel_CursorChanged);

        // Cursor Event ListView
        this.cursorEventViewer.Location = new                      ↵
System.Drawing.Point(184, 40);
        this.cursorEventViewer.Size = new                          ↵
System.Drawing.Size(256, 224);
        this.cursorEventViewer.TabIndex = 4;
        this.cursorEventViewer.View =                              ↵
System.Windows.Forms.View.List;

        // Set up how the form should be displayed                 ↵
 and add the controls to the form.
        this.ClientSize = new System.Drawing.Size(456, 286);
        this.Controls.AddRange(new System.Windows.Forms.Control[] {
                                    this.label3,                   ↵
this.cursorEventViewer,
                                    this.label2, this.label1,
                                    this.testPanel,                ↵
this.cursorSelectionComboBox});

        this.Text = "Cursors Example";

        // Add all the cursor types to the combobox.
        foreach (Cursor cursor in CursorList())
        {
            cursorSelectionComboBox.Items.Add(cursor);
        }

    }

    private Cursor [] CursorList()
    {

        // Make an array of all the types of cursors               ↵
 in Windows Forms.
        return new Cursor [] {
                                Cursors.AppStarting,               ↵
 Cursors.Arrow, Cursors.Cross,
                                Cursors.Default,                   ↵
Cursors.Hand, Cursors.Help,
                                Cursors.HSplit,                    ↵
Cursors.IBeam, Cursors.No,
                                Cursors.NoMove2D,                  ↵
Cursors.NoMoveHoriz, Cursors.NoMoveVert,
                                Cursors.PanEast,                   ↵
Cursors.PanNE, Cursors.PanNorth,
                                Cursors.PanNW,                     ↵
Cursors.PanSE, Cursors.PanSouth,
                                Cursors.PanSW,                     ↵
Cursors.PanWest, Cursors.SizeAll,
                                Cursors.SizeNESW,                  ↵
 Cursors.SizeNS, Cursors.SizeNWSE,
                                Cursors.SizeWE,                    ↵
Cursors.UpArrow, Cursors.VSplit, Cursors.WaitCursor};

    }

    private void cursorSelectionComboBox_SelectedIndexChanged(object ↵
sender,
System.EventArgs e)
    {
        // Set the cursor in the test panel to be the              ↵
 selected cursor style.
        testPanel.Cursor =                                         ↵
(Cursor)cursorSelectionComboBox.SelectedItem;
    }

    private void testPanel_CursorChanged(object sender,            ↵
System.EventArgs e)
    {
        // Build up a string containing the type of object         ↵
 sending the event, and the event.
        string cursorEvent = string.Format("[{0}]: {1}",           ↵
sender.GetType().ToString(), "Cursor changed");

        // Record this event in the list view.
        this.cursorEventViewer.Items.Add(cursorEvent);
    }
  }
}
```

[C++]

```
#using <mscorlib.dll>
#using <System.dll>
#using <System.Windows.Forms.dll>
#using <System.Drawing.dll>

using namespace System;
using namespace System::Drawing;
using namespace System::Windows::Forms;

namespace Snippet {
public __gc class Form1 : public System::Windows::Forms::Form {
private:
   System::Windows::Forms::ComboBox*  cursorSelectionComboBox;
   System::Windows::Forms::Panel*  testPanel;
   System::Windows::Forms::Label*  label1;
   System::Windows::Forms::Label*  label2;
   System::Windows::Forms::ListView*  cursorEventViewer;
   System::Windows::Forms::Label*  label3;
public:
   Form1() {
      this->cursorSelectionComboBox = new                          ↵
System::Windows::Forms::ComboBox();
      this->testPanel = new System::Windows::Forms::Panel();
      this->label1 = new System::Windows::Forms::Label();
      this->label2 = new System::Windows::Forms::Label();
      this->cursorEventViewer = new System::Windows::Forms::ListView();
      this->label3 = new System::Windows::Forms::Label();

      // Select Cursor Label
      this->label2->Location =  System::Drawing::Point(24, 16);
      this->label2->Size =  System::Drawing::Size(80, 16);
      this->label2->Text = S"Select cursor:";

      // Cursor Testing Panel Label
      this->label1->Location =  System::Drawing::Point(24, 80);
      this->label1->Size =  System::Drawing::Size(144, 23);
      this->label1->Text = S"Cursor testing panel:";

      // Cursor Changed Events Label
      this->label3->Location =  System::Drawing::Point(184, 16);
```

```
        this->label3->Size =  System::Drawing::Size(128, 16);
        this->label3->Text = S"Cursor changed events:";

        // Cursor Selection ComboBox
        this->cursorSelectionComboBox->Location =                        ↵
 System::Drawing::Point(24, 40);
        this->cursorSelectionComboBox->Size =                            ↵
 System::Drawing::Size(152, 21);
        this->cursorSelectionComboBox->TabIndex = 0;
        this->cursorSelectionComboBox->SelectedIndexChanged +=           ↵
  new System::EventHandler(this,                                         ↵
 cursorSelectionComboBox_SelectedIndexChanged);

        // Cursor Test Panel
        this->testPanel->BackColor =                                     ↵
 System::Drawing::SystemColors::ControlDark;
        this->testPanel->Location =  System::Drawing::Point(24, 104);
        this->testPanel->Size =  System::Drawing::Size(152, 160);
        this->testPanel->CursorChanged += new System::EventHandler       ↵
  (this, testPanel_CursorChanged);

        // Cursor Event ListView
        this->cursorEventViewer->Location =                              ↵
 System::Drawing::Point(184, 40);
        this->cursorEventViewer->Size =  System::Drawing::Size(256, 224);
        this->cursorEventViewer->TabIndex = 4;
        this->cursorEventViewer->View =
 System::Windows::Forms::View::List;

        // Set up how the form should be displayed and add the          ↵
  controls to the form.
        this->ClientSize =  System::Drawing::Size(456, 286);

        System::Windows::Forms::Control* temp0 [] = {this->label3,       ↵
  this->cursorEventViewer,
           this->label2, this->label1,
           this->testPanel, this->cursorSelectionComboBox};

        this->Controls->AddRange(temp0);

        this->Text = S"Cursors Example";

        // Add all the cursor types to the combobox.
        System::Collections::IEnumerator* myEnum =                       ↵
 CursorList()->GetEnumerator();
        while (myEnum->MoveNext()) {
           System::Windows::Forms::Cursor* cursor =                      ↵
 __try_cast<System::Windows::Forms::Cursor*>(myEnum->Current);
           cursorSelectionComboBox->Items->Add(cursor);
        }
    }

private:
    System::Windows::Forms::Cursor* CursorList()[] {

        // Make an array of all the types of cursors in Windows Forms.

        System::Windows::Forms::Cursor*  temp1 [] =                      ↵
 {Cursors::AppStarting, Cursors::Arrow, Cursors::Cross,
           Cursors::Default, Cursors::Hand, Cursors::Help,
           Cursors::HSplit, Cursors::IBeam, Cursors::No,
           Cursors::NoMove2D, Cursors::NoMoveHoriz, Cursors::NoMoveVert,
           Cursors::PanEast, Cursors::PanNE, Cursors::PanNorth,
           Cursors::PanNW, Cursors::PanSE, Cursors::PanSouth,
           Cursors::PanSW, Cursors::PanWest, Cursors::SizeAll,
           Cursors::SizeNESW, Cursors::SizeNS, Cursors::SizeNWSE,
           Cursors::SizeWE, Cursors::UpArrow, Cursors::VSplit,           ↵
 Cursors::WaitCursor};
        return temp1;
    }

    void cursorSelectionComboBox_SelectedIndexChanged(Object*            ↵
 sender, System::EventArgs* e) {
        // Set the cursor in the test panel to be the selected           ↵
 cursor style.
        testPanel->Cursor =                                              ↵
 dynamic_cast<System::Windows::Forms::Cursor*>(cursorSelectionComboBox-
 >SelectedItem);
    }

    void testPanel_CursorChanged(Object* sender, System::EventArgs* e) {
        // Build up a String* containing the type of Object*            ↵
  sending the event, and the event.
        String* cursorEvent = String::Format(S"[{0}]: {1}",             ↵
  sender->GetType(), S"Cursor changed");

        // Record this event in the list view.
        this->cursorEventViewer->Items->Add(cursorEvent);
    }
};
}

[STAThread]
int main() {
    Application::Run(new Snippet::Form1());
}
```

Requirements

Platforms: Windows 98, Windows NT 4.0, Windows Millennium Edition, Windows 2000, Windows XP Home Edition, Windows XP Professional, Windows Server 2003 family

Control.DockChanged Event

Occurs when the value of the **Dock** property changes.

[Visual Basic]
```
Public Event DockChanged As EventHandler
```
[C#]
```
public event EventHandler DockChanged;
```
[C++]
```
public: __event EventHandler* DockChanged;
```

[JScript] In JScript, you can handle the events defined by a class, but you cannot define your own.

Event Data

The event handler receives an argument of type **EventArgs**.

Remarks

This event is raised if the **Dock** property is changed by either a programmatic modification or user interaction.

Example

[Visual Basic, C#, C++] The example below is an event handling method that is executed when the **Text** property value changes. The **Control** class has several methods with the name pattern Property-Name **Changed** that are raised when the corresponding Property-Name value changes(PropertyName represents the name of the corresponding property).

[Visual Basic, C#, C++] The following example changes the **ForeColor** of a **TextBox** displaying currency data. The example converts the text to a decimal number and changes the **ForeColor** to **Color.Red** if the number is negative and to **Color.Black** if the number is positive. This example assumes you have a **Form** that contains a **TextBox**.

[Visual Basic]
```
Private Sub currencyTextBox_TextChanged(sender As Object, _
   e As EventArgs) Handles currencyTextBox.TextChanged
    Try
        ' Convert the text to a Double and determine if it is a       ↵
 negative number.
        If Double.Parse(currencyTextBox.Text) < 0 Then
            ' If the number is negative, display it in Red.
```

```
            currencyTextBox.ForeColor = Color.Red
        Else
            ' If the number is not negative, display it in Black.
            currencyTextBox.ForeColor = Color.Black
        End If
    Catch
        ' If there is an error, display the text using the system colors.
        currencyTextBox.ForeColor = SystemColors.ControlText
    End Try
End Sub
```

[C#]

```
private void currencyTextBox_TextChanged(object sender, EventArgs e)
{
    try
    {
        // Convert the text to a Double and determine if it is a ↵
 negative number.
        if(double.Parse(currencyTextBox.Text) < 0)
        {
            // If the number is negative, display it in Red.
            currencyTextBox.ForeColor = Color.Red;
        }
        else
        {
            // If the number is not negative, display it in Black.
            currencyTextBox.ForeColor = Color.Black;
        }
    }
    catch
    {
        // If there is an error, display the text using the ↵
 system colors.
        currencyTextBox.ForeColor = SystemColors.ControlText;
    }
}
```

[C++]

```
private:
    void currencyTextBox_TextChanged(Object* /*sender*/, ↵
EventArgs* /*e*/) {
        try {
            // Convert the text to a Double and determine if ↵
 it is a negative number.
            if (Double::Parse(currencyTextBox->Text) < 0) {
                // If the number is negative, display it in Red.
                currencyTextBox->ForeColor = Color::Red;
            } else {
                // If the number is not negative, display it in Black.
                currencyTextBox->ForeColor = Color::Black;
            }
        } catch (Exception*) {
            // If there is an error, display the text using ↵
 the system colors.
            currencyTextBox->ForeColor = SystemColors::ControlText;
        }
    }
```

Requirements

Platforms: Windows 98, Windows NT 4.0, Windows Millennium Edition, Windows 2000, Windows XP Home Edition, Windows XP Professional, Windows Server 2003 family

Control.DoubleClick Event

Occurs when the control is double-clicked.

[Visual Basic]

```
Public Event DoubleClick As EventHandler
```

[C#]

```
public event EventHandler DoubleClick;
```

[C++]

```
public: __event EventHandler* DoubleClick;
```

[JScript] In JScript, you can handle the events defined by a class, but you cannot define your own.

Event Data

The event handler receives an argument of type **EventArgs**.

Remarks

A double-click is determined by the mouse settings of the user's operating system. The user can set the time between clicks of a mouse button that should be considered a double-click rather than two clicks. The **Click** event is raised every time a control is double-clicked. For example, if you have an event-handling methods for the **Click** and **DoubleClick** events of a **Form**, the **Click** and **DoubleClick** events are raised when the form is double-clicked and both methods are called. If a control is double-clicked and that control does not support the **DoubleClick** event, the **Click** event might be raised twice.

The **ControlStyles.StandardDoubleClick** and **ControlStyles.StandardClick** bits must be set to **true** for this event to be raised. These bits might already be set to **true** if you are inheriting from existing Windows Forms controls.

Notes to Inheritors: Inheriting from a standard Windows Forms control and changing the **StandardClick** or **StandardDoubleClick** bit values to **true** can cause unexpected behavior or have no effect at all if the control does not support the **Click** or **DoubleClick** events.

Example

[Visual Basic]

```
' This example uses the DoubleClick event of a ListBox to load ↵
text files
' listed in the ListBox into a TextBox control. This example
' assumes that the ListBox, named listBox1, contains a list of ↵
valid file
' names with path and that this event handling method
' is connected to the DoublClick event of a ListBox control ↵
named listBox1.
' This example requires code access permission to access files.
Private Sub listBox1_DoubleClick(ByVal sender As Object, ByVal ↵
 e As System.EventArgs) Handles listBox1.DoubleClick
    ' Get the name of the file to open from the ListBox.
    Dim file As [String] = listBox1.SelectedItem.ToString()

    Try
        ' Determine if the file exists before loading.
        If System.IO.File.Exists(file) Then
            ' Open the file and use a TextReader to read the ↵
 contents into the TextBox.
            Dim myFile As New ↵
System.IO.FileInfo(listBox1.SelectedItem.ToString())
            Dim myData As System.IO.TextReader = myFile.OpenText()

            textBox1.Text = myData.ReadToEnd()
            myData.Close()
        End If
        ' Exception is thrown by the OpenText method of the ↵
 FileInfo class.
    Catch
        MessageBox.Show("The file you specified does not exist.")
        ' Exception is thrown by the ReadToEnd method of the ↵
 TextReader class.
    Catch
     MessageBox.Show("There was a problem loading the file ↵
 into the TextBox. Ensure that the file is a valid text file.")
    End Try
End Sub
```

[C#]
```
// This example uses the DoubleClick event of a ListBox to 
load text files
// listed in the ListBox into a TextBox control. This example
// assumes that the ListBox, named listBox1, contains a list 
 of valid file
// names with path and that this event handling method
// is connected to the DoublClick event of a ListBox control 
named listBox1.
// This example requires code access permission to access files.
private void listBox1_DoubleClick(object sender, System.EventArgs e)
{
    // Get the name of the file to open from the ListBox.
    String file = listBox1.SelectedItem.ToString();

    try
    {
        // Determine if the file exists before loading.
        if (System.IO.File.Exists(file))
        {
            // Open the file and use a TextReader to read the 
contents into the TextBox.
            System.IO.FileInfo myFile = new 
System.IO.FileInfo(listBox1.SelectedItem.ToString());
            System.IO.TextReader myData = myFile.OpenText();;

            textBox1.Text = myData.ReadToEnd();
            myData.Close();
        }
    }
        // Exception is thrown by the OpenText method of the 
FileInfo class.
    catch(System.IO.FileNotFoundException)
    {
        MessageBox.Show("The file you specified does not exist.");
    }
        // Exception is thrown by the ReadToEnd method of the 
TextReader class.
    catch(System.IO.IOException)
    {
        MessageBox.Show("There was a problem loading the file 
 into the TextBox. Ensure that the file is a valid text file.");
    }
}
```

Requirements

Platforms: Windows 98, Windows NT 4.0, Windows Millennium Edition, Windows 2000, Windows XP Home Edition, Windows XP Professional, Windows Server 2003 family

Control.DragDrop Event

Occurs when a drag-and-drop operation is completed.

[Visual Basic]
```
Public Event DragDrop As DragEventHandler
```
[C#]
```
public event DragEventHandler DragDrop;
```
[C++]
```
public: __event DragEventHandler* DragDrop;
```

[JScript] In JScript, you can handle the events defined by a class, but you cannot define your own.

Event Data

The event handler receives an argument of type **DragEventArgs** containing data related to this event. The following **DragEventArgs** properties provide information specific to this event.

Property	Description
AllowedEffect	Gets which drag-and-drop operations are allowed by the originator (or source) of the drag event.
Data	Gets the **IDataObject** that contains the data associated with this event.
Effect	Gets or sets the target drop effect in a drag-and-drop operation.
KeyState	Gets the current state of the SHIFT, CTRL, and ALT keys, as well as the state of the mouse buttons.
X	Gets the x-coordinate of the mouse pointer, in screen coordinates.
Y	Gets the y-coordinate of the mouse pointer, in screen coordinates.

Remarks

Note The **X** and **Y** properties of the **DragEventArgs** are in screen coordinates, not client coordinates. The following line of C# code converts the properties to a client **Point**:

```
Point clientPoint = targetControl.PointToClient(new Point(de.X, 
de.Y));
```

Example

[Visual Basic, C#, C++] The following example demonstrates a drag-and-drop operation between two **ListBox** controls. The example calls the **DoDragDrop** method when the drag action starts. The drag action starts if the mouse has moved more than **SystemInformation.DragSize** from the mouse location during the **MouseDown** event. The **IndexFromPoint** method is used to determine the index of the item to drag during the **MouseDown** event.

[Visual Basic, C#, C++] The example also demonstrates using custom cursors for the drag-and-drop operation. The example assumes that two cursor files, `3dwarro.cur` and `3dwno.cur`, exist in the application directory, for the custom drag and no-drop cursors, respectively. The custom cursors will be used if the `UseCustomCursorsCheck` **CheckBox** is checked. The custom cursors are set in the **GiveFeedback** event handler.

[Visual Basic, C#, C++] The keyboard state is evaluated in the **DragOver** event handler for the right **ListBox**, to determine what the drag operation will be based upon state of the SHIFT, CTRL, ALT, or CTRL+ALT keys. The location in the **ListBox** where the drop would occur is also determined during the **DragOver** event. If the data to drop is not a **String**, then the **DragEventArgs.Effect** is set to **DragDropEffects.None**. Finally, the status of the drop is displayed in the `DropLocationLabel` **Label**.

[Visual Basic, C#, C++] The data to drop for the right **ListBox** is determined in the **DragDrop** event handler and the **String** value is added at the appropriate place in the **ListBox**. If the drag operation moves outside the bounds of the form, then the drag-and-drop operation is canceled in the **QueryContinueDrag** event handler.

[Visual Basic, C#, C++] This code excerpt demonstrates using the **DragDrop** event. See the **DoDragDrop** method for the complete code example.

[Visual Basic]
```
Private Sub ListDragTarget_DragDrop(ByVal sender As Object, ↵
 ByVal e As DragEventArgs) Handles ListDragTarget.DragDrop
    ' Ensures that the list item index is contained in the data.

    If (e.Data.GetDataPresent(GetType(System.String))) Then

        Dim item As Object = ↵
CType(e.Data.GetData(GetType(System.String)), System.Object)

        ' Perform drag and drop, depending upon the effect.
        If (e.Effect = DragDropEffects.Copy Or _
            e.Effect = DragDropEffects.Move) Then

            ' Insert the item.
            If (indexOfItemUnderMouseToDrop <> ListBox.NoMatches) Then
                ListDragTarget.Items.Insert(indexOfItemUnderMouseToDrop,
item)
            Else
                ListDragTarget.Items.Add(item)

            End If
        End If
        ' Reset the label text.
        DropLocationLabel.Text = "None"
    End If
End Sub
```

[C#]
```
private void ListDragTarget_DragDrop(object sender, ↵
System.Windows.Forms.DragEventArgs e)
{
    // Ensure that the list item index is contained in the data.
    if (e.Data.GetDataPresent(typeof(System.String))) {

        Object item = (object)e.Data.GetData(typeof(System.String));

        // Perform drag and drop, depending upon the effect.
        if (e.Effect == DragDropEffects.Copy ||
            e.Effect == DragDropEffects.Move) {

            // Insert the item.
            if (indexOfItemUnderMouseToDrop != ListBox.NoMatches)
                ListDragTarget.Items.Insert(indexOfItemUnderMouseToDrop,
item);
            else
                ListDragTarget.Items.Add(item);

        }
    }
    // Reset the label text.
    DropLocationLabel.Text = "None";
}
```

[C++]
```
private:
    void ListDragTarget_DragDrop(Object* /*sender*/,
        System::Windows::Forms::DragEventArgs* e) {
        // Ensure that the list item index is contained in the data.
        if (e->Data->GetDataPresent(__typeof(System::String))) {
            Object* item = dynamic_cast<Object*>(
                e->Data->GetData(__typeof(System::String)));

            // Perform drag and drop, depending upon the effect.
            if (e->Effect == DragDropEffects::Copy ||
                e->Effect == DragDropEffects::Move) {

                    // Insert the item.
                    if (indexOfItemUnderMouseToDrop != ↵
ListBox::NoMatches)
                        ListDragTarget->Items->Insert(
                        indexOfItemUnderMouseToDrop, item);
                    else
                        ListDragTarget->Items->Add(item);

            }
        }
        // Reset the label text.
        DropLocationLabel->Text = S"None";
    }
```

Requirements

Platforms: Windows 98, Windows NT 4.0, Windows Millennium Edition, Windows 2000, Windows XP Home Edition, Windows XP Professional, Windows Server 2003 family

Control.DragEnter Event

Occurs when an object is dragged into the control's bounds.

[Visual Basic]
```
Public Event DragEnter As DragEventHandler
```
[C#]
```
public event DragEventHandler DragEnter;
```
[C++]
```
public: __event DragEventHandler* DragEnter;
```

[JScript] In JScript, you can handle the events defined by a class, but you cannot define your own.

Event Data

The event handler receives an argument of type **DragEventArgs** containing data related to this event. The following **DragEventArgs** properties provide information specific to this event.

Property	Description
AllowedEffect	Gets which drag-and-drop operations are allowed by the originator (or source) of the drag event.
Data	Gets the **IDataObject** that contains the data associated with this event.
Effect	Gets or sets the target drop effect in a drag-and-drop operation.
KeyState	Gets the current state of the SHIFT, CTRL, and ALT keys, as well as the state of the mouse buttons.
X	Gets the x-coordinate of the mouse pointer, in screen coordinates.
Y	Gets the y-coordinate of the mouse pointer, in screen coordinates.

Remarks

The **DragEnter** event is raised when the user first drags the mouse cursor over the control during a drag-and-drop operation.

The following describes how and when events related to drag-and-drop operations are raised.

The **DoDragDrop** method determines the control under the current cursor location. It then checks to see if the control is a valid drop target.

If the control is a valid drop target, the **GiveFeedback** event is raised with the drag-and-drop effect specified. For a list of drag-and-drop effects, see the **DragDropEffects** enumeration.

Changes in the mouse cursor position, keyboard state, and mouse button state are tracked.

- If the user moves out of a window, the **DragLeave** event is raised.
- If the mouse enters another control, the **DragEnter** for that control is raised.
- If the mouse moves but stays within the same control, the **DragOver** event is raised.

If there is a change in the keyboard or mouse button state, the **QueryContinueDrag** event is raised and determines whether to continue the drag, to drop the data, or to cancel the operation based on the value of the **Action** property of the event's **QueryContinueDragEventArgs**.

- If the value is **DragAction.Continue**, the **DragOver** event is raised to continue the operation and the **GiveFeedback** event is raised with the new effect so appropriate visual feedback can be set. For a list of valid drop effects, see the **DragDropEffects** enumeration.

> **Note** The **DragOver** and **GiveFeedback** events are paired so that as the mouse moves across the drop target, the user is given the most up-to-date feedback on the mouse's position.

If the value is **DragAction.Drop**, the drop effect value is returned to the source, so the source application can perform the appropriate operation on the source data; for example, cut the data if the operation was a move.

If the value is **DragAction.Cancel**, the **DragLeave** event is raised.

> **Note** The **X** and **Y** properties of the **DragEventArgs** are in screen coordinates, not client coordinates. The following line of C# code converts the properties to a client **Point**:

```
Point clientPoint = targetControl.PointToClient(new Point ↵
(de.X, de.Y));
```

Example

[Visual Basic, C#, C++] The following example demonstrates a drag-and-drop operation between two **ListBox** controls. The example calls the **DoDragDrop** method when the drag action starts. The drag action starts if the mouse has moved more than **SystemInformation.DragSize** from the mouse location during the **MouseDown** event. The **IndexFromPoint** method is used to determine the index of the item to drag during the **MouseDown** event.

[Visual Basic, C#, C++] The example also demonstrates using custom cursors for the drag-and-drop operation. The example assumes that two cursor files, `3dwarro.cur` and `3dwno.cur`, exist in the application directory, for the custom drag and no-drop cursors, respectively. The custom cursors will be used if the `UseCustomCursorsCheck` **CheckBox** is checked. The custom cursors are set in the **GiveFeedback** event handler.

[Visual Basic, C#, C++] The keyboard state is evaluated in the **DragOver** event handler for the right **ListBox**, to determine what the drag operation will be based upon state of the SHIFT, CTRL, ALT, or CTRL+ALT keys. The location in the **ListBox** where the drop would occur is also determined during the **DragOver** event. If the data to drop is not a **String**, then the **DragEventArgs.Effect** is set to **DragDropEffects.None**. Finally, the status of the drop is displayed in the `DropLocationLabel` **Label**.

[Visual Basic, C#, C++] The data to drop for the right **ListBox** is determined in the **DragDrop** event handler and the **String** value is added at the appropriate place in the **ListBox**. If the drag operation moves outside the bounds of the form, then the drag-and-drop operation is canceled in the **QueryContinueDrag** event handler.

[Visual Basic, C#, C++] This code excerpt demonstrates using the **DragEnter** event. See the **DoDragDrop** method for the complete code example.

[Visual Basic]

```
Private Sub ListDragTarget_DragEnter(ByVal sender As Object, ↵
 ByVal e As DragEventArgs) Handles ListDragTarget.DragEnter

    ' Reset the label text.
    DropLocationLabel.Text = "None"
End Sub
```

[C#]

```
private void ListDragTarget_DragEnter(object sender, ↵
System.Windows.Forms.DragEventArgs e) {
    // Reset the label text.
    DropLocationLabel.Text = "None";
}
```

[C++]

```
private:
    void ListDragTarget_DragEnter(Object* /*sender*/, ↵
System::Windows::Forms::DragEventArgs* /*e*/) {
        // Reset the label text.
        DropLocationLabel->Text = S"None";
    }
```

Requirements

Platforms: Windows 98, Windows NT 4.0, Windows Millennium Edition, Windows 2000, Windows XP Home Edition, Windows XP Professional, Windows Server 2003 family

Control.DragLeave Event

Occurs when an object is dragged out of the control's bounds.

[Visual Basic]

```
Public Event DragLeave As EventHandler
```

[C#]

```
public event EventHandler DragLeave;
```

[C++]

```
public: __event EventHandler* DragLeave;
```

[JScript] In JScript, you can handle the events defined by a class, but you cannot define your own.

Event Data

The event handler receives an argument of type **EventArgs**.

Remarks

The **DragLeave** event is raised when the user drags the cursor out of the control or the user cancels the current drag-and-drop operation.

The following describes how and when events related to drag-and-drop operations are raised.

The **DoDragDrop** method determines the control under the current cursor location. It then checks to see if the control is a valid drop target.

If the control is a valid drop target, the **GiveFeedback** event is raised with the drag-and-drop effect specified. For a list of drag-and-drop effects, see the **DragDropEffects** enumeration.

Changes in the mouse cursor position, keyboard state, and mouse button state are tracked.

- If the user moves out of a window, the **DragLeave** event is raised.
- If the mouse enters another control, the **DragEnter** for that control is raised.
- If the mouse moves but stays within the same control, the **DragOver** event is raised.

If there is a change in the keyboard or mouse button state, the **QueryContinueDrag** event is raised and determines whether to continue the drag, to drop the data, or to cancel the operation based on the value of the **Action** property of the event's **QueryContinue-DragEventArgs**.

- If the value is **DragAction.Continue**, the **DragOver** event is raised to continue the operation and the **GiveFeedback** event is raised with the new effect so appropriate visual feedback can be set. For a list of valid drop effects, see the **DragDropEffects** enumeration.

> **Note** The **DragOver** and **GiveFeedback** events are paired so that as the mouse moves across the drop target, the user is given the most up-to-date feedback on the mouse's position.

If the value is **DragAction.Drop**, the drop effect value is returned to the source, so the source application can perform the appropriate operation on the source data; for example, cut the data if the operation was a move.

If the value is **DragAction.Cancel**, the **DragLeave** event is raised.

Example

[Visual Basic, C#, C++] The following example demonstrates a drag-and-drop operation between two **ListBox** controls. The example calls the **DoDragDrop** method when the drag action starts. The drag action starts if the mouse has moved more than **System-Information.DragSize** from the mouse location during the **Mouse-Down** event. The **IndexFromPoint** method is used to determine the index of the item to drag during the **MouseDown** event.

[Visual Basic, C#, C++] The example also demonstrates using custom cursors for the drag-and-drop operation. The example assumes that two cursor files, `3dwarro.cur` and `3dwno.cur`, exist in the application directory, for the custom drag and no-drop cursors, respectively. The custom cursors will be used if the `UseCustomCursors-Check` **CheckBox** is checked. The custom cursors are set in the **GiveFeedback** event handler.

[Visual Basic, C#, C++] The keyboard state is evaluated in the **DragOver** event handler for the right **ListBox**, to determine what the drag operation will be based upon state of the SHIFT, CTRL, ALT, or CTRL+ALT keys. The location in the **ListBox** where the drop would occur is also determined during the **DragOver** event. If the data to drop is not a **String**, then the **DragEventArgs.Effect** is set to **DragDropEffects.None**. Finally, the status of the drop is displayed in the `DropLocationLabel` **Label**.

[Visual Basic, C#, C++] The data to drop for the right **ListBox** is determined in the **DragDrop** event handler and the **String** value is added at the appropriate place in the **ListBox**. If the drag operation moves outside the bounds of the form, then the drag-and-drop operation is canceled in the **QueryContinueDrag** event handler.

[Visual Basic, C#, C++] This code excerpt demonstrates using the **DragLeave** event. See the **DoDragDrop** method for the complete code example.

[Visual Basic]
```
Private Sub ListDragTarget_DragLeave(ByVal sender As Object, ↵
ByVal e As System.EventArgs) Handles ListDragTarget.DragLeave

    ' Reset the label text.
    DropLocationLabel.Text = "None"
End Sub
```

[C#]
```
private void ListDragTarget_DragLeave(object sender, ↵
System.EventArgs e) {
    // Reset the label text.
    DropLocationLabel.Text = "None";
}
```

[C++]
```
private:
    void ListDragTarget_DragLeave(Object* /*sender*/, ↵
System::EventArgs* /*e*/) {
        // Reset the label text.
        DropLocationLabel->Text = S"None";
    }
```

Requirements

Platforms: Windows 98, Windows NT 4.0, Windows Millennium Edition, Windows 2000, Windows XP Home Edition, Windows XP Professional, Windows Server 2003 family

Control.DragOver Event

Occurs when an object is dragged over the control's bounds.

[Visual Basic]
```
Public Event DragOver As DragEventHandler
```
[C#]
```
public event DragEventHandler DragOver;
```
[C++]
```
public: __event DragEventHandler* DragOver;
```

[JScript] In JScript, you can handle the events defined by a class, but you cannot define your own.

Event Data

The event handler receives an argument of type **DragEventArgs** containing data related to this event. The following **DragEventArgs** properties provide information specific to this event.

Property	Description
AllowedEffect	Gets which drag-and-drop operations are allowed by the originator (or source) of the drag event.
Data	Gets the **IDataObject** that contains the data associated with this event.
Effect	Gets or sets the target drop effect in a drag-and-drop operation.
KeyState	Gets the current state of the SHIFT, CTRL, and ALT keys, as well as the state of the mouse buttons.
X	Gets the x-coordinate of the mouse pointer, in screen coordinates.
Y	Gets the y-coordinate of the mouse pointer, in screen coordinates.

Remarks

The **DragOver** event is raised when the mouse cursor moves withing the bounds of the control during a drag-and-drop operation.

The following describes how and when events related to drag-and-drop operations are raised.

The **DoDragDrop** method determines the control under the current cursor location. It then checks to see if the control is a valid drop target.

If the control is a valid drop target, the **GiveFeedback** event is raised with the drag-and-drop effect specified. For a list of drag-and-drop effects, see the **DragDropEffects** enumeration.

Changes in the mouse cursor position, keyboard state, and mouse button state are tracked.

- If the user moves out of a window, the **DragLeave** event is raised.
- If the mouse enters another control, the **DragEnter** for that control is raised.
- If the mouse moves but stays within the same control, the **DragOver** event is raised.

If there is a change in the keyboard or mouse button state, the **QueryContinueDrag** event is raised and determines whether to continue the drag, to drop the data, or to cancel the operation based on the value of the **Action** property of the event's **QueryContinueDragEventArgs**.

- If the value is **DragAction.Continue**, the **DragOver** event is raised to continue the operation and the **GiveFeedback** event is raised with the new effect so appropriate visual feedback can be set. For a list of valid drop effects, see the **DragDropEffects** enumeration.

> **Note** The **DragOver** and **GiveFeedback** events are paired so that as the mouse moves across the drop target, the user is given the most up-to-date feedback on the mouse's position.

If the value is **DragAction.Drop**, the drop effect value is returned to the source, so the source application can perform the appropriate operation on the source data; for example, cut the data if the operation was a move.

If the value is **DragAction.Cancel**, the **DragLeave** event is raised.

> **Note** The **X** and **Y** properties of the **DragEventArgs** are in screen coordinates, not client coordinates. The following line of C# code converts the properties to a client **Point**:

```
Point clientPoint = targetControl.PointToClient(new Point ↵
 (de.X, de.Y));
```

Example

[Visual Basic, C#, C++] The following example demonstrates a drag-and-drop operation between two **ListBox** controls. The example calls the **DoDragDrop** method when the drag action starts. The drag action starts if the mouse has moved more than **SystemInformation.DragSize** from the mouse location during the **MouseDown** event. The **IndexFromPoint** method is used to determine the index of the item to drag during the **MouseDown** event.

[Visual Basic, C#, C++] The example also demonstrates using custom cursors for the drag-and-drop operation. The example assumes that two cursor files, `3dwarro.cur` and `3dwno.cur`, exist in the application directory, for the custom drag and no-drop cursors, respectively. The custom cursors will be used if the `UseCustomCursorsCheck` **CheckBox** is checked. The custom cursors are set in the **GiveFeedback** event handler.

[Visual Basic, C#, C++] The keyboard state is evaluated in the **DragOver** event handler for the right **ListBox**, to determine what the drag operation will be based upon state of the SHIFT, CTRL, ALT, or CTRL+ALT keys. The location in the **ListBox** where the drop would occur is also determined during the **DragOver** event. If the data to drop is not a **String**, then the **DragEventArgs.Effect** is set to **DragDropEffects.None**. Finally, the status of the drop is displayed in the `DropLocationLabel` **Label**.

[Visual Basic, C#, C++] The data to drop for the right **ListBox** is determined in the **DragDrop** event handler and the **String** value is added at the appropriate place in the **ListBox**. If the drag operation moves outside the bounds of the form, then the drag-and-drop operation is canceled in the **QueryContinueDrag** event handler.

[Visual Basic, C#, C++] This code excerpt demonstrates using the **DragOver** event. See the **DoDragDrop** method for the complete code example.

[Visual Basic]

```
Private Sub ListDragTarget_DragOver(ByVal sender As Object, ↵
 ByVal e As DragEventArgs) Handles ListDragTarget.DragOver
    ' Determine whether string data exists in the drop data. ↵
If not, then
    ' the drop effect reflects that the drop cannot occur.
    If Not (e.Data.GetDataPresent(GetType(System.String))) Then

        e.Effect = DragDropEffects.None
        DropLocationLabel.Text = "None - no string data."
        Return
    End If

    ' Set the effect based upon the KeyState.
    If ((e.KeyState And (8 + 32)) = (8 + 32) And _
        (e.AllowedEffect And DragDropEffects.Link) = ↵
DragDropEffects.Link) Then
        ' KeyState 8 + 32 = CTL + ALT

        ' Link drag and drop effect.
        e.Effect = DragDropEffects.Link

    ElseIf ((e.KeyState And 32) = 32 And _
        (e.AllowedEffect And DragDropEffects.Link) = ↵
DragDropEffects.Link) Then

        ' ALT KeyState for link.
        e.Effect = DragDropEffects.Link

    ElseIf ((e.KeyState And 4) = 4 And _
        (e.AllowedEffect And DragDropEffects.Move) = ↵
DragDropEffects.Move) Then

        ' SHIFT KeyState for move.
        e.Effect = DragDropEffects.Move

    ElseIf ((e.KeyState And 8) = 8 And _
        (e.AllowedEffect And DragDropEffects.Copy) = ↵
DragDropEffects.Copy) Then

        ' CTL KeyState for copy.
        e.Effect = DragDropEffects.Copy

    ElseIf ((e.AllowedEffect And DragDropEffects.Move) = ↵
DragDropEffects.Move) Then

        ' By default, the drop action should be move, if allowed.
        e.Effect = DragDropEffects.Move

    Else
        e.Effect = DragDropEffects.None
    End If

    ' Gets the index of the item the mouse is below.

    ' The mouse locations are relative to the screen, so they must be
    ' converted to client coordinates.

    indexOfItemUnderMouseToDrop = _
        ListDragTarget.IndexFromPoint ↵
(ListDragTarget.PointToClient(New Point(e.X, e.Y)))
```

```
    ' Updates the label text.
    If (indexOfItemUnderMouseToDrop <> ListBox.NoMatches) Then

        DropLocationLabel.Text = "Drops before item #" &                ↵
(indexOfItemUnderMouseToDrop + 1)
    Else
        DropLocationLabel.Text = "Drops at the end."
    End If

End Sub
```

[C#]

```
private void ListDragTarget_DragOver(object sender,                    ↵
System.Windows.Forms.DragEventArgs e)
{

    // Determine whether string data exists in the drop                ↵
 data. If not, then
    // the drop effect reflects that the drop cannot occur.
    if (!e.Data.GetDataPresent(typeof(System.String))) {

        e.Effect = DragDropEffects.None;
        DropLocationLabel.Text = "None - no string data.";
        return;
    }

    // Set the effect based upon the KeyState.
    if ((e.KeyState & (8+32)) == (8+32) &&
        (e.AllowedEffect & DragDropEffects.Link) ==                    ↵
DragDropEffects.Link) {
        // KeyState 8 + 32 = CTL + ALT

        // Link drag and drop effect.
        e.Effect = DragDropEffects.Link;

    } else if ((e.KeyState & 32) == 32 &&
        (e.AllowedEffect & DragDropEffects.Link) ==                    ↵
DragDropEffects.Link) {

        // ALT KeyState for link.
        e.Effect = DragDropEffects.Link;

    } else if ((e.KeyState & 4) == 4 &&
        (e.AllowedEffect & DragDropEffects.Move) ==                    ↵
DragDropEffects.Move) {

        // SHIFT KeyState for move.
        e.Effect = DragDropEffects.Move;

    } else if ((e.KeyState & 8) == 8 &&
        (e.AllowedEffect & DragDropEffects.Copy) ==                    ↵
DragDropEffects.Copy) {

        // CTL KeyState for copy.
        e.Effect = DragDropEffects.Copy;

    } else if ((e.AllowedEffect & DragDropEffects.Move)                ↵
== DragDropEffects.Move)  {

        // By default, the drop action should be move, if allowed.
        e.Effect = DragDropEffects.Move;

    } else
        e.Effect = DragDropEffects.None;

    // Get the index of the item the mouse is below.

    // The mouse locations are relative to the screen, so they must be
    // converted to client coordinates.

    indexOfItemUnderMouseToDrop =
        ListDragTarget.IndexFromPoint                                  ↵
 (ListDragTarget.PointToClient(new Point(e.X, e.Y)));
```

```
    // Updates the label text.
    if (indexOfItemUnderMouseToDrop != ListBox.NoMatches){

        DropLocationLabel.Text = "Drops before item #" +               ↵
(indexOfItemUnderMouseToDrop + 1);
    } else
        DropLocationLabel.Text = "Drops at the end.";

}
```

[C++]

```
private:
    void ListDragTarget_DragOver(Object* /*sender*/,
        System::Windows::Forms::DragEventArgs* e) {

        // Determine whether String* data exists in the drop           ↵
data. If not, then
        // the drop effect reflects that the drop cannot occur.
        if (!e->Data->GetDataPresent(__typeof(System::String))) {

            e->Effect = DragDropEffects::None;
            DropLocationLabel->Text = S"None - no String* data.";
            return;
        }

        // Set the effect based upon the KeyState.
        if ((e->KeyState & (8+32)) == (8+32) &&
            (e->AllowedEffect & DragDropEffects::Link) ==              ↵
DragDropEffects::Link) {
                // KeyState 8 + 32 = CTL + ALT

                // Link drag and drop effect.
                e->Effect = DragDropEffects::Link;

            } else if ((e->KeyState & 32) == 32 &&
                (e->AllowedEffect & DragDropEffects::Link) ==          ↵
DragDropEffects::Link) {

                    // ALT KeyState for link.
                    e->Effect = DragDropEffects::Link;

                } else if ((e->KeyState & 4) == 4 &&
                    (e->AllowedEffect & DragDropEffects::Move) ==
                    DragDropEffects::Move) {
                        // SHIFT KeyState for move.
                        e->Effect = DragDropEffects::Move;

                    } else if ((e->KeyState & 8) == 8 &&
                        (e->AllowedEffect & DragDropEffects::Copy) ==
                        DragDropEffects::Copy) {
                            // CTL KeyState for copy.
                            e->Effect = DragDropEffects::Copy;

                        } else if ((e->AllowedEffect &                 ↵
DragDropEffects::Move) ==
                            DragDropEffects::Move) {
                            // By default, the drop action             ↵
 should be move, if allowed.
                            e->Effect = DragDropEffects::Move;

                        } else
                            e->Effect = DragDropEffects::None;

                        // Get the index of the item the               ↵
mouse is below.

                        // The mouse locations are relative            ↵
to the screen, so they must be
                        // converted to client coordinates.

                        indexOfItemUnderMouseToDrop =
                            ListDragTarget->IndexFromPoint(
                            ListDragTarget->PointToClient              ↵
 (Point(e->X, e->Y)));
```

```
                // Updates the label text.
                if (indexOfItemUnderMouseToDrop !=                    ↵
ListBox::NoMatches) {
                    DropLocationLabel->Text =
                        String::Concat(S"Drops before item # ",
                        __box( (                                      ↵
indexOfItemUnderMouseToDrop + 1)));
                } else
                    DropLocationLabel->Text =                         ↵
S"Drops at the end.";

    }
```

Requirements

Platforms: Windows 98, Windows NT 4.0, Windows Millennium Edition, Windows 2000, Windows XP Home Edition, Windows XP Professional, Windows Server 2003 family

Control.EnabledChanged Event

Occurs when the **Enabled** property value has changed.

[Visual Basic]
```
Public Event EnabledChanged As EventHandler
```
[C#]
```
public event EventHandler EnabledChanged;
```
[C++]
```
public: __event EventHandler* EnabledChanged;
```

[JScript] In JScript, you can handle the events defined by a class, but you cannot define your own.

Event Data

The event handler receives an argument of type **EventArgs**.

Remarks

This event is raised if the **Enabled** property is changed by either a programmatic modification or user interaction.

Example

[Visual Basic, C#, C++] The example below is an event handling method that is executed when the **Text** property value changes. The **Control** class has several methods with the name pattern Property-Name **Changed** that are raised when the corresponding Property-Name value changes(PropertyName represents the name of the corresponding property).

[Visual Basic, C#, C++] The following example changes the **ForeColor** of a **TextBox** displaying currency data. The example converts the text to a decimal number and changes the **ForeColor** to **Color.Red** if the number is negative and to **Color.Black** if the number is positive. This example assumes you have a **Form** that contains a **TextBox**.

[Visual Basic]
```
Private Sub currencyTextBox_TextChanged(sender As Object, _
  e As EventArgs) Handles currencyTextBox.TextChanged
    Try
        ' Convert the text to a Double and determine if it is a       ↵
negative number.
        If Double.Parse(currencyTextBox.Text) < 0 Then
            ' If the number is negative, display it in Red.
            currencyTextBox.ForeColor = Color.Red
        Else
            ' If the number is not negative, display it in Black.
            currencyTextBox.ForeColor = Color.Black
        End If
    Catch
        ' If there is an error, display the text using the system colors.
        currencyTextBox.ForeColor = SystemColors.ControlText
    End Try
End Sub
```

[C#]
```
private void currencyTextBox_TextChanged(object sender, EventArgs e)
{
   try
   {
      // Convert the text to a Double and determine if it is a        ↵
negative number.
      if(double.Parse(currencyTextBox.Text) < 0)
      {
         // If the number is negative, display it in Red.
         currencyTextBox.ForeColor = Color.Red;
      }
      else
      {
         // If the number is not negative, display it in Black.
         currencyTextBox.ForeColor = Color.Black;
      }
   }
   catch
   {
      // If there is an error, display the text using the             ↵
system colors.
      currencyTextBox.ForeColor = SystemColors.ControlText;
   }
}
```

[C++]
```
private:
    void currencyTextBox_TextChanged(Object* /*sender*/,              ↵
EventArgs* /*e*/) {
        try {
            // Convert the text to a Double and determine if         ↵
 it is a negative number.
            if (Double::Parse(currencyTextBox->Text) < 0) {
                // If the number is negative, display it in Red.
                currencyTextBox->ForeColor = Color::Red;
            } else {
                // If the number is not negative, display it in Black.
                currencyTextBox->ForeColor = Color::Black;
            }
        } catch (Exception*) {
            // If there is an error, display the text using the      ↵
 system colors.
            currencyTextBox->ForeColor = SystemColors::ControlText;
        }
    }
```

Requirements

Platforms: Windows 98, Windows NT 4.0, Windows Millennium Edition, Windows 2000, Windows XP Home Edition, Windows XP Professional, Windows Server 2003 family

Control.Enter Event

Occurs when the control is entered.

[Visual Basic]
```
Public Event Enter As EventHandler
```
[C#]
```
public event EventHandler Enter;
```
[C++]
```
public: __event EventHandler* Enter;
```

[JScript] In JScript, you can handle the events defined by a class, but you cannot define your own.

Event Data

The event handler receives an argument of type **EventArgs**.

Remarks

Focus events occur in the following order:

1. **Enter**
2. **GotFocus**

3. **Leave**
4. **Validating**
5. **Validated**
6. **LostFocus**

If the **CausesValidation** property is set to **false**, the **Validating** and **Validated** events are suppressed.

> **Note** The **Enter** and **Leave** events are suppressed by the **Form** class. The equivalent events in the **Form** class are the **Activated** and **Deactivate** events. The **Enter** and **Leave** events are hierarchical and will cascade up and down the parent chain until the appropriate control is reached. For example, assume you have a **Form** with two **GroupBox** controls, and each **GroupBox** control has one **TextBox** control. When the caret is moved from one **TextBox** to the other, the **Leave** event is raised for the **TextBox** and **GroupBox**, and the **Enter** event is raised for the other **GroupBox** and **TextBox**.

Requirements

Platforms: Windows 98, Windows NT 4.0, Windows Millennium Edition, Windows 2000, Windows XP Home Edition, Windows XP Professional, Windows Server 2003 family

Control.FontChanged Event

Occurs when the **Font** property value changes.

[Visual Basic]
```
Public Event FontChanged As EventHandler
```
[C#]
```
public event EventHandler FontChanged;
```
[C++]
```
public: __event EventHandler* FontChanged;
```

[JScript] In JScript, you can handle the events defined by a class, but you cannot define your own.

Event Data

The event handler receives an argument of type **EventArgs**.

Remarks

This event is raised if the **Font** property is changed by either a programmatic modification or through interaction.

Example

[Visual Basic, C#, C++] The example below is an event handling method that is executed when the **Text** property value changes. The **Control** class has several methods with the name pattern PropertyName **Changed** that are raised when the corresponding PropertyName value changes(PropertyName represents the name of the corresponding property).

[Visual Basic, C#, C++] The following example changes the **ForeColor** of a **TextBox** displaying currency data. The example converts the text to a decimal number and changes the **ForeColor** to **Color.Red** if the number is negative and to **Color.Black** if the number is positive. This example assumes you have a **Form** that contains a **TextBox**.

[Visual Basic]
```
Private Sub currencyTextBox_TextChanged(sender As Object, _
  e As EventArgs) Handles currencyTextBox.TextChanged
   Try
      ' Convert the text to a Double and determine if it is a negative number.
      If Double.Parse(currencyTextBox.Text) < 0 Then
         ' If the number is negative, display it in Red.
         currencyTextBox.ForeColor = Color.Red
      Else
         ' If the number is not negative, display it in Black.
         currencyTextBox.ForeColor = Color.Black
      End If
   Catch
      ' If there is an error, display the text using the system colors.
      currencyTextBox.ForeColor = SystemColors.ControlText
   End Try
End Sub
```

[C#]
```
private void currencyTextBox_TextChanged(object sender, EventArgs e)
{
   try
   {
      // Convert the text to a Double and determine if it is a negative number.
      if(double.Parse(currencyTextBox.Text) < 0)
      {
         // If the number is negative, display it in Red.
         currencyTextBox.ForeColor = Color.Red;
      }
      else
      {
         // If the number is not negative, display it in Black.
         currencyTextBox.ForeColor = Color.Black;
      }
   }
   catch
   {
      // If there is an error, display the text using the system colors.
      currencyTextBox.ForeColor = SystemColors.ControlText;
   }
}
```

[C++]
```
private:
    void currencyTextBox_TextChanged(Object* /*sender*/, EventArgs* /*e*/) {
        try {
            // Convert the text to a Double and determine if it is a negative number.
            if (Double::Parse(currencyTextBox->Text) < 0) {
                // If the number is negative, display it in Red.
                currencyTextBox->ForeColor = Color::Red;
            } else {
                // If the number is not negative, display it in Black.
                currencyTextBox->ForeColor = Color::Black;
            }
        } catch (Exception*) {
            // If there is an error, display the text using the system colors.
            currencyTextBox->ForeColor = SystemColors::ControlText;
        }
    }
```

Requirements

Platforms: Windows 98, Windows NT 4.0, Windows Millennium Edition, Windows 2000, Windows XP Home Edition, Windows XP Professional, Windows Server 2003 family

Control.ForeColorChanged Event

Occurs when the **ForeColor** property value changes.

[Visual Basic]
```
Public Event ForeColorChanged As EventHandler
```
[C#]
```
public event EventHandler ForeColorChanged;
```
[C++]
```
public: __event EventHandler* ForeColorChanged;
```

[JScript] In JScript, you can handle the events defined by a class, but you cannot define your own.

Event Data

The event handler receives an argument of type **EventArgs**.

Remarks

This event is raised if the **ForeColor** property is changed by either a programmatic modification or through interaction.

Example

[Visual Basic, C#, C++] The example below is an event handling method that is executed when the **Text** property value changes. The **Control** class has several methods with the name pattern Property-Name **Changed** that are raised when the corresponding Property-Name value changes(PropertyName represents the name of the corresponding property).

[Visual Basic, C#, C++] The following example changes the **ForeColor** of a **TextBox** displaying currency data. The example converts the text to a decimal number and changes the **ForeColor** to **Color.Red** if the number is negative and to **Color.Black** if the number is positive. This example assumes you have a **Form** that contains a **TextBox**.

[Visual Basic]
```
Private Sub currencyTextBox_TextChanged(sender As Object, _
  e As EventArgs) Handles currencyTextBox.TextChanged
   Try
      ' Convert the text to a Double and determine if it is a
 negative number.
      If Double.Parse(currencyTextBox.Text) < 0 Then
         ' If the number is negative, display it in Red.
         currencyTextBox.ForeColor = Color.Red
      Else
         ' If the number is not negative, display it in Black.
         currencyTextBox.ForeColor = Color.Black
      End If
   Catch
      ' If there is an error, display the text using the system colors.
      currencyTextBox.ForeColor = SystemColors.ControlText
   End Try
End Sub
```

[C#]
```
private void currencyTextBox_TextChanged(object sender, EventArgs e)
{
   try
   {
      // Convert the text to a Double and determine if it is a
 negative number.
      if(double.Parse(currencyTextBox.Text) < 0)
      {
         // If the number is negative, display it in Red.
         currencyTextBox.ForeColor = Color.Red;
      }
      else
      {
         // If the number is not negative, display it in Black.
         currencyTextBox.ForeColor = Color.Black;
      }
   }
   catch
   {
      // If there is an error, display the text using the system
colors.
      currencyTextBox.ForeColor = SystemColors.ControlText;
   }
}
```

[C++]
```
private:
    void currencyTextBox_TextChanged(Object* /*sender*/,
EventArgs* /*e*/) {
        try {
            // Convert the text to a Double and determine if i
t is a negative number.
            if (Double::Parse(currencyTextBox->Text) < 0) {
                // If the number is negative, display it in Red.
                currencyTextBox->ForeColor = Color::Red;
            } else {
                // If the number is not negative, display it in Black.
                currencyTextBox->ForeColor = Color::Black;
            }
        } catch (Exception*) {
            // If there is an error, display the text using the
system colors.
            currencyTextBox->ForeColor = SystemColors::ControlText;
        }
    }
```

Requirements

Platforms: Windows 98, Windows NT 4.0, Windows Millennium Edition, Windows 2000, Windows XP Home Edition, Windows XP Professional, Windows Server 2003 family

Control.GiveFeedback Event

Occurs during a drag operation.

[Visual Basic]
```
Public Event GiveFeedback As GiveFeedbackEventHandler
```
[C#]
```
public event GiveFeedbackEventHandler GiveFeedback;
```
[C++]
```
public: __event GiveFeedbackEventHandler* GiveFeedback;
```

[JScript] In JScript, you can handle the events defined by a class, but you cannot define your own.

Event Data

The event handler receives an argument of type **GiveFeedbackEventArgs** containing data related to this event. The following **GiveFeedbackEventArgs** properties provide information specific to this event.

Property	Description
Effect	Gets the drag-and-drop operation feedback that is displayed.
UseDefaultCursors	Gets or sets whether drag operation should use the default cursors that are associated with drag-drop effects.

Remarks

The **GiveFeedback** event is raised when a drag-and-drop operation is started. The **GiveFeedback** event allows the source of a drag event to modify the appearance of the mouse pointer in order to give the user visual feedback during a drag-and-drop operation.

The following describes how and when events related to drag-and-drop operations are raised.

The **DoDragDrop** method determines the control under the current cursor location. It then checks to see if the control is a valid drop target.

If the control is a valid drop target, the **GiveFeedback** event is raised with the drag-and-drop effect specified. For a list of drag-and-drop effects, see the **DragDropEffects** enumeration.

Changes in the mouse cursor position, keyboard state, and mouse button state are tracked.

- If the user moves out of a window, the **DragLeave** event is raised.
- If the mouse enters another control, the **DragEnter** for that control is raised.
- If the mouse moves but stays within the same control, the **DragOver** event is raised.

If there is a change in the keyboard or mouse button state, the **QueryContinueDrag** event is raised and determines whether to continue the drag, to drop the data, or to cancel the operation based on the value of the **Action** property of the event's **QueryContinueDragEventArgs**.

- If the value is **DragAction.Continue**, the **DragOver** event is raised to continue the operation and the **GiveFeedback** event is raised with the new effect so appropriate visual feedback can be set. For a list of valid drop effects, see the **DragDropEffects** enumeration.

> **Note** The **DragOver** and **GiveFeedback** events are paired so that as the mouse moves across the drop target, the user is given the most up-to-date feedback on the mouse's position.

If the value is **DragAction.Drop**, the drop effect value is returned to the source, so the source application can perform the appropriate operation on the source data; for example, cut the data if the operation was a move.

If the value is **DragAction.Cancel**, the **DragLeave** event is raised.

Example

[Visual Basic, C#, C++] The following example demonstrates a drag-and-drop operation between two **ListBox** controls. The example calls the **DoDragDrop** method when the drag action starts. The drag action starts if the mouse has moved more than **SystemInformation.DragSize** from the mouse location during the **MouseDown** event. The **IndexFromPoint** method is used to determine the index of the item to drag during the **MouseDown** event.

[Visual Basic, C#, C++] The example also demonstrates using custom cursors for the drag-and-drop operation. The example assumes that two cursor files, `3dwarro.cur` and `3dwno.cur`, exist in the application directory, for the custom drag and no-drop cursors, respectively. The custom cursors will be used if the `UseCustomCursorsCheck` **CheckBox** is checked. The custom cursors are set in the **GiveFeedback** event handler.

[Visual Basic, C#, C++] The keyboard state is evaluated in the **DragOver** event handler for the right **ListBox**, to determine what the drag operation will be based upon state of the SHIFT, CTRL, ALT, or CTRL+ALT keys. The location in the **ListBox** where the drop would occur is also determined during the **DragOver** event. If the data to drop is not a **String**, then the **DragEventArgs.Effect** is set to **DragDropEffects.None**. Finally, the status of the drop is displayed in the `DropLocationLabel` **Label**.

[Visual Basic, C#, C++] The data to drop for the right **ListBox** is determined in the **DragDrop** event handler and the **String** value is added at the appropriate place in the **ListBox**. If the drag operation moves outside the bounds of the form, then the drag-and-drop operation is canceled in the **QueryContinueDrag** event handler.

[Visual Basic, C#, C++] This code excerpt demonstrates using the **GiveFeedback** event. See the **DoDragDrop** method for the complete code example.

[Visual Basic]
```
Private Sub ListDragSource_GiveFeedback(ByVal sender As Object, ↵
ByVal e As GiveFeedbackEventArgs) Handles ListDragSource.GiveFeedback

    ' Use custom cursors if the check box is checked.
    If (UseCustomCursorsCheck.Checked) Then

        ' Set the custom cursor based upon the effect.
        e.UseDefaultCursors = False
        If ((e.Effect And DragDropEffects.Move) = DragDropEffects.Move)
Then
            Cursor.Current = MyNormalCursor
        Else
            Cursor.Current = MyNoDropCursor
        End If
    End If

End Sub
```

[C#]
```
private void ListDragSource_GiveFeedback(object sender, ↵
System.Windows.Forms.GiveFeedbackEventArgs e)
{
    // Use custom cursors if the check box is checked.
    if (UseCustomCursorsCheck.Checked) {

        // Sets the custom cursor based upon the effect.
        e.UseDefaultCursors = false;
        if ((e.Effect & DragDropEffects.Move) == DragDropEffects.Move)
            Cursor.Current = MyNormalCursor;
        else
            Cursor.Current = MyNoDropCursor;
    }

}
```

[C++]
```
private:
    void ListDragSource_GiveFeedback(Object* /*sender*/,
        System::Windows::Forms::GiveFeedbackEventArgs* e) {

        // Use custom cursors if the check box is checked.
        if (UseCustomCursorsCheck->Checked) {

            // Sets the custom cursor based upon the effect.
            e->UseDefaultCursors = false;
            if ((e->Effect & DragDropEffects::Move) == ↵
DragDropEffects::Move)
                Cursor::Current = MyNormalCursor;
            else
                Cursor::Current = MyNoDropCursor;
        }

    }
```

Requirements

Platforms: Windows 98, Windows NT 4.0, Windows Millennium Edition, Windows 2000, Windows XP Home Edition, Windows XP Professional, Windows Server 2003 family

Control.GotFocus Event

Occurs when the control receives focus.

[Visual Basic]
```
Public Event GotFocus As EventHandler
```
[C#]
```
public event EventHandler GotFocus;
```
[C++]
```
public: __event EventHandler* GotFocus;
```

[JScript] In JScript, you can handle the events defined by a class, but you cannot define your own.

Event Data

The event handler receives an argument of type **EventArgs**.

Remarks

Focus events occur in the following order:

1. **Enter**
2. **GotFocus**
3. **Leave**
4. **Validating**
5. **Validated**
6. **LostFocus**

If the **CausesValidation** property is set to **false**, the **Validating** and **Validated** events are suppressed.

> **Note** The **GotFocus** and **LostFocus** events are low-level focus events that are tied to the WM_KILLFOCUS and WM_SETFOCUS Windows messages. Typically, the **GotFocus** and **LostFocus** events are only used when updating **UICues**. The **Enter** and **Leave** events should be used for all controls except the **Form** class, which uses the **Activated** and **Deactivate** events. For more information about the **GotFocus** and **LostFocus** events, see the **WM_SETFOCUS** and **WM_KILLFOCUS** topics in the Keyboard Input Reference section of the Platform SDK Documentation in the MSDN Library.

> **CAUTION** Do not attempt to set focus from within the **LostFocus** event handler. Doing so can cause your application or the operating system to stop responding. For more information about the **LostFocus** event, see the **WM_KILLFOCUS** topic in the Keyboard Input Reference section, and the **Message Deadlocks** topic in the Messages and Message Queues section of the Platform SDK Documentation in the MSDN Library.

Requirements

Platforms: Windows 98, Windows NT 4.0,
Windows Millennium Edition, Windows 2000,
Windows XP Home Edition, Windows XP Professional,
Windows Server 2003 family

Control.HandleCreated Event

Occurs when a handle is created for the control.

```
[Visual Basic]
Public Event HandleCreated As EventHandler
[C#]
public event EventHandler HandleCreated;
[C++]
public: __event EventHandler* HandleCreated;
```

[JScript] In JScript, you can handle the events defined by a class, but you cannot define your own.

Event Data

The event handler receives an argument of type **EventArgs**.

Requirements

Platforms: Windows 98, Windows NT 4.0,
Windows Millennium Edition, Windows 2000,
Windows XP Home Edition, Windows XP Professional,
Windows Server 2003 family

Control.HandleDestroyed Event

Occurs when the control's handle is in the process of being destroyed.

```
[Visual Basic]
Public Event HandleDestroyed As EventHandler
[C#]
public event EventHandler HandleDestroyed;
[C++]
public: __event EventHandler* HandleDestroyed;
```

[JScript] In JScript, you can handle the events defined by a class, but you cannot define your own.

Event Data

The event handler receives an argument of type **EventArgs**.

Remarks

During the **HandleDestroyed** event, the control is still a valid Windows control and the **Handle** can be recreated by calling the **RecreateHandle** method.

Requirements

Platforms: Windows 98, Windows NT 4.0,
Windows Millennium Edition, Windows 2000,
Windows XP Home Edition, Windows XP Professional,
Windows Server 2003 family

Control.HelpRequested Event

Occurs when the user requests help for a control.

```
[Visual Basic]
Public Event HelpRequested As HelpEventHandler
[C#]
public event HelpEventHandler HelpRequested;
[C++]
public: __event HelpEventHandler* HelpRequested;
```

[JScript] In JScript, you can handle the events defined by a class, but you cannot define your own.

Event Data

The event handler receives an argument of type **HelpEventArgs** containing data related to this event. The following **HelpEventArgs** properties provide information specific to this event.

Property	Description
Handled	Gets or sets a value indicating whether the help event was handled.
MousePos	Gets the screen coordinates of the mouse pointer.

Remarks

The **HelpRequested** event is commonly raised when the user presses the F1 key or an associated context-sensitive help button is clicked.

Example

[Visual Basic, C#, C++] The following example demonstrates handling the **HelpRequested** event to display custom Help content on a form containing four address fields. The **HelpRequested** event is raised either by pressing the F1 key with the focus in an address field, or by the using the context-sensitive Help button and clicking the Help cursor on an address field. The **Handled** property is set to true to indicate that the **HelpRequested** event is handled. The example also demonstrates storing the Help text in the **Control.Tag** property.

[Visual Basic]
```
Imports System
Imports System.Drawing
Imports System.Windows.Forms

Public Class Form1
    Inherits System.Windows.Forms.Form
    Private WithEvents addressTextBox As System.Windows.Forms.TextBox
    Private WithEvents label2 As System.Windows.Forms.Label
    Private WithEvents cityTextBox As System.Windows.Forms.TextBox
    Private WithEvents label3 As System.Windows.Forms.Label
    Private WithEvents stateTextBox As System.Windows.Forms.TextBox
    Private WithEvents zipTextBox As System.Windows.Forms.TextBox
    Private WithEvents helpLabel As System.Windows.Forms.Label

    <STAThread()> _
    Shared Sub Main()
        Application.Run(New Form1)
    End Sub 'Main

    Public Sub New()
        Me.addressTextBox = New System.Windows.Forms.TextBox
        Me.helpLabel = New System.Windows.Forms.Label
        Me.label2 = New System.Windows.Forms.Label
        Me.cityTextBox = New System.Windows.Forms.TextBox
        Me.label3 = New System.Windows.Forms.Label
        Me.stateTextBox = New System.Windows.Forms.TextBox
        Me.zipTextBox = New System.Windows.Forms.TextBox

        ' Help Label
        Me.helpLabel.BorderStyle =                                      ↵
System.Windows.Forms.BorderStyle.Fixed3D
        Me.helpLabel.Location = New System.Drawing.Point(8, 80)
        Me.helpLabel.Size = New System.Drawing.Size(272, 72)
        Me.helpLabel.Text = "Click on any control to give it              ↵
focus, and then " & _
            "press F1 to display help for that" + " control.          ↵
Alternately, you can " & _
            "click the help button at the top of the dialog and       ↵
then click on a control."

        ' Address Label
        Me.label2.Location = New System.Drawing.Point(16, 8)
        Me.label2.Size = New System.Drawing.Size(100, 16)
        Me.label2.Text = "Address:"

        ' Comma Label
        Me.label3.Location = New System.Drawing.Point(136, 56)
        Me.label3.Size = New System.Drawing.Size(16, 16)
        Me.label3.Text = ","

        ' Address TextBox
        Me.addressTextBox.Location = New System.Drawing.Point(16, 24)
        Me.addressTextBox.Size = New System.Drawing.Size(264, 20)
        Me.addressTextBox.TabIndex = 0
        Me.addressTextBox.Tag = "Enter the stree address in              ↵
this text box."
        Me.addressTextBox.Text = ""

        ' City TextBox
        Me.cityTextBox.Location = New System.Drawing.Point(16, 48)
        Me.cityTextBox.Size = New System.Drawing.Size(120, 20)
        Me.cityTextBox.TabIndex = 3
        Me.cityTextBox.Tag = "Enter the city here."
        Me.cityTextBox.Text = ""

        ' State TextBox
        Me.stateTextBox.Location = New System.Drawing.Point(152, 48)
        Me.stateTextBox.MaxLength = 2
        Me.stateTextBox.Size = New System.Drawing.Size(32, 20)
        Me.stateTextBox.TabIndex = 5
        Me.stateTextBox.Tag = "Enter the state in this text box."
        Me.stateTextBox.Text = ""

        ' Zip TextBox
        Me.zipTextBox.Location = New System.Drawing.Point(192, 48)
        Me.zipTextBox.Size = New System.Drawing.Size(88, 20)
        Me.zipTextBox.TabIndex = 6
        Me.zipTextBox.Tag = "Enter the zip code here."
        Me.zipTextBox.Text = ""

        ' Set up how the form should be displayed and add the          ↵
controls to the form.
        Me.ClientSize = New System.Drawing.Size(292, 160)
        Me.Controls.AddRange(New System.Windows.Forms.Control          ↵
() {Me.zipTextBox, _
                              Me.stateTextBox, Me.label3,             ↵
Me.cityTextBox, _
                              Me.label2, Me.helpLabel,                ↵
Me.addressTextBox})
        Me.FormBorderStyle =                                           ↵
System.Windows.Forms.FormBorderStyle.FixedDialog
        Me.HelpButton = True
        Me.MaximizeBox = False
        Me.MinimizeBox = False
        Me.Text = "Help Event Demonstration"
    End Sub 'New

    Private Sub textBox_HelpRequested(ByVal sender As Object,          ↵
ByVal hlpevent As System.Windows.Forms.HelpEventArgs) Handles         ↵
addressTextBox.HelpRequested, cityTextBox.HelpRequested,              ↵
stateTextBox.HelpRequested, zipTextBox.HelpRequested
        ' This event is raised when the F1 key is pressed or the
        ' Help cursor is clicked on any of the address fields.
        ' The Help text for the field is in the control's
        ' Tag property. It is retrieved and displayed in the label.

        Dim requestingControl As Control = CType(sender, Control)
        helpLabel.Text = CStr(requestingControl.Tag)
        hlpevent.Handled = True

    End Sub 'textBox_HelpRequested
End Class 'Form1
```

[C#]
```
using System;
using System.Drawing;
using System.Windows.Forms;

public class Form1 : System.Windows.Forms.Form
{
    private System.Windows.Forms.TextBox addressTextBox;
    private System.Windows.Forms.Label label2;
    private System.Windows.Forms.TextBox cityTextBox;
    private System.Windows.Forms.Label label3;
    private System.Windows.Forms.TextBox stateTextBox;
    private System.Windows.Forms.TextBox zipTextBox;
    private System.Windows.Forms.Label helpLabel;

    [STAThread]
    static void Main()
    {
        Application.Run(new Form1());
    }

    public Form1()
    {
        this.addressTextBox = new System.Windows.Forms.TextBox();
        this.helpLabel = new System.Windows.Forms.Label();
        this.label2 = new System.Windows.Forms.Label();
        this.cityTextBox = new System.Windows.Forms.TextBox();
        this.label3 = new System.Windows.Forms.Label();
        this.stateTextBox = new System.Windows.Forms.TextBox();
        this.zipTextBox = new System.Windows.Forms.TextBox();

        // Help Label
        this.helpLabel.BorderStyle =                                   ↵
System.Windows.Forms.BorderStyle.Fixed3D;
        this.helpLabel.Location = new System.Drawing.Point(8, 80);
        this.helpLabel.Size = new System.Drawing.Size(272, 72);
        this.helpLabel.Text = "Click on any control to give              ↵
it focus, and then " +
```

```
            "press F1 to display help for that control.        ↵
 Alternately, you can " +
            "click the help button at the top of the dialog    ↵
and then click on a control.";

        // Address Label
        this.label2.Location = new System.Drawing.Point(16, 8);
        this.label2.Size = new System.Drawing.Size(100, 16);
        this.label2.Text = "Address:";

        // Comma Label
        this.label3.Location = new System.Drawing.Point(136, 56);
        this.label3.Size = new System.Drawing.Size(16, 16);
        this.label3.Text = ",";

        // Address TextBox
        this.addressTextBox.Location = new                     ↵
System.Drawing.Point(16, 24);
        this.addressTextBox.Size = new System.Drawing.Size(264, 20);
        this.addressTextBox.TabIndex = 0;
        this.addressTextBox.Tag = "Enter the street address     ↵
in this text box.";
        this.addressTextBox.Text = "";
        this.addressTextBox.HelpRequested += new               ↵
System.Windows.Forms.HelpEventHandler(this.textBox_HelpRequested);

        // City TextBox
        this.cityTextBox.Location = new System.Drawing.Point(16, 48);
        this.cityTextBox.Size = new System.Drawing.Size(120, 20);
        this.cityTextBox.TabIndex = 3;
        this.cityTextBox.Tag = "Enter the city here.";
        this.cityTextBox.Text = "";
        this.cityTextBox.HelpRequested += new                  ↵
System.Windows.Forms.HelpEventHandler(this.textBox_HelpRequested);

        // State TextBox
        this.stateTextBox.Location = new System.Drawing.Point(152, 48);
        this.stateTextBox.MaxLength = 2;
        this.stateTextBox.Size = new System.Drawing.Size(32, 20);
        this.stateTextBox.TabIndex = 5;
        this.stateTextBox.Tag = "Enter the state in this text box.";
        this.stateTextBox.Text = "";
        this.stateTextBox.HelpRequested += new                 ↵
System.Windows.Forms.HelpEventHandler(this.textBox_HelpRequested);

        // Zip TextBox
        this.zipTextBox.Location = new System.Drawing.Point(192, 48);
        this.zipTextBox.Name = "zipTextBox";
        this.zipTextBox.Size = new System.Drawing.Size(88, 20);
        this.zipTextBox.TabIndex = 6;
        this.zipTextBox.Tag = "Enter the zip code here.";
        this.zipTextBox.Text = "";
        this.zipTextBox.HelpRequested += new                   ↵
System.Windows.Forms.HelpEventHandler(this.textBox_HelpRequested);

        // Set up how the form should be displayed and add the  ↵
controls to the form.
        this.ClientSize = new System.Drawing.Size(292, 160);
        this.Controls.AddRange(new                              ↵
System.Windows.Forms.Control[] { this.zipTextBox,
                this.stateTextBox, this.label3, this.cityTextBox,
                    this.label2, this.helpLabel, this.addressTextBox});

        this.FormBorderStyle =                                  ↵
System.Windows.Forms.FormBorderStyle.FixedDialog;
        this.HelpButton = true;
        this.MaximizeBox = false;
        this.MinimizeBox = false;
        this.Text = "Help Event Demonstration";
    }

    private void textBox_HelpRequested(object sender,           ↵
System.Windows.Forms.HelpEventArgs hlpevent)
    {
        // This event is raised when the F1 key is pressed or the
        // Help cursor is clicked on any of the address fields.
        // The Help text for the field is in the control's
        // Tag property. It is retrieved and displayed in the label.

        Control requestingControl = (Control)sender;
        helpLabel.Text = (string)requestingControl.Tag;
        hlpevent.Handled = true;
    }
}
```

[C++]

```
#using <mscorlib.dll>
#using <System.dll>
#using <System.Windows.Forms.dll>
#using <System.Drawing.dll>

using namespace System;
using namespace System::Drawing;
using namespace System::Windows::Forms;

public __gc class Form1 : public System::Windows::Forms::Form {
private:
   System::Windows::Forms::TextBox*  addressTextBox;
   System::Windows::Forms::Label*  label2;
   System::Windows::Forms::TextBox*  cityTextBox;
   System::Windows::Forms::Label*  label3;
   System::Windows::Forms::TextBox*  stateTextBox;
   System::Windows::Forms::TextBox*  zipTextBox;
   System::Windows::Forms::Label*  helpLabel;
public:
   Form1() {
      this->addressTextBox = new System::Windows::Forms::TextBox();
      this->helpLabel = new System::Windows::Forms::Label();
      this->label2 = new System::Windows::Forms::Label();
      this->cityTextBox = new System::Windows::Forms::TextBox();
      this->label3 = new System::Windows::Forms::Label();
      this->stateTextBox = new System::Windows::Forms::TextBox();
      this->zipTextBox = new System::Windows::Forms::TextBox();

      // Help Label
      this->helpLabel->BorderStyle =                            ↵
System::Windows::Forms::BorderStyle::Fixed3D;
      this->helpLabel->Location =  System::Drawing::Point(8, 80);
      this->helpLabel->Size =  System::Drawing::Size(272, 72);
      this->helpLabel->Text = S"Click on any control to give  ↵
 it focus, and then press F1 to display help for that control.   ↵
 Alternately, you can click the help button at the top of the    ↵
 dialog and then click on a control.";

      // Address Label
      this->label2->Location =  System::Drawing::Point(16, 8);
      this->label2->Size =  System::Drawing::Size(100, 16);
      this->label2->Text = S"Address:";

      // Comma Label
      this->label3->Location =  System::Drawing::Point(136, 56);
      this->label3->Size =  System::Drawing::Size(16, 16);
      this->label3->Text = S", ";

      // Address TextBox
      this->addressTextBox->Location =  System::Drawing::Point(16, 24);
      this->addressTextBox->Size =  System::Drawing::Size(264, 20);
      this->addressTextBox->TabIndex = 0;
      this->addressTextBox->Tag = S"Enter the street address   ↵
in this text box.";
      this->addressTextBox->Text = S"";
      this->addressTextBox->HelpRequested += new                ↵
System::Windows::Forms::HelpEventHandler(this, textBox_HelpRequested);

      // City TextBox
      this->cityTextBox->Location =  System::Drawing::Point(16, 48);
      this->cityTextBox->Size =  System::Drawing::Size(120, 20);
      this->cityTextBox->TabIndex = 3;
      this->cityTextBox->Tag = S"Enter the city here.";
      this->cityTextBox->Text = S"";
      this->cityTextBox->HelpRequested += new                   ↵
System::Windows::Forms::HelpEventHandler(this, textBox_HelpRequested);
```

```
      // State TextBox
      this->stateTextBox->Location =  System::Drawing::Point(152, 48);
      this->stateTextBox->MaxLength = 2;
      this->stateTextBox->Size =  System::Drawing::Size(32, 20);
      this->stateTextBox->TabIndex = 5;
      this->stateTextBox->Tag = S"Enter the state in this text box.";
      this->stateTextBox->Text = S"";
      this->stateTextBox->HelpRequested += new                          ↵
System::Windows::Forms::HelpEventHandler(this, textBox_HelpRequested);

      // Zip TextBox
      this->zipTextBox->Location =  System::Drawing::Point(192, 48);
      this->zipTextBox->Name = S"zipTextBox";
      this->zipTextBox->Size =  System::Drawing::Size(88, 20);
      this->zipTextBox->TabIndex = 6;
      this->zipTextBox->Tag = S"Enter the zip code here.";
      this->zipTextBox->Text = S"";
      this->zipTextBox->HelpRequested += new                            ↵
System::Windows::Forms::HelpEventHandler(this, textBox_HelpRequested);

      // Set up how the form should be displayed and add                ↵
 the controls to the form.
      this->ClientSize =  System::Drawing::Size(292, 160);

      System::Windows::Forms::Control* temp0 [] = {this->zipTextBox,
         this->stateTextBox, this->label3, this->cityTextBox,
         this->label2, this->helpLabel, this->addressTextBox};

      this->Controls->AddRange(temp0);

      this->FormBorderStyle =                                           ↵
System::Windows::Forms::FormBorderStyle::FixedDialog;
      this->HelpButton = true;
      this->MaximizeBox = false;
      this->MinimizeBox = false;
      this->Text = S"Help Event Demonstration";
   }

private:
   void textBox_HelpRequested(Object* sender,                           ↵
System::Windows::Forms::HelpEventArgs* hlpevent) {
      // This event is raised when the F1 key is pressed or the
      // Help cursor is clicked on any of the address fields.
      // The Help text for the field is in the control's
      // Tag property. It is retrieved and displayed in the label.

      Control* requestingControl = dynamic_cast<Control*>(sender);
      helpLabel->Text = dynamic_cast<String*>(requestingControl->Tag);
      hlpevent->Handled = true;
   }
};

[STAThread]
int main() {
   Application::Run(new Form1());
}
```

Requirements

Platforms: Windows 98, Windows NT 4.0, Windows Millennium Edition, Windows 2000, Windows XP Home Edition, Windows XP Professional, Windows Server 2003 family

Control.ImeModeChanged Event

Occurs when the **ImeMode** property has changed.

[Visual Basic]
```
Public Event ImeModeChanged As EventHandler
```
[C#]
```
public event EventHandler ImeModeChanged;
```
[C++]
```
public: __event EventHandler* ImeModeChanged;
```

[JScript] In JScript, you can handle the events defined by a class, but you cannot define your own.

Event Data

The event handler receives an argument of type **EventArgs**.

Remarks

This event is raised if the **ImeMode** property is changed by either a programmatic modification or through interaction.

Example

[Visual Basic, C#, C++] The example below is an event handling method that is executed when the **Text** property value changes. The **Control** class has several methods with the name pattern PropertyName **Changed** that are raised when the corresponding PropertyName value changes(PropertyName represents the name of the corresponding property).

[Visual Basic, C#, C++] The following example changes the **ForeColor** of a **TextBox** displaying currency data. The example converts the text to a decimal number and changes the **ForeColor** to **Color.Red** if the number is negative and to **Color.Black** if the number is positive. This example assumes you have a **Form** that contains a **TextBox**.

[Visual Basic]
```
Private Sub currencyTextBox_TextChanged(sender As Object, _
  e As EventArgs) Handles currencyTextBox.TextChanged
    Try
        ' Convert the text to a Double and determine if it is a        ↵
negative number.
        If Double.Parse(currencyTextBox.Text) < 0 Then
            ' If the number is negative, display it in Red.
            currencyTextBox.ForeColor = Color.Red
        Else
            ' If the number is not negative, display it in Black.
            currencyTextBox.ForeColor = Color.Black
        End If
    Catch
        ' If there is an error, display the text using the system colors.
        currencyTextBox.ForeColor = SystemColors.ControlText
    End Try
End Sub
```

[C#]
```
private void currencyTextBox_TextChanged(object sender, EventArgs e)
{
   try
   {
      // Convert the text to a Double and determine if it is a         ↵
negative number.
      if(double.Parse(currencyTextBox.Text) < 0)
      {
         // If the number is negative, display it in Red.
         currencyTextBox.ForeColor = Color.Red;
      }
      else
      {
         // If the number is not negative, display it in Black.
         currencyTextBox.ForeColor = Color.Black;
      }
   }
   catch
   {
      // If there is an error, display the text using the              ↵
system colors.
      currencyTextBox.ForeColor = SystemColors.ControlText;
   }
}
```

[C++]
```
private:
    void currencyTextBox_TextChanged(Object* /*sender*/,                ↵
EventArgs* /*e*/) {
```

```
        try {
            // Convert the text to a Double and determine ↵
 if it is a negative number.
            if (Double::Parse(currencyTextBox->Text) < 0) {
                // If the number is negative, display it in Red.
                currencyTextBox->ForeColor = Color::Red;
            } else {
                // If the number is not negative, display it in Black.
                currencyTextBox->ForeColor = Color::Black;
            }
        } catch (Exception*) {
            // If there is an error, display the text using ↵
the system colors.
            currencyTextBox->ForeColor = SystemColors::ControlText;
        }
    }
```

Requirements

Platforms: Windows 98, Windows NT 4.0, Windows Millennium Edition, Windows 2000, Windows XP Home Edition, Windows XP Professional, Windows Server 2003 family

Control.Invalidated Event

Occurs when a control's display requires redrawing.

[Visual Basic]
```
Public Event Invalidated As InvalidateEventHandler
```
[C#]
```
public event InvalidateEventHandler Invalidated;
```
[C++]
```
public: __event InvalidateEventHandler* Invalidated;
```

[JScript] In JScript, you can handle the events defined by a class, but you cannot define your own.

Event Data

The event handler receives an argument of type **InvalidateEventArgs** containing data related to this event. The following **InvalidateEventArgs** property provides information specific to this event.

Property	Description
InvalidRect	Gets the **Rectangle** that contains the invalidated window area.

Requirements

Platforms: Windows 98, Windows NT 4.0, Windows Millennium Edition, Windows 2000, Windows XP Home Edition, Windows XP Professional, Windows Server 2003 family

Control.KeyDown Event

Occurs when a key is pressed while the control has focus.

[Visual Basic]
```
Public Event KeyDown As KeyEventHandler
```
[C#]
```
public event KeyEventHandler KeyDown;
```
[C++]
```
public: __event KeyEventHandler* KeyDown;
```

[JScript] In JScript, you can handle the events defined by a class, but you cannot define your own.

Event Data

The event handler receives an argument of type **KeyEventArgs** containing data related to this event. The following **KeyEventArgs** properties provide information specific to this event.

Property	Description
Alt	Gets a value indicating whether the ALT key was pressed.
Control	Gets a value indicating whether the CTRL key was pressed.
Handled	Gets or sets a value indicating whether the event was handled.
KeyCode	Gets the keyboard code for a **KeyDown** or **KeyUp** event.
KeyData	Gets the key data for a **KeyDown** or **KeyUp** event.
KeyValue	Gets the keyboard value for a **KeyDown** or **KeyUp** event.
Modifiers	Gets the modifier flags for a **KeyDown** or **KeyUp** event. This indicates which combination of modifier keys (CTRL, SHIFT, and ALT) were pressed.
Shift	Gets a value indicating whether the SHIFT key was pressed.

Remarks

Key events occur in the following order:

1. KeyDown
2. **KeyPress**
3. **KeyUp**

To handle keyboard events only at the form level and not allow other controls to receive keyboard events, set the **KeyPressEventArgs.Handled** property in your form's **KeyPress** event-handling method to **true**. Certain keys, such as the TAB, RETURN, ESCAPE, and arrow keys are handled by controls automatically. In order to have these keys raise the KeyDown event, you must override the **IsInputKey** method in each control on your form. The code for the override of the IsInputKey would need to determine if one of the special keys is pressed and return a value of **true**.

Requirements

Platforms: Windows 98, Windows NT 4.0, Windows Millennium Edition, Windows 2000, Windows XP Home Edition, Windows XP Professional, Windows Server 2003 family

Control.KeyPress Event

Occurs when a key is pressed while the control has focus.

[Visual Basic]
```
Public Event KeyPress As KeyPressEventHandler
```
[C#]
```
public event KeyPressEventHandler KeyPress;
```
[C++]
```
public: __event KeyPressEventHandler* KeyPress;
```

[JScript] In JScript, you can handle the events defined by a class, but you cannot define your own.

Event Data

The event handler receives an argument of type **KeyPressEventArgs** containing data related to this event. The following **KeyPressEventArgs** properties provide information specific to this event.

Property	Description
Handled	Gets or sets a value indicating whether the **KeyPress** event was handled.
KeyChar	Gets the character corresponding to the key pressed.

Remarks

Key events occur in the following order:

1. **KeyDown**
2. **KeyPress**
3. **KeyUp**

The **KeyPress** event is not raised by noncharacter keys; however, the noncharacter keys do raise the **KeyDown** and **KeyUp** events.

To handle keyboard events only at the form level and not allow other controls to receive keyboard events, set the **KeyPressEventArgs.Handled** property in your form's **KeyPress** event-handling method to **true**.

Requirements

Platforms: Windows 98, Windows NT 4.0, Windows Millennium Edition, Windows 2000, Windows XP Home Edition, Windows XP Professional, Windows Server 2003 family

Control.KeyUp Event

Occurs when a key is released while the control has focus.

[Visual Basic]
```
Public Event KeyUp As KeyEventHandler
```
[C#]
```
public event KeyEventHandler KeyUp;
```
[C++]
```
public: __event KeyEventHandler* KeyUp;
```

[JScript] In JScript, you can handle the events defined by a class, but you cannot define your own.

Event Data

The event handler receives an argument of type **KeyEventArgs** containing data related to this event. The following **KeyEventArgs** properties provide information specific to this event.

Property	Description
Alt	Gets a value indicating whether the ALT key was pressed.
Control	Gets a value indicating whether the CTRL key was pressed.
Handled	Gets or sets a value indicating whether the event was handled.
KeyCode	Gets the keyboard code for a **KeyDown** or **KeyUp** event.
KeyData	Gets the key data for a **KeyDown** or **KeyUp** event.
KeyValue	Gets the keyboard value for a **KeyDown** or **KeyUp** event.
Modifiers	Gets the modifier flags for a **KeyDown** or **KeyUp** event. This indicates which combination of modifier keys (CTRL, SHIFT, and ALT) were pressed.
Shift	Gets a value indicating whether the SHIFT key was pressed.

Remarks

Key events occur in the following order:

1. **KeyDown**
2. **KeyPress**
3. **KeyUp**

Example

[Visual Basic]
```
' This example demonstrates how to use the KeyUp event with ↵
the Help class to display
' pop-up style help to the user of the application. When the ↵
 user presses F1, the Help
' class displays a pop-up window, similar to a ToolTip, near ↵
 the control. This example assumes
' that a TextBox control, named textBox1, has been added to ↵
 the form and its KeyUp
' event has been contected to this event handling method.
Private Sub textBox1_KeyUp(ByVal sender As Object, ByVal e As ↵
System.Windows.Forms.KeyEventArgs) Handles textBox1.KeyUp
    ' Determine whether the key entered is the F1 key. Display ↵
help if it is.
    If e.KeyCode = Keys.F1 Then
        ' Display a pop-up help topic to assist the user.
        Help.ShowPopup(textBox1, "Enter your first name", New ↵
Point(textBox1.Right, Me.textBox1.Bottom))
    End If
End Sub 'textBox1_KeyUp
```

[C#]
```
// This example demonstrates how to use the KeyUp event with ↵
the Help class to display
// pop-up style help to the user of the application. When the ↵
user presses F1, the Help
// class displays a pop-up window, similar to a ToolTip, near ↵
the control. This example assumes
// that a TextBox control, named textBox1, has been added to ↵
the form and its KeyUp
// event has been contected to this event handling method.
private void textBox1_KeyUp(object sender, ↵
System.Windows.Forms.KeyEventArgs e)
{
    // Determine whether the key entered is the F1 key. Display ↵
help if it is.
    if(e.KeyCode == Keys.F1)
    {
        // Display a pop-up help topic to assist the user.
        Help.ShowPopup(textBox1, "Enter your first name", new ↵
Point(textBox1.Right, this.textBox1.Bottom));
    }
}
```

Requirements

Platforms: Windows 98, Windows NT 4.0, Windows Millennium Edition, Windows 2000, Windows XP Home Edition, Windows XP Professional, Windows Server 2003 family

Control.Layout Event

Occurs when a control should reposition its child controls.

[Visual Basic]
```
Public Event Layout As LayoutEventHandler
```
[C#]
```
public event LayoutEventHandler Layout;
```
[C++]
```
public: __event LayoutEventHandler* Layout;
```

[JScript] In JScript, you can handle the events defined by a class, but you cannot define your own.

Event Data

The event handler receives an argument of type **LayoutEventArgs** containing data related to this event. The following **LayoutEventArgs** properties provide information specific to this event.

Property	Description
AffectedControl	Gets the child control affected by the change.
AffectedProperty	Gets the property affected by the change.

Remarks

The **Layout** event occurs when child controls are added or removed, when the bounds of the control changes, and when other changes occur that can affect the layout of the control. The layout event can be suppressed using the **SuspendLayout** and **ResumeLayout** methods. Suspending layout allows for multiple actions to be performed on a control without having to perform a layout for each change. For example, if you resize and move a control, each operation would raise a **Layout** event.

Example

[Visual Basic, C#, C++] The following example centers a **Form** on the screen in the **Layout** event. This will keep the form centered as the user resizes it. This example assumes you have created a **Form** control.

[Visual Basic]
```
    Private Sub MyForm_Layout(ByVal sender As Object, _
        ByVal e As System.Windows.Forms.LayoutEventArgs) Handles
MyBase.Layout

        ' Center the Form on the user's screen everytime it
requires a Layout.
        Me.SetBounds
 ((System.Windows.Forms.Screen.GetBounds(Me).Width / 2) -
 (Me.Width / 2), _
            (System.Windows.Forms.Screen.GetBounds(Me).Height
 / 2) - (Me.Height / 2), _
            Me.Width, Me.Height,
System.Windows.Forms.BoundsSpecified.Location)
    End Sub
```

[C#]
```
private void MyForm_Layout(object sender,
System.Windows.Forms.LayoutEventArgs e)
{
   // Center the Form on the user's screen everytime it
requires a Layout.
   this.SetBounds((Screen.GetBounds(this).Width/2) - (this.Width/2),
       (Screen.GetBounds(this).Height/2) - (this.Height/2),
       this.Width, this.Height, BoundsSpecified.Location);
}
```

[C++]
```
private:
    void MyForm_Layout(Object* sender,
System::Windows::Forms::LayoutEventArgs* e) {
        // Center the Form on the user's screen everytime it
requires a Layout.
        this->SetBounds((Screen::GetBounds(this).Width/2) -
 (this->Width/2),
            (Screen::GetBounds(this).Height/2) - (this->Height/2),
            this->Width, this->Height, BoundsSpecified::Location);
    }
```

Requirements

Platforms: Windows 98, Windows NT 4.0, Windows Millennium Edition, Windows 2000, Windows XP Home Edition, Windows XP Professional, Windows Server 2003 family

Control.Leave Event

Occurs when the input focus leaves the control.

[Visual Basic]
```
Public Event Leave As EventHandler
```
[C#]
```
public event EventHandler Leave;
```
[C++]
```
public: __event EventHandler* Leave;
```

[JScript] In JScript, you can handle the events defined by a class, but you cannot define your own.

Event Data

The event handler receives an argument of type **EventArgs**.

Remarks

Focus events occur in the following order:

1. **Enter**
2. **GotFocus**
3. **Leave**
4. **Validating**
5. **Validated**
6. **LostFocus**

If the **CausesValidation** property is set to **false**, the **Validating** and **Validated** events are suppressed.

> **Note** The **Enter** and **Leave** events are suppressed by the **Form** class. The equivalent events in the **Form** class are the **Activated** and **Deactivate** events. The **Enter** and **Leave** events are hierarchical and will cascade up and down the parent chain until the appropriate control is reached. For example, assume you have a **Form** with two **GroupBox** controls, and each **GroupBox** control has one **TextBox** control. When the caret is moved from one **TextBox** to the other, the **Leave** event is raised for the **TextBox** and **GroupBox**, and the **Enter** event is raised for the other **GroupBox** and **TextBox**.

Requirements

Platforms: Windows 98, Windows NT 4.0, Windows Millennium Edition, Windows 2000, Windows XP Home Edition, Windows XP Professional, Windows Server 2003 family

Control.LocationChanged Event

Occurs when the **Location** property value has changed.

[Visual Basic]
```
Public Event LocationChanged As EventHandler
```
[C#]
```
public event EventHandler LocationChanged;
```
[C++]
```
public: __event EventHandler* LocationChanged;
```

[JScript] In JScript, you can handle the events defined by a class, but you cannot define your own.

Event Data

The event handler receives an argument of type **EventArgs**.

Remarks

This event is raised if the **Location** property is changed by either a programmatic modification or through interaction.

Example

[Visual Basic, C#, C++] The example below is an event handling method that is executed when the **Text** property value changes. The **Control** class has several methods with the name pattern PropertyName **Changed** that are raised when the corresponding PropertyName value changes(PropertyName represents the name of the corresponding property).

[Visual Basic, C#, C++] The following example changes the **ForeColor** of a **TextBox** displaying currency data. The example converts the text to a decimal number and changes the **ForeColor** to **Color.Red** if the number is negative and to **Color.Black** if the number is positive. This example assumes you have a **Form** that contains a **TextBox**.

[Visual Basic]
```
Private Sub currencyTextBox_TextChanged(sender As Object, _
  e As EventArgs) Handles currencyTextBox.TextChanged
   Try
      ' Convert the text to a Double and determine if it is a         ↵
negative number.
      If Double.Parse(currencyTextBox.Text) < 0 Then
         ' If the number is negative, display it in Red.
         currencyTextBox.ForeColor = Color.Red
      Else
         ' If the number is not negative, display it in Black.
         currencyTextBox.ForeColor = Color.Black
      End If
   Catch
      ' If there is an error, display the text using the system colors.
      currencyTextBox.ForeColor = SystemColors.ControlText
   End Try
End Sub
```

[C#]
```
private void currencyTextBox_TextChanged(object sender, EventArgs e)
{
   try
   {
      // Convert the text to a Double and determine if it is a        ↵
negative number.
      if(double.Parse(currencyTextBox.Text) < 0)
      {
         // If the number is negative, display it in Red.
         currencyTextBox.ForeColor = Color.Red;
      }
      else
      {
         // If the number is not negative, display it in Black.
         currencyTextBox.ForeColor = Color.Black;
      }
   }
   catch
   {
      // If there is an error, display the text using the             ↵
system colors.
      currencyTextBox.ForeColor = SystemColors.ControlText;
   }
}
```

[C++]
```
private:
    void currencyTextBox_TextChanged(Object* /*sender*/,             ↵
EventArgs* /*e*/) {
        try {
            // Convert the text to a Double and determine              ↵
if it is a negative number.
            if (Double::Parse(currencyTextBox->Text) < 0) {
                // If the number is negative, display it in Red.
                currencyTextBox->ForeColor = Color::Red;
            } else {
                // If the number is not negative, display it in Black.
                currencyTextBox->ForeColor = Color::Black;
            }
        } catch (Exception*) {
            // If there is an error, display the text using            ↵
the system colors.
            currencyTextBox->ForeColor = SystemColors::ControlText;
        }
    }
```

Requirements

Platforms: Windows 98, Windows NT 4.0, Windows Millennium Edition, Windows 2000, Windows XP Home Edition, Windows XP Professional, Windows Server 2003 family

Control.LostFocus Event

Occurs when the control loses focus.

[Visual Basic]
```
Public Event LostFocus As EventHandler
```
[C#]
```
public event EventHandler LostFocus;
```
[C++]
```
public: __event EventHandler* LostFocus;
```

[JScript] In JScript, you can handle the events defined by a class, but you cannot define your own.

Event Data

The event handler receives an argument of type **EventArgs**.

Remarks

Focus events occur in the following order:

1. **Enter**
2. **GotFocus**
3. **Leave**
4. **Validating**
5. **Validated**
6. **LostFocus**

If the **CausesValidation** property is set to **false**, the **Validating** and **Validated** events are suppressed.

If the **Cancel** property of the **CancelEventArgs** object is set to **true** in the **Validating** event delegate, all events that would normally occur after the **Validating** event are suppressed.

Note The **GotFocus** and **LostFocus** events are low-level focus events that are tied to the WM_KILLFOCUS and WM_SETFOCUS Windows messages. Typically, the **GotFocus** and **LostFocus** events are only used when updating **UICues**. The **Enter** and **Leave** events should be used for all controls except the **Form** class, which uses the **Activated** and **Deactivate** events. For more information about the **GotFocus** and **LostFocus** events, see the **WM_SETFOCUS** and **WM_KILLFOCUS** topics in the Keyboard Input Reference section of the Platform SDK Documentation in the MSDN Library.

CAUTION Do not attempt to set focus from within the **LostFocus** event handler. Doing so can cause your application or the operating system to stop responding. For more information about the **LostFocus** event, see the **WM_KILLFOCUS** topic in the Keyboard Input Reference section, and the **Message Deadlocks** topic in the Messages and Message Queues section of the Platform SDK Documentation in the MSDN Library.

Requirements

Platforms: Windows 98, Windows NT 4.0, Windows Millennium Edition, Windows 2000, Windows XP Home Edition, Windows XP Professional, Windows Server 2003 family

Control.MouseDown Event

Occurs when the mouse pointer is over the control and a mouse button is pressed.

[Visual Basic]
```
Public Event MouseDown As MouseEventHandler
```
[C#]
```
public event MouseEventHandler MouseDown;
```
[C++]
```
public: __event MouseEventHandler* MouseDown;
```

[JScript] In JScript, you can handle the events defined by a class, but you cannot define your own.

Event Data

The event handler receives an argument of type **MouseEventArgs** containing data related to this event. The following **MouseEventArgs** properties provide information specific to this event.

Property	Description
Button	Gets which mouse button was pressed.
Clicks	Gets the number of times the mouse button was pressed and released.
Delta	Gets a signed count of the number of detents the mouse wheel has rotated. A detent is one notch of the mouse wheel.
X	Gets the x-coordinate of the mouse.
Y	Gets the y-coordinate of the mouse.

Remarks

Mouse events occur in the following order:

1. **MouseEnter**
2. **MouseMove**
3. **MouseHover/ MouseDown/ MouseWheel**
4. **MouseUp**
5. **MouseLeave**

Note The following events are not raised for the **TabControl** class unless there is at least one **TabPage** in the **TabControl.TabPages** collection: **Click**, **DoubleClick**, **MouseDown**, **MouseUp**, **MouseHover**, **MouseEnter**, **MouseLeave** and **MouseMove**. If there is at least one **TabPage** in the collection, and the user interacts with the tab control's header (where the **TabPage** names appear), the **TabControl** raises the appropriate event. However, if the user interaction is within the client area of the tab page, the **TabPage** raises the appropriate event.

Example

[Visual Basic, C#, C++] The following example demonstrates using different mouse events to draw the path of the mouse on a **Panel**. A line segment is added to the **GraphicsPath** for each **MouseMove** and **MouseDown** events that occur. To update the graphics, the **Invalidate** method is called for the **Panel** on each **MouseDown** and **MouseUp** event. In addition, the graphic path is scrolled up or down when the **MouseWheel** event occurs. Additional mouse events, like **MouseHover**, are identified on screen as well. Also displayed on the screen is additional information about the mouse from the **SystemInformation** class.

[Visual Basic]
```
Imports System
Imports System.Drawing
Imports System.Windows.Forms

Namespace MouseEvent
    ' Summary description for Form1.
    Public NotInheritable Class Form1
        Inherits System.Windows.Forms.Form

        Friend WithEvents panel1 As System.Windows.Forms.Panel
        Private label1 As System.Windows.Forms.Label
        Private label2 As System.Windows.Forms.Label
        Private label3 As System.Windows.Forms.Label
        Private label4 As System.Windows.Forms.Label
        Private label5 As System.Windows.Forms.Label
        Private label6 As System.Windows.Forms.Label
        Private label7 As System.Windows.Forms.Label
        Private label8 As System.Windows.Forms.Label
        Private label9 As System.Windows.Forms.Label
        Friend WithEvents clearButton As System.Windows.Forms.Button
        Private mousePath As System.Drawing.Drawing2D.GraphicsPath
        Private groupBox1 As System.Windows.Forms.GroupBox

        Private fontSize As Integer = 20

        <System.STAThread()> _
        Public Shared Sub Main()
            System.Windows.Forms.Application.Run(New Form1())
        End Sub 'Main

        Public Sub New()

            mousePath = New System.Drawing.Drawing2D.GraphicsPath()

            Me.panel1 = New System.Windows.Forms.Panel()
            Me.label1 = New System.Windows.Forms.Label()
            Me.clearButton = New System.Windows.Forms.Button()
            Me.label2 = New System.Windows.Forms.Label()
            Me.label3 = New System.Windows.Forms.Label()
            Me.label4 = New System.Windows.Forms.Label()
            Me.label5 = New System.Windows.Forms.Label()
            Me.label6 = New System.Windows.Forms.Label()
```

```
        Me.label7 = New System.Windows.Forms.Label()
        Me.label8 = New System.Windows.Forms.Label()
        Me.label9 = New System.Windows.Forms.Label()
        Me.groupBox1 = New System.Windows.Forms.GroupBox()

        ' Mouse Events Label
        Me.label1.Location = New System.Drawing.Point(24, 504)
        Me.label1.Size = New System.Drawing.Size(392, 23)
        ' DoubleClickSize Label
        Me.label2.AutoSize = True
        Me.label2.Location = New System.Drawing.Point(24, 48)
        Me.label2.Size = New System.Drawing.Size(35, 13)
        ' DoubleClickTime Label
        Me.label3.AutoSize = True
        Me.label3.Location = New System.Drawing.Point(24, 72)
        Me.label3.Size = New System.Drawing.Size(35, 13)
        ' MousePresent Label
        Me.label4.AutoSize = True
        Me.label4.Location = New System.Drawing.Point(24, 96)
        Me.label4.Size = New System.Drawing.Size(35, 13)
        ' MouseButtons Label
        Me.label5.AutoSize = True
        Me.label5.Location = New System.Drawing.Point(24, 120)
        Me.label5.Size = New System.Drawing.Size(35, 13)
        ' MouseButtonsSwapped Label
        Me.label6.AutoSize = True
        Me.label6.Location = New System.Drawing.Point(320, 48)
        Me.label6.Size = New System.Drawing.Size(35, 13)
        ' MouseWheelPresent Label
        Me.label7.AutoSize = True
        Me.label7.Location = New System.Drawing.Point(320, 72)
        Me.label7.Size = New System.Drawing.Size(35, 13)
        ' MouseWheelScrollLines Label
        Me.label8.AutoSize = True
        Me.label8.Location = New System.Drawing.Point(320, 96)
        Me.label8.Size = New System.Drawing.Size(35, 13)
        ' NativeMouseWheelSupport Label
        Me.label9.AutoSize = True
        Me.label9.Location = New System.Drawing.Point(320, 120)
        Me.label9.Size = New System.Drawing.Size(35, 13)

        ' Mouse Panel
        Me.panel1.Anchor = ↵
System.Windows.Forms.AnchorStyles.Top Or _
                                                                    ↵
System.Windows.Forms.AnchorStyles.Left Or _
                                                                    ↵
System.Windows.Forms.AnchorStyles.Right
        Me.panel1.BackColor = ↵
System.Drawing.SystemColors.ControlDark
        Me.panel1.Location = New System.Drawing.Point(16, 160)
        Me.panel1.Size = New System.Drawing.Size(664, 320)

        ' Clear Button
        Me.clearButton.Anchor = ↵
System.Windows.Forms.AnchorStyles.Top Or _
                                System.Windows.Forms.AnchorStyles.Right
        Me.clearButton.Location = ↵
New System.Drawing.Point(592, 504)
        Me.clearButton.TabIndex = 1
        Me.clearButton.Text = "Clear"

        ' GroupBox
        Me.groupBox1.Anchor = ↵
System.Windows.Forms.AnchorStyles.Top Or _
                                                                    ↵
System.Windows.Forms.AnchorStyles.Left Or _
                                                                    ↵
System.Windows.Forms.AnchorStyles.Right
        Me.groupBox1.Location = New System.Drawing.Point(16, 24)
        Me.groupBox1.Size = New System.Drawing.Size(664, 128)
        Me.groupBox1.Text = ↵
"System.Windows.Forms.SystemInformation"

        ' Set up how the form should be displayed and ↵
add the controls to the form.
        Me.ClientSize = New System.Drawing.Size(696, 534)
        Me.Controls.AddRange(New ↵
System.Windows.Forms.Control() {Me.label9, _
                        Me.label8, Me.label7, Me.label6, ↵
Me.label5, Me.label4, _
                        Me.label3, Me.label2, ↵
Me.clearButton, Me.panel1, Me.label1, Me.groupBox1})

        Me.Text = "Mouse Event Example"

        ' Display information about the system mouse.
        label2.Text = "SystemInformation.DoubleClickSize: ↵
" + SystemInformation.DoubleClickSize.ToString()
        label3.Text = "SystemInformation.DoubleClickTime: ↵
" + SystemInformation.DoubleClickTime.ToString()
        label4.Text = "SystemInformation.MousePresent: " ↵
+ SystemInformation.MousePresent.ToString()
        label5.Text = "SystemInformation.MouseButtons: " ↵
+ SystemInformation.MouseButtons.ToString()
        label6.Text = ↵
"SystemInformation.MouseButtonsSwapped: " + ↵
SystemInformation.MouseButtonsSwapped.ToString()
        label7.Text = "SystemInformation.MouseWheelPresent: ↵
" + SystemInformation.MouseWheelPresent.ToString()
        label8.Text = ↵
"SystemInformation.MouseWheelScrollLines: " + ↵
SystemInformation.MouseWheelScrollLines.ToString()
        label9.Text = ↵
"SystemInformation.NativeMouseWheelSupport: " + ↵
SystemInformation.NativeMouseWheelSupport.ToString()
    End Sub 'New

    Private Sub panel1_MouseDown(sender As Object, e As ↵
System.Windows.Forms.MouseEventArgs) Handles panel1.MouseDown
        ' Update the mouse path with the mouse information
        Dim mouseDownLocation As New Point(e.X, e.Y)

        Dim eventString As String = Nothing
        Select Case e.Button
            Case MouseButtons.Left
                eventString = "L"
            Case MouseButtons.Right
                eventString = "R"
            Case MouseButtons.Middle
                eventString = "M"
            Case MouseButtons.XButton1
                eventString = "X1"
            Case MouseButtons.XButton2
                eventString = "X2"
            Case MouseButtons.None:
                eventString = Nothing
        End Select

        If Not (eventString Is Nothing) Then
            mousePath.AddString(eventString, ↵
FontFamily.GenericSerif, CInt(FontStyle.Bold), fontSize, ↵
mouseDownLocation, StringFormat.GenericDefault)
        Else
            mousePath.AddLine(mouseDownLocation, mouseDownLocation)
        End If

        panel1.Focus()
        panel1.Invalidate()
    End Sub

    Private Sub panel1_MouseEnter(sender As Object, e As ↵
System.EventArgs) Handles panel1.MouseEnter
        ' Update the mouse event label to indicate the ↵
MouseEnter event occurred.
        label1.Text = sender.GetType().ToString() + ": MouseEnter"
    End Sub
```

```
        Private Sub panel1_MouseHover(sender As Object, e As                ↵
System.EventArgs) Handles panel1.MouseHover
            ' Update the mouse event label to indicate the                  ↵
MouseHover event occurred.
            label1.Text = sender.GetType().ToString() + ": MouseHover"
        End Sub

        Private Sub panel1_MouseLeave(sender As Object, e As                ↵
System.EventArgs) Handles panel1.MouseLeave
            ' Update the mouse event label to indicate the                  ↵
MouseLeave event occurred.
            label1.Text = sender.GetType().ToString() + ": MouseLeave"
        End Sub

        Private Sub panel1_MouseMove(sender As Object, e As                 ↵
System.Windows.Forms.MouseEventArgs) Handles panel1.MouseMove
            ' Update the mouse path that is drawn onto the Panel.
            Dim mouseX As Integer = e.X
            Dim mouseY As Integer = e.Y

            mousePath.AddLine(mouseX, mouseY, mouseX, mouseY)
        End Sub
        Private Sub panel1_MouseWheel(sender As Object, e As                ↵
System.Windows.Forms.MouseEventArgs) Handles panel1.MouseWheel
            ' Update the drawing based upon the mouse wheel scrolling.
            Dim numberOfTextLinesToMove As Integer = e.Delta *              ↵
SystemInformation.MouseWheelScrollLines / 120 ' WHEEL_DATA
            Dim numberOfPixelsToMove As Integer =                           ↵
numberOfTextLinesToMove * fontSize

            If numberOfPixelsToMove <> 0 Then
                Dim translateMatrix As New                                  ↵
System.Drawing.Drawing2D.Matrix()
                translateMatrix.Translate(0, numberOfPixelsToMove)
                mousePath.Transform(translateMatrix)
            End If

            panel1.Invalidate()
        End Sub
        Private Sub panel1_MouseUp(sender As Object, e As                   ↵
System.Windows.Forms.MouseEventArgs) Handles panel1.MouseUp
            Dim mouseUpLocation = New System.Drawing.Point(e.X, e.Y)

            ' Show the number of clicks in the path graphic.
            Dim numberOfClicks As Integer = e.Clicks
            mousePath.AddString("     " + numberOfClicks.ToString(), _
                                FontFamily.GenericSerif,                    ↵
CInt(FontStyle.Bold), _
                                fontSize, mouseUpLocation,                  ↵
StringFormat.GenericDefault)

            panel1.Invalidate()
        End Sub

        Private Sub panel1_Paint(sender As Object, e As                     ↵
System.Windows.Forms.PaintEventArgs) Handles panel1.Paint
            ' Perform the painting of the Panel.
            e.Graphics.DrawPath(System.Drawing.Pens.DarkRed, mousePath)
        End Sub

        Private Sub clearButton_Click(sender As Object, e As                ↵
System.EventArgs) Handles clearButton.Click
            ' Clear the Panel display.
            mousePath.Dispose()
            mousePath = New System.Drawing.Drawing2D.GraphicsPath()
            panel1.Invalidate()
        End Sub

    End Class 'Form1
End Namespace
```

[C#]

```
using System;
using System.Drawing;
using System.Windows.Forms;

namespace MouseEvent
{
    public class Form1 : System.Windows.Forms.Form
    {
        private System.Windows.Forms.Panel panel1;
        private System.Windows.Forms.Label label1;
        private System.Windows.Forms.Label label2;
        private System.Windows.Forms.Label label3;
        private System.Windows.Forms.Label label4;
        private System.Windows.Forms.Label label5;
        private System.Windows.Forms.Label label6;
        private System.Windows.Forms.Label label7;
        private System.Windows.Forms.Label label8;
        private System.Windows.Forms.Label label9;
        private System.Windows.Forms.Button clearButton;
        private System.Drawing.Drawing2D.GraphicsPath mousePath;
        private System.Windows.Forms.GroupBox groupBox1;

        private int fontSize = 20;

        [STAThread]
        static void Main()
        {
            Application.Run(new Form1());
        }

        public Form1()
        {
            mousePath = new System.Drawing.Drawing2D.GraphicsPath();

            this.panel1 = new System.Windows.Forms.Panel();
            this.label1 = new System.Windows.Forms.Label();
            this.clearButton = new System.Windows.Forms.Button();
            this.label2 = new System.Windows.Forms.Label();
            this.label3 = new System.Windows.Forms.Label();
            this.label4 = new System.Windows.Forms.Label();
            this.label5 = new System.Windows.Forms.Label();
            this.label6 = new System.Windows.Forms.Label();
            this.label7 = new System.Windows.Forms.Label();
            this.label8 = new System.Windows.Forms.Label();
            this.label9 = new System.Windows.Forms.Label();
            this.groupBox1 = new System.Windows.Forms.GroupBox();

            // Mouse Events Label
            this.label1.Location = new System.Drawing.Point(24, 504);
            this.label1.Size = new System.Drawing.Size(392, 23);
            // DoubleClickSize Label
            this.label2.AutoSize = true;
            this.label2.Location = new System.Drawing.Point(24, 48);
            this.label2.Size = new System.Drawing.Size(35, 13);
            // DoubleClickTime Label
            this.label3.AutoSize = true;
            this.label3.Location = new System.Drawing.Point(24, 72);
            this.label3.Size = new System.Drawing.Size(35, 13);
            // MousePresent Label
            this.label4.AutoSize = true;
            this.label4.Location = new System.Drawing.Point(24, 96);
            this.label4.Size = new System.Drawing.Size(35, 13);
            // MouseButtons Label
            this.label5.AutoSize = true;
            this.label5.Location = new System.Drawing.Point(24, 120);
            this.label5.Size = new System.Drawing.Size(35, 13);
            // MouseButtonsSwapped Label
            this.label6.AutoSize = true;
            this.label6.Location = new System.Drawing.Point(320, 48);
            this.label6.Size = new System.Drawing.Size(35, 13);
            // MouseWheelPresent Label
            this.label7.AutoSize = true;
            this.label7.Location = new System.Drawing.Point(320, 72);
            this.label7.Size = new System.Drawing.Size(35, 13);
            // MouseWheelScrollLines Label
            this.label8.AutoSize = true;
            this.label8.Location = new System.Drawing.Point(320, 96);
            this.label8.Size = new System.Drawing.Size(35, 13);
            // NativeMouseWheelSupport Label
```

```
            this.label9.AutoSize = true;
            this.label9.Location = new System.Drawing.Point(320, 120);
            this.label9.Size = new System.Drawing.Size(35, 13);

            // Mouse Panel
            this.panel1.Anchor =                                          ↵
((System.Windows.Forms.AnchorStyles.Top |                                 ↵
System.Windows.Forms.AnchorStyles.Left)
                | System.Windows.Forms.AnchorStyles.Right);
            this.panel1.BackColor =                                       ↵
System.Drawing.SystemColors.ControlDark;
            this.panel1.Location = new System.Drawing.Point(16, 160);
            this.panel1.Size = new System.Drawing.Size(664, 320);
            this.panel1.MouseUp += new                                    ↵
System.Windows.Forms.MouseEventHandler(this.panel1_MouseUp);
            this.panel1.Paint += new                                      ↵
System.Windows.Forms.PaintEventHandler(this.panel1_Paint);
            this.panel1.MouseEnter += new                                 ↵
System.EventHandler(this.panel1_MouseEnter);
            this.panel1.MouseHover += new                                 ↵
System.EventHandler(this.panel1_MouseHover);
            this.panel1.MouseMove += new                                  ↵
System.Windows.Forms.MouseEventHandler(this.panel1_MouseMove);
            this.panel1.MouseLeave += new                                 ↵
System.EventHandler(this.panel1_MouseLeave);
            this.panel1.MouseDown += new                                  ↵
System.Windows.Forms.MouseEventHandler(this.panel1_MouseDown);
            this.panel1.MouseWheel += new                                 ↵
System.Windows.Forms.MouseEventHandler(this.panel1_MouseWheel);

            // Clear Button
            this.clearButton.Anchor =                                     ↵
(System.Windows.Forms.AnchorStyles.Top |                                  ↵
System.Windows.Forms.AnchorStyles.Right);
            this.clearButton.Location = new                               ↵
System.Drawing.Point(592, 504);
            this.clearButton.TabIndex = 1;
            this.clearButton.Text = "Clear";
            this.clearButton.Click += new
System.EventHandler(this.clearButton_Click);

            // GroupBox
            this.groupBox1.Anchor =                                       ↵
((System.Windows.Forms.AnchorStyles.Top |                                 ↵
System.Windows.Forms.AnchorStyles.Left)
                | System.Windows.Forms.AnchorStyles.Right);
            this.groupBox1.Location = new System.Drawing.Point(16, 24);
            this.groupBox1.Size = new System.Drawing.Size(664, 128);
            this.groupBox1.Text =                                         ↵
"System.Windows.Forms.SystemInformation";

            // Set up how the form should be displayed and               ↵
add the controls to the form.
            this.ClientSize = new System.Drawing.Size(696, 534);
            this.Controls.AddRange(new System.Windows.Forms.Control[] {
                                                                          ↵
this.label9,this.label8,this.label7,this.label6,
                                                                          ↵
this.label5,this.label4,this.label3,this.label2,
                                                                          ↵
this.clearButton,this.panel1,this.label1,this.groupBox1});
            this.Text = "Mouse Event Example";

            // Displays information about the system mouse.
            label2.Text = "SystemInformation.DoubleClickSize:              ↵
" + SystemInformation.DoubleClickSize.ToString();
            label3.Text = "SystemInformation.DoubleClickTime:              ↵
" + SystemInformation.DoubleClickTime.ToString();
            label4.Text = "SystemInformation.MousePresent:                 ↵
" + SystemInformation.MousePresent.ToString();
            label5.Text = "SystemInformation.MouseButtons:                 ↵
" + SystemInformation.MouseButtons.ToString();
            label6.Text =                                                 ↵
"SystemInformation.MouseButtonsSwapped: " +                               ↵
SystemInformation.MouseButtonsSwapped.ToString();
            label7.Text = "SystemInformation.MouseWheelPresent:            ↵
" + SystemInformation.MouseWheelPresent.ToString();
            label8.Text =                                                 ↵
"SystemInformation.MouseWheelScrollLines: " +                             ↵
SystemInformation.MouseWheelScrollLines.ToString();
            label9.Text =                                                 ↵
"SystemInformation.NativeMouseWheelSupport: " +                           ↵
SystemInformation.NativeMouseWheelSupport.ToString();

        }

        private void panel1_MouseDown(object sender,                      ↵
System.Windows.Forms.MouseEventArgs e)
        {
            // Update the mouse path with the mouse information
            Point mouseDownLocation = new Point(e.X, e.Y);

            string eventString = null;
            switch (e.Button) {
                case MouseButtons.Left:
                    eventString = "L";
                    break;
                case MouseButtons.Right:
                    eventString = "R";
                    break;
                case MouseButtons.Middle:
                    eventString = "M";
                    break;
                case MouseButtons.XButton1:
                    eventString = "X1";
                    break;
                case MouseButtons.XButton2:
                    eventString = "X2";
                    break;
                case MouseButtons.None:
                default:
                    break;
            }

            if (eventString != null)
            {
                mousePath.AddString(eventString,                          ↵
FontFamily.GenericSerif, (int)FontStyle.Bold, fontSize,                   ↵
mouseDownLocation, StringFormat.GenericDefault);
            }
            else
            {
                mousePath.AddLine(mouseDownLocation,mouseDownLocation);
            }
            panel1.Focus();
            panel1.Invalidate();
        }

        private void panel1_MouseEnter(object sender,                     ↵
System.EventArgs e)
        {
            // Update the mouse event label to indicate the              ↵
MouseEnter event occurred.
            label1.Text = sender.GetType().ToString() + ":               ↵
MouseEnter";
        }

        private void panel1_MouseHover(object sender,                     ↵
System.EventArgs e)
        {
            // Update the mouse event label to indicate the              ↵
MouseHover event occurred.
            label1.Text = sender.GetType().ToString() + ": MouseHover";
        }

        private void panel1_MouseLeave(object sender,                     ↵
System.EventArgs e)
        {
            // Update the mouse event label to indicate the              ↵
MouseLeave event occurred.
```

```
            label1.Text = sender.GetType().ToString() + ": MouseLeave";
        }

        private void panel1_MouseMove(object sender,                      ↵
System.Windows.Forms.MouseEventArgs e)
        {
            // Update the mouse path that is drawn onto the Panel.
            int mouseX = e.X;
            int mouseY = e.Y;

            mousePath.AddLine(mouseX,mouseY,mouseX,mouseY);
        }

        private void panel1_MouseWheel(object sender,                     ↵
System.Windows.Forms.MouseEventArgs e)
        {
            // Update the drawing based upon the mouse wheel scrolling.

            int numberOfTextLinesToMove = e.Delta *                       ↵
SystemInformation.MouseWheelScrollLines / 120;
            int numberOfPixelsToMove =                                    ↵
numberOfTextLinesToMove * fontSize;

            if (numberOfPixelsToMove != 0) {
                System.Drawing.Drawing2D.Matrix translateMatrix           ↵
= new  System.Drawing.Drawing2D.Matrix();
                translateMatrix.Translate(0, numberOfPixelsToMove);
                mousePath.Transform(translateMatrix);
            }
            panel1.Invalidate();
        }
        private void panel1_MouseUp(object sender,                        ↵
System.Windows.Forms.MouseEventArgs e)
        {
            Point mouseUpLocation = new System.Drawing.Point(e.X, e.Y);

            // Show the number of clicks in the path graphic.
            int numberOfClicks = e.Clicks;
            mousePath.AddString("    " + numberOfClicks.ToString(),
                        FontFamily.GenericSerif, (int)FontStyle.Bold,
                        fontSize, mouseUpLocation,
StringFormat.GenericDefault);

            panel1.Invalidate();
        }

        private void panel1_Paint(object sender,                          ↵
System.Windows.Forms.PaintEventArgs e)
        {
            // Perform the painting of the Panel.
            e.Graphics.DrawPath(System.Drawing.Pens.DarkRed,              ↵
mousePath);
        }

        private void clearButton_Click(object sender,                     ↵
System.EventArgs e)
        {
            // Clear the Panel display.
            mousePath.Dispose();
            mousePath = new System.Drawing.Drawing2D.GraphicsPath();
            panel1.Invalidate();
        }
    }
}
```

[C++]

```
#using <mscorlib.dll>
#using <System.dll>
#using <System.Windows.Forms.dll>
#using <System.Drawing.dll>

using namespace System;
using namespace System::Drawing;
using namespace System::Windows::Forms;

namespace MouseEvent {
public __gc class Form1 : public System::Windows::Forms::Form {
private:
   System::Windows::Forms::Panel*  panel1;
   System::Windows::Forms::Label*  label1;
   System::Windows::Forms::Label*  label2;
   System::Windows::Forms::Label*  label3;
   System::Windows::Forms::Label*  label4;
   System::Windows::Forms::Label*  label5;
   System::Windows::Forms::Label*  label6;
   System::Windows::Forms::Label*  label7;
   System::Windows::Forms::Label*  label8;
   System::Windows::Forms::Label*  label9;
   System::Windows::Forms::Button*  clearButton;
   System::Drawing::Drawing2D::GraphicsPath*  mousePath;
   System::Windows::Forms::GroupBox*  groupBox1;

   int  fontSize;
public:
   Form1() {
      fontSize = 20;
      mousePath = new System::Drawing::Drawing2D::GraphicsPath();
      this->panel1 = new System::Windows::Forms::Panel();
      this->label1 = new System::Windows::Forms::Label();
      this->clearButton = new System::Windows::Forms::Button();
      this->label2 = new System::Windows::Forms::Label();
      this->label3 = new System::Windows::Forms::Label();
      this->label4 = new System::Windows::Forms::Label();
      this->label5 = new System::Windows::Forms::Label();
      this->label6 = new System::Windows::Forms::Label();
      this->label7 = new System::Windows::Forms::Label();
      this->label8 = new System::Windows::Forms::Label();
      this->label9 = new System::Windows::Forms::Label();
      this->groupBox1 = new System::Windows::Forms::GroupBox();

      // Mouse Events Label
      this->label1->Location = System::Drawing::Point(24, 504);
      this->label1->Size =  System::Drawing::Size(392, 23);
      // DoubleClickSize Label
      this->label2->AutoSize = true;
      this->label2->Location =  System::Drawing::Point(24, 48);
      this->label2->Size =  System::Drawing::Size(35, 13);
      // DoubleClickTime Label
      this->label3->AutoSize = true;
      this->label3->Location =  System::Drawing::Point(24, 72);
      this->label3->Size =  System::Drawing::Size(35, 13);
      // MousePresent Label
      this->label4->AutoSize = true;
      this->label4->Location =  System::Drawing::Point(24, 96);
      this->label4->Size =  System::Drawing::Size(35, 13);
      // MouseButtons Label
      this->label5->AutoSize = true;
      this->label5->Location =  System::Drawing::Point(24, 120);
      this->label5->Size =  System::Drawing::Size(35, 13);
      // MouseButtonsSwapped Label
      this->label6->AutoSize = true;
      this->label6->Location =  System::Drawing::Point(320, 48);
      this->label6->Size =  System::Drawing::Size(35, 13);
      // MouseWheelPresent Label
      this->label7->AutoSize = true;
      this->label7->Location =  System::Drawing::Point(320, 72);
      this->label7->Size =  System::Drawing::Size(35, 13);
      // MouseWheelScrollLines Label
      this->label8->AutoSize = true;
      this->label8->Location =  System::Drawing::Point(320, 96);
      this->label8->Size =  System::Drawing::Size(35, 13);
      // NativeMouseWheelSupport Label
      this->label9->AutoSize = true;
      this->label9->Location =  System::Drawing::Point(320, 120);
      this->label9->Size =  System::Drawing::Size(35, 13);

      // Mouse Panel
      this->panel1->Anchor =                                              ↵
static_cast<System::Windows::Forms::AnchorStyles>(System::Windows::Forms
::AnchorStyles::Top | System::Windows::Forms::AnchorStyles::Left
```

```
        | System::Windows::Forms::AnchorStyles::Right);
    this->panel1->BackColor =                                        ↵
System::Drawing::SystemColors::ControlDark;
    this->panel1->Location =  System::Drawing::Point(16, 160);
    this->panel1->Size =  System::Drawing::Size(664, 320);
    this->panel1->MouseUp += new                                      ↵
System::Windows::Forms::MouseEventHandler(this, panel1_MouseUp);
    this->panel1->Paint += new                                        ↵
System::Windows::Forms::PaintEventHandler(this, panel1_Paint);
    this->panel1->MouseEnter += new System::EventHandler              ↵
 (this, panel1_MouseEnter);
    this->panel1->MouseHover += new System::EventHandler              ↵
 (this, panel1_MouseHover);
    this->panel1->MouseMove += new                                    ↵
System::Windows::Forms::MouseEventHandler(this, panel1_MouseMove);
    this->panel1->MouseLeave += new System::EventHandler(this,
panel1_MouseLeave);
    this->panel1->MouseDown += new                                    ↵
System::Windows::Forms::MouseEventHandler(this, panel1_MouseDown);
    this->panel1->MouseWheel += new                                   ↵
System::Windows::Forms::MouseEventHandler(this, panel1_MouseWheel);

    // Clear Button
    this->clearButton->Anchor =                                       ↵
static_cast<System::Windows::Forms::AnchorStyles>(System::Windows::Forms
::AnchorStyles::Top | System::Windows::Forms::AnchorStyles::Right);
    this->clearButton->Location =  System::Drawing::Point(592, 504);
    this->clearButton->TabIndex = 1;
    this->clearButton->Text = S"Clear";
    this->clearButton->Click += new System::EventHandler              ↵
 (this, clearButton_Click);

    // GroupBox
    this->groupBox1->Anchor =                                         ↵
static_cast<System::Windows::Forms::AnchorStyles>                      ↵
 (System::Windows::Forms::AnchorStyles::Top |                          ↵
System::Windows::Forms::AnchorStyles::Left
        | System::Windows::Forms::AnchorStyles::Right);
    this->groupBox1->Location =  System::Drawing::Point(16, 24);
    this->groupBox1->Size =  System::Drawing::Size(664, 128);
    this->groupBox1->Text =                                           ↵
S"System::Windows::Forms::SystemInformation";

    // Set up how the form should be displayed and add                ↵
 the controls to the form.
    this->ClientSize =  System::Drawing::Size(696, 534);

    System::Windows::Forms::Control* temp0 [] = {this->               ↵
label9, this->label8, this->label7, this->label6,
        this->label5, this->label4, this->label3, this->label2,
        this->clearButton, this->panel1, this->label1,                ↵
this->groupBox1};

    this->Controls->AddRange(temp0);
    this->Text = S"Mouse Event Example";

    // Displays information about the system mouse.
    label2->Text = S"SystemInformation::DoubleClickSize:              ↵
 {0}", SystemInformation::DoubleClickSize;
    label3->Text = S"SystemInformation::DoubleClickTime:              ↵
 {0}", SystemInformation::DoubleClickTime;
    label4->Text = S"SystemInformation::MousePresent: {0}             ↵
", SystemInformation::MousePresent;
    label5->Text = S"SystemInformation::MouseButtons: {0}",           ↵
 SystemInformation::MouseButtons;
    label6->Text = S"SystemInformation::MouseButtonsSwapped:          ↵
 {0}", SystemInformation::MouseButtonsSwapped;
    label7->Text = S"SystemInformation::MouseWheelPresent:            ↵
 {0}", SystemInformation::MouseWheelPresent;
    label8->Text = S"SystemInformation::MouseWheelScrollLines:        ↵
 {0}", SystemInformation::MouseWheelScrollLines;
    label9->Text =                                                    ↵
 S"SystemInformation::NativeMouseWheelSupport: {0}",                  ↵
 SystemInformation::NativeMouseWheelSupport;
  }

private:
  void panel1_MouseDown(Object* sender,                               ↵
System::Windows::Forms::MouseEventArgs* e) {
      // Update the mouse path with the mouse information
      Point mouseDownLocation =  Point(e->X, e->Y);

      String* eventString = 0;
      switch (e->Button) {
      case MouseButtons::Left:
         eventString = S"L";
         break;
      case MouseButtons::Right:
         eventString = S"R";
         break;
      case MouseButtons::Middle:
         eventString = S"M";
         break;
      case MouseButtons::XButton1:
         eventString = S"X1";
         break;
      case MouseButtons::XButton2:
         eventString = S"X2";
         break;
      case MouseButtons::None:
      default:
         break;
      }

      if (eventString != 0) {
         mousePath->AddString(eventString,                            ↵
FontFamily::GenericSerif, (int)FontStyle::Bold, (float)fontSize,      ↵
mouseDownLocation, StringFormat::GenericDefault);
      } else {
         mousePath->AddLine(mouseDownLocation, mouseDownLocation);
      }
      panel1->Focus();
      panel1->Invalidate();
  }

  void panel1_MouseEnter(Object* sender, System::EventArgs* e) {
      // Update the mouse event label to indicate the MouseEnter      ↵
event occurred.
      label1->Text = String::Concat( sender->GetType(), S":           ↵
MouseEnter" );
  }

  void panel1_MouseHover(Object* sender, System::EventArgs* e) {
      // Update the mouse event label to indicate the MouseHover      ↵
event occurred.
      label1->Text = String::Concat( sender->GetType(), S":           ↵
MouseHover" );
  }

  void panel1_MouseLeave(Object* sender, System::EventArgs* e) {
      // Update the mouse event label to indicate the MouseLeave      ↵
event occurred.
      label1->Text = String::Concat( sender->GetType(), S":           ↵
MouseLeave" );
  }

  void panel1_MouseMove(Object* sender,                               ↵
System::Windows::Forms::MouseEventArgs* e) {
      // Update the mouse path that is drawn onto the Panel.
      int mouseX = e->X;
      int mouseY = e->Y;

      mousePath->AddLine(mouseX, mouseY, mouseX, mouseY);
  }

  void panel1_MouseWheel(Object* sender,                              ↵
System::Windows::Forms::MouseEventArgs* e) {
      // Update the drawing based upon the mouse wheel scrolling.
```

```
      int numberOfTextLinesToMove = e->Delta *
SystemInformation::MouseWheelScrollLines / 120;
      int numberOfPixelsToMove = numberOfTextLinesToMove * fontSize;

      if (numberOfPixelsToMove != 0) {
         System::Drawing::Drawing2D::Matrix* translateMatrix
 = new System::Drawing::Drawing2D::Matrix();
         translateMatrix->Translate(0, (float)numberOfPixelsToMove);
         mousePath->Transform(translateMatrix);
      }
      panel1->Invalidate();
   }
   void panel1_MouseUp(Object* sender,
System::Windows::Forms::MouseEventArgs* e) {
      Point mouseUpLocation =  System::Drawing::Point(e->X, e->Y);

      // Show the number of clicks in the path graphic.
      int numberOfClicks = e->Clicks;
      mousePath->AddString(String::Format( S"   {0}",
__box(numberOfClicks)),
         FontFamily::GenericSerif, (int)FontStyle::Bold,
         (float)fontSize, mouseUpLocation,
StringFormat::GenericDefault);

      panel1->Invalidate();
   }

   void panel1_Paint(Object* sender,
System::Windows::Forms::PaintEventArgs* e) {
      // Perform the painting of the Panel.
      e->Graphics->DrawPath(System::Drawing::Pens::DarkRed, mousePath);
   }

   void clearButton_Click(Object* sender, System::EventArgs* e) {
      // Clear the Panel display.
      mousePath->Dispose();
      mousePath = new System::Drawing::Drawing2D::GraphicsPath();
      panel1->Invalidate();
   }
};
}

[STAThread]
int main() {
   Application::Run(new MouseEvent::Form1());
}
```

Requirements

Platforms: Windows 98, Windows NT 4.0, Windows Millennium Edition, Windows 2000, Windows XP Home Edition, Windows XP Professional, Windows Server 2003 family

Control.MouseEnter Event

Occurs when the mouse pointer enters the control.

[Visual Basic]
```
Public Event MouseEnter As EventHandler
```
[C#]
```
public event EventHandler MouseEnter;
```
[C++]
```
public: __event EventHandler* MouseEnter;
```

[JScript] In JScript, you can handle the events defined by a class, but you cannot define your own.

Event Data

The event handler receives an argument of type **EventArgs**.

Remarks

Mouse events occur in the following order:

1. **MouseEnter**
2. **MouseMove**
3. **MouseHover/ MouseDown/ MouseWheel**
4. **MouseUp**
5. **MouseLeave**

Note The following events are not raised for the **TabControl** class unless there is at least one **TabPage** in the **TabControl.TabPages** collection: **Click**, **DoubleClick**, **MouseDown**, **MouseUp**, **MouseHover**, **MouseEnter**, **MouseLeave** and **MouseMove**. If there is at least one **TabPage** in the collection, and the user interacts with the tab control's header (where the **TabPage** names appear), the **TabControl** raises the appropriate event. However, if the user interaction is within the client area of the tab page, the **TabPage** raises the appropriate event.

Example

See related example in the **System.Windows.Forms.Control.LocationChanged** event topic.

Requirements

Platforms: Windows 98 Windows NT 4.0, Windows Millennium Edition, Windows 2000, Windows XP Home Edition, Windows XP Professional, Windows Server 2003 family

Control.MouseHover Event

Occurs when the mouse pointer hovers over the control.

[Visual Basic]
```
Public Event MouseHover As EventHandler
```
[C#]
```
public event EventHandler MouseHover;
```
[C++]
```
public: __event EventHandler* MouseHover;
```

[JScript] In JScript, you can handle the events defined by a class, but you cannot define your own.

Event Data

The event handler receives an argument of type **EventArgs**.

Remarks

Mouse events occur in the following order:

1. **MouseEnter**
2. **MouseMove**
3. **MouseHover/ MouseDown/ MouseWheel**
4. **MouseUp**
5. **MouseLeave**

Note The following events are not raised for the **TabControl** class unless there is at least one **TabPage** in the **TabControl.TabPages** collection: **Click**, **DoubleClick**, **MouseDown**, **MouseUp**, **MouseHover**, **MouseEnter**, **MouseLeave** and **MouseMove**. If there is at least one **TabPage** in the collection, and the user interacts with the tab control's header (where the **TabPage** names appear), the **TabControl** raises the appropriate event. However, if the user interaction is within the client area of the tab page, the **TabPage** raises the appropriate event.

Example

See related example in the **System.Windows.Forms.Control.LocationChanged** event topic.

Requirements

Platforms: Windows 98, Windows NT 4.0, Windows Millennium Edition, Windows 2000, Windows XP Home Edition, Windows XP Professional, Windows Server 2003 family

Control.MouseLeave Event

Occurs when the mouse pointer leaves the control.

```
[Visual Basic]
Public Event MouseLeave As EventHandler
[C#]
public event EventHandler MouseLeave;
[C++]
public: __event EventHandler* MouseLeave;
```

[JScript] In JScript, you can handle the events defined by a class, but you cannot define your own.

Event Data

The event handler receives an argument of type **EventArgs**.

Remarks

Mouse events occur in the following order:

1. **MouseEnter**
2. **MouseMove**
3. **MouseHover/ MouseDown/ MouseWheel**
4. **MouseUp**
5. **MouseLeave**

> **Note** The following events are not raised for the **TabControl** class unless there is at least one **TabPage** in the **TabControl.TabPages** collection: **Click**, **DoubleClick**, **MouseDown**, **MouseUp**, **MouseHover**, **MouseEnter**, **MouseLeave** and **MouseMove**. If there is at least one **TabPage** in the collection, and the user interacts with the tab control's header (where the **TabPage** names appear), the **TabControl** raises the appropriate event. However, if the user interaction is within the client area of the tab page, the **TabPage** raises the appropriate event.

Example

See related example in the **System.Windows.Forms.Control.LocationChanged** event topic.

Requirements

Platforms: Windows 98, Windows NT 4.0, Windows Millennium Edition, Windows 2000, Windows XP Home Edition, Windows XP Professional, Windows Server 2003 family

Control.MouseMove Event

Occurs when the mouse pointer is moved over the control.

```
[Visual Basic]
Public Event MouseMove As MouseEventHandler
[C#]
public event MouseEventHandler MouseMove;
[C++]
public: __event MouseEventHandler* MouseMove;
```

[JScript] In JScript, you can handle the events defined by a class, but you cannot define your own.

Event Data

The event handler receives an argument of type **MouseEventArgs** containing data related to this event. The following **MouseEventArgs** properties provide information specific to this event.

Property	Description
Button	Gets which mouse button was pressed.
Clicks	Gets the number of times the mouse button was pressed and released.
Delta	Gets a signed count of the number of detents the mouse wheel has rotated. A detent is one notch of the mouse wheel.
X	Gets the x-coordinate of the mouse.
Y	Gets the y-coordinate of the mouse.

Remarks

Mouse events occur in the following order:

1. **MouseEnter**
2. **MouseMove**
3. **MouseHover/ MouseDown/ MouseWheel**
4. **MouseUp**
5. **MouseLeave**

> **Note** The following events are not raised for the **TabControl** class unless there is at least one **TabPage** in the **TabControl.TabPages** collection: **Click**, **DoubleClick**, **MouseDown**, **MouseUp**, **MouseHover**, **MouseEnter**, **MouseLeave** and **MouseMove**. If there is at least one **TabPage** in the collection, and the user interacts with the tab control's header (where the **TabPage** names appear), the **TabControl** raises the appropriate event. However, if the user interaction is within the client area of the tab page, the **TabPage** raises the appropriate event.

Example

See related example in the **System.Windows.Forms.Control.LocationChanged** event topic.

Requirements

Platforms: Windows 98, Windows NT 4.0, Windows Millennium Edition, Windows 2000, Windows XP Home Edition, Windows XP Professional, Windows Server 2003 family

Control.MouseUp Event

Occurs when the mouse pointer is over the control and a mouse button is released.

```
[Visual Basic]
Public Event MouseUp As MouseEventHandler
[C#]
public event MouseEventHandler MouseUp;
[C++]
public: __event MouseEventHandler* MouseUp;
```

[JScript] In JScript, you can handle the events defined by a class, but you cannot define your own.

Event Data

The event handler receives an argument of type **MouseEventArgs** containing data related to this event. The following **MouseEvent-Args** properties provide information specific to this event.

Property	Description
Button	Gets which mouse button was pressed.
Clicks	Gets the number of times the mouse button was pressed and released.
Delta	Gets a signed count of the number of detents the mouse wheel has rotated. A detent is one notch of the mouse wheel.
X	Gets the x-coordinate of the mouse.
Y	Gets the y-coordinate of the mouse.

Remarks

Mouse events occur in the following order:

1. **MouseEnter**
2. **MouseMove**
3. **MouseHover/ MouseDown/ MouseWheel**
4. **MouseUp**
5. **MouseLeave**

> **Note** The following events are not raised for the **TabControl** class unless there is at least one **TabPage** in the **TabControl.TabPages** collection: **Click**, **DoubleClick**, **MouseDown**, **MouseUp**, **MouseHover**, **MouseEnter**, **MouseLeave** and **MouseMove**. If there is at least one **TabPage** in the collection, and the user interacts with the tab control's header (where the **TabPage** names appear), the **TabControl** raises the appropriate event. However, if the user interaction is within the client area of the tab page, the **TabPage** raises the appropriate event.

Example

See related example in the **System.Windows.Forms.Control.LocationChanged** event topic.

Requirements

Platforms: Windows 98, Windows NT 4.0, Windows Millennium Edition, Windows 2000, Windows XP Home Edition, Windows XP Professional, Windows Server 2003 family

Control.MouseWheel Event

Occurs when the mouse wheel moves while the control has focus.

```
[Visual Basic]
Public Event MouseWheel As MouseEventHandler
[C#]
public event MouseEventHandler MouseWheel;
[C++]
public: __event MouseEventHandler* MouseWheel;
```

[JScript] In JScript, you can handle the events defined by a class, but you cannot define your own.

Event Data

The event handler receives an argument of type **MouseEventArgs** containing data related to this event. The following **MouseEvent-Args** properties provide information specific to this event.

Property	Description
Button	Gets which mouse button was pressed.
Clicks	Gets the number of times the mouse button was pressed and released.
Delta	Gets a signed count of the number of detents the mouse wheel has rotated. A detent is one notch of the mouse wheel.
X	Gets the x-coordinate of the mouse.
Y	Gets the y-coordinate of the mouse.

Remarks

When handling the **MouseWheel** event it is important to follow the user interface (UI) standards associated with the mouse wheel. The **MouseEventArgs.Delta** property value indicates the amount the mouse wheel has been moved. The UI should scroll when the accumulated delta is plus or minus 120. The UI should scroll the number of logical lines returned by the **SystemInformation.MouseWheelScrollLines** property for every delta value reached. You can also scroll more smoothly in smaller that 120 unit increments, however the ratio should remain constant, that is **SystemInformation.MouseWheelScrollLines** lines scrolled per 120 delta units of wheel movement.

For more information about handling mouse wheel messages, see the **WM_MOUSEWHEEL** message documentation in the Windows Platform SDK reference located in the MSDN library.

Mouse events occur in the following order:

1. **MouseEnter**
2. **MouseMove**
3. **MouseHover/ MouseDown/ MouseWheel**
4. **MouseUp**
5. **MouseLeave**

Example

See related example in the **System.Windows.Forms.Control.LocationChanged** event topic.

Requirements

Platforms: Windows 98, Windows NT 4.0, Windows Millennium Edition, Windows 2000, Windows XP Home Edition, Windows XP Professional, Windows Server 2003 family

Control.Move Event

Occurs when the control is moved.

```
[Visual Basic]
Public Event Move As EventHandler
[C#]
public event EventHandler Move;
[C++]
public: __event EventHandler* Move;
```

[JScript] In JScript, you can handle the events defined by a class, but you cannot define your own.

Event Data

The event handler receives an argument of type **EventArgs**.

Requirements

Platforms: Windows 98, Windows NT 4.0, Windows Millennium Edition, Windows 2000, Windows XP Home Edition, Windows XP Professional, Windows Server 2003 family

Control.Paint Event

Occurs when the control is redrawn.

[Visual Basic]
```
Public Event Paint As PaintEventHandler
```
[C#]
```
public event PaintEventHandler Paint;
```
[C++]
```
public: __event PaintEventHandler* Paint;
```

[JScript] In JScript, you can handle the events defined by a class, but you cannot define your own.

Event Data

The event handler receives an argument of type **PaintEventArgs** containing data related to this event. The following **PaintEventArgs** properties provide information specific to this event.

Property	Description
ClipRectangle	Gets the rectangle in which to paint.
Graphics	Gets the graphics used to paint.

Example

See related example in the **System.Windows.Forms.Control.LocationChanged** event topic.

Requirements

Platforms: Windows 98, Windows NT 4.0, Windows Millennium Edition, Windows 2000, Windows XP Home Edition, Windows XP Professional, Windows Server 2003 family

Control.ParentChanged Event

Occurs when the **Parent** property value changes.

[Visual Basic]
```
Public Event ParentChanged As EventHandler
```
[C#]
```
public event EventHandler ParentChanged;
```
[C++]
```
public: __event EventHandler* ParentChanged;
```

[JScript] In JScript, you can handle the events defined by a class, but you cannot define your own.

Event Data

The event handler receives an argument of type **EventArgs**.

Remarks

This event is raised if the **Parent** property is changed by either a programmatic modification or user interaction.

Example

[Visual Basic, C#, C++] The example below is an event handling method that is executed when the **Text** property value changes. The **Control** class has several methods with the name pattern PropertyName **Changed** that are raised when the corresponding PropertyName value changes(PropertyName represents the name of the corresponding property).

[Visual Basic, C#, C++] The following example changes the **ForeColor** of a **TextBox** displaying currency data. The example converts the text to a decimal number and changes the **ForeColor** to **Color.Red** if the number is negative and to **Color.Black** if the number is positive. This example assumes you have a **Form** that contains a **TextBox**.

[Visual Basic]
```
Private Sub currencyTextBox_TextChanged(sender As Object, _
  e As EventArgs) Handles currencyTextBox.TextChanged
    Try
      ' Convert the text to a Double and determine if it is a     ↵
negative number.
      If Double.Parse(currencyTextBox.Text) < 0 Then
         ' If the number is negative, display it in Red.
         currencyTextBox.ForeColor = Color.Red
      Else
         ' If the number is not negative, display it in Black.
         currencyTextBox.ForeColor = Color.Black
      End If
   Catch
      ' If there is an error, display the text using the system colors.
      currencyTextBox.ForeColor = SystemColors.ControlText
   End Try
End Sub
```

[C#]
```
private void currencyTextBox_TextChanged(object sender, EventArgs e)
{
   try
   {
      // Convert the text to a Double and determine if it is a     ↵
negative number.
      if(double.Parse(currencyTextBox.Text) < 0)
      {
         // If the number is negative, display it in Red.
         currencyTextBox.ForeColor = Color.Red;
      }
      else
      {
         // If the number is not negative, display it in Black.
         currencyTextBox.ForeColor = Color.Black;
      }
   }
   catch
   {
      // If there is an error, display the text using the     ↵
system colors.
      currencyTextBox.ForeColor = SystemColors.ControlText;
   }
}
```

[C++]
```
private:
    void currencyTextBox_TextChanged(Object* /*sender*/,     ↵
EventArgs* /*e*/) {
        try {
            // Convert the text to a Double and determine if     ↵
it is a negative number.
            if (Double::Parse(currencyTextBox->Text) < 0) {
                // If the number is negative, display it in Red.
                currencyTextBox->ForeColor = Color::Red;
            } else {
                // If the number is not negative, display it in Black.
                currencyTextBox->ForeColor = Color::Black;
            }
        } catch (Exception*) {
            // If there is an error, display the text using the     ↵
system colors.
            currencyTextBox->ForeColor = SystemColors::ControlText;
        }
    }
```

Requirements

Platforms: Windows 98, Windows NT 4.0, Windows Millennium Edition, Windows 2000, Windows XP Home Edition, Windows XP Professional, Windows Server 2003 family

Control.QueryAccessibilityHelp Event

Occurs when **AccessibleObject** is providing help to accessibility applications.

[Visual Basic]
```
Public Event QueryAccessibilityHelp As _
   QueryAccessibilityHelpEventHandler
```
[C#]
```
public event QueryAccessibilityHelpEventHandler
   QueryAccessibilityHelp;
```
[C++]
```
public: __event QueryAccessibilityHelpEventHandler*
   QueryAccessibilityHelp;
```

[JScript] In JScript, you can handle the events defined by a class, but you cannot define your own.

Event Data

The event handler receives an argument of type **QueryAccessibility-HelpEventArgs** containing data related to this event. The following **QueryAccessibilityHelpEventArgs** properties provide information specific to this event.

Property	Description
HelpKeyword	Gets or sets the Help keyword for the specified control.
HelpNamespace	Gets or sets a value specifying the name of the Help file.
HelpString	Gets or sets the string defining what Help to get for the **AccessibleObject**.

Remarks

You should use the **HelpProvider** class to allow users to invoke help on your accessible object by pressing the F1 key. Using the **HelpProvider** provides you with complete information in the **QueryAccessibilityHelpEventArgs** object.

Example

See related example in the **System.Windows.Forms.Control.LocationChanged** event topic.

Requirements

Platforms: Windows 98, Windows NT 4.0, Windows Millennium Edition, Windows 2000, Windows XP Home Edition, Windows XP Professional, Windows Server 2003 family

Control.QueryContinueDrag Event

Occurs during a drag-and-drop operation and allows the drag source to determine whether the drag-and-drop operation should be canceled.

[Visual Basic]
```
Public Event QueryContinueDrag As QueryContinueDragEventHandler
```
[C#]
```
public event QueryContinueDragEventHandler QueryContinueDrag;
```
[C++]
```
public: __event QueryContinueDragEventHandler* QueryContinueDrag;
```

[JScript] In JScript, you can handle the events defined by a class, but you cannot define your own.

Event Data

The event handler receives an argument of type **QueryContinueDragEventArgs** containing data related to this event. The following **QueryContinueDragEventArgs** properties provide information specific to this event.

Property	Description
Action	Gets or sets the status of a drag-and-drop operation.
EscapePressed	Gets whether the user pressed the ESC key.
KeyState	Gets the current state of the SHIFT, CTRL, and ALT keys.

Remarks

The **QueryContinueDrag** event is raised when there is a change in the keyboard or mouse button state during a drag-and-drop operation. The **QueryContinueDrag** event allows the drag source to determine whether the drag-and-drop operation should be canceled.

The following describes how and when events related to drag-and-drop operations are raised.

The **DoDragDrop** method determines the control under the current cursor location. It then checks to see if the control is a valid drop target.

If the control is a valid drop target, the **GiveFeedback** event is raised with the drag-and-drop effect specified. For a list of drag-and-drop effects, see the **DragDropEffects** enumeration.

Changes in the mouse cursor position, keyboard state, and mouse button state are tracked.

- If the user moves out of a window, the **DragLeave** event is raised.
- If the mouse enters another control, the **DragEnter** for that control is raised.
- If the mouse moves but stays within the same control, the **DragOver** event is raised.

If there is a change in the keyboard or mouse button state, the **QueryContinueDrag** event is raised and determines whether to continue the drag, to drop the data, or to cancel the operation based on the value of the **Action** property of the event's **QueryContinueDragEventArgs**.

- If the value is **DragAction.Continue**, the **DragOver** event is raised to continue the operation and the **GiveFeedback** event is raised with the new effect so appropriate visual feedback can be set. For a list of valid drop effects, see the **DragDropEffects** enumeration.

> **Note** The **DragOver** and **GiveFeedback** events are paired so that as the mouse moves across the drop target, the user is given the most up-to-date feedback on the mouse's position.

If the value is **DragAction.Drop**, the drop effect value is returned to the source, so the source application can perform the appropriate operation on the source data; for example, cut the data if the operation was a move.

If the value is **DragAction.Cancel**, the **DragLeave** event is raised.

By default, the **QueryContinueDrag** event sets **Action** to **Drag-Action.Cancel** if the ESC key was pressed and sets **Action** to **Drag-Action.Drop** if the left, middle, or right mouse button is pressed.

Example

See related example in the **System.Windows.Forms.Control.LocationChanged** event topic.

Requirements

Platforms: Windows 98, Windows NT 4.0, Windows Millennium Edition, Windows 2000, Windows XP Home Edition, Windows XP Professional, Windows Server 2003 family

Control.Resize Event

Occurs when the control is resized.

```
[Visual Basic]
Public Event Resize As EventHandler
[C#]
public event EventHandler Resize;
[C++]
public: __event EventHandler* Resize;
```

[JScript] In JScript, you can handle the events defined by a class, but you cannot define your own.

Event Data

The event handler receives an argument of type **EventArgs**.

Remarks

To determine the **Size** of the resized control, you can cast the *sender* parameter of the **EventArgs** data to a **Control** object and get its **Size** property (or **Height** and **Width** properties individually).

To handle custom layouts, use the **Layout** event instead of the Resize event. The **Layout** event is raised in response to a **Resize** event, but also in response to other changes that affect the layout of the control.

Example

See related example in the **System.Windows.Forms.Control.LocationChanged** event topic.

Requirements

Platforms: Windows 98, Windows NT 4.0, Windows Millennium Edition, Windows 2000, Windows XP Home Edition, Windows XP Professional, Windows Server 2003 family

Control.RightToLeftChanged Event

Occurs when the **RightToLeft** property value changes.

```
[Visual Basic]
Public Event RightToLeftChanged As EventHandler
[C#]
public event EventHandler RightToLeftChanged;
[C++]
public: __event EventHandler* RightToLeftChanged;
```

[JScript] In JScript, you can handle the events defined by a class, but you cannot define your own.

Event Data

The event handler receives an argument of type **EventArgs**.

Remarks

This event is raised if the **RightToLeft** property is changed by either a programmatic modification or user interaction.

Example

See related example in the **System.Windows.Forms.Control.LocationChanged** event topic.

Requirements

Platforms: Windows 98, Windows NT 4.0, Windows Millennium Edition, Windows 2000, Windows XP Home Edition, Windows XP Professional, Windows Server 2003 family

Control.SizeChanged Event

Occurs when the **Size** property value changes.

```
[Visual Basic]
Public Event SizeChanged As EventHandler
[C#]
public event EventHandler SizeChanged;
[C++]
public: __event EventHandler* SizeChanged;
```

[JScript] In JScript, you can handle the events defined by a class, but you cannot define your own.

Event Data

The event handler receives an argument of type **EventArgs**.

Remarks

It is preferable to use the **Layout** event to handle custom layouts. The **Layout** event is raised in response to **Resize** events, but also in other conditions when layout might need to be applied.

This event is raised if the **Size** property is changed by either a programmatic modification or user interaction.

Example

See related example in the **System.Windows.Forms.Control.LocationChanged** event topic.

Requirements

Platforms: Windows 98, Windows NT 4.0, Windows Millennium Edition, Windows 2000, Windows XP Home Edition, Windows XP Professional, Windows Server 2003 family

Control.StyleChanged Event

Occurs when the control style changes.

```
[Visual Basic]
Public Event StyleChanged As EventHandler
[C#]
public event EventHandler StyleChanged;
[C++]
public: __event EventHandler* StyleChanged;
```

[JScript] In JScript, you can handle the events defined by a class, but you cannot define your own.

Event Data

The event handler receives an argument of type **EventArgs**.

Remarks

The **StyleChanged** event occurs when **ControlStyles** flags have been added or changed.

This event is raised if the cotrol style is changed by either a programmatic modification or user interaction.

Requirements

Platforms: Windows 98, Windows NT 4.0, Windows Millennium Edition, Windows 2000, Windows XP Home Edition, Windows XP Professional, Windows Server 2003 family

Control.SystemColorsChanged Event

Occurs when the system colors change.

```
[Visual Basic]
Public Event SystemColorsChanged As EventHandler
[C#]
public event EventHandler SystemColorsChanged;
[C++]
public: __event EventHandler* SystemColorsChanged;
```

[JScript] In JScript, you can handle the events defined by a class, but you cannot define your own.

Event Data

The event handler receives an argument of type **EventArgs**.

Remarks

This event is raised if the **SystemColors** is changed by either a programmatic modification or user interaction.

Requirements

Platforms: Windows 98, Windows NT 4.0,
Windows Millennium Edition, Windows 2000,
Windows XP Home Edition, Windows XP Professional,
Windows Server 2003 family

Control.TabIndexChanged Event

Occurs when the **TabIndex** property value changes.

```
[Visual Basic]
Public Event TabIndexChanged As EventHandler
[C#]
public event EventHandler TabIndexChanged;
[C++]
public: __event EventHandler* TabIndexChanged;
```

[JScript] In JScript, you can handle the events defined by a class, but you cannot define your own.

Event Data

The event handler receives an argument of type **EventArgs**.

Remarks

This event is raised if the **TabIndex** property is changed by either a programmatic modification or user interaction.

Example

See related example in the **System.Windows.Forms.Control.LocationChanged** event topic.

Requirements

Platforms: Windows 98, Windows NT 4.0,
Windows Millennium Edition, Windows 2000,
Windows XP Home Edition, Windows XP Professional,
Windows Server 2003 family

Control.TabStopChanged Event

Occurs when the **TabStop** property value changes.

```
[Visual Basic]
Public Event TabStopChanged As EventHandler
[C#]
public event EventHandler TabStopChanged;
[C++]
public: __event EventHandler* TabStopChanged;
```

[JScript] In JScript, you can handle the events defined by a class, but you cannot define your own.

Event Data

The event handler receives an argument of type **EventArgs**.

Remarks

This event is raised if the **TabStop** property is changed by either a programmatic modification or user interaction.

Example

See related example in the **System.Windows.Forms.Control.LocationChanged** event topic.

Requirements

Platforms: Windows 98, Windows NT 4.0,
Windows Millennium Edition, Windows 2000,
Windows XP Home Edition, Windows XP Professional,
Windows Server 2003 family

Control.TextChanged Event

Occurs when the **Text** property value changes.

```
[Visual Basic]
Public Event TextChanged As EventHandler
[C#]
public event EventHandler TextChanged;
[C++]
public: __event EventHandler* TextChanged;
```

[JScript] In JScript, you can handle the events defined by a class, but you cannot define your own.

Event Data

The event handler receives an argument of type **EventArgs**.

Remarks

This event is raised if the **Text** property is changed by either a programmatic modification or user interaction.

Example

See related example in the **System.Windows.Forms.Control.LocationChanged** event topic.

Requirements

Platforms: Windows 98, Windows NT 4.0,
Windows Millennium Edition, Windows 2000,
Windows XP Home Edition, Windows XP Professional,
Windows Server 2003 family

Control.Validated Event

Occurs when the control is finished validating.

```
[Visual Basic]
Public Event Validated As EventHandler
[C#]
public event EventHandler Validated;
[C++]
public: __event EventHandler* Validated;
```

[JScript] In JScript, you can handle the events defined by a class, but you cannot define your own.

Event Data

The event handler receives an argument of type **EventArgs**.

Remarks

Focus events occur in the following order:

1. **Enter**
2. **GotFocus**
3. **Leave**
4. **Validating**
5. **Validated**
6. **LostFocus**

If the **CausesValidation** property is set to **false**, the **Validating** and **Validated** events are suppressed.

If the **Cancel** property of the **CancelEventArgs** object is set to **true** in the **Validating** event delegate, all events that would normally occur after the **Validating** event are suppressed.

Example

See related example in the **System.Windows.Forms.Control.LocationChanged** event topic.

Requirements

Platforms: Windows 98, Windows NT 4.0,
Windows Millennium Edition, Windows 2000,
Windows XP Home Edition, Windows XP Professional,
Windows Server 2003 family

Control.Validating Event

Occurs when the control is validating.

[Visual Basic]
```
Public Event Validating As CancelEventHandler
```
[C#]
```
public event CancelEventHandler Validating;
```
[C++]
```
public: __event CancelEventHandler* Validating;
```

[JScript] In JScript, you can handle the events defined by a class, but you cannot define your own.

Event Data

The event handler receives an argument of type **CancelEventArgs** containing data related to this event. The following **CancelEventArgs** property provides information specific to this event.

Property	Description
Cancel	Gets or sets a value indicating whether the event should be canceled.

Remarks

Focus events occur in the following order:

1. **Enter**
2. **GotFocus**
3. **Leave**
4. **Validating**
5. **Validated**
6. **LostFocus**

If the **CausesValidation** property is set to **false**, the **Validating** and **Validated** events are suppressed.

If the **Cancel** property of the **CancelEventArgs** object is set to **true** in the **Validating** event delegate, all events that would normally occur after the **Validating** event are suppressed.

Example

See related example in the **System.Windows.Forms.Control.LocationChanged** event topic.

Requirements

Platforms: Windows 98, Windows NT 4.0,
Windows Millennium Edition, Windows 2000,
Windows XP Home Edition, Windows XP Professional,
Windows Server 2003 family

Control.VisibleChanged Event

Occurs when the **Visible** property value changes.

[Visual Basic]
```
Public Event VisibleChanged As EventHandler
```
[C#]
```
public event EventHandler VisibleChanged;
```
[C++]
```
public: __event EventHandler* VisibleChanged;
```

[JScript] In JScript, you can handle the events defined by a class, but you cannot define your own.

Event Data

The event handler receives an argument of type **EventArgs**.

Remarks

This event is raised if the **Visible** property is changed by either a programmatic modification or user interaction.

Example

See related example in the **System.Windows.Forms.Control.LocationChanged** event topic.

Requirements

Platforms: Windows 98, Windows NT 4.0,
Windows Millennium Edition, Windows 2000,
Windows XP Home Edition, Windows XP Professional,
Windows Server 2003 family

ControlBindingsCollection Class

Represents the collection of data bindings for a control.

System.Object
  System.MarshalByRefObject
    System.Windows.Forms.BaseCollection
      System.Windows.Forms.BindingsCollection
        System.Windows.Forms.ControlBindingsCollection

[Visual Basic]
```
Public Class ControlBindingsCollection
   Inherits BindingsCollection
```
[C#]
```
public class ControlBindingsCollection : BindingsCollection
```
[C++]
```
public __gc class ControlBindingsCollection : public
   BindingsCollection
```
[JScript]
```
public class ControlBindingsCollection extends BindingsCollection
```

Thread Safety

Any public static (**Shared** in Visual Basic) members of this type are safe for multithreaded operations. Any instance members are not guaranteed to be thread safe.

Remarks

Simple data binding is accomplished by adding **Binding** objects to a **ControlBindingsCollection**. Any object that inherits from the **Control** class can access the **ControlBindingsCollection** through the **DataBindings** property. For a list of Windows controls that support data binding, see the **Binding** class.

The **ControlBindingsCollection** contains standard collection methods such as **Add**, **Clear**, and **Remove**.

To get the control that the **ControlBindingsCollection** belongs to, use the **Control** property.

Example

[Visual Basic, C#] The following example adds **Binding** objects to a **ControlBindingsCollection** of five controls--four **TextBox** controls and a **DateTimePicker** control. The **ControlBindingsCollection** is accessed through the **DataBindings** property of the **Control** class.

[Visual Basic]
```
Protected Sub BindControls()
    ' Create two Binding objects for the first two TextBox
    ' controls. The data-bound property for both controls
    ' is the Text property. The data source is a DataSet
    ' (ds). The data member is the navigation path:
    ' TableName.ColumnName.
    textBox1.DataBindings.Add _
       (New Binding("Text", ds, "customers.custName"))
    textBox2.DataBindings.Add _
       (New Binding("Text", ds, "customers.custID"))

    ' Bind the DateTimePicker control by adding a new Binding.
    ' The data member of the DateTimePicker is a navigation path:
    ' TableName.RelationName.ColumnName.
    DateTimePicker1.DataBindings.Add _
       (New Binding("Value", ds, "customers.CustToOrders.OrderDate"))

    ' Create a new Binding using the DataSet and a
    ' navigation path(TableName.RelationName.ColumnName).
    ' Add event delegates for the Parse and Format events to
    ' the Binding object, and add the object to the third
    ' TextBox control's BindingsCollection. The delegates
    ' must be added before adding the Binding to the
    ' collection; otherwise, no formatting occurs until
    ' the Current object of the BindingManagerBase for
    ' the data source changes.
    Dim b As New Binding("Text", ds, ↵
"customers.custToOrders.OrderAmount")
    AddHandler b.Parse, AddressOf CurrencyStringToDecimal
    AddHandler b.Format, AddressOf DecimalToCurrencyString
    textBox3.DataBindings.Add(b)

    ' Bind the fourth TextBox to the Value of the
    ' DateTimePicker control. This demonstates how one control
    ' can be data-bound to another.
    textBox4.DataBindings.Add("Text", DateTimePicker1, "Value")

    ' Get the BindingManagerBase for the textBox4 Binding.
    Dim bmText As BindingManagerBase = ↵
Me.BindingContext(DateTimePicker1)

    ' Print the Type of the BindingManagerBase, which is
    ' a PropertyManager because the data source
    ' returns only a single property value.
    Console.WriteLine(bmText.GetType().ToString())

    ' Print the count of managed objects, which is one.
    Console.WriteLine(bmText.Count)

    ' Get the BindingManagerBase for the Customers table.
    bmCustomers = Me.BindingContext(ds, "Customers")

    ' Print the Type and count of the BindingManagerBase.
    ' Because the data source inherits from IBindingList,
    ' it is a RelatedCurrencyManager (a derived class of
    ' CurrencyManager).
    Console.WriteLine(bmCustomers.GetType().ToString())
    Console.WriteLine(bmCustomers.Count)

    ' Get the BindingManagerBase for the Orders of the current
    ' customer using a navigation path: TableName.RelationName.
    bmOrders = Me.BindingContext(ds, "customers.CustToOrders")
End Sub
```

[C#]
```
protected void BindControls()
{
   /* Create two Binding objects for the first two TextBox
   controls. The data-bound property for both controls
   is the Text property. The data source is a DataSet
   (ds). The data member is the navigation path:
   TableName.ColumnName. */
   textBox1.DataBindings.Add(new Binding
   ("Text", ds, "customers.custName"));
   textBox2.DataBindings.Add(new Binding
   ("Text", ds, "customers.custID"));

   /* Bind the DateTimePicker control by adding a new Binding.
   The data member of the DateTimePicker is a navigation path:
   TableName.RelationName.ColumnName. */
   DateTimePicker1.DataBindings.Add(new
   Binding("Value", ds, "customers.CustToOrders.OrderDate"));

   /* Create a new Binding using the DataSet and a
   navigation path(TableName.RelationName.ColumnName).
   Add event delegates for the Parse and Format events to
   the Binding object, and add the object to the third
   TextBox control's BindingsCollection. The delegates
   must be added before adding the Binding to the
   collection; otherwise, no formatting occurs until
   the Current object of the BindingManagerBase for
   the data source changes. */
   Binding b = new Binding
   ("Text", ds, "customers.custToOrders.OrderAmount");
   b.Parse+=new ConvertEventHandler(CurrencyStringToDecimal);
   b.Format+=new ConvertEventHandler(DecimalToCurrencyString);
   textBox3.DataBindings.Add(b);
```

```
   /*Bind the fourth TextBox to the Value of the
   DateTimePicker control. This demonstates how one control
   can be data-bound to another.*/
   textBox4.DataBindings.Add("Text", DateTimePicker1,"Value");

   // Get the BindingManagerBase for the textBox4 Binding.
   BindingManagerBase bmText = this.BindingContext
   [DateTimePicker1];

   /* Print the Type of the BindingManagerBase, which is
   a PropertyManager because the data source
   returns only a single property value. */
   Console.WriteLine(bmText.GetType().ToString());

   // Print the count of managed objects, which is one.
   Console.WriteLine(bmText.Count);

   // Get the BindingManagerBase for the Customers table.
   bmCustomers = this.BindingContext [ds, "Customers"];

   /* Print the Type and count of the BindingManagerBase.
   Because the data source inherits from IBindingList,
   it is a RelatedCurrencyManager (a derived class of
   CurrencyManager). */
   Console.WriteLine(bmCustomers.GetType().ToString());
   Console.WriteLine(bmCustomers.Count);

   /* Get the BindingManagerBase for the Orders of the current
   customer using a navigation path: TableName.RelationName. */
   bmOrders = this.BindingContext[ds, "customers.CustToOrders"];
}
```

Requirements

Namespace: System.Windows.Forms

Platforms: Windows 98, Windows NT 4.0, Windows Millennium Edition, Windows 2000, Windows XP Home Edition, Windows XP Professional, Windows Server 2003 family, .NET Compact Framework - Windows CE .NET

Assembly: System.Windows.Forms (in System.Windows.Forms.dll)

ControlBindingsCollection.Control Property

Gets the control that the collection belongs to.

[Visual Basic]
```
Public ReadOnly Property Control As Control
```
[C#]
```
public Control Control {get;}
```
[C++]
```
public: __property Control* get_Control();
```
[JScript]
```
public function get Control() : Control;
```

Property Value

The **Control** that the collection belongs to.

Example

[Visual Basic, C#] The following example prints information about the control to that a **ControlBindingsCollection** belongs to.

[Visual Basic]
```
Private Sub GetControl(myBindings As ControlBindingsCollection)
    Dim c As Control = myBindings.Control
    Console.WriteLine(c.ToString())
End Sub
```

[C#]
```
private void GetControl(ControlBindingsCollection myBindings)
{
   Control c = myBindings.Control;
   Console.WriteLine(c.ToString());
}
```

Requirements

Platforms: Windows 98, Windows NT 4.0, Windows Millennium Edition, Windows 2000, Windows XP Home Edition, Windows XP Professional, Windows Server 2003 family

ControlBindingsCollection.Item Property

Gets the specified **Binding** from the collection.

[C#] In C#, this property is the indexer for the **ControlBindingsCollection** class.

Overload List

Gets the **Binding** specified by the control's property name.

[Visual Basic] **Overloads Public Default ReadOnly Property Item(String) As Binding**

[C#] **public Binding this[string] {get;}**

[C++] **public: __property Binding* get_Item(String*);**

[JScript] **ControlBindingsCollection.Item (String)**

Inherited from **BindingsCollection**.

[Visual Basic] **Overloads Public Default ReadOnly Property Item(Integer) As Binding**

[C#] **public Binding this[int] {get;}**

[C++] **public: __property Binding* get_Item(int);**

[JScript] **ControlBindingsCollection.Item (int)**

Example

The following example uses the **Item** property to return the **Binding** for a **TextBox** control's **Text** property.

ControlBindingsCollection.Item Property (String)

Gets the **Binding** specified by the control's property name.

[C#] In C#, this property is the indexer for the **ControlBindingsCollection** class.

[Visual Basic]
```
Overloads Public Default ReadOnly Property Item( _
   ByVal propertyName As String _
) As Binding
```
[C#]
```
public Binding this[
   string propertyName
] {get;}
```
[C++]
```
public: __property Binding* get_Item(
   String* propertyName
);
```
[JScript]
```
returnValue = ControlBindingsCollectionObject.Item(propertyName);
-or-
returnValue = ControlBindingsCollectionObject(propertyName);
```

[JScript] In JScript, you can use the default indexed properties defined by a type, but you cannot explicitly define your own. However, specifying the **expando** attribute on a class automatically provides a default indexed property whose type is **Object** and whose index type is **String**.

Arguments [JScript]

propertyName

The name of the property on the data-bound control.

Parameters [Visual Basic, C#, C++]

propertyName

The name of the property on the data-bound control.

Property Value

The **Binding** that binds the specified control property to a data source.

Remarks

The following example returns a single **Binding** from a **ControlBindingsCollection**.

[Visual Basic]
```
Private Sub PrintValue()

   Dim myControlBindings As ControlBindingsCollection = _
   textBox1.DataBindings

   ' Get the Binding for the Text property.
   Dim myBinding As Binding = myControlBindings("Text")

   ' Assuming the data source is a DataTable.
   Dim drv As DataRowView = _
   CType( myBinding.BindingManagerBase.Current, DataRowView)

   ' Assuming a column named "custName" exists, print the value.
   Console.WriteLine(drv("custName"))
End Sub
```

[C#]
```
private void PrintValue()
{
   ControlBindingsCollection myControlBindings;
   myControlBindings = textBox1.DataBindings;

   // Get the Binding for the Text property.
   Binding myBinding = myControlBindings["Text"];

   // Assuming the data source is a DataTable.
   DataRowView drv;
   drv = (DataRowView) myBinding.BindingManagerBase.Current;

   // Assuming a column named "custName" exists, print the value.
   Console.WriteLine(drv["custName"]);
}
```

[C++]
```
private:
    void PrintValue() {
        ControlBindingsCollection* myControlBindings;
        myControlBindings = textBox1->DataBindings;

        // Get the Binding for the Text property.
        Binding* myBinding = myControlBindings->Item[S"Text"];

        // Assuming the data source is a DataTable.
        DataRowView* drv;
        drv = dynamic_cast<DataRowView*>(myBinding->
BindingManagerBase->Current);

        // Assuming a column named S"custName" exists, print the value.
        Console::WriteLine(drv->Item[S"custName"]);
    }
```

Example

The following example uses the **Item** property to return the **Binding** for a **TextBox** control's **Text** property.

Requirements

Platforms: Windows 98, Windows NT 4.0, Windows Millennium Edition, Windows 2000, Windows XP Home Edition, Windows XP Professional, Windows Server 2003 family

ControlBindingsCollection.Add Method

Adds a **Binding** to the collection.

Overload List

Adds the specified **Binding** to the collection.

Supported by the .NET Compact Framework.

[Visual Basic] **Overloads Public Shadows Sub Add(Binding)**

[C#] **public new void Add(Binding);**

[C++] **public: void Add(Binding*);**

[JScript] **public hide function Add(Binding);**

Creates a **Binding** using the specified control property name, data source, and data member, and adds it to the collection.

Supported by the .NET Compact Framework.

[Visual Basic] **Overloads Public Function Add(String, Object, String) As Binding**

[C#] **public Binding Add(string, object, string);**

[C++] **public: Binding* Add(String*, Object*, String*);**

[JScript] **public function Add(String, Object, String) : Binding;**

Example

[Visual Basic, C#] The following example uses the **Add** method to add three **Binding** objects to the **ControlBindingsCollection** of a **TextBox** control. The **ControlBindingsCollection** is accessed through the **DataBindings** property of the **Control** class.

> [Visual Basic, C#] **Note** This example shows how to use one of the overloaded versions of **Add**. For other examples that might be available, see the individual overload topics.

[Visual Basic]
```
Private Sub BindTextBoxProperties()
    ' Clear the collection before adding new Binding objects.
    textBox1.DataBindings.Clear()

    ' Create a DataTable containing Color objects.
    Dim t As DataTable = MakeTable()

    ' Bind the Text, BackColor, and ForeColor properties
    ' to columns in the DataTable.
    textBox1.DataBindings.Add("Text", t, "Text")
    textBox1.DataBindings.Add("BackColor", t, "BackColor")
    textBox1.DataBindings.Add("ForeColor", t, "ForeColor")
End Sub

Private Function MakeTable() As DataTable
    ' Create a DataTable with three columns.
    ' Two of the columns contain Color objects.

    Dim t As New DataTable("Control")
    t.Columns.Add("BackColor", GetType(Color))
    t.Columns.Add("ForeColor", GetType(Color))
    t.Columns.Add("Text")
```

```
    ' Add three rows to the table.
    Dim r As DataRow

    r = t.NewRow()
    r("BackColor") = Color.Blue
    r("ForeColor") = Color.Yellow
    r("Text") = "Yellow on Blue"
    t.Rows.Add(r)

    r = t.NewRow()
    r("BackColor") = Color.White
    r("ForeColor") = Color.Green
    r("Text") = "Green on white"
    t.Rows.Add(r)

    r = t.NewRow()
    r("BackColor") = Color.Orange
    r("ForeColor") = Color.Black
    r("Text") = "Black on Orange"
    t.Rows.Add(r)

    Return t
End Function
```

[C#]

```
private void BindTextBoxProperties()
{
   // Clear the collection before adding new Binding objects.
   textBox1.DataBindings.Clear();

   // Create a DataTable containing Color objects.
   DataTable t = MakeTable();

   /* Bind the Text, BackColor, and ForeColor properties
   to columns in the DataTable. */
   textBox1.DataBindings.Add("Text", t, "Text");
   textBox1.DataBindings.Add("BackColor", t, "BackColor");
   textBox1.DataBindings.Add("ForeColor", t, "ForeColor");
}

private DataTable MakeTable()
{
   /* Create a DataTable with three columns.
   Two of the columns contain Color objects. */

   DataTable t = new DataTable("Control");
   t.Columns.Add("BackColor", typeof(Color));
   t.Columns.Add("ForeColor", typeof(Color));
   t.Columns.Add("Text");

   // Add three rows to the table.
   DataRow r;

   r = t.NewRow();
   r["BackColor"] = Color.Blue;
   r["ForeColor"] = Color.Yellow;
   r["Text"] = "Yellow on Blue";
   t.Rows.Add(r);

   r = t.NewRow();
   r["BackColor"] = Color.White;
   r["ForeColor"] = Color.Green;
   r["Text"] = "Green on white";
   t.Rows.Add(r);

   r = t.NewRow();
   r["BackColor"] = Color.Orange;
   r["ForeColor"] = Color.Black;
   r["Text"] = "Black on Orange";
   t.Rows.Add(r);

   return t;
}
```

ControlBindingsCollection.Add Method (Binding)

Adds the specified **Binding** to the collection.

[Visual Basic]

```
Overloads Public Shadows Sub Add( _
   ByVal binding As Binding _
)
```

[C#]

```
public new void Add(
   Binding binding
);
```

[C++]

```
public: void Add(
   Binding* binding
);
```

[JScript]

```
public hide function Add(
   binding : Binding
);
```

Parameters

binding
The **Binding** to add.

Exceptions

Exception Type	Condition
ArgumentNull-Exception	The *binding* is null.
Exception	The control property is already data-bound.
Exception	The **Binding** object doesn't specify a valid column of the **DataSource**.

Remarks

The **CollectionChanged** event occurs when the change is complete.

Example

See related example in the **System.Windows.Forms.Control-BindingsCollection** class topic.

Requirements

Platforms: Windows 98, Windows NT 4.0,
Windows Millennium Edition, Windows 2000,
Windows XP Home Edition, Windows XP Professional,
Windows Server 2003 family,
.NET Compact Framework - Windows CE .NET

ControlBindingsCollection.Add Method (String, Object, String)

Creates a **Binding** using the specified control property name, data source, and data member, and adds it to the collection.

[Visual Basic]

```
Overloads Public Function Add( _
   ByVal propertyName As String, _
   ByVal dataSource As Object, _
   ByVal dataMember As String _
) As Binding
```

[C#]

```
public Binding Add(
   string propertyName,
   object dataSource,
   string dataMember
);
```

```
[C++]
public: Binding* Add(
   String* propertyName,
   Object* dataSource,
   String* dataMember
);
[JScript]
public function Add(
   propertyName : String,
   dataSource : Object,
   dataMember : String
) : Binding;
```

Parameters

propertyName

The name of the control property to bind.

dataSource

An **Object** that represents the data source.

dataMember

The property or list to bind to.

Return Value

The newly-created **Binding**.

Exceptions

Exception Type	Condition
ArgumentNull-Exception	The *binding* is null.
Exception	The *propertyName* is already data-bound.
Exception	The *dataMember* doesn't specify a valid member of the *dataSource*.

Remarks

Adding a **Binding** causes the **CollectionChanged** event to occur.

Example

See related example in the **System.Windows.Forms.Control-BindingsCollection** class topic.

Requirements

Platforms: Windows 98, Windows NT 4.0, Windows Millennium Edition, Windows 2000, Windows XP Home Edition, Windows XP Professional, Windows Server 2003 family, .NET Compact Framework - Windows CE .NET

ControlBindingsCollection.AddCore Method

This member supports the .NET Framework infrastructure and is not intended to be used directly from your code.

```
[Visual Basic]
Overrides Protected Sub AddCore( _
   ByVal dataBinding As Binding _
)
[C#]
protected override void AddCore(
   Binding dataBinding
);
[C++]
protected: void AddCore(
   Binding* dataBinding
);
[JScript]
protected override function AddCore(
   dataBinding : Binding
);
```

ControlBindingsCollection.Clear Method

Clears the collection of any bindings.

```
[Visual Basic]
Public Shadows Sub Clear()
[C#]
public new void Clear();
[C++]
public: void Clear();
[JScript]
public hide function Clear();
```

Remarks

The **CollectionChanged** event occurs when the collection is cleared.

Example

See related example in the **System.Windows.Forms.Control-BindingsCollection** class topic.

Requirements

Platforms: Windows 98, Windows NT 4.0, Windows Millennium Edition, Windows 2000, Windows XP Home Edition, Windows XP Professional, Windows Server 2003 family, .NET Compact Framework - Windows CE .NET

ControlBindingsCollection.ClearCore Method

This member supports the .NET Framework infrastructure and is not intended to be used directly from your code.

```
[Visual Basic]
Overrides Protected Sub ClearCore()
[C#]
protected override void ClearCore();
[C++]
protected: void ClearCore();
[JScript]
protected override function ClearCore();
```

ControlBindingsCollection.Remove Method

Deletes the specified **Binding** from the collection.

```
[Visual Basic]
Public Shadows Sub Remove( _
   ByVal binding As Binding _
)
[C#]
public new void Remove(
   Binding binding
);
[C++]
public: void Remove(
   Binding* binding
);
```

```
[JScript]
public hide function Remove(
   binding : Binding
);
```

Parameters

binding
The **Binding** to remove.

Exceptions

Exception Type	Condition
NullReferenceException	The *binding* is null.

Example

See related example in the **System.Windows.Forms.ControlBindingsCollection** class topic.

Requirements

Platforms: Windows 98, Windows NT 4.0, Windows Millennium Edition, Windows 2000, Windows XP Home Edition, Windows XP Professional, Windows Server 2003 family, .NET Compact Framework - Windows CE .NET

ControlBindingsCollection.RemoveAt Method

Deletes the **Binding** at the specified index.

```
[Visual Basic]
Public Shadows Sub RemoveAt( _
   ByVal index As Integer _
)
[C#]
public new void RemoveAt(
   int index
);
[C++]
public: void RemoveAt(
   int index
);
[JScript]
public hide function RemoveAt(
   index : int
);
```

Parameters

index
The zero-based index of the item to remove.

Exceptions

Exception Type	Condition
ArgumentOutOfRange-Exception	The *index* value is less than 0, or it is greater than the number of bindings in the collection.

Remarks

The **CollectionChanged** event occurs if the removal succeeds.

Example

[Visual Basic, C#] The following example uses the **Count** property to determine whether the index is within the range of the collection. If so, the third **Binding** object is removed.

```
[Visual Basic]
Private Sub RemoveThirdBinding()
    If textBox1.DataBindings.Count < 3 Then
        Return
    End If
    textBox1.DataBindings.RemoveAt(2)
End Sub

[C#]
private void RemoveThirdBinding()
{
   if(textBox1.DataBindings.Count < 3) return;
   textBox1.DataBindings.RemoveAt(2);
}
```

Requirements

Platforms: Windows 98, Windows NT 4.0, Windows Millennium Edition, Windows 2000, Windows XP Home Edition, Windows XP Professional, Windows Server 2003 family, .NET Compact Framework - Windows CE .NET

ControlBindingsCollection.RemoveCore Method

This member supports the .NET Framework infrastructure and is not intended to be used directly from your code.

```
[Visual Basic]
Overrides Protected Sub RemoveCore( _
   ByVal dataBinding As Binding _
)
[C#]
protected override void RemoveCore(
   Binding dataBinding
);
[C++]
protected: void RemoveCore(
   Binding* dataBinding
);
[JScript]
protected override function RemoveCore(
   dataBinding : Binding
);
```

Control.ControlAccessible-Object Class

Provides information about a control that can be used by an accessibility application.

System.Object
  System.MarshalByRefObject
    System.Windows.Forms.AccessibleObject
      System.Windows.Forms.Control.ControlAccessibleObject

[Visual Basic]
```
<ComVisible(True)>
Public Class Control.ControlAccessibleObject
   Inherits AccessibleObject
```
[C#]
```
[ComVisible(true)]
public class Control.ControlAccessibleObject : AccessibleObject
```
[C++]
```
[ComVisible(true)]
public __gc class Control.ControlAccessibleObject : public
   AccessibleObject
```
[JScript]
```
public
   ComVisible(true)
class Control.ControlAccessibleObject extends
   AccessibleObject
```

Thread Safety

Any public static (**Shared** in Visual Basic) members of this type are safe for multithreaded operations. Any instance members are not guaranteed to be thread safe.

Remarks

Windows Forms has accessibility support built in, and provides information about your application that allows it to work with accessibility client applications. Examples of accessibility client applications are: screen enlarger and reviewer utilities, voice input utilities, on-screen keyboards, alternative input devices, and keyboard enhancement utilities. There are instances when you will want to provide additional information to accessibility client applications. There are two ways of providing this additional information. To provide limited accessibility information for existing controls, set the control's **AccessibleName**, **AccessibleDescription**, **AccessibleDefaultActionDescription**, and **AccessibleRole** property values, which will be reported to accessibility client applications. Alternatively, if you require more accessibility information to be included with your control, you can write your own class deriving from the **AccessibleObject** or **Control.ControlAccessibleObject** classes. For example, if you are writing your own control that is not derived from the common controls or you require such operations as hit testing within your control, you should create a **Control.ControlAccessibleObject** for your control by calling the **CreateAccessibilityInstance** method.

> **Note** If you override the **AccessibleObject.GetChild** method, you must also override the **AccessibleObject.GetChildCount** method.

> **Note** To get or set the **AccessibilityObject** property, you must add a reference to the **Accessibility** assembly installed with the .NET Framework.

For more information about accessible objects, see the Active Accessibility section of the MSDN Library.

Example

[Visual Basic, C#, C++] The following example creates a check box control that derives from the **CheckBox** class and creates a custom **Control.ControlAccessibleObject** for the derived class to use. The derived class, `MyCheckBox`, has an **Appearance** of **Button** by default so it appears as a toggle button. The derived **Control.ControlAccessibleObject** class, `MyCheckBoxControlAccessibleObject`, overrides three properties to account for the difference in appearance.

[Visual Basic]
```
Imports System
Imports System.Windows.Forms
Imports Accessibility
Imports System.Drawing

Namespace MyCustomControls
   Public Class MyCheckBox
      Inherits CheckBox

      Public Sub New()
         ' Make the check box appear like a toggle button.
         Me.Appearance = Appearance.Button
         ' Center the text on the button.
         Me.TextAlign = ContentAlignment.MiddleCenter
      End Sub

      ' Create an instance of the AccessibleObject
      ' defined for the 'MyCheckBox' control
      Protected Overrides Function CreateAccessibilityInstance() _
        As AccessibleObject
         Return New MyCheckBoxAccessibleObject(Me)
      End Function
   End Class

   ' Accessible object for use with the 'MyCheckBox' control.
   Friend Class MyCheckBoxAccessibleObject
      Inherits Control.ControlAccessibleObject

      Public Sub New(owner As MyCheckBox)
         MyBase.New(owner)
      End Sub

      Public Overrides ReadOnly Property DefaultAction() As String
         Get
            ' Return the DefaultAction based upon
            ' the state of the control.
            If CType(Owner, MyCheckBox).Checked Then
               Return "Toggle button up"
            Else
               Return "Toggle button down"
            End If
         End Get
      End Property

      Public Overrides Property Name() As String
         Get
            ' Return the Text property of the control
            ' if the AccessibleName is null.
            Dim accessibleName As String = Owner.AccessibleName
            If Not (accessibleName Is Nothing) Then
               Return accessibleName
            End If
            Return CType(Owner, MyCheckBox).Text
         End Get

         Set
            MyBase.Name = value
         End Set
      End Property
```

```
      Public Overrides ReadOnly Property Role() As AccessibleRole
         Get
            ' Since the check box appears like a button,
            ' make the Role the same as a button.
            Return AccessibleRole.PushButton
         End Get
      End Property
   End Class
End Namespace
```

[C#]

```
using System;
using System.Windows.Forms;
using Accessibility;
using System.Drawing;

namespace MyCustomControls
{
   public class MyCheckBox : CheckBox
   {
      public MyCheckBox()
      {
         // Make the check box appear like a toggle button.
         this.Appearance = Appearance.Button;
         // Center the text on the button.
         this.TextAlign = ContentAlignment.MiddleCenter;
     // Set the AccessibleDescription text.
         this.AccessibleDescription = "A toggle style button.";
      }

      // Create an instance of the AccessibleObject
      // defined for the 'MyCheckBox' control
      protected override AccessibleObject CreateAccessibilityInstance()
      {
         return new MyCheckBoxAccessibleObject(this);
      }
   }

   // Accessible object for use with the 'MyCheckBox' control.
   internal class MyCheckBoxAccessibleObject :
Control.ControlAccessibleObject
   {
      public MyCheckBoxAccessibleObject(MyCheckBox owner) : base(owner)
      {

      }

      public override string DefaultAction
      {
         get
         {
            // Return the DefaultAction based upon
            // the state of the control.
            if( ((MyCheckBox)Owner).Checked )
            {
               return "Toggle button up";
            }
            else
            {
               return "Toggle button down";
            }
         }
      }

      public override string Name
      {
         get
         {
            // Return the Text property of the control
            // if the AccessibleName is null.
            string name = Owner.AccessibleName;
            if (name != null)
            {
               return name;
            }
            return ((MyCheckBox)Owner).Text;
         }

         set
         {
            base.Name = value;
         }
      }

      public override AccessibleRole Role
      {
         get
         {
            // Since the check box appears like a button,
            // make the Role the same as a button.
            return AccessibleRole.PushButton;
         }
      }
   }
}
```

[C++]

```
#using <mscorlib.dll>
#using <Accessibility.dll>
#using <System.Drawing.dll>
#using <System.dll>
#using <System.Windows.Forms.dll>

using namespace System;
using namespace System::Windows::Forms;
using namespace System::Drawing;

namespace MyCustomControls {
public __gc class MyCheckBox : public CheckBox {
public:
   MyCheckBox() {
      // Make the check box appear like a toggle button.
      this->Appearance = Appearance::Button;
      // Center the text on the button.
      this->TextAlign = ContentAlignment::MiddleCenter;
      // Set the AccessibleDescription text.
      this->AccessibleDescription = S"A toggle style button.";
   }

   // Create an instance of the AccessibleObject
   // defined for the 'MyCheckBox' control
protected:
   AccessibleObject* CreateAccessibilityInstance();
};

// Accessible Object* for use with the 'MyCheckBox' control.
private __gc class MyCheckBoxAccessibleObject : public
Control::ControlAccessibleObject {
public:
   MyCheckBoxAccessibleObject(MyCheckBox* owner) :
ControlAccessibleObject(owner) {
   }

   __property String* get_DefaultAction() {
      // Return the DefaultAction based upon
      // the state of the control.
      if ((dynamic_cast<MyCheckBox*>(Owner))->Checked) {
         return S"Toggle button up";
      } else {
         return S"Toggle button down";
      }
   }

   __property String* get_Name() {
      // Return the Text property of the control
      // if the AccessibleName is 0.
      String* name = Owner->AccessibleName;
      if (name != 0) {
         return name;
      }
```

```
      return (dynamic_cast<MyCheckBox*>(Owner))->Text;
   }
   __property void set_Name(String* value) {
      ControlAccessibleObject::set_Name(value);
   }

   __property AccessibleRole get_Role() {
      // Since the check box appears like a button,
      // make the Role the same as a button.
      return AccessibleRole::PushButton;
   }
};

AccessibleObject* MyCheckBox::CreateAccessibilityInstance() {
   return new MyCheckBoxAccessibleObject(this);
}
}
```

Requirements

Namespace: System.Windows.Forms

Platforms: Windows 98, Windows NT 4.0, Windows Millennium Edition, Windows 2000, Windows XP Home Edition, Windows XP Professional, Windows Server 2003 family

Assembly: System.Windows.Forms (in System.Windows.Forms.dll)

Control.ControlAccessibleObject Constructor

Initializes a new instance of the **Control.ControlAccessibleObject** class.

[Visual Basic]
```
Public Sub New( _
   ByVal ownerControl As Control _
)
```
[C#]
```
public Control.ControlAccessibleObject(
   Control ownerControl
);
```
[C++]
```
public: ControlAccessibleObject(
   Control* ownerControl
);
```
[JScript]
```
public function Control.ControlAccessibleObject(
   ownerControl : Control
);
```

Parameters

ownerControl

The **Control** that owns the **Control.ControlAccessibleObject**.

Exceptions

Exception Type	Condition
ArgumentNull-Exception	The *ownerControl* parameter value is a null reference (**Nothing** in Visual Basic).

Example

See related example in the **System.Windows.Forms.Control.ControlAccessibleObject** class topic.

Requirements

Platforms: Windows 98, Windows NT 4.0, Windows Millennium Edition, Windows 2000, Windows XP Home Edition, Windows XP Professional, Windows Server 2003 family

Control.ControlAccessibleObject.DefaultAction Property

This member overrides **AccessibleObject.DefaultAction**.

[Visual Basic]
```
Overrides Public ReadOnly Property DefaultAction As String
```
[C#]
```
public override string DefaultAction {get;}
```
[C++]
```
public: __property String* get_DefaultAction();
```
[JScript]
```
public override function get DefaultAction() : String;
```

Requirements

Platforms: Windows 98, Windows NT 4.0, Windows Millennium Edition, Windows 2000, Windows XP Home Edition, Windows XP Professional, Windows Server 2003 family

Control.ControlAccessibleObject.Description Property

This member overrides **AccessibleObject.Description**.

[Visual Basic]
```
Overrides Public ReadOnly Property Description As String
```
[C#]
```
public override string Description {get;}
```
[C++]
```
public: __property String* get_Description();
```
[JScript]
```
public override function get Description() : String;
```

Requirements

Platforms: Windows 98, Windows NT 4.0, Windows Millennium Edition, Windows 2000, Windows XP Home Edition, Windows XP Professional, Windows Server 2003 family

Control.ControlAccessibleObject.Handle Property

Gets or sets the handle of the accessible object.

[Visual Basic]
```
Public Property Handle As IntPtr
```
[C#]
```
public IntPtr Handle {get; set;}
```
[C++]
```
public: __property IntPtr get_Handle();
public: __property void set_Handle(IntPtr);
```
[JScript]
```
public function get Handle() : IntPtr;
public function set Handle(IntPtr);
```

Property Value

An **IntPtr** that represents the handle of the control.

Remarks

The value of the **Handle** property for the **Control.ControlAccessibleObject** is equal to the **Handle** property of the **Control** it is associated with.

Requirements

Platforms: Windows 98, Windows NT 4.0, Windows Millennium Edition, Windows 2000, Windows XP Home Edition, Windows XP Professional, Windows Server 2003 family

Control.ControlAccessibleObject.Help Property

This member overrides **AccessibleObject.Help**.

```
[Visual Basic]
Overrides Public ReadOnly Property Help As String
[C#]
public override string Help {get;}
[C++]
public: __property String* get_Help();
[JScript]
public override function get Help() : String;
```

Requirements

Platforms: Windows 98, Windows NT 4.0, Windows Millennium Edition, Windows 2000, Windows XP Home Edition, Windows XP Professional, Windows Server 2003 family

Control.ControlAccessibleObject.KeyboardShortcut Property

This member overrides **AccessibleObject.KeyboardShortcut**.

```
[Visual Basic]
Overrides Public ReadOnly Property KeyboardShortcut As String
[C#]
public override string KeyboardShortcut {get;}
[C++]
public: __property String* get_KeyboardShortcut();
[JScript]
public override function get KeyboardShortcut() : String;
```

Requirements

Platforms: Windows 98, Windows NT 4.0, Windows Millennium Edition, Windows 2000, Windows XP Home Edition, Windows XP Professional, Windows Server 2003 family

Control.ControlAccessibleObject.Name Property

This member overrides **AccessibleObject.Name**.

```
[Visual Basic]
Overrides Public Property Name As String
[C#]
public override string Name {get; set;}
[C++]
public: __property String* get_Name();
public: __property void set_Name(String*);
[JScript]
public override function get Name() : String;
public override function set Name(String);
```

Requirements

Platforms: Windows 98, Windows NT 4.0, Windows Millennium Edition, Windows 2000, Windows XP Home Edition, Windows XP Professional, Windows Server 2003 family

Control.ControlAccessibleObject.Owner Property

Gets the owner of the accessible object.

```
[Visual Basic]
Public ReadOnly Property Owner As Control
[C#]
public Control Owner {get;}
[C++]
public: __property Control* get_Owner();
[JScript]
public function get Owner() : Control;
```

Property Value

The **Control** that owns the **Control.ControlAccessibleObject**.

Example

See related example in the **System.Windows.Forms.Control.ControlAccessibleObject** class topic.

Requirements

Platforms: Windows 98, Windows NT 4.0, Windows Millennium Edition, Windows 2000, Windows XP Home Edition, Windows XP Professional, Windows Server 2003 family

Control.ControlAccessibleObject.Role Property

This member overrides **AccessibleObject.Role**.

```
[Visual Basic]
Overrides Public ReadOnly Property Role As AccessibleRole
[C#]
public override AccessibleRole Role {get;}
[C++]
public: __property AccessibleRole get_Role();
[JScript]
public override function get Role() : AccessibleRole;
```

Requirements

Platforms: Windows 98, Windows NT 4.0, Windows Millennium Edition, Windows 2000, Windows XP Home Edition, Windows XP Professional, Windows Server 2003 family

Control.ControlAccessibleObject.GetHelpTopic Method

This member overrides **AccessibleObject.GetHelpTopic**.

```
[Visual Basic]
Overrides Public Function GetHelpTopic( _
   <Out()> ByRef fileName As String _
) As Integer
[C#]
public override int GetHelpTopic(
   out string fileName
);
[C++]
public: int GetHelpTopic(
   [
   Out
] String** fileName
);
[JScript]
public override function GetHelpTopic(
   fileName : String
) : int;
```

Requirements

Platforms: Windows 98, Windows NT 4.0, Windows Millennium Edition, Windows 2000, Windows XP Home Edition, Windows XP Professional, Windows Server 2003 family

Control.ControlAccessibleObject.NotifyClients Method

Notifies accessibility client applications of **AccessibleEvents**.

Overload List

Notifies accessibility client applications of the specified **AccessibleEvents**.

[Visual Basic] **Overloads Public Sub NotifyClients(AccessibleEvents)**

[C#] **public void NotifyClients(AccessibleEvents);**

[C++] **public: void NotifyClients(AccessibleEvents);**

[JScript] **public function NotifyClients(AccessibleEvents);**

Notifies the accessibility client applications of the specified **AccessibleEvents** for the specified child control.

[Visual Basic] **Overloads Public Sub NotifyClients(AccessibleEvents, Integer)**

[C#] **public void NotifyClients(AccessibleEvents, int);**

[C++] **public: void NotifyClients(AccessibleEvents, int);**

[JScript] **public function NotifyClients(AccessibleEvents, int);**

Control.ControlAccessibleObject.NotifyClients Method (AccessibleEvents)

Notifies accessibility client applications of the specified **AccessibleEvents**.

```
[Visual Basic]
Overloads Public Sub NotifyClients( _
   ByVal accEvent As AccessibleEvents _
)
[C#]
public void NotifyClients(
   AccessibleEvents accEvent
);
[C++]
public: void NotifyClients(
   AccessibleEvents accEvent
);
[JScript]
public function NotifyClients(
   accEvent : AccessibleEvents
);
```

Parameters

accEvent

The **AccessibleEvents** object to notify the accessibility client applications of.

Remarks

You must call the **NotifyClients** method for each **AccessibleEvents** object the accessibility client applications are to be notified of. The **NotifyClients** method is typically called when a property is set or from within an event handler. For example, you might call the **NotifyClients** method and pass in **AccessibleEvents.Hide** from within the event handler for the **Control.VisibleChanged** event.

Requirements

Platforms: Windows 98, Windows NT 4.0, Windows Millennium Edition, Windows 2000, Windows XP Home Edition, Windows XP Professional, Windows Server 2003 family

Control.ControlAccessibleObject.NotifyClients Method (AccessibleEvents, Int32)

Notifies the accessibility client applications of the specified **AccessibleEvents** for the specified child control.

```
[Visual Basic]
Overloads Public Sub NotifyClients( _
   ByVal accEvent As AccessibleEvents, _
   ByVal childID As Integer _
)
[C#]
public void NotifyClients(
   AccessibleEvents accEvent,
   int childID
);
[C++]
public: void NotifyClients(
   AccessibleEvents accEvent,
   int childID
);
[JScript]
public function NotifyClients(
   accEvent : AccessibleEvents,
   childID : int
);
```

Parameters

accEvent

The **AccessibleEvents** object to notify the accessibility client applications of.

childID

The child **Control** to notify of the accessible event.

Remarks

You must call the **NotifyClients** method for each **AccessibleEvents** object the accessibility client applications are to be notified of. The **NotifyClients** method is typically called when a property is set or from within an event handler. For example, you might call the **NotifyClients** method and pass in **AccessibleEvents.Hide** from within the event handler for the **Control.VisibleChanged** event.

Requirements

Platforms: Windows 98, Windows NT 4.0, Windows Millennium Edition, Windows 2000, Windows XP Home Edition, Windows XP Professional, Windows Server 2003 family

Control.ControlAccessibleObject.ToString Method

This member overrides **Object.ToString**.

[Visual Basic]
```
Overrides Public Function ToString() As String
```
[C#]
```
public override string ToString();
```
[C++]
```
public: String* ToString();
```
[JScript]
```
public override function ToString() : String;
```

Requirements

Platforms: Windows 98, Windows NT 4.0, Windows Millennium Edition, Windows 2000, Windows XP Home Edition, Windows XP Professional, Windows Server 2003 family

Control.ControlCollection Class

Represents a collection of **Control** objects

System.Object
System.Windows.Forms.Control.ControlCollection
System.Windows.Forms.Form.ControlCollection
System.Windows.Forms.TabControl.ControlCollection
System.Windows.Forms.TabPage.TabPageControlCollection

[Visual Basic]
```
Public Class Control.ControlCollection
   Implements IList, ICollection, IEnumerable, ICloneable
```
[C#]
```
public class Control.ControlCollection : IList, ICollection,
   IEnumerable, ICloneable
```
[C++]
```
public __gc class Control.ControlCollection : public IList,
   ICollection, IEnumerable, ICloneable
```
[JScript]
```
public class Control.ControlCollection implements IList,
   ICollection, IEnumerable, ICloneable
```

Thread Safety

Any public static (**Shared** in Visual Basic) members of this type are safe for multithreaded operations. Any instance members are not guaranteed to be thread safe.

Remarks

The **Add**, **Remove**, and **RemoveAt** methods enable you to add and remove individual controls from the collection. You can also use the **AddRange** or **Clear** methods to add or remove all the controls from the collection.

You can determine if a **Control** is a member of the collection by passing the control into the **Contains** method. To get the index value of the location of a **Control** in the collection, pass the control into the **IndexOf** method. The collection can be copied into an array by calling the **CopyTo** method.

Example

[Visual Basic, C#, C++] The following example removes a **Control** from the **Control.ControlCollection** of the derived class **Panel** if it is a member of the collection. The example assumes you have created a **Panel**, a **Button**, and at least one **RadioButton** control on a **Form**. The **RadioButton** control(s) are added to the **Panel** control, and the **Panel** control added to the **Form**. When the button is clicked, the radio button named `radioButton2` is removed from the **Control.ControlCollection**.

[Visual Basic]
```
' Remove the RadioButton control if it exists.
Private Sub RemoveButton_Click(ByVal sender As System.Object, _
    ByVal e As System.EventArgs) Handles RemoveButton.Click
    If Panel1.Controls.Contains(RadioAddRangeButton) Then
        Panel1.Controls.Remove(RadioAddRangeButton)
    End If
End Sub
```

[C#]
```
// Remove the RadioButton control if it exists.
private void removeButton_Click(object sender, System.EventArgs e)
{
   if(panel1.Controls.Contains(removeButton))
   {
      panel1.Controls.Remove(removeButton);
   }
}
```

[C++]
```
// Remove the RadioButton control if it exists.
private:
void removeButton_Click(Object* sender, System::EventArgs* e) {
    if (panel1->Controls->Contains(removeButton)) {
        panel1->Controls->Remove(removeButton);
    }
}
```

Requirements

Namespace: System.Windows.Forms

Platforms: Windows 98, Windows NT 4.0, Windows Millennium Edition, Windows 2000, Windows XP Home Edition, Windows XP Professional, Windows Server 2003 family, .NET Compact Framework - Windows CE .NET

Assembly: System.Windows.Forms (in System.Windows.Forms.dll)

Control.ControlCollection Constructor

Initializes a new instance of the **Control.ControlCollection** class.

[Visual Basic]
```
Public Sub New( _
   ByVal owner As Control _
)
```
[C#]
```
public Control.ControlCollection(
   Control owner
);
```
[C++]
```
public: ControlCollection(
   Control* owner
);
```
[JScript]
```
public function Control.ControlCollection(
   owner : Control
);
```

Parameters

owner

A **Control** representing the control that owns the control collection.

Requirements

Platforms: Windows 98, Windows NT 4.0, Windows Millennium Edition, Windows 2000, Windows XP Home Edition, Windows XP Professional, Windows Server 2003 family, .NET Compact Framework - Windows CE .NET

Control.ControlCollection.Count Property

Gets the total number of **Control** objects in the collection.

```
[Visual Basic]
Public Overridable ReadOnly Property Count As Integer  Implements _
   ICollection.Count
[C#]
public virtual int Count {get;}
[C++]
public: __property virtual int get_Count();
[JScript]
public function get Count() : int;
```

Property Value

The total number of **Control** objects in the collection.

Implements

ICollection.Count

Remarks

The **Count** property holds the number of **Control** objects assigned to the collection. You can use the **Count** property value as the upper bounds of a loop to iterate through a collection.

Because the index value of a collection is a zero-based index, you must subtract one from the looping variable. If you do not account for this, you will exceed the upper bounds of the collection and throw an **IndexOutOfRangeException** exception.

Example

See related example in the **System.Windows.Forms.Control.ControlCollection** class topic.

Requirements

Platforms: Windows 98, Windows NT 4.0,
Windows Millennium Edition, Windows 2000,
Windows XP Home Edition, Windows XP Professional,
Windows Server 2003 family,
.NET Compact Framework - Windows CE .NET

Control.ControlCollection.IsReadOnly Property

Gets a value indicating whether the control collection is read-only.

```
[Visual Basic]
Public Overridable ReadOnly Property IsReadOnly As Boolean  _
   Implements IList.IsReadOnly
[C#]
public virtual bool IsReadOnly {get;}
[C++]
public: __property virtual bool get_IsReadOnly();
[JScript]
public function get IsReadOnly() : Boolean;
```

Property Value

true if the control collection is read-only; otherwise, **false**.

Implements

IList.IsReadOnly

Requirements

Platforms: Windows 98, Windows NT 4.0,
Windows Millennium Edition, Windows 2000,
Windows XP Home Edition, Windows XP Professional,
Windows Server 2003 family,
.NET Compact Framework - Windows CE .NET

Control.ControlCollection.Item Property

Indicates the **Control** at the specified indexed location in the collection.

[C#] In C#, this property is the indexer for the **Control.ControlCollection** class.

```
[Visual Basic]
Public Overridable Default ReadOnly Property Item( _
   ByVal index As Integer _
) As Control
[C#]
public virtual Control this[
   int index
] {get;}
[C++]
public: __property virtual Control* get_Item(
   int index
);
[JScript]
returnValue = ControlCollectionObject.Item(index);
-or-
returnValue = ControlCollectionObject(index);
```

[JScript] In JScript, you can use the default indexed properties defined by a type, but you cannot explicitly define your own. However, specifying the **expando** attribute on a class automatically provides a default indexed property whose type is **Object** and whose index type is **String**.

Arguments [JScript]

index
: The index of the control to retrieve from the control collection.

Parameters [Visual Basic, C#, C++]

index
: The index of the control to retrieve from the control collection.

Property Value

The **Control** located at the specified index location within the control collection.

Exceptions

Exception Type	Condition
ArgumentOutOfRange-Exception	The *index* value is less than zero or is greater than or equal to the number of controls in the collection.

Remarks

To retrieve a **Control** from the **Control.ControlCollection**, reference the collection object with a specific index value. The index value of the **Control.ControlCollection** is a zero-based index.

Requirements

Platforms: Windows 98, Windows NT 4.0,
Windows Millennium Edition, Windows 2000,
Windows XP Home Edition, Windows XP Professional,
Windows Server 2003 family

Control.ControlCollection.System.Collections.ICollection.IsSynchronized Property

Note: This namespace, class, or member is supported only in version 1.1 of the .NET Framework.

This member supports the .NET Framework infrastructure and is not intended to be used directly from your code.

```
[Visual Basic]
Private ReadOnly Property IsSynchronized As Boolean Implements _
   ICollection.IsSynchronized
[C#]
bool ICollection.IsSynchronized {get;}
[C++]
private: __property bool
   System::Collections::ICollection::get_IsSynchronized();
[JScript]
private function get ICollection.IsSynchronized() : Boolean;
```

Control.ControlCollection.System.Collections.ICollection.SyncRoot Property

Note: This namespace, class, or member is supported only in version 1.1 of the .NET Framework.

This member supports the .NET Framework infrastructure and is not intended to be used directly from your code.

```
[Visual Basic]
Private ReadOnly Property SyncRoot As Object Implements _
   ICollection.SyncRoot
[C#]
object ICollection.SyncRoot {get;}
[C++]
private: __property Object*
   System::Collections::ICollection::get_SyncRoot();
[JScript]
private function get ICollection.SyncRoot() : Object;
```

Control.ControlCollection.System.Collections.IList.IsFixedSize Property

Note: This namespace, class, or member is supported only in version 1.1 of the .NET Framework.

This member supports the .NET Framework infrastructure and is not intended to be used directly from your code.

```
[Visual Basic]
Private ReadOnly Property IsFixedSize As Boolean Implements _
   IList.IsFixedSize
[C#]
bool IList.IsFixedSize {get;}
[C++]
private: __property bool
   System::Collections::IList::get_IsFixedSize();
[JScript]
private function get IList.IsFixedSize() : Boolean;
```

Control.ControlCollection.System.Collections.IList.Item Property

Note: This namespace, class, or member is supported only in version 1.1 of the .NET Framework.

[C#] In C#, this property is the indexer for the **Control.ControlCollection** class.

```
[Visual Basic]
Private Default Property Item( _
   ByVal index As Integer _
) As Object Implements IList.Item
[C#]
object IList.this[
   int index
] {get; set;}
[C++]
private: __property Object* System::Collections::IList::get_Item(
   int index
);
private: __property void System::Collections::IList::set_Item(
   int index,
   Object*
);
[JScript]
private function get IList.get_Item(index : int) : Object;
private function set IList.set_Item(index : int, value : Object);
-or-
private function get IList.get_Item(index : int) : Object;
private function set IList.set_Item(index : int, value : Object);
```

[JScript] In JScript, you can use the default indexed properties defined by a type, but you cannot explicitly define your own. However, specifying the **expando** attribute on a class automatically provides a default indexed property whose type is **Object** and whose index type is **String**.

Arguments [JScript]

index

Parameters [Visual Basic, C#, C++]

index

Requirements

Platforms: Windows 98, Windows NT 4.0, Windows Millennium Edition, Windows 2000, Windows XP Home Edition, Windows XP Professional, Windows Server 2003 family

Control.ControlCollection.Add Method

Adds the specified control to the control collection.

```
[Visual Basic]
Public Overridable Sub Add( _
   ByVal value As Control _
)
[C#]
public virtual void Add(
   Control value
);
[C++]
public: virtual void Add(
   Control* value
);
```

```
[JScript]
public function Add(
   value : Control
);
```

Parameters

value

The **Control** to add to the control collection.

Exceptions

Exception Type	Condition
Exception	The specified control is a top-level control, or a circular control reference would result if this control were added to the control collection.
ArgumentException	The object assigned to the *value* parameter is not a **Control**.

Remarks

The **Add** method allows you to add **Control** objects to the end of the control collection.

You can also add new **Control** objects to the collection by using the **AddRange** method.

To remove a **Control** that you previously added, use the **Remove**, **RemoveAt**, or **Clear** methods.

> **Note** A **Control** object can only be assigned to one **Control.ControlCollection** at a time. If the **Control** is already a child of another control it is removed from that control before it is added to another control.

Notes to Inheritors: When overriding **Add** in a derived class, be sure to call the base class's **Add** method to ensure that the control is added to the collection.

Example

See related example in the **System.Windows.Forms.Control.ControlCollection** class topic.

Requirements

Platforms: Windows 98, Windows NT 4.0, Windows Millennium Edition, Windows 2000, Windows XP Home Edition, Windows XP Professional, Windows Server 2003 family, .NET Compact Framework - Windows CE .NET

Control.ControlCollection.AddRange Method

Adds an array of control objects to the collection.

```
[Visual Basic]
Public Overridable Sub AddRange( _
   ByVal controls() As Control _
)
[C#]
public virtual void AddRange(
   Control[] controls
);
[C++]
public: virtual void AddRange(
   Control* controls[]
);
[JScript]
public function AddRange(
   controls : Control[]
);
```

Parameters

controls

An array of **Control** objects to add to the collection.

Remarks

The **Control** objects contained in the *controls* array are appended to the end of the collection.

You can use the **AddRange** method to quickly add a group of **Control** objects to the collection instead of manually adding each **Control** to the collection using the **Add** method.

To remove a **Control** that you previously added, use the **Remove**, **RemoveAt**, or **Clear** methods.

Notes to Inheritors: When overriding **AddRange** in a derived class, be sure to call the base class's **AddRange** method to ensure that the controls are added to the collection.

Example

See related example in the **System.Windows.Forms.Control.ControlCollection** class topic.

Requirements

Platforms: Windows 98, Windows NT 4.0, Windows Millennium Edition, Windows 2000, Windows XP Home Edition, Windows XP Professional, Windows Server 2003 family

Control.ControlCollection.Clear Method

Removes all controls from the collection.

```
[Visual Basic]
Public Overridable Sub Clear() Implements IList.Clear
[C#]
public virtual void Clear();
[C++]
public: virtual void Clear();
[JScript]
public function Clear();
```

Implements

IList.Clear

Remarks

You can use the **Clear** method to remove the entire collection of controls from a parent control.

To remove an individual control from the collection, use the **Remove** or **RemoveAt** methods.

To add new **Control** objects to the collection, use the **Add** or **AddRange** methods.

Notes to Inheritors: When overriding **Clear** in a derived class, be sure to call the base class's **Clear** method to ensure that all the controls are removed from the collection.

Example

See related example in the **System.Windows.Forms.Control.ControlCollection** class topic.

Requirements

Platforms: Windows 98, Windows NT 4.0,
Windows Millennium Edition, Windows 2000,
Windows XP Home Edition, Windows XP Professional,
Windows Server 2003 family,
.NET Compact Framework - Windows CE .NET

Control.ControlCollection.Contains Method

Determines whether the specified control is a member of the collection.

```
[Visual Basic]
Public Function Contains( _
   ByVal control As Control _
) As Boolean
[C#]
public bool Contains(
   Control control
);
[C++]
public: bool Contains(
   Control* control
);
[JScript]
public function Contains(
   control : Control
) : Boolean;
```

Parameters

control
The **Control** to locate in the collection.

Return Value

true if the **Control** is a member of the collection; otherwise, **false**.

Remarks

This method enables you to determine whether a **Control** is a member of the collection before attempting to perform operations on the **Control**. You can use this method to confirm that a **Control** has been added to or is still a member of the collection.

Example

See related example in the **System.Windows.Forms.Control.ControlCollection** class topic.

Requirements

Platforms: Windows 98, Windows NT 4.0,
Windows Millennium Edition, Windows 2000,
Windows XP Home Edition, Windows XP Professional,
Windows Server 2003 family,
.NET Compact Framework - Windows CE .NET

Control.ControlCollection.CopyTo Method

Copies the entire collection into an existing array at a specified location within the array.

```
[Visual Basic]
Public Overridable Sub CopyTo( _
   ByVal dest As Array, _
   ByVal index As Integer _
) Implements ICollection.CopyTo
[C#]
public virtual void CopyTo(
   Array dest,
   int index
);
[C++]
public: virtual void CopyTo(
   Array* dest,
   int index
);
[JScript]
public function CopyTo(
   dest : Array,
   index : int
);
```

Parameters

dest
The destination array.

index
The index in the destination array at which storing begins.

Implements

ICollection.CopyTo

Remarks

CAUTION All the controls in the collection are copied into the array starting at the specified indexed location, overwriting any existing data within the range of objects copied into the array.

Requirements

Platforms: Windows 98, Windows NT 4.0,
Windows Millennium Edition, Windows 2000,
Windows XP Home Edition, Windows XP Professional,
Windows Server 2003 family,
.NET Compact Framework - Windows CE .NET

Control.ControlCollection.Equals Method

This member overrides **Object.Equals**.

```
[Visual Basic]
Overrides Public Function Equals( _
   ByVal other As Object _
) As Boolean
[C#]
public override bool Equals(
   object other
);
[C++]
public: bool Equals(
   Object* other
);
[JScript]
public override function Equals(
   other : Object
) : Boolean;
```

Requirements

Platforms: Windows 98, Windows NT 4.0,
Windows Millennium Edition, Windows 2000,
Windows XP Home Edition, Windows XP Professional,
Windows Server 2003 family,
.NET Compact Framework - Windows CE .NET

Control.ControlCollection.GetChildIndex Method

Retrieves the index of a control within the control collection.

Overload List

Retrieves the index of the specified child control within the control collection.

Supported by the .NET Compact Framework.

[Visual Basic] **Overloads Public Function GetChildIndex(Control) As Integer**

[C#] **public int GetChildIndex(Control);**

[C++] **public: int GetChildIndex(Control*);**

[JScript] **public function GetChildIndex(Control) : int;**

Retrieves the index of the specified child control within the control collection, and optionally raises an exception if the specified control is not within the control collection.

[Visual Basic] **Overloads Public Function GetChildIndex(Control, Boolean) As Integer**

[C#] **public int GetChildIndex(Control, bool);**

[C++] **public: int GetChildIndex(Control*, bool);**

[JScript] **public function GetChildIndex(Control, Boolean) : int;**

Control.ControlCollection.GetChildIndex Method (Control)

Retrieves the index of the specified child control within the control collection.

```
[Visual Basic]
Overloads Public Function GetChildIndex( _
   ByVal child As Control _
) As Integer
[C#]
public int GetChildIndex(
   Control child
);
[C++]
public: int GetChildIndex(
   Control* child
);
[JScript]
public function GetChildIndex(
   child : Control
) : int;
```

Parameters

child

The **Control** to search for in the control collection.

Return Value

A zero-based index value that represents the location of the specified child control within the control collection.

Exceptions

Exception Type	Condition
ArgumentException	The *child* **Control** is not in the **Control.ControlCollection**.

Remarks

The control with an index value of zero is at the top of the z-order, and higher numbers are closer to the bottom.

Requirements

Platforms: Windows 98, Windows NT 4.0, Windows Millennium Edition, Windows 2000, Windows XP Home Edition, Windows XP Professional, Windows Server 2003 family, .NET Compact Framework - Windows CE .NET

Control.ControlCollection.GetChildIndex Method (Control, Boolean)

Retrieves the index of the specified child control within the control collection, and optionally raises an exception if the specified control is not within the control collection.

```
[Visual Basic]
Overloads Public Function GetChildIndex( _
   ByVal child As Control, _
   ByVal throwException As Boolean _
) As Integer
[C#]
public int GetChildIndex(
   Control child,
   bool throwException
);
[C++]
public: int GetChildIndex(
   Control* child,
   bool throwException
);
[JScript]
public function GetChildIndex(
   child : Control,
   throwException : Boolean
) : int;
```

Parameters

child

The **Control** to search for in the control collection.

throwException

true to throw an exception if the **Control** specified in the *child* parameter is not a control in the **Control.ControlCollection**; otherwise, **false**.

Return Value

A zero-based index value that represents the location of the specified child control within the control collection; otherwise -1 if the specified **Control** is not found in the **Control.ControlCollection**.

Exceptions

Exception Type	Condition
ArgumentException	The *child* **Control** is not in the **Control.ControlCollection**, and the *throwException* parameter value is **true**.

Remarks

The control with an index value of zero is at the top of the z-order, and higher numbers are closer to the bottom. A return value of -1 is returned only when the *throwException* parameter is **false**.

Requirements

Platforms: Windows 98, Windows NT 4.0, Windows Millennium Edition, Windows 2000, Windows XP Home Edition, Windows XP Professional, Windows Server 2003 family

Control.ControlCollection.GetEnumerator Method

Returns an enumerator that can be used to iterate through the control collection.

```
[Visual Basic]
Public Overridable Function GetEnumerator() As IEnumerator _
   Implements IEnumerable.GetEnumerator
[C#]
public virtual IEnumerator GetEnumerator();
[C++]
public: virtual IEnumerator* GetEnumerator();
[JScript]
public function GetEnumerator() : IEnumerator;
```

Return Value

An **IEnumerator** object that represents the control collection.

Implements

IEnumerable.GetEnumerator

Requirements

Platforms: Windows 98, Windows NT 4.0, Windows Millennium Edition, Windows 2000, Windows XP Home Edition, Windows XP Professional, Windows Server 2003 family, .NET Compact Framework - Windows CE .NET

Control.ControlCollection.GetHashCode Method

This member overrides **Object.GetHashCode**.

```
[Visual Basic]
Overrides Public Function GetHashCode() As Integer
[C#]
public override int GetHashCode();
[C++]
public: int GetHashCode();
[JScript]
public override function GetHashCode() : int;
```

Requirements

Platforms: Windows 98, Windows NT 4.0, Windows Millennium Edition, Windows 2000, Windows XP Home Edition, Windows XP Professional, Windows Server 2003 family, .NET Compact Framework - Windows CE .NET

Control.ControlCollection.ICloneable.Clone Method

This member supports the .NET Framework infrastructure and is not intended to be used directly from your code.

```
[Visual Basic]
Private Function Clone() As Object Implements ICloneable.Clone
[C#]
object ICloneable.Clone();
[C++]
private: Object* ICloneable::Clone();
[JScript]
private function ICloneable.Clone() : Object;
```

Control.ControlCollection.IList.Add Method

This member supports the .NET Framework infrastructure and is not intended to be used directly from your code.

```
[Visual Basic]
Private Function Add( _
   ByVal control As Object _
) As Integer Implements IList.Add
[C#]
int IList.Add(
   object control
);
[C++]
private: int IList::Add(
   Object* control
);
[JScript]
private function IList.Add(
   control : Object
) : int;
```

Control.ControlCollection.IList.Contains Method

This member supports the .NET Framework infrastructure and is not intended to be used directly from your code.

```
[Visual Basic]
Private Function Contains( _
   ByVal control As Object _
) As Boolean Implements IList.Contains
[C#]
bool IList.Contains(
   object control
);
[C++]
private: bool IList::Contains(
   Object* control
);
[JScript]
private function IList.Contains(
   control : Object
) : Boolean;
```

Control.ControlCollection.IList.IndexOf Method

This member supports the .NET Framework infrastructure and is not intended to be used directly from your code.

```
[Visual Basic]
Private Function IndexOf( _
   ByVal control As Object _
) As Integer Implements IList.IndexOf
[C#]
int IList.IndexOf(
   object control
);
```

```
[C++]
private: int IList::IndexOf(
   Object* control
);
[JScript]
private function IList.IndexOf(
   control : Object
) : int;
```

Control.ControlCollection.IList.Insert Method

This member supports the .NET Framework infrastructure and is not intended to be used directly from your code.

```
[Visual Basic]
Private Sub Insert( _
   ByVal index As Integer, _
   ByVal value As Object _
) Implements IList.Insert
[C#]
void IList.Insert(
   int index,
   object value
);
[C++]
private: void IList::Insert(
   int index,
   Object* value
);
[JScript]
private function IList.Insert(
   index : int,
   value : Object
);
```

Control.ControlCollection.IList.Remove Method

This member supports the .NET Framework infrastructure and is not intended to be used directly from your code.

```
[Visual Basic]
Private Sub Remove( _
   ByVal control As Object _
) Implements IList.Remove
[C#]
void IList.Remove(
   object control
);
[C++]
private: void IList::Remove(
   Object* control
);
[JScript]
private function IList.Remove(
   control : Object
);
```

Control.ControlCollection.IndexOf Method

Retrieves the index of the specified control in the control collection.

```
[Visual Basic]
Public Function IndexOf( _
   ByVal control As Control _
) As Integer
[C#]
public int IndexOf(
   Control control
);
[C++]
public: int IndexOf(
   Control* control
);
[JScript]
public function IndexOf(
   control : Control
) : int;
```

Parameters

control
The **Control** to locate in the collection.

Return Value

A zero-based index value that represents the position of the specified **Control** in the **Control.ControlCollection**.

Remarks

If the control is not found in the collection, the **IndexOf** method return value is -1.

Requirements

Platforms: Windows 98, Windows NT 4.0, Windows Millennium Edition, Windows 2000, Windows XP Home Edition, Windows XP Professional, Windows Server 2003 family, .NET Compact Framework - Windows CE .NET

Control.ControlCollection.Remove Method

Removes the specified control from the control collection.

```
[Visual Basic]
Public Overridable Sub Remove( _
   ByVal value As Control _
)
[C#]
public virtual void Remove(
   Control value
);
[C++]
public: virtual void Remove(
   Control* value
);
[JScript]
public function Remove(
   value : Control
);
```

Parameters

value
The **Control** to remove from the **Control.ControlCollection**.

Remarks

When a **Control** is removed from the control collection, all subsequent controls are moved up one position in the collection.

You can also remove a **Control** by using the **RemoveAt** or **Clear** methods.

To add new **Control** objects to the collection, use the **Add** or **AddRange** methods.

Notes to Inheritors: When overriding **Remove** in a derived class, be sure to call the base class's **Remove** method to ensure that the control is removed from the collection.

Example

See related example in the **System.Windows.Forms.Control.ControlCollection** class topic.

Requirements

Platforms: Windows 98, Windows NT 4.0,
Windows Millennium Edition, Windows 2000,
Windows XP Home Edition, Windows XP Professional,
Windows Server 2003 family,
.NET Compact Framework - Windows CE .NET

Control.ControlCollection.RemoveAt Method

Removes a control from the control collection at the specified indexed location.

```
[Visual Basic]
Public Overridable Sub RemoveAt( _
   ByVal index As Integer _
) Implements IList.RemoveAt
[C#]
public virtual void RemoveAt(
   int index
);
[C++]
public: virtual void RemoveAt(
   int index
);
[JScript]
public function RemoveAt(
   index : int
);
```

Parameters

index

The index value of the **Control** to remove.

Implements

IList.RemoveAt

Remarks

When a **Control** is removed from the control collection, all subsequent controls are moved up one position in the collection.

You can also remove a **Control** that you previously added by using the **Remove** or **Clear** methods.

To add new **Control** objects to the collection, use the **Add** or **AddRange** methods.

Example

See related example in the **System.Windows.Forms.Control.ControlCollection** class topic.

Requirements

Platforms: Windows 98, Windows NT 4.0,
Windows Millennium Edition, Windows 2000,
Windows XP Home Edition, Windows XP Professional,
Windows Server 2003 family,
.NET Compact Framework - Windows CE .NET

Control.ControlCollection.SetChildIndex Method

Sets the index of the specified child control in the collection to the specified index value.

```
[Visual Basic]
Public Sub SetChildIndex( _
   ByVal child As Control, _
   ByVal newIndex As Integer _
)
[C#]
public void SetChildIndex(
   Control child,
   int newIndex
);
[C++]
public: void SetChildIndex(
   Control* child,
   int newIndex
);
[JScript]
public function SetChildIndex(
   child : Control,
   newIndex : int
);
```

Parameters

child

The *child* **Control** to search for.

newIndex

The new index value of the control.

Exceptions

Exception Type	Condition
ArgumentException	The *child* control is not in the **Control.ControlCollection**.

Remarks

When **SetChildIndex** is called, the **Control** referred to by the *child* parameter is moved to the position specified by *newIndex* and the other **Control** references in the **Control.ControlCollection** are reordered to accommodate the move. The control with an index value of zero is at the top of the z-order, and higher numbers are closer to the bottom.

Requirements

Platforms: Windows 98, Windows NT 4.0,
Windows Millennium Edition, Windows 2000,
Windows XP Home Edition, Windows XP Professional,
Windows Server 2003 family,
.NET Compact Framework - Windows CE .NET

ControlEventArgs Class

Provides data for the **ControlAdded** and **ControlRemoved** events.

System.Object
  System.EventArgs
    System.Windows.Forms.ControlEventArgs

[Visual Basic]
```
Public Class ControlEventArgs
   Inherits EventArgs
```
[C#]
```
public class ControlEventArgs : EventArgs
```
[C++]
```
public __gc class ControlEventArgs : public EventArgs
```
[JScript]
```
public class ControlEventArgs extends EventArgs
```

Thread Safety

Any public static (**Shared** in Visual Basic) members of this type are safe for multithreaded operations. Any instance members are not guaranteed to be thread safe.

Example

[Visual Basic]
```
' This example demonstrates the use of the ControlAdded and
' ControlRemoved events. This example assumes that two Button controls
' are added to the form and connected to the addControl_Click and
' removeControl_Click event handling methods.
Private Sub Form1_Load(ByVal sender As Object, ByVal e As ↵
System.EventArgs) Handles MyBase.Load
    ' Connect the ControlRemoved and ControlAdded event handlers ↵
 to the event handling methods.
    ' ControlRemoved and ControlAdded are not available at design time.
    AddHandler Me.ControlRemoved, AddressOf Me.Control_Removed
    AddHandler Me.ControlAdded, AddressOf Me.Control_Added
End Sub 'Form1_Load

Private Sub Control_Added(ByVal sender As Object, ByVal e As ↵
System.Windows.Forms.ControlEventArgs)
    MessageBox.Show(("The control named " + e.Control.Name + " ↵
has been added to the form."))
End Sub

Private Sub Control_Removed(ByVal sender As Object, ByVal e As ↵
System.Windows.Forms.ControlEventArgs)
    MessageBox.Show(("The control named " + e.Control.Name + " ↵
 has been removed from the form."))
End Sub

' Click event handler for a Button control. Adds a TextBox to the form.
Private Sub addControl_Click(ByVal sender As Object, ByVal e As ↵
System.EventArgs) Handles button1.Click
    ' Create a new TextBox control and add it to the form.
    Dim textBox1 As New TextBox()
    textBox1.Size = New Size(100, 10)
    textBox1.Location = New Point(10, 10)
    ' Name the control in order to remove it later.
    ' The name must be specified if a control is added at run time.
    textBox1.Name = "textBox1"

    ' Add the control to the form's control collection.
    Me.Controls.Add(textBox1)
End Sub

' Click event handler for a Button control.
' Removes the previously added TextBox from the form.
Private Sub removeControl_Click(ByVal sender As Object, ByVal ↵
 e As System.EventArgs) Handles button2.Click
    ' Loop through all controls in the form's control collection.
    Dim tempCtrl As Control
    For Each tempCtrl In Me.Controls
        ' Determine whether the control is textBox1,
        ' and if it is, remove it.
        If tempCtrl.Name = "textBox1" Then
            Me.Controls.Remove(tempCtrl)
        End If
    Next tempCtrl
End Sub
```

[C#]
```
// This example demonstrates the use of the ControlAdded and
// ControlRemoved events. This example assumes that two Button controls
// are added to the form and connected to the addControl_Click and
// removeControl_Click event handling methods.
private void Form1_Load(object sender, System.EventArgs e)
{
    // Connect the ControlRemoved and ControlAdded event handlers
    // to the event handling methods.
    // ControlRemoved and ControlAdded are not available at ↵
 design time.
    this.ControlRemoved += new ↵
System.Windows.Forms.ControlEventHandler(this.Control_Removed);
    this.ControlAdded += new ↵
System.Windows.Forms.ControlEventHandler(this.Control_Added);
}

private void Control_Added(object sender, ↵
System.Windows.Forms.ControlEventArgs e)
{
    MessageBox.Show("The control named " + e.Control.Name + ↵
 " has been added to the form.");
}

private void Control_Removed(object sender, ↵
System.Windows.Forms.ControlEventArgs e)
{
    MessageBox.Show("The control named " + e.Control.Name + ↵
" has been removed from the form.");
}

// Click event handler for a Button control. Adds a TextBox ↵
to the form.
private void addControl_Click(object sender, System.EventArgs e)
{
    // Create a new TextBox control and add it to the form.
    TextBox textBox1 = new TextBox();
    textBox1.Size = new Size(100,10);
    textBox1.Location = new Point(10,10);
    // Name the control in order to remove it later. The name ↵
 must be specified
    // if a control is added at run time.
    textBox1.Name = "textBox1";

    // Add the control to the form's control collection.
    this.Controls.Add(textBox1);
}

// Click event handler for a Button control.
// Removes the previously added TextBox from the form.
private void removeControl_Click(object sender, System.EventArgs e)
{
    // Loop through all controls in the form's control collection.
    foreach (Control tempCtrl in this.Controls)
    {
        // Determine whether the control is textBox1,
        // and if it is, remove it.
        if (tempCtrl.Name == "textBox1")
        {
            this.Controls.Remove(tempCtrl);
        }
    }
}
```

Requirements

Namespace: System.Windows.Forms

Platforms: Windows 98, Windows NT 4.0, Windows Millennium Edition, Windows 2000, Windows XP Home Edition, Windows XP Professional, Windows Server 2003 family

Assembly: System.Windows.Forms (in System.Windows.Forms.dll)

ControlEventArgs Constructor

Initializes a new instance of the **ControlEventArgs** class for the specified control.

```
[Visual Basic]
Public Sub New( _
   ByVal control As Control _
)
[C#]
public ControlEventArgs(
   Control control
);
[C++]
public: ControlEventArgs(
   Control* control
);
[JScript]
public function ControlEventArgs(
   control : Control
);
```

Parameters

control

The **Control** to store in this event.

Example

See related example in the **System.Windows.Forms.Control.EventArgs** class topic.

Requirements

Platforms: Windows 98, Windows NT 4.0, Windows Millennium Edition, Windows 2000, Windows XP Home Edition, Windows XP Professional, Windows Server 2003 family

ControlEventArgs.Control Property

Gets the control object used by this event.

```
[Visual Basic]
Public ReadOnly Property Control As Control
[C#]
public Control Control {get;}
[C++]
public: __property Control* get_Control();
[JScript]
public function get Control() : Control;
```

Property Value

The **Control** used by this event.

Example

See related example in the **System.Windows.Forms.Control.EventArgs** class topic.

Requirements

Platforms: Windows 98, Windows NT 4.0, Windows Millennium Edition, Windows 2000, Windows XP Home Edition, Windows XP Professional, Windows Server 2003 family

ControlEventHandler Delegate

Represents the method that will handle the **ControlAdded** and **ControlRemoved** events of the **Control** class.

[Visual Basic]
```
<Serializable>
Public Delegate Sub ControlEventHandler( _
   ByVal sender As Object, _
   ByVal e As ControlEventArgs _
)
```
[C#]
```
[Serializable]
public delegate void ControlEventHandler(
   object sender,
   ControlEventArgs e
);
```
[C++]
```
[Serializable]
public __gc __delegate void ControlEventHandler(
   Object* sender,
   ControlEventArgs* e
);
```

[JScript] In JScript, you can use the delegates in the .NET Framework, but you cannot define your own.

Parameters [Visual Basic, C#, C++]

The declaration of your event handler must have the same parameters as the **ControlEventHandler** delegate declaration.

sender
The source of the event.

e
A **ControlEventArgs** that contains the event data.

Remarks

When you create a **ControlEventArgs** delegate, you identify the method that will handle the event. To associate the event with your event handler, add an instance of the delegate to the event. The event handler is called whenever the event occurs, unless you remove the delegate. For more information about event handler delegates, see **Events and Delegates**.

Example

[Visual Basic, C#] The following example creates a **Binding**, adds a **ConvertEventHandler** delegate to both the **Parse** and **Format** events, and adds the **Binding** to the **BindingsCollection** of a **TextBox** control through the **DataBindings** property. The **DecimalToCurrencyString** event delegate, added to the **Format** event, formats the bound value (a **Decimal** type) as currency using the **ToString** method. The **CurrencyStringToDecimal** event delegate, added to the **Parse** event, converts the value displayed by the control back to the **Decimal** type.

[Visual Basic]
```
Private Sub BindControl()
    ' Create the binding first. The OrderAmount is typed as Decimal.
    Dim b As New Binding("Text", ds,
"customers.custToOrders.OrderAmount")
    ' Add the delegates to the events.
    AddHandler b.Format, AddressOf DecimalToCurrencyString
    AddHandler b.Parse, AddressOf CurrencyStringToDecimal
    text1.DataBindings.Add(b)
End Sub 'BindControl

Private Sub DecimalToCurrencyString(sender As Object,
cevent As ConvertEventArgs)
    ' Check for the appropriate DesiredType.
    If Not cevent.DesiredType Is GetType(String) Then
        Return
    End If
    ' Use the ToString method to format the value as currency ("c").
    cevent.Value = CDec(cevent.Value).ToString("c")
End Sub 'DecimalToCurrencyString

Private Sub CurrencyStringToDecimal(sender As Object,
 cevent As ConvertEventArgs)
    ' Check for the appropriate DesiredType.
    If Not cevent.DesiredType Is GetType(Decimal) Then
        Return
    End If
    ' Convert the string back to decimal using the static Parse method.
  cevent.Value = Decimal.Parse(cevent.Value.ToString, _
  NumberStyles.Currency, nothing)

End Sub 'CurrencyStringToDecimal
```
[C#]
```
private void BindControl()
{
   // Create the binding first. The OrderAmount is typed as Decimal.
   Binding b = new Binding
      ("Text", ds, "customers.custToOrders.OrderAmount");
   // Add the delegates to the events.
   b.Format += new ConvertEventHandler(DecimalToCurrencyString);
   b.Parse += new ConvertEventHandler(CurrencyStringToDecimal);
   text1.DataBindings.Add(b);
}

private void DecimalToCurrencyString(object sender,
 ConvertEventArgs cevent)
{
   // Check for the appropriate DesiredType.
   if(cevent.DesiredType != typeof(string)) return;

   // Use the ToString method to format the value as currency ("c").
   cevent.Value = ((decimal) cevent.Value).ToString("c");
}

private void CurrencyStringToDecimal(object sender,
ConvertEventArgs cevent)
{
   // Check for the appropriate DesiredType.
   if(cevent.DesiredType != typeof(decimal)) return;

   // Convert the string back to decimal using the static Parse method.
   cevent.Value = Decimal.Parse(cevent.Value.ToString(),
   NumberStyles.Currency, null);
}
```

Requirements

Namespace: System.Windows.Forms

Platforms: Windows 98, Windows NT 4.0, Windows Millennium Edition, Windows 2000, Windows XP Home Edition, Windows XP Professional, Windows Server 2003 family

Assembly: System.Windows.Forms (in System.Windows.Forms.dll)

ControlPaint Class

Provides methods used to paint common Windows controls and their elements.

System.Object
System.Windows.Forms.ControlPaint

[Visual Basic]
```
NotInheritable Public Class ControlPaint
```
[C#]
```
public sealed class ControlPaint
```
[C++]
```
public __gc __sealed class ControlPaint
```
[JScript]
```
public class ControlPaint
```

Thread Safety

Any public static (**Shared** in Visual Basic) members of this type are safe for multithreaded operations. Any instance members are not guaranteed to be thread safe.

Remarks

The methods contained in the **ControlPaint** class allow you to draw your own controls or elements of controls. You can control the drawing of your own controls if the **UserPaint** bit is set to **true** for the control. You can get or set the style bits by calling the **Control.GetStyle** or **Control.SetStyle** methods. You can set multiple style bits for any control. The **ControlStyles** enumeration members can be combined with bitwise operations.

Example

[Visual Basic]
```
Imports System
Imports System.Drawing
Imports System.Windows.Forms

    Public Class Form1
        Inherits System.Windows.Forms.Form

        Private button1 As System.Windows.Forms.Button = New Button
        Private button2 As System.Windows.Forms.Button = New Button

        <System.STAThreadAttribute()> _
        Public Shared Sub Main()
            System.Windows.Forms.Application.Run(New Form1)
        End Sub

        Public Sub New()
            Me.button2.Location = New Point(0, button1.Height + 10)
            AddHandler Me.button2.Click, AddressOf Me.button2_Click
            Me.Controls.Add(Me.button1)
            Me.Controls.Add(Me.button2)
        End Sub

        Private Sub button2_Click(sender As Object, e As ↵
System.EventArgs)
            ' Draws a flat button on button1.
            ControlPaint.DrawButton ↵
 (System.Drawing.Graphics.FromHwnd(button1.Handle), 0, 0, ↵
button1.Width, button1.Height, ButtonState.Flat)
        End Sub 'button2_Click
End Class
```

[C#]
```
using System;
using System.Drawing;
using System.Windows.Forms;

public class Form1 : Form
{
    private Button button1 = new Button();
    private Button button2 = new Button();

    [STAThread]
    static void Main()
    {
        Application.Run(new Form1());
    }

    public Form1(){
        this.button2.Location = new Point(0, button1.Height + 10);
        this.Click += new EventHandler(this.button2_Click);
        this.Controls.Add(this.button1);
        this.Controls.Add(this.button2);
    }

    private void button2_Click(object sender, System.EventArgs e)
    {
        // Draws a flat button on button1.
        ControlPaint.DrawButton(
        System.Drawing.Graphics.FromHwnd ↵
 (button1.Handle),0,0,button1.Width,button1.Height,
             ButtonState.Flat);
    }
}
```

[C++]
```
#using <mscorlib.dll>
#using <System.dll>
#using <System.Drawing.dll>
#using <System.Windows.Forms.dll>

using namespace System;
using namespace System::Drawing;
using namespace System::Windows::Forms;

public __gc class Form1 : public Form {

    private:
        Button* button1;
        Button* button2;

    public:
        Form1() {
            button1 = new Button();
            button2 = new Button();

            this->button2->Location = Point(0, button1->Height + 10);
            this->Click += new EventHandler(this, button2_Click);
            this->Controls->Add(this->button1);
            this->Controls->Add(this->button2);
        }

    private:
        void button2_Click(Object* sender, System::EventArgs* e) {
            // Draws a flat button on button1.
            ControlPaint::DrawButton ↵
 (System::Drawing::Graphics::FromHwnd(button1->Handle),
                0, 0, button1->Width, button1->Height, ↵
ButtonState::Flat);
        }
};

[STAThread]
void main() {
    Application::Run(new Form1());
}
```

Requirements

Namespace: System.Windows.Forms

Platforms: Windows 98, Windows NT 4.0, Windows Millennium Edition, Windows 2000, Windows XP Home Edition, Windows XP Professional, Windows Server 2003 family

Assembly: System.Windows.Forms (in System.Windows.Forms.dll)

ControlPaint.ContrastControlDark Property

Gets the color to use as the **ControlDark** color.

[Visual Basic]
```
Public Shared ReadOnly Property ContrastControlDark As Color
```
[C#]
```
public static Color ContrastControlDark {get;}
```
[C++]
```
public: __property static Color get_ContrastControlDark();
```
[JScript]
```
public static function get ContrastControlDark() : Color;
```

Property Value

The **Color** to use as the **ControlDark** color.

Remarks

If the user has enabled the **HighContrast** mode, this property is set to **SystemColors.WindowFrame**; otherwise, it is set to **SystemColors.ControlDark**.

Requirements

Platforms: Windows 98, Windows NT 4.0, Windows Millennium Edition, Windows 2000, Windows XP Home Edition, Windows XP Professional, Windows Server 2003 family

ControlPaint.CreateHBitmap16Bit Method

This member supports the .NET Framework infrastructure and is not intended to be used directly from your code.

[Visual Basic]
```
Public Shared Function CreateHBitmap16Bit( _
   ByVal bitmap As Bitmap, _
   ByVal background As Color _
) As IntPtr
```
[C#]
```
public static IntPtr CreateHBitmap16Bit(
   Bitmap bitmap,
   Color background
);
```
[C++]
```
public: static IntPtr CreateHBitmap16Bit(
   Bitmap* bitmap,
   Color background
);
```
[JScript]
```
public static function CreateHBitmap16Bit(
   bitmap : Bitmap,
   background : Color
) : IntPtr;
```

ControlPaint.CreateHBitmapColorMask Method

This member supports the .NET Framework infrastructure and is not intended to be used directly from your code.

[Visual Basic]
```
Public Shared Function CreateHBitmapColorMask( _
   ByVal bitmap As Bitmap, _
   ByVal monochromeMask As IntPtr _
) As IntPtr
```
[C#]
```
public static IntPtr CreateHBitmapColorMask(
   Bitmap bitmap,
   IntPtr monochromeMask
);
```
[C++]
```
public: static IntPtr CreateHBitmapColorMask(
   Bitmap* bitmap,
   IntPtr monochromeMask
);
```
[JScript]
```
public static function CreateHBitmapColorMask(
   bitmap : Bitmap,
   monochromeMask : IntPtr
) : IntPtr;
```

ControlPaint.CreateHBitmapTransparencyMask Method

This member supports the .NET Framework infrastructure and is not intended to be used directly from your code.

[Visual Basic]
```
Public Shared Function CreateHBitmapTransparencyMask( _
   ByVal bitmap As Bitmap _
) As IntPtr
```
[C#]
```
public static IntPtr CreateHBitmapTransparencyMask(
   Bitmap bitmap
);
```
[C++]
```
public: static IntPtr CreateHBitmapTransparencyMask(
   Bitmap* bitmap
);
```
[JScript]
```
public static function CreateHBitmapTransparencyMask(
   bitmap : Bitmap
) : IntPtr;
```

ControlPaint.Dark Method

Creates a new dark color object for the control.

Overload List

Creates a new dark color object for the control from the specified color.

[Visual Basic] **Overloads Public Shared Function Dark(Color) As Color**

[C#] **public static Color Dark(Color);**

[C++] **public: static Color Dark(Color);**

[JScript] **public static function Dark(Color) : Color;**

Creates a new dark color object for the control from the specified color and darkens it by the specified percentage.

[Visual Basic] **Overloads Public Shared Function Dark(Color, Single) As Color**

[C#] **public static Color Dark(Color, float);**

[C++] **public: static Color Dark(Color, float);**

[JScript] **public static function Dark(Color, float) : Color;**

ControlPaint.Dark Method (Color)

Creates a new dark color object for the control from the specified color.

[Visual Basic]
```
Overloads Public Shared Function Dark( _
   ByVal baseColor As Color _
) As Color
```
[C#]
```
public static Color Dark(
   Color baseColor
);
```
[C++]
```
public: static Color Dark(
   Color baseColor
);
```
[JScript]
```
public static function Dark(
   baseColor : Color
) : Color;
```

Parameters

baseColor

The **Color** to be darkened.

Return Value

A **Color** that represents the dark color on the control.

Remarks

If the specified **Color** is one of the **SystemColors**, the color is converted to a **SystemColors.ControlDark** color; otherwise, the color's luminosity value is decreased.

Requirements

Platforms: Windows 98, Windows NT 4.0, Windows Millennium Edition, Windows 2000, Windows XP Home Edition, Windows XP Professional, Windows Server 2003 family

ControlPaint.Dark Method (Color, Single)

Creates a new dark color object for the control from the specified color and darkens it by the specified percentage.

[Visual Basic]
```
Overloads Public Shared Function Dark( _
   ByVal baseColor As Color, _
   ByVal percOfDarkDark As Single _
) As Color
```
[C#]
```
public static Color Dark(
   Color baseColor,
   float percOfDarkDark
);
```
[C++]
```
public: static Color Dark(
   Color baseColor,
   float percOfDarkDark
);
```
[JScript]
```
public static function Dark(
   baseColor : Color,
   percOfDarkDark : float
) : Color;
```

Parameters

baseColor

The **Color** to be darkened.

percOfDarkDark

The percentage to darken the specified **Color**.

Return Value

A **Color** that represent the dark color on the control.

Remarks

If the specified **Color** is one of the **SystemColors**, the color is converted to a **SystemColors.ControlDark** color; otherwise, the color's luminosity value is decreased.

Requirements

Platforms: Windows 98, Windows NT 4.0, Windows Millennium Edition, Windows 2000, Windows XP Home Edition, Windows XP Professional, Windows Server 2003 family

ControlPaint.DarkDark Method

Creates a new dark color object for the control from the specified color.

[Visual Basic]
```
Public Shared Function DarkDark( _
   ByVal baseColor As Color _
) As Color
```
[C#]
```
public static Color DarkDark(
   Color baseColor
);
```
[C++]
```
public: static Color DarkDark(
   Color baseColor
);
```
[JScript]
```
public static function DarkDark(
   baseColor : Color
) : Color;
```

Parameters

baseColor

The **Color** to be darkened.

Return Value

A **Color** that represents the dark color on the control.

Remarks

If the specified **Color** is one of the **SystemColors**, the color is converted to the **SystemColors.ControlDarkDark** color; otherwise, the color's luminosity value is increased.

Requirements

Platforms: Windows 98, Windows NT 4.0, Windows Millennium Edition, Windows 2000, Windows XP Home Edition, Windows XP Professional, Windows Server 2003 family

ControlPaint.DrawBorder Method

Draws a border on a button-style control.

Overload List

Draws a border with the specified style and color, on the specified graphics surface, and within the specified bounds on a button-style control.

[Visual Basic] **Overloads Public Shared Sub DrawBorder(Graphics, Rectangle, Color, ButtonBorderStyle)**

[C#] **public static void DrawBorder(Graphics, Rectangle, Color, ButtonBorderStyle);**

[C++] **public: static void DrawBorder(Graphics*, Rectangle, Color, ButtonBorderStyle);**

[JScript] **public static function DrawBorder(Graphics, Rectangle, Color, ButtonBorderStyle);**

Draws a border on a button-style control with the specified styles, colors, and border widths, on the specified graphics surface, and within the specified bounds.

[Visual Basic] **Overloads Public Shared Sub DrawBorder(Graphics, Rectangle, Color, Integer, ButtonBorderStyle, Color, Integer, ButtonBorderStyle, Color, Integer, ButtonBorderStyle, Color, Integer, ButtonBorderStyle)**

[C#] **public static void DrawBorder(Graphics, Rectangle, Color, int, ButtonBorderStyle, Color, int, ButtonBorderStyle, Color, int, ButtonBorderStyle, Color, int, ButtonBorderStyle);**

[C++] **public: static void DrawBorder(Graphics*, Rectangle, Color, int, ButtonBorderStyle, Color, int, ButtonBorderStyle, Color, int, ButtonBorderStyle, Color, int, ButtonBorderStyle);**

[JScript] **public static function DrawBorder(Graphics, Rectangle, Color, int, ButtonBorderStyle, Color, int, ButtonBorderStyle, Color, int, ButtonBorderStyle, Color, int, ButtonBorderStyle);**

ControlPaint.DrawBorder Method (Graphics, Rectangle, Color, ButtonBorderStyle)

Draws a border with the specified style and color, on the specified graphics surface, and within the specified bounds on a button-style control.

[Visual Basic]
```
Overloads Public Shared Sub DrawBorder( _
   ByVal graphics As Graphics, _
   ByVal bounds As Rectangle, _
   ByVal color As Color, _
   ByVal style As ButtonBorderStyle _
)
```
[C#]
```
public static void DrawBorder(
   Graphics graphics,
   Rectangle bounds,
   Color color,
   ButtonBorderStyle style
);
```
[C++]
```
public: static void DrawBorder(
   Graphics* graphics,
   Rectangle bounds,
   Color color,
   ButtonBorderStyle style
);
```
[JScript]
```
public static function DrawBorder(
   graphics : Graphics,
   bounds : Rectangle,
   color : Color,
   style : ButtonBorderStyle
);
```

Parameters

graphics
The **Graphics** to draw on.

bounds
The **Rectangle** that represents the dimensions of the border.

color
The **Color** of the border.

style
One of the **ButtonBorderStyle** values that specifies the style of the border.

Requirements

Platforms: Windows 98, Windows NT 4.0, Windows Millennium Edition, Windows 2000, Windows XP Home Edition, Windows XP Professional, Windows Server 2003 family

ControlPaint.DrawBorder Method (Graphics, Rectangle, Color, Int32, ButtonBorderStyle, Color, Int32, ButtonBorderStyle, Color, Int32, ButtonBorderStyle, Color, Int32, ButtonBorderStyle)

Draws a border on a button-style control with the specified styles, colors, and border widths, on the specified graphics surface, and within the specified bounds.

[Visual Basic]
```
Overloads Public Shared Sub DrawBorder( _
   ByVal graphics As Graphics, _
   ByVal bounds As Rectangle, _
   ByVal leftColor As Color, _
   ByVal leftWidth As Integer, _
   ByVal leftStyle As ButtonBorderStyle, _
   ByVal topColor As Color, _
   ByVal topWidth As Integer, _
   ByVal topStyle As ButtonBorderStyle, _
   ByVal rightColor As Color, _
   ByVal rightWidth As Integer, _
   ByVal rightStyle As ButtonBorderStyle, _
   ByVal bottomColor As Color, _
   ByVal bottomWidth As Integer, _
   ByVal bottomStyle As ButtonBorderStyle _
)
```

[C#]
```
public static void DrawBorder(
   Graphics graphics,
   Rectangle bounds,
   Color leftColor,
   int leftWidth,
   ButtonBorderStyle leftStyle,
   Color topColor,
   int topWidth,
   ButtonBorderStyle topStyle,
   Color rightColor,
   int rightWidth,
   ButtonBorderStyle rightStyle,
   Color bottomColor,
   int bottomWidth,
   ButtonBorderStyle bottomStyle
);
```
[C++]
```
public: static void DrawBorder(
   Graphics* graphics,
   Rectangle bounds,
   Color leftColor,
   int leftWidth,
   ButtonBorderStyle leftStyle,
   Color topColor,
   int topWidth,
   ButtonBorderStyle topStyle,
   Color rightColor,
   int rightWidth,
   ButtonBorderStyle rightStyle,
   Color bottomColor,
   int bottomWidth,
   ButtonBorderStyle bottomStyle
);
```
[JScript]
```
public static function DrawBorder(
   graphics : Graphics,
   bounds : Rectangle,
   leftColor : Color,
   leftWidth : int,
   leftStyle : ButtonBorderStyle,
   topColor : Color,
   topWidth : int,
   topStyle : ButtonBorderStyle,
   rightColor : Color,
   rightWidth : int,
   rightStyle : ButtonBorderStyle,
   bottomColor : Color,
   bottomWidth : int,
   bottomStyle : ButtonBorderStyle
);
```

Parameters

graphics
: The **Graphics** to draw on.

bounds
: The **Rectangle** that represents the dimensions of the border.

leftColor
: The **Color** of the left of the border.

leftWidth
: The width of the left border.

leftStyle
: One of the **ButtonBorderStyle** values that specifies the style of the left border.

topColor
: The **Color** of the top of the border.

topWidth
: The width of the top border.

topStyle
: One of the **ButtonBorderStyle** values that specifies the style of the top border.

rightColor
: The **Color** of the right of the border.

rightWidth
: The width of the right border.

rightStyle
: One of the **ButtonBorderStyle** values that specifies the style of the right border.

bottomColor
: The **Color** of the bottom of the border.

bottomWidth
: The width of the left border.

bottomStyle
: One of the **ButtonBorderStyle** values that specifies the style of the bottom border.

Requirements

Platforms: Windows 98, Windows NT 4.0, Windows Millennium Edition, Windows 2000, Windows XP Home Edition, Windows XP Professional, Windows Server 2003 family

ControlPaint.DrawBorder3D Method

Draws a three-dimensional style border on a control.

Overload List

Draws a three-dimensional style border on the specified graphics surface and within the specified bounds on a control.

[Visual Basic] **Overloads Public Shared Sub DrawBorder3D(Graphics, Rectangle)**

[C#] **public static void DrawBorder3D(Graphics, Rectangle);**

[C++] **public: static void DrawBorder3D(Graphics*, Rectangle);**

[JScript] **public static function DrawBorder3D(Graphics, Rectangle);**

Draws a three-dimensional style border with the specified style, on the specified graphics surface, and within the specified bounds on a control.

[Visual Basic] **Overloads Public Shared Sub DrawBorder3D(Graphics, Rectangle, Border3DStyle)**

[C#] **public static void DrawBorder3D(Graphics, Rectangle, Border3DStyle);**

[C++] **public: static void DrawBorder3D(Graphics*, Rectangle, Border3DStyle);**

[JScript] **public static function DrawBorder3D(Graphics, Rectangle, Border3DStyle);**

Draws a three-dimensional style border with the specified style, on the specified graphics surface and sides, and within the specified bounds on a control.

[Visual Basic] **Overloads Public Shared Sub DrawBorder3D(Graphics, Rectangle, Border3DStyle, Border3DSide)**

[C#] **public static void DrawBorder3D(Graphics, Rectangle, Border3DStyle, Border3DSide);**

[C++] **public: static void DrawBorder3D(Graphics*, Rectangle, Border3DStyle, Border3DSide);**

[JScript] **public static function DrawBorder3D(Graphics, Rectangle, Border3DStyle, Border3DSide);**

Draws a three-dimensional style border on the specified graphics surface and within the specified bounds on a control.

[Visual Basic] **Overloads Public Shared Sub DrawBorder3D(Graphics, Integer, Integer, Integer, Integer)**

[C#] **public static void DrawBorder3D(Graphics, int, int, int, int);**

[C++] **public: static void DrawBorder3D(Graphics*, int, int, int, int);**

[JScript] **public static function DrawBorder3D(Graphics, int, int, int, int);**

Draws a three-dimensional style border with the specified style, on the specified graphics surface, and within the specified bounds on a control.

[Visual Basic] **Overloads Public Shared Sub DrawBorder3D(Graphics, Integer, Integer, Integer, Integer, Border3DStyle)**

[C#] **public static void DrawBorder3D(Graphics, int, int, int, int, Border3DStyle);**

[C++] **public: static void DrawBorder3D(Graphics*, int, int, int, int, Border3DStyle);**

[JScript] **public static function DrawBorder3D(Graphics, int, int, int, int, Border3DStyle);**

Draws a three-dimensional style border with the specified style, on the specified graphics surface and side, and within the specified bounds on a control.

[Visual Basic] **Overloads Public Shared Sub DrawBorder3D(Graphics, Integer, Integer, Integer, Integer, Border3DStyle, Border3DSide)**

[C#] **public static void DrawBorder3D(Graphics, int, int, int, int, Border3DStyle, Border3DSide);**

[C++] **public: static void DrawBorder3D(Graphics*, int, int, int, int, Border3DStyle, Border3DSide);**

[JScript] **public static function DrawBorder3D(Graphics, int, int, int, int, Border3DStyle, Border3DSide);**

ControlPaint.DrawBorder3D Method (Graphics, Rectangle)

Draws a three-dimensional style border on the specified graphics surface and within the specified bounds on a control.

```
[Visual Basic]
Overloads Public Shared Sub DrawBorder3D( _
   ByVal graphics As Graphics, _
   ByVal rectangle As Rectangle _
)
[C#]
public static void DrawBorder3D(
   Graphics graphics,
   Rectangle rectangle
);
[C++]
public: static void DrawBorder3D(
   Graphics* graphics,
   Rectangle rectangle
);
[JScript]
public static function DrawBorder3D(
   graphics : Graphics,
   rectangle : Rectangle
);
```

Parameters

graphics
  The **Graphics** to draw on.

rectangle
  The **Rectangle** that represents the dimensions of the border.

Remarks

The **Border3DStyle.Etched** style is used by default to draw the border.

Requirements

Platforms: Windows 98, Windows NT 4.0, Windows Millennium Edition, Windows 2000, Windows XP Home Edition, Windows XP Professional, Windows Server 2003 family

ControlPaint.DrawBorder3D Method (Graphics, Rectangle, Border3DStyle)

Draws a three-dimensional style border with the specified style, on the specified graphics surface, and within the specified bounds on a control.

```
[Visual Basic]
Overloads Public Shared Sub DrawBorder3D( _
   ByVal graphics As Graphics, _
   ByVal rectangle As Rectangle, _
   ByVal style As Border3DStyle _
)
[C#]
public static void DrawBorder3D(
   Graphics graphics,
   Rectangle rectangle,
   Border3DStyle style
);
[C++]
public: static void DrawBorder3D(
   Graphics* graphics,
   Rectangle rectangle,
   Border3DStyle style
);
[JScript]
public static function DrawBorder3D(
   graphics : Graphics,
   rectangle : Rectangle,
   style : Border3DStyle
);
```

Parameters

graphics
The **Graphics** to draw on.

rectangle
The **Rectangle** that represents the dimensions of the border.

style
One of the **Border3DStyle** values that specifies the style of the border.

Requirements

Platforms: Windows 98, Windows NT 4.0, Windows Millennium Edition, Windows 2000, Windows XP Home Edition, Windows XP Professional, Windows Server 2003 family

ControlPaint.DrawBorder3D Method (Graphics, Rectangle, Border3DStyle, Border3DSide)

Draws a three-dimensional style border with the specified style, on the specified graphics surface and sides, and within the specified bounds on a control.

```
[Visual Basic]
Overloads Public Shared Sub DrawBorder3D( _
   ByVal graphics As Graphics, _
   ByVal rectangle As Rectangle, _
   ByVal style As Border3DStyle, _
   ByVal sides As Border3DSide _
)
[C#]
public static void DrawBorder3D(
   Graphics graphics,
   Rectangle rectangle,
   Border3DStyle style,
   Border3DSide sides
);
[C++]
public: static void DrawBorder3D(
   Graphics* graphics,
   Rectangle rectangle,
   Border3DStyle style,
   Border3DSide sides
);
[JScript]
public static function DrawBorder3D(
   graphics : Graphics,
   rectangle : Rectangle,
   style : Border3DStyle,
   sides : Border3DSide
);
```

Parameters

graphics
The **Graphics** to draw on.

rectangle
The **Rectangle** that represents the dimensions of the border.

style
One of the **Border3DStyle** values that specifies the style of the border.

sides
One of the **Border3DSide** values that specifies the side of the rectangle to draw the border on.

Requirements

Platforms: Windows 98, Windows NT 4.0, Windows Millennium Edition, Windows 2000, Windows XP Home Edition, Windows XP Professional, Windows Server 2003 family

ControlPaint.DrawBorder3D Method (Graphics, Int32, Int32, Int32, Int32)

Draws a three-dimensional style border on the specified graphics surface and within the specified bounds on a control.

```
[Visual Basic]
Overloads Public Shared Sub DrawBorder3D( _
   ByVal graphics As Graphics, _
   ByVal x As Integer, _
   ByVal y As Integer, _
   ByVal width As Integer, _
   ByVal height As Integer _
)
[C#]
public static void DrawBorder3D(
   Graphics graphics,
   int x,
   int y,
   int width,
   int height
);
[C++]
public: static void DrawBorder3D(
   Graphics* graphics,
   int x,
   int y,
   int width,
   int height
);
[JScript]
public static function DrawBorder3D(
   graphics : Graphics,
   x : int,
   y : int,
   width : int,
   height : int
);
```

Parameters

graphics
The **Graphics** to draw on.

x
The x-coordinate of the top left of the border rectangle.

y
The y-coordinate of the top left of the border rectangle.

width
The width of the border rectangle.

height
The height of the border rectangle.

Remarks

The **Border3DStyle.Etched** style is used by default to draw the border.

Requirements

Platforms: Windows 98, Windows NT 4.0, Windows Millennium Edition, Windows 2000, Windows XP Home Edition, Windows XP Professional, Windows Server 2003 family

ControlPaint.DrawBorder3D Method (Graphics, Int32, Int32, Int32, Int32, Border3DStyle)

Draws a three-dimensional style border with the specified style, on the specified graphics surface, and within the specified bounds on a control.

```
[Visual Basic]
Overloads Public Shared Sub DrawBorder3D( _
   ByVal graphics As Graphics, _
   ByVal x As Integer, _
   ByVal y As Integer, _
   ByVal width As Integer, _
   ByVal height As Integer, _
   ByVal style As Border3DStyle _
)
[C#]
public static void DrawBorder3D(
   Graphics graphics,
   int x,
   int y,
   int width,
   int height,
   Border3DStyle style
);
[C++]
public: static void DrawBorder3D(
   Graphics* graphics,
   int x,
   int y,
   int width,
   int height,
   Border3DStyle style
);
[JScript]
public static function DrawBorder3D(
   graphics : Graphics,
   x : int,
   y : int,
   width : int,
   height : int,
   style : Border3DStyle
);
```

Parameters

graphics
The **Graphics** to draw on.

x
The x-coordinate of the top left of the border rectangle.

y
The y-coordinate of the top left of the border rectangle.

width
The width of the border rectangle.

height
The height of the border rectangle.

style
One of the **Border3DStyle** values that specifies the style of the border.

Requirements

Platforms: Windows 98, Windows NT 4.0, Windows Millennium Edition, Windows 2000, Windows XP Home Edition, Windows XP Professional, Windows Server 2003 family

ControlPaint.DrawBorder3D Method (Graphics, Int32, Int32, Int32, Int32, Border3DStyle, Border3DSide)

Draws a three-dimensional style border with the specified style, on the specified graphics surface and side, and within the specified bounds on a control.

```
[Visual Basic]
Overloads Public Shared Sub DrawBorder3D( _
   ByVal graphics As Graphics, _
   ByVal x As Integer, _
   ByVal y As Integer, _
   ByVal width As Integer, _
   ByVal height As Integer, _
   ByVal style As Border3DStyle, _
   ByVal sides As Border3DSide _
)
[C#]
public static void DrawBorder3D(
   Graphics graphics,
   int x,
   int y,
   int width,
   int height,
   Border3DStyle style,
   Border3DSide sides
);
[C++]
public: static void DrawBorder3D(
   Graphics* graphics,
   int x,
   int y,
   int width,
   int height,
   Border3DStyle style,
   Border3DSide sides
);
[JScript]
public static function DrawBorder3D(
   graphics : Graphics,
   x : int,
   y : int,
   width : int,
   height : int,
   style : Border3DStyle,
   sides : Border3DSide
);
```

Parameters

graphics
The **Graphics** to draw on.

x
The x-coordinate of the top left of the border rectangle.

y
The y-coordinate of the top left of the border rectangle.

width
The width of the border rectangle.

height
The height of the border rectangle.

style
One of the **Border3DStyle** values that specifies the style of the border.

sides
The **Border3DSide** of the rectangle to draw the border on.

Requirements

Platforms: Windows 98, Windows NT 4.0, Windows Millennium Edition, Windows 2000, Windows XP Home Edition, Windows XP Professional, Windows Server 2003 family

ControlPaint.DrawButton Method

Draws a button control.

Overload List

Draws a button control in the specified state, on the specified graphics surface, and within the specified bounds.

[Visual Basic] **Overloads Public Shared Sub DrawButton(Graphics, Rectangle, ButtonState)**

[C#] **public static void DrawButton(Graphics, Rectangle, ButtonState);**

[C++] **public: static void DrawButton(Graphics*, Rectangle, ButtonState);**

[JScript] **public static function DrawButton(Graphics, Rectangle, ButtonState);**

Draws a button control in the specified state, on the specified graphics surface, and within the specified bounds.

[Visual Basic] **Overloads Public Shared Sub DrawButton (Graphics, Integer, Integer, Integer, Integer, ButtonState)**

[C#] **public static void DrawButton(Graphics, int, int, int, int, ButtonState);**

[C++] **public: static void DrawButton(Graphics*, int, int, int, int, ButtonState);**

[JScript] **public static function DrawButton(Graphics, int, int, int, int, ButtonState);**

Example

See related example in the **System.Windows.Forms.Control.Paint** class topic.

ControlPaint.DrawButton Method (Graphics, Rectangle, ButtonState)

Draws a button control in the specified state, on the specified graphics surface, and within the specified bounds.

[Visual Basic]
```
Overloads Public Shared Sub DrawButton( _
   ByVal graphics As Graphics, _
   ByVal rectangle As Rectangle, _
   ByVal state As ButtonState _
)
```
[C#]
```
public static void DrawButton(
   Graphics graphics,
   Rectangle rectangle,
   ButtonState state
);
```
[C++]
```
public: static void DrawButton(
   Graphics* graphics,
   Rectangle rectangle,
   ButtonState state
);
```
[JScript]
```
public static function DrawButton(
   graphics : Graphics,
   rectangle : Rectangle,
   state : ButtonState
);
```

Parameters

graphics
The **Graphics** to draw on.

rectangle
The **Rectangle** that represents the dimensions of the button.

state
A bitwise combination of the **ButtonState** values that specifies the state to draw the button in.

Requirements

Platforms: Windows 98, Windows NT 4.0, Windows Millennium Edition, Windows 2000, Windows XP Home Edition, Windows XP Professional, Windows Server 2003 family

ControlPaint.DrawButton Method (Graphics, Int32, Int32, Int32, Int32, ButtonState)

Draws a button control in the specified state, on the specified graphics surface, and within the specified bounds.

[Visual Basic]
```
Overloads Public Shared Sub DrawButton( _
   ByVal graphics As Graphics, _
   ByVal x As Integer, _
   ByVal y As Integer, _
   ByVal width As Integer, _
   ByVal height As Integer, _
   ByVal state As ButtonState _
)
```
[C#]
```
public static void DrawButton(
   Graphics graphics,
   int x,
   int y,
   int width,
   int height,
   ButtonState state
);
```
[C++]
```
public: static void DrawButton(
   Graphics* graphics,
   int x,
   int y,
   int width,
   int height,
   ButtonState state
);
```

```
[JScript]
public static function DrawButton(
   graphics : Graphics,
   x : int,
   y : int,
   width : int,
   height : int,
   state : ButtonState
);
```

Parameters

graphics
The **Graphics** to draw on.

x
The x-coordinate of the upper left corner of the drawing rectangle.

y
The y-coordinate of the upper left corner of the drawing rectangle.

width
The widthof the button.

height
The height of the button.

state
A bitwise combination of the **ButtonState** values that specifies the state to draw the button in.

Example

See related example in the **System.Windows.Forms.Control.Paint** class topic.

Requirements

Platforms: Windows 98, Windows NT 4.0, Windows Millennium Edition, Windows 2000, Windows XP Home Edition, Windows XP Professional, Windows Server 2003 family

ControlPaint.DrawCaptionButton Method

Draws a caption button control.

Overload List

Draws the specified caption button control in the specified state, on the specified graphics surface, and within the specified bounds.

[Visual Basic] **Overloads Public Shared Sub DrawCaptionButton(Graphics, Rectangle, CaptionButton, ButtonState)**

[C#] **public static void DrawCaptionButton(Graphics, Rectangle, CaptionButton, ButtonState);**

[C++] **public: static void DrawCaptionButton(Graphics*, Rectangle, CaptionButton, ButtonState);**

[JScript] **public static function DrawCaptionButton(Graphics, Rectangle, CaptionButton, ButtonState);**

Draws the specified caption button control in the specified state, on the specified graphics surface, and within the specified bounds.

[Visual Basic] **Overloads Public Shared Sub DrawCaptionButton(Graphics, Integer, Integer, Integer, Integer, CaptionButton, ButtonState)**

[C#] **public static void DrawCaptionButton(Graphics, int, int, int, int, CaptionButton, ButtonState);**

[C++] **public: static void DrawCaptionButton(Graphics*, int, int, int, int, CaptionButton, ButtonState);**

[JScript] **public static function DrawCaptionButton (Graphics, int, int, int, int, CaptionButton, ButtonState);**

ControlPaint.DrawCaptionButton Method (Graphics, Rectangle, CaptionButton, ButtonState)

Draws the specified caption button control in the specified state, on the specified graphics surface, and within the specified bounds.

```
[Visual Basic]
Overloads Public Shared Sub DrawCaptionButton( _
   ByVal graphics As Graphics, _
   ByVal rectangle As Rectangle, _
   ByVal button As CaptionButton, _
   ByVal state As ButtonState _
)
[C#]
public static void DrawCaptionButton(
   Graphics graphics,
   Rectangle rectangle,
   CaptionButton button,
   ButtonState state
);
[C++]
public: static void DrawCaptionButton(
   Graphics* graphics,
   Rectangle rectangle,
   CaptionButton button,
   ButtonState state
);
[JScript]
public static function DrawCaptionButton(
   graphics : Graphics,
   rectangle : Rectangle,
   button : CaptionButton,
   state : ButtonState
);
```

Parameters

graphics
The **Graphics** to draw on.

rectangle
The **Rectangle** that represents the dimensions of the caption button.

button
One of the **CaptionButton** values that specifies the type of caption button to draw.

state
A bitwise combination of the **ButtonState** values that specifies the state to draw the button in.

Requirements

Platforms: Windows 98, Windows NT 4.0, Windows Millennium Edition, Windows 2000, Windows XP Home Edition, Windows XP Professional, Windows Server 2003 family

ControlPaint.DrawCaptionButton Method (Graphics, Int32, Int32, Int32, Int32, CaptionButton, ButtonState)

Draws the specified caption button control in the specified state, on the specified graphics surface, and within the specified bounds.

[Visual Basic]
```
Overloads Public Shared Sub DrawCaptionButton( _
   ByVal graphics As Graphics, _
   ByVal x As Integer, _
   ByVal y As Integer, _
   ByVal width As Integer, _
   ByVal height As Integer, _
   ByVal button As CaptionButton, _
   ByVal state As ButtonState _
)
```
[C#]
```
public static void DrawCaptionButton(
   Graphics graphics,
   int x,
   int y,
   int width,
   int height,
   CaptionButton button,
   ButtonState state
);
```
[C++]
```
public: static void DrawCaptionButton(
   Graphics* graphics,
   int x,
   int y,
   int width,
   int height,
   CaptionButton button,
   ButtonState state
);
```
[JScript]
```
public static function DrawCaptionButton(
   graphics : Graphics,
   x : int,
   y : int,
   width : int,
   height : int,
   button : CaptionButton,
   state : ButtonState
);
```

Parameters

graphics
   The **Graphics** object to draw on.

x
   The x-coordinate of the top left of the drawing rectangle.

y
   The y-coordinate of the top left of the drawing rectangle.

width
   The width of the drawing rectangle.

height
   The height of the drawing rectangle.

button
   One of the **CaptionButton** values that specifies the type of caption button to draw.

state
   A bitwise combination of the **ButtonState** values that specifies the state to draw the button in.

Requirements

Platforms: Windows 98, Windows NT 4.0, Windows Millennium Edition, Windows 2000, Windows XP Home Edition, Windows XP Professional, Windows Server 2003 family

ControlPaint.DrawCheckBox Method

Draws a check box control.

Overload List

Draws a check box control in the specified state, on the specified graphics surface, and within the specified bounds.

[Visual Basic] **Overloads Public Shared Sub DrawCheckBox(Graphics, Rectangle, ButtonState)**

[C#] **public static void DrawCheckBox(Graphics, Rectangle, ButtonState);**

[C++] **public: static void DrawCheckBox(Graphics*, Rectangle, ButtonState);**

[JScript] **public static function DrawCheckBox(Graphics, Rectangle, ButtonState);**

Draws a check box control in the specified state, on the specified graphics surface, and within the specified bounds.

[Visual Basic] **Overloads Public Shared Sub DrawCheckBox(Graphics, Integer, Integer, Integer, Integer, ButtonState)**

[C#] **public static void DrawCheckBox(Graphics, int, int, int, int, ButtonState);**

[C++] **public: static void DrawCheckBox(Graphics*, int, int, int, int, ButtonState);**

[JScript] **public static function DrawCheckBox(Graphics, int, int, int, int, ButtonState);**

ControlPaint.DrawCheckBox Method (Graphics, Rectangle, ButtonState)

Draws a check box control in the specified state, on the specified graphics surface, and within the specified bounds.

[Visual Basic]
```
Overloads Public Shared Sub DrawCheckBox( _
   ByVal graphics As Graphics, _
   ByVal rectangle As Rectangle, _
   ByVal state As ButtonState _
)
```
[C#]
```
public static void DrawCheckBox(
   Graphics graphics,
   Rectangle rectangle,
   ButtonState state
);
```
[C++]
```
public: static void DrawCheckBox(
   Graphics* graphics,
   Rectangle rectangle,
   ButtonState state
);
```
[JScript]
```
public static function DrawCheckBox(
   graphics : Graphics,
   rectangle : Rectangle,
   state : ButtonState
);
```

Parameters

graphics
: The **Graphics** to draw on.

rectangle
: The **Rectangle** that represents the dimensions of the check box.

state
: A bitwise combination of the **ButtonState** values that specifies the state to draw the check box in.

Requirements

Platforms: Windows 98, Windows NT 4.0, Windows Millennium Edition, Windows 2000, Windows XP Home Edition, Windows XP Professional, Windows Server 2003 family

ControlPaint.DrawCheckBox Method (Graphics, Int32, Int32, Int32, Int32, ButtonState)

Draws a check box control in the specified state, on the specified graphics surface, and within the specified bounds.

[Visual Basic]
```
Overloads Public Shared Sub DrawCheckBox( _
   ByVal graphics As Graphics, _
   ByVal x As Integer, _
   ByVal y As Integer, _
   ByVal width As Integer, _
   ByVal height As Integer, _
   ByVal state As ButtonState _
)
```
[C#]
```
public static void DrawCheckBox(
   Graphics graphics,
   int x,
   int y,
   int width,
   int height,
   ButtonState state
);
```
[C++]
```
public: static void DrawCheckBox(
   Graphics* graphics,
   int x,
   int y,
   int width,
   int height,
   ButtonState state
);
```
[JScript]
```
public static function DrawCheckBox(
   graphics : Graphics,
   x : int,
   y : int,
   width : int,
   height : int,
   state : ButtonState
);
```

Parameters

graphics
: The **Graphics** to draw on.

x
: The x-coordinate of the upper left corner of the drawing rectangle.

y
: The y-coordinate of the upper left corner of the drawing rectangle.

width
: The width of the check box.

height
: The height of the check box.

state
: A bitwise combination of the **ButtonState** values that specifies the state to draw the check box in.

Requirements

Platforms: Windows 98, Windows NT 4.0, Windows Millennium Edition, Windows 2000, Windows XP Home Edition, Windows XP Professional, Windows Server 2003 family

ControlPaint.DrawComboButton Method

Draws a drop-down button on a combo box control.

Overload List

Draws a drop-down button on a combo box control in the specified state, on the specified graphics surface, and within the specified bounds.

[Visual Basic] **Overloads Public Shared Sub DrawComboButton(Graphics, Rectangle, ButtonState)**

[C#] **public static void DrawComboButton(Graphics, Rectangle, ButtonState);**

[C++] **public: static void DrawComboButton(Graphics*, Rectangle, ButtonState);**

[JScript] **public static function DrawComboButton(Graphics, Rectangle, ButtonState);**

Draws a drop-down button on a combo box control in the specified state, on the specified graphics surface, and within the specified bounds.

[Visual Basic] **Overloads Public Shared Sub DrawComboButton(Graphics, Integer, Integer, Integer, Integer, ButtonState)**

[C#] **public static void DrawComboButton(Graphics, int, int, int, int, ButtonState);**

[C++] **public: static void DrawComboButton(Graphics*, int, int, int, int, ButtonState);**

[JScript] **public static function DrawComboButton(Graphics, int, int, int, int, ButtonState);**

ControlPaint.DrawComboButton Method (Graphics, Rectangle, ButtonState)

Draws a drop-down button on a combo box control in the specified state, on the specified graphics surface, and within the specified bounds.

[Visual Basic]
```
Overloads Public Shared Sub DrawComboButton( _
   ByVal graphics As Graphics, _
   ByVal rectangle As Rectangle, _
   ByVal state As ButtonState _
)
```

[C#]
```
public static void DrawComboButton(
   Graphics graphics,
   Rectangle rectangle,
   ButtonState state
);
```
[C++]
```
public: static void DrawComboButton(
   Graphics* graphics,
   Rectangle rectangle,
   ButtonState state
);
```
[JScript]
```
public static function DrawComboButton(
   graphics : Graphics,
   rectangle : Rectangle,
   state : ButtonState
);
```

Parameters

graphics
The **Graphics** to draw on.

rectangle
The **Rectangle** that represents the dimensions of the combo box.

state
A bitwise combination of the **ButtonState** values that specifies the state to draw the combo box in.

Requirements

Platforms: Windows 98, Windows NT 4.0, Windows Millennium Edition, Windows 2000, Windows XP Home Edition, Windows XP Professional, Windows Server 2003 family

ControlPaint.DrawComboButton Method (Graphics, Int32, Int32, Int32, Int32, ButtonState)

Draws a drop-down button on a combo box control in the specified state, on the specified graphics surface, and within the specified bounds.

[Visual Basic]
```
Overloads Public Shared Sub DrawComboButton( _
   ByVal graphics As Graphics, _
   ByVal x As Integer, _
   ByVal y As Integer, _
   ByVal width As Integer, _
   ByVal height As Integer, _
   ByVal state As ButtonState _
)
```
[C#]
```
public static void DrawComboButton(
   Graphics graphics,
   int x,
   int y,
   int width,
   int height,
   ButtonState state
);
```
[C++]
```
public: static void DrawComboButton(
   Graphics* graphics,
   int x,
   int y,
   int width,
   int height,
   ButtonState state
);
```
[JScript]
```
public static function DrawComboButton(
   graphics : Graphics,
   x : int,
   y : int,
   width : int,
   height : int,
   state : ButtonState
);
```

Parameters

graphics
The **Graphics** to draw on.

x
The x-coordinate of the top left of the border rectangle.

y
The y-coordinate of the top left of the border rectangle.

width
The width of the combo box.

height
The height of the combo box.

state
A bitwise combination of the **ButtonState** values that specifies the state to draw the combo box in.

Requirements

Platforms: Windows 98, Windows NT 4.0, Windows Millennium Edition, Windows 2000, Windows XP Home Edition, Windows XP Professional, Windows Server 2003 family

ControlPaint.DrawContainerGrabHandle Method

Draws a container control grab handle glyph on the specified graphics surface and within the specified bounds.

[Visual Basic]
```
Public Shared Sub DrawContainerGrabHandle( _
   ByVal graphics As Graphics, _
   ByVal bounds As Rectangle _
)
```
[C#]
```
public static void DrawContainerGrabHandle(
   Graphics graphics,
   Rectangle bounds
);
```
[C++]
```
public: static void DrawContainerGrabHandle(
   Graphics* graphics,
   Rectangle bounds
);
```

```
[JScript]
public static function DrawContainerGrabHandle(
   graphics : Graphics,
   bounds : Rectangle
);
```

Parameters

graphics
The **Graphics** to draw on.

bounds
The **Rectangle** that represents the dimensions of the grab handle glyph.

Remarks

Grab handles are used by containers to indicate to the user that the user can directly manipulate the containers. The manipulation can consist of actions such as sizing and moving.

Requirements

Platforms: Windows 98, Windows NT 4.0, Windows Millennium Edition, Windows 2000, Windows XP Home Edition, Windows XP Professional, Windows Server 2003 family

ControlPaint.DrawFocusRectangle Method

Draws a focus rectangle.

Overload List

Draws a focus rectangle on the specified graphics surface and within the specified bounds.

[Visual Basic] **Overloads Public Shared Sub DrawFocus-Rectangle(Graphics, Rectangle)**

[C#] **public static void DrawFocusRectangle(Graphics, Rectangle);**

[C++] **public: static void DrawFocusRectangle(Graphics*, Rectangle);**

[JScript] **public static function DrawFocus-Rectangle(Graphics, Rectangle);**

Draws a focus rectangle on the specified graphics surface and within the specified bounds.

[Visual Basic] **Overloads Public Shared Sub DrawFocus-Rectangle(Graphics, Rectangle, Color, Color)**

[C#] **public static void DrawFocusRectangle(Graphics, Rectangle, Color, Color);**

[C++] **public: static void DrawFocusRectangle(Graphics*, Rectangle, Color, Color);**

[JScript] **public static function DrawFocus-Rectangle(Graphics, Rectangle, Color, Color);**

ControlPaint.DrawFocusRectangle Method (Graphics, Rectangle)

Draws a focus rectangle on the specified graphics surface and within the specified bounds.

```
[Visual Basic]
Overloads Public Shared Sub DrawFocusRectangle( _
   ByVal graphics As Graphics, _
   ByVal rectangle As Rectangle _
)
[C#]
public static void DrawFocusRectangle(
   Graphics graphics,
   Rectangle rectangle
);
[C++]
public: static void DrawFocusRectangle(
   Graphics* graphics,
   Rectangle rectangle
);
[JScript]
public static function DrawFocusRectangle(
   graphics : Graphics,
   rectangle : Rectangle
);
```

Parameters

graphics
The **Graphics** to draw on.

rectangle
The **Rectangle** that represents the dimensions of the grab handle glyph.

Remarks

A focus rectangle is a dotted rectangle that Windows uses to indicate what control has the current keyboard focus.

Requirements

Platforms: Windows 98, Windows NT 4.0, Windows Millennium Edition, Windows 2000, Windows XP Home Edition, Windows XP Professional, Windows Server 2003 family

ControlPaint.DrawFocusRectangle Method (Graphics, Rectangle, Color, Color)

Draws a focus rectangle on the specified graphics surface and within the specified bounds.

```
[Visual Basic]
Overloads Public Shared Sub DrawFocusRectangle( _
   ByVal graphics As Graphics, _
   ByVal rectangle As Rectangle, _
   ByVal foreColor As Color, _
   ByVal backColor As Color _
)
[C#]
public static void DrawFocusRectangle(
   Graphics graphics,
   Rectangle rectangle,
   Color foreColor,
   Color backColor
);
[C++]
public: static void DrawFocusRectangle(
   Graphics* graphics,
   Rectangle rectangle,
   Color foreColor,
   Color backColor
);
```

```
[JScript]
public static function DrawFocusRectangle(
   graphics : Graphics,
   rectangle : Rectangle,
   foreColor : Color,
   backColor : Color
);
```

Parameters

graphics
The **Graphics** to draw on.

rectangle
The **Rectangle** that represents the dimensions of the grab handle glyph.

foreColor
The **Color** that is the foreground color of the object to draw the focus rectangle on.

backColor
The **Color** that is the foreground color of the object to draw the focus rectangle on.

Remarks

A focus rectangle is a dotted rectangle that Windows uses to indicate what control has the current keyboard focus.

Requirements

Platforms: Windows 98, Windows NT 4.0, Windows Millennium Edition, Windows 2000, Windows XP Home Edition, Windows XP Professional, Windows Server 2003 family

ControlPaint.DrawGrabHandle Method

Draws a standard selection grab handle glyph on the specified graphics surface, within the specified bounds, and in the specified state and style.

```
[Visual Basic]
Public Shared Sub DrawGrabHandle( _
   ByVal graphics As Graphics, _
   ByVal rectangle As Rectangle, _
   ByVal primary As Boolean, _
   ByVal enabled As Boolean _
)
[C#]
public static void DrawGrabHandle(
   Graphics graphics,
   Rectangle rectangle,
   bool primary,
   bool enabled
);
[C++]
public: static void DrawGrabHandle(
   Graphics* graphics,
   Rectangle rectangle,
   bool primary,
   bool enabled
);
[JScript]
public static function DrawGrabHandle(
   graphics : Graphics,
   rectangle : Rectangle,
   primary : Boolean,
   enabled : Boolean
);
```

Parameters

graphics
The **Graphics** to draw on.

rectangle
The **Rectangle** that represents the dimensions of the grab handle glyph.

primary
true to draw the handle as a primary grab handle; otherwise, **false**.

enabled
true to draw the handle in an enabled state; otherwise, **false**.

Remarks

Grab handles are used by objects to indicate to the user that the user can directly manipulate the object. The manipulation can consist of actions such as sizing and moving.

Requirements

Platforms: Windows 98, Windows NT 4.0, Windows Millennium Edition, Windows 2000, Windows XP Home Edition, Windows XP Professional, Windows Server 2003 family

ControlPaint.DrawGrid Method

Draws a grid of one-pixel dots with the specified spacing, within the specified bounds, on the specified graphics surface, and in the specified color.

```
[Visual Basic]
Public Shared Sub DrawGrid( _
   ByVal graphics As Graphics, _
   ByVal area As Rectangle, _
   ByVal pixelsBetweenDots As Size, _
   ByVal backColor As Color _
)
[C#]
public static void DrawGrid(
   Graphics graphics,
   Rectangle area,
   Size pixelsBetweenDots,
   Color backColor
);
[C++]
public: static void DrawGrid(
   Graphics* graphics,
   Rectangle area,
   Size pixelsBetweenDots,
   Color backColor
);
[JScript]
public static function DrawGrid(
   graphics : Graphics,
   area : Rectangle,
   pixelsBetweenDots : Size,
   backColor : Color
);
```

Parameters

graphics
The **Graphics** to draw on.

area
The **Rectangle** that represents the dimensions of the grab handle glyph.

pixelsBetweenDots
The **Size** that specified the height and width between the dots of the grid.

backColor
The **Color** of the background behind the grid.

Remarks

The *backColor* parameter is used to calculate the fill color of the dots so that the grid is always visible against the background.

Requirements

Platforms: Windows 98, Windows NT 4.0,
Windows Millennium Edition, Windows 2000,
Windows XP Home Edition, Windows XP Professional,
Windows Server 2003 family

ControlPaint.DrawImageDisabled Method

Draws the specified image in a disabled state.

```
[Visual Basic]
Public Shared Sub DrawImageDisabled( _
   ByVal graphics As Graphics, _
   ByVal image As Image, _
   ByVal x As Integer, _
   ByVal y As Integer, _
   ByVal background As Color _
)
[C#]
public static void DrawImageDisabled(
   Graphics graphics,
   Image image,
   int x,
   int y,
   Color background
);
[C++]
public: static void DrawImageDisabled(
   Graphics* graphics,
   Image* image,
   int x,
   int y,
   Color background
);
[JScript]
public static function DrawImageDisabled(
   graphics : Graphics,
   image : Image,
   x : int,
   y : int,
   background : Color
);
```

Parameters

graphics
The **Graphics** to draw on.

image
The **Image** to draw.

x
The x-coordinate of the top left of the border image.

y
The y-coordinate of the top left of the border image.

background
The **Color** of the background behind the image.

Remarks

The *background* parameter is used to calculate the fill color of the disabled image so that it is always visible against the background.

Requirements

Platforms: Windows 98, Windows NT 4.0,
Windows Millennium Edition, Windows 2000,
Windows XP Home Edition, Windows XP Professional,
Windows Server 2003 family

ControlPaint.DrawLockedFrame Method

Draws a locked selection frame on the screen within the specified bounds and on the specified graphics surface. Specifies whether to draw the frame with the primary selected colors.

```
[Visual Basic]
Public Shared Sub DrawLockedFrame( _
   ByVal graphics As Graphics, _
   ByVal rectangle As Rectangle, _
   ByVal primary As Boolean _
)
[C#]
public static void DrawLockedFrame(
   Graphics graphics,
   Rectangle rectangle,
   bool primary
);
[C++]
public: static void DrawLockedFrame(
   Graphics* graphics,
   Rectangle rectangle,
   bool primary
);
[JScript]
public static function DrawLockedFrame(
   graphics : Graphics,
   rectangle : Rectangle,
   primary : Boolean
);
```

Parameters

graphics
The **Graphics** to draw on.

rectangle
The **Rectangle** that represents the dimensions of the frame.

primary
true to draw this frame with the colors used for the primary selection; otherwise, **false**.

Requirements

Platforms: Windows 98, Windows NT 4.0,
Windows Millennium Edition, Windows 2000,
Windows XP Home Edition, Windows XP Professional,
Windows Server 2003 family

ControlPaint.DrawMenuGlyph Method

Draws a menu glyph on a menu item control.

Overload List

Draws the specified menu glyph on a menu item control within the specified bounds and on the specified surface.

[Visual Basic] **Overloads Public Shared Sub DrawMenuGlyph(Graphics, Rectangle, MenuGlyph)**

[C#] **public static void DrawMenuGlyph(Graphics, Rectangle, MenuGlyph);**

[C++] **public: static void DrawMenuGlyph(Graphics*, Rectangle, MenuGlyph);**

[JScript] **public static function DrawMenuGlyph(Graphics, Rectangle, MenuGlyph);**

Draws the specified menu glyph on a menu item control with the specified bounds and on the specified surface.

[Visual Basic] **Overloads Public Shared Sub DrawMenuGlyph(Graphics, Integer, Integer, Integer, Integer, MenuGlyph)**

[C#] **public static void DrawMenuGlyph(Graphics, int, int, int, int, MenuGlyph);**

[C++] **public: static void DrawMenuGlyph(Graphics*, int, int, int, int, MenuGlyph);**

[JScript] **public static function DrawMenuGlyph(Graphics, int, int, int, int, MenuGlyph);**

ControlPaint.DrawMenuGlyph Method (Graphics, Rectangle, MenuGlyph)

Draws the specified menu glyph on a menu item control within the specified bounds and on the specified surface.

```
[Visual Basic]
Overloads Public Shared Sub DrawMenuGlyph( _
   ByVal graphics As Graphics, _
   ByVal rectangle As Rectangle, _
   ByVal glyph As MenuGlyph _
)
[C#]
public static void DrawMenuGlyph(
   Graphics graphics,
   Rectangle rectangle,
   MenuGlyph glyph
);
[C++]
public: static void DrawMenuGlyph(
   Graphics* graphics,
   Rectangle rectangle,
   MenuGlyph glyph
);
[JScript]
public static function DrawMenuGlyph(
   graphics : Graphics,
   rectangle : Rectangle,
   glyph : MenuGlyph
);
```

Parameters

graphics
: The **Graphics** to draw on.

rectangle
: The **Rectangle** that represents the dimensions of the glyph.

glyph
: One of the **MenuGlyph** values that specifies the image to draw.

Remarks

When owner-drawing **MenuItem** controls, you need to verify property values to determine the correct glyph to draw or remove. For example, when the **MenuItem.Checked** property is set to **true**, you need to draw a **Checkmark** glyph on the **MenuItem**.

Requirements

Platforms: Windows 98, Windows NT 4.0, Windows Millennium Edition, Windows 2000, Windows XP Home Edition, Windows XP Professional, Windows Server 2003 family

ControlPaint.DrawMenuGlyph Method (Graphics, Int32, Int32, Int32, Int32, MenuGlyph)

Draws the specified menu glyph on a menu item control with the specified bounds and on the specified surface.

```
[Visual Basic]
Overloads Public Shared Sub DrawMenuGlyph( _
   ByVal graphics As Graphics, _
   ByVal x As Integer, _
   ByVal y As Integer, _
   ByVal width As Integer, _
   ByVal height As Integer, _
   ByVal glyph As MenuGlyph _
)
[C#]
public static void DrawMenuGlyph(
   Graphics graphics,
   int x,
   int y,
   int width,
   int height,
   MenuGlyph glyph
);
[C++]
public: static void DrawMenuGlyph(
   Graphics* graphics,
   int x,
   int y,
   int width,
   int height,
   MenuGlyph glyph
);
[JScript]
public static function DrawMenuGlyph(
   graphics : Graphics,
   x : int,
   y : int,
   width : int,
   height : int,
   glyph : MenuGlyph
);
```

Parameters

graphics
: The **Graphics** to draw on.

x
: The x-coordinate of the upper left corner of the drawing rectangle.

y
: The y-coordinate of the upper left corner of the drawing rectangle.

width
: The width of the menu glyph.

height
: The height of the menu glyph.

glyph
One of the **MenuGlyph** values that specifies the image to draw.

Remarks

When owner-drawing **MenuItem** controls, you need to verify property values to determine the correct glyph to draw or remove. For example, when the **MenuItem.Checked** property is set to **true**, you need to draw a **Checkmark** glyph on the **MenuItem**.

Requirements

Platforms: Windows 98, Windows NT 4.0, Windows Millennium Edition, Windows 2000, Windows XP Home Edition, Windows XP Professional, Windows Server 2003 family

ControlPaint.DrawMixedCheckBox Method

Draws a three-state check box control.

Overload List

Draws a three-state check box control in the specified state, on the specified graphics surface, and within the specified bounds.

[Visual Basic] **Overloads Public Shared Sub DrawMixedCheckBox(Graphics, Rectangle, ButtonState)**

[C#] **public static void DrawMixedCheckBox(Graphics, Rectangle, ButtonState);**

[C++] **public: static void DrawMixedCheckBox(Graphics*, Rectangle, ButtonState);**

[JScript] **public static function DrawMixedCheckBox(Graphics, Rectangle, ButtonState);**

Draws a three-state check box control in the specified state, on the specified graphics surface, and within the specified bounds.

[Visual Basic] **Overloads Public Shared Sub DrawMixedCheckBox(Graphics, Integer, Integer, Integer, Integer, ButtonState)**

[C#] **public static void DrawMixedCheckBox(Graphics, int, int, int, int, ButtonState);**

[C++] **public: static void DrawMixedCheckBox(Graphics*, int, int, int, int, ButtonState);**

[JScript] **public static function DrawMixedCheckBox(Graphics, int, int, int, int, ButtonState);**

ControlPaint.DrawMixedCheckBox Method (Graphics, Rectangle, ButtonState)

Draws a three-state check box control in the specified state, on the specified graphics surface, and within the specified bounds.

```
[Visual Basic]
Overloads Public Shared Sub DrawMixedCheckBox( _
   ByVal graphics As Graphics, _
   ByVal rectangle As Rectangle, _
   ByVal state As ButtonState _
)
[C#]
public static void DrawMixedCheckBox(
   Graphics graphics,
   Rectangle rectangle,
   ButtonState state
);
[C++]
public: static void DrawMixedCheckBox(
   Graphics* graphics,
   Rectangle rectangle,
   ButtonState state
);
[JScript]
public static function DrawMixedCheckBox(
   graphics : Graphics,
   rectangle : Rectangle,
   state : ButtonState
);
```

Parameters

graphics
The **Graphics** object to draw on.

rectangle
The **Rectangle** that represents the dimensions of the check box.

state
A bitwise combination of the **ButtonState** values that specifies the state to draw the check box in.

Requirements

Platforms: Windows 98, Windows NT 4.0, Windows Millennium Edition, Windows 2000, Windows XP Home Edition, Windows XP Professional, Windows Server 2003 family

ControlPaint.DrawMixedCheckBox Method (Graphics, Int32, Int32, Int32, Int32, ButtonState)

Draws a three-state check box control in the specified state, on the specified graphics surface, and within the specified bounds.

```
[Visual Basic]
Overloads Public Shared Sub DrawMixedCheckBox( _
   ByVal graphics As Graphics, _
   ByVal x As Integer, _
   ByVal y As Integer, _
   ByVal width As Integer, _
   ByVal height As Integer, _
   ByVal state As ButtonState _
)
[C#]
public static void DrawMixedCheckBox(
   Graphics graphics,
   int x,
   int y,
   int width,
   int height,
   ButtonState state
);
[C++]
public: static void DrawMixedCheckBox(
   Graphics* graphics,
   int x,
   int y,
   int width,
   int height,
   ButtonState state
);
```

```
[JScript]
public static function DrawMixedCheckBox(
   graphics : Graphics,
   x : int,
   y : int,
   width : int,
   height : int,
   state : ButtonState
);
```

Parameters

graphics
: The **Graphics** to draw on.

x
: The x-coordinate of the upper left corner of the drawing rectangle.

y
: The y-coordinate of the upper left corner of the drawing rectangle.

width
: The width of the check box.

height
: The height of the check box.

state
: A bitwise combination of the **ButtonState** values that specifies the state to draw the check box in.

Requirements

Platforms: Windows 98, Windows NT 4.0, Windows Millennium Edition, Windows 2000, Windows XP Home Edition, Windows XP Professional, Windows Server 2003 family

ControlPaint.DrawRadioButton Method

Draws a radio button control.

Overload List

Draws a radio button control in the specified state, on the specified graphics surface, and within the specified bounds.

[Visual Basic] **Overloads Public Shared Sub DrawRadioButton(Graphics, Rectangle, ButtonState)**

[C#] **public static void DrawRadioButton(Graphics, Rectangle, ButtonState);**

[C++] **public: static void DrawRadioButton(Graphics*, Rectangle, ButtonState);**

[JScript] **public static function DrawRadioButton(Graphics, Rectangle, ButtonState);**

Draws a radio button control in the specified state, on the specified graphics surface, and within the specified bounds.

[Visual Basic] **Overloads Public Shared Sub DrawRadioButton(Graphics, Integer, Integer, Integer, Integer, ButtonState)**

[C#] **public static void DrawRadioButton(Graphics, int, int, int, int, ButtonState);**

[C++] **public: static void DrawRadioButton(Graphics*, int, int, int, int, ButtonState);**

[JScript] **public static function DrawRadioButton(Graphics, int, int, int, int, ButtonState);**

ControlPaint.DrawRadioButton Method (Graphics, Rectangle, ButtonState)

Draws a radio button control in the specified state, on the specified graphics surface, and within the specified bounds.

```
[Visual Basic]
Overloads Public Shared Sub DrawRadioButton( _
   ByVal graphics As Graphics, _
   ByVal rectangle As Rectangle, _
   ByVal state As ButtonState _
)
[C#]
public static void DrawRadioButton(
   Graphics graphics,
   Rectangle rectangle,
   ButtonState state
);
[C++]
public: static void DrawRadioButton(
   Graphics* graphics,
   Rectangle rectangle,
   ButtonState state
);
[JScript]
public static function DrawRadioButton(
   graphics : Graphics,
   rectangle : Rectangle,
   state : ButtonState
);
```

Parameters

graphics
: The **Graphics** to draw on.

rectangle
: The **Rectangle** that represents the dimensions of the radio button.

state
: A bitwise combination of the **ButtonState** values that specifies the state to draw the radio button in.

Requirements

Platforms: Windows 98, Windows NT 4.0, Windows Millennium Edition, Windows 2000, Windows XP Home Edition, Windows XP Professional, Windows Server 2003 family

ControlPaint.DrawRadioButton Method (Graphics, Int32, Int32, Int32, Int32, ButtonState)

Draws a radio button control in the specified state, on the specified graphics surface, and within the specified bounds.

```
[Visual Basic]
Overloads Public Shared Sub DrawRadioButton( _
   ByVal graphics As Graphics, _
   ByVal x As Integer, _
   ByVal y As Integer, _
   ByVal width As Integer, _
   ByVal height As Integer, _
   ByVal state As ButtonState _
)
```

```
[C#]
public static void DrawRadioButton(
   Graphics graphics,
   int x,
   int y,
   int width,
   int height,
   ButtonState state
);
[C++]
public: static void DrawRadioButton(
   Graphics* graphics,
   int x,
   int y,
   int width,
   int height,
   ButtonState state
);
[JScript]
public static function DrawRadioButton(
   graphics : Graphics,
   x : int,
   y : int,
   width : int,
   height : int,
   state : ButtonState
);
```

Parameters

graphics
The **Graphics** to draw on.

x
The x-coordinate of the upper left corner of the drawing rectangle.

y
The y-coordinate of the upper left corner of the drawing rectangle.

width
The width of the radio button.

height
The height of the radio button.

state
A bitwise combination of the **ButtonState** values that specifies the state to draw the radio button in.

Requirements

Platforms: Windows 98, Windows NT 4.0, Windows Millennium Edition, Windows 2000, Windows XP Home Edition, Windows XP Professional, Windows Server 2003 family

ControlPaint.DrawReversibleFrame Method

Draws a reversible frame on the screen within the specified bounds, with the specified background color, and in the specified state.

```
[Visual Basic]
Public Shared Sub DrawReversibleFrame( _
   ByVal rectangle As Rectangle, _
   ByVal backColor As Color, _
   ByVal style As FrameStyle _
)
[C#]
public static void DrawReversibleFrame(
   Rectangle rectangle,
   Color backColor,
   FrameStyle style
);
[C++]
public: static void DrawReversibleFrame(
   Rectangle rectangle,
   Color backColor,
   FrameStyle style
);
[JScript]
public static function DrawReversibleFrame(
   rectangle : Rectangle,
   backColor : Color,
   style : FrameStyle
);
```

Parameters

rectangle
The **Rectangle** that represents the dimensions of the rectangle to draw, in screen coordinates.

backColor
The **Color** of the background behind the frame.

style
One of the **FrameStyle** values that specifies the style of the frame.

Remarks

The *backColor* parameter is used to calculate the fill color of the frame so that it is always visible against the background.

The results of this method can be reversed by drawing the same frame again. Drawing a frame using this method is similar to inverting a region of the screen, except that it provides better performance for a wider variety of colors.

Requirements

Platforms: Windows 98, Windows NT 4.0, Windows Millennium Edition, Windows 2000, Windows XP Home Edition, Windows XP Professional, Windows Server 2003 family

ControlPaint.DrawReversibleLine Method

Draws a reversible line on the screen within the specified starting and ending points and with the specified background color.

```
[Visual Basic]
Public Shared Sub DrawReversibleLine( _
   ByVal start As Point, _
   ByVal end As Point, _
   ByVal backColor As Color _
)
[C#]
public static void DrawReversibleLine(
   Point start,
   Point end,
   Color backColor
);
```

```
[C++]
public: static void DrawReversibleLine(
   Point start,
   Point end,
   Color backColor
);
[JScript]
public static function DrawReversibleLine(
   start : Point,
   end : Point,
   backColor : Color
);
```

Parameters

start
The starting **Point** of the line, in screen coordinates.

end
The ending **Point** of the line, in screen coordinates.

backColor
The **Color** of the background behind the line.

Remarks

The *backColor* parameter is used to calculate the fill color of the line so that it is always visible against the background.

The results of this method can be reversed by drawing the same line again. Drawing a line using this method is similar to inverting a region of the screen, except that it provides better performance for a wider variety of colors.

Requirements

Platforms: Windows 98, Windows NT 4.0, Windows Millennium Edition, Windows 2000, Windows XP Home Edition, Windows XP Professional, Windows Server 2003 family

ControlPaint.DrawScrollButton Method

Draws a scroll button on a scroll bar control.

Overload List

Draws the specified scroll button on a scroll bar control in the specified state, on the specified graphics surface, and within the specified bounds.

[Visual Basic] **Overloads Public Shared Sub DrawScrollButton(Graphics, Rectangle, ScrollButton, ButtonState)**

[C#] **public static void DrawScrollButton(Graphics, Rectangle, ScrollButton, ButtonState);**

[C++] **public: static void DrawScrollButton(Graphics*, Rectangle, ScrollButton, ButtonState);**

[JScript] **public static function DrawScrollButton(Graphics, Rectangle, ScrollButton, ButtonState);**

Draws the specified scroll button on a scroll bar control in the specified state, on the specified graphics surface, and within the specified bounds.

[Visual Basic] **Overloads Public Shared Sub DrawScrollButton(Graphics, Integer, Integer, Integer, Integer, ScrollButton, ButtonState)**

[C#] **public static void DrawScrollButton(Graphics, int, int, int, int, ScrollButton, ButtonState);**

[C++] **public: static void DrawScrollButton(Graphics*, int, int, int, int, ScrollButton, ButtonState);**

[JScript] **public static function DrawScrollButton(Graphics, int, int, int, int, ScrollButton, ButtonState);**

ControlPaint.DrawScrollButton Method (Graphics, Rectangle, ScrollButton, ButtonState)

Draws the specified scroll button on a scroll bar control in the specified state, on the specified graphics surface, and within the specified bounds.

```
[Visual Basic]
Overloads Public Shared Sub DrawScrollButton( _
   ByVal graphics As Graphics, _
   ByVal rectangle As Rectangle, _
   ByVal button As ScrollButton, _
   ByVal state As ButtonState _
)
[C#]
public static void DrawScrollButton(
   Graphics graphics,
   Rectangle rectangle,
   ScrollButton button,
   ButtonState state
);
[C++]
public: static void DrawScrollButton(
   Graphics* graphics,
   Rectangle rectangle,
   ScrollButton button,
   ButtonState state
);
[JScript]
public static function DrawScrollButton(
   graphics : Graphics,
   rectangle : Rectangle,
   button : ScrollButton,
   state : ButtonState
);
```

Parameters

graphics
The **Graphics** to draw on.

rectangle
The **Rectangle** that represents the dimensions of the glyph.

button
One of the **ScrollButton** values that specifies the type of scroll arrow to draw.

state
A bitwise combination of the **ButtonState** values that specifies the state to draw the scroll button in.

Requirements

Platforms: Windows 98, Windows NT 4.0, Windows Millennium Edition, Windows 2000, Windows XP Home Edition, Windows XP Professional, Windows Server 2003 family

ControlPaint.DrawScrollButton Method (Graphics, Int32, Int32, Int32, Int32, ScrollButton, ButtonState)

Draws the specified scroll button on a scroll bar control in the specified state, on the specified graphics surface, and within the specified bounds.

```
[Visual Basic]
Overloads Public Shared Sub DrawScrollButton( _
   ByVal graphics As Graphics, _
   ByVal x As Integer, _
   ByVal y As Integer, _
   ByVal width As Integer, _
   ByVal height As Integer, _
   ByVal button As ScrollButton, _
   ByVal state As ButtonState _
)
[C#]
public static void DrawScrollButton(
   Graphics graphics,
   int x,
   int y,
   int width,
   int height,
   ScrollButton button,
   ButtonState state
);
[C++]
public: static void DrawScrollButton(
   Graphics* graphics,
   int x,
   int y,
   int width,
   int height,
   ScrollButton button,
   ButtonState state
);
[JScript]
public static function DrawScrollButton(
   graphics : Graphics,
   x : int,
   y : int,
   width : int,
   height : int,
   button : ScrollButton,
   state : ButtonState
);
```

Parameters

graphics
The **Graphics** to draw on.

x
The x-coordinate of the upper left corner of the drawing rectangle.

y
The y-coordinate of the upper left corner of the drawing rectangle.

width
The width of the scroll button.

height
The height of the scroll button.

button
One of the **ScrollButton** values that specifies the type of scroll arrow to draw.

state
A bitwise combination of the **ButtonState** values that specifies the state to draw the scroll button in.

Requirements

Platforms: Windows 98, Windows NT 4.0, Windows Millennium Edition, Windows 2000, Windows XP Home Edition, Windows XP Professional, Windows Server 2003 family

ControlPaint.DrawSelectionFrame Method

Draws a standard selection frame in the specified state, on the specified graphics surface, with the specified inner and outer dimensions, and with the specified background color.

```
[Visual Basic]
Public Shared Sub DrawSelectionFrame( _
   ByVal graphics As Graphics, _
   ByVal active As Boolean, _
   ByVal outsideRect As Rectangle, _
   ByVal insideRect As Rectangle, _
   ByVal backColor As Color _
)
[C#]
public static void DrawSelectionFrame(
   Graphics graphics,
   bool active,
   Rectangle outsideRect,
   Rectangle insideRect,
   Color backColor
);
[C++]
public: static void DrawSelectionFrame(
   Graphics* graphics,
   bool active,
   Rectangle outsideRect,
   Rectangle insideRect,
   Color backColor
);
[JScript]
public static function DrawSelectionFrame(
   graphics : Graphics,
   active : Boolean,
   outsideRect : Rectangle,
   insideRect : Rectangle,
   backColor : Color
);
```

Parameters

graphics
The **Graphics** to draw on.

active
true to draw the selection frame in an active state; otherwise, **false**.

outsideRect
The **Rectangle** that represents the outer boundary of the selection frame.

insideRect
The **Rectangle** that represents the inner boundary of the selection frame.

backColor
The **Color** of the background behind the frame.

Remarks

A selection frame is a frame that is drawn around a selected component at design time.

The *backColor* parameter is used to calculate the fill color of the frame so that it is always visible against the background.

If the *active* parameter is set to **true**, the selection frame is drawn as a set of hatch marks indicating that the component has been activated; otherwise, the selection frame is drawn with a dotted pattern or nothing, depending on the implementation.

Requirements

Platforms: Windows 98, Windows NT 4.0, Windows Millennium Edition, Windows 2000, Windows XP Home Edition, Windows XP Professional, Windows Server 2003 family

ControlPaint.DrawSizeGrip Method

Draws a size grip on a form.

Overload List

Draws a size grip on a form with the specified bounds and background color and on the specified graphics surface.

[Visual Basic] **Overloads Public Shared Sub DrawSize-Grip(Graphics, Color, Rectangle)**

[C#] **public static void DrawSizeGrip(Graphics, Color, Rectangle);**

[C++] **public: static void DrawSizeGrip(Graphics*, Color, Rectangle);**

[JScript] **public static function DrawSizeGrip(Graphics, Color, Rectangle);**

Draws a size grip on a form with the specified bounds and background color and on the specified graphics surface.

[Visual Basic] **Overloads Public Shared Sub DrawSize-Grip(Graphics, Color, Integer, Integer, Integer, Integer)**

[C#] **public static void DrawSizeGrip(Graphics, Color, int, int, int, int);**

[C++] **public: static void DrawSizeGrip(Graphics*, Color, int, int, int, int);**

[JScript] **public static function DrawSizeGrip(Graphics, Color, int, int, int, int);**

ControlPaint.DrawSizeGrip Method (Graphics, Color, Rectangle)

Draws a size grip on a form with the specified bounds and background color and on the specified graphics surface.

```
[Visual Basic]
Overloads Public Shared Sub DrawSizeGrip( _
   ByVal graphics As Graphics, _
   ByVal backColor As Color, _
   ByVal bounds As Rectangle _
)
[C#]
public static void DrawSizeGrip(
   Graphics graphics,
   Color backColor,
   Rectangle bounds
);
[C++]
public: static void DrawSizeGrip(
   Graphics* graphics,
   Color backColor,
   Rectangle bounds
);
[JScript]
public static function DrawSizeGrip(
   graphics : Graphics,
   backColor : Color,
   bounds : Rectangle
);
```

Parameters

graphics
: The **Graphics** to draw on.

backColor
: The **Color** of the background used to determine the colors of the size grip.

bounds
: The **Rectangle** that represents the dimensions of the size grip.

Remarks

The *backColor* parameter is used to calculate the color of the size grip so that it is always visible against the background.

When you define a sizable window, you can include a size grip. A size grip is a special handle that enables the user to resize a window.

Requirements

Platforms: Windows 98, Windows NT 4.0, Windows Millennium Edition, Windows 2000, Windows XP Home Edition, Windows XP Professional, Windows Server 2003 family

ControlPaint.DrawSizeGrip Method (Graphics, Color, Int32, Int32, Int32, Int32)

Draws a size grip on a form with the specified bounds and background color and on the specified graphics surface.

```
[Visual Basic]
Overloads Public Shared Sub DrawSizeGrip( _
   ByVal graphics As Graphics, _
   ByVal backColor As Color, _
   ByVal x As Integer, _
   ByVal y As Integer, _
   ByVal width As Integer, _
   ByVal height As Integer _
)
[C#]
public static void DrawSizeGrip(
   Graphics graphics,
   Color backColor,
   int x,
   int y,
   int width,
   int height
);
```

```
[C++]
public: static void DrawSizeGrip(
   Graphics* graphics,
   Color backColor,
   int x,
   int y,
   int width,
   int height
);
[JScript]
public static function DrawSizeGrip(
   graphics : Graphics,
   backColor : Color,
   x : int,
   y : int,
   width : int,
   height : int
);
```

Parameters

graphics
The **Graphics** to draw on.

backColor
The **Color** of the background used to determine the colors of the size grip.

x
The x-coordinate of the upper left corner of the size grip.

y
The y-coordinate of the upper left corner of the size grip.

width
The width of the size grip.

height
The height of the size grip.

Remarks

The *backColor* parameter is used to calculate the color of the size grip so that it is always visible against the background.

When you define a sizable window, you can include a size grip. A size grip is a special handle that enables the user to resize a window.

Requirements

Platforms: Windows 98, Windows NT 4.0, Windows Millennium Edition, Windows 2000, Windows XP Home Edition, Windows XP Professional, Windows Server 2003 family

ControlPaint.DrawStringDisabled Method

Draws the specified string in a disabled state on the specified graphics surface, within the specified bounds, and in the specified font, color, and format.

```
[Visual Basic]
Public Shared Sub DrawStringDisabled( _
   ByVal graphics As Graphics, _
   ByVal s As String, _
   ByVal font As Font, _
   ByVal color As Color, _
   ByVal layoutRectangle As RectangleF, _
   ByVal format As StringFormat _
)
[C#]
public static void DrawStringDisabled(
   Graphics graphics,
   string s,
   Font font,
   Color color,
   RectangleF layoutRectangle,
   StringFormat format
);
[C++]
public: static void DrawStringDisabled(
   Graphics* graphics,
   String* s,
   Font* font,
   Color color,
   RectangleF layoutRectangle,
   StringFormat* format
);
[JScript]
public static function DrawStringDisabled(
   graphics : Graphics,
   s : String,
   font : Font,
   color : Color,
   layoutRectangle : RectangleF,
   format : StringFormat
);
```

Parameters

graphics
The **Graphics** to draw on.

s
The string to draw.

font
The **Font** to draw the string with.

color
The **Color** to draw the string with.

layoutRectangle
The **RectangleF** that represents the dimensions of the string.

format
The **StringFormat** to apply to the string.

Requirements

Platforms: Windows 98, Windows NT 4.0, Windows Millennium Edition, Windows 2000, Windows XP Home Edition, Windows XP Professional, Windows Server 2003 family

ControlPaint.FillReversibleRectangle Method

Draws a filled, reversible rectangle on the screen.

```
[Visual Basic]
Public Shared Sub FillReversibleRectangle( _
   ByVal rectangle As Rectangle, _
   ByVal backColor As Color _
)
[C#]
public static void FillReversibleRectangle(
   Rectangle rectangle,
   Color backColor
);
```

```
[C++]
public: static void FillReversibleRectangle(
   Rectangle rectangle,
   Color backColor
);
[JScript]
public static function FillReversibleRectangle(
   rectangle : Rectangle,
   backColor : Color
);
```

Parameters

rectangle
The **Rectangle** that represents the dimensions of the rectangle to fill, in screen coordinates.

backColor
The **Color** of the background behind the fill.

Remarks

The *backColor* parameter is used to calculate the fill color of the rectangle so that it is always visible against the background.

The results of this method can be reversed by drawing the same rectangle again. Drawing a rectangle using this method is similar to inverting a region of the screen except that it provides better performance for a wider variety of colors.

Requirements

Platforms: Windows 98, Windows NT 4.0, Windows Millennium Edition, Windows 2000, Windows XP Home Edition, Windows XP Professional, Windows Server 2003 family

ControlPaint.Light Method

Creates a new light color object for the control.

Overload List

Creates a new light color object for the control from the specified color.

[Visual Basic] **Overloads Public Shared Function Light(Color) As Color**

[C#] **public static Color Light(Color);**

[C++] **public: static Color Light(Color);**

[JScript] **public static function Light(Color) : Color;**

Creates a new light color object for the control from the specified color and lightens it by the specified percentage.

[Visual Basic] **Overloads Public Shared Function Light(Color, Single) As Color**

[C#] **public static Color Light(Color, float);**

[C++] **public: static Color Light(Color, float);**

[JScript] **public static function Light(Color, float) : Color;**

ControlPaint.Light Method (Color)

Creates a new light color object for the control from the specified color.

```
[Visual Basic]
Overloads Public Shared Function Light( _
   ByVal baseColor As Color _
) As Color
[C#]
public static Color Light(
   Color baseColor
);
[C++]
public: static Color Light(
   Color baseColor
);
[JScript]
public static function Light(
   baseColor : Color
) : Color;
```

Parameters

baseColor
The **Color** to be lightened.

Return Value

A **Color** that represents the light color on the control.

Remarks

If the specified **Color** is one of the **SystemColors**, the color is converted to a **SystemColors.ControlLight** color; otherwise, the color's luminosity value is decreased.

Requirements

Platforms: Windows 98, Windows NT 4.0, Windows Millennium Edition, Windows 2000, Windows XP Home Edition, Windows XP Professional, Windows Server 2003 family

ControlPaint.Light Method (Color, Single)

Creates a new light color object for the control from the specified color and lightens it by the specified percentage.

```
[Visual Basic]
Overloads Public Shared Function Light( _
   ByVal baseColor As Color, _
   ByVal percOfLightLight As Single _
) As Color
[C#]
public static Color Light(
   Color baseColor,
   float percOfLightLight
);
[C++]
public: static Color Light(
   Color baseColor,
   float percOfLightLight
);
[JScript]
public static function Light(
   baseColor : Color,
   percOfLightLight : float
) : Color;
```

Parameters

baseColor
The **Color** to be lightened.

percOfLightLight
The percentage to lighten the specified **Color**.

Return Value

A **Color** that represents the light color on the control.

Remarks

If the specified **Color** is one of the **SystemColors**, the color is converted to a **SystemColors.ControlLight** color; otherwise, the color's luminosity value is decreased.

Requirements

Platforms: Windows 98, Windows NT 4.0, Windows Millennium Edition, Windows 2000, Windows XP Home Edition, Windows XP Professional, Windows Server 2003 family

ControlPaint.LightLight Method

Creates a new light color object for the control from the specified color.

[Visual Basic]
```
Public Shared Function LightLight( _
   ByVal baseColor As Color _
) As Color
```
[C#]
```
public static Color LightLight(
   Color baseColor
);
```
[C++]
```
public: static Color LightLight(
   Color baseColor
);
```
[JScript]
```
public static function LightLight(
   baseColor : Color
) : Color;
```

Parameters

baseColor

The **Color** to be lightened.

Return Value

A **Color** that represents the light color on the control.

Remarks

If the specified **Color** is one of the **SystemColors**, the color is converted to the **SystemColors.ControlLightLight** color; otherwise, the color's luminosity value is increased.

Requirements

Platforms: Windows 98, Windows NT 4.0, Windows Millennium Edition, Windows 2000, Windows XP Home Edition, Windows XP Professional, Windows Server 2003 family

ControlStyles Enumeration

Specifies the style and behavior of a control.

This enumeration has a **FlagsAttribute** attribute that allows a bitwise combination of its member values.

[Visual Basic]
```
<Flags>
<Serializable>
Public Enum ControlStyles
```
[C#]
```
[Flags]
[Serializable]
public enum ControlStyles
```
[C++]
```
[Flags]
[Serializable]
__value public enum ControlStyles
```
[JScript]
```
public
   Flags
   Serializable
enum ControlStyles
```

Remarks

Controls use this enumeration in various properties and methods to specify functionality. A control can enable a style by calling the **SetStyle** method and passing in the appropriate **ControlStyles** bit (or bits) and the Boolean value to set the bit(s) to. For example, the following line of Visual Basic code would enable double-buffering.

```
myControl.SetStyle(UserPaint Or AllPaintingInWmPaint Or DoubleBuffer,
True)
```

If the **AllPaintingInWmPaint** bit is set to **true**, the window message WM_ERASEBKGND is ignored, and both **OnPaintBackground** and **OnPaint** methods are called directly from the window message WM_PAINT. This generally reduces flicker unless other controls send the window message WM_ERASEBKGND to the control. You might send the window message WM_ERASEBKGRND to achieve a pseudo-transparent effect similar to **SupportsTransparentBackColor**; for example, a **ToolBar** with flat appearance does this.

To fully enable double-buffering, you must set the **UserPaint**, **AllPaintingInWmPaint**, and **DoubleBuffer** bits to **true**.

If the **SupportsTransparentBackColor** bit is set to **true**, and the **BackColor** is set to a color whose alpha component is less than 255, **OnPaintBackground** will simulate transparency by asking its parent control to paint the background. This is not true transparency.

> **Note** If there is another control between the control and its parent, the current control will not show the control in the middle.

When the **UserMouse** bit is set to **true**, the following methods are still called: **Control.OnMouseDown**, **Control.OnMouseUp**, **Control.OnMouseEnter**, **Control.OnMouseMove**, **Control.OnMouseHover**, **Control.OnMouseLeave**, and **Control.OnMouseWheel**.

When the control is clicked, if the **StandardClick** bit is set to **true** the **Control.OnClick** method is called and it raises the **Control.Click** event. When the control is double-clicked, and both the **StandardClick** and **StandardDoubleClick** bits are set to **true**, the click is passed on to the **DoubleClick** event. Then the **Control.OnDoubleClick** method is called and it raises the **Control.DoubleClick** event. However, the control can call **OnClick** or **OnDoubleClick** directly regardless of the **StandardClick** and **StandardDoubleClick** bit values. For more information on control click and double click behaviors, see the **Control.Click** and **Control.DoubleClick** topics.

Notes to Inheritors: Inheriting from a standard Windows Forms control and changing the **StandardClick** or **StandardDoubleClick** bit values to **true** can cause unexpected behavior or can have no effect at all if the control does not support the **Click** or **DoubleClick** events.

Members

Member name	Description	Value
AllPaintingInWmPaint	If **true**, the control ignores the window message WM_ERASEBKGND to reduce flicker. This style should only be applied if the **UserPaint** bit is set to **true**.	8192
CacheText	If **true**, the control keeps a copy of the text rather than getting it from the **Handle** each time it is needed. This style defaults to **false**. This behavior improves performance, but makes it difficult to keep the text synchronized.	16384
ContainerControl	If **true**, the control is a container-like control.	1
DoubleBuffer	If **true**, drawing is performed in a buffer, and after it completes, the result is output to the screen. Double-buffering prevents flicker caused by the redrawing of the control. To fully enable double-buffering, you must also set the **UserPaint** and **AllPaintingInWmPaint** style bits to **true**.	65536
EnableNotifyMessage	If **true**, the **OnNotifyMessage** method is called for every message sent to the control's **WndProc**. This style defaults to **false**.	32768
FixedHeight	If **true**, the control has a fixed width when auto-scaled. For example, if a layout operation attempts to rescale the control to accommodate a new **Font**, the control's **Width** remains unchanged.	64

Member name	Description	Value
FixedWidth	If **true**, the control has a fixed height when auto-scaled. For example, if a layout operation attempts to rescale the control to accommodate a new **Font**, the control's **Height** remains unchanged.	32
Opaque	If **true**, the control is drawn opaque and the background is not painted.	4
ResizeRedraw	If **true**, the control is redrawn when it is resized.	16
Selectable	If **true**, the control can receive focus.	512
StandardClick	If **true**, the control implements the standard **Click** behavior.	256
StandardDoubleClick	If **true**, the control implements the standard **DoubleClick** behavior. This style is ignored if the **StandardClick** bit is not set to **true**.	4096
SupportsTransparentBackColor	If **true**, the control accepts a **BackColor** with an alpha component of less than 255 to simulate transparency. Transparency will be simulated only if the **UserPaint** bit is set to **true** and the parent control is derived from **Control**.	2048
UserMouse	If **true**, the control does its own mouse processing, and mouse events are not handled by the operating system.	1024
UserPaint	If **true**, the control paints itself rather than the operating system doing so. This style only applies to classes derived from **Control**.	2

Example

The following example enables double-buffering on a **Form** and updates the styles to reflect the changes.

Requirements

Namespace: System.Windows.Forms

Platforms: Windows 98, Windows NT 4.0, Windows Millennium Edition, Windows 2000, Windows XP Home Edition, Windows XP Professional, Windows Server 2003 family

Assembly: System.Windows.Forms (in System.Windows.Forms.dll)

ConvertEventArgs Class

Provides data for the **Format** and **Parse** events.

System.Object
  System.EventArgs
    System.Windows.Forms.ConvertEventArgs

[Visual Basic]
```
Public Class ConvertEventArgs
   Inherits EventArgs
```
[C#]
```
public class ConvertEventArgs : EventArgs
```
[C++]
```
public __gc class ConvertEventArgs : public EventArgs
```
[JScript]
```
public class ConvertEventArgs extends EventArgs
```

Thread Safety

Any public static (**Shared** in Visual Basic) members of this type are safe for multithreaded operations. Any instance members are not guaranteed to be thread safe.

Remarks

The **ConvertEventArgs** is used to format and unformat values displayed by a Windows Forms control that is bound to data through a **Binding** object. The **Format** event occurs whenever a control property is bound to a value, and the **Parse** event occurs whenever the bound value changes.

The **Format** and **Parse** events allow you to create custom formats for displaying data. For example, if the data in a table is of type **Decimal**, you can specify that the data should be displayed in the local currency format--by setting the **Value** property of the **ConvertEventArgs** object to the formatted value in the **Format** event. You must consequently unformat the displayed value in the **Parse** event.

Example

[Visual Basic, C#] The following example creates a **Binding**, adds a **ConvertEventHandler** delegate to both the **Parse** and **Format** events, and uses the **DataBindings** property to add the **Binding** to the **BindingsCollection** of a **TextBox** control. The **DecimalToCurrencyString** event delegate, which is added to the **Format** event, uses the **ToString** method to format the bound value (a **Decimal** type) as currency. The **CurrencyStringToDecimal** event delegate, which is added to the **Parse** event, converts the value displayed by the control back to the **Decimal** type.

[Visual Basic]
```
Private Sub DecimalToCurrencyString(sender As Object, ↵
 cevent As ConvertEventArgs)
   ' The method converts only to string type. Test this ↵
 using the DesiredType.
   If Not cevent.DesiredType Is GetType(String) Then
      Return
   End If
   ' Use the ToString method to format the value as currency ("c").
   cevent.Value = CDec(cevent.Value).ToString("c")
End Sub 'DecimalToCurrencyString

Private Sub CurrencyStringToDecimal(sender As Object, ↵
cevent As ConvertEventArgs)
   ' The method converts back to decimal type only.
   If Not cevent.DesiredType Is GetType(Decimal) Then
      Return
   End If
   ' Converts the string back to decimal using the shared Parse method.
   cevent.Value = Decimal.Parse(cevent.Value.ToString, _
   NumberStyles.Currency, nothing)

End Sub 'CurrencyStringToDecimal

Private Sub BindControl()
   ' Creates the binding first. The OrderAmount is typed as Decimal.
   Dim b As New Binding("Text", ds, ↵
"customers.custToOrders.OrderAmount")
   ' Adds the delegates to the events.
   AddHandler b.Format, AddressOf DecimalToCurrencyString
   AddHandler b.Parse, AddressOf CurrencyStringToDecimal
   text1.DataBindings.Add(b)
End Sub 'BindControl
```

[C#]
```
private void DecimalToCurrencyString(object sender, ↵
ConvertEventArgs cevent)
{
   // The method converts only to string type. Test this ↵
 using the DesiredType.
   if(cevent.DesiredType != typeof(string)) return;

   // Use the ToString method to format the value as currency ("c").
   cevent.Value = ((decimal) cevent.Value).ToString("c");
}

private void CurrencyStringToDecimal(object sender, ↵
ConvertEventArgs cevent)
{
   // The method converts back to decimal type only.
   if(cevent.DesiredType != typeof(decimal)) return;

   // Converts the string back to decimal using the static ↵
Parse method.
   cevent.Value = Decimal.Parse(cevent.Value.ToString(),
   NumberStyles.Currency, null);
}

private void BindControl()
{
   // Creates the binding first. The OrderAmount is typed as Decimal.
   Binding b = new Binding
   ("Text", ds, "customers.custToOrders.OrderAmount");
   // Adds the delegates to the events.
   b.Format += new ConvertEventHandler(DecimalToCurrencyString);
   b.Parse += new ConvertEventHandler(CurrencyStringToDecimal);
   text1.DataBindings.Add(b);
}
```

Requirements

Namespace: System.Windows.Forms

Platforms: Windows 98, Windows NT 4.0, Windows Millennium Edition, Windows 2000, Windows XP Home Edition, Windows XP Professional, Windows Server 2003 family, .NET Compact Framework - Windows CE .NET

Assembly: System.Windows.Forms (in System.Windows.Forms.dll)

ConvertEventArgs Constructor

Initializes a new instance of the **ConvertEventArgs** class.

[Visual Basic]
```
Public Sub New( _
   ByVal value As Object, _
   ByVal desiredType As Type _
)
```

```
[C#]
public ConvertEventArgs(
   object value,
   Type desiredType
);
[C++]
public: ConvertEventArgs(
   Object* value,
   Type* desiredType
);
[JScript]
public function ConvertEventArgs(
   value : Object,
   desiredType : Type
);
```

Parameters

value
An **Object** that contains the value of the current property.

desiredType
The **Type** of the value.

Requirements

Platforms: Windows 98, Windows NT 4.0, Windows Millennium Edition, Windows 2000, Windows XP Home Edition, Windows XP Professional, Windows Server 2003 family, .NET Compact Framework - Windows CE .NET

ConvertEventArgs.DesiredType Property

Gets the data type of the desired value.

```
[Visual Basic]
Public ReadOnly Property DesiredType As Type
[C#]
public Type DesiredType {get;}
[C++]
public: __property Type* get_DesiredType();
[JScript]
public function get DesiredType() : Type;
```

Property Value

The **Type** of the desired value.

Remarks

The **DesiredType** property enables you to check the type of the property that the value is being converted to.

Example

See related example in the **System.Windows.Forms.Convert.EventArgs** class topic.

Requirements

Platforms: Windows 98, Windows NT 4.0, Windows Millennium Edition, Windows 2000, Windows XP Home Edition, Windows XP Professional, Windows Server 2003 family, .NET Compact Framework - Windows CE .NET

ConvertEventArgs.Value Property

Gets or sets the value of the **ConvertEventArgs** object.

```
[Visual Basic]
Public Property Value As Object
[C#]
public object Value {get; set;}
[C++]
public: __property Object* get_Value();
public: __property void set_Value(Object*);
[JScript]
public function get Value() : Object;
public function set Value(Object);
```

Property Value

The value of the **ConvertEventArgs** object.

Remarks

The value contained by the **Value** property depends on the event in which the **ConvertEventArgs** object is returned. The **ConvertEventArgs** object can be returned in either the the **Format** event, or the **Parse** event.

When the **ConvertEventArgs** object is returned in the **Format** event, the **Value** property contains the unformatted property value of the data source. Within the **Format** event, you can read the property value, format the value, and reset the **Value** property to the new (formatted) value, thereby setting the value displayed in the data-bound control.

When the **ConvertEventArgs** object is returned in the **Parse** event, the property contains the custom-formatted value of the data-bound control. Within the **Parse** event, you must read the formatted value, parse it, and convert it back to the same data type as the data source. You can then reset the **Value** property to the unformatted value, and thereby set the value of the data source. To determine the type of the data source, examine the **DesiredType** property value.

Example

See related example in the **System.Windows.Forms.Convert.EventArgs** class topic.

Requirements

Platforms: Windows 98, Windows NT 4.0, Windows Millennium Edition, Windows 2000, Windows XP Home Edition, Windows XP Professional, Windows Server 2003 family, .NET Compact Framework - Windows CE .NET

ConvertEventHandler Delegate

Represents the method that will handle the **Parse** and **Format** events of a **Binding** object.

[Visual Basic]
```
<Serializable>
Public Delegate Sub ConvertEventHandler( _
   ByVal sender As Object, _
   ByVal e As ConvertEventArgs _
)
```
[C#]
```
[Serializable]
public delegate void ConvertEventHandler(
   object sender,
   ConvertEventArgs e
);
```
[C++]
```
[Serializable]
public __gc __delegate void ConvertEventHandler(
   Object* sender,
   ConvertEventArgs* e
);
```

[JScript] In JScript, you can use the delegates in the .NET Framework, but you cannot define your own.

Parameters [Visual Basic, C#, C++]

The declaration of your event handler must have the same parameters as the **ConvertEventHandler** delegate declaration.

sender

The source of the event.

e

A **ConvertEventArgs** that contains the event data.

Remarks

When you create a(n) **ConvertEventHandler** delegate, you identify the method that will handle the event. To associate the event with your event handler, add an instance of the delegate to the event. The event handler is called whenever the event occurs, unless you remove the delegate. For more information about event handler delegates, see **Events and Delegates**.

Example

See related example in the **System.Windows.Forms.Convert.EventArgs** class topic.

Requirements

Namespace: System.Windows.Forms

Platforms: Windows 98, Windows NT 4.0, Windows Millennium Edition, Windows 2000, Windows XP Home Edition, Windows XP Professional, Windows Server 2003 family, .NET Compact Framework - Windows CE .NET

Assembly: System.Windows.Forms (in System.Windows.Forms.dll)

CreateParams Class

Encapsulates the information needed when creating a control.

System.Object
  System.Windows.Forms.CreateParams

```
[Visual Basic]
Public Class CreateParams
[C#]
public class CreateParams
[C++]
public __gc class CreateParams
[JScript]
public class CreateParams
```

Thread Safety

Any public static (**Shared** in Visual Basic) members of this type are safe for multithreaded operations. Any instance members are not guaranteed to be thread safe.

Remarks

The information in a **CreateParams** object can be used to pass information about the initial state and appearance of a control. Most **Control** derived controls override the **CreateParams** property to pass in the appropriate values or include additional information in the **CreateParams** object.

For more information about creating control parameters, see the **CreateWindow** and **CreateWindowEx** functions and the **CREATESTRUCT** structure documentation in the Windows Platform SDK reference located in the MSDN Library.

> **Note** The constants used to set the **Style**, **ExStyle**, and **ClassStyle** properties are defined in the Winuser.h header file. This file is installed by the Platform SDK or Visual Studio .NET.

Requirements

Namespace: System.Windows.Forms

Platforms: Windows 98, Windows NT 4.0, Windows Millennium Edition, Windows 2000, Windows XP Home Edition, Windows XP Professional, Windows Server 2003 family

Assembly: System.Windows.Forms (in System.Windows.Forms.dll)

CreateParams Constructor

Initializes a new instance of the **CreateParams** class.

```
[Visual Basic]
Public Sub New()
[C#]
public CreateParams();
[C++]
public: CreateParams();
[JScript]
public function CreateParams();
```

Remarks

The default constructor initializes any fields to their default values.

Requirements

Platforms: Windows 98, Windows NT 4.0, Windows Millennium Edition, Windows 2000, Windows XP Home Edition, Windows XP Professional, Windows Server 2003 family

CreateParams.Caption Property

Gets or sets the control's initial text.

```
[Visual Basic]
Public Property Caption As String
[C#]
public string Caption {get; set;}
[C++]
public: __property String* get_Caption();
public: __property void set_Caption(String*);
[JScript]
public function get Caption() : String;
public function set Caption(String);
```

Property Value

The control's initial text.

Requirements

Platforms: Windows 98, Windows NT 4.0, Windows Millennium Edition, Windows 2000, Windows XP Home Edition, Windows XP Professional, Windows Server 2003 family

CreateParams.ClassName Property

Gets or sets the name of the Windows class to derive the control from.

```
[Visual Basic]
Public Property ClassName As String
[C#]
public string ClassName {get; set;}
[C++]
public: __property String* get_ClassName();
public: __property void set_ClassName(String*);
[JScript]
public function get ClassName() : String;
public function set ClassName(String);
```

Property Value

The name of the Windows class to derive the control from.

Remarks

The default value for this property is a null reference (**Nothing** in Visual Basic), indicating that the control is not derived from an existing control class. To derive from an existing control class, store the system class name in this property. For example, to derive from the standard **Button** control, set this property to "BUTTON".

Requirements

Platforms: Windows 98, Windows NT 4.0, Windows Millennium Edition, Windows 2000, Windows XP Home Edition, Windows XP Professional, Windows Server 2003 family

CreateParams.ClassStyle Property

Gets or sets a bitwise combination of class style values.

```
[Visual Basic]
Public Property ClassStyle As Integer
[C#]
public int ClassStyle {get; set;}
[C++]
public: __property int get_ClassStyle();
public: __property void set_ClassStyle(int);
[JScript]
public function get ClassStyle() : int;
public function set ClassStyle(int);
```

Property Value

A bitwise combination of the class style values.

Remarks

The **ClassStyle** property is ignored if the **ClassName** property is not a null reference (**Nothing** in Visual Basic).

For more information about creating control parameters, see the **CreateWindow** and **CreateWindowEx** functions and the **CREATESTRUCT** structure documentation in the Windows Platform SDK reference located in the MSDN Library.

> **Note** The constants used to set the **Style**, **ExStyle**, and **ClassStyle** properties are defined in the Winuser.h header file. This file is installed by the Platform SDK or Visual Studio .NET.

Requirements

Platforms: Windows 98, Windows NT 4.0, Windows Millennium Edition, Windows 2000, Windows XP Home Edition, Windows XP Professional, Windows Server 2003 family

CreateParams.ExStyle Property

Gets or sets a bitwise combination of extended window style values.

```
[Visual Basic]
Public Property ExStyle As Integer
[C#]
public int ExStyle {get; set;}
[C++]
public: __property int get_ExStyle();
public: __property void set_ExStyle(int);
[JScript]
public function get ExStyle() : int;
public function set ExStyle(int);
```

Property Value

A bitwise combination of the extended window style values.

Remarks

The **ExStyle** property supports extended appearance and initial state values to apply to the control.

For more information about creating control parameters, see the **CreateWindow** and **CreateWindowEx** functions and the **CREATESTRUCT** structure documentation in the Windows Platform SDK reference located in the MSDN Library.

> **Note** The constants used to set the **Style**, **ExStyle**, and **ClassStyle** properties are defined in the Winuser.h header file. This file is installed by the Platform SDK or Visual Studio .NET.

Requirements

Platforms: Windows 98, Windows NT 4.0, Windows Millennium Edition, Windows 2000, Windows XP Home Edition, Windows XP Professional, Windows Server 2003 family

CreateParams.Height Property

Gets or sets the initial height of the control.

```
[Visual Basic]
Public Property Height As Integer
[C#]
public int Height {get; set;}
[C++]
public: __property int get_Height();
public: __property void set_Height(int);
[JScript]
public function get Height() : int;
public function set Height(int);
```

Property Value

The numeric value that represents the initial height of the control.

Requirements

Platforms: Windows 98, Windows NT 4.0, Windows Millennium Edition, Windows 2000, Windows XP Home Edition, Windows XP Professional, Windows Server 2003 family

CreateParams.Param Property

Gets or sets additional parameter information needed to create the control.

```
[Visual Basic]
Public Property Param As Object
[C#]
public object Param {get; set;}
[C++]
public: __property Object* get_Param();
public: __property void set_Param(Object*);
[JScript]
public function get Param() : Object;
public function set Param(Object);
```

Property Value

The **Object** that holds additional parameter information needed to create the control.

Remarks

If you are creating a multiple document interface (MDI) client window, the **Param** property must reference a **CLIENTCREATESTRUCT** structure.

For more information about creating control parameters, see the **CreateWindow** and **CreateWindowEx** functions and the **CLIENTCREATESTRUCT** structure documentation in the Windows Platform SDK reference located in the MSDN Library.

Requirements

Platforms: Windows 98, Windows NT 4.0, Windows Millennium Edition, Windows 2000, Windows XP Home Edition, Windows XP Professional, Windows Server 2003 family

CreateParams.Parent Property

Gets or sets the control's parent.

[Visual Basic]
```
Public Property Parent As IntPtr
```
[C#]
```
public IntPtr Parent {get; set;}
```
[C++]
```
public: __property IntPtr get_Parent();
public: __property void set_Parent(IntPtr);
```
[JScript]
```
public function get Parent() : IntPtr;
public function set Parent(IntPtr);
```

Property Value

An **IntPtr** that contains the window handle of the control's parent.

Requirements

Platforms: Windows 98, Windows NT 4.0, Windows Millennium Edition, Windows 2000, Windows XP Home Edition, Windows XP Professional, Windows Server 2003 family

CreateParams.Style Property

Gets or sets a bitwise combination of window style values.

[Visual Basic]
```
Public Property Style As Integer
```
[C#]
```
public int Style {get; set;}
```
[C++]
```
public: __property int get_Style();
public: __property void set_Style(int);
```
[JScript]
```
public function get Style() : int;
public function set Style(int);
```

Property Value

A bitwise combination of the window style values.

Remarks

The **Style** property controls the appearance of the control and its initial state.

For more information about creating control parameters, see the **CreateWindow** and **CreateWindowEx** functions and the **CREATESTRUCT** structure documentation in the Windows Platform SDK reference located in the MSDN Library.

> **Note** The constants used to set the **Style**, **ExStyle**, and **ClassStyle** properties are defined in the Winuser.h header file. This file is installed by the Platform SDK or Visual Studio .NET.

Requirements

Platforms: Windows 98, Windows NT 4.0, Windows Millennium Edition, Windows 2000, Windows XP Home Edition, Windows XP Professional, Windows Server 2003 family

CreateParams.Width Property

Gets or sets the initial width of the control.

[Visual Basic]
```
Public Property Width As Integer
```
[C#]
```
public int Width {get; set;}
```
[C++]
```
public: __property int get_Width();
public: __property void set_Width(int);
```
[JScript]
```
public function get Width() : int;
public function set Width(int);
```

Property Value

The numeric value that represents the initial width of the control.

Requirements

Platforms: Windows 98, Windows NT 4.0, Windows Millennium Edition, Windows 2000, Windows XP Home Edition, Windows XP Professional, Windows Server 2003 family

CreateParams.X Property

Gets or sets the initial left position of the control.

[Visual Basic]
```
Public Property X As Integer
```
[C#]
```
public int X {get; set;}
```
[C++]
```
public: __property int get_X();
public: __property void set_X(int);
```
[JScript]
```
public function get X() : int;
public function set X(int);
```

Property Value

The numeric value that represents the initial left position of the control.

Requirements

Platforms: Windows 98, Windows NT 4.0, Windows Millennium Edition, Windows 2000, Windows XP Home Edition, Windows XP Professional, Windows Server 2003 family

CreateParams.Y Property

Gets or sets the top position of the initial location of the control.

[Visual Basic]
```
Public Property Y As Integer
```
[C#]
```
public int Y {get; set;}
```
[C++]
```
public: __property int get_Y();
public: __property void set_Y(int);
```
[JScript]
```
public function get Y() : int;
public function set Y(int);
```

Property Value

The numeric value that represents the top position of the initial location of the control.

Requirements

Platforms: Windows 98, Windows NT 4.0,
Windows Millennium Edition, Windows 2000,
Windows XP Home Edition, Windows XP Professional,
Windows Server 2003 family

CreateParams.ToString Method

This member overrides **Object.ToString**.

[Visual Basic]
```
Overrides Public Function ToString() As String
```
[C#]
```
public override string ToString();
```
[C++]
```
public: String* ToString();
```
[JScript]
```
public override function ToString() : String;
```

Requirements

Platforms: Windows 98, Windows NT 4.0,
Windows Millennium Edition, Windows 2000,
Windows XP Home Edition, Windows XP Professional,
Windows Server 2003 family

CurrencyManager Class

Manages a list of **Binding** objects.

System.Object
  System.Windows.Forms.BindingManagerBase
    System.Windows.Forms.CurrencyManager

[Visual Basic]
```
Public Class CurrencyManager
   Inherits BindingManagerBase
```
[C#]
```
public class CurrencyManager : BindingManagerBase
```
[C++]
```
public __gc class CurrencyManager : public BindingManagerBase
```
[JScript]
```
public class CurrencyManager extends BindingManagerBase
```

Thread Safety

Any public static (**Shared** in Visual Basic) members of this type are safe for multithreaded operations. Any instance members are not guaranteed to be thread safe.

Remarks

The **CurrencyManager** derives from the **BindingManagerBase** class. Use the **BindingContext** to return either a **CurrencyManager** or a **PropertyManager**. The actual object returned depends on the data source and data member passed to the **Item** property of the **BindingContext**. If the data source is an object that can only return a single property (instead of a list of objects), the type will be a **PropertyManager**. For example, if you specify a **TextBox** as the data source, a **PropertyManager** will be returned. If, on the other hand, the data source is an object that implements **IList**, **IListSource**, or **IBindingList**, a **CurrencyManager** will be returned.

The **Current** property returns the current item in the underlying list. To change the current item, set the **Position** property to a new value. The value must be greater than 0, and must be less than the value of the **Count** property.

If the underlying data source implements the **IBindingList** interface, and the **AllowNew** property is set to **true**, you can use the **AddNew** method.

Example

[Visual Basic, C#, JScript] The following example binds a **TextBox** control to a column in a **DataTable**, gets the **CurrencyManager** for the binding, and sets its position.

[Visual Basic]
```
' Place the next line into the Declarations section of the form.
 Private myCurrencyManager As CurrencyManager

 Private Sub BindControl(myTable As DataTable)
    ' Bind a TextBox control to a DataTable column in a DataSet.
    TextBox1.DataBindings.Add("Text", myTable, "CompanyName")
    ' Specify the CurrencyManager for the DataTable.
    myCurrencyManager = CType(me.BindingContext(myTable),             ↵
CurrencyManager)
    ' Set the initial Position of the control.
    myCurrencyManager.Position = 0
 End Sub

 Private Sub MoveNext(myCurrencyManager As CurrencyManager)
    If myCurrencyManager.Position = myCurrencyManager.Count - 1 Then
       MessageBox.Show("You're at end of the records")
    Else
       myCurrencyManager.Position += 1
    End If
 End Sub

 Private Sub MoveFirst(myCurrencyManager As CurrencyManager)
    myCurrencyManager.Position = 0
 End Sub

 Private Sub MovePrevious(myCurrencyManager As CurrencyManager)
    If myCurrencyManager.Position = 0 Then
       MessageBox.Show("You're at the beginning of the records.")
    Else
       myCurrencyManager.Position -= 1
    End if
 End Sub

 Private Sub MoveLast(myCurrencyManager As CurrencyManager)
    myCurrencyManager.Position = myCurrencyManager.Count - 1
 End Sub
```

[C#]
```
private CurrencyManager myCurrencyManager;

 private void BindControl(DataTable myTable){
    // Bind a TextBox control to a DataTable column in a DataSet.
    textBox1.DataBindings.Add("Text", myTable, "CompanyName");
    // Specify the CurrencyManager for the DataTable.
    myCurrencyManager = (CurrencyManager)this.BindingContext[myTable];
    // Set the initial Position of the control.
    myCurrencyManager.Position = 0;
 }

 private void MoveNext(CurrencyManager myCurrencyManager){
    if (myCurrencyManager.Position == myCurrencyManager.Count - 1){
       MessageBox.Show("You're at end of the records");
    }
    else{
      myCurrencyManager.Position += 1;
    }
 }

 private void MoveFirst(CurrencyManager myCurrencyManager){
    myCurrencyManager.Position = 0;
 }

 private void MovePrevious(CurrencyManager myCurrencyManager ){
    if(myCurrencyManager.Position == 0) {
       MessageBox.Show("You're at the beginning of the records.");
    }
    else{
       myCurrencyManager.Position -= 1;
    }
 }

 private void MoveLast(CurrencyManager myCurrencyManager){
    myCurrencyManager.Position = myCurrencyManager.Count - 1;
 }
```

[JScript]
```
private var myCurrencyManager : CurrencyManager;

private function BindControl(myTable : DataTable){
   // Bind a TextBox control to a DataTable column in a DataSet.
   textBox1.DataBindings.Add("Text", myTable, "CompanyName");
   // Specify the CurrencyManager for the DataTable.
   myCurrencyManager = CurrencyManager(this.BindingContext[myTable]);
   // Set the initial Position of the control.
   myCurrencyManager.Position = 0;
}

private function MoveNext(myCurrencyManager : CurrencyManager){
   if (myCurrencyManager.Position == myCurrencyManager.Count - 1){
      MessageBox.Show("You're at end of the records");
   }
   else{
     myCurrencyManager.Position += 1;
   }
}
```

```
private function MoveFirst(myCurrencyManager : CurrencyManager){
   myCurrencyManager.Position = 0;
}

private function MovePrevious(myCurrencyManager : CurrencyManager){
   if(myCurrencyManager.Position == 0) {
      MessageBox.Show("You're at the beginning of the records.");
   }
   else{
      myCurrencyManager.Position -= 1;
   }
}

private function MoveLast(myCurrencyManager : CurrencyManager){
   myCurrencyManager.Position = myCurrencyManager.Count - 1;
}
```

Requirements

Namespace: System.Windows.Forms

Platforms: Windows 98, Windows NT 4.0, Windows Millennium Edition, Windows 2000, Windows XP Home Edition, Windows XP Professional, Windows Server 2003 family, .NET Compact Framework - Windows CE .NET

Assembly: System.Windows.Forms (in System.Windows.Forms.dll)

CurrencyManager.finalType Field

This member supports the .NET Framework infrastructure and is not intended to be used directly from your code.

[Visual Basic]
```
Protected finalType As Type
```
[C#]
```
protected Type finalType;
```
[C++]
```
protected: Type* finalType;
```
[JScript]
```
protected var finalType : Type;
```

CurrencyManager.listposition Field

This member supports the .NET Framework infrastructure and is not intended to be used directly from your code.

[Visual Basic]
```
Protected listposition As Integer
```
[C#]
```
protected int listposition;
```
[C++]
```
protected: int listposition;
```
[JScript]
```
protected var listposition : int;
```

CurrencyManager.Count Property

This member overrides **BindingManagerBase.Count**.

[Visual Basic]
```
Overrides Public ReadOnly Property Count As Integer
```
[C#]
```
public override int Count {get;}
```
[C++]
```
public: __property int get_Count();
```
[JScript]
```
public override function get Count() : int;
```

Requirements

Platforms: Windows 98, Windows NT 4.0, Windows Millennium Edition, Windows 2000, Windows XP Home Edition, Windows XP Professional, Windows Server 2003 family, .NET Compact Framework - Windows CE .NET

CurrencyManager.Current Property

This member overrides **BindingManagerBase.Current**.

[Visual Basic]
```
Overrides Public ReadOnly Property Current As Object
```
[C#]
```
public override object Current {get;}
```
[C++]
```
public: __property Object* get_Current();
```
[JScript]
```
public override function get Current() : Object;
```

Requirements

Platforms: Windows 98, Windows NT 4.0, Windows Millennium Edition, Windows 2000, Windows XP Home Edition, Windows XP Professional, Windows Server 2003 family, .NET Compact Framework - Windows CE .NET

CurrencyManager.List Property

Gets the list for this **CurrencyManager**.

[Visual Basic]
```
Public ReadOnly Property List As IList
```
[C#]
```
public IList List {get;}
```
[C++]
```
public: __property IList* get_List();
```
[JScript]
```
public function get List() : IList;
```

Property Value

An **IList** object that contains the list.

Remarks

The object returned by the **List** property can be cast to any type that implments the **IList** interface. This will be commonly used when you know the type of the underlying list. For example, if you are data bound to a **DataSet**, the underlying list is a **DataView** (which implements **IList**). Other classes that implement the interface (this is not a complete list) include: **Array**, **ArrayList**, and **CollectionBase**.

How you use the **List** property depends on the class that implements the **IList** interface. For example, you can use the **List** property to determine the name of the list. If the data source implements the **ITypedList** interface, you can use the **GetListName** method to return the name of the current table. This is shown in the C# code below:

```
private void PrintCurrentListName(DataGrid myDataGrid){
   CurrencyManager myCM = (CurrencyManager)
   BindingContext[myDataGrid.DataSource, myDataGrid.DataMember];
   IList myList = myCM.List;
   ITypedList thisList = (ITypedList) myList;
   Console.WriteLine(thisList.GetListName(null));
}
```

Example

See related example in the **System.Windows.Forms.CurrencyManager** class topic.

Requirements

Platforms: Windows 98, Windows NT 4.0, Windows Millennium Edition, Windows 2000, Windows XP Home Edition, Windows XP Professional, Windows Server 2003 family, .NET Compact Framework - Windows CE .NET

CurrencyManager.Position Property

This member overrides **BindingManagerBase.Position**.

```
[Visual Basic]
Overrides Public Property Position As Integer
[C#]
public override int Position {get; set;}
[C++]
public: __property int get_Position();
public: __property void set_Position(int);
[JScript]
public override function get Position() : int;
public override function set Position(int);
```

Requirements

Platforms: Windows 98, Windows NT 4.0, Windows Millennium Edition, Windows 2000, Windows XP Home Edition, Windows XP Professional, Windows Server 2003 family, .NET Compact Framework - Windows CE .NET

CurrencyManager.AddNew Method

Adds a new item to the underlying list.

```
[Visual Basic]
Overrides Public Sub AddNew()
[C#]
public override void AddNew();
[C++]
public: void AddNew();
[JScript]
public override function AddNew();
```

Exceptions

Exception Type	Condition
NotSupportedException	The underlying data source does not implement **IBindingList**, or the data source has thrown an exception because the user has attempted to add a row to a read-only **DataView**.

Remarks

This method is only supported if the data source implements **IBindingList** and the data source allows adding rows.

> **Note** This property was designed to allow complex-bound controls, such as the **DataGrid** control, to add new items to list.

You typically use this property only if you are creating your own control incorporating the **CurrencyManager**. Otherwise, to add items, if the data source is a **DataView**, use the **AddNew** method of the **DataView** class. If the data source is a **DataTable**, use the **NewRow** method and add the row to the **DataRowCollection**.

Example

See related example in the **System.Windows.Forms.CurrencyManager** class topic.

Requirements

Platforms: Windows 98, Windows NT 4.0, Windows Millennium Edition, Windows 2000, Windows XP Home Edition, Windows XP Professional, Windows Server 2003 family, .NET Compact Framework - Windows CE .NET

CurrencyManager.CancelCurrentEdit Method

Cancels the current edit operation.

```
[Visual Basic]
Overrides Public Sub CancelCurrentEdit()
[C#]
public override void CancelCurrentEdit();
[C++]
public: void CancelCurrentEdit();
[JScript]
public override function CancelCurrentEdit();
```

Remarks

This method is supported only if the objects contained by the data source implement the **IEditableObject** interface. If the objects contained within the data source do not implement the **IEditableObject** interface, changes made to the data will not be discarded.

> **Note** This property was designed to be used by complex-bound controls, such as the **DataGrid** control, to cancel edits. For example, when the Esc key is pressed, the **CancelCurrentEdit** method is called on the **CurrencyManager** for the **DataGrid**. Unless you are creating a control that requires this same functionality, it is not recommended that you use this method. Instead, use the **DataRowView** class's **CancelEdit**.

Example

See related example in the **System.Windows.Forms.CurrencyManager** class topic.

Requirements

Platforms: Windows 98, Windows NT 4.0, Windows Millennium Edition, Windows 2000, Windows XP Home Edition, Windows XP Professional, Windows Server 2003 family, .NET Compact Framework - Windows CE .NET

CurrencyManager.CheckEmpty Method

Throws an exception if there is no list, or the list is empty.

```
[Visual Basic]
Protected Sub CheckEmpty()
[C#]
protected void CheckEmpty();
[C++]
protected: void CheckEmpty();
[JScript]
protected function CheckEmpty();
```

Exceptions

Exception Type	Condition
Exception	There is no list, or the list is empty.

Requirements

Platforms: Windows 98, Windows NT 4.0, Windows Millennium Edition, Windows 2000, Windows XP Home Edition, Windows XP Professional, Windows Server 2003 family, .NET Compact Framework - Windows CE .NET

CurrencyManager.EndCurrentEdit Method

Ends the current edit operation.

```
[Visual Basic]
Overrides Public Sub EndCurrentEdit()
[C#]
public override void EndCurrentEdit();
[C++]
public: void EndCurrentEdit();
[JScript]
public override function EndCurrentEdit();
```

Remarks

This method is supported only if the objects contained by the data source implement the **IEditableObject** interface.

> **Note** This property was designed to be used by complex-bound controls, such as the **DataGrid** control, to cancel edits. Unless you are creating a control that requires this same functionality, it is not recommended that you use this method. Instead, if the data source is either a **DataView** or **DataTable**, use the **DataRowView** class's **EndEdit** method.

Example

See related example in the **System.Windows.Forms.Currency-Manager** class topic.

Requirements

Platforms: Windows 98, Windows NT 4.0, Windows Millennium Edition, Windows 2000, Windows XP Home Edition, Windows XP Professional, Windows Server 2003 family, .NET Compact Framework - Windows CE .NET

CurrencyManager.GetItemProperties Method

This member supports the .NET Framework infrastructure and is not intended to be used directly from your code.

Overload List

This member overrides **BindingManagerBase.GetItemProperties**.

Supported by the .NET Compact Framework.

[Visual Basic] **Overloads Overrides Public Function GetItemProperties() As PropertyDescriptorCollection**

[C#] **public override PropertyDescriptorCollection GetItemProperties();**

[C++] **public: PropertyDescriptorCollection* GetItemProperties();**

[JScript] **public override function GetItemProperties() : PropertyDescriptorCollection;**

Inherited from **BindingManagerBase**.

[Visual Basic] **Overloads Protected Friend Overridable Function GetItemProperties(ArrayList, ArrayList) As PropertyDescriptorCollection**

[C#] **protected internal virtual PropertyDescriptorCollection GetItemProperties(ArrayList, ArrayList);**

[C++] **protected public: virtual PropertyDescriptor-Collection* GetItemProperties(ArrayList*, ArrayList*);**

[JScript] **protected internal function GetItemProperties (ArrayList, ArrayList) : PropertyDescriptorCollection;**

Inherited from **BindingManagerBase**.

Supported by the .NET Compact Framework.

[Visual Basic] **Overloads Protected Overridable Function GetItemProperties(Type, Integer, ArrayList, ArrayList) As PropertyDescriptorCollection**

[C#] **protected virtual PropertyDescriptorCollection GetItemProperties(Type, int, ArrayList, ArrayList);**

[C++] **protected: virtual PropertyDescriptorCollection* GetItemProperties(Type*, int, ArrayList*, ArrayList*);**

[JScript] **protected function GetItemProperties(Type, int, ArrayList, ArrayList) : PropertyDescriptorCollection;**

Example

See related example in the **System.Windows.Forms.Currency-Manager** class topic.

CurrencyManager.GetItemProperties Method ()

This member overrides **BindingManagerBase.GetItemProperties**.

```
[Visual Basic]
Overrides Overloads Public Function GetItemProperties() As _
   PropertyDescriptorCollection
[C#]
public override PropertyDescriptorCollection GetItemProperties();
[C++]
public: PropertyDescriptorCollection* GetItemProperties();
[JScript]
public override function GetItemProperties() :
   PropertyDescriptorCollection;
```

Requirements

Platforms: Windows 98, Windows NT 4.0, Windows Millennium Edition, Windows 2000, Windows XP Home Edition, Windows XP Professional, Windows Server 2003 family, .NET Compact Framework - Windows CE .NET

CurrencyManager.GetListName Method

This member overrides **BindingManagerBase.GetListName**.

```
[Visual Basic]
Protected Friend Overrides Function GetListName( _
   ByVal listAccessors As ArrayList _
) As String
[C#]
protected internal override string GetListName(
   ArrayList listAccessors
);
```

```
[C++]
protected public: String* GetListName(
   ArrayList* listAccessors
);
[JScript]
protected internal override function GetListName(
   listAccessors : ArrayList
) : String;
```

Requirements

Platforms: Windows 98, Windows NT 4.0, Windows Millennium Edition, Windows 2000, Windows XP Home Edition, Windows XP Professional, Windows Server 2003 family

CurrencyManager.OnCurrentChanged Method

This member overrides **BindingManagerBase.OnCurrentChanged**.

```
[Visual Basic]
Protected Friend Overrides Sub OnCurrentChanged( _
   ByVal e As EventArgs _
)
[C#]
protected internal override void OnCurrentChanged(
   EventArgs e
);
[C++]
protected public: void OnCurrentChanged(
   EventArgs* e
);
[JScript]
protected internal override function OnCurrentChanged(
   e : EventArgs
);
```

Requirements

Platforms: Windows 98, Windows NT 4.0, Windows Millennium Edition, Windows 2000, Windows XP Home Edition, Windows XP Professional, Windows Server 2003 family

CurrencyManager.OnItemChanged Method

Raises the **ItemChanged** event.

```
[Visual Basic]
Protected Overridable Sub OnItemChanged( _
   ByVal e As ItemChangedEventArgs _
)
[C#]
protected virtual void OnItemChanged(
   ItemChangedEventArgs e
);
[C++]
protected: virtual void OnItemChanged(
   ItemChangedEventArgs* e
);
[JScript]
protected function OnItemChanged(
   e : ItemChangedEventArgs
);
```

Parameters

e

An **ItemChangedEventArgs** that contains the event data.

Requirements

Platforms: Windows 98, Windows NT 4.0, Windows Millennium Edition, Windows 2000, Windows XP Home Edition, Windows XP Professional, Windows Server 2003 family, .NET Compact Framework - Windows CE .NET

CurrencyManager.OnPositionChanged Method

This member supports the .NET Framework infrastructure and is not intended to be used directly from your code.

```
[Visual Basic]
Protected Overridable Sub OnPositionChanged( _
   ByVal e As EventArgs _
)
[C#]
protected virtual void OnPositionChanged(
   EventArgs e
);
[C++]
protected: virtual void OnPositionChanged(
   EventArgs* e
);
[JScript]
protected function OnPositionChanged(
   e : EventArgs
);
```

CurrencyManager.Refresh Method

Forces a repopulation of the bound controls.

```
[Visual Basic]
Public Sub Refresh()
[C#]
public void Refresh();
[C++]
public: void Refresh();
[JScript]
public function Refresh();
```

Remarks

Use the **Refresh** method when the data source doesn't support notification when it is changed, for example an **Array**.

Example

See related example in the **System.Windows.Forms.CurrencyManager** class topic.

Requirements

Platforms: Windows 98, Windows NT 4.0, Windows Millennium Edition, Windows 2000, Windows XP Home Edition, Windows XP Professional, Windows Server 2003 family, .NET Compact Framework - Windows CE .NET

CurrencyManager.RemoveAt Method

Removes the item at the specified index.

[Visual Basic]
```
Overrides Public Sub RemoveAt( _
   ByVal index As Integer _
)
```
[C#]
```
public override void RemoveAt(
   int index
);
```
[C++]
```
public: void RemoveAt(
   int index
);
```
[JScript]
```
public override function RemoveAt(
   index : int
);
```

Parameters

index

The index of the item to remove from the list.

Exceptions

Exception Type	Condition
IndexOutOfRange-Exception	There is no row at the specified *index*.

Remarks

Note This method was designed to allow complex controls, such as the **DataGrid** control, to remove items from the list. It is not recommended that you use this method to actually remove items. Instead, use the **Delete** method of the **DataView** class to delete items.

Example

See related example in the **System.Windows.Forms.CurrencyManager** class topic.

Requirements

Platforms: Windows 98, Windows NT 4.0, Windows Millennium Edition, Windows 2000, Windows XP Home Edition, Windows XP Professional, Windows Server 2003 family, .NET Compact Framework - Windows CE .NET

CurrencyManager.ResumeBinding Method

This member overrides **BindingManagerBase.ResumeBinding**.

[Visual Basic]
```
Overrides Public Sub ResumeBinding()
```
[C#]
```
public override void ResumeBinding();
```
[C++]
```
public: void ResumeBinding();
```
[JScript]
```
public override function ResumeBinding();
```

Requirements

Platforms: Windows 98, Windows NT 4.0, Windows Millennium Edition, Windows 2000, Windows XP Home Edition, Windows XP Professional, Windows Server 2003 family

CurrencyManager.SuspendBinding Method

This member overrides **BindingManagerBase.SuspendBinding**.

[Visual Basic]
```
Overrides Public Sub SuspendBinding()
```
[C#]
```
public override void SuspendBinding();
```
[C++]
```
public: void SuspendBinding();
```
[JScript]
```
public override function SuspendBinding();
```

Requirements

Platforms: Windows 98, Windows NT 4.0, Windows Millennium Edition, Windows 2000, Windows XP Home Edition, Windows XP Professional, Windows Server 2003 family

CurrencyManager.UpdateIsBinding Method

This member overrides **BindingManagerBase.UpdateIsBinding**.

[Visual Basic]
```
Overrides Protected Sub UpdateIsBinding()
```
[C#]
```
protected override void UpdateIsBinding();
```
[C++]
```
protected: void UpdateIsBinding();
```
[JScript]
```
protected override function UpdateIsBinding();
```

Requirements

Platforms: Windows 98, Windows NT 4.0, Windows Millennium Edition, Windows 2000, Windows XP Home Edition, Windows XP Professional, Windows Server 2003 family, .NET Compact Framework - Windows CE .NET

CurrencyManager.ItemChanged Event

Occurs when the current item has been altered.

[Visual Basic]
```
Public Event ItemChanged As ItemChangedEventHandler
```
[C#]
```
public event ItemChangedEventHandler ItemChanged;
```
[C++]
```
public: __event ItemChangedEventHandler* ItemChanged;
```

[JScript] In JScript, you can handle the events defined by a class, but you cannot define your own.

Event Data

The event handler receives an argument of type **ItemChanged-EventArgs** containing data related to this event. The following **ItemChangedEventArgs** property provides information specific to this event.

Property	Description
Index	Indicates the position of the item being changed within the list.

Remarks

The **ItemChanged** event will occur when the user calls the **Resume-Binding** or **SuspendBinding** method.

The **ItemChanged** event occurs only when the item itself has been changed in some manner. For example, if the value of an item is changed from "10" to "42" the event will occur. This shouldn't be confused with the **PositionChanged** event where the item has been changed to a new item.

The event will also occur if the underlying data changes. For example, if you change the value of a **DataRowView**, the **ItemChanged** event will occur.

Note If you are creating your own control that uses the **CurrencyManager**, you should use the **ListChanged** event of the **IBindingList** class instead of the **ItemChanged** event. The **ListChangedType** property of the **ListChangedEventArgs** object enables you to determine the type of action that has occurred.

Example

See related example in the **System.Windows.Forms.CurrencyManager** class topic.

Requirements

Platforms: Windows 98, Windows NT 4.0, Windows Millennium Edition, Windows 2000, Windows XP Home Edition, Windows XP Professional, Windows Server 2003 family

CurrencyManager.MetaDataChanged Event

Note: This namespace, class, or member is supported only in version 1.1 of the .NET Framework.

Occurs when the metadata of the **List** has changed.

[Visual Basic]
```
Public Event MetaDataChanged As EventHandler
```
[C#]
```
public event EventHandler MetaDataChanged;
```
[C++]
```
public: __event EventHandler* MetaDataChanged;
```

[JScript] In JScript, you can handle the events defined by a class, but you cannot define your own.

Event Data

The event handler receives an argument of type **EventArgs**.

Remarks

The metadata of the **List** consists of the schema of the underlying **Binding.DataSource**. The **MetaDataChanged** event is raised when that schema has changed. For example, the **MetaDataChanged** event is raised when a **DataColumn** is programmatically added to a **DataTable**.

Requirements

Platforms: Windows 98, Windows NT 4.0, Windows Millennium Edition, Windows 2000, Windows XP Home Edition, Windows XP Professional, Windows Server 2003 family

Cursor Class

Represents the image used to paint the mouse pointer.

System.Object
System.Windows.Forms.Cursor

[Visual Basic]
```
<Serializable>
NotInheritable Public Class Cursor
   Implements IDisposable, ISerializable
```
[C#]
```
[Serializable]
public sealed class Cursor : IDisposable, ISerializable
```
[C++]
```
[Serializable]
public __gc __sealed class Cursor : public IDisposable,
   ISerializable
```
[JScript]
```
public
   Serializable
class Cursor implements IDisposable, ISerializable
```

Thread Safety

Any public static (**Shared** in Visual Basic) members of this type are safe for multithreaded operations. Any instance members are not guaranteed to be thread safe.

Remarks

A cursor is a small picture whose location on the screen is controlled by a pointing device, such as a mouse, pen, or trackball. When the user moves the pointing device, the operating system moves the cursor accordingly.

Different cursor shapes are used to inform the user what operation the mouse will have. For example, when editing or selecting text, a **Cursors.IBeam** cursor is typically displayed. A wait cursor is commonly used to inform the user that a process is currently running. Examples of processes you might have the user wait for are opening a file, saving a file, or filling a control such as a **DataGrid**, **ListBox** or **TreeView** with a large amount of data.

All controls that derive from the **Control** class have a **Cursor** property. To change the cursor displayed by the mouse pointer when it is within the bounds of the control, assign a **Cursor** to the **Cursor** property of the control. Alternatively, you can display cursors at the application level by assigning a **Cursor** to the **Current** property. For example, if the purpose of your application is to edit a text file, you might set the **Current** property to **Cursors.WaitCursor** to display a wait cursor over the application while the file loads or saves to prevent any mouse events from being processed. When the process is complete, set the **Current** property to **Cursors.Default** for the application to display the appropriate cursor over each control type.

> **Note** If you call **Application.DoEvents** before resetting the **Current** property back to the **Cursors.Default** cursor, the application will resume listening for mouse events and will resume displaying the appropriate **Cursor** for each control in the application.

Cursor objects can be created from several sources, such as the handle of an existing **Cursor**, a standard **Cursor** file, a resource, or a data stream.

> **Note** The **Cursor** class does not support animated cursors (.ani files) or cursors with colors other than black and white.

If the image you are using as a cursor is too small, you can use the **DrawStretched** method to force the image to fill the bounds of the cursor. You can temporarily hide the cursor by calling the **Hide** method, and restore it by calling the **Show** method.

Example

[Visual Basic, C#, C++] The following example displays a form that demonstrates using a custom cursor by using the **System.Windows.Forms.Cursor.#ctor** constructor. The custom **Cursor** is embedded in the application's resource file. The example assumes that you have a cursor contained in a cursor file named `MyCursor.cur`. To compile this example using the command line, include the following flag: **/res:MyCursor.Cur, CustomCursor.MyCursor.Cur**

[Visual Basic]
```
Imports System
Imports System.Drawing
Imports System.Windows.Forms

Namespace CustomCursor

   Public Class Form1
      Inherits System.Windows.Forms.Form

      <System.STAThread()> _
      Public Shared Sub Main()
         System.Windows.Forms.Application.Run(New Form1())
      End Sub 'Main

      Public Sub New()

         Me.ClientSize = New System.Drawing.Size(292, 266)
         Me.Text = "Cursor Example"

         ' Looks namespace.MyCursor.cur in the assemblies manifest.

         ' The following generates a cursor from an embedded resource.
         ' To add a custom cursor, create or use an existing        ↵
16x16 bitmap
         '        1. Add a new cursor file to your project:
         '                File->Add New Item->Local Project         ↵
Items->Cursor File
         '        2. Select 16x16 image type:
         '                Image->Current Icon Image Types->16x16
         ' --- To make the custom cursor an embedded resource ---
         ' In Visual Studio:
         '        1. Select the cursor file in the Solution Explorer
         '        2. Choose View->Properties.
         '        3. In the properties window switch               ↵
"Build Action" to "Embedded"
         ' On the command line:
         '        Add the following flag:
         '           /res:CursorFileName.Cur,Namespace.CursorFileName.Cur
         '
         ' The following line uses the namespace from the          ↵
passed-in type
         ' and looks for CustomCursor.MyCursor.Cur in the          ↵
assemblies manifest.
      ' NOTE: The cursor name is acase sensitive.

         Me.Cursor = New Cursor(Me.GetType(), "MyCursor.Cur")
      End Sub 'New
   End Class 'Form1
End Namespace 'CustomCursor
```

[C#]
```
using System;
using System.Drawing;
using System.Windows.Forms;

namespace CustomCursor
{
   public class Form1 : System.Windows.Forms.Form
```

```
{
    [STAThread]
    static void Main()
    {
        Application.Run(new Form1());
    }

    public Form1()
    {
        this.ClientSize = new System.Drawing.Size(292, 266);
        this.Text = "Cursor Example";

        // The following generates a cursor from an              ↵
embedded resource.

        // To add a custom cursor, create or use an              ↵
existing 16x16 bitmap
        //        1. Add a new cursor file to your project:
        //                File->Add New Item->Local Project       ↵
 Items->Cursor File
        //        2. Select 16x16 image type:
        //                Image->Current Icon Image Types->16x16

        // --- To make the custom cursor an embedded resource  ---

        // In Visual Studio:
        //        1. Select the cursor file in the Solution      ↵
Explorer
        //        2. Choose View->Properties.
        //        3. In the properties window switch             ↵
"Build Action" to "Embedded"

        // On the command line:
        //        Add the following flag:
        //                                                        ↵
/res:CursorFileName.Cur,Namespace.CursorFileName.Cur
        //
        //        Where "Namespace" is the namespace in which    ↵
 you want to use the cursor
        //        and   "CursorFileName.Cur" is the cursor       ↵
filename.

        // The following line uses the namespace from the        ↵
passed-in type
        // and looks for CustomCursor.MyCursor.Cur in the        ↵
assemblies manifest.
      // NOTE: The cursor name is acase sensitive.
        this.Cursor = new Cursor(GetType(), "MyCursor.Cur");

      }
    }
}
```

[C++]

```
using namespace System;
using namespace System::Drawing;
using namespace System::Windows::Forms;

namespace CustomCursor {
public __gc class Form1 : public System::Windows::Forms::Form {

public:
    Form1() {
        this->ClientSize = System::Drawing::Size(292, 266);
        this->Text = S"Cursor Example";

        // The following generates a cursor from an embedded resource.

        // To add a custom cursor, create or use an existing 16x16 bitmap
        //        1. Add a new cursor file to your project:
        //                File->Add New Item->Local Project       ↵
 Items->Cursor File
        //        2. Select 16x16 image type:
        //                Image->Current Icon Image Types->16x16

        // --- To make the custom cursor an embedded resource  ---

        // In Visual Studio:
        //        1. Select the cursor file in the Solution Explorer
        //        2. Choose View->Properties.
        //        3. In the properties window switch             ↵
 S"Build Action" to S"Embedded"

        // On the command line:
        //        Add the following flag:
        //            /res:CursorFileName.Cur,                   ↵
Namespace.CursorFileName.Cur
        //
        //        Where S"Namespace" is the namespace in which   ↵
you want to use the cursor
        //        and   S"CursorFileName.Cur" is the cursor filename.

        // The following line uses the namespace from the        ↵
passed-in type
        // and looks for CustomCursor.MyCursor.Cur in the        ↵
assemblies manifest.
        // NOTE: The cursor name is acase sensitive.
        this->Cursor = new System::Windows::Forms::Cursor        ↵
 (GetType(), S"MyCursor.Cur");

    }
};
}
[STAThread]
int main() {
    Application::Run(new CustomCursor::Form1());
}
```

[Visual Basic, C#, C++] The following example displays customer information in a **TreeView** control. The root tree nodes display customer names, and the child tree nodes display the order numbers assigned to each customer. In this example, 1,000 customers are displayed with 15 orders each. The repainting of the **TreeView** is suppressed by using the **BeginUpdate** and **EndUpdate** methods, and a wait **Cursor** is displayed while the **TreeView** creates and paints the **TreeNode** objects. This example assumes you have a cursor file named `MyWait.cur` in the application directory. It also assumes you have a `Customer` object that can hold a collection of `Order` objects, and that you have created an instance of a **TreeView** control on a **Form**.

[Visual Basic]

```
' Create a new ArrayList to hold the Customer objects.
Private customerArray As New ArrayList()

Private Sub FillMyTreeView()
   ' Add customers to the ArrayList of Customer objects.
   Dim x As Integer
   For x = 0 To 999
      customerArray.Add(New Customer("Customer" + x.ToString()))
   Next x

   ' Add orders to each Customer object in the ArrayList.
   Dim customer1 As Customer
   For Each customer1 In customerArray
      Dim y As Integer
      For y = 0 To 14
         customer1.CustomerOrders.Add(New Order("Order" +        ↵
y.ToString()))
      Next y
   Next customer1

   ' Display a wait cursor while the TreeNodes are being created.
   Cursor.Current = New Cursor("MyWait.cur")

   ' Suppress repainting the TreeView until all the objects have ↵
 been created.
   treeView1.BeginUpdate()

   ' Clear the TreeView each time the method is called.
   treeView1.Nodes.Clear()
```

```
    ' Add a root TreeNode for each Customer object in the ArrayList.
    Dim customer2 As Customer
    For Each customer2 In customerArray
       treeView1.Nodes.Add(New TreeNode(customer2.CustomerName))

       ' Add a child TreeNode for each Order object in the           ↵
current Customer object.
       Dim order1 As Order
       For Each order1 In customer2.CustomerOrders
          treeView1.Nodes(customerArray.IndexOf(customer2)).Nodes.Add( _
     New TreeNode(customer2.CustomerName + "." + order1.OrderID))
       Next order1
    Next customer2

    ' Reset the cursor to the default for all controls.
    Cursor.Current = System.Windows.Forms.Cursors.Default

    ' Begin repainting the TreeView.
    treeView1.EndUpdate()
End Sub 'FillMyTreeView
```

[C#]

```
// Create a new ArrayList to hold the Customer objects.
private ArrayList customerArray = new ArrayList();

private void FillMyTreeView()
{
   // Add customers to the ArrayList of Customer objects.
   for(int x=0; x<1000; x++)
   {
      customerArray.Add(new Customer("Customer" + x.ToString()));
   }

   // Add orders to each Customer object in the ArrayList.
   foreach(Customer customer1 in customerArray)
   {
      for(int y=0; y<15; y++)
      {
         customer1.CustomerOrders.Add(new Order("Order" +               ↵
y.ToString()));
      }
   }

   // Display a wait cursor while the TreeNodes are being created.
   Cursor.Current = new Cursor("MyWait.cur");

   // Suppress repainting the TreeView until all the objects            ↵
have been created.
   treeView1.BeginUpdate();

   // Clear the TreeView each time the method is called.
   treeView1.Nodes.Clear();

   // Add a root TreeNode for each Customer object in the ArrayList.
   foreach(Customer customer2 in customerArray)
   {
      treeView1.Nodes.Add(new TreeNode(customer2.CustomerName));

      // Add a child treenode for each Order object in the              ↵
current Customer object.
      foreach(Order order1 in customer2.CustomerOrders)
      {
         treeView1.Nodes[customerArray.IndexOf(customer2)].Nodes.Add(
           new TreeNode(customer2.CustomerName + "." +                  ↵
order1.OrderID));
      }
   }

   // Reset the cursor to the default for all controls.
   Cursor.Current = Cursors.Default;

   // Begin repainting the TreeView.
   treeView1.EndUpdate();
}
```

[C++]

```
void FillMyTreeView() {
    // Add customers to the ArrayList of Customer objects.
    for (int x=0; x<1000; x++) {
        customerArray->Add(new Customer(String::Concat                  ↵
 (S"Customer ", __box(x))));
    }

    // Add orders to each Customer object in the ArrayList.
    IEnumerator* myEnum = customerArray->GetEnumerator();
    while (myEnum->MoveNext()) {
        Customer* customer1 = __try_cast<Customer*>(myEnum->Current);

        for (int y=0; y<15; y++) {
            customer1->CustomerOrders->Add(new                          ↵
Order(String::Concat(S"Order ", __box(y))));
        }
    }

    // Display a wait cursor while the TreeNodes are being created.
    Cursor::Current = new                                               ↵
System::Windows::Forms::Cursor(S"MyWait.cur");

    // Suppress repainting the TreeView until all the objects           ↵
have been created.
    treeView1->BeginUpdate();

    // Clear the TreeView each time the method is called.
    treeView1->Nodes->Clear();

    // Add a root TreeNode for each Customer object in the ArrayList.
    while (myEnum->MoveNext()) {
        Customer* customer2 = __try_cast<Customer*>(myEnum->Current);

        treeView1->Nodes->Add(new TreeNode(customer2->CustomerName));

        // Add a child treenode for each Order object in the            ↵
 current Customer object.
        IEnumerator* myEnum = customer2->CustomerOrders-                ↵
>GetEnumerator();
        while (myEnum->MoveNext()) {
            Order* order1 = __try_cast<Order*>(myEnum->Current);

            treeView1->Nodes->Item[customerArray->IndexOf               ↵
 (customer2)]->Nodes->Add(
                new TreeNode(String::Concat(customer2->                 ↵
CustomerName, S".", order1->OrderID)));
        }
    }

    // Reset the cursor to the default for all controls.
    Cursor::Current = Cursors::Default;

    // Begin repainting the TreeView.
    treeView1->EndUpdate();
}
```

Requirements

Namespace: System.Windows.Forms

Platforms: Windows 98, Windows NT 4.0, Windows Millennium Edition, Windows 2000, Windows XP Home Edition, Windows XP Professional, Windows Server 2003 family, .NET Compact Framework - Windows CE .NET

Assembly: System.Windows.Forms (in System.Windows.Forms.dll)

Cursor Constructor

Initializes a new instance of the **Cursor** class.

Overload List

Initializes a new instance of the **Cursor** class from the specified Windows handle.

[Visual Basic] **Public Sub New(IntPtr)**

[C#] **public Cursor(IntPtr);**

[C++] **public: Cursor(IntPtr);**

[JScript] **public function Cursor(IntPtr);**

Initializes a new instance of the **Cursor** class from the specified data stream.

[Visual Basic] **Public Sub New(Stream)**

[C#] **public Cursor(Stream);**

[C++] **public: Cursor(Stream*);**

[JScript] **public function Cursor(Stream);**

Initializes a new instance of the **Cursor** class from the specified file.

[Visual Basic] **Public Sub New(String)**

[C#] **public Cursor(string);**

[C++] **public: Cursor(String*);**

[JScript] **public function Cursor(String);**

Initializes a new instance of the **Cursor** class from the specified resource with the specified resource type.

[Visual Basic] **Public Sub New(Type, String)**

[C#] **public Cursor(Type, string);**

[C++] **public: Cursor(Type*, String*);**

[JScript] **public function Cursor(Type, String);**

Example

See related example in the **System.Windows.Forms.Cursor** class topic.

Cursor Constructor (IntPtr)

Initializes a new instance of the **Cursor** class from the specified Windows handle.

```
[Visual Basic]
Public Sub New( _
   ByVal handle As IntPtr _
)
[C#]
public Cursor(
   IntPtr handle
);
[C++]
public: Cursor(
   IntPtr handle
);
[JScript]
public function Cursor(
   handle : IntPtr
);
```

Parameters

handle

An **IntPtr** that represents the Windows handle of the cursor to create.

Exceptions

Exception Type	Condition
ArgumentException	*handle* is **IntPtr.Zero**.

Remarks

You must free the cursor handle when you are done with it.

Example

See related example in the **System.Windows.Forms.Cursor** class topic.

Requirements

Platforms: Windows 98, Windows NT 4.0, Windows Millennium Edition, Windows 2000, Windows XP Home Edition, Windows XP Professional, Windows Server 2003 family

Cursor Constructor (Stream)

Initializes a new instance of the **Cursor** class from the specified data stream.

```
[Visual Basic]
Public Sub New( _
   ByVal stream As Stream _
)
[C#]
public Cursor(
   Stream stream
);
[C++]
public: Cursor(
   Stream* stream
);
[JScript]
public function Cursor(
   stream : Stream
);
```

Parameters

stream

The data stream to load the **Cursor** from.

Remarks

The data stream specified by *stream* must contain a cursor (.cur) file.

> **Note** Animated cursors (.ani files) are not supported by the **Cursor** class.

Example

See related example in the **System.Windows.Forms.Cursor** class topic.

Requirements

Platforms: Windows 98, Windows NT 4.0, Windows Millennium Edition, Windows 2000, Windows XP Home Edition, Windows XP Professional, Windows Server 2003 family

Cursor Constructor (String)

Initializes a new instance of the **Cursor** class from the specified file.

[Visual Basic]
```
Public Sub New( _
   ByVal fileName As String _
)
```
[C#]
```
public Cursor(
   string fileName
);
```
[C++]
```
public: Cursor(
   String* fileName
);
```
[JScript]
```
public function Cursor(
   fileName : String
);
```

Parameters

fileName
    The cursor file to load.

Remarks

The *fileName* parameter must reference a standard cursor (.cur) file.

> **Note** Animated cursors (.ani files) are not supported by the **Cursor** class.

Example

See related example in the **System.Windows.Forms.Cursor** class topic.

Requirements

Platforms: Windows 98, Windows NT 4.0, Windows Millennium Edition, Windows 2000, Windows XP Home Edition, Windows XP Professional, Windows Server 2003 family

Cursor Constructor (Type, String)

Initializes a new instance of the **Cursor** class from the specified resource with the specified resource type.

[Visual Basic]
```
Public Sub New( _
   ByVal type As Type, _
   ByVal resource As String _
)
```
[C#]
```
public Cursor(
   Type type,
   string resource
);
```
[C++]
```
public: Cursor(
   Type* type,
   String* resource
);
```
[JScript]
```
public function Cursor(
   type : Type,
   resource : String
);
```

Parameters

type
    The resource **Type**.

resource
    The name of the resource.

Remarks

The following is an example of how to embed a cursor as a resource within your application. To embed the resource, reference the resource name followed by a comma, then its full assembly path. See the Example section to learn how to load the cursor from the embedded resource.

```
Using the C# compiler:
csc /resource:"MyWaitCursor.cur","MyCursors.MyWaitCursor.cur"
MyCursor.cs
Using the Visual Basic compiler:
vbc /resource:"MyWaitCursor.cur","MyCursors.MyWaitCursor.cur"
MyCursor.vb
```

> **Note** The resource reference when compiling as well as when referencing it in code, is case sensitive for both the C# and Visual Basic compilers.

Example

See related example in the **System.Windows.Forms.Cursor** class topic.

Requirements

Platforms: Windows 98, Windows NT 4.0, Windows Millennium Edition, Windows 2000, Windows XP Home Edition, Windows XP Professional, Windows Server 2003 family

Cursor.Clip Property

Gets or sets the bounds that represents the clipping rectangle for the cursor.

[Visual Basic]
```
Public Shared Property Clip As Rectangle
```
[C#]
```
public static Rectangle Clip {get; set;}
```
[C++]
```
public: __property static Rectangle get_Clip();
public: __property static void set_Clip(Rectangle);
```
[JScript]
```
public static function get Clip() : Rectangle;
public static function set Clip(Rectangle);
```

Property Value

The **Rectangle** that represents the clipping rectangle for the **Cursor**, in screen coordinates.

Remarks

A clipped cursor is allowed to move only within its clipping rectangle. Generally, the system allows this only if the mouse is currently captured. If the cursor is not currently clipped, the resulting rectangle contains the dimensions of the entire screen.

Example

See related example in the **System.Windows.Forms.Cursor** class topic.

Requirements

Platforms: Windows 98, Windows NT 4.0,
Windows Millennium Edition, Windows 2000,
Windows XP Home Edition, Windows XP Professional,
Windows Server 2003 family

.NET Framework Security:

- **UIPermission** for all windows to set this property. Associated enumeration: **UIPermissionWindow.AllWindows**

Cursor.Current Property

Gets or sets a cursor object that represents the mouse cursor.

```
[Visual Basic]
Public Shared Property Current As Cursor
[C#]
public static Cursor Current {get; set;}
[C++]
public: __property static Cursor* get_Current();
public: __property static void set_Current(Cursor*);
[JScript]
public static function get Current() : Cursor;
public static function set Current(Cursor);
```

Property Value

A **Cursor** that represents the mouse cursor. The default is a null reference (**Nothing** in Visual Basic) if the mouse cursor is not visible.

Remarks

Setting the **Current** property changes the cursor currently displayed, and the application stops listening for mouse events. For example, you might set the **Current** property to **Cursors.WaitCursor** before you start filling a **TreeView**, **DataGrid**, or **ListBox** control with a large amount of data. After the loop is completed, set this property back to **Cursors.Default** to display the appropriate cursor for each control.

Note If you call **Application.DoEvents** before resetting the **Current** property back to the **Cursors.Default** cursor, the application will resume listening for mouse events and will resume displaying the appropriate **Cursor** for each control in the application.

Example

See related example in the **System.Windows.Forms.Cursor** class topic.

Requirements

Platforms: Windows 98, Windows NT 4.0,
Windows Millennium Edition, Windows 2000,
Windows XP Home Edition, Windows XP Professional,
Windows Server 2003 family,
.NET Compact Framework - Windows CE .NET

.NET Framework Security:

- **UIPermission** for safe subwindows to set this property. Associated enumeration: **UIPermissionWindow.SafeSubWindows**

Cursor.Handle Property

Gets the handle of the cursor.

```
[Visual Basic]
Public ReadOnly Property Handle As IntPtr
[C#]
public IntPtr Handle {get;}
[C++]
public: __property IntPtr get_Handle();
[JScript]
public function get Handle() : IntPtr;
```

Property Value

An **IntPtr** that represents the cursor's handle.

Exceptions

Exception Type	Condition
Exception	The handle value is **IntPtr.Zero**.

Remarks

This is not a copy of the handle; do not dispose of it.

Example

See related example in the **System.Windows.Forms.Cursor** class topic.

Requirements

Platforms: Windows 98, Windows NT 4.0,
Windows Millennium Edition, Windows 2000,
Windows XP Home Edition, Windows XP Professional,
Windows Server 2003 family

Cursor.Position Property

Gets or sets the cursor's position.

```
[Visual Basic]
Public Shared Property Position As Point
[C#]
public static Point Position {get; set;}
[C++]
public: __property static Point get_Position();
public: __property static void set_Position(Point);
[JScript]
public static function get Position() : Point;
public static function set Position(Point);
```

Property Value

A **Point** that represents the cursor's position in screen coordinates.

Example

See related example in the **System.Windows.Forms.Cursor** class topic.

Requirements

Platforms: Windows 98, Windows NT 4.0,
Windows Millennium Edition, Windows 2000,
Windows XP Home Edition, Windows XP Professional,
Windows Server 2003 family

Cursor.Size Property

Gets the size of the cursor object.

```
[Visual Basic]
Public ReadOnly Property Size As Size
[C#]
public Size Size {get;}
[C++]
public: __property Size get_Size();
[JScript]
public function get Size() : Size;
```

Property Value

A **Size** that represents the width and height of the **Cursor**.

Example

See related example in the **System.Windows.Forms.Cursor** class topic.

Requirements

Platforms: Windows 98, Windows NT 4.0, Windows Millennium Edition, Windows 2000, Windows XP Home Edition, Windows XP Professional, Windows Server 2003 family

Cursor.CopyHandle Method

Copies the handle of this **Cursor**.

```
[Visual Basic]
Public Function CopyHandle() As IntPtr
[C#]
public IntPtr CopyHandle();
[C++]
public: IntPtr CopyHandle();
[JScript]
public function CopyHandle() : IntPtr;
```

Return Value

An **IntPtr** that represents the cursor's handle.

Remarks

The handle created as a result of calling this method must be disposed of when you are done with it because it will not be disposed of by the garbage collector.

Requirements

Platforms: Windows 98, Windows NT 4.0, Windows Millennium Edition, Windows 2000, Windows XP Home Edition, Windows XP Professional, Windows Server 2003 family

Cursor.Dispose Method

Releases all resources used by the **Cursor**.

```
[Visual Basic]
Public Overridable Sub Dispose() Implements IDisposable.Dispose
[C#]
public virtual void Dispose();
[C++]
public: virtual void Dispose();
[JScript]
public function Dispose();
```

Implements

IDisposable.Dispose

Remarks

Call **Dispose** when you are finished using the **Cursor**. The **Dispose** method leaves the **Cursor** in an unusable state. After calling **Dispose**, you must release all references to the **Cursor** so the garbage collector can reclaim the memory that the **Cursor** was occupying.

Note Always call **Dispose** before you release your last reference to the **Cursor**. Otherwise, the resources it is using will not be freed until the garbage collector calls the **Cursor** object's **Finalize** method.

Example

See related example in the **System.Windows.Forms.Cursor** class topic.

Requirements

Platforms: Windows 98, Windows NT 4.0, Windows Millennium Edition, Windows 2000, Windows XP Home Edition, Windows XP Professional, Windows Server 2003 family

Cursor.Draw Method

Draws the cursor on the specified surface, within the specified bounds.

```
[Visual Basic]
Public Sub Draw( _
   ByVal g As Graphics, _
   ByVal targetRect As Rectangle _
)
[C#]
public void Draw(
   Graphics g,
   Rectangle targetRect
);
[C++]
public: void Draw(
   Graphics* g,
   Rectangle targetRect
);
[JScript]
public function Draw(
   g : Graphics,
   targetRect : Rectangle
);
```

Parameters

g
   The **Graphics** surface on which to draw the **Cursor**.

targetRect
   The **Rectangle** that represents the bounds of the **Cursor**.

Remarks

The drawing command originates on the graphics surface represented by the *g* parameter, but a **Graphics** does not contain information about how to render a given image, so it passes the call to the **Cursor**. The **Draw** method crops the image to the given dimensions and allows you to specify a **Rectangle** within which to draw the **Cursor**. This method is typically used if you want to draw the curso on a Graphics surface. For example, you might have a dialog that allows the user to select cursors from a **ListBox** control, or a group of **RadioButton** controls.

Example

See related example in the **System.Windows.Forms.Cursor** class topic.

Requirements

Platforms: Windows 98, Windows NT 4.0,
Windows Millennium Edition, Windows 2000,
Windows XP Home Edition, Windows XP Professional,
Windows Server 2003 family

Cursor.DrawStretched Method

Draws the cursor in a stretched format on the specified surface, within the specified bounds.

```
[Visual Basic]
Public Sub DrawStretched( _
   ByVal g As Graphics, _
   ByVal targetRect As Rectangle _
)
[C#]
public void DrawStretched(
   Graphics g,
   Rectangle targetRect
);
[C++]
public: void DrawStretched(
   Graphics* g,
   Rectangle targetRect
);
[JScript]
public function DrawStretched(
   g : Graphics,
   targetRect : Rectangle
);
```

Parameters

g
The **Graphics** surface on which to draw the **Cursor**.

targetRect
The **Rectangle** that represents the bounds of the **Cursor**.

Remarks

The drawing command originates on the graphics surface represented by the *g* parameter, but a **Graphics** object does not contain information about how to render a given image, so it passes the call to the **Cursor** object. The **DrawStretched** method stretches the image to fill the specified **Rectangle** when the cursor is drawn.

Example

See related example in the **System.Windows.Forms.Cursor** class topic.

Requirements

Platforms: Windows 98, Windows NT 4.0,
Windows Millennium Edition, Windows 2000,
Windows XP Home Edition, Windows XP Professional,
Windows Server 2003 family

Cursor.Equals Method

Returns a value indicating whether this cursor is equal to the specified **Cursor**.

```
[Visual Basic]
Overrides Public Function Equals( _
   ByVal obj As Object _
) As Boolean
[C#]
public override bool Equals(
   object obj
);
[C++]
public: bool Equals(
   Object* obj
);
[JScript]
public override function Equals(
   obj : Object
) : Boolean;
```

Parameters

obj
The **Cursor** to compare.

Return Value

true if this cursor is equal to the specified **Cursor**; otherwise, **false**.

Example

See related example in the **System.Windows.Forms.Cursor** class topic.

\

Requirements

Platforms: Windows 98, Windows NT 4.0,
Windows Millennium Edition, Windows 2000,
Windows XP Home Edition, Windows XP Professional,
Windows Server 2003 family,
.NET Compact Framework - Windows CE .NET

Cursor.Finalize Method

Releases the unmanaged resources and performs other cleanup operations before the **Cursor** is reclaimed by garbage collection.

[C#] In C#, finalizers are expressed using destructor syntax.

[C++] In C++, finalizers are expressed using destructor syntax.

```
[Visual Basic]
Overrides Protected Sub Finalize()
[C#]
~Cursor();
[C++]
~Cursor();
[JScript]
protected override function Finalize();
```

Remarks

This method overrides **Object.Finalize**. Application code should not call this method; an object's **Finalize** method is automatically invoked during garbage collection, unless finalization by the garbage collector has been disabled by a call to the **GC.SuppressFinalize** method.

Requirements

Platforms: Windows 98, Windows NT 4.0,
Windows Millennium Edition, Windows 2000,
Windows XP Home Edition, Windows XP Professional,
Windows Server 2003 family,
.NET Compact Framework - Windows CE .NET

Cursor.GetHashCode Method

This member overrides **Object.GetHashCode**.

```
[Visual Basic]
Overrides Public Function GetHashCode() As Integer
[C#]
public override int GetHashCode();
[C++]
public: int GetHashCode();
[JScript]
public override function GetHashCode() : int;
```

Requirements

Platforms: Windows 98, Windows NT 4.0,
Windows Millennium Edition, Windows 2000,
Windows XP Home Edition, Windows XP Professional,
Windows Server 2003 family,
.NET Compact Framework - Windows CE .NET

Cursor.Hide Method

Hides the cursor.

```
[Visual Basic]
Public Shared Sub Hide()
[C#]
public static void Hide();
[C++]
public: static void Hide();
[JScript]
public static function Hide();
```

Remarks

The **Show** and **Hide** method calls must be balanced. For every call to the **Hide** method there must be a corresponding call to the **Show** method.

Example

See related example in the **System.Windows.Forms.Cursor** class topic.

Requirements

Platforms: Windows 98, Windows NT 4.0,
Windows Millennium Edition, Windows 2000,
Windows XP Home Edition, Windows XP Professional,
Windows Server 2003 family,
.NET Compact Framework - Windows CE .NET

.NET Framework Security:

- **UIPermission** for all windows call this method. Associated enumeration: **UIPermissionWindow.AllWindows**

Cursor.ISerializable.GetObjectData Method

This member supports the .NET Framework infrastructure and is not intended to be used directly from your code.

```
[Visual Basic]
Private Sub GetObjectData( _
   ByVal si As SerializationInfo, _
   ByVal context As StreamingContext _
) Implements ISerializable.GetObjectData
[C#]
void ISerializable.GetObjectData(
   SerializationInfo si,
   StreamingContext context
);
[C++]
private: void ISerializable::GetObjectData(
   SerializationInfo* si,
   StreamingContext context
);
[JScript]
private function ISerializable.GetObjectData(
   si : SerializationInfo,
   context : StreamingContext
);
```

Cursor.Show Method

Displays the cursor.

```
[Visual Basic]
Public Shared Sub Show()
[C#]
public static void Show();
[C++]
public: static void Show();
[JScript]
public static function Show();
```

Remarks

The **Show** and **Hide** method calls must be balanced. For every call to the **Hide** method there must be a corresponding call to the **Show** method.

Example

See related example in the **System.Windows.Forms.Cursor** class topic.

Requirements

Platforms: Windows 98, Windows NT 4.0,
Windows Millennium Edition, Windows 2000,
Windows XP Home Edition, Windows XP Professional,
Windows Server 2003 family,
.NET Compact Framework - Windows CE .NET

Cursor.ToString Method

This member overrides **Object.ToString**.

```
[Visual Basic]
Overrides Public Function ToString() As String
[C#]
public override string ToString();
[C++]
public: String* ToString();
[JScript]
public override function ToString() : String;
```

Requirements

Platforms: Windows 98, Windows NT 4.0, Windows Millennium Edition, Windows 2000, Windows XP Home Edition, Windows XP Professional, Windows Server 2003 family, .NET Compact Framework - Windows CE .NET

Cursor Equality Operator

Returns a value indicating whether two instances of the **Cursor** class are equal.

```
[Visual Basic]
returnValue = Cursor.op_Equality(left, right)
[C#]
public static bool operator ==(
   Cursor left,
   Cursor right
);
[C++]
public: static bool op_Equality(
   Cursor* left,
   Cursor* right
);
[JScript]
returnValue = left == right;
```

[Visual Basic] In Visual Basic, you can use the operators defined by a type, but you cannot define your own. You can use the **Equals** method instead of the **Cursor** equality operator.

[JScript] In JScript, you can use the operators defined by a type, but you cannot define your own.

Arguments [Visual Basic, JScript]

left
  A **Cursor** to compare.

right
  A **Cursor** to compare.

Parameters [C#, C++]

left
  A **Cursor** to compare.

right
  A **Cursor** to compare.

Return Value

true if two instances of the **Cursor** class are equal; otherwise, **false**.

Example

See related example in the **System.Windows.Forms.Cursor** class topic.

Requirements

Platforms: Windows 98, Windows NT 4.0, Windows Millennium Edition, Windows 2000, Windows XP Home Edition, Windows XP Professional, Windows Server 2003 family

Cursor Inequality Operator

Returns a value indicating whether two instances of the **Cursor** class are not equal.

```
[Visual Basic]
returnValue = Cursor.op_Inequality(left, right)
[C#]
public static bool operator !=(
   Cursor left,
   Cursor right
);
[C++]
public: static bool op_Inequality(
   Cursor* left,
   Cursor* right
);
[JScript]
returnValue = left != right;
```

[Visual Basic] In Visual Basic, you can use the operators defined by a type, but you cannot define your own. You can use the **Equals** method instead of the **Cursor** inequality operator.

[JScript] In JScript, you can use the operators defined by a type, but you cannot define your own.

Arguments [Visual Basic, JScript]

left
  A **Cursor** to compare.

right
  A **Cursor** to compare.

Parameters [C#, C++]

left
  A **Cursor** to compare.

right
  A **Cursor** to compare.

Return Value

true if two instances of the **Cursor** class are not equal; otherwise, **false**.

Example

See related example in the **System.Windows.Forms.Cursor** class topic.

Requirements

Platforms: Windows 98, Windows NT 4.0, Windows Millennium Edition, Windows 2000, Windows XP Home Edition, Windows XP Professional, Windows Server 2003 family

CursorConverter Class

Provides a type converter to convert **Cursor** objects to and from various other representations.

System.Object
  System.ComponentModel.TypeConverter
    System.Windows.Forms.CursorConverter

```
[Visual Basic]
Public Class CursorConverter
   Inherits TypeConverter
[C#]
public class CursorConverter : TypeConverter
[C++]
public __gc class CursorConverter : public TypeConverter
[JScript]
public class CursorConverter extends TypeConverter
```

Thread Safety

Any public static (**Shared** in Visual Basic) members of this type are safe for multithreaded operations. Any instance members are not guaranteed to be thread safe.

Remarks

> **Note** You should never create an instance of the **CursorConverter** class. Instead, call the **TypeDescriptor.GetConverter** method. For more information, see the examples in the **TypeConverter** base class.

Requirements

Namespace: System.Windows.Forms

Platforms: Windows 98, Windows NT 4.0, Windows Millennium Edition, Windows 2000, Windows XP Home Edition, Windows XP Professional, Windows Server 2003 family

Assembly: System.Windows.Forms (in System.Windows.Forms.dll)

CursorConverter Constructor

Initializes a new instance of the **CursorConverter** class.

```
[Visual Basic]
Public Sub New()
[C#]
public CursorConverter();
[C++]
public: CursorConverter();
[JScript]
public function CursorConverter();
```

Remarks

The default constructor initializes any fields to their default values.

Requirements

Platforms: Windows 98, Windows NT 4.0, Windows Millennium Edition, Windows 2000, Windows XP Home Edition, Windows XP Professional, Windows Server 2003 family

CursorConverter.CanConvertFrom Method

Overload List

This member supports the .NET Framework infrastructure and is not intended to be used directly from your code.

[Visual Basic] **Overloads Overrides Public Function CanConvertFrom(ITypeDescriptorContext, Type) As Boolean**

[C#] **public override bool CanConvertFrom(ITypeDescriptorContext, Type);**

[C++] **public: bool CanConvertFrom(ITypeDescriptorContext*, Type*);**

[JScript] **public override function CanConvertFrom(ITypeDescriptorContext, Type) : Boolean;**

Inherited from **TypeConverter**.

[Visual Basic] **Overloads Public Function CanConvertFrom(Type) As Boolean**

[C#] **public bool CanConvertFrom(Type);**

[C++] **public: bool CanConvertFrom(Type*);**

[JScript] **public function CanConvertFrom(Type) : Boolean;**

CursorConverter.CanConvertFrom Method (ITypeDescriptorContext, Type)

This member overrides **TypeConverter.CanConvertFrom**.

```
[Visual Basic]
Overrides Overloads Public Function CanConvertFrom( _
   ByVal context As ITypeDescriptorContext, _
   ByVal sourceType As Type _
) As Boolean
[C#]
public override bool CanConvertFrom(
   ITypeDescriptorContext context,
   Type sourceType
);
[C++]
public: bool CanConvertFrom(
   ITypeDescriptorContext* context,
   Type* sourceType
);
[JScript]
public override function CanConvertFrom(
   context : ITypeDescriptorContext,
   sourceType : Type
) : Boolean;
```

Requirements

Platforms: Windows 98, Windows NT 4.0, Windows Millennium Edition, Windows 2000, Windows XP Home Edition, Windows XP Professional, Windows Server 2003 family

CursorConverter.CanConvertTo Method

Overload List

This member supports the .NET Framework infrastructure and is not intended to be used directly from your code.

[Visual Basic] **Overloads Overrides Public Function CanConvertTo(ITypeDescriptorContext, Type) As Boolean**

[C#] **public override bool CanConvertTo(ITypeDescriptorContext, Type);**

[C++] **public: bool CanConvertTo(ITypeDescriptorContext*, Type*);**

[JScript] **public override function CanConvertTo(ITypeDescriptorContext, Type) : Boolean;**

Inherited from **TypeConverter**.

[Visual Basic] **Overloads Public Function CanConvertTo(Type) As Boolean**

[C#] **public bool CanConvertTo(Type);**

[C++] **public: bool CanConvertTo(Type*);**

[JScript] **public function CanConvertTo(Type) : Boolean;**

CursorConverter.CanConvertTo Method (ITypeDescriptorContext, Type)

This member overrides **TypeConverter.CanConvertTo**.

[Visual Basic]
```
Overrides Overloads Public Function CanConvertTo( _
   ByVal context As ITypeDescriptorContext, _
   ByVal destinationType As Type _
) As Boolean
```
[C#]
```
public override bool CanConvertTo(
   ITypeDescriptorContext context,
   Type destinationType
);
```
[C++]
```
public: bool CanConvertTo(
   ITypeDescriptorContext* context,
   Type* destinationType
);
```
[JScript]
```
public override function CanConvertTo(
   context : ITypeDescriptorContext,
   destinationType : Type
) : Boolean;
```

Requirements

Platforms: Windows 98, Windows NT 4.0, Windows Millennium Edition, Windows 2000, Windows XP Home Edition, Windows XP Professional, Windows Server 2003 family

CursorConverter.ConvertFrom Method

Overload List

This member supports the .NET Framework infrastructure and is not intended to be used directly from your code.

[Visual Basic] **Overloads Overrides Public Function ConvertFrom(ITypeDescriptorContext, CultureInfo, Object) As Object**

[C#] **public override object ConvertFrom(ITypeDescriptorContext, CultureInfo, object);**

[C++] **public: Object* ConvertFrom(ITypeDescriptorContext*, CultureInfo*, Object*);**

[JScript] **public override function ConvertFrom(ITypeDescriptorContext, CultureInfo, Object) : Object;**

Inherited from **TypeConverter**.

[Visual Basic] **Overloads Public Function ConvertFrom(Object) As Object**

[C#] **public object ConvertFrom(object);**

[C++] **public: Object* ConvertFrom(Object*);**

[JScript] **public function ConvertFrom(Object) : Object;**

CursorConverter.ConvertFrom Method (ITypeDescriptorContext, CultureInfo, Object)

This member overrides **TypeConverter.ConvertFrom**.

[Visual Basic]
```
Overrides Overloads Public Function ConvertFrom( _
   ByVal context As ITypeDescriptorContext, _
   ByVal culture As CultureInfo, _
   ByVal value As Object _
) As Object
```
[C#]
```
public override object ConvertFrom(
   ITypeDescriptorContext context,
   CultureInfo culture,
   object value
);
```
[C++]
```
public: Object* ConvertFrom(
   ITypeDescriptorContext* context,
   CultureInfo* culture,
   Object* value
);
```
[JScript]
```
public override function ConvertFrom(
   context : ITypeDescriptorContext,
   culture : CultureInfo,
   value : Object
) : Object;
```

Requirements

Platforms: Windows 98, Windows NT 4.0, Windows Millennium Edition, Windows 2000, Windows XP Home Edition, Windows XP Professional, Windows Server 2003 family

CursorConverter.ConvertTo Method

Overload List

This member supports the .NET Framework infrastructure and is not intended to be used directly from your code.

[Visual Basic] **Overloads Overrides Public Function ConvertTo(ITypeDescriptorContext, CultureInfo, Object, Type) As Object**

[C#] **public override object ConvertTo(ITypeDescriptorContext, CultureInfo, object, Type);**

[C++] **public: Object* ConvertTo(ITypeDescriptorContext*, CultureInfo*, Object*, Type*);**

[JScript] **public override function ConvertTo(ITypeDescriptorContext, CultureInfo, Object, Type) : Object;**

Inherited from **TypeConverter**.

[Visual Basic] **Overloads Public Function ConvertTo(Object, Type) As Object**

[C#] **public object ConvertTo(object, Type);**

[C++] **public: Object* ConvertTo(Object*, Type*);**

[JScript] **public function ConvertTo(Object, Type) : Object;**

CursorConverter.ConvertTo Method (ITypeDescriptorContext, CultureInfo, Object, Type)

This member overrides **TypeConverter.ConvertTo**.

```
[Visual Basic]
Overrides Overloads Public Function ConvertTo( _
   ByVal context As ITypeDescriptorContext, _
   ByVal culture As CultureInfo, _
   ByVal value As Object, _
   ByVal destinationType As Type _
) As Object
[C#]
public override object ConvertTo(
   ITypeDescriptorContext context,
   CultureInfo culture,
   object value,
   Type destinationType
);
[C++]
public: Object* ConvertTo(
   ITypeDescriptorContext* context,
   CultureInfo* culture,
   Object* value,
   Type* destinationType
);
[JScript]
public override function ConvertTo(
   context : ITypeDescriptorContext,
   culture : CultureInfo,
   value : Object,
   destinationType : Type
) : Object;
```

Requirements

Platforms: Windows 98, Windows NT 4.0, Windows Millennium Edition, Windows 2000, Windows XP Home Edition, Windows XP Professional, Windows Server 2003 family

CursorConverter.GetStandardValues Method

Overload List

This member supports the .NET Framework infrastructure and is not intended to be used directly from your code.

[Visual Basic] **Overloads Overrides Public Function GetStandardValues(ITypeDescriptorContext) As StandardValuesCollection**

[C#] **public override StandardValuesCollection GetStandardValues(ITypeDescriptorContext);**

[C++] **public: StandardValuesCollection* GetStandardValues(ITypeDescriptorContext*);**

[JScript] **public override function GetStandardValues(ITypeDescriptorContext) : StandardValuesCollection;**

Inherited from **TypeConverter**.

[Visual Basic] **Overloads Public Function GetStandardValues() As ICollection**

[C#] **public ICollection GetStandardValues();**

[C++] **public: ICollection* GetStandardValues();**

[JScript] **public function GetStandardValues() : ICollection;**

CursorConverter.GetStandardValues Method (ITypeDescriptorContext)

This member overrides **TypeConverter.GetStandardValues**.

```
[Visual Basic]
Overrides Overloads Public Function GetStandardValues( _
   ByVal context As ITypeDescriptorContext _
) As StandardValuesCollection
[C#]
public override StandardValuesCollection GetStandardValues(
   ITypeDescriptorContext context
);
[C++]
public: StandardValuesCollection* GetStandardValues(
   ITypeDescriptorContext* context
);
[JScript]
public override function GetStandardValues(
   context : ITypeDescriptorContext
) : StandardValuesCollection;
```

Requirements

Platforms: Windows 98, Windows NT 4.0, Windows Millennium Edition, Windows 2000, Windows XP Home Edition, Windows XP Professional, Windows Server 2003 family

CursorConverter.GetStandardValuesSupported Method

Overload List

This member supports the .NET Framework infrastructure and is not intended to be used directly from your code.

[Visual Basic] **Overloads Overrides Public Function GetStandardValuesSupported(ITypeDescriptorContext) As Boolean**

[C#] **public override bool GetStandardValuesSupported(ITypeDescriptorContext);**

[C++] **public: bool GetStandardValuesSupported(ITypeDescriptorContext*);**

[JScript] **public override function GetStandardValuesSupported(ITypeDescriptorContext) : Boolean;**

Inherited from **TypeConverter**.

[Visual Basic] **Overloads Public Function GetStandardValuesSupported() As Boolean**

[C#] **public bool GetStandardValuesSupported();**

[C++] **public: bool GetStandardValuesSupported();**

[JScript] **public function GetStandardValuesSupported() : Boolean;**

CursorConverter.GetStandardValuesSupported Method (ITypeDescriptorContext)

This member overrides **TypeConverter.GetStandardValuesSupported**.

```
[Visual Basic]
Overrides Overloads Public Function GetStandardValuesSupported( _
   ByVal context As ITypeDescriptorContext _
) As Boolean
[C#]
public override bool GetStandardValuesSupported(
   ITypeDescriptorContext context
);
[C++]
public: bool GetStandardValuesSupported(
   ITypeDescriptorContext* context
);
[JScript]
public override function GetStandardValuesSupported(
   context : ITypeDescriptorContext
) : Boolean;
```

Requirements

Platforms: Windows 98, Windows NT 4.0, Windows Millennium Edition, Windows 2000, Windows XP Home Edition, Windows XP Professional, Windows Server 2003 family

Cursors Class

Provides a collection of **Cursor** objects for use by a Windows Forms application.

System.Object
  System.Windows.Forms.Cursors

[Visual Basic]
```
NotInheritable Public Class Cursors
```
[C#]
```
public sealed class Cursors
```
[C++]
```
public __gc __sealed class Cursors
```
[JScript]
```
public class Cursors
```

Thread Safety

Any public static (**Shared** in Visual Basic) members of this type are safe for multithreaded operations. Any instance members are not guaranteed to be thread safe.

Remarks

Some of the **Cursor** objects in this class can take on a different appearance than those described. The user can change the cursor appearance by adjusting the mouse pointer settings in their operating system. The panning and no move cursors are static and cannot be changed by the operating system.

The panning and no move cursors are used during mouse wheel operations. Depending on the direction the window can be scrolled, the cursor changes to the appropriate no move cursor when the mouse wheel is clicked. The cursor then changes to the appropriate panning cursor as the mouse is moved.

Example

[Visual Basic, C#, C++] The following example demonstrates changing the mouse cursor using the **Control.Cursor** property, the **Cursor** class, and the **Cursors** class. The example creates a form that contains a **ComboBox** control, a **Panel** control, and a **ListView** control. The **ComboBox** contains all cursors provided by the **Cursors** class. When the user selects a mouse cursor in the **ComboBox**, the **Control.Cursor** property is set to the selected cursor, which updates the cursor for the **Panel**. The **ListView** is updated every time the **Control.CursorChanged** event occurs.

[Visual Basic]
```
Imports System
Imports System.Drawing
Imports System.Windows.Forms

Namespace Snippet

    ' Summary description for Form1.
    Public NotInheritable Class Form1
        Inherits System.Windows.Forms.Form

        Friend WithEvents cursorSelectionComboBox As                    ↵
System.Windows.Forms.ComboBox
        Friend WithEvents testPanel As System.Windows.Forms.Panel

        Private label1 As System.Windows.Forms.Label
        Private label2 As System.Windows.Forms.Label
        Private cursorEventViewer As System.Windows.Forms.ListView
        Private label3 As System.Windows.Forms.Label

        <System.STAThread()> _
        Public Shared Sub Main()
            System.Windows.Forms.Application.Run(New Form1)
        End Sub 'Main

        Public Sub New()

            Me.cursorSelectionComboBox = New                            ↵
System.Windows.Forms.ComboBox
            Me.testPanel = New System.Windows.Forms.Panel
            Me.label1 = New System.Windows.Forms.Label
            Me.label2 = New System.Windows.Forms.Label
            Me.cursorEventViewer = New System.Windows.Forms.ListView
            Me.label3 = New System.Windows.Forms.Label

            ' Select Cursor Label
            Me.label2.Location = New System.Drawing.Point(24, 16)
            Me.label2.Size = New System.Drawing.Size(80, 16)
            Me.label2.Text = "Select cursor:"

            ' Cursor Testing Panel Label
            Me.label1.Location = New System.Drawing.Point(24, 80)
            Me.label1.Size = New System.Drawing.Size(144, 23)
            Me.label1.Text = "Cursor testing panel:"

            ' Cursor Changed Events Label
            Me.label3.Location = New System.Drawing.Point(184, 16)
            Me.label3.Size = New System.Drawing.Size(128, 16)
            Me.label3.Text = "Cursor changed events:"

            ' Cursor Selection ComboBox
            Me.cursorSelectionComboBox.Location = New                   ↵
System.Drawing.Point(24, 40)
            Me.cursorSelectionComboBox.Size = New                       ↵
System.Drawing.Size(152, 21)
            Me.cursorSelectionComboBox.TabIndex = 0

            ' Cursor Test Panel
            Me.testPanel.BackColor =                                    ↵
System.Drawing.SystemColors.ControlDark
            Me.testPanel.Location = New System.Drawing.Point(24, 104)
            Me.testPanel.Size = New System.Drawing.Size(152, 160)

            ' Cursor Event ListView
            Me.cursorEventViewer.Location = New                         ↵
System.Drawing.Point(184, 40)
            Me.cursorEventViewer.Size = New                             ↵
System.Drawing.Size(256, 224)
            Me.cursorEventViewer.TabIndex = 4
            Me.cursorEventViewer.View = System.Windows.Forms.View.List

            ' Set up how the form should be displayed and add           ↵
 the controls to the form.
            Me.ClientSize = New System.Drawing.Size(456, 286)
            Me.Controls.AddRange                                        ↵
 (New System.Windows.Forms.Control() {Me.label3, _
                Me.cursorEventViewer, Me.label2, Me.label1, _
                 Me.testPanel, Me.cursorSelectionComboBox})

            Me.Text = "Cursors Example"

            ' Add all the cursor types to the combobox.
            Dim cursor As Cursor
            For Each cursor In CursorList()
                cursorSelectionComboBox.Items.Add(cursor)
            Next cursor
        End Sub 'New

        Private Function CursorList() As Cursor()
            ' Make an array of all the types of cursors                 ↵
in Windows Forms.
            return New Cursor() {Cursors.AppStarting,                   ↵
Cursors.Arrow, Cursors.Cross, _
                                Cursors.Default,                        ↵
Cursors.Hand, Cursors.Help, _
                                Cursors.HSplit,                         ↵
Cursors.IBeam, Cursors.No, _
```

```
                                     Cursors.NoMove2D,                    ↵
Cursors.NoMoveHoriz, Cursors.NoMoveVert, _
                                     Cursors.PanEast,                     ↵
Cursors.PanNE, Cursors.PanNorth, _
                                     Cursors.PanNW,                       ↵
Cursors.PanSE, Cursors.PanSouth, _
                                     Cursors.PanSW,                       ↵
Cursors.PanWest, Cursors.SizeAll, _
                                     Cursors.SizeNESW,                    ↵
Cursors.SizeNS, Cursors.SizeNWSE, _
                                     Cursors.SizeWE,                      ↵
Cursors.UpArrow, Cursors.VSplit, Cursors.WaitCursor}
        End Function

        Private                                                           ↵
Sub cursorSelectionComboBox_SelectedIndexChanged                          ↵
 (ByVal sender As Object, ByVal e As System.EventArgs)                    ↵
 Handles cursorSelectionComboBox.SelectedIndexChanged
            ' Set the cursor in the test panel to be the                  ↵
selected cursor style.
            testPanel.Cursor =                                            ↵
CType(cursorSelectionComboBox.SelectedItem, Cursor)

        End Sub

        Private Sub testPanel_CursorChanged(ByVal sender As               ↵
 Object, ByVal e As System.EventArgs) Handles testPanel.CursorChanged
            ' Build up a string containing the type of object             ↵
 sending the event, and the event.
            Dim cursorEvent As String = String.Format("[{0}]:             ↵
 {1}", sender.GetType().ToString(), "Cursor changed")

            ' Records this event in the list view.
            Me.cursorEventViewer.Items.Add(cursorEvent)

        End Sub

    End Class 'Form1
End Namespace 'Snippet
```

[C#]

```
using System;
using System.Drawing;
using System.Windows.Forms;

namespace Snippet
{
    public class Form1 : System.Windows.Forms.Form
    {
        private System.Windows.Forms.ComboBox cursorSelectionComboBox;

        private System.Windows.Forms.Panel testPanel;
        private System.Windows.Forms.Label label1;
        private System.Windows.Forms.Label label2;
        private System.Windows.Forms.ListView cursorEventViewer;
        private System.Windows.Forms.Label label3;

        [STAThread]
        static void Main()
        {
            Application.Run(new Form1());
        }

        public Form1()
        {
            this.cursorSelectionComboBox = new                            ↵
 System.Windows.Forms.ComboBox();
            this.testPanel = new System.Windows.Forms.Panel();
            this.label1 = new System.Windows.Forms.Label();
            this.label2 = new System.Windows.Forms.Label();
            this.cursorEventViewer = new                                  ↵
 System.Windows.Forms.ListView();
            this.label3 = new System.Windows.Forms.Label();

            // Select Cursor Label
            this.label2.Location = new System.Drawing.Point(24, 16);
            this.label2.Size = new System.Drawing.Size(80, 16);
            this.label2.Text = "Select cursor:";

            // Cursor Testing Panel Label
            this.label1.Location = new System.Drawing.Point(24, 80);
            this.label1.Size = new System.Drawing.Size(144, 23);
            this.label1.Text = "Cursor testing panel:";

            // Cursor Changed Events Label
            this.label3.Location = new System.Drawing.Point(184, 16);
            this.label3.Size = new System.Drawing.Size(128, 16);
            this.label3.Text = "Cursor changed events:";

            // Cursor Selection ComboBox
            this.cursorSelectionComboBox.Location = new                   ↵
System.Drawing.Point(24, 40);
            this.cursorSelectionComboBox.Size = new                       ↵
System.Drawing.Size(152, 21);
            this.cursorSelectionComboBox.TabIndex = 0;
            this.cursorSelectionComboBox.SelectedIndexChanged +=
                new
System.EventHandler(this.cursorSelectionComboBox_SelectedIndexChanged);

            // Cursor Test Panel
            this.testPanel.BackColor =                                    ↵
System.Drawing.SystemColors.ControlDark;
            this.testPanel.Location = new                                 ↵
System.Drawing.Point(24, 104);
            this.testPanel.Size = new System.Drawing.Size(152, 160);
            this.testPanel.CursorChanged += new                           ↵
System.EventHandler(this.testPanel_CursorChanged);

            // Cursor Event ListView
            this.cursorEventViewer.Location = new                         ↵
System.Drawing.Point(184, 40);
            this.cursorEventViewer.Size = new                             ↵
System.Drawing.Size(256, 224);
            this.cursorEventViewer.TabIndex = 4;
            this.cursorEventViewer.View =                                 ↵
System.Windows.Forms.View.List;

            // Set up how the form should be displayed and                ↵
add the controls to the form.
            this.ClientSize = new System.Drawing.Size(456, 286);
            this.Controls.AddRange(new System.Windows.Forms.Control[] {
                                    this.label3,                          ↵
this.cursorEventViewer,
                                    this.label2, this.label1,
                                    this.testPanel,                       ↵
this.cursorSelectionComboBox});

            this.Text = "Cursors Example";

            // Add all the cursor types to the combobox.
            foreach (Cursor cursor in CursorList())
            {
                cursorSelectionComboBox.Items.Add(cursor);
            }

        }

        private Cursor [] CursorList()
        {

            // Make an array of all the types of cursors                  ↵
in Windows Forms.
            return new Cursor [] {
                                    Cursors.AppStarting,                  ↵
Cursors.Arrow, Cursors.Cross,
                                    Cursors.Default,                      ↵
Cursors.Hand, Cursors.Help,
                                    Cursors.HSplit,                       ↵
Cursors.IBeam, Cursors.No,
```

```
                                        Cursors.NoMove2D,                    ↵
Cursors.NoMoveHoriz, Cursors.NoMoveVert,
                                        Cursors.PanEast,                     ↵
 Cursors.PanNE, Cursors.PanNorth,
                                        Cursors.PanNW,                       ↵
Cursors.PanSE, Cursors.PanSouth,
                                        Cursors.PanSW,                       ↵
Cursors.PanWest, Cursors.SizeAll,
                                        Cursors.SizeNESW,                    ↵
Cursors.SizeNS, Cursors.SizeNWSE,
                                        Cursors.SizeWE,                      ↵
Cursors.UpArrow, Cursors.VSplit, Cursors.WaitCursor};

        }

        private void                                                         ↵
cursorSelectionComboBox_SelectedIndexChanged(object sender,                  ↵
System.EventArgs e)
        {
            // Set the cursor in the test panel to be th                     ↵
e selected cursor style.
            testPanel.Cursor =                                               ↵
 (Cursor)cursorSelectionComboBox.SelectedItem;
        }

        private void testPanel_CursorChanged(object sender,                  ↵
System.EventArgs e)
        {
            // Build up a string containing the type of                      ↵
object sending the event, and the event.
            string cursorEvent = string.Format("[{0}]: {1}",                 ↵
sender.GetType().ToString(), "Cursor changed");

            // Record this event in the list view.
            this.cursorEventViewer.Items.Add(cursorEvent);
        }
    }
}
```

[C++]

```
#using <mscorlib.dll>
#using <System.dll>
#using <System.Windows.Forms.dll>
#using <System.Drawing.dll>

using namespace System;
using namespace System::Drawing;
using namespace System::Windows::Forms;

namespace Snippet {
public __gc class Form1 : public System::Windows::Forms::Form {
private:
   System::Windows::Forms::ComboBox*  cursorSelectionComboBox;
   System::Windows::Forms::Panel*  testPanel;
   System::Windows::Forms::Label*  label1;
   System::Windows::Forms::Label*  label2;
   System::Windows::Forms::ListView*  cursorEventViewer;
   System::Windows::Forms::Label*  label3;
public:
   Form1() {
      this->cursorSelectionComboBox = new                                    ↵
System::Windows::Forms::ComboBox();
      this->testPanel = new System::Windows::Forms::Panel();
      this->label1 = new System::Windows::Forms::Label();
      this->label2 = new System::Windows::Forms::Label();
      this->cursorEventViewer = new System::Windows::Forms::ListView();
      this->label3 = new System::Windows::Forms::Label();

      // Select Cursor Label
      this->label2->Location =  System::Drawing::Point(24, 16);
      this->label2->Size =  System::Drawing::Size(80, 16);
      this->label2->Text = S"Select cursor:";

      // Cursor Testing Panel Label
      this->label1->Location =  System::Drawing::Point(24, 80);
      this->label1->Size =  System::Drawing::Size(144, 23);
      this->label1->Text = S"Cursor testing panel:";

      // Cursor Changed Events Label
      this->label3->Location =  System::Drawing::Point(184, 16);
      this->label3->Size =  System::Drawing::Size(128, 16);
      this->label3->Text = S"Cursor changed events:";

      // Cursor Selection ComboBox
      this->cursorSelectionComboBox->Location =                              ↵
System::Drawing::Point(24, 40);
      this->cursorSelectionComboBox->Size =                                  ↵
System::Drawing::Size(152, 21);
      this->cursorSelectionComboBox->TabIndex = 0;
      this->cursorSelectionComboBox->SelectedIndexChanged                    ↵
+= new System::EventHandler(this,
cursorSelectionComboBox_SelectedIndexChanged);

      // Cursor Test Panel
      this->testPanel->BackColor =                                           ↵
System::Drawing::SystemColors::ControlDark;
      this->testPanel->Location =  System::Drawing::Point(24, 104);
      this->testPanel->Size =  System::Drawing::Size(152, 160);
      this->testPanel->CursorChanged +=                                      ↵
new System::EventHandler(this, testPanel_CursorChanged);

      // Cursor Event ListView
      this->cursorEventViewer->Location =                                    ↵
System::Drawing::Point(184, 40);
      this->cursorEventViewer->Size =  System::Drawing::Size(256, 224);
      this->cursorEventViewer->TabIndex = 4;
      this->cursorEventViewer->View =                                        ↵
System::Windows::Forms::View::List;

      // Set up how the form should be displayed and add the                 ↵
 controls to the form.
      this->ClientSize =  System::Drawing::Size(456, 286);

      System::Windows::Forms::Control* temp0 [] = {this->label3,             ↵
 this->cursorEventViewer,
         this->label2, this->label1,
         this->testPanel, this->cursorSelectionComboBox};

      this->Controls->AddRange(temp0);

      this->Text = S"Cursors Example";

      // Add all the cursor types to the combobox.
      System::Collections::IEnumerator* myEnum =                             ↵
CursorList()->GetEnumerator();
      while (myEnum->MoveNext()) {
         System::Windows::Forms::Cursor* cursor =                            ↵
__try_cast<System::Windows::Forms::Cursor*>(myEnum->Current);
         cursorSelectionComboBox->Items->Add(cursor);
      }
   }

private:
   System::Windows::Forms::Cursor* CursorList()[] {

      // Make an array of all the types of cursors in Windows Forms.

      System::Windows::Forms::Cursor*  temp1 [] =                            ↵
{Cursors::AppStarting, Cursors::Arrow, Cursors::Cross,
         Cursors::Default, Cursors::Hand, Cursors::Help,
         Cursors::HSplit, Cursors::IBeam, Cursors::No,
         Cursors::NoMove2D, Cursors::NoMoveHoriz, Cursors::NoMoveVert,
         Cursors::PanEast, Cursors::PanNE, Cursors::PanNorth,
         Cursors::PanNW, Cursors::PanSE, Cursors::PanSouth,
         Cursors::PanSW, Cursors::PanWest, Cursors::SizeAll,
         Cursors::SizeNESW, Cursors::SizeNS, Cursors::SizeNWSE,
         Cursors::SizeWE, Cursors::UpArrow, Cursors::VSplit,                 ↵
Cursors::WaitCursor};
      return temp1;
   }
```

```
   void cursorSelectionComboBox_SelectedIndexChanged(Object*          ↵
sender, System::EventArgs* e) {
      // Set the cursor in the test panel to be the selected          ↵
cursor style.
      testPanel->Cursor =                                             ↵
dynamic_cast<System::Windows::Forms::Cursor*>                         ↵
 (cursorSelectionComboBox->SelectedItem);
   }

   void testPanel_CursorChanged(Object* sender, System::EventArgs* e) {
      // Build up a String* containing the type of Object*            ↵
sending the event, and the event.
      String* cursorEvent = String::Format(S"[{0}]: {1}",             ↵
sender->GetType(), S"Cursor changed");

      // Record this event in the list view.
      this->cursorEventViewer->Items->Add(cursorEvent);
   }
};
}

[STAThread]
int main() {
   Application::Run(new Snippet::Form1());
}
```

[Visual Basic, C#, C++] The following example draws the specified cursor on the form in its normal size, and in stretched mode, twice its size. This example assumes that you have a **Form** and a **Cursor** object to pass into the method when it is called.

[Visual Basic]

```
Private Sub DrawCursorsOnForm(cursor As Cursor)
   ' If the form's cursor is not the Hand cursor and the
   ' Current cursor is the Default, Draw the specified
   ' cursor on the form in normal size and twice normal size.
   If (Not Me.Cursor.Equals(Cursors.Hand)) And _
     Cursor.Current.Equals(Cursors.Default) Then

      ' Draw the cursor stretched.
      Dim graphics As Graphics = Me.CreateGraphics()
      Dim rectangle As New Rectangle(New Point(10, 10), _
        New Size(cursor.Size.Width * 2, cursor.Size.Height * 2))
      cursor.DrawStretched(graphics, rectangle)

      ' Draw the cursor in normal size.
      rectangle.Location = New Point(rectangle.Width + _
        rectangle.Location.X, rectangle.Height + rectangle.Location.Y)
      rectangle.Size = cursor.Size
      cursor.Draw(graphics, rectangle)

      ' Dispose of the cursor.
      cursor.Dispose()
   End If
End Sub
```

[C#]

```
private void DrawCursorsOnForm(Cursor cursor)
{
   // If the form's cursor is not the Hand cursor and the
   // Current cursor is the Default, Draw the specified
   // cursor on the form in normal size and twice normal size.
   if(this.Cursor != Cursors.Hand &
     Cursor.Current == Cursors.Default)
   {
      // Draw the cursor stretched.
      Graphics graphics = this.CreateGraphics();
      Rectangle rectangle = new Rectangle(
        new Point(10,10), new Size(cursor.Size.Width * 2,
        cursor.Size.Height * 2));
      cursor.DrawStretched(graphics, rectangle);

      // Draw the cursor in normal size.
      rectangle.Location = new Point(
      rectangle.Width + rectangle.Location.X,
        rectangle.Height + rectangle.Location.Y);
      rectangle.Size = cursor.Size;
      cursor.Draw(graphics, rectangle);

      // Dispose of the cursor.
      cursor.Dispose();
   }
}
```

[C++]

```
private:
   void DrawCursorsOnForm(System::Windows::Forms::Cursor* cursor) {
      // If the form's cursor is not the Hand cursor and the
      // Current cursor is the Default, Draw the specified
      // cursor on the form in normal size and twice normal size.
      if (this->Cursor != Cursors::Hand &&
         System::Windows::Forms::Cursor::Current == Cursors::Default) {
            // Draw the cursor stretched.
            Graphics* graphics = this->CreateGraphics();
            Rectangle rectangle =  Rectangle( Point(10, 10),          ↵
System::Drawing::Size(cursor->Size.Width * 2,
               cursor->Size.Height * 2));
            cursor->DrawStretched(graphics, rectangle);

            // Draw the cursor in normal size.
            rectangle.Location =  Point(rectangle.Width +             ↵
rectangle.Location.X,
               rectangle.Height + rectangle.Location.Y);
            rectangle.Size = cursor->Size;
            cursor->Draw(graphics, rectangle);

            // Dispose of the cursor.
            cursor->Dispose();
         }
   }
```

Requirements

Namespace: System.Windows.Forms

Platforms: Windows 98, Windows NT 4.0, Windows Millennium Edition, Windows 2000, Windows XP Home Edition, Windows XP Professional, Windows Server 2003 family, .NET Compact Framework - Windows CE .NET

Assembly: System.Windows.Forms (in System.Windows.Forms.dll)

Cursors.AppStarting Property

Gets the cursor that appears when an application starts.

[Visual Basic]
```
Public Shared ReadOnly Property AppStarting As Cursor
```
[C#]
```
public static Cursor AppStarting {get;}
```
[C++]
```
public: __property static Cursor* get_AppStarting();
```
[JScript]
```
public static function get AppStarting() : Cursor;
```

Property Value

The **Cursor** that represents the cursor that appears when an application starts.

Requirements

Platforms: Windows 98, Windows NT 4.0, Windows Millennium Edition, Windows 2000, Windows XP Home Edition, Windows XP Professional, Windows Server 2003 family

Cursors.Arrow Property

Gets the arrow cursor.

[Visual Basic]
```
Public Shared ReadOnly Property Arrow As Cursor
```
[C#]
```
public static Cursor Arrow {get;}
```
[C++]
```
public: __property static Cursor* get_Arrow();
```
[JScript]
```
public static function get Arrow() : Cursor;
```

Property Value

The **Cursor** that represents the arrow cursor.

Requirements

Platforms: Windows 98, Windows NT 4.0, Windows Millennium Edition, Windows 2000, Windows XP Home Edition, Windows XP Professional, Windows Server 2003 family

Cursors.Cross Property

Gets the crosshair cursor.

[Visual Basic]
```
Public Shared ReadOnly Property Cross As Cursor
```
[C#]
```
public static Cursor Cross {get;}
```
[C++]
```
public: __property static Cursor* get_Cross();
```
[JScript]
```
public static function get Cross() : Cursor;
```

Property Value

The **Cursor** that represents the crosshair cursor.

Requirements

Platforms: Windows 98, Windows NT 4.0, Windows Millennium Edition, Windows 2000, Windows XP Home Edition, Windows XP Professional, Windows Server 2003 family

Cursors.Default Property

Gets the default cursor, which is usually an arrow cursor.

[Visual Basic]
```
Public Shared ReadOnly Property Default As Cursor
```
[C#]
```
public static Cursor Default {get;}
```
[C++]
```
public: __property static Cursor* get_Default();
```
[JScript]
```
public static function get Default() : Cursor;
```

Property Value

The **Cursor** that represents the default cursor.

Requirements

Platforms: Windows 98, Windows NT 4.0, Windows Millennium Edition, Windows 2000, Windows XP Home Edition, Windows XP Professional, Windows Server 2003 family, .NET Compact Framework - Windows CE .NET

Cursors.Hand Property

Gets the hand cursor, typically used when hovering over a Web link.

[Visual Basic]
```
Public Shared ReadOnly Property Hand As Cursor
```
[C#]
```
public static Cursor Hand {get;}
```
[C++]
```
public: __property static Cursor* get_Hand();
```
[JScript]
```
public static function get Hand() : Cursor;
```

Property Value

The **Cursor** that represents the hand cursor.

Requirements

Platforms: Windows 98, Windows NT 4.0, Windows Millennium Edition, Windows 2000, Windows XP Home Edition, Windows XP Professional, Windows Server 2003 family

Cursors.Help Property

Gets the Help cursor, which is a combination of an arrow and a question mark.

[Visual Basic]
```
Public Shared ReadOnly Property Help As Cursor
```
[C#]
```
public static Cursor Help {get;}
```
[C++]
```
public: __property static Cursor* get_Help();
```
[JScript]
```
public static function get Help() : Cursor;
```

Property Value

The **Cursor** that represents the Help cursor.

Requirements

Platforms: Windows 98, Windows NT 4.0, Windows Millennium Edition, Windows 2000, Windows XP Home Edition, Windows XP Professional, Windows Server 2003 family

Cursors.HSplit Property

Gets the cursor that appears when the mouse is positioned over a horizontal splitter bar.

[Visual Basic]
```
Public Shared ReadOnly Property HSplit As Cursor
```
[C#]
```
public static Cursor HSplit {get;}
```
[C++]
```
public: __property static Cursor* get_HSplit();
```
[JScript]
```
public static function get HSplit() : Cursor;
```

Property Value

The **Cursor** that represents the cursor that appears when the mouse is positioned over a horizontal splitter bar.

Requirements

Platforms: Windows 98, Windows NT 4.0, Windows Millennium Edition, Windows 2000, Windows XP Home Edition, Windows XP Professional, Windows Server 2003 family

Cursors.IBeam Property

Gets the I-beam cursor, which is used to show where the text cursor appears when the mouse is clicked.

```
[Visual Basic]
Public Shared ReadOnly Property IBeam As Cursor
[C#]
public static Cursor IBeam {get;}
[C++]
public: __property static Cursor* get_IBeam();
[JScript]
public static function get IBeam() : Cursor;
```

Property Value

The **Cursor** that represents the I-beam cursor.

Requirements

Platforms: Windows 98, Windows NT 4.0, Windows Millennium Edition, Windows 2000, Windows XP Home Edition, Windows XP Professional, Windows Server 2003 family

Cursors.No Property

Gets the cursor that indicates that a particular region is invalid for the current operation.

```
[Visual Basic]
Public Shared ReadOnly Property No As Cursor
[C#]
public static Cursor No {get;}
[C++]
public: __property static Cursor* get_No();
[JScript]
public static function get No() : Cursor;
```

Property Value

The **Cursor** that represents the cursor that indicates that a particular region is invalid for the current operation.

Requirements

Platforms: Windows 98, Windows NT 4.0, Windows Millennium Edition, Windows 2000, Windows XP Home Edition, Windows XP Professional, Windows Server 2003 family

Cursors.NoMove2D Property

Gets the cursor that appears during wheel operations when the mouse is not moving, but the window can be scrolled in both a horizontal and vertical direction.

```
[Visual Basic]
Public Shared ReadOnly Property NoMove2D As Cursor
[C#]
public static Cursor NoMove2D {get;}
[C++]
public: __property static Cursor* get_NoMove2D();
[JScript]
public static function get NoMove2D() : Cursor;
```

Property Value

The **Cursor** that represents the cursor that appears during wheel operations when the mouse is not moving.

Requirements

Platforms: Windows 98, Windows NT 4.0, Windows Millennium Edition, Windows 2000, Windows XP Home Edition, Windows XP Professional, Windows Server 2003 family

Cursors.NoMoveHoriz Property

Gets the cursor that appears during wheel operations when the mouse is not moving, but the window can be scrolled in a horizontal direction.

```
[Visual Basic]
Public Shared ReadOnly Property NoMoveHoriz As Cursor
[C#]
public static Cursor NoMoveHoriz {get;}
[C++]
public: __property static Cursor* get_NoMoveHoriz();
[JScript]
public static function get NoMoveHoriz() : Cursor;
```

Property Value

The **Cursor** that represents the cursor that appears during wheel operations when the mouse is not moving.

Requirements

Platforms: Windows 98, Windows NT 4.0, Windows Millennium Edition, Windows 2000, Windows XP Home Edition, Windows XP Professional, Windows Server 2003 family

Cursors.NoMoveVert Property

Gets the cursor that appears during wheel operations when the mouse is not moving, but the window can be scrolled in a vertical direction.

```
[Visual Basic]
Public Shared ReadOnly Property NoMoveVert As Cursor
[C#]
public static Cursor NoMoveVert {get;}
[C++]
public: __property static Cursor* get_NoMoveVert();
[JScript]
public static function get NoMoveVert() : Cursor;
```

Property Value

The **Cursor** that represents the cursor that appears during wheel operations when the mouse is not moving.

Requirements

Platforms: Windows 98, Windows NT 4.0, Windows Millennium Edition, Windows 2000, Windows XP Home Edition, Windows XP Professional, Windows Server 2003 family

Cursors.PanEast Property

Gets the cursor that appears during wheel operations when the mouse is moving and the window is scrolling horizontally to the right.

```
[Visual Basic]
Public Shared ReadOnly Property PanEast As Cursor
[C#]
public static Cursor PanEast {get;}
[C++]
public: __property static Cursor* get_PanEast();
[JScript]
public static function get PanEast() : Cursor;
```

Property Value

The **Cursor** that represents the cursor that appears during wheel operations when the mouse is moving and the window is scrolling horizontally to the right.

Requirements

Platforms: Windows 98, Windows NT 4.0, Windows Millennium Edition, Windows 2000, Windows XP Home Edition, Windows XP Professional, Windows Server 2003 family

Cursors.PanNE Property

Gets the cursor that appears during wheel operations when the mouse is moving and the window is scrolling horizontally and vertically upward and to the right.

```
[Visual Basic]
Public Shared ReadOnly Property PanNE As Cursor
[C#]
public static Cursor PanNE {get;}
[C++]
public: __property static Cursor* get_PanNE();
[JScript]
public static function get PanNE() : Cursor;
```

Property Value

The **Cursor** that represents the cursor that appears during wheel operations when the mouse is moving and the window is scrolling horizontally and vertically upward and to the right.

Requirements

Platforms: Windows 98, Windows NT 4.0, Windows Millennium Edition, Windows 2000, Windows XP Home Edition, Windows XP Professional, Windows Server 2003 family

Cursors.PanNorth Property

Gets the cursor that appears during wheel operations when the mouse is moving and the window is scrolling vertically in an upward direction.

```
[Visual Basic]
Public Shared ReadOnly Property PanNorth As Cursor
[C#]
public static Cursor PanNorth {get;}
[C++]
public: __property static Cursor* get_PanNorth();
[JScript]
public static function get PanNorth() : Cursor;
```

Property Value

The **Cursor** that represents the cursor that appears during wheel operations when the mouse is moving and the window is scrolling vertically in an upward direction.

Requirements

Platforms: Windows 98, Windows NT 4.0, Windows Millennium Edition, Windows 2000, Windows XP Home Edition, Windows XP Professional, Windows Server 2003 family

Cursors.PanNW Property

Gets the cursor that appears during wheel operations when the mouse is moving and the window is scrolling horizontally and vertically upward and to the left.

```
[Visual Basic]
Public Shared ReadOnly Property PanNW As Cursor
[C#]
public static Cursor PanNW {get;}
[C++]
public: __property static Cursor* get_PanNW();
[JScript]
public static function get PanNW() : Cursor;
```

Property Value

The **Cursor** that represents the cursor that appears during wheel operations when the mouse is moving and the window is scrolling horizontally and vertically upward and to the left.

Requirements

Platforms: Windows 98, Windows NT 4.0, Windows Millennium Edition, Windows 2000, Windows XP Home Edition, Windows XP Professional, Windows Server 2003 family

Cursors.PanSE Property

Gets the cursor that appears during wheel operations when the mouse is moving and the window is scrolling horizontally and vertically downward and to the right.

```
[Visual Basic]
Public Shared ReadOnly Property PanSE As Cursor
[C#]
public static Cursor PanSE {get;}
[C++]
public: __property static Cursor* get_PanSE();
[JScript]
public static function get PanSE() : Cursor;
```

Property Value

The **Cursor** that represents the cursor that appears during wheel operations when the mouse is moving and the window is scrolling horizontally and vertically downward and to the right.

Requirements

Platforms: Windows 98, Windows NT 4.0, Windows Millennium Edition, Windows 2000, Windows XP Home Edition, Windows XP Professional, Windows Server 2003 family

Cursors.PanSouth Property

Gets the cursor that appears during wheel operations when the mouse is moving and the window is scrolling vertically in a downward direction.

[Visual Basic]
```
Public Shared ReadOnly Property PanSouth As Cursor
```
[C#]
```
public static Cursor PanSouth {get;}
```
[C++]
```
public: __property static Cursor* get_PanSouth();
```
[JScript]
```
public static function get PanSouth() : Cursor;
```

Property Value

The **Cursor** that represents the cursor that appears during wheel operations when the mouse is moving and the window is scrolling vertically in a downward direction.

Requirements

Platforms: Windows 98, Windows NT 4.0, Windows Millennium Edition, Windows 2000, Windows XP Home Edition, Windows XP Professional, Windows Server 2003 family

Cursors.PanSW Property

Gets the cursor that appears during wheel operations when the mouse is moving and the window is scrolling horizontally and vertically downward and to the left.

[Visual Basic]
```
Public Shared ReadOnly Property PanSW As Cursor
```
[C#]
```
public static Cursor PanSW {get;}
```
[C++]
```
public: __property static Cursor* get_PanSW();
```
[JScript]
```
public static function get PanSW() : Cursor;
```

Property Value

The **Cursor** that represents the cursor that appears during wheel operations when the mouse is moving and the window is scrolling horizontally and vertically downward and to the left.

Requirements

Platforms: Windows 98, Windows NT 4.0, Windows Millennium Edition, Windows 2000, Windows XP Home Edition, Windows XP Professional, Windows Server 2003 family

Cursors.PanWest Property

Gets the cursor that appears during wheel operations when the mouse is moving and the window is scrolling horizontally to the left.

[Visual Basic]
```
Public Shared ReadOnly Property PanWest As Cursor
```
[C#]
```
public static Cursor PanWest {get;}
```
[C++]
```
public: __property static Cursor* get_PanWest();
```
[JScript]
```
public static function get PanWest() : Cursor;
```

Property Value

The **Cursor** that represents the cursor that appears during wheel operations when the mouse is moving and the window is scrolling horizontally to the left.

Requirements

Platforms: Windows 98, Windows NT 4.0, Windows Millennium Edition, Windows 2000, Windows XP Home Edition, Windows XP Professional, Windows Server 2003 family

Cursors.SizeAll Property

Gets the four-headed sizing cursor, which consists of four joined arrows that point north, south, east, and west.

[Visual Basic]
```
Public Shared ReadOnly Property SizeAll As Cursor
```
[C#]
```
public static Cursor SizeAll {get;}
```
[C++]
```
public: __property static Cursor* get_SizeAll();
```
[JScript]
```
public static function get SizeAll() : Cursor;
```

Property Value

The **Cursor** that represents the four-headed sizing cursor.

Requirements

Platforms: Windows 98, Windows NT 4.0, Windows Millennium Edition, Windows 2000, Windows XP Home Edition, Windows XP Professional, Windows Server 2003 family

Cursors.SizeNESW Property

Gets the two-headed diagonal (northeast/southwest) sizing cursor.

[Visual Basic]
```
Public Shared ReadOnly Property SizeNESW As Cursor
```
[C#]
```
public static Cursor SizeNESW {get;}
```
[C++]
```
public: __property static Cursor* get_SizeNESW();
```
[JScript]
```
public static function get SizeNESW() : Cursor;
```

Property Value

The **Cursor** that represents two-headed diagonal (northeast/southwest) sizing cursor.

Requirements

Platforms: Windows 98, Windows NT 4.0, Windows Millennium Edition, Windows 2000, Windows XP Home Edition, Windows XP Professional, Windows Server 2003 family

Cursors.SizeNS Property

Gets the two-headed vertical (north/south) sizing cursor.

[Visual Basic]
```
Public Shared ReadOnly Property SizeNS As Cursor
```
[C#]
```
public static Cursor SizeNS {get;}
```
[C++]
```
public: __property static Cursor* get_SizeNS();
```

[JScript]
```
public static function get SizeNS() : Cursor;
```

Property Value

The **Cursor** that represents the two-headed vertical (north/south) sizing cursor.

Requirements

Platforms: Windows 98, Windows NT 4.0, Windows Millennium Edition, Windows 2000, Windows XP Home Edition, Windows XP Professional, Windows Server 2003 family

Cursors.SizeNWSE Property

Gets the two-headed diagonal (northwest/southeast) sizing cursor.

[Visual Basic]
```
Public Shared ReadOnly Property SizeNWSE As Cursor
```
[C#]
```
public static Cursor SizeNWSE {get;}
```
[C++]
```
public: __property static Cursor* get_SizeNWSE();
```
[JScript]
```
public static function get SizeNWSE() : Cursor;
```

Property Value

The **Cursor** that represents the two-headed diagonal (northwest/southeast) sizing cursor.

Requirements

Platforms: Windows 98, Windows NT 4.0, Windows Millennium Edition, Windows 2000, Windows XP Home Edition, Windows XP Professional, Windows Server 2003 family

Cursors.SizeWE Property

Gets the two-headed horizontal (west/east) sizing cursor.

[Visual Basic]
```
Public Shared ReadOnly Property SizeWE As Cursor
```
[C#]
```
public static Cursor SizeWE {get;}
```
[C++]
```
public: __property static Cursor* get_SizeWE();
```
[JScript]
```
public static function get SizeWE() : Cursor;
```

Property Value

The **Cursor** that represents the two-headed horizontal (west/east) sizing cursor.

Requirements

Platforms: Windows 98, Windows NT 4.0, Windows Millennium Edition, Windows 2000, Windows XP Home Edition, Windows XP Professional, Windows Server 2003 family

Cursors.UpArrow Property

Gets the up arrow cursor, typically used to identify an insertion point.

[Visual Basic]
```
Public Shared ReadOnly Property UpArrow As Cursor
```
[C#]
```
public static Cursor UpArrow {get;}
```
[C++]
```
public: __property static Cursor* get_UpArrow();
```
[JScript]
```
public static function get UpArrow() : Cursor;
```

Property Value

The **Cursor** that represents the up arrow cursor.

Requirements

Platforms: Windows 98, Windows NT 4.0, Windows Millennium Edition, Windows 2000, Windows XP Home Edition, Windows XP Professional, Windows Server 2003 family

Cursors.VSplit Property

Gets the cursor that appears when the mouse is positioned over a vertical splitter bar.

[Visual Basic]
```
Public Shared ReadOnly Property VSplit As Cursor
```
[C#]
```
public static Cursor VSplit {get;}
```
[C++]
```
public: __property static Cursor* get_VSplit();
```
[JScript]
```
public static function get VSplit() : Cursor;
```

Property Value

The **Cursor** that represents the cursor that appears when the mouse is positioned over a vertical splitter bar.

Requirements

Platforms: Windows 98, Windows NT 4.0, Windows Millennium Edition, Windows 2000, Windows XP Home Edition, Windows XP Professional, Windows Server 2003 family

Cursors.WaitCursor Property

Gets the wait cursor, typically an hourglass shape.

[Visual Basic]
```
Public Shared ReadOnly Property WaitCursor As Cursor
```
[C#]
```
public static Cursor WaitCursor {get;}
```
[C++]
```
public: __property static Cursor* get_WaitCursor();
```
[JScript]
```
public static function get WaitCursor() : Cursor;
```

Property Value

The **Cursor** that represents the wait cursor.

Requirements

Platforms: Windows 98, Windows NT 4.0, Windows Millennium Edition, Windows 2000, Windows XP Home Edition, Windows XP Professional, Windows Server 2003 family, .NET Compact Framework - Windows CE .NET

DataFormats Class

Provides static (**Shared** in Visual Basic), predefined **Clipboard** format names. Use them to identify the format of data that you store in an **IDataObject**.

System.Object
  System.Windows.Forms.DataFormats

[Visual Basic]
```
Public Class DataFormats
```
[C#]
```
public class DataFormats
```
[C++]
```
public __gc class DataFormats
```
[JScript]
```
public class DataFormats
```

Thread Safety

Any public static (**Shared** in Visual Basic) members of this type are safe for multithreaded operations. Any instance members are not guaranteed to be thread safe.

Remarks

The **IDataObject** and **DataObject** classes also use the static (**Shared** in Visual Basic) format list to determine the type of data that is retrieved from the system **Clipboard**, or that is transferred in a drag-and-drop operation.

The **GetFormat** method allows you to:

- Get a predefined **DataFormats.Format** object for a format name or ID number.
- Add a new format name/ID number pair to the static (**Shared** in Visual Basic) list in this class, and to register the format with the Windows registry as a **Clipboard** format when you pass it the format name.

You can get the **id** number or format **name** from the appropriate field in the **DataFormats.Format** instance.

Example

[Visual Basic, C#, JScript] The following example creates a new data format named `myFormat`. The code then creates a `MyNewObject` which it stores in a **DataObject**. The **DataObject** is copied to the **Clipboard**.

[Visual Basic, C#, JScript] Then the **DataObject** is retrieved from the **Clipboard** and the `MyNewObject` is recovered. The value of the `MyNewObject` is printed in a text box. This code assumes that `textBox1` has been created and placed on a form.

[Visual Basic]
```
Option Explicit
Option Strict

Imports System
Imports System.Windows.Forms

Public Class MyClass1
    Inherits Form
    Private textBox1 As TextBox

    Public Sub MyClipboardMethod()
        ' Creates a new data format.
        Dim myFormat As DataFormats.Format = _
            DataFormats.GetFormat("myFormat")

        ' Creates a new object and store it in a DataObject ↵
 using myFormat
        ' as the type of format.
        Dim myObject As New MyNewObject()
        Dim myDataObject As New DataObject(myFormat.Name, myObject)

        ' Copies myObject into the clipboard.
        Clipboard.SetDataObject(myDataObject)

        ' Performs some processing steps.
        ' Retrieves the data from the clipboard.
        Dim myRetrievedObject As IDataObject = ↵
Clipboard.GetDataObject()

        ' Converts the IDataObject type to MyNewObject type.
        Dim myDereferencedObject As MyNewObject = _
            CType(myRetrievedObject.GetData(myFormat.Name), ↵
MyNewObject)

        ' Print the value of the Object in a textBox.
        textBox1.Text = myDereferencedObject.MyObjectValue
    End Sub 'MyClipboardMethod
End Class 'MyClass

' Creates a new type.
<Serializable()> Public Class MyNewObject
    Inherits Object
    Private myValue As String

    ' Creates a default constructor for the class.
    Public Sub New()
        myValue = "This is the value of the class"
    End Sub 'New

    ' Creates a property to retrieve or set the value.

    Public Property MyObjectValue() As String
        Get
            Return myValue
        End Get
        Set
            myValue = value
        End Set
    End Property
End Class 'MyNewObject
```

[C#]
```
using System;
using System.Windows.Forms;

public class MyClass : Form {
    protected TextBox textBox1;

    public void MyClipboardMethod() {
       // Creates a new data format.
       DataFormats.Format myFormat = DataFormats.GetFormat("myFormat");

       /* Creates a new object and stores it in a DataObject ↵
 using myFormat
        * as the type of format. */
       MyNewObject myObject = new MyNewObject();
       DataObject myDataObject = new DataObject(myFormat.Name, ↵
myObject);

       // Copies myObject into the clipboard.
       Clipboard.SetDataObject(myDataObject);

       // Performs some processing steps.

       // Retrieves the data from the clipboard.
       IDataObject myRetrievedObject = Clipboard.GetDataObject();

       // Converts the IDataObject type to MyNewObject type.
       MyNewObject myDereferencedObject = ↵
 (MyNewObject)myRetrievedObject.GetData(myFormat.Name);

       // Prints the value of the Object in a textBox.
       textBox1.Text = myDereferencedObject.MyObjectValue;
    }
 }
```

```
// Creates a new type.
[Serializable]
public class MyNewObject : Object {
   private string myValue;

   // Creates a default constructor for the class.
   public MyNewObject() {
      myValue = "This is the value of the class";
   }

   // Creates a property to retrieve or set the value.
   public string MyObjectValue {
      get {
         return myValue;
      }
      set {
         myValue = value;
      }
   }
}
```

[JScript]

```
import System;
import System.Windows.Forms;

public class MyClass extends Form {
    protected var textBox1 : TextBox;

    public function MyClipboardMethod() {
       // Create a new data format.
       var myFormat : DataFormats.Format =
DataFormats.GetFormat("myFormat");

       /* Create a new object and store it in a DataObject
 import the myFormat
        * as the type of format. */
       var myObject : MyNewObject = new MyNewObject();
       var myDataObject : DataObject = new DataObject
("myFormat", myObject);

       // Copy myObject into the clipboard.
       Clipboard.SetDataObject(myDataObject);

       // Perform some processing steps.

       // Retrieve the data from the clipboard.
       var myRetrievedObject : IDataObject = Clipboard.GetDataObject();

       // Convert the IDataObject type to MyNewObject type.
       var myDereferencedObject : MyNewObject =
MyNewObject(myRetrievedObject.GetData("myFormat"));

       // Print the value of the Object in a textBox.
       textBox1.Text = myDereferencedObject.MyObjectValue;
    }
}

// Create a new type.
Serializable public class MyNewObject extends Object {
    private var myValue : String;

    // Create a default constructor for the class.
    public function MyNewObject() {
       myValue = "This is the value of the class";
    }

    // Create a property to retrieve or set the value.
    public function get MyObjectValue() : String {
          return myValue;
    }

    public function set MyObjectValue(value : String) {
          myValue = value;
    }
}
```

Requirements

Namespace: System.Windows.Forms

Platforms: Windows 98, Windows NT 4.0, Windows Millennium Edition, Windows 2000, Windows XP Home Edition, Windows XP Professional, Windows Server 2003 family

Assembly: System.Windows.Forms (in System.Windows.Forms.dll)

DataFormats.Bitmap Field

Specifies a Windows bitmap format. This static (**Shared** in Visual Basic) field is read-only.

[Visual Basic]

```
Public Shared ReadOnly Bitmap As String
```

[C#]

```
public static readonly string Bitmap;
```

[C++]

```
public: static String* Bitmap;
```

[JScript]

```
public static var Bitmap : String;
```

Remarks

A bitmap represents a computer graphic as an array of bits in memory, and these bits represent the attributes of the individual pixels in an image.

This field is used by the **IDataObject** interface and the **DataObject** class to specify the data type.

When adding to an **IDataObject** or to an implementation of **DataObject**, use this field as the format for the **IDataObject.SetData** and **DataObject.SetData** methods.

To see if an object of this type exists, use this field as the format for the **IDataObject.GetDataPresent** and **DataObject.GetDataPresent** methods.

To get an object of this type, use this as the format for the **IDataObject.GetData** and **DataObject.GetData** methods.

Requirements

Platforms: Windows 98, Windows NT 4.0, Windows Millennium Edition, Windows 2000, Windows XP Home Edition, Windows XP Professional, Windows Server 2003 family

DataFormats.CommaSeparatedValue Field

Specifies a comma-separated value (CSV) format, which is a common interchange format used by spreadsheets. This format is not used directly by Windows Forms. This static (**Shared** in Visual Basic) field is read-only.

[Visual Basic]

```
Public Shared ReadOnly CommaSeparatedValue As String
```

[C#]

```
public static readonly string CommaSeparatedValue;
```

[C++]

```
public: static String* CommaSeparatedValue;
```

[JScript]

```
public static var CommaSeparatedValue : String;
```

Remarks

This field is used by the **IDataObject** interface and the **DataObject** class to specify the data type.

When adding to an **IDataObject** or to an implementation of **DataObject**, use this field as the format for the **IDataObject.SetData** and **DataObject.SetData** methods.

To see if an object of this type exists, use this field as the format for the **IDataObject.GetDataPresent** and **DataObject.GetDataPresent** methods.

To get an object of this type, use this as the format for the **IDataObject.GetData** and **DataObject.GetData** methods.

Requirements

Platforms: Windows 98, Windows NT 4.0, Windows Millennium Edition, Windows 2000, Windows XP Home Edition, Windows XP Professional, Windows Server 2003 family

DataFormats.Dib Field

Specifies the Windows Device Independent Bitmap (DIB) format. This static (**Shared** in Visual Basic) field is read-only.

```
[Visual Basic]
Public Shared ReadOnly Dib As String
[C#]
public static readonly string Dib;
[C++]
public: static String* Dib;
[JScript]
public static var Dib : String;
```

Remarks

DIB is a file format designed to ensure that bitmapped graphics created using one application can be loaded and displayed in another application exactly the way they appeared in the originating application.

This field is used by the **IDataObject** interface and the **DataObject** class to specify the data type.

When adding to an **IDataObject** or to an implementation of **DataObject**, use this field as the format for the **IDataObject.SetData** and **DataObject.SetData** methods.

To see if an object of this type exists, use this field as the format for the **IDataObject.GetDataPresent** and **DataObject.GetDataPresent** methods.

To get an object of this type, use this as the format for the **IDataObject.GetData** and **DataObject.GetData** methods.

Requirements

Platforms: Windows 98, Windows NT 4.0, Windows Millennium Edition, Windows 2000, Windows XP Home Edition, Windows XP Professional, Windows Server 2003 family

DataFormats.Dif Field

Specifies the Windows Data Interchange Format (DIF), which Windows Forms does not directly use. This static (**Shared** in Visual Basic) field is read-only.

```
[Visual Basic]
Public Shared ReadOnly Dif As String
[C#]
public static readonly string Dif;
[C++]
public: static String* Dif;
[JScript]
public static var Dif : String;
```

Remarks

DIF is a format consisting of ASCII codes in which database, spreadsheet, and similar documents can be structured to facilitate their use by and transfer to other programs.

This field is used by the **IDataObject** interface and the **DataObject** class to specify the data type.

When adding to an **IDataObject** or to an implementation of **DataObject**, use this field as the format for the **IDataObject.SetData** and **DataObject.SetData** methods.

To see if an object of this type exists, use this field as the format for the **IDataObject.GetDataPresent** and **DataObject.GetDataPresent** methods.

To get an object of this type, use this as the format for the **IDataObject.GetData** and **DataObject.GetData** methods.

Example

See related example in the **System.Windows.Forms.DataFormats** class topic.

Requirements

Platforms: Windows 98, Windows NT 4.0, Windows Millennium Edition, Windows 2000, Windows XP Home Edition, Windows XP Professional, Windows Server 2003 family

DataFormats.EnhancedMetafile Field

Specifies the Windows enhanced metafile format. This static (**Shared** in Visual Basic) field is read-only.

```
[Visual Basic]
Public Shared ReadOnly EnhancedMetafile As String
[C#]
public static readonly string EnhancedMetafile;
[C++]
public: static String* EnhancedMetafile;
[JScript]
public static var EnhancedMetafile : String;
```

Remarks

The metafile format is a Windows file that stores an image in terms of graphic objects rather than pixels. When resized, a metafile preserves an image better than a bitmap.

This field is used by the **IDataObject** interface and the **DataObject** class to specify the data type.

When adding to an **IDataObject** or to an implementation of **DataObject**, use this field as the format for the **IDataObject.SetData** and **DataObject.SetData** methods.

To see if an object of this type exists, use this field as the format for the **IDataObject.GetDataPresent** and **DataObject.GetDataPresent** methods.

To get an object of this type, use this as the format for the **IDataObject.GetData** and **DataObject.GetData** methods.

Requirements

Platforms: Windows 98, Windows NT 4.0,
Windows Millennium Edition, Windows 2000,
Windows XP Home Edition, Windows XP Professional,
Windows Server 2003 family

DataFormats.FileDrop Field

Specifies the Windows file drop format, which Windows Forms does not directly use. This static (**Shared** in Visual Basic) field is read-only.

```
[Visual Basic]
Public Shared ReadOnly FileDrop As String
[C#]
public static readonly string FileDrop;
[C++]
public: static String* FileDrop;
[JScript]
public static var FileDrop : String;
```

Remarks

You can use this format to interact with shell file drags during drag-and-drop operations.

This field is used by the **IDataObject** interface and the **DataObject** class to specify the data type.

When adding to an **IDataObject** or to an implementation of **DataObject**, use this field as the format for the **IDataObject.SetData** and **DataObject.SetData** methods.

To see if an object of this type exists, use this field as the format for the **IDataObject.GetDataPresent** and **DataObject.GetDataPresent** methods.

To get an object of this type, use this as the format for the **IDataObject.GetData** and **DataObject.GetData** methods.

Requirements

Platforms: Windows 98, Windows NT 4.0,
Windows Millennium Edition, Windows 2000,
Windows XP Home Edition, Windows XP Professional,
Windows Server 2003 family

DataFormats.Html Field

Specifies text consisting of HTML data. This static (**Shared** in Visual Basic) field is read-only.

```
[Visual Basic]
Public Shared ReadOnly Html As String
[C#]
public static readonly string Html;
[C++]
public: static String* Html;
[JScript]
public static var Html : String;
```

Remarks

This field is used by the **IDataObject** interface and the **DataObject** class to specify the data type.

When adding to an **IDataObject** or to an implementation of **DataObject**, use this field as the format for the **IDataObject.SetData** and **DataObject.SetData** methods.

To see if an object of this type exists, use this field as the format for the **IDataObject.GetDataPresent** and **DataObject.GetDataPresent** methods.

To get an object of this type, use this as the format for the **IDataObject.GetData** and **DataObject.GetData** methods.

Requirements

Platforms: Windows 98, Windows NT 4.0,
Windows Millennium Edition, Windows 2000,
Windows XP Home Edition, Windows XP Professional,
Windows Server 2003 family

DataFormats.Locale Field

Specifies the Windows culture format, which Windows Forms does not directly use. This static (**Shared** in Visual Basic) field is read-only.

```
[Visual Basic]
Public Shared ReadOnly Locale As String
[C#]
public static readonly string Locale;
[C++]
public: static String* Locale;
[JScript]
public static var Locale : String;
```

Remarks

This field is used by the **IDataObject** interface and the **DataObject** class to specify the data type.

When adding to an **IDataObject** or to an implementation of **DataObject**, use this field as the format for the **IDataObject.SetData** and **DataObject.SetData** methods.

To see if an object of this type exists, use this field as the format for the **IDataObject.GetDataPresent** and **DataObject.GetDataPresent** methods.

To get an object of this type, use this as the format for the **IDataObject.GetData** and **DataObject.GetData** methods.

Requirements

Platforms: Windows 98, Windows NT 4.0,
Windows Millennium Edition, Windows 2000,
Windows XP Home Edition, Windows XP Professional,
Windows Server 2003 family

DataFormats.MetafilePict Field

Specifies the Windows metafile format, which Windows Forms does not directly use. This static (**Shared** in Visual Basic) field is read-only.

```
[Visual Basic]
Public Shared ReadOnly MetafilePict As String
[C#]
public static readonly string MetafilePict;
[C++]
public: static String* MetafilePict;
[JScript]
public static var MetafilePict : String;
```

Remarks

The metafile format is a Windows file that stores an image in terms of graphic objects rather than pixels. When resized, a metafile preserves an image better than a bitmap.

This field is used by the **IDataObject** interface and the **DataObject** class to specify the data type.

When adding to an **IDataObject** or to an implementation of **DataObject**, use this field as the format for the **IDataObject.SetData** and **DataObject.SetData** methods.

To see if an object of this type exists, use this field as the format for the **IDataObject.GetDataPresent** and **DataObject.GetDataPresent** methods.

To get an object of this type, use this as the format for the **IDataObject.GetData** and **DataObject.GetData** methods.

Requirements

Platforms: Windows 98, Windows NT 4.0, Windows Millennium Edition, Windows 2000, Windows XP Home Edition, Windows XP Professional, Windows Server 2003 family

DataFormats.OemText Field

Specifies the standard Windows original equipment manufacturer (OEM) text format. This static (**Shared** in Visual Basic) field is read-only.

```
[Visual Basic]
Public Shared ReadOnly OemText As String
[C#]
public static readonly string OemText;
[C++]
public: static String* OemText;
[JScript]
public static var OemText : String;
```

Remarks

This field is used by the **IDataObject** interface and the **DataObject** class to specify the data type.

When adding to an **IDataObject** or to an implementation of **DataObject**, use this field as the format for the **IDataObject.SetData** and **DataObject.SetData** methods.

To see if an object of this type exists, use this field as the format for the **IDataObject.GetDataPresent** and **DataObject.GetDataPresent** methods.

To get an object of this type, use this as the format for the **IDataObject.GetData** and **DataObject.GetData** methods.

Requirements

Platforms: Windows 98, Windows NT 4.0, Windows Millennium Edition, Windows 2000, Windows XP Home Edition, Windows XP Professional, Windows Server 2003 family

DataFormats.Palette Field

Specifies the Windows palette format. This static (**Shared** in Visual Basic) field is read-only.

```
[Visual Basic]
Public Shared ReadOnly Palette As String
[C#]
public static readonly string Palette;
[C++]
public: static String* Palette;
[JScript]
public static var Palette : String;
```

Remarks

Use this field to query a **DataObject** for the format of data that it contains.

This field is used by the **IDataObject** interface and the **DataObject** class to specify the data type.

When adding to an **IDataObject** or to an implementation of **DataObject**, use this field as the format for the **IDataObject.SetData** and **DataObject.SetData** methods.

To see if an object of this type exists, use this field as the format for the **IDataObject.GetDataPresent** and **DataObject.GetDataPresent** methods.

To get an object of this type, use this as the format for the **IDataObject.GetData** and **DataObject.GetData** methods.

Requirements

Platforms: Windows 98, Windows NT 4.0, Windows Millennium Edition, Windows 2000, Windows XP Home Edition, Windows XP Professional, Windows Server 2003 family

DataFormats.PenData Field

Specifies the Windows pen data format, which consists of pen strokes for handwriting software; Windows Forms does not use this format. This static (**Shared** in Visual Basic) field is read-only.

```
[Visual Basic]
Public Shared ReadOnly PenData As String
[C#]
public static readonly string PenData;
[C++]
public: static String* PenData;
[JScript]
public static var PenData : String;
```

Remarks

This field is used by the **IDataObject** interface and the **DataObject** class to specify the data type.

When adding to an **IDataObject** or to an implementation of **DataObject**, use this field as the format for the **IDataObject.SetData** and **DataObject.SetData** methods.

To see if an object of this type exists, use this field as the format for the **IDataObject.GetDataPresent** and **DataObject.GetDataPresent** methods.

To get an object of this type, use this as the format for the **IDataObject.GetData** and **DataObject.GetData** methods.

Requirements

Platforms: Windows 98, Windows NT 4.0, Windows Millennium Edition, Windows 2000, Windows XP Home Edition, Windows XP Professional, Windows Server 2003 family

DataFormats.Riff Field

Specifies the Resource Interchange File Format (RIFF) audio format, which Windows Forms does not directly use. This static (**Shared** in Visual Basic) field is read-only.

[Visual Basic]
```
Public Shared ReadOnly Riff As String
```
[C#]
```
public static readonly string Riff;
```
[C++]
```
public: static String* Riff;
```
[JScript]
```
public static var Riff : String;
```

Remarks

RIFF is a broad-based specification, designed to be used in defining standard formats for different types of multimedia files.

This field is used by the **IDataObject** interface and the **DataObject** class to specify the data type.

When adding to an **IDataObject** or to an implementation of **DataObject**, use this field as the format for the **IDataObject.SetData** and **DataObject.SetData** methods.

To see if an object of this type exists, use this field as the format for the **IDataObject.GetDataPresent** and **DataObject.GetDataPresent** methods.

To get an object of this type, use this as the format for the **IDataObject.GetData** and **DataObject.GetData** methods.

Requirements

Platforms: Windows 98, Windows NT 4.0, Windows Millennium Edition, Windows 2000, Windows XP Home Edition, Windows XP Professional, Windows Server 2003 family

DataFormats.Rtf Field

Specifies text consisting of Rich Text Format (RTF) data. This static (**Shared** in Visual Basic) field is read-only.

[Visual Basic]
```
Public Shared ReadOnly Rtf As String
```
[C#]
```
public static readonly string Rtf;
```
[C++]
```
public: static String* Rtf;
```
[JScript]
```
public static var Rtf : String;
```

Remarks

RTF is an adaptation of Document Content Architecture that is used for transferring formatted text documents between applications.

This field is used by the **IDataObject** interface and the **DataObject** class to specify the data type.

When adding to an **IDataObject** or to an implementation of **DataObject**, use this field as the format for the **IDataObject.SetData** and **DataObject.SetData** methods.

To see if an object of this type exists, use this field as the format for the **IDataObject.GetDataPresent** and **DataObject.GetDataPresent** methods.

To get an object of this type, use this as the format for the **IDataObject.GetData** and **DataObject.GetData** methods.

Requirements

Platforms: Windows 98, Windows NT 4.0, Windows Millennium Edition, Windows 2000, Windows XP Home Edition, Windows XP Professional, Windows Server 2003 family

DataFormats.Serializable Field

Specifies a format that encapsulates any type of Windows Forms object. This static (**Shared** in Visual Basic) field is read-only.

[Visual Basic]
```
Public Shared ReadOnly Serializable As String
```
[C#]
```
public static readonly string Serializable;
```
[C++]
```
public: static String* Serializable;
```
[JScript]
```
public static var Serializable : String;
```

Remarks

This field is used by the **IDataObject** interface and the **DataObject** class to specify the data type.

When adding to an **IDataObject** or to an implementation of **DataObject**, use this field as the format for the **IDataObject.SetData** and **DataObject.SetData** methods.

To see if an object of this type exists, use this field as the format for the **IDataObject.GetDataPresent** and **DataObject.GetDataPresent** methods.

To get an object of this type, use this as the format for the **IDataObject.GetData** and **DataObject.GetData** methods.

> **Note** The serializable format is specific to Windows Forms only and will not be recognized by applications created outside of Windows Forms.

Requirements

Platforms: Windows 98, Windows NT 4.0, Windows Millennium Edition, Windows 2000, Windows XP Home Edition, Windows XP Professional, Windows Server 2003 family

DataFormats.StringFormat Field

Specifies the Windows Forms string class format, which Windows Forms uses to store string objects. This static (**Shared** in Visual Basic) field is read-only.

```
[Visual Basic]
Public Shared ReadOnly StringFormat As String
[C#]
public static readonly string StringFormat;
[C++]
public: static String* StringFormat;
[JScript]
public static var StringFormat : String;
```

Remarks

This field is used by the **IDataObject** interface and the **DataObject** class to specify the data type.

When adding to an **IDataObject** or to an implementation of **DataObject**, use this field as the format for the **IDataObject.SetData** and **DataObject.SetData** methods.

To see if an object of this type exists, use this field as the format for the **IDataObject.GetDataPresent** and **DataObject.GetDataPresent** methods.

To get an object of this type, use this as the format for the **IDataObject.GetData** and **DataObject.GetData** methods.

> **Note** The string class format is specific to Windows Forms only and will not be recognized by applications created outside of Windows Forms.

Example

See related example in the **System.Windows.Forms.DataFormats** class topic.

Requirements

Platforms: Windows 98, Windows NT 4.0, Windows Millennium Edition, Windows 2000, Windows XP Home Edition, Windows XP Professional, Windows Server 2003 family

DataFormats.SymbolicLink Field

Specifies the Windows symbolic link format, which Windows Forms does not directly use. This static (**Shared** in Visual Basic) field is read-only.

```
[Visual Basic]
Public Shared ReadOnly SymbolicLink As String
[C#]
public static readonly string SymbolicLink;
[C++]
public: static String* SymbolicLink;
[JScript]
public static var SymbolicLink : String;
```

Remarks

A symbolic link is a disk directory entry that takes the place of a directory entry for a file, but is actually a reference to a file in a different directory. A symbolic link is also called an alias, shortcut, soft link, or symlink.

This field is used by the **IDataObject** interface and the **DataObject** class to specify the data type.

When adding to an **IDataObject** or to an implementation of **DataObject**, use this field as the format for the **IDataObject.SetData** and **DataObject.SetData** methods.

To see if an object of this type exists, use this field as the format for the **IDataObject.GetDataPresent** and **DataObject.GetDataPresent** methods.

To get an object of this type, use this as the format for the **IDataObject.GetData** and **DataObject.GetData** methods.

Requirements

Platforms: Windows 98, Windows NT 4.0, Windows Millennium Edition, Windows 2000, Windows XP Home Edition, Windows XP Professional, Windows Server 2003 family

DataFormats.Text Field

Specifies the standard ANSI text format. This static (**Shared** in Visual Basic) field is read-only.

```
[Visual Basic]
Public Shared ReadOnly Text As String
[C#]
public static readonly string Text;
[C++]
public: static String* Text;
[JScript]
public static var Text : String;
```

Remarks

This field is used by the **IDataObject** interface and the **DataObject** class to specify the data type.

When adding to an **IDataObject** or to an implementation of **DataObject**, use this field as the format for the **IDataObject.SetData** and **DataObject.SetData** methods.

To see if an object of this type exists, use this field as the format for the **IDataObject.GetDataPresent** and **DataObject.GetDataPresent** methods.

To get an object of this type, use this as the format for the **IDataObject.GetData** and **DataObject.GetData** methods.

Example

See related example in the **System.Windows.Forms.DataFormats** class topic.

Requirements

Platforms: Windows 98, Windows NT 4.0, Windows Millennium Edition, Windows 2000, Windows XP Home Edition, Windows XP Professional, Windows Server 2003 family

DataFormats.Tiff Field

Specifies the Tagged Image File Format (TIFF), which Windows Forms does not directly use. This static (**Shared** in Visual Basic) field is read-only.

```
[Visual Basic]
Public Shared ReadOnly Tiff As String
[C#]
public static readonly string Tiff;
[C++]
public: static String* Tiff;
[JScript]
public static var Tiff : String;
```

Remarks

TIFF is a standard file format commonly used for scanning, storage, and interchanges of gray-scale graphic images.

This field is used by the **IDataObject** interface and the **DataObject** class to specify the data type.

When adding to an **IDataObject** or to an implementation of **DataObject**, use this field as the format for the **IDataObject.SetData** and **DataObject.SetData** methods.

To see if an object of this type exists, use this field as the format for the **IDataObject.GetDataPresent** and **DataObject.GetDataPresent** methods.

To get an object of this type, use this as the format for the **IDataObject.GetData** and **DataObject.GetData** methods.

Requirements

Platforms: Windows 98, Windows NT 4.0, Windows Millennium Edition, Windows 2000, Windows XP Home Edition, Windows XP Professional, Windows Server 2003 family

DataFormats.UnicodeText Field

Specifies the standard Windows Unicode text format. This static (**Shared** in Visual Basic) field is read-only.

```
[Visual Basic]
Public Shared ReadOnly UnicodeText As String
[C#]
public static readonly string UnicodeText;
[C++]
public: static String* UnicodeText;
[JScript]
public static var UnicodeText : String;
```

Remarks

This field is used by the **IDataObject** interface and the **DataObject** class to specify the data type.

When adding to an **IDataObject** or to an implementation of **DataObject**, use this field as the format for the **IDataObject.SetData** and **DataObject.SetData** methods.

To see if an object of this type exists, use this field as the format for the **IDataObject.GetDataPresent** and **DataObject.GetDataPresent** methods.

To get an object of this type, use this as the format for the **IDataObject.GetData** and **DataObject.GetData** methods.

Example

See related example in the **System.Windows.Forms.DataFormats** class topic.

Requirements

Platforms: Windows 98, Windows NT 4.0, Windows Millennium Edition, Windows 2000, Windows XP Home Edition, Windows XP Professional, Windows Server 2003 family

DataFormats.WaveAudio Field

Specifies the wave audio format, which Windows Forms does not directly use. This static (**Shared** in Visual Basic) field is read-only.

```
[Visual Basic]
Public Shared ReadOnly WaveAudio As String
[C#]
public static readonly string WaveAudio;
[C++]
public: static String* WaveAudio;
[JScript]
public static var WaveAudio : String;
```

Remarks

This field is used by the **IDataObject** interface and the **DataObject** class to specify the data type.

When adding to an **IDataObject** or to an implementation of **DataObject**, use this field as the format for the **IDataObject.SetData** and **DataObject.SetData** methods.

To see if an object of this type exists, use this field as the format for the **IDataObject.GetDataPresent** and **DataObject.GetDataPresent** methods.

To get an object of this type, use this as the format for the **IDataObject.GetData** and **DataObject.GetData** methods.

Requirements

Platforms: Windows 98, Windows NT 4.0, Windows Millennium Edition, Windows 2000, Windows XP Home Edition, Windows XP Professional, Windows Server 2003 family

DataFormats.GetFormat Method

Returns a **DataFormats.Format** with the Windows Clipboard numeric ID and name.

Overload List

Returns a **DataFormats.Format** with the Windows Clipboard numeric ID and name for the specified ID.

[Visual Basic] **Overloads Public Shared Function GetFormat(Integer) As Format**

[C#] **public static Format GetFormat(int);**

[C++] **public: static Format* GetFormat(int);**

[JScript] **public static function GetFormat(int) : Format;**

Returns a **DataFormats.Format** with the Windows Clipboard numeric ID and name for the specified format.

[Visual Basic] **Overloads Public Shared Function GetFormat(String) As Format**

[C#] **public static Format GetFormat(string);**

[C++] **public: static Format* GetFormat(String*);**

[JScript] **public static function GetFormat(String) : Format;**

Example

See related example in the **System.Windows.Forms.DataFormats** class topic.

DataFormats.GetFormat Method (Int32)

Returns a **DataFormats.Format** with the Windows Clipboard numeric ID and name for the specified ID.

[Visual Basic]
```
Overloads Public Shared Function GetFormat( _
   ByVal id As Integer _
) As Format
```
[C#]
```
public static Format GetFormat(
   int id
);
```
[C++]
```
public: static Format* GetFormat(
   int id
);
```
[JScript]
```
public static function GetFormat(
   id : int
) : Format;
```

Parameters

id

The format ID.

Return Value

A **DataFormats.Format** that has the Windows Clipboard numeric ID and the name of the format.

Remarks

This member is typically used to register native clipboard formats.

Call **GetFormat** with an ID number when you want to retrieve a **DataFormats.Format** instance that contains the ID/format name pair. Typically, the ID name and number is published by the creator of the application that you are using the **Clipboard** to interface with. For example, the ID number for DDE conversation information in Visual Basic is &HBF00, and the format name is vbCFLink.

Call this method with a any unique ID number to add the ID/format name pair to the static (**Shared** in Visual Basic) list of format name/ID pairs in the **DataFormats** class. The new name will be created by concatenating "Format" and the ID number. This pair is not registered as a new **Clipboard** format since you have not provided a name.

Example

See related example in the **System.Windows.Forms.DataFormats** class topic.

Requirements

Platforms: Windows 98, Windows NT 4.0, Windows Millennium Edition, Windows 2000, Windows XP Home Edition, Windows XP Professional, Windows Server 2003 family

DataFormats.GetFormat Method (String)

Returns a **DataFormats.Format** with the Windows Clipboard numeric ID and name for the specified format.

[Visual Basic]
```
Overloads Public Shared Function GetFormat( _
   ByVal format As String _
) As Format
```
[C#]
```
public static Format GetFormat(
   string format
);
```
[C++]
```
public: static Format* GetFormat(
   String* format
);
```
[JScript]
```
public static function GetFormat(
   format : String
) : Format;
```

Parameters

format

The format name.

Return Value

A **DataFormats.Format** that has the Windows Clipboard numeric ID and the name of the format.

Exceptions

Exception Type	Condition
Exception	Registering a new **Clipboard** format failed.

Remarks

Call **GetFormat** with the format name when you need a Windows Clipboard numeric ID for an existing format.

Call this method with your own format name to create a new **Clipboard** format type. If the specified format does not exist, this method will register the name as a Clipboard format with the Windows registry and get a unique format identifier. This new name/ID pair will be added to the static (**Shared** in Visual Basic) list of format name/ID pairs in the **DataFormats** class.

Example

See related example in the **System.Windows.Forms.DataFormats** class topic.

Requirements

Platforms: Windows 98, Windows NT 4.0, Windows Millennium Edition, Windows 2000, Windows XP Home Edition, Windows XP Professional, Windows Server 2003 family

DataFormats.Format Class

Represents a clipboard format type.

System.Object
  System.Windows.Forms.DataFormats.Format

```
[Visual Basic]
Public Class DataFormats.Format
[C#]
public class DataFormats.Format
[C++]
public __gc class DataFormats.Format
[JScript]
public class DataFormats.Format
```

Thread Safety

Any public static (**Shared** in Visual Basic) members of this type are safe for multithreaded operations. Any instance members are not guaranteed to be thread safe.

Remarks

A format type consists of a text-based format name and an ID number. The format name/ID number pair can define a system **Clipboard** or other format.

Example

[Visual Basic, C#] The following example shows how to retrieve a **DataFormats.Format** representing a format name/ID pair. The **UnicodeText** format is requested, and the contents of the retrieved **DataFormats.Format** object are displayed in a text box.

[Visual Basic, C#] This code assumes `textBox1` has been created.

```
[Visual Basic]
Private Sub GetMyFormatInfomation()
    ' Creates a DataFormats.Format for the Unicode data format.
    Dim myFormat As DataFormats.Format = _
       DataFormats.GetFormat(DataFormats.UnicodeText)

    ' Displays the contents of myFormat.
    textBox1.Text = "ID value: " + myFormat.Id.ToString() +     ↵
ControlChars.Cr _
                  + "Format name: " + myFormat.Name
End Sub
```

```
[C#]
private void GetMyFormatInfomation() {
   // Creates a DataFormats.Format for the Unicode data format.
   DataFormats.Format myFormat =                                 ↵
DataFormats.GetFormat(DataFormats.UnicodeText);

   // Displays the contents of myFormat.
   textBox1.Text = "ID value: " + myFormat.Id + '\n' +
      "Format name: " + myFormat.Name;
}
```

Requirements

Namespace: **System.Windows.Forms**

Platforms: Windows 98, Windows NT 4.0, Windows Millennium Edition, Windows 2000, Windows XP Home Edition, Windows XP Professional, Windows Server 2003 family

Assembly: System.Windows.Forms (in System.Windows.Forms.dll)

DataFormats.Format Constructor

This member supports the .NET Framework infrastructure and is not intended to be used directly from your code.

```
[Visual Basic]
Public Sub New( _
   ByVal name As String, _
   ByVal id As Integer _
)
[C#]
public DataFormats.Format(
   string name,
   int id
);
[C++]
public: Format(
   String* name,
   int id
);
[JScript]
public function DataFormats.Format(
   name : String,
   id : int
);
```

DataFormats.Format.Id Property

Gets the ID number for this format.

```
[Visual Basic]
Public ReadOnly Property Id As Integer
[C#]
public int Id {get;}
[C++]
public: __property int get_Id();
[JScript]
public function get Id() : int;
```

Property Value

The ID number for this format.

Requirements

Platforms: Windows 98, Windows NT 4.0, Windows Millennium Edition, Windows 2000, Windows XP Home Edition, Windows XP Professional, Windows Server 2003 family

DataFormats.Format.Name Property

Gets the name of this format.

```
[Visual Basic]
Public ReadOnly Property Name As String
[C#]
public string Name {get;}
[C++]
public: __property String* get_Name();
[JScript]
public function get Name() : String;
```

Property Value

The name of this format.

Requirements

Platforms: Windows 98, Windows NT 4.0, Windows Millennium Edition, Windows 2000, Windows XP Home Edition, Windows XP Professional, Windows Server 2003 family

DataGrid Class

Displays ADO.NET data in a scrollable grid.

System.Object
  System.MarshalByRefObject
    System.ComponentModel.Component
      System.Windows.Forms.Control
        System.Windows.Forms.DataGrid

[Visual Basic]
```
Public Class DataGrid
   Inherits Control
   Implements ISupportInitialize
```
[C#]
```
public class DataGrid : Control, ISupportInitialize
```
[C++]
```
public __gc class DataGrid : public Control, ISupportInitialize
```
[JScript]
```
public class DataGrid extends Control implements ISupportInitialize
```

Thread Safety

Any public static (**Shared** in Visual Basic) members of this type are safe for multithreaded operations. Any instance members are not guaranteed to be thread safe.

Remarks

The **System.Windows.Forms.DataGrid** displays Web-like links to child tables. You can click on a link to navigate to the child table. When a child table is displayed, a back button appears in the caption that can be clicked to navigate back to the parent table. The data from the parent rows is displayed below the caption and above the column headers. You can hide the parent row information by clicking the button to the right of the back button.

To display a table in the **System.Windows.Forms.DataGrid** at run time, use the **SetDataBinding** method to set the **DataSource** and **DataMember** properties to a valid data source. The following data sources are valid:

- A **DataTable**
- A **DataView**
- A **DataSet**
- A **DataViewManager**
- A single dimension array
- Any component that implements the **IListSource** interface
- Any component that implements the **IList** interface

For more information about the **DataSet** class, see **Creating and Using DataSets**.

You can create a grid that allows users to edit data but prevents them from adding new rows by using a **DataView** as the data source and setting the **AddNew** property to **false**.

Data sources are further managed by **BindingManagerBase** objects. For each table in a data source, a **BindingManagerBase** can be returned from the form's **BindingContext**. For example, you can determine the number of rows contained by a data source by returning the associated **BindingManagerBase** object's **Count** property.

To validate data, use the underlying objects that represent data and their events. For example, if the data comes from a **DataTable** in a **DataSet**, use the **ColumnChanging** and **RowChanging** events.

Note Because the number of columns can be customized (by adding or deleting members of the **GridColumnStylesCollection**) and the rows can be sorted by column, the **RowNumber** and **ColumnNumber** property values cannot be guaranteed to correspond to **DataRow** and **DataColumn** indexes in a **DataTable**. Therefore you should avoid using those properties in the **Validating** event to validate data.

To determine which cell is selected, use the **CurrentCell** property. Change the value of any cell by using the **Item** property, which can take either the row and column indexes of the cell, or a single **DataGridCell**. Monitor the **CurrentCellChanged** event to detect when the user selects another cell.

To determine which part of the control the user clicked, use the **HitTest** method in the **MouseDown** event. The **HitTest** method returns a **DataGrid.HitTestInfo** object, which contains the row and column of a clicked area.

To manage the appearance of the control at run time, several properties for setting the color and caption attributes are available, including the **CaptionForeColor**, **CaptionBackColor**, **CaptionFont**, and so on.

The appearance of the displayed grid (or grids) can be further modified by creating **DataGridTableStyle** objects and adding them to the **GridTableStylesCollection**, which is accessed through the **TableStyles** property. For example, if the **DataSource** is set to a **DataSet** containing three **DataTable** objects, you can add three **DataGridTableStyle** objects to the collection, one for each table. To synchronize each **DataGridTableStyle** object with a **DataTable**, set the **MappingName** of the **DataGridTableStyle** to the **TableName** of the **DataTable**. For more information about binding to an array of objects, see the **DataGridTableStyle.MappingName** property.

To create a customized view of a table, create an instance of a **DataGridTextBoxColumn** or **DataGridBoolColumn** class and add the object to the **GridTableStylesCollection** accessed through the **TableStyles** property. Both classes inherit from **DataGridColumnStyle**. For each column style, set the **MappingName** to the **ColumnName** of a column that you want to show in the grid. To hide a column, set its **MappingName** to something other than a valid **ColumnName**.

To format the text of a column, set the **Format** property of the **DataGridTextBoxColumn** to one of the values found in **Date and Time Format Strings** or **Standard Numeric Format Strings**.

To bind the **DataGrid** to a strongly typed array of objects, the object must contain public properties. To create a **DataGridTableStyle** that displays such an array, set the **DataGridTableStyle.MappingName** property to *classname[]* where *classname* is replaced by the class name. Also note that the **MappingName** property is case-sensitive. See the **MappingName** property for an example.

You can also bind the **DataGrid** to an **ArrayList**. A feature of the **ArrayList** is that it can contain objects of multiple types, but the **DataGrid** can only bind to such a list when all items in the list are of the same type as the first item. This means that all objects must either be of the same type, or they must inherit from the same class as the first item in the list. For example, if the first item in a list is a **Control**, the second item could be a **TextBox** (which inherits from **Control**). If, on the other hand, the first item is a **TextBox**, the second object cannot be a **Control**. Further, the **ArrayList** must have items in it when it is bound. An empty **ArrayList** will result in an empty grid. When binding to an **ArrayList**, set the **MappingName** of the **DataGridTableStyle** to "ArrayList" (the type name).

For each **DataGridTableStyle**, you can set color and caption attributes that override the settings for the **System.Windows.Forms.DataGrid** control. However, if those properties are not set, the settings for the control are used by default. The following properties can be overridden by **DataGridTableStyle** properties:

- **AllowSorting**
- **AlternatingBackColor**
- **BackColor**
- **ColumnHeadersVisible**
- **ForeColor**
- **GridLineColor**
- **GridLineStyle**
- **HeaderBackColor**
- **HeaderFont**
- **HeaderForeColor**
- **LinkColor**
- **PreferredColumnWidth**
- **PreferredRowHeight**
- **ReadOnly**
- **RowHeadersVisible**
- **RowHeaderWidth**
- **SelectionBackColor**
- **SelectionForeColor**

To customize the appearance of individual columns, add **DataGridColumnStyle** objects to the **GridColumnStylesCollection**, which is accessed through the **GridColumnStyles** property of each **DataGridTableStyle**. To synchronize each **DataGridColumnStyle** with a **DataColumn** in the **DataTable**, set the **MappingName** to the **ColumnName** of a **DataColumn**. When constructing a **DataGridColumnStyle**, you can also set a formatting string that specifies how the column displays data. For example, you can specify that the column use a short-date format to display dates contained in the table.

> **CAUTION** Always create **DataGridColumnStyle** objects and add them to the **GridColumnStylesCollection** before adding **DataGridTableStyle** objects to the **GridTableStylesCollection**. When you add an empty **DataGridTableStyle** to the collection, **DataGridColumnStyle** objects are automatically generated for you. Consequently, an exception will be thrown if you try to add new **DataGridColumnStyle** objects with duplicate **MappingName** values to the **GridColumnStylesCollection**.

Example

[Visual Basic, C#, JScript] The following example creates a Windows form, a **DataSet** containing two **DataTable** objects, and a **DataRelation** that relates the two tables. To display the data, a **System.Windows.Forms.DataGrid** control is then bound to the **DataSet** through the **SetDataBinding** method. A button on the form changes the appearance of the grid by creating two **DataGridTableStyle** objects and setting the **MappingName** of each object to a **TableName** of one of the **DataTable** objects. The example also contains code in the **MouseUp** event that uses the **HitTest** method to print the column, row, and part of the grid that has been clicked.

[Visual Basic]
```
Option Explicit
Option Strict

Imports System
Imports System.ComponentModel
Imports System.Data
Imports System.Drawing
Imports System.Windows.Forms

Public Class Form1
   Inherits System.Windows.Forms.Form
   Private components As System.ComponentModel.Container
   Private button1 As Button
   Private button2 As Button
   Private myDataGrid As DataGrid
   Private myDataSet As DataSet
   Private TablesAlreadyAdded As Boolean

   Public Sub New()
      ' Required for Windows Form Designer support.
      InitializeComponent()
      ' Call SetUp to bind the controls.
      SetUp()
   End Sub

  Private Sub InitializeComponent()
      ' Create the form and its controls.
      Me.components = New System.ComponentModel.Container()
      Me.button1 = New System.Windows.Forms.Button()
      Me.button2 = New System.Windows.Forms.Button()
      Me.myDataGrid = New DataGrid()

      Me.AutoScaleBaseSize = New System.Drawing.Size(5, 13)
      Me.Text = "DataGrid Control Sample"
      Me.ClientSize = New System.Drawing.Size(450, 330)

      button1.Location = New Point(24, 16)
      button1.Size = New System.Drawing.Size(120, 24)
      button1.Text = "Change Appearance"
      AddHandler button1.Click, AddressOf button1_Click

      button2.Location = New Point(150, 16)
      button2.Size = New System.Drawing.Size(120, 24)
      button2.Text = "Get Binding Manager"
      AddHandler button2.Click, AddressOf button2_Click

      myDataGrid.Location = New Point(24, 50)
      myDataGrid.Size = New Size(300, 200)
      myDataGrid.CaptionText = "Microsoft DataGrid Control"
      AddHandler myDataGrid.MouseUp, AddressOf Grid_MouseUp

      Me.Controls.Add(button1)
      Me.Controls.Add(button2)
      Me.Controls.Add(myDataGrid)
   End Sub

   Public Shared Sub Main()
      Application.Run(New Form1())
   End Sub

   Private Sub SetUp()
      ' Create a DataSet with two tables and one relation.
      MakeDataSet()
      ' Bind the DataGrid to the DataSet. The dataMember
      ' specifies that the Customers table should be displayed.
      myDataGrid.SetDataBinding(myDataSet, "Customers")
   End Sub

   Protected Sub button1_Click(sender As Object, e As System.EventArgs)
      If TablesAlreadyAdded = true then exit sub
        AddCustomDataTableStyle()
   End Sub

   Private Sub AddCustomDataTableStyle()
      Dim ts1 As New DataGridTableStyle()
```

```
    ts1.MappingName = "Customers"
    ' Set other properties.
    ts1.AlternatingBackColor = Color.LightGray
    ' Add a GridColumnStyle and set its MappingName
    ' to the name of a DataColumn in the DataTable.
    ' Set the HeaderText and Width properties.

    Dim boolCol As New DataGridBoolColumn()
    boolCol.MappingName = "Current"
    boolCol.HeaderText = "IsCurrent Customer"
    boolCol.Width = 150
    ts1.GridColumnStyles.Add(boolCol)

    ' Add a second column style.
    Dim TextCol As New DataGridTextBoxColumn()
    TextCol.MappingName = "custName"
    TextCol.HeaderText = "Customer Name"
    TextCol.Width = 250
    ts1.GridColumnStyles.Add(TextCol)

    ' Create the second table style with columns.
    Dim ts2 As New DataGridTableStyle()
    ts2.MappingName = "Orders"

    ' Set other properties.
    ts2.AlternatingBackColor = Color.LightBlue

    ' Create new ColumnStyle objects
    Dim cOrderDate As New DataGridTextBoxColumn()
    cOrderDate.MappingName = "OrderDate"
    cOrderDate.HeaderText = "Order Date"
    cOrderDate.Width = 100
    ts2.GridColumnStyles.Add(cOrderDate)

    ' Use a PropertyDescriptor to create a formatted
    ' column. First get the PropertyDescriptorCollection
    ' for the data source and data member.
    Dim pcol As PropertyDescriptorCollection = _
    Me.BindingContext(myDataSet, "Customers.custToOrders"). _
    GetItemProperties()

    ' Create a formatted column using a PropertyDescriptor.
    ' The formatting character "c" specifies a currency format. */

    Dim csOrderAmount As _
    New DataGridTextBoxColumn(pcol("OrderAmount"), "c", True)
    csOrderAmount.MappingName = "OrderAmount"
    csOrderAmount.HeaderText = "Total"
    csOrderAmount.Width = 100
    ts2.GridColumnStyles.Add(csOrderAmount)

    ' Add the DataGridTableStyle instances to
    ' the GridTableStylesCollection.
    myDataGrid.TableStyles.Add(ts1)
    myDataGrid.TableStyles.Add(ts2)

   ' Sets the TablesAlreadyAdded to true so this doesn't ↵
happen again.
    TablesAlreadyAdded = true
  End Sub

  Protected Sub button2_Click(sender As Object, e As System.EventArgs)
    Dim bmGrid As BindingManagerBase
    bmGrid = BindingContext(myDataSet, "Customers")
    MessageBox.Show(("Current BindingManager Position: " & ↵
bmGrid.Position))
  End Sub

  Private Sub Grid_MouseUp(sender As Object, e As MouseEventArgs)
    ' Create a HitTestInfo object using the HitTest method.
    ' Get the DataGrid by casting sender.
    Dim myGrid As DataGrid = CType(sender, DataGrid)
    Dim myHitInfo As DataGrid.HitTestInfo = myGrid.HitTest(e.X, e.Y)
    Console.WriteLine(myHitInfo)
    Console.WriteLine(myHitInfo.Type)
    Console.WriteLine(myHitInfo.Row)
    Console.WriteLine(myHitInfo.Column)
  End Sub

  ' Create a DataSet with two tables and populate it.
  Private Sub MakeDataSet()
    ' Create a DataSet.
    myDataSet = New DataSet("myDataSet")

    ' Create two DataTables.
    Dim tCust As New DataTable("Customers")
    Dim tOrders As New DataTable("Orders")

    ' Create two columns, and add them to the first table.
    Dim cCustID As New DataColumn("CustID", GetType(Integer))
    Dim cCustName As New DataColumn("CustName")
    Dim cCurrent As New DataColumn("Current", GetType(Boolean))
    tCust.Columns.Add(cCustID)
    tCust.Columns.Add(cCustName)
    tCust.Columns.Add(cCurrent)

    ' Create three columns, and add them to the second table.
    Dim cID As New DataColumn("CustID", GetType(Integer))
    Dim cOrderDate As New DataColumn("orderDate", GetType(DateTime))
    Dim cOrderAmount As New DataColumn("OrderAmount", ↵
GetType(Decimal))
    tOrders.Columns.Add(cOrderAmount)
    tOrders.Columns.Add(cID)
    tOrders.Columns.Add(cOrderDate)

    ' Add the tables to the DataSet.
    myDataSet.Tables.Add(tCust)
    myDataSet.Tables.Add(tOrders)

    ' Create a DataRelation, and add it to the DataSet.
    Dim dr As New DataRelation("custToOrders", cCustID, cID)
    myDataSet.Relations.Add(dr)

    ' Populates the tables. For each customer and order,
    ' creates two DataRow variables.
    Dim newRow1 As DataRow
    Dim newRow2 As DataRow

    ' Create three customers in the Customers Table.
    Dim i As Integer
    For i = 1 To 3
      newRow1 = tCust.NewRow()
      newRow1("custID") = i
      ' Add the row to the Customers table.
      tCust.Rows.Add(newRow1)
    Next i
    ' Give each customer a distinct name.
    tCust.Rows(0)("custName") = "Customer1"
    tCust.Rows(1)("custName") = "Customer2"
    tCust.Rows(2)("custName") = "Customer3"

    ' Give the Current column a value.
    tCust.Rows(0)("Current") = True
    tCust.Rows(1)("Current") = True
    tCust.Rows(2)("Current") = False

    ' For each customer, create five rows in the Orders table.
    For i = 1 To 3
      Dim j As Integer
      For j = 1 To 5
        newRow2 = tOrders.NewRow()
        newRow2("CustID") = i
        newRow2("orderDate") = New DateTime(2001, i, j * 2)
        newRow2("OrderAmount") = i * 10 + j * 0.1
        ' Add the row to the Orders table.
        tOrders.Rows.Add(newRow2)
      Next j
    Next i
  End Sub
End Class
```

[C#]

```
using System;
using System.ComponentModel;
using System.Data;
using System.Drawing;
using System.Windows.Forms;

public class Form1 : System.Windows.Forms.Form
{
   private System.ComponentModel.Container components;
   private Button button1;
   private Button button2;
   private DataGrid myDataGrid;
   private DataSet myDataSet;
   private bool TablesAlreadyAdded;
   public Form1()
   {
      // Required for Windows Form Designer support.
      InitializeComponent();
      // Call SetUp to bind the controls.
      SetUp();
   }

   protected override void Dispose( bool disposing ){
      if( disposing ){
         if (components != null){
            components.Dispose();}
      }
      base.Dispose( disposing );
   }
   private void InitializeComponent()
   {
      // Create the form and its controls.
      this.components = new System.ComponentModel.Container();
      this.button1 = new System.Windows.Forms.Button();
      this.button2 = new System.Windows.Forms.Button();
      this.myDataGrid = new DataGrid();

      this.AutoScaleBaseSize = new System.Drawing.Size(5, 13);
      this.Text = "DataGrid Control Sample";
      this.ClientSize = new System.Drawing.Size(450, 330);

      button1.Location = new Point(24, 16);
      button1.Size = new System.Drawing.Size(120, 24);
      button1.Text = "Change Appearance";
      button1.Click+=new System.EventHandler(button1_Click);

      button2.Location = new Point(150, 16);
      button2.Size = new System.Drawing.Size(120, 24);
      button2.Text = "Get Binding Manager";
      button2.Click+=new System.EventHandler(button2_Click);

      myDataGrid.Location = new  Point(24, 50);
      myDataGrid.Size = new Size(300, 200);
      myDataGrid.CaptionText = "Microsoft DataGrid Control";
      myDataGrid.MouseUp += new MouseEventHandler(Grid_MouseUp);

      this.Controls.Add(button1);
      this.Controls.Add(button2);
      this.Controls.Add(myDataGrid);
   }

   public static void Main()
   {
      Application.Run(new Form1());
   }

   private void SetUp()
   {
      // Create a DataSet with two tables and one relation.
      MakeDataSet();
      /* Bind the DataGrid to the DataSet. The dataMember
      specifies that the Customers table should be displayed.*/
      myDataGrid.SetDataBinding(myDataSet, "Customers");
   }

   protected void button1_Click(object sender, System.EventArgs e)
   {
      if(TablesAlreadyAdded) return;
      AddCustomDataTableStyle();
   }

   private void AddCustomDataTableStyle()
   {
      DataGridTableStyle ts1 = new DataGridTableStyle();
      ts1.MappingName = "Customers";
      // Set other properties.
      ts1.AlternatingBackColor = Color.LightGray;

      /* Add a GridColumnStyle and set its MappingName
      to the name of a DataColumn in the DataTable.
      Set the HeaderText and Width properties. */

      DataGridColumnStyle boolCol = new DataGridBoolColumn();
      boolCol.MappingName = "Current";
      boolCol.HeaderText = "IsCurrent Customer";
      boolCol.Width = 150;
      ts1.GridColumnStyles.Add(boolCol);

      // Add a second column style.
      DataGridColumnStyle TextCol = new DataGridTextBoxColumn();
      TextCol.MappingName = "custName";
      TextCol.HeaderText = "Customer Name";
      TextCol.Width = 250;
      ts1.GridColumnStyles.Add(TextCol);

      // Create the second table style with columns.
      DataGridTableStyle ts2 = new DataGridTableStyle();
      ts2.MappingName = "Orders";

      // Set other properties.
      ts2.AlternatingBackColor = Color.LightBlue;

      // Create new ColumnStyle objects
      DataGridColumnStyle cOrderDate =
      new DataGridTextBoxColumn();
      cOrderDate.MappingName = "OrderDate";
      cOrderDate.HeaderText = "Order Date";
      cOrderDate.Width = 100;
      ts2.GridColumnStyles.Add(cOrderDate);

      /* Use a PropertyDescriptor to create a formatted
      column. First get the PropertyDescriptorCollection
      for the data source and data member. */
      PropertyDescriptorCollection pcol = this.BindingContext
      [myDataSet, "Customers.custToOrders"].GetItemProperties();

      /* Create a formatted column using a PropertyDescriptor.
      The formatting character "c" specifies a currency format. */
      DataGridColumnStyle csOrderAmount =
      new DataGridTextBoxColumn(pcol["OrderAmount"], "c", true);
      csOrderAmount.MappingName = "OrderAmount";
      csOrderAmount.HeaderText = "Total";
      csOrderAmount.Width = 100;
      ts2.GridColumnStyles.Add(csOrderAmount);

      /* Add the DataGridTableStyle instances to
      the GridTableStylesCollection. */
      myDataGrid.TableStyles.Add(ts1);
      myDataGrid.TableStyles.Add(ts2);

     // Sets the TablesAlreadyAdded to true so this doesn't ↵
happen again.
      TablesAlreadyAdded=true;
   }

   protected void button2_Click(object sender, System.EventArgs e)
   {
      BindingManagerBase bmGrid;
      bmGrid = BindingContext[myDataSet, "Customers"];
      MessageBox.Show("Current BindingManager Position: " + ↵
```

```
bmGrid.Position);
   }

   private void Grid_MouseUp(object sender, MouseEventArgs e)
   {
      // Create a HitTestInfo object using the HitTest method.

      // Get the DataGrid by casting sender.
      DataGrid myGrid = (DataGrid)sender;
      DataGrid.HitTestInfo myHitInfo = myGrid.HitTest(e.X, e.Y);
      Console.WriteLine(myHitInfo);
      Console.WriteLine(myHitInfo.Type);
      Console.WriteLine(myHitInfo.Row);
      Console.WriteLine(myHitInfo.Column);
   }

   // Create a DataSet with two tables and populate it.
   private void MakeDataSet()
   {
      // Create a DataSet.
      myDataSet = new DataSet("myDataSet");

      // Create two DataTables.
      DataTable tCust = new DataTable("Customers");
      DataTable tOrders = new DataTable("Orders");

      // Create two columns, and add them to the first table.
      DataColumn cCustID = new DataColumn("CustID", typeof(int));
      DataColumn cCustName = new DataColumn("CustName");
      DataColumn cCurrent = new DataColumn("Current", typeof(bool));
      tCust.Columns.Add(cCustID);
      tCust.Columns.Add(cCustName);
      tCust.Columns.Add(cCurrent);

      // Create three columns, and add them to the second table.
      DataColumn cID =
      new DataColumn("CustID", typeof(int));
      DataColumn cOrderDate =
      new DataColumn("orderDate",typeof(DateTime));
      DataColumn cOrderAmount =
      new DataColumn("OrderAmount", typeof(decimal));
      tOrders.Columns.Add(cOrderAmount);
      tOrders.Columns.Add(cID);
      tOrders.Columns.Add(cOrderDate);

      // Add the tables to the DataSet.
      myDataSet.Tables.Add(tCust);
      myDataSet.Tables.Add(tOrders);

      // Create a DataRelation, and add it to the DataSet.
      DataRelation dr = new DataRelation
      ("custToOrders", cCustID , cID);
      myDataSet.Relations.Add(dr);

      /* Populates the tables. For each customer and order,
      creates two DataRow variables. */
      DataRow newRow1;
      DataRow newRow2;

      // Create three customers in the Customers Table.
      for(int i = 1; i < 4; i++)
      {
         newRow1 = tCust.NewRow();
         newRow1["custID"] = i;
         // Add the row to the Customers table.
         tCust.Rows.Add(newRow1);
      }
      // Give each customer a distinct name.
      tCust.Rows[0]["custName"] = "Customer1";
      tCust.Rows[1]["custName"] = "Customer2";
      tCust.Rows[2]["custName"] = "Customer3";

      // Give the Current column a value.
      tCust.Rows[0]["Current"] = true;
      tCust.Rows[1]["Current"] = true;
      tCust.Rows[2]["Current"] = false;

      // For each customer, create five rows in the Orders table.
      for(int i = 1; i < 4; i++)
      {
         for(int j = 1; j < 6; j++)
         {
            newRow2 = tOrders.NewRow();
            newRow2["CustID"]= i;
            newRow2["orderDate"]= new DateTime(2001, i, j * 2);
            newRow2["OrderAmount"] = i * 10 + j  * .1;
            // Add the row to the Orders table.
            tOrders.Rows.Add(newRow2);
         }
      }
   }
}
```

[JScript]

```
import System;
import System.ComponentModel;
import System.Data;
import System.Drawing;
import System.Windows.Forms;

public class Form1 extends System.Windows.Forms.Form
{
   private var components : System.ComponentModel.Container;
   private var button1 : Button;
   private var button2 : Button;
   private var myDataGrid : DataGrid;
   private var myDataSet : DataSet;
   private var TablesAlreadyAdded : Boolean;
   public function Form1()
   {
      // Required for Windows Form Designer support.
      InitializeComponent();
      // Call SetUp to bind the controls.
      SetUp();
   }

   protected override function Dispose(disposing :  Boolean){
      if( disposing ){
         if (components != null){
            components.Dispose();}
      }
      super.Dispose( disposing );
   }
   private function InitializeComponent()
   {
      // Create the form and its controls.
      this.components = new System.ComponentModel.Container();
      this.button1 = new System.Windows.Forms.Button();
      this.button2 = new System.Windows.Forms.Button();
      this.myDataGrid = new DataGrid();

      this.AutoScaleBaseSize = new System.Drawing.Size(5, 13);
      this.Text = "DataGrid Control Sample";
      this.ClientSize = new System.Drawing.Size(450, 330);

      button1.Location = new Point(24, 16);
      button1.Size = new System.Drawing.Size(120, 24);
      button1.Text = "Change Appearance";
      button1.add_Click(button1_Click);

      button2.Location = new Point(150, 16);
      button2.Size = new System.Drawing.Size(120, 24);
      button2.Text = "Get Binding Manager";
      button2.add_Click(button2_Click);

      myDataGrid.Location = new  Point(24, 50);
      myDataGrid.Size = new System.Drawing.Size(300, 200);
      myDataGrid.CaptionText = "Microsoft DataGrid Control";
      myDataGrid.add_MouseUp(Grid_MouseUp);
```

```
      this.Controls.Add(button1);
      this.Controls.Add(button2);
      this.Controls.Add(myDataGrid);
   }

   public static function Main()
   {
      Application.Run(new Form1());
   }

   private function SetUp()
   {
      // Create a DataSet with two tables and one relation.
      MakeDataSet();
      /* Bind the DataGrid to the DataSet. The dataMember
      specifies that the Customers table should be displayed.*/
      myDataGrid.SetDataBinding(myDataSet, "Customers");
   }

   protected function button1_Click(sender : Object, e :                ↵
System.EventArgs)
   {
      if(TablesAlreadyAdded) return;
      AddCustomDataTableStyle();
   }

   private function AddCustomDataTableStyle()
   {
      var ts1 : DataGridTableStyle = new DataGridTableStyle();
      ts1.MappingName = "Customers";
      // Set other properties.
      ts1.AlternatingBackColor = Color.LightGray;

      /* Add a GridColumnStyle and set its MappingName
      to the name of a DataColumn in the DataTable.
      Set the HeaderText and Width properties. */

      var boolCol : DataGridColumnStyle = new DataGridBoolColumn();
      boolCol.MappingName = "Current";
      boolCol.HeaderText = "IsCurrent Customer";
      boolCol.Width = 150;
      ts1.GridColumnStyles.Add(boolCol);

      // Add a second column style.
      var TextCol : DataGridColumnStyle = new DataGridTextBoxColumn();
      TextCol.MappingName = "custName";
      TextCol.HeaderText = "Customer Name";
      TextCol.Width = 250;
      ts1.GridColumnStyles.Add(TextCol);

      // Create the second table style with columns.
      var ts2 : DataGridTableStyle = new DataGridTableStyle();
      ts2.MappingName = "Orders";

      // Set other properties.
      ts2.AlternatingBackColor = Color.LightBlue;

      // Create new ColumnStyle objects
      var cOrderDate : DataGridColumnStyle =
      new DataGridTextBoxColumn();
      cOrderDate.MappingName = "OrderDate";
      cOrderDate.HeaderText = "Order Date";
      cOrderDate.Width = 100;
      ts2.GridColumnStyles.Add(cOrderDate);

      /* Use a PropertyDescriptor to create a formatted
      column. First get the PropertyDescriptorCollection
      for the data source and data member. */
      var pcol : PropertyDescriptorCollection = this.BindingContext
      [myDataSet, "Customers.custToOrders"].GetItemProperties();

      /* Create a formatted column import a PropertyDescriptor.
      The formatting character "c" specifies a currency format. */
      var csOrderAmount : DataGridColumnStyle =
      new DataGridTextBoxColumn(pcol["OrderAmount"], "c", true);
      csOrderAmount.MappingName = "OrderAmount";
      csOrderAmount.HeaderText = "Total";
      csOrderAmount.Width = 100;
      ts2.GridColumnStyles.Add(csOrderAmount);

      /* Add the DataGridTableStyle instances to
      the GridTableStylesCollection. */
      myDataGrid.TableStyles.Add(ts1);
      myDataGrid.TableStyles.Add(ts2);

     // Sets the TablesAlreadyAdded to true so this doesn't                ↵
 happen again.
     TablesAlreadyAdded=true;
   }

   protected function button2_Click(sender : Object, e :                ↵
System.EventArgs)
   {
      var bmGrid : BindingManagerBase;
      bmGrid = BindingContext[myDataSet, "Customers"];
      MessageBox.Show("Current BindingManager Position: " +                ↵
bmGrid.Position);
   }

   private function Grid_MouseUp(sender : Object, e : MouseEventArgs)
   {
      // Create a HitTestInfo object import the HitTest method.

      // Get the DataGrid by casting sender.
      var myGrid : DataGrid = DataGrid(sender);
      var myHitInfo : DataGrid.HitTestInfo= myGrid.HitTest(e.X, e.Y);
      Console.WriteLine(myHitInfo);
      Console.WriteLine(myHitInfo.Type);
      Console.WriteLine(myHitInfo.Row);
      Console.WriteLine(myHitInfo.Column);
   }

   // Create a DataSet with two tables and populate it.
   private function MakeDataSet()
   {
      // Create a DataSet.
      myDataSet = new DataSet("myDataSet");

      // Create two DataTables.
      var tCust : DataTable = new DataTable("Customers");
      var tOrders : DataTable = new DataTable("Orders");

      // Create two columns, and add them to the first table.
      var cCustID : DataColumn = new DataColumn("CustID", int);
      var cCustName : DataColumn = new DataColumn("CustName");
      var cCurrent : DataColumn = new DataColumn("Current", Boolean);
      tCust.Columns.Add(cCustID);
      tCust.Columns.Add(cCustName);
      tCust.Columns.Add(cCurrent);

      // Create three columns, and add them to the second table.
      var cID : DataColumn =
      new DataColumn("CustID", int);
      var cOrderDate : DataColumn =
      new DataColumn("orderDate", DateTime);
      var cOrderAmount : DataColumn =
      new DataColumn("OrderAmount", decimal);
      tOrders.Columns.Add(cOrderAmount);
      tOrders.Columns.Add(cID);
      tOrders.Columns.Add(cOrderDate);

      // Add the tables to the DataSet.
      myDataSet.Tables.Add(tCust);
      myDataSet.Tables.Add(tOrders);

      // Create a DataRelation, and add it to the DataSet.
      var dr : DataRelation = new DataRelation
      ("custToOrders", cCustID , cID);
      myDataSet.Relations.Add(dr);

      /* Populates the tables. For each customer and order,
      creates two DataRow variables. */
```

```
      var newRow1 : DataRow;
      var newRow2 : DataRow;

      // Create three customers in the Customers Table.
      for(var x : int = 1; x < 4; x++)
      {
         newRow1 = tCust.NewRow();
         newRow1["custID"] = x;
         // Add the row to the Customers table.
         tCust.Rows.Add(newRow1);
      }
      // Give each customer a distinct name.
      tCust.Rows[0]["custName"] = "Customer1";
      tCust.Rows[1]["custName"] = "Customer2";
      tCust.Rows[2]["custName"] = "Customer3";

      // Give the Current column a value.
      tCust.Rows[0]["Current"] = true;
      tCust.Rows[1]["Current"] = true;
      tCust.Rows[2]["Current"] = false;

      // For each customer, create five rows in the Orders table.
      for(var i : int = 1; i < 4; i++)
      {
         for(var j : int = 1; j < 6; j++)
         {
            newRow2 = tOrders.NewRow();
            newRow2["CustID"]= i;
            newRow2["orderDate"]= new DateTime(2001, i, j * 2);
            newRow2["OrderAmount"] = i * 10 + j  * .1;
            // Add the row to the Orders table.
            tOrders.Rows.Add(newRow2);
         }
      }
   }
}

Form1.Main();
```

Requirements

Namespace: System.Windows.Forms

Platforms: Windows 98, Windows NT 4.0, Windows Millennium Edition, Windows 2000, Windows XP Home Edition, Windows XP Professional, Windows Server 2003 family, .NET Compact Framework - Windows CE .NET

Assembly: System.Windows.Forms (in System.Windows.Forms.dll)

DataGrid Constructor

Initializes a new instance of the **System.Windows.Forms.DataGrid** class.

[Visual Basic]
```
Public Sub New()
```
[C#]
```
public DataGrid();
```
[C++]
```
public: DataGrid();
```
[JScript]
```
public function DataGrid();
```

Remarks

To populate a newly created **System.Windows.Forms.DataGrid** control, set the **DataSource** property to a valid source, such as a **DataView**, **DataSet**, or **DataViewManager**.

Example

See related example in the **System.Windows.Forms.DataGrid** class topic.

Requirements

Platforms: Windows 98, Windows NT 4.0, Windows Millennium Edition, Windows 2000, Windows XP Home Edition, Windows XP Professional, Windows Server 2003 family, .NET Compact Framework - Windows CE .NET

DataGrid.AllowNavigation Property

Gets or sets a value indicating whether navigation is allowed.

[Visual Basic]
```
Public Property AllowNavigation As Boolean
```
[C#]
```
public bool AllowNavigation {get; set;}
```
[C++]
```
public: __property bool get_AllowNavigation();
public: __property void set_AllowNavigation(bool);
```
[JScript]
```
public function get AllowNavigation() : Boolean;
public function set AllowNavigation(Boolean);
```

Property Value

true if navigation is allowed; otherwise, **false**. The default is **true**.

Remarks

If this property is set to **false**, links to child tables are not shown.

Example

See related example in the **System.Windows.Forms.DataGrid** class topic.

Requirements

Platforms: Windows 98, Windows NT 4.0, Windows Millennium Edition, Windows 2000, Windows XP Home Edition, Windows XP Professional, Windows Server 2003 family

DataGrid.AllowSorting Property

Gets or sets a value indicating whether the grid can be resorted by clicking on a column header.

[Visual Basic]
```
Public Property AllowSorting As Boolean
```
[C#]
```
public bool AllowSorting {get; set;}
```
[C++]
```
public: __property bool get_AllowSorting();
public: __property void set_AllowSorting(bool);
```
[JScript]
```
public function get AllowSorting() : Boolean;
public function set AllowSorting(Boolean);
```

Property Value

true if columns can be sorted; otherwise, **false**.

Remarks

If sorting is allowed, clicking on a column header will sort the table data by that column.

You can also sort using an expression for a **DataColumn**.

If the **System.Windows.Forms.DataGrid** is bound to a **DataView**, you can set a custom sort for the table using the **DataView** class's **Sort** property. Similarly, if the **System.Windows.Forms.DataGrid** is bound to a **DataViewManager**, each table in the **DataViewManager** can have a custom sort by setting the **DataViewSettings** class's **Sort** property.

Example

See related example in the **System.Windows.Forms.DataGrid** class topic.

Requirements

Platforms: Windows 98, Windows NT 4.0, Windows Millennium Edition, Windows 2000, Windows XP Home Edition, Windows XP Professional, Windows Server 2003 family

DataGrid.AlternatingBackColor Property

Gets or sets the background color of odd-numbered rows of the grid.

[Visual Basic]
```
Public Property AlternatingBackColor As Color
```
[C#]
```
public Color AlternatingBackColor {get; set;}
```
[C++]
```
public: __property Color get_AlternatingBackColor();
public: __property void set_AlternatingBackColor(Color);
```
[JScript]
```
public function get AlternatingBackColor() : Color;
public function set AlternatingBackColor(Color);
```

Property Value

A **Color** that represents the alternating background color. The default is the system color for windows (**Window**).

Remarks

By default, both the **BackColor** and the **AlternatingBackColor** properties are set to the same color. Setting the **BackColor** property affects only even-numbered rows, while setting the **AlternatingBackColor** affects only odd-numbered rows.

Example

See related example in the **System.Windows.Forms.DataGrid** class topic.

Requirements

Platforms: Windows 98, Windows NT 4.0, Windows Millennium Edition, Windows 2000, Windows XP Home Edition, Windows XP Professional, Windows Server 2003 family

DataGrid.BackColor Property

Gets or sets the background color of even-numbered rows of the grid.

[Visual Basic]
```
Overrides Public Property BackColor As Color
```
[C#]
```
public override Color BackColor {get; set;}
```
[C++]
```
public: __property Color get_BackColor();
public: __property void set_BackColor(Color);
```
[JScript]
```
public override function get BackColor() : Color;
public override function set BackColor(Color);
```

Property Value

A **Color** that represents the color of rows in the grid. The default is the system color for windows (**Window**).

Remarks

Whereas the **BackColor** property determines the color of rows in the grid, the **BackgroundColor** determines the color of the nonrow area, which is only visible when the grid is scrolled to the bottom, or if only a few rows are contained in the grid.

By default, both the **BackColor** and the **AlternatingBackColor** properties are set to the same color. Setting the **BackColor** property affects only even-numbered rows, while setting the **AlternatingBackColor** affects only odd-numbered rows.

Example

[Visual Basic, C#] The following example sets both the **BackColor** and **BackgroundColor** properties to different values.

[Visual Basic]
```
Private Sub SetBackColorAndBackgroundColor()
   ' Set the BackColor and BackgroundColor properties.
   dataGrid1.BackColor = System.Drawing.Color.Blue
   dataGrid1.BackgroundColor = System.Drawing.Color.Red
End Sub
```

[C#]
```
private void SetBackColorAndBackgroundColor(){
   // Set the BackColor and BackgroundColor properties.
   dataGrid1.BackColor = System.Drawing.Color.Blue;
   dataGrid1.BackgroundColor = System.Drawing.Color.Red;
}
```

Requirements

Platforms: Windows 98, Windows NT 4.0, Windows Millennium Edition, Windows 2000, Windows XP Home Edition, Windows XP Professional, Windows Server 2003 family, .NET Compact Framework - Windows CE .NET

DataGrid.BackgroundColor Property

Gets or sets the color of the non-row area of the grid.

[Visual Basic]
```
Public Property BackgroundColor As Color
```
[C#]
```
public Color BackgroundColor {get; set;}
```
[C++]
```
public: __property Color get_BackgroundColor();
public: __property void set_BackgroundColor(Color);
```
[JScript]
```
public function get BackgroundColor() : Color;
public function set BackgroundColor(Color);
```

Property Value

A **Color** that represents the color of the grid's background. The default is the **AppWorkspace** color.

Remarks

The **BackgroundColor** determines the color of the nonrow area of the grid, which is only visible when no table is displayed by the **System.Windows.Forms.DataGrid**, or if the grid is scrolled to the bottom, or if only a few rows are contained in the grid.

Example

See related example in the **System.Windows.Forms.DataGrid** class topic.

Requirements

Platforms: Windows 98, Windows NT 4.0, Windows Millennium Edition, Windows 2000, Windows XP Home Edition, Windows XP Professional, Windows Server 2003 family

DataGrid.BackgroundImage Property

This member overrides **Control.BackgroundImage**.

```
[Visual Basic]
Overrides Public Property BackgroundImage As Image
[C#]
public override Image BackgroundImage {get; set;}
[C++]
public: __property Image* get_BackgroundImage();
public: __property void set_BackgroundImage(Image*);
[JScript]
public override function get BackgroundImage() : Image;
public override function set BackgroundImage(Image);
```

Requirements

Platforms: Windows 98, Windows NT 4.0, Windows Millennium Edition, Windows 2000, Windows XP Home Edition, Windows XP Professional, Windows Server 2003 family

DataGrid.BorderStyle Property

Gets or sets the grid's border style.

```
[Visual Basic]
Public Property BorderStyle As BorderStyle
[C#]
public BorderStyle BorderStyle {get; set;}
[C++]
public: __property BorderStyle get_BorderStyle();
public: __property void set_BorderStyle(BorderStyle);
[JScript]
public function get BorderStyle() : BorderStyle;
public function set BorderStyle(BorderStyle);
```

Property Value

One of the **BorderStyle** enumeration values. The default is **FixedSingle**.

Example

See related example in the **System.Windows.Forms.DataGrid** class topic.

Requirements

Platforms: Windows 98, Windows NT 4.0, Windows Millennium Edition, Windows 2000, Windows XP Home Edition, Windows XP Professional, Windows Server 2003 family

DataGrid.CaptionBackColor Property

Gets or sets the background color of the caption area.

```
[Visual Basic]
Public Property CaptionBackColor As Color
[C#]
public Color CaptionBackColor {get; set;}
[C++]
public: __property Color get_CaptionBackColor();
public: __property void set_CaptionBackColor(Color);
[JScript]
public function get CaptionBackColor() : Color;
public function set CaptionBackColor(Color);
```

Property Value

A **Color** that represents the caption's background color. The default is **ActiveCaption** color.

Example

[Visual Basic] The following example sets the **CaptionBackColor** property of the **System.Windows.Forms.DataGrid** control.

```
[Visual Basic]
Private Sub SetCaptionBackClr(ByVal myGrid As DataGrid)
   myGrid.CaptionBackColor = System.Drawing.Color.Blue
End Sub
```

Requirements

Platforms: Windows 98, Windows NT 4.0, Windows Millennium Edition, Windows 2000, Windows XP Home Edition, Windows XP Professional, Windows Server 2003 family

DataGrid.CaptionFont Property

Gets or sets the font of the grid's caption.

```
[Visual Basic]
Public Property CaptionFont As Font
[C#]
public Font CaptionFont {get; set;}
[C++]
public: __property Font* get_CaptionFont();
public: __property void set_CaptionFont(Font*);
[JScript]
public function get CaptionFont() : Font;
public function set CaptionFont(Font);
```

Property Value

A **Font** that represents the caption's font.

Remarks

A **Font** encapsulates a Windows font and provides the methods for manipulating that font.

Example

See related example in the **System.Windows.Forms.DataGrid** class topic.

Requirements

Platforms: Windows 98, Windows NT 4.0, Windows Millennium Edition, Windows 2000, Windows XP Home Edition, Windows XP Professional, Windows Server 2003 family

DataGrid.CaptionForeColor Property

Gets or sets the foreground color of the caption area.

```
[Visual Basic]
Public Property CaptionForeColor As Color
[C#]
public Color CaptionForeColor {get; set;}
[C++]
public: __property Color get_CaptionForeColor();
public: __property void set_CaptionForeColor(Color);
[JScript]
public function get CaptionForeColor() : Color;
public function set CaptionForeColor(Color);
```

Property Value

A **Color** that represents the foreground color of the caption area. The default is **ActiveCaptionText**.

Example

See related example in the **System.Windows.Forms.DataGrid** class topic.

Requirements

Platforms: Windows 98, Windows NT 4.0, Windows Millennium Edition, Windows 2000, Windows XP Home Edition, Windows XP Professional, Windows Server 2003 family

DataGrid.CaptionText Property

Gets or sets the text of the grid's window caption.

```
[Visual Basic]
Public Property CaptionText As String
[C#]
public string CaptionText {get; set;}
[C++]
public: __property String* get_CaptionText();
public: __property void set_CaptionText(String*);
[JScript]
public function get CaptionText() : String;
public function set CaptionText(String);
```

Property Value

A string to be displayed as the grid's window caption. The default is an empty string ("").

Example

[Visual Basic, C#] The following example sets the caption of a **System.Windows.Forms.DataGrid**.

```
[Visual Basic]
If DataGrid1.CaptionText = "" Then
    DataGrid1.CaptionText = "Microsoft DataGrid"
End If
```

```
[C#]
if(dataGrid1.CaptionText == "")
dataGrid1.CaptionText = "Microsoft DataGrid";
```

Requirements

Platforms: Windows 98, Windows NT 4.0, Windows Millennium Edition, Windows 2000, Windows XP Home Edition, Windows XP Professional, Windows Server 2003 family

DataGrid.CaptionVisible Property

Gets or sets a value that indicates whether the grid's caption is visible.

```
[Visual Basic]
Public Property CaptionVisible As Boolean
[C#]
public bool CaptionVisible {get; set;}
[C++]
public: __property bool get_CaptionVisible();
public: __property void set_CaptionVisible(bool);
[JScript]
public function get CaptionVisible() : Boolean;
public function set CaptionVisible(Boolean);
```

Property Value

true if the caption is visible; otherwise, **false**. The default is **true**.

Remarks

If **CaptionVisible** is **false**, the **Back** button, **ParentRow** button, and caption will not be seen. Because navigation is limited, links to child tables will also not be visible and **AllowNavigation** will be set to **None.**

Example

[Visual Basic] The following example toggles the **CaptionVisible** property.

```
[Visual Basic]
Private Sub ToggleCaptionVisible(ByVal myGrid As DataGrid)
    ' Toggle the CaptionVisibleProperty.
    myGrid.CaptionVisible = myGrid.CaptionVisible Xor True
End Sub
```

Requirements

Platforms: Windows 98, Windows NT 4.0, Windows Millennium Edition, Windows 2000, Windows XP Home Edition, Windows XP Professional, Windows Server 2003 family

DataGrid.ColumnHeadersVisible Property

Gets or sets a value indicating whether the column headers a table are visible.

```
[Visual Basic]
Public Property ColumnHeadersVisible As Boolean
[C#]
public bool ColumnHeadersVisible {get; set;}
[C++]
public: __property bool get_ColumnHeadersVisible();
public: __property void set_ColumnHeadersVisible(bool);
[JScript]
public function get ColumnHeadersVisible() : Boolean;
public function set ColumnHeadersVisible(Boolean);
```

Property Value

true if the column headers are visible; otherwise, **false**. The default is **true**.

Example

[Visual Basic] The following example toggles the **ColumnHeaders-Visible** property.

```
[Visual Basic]
Private Sub ToggleColumnHeadersVisible(ByVal myGrid As DataGrid)
    myGrid.ColumnHeadersVisible = myGrid.ColumnHeadersVisible Xor True
End Sub
```

Requirements

Platforms: Windows 98, Windows NT 4.0, Windows Millennium Edition, Windows 2000, Windows XP Home Edition, Windows XP Professional, Windows Server 2003 family, .NET Compact Framework - Windows CE .NET

DataGrid.CurrentCell Property

Gets or sets which cell has the focus. Not available at design time.

```
[Visual Basic]
Public Property CurrentCell As DataGridCell
[C#]
public DataGridCell CurrentCell {get; set;}
[C++]
public: __property DataGridCell get_CurrentCell();
public: __property void set_CurrentCell(DataGridCell);
[JScript]
public function get CurrentCell() : DataGridCell;
public function set CurrentCell(DataGridCell);
```

Property Value

The **DataGridCell** with the focus.

Remarks

Setting the **CurrentCell** property will cause the grid to scroll and show the cell if it is not already visible.

Example

See related example in the **System.Windows.Forms.DataGrid** class topic.

Requirements

Platforms: Windows 98, Windows NT 4.0, Windows Millennium Edition, Windows 2000, Windows XP Home Edition, Windows XP Professional, Windows Server 2003 family, .NET Compact Framework - Windows CE .NET

DataGrid.CurrentRowIndex Property

Gets or sets index of the selected row.

```
[Visual Basic]
Public Property CurrentRowIndex As Integer
[C#]
public int CurrentRowIndex {get; set;}
[C++]
public: __property int get_CurrentRowIndex();
public: __property void set_CurrentRowIndex(int);
[JScript]
public function get CurrentRowIndex() : int;
public function set CurrentRowIndex(int);
```

Property Value

The zero-based index of the selected row.

Exceptions

Exception Type	Condition
Exception	There is no **CurrencyManager**.

Remarks

The **CurrentRowIndex** property allows you to iterate through a parent table's rows even if you are viewing the child table rows. For example, if you are viewing a child table, incrementing the **CurrentRowIndex** will cause the **System.Windows.Forms.DataGrid** to display the next set of records in the child table that are linked to the parent table.

If the user is viewing a parent table, or a table with no child relations, then the property returns the zero-based index of the current row.

Example

See related example in the **System.Windows.Forms.DataGrid** class topic.

Requirements

Platforms: Windows 98, Windows NT 4.0, Windows Millennium Edition, Windows 2000, Windows XP Home Edition, Windows XP Professional, Windows Server 2003 family, .NET Compact Framework - Windows CE .NET

DataGrid.Cursor Property

This member overrides **Control.Cursor**.

```
[Visual Basic]
Overrides Public Property Cursor As Cursor
[C#]
public override Cursor Cursor {get; set;}
[C++]
public: __property Cursor* get_Cursor();
public: __property void set_Cursor(Cursor*);
[JScript]
public override function get Cursor() : Cursor;
public override function set Cursor(Cursor);
```

Requirements

Platforms: Windows 98, Windows NT 4.0, Windows Millennium Edition, Windows 2000, Windows XP Home Edition, Windows XP Professional, Windows Server 2003 family

DataGrid.DataMember Property

Gets or sets the specific list in a **DataSource** for which the **System.Windows.Forms.DataGrid** control displays a grid.

```
[Visual Basic]
Public Property DataMember As String
[C#]
public string DataMember {get; set;}
[C++]
public: __property String* get_DataMember();
public: __property void set_DataMember(String*);
[JScript]
public function get DataMember() : String;
public function set DataMember(String);
```

Property Value

A list in a **DataSource**. The default is an empty string ("").

Remarks

If a **DataSource** contains multiple sources of data, you should set the **DataMember** to one of the sources. For example, if the **DataSource** is a **DataSet** or **DataViewManager** that contains three tables named Customers, Orders, and OrderDetails, you must specify one of the tables to bind to. If the **DataSet** or **DataViewManager** contains only one **DataTable**, you should set the **DataMember** to the **TableName** of that **DataTable**.

If the **DataSource** is set to a **DataSet** that contains **DataRelation** objects, parent tables will appear with a plus sign (+) in each row header. Clicking the plus sign causes a node to appear that contains links to child tables. For example, if a **DataSet** contains two **DataTable** objects named Customers and Orders, setting the **DataMember** to the Customers table causes the **System.Windows.Forms.DataGrid** to display a parent table with a plus sign visible on each row header. If the **DataMember** is set to Orders, however, the row headers will be blank.

If the **DataSource** is a **DataTable**, **DataView**, collection, or array, setting the **DataMember** property throws an exception.

> **Note** At run time, you must use the **SetDataBinding** method to reset the **DataSource** property. However, the **DataMember** property alone can be reset at any time to a valid table name.

Example

See related example in the **System.Windows.Forms.DataGrid** class topic.

Requirements

Platforms: Windows 98, Windows NT 4.0, Windows Millennium Edition, Windows 2000, Windows XP Home Edition, Windows XP Professional, Windows Server 2003 family

DataGrid.DataSource Property

Gets or sets the data source that the grid is displaying data for.

```
[Visual Basic]
Public Property DataSource As Object
[C#]
public object DataSource {get; set;}
[C++]
public: __property Object* get_DataSource();
public: __property void set_DataSource(Object*);
[JScript]
public function get DataSource() : Object;
public function set DataSource(Object);
```

Property Value

An object that functions as a data source.

Remarks

At run time, use the **SetDataBinding** method to set the **DataSource** and **DataMember** properties.

The following data sources are valid:

- A **DataTable**
- A **DataView**
- A **DataSet**
- A **DataViewManager**
- Any component that implements the **IListSource** interface
- Any component that implements the **IList** interface

See the **Binding** class overview for more information on data sources.

If the **DataSource** reference contains more than one table, you must set the **DataMember** property a string that specifies the table to bind to. For example, if the **DataSource** is a **DataSet** or **DataViewManager** that contains three tables named Customers, Orders, and OrderDetails, you must specify the table to bind to.

Setting the **DataSource** to an object that does not implement the **IList** interface or an **IListSource** will cause the grid to throw an exception.

You can create a grid that allows users to edit data but prevents them from adding new rows by using a **DataView** as the data source and setting the **AddNew** property to **false**.

To bind the **DataGrid** to a strongly typed array of objects, the object must contain public properties. To create a **DataGridTableStyle** that displays such an array, set the **MappingName** property to *classname[]* where *classname* is replaced by the class name. Also note that the **MappingName** property is case-sensitive. See the **MappingName** property for an example.

You can also bind the **DataGrid** to an **ArrayList**. A feature of the **ArrayList** is that it can contain objects of multiple types, but the **DataGrid** can only bind to such a list when all items in the list are of the same type as the first item. This means that all objects must either be of the same type, or they must inherit from the same class as the first item in the list. For example, if the first item in a list is a **Control**, the second item could be a **TextBox** (which inherits from **Control**). If, on the other hand, the first item is a **TextBox**, the second object cannot be a **Control**. Further, the **ArrayList** must have items in it when it is bound. An empty **ArrayList** will result in an empty grid. When binding to an **ArrayList**, set the **MappingName** of the **DataGridTableStyle** to "ArrayList" (the type name).

Example

See related example in the **System.Windows.Forms.DataGrid** class topic.

Requirements

Platforms: Windows 98, Windows NT 4.0, Windows Millennium Edition, Windows 2000, Windows XP Home Edition, Windows XP Professional, Windows Server 2003 family, .NET Compact Framework - Windows CE .NET

DataGrid.DefaultSize Property

Gets the default size of the control.

```
[Visual Basic]
Overrides Protected ReadOnly Property DefaultSize As Size
[C#]
protected override Size DefaultSize {get;}
[C++]
protected: __property Size get_DefaultSize();
[JScript]
protected override function get DefaultSize() : Size;
```

Property Value

The default size of the control.

Requirements

Platforms: Windows 98, Windows NT 4.0, Windows Millennium Edition, Windows 2000, Windows XP Home Edition, Windows XP Professional, Windows Server 2003 family

DataGrid.FirstVisibleColumn Property

Gets the index of the first visible column in a grid.

```
[Visual Basic]
Public ReadOnly Property FirstVisibleColumn As Integer
[C#]
public int FirstVisibleColumn {get;}
[C++]
public: __property int get_FirstVisibleColumn();
[JScript]
public function get FirstVisibleColumn() : int;
```

Property Value

The index of a **DataGridColumnStyle**.

Remarks

A column is considered visible even if it is partially concealed.

If a particular column is not visible, set the **CurrentCell** property to the cell that should be visible.

Example

See related example in the **System.Windows.Forms.DataGrid** class topic.

Requirements

Platforms: Windows 98, Windows NT 4.0, Windows Millennium Edition, Windows 2000, Windows XP Home Edition, Windows XP Professional, Windows Server 2003 family, .NET Compact Framework - Windows CE .NET

DataGrid.FlatMode Property

Gets or sets a value indicating whether the grid displays in flat mode.

```
[Visual Basic]
Public Property FlatMode As Boolean
[C#]
public bool FlatMode {get; set;}
[C++]
public: __property bool get_FlatMode();
public: __property void set_FlatMode(bool);
[JScript]
public function get FlatMode() : Boolean;
public function set FlatMode(Boolean);
```

Property Value

true if the grid is displayed flat; otherwise, **false**. The default is **false**.

Example

See related example in the **System.Windows.Forms.DataGrid** class topic.

Requirements

Platforms: Windows 98, Windows NT 4.0, Windows Millennium Edition, Windows 2000, Windows XP Home Edition, Windows XP Professional, Windows Server 2003 family

DataGrid.ForeColor Property

Gets or sets the foreground color (typically the color of the text) property of the **System.Windows.Forms.DataGrid** control.

```
[Visual Basic]
Overrides Public Property ForeColor As Color
[C#]
public override Color ForeColor {get; set;}
[C++]
public: __property Color get_ForeColor();
public: __property void set_ForeColor(Color);
[JScript]
public override function get ForeColor() : Color;
public override function set ForeColor(Color);
```

Property Value

A **Color** that represents the foreground color. The default is **WindowText** color.

Example

See related example in the **System.Windows.Forms.DataGrid** class topic.

Requirements

Platforms: Windows 98, Windows NT 4.0, Windows Millennium Edition, Windows 2000, Windows XP Home Edition, Windows XP Professional, Windows Server 2003 family, .NET Compact Framework - Windows CE .NET

DataGrid.GridLineColor Property

Gets or sets the color of the grid lines.

```
[Visual Basic]
Public Property GridLineColor As Color
[C#]
public Color GridLineColor {get; set;}
[C++]
public: __property Color get_GridLineColor();
public: __property void set_GridLineColor(Color);
[JScript]
public function get GridLineColor() : Color;
public function set GridLineColor(Color);
```

Property Value

A **Color** that represents the color of the grid lines. The default is the system color for controls (**Control**).

Exceptions

Exception Type	Condition
ArgumentException	The value is not set.

Remarks

No grid line is displayed if the **GridLineStyle** property is set to **DataGridLineStyle.None**.

Example

See related example in the **System.Windows.Forms.DataGrid** class topic.

Requirements

Platforms: Windows 98, Windows NT 4.0, Windows Millennium Edition, Windows 2000, Windows XP Home Edition, Windows XP Professional, Windows Server 2003 family, .NET Compact Framework - Windows CE .NET

DataGrid.GridLineStyle Property

Gets or sets the line style of the grid.

```
[Visual Basic]
Public Property GridLineStyle As DataGridLineStyle
[C#]
public DataGridLineStyle GridLineStyle {get; set;}
[C++]
public: __property DataGridLineStyle get_GridLineStyle();
public: __property void set_GridLineStyle(DataGridLineStyle);
[JScript]
public function get GridLineStyle() : DataGridLineStyle;
public function set GridLineStyle(DataGridLineStyle);
```

Property Value

One of the **DataGridLineStyle** values. The default is **Solid**.

Example

[Visual Basic] The following example changes the **GridLineStyle** property to show no lines.

```
[Visual Basic]
DataGrid1.GridLineStyle = DataGridLineStyle.None
```

Requirements

Platforms: Windows 98, Windows NT 4.0, Windows Millennium Edition, Windows 2000, Windows XP Home Edition, Windows XP Professional, Windows Server 2003 family

DataGrid.HeaderBackColor Property

Gets or sets the background color of all row and column headers.

```
[Visual Basic]
Public Property HeaderBackColor As Color
[C#]
public Color HeaderBackColor {get; set;}
[C++]
public: __property Color get_HeaderBackColor();
public: __property void set_HeaderBackColor(Color);
[JScript]
public function get HeaderBackColor() : Color;
public function set HeaderBackColor(Color);
```

Property Value

A **Color** that represents the background color of row and column headers. The default is the system color for controls, **Control**.

Exceptions

Exception Type	Condition
ArgumentNull-Exception	While trying to set the property, a **Color.Empty** was passed.

Example

[Visual Basic] The following example sets the background color of column headers using a value passed to the method.

```
[Visual Basic]
Private Sub SetHeaderBackClr(Byval myGrid As DataGrid)
   myGrid.HeaderBackColor = System.Drawing.Color.CadetBlue
End Sub
```

Requirements

Platforms: Windows 98, Windows NT 4.0, Windows Millennium Edition, Windows 2000, Windows XP Home Edition, Windows XP Professional, Windows Server 2003 family, .NET Compact Framework - Windows CE .NET

DataGrid.HeaderFont Property

Gets or sets the font used for column headers.

```
[Visual Basic]
Public Property HeaderFont As Font
[C#]
public Font HeaderFont {get; set;}
[C++]
public: __property Font* get_HeaderFont();
public: __property void set_HeaderFont(Font*);
[JScript]
public function get HeaderFont() : Font;
public function set HeaderFont(Font);
```

Property Value

The **Font** object that represents the header text.

Remarks

You typically use this method only if you are either creating a designer for the **System.Windows.Forms.DataGrid**, or creating your own control incorporating the **System.Windows.Forms.DataGrid**.

Requirements

Platforms: Windows 98, Windows NT 4.0, Windows Millennium Edition, Windows 2000, Windows XP Home Edition, Windows XP Professional, Windows Server 2003 family

DataGrid.HeaderForeColor Property

Gets or sets the foreground color of headers.

```
[Visual Basic]
Public Property HeaderForeColor As Color
[C#]
public Color HeaderForeColor {get; set;}
[C++]
public: __property Color get_HeaderForeColor();
public: __property void set_HeaderForeColor(Color);
[JScript]
public function get HeaderForeColor() : Color;
public function set HeaderForeColor(Color);
```

Property Value

A **Color** that represents the foreground color of the grid's column headers, including the column header text and the plus/minus glyphs. The default is **ControlText** color.

Example

See related example in the **System.Windows.Forms.DataGrid** class topic.

Requirements

Platforms: Windows 98, Windows NT 4.0, Windows Millennium Edition, Windows 2000, Windows XP Home Edition, Windows XP Professional, Windows Server 2003 family, .NET Compact Framework - Windows CE .NET

DataGrid.HorizScrollBar Property

Gets the horizontal scrollbar for the grid.

```
[Visual Basic]
Protected ReadOnly Property HorizScrollBar As ScrollBar
[C#]
protected ScrollBar HorizScrollBar {get;}
[C++]
protected: __property ScrollBar* get_HorizScrollBar();
[JScript]
protected function get HorizScrollBar() : ScrollBar;
```

Property Value

The **ScrollBar** for the grid.

Requirements

Platforms: Windows 98, Windows NT 4.0, Windows Millennium Edition, Windows 2000, Windows XP Home Edition, Windows XP Professional, Windows Server 2003 family

DataGrid.Item Property

Gets or sets the value of a specified cell.

[C#] In C#, this property is the indexer for the **DataGrid** class.

Overload List

Gets or sets the value of a specified **DataGridCell**.

[Visual Basic] **Overloads Public Default Property Item(DataGridCell) As Object**

[C#] **public object this[DataGridCell] {get; set;}**

[C++] **public: __property Object* get_Item(DataGridCell); public: __property void set_Item(DataGridCell, Object*);**

[JScript] **DataGrid.Item (DataGridCell)**

Gets or sets the value of the cell at the specified the row and column.

[Visual Basic] **Overloads Public Default Property Item(Integer, Integer) As Object**

[C#] **public object this[int, int] {get; set;}**

[C++] **public: __property Object* get_Item(int, int); public: __property void set_Item(int, int, Object*);**

[JScript] **DataGrid.Item (int, int)**

Example

See related example in the **System.Windows.Forms.DataGrid** class topic.

DataGrid.Item Property (DataGridCell)

Gets or sets the value of a specified **DataGridCell**.

[C#] In C#, this property is the indexer for the **DataGrid** class.

```
[Visual Basic]
Overloads Public Default Property Item( _
   ByVal cell As DataGridCell _
) As Object
[C#]
public object this[
   DataGridCell cell
] {get; set;}
[C++]
public: __property Object* get_Item(
   DataGridCell cell
);
public: __property void set_Item(
   DataGridCell cell,
   Object*
);
[JScript]
returnValue = DataGridObject.Item(cell);
DataGridObject.Item(cell) = returnValue;
-or-
returnValue = DataGridObject(cell);
DataGridObject(cell) = returnValue;
```

[JScript] In JScript, you can use the default indexed properties defined by a type, but you cannot explicitly define your own. However, specifying the **expando** attribute on a class automatically provides a default indexed property whose type is **Object** and whose index type is **String**.

Arguments [JScript]

cell
: A **DataGridCell** that represents a cell in the grid.

Parameters [Visual Basic, C#, C++]

cell
: A **DataGridCell** that represents a cell in the grid.

Property Value

The value, typed as **object**, of the cell.

Remarks

Setting this property changes the position of the **DataView** to the specified row.

Example

See related example in the **System.Windows.Forms.DataGrid** class topic.

Requirements

Platforms: Windows 98, Windows NT 4.0, Windows Millennium Edition, Windows 2000, Windows XP Home Edition, Windows XP Professional, Windows Server 2003 family

DataGrid.Item Property (Int32, Int32)

Gets or sets the value of the cell at the specified the row and column.

[C#] In C#, this property is the indexer for the **DataGrid** class.

[Visual Basic]
```
Overloads Public Default Property Item( _
   ByVal rowIndex As Integer, _
   ByVal columnIndex As Integer _
) As Object
```
[C#]
```
public object this[
   int rowIndex,
   int columnIndex
] {get; set;}
```
[C++]
```
public: __property Object* get_Item(
   int rowIndex,
   int columnIndex
);
public: __property void set_Item(
   int rowIndex,
   int columnIndex,
   Object*
);
```
[JScript]
```
returnValue = DataGridObject.Item(rowIndex, columnIndex);
DataGridObject.Item(rowIndex, columnIndex) = returnValue;
-or-
returnValue = DataGridObject(rowIndex, columnIndex);
DataGridObject(rowIndex, columnIndex) = returnValue;
```

[JScript] In JScript, you can use the default indexed properties defined by a type, but you cannot explicitly define your own. However, specifying the **expando** attribute on a class automatically provides a default indexed property whose type is **Object** and whose index type is **String**.

Arguments [JScript]

rowIndex

The zero-based index of the row containing the value.

columnIndex

The zero-based index of the column containing the value.

Parameters [Visual Basic, C#, C++]

rowIndex

The zero-based index of the row containing the value.

columnIndex

The zero-based index of the column containing the value.

Property Value

The value, typed as **object**, of the cell.

Exceptions

Exception Type	Condition
ArgumentOutOfRange-Exception	While getting or setting, the *rowIndex* is out of range. While getting or setting, the *columnIndex* is out of range.

Remarks

Setting this property changes the position of the **DataView** to the specified row.

Example

See related example in the **System.Windows.Forms.DataGrid** class topic.

Requirements

Platforms: Windows 98, Windows NT 4.0, Windows Millennium Edition, Windows 2000, Windows XP Home Edition, Windows XP Professional, Windows Server 2003 family

DataGrid.LinkColor Property

Gets or sets the color of the text that you can click to navigate to a child table.

[Visual Basic]
```
Public Property LinkColor As Color
```
[C#]
```
public Color LinkColor {get; set;}
```
[C++]
```
public: __property Color get_LinkColor();
public: __property void set_LinkColor(Color);
```
[JScript]
```
public function get LinkColor() : Color;
public function set LinkColor(Color);
```

Property Value

A **Color** that represents the color of text that is clicked to navigate to a child table. The default is **HotTrack**.

Remarks

You typically use this method only if you are either creating a designer for the **System.Windows.Forms.DataGrid**, or creating your own control incorporating the **System.Windows.Forms.DataGrid**.

Requirements

Platforms: Windows 98, Windows NT 4.0, Windows Millennium Edition, Windows 2000, Windows XP Home Edition, Windows XP Professional, Windows Server 2003 family

DataGrid.LinkHoverColor Property

Gets or sets the color a link changes to when the mouse pointer moves over it.

[Visual Basic]
```
<ComVisible(False)>
Public Property LinkHoverColor As Color
```
[C#]
```
[ComVisible(false)]
public Color LinkHoverColor {get; set;}
```
[C++]
```
[ComVisible(false)]
public: __property Color get_LinkHoverColor();
public: __property void set_LinkHoverColor(Color);
```
[JScript]
```
public
   ComVisible(false)
function get LinkHoverColor() : Color;
public function set LinkHoverColor(Color);
```

Property Value

A **Color** that represents the color of a link when the mouse pointer moves over it. The default is **HotTrack**.

Example

[Visual Basic] The following example sets the **LinkHoverColor**.

```
[Visual Basic]
Private Sub SetLinkHoverClr(ByRef myGrid As DataGrid)
    myGrid.LinkHoverColor = System.Drawing.Color.Tomato
End Sub
```

Requirements

Platforms: Windows 98, Windows NT 4.0, Windows Millennium Edition, Windows 2000, Windows XP Home Edition, Windows XP Professional, Windows Server 2003 family

DataGrid.ListManager Property

Gets the **CurrencyManager** for this **System.Windows.Forms.DataGrid** control.

```
[Visual Basic]
Protected Friend Property ListManager As CurrencyManager
[C#]
protected internal CurrencyManager ListManager {get; set;}
[C++]
protected public: __property CurrencyManager* get_ListManager();
protected public: __property void set_ListManager(CurrencyManager*);
[JScript]
protected internal function get ListManager() : CurrencyManager;
protected internal function set ListManager(CurrencyManager);
```

Property Value

The **CurrencyManager** for this **System.Windows.Forms.DataGrid** control.

Requirements

Platforms: Windows 98, Windows NT 4.0, Windows Millennium Edition, Windows 2000, Windows XP Home Edition, Windows XP Professional, Windows Server 2003 family

DataGrid.ParentRowsBackColor Property

Gets or sets the background color of parent rows.

```
[Visual Basic]
Public Property ParentRowsBackColor As Color
[C#]
public Color ParentRowsBackColor {get; set;}
[C++]
public: __property Color get_ParentRowsBackColor();
public: __property void set_ParentRowsBackColor(Color);
[JScript]
public function get ParentRowsBackColor() : Color;
public function set ParentRowsBackColor(Color);
```

Property Value

A **Color** that represents the color of parent rows. The default is the **Control** color.

Example

[Visual Basic] The following example sets the **ParentRowsBackColor** property to a new color.

```
[Visual Basic]
Private Sub SetParentRowBackClr(ByVal myGrid As DataGrid)
    myGrid.ParentRowsBackColor = System.Drawing.Color.Beige
End Sub
```

Requirements

Platforms: Windows 98, Windows NT 4.0, Windows Millennium Edition, Windows 2000, Windows XP Home Edition, Windows XP Professional, Windows Server 2003 family

DataGrid.ParentRowsForeColor Property

Gets or sets the foreground color of parent rows.

```
[Visual Basic]
Public Property ParentRowsForeColor As Color
[C#]
public Color ParentRowsForeColor {get; set;}
[C++]
public: __property Color get_ParentRowsForeColor();
public: __property void set_ParentRowsForeColor(Color);
[JScript]
public function get ParentRowsForeColor() : Color;
public function set ParentRowsForeColor(Color);
```

Property Value

A **Color** that represents the foreground color of parent rows. The default is the **WindowText** color.

Example

[Visual Basic] The following example sets the **ParentRowsForeColor** property to a new color.

```
[Visual Basic]
Private Sub SetParentRowsForeClr(ByVal myGrid As DataGrid)
    myGrid.ParentRowsForeColor = System.Drawing.Color.Tomato
End Sub
```

Requirements

Platforms: Windows 98, Windows NT 4.0, Windows Millennium Edition, Windows 2000, Windows XP Home Edition, Windows XP Professional, Windows Server 2003 family

DataGrid.ParentRowsLabelStyle Property

Gets or sets the way parent row labels are displayed.

```
[Visual Basic]
Public Property ParentRowsLabelStyle As _
   DataGridParentRowsLabelStyle
[C#]
public DataGridParentRowsLabelStyle ParentRowsLabelStyle {get;
   set;}
[C++]
public: __property DataGridParentRowsLabelStyle
get_ParentRowsLabelStyle();
public: __property void
set_ParentRowsLabelStyle(DataGridParentRowsLabelStyle);
```

[JScript]
```
public function get ParentRowsLabelStyle() :
DataGridParentRowsLabelStyle;
public function set
ParentRowsLabelStyle(DataGridParentRowsLabelStyle);
```

Property Value

One of the **DataGridParentRowsLabelStyle** values. The default is **Both**.

Exceptions

Exception Type	Condition
InvalidEnumArgument-Exception	The enumator was not valid.

Example

See related example in the **System.Windows.Forms.DataGrid** class topic.

Requirements

Platforms: Windows 98, Windows NT 4.0, Windows Millennium Edition, Windows 2000, Windows XP Home Edition, Windows XP Professional, Windows Server 2003 family

DataGrid.ParentRowsVisible Property

Gets or sets a value indicating whether the parent rows of a table are visible.

[Visual Basic]
```
Public Property ParentRowsVisible As Boolean
```
[C#]
```
public bool ParentRowsVisible {get; set;}
```
[C++]
```
public: __property bool get_ParentRowsVisible();
public: __property void set_ParentRowsVisible(bool);
```
[JScript]
```
public function get ParentRowsVisible() : Boolean;
public function set ParentRowsVisible(Boolean);
```

Property Value

true if the parent rows are visible; otherwise, **false**. The default is **true**.

Example

See related example in the **System.Windows.Forms.DataGrid** class topic.

Requirements

Platforms: Windows 98, Windows NT 4.0, Windows Millennium Edition, Windows 2000, Windows XP Home Edition, Windows XP Professional, Windows Server 2003 family

DataGrid.PreferredColumnWidth Property

Gets or sets the default width of the grid columns in pixels.

[Visual Basic]
```
Public Property PreferredColumnWidth As Integer
```
[C#]
```
public int PreferredColumnWidth {get; set;}
```
[C++]
```
public: __property int get_PreferredColumnWidth();
public: __property void set_PreferredColumnWidth(int);
```
[JScript]
```
public function get PreferredColumnWidth() : int;
public function set PreferredColumnWidth(int);
```

Property Value

The default width (in pixels) of columns in the grid.

Exceptions

Exception Type	Condition
ArgumentException	The property value is less than 0.

Remarks

Set this property before resetting the **DataSource** and **DataMember** properties (either separately, or through the **SetDataBinding** method), or the property will have no effect.

The property cannot be set to a value less than 0.

Example

See related example in the **System.Windows.Forms.DataGrid** class topic.

Requirements

Platforms: Windows 98, Windows NT 4.0, Windows Millennium Edition, Windows 2000, Windows XP Home Edition, Windows XP Professional, Windows Server 2003 family

DataGrid.PreferredRowHeight Property

Gets or sets the preferred row height for the **System.Windows.Forms.DataGrid** control.

[Visual Basic]
```
Public Property PreferredRowHeight As Integer
```
[C#]
```
public int PreferredRowHeight {get; set;}
```
[C++]
```
public: __property int get_PreferredRowHeight();
public: __property void set_PreferredRowHeight(int);
```
[JScript]
```
public function get PreferredRowHeight() : int;
public function set PreferredRowHeight(int);
```

Property Value

The height of a row.

Remarks

Set this property before resetting the **DataSource** and **DataMember** properties (either separately, or through the **SetDataBinding** method), or the property will have no effect.

Example

See related example in the **System.Windows.Forms.DataGrid** class topic.

Requirements

Platforms: Windows 98, Windows NT 4.0, Windows Millennium Edition, Windows 2000, Windows XP Home Edition, Windows XP Professional, Windows Server 2003 family

DataGrid.ReadOnly Property

Gets or sets a value indicating whether the grid is in read-only mode.

```
[Visual Basic]
Public Property ReadOnly As Boolean
[C#]
public bool ReadOnly {get; set;}
[C++]
public: __property bool get_ReadOnly();
public: __property void set_ReadOnly(bool);
[JScript]
public function get ReadOnly() : Boolean;
public function set ReadOnly(Boolean);
```

Property Value

true if the grid is in read-only mode; otherwise, **false**. The default is **false**.

Remarks

In read-only mode, the grid can be scrolled, nodes can be expanded or collapsed, and so on, However, no additions, edits, or deletes can take place.

The **DataGridColumnStyle** also has a **ReadOnly** property that can be set to true to prevent data from being edited, on a column-by-column basis.

The **ReadOnly** can be set to true if you want to prohibit the user from editing the data directly in the **System.Windows.Forms.DataGrid**. For example, you might want to let users to see all columns in a table, but allow them to edit specific fields only through **TextBox** controls on a different form.

Example

[Visual Basic] The following example toggles the **ReadOnly** property.

```
[Visual Basic]
Private Sub ToggleReadOnly(ByVal myGrid As DataGrid)
    myGrid.ReadOnly = myGrid.ReadOnly Xor True
End Sub
```

Requirements

Platforms: Windows 98, Windows NT 4.0, Windows Millennium Edition, Windows 2000, Windows XP Home Edition, Windows XP Professional, Windows Server 2003 family

DataGrid.RowHeadersVisible Property

Gets or sets a value that specifies whether row headers are visible.

```
[Visual Basic]
Public Property RowHeadersVisible As Boolean
[C#]
public bool RowHeadersVisible {get; set;}
[C++]
public: __property bool get_RowHeadersVisible();
public: __property void set_RowHeadersVisible(bool);
[JScript]
public function get RowHeadersVisible() : Boolean;
public function set RowHeadersVisible(Boolean);
```

Property Value

true if row headers are visible; otherwise, **false**.

Requirements

Platforms: Windows 98, Windows NT 4.0, Windows Millennium Edition, Windows 2000, Windows XP Home Edition, Windows XP Professional, Windows Server 2003 family, .NET Compact Framework - Windows CE .NET

DataGrid.RowHeaderWidth Property

Gets or sets the width of row headers.

```
[Visual Basic]
Public Property RowHeaderWidth As Integer
[C#]
public int RowHeaderWidth {get; set;}
[C++]
public: __property int get_RowHeaderWidth();
public: __property void set_RowHeaderWidth(int);
[JScript]
public function get RowHeaderWidth() : int;
public function set RowHeaderWidth(int);
```

Property Value

The width of row headers in the **System.Windows.Forms.DataGrid**. The default is 50.

Example

See related example in the **System.Windows.Forms.DataGrid** class topic.

Requirements

Platforms: Windows 98, Windows NT 4.0, Windows Millennium Edition, Windows 2000, Windows XP Home Edition, Windows XP Professional, Windows Server 2003 family

DataGrid.SelectionBackColor Property

Gets or sets the background color of selected rows.

```
[Visual Basic]
Public Property SelectionBackColor As Color
[C#]
public Color SelectionBackColor {get; set;}
[C++]
public: __property Color get_SelectionBackColor();
public: __property void set_SelectionBackColor(Color);
[JScript]
public function get SelectionBackColor() : Color;
public function set SelectionBackColor(Color);
```

Property Value

A **Color** that represents the background color of selected rows. The default is the **ActiveCaption** color.

Remarks

You typically use this method if you are either creating a designer for the **System.Windows.Forms.DataGrid** or creating your own control incorporating the **System.Windows.Forms.DataGrid**.

Example

See related example in the **System.Windows.Forms.DataGrid** class topic.

Requirements

Platforms: Windows 98, Windows NT 4.0, Windows Millennium Edition, Windows 2000, Windows XP Home Edition, Windows XP Professional, Windows Server 2003 family, .NET Compact Framework - Windows CE .NET

DataGrid.SelectionForeColor Property

Gets or set the foreground color of selected rows.

```
[Visual Basic]
Public Property SelectionForeColor As Color
[C#]
public Color SelectionForeColor {get; set;}
[C++]
public: __property Color get_SelectionForeColor();
public: __property void set_SelectionForeColor(Color);
[JScript]
public function get SelectionForeColor() : Color;
public function set SelectionForeColor(Color);
```

Property Value

A **Color** representing the foreground color of selected rows. The default is the **ActiveCaptionText** color.

Example

See related example in the **System.Windows.Forms.DataGrid** class topic.

Requirements

Platforms: Windows 98, Windows NT 4.0, Windows Millennium Edition, Windows 2000, Windows XP Home Edition, Windows XP Professional, Windows Server 2003 family, .NET Compact Framework - Windows CE .NET

DataGrid.Site Property

This member overrides **Control.Site**.

```
[Visual Basic]
Overrides Public Property Site As ISite  Implements IComponent.Site
[C#]
public override ISite Site {get; set;}
[C++]
public: __property ISite* get_Site();
public: __property void set_Site(ISite*);
[JScript]
public override function get Site() : ISite;
public override function set Site(ISite);
```

Requirements

Platforms: Windows 98, Windows NT 4.0, Windows Millennium Edition, Windows 2000, Windows XP Home Edition, Windows XP Professional, Windows Server 2003 family

DataGrid.TableStyles Property

Gets the collection of **DataGridTableStyle** objects for the grid.

```
[Visual Basic]
Public ReadOnly Property TableStyles As GridTableStylesCollection
[C#]
public GridTableStylesCollection TableStyles {get;}
[C++]
public: __property GridTableStylesCollection* get_TableStyles();
[JScript]
public function get TableStyles() : GridTableStylesCollection;
```

Property Value

A **GridTableStylesCollection** that represents the collection of **DataGridTableStyle** objects.

Remarks

Use the **GridTableStylesCollection** to create customized views of each table displayed by the **System.Windows.Forms.DataGrid** control.

By default, the collection returned by **TableStyles** property does not contain any **DataGridTableStyle** objects. To create a set of customized views:

1. Create a **DataGridTableStyle** object.
2. Set the grid table object's **MappingName** to a **DataTable** object's **TableName**.
3. Add **DataGridColumnStyle** objects, one for each grid column you want to show, to the **GridColumnStylesCollection** returned by the **GridColumnStyles** property.
4. Set the **MappingName** of each **DataGridColumnStyle** object to the **ColumnName** of a **DataColumn**.
5. Add the **DataGridTableStyle** object to the collection returned by **TableStyles** property.

CAUTION Always create **DataGridColumnStyle** objects and add them to the **GridColumnStylesCollection** before adding **DataGridTableStyle** objects to the **GridTableStylesCollection**. When you add an empty **DataGridTableStyle** to the collection, **DataGridColumnStyle** objects are automatically generated for you. Consequently, an exception will be thrown if you try to add new **DataGridColumnStyle** objects with duplicate **MappingName** values to the **GridColumnStylesCollection**.

Example

See related example in the **System.Windows.Forms.DataGrid** class topic.

Requirements

Platforms: Windows 98, Windows NT 4.0, Windows Millennium Edition, Windows 2000, Windows XP Home Edition, Windows XP Professional, Windows Server 2003 family, .NET Compact Framework - Windows CE .NET

DataGrid.Text Property

This member overrides **Control.Text**.

```
[Visual Basic]
Overrides Public Property Text As String
[C#]
public override string Text {get; set;}
[C++]
public: __property String* get_Text();
public: __property void set_Text(String*);
[JScript]
public override function get Text() : String;
public override function set Text(String);
```

Requirements

Platforms: Windows 98, Windows NT 4.0, Windows Millennium Edition, Windows 2000, Windows XP Home Edition, Windows XP Professional, Windows Server 2003 family, .NET Compact Framework - Windows CE .NET

DataGrid.VertScrollBar Property

Gets the vertical scroll bar of the control.

```
[Visual Basic]
Protected ReadOnly Property VertScrollBar As ScrollBar
[C#]
protected ScrollBar VertScrollBar {get;}
[C++]
protected: __property ScrollBar* get_VertScrollBar();
[JScript]
protected function get VertScrollBar() : ScrollBar;
```

Property Value

The grid's vertical **ScrollBar**.

Requirements

Platforms: Windows 98, Windows NT 4.0, Windows Millennium Edition, Windows 2000, Windows XP Home Edition, Windows XP Professional, Windows Server 2003 family

DataGrid.VisibleColumnCount Property

Gets the number of visible columns.

```
[Visual Basic]
Public ReadOnly Property VisibleColumnCount As Integer
[C#]
public int VisibleColumnCount {get;}
[C++]
public: __property int get_VisibleColumnCount();
[JScript]
public function get VisibleColumnCount() : int;
```

Property Value

The number of columns visible in the viewport. The viewport is the rectangular area through which the grid is visible. The viewport's size depends on the size of the **System.Windows.Forms.DataGrid** control; if you allow users to resize the control, the viewport will also be affected.

Remarks

The number of visible columns can change depending on their width. For example, if a default width for all columns is set, but a new column's width is set twice as large, the number of visible columns can be reduced by at least one.

Example

[Visual Basic] The following example returns the number of visible columns.

```
[Visual Basic]
Private Function ReturnVisibleCols(ByVal myGrid As DataGrid) As Integer
    ReturnVisibleCols = myGrid.VisibleColumnCount
 End Function
```

Requirements

Platforms: Windows 98, Windows NT 4.0, Windows Millennium Edition, Windows 2000, Windows XP Home Edition, Windows XP Professional, Windows Server 2003 family, .NET Compact Framework - Windows CE .NET

DataGrid.VisibleRowCount Property

Gets the number of rows visible.

```
[Visual Basic]
Public ReadOnly Property VisibleRowCount As Integer
[C#]
public int VisibleRowCount {get;}
[C++]
public: __property int get_VisibleRowCount();
[JScript]
public function get VisibleRowCount() : int;
```

Property Value

The number of rows visible in the viewport. The viewport is the rectangular area through which the grid is visible. The viewport's size depends on the size of the **System.Windows.Forms.DataGrid** control; if you allow users to resize the control, the viewport will also be affected.

Remarks

The number of visible rows can be changed at run time if the user is allowed to resize the **System.Windows.Forms.DataGrid** control.

Example

[Visual Basic] The following example returns the number of rows visible in a **System.Windows.Forms.DataGrid** control.

```
[Visual Basic]
Private Function ReturnVisibleRows(ByVal myGrid As DataGrid)As Integer
    ReturnVisibleRows = myGrid.VisibleRowCount
 End Function
```

Requirements

Platforms: Windows 98, Windows NT 4.0, Windows Millennium Edition, Windows 2000, Windows XP Home Edition, Windows XP Professional, Windows Server 2003 family, .NET Compact Framework - Windows CE .NET

DataGrid.BeginEdit Method

Attempts to put the grid into a state where editing is allowed.

```
[Visual Basic]
Public Overridable Function BeginEdit( _
   ByVal gridColumn As DataGridColumnStyle, _
   ByVal rowNumber As Integer _
) As Boolean Implements IDataGridEditingService.BeginEdit
[C#]
public virtual bool BeginEdit(
   DataGridColumnStyle gridColumn,
   int rowNumber
);
[C++]
public: virtual bool BeginEdit(
   DataGridColumnStyle* gridColumn,
   int rowNumber
);
```

```
[JScript]
public function BeginEdit(
   gridColumn : DataGridColumnStyle,
   rowNumber : int
) : Boolean;
```

Parameters

gridColumn

A **DataGridColumnStyle** to edit.

rowNumber

The number of the row to edit.

Return Value

true if the method is successful; otherwise, **false**.

Implements

IDataGridEditingService.BeginEdit

Remarks

The grid will deny edit requests if the user already started typing into a cell. In that case, the **BeginEdit** method will return **false**.

Example

See related example in the **System.Windows.Forms.DataGrid** class topic.

Requirements

Platforms: Windows 98, Windows NT 4.0,
Windows Millennium Edition, Windows 2000,
Windows XP Home Edition, Windows XP Professional,
Windows Server 2003 family

DataGrid.BeginInit Method

Begins the initialization of a **System.Windows.Forms.DataGrid** that is used on a form or used by another component. The initialization occurs at run time.

```
[Visual Basic]
Public Overridable Sub BeginInit() Implements _
   ISupportInitialize.BeginInit
[C#]
public virtual void BeginInit();
[C++]
public: virtual void BeginInit();
[JScript]
public function BeginInit();
```

Implements

ISupportInitialize.BeginInit

Remarks

The Visual Studio .NET design environment uses this method to start the initialization of a component that is used on a form or used by another component. The **EndInit** method ends the initialization. Using the **BeginInit** and **EndInit** methods prevents the control from being used before it is fully initialized.

Requirements

Platforms: Windows 98, Windows NT 4.0,
Windows Millennium Edition, Windows 2000,
Windows XP Home Edition, Windows XP Professional,
Windows Server 2003 family

DataGrid.CancelEditing Method

Cancels the current edit operation and rolls back all changes.

```
[Visual Basic]
Protected Overridable Sub CancelEditing()
[C#]
protected virtual void CancelEditing();
[C++]
protected: virtual void CancelEditing();
[JScript]
protected function CancelEditing();
```

Requirements

Platforms: Windows 98, Windows NT 4.0,
Windows Millennium Edition, Windows 2000,
Windows XP Home Edition, Windows XP Professional,
Windows Server 2003 family

DataGrid.Collapse Method

Collapses child relations, if any exist for all rows, or for a specified row.

```
[Visual Basic]
Public Sub Collapse( _
   ByVal row As Integer _
)
[C#]
public void Collapse(
   int row
);
[C++]
public: void Collapse(
   int row
);
[JScript]
public function Collapse(
   row : int
);
```

Parameters

row

The number of the row to collapse. If set to -1, all rows are collapsed.

Remarks

Use the **IsExpanded** method to determine if a row is expanded.

Example

[Visual Basic] The following example collapses all rows in the **System.Windows.Forms.DataGrid** control.

```
[Visual Basic]
DataGrid1.Collapse( -1 )
```

Requirements

Platforms: Windows 98, Windows NT 4.0,
Windows Millennium Edition, Windows 2000,
Windows XP Home Edition, Windows XP Professional,
Windows Server 2003 family

DataGrid.ColumnStartedEditing Method

Informs the **System.Windows.Forms.DataGrid** control that the user has begun editing a column.

Overload List

Informs the **System.Windows.Forms.DataGrid** control when the user begins to edit a column using the specified control.

[Visual Basic] **Overloads Protected Friend Overridable Sub ColumnStartedEditing(Control)**

[C#] **protected internal virtual void ColumnStarted-Editing(Control);**

[C++] **protected public: virtual void ColumnStarted-Editing(Control*);**

[JScript] **protected internal function ColumnStarted-Editing(Control);**

Informs the **System.Windows.Forms.DataGrid** control when the user begins to edit the column at the specified location.

[Visual Basic] **Overloads Protected Friend Overridable Sub ColumnStartedEditing(Rectangle)**

[C#] **protected internal virtual void ColumnStarted-Editing(Rectangle);**

[C++] **protected public: virtual void ColumnStarted-Editing(Rectangle);**

[JScript] **protected internal function ColumnStarted-Editing(Rectangle);**

DataGrid.ColumnStartedEditing Method (Control)

Informs the **System.Windows.Forms.DataGrid** control when the user begins to edit a column using the specified control.

```
[Visual Basic]
Overloads Protected Friend Overridable Sub ColumnStartedEditing( _
   ByVal editingControl As Control _
)
[C#]
protected internal virtual void ColumnStartedEditing(
   Control editingControl
);
[C++]
protected public: virtual void ColumnStartedEditing(
   Control* editingControl
);
[JScript]
protected internal function ColumnStartedEditing(
   editingControl : Control
);
```

Parameters

editingControl

The **Control** used to edit the column.

Remarks

When called, the **ColumnStartedEditing** method allows the **System.Windows.Forms.DataGrid** control to show a pencil in the row header.

Requirements

Platforms: Windows 98, Windows NT 4.0, Windows Millennium Edition, Windows 2000, Windows XP Home Edition, Windows XP Professional, Windows Server 2003 family

DataGrid.ColumnStartedEditing Method (Rectangle)

Informs the **System.Windows.Forms.DataGrid** control when the user begins to edit the column at the specified location.

```
[Visual Basic]
Overloads Protected Friend Overridable Sub ColumnStartedEditing( _
   ByVal bounds As Rectangle _
)
[C#]
protected internal virtual void ColumnStartedEditing(
   Rectangle bounds
);
[C++]
protected public: virtual void ColumnStartedEditing(
   Rectangle bounds
);
[JScript]
protected internal function ColumnStartedEditing(
   bounds : Rectangle
);
```

Parameters

bounds

The **Rectangle** that defines the location of the edited column.

Remarks

When called, the **ColumnStartedEditing** method allows the **System.Windows.Forms.DataGrid** control to show a pencil in the row header.

Requirements

Platforms: Windows 98, Windows NT 4.0, Windows Millennium Edition, Windows 2000, Windows XP Home Edition, Windows XP Professional, Windows Server 2003 family

DataGrid.CreateAccessibilityInstance Method

Constructs a new instance of the accessibility object for this control.

```
[Visual Basic]
Overrides Protected Function CreateAccessibilityInstance() As _
   AccessibleObject
[C#]
protected override AccessibleObject CreateAccessibilityInstance();
[C++]
protected: AccessibleObject* CreateAccessibilityInstance();
[JScript]
protected override function CreateAccessibilityInstance() :
   AccessibleObject;
```

Return Value

The **Control.ControlAccessibleObject** for this control.

Remarks

Derived classes should not call the base class's **CreateAccessibilityInstance** method.

The only properties of the **AccessibleObject** that should be set are:

- **Role**
- **Description**
- **Name**

All other properties are handled by the **System.Windows.Forms.DataGrid** itself.

Requirements

Platforms: Windows 98, Windows NT 4.0, Windows Millennium Edition, Windows 2000, Windows XP Home Edition, Windows XP Professional, Windows Server 2003 family

DataGrid.CreateGridColumn Method

Creates a new **DataGridColumnStyle** that is added to the control.

Overload List

Creates a new **DataGridColumnStyle** with the specified **PropertyDescriptor**.

[Visual Basic] **Overloads Protected Overridable Function CreateGridColumn(PropertyDescriptor) As DataGridColumnStyle**

[C#] **protected virtual DataGridColumnStyle CreateGridColumn(PropertyDescriptor);**

[C++] **protected: virtual DataGridColumnStyle* CreateGridColumn(PropertyDescriptor*);**

[JScript] **protected function CreateGridColumn(PropertyDescriptor) : DataGridColumnStyle;**

Creates a **DataGridColumnStyle** using the specified **PropertyDescriptor**.

[Visual Basic] **Overloads Protected Overridable Function CreateGridColumn(PropertyDescriptor, Boolean) As DataGridColumnStyle**

[C#] **protected virtual DataGridColumnStyle CreateGridColumn(PropertyDescriptor, bool);**

[C++] **protected: virtual DataGridColumnStyle* CreateGridColumn(PropertyDescriptor*, bool);**

[JScript] **protected function CreateGridColumn(PropertyDescriptor, Boolean) : DataGridColumnStyle;**

DataGrid.CreateGridColumn Method (PropertyDescriptor)

Creates a new **DataGridColumnStyle** with the specified **PropertyDescriptor**.

```
[Visual Basic]
Overloads Protected Overridable Function CreateGridColumn( _
   ByVal prop As PropertyDescriptor _
) As DataGridColumnStyle
[C#]
protected virtual DataGridColumnStyle CreateGridColumn(
   PropertyDescriptor prop
);
[C++]
protected: virtual DataGridColumnStyle* CreateGridColumn(
   PropertyDescriptor* prop
);
[JScript]
protected function CreateGridColumn(
   prop : PropertyDescriptor
) : DataGridColumnStyle;
```

Parameters

prop

The **PropertyDescriptor** to use for creating the grid column style.

Return Value

The new **DataGridColumnStyle**.

Requirements

Platforms: Windows 98, Windows NT 4.0, Windows Millennium Edition, Windows 2000, Windows XP Home Edition, Windows XP Professional, Windows Server 2003 family

DataGrid.CreateGridColumn Method (PropertyDescriptor, Boolean)

Creates a **DataGridColumnStyle** using the specified **PropertyDescriptor**.

```
[Visual Basic]
Overloads Protected Overridable Function CreateGridColumn( _
   ByVal prop As PropertyDescriptor, _
   ByVal isDefault As Boolean _
) As DataGridColumnStyle
[C#]
protected virtual DataGridColumnStyle CreateGridColumn(
   PropertyDescriptor prop,
   bool isDefault
);
[C++]
protected: virtual DataGridColumnStyle* CreateGridColumn(
   PropertyDescriptor* prop,
   bool isDefault
);
[JScript]
protected function CreateGridColumn(
   prop : PropertyDescriptor,
   isDefault : Boolean
) : DataGridColumnStyle;
```

Parameters

prop

The **PropertyDescriptor** to use for creating the grid column style.

isDefault

true to set the column style as the default; otherwise, **false**.

Return Value

The new **DataGridColumnStyle**.

Requirements

Platforms: Windows 98, Windows NT 4.0, Windows Millennium Edition, Windows 2000, Windows XP Home Edition, Windows XP Professional, Windows Server 2003 family

DataGrid.Dispose Method

Overload List

This member supports the .NET Framework infrastructure and is not intended to be used directly from your code.

Supported by the .NET Compact Framework.

[Visual Basic] **Overloads Overrides Protected Sub Dispose(Boolean)**

[C#] **protected override void Dispose(bool);**

[C++] **protected: void Dispose(bool);**

[JScript] **protected override function Dispose(Boolean);**

Inherited from **Component**.

Supported by the .NET Compact Framework.

[Visual Basic] **Overloads Public Overridable Sub Dispose() Implements IDisposable.Dispose**

[C#] **public virtual void Dispose();**

[C++] **public: virtual void Dispose();**

[JScript] **public function Dispose();**

Example

[Visual Basic] The following example uses the **Dispose** method to free resources.

> [Visual Basic] **Note** This example shows how to use one of the overloaded versions of **Dispose**. For other examples that might be available, see the individual overload topics.

[Visual Basic]

```
Private Sub DisposeGridResources(ByVal myGrid As DataGrid)
   myGrid.Dispose
   myGrid = Nothing
End Sub
```

DataGrid.Dispose Method (Boolean)

This member overrides **Control.Dispose**.

```
[Visual Basic]
Overrides Overloads Protected Sub Dispose( _
   ByVal disposing As Boolean _
)
[C#]
protected override void Dispose(
   bool disposing
);
[C++]
protected: void Dispose(
   bool disposing
);
[JScript]
protected override function Dispose(
   disposing : Boolean
);
```

Requirements

Platforms: Windows 98, Windows NT 4.0, Windows Millennium Edition, Windows 2000, Windows XP Home Edition, Windows XP Professional, Windows Server 2003 family, .NET Compact Framework - Windows CE .NET

DataGrid.EndEdit Method

Requests an end to an edit operation taking place on the **System.Windows.Forms.DataGrid** control.

```
[Visual Basic]
Public Overridable Function EndEdit( _
   ByVal gridColumn As DataGridColumnStyle, _
   ByVal rowNumber As Integer, _
   ByVal shouldAbort As Boolean _
) As Boolean Implements IDataGridEditingService.EndEdit
[C#]
public virtual bool EndEdit(
   DataGridColumnStyle gridColumn,
   int rowNumber,
   bool shouldAbort
);
[C++]
public: virtual bool EndEdit(
   DataGridColumnStyle* gridColumn,
   int rowNumber,
   bool shouldAbort
);
[JScript]
public function EndEdit(
   gridColumn : DataGridColumnStyle,
   rowNumber : int,
   shouldAbort : Boolean
) : Boolean;
```

Parameters

gridColumn
The **DataGridColumnStyle** to cease editing.

rowNumber
The number of the row to cease editing.

shouldAbort
Set to **true** if the current operation should be stopped.

Return Value

true if the editing operation ceases; otherwise, **false**.

Implements

IDataGridEditingService.EndEdit

Remarks

The **EndEdit** method returns **false** if the user is not editing (typing into) a cell.

Example

See related example in the **System.Windows.Forms.DataGrid** class topic.

Requirements

Platforms: Windows 98, Windows NT 4.0, Windows Millennium Edition, Windows 2000, Windows XP Home Edition, Windows XP Professional, Windows Server 2003 family

DataGrid.EndInit Method

Ends the initialization of a **System.Windows.Forms.DataGrid** that is used on a form or used by another component. The initialization occurs at run time.

```
[Visual Basic]
Public Overridable Sub EndInit() Implements _
   ISupportInitialize.EndInit
[C#]
public virtual void EndInit();
[C++]
public: virtual void EndInit();
[JScript]
public function EndInit();
```

Implements

ISupportInitialize.EndInit

Remarks

The Visual Studio .NET design environment uses this method to end the initialization of a component that is used on a form or used by another component. The **BeginInit** method starts the initialization. Using the **BeginInit** and **EndInit** methods prevents the control from being used before it is fully initialized.

Requirements

Platforms: Windows 98, Windows NT 4.0, Windows Millennium Edition, Windows 2000, Windows XP Home Edition, Windows XP Professional, Windows Server 2003 family

DataGrid.Expand Method

Displays child relations, if any exist, for all rows or a specific row.

[Visual Basic]
```
Public Sub Expand( _
   ByVal row As Integer _
)
```
[C#]
```
public void Expand(
   int row
);
```
[C++]
```
public: void Expand(
   int row
);
```
[JScript]
```
public function Expand(
   row : int
);
```

Parameters

row

The number of the row to expand. If set to -1, all rows are expanded.

Example

[Visual Basic]
```
Private Sub ExpandRow(ByVal myGrid As DataGrid, row As Integer)
   myGrid.Expand( row )
End Sub
```

Requirements

Platforms: Windows 98, Windows NT 4.0, Windows Millennium Edition, Windows 2000, Windows XP Home Edition, Windows XP Professional, Windows Server 2003 family

DataGrid.GetCellBounds Method

Gets the **Rectangle** that specifies the four corners of a cell.

Overload List

Gets the **Rectangle** of the cell specified by **DataGridCell**.

[Visual Basic] **Overloads Public Function GetCellBounds(DataGridCell) As Rectangle**

[C#] **public Rectangle GetCellBounds(DataGridCell);**

[C++] **public: Rectangle GetCellBounds(DataGridCell);**

[JScript] **public function GetCellBounds(DataGridCell) : Rectangle;**

Gets the **Rectangle** of the cell specified by row and column number.

Supported by the .NET Compact Framework.

[Visual Basic] **Overloads Public Function GetCellBounds(Integer, Integer) As Rectangle**

[C#] **public Rectangle GetCellBounds(int, int);**

[C++] **public: Rectangle GetCellBounds(int, int);**

[JScript] **public function GetCellBounds(int, int) : Rectangle;**

Example

See related example in the **System.Windows.Forms.DataGrid** class topic.

DataGrid.GetCellBounds Method (DataGridCell)

Gets the **Rectangle** of the cell specified by **DataGridCell**.

[Visual Basic]
```
Overloads Public Function GetCellBounds( _
   ByVal dgc As DataGridCell _
) As Rectangle
```
[C#]
```
public Rectangle GetCellBounds(
   DataGridCell dgc
);
```
[C++]
```
public: Rectangle GetCellBounds(
   DataGridCell dgc
);
```
[JScript]
```
public function GetCellBounds(
   dgc : DataGridCell
) : Rectangle;
```

Parameters

dgc

The **DataGridCell** to look up.

Return Value

A **Rectangle** that defines the current cell's corners.

Example

See related example in the **System.Windows.Forms.DataGrid** class topic.

Requirements

Platforms: Windows 98, Windows NT 4.0, Windows Millennium Edition, Windows 2000, Windows XP Home Edition, Windows XP Professional, Windows Server 2003 family

DataGrid.GetCellBounds Method (Int32, Int32)

Gets the **Rectangle** of the cell specified by row and column number.

[Visual Basic]
```
Overloads Public Function GetCellBounds( _
   ByVal row As Integer, _
   ByVal col As Integer _
) As Rectangle
```
[C#]
```
public Rectangle GetCellBounds(
   int row,
   int col
);
```

```
[C++]
public: Rectangle GetCellBounds(
   int row,
   int col
);
[JScript]
public function GetCellBounds(
   row : int,
   col : int
) : Rectangle;
```

Parameters

row
The number of the cell's row.

col
The number of the cell's column.

Return Value

A **Rectangle** that defines the current cell's corners.

Example

See related example in the **System.Windows.Forms.DataGrid** class topic.

Requirements

Platforms: Windows 98, Windows NT 4.0, Windows Millennium Edition, Windows 2000, Windows XP Home Edition, Windows XP Professional, Windows Server 2003 family, .NET Compact Framework - Windows CE .NET

DataGrid.GetCurrentCellBounds Method

Gets a **Rectangle** that specifies the four corners of the selected cell.

```
[Visual Basic]
Public Function GetCurrentCellBounds() As Rectangle
[C#]
public Rectangle GetCurrentCellBounds();
[C++]
public: Rectangle GetCurrentCellBounds();
[JScript]
public function GetCurrentCellBounds() : Rectangle;
```

Return Value

A **Rectangle** that defines the current cell's corners.

Example

See related example in the **System.Windows.Forms.DataGrid** class topic.

Requirements

Platforms: Windows 98, Windows NT 4.0, Windows Millennium Edition, Windows 2000, Windows XP Home Edition, Windows XP Professional, Windows Server 2003 family

DataGrid.GetOutputTextDelimiter Method

This member supports the .NET Framework infrastructure and is not intended to be used directly from your code.

```
[Visual Basic]
Protected Overridable Function GetOutputTextDelimiter() As String
[C#]
protected virtual string GetOutputTextDelimiter();
[C++]
protected: virtual String* GetOutputTextDelimiter();
[JScript]
protected function GetOutputTextDelimiter() : String;
```

DataGrid.GridHScrolled Method

Listens for the horizontal scrollbar's scroll event.

```
[Visual Basic]
Protected Overridable Sub GridHScrolled( _
   ByVal sender As Object, _
   ByVal se As ScrollEventArgs _
)
[C#]
protected virtual void GridHScrolled(
   object sender,
   ScrollEventArgs se
);
[C++]
protected: virtual void GridHScrolled(
   Object* sender,
   ScrollEventArgs* se
);
[JScript]
protected function GridHScrolled(
   sender : Object,
   se : ScrollEventArgs
);
```

Parameters

sender
An **Object** that contains data about the control.

se
A **ScrollEventArgs** that contains the event data.

Requirements

Platforms: Windows 98, Windows NT 4.0, Windows Millennium Edition, Windows 2000, Windows XP Home Edition, Windows XP Professional, Windows Server 2003 family

DataGrid.GridVScrolled Method

Listens for the vertical scrollbar's scroll event.

```
[Visual Basic]
Protected Overridable Sub GridVScrolled( _
   ByVal sender As Object, _
   ByVal se As ScrollEventArgs _
)
[C#]
protected virtual void GridVScrolled(
   object sender,
   ScrollEventArgs se
);
[C++]
protected: virtual void GridVScrolled(
   Object* sender,
   ScrollEventArgs* se
);
```

```
[JScript]
protected function GridVScrolled(
   sender : Object,
   se : ScrollEventArgs
);
```

Parameters

sender

An **Object** that contains data about the control.

se

A **ScrollEventArgs** that contains the event data.

Requirements

Platforms: Windows 98, Windows NT 4.0, Windows Millennium Edition, Windows 2000, Windows XP Home Edition, Windows XP Professional, Windows Server 2003 family

DataGrid.HitTest Method

Gets information about the **System.Windows.Forms.DataGrid** control at a specified point on the screen.

Overload List

Gets information, such as row and column number of a clicked point on the grid, about the grid using a specific **Point**.

[Visual Basic] **Overloads Public Function HitTest(Point) As HitTestInfo**

[C#] **public HitTestInfo HitTest(Point);**

[C++] **public: HitTestInfo* HitTest(Point);**

[JScript] **public function HitTest(Point) : HitTestInfo;**

Gets information, such as row and column number of a clicked point on the grid, using the x and y coordinate passed to the method.

Supported by the .NET Compact Framework.

[Visual Basic] **Overloads Public Function HitTest(Integer, Integer) As HitTestInfo**

[C#] **public HitTestInfo HitTest(int, int);**

[C++] **public: HitTestInfo* HitTest(int, int);**

[JScript] **public function HitTest(int, int) : HitTestInfo;**

Example

See related example in the **System.Windows.Forms.DataGrid** class topic.

DataGrid.HitTest Method (Point)

Gets information, such as row and column number of a clicked point on the grid, about the grid using a specific **Point**.

```
[Visual Basic]
Overloads Public Function HitTest( _
   ByVal position As Point _
) As HitTestInfo
[C#]
public HitTestInfo HitTest(
   Point position
);
[C++]
public: HitTestInfo* HitTest(
   Point position
);
[JScript]
public function HitTest(
   position : Point
) : HitTestInfo;
```

Parameters

position

A **Point** that represents single x,y coordinate.

Return Value

A **DataGrid.HitTestInfo** that contains specific information about the grid.

Remarks

The **DataGrid.HitTestInfo**, in conjunction with the **HitTest** method of the **System.Windows.Forms.DataGrid** control, is used to determine which part of a **System.Windows.Forms.DataGrid** control the user has clicked. The **DataGrid.HitTestInfo** contains both the row, column and part of the grid that was clicked. Additionally, the **Type** property returns a **DataGrid.HitTestType** enumeration.

The **HitTest** method takes an **x** and **y** argument supplied by the **System.Windows.Forms.DataGrid** control's **DragDrop**, **DragEnter**, **DragOver**, **MouseDown**, **MouseMove**, **MouseUp** and **MouseWheel** events.

Example

See related example in the **System.Windows.Forms.DataGrid** class topic.

Requirements

Platforms: Windows 98, Windows NT 4.0, Windows Millennium Edition, Windows 2000, Windows XP Home Edition, Windows XP Professional, Windows Server 2003 family

DataGrid.HitTest Method (Int32, Int32)

Gets information, such as row and column number of a clicked point on the grid, using the x and y coordinate passed to the method.

```
[Visual Basic]
Overloads Public Function HitTest( _
   ByVal x As Integer, _
   ByVal y As Integer _
) As HitTestInfo
[C#]
public HitTestInfo HitTest(
   int x,
   int y
);
[C++]
public: HitTestInfo* HitTest(
   int x,
   int y
);
[JScript]
public function HitTest(
   x : int,
   y : int
) : HitTestInfo;
```

Parameters

x

The horizontal position of the coordinate.

y

The vertical position of the coordinate.

Return Value

A **DataGrid.HitTestInfo** that contains information about the clicked part of the grid.

Remarks

The **DataGrid.HitTestInfo**, in conjunction with the **HitTest** method of the **System.Windows.Forms.DataGrid** control, is used to determine which part of a **System.Windows.Forms.DataGrid** control the user has clicked. The **DataGrid.HitTestInfo** contains both the row, column and part of the grid that was clicked. Additionally, the **Type** property returns a **DataGrid.HitTestType** enumeration.

The **HitTest** method takes an **x** and **y** argument supplied by the **System.Windows.Forms.DataGrid** control's **DragDrop**, **DragEnter**, **DragOver**, **MouseDown**, **MouseMove**, **MouseUp** and **MouseWheel** events.

Example

See related example in the **System.Windows.Forms.DataGrid** class topic.

Requirements

Platforms: Windows 98, Windows NT 4.0, Windows Millennium Edition, Windows 2000, Windows XP Home Edition, Windows XP Professional, Windows Server 2003 family, .NET Compact Framework - Windows CE .NET

DataGrid.IsExpanded Method

Gets a value that indicates whether a specified row's node is expanded or collapsed.

```
[Visual Basic]
Public Function IsExpanded( _
   ByVal rowNumber As Integer _
) As Boolean
[C#]
public bool IsExpanded(
   int rowNumber
);
[C++]
public: bool IsExpanded(
   int rowNumber
);
[JScript]
public function IsExpanded(
   rowNumber : int
) : Boolean;
```

Parameters

rowNumber

The number of the row in question.

Return Value

true if the node is expanded; otherwise, **false**.

Example

See related example in the **System.Windows.Forms.DataGrid** class topic.

Requirements

Platforms: Windows 98, Windows NT 4.0, Windows Millennium Edition, Windows 2000, Windows XP Home Edition, Windows XP Professional, Windows Server 2003 family

DataGrid.IsSelected Method

Gets a value indicating whether a specified row is selected.

```
[Visual Basic]
Public Function IsSelected( _
   ByVal row As Integer _
) As Boolean
[C#]
public bool IsSelected(
   int row
);
[C++]
public: bool IsSelected(
   int row
);
[JScript]
public function IsSelected(
   row : int
) : Boolean;
```

Parameters

row

The number of the row you are interested in.

Return Value

true if the row is selected; otherwise, **false**.

Example

See related example in the **System.Windows.Forms.DataGrid** class topic.

Requirements

Platforms: Windows 98, Windows NT 4.0, Windows Millennium Edition, Windows 2000, Windows XP Home Edition, Windows XP Professional, Windows Server 2003 family, .NET Compact Framework - Windows CE .NET

DataGrid.NavigateBack Method

Navigates back to the table previously displayed in the grid.

```
[Visual Basic]
Public Sub NavigateBack()
[C#]
public void NavigateBack();
[C++]
public: void NavigateBack();
[JScript]
public function NavigateBack();
```

Remarks

If the grid has no parent rows, no change occurs.

Example

See related example in the **System.Windows.Forms.DataGrid** class topic.

Requirements

Platforms: Windows 98, Windows NT 4.0, Windows Millennium Edition, Windows 2000, Windows XP Home Edition, Windows XP Professional, Windows Server 2003 family

DataGrid.NavigateTo Method

Navigates to the table specified by row and relation name.

```
[Visual Basic]
Public Sub NavigateTo( _
   ByVal rowNumber As Integer, _
   ByVal relationName As String _
)
[C#]
public void NavigateTo(
   int rowNumber,
   string relationName
);
[C++]
public: void NavigateTo(
   int rowNumber,
   String* relationName
);
[JScript]
public function NavigateTo(
   rowNumber : int,
   relationName : String
);
```

Parameters

rowNumber

The number of the row to navigate to.

relationName

The name of the child relation to navigate to.

Example

[Visual Basic] The following example navigates to the specified row number, in the table specified by child relationship name.

```
[Visual Basic]
Private Sub NavToGrid(ByVal myGrid As DataGrid)
   ' Presumes a relationship named OrderDetails exists.
   myGrid.NavigateTo( 2, "OrderDetails" )
End Sub
```

Requirements

Platforms: Windows 98, Windows NT 4.0, Windows Millennium Edition, Windows 2000, Windows XP Home Edition, Windows XP Professional, Windows Server 2003 family

DataGrid.OnAllowNavigationChanged Method

Raises the **AllowNavigationChanged** event.

```
[Visual Basic]
Protected Overridable Sub OnAllowNavigationChanged( _
   ByVal e As EventArgs _
)
[C#]
protected virtual void OnAllowNavigationChanged(
   EventArgs e
);
[C++]
protected: virtual void OnAllowNavigationChanged(
   EventArgs* e
);
[JScript]
protected function OnAllowNavigationChanged(
   e : EventArgs
);
```

Parameters

e

An **EventArgs** that contains the event data.

Requirements

Platforms: Windows 98, Windows NT 4.0, Windows Millennium Edition, Windows 2000, Windows XP Home Edition, Windows XP Professional, Windows Server 2003 family

DataGrid.OnBackButtonClicked Method

Listens for the caption's back button clicked event.

```
[Visual Basic]
Protected Sub OnBackButtonClicked( _
   ByVal sender As Object, _
   ByVal e As EventArgs _
)
[C#]
protected void OnBackButtonClicked(
   object sender,
   EventArgs e
);
[C++]
protected: void OnBackButtonClicked(
   Object* sender,
   EventArgs* e
);
[JScript]
protected function OnBackButtonClicked(
   sender : Object,
   e : EventArgs
);
```

Parameters

sender

An **Object** that contains data about the control.

e

An **EventArgs** that contains data about the event.

Requirements

Platforms: Windows 98, Windows NT 4.0, Windows Millennium Edition, Windows 2000, Windows XP Home Edition, Windows XP Professional, Windows Server 2003 family

DataGrid.OnBackColorChanged Method

Raises the **BackColorChanged** event.

[Visual Basic]
```
Overrides Protected Sub OnBackColorChanged( _
   ByVal e As EventArgs _
)
```
[C#]
```
protected override void OnBackColorChanged(
   EventArgs e
);
```
[C++]
```
protected: void OnBackColorChanged(
   EventArgs* e
);
```
[JScript]
```
protected override function OnBackColorChanged(
   e : EventArgs
);
```

Parameters

e

An **EventArgs** that contains the event data.

Remarks

Raising an event invokes the event handler through a delegate.

The **OnBackColorChanged** method also allows derived classes to handle the event without attaching a delegate. This is the preferred technique for handling the event in a derived class.

Notes to Inheritors: When overriding **OnBackColorChanged** in a derived class, be sure to call the base class's **OnBackColorChanged** method so that registered delegates receive the event.

Requirements

Platforms: Windows 98, Windows NT 4.0, Windows Millennium Edition, Windows 2000, Windows XP Home Edition, Windows XP Professional, Windows Server 2003 family

DataGrid.OnBackgroundColorChanged Method

Raises the **BackgroundColorChanged** event.

[Visual Basic]
```
Protected Overridable Sub OnBackgroundColorChanged( _
   ByVal e As EventArgs _
)
```
[C#]
```
protected virtual void OnBackgroundColorChanged(
   EventArgs e
);
```
[C++]
```
protected: virtual void OnBackgroundColorChanged(
   EventArgs* e
);
```
[JScript]
```
protected function OnBackgroundColorChanged(
   e : EventArgs
);
```

Parameters

e

An **EventArgs** that contains the event data.

Requirements

Platforms: Windows 98, Windows NT 4.0, Windows Millennium Edition, Windows 2000, Windows XP Home Edition, Windows XP Professional, Windows Server 2003 family

DataGrid.OnBindingContextChanged Method

Raises the **BindingContextChanged** event.

[Visual Basic]
```
Overrides Protected Sub OnBindingContextChanged( _
   ByVal e As EventArgs _
)
```
[C#]
```
protected override void OnBindingContextChanged(
   EventArgs e
);
```
[C++]
```
protected: void OnBindingContextChanged(
   EventArgs* e
);
```
[JScript]
```
protected override function OnBindingContextChanged(
   e : EventArgs
);
```

Parameters

e

An **EventArgs** that contains the event data.

Remarks

Raising an event invokes the event handler through a delegate.

The **OnBindingContextChanged** method also allows derived classes to handle the event without attaching a delegate. This is the preferred technique for handling the event in a derived class.

Notes to Inheritors: When overriding **OnBindingContext-Changed** in a derived class, be sure to call the base class's **OnBindingContextChanged** method so that registered delegates receive the event.

Requirements

Platforms: Windows 98, Windows NT 4.0, Windows Millennium Edition, Windows 2000, Windows XP Home Edition, Windows XP Professional, Windows Server 2003 family, .NET Compact Framework - Windows CE .NET

DataGrid.OnBorderStyleChanged Method

Raises the **BorderStyleChanged** event.

[Visual Basic]
```
Protected Overridable Sub OnBorderStyleChanged( _
   ByVal e As EventArgs _
)
```
[C#]
```
protected virtual void OnBorderStyleChanged(
   EventArgs e
);
```
[C++]
```
protected: virtual void OnBorderStyleChanged(
   EventArgs* e
);
```

[JScript]
```
protected function OnBorderStyleChanged(
   e : EventArgs
);
```

Parameters

e

An **EventArgs** that contains the event data.

Requirements

Platforms: Windows 98, Windows NT 4.0, Windows Millennium Edition, Windows 2000, Windows XP Home Edition, Windows XP Professional, Windows Server 2003 family

DataGrid.OnCaptionVisibleChanged Method

Raises the **CaptionVisibleChanged** event.

[Visual Basic]
```
Protected Overridable Sub OnCaptionVisibleChanged( _
   ByVal e As EventArgs _
)
```
[C#]
```
protected virtual void OnCaptionVisibleChanged(
   EventArgs e
);
```
[C++]
```
protected: virtual void OnCaptionVisibleChanged(
   EventArgs* e
);
```
[JScript]
```
protected function OnCaptionVisibleChanged(
   e : EventArgs
);
```

Parameters

e

An **EventArgs** that contains the event data.

Requirements

Platforms: Windows 98, Windows NT 4.0, Windows Millennium Edition, Windows 2000, Windows XP Home Edition, Windows XP Professional, Windows Server 2003 family

DataGrid.OnCurrentCellChanged Method

Raises the **CurrentCellChanged** event.

[Visual Basic]
```
Protected Overridable Sub OnCurrentCellChanged( _
   ByVal e As EventArgs _
)
```
[C#]
```
protected virtual void OnCurrentCellChanged(
   EventArgs e
);
```
[C++]
```
protected: virtual void OnCurrentCellChanged(
   EventArgs* e
);
```
[JScript]
```
protected function OnCurrentCellChanged(
   e : EventArgs
);
```

Parameters

e

An **EventArgs** that contains the event data.

Requirements

Platforms: Windows 98, Windows NT 4.0, Windows Millennium Edition, Windows 2000, Windows XP Home Edition, Windows XP Professional, Windows Server 2003 family, .NET Compact Framework - Windows CE .NET

DataGrid.OnDataSourceChanged Method

Raises the **DataSourceChanged** event.

[Visual Basic]
```
Protected Overridable Sub OnDataSourceChanged( _
   ByVal e As EventArgs _
)
```
[C#]
```
protected virtual void OnDataSourceChanged(
   EventArgs e
);
```
[C++]
```
protected: virtual void OnDataSourceChanged(
   EventArgs* e
);
```
[JScript]
```
protected function OnDataSourceChanged(
   e : EventArgs
);
```

Parameters

e

An **EventArgs** that contains the event data.

Remarks

Raising an event invokes the event handler through a delegate.

The **OnDataSourceChanged** method also allows derived classes to handle the event without attaching a delegate. This is the preferred technique for handling the event in a derived class.

Notes to Inheritors: When overriding **OnDataSourceChanged** in a derived class, be sure to call the base class's **OnDataSourceChanged** method so that registered delegates receive the event.

Requirements

Platforms: Windows 98, Windows NT 4.0, Windows Millennium Edition, Windows 2000, Windows XP Home Edition, Windows XP Professional, Windows Server 2003 family

DataGrid.OnEnter Method

Raises the **Enter** event.

[Visual Basic]
```
Overrides Protected Sub OnEnter( _
   ByVal e As EventArgs _
)
```

```
[C#]
protected override void OnEnter(
   EventArgs e
);
[C++]
protected: void OnEnter(
   EventArgs* e
);
[JScript]
protected override function OnEnter(
   e : EventArgs
);
```

Parameters

e

An **EventArgs** that contains the event data.

Requirements

Platforms: Windows 98, Windows NT 4.0, Windows Millennium Edition, Windows 2000, Windows XP Home Edition, Windows XP Professional, Windows Server 2003 family

DataGrid.OnFlatModeChanged Method

Raises the **FlatModeChanged** event.

```
[Visual Basic]
Protected Overridable Sub OnFlatModeChanged( _
   ByVal e As EventArgs _
)
[C#]
protected virtual void OnFlatModeChanged(
   EventArgs e
);
[C++]
protected: virtual void OnFlatModeChanged(
   EventArgs* e
);
[JScript]
protected function OnFlatModeChanged(
   e : EventArgs
);
```

Parameters

e

An **EventArgs** that contains the event data.

Requirements

Platforms: Windows 98, Windows NT 4.0, Windows Millennium Edition, Windows 2000, Windows XP Home Edition, Windows XP Professional, Windows Server 2003 family

DataGrid.OnFontChanged Method

Raises the **FontChanged** event.

```
[Visual Basic]
Overrides Protected Sub OnFontChanged( _
   ByVal e As EventArgs _
)
[C#]
protected override void OnFontChanged(
   EventArgs e
);
[C++]
protected: void OnFontChanged(
   EventArgs* e
);
[JScript]
protected override function OnFontChanged(
   e : EventArgs
);
```

Parameters

e

An **EventArgs** that contains the event data.

Remarks

Raising an event invokes the event handler through a delegate.

The **OnFontChanged** method also allows derived classes to handle the event without attaching a delegate. This is the preferred technique for handling the event in a derived class.

Notes to Inheritors: When overriding **OnFontChanged** in a derived class, be sure to call the base class's **OnFontChanged** method so that registered delegates receive the event.

Requirements

Platforms: Windows 98, Windows NT 4.0, Windows Millennium Edition, Windows 2000, Windows XP Home Edition, Windows XP Professional, Windows Server 2003 family

DataGrid.OnForeColorChanged Method

Raises the **ForeColorChanged** event.

```
[Visual Basic]
Overrides Protected Sub OnForeColorChanged( _
   ByVal e As EventArgs _
)
[C#]
protected override void OnForeColorChanged(
   EventArgs e
);
[C++]
protected: void OnForeColorChanged(
   EventArgs* e
);
[JScript]
protected override function OnForeColorChanged(
   e : EventArgs
);
```

Parameters

e

An **EventArgs** that contains the event data.

Remarks

Raising an event invokes the event handler through a delegate.

The **OnForeColorChanged** method also allows derived classes to handle the event without attaching a delegate. This is the preferred technique for handling the event in a derived class.

Notes to Inheritors: When overriding **OnForeColorChanged** in a derived class, be sure to call the base class's **OnForeColorChanged** method so that registered delegates receive the event.

Requirements

Platforms: Windows 98, Windows NT 4.0, Windows Millennium Edition, Windows 2000, Windows XP Home Edition, Windows XP Professional, Windows Server 2003 family

DataGrid.OnHandleCreated Method

Raises the **CreateHandle** event.

```
[Visual Basic]
Overrides Protected Sub OnHandleCreated( _
   ByVal e As EventArgs _
)
[C#]
protected override void OnHandleCreated(
   EventArgs e
);
[C++]
protected: void OnHandleCreated(
   EventArgs* e
);
[JScript]
protected override function OnHandleCreated(
   e : EventArgs
);
```

Parameters

e

An **EventArgs** that contains the event data.

Remarks

Raising an event invokes the event handler through a delegate.

The **OnHandleCreated** method also allows derived classes to handle the event without attaching a delegate. This is the preferred technique for handling the event in a derived class.

Notes to Inheritors: When overriding **OnHandleCreated** in a derived class, be sure to call the base class's **OnHandleCreated** method so that registered delegates receive the event.

Requirements

Platforms: Windows 98, Windows NT 4.0, Windows Millennium Edition, Windows 2000, Windows XP Home Edition, Windows XP Professional, Windows Server 2003 family

DataGrid.OnHandleDestroyed Method

Raises the **DestroyHandle** event.

```
[Visual Basic]
Overrides Protected Sub OnHandleDestroyed( _
   ByVal e As EventArgs _
)
[C#]
protected override void OnHandleDestroyed(
   EventArgs e
);
[C++]
protected: void OnHandleDestroyed(
   EventArgs* e
);
[JScript]
protected override function OnHandleDestroyed(
   e : EventArgs
);
```

Parameters

e

An **EventArgs** containing the event data.

Remarks

Raising an event invokes the event handler through a delegate.

The **OnHandleDestroyed** method also allows derived classes to handle the event without attaching a delegate. This is the preferred technique for handling the event in a derived class.

Notes to Inheritors: When overriding **OnHandleDestroyed** in a derived class, be sure to call the base class's **OnHandleDestroyed** method so that registered delegates receive the event.

Requirements

Platforms: Windows 98, Windows NT 4.0, Windows Millennium Edition, Windows 2000, Windows XP Home Edition, Windows XP Professional, Windows Server 2003 family

DataGrid.OnKeyDown Method

Raises the **KeyDown** event.

```
[Visual Basic]
Overrides Protected Sub OnKeyDown( _
   ByVal ke As KeyEventArgs _
)
[C#]
protected override void OnKeyDown(
   KeyEventArgs ke
);
[C++]
protected: void OnKeyDown(
   KeyEventArgs* ke
);
[JScript]
protected override function OnKeyDown(
   ke : KeyEventArgs
);
```

Parameters

ke

A **KeyEventArgs** that provides data about the **OnKeyDown** event.

Remarks

Raising an event invokes the event handler through a delegate.

The **OnKeyDown** method also allows derived classes to handle the event without attaching a delegate. This is the preferred technique for handling the event in a derived class.

Notes to Inheritors: When overriding **OnKeyDown** in a derived class, be sure to call the base class's **OnKeyDown** method so that registered delegates receive the event.

Requirements

Platforms: Windows 98, Windows NT 4.0, Windows Millennium Edition, Windows 2000, Windows XP Home Edition, Windows XP Professional, Windows Server 2003 family, .NET Compact Framework - Windows CE .NET

DataGrid.OnKeyPress Method

Raises the **KeyPress** event.

[Visual Basic]
```
Overrides Protected Sub OnKeyPress( _
   ByVal kpe As KeyPressEventArgs _
)
```
[C#]
```
protected override void OnKeyPress(
   KeyPressEventArgs kpe
);
```
[C++]
```
protected: void OnKeyPress(
   KeyPressEventArgs* kpe
);
```
[JScript]
```
protected override function OnKeyPress(
   kpe : KeyPressEventArgs
);
```

Parameters

kpe

A **KeyPressEventArgs** that contains data about the **OnKeyPress** event

Remarks

Raising an event invokes the event handler through a delegate.

The **OnKeyPress** method also allows derived classes to handle the event without attaching a delegate. This is the preferred technique for handling the event in a derived class.

Notes to Inheritors: When overriding **OnKeyPress** in a derived class, be sure to call the base class's **OnKeyPress** method so that registered delegates receive the event.

Requirements

Platforms: Windows 98, Windows NT 4.0,
Windows Millennium Edition, Windows 2000,
Windows XP Home Edition, Windows XP Professional,
Windows Server 2003 family,
.NET Compact Framework - Windows CE .NET

DataGrid.OnLayout Method

Raises the **Layout** event that repositions controls and updates scroll bars.

[Visual Basic]
```
Overrides Protected Sub OnLayout( _
   ByVal levent As LayoutEventArgs _
)
```
[C#]
```
protected override void OnLayout(
   LayoutEventArgs levent
);
```
[C++]
```
protected: void OnLayout(
   LayoutEventArgs* levent
);
```
[JScript]
```
protected override function OnLayout(
   levent : LayoutEventArgs
);
```

Parameters

levent

A **LayoutEventArgs** that contains the event data.

Remarks

Raising an event invokes the event handler through a delegate.

The **OnLayout** method also allows derived classes to handle the event without attaching a delegate. This is the preferred technique for handling the event in a derived class.

Notes to Inheritors: When overriding **OnLayout** in a derived class, be sure to call the base class's **OnLayout** method so that registered delegates receive the event.

Requirements

Platforms: Windows 98, Windows NT 4.0,
Windows Millennium Edition, Windows 2000,
Windows XP Home Edition, Windows XP Professional,
Windows Server 2003 family

DataGrid.OnLeave Method

Raises the **Leave** event.

[Visual Basic]
```
Overrides Protected Sub OnLeave( _
   ByVal e As EventArgs _
)
```
[C#]
```
protected override void OnLeave(
   EventArgs e
);
```
[C++]
```
protected: void OnLeave(
   EventArgs* e
);
```
[JScript]
```
protected override function OnLeave(
   e : EventArgs
);
```

Parameters

e

An **EventArgs** that contains the event data.

Remarks

Raising an event invokes the event handler through a delegate.

The **OnLeave** method also allows derived classes to handle the event without attaching a delegate. This is the preferred technique for handling the event in a derived class.

Notes to Inheritors: When overriding **OnLeave** in a derived class, be sure to call the base class's **OnLeave** method so that registered delegates receive the event.

Requirements

Platforms: Windows 98, Windows NT 4.0,
Windows Millennium Edition, Windows 2000,
Windows XP Home Edition, Windows XP Professional,
Windows Server 2003 family

DataGrid.OnMouseDown Method

Raises the **MouseDown** event.

```
[Visual Basic]
Overrides Protected Sub OnMouseDown( _
   ByVal e As MouseEventArgs _
)
[C#]
protected override void OnMouseDown(
   MouseEventArgs e
);
[C++]
protected: void OnMouseDown(
   MouseEventArgs* e
);
[JScript]
protected override function OnMouseDown(
   e : MouseEventArgs
);
```

Parameters

e

A **MouseEventArgs** that contains data about the **OnMouseDown** event.

Remarks

Raising an event invokes the event handler through a delegate.

Notes to Inheritors: When overriding **OnMouseDown** in a derived class, be sure to call the base class's **OnMouseDown** method.

Example

See related example in the **System.Windows.Forms.DataGrid** class topic.

Requirements

Platforms: Windows 98, Windows NT 4.0, Windows Millennium Edition, Windows 2000, Windows XP Home Edition, Windows XP Professional, Windows Server 2003 family, .NET Compact Framework - Windows CE .NET

DataGrid.OnMouseLeave Method

Creates the **MouseLeave** event.

```
[Visual Basic]
Overrides Protected Sub OnMouseLeave( _
   ByVal e As EventArgs _
)
[C#]
protected override void OnMouseLeave(
   EventArgs e
);
[C++]
protected: void OnMouseLeave(
   EventArgs* e
);
[JScript]
protected override function OnMouseLeave(
   e : EventArgs
);
```

Parameters

e

An **EventArgs** that contains data about the **OnMouseLeave** event.

Remarks

Raising an event invokes the event handler through a delegate.

Notes to Inheritors: When overriding **OnMouseLeave** in a derived class, be sure to call the base class's **OnMouseLeave** method.

Requirements

Platforms: Windows 98, Windows NT 4.0, Windows Millennium Edition, Windows 2000, Windows XP Home Edition, Windows XP Professional, Windows Server 2003 family

DataGrid.OnMouseMove Method

Raises the **MouseMove** event.

```
[Visual Basic]
Overrides Protected Sub OnMouseMove( _
   ByVal e As MouseEventArgs _
)
[C#]
protected override void OnMouseMove(
   MouseEventArgs e
);
[C++]
protected: void OnMouseMove(
   MouseEventArgs* e
);
[JScript]
protected override function OnMouseMove(
   e : MouseEventArgs
);
```

Parameters

e

A **MouseEventArgs** that contains data about the **OnMouseMove** event.

Remarks

Raising an event invokes the event handler through a delegate.

Notes to Inheritors: When overriding **OnMouseMove** in a derived class, be sure to call the base class's **OnMouseMove** method.

Requirements

Platforms: Windows 98, Windows NT 4.0, Windows Millennium Edition, Windows 2000, Windows XP Home Edition, Windows XP Professional, Windows Server 2003 family, .NET Compact Framework - Windows CE .NET

DataGrid.OnMouseUp Method

Raises the **MouseUp** event.

```
[Visual Basic]
Overrides Protected Sub OnMouseUp( _
   ByVal e As MouseEventArgs _
)
```

```
[C#]
protected override void OnMouseUp(
   MouseEventArgs e
);
[C++]
protected: void OnMouseUp(
   MouseEventArgs* e
);
[JScript]
protected override function OnMouseUp(
   e : MouseEventArgs
);
```

Parameters

e

A **MouseEventArgs** that contains data about the **OnMouseUp** event.

Remarks

Raising an event invokes the event handler through a delegate.

Notes to Inheritors: When overriding **OnMouseUp** in a derived class, be sure to call the base class's **OnMouseUp** method.

Requirements

Platforms: Windows 98, Windows NT 4.0, Windows Millennium Edition, Windows 2000, Windows XP Home Edition, Windows XP Professional, Windows Server 2003 family, .NET Compact Framework - Windows CE .NET

DataGrid.OnMouseWheel Method

Raises the **MouseWheel** event.

```
[Visual Basic]
Overrides Protected Sub OnMouseWheel( _
   ByVal e As MouseEventArgs _
)
[C#]
protected override void OnMouseWheel(
   MouseEventArgs e
);
[C++]
protected: void OnMouseWheel(
   MouseEventArgs* e
);
[JScript]
protected override function OnMouseWheel(
   e : MouseEventArgs
);
```

Parameters

e

A **MouseEventArgs** that contains data about the **OnMouseUp** event.

Remarks

Raising an event invokes the event handler through a delegate.

Notes to Inheritors: When overriding **OnMouseWheel** in a derived class, be sure to call the base class's **OnMouseWheel** method.

Requirements

Platforms: Windows 98, Windows NT 4.0, Windows Millennium Edition, Windows 2000, Windows XP Home Edition, Windows XP Professional, Windows Server 2003 family

DataGrid.OnNavigate Method

Raises the **Navigate** event.

```
[Visual Basic]
Protected Sub OnNavigate( _
   ByVal e As NavigateEventArgs _
)
[C#]
protected void OnNavigate(
   NavigateEventArgs e
);
[C++]
protected: void OnNavigate(
   NavigateEventArgs* e
);
[JScript]
protected function OnNavigate(
   e : NavigateEventArgs
);
```

Parameters

e

A **NavigateEventArgs** that contains the event data.

Requirements

Platforms: Windows 98, Windows NT 4.0, Windows Millennium Edition, Windows 2000, Windows XP Home Edition, Windows XP Professional, Windows Server 2003 family

DataGrid.OnPaint Method

Raises the **Paint** event.

```
[Visual Basic]
Overrides Protected Sub OnPaint( _
   ByVal pe As PaintEventArgs _
)
[C#]
protected override void OnPaint(
   PaintEventArgs pe
);
[C++]
protected: void OnPaint(
   PaintEventArgs* pe
);
[JScript]
protected override function OnPaint(
   pe : PaintEventArgs
);
```

Parameters

pe

A **PaintEventArgs** which contains data about the event.

Remarks

Raising an event invokes the event handler through a delegate.

Notes to Inheritors: When overriding **OnPaint** in a derived class, be sure to call the base class's **OnPaint** method.

Requirements

Platforms: Windows 98, Windows NT 4.0, Windows Millennium Edition, Windows 2000, Windows XP Home Edition, Windows XP Professional, Windows Server 2003 family, .NET Compact Framework - Windows CE .NET

DataGrid.OnPaintBackground Method

Overrides **Control.OnPaintBackground** to prevent painting the background of the **System.Windows.Forms.DataGrid** control.

```
[Visual Basic]
Overrides Protected Sub OnPaintBackground( _
   ByVal ebe As PaintEventArgs _
)
[C#]
protected override void OnPaintBackground(
   PaintEventArgs ebe
);
[C++]
protected: void OnPaintBackground(
   PaintEventArgs* ebe
);
[JScript]
protected override function OnPaintBackground(
   ebe : PaintEventArgs
);
```

Parameters

ebe

A **PaintEventArgs** that contains information about the control to paint.

Remarks

Because the **System.Windows.Forms.DataGrid** is a complex control, this override is implemented to have no action. Therefore, calling this method will have no effect.

Requirements

Platforms: Windows 98, Windows NT 4.0, Windows Millennium Edition, Windows 2000, Windows XP Home Edition, Windows XP Professional, Windows Server 2003 family, .NET Compact Framework - Windows CE .NET

DataGrid.OnParentRowsLabelStyleChanged Method

Raises the **ParentRowsLabelStyleChanged** event.

```
[Visual Basic]
Protected Overridable Sub OnParentRowsLabelStyleChanged( _
   ByVal e As EventArgs _
)
[C#]
protected virtual void OnParentRowsLabelStyleChanged(
   EventArgs e
);
[C++]
protected: virtual void OnParentRowsLabelStyleChanged(
   EventArgs* e
);
[JScript]
protected function OnParentRowsLabelStyleChanged(
   e : EventArgs
);
```

Parameters

e

An **EventArgs** that contains the event data.

Remarks

Raising an event invokes the event handler through a delegate.

The **OnParentRowsLabelStyleChanged** method also allows derived classes to handle the event without attaching a delegate. This is the preferred technique for handling the event in a derived class.

Notes to Inheritors: When overriding **OnParentRowsLabelStyleChanged** in a derived class, be sure to call the base class's **OnParentRowsLabelStyleChanged** method so that registered delegates receive the event.

Requirements

Platforms: Windows 98, Windows NT 4.0, Windows Millennium Edition, Windows 2000, Windows XP Home Edition, Windows XP Professional, Windows Server 2003 family

DataGrid.OnParentRowsVisibleChanged Method

Raises the **ParentRowsVisibleChanged** event.

```
[Visual Basic]
Protected Overridable Sub OnParentRowsVisibleChanged( _
   ByVal e As EventArgs _
)
[C#]
protected virtual void OnParentRowsVisibleChanged(
   EventArgs e
);
[C++]
protected: virtual void OnParentRowsVisibleChanged(
   EventArgs* e
);
[JScript]
protected function OnParentRowsVisibleChanged(
   e : EventArgs
);
```

Parameters

e

An **EventArgs** that contains the event data.

Requirements

Platforms: Windows 98, Windows NT 4.0, Windows Millennium Edition, Windows 2000, Windows XP Home Edition, Windows XP Professional, Windows Server 2003 family

DataGrid.OnReadOnlyChanged Method

Raises the **ReadOnlyChanged** event

```
[Visual Basic]
Protected Overridable Sub OnReadOnlyChanged( _
   ByVal e As EventArgs _
)
[C#]
protected virtual void OnReadOnlyChanged(
   EventArgs e
);
[C++]
protected: virtual void OnReadOnlyChanged(
   EventArgs* e
);
[JScript]
protected function OnReadOnlyChanged(
   e : EventArgs
);
```

Parameters

e

An **EventArgs** that contains the event data.

Remarks

Raising an event invokes the event handler through a delegate.

The **OnReadOnlyChanged** method also allows derived classes to handle the event without attaching a delegate. This is the preferred technique for handling the event in a derived class.

Notes to Inheritors: When overriding **OnReadOnlyChanged** in a derived class, be sure to call the base class's **OnReadOnlyChanged** method so that registered delegates receive the event.

Requirements

Platforms: Windows 98, Windows NT 4.0, Windows Millennium Edition, Windows 2000, Windows XP Home Edition, Windows XP Professional, Windows Server 2003 family

DataGrid.OnResize Method

Raises the **Resize** event.

```
[Visual Basic]
Overrides Protected Sub OnResize( _
   ByVal e As EventArgs _
)
[C#]
protected override void OnResize(
   EventArgs e
);
[C++]
protected: void OnResize(
   EventArgs* e
);
[JScript]
protected override function OnResize(
   e : EventArgs
);
```

Parameters

e

An **EventArgs** that contains the event data.

Remarks

Raising an event invokes the event handler through a delegate.

Notes to Inheritors: When overriding **OnResize** in a derived class, be sure to call the base class's **OnResize** method.

Requirements

Platforms: Windows 98, Windows NT 4.0, Windows Millennium Edition, Windows 2000, Windows XP Home Edition, Windows XP Professional, Windows Server 2003 family, .NET Compact Framework - Windows CE .NET

DataGrid.OnRowHeaderClick Method

Raises the **RowHeaderClick** event.

```
[Visual Basic]
Protected Sub OnRowHeaderClick( _
   ByVal e As EventArgs _
)
[C#]
protected void OnRowHeaderClick(
   EventArgs e
);
[C++]
protected: void OnRowHeaderClick(
   EventArgs* e
);
[JScript]
protected function OnRowHeaderClick(
   e : EventArgs
);
```

Parameters

e

An **EventArgs** that contains the event data.

Requirements

Platforms: Windows 98, Windows NT 4.0, Windows Millennium Edition, Windows 2000, Windows XP Home Edition, Windows XP Professional, Windows Server 2003 family

.NET Framework Security:

- **UIPermission** You must have the **UIPermission** for safe subwindows to set this property.

DataGrid.OnScroll Method

Raises the **Scroll** event.

```
[Visual Basic]
Protected Sub OnScroll( _
   ByVal e As EventArgs _
)
[C#]
protected void OnScroll(
   EventArgs e
);
[C++]
protected: void OnScroll(
   EventArgs* e
);
```

```
[JScript]
protected function OnScroll(
   e : EventArgs
);
```

Parameters

e

An **EventArgs** that contains the event data.

Requirements

Platforms: Windows 98, Windows NT 4.0, Windows Millennium Edition, Windows 2000, Windows XP Home Edition, Windows XP Professional, Windows Server 2003 family

DataGrid.OnShowParentDetailsButtonClicked Method

Raises the **ShowParentDetailsButtonClick** event.

```
[Visual Basic]
Protected Sub OnShowParentDetailsButtonClicked( _
   ByVal sender As Object, _
   ByVal e As EventArgs _
)
[C#]
protected void OnShowParentDetailsButtonClicked(
   object sender,
   EventArgs e
);
[C++]
protected: void OnShowParentDetailsButtonClicked(
   Object* sender,
   EventArgs* e
);
[JScript]
protected function OnShowParentDetailsButtonClicked(
   sender : Object,
   e : EventArgs
);
```

Parameters

sender

The source of the event.

e

An **EventArgs** that contains the event data.

Requirements

Platforms: Windows 98, Windows NT 4.0, Windows Millennium Edition, Windows 2000, Windows XP Home Edition, Windows XP Professional, Windows Server 2003 family

DataGrid.ProcessDialogKey Method

Gets or sets a value that indicates whether a key should be processed further.

```
[Visual Basic]
Overrides Protected Function ProcessDialogKey( _
   ByVal keyData As Keys _
) As Boolean
[C#]
protected override bool ProcessDialogKey(
   Keys keyData
);
[C++]
protected: bool ProcessDialogKey(
   Keys keyData
);
[JScript]
protected override function ProcessDialogKey(
   keyData : Keys
) : Boolean;
```

Parameters

keyData

A **Keys** that contains data about the pressed key.

Return Value

true, the key should be processed; otherwise, **false**.

Remarks

The method overrides the **ProcessDialogKey** method to implement keyboard navigation of the grid.

Requirements

Platforms: Windows 98, Windows NT 4.0, Windows Millennium Edition, Windows 2000, Windows XP Home Edition, Windows XP Professional, Windows Server 2003 family

DataGrid.ProcessGridKey Method

Processes keys for grid navigation.

```
[Visual Basic]
Protected Function ProcessGridKey( _
   ByVal ke As KeyEventArgs _
) As Boolean
[C#]
protected bool ProcessGridKey(
   KeyEventArgs ke
);
[C++]
protected: bool ProcessGridKey(
   KeyEventArgs* ke
);
[JScript]
protected function ProcessGridKey(
   ke : KeyEventArgs
) : Boolean;
```

Parameters

ke

A **KeyEventArgs** that contains data about the key up or key down event.

Return Value

true, if the key was processed; otherwise **false**.

Requirements

Platforms: Windows 98, Windows NT 4.0, Windows Millennium Edition, Windows 2000, Windows XP Home Edition, Windows XP Professional, Windows Server 2003 family

DataGrid.ProcessKeyPreview Method

Previews a keyboard message and returns a value indicating if the key was consumed.

```
[Visual Basic]
Overrides Protected Function ProcessKeyPreview( _
   ByRef m As Message _
) As Boolean
[C#]
protected override bool ProcessKeyPreview(
   ref Message m
);
[C++]
protected: bool ProcessKeyPreview(
   Message* m
);
[JScript]
protected override function ProcessKeyPreview(
   m : Message
) : Boolean;
```

Parameters

m
A **Message** that contains data about the event. The parameter is passed by reference.

Return Value

true, if the key was consumed; otherwise, **false**.

Remarks

This method is called by a child control when the child control receives a keyboard message. The child control calls this method before generating any keyboard events for the message. If this method returns **true**, the child control considers the message consumed and does not generate any keyboard events.

Requirements

Platforms: Windows 98, Windows NT 4.0, Windows Millennium Edition, Windows 2000, Windows XP Home Edition, Windows XP Professional, Windows Server 2003 family

DataGrid.ProcessTabKey Method

Gets a value indicating whether the Tab key should be processed.

```
[Visual Basic]
Protected Function ProcessTabKey( _
   ByVal keyData As Keys _
) As Boolean
[C#]
protected bool ProcessTabKey(
   Keys keyData
);
[C++]
protected: bool ProcessTabKey(
   Keys keyData
);
[JScript]
protected function ProcessTabKey(
   keyData : Keys
) : Boolean;
```

Parameters

keyData
A **Keys** that contains data about which the pressed key.

Return Value

true if the Tab key should be processed; otherwise, **false**.

Requirements

Platforms: Windows 98, Windows NT 4.0, Windows Millennium Edition, Windows 2000, Windows XP Home Edition, Windows XP Professional, Windows Server 2003 family

.NET Framework Security:

- **UIPermission** for drawing UI. Associated enumeration: **UIPermissionWindow.AllWindows**.

DataGrid.ResetAlternatingBackColor Method

Resets the **AlternatingBackColor** property to its default color.

```
[Visual Basic]
Public Sub ResetAlternatingBackColor()
[C#]
public void ResetAlternatingBackColor();
[C++]
public: void ResetAlternatingBackColor();
[JScript]
public function ResetAlternatingBackColor();
```

Remarks

You typically use this method if you are either creating a designer for the **System.Windows.Forms.DataGrid** or creating your own control incorporating the **System.Windows.Forms.DataGrid**. You can use the **ShouldSerializeAlternatingBackColor** method to determine whether the property value has changed from its default.

Example

See related example in the **System.Windows.Forms.DataGrid** class topic.

Requirements

Platforms: Windows 98, Windows NT 4.0, Windows Millennium Edition, Windows 2000, Windows XP Home Edition, Windows XP Professional, Windows Server 2003 family

DataGrid.ResetBackColor Method

Resets the **BackColor** property to its default value.

```
[Visual Basic]
Overrides Public Sub ResetBackColor()
[C#]
public override void ResetBackColor();
[C++]
public: void ResetBackColor();
[JScript]
public override function ResetBackColor();
```

Remarks

You typically use this method if you are either creating a designer for the **System.Windows.Forms.DataGrid** or creating your own control incorporating the **System.Windows.Forms.DataGrid**.

Example

See related example in the **System.Windows.Forms.DataGrid** class topic.

Requirements

Platforms: Windows 98, Windows NT 4.0, Windows Millennium Edition, Windows 2000, Windows XP Home Edition, Windows XP Professional, Windows Server 2003 family

DataGrid.ResetForeColor Method

Resets the **ForeColor** property to its default value.

```
[Visual Basic]
Overrides Public Sub ResetForeColor()
[C#]
public override void ResetForeColor();
[C++]
public: void ResetForeColor();
[JScript]
public override function ResetForeColor();
```

Remarks

You typically use this method if you are either creating a designer for the **System.Windows.Forms.DataGrid** or creating your own control incorporating the **System.Windows.Forms.DataGrid**.

Example

See related example in the **System.Windows.Forms.DataGrid** class topic.

Requirements

Platforms: Windows 98, Windows NT 4.0, Windows Millennium Edition, Windows 2000, Windows XP Home Edition, Windows XP Professional, Windows Server 2003 family

DataGrid.ResetGridLineColor Method

Resets the **GridLineColor** property to its default value.

```
[Visual Basic]
Public Sub ResetGridLineColor()
[C#]
public void ResetGridLineColor();
[C++]
public: void ResetGridLineColor();
[JScript]
public function ResetGridLineColor();
```

Remarks

You typically use this method if you are either creating a designer for the **System.Windows.Forms.DataGrid** or creating your own control incorporating the **System.Windows.Forms.DataGrid**. You can use the **ShouldSerializeGridLineColor** method to determine whether the property value has changed from its default.

Example

See related example in the **System.Windows.Forms.DataGrid** class topic.

Requirements

Platforms: Windows 98, Windows NT 4.0, Windows Millennium Edition, Windows 2000, Windows XP Home Edition, Windows XP Professional, Windows Server 2003 family

DataGrid.ResetHeaderBackColor Method

Resets the **HeaderBackColor** property to its default value.

```
[Visual Basic]
Public Sub ResetHeaderBackColor()
[C#]
public void ResetHeaderBackColor();
[C++]
public: void ResetHeaderBackColor();
[JScript]
public function ResetHeaderBackColor();
```

Remarks

You typically use this method if you are either creating a designer for the **System.Windows.Forms.DataGrid** or creating your own control incorporating the **System.Windows.Forms.DataGrid**. You can use the **ShouldSerializeHeaderBackColor** method to determine whether the property value has changed from its default.

Example

See related example in the **System.Windows.Forms.DataGrid** class topic.

Requirements

Platforms: Windows 98, Windows NT 4.0, Windows Millennium Edition, Windows 2000, Windows XP Home Edition, Windows XP Professional, Windows Server 2003 family

DataGrid.ResetHeaderFont Method

Resets the **HeaderFont** property to its default value.

```
[Visual Basic]
Public Sub ResetHeaderFont()
[C#]
public void ResetHeaderFont();
[C++]
public: void ResetHeaderFont();
[JScript]
public function ResetHeaderFont();
```

Remarks

You typically use this method if you are either creating a designer for the **System.Windows.Forms.DataGrid** or creating your own control incorporating the **System.Windows.Forms.DataGrid**. You can use the **ShouldSerializeHeaderFont** method to determine whether the property value has changed from its default.

Example

See related example in the **System.Windows.Forms.DataGrid** class topic.

Requirements

Platforms: Windows 98, Windows NT 4.0, Windows Millennium Edition, Windows 2000, Windows XP Home Edition, Windows XP Professional, Windows Server 2003 family

DataGrid.ResetHeaderForeColor Method

Resets the **HeaderForeColor** property to its default value.

```
[Visual Basic]
Public Sub ResetHeaderForeColor()
[C#]
public void ResetHeaderForeColor();
[C++]
public: void ResetHeaderForeColor();
[JScript]
public function ResetHeaderForeColor();
```

Remarks

You typically use this method if you are either creating a designer for the **System.Windows.Forms.DataGrid** or creating your own control incorporating the **System.Windows.Forms.DataGrid**. You can use the **ShouldSerializeHeaderForeColor** method to determine whether the property value has changed from its default.

Example

See related example in the **System.Windows.Forms.DataGrid** class topic.

Requirements

Platforms: Windows 98, Windows NT 4.0, Windows Millennium Edition, Windows 2000, Windows XP Home Edition, Windows XP Professional, Windows Server 2003 family

DataGrid.ResetLinkColor Method

Resets the **LinkColor** property to its default value.

```
[Visual Basic]
Public Sub ResetLinkColor()
[C#]
public void ResetLinkColor();
[C++]
public: void ResetLinkColor();
[JScript]
public function ResetLinkColor();
```

Remarks

You typically use this method if you are either creating a designer for the **System.Windows.Forms.DataGrid** or creating your own control incorporating the **System.Windows.Forms.DataGrid**.

Example

See related example in the **System.Windows.Forms.DataGrid** class topic.

Requirements

Platforms: Windows 98, Windows NT 4.0, Windows Millennium Edition, Windows 2000, Windows XP Home Edition, Windows XP Professional, Windows Server 2003 family

DataGrid.ResetLinkHoverColor Method

This member supports the .NET Framework infrastructure and is not intended to be used directly from your code.

```
[Visual Basic]
Public Sub ResetLinkHoverColor()
[C#]
public void ResetLinkHoverColor();
[C++]
public: void ResetLinkHoverColor();
[JScript]
public function ResetLinkHoverColor();
```

DataGrid.ResetSelection Method

Turns off selection for all rows that are selected.

```
[Visual Basic]
Protected Sub ResetSelection()
[C#]
protected void ResetSelection();
[C++]
protected: void ResetSelection();
[JScript]
protected function ResetSelection();
```

Requirements

Platforms: Windows 98, Windows NT 4.0, Windows Millennium Edition, Windows 2000, Windows XP Home Edition, Windows XP Professional, Windows Server 2003 family

DataGrid.ResetSelectionBackColor Method

Resets the **SelectionBackColor** property to its default value.

```
[Visual Basic]
Public Sub ResetSelectionBackColor()
[C#]
public void ResetSelectionBackColor();
[C++]
public: void ResetSelectionBackColor();
[JScript]
public function ResetSelectionBackColor();
```

Remarks

You typically use this method if you are either creating a designer for the **System.Windows.Forms.DataGrid** or creating your own control incorporating the **System.Windows.Forms.DataGrid**. You can use the **ShouldSerializeSelectionBackColor** method to determine whether the property value has changed from its default.

Example

See related example in the **System.Windows.Forms.DataGrid** class topic.

Requirements

Platforms: Windows 98, Windows NT 4.0, Windows Millennium Edition, Windows 2000, Windows XP Home Edition, Windows XP Professional, Windows Server 2003 family

DataGrid.ResetSelectionForeColor Method

Resets the **SelectionForeColor** property to its default value.

```
[Visual Basic]
Public Sub ResetSelectionForeColor()
[C#]
public void ResetSelectionForeColor();
[C++]
public: void ResetSelectionForeColor();
```

```
[JScript]
public function ResetSelectionForeColor();
```

Remarks

You typically use this method if you are either creating a designer for the **System.Windows.Forms.DataGrid** or creating your own control incorporating the **System.Windows.Forms.DataGrid**. You can use the **ShouldSerializeSelectionForeColor** method to determine whether the property value has changed from its default.

Example

See related example in the **System.Windows.Forms.DataGrid** class topic.

Requirements

Platforms: Windows 98, Windows NT 4.0, Windows Millennium Edition, Windows 2000, Windows XP Home Edition, Windows XP Professional, Windows Server 2003 family

DataGrid.Select Method

Selects a specified row.

Overload List

Selects a specified row.

Supported by the .NET Compact Framework.

[Visual Basic] **Overloads Public Sub Select(Integer)**

[C#] **public void Select(int);**

[C++] **public: void Select(int);**

[JScript] **public function Select(int);**

Inherited from **Control**.

[Visual Basic] **Overloads Public Sub Select()**

[C#] **public void Select();**

[C++] **public: void Select();**

[JScript] **public function Select();**

Inherited from **Control**.

[Visual Basic] **Overloads Protected Overridable Sub Select(Boolean, Boolean)**

[C#] **protected virtual void Select(bool, bool);**

[C++] **protected: virtual void Select(bool, bool);**

[JScript] **protected function Select(Boolean, Boolean);**

Example

See related example in the **System.Windows.Forms.DataGrid** class topic.

DataGrid.Select Method (Int32)

Selects a specified row.

```
[Visual Basic]
Overloads Public Sub Select( _
   ByVal row As Integer _
)
[C#]
public void Select(
   int row
);
[C++]
public: void Select(
   int row
);
[JScript]
public function Select(
   row : int
);
```

Parameters

row
The index of the row to select.

Example

See related example in the **System.Windows.Forms.DataGrid** class topic.

Requirements

Platforms: Windows 98, Windows NT 4.0, Windows Millennium Edition, Windows 2000, Windows XP Home Edition, Windows XP Professional, Windows Server 2003 family, .NET Compact Framework - Windows CE .NET

DataGrid.SetDataBinding Method

Sets the **DataSource** and **DataMember** properties at run time.

```
[Visual Basic]
Public Sub SetDataBinding( _
   ByVal dataSource As Object, _
   ByVal dataMember As String _
)
[C#]
public void SetDataBinding(
   object dataSource,
   string dataMember
);
[C++]
public: void SetDataBinding(
   Object* dataSource,
   String* dataMember
);
[JScript]
public function SetDataBinding(
   dataSource : Object,
   dataMember : String
);
```

Parameters

dataSource
The data source for the **System.Windows.Forms.DataGrid** control.

dataMember
The **DataMember** string that specifies the table to bind to within the object returned by the **DataSource** property.

Exceptions

Exception Type	Condition
ArgumentException	One or more of the arguments are invalid.
ArgumentNull-Exception	The *dataSource* argument is a null reference (**Nothing** in Visual Basic).

Remarks

You must use the **SetDataBinding** method at run time to reset the **DataSource** property.

See the **DataSource** property for more details about setting a valid data source.

You can create a grid that allows users to edit data but prevents them from adding new rows by using a **DataView** as the data source and setting the **AddNew** property to **false**. When the **DataSource** is a **DataView** or **DataTable**, set the **DataMember** to an empty string ("").

Example

See related example in the **System.Windows.Forms.DataGrid** class topic.

Requirements

Platforms: Windows 98, Windows NT 4.0, Windows Millennium Edition, Windows 2000, Windows XP Home Edition, Windows XP Professional, Windows Server 2003 family

DataGrid.ShouldSerializeAlternatingBackColor Method

Indicates whether the **AlternatingBackColor** property should be persisted.

```
[Visual Basic]
Protected Overridable Function _
   ShouldSerializeAlternatingBackColor() _
   As Boolean
[C#]
protected virtual bool ShouldSerializeAlternatingBackColor();
[C++]
protected: virtual bool ShouldSerializeAlternatingBackColor();
[JScript]
protected function ShouldSerializeAlternatingBackColor() : Boolean;
```

Return Value

true if the property value has changed from its default; otherwise, **false**.

Remarks

You typically use this method if you are either creating a designer for the **System.Windows.Forms.DataGrid** or creating your own control incorporating the **System.Windows.Forms.DataGrid**.

Requirements

Platforms: Windows 98, Windows NT 4.0, Windows Millennium Edition, Windows 2000, Windows XP Home Edition, Windows XP Professional, Windows Server 2003 family

DataGrid.ShouldSerializeBackgroundColor Method

Indicates whether the **BackgroundColor** property should be persisted.

```
[Visual Basic]
Protected Overridable Function ShouldSerializeBackgroundColor() As _
   _
   Boolean
[C#]
protected virtual bool ShouldSerializeBackgroundColor();
[C++]
protected: virtual bool ShouldSerializeBackgroundColor();
[JScript]
protected function ShouldSerializeBackgroundColor() : Boolean;
```

Return Value

true if the property value has changed from its default; otherwise, **false**.

Remarks

You typically use this method if you are either creating a designer for the **System.Windows.Forms.DataGrid** or creating your own control incorporating the **System.Windows.Forms.DataGrid**.

Requirements

Platforms: Windows 98, Windows NT 4.0, Windows Millennium Edition, Windows 2000, Windows XP Home Edition, Windows XP Professional, Windows Server 2003 family

DataGrid.ShouldSerializeCaptionBackColor Method

Gets a value indicating whether the **CaptionBackColor** property should be persisted.

```
[Visual Basic]
Protected Overridable Function ShouldSerializeCaptionBackColor() As _
   _
   Boolean
[C#]
protected virtual bool ShouldSerializeCaptionBackColor();
[C++]
protected: virtual bool ShouldSerializeCaptionBackColor();
[JScript]
protected function ShouldSerializeCaptionBackColor() : Boolean;
```

Return Value

true if the property value has been changed from its default; otherwise, **false**.

Remarks

You typically use this method only if you are either creating a designer for the **System.Windows.Forms.DataGrid**, or creating your own control incorporating the **System.Windows.Forms.DataGrid**.

Requirements

Platforms: Windows 98, Windows NT 4.0, Windows Millennium Edition, Windows 2000, Windows XP Home Edition, Windows XP Professional, Windows Server 2003 family

DataGrid.ShouldSerializeCaptionForeColor Method

Gets a value indicating whether the **CaptionForeColor** property should be persisted.

```
[Visual Basic]
Protected Overridable Function ShouldSerializeCaptionForeColor() As _
   _
   Boolean
```

[C#]
```
protected virtual bool ShouldSerializeCaptionForeColor();
```
[C++]
```
protected: virtual bool ShouldSerializeCaptionForeColor();
```
[JScript]
```
protected function ShouldSerializeCaptionForeColor() : Boolean;
```

Return Value

true if the property value has been changed from its default; otherwise, **false**.

Remarks

You typically use this method only if you are either creating a designer for the **System.Windows.Forms.DataGrid**, or creating your own control incorporating the **System.Windows.Forms.DataGrid**.

Requirements

Platforms: Windows 98, Windows NT 4.0, Windows Millennium Edition, Windows 2000, Windows XP Home Edition, Windows XP Professional, Windows Server 2003 family

DataGrid.ShouldSerializeGridLineColor Method

Indicates whether the **GridLineColor** property should be persisted.

[Visual Basic]
```
Protected Overridable Function ShouldSerializeGridLineColor() As _
   Boolean
```
[C#]
```
protected virtual bool ShouldSerializeGridLineColor();
```
[C++]
```
protected: virtual bool ShouldSerializeGridLineColor();
```
[JScript]
```
protected function ShouldSerializeGridLineColor() : Boolean;
```

Return Value

true if the property value has changed from its default; otherwise, **false**.

Remarks

You typically use this method if you are either creating a designer for the **System.Windows.Forms.DataGrid** or creating your own control incorporating the **System.Windows.Forms.DataGrid**.

Requirements

Platforms: Windows 98, Windows NT 4.0, Windows Millennium Edition, Windows 2000, Windows XP Home Edition, Windows XP Professional, Windows Server 2003 family

DataGrid.ShouldSerializeHeaderBackColor Method

Indicates whether the **HeaderBackColor** property should be persisted.

[Visual Basic]
```
Protected Overridable Function ShouldSerializeHeaderBackColor() As _
_
   Boolean
```
[C#]
```
protected virtual bool ShouldSerializeHeaderBackColor();
```
[C++]
```
protected: virtual bool ShouldSerializeHeaderBackColor();
```
[JScript]
```
protected function ShouldSerializeHeaderBackColor() : Boolean;
```

Return Value

true if the property value has changed from its default; otherwise, **false**.

Remarks

You typically use this method if you are either creating a designer for the **System.Windows.Forms.DataGrid** or creating your own control incorporating the **System.Windows.Forms.DataGrid**.

Requirements

Platforms: Windows 98, Windows NT 4.0, Windows Millennium Edition, Windows 2000, Windows XP Home Edition, Windows XP Professional, Windows Server 2003 family

DataGrid.ShouldSerializeHeaderFont Method

Indicates whether the **HeaderFont** property should be persisted.

[Visual Basic]
```
Protected Function ShouldSerializeHeaderFont() As Boolean
```
[C#]
```
protected bool ShouldSerializeHeaderFont();
```
[C++]
```
protected: bool ShouldSerializeHeaderFont();
```
[JScript]
```
protected function ShouldSerializeHeaderFont() : Boolean;
```

Return Value

true if the property value has changed from its default; otherwise, **false**.

Remarks

You typically use this method if you are either creating a designer for the **System.Windows.Forms.DataGrid** or creating your own control incorporating the **System.Windows.Forms.DataGrid**.

Requirements

Platforms: Windows 98, Windows NT 4.0, Windows Millennium Edition, Windows 2000, Windows XP Home Edition, Windows XP Professional, Windows Server 2003 family

DataGrid.ShouldSerializeHeaderForeColor Method

Indicates whether the **HeaderForeColor** property should be persisted.

[Visual Basic]
```
Protected Overridable Function ShouldSerializeHeaderForeColor() As _
_
   Boolean
```
[C#]
```
protected virtual bool ShouldSerializeHeaderForeColor();
```
[C++]
```
protected: virtual bool ShouldSerializeHeaderForeColor();
```
[JScript]
```
protected function ShouldSerializeHeaderForeColor() : Boolean;
```

Return Value

true if the property value has changed from its default; otherwise, **false**.

Remarks

You typically use this method if you are either creating a designer for the **System.Windows.Forms.DataGrid** or creating your own control incorporating the **System.Windows.Forms.DataGrid**.

Requirements

Platforms: Windows 98, Windows NT 4.0,
Windows Millennium Edition, Windows 2000,
Windows XP Home Edition, Windows XP Professional,
Windows Server 2003 family

DataGrid.ShouldSerializeLinkHoverColor Method

Indicates whether the **LinkHoverColor** property should be persisted.

[Visual Basic]
```
Protected Overridable Function ShouldSerializeLinkHoverColor() As _
   Boolean
```
[C#]
```
protected virtual bool ShouldSerializeLinkHoverColor();
```
[C++]
```
protected: virtual bool ShouldSerializeLinkHoverColor();
```
[JScript]
```
protected function ShouldSerializeLinkHoverColor() : Boolean;
```

Return Value

true if the property value has changed from its default; otherwise, **false**.

Remarks

You typically use this method if you are either creating a designer for the **System.Windows.Forms.DataGrid** or creating your own control incorporating the **System.Windows.Forms.DataGrid**.

Requirements

Platforms: Windows 98, Windows NT 4.0,
Windows Millennium Edition, Windows 2000,
Windows XP Home Edition, Windows XP Professional,
Windows Server 2003 family

DataGrid.ShouldSerializeParentRowsBackColor Method

Indicates whether the **ParentRowsBackColor** property should be persisted.

[Visual Basic]
```
Protected Overridable Function ShouldSerializeParentRowsBackColor() _
   _
   As Boolean
```
[C#]
```
protected virtual bool ShouldSerializeParentRowsBackColor();
```
[C++]
```
protected: virtual bool ShouldSerializeParentRowsBackColor();
```
[JScript]
```
protected function ShouldSerializeParentRowsBackColor() : Boolean;
```

Return Value

true if the property value has been changed from its default; otherwise, **false**.

Remarks

You typically use this method only if you are either creating a designer for the **System.Windows.Forms.DataGrid**, or creating your own control incorporating the **System.Windows.Forms.DataGrid**.

Requirements

Platforms: Windows 98, Windows NT 4.0,
Windows Millennium Edition, Windows 2000,
Windows XP Home Edition, Windows XP Professional,
Windows Server 2003 family

DataGrid.ShouldSerializeParentRowsForeColor Method

Indicates whether the **ParentRowsForeColor** property should be persisted.

[Visual Basic]
```
Protected Overridable Function ShouldSerializeParentRowsForeColor() _
   _
   As Boolean
```
[C#]
```
protected virtual bool ShouldSerializeParentRowsForeColor();
```
[C++]
```
protected: virtual bool ShouldSerializeParentRowsForeColor();
```
[JScript]
```
protected function ShouldSerializeParentRowsForeColor() : Boolean;
```

Return Value

true if the property value has been changed from its default; otherwise, **false**.

Remarks

You typically use this method only if you are either creating a designer for the **System.Windows.Forms.DataGrid**, or creating your own control incorporating the **System.Windows.Forms.DataGrid**.

Requirements

Platforms: Windows 98, Windows NT 4.0,
Windows Millennium Edition, Windows 2000,
Windows XP Home Edition, Windows XP Professional,
Windows Server 2003 family

DataGrid.ShouldSerializePreferredRowHeight Method

Indicates whether the **PreferredRowHeight** property should be persisted.

[Visual Basic]
```
Protected Function ShouldSerializePreferredRowHeight() As Boolean
```
[C#]
```
protected bool ShouldSerializePreferredRowHeight();
```
[C++]
```
protected: bool ShouldSerializePreferredRowHeight();
```
[JScript]
```
protected function ShouldSerializePreferredRowHeight() : Boolean;
```

Return Value

true if the property value has changed from its default; otherwise, **false**.

Remarks

You typically use this method if you are either creating a designer for the **System.Windows.Forms.DataGrid** or creating your own control incorporating the **System.Windows.Forms.DataGrid**.

Requirements

Platforms: Windows 98, Windows NT 4.0, Windows Millennium Edition, Windows 2000, Windows XP Home Edition, Windows XP Professional, Windows Server 2003 family

DataGrid.ShouldSerializeSelectionBackColor Method

Indicates whether the **SelectionBackColor** property should be persisted.

```
[Visual Basic]
Protected Function ShouldSerializeSelectionBackColor() As Boolean
[C#]
protected bool ShouldSerializeSelectionBackColor();
[C++]
protected: bool ShouldSerializeSelectionBackColor();
[JScript]
protected function ShouldSerializeSelectionBackColor() : Boolean;
```

Return Value

true if the property value has changed from its default; otherwise, **false**.

Remarks

You typically use this method if you are either creating a designer for the **System.Windows.Forms.DataGrid** or creating your own control incorporating the **System.Windows.Forms.DataGrid**.

Requirements

Platforms: Windows 98, Windows NT 4.0, Windows Millennium Edition, Windows 2000, Windows XP Home Edition, Windows XP Professional, Windows Server 2003 family

DataGrid.ShouldSerializeSelectionForeColor Method

Indicates whether the **SelectionForeColor** property should be persisted.

```
[Visual Basic]
Protected Overridable Function ShouldSerializeSelectionForeColor() _
_
   As Boolean
[C#]
protected virtual bool ShouldSerializeSelectionForeColor();
[C++]
protected: virtual bool ShouldSerializeSelectionForeColor();
[JScript]
protected function ShouldSerializeSelectionForeColor() : Boolean;
```

Return Value

true if the property value has changed from its default; otherwise, **false**.

Remarks

You typically use this method if you are either creating a designer for the **System.Windows.Forms.DataGrid** or creating your own control incorporating the **System.Windows.Forms.DataGrid**.

Requirements

Platforms: Windows 98, Windows NT 4.0, Windows Millennium Edition, Windows 2000, Windows XP Home Edition, Windows XP Professional, Windows Server 2003 family

DataGrid.SubObjectsSiteChange Method

This member supports the .NET Framework infrastructure and is not intended to be used directly from your code.

```
[Visual Basic]
Public Sub SubObjectsSiteChange( _
   ByVal site As Boolean _
)
[C#]
public void SubObjectsSiteChange(
   bool site
);
[C++]
public: void SubObjectsSiteChange(
   bool site
);
[JScript]
public function SubObjectsSiteChange(
   site : Boolean
);
```

DataGrid.UnSelect Method

Unselects a specified row.

```
[Visual Basic]
Public Sub UnSelect( _
   ByVal row As Integer _
)
[C#]
public void UnSelect(
   int row
);
[C++]
public: void UnSelect(
   int row
);
[JScript]
public function UnSelect(
   row : int
);
```

Parameters

row
: The index of the row to deselect.

Example

See related example in the **System.Windows.Forms.DataGrid** class topic.

Requirements

Platforms: Windows 98, Windows NT 4.0, Windows Millennium Edition, Windows 2000, Windows XP Home Edition, Windows XP Professional, Windows Server 2003 family, .NET Compact Framework - Windows CE .NET

DataGrid.AllowNavigationChanged Event

Occurs when the **AllowNavigation** property has changed.

[Visual Basic]
```
Public Event AllowNavigationChanged As EventHandler
```
[C#]
```
public event EventHandler AllowNavigationChanged;
```
[C++]
```
public: __event EventHandler* AllowNavigationChanged;
```

[JScript] In JScript, you can handle the events defined by a class, but you cannot define your own.

Event Data

The event handler receives an argument of type **EventArgs**.

Remarks

If the **AllowNavigation** property is set to **false**, then no links to child tables are shown.For more information about handling events, see **Consuming Events**.

Example

See related example in the **System.Windows.Forms.DataGrid** class topic.

Requirements

Platforms: Windows 98, Windows NT 4.0, Windows Millennium Edition, Windows 2000, Windows XP Home Edition, Windows XP Professional, Windows Server 2003 family

DataGrid.BackButtonClick Event

Occurs when the **Back** button on a child table is clicked.

[Visual Basic]
```
Public Event BackButtonClick As EventHandler
```
[C#]
```
public event EventHandler BackButtonClick;
```
[C++]
```
public: __event EventHandler* BackButtonClick;
```

[JScript] In JScript, you can handle the events defined by a class, but you cannot define your own.

Event Data

The event handler receives an argument of type **EventArgs**.

Remarks

The **Back** button becomes visible when a child table is displayed. Clicking the button will cause the grid to display the parent table.

Example

See related example in the **System.Windows.Forms.DataGrid** class topic.

Requirements

Platforms: Windows 98, Windows NT 4.0, Windows Millennium Edition, Windows 2000, Windows XP Home Edition, Windows XP Professional, Windows Server 2003 family

DataGrid.BackgroundColorChanged Event

Occurs when the **BackgroundColor** has changed.

[Visual Basic]
```
Public Event BackgroundColorChanged As EventHandler
```
[C#]
```
public event EventHandler BackgroundColorChanged;
```
[C++]
```
public: __event EventHandler* BackgroundColorChanged;
```

[JScript] In JScript, you can handle the events defined by a class, but you cannot define your own.

Event Data

The event handler receives an argument of type **EventArgs**.

Remarks

For more information about handling events, see **Consuming Events**.

Example

See related example in the **System.Windows.Forms.DataGrid** class topic.

Requirements

Platforms: Windows 98, Windows NT 4.0, Windows Millennium Edition, Windows 2000, Windows XP Home Edition, Windows XP Professional, Windows Server 2003 family

DataGrid.BackgroundImageChanged Event

This member supports the .NET Framework infrastructure and is not intended to be used directly from your code.

[Visual Basic]
```
Public Shadows Event BackgroundImageChanged As EventHandler
```
[C#]
```
public new event EventHandler BackgroundImageChanged;
```
[C++]
```
public: __event EventHandler* BackgroundImageChanged;
```

[JScript] In JScript, you can handle the events defined by a class, but you cannot define your own.

DataGrid.BorderStyleChanged Event

Occurs when the **BorderStyle** has changed.

[Visual Basic]
```
Public Event BorderStyleChanged As EventHandler
```
[C#]
```
public event EventHandler BorderStyleChanged;
```
[C++]
```
public: __event EventHandler* BorderStyleChanged;
```

[JScript] In JScript, you can handle the events defined by a class, but you cannot define your own.

Event Data

The event handler receives an argument of type **EventArgs**.

Remarks

Possible values include **None**, **FixedSingle**, and **Fixed3D**.

Requirements

Platforms: Windows 98, Windows NT 4.0, Windows Millennium Edition, Windows 2000, Windows XP Home Edition, Windows XP Professional, Windows Server 2003 family

DataGrid.CaptionVisibleChanged Event

Occurs when the **CaptionVisible** property has changed.

```
[Visual Basic]
Public Event CaptionVisibleChanged As EventHandler
[C#]
public event EventHandler CaptionVisibleChanged;
[C++]
public: __event EventHandler* CaptionVisibleChanged;
```

[JScript] In JScript, you can handle the events defined by a class, but you cannot define your own.

Event Data

The event handler receives an argument of type **EventArgs**.

Remarks

For more information about handling events, see **Consuming Events**.

Example

See related example in the **System.Windows.Forms.DataGrid** class topic.

Requirements

Platforms: Windows 98, Windows NT 4.0, Windows Millennium Edition, Windows 2000, Windows XP Home Edition, Windows XP Professional, Windows Server 2003 family

DataGrid.CurrentCellChanged Event

Occurs when the **CurrentCell** property has changed.

```
[Visual Basic]
Public Event CurrentCellChanged As EventHandler
[C#]
public event EventHandler CurrentCellChanged;
[C++]
public: __event EventHandler* CurrentCellChanged;
```

[JScript] In JScript, you can handle the events defined by a class, but you cannot define your own.

Event Data

The event handler receives an argument of type **EventArgs**.

Remarks

To determine the current cell, use the **CurrentCell** property.

Example

Requirements

Platforms: Windows 98, Windows NT 4.0, Windows Millennium Edition, Windows 2000, Windows XP Home Edition, Windows XP Professional, Windows Server 2003 family

DataGrid.CursorChanged Event

This member supports the .NET Framework infrastructure and is not intended to be used directly from your code.

```
[Visual Basic]
Public Shadows Event CursorChanged As EventHandler
[C#]
public new event EventHandler CursorChanged;
[C++]
public: __event EventHandler* CursorChanged;
```

[JScript] In JScript, you can handle the events defined by a class, but you cannot define your own.

DataGrid.DataSourceChanged Event

Occurs when the **DataSource** property value has changed.

```
[Visual Basic]
Public Event DataSourceChanged As EventHandler
[C#]
public event EventHandler DataSourceChanged;
[C++]
public: __event EventHandler* DataSourceChanged;
```

[JScript] In JScript, you can handle the events defined by a class, but you cannot define your own.

Event Data

The event handler receives an argument of type **EventArgs**.

Remarks

The **DataSourceChanged** event occurs when the **DataMember** value changes, or when the **BindingContext** of the **DataGrid** changes.

Example

See related example in the **System.Windows.Forms.DataGrid** class topic.

Requirements

Platforms: Windows 98, Windows NT 4.0, Windows Millennium Edition, Windows 2000, Windows XP Home Edition, Windows XP Professional, Windows Server 2003 family

DataGrid.FlatModeChanged Event

Occurs when the **FlatMode** has changed.

```
[Visual Basic]
Public Event FlatModeChanged As EventHandler
[C#]
public event EventHandler FlatModeChanged;
[C++]
public: __event EventHandler* FlatModeChanged;
```

[JScript] In JScript, you can handle the events defined by a class, but you cannot define your own.

Event Data

The event handler receives an argument of type **EventArgs**.

Example

See related example in the **System.Windows.Forms.DataGrid** class topic.

Requirements

Platforms: Windows 98, Windows NT 4.0, Windows Millennium Edition, Windows 2000, Windows XP Home Edition, Windows XP Professional, Windows Server 2003 family

DataGrid.Navigate Event

Occurs when the user navigates to a new table.

[Visual Basic]
```
Public Event Navigate As NavigateEventHandler
```
[C#]
```
public event NavigateEventHandler Navigate;
```
[C++]
```
public: __event NavigateEventHandler* Navigate;
```

[JScript] In JScript, you can handle the events defined by a class, but you cannot define your own.

Event Data

The event handler receives an argument of type **NavigateEventArgs** containing data related to this event. The following **NavigateEventArgs** property provides information specific to this event.

Property	Description
Forward	Gets a value indicating whether to navigate in a forward direction.

Remarks

Use the **Navigate** event to reset individual column properties, such as Width, as appropriate to the table.

For more information about handling events, see **Consuming Events**.

Example

See related example in the **System.Windows.Forms.DataGrid** class topic.

Requirements

Platforms: Windows 98, Windows NT 4.0, Windows Millennium Edition, Windows 2000, Windows XP Home Edition, Windows XP Professional, Windows Server 2003 family

DataGrid.ParentRowsLabelStyleChanged Event

Occurs when the label style of the parent row is changed.

[Visual Basic]
```
Public Event ParentRowsLabelStyleChanged As EventHandler
```
[C#]
```
public event EventHandler ParentRowsLabelStyleChanged;
```
[C++]
```
public: __event EventHandler* ParentRowsLabelStyleChanged;
```

[JScript] In JScript, you can handle the events defined by a class, but you cannot define your own.

Event Data

The event handler receives an argument of type **EventArgs**.

Example

See related example in the **System.Windows.Forms.DataGrid** class topic.

Requirements

Platforms: Windows 98, Windows NT 4.0, Windows Millennium Edition, Windows 2000, Windows XP Home Edition, Windows XP Professional, Windows Server 2003 family

DataGrid.ParentRowsVisibleChanged Event

Occurs when the **ParentRowsVisible** property value changes.

[Visual Basic]
```
Public Event ParentRowsVisibleChanged As EventHandler
```
[C#]
```
public event EventHandler ParentRowsVisibleChanged;
```
[C++]
```
public: __event EventHandler* ParentRowsVisibleChanged;
```

[JScript] In JScript, you can handle the events defined by a class, but you cannot define your own.

Event Data

The event handler receives an argument of type **EventArgs**.

Requirements

Platforms: Windows 98, Windows NT 4.0, Windows Millennium Edition, Windows 2000, Windows XP Home Edition, Windows XP Professional, Windows Server 2003 family

DataGrid.ReadOnlyChanged Event

Occurs when the **ReadOnly** property value changes.

[Visual Basic]
```
Public Event ReadOnlyChanged As EventHandler
```
[C#]
```
public event EventHandler ReadOnlyChanged;
```
[C++]
```
public: __event EventHandler* ReadOnlyChanged;
```

[JScript] In JScript, you can handle the events defined by a class, but you cannot define your own.

Event Data

The event handler receives an argument of type **EventArgs**.

Example

See related example in the **System.Windows.Forms.DataGrid** class topic.

Requirements

Platforms: Windows 98, Windows NT 4.0, Windows Millennium Edition, Windows 2000, Windows XP Home Edition, Windows XP Professional, Windows Server 2003 family

DataGrid.RowHeaderClick Event

Occurs when a row header is clicked.

[Visual Basic]
```
Protected Event RowHeaderClick As EventHandler
```
[C#]
```
protected event EventHandler RowHeaderClick;
```
[C++]
```
protected: __event EventHandler* RowHeaderClick;
```

[JScript] In JScript, you can handle the events defined by a class, but you cannot define your own.

Event Data

The event handler receives an argument of type **EventArgs**.

Requirements

Platforms: Windows 98, Windows NT 4.0,
Windows Millennium Edition, Windows 2000,
Windows XP Home Edition, Windows XP Professional,
Windows Server 2003 family

DataGrid.Scroll Event

Occurs when the user scrolls the **System.Windows.Forms.DataGrid** control.

[Visual Basic]
```
Public Event Scroll As EventHandler
```
[C#]
```
public event EventHandler Scroll;
```
[C++]
```
public: __event EventHandler* Scroll;
```

[JScript] In JScript, you can handle the events defined by a class, but you cannot define your own.

Event Data

The event handler receives an argument of type **EventArgs**.

Example

See related example in the **System.Windows.Forms.DataGrid** class topic.

Requirements

Platforms: Windows 98, Windows NT 4.0,
Windows Millennium Edition, Windows 2000,
Windows XP Home Edition, Windows XP Professional,
Windows Server 2003 family

DataGrid.ShowParentDetailsButtonClick Event

Occurs when the ShowParentDetails button is clicked.

[Visual Basic]
```
Public Event ShowParentDetailsButtonClick As EventHandler
```
[C#]
```
public event EventHandler ShowParentDetailsButtonClick;
```
[C++]
```
public: __event EventHandler* ShowParentDetailsButtonClick;
```

[JScript] In JScript, you can handle the events defined by a class, but you cannot define your own.

Event Data

The event handler receives an argument of type **EventArgs**.

Example

See related example in the **System.Windows.Forms.DataGrid** class topic.

Requirements

Platforms: Windows 98, Windows NT 4.0,
Windows Millennium Edition, Windows 2000,
Windows XP Home Edition, Windows XP Professional,
Windows Server 2003 family

DataGrid.TextChanged Event

This member supports the .NET Framework infrastructure and is not intended to be used directly from your code.

[Visual Basic]
```
Public Shadows Event TextChanged As EventHandler
```
[C#]
```
public new event EventHandler TextChanged;
```
[C++]
```
public: __event EventHandler* TextChanged;
```

[JScript] In JScript, you can handle the events defined by a class, but you cannot define your own.

DataGridBoolColumn Class

Specifies a column in which each cell contains a check box for representing a Boolean value.

System.Object
  System.MarshalByRefObject
    System.ComponentModel.Component
      System.Windows.Forms.DataGridColumnStyle
        System.Windows.Forms.DataGridBoolColumn

[Visual Basic]
```
Public Class DataGridBoolColumn
   Inherits DataGridColumnStyle
```
[C#]
```
public class DataGridBoolColumn : DataGridColumnStyle
```
[C++]
```
public __gc class DataGridBoolColumn : public DataGridColumnStyle
```
[JScript]
```
public class DataGridBoolColumn extends DataGridColumnStyle
```

Thread Safety

Any public static (**Shared** in Visual Basic) members of this type are safe for multithreaded operations. Any instance members are not guaranteed to be thread safe.

Remarks

The **DataGridBoolColumn** derives from the abstract (**MustInherit** in Visual Basic) class **DataGridColumnStyle**. At run time, the **DataGridBoolColumn** contains check boxes in each cell that have three states: checked (**true**), unchecked (**false**), and **DBNull.Value**.

Properties added to the class include **FalseValue**, **NullValue**, and **TrueValue**. These properties specify the value underlying each of the column's states.

Example

[Visual Basic, C#, C++] The following example first creates a new **DataGridBoolColumn** object and adds it to the **GridColumnStylesCollection** of a **DataGridTableStyle** object.

[Visual Basic]
```
Imports System
Imports System.Data
Imports System.Windows.Forms
Imports System.Drawing
Imports System.ComponentModel

Public Class MyForm
    Inherits System.Windows.Forms.Form
    Private components As System.ComponentModel.Container
    Private myTable As DataTable
    Private myGrid As DataGrid = New DataGrid()

    Public Shared Sub Main()
        Application.Run(New MyForm())
    End Sub

    Public Sub New()
        Try
            InitializeComponent()
            myTable = New DataTable("NamesTable")
            myTable.Columns.Add(New DataColumn("Name"))
            Dim column As DataColumn = New DataColumn _
            ("id", GetType(System.Int32))
            myTable.Columns.Add(column)
            myTable.Columns.Add(New DataColumn _
            ("calculatedField", GetType(Boolean)))
            Dim namesDataSet As DataSet = New DataSet("myDataSet")
            namesDataSet.Tables.Add(myTable)
            myGrid.SetDataBinding(namesDataSet, "NamesTable")
            AddData()
            AddTableStyle()

        Catch exc As System.Exception
            Console.WriteLine(exc.ToString)
        End Try
    End Sub

    Private Sub AddTableStyle()
        ' Map a new  TableStyle to the DataTable. Then
        ' add DataGridColumnStyle objects to the collection
        ' of column styles with appropriate mappings.
        Dim dgt As DataGridTableStyle = New DataGridTableStyle()
        dgt.MappingName = "NamesTable"

        Dim dgtbc As DataGridTextBoxColumn = _
        New DataGridTextBoxColumn()
        dgtbc.MappingName = "Name"
        dgtbc.HeaderText = "Name"
        dgt.GridColumnStyles.Add(dgtbc)

        dgtbc = New DataGridTextBoxColumn()
        dgtbc.MappingName = "id"
        dgtbc.HeaderText = "id"
        dgt.GridColumnStyles.Add(dgtbc)

        Dim db As DataGridBoolColumnInherit = _
        New DataGridBoolColumnInherit()
        db.HeaderText = "less than 1000 = blue"
        db.Width = 150
        db.MappingName = "calculatedField"
        dgt.GridColumnStyles.Add(db)

        myGrid.TableStyles.Add(dgt)

        ' This expression instructs the grid to change
        ' the color of the inherited DataGridBoolColumn
        ' according to the value of the id field. If it's
        ' less than 1000, the row is blue. Otherwise,
        ' the color is yellow.
        db.Expression = "id < 1000"
    End Sub

    Private Sub AddData()

        ' Add data with varying numbers for the id field.
        ' If the number is over 1000, the cell will paint
        ' yellow. Otherwise, it will be blue.
        Dim dRow As DataRow

        dRow = myTable.NewRow()
        dRow("Name") = "name 1"
        dRow("id") = 999
        myTable.Rows.Add(dRow)

        dRow = myTable.NewRow()
        dRow("Name") = "name 2"
        dRow("id") = 2300
        myTable.Rows.Add(dRow)

        dRow = myTable.NewRow()
        dRow("Name") = "name 3"
        dRow("id") = 120
        myTable.Rows.Add(dRow)

        dRow = myTable.NewRow()
        dRow("Name") = "name 4"
        dRow("id") = 4023
        myTable.Rows.Add(dRow)

        dRow = myTable.NewRow()
        dRow("Name") = "name 5"
        dRow("id") = 2345
        myTable.Rows.Add(dRow)
```

```
        myTable.AcceptChanges()
    End Sub

    Private Sub InitializeComponent()
        Me.Size = New Size(500, 500)
        myGrid.Size = New Size(350, 250)
        myGrid.TabStop = True
        myGrid.TabIndex = 1
        Me.StartPosition = FormStartPosition.CenterScreen
        Me.Controls.Add(myGrid)
    End Sub

End Class

Public Class DataGridBoolColumnInherit
    Inherits DataGridBoolColumn

    Private trueBrush As SolidBrush = Brushes.Blue
    Private falseBrush As SolidBrush = Brushes.Yellow
    Private expressionColumn As DataColumn = Nothing
    Shared count As Int32 = 0

    Public Property FalseColor() As Color
        Get
            Return falseBrush.Color
        End Get

        Set(ByVal Value As Color)

            falseBrush = New SolidBrush(Value)
            Invalidate()
        End Set
    End Property

    Public Property TrueColor() As Color
        Get
            Return trueBrush.Color
        End Get

        Set(ByVal Value As Color)

            trueBrush = New SolidBrush(Value)
            Invalidate()
        End Set
    End Property

    Public Sub New()
        count += 1
    End Sub

    ' This will work only with a DataSet or DataTable.
    ' The code is not compatible with IBindingList implementations.
    Public Property Expression() As String
        Get
            If Me.expressionColumn Is Nothing Then
                Return String.Empty
            Else
                Return Me.expressionColumn.Expression
            End If
        End Get
        Set(ByVal Value As String)
            If expressionColumn Is Nothing Then
                AddExpressionColumn(Value)
            Else
                expressionColumn.Expression = Value
            End If
            If Not (expressionColumn Is Nothing) And expressionColumn.Expression.Equals(Value) Then
                Return
            End If
            Invalidate()
        End Set
    End Property

    Private Sub AddExpressionColumn(ByVal value As String)
        ' Get the grid's data source. First check for a null
        ' table or data grid.
        If Me.DataGridTableStyle Is Nothing Or _
        Me.DataGridTableStyle.DataGrid Is Nothing Then
            Return
        End If

        Dim dg As DataGrid = Me.DataGridTableStyle.DataGrid
        Dim dv As DataView = CType(dg.BindingContext(dg.DataSource, dg.DataMember), CurrencyManager).List

        ' This works only with System.Data.DataTable.
        If dv Is Nothing Then
            Return
        End If

        ' If the user already added a column with the name
        ' then exit. Otherwise, add the column and set the
        ' expression to the value passed to this function.
        Dim col As DataColumn = dv.Table.Columns("__Computed__Column__")
        If Not (col Is Nothing) Then
            Return
        End If
        col = New DataColumn("__Computed__Column__" + count.ToString())

        dv.Table.Columns.Add(col)

        col.Expression = value
        expressionColumn = col
    End Sub

    ' Override the OnPaint method to paint the cell based on the expression.
    Protected Overloads Overrides Sub Paint _
    (ByVal g As Graphics, _
    ByVal bounds As Rectangle, _
    ByVal [source] As CurrencyManager, _
    ByVal rowNum As Integer, _
    ByVal backBrush As Brush, _
    ByVal foreBrush As Brush, _
    ByVal alignToRight As Boolean)
        Dim trueExpression As Boolean = False
        Dim hasExpression As Boolean = False
        Dim drv As DataRowView = [source].List(rowNum)
        hasExpression = Not (Me.expressionColumn Is Nothing) And Not (Me.expressionColumn.Expression Is Nothing) And Not Me.expressionColumn.Expression.Equals([String].Empty)

        ' Get the value from the expression column.
        ' For simplicity, we assume a True/False value for the
        ' expression column.
        If hasExpression Then
            Dim expr As Object = drv.Row(expressionColumn.ColumnName)
            trueExpression = expr.Equals("True")
        End If

        ' Let the DataGridBoolColumn do the painting.
        If Not hasExpression Then
            MyBase.Paint(g, bounds, [source], rowNum, backBrush, foreBrush, alignToRight)
        End If

        ' Paint using the expression color for true or false, as calculated.
        If trueExpression Then
            MyBase.Paint(g, bounds, [source], rowNum, trueBrush, foreBrush, alignToRight)
        Else
            MyBase.Paint(g, bounds, [source], rowNum, falseBrush, foreBrush, alignToRight)
        End If
    End Sub
End Class
```

[C#]

```
using System;
using System.Data;
```

```
using System.Windows.Forms;
using System.Drawing;
using System.ComponentModel;

public class MyForm : Form
{
    private DataTable myTable;
    private DataGrid myGrid = new DataGrid();

    public MyForm() : base()
    {
        try
        {
            InitializeComponent();

            myTable = new DataTable("NamesTable");
            myTable.Columns.Add(new DataColumn("Name"));
            DataColumn column = new DataColumn
                ("id", typeof(System.Int32));
            myTable.Columns.Add(column);
            myTable.Columns.Add(new
                DataColumn("calculatedField", typeof(bool)));
            DataSet namesDataSet = new DataSet();
            namesDataSet.Tables.Add(myTable);
            myGrid.SetDataBinding(namesDataSet, "NamesTable");

            AddTableStyle();
            AddData();
        }
        catch (System.Exception exc)
        {
            Console.WriteLine(exc.ToString());
        }
    }

    private void grid_Enter(object sender, EventArgs e)
    {
        myGrid.CurrentCell = new DataGridCell(2,2);
    }

    private void AddTableStyle()
    {
        // Map a new  TableStyle to the DataTable. Then
        // add DataGridColumnStyle objects to the collection
        // of column styles with appropriate mappings.
        DataGridTableStyle dgt = new DataGridTableStyle();
        dgt.MappingName = "NamesTable";

        DataGridTextBoxColumn dgtbc = new DataGridTextBoxColumn();
        dgtbc.MappingName = "Name";
        dgtbc.HeaderText= "Name";
        dgt.GridColumnStyles.Add(dgtbc);

        dgtbc = new DataGridTextBoxColumn();
        dgtbc.MappingName = "id";
        dgtbc.HeaderText= "id";
        dgt.GridColumnStyles.Add(dgtbc);

        DataGridBoolColumnInherit db =
            new DataGridBoolColumnInherit();
        db.HeaderText= "less than 1000 = blue";
        db.Width= 150;
        db.MappingName = "calculatedField";
        dgt.GridColumnStyles.Add(db);

        myGrid.TableStyles.Add(dgt);

        // This expression instructs the grid to change
        // the color of the inherited DataGridBoolColumn
        // according to the value of the id field. If it's
        // less than 1000, the row is blue. Otherwise,
        // the color is yellow.
        db.Expression = "id < 1000";
    }

    private void AddData()
    {
        // Add data with varying numbers for the id field.
        // If the number is over 1000, the cell will paint
        // yellow. Otherwise, it will be blue.
        DataRow dRow = myTable.NewRow();

        dRow["Name"] = "name 1 ";
        dRow["id"] = 999;
        myTable.Rows.Add(dRow);

        dRow = myTable.NewRow();
        dRow["Name"] = "name 2";
        dRow["id"] = 2300;
        myTable.Rows.Add(dRow);

        dRow = myTable.NewRow();
        dRow["Name"] = "name 3";
        dRow["id"] = 120;
        myTable.Rows.Add(dRow);

        dRow = myTable.NewRow();
        dRow["Name"] = "name 4";
        dRow["id"] = 4023;
        myTable.Rows.Add(dRow);

        dRow = myTable.NewRow();
        dRow["Name"] = "name 5";
        dRow["id"] = 2345;
        myTable.Rows.Add(dRow);

        myTable.AcceptChanges();
    }

    private void InitializeComponent()
    {
        this.Size = new Size(500, 500);
        myGrid.Size = new Size(350, 250);
        myGrid.TabStop = true;
        myGrid.TabIndex = 1;

        this.StartPosition = FormStartPosition.CenterScreen;
        this.Controls.Add(myGrid);
    }
    [STAThread]
    public static void Main()
    {
        MyForm myGridForm = new MyForm();
        myGridForm.ShowDialog();
    }
}

public class DataGridBoolColumnInherit : DataGridBoolColumn
{
    private SolidBrush trueBrush = Brushes.Blue as SolidBrush;
    private SolidBrush falseBrush = Brushes.Yellow as SolidBrush;
    private DataColumn expressionColumn = null;
    private static int count = 0;

    public Color FalseColor
    {
        get
        {
            return falseBrush.Color;
        }
        set
        {
            falseBrush = new SolidBrush(value);
            Invalidate();
        }
    }

    public Color TrueColor
    {
        get
        {
```

```
            return trueBrush.Color;
        }
        set
        {
            trueBrush = new SolidBrush(value);
            Invalidate();
        }
    }

    public DataGridBoolColumnInherit() : base ()
    {
        count ++;
    }

    // This will work only with a DataSet or DataTable.
    // The code is not compatible with IBindingList implementations.
    public string Expression
    {
        get
        {
            return this.expressionColumn == null ? String.Empty :
                this.expressionColumn.Expression;
        }
        set
        {
            if (expressionColumn == null)
                AddExpressionColumn(value);
            else
                expressionColumn.Expression = value;
            if (expressionColumn != null &&
                expressionColumn.Expression.Equals(value))
                return;
            Invalidate();
        }
    }

    private void AddExpressionColumn(string value)
    {
        // Get the grid's data source. First check for a null
        // table or data grid.
        if (this.DataGridTableStyle == null ||
            this.DataGridTableStyle.DataGrid == null)
            return;

        DataGrid myGrid = this.DataGridTableStyle.DataGrid;
        DataView myDataView = ((CurrencyManager)
            myGrid.BindingContext[myGrid.DataSource,
            myGrid.DataMember]).List
            as DataView;

        // This works only with System.Data.DataTable.
        if (myDataView == null)
            return;

        // If the user already added a column with the name
        // then exit. Otherwise, add the column and set the
        // expression to the value passed to this function.
        DataColumn col =
myDataView.Table.Columns["__Computed__Column__"];
        if (col != null)
            return;
        col = new DataColumn("__Computed__Column__" +                ↵
count.ToString());

        myDataView.Table.Columns.Add(col);
        col.Expression = value;
        expressionColumn = col;
    }

    // override the OnPaint method to paint the cell based            ↵
 on the expression.
    protected override void Paint(Graphics g, Rectangle bounds,
        CurrencyManager source, int rowNum,
        Brush backBrush, Brush foreBrush,
        bool alignToRight)
    {
        bool trueExpression = false;
        bool hasExpression = false;
        DataRowView drv = source.List[rowNum] as DataRowView;

        hasExpression = this.expressionColumn != null &&
            this.expressionColumn.Expression != null &&
            !this.expressionColumn.Expression.Equals(String.Empty);

        Console.WriteLine(string.Format("hasExpressionValue            ↵
{0}",hasExpression));
        // Get the value from the expression column.
        // For simplicity, we assume a True/False value for the
        // expression column.
        if (hasExpression)
        {
            object expr = drv.Row[expressionColumn.ColumnName];
            trueExpression = expr.Equals("True");
        }

        // Let the DataGridBoolColumn do the painting.
        if (!hasExpression)
            base.Paint(g, bounds, source, rowNum,
                backBrush, foreBrush, alignToRight);

        // Paint using the expression color for true or false,        ↵
 as calculated.
        if (trueExpression)
            base.Paint(g, bounds, source, rowNum,
                trueBrush, foreBrush, alignToRight);
        else
            base.Paint(g, bounds, source, rowNum,
                falseBrush, foreBrush, alignToRight);
    }
}
```

[C++]

```
using namespace System;
using namespace System::Data;
using namespace System::Windows::Forms;
using namespace System::Drawing;
using namespace System::ComponentModel;

    public __gc class DataGridBoolColumnInherit : public              ↵
DataGridBoolColumn {
    private:
        SolidBrush*  trueBrush;
        SolidBrush*  falseBrush;
        DataColumn* expressionColumn;
        static int  count = 0;

    public:
        DataGridBoolColumnInherit() : DataGridBoolColumn() {
            trueBrush = dynamic_cast<SolidBrush*>(Brushes::Blue);
            falseBrush = dynamic_cast<SolidBrush*>(Brushes::Yellow);
            expressionColumn = 0;
            count ++;
        }
        __property Color get_FalseColor() {
                return falseBrush->Color;
            }

        __property void set_FalseColor(Color value) {
            falseBrush = new System::Drawing::SolidBrush(value);
                Invalidate();
            }

        __property Color get_TrueColor() {
                return trueBrush->Color;
            }

        __property void set_TrueColor(Color value) {
                trueBrush = new System::Drawing::SolidBrush(value);
                Invalidate();
            }
```

```
        // This will work only with a DataSet or DataTable.
        // The code is not compatible with IBindingList*                  ↵
implementations.
        __property String* get_Expression() {
                return this->expressionColumn == 0 ? String::Empty :
                this->expressionColumn->Expression;
            }

        __property void set_Expression(String* value) {
                if (expressionColumn == 0)
                    AddExpressionColumn(value);
                else
                    expressionColumn->Expression = value;
                if (expressionColumn != 0 &&
                    expressionColumn->Expression->Equals(value))
                    return;
                Invalidate();
            }

    private:
        void AddExpressionColumn(String* value) {
            // Get the grid's data source. First check for a 0
            // table or data grid.
            if (this->DataGridTableStyle == 0 ||
                this->DataGridTableStyle->DataGrid == 0)
                return;

            DataGrid* myGrid = this->DataGridTableStyle->DataGrid;
            DataView* myDataView = dynamic_cast<DataView*>(
                (dynamic_cast<CurrencyManager*>(
                myGrid->BindingContext->Item[myGrid->DataSource,
                myGrid->DataMember]))->List);

            // This works only with System::Data::DataTable.
            if (myDataView == 0)
                return;

            // If the user already added a column with the name
            // then exit. Otherwise, add the column and set the
            // expression to the value passed to this function.
            DataColumn* col =
                myDataView->Table->Columns-                               ↵
>Item[S"__Computed__Column__"];
            if (col != 0)
                return;
            col = new DataColumn(String::Concat(
                S"__Computed__Column__", __box(count)));

            myDataView->Table->Columns->Add(col);
            col->Expression = value;
            expressionColumn = col;
        }

        //  the OnPaint method to paint the cell based                   ↵
 on the expression.
    protected:
        void Paint(Graphics* g, Rectangle bounds,
            CurrencyManager* source, int rowNum,
            Brush* backBrush, Brush* foreBrush,
            bool alignToRight) {
                bool trueExpression = false;
                bool hasExpression = false;
                DataRowView* drv = dynamic_cast<DataRowView*>             ↵
 (source->List->Item[rowNum]);

                hasExpression = this->expressionColumn != 0 &&
                    this->expressionColumn->Expression != 0 &&
                    !this->expressionColumn->Expression-                  ↵
>Equals(String::Empty);

                Console::WriteLine(String::Format                         ↵
 (S"hasExpressionValue {0}", __box(hasExpression)));
                // Get the value from the expression column.
                // For simplicity, we assume a True/False value for the
                // expression column.
                if (hasExpression) {
                    Object* expr = drv->Row->Item                         ↵
[expressionColumn->ColumnName];
                    trueExpression = expr->Equals(S"True");
                }

                // Let the DataGridBoolColumn do the painting.
                if (!hasExpression)
                    DataGridBoolColumn::Paint(g, bounds,                  ↵
source, rowNum,
                    backBrush, foreBrush, alignToRight);

                // Paint using the expression color for                  ↵
true or false, as calculated.
                if (trueExpression)
                    DataGridBoolColumn::Paint(g, bounds,                  ↵
source, rowNum,
                    trueBrush, foreBrush, alignToRight);
                else
                    DataGridBoolColumn::Paint(g, bounds,                  ↵
 source, rowNum,
                    falseBrush, foreBrush, alignToRight);
            }
    };

    public __gc class MyForm : public Form {
    private:
        DataTable*  myTable;
        DataGrid* myGrid;

    public:
        MyForm() {
            myGrid = new DataGrid();

            try {
                InitializeComponent();
                myTable = new DataTable(S"NamesTable");
                myTable->Columns->Add(new DataColumn(S"Name"));
                DataColumn* column = new DataColumn
                    (S"id", __typeof(System::Int32));
                myTable->Columns->Add(column);
                myTable->Columns->Add(new
                    DataColumn(S"calculatedField", __typeof(bool)));
                DataSet* namesDataSet = new DataSet();
                namesDataSet->Tables->Add(myTable);
                myGrid->SetDataBinding(namesDataSet, S"NamesTable");

                AddTableStyle();
                AddData();
            } catch (System::Exception* exc) {
                Console::WriteLine(exc);
            }
        }

    private:
        void grid_Enter(Object* sender, EventArgs* e) {
            myGrid->CurrentCell = DataGridCell(2, 2);
        }

        void AddTableStyle() {
            // Map a new  TableStyle to the DataTable. Then
            // add DataGridColumnStyle objects to the collection
            // of column styles with appropriate mappings.
            DataGridTableStyle* dgt = new DataGridTableStyle();
            dgt->MappingName = S"NamesTable";

            DataGridTextBoxColumn* dgtbc = new DataGridTextBoxColumn();
            dgtbc->MappingName = S"Name";
            dgtbc->HeaderText= S"Name";
            dgt->GridColumnStyles->Add(dgtbc);
            dgtbc = new DataGridTextBoxColumn();
            dgtbc->MappingName = S"id";
            dgtbc->HeaderText= S"id";
            dgt->GridColumnStyles->Add(dgtbc);

            DataGridBoolColumnInherit* db = new                           ↵
DataGridBoolColumnInherit();
```

```
        db->HeaderText= S"less than 1000 = blue";
        db->Width= 150;
        db->MappingName = S"calculatedField";
        dgt->GridColumnStyles->Add(db);

        myGrid->TableStyles->Add(dgt);

        // This expression instructs the grid to change
        // the color of the inherited DataGridBoolColumn
        // according to the value of the id field. If it's
        // less than 1000, the row is blue. Otherwise,
        // the color is yellow.
        db->Expression = S"id < 1000";
    }

    void AddData() {
        // Add data with varying numbers for the id field.
        // If the number is over 1000, the cell will paint
        // yellow. Otherwise, it will be blue.
        DataRow* dRow = myTable->NewRow();

        dRow->Item[S"Name"] = S"name 1 ";
        dRow->Item[S"id"] = __box(999);
        myTable->Rows->Add(dRow);

        dRow = myTable->NewRow();
        dRow->Item[S"Name"] = S"name 2";
        dRow->Item[S"id"] = __box(2300);
        myTable->Rows->Add(dRow);

        dRow = myTable->NewRow();
        dRow->Item[S"Name"] = S"name 3";
        dRow->Item[S"id"] = __box(120);
        myTable->Rows->Add(dRow);

        dRow = myTable->NewRow();
        dRow->Item[S"Name"] = S"name 4";
        dRow->Item[S"id"] = __box(4023);
        myTable->Rows->Add(dRow);

        dRow = myTable->NewRow();
        dRow->Item[S"Name"] = S"name 5";
        dRow->Item[S"id"] = __box(2345);
        myTable->Rows->Add(dRow);

        myTable->AcceptChanges();
    }

    void InitializeComponent() {
        this->Size = System::Drawing::Size(500, 500);
        myGrid->Size = System::Drawing::Size(350, 250);
        myGrid->TabStop = true;
        myGrid->TabIndex = 1;

        this->StartPosition = FormStartPosition::CenterScreen;
        this->Controls->Add(myGrid);
    }
};

[STAThread]
int main() {
    MyForm* myGridForm = new MyForm();
    myGridForm->ShowDialog();
}
```

Requirements

Namespace: System.Windows.Forms

Platforms: Windows 98, Windows NT 4.0, Windows Millennium Edition, Windows 2000, Windows XP Home Edition, Windows XP Professional, Windows Server 2003 family

Assembly: System.Windows.Forms (in System.Windows.Forms.dll)

DataGridBoolColumn Constructor

Initializes a new instance of the **DataGridBoolColumn** class.

Overload List

Initializes a new instance of the **DataGridBoolColumn** class.

[Visual Basic] **Public Sub New()**

[C#] **public DataGridBoolColumn();**

[C++] **public: DataGridBoolColumn();**

[JScript] **public function DataGridBoolColumn();**

Initializes a new instance of a **DataGridBoolColumn** with the specified **PropertyDescriptor**.

[Visual Basic] **Public Sub New(PropertyDescriptor)**

[C#] **public DataGridBoolColumn(PropertyDescriptor);**

[C++] **public: DataGridBoolColumn(PropertyDescriptor*);**

[JScript] **public function DataGridBoolColumn(PropertyDescriptor);**

This member supports the .NET Framework infrastructure and is not intended to be used directly from your code.

[Visual Basic] **Public Sub New(PropertyDescriptor, Boolean)**

[C#] **public DataGridBoolColumn(PropertyDescriptor, bool);**

[C++] **public: DataGridBoolColumn(PropertyDescriptor*, bool);**

[JScript] **public function DataGridBoolColumn(PropertyDescriptor, Boolean);**

Example

See related example in the **System.Windows.Forms.DataGridBoolColumn** class topic.

DataGridBoolColumn Constructor ()

Initializes a new instance of the **DataGridBoolColumn** class.

[Visual Basic]
```
Public Sub New()
```
[C#]
```
public DataGridBoolColumn();
```
[C++]
```
public: DataGridBoolColumn();
```
[JScript]
```
public function DataGridBoolColumn();
```

Remarks

When using this overload to create a **DataGridBoolColumn**, be sure to set the **MappingName** value to the **ColumnName** of a **DataColumn**.

Example

See related example in the **System.Windows.Forms.DataGridBoolColumn** class topic.

Requirements

Platforms: Windows 98, Windows NT 4.0, Windows Millennium Edition, Windows 2000, Windows XP Home Edition, Windows XP Professional, Windows Server 2003 family

DataGridBoolColumn Constructor (PropertyDescriptor)

Initializes a new instance of a **DataGridBoolColumn** with the specified **PropertyDescriptor**.

```
[Visual Basic]
Public Sub New( _
   ByVal prop As PropertyDescriptor _
)
[C#]
public DataGridBoolColumn(
   PropertyDescriptor prop
);
[C++]
public: DataGridBoolColumn(
   PropertyDescriptor* prop
);
[JScript]
public function DataGridBoolColumn(
   prop : PropertyDescriptor
);
```

Parameters

prop
The **PropertyDescriptor** associated with the column.

Remarks

The **DataGridBoolColumn** must be associated with a data source that contains Boolean values.

To get a **PropertyDescriptor**, first use the **BindingContext** to return the appropriate **BindingManagerBase** object. Then use the **GetItemProperties** method of the **BindingManagerBase** to return a **PropertyDescriptorCollection**. Finally, use the this property of the **PropertyDescriptorCollection** to return the specific **PropertyDescriptor** for the column.

Example

See related example in the **System.Windows.Forms.DataGridBoolColumn** class topic.

Requirements

Platforms: Windows 98, Windows NT 4.0, Windows Millennium Edition, Windows 2000, Windows XP Home Edition, Windows XP Professional, Windows Server 2003 family

DataGridBoolColumn Constructor (PropertyDescriptor, Boolean)

This member supports the .NET Framework infrastructure and is not intended to be used directly from your code.

```
[Visual Basic]
Public Sub New( _
   ByVal prop As PropertyDescriptor, _
   ByVal isDefault As Boolean _
)
[C#]
public DataGridBoolColumn(
   PropertyDescriptor prop,
   bool isDefault
);
[C++]
public: DataGridBoolColumn(
   PropertyDescriptor* prop,
   bool isDefault
);
[JScript]
public function DataGridBoolColumn(
   prop : PropertyDescriptor,
   isDefault : Boolean
);
```

DataGridBoolColumn.AllowNull Property

Gets or sets a value indicating whether null values are allowed.

```
[Visual Basic]
Public Property AllowNull As Boolean
[C#]
public bool AllowNull {get; set;}
[C++]
public: __property bool get_AllowNull();
public: __property void set_AllowNull(bool);
[JScript]
public function get AllowNull() : Boolean;
public function set AllowNull(Boolean);
```

Property Value

true if null values are allowed, otherwise, **false**.

Example

See related example in the **System.Windows.Forms.DataGridBoolColumn** class topic.

Requirements

Platforms: Windows 98, Windows NT 4.0, Windows Millennium Edition, Windows 2000, Windows XP Home Edition, Windows XP Professional, Windows Server 2003 family

DataGridBoolColumn.FalseValue Property

Gets or sets the actual value used when setting the value of the column to **false**.

```
[Visual Basic]
Public Property FalseValue As Object
[C#]
public object FalseValue {get; set;}
[C++]
public: __property Object* get_FalseValue();
public: __property void set_FalseValue(Object*);
[JScript]
public function get FalseValue() : Object;
public function set FalseValue(Object);
```

Property Value

The value, typed as **Object**.

Remarks

The **FalseValue**, **NullValue**, and **TrueValue** properties determine the actual values pushed into the data source.

Example

See related example in the **System.Windows.Forms.DataGrid-BoolColumn** class topic.

Requirements

Platforms: Windows 98, Windows NT 4.0, Windows Millennium Edition, Windows 2000, Windows XP Home Edition, Windows XP Professional, Windows Server 2003 family

DataGridBoolColumn.NullValue Property

Gets or sets the actual value used when setting the value of the column to **Value**.

```
[Visual Basic]
Public Property NullValue As Object
[C#]
public object NullValue {get; set;}
[C++]
public: __property Object* get_NullValue();
public: __property void set_NullValue(Object*);
[JScript]
public function get NullValue() : Object;
public function set NullValue(Object);
```

Property Value

The value, typed as **Object**.

Remarks

You can also specify what text will be displayed by setting the **NullText** property.

The **AllowNull** property must be set to true to enter a null reference (**Nothing** in Visual Basic) values.

The **FalseValue**, **NullValue**, and **TrueValue** properties determine the actual values pushed into the data source.

Example

See related example in the **System.Windows.Forms.DataGrid-BoolColumn** class topic.

Requirements

Platforms: Windows 98, Windows NT 4.0, Windows Millennium Edition, Windows 2000, Windows XP Home Edition, Windows XP Professional, Windows Server 2003 family

DataGridBoolColumn.TrueValue Property

Gets or sets the actual value used when setting the value of the column to **true**.

```
[Visual Basic]
Public Property TrueValue As Object
[C#]
public object TrueValue {get; set;}
[C++]
public: __property Object* get_TrueValue();
public: __property void set_TrueValue(Object*);
[JScript]
public function get TrueValue() : Object;
public function set TrueValue(Object);
```

Property Value

The value, typed as **Object**.

Remarks

The **FalseValue**, **NullValue**, and **TrueValue** properties determine the actual values pushed into the data source.

Example

See related example in the **System.Windows.Forms.DataGrid-BoolColumn** class topic.

Requirements

Platforms: Windows 98, Windows NT 4.0, Windows Millennium Edition, Windows 2000, Windows XP Home Edition, Windows XP Professional, Windows Server 2003 family

DataGridBoolColumn.Abort Method

This member overrides **DataGridColumnStyle.Abort**.

```
[Visual Basic]
Protected Friend Overrides Sub Abort( _
   ByVal rowNum As Integer _
)
[C#]
protected internal override void Abort(
   int rowNum
);
[C++]
protected public: void Abort(
   int rowNum
);
[JScript]
protected internal override function Abort(
   rowNum : int
);
```

Requirements

Platforms: Windows 98, Windows NT 4.0, Windows Millennium Edition, Windows 2000, Windows XP Home Edition, Windows XP Professional, Windows Server 2003 family

DataGridBoolColumn.Commit Method

This member overrides **DataGridColumnStyle.Commit**.

```
[Visual Basic]
Protected Friend Overrides Function Commit( _
   ByVal dataSource As CurrencyManager, _
   ByVal rowNum As Integer _
) As Boolean
[C#]
protected internal override bool Commit(
   CurrencyManager dataSource,
   int rowNum
);
[C++]
protected public: bool Commit(
   CurrencyManager* dataSource,
   int rowNum
);
```

```
[JScript]
protected internal override function Commit(
   dataSource : CurrencyManager,
   rowNum : int
) : Boolean;
```

Requirements

Platforms: Windows 98, Windows NT 4.0, Windows Millennium Edition, Windows 2000, Windows XP Home Edition, Windows XP Professional, Windows Server 2003 family

DataGridBoolColumn.ConcedeFocus Method

This member overrides **DataGridColumnStyle.ConcedeFocus**.

```
[Visual Basic]
Protected Friend Overrides Sub ConcedeFocus()
[C#]
protected internal override void ConcedeFocus();
[C++]
protected public: void ConcedeFocus();
[JScript]
protected internal override function ConcedeFocus();
```

Requirements

Platforms: Windows 98, Windows NT 4.0, Windows Millennium Edition, Windows 2000, Windows XP Home Edition, Windows XP Professional, Windows Server 2003 family

DataGridBoolColumn.Edit Method

Prepares the cell for editing a value.

Overload List

This member supports the .NET Framework infrastructure and is not intended to be used directly from your code.

[Visual Basic] **Overloads Protected Friend Overrides Sub Edit(CurrencyManager, Integer, Rectangle, Boolean, String, Boolean)**

[C#] **protected internal override void Edit(CurrencyManager, int, Rectangle, bool, string, bool);**

[C++] **protected public: void Edit(CurrencyManager*, int, Rectangle, bool, String*, bool);**

[JScript] **protected internal override function Edit(CurrencyManager, int, Rectangle, Boolean, String, Boolean);**

Inherited from **DataGridColumnStyle**.

[Visual Basic] **Overloads Protected Friend Overridable Sub Edit(CurrencyManager, Integer, Rectangle, Boolean)**

[C#] **protected internal virtual void Edit(CurrencyManager, int, Rectangle, bool);**

[C++] **protected public: virtual void Edit(CurrencyManager*, int, Rectangle, bool);**

[JScript] **protected internal function Edit(CurrencyManager, int, Rectangle, Boolean);**

Inherited from **DataGridColumnStyle**.

[Visual Basic] **Overloads Protected Friend Overridable Sub Edit(CurrencyManager, Integer, Rectangle, Boolean, String)**

[C#] **protected internal virtual void Edit(CurrencyManager, int, Rectangle, bool, string);**

[C++] **protected public: virtual void Edit(CurrencyManager*, int, Rectangle, bool, String*);**

[JScript] **protected internal function Edit(CurrencyManager, int, Rectangle, Boolean, String);**

Example

The following example invokes the **Edit** method to edit the value of a cell in the column.

DataGridBoolColumn.Edit Method (CurrencyManager, Int32, Rectangle, Boolean, String, Boolean)

This member overrides **DataGridColumnStyle.Edit**.

```
[Visual Basic]
Overloads Protected Friend Overrides Sub Edit( _
   ByVal source As CurrencyManager, _
   ByVal rowNum As Integer, _
   ByVal bounds As Rectangle, _
   ByVal readOnly As Boolean, _
   ByVal instantText As String, _
   ByVal cellIsVisible As Boolean _
)
[C#]
protected internal override void Edit(
   CurrencyManager source,
   int rowNum,
   Rectangle bounds,
   bool readOnly,
   string instantText,
   bool cellIsVisible
);
[C++]
protected public: void Edit(
   CurrencyManager* source,
   int rowNum,
   Rectangle bounds,
   bool readOnly,
   String* instantText,
   bool cellIsVisible
);
[JScript]
protected internal override function Edit(
   source : CurrencyManager,
   rowNum : int,
   bounds : Rectangle,
   readOnly : Boolean,
   instantText : String,
   cellIsVisible : Boolean
);
```

Requirements

Platforms: Windows 98, Windows NT 4.0, Windows Millennium Edition, Windows 2000, Windows XP Home Edition, Windows XP Professional, Windows Server 2003 family

DataGridBoolColumn.EnterNullValue Method

This member overrides **DataGridColumnStyle.EnterNullValue**.

[Visual Basic]
```
Protected Friend Overrides Sub EnterNullValue()
```
[C#]
```
protected internal override void EnterNullValue();
```
[C++]
```
protected public: void EnterNullValue();
```
[JScript]
```
protected internal override function EnterNullValue();
```

Requirements

Platforms: Windows 98, Windows NT 4.0, Windows Millennium Edition, Windows 2000, Windows XP Home Edition, Windows XP Professional, Windows Server 2003 family

DataGridBoolColumn.GetColumnValueAtRow Method

This member overrides **DataGridColumnStyle.GetColumnValueAtRow**.

[Visual Basic]
```
Protected Friend Overrides Function GetColumnValueAtRow( _
   ByVal lm As CurrencyManager, _
   ByVal row As Integer _
) As Object
```
[C#]
```
protected internal override object GetColumnValueAtRow(
   CurrencyManager lm,
   int row
);
```
[C++]
```
protected public: Object* GetColumnValueAtRow(
   CurrencyManager* lm,
   int row
);
```
[JScript]
```
protected internal override function GetColumnValueAtRow(
   lm : CurrencyManager,
   row : int
) : Object;
```

Requirements

Platforms: Windows 98, Windows NT 4.0, Windows Millennium Edition, Windows 2000, Windows XP Home Edition, Windows XP Professional, Windows Server 2003 family

DataGridBoolColumn.GetMinimumHeight Method

This member overrides **DataGridColumnStyle.GetMinimumHeight**.

[Visual Basic]
```
Protected Friend Overrides Function GetMinimumHeight() As Integer
```
[C#]
```
protected internal override int GetMinimumHeight();
```
[C++]
```
protected public: int GetMinimumHeight();
```
[JScript]
```
protected internal override function GetMinimumHeight() : int;
```

Requirements

Platforms: Windows 98, Windows NT 4.0, Windows Millennium Edition, Windows 2000, Windows XP Home Edition, Windows XP Professional, Windows Server 2003 family

DataGridBoolColumn.GetPreferredHeight Method

This member overrides **DataGridColumnStyle.GetPreferredHeight**.

[Visual Basic]
```
Protected Friend Overrides Function GetPreferredHeight( _
   ByVal g As Graphics, _
   ByVal value As Object _
) As Integer
```
[C#]
```
protected internal override int GetPreferredHeight(
   Graphics g,
   object value
);
```
[C++]
```
protected public: int GetPreferredHeight(
   Graphics* g,
   Object* value
);
```
[JScript]
```
protected internal override function GetPreferredHeight(
   g : Graphics,
   value : Object
) : int;
```

Requirements

Platforms: Windows 98, Windows NT 4.0, Windows Millennium Edition, Windows 2000, Windows XP Home Edition, Windows XP Professional, Windows Server 2003 family

DataGridBoolColumn.GetPreferredSize Method

This member overrides **DataGridColumnStyle.GetPreferredSize**.

[Visual Basic]
```
Protected Friend Overrides Function GetPreferredSize( _
   ByVal g As Graphics, _
   ByVal value As Object _
) As Size
```
[C#]
```
protected internal override Size GetPreferredSize(
   Graphics g,
   object value
);
```
[C++]
```
protected public: Size GetPreferredSize(
   Graphics* g,
   Object* value
);
```

```
[JScript]
protected internal override function GetPreferredSize(
   g : Graphics,
   value : Object
) : Size;
```

Requirements

Platforms: Windows 98, Windows NT 4.0, Windows Millennium Edition, Windows 2000, Windows XP Home Edition, Windows XP Professional, Windows Server 2003 family

DataGridBoolColumn.Paint Method

This member supports the .NET Framework infrastructure and is not intended to be used directly from your code.

Overload List

This member overrides **DataGridColumnStyle.Paint**.

[Visual Basic] **Overloads Protected Friend Overrides Sub Paint(Graphics, Rectangle, CurrencyManager, Integer)**

[C#] **protected internal override void Paint(Graphics, Rectangle, CurrencyManager, int);**

[C++] **protected public: void Paint(Graphics*, Rectangle, CurrencyManager*, int);**

[JScript] **protected internal override function Paint(Graphics, Rectangle, CurrencyManager, int);**

This member overrides **DataGridColumnStyle.Paint**.

[Visual Basic] **Overloads Protected Friend Overrides Sub Paint(Graphics, Rectangle, CurrencyManager, Integer, Boolean)**

[C#] **protected internal override void Paint(Graphics, Rectangle, CurrencyManager, int, bool);**

[C++] **protected public: void Paint(Graphics*, Rectangle, CurrencyManager*, int, bool);**

[JScript] **protected internal override function Paint(Graphics, Rectangle, CurrencyManager, int, Boolean);**

This member overrides **DataGridColumnStyle.Paint**.

[Visual Basic] **Overloads Protected Friend Overrides Sub Paint(Graphics, Rectangle, CurrencyManager, Integer, Brush, Brush, Boolean)**

[C#] **protected internal override void Paint(Graphics, Rectangle, CurrencyManager, int, Brush, Brush, bool);**

[C++] **protected public: void Paint(Graphics*, Rectangle, CurrencyManager*, int, Brush*, Brush*, bool);**

[JScript] **protected internal override function Paint(Graphics, Rectangle, CurrencyManager, int, Brush, Brush, Boolean);**

DataGridBoolColumn.Paint Method (Graphics, Rectangle, CurrencyManager, Int32)

This member overrides **DataGridColumnStyle.Paint**.

```
[Visual Basic]
Overloads Protected Friend Overrides Sub Paint( _
   ByVal g As Graphics, _
   ByVal bounds As Rectangle, _
   ByVal source As CurrencyManager, _
   ByVal rowNum As Integer _
)
[C#]
protected internal override void Paint(
   Graphics g,
   Rectangle bounds,
   CurrencyManager source,
   int rowNum
);
[C++]
protected public: void Paint(
   Graphics* g,
   Rectangle bounds,
   CurrencyManager* source,
   int rowNum
);
[JScript]
protected internal override function Paint(
   g : Graphics,
   bounds : Rectangle,
   source : CurrencyManager,
   rowNum : int
);
```

Requirements

Platforms: Windows 98, Windows NT 4.0, Windows Millennium Edition, Windows 2000, Windows XP Home Edition, Windows XP Professional, Windows Server 2003 family

DataGridBoolColumn.Paint Method (Graphics, Rectangle, CurrencyManager, Int32, Boolean)

This member overrides **DataGridColumnStyle.Paint**.

```
[Visual Basic]
Overloads Protected Friend Overrides Sub Paint( _
   ByVal g As Graphics, _
   ByVal bounds As Rectangle, _
   ByVal source As CurrencyManager, _
   ByVal rowNum As Integer, _
   ByVal alignToRight As Boolean _
)
[C#]
protected internal override void Paint(
   Graphics g,
   Rectangle bounds,
   CurrencyManager source,
   int rowNum,
   bool alignToRight
);
[C++]
protected public: void Paint(
   Graphics* g,
   Rectangle bounds,
   CurrencyManager* source,
   int rowNum,
   bool alignToRight
);
```

```
[JScript]
protected internal override function Paint(
   g : Graphics,
   bounds : Rectangle,
   source : CurrencyManager,
   rowNum : int,
   alignToRight : Boolean
);
```

Requirements

Platforms: Windows 98, Windows NT 4.0, Windows Millennium Edition, Windows 2000, Windows XP Home Edition, Windows XP Professional, Windows Server 2003 family

DataGridBoolColumn.Paint Method (Graphics, Rectangle, CurrencyManager, Int32, Brush, Brush, Boolean)

This member overrides **DataGridColumnStyle.Paint**.

```
[Visual Basic]
Overloads Protected Friend Overrides Sub Paint( _
   ByVal g As Graphics, _
   ByVal bounds As Rectangle, _
   ByVal source As CurrencyManager, _
   ByVal rowNum As Integer, _
   ByVal backBrush As Brush, _
   ByVal foreBrush As Brush, _
   ByVal alignToRight As Boolean _
)
[C#]
protected internal override void Paint(
   Graphics g,
   Rectangle bounds,
   CurrencyManager source,
   int rowNum,
   Brush backBrush,
   Brush foreBrush,
   bool alignToRight
);
[C++]
protected public: void Paint(
   Graphics* g,
   Rectangle bounds,
   CurrencyManager* source,
   int rowNum,
   Brush* backBrush,
   Brush* foreBrush,
   bool alignToRight
);
[JScript]
protected internal override function Paint(
   g : Graphics,
   bounds : Rectangle,
   source : CurrencyManager,
   rowNum : int,
   backBrush : Brush,
   foreBrush : Brush,
   alignToRight : Boolean
);
```

Requirements

Platforms: Windows 98, Windows NT 4.0, Windows Millennium Edition, Windows 2000, Windows XP Home Edition, Windows XP Professional, Windows Server 2003 family

DataGridBoolColumn.SetColumnValueAtRow Method

This member overrides **DataGridColumnStyle.SetColumnValueAtRow**.

```
[Visual Basic]
Protected Friend Overrides Sub SetColumnValueAtRow( _
   ByVal lm As CurrencyManager, _
   ByVal row As Integer, _
   ByVal value As Object _
)
[C#]
protected internal override void SetColumnValueAtRow(
   CurrencyManager lm,
   int row,
   object value
);
[C++]
protected public: void SetColumnValueAtRow(
   CurrencyManager* lm,
   int row,
   Object* value
);
[JScript]
protected internal override function SetColumnValueAtRow(
   lm : CurrencyManager,
   row : int,
   value : Object
);
```

Requirements

Platforms: Windows 98, Windows NT 4.0, Windows Millennium Edition, Windows 2000, Windows XP Home Edition, Windows XP Professional, Windows Server 2003 family

DataGridBoolColumn.AllowNullChanged Event

Occurs when the **AllowNull** property is changed.

```
[Visual Basic]
Public Event AllowNullChanged As EventHandler
[C#]
public event EventHandler AllowNullChanged;
[C++]
public: __event EventHandler* AllowNullChanged;
```

[JScript] In JScript, you can handle the events defined by a class, but you cannot define your own.

Event Data

The event handler receives an argument of type **EventArgs**.

Example

See related example in the **System.Windows.Forms.DataGridBoolColumn** class topic.

Requirements

Platforms: Windows 98, Windows NT 4.0, Windows Millennium Edition, Windows 2000, Windows XP Home Edition, Windows XP Professional, Windows Server 2003 family

DataGridBoolColumn.FalseValueChanged Event

Occurs when the **FalseValue** property is changed.

```
[Visual Basic]
Public Event FalseValueChanged As EventHandler
[C#]
public event EventHandler FalseValueChanged;
[C++]
public: __event EventHandler* FalseValueChanged;
```

[JScript] In JScript, you can handle the events defined by a class, but you cannot define your own.

Event Data

The event handler receives an argument of type **EventArgs**.

Example

See related example in the **System.Windows.Forms.DataGrid-BoolColumn** class topic.

Requirements

Platforms: Windows 98, Windows NT 4.0, Windows Millennium Edition, Windows 2000, Windows XP Home Edition, Windows XP Professional, Windows Server 2003 family

DataGridBoolColumn.TrueValueChanged Event

Occurs when the **TrueValue** property value is changed.

```
[Visual Basic]
Public Event TrueValueChanged As EventHandler
[C#]
public event EventHandler TrueValueChanged;
[C++]
public: __event EventHandler* TrueValueChanged;
```

[JScript] In JScript, you can handle the events defined by a class, but you cannot define your own.

Event Data

The event handler receives an argument of type **EventArgs**.

Example

See related example in the **System.Windows.Forms.DataGrid-BoolColumn** class topic.

Requirements

Platforms: Windows 98, Windows NT 4.0, Windows Millennium Edition, Windows 2000, Windows XP Home Edition, Windows XP Professional, Windows Server 2003 family

DataGridCell Structure

Identifies a cell in the grid.

System.Object
  System.ValueType
    System.Windows.Forms.DataGridCell

[Visual Basic]
```
Public Structure DataGridCell
```
[C#]
```
public struct DataGridCell
```
[C++]
```
public __value struct DataGridCell
```

[JScript] In JScript, you can use the structures in the .NET Framework, but you cannot define your own.

Thread Safety

Any public static (**Shared** in Visual Basic) members of this type are safe for multithreaded operations. Any instance members are not guaranteed to be thread safe.

Remarks

The **DataGridCell** can be used in conjunction with the **System.Windows.Forms.DataGrid** control's **CurrentCell** property to get or set the value of any cell. Setting the **System.Windows.Forms.DataGrid** control's **CurrentCell** property to a **DataGridCell** causes the focus to move to the cell specified by the **DataGridCell**.

Example

[Visual Basic, C#] The following example assigns the **DataGridCell** to the **CurrentCell** of a **System.Windows.Forms.DataGrid** and returns the column and row number of the selected cell. The value stored in the **DataTable** is also printed using the **DataGridCell** object's **RowNumber** and **ColumnNumber**.

[Visual Basic]
```
Private Sub PrintCellRowAndCol()
    Dim myCell As DataGridCell
    myCell = DataGrid1.CurrentCell
    Console.WriteLine(myCell.RowNumber)
    Console.WriteLine(myCell.ColumnNumber)
    ' Prints the value of the cell through the DataTable.
    Dim myTable As DataTable
    ' Assumes the DataGrid is bound to a DataTable.
    myTable = CType(DataGrid1.DataSource, DataTable)

Console.WriteLine(myTable.Rows(myCell.RowNumber)(myCell.ColumnNumber))
 End Sub
```

[C#]
```
private void PrintCellRowAndCol()
{
   DataGridCell myCell;
   myCell = DataGrid1.CurrentCell;
   Console.WriteLine(myCell.RowNumber);
   Console.WriteLine(myCell.ColumnNumber);
   // Prints the value of the cell through the DataTable.
   DataTable myTable;
   // Assumes the DataGrid is bound to a DataTable.
   myTable = (DataTable) DataGrid1.DataSource;
   Console.WriteLine(myTable.Rows[myCell.RowNumber]
   [myCell.ColumnNumber]);
}
```

Requirements

Namespace: System.Windows.Forms

Platforms: Windows 98, Windows NT 4.0, Windows Millennium Edition, Windows 2000, Windows XP Home Edition, Windows XP Professional, Windows Server 2003 family, .NET Compact Framework - Windows CE .NET

Assembly: System.Windows.Forms (in System.Windows.Forms.dll)

DataGridCell Constructor

Initializes a new instance of the **DataGridCell** class.

[Visual Basic]
```
Public Sub New( _
   ByVal r As Integer, _
   ByVal c As Integer _
)
```
[C#]
```
public DataGridCell(
   int r,
   int c
);
```
[C++]
```
public: DataGridCell(
   int r,
   int c
);
```
[JScript]
```
public function DataGridCell(
   r : int,
   c : int
);
```

Parameters

r

The number of a row in the **System.Windows.Forms.DataGrid**.

c

The number of a column in the **System.Windows.Forms.DataGrid**.

Example

[Visual Basic, C#] The following example creates a **DataGridCell** and sets the new instance to the **CurrentCell** of a **System.Windows.Forms.DataGrid** control.

[Visual Basic]
```
Private Sub SetCell()
   ' Set the focus to the cell specified by the DataGridCell.
   Dim dc As DataGridCell
   dc.RowNumber = 1
   dc.ColumnNumber = 1
   DataGrid1.CurrentCell = dc
End Sub
```

[C#]
```
private void SetCell()
{
   // Set the focus to the cell specified by the DataGridCell.
   DataGridCell dc = new DataGridCell();
   dc.RowNumber = 1;
   dc.ColumnNumber = 1;
   dataGrid1.CurrentCell = dc;
}
```

Requirements

Platforms: Windows 98, Windows NT 4.0, Windows Millennium Edition, Windows 2000, Windows XP Home Edition, Windows XP Professional, Windows Server 2003 family, .NET Compact Framework - Windows CE .NET

DataGridCell.ColumnNumber Property

Gets or sets the number of a column in the **System.Windows.Forms.DataGrid** control.

[Visual Basic]
```
Public Property ColumnNumber As Integer
```
[C#]
```
public int ColumnNumber {get; set;}
```
[C++]
```
public: __property int get_ColumnNumber();
public: __property void set_ColumnNumber(int);
```
[JScript]
```
public function get ColumnNumber() : int;
public function set ColumnNumber(int);
```

Property Value

The number of the column.

Remarks

You can use the **ColumnNumber** value to specify a **DataColumn** in the **DataTable** associated with the **System.Windows.Forms.DataGrid** control.

Example

[Visual Basic, C#] The following example assigns the **CurrentCell** property of a **System.Windows.Forms.DataGrid** to a **DataGridCell**. The value stored in the **DataTable** is returned by specifying **DataRow** and **DataColumn** objects through the **RowNumber** and **ColumnNumber** properties.

[Visual Basic]
```
Private Sub PrintCell(sender As Object, e As MouseEventArgs)
   Dim thisGrid As DataGrid = CType(sender, DataGrid)
   Dim myDataGridCell As DataGridCell = thisGrid.CurrentCell
   Dim bm As BindingManagerBase = _
   BindingContext (thisGrid.DataSource, thisGrid.DataMember)
   Dim drv As DataRowView = CType(bm.Current, DataRowView)
   Console.WriteLine(drv(myDataGridCell.ColumnNumber))
   Console.WriteLine(myDataGridCell.RowNumber)
End Sub
```

[C#]
```
private void PrintCell(object sender, MouseEventArgs e)
{
   DataGrid thisGrid = (DataGrid) sender;
   DataGridCell myDataGridCell = thisGrid.CurrentCell;
   BindingManagerBase bm = BindingContext                          ↵
[thisGrid.DataSource, thisGrid.DataMember];
   DataRowView drv = (DataRowView) bm.Current;
   Console.WriteLine(drv [myDataGridCell.ColumnNumber]);
   Console.WriteLine(myDataGridCell.RowNumber);
}
```

Requirements

Platforms: Windows 98, Windows NT 4.0, Windows Millennium Edition, Windows 2000, Windows XP Home Edition, Windows XP Professional, Windows Server 2003 family, .NET Compact Framework - Windows CE .NET

DataGridCell.RowNumber Property

Gets or sets the number of a row in the **System.Windows.Forms.DataGrid** control.

[Visual Basic]
```
Public Property RowNumber As Integer
```
[C#]
```
public int RowNumber {get; set;}
```
[C++]
```
public: __property int get_RowNumber();
public: __property void set_RowNumber(int);
```
[JScript]
```
public function get RowNumber() : int;
public function set RowNumber(int);
```

Property Value

The number of the row.

Remarks

You can use the **RowNumber** value to specify a **DataRow** in the **DataTable** associated with the **System.Windows.Forms.DataGrid** control.

Example

[Visual Basic, C#] The following example assigns the **CurrentCell** property of a **System.Windows.Forms.DataGrid** to a **DataGridCell** and returns the value stored in the **DataTable** object's **RowNumber** and **ColumnNumber** properties.

[Visual Basic]
```
Private Sub PrintCell(sender As Object, e As MouseEventArgs)
   Dim thisGrid As DataGrid = CType(sender, DataGrid)
   Dim myDataGridCell As DataGridCell = thisGrid.CurrentCell
   Dim bm As BindingManagerBase = _
   BindingContext (thisGrid.DataSource, thisGrid.DataMember)
   Dim drv As DataRowView = CType(bm.Current, DataRowView)
   Console.WriteLine(drv(myDataGridCell.ColumnNumber))
   Console.WriteLine(myDataGridCell.RowNumber)
End Sub
```

[C#]
```
private void PrintCell(object sender, MouseEventArgs e)
{
   DataGrid thisGrid = (DataGrid) sender;
   DataGridCell myDataGridCell = thisGrid.CurrentCell;
   BindingManagerBase bm = BindingContext                          ↵
 [thisGrid.DataSource, thisGrid.DataMember];
   DataRowView drv = (DataRowView) bm.Current;
   Console.WriteLine(drv [myDataGridCell.ColumnNumber]);
   Console.WriteLine(myDataGridCell.RowNumber);
}
```

Requirements

Platforms: Windows 98, Windows NT 4.0, Windows Millennium Edition, Windows 2000, Windows XP Home Edition, Windows XP Professional, Windows Server 2003 family, .NET Compact Framework - Windows CE .NET

DataGridCell.Equals Method

This member overrides **ValueType.Equals**.

[Visual Basic]
```
Overrides Public Function Equals( _
   ByVal o As Object _
) As Boolean
```
[C#]
```
public override bool Equals(
   object o
);
```
[C++]
```
public: bool Equals(
   Object* o
);
```
[JScript]
```
public override function Equals(
   o : Object
) : Boolean;
```

Requirements

Platforms: Windows 98, Windows NT 4.0, Windows Millennium Edition, Windows 2000, Windows XP Home Edition, Windows XP Professional, Windows Server 2003 family, .NET Compact Framework - Windows CE .NET

DataGridCell.GetHashCode Method

This member overrides **ValueType.GetHashCode**.

[Visual Basic]
```
Overrides Public Function GetHashCode() As Integer
```
[C#]
```
public override int GetHashCode();
```
[C++]
```
public: int GetHashCode();
```
[JScript]
```
public override function GetHashCode() : int;
```

Requirements

Platforms: Windows 98, Windows NT 4.0, Windows Millennium Edition, Windows 2000, Windows XP Home Edition, Windows XP Professional, Windows Server 2003 family, .NET Compact Framework - Windows CE .NET

DataGridCell.ToString Method

Gets the row number and column number of the cell.

[Visual Basic]
```
Overrides Public Function ToString() As String
```
[C#]
```
public override string ToString();
```
[C++]
```
public: String* ToString();
```
[JScript]
```
public override function ToString() : String;
```

Return Value

A string containing the row number and column number.

Example

[Visual Basic, C#] The following example returns the row number of the **System.Windows.Forms.DataGrid** control's **CurrentCell** using the **DataGridCell** object's **ToString** method.

[Visual Basic]
```
Public Sub DataGrid1_MouseUp(ByVal sender As Object,ByVal ↵
e As System.Windows.Forms.MouseEventArgs)
   Dim myGrid As DataGrid = CType(sender, DataGrid)
   Dim myCell As DataGridCell = myGrid.CurrentCell
   Console.WriteLine(myCell.ToString)
End Sub
```

[C#]
```
private void Grid_MouseUp
(object sender, System.Windows.Forms.MouseEventArgs e)
{
   DataGrid dg = (DataGrid)sender;
   DataGridCell myCell = dg.CurrentCell;
   Console.WriteLine(myCell.ToString());
}
```

Requirements

Platforms: Windows 98, Windows NT 4.0, Windows Millennium Edition, Windows 2000, Windows XP Home Edition, Windows XP Professional, Windows Server 2003 family, .NET Compact Framework - Windows CE .NET

DataGridColumnStyle Class

Specifies the appearance and text formatting and behavior of a **System.Windows.Forms.DataGrid** control column. This class is abstract.

System.Object
  System.MarshalByRefObject
    System.ComponentModel.Component
      System.Windows.Forms.DataGridColumnStyle
        System.Windows.Forms.DataGridBoolColumn
        System.Windows.Forms.DataGridTextBoxColumn

[Visual Basic]
```
MustInherit Public Class DataGridColumnStyle
   Inherits Component
   Implements IDataGridColumnStyleEditingNotificationService
```
[C#]
```
public abstract class DataGridColumnStyle : Component,
   IDataGridColumnStyleEditingNotificationService
```
[C++]
```
public __gc __abstract class DataGridColumnStyle : public
   Component, IDataGridColumnStyleEditingNotificationService
```
[JScript]
```
public abstract class DataGridColumnStyle extends Component
   implements IDataGridColumnStyleEditingNotificationService
```

Thread Safety

Any public static (**Shared** in Visual Basic) members of this type are safe for multithreaded operations. Any instance members are not guaranteed to be thread safe.

Remarks

The collection of **DataGridColumnStyle** objects (the **GridColumnStylesCollection**) is accessed through the **System.Windows.Forms.DataGrid** control's **TableStyles** property.

The **System.Windows.Forms.DataGrid** control automatically creates a collection of **DataGridColumnStyle** objects for you when you set the **DataSource** property to an appropriate data source. The objects created actually are instances of one of the following classes that inherit from **DataGridColumnStyle**: **DataGridBoolColumn** or **DataGridTextBoxColumn** class.

To format the data display, set the **Format** property of the **DataGridTextBoxColumn** class to one of the formatting values. For more information about valid formatting values, see **Date and Time Format Strings** and **Standard Numeric Format Strings**.

You can also create your own set of **DataGridColumnStyle** objects and add them to the **GridColumnStylesCollection**. When you do so, you must set the **MappingName** of each column style to the **ColumnName** of a **DataColumn** to synchronize the display of columns with the actual data.

CAUTION Always create **DataGridColumnStyle** objects and add them to the **GridColumnStylesCollection** before adding **DataGridTableStyle** objects to the **GridTableStylesCollection**. When you add an empty **DataGridTableStyle** to the collection, **DataGridColumnStyle** objects are automatically generated for you. Consequently, an exception will be thrown if you try to add new **DataGridColumnStyle** objects with duplicate **MappingName** values to the **GridColumnStylesCollection**.

When one of the derived classes is instantiated by a **System.Windows.Forms.DataGrid** control, the class created depends on the **DataType** of the **DataColumn** associated with the **DataGridColumnStyle** object. For example, a **DataColumn** with its **DataType** set to **System.Boolean** will be associated with a **DataGridBoolColumn**. To determine the type of any **DataGridColumnStyle**, use the **GetType** method.

To create your own column classes, you can inherit from **DataGridColumnStyle**. You might want to do this in order to create special columns that host controls, as exemplified by the **DataGridTextBox** class, which hosts the **TextBox** control. For example, you can host an **Image** control to show pictures in columns, or you can create your own user control to host in the column.

The functionality of the **DataGridColumnStyle** shouldn't be confused with that of the **DataColumn**. Whereas the **DataColumn** contains the properties and methods appropriate to creating a data table's schema, the **DataGridColumnStyle** contains the properties and methods related to the appearance of an individual column on the screen.

If a row contains a **DBNull.Value**, the text displayed in the column can be set with the **NullText** property.

The **DataGridColumnStyle** class also allows you to specify the behavior of a column while its data is being changed. The **BeginUpdate** and **EndUpdate** methods temporarily suspend the drawing of the column while large updates are being made to the column's data. Without this functionality, every change in every cell of the grid would be immediately drawn; this could be distracting to the user and a performance liability.

Several methods allow monitoring of the column as it is edited by the user, including the **Edit** and **Commit** events.

Most of the properties and methods of the class are tailored to controlling a column's appearance. But a few, such as the **GetColumnValueAtRow** and **SetColumnValueAtRow** allow you to examine and change the value in a specified cell.

Notes to Implementers: When you inherit from **DataGridColumnStyle**, you must override the following members: **Abort**, **Commit**, **Edit**, and **Paint** (twice).

Example

[Visual Basic, C#, C++] The following example creates a **DataGridColumnStyle** that hosts a **DateTimePicker** control.

[Visual Basic]
```
Imports System
Imports System.Data
Imports System.Windows.Forms
Imports System.Drawing
Imports System.ComponentModel

' This example shows how to create your own column style that
' hosts a control, in this case, a DateTimePicker.
Public Class DataGridTimePickerColumn
    Inherits DataGridColumnStyle
    Private timePicker As New DateTimePicker()
    ' The isEditing field tracks whether or not the user is
    ' editing data with the hosted control.
    Private isEditing As Boolean

    Public Sub New()
        timePicker.Visible = False
    End Sub

    Protected Overrides Sub Abort(ByVal rowNum As Integer)
        isEditing = False
        RemoveHandler timePicker.ValueChanged, _
```

```
        AddressOf TimePickerValueChanged
        Invalidate()
    End Sub

    Protected Overrides Function Commit _
    (ByVal dataSource As CurrencyManager, ByVal rowNum As Integer) _
    As Boolean
        timePicker.Bounds = Rectangle.Empty

        AddHandler timePicker.ValueChanged, _
        AddressOf TimePickerValueChanged

        If Not isEditing Then
            Return True
        End If
        isEditing = False

        Try
            Dim value As DateTime = timePicker.Value
            SetColumnValueAtRow(dataSource, rowNum, value)
        Catch
        End Try

        Invalidate()
        Return True
    End Function

    Protected Overloads Overrides Sub Edit( _
    ByVal [source] As CurrencyManager, _
    ByVal rowNum As Integer, _
    ByVal bounds As Rectangle, _
    ByVal [readOnly] As Boolean, _
    ByVal instantText As String, _
    ByVal cellIsVisible As Boolean)
        Dim value As DateTime = _
        CType(GetColumnValueAtRow([source], rowNum), DateTime)
        If cellIsVisible Then
            timePicker.Bounds = New Rectangle _
            (bounds.X + 2, bounds.Y + 2, bounds.Width - 4, _
            bounds.Height - 4)

            timePicker.Value = value
            timePicker.Visible = True
            AddHandler timePicker.ValueChanged, _
            AddressOf TimePickerValueChanged
        Else
            timePicker.Value = value
            timePicker.Visible = False
        End If

        If timePicker.Visible Then
            DataGridTableStyle.DataGrid.Invalidate(bounds)
        End If
    End Sub

    Protected Overrides Function GetPreferredSize( _
    ByVal g As Graphics, _
    ByVal value As Object) As Size
        Return New Size(100, timePicker.PreferredHeight + 4)
    End Function

    Protected Overrides Function GetMinimumHeight() As Integer
        Return timePicker.PreferredHeight + 4
    End Function

    Protected Overrides Function GetPreferredHeight                    ↵
(ByVal g As Graphics, ByVal value As Object) As Integer
        Return timePicker.PreferredHeight + 4
    End Function

    Protected Overloads Overrides Sub Paint(ByVal g As Graphics,       ↵
 ByVal bounds As Rectangle, ByVal [source] As CurrencyManager,         ↵
ByVal rowNum As Integer)
        Paint(g, bounds, [source], rowNum, False)
    End Sub

    Protected Overloads Overrides Sub Paint(ByVal g As Graphics,       ↵
 ByVal bounds As Rectangle, ByVal [source] As CurrencyManager,         ↵
 ByVal rowNum As Integer, ByVal alignToRight As Boolean)
        Paint(g, bounds, [source], rowNum, Brushes.Red,                ↵
Brushes.Blue, alignToRight)
    End Sub

    Protected Overloads Overrides Sub Paint(ByVal g As Graphics,       ↵
 ByVal bounds As Rectangle, ByVal [source] As CurrencyManager,         ↵
ByVal rowNum As Integer, ByVal backBrush As Brush, ByVal               ↵
foreBrush As Brush, ByVal alignToRight As Boolean)
        Dim [date] As DateTime = CType(GetColumnValueAtRow             ↵
 ([source], rowNum), DateTime)
        Dim rect As Rectangle = bounds
        g.FillRectangle(backBrush, rect)
        rect.Offset(0, 2)
        rect.Height -= 2
        g.DrawString([date].ToString("d"),                             ↵
Me.DataGridTableStyle.DataGrid.Font, foreBrush,                        ↵
RectangleF.FromLTRB(rect.X, rect.Y, rect.Right, rect.Bottom))
    End Sub

    Protected Overrides Sub SetDataGridInColumn(ByVal value            ↵
 As DataGrid)
        MyBase.SetDataGridInColumn(value)
        If Not (timePicker.Parent Is Nothing) Then
            timePicker.Parent.Controls.Remove(timePicker)
        End If
        If Not (value Is Nothing) Then
            value.Controls.Add(timePicker)
        End If
    End Sub

    Private Sub TimePickerValueChanged(ByVal sender As Object,         ↵
 ByVal e As EventArgs)
        Me.isEditing = True
        MyBase.ColumnStartedEditing(timePicker)
    End Sub
End Class

Namespace DataGridColumnStyleExample
    Public Class MyForm
        Inherits Form

        Private namesDataTable As dataTable
        Private myGrid As DataGrid = New DataGrid()
        Public Sub New()

            InitForm()

            namesDataTable = New DataTable("NamesTable")
            namesDataTable.Columns.Add(New DataColumn("Name"))
            Dim dateColumn As DataColumn = _
            New DataColumn("Date", GetType(DateTime))
            namesDataTable.Columns.Add(dateColumn)
            Dim namesDataSet As DataSet = New DataSet()
            namesDataSet.Tables.Add(namesDataTable)
            myGrid.DataSource = namesDataSet
            myGrid.DataMember = "NamesTable"
            AddGridStyle()
            AddData()
        End Sub

        Private Sub AddGridStyle()
            Dim myGridStyle As DataGridTableStyle = _
                        New DataGridTableStyle()
            myGridStyle.MappingName = "NamesTable"

            Dim nameColumnStyle As DataGridTextBoxColumn = _
                New DataGridTextBoxColumn()
            nameColumnStyle.MappingName = "Name"
            nameColumnStyle.HeaderText = "Name"
            myGridStyle.GridColumnStyles.Add(nameColumnStyle)

            Dim timePickerColumnStyle As DataGridTimePickerColumn = _
                New DataGridTimePickerColumn()
```

```
        timePickerColumnStyle.MappingName = "Date"
        timePickerColumnStyle.HeaderText = "Date"
        timePickerColumnStyle.Width = 100
        myGridStyle.GridColumnStyles.Add(timePickerColumnStyle)

        myGrid.TableStyles.Add(myGridStyle)
    End Sub

    Private Sub AddData()
        Dim dRow As DataRow = namesDataTable.NewRow()
        dRow("Name") = "Name 1"
        dRow("Date") = New DateTime(2001, 12, 1)
        namesDataTable.Rows.Add(dRow)

        dRow = namesDataTable.NewRow()
        dRow("Name") = "Name 2"
        dRow("Date") = New DateTime(2001, 12, 4)
        namesDataTable.Rows.Add(dRow)

        dRow = namesDataTable.NewRow()
        dRow("Name") = "Name 3"
        dRow("Date") = New DateTime(2001, 12, 29)
        namesDataTable.Rows.Add(dRow)

        dRow = namesDataTable.NewRow()
        dRow("Name") = "Name 4"
        dRow("Date") = New DateTime(2001, 12, 13)
        namesDataTable.Rows.Add(dRow)

        dRow = namesDataTable.NewRow()
        dRow("Name") = "Name 5"
        dRow("Date") = New DateTime(2001, 12, 21)
        namesDataTable.Rows.Add(dRow)

        namesDataTable.AcceptChanges()
    End Sub

    Private Sub InitForm()

        Me.Size = New Size(500, 500)
        myGrid.Size = New Size(350, 250)
        myGrid.TabStop = True
        myGrid.TabIndex = 1
        Me.StartPosition = FormStartPosition.CenterScreen
        Me.Controls.Add(myGrid)
    End Sub

    <STAThread()> _
    Public Shared Sub Main()
        Application.Run(New MyForm())
    End Sub
  End Class
End Namespace
```

[C#]

```
using System;
using System.Data;
using System.Windows.Forms;
using System.Drawing;

// This example shows how to create your own column style that
// hosts a control, in this case, a DateTimePicker.
public class DataGridTimePickerColumn : DataGridColumnStyle
{
    private DateTimePicker myDateTimePicker = new DateTimePicker();
    // The isEditing field tracks whether or not the user is
    // editing data with the hosted control.
    private bool isEditing;

    public DataGridTimePickerColumn() : base()
    {
        myDateTimePicker.Visible = false;
    }

    protected override void Abort(int rowNum)
    {
        isEditing = false;
        myDateTimePicker.ValueChanged -=
            new EventHandler(TimePickerValueChanged);
        Invalidate();
    }

    protected override bool Commit
        (CurrencyManager dataSource, int rowNum)
    {
        myDateTimePicker.Bounds = Rectangle.Empty;

        myDateTimePicker.ValueChanged -=
            new EventHandler(TimePickerValueChanged);

        if (!isEditing)
            return true;

        isEditing = false;

        try
        {
            DateTime value = myDateTimePicker.Value;
            SetColumnValueAtRow(dataSource, rowNum, value);
        }
        catch (Exception)
        {
            Abort(rowNum);
            return false;
        }

        Invalidate();
        return true;
    }

    protected override void Edit(
        CurrencyManager source,
        int rowNum,
        Rectangle bounds,
        bool readOnly,
        string instantText,
        bool cellIsVisible)
    {
        DateTime value = (DateTime)
            GetColumnValueAtRow(source, rowNum);
        if (cellIsVisible)
        {
            myDateTimePicker.Bounds = new Rectangle
                (bounds.X + 2, bounds.Y + 2,
                bounds.Width - 4, bounds.Height - 4);
            myDateTimePicker.Value = value;
            myDateTimePicker.Visible = true;
            myDateTimePicker.ValueChanged +=
                new EventHandler(TimePickerValueChanged);
        }
        else
        {
            myDateTimePicker.Value = value;
            myDateTimePicker.Visible = false;
        }

        if (myDateTimePicker.Visible)
            DataGridTableStyle.DataGrid.Invalidate(bounds);
    }

    protected override Size GetPreferredSize(
        Graphics g,
        object value)
    {
        return new Size(100, myDateTimePicker.PreferredHeight + 4);
    }

    protected override int GetMinimumHeight()
    {
        return myDateTimePicker.PreferredHeight + 4;
    }
```

```
    protected override int GetPreferredHeight(Graphics g,
        object value)
    {
        return myDateTimePicker.PreferredHeight + 4;
    }

    protected override void Paint(Graphics g,
        Rectangle bounds,
        CurrencyManager source,
        int rowNum)
    {
        Paint(g, bounds, source, rowNum, false);
    }
    protected override void Paint(
        Graphics g,
        Rectangle bounds,
        CurrencyManager source,
        int rowNum,
        bool alignToRight)
    {
        Paint(
            g,bounds,
            source,
            rowNum,
            Brushes.Red,
            Brushes.Blue,
            alignToRight);
    }
    protected override void Paint(
        Graphics g,
        Rectangle bounds,
        CurrencyManager source,
        int rowNum,
        Brush backBrush,
        Brush foreBrush,
        bool alignToRight)
    {
        DateTime date = (DateTime)
            GetColumnValueAtRow(source, rowNum);
        Rectangle rect = bounds;
        g.FillRectangle(backBrush,rect);
        rect.Offset(0, 2);
        rect.Height -= 2;
        g.DrawString(date.ToString("d"),
            this.DataGridTableStyle.DataGrid.Font,
            foreBrush, rect);
    }

    protected override void SetDataGridInColumn(DataGrid value)
    {
        base.SetDataGridInColumn(value);
        if (myDateTimePicker.Parent != null)
        {
            myDateTimePicker.Parent.Controls.Remove
                (myDateTimePicker);
        }
        if (value != null)
        {
            value.Controls.Add(myDateTimePicker);
        }
    }

    private void TimePickerValueChanged(object sender, EventArgs e)
    {
        this.isEditing = true;
        base.ColumnStartedEditing(myDateTimePicker);
    }
}
namespace DataGridColumnStyleExample
{
    using System;
    using System.Data;
    using System.Windows.Forms;
    using System.Drawing;
    using System.ComponentModel;

    public class MyForm : Form
    {
        private DataTable namesDataTable;
        private DataGrid grid = new DataGrid();
        public MyForm() : base()
        {
            InitForm();

            namesDataTable = new DataTable("NamesTable");
            namesDataTable.Columns.Add(new DataColumn("Name"));
            DataColumn dateColumn = new DataColumn
                ("Date", typeof(DateTime));
            namesDataTable.Columns.Add(dateColumn);
            DataSet namesDataSet = new DataSet();
            namesDataSet.Tables.Add(namesDataTable);
            grid.DataSource = namesDataSet;
            grid.DataMember = "NamesTable";
            AddGridStyle();
            AddData();
        }

        private void AddGridStyle()
        {
            DataGridTableStyle myGridStyle = new DataGridTableStyle();
            myGridStyle.MappingName = "NamesTable";

            DataGridTextBoxColumn nameColumnStyle =
                new DataGridTextBoxColumn();
            nameColumnStyle.MappingName = "Name";
            nameColumnStyle.HeaderText= "Name";
            myGridStyle.GridColumnStyles.Add(nameColumnStyle);

            DataGridTimePickerColumn timePickerColumnStyle =
                new DataGridTimePickerColumn();
            timePickerColumnStyle.MappingName = "Date";
            timePickerColumnStyle.HeaderText = "Date";
            timePickerColumnStyle.Width = 100;
            myGridStyle.GridColumnStyles.Add(timePickerColumnStyle);

            grid.TableStyles.Add(myGridStyle);
        }

        private void AddData()
        {

            DataRow dRow = namesDataTable.NewRow();
            dRow["Name"] = "Name 1";
            dRow["Date"] = new DateTime(2001, 12, 01);
            namesDataTable.Rows.Add(dRow);

            dRow = namesDataTable.NewRow();
            dRow["Name"] = "Name 2";
            dRow["Date"] = new DateTime(2001, 12, 04);
            namesDataTable.Rows.Add(dRow);

            dRow = namesDataTable.NewRow();
            dRow["Name"] = "Name 3";
            dRow["Date"] = new DateTime(2001, 12, 29);
            namesDataTable.Rows.Add(dRow);

            dRow = namesDataTable.NewRow();
            dRow["Name"] = "Name 4";
            dRow["Date"] = new DateTime(2001, 12, 13);
            namesDataTable.Rows.Add(dRow);

            dRow = namesDataTable.NewRow();
            dRow["Name"] = "Name 5";
            dRow["Date"] = new DateTime(2001, 12, 21);
            namesDataTable.Rows.Add(dRow);

            namesDataTable.AcceptChanges();
        }

        private void InitForm()
        {
            this.Size = new Size(500, 500);
```

```
            grid.Size = new Size(350, 250);
            grid.TabStop = true;
            grid.TabIndex = 1;
            this.StartPosition = FormStartPosition.CenterScreen;
            this.Controls.Add(grid);
        }
        [STAThread]
        public static void Main()
        {
            MyForm myForm1= new MyForm();
            myForm1.ShowDialog();
        }
    }
}
```

[C++]

```
using namespace System;
using namespace System::Data;
using namespace System::Windows::Forms;
using namespace System::Drawing;
using namespace System::ComponentModel;

// This example shows how to create your own column style that
// hosts a control, in this case, a DateTimePicker.
public __gc class DataGridTimePickerColumn : public
 DataGridColumnStyle {
private:
    DateTimePicker* myDateTimePicker;

    // The isEditing field tracks whether or not the user is
    // editing data with the hosted control.
    bool*  isEditing;

public:
    DataGridTimePickerColumn() {
        myDateTimePicker = new DateTimePicker();
        myDateTimePicker->Visible = false;
    }

protected:
    void Abort(int /*rowNum*/) {
        isEditing = false;
        myDateTimePicker->ValueChanged -=
            new EventHandler(this, TimePickerValueChanged);
        Invalidate();
    }

    bool Commit
        (CurrencyManager* dataSource, int rowNum) {
            myDateTimePicker->Bounds = Rectangle::Empty;

            myDateTimePicker->ValueChanged -=
                new EventHandler(this, TimePickerValueChanged);

            if (!isEditing)
                return true;

            isEditing = false;

            try {
                DateTime value = myDateTimePicker->Value;
                SetColumnValueAtRow(dataSource, rowNum, __box(value));
            } catch (Exception*) {
                Abort(rowNum);
                return false;
            }

            Invalidate();
            return true;
        }

    void Edit(CurrencyManager* source,
        int rowNum,
        Rectangle bounds,
        bool /*readOnly*/,
        String* /*instantText*/,
            bool cellIsVisible) {
                DateTime value =
*dynamic_cast<DateTime*>(GetColumnValueAtRow(source, rowNum));
                if (cellIsVisible) {
                    myDateTimePicker->Bounds = Rectangle
                        (bounds.X + 2, bounds.Y + 2,
                        bounds.Width - 4, bounds.Height - 4);
                    myDateTimePicker->Value = value;
                    myDateTimePicker->Visible = true;
                    myDateTimePicker->ValueChanged += new
EventHandler(this, TimePickerValueChanged);
                } else {
                    myDateTimePicker->Value = value;
                    myDateTimePicker->Visible = false;
                }

                if (myDateTimePicker->Visible)
                    DataGridTableStyle->DataGrid->Invalidate(bounds);
            }

        System::Drawing::Size GetPreferredSize(Graphics* /*g*/,
            Object* /*value*/) {
                return Size(100, myDateTimePicker->PreferredHeight + 4);
            }

        int GetMinimumHeight() {
            return myDateTimePicker->PreferredHeight + 4;
        }

        int GetPreferredHeight(Graphics* /*g*/,
            Object* /*value*/) {
                return myDateTimePicker->PreferredHeight + 4;
            }

        void Paint(Graphics* g,
            Rectangle bounds,
            CurrencyManager* source,
            int rowNum) {
                Paint(g, bounds, source, rowNum, false);
            }

        void Paint(Graphics* g,
            Rectangle bounds,
            CurrencyManager* source,
            int rowNum,
            bool alignToRight) {
                Paint(g, bounds,
                    source,
                    rowNum,
                    Brushes::Red,
                    Brushes::Blue,
                    alignToRight);
            }

        void Paint(Graphics* g,
            Rectangle bounds,
            CurrencyManager* source,
            int rowNum,
            Brush* backBrush,
            Brush* foreBrush,
            bool /*alignToRight*/) {
                DateTime date = *dynamic_cast<DateTime*>
                    (GetColumnValueAtRow(source, rowNum));
                Rectangle rect = bounds;
                g->FillRectangle(backBrush, rect);
                rect.Offset(0, 2);
                rect.Height -= 2;
                g->DrawString(date.ToString(S"d"),
                    this->DataGridTableStyle->DataGrid->Font,
                    foreBrush, RectangleF::op_Implicit(rect));
            }

        void SetDataGridInColumn(DataGrid* value) {
            DataGridColumnStyle::SetDataGridInColumn(value);
            if (myDateTimePicker->Parent != 0) {
                myDateTimePicker->Parent->Controls->Remove
```

```
                (myDateTimePicker);
        }
        if (value != 0) {
            value->Controls->Add(myDateTimePicker);
        }
    }

private:
    void TimePickerValueChanged(Object* /*sender*/, EventArgs* /*e*/) {
        this->isEditing = (bool*)true;
        DataGridColumnStyle::ColumnStartedEditing(myDateTimePicker);
    }
};

namespace DataGridColumnStyleExample {
public __gc class MyForm : public Form {
private:
    DataTable*  namesDataTable;
    DataGrid* grid;

public:
    MyForm() {
        grid = new DataGrid();

        InitForm();
        namesDataTable = new DataTable(S"NamesTable");
        namesDataTable->Columns->Add(new DataColumn(S"Name"));
        DataColumn* dateColumn = new DataColumn
            (S"Date", __typeof(DateTime));
        namesDataTable->Columns->Add(dateColumn);
        DataSet* namesDataSet = new DataSet();
        namesDataSet->Tables->Add(namesDataTable);
        grid->DataSource = namesDataSet;
        grid->DataMember = S"NamesTable";
        AddGridStyle();
        AddData();
    }

private:
    void AddGridStyle() {
        DataGridTableStyle* myGridStyle = new DataGridTableStyle();
        myGridStyle->MappingName = S"NamesTable";

        DataGridTextBoxColumn* nameColumnStyle = new                        ↵
DataGridTextBoxColumn();
        nameColumnStyle->MappingName = S"Name";
        nameColumnStyle->HeaderText= S"Name";
        myGridStyle->GridColumnStyles->Add(nameColumnStyle);

        DataGridTimePickerColumn* timePickerColumnStyle =                    ↵
 new DataGridTimePickerColumn();
        timePickerColumnStyle->MappingName = S"Date";
        timePickerColumnStyle->HeaderText = S"Date";
        timePickerColumnStyle->Width = 100;
        myGridStyle->GridColumnStyles->Add(timePickerColumnStyle);

        grid->TableStyles->Add(myGridStyle);
    }

private:
    void AddData() {

        DataRow* dRow = namesDataTable->NewRow();
        dRow->Item[S"Name"] = S"Name 1";
        dRow->Item[S"Date"] = __box(DateTime(2001, 12, 01));
        namesDataTable->Rows->Add(dRow);

        dRow = namesDataTable->NewRow();
        dRow->Item[S"Name"] = S"Name 2";
        dRow->Item[S"Date"] = __box(DateTime(2001, 12, 04));
        namesDataTable->Rows->Add(dRow);

        dRow = namesDataTable->NewRow();
        dRow->Item[S"Name"] = S"Name 3";
        dRow->Item[S"Date"] = __box(DateTime(2001, 12, 29));
        namesDataTable->Rows->Add(dRow);

        dRow = namesDataTable->NewRow();
        dRow->Item[S"Name"] = S"Name 4";
        dRow->Item[S"Date"] = __box(DateTime(2001, 12, 13));
        namesDataTable->Rows->Add(dRow);

        dRow = namesDataTable->NewRow();
        dRow->Item[S"Name"] = S"Name 5";
        dRow->Item[S"Date"] = __box(DateTime(2001, 12, 21));
        namesDataTable->Rows->Add(dRow);

        namesDataTable->AcceptChanges();
    }

private:
    void InitForm() {
        this->Size = System::Drawing::Size(500, 500);
        grid->Size = System::Drawing::Size(350, 250);
        grid->TabStop = true;
        grid->TabIndex = 1;
        this->StartPosition = FormStartPosition::CenterScreen;
        this->Controls->Add(grid);
    }
};
}

[STAThread]
int main() {
    DataGridColumnStyleExample::MyForm* myForm1 =
        new DataGridColumnStyleExample::MyForm();
    myForm1->ShowDialog();
}
```

Requirements

Namespace: System.Windows.Forms

Platforms: Windows 98, Windows NT 4.0, Windows Millennium Edition, Windows 2000, Windows XP Home Edition, Windows XP Professional, Windows Server 2003 family, .NET Compact Framework - Windows CE .NET

Assembly: System.Windows.Forms (in System.Windows.Forms.dll)

DataGridColumnStyle Constructor

Initializes a new instance of the **DataGridColumnStyle** class.

Overload List

In a derived class, initializes a new instance of the **DataGrid-ColumnStyle** class.

Supported by the .NET Compact Framework.

[Visual Basic] **Public Sub New()**

[C#] **public DataGridColumnStyle();**

[C++] **public: DataGridColumnStyle();**

[JScript] **public function DataGridColumnStyle();**

Initializes a new instance of the **DataGridColumnStyle** class with the specified **PropertyDescriptor**.

[Visual Basic] **Public Sub New(PropertyDescriptor)**

[C#] **public DataGridColumnStyle(PropertyDescriptor);**

[C++] **public: DataGridColumnStyle(PropertyDescriptor*);**

[JScript] **public function DataGridColumnStyle(PropertyDescriptor);**

Example

See related example in the **System.Windows.Forms.DataGrid-ColumnStyle** class topic.

DataGridColumnStyle Constructor ()

In a derived class, initializes a new instance of the **DataGridColumnStyle** class.

```
[Visual Basic]
Public Sub New()
[C#]
public DataGridColumnStyle();
[C++]
public: DataGridColumnStyle();
[JScript]
public function DataGridColumnStyle();
```

Remarks

When you create an instance of a **DataGridColumnStyle**, the following properties are initialized.

Property	Default Value
Alignment	**HorizontalAlignment.Left**
DataGridTableStyle	A null reference (**Nothing** in Visual Basic)
FontHeight	-1
Invalidate	**false**
NullText	The string "(null)".
ReadOnly	**false**

Requirements

Platforms: Windows 98, Windows NT 4.0, Windows Millennium Edition, Windows 2000, Windows XP Home Edition, Windows XP Professional, Windows Server 2003 family, .NET Compact Framework - Windows CE .NET

DataGridColumnStyle Constructor (PropertyDescriptor)

Initializes a new instance of the **DataGridColumnStyle** class with the specified **PropertyDescriptor**.

```
[Visual Basic]
Public Sub New( _
   ByVal prop As PropertyDescriptor _
)
[C#]
public DataGridColumnStyle(
   PropertyDescriptor prop
);
[C++]
public: DataGridColumnStyle(
   PropertyDescriptor* prop
);
[JScript]
public function DataGridColumnStyle(
   prop : PropertyDescriptor
);
```

Parameters

prop

A that **PropertyDescriptor** that provides the attributes for the column.

Remarks

To create a new **DataGridColumnStyle**, you must first get the **CurrencyManager** for the data source of the table to which the column will be added. See the CurrencyManager and BindingManager for details on getting specific CurrencyManager objects for a form.

From the **CurrencyManager**, you can then get the **PropertyDescriptor** for the **DataColumn** that will supply the data for the column.

When you create an instance of a **DataGridColumnStyle**, the following read/write properties are initialized.

Property	Initial Value
Alignment	**HorizontalAlignment.Left**
DataGridTableStyle	A null reference (**Nothing** in Visual Basic)
FontHeight	-1
Invalidate	**false**
NullText	"(null)"
ReadOnly	**false**

Example

See related example in the **System.Windows.Forms.DataGridColumnStyle** class topic.

Requirements

Platforms: Windows 98, Windows NT 4.0, Windows Millennium Edition, Windows 2000, Windows XP Home Edition, Windows XP Professional, Windows Server 2003 family

DataGridColumnStyle.Alignment Property

Gets or sets the alignment of text in a column.

```
[Visual Basic]
Public Overridable Property Alignment As HorizontalAlignment
[C#]
public virtual HorizontalAlignment Alignment {get; set;}
[C++]
public: __property virtual HorizontalAlignment get_Alignment();
public: __property virtual void set_Alignment(HorizontalAlignment);
[JScript]
public function get Alignment() : HorizontalAlignment;
public function set Alignment(HorizontalAlignment);
```

Property Value

One of the **HorizontalAlignment** values. The default is **Left**. Valid options include **Left**, **Center**, and **Right**.

Example

See related example in the **System.Windows.Forms.DataGridColumnStyle** class topic.

Requirements

Platforms: Windows 98, Windows NT 4.0, Windows Millennium Edition, Windows 2000, Windows XP Home Edition, Windows XP Professional, Windows Server 2003 family

DataGridColumnStyle.DataGridTableStyle Property

Gets the **DataGridTableStyle** for the column.

```
[Visual Basic]
Public Overridable ReadOnly Property DataGridTableStyle As _
   DataGridTableStyle
[C#]
public virtual DataGridTableStyle DataGridTableStyle {get;}
[C++]
public: __property virtual DataGridTableStyle*
   get_DataGridTableStyle();
[JScript]
public function get DataGridTableStyle() : DataGridTableStyle;
```

Property Value

The **DataGridTableStyle** that contains the current **DataGrid-ColumnStyle**.

Example

See related example in the **System.Windows.Forms.DataGrid-ColumnStyle** class topic.

Requirements

Platforms: Windows 98, Windows NT 4.0, Windows Millennium Edition, Windows 2000, Windows XP Home Edition, Windows XP Professional, Windows Server 2003 family

DataGridColumnStyle.FontHeight Property

Gets the height of the column's font.

```
[Visual Basic]
Protected ReadOnly Property FontHeight As Integer
[C#]
protected int FontHeight {get;}
[C++]
protected: __property int get_FontHeight();
[JScript]
protected function get FontHeight() : int;
```

Property Value

The height of the font in pixels. If no font height has been set, the property returns the **System.Windows.Forms.DataGrid** control's font height; if that property hasn't been set, the default font height value for the **System.Windows.Forms.DataGrid** control is returned.

Requirements

Platforms: Windows 98, Windows NT 4.0, Windows Millennium Edition, Windows 2000, Windows XP Home Edition, Windows XP Professional, Windows Server 2003 family

DataGridColumnStyle.HeaderAccessibleObject Property

This member supports the .NET Framework infrastructure and is not intended to be used directly from your code.

```
[Visual Basic]
Public ReadOnly Property HeaderAccessibleObject As AccessibleObject
[C#]
public AccessibleObject HeaderAccessibleObject {get;}
[C++]
public: __property AccessibleObject* get_HeaderAccessibleObject();
[JScript]
public function get HeaderAccessibleObject() : AccessibleObject;
```

DataGridColumnStyle.HeaderText Property

Gets or sets the text of the column header.

```
[Visual Basic]
Public Overridable Property HeaderText As String
[C#]
public virtual string HeaderText {get; set;}
[C++]
public: __property virtual String* get_HeaderText();
public: __property virtual void set_HeaderText(String*);
[JScript]
public function get HeaderText() : String;
public function set HeaderText(String);
```

Property Value

A string that is displayed as the column header. If it is created by the **DataGrid**, the default value is the name of the **PropertyDescriptor** used to create the column. If it is created by the user, the default is an empty string ("").

Remarks

The **HeaderText** property is typically used to display a caption that is different from the **MappingName** value when the **MappingName** value isn't easily understandable. For example, you can change the **HeaderText** to "First Name" when the is "FName".

Example

See related example in the **System.Windows.Forms.DataGrid-ColumnStyle** class topic.

Requirements

Platforms: Windows 98, Windows NT 4.0, Windows Millennium Edition, Windows 2000, Windows XP Home Edition, Windows XP Professional, Windows Server 2003 family, .NET Compact Framework - Windows CE .NET

DataGridColumnStyle.MappingName Property

Gets or sets the name used to map the column style to a data member.

```
[Visual Basic]
Public Property MappingName As String
[C#]
public string MappingName {get; set;}
[C++]
public: __property String* get_MappingName();
public: __property void set_MappingName(String*);
[JScript]
public function get MappingName() : String;
public function set MappingName(String);
```

Property Value

The name used to map the column style to a data member.

Remarks

The **MappingName** property is usually set to the **ColumnName** of a **DataColumn**. Whenever the **DataTable** containing the **DataColumn** is displayed, the **DataGridColumnStyle** with the same **MappingName** will be used to display the data.

The comparison used to match the **MappingName** to the **ColumnName** is case-insensitive.

Example

See related example in the **System.Windows.Forms.DataGridColumnStyle** class topic.

Requirements

Platforms: Windows 98, Windows NT 4.0,
Windows Millennium Edition, Windows 2000,
Windows XP Home Edition, Windows XP Professional,
Windows Server 2003 family,
.NET Compact Framework - Windows CE .NET

DataGridColumnStyle.NullText Property

Gets or sets the text that is displayed when the column contains a null reference (**Nothing** in Visual Basic).

[Visual Basic]
```
Public Overridable Property NullText As String
```
[C#]
```
public virtual string NullText {get; set;}
```
[C++]
```
public: __property virtual String* get_NullText();
public: __property virtual void set_NullText(String*);
```
[JScript]
```
public function get NullText() : String;
public function set NullText(String);
```

Property Value

A string displayed in a column containing a **DBNull.Value**.

Remarks

The **DataColumn** class's **AllowDBNull** property determines if a column can contain null values.

Example

See related example in the **System.Windows.Forms.DataGridColumnStyle** class topic.

Requirements

Platforms: Windows 98, Windows NT 4.0,
Windows Millennium Edition, Windows 2000,
Windows XP Home Edition, Windows XP Professional,
Windows Server 2003 family,
.NET Compact Framework - Windows CE .NET

DataGridColumnStyle.PropertyDescriptor Property

Gets or sets the **PropertyDescriptor** that determines the attributes of data displayed by the **DataGridColumnStyle**.

[Visual Basic]
```
Public Overridable Property PropertyDescriptor As _
   PropertyDescriptor
```
[C#]
```
public virtual PropertyDescriptor PropertyDescriptor {get; set;}
```
[C++]
```
public: __property virtual PropertyDescriptor*
get_PropertyDescriptor();
public: __property virtual void
set_PropertyDescriptor(PropertyDescriptor*);
```
[JScript]
```
public function get PropertyDescriptor() : PropertyDescriptor;
public function set PropertyDescriptor(PropertyDescriptor);
```

Property Value

A **PropertyDescriptor** that contains data about the attributes of the column.

Remarks

The **PropertyDescriptor** for a column is set using the **GetItemProperties** method of the **BindingManagerBase**. See the **DataGridColumnStyle** constructor for an example of using the **PropertyDescriptor** to create a new **DataGridColumnStyle** object.

Example

See related example in the **System.Windows.Forms.DataGridColumnStyle** class topic.

Requirements

Platforms: Windows 98, Windows NT 4.0,
Windows Millennium Edition, Windows 2000,
Windows XP Home Edition, Windows XP Professional,
Windows Server 2003 family

DataGridColumnStyle.ReadOnly Property

Gets or sets a value indicating whether the data in the column can be edited.

[Visual Basic]
```
Public Overridable Property ReadOnly As Boolean
```
[C#]
```
public virtual bool ReadOnly {get; set;}
```
[C++]
```
public: __property virtual bool get_ReadOnly();
public: __property virtual void set_ReadOnly(bool);
```
[JScript]
```
public function get ReadOnly() : Boolean;
public function set ReadOnly(Boolean);
```

Property Value

true, if the data can't be edited; otherwise, **false**.

Remarks

Make a column read-only if it contains a primary key or if its value is generated automatically (as when the **DataColumn** object's **AutoIncrement** property is set to **true**).

Similar read only properties exist on other classes, each allowing more control over the access to data. For example, the **System.Windows.Forms.DataGrid** control can be set to read-only mode with by using its **ReadOnly** property; the **DataGridTableStyle** also has a **ReadOnly** property, and the **DataColumn** class has a **ReadOnly** property for restricting data updates.

Example

See related example in the **System.Windows.Forms.DataGridColumnStyle** class topic.

Requirements

Platforms: Windows 98, Windows NT 4.0,
Windows Millennium Edition, Windows 2000,
Windows XP Home Edition, Windows XP Professional,
Windows Server 2003 family

DataGridColumnStyle.Width Property

Gets or sets the width of the column.

[Visual Basic]
```
Public Overridable Property Width As Integer
```
[C#]
```
public virtual int Width {get; set;}
```
[C++]
```
public: __property virtual int get_Width();
public: __property virtual void set_Width(int);
```
[JScript]
```
public function get Width() : int;
public function set Width(int);
```

Property Value

The width of the column in pixels.

Example

See related example in the **System.Windows.Forms.DataGridColumnStyle** class topic.

Requirements

Platforms: Windows 98, Windows NT 4.0,
Windows Millennium Edition, Windows 2000,
Windows XP Home Edition, Windows XP Professional,
Windows Server 2003 family,
.NET Compact Framework - Windows CE .NET

DataGridColumnStyle.Abort Method

When overridden in a derived class, initiates a request to interrupt an edit procedure.

[Visual Basic]
```
Protected Friend MustOverride Sub Abort( _
   ByVal rowNum As Integer _
)
```
[C#]
```
protected internal abstract void Abort(
   int rowNum
);
```
[C++]
```
protected public: virtual void Abort(
   int rowNum
) = 0;
```
[JScript]
```
protected internal abstract function Abort(
   rowNum : int
);
```

Parameters

rowNum

The row number upon which an operation is being interrupted.

Remarks

The **Abort** method is used by the **DataGrid** when the **Commit** method of the **DataGridColumnStyle** method returns **false**. In that case, the column value is rolled back to its previous value.

The **DataGridColumnStyle** must end any editing operations before returning. Use the **Abort** method to accomplish this.

The **System.Windows.Forms.DataGrid** control's **EndEdit** method indirectly invokes **Abort** if its *ShouldAbort* parameter is set to **true**.

Requirements

Platforms: Windows 98, Windows NT 4.0,
Windows Millennium Edition, Windows 2000,
Windows XP Home Edition, Windows XP Professional,
Windows Server 2003 family

DataGridColumnStyle.BeginUpdate Method

Suspends the painting of the column until the **EndUpdate** method is called.

[Visual Basic]
```
Protected Sub BeginUpdate()
```
[C#]
```
protected void BeginUpdate();
```
[C++]
```
protected: void BeginUpdate();
```
[JScript]
```
protected function BeginUpdate();
```

Remarks

When many changes are made to the appearance of a **System.Windows.Forms.DataGrid** control (whether the changes are in the attributes of the column or the data displayed by the control), you should invoke the **BeginUpdate** method to temporarily freeze the drawing of the control. This results in less distraction to the user, and a performance gain. After all updates have been made, invoke the **EndUpdate** method to resume drawing of the control.

Example

See related example in the **System.Windows.Forms.DataGridColumnStyle** class topic.

Requirements

Platforms: Windows 98, Windows NT 4.0,
Windows Millennium Edition, Windows 2000,
Windows XP Home Edition, Windows XP Professional,
Windows Server 2003 family

DataGridColumnStyle.CheckValidDataSource Method

Throws an exception if the **System.Windows.Forms.DataGrid** does not have a valid data source, or if this column is not mapped to a valid property in the data source.

[Visual Basic]
```
Protected Sub CheckValidDataSource( _
   ByVal value As CurrencyManager _
)
```
[C#]
```
protected void CheckValidDataSource(
   CurrencyManager value
);
```

```
[C++]
protected: void CheckValidDataSource(
   CurrencyManager* value
);
[JScript]
protected function CheckValidDataSource(
   value : CurrencyManager
);
```

Parameters

value

A **CurrencyManager** to check.

Exceptions

Exception Type	Condition
ArgumentNull-Exception	The *value* is a null reference (**Nothing** in Visual Basic).
ApplicationException	The **PropertyDescriptor** for this column is a null reference (**Nothing** in Visual Basic).

Example

See related example in the **System.Windows.Forms.DataGrid-ColumnStyle** class topic.

Requirements

Platforms: Windows 98, Windows NT 4.0, Windows Millennium Edition, Windows 2000, Windows XP Home Edition, Windows XP Professional, Windows Server 2003 family

DataGridColumnStyle.ColumnStartedEditing Method

Informs the **System.Windows.Forms.DataGrid** that the user has begun editing the column.

```
[Visual Basic]
Protected Friend Overridable Sub ColumnStartedEditing( _
   ByVal editingControl As Control _
)
[C#]
protected internal virtual void ColumnStartedEditing(
   Control editingControl
);
[C++]
protected public: virtual void ColumnStartedEditing(
   Control* editingControl
);
[JScript]
protected internal function ColumnStartedEditing(
   editingControl : Control
);
```

Parameters

editingControl

The **Control** that hosted by the column.

Remarks

When called, the **ColumnStartedEditing** method allows the **System.Windows.Forms.DataGrid** control to show a pencil in the row header indicating the row is being edited.

Requirements

Platforms: Windows 98, Windows NT 4.0, Windows Millennium Edition, Windows 2000, Windows XP Home Edition, Windows XP Professional, Windows Server 2003 family

DataGridColumnStyle.Commit Method

When overridden in a derived class, initiates a request to complete an editing procedure.

```
[Visual Basic]
Protected Friend MustOverride Function Commit( _
   ByVal dataSource As CurrencyManager, _
   ByVal rowNum As Integer _
) As Boolean
[C#]
protected internal abstract bool Commit(
   CurrencyManager dataSource,
   int rowNum
);
[C++]
protected public: virtual bool Commit(
   CurrencyManager* dataSource,
   int rowNum
) = 0;
[JScript]
protected internal abstract function Commit(
   dataSource : CurrencyManager,
   rowNum : int
) : Boolean;
```

Parameters

dataSource

The **CurrencyManager** for the **DataGridColumnStyle**.

rowNum

The number of the row being edited.

Return Value

true if the editing procedure committed successfully; otherwise, **false**.

Remarks

Notes to Inheritors: The **Commit** method should be used by classes derived from the **DataGridColumnStyle** class to reset their editing state, for example, to concede the focus if the **DataGrid-ColumnStyle** hosts an editing control. See the **ConcedeFocus** method.

Call the **Commit** method when the **DataGridColumnStyle** receives a request to complete editing. If this is not possible without error, return **false**.

The **Commit** method is called by the **System.Windows.Forms.Data-Grid** control's public method **OnMouseDown**. The method is also called by other private methods, for example, when the current row is changed.

Example

See related example in the **System.Windows.Forms.DataGrid-ColumnStyle** class topic.

Requirements

Platforms: Windows 98, Windows NT 4.0, Windows Millennium Edition, Windows 2000, Windows XP Home Edition, Windows XP Professional, Windows Server 2003 family

DataGridColumnStyle.ConcedeFocus Method

Notifies a column that it must relinquish the focus to the control it is hosting.

```
[Visual Basic]
Protected Friend Overridable Sub ConcedeFocus()
[C#]
protected internal virtual void ConcedeFocus();
[C++]
protected public: virtual void ConcedeFocus();
[JScript]
protected internal function ConcedeFocus();
```

Remarks

Use this method to determine when a further action is required in a derived class. For example, this method is overridden by the **DataGridTextBoxColumn** to hide the **DataGridTextBox**.

Example

See related example in the **System.Windows.Forms.DataGridColumnStyle** class topic.

Requirements

Platforms: Windows 98, Windows NT 4.0, Windows Millennium Edition, Windows 2000, Windows XP Home Edition, Windows XP Professional, Windows Server 2003 family

DataGridColumnStyle.CreateHeaderAccessibleObject Method

This member supports the .NET Framework infrastructure and is not intended to be used directly from your code.

```
[Visual Basic]
Protected Overridable Function CreateHeaderAccessibleObject() As _
   AccessibleObject
[C#]
protected virtual AccessibleObject CreateHeaderAccessibleObject();
[C++]
protected: virtual AccessibleObject* CreateHeaderAccessibleObject();
[JScript]
protected function CreateHeaderAccessibleObject() :
   AccessibleObject;
```

DataGridColumnStyle.Edit Method

Prepares the cell for editing a value.

Overload List

Prepares a cell for editing.

[Visual Basic] **Overloads Protected Friend Overridable Sub Edit(CurrencyManager, Integer, Rectangle, Boolean)**

[C#] **protected internal virtual void Edit(CurrencyManager, int, Rectangle, bool);**

[C++] **protected public: virtual void Edit(CurrencyManager*, int, Rectangle, bool);**

[JScript] **protected internal function Edit(CurrencyManager, int, Rectangle, Boolean);**

Prepares the cell for editing using the specified **CurrencyManager**, row number, and **Rectangle** parameters.

[Visual Basic] **Overloads Protected Friend Overridable Sub Edit(CurrencyManager, Integer, Rectangle, Boolean, String)**

[C#] **protected internal virtual void Edit(CurrencyManager, int, Rectangle, bool, string);**

[C++] **protected public: virtual void Edit(CurrencyManager*, int, Rectangle, bool, String*);**

[JScript] **protected internal function Edit(CurrencyManager, int, Rectangle, Boolean, String);**

When overridden in a deriving class, prepares a cell for editing.

[Visual Basic] **Overloads Protected Friend MustOverride Sub Edit(CurrencyManager, Integer, Rectangle, Boolean, String, Boolean)**

[C#] **protected internal abstract void Edit(CurrencyManager, int, Rectangle, bool, string, bool);**

[C++] **protected public: virtual void Edit(CurrencyManager*, int, Rectangle, bool, String*, bool) = 0;**

[JScript] **protected internal abstract function Edit(CurrencyManager, int, Rectangle, Boolean, String, Boolean);**

Example

See related example in the **System.Windows.Forms.DataGridColumnStyle** class topic.

DataGridColumnStyle.Edit Method (CurrencyManager, Int32, Rectangle, Boolean)

Prepares a cell for editing.

```
[Visual Basic]
Overloads Protected Friend Overridable Sub Edit( _
   ByVal source As CurrencyManager, _
   ByVal rowNum As Integer, _
   ByVal bounds As Rectangle, _
   ByVal readOnly As Boolean _
)
[C#]
protected internal virtual void Edit(
   CurrencyManager source,
   int rowNum,
   Rectangle bounds,
   bool readOnly
);
[C++]
protected public: virtual void Edit(
   CurrencyManager* source,
   int rowNum,
   Rectangle bounds,
   bool readOnly
);
[JScript]
protected internal function Edit(
   source : CurrencyManager,
   rowNum : int,
   bounds : Rectangle,
   readOnly : Boolean
);
```

Parameters

source

The **CurrencyManager** for the **DataGridColumnStyle**.

rowNum

The row number to edit.

bounds

The bounding **Rectangle** in which the control is to be sited.

readOnly

A value indicating whether the column is a read-only. **true** if the value is read-only; otherwise, **false**.

Remarks

Typically, the **Edit** method sites a control onto the grid at the location of the cell being edited.

Example

See related example in the **System.Windows.Forms.DataGridColumnStyle** class topic.

Requirements

Platforms: Windows 98, Windows NT 4.0, Windows Millennium Edition, Windows 2000, Windows XP Home Edition, Windows XP Professional, Windows Server 2003 family

DataGridColumnStyle.Edit Method (CurrencyManager, Int32, Rectangle, Boolean, String)

Prepares the cell for editing using the specified **CurrencyManager**, row number, and **Rectangle** parameters.

[Visual Basic]
```
Overloads Protected Friend Overridable Sub Edit( _
   ByVal source As CurrencyManager, _
   ByVal rowNum As Integer, _
   ByVal bounds As Rectangle, _
   ByVal readOnly As Boolean, _
   ByVal instantText As String _
)
```
[C#]
```
protected internal virtual void Edit(
   CurrencyManager source,
   int rowNum,
   Rectangle bounds,
   bool readOnly,
   string instantText
);
```
[C++]
```
protected public: virtual void Edit(
   CurrencyManager* source,
   int rowNum,
   Rectangle bounds,
   bool readOnly,
   String* instantText
);
```
[JScript]
```
protected internal function Edit(
   source : CurrencyManager,
   rowNum : int,
   bounds : Rectangle,
   readOnly : Boolean,
   instantText : String
);
```

Parameters

source

The **CurrencyManager** for the **DataGridColumnStyle**.

rowNum

The row number in this column which is being edited.

bounds

The **Rectangle** in which the control is to be sited.

readOnly

A value indicating whether the column is a read-only. **true** if the value is read-only; otherwise, **false**.

instantText

The text to display in the control.

Remarks

Typically, the **Edit** method sites a control onto the grid at the location of the cell being edited.

Example

See related example in the **System.Windows.Forms.DataGridColumnStyle** class topic.

Requirements

Platforms: Windows 98, Windows NT 4.0, Windows Millennium Edition, Windows 2000, Windows XP Home Edition, Windows XP Professional, Windows Server 2003 family

DataGridColumnStyle.Edit Method (CurrencyManager, Int32, Rectangle, Boolean, String, Boolean)

When overridden in a deriving class, prepares a cell for editing.

[Visual Basic]
```
Overloads Protected Friend MustOverride Sub Edit( _
   ByVal source As CurrencyManager, _
   ByVal rowNum As Integer, _
   ByVal bounds As Rectangle, _
   ByVal readOnly As Boolean, _
   ByVal instantText As String, _
   ByVal cellIsVisible As Boolean _
)
```
[C#]
```
protected internal abstract void Edit(
   CurrencyManager source,
   int rowNum,
   Rectangle bounds,
   bool readOnly,
   string instantText,
   bool cellIsVisible
);
```
[C++]
```
protected public: virtual void Edit(
   CurrencyManager* source,
   int rowNum,
   Rectangle bounds,
   bool readOnly,
   String* instantText,
   bool cellIsVisible
) = 0;
```

```
[JScript]
protected internal abstract function Edit(
   source : CurrencyManager,
   rowNum : int,
   bounds : Rectangle,
   readOnly : Boolean,
   instantText : String,
   cellIsVisible : Boolean
);
```

Parameters

source
The **CurrencyManager** for the **DataGridColumnStyle**.

rowNum
The row number in this column which is being edited.

bounds
The **Rectangle** in which the control is to be sited.

readOnly
A value indicating whether the column is a read-only. **true** if the value is read-only; otherwise, **false**.

instantText
The text to display in the control.

cellIsVisible
A value indicating whether the cell is visible. **true** if the cell is visible; otherwise, **false**.

Remarks

Typically, the **Edit** method sites a control onto the grid at the location of the cell being edited.

Example

See related example in the **System.Windows.Forms.DataGridColumnStyle** class topic.

Requirements

Platforms: Windows 98, Windows NT 4.0, Windows Millennium Edition, Windows 2000, Windows XP Home Edition, Windows XP Professional, Windows Server 2003 family

DataGridColumnStyle.EndUpdate Method

Resumes the painting of columns suspended by calling the **BeginUpdate** method.

```
[Visual Basic]
Protected Sub EndUpdate()
[C#]
protected void EndUpdate();
[C++]
protected: void EndUpdate();
[JScript]
protected function EndUpdate();
```

Remarks

When many changes are made to the appearance of a **System.Windows.Forms.DataGrid** control (whether the changes are in the attributes of the column or the data displayed by the control), you should invoke the **BeginUpdate** method to temporarily freeze the drawing of the control. This results in less distraction to the user, and a performance gain. After all updates have been made, invoke the **EndUpdate** method to resume drawing of the control.

Example

See related example in the **System.Windows.Forms.DataGridColumnStyle** class topic.

Requirements

Platforms: Windows 98, Windows NT 4.0, Windows Millennium Edition, Windows 2000, Windows XP Home Edition, Windows XP Professional, Windows Server 2003 family

DataGridColumnStyle.EnterNullValue Method

Enters a **DBNull.Value** into the column.

```
[Visual Basic]
Protected Friend Overridable Sub EnterNullValue()
[C#]
protected internal virtual void EnterNullValue();
[C++]
protected public: virtual void EnterNullValue();
[JScript]
protected internal function EnterNullValue();
```

Remarks

This method is called when the user presses Alt+0 to allow a column to enter the appropriate null value. For example, when called on a **DataGridTextBoxColumn**, the appropriate **NullText** value is inserted into the column.

The **EnterNullValue** has no default behavior. When inheriting from **DataGridColumnStyle**, override the method to enter a null reference (**Nothing** in Visual Basic) in a column.

Example

[Visual Basic] The following example shows a possible override of the **EnterNullValue** method.

```
[Visual Basic]
Overrides Protected Sub EnterNullValue()
   ' Enter the NullText value into a hosted TextBox control.
   Me.TextBox.Text = Me.NullText
End Sub
```

Requirements

Platforms: Windows 98, Windows NT 4.0, Windows Millennium Edition, Windows 2000, Windows XP Home Edition, Windows XP Professional, Windows Server 2003 family

DataGridColumnStyle.GetColumnValueAtRow Method

Gets the value in the specified row from the specified **CurrencyManager**.

```
[Visual Basic]
Protected Friend Overridable Function GetColumnValueAtRow( _
   ByVal source As CurrencyManager, _
   ByVal rowNum As Integer _
) As Object
[C#]
protected internal virtual object GetColumnValueAtRow(
   CurrencyManager source,
   int rowNum
);
```

[C++]
```
protected public: virtual Object* GetColumnValueAtRow(
   CurrencyManager* source,
   int rowNum
);
```
[JScript]
```
protected internal function GetColumnValueAtRow(
   source : CurrencyManager,
   rowNum : int
) : Object;
```

Parameters

source
The **CurrencyManager** containing the data.

rowNum
The row number containing the data.

Return Value

An **Object** containing the value.

Exceptions

Exception Type	Condition
ApplicationException	The **DataColumn** for this **DataGridColumnStyle** hasn't been set yet.

Remarks

If the data source for the column is a **DataTable**, use the **Column-Changing** or **RowChanging** events to determine when a row or column value has changed.

Example

See related example in the **System.Windows.Forms.DataGrid-ColumnStyle** class topic.

Requirements

Platforms: Windows 98, Windows NT 4.0, Windows Millennium Edition, Windows 2000, Windows XP Home Edition, Windows XP Professional, Windows Server 2003 family

DataGridColumnStyle.GetMinimumHeight Method

When overridden in a derived class, gets the minimum height of a row.

[Visual Basic]
```
Protected Friend MustOverride Function GetMinimumHeight() As Integer
```
[C#]
```
protected internal abstract int GetMinimumHeight();
```
[C++]
```
protected public: virtual int GetMinimumHeight() = 0;
```
[JScript]
```
protected internal abstract function GetMinimumHeight() : int;
```

Return Value

The minimum height of a row.

Example

See related example in the **System.Windows.Forms.DataGrid-ColumnStyle** class topic.

Requirements

Platforms: Windows 98, Windows NT 4.0, Windows Millennium Edition, Windows 2000, Windows XP Home Edition, Windows XP Professional, Windows Server 2003 family

DataGridColumnStyle.GetPreferredHeight Method

When overridden in a derived class, gets the height used for automatically resizing columns.

[Visual Basic]
```
Protected Friend MustOverride Function GetPreferredHeight( _
   ByVal g As Graphics, _
   ByVal value As Object _
) As Integer
```
[C#]
```
protected internal abstract int GetPreferredHeight(
   Graphics g,
   object value
);
```
[C++]
```
protected public: virtual int GetPreferredHeight(
   Graphics* g,
   Object* value
) = 0;
```
[JScript]
```
protected internal abstract function GetPreferredHeight(
   g : Graphics,
   value : Object
) : int;
```

Parameters

g
A **Graphics** object.

value
A object value for which you want to know the screen height and width.

Return Value

The height used for auto resizing a cell.

Remarks

The **GetPreferredSize** will usually be invoked from a mouse down event to resize a column's height for a long string.

Example

See related example in the **System.Windows.Forms.DataGrid-ColumnStyle** class topic.

Requirements

Platforms: Windows 98, Windows NT 4.0, Windows Millennium Edition, Windows 2000, Windows XP Home Edition, Windows XP Professional, Windows Server 2003 family

DataGridColumnStyle.GetPreferredSize Method

When overridden in a derived class, gets the width and height of the specified value. The width and height are used when the user navigates to **DataGridTableStyle** using the **DataGridColumnStyle**.

[Visual Basic]
```
Protected Friend MustOverride Function GetPreferredSize( _
   ByVal g As Graphics, _
   ByVal value As Object _
) As Size
```
[C#]
```
protected internal abstract Size GetPreferredSize(
   Graphics g,
   object value
);
```
[C++]
```
protected public: virtual Size GetPreferredSize(
   Graphics* g,
   Object* value
) = 0;
```
[JScript]
```
protected internal abstract function GetPreferredSize(
   g : Graphics,
   value : Object
) : Size;
```

Parameters

g

A **Graphics** object.

value

An object value for which you want to know the screen height and width.

Return Value

A **Size** that contains the dimensions of the cell.

Remarks

Use **GetPreferredSize** to determine the width a column should resize to, given a particular string or numeral.

Example

See related example in the **System.Windows.Forms.DataGridColumnStyle** class topic.

Requirements

Platforms: Windows 98, Windows NT 4.0, Windows Millennium Edition, Windows 2000, Windows XP Home Edition, Windows XP Professional, Windows Server 2003 family

DataGridColumnStyle.IDataGridColumnStyleEditingNotificationService.ColumnStartedEditing Method

This member supports the .NET Framework infrastructure and is not intended to be used directly from your code.

[Visual Basic]
```
Private Sub ColumnStartedEditing( _
   ByVal editingControl As Control _
) Implements _
   IDataGridColumnStyleEditingNotificationService.ColumnStartedEditing
```
[C#]
```
void

IDataGridColumnStyleEditingNotificationService.ColumnStartedEditing(
   Control editingControl
);
```
[C++]
```
private: void
IDataGridColumnStyleEditingNotificationService::ColumnStartedEditing(
   Control* editingControl
);
```
[JScript]
```
private function

IDataGridColumnStyleEditingNotificationService.ColumnStartedEditing(
   editingControl : Control
);
```

DataGridColumnStyle.Invalidate Method

Redraws the column and causes a paint message to be sent to the control.

[Visual Basic]
```
Protected Overridable Sub Invalidate()
```
[C#]
```
protected virtual void Invalidate();
```
[C++]
```
protected: virtual void Invalidate();
```
[JScript]
```
protected function Invalidate();
```

Remarks

The **Invalidate** method is typically called after an editing operation is interrupted. For example, you can call the method when implementing the **Abort** method.

Requirements

Platforms: Windows 98, Windows NT 4.0, Windows Millennium Edition, Windows 2000, Windows XP Home Edition, Windows XP Professional, Windows Server 2003 family

DataGridColumnStyle.Paint Method

When overridden in a derived class, paints the column in a **System.Windows.Forms.DataGrid** control.

Overload List

Paints the a **DataGridColumnStyle** with the specified **Graphics**, **Rectangle**, **CurrencyManager**, and row number.

[Visual Basic] **Overloads Protected Friend MustOverride Sub Paint(Graphics, Rectangle, CurrencyManager, Integer)**

[C#] **protected internal abstract void Paint(Graphics, Rectangle, CurrencyManager, int);**

[C++] **protected public: virtual void Paint(Graphics*, Rectangle, CurrencyManager*, int) = 0;**

[JScript] **protected internal abstract function Paint(Graphics, Rectangle, CurrencyManager, int);**

When overridden in a derived class, paints a **DataGridColumnStyle** with the specified **Graphics**, **Rectangle**, **CurrencyManager**, row number, and alignment.

[Visual Basic] **Overloads Protected Friend MustOverride Sub Paint(Graphics, Rectangle, CurrencyManager, Integer, Boolean)**

[C#] **protected internal abstract void Paint(Graphics, Rectangle, CurrencyManager, int, bool);**

[C++] **protected public: virtual void Paint(Graphics*, Rectangle, CurrencyManager*, int, bool) = 0;**

[JScript] **protected internal abstract function Paint(Graphics, Rectangle, CurrencyManager, int, Boolean);**

Paints a **DataGridColumnStyle** with the specified **Graphics**, **Rectangle**, **CurrencyManager**, row number, background color, foreground color, and alignment.

[Visual Basic] **Overloads Protected Friend Overridable Sub Paint(Graphics, Rectangle, CurrencyManager, Integer, Brush, Brush, Boolean)**

[C#] **protected internal virtual void Paint(Graphics, Rectangle, CurrencyManager, int, Brush, Brush, bool);**

[C++] **protected public: virtual void Paint(Graphics*, Rectangle, CurrencyManager*, int, Brush*, Brush*, bool);**

[JScript] **protected internal function Paint(Graphics, Rectangle, CurrencyManager, int, Brush, Brush, Boolean);**

DataGridColumnStyle.Paint Method (Graphics, Rectangle, CurrencyManager, Int32)

Paints the a **DataGridColumnStyle** with the specified **Graphics**, **Rectangle**, **CurrencyManager**, and row number.

```
[Visual Basic]
Overloads Protected Friend MustOverride Sub Paint( _
   ByVal g As Graphics, _
   ByVal bounds As Rectangle, _
   ByVal source As CurrencyManager, _
   ByVal rowNum As Integer _
)
[C#]
protected internal abstract void Paint(
   Graphics g,
   Rectangle bounds,
   CurrencyManager source,
   int rowNum
);
[C++]
protected public: virtual void Paint(
   Graphics* g,
   Rectangle bounds,
   CurrencyManager* source,
   int rowNum
) = 0;
[JScript]
protected internal abstract function Paint(
   g : Graphics,
   bounds : Rectangle,
   source : CurrencyManager,
   rowNum : int
);
```

Parameters

g
: The **Graphics** object to draw to.

bounds
: The bounding **Rectangle** to paint into.

source
: The **CurrencyManager** of the **System.Windows.Forms.DataGrid** control the column belongs to.

rowNum
: The number of the row in the underlying data being referred to.

Remarks

This method will be called very often with state = **DataGridColumnStyleState.Normal**, so inheriting classes should heavily optimize that type of call. When painting a cell, keep in mind the following: the border painting logic is handled elsewhere. Callers should save all Pens, Brushes, and so forth before passing their **Graphics** object to this method.

Requirements

Platforms: Windows 98, Windows NT 4.0, Windows Millennium Edition, Windows 2000, Windows XP Home Edition, Windows XP Professional, Windows Server 2003 family

DataGridColumnStyle.Paint Method (Graphics, Rectangle, CurrencyManager, Int32, Boolean)

When overridden in a derived class, paints a **DataGridColumnStyle** with the specified **Graphics**, **Rectangle**, **CurrencyManager**, row number, and alignment.

```
[Visual Basic]
Overloads Protected Friend MustOverride Sub Paint( _
   ByVal g As Graphics, _
   ByVal bounds As Rectangle, _
   ByVal source As CurrencyManager, _
   ByVal rowNum As Integer, _
   ByVal alignToRight As Boolean _
)
[C#]
protected internal abstract void Paint(
   Graphics g,
   Rectangle bounds,
   CurrencyManager source,
   int rowNum,
   bool alignToRight
);
[C++]
protected public: virtual void Paint(
   Graphics* g,
   Rectangle bounds,
   CurrencyManager* source,
   int rowNum,
   bool alignToRight
) = 0;
```

```
[JScript]
protected internal abstract function Paint(
   g : Graphics,
   bounds : Rectangle,
   source : CurrencyManager,
   rowNum : int,
   alignToRight : Boolean
);
```

Parameters

g
The **Graphics** object to draw to.

bounds
The bounding **Rectangle** to paint into.

source
The **CurrencyManager** of the **System.Windows.Forms.DataGrid** control the column belongs to.

rowNum
The number of the row in the underlying data being referred to.

alignToRight
A value indicating whether to align the column's content to the right. **true** if the content should be aligned to the right; otherwise **false**.

Requirements

Platforms: Windows 98, Windows NT 4.0, Windows Millennium Edition, Windows 2000, Windows XP Home Edition, Windows XP Professional, Windows Server 2003 family

DataGridColumnStyle.Paint Method (Graphics, Rectangle, CurrencyManager, Int32, Brush, Brush, Boolean)

Paints a **DataGridColumnStyle** with the specified **Graphics**, **Rectangle**, **CurrencyManager**, row number, background color, foreground color, and alignment.

```
[Visual Basic]
Overloads Protected Friend Overridable Sub Paint( _
   ByVal g As Graphics, _
   ByVal bounds As Rectangle, _
   ByVal source As CurrencyManager, _
   ByVal rowNum As Integer, _
   ByVal backBrush As Brush, _
   ByVal foreBrush As Brush, _
   ByVal alignToRight As Boolean _
)
[C#]
protected internal virtual void Paint(
   Graphics g,
   Rectangle bounds,
   CurrencyManager source,
   int rowNum,
   Brush backBrush,
   Brush foreBrush,
   bool alignToRight
);
[C++]
protected public: virtual void Paint(
   Graphics* g,
   Rectangle bounds,
   CurrencyManager* source,
   int rowNum,
   Brush* backBrush,
   Brush* foreBrush,
   bool alignToRight
);
[JScript]
protected internal function Paint(
   g : Graphics,
   bounds : Rectangle,
   source : CurrencyManager,
   rowNum : int,
   backBrush : Brush,
   foreBrush : Brush,
   alignToRight : Boolean
);
```

Parameters

g
The **Graphics** object to draw to.

bounds
The bounding **Rectangle** to paint into.

source
The **CurrencyManager** of the **System.Windows.Forms.DataGrid** control the column belongs to.

rowNum
The number of the row in the underlying data table being referred to.

backBrush
A **Brush** used to paint the background color.

foreBrush
A **Color** used to paint the foreground color.

alignToRight
A value indicating whether to align the content to the right. **true** if the content is aligned to the right, otherwise, **false**.

Requirements

Platforms: Windows 98, Windows NT 4.0, Windows Millennium Edition, Windows 2000, Windows XP Home Edition, Windows XP Professional, Windows Server 2003 family

DataGridColumnStyle.ReleaseHostedControl Method

Note: This namespace, class, or member is supported only in version 1.1 of the .NET Framework.

Allows the column to free resources when the control it hosts is not needed.

```
[Visual Basic]
Protected Friend Overridable Sub ReleaseHostedControl()
[C#]
protected internal virtual void ReleaseHostedControl();
[C++]
protected public: virtual void ReleaseHostedControl();
[JScript]
protected internal function ReleaseHostedControl();
```

Remarks

If you create a class that derives from **DataGridColumnStyle**, you will often use the derived class to host a control that is used to edit data. You should override the **ReleaseHostedControl** method to release any references to the control in order to free system resources. For example, the **DataGridTextBoxColumn** derived class uses this method to release the reference to the hosted **DataGridTextBox**.

Requirements

Platforms: Windows 98, Windows NT 4.0, Windows Millennium Edition, Windows 2000, Windows XP Home Edition, Windows XP Professional, Windows Server 2003 family

DataGridColumnStyle.ResetHeaderText Method

Resets the **HeaderText** to its default value, a null reference (**Nothing** in Visual Basic).

```
[Visual Basic]
Public Sub ResetHeaderText()
[C#]
public void ResetHeaderText();
[C++]
public: void ResetHeaderText();
[JScript]
public function ResetHeaderText();
```

Remarks

You typically use this method if you are either creating a designer for the **System.Windows.Forms.DataGrid**, or creating your own control incorporating the **System.Windows.Forms.DataGrid**.

Example

See related example in the **System.Windows.Forms.DataGridColumnStyle** class topic.

Requirements

Platforms: Windows 98, Windows NT 4.0, Windows Millennium Edition, Windows 2000, Windows XP Home Edition, Windows XP Professional, Windows Server 2003 family

DataGridColumnStyle.SetColumnValueAtRow Method

Sets the value in a specified row with the value from a specified **CurrencyManager**.

```
[Visual Basic]
Protected Friend Overridable Sub SetColumnValueAtRow( _
   ByVal source As CurrencyManager, _
   ByVal rowNum As Integer, _
   ByVal value As Object _
)
[C#]
protected internal virtual void SetColumnValueAtRow(
   CurrencyManager source,
   int rowNum,
   object value
);
[C++]
protected public: virtual void SetColumnValueAtRow(
   CurrencyManager* source,
   int rowNum,
   Object* value
);
[JScript]
protected internal function SetColumnValueAtRow(
   source : CurrencyManager,
   rowNum : int,
   value : Object
);
```

Parameters

source
A **CurrencyManager** associated with the **DataGridColumnStyle**.

rowNum
The number of the row.

value
The value to set.

Exceptions

Exception Type	Condition
ArgumentException	The **CurrencyManager** object's **Position** doesn't match *rowNum*.

Requirements

Platforms: Windows 98, Windows NT 4.0, Windows Millennium Edition, Windows 2000, Windows XP Home Edition, Windows XP Professional, Windows Server 2003 family

DataGridColumnStyle.SetDataGrid Method

Sets the **System.Windows.Forms.DataGrid** control that this column belongs to.

```
[Visual Basic]
Protected Overridable Sub SetDataGrid( _
   ByVal value As DataGrid _
)
[C#]
protected virtual void SetDataGrid(
   DataGrid value
);
[C++]
protected: virtual void SetDataGrid(
   DataGrid* value
);
[JScript]
protected function SetDataGrid(
   value : DataGrid
);
```

Parameters

value
The **System.Windows.Forms.DataGrid** control that this column belongs to.

Remarks

Typically, you should use the **SetDataGridInColumn** method.

Requirements

Platforms: Windows 98, Windows NT 4.0, Windows Millennium Edition, Windows 2000, Windows XP Home Edition, Windows XP Professional, Windows Server 2003 family

DataGridColumnStyle.SetDataGridInColumn Method

Sets the **System.Windows.Forms.DataGrid** for the column.

```
[Visual Basic]
Protected Overridable Sub SetDataGridInColumn( _
   ByVal value As DataGrid _
)
[C#]
protected virtual void SetDataGridInColumn(
   DataGrid value
);
[C++]
protected: virtual void SetDataGridInColumn(
   DataGrid* value
);
[JScript]
protected function SetDataGridInColumn(
   value : DataGrid
);
```

Parameters

value

A **System.Windows.Forms.DataGrid**.

Remarks

This method is typically overridden by derived classes to do special processing when the **DataGridColumnStyle** is added to **System.Windows.Forms.DataGrid**. For example, the **DataGridTextBoxColumn** uses this method to add the **DataGridTextBox** as a child of the **System.Windows.Forms.DataGrid**.

Requirements

Platforms: Windows 98, Windows NT 4.0, Windows Millennium Edition, Windows 2000, Windows XP Home Edition, Windows XP Professional, Windows Server 2003 family

DataGridColumnStyle.UpdateUI Method

Updates the value of a specified row with the given text.

```
[Visual Basic]
Protected Friend Overridable Sub UpdateUI( _
   ByVal source As CurrencyManager, _
   ByVal rowNum As Integer, _
   ByVal instantText As String _
)
[C#]
protected internal virtual void UpdateUI(
   CurrencyManager source,
   int rowNum,
   string instantText
);
[C++]
protected public: virtual void UpdateUI(
   CurrencyManager* source,
   int rowNum,
   String* instantText
);
[JScript]
protected internal function UpdateUI(
   source : CurrencyManager,
   rowNum : int,
   instantText : String
);
```

Parameters

source

The **CurrencyManager** associated with the **DataGridColumnStyle**.

rowNum

The row to update.

instantText

The new value.

Example

See related example in the **System.Windows.Forms.DataGridColumnStyle** class topic.

Requirements

Platforms: Windows 98, Windows NT 4.0, Windows Millennium Edition, Windows 2000, Windows XP Home Edition, Windows XP Professional, Windows Server 2003 family

DataGridColumnStyle.AlignmentChanged Event

Occurs when the **Alignment** property value changes.

```
[Visual Basic]
Public Event AlignmentChanged As EventHandler
[C#]
public event EventHandler AlignmentChanged;
[C++]
public: __event EventHandler* AlignmentChanged;
```

[JScript] In JScript, you can handle the events defined by a class, but you cannot define your own.

Event Data

The event handler receives an argument of type **EventArgs**.

Example

See related example in the **System.Windows.Forms.DataGridColumnStyle** class topic.

Requirements

Platforms: Windows 98, Windows NT 4.0, Windows Millennium Edition, Windows 2000, Windows XP Home Edition, Windows XP Professional, Windows Server 2003 family

DataGridColumnStyle.FontChanged Event

This member supports the .NET Framework infrastructure and is not intended to be used directly from your code.

[Visual Basic]
```
Public Event FontChanged As EventHandler
```
[C#]
```
public event EventHandler FontChanged;
```
[C++]
```
public: __event EventHandler* FontChanged;
```

[JScript] In JScript, you can handle the events defined by a class, but you cannot define your own.

DataGridColumnStyle.HeaderTextChanged Event

Occurs when the **HeaderText** property value changes.

[Visual Basic]
```
Public Event HeaderTextChanged As EventHandler
```
[C#]
```
public event EventHandler HeaderTextChanged;
```
[C++]
```
public: __event EventHandler* HeaderTextChanged;
```

[JScript] In JScript, you can handle the events defined by a class, but you cannot define your own.

Event Data

The event handler receives an argument of type **EventArgs**.

Example

See related example in the **System.Windows.Forms.DataGridColumnStyle** class topic.

Requirements

Platforms: Windows 98, Windows NT 4.0, Windows Millennium Edition, Windows 2000, Windows XP Home Edition, Windows XP Professional, Windows Server 2003 family

DataGridColumnStyle.MappingNameChanged Event

Occurs when the **MappingName** value changes.

[Visual Basic]
```
Public Event MappingNameChanged As EventHandler
```
[C#]
```
public event EventHandler MappingNameChanged;
```
[C++]
```
public: __event EventHandler* MappingNameChanged;
```

[JScript] In JScript, you can handle the events defined by a class, but you cannot define your own.

Event Data

The event handler receives an argument of type **EventArgs**.

Example

See related example in the **System.Windows.Forms.DataGridColumnStyle** class topic.

Requirements

Platforms: Windows 98, Windows NT 4.0, Windows Millennium Edition, Windows 2000, Windows XP Home Edition, Windows XP Professional, Windows Server 2003 family

DataGridColumnStyle.NullTextChanged Event

Occurs when the **NullText** value changes.

[Visual Basic]
```
Public Event NullTextChanged As EventHandler
```
[C#]
```
public event EventHandler NullTextChanged;
```
[C++]
```
public: __event EventHandler* NullTextChanged;
```

[JScript] In JScript, you can handle the events defined by a class, but you cannot define your own.

Event Data

The event handler receives an argument of type **EventArgs**.

Example

See related example in the **System.Windows.Forms.DataGridColumnStyle** class topic.

Requirements

Platforms: Windows 98, Windows NT 4.0, Windows Millennium Edition, Windows 2000, Windows XP Home Edition, Windows XP Professional, Windows Server 2003 family

DataGridColumnStyle.PropertyDescriptorChanged Event

Occurs when the **PropertyDescriptor** property value changes.

[Visual Basic]
```
Public Event PropertyDescriptorChanged As EventHandler
```
[C#]
```
public event EventHandler PropertyDescriptorChanged;
```
[C++]
```
public: __event EventHandler* PropertyDescriptorChanged;
```

[JScript] In JScript, you can handle the events defined by a class, but you cannot define your own.

Event Data

The event handler receives an argument of type **EventArgs**.

Example

See related example in the **System.Windows.Forms.DataGridColumnStyle** class topic.

Requirements

Platforms: Windows 98, Windows NT 4.0, Windows Millennium Edition, Windows 2000, Windows XP Home Edition, Windows XP Professional, Windows Server 2003 family

DataGridColumnStyle.ReadOnlyChanged Event

Occurs when the **ReadOnly** property value changes.

[Visual Basic]
```
Public Event ReadOnlyChanged As EventHandler
```
[C#]
```
public event EventHandler ReadOnlyChanged;
```
[C++]
```
public: __event EventHandler* ReadOnlyChanged;
```

[JScript] In JScript, you can handle the events defined by a class, but you cannot define your own.

Event Data

The event handler receives an argument of type **EventArgs**.

Example

See related example in the **System.Windows.Forms.DataGrid-ColumnStyle** class topic.

Requirements

Platforms: Windows 98, Windows NT 4.0,
Windows Millennium Edition, Windows 2000,
Windows XP Home Edition, Windows XP Professional,
Windows Server 2003 family

DataGridColumnStyle.WidthChanged Event

Occurs when the **Width** property value changes.

[Visual Basic]
```
Public Event WidthChanged As EventHandler
```
[C#]
```
public event EventHandler WidthChanged;
```
[C++]
```
public: __event EventHandler* WidthChanged;
```

[JScript] In JScript, you can handle the events defined by a class, but you cannot define your own.

Event Data

The event handler receives an argument of type **EventArgs**.

Example

See related example in the **System.Windows.Forms.DataGrid-ColumnStyle** class topic.

Requirements

Platforms: Windows 98, Windows NT 4.0,
Windows Millennium Edition, Windows 2000,
Windows XP Home Edition, Windows XP Professional,
Windows Server 2003 family

DataGridColumnStyle.CompModSwitches Class

This type supports the .NET Framework infrastructure and is not intended to be used directly from your code.

[Visual Basic]
```
Protected Class DataGridColumnStyle.CompModSwitches
```
[C#]
```
protected class DataGridColumnStyle.CompModSwitches
```
[C++]
```
protected __gc class DataGridColumnStyle.CompModSwitches
```
[JScript]
```
protected class DataGridColumnStyle.CompModSwitches
```

DataGridColumnStyle.CompModSwitches Constructor

This member supports the .NET Framework infrastructure and is not intended to be used directly from your code.

[Visual Basic]
```
Public Sub New()
```
[C#]
```
public DataGridColumnStyle.CompModSwitches();
```
[C++]
```
public: CompModSwitches();
```
[JScript]
```
public function DataGridColumnStyle.CompModSwitches();
```

DataGridColumnStyle.CompModSwitches.DGEditColumnEditing Property

This member supports the .NET Framework infrastructure and is not intended to be used directly from your code.

[Visual Basic]
```
Public Shared ReadOnly Property DGEditColumnEditing As TraceSwitch
```
[C#]
```
public static TraceSwitch DGEditColumnEditing {get;}
```
[C++]
```
public: __property static TraceSwitch* get_DGEditColumnEditing();
```
[JScript]
```
public static function get DGEditColumnEditing() : TraceSwitch;
```

DataGridColumnStyle.DataGridColumnHeaderAccessibleObject Class

This type supports the .NET Framework infrastructure and is not intended to be used directly from your code.

```
[Visual Basic]
<ComVisible(True)>
Protected Class _
   DataGridColumnStyle.DataGridColumnHeaderAccessibleObject
   Inherits AccessibleObject
[C#]
[ComVisible(true)]
protected class
   DataGridColumnStyle.DataGridColumnHeaderAccessibleObject :
   AccessibleObject
[C++]
[ComVisible(true)]
protected __gc class
   DataGridColumnStyle.DataGridColumnHeaderAccessibleObject :
   public
   AccessibleObject
[JScript]
protected
   ComVisible(true)
class
   DataGridColumnStyle.DataGridColumnHeaderAccessibleObject extends
   AccessibleObject
```

DataGridColumnStyle.DataGridColumnHeaderAccessibleObject Constructor

This member supports the .NET Framework infrastructure and is not intended to be used directly from your code.

```
[Visual Basic]
Public Sub New( _
   ByVal owner As DataGridColumnStyle _
)
[C#]
public DataGridColumnStyle.DataGridColumnHeaderAccessibleObject(
   DataGridColumnStyle owner
);
[C++]
public: DataGridColumnHeaderAccessibleObject(
   DataGridColumnStyle* owner
);
[JScript]
public function
   DataGridColumnStyle.DataGridColumnHeaderAccessibleObject(
   owner : DataGridColumnStyle
);
```

DataGridColumnStyle.DataGridColumnHeaderAccessibleObject.Bounds Property

This member supports the .NET Framework infrastructure and is not intended to be used directly from your code.

```
[Visual Basic]
Overrides Public ReadOnly Property Bounds As Rectangle
[C#]
public override Rectangle Bounds {get;}
[C++]
public: __property Rectangle get_Bounds();
[JScript]
public override function get Bounds() : Rectangle;
```

DataGridColumnStyle.DataGridColumnHeaderAccessibleObject.Name Property

This member supports the .NET Framework infrastructure and is not intended to be used directly from your code.

```
[Visual Basic]
Overrides Public ReadOnly Property Name As String
[C#]
public override string Name {get;}
[C++]
public: __property String* get_Name();
[JScript]
public override function get Name() : String;
```

DataGridColumnStyle.DataGridColumnHeaderAccessibleObject.Owner Property

This member supports the .NET Framework infrastructure and is not intended to be used directly from your code.

```
[Visual Basic]
Protected ReadOnly Property Owner As DataGridColumnStyle
[C#]
protected DataGridColumnStyle Owner {get;}
[C++]
protected: __property DataGridColumnStyle* get_Owner();
[JScript]
protected function get Owner() : DataGridColumnStyle;
```

DataGridColumnStyle.DataGridColumnHeaderAccessibleObject.Parent Property

This member supports the .NET Framework infrastructure and is not intended to be used directly from your code.

```
[Visual Basic]
Overrides Public ReadOnly Property Parent As AccessibleObject
[C#]
public override AccessibleObject Parent {get;}
[C++]
public: __property AccessibleObject* get_Parent();
[JScript]
public override function get Parent() : AccessibleObject;
```

DataGridColumnStyle.DataGridColumnHeader-AccessibleObject.Role Property

This member supports the .NET Framework infrastructure and is not intended to be used directly from your code.

[Visual Basic]
```
Overrides Public ReadOnly Property Role As AccessibleRole
```
[C#]
```
public override AccessibleRole Role {get;}
```
[C++]
```
public: __property AccessibleRole get_Role();
```
[JScript]
```
public override function get Role() : AccessibleRole;
```

DataGridColumnStyle.DataGridColumnHeader-AccessibleObject.Navigate Method

This member supports the .NET Framework infrastructure and is not intended to be used directly from your code.

[Visual Basic]
```
Overrides Public Function Navigate( _
   ByVal navdir As AccessibleNavigation _
) As AccessibleObject
```
[C#]
```
public override AccessibleObject Navigate(
   AccessibleNavigation navdir
);
```
[C++]
```
public: AccessibleObject* Navigate(
   AccessibleNavigation navdir
);
```
[JScript]
```
public override function Navigate(
   navdir : AccessibleNavigation
) : AccessibleObject;
```

DataGrid.HitTestInfo Class

Contains information about a part of the **System.Windows.Forms.DataGrid** at a specified coordinate. This class cannot be inherited.

System.Object
System.Windows.Forms.DataGrid.HitTestInfo

[Visual Basic]
```
NotInheritable Public Class DataGrid.HitTestInfo
```
[C#]
```
public sealed class DataGrid.HitTestInfo
```
[C++]
```
public __gc __sealed class DataGrid.HitTestInfo
```
[JScript]
```
public class DataGrid.HitTestInfo
```

Thread Safety

Any public static (**Shared** in Visual Basic) members of this type are safe for multithreaded operations. Any instance members are not guaranteed to be thread safe.

Remarks

The **DataGrid.HitTestInfo** class, in conjunction with the **HitTest** method of the **DataGrid** control, is used to determine which part of a **DataGrid** control the user has clicked. The **DataGrid.HitTestInfo** class contains the row, column, and part of the grid that was clicked. See the **DataGrid.HitTestType** enumeration returned by the **Type** property for a complete list of grid parts.

To return a **DataGrid.HitTestInfo**, invoke the **HitTest** method from the **MouseDown** event of **DataGrid** control. Pass the *x* and *y* properties of the **MouseEventArgs** to the **HitTest** method.

Example

See related example in the **System.Windows.Forms.DataGrid-HitTestInfo** class topic.

Requirements

Namespace: System.Windows.Forms

Platforms: Windows 98, Windows NT 4.0, Windows Millennium Edition, Windows 2000, Windows XP Home Edition, Windows XP Professional, Windows Server 2003 family, .NET Compact Framework - Windows CE .NET

Assembly: System.Windows.Forms (in System.Windows.Forms.dll)

DataGrid.HitTestInfo.Nowhere Field

Indicates that a coordinate corresponds to part of the **System.Windows.Forms.DataGrid** control that is not functioning.

[Visual Basic]
```
Public Shared ReadOnly Nowhere As DataGrid.HitTestInfo
```
[C#]
```
public static readonly DataGrid.HitTestInfo Nowhere;
```
[C++]
```
public: static DataGrid.HitTestInfo* Nowhere;
```
[JScript]
```
public static var Nowhere : DataGrid.HitTestInfo;
```

Remarks

Other parts of the **System.Windows.Forms.DataGrid**, such as the **Caption**, can return useful information. If the part of the grid has no function (such as the gray area behind a sparsely populated grid table), the **Nowhere** field is returned.

Example

See related example in the **System.Windows.Forms.DataGrid-HitTestInfo** class topic.

Requirements

Platforms: Windows 98, Windows NT 4.0, Windows Millennium Edition, Windows 2000, Windows XP Home Edition, Windows XP Professional, Windows Server 2003 family, .NET Compact Framework - Windows CE .NET

DataGrid.HitTestInfo.Column Property

Gets the number of the column the user has clicked.

[Visual Basic]
```
Public ReadOnly Property Column As Integer
```
[C#]
```
public int Column {get;}
```
[C++]
```
public: __property int get_Column();
```
[JScript]
```
public function get Column() : int;
```

Property Value

The number of the column.

Remarks

If the coordinate is not a cell, the property returns -1.

Example

See related example in the **System.Windows.Forms.DataGrid-HitTestInfo** class topic.

Requirements

Platforms: Windows 98, Windows NT 4.0, Windows Millennium Edition, Windows 2000, Windows XP Home Edition, Windows XP Professional, Windows Server 2003 family, .NET Compact Framework - Windows CE .NET

DataGrid.HitTestInfo.Row Property

Gets the number of the row the user has clicked.

[Visual Basic]
```
Public ReadOnly Property Row As Integer
```
[C#]
```
public int Row {get;}
```
[C++]
```
public: __property int get_Row();
```
[JScript]
```
public function get Row() : int;
```

Property Value

The number of the clicked row.

Remarks

If the coordinate is not a cell, the property returns -1. If the coordinate is a **RowHeader**, the property returns the row number of the header, but the **Column** property will return -1.

Example

See related example in the **System.Windows.Forms.DataGrid-HitTestInfo** class topic.

Requirements

Platforms: Windows 98, Windows NT 4.0, Windows Millennium Edition, Windows 2000, Windows XP Home Edition, Windows XP Professional, Windows Server 2003 family, .NET Compact Framework - Windows CE .NET

DataGrid.HitTestInfo.Type Property

Gets the part of the **System.Windows.Forms.DataGrid** control, other than the row or column, that was clicked.

```
[Visual Basic]
Public ReadOnly Property Type As DataGrid.HitTestType
[C#]
public DataGrid.HitTestType Type {get;}
[C++]
public: __property DataGrid.HitTestType get_Type();
[JScript]
public function get Type() : DataGrid.HitTestType;
```

Property Value

One of the **DataGrid.HitTestType** enumerations.

Example

See related example in the **System.Windows.Forms.DataGrid-HitTestInfo** class topic.

Requirements

Platforms: Windows 98, Windows NT 4.0, Windows Millennium Edition, Windows 2000, Windows XP Home Edition, Windows XP Professional, Windows Server 2003 family, .NET Compact Framework - Windows CE .NET

DataGrid.HitTestInfo.Equals Method

Indicates whether two objects are identical.

```
[Visual Basic]
Overrides Public Function Equals( _
   ByVal value As Object _
) As Boolean
[C#]
public override bool Equals(
   object value
);
[C++]
public: bool Equals(
   Object* value
);
[JScript]
public override function Equals(
   value : Object
) : Boolean;
```

Parameters

value
The second object to compare, typed as **Object**.

Return Value

true if the objects are equal; otherwise, **false**.

Example

See related example in the **System.Windows.Forms.DataGrid-HitTestInfo** class topic.

Requirements

Platforms: Windows 98, Windows NT 4.0, Windows Millennium Edition, Windows 2000, Windows XP Home Edition, Windows XP Professional, Windows Server 2003 family, .NET Compact Framework - Windows CE .NET

DataGrid.HitTestInfo.GetHashCode Method

Gets the hash code for the **DataGrid.HitTestInfo** instance.

```
[Visual Basic]
Overrides Public Function GetHashCode() As Integer
[C#]
public override int GetHashCode();
[C++]
public: int GetHashCode();
[JScript]
public override function GetHashCode() : int;
```

Return Value

The hash code for this instance.

Remarks

This method overrides **GetHashCode**.

Example

See related example in the **System.Windows.Forms.DataGrid-HitTestInfo** class topic.

Requirements

Platforms: Windows 98, Windows NT 4.0, Windows Millennium Edition, Windows 2000, Windows XP Home Edition, Windows XP Professional, Windows Server 2003 family, .NET Compact Framework - Windows CE .NET

DataGrid.HitTestInfo.ToString Method

Gets the type, row number, and column number.

```
[Visual Basic]
Overrides Public Function ToString() As String
[C#]
public override string ToString();
[C++]
public: String* ToString();
[JScript]
public override function ToString() : String;
```

Return Value

The type, row number, and column number.

Example

See related example in the **System.Windows.Forms.DataGrid-HitTestInfo** class topic.

Requirements

Platforms: Windows 98, Windows NT 4.0, Windows Millennium Edition, Windows 2000, Windows XP Home Edition, Windows XP Professional, Windows Server 2003 family, .NET Compact Framework - Windows CE .NET

DataGrid.HitTestType Enumeration

Specifies the part of the **System.Windows.Forms.DataGrid** control the user has clicked.

This enumeration has a **FlagsAttribute** attribute that allows a bitwise combination of its member values.

```
[Visual Basic]
<Flags>
<Serializable>
Public Enum DataGrid.HitTestType
[C#]
[Flags]
[Serializable]
public enum DataGrid.HitTestType
[C++]
[Flags]
[Serializable]
__value public enum DataGrid.HitTestType
[JScript]
public
   Flags
   Serializable
enum DataGrid.HitTestType
```

Remarks

Use the members of this enumeration to determine which part of the grid has been clicked. The **Type** property of a **DataGrid.HitTestInfo** returns a **DataGrid.HitTestType**. The **DataGrid.HitTestInfo** is created by invoking the **HitTest** method of a **System.Windows.Forms.DataGrid** control.

Members

Member name	Description	Value
Caption	The caption of the **System.Windows.Forms.DataGrid** control.	32
Cell Supported by the .NET Compact Framework.	A cell in the **System.Windows.Forms.DataGrid** control.	1
ColumnHeader Supported by the .NET Compact Framework.	A column header in the **System.Windows.Forms.DataGrid** control.	2
ColumnResize Supported by the .NET Compact Framework.	The column border, which is the line between column headers. It can be dragged to resize a column's width.	8
None Supported by the .NET Compact Framework.	The background area, visible when the control contains no table, few rows, or when a table is scrolled to its bottom.	0
ParentRows	The parent row section of the **System.Windows.Forms.DataGrid** control. The parent row displays information from or about the parent table of the currently displayed child table, such as the name of the parent table, column names and values of the parent record.	64
RowHeader Supported by the .NET Compact Framework.	A row header in the **System.Windows.Forms.DataGrid** control.	4
RowResize Supported by the .NET Compact Framework.	The row border, which is the line between grid row headers. It can be dragged to resize a row's height.	16

Example

See related example in the **System.Windows.Forms.DataGrid-HitTestInfo** class topic.

Requirements

Namespace: System.Windows.Forms

Platforms: Windows 98, Windows NT 4.0, Windows Millennium Edition, Windows 2000, Windows XP Home Edition, Windows XP Professional, Windows Server 2003 family, .NET Compact Framework - Windows CE .NET

Assembly: System.Windows.Forms (in System.Windows.Forms.dll)

DataGridLineStyle Enumeration

Specifies the style of gridlines in a **System.Windows.Forms.DataGrid**.

[Visual Basic]
```
<Serializable>
Public Enum DataGridLineStyle
```
[C#]
```
[Serializable]
public enum DataGridLineStyle
```
[C++]
```
[Serializable]
__value public enum DataGridLineStyle
```
[JScript]
```
public
   Serializable
enum DataGridLineStyle
```

Remarks

Use the members of this enumeration to set the value of the **GridLineStyle** property of the **System.Windows.Forms.DataGrid** class. The default is **Solid**.

Members

Member name	Description
None	No gridlines between cells.
Solid	Solid gridlines between cells.

Example

[Visual Basic, C#] The following example sets the **GridLineStyle** property to **DataGridLineStyle.None**.

[Visual Basic]
```
Private Sub SetGridLineAttributes()
    dataGrid1.GridLineStyle = DataGridLineStyle.None
End Sub 'SetGridLineAttributes
```

[C#]
```
private void SetGridLineAttributes()
{
   dataGrid1.GridLineStyle = DataGridLineStyle.None;
}
```

Requirements

Namespace: System.Windows.Forms

Platforms: Windows 98, Windows NT 4.0, Windows Millennium Edition, Windows 2000, Windows XP Home Edition, Windows XP Professional, Windows Server 2003 family

Assembly: System.Windows.Forms (in System.Windows.Forms.dll)

DataGridParentRowsLabelStyle Enumeration

Specifies how the parent row labels of a **DataGrid** control are displayed.

[Visual Basic]
```
<Serializable>
Public Enum DataGridParentRowsLabelStyle
```
[C#]
```
[Serializable]
public enum DataGridParentRowsLabelStyle
```
[C++]
```
[Serializable]
__value public enum DataGridParentRowsLabelStyle
```
[JScript]
```
public
   Serializable
enum DataGridParentRowsLabelStyle
```

Remarks

Use the members of this enumeration to set the value of the **ParentRowsLabelStyle** property.

Parent rows can be displayed only if the **DataGrid** contains at least one **DataRelation** to a second **DataTable**, and if the **AllowNavigation** property is set to a value that allows navigation.

Members

Member name	Description
Both	Displays both the parent table and column names.
ColumnName	Displays the parent column name.
None	Display no parent row labels.
TableName	Displays the parent table name.

Example

See related example in the **System.Windows.Forms.DataGridParentRowsLabelStyle** class topic.

Requirements

Namespace: System.Windows.Forms

Platforms: Windows 98, Windows NT 4.0,
Windows Millennium Edition, Windows 2000,
Windows XP Home Edition, Windows XP Professional,
Windows Server 2003 family

Assembly: System.Windows.Forms (in System.Windows.Forms.dll)

DataGridPreferredColumnWidthTypeConverter Class

Converts the value of an object to a different data type.

System.Object
System.ComponentModel.TypeConverter
System.Windows.Forms.DataGridPreferredColumnWidthTypeConverter

```
[Visual Basic]
Public Class DataGridPreferredColumnWidthTypeConverter
   Inherits TypeConverter
[C#]
public class DataGridPreferredColumnWidthTypeConverter :
   TypeConverter
[C++]
public __gc class DataGridPreferredColumnWidthTypeConverter :
   public TypeConverter
[JScript]
public class DataGridPreferredColumnWidthTypeConverter extends
   TypeConverter
```

Thread Safety

Any public static (**Shared** in Visual Basic) members of this type are safe for multithreaded operations. Any instance members are not guaranteed to be thread safe.

Requirements

Namespace: System.Windows.Forms

Platforms: Windows 98, Windows NT 4.0, Windows Millennium Edition, Windows 2000, Windows XP Home Edition, Windows XP Professional, Windows Server 2003 family

Assembly: System.Windows.Forms (in System.Windows.Forms.dll)

DataGridPreferredColumnWidthTypeConverter Constructor

Initializes a new instance of the **DataGridPreferredColumnWidthTypeConverter** class.

```
[Visual Basic]
Public Sub New()
[C#]
public DataGridPreferredColumnWidthTypeConverter();
[C++]
public: DataGridPreferredColumnWidthTypeConverter();
[JScript]
public function DataGridPreferredColumnWidthTypeConverter();
```

Remarks

The default constructor initializes any fields to their default values.

Requirements

Platforms: Windows 98, Windows NT 4.0, Windows Millennium Edition, Windows 2000, Windows XP Home Edition, Windows XP Professional, Windows Server 2003 family

DataGridPreferredColumnWidthTypeConverter.CanConvertFrom Method

Overload List

This member supports the .NET Framework infrastructure and is not intended to be used directly from your code.

[Visual Basic] **Overloads Overrides Public Function CanConvertFrom(ITypeDescriptorContext, Type) As Boolean**

[C#] **public override bool CanConvertFrom(ITypeDescriptorContext, Type);**

[C++] **public: bool CanConvertFrom(ITypeDescriptorContext*, Type*);**

[JScript] **public override function CanConvertFrom(ITypeDescriptorContext, Type) : Boolean;**

Inherited from **TypeConverter**.

[Visual Basic] **Overloads Public Function CanConvertFrom(Type) As Boolean**

[C#] **public bool CanConvertFrom(Type);**

[C++] **public: bool CanConvertFrom(Type*);**

[JScript] **public function CanConvertFrom(Type) : Boolean;**

DataGridPreferredColumnWidthTypeConverter.CanConvertFrom Method (ITypeDescriptorContext, Type)

This member overrides **TypeConverter.CanConvertFrom**.

```
[Visual Basic]
Overrides Overloads Public Function CanConvertFrom( _
   ByVal context As ITypeDescriptorContext, _
   ByVal sourceType As Type _
) As Boolean
[C#]
public override bool CanConvertFrom(
   ITypeDescriptorContext context,
   Type sourceType
);
[C++]
public: bool CanConvertFrom(
   ITypeDescriptorContext* context,
   Type* sourceType
);
[JScript]
public override function CanConvertFrom(
   context : ITypeDescriptorContext,
   sourceType : Type
) : Boolean;
```

Requirements

Platforms: Windows 98, Windows NT 4.0, Windows Millennium Edition, Windows 2000, Windows XP Home Edition, Windows XP Professional, Windows Server 2003 family

DataGridPreferredColumnWidthTypeConverter.ConvertFrom Method

Overload List

This member supports the .NET Framework infrastructure and is not intended to be used directly from your code.

[Visual Basic] **Overloads Overrides Public Function ConvertFrom(ITypeDescriptorContext, CultureInfo, Object) As Object**

[C#] **public override object ConvertFrom(ITypeDescriptorContext, CultureInfo, object);**

[C++] **public: Object* ConvertFrom(ITypeDescriptorContext*, CultureInfo*, Object*);**

[JScript] **public override function ConvertFrom(ITypeDescriptorContext, CultureInfo, Object) : Object;**

Inherited from **TypeConverter**.

[Visual Basic] **Overloads Public Function ConvertFrom(Object) As Object**

[C#] **public object ConvertFrom(object);**

[C++] **public: Object* ConvertFrom(Object*);**

[JScript] **public function ConvertFrom(Object) : Object;**

DataGridPreferredColumnWidthTypeConverter.ConvertFrom Method (ITypeDescriptorContext, CultureInfo, Object)

This member overrides **TypeConverter.ConvertFrom**.

[Visual Basic]
```
Overrides Overloads Public Function ConvertFrom( _
   ByVal context As ITypeDescriptorContext, _
   ByVal culture As CultureInfo, _
   ByVal value As Object _
) As Object
```
[C#]
```
public override object ConvertFrom(
   ITypeDescriptorContext context,
   CultureInfo culture,
   object value
);
```
[C++]
```
public: Object* ConvertFrom(
   ITypeDescriptorContext* context,
   CultureInfo* culture,
   Object* value
);
```
[JScript]
```
public override function ConvertFrom(
   context : ITypeDescriptorContext,
   culture : CultureInfo,
   value : Object
) : Object;
```

Requirements

Platforms: Windows 98, Windows NT 4.0, Windows Millennium Edition, Windows 2000, Windows XP Home Edition, Windows XP Professional, Windows Server 2003 family

DataGridPreferredColumnWidthTypeConverter.ConvertTo Method

Overload List

This member supports the .NET Framework infrastructure and is not intended to be used directly from your code.

[Visual Basic] **Overloads Overrides Public Function ConvertTo(ITypeDescriptorContext, CultureInfo, Object, Type) As Object**

[C#] **public override object ConvertTo(ITypeDescriptorContext, CultureInfo, object, Type);**

[C++] **public: Object* ConvertTo(ITypeDescriptorContext*, CultureInfo*, Object*, Type*);**

[JScript] **public override function ConvertTo(ITypeDescriptorContext, CultureInfo, Object, Type) : Object;**

Inherited from **TypeConverter**.

[Visual Basic] **Overloads Public Function ConvertTo(Object, Type) As Object**

[C#] **public object ConvertTo(object, Type);**

[C++] **public: Object* ConvertTo(Object*, Type*);**

[JScript] **public function ConvertTo(Object, Type) : Object;**

DataGridPreferredColumnWidthTypeConverter.ConvertTo Method (ITypeDescriptorContext, CultureInfo, Object, Type)

This member overrides **TypeConverter.ConvertTo**.

[Visual Basic]
```
Overrides Overloads Public Function ConvertTo( _
   ByVal context As ITypeDescriptorContext, _
   ByVal culture As CultureInfo, _
   ByVal value As Object, _
   ByVal destinationType As Type _
) As Object
```
[C#]
```
public override object ConvertTo(
   ITypeDescriptorContext context,
   CultureInfo culture,
   object value,
   Type destinationType
);
```
[C++]
```
public: Object* ConvertTo(
   ITypeDescriptorContext* context,
   CultureInfo* culture,
   Object* value,
   Type* destinationType
);
```
[JScript]
```
public override function ConvertTo(
   context : ITypeDescriptorContext,
   culture : CultureInfo,
   value : Object,
   destinationType : Type
) : Object;
```

Requirements

Platforms: Windows 98, Windows NT 4.0, Windows Millennium Edition, Windows 2000, Windows XP Home Edition, Windows XP Professional, Windows Server 2003 family

DataGridTableStyle Class

Represents the table drawn by the **System.Windows.Forms.DataGrid** control at run time.

System.Object
  System.MarshalByRefObject
    System.ComponentModel.Component
      System.Windows.Forms.DataGridTableStyle

[Visual Basic]
```
Public Class DataGridTableStyle
   Inherits Component
```
[C#]
```
public class DataGridTableStyle : Component
```
[C++]
```
public __gc class DataGridTableStyle : public Component
```
[JScript]
```
public class DataGridTableStyle extends Component
```

Thread Safety

Any public static (**Shared** in Visual Basic) members of this type are safe for multithreaded operations. Any instance members are not guaranteed to be thread safe.

Remarks

The **System.Windows.Forms.DataGrid** control displays data in the form of a grid. The **DataGridTableStyle** is a class that represents the drawn grid only. This grid should not be confused with the **DataTable** class, which is a possible source of data for the grid. Instead, the **DataGridTableStyle** strictly represents the grid as it is painted in the control. Therefore, through the **DataGridTableStyle** you can control the appearance of the grid for each **DataTable**. To specify which **DataGridTableStyle** is used when displaying data from a particular **DataTable**, set the **MappingName** to the **TableName** of a **DataTable**.

The **GridTableStylesCollection** contains all the **DataGridTableStyle** objects used by a **System.Windows.Forms.DataGrid** control. The collection can contain as many **DataGridTableStyle** objects as you need, however the **MappingName** of each must be unique. At run time, this allows you to substitute a different **DataGridTableStyle** for the same data, depending on the user's preference. To do this:

1. Populate the **GridTableStylesCollection** with **DataGridTableStyle** objects. If a **DataGridTableStyle** exists in the **GridTableStylesCollection** whose **MappingName** property value equals the **DataTable** object's **TableName** property, the **DataTable** is displayed with this **DataGridTableStyle**. If no **DataGridTableStyle** exists with a matching **MappingName**, the **DataTable** is displayed with the default style for data grid tables.
2. When a different grid style is needed, use the Item property to select the appropriate **DataGridTableStyle** (pass the **TableName** to the **Item** property) and set the **MappingName** of the returned object to a new value.
3. Use the **Item** property to select the desired **DataGridTableStyle**, and set its **MappingName** to the **TableName** of the **DataTable**.

To determine which **DataGridTableStyle** is currently displayed, use the **DataSource** and **DataMember** properties of the **System.Windows.Forms.DataGrid** to return a **CurrencyManager**. If the data source implements the **ITypedList** interface, you can use the **GetListName** method to return the **MappingName** of the current table. This is shown in the C# code below:

```
private void PrintCurrentListName(DataGrid myDataGrid){
 CurrencyManager myCM = (CurrencyManager)
 BindingContext[myDataGrid.DataSource, myDataGrid.DataMember];
 IList myList = myCM.List;
 ITypedList thisList = (ITypedList) myList;
 Console.WriteLine(thisList.GetListName(null));
}
```

If the **DataSet** contains **DataTable** objects related through **DataRelation** objects, and the currently displayed **DataTable** is a child table, the **DataMember** will return a string in the form of TableName.RelationName (in the simplest case). If the **DataTable** is further down in the hierarchy, the string will consist of the parent table's name followed by the necessary **RelationName** values required to reach the table's level. For example, imagine three **DataTable** objects in a hierarchical relationship named (top to bottom) Regions, Customers, and Orders, and two **DataRelation** objects named RegionsToCustomers and CustomersToOrders, the **DataMember** property will return "Regions.RegionsToCustomers.CustomersToOrders". However, the **MappingName** will then be "Orders".

The collection of **DataGridTableStyle** objects is returned through the **TableStyles** property of the **System.Windows.Forms.DataGrid**.

When a **DataGridTableStyle** is displayed, the settings for the **DataGridTableStyle** will override the settings for the **System.Windows.Forms.DataGrid** control. If a value is not set for a particular **DataGridTableStyle** property, the **System.Windows.Forms.DataGrid** control's value will be used instead. The following list shows the **DataGridColumnStyle** properties that can be set to override **System.Windows.Forms.DataGrid** control properties:

- **AllowSorting**
- **AlternatingBackColor**
- **BackColor**
- **ColumnHeadersVisible**
- **ForeColor**
- **GridLineColor**
- **GridLineStyle**
- **HeaderBackColor**
- **HeaderFont**
- **HeaderForeColor**
- **LinkColor**
- **PreferredColumnWidth**
- **PreferredRowHeight**
- **ReadOnly**
- **RowHeadersVisible**
- **RowHeaderWidth**
- **SelectionBackColor**
- **SelectionForeColor**

To bind the **DataGrid** to a strongly typed array of objects, the object must contain public properties. To create a **DataGridTableStyle** that displays such an array, set the **MappingName** property to *classname[]* where *classname* is replaced by the class name. Also note that the **MappingName** property is case-sensitive. See the **MappingName** property for an example.

You can also bind the **DataGrid** to an **ArrayList**. A feature of the **ArrayList** is that it can contain objects of multiple types, but the **DataGrid** can only bind to such a list when all items in the list are of the same type as the first item. This means that all objects must either be of the same type, or they must inherit from the same class as the first item in the list. For example, if the first item in a list is a **Control**, the second item could be a **TextBox** (which inherits from **Control**). If, on the other hand, the first item is a **TextBox**, the second object cannot be a **Control**. Further, the **ArrayList** must have items in it when it is bound. An empty **ArrayList** will result in an empty grid. When binding to an **ArrayList**, set the **MappingName** of the **DataGridTableStyle** to "ArrayList" (the type name).

Example

[Visual Basic, C#] The following example sets creates two **DataGridTableStyle** instances and sets the **MappingName** of each object to the **TableName** of a **DataTable** in a **DataSet**. The example then adds **DataGridColumnStyle** objects to the **GridColumnStylesCollection** of each **DataGridTableStyle**. For an example that runs, see the **System.Windows.Forms.DataGrid** example.

[Visual Basic]

```
Private Sub AddCustomDataTableStyle()
    ' Create a new DataGridTableStyle and set
    ' its MappingName to the TableName of a DataTable.
    Dim ts1 As New DataGridTableStyle()
    ts1.MappingName = "Customers"

    ' Add a GridColumnStyle and set its MappingName
    ' to the name of a DataColumn in the DataTable.
    ' Set the HeaderText and Width properties.

    Dim boolCol As New DataGridBoolColumn()
    boolCol.MappingName = "Current"
    boolCol.HeaderText = "IsCurrent Customer"
    boolCol.Width = 150
    ts1.GridColumnStyles.Add(boolCol)

    ' Add a second column style.
    Dim TextCol As New DataGridTextBoxColumn()
    TextCol.MappingName = "custName"
    TextCol.HeaderText = "Customer Name"
    TextCol.Width = 250
    ts1.GridColumnStyles.Add(TextCol)

    ' Create the second table style with columns.
    Dim ts2 As New DataGridTableStyle()
    ts2.MappingName = "Orders"

    ' Change the colors.
    ts2.ForeColor = Color.Yellow
    ts2.AlternatingBackColor = Color.Blue
    ts2.BackColor = Color.Blue

    ' Create new DataGridColumnStyle objects.
    Dim cOrderDate As New DataGridTextBoxColumn()
    cOrderDate.MappingName = "OrderDate"
    cOrderDate.HeaderText = "Order Date"
    cOrderDate.Width = 100
    ts2.GridColumnStyles.Add(cOrderDate)

    Dim pcol As PropertyDescriptorCollection =                          ↵
Me.BindingContext(myDataSet,                                            ↵
"Customers.custToOrders").GetItemProperties()

    Dim csOrderAmount As New DataGridTextBoxColumn(pcol                 ↵
 ("OrderAmount"), "c", True)
    csOrderAmount.MappingName = "OrderAmount"
    csOrderAmount.HeaderText = "Total"
    csOrderAmount.Width = 100
    ts2.GridColumnStyles.Add(csOrderAmount)

    ' Add the DataGridTableStyle objects to the collection.
    myDataGrid.TableStyles.Add(ts1)
    myDataGrid.TableStyles.Add(ts2)
End Sub 'AddCustomDataTableStyle
```

[C#]

```
private void AddCustomDataTableStyle()
   {
      /* Create a new DataGridTableStyle and set
      its MappingName to the TableName of a DataTable. */
      DataGridTableStyle ts1 = new DataGridTableStyle();
      ts1.MappingName = "Customers";

      /* Add a GridColumnStyle and set its MappingName
      to the name of a DataColumn in the DataTable.
      Set the HeaderText and Width properties. */

      DataGridColumnStyle boolCol = new DataGridBoolColumn();
      boolCol.MappingName = "Current";
      boolCol.HeaderText = "IsCurrent Customer";
      boolCol.Width = 150;
      ts1.GridColumnStyles.Add(boolCol);

      // Add a second column style.
      DataGridColumnStyle TextCol = new DataGridTextBoxColumn();
      TextCol.MappingName = "custName";
      TextCol.HeaderText = "Customer Name";
      TextCol.Width = 250;
      ts1.GridColumnStyles.Add(TextCol);

      // Create the second table style with columns.
      DataGridTableStyle ts2 = new DataGridTableStyle();
      ts2.MappingName = "Orders";
      // Change the colors.
      ts2.ForeColor = Color.Yellow;
      ts2.AlternatingBackColor = Color.Blue;
      ts2.BackColor = Color.Blue;

      // Create new DataGridColumnStyle objects.
      DataGridColumnStyle cOrderDate =
      new DataGridTextBoxColumn();
      cOrderDate.MappingName = "OrderDate";
      cOrderDate.HeaderText = "Order Date";
      cOrderDate.Width = 100;
      ts2.GridColumnStyles.Add(cOrderDate);

      PropertyDescriptorCollection pcol = this.BindingContext
      [myDataSet, "Customers.custToOrders"].GetItemProperties();

      DataGridColumnStyle csOrderAmount =
      new DataGridTextBoxColumn(pcol["OrderAmount"], "c", true);
      csOrderAmount.MappingName = "OrderAmount";
      csOrderAmount.HeaderText = "Total";
      csOrderAmount.Width = 100;
      ts2.GridColumnStyles.Add(csOrderAmount);

      // Add the DataGridTableStyle objects to the collection.
      myDataGrid.TableStyles.Add(ts1);
      myDataGrid.TableStyles.Add(ts2);
   }
```

Requirements

Namespace: System.Windows.Forms

Platforms: Windows 98, Windows NT 4.0, Windows Millennium Edition, Windows 2000, Windows XP Home Edition, Windows XP Professional, Windows Server 2003 family, .NET Compact Framework - Windows CE .NET

Assembly: System.Windows.Forms (in System.Windows.Forms.dll)

DataGridTableStyle Constructor

Initializes a new instance of the **DataGridTableStyle** class.

Overload List

Initializes a new instance of the **DataGridTableStyle** class.

Supported by the .NET Compact Framework.

[Visual Basic] **Public Sub New()**

[C#] **public DataGridTableStyle();**

[C++] **public: DataGridTableStyle();**

[JScript] **public function DataGridTableStyle();**

This member supports the .NET Framework infrastructure and is not intended to be used directly from your code.

[Visual Basic] **Public Sub New(Boolean)**

[C#] **public DataGridTableStyle(bool);**

[C++] **public: DataGridTableStyle(bool);**

[JScript] **public function DataGridTableStyle(Boolean);**

Initializes a new instance of the **DataGridTableStyle** class with the specified **CurrencyManager**.

[Visual Basic] **Public Sub New(CurrencyManager)**

[C#] **public DataGridTableStyle(CurrencyManager);**

[C++] **public: DataGridTableStyle(CurrencyManager*);**

[JScript] **public function DataGridTableStyle(Currency-Manager);**

Example

See related example in the **System.Windows.Forms.DataGrid-TableStyle** class topic.

DataGridTableStyle Constructor ()

Initializes a new instance of the **DataGridTableStyle** class.

```
[Visual Basic]
Public Sub New()
[C#]
public DataGridTableStyle();
[C++]
public: DataGridTableStyle();
[JScript]
public function DataGridTableStyle();
```

Example

See related example in the **System.Windows.Forms.DataGrid-TableStyle** class topic.

Requirements

Platforms: Windows 98, Windows NT 4.0, Windows Millennium Edition, Windows 2000, Windows XP Home Edition, Windows XP Professional, Windows Server 2003 family, .NET Compact Framework - Windows CE .NET

DataGridTableStyle Constructor (Boolean)

This member supports the .NET Framework infrastructure and is not intended to be used directly from your code.

```
[Visual Basic]
Public Sub New( _
   ByVal isDefaultTableStyle As Boolean _
)
[C#]
public DataGridTableStyle(
   bool isDefaultTableStyle
);
[C++]
public: DataGridTableStyle(
   bool isDefaultTableStyle
);
[JScript]
public function DataGridTableStyle(
   isDefaultTableStyle : Boolean
);
```

DataGridTableStyle Constructor (CurrencyManager)

Initializes a new instance of the **DataGridTableStyle** class with the specified **CurrencyManager**.

```
[Visual Basic]
Public Sub New( _
   ByVal listManager As CurrencyManager _
)
[C#]
public DataGridTableStyle(
   CurrencyManager listManager
);
[C++]
public: DataGridTableStyle(
   CurrencyManager* listManager
);
[JScript]
public function DataGridTableStyle(
   listManager : CurrencyManager
);
```

Parameters

listManager

The **CurrencyManager** to use.

Example

See related example in the **System.Windows.Forms.DataGrid-TableStyle** class topic.

Requirements

Platforms: Windows 98, Windows NT 4.0, Windows Millennium Edition, Windows 2000, Windows XP Home Edition, Windows XP Professional, Windows Server 2003 family

DataGridTableStyle.DefaultTableStyle Field

This member supports the .NET Framework infrastructure and is not intended to be used directly from your code.

```
[Visual Basic]
Public Shared DefaultTableStyle As DataGridTableStyle
[C#]
public static DataGridTableStyle DefaultTableStyle;
[C++]
public: static DataGridTableStyle* DefaultTableStyle;
[JScript]
public static var DefaultTableStyle : DataGridTableStyle;
```

DataGridTableStyle.AllowSorting Property

Indicates whether sorting is allowed on the grid table when this **DataGridTableStyle** is used.

[Visual Basic]
```
Public Property AllowSorting As Boolean
```
[C#]
```
public bool AllowSorting {get; set;}
```
[C++]
```
public: __property bool get_AllowSorting();
public: __property void set_AllowSorting(bool);
```
[JScript]
```
public function get AllowSorting() : Boolean;
public function set AllowSorting(Boolean);
```

Property Value

true if sorting is allowed; otherwise, **false**. The default is **true**.

Remarks

When the **AllowSorting** property is set to **true**, a triangle appears in each column header indicating the direction of the sort. The user can click on any column header to sort the grid by that column. Clicking the column a second time changes the direction of the sort.

Example

See related example in the **System.Windows.Forms.DataGrid-TableStyle** class topic.

Requirements

Platforms: Windows 98, Windows NT 4.0,
Windows Millennium Edition, Windows 2000,
Windows XP Home Edition, Windows XP Professional,
Windows Server 2003 family

DataGridTableStyle.AlternatingBackColor Property

Gets or sets the background color of odd-numbered rows of the grid.

[Visual Basic]
```
Public Property AlternatingBackColor As Color
```
[C#]
```
public Color AlternatingBackColor {get; set;}
```
[C++]
```
public: __property Color get_AlternatingBackColor();
public: __property void set_AlternatingBackColor(Color);
```
[JScript]
```
public function get AlternatingBackColor() : Color;
public function set AlternatingBackColor(Color);
```

Property Value

A **Color** that represents the background color of odd-numbered rows. The default is **Window**

Example

See related example in the **System.Windows.Forms.DataGrid-TableStyle** class topic.

Requirements

Platforms: Windows 98, Windows NT 4.0,
Windows Millennium Edition, Windows 2000,
Windows XP Home Edition, Windows XP Professional,
Windows Server 2003 family

DataGridTableStyle.BackColor Property

Gets or sets the background color of odd-numbered rows of the grid.

[Visual Basic]
```
Public Property BackColor As Color
```
[C#]
```
public Color BackColor {get; set;}
```
[C++]
```
public: __property Color get_BackColor();
public: __property void set_BackColor(Color);
```
[JScript]
```
public function get BackColor() : Color;
public function set BackColor(Color);
```

Property Value

A **Color** that represents the background color of odd-numbered rows.

Remarks

The **AlternatingBackColor** property can also be set to create a ledger-like appearance.

Example

See related example in the **System.Windows.Forms.DataGrid-TableStyle** class topic.

Requirements

Platforms: Windows 98, Windows NT 4.0,
Windows Millennium Edition, Windows 2000,
Windows XP Home Edition, Windows XP Professional,
Windows Server 2003 family

DataGridTableStyle.ColumnHeadersVisible Property

Gets or sets a value indicating whether column headers are visible.

[Visual Basic]
```
Public Property ColumnHeadersVisible As Boolean
```
[C#]
```
public bool ColumnHeadersVisible {get; set;}
```
[C++]
```
public: __property bool get_ColumnHeadersVisible();
public: __property void set_ColumnHeadersVisible(bool);
```
[JScript]
```
public function get ColumnHeadersVisible() : Boolean;
public function set ColumnHeadersVisible(Boolean);
```

Property Value

true if column headers are visible; otherwise, **false**. The default is **true**.

Remarks

To set header caption text, use the **HeaderText** property of the **DataGridColumnStyle** class.

Example

See related example in the **System.Windows.Forms.DataGrid-TableStyle** class topic.

Requirements

Platforms: Windows 98, Windows NT 4.0,
Windows Millennium Edition, Windows 2000,
Windows XP Home Edition, Windows XP Professional,
Windows Server 2003 family

DataGridTableStyle.DataGrid Property

Gets or sets the **System.Windows.Forms.DataGrid** control for the drawn table.

```
[Visual Basic]
Public Overridable Property DataGrid As DataGrid
[C#]
public virtual DataGrid DataGrid {get; set;}
[C++]
public: __property virtual DataGrid* get_DataGrid();
public: __property virtual void set_DataGrid(DataGrid*);
[JScript]
public function get DataGrid() : DataGrid;
public function set DataGrid(DataGrid);
```

Property Value

The **System.Windows.Forms.DataGrid** control that displays the table.

Remarks

The **System.Windows.Forms.DataGrid** control displays data in the form of a grid. The **DataGridTableStyle** is an object that represents the drawn grid. The **System.Windows.Forms.DataGrid** property returns a reference to the control that is displaying the grid.

The **DataGrid** property is set when a **DataGridTableStyle** is added to a **System.Windows.Forms.DataGrid** control's **GridTableStylesCollection**. You should not try to set this property unless you are overriding it and creating a designer for a user control that incorporates the **DataGrid** control.

Example

See related example in the **System.Windows.Forms.DataGridTableStyle** class topic.

Requirements

Platforms: Windows 98, Windows NT 4.0, Windows Millennium Edition, Windows 2000, Windows XP Home Edition, Windows XP Professional, Windows Server 2003 family

DataGridTableStyle.ForeColor Property

Gets or sets the foreground color of the grid table.

```
[Visual Basic]
Public Property ForeColor As Color
[C#]
public Color ForeColor {get; set;}
[C++]
public: __property Color get_ForeColor();
public: __property void set_ForeColor(Color);
[JScript]
public function get ForeColor() : Color;
public function set ForeColor(Color);
```

Property Value

A **Color** that represents the foreground color of the grid table.

Example

See related example in the **System.Windows.Forms.DataGridTableStyle** class topic.

Requirements

Platforms: Windows 98, Windows NT 4.0, Windows Millennium Edition, Windows 2000, Windows XP Home Edition, Windows XP Professional, Windows Server 2003 family

DataGridTableStyle.GridColumnStyles Property

Gets the collection of columns drawn for this table.

```
[Visual Basic]
Public Overridable ReadOnly Property GridColumnStyles As _
   GridColumnStylesCollection
[C#]
public virtual GridColumnStylesCollection GridColumnStyles {get;}
[C++]
public: __property virtual GridColumnStylesCollection*
   get_GridColumnStyles();
[JScript]
public function get GridColumnStyles() : GridColumnStylesCollection;
```

Property Value

A **GridColumnStylesCollection** that contains all **DataGridColumnStyle** objects for the table.

Remarks

The **GridColumnStylesCollection** returned by the **GridColumnStyles** property allows you to create a customized set of column styles. For each **DataColumn** in a **DataTable**, set the **MappingName** of a **DataGridColumnStyle** object to the **ColumnName**. That column style will automatically be used when this **DataGridTableStyle** is displayed.

If you create a **DataGridTableStyle** object without adding any **DataGridColumnStyle** objects to the **GridColumnStylesCollection**, a collection of **DataGridColumnStyle** objects will be created automatically when the **DataGridTableStyle** object is added to the **GridTableStylesCollection**. An exception will be thrown if you attempt to add **DataGridColumnStyle** objects with duplicate **MappingName** values to the collection.

Example

See related example in the **System.Windows.Forms.DataGridTableStyle** class topic.

Requirements

Platforms: Windows 98, Windows NT 4.0, Windows Millennium Edition, Windows 2000, Windows XP Home Edition, Windows XP Professional, Windows Server 2003 family, .NET Compact Framework - Windows CE .NET

DataGridTableStyle.GridLineColor Property

Gets or sets the color of grid lines.

```
[Visual Basic]
Public Property GridLineColor As Color
[C#]
public Color GridLineColor {get; set;}
[C++]
public: __property Color get_GridLineColor();
public: __property void set_GridLineColor(Color);
```

```
[JScript]
public function get GridLineColor() : Color;
public function set GridLineColor(Color);
```

Property Value

A **Color** that represents the grid line color.

Example

See related example in the **System.Windows.Forms.DataGrid-TableStyle** class topic.

Requirements

Platforms: Windows 98, Windows NT 4.0, Windows Millennium Edition, Windows 2000, Windows XP Home Edition, Windows XP Professional, Windows Server 2003 family

DataGridTableStyle.GridLineStyle Property

Gets or sets the style of grid lines.

```
[Visual Basic]
Public Property GridLineStyle As DataGridLineStyle
[C#]
public DataGridLineStyle GridLineStyle {get; set;}
[C++]
public: __property DataGridLineStyle get_GridLineStyle();
public: __property void set_GridLineStyle(DataGridLineStyle);
[JScript]
public function get GridLineStyle() : DataGridLineStyle;
public function set GridLineStyle(DataGridLineStyle);
```

Property Value

One of the **DataGridLineStyle** values. The default is **DataGridLineStyle.Solid**.

Requirements

Platforms: Windows 98, Windows NT 4.0, Windows Millennium Edition, Windows 2000, Windows XP Home Edition, Windows XP Professional, Windows Server 2003 family

DataGridTableStyle.HeaderBackColor Property

Gets or sets the background color of headers.

```
[Visual Basic]
Public Property HeaderBackColor As Color
[C#]
public Color HeaderBackColor {get; set;}
[C++]
public: __property Color get_HeaderBackColor();
public: __property void set_HeaderBackColor(Color);
[JScript]
public function get HeaderBackColor() : Color;
public function set HeaderBackColor(Color);
```

Property Value

A **Color** that represents the background color of headers.

Example

See related example in the **System.Windows.Forms.DataGrid-TableStyle** class topic.

Requirements

Platforms: Windows 98, Windows NT 4.0, Windows Millennium Edition, Windows 2000, Windows XP Home Edition, Windows XP Professional, Windows Server 2003 family

DataGridTableStyle.HeaderFont Property

Gets or sets the font used for header captions.

```
[Visual Basic]
Public Property HeaderFont As Font
[C#]
public Font HeaderFont {get; set;}
[C++]
public: __property Font* get_HeaderFont();
public: __property void set_HeaderFont(Font*);
[JScript]
public function get HeaderFont() : Font;
public function set HeaderFont(Font);
```

Property Value

The **Font** used for captions.

Remarks

To set header caption text, use the **HeaderText** property of the **DataGridColumnStyle** class.

Example

See related example in the **System.Windows.Forms.DataGrid-TableStyle** class topic.

Requirements

Platforms: Windows 98, Windows NT 4.0, Windows Millennium Edition, Windows 2000, Windows XP Home Edition, Windows XP Professional, Windows Server 2003 family

DataGridTableStyle.HeaderForeColor Property

Gets or sets the foreground color of headers.

```
[Visual Basic]
Public Property HeaderForeColor As Color
[C#]
public Color HeaderForeColor {get; set;}
[C++]
public: __property Color get_HeaderForeColor();
public: __property void set_HeaderForeColor(Color);
[JScript]
public function get HeaderForeColor() : Color;
public function set HeaderForeColor(Color);
```

Property Value

A **Color** that represents the foreground color of headers.

Example

See related example in the **System.Windows.Forms.DataGrid-TableStyle** class topic.

Requirements

Platforms: Windows 98, Windows NT 4.0, Windows Millennium Edition, Windows 2000, Windows XP Home Edition, Windows XP Professional, Windows Server 2003 family

DataGridTableStyle.LinkColor Property

Gets or sets the color of link text.

```
[Visual Basic]
Public Property LinkColor As Color
[C#]
public Color LinkColor {get; set;}
[C++]
public: __property Color get_LinkColor();
public: __property void set_LinkColor(Color);
[JScript]
public function get LinkColor() : Color;
public function set LinkColor(Color);
```

Property Value

The **Color** of link text.

Example

See related example in the **System.Windows.Forms.DataGrid-TableStyle** class topic.

Requirements

Platforms: Windows 98, Windows NT 4.0, Windows Millennium Edition, Windows 2000, Windows XP Home Edition, Windows XP Professional, Windows Server 2003 family

DataGridTableStyle.LinkHoverColor Property

This member supports the .NET Framework infrastructure and is not intended to be used directly from your code.

```
[Visual Basic]
<ComVisible(False)>
Public Property LinkHoverColor As Color
[C#]
[ComVisible(false)]
public Color LinkHoverColor {get; set;}
[C++]
[ComVisible(false)]
public: __property Color get_LinkHoverColor();
public: __property void set_LinkHoverColor(Color);
[JScript]
public
   ComVisible(false)
function get LinkHoverColor() : Color;
public function set LinkHoverColor(Color);
```

DataGridTableStyle.MappingName Property

Gets or sets the name used to map this table to a specific data source.

```
[Visual Basic]
Public Property MappingName As String
[C#]
public string MappingName {get; set;}
[C++]
public: __property String* get_MappingName();
public: __property void set_MappingName(String*);
[JScript]
public function get MappingName() : String;
public function set MappingName(String);
```

Property Value

The name used to map this grid to a specific data source.

Remarks

To bind the **System.Windows.Forms.DataGrid** to a strongly typed array of objects, the object must contain public properties. To create a **DataGridTableStyle** that displays such an array, set the **Mapping-Name** property to *classname[ ]* where *classname* is replaced by the class name. Also note that the **MappingName** property is case-sensitive.

You can also bind the **DataGrid** to an **ArrayList**. A feature of the **ArrayList** is that it can contain objects of multiple types, but the **DataGrid** can only bind to such a list when all items in the list are of the same type as the first item. This means that all objects must either be of the same type, or they must inherit from the same class as the first item in the list. For example, if the first item in a list is a **Control** object, the second item could be a **TextBox** (which inherits from **Control**). If, on the other hand, the first item is a **TextBox**, the second object cannot be a **Control**. Further, the **ArrayList** must have items in it when it is bound. An empty **ArrayList** will result in an empty grid. When binding to an **ArrayList**, set the **Mapping-Name** of the **DataGridTableStyle** to "ArrayList" (the type name).

The default is the name of the list managed by the **Currency-Manager** for this grid. The **CurrencyManager** for the **DataGrid-TableStyle** is set using the **DataGridTableStyle** constructor.

The **MappingNameChanged** event occurs when the **Mapping-Name** value changes.

Example

See related example in the **System.Windows.Forms.DataGrid-TableStyle** class topic.

Requirements

Platforms: Windows 98, Windows NT 4.0, Windows Millennium Edition, Windows 2000, Windows XP Home Edition, Windows XP Professional, Windows Server 2003 family, .NET Compact Framework - Windows CE .NET

DataGridTableStyle.PreferredColumnWidth Property

Gets or sets the width used to create columns when a new grid is displayed.

```
[Visual Basic]
Public Property PreferredColumnWidth As Integer
[C#]
public int PreferredColumnWidth {get; set;}
[C++]
public: __property int get_PreferredColumnWidth();
public: __property void set_PreferredColumnWidth(int);
[JScript]
public function get PreferredColumnWidth() : int;
public function set PreferredColumnWidth(int);
```

Property Value

The width used to create columns when a new grid is displayed.

Example

See related example in the **System.Windows.Forms.DataGrid-TableStyle** class topic.

Requirements

Platforms: Windows 98, Windows NT 4.0, Windows Millennium Edition, Windows 2000, Windows XP Home Edition, Windows XP Professional, Windows Server 2003 family

DataGridTableStyle.PreferredRowHeight Property

Gets or sets the height used to create a row when a new grid is displayed.

```
[Visual Basic]
Public Property PreferredRowHeight As Integer
[C#]
public int PreferredRowHeight {get; set;}
[C++]
public: __property int get_PreferredRowHeight();
public: __property void set_PreferredRowHeight(int);
[JScript]
public function get PreferredRowHeight() : int;
public function set PreferredRowHeight(int);
```

Property Value

The height of a row in pixels.

Remarks

The preferred height is the minimum height needed to accommodate the displayed text with the assigned **HeaderFont**.

Example

See related example in the **System.Windows.Forms.DataGrid-TableStyle** class topic.

Requirements

Platforms: Windows 98, Windows NT 4.0, Windows Millennium Edition, Windows 2000, Windows XP Home Edition, Windows XP Professional, Windows Server 2003 family

DataGridTableStyle.ReadOnly Property

Gets or sets a value indicating whether columns can be edited.

```
[Visual Basic]
Public Overridable Property ReadOnly As Boolean
[C#]
public virtual bool ReadOnly {get; set;}
[C++]
public: __property virtual bool get_ReadOnly();
public: __property virtual void set_ReadOnly(bool);
[JScript]
public function get ReadOnly() : Boolean;
public function set ReadOnly(Boolean);
```

Property Value

true, if columns can be edited; otherwise, **false**.

Remarks

You can also specify whether individual columns within the table are editable by setting the **DataGridColumnStyle** class's **DataGrid-ColumnStyle.ReadOnly** property to an appropriate value, **true** or **false**.

Alternatively, to ensure that the data is not edited, you can set the **DataColumn** class's **ReadOnly** property to **true**.

Example

See related example in the **System.Windows.Forms.DataGrid-TableStyle** class topic.

Requirements

Platforms: Windows 98, Windows NT 4.0, Windows Millennium Edition, Windows 2000, Windows XP Home Edition, Windows XP Professional, Windows Server 2003 family

DataGridTableStyle.RowHeadersVisible Property

Gets or sets a value indicating whether row headers are visible.

```
[Visual Basic]
Public Property RowHeadersVisible As Boolean
[C#]
public bool RowHeadersVisible {get; set;}
[C++]
public: __property bool get_RowHeadersVisible();
public: __property void set_RowHeadersVisible(bool);
[JScript]
public function get RowHeadersVisible() : Boolean;
public function set RowHeadersVisible(Boolean);
```

Property Value

true if row headers are visible; otherwise, **false**. The default is **true**.

Remarks

When row headers are visible, a plus sign is displayed in each row header if the underlying **DataTable** has a related child table.

This property will not function until you add **DataGridTableStyle** objects to the **GridTableStylesCollection**. Until then, setting this property will have no effect.

Example

See related example in the **System.Windows.Forms.DataGrid-TableStyle** class topic.

Requirements

Platforms: Windows 98, Windows NT 4.0, Windows Millennium Edition, Windows 2000, Windows XP Home Edition, Windows XP Professional, Windows Server 2003 family

DataGridTableStyle.RowHeaderWidth Property

Gets or sets the width of row headers.

```
[Visual Basic]
Public Property RowHeaderWidth As Integer
[C#]
public int RowHeaderWidth {get; set;}
[C++]
public: __property int get_RowHeaderWidth();
public: __property void set_RowHeaderWidth(int);
[JScript]
public function get RowHeaderWidth() : int;
public function set RowHeaderWidth(int);
```

Property Value

The width of row headers in pixels.

Remarks

When row headers are visible a plus sign is displayed in each row header if the underlying data has a related child table.

This property will not function until you add **DataGridTableStyle** objects to the **GridTableStylesCollection**. Until then, setting this property will have no effect.

Example

See related example in the **System.Windows.Forms.DataGrid-TableStyle** class topic.

Requirements

Platforms: Windows 98, Windows NT 4.0, Windows Millennium Edition, Windows 2000, Windows XP Home Edition, Windows XP Professional, Windows Server 2003 family

DataGridTableStyle.SelectionBackColor Property

Gets or sets the background color of selected cells.

```
[Visual Basic]
Public Property SelectionBackColor As Color
[C#]
public Color SelectionBackColor {get; set;}
[C++]
public: __property Color get_SelectionBackColor();
public: __property void set_SelectionBackColor(Color);
[JScript]
public function get SelectionBackColor() : Color;
public function set SelectionBackColor(Color);
```

Property Value

The **Color** that represents the background color of selected cells.

Example

See related example in the **System.Windows.Forms.DataGrid-TableStyle** class topic.

Requirements

Platforms: Windows 98, Windows NT 4.0, Windows Millennium Edition, Windows 2000, Windows XP Home Edition, Windows XP Professional, Windows Server 2003 family

DataGridTableStyle.SelectionForeColor Property

Gets or sets the foreground color of selected cells.

```
[Visual Basic]
Public Property SelectionForeColor As Color
[C#]
public Color SelectionForeColor {get; set;}
[C++]
public: __property Color get_SelectionForeColor();
public: __property void set_SelectionForeColor(Color);
[JScript]
public function get SelectionForeColor() : Color;
public function set SelectionForeColor(Color);
```

Property Value

The **Color** that represents the foreground color of selected cells.

Example

See related example in the **System.Windows.Forms.DataGrid-TableStyle** class topic.

Requirements

Platforms: Windows 98, Windows NT 4.0, Windows Millennium Edition, Windows 2000, Windows XP Home Edition, Windows XP Professional, Windows Server 2003 family

DataGridTableStyle.BeginEdit Method

Requests an edit operation.

```
[Visual Basic]
Public Overridable Function BeginEdit( _
   ByVal gridColumn As DataGridColumnStyle, _
   ByVal rowNumber As Integer _
) As Boolean Implements IDataGridEditingService.BeginEdit
[C#]
public virtual bool BeginEdit(
   DataGridColumnStyle gridColumn,
   int rowNumber
);
[C++]
public: virtual bool BeginEdit(
   DataGridColumnStyle* gridColumn,
   int rowNumber
);
[JScript]
public function BeginEdit(
   gridColumn : DataGridColumnStyle,
   rowNumber : int
) : Boolean;
```

Parameters

gridColumn

The **DataGridColumnStyle** to edit.

rowNumber

The number of the edited row.

Return Value

true, if the operation succeeds; otherwise, **false**.

Implements

IDataGridEditingService.BeginEdit

Remarks

The **BeginEdit** method is intended to notify the **System.Windows.Forms.DataGrid** control when the user has begun an editing operation. When the controls is in edit mode, multiple edits can be made and the constraints will be temporarily unenforced.

Call the **EndEdit** method to quit the edit mode.

Example

See related example in the **System.Windows.Forms.DataGrid-TableStyle** class topic.

Requirements

Platforms: Windows 98, Windows NT 4.0, Windows Millennium Edition, Windows 2000, Windows XP Home Edition, Windows XP Professional, Windows Server 2003 family

DataGridTableStyle.CreateGridColumn Method

Creates a **DataGridColumnStyle**.

Overload List

Creates a **DataGridColumnStyle**. using the specified property descriptor.

[Visual Basic] **Overloads Protected Friend Overridable Function CreateGridColumn(PropertyDescriptor) As DataGridColumnStyle**

[C#] **protected internal virtual DataGridColumnStyle CreateGridColumn(PropertyDescriptor);**

[C++] **protected public: virtual DataGridColumnStyle* CreateGridColumn(PropertyDescriptor*);**

[JScript] **protected internal function CreateGrid-Column(PropertyDescriptor) : DataGridColumnStyle;**

Creates a **DataGridColumnStyle** using the specified property descriptor. Specifies whether the **DataGridColumnStyle** is a default column style.

[Visual Basic] **Overloads Protected Friend Overridable Function CreateGridColumn(PropertyDescriptor, Boolean) As DataGridColumnStyle**

[C#] **protected internal virtual DataGridColumnStyle CreateGridColumn(PropertyDescriptor, bool);**

[C++] **protected public: virtual DataGridColumnStyle* CreateGridColumn(PropertyDescriptor*, bool);**

[JScript] **protected internal function CreateGrid-Column(PropertyDescriptor, Boolean) : DataGridColumnStyle;**

DataGridTableStyle.CreateGridColumn Method (PropertyDescriptor)

Creates a **DataGridColumnStyle**. using the specified property descriptor.

[Visual Basic]
```
Overloads Protected Friend Overridable Function CreateGridColumn( _
   ByVal prop As PropertyDescriptor _
) As DataGridColumnStyle
```
[C#]
```
protected internal virtual DataGridColumnStyle CreateGridColumn(
   PropertyDescriptor prop
);
```
[C++]
```
protected public: virtual DataGridColumnStyle* CreateGridColumn(
   PropertyDescriptor* prop
);
```
[JScript]
```
protected internal function CreateGridColumn(
   prop : PropertyDescriptor
) : DataGridColumnStyle;
```

Parameters

prop

The **PropertyDescriptor** used to create the column style object.

Return Value

The newly created **DataGridColumnStyle** object.

Requirements

Platforms: Windows 98, Windows NT 4.0, Windows Millennium Edition, Windows 2000, Windows XP Home Edition, Windows XP Professional, Windows Server 2003 family

DataGridTableStyle.CreateGridColumn Method (PropertyDescriptor, Boolean)

Creates a **DataGridColumnStyle** using the specified property descriptor. Specifies whether the **DataGridColumnStyle** is a default column style.

[Visual Basic]
```
Overloads Protected Friend Overridable Function CreateGridColumn( _
   ByVal prop As PropertyDescriptor, _
   ByVal isDefault As Boolean _
) As DataGridColumnStyle
```
[C#]
```
protected internal virtual DataGridColumnStyle CreateGridColumn(
   PropertyDescriptor prop,
   bool isDefault
);
```
[C++]
```
protected public: virtual DataGridColumnStyle* CreateGridColumn(
   PropertyDescriptor* prop,
   bool isDefault
);
```
[JScript]
```
protected internal function CreateGridColumn(
   prop : PropertyDescriptor,
   isDefault : Boolean
) : DataGridColumnStyle;
```

Parameters

prop

The **PropertyDescriptor** used to create the column style object.

isDefault

Specifies whether the **DataGridColumnStyle** object is a default column style. This parameter is read-only.

Return Value

The newly created **DataGridColumnStyle** object.

Requirements

Platforms: Windows 98, Windows NT 4.0, Windows Millennium Edition, Windows 2000, Windows XP Home Edition, Windows XP Professional, Windows Server 2003 family

DataGridTableStyle.Dispose Method

Overload List

This member supports the .NET Framework infrastructure and is not intended to be used directly from your code.

Supported by the .NET Compact Framework.

[Visual Basic] **Overloads Overrides Protected Sub Dispose(Boolean)**

[C#] **protected override void Dispose(bool);**

[C++] **protected: void Dispose(bool);**

[JScript] **protected override function Dispose(Boolean);**

Inherited from **Component**.

[Visual Basic] **Overloads Public Overridable Sub Dispose() Implements IDisposable.Dispose**

[C#] **public virtual void Dispose();**

[C++] **public: virtual void Dispose();**

[JScript] **public function Dispose();**

DataGridTableStyle.Dispose Method (Boolean)

This member overrides **Component.Dispose**.

```
[Visual Basic]
Overrides Overloads Protected Sub Dispose( _
   ByVal disposing As Boolean _
)
[C#]
protected override void Dispose(
   bool disposing
);
[C++]
protected: void Dispose(
   bool disposing
);
[JScript]
protected override function Dispose(
   disposing : Boolean
);
```

Requirements

Platforms: Windows 98, Windows NT 4.0, Windows Millennium Edition, Windows 2000, Windows XP Home Edition, Windows XP Professional, Windows Server 2003 family, .NET Compact Framework - Windows CE .NET

DataGridTableStyle.EndEdit Method

Requests an end to an edit operation.

```
[Visual Basic]
Public Overridable Function EndEdit( _
   ByVal gridColumn As DataGridColumnStyle, _
   ByVal rowNumber As Integer, _
   ByVal shouldAbort As Boolean _
) As Boolean Implements IDataGridEditingService.EndEdit
[C#]
public virtual bool EndEdit(
   DataGridColumnStyle gridColumn,
   int rowNumber,
   bool shouldAbort
);
[C++]
public: virtual bool EndEdit(
   DataGridColumnStyle* gridColumn,
   int rowNumber,
   bool shouldAbort
);
[JScript]
public function EndEdit(
   gridColumn : DataGridColumnStyle,
   rowNumber : int,
   shouldAbort : Boolean
) : Boolean;
```

Parameters

gridColumn
: The **DataGridColumnStyle** to edit.

rowNumber
: The number of the edited row.

shouldAbort
: A value indicating whether the operation should be stopped; **true** if it should stop; otherwise, **false**.

Return Value

true if the edit operation ends successfully; otherwise, **false**.

Implements

IDataGridEditingService.EndEdit

Remarks

Similar to the **BeginEdit** method, the **EndEdit** method is intended to notify the **System.Windows.Forms.DataGrid** when an edit operation is ending.

Example

See related example in the **System.Windows.Forms.DataGridTableStyle** class topic.

Requirements

Platforms: Windows 98, Windows NT 4.0, Windows Millennium Edition, Windows 2000, Windows XP Home Edition, Windows XP Professional, Windows Server 2003 family

DataGridTableStyle.OnAllowSortingChanged Method

Raises the **AllowSortingChanged** event.

```
[Visual Basic]
Protected Overridable Sub OnAllowSortingChanged( _
   ByVal e As EventArgs _
)
[C#]
protected virtual void OnAllowSortingChanged(
   EventArgs e
);
[C++]
protected: virtual void OnAllowSortingChanged(
   EventArgs* e
);
[JScript]
protected function OnAllowSortingChanged(
   e : EventArgs
);
```

Parameters

e
: An **EventArgs** that contains the event data.

Remarks

Raising an event invokes the event handler through a delegate.

The **OnAllowSortingChanged** method also allows derived classes to handle the event without attaching a delegate. This is the preferred technique for handling the event in a derived class.

Notes to Inheritors: When overriding **OnAllowSortingChanged** in a derived class, be sure to call the base class's **OnAllowSortingChanged** method so that registered delegates receive the event.

Requirements

Platforms: Windows 98, Windows NT 4.0, Windows Millennium Edition, Windows 2000, Windows XP Home Edition, Windows XP Professional, Windows Server 2003 family

DataGridTableStyle.OnAlternatingBackColorChanged Method

Raises the **AlternatingBackColorChanged** event.

```
[Visual Basic]
Protected Overridable Sub OnAlternatingBackColorChanged( _
   ByVal e As EventArgs _
)
[C#]
protected virtual void OnAlternatingBackColorChanged(
   EventArgs e
);
[C++]
protected: virtual void OnAlternatingBackColorChanged(
   EventArgs* e
);
[JScript]
protected function OnAlternatingBackColorChanged(
   e : EventArgs
);
```

Parameters

e

An **EventArgs** that contains the event data.

Remarks

Raising an event invokes the event handler through a delegate.

The **OnAlternatingBackColorChanged** method also allows derived classes to handle the event without attaching a delegate. This is the preferred technique for handling the event in a derived class.

Notes to Inheritors: When overriding **OnAlternatingBackColorChanged** in a derived class, be sure to call the base class's **OnAlternatingBackColorChanged** method so that registered delegates receive the event.

Requirements

Platforms: Windows 98, Windows NT 4.0, Windows Millennium Edition, Windows 2000, Windows XP Home Edition, Windows XP Professional, Windows Server 2003 family

DataGridTableStyle.OnBackColorChanged Method

Raises the **BackColorChanged** event.

```
[Visual Basic]
Protected Overridable Sub OnBackColorChanged( _
   ByVal e As EventArgs _
)
[C#]
protected virtual void OnBackColorChanged(
   EventArgs e
);
[C++]
protected: virtual void OnBackColorChanged(
   EventArgs* e
);
[JScript]
protected function OnBackColorChanged(
   e : EventArgs
);
```

Parameters

e

An **EventArgs** that contains the event data.

Remarks

Raising an event invokes the event handler through a delegate.

The **OnBackColorChanged** method also allows derived classes to handle the event without attaching a delegate. This is the preferred technique for handling the event in a derived class.

Notes to Inheritors: When overriding **OnBackColorChanged** in a derived class, be sure to call the base class's **OnBackColorChanged** method so that registered delegates receive the event.

Requirements

Platforms: Windows 98, Windows NT 4.0, Windows Millennium Edition, Windows 2000, Windows XP Home Edition, Windows XP Professional, Windows Server 2003 family

DataGridTableStyle.OnColumnHeadersVisibleChanged Method

Raises the **ColumnHeadersVisibleChanged** event.

```
[Visual Basic]
Protected Overridable Sub OnColumnHeadersVisibleChanged( _
   ByVal e As EventArgs _
)
[C#]
protected virtual void OnColumnHeadersVisibleChanged(
   EventArgs e
);
[C++]
protected: virtual void OnColumnHeadersVisibleChanged(
   EventArgs* e
);
[JScript]
protected function OnColumnHeadersVisibleChanged(
   e : EventArgs
);
```

Parameters

e

An **EventArgs** that contains the event data.

Remarks

Raising an event invokes the event handler through a delegate.

The **OnColumnHeadersVisibleChanged** method also allows derived classes to handle the event without attaching a delegate. This is the preferred technique for handling the event in a derived class.

Notes to Inheritors: When overriding **OnColumnHeadersVisibleChanged** in a derived class, be sure to call the base class's **OnColumnHeadersVisibleChanged** method so that registered delegates receive the event.

Requirements

Platforms: Windows 98, Windows NT 4.0, Windows Millennium Edition, Windows 2000, Windows XP Home Edition, Windows XP Professional, Windows Server 2003 family

DataGridTableStyle.OnForeColorChanged Method

Raises the **ForeColorChanged** event.

[Visual Basic]
```
Protected Overridable Sub OnForeColorChanged( _
   ByVal e As EventArgs _
)
```
[C#]
```
protected virtual void OnForeColorChanged(
   EventArgs e
);
```
[C++]
```
protected: virtual void OnForeColorChanged(
   EventArgs* e
);
```
[JScript]
```
protected function OnForeColorChanged(
   e : EventArgs
);
```

Parameters

e

An **EventArgs** that contains the event data.

Remarks

Raising an event invokes the event handler through a delegate.

The **OnForeColorChanged** method also allows derived classes to handle the event without attaching a delegate. This is the preferred technique for handling the event in a derived class.

Notes to Inheritors: When overriding **OnForeColorChanged** in a derived class, be sure to call the base class's **OnForeColorChanged** method so that registered delegates receive the event.

Requirements

Platforms: Windows 98, Windows NT 4.0, Windows Millennium Edition, Windows 2000, Windows XP Home Edition, Windows XP Professional, Windows Server 2003 family

DataGridTableStyle.OnGridLineColorChanged Method

Raises the **GridLineColorChanged** event.

[Visual Basic]
```
Protected Overridable Sub OnGridLineColorChanged( _
   ByVal e As EventArgs _
)
```
[C#]
```
protected virtual void OnGridLineColorChanged(
   EventArgs e
);
```
[C++]
```
protected: virtual void OnGridLineColorChanged(
   EventArgs* e
);
```
[JScript]
```
protected function OnGridLineColorChanged(
   e : EventArgs
);
```

Parameters

e

An **EventArgs** that contains the event data.

Remarks

Raising an event invokes the event handler through a delegate.

The **OnGridLineColorChanged** method also allows derived classes to handle the event without attaching a delegate. This is the preferred technique for handling the event in a derived class.

Notes to Inheritors: When overriding **OnGridLineColor-Changed** in a derived class, be sure to call the base class's **OnGridLineColorChanged** method so that registered delegates receive the event.

Requirements

Platforms: Windows 98, Windows NT 4.0, Windows Millennium Edition, Windows 2000, Windows XP Home Edition, Windows XP Professional, Windows Server 2003 family

DataGridTableStyle.OnGridLineStyleChanged Method

Raises the **GridLineStyleChanged** event.

[Visual Basic]
```
Protected Overridable Sub OnGridLineStyleChanged( _
   ByVal e As EventArgs _
)
```
[C#]
```
protected virtual void OnGridLineStyleChanged(
   EventArgs e
);
```
[C++]
```
protected: virtual void OnGridLineStyleChanged(
   EventArgs* e
);
```
[JScript]
```
protected function OnGridLineStyleChanged(
   e : EventArgs
);
```

Parameters

e

An **EventArgs** that contains the event data.

Remarks

Raising an event invokes the event handler through a delegate.

The **OnGridLineStyleChanged** method also allows derived classes to handle the event without attaching a delegate. This is the preferred technique for handling the event in a derived class.

Notes to Inheritors: When overriding **OnGridLineStyleChanged** in a derived class, be sure to call the base class's **OnGridLineStyle-Changed** method so that registered delegates receive the event.

Requirements

Platforms: Windows 98, Windows NT 4.0, Windows Millennium Edition, Windows 2000, Windows XP Home Edition, Windows XP Professional, Windows Server 2003 family

DataGridTableStyle.OnHeaderBackColorChanged Method

Raises the **HeaderBackColorChanged** event.

```
[Visual Basic]
Protected Overridable Sub OnHeaderBackColorChanged( _
   ByVal e As EventArgs _
)
[C#]
protected virtual void OnHeaderBackColorChanged(
   EventArgs e
);
[C++]
protected: virtual void OnHeaderBackColorChanged(
   EventArgs* e
);
[JScript]
protected function OnHeaderBackColorChanged(
   e : EventArgs
);
```

Parameters

e

An **EventArgs** that contains the event data.

Remarks

Raising an event invokes the event handler through a delegate.

The **OnHeaderBackColorChanged** method also allows derived classes to handle the event without attaching a delegate. This is the preferred technique for handling the event in a derived class.

Notes to Inheritors: When overriding **OnHeaderBackColor-Changed** in a derived class, be sure to call the base class's **OnHeaderBackColorChanged** method so that registered delegates receive the event.

Requirements

Platforms: Windows 98, Windows NT 4.0, Windows Millennium Edition, Windows 2000, Windows XP Home Edition, Windows XP Professional, Windows Server 2003 family

DataGridTableStyle.OnHeaderFontChanged Method

Raises the **HeaderFontChanged** event.

```
[Visual Basic]
Protected Overridable Sub OnHeaderFontChanged( _
   ByVal e As EventArgs _
)
[C#]
protected virtual void OnHeaderFontChanged(
   EventArgs e
);
[C++]
protected: virtual void OnHeaderFontChanged(
   EventArgs* e
);
[JScript]
protected function OnHeaderFontChanged(
   e : EventArgs
);
```

Parameters

e

An **EventArgs** that contains the event data.

Remarks

Raising an event invokes the event handler through a delegate.

The **OnHeaderFontChanged** method also allows derived classes to handle the event without attaching a delegate. This is the preferred technique for handling the event in a derived class.

Notes to Inheritors: When overriding **OnHeaderFontChanged** in a derived class, be sure to call the base class's **OnHeaderFont-Changed** method so that registered delegates receive the event.

Requirements

Platforms: Windows 98, Windows NT 4.0, Windows Millennium Edition, Windows 2000, Windows XP Home Edition, Windows XP Professional, Windows Server 2003 family

DataGridTableStyle.OnHeaderForeColorChanged Method

Raises the **HeaderForeColorChanged** event.

```
[Visual Basic]
Protected Overridable Sub OnHeaderForeColorChanged( _
   ByVal e As EventArgs _
)
[C#]
protected virtual void OnHeaderForeColorChanged(
   EventArgs e
);
[C++]
protected: virtual void OnHeaderForeColorChanged(
   EventArgs* e
);
[JScript]
protected function OnHeaderForeColorChanged(
   e : EventArgs
);
```

Parameters

e

An **EventArgs** that contains the event data.

Remarks

Raising an event invokes the event handler through a delegate.

The **OnHeaderForeColorChanged** method also allows derived classes to handle the event without attaching a delegate. This is the preferred technique for handling the event in a derived class.

Notes to Inheritors: When overriding **OnHeaderForeColor-Changed** in a derived class, be sure to call the base class's **OnHeaderForeColorChanged** method so that registered delegates receive the event.

Requirements

Platforms: Windows 98, Windows NT 4.0, Windows Millennium Edition, Windows 2000, Windows XP Home Edition, Windows XP Professional, Windows Server 2003 family

DataGridTableStyle.OnLinkColorChanged Method

Raises the **LinkColorChanged** event.

```
[Visual Basic]
Protected Overridable Sub OnLinkColorChanged( _
   ByVal e As EventArgs _
)
[C#]
protected virtual void OnLinkColorChanged(
   EventArgs e
);
[C++]
protected: virtual void OnLinkColorChanged(
   EventArgs* e
);
[JScript]
protected function OnLinkColorChanged(
   e : EventArgs
);
```

Parameters

e

An **EventArgs** that contains the event data.

Remarks

Raising an event invokes the event handler through a delegate.

The **OnLinkColorChanged** method also allows derived classes to handle the event without attaching a delegate. This is the preferred technique for handling the event in a derived class.

Notes to Inheritors: When overriding **OnLinkColorChanged** in a derived class, be sure to call the base class's **OnLinkColorChanged** method so that registered delegates receive the event.

Requirements

Platforms: Windows 98, Windows NT 4.0, Windows Millennium Edition, Windows 2000, Windows XP Home Edition, Windows XP Professional, Windows Server 2003 family

DataGridTableStyle.OnLinkHoverColorChanged Method

Raises the LinkHoverColorChanged event.

```
[Visual Basic]
Protected Overridable Sub OnLinkHoverColorChanged( _
   ByVal e As EventArgs _
)
[C#]
protected virtual void OnLinkHoverColorChanged(
   EventArgs e
);
[C++]
protected: virtual void OnLinkHoverColorChanged(
   EventArgs* e
);
[JScript]
protected function OnLinkHoverColorChanged(
   e : EventArgs
);
```

Parameters

e

An **EventArgs** that contains the event data.

Remarks

Raising an event invokes the event handler through a delegate.

The **OnLinkHoverColorChanged** method also allows derived classes to handle the event without attaching a delegate. This is the preferred technique for handling the event in a derived class.

Notes to Inheritors: When overriding **OnLinkHoverColor-Changed** in a derived class, be sure to call the base class's **OnLink-HoverColorChanged** method so that registered delegates receive the event.

Requirements

Platforms: Windows 98, Windows NT 4.0, Windows Millennium Edition, Windows 2000, Windows XP Home Edition, Windows XP Professional, Windows Server 2003 family

DataGridTableStyle.OnMappingNameChanged Method

Raises the **MappingNameChanged** event

```
[Visual Basic]
Protected Overridable Sub OnMappingNameChanged( _
   ByVal e As EventArgs _
)
[C#]
protected virtual void OnMappingNameChanged(
   EventArgs e
);
[C++]
protected: virtual void OnMappingNameChanged(
   EventArgs* e
);
[JScript]
protected function OnMappingNameChanged(
   e : EventArgs
);
```

Parameters

e

An **EventArgs** that contains the event data.

Remarks

Raising an event invokes the event handler through a delegate.

The **OnMappingNameChanged** method also allows derived classes to handle the event without attaching a delegate. This is the preferred technique for handling the event in a derived class.

Notes to Inheritors: When overriding **OnMappingNameChanged** in a derived class, be sure to call the base class's **OnMappingName-Changed** method so that registered delegates receive the event.

Requirements

Platforms: Windows 98, Windows NT 4.0, Windows Millennium Edition, Windows 2000, Windows XP Home Edition, Windows XP Professional, Windows Server 2003 family

DataGridTableStyle.OnPreferredColumnWidthChanged Method

Raises the **PreferredColumnWidthChanged** event.

```
[Visual Basic]
Protected Overridable Sub OnPreferredColumnWidthChanged( _
   ByVal e As EventArgs _
)
[C#]
protected virtual void OnPreferredColumnWidthChanged(
   EventArgs e
);
[C++]
protected: virtual void OnPreferredColumnWidthChanged(
   EventArgs* e
);
[JScript]
protected function OnPreferredColumnWidthChanged(
   e : EventArgs
);
```

Parameters

e

An **EventArgs** that contains the event data.

Remarks

Raising an event invokes the event handler through a delegate.

The **OnPreferredColumnWidthChanged** method also allows derived classes to handle the event without attaching a delegate. This is the preferred technique for handling the event in a derived class.

Notes to Inheritors: When overriding **OnPreferredColumnWidthChanged** in a derived class, be sure to call the base class's **OnPreferredColumnWidthChanged** method so that registered delegates receive the event.

Requirements

Platforms: Windows 98, Windows NT 4.0, Windows Millennium Edition, Windows 2000, Windows XP Home Edition, Windows XP Professional, Windows Server 2003 family

DataGridTableStyle.OnPreferredRowHeightChanged Method

Raises the **PreferredRowHeightChanged** event.

```
[Visual Basic]
Protected Overridable Sub OnPreferredRowHeightChanged( _
   ByVal e As EventArgs _
)
[C#]
protected virtual void OnPreferredRowHeightChanged(
   EventArgs e
);
[C++]
protected: virtual void OnPreferredRowHeightChanged(
   EventArgs* e
);
[JScript]
protected function OnPreferredRowHeightChanged(
   e : EventArgs
);
```

Parameters

e

An **EventArgs** that contains the event data.

Remarks

Raising an event invokes the event handler through a delegate.

The **OnPreferredRowHeightChanged** method also allows derived classes to handle the event without attaching a delegate. This is the preferred technique for handling the event in a derived class.

Notes to Inheritors: When overriding **OnPreferredRowHeightChanged** in a derived class, be sure to call the base class's **OnPreferredRowHeightChanged** method so that registered delegates receive the event.

Requirements

Platforms: Windows 98, Windows NT 4.0, Windows Millennium Edition, Windows 2000, Windows XP Home Edition, Windows XP Professional, Windows Server 2003 family

DataGridTableStyle.OnReadOnlyChanged Method

Raises the **ReadOnlyChanged** event.

```
[Visual Basic]
Protected Overridable Sub OnReadOnlyChanged( _
   ByVal e As EventArgs _
)
[C#]
protected virtual void OnReadOnlyChanged(
   EventArgs e
);
[C++]
protected: virtual void OnReadOnlyChanged(
   EventArgs* e
);
[JScript]
protected function OnReadOnlyChanged(
   e : EventArgs
);
```

Parameters

e

An **EventArgs** that contains the event data.

Remarks

Raising an event invokes the event handler through a delegate.

The **OnReadOnlyChanged** method also allows derived classes to handle the event without attaching a delegate. This is the preferred technique for handling the event in a derived class.

Notes to Inheritors: When overriding **OnReadOnlyChanged** in a derived class, be sure to call the base class's **OnReadOnlyChanged** method so that registered delegates receive the event.

Requirements

Platforms: Windows 98, Windows NT 4.0, Windows Millennium Edition, Windows 2000, Windows XP Home Edition, Windows XP Professional, Windows Server 2003 family

DataGridTableStyle.OnRowHeadersVisibleChanged Method

Raises the **RowHeadersVisibleChanged** event.

```
[Visual Basic]
Protected Overridable Sub OnRowHeadersVisibleChanged( _
   ByVal e As EventArgs _
)
[C#]
protected virtual void OnRowHeadersVisibleChanged(
   EventArgs e
);
[C++]
protected: virtual void OnRowHeadersVisibleChanged(
   EventArgs* e
);
[JScript]
protected function OnRowHeadersVisibleChanged(
   e : EventArgs
);
```

Parameters

e

An **EventArgs** that contains the event data.

Remarks

Raising an event invokes the event handler through a delegate.

The **OnRowHeadersVisibleChanged** method also allows derived classes to handle the event without attaching a delegate. This is the preferred technique for handling the event in a derived class.

Notes to Inheritors: When overriding **OnRowHeadersVisibleChanged** in a derived class, be sure to call the base class's **OnRowHeadersVisibleChanged** method so that registered delegates receive the event.

Requirements

Platforms: Windows 98, Windows NT 4.0, Windows Millennium Edition, Windows 2000, Windows XP Home Edition, Windows XP Professional, Windows Server 2003 family

DataGridTableStyle.OnRowHeaderWidthChanged Method

Raises the **RowHeaderWidthChanged** event.

```
[Visual Basic]
Protected Overridable Sub OnRowHeaderWidthChanged( _
   ByVal e As EventArgs _
)
[C#]
protected virtual void OnRowHeaderWidthChanged(
   EventArgs e
);
[C++]
protected: virtual void OnRowHeaderWidthChanged(
   EventArgs* e
);
[JScript]
protected function OnRowHeaderWidthChanged(
   e : EventArgs
);
```

Parameters

e

An **EventArgs** that contains the event data.

Remarks

Raising an event invokes the event handler through a delegate.

The **OnRowHeaderWidthChanged** method also allows derived classes to handle the event without attaching a delegate. This is the preferred technique for handling the event in a derived class.

Notes to Inheritors: When overriding **OnRowHeaderWidthChanged** in a derived class, be sure to call the base class's **OnRowHeaderWidthChanged** method so that registered delegates receive the event.

Requirements

Platforms: Windows 98, Windows NT 4.0, Windows Millennium Edition, Windows 2000, Windows XP Home Edition, Windows XP Professional, Windows Server 2003 family

DataGridTableStyle.OnSelectionBackColorChanged Method

Raises the **SelectionBackColorChanged** event.

```
[Visual Basic]
Protected Overridable Sub OnSelectionBackColorChanged( _
   ByVal e As EventArgs _
)
[C#]
protected virtual void OnSelectionBackColorChanged(
   EventArgs e
);
[C++]
protected: virtual void OnSelectionBackColorChanged(
   EventArgs* e
);
[JScript]
protected function OnSelectionBackColorChanged(
   e : EventArgs
);
```

Parameters

e

An **EventArgs** that contains the event data.

Remarks

Raising an event invokes the event handler through a delegate.

The **OnSelectionBackColorChanged** method also allows derived classes to handle the event without attaching a delegate. This is the preferred technique for handling the event in a derived class.

Notes to Inheritors: When overriding **OnSelectionBackColorChanged** in a derived class, be sure to call the base class's **OnSelectionBackColorChanged** method so that registered delegates receive the event.

Requirements

Platforms: Windows 98, Windows NT 4.0, Windows Millennium Edition, Windows 2000, Windows XP Home Edition, Windows XP Professional, Windows Server 2003 family

DataGridTableStyle.OnSelectionForeColorChanged Method

Raises the **SelectionForeColorChanged** event.

[Visual Basic]
```
Protected Overridable Sub OnSelectionForeColorChanged( _
   ByVal e As EventArgs _
)
```
[C#]
```
protected virtual void OnSelectionForeColorChanged(
   EventArgs e
);
```
[C++]
```
protected: virtual void OnSelectionForeColorChanged(
   EventArgs* e
);
```
[JScript]
```
protected function OnSelectionForeColorChanged(
   e : EventArgs
);
```

Parameters

e

An **EventArgs** that contains the event data.

Remarks

Raising an event invokes the event handler through a delegate.

The **OnSelectionForeColorChanged** method also allows derived classes to handle the event without attaching a delegate. This is the preferred technique for handling the event in a derived class.

Notes to Inheritors: When overriding **OnSelectionForeColorChanged** in a derived class, be sure to call the base class's **OnSelectionForeColorChanged** method so that registered delegates receive the event.

Requirements

Platforms: Windows 98, Windows NT 4.0, Windows Millennium Edition, Windows 2000, Windows XP Home Edition, Windows XP Professional, Windows Server 2003 family

DataGridTableStyle.ResetAlternatingBackColor Method

Resets the **AlternatingBackColor** property to its default value.

[Visual Basic]
```
Public Sub ResetAlternatingBackColor()
```
[C#]
```
public void ResetAlternatingBackColor();
```
[C++]
```
public: void ResetAlternatingBackColor();
```
[JScript]
```
public function ResetAlternatingBackColor();
```

Remarks

You typically use this method if you are either creating a designer for the **DataGridTableStyle** or creating your own control incorporating the **DataGridTableStyle**. You can use the **ShouldSerializeAlternatingBackColor** method to determine whether the property value has changed from its default.

Example

See related example in the **System.Windows.Forms.DataGridTableStyle** class topic.

\

Requirements

Platforms: Windows 98, Windows NT 4.0, Windows Millennium Edition, Windows 2000, Windows XP Home Edition, Windows XP Professional, Windows Server 2003 family

DataGridTableStyle.ResetBackColor Method

Resets the **BackColor** property to its default value.

[Visual Basic]
```
Public Sub ResetBackColor()
```
[C#]
```
public void ResetBackColor();
```
[C++]
```
public: void ResetBackColor();
```
[JScript]
```
public function ResetBackColor();
```

Remarks

You typically use this method if you are either creating a designer for the **DataGridTableStyle** or creating your own control incorporating the **DataGridTableStyle**.

Example

See related example in the **System.Windows.Forms.DataGridTableStyle** class topic.

Requirements

Platforms: Windows 98, Windows NT 4.0, Windows Millennium Edition, Windows 2000, Windows XP Home Edition, Windows XP Professional, Windows Server 2003 family

DataGridTableStyle.ResetForeColor Method

Resets the **ForeColor** property to its default value.

[Visual Basic]
```
Public Sub ResetForeColor()
```
[C#]
```
public void ResetForeColor();
```
[C++]
```
public: void ResetForeColor();
```
[JScript]
```
public function ResetForeColor();
```

Remarks

You typically use this method if you are either creating a designer for the **DataGridTableStyle** or creating your own control incorporating the **DataGridTableStyle**. You can use the **ShouldSerializeForeColor** method to determine whether the property value has changed from its default.

Example

See related example in the **System.Windows.Forms.DataGrid-TableStyle** class topic.

Requirements

Platforms: Windows 98, Windows NT 4.0, Windows Millennium Edition, Windows 2000, Windows XP Home Edition, Windows XP Professional, Windows Server 2003 family

DataGridTableStyle.ResetGridLineColor Method

Resets the **GridLineColor** property to its default value.

```
[Visual Basic]
Public Sub ResetGridLineColor()
[C#]
public void ResetGridLineColor();
[C++]
public: void ResetGridLineColor();
[JScript]
public function ResetGridLineColor();
```

Remarks

You typically use this method if you are either creating a designer for the **DataGridTableStyle** or creating your own control incorporating the **DataGridTableStyle**. You can use the **Should-SerializeGridLineColor** method to determine whether the property value has changed from its default.

Example

See related example in the **System.Windows.Forms.DataGrid-TableStyle** class topic.

Requirements

Platforms: Windows 98, Windows NT 4.0, Windows Millennium Edition, Windows 2000, Windows XP Home Edition, Windows XP Professional, Windows Server 2003 family

DataGridTableStyle.ResetHeaderBackColor Method

Resets the **HeaderBackColor** property to its default value.

```
[Visual Basic]
Public Sub ResetHeaderBackColor()
[C#]
public void ResetHeaderBackColor();
[C++]
public: void ResetHeaderBackColor();
[JScript]
public function ResetHeaderBackColor();
```

Remarks

You typically use this method if you are either creating a designer for the **DataGridTableStyle** or creating your own control incorporating the **DataGridTableStyle**. You can use the **Should-SerializeHeaderBackColor** method to determine whether the property value has changed from its default.

Example

See related example in the **System.Windows.Forms.DataGrid-TableStyle** class topic.

Requirements

Platforms: Windows 98, Windows NT 4.0, Windows Millennium Edition, Windows 2000, Windows XP Home Edition, Windows XP Professional, Windows Server 2003 family

DataGridTableStyle.ResetHeaderFont Method

Resets the **HeaderFont** property to its default value.

```
[Visual Basic]
Public Sub ResetHeaderFont()
[C#]
public void ResetHeaderFont();
[C++]
public: void ResetHeaderFont();
[JScript]
public function ResetHeaderFont();
```

Remarks

You typically use this method if you are either creating a designer for the **DataGridTableStyle** or creating your own control incorporating the **DataGridTableStyle**.

Example

See related example in the **System.Windows.Forms.DataGrid-TableStyle** class topic.

Requirements

Platforms: Windows 98, Windows NT 4.0, Windows Millennium Edition, Windows 2000, Windows XP Home Edition, Windows XP Professional, Windows Server 2003 family

DataGridTableStyle.ResetHeaderForeColor Method

Resets the **HeaderForeColor** property to its default value.

```
[Visual Basic]
Public Sub ResetHeaderForeColor()
[C#]
public void ResetHeaderForeColor();
[C++]
public: void ResetHeaderForeColor();
[JScript]
public function ResetHeaderForeColor();
```

Remarks

You typically use this method if you are either creating a designer for the **DataGridTableStyle** or creating your own control incorporating the **DataGridTableStyle**. You can use the **Should-SerializeHeaderForeColor** method to determine whether the property value has changed from its default.

Example

See related example in the **System.Windows.Forms.DataGrid-TableStyle** class topic.

Requirements

Platforms: Windows 98, Windows NT 4.0, Windows Millennium Edition, Windows 2000, Windows XP Home Edition, Windows XP Professional, Windows Server 2003 family

DataGridTableStyle.ResetLinkColor Method

Resets the **LinkColor** property to its default value.

```
[Visual Basic]
Public Sub ResetLinkColor()
[C#]
public void ResetLinkColor();
[C++]
public: void ResetLinkColor();
[JScript]
public function ResetLinkColor();
```

Remarks

You typically use this method if you are either creating a designer for the **DataGridTableStyle** or creating your own control incorporating the **DataGridTableStyle**. You can use the **ShouldSerializeLinkColor** method to determine whether the property value has changed from its default.

Example

See related example in the **System.Windows.Forms.DataGridTableStyle** class topic.

Requirements

Platforms: Windows 98, Windows NT 4.0, Windows Millennium Edition, Windows 2000, Windows XP Home Edition, Windows XP Professional, Windows Server 2003 family

DataGridTableStyle.ResetLinkHoverColor Method

This member supports the .NET Framework infrastructure and is not intended to be used directly from your code.

```
[Visual Basic]
Public Sub ResetLinkHoverColor()
[C#]
public void ResetLinkHoverColor();
[C++]
public: void ResetLinkHoverColor();
[JScript]
public function ResetLinkHoverColor();
```

DataGridTableStyle.ResetSelectionBackColor Method

Resets the **SelectionBackColor** property to its default value.

```
[Visual Basic]
Public Sub ResetSelectionBackColor()
[C#]
public void ResetSelectionBackColor();
[C++]
public: void ResetSelectionBackColor();
[JScript]
public function ResetSelectionBackColor();
```

Remarks

You typically use this method if you are either creating a designer for the **DataGridTableStyle** or creating your own control incorporating the **DataGridTableStyle**. You can use the **ShouldSerializeSelectionBackColor** method to determine whether the property value has changed from its default.

Requirements

Platforms: Windows 98, Windows NT 4.0, Windows Millennium Edition, Windows 2000, Windows XP Home Edition, Windows XP Professional, Windows Server 2003 family

DataGridTableStyle.ResetSelectionForeColor Method

Resets the **SelectionForeColor** property to its default value.

```
[Visual Basic]
Public Sub ResetSelectionForeColor()
[C#]
public void ResetSelectionForeColor();
[C++]
public: void ResetSelectionForeColor();
[JScript]
public function ResetSelectionForeColor();
```

Remarks

You typically use this method if you are either creating a designer for the **DataGridTableStyle** or creating your own control incorporating the **DataGridTableStyle**. You can use the **ShouldSerializeSelectionForeColor** method to determine whether the property value has changed from its default.

Example

See related example in the **System.Windows.Forms.DataGridTableStyle** class topic.

Requirements

Platforms: Windows 98, Windows NT 4.0, Windows Millennium Edition, Windows 2000, Windows XP Home Edition, Windows XP Professional, Windows Server 2003 family

DataGridTableStyle.ShouldSerializeAlternatingBackColor Method

Indicates whether the **AlternatingBackColor** property should be persisted.

```
[Visual Basic]
Protected Overridable Function _
   ShouldSerializeAlternatingBackColor() _
   As Boolean
[C#]
protected virtual bool ShouldSerializeAlternatingBackColor();
[C++]
protected: virtual bool ShouldSerializeAlternatingBackColor();
[JScript]
protected function ShouldSerializeAlternatingBackColor() : Boolean;
```

Return Value

true if the property value has changed from its default; otherwise, **false**.

Remarks

You typically use this method if you are either creating a designer for the **DataGridTableStyle** or creating your own control incorporating the **DataGridTableStyle**.

Requirements

Platforms: Windows 98, Windows NT 4.0, Windows Millennium Edition, Windows 2000, Windows XP Home Edition, Windows XP Professional, Windows Server 2003 family

DataGridTableStyle.ShouldSerializeBackColor Method

Indicates whether the **BackColor** property should be persisted.

[Visual Basic]
```
Protected Function ShouldSerializeBackColor() As Boolean
```
[C#]
```
protected bool ShouldSerializeBackColor();
```
[C++]
```
protected: bool ShouldSerializeBackColor();
```
[JScript]
```
protected function ShouldSerializeBackColor() : Boolean;
```

Return Value

true if the property value has changed from its default; otherwise, **false**.

Remarks

You typically use this method if you are either creating a designer for the **DataGridTableStyle** or creating your own control incorporating the **DataGridTableStyle**.

Requirements

Platforms: Windows 98, Windows NT 4.0, Windows Millennium Edition, Windows 2000, Windows XP Home Edition, Windows XP Professional, Windows Server 2003 family

DataGridTableStyle.ShouldSerializeForeColor Method

Indicates whether the **ForeColor** property should be persisted.

[Visual Basic]
```
Protected Function ShouldSerializeForeColor() As Boolean
```
[C#]
```
protected bool ShouldSerializeForeColor();
```
[C++]
```
protected: bool ShouldSerializeForeColor();
```
[JScript]
```
protected function ShouldSerializeForeColor() : Boolean;
```

Return Value

true if the property value has changed from its default; otherwise, **false**.

Remarks

You typically use this method if you are either creating a designer for the **DataGridTableStyle** or creating your own control incorporating the **DataGridTableStyle**.

Requirements

Platforms: Windows 98, Windows NT 4.0, Windows Millennium Edition, Windows 2000, Windows XP Home Edition, Windows XP Professional, Windows Server 2003 family

DataGridTableStyle.ShouldSerializeGridLineColor Method

Indicates whether the **GridLineColor** property should be persisted.

[Visual Basic]
```
Protected Overridable Function ShouldSerializeGridLineColor() As _
   Boolean
```
[C#]
```
protected virtual bool ShouldSerializeGridLineColor();
```
[C++]
```
protected: virtual bool ShouldSerializeGridLineColor();
```
[JScript]
```
protected function ShouldSerializeGridLineColor() : Boolean;
```

Return Value

true if the property value has changed from its default; otherwise, **false**.

Remarks

You typically use this method if you are either creating a designer for the **DataGridTableStyle** or creating your own control incorporating the **DataGridTableStyle**.

Requirements

Platforms: Windows 98, Windows NT 4.0, Windows Millennium Edition, Windows 2000, Windows XP Home Edition, Windows XP Professional, Windows Server 2003 family

DataGridTableStyle.ShouldSerializeHeaderBackColor Method

Indicates whether the **HeaderBackColor** property should be persisted.

[Visual Basic]
```
Protected Overridable Function ShouldSerializeHeaderBackColor() As _
   _
   Boolean
```
[C#]
```
protected virtual bool ShouldSerializeHeaderBackColor();
```
[C++]
```
protected: virtual bool ShouldSerializeHeaderBackColor();
```
[JScript]
```
protected function ShouldSerializeHeaderBackColor() : Boolean;
```

Return Value

true if the property value has changed from its default; otherwise, **false**.

Remarks

You typically use this method if you are either creating a designer for the **DataGridTableStyle** or creating your own control incorporating the **DataGridTableStyle**.

Requirements

Platforms: Windows 98, Windows NT 4.0, Windows Millennium Edition, Windows 2000, Windows XP Home Edition, Windows XP Professional, Windows Server 2003 family

DataGridTableStyle.ShouldSerializeHeaderForeColor Method

Indicates whether the **HeaderForeColor** property should be persisted.

[Visual Basic]
```
Protected Overridable Function ShouldSerializeHeaderForeColor() As _
   _
   Boolean
```
[C#]
```
protected virtual bool ShouldSerializeHeaderForeColor();
```
[C++]
```
protected: virtual bool ShouldSerializeHeaderForeColor();
```
[JScript]
```
protected function ShouldSerializeHeaderForeColor() : Boolean;
```

Return Value

true if the property value has changed from its default; otherwise, **false**.

Remarks

You typically use this method if you are either creating a designer for the **DataGridTableStyle** or creating your own control incorporating the **DataGridTableStyle**.

Requirements

Platforms: Windows 98, Windows NT 4.0, Windows Millennium Edition, Windows 2000, Windows XP Home Edition, Windows XP Professional, Windows Server 2003 family

DataGridTableStyle.ShouldSerializeLinkColor Method

Indicates whether the **LinkColor** property should be persisted.

[Visual Basic]
```
Protected Overridable Function ShouldSerializeLinkColor() As Boolean
```
[C#]
```
protected virtual bool ShouldSerializeLinkColor();
```
[C++]
```
protected: virtual bool ShouldSerializeLinkColor();
```
[JScript]
```
protected function ShouldSerializeLinkColor() : Boolean;
```

Return Value

true if the property value has changed from its default; otherwise, **false**.

Remarks

You typically use this method if you are either creating a designer for the **DataGridTableStyle** or creating your own control incorporating the **DataGridTableStyle**.

Requirements

Platforms: Windows 98, Windows NT 4.0, Windows Millennium Edition, Windows 2000, Windows XP Home Edition, Windows XP Professional, Windows Server 2003 family

DataGridTableStyle.ShouldSerializeLinkHoverColor Method

This member supports the .NET Framework infrastructure and is not intended to be used directly from your code.

[Visual Basic]
```
Protected Overridable Function ShouldSerializeLinkHoverColor() As _
   Boolean
```
[C#]
```
protected virtual bool ShouldSerializeLinkHoverColor();
```
[C++]
```
protected: virtual bool ShouldSerializeLinkHoverColor();
```
[JScript]
```
protected function ShouldSerializeLinkHoverColor() : Boolean;
```

DataGridTableStyle.ShouldSerializePreferredRowHeight Method

Indicates whether the **PreferredRowHeight** property should be persisted.

[Visual Basic]
```
Protected Function ShouldSerializePreferredRowHeight() As Boolean
```
[C#]
```
protected bool ShouldSerializePreferredRowHeight();
```
[C++]
```
protected: bool ShouldSerializePreferredRowHeight();
```
[JScript]
```
protected function ShouldSerializePreferredRowHeight() : Boolean;
```

Return Value

true if the property value has changed from its default; otherwise, **false**.

Remarks

You typically use this method if you are either creating a designer for the **DataGridTableStyle** or creating your own control incorporating the **DataGridTableStyle**.

Requirements

Platforms: Windows 98, Windows NT 4.0, Windows Millennium Edition, Windows 2000, Windows XP Home Edition, Windows XP Professional, Windows Server 2003 family

DataGridTableStyle.ShouldSerializeSelectionBackColor Method

Indicates whether the **SelectionBackColor** property should be persisted.

[Visual Basic]
```
Protected Function ShouldSerializeSelectionBackColor() As Boolean
```
[C#]
```
protected bool ShouldSerializeSelectionBackColor();
```
[C++]
```
protected: bool ShouldSerializeSelectionBackColor();
```
[JScript]
```
protected function ShouldSerializeSelectionBackColor() : Boolean;
```

Return Value

true if the property value has changed from its default; otherwise, **false**.

Remarks

You typically use this method if you are either creating a designer for the **DataGridTableStyle** or creating your own control incorporating the **DataGridTableStyle**.

Requirements

Platforms: Windows 98, Windows NT 4.0, Windows Millennium Edition, Windows 2000, Windows XP Home Edition, Windows XP Professional, Windows Server 2003 family

DataGridTableStyle.ShouldSerializeSelectionForeColor Method

Indicates whether the **SelectionForeColor** property should be persisted.

```
[Visual Basic]
Protected Overridable Function ShouldSerializeSelectionForeColor() _
   _
   As Boolean
[C#]
protected virtual bool ShouldSerializeSelectionForeColor();
[C++]
protected: virtual bool ShouldSerializeSelectionForeColor();
[JScript]
protected function ShouldSerializeSelectionForeColor() : Boolean;
```

Return Value

true if the property value has changed from its default; otherwise, **false**.

Remarks

You typically use this method if you are either creating a designer for the **DataGridTableStyle** or creating your own control incorporating the **DataGridTableStyle**.

Requirements

Platforms: Windows 98, Windows NT 4.0, Windows Millennium Edition, Windows 2000, Windows XP Home Edition, Windows XP Professional, Windows Server 2003 family

DataGridTableStyle.AllowSortingChanged Event

Occurs when the **AllowSorting** property value changes.

```
[Visual Basic]
Public Event AllowSortingChanged As EventHandler
[C#]
public event EventHandler AllowSortingChanged;
[C++]
public: __event EventHandler* AllowSortingChanged;
```

[JScript] In JScript, you can handle the events defined by a class, but you cannot define your own.

Event Data

The event handler receives an argument of type **EventArgs**.

Example

See related example in the **System.Windows.Forms.DataGridTableStyle** class topic.

Requirements

Platforms: Windows 98, Windows NT 4.0, Windows Millennium Edition, Windows 2000, Windows XP Home Edition, Windows XP Professional, Windows Server 2003 family

DataGridTableStyle.AlternatingBackColorChanged Event

Occurs when the **AlternatingBackColor** value changes.

```
[Visual Basic]
Public Event AlternatingBackColorChanged As EventHandler
[C#]
public event EventHandler AlternatingBackColorChanged;
[C++]
public: __event EventHandler* AlternatingBackColorChanged;
```

[JScript] In JScript, you can handle the events defined by a class, but you cannot define your own.

Event Data

The event handler receives an argument of type **EventArgs**.

Requirements

Platforms: Windows 98, Windows NT 4.0, Windows Millennium Edition, Windows 2000, Windows XP Home Edition, Windows XP Professional, Windows Server 2003 family

DataGridTableStyle.BackColorChanged Event

Occurs when the **BackColor** value changes.

```
[Visual Basic]
Public Event BackColorChanged As EventHandler
[C#]
public event EventHandler BackColorChanged;
[C++]
public: __event EventHandler* BackColorChanged;
```

[JScript] In JScript, you can handle the events defined by a class, but you cannot define your own.

Event Data

The event handler receives an argument of type **EventArgs**.

Requirements

Platforms: Windows 98, Windows NT 4.0, Windows Millennium Edition, Windows 2000, Windows XP Home Edition, Windows XP Professional, Windows Server 2003 family

DataGridTableStyle.ColumnHeadersVisibleChanged Event

Occurs when the **ColumnHeadersVisible** value changes.

```
[Visual Basic]
Public Event ColumnHeadersVisibleChanged As EventHandler
[C#]
public event EventHandler ColumnHeadersVisibleChanged;
[C++]
public: __event EventHandler* ColumnHeadersVisibleChanged;
```

[JScript] In JScript, you can handle the events defined by a class, but you cannot define your own.

Event Data

The event handler receives an argument of type **EventArgs**.

Remarks

To set the caption text for each column in a grid, set the **HeaderText** property of the **DataGridColumnStyle** class.

Example

See related example in the **System.Windows.Forms.DataGridTableStyle** class topic.

Requirements

Platforms: Windows 98, Windows NT 4.0, Windows Millennium Edition, Windows 2000, Windows XP Home Edition, Windows XP Professional, Windows Server 2003 family

DataGridTableStyle.ForeColorChanged Event

Occurs when the **ForeColor** value changes.

```
[Visual Basic]
Public Event ForeColorChanged As EventHandler
[C#]
public event EventHandler ForeColorChanged;
[C++]
public: __event EventHandler* ForeColorChanged;
```

[JScript] In JScript, you can handle the events defined by a class, but you cannot define your own.

Event Data

The event handler receives an argument of type **EventArgs**.

Requirements

Platforms: Windows 98, Windows NT 4.0, Windows Millennium Edition, Windows 2000, Windows XP Home Edition, Windows XP Professional, Windows Server 2003 family

DataGridTableStyle.GridLineColorChanged Event

Occurs when the **GridLineColor** value changes.

```
[Visual Basic]
Public Event GridLineColorChanged As EventHandler
[C#]
public event EventHandler GridLineColorChanged;
[C++]
public: __event EventHandler* GridLineColorChanged;
```

[JScript] In JScript, you can handle the events defined by a class, but you cannot define your own.

Event Data

The event handler receives an argument of type **EventArgs**.

Example

See related example in the **System.Windows.Forms.DataGridTableStyle** class topic.

Requirements

Platforms: Windows 98, Windows NT 4.0, Windows Millennium Edition, Windows 2000, Windows XP Home Edition, Windows XP Professional, Windows Server 2003 family

DataGridTableStyle.GridLineStyleChanged Event

Occurs when the **GridLineStyle** value changes.

```
[Visual Basic]
Public Event GridLineStyleChanged As EventHandler
[C#]
public event EventHandler GridLineStyleChanged;
[C++]
public: __event EventHandler* GridLineStyleChanged;
```

[JScript] In JScript, you can handle the events defined by a class, but you cannot define your own.

Event Data

The event handler receives an argument of type **EventArgs**.

Example

See related example in the **System.Windows.Forms.DataGridTableStyle** class topic.

Requirements

Platforms: Windows 98, Windows NT 4.0, Windows Millennium Edition, Windows 2000, Windows XP Home Edition, Windows XP Professional, Windows Server 2003 family

DataGridTableStyle.HeaderBackColorChanged Event

Occurs when the **HeaderBackColor** value changes.

```
[Visual Basic]
Public Event HeaderBackColorChanged As EventHandler
[C#]
public event EventHandler HeaderBackColorChanged;
[C++]
public: __event EventHandler* HeaderBackColorChanged;
```

[JScript] In JScript, you can handle the events defined by a class, but you cannot define your own.

Event Data

The event handler receives an argument of type **EventArgs**.

Example

See related example in the **System.Windows.Forms.DataGridTableStyle** class topic.

Requirements

Platforms: Windows 98, Windows NT 4.0, Windows Millennium Edition, Windows 2000, Windows XP Home Edition, Windows XP Professional, Windows Server 2003 family

DataGridTableStyle.HeaderFontChanged Event

Occurs when the **HeaderFont** value changes.

```
[Visual Basic]
Public Event HeaderFontChanged As EventHandler
[C#]
public event EventHandler HeaderFontChanged;
[C++]
public: __event EventHandler* HeaderFontChanged;
```

[JScript] In JScript, you can handle the events defined by a class, but you cannot define your own.

Event Data

The event handler receives an argument of type **EventArgs**.

Example

See related example in the **System.Windows.Forms.DataGrid-TableStyle** class topic.

Requirements

Platforms: Windows 98, Windows NT 4.0, Windows Millennium Edition, Windows 2000, Windows XP Home Edition, Windows XP Professional, Windows Server 2003 family

DataGridTableStyle.HeaderForeColorChanged Event

Occurs when the **HeaderForeColor** value changes.

[Visual Basic]
```
Public Event HeaderForeColorChanged As EventHandler
```
[C#]
```
public event EventHandler HeaderForeColorChanged;
```
[C++]
```
public: __event EventHandler* HeaderForeColorChanged;
```

[JScript] In JScript, you can handle the events defined by a class, but you cannot define your own.

Event Data

The event handler receives an argument of type **EventArgs**.

Example

See related example in the **System.Windows.Forms.DataGrid-TableStyle** class topic.

Requirements

Platforms: Windows 98, Windows NT 4.0, Windows Millennium Edition, Windows 2000, Windows XP Home Edition, Windows XP Professional, Windows Server 2003 family

DataGridTableStyle.LinkColorChanged Event

Occurs when the **LinkColor** value changes.

[Visual Basic]
```
Public Event LinkColorChanged As EventHandler
```
[C#]
```
public event EventHandler LinkColorChanged;
```
[C++]
```
public: __event EventHandler* LinkColorChanged;
```

[JScript] In JScript, you can handle the events defined by a class, but you cannot define your own.

Event Data

The event handler receives an argument of type **EventArgs**.

Example

See related example in the **System.Windows.Forms.DataGrid-TableStyle** class topic.

Requirements

Platforms: Windows 98, Windows NT 4.0, Windows Millennium Edition, Windows 2000, Windows XP Home Edition, Windows XP Professional, Windows Server 2003 family

DataGridTableStyle.LinkHoverColorChanged Event

This member supports the .NET Framework infrastructure and is not intended to be used directly from your code.

[Visual Basic]
```
Public Event LinkHoverColorChanged As EventHandler
```
[C#]
```
public event EventHandler LinkHoverColorChanged;
```
[C++]
```
public: __event EventHandler* LinkHoverColorChanged;
```

[JScript] In JScript, you can handle the events defined by a class, but you cannot define your own.

DataGridTableStyle.MappingNameChanged Event

Occurs when the **MappingName** value changes.

[Visual Basic]
```
Public Event MappingNameChanged As EventHandler
```
[C#]
```
public event EventHandler MappingNameChanged;
```
[C++]
```
public: __event EventHandler* MappingNameChanged;
```

[JScript] In JScript, you can handle the events defined by a class, but you cannot define your own.

Event Data

The event handler receives an argument of type **EventArgs**.

Example

See related example in the **System.Windows.Forms.DataGrid-TableStyle** class topic.

Requirements

Platforms: Windows 98, Windows NT 4.0, Windows Millennium Edition, Windows 2000, Windows XP Home Edition, Windows XP Professional, Windows Server 2003 family

DataGridTableStyle.PreferredColumnWidth-Changed Event

Occurs when the **PreferredColumnWidth** property value changes.

[Visual Basic]
```
Public Event PreferredColumnWidthChanged As EventHandler
```
[C#]
```
public event EventHandler PreferredColumnWidthChanged;
```
[C++]
```
public: __event EventHandler* PreferredColumnWidthChanged;
```

[JScript] In JScript, you can handle the events defined by a class, but you cannot define your own.

Event Data

The event handler receives an argument of type **EventArgs**.

Requirements

Platforms: Windows 98, Windows NT 4.0, Windows Millennium Edition, Windows 2000, Windows XP Home Edition, Windows XP Professional, Windows Server 2003 family

DataGridTableStyle.PreferredRowHeightChanged Event

Occurs when the **PreferredRowHeight** value changes.

[Visual Basic]
```
Public Event PreferredRowHeightChanged As EventHandler
```
[C#]
```
public event EventHandler PreferredRowHeightChanged;
```
[C++]
```
public: __event EventHandler* PreferredRowHeightChanged;
```

[JScript] In JScript, you can handle the events defined by a class, but you cannot define your own.

Event Data

The event handler receives an argument of type **EventArgs**.

Example

See related example in the **System.Windows.Forms.DataGridTableStyle** class topic.

Requirements

Platforms: Windows 98, Windows NT 4.0, Windows Millennium Edition, Windows 2000, Windows XP Home Edition, Windows XP Professional, Windows Server 2003 family

DataGridTableStyle.ReadOnlyChanged Event

Occurs when the **ReadOnly** value changes.

[Visual Basic]
```
Public Event ReadOnlyChanged As EventHandler
```
[C#]
```
public event EventHandler ReadOnlyChanged;
```
[C++]
```
public: __event EventHandler* ReadOnlyChanged;
```

[JScript] In JScript, you can handle the events defined by a class, but you cannot define your own.

Event Data

The event handler receives an argument of type **EventArgs**.

Example

See related example in the **System.Windows.Forms.DataGridTableStyle** class topic.

Requirements

Platforms: Windows 98, Windows NT 4.0, Windows Millennium Edition, Windows 2000, Windows XP Home Edition, Windows XP Professional, Windows Server 2003 family

DataGridTableStyle.RowHeadersVisibleChanged Event

Occurs when the **RowHeadersVisible** value changes.

[Visual Basic]
```
Public Event RowHeadersVisibleChanged As EventHandler
```
[C#]
```
public event EventHandler RowHeadersVisibleChanged;
```
[C++]
```
public: __event EventHandler* RowHeadersVisibleChanged;
```

[JScript] In JScript, you can handle the events defined by a class, but you cannot define your own.

Event Data

The event handler receives an argument of type **EventArgs**.

Example

See related example in the **System.Windows.Forms.DataGridTableStyle** class topic.

Requirements

Platforms: Windows 98, Windows NT 4.0, Windows Millennium Edition, Windows 2000, Windows XP Home Edition, Windows XP Professional, Windows Server 2003 family

DataGridTableStyle.RowHeaderWidthChanged Event

Occurs when the **RowHeaderWidth** value changes.

[Visual Basic]
```
Public Event RowHeaderWidthChanged As EventHandler
```
[C#]
```
public event EventHandler RowHeaderWidthChanged;
```
[C++]
```
public: __event EventHandler* RowHeaderWidthChanged;
```

[JScript] In JScript, you can handle the events defined by a class, but you cannot define your own.

Event Data

The event handler receives an argument of type **EventArgs**.

Example

See related example in the **System.Windows.Forms.DataGridTableStyle** class topic.

Requirements

Platforms: Windows 98, Windows NT 4.0, Windows Millennium Edition, Windows 2000, Windows XP Home Edition, Windows XP Professional, Windows Server 2003 family

DataGridTableStyle.SelectionBackColorChanged Event

Occurs when the **SelectionBackColor** value changes.

[Visual Basic]
```
Public Event SelectionBackColorChanged As EventHandler
```
[C#]
```
public event EventHandler SelectionBackColorChanged;
```
[C++]
```
public: __event EventHandler* SelectionBackColorChanged;
```

[JScript] In JScript, you can handle the events defined by a class, but you cannot define your own.

Event Data

The event handler receives an argument of type **EventArgs**.

Example

See related example in the **System.Windows.Forms.DataGridTableStyle** class topic.

Requirements

Platforms: Windows 98, Windows NT 4.0, Windows Millennium Edition, Windows 2000, Windows XP Home Edition, Windows XP Professional, Windows Server 2003 family

DataGridTableStyle.SelectionForeColorChanged Event

Occurs when the **SelectionForeColor** value changes.

[Visual Basic]
```
Public Event SelectionForeColorChanged As EventHandler
```
[C#]
```
public event EventHandler SelectionForeColorChanged;
```
[C++]
```
public: __event EventHandler* SelectionForeColorChanged;
```

[JScript] In JScript, you can handle the events defined by a class, but you cannot define your own.

Event Data

The event handler receives an argument of type **EventArgs**.

Requirements

Platforms: Windows 98, Windows NT 4.0, Windows Millennium Edition, Windows 2000, Windows XP Home Edition, Windows XP Professional, Windows Server 2003 family

DataGridTextBox Class

Represents a **TextBox** control that is hosted in a **DataGridTextBoxColumn**.

System.Object
  System.MarshalByRefObject
    System.ComponentModel.Component
      System.Windows.Forms.Control
        System.Windows.Forms.TextBoxBase
          System.Windows.Forms.TextBox
            System.Windows.Forms.DataGridTextBox

[Visual Basic]
```
Public Class DataGridTextBox
   Inherits TextBox
```
[C#]
```
public class DataGridTextBox : TextBox
```
[C++]
```
public __gc class DataGridTextBox : public TextBox
```
[JScript]
```
public class DataGridTextBox extends TextBox
```

Thread Safety

Any public static (**Shared** in Visual Basic) members of this type are safe for multithreaded operations. Any instance members are not guaranteed to be thread safe.

Remarks

The **DataGridTextBox** and the **DataGridTextBoxColumn** work together to allow users to directly edit values in a **DataGrid** control column. The **DataGridTextBoxColumn** derives from **DataGridColumnStyle**, and is designed to host the **DataGridTextBox**, which derives from the **TextBox** control.

In addition to the properties, events, and methods of the base control, you can call the **KeyPress** and **KeyDown** events with the **OnKeyPress** and **OnMouseDown** methods.

Example

[Visual Basic, C#] The following example returns the **DataGridTextBox** hosted by a **DataGridTextBoxColumn**.

[Visual Basic]
```
private Sub CreateDataGridTextBoxColumn()
   Dim myTextBoxColumn As DataGridTextBoxColumn  = _
   New DataGridTextBoxColumn()
   ' Set the MappingName and Format properties.
   myTextBoxColumn.MappingName = "OrderDate"
   ' The character "D" means use the long date format.
   myTextBoxColumn.Format = "D"
   ' Add the column to the DataGridTableStyle object.
   dataGrid1.TableStyles("Orders").GridColumnStyles. _
   Add(myTextBoxColumn)

End Sub
```

[C#]
```
private void GetDataGridTextBox()
{
   // Gets the DataGridTextBoxColumn from the DataGrid control.
   DataGridTextBoxColumn myTextBoxColumn;
   // Assumes the CompanyName column is a DataGridTextBoxColumn.
    myTextBoxColumn = (DataGridTextBoxColumn)dataGrid1.
   TableStyles[0].GridColumnStyles["CompanyName"];
   // Gets the DataGridTextBox for the column.
   DataGridTextBox myGridTextBox;
   myGridTextBox = (DataGridTextBox) myTextBoxColumn.TextBox;
}
```

Requirements

Namespace: System.Windows.Forms

Platforms: Windows 98, Windows NT 4.0, Windows Millennium Edition, Windows 2000, Windows XP Home Edition, Windows XP Professional, Windows Server 2003 family

Assembly: System.Windows.Forms (in System.Windows.Forms.dll)

DataGridTextBox Constructor

Initializes a new instance of the **DataGridTextBox** class.

[Visual Basic]
```
Public Sub New()
```
[C#]
```
public DataGridTextBox();
```
[C++]
```
public: DataGridTextBox();
```
[JScript]
```
public function DataGridTextBox();
```

Remarks

The default constructor initializes any fields to their default values.

Requirements

Platforms: Windows 98, Windows NT 4.0, Windows Millennium Edition, Windows 2000, Windows XP Home Edition, Windows XP Professional, Windows Server 2003 family

DataGridTextBox.IsInEditOrNavigateMode Property

Gets or sets a value indicating whether the **DataGridTextBox** is in a mode that allows either editing or navigating.

[Visual Basic]
```
Public Property IsInEditOrNavigateMode As Boolean
```
[C#]
```
public bool IsInEditOrNavigateMode {get; set;}
```
[C++]
```
public: __property bool get_IsInEditOrNavigateMode();
public: __property void set_IsInEditOrNavigateMode(bool);
```
[JScript]
```
public function get IsInEditOrNavigateMode() : Boolean;
public function set IsInEditOrNavigateMode(Boolean);
```

Property Value

true if the controls is in navigation mode, and editing has not begun; otherwise, **false**. The default is **true**.

Remarks

The **IsInEditOrNavigateMode** property is used within the **ProcessKeyMessage** to determine how to process key press events, to check the state of the **DataGridTextBox**. For example, if one of the navigation (arrow) keys is pressed, the appropriate action for the state of the control must occur.

Example

[Visual Basic]
```
' Handle event to show the state of 'IsInEditOrNavigateMode'.
Private Sub Button_ClickEvent(sender As Object, e As EventArgs)

   If myDataGridTextBox.IsInEditOrNavigateMode Then
      ' DataGridTextBox has not been edited.
      MessageBox.Show("Editing of DataGridTextBox not ↵
begun,IsInEditOrNavigateMode = True")
   Else
      ' DataGridTextBox has been edited.
      MessageBox.Show("Editing of DataGridTextBox ↵
begun,IsInEditOrNavigateMode = False")
   End If
End Sub 'Button_ClickEvent
```

[C#]
```
// Handle event to show the state of 'IsInEditOrNavigateMode'.
private void Button_ClickEvent(object sender, EventArgs e)
{

   if (myDataGridTextBox.IsInEditOrNavigateMode)
   {
      // DataGridTextBox has not been edited.
      MessageBox.Show("Editing of DataGridTextBox not ↵
begun, IsInEditOrNavigateMode = True");
   }
   else
   {
      // DataGridTextBox has been edited.
      MessageBox.Show("Editing of DataGridTextBox begun, ↵
IsInEditOrNavigateMode = False");
   }
}
```

[C++]
```
// Handle event to show the state of 'IsInEditOrNavigateMode'.
private:
void Button_ClickEvent(Object* /*sender*/, EventArgs* /*e*/) {

    if (myDataGridTextBox->IsInEditOrNavigateMode) {
        // DataGridTextBox has not been edited.
        MessageBox::Show(S"Editing of DataGridTextBox not ↵
begun, IsInEditOrNavigateMode = True");
    } else {
        // DataGridTextBox has been edited.
        MessageBox::Show(S"Editing of DataGridTextBox ↵
begun, IsInEditOrNavigateMode = False");
    }
}
```

Requirements

Platforms: Windows 98, Windows NT 4.0, Windows Millennium Edition, Windows 2000, Windows XP Home Edition, Windows XP Professional, Windows Server 2003 family

DataGridTextBox.OnKeyPress Method

This member overrides **Control.OnKeyPress**.

[Visual Basic]
```
Overrides Protected Sub OnKeyPress( _
   ByVal e As KeyPressEventArgs _
)
```
[C#]
```
protected override void OnKeyPress(
   KeyPressEventArgs e
);
```
[C++]
```
protected: void OnKeyPress(
   KeyPressEventArgs* e
);
```
[JScript]
```
protected override function OnKeyPress(
   e : KeyPressEventArgs
);
```

Requirements

Platforms: Windows 98, Windows NT 4.0, Windows Millennium Edition, Windows 2000, Windows XP Home Edition, Windows XP Professional, Windows Server 2003 family

DataGridTextBox.OnMouseWheel Method

This member overrides **Control.OnMouseWheel**.

[Visual Basic]
```
Overrides Protected Sub OnMouseWheel( _
   ByVal e As MouseEventArgs _
)
```
[C#]
```
protected override void OnMouseWheel(
   MouseEventArgs e
);
```
[C++]
```
protected: void OnMouseWheel(
   MouseEventArgs* e
);
```
[JScript]
```
protected override function OnMouseWheel(
   e : MouseEventArgs
);
```

Requirements

Platforms: Windows 98, Windows NT 4.0, Windows Millennium Edition, Windows 2000, Windows XP Home Edition, Windows XP Professional, Windows Server 2003 family

DataGridTextBox.ProcessKeyMessage Method

This member overrides **Control.ProcessKeyMessage**.

[Visual Basic]
```
Protected Friend Overrides Function ProcessKeyMessage( _
   ByRef m As Message _
) As Boolean
```
[C#]
```
protected internal override bool ProcessKeyMessage(
   ref Message m
);
```
[C++]
```
protected public: bool ProcessKeyMessage(
   Message* m
);
```
[JScript]
```
protected internal override function ProcessKeyMessage(
   m : Message
) : Boolean;
```

Requirements

Platforms: Windows 98, Windows NT 4.0, Windows Millennium Edition, Windows 2000, Windows XP Home Edition, Windows XP Professional, Windows Server 2003 family

DataGridTextBox.SetDataGrid Method

Sets the **DataGrid** to which this **TextBox** control belongs.

[Visual Basic]
```
Public Sub SetDataGrid( _
   ByVal parentGrid As DataGrid _
)
```
[C#]
```
public void SetDataGrid(
   DataGrid parentGrid
);
```
[C++]
```
public: void SetDataGrid(
   DataGrid* parentGrid
);
```
[JScript]
```
public function SetDataGrid(
   parentGrid : DataGrid
);
```

Parameters

parentGrid
The **DataGrid** control that hosts the control.

Example

[Visual Basic]
```
' Create a DataSet with a table and populate it.
Private Sub MakeDataSet()
   myDataSet = New DataSet("myDataSet")
   Dim tPer As New DataTable("Person")
   Dim cPerName As New DataColumn("PersonName")

   tPer.Columns.Add(cPerName)
   myDataSet.Tables.Add(tPer)

   Dim newRow1 As DataRow
   Dim i As Integer
   For i = 1 To 5
      newRow1 = tPer.NewRow()
      tPer.Rows.Add(newRow1)
   Next i

   tPer.Rows(0)("PersonName") = "Robert"
   tPer.Rows(1)("PersonName") = "Michael"
   tPer.Rows(2)("PersonName") = "John"
   tPer.Rows(3)("PersonName") = "Walter"
   tPer.Rows(4)("PersonName") = "Simon"

   ' Bind the 'DataSet' to the 'DataGrid'.
   myDataGrid.SetDataBinding(myDataSet, "Person")
   myDataGridTextBox.DataBindings.Add("Text", myDataSet, ┘
"Person.PersonName")
   ' Set the DataGrid to the DataGridTextBox.
   myDataGridTextBox.SetDataGrid(myDataGrid)
End Sub 'MakeDataSet
```

[C#]
```
// Create a DataSet with a table and populate it.
private void MakeDataSet()
{
   myDataSet = new DataSet("myDataSet");

   DataTable tPer = new DataTable("Person");

   DataColumn cPerName = new DataColumn("PersonName");
   tPer.Columns.Add(cPerName);

   myDataSet.Tables.Add(tPer);

   DataRow newRow1;

   for(int i = 1; i < 6; i++)
   {
      newRow1 = tPer.NewRow();
      tPer.Rows.Add(newRow1);
   }

   tPer.Rows[0]["PersonName"] = "Robert";
   tPer.Rows[1]["PersonName"] = "Michael";
   tPer.Rows[2]["PersonName"] = "John";
   tPer.Rows[3]["PersonName"] = "Walter";
   tPer.Rows[4]["PersonName"] = "Simon";

   // Bind the 'DataSet' to the 'DataGrid'.
   myDataGrid.SetDataBinding(myDataSet, "Person");
   myDataGridTextBox.DataBindings.Add("Text",myDataSet,    ┘
"Person.PersonName");
   // Set the DataGrid to the DataGridTextBox.
   myDataGridTextBox.SetDataGrid(myDataGrid);
}
```

[C++]
```
// Create a DataSet with a table and populate it.
private:
void MakeDataSet() {
    myDataSet = new DataSet(S"myDataSet");

    DataTable* tPer = new DataTable(S"Person");

    DataColumn* cPerName = new DataColumn(S"PersonName");
    tPer->Columns->Add(cPerName);

    myDataSet->Tables->Add(tPer);

    DataRow* newRow1;

    for (int i = 1; i < 6; i++) {
        newRow1 = tPer->NewRow();
        tPer->Rows->Add(newRow1);
    }

    tPer->Rows->Item[0]->Item[S"PersonName"] = S"Robert";
    tPer->Rows->Item[1]->Item[S"PersonName"] = S"Michael";
    tPer->Rows->Item[2]->Item[S"PersonName"] = S"John";
    tPer->Rows->Item[3]->Item[S"PersonName"] = S"Walter";
    tPer->Rows->Item[4]->Item[S"PersonName"] = S"Simon";

    // Bind the 'DataSet' to the 'DataGrid'.
    myDataGrid->SetDataBinding(myDataSet, S"Person");
    myDataGridTextBox->DataBindings->Add(S"Text", myDataSet,    ┘
S"Person::PersonName");
    // Set the DataGrid to the DataGridTextBox.
    myDataGridTextBox->SetDataGrid(myDataGrid);
}
```

Requirements

Platforms: Windows 98, Windows NT 4.0, Windows Millennium Edition, Windows 2000, Windows XP Home Edition, Windows XP Professional, Windows Server 2003 family

DataGridTextBox.WndProc Method

This member overrides **Control.WndProc**.

[Visual Basic]
```
Overrides Protected Sub WndProc( _
   ByRef m As Message _
)
```
[C#]
```
protected override void WndProc(
   ref Message m
);
```
[C++]
```
protected: void WndProc(
   Message* m
);
```
[JScript]
```
protected override function WndProc(
   m : Message
);
```

Requirements

Platforms: Windows 98, Windows NT 4.0, Windows Millennium Edition, Windows 2000, Windows XP Home Edition, Windows XP Professional, Windows Server 2003 family

DataGridTextBoxColumn Class

Hosts a **TextBox** control in a cell of a **DataGridColumnStyle** for editing strings.

System.Object
System.MarshalByRefObject
System.ComponentModel.Component
System.Windows.Forms.DataGridColumnStyle
System.Windows.Forms.DataGridTextBoxColumn

[Visual Basic]
```
Public Class DataGridTextBoxColumn
   Inherits DataGridColumnStyle
```
[C#]
```
public class DataGridTextBoxColumn : DataGridColumnStyle
```
[C++]
```
public __gc class DataGridTextBoxColumn : public
   DataGridColumnStyle
```
[JScript]
```
public class DataGridTextBoxColumn extends DataGridColumnStyle
```

Thread Safety

Any public static (**Shared** in Visual Basic) members of this type are safe for multithreaded operations. Any instance members are not guaranteed to be thread safe.

Remarks

The **DataGridTextBoxColumn** class derives from the abstract (**MustInherit** in Visual Basic) class **DataGridColumnStyle**. At run time, the **DataGridTextBoxColumn** hosts a **DataGridTextBox** control that allows users to edit text.

Special properties added to the class include **Format**, and **HideEditBox**. These properties allow you to access the hosted **DataGridTextBox** control and its attributes, and set the format for displaying values.

If the data source is a **DataTable** containing **DataColumn** objects, the **DataType** property of the **DataColumn** should be set to a data type that can logically be edited in a text box control. The following data types are automatically associated with a **DataGridTextBoxColumn**: **Byte**, **DateTime**, **Decimal**, **Double**, **Int16**, **Int32**, **Int64**, **UInt16**, **UInt32**, **UInt64**, **Single**, and **String**.

> [Visual Basic] **Note** The following types are not fully supported by Visual Basic: **DateTime**, **UInt16**, **UInt32**, **UInt64**, and **TimeSpan**. (Operators are not allowed.)

Example

[Visual Basic, C#] The following example creates a **DataGridTextBoxColumn** is and adds it to the **GridColumnStylesCollection**. For this code example to run, you must provide the fully qualified assembly name.

[Visual Basic]
```
Private Sub AddColumn()
    Dim myTable As New DataTable()

    ' Add a new DataColumn to the DataTable.
    Dim myColumn As New DataColumn("myTextBoxColumn")
    myColumn.DataType = System.Type.GetType("System.String")
    myColumn.DefaultValue = "default string"
    myTable.Columns.Add(myColumn)
    ' Get the CurrencyManager for the DataTable.
    Dim cm As CurrencyManager = CType(Me.BindingContext ↵
(myTable), CurrencyManager)
    ' Use the CurrencyManager to get the PropertyDescriptor ↵
for the new column.
    Dim pd As PropertyDescriptor = ↵
cm.GetItemProperties()("myTextBoxColumn")
    Dim myColumnTextColumn As DataGridTextBoxColumn
    ' Create the DataGridTextBoxColumn with the PropertyDescriptor.
    myColumnTextColumn = New DataGridTextBoxColumn(pd)
    ' Add the new DataGridColumn to the GridColumnsCollection.
    dataGrid1.DataSource = myTable
    dataGrid1.TableStyles.Add(New DataGridTableStyle())
    dataGrid1.TableStyles(0).GridColumnStyles.Add(myColumnTextColumn)
End Sub 'AddColumn
```

[C#]
```
private void AddColumn()
{
     DataTable myTable= new DataTable();

     // Add a new DataColumn to the DataTable.
     DataColumn myColumn = new DataColumn("myTextBoxColumn");
     myColumn.DataType = System.Type.GetType("System.String");
     myColumn.DefaultValue="default string";
     myTable.Columns.Add(myColumn);
     // Get the CurrencyManager for the DataTable.
     CurrencyManager cm = ↵
 (CurrencyManager)this.BindingContext[myTable];
     // Use the CurrencyManager to get the PropertyDescriptor ↵
for the new column.
     PropertyDescriptor pd = cm.GetItemProperties()["myTextBoxColumn"];
     DataGridTextBoxColumn myColumnTextColumn;
     // Create the DataGridTextBoxColumn with the PropertyDescriptor.
     myColumnTextColumn = new DataGridTextBoxColumn(pd);
     // Add the new DataGridColumn to the GridColumnsCollection.
     dataGrid1.DataSource= myTable;
     dataGrid1.TableStyles.Add(new DataGridTableStyle());
     dataGrid1.TableStyles[0].GridColumnStyles.Add(myColumnTextColumn);
 }
```

Requirements

Namespace: System.Windows.Forms

Platforms: Windows 98, Windows NT 4.0, Windows Millennium Edition, Windows 2000, Windows XP Home Edition, Windows XP Professional, Windows Server 2003 family, .NET Compact Framework - Windows CE .NET

Assembly: System.Windows.Forms (in System.Windows.Forms.dll)

DataGridTextBoxColumn Constructor

Initializes a new instance of the **DataGridTextBoxColumn** class.

Overload List

Initializes a new instance of the **DataGridTextBoxColumn** class.

Supported by the .NET Compact Framework.

[Visual Basic] **Public Sub New()**

[C#] **public DataGridTextBoxColumn();**

[C++] **public: DataGridTextBoxColumn();**

[JScript] **public function DataGridTextBoxColumn();**

Initializes a new instance of a **DataGridTextBoxColumn** with a specified **PropertyDescriptor**.

[Visual Basic] **Public Sub New(PropertyDescriptor)**

[C#] **public DataGridTextBoxColumn(PropertyDescriptor);**

[C++] **public: DataGridTextBoxColumn(PropertyDescriptor*);**

[JScript] **public function DataGridTextBoxColumn(PropertyDescriptor);**

This member supports the .NET Framework infrastructure and is not intended to be used directly from your code.

[Visual Basic] **Public Sub New(PropertyDescriptor, Boolean)**

[C#] **public DataGridTextBoxColumn(PropertyDescriptor, bool);**

[C++] **public: DataGridTextBoxColumn(PropertyDescriptor*, bool);**

[JScript] **public function DataGridTextBoxColumn(PropertyDescriptor, Boolean);**

Initializes a new instance of a **DataGridTextBoxColumn** with the specified **PropertyDescriptor** and format.

[Visual Basic] **Public Sub New(PropertyDescriptor, String)**

[C#] **public DataGridTextBoxColumn(PropertyDescriptor, string);**

[C++] **public: DataGridTextBoxColumn(PropertyDescriptor*, String*);**

[JScript] **public function DataGridTextBoxColumn(PropertyDescriptor, String);**

This member supports the .NET Framework infrastructure and is not intended to be used directly from your code.

[Visual Basic] **Public Sub New(PropertyDescriptor, String, Boolean)**

[C#] **public DataGridTextBoxColumn(PropertyDescriptor, string, bool);**

[C++] **public: DataGridTextBoxColumn(PropertyDescriptor*, String*, bool);**

[JScript] **public function DataGridTextBoxColumn(PropertyDescriptor, String, Boolean);**

Example

See related example in the **System.Windows.Forms.DataGridTextBoxColumn** class topic.

DataGridTextBoxColumn Constructor ()

Initializes a new instance of the **DataGridTextBoxColumn** class.

```
[Visual Basic]
Public Sub New()
[C#]
public DataGridTextBoxColumn();
[C++]
public: DataGridTextBoxColumn();
[JScript]
public function DataGridTextBoxColumn();
```

Example

See related example in the **System.Windows.Forms.DataGridTextBoxColumn** class topic.

Requirements

Platforms: Windows 98, Windows NT 4.0, Windows Millennium Edition, Windows 2000, Windows XP Home Edition, Windows XP Professional, Windows Server 2003 family, .NET Compact Framework - Windows CE .NET

DataGridTextBoxColumn Constructor (PropertyDescriptor)

Initializes a new instance of a **DataGridTextBoxColumn** with a specified **PropertyDescriptor**.

```
[Visual Basic]
Public Sub New( _
   ByVal prop As PropertyDescriptor _
)
[C#]
public DataGridTextBoxColumn(
   PropertyDescriptor prop
);
[C++]
public: DataGridTextBoxColumn(
   PropertyDescriptor* prop
);
[JScript]
public function DataGridTextBoxColumn(
   prop : PropertyDescriptor
);
```

Parameters

prop
The **PropertyDescriptor** for the column with which the **DataGridTextBoxColumn** will be associated.

Remarks

The **DataGridColumnStyle** uses a **PropertyDescriptor** to determine the type of data displayed in the column. To return a **PropertyDescriptorCollection**, use the **GetItemProperties** method of the **BindingManagerBase** class.

Example

See related example in the **System.Windows.Forms.DataGridTextBoxColumn** class topic.

Requirements

Platforms: Windows 98, Windows NT 4.0, Windows Millennium Edition, Windows 2000, Windows XP Home Edition, Windows XP Professional, Windows Server 2003 family

DataGridTextBoxColumn Constructor (PropertyDescriptor, Boolean)

This member supports the .NET Framework infrastructure and is not intended to be used directly from your code.

```
[Visual Basic]
Public Sub New( _
   ByVal prop As PropertyDescriptor, _
   ByVal isDefault As Boolean _
)
[C#]
public DataGridTextBoxColumn(
   PropertyDescriptor prop,
   bool isDefault
);
[C++]
public: DataGridTextBoxColumn(
   PropertyDescriptor* prop,
   bool isDefault
);
```

```
[JScript]
public function DataGridTextBoxColumn(
   prop : PropertyDescriptor,
   isDefault : Boolean
);
```

DataGridTextBoxColumn Constructor (PropertyDescriptor, String)

Initializes a new instance of a **DataGridTextBoxColumn** with the specified **PropertyDescriptor** and format.

```
[Visual Basic]
Public Sub New( _
   ByVal prop As PropertyDescriptor, _
   ByVal format As String _
)
[C#]
public DataGridTextBoxColumn(
   PropertyDescriptor prop,
   string format
);
[C++]
public: DataGridTextBoxColumn(
   PropertyDescriptor* prop,
   String* format
);
[JScript]
public function DataGridTextBoxColumn(
   prop : PropertyDescriptor,
   format : String
);
```

Parameters

prop

The **PropertyDescriptor** for the column with which the **DataGridTextBoxColumn** will be associated.

format

The format used to format the column values.

Remarks

Use this constructor to create a custom format for the displayed data.

The **DataGridColumnStyle** uses a **PropertyDescriptor** to determine the type of data displayed in the column. To return a **PropertyDescriptorCollection**, use the **GetItemProperties** method of the **BindingManagerBase** class.

Example

See related example in the **System.Windows.Forms.DataGrid-TextBoxColumn** class topic.

Requirements

Platforms: Windows 98, Windows NT 4.0, Windows Millennium Edition, Windows 2000, Windows XP Home Edition, Windows XP Professional, Windows Server 2003 family

DataGridTextBoxColumn Constructor (PropertyDescriptor, String, Boolean)

This member supports the .NET Framework infrastructure and is not intended to be used directly from your code.

```
[Visual Basic]
Public Sub New( _
   ByVal prop As PropertyDescriptor, _
   ByVal format As String, _
   ByVal isDefault As Boolean _
)
[C#]
public DataGridTextBoxColumn(
   PropertyDescriptor prop,
   string format,
   bool isDefault
);
[C++]
public: DataGridTextBoxColumn(
   PropertyDescriptor* prop,
   String* format,
   bool isDefault
);
[JScript]
public function DataGridTextBoxColumn(
   prop : PropertyDescriptor,
   format : String,
   isDefault : Boolean
);
```

DataGridTextBoxColumn.Format Property

Gets or sets the character(s) that specify how text is formatted.

```
[Visual Basic]
Public Property Format As String
[C#]
public string Format {get; set;}
[C++]
public: __property String* get_Format();
public: __property void set_Format(String*);
[JScript]
public function get Format() : String;
public function set Format(String);
```

Property Value

The character or characters that specify how text is formatted.

Remarks

The **Format** property specifies how values are displayed in the column. For example, set the property to "c" to specify that the values will be formatted as the local currency. The **CultureInfo** for the computer is used to determine the actual currency format. The values are automatically unformatted to the native type when data is changed.

The format you apply should be appropriate to the data type. For example, if the data is numeric in nature use one of the numeric format strings.

You can change the **CultureInfo** for a **DataGridTextBoxColumn** by setting the **FormatInfo** property to a new **CultureInfo** instance constructed with an appropriate culture ID.

To set the **CultureInfo** for the application, set the **CurrentCulture** property of the **Application** object to a new **CultureInfo** instance constructed with an appropriate culture ID.

Example

See related example in the **System.Windows.Forms.DataGrid-TextBoxColumn** class topic.

Requirements

Platforms: Windows 98, Windows NT 4.0, Windows Millennium Edition, Windows 2000, Windows XP Home Edition, Windows XP Professional, Windows Server 2003 family

DataGridTextBoxColumn.FormatInfo Property

Gets or sets the culture specific information used to determine how values are formatted.

```
[Visual Basic]
Public Property FormatInfo As IFormatProvider
[C#]
public IFormatProvider FormatInfo {get; set;}
[C++]
public: __property IFormatProvider* get_FormatInfo();
public: __property void set_FormatInfo(IFormatProvider*);
[JScript]
public function get FormatInfo() : IFormatProvider;
public function set FormatInfo(IFormatProvider);
```

Property Value

An object that implements the **IFormatProvider** interface, such as the **CultureInfo** class.

Remarks

When setting the **Format** property to one of the formatting characters, the **DataGridTextBoxColumn** uses the information provided by the **FormatInfo** property to further specify what cultural-specific formatting to use. For example, when the **Format** property is set to the format character "c" (for currency), you can further specify that the symbol for the lira be used. To do this, create a new **CultureInfo** object with the locale ID for Italy, and set the **FormatInfo** property to the new **CultureInfo** object.

Example

See related example in the **System.Windows.Forms.DataGrid-TextBoxColumn** class topic.

Requirements

Platforms: Windows 98, Windows NT 4.0, Windows Millennium Edition, Windows 2000, Windows XP Home Edition, Windows XP Professional, Windows Server 2003 family

DataGridTextBoxColumn.PropertyDescriptor Property

This member overrides **DataGridColumnStyle.Property-Descriptor**.

```
[Visual Basic]
Property PropertyDescriptor As PropertyDescriptor
[C#]
PropertyDescriptor PropertyDescriptor {set;}
[C++]
public: __property void set_PropertyDescriptor(PropertyDescriptor*);
[JScript]
public override function set PropertyDescriptor(PropertyDescriptor);
```

Requirements

Platforms: Windows 98, Windows NT 4.0, Windows Millennium Edition, Windows 2000, Windows XP Home Edition, Windows XP Professional, Windows Server 2003 family

DataGridTextBoxColumn.ReadOnly Property

This member overrides **DataGridColumnStyle.ReadOnly**.

```
[Visual Basic]
Overrides Public Property ReadOnly As Boolean
[C#]
public override bool ReadOnly {get; set;}
[C++]
public: __property bool get_ReadOnly();
public: __property void set_ReadOnly(bool);
[JScript]
public override function get ReadOnly() : Boolean;
public override function set ReadOnly(Boolean);
```

Requirements

Platforms: Windows 98, Windows NT 4.0, Windows Millennium Edition, Windows 2000, Windows XP Home Edition, Windows XP Professional, Windows Server 2003 family

DataGridTextBoxColumn.TextBox Property

Gets the hosted **TextBox** control.

```
[Visual Basic]
Public Overridable ReadOnly Property TextBox As TextBox
[C#]
public virtual TextBox TextBox {get;}
[C++]
public: __property virtual TextBox* get_TextBox();
[JScript]
public function get TextBox() : TextBox;
```

Property Value

A **TextBox** control hosted by the column.

Example

See related example in the **System.Windows.Forms.DataGrid-TextBoxColumn** class topic.

Requirements

Platforms: Windows 98, Windows NT 4.0, Windows Millennium Edition, Windows 2000, Windows XP Home Edition, Windows XP Professional, Windows Server 2003 family

DataGridTextBoxColumn.Abort Method

This member overrides **DataGridColumnStyle.Abort**.

```
[Visual Basic]
Protected Friend Overrides Sub Abort( _
   ByVal rowNum As Integer _
)
```

[C#]
```
protected internal override void Abort(
   int rowNum
);
```
[C++]
```
protected public: void Abort(
   int rowNum
);
```
[JScript]
```
protected internal override function Abort(
   rowNum : int
);
```

Requirements

Platforms: Windows 98, Windows NT 4.0, Windows Millennium Edition, Windows 2000, Windows XP Home Edition, Windows XP Professional, Windows Server 2003 family

DataGridTextBoxColumn.Commit Method

This member overrides **DataGridColumnStyle.Commit**.

[Visual Basic]
```
Protected Friend Overrides Function Commit( _
   ByVal dataSource As CurrencyManager, _
   ByVal rowNum As Integer _
) As Boolean
```
[C#]
```
protected internal override bool Commit(
   CurrencyManager dataSource,
   int rowNum
);
```
[C++]
```
protected public: bool Commit(
   CurrencyManager* dataSource,
   int rowNum
);
```
[JScript]
```
protected internal override function Commit(
   dataSource : CurrencyManager,
   rowNum : int
) : Boolean;
```

Requirements

Platforms: Windows 98, Windows NT 4.0, Windows Millennium Edition, Windows 2000, Windows XP Home Edition, Windows XP Professional, Windows Server 2003 family

DataGridTextBoxColumn.ConcedeFocus Method

This member overrides **DataGridColumnStyle.ConcedeFocus**.

[Visual Basic]
```
Protected Friend Overrides Sub ConcedeFocus()
```
[C#]
```
protected internal override void ConcedeFocus();
```
[C++]
```
protected public: void ConcedeFocus();
```
[JScript]
```
protected internal override function ConcedeFocus();
```

Requirements

Platforms: Windows 98, Windows NT 4.0, Windows Millennium Edition, Windows 2000, Windows XP Home Edition, Windows XP Professional, Windows Server 2003 family

DataGridTextBoxColumn.Edit Method

Overload List

This member supports the .NET Framework infrastructure and is not intended to be used directly from your code.

[Visual Basic] **Overloads Protected Friend Overrides Sub Edit(CurrencyManager, Integer, Rectangle, Boolean, String, Boolean)**

[C#] **protected internal override void Edit(CurrencyManager, int, Rectangle, bool, string, bool);**

[C++] **protected public: void Edit(CurrencyManager*, int, Rectangle, bool, String*, bool);**

[JScript] **protected internal override function Edit(CurrencyManager, int, Rectangle, Boolean, String, Boolean);**

Inherited from **DataGridColumnStyle**.

[Visual Basic] **Overloads Protected Friend Overridable Sub Edit(CurrencyManager, Integer, Rectangle, Boolean)**

[C#] **protected internal virtual void Edit(CurrencyManager, int, Rectangle, bool);**

[C++] **protected public: virtual void Edit(CurrencyManager*, int, Rectangle, bool);**

[JScript] **protected internal function Edit(CurrencyManager, int, Rectangle, Boolean);**

Inherited from **DataGridColumnStyle**.

[Visual Basic] **Overloads Protected Friend Overridable Sub Edit(CurrencyManager, Integer, Rectangle, Boolean, String)**

[C#] **protected internal virtual void Edit(CurrencyManager, int, Rectangle, bool, string);**

[C++] **protected public: virtual void Edit(CurrencyManager*, int, Rectangle, bool, String*);**

[JScript] **protected internal function Edit(CurrencyManager, int, Rectangle, Boolean, String);**

Example

See related example in the **System.Windows.Forms.DataGridTextBoxColumn** class topic.

DataGridTextBoxColumn.Edit Method (CurrencyManager, Int32, Rectangle, Boolean, String, Boolean)

This member overrides **DataGridColumnStyle.Edit**.

[Visual Basic]
```
Overloads Protected Friend Overrides Sub Edit( _
   ByVal source As CurrencyManager, _
   ByVal rowNum As Integer, _
   ByVal bounds As Rectangle, _
   ByVal readOnly As Boolean, _
   ByVal instantText As String, _
   ByVal cellIsVisible As Boolean _
)
```

```
[C#]
protected internal override void Edit(
   CurrencyManager source,
   int rowNum,
   Rectangle bounds,
   bool readOnly,
   string instantText,
   bool cellIsVisible
);
[C++]
protected public: void Edit(
   CurrencyManager* source,
   int rowNum,
   Rectangle bounds,
   bool readOnly,
   String* instantText,
   bool cellIsVisible
);
[JScript]
protected internal override function Edit(
   source : CurrencyManager,
   rowNum : int,
   bounds : Rectangle,
   readOnly : Boolean,
   instantText : String,
   cellIsVisible : Boolean
);
```

Requirements

Platforms: Windows 98, Windows NT 4.0, Windows Millennium Edition, Windows 2000, Windows XP Home Edition, Windows XP Professional, Windows Server 2003 family

DataGridTextBoxColumn.EndEdit Method

This member supports the .NET Framework infrastructure and is not intended to be used directly from your code.

```
[Visual Basic]
Protected Sub EndEdit()
[C#]
protected void EndEdit();
[C++]
protected: void EndEdit();
[JScript]
protected function EndEdit();
```

DataGridTextBoxColumn.EnterNullValue Method

This member overrides **DataGridColumnStyle.EnterNullValue**.

```
[Visual Basic]
Protected Friend Overrides Sub EnterNullValue()
[C#]
protected internal override void EnterNullValue();
[C++]
protected public: void EnterNullValue();
[JScript]
protected internal override function EnterNullValue();
```

Requirements

Platforms: Windows 98, Windows NT 4.0, Windows Millennium Edition, Windows 2000, Windows XP Home Edition, Windows XP Professional, Windows Server 2003 family

DataGridTextBoxColumn.GetMinimumHeight Method

This member overrides **DataGridColumnStyle.GetMinimumHeight**.

```
[Visual Basic]
Protected Friend Overrides Function GetMinimumHeight() As Integer
[C#]
protected internal override int GetMinimumHeight();
[C++]
protected public: int GetMinimumHeight();
[JScript]
protected internal override function GetMinimumHeight() : int;
```

Requirements

Platforms: Windows 98, Windows NT 4.0, Windows Millennium Edition, Windows 2000, Windows XP Home Edition, Windows XP Professional, Windows Server 2003 family

DataGridTextBoxColumn.GetPreferredHeight Method

This member overrides **DataGridColumnStyle.GetPreferredHeight**.

```
[Visual Basic]
Protected Friend Overrides Function GetPreferredHeight( _
   ByVal g As Graphics, _
   ByVal value As Object _
) As Integer
[C#]
protected internal override int GetPreferredHeight(
   Graphics g,
   object value
);
[C++]
protected public: int GetPreferredHeight(
   Graphics* g,
   Object* value
);
[JScript]
protected internal override function GetPreferredHeight(
   g : Graphics,
   value : Object
) : int;
```

Requirements

Platforms: Windows 98, Windows NT 4.0, Windows Millennium Edition, Windows 2000, Windows XP Home Edition, Windows XP Professional, Windows Server 2003 family

DataGridTextBoxColumn.GetPreferredSize Method

This member overrides **DataGridColumnStyle.GetPreferredSize**.

```
[Visual Basic]
Protected Friend Overrides Function GetPreferredSize( _
   ByVal g As Graphics, _
   ByVal value As Object _
) As Size
[C#]
protected internal override Size GetPreferredSize(
   Graphics g,
   object value
);
[C++]
protected public: Size GetPreferredSize(
   Graphics* g,
   Object* value
);
[JScript]
protected internal override function GetPreferredSize(
   g : Graphics,
   value : Object
) : Size;
```

Requirements

Platforms: Windows 98, Windows NT 4.0, Windows Millennium Edition, Windows 2000, Windows XP Home Edition, Windows XP Professional, Windows Server 2003 family

DataGridTextBoxColumn.HideEditBox Method

Hides the **DataGridTextBox** control and moves the focus to the **DataGrid** control.

```
[Visual Basic]
Protected Sub HideEditBox()
[C#]
protected void HideEditBox();
[C++]
protected: void HideEditBox();
[JScript]
protected function HideEditBox();
```

Requirements

Platforms: Windows 98, Windows NT 4.0, Windows Millennium Edition, Windows 2000, Windows XP Home Edition, Windows XP Professional, Windows Server 2003 family

DataGridTextBoxColumn.Paint Method

This member supports the .NET Framework infrastructure and is not intended to be used directly from your code.

Overload List

This member overrides **DataGridColumnStyle.Paint**.

[Visual Basic] **Overloads Protected Friend Overrides Sub Paint(Graphics, Rectangle, CurrencyManager, Integer)**

[C#] **protected internal override void Paint(Graphics, Rectangle, CurrencyManager, int);**

[C++] **protected public: void Paint(Graphics*, Rectangle, CurrencyManager*, int);**

[JScript] **protected internal override function Paint(Graphics, Rectangle, CurrencyManager, int);**

This member overrides **DataGridColumnStyle.Paint**.

[Visual Basic] **Overloads Protected Friend Overrides Sub Paint(Graphics, Rectangle, CurrencyManager, Integer, Boolean)**

[C#] **protected internal override void Paint(Graphics, Rectangle, CurrencyManager, int, bool);**

[C++] **protected public: void Paint(Graphics*, Rectangle, CurrencyManager*, int, bool);**

[JScript] **protected internal override function Paint(Graphics, Rectangle, CurrencyManager, int, Boolean);**

This member overrides **DataGridColumnStyle.Paint**.

[Visual Basic] **Overloads Protected Friend Overrides Sub Paint(Graphics, Rectangle, CurrencyManager, Integer, Brush, Brush, Boolean)**

[C#] **protected internal override void Paint(Graphics, Rectangle, CurrencyManager, int, Brush, Brush, bool);**

[C++] **protected public: void Paint(Graphics*, Rectangle, CurrencyManager*, int, Brush*, Brush*, bool);**

[JScript] **protected internal override function Paint(Graphics, Rectangle, CurrencyManager, int, Brush, Brush, Boolean);**

Example

See related example in the **System.Windows.Forms.DataGridTextBoxColumn** class topic.

DataGridTextBoxColumn.Paint Method (Graphics, Rectangle, CurrencyManager, Int32)

This member overrides **DataGridColumnStyle.Paint**.

```
[Visual Basic]
Overloads Protected Friend Overrides Sub Paint( _
   ByVal g As Graphics, _
   ByVal bounds As Rectangle, _
   ByVal source As CurrencyManager, _
   ByVal rowNum As Integer _
)
[C#]
protected internal override void Paint(
   Graphics g,
   Rectangle bounds,
   CurrencyManager source,
   int rowNum
);
[C++]
protected public: void Paint(
   Graphics* g,
   Rectangle bounds,
   CurrencyManager* source,
   int rowNum
);
[JScript]
protected internal override function Paint(
   g : Graphics,
   bounds : Rectangle,
   source : CurrencyManager,
   rowNum : int
);
```

Requirements

Platforms: Windows 98, Windows NT 4.0, Windows Millennium Edition, Windows 2000, Windows XP Home Edition, Windows XP Professional, Windows Server 2003 family

DataGridTextBoxColumn.Paint Method (Graphics, Rectangle, CurrencyManager, Int32, Boolean)

This member overrides **DataGridColumnStyle.Paint**.

[Visual Basic]
```
Overloads Protected Friend Overrides Sub Paint( _
   ByVal g As Graphics, _
   ByVal bounds As Rectangle, _
   ByVal source As CurrencyManager, _
   ByVal rowNum As Integer, _
   ByVal alignToRight As Boolean _
)
```
[C#]
```
protected internal override void Paint(
   Graphics g,
   Rectangle bounds,
   CurrencyManager source,
   int rowNum,
   bool alignToRight
);
```
[C++]
```
protected public: void Paint(
   Graphics* g,
   Rectangle bounds,
   CurrencyManager* source,
   int rowNum,
   bool alignToRight
);
```
[JScript]
```
protected internal override function Paint(
   g : Graphics,
   bounds : Rectangle,
   source : CurrencyManager,
   rowNum : int,
   alignToRight : Boolean
);
```

Requirements

Platforms: Windows 98, Windows NT 4.0, Windows Millennium Edition, Windows 2000, Windows XP Home Edition, Windows XP Professional, Windows Server 2003 family

DataGridTextBoxColumn.Paint Method (Graphics, Rectangle, CurrencyManager, Int32, Brush, Brush, Boolean)

This member overrides **DataGridColumnStyle.Paint**.

[Visual Basic]
```
Overloads Protected Friend Overrides Sub Paint( _
   ByVal g As Graphics, _
   ByVal bounds As Rectangle, _
   ByVal source As CurrencyManager, _
   ByVal rowNum As Integer, _
   ByVal backBrush As Brush, _
   ByVal foreBrush As Brush, _
   ByVal alignToRight As Boolean _
)
```
[C#]
```
protected internal override void Paint(
   Graphics g,
   Rectangle bounds,
   CurrencyManager source,
   int rowNum,
   Brush backBrush,
   Brush foreBrush,
   bool alignToRight
);
```
[C++]
```
protected public: void Paint(
   Graphics* g,
   Rectangle bounds,
   CurrencyManager* source,
   int rowNum,
   Brush* backBrush,
   Brush* foreBrush,
   bool alignToRight
);
```
[JScript]
```
protected internal override function Paint(
   g : Graphics,
   bounds : Rectangle,
   source : CurrencyManager,
   rowNum : int,
   backBrush : Brush,
   foreBrush : Brush,
   alignToRight : Boolean
);
```

Requirements

Platforms: Windows 98, Windows NT 4.0, Windows Millennium Edition, Windows 2000, Windows XP Home Edition, Windows XP Professional, Windows Server 2003 family

DataGridTextBoxColumn.PaintText Method

Draws the specified text and surrounding rectangle at the specified location.

Overload List

Draws the text and rectangle at the given location with the specified alignment.

[Visual Basic] **Overloads Protected Sub PaintText(Graphics, Rectangle, String, Boolean)**

[C#] **protected void PaintText(Graphics, Rectangle, string, bool);**

[C++] **protected: void PaintText(Graphics*, Rectangle, String*, bool);**

[JScript] **protected function PaintText(Graphics, Rectangle, String, Boolean);**

Draws the text and rectangle at the specified location with the specified colors and alignment.

[Visual Basic] **Overloads Protected Sub PaintText(Graphics, Rectangle, String, Brush, Brush, Boolean)**

[C#] **protected void PaintText(Graphics, Rectangle, string, Brush, Brush, bool);**

[C++] **protected: void PaintText(Graphics*, Rectangle, String*, Brush*, Brush*, bool);**

[JScript] **protected function PaintText(Graphics, Rectangle, String, Brush, Brush, Boolean);**

DataGridTextBoxColumn.PaintText Method (Graphics, Rectangle, String, Boolean)

Draws the text and rectangle at the given location with the specified alignment.

```
[Visual Basic]
Overloads Protected Sub PaintText( _
   ByVal g As Graphics, _
   ByVal bounds As Rectangle, _
   ByVal text As String, _
   ByVal alignToRight As Boolean _
)
[C#]
protected void PaintText(
   Graphics g,
   Rectangle bounds,
   string text,
   bool alignToRight
);
[C++]
protected: void PaintText(
   Graphics* g,
   Rectangle bounds,
   String* text,
   bool alignToRight
);
[JScript]
protected function PaintText(
   g : Graphics,
   bounds : Rectangle,
   text : String,
   alignToRight : Boolean
);
```

Parameters

g
  A **Graphics** object used to draw the string.

bounds
  A **Rectangle** which contains the boundary data of the rectangle.

text
  The string to be drawn to the screen.

alignToRight
  A value indicating whether the text is right-aligned.

Remarks

The **PaintText** method uses the **DataFormats.Format** object set with the **Format** property to format the value before drawing it to the screen.

The **Paint** method calls the **PaintText** method.

Requirements

Platforms: Windows 98, Windows NT 4.0, Windows Millennium Edition, Windows 2000, Windows XP Home Edition, Windows XP Professional, Windows Server 2003 family

DataGridTextBoxColumn.PaintText Method (Graphics, Rectangle, String, Brush, Brush, Boolean)

Draws the text and rectangle at the specified location with the specified colors and alignment.

```
[Visual Basic]
Overloads Protected Sub PaintText( _
   ByVal g As Graphics, _
   ByVal textBounds As Rectangle, _
   ByVal text As String, _
   ByVal backBrush As Brush, _
   ByVal foreBrush As Brush, _
   ByVal alignToRight As Boolean _
)
[C#]
protected void PaintText(
   Graphics g,
   Rectangle textBounds,
   string text,
   Brush backBrush,
   Brush foreBrush,
   bool alignToRight
);
[C++]
protected: void PaintText(
   Graphics* g,
   Rectangle textBounds,
   String* text,
   Brush* backBrush,
   Brush* foreBrush,
   bool alignToRight
);
[JScript]
protected function PaintText(
   g : Graphics,
   textBounds : Rectangle,
   text : String,
   backBrush : Brush,
   foreBrush : Brush,
   alignToRight : Boolean
);
```

Parameters

g
  A **Graphics** object used to draw the string.

textBounds
  A **Rectangle** which contains the boundary data of the rectangle.

text
  The string to be drawn to the screen.

backBrush
  A **Brush** that determines the rectangle's background color

foreBrush
  A **Brush** that determines the rectangles foreground color.

alignToRight
  A value indicating whether the text is right-aligned.

Remarks

The **PaintText** method uses the **Format** property to format the value before drawing it to the screen.

The **Paint** method calls the **PaintText** method.

Requirements

Platforms: Windows 98, Windows NT 4.0, Windows Millennium Edition, Windows 2000, Windows XP Home Edition, Windows XP Professional, Windows Server 2003 family

DataGridTextBoxColumn.ReleaseHostedControl Method

Note: This namespace, class, or member is supported only in version 1.1 of the .NET Framework.

Removes the reference that the **DataGrid** holds to the control used to edit data.

```
[Visual Basic]
Protected Friend Overrides Sub ReleaseHostedControl()
[C#]
protected internal override void ReleaseHostedControl();
[C++]
protected public: void ReleaseHostedControl();
[JScript]
protected internal override function ReleaseHostedControl();
```

Remarks

This method removes the reference that the **DataGrid** holds to the **DataGridTextBox** control, in order to free system resources.

Requirements

Platforms: Windows 98, Windows NT 4.0, Windows Millennium Edition, Windows 2000, Windows XP Home Edition, Windows XP Professional, Windows Server 2003 family

DataGridTextBoxColumn.SetDataGridInColumn Method

Adds a **TextBox** control to the **DataGrid** control's **Control.ControlCollection**.

```
[Visual Basic]
Overrides Protected Sub SetDataGridInColumn( _
   ByVal value As DataGrid _
)
[C#]
protected override void SetDataGridInColumn(
   DataGrid value
);
[C++]
protected: void SetDataGridInColumn(
   DataGrid* value
);
[JScript]
protected override function SetDataGridInColumn(
   value : DataGrid
);
```

Parameters

value

The **DataGrid** control the **TextBox** control is added to.

Remarks

When this methods is called, the hosted **TextBox** control is added to the **DataGrid** control's **Control.ControlCollection**. This allows the **CurrencyManager** to associate both controls with the same data source.

Requirements

Platforms: Windows 98, Windows NT 4.0, Windows Millennium Edition, Windows 2000, Windows XP Home Edition, Windows XP Professional, Windows Server 2003 family

DataGridTextBoxColumn.UpdateUI Method

This member overrides **DataGridColumnStyle.UpdateUI**.

```
[Visual Basic]
Protected Friend Overrides Sub UpdateUI( _
   ByVal source As CurrencyManager, _
   ByVal rowNum As Integer, _
   ByVal instantText As String _
)
[C#]
protected internal override void UpdateUI(
   CurrencyManager source,
   int rowNum,
   string instantText
);
[C++]
protected public: void UpdateUI(
   CurrencyManager* source,
   int rowNum,
   String* instantText
);
[JScript]
protected internal override function UpdateUI(
   source : CurrencyManager,
   rowNum : int,
   instantText : String
);
```

Requirements

Platforms: Windows 98, Windows NT 4.0, Windows Millennium Edition, Windows 2000, Windows XP Home Edition, Windows XP Professional, Windows Server 2003 family

DataObject Class

Implements a basic data transfer mechanism.

System.Object
 System.Windows.Forms.DataObject

[Visual Basic]
```
<ClassInterface(ClassInterfaceType.None)>
Public Class DataObject
   Implements IDataObject
```
[C#]
```
[ClassInterface(ClassInterfaceType.None)]
public class DataObject : IDataObject
```
[C++]
```
[ClassInterface(ClassInterfaceType::None)]
public __gc class DataObject : public IDataObject
```
[JScript]
```
public
   ClassInterface(ClassInterfaceType.None)
class DataObject implements IDataObject
```

Thread Safety

Any public static (**Shared** in Visual Basic) members of this type are safe for multithreaded operations. Any instance members are not guaranteed to be thread safe.

Remarks

DataObject implements the **IDataObject** interface, whose methods provide a format-independent mechanism for data transfer.

A **DataObject** is typically used with the **Clipboard** and in drag-and-drop operations. The **DataObject** class provides the recommended implementation of the **IDataObject** interface. It is suggested that you use the **DataObject** class rather than implementing **IDataObject** yourself.

Multiple pieces of data in different formats can be stored in an instance of **DataObject**. Data is retrieved from the instance by its associated format. Because the target application might not be known, you can increase the likelihood that the data will be in the appropriate format for an application by placing the data in a **DataObject** in multiple formats. See **DataFormats** for the pre-defined formats. You can implement your own format by creating an instance of the **DataFormats.Format** class.

To store data in an instance of this class, pass the data to the constructor or call **SetData**. You can add data in other formats to an instance of this class. If you want the data you add always to be retrieved in its native format, call **SetData** with the *autoConvert* parameter set to **false**.

Data can be retrieved from a **DataObject** in any format which is compatible with **GetData**. For example, text can be converted to Unicode. To retrieve data in the format in which it was stored, call **GetData** with the *autoConvert* parameter set to **false**.

To determine what formats the data is stored in, call **GetFormats**. To determine if a format is available, call **GetDataPresent** with the desired format.

Example

See related example in the **System.Windows.Forms.DataObject** class topic.

Requirements

Namespace: System.Windows.Forms

Platforms: Windows 98, Windows NT 4.0, Windows Millennium Edition, Windows 2000, Windows XP Home Edition, Windows XP Professional, Windows Server 2003 family

Assembly: System.Windows.Forms (in System.Windows.Forms.dll)

DataObject Constructor

Initializes a new instance of the **DataObject** class.

Overload List

Initializes a new instance of the **DataObject** class, which can store arbitrary data.

[Visual Basic] **Public Sub New()**

[C#] **public DataObject();**

[C++] **public: DataObject();**

[JScript] **public function DataObject();**

Initializes a new instance of the **DataObject** class, containing the specified data.

[Visual Basic] **Public Sub New(Object)**

[C#] **public DataObject(object);**

[C++] **public: DataObject(Object*);**

[JScript] **public function DataObject(Object);**

Initializes a new instance of the **DataObject** class, containing the specified data and its associated format.

[Visual Basic] **Public Sub New(String, Object)**

[C#] **public DataObject(string, object);**

[C++] **public: DataObject(String*, Object*);**

[JScript] **public function DataObject(String, Object);**

Example

See related example in the **System.Windows.Forms.DataObject** class topic.

DataObject Constructor ()

Initializes a new instance of the **DataObject** class, which can store arbitrary data.

[Visual Basic]
```
Public Sub New()
```
[C#]
```
public DataObject();
```
[C++]
```
public: DataObject();
```
[JScript]
```
public function DataObject();
```

Example

See related example in the **System.Windows.Forms.DataObject** class topic.

Requirements

Platforms: Windows 98, Windows NT 4.0, Windows Millennium Edition, Windows 2000, Windows XP Home Edition, Windows XP Professional, Windows Server 2003 family

DataObject Constructor (Object)

Initializes a new instance of the **DataObject** class, containing the specified data.

```
[Visual Basic]
Public Sub New( _
   ByVal data As Object _
)
[C#]
public DataObject(
   object data
);
[C++]
public: DataObject(
   Object* data
);
[JScript]
public function DataObject(
   data : Object
);
```

Parameters

data
The data to store.

Example

See related example in the **System.Windows.Forms.DataObject** class topic.

Requirements

Platforms: Windows 98, Windows NT 4.0, Windows Millennium Edition, Windows 2000, Windows XP Home Edition, Windows XP Professional, Windows Server 2003 family

DataObject Constructor (String, Object)

Initializes a new instance of the **DataObject** class, containing the specified data and its associated format.

```
[Visual Basic]
Public Sub New( _
   ByVal format As String, _
   ByVal data As Object _
)
[C#]
public DataObject(
   string format,
   object data
);
[C++]
public: DataObject(
   String* format,
   Object* data
);
[JScript]
public function DataObject(
   format : String,
   data : Object
);
```

Parameters

format
The class type associated with the data. See **DataFormats** for the predefined formats.

data
The data to store.

Example

See related example in the **System.Windows.Forms.DataObject** class topic.

Requirements

Platforms: Windows 98, Windows NT 4.0, Windows Millennium Edition, Windows 2000, Windows XP Home Edition, Windows XP Professional, Windows Server 2003 family

DataObject.GetData Method

Returns the data associated with the specified data format.

Overload List

Returns the data associated with the specified data format.

[Visual Basic] **Overloads Public Overridable Function GetData(String) As Object Implements IDataObject.GetData**

[C#] **public virtual object GetData(string);**

[C++] **public: virtual Object* GetData(String*);**

[JScript] **public function GetData(String) : Object;**

Returns the data associated with the specified class type format.

[Visual Basic] **Overloads Public Overridable Function GetData(Type) As Object Implements IDataObject.GetData**

[C#] **public virtual object GetData(Type);**

[C++] **public: virtual Object* GetData(Type*);**

[JScript] **public function GetData(Type) : Object;**

Returns the data associated with the specified data format, using an automated conversion parameter to determine whether to convert the data to the format.

[Visual Basic] **Overloads Public Overridable Function GetData(String, Boolean) As Object Implements IDataObject.GetData**

[C#] **public virtual object GetData(string, bool);**

[C++] **public: virtual Object* GetData(String*, bool);**

[JScript] **public function GetData(String, Boolean) : Object;**

Example

See related example in the **System.Windows.Forms.DataObject** class topic.

DataObject.GetData Method (String)

Returns the data associated with the specified data format.

```
[Visual Basic]
Overloads Public Overridable Function GetData( _
   ByVal format As String _
) As Object Implements IDataObject.GetData
[C#]
public virtual object GetData(
   string format
);
```

```
[C++]
public: virtual Object* GetData(
   String* format
);
[JScript]
public function GetData(
   format : String
) : Object;
```

Parameters

format

The format of the data to retrieve. See **DataFormats** for predefined formats.

Return Value

The data associated with the specified format, or a null reference (**Nothing** in Visual Basic).

Implements

IDataObject.GetData

Remarks

If this method cannot find data in the specified format, it attempts to convert the data to the format. If the data cannot be converted to the specified format, or if the data was stored with automatic conversion set to **false**, this method returns a null reference (**Nothing** in Visual Basic).

To determine whether data is associated with, or can be converted to, a format, call **GetDataPresent** before calling **GetData**. Call **GetFormats** for a list of valid formats for the data stored in this instance.

> **Note** Data can be converted to another format if it was stored specifying that conversion is allowed, and if the requested format is compatible with the stored format. For example, data stored as Unicode can be converted to text.

Example

See related example in the **System.Windows.Forms.DataObject** class topic.

Requirements

Platforms: Windows 98, Windows NT 4.0, Windows Millennium Edition, Windows 2000, Windows XP Home Edition, Windows XP Professional, Windows Server 2003 family

DataObject.GetData Method (Type)

Returns the data associated with the specified class type format.

```
[Visual Basic]
Overloads Public Overridable Function GetData( _
   ByVal format As Type _
) As Object Implements IDataObject.GetData
[C#]
public virtual object GetData(
   Type format
);
[C++]
public: virtual Object* GetData(
   Type* format
);
[JScript]
public function GetData(
   format : Type
) : Object;
```

Parameters

format

A **Type** representing the format of the data to retrieve.

Return Value

The data associated with the specified format, or a null reference (**Nothing** in Visual Basic).

Implements

IDataObject.GetData

Remarks

If this method cannot find data in the specified format, it attempts to convert the data to the format. If the data cannot be converted to the specified format, or if the data was stored with automatic conversion set to **false**, this method returns a null reference (**Nothing** in Visual Basic).

To determine whether data is associated with, or can be converted to, a format, call **GetDataPresent** before calling **GetData**. Call **GetFormats** for a list of valid formats for the data stored in this instance.

> **Note** Data can be converted to another format if it was stored specifying that conversion is allowed, and if the requested format is compatible with the stored format. For example, data stored as Unicode can be converted to text.

Example

See related example in the **System.Windows.Forms.DataObject** class topic.

Requirements

Platforms: Windows 98, Windows NT 4.0, Windows Millennium Edition, Windows 2000, Windows XP Home Edition, Windows XP Professional, Windows Server 2003 family

DataObject.GetData Method (String, Boolean)

Returns the data associated with the specified data format, using an automated conversion parameter to determine whether to convert the data to the format.

```
[Visual Basic]
Overloads Public Overridable Function GetData( _
   ByVal format As String, _
   ByVal autoConvert As Boolean _
) As Object Implements IDataObject.GetData
[C#]
public virtual object GetData(
   string format,
   bool autoConvert
);
[C++]
public: virtual Object* GetData(
   String* format,
   bool autoConvert
);
```

```
[JScript]
public function GetData(
   format : String,
   autoConvert : Boolean
) : Object;
```

Parameters

format
The format of the data to retrieve. See **DataFormats** for predefined formats.

autoConvert
true to the convert data to the specified format; otherwise, **false**.

Return Value

The data associated with the specified format, or a null reference (**Nothing** in Visual Basic).

Implements

IDataObject.GetData

Remarks

If the *autoConvert* parameter is **true** and this method cannot find data in the specified format, it attempts to convert the data to the format. If the data cannot be converted to the specified format, or if the data was stored with the automatic conversion set to **false**, this method returns a null reference (**Nothing** in Visual Basic).

If the *autoConvert* parameter is **false**, this method returns data in the specified format, or a null reference (**Nothing**) if no data in this format can be found.

To determine whether data is associated with, or can be converted to, a format, call **GetDataPresent** before calling **GetData**. Call **GetFormats** for a list of valid formats for the data stored in this instance.

> **Note** Data can be converted to another format if it was stored specifying that conversion is allowed, and if the requested format is compatible with the stored format. For example, data stored as Unicode can be converted to text.

Example

See related example in the **System.Windows.Forms.DataObject** class topic.

Requirements

Platforms: Windows 98, Windows NT 4.0, Windows Millennium Edition, Windows 2000, Windows XP Home Edition, Windows XP Professional, Windows Server 2003 family

DataObject.GetDataPresent Method

Determines whether data stored in this instance is associated with the specified format.

Overload List

Determines whether data stored in this instance is associated with, or can be converted to, the specified format.

[Visual Basic] **Overloads Public Overridable Function GetDataPresent(String) As Boolean Implements IDataObject.GetDataPresent**

[C#] **public virtual bool GetDataPresent(string);**

[C++] **public: virtual bool GetDataPresent(String*);**

[JScript] **public function GetDataPresent(String) : Boolean;**

Determines whether data stored in this instance is associated with, or can be converted to, the specified format.

[Visual Basic] **Overloads Public Overridable Function GetDataPresent(Type) As Boolean Implements IDataObject.GetDataPresent**

[C#] **public virtual bool GetDataPresent(Type);**

[C++] **public: virtual bool GetDataPresent(Type*);**

[JScript] **public function GetDataPresent(Type) : Boolean;**

Determines whether data stored in this instance is associated with the specified format, using an automatic conversion parameter to determine whether to convert the data to the format.

[Visual Basic] **Overloads Public Overridable Function GetDataPresent(String, Boolean) As Boolean Implements IDataObject.GetDataPresent**

[C#] **public virtual bool GetDataPresent(string, bool);**

[C++] **public: virtual bool GetDataPresent(String*, bool);**

[JScript] **public function GetDataPresent(String, Boolean) : Boolean;**

Example

See related example in the **System.Windows.Forms.DataObject** class topic.

DataObject.GetDataPresent Method (String)

Determines whether data stored in this instance is associated with, or can be converted to, the specified format.

```
[Visual Basic]
Overloads Public Overridable Function GetDataPresent( _
   ByVal format As String _
) As Boolean Implements IDataObject.GetDataPresent
[C#]
public virtual bool GetDataPresent(
   string format
);
[C++]
public: virtual bool GetDataPresent(
   String* format
);
[JScript]
public function GetDataPresent(
   format : String
) : Boolean;
```

Parameters

format
The format to check for. See **DataFormats** for predefined formats.

Return Value

true if data stored in this instance is associated with, or can be converted to, the specified format; otherwise, **false**.

Implements

IDataObject.GetDataPresent

Remarks

Call this method to determine whether a format exists before calling **GetData**. Call **GetFormats** for the formats that are available in this instance.

> **Note** Data can be converted to another format if it was stored specifying that conversion is allowed, and if the requested format is compatible with the stored format. For example, data stored as Unicode can be converted to text.

> **Note** If no data can be retrieved, no exception will be thrown. Instead, **false** will be returned.

Example

See related example in the **System.Windows.Forms.DataObject** class topic.

Requirements

Platforms: Windows 98, Windows NT 4.0, Windows Millennium Edition, Windows 2000, Windows XP Home Edition, Windows XP Professional, Windows Server 2003 family

DataObject.GetDataPresent Method (Type)

Determines whether data stored in this instance is associated with, or can be converted to, the specified format.

[Visual Basic]
```
Overloads Public Overridable Function GetDataPresent( _
   ByVal format As Type _
) As Boolean Implements IDataObject.GetDataPresent
```
[C#]
```
public virtual bool GetDataPresent(
   Type format
);
```
[C++]
```
public: virtual bool GetDataPresent(
   Type* format
);
```
[JScript]
```
public function GetDataPresent(
   format : Type
) : Boolean;
```

Parameters

format

A **Type** representing the format to check for.

Return Value

true if data stored in this instance is associated with, or can be converted to, the specified format; otherwise, **false**.

Implements

IDataObject.GetDataPresent

Remarks

Call this method to determine whether a format exists before calling **GetData**. Call **GetFormats** for the formats that are available in this instance.

> **Note** Data can be converted to another format if it was stored specifying that conversion is allowed, and if the requested format is compatible with the stored format. For example, data stored as Unicode can be converted to text.

> **Note** If no data can be retrieved, no exception will be thrown. Instead, **false** will be returned.

Example

See related example in the **System.Windows.Forms.DataObject** class topic.

Requirements

Platforms: Windows 98, Windows NT 4.0, Windows Millennium Edition, Windows 2000, Windows XP Home Edition, Windows XP Professional, Windows Server 2003 family

DataObject.GetDataPresent Method (String, Boolean)

Determines whether data stored in this instance is associated with the specified format, using an automatic conversion parameter to determine whether to convert the data to the format.

[Visual Basic]
```
Overloads Public Overridable Function GetDataPresent( _
   ByVal format As String, _
   ByVal autoConvert As Boolean _
) As Boolean Implements IDataObject.GetDataPresent
```
[C#]
```
public virtual bool GetDataPresent(
   string format,
   bool autoConvert
);
```
[C++]
```
public: virtual bool GetDataPresent(
   String* format,
   bool autoConvert
);
```
[JScript]
```
public function GetDataPresent(
   format : String,
   autoConvert : Boolean
) : Boolean;
```

Parameters

format

The format to check for. See **DataFormats** for predefined formats.

autoConvert

true to determine whether data stored in this instance can be converted to the specified format; **false** to check whether the data is in the specified format.

Return Value

true if the data is in, or can be converted to, the specified format; otherwise, **false**.

Implements

IDataObject.GetDataPresent

Remarks

Call this method to determine whether a format exists before calling **GetData**. Call **GetFormats** for the formats that are available in this instance.

This method returns **true** when:

- *autoConvert* parameter is **true** and the data is in a format that can be converted to the appropriate format.
- *autoConvert* parameter is **false** and the data is in the appropriate format.

This method returns **false** when:

- *autoConvert* parameter is **true** and this method cannot find data in the specified format, and it cannot convert data to the specified format, or the data was stored with automatic conversion set to **false**.
- *autoConvert* parameter is **false**, and data does not exist in this instance in the specified format.

> **Note** Data can be converted to another format if it was stored specifying that conversion is allowed and if the requested format is compatible with the stored format. For example, data stored as Unicode can be converted to text.

> **Note** If no data can be retrieved, no exception will be thrown. Instead, **false** will be returned.

Example

See related example in the **System.Windows.Forms.DataObject** class topic.

Requirements

Platforms: Windows 98, Windows NT 4.0, Windows Millennium Edition, Windows 2000, Windows XP Home Edition, Windows XP Professional, Windows Server 2003 family

DataObject.GetFormats Method

Returns a list of all formats that data stored in this instance is associated with or can be converted to.

Overload List

Returns a list of all formats that data stored in this instance is associated with or can be converted to.

[Visual Basic] **Overloads Public Overridable Function GetFormats() As String() Implements IDataObject.GetFormats**

[C#] **public virtual string[] GetFormats();**

[C++] **public: virtual String* GetFormats() __gc[];**

[JScript] **public function GetFormats() : String[];**

Returns a list of all formats that data stored in this instance is associated with or can be converted to, using an automatic conversion parameter to determine whether to retrieve only native data formats or all formats that the data can be converted to.

[Visual Basic] **Overloads Public Overridable Function GetFormats(Boolean) As String() Implements IDataObject.GetFormats**

[C#] **public virtual string[] GetFormats(bool);**

[C++] **public: virtual String* GetFormats(bool) __gc[];**

[JScript] **public function GetFormats(Boolean) : String[];**

Example

See related example in the **System.Windows.Forms.DataObject** class topic.

DataObject.GetFormats Method ()

Returns a list of all formats that data stored in this instance is associated with or can be converted to.

```
[Visual Basic]
Overloads Public Overridable Function GetFormats() As String()
Implements _
   IDataObject.GetFormats
[C#]
public virtual string[] GetFormats();
[C++]
public: virtual String* GetFormats()  __gc[];
[JScript]
public function GetFormats() : String[];
```

Return Value

An array of type **String**, containing a list of all formats that are supported by the data stored in this object.

Implements

IDataObject.GetFormats

Remarks

Call this method to get the supported data formats before calling **GetData**. See **DataFormats** for the predefined formats.

> **Note** Data can be converted to another format if it was stored specifying that conversion is allowed and if the requested format is compatible with the stored format. For example, data stored as Unicode can be converted to text.

Example

See related example in the **System.Windows.Forms.DataObject** class topic.

Requirements

Platforms: Windows 98, Windows NT 4.0, Windows Millennium Edition, Windows 2000, Windows XP Home Edition, Windows XP Professional, Windows Server 2003 family

DataObject.GetFormats Method (Boolean)

Returns a list of all formats that data stored in this instance is associated with or can be converted to, using an automatic conversion parameter to determine whether to retrieve only native data formats or all formats that the data can be converted to.

```
[Visual Basic]
Overloads Public Overridable Function GetFormats( _
   ByVal autoConvert As Boolean _
) As String() Implements IDataObject.GetFormats
[C#]
public virtual string[] GetFormats(
   bool autoConvert
);
[C++]
public: virtual String* GetFormats(
   bool autoConvert
)  __gc[];
[JScript]
public function GetFormats(
   autoConvert : Boolean
) : String[];
```

Parameters

autoConvert

true to retrieve all formats that data stored in this instance is associated with, or can be converted to; **false** to retrieve only native data formats.

Return Value

An array of type **String**, containing a list of all formats that are supported by the data stored in this object.

Implements

IDataObject.GetFormats

Remarks

Call this method to get the supported data formats before calling **GetData**. See **DataFormats** for the predefined formats.

> **Note** Data can be converted to another format if it was stored specifying that conversion is allowed and if the requested format is compatible with the stored format. For example, data stored as Unicode can be converted to text.

Example

See related example in the **System.Windows.Forms.DataObject** class topic.

Requirements

Platforms: Windows 98, Windows NT 4.0,
Windows Millennium Edition, Windows 2000,
Windows XP Home Edition, Windows XP Professional,
Windows Server 2003 family

DataObject.SetData Method

Stores the specified format and data in this instance.

Overload List

Stores the specified data in this instance, using the class of the data for the format.

[Visual Basic] **Overloads Public Overridable Sub SetData(Object) Implements IDataObject.SetData**

[C#] **public virtual void SetData(object);**

[C++] **public: virtual void SetData(Object*);**

[JScript] **public function SetData(Object);**

Stores the specified format and data in this instance.

[Visual Basic] **Overloads Public Overridable Sub SetData(String, Object) Implements IDataObject.SetData**

[C#] **public virtual void SetData(string, object);**

[C++] **public: virtual void SetData(String*, Object*);**

[JScript] **public function SetData(String, Object);**

Stores the specified data and its associated class type in this instance.

[Visual Basic] **Overloads Public Overridable Sub SetData(Type, Object) Implements IDataObject.SetData**

[C#] **public virtual void SetData(Type, object);**

[C++] **public: virtual void SetData(Type*, Object*);**

[JScript] **public function SetData(Type, Object);**

Stores the specified format and data in this instance, using the automatic conversion parameter to specify whether the data can be converted to another format.

[Visual Basic] **Overloads Public Overridable Sub SetData(String, Boolean, Object) Implements IDataObject.SetData**

[C#] **public virtual void SetData(string, bool, object);**

[C++] **public: virtual void SetData(String*, bool, Object*);**

[JScript] **public function SetData(String, Boolean, Object);**

Example

See related example in the **System.Windows.Forms.DataObject** class topic.

DataObject.SetData Method (Object)

Stores the specified data in this instance, using the class of the data for the format.

```
[Visual Basic]
Overloads Public Overridable Sub SetData( _
   ByVal data As Object _
) Implements IDataObject.SetData
[C#]
public virtual void SetData(
   object data
);
[C++]
public: virtual void SetData(
   Object* data
);
[JScript]
public function SetData(
   data : Object
);
```

Parameters

data
The data to store.

Implements

IDataObject.SetData

Remarks

The data format is its class. If you do not know the format of the target application, you can store data in multiple formats using this method.

Data stored using this method can be converted to a compatible format when it is retrieved.

Example

See related example in the **System.Windows.Forms.DataObject** class topic.

Requirements

Platforms: Windows 98, Windows NT 4.0,
Windows Millennium Edition, Windows 2000,
Windows XP Home Edition, Windows XP Professional,
Windows Server 2003 family

DataObject.SetData Method (String, Object)

Stores the specified format and data in this instance.

```
[Visual Basic]
Overloads Public Overridable Sub SetData( _
   ByVal format As String, _
   ByVal data As Object _
) Implements IDataObject.SetData
[C#]
public virtual void SetData(
   string format,
   object data
);
```

[C++]
```
public: virtual void SetData(
   String* format,
   Object* data
);
```
[JScript]
```
public function SetData(
   format : String,
   data : Object
);
```

Parameters

format
The format associated with the data. See **DataFormats** for predefined formats.

data
The data to store.

Implements

IDataObject.SetData

Remarks

If you do not know the format of the target application, you can store data in multiple formats using this method.

Data stored using this method can be converted to a compatible format when it is retrieved.

Example

See related example in the **System.Windows.Forms.DataObject** class topic.

Requirements

Platforms: Windows 98, Windows NT 4.0, Windows Millennium Edition, Windows 2000, Windows XP Home Edition, Windows XP Professional, Windows Server 2003 family

DataObject.SetData Method (Type, Object)

Stores the specified data and its associated class type in this instance.

[Visual Basic]
```
Overloads Public Overridable Sub SetData( _
   ByVal format As Type, _
   ByVal data As Object _
) Implements IDataObject.SetData
```
[C#]
```
public virtual void SetData(
   Type format,
   object data
);
```
[C++]
```
public: virtual void SetData(
   Type* format,
   Object* data
);
```
[JScript]
```
public function SetData(
   format : Type,
   data : Object
);
```

Parameters

format
A **Type** representing the format associated with the data.

data
The data to store.

Implements

IDataObject.SetData

Remarks

If you do not know the format of the target application, you can store data in multiple formats using this method.

Data stored using this method can be converted to a compatible format when it is retrieved.

Example

See related example in the **System.Windows.Forms.DataObject** class topic.

Requirements

Platforms: Windows 98, Windows NT 4.0, Windows Millennium Edition, Windows 2000, Windows XP Home Edition, Windows XP Professional, Windows Server 2003 family

DataObject.SetData Method (String, Boolean, Object)

Stores the specified format and data in this instance, using the automatic conversion parameter to specify whether the data can be converted to another format.

[Visual Basic]
```
Overloads Public Overridable Sub SetData( _
   ByVal format As String, _
   ByVal autoConvert As Boolean, _
   ByVal data As Object _
) Implements IDataObject.SetData
```
[C#]
```
public virtual void SetData(
   string format,
   bool autoConvert,
   object data
);
```
[C++]
```
public: virtual void SetData(
   String* format,
   bool autoConvert,
   Object* data
);
```
[JScript]
```
public function SetData(
   format : String,
   autoConvert : Boolean,
   data : Object
);
```

Parameters

format

The format associated with the data. See **DataFormats** for predefined formats.

autoConvert

true to allow the data to be converted to another format; otherwise, **false**.

data

The data to store.

Implements

IDataObject.SetData

Remarks

If you do not know the format of the target application, you can store data in multiple formats using this method.

Example

See related example in the **System.Windows.Forms.DataObject** class topic.

Requirements

Platforms: Windows 98, Windows NT 4.0,
Windows Millennium Edition, Windows 2000,
Windows XP Home Edition, Windows XP Professional,
Windows Server 2003 family

DateBoldEventArgs Class

This type supports the .NET Framework infrastructure and is not intended to be used directly from your code.

[Visual Basic]
```
Public Class DateBoldEventArgs
   Inherits EventArgs
```
[C#]
```
public class DateBoldEventArgs : EventArgs
```
[C++]
```
public __gc class DateBoldEventArgs : public EventArgs
```
[JScript]
```
public class DateBoldEventArgs extends EventArgs
```

DateBoldEventArgs.DaysToBold Property

This member supports the .NET Framework infrastructure and is not intended to be used directly from your code.

[Visual Basic]
```
Public Property DaysToBold As Integer ()
```
[C#]
```
public int[] DaysToBold {get; set;}
```
[C++]
```
public: __property int get_DaysToBold();
public: __property void set_DaysToBold(int __gc[]);
```
[JScript]
```
public function get DaysToBold() : int[];
public function set DaysToBold(int[]);
```

DateBoldEventArgs.Size Property

This member supports the .NET Framework infrastructure and is not intended to be used directly from your code.

[Visual Basic]
```
Public ReadOnly Property Size As Integer
```
[C#]
```
public int Size {get;}
```
[C++]
```
public: __property int get_Size();
```
[JScript]
```
public function get Size() : int;
```

DateBoldEventArgs.StartDate Property

This member supports the .NET Framework infrastructure and is not intended to be used directly from your code.

[Visual Basic]
```
Public ReadOnly Property StartDate As DateTime
```
[C#]
```
public DateTime StartDate {get;}
```
[C++]
```
public: __property DateTime get_StartDate();
```
[JScript]
```
public function get StartDate() : DateTime;
```

DateBoldEventHandler Delegate

This type supports the .NET Framework infrastructure and is not intended to be used directly from your code.

[Visual Basic]

```
<Serializable>
Public Delegate Sub DateBoldEventHandler( _
   ByVal sender As Object, _
   ByVal e As DateBoldEventArgs _
)
```

[C#]

```
[Serializable]
public delegate void DateBoldEventHandler(
   object sender,
   DateBoldEventArgs e
);
```

[C++]

```
[Serializable]
public __gc __delegate void DateBoldEventHandler(
   Object* sender,
   DateBoldEventArgs* e
);
```

[JScript] In JScript, you can use the delegates in the .NET Framework, but you cannot define your own.

DateRangeEventArgs Class

Provides data for the **DateChanged** or **DateSelected** events of the **MonthCalendar** control.

System.Object
  System.EventArgs
    System.Windows.Forms.DateRangeEventArgs

[Visual Basic]
```
Public Class DateRangeEventArgs
   Inherits EventArgs
```
[C#]
```
public class DateRangeEventArgs : EventArgs
```
[C++]
```
public __gc class DateRangeEventArgs : public EventArgs
```
[JScript]
```
public class DateRangeEventArgs extends EventArgs
```

Thread Safety

Any public static (**Shared** in Visual Basic) members of this type are safe for multithreaded operations. Any instance members are not guaranteed to be thread safe.

Remarks

The **DateChanged** event occurs when the currently selected date or range of dates changes; for example, when the user explicitly changes a selection within the current month or when the selection is implicitly changed in response to next/previous month navigation. The **DateSelected** event occurs when the user explicitly changes a selection. The **DateRangeEventArgs** constructor specifies the start and end for the new date range that has been selected.

Note If a single date is selected, the **Start** and **End** property values will be equal.

Example

[Visual Basic, C#, C++] The following example displays a form containing a **MonthCalendar** control that displays one calendar year. The example demonstrates setting properties like **BackColor**, **ForeColor**, **TitleBackColor**, **TitleForeColor**, **CalendarDimensions**, and **TrailingForeColor** to customize the look of the calendar control. Other properties like **AnnuallyBoldedDates**, **BoldedDates**, and **MonthlyBoldedDates** are set to customize which dates are bolded. The example also sets properties to change the calendar format, including **FirstDayOfWeek**, **MaxDate**, **MinDate**, and **MaxSelectionCount**. The **DateSelected** and **DateChanged** events are also handled and their status displayed on the form.

[Visual Basic]
```
Imports System
Imports System.Drawing
Imports System.Windows.Forms

Public NotInheritable Class Form1
    Inherits System.Windows.Forms.Form

    Friend WithEvents MonthCalendar1 As                          ↵
System.Windows.Forms.MonthCalendar
    Friend WithEvents TextBox1 As System.Windows.Forms.TextBox

    <System.STAThread()> _
    Public Shared Sub Main()
        System.Windows.Forms.Application.Run(New Form1)
    End Sub 'Main

    Public Sub New()
        MyBase.New()

        Me.TextBox1 = New System.Windows.Forms.TextBox
        Me.TextBox1.BorderStyle =                                 ↵
System.Windows.Forms.BorderStyle.FixedSingle
        Me.TextBox1.Location = New System.Drawing.Point(48, 488)
        Me.TextBox1.Multiline = True
        Me.TextBox1.ReadOnly = True
        Me.TextBox1.Size = New System.Drawing.Size(824, 32)

        ' Create the calendar.
        Me.MonthCalendar1 = New System.Windows.Forms.MonthCalendar

        ' Set the calendar location.
        Me.MonthCalendar1.Location = New System.Drawing.Point(47, 16)

        ' Change the color.
        Me.MonthCalendar1.BackColor = System.Drawing.SystemColors.Info
        Me.MonthCalendar1.ForeColor = System.Drawing.Color.FromArgb( _
                            CType(192, System.Byte),               ↵
CType(0, System.Byte), CType(192, System.Byte))
        Me.MonthCalendar1.TitleBackColor = System.Drawing.Color.Purple
        Me.MonthCalendar1.TitleForeColor = System.Drawing.Color.Yellow
        Me.MonthCalendar1.TrailingForeColor =                     ↵
System.Drawing.Color.FromArgb( _
                            CType(192, System.Byte),               ↵
CType(192, System.Byte), CType(0, System.Byte))

        ' Add dates to the AnnuallyBoldedDates array.
        Me.MonthCalendar1.AnnuallyBoldedDates = New System.DateTime() _
                    {New System.DateTime(2002, 4, 20, 0, 0, 0, 0), _
                     New System.DateTime(2002, 4, 28, 0, 0, 0, 0), _
                     New System.DateTime(2002, 5, 5, 0, 0, 0, 0), _
                     New System.DateTime(2002, 7, 4, 0, 0, 0, 0), _
                     New System.DateTime(2002, 12, 15, 0, 0, 0, 0), _
                     New System.DateTime(2002, 12, 18, 0, 0, 0, 0)}

        ' Add dates to BoldedDates array.
        Me.MonthCalendar1.BoldedDates = New System.DateTime()     ↵
 {New System.DateTime(2002, 9, 26, 0, 0, 0, 0)}

        ' Add dates to MonthlyBoldedDates array.
        Me.MonthCalendar1.MonthlyBoldedDates = New System.DateTime() _
                    {New System.DateTime(2002, 1, 15, 0, 0, 0, 0), _
                     New System.DateTime(2002, 1, 30, 0, 0, 0, 0)}

        ' Configure the calendar to display 3 rows by 4            ↵
 columns of months.
        Me.MonthCalendar1.CalendarDimensions = New                 ↵
System.Drawing.Size(4, 3)

        ' Set the week to begin on Monday.
        Me.MonthCalendar1.FirstDayOfWeek =                         ↵
System.Windows.Forms.Day.Monday

        ' Sets the maximum visible date on the calendar to 12/31/2010.
        Me.MonthCalendar1.MaxDate = New System.DateTime            ↵
 (2010, 12, 31, 0, 0, 0, 0)

        ' Set the minimum visible date on the calendar to 12/31/2010.
        Me.MonthCalendar1.MinDate = New System.DateTime(1999,      ↵
 1, 1, 0, 0, 0, 0)

        ' Only allow 21 days to be selected at the same time.
        Me.MonthCalendar1.MaxSelectionCount = 21

        ' Set the calendar to move one month at a time when          ↵
 navigating using the arrows.
        Me.MonthCalendar1.ScrollChange = 1

        ' Do not show the "Today" banner.
        Me.MonthCalendar1.ShowToday = False

        ' Do not circle today's date.
        Me.MonthCalendar1.ShowTodayCircle = False
```

```
        ' Show the week numbers to the left of each week.
        Me.MonthCalendar1.ShowWeekNumbers = True

        ' Set up how the form should be displayed and add the
 controls to the form.
        Me.ClientSize = New System.Drawing.Size(920, 566)
        Me.Controls.AddRange(New System.Windows.Forms.Control()
{Me.TextBox1, Me.MonthCalendar1})
        Me.Text = "Month Calendar Example"

    End Sub

    Private Sub monthCalendar1_DateSelected(ByVal sender As Object, _
                ByVal e As
System.Windows.Forms.DateRangeEventArgs) Handles
MonthCalendar1.DateSelected

        ' Show the start and end dates in the text box.
        Me.TextBox1.Text = "Date Selected: Start = " + _
            e.Start.ToShortDateString() + " : End = " +
e.End.ToShortDateString()
    End Sub

    Private Sub monthCalendar1_DateChanged(ByVal sender As Object, _
                ByVal e As
System.Windows.Forms.DateRangeEventArgs) Handles
MonthCalendar1.DateChanged

        ' Show the start and end dates in the text box.
        Me.TextBox1.Text = "Date Changed: Start = " + _
            e.Start.ToShortDateString() + " : End = " +
e.End.ToShortDateString()
    End Sub
End Class
```

[C#]

```
using System;
using System.Drawing;
using System.Windows.Forms;

public class Form1 : System.Windows.Forms.Form
{
    private System.Windows.Forms.MonthCalendar monthCalendar1;
    private System.Windows.Forms.TextBox textBox1;

    [STAThread]
    static void Main()
    {
        Application.Run(new Form1());
    }

    public Form1()
    {
        this.textBox1 = new System.Windows.Forms.TextBox();
        this.textBox1.BorderStyle =
System.Windows.Forms.BorderStyle.FixedSingle;
        this.textBox1.Location = new System.Drawing.Point(48, 488);
        this.textBox1.Multiline = true;
        this.textBox1.ReadOnly = true;
        this.textBox1.Size = new System.Drawing.Size(824, 32);

        // Create the calendar.
        this.monthCalendar1 = new System.Windows.Forms.MonthCalendar();

        // Set the calendar location.
        this.monthCalendar1.Location = new System.Drawing.Point
(47, 16);

        // Change the color.
        this.monthCalendar1.BackColor =
System.Drawing.SystemColors.Info;
        this.monthCalendar1.ForeColor = System.Drawing.Color.FromArgb(
                        ((System.Byte)(192)),
((System.Byte)(0)), ((System.Byte)(192)));
        this.monthCalendar1.TitleBackColor =
System.Drawing.Color.Purple;
        this.monthCalendar1.TitleForeColor =
System.Drawing.Color.Yellow;
        this.monthCalendar1.TrailingForeColor =
System.Drawing.Color.FromArgb(
                        ((System.Byte)(192)),
((System.Byte)(192)), ((System.Byte)(0)));

        // Add dates to the AnnuallyBoldedDates array.
        this.monthCalendar1.AnnuallyBoldedDates =
           new System.DateTime[] { new System.DateTime(2002,
4, 20, 0, 0, 0, 0),
                                   new System.DateTime(2002,
4, 28, 0, 0, 0, 0),
                                   new System.DateTime(2002,
5, 5, 0, 0, 0, 0),
                                   new System.DateTime(2002,
7, 4, 0, 0, 0, 0),
                                   new System.DateTime(2002,
12, 15, 0, 0, 0, 0),
                                   new System.DateTime(2002,
12, 18, 0, 0, 0, 0)};

        // Add dates to BoldedDates array.
        this.monthCalendar1.BoldedDates = new System.DateTime[]
{new System.DateTime(2002, 9, 26, 0, 0, 0, 0)};

        // Add dates to MonthlyBoldedDates array.
        this.monthCalendar1.MonthlyBoldedDates =
           new System.DateTime[] {new System.DateTime(2002, 1,
15, 0, 0, 0, 0),
                                  new System.DateTime(2002, 1,
30, 0, 0, 0, 0)};

        // Configure the calendar to display 3 rows by 4 columns
 of months.
        this.monthCalendar1.CalendarDimensions = new
System.Drawing.Size(4, 3);

        // Set week to begin on Monday.
        this.monthCalendar1.FirstDayOfWeek =
System.Windows.Forms.Day.Monday;

        // Set the maximum visible date on the calendar to 12/31/2010.
        this.monthCalendar1.MaxDate = new System.DateTime(2010,
 12, 31, 0, 0, 0, 0);

        // Set the minimum visible date on calendar to 12/31/2010.
        this.monthCalendar1.MinDate = new System.DateTime(1999,
 1, 1, 0, 0, 0, 0);

        // Only allow 21 days to be selected at the same time.
        this.monthCalendar1.MaxSelectionCount = 21;

        // Set the calendar to move one month at a time when
navigating using the arrows.
        this.monthCalendar1.ScrollChange = 1;

        // Do not show the "Today" banner.
        this.monthCalendar1.ShowToday = false;

        // Do not circle today's date.
        this.monthCalendar1.ShowTodayCircle = false;

        // Show the week numbers to the left of each week.
        this.monthCalendar1.ShowWeekNumbers = true;

        // Add event handlers for the DateSelected and
DateChanged events
        this.monthCalendar1.DateSelected += new
System.Windows.Forms.DateRangeEventHandler
(this.monthCalendar1_DateSelected);
        this.monthCalendar1.DateChanged += new
System.Windows.Forms.DateRangeEventHandler
(this.monthCalendar1_DateChanged);
```

```
        // Set up how the form should be displayed and add ↵
the controls to the form.
        this.ClientSize = new System.Drawing.Size(920, 566);
        this.Controls.AddRange(new System.Windows.Forms.Control[] ↵
{this.textBox1, this.monthCalendar1});
        this.Text = "Month Calendar Example";
    }

    private void monthCalendar1_DateSelected(object sender, ↵
System.Windows.Forms.DateRangeEventArgs e)
    {
        // Show the start and end dates in the text box.
        this.textBox1.Text = "Date Selected: Start = " +
            e.Start.ToShortDateString() + " : End = " + ↵
e.End.ToShortDateString();
    }

    private void monthCalendar1_DateChanged(object sender, ↵
System.Windows.Forms.DateRangeEventArgs e)
    {
        // Show the start and end dates in the text box.
        this.textBox1.Text = "Date Changed: Start =  " +
            e.Start.ToShortDateString() + " : End = " + ↵
e.End.ToShortDateString();
    }
}
```

[C++]

```
#using <mscorlib.dll>
#using <System.dll>
#using <System.Windows.Forms.dll>
#using <System.Drawing.dll>

using namespace System;
using namespace System::Drawing;
using namespace System::Windows::Forms;

public __gc class Form1 : public System::Windows::Forms::Form {
private:
   System::Windows::Forms::MonthCalendar*  monthCalendar1;
   System::Windows::Forms::TextBox*  textBox1;
public:
   Form1() {
      this->textBox1 = new System::Windows::Forms::TextBox();
      this->textBox1->BorderStyle = ↵
System::Windows::Forms::BorderStyle::FixedSingle;
      this->textBox1->Location =  System::Drawing::Point(48, 488);
      this->textBox1->Multiline = true;
      this->textBox1->ReadOnly = true;
      this->textBox1->Size =  System::Drawing::Size(824, 32);

      // Create the calendar.
      this->monthCalendar1 = new ↵
System::Windows::Forms::MonthCalendar();

      // Set the calendar location.
      this->monthCalendar1->Location =  System::Drawing::Point(47, 16);

      // Change the color.
      this->monthCalendar1->BackColor = ↵
System::Drawing::SystemColors::Info;
      this->monthCalendar1->ForeColor = ↵
System::Drawing::Color::FromArgb(((System::Byte)(192)), ↵
((System::Byte)(0)), ((System::Byte)(192)));
      this->monthCalendar1->TitleBackColor = ↵
System::Drawing::Color::Purple;
      this->monthCalendar1->TitleForeColor = ↵
System::Drawing::Color::Yellow;
      this->monthCalendar1->TrailingForeColor = ↵
System::Drawing::Color::FromArgb(((System::Byte)(192)), ↵
((System::Byte)(192)), ((System::Byte)(0)));

      // Add dates to the AnnuallyBoldedDates array.

      System::DateTime temp1 [] = {System::DateTime(2002, ↵
4, 20, 0, 0, 0, 0),
         System::DateTime(2002, 4, 28, 0, 0, 0, 0),
         System::DateTime(2002, 5, 5, 0, 0, 0, 0),
         System::DateTime(2002, 7, 4, 0, 0, 0, 0),
         System::DateTime(2002, 12, 15, 0, 0, 0, 0),
         System::DateTime(2002, 12, 18, 0, 0, 0, 0)};

      this->monthCalendar1->AnnuallyBoldedDates = temp1;

      // Add dates to BoldedDates array.

      System::DateTime temp2 [] = {System::DateTime(2002, ↵
9, 26, 0, 0, 0, 0)};

      this->monthCalendar1->BoldedDates = temp2;

      // Add dates to MonthlyBoldedDates array.

      System::DateTime temp5 [] = {System::DateTime(2002, ↵
1, 15, 0, 0, 0, 0),
         System::DateTime(2002, 1, 30, 0, 0, 0, 0)};

      this->monthCalendar1->MonthlyBoldedDates = temp5;

      // Configure the calendar to display 3 rows by 4 ↵
columns of months.
      this->monthCalendar1->CalendarDimensions = ↵
System::Drawing::Size(4, 3);

      // Set week to begin on Monday.
      this->monthCalendar1->FirstDayOfWeek = ↵
System::Windows::Forms::Day::Monday;

      // Set the maximum visible date on the calendar to 12/31/2010.
      this->monthCalendar1->MaxDate = System::DateTime ↵
(2010, 12, 31, 0, 0, 0, 0);

      // Set the minimum visible date on calendar to 12/31/2010.
      this->monthCalendar1->MinDate = System::DateTime ↵
(1999, 1, 1, 0, 0, 0, 0);

      // Only allow 21 days to be selected at the same time.
      this->monthCalendar1->MaxSelectionCount = 21;

      // Set the calendar to move one month at a time when ↵
navigating using the arrows.
      this->monthCalendar1->ScrollChange = 1;

      // Do not show the S"Today" banner.
      this->monthCalendar1->ShowToday = false;

      // Do not circle today's date.
      this->monthCalendar1->ShowTodayCircle = false;

      // Show the week numbers to the left of each week.
      this->monthCalendar1->ShowWeekNumbers = true;

      // Add event handlers for the DateSelected and DateChanged events ↵
      this->monthCalendar1->DateSelected += new ↵
System::Windows::Forms::DateRangeEventHandler(this, ↵
monthCalendar1_DateSelected);
      this->monthCalendar1->DateChanged += new ↵
System::Windows::Forms::DateRangeEventHandler(this, ↵
monthCalendar1_DateChanged);

      // Set up how the form should be displayed and ↵
add the controls to the form.
      this->ClientSize =  System::Drawing::Size(920, 566);

      System::Windows::Forms::Control* temp0 [] = ↵
{this->textBox1, this->monthCalendar1};

      this->Controls->AddRange(temp0);
      this->Text = S"Month Calendar Example";
   }

private:
   void monthCalendar1_DateSelected(Object* sender, ↵
```

```
System::Windows::Forms::DateRangeEventArgs* e) {
      // Show the start and end dates in the text box.
      this->textBox1->Text = String::Format( S"Date ↵
Selected: Start = {0} : End = {1}", e-> ↵
Start.ToShortDateString(), e->End.ToShortDateString() );
   }

private:
   void monthCalendar1_DateChanged(Object* sender, ↵
System::Windows::Forms::DateRangeEventArgs* e) {
      // Show the start and end dates in the text box.
      this->textBox1->Text = String::Format( S"Date ↵
Changed: Start = {0} : End = {1}", e->Start.ToShortDateString(), ↵
 e->End.ToShortDateString() );
   }
};

[STAThread]
int main() {
   Application::Run(new Form1());
}
```

Requirements

Namespace: System.Windows.Forms

Platforms: Windows 98, Windows NT 4.0, Windows Millennium Edition, Windows 2000, Windows XP Home Edition, Windows XP Professional, Windows Server 2003 family

Assembly: System.Windows.Forms (in System.Windows.Forms.dll)

DateRangeEventArgs Constructor

Initializes a new instance of the **DateRangeEventArgs** class.

```
[Visual Basic]
Public Sub New( _
   ByVal start As DateTime, _
   ByVal end As DateTime _
)
[C#]
public DateRangeEventArgs(
   DateTime start,
   DateTime end
);
[C++]
public: DateRangeEventArgs(
   DateTime start,
   DateTime end
);
[JScript]
public function DateRangeEventArgs(
   start : DateTime,
   end : DateTime
);
```

Parameters

start

The first date/time value in the range that the user has selected.

end

The last date/time value in the range that the user has selected.

Remarks

The **Start** and **End** property values are set by the *start* and *end* parameter values of this constructor.

Requirements

Platforms: Windows 98, Windows NT 4.0, Windows Millennium Edition, Windows 2000, Windows XP Home Edition, Windows XP Professional, Windows Server 2003 family

DateRangeEventArgs.End Property

Gets the last date/time value in the range that the user has selected.

```
[Visual Basic]
Public ReadOnly Property End As DateTime
[C#]
public DateTime End {get;}
[C++]
public: __property DateTime get_End();
[JScript]
public function get End() : DateTime;
```

Property Value

A **DateTime** that represents the last date in the date range that the user has selected.

Example

See related example in the **System.Windows.Forms.DateRangeEventArgs** class topic.

Requirements

Platforms: Windows 98, Windows NT 4.0, Windows Millennium Edition, Windows 2000, Windows XP Home Edition, Windows XP Professional, Windows Server 2003 family

DateRangeEventArgs.Start Property

Gets the first date/time value in the range that the user has selected.

```
[Visual Basic]
Public ReadOnly Property Start As DateTime
[C#]
public DateTime Start {get;}
[C++]
public: __property DateTime get_Start();
[JScript]
public function get Start() : DateTime;
```

Property Value

A **DateTime** that represents the first date in the date range that the user has selected.

Example

See related example in the **System.Windows.Forms.DateRangeEventArgs** class topic.

Requirements

Platforms: Windows 98, Windows NT 4.0, Windows Millennium Edition, Windows 2000, Windows XP Home Edition, Windows XP Professional, Windows Server 2003 family

DateRangeEventHandler Delegate

Represents the method that will handle the **DateChanged** or **DateSelected** event of a **MonthCalendar**.

[Visual Basic]
```
<Serializable>
Public Delegate Sub DateRangeEventHandler( _
   ByVal sender As Object, _
   ByVal e As DateRangeEventArgs _
)
```
[C#]
```
[Serializable]
public delegate void DateRangeEventHandler(
   object sender,
   DateRangeEventArgs e
);
```
[C++]
```
[Serializable]
public __gc __delegate void DateRangeEventHandler(
   Object* sender,
   DateRangeEventArgs* e
);
```

[JScript] In JScript, you can use the delegates in the .NET Framework, but you cannot define your own.

Parameters [Visual Basic, C#, C++]

The declaration of your event handler must have the same parameters as the **DateRangeEventHandler** delegate declaration.

sender
: The source of the event.

e
: A **DateRangeEventArgs** that contains the event data.

Remarks

When you create a **DateRangeEventArgs** delegate, you identify the method that will handle the event. To associate the event with your event handler, add an instance of the delegate to the event. The event handler is called whenever the event occurs, unless you remove the delegate. For more information about event handler delegates, see **Events and Delegates**.

Example

[Visual Basic, C#, C++] The following example displays a form containing a **MonthCalendar** control that displays one calendar year. The example demonstrates setting properties like **BackColor**, **ForeColor**, **TitleBackColor**, **TitleForeColor**, **CalendarDimensions**, and **TrailingForeColor** to customize the look of the calendar control. Other properties like **AnnuallyBoldedDates**, **BoldedDates**, and **MonthlyBoldedDates** are set to customize which dates are bolded. The example also sets properties to change the calendar format, including **FirstDayOfWeek**, **MaxDate**, **MinDate**, and **MaxSelectionCount**. The **DateSelected** and **DateChanged** events are also handled and their status displayed on the form.

[Visual Basic]
```
Imports System
Imports System.Drawing
Imports System.Windows.Forms

Public NotInheritable Class Form1
    Inherits System.Windows.Forms.Form

    Friend WithEvents MonthCalendar1 As                              ↵
System.Windows.Forms.MonthCalendar
    Friend WithEvents TextBox1 As System.Windows.Forms.TextBox

    <System.STAThread()> _
    Public Shared Sub Main()
        System.Windows.Forms.Application.Run(New Form1)
    End Sub 'Main

    Public Sub New()
        MyBase.New()

        Me.TextBox1 = New System.Windows.Forms.TextBox
        Me.TextBox1.BorderStyle =                                    ↵
System.Windows.Forms.BorderStyle.FixedSingle
        Me.TextBox1.Location = New System.Drawing.Point(48, 488)
        Me.TextBox1.Multiline = True
        Me.TextBox1.ReadOnly = True
        Me.TextBox1.Size = New System.Drawing.Size(824, 32)

        ' Create the calendar.
        Me.MonthCalendar1 = New System.Windows.Forms.MonthCalendar

        ' Set the calendar location.
        Me.MonthCalendar1.Location = New System.Drawing.Point(47, 16)

        ' Change the color.
        Me.MonthCalendar1.BackColor = System.Drawing.SystemColors.Info
        Me.MonthCalendar1.ForeColor = System.Drawing.Color.FromArgb( _
                        CType(192, System.Byte), CType               ↵
(0, System.Byte), CType(192, System.Byte))
        Me.MonthCalendar1.TitleBackColor = System.Drawing.Color.Purple
        Me.MonthCalendar1.TitleForeColor = System.Drawing.Color.Yellow
        Me.MonthCalendar1.TrailingForeColor =                        ↵
System.Drawing.Color.FromArgb( _
                        CType(192, System.Byte),                     ↵
CType(192, System.Byte), CType(0, System.Byte))

        ' Add dates to the AnnuallyBoldedDates array.
        Me.MonthCalendar1.AnnuallyBoldedDates = New System.DateTime() _
                {New System.DateTime(2002, 4, 20, 0, 0, 0, 0), _
                 New System.DateTime(2002, 4, 28, 0, 0, 0, 0), _
                 New System.DateTime(2002, 5, 5, 0, 0, 0, 0), _
                 New System.DateTime(2002, 7, 4, 0, 0, 0, 0), _
                 New System.DateTime(2002, 12, 15, 0, 0, 0, 0), _
                 New System.DateTime(2002, 12, 18, 0, 0, 0, 0)}

        ' Add dates to BoldedDates array.
        Me.MonthCalendar1.BoldedDates = New System.DateTime()        ↵
{New System.DateTime(2002, 9, 26, 0, 0, 0, 0)}

        ' Add dates to MonthlyBoldedDates array.
        Me.MonthCalendar1.MonthlyBoldedDates = New System.DateTime() _
                {New System.DateTime(2002, 1, 15, 0, 0, 0, 0), _
                 New System.DateTime(2002, 1, 30, 0, 0, 0, 0)}

        ' Configure the calendar to display 3 rows by 4              ↵
columns of months.
        Me.MonthCalendar1.CalendarDimensions = New                   ↵
System.Drawing.Size(4, 3)

        ' Set the week to begin on Monday.
        Me.MonthCalendar1.FirstDayOfWeek =                           ↵
System.Windows.Forms.Day.Monday
```

```
        ' Sets the maximum visible date on the calendar to 12/31/2010.
        Me.MonthCalendar1.MaxDate = New System.DateTime(2010, ↵
 12, 31, 0, 0, 0, 0)

        ' Set the minimum visible date on the calendar to 12/31/2010.
        Me.MonthCalendar1.MinDate = New System.DateTime(1999, ↵
 1, 1, 0, 0, 0, 0)

        ' Only allow 21 days to be selected at the same time.
        Me.MonthCalendar1.MaxSelectionCount = 21

        ' Set the calendar to move one month at a time when ↵
navigating using the arrows.
        Me.MonthCalendar1.ScrollChange = 1

        ' Do not show the "Today" banner.
        Me.MonthCalendar1.ShowToday = False

        ' Do not circle today's date.
        Me.MonthCalendar1.ShowTodayCircle = False

        ' Show the week numbers to the left of each week.
        Me.MonthCalendar1.ShowWeekNumbers = True

        ' Set up how the form should be displayed and add the ↵
 controls to the form.
        Me.ClientSize = New System.Drawing.Size(920, 566)
        Me.Controls.AddRange(New System.Windows.Forms.Control() ↵
{Me.TextBox1, Me.MonthCalendar1})
        Me.Text = "Month Calendar Example"

    End Sub

    Private Sub monthCalendar1_DateSelected(ByVal sender As Object, _
                    ByVal e As ↵
System.Windows.Forms.DateRangeEventArgs) Handles ↵
MonthCalendar1.DateSelected

        ' Show the start and end dates in the text box.
        Me.TextBox1.Text = "Date Selected: Start = " + _
                e.Start.ToShortDateString() + " : End = " + ↵
e.End.ToShortDateString()
    End Sub

    Private Sub monthCalendar1_DateChanged(ByVal sender As Object, _
                    ByVal e As ↵
System.Windows.Forms.DateRangeEventArgs) Handles ↵
MonthCalendar1.DateChanged

        ' Show the start and end dates in the text box.
        Me.TextBox1.Text = "Date Changed: Start = " + _
                e.Start.ToShortDateString() + " : End = " + ↵
e.End.ToShortDateString()
    End Sub
End Class
```

[C#]

```
using System;
using System.Drawing;
using System.Windows.Forms;

public class Form1 : System.Windows.Forms.Form
{
    private System.Windows.Forms.MonthCalendar monthCalendar1;
    private System.Windows.Forms.TextBox textBox1;

    [STAThread]
    static void Main()
    {
        Application.Run(new Form1());
    }

    public Form1()
    {
        this.textBox1 = new System.Windows.Forms.TextBox();
        this.textBox1.BorderStyle = ↵
System.Windows.Forms.BorderStyle.FixedSingle;
        this.textBox1.Location = new System.Drawing.Point(48, 488);
        this.textBox1.Multiline = true;
        this.textBox1.ReadOnly = true;
        this.textBox1.Size = new System.Drawing.Size(824, 32);

        // Create the calendar.
        this.monthCalendar1 = new System.Windows.Forms.MonthCalendar();

        // Set the calendar location.
        this.monthCalendar1.Location = new ↵
System.Drawing.Point(47, 16);

        // Change the color.
        this.monthCalendar1.BackColor = ↵
System.Drawing.SystemColors.Info;
        this.monthCalendar1.ForeColor = System.Drawing.Color.FromArgb(
                                 ((System.Byte)(192)), ↵
 ((System.Byte)(0)), ((System.Byte)(192)));
        this.monthCalendar1.TitleBackColor = ↵
System.Drawing.Color.Purple;
        this.monthCalendar1.TitleForeColor = ↵
System.Drawing.Color.Yellow;
        this.monthCalendar1.TrailingForeColor = ↵
System.Drawing.Color.FromArgb(
                                 ((System.Byte)(192)), ↵
 ((System.Byte)(192)), ((System.Byte)(0)));

        // Add dates to the AnnuallyBoldedDates array.
        this.monthCalendar1.AnnuallyBoldedDates =
           new System.DateTime[] { new System.DateTime(2002, ↵
 4, 20, 0, 0, 0, 0),
                                   new System.DateTime(2002, ↵
 4, 28, 0, 0, 0, 0),
                                   new System.DateTime(2002, ↵
 5, 5, 0, 0, 0, 0),
                                   new System.DateTime(2002, ↵
 7, 4, 0, 0, 0, 0),
                                   new System.DateTime(2002, ↵
12, 15, 0, 0, 0, 0),
                                   new System.DateTime(2002, ↵
12, 18, 0, 0, 0, 0)};

        // Add dates to BoldedDates array.
        this.monthCalendar1.BoldedDates = new System.DateTime[] ↵
 {new System.DateTime(2002, 9, 26, 0, 0, 0, 0)};

        // Add dates to MonthlyBoldedDates array.
        this.monthCalendar1.MonthlyBoldedDates =
           new System.DateTime[] {new System.DateTime(2002, 1, ↵
 15, 0, 0, 0, 0),
                                 new System.DateTime(2002, 1, ↵
30, 0, 0, 0, 0)};

        // Configure the calendar to display 3 rows by 4 columns ↵
 of months.
        this.monthCalendar1.CalendarDimensions = new ↵
System.Drawing.Size(4, 3);

        // Set week to begin on Monday.
        this.monthCalendar1.FirstDayOfWeek = ↵
System.Windows.Forms.Day.Monday;

        // Set the maximum visible date on the calendar to 12/31/2010.
        this.monthCalendar1.MaxDate = new System.DateTime(2010, ↵
 12, 31, 0, 0, 0, 0);

        // Set the minimum visible date on calendar to 12/31/2010.
        this.monthCalendar1.MinDate = new System.DateTime(1999, ↵
 1, 1, 0, 0, 0, 0);

        // Only allow 21 days to be selected at the same time.
        this.monthCalendar1.MaxSelectionCount = 21;
```

```
        // Set the calendar to move one month at a time when          ↵
navigating using the arrows.
        this.monthCalendar1.ScrollChange = 1;

        // Do not show the "Today" banner.
        this.monthCalendar1.ShowToday = false;

        // Do not circle today's date.
        this.monthCalendar1.ShowTodayCircle = false;

        // Show the week numbers to the left of each week.
        this.monthCalendar1.ShowWeekNumbers = true;

        // Add event handlers for the DateSelected and                ↵
DateChanged events
        this.monthCalendar1.DateSelected += new                       ↵
System.Windows.Forms.DateRangeEventHandler                            ↵
 (this.monthCalendar1_DateSelected);
        this.monthCalendar1.DateChanged += new                        ↵
System.Windows.Forms.DateRangeEventHandler                            ↵
 (this.monthCalendar1_DateChanged);

        // Set up how the form should be displayed and add the        ↵
controls to the form.
        this.ClientSize = new System.Drawing.Size(920, 566);
        this.Controls.AddRange(new System.Windows.Forms.Control[]     ↵
{this.textBox1, this.monthCalendar1});
        this.Text = "Month Calendar Example";
    }

    private void monthCalendar1_DateSelected(object sender,           ↵
System.Windows.Forms.DateRangeEventArgs e)
    {
        // Show the start and end dates in the text box.
        this.textBox1.Text = "Date Selected: Start = " +
            e.Start.ToShortDateString() + " : End = " +               ↵
e.End.ToShortDateString();
    }

    private void monthCalendar1_DateChanged(object sender,            ↵
System.Windows.Forms.DateRangeEventArgs e)
    {
        // Show the start and end dates in the text box.
        this.textBox1.Text = "Date Changed: Start =  " +
            e.Start.ToShortDateString() + " : End = " +               ↵
e.End.ToShortDateString();
    }
}
```

[C++]

```
#using <mscorlib.dll>
#using <System.dll>
#using <System.Windows.Forms.dll>
#using <System.Drawing.dll>

using namespace System;
using namespace System::Drawing;
using namespace System::Windows::Forms;

public __gc class Form1 : public System::Windows::Forms::Form {
private:
   System::Windows::Forms::MonthCalendar*  monthCalendar1;
   System::Windows::Forms::TextBox*  textBox1;
public:
   Form1() {
      this->textBox1 = new System::Windows::Forms::TextBox();
      this->textBox1->BorderStyle =                                   ↵
System::Windows::Forms::BorderStyle::FixedSingle;
      this->textBox1->Location =  System::Drawing::Point(48, 488);
      this->textBox1->Multiline = true;
      this->textBox1->ReadOnly = true;
      this->textBox1->Size =  System::Drawing::Size(824, 32);

      // Create the calendar.
      this->monthCalendar1 = new                                      ↵
System::Windows::Forms::MonthCalendar();

      // Set the calendar location.
      this->monthCalendar1->Location =  System::Drawing::Point(47, 16);

      // Change the color.
      this->monthCalendar1->BackColor =                               ↵
System::Drawing::SystemColors::Info;
      this->monthCalendar1->ForeColor =                               ↵
System::Drawing::Color::FromArgb(((System::Byte)(192)),               ↵
 ((System::Byte)(0)), ((System::Byte)(192)));
      this->monthCalendar1->TitleBackColor =                          ↵
System::Drawing::Color::Purple;
      this->monthCalendar1->TitleForeColor =                          ↵
System::Drawing::Color::Yellow;
      this->monthCalendar1->TrailingForeColor =                       ↵
System::Drawing::Color::FromArgb(((System::Byte)(192)),               ↵
 ((System::Byte)(192)), ((System::Byte)(0)));

      // Add dates to the AnnuallyBoldedDates array.

      System::DateTime temp1 [] = {System::DateTime(2002,             ↵
4, 20, 0, 0, 0, 0),
          System::DateTime(2002, 4, 28, 0, 0, 0, 0),
          System::DateTime(2002, 5, 5, 0, 0, 0, 0),
          System::DateTime(2002, 7, 4, 0, 0, 0, 0),
          System::DateTime(2002, 12, 15, 0, 0, 0, 0),
          System::DateTime(2002, 12, 18, 0, 0, 0, 0)};

      this->monthCalendar1->AnnuallyBoldedDates = temp1;

      // Add dates to BoldedDates array.

      System::DateTime temp2 [] = {System::DateTime(2002, 9,          ↵
26, 0, 0, 0, 0)};

      this->monthCalendar1->BoldedDates = temp2;

      // Add dates to MonthlyBoldedDates array.

      System::DateTime temp5 [] = {System::DateTime(2002, 1,          ↵
15, 0, 0, 0, 0),
          System::DateTime(2002, 1, 30, 0, 0, 0, 0)};

      this->monthCalendar1->MonthlyBoldedDates = temp5;

      // Configure the calendar to display 3 rows by 4                ↵
columns of months.
      this->monthCalendar1->CalendarDimensions =                      ↵
System::Drawing::Size(4, 3);

      // Set week to begin on Monday.
      this->monthCalendar1->FirstDayOfWeek =                          ↵
System::Windows::Forms::Day::Monday;

      // Set the maximum visible date on the calendar to 12/31/2010.
      this->monthCalendar1->MaxDate = System::DateTime                ↵
 (2010, 12, 31, 0, 0, 0, 0);

      // Set the minimum visible date on calendar to 12/31/2010.
      this->monthCalendar1->MinDate = System::DateTime(1999,          ↵
 1, 1, 0, 0, 0, 0);

      // Only allow 21 days to be selected at the same time.
      this->monthCalendar1->MaxSelectionCount = 21;

      // Set the calendar to move one month at a time when            ↵
navigating using the arrows.
      this->monthCalendar1->ScrollChange = 1;

      // Do not show the S"Today" banner.
      this->monthCalendar1->ShowToday = false;
```

```
      // Do not circle today's date.
      this->monthCalendar1->ShowTodayCircle = false;

      // Show the week numbers to the left of each week.
      this->monthCalendar1->ShowWeekNumbers = true;

      // Add event handlers for the DateSelected and DateChanged events
      this->monthCalendar1->DateSelected += new                    ↵
System::Windows::Forms::DateRangeEventHandler(this,                ↵
monthCalendar1_DateSelected);
      this->monthCalendar1->DateChanged += new                     ↵
System::Windows::Forms::DateRangeEventHandler(this,                ↵
monthCalendar1_DateChanged);

      // Set up how the form should be displayed and add           ↵
the controls to the form.
      this->ClientSize =  System::Drawing::Size(920, 566);

      System::Windows::Forms::Control* temp0 [] = {this->          ↵
textBox1, this->monthCalendar1};

      this->Controls->AddRange(temp0);
      this->Text = S"Month Calendar Example";
   }

private:
   void monthCalendar1_DateSelected(Object* sender,                ↵
System::Windows::Forms::DateRangeEventArgs* e) {
      // Show the start and end dates in the text box.
      this->textBox1->Text = String::Format( S"Date Selected:      ↵
Start = {0} : End = {1}", e->Start.ToShortDateString(), e-         ↵
>End.ToShortDateString() );
   }

private:
   void monthCalendar1_DateChanged(Object* sender,                 ↵
System::Windows::Forms::DateRangeEventArgs* e) {
      // Show the start and end dates in the text box.
      this->textBox1->Text = String::Format( S"Date Changed:       ↵
Start = {0} : End = {1}", e->Start.ToShortDateString(), e-         ↵
>End.ToShortDateString() );
   }
};

[STAThread]
int main() {
   Application::Run(new Form1());
}
```

Requirements

Namespace: System.Windows.Forms

Platforms: Windows 98, Windows NT 4.0, Windows Millennium Edition, Windows 2000, Windows XP Home Edition, Windows XP Professional, Windows Server 2003 family

Assembly: System.Windows.Forms (in System.Windows.Forms.dll)

DateTimePicker Class

Represents a Windows date/time picker control.

System.Object
  System.MarshalByRefObject
    System.ComponentModel.Component
      System.Windows.Forms.Control
        System.Windows.Forms.DateTimePicker

[Visual Basic]
```
Public Class DateTimePicker
   Inherits Control
```
[C#]
```
public class DateTimePicker : Control
```
[C++]
```
public __gc class DateTimePicker : public Control
```
[JScript]
```
public class DateTimePicker extends Control
```

Thread Safety

Any public static (**Shared** in Visual Basic) members of this type are safe for multithreaded operations. Any instance members are not guaranteed to be thread safe.

Remarks

The **DateTimePicker** control is used to allow the user to select a date and time, and to display that date/time in the specified format. You can limit the dates and times that can be selected by setting the **MinDate** and **MaxDate** properties.

You can change the look of the calendar portion of the control by setting the **CalendarForeColor**, **CalendarFont**, **CalendarTitleBackColor**, **CalendarTitleForeColor**, **CalendarTrailingForeColor**, and **CalendarMonthBackground** properties.

The **Format** property sets the **DateTimePickerFormat** of the control. The default date **Format** is **DateTimePickerFormat.Long**. If the **Format** property is set to **DateTimePickerFormat.Custom**, you can create your own format style by setting the **CustomFormat** property and building a custom format string. The custom format string can be a combination of custom field characters and other literal characters. For example, you can display the date as "June 01, 2001 - Friday" by setting the **CustomFormat** property to "MMMM dd, yyyy - dddd". For more information, see **Date and Time Format Strings**.

To use an up-down style control to adjust the date/time value, set the **ShowUpDown** property to **true**. The calendar control will not drop down when the control is selected. The date/time can be adjusted by selecting each element individually and using the up and down buttons to change the value.

You might consider using a **DateTimePicker** control instead of a **MonthCalendar** if you have a need for custom date formatting and limiting a selection to just one date. Using the **DateTimePicker** will limit the need for much data validation of date/time values.

> **Note** The **DateTimePicker** control only supports Gregorian calendars.

Example

[Visual Basic, C#] The following example creates an new instance of a **DateTimePicker** control and initializes it. The control's **CustomFormat** property is set. Also, the **ShowCheckBox** property is set so that the control displays a **CheckBox**, and the **ShowUpDown** property is set so that the control is displayed as an up-down control.

[Visual Basic]
```
Public Sub CreateMyDateTimePicker()
    ' Create a new DateTimePicker control and initialize it.
    Dim dateTimePicker1 As New DateTimePicker()

    ' Set the MinDate and MaxDate.
    dateTimePicker1.MinDate = New DateTime(1985, 6, 20)
    dateTimePicker1.MaxDate = DateTime.Today

    ' Set the CustomFormat string.
    dateTimePicker1.CustomFormat = "MMMM dd, yyyy - dddd"
    dateTimePicker1.Format = DateTimePickerFormat.Custom

    ' Show the CheckBox and display the control as an up-down control.
    dateTimePicker1.ShowCheckBox = True
    dateTimePicker1.ShowUpDown = True
End Sub 'CreateMyDateTimePicker
```

[C#]
```
public void CreateMyDateTimePicker()
{
   // Create a new DateTimePicker control and initialize it.
   DateTimePicker dateTimePicker1 = new DateTimePicker();

   // Set the MinDate and MaxDate.
   dateTimePicker1.MinDate = new DateTime(1985, 6, 20);
   dateTimePicker1.MaxDate = DateTime.Today;

   // Set the CustomFormat string.
   dateTimePicker1.CustomFormat = "MMMM dd, yyyy - dddd";
   dateTimePicker1.Format = DateTimePickerFormat.Custom;

   // Show the CheckBox and display the control as an up-down control.
   dateTimePicker1.ShowCheckBox = true;
   dateTimePicker1.ShowUpDown = true;
}
```

Requirements

Namespace: System.Windows.Forms

Platforms: Windows 98, Windows NT 4.0, Windows Millennium Edition, Windows 2000, Windows XP Home Edition, Windows XP Professional, Windows Server 2003 family

Assembly: System.Windows.Forms (in System.Windows.Forms.dll)

DateTimePicker Constructor

Initializes a new instance of the **DateTimePicker** class.

[Visual Basic]
```
Public Sub New()
```
[C#]
```
public DateTimePicker();
```
[C++]
```
public: DateTimePicker();
```
[JScript]
```
public function DateTimePicker();
```

Example

[Visual Basic, C#] The following example creates an new instance of a **DateTimePicker** control and initializes it. The control's **CustomFormat** property is set. Also, the **ShowCheckBox** property is set so that the control displays a **CheckBox**, and the **ShowUpDown** property is set so that the control is displayed as an up-down control.

[Visual Basic]
```
Public Sub CreateMyDateTimePicker()
    ' Create a new DateTimePicker control and initialize it.
    Dim dateTimePicker1 As New DateTimePicker()

    ' Set the MinDate and MaxDate.
    dateTimePicker1.MinDate = New DateTime(1985, 6, 20)
    dateTimePicker1.MaxDate = DateTime.Today

    ' Set the CustomFormat string.
    dateTimePicker1.CustomFormat = "MMMM dd, yyyy - dddd"
    dateTimePicker1.Format = DateTimePickerFormat.Custom

    ' Show the CheckBox and display the control as an up-down control.
    dateTimePicker1.ShowCheckBox = True
    dateTimePicker1.ShowUpDown = True
End Sub 'CreateMyDateTimePicker
```

[C#]
```
public void CreateMyDateTimePicker()
{
   // Create a new DateTimePicker control and initialize it.
   DateTimePicker dateTimePicker1 = new DateTimePicker();

   // Set the MinDate and MaxDate.
   dateTimePicker1.MinDate = new DateTime(1985, 6, 20);
   dateTimePicker1.MaxDate = DateTime.Today;

   // Set the CustomFormat string.
   dateTimePicker1.CustomFormat = "MMMM dd, yyyy - dddd";
   dateTimePicker1.Format = DateTimePickerFormat.Custom;

   // Show the CheckBox and display the control as an up-down control.
   dateTimePicker1.ShowCheckBox = true;
   dateTimePicker1.ShowUpDown = true;
}
```

Requirements

Platforms: Windows 98, Windows NT 4.0, Windows Millennium Edition, Windows 2000, Windows XP Home Edition, Windows XP Professional, Windows Server 2003 family

DateTimePicker.DefaultMonthBackColor Field

Specifies the default month background color of the date/time picker control. This field is read-only.

[Visual Basic]
```
Protected Shared ReadOnly DefaultMonthBackColor As Color
```
[C#]
```
protected static readonly Color DefaultMonthBackColor;
```
[C++]
```
protected: static Color DefaultMonthBackColor;
```
[JScript]
```
protected static var DefaultMonthBackColor : Color;
```

Requirements

Platforms: Windows 98, Windows NT 4.0, Windows Millennium Edition, Windows 2000, Windows XP Home Edition, Windows XP Professional, Windows Server 2003 family

DateTimePicker.DefaultTitleBackColor Field

Specifies the default title back color of the date/time picker control. This field is read-only.

[Visual Basic]
```
Protected Shared ReadOnly DefaultTitleBackColor As Color
```
[C#]
```
protected static readonly Color DefaultTitleBackColor;
```
[C++]
```
protected: static Color DefaultTitleBackColor;
```
[JScript]
```
protected static var DefaultTitleBackColor : Color;
```

Requirements

Platforms: Windows 98, Windows NT 4.0, Windows Millennium Edition, Windows 2000, Windows XP Home Edition, Windows XP Professional, Windows Server 2003 family

DateTimePicker.DefaultTitleForeColor Field

Specifies the default title foreground color of the date/time picker control. This field is read-only.

[Visual Basic]
```
Protected Shared ReadOnly DefaultTitleForeColor As Color
```
[C#]
```
protected static readonly Color DefaultTitleForeColor;
```
[C++]
```
protected: static Color DefaultTitleForeColor;
```
[JScript]
```
protected static var DefaultTitleForeColor : Color;
```

Requirements

Platforms: Windows 98, Windows NT 4.0, Windows Millennium Edition, Windows 2000, Windows XP Home Edition, Windows XP Professional, Windows Server 2003 family

DateTimePicker.DefaultTrailingForeColor Field

Specifies the default trailing foreground color of the date/time picker control. This field is read-only.

[Visual Basic]
```
Protected Shared ReadOnly DefaultTrailingForeColor As Color
```
[C#]
```
protected static readonly Color DefaultTrailingForeColor;
```
[C++]
```
protected: static Color DefaultTrailingForeColor;
```
[JScript]
```
protected static var DefaultTrailingForeColor : Color;
```

Requirements

Platforms: Windows 98, Windows NT 4.0, Windows Millennium Edition, Windows 2000, Windows XP Home Edition, Windows XP Professional, Windows Server 2003 family

DateTimePicker.MaxDateTime Field

Specifies the maximum date value of the date/time picker control. This field is read-only.

```
[Visual Basic]
Public Shared ReadOnly MaxDateTime As DateTime
[C#]
public static readonly DateTime MaxDateTime;
[C++]
public: static DateTime MaxDateTime;
[JScript]
public static var MaxDateTime : DateTime;
```

Remarks

The maximum date is set to 12/31/9998 23:59:59.

Requirements

Platforms: Windows 98, Windows NT 4.0, Windows Millennium Edition, Windows 2000, Windows XP Home Edition, Windows XP Professional, Windows Server 2003 family

DateTimePicker.MinDateTime Field

Specifies the minimum date value of the date/time picker control. This field is read-only.

```
[Visual Basic]
Public Shared ReadOnly MinDateTime As DateTime
[C#]
public static readonly DateTime MinDateTime;
[C++]
public: static DateTime MinDateTime;
[JScript]
public static var MinDateTime : DateTime;
```

Remarks

The minimum date is set to 1/1/1753 00:00:00.

Requirements

Platforms: Windows 98, Windows NT 4.0, Windows Millennium Edition, Windows 2000, Windows XP Home Edition, Windows XP Professional, Windows Server 2003 family

DateTimePicker.BackColor Property

This member overrides **Control.BackColor**.

```
[Visual Basic]
Overrides Public Property BackColor As Color
[C#]
public override Color BackColor {get; set;}
[C++]
public: __property Color get_BackColor();
public: __property void set_BackColor(Color);
[JScript]
public override function get BackColor() : Color;
public override function set BackColor(Color);
```

Requirements

Platforms: Windows 98, Windows NT 4.0, Windows Millennium Edition, Windows 2000, Windows XP Home Edition, Windows XP Professional, Windows Server 2003 family

DateTimePicker.BackgroundImage Property

This member overrides **Control.BackgroundImage**.

```
[Visual Basic]
Overrides Public Property BackgroundImage As Image
[C#]
public override Image BackgroundImage {get; set;}
[C++]
public: __property Image* get_BackgroundImage();
public: __property void set_BackgroundImage(Image*);
[JScript]
public override function get BackgroundImage() : Image;
public override function set BackgroundImage(Image);
```

Requirements

Platforms: Windows 98, Windows NT 4.0, Windows Millennium Edition, Windows 2000, Windows XP Home Edition, Windows XP Professional, Windows Server 2003 family

DateTimePicker.CalendarFont Property

Gets or sets the font style applied to the calendar.

```
[Visual Basic]
Public Property CalendarFont As Font
[C#]
public Font CalendarFont {get; set;}
[C++]
public: __property Font* get_CalendarFont();
public: __property void set_CalendarFont(Font*);
[JScript]
public function get CalendarFont() : Font;
public function set CalendarFont(Font);
```

Property Value

A **Font** that represents the font style applied to the calendar.

Example

[Visual Basic, C#, C++] The following example demonstrates how to initialize the **CalendarFont** property. This example creates a new **DateTimePicker** control, adds it to the **Controls** collection of a **Form**, and then initializes the **CalendarFont** property to a dynamically defined **Font**.

```
[Visual Basic]
Public Sub New()
   ' Create a new DateTimePicker.
   Dim dateTimePicker1 As New DateTimePicker()
   Controls.AddRange(New Control() {dateTimePicker1})
   dateTimePicker1.CalendarFont = New Font("Courier New", ↵
8.25F, FontStyle.Italic, GraphicsUnit.Point, CType(0, [Byte]))
End Sub
```

```
[C#]
public MyClass()
{
   // Create a new DateTimePicker.
   DateTimePicker dateTimePicker1 = new DateTimePicker();
   Controls.AddRange(new Control[] {dateTimePicker1});
   dateTimePicker1.CalendarFont = new Font("Courier New", ↵
 8.25F, FontStyle.Italic, GraphicsUnit.Point, ((Byte)(0)));
}
```

[C++]
```
public:
    MyClass() {
        // Create a new DateTimePicker.
        DateTimePicker* dateTimePicker1 = new DateTimePicker();
        Control* myClassControls[] = {dateTimePicker1};
        Controls->AddRange(myClassControls);
        dateTimePicker1->CalendarFont = new                    ↵
System::Drawing::Font(S"Courier New",
          8.25F, FontStyle::Italic, GraphicsUnit::Point,       ↵
 ((Byte)(0)));
    }
```

Requirements

Platforms: Windows 98, Windows NT 4.0, Windows Millennium Edition, Windows 2000, Windows XP Home Edition, Windows XP Professional, Windows Server 2003 family

DateTimePicker.CalendarForeColor Property

Gets or sets the foreground color of the calendar.

[Visual Basic]
```
Public Property CalendarForeColor As Color
```
[C#]
```
public Color CalendarForeColor {get; set;}
```
[C++]
```
public: __property Color get_CalendarForeColor();
public: __property void set_CalendarForeColor(Color);
```
[JScript]
```
public function get CalendarForeColor() : Color;
public function set CalendarForeColor(Color);
```

Property Value

A **Color** that represents the foreground color of the calendar.

Exceptions

Exception Type	Condition
ArgumentException	The value assigned is a null reference (**Nothing** in Visual Basic).

Remarks

When a **DateTimePicker** is created, this property is initially set equal to the **ForeColor** property value.

Example

[Visual Basic, C#, C++] The following example demonstrates how to initialize the **CalendarForeColor** property. This example creates a new **DateTimePicker**, adds it to the **Controls** collection, and then initializes its **CalendarForeColor** property to the **Aqua** constant.

[Visual Basic]
```
Public Sub New()
   Dim dateTimePicker1 As New DateTimePicker()
   Controls.AddRange(New Control() {dateTimePicker1})
   dateTimePicker1.CalendarForeColor = Color.Aqua
End Sub
```

[C#]
```
public MyClass()
{
   DateTimePicker dateTimePicker1 = new DateTimePicker();
   Controls.AddRange(new Control[] {dateTimePicker1});
   dateTimePicker1.CalendarForeColor = Color.Aqua;
}
```

[C++]
```
public:
    MyClass() {
        DateTimePicker* dateTimePicker1 = new DateTimePicker();
        Control* myClassControls[] = {dateTimePicker1};
        Controls->AddRange(myClassControls);
        dateTimePicker1->CalendarForeColor = Color::Aqua;
    }
```

Requirements

Platforms: Windows 98, Windows NT 4.0, Windows Millennium Edition, Windows 2000, Windows XP Home Edition, Windows XP Professional, Windows Server 2003 family

DateTimePicker.CalendarMonthBackground Property

Gets or sets the background color of the calendar month.

[Visual Basic]
```
Public Property CalendarMonthBackground As Color
```
[C#]
```
public Color CalendarMonthBackground {get; set;}
```
[C++]
```
public: __property Color get_CalendarMonthBackground();
public: __property void set_CalendarMonthBackground(Color);
```
[JScript]
```
public function get CalendarMonthBackground() : Color;
public function set CalendarMonthBackground(Color);
```

Property Value

A **Color** that represents the background color of the calendar month.

Exceptions

Exception Type	Condition
ArgumentException	The value assigned is a null reference (**Nothing** in Visual Basic).

Remarks

When a **DateTimePicker** is created, this property is initially set equal to the **DefaultMonthBackColor** field value.

Example

[Visual Basic, C#, C++] The following example demonstrates how to initialize the **CalendarMonthBackground** property. After creating a **DateTimePicker** and adding it to a **Form**, the example initializes the **CalendarMonthBackground** property to a **Color** constant.

[Visual Basic]
```
Public Sub New()
   Dim dateTimePicker1 As New DateTimePicker()
   Controls.AddRange(New Control() {dateTimePicker1})
   dateTimePicker1.CalendarMonthBackground = Color.Aqua
End Sub
```

[C#]
```
public MyClass()
{
   DateTimePicker dateTimePicker1 = new DateTimePicker();
   Controls.AddRange(new Control[] {dateTimePicker1});
   dateTimePicker1.CalendarMonthBackground = Color.Aqua;
}
```

[C++]
```
public:
    MyClass() {
        DateTimePicker* dateTimePicker1 = new DateTimePicker();
        Control* myClassControls[] = {dateTimePicker1};
        Controls->AddRange(myClassControls);
        dateTimePicker1->CalendarMonthBackground = Color::Aqua;
    }
```

Requirements

Platforms: Windows 98, Windows NT 4.0, Windows Millennium Edition, Windows 2000, Windows XP Home Edition, Windows XP Professional, Windows Server 2003 family

DateTimePicker.CalendarTitleBackColor Property

Gets or sets the background color of the calendar title.

[Visual Basic]
```
Public Property CalendarTitleBackColor As Color
```
[C#]
```
public Color CalendarTitleBackColor {get; set;}
```
[C++]
```
public: __property Color get_CalendarTitleBackColor();
public: __property void set_CalendarTitleBackColor(Color);
```
[JScript]
```
public function get CalendarTitleBackColor() : Color;
public function set CalendarTitleBackColor(Color);
```

Property Value

A **Color** that represents the background color of the calendar title.

Exceptions

Exception Type	Condition
ArgumentException	The value assigned is a null reference (**Nothing** in Visual Basic).

Remarks

When a **DateTimePicker** is created, this property is initially set equal to the **DefaultTitleBackColor** field value.

Requirements

Platforms: Windows 98, Windows NT 4.0, Windows Millennium Edition, Windows 2000, Windows XP Home Edition, Windows XP Professional, Windows Server 2003 family

DateTimePicker.CalendarTitleForeColor Property

Gets or sets the foreground color of the calendar title.

[Visual Basic]
```
Public Property CalendarTitleForeColor As Color
```
[C#]
```
public Color CalendarTitleForeColor {get; set;}
```
[C++]
```
public: __property Color get_CalendarTitleForeColor();
public: __property void set_CalendarTitleForeColor(Color);
```
[JScript]
```
public function get CalendarTitleForeColor() : Color;
public function set CalendarTitleForeColor(Color);
```

Property Value

A **Color** that represents the foreground color of the calendar title.

Exceptions

Exception Type	Condition
ArgumentException	The value assigned is a null reference (**Nothing** in Visual Basic).

Remarks

When a **DateTimePicker** is created, this property is initially set equal to the **DefaultTitleForeColor** field value.

Requirements

Platforms: Windows 98, Windows NT 4.0, Windows Millennium Edition, Windows 2000, Windows XP Home Edition, Windows XP Professional, Windows Server 2003 family

DateTimePicker.CalendarTrailingForeColor Property

Gets or sets the foreground color of the calendar trailing dates.

[Visual Basic]
```
Public Property CalendarTrailingForeColor As Color
```
[C#]
```
public Color CalendarTrailingForeColor {get; set;}
```
[C++]
```
public: __property Color get_CalendarTrailingForeColor();
public: __property void set_CalendarTrailingForeColor(Color);
```
[JScript]
```
public function get CalendarTrailingForeColor() : Color;
public function set CalendarTrailingForeColor(Color);
```

Property Value

A **Color** that represents the foreground color of the calendar trailing dates.

Exceptions

Exception Type	Condition
ArgumentException	The value assigned is a null reference (**Nothing** in Visual Basic).

Remarks

When a **DateTimePicker** is created, this property is initially set equal to the **DefaultTrailingForeColor** field value.

The trailing dates are the ending dates from the previous month or the beginning dates from the next month used to fill the calendar grid.

Requirements

Platforms: Windows 98, Windows NT 4.0, Windows Millennium Edition, Windows 2000, Windows XP Home Edition, Windows XP Professional, Windows Server 2003 family

DateTimePicker.Checked Property

Gets or sets a value indicating whether the **Value** property has been set with a valid date/time value and the displayed value is able to be updated.

```
[Visual Basic]
Public Property Checked As Boolean
[C#]
public bool Checked {get; set;}
[C++]
public: __property bool get_Checked();
public: __property void set_Checked(bool);
[JScript]
public function get Checked() : Boolean;
public function set Checked(Boolean);
```

Property Value

true if the **Value** property has been set with a valid **DateTime** value and the displayed value is able to be updated; otherwise, **false**. The default is **true**.

Remarks

This parameter is used to obtain the state of the check box that is displayed if the **ShowCheckBox** property value is **true**. If the **Checked** property value is **true**, the date/time picker control displays the properly formatted **Value** property value; otherwise, the control displays either the current date and time (**DateTime.Now**) or the last valid date/time value assigned to the **Value** property.

Requirements

Platforms: Windows 98, Windows NT 4.0, Windows Millennium Edition, Windows 2000, Windows XP Home Edition, Windows XP Professional, Windows Server 2003 family

DateTimePicker.CreateParams Property

This member overrides **Control.CreateParams**.

```
[Visual Basic]
Overrides Protected ReadOnly Property CreateParams As CreateParams
[C#]
protected override CreateParams CreateParams {get;}
[C++]
protected: __property CreateParams* get_CreateParams();
[JScript]
protected override function get CreateParams() : CreateParams;
```

Requirements

Platforms: Windows 98, Windows NT 4.0, Windows Millennium Edition, Windows 2000, Windows XP Home Edition, Windows XP Professional, Windows Server 2003 family

DateTimePicker.CustomFormat Property

Gets or sets the custom date/time format string.

```
[Visual Basic]
Public Property CustomFormat As String
[C#]
public string CustomFormat {get; set;}
[C++]
public: __property String* get_CustomFormat();
public: __property void set_CustomFormat(String*);
[JScript]
public function get CustomFormat() : String;
public function set CustomFormat(String);
```

Property Value

A string that represents the custom date/time format. The default is a null reference (**Nothing** in Visual Basic).

Remarks

To display string literals that contain date and time separators or format strings you must use escape characters in the substring. For example, to display the date as "June 06 at 3:00 PM", set the **CustomFormat** property to "MMMM dd 'at' t:mm tt". If the "at" substring is not enclosed by escape characters, the result is a "June 06 aP 3:00PM" because the "t" character is read as the one-letter AM/PM format string (see the format string table below).

The format strings can be combined to format the date and time. For example, to display the date and time as 06/01/2001 12:00 PM, this property should be set to "dd'/'MM'/'yyyy hh':'mm tt". For more information, see **Date and Time Format Strings**.

> **Note** The **Format** property must be set to **DateTimePickerFormat.Custom** for this property to affect the formatting of the displayed date/time.

The following table lists all the valid format strings and their descriptions.

Format String	Description
d	The one or two-digit day.
dd	The two-digit day. Single digit day values are preceded by a zero.
ddd	The three-character day-of-week abbreviation.
dddd	The full day-of-week name.
h	The one or two-digit hour in 12-hour format.
hh	The two-digit hour in 12-hour format. Single digit values are preceded by a zero.
H	The one or two-digit hour in 24-hour format.
HH	The two-digit hour in 24-hour format. Single digit values are preceded by a zero.
m	The one or two-digit minute.
mm	The two-digit minute. Single digit values are preceded by a zero.
M	The one or two-digit month number.
MM	The two-digit month number. Single digit values are preceded by a zero.
MMM	The three-character month abbreviation.
MMMM	The full month name.
s	The one or two-digit seconds.
ss	The two-digit seconds. Single digit values are preceded by a zero.
t	The one-letter AM/PM abbreviation ("AM" is displayed as "A").

Format String	Description
tt	The two-letter AM/PM abbreviation ("AM" is displayed as "AM").
y	The one-digit year (2001 is displayed as "1").
yy	The last two digits of the year (2001 is displayed as "01").
yyyy	The full year (2001 is displayed as "2001").

Example

[Visual Basic, C#] The following example sets the **CustomFormat** property so that the **DateTimePicker** will display the date as "June 01, 2001 - Friday". This code assumes that an instance of a **DateTimePicker** control has been created on a **Form**.

[Visual Basic]
```
Public Sub SetMyCustomFormat()
    ' Set the Format type and the CustomFormat string.
    dateTimePicker1.Format = DateTimePickerFormat.Custom
    dateTimePicker1.CustomFormat = "MMMM dd, yyyy - dddd"
End Sub 'SetMyCustomFormat
```

[C#]
```
public void SetMyCustomFormat()
{
   // Set the Format type and the CustomFormat string.
   dateTimePicker1.Format = DateTimePickerFormat.Custom;
   dateTimePicker1.CustomFormat = "MMMM dd, yyyy - dddd";
}
```

Requirements

Platforms: Windows 98, Windows NT 4.0, Windows Millennium Edition, Windows 2000, Windows XP Home Edition, Windows XP Professional, Windows Server 2003 family

DateTimePicker.DefaultSize Property

This member overrides **Control.DefaultSize**.

[Visual Basic]
```
Overrides Protected ReadOnly Property DefaultSize As Size
```
[C#]
```
protected override Size DefaultSize {get;}
```
[C++]
```
protected: __property Size get_DefaultSize();
```
[JScript]
```
protected override function get DefaultSize() : Size;
```

Requirements

Platforms: Windows 98, Windows NT 4.0, Windows Millennium Edition, Windows 2000, Windows XP Home Edition, Windows XP Professional, Windows Server 2003 family

DateTimePicker.DropDownAlign Property

Gets or sets the alignment of the drop-down calendar on the date/time picker control.

[Visual Basic]
```
Public Property DropDownAlign As LeftRightAlignment
```
[C#]
```
public LeftRightAlignment DropDownAlign {get; set;}
```
[C++]
```
public: __property LeftRightAlignment get_DropDownAlign();
public: __property void set_DropDownAlign(LeftRightAlignment);
```
[JScript]
```
public function get DropDownAlign() : LeftRightAlignment;
public function set DropDownAlign(LeftRightAlignment);
```

Property Value

The alignment of the drop-down calendar on the control. The default is **Left**.

Exceptions

Exception Type	Condition
InvalidEnumArgumentException	The value assigned is not one of the **LeftRightAlignment** values.

Remarks

The calendar drop-down can be aligned to the left or right of the control.

Requirements

Platforms: Windows 98, Windows NT 4.0, Windows Millennium Edition, Windows 2000, Windows XP Home Edition, Windows XP Professional, Windows Server 2003 family

DateTimePicker.ForeColor Property

This member overrides **Control.ForeColor**.

[Visual Basic]
```
Overrides Public Property ForeColor As Color
```
[C#]
```
public override Color ForeColor {get; set;}
```
[C++]
```
public: __property Color get_ForeColor();
public: __property void set_ForeColor(Color);
```
[JScript]
```
public override function get ForeColor() : Color;
public override function set ForeColor(Color);
```

Requirements

Platforms: Windows 98, Windows NT 4.0, Windows Millennium Edition, Windows 2000, Windows XP Home Edition, Windows XP Professional, Windows Server 2003 family

DateTimePicker.Format Property

Gets or sets the format of the date and time displayed in the control.

[Visual Basic]
```
Public Property Format As DateTimePickerFormat
```
[C#]
```
public DateTimePickerFormat Format {get; set;}
```
[C++]
```
public: __property DateTimePickerFormat get_Format();
public: __property void set_Format(DateTimePickerFormat);
```
[JScript]
```
public function get Format() : DateTimePickerFormat;
public function set Format(DateTimePickerFormat);
```

Property Value

One of the **DateTimePickerFormat** values. The default is **Long**.

Exceptions

Exception Type	Condition
InvalidEnumArgument-Exception	The value assigned is not one of the **DateTimePickerFormat** values.

Remarks

This property determines the date/time format the date is displayed in. The date/time format is based on the user's regional settings in their operating system.

> **Note** The **Format** property must be set to **DateTimePicker-Format.Custom** for the **CustomFormat** property to affect the formatting of the displayed date/time.

Example

[Visual Basic, C#] The following example sets the **CustomFormat** property so that the **DateTimePicker** will display the date as "June 01, 2001 - Friday". This code assumes that an instance of a **DateTimePicker** control has been created on a **Form**.

[Visual Basic]
```
Public Sub SetMyCustomFormat()
    ' Set the Format type and the CustomFormat string.
    dateTimePicker1.Format = DateTimePickerFormat.Custom
    dateTimePicker1.CustomFormat = "MMMM dd, yyyy - dddd"
End Sub 'SetMyCustomFormat
```

[C#]
```
public void SetMyCustomFormat()
{
   // Set the Format type and the CustomFormat string.
   dateTimePicker1.Format = DateTimePickerFormat.Custom;
   dateTimePicker1.CustomFormat = "MMMM dd, yyyy - dddd";
}
```

Requirements

Platforms: Windows 98, Windows NT 4.0, Windows Millennium Edition, Windows 2000, Windows XP Home Edition, Windows XP Professional, Windows Server 2003 family

DateTimePicker.MaxDate Property

Gets or sets the maximum date and time that can be selected in the control.

[Visual Basic]
```
Public Property MaxDate As DateTime
```
[C#]
```
public DateTime MaxDate {get; set;}
```
[C++]
```
public: __property DateTime get_MaxDate();
public: __property void set_MaxDate(DateTime);
```
[JScript]
```
public function get MaxDate() : DateTime;
public function set MaxDate(DateTime);
```

Property Value

The maximum date and time that can be selected in the control. The default is 12/31/9998 23:59:59.

Exceptions

Exception Type	Condition
ArgumentException	The value assigned is less than **MinDate** value.
SystemException	The value assigned is greater than the **MaxDateTime** value.

Example

[Visual Basic, C#] The following example creates an new instance of a **DateTimePicker** control and initializes it. The control's **CustomFormat** property is set. Also, the **ShowCheckBox** property is set so that the control displays a **CheckBox**, and the **ShowUp-Down** property is set so that the control is displayed as an up-down control.

[Visual Basic]
```
Public Sub CreateMyDateTimePicker()
    ' Create a new DateTimePicker control and initialize it.
    Dim dateTimePicker1 As New DateTimePicker()

    ' Set the MinDate and MaxDate.
    dateTimePicker1.MinDate = New DateTime(1985, 6, 20)
    dateTimePicker1.MaxDate = DateTime.Today

    ' Set the CustomFormat string.
    dateTimePicker1.CustomFormat = "MMMM dd, yyyy - dddd"
    dateTimePicker1.Format = DateTimePickerFormat.Custom

    ' Show the CheckBox and display the control as an up-down control.
    dateTimePicker1.ShowCheckBox = True
    dateTimePicker1.ShowUpDown = True
End Sub 'CreateMyDateTimePicker
```

[C#]
```
public void CreateMyDateTimePicker()
{
   // Create a new DateTimePicker control and initialize it.
   DateTimePicker dateTimePicker1 = new DateTimePicker();

   // Set the MinDate and MaxDate.
   dateTimePicker1.MinDate = new DateTime(1985, 6, 20);
   dateTimePicker1.MaxDate = DateTime.Today;

   // Set the CustomFormat string.
   dateTimePicker1.CustomFormat = "MMMM dd, yyyy - dddd";
   dateTimePicker1.Format = DateTimePickerFormat.Custom;

   // Show the CheckBox and display the control as an up-down control.
   dateTimePicker1.ShowCheckBox = true;
   dateTimePicker1.ShowUpDown = true;
}
```

Requirements

Platforms: Windows 98, Windows NT 4.0, Windows Millennium Edition, Windows 2000, Windows XP Home Edition, Windows XP Professional, Windows Server 2003 family

DateTimePicker.MinDate Property

Gets or sets the minimum date and time that can be selected in the control.

[Visual Basic]
```
Public Property MinDate As DateTime
```
[C#]
```
public DateTime MinDate {get; set;}
```
[C++]
```
public: __property DateTime get_MinDate();
public: __property void set_MinDate(DateTime);
```

```
[JScript]
public function get MinDate() : DateTime;
public function set MinDate(DateTime);
```

Property Value

The minimum date and time that can be selected in the control. The default is 1/1/1753 00:00:00.

Exceptions

Exception Type	Condition
ArgumentException	The value assigned is not less than the **MaxDate** value.
SystemException	The value assigned is less than the **MinDateTime** value.

Example

[Visual Basic, C#] The following example creates an new instance of a **DateTimePicker** control and initializes it. The control's **CustomFormat** property is set. Also, the **ShowCheckBox** property is set so that the control displays a **CheckBox**, and the **ShowUpDown** property is set so that the control is displayed as an up-down control.

```
[Visual Basic]
Public Sub CreateMyDateTimePicker()
    ' Create a new DateTimePicker control and initialize it.
    Dim dateTimePicker1 As New DateTimePicker()

    ' Set the MinDate and MaxDate.
    dateTimePicker1.MinDate = New DateTime(1985, 6, 20)
    dateTimePicker1.MaxDate = DateTime.Today

    ' Set the CustomFormat string.
    dateTimePicker1.CustomFormat = "MMMM dd, yyyy - dddd"
    dateTimePicker1.Format = DateTimePickerFormat.Custom

    ' Show the CheckBox and display the control as an up-down control.
    dateTimePicker1.ShowCheckBox = True
    dateTimePicker1.ShowUpDown = True
End Sub 'CreateMyDateTimePicker
```

```
[C#]
public void CreateMyDateTimePicker()
{
   // Create a new DateTimePicker control and initialize it.
   DateTimePicker dateTimePicker1 = new DateTimePicker();

   // Set the MinDate and MaxDate.
   dateTimePicker1.MinDate = new DateTime(1985, 6, 20);
   dateTimePicker1.MaxDate = DateTime.Today;

   // Set the CustomFormat string.
   dateTimePicker1.CustomFormat = "MMMM dd, yyyy - dddd";
   dateTimePicker1.Format = DateTimePickerFormat.Custom;

   // Show the CheckBox and display the control as an up-down control.
   dateTimePicker1.ShowCheckBox = true;
   dateTimePicker1.ShowUpDown = true;
}
```

Requirements

Platforms: Windows 98, Windows NT 4.0, Windows Millennium Edition, Windows 2000, Windows XP Home Edition, Windows XP Professional, Windows Server 2003 family

DateTimePicker.PreferredHeight Property

Gets the preferred height of the date/time picker control.

```
[Visual Basic]
Public ReadOnly Property PreferredHeight As Integer
[C#]
public int PreferredHeight {get;}
[C++]
public: __property int get_PreferredHeight();
[JScript]
public function get PreferredHeight() : int;
```

Property Value

The preferred height of the date/time picker control in pixels.

Remarks

The preferred height is the minimum height needed to accommodate the displayed text with the assigned **Font** applied.

Requirements

Platforms: Windows 98, Windows NT 4.0, Windows Millennium Edition, Windows 2000, Windows XP Home Edition, Windows XP Professional, Windows Server 2003 family

DateTimePicker.ShowCheckBox Property

Gets or sets a value indicating whether a check box is displayed to the left of the selected date.

```
[Visual Basic]
Public Property ShowCheckBox As Boolean
[C#]
public bool ShowCheckBox {get; set;}
[C++]
public: __property bool get_ShowCheckBox();
public: __property void set_ShowCheckBox(bool);
[JScript]
public function get ShowCheckBox() : Boolean;
public function set ShowCheckBox(Boolean);
```

Property Value

true if a check box is displayed to the left of the selected date; otherwise, **false**. The default is **false**.

Remarks

When **ShowCheckBox** is set to **true**, a check box is displayed to the left of the date in the control. When the check box is checked, the date/time value can be updated. When the check box is empty, the date/time value is unable to be changed.

Example

[Visual Basic, C#] The following example creates an new instance of a **DateTimePicker** control and initializes it. The control's **CustomFormat** property is set. Also, the **ShowCheckBox** property is set so that the control displays a **CheckBox**, and the **ShowUpDown** property is set so that the control is displayed as an up-down control.

[Visual Basic]
```
Public Sub CreateMyDateTimePicker()
    ' Create a new DateTimePicker control and initialize it.
    Dim dateTimePicker1 As New DateTimePicker()

    ' Set the MinDate and MaxDate.
    dateTimePicker1.MinDate = New DateTime(1985, 6, 20)
    dateTimePicker1.MaxDate = DateTime.Today

    ' Set the CustomFormat string.
    dateTimePicker1.CustomFormat = "MMMM dd, yyyy - dddd"
    dateTimePicker1.Format = DateTimePickerFormat.Custom

    ' Show the CheckBox and display the control as an up-down control.
    dateTimePicker1.ShowCheckBox = True
    dateTimePicker1.ShowUpDown = True
End Sub 'CreateMyDateTimePicker
```

[C#]
```
public void CreateMyDateTimePicker()
{
   // Create a new DateTimePicker control and initialize it.
   DateTimePicker dateTimePicker1 = new DateTimePicker();

   // Set the MinDate and MaxDate.
   dateTimePicker1.MinDate = new DateTime(1985, 6, 20);
   dateTimePicker1.MaxDate = DateTime.Today;

   // Set the CustomFormat string.
   dateTimePicker1.CustomFormat = "MMMM dd, yyyy - dddd";
   dateTimePicker1.Format = DateTimePickerFormat.Custom;

   // Show the CheckBox and display the control as an up-down control.
   dateTimePicker1.ShowCheckBox = true;
   dateTimePicker1.ShowUpDown = true;
}
```

Requirements

Platforms: Windows 98, Windows NT 4.0, Windows Millennium Edition, Windows 2000, Windows XP Home Edition, Windows XP Professional, Windows Server 2003 family

DateTimePicker.ShowUpDown Property

Gets or sets a value indicating whether an up-down control is used to adjust the date/time value.

[Visual Basic]
```
Public Property ShowUpDown As Boolean
```
[C#]
```
public bool ShowUpDown {get; set;}
```
[C++]
```
public: __property bool get_ShowUpDown();
public: __property void set_ShowUpDown(bool);
```
[JScript]
```
public function get ShowUpDown() : Boolean;
public function set ShowUpDown(Boolean);
```

Property Value

true if an up-down control is used to adjust the date/time value; otherwise, **false**. The default is **false**.

Remarks

When **ShowUpDown** is set to **true**, an up-down control is used to adjust time values instead of the drop-down calendar. The date/time can be adjusted by selecting each element individually and using the up and down buttons to change the value.

Example

[Visual Basic, C#] The following example creates an new instance of a **DateTimePicker** control and initializes it. The control's **CustomFormat** property is set. Also, the **ShowCheckBox** property is set so that the control displays a **CheckBox**, and the **ShowUpDown** property is set so that the control is displayed as an up-down control.

[Visual Basic]
```
Public Sub CreateMyDateTimePicker()
    ' Create a new DateTimePicker control and initialize it.
    Dim dateTimePicker1 As New DateTimePicker()

    ' Set the MinDate and MaxDate.
    dateTimePicker1.MinDate = New DateTime(1985, 6, 20)
    dateTimePicker1.MaxDate = DateTime.Today

    ' Set the CustomFormat string.
    dateTimePicker1.CustomFormat = "MMMM dd, yyyy - dddd"
    dateTimePicker1.Format = DateTimePickerFormat.Custom

    ' Show the CheckBox and display the control as an up-down control.
    dateTimePicker1.ShowCheckBox = True
    dateTimePicker1.ShowUpDown = True
End Sub 'CreateMyDateTimePicker
```

[C#]
```
public void CreateMyDateTimePicker()
{
   // Create a new DateTimePicker control and initialize it.
   DateTimePicker dateTimePicker1 = new DateTimePicker();

   // Set the MinDate and MaxDate.
   dateTimePicker1.MinDate = new DateTime(1985, 6, 20);
   dateTimePicker1.MaxDate = DateTime.Today;

   // Set the CustomFormat string.
   dateTimePicker1.CustomFormat = "MMMM dd, yyyy - dddd";
   dateTimePicker1.Format = DateTimePickerFormat.Custom;

   // Show the CheckBox and display the control as an up-down control.
   dateTimePicker1.ShowCheckBox = true;
   dateTimePicker1.ShowUpDown = true;
}
```

Requirements

Platforms: Windows 98, Windows NT 4.0, Windows Millennium Edition, Windows 2000, Windows XP Home Edition, Windows XP Professional, Windows Server 2003 family

DateTimePicker.Text Property

Gets or sets the text associated with this control.

[Visual Basic]
```
Overrides Public Property Text As String
```
[C#]
```
public override string Text {get; set;}
```
[C++]
```
public: __property String* get_Text();
public: __property void set_Text(String*);
```
[JScript]
```
public override function get Text() : String;
public override function set Text(String);
```

Property Value

A string that represents the text associated with this control.

Remarks

The string returned by this property is equivalent to the **Value** property with the appropriate formatting or custom formatting applied. For example, if the **Value** property is set to 06/01/2001 12:00:00 AM while the **CustomFormat** property is set to "dddd, MMMM dd, yyyy", the **Text** property value is "Friday, June 01, 2001".

When setting this property, the string must be convertible to an instance of the **DateTime** class. It is possible to define a custom format that results in a string that cannot be converted to a valid **DateTime** value. Because of this, the string returned from the **Text** property might cause an error if it is passed back to the **Text** property. If the string cannot be converted to a date/time value, the **DateTime** class throws a **FormatException**.

Requirements

Platforms: Windows 98, Windows NT 4.0, Windows Millennium Edition, Windows 2000, Windows XP Home Edition, Windows XP Professional, Windows Server 2003 family

DateTimePicker.Value Property

Gets or sets the date/time value assigned to the control.

[Visual Basic]
```
Public Property Value As DateTime
```
[C#]
```
public DateTime Value {get; set;}
```
[C++]
```
public: __property DateTime get_Value();
public: __property void set_Value(DateTime);
```
[JScript]
```
public function get Value() : DateTime;
public function set Value(DateTime);
```

Property Value

The **DateTime** value assign to the control.

Remarks

If the **Value** property has not been changed in code or by the user, it is set to the current date and time (**DateTime.Now**).

Example

[Visual Basic, C#, C++] The following example demonstrates how use the **Value** property to retrieve the current date value. First, the example displays the **Value** property. The example then increments the **Value** property by one day and displays the property value again.

[Visual Basic]
```
Public Sub New()
   ' Create a new DateTimePicker
   Dim dateTimePicker1 As New DateTimePicker()
   Controls.AddRange(New Control() {dateTimePicker1})
   MessageBox.Show(dateTimePicker1.Value.ToString())

   dateTimePicker1.Value = DateTime.Now.AddDays(1)
   MessageBox.Show(dateTimePicker1.Value.ToString())
End Sub 'New
```

[C#]
```
public MyClass()
{
   // Create a new DateTimePicker
   DateTimePicker dateTimePicker1 = new DateTimePicker();
   Controls.AddRange(new Control[] {dateTimePicker1});
   MessageBox.Show(dateTimePicker1.Value.ToString());

   dateTimePicker1.Value = DateTime.Now.AddDays(1);
   MessageBox.Show(dateTimePicker1.Value.ToString());
}
```

[C++]
```
public:
    MyClass() {
        // Create a new DateTimePicker
        DateTimePicker* dateTimePicker1 = new DateTimePicker();
        Control* myClassControls[] = {dateTimePicker1};
        Controls->AddRange(myClassControls);
        MessageBox::Show(dateTimePicker1->Value.ToString());

        dateTimePicker1->Value = (System::DateTime::Now).AddDays(1);
        MessageBox::Show(dateTimePicker1->Value.ToString());
    }
```

Requirements

Platforms: Windows 98, Windows NT 4.0, Windows Millennium Edition, Windows 2000, Windows XP Home Edition, Windows XP Professional, Windows Server 2003 family

DateTimePicker.CreateAccessibilityInstance Method

This member overrides **Control.CreateAccessibilityInstance**.

[Visual Basic]
```
Overrides Protected Function CreateAccessibilityInstance() As _
   AccessibleObject
```
[C#]
```
protected override AccessibleObject CreateAccessibilityInstance();
```
[C++]
```
protected: AccessibleObject* CreateAccessibilityInstance();
```
[JScript]
```
protected override function CreateAccessibilityInstance() :
   AccessibleObject;
```

Requirements

Platforms: Windows 98, Windows NT 4.0, Windows Millennium Edition, Windows 2000, Windows XP Home Edition, Windows XP Professional, Windows Server 2003 family

DateTimePicker.CreateHandle Method

This member overrides **Control.CreateHandle**.

[Visual Basic]
```
Overrides Protected Sub CreateHandle()
```
[C#]
```
protected override void CreateHandle();
```
[C++]
```
protected: void CreateHandle();
```
[JScript]
```
protected override function CreateHandle();
```

Requirements

Platforms: Windows 98, Windows NT 4.0, Windows Millennium Edition, Windows 2000, Windows XP Home Edition, Windows XP Professional, Windows Server 2003 family

DateTimePicker.DestroyHandle Method

This member overrides **Control.DestroyHandle**.

```
[Visual Basic]
Overrides Protected Sub DestroyHandle()
[C#]
protected override void DestroyHandle();
[C++]
protected: void DestroyHandle();
[JScript]
protected override function DestroyHandle();
```

Requirements

Platforms: Windows 98, Windows NT 4.0, Windows Millennium Edition, Windows 2000, Windows XP Home Edition, Windows XP Professional, Windows Server 2003 family

DateTimePicker.Dispose Method

Overload List

This member supports the .NET Framework infrastructure and is not intended to be used directly from your code.

[Visual Basic] **Overloads Overrides Protected Sub Dispose(Boolean)**

[C#] **protected override void Dispose(bool);**

[C++] **protected: void Dispose(bool);**

[JScript] **protected override function Dispose(Boolean);**

Inherited from **Component**.

[Visual Basic] **Overloads Public Overridable Sub Dispose() Implements IDisposable.Dispose**

[C#] **public virtual void Dispose();**

[C++] **public: virtual void Dispose();**

[JScript] **public function Dispose();**

DateTimePicker.Dispose Method (Boolean)

This member overrides **Control.Dispose**.

```
[Visual Basic]
Overrides Overloads Protected Sub Dispose( _
   ByVal disposing As Boolean _
)
[C#]
protected override void Dispose(
   bool disposing
);
[C++]
protected: void Dispose(
   bool disposing
);
[JScript]
protected override function Dispose(
   disposing : Boolean
);
```

Requirements

Platforms: Windows 98, Windows NT 4.0, Windows Millennium Edition, Windows 2000, Windows XP Home Edition, Windows XP Professional, Windows Server 2003 family

DateTimePicker.IsInputKey Method

This member overrides **Control.IsInputKey**.

```
[Visual Basic]
Overrides Protected Function IsInputKey( _
   ByVal keyData As Keys _
) As Boolean
[C#]
protected override bool IsInputKey(
   Keys keyData
);
[C++]
protected: bool IsInputKey(
   Keys keyData
);
[JScript]
protected override function IsInputKey(
   keyData : Keys
) : Boolean;
```

Requirements

Platforms: Windows 98, Windows NT 4.0, Windows Millennium Edition, Windows 2000, Windows XP Home Edition, Windows XP Professional, Windows Server 2003 family

DateTimePicker.OnCloseUp Method

Raises the **CloseUp** event.

```
[Visual Basic]
Protected Overridable Sub OnCloseUp( _
   ByVal eventargs As EventArgs _
)
[C#]
protected virtual void OnCloseUp(
   EventArgs eventargs
);
[C++]
protected: virtual void OnCloseUp(
   EventArgs* eventargs
);
[JScript]
protected function OnCloseUp(
   eventargs : EventArgs
);
```

Parameters

eventargs

An **EventArgs** that contains the event data.

Remarks

The **CloseUp** event occurs when the drop-down calendar is dismissed and disappears.

Raising an event invokes the event handler through a delegate. For more information, see **Raising an Event**.

The **OnCloseUp** method also allows derived classes to handle the event without attaching a delegate. This is the preferred technique for handling the event in a derived class.

Notes to Inheritors: When overriding **OnCloseUp** in a derived class, be sure to call the base class's **OnCloseUp** method so that registered delegates receive the event.

Requirements

Platforms: Windows 98, Windows NT 4.0, Windows Millennium Edition, Windows 2000, Windows XP Home Edition, Windows XP Professional, Windows Server 2003 family

DateTimePicker.OnDropDown Method

Raises the **DropDown** event.

```
[Visual Basic]
Protected Overridable Sub OnDropDown( _
   ByVal eventargs As EventArgs _
)
[C#]
protected virtual void OnDropDown(
   EventArgs eventargs
);
[C++]
protected: virtual void OnDropDown(
   EventArgs* eventargs
);
[JScript]
protected function OnDropDown(
   eventargs : EventArgs
);
```

Parameters

eventargs

An **EventArgs** that contains the event data.

Remarks

The **DropDown** event occurs when the drop-down calendar is shown.

Raising an event invokes the event handler through a delegate. For more information, see **Raising an Event**.

The **OnDropDown** method also allows derived classes to handle the event without attaching a delegate. This is the preferred technique for handling the event in a derived class.

Notes to Inheritors: When overriding **OnDropDown** in a derived class, be sure to call the base class's **OnDropDown** method so that registered delegates receive the event.

Requirements

Platforms: Windows 98, Windows NT 4.0, Windows Millennium Edition, Windows 2000, Windows XP Home Edition, Windows XP Professional, Windows Server 2003 family

DateTimePicker.OnFontChanged Method

This member overrides **Control.OnFontChanged**.

```
[Visual Basic]
Overrides Protected Sub OnFontChanged( _
   ByVal e As EventArgs _
)
[C#]
protected override void OnFontChanged(
   EventArgs e
);
[C++]
protected: void OnFontChanged(
   EventArgs* e
);
[JScript]
protected override function OnFontChanged(
   e : EventArgs
);
```

Requirements

Platforms: Windows 98, Windows NT 4.0, Windows Millennium Edition, Windows 2000, Windows XP Home Edition, Windows XP Professional, Windows Server 2003 family

DateTimePicker.OnFormatChanged Method

Raises the **FormatChanged** event.

```
[Visual Basic]
Protected Overridable Sub OnFormatChanged( _
   ByVal e As EventArgs _
)
[C#]
protected virtual void OnFormatChanged(
   EventArgs e
);
[C++]
protected: virtual void OnFormatChanged(
   EventArgs* e
);
[JScript]
protected function OnFormatChanged(
   e : EventArgs
);
```

Parameters

e

An **EventArgs** that contains the event data.

Remarks

The **FormatChanged** event occurs when the **Format** property value has changed.

Raising an event invokes the event handler through a delegate.

The **OnFormatChanged** method also allows derived classes to handle the event without attaching a delegate. This is the preferred technique for handling the event in a derived class.

Notes to Inheritors: When overriding **OnFormatChanged** in a derived class, be sure to call the base class's **OnFormatChanged** method so that registered delegates receive the event.

Requirements

Platforms: Windows 98, Windows NT 4.0, Windows Millennium Edition, Windows 2000, Windows XP Home Edition, Windows XP Professional, Windows Server 2003 family

DateTimePicker.OnSystemColorsChanged Method

This member overrides **Control.OnSystemColorsChanged**.

```
[Visual Basic]
Overrides Protected Sub OnSystemColorsChanged( _
   ByVal e As EventArgs _
)
```

```
[C#]
protected override void OnSystemColorsChanged(
   EventArgs e
);
[C++]
protected: void OnSystemColorsChanged(
   EventArgs* e
);
[JScript]
protected override function OnSystemColorsChanged(
   e : EventArgs
);
```

Requirements

Platforms: Windows 98, Windows NT 4.0, Windows Millennium Edition, Windows 2000, Windows XP Home Edition, Windows XP Professional, Windows Server 2003 family

DateTimePicker.OnValueChanged Method

Raises the **ValueChanged** event.

```
[Visual Basic]
Protected Overridable Sub OnValueChanged( _
   ByVal eventargs As EventArgs _
)
[C#]
protected virtual void OnValueChanged(
   EventArgs eventargs
);
[C++]
protected: virtual void OnValueChanged(
   EventArgs* eventargs
);
[JScript]
protected function OnValueChanged(
   eventargs : EventArgs
);
```

Parameters

eventargs
An **EventArgs** that contains the event data.

Remarks

The **ValueChanged** event occurs when the value for the control changes.

Raising an event invokes the event handler through a delegate.

The **OnValueChanged** method also allows derived classes to handle the event without attaching a delegate. This is the preferred technique for handling the event in a derived class.

Notes to Inheritors: When overriding **OnValueChanged** in a derived class, be sure to call the base class's **OnValueChanged** method so that registered delegates receive the event.

Requirements

Platforms: Windows 98, Windows NT 4.0, Windows Millennium Edition, Windows 2000, Windows XP Home Edition, Windows XP Professional, Windows Server 2003 family

DateTimePicker.SetBoundsCore Method

This member overrides **Control.SetBoundsCore**.

```
[Visual Basic]
Overrides Protected Sub SetBoundsCore( _
   ByVal x As Integer, _
   ByVal y As Integer, _
   ByVal width As Integer, _
   ByVal height As Integer, _
   ByVal specified As BoundsSpecified _
)
[C#]
protected override void SetBoundsCore(
   int x,
   int y,
   int width,
   int height,
   BoundsSpecified specified
);
[C++]
protected: void SetBoundsCore(
   int x,
   int y,
   int width,
   int height,
   BoundsSpecified specified
);
[JScript]
protected override function SetBoundsCore(
   x : int,
   y : int,
   width : int,
   height : int,
   specified : BoundsSpecified
);
```

Requirements

Platforms: Windows 98, Windows NT 4.0, Windows Millennium Edition, Windows 2000, Windows XP Home Edition, Windows XP Professional, Windows Server 2003 family

DateTimePicker.ToString Method

This member overrides **Object.ToString**.

```
[Visual Basic]
Overrides Public Function ToString() As String
[C#]
public override string ToString();
[C++]
public: String* ToString();
[JScript]
public override function ToString() : String;
```

Requirements

Platforms: Windows 98, Windows NT 4.0, Windows Millennium Edition, Windows 2000, Windows XP Home Edition, Windows XP Professional, Windows Server 2003 family

DateTimePicker.WndProc Method

This member overrides **Control.WndProc**.

```
[Visual Basic]
Overrides Protected Sub WndProc( _
   ByRef m As Message _
)
[C#]
protected override void WndProc(
   ref Message m
);
[C++]
protected: void WndProc(
   Message* m
);
[JScript]
protected override function WndProc(
   m : Message
);
```

Requirements

Platforms: Windows 98, Windows NT 4.0, Windows Millennium Edition, Windows 2000, Windows XP Home Edition, Windows XP Professional, Windows Server 2003 family

DateTimePicker.BackColorChanged Event

This member supports the .NET Framework infrastructure and is not intended to be used directly from your code.

```
[Visual Basic]
Public Shadows Event BackColorChanged As EventHandler
[C#]
public new event EventHandler BackColorChanged;
[C++]
public: __event EventHandler* BackColorChanged;
```

[JScript] In JScript, you can handle the events defined by a class, but you cannot define your own.

DateTimePicker.BackgroundImageChanged Event

This member supports the .NET Framework infrastructure and is not intended to be used directly from your code.

```
[Visual Basic]
Public Shadows Event BackgroundImageChanged As EventHandler
[C#]
public new event EventHandler BackgroundImageChanged;
[C++]
public: __event EventHandler* BackgroundImageChanged;
```

[JScript] In JScript, you can handle the events defined by a class, but you cannot define your own.

DateTimePicker.CloseUp Event

Occurs when the drop-down calendar is dismissed and disappears.

```
[Visual Basic]
Public Event CloseUp As EventHandler
[C#]
public event EventHandler CloseUp;
[C++]
public: __event EventHandler* CloseUp;
```

[JScript] In JScript, you can handle the events defined by a class, but you cannot define your own.

Event Data

The event handler receives an argument of type **EventArgs**.

Requirements

Platforms: Windows 98, Windows NT 4.0, Windows Millennium Edition, Windows 2000, Windows XP Home Edition, Windows XP Professional, Windows Server 2003 family

DateTimePicker.DropDown Event

Occurs when the drop-down calendar is shown.

```
[Visual Basic]
Public Event DropDown As EventHandler
[C#]
public event EventHandler DropDown;
[C++]
public: __event EventHandler* DropDown;
```

[JScript] In JScript, you can handle the events defined by a class, but you cannot define your own.

Event Data

The event handler receives an argument of type **EventArgs**.

Requirements

Platforms: Windows 98, Windows NT 4.0, Windows Millennium Edition, Windows 2000, Windows XP Home Edition, Windows XP Professional, Windows Server 2003 family

DateTimePicker.ForeColorChanged Event

This member supports the .NET Framework infrastructure and is not intended to be used directly from your code.

```
[Visual Basic]
Public Shadows Event ForeColorChanged As EventHandler
[C#]
public new event EventHandler ForeColorChanged;
[C++]
public: __event EventHandler* ForeColorChanged;
```

[JScript] In JScript, you can handle the events defined by a class, but you cannot define your own.

DateTimePicker.FormatChanged Event

Occurs when the **Format** property value has changed.

```
[Visual Basic]
Public Event FormatChanged As EventHandler
[C#]
public event EventHandler FormatChanged;
[C++]
public: __event EventHandler* FormatChanged;
```

[JScript] In JScript, you can handle the events defined by a class, but you cannot define your own.

Event Data

The event handler receives an argument of type **EventArgs**.

Requirements

Platforms: Windows 98, Windows NT 4.0,
Windows Millennium Edition, Windows 2000,
Windows XP Home Edition, Windows XP Professional,
Windows Server 2003 family

DateTimePicker.Paint Event

This member supports the .NET Framework infrastructure and is not intended to be used directly from your code.

```
[Visual Basic]
Public Shadows Event Paint As PaintEventHandler
[C#]
public new event PaintEventHandler Paint;
[C++]
public: __event PaintEventHandler* Paint;
```

[JScript] In JScript, you can handle the events defined by a class, but you cannot define your own.

DateTimePicker.TextChanged Event

This member supports the .NET Framework infrastructure and is not intended to be used directly from your code.

```
[Visual Basic]
Public Shadows Event TextChanged As EventHandler
[C#]
public new event EventHandler TextChanged;
[C++]
public: __event EventHandler* TextChanged;
```

[JScript] In JScript, you can handle the events defined by a class, but you cannot define your own.

DateTimePicker.ValueChanged Event

Occurs when the **Value** property changes.

```
[Visual Basic]
Public Event ValueChanged As EventHandler
[C#]
public event EventHandler ValueChanged;
[C++]
public: __event EventHandler* ValueChanged;
```

[JScript] In JScript, you can handle the events defined by a class, but you cannot define your own.

Event Data

The event handler receives an argument of type **EventArgs**.

Requirements

Platforms: Windows 98, Windows NT 4.0,
Windows Millennium Edition, Windows 2000,
Windows XP Home Edition, Windows XP Professional,
Windows Server 2003 family

DateTimePicker.DateTime-PickerAccessibleObject Class

This type supports the .NET Framework infrastructure and is not intended to be used directly from your code.

```
[Visual Basic]
<ComVisible(True)>
Public Class DateTimePicker.DateTimePickerAccessibleObject
   Inherits Control.ControlAccessibleObject
[C#]
[ComVisible(true)]
public class DateTimePicker.DateTimePickerAccessibleObject :
   Control.ControlAccessibleObject
[C++]
[ComVisible(true)]
public __gc class DateTimePicker.DateTimePickerAccessibleObject :
   public Control.ControlAccessibleObject
[JScript]
public
   ComVisible(true)
class DateTimePicker.DateTimePickerAccessibleObject extends
   Control.ControlAccessibleObject
```

DateTimePicker.DateTimePicker-AccessibleObject Constructor

This member supports the .NET Framework infrastructure and is not intended to be used directly from your code.

```
[Visual Basic]
Public Sub New( _
   ByVal owner As DateTimePicker _
)
[C#]
public DateTimePicker.DateTimePickerAccessibleObject(
   DateTimePicker owner
);
[C++]
public: DateTimePickerAccessibleObject(
   DateTimePicker* owner
);
[JScript]
public function DateTimePicker.DateTimePickerAccessibleObject(
   owner : DateTimePicker
);
```

DateTimePicker.DateTimePickerAccessible-Object.State Property

This member overrides **AccessibleObject.State**.

```
[Visual Basic]
Overrides Public ReadOnly Property State As AccessibleStates
[C#]
public override AccessibleStates State {get;}
[C++]
public: __property AccessibleStates get_State();
[JScript]
public override function get State() : AccessibleStates;
```

Requirements

Platforms: Windows 98, Windows NT 4.0, Windows Millennium Edition, Windows 2000, Windows XP Home Edition, Windows XP Professional, Windows Server 2003 family

DateTimePicker.DateTimePickerAccessible-Object.Value Property

This member overrides **AccessibleObject.Value**.

```
[Visual Basic]
Overrides Public ReadOnly Property Value As String
[C#]
public override string Value {get;}
[C++]
public: __property String* get_Value();
[JScript]
public override function get Value() : String;
```

Requirements

Platforms: Windows 98, Windows NT 4.0, Windows Millennium Edition, Windows 2000, Windows XP Home Edition, Windows XP Professional, Windows Server 2003 family

DateTimePickerFormat Enumeration

Specifies the date and time format the **DateTimePicker** control displays.

[Visual Basic]
```
<Serializable>
Public Enum DateTimePickerFormat
```
[C#]
```
[Serializable]
public enum DateTimePickerFormat
```
[C++]
```
[Serializable]
__value public enum DateTimePickerFormat
```
[JScript]
```
public
   Serializable
enum DateTimePickerFormat
```

Remarks

This enumeration is used by members such as **DateTimePicker.Format**.

Note The actual date/time formats are determined by the date, time, and regional settings set in the user's operating system.

Members

Member name	Description
Custom	The **DateTimePicker** control displays the date/time value in a custom format.
Long	The **DateTimePicker** control displays the date/time value in the long date format set by the user's operating system.
Short	The **DateTimePicker** control displays the date/time value in the short date format set by the user's operating system.
Time	The **DateTimePicker** control displays the date/time value in the time format set by the user's operating system.

Requirements

Namespace: System.Windows.Forms

Platforms: Windows 98, Windows NT 4.0, Windows Millennium Edition, Windows 2000, Windows XP Home Edition, Windows XP Professional, Windows Server 2003 family

Assembly: System.Windows.Forms (in System.Windows.Forms.dll)

Day Enumeration

Specifies the day of the week.

[Visual Basic]

```
<Serializable>
Public Enum Day
```

[C#]

```
[Serializable]
public enum Day
```

[C++]

```
[Serializable]
__value public enum Day
```

[JScript]

```
public
   Serializable
enum Day
```

Remarks

This class is used by **MonthCalendar**.

Members

Member name	Description
Default	A default day of the week specified by the application.
Friday	The day Friday.
Monday	The day Monday.
Saturday	The day Saturday.
Sunday	The day Sunday.
Thursday	The day Thursday.
Tuesday	The day Tuesday.
Wednesday	The day Wednesday.

Requirements

Namespace: System.Windows.Forms

Platforms: Windows 98, Windows NT 4.0, Windows Millennium Edition, Windows 2000, Windows XP Home Edition, Windows XP Professional, Windows Server 2003 family

Assembly: System.Windows.Forms (in System.Windows.Forms.dll)

DialogResult Enumeration

Specifies identifiers to indicate the return value of a dialog box.

[Visual Basic]
```
<Serializable>
<ComVisible(True)>
Public Enum DialogResult
```
[C#]
```
[Serializable]
[ComVisible(true)]
public enum DialogResult
```
[C++]
```
[Serializable]
[ComVisible(true)]
__value public enum DialogResult
```
[JScript]
```
public
   Serializable
   ComVisible(true)
enum DialogResult
```

Remarks

The **Button.DialogResult** property and the **Form.ShowDialog** method use this enumeration.

Members

Member name	Description
Abort Supported by the .NET Compact Framework.	The dialog box return value is **Abort** (usually sent from a button labeled **Abort**).
Cancel Supported by the .NET Compact Framework.	The dialog box return value is **Cancel** (usually sent from a button labeled **Cancel**).
Ignore Supported by the .NET Compact Framework.	The dialog box return value is **Ignore** (usually sent from a button labeled **Ignore**).
No Supported by the .NET Compact Framework.	The dialog box return value is **No** (usually sent from a button labeled **No**).
None Supported by the .NET Compact Framework.	**Nothing** is returned from the dialog box. This means that the modal dialog continues running.
OK Supported by the .NET Compact Framework.	The dialog box return value is **OK** (usually sent from a button labeled **OK**).
Retry Supported by the .NET Compact Framework.	The dialog box return value is **Retry** (usually sent from a button labeled **Retry**).
Yes Supported by the .NET Compact Framework.	The dialog box return value is **Yes** (usually sent from a button labeled **Yes**).

Example

[Visual Basic]
```
Private Sub ValidateUserEntry5()

    ' Checks the value of the text.

    If ServerName.Text.Length = 0 Then

        ' Initializes variables to pass to the MessageBox.Show method.

        Dim Message As String = "You did not enter a server ↵
 name. Cancel this operation?"
        Dim Caption As String = "No Server Name Specified"
        Dim Buttons As Integer = MessageBoxButtons.YesNo

        Dim Result As DialogResult

        'Displays a MessageBox using the Question icon and ↵
 specifying the No button as the default.

        Result = MessageBox.Show(Me, Message, Caption, ↵
MessageBoxButtons.YesNo)

        ' Gets the result of the MessageBox display.

        If Result = DialogResult.Yes Then

            ' Closes the parent form.

            Me.Close()

        End If

    End If

End Sub
```
[C#]
```
private void validateUserEntry5()
{

    // Checks the value of the text.

    if(serverName.Text.Length == 0)
    {

        // Initializes the variables to pass to the ↵
MessageBox.Show method.

        string message = "You did not enter a server name. ↵
Cancel this operation?";
        string caption = "No Server Name Specified";
        MessageBoxButtons buttons = MessageBoxButtons.YesNo;
        DialogResult result;

        // Displays the MessageBox.

        result = MessageBox.Show(this, message, caption, buttons);

        if(result == DialogResult.Yes)
        {

            // Closes the parent form.

            this.Close();

        }

    }

}
```

[C++]
```
private:
    void validateUserEntry5() {
        // Checks the value of the text.
        if (serverName->Text->Length == 0) {

            // Initializes the variables to pass to the
MessageBox::Show method.
            String* message = S"You did not enter a server name.
 Cancel this operation?";
            String* caption = S"No Server Name Specified";
            MessageBoxButtons buttons = MessageBoxButtons::YesNo;
            System::Windows::Forms::DialogResult result;

            // Displays the MessageBox.
            result = MessageBox::Show(this, message, caption, buttons);

            if (result == DialogResult::Yes) {
                // Closes the parent form.
                this->Close();
            }
        }
    }
```

Requirements

Namespace: System.Windows.Forms

Platforms: Windows 98, Windows NT 4.0, Windows Millennium Edition, Windows 2000, Windows XP Home Edition, Windows XP Professional, Windows Server 2003 family, .NET Compact Framework - Windows CE .NET

Assembly: System.Windows.Forms (in System.Windows.Forms.dll)

DockStyle Enumeration

Specifies the position and manner in which a control is docked.

[Visual Basic]
```
<Serializable>
Public Enum DockStyle
```
[C#]
```
[Serializable]
public enum DockStyle
```
[C++]
```
[Serializable]
__value public enum DockStyle
```
[JScript]
```
public
   Serializable
enum DockStyle
```

Remarks

When a control is docked to an edge of its container, it is always positioned flush against that edge when the container is resized. If more than one control is docked to an edge, the controls appear side by side according to their z-order; controls higher in the z-order are positioned farther from the container's edge.

If **Left**, **Right**, **Top**, or **Bottom** is selected, the specified and opposite edges of the control are resized to the size of the containing control's corresponding edges. If **Fill** is selected, all four sides of the control are resized to match the containing control's edges.

Members

Member name	Description
Bottom	The control's bottom edge is docked to the bottom of its containing control.
Fill	All the control's edges are docked to the all edges of its containing control and sized appropriately.
Left	The control's left edge is docked to the left edge of its containing control.
None	The control is not docked.
Right	The control's right edge is docked to the right edge of its containing control.
Top	The control's top edge is docked to the top of its containing control.

Example

[Visual Basic, C#, C++] The following example creates a **GroupBox** and sets some of its common properties. The example creates a **TextBox** and sets its **Location** within the group box. Next, it sets the **Text** property of the group box, and docks the group box to the top of the form. Lastly, it disables the group box by setting the **Enabled** property to **false**, which causes all controls contained within the group box to be disabled.

[Visual Basic]
```
' Add a GroupBox to a form and set some of its common properties.
Private Sub AddMyGroupBox()
   ' Create a GroupBox and add a TextBox to it.
   Dim groupBox1 As New GroupBox()
   Dim textBox1 As New TextBox()
   textBox1.Location = New Point(15, 15)
   groupBox1.Controls.Add(textBox1)

   ' Set the Text and Dock properties of the GroupBox.
   groupBox1.Text = "MyGroupBox"
   groupBox1.Dock = DockStyle.Top

   ' Disable the GroupBox (which disables all its child controls)
   groupBox1.Enabled = False

   ' Add the Groupbox to the form.
   Me.Controls.Add(groupBox1)
End Sub
```

[C#]
```
// Add a GroupBox to a form and set some of its common properties.
private void AddMyGroupBox()
{
   // Create a GroupBox and add a TextBox to it.
   GroupBox groupBox1 = new GroupBox();
   TextBox textBox1 = new TextBox();
   textBox1.Location = new Point(15, 15);
   groupBox1.Controls.Add(textBox1);

   // Set the Text and Dock properties of the GroupBox.
   groupBox1.Text = "MyGroupBox";
   groupBox1.Dock = DockStyle.Top;

   // Disable the GroupBox (which disables all its child controls)
   groupBox1.Enabled = false;

   // Add the Groupbox to the form.
   this.Controls.Add(groupBox1);
}
```

[C++]
```
// Add a GroupBox to a form and set some of its common properties.
private:
void AddMyGroupBox() {
   // Create a GroupBox and add a TextBox to it.
   GroupBox* groupBox1 = new GroupBox();
   TextBox* textBox1 = new TextBox();
   textBox1->Location =  Point(15, 15);
   groupBox1->Controls->Add(textBox1);

   // Set the Text and Dock properties of the GroupBox.
   groupBox1->Text = S"MyGroupBox";
   groupBox1->Dock = DockStyle::Top;

   // Disable the GroupBox (which disables all its child controls)
   groupBox1->Enabled = false;

   // Add the Groupbox to the form.
   this->Controls->Add(groupBox1);
}
```

Requirements

Namespace: System.Windows.Forms

Platforms: Windows 98, Windows NT 4.0, Windows Millennium Edition, Windows 2000, Windows XP Home Edition, Windows XP Professional, Windows Server 2003 family

Assembly: System.Windows.Forms (in System.Windows.Forms.dll)

DomainUpDown Class

Represents a Windows up-down control that displays string values.

System.Object
System.MarshalByRefObject
System.ComponentModel.Component
System.Windows.Forms.Control
System.Windows.Forms.ScrollableControl
System.Windows.Forms.ContainerControl
System.Windows.Forms.UpDownBase
System.Windows.Forms.DomainUpDown

[Visual Basic]
```
Public Class DomainUpDown
   Inherits UpDownBase
```
[C#]
```
public class DomainUpDown : UpDownBase
```
[C++]
```
public __gc class DomainUpDown : public UpDownBase
```
[JScript]
```
public class DomainUpDown extends UpDownBase
```

Thread Safety

Any public static (**Shared** in Visual Basic) members of this type are safe for multithreaded operations. Any instance members are not guaranteed to be thread safe.

Remarks

A **DomainUpDown** control displays a single string value that is selected from an **Object** collection by clicking the up or down buttons of the control. The user can also enter text in the control, unless the **ReadOnly** property is set to **true** (the string typed in must match an item in the collection to be accepted). When an item is selected, the object is converted to a string value so it can be displayed in the up-down control.

To create a collection of objects to display in the **DomainUpDown** control, you can add or remove the items individually by using the **Add** and **Remove** methods. This can be called in an event handler, such as the **Click** of a button. The object collection can be sorted alphabetically by setting the **Sorted** property to **true**. When **Wrap** is set to **true**, if you scroll past the last or first object in the collection, the list will start over with the first or last object respectively and appear to roll in a continuous list.

When the **UpButton** or **DownButton** methods are called, either in code or by the click of the up or down buttons, **UpdateEditText** is called to update the control with the new string. If **UserEdit** is set to **true**, the string is matched to one of the values in the collection prior to updating the control's text display.

Example

[Visual Basic, C#] The following example creates and initializes a **DomainUpDown** control. The example allows you to set some of its properties and create a collection of strings for display in the up-down control. The code assumes that a **TextBox**, **CheckBox** and a **Button** have been instantiated on a form. The example also assumes that you have a member variable at the class level declared as a 32-bit signed integer named `myCounter`. You can enter a string in the text box and add it to the **Items** collection when the button is clicked. By clicking the check box, you can toggle the **Sorted** property and observe the difference in the collection of items in the up-down control.

[Visual Basic]
```
Protected domainUpDown1 As DomainUpDown

Private Sub MySub()
    ' Create and initialize the DomainUpDown control.
    domainUpDown1 = New System.Windows.Forms.DomainUpDown()

    ' Add the DomainUpDown control to the form.
    Controls.Add(domainUpDown1)
End Sub 'MySub

Private Sub button1_Click(sender As System.Object, e As ↵
System.EventArgs)
    ' Add the text box contents and initial location in the collection
    ' to the DomainUpDown control.
    domainUpDown1.Items.Add((textBox1.Text.Trim() & " - " & myCounter))

    ' Increment the counter variable.
    myCounter = myCounter + 1

    ' Clear the TextBox.
    textBox1.Text = ""
End Sub 'button1_Click

Private Sub checkBox1_Click(sender As System.Object, e As ↵
System.EventArgs)
    ' If Sorted is set to true, set it to false;
    ' otherwise set it to true.
    If domainUpDown1.Sorted Then
        domainUpDown1.Sorted = False
    Else
        domainUpDown1.Sorted = True
    End If
End Sub 'checkBox1_Click

Private Sub domainUpDown1_SelectedItemChanged _
    (sender As System.Object, e As System.EventArgs)

    ' Display the SelectedIndex and SelectedItem property ↵
 values in a MessageBox.
    MessageBox.Show(("SelectedIndex: " & ↵
domainUpDown1.SelectedIndex.ToString() & _
        ControlChars.Cr & "SelectedItem: " & ↵
domainUpDown1.SelectedItem.ToString()))
End Sub 'domainUpDown1_SelectedItemChanged
```

[C#]
```
protected DomainUpDown domainUpDown1;

private void MySub()
 {
    // Create and initialize the DomainUpDown control.
    domainUpDown1 = new System.Windows.Forms.DomainUpDown();

    // Add the DomainUpDown control to the form.
    Controls.Add(domainUpDown1);
 }

 private void button1_Click(System.Object sender,
                            System.EventArgs e)
 {
    // Add the text box contents and initial location in the collection
    // to the DomainUpDown control.
    domainUpDown1.Items.Add((textBox1.Text.Trim()) + " - " + ↵
myCounter);

    // Increment the counter variable.
    myCounter = myCounter + 1;

    // Clear the TextBox.
    textBox1.Text = "";
 }

 private void checkBox1_Click(System.Object sender,
                              System.EventArgs e)
```

```
{
   // If Sorted is set to true, set it to false;
   // otherwise set it to true.
   if (domainUpDown1.Sorted)
   {
      domainUpDown1.Sorted = false;
   }
   else
   {
      domainUpDown1.Sorted = true;
   }
}

private void domainUpDown1_SelectedItemChanged(System.Object sender,
                                                System.EventArgs e)
{
   // Display the SelectedIndex and SelectedItem property         ↵
values in a MessageBox.
   MessageBox.Show("SelectedIndex: " +                            ↵
domainUpDown1.SelectedIndex.ToString()
      + "\n" + "SelectedItem: " +
domainUpDown1.SelectedItem.ToString());
}
```

Requirements

Namespace: System.Windows.Forms

Platforms: Windows 98, Windows NT 4.0,
Windows Millennium Edition, Windows 2000,
Windows XP Home Edition, Windows XP Professional,
Windows Server 2003 family,
.NET Compact Framework - Windows CE .NET

Assembly: System.Windows.Forms (in System.Windows.Forms.dll)

DomainUpDown Constructor

Initializes a new instance of the **DomainUpDown** class.

[Visual Basic]
```
Public Sub New()
```
[C#]
```
public DomainUpDown();
```
[C++]
```
public: DomainUpDown();
```
[JScript]
```
public function DomainUpDown();
```

Example

See related example in the **System.Windows.Forms.DomainUpDown** class topic.

Requirements

Platforms: Windows 98, Windows NT 4.0,
Windows Millennium Edition, Windows 2000,
Windows XP Home Edition, Windows XP Professional,
Windows Server 2003 family,
.NET Compact Framework - Windows CE .NET

DomainUpDown.Items Property

A collection of objects assigned to the up-down control.

[Visual Basic]
```
Public ReadOnly Property Items As _
   DomainUpDown.DomainUpDownItemCollection
```
[C#]
```
public DomainUpDown.DomainUpDownItemCollection Items {get;}
```
[C++]
```
public: __property DomainUpDown.DomainUpDownItemCollection*
   get_Items();
```
[JScript]
```
public function get Items() :
   DomainUpDown.DomainUpDownItemCollection;
```

Property Value

A **DomainUpDown.DomainUpDownItemCollection** object that contains an **Object** collection.

Remarks

The **Object** collection can be built and made available to the **DomainUpDown** control in two ways. You can add items to the collection by using the **Add** or **Insert** methods.

Example

See related example in the **System.Windows.Forms.DomainUpDown** class topic.

Requirements

Platforms: Windows 98, Windows NT 4.0,
Windows Millennium Edition, Windows 2000,
Windows XP Home Edition, Windows XP Professional,
Windows Server 2003 family,
.NET Compact Framework - Windows CE .NET

DomainUpDown.SelectedIndex Property

Gets or sets the index value of the selected item.

[Visual Basic]
```
Public Property SelectedIndex As Integer
```
[C#]
```
public int SelectedIndex {get; set;}
```
[C++]
```
public: __property int get_SelectedIndex();
public: __property void set_SelectedIndex(int);
```
[JScript]
```
public function get SelectedIndex() : int;
public function set SelectedIndex(int);
```

Property Value

The zero-based index value of the selected item. The default value is -1.

Exceptions

Exception Type	Condition
ArgumentException	The assigned value is less than the default, -1. -or- The assigned value is greater than the **Items** count.

Remarks

The **SelectedIndex** property holds the index value of the item in the collection that is currently selected in the up-down control. Collection items can be re-assigned new index values if the **Sorted** property has been changed from **false** to **true**. As the collection is re-sorted alphabetically, the items will be assigned a new index value.

Note If the user has entered an item in the up-down control, or if no item has been selected, the **SelectedIndex** value will be the default value, -1.

Example

See related example in the **System.Windows.Forms.DomainUpDown** class topic.

Requirements

Platforms: Windows 98, Windows NT 4.0, Windows Millennium Edition, Windows 2000, Windows XP Home Edition, Windows XP Professional, Windows Server 2003 family, .NET Compact Framework - Windows CE .NET

DomainUpDown.SelectedItem Property

Gets or sets the selected item based on the index value of the selected item in the collection.

```
[Visual Basic]
Public Property SelectedItem As Object
[C#]
public object SelectedItem {get; set;}
[C++]
public: __property Object* get_SelectedItem();
public: __property void set_SelectedItem(Object*);
[JScript]
public function get SelectedItem() : Object;
public function set SelectedItem(Object);
```

Property Value

The selected item based on the **SelectedIndex** value. The default value is a null reference (**Nothing** in Visual Basic).

Remarks

When this property is set, the value is validated to be one of the items in the collection, and the **SelectedIndex** property is set to the appropriate index value.

Example

See related example in the **System.Windows.Forms.DomainUpDown** class topic.

Requirements

Platforms: Windows 98, Windows NT 4.0, Windows Millennium Edition, Windows 2000, Windows XP Home Edition, Windows XP Professional, Windows Server 2003 family

DomainUpDown.Sorted Property

Gets or sets a value indicating whether the item collection is sorted.

```
[Visual Basic]
Public Property Sorted As Boolean
[C#]
public bool Sorted {get; set;}
[C++]
public: __property bool get_Sorted();
public: __property void set_Sorted(bool);
[JScript]
public function get Sorted() : Boolean;
public function set Sorted(Boolean);
```

Property Value

true if the item collection is sorted; otherwise, **false**. The default value is **false**.

Remarks

When **Sorted** is set to **true**, the collection is sorted in alphabetical order.

Example

See related example in the **System.Windows.Forms.DomainUpDown** class topic.

Requirements

Platforms: Windows 98, Windows NT 4.0, Windows Millennium Edition, Windows 2000, Windows XP Home Edition, Windows XP Professional, Windows Server 2003 family

DomainUpDown.Wrap Property

Gets or sets a value indicating whether the collection of items continues to the first or last item if the user continues past the end of the list.

```
[Visual Basic]
Public Property Wrap As Boolean
[C#]
public bool Wrap {get; set;}
[C++]
public: __property bool get_Wrap();
public: __property void set_Wrap(bool);
[JScript]
public function get Wrap() : Boolean;
public function set Wrap(Boolean);
```

Property Value

true if the list starts again when the user reaches the beginning or end of the collection; otherwise, **false**. The default value is **false**.

Remarks

When **Wrap** is set to **true**, if you reach the last item in the collection and continue, the list will start over with the first item and appear to be continuous. This behavior works in reverse as well.

Example

See related example in the **System.Windows.Forms.DomainUpDown** class topic.

Requirements

Platforms: Windows 98, Windows NT 4.0, Windows Millennium Edition, Windows 2000, Windows XP Home Edition, Windows XP Professional, Windows Server 2003 family, .NET Compact Framework - Windows CE .NET

DomainUpDown.CreateAccessibilityInstance Method

This member overrides **Control.CreateAccessibilityInstance**.

```
[Visual Basic]
Overrides Protected Function CreateAccessibilityInstance() As _
   AccessibleObject
[C#]
protected override AccessibleObject CreateAccessibilityInstance();
```

```
[C++]
protected: AccessibleObject* CreateAccessibilityInstance();
[JScript]
protected override function CreateAccessibilityInstance() :
   AccessibleObject;
```

Requirements

Platforms: Windows 98, Windows NT 4.0, Windows Millennium Edition, Windows 2000, Windows XP Home Edition, Windows XP Professional, Windows Server 2003 family

DomainUpDown.DownButton Method

Displays the next item in the object collection.

```
[Visual Basic]
Overrides Public Sub DownButton()
[C#]
public override void DownButton();
[C++]
public: void DownButton();
[JScript]
public override function DownButton();
```

Remarks

As you move through the collection of items in the **DomainUp-Down** control using the down button, you will eventually reach the last item in the collection. If you continue, and **Wrap** is set to **true**, the list will start over with the first item in the collection and appear to be continuous. This behavior is also true when moving through the collection using the up button.

Requirements

Platforms: Windows 98, Windows NT 4.0, Windows Millennium Edition, Windows 2000, Windows XP Home Edition, Windows XP Professional, Windows Server 2003 family

DomainUpDown.OnChanged Method

This member supports the .NET Framework infrastructure and is not intended to be used directly from your code.

```
[Visual Basic]
Overrides Protected Sub OnChanged( _
   ByVal source As Object, _
   ByVal e As EventArgs _
)
[C#]
protected override void OnChanged(
   object source,
   EventArgs e
);
[C++]
protected: void OnChanged(
   Object* source,
   EventArgs* e
);
[JScript]
protected override function OnChanged(
   source : Object,
   e : EventArgs
);
```

DomainUpDown.OnSelectedItemChanged Method

Raises the **SelectedItemChanged** event.

```
[Visual Basic]
Protected Sub OnSelectedItemChanged( _
   ByVal source As Object, _
   ByVal e As EventArgs _
)
[C#]
protected void OnSelectedItemChanged(
   object source,
   EventArgs e
);
[C++]
protected: void OnSelectedItemChanged(
   Object* source,
   EventArgs* e
);
[JScript]
protected function OnSelectedItemChanged(
   source : Object,
   e : EventArgs
);
```

Parameters

source

The source of the event.

e

An **EventArgs** that contains the event data.

Remarks

Raising an event invokes the event handler through a delegate.

The **OnSelectedItemChanged** method also allows derived classes to handle the event without attaching a delegate. This is the preferred technique for handling the event in a derived class.

Notes to Inheritors: When overriding **OnSelectedItemChanged** in a derived class, be sure to call the base class's **OnSelected-ItemChanged** method so that registered delegates receive the event.

Example

See related example in the **System.Windows.Forms.DomainUpDown** class topic.

Requirements

Platforms: Windows 98, Windows NT 4.0, Windows Millennium Edition, Windows 2000, Windows XP Home Edition, Windows XP Professional, Windows Server 2003 family, .NET Compact Framework - Windows CE .NET

DomainUpDown.OnTextBoxKeyDown Method

This member overrides **UpDownBase.OnTextBoxKeyDown**.

```
[Visual Basic]
Overrides Protected Sub OnTextBoxKeyDown( _
   ByVal source As Object, _
   ByVal e As KeyEventArgs _
)
```

```
[C#]
protected override void OnTextBoxKeyDown(
   object source,
   KeyEventArgs e
);
[C++]
protected: void OnTextBoxKeyDown(
   Object* source,
   KeyEventArgs* e
);
[JScript]
protected override function OnTextBoxKeyDown(
   source : Object,
   e : KeyEventArgs
);
```

Requirements

Platforms: Windows 98, Windows NT 4.0, Windows Millennium Edition, Windows 2000, Windows XP Home Edition, Windows XP Professional, Windows Server 2003 family

DomainUpDown.ToString Method

This member overrides **Object.ToString**.

```
[Visual Basic]
Overrides Public Function ToString() As String
[C#]
public override string ToString();
[C++]
public: String* ToString();
[JScript]
public override function ToString() : String;
```

Requirements

Platforms: Windows 98, Windows NT 4.0, Windows Millennium Edition, Windows 2000, Windows XP Home Edition, Windows XP Professional, Windows Server 2003 family, .NET Compact Framework - Windows CE .NET

DomainUpDown.UpButton Method

Displays the previous item in the collection.

```
[Visual Basic]
Overrides Public Sub UpButton()
[C#]
public override void UpButton();
[C++]
public: void UpButton();
[JScript]
public override function UpButton();
```

Remarks

As you move through the collection of items in the **DomainUpDown** control using the up button, you will eventually reach the first item in the collection. If you continue, and **Wrap** is set to **true**, the list will start over with the last item in the collection and appear to be continuous. This behavior is also true when moving through the collection using the down button.

Requirements

Platforms: Windows 98, Windows NT 4.0, Windows Millennium Edition, Windows 2000, Windows XP Home Edition, Windows XP Professional, Windows Server 2003 family

DomainUpDown.UpdateEditText Method

Updates the text in the up-down control to display the selected item.

```
[Visual Basic]
Overrides Protected Sub UpdateEditText()
[C#]
protected override void UpdateEditText();
[C++]
protected: void UpdateEditText();
[JScript]
protected override function UpdateEditText();
```

Requirements

Platforms: Windows 98, Windows NT 4.0, Windows Millennium Edition, Windows 2000, Windows XP Home Edition, Windows XP Professional, Windows Server 2003 family

DomainUpDown.SelectedItemChanged Event

Occurs when the **SelectedItem** property has been changed.

```
[Visual Basic]
Public Event SelectedItemChanged As EventHandler
[C#]
public event EventHandler SelectedItemChanged;
[C++]
public: __event EventHandler* SelectedItemChanged;
```

[JScript] In JScript, you can handle the events defined by a class, but you cannot define your own.

Event Data

The event handler receives an argument of type **EventArgs**.

Remarks

For the **SelectedItemChanged** event to occur, the **SelectedItem** property can be changed in code, by the user typing in a new value or clicking the control's up or down buttons.

Requirements

Platforms: Windows 98, Windows NT 4.0, Windows Millennium Edition, Windows 2000, Windows XP Home Edition, Windows XP Professional, Windows Server 2003 family

DomainUpDown.DomainItemAccessibleObject Class

This type supports the .NET Framework infrastructure and is not intended to be used directly from your code.

```
[Visual Basic]
<ComVisible(True)>
Public Class DomainUpDown.DomainItemAccessibleObject
   Inherits AccessibleObject
[C#]
[ComVisible(true)]
public class DomainUpDown.DomainItemAccessibleObject :
   AccessibleObject
[C++]
[ComVisible(true)]
public __gc class DomainUpDown.DomainItemAccessibleObject : public
   AccessibleObject
[JScript]
public
   ComVisible(true)
class DomainUpDown.DomainItemAccessibleObject extends
   AccessibleObject
```

DomainUpDown.DomainItemAccessibleObject Constructor

This member supports the .NET Framework infrastructure and is not intended to be used directly from your code.

```
[Visual Basic]
Public Sub New( _
   ByVal name As String, _
   ByVal parent As AccessibleObject _
)
[C#]
public DomainUpDown.DomainItemAccessibleObject(
   string name,
   AccessibleObject parent
);
[C++]
public: DomainItemAccessibleObject(
   String* name,
   AccessibleObject* parent
);
[JScript]
public function DomainUpDown.DomainItemAccessibleObject(
   name : String,
   parent : AccessibleObject
);
```

DomainUpDown.DomainItemAccessibleObject.Name Property

This member overrides **AccessibleObject.Name**.

```
[Visual Basic]
Overrides Public Property Name As String
[C#]
public override string Name {get; set;}
[C++]
public: __property String* get_Name();
public: __property void set_Name(String*);
[JScript]
public override function get Name() : String;
public override function set Name(String);
```

Requirements

Platforms: Windows 98, Windows NT 4.0, Windows Millennium Edition, Windows 2000, Windows XP Home Edition, Windows XP Professional, Windows Server 2003 family

DomainUpDown.DomainItemAccessibleObject.Parent Property

This member overrides **AccessibleObject.Parent**.

```
[Visual Basic]
Overrides Public ReadOnly Property Parent As AccessibleObject
[C#]
public override AccessibleObject Parent {get;}
[C++]
public: __property AccessibleObject* get_Parent();
[JScript]
public override function get Parent() : AccessibleObject;
```

Requirements

Platforms: Windows 98, Windows NT 4.0, Windows Millennium Edition, Windows 2000, Windows XP Home Edition, Windows XP Professional, Windows Server 2003 family

DomainUpDown.DomainItemAccessibleObject.Role Property

This member overrides **AccessibleObject.Role**.

```
[Visual Basic]
Overrides Public ReadOnly Property Role As AccessibleRole
[C#]
public override AccessibleRole Role {get;}
[C++]
public: __property AccessibleRole get_Role();
[JScript]
public override function get Role() : AccessibleRole;
```

Requirements

Platforms: Windows 98, Windows NT 4.0, Windows Millennium Edition, Windows 2000, Windows XP Home Edition, Windows XP Professional, Windows Server 2003 family

DomainUpDown.DomainItemAccessibleObject.State Property

This member overrides **AccessibleObject.State**.

[Visual Basic]
```
Overrides Public ReadOnly Property State As AccessibleStates
```
[C#]
```
public override AccessibleStates State {get;}
```
[C++]
```
public: __property AccessibleStates get_State();
```
[JScript]
```
public override function get State() : AccessibleStates;
```

Requirements

Platforms: Windows 98, Windows NT 4.0, Windows Millennium Edition, Windows 2000, Windows XP Home Edition, Windows XP Professional, Windows Server 2003 family

DomainUpDown.DomainItemAccessibleObject.Value Property

This member overrides **AccessibleObject.Value**.

[Visual Basic]
```
Overrides Public ReadOnly Property Value As String
```
[C#]
```
public override string Value {get;}
```
[C++]
```
public: __property String* get_Value();
```
[JScript]
```
public override function get Value() : String;
```

Requirements

Platforms: Windows 98, Windows NT 4.0, Windows Millennium Edition, Windows 2000, Windows XP Home Edition, Windows XP Professional, Windows Server 2003 family

DomainUpDown.DomainUpDownAccessibleObject Class

This type supports the .NET Framework infrastructure and is not intended to be used directly from your code.

[Visual Basic]
```
<ComVisible(True)>
Public Class DomainUpDown.DomainUpDownAccessibleObject
   Inherits Control.ControlAccessibleObject
```
[C#]
```
[ComVisible(true)]
public class DomainUpDown.DomainUpDownAccessibleObject :
   Control.ControlAccessibleObject
```
[C++]
```
[ComVisible(true)]
public __gc class DomainUpDown.DomainUpDownAccessibleObject :
   public Control.ControlAccessibleObject
```
[JScript]
```
public
   ComVisible(true)
class DomainUpDown.DomainUpDownAccessibleObject extends
   Control.ControlAccessibleObject
```

DomainUpDown.DomainUpDownAccessibleObject Constructor

This member supports the .NET Framework infrastructure and is not intended to be used directly from your code.

[Visual Basic]
```
Public Sub New( _
   ByVal owner As Control _
)
```
[C#]
```
public DomainUpDown.DomainUpDownAccessibleObject(
   Control owner
);
```
[C++]
```
public: DomainUpDownAccessibleObject(
   Control* owner
);
```
[JScript]
```
public function DomainUpDown.DomainUpDownAccessibleObject(
   owner : Control
);
```

DomainUpDown.DomainUpDownAccessibleObject.Role Property

This member overrides **AccessibleObject.Role**.

[Visual Basic]
```
Overrides Public ReadOnly Property Role As AccessibleRole
```
[C#]
```
public override AccessibleRole Role {get;}
```
[C++]
```
public: __property AccessibleRole get_Role();
```
[JScript]
```
public override function get Role() : AccessibleRole;
```

Requirements

Platforms: Windows 98, Windows NT 4.0, Windows Millennium Edition, Windows 2000, Windows XP Home Edition, Windows XP Professional, Windows Server 2003 family

DomainUpDown.DomainUpDownAccessibleObject.GetChild Method

This member overrides **AccessibleObject.GetChild**.

[Visual Basic]
```
Overrides Public Function GetChild( _
   ByVal index As Integer _
) As AccessibleObject
```
[C#]
```
public override AccessibleObject GetChild(
   int index
);
```
[C++]
```
public: AccessibleObject* GetChild(
   int index
);
```
[JScript]
```
public override function GetChild(
   index : int
) : AccessibleObject;
```

Requirements

Platforms: Windows 98, Windows NT 4.0, Windows Millennium Edition, Windows 2000, Windows XP Home Edition, Windows XP Professional, Windows Server 2003 family

DomainUpDown.DomainUpDownAccessibleObject.GetChildCount Method

This member overrides **AccessibleObject.GetChildCount**.

[Visual Basic]
```
Overrides Public Function GetChildCount() As Integer
```
[C#]
```
public override int GetChildCount();
```
[C++]
```
public: int GetChildCount();
```
[JScript]
```
public override function GetChildCount() : int;
```

Requirements

Platforms: Windows 98, Windows NT 4.0, Windows Millennium Edition, Windows 2000, Windows XP Home Edition, Windows XP Professional, Windows Server 2003 family

DomainUpDown.DomainUpDownItemCollection Class

Encapsulates a collection of objects for use by the **DomainUpDown** class.

System.Object
  System.Collections.ArrayList
    System.Windows.Forms.DomainUpDown.DomainUpDownItemCollection

[Visual Basic]
```
Public Class DomainUpDown.DomainUpDownItemCollection
   Inherits ArrayList
```
[C#]
```
public class DomainUpDown.DomainUpDownItemCollection : ArrayList
```
[C++]
```
public __gc class DomainUpDown.DomainUpDownItemCollection : public
   ArrayList
```
[JScript]
```
public class DomainUpDown.DomainUpDownItemCollection extends
   ArrayList
```

Thread Safety

Any public static (**Shared** in Visual Basic) members of this type are safe for multithreaded operations. Any instance members are not guaranteed to be thread safe.

Remarks

To create a collection of objects to display in the **DomainUpDown** control, you can add or remove the items individually by using the **Add** and **Remove** methods. The collection is accessed from the parent control, **DomainUpDown**, by the **Items** property.

Example

[Visual Basic, C#] The following example creates and initializes a **DomainUpDown** control. The example allows you to set some of its properties and create a collection of strings for display in the up-down control. The code assumes that a **TextBox**, **CheckBox** and a **Button** have been instantiated on a form. The example also assumes that you have a member variable at the class level declared as a 32-bit signed integer named `myCounter`. You can enter a string in the text box and add it to the **Items** collection when the button is clicked. By clicking the check box, you can toggle the **Sorted** property and observe the difference in the collection of items in the up-down control.

[Visual Basic]
```
Protected domainUpDown1 As DomainUpDown

Private Sub InitializeMyDomainUpDown()
    ' Create and initialize the DomainUpDown control.
    domainUpDown1 = New DomainUpDown()

    ' Add the DomainUpDown control to the form.
    Controls.Add(domainUpDown1)
End Sub 'InitializeMyDomainUpDown

Private Sub button1_Click(sender As Object, e As EventArgs)
    ' Add the text box contents and initial location in the collection
    ' to the DomainUpDown control.
    domainUpDown1.Items.Add((textBox1.Text.Trim() & " - " & myCounter))

    ' Increment the counter variable.
    myCounter = myCounter + 1

    ' Clear the TextBox.
    textBox1.Text = ""
End Sub 'button1_Click

Private Sub checkBox1_Click(sender As Object, e As EventArgs)
    ' If Sorted is set to true, set it to false;
    ' otherwise set it to true.
    If domainUpDown1.Sorted Then
        domainUpDown1.Sorted = False
    Else
        domainUpDown1.Sorted = True
    End If
End Sub 'checkBox1_Click

Private Sub domainUpDown1_SelectedItemChanged _
    (sender As Object, e As EventArgs)

    ' Display the SelectedIndex and
    ' SelectedItem property values in a MessageBox.
    MessageBox.Show(("SelectedIndex: " &                              ↵
domainUpDown1.SelectedIndex.ToString() & _
        ControlChars.Cr & "SelectedItem: " &                          ↵
domainUpDown1.SelectedItem.ToString()))
End Sub 'domainUpDown1_SelectedItemChanged
```

[C#]
```
protected DomainUpDown domainUpDown1;

private void InitializeMyDomainUpDown()
 {
    // Create and initialize the DomainUpDown control.
    domainUpDown1 = new DomainUpDown();

    // Add the DomainUpDown control to the form.
    Controls.Add(domainUpDown1);
 }

 private void button1_Click(Object sender,
                            EventArgs e)
 {
    // Add the text box contents and initial location in the collection
    // to the DomainUpDown control.
    domainUpDown1.Items.Add((textBox1.Text.Trim()) + " - " +          ↵
myCounter);

    // Increment the counter variable.
    myCounter = myCounter + 1;

    // Clear the TextBox.
    textBox1.Text = "";
 }

 private void checkBox1_Click(Object sender,
                              EventArgs e)
 {
    // If Sorted is set to true, set it to false;
    // otherwise set it to true.
    if (domainUpDown1.Sorted)
    {
       domainUpDown1.Sorted = false;
    }
    else
    {
       domainUpDown1.Sorted = true;
    }
 }

 private void domainUpDown1_SelectedItemChanged(Object sender,
                                                 EventArgs e)
 {
    // Display the SelectedIndex and
    // SelectedItem property values in a MessageBox.
    MessageBox.Show("SelectedIndex: " +                               ↵
domainUpDown1.SelectedIndex.ToString()
       + "\n" + "SelectedItem: " +
domainUpDown1.SelectedItem.ToString());
 }
```

Requirements

Namespace: System.Windows.Forms

Platforms: Windows 98, Windows NT 4.0,
Windows Millennium Edition, Windows 2000,
Windows XP Home Edition, Windows XP Professional,
Windows Server 2003 family,
.NET Compact Framework - Windows CE .NET

Assembly: System.Windows.Forms (in System.Windows.Forms.dll)

DomainUpDown.DomainUpDownItemCollection.Item Property

Gets or sets the item at the specified indexed location in the collection.

[C#] In C#, this property is the indexer for the **DomainUpDown.DomainUpDownItemCollection** class.

```
[Visual Basic]
Overrides Public Default Property Item( _
   ByVal index As Integer _
) As Object  Implements IList.Item
[C#]
public override object this[
   int index
] {get; set;}
[C++]
public: __property Object* get_Item(
   int index
);
public: __property void set_Item(
   int index,
   Object*
);
[JScript]
returnValue = DomainUpDownItemCollectionObject.Item(index);
DomainUpDownItemCollectionObject.Item(index) = returnValue;
-or-
returnValue = DomainUpDownItemCollectionObject(index);
DomainUpDownItemCollectionObject(index) = returnValue;
```

[JScript] In JScript, you can use the default indexed properties defined by a type, but you cannot explicitly define your own. However, specifying the **expando** attribute on a class automatically provides a default indexed property whose type is **Object** and whose index type is **String**.

Arguments [JScript]

index

The indexed location of the item in the collection.

Parameters [Visual Basic, C#, C++]

index

The indexed location of the item in the collection.

Property Value

An **Object** that represents the item at the specified indexed location.

Implements

IList.Item

Remarks

To assign items to a specific location, or to retrieve them from the **DomainUpDown.DomainUpDownItemCollection**, you can reference the collection object with a specific index value. The index value of the **DomainUpDown.DomainUpDownItemCollection** is a zero-based index.

Requirements

Platforms: Windows 98, Windows NT 4.0,
Windows Millennium Edition, Windows 2000,
Windows XP Home Edition, Windows XP Professional,
Windows Server 2003 family

DomainUpDown.DomainUpDownItemCollection.Add Method

Adds the specified object to the end of the collection.

```
[Visual Basic]
Overrides Public Function Add( _
   ByVal item As Object _
) As Integer Implements IList.Add
[C#]
public override int Add(
   object item
);
[C++]
public: int Add(
   Object* item
);
[JScript]
public override function Add(
   item : Object
) : int;
```

Parameters

item

The **Object** to be added to the end of the collection.

Return Value

The zero-based index value of the **Object** added to the collection.

Implements

IList.Add

Remarks

You can also add a new **Object** to the collection by using the **Insert** method.

To remove an **Object** that you have previously added, use the **Remove** or **RemoveAt** methods.

Example

[Visual Basic, C#] The following example creates and initializes a **DomainUpDown** control. The example allows you to set some of its properties and create a collection of strings for display in the up-down control. The code assumes that a **TextBox**, **CheckBox** and a **Button** have been instantiated on a form. The example also assumes that you have a member variable at the class level declared as a 32-bit signed integer named `myCounter`. You can enter a string in the text box and add it to the **Items** collection when the button is clicked. By clicking the check box, you can toggle the **Sorted** property and observe the difference in the collection of items in the up-down control.

[Visual Basic]
```
Protected domainUpDown1 As DomainUpDown

Private Sub InitializeMyDomainUpDown()
    ' Create and initialize the DomainUpDown control.
    domainUpDown1 = New DomainUpDown()

    ' Add the DomainUpDown control to the form.
    Controls.Add(domainUpDown1)
End Sub 'InitializeMyDomainUpDown

Private Sub button1_Click(sender As Object, e As EventArgs)
    ' Add the text box contents and initial location in the collection
    ' to the DomainUpDown control.
    domainUpDown1.Items.Add((textBox1.Text.Trim() & " - " & myCounter))

    ' Increment the counter variable.
    myCounter = myCounter + 1

    ' Clear the TextBox.
    textBox1.Text = ""
End Sub 'button1_Click

Private Sub checkBox1_Click(sender As Object, e As EventArgs)
    ' If Sorted is set to true, set it to false;
    ' otherwise set it to true.
    If domainUpDown1.Sorted Then
        domainUpDown1.Sorted = False
    Else
        domainUpDown1.Sorted = True
    End If
End Sub 'checkBox1_Click

Private Sub domainUpDown1_SelectedItemChanged _
    (sender As Object, e As EventArgs)

    ' Display the SelectedIndex and
    ' SelectedItem property values in a MessageBox.
    MessageBox.Show(("SelectedIndex: " &                              ↵
domainUpDown1.SelectedIndex.ToString() & _
        ControlChars.Cr & "SelectedItem: " &                          ↵
domainUpDown1.SelectedItem.ToString()))
End Sub 'domainUpDown1_SelectedItemChanged
```

[C#]
```
protected DomainUpDown domainUpDown1;

private void InitializeMyDomainUpDown()
 {
    // Create and initialize the DomainUpDown control.
    domainUpDown1 = new DomainUpDown();

    // Add the DomainUpDown control to the form.
    Controls.Add(domainUpDown1);
 }

 private void button1_Click(Object sender,
                            EventArgs e)
 {
    // Add the text box contents and initial location in the collection
    // to the DomainUpDown control.
    domainUpDown1.Items.Add((textBox1.Text.Trim()) + " - " +          ↵
myCounter);

    // Increment the counter variable.
    myCounter = myCounter + 1;

    // Clear the TextBox.
    textBox1.Text = "";
 }

 private void checkBox1_Click(Object sender,
                              EventArgs e)
 {
    // If Sorted is set to true, set it to false;
    // otherwise set it to true.
    if (domainUpDown1.Sorted)
    {
       domainUpDown1.Sorted = false;
    }
    else
    {
       domainUpDown1.Sorted = true;
    }
 }

 private void domainUpDown1_SelectedItemChanged(Object sender,
                                                 EventArgs e)
 {
    // Display the SelectedIndex and
    // SelectedItem property values in a MessageBox.
    MessageBox.Show("SelectedIndex: " +                               ↵
domainUpDown1.SelectedIndex.ToString()
       + "\n" + "SelectedItem: " +                                    ↵
domainUpDown1.SelectedItem.ToString());
 }
```

Requirements

Platforms: Windows 98, Windows NT 4.0, Windows Millennium Edition, Windows 2000, Windows XP Home Edition, Windows XP Professional, Windows Server 2003 family, .NET Compact Framework - Windows CE .NET

DomainUpDown.DomainUpDownItemCollection.Insert Method

Inserts the specified object into the collection at the specified location.

[Visual Basic]
```
Overrides Public Sub Insert( _
   ByVal index As Integer, _
   ByVal item As Object _
) Implements IList.Insert
```
[C#]
```
public override void Insert(
   int index,
   object item
);
```
[C++]
```
public: void Insert(
   int index,
   Object* item
);
```
[JScript]
```
public override function Insert(
   index : int,
   item : Object
);
```

Parameters

index
: The indexed location within the collection to insert the **Object**.

item
: The **Object** to insert.

Implements

IList.Insert

Remarks

You can also add a new **Object** to the collection by using the **Add** method.

To remove an **Object** that you have previously added, use the **Remove** or **RemoveAt** methods.

Requirements

Platforms: Windows 98, Windows NT 4.0,
Windows Millennium Edition, Windows 2000,
Windows XP Home Edition, Windows XP Professional,
Windows Server 2003 family,
.NET Compact Framework - Windows CE .NET

DomainUpDown.DomainUpDownItemCollection.Remove Method

Removes the specified item from the collection.

```
[Visual Basic]
Overrides Public Sub Remove( _
   ByVal item As Object _
) Implements IList.Remove
[C#]
public override void Remove(
   object item
);
[C++]
public: void Remove(
   Object* item
);
[JScript]
public override function Remove(
   item : Object
);
```

Parameters

item

The **Object** to remove from the collection.

Implements

IList.Remove

Remarks

You can also remove an **Object** that you have previously added by using the **RemoveAt** method.

To add a new **Object** to the collection, use the **Insert** or **Add** methods.

Requirements

Platforms: Windows 98, Windows NT 4.0,
Windows Millennium Edition, Windows 2000,
Windows XP Home Edition, Windows XP Professional,
Windows Server 2003 family,
.NET Compact Framework - Windows CE .NET

DomainUpDown.DomainUpDownItemCollection.RemoveAt Method

Removes the item from the specified location in the collection.

```
[Visual Basic]
Overrides Public Sub RemoveAt( _
   ByVal item As Integer _
) Implements IList.RemoveAt
[C#]
public override void RemoveAt(
   int item
);
[C++]
public: void RemoveAt(
   int item
);
[JScript]
public override function RemoveAt(
   item : int
);
```

Parameters

item

The indexed location of the **Object** in the collection.

Implements

IList.RemoveAt

Remarks

You can also remove an **Object** that you have previously added by using the **Remove** method.

To add a new **Object** to the collection, use the **Insert** or **Add** methods.

Requirements

Platforms: Windows 98, Windows NT 4.0,
Windows Millennium Edition, Windows 2000,
Windows XP Home Edition, Windows XP Professional,
Windows Server 2003 family,
.NET Compact Framework - Windows CE .NET

DragAction Enumeration

Specifies how and if a drag-and-drop operation should continue.

[Visual Basic]
```
<Serializable>
<ComVisible(True)>
Public Enum DragAction
```
[C#]
```
[Serializable]
[ComVisible(true)]
public enum DragAction
```
[C++]
```
[Serializable]
[ComVisible(true)]
__value public enum DragAction
```
[JScript]
```
public
   Serializable
   ComVisible(true)
enum DragAction
```

Remarks

This enumeration is used by **QueryContinueDragEventArgs**.

Members

Member name	Description
Cancel	The operation is canceled with no drop message.
Continue	The operation will continue.
Drop	The operation will stop with a drop.

Example

[Visual Basic, C#, C++] The following example demonstrates a drag-and-drop operation between two **ListBox** controls. The example calls the **DoDragDrop** method when the drag action starts. The drag action starts if the mouse has moved more than **SystemInformation.DragSize** from the mouse location during the **MouseDown** event. The **IndexFromPoint** method is used to determine the index of the item to drag during the **MouseDown** event.

[Visual Basic, C#, C++] The example also demonstrates using custom cursors for the drag-and-drop operation. The example assumes that two cursor files, `3dwarro.cur` and `3dwno.cur`, exist in the application directory, for the custom drag and no-drop cursors, respectively. The custom cursors will be used if the `UseCustomCursorsCheck` **CheckBox** is checked. The custom cursors are set in the **GiveFeedback** event handler.

[Visual Basic, C#, C++] The keyboard state is evaluated in the **DragOver** event handler for the right **ListBox**, to determine what the drag operation will be based upon state of the SHIFT, CTRL, ALT, or CTRL+ALT keys. The location in the **ListBox** where the drop would occur is also determined during the **DragOver** event. If the data to drop is not a **String**, then the **DragEventArgs.Effect** is set to **DragDropEffects.None**. Finally, the status of the drop is displayed in the `DropLocationLabel` **Label**.

[Visual Basic, C#, C++] The data to drop for the right **ListBox** is determined in the **DragDrop** event handler and the **String** value is added at the appropriate place in the **ListBox**. If the drag operation moves outside the bounds of the form, then the drag-and-drop operation is canceled in the **QueryContinueDrag** event handler.

[Visual Basic, C#, C++] This code excerpt demonstrates using the **DragAction** enumeration. See the **DoDragDrop** method for the complete code example.

[Visual Basic]
```
Private Sub ListDragSource_QueryContinueDrag(ByVal sender As 
Object, ByVal e As QueryContinueDragEventArgs) Handles 
ListDragSource.QueryContinueDrag
    ' Cancel the drag if the mouse moves off the form.
    Dim lb as ListBox = CType(sender, System.Windows.Forms.ListBox)

    If Not (lb is nothing) Then

        Dim f as Form = lb.FindForm()

        ' Cancel the drag if the mouse moves off the form. 
 The screenOffset
        ' takes into account any desktop bands that may be 
 at the top or left
        ' side of the screen.
        If (((Control.MousePosition.X - screenOffset.X) < 
f.DesktopBounds.Left) Or _
            ((Control.MousePosition.X - screenOffset.X) > 
f.DesktopBounds.Right) Or _
            ((Control.MousePosition.Y - screenOffset.Y) < 
f.DesktopBounds.Top) Or _
            ((Control.MousePosition.Y - screenOffset.Y) > 
f.DesktopBounds.Bottom)) Then

            e.Action = DragAction.Cancel
        End If
    End if
End Sub
```

[C#]
```
private void ListDragSource_QueryContinueDrag(object 
sender, System.Windows.Forms.QueryContinueDragEventArgs e) {
    // Cancel the drag if the mouse moves off the form.
    ListBox lb = sender as ListBox;

    if (lb != null) {

        Form f = lb.FindForm();

        // Cancel the drag if the mouse moves off the form. 
 The screenOffset
        // takes into account any desktop bands that may be 
 at the top or left
        // side of the screen.
        if (((Control.MousePosition.X - screenOffset.X) < 
f.DesktopBounds.Left) ||
            ((Control.MousePosition.X - screenOffset.X) > 
f.DesktopBounds.Right) ||
            ((Control.MousePosition.Y - screenOffset.Y) < 
f.DesktopBounds.Top) ||
            ((Control.MousePosition.Y - screenOffset.Y) > 
f.DesktopBounds.Bottom)) {

            e.Action = DragAction.Cancel;
        }
    }
}
```

[C++]
```
private:
    void ListDragSource_QueryContinueDrag(Object* sender,
        System::Windows::Forms::QueryContinueDragEventArgs* e) {
        // Cancel the drag if the mouse moves off the form.
        ListBox* lb = dynamic_cast<ListBox*>(sender);

        if (lb != 0) {

            Form* f = lb->FindForm();

            // Cancel the drag if the mouse moves off the                ↵
 form. The screenOffset
            // takes into account any desktop bands that may             ↵
 be at the top or left
            // side of the screen.
            if (((Control::MousePosition.X - screenOffset.X)             ↵
 < f->DesktopBounds.Left) ||
                ((Control::MousePosition.X - screenOffset.X)             ↵
 > f->DesktopBounds.Right) ||
                ((Control::MousePosition.Y - screenOffset.Y)             ↵
 < f->DesktopBounds.Top) ||
                ((Control::MousePosition.Y - screenOffset.Y)             ↵
 > f->DesktopBounds.Bottom)) {

                    e->Action = DragAction::Cancel;
                }
        }
    }
```

Requirements

Namespace: System.Windows.Forms

Platforms: Windows 98, Windows NT 4.0, Windows Millennium Edition, Windows 2000, Windows XP Home Edition, Windows XP Professional, Windows Server 2003 family

Assembly: System.Windows.Forms (in System.Windows.Forms.dll)

DragDropEffects Enumeration

Specifies the effects of a drag-and-drop operation.

This enumeration has a **FlagsAttribute** attribute that allows a bitwise combination of its member values.

[Visual Basic]
```
<Flags>
<Serializable>
Public Enum DragDropEffects
```
[C#]
```
[Flags]
[Serializable]
public enum DragDropEffects
```
[C++]
```
[Flags]
[Serializable]
__value public enum DragDropEffects
```
[JScript]
```
public
   Flags
   Serializable
enum DragDropEffects
```

Remarks

This enumeration is used by the following classes: **DragEventArgs**, **GiveFeedbackEventArgs**, and **Control**.

Members

Member name	Description	Value
All	The data is copied, removed from the drag source, and scrolled in the drop target.	-2147483645
Copy	The data is copied to the drop target.	1
Link	The data from the drag source is linked to the drop target.	4
Move	The data from the drag source is moved to the drop target.	2
None	The drop target does not accept the data.	0
Scroll	Scrolling is about to start or is currently occurring in the drop target.	-2147483648

Example

[Visual Basic, C#, C++] The following example demonstrates a drag-and-drop operation between two **ListBox** controls. The example calls the **DoDragDrop** method when the drag action starts. The drag action starts if the mouse has moved more than **SystemInformation.DragSize** from the mouse location during the **MouseDown** event. The **IndexFromPoint** method is used to determine the index of the item to drag during the **MouseDown** event.

[Visual Basic, C#, C++] The example also demonstrates using custom cursors for the drag-and-drop operation. The example assumes that two cursor files, `3dwarro.cur` and `3dwno.cur`, exist in the application directory, for the custom drag and no-drop cursors, respectively. The custom cursors will be used if the `UseCustomCursorsCheck` **CheckBox** is checked. The custom cursors are set in the **GiveFeedback** event handler.

[Visual Basic, C#, C++] The keyboard state is evaluated in the **DragOver** event handler for the right **ListBox**, to determine what the drag operation will be based upon state of the SHIFT, CTRL, ALT, or CTRL+ALT keys. The location in the **ListBox** where the drop would occur is also determined during the **DragOver** event. If the data to drop is not a **String**, then the **DragEventArgs.Effect** is set to **DragDropEffects.None**. Finally, the status of the drop is displayed in the `DropLocationLabel` **Label**.

[Visual Basic, C#, C++] The data to drop for the right **ListBox** is determined in the **DragDrop** event handler and the **String** value is added at the appropriate place in the **ListBox**. If the drag operation moves outside the bounds of the form, then the drag-and-drop operation is canceled in the **QueryContinueDrag** event handler.

[Visual Basic, C#, C++] This code excerpt demonstrates using the **DragDropEffects** enumeration. See the **DoDragDrop** method for the complete code example.

[Visual Basic]
```
Private Sub ListDragTarget_DragOver(ByVal sender As Object, ↵
 ByVal e As DragEventArgs) Handles ListDragTarget.DragOver
    ' Determine whether string data exists in the drop data. ↵
 If not, then
    ' the drop effect reflects that the drop cannot occur.
    If Not (e.Data.GetDataPresent(GetType(System.String))) Then

        e.Effect = DragDropEffects.None
        DropLocationLabel.Text = "None - no string data."
        Return
    End If

    ' Set the effect based upon the KeyState.
    If ((e.KeyState And (8 + 32)) = (8 + 32) And _
        (e.AllowedEffect And DragDropEffects.Link) = ↵
DragDropEffects.Link) Then
        ' KeyState 8 + 32 = CTL + ALT

        ' Link drag and drop effect.
        e.Effect = DragDropEffects.Link

    ElseIf ((e.KeyState And 32) = 32 And _
        (e.AllowedEffect And DragDropEffects.Link) = ↵
DragDropEffects.Link) Then

        ' ALT KeyState for link.
        e.Effect = DragDropEffects.Link

    ElseIf ((e.KeyState And 4) = 4 And _
        (e.AllowedEffect And DragDropEffects.Move) = ↵
DragDropEffects.Move) Then

        ' SHIFT KeyState for move.
        e.Effect = DragDropEffects.Move

    ElseIf ((e.KeyState And 8) = 8 And _
        (e.AllowedEffect And DragDropEffects.Copy) = ↵
DragDropEffects.Copy) Then

        ' CTL KeyState for copy.
        e.Effect = DragDropEffects.Copy

    ElseIf ((e.AllowedEffect And DragDropEffects.Move) = ↵
DragDropEffects.Move) Then

        ' By default, the drop action should be move, if allowed.
        e.Effect = DragDropEffects.Move

    Else
        e.Effect = DragDropEffects.None
    End If

    ' Gets the index of the item the mouse is below.
```

```
    ' The mouse locations are relative to the screen, so they must be
    ' converted to client coordinates.

    indexOfItemUnderMouseToDrop = _
        ListDragTarget.IndexFromPoint                                    ↵
(ListDragTarget.PointToClient(New Point(e.X, e.Y)))

    ' Updates the label text.
    If (indexOfItemUnderMouseToDrop <> ListBox.NoMatches) Then

        DropLocationLabel.Text = "Drops before item #" &                 ↵
(indexOfItemUnderMouseToDrop + 1)
    Else
        DropLocationLabel.Text = "Drops at the end."
    End If

End Sub
```

[C#]

```
private void ListDragTarget_DragOver(object sender,                      ↵
System.Windows.Forms.DragEventArgs e)
{

    // Determine whether string data exists in the drop data.            ↵
If not, then
    // the drop effect reflects that the drop cannot occur.
    if (!e.Data.GetDataPresent(typeof(System.String))) {

        e.Effect = DragDropEffects.None;
        DropLocationLabel.Text = "None - no string data.";
        return;
    }

    // Set the effect based upon the KeyState.
    if ((e.KeyState & (8+32)) == (8+32) &&
        (e.AllowedEffect & DragDropEffects.Link) ==                      ↵
DragDropEffects.Link) {
        // KeyState 8 + 32 = CTL + ALT

        // Link drag and drop effect.
        e.Effect = DragDropEffects.Link;

    } else if ((e.KeyState & 32) == 32 &&
        (e.AllowedEffect & DragDropEffects.Link) ==                      ↵
DragDropEffects.Link) {

        // ALT KeyState for link.
        e.Effect = DragDropEffects.Link;

    } else if ((e.KeyState & 4) == 4 &&
        (e.AllowedEffect & DragDropEffects.Move) ==                      ↵
DragDropEffects.Move) {

        // SHIFT KeyState for move.
        e.Effect = DragDropEffects.Move;

    } else if ((e.KeyState & 8) == 8 &&
        (e.AllowedEffect & DragDropEffects.Copy) ==                      ↵
DragDropEffects.Copy) {

        // CTL KeyState for copy.
        e.Effect = DragDropEffects.Copy;

    } else if ((e.AllowedEffect & DragDropEffects.Move) ==               ↵
DragDropEffects.Move)  {

        // By default, the drop action should be move, if allowed.
        e.Effect = DragDropEffects.Move;

    } else
        e.Effect = DragDropEffects.None;

    // Get the index of the item the mouse is below.

    // The mouse locations are relative to the screen, so they must be
    // converted to client coordinates.

    indexOfItemUnderMouseToDrop =
        ListDragTarget.IndexFromPoint                                    ↵
(ListDragTarget.PointToClient(new Point(e.X, e.Y)));

    // Updates the label text.
    if (indexOfItemUnderMouseToDrop != ListBox.NoMatches){

        DropLocationLabel.Text = "Drops before item #" +                 ↵
(indexOfItemUnderMouseToDrop + 1);
    } else
        DropLocationLabel.Text = "Drops at the end.";

}
```

[C++]

```
private:
    void ListDragTarget_DragOver(Object* /*sender*/,
        System::Windows::Forms::DragEventArgs* e) {

        // Determine whether String* data exists in the                  ↵
 drop data. If not, then
        // the drop effect reflects that the drop cannot occur.
        if (!e->Data->GetDataPresent(__typeof(System::String))) {

            e->Effect = DragDropEffects::None;
            DropLocationLabel->Text = S"None - no String* data.";
            return;
        }

        // Set the effect based upon the KeyState.
        if ((e->KeyState & (8+32)) == (8+32) &&
            (e->AllowedEffect & DragDropEffects::Link) ==                ↵
DragDropEffects::Link) {
                // KeyState 8 + 32 = CTL + ALT

                // Link drag and drop effect.
                e->Effect = DragDropEffects::Link;

            } else if ((e->KeyState & 32) == 32 &&
                (e->AllowedEffect & DragDropEffects::Link) ==            ↵
DragDropEffects::Link) {

                    // ALT KeyState for link.
                    e->Effect = DragDropEffects::Link;

                } else if ((e->KeyState & 4) == 4 &&
                    (e->AllowedEffect & DragDropEffects::Move) ==
                    DragDropEffects::Move) {
                        // SHIFT KeyState for move.
                        e->Effect = DragDropEffects::Move;

                    } else if ((e->KeyState & 8) == 8 &&
                        (e->AllowedEffect & DragDropEffects::Copy) ==
                        DragDropEffects::Copy) {
                            // CTL KeyState for copy.
                            e->Effect = DragDropEffects::Copy;

                        } else if ((e->AllowedEffect &                   ↵
DragDropEffects::Move) ==
                            DragDropEffects::Move) {
                            // By default, the drop action               ↵
should be move, if allowed.
                            e->Effect = DragDropEffects::Move;

                        } else
                            e->Effect = DragDropEffects::None;

                        // Get the index of the item the                 ↵
 mouse is below.
```

```
                    // The mouse locations are relative           ↵
to the screen, so they must be
                    // converted to client coordinates.

                    indexOfItemUnderMouseToDrop =
                        ListDragTarget->IndexFromPoint(
                        ListDragTarget->PointToClient             ↵
(Point(e->X, e->Y)));

                    // Updates the label text.
                    if (indexOfItemUnderMouseToDrop !=            ↵
ListBox::NoMatches) {

                        DropLocationLabel->Text =
                            String::Concat(S"Drops before item # ",
                            __box(                                ↵
(indexOfItemUnderMouseToDrop + 1)));
                    } else
                        DropLocationLabel->Text = S"Drops         ↵
at the end.";

    }
```

Requirements

Namespace: System.Windows.Forms

Platforms: Windows 98, Windows NT 4.0, Windows Millennium Edition, Windows 2000, Windows XP Home Edition, Windows XP Professional, Windows Server 2003 family

Assembly: System.Windows.Forms (in System.Windows.Forms.dll)

DragEventArgs Class

Provides data for the **DragDrop**, **DragEnter**, or **DragOver** event.

System.Object
  System.EventArgs
    System.Windows.Forms.DragEventArgs

[Visual Basic]
```
<ComVisible(True)>
Public Class DragEventArgs
   Inherits EventArgs
```
[C#]
```
[ComVisible(true)]
public class DragEventArgs : EventArgs
```
[C++]
```
[ComVisible(true)]
public __gc class DragEventArgs : public EventArgs
```
[JScript]
```
public
   ComVisible(true)
class DragEventArgs extends EventArgs
```

Thread Safety

Any public static (**Shared** in Visual Basic) members of this type are safe for multithreaded operations. Any instance members are not guaranteed to be thread safe.

Remarks

The **DragDrop** event occurs when the user completes a drag-and-drop operation by dragging an object over the control and then dropping it onto the control by releasing the mouse button. The **DragEnter** event occurs when the user moves the mouse pointer onto the control while dragging an object with the mouse. The **DragOver** event occurs when the user moves the mouse pointer over the control while dragging an object with the mouse.

A **DragEventArgs** object specifies any data associated with this event; the current state of the SHIFT, CTRL, and ALT keys; the location of the mouse pointer; and the drag-and-drop effects allowed by the source and target of the drag event.

Example

[Visual Basic, C#, C++] The following example demonstrates a drag-and-drop operation between two **ListBox** controls. The example calls the **DoDragDrop** method when the drag action starts. The drag action starts if the mouse has moved more than **SystemInformation.DragSize** from the mouse location during the **MouseDown** event. The **IndexFromPoint** method is used to determine the index of the item to drag during the **MouseDown** event.

[Visual Basic, C#, C++] The example also demonstrates using custom cursors for the drag-and-drop operation. The example assumes that two cursor files, `3dwarro.cur` and `3dwno.cur`, exist in the application directory, for the custom drag and no-drop cursors, respectively. The custom cursors will be used if the `UseCustomCursorsCheck` **CheckBox** is checked. The custom cursors are set in the **GiveFeedback** event handler.

[Visual Basic, C#, C++] The keyboard state is evaluated in the **DragOver** event handler for the right **ListBox**, to determine what the drag operation will be based upon state of the SHIFT, CTRL, ALT, or CTRL+ALT keys. The location in the **ListBox** where the drop would occur is also determined during the **DragOver** event. If the data to drop is not a **String**, then the **DragEventArgs.Effect** is set to **DragDropEffects.None**. Finally, the status of the drop is displayed in the `DropLocationLabel` **Label**.

[Visual Basic, C#, C++] The data to drop for the right **ListBox** is determined in the **DragDrop** event handler and the **String** value is added at the appropriate place in the **ListBox**. If the drag operation moves outside the bounds of the form, then the drag-and-drop operation is canceled in the **QueryContinueDrag** event handler.

[Visual Basic, C#, C++] This code excerpt demonstrates using the **DragEventArgs** class. See the **DoDragDrop** method for the complete code example.

[Visual Basic]
```
Private Sub ListDragTarget_DragOver(ByVal sender As Object, ByVal e As DragEventArgs) Handles ListDragTarget.DragOver
    ' Determine whether string data exists in the drop data. If not, then
    ' the drop effect reflects that the drop cannot occur.
    If Not (e.Data.GetDataPresent(GetType(System.String))) Then

        e.Effect = DragDropEffects.None
        DropLocationLabel.Text = "None - no string data."
        Return
    End If

    ' Set the effect based upon the KeyState.
    If ((e.KeyState And (8 + 32)) = (8 + 32) And _
        (e.AllowedEffect And DragDropEffects.Link) = DragDropEffects.Link) Then
        ' KeyState 8 + 32 = CTL + ALT

        ' Link drag and drop effect.
        e.Effect = DragDropEffects.Link

    ElseIf ((e.KeyState And 32) = 32 And _
        (e.AllowedEffect And DragDropEffects.Link) = DragDropEffects.Link) Then

        ' ALT KeyState for link.
        e.Effect = DragDropEffects.Link

    ElseIf ((e.KeyState And 4) = 4 And _
        (e.AllowedEffect And DragDropEffects.Move) = DragDropEffects.Move) Then

        ' SHIFT KeyState for move.
        e.Effect = DragDropEffects.Move

    ElseIf ((e.KeyState And 8) = 8 And _
        (e.AllowedEffect And DragDropEffects.Copy) = DragDropEffects.Copy) Then

        ' CTL KeyState for copy.
        e.Effect = DragDropEffects.Copy

    ElseIf ((e.AllowedEffect And DragDropEffects.Move) = DragDropEffects.Move) Then

        ' By default, the drop action should be move, if allowed.
        e.Effect = DragDropEffects.Move

    Else
        e.Effect = DragDropEffects.None
    End If

    ' Gets the index of the item the mouse is below.

    ' The mouse locations are relative to the screen, so they must be
    ' converted to client coordinates.

    indexOfItemUnderMouseToDrop = _
        ListDragTarget.IndexFromPoint(ListDragTarget.PointToClient(New Point(e.X, e.Y)))

    ' Updates the label text.
    If (indexOfItemUnderMouseToDrop <> ListBox.NoMatches) Then

        DropLocationLabel.Text = "Drops before item #" & (indexOfItemUnderMouseToDrop + 1)
```

```
    Else
        DropLocationLabel.Text = "Drops at the end."
    End If

End Sub
```

[C#]

```
private void ListDragTarget_DragOver(object sender, ↵
System.Windows.Forms.DragEventArgs e)
{

    // Determine whether string data exists in the drop ↵
data. If not, then
    // the drop effect reflects that the drop cannot occur.
    if (!e.Data.GetDataPresent(typeof(System.String))) {

        e.Effect = DragDropEffects.None;
        DropLocationLabel.Text = "None - no string data.";
        return;
    }

    // Set the effect based upon the KeyState.
    if ((e.KeyState & (8+32)) == (8+32) &&
        (e.AllowedEffect & DragDropEffects.Link) == ↵
DragDropEffects.Link) {
        // KeyState 8 + 32 = CTL + ALT

        // Link drag and drop effect.
        e.Effect = DragDropEffects.Link;

    } else if ((e.KeyState & 32) == 32 &&
        (e.AllowedEffect & DragDropEffects.Link) == ↵
DragDropEffects.Link) {

        // ALT KeyState for link.
        e.Effect = DragDropEffects.Link;

    } else if ((e.KeyState & 4) == 4 &&
        (e.AllowedEffect & DragDropEffects.Move) == ↵
DragDropEffects.Move) {

        // SHIFT KeyState for move.
        e.Effect = DragDropEffects.Move;

    } else if ((e.KeyState & 8) == 8 &&
        (e.AllowedEffect & DragDropEffects.Copy) == ↵
DragDropEffects.Copy) {

        // CTL KeyState for copy.
        e.Effect = DragDropEffects.Copy;

    } else if ((e.AllowedEffect & DragDropEffects.Move) == ↵
DragDropEffects.Move)  {

        // By default, the drop action should be move, if allowed.
        e.Effect = DragDropEffects.Move;

    } else
        e.Effect = DragDropEffects.None;

    // Get the index of the item the mouse is below.

    // The mouse locations are relative to the screen, so they must be
    // converted to client coordinates.

    indexOfItemUnderMouseToDrop =
        ListDragTarget.IndexFromPoint ↵
 (ListDragTarget.PointToClient(new Point(e.X, e.Y)));

    // Updates the label text.
    if (indexOfItemUnderMouseToDrop != ListBox.NoMatches){

        DropLocationLabel.Text = "Drops before item #" + ↵
 (indexOfItemUnderMouseToDrop + 1);
    } else
        DropLocationLabel.Text = "Drops at the end.";

}
```

[C++]

```
private:
    void ListDragTarget_DragOver(Object* /*sender*/,
        System::Windows::Forms::DragEventArgs* e) {

        // Determine whether String* data exists in the drop ↵
 data. If not, then
        // the drop effect reflects that the drop cannot occur.
        if (!e->Data->GetDataPresent ↵
 (__typeof(System::String))) {

            e->Effect = DragDropEffects::None;
            DropLocationLabel->Text = S"None - no String* data.";
            return;
        }

        // Set the effect based upon the KeyState.
        if ((e->KeyState & (8+32)) == (8+32) &&
            (e->AllowedEffect & DragDropEffects::Link) == ↵
DragDropEffects::Link) {
                // KeyState 8 + 32 = CTL + ALT

                // Link drag and drop effect.
                e->Effect = DragDropEffects::Link;

            } else if ((e->KeyState & 32) == 32 &&
                (e->AllowedEffect & DragDropEffects::Link) ↵
 == DragDropEffects::Link) {

                    // ALT KeyState for link.
                    e->Effect = DragDropEffects::Link;

                } else if ((e->KeyState & 4) == 4 &&
                    (e->AllowedEffect & DragDropEffects::Move) ==
                    DragDropEffects::Move) {
                        // SHIFT KeyState for move.
                        e->Effect = DragDropEffects::Move;

                    } else if ((e->KeyState & 8) == 8 &&
                        (e->AllowedEffect & DragDropEffects::Copy) ==
                        DragDropEffects::Copy) {
                            // CTL KeyState for copy.
                            e->Effect = DragDropEffects::Copy;

                        } else if ((e->AllowedEffect & ↵
DragDropEffects::Move) ==
                            DragDropEffects::Move) {
                            // By default, the drop action ↵
 should be move, if allowed.
                            e->Effect = DragDropEffects::Move;

                        } else
                            e->Effect = DragDropEffects::None;

                        // Get the index of the item the ↵
 mouse is below.

                        // The mouse locations are ↵
relative to the screen, so they must be
                        // converted to client coordinates.

                        indexOfItemUnderMouseToDrop =
                            ListDragTarget->IndexFromPoint(
                            ListDragTarget->PointToClient ↵
 (Point(e->X, e->Y)));

                        // Updates the label text.
                        if (indexOfItemUnderMouseToDrop != ↵
ListBox::NoMatches) {

                            DropLocationLabel->Text =
                                String::Concat(S"Drops before item # ",
                                __box( ↵
 (indexOfItemUnderMouseToDrop + 1)));
                        } else
                            DropLocationLabel->Text = ↵
S"Drops at the end.";

    }
```

[Visual Basic, C#, C++] The following example illustrates how **DragEventArgs** are passed between the source and target of a drag-and-drop operation. In this example, a **ListBox** control is the source of the data, and the **RichTextBox** control is the target. The example assumes that the **ListBox** control has been populated with a list of valid filenames. When the user drags one of the displayed filenames from the **ListBox** control onto the **RichTextBox** control, the file referenced in the filename is opened.

[Visual Basic, C#, C++] The operation is initiated in the **ListBox** control's MouseDown event. In the **DragEnter** event handler, the example uses the **GetDataPresent** method to verify that the data is in a format that the **RichTextBox** control can display and then sets the **DragDropEffects** property to specify that data should be copied from the source control to the target control. Finally, the **RichTextBox** control's DragDrop event handler uses the **GetData** method to retrieve the filename to open.

[Visual Basic]
```
Private Sub Form1_Load(ByVal sender As System.Object, ByVal e As ↵
System.EventArgs) Handles MyBase.Load
   ' Sets the AllowDrop property so that data can be dragged onto ↵
 the control.
   RichTextBox1.AllowDrop = True

   ' Add code here to populate the ListBox1 with paths to text files.

End Sub

Private Sub RichTextBox1_DragEnter(ByVal sender As Object, ByVal ↵
 e As System.Windows.Forms.DragEventArgs) Handles ↵
RichTextBox1.DragEnter
   ' If the data is text, copy the data to the RichTextBox control.
   If (e.Data.GetDataPresent("Text")) Then
      e.Effect = DragDropEffects.Copy
   End If
End Sub

Private Overloads Sub RichTextBox1_DragDrop(ByVal sender ↵
 As Object, ByVal e As System.Windows.Forms.DragEventArgs) ↵
Handles RichTextBox1.DragDrop
   ' Loads the file into the control.
   RichTextBox1.LoadFile(e.Data.GetData("Text"), ↵
System.Windows.Forms.RichTextBoxStreamType.RichText)
End Sub

Private Sub ListBox1_MouseDown(ByVal sender As Object, ↵
 ByVal e As System.Windows.Forms.MouseEventArgs) Handles ↵
ListBox1.MouseDown
   Dim Lb As ListBox
   Dim Pt As New Point(e.X, e.Y)
   Dim Index As Integer

   ' Determines which item was selected.
   Lb = sender
   Index = Lb.IndexFromPoint(Pt)

   ' Starts a drag-and-drop operation with that item.
   If Index >= 0 Then
      Lb.DoDragDrop(Lb.Items(Index), DragDropEffects.Link)
   End If
End Sub
```

[C#]
```
private void Form1_Load(object sender, EventArgs e)
{
   // Sets the AllowDrop property so that data can be ↵
dragged onto the control.
   richTextBox1.AllowDrop = true;

   // Add code here to populate the ListBox1 with paths to text files.

}

private void listBox1_MouseDown(object sender, ↵
System.Windows.Forms.MouseEventArgs e)
{
   // Determines which item was selected.
   ListBox lb =( (ListBox)sender);
   Point pt = new Point(e.X,e.Y);
   int index = lb.IndexFromPoint(pt);

   // Starts a drag-and-drop operation with that item.
   if(index>=0)
   {
      lb.DoDragDrop(lb.Items[index].ToString(), DragDropEffects.Link);
   }
}

private void richTextBox1_DragEnter(object sender, DragEventArgs e)
{
   // If the data is text, copy the data to the RichTextBox control.
   if(e.Data.GetDataPresent("Text"))
      e.Effect = DragDropEffects.Copy;
}

private void richTextBox1_DragDrop(object sender, DragEventArgs e)
{
   // Loads the file into the control.
   richTextBox1.LoadFile((String)e.Data.GetData("Text"), ↵
System.Windows.Forms.RichTextBoxStreamType.RichText);
}
```

[C++]
```
private:
    void Form1_Load(Object* /*sender*/, EventArgs* /*e*/) {
        // Sets the AllowDrop property so that data can be ↵
 dragged onto the control.
        richTextBox1->AllowDrop = true;

        // Add code here to populate the ListBox1 with paths ↵
 to text files.
    }

    void listBox1_MouseDown(Object* sender, ↵
 System::Windows::Forms::MouseEventArgs* e) {
        // Determines which item was selected.
        ListBox* lb =(dynamic_cast<ListBox*>(sender));
        Point pt = Point(e->X, e->Y);
        int index = lb->IndexFromPoint(pt);

        // Starts a drag-and-drop operation with that item.
        if (index>=0) {
            lb->DoDragDrop(lb->Items->Item[index], ↵
DragDropEffects::Link);
        }
    }

    void richTextBox1_DragEnter(Object* /*sender*/, DragEventArgs* e) {
        // If the data is text, copy the data to the ↵
RichTextBox control.
        if (e->Data->GetDataPresent(S"Text"))
            e->Effect = DragDropEffects::Copy;
    }

    void richTextBox1_DragDrop(Object* /*sender*/, DragEventArgs* e) {
        // Loads the file into the control.
        richTextBox1->LoadFile(dynamic_cast<String*>(e->Data- ↵
>GetData(S"Text")),
            System::Windows::Forms::RichTextBoxStreamType::RichText);
    }
```

Requirements

Namespace: System.Windows.Forms

Platforms: Windows 98, Windows NT 4.0, Windows Millennium Edition, Windows 2000, Windows XP Home Edition, Windows XP Professional, Windows Server 2003 family

Assembly: System.Windows.Forms (in System.Windows.Forms.dll)

DragEventArgs Constructor

Initializes a new instance of the **DragEventArgs** class.

[Visual Basic]
```
Public Sub New( _
   ByVal data As IDataObject, _
   ByVal keyState As Integer, _
   ByVal x As Integer, _
   ByVal y As Integer, _
   ByVal allowedEffect As DragDropEffects, _
   ByVal effect As DragDropEffects _
)
```
[C#]
```
public DragEventArgs(
   IDataObject data,
   int keyState,
   int x,
   int y,
   DragDropEffects allowedEffect,
   DragDropEffects effect
);
```
[C++]
```
public: DragEventArgs(
   IDataObject* data,
   int keyState,
   int x,
   int y,
   DragDropEffects allowedEffect,
   DragDropEffects effect
);
```
[JScript]
```
public function DragEventArgs(
   data : IDataObject,
   keyState : int,
   x : int,
   y : int,
   allowedEffect : DragDropEffects,
   effect : DragDropEffects
);
```

Parameters

data
  The data associated with this event.

keyState
  The current state of the SHIFT, CTRL, and ALT keys.

x
  The x-coordinate of the mouse cursor in pixels.

y
  The y-coordinate of the mouse cursor in pixels.

allowedEffect
  One of the **DragDropEffects** values.

effect
  One of the **DragDropEffects** values.

Requirements

Platforms: Windows 98, Windows NT 4.0,
Windows Millennium Edition, Windows 2000,
Windows XP Home Edition, Windows XP Professional,
Windows Server 2003 family

DragEventArgs.AllowedEffect Property

Gets which drag-and-drop operations are allowed by the originator (or source) of the drag event.

[Visual Basic]
```
Public ReadOnly Property AllowedEffect As DragDropEffects
```
[C#]
```
public DragDropEffects AllowedEffect {get;}
```
[C++]
```
public: __property DragDropEffects get_AllowedEffect();
```
[JScript]
```
public function get AllowedEffect() : DragDropEffects;
```

Property Value

One of the **DragDropEffects** values.

Remarks

When a control initiates a drag-and-drop operation by calling the **Control.DoDragDrop** method, it specifies the permissible effects of the operation. For example, when you drag a file from a source, if the file is read-only (or from a read-only storage medium such as a CD), the source will indicate that the file can be copied, but not transferred, to the target.

Before attempting to perform an operation on the dragged data, you should examine this property to ensure that the operation is allowed.

Example

See related example in the **System.Windows.Forms.DragEventArgs** class topic.

Requirements

Platforms: Windows 98, Windows NT 4.0,
Windows Millennium Edition, Windows 2000,
Windows XP Home Edition, Windows XP Professional,
Windows Server 2003 family

DragEventArgs.Data Property

Gets the **IDataObject** that contains the data associated with this event.

[Visual Basic]
```
Public ReadOnly Property Data As IDataObject
```
[C#]
```
public IDataObject Data {get;}
```
[C++]
```
public: __property IDataObject* get_Data();
```
[JScript]
```
public function get Data() : IDataObject;
```

Property Value

The data associated with this event.

Remarks

In the body of your event handler, you can use the **GetDataPresent** method to determine whether the data matches the format requirements of the control onto which the data is being dragged. You also can specify whether you want to attempt to convert the data to meet your format requirements. If the dragged data meets your format requirements, use the **GetData** method to retrieve the data.

Example

See related example in the **System.Windows.Forms.DragEventArgs** class topic.

Requirements

Platforms: Windows 98, Windows NT 4.0, Windows Millennium Edition, Windows 2000, Windows XP Home Edition, Windows XP Professional, Windows Server 2003 family

DragEventArgs.Effect Property

Gets or sets the target drop effect in a drag-and-drop operation.

```
[Visual Basic]
Public Property Effect As DragDropEffects
[C#]
public DragDropEffects Effect {get; set;}
[C++]
public: __property DragDropEffects get_Effect();
public: __property void set_Effect(DragDropEffects);
[JScript]
public function get Effect() : DragDropEffects;
public function set Effect(DragDropEffects);
```

Property Value

One of the **DragDropEffects** values.

Remarks

By default, the effect applied determines the mouse cursor for the target of a drag-and-drop operation. This is useful to provide feedback to the user on the operation that will occur. For example, if you press the CTRL key when you drag a file from a source, specify **DragDropEffects.Copy** to indicate the target will try to perform a copy operation.

Example

Requirements

Platforms: Windows 98, Windows NT 4.0, Windows Millennium Edition, Windows 2000, Windows XP Home Edition, Windows XP Professional, Windows Server 2003 family

DragEventArgs.KeyState Property

Gets the current state of the SHIFT, CTRL, and ALT keys, as well as the state of the mouse buttons.

```
[Visual Basic]
Public ReadOnly Property KeyState As Integer
[C#]
public int KeyState {get;}
[C++]
public: __property int get_KeyState();
[JScript]
public function get KeyState() : int;
```

Property Value

The current state of the SHIFT, CTRL, and ALT keys and of the mouse buttons.

Remarks

You can make the effect of a drag-and-drop operation to depend on the state of a particular key. For example, you may decide to copy or move data depending on whether the CTRL or SHIFT keys are pressed during the drag-and-drop operation.

The bits that are set in the **KeyState** property identify the keys or mouse buttons that were pressed during the operation. For example, if the left mouse button is pressed, the first bit in the **KeyState** property is set. You can use the bitwise AND operator to test for a given key state.

The following table lists the bits that are set for a specified event.

Bit	Key
1	The left mouse button.
2	The right mouse button.
4	The SHIFT key.
8	The CTRL key.
16	The middle mouse button.
32	The ALT key.

Example

See related example in the **System.Windows.Forms.DragEventArgs** class topic.

Requirements

Platforms: Windows 98, Windows NT 4.0, Windows Millennium Edition, Windows 2000, Windows XP Home Edition, Windows XP Professional, Windows Server 2003 family

DragEventArgs.X Property

Gets the x-coordinate of the mouse pointer, in screen coordinates.

```
[Visual Basic]
Public ReadOnly Property X As Integer
[C#]
public int X {get;}
[C++]
public: __property int get_X();
[JScript]
public function get X() : int;
```

Property Value

The x-coordinate of the mouse pointer in pixels.

Example

See related example in the **System.Windows.Forms.DragEventArgs** class topic.

Requirements

Platforms: Windows 98, Windows NT 4.0, Windows Millennium Edition, Windows 2000, Windows XP Home Edition, Windows XP Professional, Windows Server 2003 family

DragEventArgs.Y Property

Gets the y-coordinate of the mouse pointer, in screen coordinates.

```
[Visual Basic]
Public ReadOnly Property Y As Integer
[C#]
public int Y {get;}
[C++]
public: __property int get_Y();
[JScript]
public function get Y() : int;
```

Property Value

The y-coordinate of the mouse pointer in pixels.

Example

See related example in the **System.Windows.Forms.DragEventArgs** class topic.

Requirements

Platforms: Windows 98, Windows NT 4.0, Windows Millennium Edition, Windows 2000, Windows XP Home Edition, Windows XP Professional, Windows Server 2003 family

DragEventHandler Delegate

Represents the method that will handle the **DragDrop**, **DragEnter**, or **DragOver** event of a **Control**.

[Visual Basic]
```
<Serializable>
Public Delegate Sub DragEventHandler( _
   ByVal sender As Object, _
   ByVal e As DragEventArgs _
)
```
[C#]
```
[Serializable]
public delegate void DragEventHandler(
   object sender,
   DragEventArgs e
);
```
[C++]
```
[Serializable]
public __gc __delegate void DragEventHandler(
   Object* sender,
   DragEventArgs* e
);
```

[JScript] In JScript, you can use the delegates in the .NET Framework, but you cannot define your own.

Parameters [Visual Basic, C#, C++]

The declaration of your event handler must have the same parameters as the **DragEventHandler** delegate declaration.

sender

The source of the event.

e

A **DragEventArgs** that contains the event data.

Example

See related example in the **System.Windows.Forms.DragEventArgs** class topic.

Requirements

Namespace: System.Windows.Forms

Platforms: Windows 98, Windows NT 4.0, Windows Millennium Edition, Windows 2000, Windows XP Home Edition, Windows XP Professional, Windows Server 2003 family

Assembly: System.Windows.Forms (in System.Windows.Forms.dll)

DrawItemEventArgs Class

Provides data for the **DrawItem** event.

System.Object
  System.EventArgs
    System.Windows.Forms.DrawItemEventArgs
      System.Windows.Forms.StatusBarDrawItemEventArgs

[Visual Basic]
```
Public Class DrawItemEventArgs
   Inherits EventArgs
```
[C#]
```
public class DrawItemEventArgs : EventArgs
```
[C++]
```
public __gc class DrawItemEventArgs : public EventArgs
```
[JScript]
```
public class DrawItemEventArgs extends EventArgs
```

Thread Safety

Any public static (**Shared** in Visual Basic) members of this type are safe for multithreaded operations. Any instance members are not guaranteed to be thread safe.

Remarks

The **DrawItem** event is raised by owner draw controls, such as **ListBox** and **ComboBox** controls. It contains all the information needed for the user to paint the specified item, including the item index, the **Rectangle**, and the **Graphics** on which the drawing should be done.

Example

[Visual Basic, C#] The following example demonstrates how to create owner-drawn **ListBox** items. The code uses the **DrawMode** property to specify that the items drawn are fixed sized and the **DrawItem** event to perform the drawing of each item into the **ListBox**. The example code uses the properties and methods of the **DrawItemEventArgs** class passed as a parameter to the event handler to draw the items. This example assumes that a **ListBox** control called `listBox1` has been added to a form and that the **DrawItem** event is handled by the event handler defined in the example code. The example also assumes that items have been added to the **ListBox** with the text of "Apple", "Orange", and "Plum" in that order.

[Visual Basic]
```
Private Sub listBox1_DrawItem(ByVal sender As System.Object, ↵
ByVal e As System.Windows.Forms.DrawItemEventArgs) Handles ↵
ListBox1.DrawItem
   ' Set the DrawMode property to draw fixed sized items.
   ListBox1.DrawMode = DrawMode.OwnerDrawFixed
   ' Draw the background of the ListBox control for each item.
   e.DrawBackground()
   ' Create a new Brush and initialize to a Black colored brush ↵
by default.
   Dim myBrush As Brush

   ' Determine the color of the brush to draw each item based ↵
on the index of the item to draw.
   Select Case (e.Index)
      Case 0
         myBrush = Brushes.Red
      Case 1
         myBrush = Brushes.Orange
      Case 2
         myBrush = Brushes.Purple
   End Select

   ' Draw the current item text based on the current Font and ↵
the custom brush settings.
   e.Graphics.DrawString(ListBox1.Items(e.Index), e.Font, ↵
myBrush, New RectangleF(e.Bounds.X, e.Bounds.Y, e.Bounds.Width, ↵
e.Bounds.Height))
   ' If the ListBox has focus, draw a focus rectangle around the ↵
selected item.
   e.DrawFocusRectangle()
End Sub
```

[C#]
```
private void listBox1_DrawItem(object sender, ↵
System.Windows.Forms.DrawItemEventArgs e)
{
   // Set the DrawMode property to draw fixed sized items.
   listBox1.DrawMode = DrawMode.OwnerDrawFixed;
   // Draw the background of the ListBox control for each item.
   e.DrawBackground();
   // Create a new Brush and initialize to a Black colored ↵
brush by default.
   Brush myBrush = Brushes.Black;

   // Determine the color of the brush to draw each item ↵
based on the index of the item to draw.
   switch (e.Index)
   {
      case 0:
         myBrush = Brushes.Red;
         break;
      case 1:
         myBrush = Brushes.Orange;
         break;
      case 2:
         myBrush = Brushes.Purple;
         break;
   }

   // Draw the current item text based on the current Font ↵
and the custom brush settings.
   e.Graphics.DrawString(listBox1.Items[e.Index].ToString(), ↵
e.Font, myBrush,e.Bounds,StringFormat.GenericDefault);
   // If the ListBox has focus, draw a focus rectangle around ↵
the selected item.
   e.DrawFocusRectangle();
}
```

Requirements

Namespace: System.Windows.Forms

Platforms: Windows 98, Windows NT 4.0, Windows Millennium Edition, Windows 2000, Windows XP Home Edition, Windows XP Professional, Windows Server 2003 family

Assembly: System.Windows.Forms (in System.Windows.Forms.dll)

DrawItemEventArgs Constructor

Initializes a new instance of the **DrawItemEventArgs** class.

Overload List

Initializes a new instance of the **DrawItemEventArgs** class for the specified control with the specified font, state, surface to draw on, and the bounds to draw within.

[Visual Basic] **Public Sub New(Graphics, Font, Rectangle, Integer, DrawItemState)**

[C#] **public DrawItemEventArgs(Graphics, Font, Rectangle, int, DrawItemState);**

[C++] **public: DrawItemEventArgs(Graphics*, Font*, Rectangle, int, DrawItemState);**

[JScript] **public function DrawItemEventArgs(Graphics, Font, Rectangle, int, DrawItemState);**

Initializes a new instance of the **DrawItemEventArgs** class for the specified control with the specified font, state, foreground color, background color, surface to draw on, and the bounds to draw within.

[Visual Basic] **Public Sub New(Graphics, Font, Rectangle, Integer, DrawItemState, Color, Color)**

[C#] **public DrawItemEventArgs(Graphics, Font, Rectangle, int, DrawItemState, Color, Color);**

[C++] **public: DrawItemEventArgs(Graphics*, Font*, Rectangle, int, DrawItemState, Color, Color);**

[JScript] **public function DrawItemEventArgs(Graphics, Font, Rectangle, int, DrawItemState, Color, Color);**

DrawItemEventArgs Constructor (Graphics, Font, Rectangle, Int32, DrawItemState)

Initializes a new instance of the **DrawItemEventArgs** class for the specified control with the specified font, state, surface to draw on, and the bounds to draw within.

[Visual Basic]
```
Public Sub New( _
   ByVal graphics As Graphics, _
   ByVal font As Font, _
   ByVal rect As Rectangle, _
   ByVal index As Integer, _
   ByVal state As DrawItemState _
)
```
[C#]
```
public DrawItemEventArgs(
   Graphics graphics,
   Font font,
   Rectangle rect,
   int index,
   DrawItemState state
);
```
[C++]
```
public: DrawItemEventArgs(
   Graphics* graphics,
   Font* font,
   Rectangle rect,
   int index,
   DrawItemState state
);
```
[JScript]
```
public function DrawItemEventArgs(
   graphics : Graphics,
   font : Font,
   rect : Rectangle,
   index : int,
   state : DrawItemState
);
```

Parameters

graphics

The **Graphics** surface on which to draw.

font

The **Font** to use, usually the parent control's **Font** property.

rect

The **Rectangle** bounds to draw within.

index

The **System.Windows.Forms.Control.ControlCollection** index value of the item that is being drawn.

state

The control's **DrawItemState** information.

Requirements

Platforms: Windows 98, Windows NT 4.0, Windows Millennium Edition, Windows 2000, Windows XP Home Edition, Windows XP Professional, Windows Server 2003 family

DrawItemEventArgs Constructor (Graphics, Font, Rectangle, Int32, DrawItemState, Color, Color)

Initializes a new instance of the **DrawItemEventArgs** class for the specified control with the specified font, state, foreground color, background color, surface to draw on, and the bounds to draw within.

[Visual Basic]
```
Public Sub New( _
   ByVal graphics As Graphics, _
   ByVal font As Font, _
   ByVal rect As Rectangle, _
   ByVal index As Integer, _
   ByVal state As DrawItemState, _
   ByVal foreColor As Color, _
   ByVal backColor As Color _
)
```
[C#]
```
public DrawItemEventArgs(
   Graphics graphics,
   Font font,
   Rectangle rect,
   int index,
   DrawItemState state,
   Color foreColor,
   Color backColor
);
```
[C++]
```
public: DrawItemEventArgs(
   Graphics* graphics,
   Font* font,
   Rectangle rect,
   int index,
   DrawItemState state,
   Color foreColor,
   Color backColor
);
```
[JScript]
```
public function DrawItemEventArgs(
   graphics : Graphics,
   font : Font,
   rect : Rectangle,
   index : int,
   state : DrawItemState,
   foreColor : Color,
   backColor : Color
);
```

Parameters

graphics
The **Graphics** surface on which to draw.

font
The **Font** to use, usually the parent control's **Font** property.

rect
The **Rectangle** bounds to draw within.

index
The **System.Windows.Forms.Control.ControlCollection** index value of the item that is being drawn.

state
The control's **DrawItemState** information.

foreColor
The foreground **Color** to draw the control with.

backColor
The background **Color** to draw the control with.

Requirements

Platforms: Windows 98, Windows NT 4.0, Windows Millennium Edition, Windows 2000, Windows XP Home Edition, Windows XP Professional, Windows Server 2003 family

DrawItemEventArgs.BackColor Property

Gets the background color of the item that is being drawn.

[Visual Basic]
```
Public ReadOnly Property BackColor As Color
```
[C#]
```
public Color BackColor {get;}
```
[C++]
```
public: __property Color get_BackColor();
```
[JScript]
```
public function get BackColor() : Color;
```

Property Value

The background **Color** of the item that is being drawn.

Remarks

If the item's state is **DrawItemState.Selected**, the **BackColor** is set to **SystemColors.HighlightText**. If the item's state is not **Selected**, then the **BackColor** property is set to **SystemColors.Window**.

Requirements

Platforms: Windows 98, Windows NT 4.0, Windows Millennium Edition, Windows 2000, Windows XP Home Edition, Windows XP Professional, Windows Server 2003 family

DrawItemEventArgs.Bounds Property

Gets the rectangle that represents the bounds of the item that is being drawn.

[Visual Basic]
```
Public ReadOnly Property Bounds As Rectangle
```
[C#]
```
public Rectangle Bounds {get;}
```
[C++]
```
public: __property Rectangle get_Bounds();
```
[JScript]
```
public function get Bounds() : Rectangle;
```

Property Value

The **Rectangle** that represents the bounds of the item that is being drawn.

Example

See related example in the **System.Windows.Forms.DrawItem-EventArgs** class topic.

Requirements

Platforms: Windows 98, Windows NT 4.0, Windows Millennium Edition, Windows 2000, Windows XP Home Edition, Windows XP Professional, Windows Server 2003 family

DrawItemEventArgs.Font Property

Gets the font assigned to the item being drawn.

[Visual Basic]
```
Public ReadOnly Property Font As Font
```
[C#]
```
public Font Font {get;}
```
[C++]
```
public: __property Font* get_Font();
```
[JScript]
```
public function get Font() : Font;
```

Property Value

The **Font** assigned to the item being drawn.

Remarks

A suggested **Font**, usually the parent control's **Font** property.

Example

See related example in the **System.Windows.Forms.DrawItem-EventArgs** class topic.

Requirements

Platforms: Windows 98, Windows NT 4.0, Windows Millennium Edition, Windows 2000, Windows XP Home Edition, Windows XP Professional, Windows Server 2003 family

DrawItemEventArgs.ForeColor Property

Gets the foreground color of the of the item being drawn.

[Visual Basic]
```
Public ReadOnly Property ForeColor As Color
```
[C#]
```
public Color ForeColor {get;}
```
[C++]
```
public: __property Color get_ForeColor();
```
[JScript]
```
public function get ForeColor() : Color;
```

Property Value

The foreground **Color** of the item being drawn.

Remarks

If the item's state is **DrawItemState.Selected**, the **ForeColor** is set to **SystemColors.HighlightText**. If the item's state is not **Selected**, then the **ForeColor** property is set to **SystemColors.WindowText**.

Requirements

Platforms: Windows 98, Windows NT 4.0, Windows Millennium Edition, Windows 2000, Windows XP Home Edition, Windows XP Professional, Windows Server 2003 family

DrawItemEventArgs.Graphics Property

Gets the graphics surface to draw the item on.

```
[Visual Basic]
Public ReadOnly Property Graphics As Graphics
[C#]
public Graphics Graphics {get;}
[C++]
public: __property Graphics* get_Graphics();
[JScript]
public function get Graphics() : Graphics;
```

Property Value

The **Graphics** surface to draw the item on.

Example

See related example in the **System.Windows.Forms.DrawItem-EventArgs** class topic.

Requirements

Platforms: Windows 98, Windows NT 4.0, Windows Millennium Edition, Windows 2000, Windows XP Home Edition, Windows XP Professional, Windows Server 2003 family

DrawItemEventArgs.Index Property

Gets the index value of the item that is being drawn.

```
[Visual Basic]
Public ReadOnly Property Index As Integer
[C#]
public int Index {get;}
[C++]
public: __property int get_Index();
[JScript]
public function get Index() : int;
```

Property Value

The numeric value that represents the **Item** value of the item being drawn.

Remarks

This property returns the **Item** value of the item being drawn in the **System.Windows.Forms.Control.ControlCollection**.

Example

See related example in the **System.Windows.Forms.DrawItem-EventArgs** class topic.

Requirements

Platforms: Windows 98, Windows NT 4.0, Windows Millennium Edition, Windows 2000, Windows XP Home Edition, Windows XP Professional, Windows Server 2003 family

DrawItemEventArgs.State Property

Gets the state of the item being drawn.

```
[Visual Basic]
Public ReadOnly Property State As DrawItemState
[C#]
public DrawItemState State {get;}
[C++]
public: __property DrawItemState get_State();
[JScript]
public function get State() : DrawItemState;
```

Property Value

The **DrawItemState** that represents the state of the item being drawn.

Remarks

This property value can be a combination of the **DrawItemState** enumeration members. The members can be combined using bitwise operators.

Requirements

Platforms: Windows 98, Windows NT 4.0, Windows Millennium Edition, Windows 2000, Windows XP Home Edition, Windows XP Professional, Windows Server 2003 family

DrawItemEventArgs.DrawBackground Method

Draws the background within the bounds specified in the **DrawItemEventArgs** constructor and with the appropriate color.

```
[Visual Basic]
Public Overridable Sub DrawBackground()
[C#]
public virtual void DrawBackground();
[C++]
public: virtual void DrawBackground();
[JScript]
public function DrawBackground();
```

Remarks

If the item being drawn is **Selected**, the background is drawn with the text highlighted.

Notes to Inheritors: When overriding **DrawBackground** in a derived class, be sure to call the base class's **DrawBackground** method.

Example

See related example in the **System.Windows.Forms.DrawItem-EventArgs** class topic.

Requirements

Platforms: Windows 98, Windows NT 4.0, Windows Millennium Edition, Windows 2000, Windows XP Home Edition, Windows XP Professional, Windows Server 2003 family

DrawItemEventArgs.DrawFocusRectangle Method

Draws a focus rectangle within the bounds specified in the **DrawItemEventArgs** constructor.

[Visual Basic]
```
Public Overridable Sub DrawFocusRectangle()
```
[C#]
```
public virtual void DrawFocusRectangle();
```
[C++]
```
public: virtual void DrawFocusRectangle();
```
[JScript]
```
public function DrawFocusRectangle();
```

Remarks

If the item being drawn has **Focus**, the focus rectangle is drawn.

Notes to Inheritors: When overriding **DrawFocusRectangle** in a derived class, be sure to call the base class's **DrawFocusRectangle** method.

Example

See related example in the **System.Windows.Forms.DrawItem-EventArgs** class topic.

Requirements

Platforms: Windows 98, Windows NT 4.0,
Windows Millennium Edition, Windows 2000,
Windows XP Home Edition, Windows XP Professional,
Windows Server 2003 family

DrawItemEventHandler Delegate

Represents the method that will handle the **DrawItem** event of a **ComboBox**, **ListBox**, **MenuItem**, or **TabControl** control.

[Visual Basic]
```
<Serializable>
Public Delegate Sub DrawItemEventHandler( _
   ByVal sender As Object, _
   ByVal e As DrawItemEventArgs _
)
```
[C#]
```
[Serializable]
public delegate void DrawItemEventHandler(
   object sender,
   DrawItemEventArgs e
);
```
[C++]
```
[Serializable]
public __gc __delegate void DrawItemEventHandler(
   Object* sender,
   DrawItemEventArgs* e
);
```

[JScript] In JScript, you can use the delegates in the .NET Framework, but you cannot define your own.

Parameters [Visual Basic, C#, C++]

The declaration of your event handler must have the same parameters as the **DrawItemEventHandler** delegate declaration.

sender

The source of the event.

e

A **DrawItemEventArgs** that contains the event data.

Remarks

When you create a **DrawItemEventArgs** delegate, you identify the method that will handle the event. To associate the event with your event handler, add an instance of the delegate to the event. The event handler is called whenever the event occurs, unless you remove the delegate.

Requirements

Namespace: System.Windows.Forms

Platforms: Windows 98, Windows NT 4.0, Windows Millennium Edition, Windows 2000, Windows XP Home Edition, Windows XP Professional, Windows Server 2003 family

Assembly: System.Windows.Forms (in System.Windows.Forms.dll)

DrawItemState Enumeration

Specifies the state of an item that is being drawn.

This enumeration has a **FlagsAttribute** attribute that allows a bitwise combination of its member values.

[Visual Basic]
```
<Flags>
<Serializable>
Public Enum DrawItemState
```
[C#]
```
[Flags]
[Serializable]
public enum DrawItemState
```
[C++]
```
[Flags]
[Serializable]
__value public enum DrawItemState
```
[JScript]
```
public
   Flags
   Serializable
enum DrawItemState
```

Remarks

This enumeration is used by members such as **DrawItem-EventArgs.State**.

Members

Member name	Description	Value
Checked	The item is checked. Only menu controls use this value.	8
ComboBoxEdit	The item is the editing portion of a **ComboBox**.	4096
Default	The item is in its default visual state.	32
Disabled	The item is disabled.	4
Focus	The item has focus.	16
Grayed	The item is grayed. Only menu controls use this value.	2
HotLight	The item is being hot-tracked (the item is highlighted as the mouse pointer passes over it).	64
Inactive	The item is inactive.	128
NoAccelerator	The item displays without a keyboard accelerator.	256
NoFocusRect	The item displays without the visual cue that indicates it has focus.	512
None	The item currently has no state.	0
Selected	The item is selected.	1

Example

[Visual Basic]
```
Public Class Form1
   Inherits System.Windows.Forms.Form
   Private WithEvents listBox1 As System.Windows.Forms.ListBox
   Private components As System.ComponentModel.Container = Nothing

   Private FontSize As Single = 12.0F

   '
   ' This sample displays a ListBox that contains a list of ↵
all the fonts
   ' installed on the system and draws each item in its ↵
respective font.
   '
   Public Sub New()
      InitializeComponent()

      ' Populate control with the fonts installed on the system.
      Dim families As FontFamily() = FontFamily.Families

      Dim family As FontFamily
      For Each family In families
         Dim style As FontStyle = FontStyle.Regular

         ' Monotype Corsiva is only available in italic
         If family.Name = "Monotype Corsiva" Then
            style = style Or FontStyle.Italic
         End If

         listBox1.Items.Add(New ListBoxFontItem(New ↵
Font(family.Name, FontSize, style, GraphicsUnit.Point)))
      Next family
   End Sub

   Protected Overloads Overrides Sub Dispose(ByVal ↵
disposing As Boolean)
      If disposing Then
         If Not (components Is Nothing) Then
            components.Dispose()
         End If

         If Not (foreColorBrush Is Nothing) Then
            foreColorBrush.Dispose()
         End If
      End If

      MyBase.Dispose(disposing)
   End Sub

   Private Sub InitializeComponent()
      Me.listBox1 = New System.Windows.Forms.ListBox()
      Me.SuspendLayout()
      '
      ' listBox1
      '
      Me.listBox1.DrawMode = ↵
System.Windows.Forms.DrawMode.OwnerDrawVariable
      Me.listBox1.Location = New System.Drawing.Point(16, 48)
      Me.listBox1.Name = "listBox1"
      Me.listBox1.SelectionMode = ↵
System.Windows.Forms.SelectionMode.MultiExtended
      Me.listBox1.Size = New System.Drawing.Size(256, 134)
      Me.listBox1.TabIndex = 0
      '
      ' Form1
      '
      Me.AutoScaleBaseSize = New System.Drawing.Size(5, 13)
      Me.ClientSize = New System.Drawing.Size(292, 273)
      Me.Controls.AddRange ↵
(New System.Windows.Forms.Control() {Me.listBox1})
      Me.Name = "Form1"
      Me.Text = "Form1"
      Me.ResumeLayout(False)
   End Sub

   <STAThread()> Shared Sub Main()
      Application.Run(New Form1())
   End Sub

   Private Sub listBox1_MeasureItem(ByVal sender As Object, ↵
ByVal e As System.Windows.Forms.MeasureItemEventArgs) ↵
Handles listBox1.MeasureItem
      Dim font As Font = CType(listBox1.Items(e.Index), ↵
```

```
ListBoxFontItem).Font
      Dim stringSize As SizeF = e.Graphics.MeasureString      ↵
 (font.Name, font)

      ' Set the height and width of the item
      e.ItemHeight = CInt(stringSize.Height)
      e.ItemWidth = CInt(stringSize.Width)
   End Sub

   ' For efficiency, cache the brush used for drawing.
   Private foreColorBrush As SolidBrush

   Private Sub listBox1_DrawItem(ByVal sender As Object,      ↵
ByVal e As System.Windows.Forms.DrawItemEventArgs) Handles    ↵
listBox1.DrawItem
      Dim brush As Brush

      ' Create the brush using the ForeColor specified by     ↵
the DrawItemEventArgs
      If foreColorBrush Is Nothing Then
         foreColorBrush = New SolidBrush(e.ForeColor)
      Else
         If Not foreColorBrush.Color.Equals(e.ForeColor) Then
            ' The control's ForeColor has changed, so dispose  ↵
of the cached brush and
            ' create a new one.
            foreColorBrush.Dispose()
            foreColorBrush = New SolidBrush(e.ForeColor)
         End If
      End If

      ' Select the appropriate brush depending on if the      ↵
item is selected.
      ' Since State can be a combinateion (bit-flag) of       ↵
enum values, you can't use
      ' "==" to compare them.
      If (e.State And DrawItemState.Selected) =               ↵
DrawItemState.Selected Then
         brush = SystemBrushes.HighlightText
      Else
         brush = foreColorBrush
      End If

      ' Perform the painting.
      Dim font As Font = CType(listBox1.Items(e.Index),       ↵
ListBoxFontItem).Font
      e.DrawBackground()
      e.Graphics.DrawString(font.Name, font, brush,           ↵
e.Bounds.X, e.Bounds.Y)
      e.DrawFocusRectangle()
   End Sub

   '
   ' A wrapper class for use with storing Fonts in a          ↵
ListBox.  Since ListBox uses the
   ' ToString() of its items for the text it displays,        ↵
this class is needed to return
   ' the name of the font, rather than its ToString() value.
   '
   Public Class ListBoxFontItem
      Public Font As Font

      Public Sub New(ByVal f As Font)
         Font = f
      End Sub

      Public Overrides Function ToString() As String
         Return Font.Name
      End Function
   End Class
End Class
```

[C#]

```
public class Form1 : System.Windows.Forms.Form
{
   private System.Windows.Forms.ListBox listBox1;
   private System.ComponentModel.Container components = null;

   protected override void Dispose(bool disposing)
   {
      if( disposing )
      {
         if ( components != null )
            components.Dispose();

         if ( foreColorBrush != null )
            foreColorBrush.Dispose();
      }
      base.Dispose(disposing);
   }

    #region Windows Form Designer generated code
   /// <summary>
   /// Required method for Designer support - do not modify
   /// the contents of this method with the code editor.
   /// </summary>
   private void InitializeComponent()
   {
      this.listBox1 = new System.Windows.Forms.ListBox();
      this.SuspendLayout();
      //
      // listBox1
      //
      this.listBox1.DrawMode =                                 ↵
System.Windows.Forms.DrawMode.OwnerDrawVariable;
      this.listBox1.Location = new System.Drawing.Point(16, 48);
      this.listBox1.Name = "listBox1";
      this.listBox1.SelectionMode =                            ↵
System.Windows.Forms.SelectionMode.MultiExtended;
      this.listBox1.Size = new System.Drawing.Size(256, 134);
      this.listBox1.TabIndex = 0;
      this.listBox1.MeasureItem += new                         ↵
System.Windows.Forms.MeasureItemEventHandler                   ↵
(this.listBox1_MeasureItem);
      this.listBox1.DrawItem += new                            ↵
System.Windows.Forms.DrawItemEventHandler(this.listBox1_DrawItem);
      //
      // Form1
      //
      this.AutoScaleBaseSize = new System.Drawing.Size(5, 13);
      this.ClientSize = new System.Drawing.Size(292, 273);
      this.Controls.AddRange(new System.Windows.Forms.Control[] {
                                    this.listBox1});
      this.Name = "Form1";
      this.Text = "Form1";
      this.ResumeLayout(false);

   }
    #endregion

   [STAThread]
   static void Main()
   {
      Application.Run(new Form1());
   }

   private void listBox1_MeasureItem(object sender,            ↵
System.Windows.Forms.MeasureItemEventArgs e)
   {
      Font font = ((ListBoxFontItem)listBox1.Items[e.Index]).Font;
      SizeF stringSize = e.Graphics.MeasureString(font.Name, font);

      // Set the height and width of the item
      e.ItemHeight = (int)stringSize.Height;
      e.ItemWidth = (int)stringSize.Width;
   }
```

```
   // For efficiency, cache the brush to use for drawing.
   private SolidBrush foreColorBrush;

   private void listBox1_DrawItem(object sender,                    ↵
System.Windows.Forms.DrawItemEventArgs e)
   {
      Brush brush;

      // Create the brush using the ForeColor specified by           ↵
the DrawItemEventArgs
      if ( foreColorBrush == null )
         foreColorBrush = new SolidBrush(e.ForeColor);
      else if ( foreColorBrush.Color != e.ForeColor )
      {
         // The control's ForeColor has changed, so dispose          ↵
of the cached brush and
         // create a new one.
         foreColorBrush.Dispose();
         foreColorBrush = new SolidBrush(e.ForeColor);
      }

      // Select the appropriate brush depending on if the            ↵
item is selected.
      // Since State can be a combinateion (bit-flag) of             ↵
enum values, you can't use
      // "==" to compare them.
      if ( (e.State & DrawItemState.Selected) ==                     ↵
DrawItemState.Selected )
         brush = SystemBrushes.HighlightText;
      else
         brush = foreColorBrush;

      // Perform the painting.
      Font font = ((ListBoxFontItem)listBox1.Items[e.Index]).Font;
      e.DrawBackground();
      e.Graphics.DrawString(font.Name, font, brush, e.Bounds);
      e.DrawFocusRectangle();
   }

   /// <summary>
   ///  A wrapper class for use with storing Fonts in a ListBox.     ↵
  Since ListBox uses the
   ///  ToString() of its items for the text it displays, this       ↵
 class is needed to return
   ///  the name of the font, rather than its ToString() value.
   /// </summary>
   public class ListBoxFontItem
   {
      public Font Font;

      public ListBoxFontItem(Font f)
      {
         Font = f;
      }

      public override string ToString()
      {
         return Font.Name;
      }
   }
}
```

Requirements

Namespace: System.Windows.Forms

Platforms: Windows 98, Windows NT 4.0, Windows Millennium Edition, Windows 2000, Windows XP Home Edition, Windows XP Professional, Windows Server 2003 family

Assembly: System.Windows.Forms (in System.Windows.Forms.dll)

DrawMode Enumeration

Specifies how the elements of a control are drawn.

[Visual Basic]
```
<Serializable>
Public Enum DrawMode
```
[C#]
```
[Serializable]
public enum DrawMode
```
[C++]
```
[Serializable]
__value public enum DrawMode
```
[JScript]
```
public
   Serializable
enum DrawMode
```

Remarks

This enumeration is used by members such as **DrawMode** in the **ListBox**, **CheckedListBox**, and **ComboBox** classes.

You can override the drawing of some controls or certain elements. This enumeration is used to specify if a control is drawn by the operating system or if your own code handles the drawing of the control.

> **Note** The **CheckedListBox** class only supports **DrawMode.Normal**; owner draw modes are ignored.

For more information about using the **DrawMode** enumeration, see the **MeasureItem** and **DrawItem** events, and the **ItemHeight** property.

Members

Member name	Description
Normal	All the elements in a control are drawn by the operating system and are of the same size.
OwnerDrawFixed	All the elements in the control are drawn manually and are of the same size.
OwnerDrawVariable	All the elements in the control are drawn manually and can differ in size.

Example

See related example in the **System.Windows.Forms.DrawItem-State** enumeration topic.

Requirements

Namespace: System.Windows.Forms

Platforms: Windows 98, Windows NT 4.0, Windows Millennium Edition, Windows 2000, Windows XP Home Edition, Windows XP Professional, Windows Server 2003 family

Assembly: System.Windows.Forms (in System.Windows.Forms.dll)

ErrorBlinkStyle Enumeration

Specifies constants indicating when the error icon, supplied by an **ErrorProvider**, should blink to alert the user that an error has occurred.

[Visual Basic]
```
<Serializable>
Public Enum ErrorBlinkStyle
```
[C#]
```
[Serializable]
public enum ErrorBlinkStyle
```
[C++]
```
[Serializable]
__value public enum ErrorBlinkStyle
```
[JScript]
```
public
   Serializable
enum ErrorBlinkStyle
```

Remarks

This enumeration is used by **ErrorProvider**.

Members

Member name	Description
AlwaysBlink	Always blink when the error icon is first displayed, or when a error description string is set for the control and the error icon is already displayed.
BlinkIfDifferentError	Blinks when the icon is already displayed and a new error string is set for the control.
NeverBlink	Never blink the error icon.

Example

[Visual Basic, C#, C++] The following example demonstrates using the **ErrorProvider** class to notify the user of a data entry error. The example creates a **Form** that contains a **TextBox** control, a **NumericUpDown** control, and a **ComboBox** control, each validating its content, and an **ErrorProvider** for each control. The example sets error icon options using the **BlinkRate** and **BlinkStyle** properties and the **SetIconAlignment** and **SetIconPadding** methods. The **SetError** method is called with or without appropriate error text during a control's **Validated** event, depending upon the content in the control.

[Visual Basic]
```
Imports System
Imports System.Drawing
Imports System.Windows.Forms

Namespace ErrorProvider

    Public NotInheritable Class Form1
        Inherits System.Windows.Forms.Form

        Private label1 As System.Windows.Forms.Label
        Private label2 As System.Windows.Forms.Label
        Private label3 As System.Windows.Forms.Label
        Private label4 As System.Windows.Forms.Label
        Private label5 As System.Windows.Forms.Label
        Private label6 As System.Windows.Forms.Label
        Friend WithEvents favoriteColorComboBox As ↵
System.Windows.Forms.ComboBox
        Friend WithEvents nameTextBox1 As System.Windows.Forms.TextBox
        Friend WithEvents ageUpDownPicker As ↵
System.Windows.Forms.NumericUpDown
        Private ageErrorProvider As System.Windows.Forms.ErrorProvider
        Private nameErrorProvider As System.Windows.Forms.ErrorProvider
        Private favoriteColorErrorProvider As ↵
System.Windows.Forms.ErrorProvider

        <System.STAThread()> _
        Public Shared Sub Main()
            System.Windows.Forms.Application.Run(New Form1())
        End Sub 'Main

        Public Sub New()

            Me.nameTextBox1 = New System.Windows.Forms.TextBox()
            Me.label1 = New System.Windows.Forms.Label()
            Me.label2 = New System.Windows.Forms.Label()
            Me.ageUpDownPicker = New ↵
System.Windows.Forms.NumericUpDown()
            Me.favoriteColorComboBox = New ↵
System.Windows.Forms.ComboBox()
            Me.label3 = New System.Windows.Forms.Label()
            Me.label4 = New System.Windows.Forms.Label()
            Me.label5 = New System.Windows.Forms.Label()
            Me.label6 = New System.Windows.Forms.Label()

            ' Name Label
            Me.label1.Location = New System.Drawing.Point(56, 32)
            Me.label1.Size = New System.Drawing.Size(40, 23)
            Me.label1.Text = "Name:"

            ' Age Label
            Me.label2.Location = New System.Drawing.Point(40, 64)
            Me.label2.Size = New System.Drawing.Size(56, 23)
            Me.label2.Text = "Age (3-5)"

            ' Favorite Color Label
            Me.label3.Location = New System.Drawing.Point(24, 96)
            Me.label3.Size = New System.Drawing.Size(80, 24)
            Me.label3.Text = "Favorite color"

            ' ErrorBlinkStyle.AlwaysBlink Label
            Me.label4.Location = New System.Drawing.Point(264, 32)
            Me.label4.Size = New System.Drawing.Size(160, 23)
            Me.label4.Text = "ErrorBlinkStyle.AlwaysBlink"

            ' ErrorBlinkStyle.BlinkIfDifferentError Label
            Me.label5.Location = New System.Drawing.Point(264, 64)
            Me.label5.Size = New System.Drawing.Size(200, 23)
            Me.label5.Text = "ErrorBlinkStyle.BlinkIfDifferentError"

            ' ErrorBlinkStyle.NeverBlink Label
            Me.label6.Location = New System.Drawing.Point(264, 96)
            Me.label6.Size = New System.Drawing.Size(200, 23)
            Me.label6.Text = "ErrorBlinkStyle.NeverBlink"

            ' Name TextBox
            Me.nameTextBox1.Location = New ↵
System.Drawing.Point(112, 32)
            Me.nameTextBox1.Size = New System.Drawing.Size(120, 20)
            Me.nameTextBox1.TabIndex = 0

            ' Age NumericUpDown
            Me.ageUpDownPicker.Location = New ↵
System.Drawing.Point(112, 64)
            Me.ageUpDownPicker.Maximum = New ↵
System.Decimal(New Integer() {150, 0, 0, 0})
            Me.ageUpDownPicker.TabIndex = 4

            ' Favorite Color ComboBox
            Me.favoriteColorComboBox.Items.AddRange(New Object() ↵
{"None", "Red", "Yellow", _
                                              "Green", "Blue", "Purple"})
            Me.favoriteColorComboBox.Location = New ↵
System.Drawing.Point(112, 96)
            Me.favoriteColorComboBox.Size = New ↵
```

```
System.Drawing.Size(120, 21)
            Me.favoriteColorComboBox.TabIndex = 5

            ' Set up how the form should be displayed ↵
 and add the controls to the form.
            Me.ClientSize = New System.Drawing.Size(464, 150)
            Me.Controls.AddRange(New ↵
 System.Windows.Forms.Control() {Me.label6, Me.label5, Me.label4, _
                                           Me.label3, ↵
Me.favoriteColorComboBox, Me.ageUpDownPicker, Me.label2, _
                                           Me.label1, Me.nameTextBox1})

            Me.Text = "Error Provider Example"

            ' Create and set the ErrorProvider for each ↵
data entry control.

            nameErrorProvider = New ↵
System.Windows.Forms.ErrorProvider()
            nameErrorProvider.SetIconAlignment ↵
 (Me.nameTextBox1, ErrorIconAlignment.MiddleRight)
            nameErrorProvider.SetIconPadding(Me.nameTextBox1, 2)
            nameErrorProvider.BlinkRate = 1000
            nameErrorProvider.BlinkStyle = ↵
System.Windows.Forms.ErrorBlinkStyle.AlwaysBlink

            ageErrorProvider = New System.Windows.Forms.ErrorProvider()
            ageErrorProvider.SetIconAlignment ↵
 (Me.ageUpDownPicker, ErrorIconAlignment.MiddleRight)
            ageErrorProvider.SetIconPadding(Me.ageUpDownPicker, 2)
            ageErrorProvider.BlinkStyle = ↵
System.Windows.Forms.ErrorBlinkStyle.BlinkIfDifferentError

            favoriteColorErrorProvider = New ↵
System.Windows.Forms.ErrorProvider()
            favoriteColorErrorProvider.SetIconAlignment ↵
 (Me.ageUpDownPicker, ErrorIconAlignment.MiddleRight)
          favoriteColorErrorProvider.SetIconPadding(Me.ageUpDownPicker,
2)
            favoriteColorErrorProvider.BlinkRate = 1000
            favoriteColorErrorProvider.BlinkStyle = ↵
System.Windows.Forms.ErrorBlinkStyle.NeverBlink
        End Sub 'New

        Private Sub nameTextBox1_Validated(sender As Object, ↵
 e As System.EventArgs) Handles nameTextBox1.Validated
            If IsNameValid() Then
                ' Clear the error, if any, in the error provider.
                nameErrorProvider.SetError(Me.nameTextBox1, "")
            Else
                ' Set the error if the name is not valid.
                nameErrorProvider.SetError(Me.nameTextBox1, ↵
 "Name is required.")
            End If
        End Sub

        Private Sub ageUpDownPicker_Validated(sender As ↵
 Object, e As System.EventArgs) Handles ageUpDownPicker.Validated
            If IsAgeTooYoung() Then
                ' Set the error if the age is too young.
                ageErrorProvider.SetError(Me.ageUpDownPicker, ↵
"Age not old enough")
            ElseIf IsAgeTooOld() Then
                ' Set the error if the age is too old.
                ageErrorProvider.SetError(Me.ageUpDownPicker, ↵
"Age is too old")
            Else
                ' Clear the error, if any, in the error provider.
                ageErrorProvider.SetError(Me.ageUpDownPicker, "")
            End If
        End Sub

        Private Sub favoriteColorComboBox_Validated(sender As ↵
 Object, e As System.EventArgs) Handles favoriteColorComboBox.Validated
            If Not IsColorValid() Then
                ' Set the error if the favorite color is not valid.

favoriteColorErrorProvider.SetError(Me.favoriteColorComboBox, ↵
 "Must select a color.")
            Else
                ' Clear the error, if any, in the error provider.

favoriteColorErrorProvider.SetError(Me.favoriteColorComboBox, "")
            End If
        End Sub

        ' Functions to verify data.
        Private Function IsNameValid() As Boolean
            ' Determine whether the text box contains a ↵
zero-length string.
            Return nameTextBox1.Text.Length > 0
        End Function

        Private Function IsAgeTooYoung() As Boolean
            ' Determine whether the age value is less than three.
            Return ageUpDownPicker.Value < 3
        End Function


        Private Function IsAgeTooOld() As Boolean
            ' Determine whether the age value is greater than five.
            Return ageUpDownPicker.Value > 5
        End Function

        Private Function IsColorValid() As Boolean
            ' Determine whether the favorite color has a valid value.
            If Not (favoriteColorComboBox.SelectedItem Is Nothing) Then
                If ↵
Not(favoriteColorComboBox.SelectedItem.ToString().Equals("None")) Then
                    Return true
                End If
            End If
            Return false
        End Function

    End Class 'Form1
End Namespace 'ErrorProvider
```

[C#]

```
using System;
using System.Drawing;
using System.Windows.Forms;

namespace ErrorProvider
{
    public class Form1 : System.Windows.Forms.Form
    {
        private System.Windows.Forms.Label label1;
        private System.Windows.Forms.Label label2;
        private System.Windows.Forms.Label label4;
        private System.Windows.Forms.Label label5;
        private System.Windows.Forms.Label label6;
        private System.Windows.Forms.Label label3;
        private System.Windows.Forms.TextBox nameTextBox1;
        private System.Windows.Forms.NumericUpDown ageUpDownPicker;
        private System.Windows.Forms.ComboBox favoriteColorComboBox;
        private System.Windows.Forms.ErrorProvider ageErrorProvider;
        private System.Windows.Forms.ErrorProvider nameErrorProvider;
        private System.Windows.Forms.ErrorProvider ↵
favoriteColorErrorProvider;

        [STAThread]
        static void Main()
        {
            Application.Run(new Form1());
        }

        public Form1()
        {
            this.nameTextBox1 = new System.Windows.Forms.TextBox();
```

```
            this.label1 = new System.Windows.Forms.Label();
            this.label2 = new System.Windows.Forms.Label();
            this.ageUpDownPicker = new ↵
System.Windows.Forms.NumericUpDown();
            this.favoriteColorComboBox = new ↵
System.Windows.Forms.ComboBox();
            this.label3 = new System.Windows.Forms.Label();
            this.label4 = new System.Windows.Forms.Label();
            this.label5 = new System.Windows.Forms.Label();
            this.label6 = new System.Windows.Forms.Label();

            // Name Label
            this.label1.Location = new System.Drawing.Point(56, 32);
            this.label1.Size = new System.Drawing.Size(40, 23);
            this.label1.Text = "Name:";

            // Age Label
            this.label2.Location = new System.Drawing.Point(40, 64);
            this.label2.Size = new System.Drawing.Size(56, 23);
            this.label2.Text = "Age (3-5)";

            // Favorite Color Label
            this.label3.Location = new System.Drawing.Point(24, 96);
            this.label3.Size = new System.Drawing.Size(80, 24);
            this.label3.Text = "Favorite color";

            // ErrorBlinkStyle.AlwaysBlink Label
            this.label4.Location = new System.Drawing.Point(264, 32);
            this.label4.Size = new System.Drawing.Size(160, 23);
            this.label4.Text = "ErrorBlinkStyle.AlwaysBlink";

            // ErrorBlinkStyle.BlinkIfDifferentError Label
            this.label5.Location = new System.Drawing.Point(264, 64);
            this.label5.Size = new System.Drawing.Size(200, 23);
            this.label5.Text = "ErrorBlinkStyle.BlinkIfDifferentError";

            // ErrorBlinkStyle.NeverBlink Label
            this.label6.Location = new System.Drawing.Point(264, 96);
            this.label6.Size = new System.Drawing.Size(200, 23);
            this.label6.Text = "ErrorBlinkStyle.NeverBlink";

            // Name TextBox
            this.nameTextBox1.Location = new ↵
System.Drawing.Point(112, 32);
            this.nameTextBox1.Size = new System.Drawing.Size(120, 20);
            this.nameTextBox1.TabIndex = 0;
            this.nameTextBox1.Validated += new ↵
System.EventHandler(this.nameTextBox1_Validated);

            // Age NumericUpDown
            this.ageUpDownPicker.Location = new ↵
System.Drawing.Point(112, 64);
            this.ageUpDownPicker.Maximum = new ↵
System.Decimal(new int[] {150,0,0,0});
            this.ageUpDownPicker.TabIndex = 4;
            this.ageUpDownPicker.Validated += new ↵
System.EventHandler(this.ageUpDownPicker_Validated);

            // Favorite Color ComboBox
            this.favoriteColorComboBox.Items.AddRange ↵
 (new object[] {"None","Red","Yellow",
                                "Green","Blue","Purple"});
            this.favoriteColorComboBox.Location = new ↵
System.Drawing.Point(112, 96);
            this.favoriteColorComboBox.Size = new ↵
System.Drawing.Size(120, 21);
            this.favoriteColorComboBox.TabIndex = 5;
            this.favoriteColorComboBox.Validated += new ↵
System.EventHandler(this.favoriteColorComboBox_Validated);

            // Set up how the form should be displayed ↵
 and add the controls to the form.
            this.ClientSize = new System.Drawing.Size(464, 150);
            this.Controls.AddRange(new System.Windows.Forms.Control[] {
                this.label6,this.label5,this.label4,this.label3,
                this.favoriteColorComboBox,this.ageUpDownPicker,
                this.label2,this.label1,this.nameTextBox1});
            this.Text = "Error Provider Example";

            // Create and set the ErrorProvider for each ↵
data entry control.

            nameErrorProvider = new ↵
System.Windows.Forms.ErrorProvider();
            nameErrorProvider.SetIconAlignment ↵
 (this.nameTextBox1, ErrorIconAlignment.MiddleRight);
            nameErrorProvider.SetIconPadding (this.nameTextBox1, 2);
            nameErrorProvider.BlinkRate = 1000;
            nameErrorProvider.BlinkStyle = ↵
System.Windows.Forms.ErrorBlinkStyle.AlwaysBlink;

            ageErrorProvider = new ↵
System.Windows.Forms.ErrorProvider();
            ageErrorProvider.SetIconAlignment ↵
 (this.ageUpDownPicker, ErrorIconAlignment.MiddleRight);
            ageErrorProvider.SetIconPadding (this.ageUpDownPicker, 2);
            ageErrorProvider.BlinkStyle = ↵
System.Windows.Forms.ErrorBlinkStyle.BlinkIfDifferentError;

            favoriteColorErrorProvider = new ↵
System.Windows.Forms.ErrorProvider();
            favoriteColorErrorProvider.SetIconAlignment ↵
 (this.ageUpDownPicker, ErrorIconAlignment.MiddleRight);
            favoriteColorErrorProvider.SetIconPadding ↵
 (this.ageUpDownPicker, 2);
            favoriteColorErrorProvider.BlinkRate = 1000;
            favoriteColorErrorProvider.BlinkStyle = ↵
System.Windows.Forms.ErrorBlinkStyle.NeverBlink;
        }

        private void nameTextBox1_Validated(object ↵
 sender, System.EventArgs e)
        {
            if(IsNameValid())
            {
                // Clear the error, if any, in the error provider.
                nameErrorProvider.SetError(this.nameTextBox1, "");
            }
            else
            {
                // Set the error if the name is not valid.
                nameErrorProvider.SetError(this.nameTextBox1, ↵
 "Name is required.");
            }
        }

        private void ageUpDownPicker_Validated(object sender, ↵
 System.EventArgs e)
        {
            if (IsAgeTooYoung())
            {
                // Set the error if the age is too young.
                ageErrorProvider.SetError(this.ageUpDownPicker, ↵
 "Age not old enough");
            }
            else if (IsAgeTooOld())
            {
                // Set the error if the age is too old.
                ageErrorProvider.SetError(this.ageUpDownPicker, ↵
 "Age is too old");
            }
            else
            {
                // Clear the error, if any, in the error provider.
                ageErrorProvider.SetError(this.ageUpDownPicker, "");
            }
        }

        private void favoriteColorComboBox_Validated(object ↵
 sender, System.EventArgs e)
```

```
        {
            if (!IsColorValid())
            {
                // Set the error if the favorite color is not valid.
                
favoriteColorErrorProvider.SetError(this.favoriteColorComboBox,            ↵
"Must select a color.");
            }
            else
            {
                // Clear the error, if any, in the error provider.
                
favoriteColorErrorProvider.SetError(this.favoriteColorComboBox, "");
            }
        }

        // Functions to verify data.
        private bool IsNameValid()
        {
            // Determine whether the text box contains a                   ↵
zero-length string.
            return (nameTextBox1.Text.Length > 0);
        }

        private bool IsAgeTooYoung()
        {
            // Determine whether the age value is less than three.
            return (ageUpDownPicker.Value < 3);
        }

        private bool IsAgeTooOld()
        {
            // Determine whether the age value is greater than five.
            return (ageUpDownPicker.Value > 5 );
        }

        private bool IsColorValid()
        {
            // Determine whether the favorite color has a valid value.
            return ((favoriteColorComboBox.SelectedItem != null) &&
            
(!favoriteColorComboBox.SelectedItem.ToString().Equals("None")));
        }
    }
}
```

[C++]

```
#using <mscorlib.dll>
#using <System.dll>
#using <System.Windows.Forms.dll>
#using <System.Drawing.dll>

using namespace System;
using namespace System::Drawing;
using namespace System::Windows::Forms;

public __gc class Form1 : public System::Windows::Forms::Form {
private:
   System::Windows::Forms::Label*  label1;
   System::Windows::Forms::Label*  label2;
   System::Windows::Forms::Label*  label4;
   System::Windows::Forms::Label*  label5;
   System::Windows::Forms::Label*  label6;
   System::Windows::Forms::Label*  label3;
   System::Windows::Forms::TextBox*  nameTextBox1;
   System::Windows::Forms::NumericUpDown*  ageUpDownPicker;
   System::Windows::Forms::ComboBox*  favoriteColorComboBox;
   System::Windows::Forms::ErrorProvider*  ageErrorProvider;
   System::Windows::Forms::ErrorProvider*  nameErrorProvider;
   System::Windows::Forms::ErrorProvider*  favoriteColorErrorProvider;

public:
   Form1() {
      this->nameTextBox1 = new System::Windows::Forms::TextBox();
      this->label1 = new System::Windows::Forms::Label();
      this->label2 = new System::Windows::Forms::Label();
      this->ageUpDownPicker = new                                          ↵
System::Windows::Forms::NumericUpDown();
      this->favoriteColorComboBox = new                                    ↵
System::Windows::Forms::ComboBox();
      this->label3 = new System::Windows::Forms::Label();
      this->label4 = new System::Windows::Forms::Label();
      this->label5 = new System::Windows::Forms::Label();
      this->label6 = new System::Windows::Forms::Label();

      // Name Label
      this->label1->Location =  System::Drawing::Point(56, 32);
      this->label1->Size =  System::Drawing::Size(40, 23);
      this->label1->Text = S"Name:";

      // Age Label
      this->label2->Location =  System::Drawing::Point(40, 64);
      this->label2->Size =  System::Drawing::Size(56, 23);
      this->label2->Text = S"Age (3-5)";

      // Favorite Color Label
      this->label3->Location =  System::Drawing::Point(24, 96);
      this->label3->Size =  System::Drawing::Size(80, 24);
      this->label3->Text = S"Favorite color";

      // ErrorBlinkStyle::AlwaysBlink Label
      this->label4->Location =  System::Drawing::Point(264, 32);
      this->label4->Size =  System::Drawing::Size(160, 23);
      this->label4->Text = S"ErrorBlinkStyle::AlwaysBlink";

      // ErrorBlinkStyle::BlinkIfDifferentError Label
      this->label5->Location =  System::Drawing::Point(264, 64);
      this->label5->Size =  System::Drawing::Size(200, 23);
      this->label5->Text = S"ErrorBlinkStyle::BlinkIfDifferentError";

      // ErrorBlinkStyle::NeverBlink Label
      this->label6->Location =  System::Drawing::Point(264, 96);
      this->label6->Size =  System::Drawing::Size(200, 23);
      this->label6->Text = S"ErrorBlinkStyle::NeverBlink";

      // Name TextBox
      this->nameTextBox1->Location =  System::Drawing::Point(112, 32);
      this->nameTextBox1->Size =  System::Drawing::Size(120, 20);
      this->nameTextBox1->TabIndex = 0;
      this->nameTextBox1->Validated += new                                 ↵
System::EventHandler(this, nameTextBox1_Validated);

      // Age NumericUpDown
      this->ageUpDownPicker->Location =                                    ↵
System::Drawing::Point(112, 64);

      int temp0 __gc [] = {150, 0, 0, 0};

      this->ageUpDownPicker->Maximum =  System::Decimal(temp0);
      this->ageUpDownPicker->TabIndex = 4;
      this->ageUpDownPicker->Validated += new                              ↵
System::EventHandler(this, ageUpDownPicker_Validated);

      // Favorite Color ComboBox

      Object* temp1 [] = {S"None", S"Red", S"Yellow",                      ↵
 S"Green", S"Blue", S"Purple"};

      this->favoriteColorComboBox->Items->AddRange(temp1);
      this->favoriteColorComboBox->Location =                              ↵
System::Drawing::Point(112, 96);
      this->favoriteColorComboBox->Size =                                  ↵
System::Drawing::Size(120, 21);
      this->favoriteColorComboBox->TabIndex = 5;
      this->favoriteColorComboBox->Validated += new                        ↵
System::EventHandler(this, favoriteColorComboBox_Validated);

      // Set up how the form should be displayed and                       ↵
add the controls to the form.
      this->ClientSize =  System::Drawing::Size(464, 150);
```

```
      System::Windows::Forms::Control* temp2 [] =                          ↵
{this->label6, this->label5, this->label4, this->label3,
         this->favoriteColorComboBox, this->ageUpDownPicker,
         this->label2, this->label1, this->nameTextBox1};

      this->Controls->AddRange(temp2);
      this->Text = S"Error Provider Example";

      // Create and set the ErrorProvider for each data entry control.
      nameErrorProvider = new System::Windows::Forms::ErrorProvider();
      nameErrorProvider->SetIconAlignment (this->nameTextBox1,            ↵
ErrorIconAlignment::MiddleRight);
      nameErrorProvider->SetIconPadding (this->nameTextBox1, 2);
      nameErrorProvider->BlinkRate = 1000;
      nameErrorProvider->BlinkStyle =                                     ↵
System::Windows::Forms::ErrorBlinkStyle::AlwaysBlink;
      ageErrorProvider = new System::Windows::Forms::ErrorProvider();
      ageErrorProvider->SetIconAlignment (this->ageUpDownPicker,          ↵
ErrorIconAlignment::MiddleRight);
      ageErrorProvider->SetIconPadding (this->ageUpDownPicker, 2);
      ageErrorProvider->BlinkStyle =                                      ↵
System::Windows::Forms::ErrorBlinkStyle::BlinkIfDifferentError;
      favoriteColorErrorProvider = new                                    ↵
System::Windows::Forms::ErrorProvider();
      favoriteColorErrorProvider->SetIconAlignment (this-                 ↵
>ageUpDownPicker, ErrorIconAlignment::MiddleRight);
      favoriteColorErrorProvider->SetIconPadding (this-                   ↵
>ageUpDownPicker, 2);
      favoriteColorErrorProvider->BlinkRate = 1000;
      favoriteColorErrorProvider->BlinkStyle =                            ↵
System::Windows::Forms::ErrorBlinkStyle::NeverBlink;
   }

private:
   void nameTextBox1_Validated(Object* sender, System::EventArgs* e) {
      if (IsNameValid()) {
         // Clear the error, if any, in the error provider.
         nameErrorProvider->SetError(this->nameTextBox1, S"");
      } else {
         // Set the error if the name is not valid.
         nameErrorProvider->SetError(this->nameTextBox1,                  ↵
S"Name is required.");
      }
   }

   void ageUpDownPicker_Validated(Object* sender,                         ↵
System::EventArgs* e) {
      if (IsAgeTooYoung()) {
         // Set the error if the age is too young.
         ageErrorProvider->SetError(this->ageUpDownPicker,                ↵
S"Age not old enough");
      } else if (IsAgeTooOld()) {
         // Set the error if the age is too old.
         ageErrorProvider->SetError(this->ageUpDownPicker,                ↵
S"Age is too old");
      } else {
         // Clear the error, if any, in the error provider.
         ageErrorProvider->SetError(this->ageUpDownPicker, S"");
      }
   }

   void favoriteColorComboBox_Validated(Object* sender,                   ↵
System::EventArgs* e) {
      if (!IsColorValid()) {
         // Set the error if the favorite color is not valid.
         favoriteColorErrorProvider->SetError(this-                       ↵
>favoriteColorComboBox, S"Must select a color.");
      } else {
         // Clear the error, if any, in the error provider.
         favoriteColorErrorProvider->SetError(this-                       ↵
>favoriteColorComboBox, S"");
      }
   }

   // Functions to verify data.
   bool IsNameValid() {
      // Determine whether the text box contains a zero-length String*.
      return (nameTextBox1->Text->Length > 0);
   }

   bool IsAgeTooYoung() {
      // Determine whether the age value is less than three.
      return (ageUpDownPicker->Value < 3);
   }

   bool IsAgeTooOld() {
      // Determine whether the age value is greater than five.
      return (ageUpDownPicker->Value > 5);
   }

   bool IsColorValid() {
      // Determine whether the favorite color has a valid value.
      return ((favoriteColorComboBox->SelectedItem != 0) &&
         (!favoriteColorComboBox->SelectedItem->Equals(S"None")));
   }
};

[STAThread]
int main() {
   Application::Run(new Form1());
}
```

Requirements

Namespace: System.Windows.Forms

Platforms: Windows 98, Windows NT 4.0, Windows Millennium Edition, Windows 2000, Windows XP Home Edition, Windows XP Professional, Windows Server 2003 family

Assembly: System.Windows.Forms (in System.Windows.Forms.dll)

ErrorIconAlignment Enumeration

Specifies constants indicating the locations that an error icon can appear in relation to the control with an error.

[Visual Basic]
```
<Serializable>
Public Enum ErrorIconAlignment
```
[C#]
```
[Serializable]
public enum ErrorIconAlignment
```
[C++]
```
[Serializable]
__value public enum ErrorIconAlignment
```
[JScript]
```
public
   Serializable
enum ErrorIconAlignment
```

Remarks

This enumeration is used by **ErrorProvider**.

Members

Member name	Description
BottomLeft	The icon appears aligned with the bottom of the control and the left of the control.
BottomRight	The icon appears aligned with the bottom of the control and the right of the control.
MiddleLeft	The icon appears aligned with the middle of the control and the left of the control.
MiddleRight	The icon appears aligned with the middle of the control and the right of the control.
TopLeft	The icon appears aligned with the top of the control and to the left of the control.
TopRight	The icon appears aligned with the top of the control and to the right of the control.

Example

See related example in the **System.Windows.Forms.ErrorBlinkStyle** enumeration topic.

Requirements

Namespace: System.Windows.Forms

Platforms: Windows 98, Windows NT 4.0, Windows Millennium Edition, Windows 2000, Windows XP Home Edition, Windows XP Professional, Windows Server 2003 family

Assembly: System.Windows.Forms (in System.Windows.Forms.dll)

ErrorProvider Class

Provides a user interface for indicating that a control on a form has an error associated with it.

System.Object
  System.MarshalByRefObject
    System.ComponentModel.Component
      System.Windows.Forms.ErrorProvider

[Visual Basic]
```
Public Class ErrorProvider
   Inherits Component
   Implements IExtenderProvider
```
[C#]
```
public class ErrorProvider : Component, IExtenderProvider
```
[C++]
```
public __gc class ErrorProvider : public Component,
   IExtenderProvider
```
[JScript]
```
public class ErrorProvider extends Component implements
   IExtenderProvider
```

Thread Safety

Any public static (**Shared** in Visual Basic) members of this type are safe for multithreaded operations. Any instance members are not guaranteed to be thread safe.

Remarks

ErrorProvider presents a simple mechanism for indicating to the end user that a control on a form has an error associated with it. If an error description string is specified for the control, an icon appears next to the control. The icon flashes in the manner specified by **BlinkStyle**, at the rate specified by **BlinkRate**. When the mouse hovers over the icon, a ToolTip appears showing the error description string.

Typically, you use **ErrorProvider** in association with data-bound controls. When using **ErrorProvider** with data-bound controls, you must specify the **ContainerControl**, either in the constructor or by setting the **ContainerControl** property.

Example

[Visual Basic, C#, C++] The following example demonstrates using the **ErrorProvider** class to notify the user of a data entry error. The example creates a **Form** that contains a **TextBox** control, a **Numeric-UpDown** control, and a **ComboBox** control, each validating its content, and an **ErrorProvider** for each control. The example sets error icon options using the **BlinkRate** and **BlinkStyle** properties and the **SetIconAlignment** and **SetIconPadding** methods. The **SetError** method is called with or without appropriate error text during a control's **Validated** event, depending upon the content in the control.

[Visual Basic]
```
Imports System
Imports System.Drawing
Imports System.Windows.Forms

Namespace ErrorProvider

    Public NotInheritable Class Form1
        Inherits System.Windows.Forms.Form

        Private label1 As System.Windows.Forms.Label
        Private label2 As System.Windows.Forms.Label
        Private label3 As System.Windows.Forms.Label
        Private label4 As System.Windows.Forms.Label
        Private label5 As System.Windows.Forms.Label
        Private label6 As System.Windows.Forms.Label
        Friend WithEvents favoriteColorComboBox As ↵
System.Windows.Forms.ComboBox
        Friend WithEvents nameTextBox1 As System.Windows.Forms.TextBox
        Friend WithEvents ageUpDownPicker As ↵
System.Windows.Forms.NumericUpDown
        Private ageErrorProvider As System.Windows.Forms.ErrorProvider
        Private nameErrorProvider As System.Windows.Forms.ErrorProvider
        Private favoriteColorErrorProvider As ↵
System.Windows.Forms.ErrorProvider

        <System.STAThread()> _
        Public Shared Sub Main()
            System.Windows.Forms.Application.Run(New Form1())
        End Sub 'Main

        Public Sub New()

            Me.nameTextBox1 = New System.Windows.Forms.TextBox()
            Me.label1 = New System.Windows.Forms.Label()
            Me.label2 = New System.Windows.Forms.Label()
            Me.ageUpDownPicker = New ↵
System.Windows.Forms.NumericUpDown()
            Me.favoriteColorComboBox = New ↵
System.Windows.Forms.ComboBox()
            Me.label3 = New System.Windows.Forms.Label()
            Me.label4 = New System.Windows.Forms.Label()
            Me.label5 = New System.Windows.Forms.Label()
            Me.label6 = New System.Windows.Forms.Label()

            ' Name Label
            Me.label1.Location = New System.Drawing.Point(56, 32)
            Me.label1.Size = New System.Drawing.Size(40, 23)
            Me.label1.Text = "Name:"

            ' Age Label
            Me.label2.Location = New System.Drawing.Point(40, 64)
            Me.label2.Size = New System.Drawing.Size(56, 23)
            Me.label2.Text = "Age (3-5)"

            ' Favorite Color Label
            Me.label3.Location = New System.Drawing.Point(24, 96)
            Me.label3.Size = New System.Drawing.Size(80, 24)
            Me.label3.Text = "Favorite color"

            ' ErrorBlinkStyle.AlwaysBlink Label
            Me.label4.Location = New System.Drawing.Point(264, 32)
            Me.label4.Size = New System.Drawing.Size(160, 23)
            Me.label4.Text = "ErrorBlinkStyle.AlwaysBlink"

            ' ErrorBlinkStyle.BlinkIfDifferentError Label
            Me.label5.Location = New System.Drawing.Point(264, 64)
            Me.label5.Size = New System.Drawing.Size(200, 23)
            Me.label5.Text = "ErrorBlinkStyle.BlinkIfDifferentError"

            ' ErrorBlinkStyle.NeverBlink Label
            Me.label6.Location = New System.Drawing.Point(264, 96)
            Me.label6.Size = New System.Drawing.Size(200, 23)
            Me.label6.Text = "ErrorBlinkStyle.NeverBlink"

            ' Name TextBox
            Me.nameTextBox1.Location = New ↵
System.Drawing.Point(112, 32)
            Me.nameTextBox1.Size = New ↵
System.Drawing.Size(120, 20)
            Me.nameTextBox1.TabIndex = 0

            ' Age NumericUpDown
            Me.ageUpDownPicker.Location = New ↵
System.Drawing.Point(112, 64)
            Me.ageUpDownPicker.Maximum = New ↵
System.Decimal(New Integer() {150, 0, 0, 0})
            Me.ageUpDownPicker.TabIndex = 4
```

```
            ' Favorite Color ComboBox
            Me.favoriteColorComboBox.Items.AddRange                    ↵
 (New Object() {"None", "Red", "Yellow", _
                                "Green", "Blue", "Purple"})
            Me.favoriteColorComboBox.Location = New                    ↵
System.Drawing.Point(112, 96)
            Me.favoriteColorComboBox.Size = New                        ↵
System.Drawing.Size(120, 21)
            Me.favoriteColorComboBox.TabIndex = 5

            ' Set up how the form should be displayed and              ↵
add the controls to the form.
            Me.ClientSize = New System.Drawing.Size(464, 150)
            Me.Controls.AddRange(New                                   ↵
System.Windows.Forms.Control() {Me.label6, Me.label5, Me.label4, _
         Me.label3, Me.favoriteColorComboBox,                          ↵
Me.ageUpDownPicker, Me.label2, _
                                         Me.label1, Me.nameTextBox1})

            Me.Text = "Error Provider Example"

            ' Create and set the ErrorProvider for each                ↵
 data entry control.

            nameErrorProvider = New                                    ↵
System.Windows.Forms.ErrorProvider()
            nameErrorProvider.SetIconAlignment                         ↵
 (Me.nameTextBox1, ErrorIconAlignment.MiddleRight)
            nameErrorProvider.SetIconPadding(Me.nameTextBox1, 2)
            nameErrorProvider.BlinkRate = 1000
            nameErrorProvider.BlinkStyle =                             ↵
System.Windows.Forms.ErrorBlinkStyle.AlwaysBlink

            ageErrorProvider = New System.Windows.Forms.ErrorProvider()
            ageErrorProvider.SetIconAlignment                          ↵
 (Me.ageUpDownPicker, ErrorIconAlignment.MiddleRight)
            ageErrorProvider.SetIconPadding(Me.ageUpDownPicker, 2)
            ageErrorProvider.BlinkStyle =                              ↵
System.Windows.Forms.ErrorBlinkStyle.BlinkIfDifferentError

            favoriteColorErrorProvider = New                           ↵
System.Windows.Forms.ErrorProvider()
            favoriteColorErrorProvider.SetIconAlignment                ↵
 (Me.ageUpDownPicker, ErrorIconAlignment.MiddleRight)
          favoriteColorErrorProvider.SetIconPadding(Me.ageUpDownPicker,
2)
            favoriteColorErrorProvider.BlinkRate = 1000
            favoriteColorErrorProvider.BlinkStyle =                    ↵
System.Windows.Forms.ErrorBlinkStyle.NeverBlink
        End Sub 'New

        Private Sub nameTextBox1_Validated(sender As                   ↵
Object, e As System.EventArgs) Handles nameTextBox1.Validated
            If IsNameValid() Then
                ' Clear the error, if any, in the error provider.
                nameErrorProvider.SetError(Me.nameTextBox1, "")
            Else
                ' Set the error if the name is not valid.
                nameErrorProvider.SetError(Me.nameTextBox1,            ↵
 "Name is required.")
            End If
        End Sub

        Private Sub ageUpDownPicker_Validated(sender As Object,        ↵
 e As System.EventArgs) Handles ageUpDownPicker.Validated
            If IsAgeTooYoung() Then
                ' Set the error if the age is too young.
                ageErrorProvider.SetError(Me.ageUpDownPicker,          ↵
 "Age not old enough")
            ElseIf IsAgeTooOld() Then
                ' Set the error if the age is too old.
                ageErrorProvider.SetError(Me.ageUpDownPicker,          ↵
 "Age is too old")
            Else
                ' Clear the error, if any, in the error provider.
                ageErrorProvider.SetError(Me.ageUpDownPicker, "")
            End If
        End Sub

        Private Sub favoriteColorComboBox_Validated(sender             ↵
 As Object, e As System.EventArgs) Handles                             ↵
 favoriteColorComboBox.Validated
            If Not IsColorValid() Then
                ' Set the error if the favorite color is not valid.

favoriteColorErrorProvider.SetError(Me.favoriteColorComboBox,          ↵
 "Must select a color.")
            Else
                ' Clear the error, if any, in the error provider.

favoriteColorErrorProvider.SetError(Me.favoriteColorComboBox, "")
            End If
        End Sub

        ' Functions to verify data.
        Private Function IsNameValid() As Boolean
            ' Determine whether the text box contains a                ↵
zero-length string.
            Return nameTextBox1.Text.Length > 0
        End Function

        Private Function IsAgeTooYoung() As Boolean
            ' Determine whether the age value is less than three.
            Return ageUpDownPicker.Value < 3
        End Function

        Private Function IsAgeTooOld() As Boolean
            ' Determine whether the age value is greater than five.
            Return ageUpDownPicker.Value > 5
        End Function

        Private Function IsColorValid() As Boolean
            ' Determine whether the favorite color has a valid value.
            If Not (favoriteColorComboBox.SelectedItem Is Nothing) Then
                If                                                     ↵
Not(favoriteColorComboBox.SelectedItem.ToString().Equals("None")) Then
                    Return true
                End If
            End If
            Return false
        End Function

    End Class 'Form1
End Namespace 'ErrorProvider
```

[C#]

```
using System;
using System.Drawing;
using System.Windows.Forms;

namespace ErrorProvider
{
    public class Form1 : System.Windows.Forms.Form
    {
        private System.Windows.Forms.Label label1;
        private System.Windows.Forms.Label label2;
        private System.Windows.Forms.Label label4;
        private System.Windows.Forms.Label label5;
        private System.Windows.Forms.Label label6;
        private System.Windows.Forms.Label label3;
        private System.Windows.Forms.TextBox nameTextBox1;
        private System.Windows.Forms.NumericUpDown ageUpDownPicker;
        private System.Windows.Forms.ComboBox favoriteColorComboBox;
        private System.Windows.Forms.ErrorProvider ageErrorProvider;
        private System.Windows.Forms.ErrorProvider nameErrorProvider;
        private System.Windows.Forms.ErrorProvider
favoriteColorErrorProvider;

        [STAThread]
        static void Main()
```

```
        {
            Application.Run(new Form1());
        }

        public Form1()
        {
            this.nameTextBox1 = new System.Windows.Forms.TextBox();
            this.label1 = new System.Windows.Forms.Label();
            this.label2 = new System.Windows.Forms.Label();
            this.ageUpDownPicker = new                                  ↵
System.Windows.Forms.NumericUpDown();
            this.favoriteColorComboBox = new                            ↵
System.Windows.Forms.ComboBox();
            this.label3 = new System.Windows.Forms.Label();
            this.label4 = new System.Windows.Forms.Label();
            this.label5 = new System.Windows.Forms.Label();
            this.label6 = new System.Windows.Forms.Label();

            // Name Label
            this.label1.Location = new System.Drawing.Point(56, 32);
            this.label1.Size = new System.Drawing.Size(40, 23);
            this.label1.Text = "Name:";

            // Age Label
            this.label2.Location = new System.Drawing.Point(40, 64);
            this.label2.Size = new System.Drawing.Size(56, 23);
            this.label2.Text = "Age (3-5)";

            // Favorite Color Label
            this.label3.Location = new System.Drawing.Point(24, 96);
            this.label3.Size = new System.Drawing.Size(80, 24);
            this.label3.Text = "Favorite color";

            // ErrorBlinkStyle.AlwaysBlink Label
            this.label4.Location = new System.Drawing.Point(264, 32);
            this.label4.Size = new System.Drawing.Size(160, 23);
            this.label4.Text = "ErrorBlinkStyle.AlwaysBlink";

            // ErrorBlinkStyle.BlinkIfDifferentError Label
            this.label5.Location = new System.Drawing.Point(264, 64);
            this.label5.Size = new System.Drawing.Size(200, 23);
            this.label5.Text = "ErrorBlinkStyle.BlinkIfDifferentError";

            // ErrorBlinkStyle.NeverBlink Label
            this.label6.Location = new System.Drawing.Point(264, 96);
            this.label6.Size = new System.Drawing.Size(200, 23);
            this.label6.Text = "ErrorBlinkStyle.NeverBlink";

            // Name TextBox
            this.nameTextBox1.Location = new                            ↵
System.Drawing.Point(112, 32);
            this.nameTextBox1.Size = new System.Drawing.Size(120, 20);
            this.nameTextBox1.TabIndex = 0;
            this.nameTextBox1.Validated += new                          ↵
System.EventHandler(this.nameTextBox1_Validated);

            // Age NumericUpDown
            this.ageUpDownPicker.Location = new                         ↵
System.Drawing.Point(112, 64);
            this.ageUpDownPicker.Maximum = new                          ↵
System.Decimal(new int[] {150,0,0,0});
            this.ageUpDownPicker.TabIndex = 4;
            this.ageUpDownPicker.Validated += new                       ↵
System.EventHandler(this.ageUpDownPicker_Validated);

            // Favorite Color ComboBox
            this.favoriteColorComboBox.Items.AddRange                   ↵
 (new object[] {"None","Red","Yellow",
                                "Green","Blue","Purple"});
            this.favoriteColorComboBox.Location = new                   ↵
System.Drawing.Point(112, 96);
            this.favoriteColorComboBox.Size = new                       ↵
System.Drawing.Size(120, 21);
            this.favoriteColorComboBox.TabIndex = 5;
            this.favoriteColorComboBox.Validated += new                 ↵
System.EventHandler(this.favoriteColorComboBox_Validated);

            // Set up how the form should be displayed                  ↵
 and add the controls to the form.
            this.ClientSize = new System.Drawing.Size(464, 150);
            this.Controls.AddRange(new System.Windows.Forms.Control[] {
 this.label6,this.label5,this.label4,this.label3,
 this.favoriteColorComboBox,this.ageUpDownPicker,
 this.label2,this.label1,this.nameTextBox1});
            this.Text = "Error Provider Example";

    // Create and set the ErrorProvider for each data entry control.

            nameErrorProvider = new                                     ↵
System.Windows.Forms.ErrorProvider();
            nameErrorProvider.SetIconAlignment                          ↵
 (this.nameTextBox1, ErrorIconAlignment.MiddleRight);
            nameErrorProvider.SetIconPadding (this.nameTextBox1, 2);
            nameErrorProvider.BlinkRate = 1000;
            nameErrorProvider.BlinkStyle =                              ↵
System.Windows.Forms.ErrorBlinkStyle.AlwaysBlink;

            ageErrorProvider = new                                      ↵
System.Windows.Forms.ErrorProvider();
            ageErrorProvider.SetIconAlignment                           ↵
 (this.ageUpDownPicker, ErrorIconAlignment.MiddleRight);
            ageErrorProvider.SetIconPadding (this.ageUpDownPicker, 2);
            ageErrorProvider.BlinkStyle =                               ↵
System.Windows.Forms.ErrorBlinkStyle.BlinkIfDifferentError;

            favoriteColorErrorProvider = new                            ↵
System.Windows.Forms.ErrorProvider();
            favoriteColorErrorProvider.SetIconAlignment                 ↵
 (this.ageUpDownPicker, ErrorIconAlignment.MiddleRight);
            favoriteColorErrorProvider.SetIconPadding                   ↵
 (this.ageUpDownPicker, 2);
            favoriteColorErrorProvider.BlinkRate = 1000;
            favoriteColorErrorProvider.BlinkStyle =                     ↵
System.Windows.Forms.ErrorBlinkStyle.NeverBlink;
        }

        private void nameTextBox1_Validated(object sender,              ↵
System.EventArgs e)
        {
            if(IsNameValid())
            {
                // Clear the error, if any, in the error provider.
                nameErrorProvider.SetError(this.nameTextBox1, "");
            }
            else
            {
                // Set the error if the name is not valid.
                nameErrorProvider.SetError(this.nameTextBox1,           ↵
 "Name is required.");
            }
        }

        private void ageUpDownPicker_Validated(object sender,           ↵
System.EventArgs e)
        {
            if (IsAgeTooYoung())
            {
                // Set the error if the age is too young.
                ageErrorProvider.SetError(this.ageUpDownPicker,         ↵
 "Age not old enough");
            }
            else if (IsAgeTooOld())
            {
                // Set the error if the age is too old.
                ageErrorProvider.SetError(this.ageUpDownPicker,         ↵
 "Age is too old");
            }
            else
            {
```

```
                // Clear the error, if any, in the error provider.
                ageErrorProvider.SetError(this.ageUpDownPicker, "");
            }
        }

        private void favoriteColorComboBox_Validated(object          ↵
sender, System.EventArgs e)
        {
            if (!IsColorValid())
            {
                // Set the error if the favorite color is not valid.

favoriteColorErrorProvider.SetError(this.favoriteColorComboBox,          ↵
"Must select a color.");
            }
            else
            {
                // Clear the error, if any, in the error provider.
favoriteColorErrorProvider.SetError(this.favoriteColorComboBox, "");
            }
        }

        // Functions to verify data.
        private bool IsNameValid()
        {
            // Determine whether the text box contains a          ↵
zero-length string.
            return (nameTextBox1.Text.Length > 0);
        }

        private bool IsAgeTooYoung()
        {
            // Determine whether the age value is less than three.
            return (ageUpDownPicker.Value < 3);
        }

        private bool IsAgeTooOld()
        {
            // Determine whether the age value is greater than five.
            return (ageUpDownPicker.Value > 5 );
        }

        private bool IsColorValid()
        {
            // Determine whether the favorite color has a valid value.
            return ((favoriteColorComboBox.SelectedItem != null) &&

(!favoriteColorComboBox.SelectedItem.ToString().Equals("None")));
        }
    }
}
```

[C++]

```
#using <mscorlib.dll>
#using <System.dll>
#using <System.Windows.Forms.dll>
#using <System.Drawing.dll>

using namespace System;
using namespace System::Drawing;
using namespace System::Windows::Forms;

public __gc class Form1 : public System::Windows::Forms::Form {
private:
   System::Windows::Forms::Label*  label1;
   System::Windows::Forms::Label*  label2;
   System::Windows::Forms::Label*  label4;
   System::Windows::Forms::Label*  label5;
   System::Windows::Forms::Label*  label6;
   System::Windows::Forms::Label*  label3;
   System::Windows::Forms::TextBox*  nameTextBox1;
   System::Windows::Forms::NumericUpDown*  ageUpDownPicker;
   System::Windows::Forms::ComboBox*  favoriteColorComboBox;
   System::Windows::Forms::ErrorProvider*  ageErrorProvider;
   System::Windows::Forms::ErrorProvider*  nameErrorProvider;
   System::Windows::Forms::ErrorProvider*  favoriteColorErrorProvider;

public:
   Form1() {
      this->nameTextBox1 = new System::Windows::Forms::TextBox();
      this->label1 = new System::Windows::Forms::Label();
      this->label2 = new System::Windows::Forms::Label();
      this->ageUpDownPicker = new          ↵
System::Windows::Forms::NumericUpDown();
      this->favoriteColorComboBox = new          ↵
System::Windows::Forms::ComboBox();
      this->label3 = new System::Windows::Forms::Label();
      this->label4 = new System::Windows::Forms::Label();
      this->label5 = new System::Windows::Forms::Label();
      this->label6 = new System::Windows::Forms::Label();

      // Name Label
      this->label1->Location =  System::Drawing::Point(56, 32);
      this->label1->Size =  System::Drawing::Size(40, 23);
      this->label1->Text = S"Name:";

      // Age Label
      this->label2->Location =  System::Drawing::Point(40, 64);
      this->label2->Size =  System::Drawing::Size(56, 23);
      this->label2->Text = S"Age (3-5)";

      // Favorite Color Label
      this->label3->Location =  System::Drawing::Point(24, 96);
      this->label3->Size =  System::Drawing::Size(80, 24);
      this->label3->Text = S"Favorite color";

      // ErrorBlinkStyle::AlwaysBlink Label
      this->label4->Location =  System::Drawing::Point(264, 32);
      this->label4->Size =  System::Drawing::Size(160, 23);
      this->label4->Text = S"ErrorBlinkStyle::AlwaysBlink";

      // ErrorBlinkStyle::BlinkIfDifferentError Label
      this->label5->Location =  System::Drawing::Point(264, 64);
      this->label5->Size =  System::Drawing::Size(200, 23);
      this->label5->Text = S"ErrorBlinkStyle::BlinkIfDifferentError";

      // ErrorBlinkStyle::NeverBlink Label
      this->label6->Location =  System::Drawing::Point(264, 96);
      this->label6->Size =  System::Drawing::Size(200, 23);
      this->label6->Text = S"ErrorBlinkStyle::NeverBlink";

      // Name TextBox
      this->nameTextBox1->Location =  System::Drawing::Point(112, 32);
      this->nameTextBox1->Size =  System::Drawing::Size(120, 20);
      this->nameTextBox1->TabIndex = 0;
      this->nameTextBox1->Validated += new          ↵
System::EventHandler(this, nameTextBox1_Validated);

      // Age NumericUpDown
      this->ageUpDownPicker->Location =          ↵
System::Drawing::Point(112, 64);

      int temp0 __gc [] = {150, 0, 0, 0};

      this->ageUpDownPicker->Maximum =  System::Decimal(temp0);
      this->ageUpDownPicker->TabIndex = 4;
      this->ageUpDownPicker->Validated += new          ↵
System::EventHandler(this, ageUpDownPicker_Validated);

      // Favorite Color ComboBox

      Object* temp1 [] = {S"None", S"Red", S"Yellow",          ↵
 S"Green", S"Blue", S"Purple"};

      this->favoriteColorComboBox->Items->AddRange(temp1);
      this->favoriteColorComboBox->Location =          ↵
System::Drawing::Point(112, 96);
      this->favoriteColorComboBox->Size =          ↵
System::Drawing::Size(120, 21);
```

```
      this->favoriteColorComboBox->TabIndex = 5;
      this->favoriteColorComboBox->Validated += new ↵
System::EventHandler(this, favoriteColorComboBox_Validated);

      // Set up how the form should be displayed and ↵
 add the controls to the form.
      this->ClientSize =  System::Drawing::Size(464, 150);

      System::Windows::Forms::Control* temp2 [] = ↵
 {this->label6, this->label5, this->label4, this->label3,
         this->favoriteColorComboBox, this->ageUpDownPicker,
         this->label2, this->label1, this->nameTextBox1};

      this->Controls->AddRange(temp2);
      this->Text = S"Error Provider Example";

      // Create and set the ErrorProvider for each data entry control.
      nameErrorProvider = new System::Windows::Forms::ErrorProvider();
      nameErrorProvider->SetIconAlignment ↵
 (this->nameTextBox1, ErrorIconAlignment::MiddleRight);
      nameErrorProvider->SetIconPadding (this->nameTextBox1, 2);
      nameErrorProvider->BlinkRate = 1000;
      nameErrorProvider->BlinkStyle = ↵
System::Windows::Forms::ErrorBlinkStyle::AlwaysBlink;
      ageErrorProvider = new System::Windows::Forms::ErrorProvider();
      ageErrorProvider->SetIconAlignment ↵
 (this->ageUpDownPicker, ErrorIconAlignment::MiddleRight);
      ageErrorProvider->SetIconPadding (this->ageUpDownPicker, 2);
      ageErrorProvider->BlinkStyle = ↵
System::Windows::Forms::ErrorBlinkStyle::BlinkIfDifferentError;
      favoriteColorErrorProvider = new ↵
System::Windows::Forms::ErrorProvider();
      favoriteColorErrorProvider->SetIconAlignment (this-
>ageUpDownPicker, ErrorIconAlignment::MiddleRight);
      favoriteColorErrorProvider->SetIconPadding (this- ↵
>ageUpDownPicker, 2);
      favoriteColorErrorProvider->BlinkRate = 1000;
      favoriteColorErrorProvider->BlinkStyle = ↵
System::Windows::Forms::ErrorBlinkStyle::NeverBlink;
   }

private:
   void nameTextBox1_Validated(Object* sender, System::EventArgs* e) {
      if (IsNameValid()) {
         // Clear the error, if any, in the error provider.
         nameErrorProvider->SetError(this->nameTextBox1, S"");
      } else {
         // Set the error if the name is not valid.
         nameErrorProvider->SetError(this->nameTextBox1, ↵
 S"Name is required.");
      }
   }

   void ageUpDownPicker_Validated(Object* sender, ↵
 System::EventArgs* e) {
      if (IsAgeTooYoung()) {
         // Set the error if the age is too young.
         ageErrorProvider->SetError(this->ageUpDownPicker, ↵
 S"Age not old enough");
      } else if (IsAgeTooOld()) {
         // Set the error if the age is too old.
         ageErrorProvider->SetError(this->ageUpDownPicker, ↵
 S"Age is too old");
      } else {
         // Clear the error, if any, in the error provider.
         ageErrorProvider->SetError(this->ageUpDownPicker, S"");
      }
   }

   void favoriteColorComboBox_Validated(Object* sender, ↵
 System::EventArgs* e) {
      if (!IsColorValid()) {
         // Set the error if the favorite color is not valid.
         favoriteColorErrorProvider->SetError(this- ↵
>favoriteColorComboBox, S"Must select a color.");
      } else {
         // Clear the error, if any, in the error provider.
         favoriteColorErrorProvider->SetError(this- ↵
>favoriteColorComboBox, S"");
      }
   }

   // Functions to verify data.
   bool IsNameValid() {
      // Determine whether the text box contains a zero-length String*.
      return (nameTextBox1->Text->Length > 0);
   }

   bool IsAgeTooYoung() {
      // Determine whether the age value is less than three.
      return (ageUpDownPicker->Value < 3);
   }

   bool IsAgeTooOld() {
      // Determine whether the age value is greater than five.
      return (ageUpDownPicker->Value > 5);
   }

   bool IsColorValid() {
      // Determine whether the favorite color has a valid value.
      return ((favoriteColorComboBox->SelectedItem != 0) &&
         (!favoriteColorComboBox->SelectedItem->Equals(S"None")));
   }
};

[STAThread]
int main() {
   Application::Run(new Form1());
}
```

[Visual Basic, C#, C++] The following example shows how to use the **ErrorProvider** with a **DataSource** and **DataMember** to indicate a data error to the user.

[Visual Basic]

```
Private Sub InitializeComponent()
    ' Standard control setup.
    '....
    ' You set the DataSource to a data set, and the DataMember ↵
 to a table.
    errorProvider1.DataSource = dataSet1
    errorProvider1.DataMember = dataTable1.TableName
    errorProvider1.ContainerControl = Me
    errorProvider1.BlinkRate = 200
End Sub 'InitializeComponent
 '...
' Since the ErrorProvider control does not have a visible component,
' it does not need to be added to the form.

Protected Sub buttonSave_Click(sender As Object, e As System.EventArgs)
    ' Checks for a bad post code.
    Dim CustomersTable As DataTable
    CustomersTable = customersDataSet1.Tables("Customers")
    Dim row As DataRow
    For Each row In  CustomersTable.Rows
        If Convert.ToBoolean(row("PostalCodeIsNull")) Then
            row.RowError = "The Customer details contain errors"
            row.SetColumnError("PostalCode", "Postal Code required")
        End If
    Next row
End Sub 'buttonSave_Click
```

[C#]

```
private void InitializeComponent()
 {
     // Standard control setup.
     //....
     // You set the DataSource to a data set, and the ↵
DataMember to a table.
     errorProvider1.DataSource = dataSet1 ;
```

```
    errorProvider1.DataMember = dataTable1.TableName ;
    errorProvider1.ContainerControl = this ;
    errorProvider1.BlinkRate = 200 ;
    //...
    // Since the ErrorProvider control does not have a                ↵
visible component,
    // it does not need to be added to the form.
}

protected void buttonSave_Click(object sender, System.EventArgs e)
{
    // Checks for a bad post code.
    DataTable CustomersTable;
    CustomersTable = customersDataSet1.Tables["Customers"];
    foreach (DataRow row in (CustomersTable.Rows))
    {
        if (Convert.ToBoolean(row["PostalCodeIsNull"]))
        {
            row.RowError="The Customer details contain errors";
            row.SetColumnError("PostalCode", "Postal Code required");
        }
    }
}
```

Requirements

Namespace: System.Windows.Forms

Platforms: Windows 98, Windows NT 4.0, Windows Millennium Edition, Windows 2000, Windows XP Home Edition, Windows XP Professional, Windows Server 2003 family

Assembly: System.Windows.Forms (in System.Windows.Forms.dll)

ErrorProvider Constructor

Initializes a new instance of the **ErrorProvider** class.

Overload List

Initializes a new instance of the **ErrorProvider** class and initializes the default settings for **BlinkRate**, **BlinkStyle**, and the **Icon**.

[Visual Basic] **Public Sub New()**

[C#] **public ErrorProvider();**

[C++] **public: ErrorProvider();**

[JScript] **public function ErrorProvider();**

Initializes a new instance of the **ErrorProvider** class attached to a container.

[Visual Basic] **Public Sub New(ContainerControl)**

[C#] **public ErrorProvider(ContainerControl);**

[C++] **public: ErrorProvider(ContainerControl*);**

[JScript] **public function ErrorProvider(ContainerControl);**

ErrorProvider Constructor ()

Initializes a new instance of the **ErrorProvider** class and initializes the default settings for **BlinkRate**, **BlinkStyle**, and the **Icon**.

```
[Visual Basic]
Public Sub New()
[C#]
public ErrorProvider();
[C++]
public: ErrorProvider();
[JScript]
public function ErrorProvider();
```

Remarks

The following table shows initial property values for an instance of **ErrorProvider**.

Property	Value
Icon	An icon that consists of an exclamation point in a circle with a red background.
BlinkRate	250
BlinkStyle	**BlinkIfDifferentError**

Requirements

Platforms: Windows 98, Windows NT 4.0, Windows Millennium Edition, Windows 2000, Windows XP Home Edition, Windows XP Professional, Windows Server 2003 family

ErrorProvider Constructor (ContainerControl)

Initializes a new instance of the **ErrorProvider** class attached to a container.

```
[Visual Basic]
Public Sub New( _
   ByVal parentControl As ContainerControl _
)
[C#]
public ErrorProvider(
   ContainerControl parentControl
);
[C++]
public: ErrorProvider(
   ContainerControl* parentControl
);
[JScript]
public function ErrorProvider(
   parentControl : ContainerControl
);
```

Parameters

parentControl

The container of the control to monitor for errors.

Remarks

The **Control** specified by **ContainerControl** is the container object for the data-bound controls to associate the error provider with.

Requirements

Platforms: Windows 98, Windows NT 4.0, Windows Millennium Edition, Windows 2000, Windows XP Home Edition, Windows XP Professional, Windows Server 2003 family

ErrorProvider.BlinkRate Property

Gets or sets the rate at which the error icon flashes.

```
[Visual Basic]
Public Property BlinkRate As Integer
[C#]
public int BlinkRate {get; set;}
[C++]
public: __property int get_BlinkRate();
public: __property void set_BlinkRate(int);
```

[JScript]
```
public function get BlinkRate() : int;
public function set BlinkRate(int);
```

Property Value

The rate at which the error icon should flash. The rate is expressed in milliseconds. The default is 250 milliseconds.

Exceptions

Exception Type	Condition
ArgumentOutOfRange-Exception	The value is less than zero.

Remarks

The error icon flashes at the specified rate. A value of zero sets **BlinkStyle** to **NeverBlink**.

Example

See related example in the **System.Windows.Forms.Error-Provider** class topic.

Requirements

Platforms: Windows 98, Windows NT 4.0, Windows Millennium Edition, Windows 2000, Windows XP Home Edition, Windows XP Professional, Windows Server 2003 family

ErrorProvider.BlinkStyle Property

Gets or sets a value indicating when the error icon flashes.

[Visual Basic]
```
Public Property BlinkStyle As ErrorBlinkStyle
```
[C#]
```
public ErrorBlinkStyle BlinkStyle {get; set;}
```
[C++]
```
public: __property ErrorBlinkStyle get_BlinkStyle();
public: __property void set_BlinkStyle(ErrorBlinkStyle);
```
[JScript]
```
public function get BlinkStyle() : ErrorBlinkStyle;
public function set BlinkStyle(ErrorBlinkStyle);
```

Property Value

One of the **ErrorBlinkStyle** values. The default is **BlinkIfDifferentError**.

Exceptions

Exception Type	Condition
InvalidEnumArgument-Exception	The assigned value is not one of the **ErrorBlinkStyle** values.

Remarks

The error icon flashes in the manner specified by the assigned **ErrorBlinkStyle** when an error occurs. Setting the **BlinkRate** to zero sets the **BlinkStyle** to **NeverBlink**.

Example

See related example in the **System.Windows.Forms.Error-Provider** class topic.

Requirements

Platforms: Windows 98, Windows NT 4.0, Windows Millennium Edition, Windows 2000, Windows XP Home Edition, Windows XP Professional, Windows Server 2003 family

ErrorProvider.ContainerControl Property

Gets or sets a value indicating the parent control for this **ErrorProvider**.

[Visual Basic]
```
Public Property ContainerControl As ContainerControl
```
[C#]
```
public ContainerControl ContainerControl {get; set;}
```
[C++]
```
public: __property ContainerControl* get_ContainerControl();
public: __property void set_ContainerControl(ContainerControl*);
```
[JScript]
```
public function get ContainerControl() : ContainerControl;
public function set ContainerControl(ContainerControl);
```

Property Value

The **ContainerControl** that contains the controls that the **ErrorProvider** is attached to.

Remarks

Typically, this is the **Form** the data-bound controls reside on.

Requirements

Platforms: Windows 98, Windows NT 4.0, Windows Millennium Edition, Windows 2000, Windows XP Home Edition, Windows XP Professional, Windows Server 2003 family

ErrorProvider.DataMember Property

Gets or sets the data table to monitor.

[Visual Basic]
```
Public Property DataMember As String
```
[C#]
```
public string DataMember {get; set;}
```
[C++]
```
public: __property String* get_DataMember();
public: __property void set_DataMember(String*);
```
[JScript]
```
public function get DataMember() : String;
public function set DataMember(String);
```

Property Value

The string that represents a data table within the data set specified by the **DataSource** to be monitored. Typically, this will be a **DataTable**.

Remarks

The **DataMember** is a navigation string based on **DataSource**.

To avoid conflicts at run time that can occur when changing **Data-Source** and **DataMember**, you should use **BindToDataAndErrors** instead of setting **DataSource** and **DataMember** individually.

Example

See related example in the **System.Windows.Forms.Error-Provider** class topic.

Requirements

Platforms: Windows 98, Windows NT 4.0, Windows Millennium Edition, Windows 2000, Windows XP Home Edition, Windows XP Professional, Windows Server 2003 family

ErrorProvider.DataSource Property

Gets or sets the data set the **ErrorProvider** monitors.

```
[Visual Basic]
Public Property DataSource As Object
[C#]
public object DataSource {get; set;}
[C++]
public: __property Object* get_DataSource();
public: __property void set_DataSource(Object*);
[JScript]
public function get DataSource() : Object;
public function set DataSource(Object);
```

Property Value

A data set based on the **IList** interface to be monitored for errors. Typically, this is a **DataSet** to be monitored for errors.

Remarks

The **DataSource** is a **DataSet** containing tables with the fields that you can attach to a control and that you want to monitor for errors. **DataSource** can be set to any collection that implements **IList**.

To avoid conflicts at run time that can occur when changing **DataSource** and **DataMember**, you should use **BindToDataAndErrors** instead of setting **DataSource** and **DataMember** individually.

Example

See related example in the **System.Windows.Forms.ErrorProvider** class topic.

Requirements

Platforms: Windows 98, Windows NT 4.0, Windows Millennium Edition, Windows 2000, Windows XP Home Edition, Windows XP Professional, Windows Server 2003 family

ErrorProvider.Icon Property

Gets or sets the **Icon** that is displayed next to a control when an error description string has been set for the control.

```
[Visual Basic]
Public Property Icon As Icon
[C#]
public Icon Icon {get; set;}
[C++]
public: __property Icon* get_Icon();
public: __property void set_Icon(Icon*);
[JScript]
public function get Icon() : Icon;
public function set Icon(Icon);
```

Property Value

An **Icon** that signals an error has occurred. The default icon consists of an exclamation point in a circle with a red background.

Exceptions

Exception Type	Condition
ArgumentNullException	The assigned value of the **Icon** is a null reference (**Nothing** in Visual Basic).

Remarks

For best results, using an icon of the size 16 by 16 pixels. If the specified icon is not 16 by 16, it is resized to 16 by 16.

Requirements

Platforms: Windows 98, Windows NT 4.0, Windows Millennium Edition, Windows 2000, Windows XP Home Edition, Windows XP Professional, Windows Server 2003 family

ErrorProvider.Site Property

This member overrides **Component.Site**.

```
[Visual Basic]
Property Site As ISite  Implements IComponent.Site
[C#]
ISite Site {set;}
[C++]
public: __property void set_Site(ISite*);
[JScript]
public override function set Site(ISite);
```

Requirements

Platforms: Windows 98, Windows NT 4.0, Windows Millennium Edition, Windows 2000, Windows XP Home Edition, Windows XP Professional, Windows Server 2003 family

ErrorProvider.BindToDataAndErrors Method

Provides a method to set both the **DataSource** and **DataMember** at run time.

```
[Visual Basic]
Public Sub BindToDataAndErrors( _
   ByVal newDataSource As Object, _
   ByVal newDataMember As String _
)
[C#]
public void BindToDataAndErrors(
   object newDataSource,
   string newDataMember
);
[C++]
public: void BindToDataAndErrors(
   Object* newDataSource,
   String* newDataMember
);
[JScript]
public function BindToDataAndErrors(
   newDataSource : Object,
   newDataMember : String
);
```

Parameters

newDataSource

A data set based on the **IList** interface to be monitored for errors. Typically, this is a **DataSet** to be monitored for errors.

newDataMember

A collection within the *newDataSource* to monitor for errors. Typically, this will be a **DataTable**.

Remarks

To avoid conflicts at run time that can occur when changing **DataSource** and **DataMember**, you should use **BindToDataAndErrors** instead of setting **DataSource** and **DataMember** individually.

Requirements

Platforms: Windows 98, Windows NT 4.0,
Windows Millennium Edition, Windows 2000,
Windows XP Home Edition, Windows XP Professional,
Windows Server 2003 family

ErrorProvider.CanExtend Method

Gets a value indicating whether a control can be extended.

```
[Visual Basic]
Public Overridable Function CanExtend( _
   ByVal extendee As Object _
) As Boolean Implements IExtenderProvider.CanExtend
[C#]
public virtual bool CanExtend(
   object extendee
);
[C++]
public: virtual bool CanExtend(
   Object* extendee
);
[JScript]
public function CanExtend(
   extendee : Object
) : Boolean;
```

Parameters

extendee
The control to be extended.

Return Value

true if the control can be extended; otherwise, **false**.

This property will be **true** if the object is a **Control** and is not a **Form** or **ToolBar**.

Implements

IExtenderProvider.CanExtend

Remarks

Typically, you will use **CanExtend** to determine whether you can attach an **ErrorProvider** to the specified control.

Requirements

Platforms: Windows 98, Windows NT 4.0,
Windows Millennium Edition, Windows 2000,
Windows XP Home Edition, Windows XP Professional,
Windows Server 2003 family

ErrorProvider.Dispose Method

Overload List

This member supports the .NET Framework infrastructure and is not intended to be used directly from your code.

[Visual Basic] **Overloads Overrides Protected Sub Dispose(Boolean)**

[C#] **protected override void Dispose(bool);**

[C++] **protected: void Dispose(bool);**

[JScript] **protected override function Dispose(Boolean);**

Inherited from **Component**.

[Visual Basic] **Overloads Public Overridable Sub Dispose() Implements IDisposable.Dispose**

[C#] **public virtual void Dispose();**

[C++] **public: virtual void Dispose();**

[JScript] **public function Dispose();**

ErrorProvider.Dispose Method (Boolean)

This member overrides **Component.Dispose**.

```
[Visual Basic]
Overrides Overloads Protected Sub Dispose( _
   ByVal disposing As Boolean _
)
[C#]
protected override void Dispose(
   bool disposing
);
[C++]
protected: void Dispose(
   bool disposing
);
[JScript]
protected override function Dispose(
   disposing : Boolean
);
```

Requirements

Platforms: Windows 98, Windows NT 4.0,
Windows Millennium Edition, Windows 2000,
Windows XP Home Edition, Windows XP Professional,
Windows Server 2003 family

ErrorProvider.GetError Method

Returns the current error description string for the specified control.

```
[Visual Basic]
Public Function GetError( _
   ByVal control As Control _
) As String
[C#]
public string GetError(
   Control control
);
[C++]
public: String* GetError(
   Control* control
);
[JScript]
public function GetError(
   control : Control
) : String;
```

Parameters

control
The item to get the error description string for.

Return Value

The error description string for the specified control.

Requirements

Platforms: Windows 98, Windows NT 4.0, Windows Millennium Edition, Windows 2000, Windows XP Home Edition, Windows XP Professional, Windows Server 2003 family

ErrorProvider.GetIconAlignment Method

Gets a value indicating where the error icon should be placed in relation to the control.

[Visual Basic]
```
Public Function GetIconAlignment( _
   ByVal control As Control _
) As ErrorIconAlignment
```
[C#]
```
public ErrorIconAlignment GetIconAlignment(
   Control control
);
```
[C++]
```
public: ErrorIconAlignment GetIconAlignment(
   Control* control
);
```
[JScript]
```
public function GetIconAlignment(
   control : Control
) : ErrorIconAlignment;
```

Parameters

control
The control to get the icon location for.

Return Value

One of the **ErrorIconAlignment** values. The default icon alignment is **MiddleRight**.

Requirements

Platforms: Windows 98, Windows NT 4.0, Windows Millennium Edition, Windows 2000, Windows XP Home Edition, Windows XP Professional, Windows Server 2003 family

ErrorProvider.GetIconPadding Method

Returns the amount of extra space to leave next to the error icon.

[Visual Basic]
```
Public Function GetIconPadding( _
   ByVal control As Control _
) As Integer
```
[C#]
```
public int GetIconPadding(
   Control control
);
```
[C++]
```
public: int GetIconPadding(
   Control* control
);
```
[JScript]
```
public function GetIconPadding(
   control : Control
) : int;
```

Parameters

control
The control to get the padding for.

Return Value

The number of pixels to leave between the icon and the control. Many icons normally have extra space around their central images, so the padding value is only necessary if additional space is necessary. Padding values can be positive or negative. Negative values cause the icon to overlap the edge of the control. The default icon padding is 0.

Requirements

Platforms: Windows 98, Windows NT 4.0, Windows Millennium Edition, Windows 2000, Windows XP Home Edition, Windows XP Professional, Windows Server 2003 family

ErrorProvider.SetError Method

Sets the error description string for the specified control.

[Visual Basic]
```
Public Sub SetError( _
   ByVal control As Control, _
   ByVal value As String _
)
```
[C#]
```
public void SetError(
   Control control,
   string value
);
```
[C++]
```
public: void SetError(
   Control* control,
   String* value
);
```
[JScript]
```
public function SetError(
   control : Control,
   value : String
);
```

Parameters

control
The control to set the error description string for.

value
The error description string.

Remarks

If the string length is greater than zero, then the error icon is displayed, and the ToolTip for the error icon is the error description text. If the string length is zero, the error icon is hidden.

Example

See related example in the **System.Windows.Forms.ErrorProvider** class topic.

Requirements

Platforms: Windows 98, Windows NT 4.0, Windows Millennium Edition, Windows 2000, Windows XP Home Edition, Windows XP Professional, Windows Server 2003 family

ErrorProvider.SetIconAlignment Method

Sets the location where the error icon should be placed in relation to the control.

```
[Visual Basic]
Public Sub SetIconAlignment( _
   ByVal control As Control, _
   ByVal value As ErrorIconAlignment _
)
[C#]
public void SetIconAlignment(
   Control control,
   ErrorIconAlignment value
);
[C++]
public: void SetIconAlignment(
   Control* control,
   ErrorIconAlignment value
);
[JScript]
public function SetIconAlignment(
   control : Control,
   value : ErrorIconAlignment
);
```

Parameters

control

The control to set the icon location for.

value

One of the **ErrorIconAlignment** values.

Remarks

The final placement of the icon is modified by the icon padding values.

Example

See related example in the **System.Windows.Forms.ErrorProvider** class topic.

Requirements

Platforms: Windows 98, Windows NT 4.0, Windows Millennium Edition, Windows 2000, Windows XP Home Edition, Windows XP Professional, Windows Server 2003 family

ErrorProvider.SetIconPadding Method

Sets the amount of extra space to leave between the specified control and the error icon.

```
[Visual Basic]
Public Sub SetIconPadding( _
   ByVal control As Control, _
   ByVal padding As Integer _
)
[C#]
public void SetIconPadding(
   Control control,
   int padding
);
[C++]
public: void SetIconPadding(
   Control* control,
   int padding
);
[JScript]
public function SetIconPadding(
   control : Control,
   padding : int
);
```

Parameters

control

The *control* to set the padding for.

padding

The number of pixels to add between the icon and the *control*.

Remarks

Many icons normally have extra space around their central images, so the padding value is only necessary when additional space is necessary. Padding values can be positive or negative. Negative values cause the icon to overlap the edge of the control.

Example

See related example in the **System.Windows.Forms.ErrorProvider** class topic.

Requirements

Platforms: Windows 98, Windows NT 4.0, Windows Millennium Edition, Windows 2000, Windows XP Home Edition, Windows XP Professional, Windows Server 2003 family

ErrorProvider.UpdateBinding Method

Provides a method to update the bindings of the **DataSource**, **DataMember**, and the error text.

```
[Visual Basic]
Public Sub UpdateBinding()
[C#]
public void UpdateBinding();
[C++]
public: void UpdateBinding();
[JScript]
public function UpdateBinding();
```

Remarks

Typically, you call this method after you have called **BindToDataAndErrors**.

Requirements

Platforms: Windows 98, Windows NT 4.0, Windows Millennium Edition, Windows 2000, Windows XP Home Edition, Windows XP Professional, Windows Server 2003 family

FeatureSupport Class

Provides static (**Shared** in Visual Basic) methods for retrieving feature information from the current system.

System.Object
  System.Windows.Forms.FeatureSupport
    System.Windows.Forms.OSFeature

[Visual Basic]
```
MustInherit Public Class FeatureSupport
   Implements IFeatureSupport
```
[C#]
```
public abstract class FeatureSupport : IFeatureSupport
```
[C++]
```
public __gc __abstract class FeatureSupport : public
   IFeatureSupport
```
[JScript]
```
public abstract class FeatureSupport implements IFeatureSupport
```

Thread Safety

Any public static (**Shared** in Visual Basic) members of this type are safe for multithreaded operations. Any instance members are not guaranteed to be thread safe.

Remarks

Use the static (**Shared** in Visual Basic) methods of this class when the classes you query for feature information implement the **IFeatureSupport** interface. Otherwise, inherit from **FeatureSupport** and provide your own implementation. For an implementation of this class, see **OSFeature**.

To get the version number of a feature, call **GetVersionPresent**. Call **IsPresent** to determine if a particular feature or version of a feature is installed.

Notes to Inheritors: When you inherit from **FeatureSupport**, you must override the **GetVersionPresent** method. When you override this method, check that the class that you use for the *feature* parameter is the same as the class used for this parameter in the **IsPresent** method. If the two *feature* parameters differ, you also must override **IsPresent**.

Example

[Visual Basic, C#] The following example uses the **OSFeature** implementation of **FeatureSupport** and queries for the **LayeredWindows** feature. The version is checked to see if it is a null reference (**Nothing** in Visual Basic), to determine whether the feature is present. The result is displayed in a text box. This code assumes `textBox1` has been created and placed on a form.

[Visual Basic]
```
Private Sub LayeredWindows()
    ' Gets the version of the layered windows feature.
    Dim myVersion As Version = _
       OSFeature.Feature.GetVersionPresent(OSFeature.LayeredWindows)

    ' Prints whether the feature is available.
    If Not (myVersion Is Nothing) Then
        textBox1.Text = "Layered windows feature is installed." & _
           ControlChars.CrLf
    Else
        textBox1.Text = "Layered windows feature is not installed." & _
           ControlChars.CrLf
    End If
    'This is an alternate way to check whether a feature is present.
    If OSFeature.Feature.IsPresent(OSFeature.LayeredWindows) Then
        textBox1.Text &= "Again, layered windows feature is installed."
    Else
        textBox1.Text &= "Again, layered windows feature is not        ↵
installed."
    End If
End Sub
```

[C#]
```
private void LayeredWindows() {
   // Gets the version of the layered windows feature.
   Version myVersion =                                                 ↵
OSFeature.Feature.GetVersionPresent(OSFeature.LayeredWindows);

   // Prints whether the feature is available.
   if (myVersion != null)
      textBox1.Text = "Layered windows feature is installed." + '\n';
   else
      textBox1.Text = "Layered windows feature is not                  ↵
installed." + '\n';

   // This is an alternate way to check whether a feature is present.
   if (OSFeature.Feature.IsPresent(OSFeature.LayeredWindows))
      textBox1.Text += "Again, layered windows feature is installed.";
   else
      textBox1.Text += "Again, layered windows feature is              ↵
 not installed.";
}
```

Requirements

Namespace: System.Windows.Forms

Platforms: Windows 98, Windows NT 4.0, Windows Millennium Edition, Windows 2000, Windows XP Home Edition, Windows XP Professional, Windows Server 2003 family

Assembly: System.Windows.Forms (in System.Windows.Forms.dll)

FeatureSupport Constructor

Initializes a new instance of the **FeatureSupport** class.

[Visual Basic]
```
Protected Sub New()
```
[C#]
```
protected FeatureSupport();
```
[C++]
```
protected: FeatureSupport();
```
[JScript]
```
protected function FeatureSupport();
```

Remarks

This constructor is called by derived class constructors to initialize state in this type.

Requirements

Platforms: Windows 98, Windows NT 4.0, Windows Millennium Edition, Windows 2000, Windows XP Home Edition, Windows XP Professional, Windows Server 2003 family

FeatureSupport.GetVersionPresent Method

Gets the version of the specified feature that is available on the system.

Overload List

When overridden in a derived class, gets the version of the specified feature that is available on the system.

[Visual Basic] **Overloads Public MustOverride Function GetVersionPresent(Object) As Version Implements IFeatureSupport.GetVersionPresent**

[C#] **public abstract Version GetVersionPresent(object);**

[C++] **public: virtual Version* GetVersionPresent(Object*) = 0;**

[JScript] **public abstract function GetVersionPresent(Object) : Version;**

Gets the version of the specified feature that is available on the system.

[Visual Basic] **Overloads Public Shared Function GetVersionPresent(String, String) As Version**

[C#] **public static Version GetVersionPresent(string, string);**

[C++] **public: static Version* GetVersionPresent(String*, String*);**

[JScript] **public static function GetVersionPresent(String, String) : Version;**

Example

See related example in the **System.Windows.Forms.FeatureSupport** class topic.

FeatureSupport.GetVersionPresent Method (Object)

When overridden in a derived class, gets the version of the specified feature that is available on the system.

```
[Visual Basic]
Overloads Public MustOverride Function GetVersionPresent( _
   ByVal feature As Object _
) As Version Implements IFeatureSupport.GetVersionPresent
[C#]
public abstract Version GetVersionPresent(
   object feature
);
[C++]
public: virtual Version* GetVersionPresent(
   Object* feature
) = 0;
[JScript]
public abstract function GetVersionPresent(
   feature : Object
) : Version;
```

Parameters

feature

The feature whose version is requested.

Return Value

A **Version** representing the version number of the specified feature available on the system; or a null reference (**Nothing** in Visual Basic) if the feature is not installed.

Implements

IFeatureSupport.GetVersionPresent

Remarks

Version numbers consist of three parts: major, minor, and build. Typically, a version number is displayed as "major number.minor number.build number".

Notes to Inheritors: When you inherit from **FeatureSupport**, you must override this method. When you override this method, check that the class that you use for the *feature* parameter is the same as the class used for this parameter in the **IsPresent** method. If the two *feature* parameters differ, you must also override **IsPresent**.

See **OSFeature.GetVersionPresent** for an implementation of this method.

Example

See related example in the **System.Windows.Forms.FeatureSupport** class topic.

Requirements

Platforms: Windows 98, Windows NT 4.0, Windows Millennium Edition, Windows 2000, Windows XP Home Edition, Windows XP Professional, Windows Server 2003 family

FeatureSupport.GetVersionPresent Method (String, String)

Gets the version of the specified feature that is available on the system.

```
[Visual Basic]
Overloads Public Shared Function GetVersionPresent( _
   ByVal featureClassName As String, _
   ByVal featureConstName As String _
) As Version
[C#]
public static Version GetVersionPresent(
   string featureClassName,
   string featureConstName
);
[C++]
public: static Version* GetVersionPresent(
   String* featureClassName,
   String* featureConstName
);
[JScript]
public static function GetVersionPresent(
   featureClassName : String,
   featureConstName : String
) : Version;
```

Parameters

featureClassName

The fully qualified name of the class to query for information about the specified feature. This class must implement the **IFeatureSupport** interface or inherit from a class that implements this interface.

featureConstName

The fully qualified name of the feature to look for.

Return Value

A **Version** with the version number of the specified feature available on the system; or a null reference (**Nothing** in Visual Basic) if the feature is not installed.

Remarks

Version numbers consist of three parts: major, minor, and build. Typically, a version number is displayed as "major number.minor number.build number".

See the documentation for the product containing the feature to determine the names to pass to the *featureClassName* and the *featureConstName* parameters.

Requirements

Platforms: Windows 98, Windows NT 4.0, Windows Millennium Edition, Windows 2000, Windows XP Home Edition, Windows XP Professional, Windows Server 2003 family

FeatureSupport.IsPresent Method

Determines whether the specified feature is installed in the system.

Overload List

Determines whether any version of the specified feature is installed in the system.

[Visual Basic] **Overloads Public Overridable Function IsPresent(Object) As Boolean Implements IFeatureSupport.IsPresent**

[C#] **public virtual bool IsPresent(object);**

[C++] **public: virtual bool IsPresent(Object*);**

[JScript] **public function IsPresent(Object) : Boolean;**

Determines whether the specified or newer version of the specified feature is installed in the system.

[Visual Basic] **Overloads Public Overridable Function IsPresent(Object, Version) As Boolean Implements IFeatureSupport.IsPresent**

[C#] **public virtual bool IsPresent(object, Version);**

[C++] **public: virtual bool IsPresent(Object*, Version*);**

[JScript] **public function IsPresent(Object, Version) : Boolean;**

Determines whether any version of the specified feature is installed in the system. This method is static (**Shared** in Visual Basic) .

[Visual Basic] **Overloads Public Shared Function IsPresent(String, String) As Boolean**

[C#] **public static bool IsPresent(string, string);**

[C++] **public: static bool IsPresent(String*, String*);**

[JScript] **public static function IsPresent(String, String) : Boolean;**

Determines whether the specified or newer version of the specified feature is installed in the system. This method is static (**Shared** in Visual Basic) .

[Visual Basic] **Overloads Public Shared Function IsPresent(String, String, Version) As Boolean**

[C#] **public static bool IsPresent(string, string, Version);**

[C++] **public: static bool IsPresent(String*, String*, Version*);**

[JScript] **public static function IsPresent(String, String, Version) : Boolean;**

Example

See related example in the **System.Windows.Forms.FeatureSupport** class topic.

FeatureSupport.IsPresent Method (Object)

Determines whether any version of the specified feature is installed in the system.

```
[Visual Basic]
Overloads Public Overridable Function IsPresent( _
   ByVal feature As Object _
) As Boolean Implements IFeatureSupport.IsPresent
[C#]
public virtual bool IsPresent(
   object feature
);
[C++]
public: virtual bool IsPresent(
   Object* feature
);
[JScript]
public function IsPresent(
   feature : Object
) : Boolean;
```

Parameters

feature
The feature to look for.

Return Value

true if the feature is present; otherwise, **false**.

Implements

IFeatureSupport.IsPresent

Remarks

Notes to Inheritors: When you inherit from **FeatureSupport**, you must override the **GetVersionPresent** method. When you override this method, check that the class that you use for the *feature* parameter is the same as the class used for this parameter in the **IsPresent** method. If the two *feature* parameters differ, you must also override **IsPresent**.

Example

See related example in the **System.Windows.Forms.FeatureSupport** class topic.

Requirements

Platforms: Windows 98, Windows NT 4.0, Windows Millennium Edition, Windows 2000, Windows XP Home Edition, Windows XP Professional, Windows Server 2003 family

FeatureSupport.IsPresent Method (Object, Version)

Determines whether the specified or newer version of the specified feature is installed in the system.

```
[Visual Basic]
Overloads Public Overridable Function IsPresent( _
   ByVal feature As Object, _
   ByVal minimumVersion As Version _
) As Boolean Implements IFeatureSupport.IsPresent
[C#]
public virtual bool IsPresent(
   object feature,
   Version minimumVersion
);
```

```
[C++]
public: virtual bool IsPresent(
   Object* feature,
   Version* minimumVersion
);
[JScript]
public function IsPresent(
   feature : Object,
   minimumVersion : Version
) : Boolean;
```

Parameters

feature
: The feature to look for.

minimumVersion
: A **Version** representing the minimum version number of the feature to look for.

Return Value

true if the feature is present and its version number is greater than or equal to the specified minimum version number; **false** if the feature is not installed or its version number is below the specified minimum number.

Implements

IFeatureSupport.IsPresent

Remarks

Notes to Inheritors: When you inherit from **FeatureSupport**, you must override the **GetVersionPresent** method. When you override this method, check that the class that you use for the *feature* parameter is the same as the class used for this parameter in the **IsPresent** method. If the two *feature* parameters differ, you must also override **IsPresent**.

Requirements

Platforms: Windows 98, Windows NT 4.0, Windows Millennium Edition, Windows 2000, Windows XP Home Edition, Windows XP Professional, Windows Server 2003 family

FeatureSupport.IsPresent Method (String, String)

Determines whether any version of the specified feature is installed in the system. This method is static (**Shared** in Visual Basic) .

```
[Visual Basic]
Overloads Public Shared Function IsPresent( _
   ByVal featureClassName As String, _
   ByVal featureConstName As String _
) As Boolean
[C#]
public static bool IsPresent(
   string featureClassName,
   string featureConstName
);
[C++]
public: static bool IsPresent(
   String* featureClassName,
   String* featureConstName
);
[JScript]
public static function IsPresent(
   featureClassName : String,
   featureConstName : String
) : Boolean;
```

Parameters

featureClassName
: The fully qualified name of the class to query for information about the specified feature. This class must implement the **IFeatureSupport** interface or inherit from a class that implements this interface.

featureConstName
: The fully qualified name of the feature to look for.

Return Value

true if the specified feature is present; **false** if the specified feature is not present or if the product containing the feature is not installed.

Remarks

See the documentation for the product containing the feature to determine the names to pass to the *featureClassName* and the *featureConstName* parameters.

Requirements

Platforms: Windows 98, Windows NT 4.0, Windows Millennium Edition, Windows 2000, Windows XP Home Edition, Windows XP Professional, Windows Server 2003 family

FeatureSupport.IsPresent Method (String, String, Version)

Determines whether the specified or newer version of the specified feature is installed in the system. This method is static (**Shared** in Visual Basic) .

```
[Visual Basic]
Overloads Public Shared Function IsPresent( _
   ByVal featureClassName As String, _
   ByVal featureConstName As String, _
   ByVal minimumVersion As Version _
) As Boolean
[C#]
public static bool IsPresent(
   string featureClassName,
   string featureConstName,
   Version minimumVersion
);
[C++]
public: static bool IsPresent(
   String* featureClassName,
   String* featureConstName,
   Version* minimumVersion
);
[JScript]
public static function IsPresent(
   featureClassName : String,
   featureConstName : String,
   minimumVersion : Version
) : Boolean;
```

Parameters

featureClassName

The fully qualified name of the class to query for information about the specified feature. This class must implement the **IFeatureSupport** interface or inherit from a class that implements this interface.

featureConstName

The fully qualified name of the feature to look for.

minimumVersion

A **Version** representing the minimum version number of the feature.

Return Value

true if the feature is present and its version number is greater than or equal to the specified minimum version number; **false** if the feature is not installed or its version number is below the specified minimum number.

Remarks

See the documentation for the product containing the feature to determine the names to pass to the *featureClassName* and the *featureConstName* parameters.

Requirements

Platforms: Windows 98, Windows NT 4.0,
Windows Millennium Edition, Windows 2000,
Windows XP Home Edition, Windows XP Professional,
Windows Server 2003 family

FileDialog Class

Displays a dialog box from which the user can select a file.

System.Object
  System.MarshalByRefObject
    System.ComponentModel.Component
      System.Windows.Forms.CommonDialog
        System.Windows.Forms.FileDialog
          System.Windows.Forms.OpenFileDialog
          System.Windows.Forms.SaveFileDialog

[Visual Basic]
```
MustInherit Public Class FileDialog
   Inherits CommonDialog
```
[C#]
```
public abstract class FileDialog : CommonDialog
```
[C++]
```
public __gc __abstract class FileDialog : public CommonDialog
```
[JScript]
```
public abstract class FileDialog extends CommonDialog
```

Thread Safety

Any public static (**Shared** in Visual Basic) members of this type are safe for multithreaded operations. Any instance members are not guaranteed to be thread safe.

Remarks

FileDialog is an abstract class, and cannot be created directly. Additionally, you cannot inherit from this class. To create a dialog box to select or save a file, use **OpenFileDialog** or **SaveFileDialog**.

FileDialog is a modal dialog box; therefore, when shown, it blocks the rest of the application until the user has chosen a file. When a dialog box is displayed modally, no input (keyboard or mouse click) can occur except to objects on the dialog box. The program must hide or close the dialog box (usually in response to some user action) before input to the calling program can occur.

Example

[Visual Basic, C#] The following example uses the **OpenFileDialog** implementation of **FileDialog** and illustrates creating, setting of properties, and showing the dialog box. The example uses the **ShowDialog** method to display the dialog box and return the **DialogResult**. The example assumes a form with a **Button** placed on it and the **System.IO** namespace added to it.

[Visual Basic]
```
Protected Sub button1_Click(sender As Object, e As System.EventArgs)
    Dim myStream As Stream
    Dim openFileDialog1 As New OpenFileDialog()

    openFileDialog1.InitialDirectory = "c:\"
    openFileDialog1.Filter = "txt files (*.txt)|*.txt|All files        ↵
(*.*)|*.*"
    openFileDialog1.FilterIndex = 2
    openFileDialog1.RestoreDirectory = True

    If openFileDialog1.ShowDialog() = DialogResult.OK Then
        myStream = openFileDialog1.OpenFile()
        If Not (myStream Is Nothing) Then
            ' Insert code to read the stream here.
            myStream.Close()
        End If
    End If
End Sub
```

[C#]
```
protected void button1_Click(object sender, System.EventArgs e)
{
    Stream myStream;
    OpenFileDialog openFileDialog1 = new OpenFileDialog();

    openFileDialog1.InitialDirectory = "c:\\" ;
    openFileDialog1.Filter = "txt files (*.txt)|*.txt|All              ↵
 files (*.*)|*.*" ;
    openFileDialog1.FilterIndex = 2 ;
    openFileDialog1.RestoreDirectory = true ;

    if(openFileDialog1.ShowDialog() == DialogResult.OK)
    {
        if((myStream = openFileDialog1.OpenFile())!= null)
        {
            // Insert code to read the stream here.
            myStream.Close();
        }
    }
}
```

Requirements

Namespace: System.Windows.Forms

Platforms: Windows 98, Windows NT 4.0, Windows Millennium Edition, Windows 2000, Windows XP Home Edition, Windows XP Professional, Windows Server 2003 family, .NET Compact Framework - Windows CE .NET

Assembly: System.Windows.Forms (in System.Windows.Forms.dll)

FileDialog.EventFileOk Field

This member supports the .NET Framework infrastructure and is not intended to be used directly from your code.

[Visual Basic]
```
Protected Shared ReadOnly EventFileOk As Object
```
[C#]
```
protected static readonly object EventFileOk;
```
[C++]
```
protected: static Object* EventFileOk;
```
[JScript]
```
protected static var EventFileOk : Object;
```

FileDialog.AddExtension Property

Gets or sets a value indicating whether the dialog box automatically adds an extension to a file name if the user omits the extension.

[Visual Basic]
```
Public Property AddExtension As Boolean
```
[C#]
```
public bool AddExtension {get; set;}
```
[C++]
```
public: __property bool get_AddExtension();
public: __property void set_AddExtension(bool);
```
[JScript]
```
public function get AddExtension() : Boolean;
public function set AddExtension(Boolean);
```

Property Value

true if the dialog box adds an extension to a file name if the user omits the extension; otherwise, **false**. The default value is **true**.

Remarks

The extension added to a file name depends on the currently selected file filter and the value of the **CheckFileExists** property.

If the **CheckFileExists** property is **true**, the dialog box adds the first extension from the current file filter that matches an existing file. If no files match the current file filter, the dialog box adds the extension specified in the **DefaultExt** property.

If the **CheckFileExists** property is **false**, the dialog box adds the first valid file name extension from the current file filter. If the current file filter contains no valid file name extensions, the dialog box adds the extension specified in the **DefaultExt** property.

Requirements

Platforms: Windows 98, Windows NT 4.0, Windows Millennium Edition, Windows 2000, Windows XP Home Edition, Windows XP Professional, Windows Server 2003 family

.NET Framework Security:

- **FileIOPermission** for adding an extension if the user omits it. Associated enumeration: **PermissionState.Unrestricted**.

FileDialog.CheckFileExists Property

Gets or sets a value indicating whether the dialog box displays a warning if the user specifies a file name that does not exist.

[Visual Basic]
```
Public Overridable Property CheckFileExists As Boolean
```
[C#]
```
public virtual bool CheckFileExists {get; set;}
```
[C++]
```
public: __property virtual bool get_CheckFileExists();
public: __property virtual void set_CheckFileExists(bool);
```
[JScript]
```
public function get CheckFileExists() : Boolean;
public function set CheckFileExists(Boolean);
```

Property Value

true if the dialog box displays a warning if the user specifies a file name that does not exist; otherwise, **false**. The default value is **false**.

Remarks

The default value is **true** for an inheriting **OpenFileDialog** and **false** for an inheriting **SaveFileDialog**.

Requirements

Platforms: Windows 98, Windows NT 4.0, Windows Millennium Edition, Windows 2000, Windows XP Home Edition, Windows XP Professional, Windows Server 2003 family

.NET Framework Security:

- **FileIOPermission** to display a warning if the file already exists. Associated enumeration: **PermissionState.Unrestricted**.

FileDialog.CheckPathExists Property

Gets or sets a value indicating whether the dialog box displays a warning if the user specifies a path that does not exist.

[Visual Basic]
```
Public Property CheckPathExists As Boolean
```
[C#]
```
public bool CheckPathExists {get; set;}
```
[C++]
```
public: __property bool get_CheckPathExists();
public: __property void set_CheckPathExists(bool);
```
[JScript]
```
public function get CheckPathExists() : Boolean;
public function set CheckPathExists(Boolean);
```

Property Value

true if the dialog box displays a warning when the user specifies a path that does not exist; otherwise, **false**. The default value is **true**.

Requirements

Platforms: Windows 98, Windows NT 4.0, Windows Millennium Edition, Windows 2000, Windows XP Home Edition, Windows XP Professional, Windows Server 2003 family

.NET Framework Security:

- **FileIOPermission** to display a warning if the user specifies a path that already exists. Associated enumeration: **PermissionState.Unrestricted**.

FileDialog.DefaultExt Property

Gets or sets the default file name extension.

[Visual Basic]
```
Public Property DefaultExt As String
```
[C#]
```
public string DefaultExt {get; set;}
```
[C++]
```
public: __property String* get_DefaultExt();
public: __property void set_DefaultExt(String*);
```
[JScript]
```
public function get DefaultExt() : String;
public function set DefaultExt(String);
```

Property Value

The default file name extension. The returned string does not include the period (.). The default value is an empty string("").

Requirements

Platforms: Windows 98, Windows NT 4.0, Windows Millennium Edition, Windows 2000, Windows XP Home Edition, Windows XP Professional, Windows Server 2003 family

FileDialog.DereferenceLinks Property

Gets or sets a value indicating whether the dialog box returns the location of the file referenced by the shortcut or whether it returns the location of the shortcut (.lnk).

[Visual Basic]
```
Public Property DereferenceLinks As Boolean
```
[C#]
```
public bool DereferenceLinks {get; set;}
```
[C++]
```
public: __property bool get_DereferenceLinks();
public: __property void set_DereferenceLinks(bool);
```
[JScript]
```
public function get DereferenceLinks() : Boolean;
public function set DereferenceLinks(Boolean);
```

Property Value

true if the dialog box returns the location of the file referenced by the shortcut; otherwise, **false**. The default value is **true**.

Requirements

Platforms: Windows 98, Windows NT 4.0, Windows Millennium Edition, Windows 2000, Windows XP Home Edition, Windows XP Professional, Windows Server 2003 family

.NET Framework Security:

- **FileIOPermission** to set the property. Associated enumeration: **PermissionState.Unrestricted**.

FileDialog.FileName Property

Gets or sets a string containing the file name selected in the file dialog box.

[Visual Basic]
```
Public Property FileName As String
```
[C#]
```
public string FileName {get; set;}
```
[C++]
```
public: __property String* get_FileName();
public: __property void set_FileName(String*);
```
[JScript]
```
public function get FileName() : String;
public function set FileName(String);
```

Property Value

The file name selected in the file dialog box. The default value is an empty string ("").

Remarks

The file name includes both the file path and the extension. If no files are selected, this method returns an empty string ("").

This method can return only the name of one selected file. If you want to return an array containing the names of all selected files in a multiple-selection dialog box, use **FileNames**.

Requirements

Platforms: Windows 98, Windows NT 4.0, Windows Millennium Edition, Windows 2000, Windows XP Home Edition, Windows XP Professional, Windows Server 2003 family, .NET Compact Framework - Windows CE .NET

.NET Framework Security:

- **FileIOPermission** to get or set the file name. Associated enumeration: **PermissionState.Unrestricted**.

FileDialog.FileNames Property

Gets the file names of all selected files in the dialog box.

[Visual Basic]
```
Public ReadOnly Property FileNames As String ()
```
[C#]
```
public string[] FileNames {get;}
```
[C++]
```
public: __property String* get_FileNames();
```
[JScript]
```
public function get FileNames() : String[];
```

Property Value

An array of type **String**, containing the file names of all selected files in the dialog box.

Remarks

Each file name includes both the file path and the extension. If no files are selected, this method returns an empty array.

Requirements

Platforms: Windows 98, Windows NT 4.0, Windows Millennium Edition, Windows 2000, Windows XP Home Edition, Windows XP Professional, Windows Server 2003 family

.NET Framework Security:

- **FileIOPermission** to get the file names. Associated enumeration: **FileIOPermissionAccess.AllAccess**.

FileDialog.Filter Property

Gets or sets the current file name filter string, which determines the choices that appear in the "Save as file type" or "Files of type" box in the dialog box.

[Visual Basic]
```
Public Property Filter As String
```
[C#]
```
public string Filter {get; set;}
```
[C++]
```
public: __property String* get_Filter();
public: __property void set_Filter(String*);
```
[JScript]
```
public function get Filter() : String;
public function set Filter(String);
```

Property Value

The file filtering options available in the dialog box.

Exceptions

Exception Type	Condition
ArgumentException	*Filter* format is invalid.

Remarks

For each filtering option, the filter string contains a description of the filter, followed by the vertical bar (|) and the filter pattern. The strings for different filtering options are separated by the vertical bar.

The following is an example of a filter string: "Text files (*.txt)|*.txt|All files (*.*)|*.*"

You can add several filter patterns to a filter by separating the file types with semicolons. For example: "Image Files(*.BMP;*.JPG;*.GIF)|*.BMP;*.JPG;*.GIF|All files (*.*)|*.*"

Use the **FilterIndex** property to set which filtering option is shown first to the user.

Example

See related example in the **System.Windows.Forms.FileDialog** class topic.

Requirements

Platforms: Windows 98, Windows NT 4.0, Windows Millennium Edition, Windows 2000, Windows XP Home Edition, Windows XP Professional, Windows Server 2003 family, .NET Compact Framework - Windows CE .NET

FileDialog.FilterIndex Property

Gets or sets the index of the filter currently selected in the file dialog box.

```
[Visual Basic]
Public Property FilterIndex As Integer
[C#]
public int FilterIndex {get; set;}
[C++]
public: __property int get_FilterIndex();
public: __property void set_FilterIndex(int);
[JScript]
public function get FilterIndex() : int;
public function set FilterIndex(int);
```

Property Value

A value containing the index of the filter currently selected in the file dialog box. The default value is 1.

Remarks

Use the **FilterIndex** property to set which filtering option is shown first to the user. You can also use the value of **FilterIndex** after showing the file dialog to perform special file operations depending upon the filter chosen.

Note The index value of the first filter entry is 1.

Example

See related example in the **System.Windows.Forms.FileDialog** class topic.

Requirements

Platforms: Windows 98, Windows NT 4.0, Windows Millennium Edition, Windows 2000, Windows XP Home Edition, Windows XP Professional, Windows Server 2003 family, .NET Compact Framework - Windows CE .NET

FileDialog.InitialDirectory Property

Gets or sets the initial directory displayed by the file dialog box.

```
[Visual Basic]
Public Property InitialDirectory As String
[C#]
public string InitialDirectory {get; set;}
[C++]
public: __property String* get_InitialDirectory();
public: __property void set_InitialDirectory(String*);
[JScript]
public function get InitialDirectory() : String;
public function set InitialDirectory(String);
```

Property Value

The initial directory displayed by the file dialog box. The default is an empty string ("").

Example

See related example in the **System.Windows.Forms.FileDialog** class topic.

Requirements

Platforms: Windows 98, Windows NT 4.0, Windows Millennium Edition, Windows 2000, Windows XP Home Edition, Windows XP Professional, Windows Server 2003 family, .NET Compact Framework - Windows CE .NET

.NET Framework Security:

- **FileIOPermission** to set the initial directory. Associated enumeration: **PermissionState.Unrestricted**.

FileDialog.Instance Property

This member supports the .NET Framework infrastructure and is not intended to be used directly from your code.

```
[Visual Basic]
Protected Overridable ReadOnly Property Instance As IntPtr
[C#]
protected virtual IntPtr Instance {get;}
[C++]
protected: __property virtual IntPtr get_Instance();
[JScript]
protected function get Instance() : IntPtr;
```

FileDialog.Options Property

This member supports the .NET Framework infrastructure and is not intended to be used directly from your code.

```
[Visual Basic]
Protected ReadOnly Property Options As Integer
[C#]
protected int Options {get;}
[C++]
protected: __property int get_Options();
[JScript]
protected function get Options() : int;
```

FileDialog.RestoreDirectory Property

Gets or sets a value indicating whether the dialog box restores the current directory before closing.

```
[Visual Basic]
Public Property RestoreDirectory As Boolean
[C#]
public bool RestoreDirectory {get; set;}
[C++]
public: __property bool get_RestoreDirectory();
public: __property void set_RestoreDirectory(bool);
[JScript]
public function get RestoreDirectory() : Boolean;
public function set RestoreDirectory(Boolean);
```

Property Value

true if the dialog box restores the current directory to its original value if the user changed the directory while searching for files; otherwise, **false**. The default value is **false**.

Example

See related example in the **System.Windows.Forms.FileDialog** class topic.

Requirements

Platforms: Windows 98, Windows NT 4.0, Windows Millennium Edition, Windows 2000, Windows XP Home Edition, Windows XP Professional, Windows Server 2003 family

.NET Framework Security:

- **FileIOPermission** to set the property. Associated enumeration: **PermissionState.Unrestricted**.

FileDialog.ShowHelp Property

Gets or sets a value indicating whether the **Help** button is displayed in the file dialog.

```
[Visual Basic]
Public Property ShowHelp As Boolean
[C#]
public bool ShowHelp {get; set;}
[C++]
public: __property bool get_ShowHelp();
public: __property void set_ShowHelp(bool);
[JScript]
public function get ShowHelp() : Boolean;
public function set ShowHelp(Boolean);
```

Property Value

true if the dialog box includes a help button; otherwise, **false.** The default value is **false**.

Remarks

A **HelpRequested** event is raised when the user clicks the **Help** button.

Requirements

Platforms: Windows 98, Windows NT 4.0, Windows Millennium Edition, Windows 2000, Windows XP Home Edition, Windows XP Professional, Windows Server 2003 family

FileDialog.Title Property

Gets or sets the file dialog box title.

```
[Visual Basic]
Public Property Title As String
[C#]
public string Title {get; set;}
[C++]
public: __property String* get_Title();
public: __property void set_Title(String*);
[JScript]
public function get Title() : String;
public function set Title(String);
```

Property Value

The file dialog box title. The default value is an empty string ("").

Remarks

The string is placed in the title bar of the dialog box. If the title is an empty string, the system uses a default title, which is either "Save As" or "Open".

Requirements

Platforms: Windows 98, Windows NT 4.0, Windows Millennium Edition, Windows 2000, Windows XP Home Edition, Windows XP Professional, Windows Server 2003 family

.NET Framework Security:

- **FileIOPermission** to set the file dialog box title. Associated enumeration: **PermissionState.Unrestricted**.

FileDialog.ValidateNames Property

Gets or sets a value indicating whether the dialog box accepts only valid Win32 file names.

```
[Visual Basic]
Public Property ValidateNames As Boolean
[C#]
public bool ValidateNames {get; set;}
[C++]
public: __property bool get_ValidateNames();
public: __property void set_ValidateNames(bool);
[JScript]
public function get ValidateNames() : Boolean;
public function set ValidateNames(Boolean);
```

Property Value

true if the dialog box accepts only valid Win32 file names; otherwise, **false**. The default value is **true**.

Remarks

If the edit control contains anything but spaces when the user clicks **OK**, the dialog returns the file name, whether it is valid or not. No default extension is added to the text.

Requirements

Platforms: Windows 98, Windows NT 4.0, Windows Millennium Edition, Windows 2000, Windows XP Home Edition, Windows XP Professional, Windows Server 2003 family

.NET Framework Security:

- **FileIOPermission** to set the property. Associated enumeration: **PermissionState.Unrestricted**.

FileDialog.HookProc Method

This member overrides **CommonDialog.HookProc**.

```
[Visual Basic]
Overrides Protected Function HookProc( _
   ByVal hWnd As IntPtr, _
   ByVal msg As Integer, _
   ByVal wparam As IntPtr, _
   ByVal lparam As IntPtr _
) As IntPtr
[C#]
protected override IntPtr HookProc(
   IntPtr hWnd,
   int msg,
   IntPtr wparam,
   IntPtr lparam
);
[C++]
protected: IntPtr HookProc(
   IntPtr hWnd,
   int msg,
   IntPtr wparam,
   IntPtr lparam
);
[JScript]
protected override function HookProc(
   hWnd : IntPtr,
   msg : int,
   wparam : IntPtr,
   lparam : IntPtr
) : IntPtr;
```

Requirements

Platforms: Windows 98, Windows NT 4.0, Windows Millennium Edition, Windows 2000, Windows XP Home Edition, Windows XP Professional, Windows Server 2003 family

FileDialog.OnFileOk Method

Raises the **FileOk** event.

```
[Visual Basic]
Protected Sub OnFileOk( _
   ByVal e As CancelEventArgs _
)
[C#]
protected void OnFileOk(
   CancelEventArgs e
);
[C++]
protected: void OnFileOk(
   CancelEventArgs* e
);
[JScript]
protected function OnFileOk(
   e : CancelEventArgs
);
```

Parameters

e

A **CancelEventArgs** that contains the event data.

Requirements

Platforms: Windows 98, Windows NT 4.0, Windows Millennium Edition, Windows 2000, Windows XP Home Edition, Windows XP Professional, Windows Server 2003 family

FileDialog.Reset Method

Resets all properties to their default values.

```
[Visual Basic]
Overrides Public Sub Reset()
[C#]
public override void Reset();
[C++]
public: void Reset();
[JScript]
public override function Reset();
```

Remarks

Notes to Inheritors: When overriding **Reset** in a derived class, be sure to call the base class's **Reset** method.

Requirements

Platforms: Windows 98, Windows NT 4.0, Windows Millennium Edition, Windows 2000, Windows XP Home Edition, Windows XP Professional, Windows Server 2003 family

FileDialog.RunDialog Method

This member overrides **CommonDialog.RunDialog**.

```
[Visual Basic]
Overrides Protected Function RunDialog( _
   ByVal hWndOwner As IntPtr _
) As Boolean
[C#]
protected override bool RunDialog(
   IntPtr hWndOwner
);
[C++]
protected: bool RunDialog(
   IntPtr hWndOwner
);
[JScript]
protected override function RunDialog(
   hWndOwner : IntPtr
) : Boolean;
```

Requirements

Platforms: Windows 98, Windows NT 4.0, Windows Millennium Edition, Windows 2000, Windows XP Home Edition, Windows XP Professional, Windows Server 2003 family

FileDialog.ToString Method

This member overrides **Object.ToString**.

```
[Visual Basic]
Overrides Public Function ToString() As String
[C#]
public override string ToString();
[C++]
public: String* ToString();
[JScript]
public override function ToString() : String;
```

Requirements

Platforms: Windows 98, Windows NT 4.0, Windows Millennium Edition, Windows 2000, Windows XP Home Edition, Windows XP Professional, Windows Server 2003 family, .NET Compact Framework - Windows CE .NET

FileDialog.FileOk Event

Occurs when the user clicks on the **Open** or **Save** button on a file dialog box.

```
[Visual Basic]
Public Event FileOk As CancelEventHandler
[C#]
public event CancelEventHandler FileOk;
[C++]
public: __event CancelEventHandler* FileOk;
```

[JScript] In JScript, you can handle the events defined by a class, but you cannot define your own.

Event Data

The event handler receives an argument of type **CancelEventArgs** containing data related to this event. The following **CancelEventArgs** property provides information specific to this event.

Property	Description
Cancel	Gets or sets a value indicating whether the event should be canceled.

Requirements

Platforms: Windows 98, Windows NT 4.0, Windows Millennium Edition, Windows 2000, Windows XP Home Edition, Windows XP Professional, Windows Server 2003 family

FlatStyle Enumeration

Specifies the appearance of a control.

[Visual Basic]
```
<Serializable>
Public Enum FlatStyle
```
[C#]
```
[Serializable]
public enum FlatStyle
```
[C++]
```
[Serializable]
__value public enum FlatStyle
```
[JScript]
```
public
   Serializable
enum FlatStyle
```

Remarks

This enumeration is used by members such as **ButtonBase.FlatStyle**, **GroupBox.FlatStyle**, and **Label.FlatStyle**.

In the case of the **Popup** style button, this enumeration controls some behavior as well as appearance. The **Popup** style control initially appears **Flat** until the mouse pointer moves over it. When the mouse pointer moves over the **Popup** control, it appears as a **Standard** style control until the mouse pointer is moved off of it again.

If the **System** style is used, the appearance of the control is determined by the user's operating system and the following property values will be ignored: **Control.BackgroundImage**, **ImageAlign**, **Image**, **ImageIndex**, **ImageList**, and **TextAlign**. In addition, the **Control.BackColor** property will be ignored for button controls. If supported, users can change the appearance of controls by adjusting the appearance settings of their operating system.

Note When the **FlatStyle** property of the **RadioButton** and **CheckBox** classes is set to **FlatStyle.System**, the control is drawn by the user's operating system and the check alignment is based upon the **CheckAlign** and **ButtonBase.TextAlign** property values. The **CheckAlign** property value is not changed, but the appearance of the control can be affected. The check box is horizontally aligned with either the left or right edge of the control (a left or center alignment appears left aligned, right remains unchanged), and vertically aligned the same as the descriptive text. For example, if you have a **CheckBox** control with a **CheckAlign** property value of **ContentAlignment.MiddleCenter** and a **TextAlign** property value of **ContentAlignment.TopRight**, and the **FlatStyle** property value is set to **FlatStyle.System**, the check box alignment will appear to be **ContentAlignment.TopLeft** while the text alignment remains unchanged.

CAUTION Setting the **FlatStyle** property to **FlatStyle.System** is not advisable if you need to display an image on a control, display an image as a control's background, or perform precise text alignment.

Windows Server 2003 family Platform Note: To make your Windows Forms application support Windows XP visual styles, be sure to set the **FlatStyle** property to **FlatStyle.System** and include a manifest with your executable. A manifest is an XML file that is included either as a resource within your application executable or as a separate file that resides in the same directory as the executable file. For an example of a manifest, see the Example section. For more information about using the visual styles available in Windows XP, see the Using Windows XP Visual Styles in the User Interface Design and Development section of the MSDN Library.

Members

Member name	Description
Flat	The control appears flat.
Popup	A control appears flat until the mouse pointer moves over it, at which point it appears three-dimensional.
Standard	The control appears three-dimensional.
System	The appearance of the control is determined by the user's operating system.

Example

The following is an example of a manifest to allow your application to support the visual styles available in Windows XP. The manifest can be added to your application as a resource or as a stand-alone text file. The manifest file resides in the same directory as the executable file, and the name of the text file must be the complete name of the executable file with an additional file name extension of .manifest. For example, the manifest file for MyApp.exe would be MyApp.exe.manifest. This example assumes that the **FlatStyle** properties of the controls in your application are set to **FlatStyle.System**.

```
<?xml version="1.0" encoding="UTF-8" standalone="yes"?>
<assembly xmlns="urn:schemas-microsoft-com:asm.v1" ↵
manifestVersion="1.0">
<assemblyIdentity
    version="1.0.0.0"
    processorArchitecture="X86"
    name="CompanyName.ProductName.YourApplication"
    type="win32"
/>
<description>Your application description here.</description>
<dependency>
    <dependentAssembly>
        <assemblyIdentity
            type="win32"
            name="Microsoft.Windows.Common-Controls"
            version="6.0.0.0"
            processorArchitecture="X86"
            publicKeyToken="6595b64144ccf1df"
            language="*"
        />
    </dependentAssembly>
</dependency>
</assembly>
```

Requirements

Namespace: System.Windows.Forms

Platforms: Windows 98, Windows NT 4.0, Windows Millennium Edition, Windows 2000, Windows XP Home Edition, Windows XP Professional, Windows Server 2003 family

Assembly: System.Windows.Forms (in System.Windows.Forms.dll)

FolderBrowserDialog Class

Note: This namespace, class, or member is supported only in version 1.1 of the .NET Framework.

Represents a common dialog box that allows the user to choose a folder. This class cannot be inherited.

System.Object
  System.MarshalByRefObject
    System.ComponentModel.Component
      System.Windows.Forms.CommonDialog
        System.Windows.Forms.FolderBrowserDialog

[Visual Basic]
```
NotInheritable Public Class FolderBrowserDialog
   Inherits CommonDialog
```
[C#]
```
public sealed class FolderBrowserDialog : CommonDialog
```
[C++]
```
public __gc __sealed class FolderBrowserDialog : public
   CommonDialog
```
[JScript]
```
public class FolderBrowserDialog extends CommonDialog
```

Thread Safety

Any public static (**Shared** in Visual Basic) members of this type are safe for multithreaded operations. Any instance members are not guaranteed to be thread safe.

Remarks

This class provides a way to prompt the user to browse, create, and eventually select a folder. Use this class when you only want to allow the user to select folders, not files. Browsing of the folders is done through a tree control. Only folders from the file system can be selected. Virtual folders cannot.

Typically, after creating a new **FolderBrowserDialog**, you set the **RootFolder** to the location from which to start browsing. Optionally, you can set the **SelectedPath** to an absolute path of a subfolder of **RootFolder** that will initially be selected. You can also optionally set the **Description** property to provide additional instructions to the user. Finally, call the **ShowDialog** method to display the dialog box to the user. When the dialog box is closed and the dialog result from **ShowDialog** is **DialogResult.OK**, the **SelectedPath** will be a string containing the path to the selected folder.

You can use the **ShowNewFolderButton** property to control if the user is able to create new folders via the **New Folder** button.

FolderBrowserDialog is a modal dialog box; therefore, when shown, it blocks the rest of the application until the user has chosen a folder. When a dialog box is displayed modally, no input (keyboard or mouse click) can occur except to objects on the dialog box. The program must hide or close the dialog box (usually in response to some user action) before input to the calling program can occur.

Example

[Visual Basic]
```
' The following example displays an application that          ↵
 provides the ability to
' open rich text files (rtf) into the RichTextBox. The         ↵
example demonstrates
' using the FolderBrowserDialog to set the default             ↵
 directory for opening files.
' The OpenFileDialog class is used to open the file.
Imports System
Imports System.Drawing
Imports System.Windows.Forms
Imports System.IO

Public Class FolderBrowserDialogExampleForm
    Inherits Form

    Private folderBrowserDialog1 As FolderBrowserDialog
    Private openFileDialog1 As OpenFileDialog

    Private richTextBox1 As RichTextBox

    Private mainMenu1 As MainMenu
    Private fileMenuItem As MenuItem
    Private WithEvents folderMenuItem As MenuItem, _
                   closeMenuItem As MenuItem, _
                   openMenuItem As MenuItem

    Private openFileName As String, folderName As String

    Private fileOpened As Boolean = False

    Public Sub New()
        Me.mainMenu1 = New System.Windows.Forms.MainMenu()
        Me.fileMenuItem = New System.Windows.Forms.MenuItem()
        Me.openMenuItem = New System.Windows.Forms.MenuItem()
        Me.folderMenuItem = New System.Windows.Forms.MenuItem()
        Me.closeMenuItem = New System.Windows.Forms.MenuItem()

        Me.openFileDialog1 = New System.Windows.Forms.OpenFileDialog()
        Me.folderBrowserDialog1 = New                            ↵
System.Windows.Forms.FolderBrowserDialog()
        Me.richTextBox1 = New System.Windows.Forms.RichTextBox()

        Me.mainMenu1.MenuItems.Add(Me.fileMenuItem)
        Me.fileMenuItem.MenuItems.AddRange( _
                New System.Windows.Forms.MenuItem()              ↵
{Me.openMenuItem, _
                            Me.closeMenuItem, _
                           Me.folderMenuItem})
        Me.fileMenuItem.Text = "File"

        Me.openMenuItem.Text = "Open..."

        Me.folderMenuItem.Text = "Select Directory..."

        Me.closeMenuItem.Text = "Close"
        Me.closeMenuItem.Enabled = False

        Me.openFileDialog1.DefaultExt = "rtf"
        Me.openFileDialog1.Filter = "rtf files (*.rtf)|*.rtf"

        ' Set the Help text description for the FolderBrowserDialog.
        Me.folderBrowserDialog1.Description = _
            "Select the directory that you want to use As the default."

        ' Do not allow the user to create New files via the      ↵
FolderBrowserDialog.
        Me.folderBrowserDialog1.ShowNewFolderButton = False

        ' Default to the My Documents folder.
        Me.folderBrowserDialog1.RootFolder =                     ↵
Environment.SpecialFolder.Personal

        Me.richTextBox1.AcceptsTab = True
        Me.richTextBox1.Location = New System.Drawing.Point(8, 8)
        Me.richTextBox1.Size = New System.Drawing.Size(280, 344)
       Me.richTextBox1.Anchor = AnchorStyles.Top Or AnchorStyles.Left Or
_
            AnchorStyles.Bottom Or AnchorStyles.Right

        Me.AutoScaleBaseSize = New System.Drawing.Size(5, 13)
        Me.ClientSize = New System.Drawing.Size(296, 360)
        Me.Controls.Add(Me.richTextBox1)
        Me.Menu = Me.mainMenu1
        Me.Text = "RTF Document Browser"
    End Sub
```

```
    <STAThread()> _
    Shared Sub Main()
        Application.Run(New FolderBrowserDialogExampleForm())
    End Sub

    ' Bring up a dialog to open a file.
    Private Sub openMenuItem_Click(sender As object, e As ↵
System.EventArgs) _
        Handles openMenuItem.Click
        ' If a file is not opened, then set the initial ↵
directory to the
        ' FolderBrowserDialog.SelectedPath value.
        If (not fileOpened) Then
            openFileDialog1.InitialDirectory = ↵
folderBrowserDialog1.SelectedPath
            openFileDialog1.FileName = nothing
        End If

        ' Display the openFile dialog.
        Dim result As DialogResult = openFileDialog1.ShowDialog()

        ' OK button was pressed.
        If (result = DialogResult.OK) Then
            openFileName = openFileDialog1.FileName
            Try
                ' Output the requested file in richTextBox1.
                Dim s As Stream = openFileDialog1.OpenFile()
                richTextBox1.LoadFile(s, ↵
RichTextBoxStreamType.RichText)
                s.Close()

                fileOpened = True

            Catch exp As Exception
                MessageBox.Show("An error occurred while ↵
 attempting to load the file. The error is:" _
                                + System.Environment.NewLine ↵
 + exp.ToString() + System.Environment.NewLine)
                fileOpened = False
            End Try
            Invalidate()

            closeMenuItem.Enabled = fileOpened

        ' Cancel button was pressed.
        ElseIf (result = DialogResult.Cancel) Then
            return
        End If
    End Sub

    ' Close the current file.
    Private Sub closeMenuItem_Click(sender As object, e As ↵
System.EventArgs) _
        Handles closeMenuItem.Click
        richTextBox1.Text = ""
        fileOpened = False

        closeMenuItem.Enabled = False
    End Sub

    ' Bring up a dialog to chose a folder path in which to ↵
 open or save a file.
    Private Sub folderMenuItem_Click(sender As object, ↵
e As System.EventArgs) _
        Handles folderMenuItem.Click
        ' Show the FolderBrowserDialog.
        Dim result As DialogResult = folderBrowserDialog1.ShowDialog()

        If ( result = DialogResult.OK ) Then
            folderName = folderBrowserDialog1.SelectedPath
            If (not fileOpened) Then
                ' No file is opened, bring up openFileDialog ↵
 in selected path.
                openFileDialog1.InitialDirectory = folderName
                openFileDialog1.FileName = nothing
                openMenuItem.PerformClick()
            End If
        End If
    End Sub

End Class
```

[C#]

```
// The following example displays an application that ↵
provides the ability to
// open rich text files (rtf) into the RichTextBox. The ↵
 example demonstrates
// using the FolderBrowserDialog to set the default ↵
directory for opening files.
// The OpenFileDialog class is used to open the file.
using System;
using System.Drawing;
using System.Windows.Forms;
using System.IO;

public class FolderBrowserDialogExampleForm : System.Windows.Forms.Form
{
    private FolderBrowserDialog folderBrowserDialog1;
    private OpenFileDialog openFileDialog1;

    private RichTextBox richTextBox1;

    private MainMenu mainMenu1;
    private MenuItem fileMenuItem, openMenuItem;
    private MenuItem folderMenuItem, closeMenuItem;

    private string openFileName, folderName;

    private bool fileOpened = false;

    // The main entry point for the application.
    static void Main()
    {
        Application.Run(new FolderBrowserDialogExampleForm());
    }

    // Constructor.
    public FolderBrowserDialogExampleForm()
    {
        this.mainMenu1 = new System.Windows.Forms.MainMenu();
        this.fileMenuItem = new System.Windows.Forms.MenuItem();
        this.openMenuItem = new System.Windows.Forms.MenuItem();
        this.folderMenuItem = new System.Windows.Forms.MenuItem();
        this.closeMenuItem = new System.Windows.Forms.MenuItem();

        this.openFileDialog1 = new ↵
System.Windows.Forms.OpenFileDialog();
        this.folderBrowserDialog1 = new ↵
System.Windows.Forms.FolderBrowserDialog();
        this.richTextBox1 = new System.Windows.Forms.RichTextBox();

        this.mainMenu1.MenuItems.Add(this.fileMenuItem);
        this.fileMenuItem.MenuItems.AddRange(
                            new System.Windows.Forms.MenuItem[] ↵
{this.openMenuItem,
                                 this.closeMenuItem,
                                 this.folderMenuItem});
        this.fileMenuItem.Text = "File";

        this.openMenuItem.Text = "Open...";
        this.openMenuItem.Click += new ↵
System.EventHandler(this.openMenuItem_Click);

        this.folderMenuItem.Text = "Select Directory...";
        this.folderMenuItem.Click += new ↵
System.EventHandler(this.folderMenuItem_Click);

        this.closeMenuItem.Text = "Close";
        this.closeMenuItem.Click += new ↵
System.EventHandler(this.closeMenuItem_Click);
        this.closeMenuItem.Enabled = false;
```

```
        this.openFileDialog1.DefaultExt = "rtf";
        this.openFileDialog1.Filter = "rtf files (*.rtf)|*.rtf";

        // Set the help text description for the FolderBrowserDialog.
        this.folderBrowserDialog1.Description =
            "Select the directory that you want to use ↵
 as the default.";

        // Do not allow the user to create new files ↵
via the FolderBrowserDialog.
        this.folderBrowserDialog1.ShowNewFolderButton = false;

        // Default to the My Documents folder.
        this.folderBrowserDialog1.RootFolder = ↵
Environment.SpecialFolder.Personal;

        this.richTextBox1.AcceptsTab = true;
        this.richTextBox1.Location = new System.Drawing.Point(8, 8);
        this.richTextBox1.Size = new System.Drawing.Size(280, 344);
        this.richTextBox1.Anchor = AnchorStyles.Top | ↵
AnchorStyles.Left |
                AnchorStyles.Bottom | AnchorStyles.Right;

        this.AutoScaleBaseSize = new System.Drawing.Size(5, 13);
        this.ClientSize = new System.Drawing.Size(296, 360);
        this.Controls.Add(this.richTextBox1);
        this.Menu = this.mainMenu1;
        this.Text = "RTF Document Browser";
    }

    // Bring up a dialog to open a file.
    private void openMenuItem_Click(object sender, System.EventArgs e)
    {
        // If a file is not opened, then set the initial ↵
 directory to the
        // FolderBrowserDialog.SelectedPath value.
        if (!fileOpened) {
            openFileDialog1.InitialDirectory = ↵
 folderBrowserDialog1.SelectedPath;
            openFileDialog1.FileName = null;
        }

        // Display the openFile dialog.
        DialogResult result = openFileDialog1.ShowDialog();

        // OK button was pressed.
        if(result == DialogResult.OK)
        {
            openFileName = openFileDialog1.FileName;
            try
            {
                // Output the requested file in richTextBox1.
                Stream s = openFileDialog1.OpenFile();
                richTextBox1.LoadFile(s, ↵
 RichTextBoxStreamType.RichText);
                s.Close();

                fileOpened = true;

            }
            catch(Exception exp)
            {
                MessageBox.Show("An error occurred while ↵
 attempting to load the file. The error is:"
                                + System.Environment.NewLine + ↵
 exp.ToString() + System.Environment.NewLine);
                fileOpened = false;
            }
            Invalidate();

            closeMenuItem.Enabled = fileOpened;
        }

        // Cancel button was pressed.
        else if(result == DialogResult.Cancel)
        {
            return;
        }
    }

    // Close the current file.
    private void closeMenuItem_Click(object sender, System.EventArgs e)
    {
        richTextBox1.Text = "";
        fileOpened = false;

        closeMenuItem.Enabled = false;
    }

    // Bring up a dialog to chose a folder path in which ↵
to open or save a file.
    private void folderMenuItem_Click(object sender, ↵
System.EventArgs e)
    {
        // Show the FolderBrowserDialog.
        DialogResult result = folderBrowserDialog1.ShowDialog();
        if( result == DialogResult.OK )
        {
            folderName = folderBrowserDialog1.SelectedPath;
            if(!fileOpened)
            {
                // No file is opened, bring up openFileDialog ↵
 in selected path.
                openFileDialog1.InitialDirectory = folderName;
                openFileDialog1.FileName = null;
                openMenuItem.PerformClick();
            }
        }
    }
}
```

[C++]

```
// The following example displays an application that ↵
provides the ability to
// open rich text files (rtf) into the RichTextBox. ↵
 The example demonstrates
// using the FolderBrowserDialog to set the default ↵
directory for opening files.
// The OpenFileDialog is used to open the file.
#using <mscorlib.dll>
#using <System.dll>
#using <System.Windows.Forms.dll>
#using <System.Drawing.dll>

using namespace System;
using namespace System::Drawing;
using namespace System::Windows::Forms;
using namespace System::IO;

public __gc class FolderBrowserDialogExampleForm : ↵
public System::Windows::Forms::Form {
private:
    FolderBrowserDialog*  folderBrowserDialog1;
    OpenFileDialog*  openFileDialog1;
    RichTextBox*  richTextBox1;
    MainMenu*  mainMenu1;
    MenuItem* fileMenuItem;
    MenuItem* openMenuItem;
    MenuItem* folderMenuItem;
    MenuItem* closeMenuItem;
    String* openFileName;
    String*     folderName;
    bool  fileOpened;

public:
    // Constructor.
    FolderBrowserDialogExampleForm() {
        fileOpened = false;
        this->mainMenu1 = new System::Windows::Forms::MainMenu();
        this->fileMenuItem = new System::Windows::Forms::MenuItem();
        this->openMenuItem = new System::Windows::Forms::MenuItem();
        this->folderMenuItem = new System::Windows::Forms::MenuItem();
```

```
        this->closeMenuItem = new System::Windows::Forms::MenuItem();
        this->openFileDialog1 = new                                  ↵
System::Windows::Forms::OpenFileDialog();
        this->folderBrowserDialog1 = new                             ↵
System::Windows::Forms::FolderBrowserDialog();
        this->richTextBox1 = new System::Windows::Forms::RichTextBox();

        this->mainMenu1->MenuItems->Add(this->fileMenuItem);
        System::Windows::Forms::MenuItem* temp0 [] =                 ↵
{this->openMenuItem,
            this->closeMenuItem,
            this->folderMenuItem};

        this->fileMenuItem->MenuItems->AddRange(temp0);
        this->fileMenuItem->Text = S"File";

        this->openMenuItem->Text = S"Open...";
        this->openMenuItem->Click += new                             ↵
System::EventHandler(this, openMenuItem_Click);

        this->folderMenuItem->Text = S"Select Directory...";
        this->folderMenuItem->Click += new                           ↵
System::EventHandler(this, folderMenuItem_Click);

        this->closeMenuItem->Text = S"Close";
        this->closeMenuItem->Click += new                            ↵
System::EventHandler(this, closeMenuItem_Click);
        this->closeMenuItem->Enabled = false;

        this->openFileDialog1->DefaultExt = S"rtf";
        this->openFileDialog1->Filter = S"rtf files (*.rtf)|*.rtf";

        // Set the help text description for the FolderBrowserDialog.
        this->folderBrowserDialog1->Description =                    ↵
S"Select the directory that you want to use as the default.";

        // Do not allow the user to create new files                 ↵
via the FolderBrowserDialog.
        this->folderBrowserDialog1->ShowNewFolderButton = false;

        // Default to the My Documents folder.
        this->folderBrowserDialog1->RootFolder =                     ↵
Environment::SpecialFolder::Personal;

        this->richTextBox1->AcceptsTab = true;
        this->richTextBox1->Location =  System::Drawing::Point(8, 8);
        this->richTextBox1->Size =  System::Drawing::Size(280, 344);
        this->richTextBox1->Anchor =                                 ↵
static_cast<AnchorStyles>(AnchorStyles::Top | AnchorStyles::Left |
            AnchorStyles::Bottom | AnchorStyles::Right);
        this->AutoScaleBaseSize =  System::Drawing::Size(5, 13);
        this->ClientSize =  System::Drawing::Size(296, 360);
        this->Controls->Add(this->richTextBox1);
        this->Menu = this->mainMenu1;
        this->Text = S"RTF Document Browser";
    }

private:
    // Bring up a dialog to open a file.
    void openMenuItem_Click(Object* /*sender*/,                      ↵
System::EventArgs* /*e*/) {
        // If a file is not opened then set the                      ↵
initial directory to the
        // FolderBrowserDialog::SelectedPath value.
        if (!fileOpened) {
            openFileDialog1->InitialDirectory =                      ↵
folderBrowserDialog1->SelectedPath;
            openFileDialog1->FileName = 0;
        }

        // Display the openFile Dialog.
        System::Windows::Forms::DialogResult result =                ↵
openFileDialog1->ShowDialog();

        // OK button was pressed.
        if (result == DialogResult::OK) {
            openFileName = openFileDialog1->FileName;
            try {
                // Output the requested file in richTextBox1.
                Stream*  s = openFileDialog1->OpenFile();
                richTextBox1->LoadFile(s,                            ↵
RichTextBoxStreamType::RichText);
                s->Close();

                fileOpened = true;

            } catch (Exception* exp) {
                MessageBox::Show(String::Concat(
                    S"An error occurred while attempting             ↵
 to load the file. The error is: ",
                    System::Environment::NewLine, exp,               ↵
System::Environment::NewLine));
                fileOpened = false;
            }
            Invalidate();

            closeMenuItem->Enabled = fileOpened;
        }

        // Cancel button was pressed.
        else if (result == DialogResult::Cancel) {
            return;
        }
    }

    // Close the current file.
    void closeMenuItem_Click(Object* /*sender*/,                     ↵
System::EventArgs* /*e*/) {
        richTextBox1->Text = S"";
        fileOpened = false;

        closeMenuItem->Enabled = false;
    }

    // Bring up a dialog to chose a folder path in which             ↵
to open/save a file.
    void folderMenuItem_Click(Object* /*sender*/,                    ↵
System::EventArgs* /*e*/) {
        // Show the FolderBrowserDialog.
        System::Windows::Forms::DialogResult result =                ↵
folderBrowserDialog1->ShowDialog();
        if (result == DialogResult::OK) {
            folderName = folderBrowserDialog1->SelectedPath;
            if (!fileOpened) {
                // No file is opened, bring up                       ↵
openFileDialog in selected path.
                openFileDialog1->InitialDirectory = folderName;
                openFileDialog1->FileName = 0;
                openMenuItem->PerformClick();
            }
        }
    }
};

// The main entry point for the application.
int main() {
    Application::Run(new FolderBrowserDialogExampleForm());
}
```

Requirements

Namespace: System.Windows.Forms

Platforms: Windows 98, Windows NT 4.0, Windows Millennium Edition, Windows 2000, Windows XP Home Edition, Windows XP Professional, Windows Server 2003 family

Assembly: System.Windows.Forms (in System.Windows.Forms.dll)

FolderBrowserDialog Constructor

Note: This namespace, class, or member is supported only in version 1.1 of the .NET Framework.

Initializes a new instance of the **FolderBrowserDialog** class.

```
[Visual Basic]
Public Sub New()
[C#]
public FolderBrowserDialog();
[C++]
public: FolderBrowserDialog();
[JScript]
public function FolderBrowserDialog();
```

Remarks

The default constructor initializes properties to their default values.

When a new **FolderBrowserDialog** is created, the **RootFolder** property is set to **SpecialFolder.Desktop**, the **Description** property is set to an empty string (""), the **SelectedPath** property is set to an empty string, and the **ShowNewFolderButton** property is set to **true**.

Typically, after creating a new **FolderBrowserDialog**, you set the **RootFolder** to the location from which to start browsing. Optionally, you can set the **SelectedPath** to the path of a subfolder of **RootFolder** that will initially be selected. You can also optionally set the **Description** property to provide additional instructions to the user. Finally, call the **ShowDialog** method to display the dialog box to the user. When the dialog box is closed and the dialog result from **ShowDialog** is **DialogResult.OK**, the **SelectedPath** will be a string containing the path to the selected folder.

FolderBrowserDialog is a modal dialog box; therefore, when shown, it blocks the rest of the application until the user has chosen a folder. When a dialog box is displayed modally, no input (keyboard or mouse click) can occur except to objects on the dialog box. The program must hide or close the dialog box (usually in response to some user action) before input to the calling program can occur.

Example

See related example in the System.Windows.Forms.Folder-BrowserDialog class topic.

Requirements

Platforms: Windows 98, Windows NT 4.0, Windows Millennium Edition, Windows 2000, Windows XP Home Edition, Windows XP Professional, Windows Server 2003 family

FolderBrowserDialog.Description Property

Note: This namespace, class, or member is supported only in version 1.1 of the .NET Framework.

Gets or sets the descriptive text displayed above the tree view control in the dialog box.

```
[Visual Basic]
Public Property Description As String
[C#]
public string Description {get; set;}
[C++]
public: __property String* get_Description();
public: __property void set_Description(String*);
[JScript]
public function get Description() : String;
public function set Description(String);
```

Property Value

The description to display. The default is an empty string ("").

Remarks

The **Description** property can be used to specify additional information to the user, like instructions.

Example

See related example in the System.Windows.Forms.Folder-BrowserDialog class topic.

Requirements

Platforms: Windows 98, Windows NT 4.0, Windows Millennium Edition, Windows 2000, Windows XP Home Edition, Windows XP Professional, Windows Server 2003 family

FolderBrowserDialog.RootFolder Property

Note: This namespace, class, or member is supported only in version 1.1 of the .NET Framework.

Gets or sets the root folder where the browsing starts from.

```
[Visual Basic]
Public Property RootFolder As Environment.SpecialFolder
[C#]
public Environment.SpecialFolder RootFolder {get; set;}
[C++]
public: __property Environment.SpecialFolder get_RootFolder();
public: __property void set_RootFolder(Environment.SpecialFolder);
[JScript]
public function get RootFolder() : Environment.SpecialFolder;
public function set RootFolder(Environment.SpecialFolder);
```

Property Value

One of the **Environment.SpecialFolder** values. The default is **Desktop**.

Exceptions

Exception Type	Condition
InvalidEnumArgument-Exception	The value assigned is not one of the **Environment.SpecialFolder** values.

Remarks

Only the specified folder and any subfolders that are beneath it will appear in the dialog box and be selectable. The **SelectedPath** property, along with **RootFolder**, determines what the selected folder will be when the dialog box is displayed, as long as **Selected-Path** is an absolute path that is a subfolder of **RootFolder** (or more accurately, points to a subfolder of the shell namespace represented by **RootFolder**).

Example

See related example in the System.Windows.Forms.Folder-BrowserDialog class topic.

Requirements

Platforms: Windows 98, Windows NT 4.0, Windows Millennium Edition, Windows 2000, Windows XP Home Edition, Windows XP Professional, Windows Server 2003 family

FolderBrowserDialog.SelectedPath Property

Note: This namespace, class, or member is supported only in version 1.1 of the .NET Framework.

Gets or sets the path selected by the user.

```
[Visual Basic]
Public Property SelectedPath As String
[C#]
public string SelectedPath {get; set;}
[C++]
public: __property String* get_SelectedPath();
public: __property void set_SelectedPath(String*);
[JScript]
public function get SelectedPath() : String;
public function set SelectedPath(String);
```

Property Value

The path of the folder first selected in the dialog box or the last folder selected by the user. The default is an empty string ("").

Remarks

If the **SelectedPath** property is set before showing the dialog box, the folder with this path will be the selected folder, as long as **SelectedPath** is set to an absolute path that is a subfolder of **RootFolder** (or more accurately, points to a subfolder of the shell namespace represented by **RootFolder**).

If the **ShowDialog** returns **DialogResult.OK**, meaning the user clicked the **OK** button, the **SelectedPath** property will return a string containing the path to the selected folder. If **ShowDialog** returns **DialogResult.Cancel**, meaning the user canceled out of the dialog box, this property will have the same value that it had prior to displaying the dialog box. If the user selects a folder that does not have a physical path (for example, **My Computer**), the **OK** button on the dialog box will be disabled.

Example

See related example in the System.Windows.Forms.Folder-BrowserDialog class topic.

Requirements

Platforms: Windows 98, Windows NT 4.0, Windows Millennium Edition, Windows 2000, Windows XP Home Edition, Windows XP Professional, Windows Server 2003 family

.NET Framework Security:

- **FileIOPermission** for getting the path. Associated enumeration: **FileIOPermissionAccess.PathDiscovery**

FolderBrowserDialog.ShowNewFolderButton Property

Note: This namespace, class, or member is supported only in version 1.1 of the .NET Framework.

Gets or sets a value indicating whether the **New Folder** button appears in the folder browser dialog box.

```
[Visual Basic]
Public Property ShowNewFolderButton As Boolean
[C#]
public bool ShowNewFolderButton {get; set;}
[C++]
public: __property bool get_ShowNewFolderButton();
public: __property void set_ShowNewFolderButton(bool);
[JScript]
public function get ShowNewFolderButton() : Boolean;
public function set ShowNewFolderButton(Boolean);
```

Property Value

true if the **New Folder** button is shown in the dialog box; otherwise, **false**. The default is **true**.

Remarks

When **ShowNewFolderButton** is true, the **New Folder** button is visible, giving the user a chance to create a folder. When the user clicks the **New Folder** button, a new folder is created and the user is prompted to specify the folder name. The selected node in the tree becomes the parent of the new folder.

> **Note** The actual caption of the **New Folder** button can vary depending upon the operation system.

Example

See related example in the **System.Windows.Forms.Folder-BrowserDialog** class topic.

Requirements

Platforms: Windows 98, Windows NT 4.0, Windows Millennium Edition, Windows 2000, Windows XP Home Edition, Windows XP Professional, Windows Server 2003 family

FolderBrowserDialog.Reset Method

Note: This namespace, class, or member is supported only in version 1.1 of the .NET Framework.

Resets properties to their default values.

```
[Visual Basic]
Overrides Public Sub Reset()
[C#]
public override void Reset();
[C++]
public: void Reset();
[JScript]
public override function Reset();
```

Remarks

Resets the **Description**, **ShowNewFolderButton**, **SelectedPath** and **RootFolder** properties to their default values. For a list of default values, see the **FolderBrowserDialog** constructor.

Requirements

Platforms: Windows 98, Windows NT 4.0, Windows Millennium Edition, Windows 2000, Windows XP Home Edition, Windows XP Professional, Windows Server 2003 family

FolderBrowserDialog.RunDialog Method

Note: This namespace, class, or member is supported only in version 1.1 of the .NET Framework.

This member overrides **CommonDialog.RunDialog**.

[Visual Basic]
```
Overrides Protected Function RunDialog( _
   ByVal hWndOwner As IntPtr _
) As Boolean
```
[C#]
```
protected override bool RunDialog(
   IntPtr hWndOwner
);
```
[C++]
```
protected: bool RunDialog(
   IntPtr hWndOwner
);
```
[JScript]
```
protected override function RunDialog(
   hWndOwner : IntPtr
) : Boolean;
```

Requirements

Platforms: Windows 98, Windows NT 4.0, Windows Millennium Edition, Windows 2000, Windows XP Home Edition, Windows XP Professional, Windows Server 2003 family

FolderBrowserDialog.HelpRequest Event

Note: This namespace, class, or member is supported only in version 1.1 of the .NET Framework.

This member supports the .NET Framework infrastructure and is not intended to be used directly from your code.

[Visual Basic]
```
Public Shadows Event HelpRequest As EventHandler
```
[C#]
```
public new event EventHandler HelpRequest;
```
[C++]
```
public: __event EventHandler* HelpRequest;
```

[JScript] In JScript, you can handle the events defined by a class, but you cannot define your own.

FontDialog Class

Represents a common dialog box that displays a list of fonts that are currently installed on the system.

System.Object
  System.MarshalByRefObject
    System.ComponentModel.Component
      System.Windows.Forms.CommonDialog
        System.Windows.Forms.FontDialog

[Visual Basic]
```
Public Class FontDialog
   Inherits CommonDialog
```
[C#]
```
public class FontDialog : CommonDialog
```
[C++]
```
public __gc class FontDialog : public CommonDialog
```
[JScript]
```
public class FontDialog extends CommonDialog
```

Thread Safety

Any public static (**Shared** in Visual Basic) members of this type are safe for multithreaded operations. Any instance members are not guaranteed to be thread safe.

Remarks

The inherited member **ShowDialog** must be invoked to create this specific common dialog box. **HookProc** can be overridden to implement specific dialog box hook functionality.

When you create an instance of **FontDialog**, some of the read/write properties are set to initial values. For a list of these values, see the **FontDialog** constructor.

Example

[Visual Basic, C#] The following example uses **ShowDialog** to display a **FontDialog**. This code assumes that a **Form** has already been created with a **TextBox** and button placed on it. It also assumes the `fontDialog1` has been created. The **Font** contains the size information but not the color information.

[Visual Basic]
```
Protected Sub button1_Click(sender As Object, e As System.EventArgs)
    fontDialog1.ShowColor = True

    fontDialog1.Font = textBox1.Font
    fontDialog1.Color = textBox1.ForeColor

    If fontDialog1.ShowDialog() <> DialogResult.Cancel Then
        textBox1.Font = fontDialog1.Font
        textBox1.ForeColor = fontDialog1.Color
    End If
End Sub 'button1_Click
```

[C#]
```
protected void button1_Click(object sender, System.EventArgs e)
 {
    fontDialog1.ShowColor = true;

    fontDialog1.Font = textBox1.Font;
    fontDialog1.Color = textBox1.ForeColor;

    if(fontDialog1.ShowDialog() != DialogResult.Cancel )
    {
       textBox1.Font = fontDialog1.Font ;
       textBox1.ForeColor = fontDialog1.Color;
    }
 }
```

Requirements

Namespace: System.Windows.Forms

Platforms: Windows 98, Windows NT 4.0, Windows Millennium Edition, Windows 2000, Windows XP Home Edition, Windows XP Professional, Windows Server 2003 family

Assembly: System.Windows.Forms (in System.Windows.Forms.dll)

FontDialog Constructor

Initializes a new instance of the **FontDialog** class.

[Visual Basic]
```
Public Sub New()
```
[C#]
```
public FontDialog();
```
[C++]
```
public: FontDialog();
```
[JScript]
```
public function FontDialog();
```

Remarks

When you create an instance of **FontDialog**, the following read/write properties are initialized.

Property	Initial Value
AllowSimulations	**true**
AllowVectorFonts	**true**
AllowVerticalFonts	**true**
AllowScriptChange	**true**
Color	**Color.Black**
FixedPitchOnly	**false**
MaxSize	0
MinSize	0
ScriptsOnly	**false**
ShowApply	**false**
ShowColor	**false**
ShowEffects	**true**
ShowHelp	**false**

You can change the value for any of these properties through a separate call to the property.

Requirements

Platforms: Windows 98, Windows NT 4.0, Windows Millennium Edition, Windows 2000, Windows XP Home Edition, Windows XP Professional, Windows Server 2003 family

FontDialog.EventApply Field

This member supports the .NET Framework infrastructure and is not intended to be used directly from your code.

[Visual Basic]
```
Protected Shared ReadOnly EventApply As Object
```
[C#]
```
protected static readonly object EventApply;
```

```
[C++]
protected: static Object* EventApply;
[JScript]
protected static var EventApply : Object;
```

FontDialog.AllowScriptChange Property

Gets or sets a value indicating whether the user can change the character set specified in the **Script** combo box to display a character set other than the one currently displayed.

```
[Visual Basic]
Public Property AllowScriptChange As Boolean
[C#]
public bool AllowScriptChange {get; set;}
[C++]
public: __property bool get_AllowScriptChange();
public: __property void set_AllowScriptChange(bool);
[JScript]
public function get AllowScriptChange() : Boolean;
public function set AllowScriptChange(Boolean);
```

Property Value

true if the user can change the character set specified in the **Script** combo box; otherwise, **false**. The default value is **true**.

Remarks

The **Script** combo box found on the font dialog box contains character sets associated with the selected font.

Requirements

Platforms: Windows 98, Windows NT 4.0, Windows Millennium Edition, Windows 2000, Windows XP Home Edition, Windows XP Professional, Windows Server 2003 family

FontDialog.AllowSimulations Property

Gets or sets a value indicating whether the dialog box allows graphics device interface (GDI) font simulations.

```
[Visual Basic]
Public Property AllowSimulations As Boolean
[C#]
public bool AllowSimulations {get; set;}
[C++]
public: __property bool get_AllowSimulations();
public: __property void set_AllowSimulations(bool);
[JScript]
public function get AllowSimulations() : Boolean;
public function set AllowSimulations(Boolean);
```

Property Value

true if font simulations are allowed; otherwise, **false**. The default value is **true**.

Requirements

Platforms: Windows 98, Windows NT 4.0, Windows Millennium Edition, Windows 2000, Windows XP Home Edition, Windows XP Professional, Windows Server 2003 family

FontDialog.AllowVectorFonts Property

Gets or sets a value indicating whether the dialog box allows vector font selections.

```
[Visual Basic]
Public Property AllowVectorFonts As Boolean
[C#]
public bool AllowVectorFonts {get; set;}
[C++]
public: __property bool get_AllowVectorFonts();
public: __property void set_AllowVectorFonts(bool);
[JScript]
public function get AllowVectorFonts() : Boolean;
public function set AllowVectorFonts(Boolean);
```

Property Value

true if vector fonts are allowed; otherwise, **false**. The default value is **true**.

Requirements

Platforms: Windows 98, Windows NT 4.0, Windows Millennium Edition, Windows 2000, Windows XP Home Edition, Windows XP Professional, Windows Server 2003 family

FontDialog.AllowVerticalFonts Property

Gets or sets a value indicating whether the dialog box displays both vertical and horizontal fonts or only horizontal fonts.

```
[Visual Basic]
Public Property AllowVerticalFonts As Boolean
[C#]
public bool AllowVerticalFonts {get; set;}
[C++]
public: __property bool get_AllowVerticalFonts();
public: __property void set_AllowVerticalFonts(bool);
[JScript]
public function get AllowVerticalFonts() : Boolean;
public function set AllowVerticalFonts(Boolean);
```

Property Value

true if both vertical and horizontal fonts are allowed; otherwise, **false**. The default value is **true**.

Requirements

Platforms: Windows 98, Windows NT 4.0, Windows Millennium Edition, Windows 2000, Windows XP Home Edition, Windows XP Professional, Windows Server 2003 family

FontDialog.Color Property

Gets or sets the selected font color.

```
[Visual Basic]
Public Property Color As Color
[C#]
public Color Color {get; set;}
[C++]
public: __property Color get_Color();
public: __property void set_Color(Color);
[JScript]
public function get Color() : Color;
public function set Color(Color);
```

Property Value

The color of the selected font. The default value is **Black**.

Example

See related example in the **System.Windows.Forms.FontDialog** class topic.

Requirements

Platforms: Windows 98, Windows NT 4.0, Windows Millennium Edition, Windows 2000, Windows XP Home Edition, Windows XP Professional, Windows Server 2003 family

FontDialog.FixedPitchOnly Property

Gets or sets a value indicating whether the dialog box allows only the selection of fixed-pitch fonts.

```
[Visual Basic]
Public Property FixedPitchOnly As Boolean
[C#]
public bool FixedPitchOnly {get; set;}
[C++]
public: __property bool get_FixedPitchOnly();
public: __property void set_FixedPitchOnly(bool);
[JScript]
public function get FixedPitchOnly() : Boolean;
public function set FixedPitchOnly(Boolean);
```

Property Value

true if only fixed-pitch fonts can be selected; otherwise, **false**. The default value is **false**.

Requirements

Platforms: Windows 98, Windows NT 4.0, Windows Millennium Edition, Windows 2000, Windows XP Home Edition, Windows XP Professional, Windows Server 2003 family

FontDialog.Font Property

Gets or sets the selected font.

```
[Visual Basic]
Public Property Font As Font
[C#]
public Font Font {get; set;}
[C++]
public: __property Font* get_Font();
public: __property void set_Font(Font*);
[JScript]
public function get Font() : Font;
public function set Font(Font);
```

Property Value

The selected font.

Example

See related example in the **System.Windows.Forms.FontDialog** class topic.

Requirements

Platforms: Windows 98, Windows NT 4.0, Windows Millennium Edition, Windows 2000, Windows XP Home Edition, Windows XP Professional, Windows Server 2003 family

FontDialog.FontMustExist Property

Gets or sets a value indicating whether the dialog box specifies an error condition if the user attempts to select a font or style that does not exist.

```
[Visual Basic]
Public Property FontMustExist As Boolean
[C#]
public bool FontMustExist {get; set;}
[C++]
public: __property bool get_FontMustExist();
public: __property void set_FontMustExist(bool);
[JScript]
public function get FontMustExist() : Boolean;
public function set FontMustExist(Boolean);
```

Property Value

true if the dialog box specifies an error condition when the user tries to select a font or style that does not exist; otherwise, **false**. The default is **false**.

Requirements

Platforms: Windows 98, Windows NT 4.0, Windows Millennium Edition, Windows 2000, Windows XP Home Edition, Windows XP Professional, Windows Server 2003 family

FontDialog.MaxSize Property

Gets or sets the maximum point size a user can select.

```
[Visual Basic]
Public Property MaxSize As Integer
[C#]
public int MaxSize {get; set;}
[C++]
public: __property int get_MaxSize();
public: __property void set_MaxSize(int);
[JScript]
public function get MaxSize() : int;
public function set MaxSize(int);
```

Property Value

The maximum point size a user can select. The default is 0.

Remarks

In order for the maximum and minimum size settings to take effect, **MaxSize** must be greater than **MinSize**, and both must be greater than 0.

Attempts to set this property to values less than 0 will result in a value of 0 being used. If you set **MaxSize** to a value less than **MinSize**, **MinSize** is set to **MaxSize**. The effect of setting **MinSize** and **MaxSize** to the same values is to limit the size selection to a single font size.

When the point size is 0, there are no font size limits.

Requirements

Platforms: Windows 98, Windows NT 4.0, Windows Millennium Edition, Windows 2000, Windows XP Home Edition, Windows XP Professional, Windows Server 2003 family

FontDialog.MinSize Property

Gets or sets the minimum point size a user can select.

```
[Visual Basic]
Public Property MinSize As Integer
[C#]
public int MinSize {get; set;}
[C++]
public: __property int get_MinSize();
public: __property void set_MinSize(int);
[JScript]
public function get MinSize() : int;
public function set MinSize(int);
```

Property Value

The minimum point size a user can select. The default is 0.

Remarks

In order for the maximum and minimum size settings to take effect, **MaxSize** must be greater than **MinSize**, and both must be greater than 0.

Attempts to set this property to values less than 0 will result in a value of 0 being used. If you set **MinSize** to a value greater than **MaxSize**, **MaxSize** is set to the value of **MinSize**. The effect of setting **MinSize** and **MaxSize** to the same value is to limit the size selection to a single font size.

When the point size is 0, there are no font size limits.

Requirements

Platforms: Windows 98, Windows NT 4.0, Windows Millennium Edition, Windows 2000, Windows XP Home Edition, Windows XP Professional, Windows Server 2003 family

FontDialog.Options Property

This member supports the .NET Framework infrastructure and is not intended to be used directly from your code.

```
[Visual Basic]
Protected ReadOnly Property Options As Integer
[C#]
protected int Options {get;}
[C++]
protected: __property int get_Options();
[JScript]
protected function get Options() : int;
```

FontDialog.ScriptsOnly Property

Gets or sets a value indicating whether the dialog box allows selection of fonts for all non-OEM and Symbol character sets, as well as the ANSI character set.

```
[Visual Basic]
Public Property ScriptsOnly As Boolean
[C#]
public bool ScriptsOnly {get; set;}
[C++]
public: __property bool get_ScriptsOnly();
public: __property void set_ScriptsOnly(bool);
[JScript]
public function get ScriptsOnly() : Boolean;
public function set ScriptsOnly(Boolean);
```

Property Value

true if selection of fonts for all non-OEM and Symbol character sets, as well as the ANSI character set, is allowed; otherwise, **false**. The default value is **false**.

Requirements

Platforms: Windows 98, Windows NT 4.0, Windows Millennium Edition, Windows 2000, Windows XP Home Edition, Windows XP Professional, Windows Server 2003 family

FontDialog.ShowApply Property

Gets or sets a value indicating whether the dialog box contains an **Apply** button.

```
[Visual Basic]
Public Property ShowApply As Boolean
[C#]
public bool ShowApply {get; set;}
[C++]
public: __property bool get_ShowApply();
public: __property void set_ShowApply(bool);
[JScript]
public function get ShowApply() : Boolean;
public function set ShowApply(Boolean);
```

Property Value

true if the dialog box contains an **Apply** button; otherwise, **false**. The default value is **false**.

Example

See related example in the **System.Windows.Forms.FontDialog** class topic.

Requirements

Platforms: Windows 98, Windows NT 4.0, Windows Millennium Edition, Windows 2000, Windows XP Home Edition, Windows XP Professional, Windows Server 2003 family

FontDialog.ShowColor Property

Gets or sets a value indicating whether the dialog box displays the color choice.

```
[Visual Basic]
Public Property ShowColor As Boolean
[C#]
public bool ShowColor {get; set;}
[C++]
public: __property bool get_ShowColor();
public: __property void set_ShowColor(bool);
[JScript]
public function get ShowColor() : Boolean;
public function set ShowColor(Boolean);
```

Property Value

true if the dialog box displays the color choice; otherwise, **false**. The default value is **false**.

Example

See related example in the **System.Windows.Forms.FontDialog** class topic.

Requirements

Platforms: Windows 98, Windows NT 4.0,
Windows Millennium Edition, Windows 2000,
Windows XP Home Edition, Windows XP Professional,
Windows Server 2003 family

FontDialog.ShowEffects Property

Gets or sets a value indicating whether the dialog box contains controls that allow the user to specify strikethrough, underline, and text color options.

```
[Visual Basic]
Public Property ShowEffects As Boolean
[C#]
public bool ShowEffects {get; set;}
[C++]
public: __property bool get_ShowEffects();
public: __property void set_ShowEffects(bool);
[JScript]
public function get ShowEffects() : Boolean;
public function set ShowEffects(Boolean);
```

Property Value

true if the dialog box contains controls to set strikethrough, underline, and text color options; otherwise, **false**. The default value is **true**.

Requirements

Platforms: Windows 98, Windows NT 4.0,
Windows Millennium Edition, Windows 2000,
Windows XP Home Edition, Windows XP Professional,
Windows Server 2003 family

FontDialog.ShowHelp Property

Gets or sets a value indicating whether the dialog box displays a Help button.

```
[Visual Basic]
Public Property ShowHelp As Boolean
[C#]
public bool ShowHelp {get; set;}
[C++]
public: __property bool get_ShowHelp();
public: __property void set_ShowHelp(bool);
[JScript]
public function get ShowHelp() : Boolean;
public function set ShowHelp(Boolean);
```

Property Value

true if the dialog box displays a Help button; otherwise, **false**. The default value is **false**.

Requirements

Platforms: Windows 98, Windows NT 4.0,
Windows Millennium Edition, Windows 2000,
Windows XP Home Edition, Windows XP Professional,
Windows Server 2003 family

FontDialog.HookProc Method

Specifies the common dialog box hook procedure that is overridden to add specific functionality to a common dialog box.

```
[Visual Basic]
Overrides Protected Function HookProc( _
   ByVal hWnd As IntPtr, _
   ByVal msg As Integer, _
   ByVal wparam As IntPtr, _
   ByVal lparam As IntPtr _
) As IntPtr
[C#]
protected override IntPtr HookProc(
   IntPtr hWnd,
   int msg,
   IntPtr wparam,
   IntPtr lparam
);
[C++]
protected: IntPtr HookProc(
   IntPtr hWnd,
   int msg,
   IntPtr wparam,
   IntPtr lparam
);
[JScript]
protected override function HookProc(
   hWnd : IntPtr,
   msg : int,
   wparam : IntPtr,
   lparam : IntPtr
) : IntPtr;
```

Parameters

hWnd
The handle to the dialog box window.

msg
The message being received.

wparam
Additional information about the message.

lparam
Additional information about the message.

Return Value

A zero value if the default dialog box procedure processes the message; a nonzero value if the default dialog box procedure ignores the message.

Remarks

A hook procedure is a mechanism by which a function can intercept events before they reach an application. When you override the **CommonDialog.HookProc** method for a **CommonDialog** class, the operating system invokes your override of the function to post operating system messages to the window.

Notes to Inheritors: When overriding **HookProc** in a derived class, be sure to call the base class's **HookProc** method.

Example

See related example in the **System.Windows.Forms.FontDialog** class topic.

Requirements

Platforms: Windows 98, Windows NT 4.0,
Windows Millennium Edition, Windows 2000,
Windows XP Home Edition, Windows XP Professional,
Windows Server 2003 family

FontDialog.OnApply Method

Raises the **Apply** event.

[Visual Basic]
```
Protected Overridable Sub OnApply( _
   ByVal e As EventArgs _
)
```
[C#]
```
protected virtual void OnApply(
   EventArgs e
);
```
[C++]
```
protected: virtual void OnApply(
   EventArgs* e
);
```
[JScript]
```
protected function OnApply(
   e : EventArgs
);
```

Parameters

e

An **EventArgs** that contains the data.

Remarks

Raising an event invokes the event handler through a delegate.

Notes to Inheritors: When overriding **OnApply** in a derived class, be sure to call the base class's **OnApply** method.

Requirements

Platforms: Windows 98, Windows NT 4.0, Windows Millennium Edition, Windows 2000, Windows XP Home Edition, Windows XP Professional, Windows Server 2003 family

FontDialog.Reset Method

Resets all dialog box options to their default values.

[Visual Basic]
```
Overrides Public Sub Reset()
```
[C#]
```
public override void Reset();
```
[C++]
```
public: void Reset();
```
[JScript]
```
public override function Reset();
```

Remarks

When the options are reset, the strikethrough, underline, and color effects are enabled. The fonts listed include only the screen fonts supported by the system.

Requirements

Platforms: Windows 98, Windows NT 4.0, Windows Millennium Edition, Windows 2000, Windows XP Home Edition, Windows XP Professional, Windows Server 2003 family

FontDialog.RunDialog Method

This member overrides **CommonDialog.RunDialog**.

[Visual Basic]
```
Overrides Protected Function RunDialog( _
   ByVal hWndOwner As IntPtr _
) As Boolean
```
[C#]
```
protected override bool RunDialog(
   IntPtr hWndOwner
);
```
[C++]
```
protected: bool RunDialog(
   IntPtr hWndOwner
);
```
[JScript]
```
protected override function RunDialog(
   hWndOwner : IntPtr
) : Boolean;
```

Requirements

Platforms: Windows 98, Windows NT 4.0, Windows Millennium Edition, Windows 2000, Windows XP Home Edition, Windows XP Professional, Windows Server 2003 family

FontDialog.ToString Method

This member overrides **Object.ToString**.

[Visual Basic]
```
Overrides Public Function ToString() As String
```
[C#]
```
public override string ToString();
```
[C++]
```
public: String* ToString();
```
[JScript]
```
public override function ToString() : String;
```

Requirements

Platforms: Windows 98, Windows NT 4.0, Windows Millennium Edition, Windows 2000, Windows XP Home Edition, Windows XP Professional, Windows Server 2003 family

FontDialog.Apply Event

Occurs when the user clicks the Apply button in the font dialog box.

[Visual Basic]
```
Public Event Apply As EventHandler
```
[C#]
```
public event EventHandler Apply;
```
[C++]
```
public: __event EventHandler* Apply;
```

[JScript] In JScript, you can handle the events defined by a class, but you cannot define your own.

Event Data

The event handler receives an argument of type **EventArgs**.

Remarks

Every time the Apply button is clicked, another **Apply** event is raised.

Requirements

Platforms: Windows 98, Windows NT 4.0, Windows Millennium Edition, Windows 2000, Windows XP Home Edition, Windows XP Professional, Windows Server 2003 family

Form Class

Represents a window or dialog box that makes up an application's user interface.

System.Object
  System.MarshalByRefObject
    System.ComponentModel.Component
      System.Windows.Forms.Control
        System.Windows.Forms.ScrollableControl
          System.Windows.Forms.ContainerControl
            System.Windows.Forms.Form
              System.ComponentModel.Design.CollectionEditor.CollectionForm
              System.Web.UI.Design.WebControls.CalendarAutoFormatDialog
              System.Windows.Forms.Design.ComponentEditorForm
              System.Windows.Forms.PrintPreviewDialog

[Visual Basic]

```
Public Class Form
   Inherits ContainerControl
```

[C#]

```
public class Form : ContainerControl
```

[C++]

```
public __gc class Form : public ContainerControl
```

[JScript]

```
public class Form extends ContainerControl
```

Thread Safety

Any public static (**Shared** in Visual Basic) members of this type are safe for multithreaded operations. Any instance members are not guaranteed to be thread safe.

Remarks

A **Form** is a representation of any window displayed in your application. The **Form** class can be used to create standard, tool, borderless, and floating windows. You can also use the **Form** class to create modal windows such as a dialog box. A special kind of form, the multiple document interface (MDI) form, can contain other forms called MDI child forms. An MDI form is created by setting the **IsMdiContainer** property to **true**. MDI child forms are created by setting the **MdiParent** property to the MDI parent form that will contain the child form.

Using the properties available in the **Form** class, you can determine the appearance, size, color, and window management features of the window or dialog box you are creating. The **Text** property allows you to specify the caption of the window in the title bar. The **Size** and **DesktopLocation** properties allow you to define the size and position of the window when it is displayed. You can use the **ForeColor** color property to change the default foreground color of all controls placed on the form. The **FormBorderStyle**, **MinimizeBox**, and **MaximizeBox** properties allow you to control whether the form can be minimized, maximized, or resized at run time.

In addition to properties, you can use the methods of the class to manipulate a form. For example, you can use the **ShowDialog** method to show a form as a modal dialog box. You can use the **SetDesktopLocation** method to position the form on the desktop.

The events of the **Form** class allow you to respond to actions performed on the form. You can use the **Activated** event to perform operations such as updating the data displayed in the controls of the form when the form is activated.

You can use a form as the starting class in your application by placing a method called `Main` in the class. In the `Main` method add code to create and show the form. You will also need to add the `[STAThread]` attribute to the `Main` method in order for the form to run. When the starting form is closed, the application is also closed.

Example

[Visual Basic, C#] The following example creates a new instance of a **Form** and calls the **ShowDialog** method to display the form as a dialog box. The example sets the **FormBorderStyle**, **AcceptButton**, **CancelButton**, **MinimizeBox**, **MaximizeBox**, and **StartPosition** properties to change the appearance and functionality of the form to a dialog box. The example also uses the **Add** method of the form's **Controls** collection to add two **Button** controls. The example uses the **HelpButton** property to display a help button in the caption bar of the dialog box.

[Visual Basic]

```
Public Sub CreateMyForm()
    ' Create a new instance of the form.
    Dim form1 As New Form()
    ' Create two buttons to use as the accept and cancel buttons.
    Dim button1 As New Button()
    Dim button2 As New Button()

    ' Set the text of button1 to "OK".
    button1.Text = "OK"
    ' Set the position of the button on the form.
    button1.Location = New Point(10, 10)
    ' Set the text of button2 to "Cancel".
    button2.Text = "Cancel"
    ' Set the position of the button based on the location of button1.
    button2.Location = _
       New Point(button1.Left, button1.Height + button1.Top + 10)
    ' Set the caption bar text of the form.
    form1.Text = "My Dialog Box"
    ' Display a help button on the form.
    form1.HelpButton = True

    ' Define the border style of the form to a dialog box.
    form1.FormBorderStyle = FormBorderStyle.FixedDialog
    ' Set the MaximizeBox to false to remove the maximize box.
    form1.MaximizeBox = False
    ' Set the MinimizeBox to false to remove the minimize box.
    form1.MinimizeBox = False
    ' Set the accept button of the form to button1.
    form1.AcceptButton = button1
    ' Set the cancel button of the form to button2.
    form1.CancelButton = button2
    ' Set the start position of the form to the center of the screen.
    form1.StartPosition = FormStartPosition.CenterScreen

    ' Add button1 to the form.
    form1.Controls.Add(button1)
    ' Add button2 to the form.
    form1.Controls.Add(button2)

    ' Display the form as a modal dialog box.
    form1.ShowDialog()
End Sub
```

[C#]

```
public void CreateMyForm()
{
   // Create a new instance of the form.
   Form form1 = new Form();
   // Create two buttons to use as the accept and cancel buttons.
   Button button1 = new Button ();
   Button button2 = new Button ();

   // Set the text of button1 to "OK".
   button1.Text = "OK";
   // Set the position of the button on the form.
   button1.Location = new Point (10, 10);
```

```
    // Set the text of button2 to "Cancel".
    button2.Text = "Cancel";
    // Set the position of the button based on the location of button1.
    button2.Location
       = new Point (button1.Left, button1.Height + button1.Top + 10);
    // Set the caption bar text of the form.
    form1.Text = "My Dialog Box";
    // Display a help button on the form.
    form1.HelpButton = true;

    // Define the border style of the form to a dialog box.
    form1.FormBorderStyle = FormBorderStyle.FixedDialog;
    // Set the MaximizeBox to false to remove the maximize box.
    form1.MaximizeBox = false;
    // Set the MinimizeBox to false to remove the minimize box.
    form1.MinimizeBox = false;
    // Set the accept button of the form to button1.
    form1.AcceptButton = button1;
    // Set the cancel button of the form to button2.
    form1.CancelButton = button2;
    // Set the start position of the form to the center of the screen.
    form1.StartPosition = FormStartPosition.CenterScreen;

    // Add button1 to the form.
    form1.Controls.Add(button1);
    // Add button2 to the form.
    form1.Controls.Add(button2);

    // Display the form as a modal dialog box.
    form1.ShowDialog();
}
```

Requirements

Namespace: System.Windows.Forms

Platforms: Windows 98, Windows NT 4.0, Windows Millennium Edition, Windows 2000, Windows XP Home Edition, Windows XP Professional, Windows Server 2003 family, .NET Compact Framework - Windows CE .NET

Assembly: System.Windows.Forms (in System.Windows.Forms.dll)

Form Constructor

Initializes a new instance of the **Form** class.

[Visual Basic]
```
Public Sub New()
```
[C#]
```
public Form();
```
[C++]
```
public: Form();
```
[JScript]
```
public function Form();
```

Remarks

The default size of a form is 300 pixels in height and 300 pixels in width.

Example

See related example in the **System.Windows.Forms.Form** class topic.

Requirements

Platforms: Windows 98, Windows NT 4.0, Windows Millennium Edition, Windows 2000, Windows XP Home Edition, Windows XP Professional, Windows Server 2003 family, .NET Compact Framework - Windows CE .NET

Form.AcceptButton Property

Gets or sets the button on the form that is clicked when the user presses the ENTER key.

[Visual Basic]
```
Public Property AcceptButton As IButtonControl
```
[C#]
```
public IButtonControl AcceptButton {get; set;}
```
[C++]
```
public: __property IButtonControl* get_AcceptButton();
public: __property void set_AcceptButton(IButtonControl*);
```
[JScript]
```
public function get AcceptButton() : IButtonControl;
public function set AcceptButton(IButtonControl);
```

Property Value

An **IButtonControl** that represents the button to use as the accept button for the form.

Remarks

This property allows you to designate a default action to occur when the user presses the ENTER key in your application. The button assigned to this property must be an **IButtonControl** that is on the current form or located within a container on the current form.

You can use this property to allow the user to quickly navigate a simple form by allowing them to simply press the ENTER key when they are finished instead of manually clicking the accept button with their mouse.

The accept button might not be activated if the currently selected control on the form intercepts the ENTER key and processes it. For example, a multiline text box control allows the ENTER key to be pressed when it is selected to insert a new line character in the control.

Example

See related example in the **System.Windows.Forms.Form** class topic.

Requirements

Platforms: Windows 98, Windows NT 4.0, Windows Millennium Edition, Windows 2000, Windows XP Home Edition, Windows XP Professional, Windows Server 2003 family

Form.ActiveForm Property

Gets the currently active form for this application.

[Visual Basic]
```
Public Shared ReadOnly Property ActiveForm As Form
```
[C#]
```
public static Form ActiveForm {get;}
```
[C++]
```
public: __property static Form* get_ActiveForm();
```
[JScript]
```
public static function get ActiveForm() : Form;
```

Property Value

A **Form** that represents the currently active form, or a null reference (**Nothing** in Visual Basic) if there is no active form.

Remarks

You can use this method to obtain a reference to the currently active form to perform actions on the form or its controls.

If your application is a multiple document interface (MDI) application, use the **ActiveMdiChild** property to obtain the currently active MDI child form.

Example

See related example in the **System.Windows.Forms.Form** class topic.

Requirements

Platforms: Windows 98, Windows NT 4.0, Windows Millennium Edition, Windows 2000, Windows XP Home Edition, Windows XP Professional, Windows Server 2003 family

.NET Framework Security:

- **UIPermission** for requesting a form. Associated enumeration: **UIPermissionWindow.AllWindows**.

Form.ActiveMdiChild Property

Gets the currently active multiple document interface (MDI) child window.

```
[Visual Basic]
Public ReadOnly Property ActiveMdiChild As Form
[C#]
public Form ActiveMdiChild {get;}
[C++]
public: __property Form* get_ActiveMdiChild();
[JScript]
public function get ActiveMdiChild() : Form;
```

Property Value

Returns a **Form** that represents the currently active MDI child window, or a null reference (**Nothing** in Visual Basic) if there are currently no child windows present.

Remarks

You can use this method to determine whether there are any MDI child forms open in your MDI application. You can also use this method to perform operations on an MDI child window from its MDI parent form or from another form that is displayed in your application.

If the currently active form is not an MDI child form, you can use the **ActiveForm** property to obtain a reference to it.

Example

See related example in the **System.Windows.Forms.Form** class topic.

Requirements

Platforms: Windows 98, Windows NT 4.0, Windows Millennium Edition, Windows 2000, Windows XP Home Edition, Windows XP Professional, Windows Server 2003 family

Form.AllowTransparency Property

This member supports the .NET Framework infrastructure and is not intended to be used directly from your code.

```
[Visual Basic]
Public Property AllowTransparency As Boolean
[C#]
public bool AllowTransparency {get; set;}
[C++]
public: __property bool get_AllowTransparency();
public: __property void set_AllowTransparency(bool);
[JScript]
public function get AllowTransparency() : Boolean;
public function set AllowTransparency(Boolean);
```

Form.AutoScale Property

Gets or sets a value indicating whether the form adjusts its size to fit the height of the font used on the form and scales its controls.

```
[Visual Basic]
Public Property AutoScale As Boolean
[C#]
public bool AutoScale {get; set;}
[C++]
public: __property bool get_AutoScale();
public: __property void set_AutoScale(bool);
[JScript]
public function get AutoScale() : Boolean;
public function set AutoScale(Boolean);
```

Property Value

true if the form will automatically scale itself and its controls based on the current font assigned to the form; otherwise, **false**. The default is **true**.

Remarks

You can use this property to allow your form and its controls to automatically adjust based on changes in the font. This can be useful in applications where the font might increase or decrease based on the language specified for use by Windows.

To obtain the size the form will auto scale to, use the **AutoScaleBaseSize** property. If you want to determine the size the form will auto scale to based on a specific font, use the **GetAutoScaleSize** method.

Requirements

Platforms: Windows 98, Windows NT 4.0, Windows Millennium Edition, Windows 2000, Windows XP Home Edition, Windows XP Professional, Windows Server 2003 family

Form.AutoScaleBaseSize Property

Gets or sets the base size used for autoscaling of the form.

```
[Visual Basic]
Public Overridable Property AutoScaleBaseSize As Size
[C#]
public virtual Size AutoScaleBaseSize {get; set;}
[C++]
public: __property virtual Size get_AutoScaleBaseSize();
public: __property virtual void set_AutoScaleBaseSize(Size);
```

```
[JScript]
public function get AutoScaleBaseSize() : Size;
public function set AutoScaleBaseSize(Size);
```

Property Value

A **Size** that represents the base size that this form uses for autoscailing.

Remarks

The value of the **AutoScaleBaseSize** property is used at form-display time to compute the scaling factor for the form. The autoscaling base size is used by the form as a baseline for comparison to the system's font size to determine how much to scale the form when autoscaling is used. If you want to determine the size a form will auto scale to based on a specific font, use the **GetAutoScaleSize** method.

> **Note** The value of this property is used when the form is initially created. Once the property is set, it cannot be changed.

Requirements

Platforms: Windows 98, Windows NT 4.0, Windows Millennium Edition, Windows 2000, Windows XP Home Edition, Windows XP Professional, Windows Server 2003 family

Form.AutoScroll Property

Gets or sets a value indicating whether the form enables autoscrolling.

```
[Visual Basic]
Overrides Public Property AutoScroll As Boolean
[C#]
public override bool AutoScroll {get; set;}
[C++]
public: __property bool get_AutoScroll();
public: __property void set_AutoScroll(bool);
[JScript]
public override function get AutoScroll() : Boolean;
public override function set AutoScroll(Boolean);
```

Property Value

true to enable autoscrolling on the form; otherwise, **false**. The default is **true**.

Remarks

If this property is set to **true**, scroll bars are displayed on the form if any controls are located outside the form's client region. Additionally, when autoscrolling is on, the client area of the form automatically scrolls to make the control with input focus visible.

You can use this property to prevent users from losing the ability to view controls when their video resolution settings are set to a low resolution.

Example

See related example in the **System.Windows.Forms.Form** class topic.

Requirements

Platforms: Windows 98, Windows NT 4.0, Windows Millennium Edition, Windows 2000, Windows XP Home Edition, Windows XP Professional, Windows Server 2003 family

Form.BackColor Property

This member overrides **Control.BackColor**.

```
[Visual Basic]
Overrides Public Property BackColor As Color
[C#]
public override Color BackColor {get; set;}
[C++]
public: __property Color get_BackColor();
public: __property void set_BackColor(Color);
[JScript]
public override function get BackColor() : Color;
public override function set BackColor(Color);
```

Requirements

Platforms: Windows 98, Windows NT 4.0, Windows Millennium Edition, Windows 2000, Windows XP Home Edition, Windows XP Professional, Windows Server 2003 family, .NET Compact Framework - Windows CE .NET

Form.CancelButton Property

Gets or sets the button control that is clicked when the user presses the ESC key.

```
[Visual Basic]
Public Property CancelButton As IButtonControl
[C#]
public IButtonControl CancelButton {get; set;}
[C++]
public: __property IButtonControl* get_CancelButton();
public: __property void set_CancelButton(IButtonControl*);
[JScript]
public function get CancelButton() : IButtonControl;
public function set CancelButton(IButtonControl);
```

Property Value

An **IButtonControl** that represents the cancel button for the form.

Remarks

The cancel button for a form is the button control that is clicked whenever the user presses the ESC key. The button assigned to this property must be an **IButtonControl** that is on the current form or located within a container on the current form.

This property allows you to designate a default action to occur when the user presses the ESC key in your application. You can use this property to allow the user to quickly navigate a simple form by allowing them to simply press the ESC key to close a window without committing changes instead of manually clicking the cancel button with their mouse.

Example

See related example in the **System.Windows.Forms.Form** class topic.

Requirements

Platforms: Windows 98, Windows NT 4.0, Windows Millennium Edition, Windows 2000, Windows XP Home Edition, Windows XP Professional, Windows Server 2003 family

Form.ClientSize Property

Gets or sets the size of the client area of the form.

[Visual Basic]
```
Public Shadows Property ClientSize As Size
```
[C#]
```
public new Size ClientSize {get; set;}
```
[C++]
```
public: __property Size get_ClientSize();
public: __property void set_ClientSize(Size);
```
[JScript]
```
public hide function get ClientSize() : Size;
public hide function set ClientSize(Size);
```

Property Value

A **Size** that represents the size of the form's client area.

Remarks

The size of the client area of the form is the size of the form excluding the borders and the title bar. The client area of a form is the area within a form where controls can be placed. You can use this property to get the proper dimensions when performing graphics operations or when sizing and positioning controls on the form. To get the size of the entire form, use the **Size** property or use the individual properties **Height** and **Width**.

Example

See related example in the **System.Windows.Forms.Form** class topic.

Requirements

Platforms: Windows 98, Windows NT 4.0,
Windows Millennium Edition, Windows 2000,
Windows XP Home Edition, Windows XP Professional,
Windows Server 2003 family,
.NET Compact Framework - Windows CE .NET

Form.ControlBox Property

Gets or sets a value indicating whether a control box is displayed in the caption bar of the form.

[Visual Basic]
```
Public Property ControlBox As Boolean
```
[C#]
```
public bool ControlBox {get; set;}
```
[C++]
```
public: __property bool get_ControlBox();
public: __property void set_ControlBox(bool);
```
[JScript]
```
public function get ControlBox() : Boolean;
public function set ControlBox(Boolean);
```

Property Value

true if the form displays a control box in the upper left corner of the form; otherwise, **false**. The default is **true**.

Remarks

If the **ControlBox** property is set to **true**, the control box is displayed in the upper-left corner of the caption bar. The control box is where the user can click to access the system menu.

> **Note** If your form does not display a control box, the form is not able to close using the ALT+F4 keyboard combination.

> **Note** When set to **false**, the **ControlBox** property has no effect on a Multiple Document Interface (MDI) child form that is displayed maximized at time of creation.

Example

See related example in the **System.Windows.Forms.Form** class topic.

Requirements

Platforms: Windows 98, Windows NT 4.0,
Windows Millennium Edition, Windows 2000,
Windows XP Home Edition, Windows XP Professional,
Windows Server 2003 family,
.NET Compact Framework - Windows CE .NET

Form.CreateParams Property

This member overrides **Control.CreateParams**.

[Visual Basic]
```
Overrides Protected ReadOnly Property CreateParams As CreateParams
```
[C#]
```
protected override CreateParams CreateParams {get;}
```
[C++]
```
protected: __property CreateParams* get_CreateParams();
```
[JScript]
```
protected override function get CreateParams() : CreateParams;
```

Requirements

Platforms: Windows 98, Windows NT 4.0,
Windows Millennium Edition, Windows 2000,
Windows XP Home Edition, Windows XP Professional,
Windows Server 2003 family

Form.DefaultImeMode Property

Gets the default Input Method Editor (IME) mode supported by the control.

[Visual Basic]
```
Overrides Protected ReadOnly Property DefaultImeMode As ImeMode
```
[C#]
```
protected override ImeMode DefaultImeMode {get;}
```
[C++]
```
protected: __property ImeMode get_DefaultImeMode();
```
[JScript]
```
protected override function get DefaultImeMode() : ImeMode;
```

Property Value

One of the **ImeMode** values.

Remarks

An input method editor (IME) is a program that allows users to enter complex characters and symbols, such as Japanese Kanji characters, by using a standard keyboard.

As implemented in the **Form** class, this property always returns the **ImeMode.NoControl** value. The value of this property is assigned to the **Control.ImeMode** property.

Requirements

Platforms: Windows 98, Windows NT 4.0,
Windows Millennium Edition, Windows 2000,
Windows XP Home Edition, Windows XP Professional,
Windows Server 2003 family

Form.DefaultSize Property

This member overrides **Control.DefaultSize**.

[Visual Basic]
```
Overrides Protected ReadOnly Property DefaultSize As Size
```
[C#]
```
protected override Size DefaultSize {get;}
```
[C++]
```
protected: __property Size get_DefaultSize();
```
[JScript]
```
protected override function get DefaultSize() : Size;
```

Requirements

Platforms: Windows 98, Windows NT 4.0, Windows Millennium Edition, Windows 2000, Windows XP Home Edition, Windows XP Professional, Windows Server 2003 family

Form.DesktopBounds Property

Gets or sets the size and location of the form on the Windows desktop.

[Visual Basic]
```
Public Property DesktopBounds As Rectangle
```
[C#]
```
public Rectangle DesktopBounds {get; set;}
```
[C++]
```
public: __property Rectangle get_DesktopBounds();
public: __property void set_DesktopBounds(Rectangle);
```
[JScript]
```
public function get DesktopBounds() : Rectangle;
public function set DesktopBounds(Rectangle);
```

Property Value

A **Rectangle** that represents the bounds of the form on the Windows desktop using desktop coordinates.

Remarks

Desktop coordinates are based on the working area of the screen, which excludes the taskbar. The coordinate system of the desktop is pixel based. If your application is running on a multiple monitor system, the coordinates of the form are the coordinates for the combined desktop.

You can use this property to size and position a form relative to other forms or applications on the Windows desktop.

Example

See related example in the **System.Windows.Forms.Form** class topic.

Requirements

Platforms: Windows 98, Windows NT 4.0, Windows Millennium Edition, Windows 2000, Windows XP Home Edition, Windows XP Professional, Windows Server 2003 family

Form.DesktopLocation Property

Gets or sets the location of the form on the Windows desktop.

[Visual Basic]
```
Public Property DesktopLocation As Point
```
[C#]
```
public Point DesktopLocation {get; set;}
```
[C++]
```
public: __property Point get_DesktopLocation();
public: __property void set_DesktopLocation(Point);
```
[JScript]
```
public function get DesktopLocation() : Point;
public function set DesktopLocation(Point);
```

Property Value

A **Point** that represents the location of the form on the desktop.

Remarks

Desktop coordinates are based on the working area of the screen, which excludes the taskbar. The coordinate system of the desktop is pixel based. If your application is running on a multimonitor system, the coordinates of the form are the coordinates for the combined desktop.

You can use this property to position your form relative to other forms and applications on the Windows desktop.

Example

See related example in the **System.Windows.Forms.Form** class topic.

Requirements

Platforms: Windows 98, Windows NT 4.0, Windows Millennium Edition, Windows 2000, Windows XP Home Edition, Windows XP Professional, Windows Server 2003 family

Form.DialogResult Property

Gets or sets the dialog result for the form.

[Visual Basic]
```
Public Property DialogResult As DialogResult
```
[C#]
```
public DialogResult DialogResult {get; set;}
```
[C++]
```
public: __property DialogResult get_DialogResult();
public: __property void set_DialogResult(DialogResult);
```
[JScript]
```
public function get DialogResult() : DialogResult;
public function set DialogResult(DialogResult);
```

Property Value

A **DialogResult** that represents the result of the form when used as a dialog box.

Exceptions

Exception Type	Condition
InvalidEnumArgumentException	The value specified is outside the range of valid values.

Remarks

The dialog result of a form is the value that is returned from the form when it is displayed as a modal dialog. If the form is displayed as a dialog box, setting this property with a value from the **DialogResult** enumeration sets the value of the dialog result for the form, hides the modal dialog, and returns control to the calling form. This property is typically set by the **DialogResult** property of a **Button** control on the form. When the user clicks the **Button** control, the value assigned to the **DialogResult** property of the **Button** is assigned to the **DialogResult** property of the form.

When a form is displayed as a modal dialog box, clicking the Close button (the button with an *X* in the top-right corner of the form) causes the form to be hidden and the **DialogResult** property to be set to **DialogResult.Cancel**. The **Close** method is not automatically called when the user clicks the Close button of a dialog box or sets the value of the **DialogResult** property. Instead, the form is hidden and can be shown again without creating a new instance of the dialog box. Because of this behavior, you must call the **Dispose** method of the form when the form is no longer needed by your application.

You can use this property to determine how a dialog box is closed in order to properly process the actions performed in the dialog box.

Note You can override the value assigned to the **DialogResult** property when the user clicks the Close button by setting the **DialogResult** property in an event handler for the **Closing** event of the form.

Note If a **Form** is displayed as a modeless window, the value returned by the **DialogResult** property might not return a value assigned to the form because the form's resources are automatically released when the form is closed.

Example

See related example in the **System.Windows.Forms.Form** class topic.

Requirements

Platforms: Windows 98, Windows NT 4.0,
Windows Millennium Edition, Windows 2000,
Windows XP Home Edition, Windows XP Professional,
Windows Server 2003 family,
.NET Compact Framework - Windows CE .NET

Form.FormBorderStyle Property

Gets or sets the border style of the form.

```
[Visual Basic]
Public Property FormBorderStyle As FormBorderStyle
[C#]
public FormBorderStyle FormBorderStyle {get; set;}
[C++]
public: __property FormBorderStyle get_FormBorderStyle();
public: __property void set_FormBorderStyle(FormBorderStyle);
[JScript]
public function get FormBorderStyle() : FormBorderStyle;
public function set FormBorderStyle(FormBorderStyle);
```

Property Value

A **FormBorderStyle** that represents the style of border to display for the form. The default is **FormBorderStyle.Sizable**.

Exceptions

Exception Type	Condition
InvalidEnumArgument-Exception	The value specified is outside the range of valid values.

Remarks

The border style of the form determines how the outer edge of the form appears. In addition to changing the border display for a form, certain border styles prevent the form from being sized. For example, the **FormBorderStyle.FixedDialog** border style changes the border of the form to that of a dialog box and prevents the form from being resized. The border style can also affect the size or availability of the caption bar section of a form.

Example

See related example in the **System.Windows.Forms.Form** class topic.

Requirements

Platforms: Windows 98, Windows NT 4.0,
Windows Millennium Edition, Windows 2000,
Windows XP Home Edition, Windows XP Professional,
Windows Server 2003 family,
.NET Compact Framework - Windows CE .NET

Form.HelpButton Property

Gets or sets a value indicating whether a Help button should be displayed in the caption box of the form.

```
[Visual Basic]
Public Property HelpButton As Boolean
[C#]
public bool HelpButton {get; set;}
[C++]
public: __property bool get_HelpButton();
public: __property void set_HelpButton(bool);
[JScript]
public function get HelpButton() : Boolean;
public function set HelpButton(Boolean);
```

Property Value

true to display a Help button in the form's caption bar; otherwise, **false**. The default is **false**.

Remarks

When this property is set to **true**, a small button with a question mark appears in the caption bar to the left of the close button. You can use this button to display help for your application. You can create an event handler for the **HelpRequested** event of the **Control** class to display Help information to the user when the Help button of the form is clicked.

The value of the **HelpButton** property is ignored if the maximize or minimize boxes are shown.

Example

See related example in the **System.Windows.Forms.Form** class topic.

Requirements

Platforms: Windows 98, Windows NT 4.0,
Windows Millennium Edition, Windows 2000,
Windows XP Home Edition, Windows XP Professional,
Windows Server 2003 family

Form.Icon Property

Gets or sets the icon for the form.

[Visual Basic]
```
Public Property Icon As Icon
```
[C#]
```
public Icon Icon {get; set;}
```
[C++]
```
public: __property Icon* get_Icon();
public: __property void set_Icon(Icon*);
```
[JScript]
```
public function get Icon() : Icon;
public function set Icon(Icon);
```

Property Value

An **Icon** that represents the icon for the form.

Remarks

A form's icon designates the picture that represents the form in the taskbar as well as the icon that is displayed for the control box of the form.

Requirements

Platforms: Windows 98, Windows NT 4.0,
Windows Millennium Edition, Windows 2000,
Windows XP Home Edition, Windows XP Professional,
Windows Server 2003 family,
.NET Compact Framework - Windows CE .NET

Form.IsMdiChild Property

Gets a value indicating whether the form is a multiple document interface (MDI) child form.

[Visual Basic]
```
Public ReadOnly Property IsMdiChild As Boolean
```
[C#]
```
public bool IsMdiChild {get;}
```
[C++]
```
public: __property bool get_IsMdiChild();
```
[JScript]
```
public function get IsMdiChild() : Boolean;
```

Property Value

true if the form is an MDI child form; otherwise, **false**.

Remarks

At run time, MDI child forms are displayed inside the client area of an MDI parent form. An MDI child form can be maximized, minimized, and moved within the MDI parent form. To create an MDI child form, assign the **Form** that will be the MDI parent form to the **MdiParent** property of the child form. You can use the **IsMdiContainer** property to determine whether a form is an MDI parent form.

You can use the **IsMdiChild** property to determine whether a form returned by a method or property is an MDI child form or a standard form in your application such as a dialog box.

> **Note** All MDI child forms have sizable borders, a control-menu box, and minimize and maximize buttons, regardless of the settings of the **FormBorderStyle**, **ControlBox**, **MinimizeBox**, and **MaximizeBox** properties.

Requirements

Platforms: Windows 98, Windows NT 4.0,
Windows Millennium Edition, Windows 2000,
Windows XP Home Edition, Windows XP Professional,
Windows Server 2003 family

Form.IsMdiContainer Property

Gets or sets a value indicating whether the form is a container for multiple document interface (MDI) child forms.

[Visual Basic]
```
Public Property IsMdiContainer As Boolean
```
[C#]
```
public bool IsMdiContainer {get; set;}
```
[C++]
```
public: __property bool get_IsMdiContainer();
public: __property void set_IsMdiContainer(bool);
```
[JScript]
```
public function get IsMdiContainer() : Boolean;
public function set IsMdiContainer(Boolean);
```

Property Value

true if the form is a container for MDI child forms; otherwise, **false**. The default is **false**.

Remarks

This property changes the display and behavior of the form to an MDI parent form. When this property is set to **true**, the form displays a sunken client area with a raised border. All MDI child forms assigned to the parent form are displayed within its client area.

When an MDI parent form is closed, the **Closing** events of all MDI child forms are raised before the MDI parent form's **Closing** event is raised. In addition, the **Closed** events of all MDI child forms are raised before the **Closed** event of the MDI parent form is raised.

Requirements

Platforms: Windows 98, Windows NT 4.0,
Windows Millennium Edition, Windows 2000,
Windows XP Home Edition, Windows XP Professional,
Windows Server 2003 family

Form.IsRestrictedWindow Property

This member supports the .NET Framework infrastructure and is not intended to be used directly from your code.

[Visual Basic]
```
Public ReadOnly Property IsRestrictedWindow As Boolean
```
[C#]
```
public bool IsRestrictedWindow {get;}
```
[C++]
```
public: __property bool get_IsRestrictedWindow();
```
[JScript]
```
public function get IsRestrictedWindow() : Boolean;
```

Form.KeyPreview Property

Gets or sets a value indicating whether the form will receive key events before the event is passed to the control that has focus.

[Visual Basic]
```
Public Property KeyPreview As Boolean
```
[C#]
```
public bool KeyPreview {get; set;}
```

[C++]
```
public: __property bool get_KeyPreview();
public: __property void set_KeyPreview(bool);
```
[JScript]
```
public function get KeyPreview() : Boolean;
public function set KeyPreview(Boolean);
```

Property Value

true if the form will receive all key events; **false** if the currently selected control on the form receives key events. The default is **false**.

Remarks

When this property is set to **true**, the form will receive all **KeyPress**, **KeyDown**, and **KeyUp** events. After the form's event handlers have completed processing the keystroke, the keystroke is then assigned to the control with focus. For example, if the **KeyPreview** property is set to **true** and the currently selected control is a **TextBox**, after the keystroke is handled by the event-handling methods of the form the **TextBox** control will receive the key that was pressed. To handle keyboard events only at the form level and not allow controls to receive keyboard events, set the **KeyPressEventArgs.Handled** property in your form's **KeyPress** event-handling method to **true**.

You can use this property to process all keystrokes in your application and either handle the keystroke or call the appropriate control to handle the keystroke. For example, when an application uses function keys, you might want to process the keystrokes at the form level rather than writing code for each control that might receive keystroke events.

> **Note** If a form has no visible or enabled controls, it automatically receives all keyboard events.

Requirements

Platforms: Windows 98, Windows NT 4.0,
Windows Millennium Edition, Windows 2000,
Windows XP Home Edition, Windows XP Professional,
Windows Server 2003 family

Form.MaximizeBox Property

Gets or sets a value indicating whether the maximize button is displayed in the caption bar of the form.

[Visual Basic]
```
Public Property MaximizeBox As Boolean
```
[C#]
```
public bool MaximizeBox {get; set;}
```
[C++]
```
public: __property bool get_MaximizeBox();
public: __property void set_MaximizeBox(bool);
```
[JScript]
```
public function get MaximizeBox() : Boolean;
public function set MaximizeBox(Boolean);
```

Property Value

true to display a maximize button for the form; otherwise, **false**. The default is **true**.

Remarks

A maximize button enables users to enlarge a window to full-screen size. To display a maximize button, you must also set the form's **FormBorderStyle** property to either **FormBorderStyle.FixedSingle**, **FormBorderStyle.Sizable**, **FormBorderStyle.Fixed3D**, or **FormBorderStyle.FixedDialog**.

A maximize button automatically becomes a restore button when a window is maximized. Minimizing or restoring a window automatically changes the restore button back to a maximize button.

> **Note** Maximizing a form at run time generates a **Resize** event. The **WindowState** property reflects the current state of the window. If you set the **WindowState** property to **FormWindowState.Maximized**, the form is maximized independently of whatever settings are in effect for the **MaximizeBox** and **FormBorderStyle** properties.

Example

See related example in the **System.Windows.Forms.Form** class topic.

Requirements

Platforms: Windows 98, Windows NT 4.0,
Windows Millennium Edition, Windows 2000,
Windows XP Home Edition, Windows XP Professional,
Windows Server 2003 family,
.NET Compact Framework - Windows CE .NET

Form.MaximizedBounds Property

Gets and sets the size of the form when it is maximized.

[Visual Basic]
```
Protected Property MaximizedBounds As Rectangle
```
[C#]
```
protected Rectangle MaximizedBounds {get; set;}
```
[C++]
```
protected: __property Rectangle get_MaximizedBounds();
protected: __property void set_MaximizedBounds(Rectangle);
```
[JScript]
```
protected function get MaximizedBounds() : Rectangle;
protected function set MaximizedBounds(Rectangle);
```

Property Value

A **Rectangle** that represents the bounds of the form when it is maximized.

Exceptions

Exception Type	Condition
ArgumentOutOfRange-Exception	The value of the **Top** property is greater than the height of the form. -or- The value of the **Left** property is greater than the width of the form.

Remarks

Notes to Inheritors: Classes that inherit from **Form** can override this method to provide new bounds for the form when it is maximized. The class sets this property internally when the form's maximize box button is clicked.

Requirements

Platforms: Windows 98, Windows NT 4.0,
Windows Millennium Edition, Windows 2000,
Windows XP Home Edition, Windows XP Professional,
Windows Server 2003 family

Form.MaximumSize Property

Gets the maximum size the form can be resized to.

```
[Visual Basic]
Public Property MaximumSize As Size
[C#]
public Size MaximumSize {get; set;}
[C++]
public: __property Size get_MaximumSize();
public: __property void set_MaximumSize(Size);
[JScript]
public function get MaximumSize() : Size;
public function set MaximumSize(Size);
```

Property Value

A **Size** that represents the maximum size for the form.

Exceptions

Exception Type	Condition
ArgumentOutOfRange-Exception	The values of the height or width within the **Size** object are less than zero.

Remarks

This property enables you to limit the size of a form to a specified maximum size. You can use this feature when displaying multiple windows at the same time, to ensure that a single window does not cause other windows to be hidden. If this property is set to a **Size** object that is 0 in height and 0 in width, the form will have no maximum size beyond the limits set by Windows.

Requirements

Platforms: Windows 98, Windows NT 4.0, Windows Millennium Edition, Windows 2000, Windows XP Home Edition, Windows XP Professional, Windows Server 2003 family

Form.MdiChildren Property

Gets an array of forms that represent the multiple document interface (MDI) child forms that are parented to this form.

```
[Visual Basic]
Public ReadOnly Property MdiChildren As Form ()
[C#]
public Form[] MdiChildren {get;}
[C++]
public: __property Form* get_MdiChildren();
[JScript]
public function get MdiChildren() : Form[];
```

Property Value

An array of **Form** objects, each of which identifies one of this form's MDI child forms.

Remarks

This property allows you to obtain references to all the MDI child forms currently opened in an MDI parent form. To create an MDI child form, assign the **Form** that will be the MDI parent form to the **MdiParent** property of the child form.

You can use this property to loop through all the MDI child forms to perform operations such as saving data to a database when the MDI parent form closes or to update fields on the child forms based on actions performed in your application.

Example

See related example in the **System.Windows.Forms.Form** class topic.

Requirements

Platforms: Windows 98, Windows NT 4.0, Windows Millennium Edition, Windows 2000, Windows XP Home Edition, Windows XP Professional, Windows Server 2003 family

Form.MdiParent Property

Gets or sets the current multiple document interface (MDI) parent form of this form.

```
[Visual Basic]
Public Property MdiParent As Form
[C#]
public Form MdiParent {get; set;}
[C++]
public: __property Form* get_MdiParent();
public: __property void set_MdiParent(Form*);
[JScript]
public function get MdiParent() : Form;
public function set MdiParent(Form);
```

Property Value

A **Form** that represents the MDI parent form.

Exceptions

Exception Type	Condition
Exception	The **Form** assigned to this property is not marked as an MDI container. -or- The **Form** assigned to this property is both a child and an MDI container form. -or- The **Form** assigned to this property is located on a different thread.

Remarks

To create an MDI child form, assign the **Form** that will be the MDI parent form to the **MdiParent** property of the child form. You can use this property from an MDI child form to obtain global information that all child forms need or to invoke methods that perform actions to all child forms.

Example

See related example in the **System.Windows.Forms.Form** class topic.

Requirements

Platforms: Windows 98, Windows NT 4.0, Windows Millennium Edition, Windows 2000, Windows XP Home Edition, Windows XP Professional, Windows Server 2003 family

.NET Framework Security:

- **UIPermission** for requesting a form. Associated enumeration: **UIPermissionWindow.AllWindows**.

Form.Menu Property

Gets or sets the **MainMenu** that is displayed in the form.

```
[Visual Basic]
Public Property Menu As MainMenu
[C#]
public MainMenu Menu {get; set;}
[C++]
public: __property MainMenu* get_Menu();
public: __property void set_Menu(MainMenu*);
[JScript]
public function get Menu() : MainMenu;
public function set Menu(MainMenu);
```

Property Value

A **MainMenu** that represents the menu to display in the form.

Remarks

You can use this property to switch between complete menu sets at run time. For example, you can define one **MainMenu** to be displayed when your multiple document interface (MDI) form has no active MDI child forms and another **MainMenu** to display when a child window is displayed. You can also use a different **MainMenu** when specific conditions exist in your application that require displaying a different menu set.

Example

See related example in the **System.Windows.Forms.Form** class topic.

Requirements

Platforms: Windows 98, Windows NT 4.0,
Windows Millennium Edition, Windows 2000,
Windows XP Home Edition, Windows XP Professional,
Windows Server 2003 family,
.NET Compact Framework - Windows CE .NET

Form.MergedMenu Property

Gets the merged menu for the form.

```
[Visual Basic]
Public ReadOnly Property MergedMenu As MainMenu
[C#]
public MainMenu MergedMenu {get;}
[C++]
public: __property MainMenu* get_MergedMenu();
[JScript]
public function get MergedMenu() : MainMenu;
```

Property Value

A **MainMenu** that represents the merged menu of the form.

Remarks

This property is primarily used when the form is a multiple document interface (MDI) child form that merges its menu with its parent form's menu. You can use this property to obtain the current menu structure in an MDI application to make changes or additions to the menu structure. To obtain the nonmerged **MainMenu** assigned to a form, use the **Menu** property.

Requirements

Platforms: Windows 98, Windows NT 4.0,
Windows Millennium Edition, Windows 2000,
Windows XP Home Edition, Windows XP Professional,
Windows Server 2003 family

Form.MinimizeBox Property

Gets or sets a value indicating whether the minimize button is displayed in the caption bar of the form.

```
[Visual Basic]
Public Property MinimizeBox As Boolean
[C#]
public bool MinimizeBox {get; set;}
[C++]
public: __property bool get_MinimizeBox();
public: __property void set_MinimizeBox(bool);
[JScript]
public function get MinimizeBox() : Boolean;
public function set MinimizeBox(Boolean);
```

Property Value

true to display a minimize button for the form; otherwise, **false**. The default is **true**.

Remarks

A minimize button enables users to minimize a window to an icon. To display a minimize button, you must also set the form's **FormBorderStyle** property to either **FormBorderStyle.FixedSingle**, **FormBorderStyle.Sizable**, **FormBorderStyle.Fixed3D**, or **FormBorderStyle.FixedDialog**.

> **Note** Minimizing a form at run time generates a **Resize** event. The **WindowState** property reflects the current state of the window. If you set the **WindowState** property to **FormWindowState.Minimized**, the form is minimized independently of whatever settings are in effect for the **MinimizeBox** and **FormBorderStyle** properties.

Example

See related example in the **System.Windows.Forms.Form** class topic.

Requirements

Platforms: Windows 98, Windows NT 4.0,
Windows Millennium Edition, Windows 2000,
Windows XP Home Edition, Windows XP Professional,
Windows Server 2003 family,
.NET Compact Framework - Windows CE .NET

Form.MinimumSize Property

Gets or sets the minimum size the form can be resized to.

```
[Visual Basic]
Public Property MinimumSize As Size
[C#]
public Size MinimumSize {get; set;}
[C++]
public: __property Size get_MinimumSize();
public: __property void set_MinimumSize(Size);
[JScript]
public function get MinimumSize() : Size;
public function set MinimumSize(Size);
```

Property Value

A **Size** that represents the minimum size for the form.

Exceptions

Exception Type	Condition
ArgumentOutOfRange-Exception	The values of the height or width within the **Size** object are less than zero.

Remarks

This property enables you to limit the size of a form to a specified minimum size. You can use this feature to prevent a user from sizing a window to an undesirable size. If this property is set to a **Size** object that is 0 in height and 0 in width, the form will have no minimum size beyond the limits set by Windows.

Requirements

Platforms: Windows 98, Windows NT 4.0, Windows Millennium Edition, Windows 2000, Windows XP Home Edition, Windows XP Professional, Windows Server 2003 family

Form.Modal Property

Gets a value indicating whether this form is displayed modally.

```
[Visual Basic]
Public ReadOnly Property Modal As Boolean
[C#]
public bool Modal {get;}
[C++]
public: __property bool get_Modal();
[JScript]
public function get Modal() : Boolean;
```

Property Value

true if the form is displayed modally; otherwise, **false**.

Remarks

When a form is displayed modally, no input (keyboard or mouse click) can occur except to objects on the modal form. The program must hide or close a modal form (usually in response to some user action) before input to another form can occur. Forms that are displayed modally are typically used as dialog boxes in an application.

You can use this property to determine whether a form that you have obtained from a method or property has been displayed modally.

To display a form modally use the **ShowDialog** method.

Example

See related example in the **System.Windows.Forms.Form** class topic.

Requirements

Platforms: Windows 98, Windows NT 4.0, Windows Millennium Edition, Windows 2000, Windows XP Home Edition, Windows XP Professional, Windows Server 2003 family

Form.Opacity Property

Gets or sets the opacity level of the form.

```
[Visual Basic]
Public Property Opacity As Double
[C#]
public double Opacity {get; set;}
[C++]
public: __property double get_Opacity();
public: __property void set_Opacity(double);
[JScript]
public function get Opacity() : double;
public function set Opacity(double);
```

Property Value

The level of opacity for the form. The default is 1.00.

Remarks

This property enables you to specify a level of transparency for the form and its controls. This property differs from transparency provided by the **TransparencyKey** which only makes a form and its controls completely transparent if they are the same color as the value specified in the **TransparencyKey** property. When this property is set to a value less than 100% (1.00), the entire form, including borders, is made more transparent. Setting this property to a value of 0% (0.00) makes the form completely invisible. You can use this property to provide different levels of transparency or to provide effects such as phasing a form in or out of view. For example, you can phase a form into view by setting the **Opacity** property to a value of 0% (0.00) and gradually increasing the value until it reaches 100% (1.00).

Windows 2000, Windows Server 2003 family Platform Note: This property has no effect on platforms that cannot display layered windows.

Example

See related example in the **System.Windows.Forms.Form** class topic.

Requirements

Platforms: Windows 2000, Windows XP Home Edition, Windows XP Professional, Windows Server 2003 family

Form.OwnedForms Property

Gets an array of **Form** objects that represent all forms that are owned by this form.

```
[Visual Basic]
Public ReadOnly Property OwnedForms As Form ()
[C#]
public Form[] OwnedForms {get;}
[C++]
public: __property Form* get_OwnedForms();
[JScript]
public function get OwnedForms() : Form[];
```

Property Value

A **Form** array that represents the owned forms for this form.

Remarks

This property returns an array that contains all forms that are owned by this form. To make a form owned by another form, call the **AddOwnedForm** method. The form assigned to the owner form will remain owned until the **RemoveOwnedForm** method is called. You can also make a form owned by another by setting the **Owner** property with a reference to its owner form.

When a form is owned by another form, it is minimized and closed with the owner form. For example, if `Form2` is owned by form `Form1`, if `Form1` is closed or minimized, `Form2` is also closed or minimized.

Owned forms are also never displayed behind their owner form. You can use owned forms for windows such as find and replace windows, which should not be displayed behind the owner form when the owner form is selected.

> **Note** If the form is a multiple document interface (MDI) parent form, this property will return all forms that are displayed with the exception of any MDI child forms that are currently open. To obtain the MDI child forms opened in an MDI parent form, use the **MdiChildren** property.

Example

See related example in the **System.Windows.Forms.Form** class topic.

\

Requirements

Platforms: Windows 98, Windows NT 4.0,
Windows Millennium Edition, Windows 2000,
Windows XP Home Edition, Windows XP Professional,
Windows Server 2003 family

Form.Owner Property

Gets or sets the form that owns this form.

```
[Visual Basic]
Public Property Owner As Form
[C#]
public Form Owner {get; set;}
[C++]
public: __property Form* get_Owner();
public: __property void set_Owner(Form*);
[JScript]
public function get Owner() : Form;
public function set Owner(Form);
```

Property Value

A **Form** that represents the form that is the owner of this form.

Exceptions

Exception Type	Condition
Exception	A window that is not a top-level window cannot have an owner.

Remarks

To make a form owned by another form, assign its **Owner** property a reference to the form that will be the owner.

When a form is owned by another form, it is minimized and closed with the owner form. For example, if `Form2` is owned by form `Form1`, if `Form1` is closed or minimized, `Form2` is also closed or minimized. Owned forms are also never displayed behind their owner form. You can use owned forms for windows such as find and replace windows, which should not disappear when the owner form is selected. To determine the forms that are owned by a parent form, use the **OwnedForms** property.

Requirements

Platforms: Windows 98, Windows NT 4.0,
Windows Millennium Edition, Windows 2000,
Windows XP Home Edition, Windows XP Professional,
Windows Server 2003 family

Form.ShowInTaskbar Property

Gets or sets a value indicating whether the form is displayed in the Windows taskbar.

```
[Visual Basic]
Public Property ShowInTaskbar As Boolean
[C#]
public bool ShowInTaskbar {get; set;}
[C++]
public: __property bool get_ShowInTaskbar();
public: __property void set_ShowInTaskbar(bool);
[JScript]
public function get ShowInTaskbar() : Boolean;
public function set ShowInTaskbar(Boolean);
```

Property Value

true to display the form in the Windows taskbar at run time; otherwise, **false**. The default is **true**.

Remarks

If a form is parented within another form, the parented form is not displayed in the Windows taskbar.

You can use this property to prevent users from selecting your form through the Windows taskbar. For example, if you display a Find and Replace tool window in your application, you might want to prevent that window from being selected through the Windows taskbar since you would need both the application's main window and the Find and Replace tool window displayed in order to process searches appropriately.

Example

See related example in the **System.Windows.Forms.Form** class topic.

Requirements

Platforms: Windows 98, Windows NT 4.0,
Windows Millennium Edition, Windows 2000,
Windows XP Home Edition, Windows XP Professional,
Windows Server 2003 family

Form.Size Property

Gets or sets the size of the form.

```
[Visual Basic]
Public Shadows Property Size As Size
[C#]
public new Size Size {get; set;}
[C++]
public: __property Size get_Size();
public: __property void set_Size(Size);
[JScript]
public hide function get Size() : Size;
public hide function set Size(Size);
```

Property Value

A **Size** that represents the size of the form.

Remarks

This property allows you to set both the height and width of the form at the same time instead of setting the **Height** and **Width** properties individually. If you want to set the size and location of a form, you can use the **DesktopBounds** property to size and locate the form based on desktop coordinates or use the **Bounds** property of the **Control** class to set the size and location of the form based on screen coordinates.

Example

See related example in the **System.Windows.Forms.Form** class topic.

Requirements

Platforms: Windows 98, Windows NT 4.0, Windows Millennium Edition, Windows 2000, Windows XP Home Edition, Windows XP Professional, Windows Server 2003 family, .NET Compact Framework - Windows CE .NET

Form.SizeGripStyle Property

Gets or sets the style of the size grip to display in the lower-right corner of the form.

```
[Visual Basic]
Public Property SizeGripStyle As SizeGripStyle
[C#]
public SizeGripStyle SizeGripStyle {get; set;}
[C++]
public: __property SizeGripStyle get_SizeGripStyle();
public: __property void set_SizeGripStyle(SizeGripStyle);
[JScript]
public function get SizeGripStyle() : SizeGripStyle;
public function set SizeGripStyle(SizeGripStyle);
```

Property Value

A **SizeGripStyle** that represents the style of the size grip to display. The default is **SizeGripStyle.Auto**

Exceptions

Exception Type	Condition
InvalidEnumArgumentException	The value specified is outside the range of valid values.

Remarks

This property enables you to determine when the sizing grip is displayed on the form. You can set this property to display the sizing grip or have it automatically displayed based on the setting of the **FormBorderStyle** property.

Example

See related example in the **System.Windows.Forms.Form** class topic.

Requirements

Platforms: Windows 98, Windows NT 4.0, Windows Millennium Edition, Windows 2000, Windows XP Home Edition, Windows XP Professional, Windows Server 2003 family

Form.StartPosition Property

Gets or sets the starting position of the form at run time.

```
[Visual Basic]
Public Property StartPosition As FormStartPosition
[C#]
public FormStartPosition StartPosition {get; set;}
[C++]
public: __property FormStartPosition get_StartPosition();
public: __property void set_StartPosition(FormStartPosition);
[JScript]
public function get StartPosition() : FormStartPosition;
public function set StartPosition(FormStartPosition);
```

Property Value

A **FormStartPosition** that represents the starting position of the form.

Exceptions

Exception Type	Condition
InvalidEnumArgumentException	The value specified is outside the range of valid values.

Remarks

This property enables you to set the starting position of the form when it is displayed at run time. The form can be displayed manually or in the default location specified by Windows. You can also position the form to display in the center of the screen or in the center of its parent form for forms such as multiple document interface (MDI) child forms.

Example

See related example in the **System.Windows.Forms.Form** class topic.

Requirements

Platforms: Windows 98, Windows NT 4.0, Windows Millennium Edition, Windows 2000, Windows XP Home Edition, Windows XP Professional, Windows Server 2003 family

Form.TabIndex Property

This member supports the .NET Framework infrastructure and is not intended to be used directly from your code.

```
[Visual Basic]
Public Shadows Property TabIndex As Integer
[C#]
public new int TabIndex {get; set;}
[C++]
public: __property int get_TabIndex();
public: __property void set_TabIndex(int);
[JScript]
public hide function get TabIndex() : int;
public hide function set TabIndex(int);
```

Form.TopLevel Property

Gets or sets a value indicating whether to display the form as a top-level window.

```
[Visual Basic]
Public Property TopLevel As Boolean
[C#]
public bool TopLevel {get; set;}
[C++]
public: __property bool get_TopLevel();
public: __property void set_TopLevel(bool);
[JScript]
public function get TopLevel() : Boolean;
public function set TopLevel(Boolean);
```

Property Value

true to display the form as a top-level window; otherwise, **false**. The default is **true**.

Exceptions

Exception Type	Condition
Exception	A Multiple Document Interface (MDI) parent form must be a top-level window.

Remarks

A top-level form is a window that has no parent form, or whose parent form is the desktop window. Top-level windows are typically used as the main form in an application.

Example

See related example in the **System.Windows.Forms.Form** class topic.

Requirements

Platforms: Windows 98, Windows NT 4.0,
Windows Millennium Edition, Windows 2000,
Windows XP Home Edition, Windows XP Professional,
Windows Server 2003 family

Form.TopMost Property

Gets or sets a value indicating whether the form should be displayed as the top-most form of your application.

```
[Visual Basic]
Public Property TopMost As Boolean
[C#]
public bool TopMost {get; set;}
[C++]
public: __property bool get_TopMost();
public: __property void set_TopMost(bool);
[JScript]
public function get TopMost() : Boolean;
public function set TopMost(Boolean);
```

Property Value

true to display the form as a top-most form; otherwise, **false**. The default is **false**.

Remarks

A top-most form is a form that overlaps all the other forms even if it is not the active or foreground form. Top-most forms are always displayed at the highest point in the Z-order of an application. You can use this method to create a form that is always displayed in your application, such as a Find and Replace tool window.

Example

See related example in the **System.Windows.Forms.Form** class topic.

Requirements

Platforms: Windows 98, Windows NT 4.0,
Windows Millennium Edition, Windows 2000,
Windows XP Home Edition, Windows XP Professional,
Windows Server 2003 family

Form.TransparencyKey Property

Gets or sets the color that will represent transparent areas of the form.

```
[Visual Basic]
Public Property TransparencyKey As Color
[C#]
public Color TransparencyKey {get; set;}
[C++]
public: __property Color get_TransparencyKey();
public: __property void set_TransparencyKey(Color);
[JScript]
public function get TransparencyKey() : Color;
public function set TransparencyKey(Color);
```

Property Value

A **Color** that represents the color to display transparently on the form.

Remarks

When the **TransparencyKey** property is assigned a **Color**, the areas of the form that have the same **BackColor** will be displayed transparently. Any mouse actions, such as the click of the mouse, that are performed on the transparent areas of the form will be transferred to the windows below the transparent area. For example, if the client region of a form is made transparent, clicking the mouse on that area would send the event notification of the click to any window that is below it. If the color assigned to the **TransparencyKey** property is the same as any controls on the form, they also will be displayed transparently. For example, if you have a **Button** control on a form that has its **TransparencyKey** property set to **SystemColors.Control**, the control will be displayed transparently unless the **BackColor** property of the **Button** control is changed to a different color.

Windows 2000 Platform Note: Transparent windows and regions are only supported under the Windows 2000 operating system.

Example

See related example in the **System.Windows.Forms.Form** class topic.

Requirements

Platforms: Windows 98, Windows NT 4.0,
Windows Millennium Edition, Windows 2000,
Windows XP Home Edition, Windows XP Professional,
Windows Server 2003 family

Form.WindowState Property

Gets or sets the form's window state.

```
[Visual Basic]
Public Property WindowState As FormWindowState
[C#]
public FormWindowState WindowState {get; set;}
[C++]
public: __property FormWindowState get_WindowState();
public: __property void set_WindowState(FormWindowState);
[JScript]
public function get WindowState() : FormWindowState;
public function set WindowState(FormWindowState);
```

Property Value

A **FormWindowState** that represents the window state of the form. The default is **FormWindowState.Normal**.

Exceptions

Exception Type	Condition
InvalidEnumArgument-Exception	The value specified is outside the range of valid values.

Remarks

Before a form is displayed, the **WindowState** property is always set to **FormWindowState.Normal**, regardless of its initial setting. This is reflected in the **Height**, **Left**, **Top**, and **Width** property settings. If a form is hidden after it has been shown, these properties reflect the previous state until the form is shown again, regardless of any changes made to the **WindowState** property.

Example

See related example in the **System.Windows.Forms.Form** class topic.

Requirements

Platforms: Windows 98, Windows NT 4.0, Windows Millennium Edition, Windows 2000, Windows XP Home Edition, Windows XP Professional, Windows Server 2003 family, .NET Compact Framework - Windows CE .NET

Form.Activate Method

Activates the form and gives it focus.

```
[Visual Basic]
Public Sub Activate()
[C#]
public void Activate();
[C++]
public: void Activate();
[JScript]
public function Activate();
```

Remarks

Activating a form brings it to the front if this is the active application, or it flashes the window caption if this is not the active application. The form must be visible for this method to have any effect. To determine the active form in an application, use the **ActiveForm** property or the **ActiveMdiChild** property if your forms are in a Multiple Document Interface (MDI) application.

Requirements

Platforms: Windows 98, Windows NT 4.0, Windows Millennium Edition, Windows 2000, Windows XP Home Edition, Windows XP Professional, Windows Server 2003 family

.NET Framework Security:

- **UIPermission** for changing focus. Associated enumeration: **UIPermissionWindow.AllWindows**.

Form.ActivateMdiChild Method

This member supports the .NET Framework infrastructure and is not intended to be used directly from your code.

```
[Visual Basic]
Protected Sub ActivateMdiChild( _
   ByVal form As Form _
)
[C#]
protected void ActivateMdiChild(
   Form form
);
[C++]
protected: void ActivateMdiChild(
   Form* form
);
[JScript]
protected function ActivateMdiChild(
   form : Form
);
```

Form.AddOwnedForm Method

Adds an owned form to this form.

```
[Visual Basic]
Public Sub AddOwnedForm( _
   ByVal ownedForm As Form _
)
[C#]
public void AddOwnedForm(
   Form ownedForm
);
[C++]
public: void AddOwnedForm(
   Form* ownedForm
);
[JScript]
public function AddOwnedForm(
   ownedForm : Form
);
```

Parameters

ownedForm

The **Form** that this form will own.

Remarks

The form assigned to the owner form remains owned until the **RemoveOwnedForm** method is called. You can also make a form owned by another by setting the **Owner** property with a reference to its owner form.

When a form is owned by another form, it is minimized and closed with the owner form. For example, if `Form2` is owned by form `Form1`, if `Form1` is closed or minimized, `Form2` is also closed or minimized. Owned forms are also never displayed behind their owner form. You can use owned forms for windows such as find and replace windows, which should not be displayed behind the owner form when the owner form is selected.

> **Note** If the form is a multiple document interface (MDI) parent form, this property returns all forms that are displayed with the exception of any MDI child forms that are currently open. To obtain the MDI child forms opened in an MDI parent form, use the **MdiChildren** property.

Example

See related example in the **System.Windows.Forms.Form** class topic.

Requirements

Platforms: Windows 98, Windows NT 4.0, Windows Millennium Edition, Windows 2000, Windows XP Home Edition, Windows XP Professional, Windows Server 2003 family

Form.AdjustFormScrollbars Method

This member supports the .NET Framework infrastructure and is not intended to be used directly from your code.

```
[Visual Basic]
Overrides Protected Sub AdjustFormScrollbars( _
   ByVal displayScrollbars As Boolean _
)
[C#]
protected override void AdjustFormScrollbars(
   bool displayScrollbars
);
[C++]
protected: void AdjustFormScrollbars(
   bool displayScrollbars
);
[JScript]
protected override function AdjustFormScrollbars(
   displayScrollbars : Boolean
);
```

Form.ApplyAutoScaling Method

This member supports the .NET Framework infrastructure and is not intended to be used directly from your code.

```
[Visual Basic]
Protected Sub ApplyAutoScaling()
[C#]
protected void ApplyAutoScaling();
[C++]
protected: void ApplyAutoScaling();
[JScript]
protected function ApplyAutoScaling();
```

Form.CenterToParent Method

This member supports the .NET Framework infrastructure and is not intended to be used directly from your code.

```
[Visual Basic]
Protected Sub CenterToParent()
[C#]
protected void CenterToParent();
[C++]
protected: void CenterToParent();
[JScript]
protected function CenterToParent();
```

Form.CenterToScreen Method

This member supports the .NET Framework infrastructure and is not intended to be used directly from your code.

```
[Visual Basic]
Protected Sub CenterToScreen()
[C#]
protected void CenterToScreen();
[C++]
protected: void CenterToScreen();
[JScript]
protected function CenterToScreen();
```

Form.Close Method

Closes the form.

```
[Visual Basic]
Public Sub Close()
[C#]
public void Close();
[C++]
public: void Close();
[JScript]
public function Close();
```

Exceptions

Exception Type	Condition
InvalidOperation-Exception	The form was closed while a handle was being created.

Remarks

When a form is closed, all resources created within the object are closed and the form is disposed. You can prevent the closing of a form at run time by handling the **Closing** event and setting the **Cancel** property of the **CancelEventArgs** passed as a parameter to your event-handling method. If the form you are closing is the startup form of your application, your application ends.

Note When the **Close** method is called on a **Form** displayed as a modeless window, you cannot call the **Show** method to make the form visible, because the form's resources have already been released. To hide a form and then make it visible, use the **Control.Hide** method.

CAUTION The **Form.Closed** and **Form.Closing** events are not raised when the **Application.Exit** method is called to exit your application. If you have validation code in either of these events that must be executed, you should call the **Form.Close** method for each open form individually before calling the **Exit** method.

Requirements

Platforms: Windows 98, Windows NT 4.0, Windows Millennium Edition, Windows 2000, Windows XP Home Edition, Windows XP Professional, Windows Server 2003 family, .NET Compact Framework - Windows CE .NET

Form.CreateControlsInstance Method

This member overrides **Control.CreateControlsInstance**.

```
[Visual Basic]
Overrides Protected Function CreateControlsInstance() As _
   ControlCollection
[C#]
protected override ControlCollection CreateControlsInstance();
[C++]
protected: ControlCollection* CreateControlsInstance();
[JScript]
protected override function CreateControlsInstance() :
   ControlCollection;
```

Requirements

Platforms: Windows 98, Windows NT 4.0, Windows Millennium Edition, Windows 2000, Windows XP Home Edition, Windows XP Professional, Windows Server 2003 family

Form.CreateHandle Method

This member overrides **Control.CreateHandle**.

```
[Visual Basic]
Overrides Protected Sub CreateHandle()
[C#]
protected override void CreateHandle();
[C++]
protected: void CreateHandle();
[JScript]
protected override function CreateHandle();
```

Requirements

Platforms: Windows 98, Windows NT 4.0, Windows Millennium Edition, Windows 2000, Windows XP Home Edition, Windows XP Professional, Windows Server 2003 family

Form.DefWndProc Method

This member overrides **Control.DefWndProc**.

```
[Visual Basic]
Overrides Protected Sub DefWndProc( _
   ByRef m As Message _
)
[C#]
protected override void DefWndProc(
   ref Message m
);
[C++]
protected: void DefWndProc(
   Message* m
);
[JScript]
protected override function DefWndProc(
   m : Message
);
```

Requirements

Platforms: Windows 98, Windows NT 4.0, Windows Millennium Edition, Windows 2000, Windows XP Home Edition, Windows XP Professional, Windows Server 2003 family

Form.Dispose Method

Overload List

Disposes of the resources (other than memory) used by the **Form**.

Supported by the .NET Compact Framework.

[Visual Basic] **Overloads Overrides Protected Sub Dispose(Boolean)**

[C#] **protected override void Dispose(bool);**

[C++] **protected: void Dispose(bool);**

[JScript] **protected override function Dispose(Boolean);**

Inherited from **Component**.

Supported by the .NET Compact Framework.

[Visual Basic] **Overloads Public Overridable Sub Dispose() Implements IDisposable.Dispose**

[C#] **public virtual void Dispose();**

[C++] **public: virtual void Dispose();**

[JScript] **public function Dispose();**

Form.Dispose Method (Boolean)

Disposes of the resources (other than memory) used by the **Form**.

```
[Visual Basic]
Overrides Overloads Protected Sub Dispose( _
   ByVal disposing As Boolean _
)
[C#]
protected override void Dispose(
   bool disposing
);
[C++]
protected: void Dispose(
   bool disposing
);
[JScript]
protected override function Dispose(
   disposing : Boolean
);
```

Parameters

disposing
: **true** to release both managed and unmanaged resources; **false** to release only unmanaged resources.

Remarks

This method is called by the public **Dispose()** method and the **Finalize** method. **Dispose()** invokes the protected **Dispose(Boolean)** method with the *disposing* parameter set to **true**. **Finalize** invokes **Dispose** with *disposing* set to **false**.

When the *disposing* parameter is **true**, this method releases all resources held by any managed objects that this **Form** references. This method invokes the **Dispose()** method of each referenced object.

Notes to Inheritors: **Dispose** can be called multiple times by other objects. When overriding **Dispose(Boolean)**, be careful not to reference objects that have been previously disposed of in an earlier call to **Dispose**.

Requirements

Platforms: Windows 98, Windows NT 4.0, Windows Millennium Edition, Windows 2000, Windows XP Home Edition, Windows XP Professional, Windows Server 2003 family, .NET Compact Framework - Windows CE .NET

Form.GetAutoScaleSize Method

Gets the sized when autoscaling the form based on a specified font.

```
[Visual Basic]
Public Shared Function GetAutoScaleSize( _
   ByVal font As Font _
) As SizeF
[C#]
public static SizeF GetAutoScaleSize(
   Font font
);
[C++]
public: static SizeF GetAutoScaleSize(
   Font* font
);
[JScript]
public static function GetAutoScaleSize(
   font : Font
) : SizeF;
```

Parameters

font

A **Font** representing the font to determine the autoscaled base size of the form.

Return Value

A **SizeF** representing the autoscaled size of the form.

Remarks

You can use this method to determine the size a form would autoscale to for a specific font before applying the font to the form. If you want to determine the size a form is autoscaled to based on the font currently assigned to the form, use the **AutoScaleBaseSize** property.

Requirements

Platforms: Windows 98, Windows NT 4.0, Windows Millennium Edition, Windows 2000, Windows XP Home Edition, Windows XP Professional, Windows Server 2003 family

Form.LayoutMdi Method

Arranges the multiple document interface (MDI) child forms within the MDI parent form.

```
[Visual Basic]
Public Sub LayoutMdi( _
   ByVal value As MdiLayout _
)
[C#]
public void LayoutMdi(
   MdiLayout value
);
[C++]
public: void LayoutMdi(
   MdiLayout value
);
[JScript]
public function LayoutMdi(
   value : MdiLayout
);
```

Parameters

value

One of the **MdiLayout** values that defines the layout of MDI child forms.

Remarks

You can use this method to arrange the MDI child forms in your MDI parent form to allow for easier navigation and manipulation of MDI child forms. MDI child forms can be tiled horizontally and vertically, cascaded, or as icons within the MDI parent form.

Example

See related example in the **System.Windows.Forms.Form** class topic.

Requirements

Platforms: Windows 98, Windows NT 4.0, Windows Millennium Edition, Windows 2000, Windows XP Home Edition, Windows XP Professional, Windows Server 2003 family

Form.OnActivated Method

Raises the **Activated** event.

```
[Visual Basic]
Protected Overridable Sub OnActivated( _
   ByVal e As EventArgs _
)
[C#]
protected virtual void OnActivated(
   EventArgs e
);
[C++]
protected: virtual void OnActivated(
   EventArgs* e
);
[JScript]
protected function OnActivated(
   e : EventArgs
);
```

Parameters

e

An **EventArgs** that contains the event data.

Remarks

Raising an event invokes the event handler through a delegate. For more information, see **Raising an Event**.

The **OnActivated** method also allows derived classes to handle the event without attaching a delegate. This is the preferred technique for handling the event in a derived class.

Notes to Inheritors: When overriding **OnActivated** in a derived class, be sure to call the base class's **OnActivated** method so that registered delegates receive the event.

Requirements

Platforms: Windows 98, Windows NT 4.0,
Windows Millennium Edition, Windows 2000,
Windows XP Home Edition, Windows XP Professional,
Windows Server 2003 family,
.NET Compact Framework - Windows CE .NET

Form.OnClosed Method

Raises the **Closed** event.

```
[Visual Basic]
Protected Overridable Sub OnClosed( _
   ByVal e As EventArgs _
)
[C#]
protected virtual void OnClosed(
   EventArgs e
);
[C++]
protected: virtual void OnClosed(
   EventArgs* e
);
[JScript]
protected function OnClosed(
   e : EventArgs
);
```

Parameters

e

The **EventArgs** that contains the event data.

Remarks

Raising an event invokes the event handler through a delegate. For more information, see **Raising an Event**.

The **OnClosed** method also allows derived classes to handle the event without attaching a delegate. This is the preferred technique for handling the event in a derived class.

Notes to Inheritors: When overriding **OnClosed** in a derived class, be sure to call the base class's **OnClosed** method so that registered delegates receive the event.

Requirements

Platforms: Windows 98, Windows NT 4.0,
Windows Millennium Edition, Windows 2000,
Windows XP Home Edition, Windows XP Professional,
Windows Server 2003 family,
.NET Compact Framework - Windows CE .NET

Form.OnClosing Method

Raises the **Closing** event.

```
[Visual Basic]
Protected Overridable Sub OnClosing( _
   ByVal e As CancelEventArgs _
)
[C#]
protected virtual void OnClosing(
   CancelEventArgs e
);
[C++]
protected: virtual void OnClosing(
   CancelEventArgs* e
);
[JScript]
protected function OnClosing(
   e : CancelEventArgs
);
```

Parameters

e

A **CancelEventArgs** that contains the event data.

Remarks

Raising an event invokes the event handler through a delegate.

The **OnClosing** method also allows derived classes to handle the event without attaching a delegate. This is the preferred technique for handling the event in a derived class.

Notes to Inheritors: When overriding **OnClosing** in a derived class, be sure to call the base class's **OnClosing** method so that registered delegates receive the event.

Example

See related example in the **System.Windows.Forms.Form** class topic.

Requirements

Platforms: Windows 98, Windows NT 4.0,
Windows Millennium Edition, Windows 2000,
Windows XP Home Edition, Windows XP Professional,
Windows Server 2003 family,
.NET Compact Framework - Windows CE .NET

Form.OnCreateControl Method

This member overrides **Control.OnCreateControl**.

```
[Visual Basic]
Overrides Protected Sub OnCreateControl()
[C#]
protected override void OnCreateControl();
[C++]
protected: void OnCreateControl();
[JScript]
protected override function OnCreateControl();
```

Requirements

Platforms: Windows 98, Windows NT 4.0,
Windows Millennium Edition, Windows 2000,
Windows XP Home Edition, Windows XP Professional,
Windows Server 2003 family

Form.OnDeactivate Method

Raises the **Deactivate** event.

```
[Visual Basic]
Protected Overridable Sub OnDeactivate( _
   ByVal e As EventArgs _
)
[C#]
protected virtual void OnDeactivate(
   EventArgs e
);
```

[C++]
```
protected: virtual void OnDeactivate(
   EventArgs* e
);
```
[JScript]
```
protected function OnDeactivate(
   e : EventArgs
);
```

Parameters

e

The **EventArgs** that contains the event data.

Remarks

Raising an event invokes the event handler through a delegate. For more information, see **Raising an Event**.

The **OnDeactivate** method also allows derived classes to handle the event without attaching a delegate. This is the preferred technique for handling the event in a derived class.

Notes to Inheritors: When overriding **OnDeactivate** in a derived class, be sure to call the base class's **OnDeactivate** method so that registered delegates receive the event.

Requirements

Platforms: Windows 98, Windows NT 4.0, Windows Millennium Edition, Windows 2000, Windows XP Home Edition, Windows XP Professional, Windows Server 2003 family, .NET Compact Framework - Windows CE .NET

Form.OnFontChanged Method

This member overrides **Control.OnFontChanged**.

[Visual Basic]
```
Overrides Protected Sub OnFontChanged( _
   ByVal e As EventArgs _
)
```
[C#]
```
protected override void OnFontChanged(
   EventArgs e
);
```
[C++]
```
protected: void OnFontChanged(
   EventArgs* e
);
```
[JScript]
```
protected override function OnFontChanged(
   e : EventArgs
);
```

Requirements

Platforms: Windows 98, Windows NT 4.0, Windows Millennium Edition, Windows 2000, Windows XP Home Edition, Windows XP Professional, Windows Server 2003 family

Form.OnHandleCreated Method

This member overrides **Control.OnHandleCreated**.

[Visual Basic]
```
Overrides Protected Sub OnHandleCreated( _
   ByVal e As EventArgs _
)
```
[C#]
```
protected override void OnHandleCreated(
   EventArgs e
);
```
[C++]
```
protected: void OnHandleCreated(
   EventArgs* e
);
```
[JScript]
```
protected override function OnHandleCreated(
   e : EventArgs
);
```

Requirements

Platforms: Windows 98, Windows NT 4.0, Windows Millennium Edition, Windows 2000, Windows XP Home Edition, Windows XP Professional, Windows Server 2003 family

Form.OnHandleDestroyed Method

This member overrides **Control.OnHandleDestroyed**.

[Visual Basic]
```
Overrides Protected Sub OnHandleDestroyed( _
   ByVal e As EventArgs _
)
```
[C#]
```
protected override void OnHandleDestroyed(
   EventArgs e
);
```
[C++]
```
protected: void OnHandleDestroyed(
   EventArgs* e
);
```
[JScript]
```
protected override function OnHandleDestroyed(
   e : EventArgs
);
```

Requirements

Platforms: Windows 98, Windows NT 4.0, Windows Millennium Edition, Windows 2000, Windows XP Home Edition, Windows XP Professional, Windows Server 2003 family

Form.OnInputLanguageChanged Method

Raises the **InputLanguageChanged** event.

[Visual Basic]
```
Protected Overridable Sub OnInputLanguageChanged( _
   ByVal e As InputLanguageChangedEventArgs _
)
```
[C#]
```
protected virtual void OnInputLanguageChanged(
   InputLanguageChangedEventArgs e
);
```
[C++]
```
protected: virtual void OnInputLanguageChanged(
   InputLanguageChangedEventArgs* e
);
```

```
[JScript]
protected function OnInputLanguageChanged(
   e : InputLanguageChangedEventArgs
);
```

Parameters

e

The **InputLanguageChangedEventArgs** that contains the event data.

Remarks

Raising an event invokes the event handler through a delegate.

The **OnInputLanguageChanged** method also allows derived classes to handle the event without attaching a delegate. This is the preferred technique for handling the event in a derived class.

Notes to Inheritors: When overriding **OnInputLanguageChanged** in a derived class, be sure to call the base class's **OnInputLanguageChanged** method so that registered delegates receive the event.

Requirements

Platforms: Windows 98, Windows NT 4.0, Windows Millennium Edition, Windows 2000, Windows XP Home Edition, Windows XP Professional, Windows Server 2003 family

Form.OnInputLanguageChanging Method

Raises the **InputLanguageChanging** event.

```
[Visual Basic]
Protected Overridable Sub OnInputLanguageChanging( _
   ByVal e As InputLanguageChangingEventArgs _
)
[C#]
protected virtual void OnInputLanguageChanging(
   InputLanguageChangingEventArgs e
);
[C++]
protected: virtual void OnInputLanguageChanging(
   InputLanguageChangingEventArgs* e
);
[JScript]
protected function OnInputLanguageChanging(
   e : InputLanguageChangingEventArgs
);
```

Parameters

e

The **InputLanguageChangingEventArgs** that contains the event data.

Remarks

Raising an event invokes the event handler through a delegate. For more information, see **Raising an Event**.

The **OnInputLanguageChanging** method also allows derived classes to handle the event without attaching a delegate. This is the preferred technique for handling the event in a derived class.

Notes to Inheritors: When overriding **OnInputLanguageChanging** in a derived class, be sure to call the base class's **OnInputLanguageChanging** method so that registered delegates receive the event.

Requirements

Platforms: Windows 98, Windows NT 4.0, Windows Millennium Edition, Windows 2000, Windows XP Home Edition, Windows XP Professional, Windows Server 2003 family

Form.OnLoad Method

Raises the **Load** event.

```
[Visual Basic]
Protected Overridable Sub OnLoad( _
   ByVal e As EventArgs _
)
[C#]
protected virtual void OnLoad(
   EventArgs e
);
[C++]
protected: virtual void OnLoad(
   EventArgs* e
);
[JScript]
protected function OnLoad(
   e : EventArgs
);
```

Parameters

e

An **EventArgs** that contains the event data.

Remarks

Raising an event invokes the event handler through a delegate. For more information, see **Raising an Event**.

The **OnLoad** method also allows derived classes to handle the event without attaching a delegate. This is the preferred technique for handling the event in a derived class.

Notes to Inheritors: When overriding **OnLoad** in a derived class, be sure to call the base class's **OnLoad** method so that registered delegates receive the event.

Requirements

Platforms: Windows 98, Windows NT 4.0, Windows Millennium Edition, Windows 2000, Windows XP Home Edition, Windows XP Professional, Windows Server 2003 family, .NET Compact Framework - Windows CE .NET

Form.OnMaximizedBoundsChanged Method

Raises the **MaximizedBoundsChanged** event.

```
[Visual Basic]
Protected Overridable Sub OnMaximizedBoundsChanged( _
   ByVal e As EventArgs _
)
[C#]
protected virtual void OnMaximizedBoundsChanged(
   EventArgs e
);
[C++]
protected: virtual void OnMaximizedBoundsChanged(
   EventArgs* e
);
```

```
[JScript]
protected function OnMaximizedBoundsChanged(
   e : EventArgs
);
```

Parameters

e

The **EventArgs** that contains the event data.

Remarks

Raising an event invokes the event handler through a delegate. For more information, see **Raising an Event**.

The **OnMaximizedBoundsChanged** method also allows derived classes to handle the event without attaching a delegate. This is the preferred technique for handling the event in a derived class.

Notes to Inheritors: When overriding **OnMaximizedBounds-Changed** in a derived class, be sure to call the base class's **OnMaximizedBoundsChanged** method so that registered delegates receive the event.

Requirements

Platforms: Windows 98, Windows NT 4.0, Windows Millennium Edition, Windows 2000, Windows XP Home Edition, Windows XP Professional, Windows Server 2003 family

Form.OnMaximumSizeChanged Method

Raises the **MaximumSizeChanged** event.

```
[Visual Basic]
Protected Overridable Sub OnMaximumSizeChanged( _
   ByVal e As EventArgs _
)
[C#]
protected virtual void OnMaximumSizeChanged(
   EventArgs e
);
[C++]
protected: virtual void OnMaximumSizeChanged(
   EventArgs* e
);
[JScript]
protected function OnMaximumSizeChanged(
   e : EventArgs
);
```

Parameters

e

The **EventArgs** that contains the event data.

Remarks

Raising an event invokes the event handler through a delegate. For more information, see **Raising an Event**.

The **OnMaximumSizeChanged** method also allows derived classes to handle the event without attaching a delegate. This is the preferred technique for handling the event in a derived class.

Notes to Inheritors: When overriding **OnMaximumSizeChanged** in a derived class, be sure to call the base class's **OnMaximum-SizeChanged** method so that registered delegates receive the event.

Requirements

Platforms: Windows 98, Windows NT 4.0, Windows Millennium Edition, Windows 2000, Windows XP Home Edition, Windows XP Professional, Windows Server 2003 family

Form.OnMdiChildActivate Method

Raises the **MdiChildActivate** event.

```
[Visual Basic]
Protected Overridable Sub OnMdiChildActivate( _
   ByVal e As EventArgs _
)
[C#]
protected virtual void OnMdiChildActivate(
   EventArgs e
);
[C++]
protected: virtual void OnMdiChildActivate(
   EventArgs* e
);
[JScript]
protected function OnMdiChildActivate(
   e : EventArgs
);
```

Parameters

e

The **EventArgs** that contains the event data.

Remarks

Raising an event invokes the event handler through a delegate. For more information, see **Raising an Event**.

The **OnMdiChildActivate** method also allows derived classes to handle the event without attaching a delegate. This is the preferred technique for handling the event in a derived class.

Notes to Inheritors: When overriding **OnMdiChildActivate** in a derived class, be sure to call the base class's **OnMdiChildActivate** method so that registered delegates receive the event.

Requirements

Platforms: Windows 98, Windows NT 4.0, Windows Millennium Edition, Windows 2000, Windows XP Home Edition, Windows XP Professional, Windows Server 2003 family

Form.OnMenuComplete Method

Raises the **MenuComplete** event.

```
[Visual Basic]
Protected Overridable Sub OnMenuComplete( _
   ByVal e As EventArgs _
)
[C#]
protected virtual void OnMenuComplete(
   EventArgs e
);
[C++]
protected: virtual void OnMenuComplete(
   EventArgs* e
);
```

```
[JScript]
protected function OnMenuComplete(
   e : EventArgs
);
```

Parameters

e

The **EventArgs** that contains the event data.

Remarks

Raising an event invokes the event handler through a delegate.

The **OnMenuComplete** method also allows derived classes to handle the event without attaching a delegate. This is the preferred technique for handling the event in a derived class.

Notes to Inheritors: When overriding **OnMenuComplete** in a derived class, be sure to call the base class's **OnMenuComplete** method so that registered delegates receive the event.

Requirements

Platforms: Windows 98, Windows NT 4.0, Windows Millennium Edition, Windows 2000, Windows XP Home Edition, Windows XP Professional, Windows Server 2003 family

Form.OnMenuStart Method

Raises the **MenuStart** event.

```
[Visual Basic]
Protected Overridable Sub OnMenuStart( _
   ByVal e As EventArgs _
)
[C#]
protected virtual void OnMenuStart(
   EventArgs e
);
[C++]
protected: virtual void OnMenuStart(
   EventArgs* e
);
[JScript]
protected function OnMenuStart(
   e : EventArgs
);
```

Parameters

e

The **EventArgs** that contains the event data.

Remarks

Raising an event invokes the event handler through a delegate. For more information, see **Raising an Event**.

The **OnMenuStart** method also allows derived classes to handle the event without attaching a delegate. This is the preferred technique for handling the event in a derived class.

Notes to Inheritors: When overriding **OnMenuStart** in a derived class, be sure to call the base class's **OnMenuStart** method so that registered delegates receive the event.

Requirements

Platforms: Windows 98, Windows NT 4.0, Windows Millennium Edition, Windows 2000, Windows XP Home Edition, Windows XP Professional, Windows Server 2003 family

Form.OnMinimumSizeChanged Method

Raises the **MinimumSizeChanged** event.

```
[Visual Basic]
Protected Overridable Sub OnMinimumSizeChanged( _
   ByVal e As EventArgs _
)
[C#]
protected virtual void OnMinimumSizeChanged(
   EventArgs e
);
[C++]
protected: virtual void OnMinimumSizeChanged(
   EventArgs* e
);
[JScript]
protected function OnMinimumSizeChanged(
   e : EventArgs
);
```

Parameters

e

An **EventArgs** that contains the event data.

Remarks

Raising an event invokes the event handler through a delegate.

The **OnMinimumSizeChanged** method also allows derived classes to handle the event without attaching a delegate. This is the preferred technique for handling the event in a derived class.

Notes to Inheritors: When overriding **OnMinimumSizeChanged** in a derived class, be sure to call the base class's **OnMinimumSize-Changed** method so that registered delegates receive the event.

Requirements

Platforms: Windows 98, Windows NT 4.0, Windows Millennium Edition, Windows 2000, Windows XP Home Edition, Windows XP Professional, Windows Server 2003 family

Form.OnPaint Method

This member overrides **Control.OnPaint**.

```
[Visual Basic]
Overrides Protected Sub OnPaint( _
   ByVal e As PaintEventArgs _
)
[C#]
protected override void OnPaint(
   PaintEventArgs e
);
[C++]
protected: void OnPaint(
   PaintEventArgs* e
);
[JScript]
protected override function OnPaint(
   e : PaintEventArgs
);
```

Requirements

Platforms: Windows 98, Windows NT 4.0, Windows Millennium Edition, Windows 2000, Windows XP Home Edition, Windows XP Professional, Windows Server 2003 family, .NET Compact Framework - Windows CE .NET

Form.OnResize Method

This member overrides **Control.OnResize**.

[Visual Basic]
```
Overrides Protected Sub OnResize( _
   ByVal e As EventArgs _
)
```
[C#]
```
protected override void OnResize(
   EventArgs e
);
```
[C++]
```
protected: void OnResize(
   EventArgs* e
);
```
[JScript]
```
protected override function OnResize(
   e : EventArgs
);
```

Requirements

Platforms: Windows 98, Windows NT 4.0, Windows Millennium Edition, Windows 2000, Windows XP Home Edition, Windows XP Professional, Windows Server 2003 family, .NET Compact Framework - Windows CE .NET

Form.OnStyleChanged Method

This member overrides **Control.OnStyleChanged**.

[Visual Basic]
```
Overrides Protected Sub OnStyleChanged( _
   ByVal e As EventArgs _
)
```
[C#]
```
protected override void OnStyleChanged(
   EventArgs e
);
```
[C++]
```
protected: void OnStyleChanged(
   EventArgs* e
);
```
[JScript]
```
protected override function OnStyleChanged(
   e : EventArgs
);
```

Requirements

Platforms: Windows 98, Windows NT 4.0, Windows Millennium Edition, Windows 2000, Windows XP Home Edition, Windows XP Professional, Windows Server 2003 family

Form.OnTextChanged Method

This member overrides **Control.OnTextChanged**.

[Visual Basic]
```
Overrides Protected Sub OnTextChanged( _
   ByVal e As EventArgs _
)
```
[C#]
```
protected override void OnTextChanged(
   EventArgs e
);
```
[C++]
```
protected: void OnTextChanged(
   EventArgs* e
);
```
[JScript]
```
protected override function OnTextChanged(
   e : EventArgs
);
```

Requirements

Platforms: Windows 98, Windows NT 4.0, Windows Millennium Edition, Windows 2000, Windows XP Home Edition, Windows XP Professional, Windows Server 2003 family, .NET Compact Framework - Windows CE .NET

Form.OnVisibleChanged Method

This member overrides **Control.OnVisibleChanged**.

[Visual Basic]
```
Overrides Protected Sub OnVisibleChanged( _
   ByVal e As EventArgs _
)
```
[C#]
```
protected override void OnVisibleChanged(
   EventArgs e
);
```
[C++]
```
protected: void OnVisibleChanged(
   EventArgs* e
);
```
[JScript]
```
protected override function OnVisibleChanged(
   e : EventArgs
);
```

Requirements

Platforms: Windows 98, Windows NT 4.0, Windows Millennium Edition, Windows 2000, Windows XP Home Edition, Windows XP Professional, Windows Server 2003 family

Form.ProcessCmdKey Method

This member overrides **Control.ProcessCmdKey**.

[Visual Basic]
```
Overrides Protected Function ProcessCmdKey( _
   ByRef msg As Message, _
   ByVal keyData As Keys _
) As Boolean
```

```
[C#]
protected override bool ProcessCmdKey(
   ref Message msg,
   Keys keyData
);
[C++]
protected: bool ProcessCmdKey(
   Message* msg,
   Keys keyData
);
[JScript]
protected override function ProcessCmdKey(
   msg : Message,
   keyData : Keys
) : Boolean;
```

Requirements

Platforms: Windows 98, Windows NT 4.0, Windows Millennium Edition, Windows 2000, Windows XP Home Edition, Windows XP Professional, Windows Server 2003 family

Form.ProcessDialogKey Method

This member overrides **Control.ProcessDialogKey**.

```
[Visual Basic]
Overrides Protected Function ProcessDialogKey( _
   ByVal keyData As Keys _
) As Boolean
[C#]
protected override bool ProcessDialogKey(
   Keys keyData
);
[C++]
protected: bool ProcessDialogKey(
   Keys keyData
);
[JScript]
protected override function ProcessDialogKey(
   keyData : Keys
) : Boolean;
```

Requirements

Platforms: Windows 98, Windows NT 4.0, Windows Millennium Edition, Windows 2000, Windows XP Home Edition, Windows XP Professional, Windows Server 2003 family

Form.ProcessKeyPreview Method

This member overrides **Control.ProcessKeyPreview**.

```
[Visual Basic]
Overrides Protected Function ProcessKeyPreview( _
   ByRef m As Message _
) As Boolean
[C#]
protected override bool ProcessKeyPreview(
   ref Message m
);
[C++]
protected: bool ProcessKeyPreview(
   Message* m
);
[JScript]
protected override function ProcessKeyPreview(
   m : Message
) : Boolean;
```

Requirements

Platforms: Windows 98, Windows NT 4.0, Windows Millennium Edition, Windows 2000, Windows XP Home Edition, Windows XP Professional, Windows Server 2003 family

Form.ProcessTabKey Method

This member overrides **ContainerControl.ProcessTabKey**.

```
[Visual Basic]
Overrides Protected Function ProcessTabKey( _
   ByVal forward As Boolean _
) As Boolean
[C#]
protected override bool ProcessTabKey(
   bool forward
);
[C++]
protected: bool ProcessTabKey(
   bool forward
);
[JScript]
protected override function ProcessTabKey(
   forward : Boolean
) : Boolean;
```

Requirements

Platforms: Windows 98, Windows NT 4.0, Windows Millennium Edition, Windows 2000, Windows XP Home Edition, Windows XP Professional, Windows Server 2003 family

Form.RemoveOwnedForm Method

Removes an owned form from this form.

```
[Visual Basic]
Public Sub RemoveOwnedForm( _
   ByVal ownedForm As Form _
)
[C#]
public void RemoveOwnedForm(
   Form ownedForm
);
[C++]
public: void RemoveOwnedForm(
   Form* ownedForm
);
[JScript]
public function RemoveOwnedForm(
   ownedForm : Form
);
```

Parameters

ownedForm

A **Form** representing the form to remove from the list of owned forms for this form.

Remarks

The form assigned to the owner form remains owned until the **RemoveOwnedForm** method is called. In addition to removing the owned form from the list of owned form, this method also sets the owner form to a null reference (**Nothing** in Visual Basic).

Requirements

Platforms: Windows 98, Windows NT 4.0, Windows Millennium Edition, Windows 2000, Windows XP Home Edition, Windows XP Professional, Windows Server 2003 family

Form.ScaleCore Method

This member overrides **Control.ScaleCore**.

```
[Visual Basic]
Overrides Protected Sub ScaleCore( _
   ByVal x As Single, _
   ByVal y As Single _
)
[C#]
protected override void ScaleCore(
   float x,
   float y
);
[C++]
protected: void ScaleCore(
   float x,
   float y
);
[JScript]
protected override function ScaleCore(
   x : float,
   y : float
);
```

Requirements

Platforms: Windows 98, Windows NT 4.0, Windows Millennium Edition, Windows 2000, Windows XP Home Edition, Windows XP Professional, Windows Server 2003 family

Form.Select Method

Overload List

This member supports the .NET Framework infrastructure and is not intended to be used directly from your code.

[Visual Basic] **Overloads Overrides Protected Sub Select(Boolean, Boolean)**

[C#] **protected override void Select(bool, bool);**

[C++] **protected: void Select(bool, bool);**

[JScript] **protected override function Select(Boolean, Boolean);**

Inherited from **Control**.

[Visual Basic] **Overloads Public Sub Select()**

[C#] **public void Select();**

[C++] **public: void Select();**

[JScript] **public function Select();**

Form.Select Method (Boolean, Boolean)

This member overrides **Control.Select**.

```
[Visual Basic]
Overrides Overloads Protected Sub Select( _
   ByVal directed As Boolean, _
   ByVal forward As Boolean _
)
[C#]
protected override void Select(
   bool directed,
   bool forward
);
[C++]
protected: void Select(
   bool directed,
   bool forward
);
[JScript]
protected override function Select(
   directed : Boolean,
   forward : Boolean
);
```

Requirements

Platforms: Windows 98, Windows NT 4.0, Windows Millennium Edition, Windows 2000, Windows XP Home Edition, Windows XP Professional, Windows Server 2003 family

.NET Framework Security:

- **UIPermission** for changing focus. Associated enumeration: **UIPermissionWindow.AllWindows**.

Form.SetBoundsCore Method

This member overrides **Control.SetBoundsCore**.

```
[Visual Basic]
Overrides Protected Sub SetBoundsCore( _
   ByVal x As Integer, _
   ByVal y As Integer, _
   ByVal width As Integer, _
   ByVal height As Integer, _
   ByVal specified As BoundsSpecified _
)
[C#]
protected override void SetBoundsCore(
   int x,
   int y,
   int width,
   int height,
   BoundsSpecified specified
);
```

[C++]
```
protected: void SetBoundsCore(
   int x,
   int y,
   int width,
   int height,
   BoundsSpecified specified
);
```
[JScript]
```
protected override function SetBoundsCore(
   x : int,
   y : int,
   width : int,
   height : int,
   specified : BoundsSpecified
);
```

Requirements

Platforms: Windows 98, Windows NT 4.0, Windows Millennium Edition, Windows 2000, Windows XP Home Edition, Windows XP Professional, Windows Server 2003 family

Form.SetClientSizeCore Method

This member overrides **Control.SetClientSizeCore**.

[Visual Basic]
```
Overrides Protected Sub SetClientSizeCore( _
   ByVal x As Integer, _
   ByVal y As Integer _
)
```
[C#]
```
protected override void SetClientSizeCore(
   int x,
   int y
);
```
[C++]
```
protected: void SetClientSizeCore(
   int x,
   int y
);
```
[JScript]
```
protected override function SetClientSizeCore(
   x : int,
   y : int
);
```

Requirements

Platforms: Windows 98, Windows NT 4.0, Windows Millennium Edition, Windows 2000, Windows XP Home Edition, Windows XP Professional, Windows Server 2003 family

Form.SetDesktopBounds Method

Sets the bounds of the form in desktop coordinates.

[Visual Basic]
```
Public Sub SetDesktopBounds( _
   ByVal x As Integer, _
   ByVal y As Integer, _
   ByVal width As Integer, _
   ByVal height As Integer _
)
```
[C#]
```
public void SetDesktopBounds(
   int x,
   int y,
   int width,
   int height
);
```
[C++]
```
public: void SetDesktopBounds(
   int x,
   int y,
   int width,
   int height
);
```
[JScript]
```
public function SetDesktopBounds(
   x : int,
   y : int,
   width : int,
   height : int
);
```

Parameters

x
: The x-coordinate of the form's location.

y
: The y-coordinate of the form's location.

width
: The width of the form.

height
: The height of the form.

Remarks

Desktop coordinates are based on the working area of the screen, which excludes the taskbar. You can use this method to set the position and size of your form on the desktop. Since desktop coordinates are based on the working area of the form, you can use this method to ensure that your form is completely visible on the desktop.

Requirements

Platforms: Windows 98, Windows NT 4.0, Windows Millennium Edition, Windows 2000, Windows XP Home Edition, Windows XP Professional, Windows Server 2003 family

Form.SetDesktopLocation Method

Sets the location of the form in desktop coordinates.

[Visual Basic]
```
Public Sub SetDesktopLocation( _
   ByVal x As Integer, _
   ByVal y As Integer _
)
```
[C#]
```
public void SetDesktopLocation(
   int x,
   int y
);
```

[C++]
```
public: void SetDesktopLocation(
   int x,
   int y
);
```
[JScript]
```
public function SetDesktopLocation(
   x : int,
   y : int
);
```

Parameters

x

The x-coordinate of the form's location.

y

The y-coordinate of the form's location.

Remarks

Desktop coordinates are based on the working area of the screen, which excludes the taskbar. You can use this method to position your form on the desktop. Since desktop coordinates are based on the working area of the form, you can use this method to ensure that your form is completely visible on the desktop.

Requirements

Platforms: Windows 98, Windows NT 4.0, Windows Millennium Edition, Windows 2000, Windows XP Home Edition, Windows XP Professional, Windows Server 2003 family

Form.SetVisibleCore Method

This member overrides **Control.SetVisibleCore**.

[Visual Basic]
```
Overrides Protected Sub SetVisibleCore( _
   ByVal value As Boolean _
)
```
[C#]
```
protected override void SetVisibleCore(
   bool value
);
```
[C++]
```
protected: void SetVisibleCore(
   bool value
);
```
[JScript]
```
protected override function SetVisibleCore(
   value : Boolean
);
```

Requirements

Platforms: Windows 98, Windows NT 4.0, Windows Millennium Edition, Windows 2000, Windows XP Home Edition, Windows XP Professional, Windows Server 2003 family

Form.ShowDialog Method

Shows the form as a modal dialog box.

Overload List

Shows the form as a modal dialog box with no owner window.

Supported by the .NET Compact Framework.

[Visual Basic] **Overloads Public Function ShowDialog() As DialogResult**

[C#] **public DialogResult ShowDialog();**

[C++] **public: DialogResult ShowDialog();**

[JScript] **public function ShowDialog() : DialogResult;**

Shows the form as a modal dialog with the specified owner.

[Visual Basic] **Overloads Public Function ShowDialog(IWin32Window) As DialogResult**

[C#] **public DialogResult ShowDialog(IWin32Window);**

[C++] **public: DialogResult ShowDialog(IWin32Window*);**

[JScript] **public function ShowDialog(IWin32Window) : DialogResult;**

Example

See related example in the **System.Windows.Forms.Form** class topic.

Form.ShowDialog Method ()

Shows the form as a modal dialog box with no owner window.

[Visual Basic]
```
Overloads Public Function ShowDialog() As DialogResult
```
[C#]
```
public DialogResult ShowDialog();
```
[C++]
```
public: DialogResult ShowDialog();
```
[JScript]
```
public function ShowDialog() : DialogResult;
```

Return Value

One of the **DialogResult** values.

Exceptions

Exception Type	Condition
Exception	The form specified in the *owner* parameter is the same as the form being shown. -or- The form being shown is already visible. -or- The form being shown is disabled. -or- The form being shown is not a top-level window. -or- The form being shown as a dialog box is already a modal form.

Remarks

You can use this method to display a modal dialog box in your application. When this method is called, the code following it is not executed until after the dialog box is closed. The dialog box can be assigned one of the values of the **DialogResult** enumeration by assigning it to the **DialogResult** property of a **Button** on the form or by setting the **DialogResult** property of the form in code. This value is then returned by this method. You can use this return value to determine how to process the actions that occurred in the dialog box. For example, if the dialog box was closed and returned the **Dialog-Result.Cancel** value through this method, you could prevent code following the call to **ShowDialog** from executing.

When a form is displayed as a modal dialog box, clicking the close form button (the button with an "X" at the top right of the form) causes the form to be hidden and the **DialogResult** property to be set to **DialogResult.Cancel**. Unlike modeless forms, the **Close** method is not called by the .NET Framework when the user clicks the close form button of a dialog box or sets the value of the **DialogResult** property. Instead the form is hidden and can be shown again without creating a new instance of the dialog box. Because a form displayed as a dialog box is not closed, you must call the **Dispose** method of the form when the form is no longer needed by your application.

This version of the **ShowDialog** method does not specify a form or control as its owner. When this version is called, the currently active window is made the owner of the dialog box. If you want to specify a specific owner, use the other version of this method.

Example

See related example in the **System.Windows.Forms.Form** class topic.

Requirements

Platforms: Windows 98, Windows NT 4.0, Windows Millennium Edition, Windows 2000, Windows XP Home Edition, Windows XP Professional, Windows Server 2003 family, .NET Compact Framework - Windows CE .NET

Form.ShowDialog Method (IWin32Window)

Shows the form as a modal dialog with the specified owner.

[Visual Basic]
```
Overloads Public Function ShowDialog( _
   ByVal owner As IWin32Window _
) As DialogResult
```
[C#]
```
public DialogResult ShowDialog(
   IWin32Window owner
);
```
[C++]
```
public: DialogResult ShowDialog(
   IWin32Window* owner
);
```
[JScript]
```
public function ShowDialog(
   owner : IWin32Window
) : DialogResult;
```

Parameters

owner
: Any object that implements **IWin32Window** that represents the top-level window that will own the modal dialog.

Return Value

One of the **DialogResult** values.

Exceptions

Exception Type	Condition
Exception	The form specified in the *owner* parameter is the same as the form being shown. -or- The form being shown is already visible. -or- The form being shown is disabled. -or- The form being shown is not a top-level window. -or- The form being shown as a dialog box is already a modal form.

Remarks

You can use this method to display a modal dialog box in your application. When this method is called, the code following it is not executed until after the dialog box is closed. The dialog box can be assigned one of the values of **DialogResult** by assigning it to the **DialogResult** property of a **Button** on the form or by setting the **DialogResult** property of the form in code. This value is then returned by this method. You can use this return value to determine how to process the actions that occurred in the dialog box. For example, if the dialog box was closed and returned the **Dialog-Result.Cancel** value through this method, you could prevent code following the call to **ShowDialog** from executing.

When a form is displayed as a modal dialog box, clicking the close form button (the button with an "X" at the top right of the form) causes the form to be hidden and the **DialogResult** property to be set to **DialogResult.Cancel**. Unlike modeless forms, the **Close** method is not called by the .NET Framework when the user clicks the close form button of a dialog box or sets the value of the **DialogResult** property. Instead the form is hidden and can be shown again without creating a new instance of the dialog box. Because a form displayed as a dialog box is not closed, you must call the **Dispose** method of the form when the form is no longer needed by your application.

This version of the **ShowDialog** method allows you to specify a specific form or control that will own the dialog box that is shown. If you use the version of this method that has no parameters, the dialog box being shown would be owned automatically by the currently active window of your application.

Example

See related example in the **System.Windows.Forms.Form** class topic.

Requirements

Platforms: Windows 98, Windows NT 4.0, Windows Millennium Edition, Windows 2000, Windows XP Home Edition, Windows XP Professional, Windows Server 2003 family

Form.ToString Method

This member overrides **Object.ToString**.

```
[Visual Basic]
Overrides Public Function ToString() As String
[C#]
public override string ToString();
[C++]
public: String* ToString();
[JScript]
public override function ToString() : String;
```

Requirements

Platforms: Windows 98, Windows NT 4.0, Windows Millennium Edition, Windows 2000, Windows XP Home Edition, Windows XP Professional, Windows Server 2003 family, .NET Compact Framework - Windows CE .NET

Form.UpdateDefaultButton Method

This member supports the .NET Framework infrastructure and is not intended to be used directly from your code.

```
[Visual Basic]
Overrides Protected Sub UpdateDefaultButton()
[C#]
protected override void UpdateDefaultButton();
[C++]
protected: void UpdateDefaultButton();
[JScript]
protected override function UpdateDefaultButton();
```

Form.WndProc Method

This member overrides **Control.WndProc**.

```
[Visual Basic]
Overrides Protected Sub WndProc( _
   ByRef m As Message _
)
[C#]
protected override void WndProc(
   ref Message m
);
[C++]
protected: void WndProc(
   Message* m
);
[JScript]
protected override function WndProc(
   m : Message
);
```

Requirements

Platforms: Windows 98, Windows NT 4.0, Windows Millennium Edition, Windows 2000, Windows XP Home Edition, Windows XP Professional, Windows Server 2003 family

Form.Activated Event

Occurs when the form is activated in code or by the user.

```
[Visual Basic]
Public Event Activated As EventHandler
[C#]
public event EventHandler Activated;
[C++]
public: __event EventHandler* Activated;
```

[JScript] In JScript, you can handle the events defined by a class, but you cannot define your own.

Event Data

The event handler receives an argument of type **EventArgs**.

Remarks

To activate a form at run time using code, call the **Activate** method. You can use this event for tasks such as updating the contents of the form based on changes made to the form's data when the form was not activated.

Requirements

Platforms: Windows 98, Windows NT 4.0, Windows Millennium Edition, Windows 2000, Windows XP Home Edition, Windows XP Professional, Windows Server 2003 family

Form.Closed Event

Occurs when the form is closed.

```
[Visual Basic]
Public Event Closed As EventHandler
[C#]
public event EventHandler Closed;
[C++]
public: __event EventHandler* Closed;
```

[JScript] In JScript, you can handle the events defined by a class, but you cannot define your own.

Event Data

The event handler receives an argument of type **EventArgs**.

Remarks

This event occurs after the form has been closed by the user or by the **Close** method of the form. To prevent a form from closing, handle the **Closing** event and set the **Cancel** property of the **CancelEventArgs** passed to your event-handling method to **true**.

You can use this event to perform tasks such as freeing resources used by the form and to save information entered in the form or to update its parent form.

> **CAUTION** The **Form.Closed** and **Form.Closing** events are not raised when the **Application.Exit** method is called to exit your application. If you have validation code in either of these events that must be executed, you should call the **Form.Close** method for each open form individually before calling the **Exit** method.

If the form is an MDI parent form, the **Closing** events of all MDI child forms are raised before the MDI parent form's **Closing** event is raised. In addition, the **Closed** events of all MDI child forms are raised before the **Closed** event of the MDI parent form is raised.

Requirements

Platforms: Windows 98, Windows NT 4.0, Windows Millennium Edition, Windows 2000, Windows XP Home Edition, Windows XP Professional, Windows Server 2003 family

Form.Closing Event

Occurs when the form is closing.

[Visual Basic]
```
Public Event Closing As CancelEventHandler
```
[C#]
```
public event CancelEventHandler Closing;
```
[C++]
```
public: __event CancelEventHandler* Closing;
```

[JScript] In JScript, you can handle the events defined by a class, but you cannot define your own.

Event Data

The event handler receives an argument of type **CancelEventArgs** containing data related to this event. The following **CancelEventArgs** property provides information specific to this event.

Property	Description
Cancel	Gets or sets a value indicating whether the event should be canceled.

Remarks

The **Closing** event occurs as the form is being closed. When a form is closed, all resources created within the object are released and the form is disposed. If you cancel this event, the form remains opened. To cancel the closure of a form, set the **Cancel** property of the **CancelEventArgs** passed to your event handler to **true**.

When a form is displayed as a modal dialog box, clicking the Close button (the button with an *X* at the upper-right corner of the form) causes the form to be hidden and the **DialogResult** property to be set to **DialogResult.Cancel**. You can override the value assigned to the **DialogResult** property when the user clicks the Close button by setting the **DialogResult** property in an event handler for the **Closing** event of the form.

Note When the **Close** method is called on a **Form** displayed as a modeless window, you cannot call the **Show** method to make the form visible, because the form's resources have already been released. To hide a form and then make it visible, use the **Control.Hide** method.

CAUTION The **Form.Closed** and **Form.Closing** events are not raised when the **Application.Exit** method is called to exit your application. If you have validation code in either of these events that must be executed, you should call the **Form.Close** method for each open form individually before calling the **Exit** method.

If the form is an MDI parent form, the **Closing** events of all MDI child forms are raised before the MDI parent form's **Closing** event is raised. In addition, the **Closed** events of all MDI child forms are raised before the **Closed** event of the MDI parent form is raised. Canceling the **Closing** event of an MDI child form does not prevent the **Closing** event of the MDI parent form from being raised. However, cancelling the event will set to **false** the **System.Windows.Forms.ClosingEventArgs.Cancel** property of the **System.Windows.Forms.ClosingEventArgs** that is passed as a parameter to the parent form. To force all MDI parent and child forms to close, set the **System.Windows.Forms.ClosingEventArgs.Cancel** property to **false** in the MDI parent form.

Example

See related example in the **System.Windows.Forms.Form** class topic.

Requirements

Platforms: Windows 98, Windows NT 4.0, Windows Millennium Edition, Windows 2000, Windows XP Home Edition, Windows XP Professional, Windows Server 2003 family

Form.Deactivate Event

Occurs when the form loses focus and is not the active form.

[Visual Basic]
```
Public Event Deactivate As EventHandler
```
[C#]
```
public event EventHandler Deactivate;
```
[C++]
```
public: __event EventHandler* Deactivate;
```

[JScript] In JScript, you can handle the events defined by a class, but you cannot define your own.

Event Data

The event handler receives an argument of type **EventArgs**.

Remarks

You can use this event to perform tasks such as updating another window in your application with data from the deactivated form.

Requirements

Platforms: Windows 98, Windows NT 4.0, Windows Millennium Edition, Windows 2000, Windows XP Home Edition, Windows XP Professional, Windows Server 2003 family

Form.InputLanguageChanged Event

Occurs after the input language of the form has changed.

[Visual Basic]
```
Public Event InputLanguageChanged As _
   InputLanguageChangedEventHandler
```
[C#]
```
public event InputLanguageChangedEventHandler InputLanguageChanged;
```
[C++]
```
public: __event InputLanguageChangedEventHandler*
   InputLanguageChanged;
```

[JScript] In JScript, you can handle the events defined by a class, but you cannot define your own.

Event Data

The event handler receives an argument of type **InputLanguageChangedEventArgs** containing data related to this event. The following **InputLanguageChangedEventArgs** properties provide information specific to this event.

Property	Description
CharSet	Gets the character set associated with the new input language.
Culture	Gets the locale of the input language.
InputLanguage	Gets a value indicating the input language.

Remarks

You can use this event to make changes to your form's appearance and text based on changes made to the input language of the form.

Requirements

Platforms: Windows 98, Windows NT 4.0, Windows Millennium Edition, Windows 2000, Windows XP Home Edition, Windows XP Professional, Windows Server 2003 family

Form.InputLanguageChanging Event

Occurs when the user attempts to change the input language for the form.

```
[Visual Basic]
Public Event InputLanguageChanging As _
   InputLanguageChangingEventHandler
[C#]
public event InputLanguageChangingEventHandler
   InputLanguageChanging;
[C++]
public: __event InputLanguageChangingEventHandler*
   InputLanguageChanging;
```

[JScript] In JScript, you can handle the events defined by a class, but you cannot define your own.

Event Data

The event handler receives an argument of type **InputLanguage-ChangingEventArgs** containing data related to this event. The following **InputLanguageChangingEventArgs** properties provide information specific to this event.

Property	Description
Cancel (inherited from **CancelEventArgs**)	Gets or sets a value indicating whether the event should be canceled.
Culture	Gets the locale of the requested input language.
InputLanguage	Gets a value indicating the input language.
SysCharSet	Gets a value indicating whether the system default font supports the character set required for the requested input language.

Remarks

This event occurs before the change of input language is made for the form. You can cancel the language change by setting the **Cancel** property of the **InputLanguageChangingEventArgs** passed to your event-handling method to **false**. If the event is canceled, the input language is not changed. You can use this event to determine whether the requested input language change is appropriate for your application.

Requirements

Platforms: Windows 98, Windows NT 4.0, Windows Millennium Edition, Windows 2000, Windows XP Home Edition, Windows XP Professional, Windows Server 2003 family

Form.Load Event

Occurs before a form is displayed for the first time.

```
[Visual Basic]
Public Event Load As EventHandler
[C#]
public event EventHandler Load;
[C++]
public: __event EventHandler* Load;
```

[JScript] In JScript, you can handle the events defined by a class, but you cannot define your own.

Event Data

The event handler receives an argument of type **EventArgs**.

Remarks

You can use this event to perform tasks such as allocating resources used by the form.

Requirements

Platforms: Windows 98, Windows NT 4.0, Windows Millennium Edition, Windows 2000, Windows XP Home Edition, Windows XP Professional, Windows Server 2003 family

Form.MaximizedBoundsChanged Event

Occurs when the value of the **MaximizedBounds** property has changed.

```
[Visual Basic]
Public Event MaximizedBoundsChanged As EventHandler
[C#]
public event EventHandler MaximizedBoundsChanged;
[C++]
public: __event EventHandler* MaximizedBoundsChanged;
```

[JScript] In JScript, you can handle the events defined by a class, but you cannot define your own.

Event Data

The event handler receives an argument of type **EventArgs**.

Remarks

Requirements

Platforms: Windows 98, Windows NT 4.0, Windows Millennium Edition, Windows 2000, Windows XP Home Edition, Windows XP Professional, Windows Server 2003 family

Form.MaximumSizeChanged Event

Occurs when the value of the **MaximumSize** property has changed.

```
[Visual Basic]
Public Event MaximumSizeChanged As EventHandler
[C#]
public event EventHandler MaximumSizeChanged;
[C++]
public: __event EventHandler* MaximumSizeChanged;
```

[JScript] In JScript, you can handle the events defined by a class, but you cannot define your own.

Event Data

The event handler receives an argument of type **EventArgs**.

Requirements

Platforms: Windows 98, Windows NT 4.0, Windows Millennium Edition, Windows 2000, Windows XP Home Edition, Windows XP Professional, Windows Server 2003 family

Form.MdiChildActivate Event

Occurs when a multiple document interface (MDI) child form is activated or closed within an MDI application.

```
[Visual Basic]
Public Event MdiChildActivate As EventHandler
[C#]
public event EventHandler MdiChildActivate;
[C++]
public: __event EventHandler* MdiChildActivate;
```

[JScript] In JScript, you can handle the events defined by a class, but you cannot define your own.

Event Data

The event handler receives an argument of type **EventArgs**.

Remarks

You can use this event to perform tasks such as updating the contents of the MDI child form and changing the menu options available in the MDI parent form based on the status of the MDI child form that is activated.

Requirements

Platforms: Windows 98, Windows NT 4.0, Windows Millennium Edition, Windows 2000, Windows XP Home Edition, Windows XP Professional, Windows Server 2003 family

Form.MenuComplete Event

Occurs when the menu of a form loses focus.

```
[Visual Basic]
Public Event MenuComplete As EventHandler
[C#]
public event EventHandler MenuComplete;
[C++]
public: __event EventHandler* MenuComplete;
```

[JScript] In JScript, you can handle the events defined by a class, but you cannot define your own.

Event Data

The event handler receives an argument of type **EventArgs**.

Remarks

This event is raised when you click on any menu item in a menu that results in a command being performed and the menu losing focus. You can use this event to perform tasks such as updating the text of a **StatusBar** control or enabling and disabling buttons on a **ToolBar**.

Requirements

Platforms: Windows 98, Windows NT 4.0, Windows Millennium Edition, Windows 2000, Windows XP Home Edition, Windows XP Professional, Windows Server 2003 family

Form.MenuStart Event

Occurs when the menu of a form receives focus.

```
[Visual Basic]
Public Event MenuStart As EventHandler
[C#]
public event EventHandler MenuStart;
[C++]
public: __event EventHandler* MenuStart;
```

[JScript] In JScript, you can handle the events defined by a class, but you cannot define your own.

Event Data

The event handler receives an argument of type **EventArgs**.

Remarks

This event is raised when any menu item in the menu is clicked by the user. You can use this event to perform tasks such as enabling and disabling controls on the form that should not be accessed by the user when the menus are being accessed.

Requirements

Platforms: Windows 98, Windows NT 4.0, Windows Millennium Edition, Windows 2000, Windows XP Home Edition, Windows XP Professional, Windows Server 2003 family

Form.MinimumSizeChanged Event

Occurs when the value of the **MinimumSize** property has changed.

```
[Visual Basic]
Public Event MinimumSizeChanged As EventHandler
[C#]
public event EventHandler MinimumSizeChanged;
[C++]
public: __event EventHandler* MinimumSizeChanged;
```

[JScript] In JScript, you can handle the events defined by a class, but you cannot define your own.

Event Data

The event handler receives an argument of type **EventArgs**.

Requirements

Platforms: Windows 98, Windows NT 4.0, Windows Millennium Edition, Windows 2000, Windows XP Home Edition, Windows XP Professional, Windows Server 2003 family

Form.TabIndexChanged Event

This member supports the .NET Framework infrastructure and is not intended to be used directly from your code.

```
[Visual Basic]
Public Shadows Event TabIndexChanged As EventHandler
[C#]
public new event EventHandler TabIndexChanged;
[C++]
public: __event EventHandler* TabIndexChanged;
```

[JScript] In JScript, you can handle the events defined by a class, but you cannot define your own.

FormBorderStyle Enumeration

Specifies the border styles for a form.

[Visual Basic]
```
<Serializable>
<ComVisible(True)>
Public Enum FormBorderStyle
```
[C#]
```
[Serializable]
[ComVisible(true)]
public enum FormBorderStyle
```
[C++]
```
[Serializable]
[ComVisible(true)]
__value public enum FormBorderStyle
```
[JScript]
```
public
   Serializable
   ComVisible(true)
enum FormBorderStyle
```

Remarks

This enumeration is used by the **Form** class. It represents the different styles of the form. The default style is **Sizable**.

Members

Member name	Description
Fixed3D Supported by the .NET Compact Framework.	A fixed, three-dimensional border.
FixedDialog Supported by the .NET Compact Framework.	A thick, fixed dialog-style border.
FixedSingle Supported by the .NET Compact Framework.	A fixed, single-line border.
FixedToolWindow Supported by the .NET Compact Framework.	A tool window border that is not resizable. A tool window does not appear in the taskbar or in the window that appears when the user presses ALT+TAB.
None Supported by the .NET Compact Framework.	No border.
Sizable Supported by the .NET Compact Framework.	A resizable border.
SizableToolWindow Supported by the .NET Compact Framework.	A resizable tool window border. A tool window does not appear in the taskbar or in the window that appears when the user presses ALT+TAB.

Example

[Visual Basic, C#] In this example, you change the form border style to **Fixed3d** and display the border's information using a label. This example assumes that you have already created a **Form** named `Form1`.

[Visual Basic]
```
Public Sub InitMyForm()
   ' Adds a label to the form.
   Dim label1 As New Label()
   label1.Location = New System.Drawing.Point(80, 80)
   label1.Name = "label1"
   label1.Size = New System.Drawing.Size(132, 80)
   label1.Text = "Start Position Information"
   Me.Controls.Add(label1)

   ' Changes the border to Fixed3D.
   FormBorderStyle = FormBorderStyle.Fixed3D

   ' Displays the border information.
   label1.Text = "The border is " + FormBorderStyle
End Sub 'InitMyForm
```
[C#]
```
public void InitMyForm()
{
    // Adds a label to the form.
    Label label1 = new Label();
    label1.Location = new System.Drawing.Point(80,80);
    label1.Name = "label1";
    label1.Size = new System.Drawing.Size(132,80);
    label1.Text = "Start Position Information";
    this.Controls.Add(label1);

    // Changes the border to Fixed3D.
    FormBorderStyle = FormBorderStyle.Fixed3D;

    // Displays the border information.
    label1.Text = "The border is " + FormBorderStyle;
}
```

Requirements

Namespace: System.Windows.Forms

Platforms: Windows 98, Windows NT 4.0, Windows Millennium Edition, Windows 2000, Windows XP Home Edition, Windows XP Professional, Windows Server 2003 family, .NET Compact Framework - Windows CE .NET

Assembly: System.Windows.Forms (in System.Windows.Forms.dll)

Form.ControlCollection Class

Represents a collection of controls on the form.

For a list of all members of this type, see **Form.ControlCollection Members**.

System.Object
  System.Windows.Forms.Control.ControlCollection
    System.Windows.Forms.Form.ControlCollection

```
[Visual Basic]
Public Class Form.ControlCollection
   Inherits Control.ControlCollection
[C#]
public class Form.ControlCollection : Control.ControlCollection
[C++]
public __gc class Form.ControlCollection : public
   Control.ControlCollection
[JScript]
public class Form.ControlCollection extends
   Control.ControlCollection
```

Thread Safety

Any public static (**Shared** in Visual Basic) members of this type are safe for multithreaded operations. Any instance members are not guaranteed to be thread safe.

Remarks

This class represents the collection of controls contained within a form. You can use the **Add** method to add a control to the form and the **Remove** method to remove the method from the form. The control collection represented by this class cannot be created without binding it to a specific form. As a result, you cannot create multiple instances of this control collection and interchange them with an active form to provide different control layouts.

Example

See related example in the **System.Windows.Forms.Form** class topic.

Requirements

Namespace: System.Windows.Forms

Platforms: Windows 98, Windows NT 4.0, Windows Millennium Edition, Windows 2000, Windows XP Home Edition, Windows XP Professional, Windows Server 2003 family

Assembly: System.Windows.Forms (in System.Windows.Forms.dll)

Form.ControlCollection Constructor

Initializes a new instance of the **Form.ControlCollection** class.

```
[Visual Basic]
Public Sub New( _
   ByVal owner As Form _
)
[C#]
public Form.ControlCollection(
   Form owner
);
[C++]
public: ControlCollection(
   Form* owner
);
[JScript]
public function Form.ControlCollection(
   owner : Form
);
```

Parameters

owner

The **Form** to contain the controls added to the control collection.

Remarks

This constructor allows you to properly bind the control collection to the form to enable controls to be added to the form.

> **Note** Because the control collection must be created with a specified form, you cannot create multiple collections of controls and interchange them with the form.

Requirements

Platforms: Windows 98, Windows NT 4.0, Windows Millennium Edition, Windows 2000, Windows XP Home Edition, Windows XP Professional, Windows Server 2003 family

Form.ControlCollection.Add Method

Adds a control to the form.

```
[Visual Basic]
Overrides Public Sub Add( _
   ByVal value As Control _
)
[C#]
public override void Add(
   Control value
);
[C++]
public: void Add(
   Control* value
);
[JScript]
public override function Add(
   value : Control
);
```

Parameters

value

The **Control** to add to the form.

Exceptions

Exception Type	Condition
Exception	A Multiple Document Interface (MDI) parent form cannot have controls added to it.

Remarks

You can use this method to adds controls to the form. If you want to add a group of already created controls to the form, use the **Control-Collection.AddRange** method of the **Control.ControlCollection** class.

Example

See related example in the **System.Windows.Forms.Form** class topic.

Requirements

Platforms: Windows 98, Windows NT 4.0, Windows Millennium Edition, Windows 2000, Windows XP Home Edition, Windows XP Professional, Windows Server 2003 family

Form.ControlCollection.Remove Method

Removes a control from the form.

```
[Visual Basic]
Overrides Public Sub Remove( _
   ByVal value As Control _
)
[C#]
public override void Remove(
   Control value
);
[C++]
public: void Remove(
   Control* value
);
[JScript]
public override function Remove(
   value : Control
);
```

Parameters

value

A **Control** to remove from the form.

Remarks

You can use this method to remove controls that you no longer need in your form. If you want to display a control after it is removed, you will need to add the control back to the form using the **Add** method. To have a control remain on the form but not displayed, use the **Visible** property of the control.

Requirements

Platforms: Windows 98, Windows NT 4.0, Windows Millennium Edition, Windows 2000, Windows XP Home Edition, Windows XP Professional, Windows Server 2003 family

FormStartPosition Enumeration

Specifies the initial position of a form.

[Visual Basic]
```
<Serializable>
<ComVisible(True)>
Public Enum FormStartPosition
```
[C#]
```
[Serializable]
[ComVisible(true)]
public enum FormStartPosition
```
[C++]
```
[Serializable]
[ComVisible(true)]
__value public enum FormStartPosition
```
[JScript]
```
public
   Serializable
   ComVisible(true)
enum FormStartPosition
```

Remarks

This enumeration is used by the **Form** class. It represents the different start positions of the form. The default start position is **WindowsDefaultLocation**.

Members

Member name	Description
CenterParent	The form is centered within the bounds of its parent form.
CenterScreen	The form is centered on the current display, and has the dimensions specified in the form's size.
Manual	The position of the form is determined by the **Location** property.
WindowsDefaultBounds	The form is positioned at the Windows default location and has the bounds determined by Windows default.
WindowsDefault-Location	The form is positioned at the Windows default location and has the dimensions specified in the form's size.

Example

See related example in the **System.Windows.Forms.Form** class topic.

Requirements

Namespace: System.Windows.Forms

Platforms: Windows 98, Windows NT 4.0, Windows Millennium Edition, Windows 2000, Windows XP Home Edition, Windows XP Professional, Windows Server 2003 family

Assembly: System.Windows.Forms (in System.Windows.Forms.dll)

FormWindowState Enumeration

Specifies how a form window is displayed.

[Visual Basic]
```
<Serializable>
<ComVisible(True)>
Public Enum FormWindowState
```
[C#]
```
[Serializable]
[ComVisible(true)]
public enum FormWindowState
```
[C++]
```
[Serializable]
[ComVisible(true)]
__value public enum FormWindowState
```
[JScript]
```
public
   Serializable
   ComVisible(true)
enum FormWindowState
```

Remarks

This enumeration is used by the **Form** class. It represents the different states of the form. The default state is **Normal**.

Members

Member name	Description
Maximized Supported by the .NET Compact Framework.	A maximized window.
Minimized	A minimized window.
Normal Supported by the .NET Compact Framework.	A default sized window.

Example

See related example in the **System.Windows.Forms.Form** class topic.

Requirements

Namespace: System.Windows.Forms

Platforms: Windows 98, Windows NT 4.0, Windows Millennium Edition, Windows 2000, Windows XP Home Edition, Windows XP Professional, Windows Server 2003 family, .NET Compact Framework - Windows CE .NET

Assembly: System.Windows.Forms (in System.Windows.Forms.dll)

FrameStyle Enumeration

Specifies the frame style of the selected control.

[Visual Basic]

```
<Serializable>
Public Enum FrameStyle
```

[C#]

```
[Serializable]
public enum FrameStyle
```

[C++]

```
[Serializable]
__value public enum FrameStyle
```

[JScript]

```
public
   Serializable
enum FrameStyle
```

Remarks

This enumeration is used by **ControlPaint.DrawReversibleFrame**.

DrawReversibleFrame is used when selecting objects or during drag-and-drop operations.

Members

Member name	Description
Dashed	A thin, dashed border.
Thick	A thick, solid border.

Requirements

Namespace: System.Windows.Forms

Platforms: Windows 98, Windows NT 4.0, Windows Millennium Edition, Windows 2000, Windows XP Home Edition, Windows XP Professional, Windows Server 2003 family

Assembly: System.Windows.Forms (in System.Windows.Forms.dll)

GiveFeedbackEventArgs Class

Provides data for the **GiveFeedback** event, which occurs during a drag operation.

System.Object
  System.EventArgs
    System.Windows.Forms.GiveFeedbackEventArgs

```
[Visual Basic]
<ComVisible(True)>
Public Class GiveFeedbackEventArgs
   Inherits EventArgs
[C#]
[ComVisible(true)]
public class GiveFeedbackEventArgs : EventArgs
[C++]
[ComVisible(true)]
public __gc class GiveFeedbackEventArgs : public EventArgs
[JScript]
public
   ComVisible(true)
class GiveFeedbackEventArgs extends EventArgs
```

Thread Safety

Any public static (**Shared** in Visual Basic) members of this type are safe for multithreaded operations. Any instance members are not guaranteed to be thread safe.

Remarks

The **GiveFeedback** event occurs during a drag operation. It allows the source of a drag event to modify the appearance of the mouse pointer in order to give the user visual feedback during a drag-and-drop operation. A **GiveFeedbackEventArgs** object specifies the type of drag-and-drop operation and whether default cursors are used.

Example

See related example in the **Windows.Forms.DragEventArgs** class topic.

Requirements

Namespace: System.Windows.Forms

Platforms: Windows 98, Windows NT 4.0, Windows Millennium Edition, Windows 2000, Windows XP Home Edition, Windows XP Professional, Windows Server 2003 family

Assembly: System.Windows.Forms (in System.Windows.Forms.dll)

GiveFeedbackEventArgs Constructor

Initializes a new instance of the **GiveFeedbackEventArgs** class.

```
[Visual Basic]
Public Sub New( _
   ByVal effect As DragDropEffects, _
   ByVal useDefaultCursors As Boolean _
)
[C#]
public GiveFeedbackEventArgs(
   DragDropEffects effect,
   bool useDefaultCursors
);
[C++]
public: GiveFeedbackEventArgs(
   DragDropEffects effect,
   bool useDefaultCursors
);
[JScript]
public function GiveFeedbackEventArgs(
   effect : DragDropEffects,
   useDefaultCursors : Boolean
);
```

Parameters

effect
  The type of drag-and-drop operation. Possible values are obtained by applying the bitwise OR (|) operation to the constants defined in the **DragDropEffects**.

useDefaultCursors
  true if default pointers are used; otherwise, **false**.

Requirements

Platforms: Windows 98, Windows NT 4.0, Windows Millennium Edition, Windows 2000, Windows XP Home Edition, Windows XP Professional, Windows Server 2003 family

GiveFeedbackEventArgs.Effect Property

Gets the drag-and-drop operation feedback that is displayed.

```
[Visual Basic]
Public ReadOnly Property Effect As DragDropEffects
[C#]
public DragDropEffects Effect {get;}
[C++]
public: __property DragDropEffects get_Effect();
[JScript]
public function get Effect() : DragDropEffects;
```

Property Value

One of the **DragDropEffects** values.

Example

See related example in the **Windows.Forms.DragEventArgs** class topic.

Requirements

Platforms: Windows 98, Windows NT 4.0, Windows Millennium Edition, Windows 2000, Windows XP Home Edition, Windows XP Professional, Windows Server 2003 family

GiveFeedbackEventArgs.UseDefaultCursors Property

Gets or sets whether drag operation should use the default cursors that are associated with drag-drop effects.

[Visual Basic]
```
Public Property UseDefaultCursors As Boolean
```
[C#]
```
public bool UseDefaultCursors {get; set;}
```
[C++]
```
public: __property bool get_UseDefaultCursors();
public: __property void set_UseDefaultCursors(bool);
```
[JScript]
```
public function get UseDefaultCursors() : Boolean;
public function set UseDefaultCursors(Boolean);
```

Property Value

true if the default pointers are used; otherwise, **false**.

Remarks

The system provides default drag-drop cursors for different drag-drop operations such as move or copy. If **UseDefaultCursors** is set to **false**, it is the responsibility of the event source to set the appropriate cursor.

Example

See related example in the **Windows.Forms.DragEventArgs** class topic.

Requirements

Platforms: Windows 98, Windows NT 4.0, Windows Millennium Edition, Windows 2000, Windows XP Home Edition, Windows XP Professional, Windows Server 2003 family

GiveFeedbackEventHandler Delegate

Represents the method that handles the **GiveFeedback** event of a **Control**.

[Visual Basic]
```
<Serializable>
Public Delegate Sub GiveFeedbackEventHandler( _
   ByVal sender As Object, _
   ByVal e As GiveFeedbackEventArgs _
)
```
[C#]
```
[Serializable]
public delegate void GiveFeedbackEventHandler(
   object sender,
   GiveFeedbackEventArgs e
);
```
[C++]
```
[Serializable]
public __gc __delegate void GiveFeedbackEventHandler(
   Object* sender,
   GiveFeedbackEventArgs* e
);
```

[JScript] In JScript, you can use the delegates in the .NET Framework, but you cannot define your own.

Parameters [Visual Basic, C#, C++]

The declaration of your event handler must have the same parameters as the **GiveFeedbackEventHandler** delegate declaration.

sender

The source of the event.

e

A **GiveFeedbackEventArgs** that contains the event data.

Remarks

When you create a **GiveFeedbackEventHandler** delegate, you identify the method that will handle the event. To associate the event with your event handler, add an instance of the delegate to the event. The event handler is called whenever the event occurs, unless you remove the delegate.

Example

See related example in the **System.Windows.Forms.DragEventArgs** class topic.

Requirements

Namespace: System.Windows.Forms

Platforms: Windows 98, Windows NT 4.0, Windows Millennium Edition, Windows 2000, Windows XP Home Edition, Windows XP Professional, Windows Server 2003 family

Assembly: System.Windows.Forms (in System.Windows.Forms.dll)

GridColumnStylesCollection Class

Represents a collection of **DataGridColumnStyle** objects in the **System.Windows.Forms.DataGrid** control.

System.Object
  System.MarshalByRefObject
    System.Windows.Forms.BaseCollection
      System.Windows.Forms.GridColumnStylesCollection

[Visual Basic]
```
Public Class GridColumnStylesCollection
   Inherits BaseCollection
   Implements IList
```
[C#]
```
public class GridColumnStylesCollection : BaseCollection, IList
```
[C++]
```
public __gc class GridColumnStylesCollection : public
   BaseCollection, IList
```
[JScript]
```
public class GridColumnStylesCollection extends BaseCollection
   implements IList
```

Thread Safety

Any public static (**Shared** in Visual Basic) members of this type are safe for multithreaded operations. Any instance members are not guaranteed to be thread safe.

Remarks

On the **DataGridTableStyle**, you access the **GridColumnStyles-Collection** through the **GridColumnStyles** property.

The **GridColumnStylesCollection** uses standard **Add** and **Remove** methods to manipulate the collection.

Use the **Contains** method to determine if a specific property value exists in the collection. Additionally, use the **IndexOf** method to determine the index of any **DataGridColumnStyle** object within the collection.

> **CAUTION** Always create **DataGridColumnStyle** objects and add them to the **GridColumnStylesCollection** before adding **DataGridTableStyle** objects to the **GridTableStylesCollection**. When you add an empty **DataGridTableStyle** to the collection, **DataGridColumnStyle** objects are automatically generated for you. Consequently, an exception will be thrown if you try to add new **DataGridColumnStyle** objects with duplicate **Mapping-Name** values to the **GridColumnStylesCollection**.

Example

[Visual Basic, C#, JScript] The following example example prints information about each **DataGridColumnStyle** in a **GridColumn-StylesCollection**.

[Visual Basic]
```
Private Sub PrintColumnInformation(grid as DataGrid)
   Console.WriteLine("Count: " & grid.TableStyles.Count)
   Dim myTableStyle As DataGridTableStyle
   Dim myColumns As GridColumnStylesCollection
   Dim dgCol As DataGridColumnStyle
   For Each myTableStyle in grid.TableStyles
      myColumns = myTableStyle.GridColumnStyles

      ' Iterate through the collection and print each
      ' object's type and width.
      For Each dgCol in myColumns
         Console.WriteLine(dgCol.MappingName)
         Console.WriteLine(dgCol.GetType.ToString())
         Console.WriteLine(dgCol.Width)
      Next
   Next
End Sub
```

[C#]
```
private void PrintColumnInformation(DataGrid grid){
   Console.WriteLine("Count: " + grid.TableStyles.Count);
   GridColumnStylesCollection myColumns;
   foreach(DataGridTableStyle myTableStyle in grid.TableStyles){

      myColumns = myTableStyle.GridColumnStyles;

      /* Iterate through the collection and print each
      object's type and width. */
      foreach (DataGridColumnStyle dgCol in myColumns){
         Console.WriteLine(dgCol.MappingName);
         Console.WriteLine(dgCol.GetType().ToString());
         Console.WriteLine(dgCol.Width);
      }
   }
}
```

[JScript]
```
function PrintColumnInformation(grid: DataGrid){
   Console.WriteLine("Count: " + grid.TableStyles.Count);
   var myColumns: GridColumnStylesCollection;
   for(var myTableStyle in grid.TableStyles){

      myColumns = myTableStyle.GridColumnStyles;

      // Iterate through the collection and print each
      // object's type and width.
      for (var dgCol in myColumns){
         Console.WriteLine(dgCol.MappingName);
         Console.WriteLine(dgCol.GetType().ToString());
         Console.WriteLine(dgCol.Width);
      }
   }
}
```

Requirements

Namespace: System.Windows.Forms

Platforms: Windows 98, Windows NT 4.0, Windows Millennium Edition, Windows 2000, Windows XP Home Edition, Windows XP Professional, Windows Server 2003 family, .NET Compact Framework - Windows CE .NET

Assembly: System.Windows.Forms (in System.Windows.Forms.dll)

GridColumnStylesCollection.Item Property

Gets a specified **DataGridColumnStyle** in the **GridColumn-StylesCollection**.

[C#] In C#, this property is the indexer for the **GridColumn-StylesCollection** class.

Overload List

Gets the **DataGridColumnStyle** at a specified index.

[Visual Basic] **Overloads Public Default ReadOnly Property Item(Integer) As DataGridColumnStyle**

[C#] **public DataGridColumnStyle this[int] {get;}**

[C++] **public: __property DataGridColumnStyle* get_Item(int);**

[JScript] **GridColumnStylesCollection.Item (int)**

Gets the **DataGridColumnStyle** associated with the specified **PropertyDescriptor**.

[Visual Basic] **Overloads Public Default ReadOnly Property Item(PropertyDescriptor) As DataGridColumnStyle**

[C#] **public DataGridColumnStyle this[PropertyDescriptor] {get;}**

[C++] **public: __property DataGridColumnStyle* get_Item(PropertyDescriptor*);**

[JScript] **GridColumnStylesCollection.Item (PropertyDescriptor)**

Gets the **DataGridColumnStyle** with the specified name.

[Visual Basic] **Overloads Public Default ReadOnly Property Item(String) As DataGridColumnStyle**

[C#] **public DataGridColumnStyle this[string] {get;}**

[C++] **public: __property DataGridColumnStyle* get_Item(String*);**

[JScript] **GridColumnStylesCollection.Item (String)**

Example

See related example in the **System.Windows.Forms.GridColumnStylesCollection** class topic.

GridColumnStylesCollection.Item Property (Int32)

Gets the **DataGridColumnStyle** at a specified index.

[C#] In C#, this property is the indexer for the **GridColumnStylesCollection** class.

[Visual Basic]
```
Overloads Public Default ReadOnly Property Item( _
   ByVal index As Integer _
) As DataGridColumnStyle
```
[C#]
```
public DataGridColumnStyle this[
   int index
] {get;}
```
[C++]
```
public: __property DataGridColumnStyle* get_Item(
   int index
);
```
[JScript]
```
returnValue = GridColumnStylesCollectionObject.Item(index);
-or-
returnValue = GridColumnStylesCollectionObject(index);
```

[JScript] In JScript, you can use the default indexed properties defined by a type, but you cannot explicitly define your own. However, specifying the **expando** attribute on a class automatically provides a default indexed property whose type is **Object** and whose index type is **String**.

Arguments [JScript]

index

The zero-based index of the **DataGridColumnStyle** to return.

Parameters [Visual Basic, C#, C++]

index

The zero-based index of the **DataGridColumnStyle** to return.

Property Value

The specified **DataGridColumnStyle**.

Remarks

Use the **IndexOf** method to determine the index of any element in the collection.

Example

See related example in the **System.Windows.Forms.GridColumnStylesCollection** class topic.

Requirements

Platforms: Windows 98, Windows NT 4.0, Windows Millennium Edition, Windows 2000, Windows XP Home Edition, Windows XP Professional, Windows Server 2003 family

GridColumnStylesCollection.Item Property (PropertyDescriptor)

Gets the **DataGridColumnStyle** associated with the specified **PropertyDescriptor**.

[C#] In C#, this property is the indexer for the **GridColumnStylesCollection** class.

[Visual Basic]
```
Overloads Public Default ReadOnly Property Item( _
   ByVal propDesc As PropertyDescriptor _
) As DataGridColumnStyle
```
[C#]
```
public DataGridColumnStyle this[
   PropertyDescriptor propDesc
] {get;}
```
[C++]
```
public: __property DataGridColumnStyle* get_Item(
   PropertyDescriptor* propDesc
);
```
[JScript]
```
returnValue = GridColumnStylesCollectionObject.Item(propDesc);
-or-
returnValue = GridColumnStylesCollectionObject(propDesc);
```

[JScript] In JScript, you can use the default indexed properties defined by a type, but you cannot explicitly define your own. However, specifying the **expando** attribute on a class automatically provides a default indexed property whose type is **Object** and whose index type is **String**.

Arguments [JScript]

propDesc

The **PropertyDescriptor** associated with the **DataGridColumnStyle**.

Parameters [Visual Basic, C#, C++]

propDesc

The **PropertyDescriptor** associated with the **DataGridColumnStyle**.

Property Value

The **DataGridColumnStyle** associated the specified **PropertyDescriptor**.

Remarks

Each **DataGridColumnStyle** object is created using a **PropertyDescriptor**. The **PropertyDescriptor** can be returned using the **PropertyDescriptor** property.

To get the **PropertyDescriptorCollection** object for a specific data source, use the **GetItemProperties** method of the **Binding-ManagerBase** class. Pass the **MappingName** to the **Item** property of the **PropertyDescriptorCollection** to return a **Property-Descriptor** for a specific column.

Example

See related example in the **System.Windows.Forms.GridColumn-StylesCollection** class topic.

Requirements

Platforms: Windows 98, Windows NT 4.0,
Windows Millennium Edition, Windows 2000,
Windows XP Home Edition, Windows XP Professional,
Windows Server 2003 family

GridColumnStylesCollection.Item Property (String)

Gets the **DataGridColumnStyle** with the specified name.

[C#] In C#, this property is the indexer for the **GridColumn-StylesCollection** class.

[Visual Basic]
```
Overloads Public Default ReadOnly Property Item( _
   ByVal columnName As String _
) As DataGridColumnStyle
```
[C#]
```
public DataGridColumnStyle this[
   string columnName
] {get;}
```
[C++]
```
public: __property DataGridColumnStyle* get_Item(
   String* columnName
);
```
[JScript]
```
returnValue = GridColumnStylesCollectionObject.Item(columnName);
-or-
returnValue = GridColumnStylesCollectionObject(columnName);
```

[JScript] In JScript, you can use the default indexed properties defined by a type, but you cannot explicitly define your own. However, specifying the **expando** attribute on a class automatically provides a default indexed property whose type is **Object** and whose index type is **String**.

Arguments [JScript]

columnName
The **MappingName** of the **DataGridColumnStyle** retrieve.

Parameters [Visual Basic, C#, C++]

columnName
The **MappingName** of the **DataGridColumnStyle** retrieve.

Property Value

The **DataGridColumnStyle** with the specified column header.

Remarks

The column header of a **DataGridColumnStyle** can be set explicitly by setting the **HeaderText** property. By default, the **HeaderText** is set using uses **MappingName** property value.

The comparison between column headers and the value to look for is not case-sensitive.

Example

See related example in the **System.Windows.Forms.GridColumn-StylesCollection** class topic.

Requirements

Platforms: Windows 98, Windows NT 4.0,
Windows Millennium Edition, Windows 2000,
Windows XP Home Edition, Windows XP Professional,
Windows Server 2003 family

GridColumnStylesCollection.List Property

This member overrides **BaseCollection.List**.

[Visual Basic]
```
Overrides Protected ReadOnly Property List As ArrayList
```
[C#]
```
protected override ArrayList List {get;}
```
[C++]
```
protected: __property ArrayList* get_List();
```
[JScript]
```
protected override function get List() : ArrayList;
```

Requirements

Platforms: Windows 98, Windows NT 4.0,
Windows Millennium Edition, Windows 2000,
Windows XP Home Edition, Windows XP Professional,
Windows Server 2003 family,
.NET Compact Framework - Windows CE .NET

GridColumnStylesCollection.System.Collections.ICollection.Count Property

Note: This namespace, class, or member is supported only in version 1.1 of the .NET Framework.

This member supports the .NET Framework infrastructure and is not intended to be used directly from your code.

[Visual Basic]
```
Private ReadOnly Property Count As Integer Implements _
   ICollection.Count
```
[C#]
```
int ICollection.Count {get;}
```
[C++]
```
private: __property int
   System::Collections::ICollection::get_Count();
```
[JScript]
```
private function get ICollection.Count() : int;
```

GridColumnStylesCollection.System.Collections.ICollection.IsSynchronized Property

Note: This namespace, class, or member is supported only in version 1.1 of the .NET Framework.

This member supports the .NET Framework infrastructure and is not intended to be used directly from your code.

[Visual Basic]
```
Private ReadOnly Property IsSynchronized As Boolean Implements _
   ICollection.IsSynchronized
```
[C#]
```
bool ICollection.IsSynchronized {get;}
```

[C++]
```
private: __property bool
   System::Collections::ICollection::get_IsSynchronized();
```
[JScript]
```
private function get ICollection.IsSynchronized() : Boolean;
```

GridColumnStylesCollection.System.Collections.ICollection.SyncRoot Property

Note: This namespace, class, or member is supported only in version 1.1 of the .NET Framework.

This member supports the .NET Framework infrastructure and is not intended to be used directly from your code.

[Visual Basic]
```
Private ReadOnly Property SyncRoot As Object Implements _
   ICollection.SyncRoot
```
[C#]
```
object ICollection.SyncRoot {get;}
```
[C++]
```
private: __property Object*
   System::Collections::ICollection::get_SyncRoot();
```
[JScript]
```
private function get ICollection.SyncRoot() : Object;
```

GridColumnStylesCollection.System.Collections.IList.IsFixedSize Property

Note: This namespace, class, or member is supported only in version 1.1 of the .NET Framework.

This member supports the .NET Framework infrastructure and is not intended to be used directly from your code.

[Visual Basic]
```
Private ReadOnly Property IsFixedSize As Boolean Implements _
   IList.IsFixedSize
```
[C#]
```
bool IList.IsFixedSize {get;}
```
[C++]
```
private: __property bool
   System::Collections::IList::get_IsFixedSize();
```
[JScript]
```
private function get IList.IsFixedSize() : Boolean;
```

GridColumnStylesCollection.System.Collections.IList.IsReadOnly Property

<Font color="red"><I>Note: This namespace, class, or member is supported only in version 1.1 of the .NET Framework.</I></Font>

This member supports the .NET Framework infrastructure and is not intended to be used directly from your code.

[Visual Basic]
```
Private ReadOnly Property IsReadOnly As Boolean Implements _
   IList.IsReadOnly
```
[C#]
```
bool IList.IsReadOnly {get;}
```
[C++]
```
private: __property bool
   System::Collections::IList::get_IsReadOnly();
```
[JScript]
```
private function get IList.IsReadOnly() : Boolean;
```

GridColumnStylesCollection.System.Collections.IList.Item Property

Note: This namespace, class, or member is supported only in version 1.1 of the .NET Framework.

[C#] In C#, this property is the indexer for the **GridColumnStylesCollection** class.

[Visual Basic]
```
Private Default Property Item( _
   ByVal i As Integer _
) As Object Implements IList.Item
```
[C#]
```
object IList.this[
   int i
] {get; set;}
```
[C++]
```
private: __property Object* System::Collections::IList::get_Item(
   int i
);
private: __property void System::Collections::IList::set_Item(
   int i,
   Object*
);
```
[JScript]
```
private function get IList.get_Item(i : int) : Object;
private function set IList.set_Item(i : int, value : Object);
-or-
private function get IList.get_Item(i : int) : Object;
private function set IList.set_Item(i : int, value : Object);
```

[JScript] In JScript, you can use the default indexed properties defined by a type, but you cannot explicitly define your own. However, specifying the **expando** attribute on a class automatically provides a default indexed property whose type is **Object** and whose index type is **String**.

Arguments [JScript]

i

Parameters [Visual Basic, C#, C++]

i

Requirements

Platforms: Windows 98, Windows NT 4.0, Windows Millennium Edition, Windows 2000, Windows XP Home Edition, Windows XP Professional, Windows Server 2003 family

GridColumnStylesCollection.Add Method

Adds a column style to the collection.

[Visual Basic]
```
Public Overridable Function Add( _
   ByVal column As DataGridColumnStyle _
) As Integer
```
[C#]
```
public virtual int Add(
   DataGridColumnStyle column
);
```

```
[C++]
public: virtual int Add(
   DataGridColumnStyle* column
);
[JScript]
public function Add(
   column : DataGridColumnStyle
) : int;
```

Parameters

column
The **DataGridColumnStyle** to add.

Return Value

The index of the new **DataGridColumnStyle** object.

Example

See related example in the **System.Windows.Forms.GridColumnStylesCollection** class topic.

Requirements

Platforms: Windows 98, Windows NT 4.0,
Windows Millennium Edition, Windows 2000,
Windows XP Home Edition, Windows XP Professional,
Windows Server 2003 family,
.NET Compact Framework - Windows CE .NET

GridColumnStylesCollection.AddRange Method

Adds an array of column style objects to the collection.

```
[Visual Basic]
Public Sub AddRange( _
   ByVal columns() As DataGridColumnStyle _
)
[C#]
public void AddRange(
   DataGridColumnStyle[] columns
);
[C++]
public: void AddRange(
   DataGridColumnStyle* columns[]
);
[JScript]
public function AddRange(
   columns : DataGridColumnStyle[]
);
```

Parameters

columns
An array of **DataGridColumnStyle** objects to add to the collection.

Example

See related example in the **System.Windows.Forms.GridColumnStylesCollection** class topic.

Requirements

Platforms: Windows 98, Windows NT 4.0,
Windows Millennium Edition, Windows 2000,
Windows XP Home Edition, Windows XP Professional,
Windows Server 2003 family

GridColumnStylesCollection.Clear Method

Clears the collection of **DataGridColumnStyle** objects.

```
[Visual Basic]
Public Sub Clear()
[C#]
public void Clear();
[C++]
public: void Clear();
[JScript]
public function Clear();
```

Example

See related example in the **System.Windows.Forms.GridColumnStylesCollection** class topic.

Requirements

Platforms: Windows 98, Windows NT 4.0,
Windows Millennium Edition, Windows 2000,
Windows XP Home Edition, Windows XP Professional,
Windows Server 2003 family,
.NET Compact Framework - Windows CE .NET

GridColumnStylesCollection.Contains Method

Gets a value indicating whether the **GridColumnStylesCollection** contains a specific **DataGridColumnStyle**.

Overload List

Gets a value indicating whether the **GridColumnStylesCollection** contains the specified **DataGridColumnStyle**.

Supported by the .NET Compact Framework.

[Visual Basic] **Overloads Public Function Contains(DataGridColumnStyle) As Boolean**

[C#] **public bool Contains(DataGridColumnStyle);**

[C++] **public: bool Contains(DataGridColumnStyle*);**

[JScript] **public function Contains(DataGridColumnStyle) : Boolean;**

Gets a value indicating whether the **GridColumnStylesCollection** contains a **DataGridColumnStyle** associated with the specified **PropertyDescriptor**.

[Visual Basic] **Overloads Public Function Contains(PropertyDescriptor) As Boolean**

[C#] **public bool Contains(PropertyDescriptor);**

[C++] **public: bool Contains(PropertyDescriptor*);**

[JScript] **public function Contains(PropertyDescriptor) : Boolean;**

Gets a value indicating whether the **GridColumnStylesCollection** contains the **DataGridColumnStyle** with the specified name.

Supported by the .NET Compact Framework.

[Visual Basic] **Overloads Public Function Contains(String) As Boolean**

[C#] **public bool Contains(string);**

[C++] **public: bool Contains(String*);**

[JScript] **public function Contains(String) : Boolean;**

Example

See related example in the **System.Windows.Forms.GridColumnStylesCollection** class topic.

GridColumnStylesCollection.Contains Method (DataGridColumnStyle)

Gets a value indicating whether the **GridColumnStylesCollection** contains the specified **DataGridColumnStyle**.

```
[Visual Basic]
Overloads Public Function Contains( _
   ByVal column As DataGridColumnStyle _
) As Boolean
[C#]
public bool Contains(
   DataGridColumnStyle column
);
[C++]
public: bool Contains(
   DataGridColumnStyle* column
);
[JScript]
public function Contains(
   column : DataGridColumnStyle
) : Boolean;
```

Parameters

column

The desired **DataGridColumnStyle**.

Return Value

true if the collection contains the **DataGridColumnStyle**; otherwise, **false**.

Remarks

Use the **Contains** method to determine if a particular **DataGridColumnStyle** object exists before invoking the **Remove** method to remove the item. If you need to know the index of a particular **DataGridColumnStyle**, use the **IndexOf** method.

Example

The following example uses the **Contains** method to determine if a **GridColumnStylesCollection** contains a specific **DataGridColumnStyle**.

Requirements

Platforms: Windows 98, Windows NT 4.0, Windows Millennium Edition, Windows 2000, Windows XP Home Edition, Windows XP Professional, Windows Server 2003 family, .NET Compact Framework - Windows CE .NET

GridColumnStylesCollection.Contains Method (PropertyDescriptor)

Gets a value indicating whether the **GridColumnStylesCollection** contains a **DataGridColumnStyle** associated with the specified **PropertyDescriptor**.

```
[Visual Basic]
Overloads Public Function Contains( _
   ByVal propDesc As PropertyDescriptor _
) As Boolean
[C#]
public bool Contains(
   PropertyDescriptor propDesc
);
[C++]
public: bool Contains(
   PropertyDescriptor* propDesc
);
[JScript]
public function Contains(
   propDesc : PropertyDescriptor
) : Boolean;
```

Parameters

propDesc

The **PropertyDescriptor** associated with the desired **DataGridColumnStyle**.

Return Value

true if the collection contains the **DataGridColumnStyle**; otherwise, **false**.

Remarks

To get a **PropertyDescriptorCollection**, use the **GetItemProperties** method of the **BindingManagerBase** class. Pass the **MappingName** of the **DataGridColumnStyle** to the **Item** property of the **PropertyDescriptorCollection** to return the **PropertyDescriptor** for a specific column.

Use the **Contains** method to determine if a particular **DataGridColumnStyle** object exists before invoking the **Remove** method to remove the item. If you need to know the index of a particular **DataGridColumnStyle**, use the **IndexOf** method.

Example

See related example in the **System.Windows.Forms.GridColumnStylesCollection** class topic.

Requirements

Platforms: Windows 98, Windows NT 4.0, Windows Millennium Edition, Windows 2000, Windows XP Home Edition, Windows XP Professional, Windows Server 2003 family

GridColumnStylesCollection.Contains Method (String)

Gets a value indicating whether the **GridColumnStylesCollection** contains the **DataGridColumnStyle** with the specified name.

```
[Visual Basic]
Overloads Public Function Contains( _
   ByVal name As String _
) As Boolean
[C#]
public bool Contains(
   string name
);
[C++]
public: bool Contains(
   String* name
);
[JScript]
public function Contains(
   name : String
) : Boolean;
```

Parameters

name

The **MappingName** of the desired **DataGridColumnStyle**.

Return Value

true if the collection contains the **DataGridColumnStyle**; otherwise, **false**.

Remarks

The caption of a **DataGridColumnStyle** is set with the **HeaderText** property.

Use the **Contains** method to determine if a particular **DataGrid-ColumnStyle** object exists before invoking the **Remove** method to remove the item. If you need to know the index of a particular **DataGridColumnStyle**, use the **IndexOf** method.

Example

See related example in the **System.Windows.Forms.GridColumn-StylesCollection** class topic.

Requirements

Platforms: Windows 98, Windows NT 4.0, Windows Millennium Edition, Windows 2000, Windows XP Home Edition, Windows XP Professional, Windows Server 2003 family, .NET Compact Framework - Windows CE .NET

GridColumnStylesCollection.ICollection.CopyTo Method

This member supports the .NET Framework infrastructure and is not intended to be used directly from your code.

```
[Visual Basic]
Private Sub CopyTo( _
   ByVal array As Array, _
   ByVal index As Integer _
) Implements ICollection.CopyTo
[C#]
void ICollection.CopyTo(
   Array array,
   int index
);
[C++]
private: void ICollection::CopyTo(
   Array* array,
   int index
);
[JScript]
private function ICollection.CopyTo(
   array : Array,
   index : int
);
```

GridColumnStylesCollection.IEnumerable.Get-Enumerator Method

This member supports the .NET Framework infrastructure and is not intended to be used directly from your code.

```
[Visual Basic]
Private Function GetEnumerator() As IEnumerator Implements _
   IEnumerable.GetEnumerator
[C#]
IEnumerator IEnumerable.GetEnumerator();
[C++]
private: IEnumerator* IEnumerable::GetEnumerator();
[JScript]
private function IEnumerable.GetEnumerator() : IEnumerator;
```

GridColumnStylesCollection.IList.Add Method

This member supports the .NET Framework infrastructure and is not intended to be used directly from your code.

```
[Visual Basic]
Private Function Add( _
   ByVal value As Object _
) As Integer Implements IList.Add
[C#]
int IList.Add(
   object value
);
[C++]
private: int IList::Add(
   Object* value
);
[JScript]
private function IList.Add(
   value : Object
) : int;
```

GridColumnStylesCollection.IList.Clear Method

This member supports the .NET Framework infrastructure and is not intended to be used directly from your code.

```
[Visual Basic]
Private Sub Clear() Implements IList.Clear
[C#]
void IList.Clear();
[C++]
private: void IList::Clear();
[JScript]
private function IList.Clear();
```

GridColumnStylesCollection.IList.Contains Method

This member supports the .NET Framework infrastructure and is not intended to be used directly from your code.

```
[Visual Basic]
Private Function Contains( _
   ByVal value As Object _
) As Boolean Implements IList.Contains
[C#]
bool IList.Contains(
   object value
);
[C++]
private: bool IList::Contains(
   Object* value
);
[JScript]
private function IList.Contains(
   value : Object
) : Boolean;
```

GridColumnStylesCollection.IList.IndexOf Method

This member supports the .NET Framework infrastructure and is not intended to be used directly from your code.

```
[Visual Basic]
Private Function IndexOf( _
   ByVal value As Object _
) As Integer Implements IList.IndexOf
[C#]
int IList.IndexOf(
   object value
);
[C++]
private: int IList::IndexOf(
   Object* value
);
[JScript]
private function IList.IndexOf(
   value : Object
) : int;
```

GridColumnStylesCollection.IList.Insert Method

This member supports the .NET Framework infrastructure and is not intended to be used directly from your code.

```
[Visual Basic]
Private Sub Insert( _
   ByVal index As Integer, _
   ByVal value As Object _
) Implements IList.Insert
[C#]
void IList.Insert(
   int index,
   object value
);
[C++]
private: void IList::Insert(
   int index,
   Object* value
);
[JScript]
private function IList.Insert(
   index : int,
   value : Object
);
```

GridColumnStylesCollection.IList.Remove Method

This member supports the .NET Framework infrastructure and is not intended to be used directly from your code.

```
[Visual Basic]
Private Sub Remove( _
   ByVal value As Object _
) Implements IList.Remove
[C#]
void IList.Remove(
   object value
);
[C++]
private: void IList::Remove(
   Object* value
);
[JScript]
private function IList.Remove(
   value : Object
);
```

GridColumnStylesCollection.IList.RemoveAt Method

This member supports the .NET Framework infrastructure and is not intended to be used directly from your code.

```
[Visual Basic]
Private Sub RemoveAt( _
   ByVal index As Integer _
) Implements IList.RemoveAt
[C#]
void IList.RemoveAt(
   int index
);
[C++]
private: void IList::RemoveAt(
   int index
);
[JScript]
private function IList.RemoveAt(
   index : int
);
```

GridColumnStylesCollection.IndexOf Method

Gets the index of a specified **DataGridColumnStyle**.

```
[Visual Basic]
Public Function IndexOf( _
   ByVal element As DataGridColumnStyle _
) As Integer
[C#]
public int IndexOf(
   DataGridColumnStyle element
);
[C++]
public: int IndexOf(
   DataGridColumnStyle* element
);
[JScript]
public function IndexOf(
   element : DataGridColumnStyle
) : int;
```

Parameters

element

The **DataGridColumnStyle** to find.

Return Value

The zero-based index of the **DataGridColumnStyle** within the **GridColumnStylesCollection** or -1 if no corresponding **DataGridColumnStyle** exists.

Remarks

Use the **Contains** method to determine if a specific **DataGridColumnStyle** exists. If so, and you need the index of the element within the collection, use the **IndexOf** method.

Example

See related example in the **System.Windows.Forms.GridColumnStylesCollection** class topic.

Requirements

Platforms: Windows 98, Windows NT 4.0, Windows Millennium Edition, Windows 2000, Windows XP Home Edition, Windows XP Professional, Windows Server 2003 family, .NET Compact Framework - Windows CE .NET

GridColumnStylesCollection.OnCollectionChanged Method

Raises the **CollectionChanged** event.

```
[Visual Basic]
Protected Sub OnCollectionChanged( _
   ByVal ccevent As CollectionChangeEventArgs _
)
[C#]
protected void OnCollectionChanged(
   CollectionChangeEventArgs ccevent
);
[C++]
protected: void OnCollectionChanged(
   CollectionChangeEventArgs* ccevent
);
[JScript]
protected function OnCollectionChanged(
   ccevent : CollectionChangeEventArgs
);
```

Parameters

ccevent

A **CollectionChangeEventArgs** that contains the event data event.

Remarks

Raising an event invokes the event handler through a delegate.

Notes to Inheritors: When overriding **OnCollectionChanged** in a derived class, be sure to call the base class's **OnCollectionChanged** method.

Requirements

Platforms: Windows 98, Windows NT 4.0, Windows Millennium Edition, Windows 2000, Windows XP Home Edition, Windows XP Professional, Windows Server 2003 family

GridColumnStylesCollection.Remove Method

Removes the specified **DataGridColumnStyle** from the **GridColumnStylesCollection**.

```
[Visual Basic]
Public Sub Remove( _
   ByVal column As DataGridColumnStyle _
)
[C#]
public void Remove(
   DataGridColumnStyle column
);
[C++]
public: void Remove(
   DataGridColumnStyle* column
);
[JScript]
public function Remove(
   column : DataGridColumnStyle
);
```

Parameters

column

The **DataGridColumnStyle** to remove from the collection.

Remarks

Use the **Contains** method to determine whether the **DataGridColumnStyle** exists in the collection.

Example

See related example in the **System.Windows.Forms.GridColumnStylesCollection** class topic.

Requirements

Platforms: Windows 98, Windows NT 4.0, Windows Millennium Edition, Windows 2000, Windows XP Home Edition, Windows XP Professional, Windows Server 2003 family, .NET Compact Framework - Windows CE .NET

GridColumnStylesCollection.RemoveAt Method

Removes the **DataGridColumnStyle** with the specified index from the **GridColumnStylesCollection**.

```
[Visual Basic]
Public Sub RemoveAt( _
   ByVal index As Integer _
)
[C#]
public void RemoveAt(
   int index
);
[C++]
public: void RemoveAt(
   int index
);
[JScript]
public function RemoveAt(
   index : int
);
```

Parameters

index

The zero-based index of the **DataGridColumnStyle** to remove.

Remarks

Use the **Contains** method to determine whether the **DataGridColumnStyle** exists in the collection.

Use the **IndexOf** method to determine the index of any element in the collection.

Example

See related example in the **System.Windows.Forms.GridColumnStylesCollection** class topic.

Requirements

Platforms: Windows 98, Windows NT 4.0, Windows Millennium Edition, Windows 2000, Windows XP Home Edition, Windows XP Professional, Windows Server 2003 family, .NET Compact Framework - Windows CE .NET

GridColumnStylesCollection.ResetPropertyDescriptors Method

Sets the **PropertyDescriptor** for each column style in the collection to a null reference (**Nothing** in Visual Basic).

```
[Visual Basic]
Public Sub ResetPropertyDescriptors()
[C#]
public void ResetPropertyDescriptors();
[C++]
public: void ResetPropertyDescriptors();
[JScript]
public function ResetPropertyDescriptors();
```

Example

See related example in the **System.Windows.Forms.GridColumnStylesCollection** class topic.

Requirements

Platforms: Windows 98, Windows NT 4.0, Windows Millennium Edition, Windows 2000, Windows XP Home Edition, Windows XP Professional, Windows Server 2003 family

GridColumnStylesCollection.CollectionChanged Event

Occurs when a change is made to the **GridColumnStylesCollection**.

```
[Visual Basic]
Public Event CollectionChanged As CollectionChangeEventHandler
[C#]
public event CollectionChangeEventHandler CollectionChanged;
[C++]
public: __event CollectionChangeEventHandler* CollectionChanged;
```

[JScript] In JScript, you can handle the events defined by a class, but you cannot define your own.

Event Data

The event handler receives an argument of type **CollectionChangeEventArgs** containing data related to this event. The following **CollectionChangeEventArgs** properties provide information specific to this event.

Property	Description
Action	Gets an action that specifies how the collection changed.
Element	Gets the instance of the collection with the change.

Example

See related example in the **System.Windows.Forms.GridColumnStylesCollection** class topic.

Requirements

Platforms: Windows 98, Windows NT 4.0, Windows Millennium Edition, Windows 2000, Windows XP Home Edition, Windows XP Professional, Windows Server 2003 family

GridItem Class

Implements one row in a **PropertyGrid**.

System.Object
  System.Windows.Forms.GridItem

[Visual Basic]
```
MustInherit Public Class GridItem
```
[C#]
```
public abstract class GridItem
```
[C++]
```
public __gc __abstract class GridItem
```
[JScript]
```
public abstract class GridItem
```

Thread Safety

Any public static (**Shared** in Visual Basic) members of this type are safe for multithreaded operations. Any instance members are not guaranteed to be thread safe.

Remarks

Grid items represent the hierarchy of the view into a **PropertyGrid**. You can use a **GridItem** to obtain information about the grid's state and contents. **GridItem** objects should not be cached because they represent a snapshot of the state of the **PropertyGrid** at the time they are accessed, and grid activity might dispose them. The **PropertyGrid** often recreates **GridItem** objects internally without changing the view to the user.

Requirements

Namespace: System.Windows.Forms

Platforms: Windows 98, Windows NT 4.0, Windows Millennium Edition, Windows 2000, Windows XP Home Edition, Windows XP Professional, Windows Server 2003 family

Assembly: System.Windows.Forms (in System.Windows.Forms.dll)

GridItem Constructor

Initializes a new instance of the **GridItem** class.

[Visual Basic]
```
Protected Sub New()
```
[C#]
```
protected GridItem();
```
[C++]
```
protected: GridItem();
```
[JScript]
```
protected function GridItem();
```

Remarks

This constructor is called by derived class constructors to initialize state in this type.

Requirements

Platforms: Windows 98, Windows NT 4.0, Windows Millennium Edition, Windows 2000, Windows XP Home Edition, Windows XP Professional, Windows Server 2003 family

GridItem.Expandable Property

When overridden in a derived class, gets a value indicating whether the specified property is expandable to show nested properties.

[Visual Basic]
```
Public Overridable ReadOnly Property Expandable As Boolean
```
[C#]
```
public virtual bool Expandable {get;}
```
[C++]
```
public: __property virtual bool get_Expandable();
```
[JScript]
```
public function get Expandable() : Boolean;
```

Property Value

true if the specified property can be expanded; otherwise, **false**. The default is false.

Remarks

If a property is expandable, a plus (+) sign is displayed by the property name in the **PropertyGrid**. If the plus sign is clicked and no nested properties are available, the plus sign is then removed.

Requirements

Platforms: Windows 98, Windows NT 4.0, Windows Millennium Edition, Windows 2000, Windows XP Home Edition, Windows XP Professional, Windows Server 2003 family

GridItem.Expanded Property

When overridden in a derived class, gets or sets a value indicating whether the **GridItem** is in an expanded state.

[Visual Basic]
```
Public Overridable Property Expanded As Boolean
```
[C#]
```
public virtual bool Expanded {get; set;}
```
[C++]
```
public: __property virtual bool get_Expanded();
public: __property virtual void set_Expanded(bool);
```
[JScript]
```
public function get Expanded() : Boolean;
public function set Expanded(Boolean);
```

Property Value

true if the grid item is expanded; otherwise, **false**. The default is **false**.

Requirements

Platforms: Windows 98, Windows NT 4.0, Windows Millennium Edition, Windows 2000, Windows XP Home Edition, Windows XP Professional, Windows Server 2003 family

GridItem.GridItems Property

When overridden in a derived class, gets the collection of **GridItem** objects, if any, associated as a child of this **GridItem**.

[Visual Basic]
```
Public MustOverride ReadOnly Property GridItems As _
   GridItemCollection
```
[C#]
```
public abstract GridItemCollection GridItems {get;}
```

```
[C++]
public: __property virtual GridItemCollection* get_GridItems() = 0;
[JScript]
public abstract function get GridItems() : GridItemCollection;
```

Property Value

A **GridItemCollection** object.

Requirements

Platforms: Windows 98, Windows NT 4.0,
Windows Millennium Edition, Windows 2000,
Windows XP Home Edition, Windows XP Professional,
Windows Server 2003 family

GridItem.GridItemType Property

When overridden in a derived class, gets the type of this **GridItem**.

```
[Visual Basic]
Public MustOverride ReadOnly Property GridItemType As GridItemType
[C#]
public abstract GridItemType GridItemType {get;}
[C++]
public: __property virtual GridItemType get_GridItemType() = 0;
[JScript]
public abstract function get GridItemType() : GridItemType;
```

Property Value

One of the **GridItemType** values.

Remarks

For a **GridItem** of type **GridItemType.Property**, you must also ensure that the **PropertyDescriptor** has a valid value. For a **GridItem** of type **GridItemType.Root** the **Parent** property must be a null reference (**Nothing** in Visual Basic).

Requirements

Platforms: Windows 98, Windows NT 4.0,
Windows Millennium Edition, Windows 2000,
Windows XP Home Edition, Windows XP Professional,
Windows Server 2003 family

GridItem.Label Property

When overridden in a derived class, gets the text of this **GridItem**.

```
[Visual Basic]
Public MustOverride ReadOnly Property Label As String
[C#]
public abstract string Label {get;}
[C++]
public: __property virtual String* get_Label() = 0;
[JScript]
public abstract function get Label() : String;
```

Property Value

A **String** representing the text associated with this **GridItem**.

Remarks

This class gets the text that displays in the left column of the grid. The text retrieved can be different from the actual property name of the property represented by this **GridItem**. You can get the name for a **GridItem** of type **GridItemType.Property** by retrieving the **PropertyDescriptor** and checking its **Name** property.

Requirements

Platforms: Windows 98, Windows NT 4.0,
Windows Millennium Edition, Windows 2000,
Windows XP Home Edition, Windows XP Professional,
Windows Server 2003 family

GridItem.Parent Property

When overridden in a derived class, gets the parent **GridItem** of this **GridItem**, if any.

```
[Visual Basic]
Public MustOverride ReadOnly Property Parent As GridItem
[C#]
public abstract GridItem Parent {get;}
[C++]
public: __property virtual GridItem* get_Parent() = 0;
[JScript]
public abstract function get Parent() : GridItem;
```

Property Value

A **GridItem** representing the parent of the **GridItem**.

Remarks

If the **GridItemType** for the **GridItem** is **GridItemType.Root**, this value will be a null reference (**Nothing** in Visual Basic).

Requirements

Platforms: Windows 98, Windows NT 4.0,
Windows Millennium Edition, Windows 2000,
Windows XP Home Edition, Windows XP Professional,
Windows Server 2003 family

GridItem.PropertyDescriptor Property

When overridden in a derived class, gets the **PropertyDescriptor** that is associated with this **GridItem**.

```
[Visual Basic]
Public MustOverride ReadOnly Property PropertyDescriptor As _
   PropertyDescriptor
[C#]
public abstract PropertyDescriptor PropertyDescriptor {get;}
[C++]
public: __property virtual PropertyDescriptor*
   get_PropertyDescriptor() = 0;
[JScript]
public abstract function get PropertyDescriptor() :
   PropertyDescriptor;
```

Property Value

The **PropertyDescriptor** associated with this **GridItem**.

Remarks

This property is only valid for a **GridItem** of type **GridItemType.Property**.

You can use this property to retrieve information such as the property type of the grid item, the name of the grid item, or the type converter for the grid item.

Requirements

Platforms: Windows 98, Windows NT 4.0,
Windows Millennium Edition, Windows 2000,
Windows XP Home Edition, Windows XP Professional,
Windows Server 2003 family

GridItem.Value Property

When overridden in a derived class, gets the current value of this **GridItem**.

[Visual Basic]
```
Public MustOverride ReadOnly Property Value As Object
```
[C#]
```
public abstract object Value {get;}
```
[C++]
```
public: __property virtual Object* get_Value() = 0;
```
[JScript]
```
public abstract function get Value() : Object;
```

Property Value

The current value of this **GridItem**. This can be a null reference (**Nothing** in Visual Basic).

Requirements

Platforms: Windows 98, Windows NT 4.0, Windows Millennium Edition, Windows 2000, Windows XP Home Edition, Windows XP Professional, Windows Server 2003 family

GridItem.Select Method

When overridden in a derived class, selects this **GridItem** in the **PropertyGrid**.

[Visual Basic]
```
Public MustOverride Function Select() As Boolean
```
[C#]
```
public abstract bool Select();
```
[C++]
```
public: virtual bool Select() = 0;
```
[JScript]
```
public abstract function Select() : Boolean;
```

Return Value

true if the selection is successful; otherwise, **false**.

Requirements

Platforms: Windows 98, Windows NT 4.0, Windows Millennium Edition, Windows 2000, Windows XP Home Edition, Windows XP Professional, Windows Server 2003 family

GridItemCollection Class

Contains a collection of **GridItem** objects.

System.Object
System.Windows.Forms.GridItemCollection

```
[Visual Basic]
Public Class GridItemCollection
   Implements ICollection, IEnumerable
[C#]
public class GridItemCollection : ICollection, IEnumerable
[C++]
public __gc class GridItemCollection : public ICollection,
   IEnumerable
[JScript]
public class GridItemCollection implements ICollection, IEnumerable
```

Thread Safety

Any public static (**Shared** in Visual Basic) members of this type are safe for multithreaded operations. Any instance members are not guaranteed to be thread safe.

Remarks

This class represents a collection of **GridItem** objects stored in a **PropertyGrid**.

You can retrieve a specific **GridItem** by using either an index into the collection or the label of a grid item in the collection that you access through the indexer.

Requirements

Namespace: System.Windows.Forms

Platforms: Windows 98, Windows NT 4.0,
Windows Millennium Edition, Windows 2000,
Windows XP Home Edition, Windows XP Professional,
Windows Server 2003 family

Assembly: System.Windows.Forms (in System.Windows.Forms.dll)

GridItemCollection.Empty Field

This member supports the .NET Framework infrastructure and is not intended to be used directly from your code.

```
[Visual Basic]
Public Shared Empty As GridItemCollection
[C#]
public static GridItemCollection Empty;
[C++]
public: static GridItemCollection* Empty;
[JScript]
public static var Empty : GridItemCollection;
```

GridItemCollection.Count Property

Gets the number of grid items in the collection.

```
[Visual Basic]
Public Overridable ReadOnly Property Count As Integer  Implements _
   ICollection.Count
[C#]
public virtual int Count {get;}
[C++]
public: __property virtual int get_Count();
[JScript]
public function get Count() : int;
```

Property Value

The number of grid items in the collection.

Implements

ICollection.Count

Requirements

Platforms: Windows 98, Windows NT 4.0,
Windows Millennium Edition, Windows 2000,
Windows XP Home Edition, Windows XP Professional,
Windows Server 2003 family

GridItemCollection.Item Property

Gets a **GridItem** from the collection.

[C#] In C#, this property is the indexer for the **GridItemCollection** class.

Overload List

Gets the **GridItem** with the matching label.

[Visual Basic] **Overloads Public Default ReadOnly Property Item(String) As GridItem**

[C#] **public GridItem this[string] {get;}**

[C++] **public: __property GridItem* get_Item(String*);**

[JScript] **GridItemCollection.Item (String)**

Gets the **GridItem** at the specified index.

[Visual Basic] **Overloads Public Default ReadOnly Property Item(Integer) As GridItem**

[C#] **public GridItem this[int] {get;}**

[C++] **public: __property GridItem* get_Item(int);**

[JScript] **GridItemCollection.Item (int)**

GridItemCollection.Item Property (String)

Gets the **GridItem** with the matching label.

[C#] In C#, this property is the indexer for the **GridItemCollection** class.

```
[Visual Basic]
Overloads Public Default ReadOnly Property Item( _
   ByVal label As String _
) As GridItem
[C#]
public GridItem this[
   string label
] {get;}
[C++]
public: __property GridItem* get_Item(
   String* label
);
[JScript]
returnValue = GridItemCollectionObject.Item(label);
-or-
returnValue = GridItemCollectionObject(label);
```

[JScript] In JScript, you can use the default indexed properties defined by a type, but you cannot explicitly define your own. However, specifying the **expando** attribute on a class automatically provides a default indexed property whose type is **Object** and whose index type is **String**.

Arguments [JScript]

label

A string value to match to a grid item label

Parameters [Visual Basic, C#, C++]

label

A string value to match to a grid item label

Property Value

The grid item whose label matches the *label* parameter.

Requirements

Platforms: Windows 98, Windows NT 4.0, Windows Millennium Edition, Windows 2000, Windows XP Home Edition, Windows XP Professional, Windows Server 2003 family

GridItemCollection.Item Property (Int32)

Gets the **GridItem** at the specified index.

[C#] In C#, this property is the indexer for the **GridItemCollection** class.

```
[Visual Basic]
Overloads Public Default ReadOnly Property Item( _
   ByVal index As Integer _
) As GridItem
[C#]
public GridItem this[
   int index
] {get;}
[C++]
public: __property GridItem* get_Item(
   int index
);
[JScript]
returnValue = GridItemCollectionObject.Item(index);
-or-
returnValue = GridItemCollectionObject(index);
```

[JScript] In JScript, you can use the default indexed properties defined by a type, but you cannot explicitly define your own. However, specifying the **expando** attribute on a class automatically provides a default indexed property whose type is **Object** and whose index type is **String**.

Arguments [JScript]

index

The index of the grid item to return.

Parameters [Visual Basic, C#, C++]

index

The index of the grid item to return.

Property Value

The **GridItem** at the specified index.

Requirements

Platforms: Windows 98, Windows NT 4.0, Windows Millennium Edition, Windows 2000, Windows XP Home Edition, Windows XP Professional, Windows Server 2003 family

GridItemCollection.GetEnumerator Method

Returns an enumeration of all the grid items in the collection.

```
[Visual Basic]
Public Overridable Function GetEnumerator() As IEnumerator _
   Implements IEnumerable.GetEnumerator
[C#]
public virtual IEnumerator GetEnumerator();
[C++]
public: virtual IEnumerator* GetEnumerator();
[JScript]
public function GetEnumerator() : IEnumerator;
```

Return Value

An **IEnumerator** for the **GridItemCollection**.

Implements

IEnumerable.GetEnumerator

Requirements

Platforms: Windows 98, Windows NT 4.0, Windows Millennium Edition, Windows 2000, Windows XP Home Edition, Windows XP Professional, Windows Server 2003 family

GridItemCollection.ICollection.CopyTo Method

This member supports the .NET Framework infrastructure and is not intended to be used directly from your code.

```
[Visual Basic]
Private Sub CopyTo( _
   ByVal dest As Array, _
   ByVal index As Integer _
) Implements ICollection.CopyTo
[C#]
void ICollection.CopyTo(
   Array dest,
   int index
);
[C++]
private: void ICollection::CopyTo(
   Array* dest,
   int index
);
[JScript]
private function ICollection.CopyTo(
   dest : Array,
   index : int
);
```

GridItemType Enumeration

Specifies the valid grid item types for a **PropertyGrid**.

[Visual Basic]
```
<Serializable>
Public Enum GridItemType
```
[C#]
```
[Serializable]
public enum GridItemType
```
[C++]
```
[Serializable]
__value public enum GridItemType
```
[JScript]
```
public
   Serializable
enum GridItemType
```

Members

Member name	Description
ArrayValue	The **GridItem** is an element of an array.
Category	A grid entry that is a category name. A category is a descriptive grouping for groups of **GridItem** rows. Typical categories include the following Behavior, Layout, Data, and Appearance.
Property	A grid entry that corresponds to a property.
Root	A root item in the grid hierarchy.

Requirements

Namespace: System.Windows.Forms

Platforms: Windows 98, Windows NT 4.0, Windows Millennium Edition, Windows 2000, Windows XP Home Edition, Windows XP Professional, Windows Server 2003 family

Assembly: System.Windows.Forms (in System.Windows.Forms.dll)

GridTablesFactory Class

This type supports the .NET Framework infrastructure and is not intended to be used directly from your code.

[Visual Basic]
```
Public Class GridTablesFactory
```
[C#]
```
public class GridTablesFactory
```
[C++]
```
public __gc class GridTablesFactory
```
[JScript]
```
public class GridTablesFactory
```

GridTablesFactory.CreateGridTables Method

This member supports the .NET Framework infrastructure and is not intended to be used directly from your code.

[Visual Basic]
```
Public Shared Function CreateGridTables( _
   ByVal gridTable As DataGridTableStyle, _
   ByVal dataSource As Object, _
   ByVal dataMember As String, _
   ByVal bindingManager As BindingContext _
) As DataGridTableStyle()
```
[C#]
```
public static DataGridTableStyle[] CreateGridTables(
   DataGridTableStyle gridTable,
   object dataSource,
   string dataMember,
   BindingContext bindingManager
);
```
[C++]
```
public: static DataGridTableStyle* CreateGridTables(
   DataGridTableStyle* gridTable,
   Object* dataSource,
   String* dataMember,
   BindingContext* bindingManager
) [];
```
[JScript]
```
public static function CreateGridTables(
   gridTable : DataGridTableStyle,
   dataSource : Object,
   dataMember : String,
   bindingManager : BindingContext
) : DataGridTableStyle[];
```

GridTableStylesCollection Class

Represents a collection of **DataGridTableStyle** objects in the **DataGrid** control.

System.Object
  System.MarshalByRefObject
    System.Windows.Forms.BaseCollection
      System.Windows.Forms.GridTableStylesCollection

[Visual Basic]
```
Public Class GridTableStylesCollection
   Inherits BaseCollection
   Implements IList
```
[C#]
```
public class GridTableStylesCollection : BaseCollection, IList
```
[C++]
```
public __gc class GridTableStylesCollection : public
   BaseCollection, IList
```
[JScript]
```
public class GridTableStylesCollection extends BaseCollection
   implements IList
```

Thread Safety

Any public static (**Shared** in Visual Basic) members of this type are safe for multithreaded operations. Any instance members are not guaranteed to be thread safe.

Remarks

The **GridTableStylesCollection** contains **DataGridTableStyle** objects that allows the **DataGrid** control to display a customized grid style for each **DataTable** in a **DataSet**.

On the **DataGrid** control, the **TableStyles** property returns the **GridTableStylesCollection** object.

By default, the **GridTableStylesCollection** does not contain any **DataGridTableStyle** objects. Instead, the **DataGrid** displays each table using default settings for color, width, and formatting. All columns of each table are displayed. When a **DataGridTableStyle** object is added to the collection, the **DataGrid** uses the **MappingName** to determine which object supplies the data for the grid. For example, if the data source is a **DataSet** that contains three **DataTable** objects, the **MappingName** must match the **TableName** of one of the objects. If the **MappingName** does not match any of the **TableName** values, the default settings will be used to display data for each table, and the **DataGridTableStyle** settings will be ignored.

CAUTION Always create **DataGridColumnStyle** objects and add them to the **GridColumnStylesCollection** before adding **DataGridTableStyle** objects to the **GridTableStylesCollection**. When you add an empty **DataGridTableStyle** to the collection, **DataGridColumnStyle** objects are automatically generated for you. Consequently, an exception will be thrown if you try to add new **DataGridColumnStyle** objects with duplicate **MappingName** values to the **GridColumnStylesCollection**. Alternatively, clear the **GridColumnStylesCollection** using the **Clear** method.

Example

[Visual Basic, C#, C++] The following example creates two **DataGridTableStyle** objects and adds each to the **GridTableStylesCollection** returned by the **TableStyles** property of a **DataGrid** control.

[Visual Basic]
```
Private Sub AddCustomDataTableStyle()
   Dim ts1 As New DataGridTableStyle()
   ts1.MappingName = "Customers"
   ' Set other properties.
   ts1.AlternatingBackColor = Color.LightGray
   ' Add a GridColumnStyle and set its MappingName
   ' to the name of a DataColumn in the DataTable.
   ' Set the HeaderText and Width properties.

   Dim boolCol As New DataGridBoolColumn()
   boolCol.MappingName = "Current"
   boolCol.HeaderText = "IsCurrent Customer"
   boolCol.Width = 150
   ts1.GridColumnStyles.Add(boolCol)

   ' Add a second column style.
   Dim TextCol As New DataGridTextBoxColumn()
   TextCol.MappingName = "custName"
   TextCol.HeaderText = "Customer Name"
   TextCol.Width = 250
   ts1.GridColumnStyles.Add(TextCol)

   ' Create the second table style with columns.
   Dim ts2 As New DataGridTableStyle()
   ts2.MappingName = "Orders"

   ' Set other properties.
   ts2.AlternatingBackColor = Color.LightBlue

   ' Create new ColumnStyle objects.
   Dim cOrderDate As New DataGridTextBoxColumn()
   cOrderDate.MappingName = "OrderDate"
   cOrderDate.HeaderText = "Order Date"
   cOrderDate.Width = 100
   ts2.GridColumnStyles.Add(cOrderDate)

   ' Use a PropertyDescriptor to create a formatted
   ' column. First get the PropertyDescriptorCollection
   ' for the data source and data member.
   Dim pcol As PropertyDescriptorCollection = _
   Me.BindingContext(myDataSet, "Customers.custToOrders"). _
   GetItemProperties()

   ' Create a formatted column using a PropertyDescriptor.
   ' The formatting character "c" specifies a currency format. */

   Dim csOrderAmount As _
   New DataGridTextBoxColumn(pcol("OrderAmount"), "c", True)
   csOrderAmount.MappingName = "OrderAmount"
   csOrderAmount.HeaderText = "Total"
   csOrderAmount.Width = 100
   ts2.GridColumnStyles.Add(csOrderAmount)

   ' Add the DataGridTableStyle instances to
   ' the GridTableStylesCollection.
   myDataGrid.TableStyles.Add(ts1)
   myDataGrid.TableStyles.Add(ts2)
End Sub 'AddCustomDataTableStyle
```

[C#]
```
private void AddCustomDataTableStyle(){
   DataGridTableStyle ts1 = new DataGridTableStyle();
   ts1.MappingName = "Customers";
   // Set other properties.
   ts1.AlternatingBackColor = Color.LightGray;
```

```
    /* Add a GridColumnStyle and set its MappingName
    to the name of a DataColumn in the DataTable.
    Set the HeaderText and Width properties. */

    DataGridColumnStyle boolCol = new DataGridBoolColumn();
    boolCol.MappingName = "Current";
    boolCol.HeaderText = "IsCurrent Customer";
    boolCol.Width = 150;
    ts1.GridColumnStyles.Add(boolCol);

    // Add a second column style.
    DataGridColumnStyle TextCol = new DataGridTextBoxColumn();
    TextCol.MappingName = "custName";
    TextCol.HeaderText = "Customer Name";
    TextCol.Width = 250;
    ts1.GridColumnStyles.Add(TextCol);

    // Create the second table style with columns.
    DataGridTableStyle ts2 = new DataGridTableStyle();
    ts2.MappingName = "Orders";

    // Set other properties.
    ts2.AlternatingBackColor = Color.LightBlue;

    // Create new ColumnStyle objects.
    DataGridColumnStyle cOrderDate =
    new DataGridTextBoxColumn();
    cOrderDate.MappingName = "OrderDate";
    cOrderDate.HeaderText = "Order Date";
    cOrderDate.Width = 100;
    ts2.GridColumnStyles.Add(cOrderDate);

    /*Use a PropertyDescriptor to create a formatted
    column. First get the PropertyDescriptorCollection
    for the data source and data member. */
    PropertyDescriptorCollection pcol = this.BindingContext
    [myDataSet, "Customers.custToOrders"].GetItemProperties();

    /* Create a formatted column using a PropertyDescriptor.
    The formatting character "c" specifies a currency format. */
    DataGridColumnStyle csOrderAmount =
    new DataGridTextBoxColumn(pcol["OrderAmount"], "c", true);
    csOrderAmount.MappingName = "OrderAmount";
    csOrderAmount.HeaderText = "Total";
    csOrderAmount.Width = 100;
    ts2.GridColumnStyles.Add(csOrderAmount);

    /* Add the DataGridTableStyle instances to
    the GridTableStylesCollection. */
    myDataGrid.TableStyles.Add(ts1);
    myDataGrid.TableStyles.Add(ts2);
}
```

[C++]

```
private:
    void AddCustomDataTableStyle() {
        DataGridTableStyle* ts1 = new DataGridTableStyle();
        ts1->MappingName = S"Customers";
        // Set other properties.
        ts1->AlternatingBackColor = Color::LightGray;

        /* Add a GridColumnStyle and set its MappingName
        to the name of a DataColumn in the DataTable.
        Set the HeaderText and Width properties. */

        DataGridColumnStyle* boolCol = new DataGridBoolColumn();
        boolCol->MappingName = S"Current";
        boolCol->HeaderText = S"IsCurrent Customer";
        boolCol->Width = 150;
        ts1->GridColumnStyles->Add(boolCol);

        // Add a second column style.
        DataGridColumnStyle* TextCol = new DataGridTextBoxColumn();
        TextCol->MappingName = S"custName";
        TextCol->HeaderText = S"Customer Name";
        TextCol->Width = 250;
        ts1->GridColumnStyles->Add(TextCol);

        // Create the second table style with columns.
        DataGridTableStyle* ts2 = new DataGridTableStyle();
        ts2->MappingName = S"Orders";

        // Set other properties.
        ts2->AlternatingBackColor = Color::LightBlue;

        // Create new ColumnStyle objects.
        DataGridColumnStyle* cOrderDate = new DataGridTextBoxColumn();
        cOrderDate->MappingName = S"OrderDate";
        cOrderDate->HeaderText = S"Order Date";
        cOrderDate->Width = 100;
        ts2->GridColumnStyles->Add(cOrderDate);

        /*Use a PropertyDescriptor to create a formatted
        column. First get the PropertyDescriptorCollection
        for the data source and data member. */
        PropertyDescriptorCollection* pcol = this->
BindingContext->get_Item
            (myDataSet, S"Customers::custToOrders")-
>GetItemProperties();

        /* Create a formatted column using a PropertyDescriptor.
        The formatting character S"c" specifies a currency format. */
        DataGridColumnStyle* csOrderAmount =
            new DataGridTextBoxColumn(pcol->Item
 [S"OrderAmount"], S"c", true);
        csOrderAmount->MappingName = S"OrderAmount";
        csOrderAmount->HeaderText = S"Total";
        csOrderAmount->Width = 100;
        ts2->GridColumnStyles->Add(csOrderAmount);

        /* Add the DataGridTableStyle instances to
        the GridTableStylesCollection. */
        myDataGrid->TableStyles->Add(ts1);
        myDataGrid->TableStyles->Add(ts2);
    }
```

Requirements

Namespace: System.Windows.Forms

Platforms: Windows 98, Windows NT 4.0, Windows Millennium Edition, Windows 2000, Windows XP Home Edition, Windows XP Professional, Windows Server 2003 family, .NET Compact Framework - Windows CE .NET

Assembly: System.Windows.Forms (in System.Windows.Forms.dll)

GridTableStylesCollection.Item Property

Gets the specified **DataGridTableStyle**.

[C#] In C#, this property is the indexer for the **GridTableStylesCollection** class.

Overload List

Gets the **DataGridTableStyle** specified by index.

[Visual Basic] **Overloads Public Default ReadOnly Property Item(Integer) As DataGridTableStyle**

[C#] **public DataGridTableStyle this[int] {get;}**

[C++] **public: __property DataGridTableStyle* get_Item(int);**

[JScript] **GridTableStylesCollection.Item (int)**

Gets the **DataGridTableStyle** with the specified name.

[Visual Basic] **Overloads Public Default ReadOnly Property Item(String) As DataGridTableStyle**

[C#] **public DataGridTableStyle this[string] {get;}**

[C++] **public: __property DataGridTableStyle* get_Item(String*);**

[JScript] **GridTableStylesCollection.Item (String)**

Example

See related example in the **System.Windows.Forms.GridTableStylesCollection** class topic.

GridTableStylesCollection.Item Property (Int32)

Gets the **DataGridTableStyle** specified by index.

[C#] In C#, this property is the indexer for the **GridTableStylesCollection** class.

```
[Visual Basic]
Overloads Public Default ReadOnly Property Item( _
   ByVal index As Integer _
) As DataGridTableStyle
[C#]
public DataGridTableStyle this[
   int index
] {get;}
[C++]
public: __property DataGridTableStyle* get_Item(
   int index
);
[JScript]
returnValue = GridTableStylesCollectionObject.Item(index);
-or-
returnValue = GridTableStylesCollectionObject(index);
```

[JScript] In JScript, you can use the default indexed properties defined by a type, but you cannot explicitly define your own. However, specifying the **expando** attribute on a class automatically provides a default indexed property whose type is **Object** and whose index type is **String**.

Arguments [JScript]

index

The index of the **DataGridTableStyle** to get.

Parameters [Visual Basic, C#, C++]

index

The index of the **DataGridTableStyle** to get.

Property Value

The **DataGridTableStyle** at the specified index.

Exceptions

Exception Type	Condition
ArgumentOutOfRangeException	No item exists at the specified index.

Remarks

Use the **Add** or **AddRange** method to add items to the collection.

Example

See related example in the **System.Windows.Forms.GridTableStylesCollection** class topic.

Requirements

Platforms: Windows 98, Windows NT 4.0, Windows Millennium Edition, Windows 2000, Windows XP Home Edition, Windows XP Professional, Windows Server 2003 family

GridTableStylesCollection.Item Property (String)

Gets the **DataGridTableStyle** with the specified name.

[C#] In C#, this property is the indexer for the **GridTableStylesCollection** class.

```
[Visual Basic]
Overloads Public Default ReadOnly Property Item( _
   ByVal tableName As String _
) As DataGridTableStyle
[C#]
public DataGridTableStyle this[
   string tableName
] {get;}
[C++]
public: __property DataGridTableStyle* get_Item(
   String* tableName
);
[JScript]
returnValue = GridTableStylesCollectionObject.Item(tableName);
-or-
returnValue = GridTableStylesCollectionObject(tableName);
```

[JScript] In JScript, you can use the default indexed properties defined by a type, but you cannot explicitly define your own. However, specifying the **expando** attribute on a class automatically provides a default indexed property whose type is **Object** and whose index type is **String**.

Arguments [JScript]

tableName

The **MappingName** of the **DataGridTableStyle** to retrieve.

Parameters [Visual Basic, C#, C++]

tableName

The **MappingName** of the **DataGridTableStyle** to retrieve.

Property Value

The **DataGridTableStyle** with the specified **MappingName**.

Remarks

When retrieving a **DataGridTableStyle** by **MappingName**, the **Item** property uses a case-insensitive comparison.

Use the **Add** or **AddRange** method to add items to the collection.

Example

See related example in the **System.Windows.Forms.GridTableStylesCollection** class topic.

Requirements

Platforms: Windows 98, Windows NT 4.0, Windows Millennium Edition, Windows 2000, Windows XP Home Edition, Windows XP Professional, Windows Server 2003 family

GridTableStylesCollection.List Property

This member overrides **BaseCollection.List**.

```
[Visual Basic]
Overrides Protected ReadOnly Property List As ArrayList
[C#]
protected override ArrayList List {get;}
[C++]
protected: __property ArrayList* get_List();
[JScript]
protected override function get List() : ArrayList;
```

Requirements

Platforms: Windows 98, Windows NT 4.0, Windows Millennium Edition, Windows 2000, Windows XP Home Edition, Windows XP Professional, Windows Server 2003 family, .NET Compact Framework - Windows CE .NET

GridTableStylesCollection.System.Collections.ICollection.Count Property

Note: This namespace, class, or member is supported only in version 1.1 of the .NET Framework.

This member supports the .NET Framework infrastructure and is not intended to be used directly from your code.

```
[Visual Basic]
Private ReadOnly Property Count As Integer Implements _
   ICollection.Count
[C#]
int ICollection.Count {get;}
[C++]
private: __property int
   System::Collections::ICollection::get_Count();
[JScript]
private function get ICollection.Count() : int;
```

GridTableStylesCollection.System.Collections.ICollection.IsSynchronized Property

Note: This namespace, class, or member is supported only in version 1.1 of the .NET Framework.

This member supports the .NET Framework infrastructure and is not intended to be used directly from your code.

```
[Visual Basic]
Private ReadOnly Property IsSynchronized As Boolean Implements _
   ICollection.IsSynchronized
[C#]
bool ICollection.IsSynchronized {get;}
[C++]
private: __property bool
   System::Collections::ICollection::get_IsSynchronized();
[JScript]
private function get ICollection.IsSynchronized() : Boolean;
```

GridTableStylesCollection.System.Collections.ICollection.SyncRoot Property

Note: This namespace, class, or member is supported only in version 1.1 of the .NET Framework.

This member supports the .NET Framework infrastructure and is not intended to be used directly from your code.

```
[Visual Basic]
Private ReadOnly Property SyncRoot As Object Implements _
   ICollection.SyncRoot
[C#]
object ICollection.SyncRoot {get;}
[C++]
private: __property Object*
   System::Collections::ICollection::get_SyncRoot();
[JScript]
private function get ICollection.SyncRoot() : Object;
```

GridTableStylesCollection.System.Collections.IList.IsFixedSize Property

Note: This namespace, class, or member is supported only in version 1.1 of the .NET Framework.

This member supports the .NET Framework infrastructure and is not intended to be used directly from your code.

```
[Visual Basic]
Private ReadOnly Property IsFixedSize As Boolean Implements _
   IList.IsFixedSize
[C#]
bool IList.IsFixedSize {get;}
[C++]
private: __property bool
   System::Collections::IList::get_IsFixedSize();
[JScript]
private function get IList.IsFixedSize() : Boolean;
```

GridTableStylesCollection.System.Collections.IList.IsReadOnly Property

Note: This namespace, class, or member is supported only in version 1.1 of the .NET Framework.

This member supports the .NET Framework infrastructure and is not intended to be used directly from your code.

```
[Visual Basic]
Private ReadOnly Property IsReadOnly As Boolean Implements _
   IList.IsReadOnly
[C#]
bool IList.IsReadOnly {get;}
[C++]
private: __property bool
   System::Collections::IList::get_IsReadOnly();
[JScript]
private function get IList.IsReadOnly() : Boolean;
```

GridTableStylesCollection.System.Collections.IList.Item Property

Note: This namespace, class, or member is supported only in version 1.1 of the .NET Framework.

[C#] In C#, this property is the indexer for the **GridTableStylesCollection** class.

```
[Visual Basic]
Private Default Property Item( _
   ByVal i As Integer _
) As Object Implements IList.Item
[C#]
object IList.this[
   int i
] {get; set;}
[C++]
private: __property Object* System::Collections::IList::get_Item(
   int i
);
private: __property void System::Collections::IList::set_Item(
   int i,
   Object*
);
[JScript]
private function get IList.get_Item(i : int) : Object;
private function set IList.set_Item(i : int, value : Object);
-or-
private function get IList.get_Item(i : int) : Object;
private function set IList.set_Item(i : int, value : Object);
```

[JScript] In JScript, you can use the default indexed properties defined by a type, but you cannot explicitly define your own. However, specifying the **expando** attribute on a class automatically provides a default indexed property whose type is **Object** and whose index type is **String**.

Arguments [JScript]

i

Parameters [Visual Basic, C#, C++]

i

Requirements

Platforms: Windows 98, Windows NT 4.0,
Windows Millennium Edition, Windows 2000,
Windows XP Home Edition, Windows XP Professional,
Windows Server 2003 family

GridTableStylesCollection.Add Method

Adds a **DataGridTableStyle** to this collection.

```
[Visual Basic]
Public Overridable Function Add( _
   ByVal table As DataGridTableStyle _
) As Integer
[C#]
public virtual int Add(
   DataGridTableStyle table
);
[C++]
public: virtual int Add(
   DataGridTableStyle* table
);
[JScript]
public function Add(
   table : DataGridTableStyle
) : int;
```

Parameters

table

The **DataGridTableStyle** to add to the collection.

Return Value

The index of the newly added object.

Example

See related example in the **System.Windows.Forms.GridTableStylesCollection** class topic.

Requirements

Platforms: Windows 98, Windows NT 4.0,
Windows Millennium Edition, Windows 2000,
Windows XP Home Edition, Windows XP Professional,
Windows Server 2003 family,
.NET Compact Framework - Windows CE .NET

GridTableStylesCollection.AddRange Method

Adds an array of table styles to the collection.

```
[Visual Basic]
Public Overridable Sub AddRange( _
   ByVal tables() As DataGridTableStyle _
)
[C#]
public virtual void AddRange(
   DataGridTableStyle[] tables
);
[C++]
public: virtual void AddRange(
   DataGridTableStyle* tables[]
);
[JScript]
public function AddRange(
   tables : DataGridTableStyle[]
);
```

Parameters

tables

An array of **DataGridTableStyle** objects.

Example

See related example in the **System.Windows.Forms.GridTableStylesCollection** class topic.

Requirements

Platforms: Windows 98, Windows NT 4.0,
Windows Millennium Edition, Windows 2000,
Windows XP Home Edition, Windows XP Professional,
Windows Server 2003 family

GridTableStylesCollection.Clear Method

Clears the collection.

```
[Visual Basic]
Public Sub Clear()
[C#]
public void Clear();
```

```
[C++]
public: void Clear();
[JScript]
public function Clear();
```

Example

See related example in the **System.Windows.Forms.GridTableStylesCollection** class topic.

Requirements

Platforms: Windows 98, Windows NT 4.0, Windows Millennium Edition, Windows 2000, Windows XP Home Edition, Windows XP Professional, Windows Server 2003 family, .NET Compact Framework - Windows CE .NET

GridTableStylesCollection.Contains Method

Gets a value indicating whether the **GridTableStylesCollection** contains the specified **DataGridTableStyle**.

Overload List

Gets a value indicating whether the **GridTableStylesCollection** contains the specified **DataGridTableStyle**.

Supported by the .NET Compact Framework.

[Visual Basic] **Overloads Public Function Contains(DataGridTableStyle) As Boolean**

[C#] **public bool Contains(DataGridTableStyle);**

[C++] **public: bool Contains(DataGridTableStyle*);**

[JScript] **public function Contains(DataGridTableStyle) : Boolean;**

Gets a value indicating whether the **GridTableStylesCollection** contains the **DataGridTableStyle** specified by name.

Supported by the .NET Compact Framework.

[Visual Basic] **Overloads Public Function Contains(String) As Boolean**

[C#] **public bool Contains(string);**

[C++] **public: bool Contains(String*);**

[JScript] **public function Contains(String) : Boolean;**

Example

See related example in the **System.Windows.Forms.GridTableStylesCollection** class topic.

GridTableStylesCollection.Contains Method (DataGridTableStyle)

Gets a value indicating whether the **GridTableStylesCollection** contains the specified **DataGridTableStyle**.

```
[Visual Basic]
Overloads Public Function Contains( _
   ByVal table As DataGridTableStyle _
) As Boolean
[C#]
public bool Contains(
   DataGridTableStyle table
);
[C++]
public: bool Contains(
   DataGridTableStyle* table
);
[JScript]
public function Contains(
   table : DataGridTableStyle
) : Boolean;
```

Parameters

table
The **DataGridTableStyle** to look for.

Return Value

true if the specified table style exists in the collection; otherwise, **false**.

Requirements

Platforms: Windows 98, Windows NT 4.0, Windows Millennium Edition, Windows 2000, Windows XP Home Edition, Windows XP Professional, Windows Server 2003 family, .NET Compact Framework - Windows CE .NET

GridTableStylesCollection.Contains Method (String)

Gets a value indicating whether the **GridTableStylesCollection** contains the **DataGridTableStyle** specified by name.

```
[Visual Basic]
Overloads Public Function Contains( _
   ByVal name As String _
) As Boolean
[C#]
public bool Contains(
   string name
);
[C++]
public: bool Contains(
   String* name
);
[JScript]
public function Contains(
   name : String
) : Boolean;
```

Parameters

name
The **MappingName** of the **DataGridTableStyle** to look for.

Return Value

true if the specified table style exists in the collection; otherwise, **false**.

Example

See related example in the **System.Windows.Forms.GridTableStylesCollection** class topic.

Requirements

Platforms: Windows 98, Windows NT 4.0, Windows Millennium Edition, Windows 2000, Windows XP Home Edition, Windows XP Professional, Windows Server 2003 family, .NET Compact Framework - Windows CE .NET

GridTableStylesCollection.ICollection.CopyTo Method

This member supports the .NET Framework infrastructure and is not intended to be used directly from your code.

```
[Visual Basic]
Private Sub CopyTo( _
   ByVal array As Array, _
   ByVal index As Integer _
) Implements ICollection.CopyTo
[C#]
void ICollection.CopyTo(
   Array array,
   int index
);
[C++]
private: void ICollection::CopyTo(
   Array* array,
   int index
);
[JScript]
private function ICollection.CopyTo(
   array : Array,
   index : int
);
```

GridTableStylesCollection.IEnumerable.GetEnumerator Method

This member supports the .NET Framework infrastructure and is not intended to be used directly from your code.

```
[Visual Basic]
Private Function GetEnumerator() As IEnumerator Implements _
   IEnumerable.GetEnumerator
[C#]
IEnumerator IEnumerable.GetEnumerator();
[C++]
private: IEnumerator* IEnumerable::GetEnumerator();
[JScript]
private function IEnumerable.GetEnumerator() : IEnumerator;
```

GridTableStylesCollection.IList.Add Method

This member supports the .NET Framework infrastructure and is not intended to be used directly from your code.

```
[Visual Basic]
Private Function Add( _
   ByVal value As Object _
) As Integer Implements IList.Add
[C#]
int IList.Add(
   object value
);
[C++]
private: int IList::Add(
   Object* value
);
[JScript]
private function IList.Add(
   value : Object
) : int;
```

GridTableStylesCollection.IList.Clear Method

This member supports the .NET Framework infrastructure and is not intended to be used directly from your code.

```
[Visual Basic]
Private Sub Clear() Implements IList.Clear
[C#]
void IList.Clear();
[C++]
private: void IList::Clear();
[JScript]
private function IList.Clear();
```

GridTableStylesCollection.IList.Contains Method

This member supports the .NET Framework infrastructure and is not intended to be used directly from your code.

```
[Visual Basic]
Private Function Contains( _
   ByVal value As Object _
) As Boolean Implements IList.Contains
[C#]
bool IList.Contains(
   object value
);
[C++]
private: bool IList::Contains(
   Object* value
);
[JScript]
private function IList.Contains(
   value : Object
) : Boolean;
```

GridTableStylesCollection.IList.IndexOf Method

This member supports the .NET Framework infrastructure and is not intended to be used directly from your code.

```
[Visual Basic]
Private Function IndexOf( _
   ByVal value As Object _
) As Integer Implements IList.IndexOf
[C#]
int IList.IndexOf(
   object value
);
[C++]
private: int IList::IndexOf(
   Object* value
);
[JScript]
private function IList.IndexOf(
   value : Object
) : int;
```

GridTableStylesCollection.IList.Insert Method

This member supports the .NET Framework infrastructure and is not intended to be used directly from your code.

```
[Visual Basic]
Private Sub Insert( _
   ByVal index As Integer, _
   ByVal value As Object _
) Implements IList.Insert
[C#]
void IList.Insert(
   int index,
   object value
);
[C++]
private: void IList::Insert(
   int index,
   Object* value
);
[JScript]
private function IList.Insert(
   index : int,
   value : Object
);
```

GridTableStylesCollection.IList.Remove Method

This member supports the .NET Framework infrastructure and is not intended to be used directly from your code.

```
[Visual Basic]
Private Sub Remove( _
   ByVal value As Object _
) Implements IList.Remove
[C#]
void IList.Remove(
   object value
);
[C++]
private: void IList::Remove(
   Object* value
);
[JScript]
private function IList.Remove(
   value : Object
);
```

GridTableStylesCollection.IList.RemoveAt Method

This member supports the .NET Framework infrastructure and is not intended to be used directly from your code.

```
[Visual Basic]
Private Sub RemoveAt( _
   ByVal index As Integer _
) Implements IList.RemoveAt
[C#]
void IList.RemoveAt(
   int index
);
[C++]
private: void IList::RemoveAt(
   int index
);
[JScript]
private function IList.RemoveAt(
   index : int
);
```

GridTableStylesCollection.OnCollectionChanged Method

Raises the **CollectionChanged** event.

```
[Visual Basic]
Protected Sub OnCollectionChanged( _
   ByVal ccevent As CollectionChangeEventArgs _
)
[C#]
protected void OnCollectionChanged(
   CollectionChangeEventArgs ccevent
);
[C++]
protected: void OnCollectionChanged(
   CollectionChangeEventArgs* ccevent
);
[JScript]
protected function OnCollectionChanged(
   ccevent : CollectionChangeEventArgs
);
```

Parameters

ccevent
   A **CollectionChangeEventArgs** containing the event data.

Requirements

Platforms: Windows 98, Windows NT 4.0, Windows Millennium Edition, Windows 2000, Windows XP Home Edition, Windows XP Professional, Windows Server 2003 family

GridTableStylesCollection.Remove Method

Removes the specified **DataGridTableStyle**.

```
[Visual Basic]
Public Sub Remove( _
   ByVal table As DataGridTableStyle _
)
[C#]
public void Remove(
   DataGridTableStyle table
);
[C++]
public: void Remove(
   DataGridTableStyle* table
);
[JScript]
public function Remove(
   table : DataGridTableStyle
);
```

Parameters

table

The **DataGridTableStyle** to remove.

Remarks

Use the **Contains** method to determine if a specific **DataGridTableStyle** object exists before using the **Remove** method.

Requirements

Platforms: Windows 98, Windows NT 4.0, Windows Millennium Edition, Windows 2000, Windows XP Home Edition, Windows XP Professional, Windows Server 2003 family, .NET Compact Framework - Windows CE .NET

GridTableStylesCollection.RemoveAt Method

Removes a **DataGridTableStyle** at the specified index.

```
[Visual Basic]
Public Sub RemoveAt( _
   ByVal index As Integer _
)
[C#]
public void RemoveAt(
   int index
);
[C++]
public: void RemoveAt(
   int index
);
[JScript]
public function RemoveAt(
   index : int
);
```

Parameters

index

The index of the **DataGridTableStyle** to remove.

Remarks

Use the **Contains** method to determine if a specific **DataGridTableStyle** object exists before using the **Remove** method.

Requirements

Platforms: Windows 98, Windows NT 4.0, Windows Millennium Edition, Windows 2000, Windows XP Home Edition, Windows XP Professional, Windows Server 2003 family, .NET Compact Framework - Windows CE .NET

GridTableStylesCollection.CollectionChanged Event

Occurs when the collection has changed.

```
[Visual Basic]
Public Event CollectionChanged As CollectionChangeEventHandler
[C#]
public event CollectionChangeEventHandler CollectionChanged;
[C++]
public: __event CollectionChangeEventHandler* CollectionChanged;
```

[JScript] In JScript, you can handle the events defined by a class, but you cannot define your own.

Event Data

The event handler receives an argument of type **CollectionChangeEventArgs** containing data related to this event. The following **CollectionChangeEventArgs** properties provide information specific to this event.

Property	Description
Action	Gets an action that specifies how the collection changed.
Element	Gets the instance of the collection with the change.

Remarks

For more information about handling events, see **Consuming Events**.

Example

See related example in the **System.Windows.Forms.GridTableStylesCollection** class topic.

Requirements

Platforms: Windows 98, Windows NT 4.0, Windows Millennium Edition, Windows 2000, Windows XP Home Edition, Windows XP Professional, Windows Server 2003 family

GroupBox Class

Represents a Windows group box.

System.Object
  System.MarshalByRefObject
    System.ComponentModel.Component
      System.Windows.Forms.Control
        System.Windows.Forms.GroupBox

[Visual Basic]
```
Public Class GroupBox
   Inherits Control
```
[C#]
```
public class GroupBox : Control
```
[C++]
```
public __gc class GroupBox : public Control
```
[JScript]
```
public class GroupBox extends Control
```

Thread Safety

Any public static (**Shared** in Visual Basic) members of this type are safe for multithreaded operations. Any instance members are not guaranteed to be thread safe.

Remarks

The **GroupBox** displays a frame around a group of controls with or without a caption. Use a **GroupBox** to logically group a collection of controls on a form. The group box is a container control that can be used to define groups of controls.

The typical use for a group box is to contain a logical group of **RadioButton** controls. If you have two group boxes, each containing several radio buttons, each group of buttons is mutually exclusive, setting one option value per group.

You can add controls to the **GroupBox** by using the **Add** method of the **Controls** property.

> **Note** Only controls contained within the **GroupBox** control can be selected or receive focus. The entire **GroupBox** itself cannot be selected or receive focus. For more information about how this control responds to the **Focus** and **Select** methods, see the following **Control** members: **CanFocus**, **CanSelect**, **Focused**, **ContainsFocus**, **Focus**, **Select**.

Example

[Visual Basic, C#, JScript] The following example instantiates and creates a **GroupBox** and two **RadioButton** controls. The radio buttons are added to the group box and the group box is added to the **Form**.

[Visual Basic]
```
Private Sub InitializeMyGroupBox()
   ' Create and initialize a GroupBox and two RadioButton controls.
   Dim groupBox1 As New GroupBox()
   Dim radioButton1 As New RadioButton()
   Dim radioButton2 As New RadioButton()

   ' Set the FlatStyle of the GroupBox.
   groupBox1.FlatStyle = FlatStyle.System

   ' Add the RadioButtons to the GroupBox.
   groupBox1.Controls.Add(radioButton1)
   groupBox1.Controls.Add(radioButton2)

   ' Add the GroupBox to the Form.
    Controls.Add(groupBox1)
End Sub 'InitializeMyGroupBox
```

[C#]
```
private void InitializeMyGroupBox()
{
   // Create and initialize a GroupBox and two RadioButton controls.
   GroupBox groupBox1 = new GroupBox();
   RadioButton radioButton1 = new RadioButton();
   RadioButton radioButton2 = new RadioButton();

   // Set the FlatStyle of the GroupBox.
   groupBox1.FlatStyle = FlatStyle.System;

   // Add the RadioButtons to the GroupBox.
   groupBox1.Controls.Add(radioButton1);
   groupBox1.Controls.Add(radioButton2);

   // Add the GroupBox to the Form.
   Controls.Add(groupBox1);
}
```

[JScript]
```
function InitializeMyGroupBox(){
   // Create and initialize a GroupBox and two RadioButton controls.
   var groupBox1 : GroupBox = new GroupBox()
   var radioButton1 : RadioButton = new RadioButton()
   var radioButton2 : RadioButton = new RadioButton()

   // Set the FlatStyle of the GroupBox.
   groupBox1.FlatStyle = FlatStyle.System

   // Add the RadioButtons to the GroupBox.
   groupBox1.Controls.Add(radioButton1)
   groupBox1.Controls.Add(radioButton2)

   // Add the GroupBox to the Form.
    Controls.Add(groupBox1)
}
```

Requirements

Namespace: System.Windows.Forms

Platforms: Windows 98, Windows NT 4.0, Windows Millennium Edition, Windows 2000, Windows XP Home Edition, Windows XP Professional, Windows Server 2003 family

Assembly: System.Windows.Forms (in System.Windows.Forms.dll)

GroupBox Constructor

Initializes a new instance of the **GroupBox** class.

[Visual Basic]
```
Public Sub New()
```
[C#]
```
public GroupBox();
```
[C++]
```
public: GroupBox();
```
[JScript]
```
public function GroupBox();
```

Remarks

By default, the **TabStop** property is set to **false** when a new **GroupBox** is created. The group box has an initial height of 100 pixels and width of 200 pixels.

Example

See related example in the **System.Windows.Forms.GroupBox** class topic.

Requirements

Platforms: Windows 98, Windows NT 4.0, Windows Millennium Edition, Windows 2000, Windows XP Home Edition, Windows XP Professional, Windows Server 2003 family

GroupBox.AllowDrop Property

This member overrides **Control.AllowDrop**.

```
[Visual Basic]
Overrides Public Property AllowDrop As Boolean
[C#]
public override bool AllowDrop {get; set;}
[C++]
public: __property bool get_AllowDrop();
public: __property void set_AllowDrop(bool);
[JScript]
public override function get AllowDrop() : Boolean;
public override function set AllowDrop(Boolean);
```

Requirements

Platforms: Windows 98, Windows NT 4.0, Windows Millennium Edition, Windows 2000, Windows XP Home Edition, Windows XP Professional, Windows Server 2003 family

GroupBox.CreateParams Property

This member overrides **Control.CreateParams**.

```
[Visual Basic]
Overrides Protected ReadOnly Property CreateParams As CreateParams
[C#]
protected override CreateParams CreateParams {get;}
[C++]
protected: __property CreateParams* get_CreateParams();
[JScript]
protected override function get CreateParams() : CreateParams;
```

Requirements

Platforms: Windows 98, Windows NT 4.0, Windows Millennium Edition, Windows 2000, Windows XP Home Edition, Windows XP Professional, Windows Server 2003 family

GroupBox.DefaultSize Property

This member overrides **Control.DefaultSize**.

```
[Visual Basic]
Overrides Protected ReadOnly Property DefaultSize As Size
[C#]
protected override Size DefaultSize {get;}
[C++]
protected: __property Size get_DefaultSize();
[JScript]
protected override function get DefaultSize() : Size;
```

Requirements

Platforms: Windows 98, Windows NT 4.0, Windows Millennium Edition, Windows 2000, Windows XP Home Edition, Windows XP Professional, Windows Server 2003 family

GroupBox.DisplayRectangle Property

This member overrides **Control.DisplayRectangle**.

```
[Visual Basic]
Overrides Public ReadOnly Property DisplayRectangle As Rectangle
[C#]
public override Rectangle DisplayRectangle {get;}
[C++]
public: __property Rectangle get_DisplayRectangle();
[JScript]
public override function get DisplayRectangle() : Rectangle;
```

Requirements

Platforms: Windows 98, Windows NT 4.0, Windows Millennium Edition, Windows 2000, Windows XP Home Edition, Windows XP Professional, Windows Server 2003 family

GroupBox.FlatStyle Property

Gets or sets the flat style appearance of the group box control.

```
[Visual Basic]
Public Property FlatStyle As FlatStyle
[C#]
public FlatStyle FlatStyle {get; set;}
[C++]
public: __property FlatStyle get_FlatStyle();
public: __property void set_FlatStyle(FlatStyle);
[JScript]
public function get FlatStyle() : FlatStyle;
public function set FlatStyle(FlatStyle);
```

Property Value

One of the **FlatStyle** values. The default value is **Standard**.

Exceptions

Exception Type	Condition
InvalidEnumArgument-Exception	The value assigned is not one of the **FlatStyle** values.

Example

See related example in the **System.Windows.Forms.GroupBox** class topic.

Requirements

Platforms: Windows 98, Windows NT 4.0, Windows Millennium Edition, Windows 2000, Windows XP Home Edition, Windows XP Professional, Windows Server 2003 family

GroupBox.TabStop Property

This member supports the .NET Framework infrastructure and is not intended to be used directly from your code.

```
[Visual Basic]
Public Shadows Property TabStop As Boolean
[C#]
public new bool TabStop {get; set;}
[C++]
public: __property bool get_TabStop();
public: __property void set_TabStop(bool);
```

[JScript]
```
public hide function get TabStop() : Boolean;
public hide function set TabStop(Boolean);
```

GroupBox.Text Property

This member overrides **Control.Text**.

[Visual Basic]
```
Overrides Public Property Text As String
```
[C#]
```
public override string Text {get; set;}
```
[C++]
```
public: __property String* get_Text();
public: __property void set_Text(String*);
```
[JScript]
```
public override function get Text() : String;
public override function set Text(String);
```

Requirements

Platforms: Windows 98, Windows NT 4.0, Windows Millennium Edition, Windows 2000, Windows XP Home Edition, Windows XP Professional, Windows Server 2003 family

GroupBox.OnFontChanged Method

This member overrides **Control.OnFontChanged**.

[Visual Basic]
```
Overrides Protected Sub OnFontChanged( _
   ByVal e As EventArgs _
)
```
[C#]
```
protected override void OnFontChanged(
   EventArgs e
);
```
[C++]
```
protected: void OnFontChanged(
   EventArgs* e
);
```
[JScript]
```
protected override function OnFontChanged(
   e : EventArgs
);
```

Requirements

Platforms: Windows 98, Windows NT 4.0, Windows Millennium Edition, Windows 2000, Windows XP Home Edition, Windows XP Professional, Windows Server 2003 family

GroupBox.OnPaint Method

This member overrides **Control.OnPaint**.

[Visual Basic]
```
Overrides Protected Sub OnPaint( _
   ByVal e As PaintEventArgs _
)
```
[C#]
```
protected override void OnPaint(
   PaintEventArgs e
);
```
[C++]
```
protected: void OnPaint(
   PaintEventArgs* e
);
```
[JScript]
```
protected override function OnPaint(
   e : PaintEventArgs
);
```

Requirements

Platforms: Windows 98, Windows NT 4.0, Windows Millennium Edition, Windows 2000, Windows XP Home Edition, Windows XP Professional, Windows Server 2003 family

GroupBox.ProcessMnemonic Method

This member overrides **Control.ProcessMnemonic**.

[Visual Basic]
```
Overrides Protected Function ProcessMnemonic( _
   ByVal charCode As Char _
) As Boolean
```
[C#]
```
protected override bool ProcessMnemonic(
   char charCode
);
```
[C++]
```
protected: bool ProcessMnemonic(
   __wchar_t charCode
);
```
[JScript]
```
protected override function ProcessMnemonic(
   charCode : Char
) : Boolean;
```

Requirements

Platforms: Windows 98, Windows NT 4.0, Windows Millennium Edition, Windows 2000, Windows XP Home Edition, Windows XP Professional, Windows Server 2003 family

GroupBox.ToString Method

This member overrides **Object.ToString**.

[Visual Basic]
```
Overrides Public Function ToString() As String
```
[C#]
```
public override string ToString();
```
[C++]
```
public: String* ToString();
```
[JScript]
```
public override function ToString() : String;
```

Requirements

Platforms: Windows 98, Windows NT 4.0, Windows Millennium Edition, Windows 2000, Windows XP Home Edition, Windows XP Professional, Windows Server 2003 family

GroupBox.WndProc Method

This member overrides **Control.WndProc**.

[Visual Basic]
```
Overrides Protected Sub WndProc( _
   ByRef m As Message _
)
```
[C#]
```
protected override void WndProc(
   ref Message m
);
```
[C++]
```
protected: void WndProc(
   Message* m
);
```
[JScript]
```
protected override function WndProc(
   m : Message
);
```

Requirements

Platforms: Windows 98, Windows NT 4.0, Windows Millennium Edition, Windows 2000, Windows XP Home Edition, Windows XP Professional, Windows Server 2003 family

GroupBox.Click Event

This member supports the .NET Framework infrastructure and is not intended to be used directly from your code.

[Visual Basic]
```
Public Shadows Event Click As EventHandler
```
[C#]
```
public new event EventHandler Click;
```
[C++]
```
public: __event EventHandler* Click;
```

[JScript] In JScript, you can handle the events defined by a class, but you cannot define your own.

GroupBox.DoubleClick Event

This member supports the .NET Framework infrastructure and is not intended to be used directly from your code.

[Visual Basic]
```
Public Shadows Event DoubleClick As EventHandler
```
[C#]
```
public new event EventHandler DoubleClick;
```
[C++]
```
public: __event EventHandler* DoubleClick;
```

[JScript] In JScript, you can handle the events defined by a class, but you cannot define your own.

GroupBox.KeyDown Event

This member supports the .NET Framework infrastructure and is not intended to be used directly from your code.

[Visual Basic]
```
Public Shadows Event KeyDown As KeyEventHandler
```
[C#]
```
public new event KeyEventHandler KeyDown;
```
[C++]
```
public: __event KeyEventHandler* KeyDown;
```

[JScript] In JScript, you can handle the events defined by a class, but you cannot define your own.

GroupBox.KeyPress Event

This member supports the .NET Framework infrastructure and is not intended to be used directly from your code.

[Visual Basic]
```
Public Shadows Event KeyPress As KeyPressEventHandler
```
[C#]
```
public new event KeyPressEventHandler KeyPress;
```
[C++]
```
public: __event KeyPressEventHandler* KeyPress;
```

[JScript] In JScript, you can handle the events defined by a class, but you cannot define your own.

GroupBox.KeyUp Event

This member supports the .NET Framework infrastructure and is not intended to be used directly from your code.

[Visual Basic]
```
Public Shadows Event KeyUp As KeyEventHandler
```
[C#]
```
public new event KeyEventHandler KeyUp;
```
[C++]
```
public: __event KeyEventHandler* KeyUp;
```

[JScript] In JScript, you can handle the events defined by a class, but you cannot define your own.

GroupBox.MouseDown Event

This member supports the .NET Framework infrastructure and is not intended to be used directly from your code.

[Visual Basic]
```
Public Shadows Event MouseDown As MouseEventHandler
```
[C#]
```
public new event MouseEventHandler MouseDown;
```
[C++]
```
public: __event MouseEventHandler* MouseDown;
```

[JScript] In JScript, you can handle the events defined by a class, but you cannot define your own.

GroupBox.MouseEnter Event

This member supports the .NET Framework infrastructure and is not intended to be used directly from your code.

[Visual Basic]
```
Public Shadows Event MouseEnter As EventHandler
```
[C#]
```
public new event EventHandler MouseEnter;
```
[C++]
```
public: __event EventHandler* MouseEnter;
```

[JScript] In JScript, you can handle the events defined by a class, but you cannot define your own.

GroupBox.MouseLeave Event

This member supports the .NET Framework infrastructure and is not intended to be used directly from your code.

[Visual Basic]
```
Public Shadows Event MouseLeave As EventHandler
```
[C#]
```
public new event EventHandler MouseLeave;
```
[C++]
```
public: __event EventHandler* MouseLeave;
```

[JScript] In JScript, you can handle the events defined by a class, but you cannot define your own.

GroupBox.MouseMove Event

This member supports the .NET Framework infrastructure and is not intended to be used directly from your code.

[Visual Basic]
```
Public Shadows Event MouseMove As MouseEventHandler
```
[C#]
```
public new event MouseEventHandler MouseMove;
```
[C++]
```
public: __event MouseEventHandler* MouseMove;
```

[JScript] In JScript, you can handle the events defined by a class, but you cannot define your own.

GroupBox.MouseUp Event

This member supports the .NET Framework infrastructure and is not intended to be used directly from your code.

[Visual Basic]
```
Public Shadows Event MouseUp As MouseEventHandler
```
[C#]
```
public new event MouseEventHandler MouseUp;
```
[C++]
```
public: __event MouseEventHandler* MouseUp;
```

[JScript] In JScript, you can handle the events defined by a class, but you cannot define your own.

GroupBox.TabStopChanged Event

This member supports the .NET Framework infrastructure and is not intended to be used directly from your code.

[Visual Basic]
```
Public Shadows Event TabStopChanged As EventHandler
```
[C#]
```
public new event EventHandler TabStopChanged;
```
[C++]
```
public: __event EventHandler* TabStopChanged;
```

[JScript] In JScript, you can handle the events defined by a class, but you cannot define your own.

Help Class

Encapsulates the HTML Help 1.0 engine.

System.Object
  System.Windows.Forms.Help

[Visual Basic]
```
Public Class Help
```
[C#]
```
public class Help
```
[C++]
```
public __gc class Help
```
[JScript]
```
public class Help
```

Thread Safety

Any public static (**Shared** in Visual Basic) members of this type are safe for multithreaded operations. Any instance members are not guaranteed to be thread safe.

Remarks

You cannot create a new instance of the **Help** class. To provide Help to an application, call the static **ShowHelp** and **ShowHelpIndex** methods.

You can use the **Help** object to show compiled Help files (.chm) or HTML files in the HTML Help format. Compiled Help files provide table of contents, index, search, and keyword links in pages. Shortcuts work only in compiled Help files.

You can generate HTML Help 1.x files with the HTML Help Workshop. For more information on HTML Help, see the "HTML Help Workshop" or the other "HTML Help" topics in MSDN.

Example

[Visual Basic, C#, C++] The following example displays a form with three buttons that can be used to interact with the `mspaint.chm` Help file. The **Show Help Index** button displays the **Index** tab for the Help file. The **Show Help** button displays content in the Help file based on the value selected in the **Help Navigator** list. The **Show Keyword** button displays content in the Help file based on the keyword specified in the **Keyword** text box.

[Visual Basic, C#, C++] For example, to show the Ovals Help page by the index value, select the **HelpNavigator.KeywordIndex** value in the **Help Navigator** drop-down list, type "ovals" (without the quotation marks) in the **Parameter** text box, and click the **Show Help** button. To show the "To paint with a brush" Help topic by the keyword, type "mspaint.chm::/paint_brush.htm" (without the quotation marks) in the **Keyword** text box and click the **Show Keyword** button.

[Visual Basic, C#, C++] The example uses the **ShowHelp** method to display the different Help tabs and Help topics, and the **ShowHelp-Index** method to display the Help index.

[Visual Basic]
```
Imports System
Imports System.Drawing
Imports System.ComponentModel
Imports System.Windows.Forms

Public Class Form1
    Inherits System.Windows.Forms.Form
    Private helpfile As String = "mspaint.chm"
    Private WithEvents showIndex As System.Windows.Forms.Button
    Private WithEvents showHelp As System.Windows.Forms.Button
    Private WithEvents label1 As System.Windows.Forms.Label
    Private WithEvents navigatorCombo As System.Windows.Forms.ComboBox
    Private WithEvents showKeyword As System.Windows.Forms.Button
    Private WithEvents keyword As System.Windows.Forms.TextBox
    Private WithEvents label2 As System.Windows.Forms.Label
    Private WithEvents label3 As System.Windows.Forms.Label
    Private WithEvents parameterTextBox As System.Windows.Forms.TextBox

    <STAThread()> _
    Shared Sub Main()
        Application.Run(New Form1)
    End Sub 'Main

    Public Sub New()
        Me.showIndex = New System.Windows.Forms.Button
        Me.showHelp = New System.Windows.Forms.Button
        Me.navigatorCombo = New System.Windows.Forms.ComboBox
        Me.label1 = New System.Windows.Forms.Label
        Me.showKeyword = New System.Windows.Forms.Button
        Me.keyword = New System.Windows.Forms.TextBox
        Me.label2 = New System.Windows.Forms.Label
        Me.label3 = New System.Windows.Forms.Label
        Me.parameterTextBox = New System.Windows.Forms.TextBox

        ' Help Navigator Label
        Me.label1.Location = New System.Drawing.Point(112, 64)
        Me.label1.Size = New System.Drawing.Size(168, 16)
        Me.label1.Text = "Help Navigator:"

        ' Keyword Label
        Me.label2.Location = New System.Drawing.Point(120, 184)
        Me.label2.Size = New System.Drawing.Size(100, 16)
        Me.label2.Text = "Keyword:"

        ' Parameter Label
        Me.label3.Location = New System.Drawing.Point(112, 120)
        Me.label3.Size = New System.Drawing.Size(168, 16)
        Me.label3.Text = "Parameter:"

        ' Show Index Button
        Me.showIndex.Location = New System.Drawing.Point(16, 16)
        Me.showIndex.Size = New System.Drawing.Size(264, 32)
        Me.showIndex.TabIndex = 0
        Me.showIndex.Text = "Show Help Index"

        ' Show Help Button
        Me.showHelp.Location = New System.Drawing.Point(16, 80)
        Me.showHelp.Size = New System.Drawing.Size(80, 80)
        Me.showHelp.TabIndex = 1
        Me.showHelp.Text = "Show Help"

        ' Show Keyword Button
        Me.showKeyword.Location = New System.Drawing.Point(16, 192)
        Me.showKeyword.Size = New System.Drawing.Size(88, 32)
        Me.showKeyword.TabIndex = 4
        Me.showKeyword.Text = "Show Keyword"

        ' Help Navigator Combo
        '
        Me.navigatorCombo.DropDownStyle = ↵
System.Windows.Forms.ComboBoxStyle.DropDownList
        Me.navigatorCombo.Location = New System.Drawing.Point(112, 80)
        Me.navigatorCombo.Size = New System.Drawing.Size(168, 21)
        Me.navigatorCombo.TabIndex = 2

        ' Keyword TextBox
        Me.keyword.Location = New System.Drawing.Point(120, 200)
        Me.keyword.Size = New System.Drawing.Size(160, 20)
        Me.keyword.TabIndex = 5
        Me.keyword.Text = ""
        '
        ' Parameter TextBox
        '
        Me.parameterTextBox.Location = New ↵
System.Drawing.Point(112, 136)
        Me.parameterTextBox.Size = New System.Drawing.Size(168, 20)
```

```
        Me.parameterTextBox.TabIndex = 8
        Me.parameterTextBox.Text = ""

        ' Set up how the form should be displayed and add the         ↵
controls to the form.
        Me.ClientSize = New System.Drawing.Size(292, 266)
        Me.Controls.AddRange(New System.Windows.Forms.Control         ↵
 () {Me.parameterTextBox, _
                                Me.label3, Me.label2,                 ↵
 Me.keyword, Me.showKeyword, _
                                Me.label1, Me.navigatorCombo,         ↵
Me.showHelp, Me.showIndex})
        Me.FormBorderStyle =
System.Windows.Forms.FormBorderStyle.FixedDialog
        Me.Text = "Help App"

        ' Load the various values of the HelpNavigator enumeration
        ' into the combo box.
        Dim converter As TypeConverter
        converter = TypeDescriptor.GetConverter(GetType(HelpNavigator))

        Dim value As Object
        For Each value In converter.GetStandardValues()
            navigatorCombo.Items.Add(value)
        Next value
    End Sub 'New

    Private Sub showIndex_Click(ByVal sender As Object,               ↵
 ByVal e As System.EventArgs) Handles showIndex.Click
        ' Display the index for the Help file.
        Help.ShowHelpIndex(Me, helpfile)
    End Sub 'showIndex_Click
    Private Sub showHelp_Click(ByVal sender As Object,                ↵
 ByVal e As System.EventArgs) Handles showHelp.Click
        ' Display Help using the Help navigator enumeration
        ' that is selected in the combo box. Some enumeration
        ' values make use of an extra parameter, which can
        ' be passed in through the Parameter text box.
        Dim navigator As HelpNavigator = HelpNavigator.TableOfContents
        If Not (navigatorCombo.SelectedItem Is Nothing) Then
            navigator = CType(navigatorCombo.SelectedItem,            ↵
HelpNavigator)
        End If
        Help.ShowHelp(Me, helpfile, navigator, parameterTextBox.Text)
    End Sub 'showHelp_Click
    Private Sub showKeyword_Click(ByVal sender As Object,             ↵
ByVal e As System.EventArgs) Handles showKeyword.Click
        ' Display Help using the provided keyword.
        Help.ShowHelp(Me, helpfile, keyword.Text)
    End Sub 'showKeyword_Click
End Class 'Form1
```

[C#]

```
using System;
using System.Drawing;
using System.ComponentModel;
using System.Windows.Forms;

public class Form1 : System.Windows.Forms.Form
{
    private const string helpfile = "mspaint.chm";
    private System.Windows.Forms.Button showIndex;
    private System.Windows.Forms.Button showHelp;
    private System.Windows.Forms.Label label1;
    private System.Windows.Forms.ComboBox navigatorCombo;
    private System.Windows.Forms.Button showKeyword;
    private System.Windows.Forms.TextBox keyword;
    private System.Windows.Forms.Label label2;
    private System.Windows.Forms.Label label3;
    private System.Windows.Forms.TextBox parameterTextBox;

    [STAThread]
    static void Main()
    {
        Application.Run(new Form1());
    }

    public Form1()
    {
        this.showIndex = new System.Windows.Forms.Button();
        this.showHelp = new System.Windows.Forms.Button();
        this.navigatorCombo = new System.Windows.Forms.ComboBox();
        this.label1 = new System.Windows.Forms.Label();
        this.showKeyword = new System.Windows.Forms.Button();
        this.keyword = new System.Windows.Forms.TextBox();
        this.label2 = new System.Windows.Forms.Label();
        this.label3 = new System.Windows.Forms.Label();
        this.parameterTextBox = new System.Windows.Forms.TextBox();

        // Help Navigator Label
        this.label1.Location = new System.Drawing.Point(112, 64);
        this.label1.Size = new System.Drawing.Size(168, 16);
        this.label1.Text = "Help Navigator:";

        // Keyword Label
        this.label2.Location = new System.Drawing.Point(120, 184);
        this.label2.Size = new System.Drawing.Size(100, 16);
        this.label2.Text = "Keyword:";

        // Parameter Label
        this.label3.Location = new System.Drawing.Point(112, 120);
        this.label3.Size = new System.Drawing.Size(168, 16);
        this.label3.Text = "Parameter:";

        // Show Index Button
        this.showIndex.Location = new System.Drawing.Point(16, 16);
        this.showIndex.Size = new System.Drawing.Size(264, 32);
        this.showIndex.TabIndex = 0;
        this.showIndex.Text = "Show Help Index";
        this.showIndex.Click += new                                   ↵
System.EventHandler(this.showIndex_Click);

        // Show Help Button
        this.showHelp.Location = new System.Drawing.Point(16, 80);
        this.showHelp.Size = new System.Drawing.Size(80, 80);
        this.showHelp.TabIndex = 1;
        this.showHelp.Text = "Show Help";
        this.showHelp.Click += new
System.EventHandler(this.showHelp_Click);

        // Show Keyword Button
        this.showKeyword.Location = new System.Drawing.Point(16, 192);
        this.showKeyword.Size = new System.Drawing.Size(88, 32);
        this.showKeyword.TabIndex = 4;
        this.showKeyword.Text = "Show Keyword";
        this.showKeyword.Click += new                                 ↵
System.EventHandler(this.showKeyword_Click);

        // Help Navigator ComboBox
        this.navigatorCombo.DropDownStyle =                           ↵
System.Windows.Forms.ComboBoxStyle.DropDownList;
        this.navigatorCombo.Location = new                            ↵
System.Drawing.Point(112, 80);
        this.navigatorCombo.Size = new System.Drawing.Size(168, 21);
        this.navigatorCombo.TabIndex = 2;

        // Keyword TextBox
        this.keyword.Location = new System.Drawing.Point(120, 200);
        this.keyword.Size = new System.Drawing.Size(160, 20);
        this.keyword.TabIndex = 5;
        this.keyword.Text = "";

        // Parameter TextBox
        this.parameterTextBox.Location = new                          ↵
System.Drawing.Point(112, 136);
        this.parameterTextBox.Size = new System.Drawing.Size(168, 20);
        this.parameterTextBox.TabIndex = 8;
        this.parameterTextBox.Text = "";
```

```
        // Set up how the form should be displayed and add the         ↵
controls to the form.
        this.ClientSize = new System.Drawing.Size(292, 266);
        this.Controls.AddRange(new System.Windows.Forms.Control[] {
                                        this.parameterTextBox,         ↵
this.label3,
                                        this.label2, this.keyword,
                                        this.showKeyword, this.label1,
                                        this.navigatorCombo,           ↵
this.showHelp,
                                        this.showIndex});
        this.FormBorderStyle =                                         ↵
System.Windows.Forms.FormBorderStyle.FixedDialog;
        this.Text = "Help App";

        // Load the various values of the HelpNavigator enumeration
        // into the combo box.
        TypeConverter converter;
        converter = TypeDescriptor.GetConverter(typeof(HelpNavigator));
        foreach(object value in converter.GetStandardValues())
        {
            navigatorCombo.Items.Add(value);
        }
    }

    private void showIndex_Click(object sender, System.EventArgs e)
    {
        // Display the index for the help file.
        Help.ShowHelpIndex(this, helpfile);
    }
    private void showHelp_Click(object sender, System.EventArgs e)
    {
        // Display Help using the Help navigator enumeration
        // that is selected in the combo box. Some enumeration
        // values make use of an extra parameter, which can
        // be passed in through the Parameter text box.
        HelpNavigator navigator = HelpNavigator.TableOfContents;
        if (navigatorCombo.SelectedItem != null)
        {
            navigator = (HelpNavigator)navigatorCombo.SelectedItem;
        }
        Help.ShowHelp(this, helpfile, navigator,                       ↵
parameterTextBox.Text);
    }
    private void showKeyword_Click(object sender, System.EventArgs e)
    {
        // Display help using the provided keyword.
        Help.ShowHelp(this, helpfile, keyword.Text);
    }
}
```

[C++]

```
#using <mscorlib.dll>
#using <System.dll>
#using <System.Drawing.dll>
#using <System.Windows.Forms.dll>

using namespace System;
using namespace System::Drawing;
using namespace System::ComponentModel;
using namespace System::Windows::Forms;

public __gc class Form1 : public System::Windows::Forms::Form {
private:
    const String* helpfile;
    System::Windows::Forms::Button*  showIndex;
    System::Windows::Forms::Button*  showHelp;
    System::Windows::Forms::Label*  label1;
    System::Windows::Forms::ComboBox*  navigatorCombo;
    System::Windows::Forms::Button*  showKeyword;
    System::Windows::Forms::TextBox*  keyword;
    System::Windows::Forms::Label*  label2;
    System::Windows::Forms::Label*  label3;
    System::Windows::Forms::TextBox*  parameterTextBox;
public:
    Form1() {

        helpfile = S"mspaint.chm";

        this->showIndex = new System::Windows::Forms::Button();
        this->showHelp = new System::Windows::Forms::Button();
        this->navigatorCombo = new System::Windows::Forms::ComboBox();
        this->label1 = new System::Windows::Forms::Label();
        this->showKeyword = new System::Windows::Forms::Button();
        this->keyword = new System::Windows::Forms::TextBox();
        this->label2 = new System::Windows::Forms::Label();
        this->label3 = new System::Windows::Forms::Label();
        this->parameterTextBox = new System::Windows::Forms::TextBox();

        // Help Navigator Label
        this->label1->Location = System::Drawing::Point(112, 64);
        this->label1->Size = System::Drawing::Size(168, 16);
        this->label1->Text = S"Help Navigator:";

        // Keyword Label
        this->label2->Location = System::Drawing::Point(120, 184);
        this->label2->Size = System::Drawing::Size(100, 16);
        this->label2->Text = S"Keyword:";

        // Parameter Label
        this->label3->Location = System::Drawing::Point(112, 120);
        this->label3->Size = System::Drawing::Size(168, 16);
        this->label3->Text = S"Parameter:";

        // Show Index Button
        this->showIndex->Location = System::Drawing::Point(16, 16);
        this->showIndex->Size = System::Drawing::Size(264, 32);
        this->showIndex->TabIndex = 0;
        this->showIndex->Text = S"Show Help Index";
        this->showIndex->Click +=
            new System::EventHandler(this, showIndex_Click);

        // Show Help Button
        this->showHelp->Location = System::Drawing::Point(16, 80);
        this->showHelp->Size = System::Drawing::Size(80, 80);
        this->showHelp->TabIndex = 1;
        this->showHelp->Text = S"Show Help";
        this->showHelp->Click +=
            new System::EventHandler(this, showHelp_Click);

        // Show Keyword Button
        this->showKeyword->Location = System::Drawing::Point(16, 192);
        this->showKeyword->Size = System::Drawing::Size(88, 32);
        this->showKeyword->TabIndex = 4;
        this->showKeyword->Text = S"Show Keyword";
        this->showKeyword->Click +=
            new System::EventHandler(this, showKeyword_Click);

        // Help Navigator ComboBox
        this->navigatorCombo->DropDownStyle =
            System::Windows::Forms::ComboBoxStyle::DropDownList;
        this->navigatorCombo->Location =                               ↵
System::Drawing::Point(112, 80);
        this->navigatorCombo->Size = System::Drawing::Size(168, 21);
        this->navigatorCombo->TabIndex = 2;

        // Keyword TextBox
        this->keyword->Location = System::Drawing::Point(120, 200);
        this->keyword->Size = System::Drawing::Size(160, 20);
        this->keyword->TabIndex = 5;
        this->keyword->Text = S"";

        // Parameter TextBox
        this->parameterTextBox->Location =                             ↵
System::Drawing::Point(112, 136);
        this->parameterTextBox->Size = System::Drawing::Size(168, 20);
        this->parameterTextBox->TabIndex = 8;
        this->parameterTextBox->Text = S"";
```

```
        // Set up how the form should be displayed and add ↵
the controls to the form.
        this->ClientSize = System::Drawing::Size(292, 266);
        System::Windows::Forms::Control* formControls[] = {
            this->parameterTextBox, this->label3,
            this->label2, this->keyword,
            this->showKeyword, this->label1,
            this->navigatorCombo, this->showHelp,
            this->showIndex};
        this->Controls->AddRange(formControls);
        this->FormBorderStyle =
            System::Windows::Forms::FormBorderStyle::FixedDialog;
        this->Text = S"Help App";

        // Load the various values of the HelpNavigator enumeration
        // into the combo box.
        TypeConverter* converter;
        converter =
TypeDescriptor::GetConverter(__typeof(HelpNavigator));
        System::Collections::IEnumerator* myEnum =
            converter->GetStandardValues()->GetEnumerator();
        while (myEnum->MoveNext()) {
            Object* value = __try_cast<Object*>(myEnum->Current);
            navigatorCombo->Items->Add(value);
        }
    }

private:
    void showIndex_Click(Object* /*sender*/, System::EventArgs* ↵
/*e*/) {
        // Display the index for the help file.
        Help::ShowHelpIndex(this, const_cast<String*>(helpfile));
    }
private:
    void showHelp_Click(Object* /*sender*/, System::EventArgs* /*e*/) {
        // Display Help using the Help navigator enumeration
        // that is selected in the combo box. Some enumeration
        // values make use of an extra parameter, which can
        // be passed in through the Parameter text box.
        HelpNavigator navigator = HelpNavigator::TableOfContents;
        if (navigatorCombo->SelectedItem != 0) {
            navigator = *__try_cast<__box HelpNavigator*>(
                navigatorCombo->SelectedItem);
        }
        Help::ShowHelp(this, const_cast<String*>(helpfile), navigator,
            parameterTextBox->Text);
    }
private:
    void showKeyword_Click(Object* /*sender*/, ↵
System::EventArgs* /*e*/) {
        // Display help using the provided keyword.
        Help::ShowHelp(this, const_cast<String*>(helpfile), ↵
keyword->Text);
    }
};

[STAThread]
int main() {
    Application::Run(new Form1());
}
```

Requirements

Namespace: System.Windows.Forms

Platforms: Windows 98, Windows NT 4.0, Windows Millennium Edition, Windows 2000, Windows XP Home Edition, Windows XP Professional, Windows Server 2003 family

Assembly: System.Windows.Forms (in System.Windows.Forms.dll)

Help.ShowHelp Method

Displays the contents of a Help file.

Overload List

Displays the contents of the Help file at the specified URL.

[Visual Basic] **Overloads Public Shared Sub ShowHelp(Control, String)**

[C#] **public static void ShowHelp(Control, string);**

[C++] **public: static void ShowHelp(Control*, String*);**

[JScript] **public static function ShowHelp(Control, String);**

Displays the contents of the Help file found at the specified URL for a specific topic.

[Visual Basic] **Overloads Public Shared Sub ShowHelp(Control, String, HelpNavigator)**

[C#] **public static void ShowHelp(Control, string, HelpNavigator);**

[C++] **public: static void ShowHelp(Control*, String*, HelpNavigator);**

[JScript] **public static function ShowHelp(Control, String, HelpNavigator);**

Displays the contents of the Help file found at the specified URL for a specific keyword.

[Visual Basic] **Overloads Public Shared Sub ShowHelp(Control, String, String)**

[C#] **public static void ShowHelp(Control, string, string);**

[C++] **public: static void ShowHelp(Control*, String*, String*);**

[JScript] **public static function ShowHelp(Control, String, String);**

Displays the contents of the Help file located at the URL supplied by the user.

[Visual Basic] **Overloads Public Shared Sub ShowHelp(Control, String, HelpNavigator, Object)**

[C#] **public static void ShowHelp(Control, string, HelpNavigator, object);**

[C++] **public: static void ShowHelp(Control*, String*, HelpNavigator, Object*);**

[JScript] **public static function ShowHelp(Control, String, HelpNavigator, Object);**

Example

See related example in the **System.Windows.Forms.Help** class topic.

Help.ShowHelp Method (Control, String)

Displays the contents of the Help file at the specified URL.

[Visual Basic]
```
Overloads Public Shared Sub ShowHelp( _
   ByVal parent As Control, _
   ByVal url As String _
)
```
[C#]
```
public static void ShowHelp(
   Control parent,
   string url
);
```

```
[C++]
public: static void ShowHelp(
   Control* parent,
   String* url
);
[JScript]
public static function ShowHelp(
   parent : Control,
   url : String
);
```

Parameters

parent

A **Control** that identifies the parent of the Help dialog box.

url

The path and name of the Help file.

Remarks

The *url* parameter can be of the form C:\path\sample.chm or/folder/file.htm.

Requirements

Platforms: Windows 98, Windows NT 4.0, Windows Millennium Edition, Windows 2000, Windows XP Home Edition, Windows XP Professional, Windows Server 2003 family

.NET Framework Security:

- **WebPermission** to access a HTML help file through a HTTP request. Associated enumeration: **NetworkAccess.Connect**
- **SecurityPermission** to access a HTML help file not served from a HTTP Server. Associated enumeration: **UnmanagedCode**

Help.ShowHelp Method (Control, String, HelpNavigator)

Displays the contents of the Help file found at the specified URL for a specific topic.

```
[Visual Basic]
Overloads Public Shared Sub ShowHelp( _
   ByVal parent As Control, _
   ByVal url As String, _
   ByVal navigator As HelpNavigator _
)
[C#]
public static void ShowHelp(
   Control parent,
   string url,
   HelpNavigator navigator
);
[C++]
public: static void ShowHelp(
   Control* parent,
   String* url,
   HelpNavigator navigator
);
[JScript]
public static function ShowHelp(
   parent : Control,
   url : String,
   navigator : HelpNavigator
);
```

Parameters

parent

A **Control** that identifies the parent of the Help dialog box.

url

The path and name of the Help file.

navigator

One of the **HelpNavigator** values.

Remarks

The *url* parameter can be of the form C:\path\sample.chm or/folder/file.htm.Compiled Help files provide table of contents, index, search, and keyword links in pages. You can use the following values for *navigator*: **TableOfContents**, **Find**, **Index**, or **Topic**.

Requirements

Platforms: Windows 98, Windows NT 4.0, Windows Millennium Edition, Windows 2000, Windows XP Home Edition, Windows XP Professional, Windows Server 2003 family

.NET Framework Security:

- **WebPermission** to access a HTML help file through a HTTP request. Associated enumeration: **NetworkAccess.Connect**
- **SecurityPermission** to access a HTML help file not served from a HTTP Server. Associated enumeration: **UnmanagedCode**

Help.ShowHelp Method (Control, String, String)

Displays the contents of the Help file found at the specified URL for a specific keyword.

```
[Visual Basic]
Overloads Public Shared Sub ShowHelp( _
   ByVal parent As Control, _
   ByVal url As String, _
   ByVal keyword As String _
)
[C#]
public static void ShowHelp(
   Control parent,
   string url,
   string keyword
);
[C++]
public: static void ShowHelp(
   Control* parent,
   String* url,
   String* keyword
);
[JScript]
public static function ShowHelp(
   parent : Control,
   url : String,
   keyword : String
);
```

Parameters

parent

A **Control** that identifies the parent of the Help dialog box.

url

The path and name of the Help file.

keyword

The keyword to display Help for.

Remarks

The *url* parameter can be of the form C:\path\sample.chm or/folder/file.htm.

If you provide the keyword a null reference (**Nothing** in Visual Basic), the table of contents for the Help file will be displayed.

Example

See related example in the **System.Windows.Forms.Help** class topic.

Requirements

Platforms: Windows 98, Windows NT 4.0, Windows Millennium Edition, Windows 2000, Windows XP Home Edition, Windows XP Professional, Windows Server 2003 family

.NET Framework Security:

- **WebPermission** to access a HTML help file through a HTTP request. Associated enumeration: **NetworkAccess.Connect**
- **SecurityPermission** to access a HTML help file not served from a HTTP Server. Associated enumeration: **UnmanagedCode**

Help.ShowHelp Method (Control, String, HelpNavigator, Object)

Displays the contents of the Help file located at the URL supplied by the user.

[Visual Basic]
```
Overloads Public Shared Sub ShowHelp( _
   ByVal parent As Control, _
   ByVal url As String, _
   ByVal command As HelpNavigator, _
   ByVal param As Object _
)
```
[C#]
```
public static void ShowHelp(
   Control parent,
   string url,
   HelpNavigator command,
   object param
);
```
[C++]
```
public: static void ShowHelp(
   Control* parent,
   String* url,
   HelpNavigator command,
   Object* param
);
```
[JScript]
```
public static function ShowHelp(
   parent : Control,
   url : String,
   command : HelpNavigator,
   param : Object
);
```

Parameters

parent
: A **Control** that identifies the parent of the Help dialog box.

url
: The path and name of the Help file.

command
: One of the **HelpNavigator** values.

param
: The numeric id of the topic to display.

Remarks

Compiled help files provide table of contents, index, search, and keyword links in pages. You can use the following values for *command*: **TableOfContents**, **Find**, **Index**, or **Topic**.

You can use *param* to provide further refinement of the **Topic** command. If the value specified in the *command* parameter is **TableOfContents**, **Index**, or **Find**, this value should be a null reference (**Nothing** in Visual Basic). If the *command* parameter references **Topic**, this value should reference an object that contains the numeric value of the topic to display.

The *url* parameter can be of the form C:\path\sample.chm or/folder/file.htm.

Example

See related example in the **System.Windows.Forms.Help** class topic.

Requirements

Platforms: Windows 98, Windows NT 4.0, Windows Millennium Edition, Windows 2000, Windows XP Home Edition, Windows XP Professional, Windows Server 2003 family

.NET Framework Security:

- **WebPermission** to access a HTML help file through a HTTP request. Associated enumeration: **NetworkAccess.Connect**
- **SecurityPermission** to access a HTML help file not served from a HTTP Server. Associated enumeration: **UnmanagedCode**

Help.ShowHelpIndex Method

Displays the index of the specified Help file.

[Visual Basic]
```
Public Shared Sub ShowHelpIndex( _
   ByVal parent As Control, _
   ByVal url As String _
)
```
[C#]
```
public static void ShowHelpIndex(
   Control parent,
   string url
);
```
[C++]
```
public: static void ShowHelpIndex(
   Control* parent,
   String* url
);
```
[JScript]
```
public static function ShowHelpIndex(
   parent : Control,
   url : String
);
```

Parameters

parent

A **Control** that identifies the parent of the Help dialog box.

url

The path and name of the Help file.

Remarks

The *url* parameter can be of the form C:\path\sample.chm or/folder/file.htm.

Example

See related example in the **System.Windows.Forms.Help** class topic.

Requirements

Platforms: Windows 98, Windows NT 4.0, Windows Millennium Edition, Windows 2000, Windows XP Home Edition, Windows XP Professional, Windows Server 2003 family

.NET Framework Security:

- **WebPermission** to access a HTML help file through a HTTP request. Associated enumeration: **NetworkAccess.Connect**
- **SecurityPermission** to access a HTML help file not served from a HTTP Server. Associated enumeration: **UnmanagedCode**

Help.ShowPopup Method

This member supports the .NET Framework infrastructure and is not intended to be used directly from your code.

```
[Visual Basic]
Public Shared Sub ShowPopup( _
   ByVal parent As Control, _
   ByVal caption As String, _
   ByVal location As Point _
)
[C#]
public static void ShowPopup(
   Control parent,
   string caption,
   Point location
);
[C++]
public: static void ShowPopup(
   Control* parent,
   String* caption,
   Point location
);
[JScript]
public static function ShowPopup(
   parent : Control,
   caption : String,
   location : Point
);
```

HelpEventArgs Class

Provides data for the **HelpRequested** event.

System.Object
  System.EventArgs
    System.Windows.Forms.HelpEventArgs

```
[Visual Basic]
<ComVisible(True)>
Public Class HelpEventArgs
   Inherits EventArgs
[C#]
[ComVisible(true)]
public class HelpEventArgs : EventArgs
[C++]
[ComVisible(true)]
public __gc class HelpEventArgs : public EventArgs
[JScript]
public
   ComVisible(true)
class HelpEventArgs extends EventArgs
```

Thread Safety

Any public static (**Shared** in Visual Basic) members of this type are safe for multithreaded operations. Any instance members are not guaranteed to be thread safe.

Remarks

The **HelpRequested** event occurs when the user requests help for a control. A **HelpEventArgs** object specifies the screen coordinates of the mouse pointer and whether the event was handled.

Example

See related example in the **System.Windows.Forms.Help** class topic.

Requirements

Namespace: System.Windows.Forms

Platforms: Windows 98, Windows NT 4.0, Windows Millennium Edition, Windows 2000, Windows XP Home Edition, Windows XP Professional, Windows Server 2003 family

Assembly: System.Windows.Forms (in System.Windows.Forms.dll)

HelpEventArgs Constructor

Initializes a new instance of the **HelpEventArgs** class.

```
[Visual Basic]
Public Sub New( _
   ByVal mousePos As Point _
)
[C#]
public HelpEventArgs(
   Point mousePos
);
[C++]
public: HelpEventArgs(
   Point mousePos
);
[JScript]
public function HelpEventArgs(
   mousePos : Point
);
```

Parameters

mousePos
    The coordinates of the mouse pointer.

Requirements

Platforms: Windows 98, Windows NT 4.0, Windows Millennium Edition, Windows 2000, Windows XP Home Edition, Windows XP Professional, Windows Server 2003 family

HelpEventArgs.Handled Property

Gets or sets a value indicating whether the help event was handled.

```
[Visual Basic]
Public Property Handled As Boolean
[C#]
public bool Handled {get; set;}
[C++]
public: __property bool get_Handled();
public: __property void set_Handled(bool);
[JScript]
public function get Handled() : Boolean;
public function set Handled(Boolean);
```

Property Value

true if the event is handled; otherwise, **false**. The default is **false**.

Remarks

If you do not set this property to **true** the event will be passed to Windows for additional processing.

Example

See related example in the **System.Windows.Forms.Help** class topic.

Requirements

Platforms: Windows 98, Windows NT 4.0, Windows Millennium Edition, Windows 2000, Windows XP Home Edition, Windows XP Professional, Windows Server 2003 family

HelpEventArgs.MousePos Property

Gets the screen coordinates of the mouse pointer.

```
[Visual Basic]
Public ReadOnly Property MousePos As Point
[C#]
public Point MousePos {get;}
[C++]
public: __property Point get_MousePos();
[JScript]
public function get MousePos() : Point;
```

Property Value

A **Point** representing the screen coordinates of the mouse pointer.

Remarks

You can use this information to provide help based on the position of the mouse pointer.

Requirements

Platforms: Windows 98, Windows NT 4.0, Windows Millennium Edition, Windows 2000, Windows XP Home Edition, Windows XP Professional, Windows Server 2003 family

HelpEventHandler Delegate

Represents the method that will handle the **HelpRequested** event of a **Control**.

[Visual Basic]
```
<Serializable>
Public Delegate Sub HelpEventHandler( _
   ByVal sender As Object, _
   ByVal hlpevent As HelpEventArgs _
)
```
[C#]
```
[Serializable]
public delegate void HelpEventHandler(
   object sender,
   HelpEventArgs hlpevent
);
```
[C++]
```
[Serializable]
public __gc __delegate void HelpEventHandler(
   Object* sender,
   HelpEventArgs* hlpevent
);
```

[JScript] In JScript, you can use the delegates in the .NET Framework, but you cannot define your own.

Parameters [Visual Basic, C#, C++]

The declaration of your event handler must have the same parameters as the **HelpEventHandler** delegate declaration.

sender
   The source of the event.

hlpevent
   A **HelpEventArgs** that contains the event data.

Remarks

When you create a **HelpEventHandler** delegate, you identify the method that will handle the event. To associate the event with your event handler, add an instance of the delegate to the event. The event handler is called whenever the event occurs, unless you remove the delegate.

Example

See related example in the **System.Windows.Forms.Help** topic.

Requirements

Namespace: System.Windows.Forms

Platforms: Windows 98, Windows NT 4.0, Windows Millennium Edition, Windows 2000, Windows XP Home Edition, Windows XP Professional, Windows Server 2003 family

Assembly: System.Windows.Forms (in System.Windows.Forms.dll)

HelpNavigator Enumeration

Specifies constants indicating which elements of the Help file to display.

[Visual Basic]
```
<Serializable>
Public Enum HelpNavigator
```
[C#]
```
[Serializable]
public enum HelpNavigator
```
[C++]
```
[Serializable]
__value public enum HelpNavigator
```
[JScript]
```
public
   Serializable
enum HelpNavigator
```

Remarks

This enumeration is used by **Help** and **HelpProvider** to provide access to specific elements of the Help file.

Members

Member name	Description
AssociateIndex	Specifies that the index for a specified topic is performed in the specified URL.
Find	Specifies that the search page of a specified URL is displayed.
Index	Specifies that the index of a specified URL is displayed.
KeywordIndex	Specifies a keyword to search for and the action to take in the specified URL.
TableOfContents	Specifies that the table of contents of the specfied URL is displayed.
Topic	Specifies that the topic referenced by the specified URL is displayed.

Example

See related example in the **System.Windows.Forms.Help** class topic.

Requirements

Namespace: System.Windows.Forms

Platforms: Windows 98, Windows NT 4.0, Windows Millennium Edition, Windows 2000, Windows XP Home Edition, Windows XP Professional, Windows Server 2003 family

Assembly: System.Windows.Forms (in System.Windows.Forms.dll)

HelpProvider Class

Provides pop-up or online Help for controls.

System.Object
  System.MarshalByRefObject
    System.ComponentModel.Component
      System.Windows.Forms.HelpProvider

[Visual Basic]
```
Public Class HelpProvider
   Inherits Component
   Implements IExtenderProvider
```
[C#]
```
public class HelpProvider : Component, IExtenderProvider
```
[C++]
```
public __gc class HelpProvider : public Component,
   IExtenderProvider
```
[JScript]
```
public class HelpProvider extends Component implements
   IExtenderProvider
```

Thread Safety

Any public static (**Shared** in Visual Basic) members of this type are safe for multithreaded operations. Any instance members are not guaranteed to be thread safe.

Remarks

Each instance of **HelpProvider** maintains a collection of references to controls associated with it. To associate a Help file with the **HelpProvider** object, set the **HelpNamespace** property. You specify the type of Help provided by calling **SetHelpNavigator** and providing a **HelpNavigator** value for the specified control. You provide the keyword or topic for the Help by calling **SetHelpKeyword**.

To associate a specific Help string with a control, use the **SetHelpString** method. The string that you associate with a control using this method is displayed in a pop-up window when the user presses the F1 key while the control has focus.

If **HelpNamespace** has not been set, you must use **SetHelpString** to provide the Help text. If you have set both **HelpNamespace** and the Help string, Help based on the **HelpNamespace** will take precedence.

HelpProvider calls methods on **Help** to provide help functionality.

Example

See related example in the **System.Windows.Forms.Help** class topic.

Requirements

Namespace: System.Windows.Forms

Platforms: Windows 98, Windows NT 4.0, Windows Millennium Edition, Windows 2000, Windows XP Home Edition, Windows XP Professional, Windows Server 2003 family

Assembly: System.Windows.Forms (in System.Windows.Forms.dll)

HelpProvider Constructor

Initializes a new instance of the **HelpProvider** class.

[Visual Basic]
```
Public Sub New()
```
[C#]
```
public HelpProvider();
```
[C++]
```
public: HelpProvider();
```
[JScript]
```
public function HelpProvider();
```

Remarks

Once you have created an instance of **HelpProvider**, use **HelpNamespace**, **SetHelpKeyword**, and **SetHelpNavigator** to associate your help topics with a control.

Example

See related example in the **System.Windows.Forms.Help** class topic.

Requirements

Platforms: Windows 98, Windows NT 4.0, Windows Millennium Edition, Windows 2000, Windows XP Home Edition, Windows XP Professional, Windows Server 2003 family

HelpProvider.HelpNamespace Property

Gets or sets a value specifying the name of the Help file associated with this **HelpProvider** object.

[Visual Basic]
```
Public Overridable Property HelpNamespace As String
```
[C#]
```
public virtual string HelpNamespace {get; set;}
```
[C++]
```
public: __property virtual String* get_HelpNamespace();
public: __property virtual void set_HelpNamespace(String*);
```
[JScript]
```
public function get HelpNamespace() : String;
public function set HelpNamespace(String);
```

Property Value

The name of the Help file. This can be of the form C:\path\sample.chm or/folder/file.htm.

Remarks

The file name retrieved by this method identifies the file that provides Help support for all the controls for which this object provides Help. This file name can designate either a compiled Help file (.chm) or a raw HTML file.

Example

See related example in the **System.Windows.Forms.Help** class topic.

Requirements

Platforms: Windows 98, Windows NT 4.0, Windows Millennium Edition, Windows 2000, Windows XP Home Edition, Windows XP Professional, Windows Server 2003 family

HelpProvider.CanExtend Method

This member supports the .NET Framework infrastructure and is not intended to be used directly from your code.

[Visual Basic]
```
Public Overridable Function CanExtend( _
   ByVal target As Object _
) As Boolean Implements IExtenderProvider.CanExtend
```
[C#]
```
public virtual bool CanExtend(
   object target
);
```
[C++]
```
public: virtual bool CanExtend(
   Object* target
);
```

```
[JScript]
public function CanExtend(
   target : Object
) : Boolean;
```

HelpProvider.GetHelpKeyword Method

Gets the Help keyword for the specified control.

```
[Visual Basic]
Public Overridable Function GetHelpKeyword( _
   ByVal ctl As Control _
) As String
[C#]
public virtual string GetHelpKeyword(
   Control ctl
);
[C++]
public: virtual String* GetHelpKeyword(
   Control* ctl
);
[JScript]
public function GetHelpKeyword(
   ctl : Control
) : String;
```

Parameters

ctl

A **Control** from which to retrieve the Help topic.

Return Value

The Help topic associated with this control. If the **HelpProvider** object is currently configured to display the entire Help file or is configured to provide a Help string, this method returns a null reference (**Nothing** in Visual Basic).

Requirements

Platforms: Windows 98, Windows NT 4.0, Windows Millennium Edition, Windows 2000, Windows XP Home Edition, Windows XP Professional, Windows Server 2003 family

HelpProvider.GetHelpNavigator Method

Gets the current **HelpNavigator** setting for the specified control.

```
[Visual Basic]
Public Overridable Function GetHelpNavigator( _
   ByVal ctl As Control _
) As HelpNavigator
[C#]
public virtual HelpNavigator GetHelpNavigator(
   Control ctl
);
[C++]
public: virtual HelpNavigator GetHelpNavigator(
   Control* ctl
);
[JScript]
public function GetHelpNavigator(
   ctl : Control
) : HelpNavigator;
```

Parameters

ctl

A **Control** from which to retrieve the Help navigator.

Return Value

The **HelpNavigator** setting for the specified control. The default is **AssociateIndex**.

Requirements

Platforms: Windows 98, Windows NT 4.0, Windows Millennium Edition, Windows 2000, Windows XP Home Edition, Windows XP Professional, Windows Server 2003 family

HelpProvider.GetHelpString Method

Gets the contents of the pop-up Help window for the specified control.

```
[Visual Basic]
Public Overridable Function GetHelpString( _
   ByVal ctl As Control _
) As String
[C#]
public virtual string GetHelpString(
   Control ctl
);
[C++]
public: virtual String* GetHelpString(
   Control* ctl
);
[JScript]
public function GetHelpString(
   ctl : Control
) : String;
```

Parameters

ctl

A **Control** from which to retrieve the Help string.

Return Value

The Help string associated with this control. The default value is a null reference (**Nothing** in Visual Basic).

Remarks

To display this Help string at run time, the user presses the F1 Key while the specified control has the input focus.

Requirements

Platforms: Windows 98, Windows NT 4.0, Windows Millennium Edition, Windows 2000, Windows XP Home Edition, Windows XP Professional, Windows Server 2003 family

HelpProvider.GetShowHelp Method

Gets a value indicating whether the specified control's help should be displayed.

```
[Visual Basic]
Public Overridable Function GetShowHelp( _
   ByVal ctl As Control _
) As Boolean
[C#]
public virtual bool GetShowHelp(
   Control ctl
);
```

[C++]
```
public: virtual bool GetShowHelp(
   Control* ctl
);
```
[JScript]
```
public function GetShowHelp(
   ctl : Control
) : Boolean;
```

Parameters

ctl

A **Control** for which Help will be displayed.

Return Value

true if Help will be displayed for the control; otherwise, **false**.

Remarks

When you use the **SetHelpKeyword** or **SetHelpString** method to associate a keyword or prompt with a specified control, calling this method automatically returns **true**. You can override this behavior by passing **false** to the **SetShowHelp** method.

Requirements

Platforms: Windows 98, Windows NT 4.0, Windows Millennium Edition, Windows 2000, Windows XP Home Edition, Windows XP Professional, Windows Server 2003 family

HelpProvider.ResetShowHelp Method

This member supports the .NET Framework infrastructure and is not intended to be used directly from your code.

[Visual Basic]
```
Public Overridable Sub ResetShowHelp( _
   ByVal ctl As Control _
)
```
[C#]
```
public virtual void ResetShowHelp(
   Control ctl
);
```
[C++]
```
public: virtual void ResetShowHelp(
   Control* ctl
);
```
[JScript]
```
public function ResetShowHelp(
   ctl : Control
);
```

HelpProvider.SetHelpKeyword Method

Specifies the keyword used to retrieve Help when the user invokes Help for the specified control.

[Visual Basic]
```
Public Overridable Sub SetHelpKeyword( _
   ByVal ctl As Control, _
   ByVal keyword As String _
)
```
[C#]
```
public virtual void SetHelpKeyword(
   Control ctl,
   string keyword
);
```
[C++]
```
public: virtual void SetHelpKeyword(
   Control* ctl,
   String* keyword
);
```
[JScript]
```
public function SetHelpKeyword(
   ctl : Control,
   keyword : String
);
```

Parameters

ctl

A **Control** that specifies the control for which to set the Help topic.

keyword

The Help keyword to associate with the control.

Remarks

The Help keyword provides the key information to retrieve the help associated with this control from the Help file specified by **HelpNamespace**. To clear the keyword call **SetHelpKeyword** with a *keyword* value of a null reference (**Nothing** in Visual Basic).

Requirements

Platforms: Windows 98, Windows NT 4.0, Windows Millennium Edition, Windows 2000, Windows XP Home Edition, Windows XP Professional, Windows Server 2003 family

HelpProvider.SetHelpNavigator Method

Specifies the Help command to use when retrieving Help from the Help file for the specified contol.

[Visual Basic]
```
Public Overridable Sub SetHelpNavigator( _
   ByVal ctl As Control, _
   ByVal navigator As HelpNavigator _
)
```
[C#]
```
public virtual void SetHelpNavigator(
   Control ctl,
   HelpNavigator navigator
);
```
[C++]
```
public: virtual void SetHelpNavigator(
   Control* ctl,
   HelpNavigator navigator
);
```
[JScript]
```
public function SetHelpNavigator(
   ctl : Control,
   navigator : HelpNavigator
);
```

Parameters

ctl

A **Control** for which to set the Help keyword.

navigator

One of the **HelpNavigator** values.

Exceptions

Exception Type	Condition
InvalidEnumArgument-Exception	The value of *navigator* is not one of the **HelpNavigator** values.

Requirements

Platforms: Windows 98, Windows NT 4.0, Windows Millennium Edition, Windows 2000, Windows XP Home Edition, Windows XP Professional, Windows Server 2003 family

HelpProvider.SetHelpString Method

Specifies the Help string associated with the specified control.

```
[Visual Basic]
Public Overridable Sub SetHelpString( _
   ByVal ctl As Control, _
   ByVal helpString As String _
)
[C#]
public virtual void SetHelpString(
   Control ctl,
   string helpString
);
[C++]
public: virtual void SetHelpString(
   Control* ctl,
   String* helpString
);
[JScript]
public function SetHelpString(
   ctl : Control,
   helpString : String
);
```

Parameters

ctl

A **Control** with which to associate the Help string.

helpString

The Help string associated with the control.

Remarks

The Help string that you specify in the *helpString* parameter is displayed in a pop-up window when the user presses the F1 Key while the specified control has focus.

Example

See related example in the **System.Windows.Forms.Help** class topic.

Requirements

Platforms: Windows 98, Windows NT 4.0, Windows Millennium Edition, Windows 2000, Windows XP Home Edition, Windows XP Professional, Windows Server 2003 family

HelpProvider.SetShowHelp Method

Specifies whether Help is displayed for the specified control.

```
[Visual Basic]
Public Overridable Sub SetShowHelp( _
   ByVal ctl As Control, _
   ByVal value As Boolean _
)
[C#]
public virtual void SetShowHelp(
   Control ctl,
   bool value
);
[C++]
public: virtual void SetShowHelp(
   Control* ctl,
   bool value
);
[JScript]
public function SetShowHelp(
   ctl : Control,
   value : Boolean
);
```

Parameters

ctl

A **Control** for which Help is turned on or off.

value

true if Help displays for the control; otherwise, **false**.

Remarks

If you previously called the **SetHelpString** or **SetHelpKeyword** for the control specified in the *ctl* parameter, the **HelpProvider** object automatically displays Help for that control. To modify this behavior, call the **SetShowHelp** method, specifying **false** in the *value* parameter.

Example

See related example in the **System.Windows.Forms.Help** class topic.

Requirements

Platforms: Windows 98, Windows NT 4.0, Windows Millennium Edition, Windows 2000, Windows XP Home Edition, Windows XP Professional, Windows Server 2003 family

HelpProvider.ToString Method

This member overrides **Object.ToString**.

```
[Visual Basic]
Overrides Public Function ToString() As String
[C#]
public override string ToString();
[C++]
public: String* ToString();
[JScript]
public override function ToString() : String;
```

Requirements

Platforms: Windows 98, Windows NT 4.0, Windows Millennium Edition, Windows 2000, Windows XP Home Edition, Windows XP Professional, Windows Server 2003 family

HorizontalAlignment Enumeration

Specifies how an object or text in a control is horizontally aligned relative to an element of the control.

[Visual Basic]
```
<Serializable>
<ComVisible(True)>
Public Enum HorizontalAlignment
```
[C#]
```
[Serializable]
[ComVisible(true)]
public enum HorizontalAlignment
```
[C++]
```
[Serializable]
[ComVisible(true)]
__value public enum HorizontalAlignment
```
[JScript]
```
public
   Serializable
   ComVisible(true)
enum HorizontalAlignment
```

Remarks

This enumeration is used in numerous classes. A partial list of these classes is **CheckedListBox**, **ColumnHeader**, **ComboBox**, **ControlPaint**, **Label**, **ListBox**, **Control**, **RichTextBox**, and **TextBox**.

Members

Member name	Description
Center Supported by the .NET Compact Framework.	The object or text is aligned in the center of the control element.
Left Supported by the .NET Compact Framework.	The object or text is aligned on the left of the control element.
Right Supported by the .NET Compact Framework.	The object or text is aligned on the right of the control element.

Example

[Visual Basic, C#, C++] This example shows how to use the **HorizontalAlignment** enumeration to align the text to the left, right, or in the center of a control element. First, create a **TextBox** with a specific size, and add a text string to it. Then, use the enumeration member **Center** to align the text in the center of the **TextBox**. The example assumes that you have created a **Form** named `Form1` and a **TextBox** named `textBox1`.

[Visual Basic]
```
Private Sub Form1_Load(ByVal sender As System.Object, ByVal
e As System.EventArgs) Handles MyBase.Load
    ' Add a text string to the TextBox.
    TextBox1.Text = "Hello World!"

    ' Set the size of the TextBox.
    TextBox1.AutoSize = False
    TextBox1.Size = New Size(Width, Height/3)

    ' Align the text in the center of the control element.
    TextBox1.TextAlign = HorizontalAlignment.Center
End Sub
```

[C#]
```
private void Form1_Load(object sender, System.EventArgs e)
{
    // Add a text string to the TextBox.
    textBox1.Text = "Hello World!";

    // Set the size of the TextBox.
    textBox1.AutoSize = false;
    textBox1.Size = new Size(Width, Height/3);

    // Align the text in the center of the control element.
    textBox1.TextAlign = HorizontalAlignment.Center;
}
```

[C++]
```
private:
    void Form1_Load(Object* /*sender*/, System::EventArgs* /*e*/) {
        // Add a text String* to the TextBox.
        textBox1->Text = S"Hello World!";

        // Set the size of the TextBox.
        textBox1->AutoSize = false;
        textBox1->Size = System::Drawing::Size(Width, Height/3);

        // Align the text in the center of the control element.
        textBox1->TextAlign = HorizontalAlignment::Center;
    }
```

Requirements

Namespace: System.Windows.Forms

Platforms: Windows 98, Windows NT 4.0, Windows Millennium Edition, Windows 2000, Windows XP Home Edition, Windows XP Professional, Windows Server 2003 family, .NET Compact Framework - Windows CE .NET

Assembly: System.Windows.Forms (in System.Windows.Forms.dll)

HScrollBar Class

Represents a standard Windows horizontal scroll bar.

System.Object
  System.MarshalByRefObject
    System.ComponentModel.Component
      System.Windows.Forms.Control
        System.Windows.Forms.ScrollBar
          System.Windows.Forms.HScrollBar

[Visual Basic]
```
Public Class HScrollBar
   Inherits ScrollBar
```
[C#]
```
public class HScrollBar : ScrollBar
```
[C++]
```
public __gc class HScrollBar : public ScrollBar
```
[JScript]
```
public class HScrollBar extends ScrollBar
```

Thread Safety

Any public static (**Shared** in Visual Basic) members of this type are safe for multithreaded operations. Any instance members are not guaranteed to be thread safe.

Remarks

Most controls that need scroll bars already provide them and do not require this control. This is true of a multiline **TextBox** control, a **ListBox**, and a **ComboBox**, for example.

You can use this control to implement scrolling in containers that do not provide their own scroll bars such as a **PictureBox** or for user input of numeric data. The numeric data can be displayed in a control or used in code. The **Minimum** and **Maximum** properties determine the range of values the user can select. The **LargeChange** property determines the effect of clicking within the scroll bar but outside the scroll box. The **SmallChange** property determines the effect of clicking the scroll arrows at each end of the control.

Example

[Visual Basic, C#, JScript] The following example creates and initializes an **HScrollBar** and adds it to a **Form**.

[Visual Basic]
```
Private Sub InitializeMyScrollBar()
    ' Create and initialize an HScrollBar.
    Dim hScrollBar1 As New HScrollBar()

    ' Dock the scroll bar to the bottom of the form.
    hScrollBar1.Dock = DockStyle.Bottom

    ' Add the scroll bar to the form.
    Controls.Add(hScrollBar1)
End Sub 'InitializeMyScrollBar
```

[C#]
```
private void InitializeMyScrollBar()
 {
    // Create and initialize an HScrollBar.
    HScrollBar hScrollBar1 = new HScrollBar();

    // Dock the scroll bar to the bottom of the form.
    hScrollBar1.Dock = DockStyle.Bottom;

    // Add the scroll bar to the form.
    Controls.Add(hScrollBar1);
 }
```

[JScript]
```
function InitializeMyScrollBar(){
    // Create and initialize an HScrollBar.
    var hScrollBar1 : HScrollBar = new HScrollBar()

    // Dock the scroll bar to the bottom of the form.
    hScrollBar1.Dock = DockStyle.Bottom

    // Add the scroll bar to the form.
    Controls.Add(hScrollBar1)
}
```

Requirements

Namespace: System.Windows.Forms

Platforms: Windows 98, Windows NT 4.0, Windows Millennium Edition, Windows 2000, Windows XP Home Edition, Windows XP Professional, Windows Server 2003 family, .NET Compact Framework - Windows CE .NET

Assembly: System.Windows.Forms (in System.Windows.Forms.dll)

HScrollBar Constructor

Initializes a new instance of the **HScrollBar** class.

[Visual Basic]
```
Public Sub New()
```
[C#]
```
public HScrollBar();
```
[C++]
```
public: HScrollBar();
```
[JScript]
```
public function HScrollBar();
```

Remarks

The default constructor initializes any fields to their default values.

Requirements

Platforms: Windows 98, Windows NT 4.0, Windows Millennium Edition, Windows 2000, Windows XP Home Edition, Windows XP Professional, Windows Server 2003 family, .NET Compact Framework - Windows CE .NET

HScrollBar.CreateParams Property

This member overrides **Control.CreateParams**.

[Visual Basic]
```
Overrides Protected ReadOnly Property CreateParams As CreateParams
```
[C#]
```
protected override CreateParams CreateParams {get;}
```
[C++]
```
protected: __property CreateParams* get_CreateParams();
```
[JScript]
```
protected override function get CreateParams() : CreateParams;
```

Requirements

Platforms: Windows 98, Windows NT 4.0, Windows Millennium Edition, Windows 2000, Windows XP Home Edition, Windows XP Professional, Windows Server 2003 family

HScrollBar.DefaultSize Property

This member overrides **Control.DefaultSize**.

[Visual Basic]

```
Overrides Protected ReadOnly Property DefaultSize As Size
```

[C#]

```
protected override Size DefaultSize {get;}
```

[C++]

```
protected: __property Size get_DefaultSize();
```

[JScript]

```
protected override function get DefaultSize() : Size;
```

Requirements

Platforms: Windows 98, Windows NT 4.0, Windows Millennium Edition, Windows 2000, Windows XP Home Edition, Windows XP Professional, Windows Server 2003 family

IButtonControl Interface

Allows a control to act like a button on a form.

[Visual Basic]
```
Public Interface IButtonControl
```
[C#]
```
public interface IButtonControl
```
[C++]
```
public __gc __interface IButtonControl
```
[JScript]
```
public interface IButtonControl
```

Classes that Implement IButtonControl

Class	Description
Button	Represents a Windows button control.
LinkLabel	Represents a Windows label control that can display hyperlinks.

Remarks

An example of where this interface might be implemented is default and cancel button processing. Default buttons are notified when an unprocessed ENTER key is entered for a form, just like a dialog box would be closed. Similarly, cancel buttons are notified whenever an unprocessed ESC key is entered on a form, much like a dialog box would be dismissed.

Notes to Implementers: Implement this interface in classes that act as button controls. The members of this interface will provide basic button functionality, such as providing a **DialogResult** to the parent form or the ability to perform a **Click** event, or acting as the default button of a form.

Example

[Visual Basic, C#, C++] The following example inherits from the **ButtonBase** class and implements the **IButtonControl** interface. Implementation is added to the **DialogResult** property and the **NotifyDefault** and **PerformClick** methods.

[Visual Basic]
```
Imports System
Imports System.Windows.Forms
Imports System.Drawing

Public Class MyButton
   Inherits ButtonBase
   Implements IButtonControl
   Private myDialogResult As DialogResult

   Public Sub New()
      ' Make the button White and a Popup style
      ' so it can be distinguished on the form.
      Me.FlatStyle = FlatStyle.Popup
      Me.BackColor = Color.White
   End Sub

   ' Add implementation to the IButtonControl.DialogResult property.
   Public Property DialogResult() As DialogResult Implements
IButtonControl.DialogResult
      Get
         Return Me.myDialogResult
      End Get

      Set
         If [Enum].IsDefined(GetType(DialogResult), value) Then
            Me.myDialogResult = value
         End If
      End Set
   End Property

   ' Add implementation to the IButtonControl.NotifyDefault method.
   Public Sub NotifyDefault(value As Boolean) Implements
IButtonControl.NotifyDefault
      If Me.IsDefault <> value Then
         Me.IsDefault = value
      End If
   End Sub

   ' Add implementation to the IButtonControl.PerformClick method.
   Public Sub PerformClick() Implements IButtonControl.PerformClick
      If Me.CanSelect Then
         Me.OnClick(EventArgs.Empty)
      End If
   End Sub

End Class
```

[C#]
```
using System;
using System.Windows.Forms;
using System.Drawing;

public class MyButton : ButtonBase, IButtonControl
{
    private DialogResult myDialogResult;

    public MyButton()
    {
        // Make the button White and a Popup style
        // so it can be distinguished on the form.
        this.FlatStyle = FlatStyle.Popup;
        this.BackColor = Color.White;
    }

    // Add implementation to the IButtonControl.DialogResult property.
    public DialogResult DialogResult
    {
        get
        {
            return this.myDialogResult;
        }

        set
        {
            if(Enum.IsDefined(typeof(DialogResult), value))
            {
                this.myDialogResult = value;
            }
        }
    }

    // Add implementation to the IButtonControl.NotifyDefault method.
    public void NotifyDefault(bool value)
    {
        if(this.IsDefault != value)
        {
            this.IsDefault = value;
        }
    }

    // Add implementation to the IButtonControl.PerformClick method.
    public void PerformClick()
    {
        if(this.CanSelect)
        {
            this.OnClick(EventArgs.Empty);
        }
    }
}
```

[C++]
```
using namespace System;
using namespace System::Windows::Forms;
using namespace System::Drawing;

public __gc class MyButton : public ButtonBase, public IButtonControl {
private:
    System::Windows::Forms::DialogResult myDialogResult;

public:
    MyButton() {
        // Make the button White and a Popup style
        // so it can be distinguished on the form.
        this->FlatStyle = FlatStyle::Popup;
        this->BackColor = Color::White;
    }

    // Add implementation to the IButtonControl.DialogResult property.
    __property System::Windows::Forms::DialogResult                  ↵
get_DialogResult() {
            return this->myDialogResult;
    }

    __property void
set_DialogResult(System::Windows::Forms::DialogResult value) {
            if                                                        ↵
 (Enum::IsDefined(__typeof(System::Windows::Forms::DialogResult),
                                                                      ↵
__box(static_cast<System::Windows::Forms::DialogResult>(value)))) {
                this->myDialogResult = value;
            }
    }

    // Add implementation to the IButtonControl.NotifyDefault method.
    void NotifyDefault(bool value) {
        if (this->IsDefault != value) {
            this->IsDefault = value;
        }
    }

    // Add implementation to the IButtonControl.PerformClick method.
    void PerformClick() {
        if (this->CanSelect) {
            this->OnClick(EventArgs::Empty);
        }
    }
};
```

Requirements

Namespace: System.Windows.Forms

Platforms: Windows 98, Windows NT 4.0, Windows Millennium Edition, Windows 2000, Windows XP Home Edition, Windows XP Professional, Windows Server 2003 family

Assembly: System.Windows.Forms (in System.Windows.Forms.dll)

IButtonControl.DialogResult Property

Gets or sets the value returned to the parent form when the button is clicked.

[Visual Basic]
```
Property DialogResult As DialogResult
```
[C#]
```
DialogResult DialogResult {get; set;}
```
[C++]
```
__property DialogResult get_DialogResult();
__property void set_DialogResult(DialogResult);
```
[JScript]
```
function get DialogResult() : DialogResult;function set
DialogResult(DialogResult);
```

Property Value

One of the **DialogResult** values.

Remarks

When a form is shown as a dialog box using the **ShowDialog** method and one of its buttons is clicked, the button's **DialogResult** value is assigned to the form's **DialogResult** property.

Example

See related example in the **System.Windows.Forms.IButton-Control** class topic.

Requirements

Platforms: Windows 98, Windows NT 4.0, Windows Millennium Edition, Windows 2000, Windows XP Home Edition, Windows XP Professional, Windows Server 2003 family

IButtonControl.NotifyDefault Method

Notifies a control that it is the default button so that its appearance and behavior is adjusted accordingly.

[Visual Basic]
```
Sub NotifyDefault( _
   ByVal value As Boolean _
)
```
[C#]
```
void NotifyDefault(
   bool value
);
```
[C++]
```
void NotifyDefault(
   bool value
);
```
[JScript]
```
function NotifyDefault(
   value : Boolean
);
```

Parameters

value

true if the control should behave as a default button; otherwise **false**.

Remarks

This method is called by a parent form to make a control the default button. Default buttons are set to have an extra thick border.

Example

See related example in the **System.Windows.Forms.IButton-Control** class topic.

Requirements

Platforms: Windows 98, Windows NT 4.0, Windows Millennium Edition, Windows 2000, Windows XP Home Edition, Windows XP Professional, Windows Server 2003 family

IButtonControl.PerformClick Method

Generates a **Click** event for the control.

[Visual Basic]
```
Sub PerformClick()
```
[C#]
```
void PerformClick();
```
[C++]
```
void PerformClick();
```
[JScript]
```
function PerformClick();
```

Remarks

This method is called for the button that has focus, or for the default button (if no other button has focus) when the user presses the ENTER key. This method is also called when the user presses the ESC key if the button is set as the cancel button.

Example

See related example in the **System.Windows.Forms.IButtonControl** class topic.

Requirements

Platforms: Windows 98, Windows NT 4.0, Windows Millennium Edition, Windows 2000, Windows XP Home Edition, Windows XP Professional, Windows Server 2003 family

ICommandExecutor Interface

This type supports the .NET Framework infrastructure and is not intended to be used directly from your code.

[Visual Basic]
```
Public Interface ICommandExecutor
```
[C#]
```
public interface ICommandExecutor
```
[C++]
```
public __gc __interface ICommandExecutor
```
[JScript]
```
public interface ICommandExecutor
```

ICommandExecutor.Execute Method

This member supports the .NET Framework infrastructure and is not intended to be used directly from your code.

[Visual Basic]
```
Sub Execute()
```
[C#]
```
void Execute();
```
[C++]
```
void Execute();
```
[JScript]
```
function Execute();
```

IComponentEditorPageSite Interface

This type supports the .NET Framework infrastructure and is not intended to be used directly from your code.

[Visual Basic]
```
Public Interface IComponentEditorPageSite
```
[C#]
```
public interface IComponentEditorPageSite
```
[C++]
```
public __gc __interface IComponentEditorPageSite
```
[JScript]
```
public interface IComponentEditorPageSite
```

IComponentEditorPageSite.GetControl Method

This member supports the .NET Framework infrastructure and is not intended to be used directly from your code.

[Visual Basic]
```
Function GetControl() As Control
```
[C#]
```
Control GetControl();
```
[C++]
```
Control* GetControl();
```
[JScript]
```
function GetControl() : Control;
```

IComponentEditorPageSite.SetDirty Method

This member supports the .NET Framework infrastructure and is not intended to be used directly from your code.

[Visual Basic]
```
Sub SetDirty()
```
[C#]
```
void SetDirty();
```
[C++]
```
void SetDirty();
```
[JScript]
```
function SetDirty();
```

IContainerControl Interface

Provides the functionality for a control to act as a parent for other controls.

[Visual Basic]
```
Public Interface IContainerControl
```
[C#]
```
public interface IContainerControl
```
[C++]
```
public __gc __interface IContainerControl
```
[JScript]
```
public interface IContainerControl
```

Classes that Implement IContainerControl

Class	Description
ContainerControl	Provides focus management functionality for controls that can function as a container for other controls.

Remarks

Notes to Implementers: Implement this interface in classes that you want to parent a collection of controls. The members of this interface allow you to activate a child control, or determine which control is currently active. When implemented in a class, **ActivateControl** takes a **Control** as a parameter and activates the specified control. The **ActiveControl** property activates or retrieves the control that is active.

In most common scenarios, you do not need to directly implement this interface. For example, if you create a Windows Control Library project, Visual Studio generates an initial class for you. That class inherits from the **UserControl** class, and **UserControl** implements **IContainerControl** for you.

Example

[Visual Basic, C#, C++] The following example inherits from the **ScrollableControl** class and implements the **IContainerControl** interface. Implementation is added to the **ActiveControl** property and the **ActivateControl** method.

[Visual Basic]
```
Imports System
Imports System.Windows.Forms
Imports System.Drawing

   Public Class MyContainerControl
      Inherits ScrollableControl
      Implements IContainerControl

      Private myActiveControl As Control

      Public Sub New()
         ' Make the container control Blue so it can be
distinguished on the form.
         Me.BackColor = Color.Blue

         ' Make the container scrollable.
         Me.AutoScroll = True
      End Sub

      ' Add implementation to the
IContainerControl.ActiveControl property.
      Public Property ActiveControl() As Control
Implements IContainerControl.ActiveControl
         Get
            Return Me.myActiveControl
         End Get
         Set
            ' Make sure the control is a member of
the ControlCollection.
            If Me.Controls.Contains(value) Then
               Me.myActiveControl = value
            End If
         End Set
      End Property

      ' Add implementation to the
IContainerControl.ActivateControl(Control) method.
      public Function ActivateControl(active As Control)
As Boolean Implements IContainerControl.ActivateControl
         If Me.Controls.Contains(active) Then
            ' Select the control and scroll the control into
view if needed.
            active.Select()
            Me.ScrollControlIntoView(active)
            Me.myActiveControl = active
            Return True
         End If
         Return False
      End Function

   End Class
```

[C#]
```
using System;
using System.Windows.Forms;
using System.Drawing;

    public class MyContainer : ScrollableControl, IContainerControl
    {
        private Control activeControl;
        public MyContainer()
        {
            // Make the container control Blue so it can be
distinguished on the form.
            this.BackColor = Color.Blue;

            // Make the container scrollable.
            this.AutoScroll = true;
        }

        // Add implementation to the
IContainerControl.ActiveControl property.
        public Control ActiveControl
        {
            get
            {
                return activeControl;
            }

            set
            {
                // Make sure the control is a member
of the ControlCollection.
                if(this.Controls.Contains(value))
                {
                    activeControl = value;
                }
            }
        }

        // Add implementations to the
IContainerControl.ActivateControl(Control) method.
        public bool ActivateControl(Control active)
        {
            if(this.Controls.Contains(active))
            {
                // Select the control and scroll the control
into view if needed.
                active.Select();
                this.ScrollControlIntoView(active);
                this.activeControl = active;
                return true;
            }
            return false;
        }
    }
```

[C++]
```
using namespace System;
using namespace System::Windows::Forms;
using namespace System::Drawing;

    public __gc class MyContainer : public ScrollableControl, ↵
 public IContainerControl {
    private:
        Control*  activeControl;

    public:
        MyContainer() {
            // Make the container control Blue so it ↵
can be distinguished on the form.
            this->BackColor = Color::Blue;

            // Make the container scrollable.
            this->AutoScroll = true;
        }

        // Add implementation to the IContainerControl* ↵
.ActiveControl property.
        __property Control* get_ActiveControl() {
            return activeControl;
        }

        __property void set_ActiveControl(Control* value) {
            // Make sure the control is a member of the ↵
ControlCollection.
            if (this->Controls->Contains(value)) {
                activeControl = value;
            }
        }

        // Add implementations to the ↵
IContainerControl*.ActivateControl(Control) method.
        bool ActivateControl(Control* active) {
            if (this->Controls->Contains(active)) {
                // Select the control and scroll the control ↵
into view if needed.
                active->Select();
                this->ScrollControlIntoView(active);
                this->activeControl = active;
                return true;
            }
            return false;
        }
    };
```

Requirements

Namespace: System.Windows.Forms

Platforms: Windows 98, Windows NT 4.0, Windows Millennium Edition, Windows 2000, Windows XP Home Edition, Windows XP Professional, Windows Server 2003 family

Assembly: System.Windows.Forms (in System.Windows.Forms.dll)

IContainerControl.ActiveControl Property

Gets or sets the control that is active on the container control.

[Visual Basic]
```
Property ActiveControl As Control
```
[C#]
```
Control ActiveControl {get; set;}
```
[C++]
```
__property Control* get_ActiveControl();
__property void set_ActiveControl(Control*);
```
[JScript]
```
function get ActiveControl() : Control;function set
ActiveControl(Control);
```

Property Value

The **Control** that is currently active on the container control.

Remarks

Notes to Implementers: When implemented in a class, this property activates or retrieves the active control on the container control.

Example

See related example in the **System.Windows.Forms.IContainerControl** interface topic.

Requirements

Platforms: Windows 98, Windows NT 4.0, Windows Millennium Edition, Windows 2000, Windows XP Home Edition, Windows XP Professional, Windows Server 2003 family

IContainerControl.ActivateControl Method

Activates a specified control.

[Visual Basic]
```
Function ActivateControl( _
   ByVal active As Control _
) As Boolean
```
[C#]
```
bool ActivateControl(
   Control active
);
```
[C++]
```
bool ActivateControl(
   Control* active
);
```
[JScript]
```
function ActivateControl(
   active : Control
) : Boolean;
```

Parameters

active
  The **Control** being activated.

Return Value

true if the control is successfully activated; otherwise, **false**.

Remarks

Notes to Implementers: When implemented in a class, this method activates the specified **Control**. The control must be a child of the container control.

Example

See related example in the **System.Windows.Forms.IContainerControl** interface topic.

Requirements

Platforms: Windows 98, Windows NT 4.0, Windows Millennium Edition, Windows 2000, Windows XP Home Edition, Windows XP Professional, Windows Server 2003 family

IDataGridColumnStyleEditing-NotificationService Interface

Provides an editing notification interface.

```
[Visual Basic]
Public Interface IDataGridColumnStyleEditingNotificationService
[C#]
public interface IDataGridColumnStyleEditingNotificationService
[C++]
public __gc __interface
   IDataGridColumnStyleEditingNotificationService
[JScript]
public interface IDataGridColumnStyleEditingNotificationService
```

Classes that Implement IDataGridColumnStyleEditingNotificationService

Class	Description
DataGridColumnStyle	Specifies the appearance and text formatting and behavior of a **System.Windows.Forms.DataGrid** control column. This class is abstract.

Remarks

To create a new **System.Windows.Forms.DataGrid** column with special properties, you must first inherit from the **DataGridColumnStyle** class. The **IDataGridColumnStyle-EditingNotificationService** interface is provided to notify the **System.Windows.Forms.DataGrid** when a column is being edited.

Requirements

Namespace: System.Windows.Forms

Platforms: Windows 98, Windows NT 4.0, Windows Millennium Edition, Windows 2000, Windows XP Home Edition, Windows XP Professional, Windows Server 2003 family

Assembly: System.Windows.Forms (in System.Windows.Forms.dll)

IDataGridColumnStyleEditingNotification-Service.ColumnStartedEditing Method

Informs the **System.Windows.Forms.DataGrid** that the user has begun editing the column.

```
[Visual Basic]
Sub ColumnStartedEditing( _
   ByVal editingControl As Control _
)
[C#]
void ColumnStartedEditing(
   Control editingControl
);
[C++]
void ColumnStartedEditing(
   Control* editingControl
);
[JScript]
function ColumnStartedEditing(
   editingControl : Control
);
```

Parameters

editingControl

The **Control** that is editing the column.

Remarks

When called, the **ColumnStartedEditing** method allows the **System.Windows.Forms.DataGrid** control to show a pencil in the row header indicating the row is being edited.

Requirements

Platforms: Windows 98, Windows NT 4.0, Windows Millennium Edition, Windows 2000, Windows XP Home Edition, Windows XP Professional, Windows Server 2003 family

IDataGridEditingService Interface

This type supports the .NET Framework infrastructure and is not intended to be used directly from your code.

[Visual Basic]
```
Public Interface IDataGridEditingService
```
[C#]
```
public interface IDataGridEditingService
```
[C++]
```
public __gc __interface IDataGridEditingService
```
[JScript]
```
public interface IDataGridEditingService
```

IDataGridEditingService.BeginEdit Method

This member supports the .NET Framework infrastructure and is not intended to be used directly from your code.

[Visual Basic]
```
Function BeginEdit( _
   ByVal gridColumn As DataGridColumnStyle, _
   ByVal rowNumber As Integer _
) As Boolean
```
[C#]
```
bool BeginEdit(
   DataGridColumnStyle gridColumn,
   int rowNumber
);
```
[C++]
```
bool BeginEdit(
   DataGridColumnStyle* gridColumn,
   int rowNumber
);
```
[JScript]
```
function BeginEdit(
   gridColumn : DataGridColumnStyle,
   rowNumber : int
) : Boolean;
```

IDataGridEditingService.EndEdit Method

This member supports the .NET Framework infrastructure and is not intended to be used directly from your code.

[Visual Basic]
```
Function EndEdit( _
   ByVal gridColumn As DataGridColumnStyle, _
   ByVal rowNumber As Integer, _
   ByVal shouldAbort As Boolean _
) As Boolean
```
[C#]
```
bool EndEdit(
   DataGridColumnStyle gridColumn,
   int rowNumber,
   bool shouldAbort
);
```
[C++]
```
bool EndEdit(
   DataGridColumnStyle* gridColumn,
   int rowNumber,
   bool shouldAbort
);
```
[JScript]
```
function EndEdit(
   gridColumn : DataGridColumnStyle,
   rowNumber : int,
   shouldAbort : Boolean
) : Boolean;
```

IDataObject Interface

Provides a format-independent mechanism for transferring data.

[Visual Basic]
```
<ComVisible(True)>
Public Interface IDataObject
```
[C#]
```
[ComVisible(true)]
public interface IDataObject
```
[C++]
```
[ComVisible(true)]
public __gc __interface IDataObject
```
[JScript]
```
public
   ComVisible(true)
interface IDataObject
```

Classes that Implement IDataObject

Class	Description
DataObject	Implements a basic data transfer mechanism.

Remarks

The **IDataObject** interface is used by the **Clipboard** class and in drag-and-drop operations.

When implemented in a class, the **IDataObject** methods allow the user to store data in multiple formats in an instance of the class. Storing data in more than one format increases the chance that a target application, whose format requirements you might not know, can retrieve the stored data. To store data in an instance of **IDataObject**, call the **SetData** method and specify the data format in the *format* parameter. Set the *autoConvert* parameter to **false** if you do not want stored data to be converted to another format when it is retrieved. Invoke **SetData** multiple times on one instance of **IDataObject** to store data in more than one format.

You retrieve stored data from an **IDataObject** by calling the **GetData** method and specifying the data format in the *format* parameter. Set the *autoConvert* parameter to **false** to retrieve only data that was stored in the specified format. To convert the stored data to the specified format, set *autoConvert* to **true**, or do not use *autoConvert*.

To determine the formats of the data stored in an **IDataObject**, use the following **IDataObject** methods.

- Call the **GetFormats** method to retrieve an array of all the formats in which the data is available. Set the *autoConvert* parameter to **false** to get only the formats in which the data is stored. To get all the formats in which the data is available, set *autoConvert* to **true**, or do not use this parameter.
- Call the **GetDataPresent** method to determine whether stored data is available in a certain format. If you do not want stored data to be converted to the specified format, set the *autoConvert* parameter to **false**.

See the **DataObject** class for an implementation of this interface. See the **DataFormats** class for the predefined **Clipboard** data formats.

Requirements

Namespace: System.Windows.Forms

Platforms: Windows 98, Windows NT 4.0, Windows Millennium Edition, Windows 2000, Windows XP Home Edition, Windows XP Professional, Windows Server 2003 family

Assembly: System.Windows.Forms (in System.Windows.Forms.dll)

IDataObject.GetData Method

Retrieves the data associated with the specified data format.

Overload List

Retrieves the data associated with the specified data format.

[Visual Basic] **Overloads Function GetData(String) As Object**

[C#] **object GetData(string);**

[C++] **Object* GetData(String*);**

[JScript] **function GetData(String) : Object;**

Retrieves the data associated with the specified class type format.

[Visual Basic] **Overloads Function GetData(Type) As Object**

[C#] **object GetData(Type);**

[C++] **Object* GetData(Type*);**

[JScript] **function GetData(Type) : Object;**

Retrieves the data associated with the specified data format, using a Boolean to determine whether to convert the data to the format.

[Visual Basic] **Overloads Function GetData(String, Boolean) As Object**

[C#] **object GetData(string, bool);**

[C++] **Object* GetData(String*, bool);**

[JScript] **function GetData(String, Boolean) : Object;**

Example

[Visual Basic, C#, C++] This example uses the **DataObject** class, which implements **IDataObject**, to demonstrate the use of the **GetData** method. The example retrieves the data stored in a **DataObject**, using the *autoConvert* parameter to specify whether or not to convert the data format. First, `myDataObject` is created with text data. Then the example tries twice to retrieve the data. In the first trial, it specifies its format as a string and sets the *autoConvert* parameter to **false**. This trial fails, and the result is displayed in a message box labeled "Message #1." In the second trial, the example retrieves the same data with the *autoConvert* parameter set to **true**. This trial succeeds, and the result is displayed in a message box labeled "Message #2." The example assumes that you have created a **Form** named `Form1`.

> [Visual Basic, C#, C++] **Note** This example shows how to use one of the overloaded versions of **GetData**. For other examples that might be available, see the individual overload topics.

[Visual Basic]
```
Private Sub GetData3()
    ' Creates a new data object using a text string.
    Dim myString As String = "Hello World!"
    Dim myDataObject As New DataObject(DataFormats.Text, myString)

    ' Displays the string with autoConvert equal to false.
    If Not (myDataObject.GetData("System.String", False)          ↵
Is Nothing) Then
        ' Displays the string in a message box.
        MessageBox.Show(myDataObject.GetData("System.String",      ↵
False).ToString() + ".", "Message #1")
        ' Displays a not found message in a message box.
    Else
        MessageBox.Show("Could not find data of the specified      ↵
format.", "Message #1")
    End If

    ' Displays the string in a text box with autoConvert equal to true.
    Dim myData As String = "The data is " +                        ↵
myDataObject.GetData("System.String", True).ToString()
```

```
    MessageBox.Show(myData, "Message #2")
End Sub 'GetData3
```

[C#]
```
private void GetData3()
{
    // Creates a new data object using a text string.
    string myString = "Hello World!";
    DataObject myDataObject = new DataObject
 (DataFormats.Text, myString);

    // Displays the string with autoConvert equal to false.
    if (myDataObject.GetData("System.String", false) != null)
    {
        // Displays the string in a message box.
        MessageBox.Show(myDataObject.GetData
 ("System.String", false).ToString() + ".", "Message #1");
    }
    else
        // Displays a not found message in a message box.
        MessageBox.Show("Could not find data of the specified
format.", "Message #1");

    // Displays the string in a text box with autoConvert
equal to true.
    string myData = "The data is " +
myDataObject.GetData("System.String", true).ToString() +".";
    MessageBox.Show(myData,"Message #2");
}
```

[C++]
```
private:
    void GetData3() {
        // Creates a new data object using a text string.
        String* myString = S"Hello World!";
        DataObject* myDataObject =
            new DataObject(DataFormats::Text, myString);

        // Displays the string with autoConvert equal to false.
        if (myDataObject->GetData(S"System::String", false) != 0) {
            // Displays the string in a message box.
            MessageBox::Show(String::Concat(
                myDataObject->GetData(S"System::String", false),
                S"."), S"Message #1");
        } else
            // Displays a not found message in a message box.
            MessageBox::Show(
                S"Could not find data of the specified format.",
                S"Message #1");

        // Displays the string in a text box with autoConvert
equal to true.
        String* myData = String::Concat(S"The data is ",
            myDataObject->GetData(S"System::String", true), S".");
        MessageBox::Show(myData, S"Message #2");
    }
```

IDataObject.GetData Method (String)

Retrieves the data associated with the specified data format.

[Visual Basic]
```
Function GetData( _
   ByVal format As String _
) As Object
```
[C#]
```
object GetData(
   string format
);
```
[C++]
```
Object* GetData(
   String* format
);
```
[JScript]
```
function GetData(
   format : String
) : Object;
```

Parameters

format
: The format of the data to retrieve. See **DataFormats** for predefined formats.

Return Value

The data associated with the specified format, or a null reference (**Nothing** in Visual Basic).

Remarks

If this method cannot find data in the specified format, it attempts to convert the data to the format. If the data cannot be converted to the specified format, this method returns a null reference (**Nothing** in Visual Basic).

To determine whether data is associated with, or can be converted to, a format, call **GetDataPresent** before calling **GetData**. Call **GetFormats** for a list of valid formats for the data stored in this instance.

> **Note** Data can be converted to another format if it was stored specifying that conversion is allowed, and if the requested format is compatible with the stored format. For example, data stored as Unicode can be converted to text.

For an implementation of this method, see **DataObject.GetData**.

Example

See related example in the **System.Windows.Forms.IDataObject** interface topic.

Requirements

Platforms: Windows 98, Windows NT 4.0, Windows Millennium Edition, Windows 2000, Windows XP Home Edition, Windows XP Professional, Windows Server 2003 family

IDataObject.GetData Method (Type)

Retrieves the data associated with the specified class type format.

[Visual Basic]
```
Function GetData( _
   ByVal format As Type _
) As Object
```
[C#]
```
object GetData(
   Type format
);
```
[C++]
```
Object* GetData(
   Type* format
);
```
[JScript]
```
function GetData(
   format : Type
) : Object;
```

Parameters

format
: A **Type** representing the format of the data to retrieve. See **DataFormats** for predefined formats.

Return Value

The data associated with the specified format, or a null reference (**Nothing** in Visual Basic).

Remarks

If this method cannot find data in the specified format, it attempts to convert the data to the format. If the data cannot be converted to the specified format, this method returns a null reference (**Nothing** in Visual Basic).

To determine whether data is associated with, or can be converted to, a format, call **GetDataPresent** before calling **GetData**. Call **GetFormats** for a list of valid formats for the data stored in this instance.

> **Note** Data can be converted to another format if it was stored specifying that conversion is allowed, and if the requested format is compatible with the stored format. For example, data stored as Unicode can be converted to text.

Example

See related example in the **System.Windows.Forms.IDataObject** interface topic.

Requirements

Platforms: Windows 98, Windows NT 4.0, Windows Millennium Edition, Windows 2000, Windows XP Home Edition, Windows XP Professional, Windows Server 2003 family

IDataObject.GetData Method (String, Boolean)

Retrieves the data associated with the specified data format, using a Boolean to determine whether to convert the data to the format.

```
[Visual Basic]
Function GetData( _
   ByVal format As String, _
   ByVal autoConvert As Boolean _
) As Object
[C#]
object GetData(
   string format,
   bool autoConvert
);
[C++]
Object* GetData(
   String* format,
   bool autoConvert
);
[JScript]
function GetData(
   format : String,
   autoConvert : Boolean
) : Object;
```

Parameters

format

The format of the data to retrieve. See **DataFormats** for predefined formats.

autoConvert

true to convert the data to the specified format; otherwise, **false**.

Return Value

The data associated with the specified format, or a null reference (**Nothing** in Visual Basic).

Remarks

If the *autoConvert* parameter is **true** and this method cannot find data in the specified format, it attempts to convert the data to the format. If the data cannot be converted to the specified format, or if the data was stored with the *autoConvert* parameter set to **false**, this method returns a null reference (**Nothing** in Visual Basic).

If the *autoConvert* parameter is **false**, this method returns data in the specified format, or a null reference (**Nothing**) if no data in this format can be found.

To determine whether data is associated with, or can be converted to, a format, call **GetDataPresent** before calling **GetData**. Call **GetFormats** for a list of valid formats for the data stored in this instance.

> **Note** Data can be converted to another format if it was stored specifying that conversion is allowed, and if the requested format is compatible with the stored format. For example, data stored as Unicode can be converted to text.

Example

See related example in the **System.Windows.Forms.IDataObject** interface topic.

Requirements

Platforms: Windows 98, Windows NT 4.0, Windows Millennium Edition, Windows 2000, Windows XP Home Edition, Windows XP Professional, Windows Server 2003 family

IDataObject.GetDataPresent Method

Determines whether data stored in this instance is associated with the specified format.

Overload List

Determines whether data stored in this instance is associated with, or can be converted to, the specified format.

[Visual Basic] **Overloads Function GetDataPresent(String) As Boolean**

[C#] **bool GetDataPresent(string);**

[C++] **bool GetDataPresent(String*);**

[JScript] **function GetDataPresent(String) : Boolean;**

Determines whether data stored in this instance is associated with, or can be converted to, the specified format.

[Visual Basic] **Overloads Function GetDataPresent(Type) As Boolean**

[C#] **bool GetDataPresent(Type);**

[C++] **bool GetDataPresent(Type*);**

[JScript] **function GetDataPresent(Type) : Boolean;**

Determines whether data stored in this instance is associated with the specified format, using a Boolean value to determine whether to convert the data to the format.

[Visual Basic] **Overloads Function GetDataPresent(String, Boolean) As Boolean**

[C#] **bool GetDataPresent(string, bool);**

[C++] **bool GetDataPresent(String*, bool);**

[JScript] **function GetDataPresent(String, Boolean) : Boolean;**

Example

See related example in the **System.Windows.Forms.IDataObject** interface topic.

IDataObject.GetDataPresent Method (String)

Determines whether data stored in this instance is associated with, or can be converted to, the specified format.

```
[Visual Basic]
Function GetDataPresent( _
   ByVal format As String _
) As Boolean
[C#]
bool GetDataPresent(
   string format
);
[C++]
bool GetDataPresent(
   String* format
);
[JScript]
function GetDataPresent(
   format : String
) : Boolean;
```

Parameters

format
: The format for which to check. See **DataFormats** for predefined formats.

Return Value

true if data stored in this instance is associated with, or can be converted to, the specified format; otherwise **false**.

Remarks

Call this method to determine whether a format exists in this **DataObject** before calling **GetData**. Call **GetFormats** for the formats that are available in this instance.

> **Note** Data can be converted to another format if it was stored specifying that conversion is allowed, and if the requested format is compatible with the stored format. For example, data stored as Unicode can be converted to text.

Example

See related example in the **System.Windows.Forms.IDataObject** interface topic.

Requirements

Platforms: Windows 98, Windows NT 4.0, Windows Millennium Edition, Windows 2000, Windows XP Home Edition, Windows XP Professional, Windows Server 2003 family

IDataObject.GetDataPresent Method (Type)

Determines whether data stored in this instance is associated with, or can be converted to, the specified format.

```
[Visual Basic]
Function GetDataPresent( _
   ByVal format As Type _
) As Boolean
[C#]
bool GetDataPresent(
   Type format
);
[C++]
bool GetDataPresent(
   Type* format
);
[JScript]
function GetDataPresent(
   format : Type
) : Boolean;
```

Parameters

format
: A **Type** representing the format for which to check. See **DataFormats** for predefined formats.

Return Value

true if data stored in this instance is associated with, or can be converted to, the specified format; otherwise, **false**.

Remarks

Call this method to determine whether a format exists in this **DataObject** before calling **GetData**. Call **GetFormats** for the formats that are available in this instance.

> **Note** Data can be converted to another format if it was stored specifying that conversion is allowed, and if the requested format is compatible with the stored format. For example, data stored as Unicode can be converted to text.

Example

See related example in the **System.Windows.Forms.IDataObject** interface topic.

Requirements

Platforms: Windows 98, Windows NT 4.0, Windows Millennium Edition, Windows 2000, Windows XP Home Edition, Windows XP Professional, Windows Server 2003 family

IDataObject.GetDataPresent Method (String, Boolean)

Determines whether data stored in this instance is associated with the specified format, using a Boolean value to determine whether to convert the data to the format.

```
[Visual Basic]
Function GetDataPresent( _
   ByVal format As String, _
   ByVal autoConvert As Boolean _
) As Boolean
[C#]
bool GetDataPresent(
   string format,
   bool autoConvert
);
[C++]
bool GetDataPresent(
   String* format,
   bool autoConvert
);
[JScript]
function GetDataPresent(
   format : String,
   autoConvert : Boolean
) : Boolean;
```

Parameters

format
: The format for which to check. See **DataFormats** for predefined formats.

autoConvert
true to determine whether data stored in this instance can be converted to the specified format; **false** to check whether the data is in the specified format.

Return Value

true if the data is in, or can be converted to, the specified format; otherwise, **false**.

Remarks

Call this method to determine whether a format exists in this **DataObject** before calling **GetData**. Call **GetFormats** for the formats that are available in this instance.

This method returns **true** when:

- The *autoConvert* parameter is **true** and the data is in a format that can be converted to the appropriate format.
- The *autoConvert* parameter is **false** and the data is in the appropriate format.

This method returns **false** when:

- The *autoConvert* parameter is **true** and this method cannot find data in the specified format, and it cannot convert data to the specified format, or the data was stored with *autoConvert* set to **false**.
- The *autoConvert* parameter is **false**, and data does not exist in this instance in the specified format.

> **Note** Data can be converted to another format if it was stored specifying that conversion is allowed, and if the requested format is compatible with the stored format. For example, data stored as Unicode can be converted to text.

Example

See related example in the **System.Windows.Forms.IDataObject** interface topic.

Requirements

Platforms: Windows 98, Windows NT 4.0, Windows Millennium Edition, Windows 2000, Windows XP Home Edition, Windows XP Professional, Windows Server 2003 family

IDataObject.GetFormats Method

Returns a list of all formats that data stored in this instance is associated with or can be converted to.

Overload List

Returns a list of all formats that data stored in this instance is associated with or can be converted to.

[Visual Basic] **Overloads Function GetFormats() As String()**

[C#] **string[] GetFormats();**

[C++] **String* GetFormats() __gc[];**

[JScript] **function GetFormats() : String[];**

Gets a list of all formats that data stored in this instance is associated with or can be converted to, using a Boolean value to determine whether to retrieve all formats that the data can be converted to or only native data formats.

[Visual Basic] **Overloads Function GetFormats(Boolean) As String()**

[C#] **string[] GetFormats(bool);**

[C++] **String* GetFormats(bool) __gc[];**

[JScript] **function GetFormats(Boolean) : String[];**

Example

See related example in the **System.Windows.Forms.IDataObject** interface topic.

IDataObject.GetFormats Method ()

Returns a list of all formats that data stored in this instance is associated with or can be converted to.

```
[Visual Basic]
Function GetFormats() As String()
[C#]
string[] GetFormats();
[C++]
String* GetFormats() __gc[];
[JScript]
function GetFormats() : String[];
```

Return Value

An array of the names that represents a list of all formats that are supported by the data stored in this object.

Remarks

Call this method to get the supported data formats before calling the **GetData** method. See the **DataFormats** class for the predefined formats.

> **Note** Data can be converted to another format if it was stored specifying that conversion is allowed, and if the requested format is compatible with the stored format. For example, data stored as Unicode can be converted to text.

Example

See related example in the **System.Windows.Forms.IDataObject** interface topic.

Requirements

Platforms: Windows 98, Windows NT 4.0, Windows Millennium Edition, Windows 2000, Windows XP Home Edition, Windows XP Professional, Windows Server 2003 family

IDataObject.GetFormats Method (Boolean)

Gets a list of all formats that data stored in this instance is associated with or can be converted to, using a Boolean value to determine whether to retrieve all formats that the data can be converted to or only native data formats.

```
[Visual Basic]
Function GetFormats( _
   ByVal autoConvert As Boolean _
) As String()
[C#]
string[] GetFormats(
   bool autoConvert
);
[C++]
String* GetFormats(
   bool autoConvert
) __gc[];
[JScript]
function GetFormats(
   autoConvert : Boolean
) : String[];
```

Parameters

autoConvert

true to retrieve all formats that data stored in this instance is associated with or can be converted to; **false** to retrieve only native data formats.

Return Value

An array of the names that represents a list of all formats that are supported by the data stored in this object.

Remarks

Call this method to get the supported data formats before calling the **GetData** method. See the **DataFormats** class for the predefined formats.

> **Note** Data can be converted to another format if it was stored specifying that conversion is allowed, and if the requested format is compatible with the stored format. For example, data stored as Unicode can be converted to text.

Example

See related example in the **System.Windows.Forms.IDataObject** interface topic.

Requirements

Platforms: Windows 98, Windows NT 4.0, Windows Millennium Edition, Windows 2000, Windows XP Home Edition, Windows XP Professional, Windows Server 2003 family

IDataObject.SetData Method

Stores the specified data and its associated format in this instance.

Overload List

Stores the specified data in this instance, using the class of the data for the format.

[Visual Basic] **Overloads Sub SetData(Object)**

[C#] **void SetData(object);**

[C++] **void SetData(Object*);**

[JScript] **function SetData(Object);**

Stores the specified data and its associated format in this instance.

[Visual Basic] **Overloads Sub SetData(String, Object)**

[C#] **void SetData(string, object);**

[C++] **void SetData(String*, Object*);**

[JScript] **function SetData(String, Object);**

Stores the specified data and its associated class type in this instance.

[Visual Basic] **Overloads Sub SetData(Type, Object)**

[C#] **void SetData(Type, object);**

[C++] **void SetData(Type*, Object*);**

[JScript] **function SetData(Type, Object);**

Stores the specified data and its associated format in this instance, using a Boolean value to specify whether the data can be converted to another format.

[Visual Basic] **Overloads Sub SetData(String, Boolean, Object)**

[C#] **void SetData(string, bool, object);**

[C++] **void SetData(String*, bool, Object*);**

[JScript] **function SetData(String, Boolean, Object);**

Example

See related example in the **System.Windows.Forms.IDataObject** interface topic.

IDataObject.SetData Method (Object)

Stores the specified data in this instance, using the class of the data for the format.

```
[Visual Basic]
Sub SetData( _
   ByVal data As Object _
)
[C#]
void SetData(
   object data
);
[C++]
void SetData(
   Object* data
);
[JScript]
function SetData(
   data : Object
);
```

Parameters

data

The data to store.

Remarks

The format is derived from the data class.

Data stored using this method can be converted to a compatible format when it is retrieved.

Example

See related example in the **System.Windows.Forms.IDataObject** interface topic.

Requirements

Platforms: Windows 98, Windows NT 4.0, Windows Millennium Edition, Windows 2000, Windows XP Home Edition, Windows XP Professional, Windows Server 2003 family

IDataObject.SetData Method (String, Object)

Stores the specified data and its associated format in this instance.

```
[Visual Basic]
Sub SetData( _
   ByVal format As String, _
   ByVal data As Object _
)
[C#]
void SetData(
   string format,
   object data
);
[C++]
void SetData(
   String* format,
   Object* data
);
[JScript]
function SetData(
   format : String,
   data : Object
);
```

Parameters

format

The format associated with the data. See **DataFormats** for predefined formats.

data

The data to store.

Remarks

If you do not know the format of the target application, you can store data in multiple formats using this method.

Data stored using this method can be converted to a compatible format when it is retrieved.

Example

See related example in the **System.Windows.Forms.IDataObject** interface topic.

Requirements

Platforms: Windows 98, Windows NT 4.0,
Windows Millennium Edition, Windows 2000,
Windows XP Home Edition, Windows XP Professional,
Windows Server 2003 family

IDataObject.SetData Method (Type, Object)

Stores the specified data and its associated class type in this instance.

```
[Visual Basic]
Sub SetData( _
   ByVal format As Type, _
   ByVal data As Object _
)
[C#]
void SetData(
   Type format,
   object data
);
[C++]
void SetData(
   Type* format,
   Object* data
);
[JScript]
function SetData(
   format : Type,
   data : Object
);
```

Parameters

format

A **Type** representing the format associated with the data. See **DataFormats** for predefined formats.

data

The data to store.

Remarks

If you do not know the format of the target application, you can store data in multiple formats using this method.

Data stored using this method can be converted to a compatible format when it is retrieved.

Example

See related example in the **System.Windows.Forms.IDataObject** interface topic.

Requirements

Platforms: Windows 98, Windows NT 4.0,
Windows Millennium Edition, Windows 2000,
Windows XP Home Edition, Windows XP Professional,
Windows Server 2003 family

IDataObject.SetData Method (String, Boolean, Object)

Stores the specified data and its associated format in this instance, using a Boolean value to specify whether the data can be converted to another format.

```
[Visual Basic]
Sub SetData( _
   ByVal format As String, _
   ByVal autoConvert As Boolean, _
   ByVal data As Object _
)
[C#]
void SetData(
   string format,
   bool autoConvert,
   object data
);
[C++]
void SetData(
   String* format,
   bool autoConvert,
   Object* data
);
[JScript]
function SetData(
   format : String,
   autoConvert : Boolean,
   data : Object
);
```

Parameters

format

The format associated with the data. See **DataFormats** for predefined formats.

autoConvert

true to allow the data to be converted to another format; otherwise, **false**.

data

The data to store.

Remarks

If you do not know the format of the target application, you can store data in multiple formats using this method.

Example

See related example in the **System.Windows.Forms.IDataObject** interface topic.

Requirements

Platforms: Windows 98, Windows NT 4.0,
Windows Millennium Edition, Windows 2000,
Windows XP Home Edition, Windows XP Professional,
Windows Server 2003 family

IFeatureSupport Interface

Specifies a standard interface for retrieving feature information from the current system.

[Visual Basic]
```
Public Interface IFeatureSupport
```
[C#]
```
public interface IFeatureSupport
```
[C++]
```
public __gc __interface IFeatureSupport
```
[JScript]
```
public interface IFeatureSupport
```

Classes that Implement IFeatureSupport

Class	Description
FeatureSupport	Provides static (**Shared** in Visual Basic) methods for retrieving feature information from the current system.

Remarks

When implemented in a class, **IFeatureSupport** provides methods you can use to determine whether a feature is currently installed on the system and to get the version number of a feature. Call **IsPresent** to determine whether a feature, or a specific version of a feature, is currently installed. Call **GetVersionPresent** to determine the version number of an installed feature.

Example

[Visual Basic, C#] The following example uses the **OSFeature** implementation of **IFeatureSupport** and queries for the **LayeredWindows** feature. The version is checked to see if it is a null reference (**Nothing** in Visual Basic), to determine whether the feature is present. The result is displayed in a text box. This code assumes `textBox1` has been created and placed on a form.

[Visual Basic]
```
Private Sub LayeredWindows()
    ' Gets the version of the layered windows feature.
    Dim myVersion As Version = _
       OSFeature.Feature.GetVersionPresent(OSFeature.LayeredWindows)

    ' Prints whether the feature is available.
    If Not (myVersion Is Nothing) Then
        textBox1.Text = "Layered windows feature is installed." & _
           ControlChars.CrLf
    Else
        textBox1.Text = "Layered windows feature is not installed." & _
           ControlChars.CrLf
    End If
    'This is an alternate way to check whether a feature is present.
    If OSFeature.Feature.IsPresent(OSFeature.LayeredWindows) Then
        textBox1.Text &= "Again, layered windows feature is installed."
    Else
        textBox1.Text &= "Again, layered windows feature is not
installed."
    End If
End Sub
```

[C#]
```
private void LayeredWindows() {
   // Gets the version of the layered windows feature.
   Version myVersion =
OSFeature.Feature.GetVersionPresent(OSFeature.LayeredWindows);

   // Prints whether the feature is available.
   if (myVersion != null)
      textBox1.Text = "Layered windows feature is installed." + '\n';
   else
      textBox1.Text = "Layered windows feature is not
installed." + '\n';

   // This is an alternate way to check whether a feature is present.
   if (OSFeature.Feature.IsPresent(OSFeature.LayeredWindows))
      textBox1.Text += "Again, layered windows feature is installed.";
   else
      textBox1.Text += "Again, layered windows feature is not
installed.";
}
```

Requirements

Namespace: System.Windows.Forms

Platforms: Windows 98, Windows NT 4.0, Windows Millennium Edition, Windows 2000, Windows XP Home Edition, Windows XP Professional, Windows Server 2003 family

Assembly: System.Windows.Forms (in System.Windows.Forms.dll)

IFeatureSupport.GetVersionPresent Method

Retrieves the version of the specified feature.

[Visual Basic]
```
Function GetVersionPresent( _
   ByVal feature As Object _
) As Version
```
[C#]
```
Version GetVersionPresent(
   object feature
);
```
[C++]
```
Version* GetVersionPresent(
   Object* feature
);
```
[JScript]
```
function GetVersionPresent(
   feature : Object
) : Version;
```

Parameters

feature
The feature whose version is requested.

Return Value

A **Version** representing the version number of the specified feature; or a null reference (**Nothing** in Visual Basic) if the feature is not installed.

Example

See related example in the **System.Windows.Forms.IFeatureSupport** interface topic.

Requirements

Platforms: Windows 98, Windows NT 4.0, Windows Millennium Edition, Windows 2000, Windows XP Home Edition, Windows XP Professional, Windows Server 2003 family

IFeatureSupport.IsPresent Method

Determines whether the specified feature is currently available on the system.

Overload List

Determines whether any version of the specified feature is currently available on the system.

[Visual Basic] **Overloads Function IsPresent(Object) As Boolean**

[C#] **bool IsPresent(object);**

[C++] **bool IsPresent(Object*);**

[JScript] **function IsPresent(Object) : Boolean;**

Determines whether the specified or newer version of the specified feature is currently available on the system.

[Visual Basic] **Overloads Function IsPresent(Object, Version) As Boolean**

[C#] **bool IsPresent(object, Version);**

[C++] **bool IsPresent(Object*, Version*);**

[JScript] **function IsPresent(Object, Version) : Boolean;**

Example

See related example in the **System.Windows.Forms.IFeature-Support** interface topic.

IFeatureSupport.IsPresent Method (Object)

Determines whether any version of the specified feature is currently available on the system.

```
[Visual Basic]
Function IsPresent( _
   ByVal feature As Object _
) As Boolean
[C#]
bool IsPresent(
   object feature
);
[C++]
bool IsPresent(
   Object* feature
);
[JScript]
function IsPresent(
   feature : Object
) : Boolean;
```

Parameters

feature

The feature to look for.

Return Value

true if the feature is present; otherwise, **false**.

Example

See related example in the **System.Windows.Forms.IFeature-Support** interface topic.

Requirements

Platforms: Windows 98, Windows NT 4.0, Windows Millennium Edition, Windows 2000, Windows XP Home Edition, Windows XP Professional, Windows Server 2003 family

IFeatureSupport.IsPresent Method (Object, Version)

Determines whether the specified or newer version of the specified feature is currently available on the system.

```
[Visual Basic]
Function IsPresent( _
   ByVal feature As Object, _
   ByVal minimumVersion As Version _
) As Boolean
[C#]
bool IsPresent(
   object feature,
   Version minimumVersion
);
[C++]
bool IsPresent(
   Object* feature,
   Version* minimumVersion
);
[JScript]
function IsPresent(
   feature : Object,
   minimumVersion : Version
) : Boolean;
```

Parameters

feature

The feature to look for.

minimumVersion

A **Version** representing the minimum version number of the feature to look for.

Return Value

true if the requested version of the feature is present; otherwise, **false**.

Example

See related example in the **System.Windows.Forms.IFeature-Support** interface topic.

Requirements

Platforms: Windows 98, Windows NT 4.0, Windows Millennium Edition, Windows 2000, Windows XP Home Edition, Windows XP Professional, Windows Server 2003 family

IFileReaderService Interface

This type supports the .NET Framework infrastructure and is not intended to be used directly from your code.

[Visual Basic]
```
Public Interface IFileReaderService
```
[C#]
```
public interface IFileReaderService
```
[C++]
```
public __gc __interface IFileReaderService
```
[JScript]
```
public interface IFileReaderService
```

IFileReaderService.OpenFileFromSource Method

This member supports the .NET Framework infrastructure and is not intended to be used directly from your code.

[Visual Basic]
```
Function OpenFileFromSource( _
   ByVal relativePath As String _
) As Stream
```
[C#]
```
Stream OpenFileFromSource(
   string relativePath
);
```
[C++]
```
Stream* OpenFileFromSource(
   String* relativePath
);
```
[JScript]
```
function OpenFileFromSource(
   relativePath : String
) : Stream;
```

ImageIndexConverter Class

Provides a type converter to convert data for an image index to and from a string.

System.Object
  System.ComponentModel.TypeConverter
    System.ComponentModel.BaseNumberConverter
      System.ComponentModel.Int32Converter
        System.Windows.Forms.ImageIndexConverter
          System.Windows.Forms.TreeViewImageIndex-Converter

[Visual Basic]
```
Public Class ImageIndexConverter
   Inherits Int32Converter
```
[C#]
```
public class ImageIndexConverter : Int32Converter
```
[C++]
```
public __gc class ImageIndexConverter : public Int32Converter
```
[JScript]
```
public class ImageIndexConverter extends Int32Converter
```

Thread Safety

Any public static (**Shared** in Visual Basic) members of this type are safe for multithreaded operations. Any instance members are not guaranteed to be thread safe.

Remarks

> **Note** Typically, you do not directly create an instance of an **ImageIndexConverter**. Instead, call the **GetConverter** method of **TypeDescriptor**. For more information, see the examples in the **TypeConverter** base class.

Requirements

Namespace: System.Windows.Forms

Platforms: Windows 98, Windows NT 4.0, Windows Millennium Edition, Windows 2000, Windows XP Home Edition, Windows XP Professional, Windows Server 2003 family

Assembly: System.Windows.Forms (in System.Windows.Forms.dll)

ImageIndexConverter Constructor

Initializes a new instance of the **ImageIndexConverter** class.

[Visual Basic]
```
Public Sub New()
```
[C#]
```
public ImageIndexConverter();
```
[C++]
```
public: ImageIndexConverter();
```
[JScript]
```
public function ImageIndexConverter();
```

Remarks

The default constructor initializes any fields to their default values.

Requirements

Platforms: Windows 98, Windows NT 4.0, Windows Millennium Edition, Windows 2000, Windows XP Home Edition, Windows XP Professional, Windows Server 2003 family

ImageIndexConverter.IncludeNoneAsStandardValue Property

Gets or sets a value indicating whether a **none** or a null reference (**Nothing** in Visual Basic) value is valid in the **TypeConverter.StandardValuesCollection** collection.

[Visual Basic]
```
Protected Overridable ReadOnly Property IncludeNoneAsStandardValue _
   _
   As Boolean
```
[C#]
```
protected virtual bool IncludeNoneAsStandardValue {get;}
```
[C++]
```
protected: __property virtual bool get_IncludeNoneAsStandardValue();
```
[JScript]
```
protected function get IncludeNoneAsStandardValue() : Boolean;
```

Property Value

true if a **none** or a null reference (**Nothing** in Visual Basic) value is valid in the standard values collection; otherwise, **false**.

Remarks

As implemented in this class is always returns **true**.

Requirements

Platforms: Windows 98, Windows NT 4.0, Windows Millennium Edition, Windows 2000, Windows XP Home Edition, Windows XP Professional, Windows Server 2003 family

ImageIndexConverter.ConvertFrom Method

Converts the given value to the native type of the converter.

Overload List

This member supports the .NET Framework infrastructure and is not intended to be used directly from your code.

[Visual Basic] **Overloads Overrides Public Function ConvertFrom(ITypeDescriptorContext, CultureInfo, Object) As Object**

[C#] **public override object ConvertFrom(ITypeDescriptorContext, CultureInfo, object);**

[C++] **public: Object* ConvertFrom(ITypeDescriptorContext*, CultureInfo*, Object*);**

[JScript] **public override function ConvertFrom(ITypeDescriptorContext, CultureInfo, Object) : Object;**

Inherited from **TypeConverter**.

[Visual Basic] **Overloads Public Function ConvertFrom(Object) As Object**

[C#] **public object ConvertFrom(object);**

[C++] **public: Object* ConvertFrom(Object*);**

[JScript] **public function ConvertFrom(Object) : Object;**

ImageIndexConverter.ConvertFrom Method (ITypeDescriptorContext, CultureInfo, Object)

This member overrides **TypeConverter.ConvertFrom**.

```
[Visual Basic]
Overrides Overloads Public Function ConvertFrom( _
   ByVal context As ITypeDescriptorContext, _
   ByVal culture As CultureInfo, _
   ByVal value As Object _
) As Object
[C#]
public override object ConvertFrom(
   ITypeDescriptorContext context,
   CultureInfo culture,
   object value
);
[C++]
public: Object* ConvertFrom(
   ITypeDescriptorContext* context,
   CultureInfo* culture,
   Object* value
);
[JScript]
public override function ConvertFrom(
   context : ITypeDescriptorContext,
   culture : CultureInfo,
   value : Object
) : Object;
```

Requirements

Platforms: Windows 98, Windows NT 4.0, Windows Millennium Edition, Windows 2000, Windows XP Home Edition, Windows XP Professional, Windows Server 2003 family

ImageIndexConverter.ConvertTo Method

Converts the given value object to the specified destination type.

Overload List

This member supports the .NET Framework infrastructure and is not intended to be used directly from your code.

[Visual Basic] **Overloads Overrides Public Function ConvertTo(ITypeDescriptorContext, CultureInfo, Object, Type) As Object**

[C#] **public override object ConvertTo(ITypeDescriptorContext, CultureInfo, object, Type);**

[C++] **public: Object* ConvertTo(ITypeDescriptorContext*, CultureInfo*, Object*, Type*);**

[JScript] **public override function ConvertTo(ITypeDescriptorContext, CultureInfo, Object, Type) : Object;**

Inherited from **TypeConverter**.

[Visual Basic] **Overloads Public Function ConvertTo(Object, Type) As Object**

[C#] **public object ConvertTo(object, Type);**

[C++] **public: Object* ConvertTo(Object*, Type*);**

[JScript] **public function ConvertTo(Object, Type) : Object;**

ImageIndexConverter.ConvertTo Method (ITypeDescriptorContext, CultureInfo, Object, Type)

This member overrides **TypeConverter.ConvertTo**.

```
[Visual Basic]
Overrides Overloads Public Function ConvertTo( _
   ByVal context As ITypeDescriptorContext, _
   ByVal culture As CultureInfo, _
   ByVal value As Object, _
   ByVal destinationType As Type _
) As Object
[C#]
public override object ConvertTo(
   ITypeDescriptorContext context,
   CultureInfo culture,
   object value,
   Type destinationType
);
[C++]
public: Object* ConvertTo(
   ITypeDescriptorContext* context,
   CultureInfo* culture,
   Object* value,
   Type* destinationType
);
[JScript]
public override function ConvertTo(
   context : ITypeDescriptorContext,
   culture : CultureInfo,
   value : Object,
   destinationType : Type
) : Object;
```

Requirements

Platforms: Windows 98, Windows NT 4.0, Windows Millennium Edition, Windows 2000, Windows XP Home Edition, Windows XP Professional, Windows Server 2003 family

ImageIndexConverter.GetStandardValues Method

Returns a collection of standard values for the data type this type converter is designed for.

Overload List

This member supports the .NET Framework infrastructure and is not intended to be used directly from your code.

[Visual Basic] **Overloads Overrides Public Function GetStandardValues(ITypeDescriptorContext) As StandardValuesCollection**

[C#] **public override StandardValuesCollection GetStandardValues(ITypeDescriptorContext);**

[C++] **public: StandardValuesCollection* GetStandardValues(ITypeDescriptorContext*);**

[JScript] **public override function GetStandardValues(ITypeDescriptorContext) : StandardValuesCollection;**

Inherited from **TypeConverter**.

[Visual Basic] **Overloads Public Function GetStandardValues() As ICollection**

[C#] **public ICollection GetStandardValues();**

[C++] **public: ICollection* GetStandardValues();**

[JScript] **public function GetStandardValues() : ICollection;**

ImageIndexConverter.GetStandardValues Method (ITypeDescriptorContext)

This member overrides **TypeConverter.GetStandardValues**.

```
[Visual Basic]
Overrides Overloads Public Function GetStandardValues( _
   ByVal context As ITypeDescriptorContext _
) As StandardValuesCollection
[C#]
public override StandardValuesCollection GetStandardValues(
   ITypeDescriptorContext context
);
[C++]
public: StandardValuesCollection* GetStandardValues(
   ITypeDescriptorContext* context
);
[JScript]
public override function GetStandardValues(
   context : ITypeDescriptorContext
) : StandardValuesCollection;
```

Requirements

Platforms: Windows 98, Windows NT 4.0, Windows Millennium Edition, Windows 2000, Windows XP Home Edition, Windows XP Professional, Windows Server 2003 family

ImageIndexConverter.GetStandardValues-Exclusive Method

Overload List

This member supports the .NET Framework infrastructure and is not intended to be used directly from your code.

[Visual Basic] **Overloads Overrides Public Function GetStandardValuesExclusive(ITypeDescriptorContext) As Boolean**

[C#] **public override bool GetStandardValues-Exclusive(ITypeDescriptorContext);**

[C++] **public: bool GetStandardValues-Exclusive(ITypeDescriptorContext*);**

[JScript] **public override function GetStandardValues-Exclusive(ITypeDescriptorContext) : Boolean;**

Inherited from **TypeConverter**.

[Visual Basic] **Overloads Public Function GetStandardValuesExclusive() As Boolean**

[C#] **public bool GetStandardValuesExclusive();**

[C++] **public: bool GetStandardValuesExclusive();**

[JScript] **public function GetStandardValuesExclusive() : Boolean;**

ImageIndexConverter.GetStandardValuesExclusive Method (ITypeDescriptorContext)

This member overrides **TypeConverter.GetStandardValuesExclusive**.

```
[Visual Basic]
Overrides Overloads Public Function GetStandardValuesExclusive( _
   ByVal context As ITypeDescriptorContext _
) As Boolean
[C#]
public override bool GetStandardValuesExclusive(
   ITypeDescriptorContext context
);
[C++]
public: bool GetStandardValuesExclusive(
   ITypeDescriptorContext* context
);
[JScript]
public override function GetStandardValuesExclusive(
   context : ITypeDescriptorContext
) : Boolean;
```

Requirements

Platforms: Windows 98, Windows NT 4.0, Windows Millennium Edition, Windows 2000, Windows XP Home Edition, Windows XP Professional, Windows Server 2003 family

ImageIndexConverter.GetStandardValues-Supported Method

Returns whether this object supports a standard set of values that can be picked from a list.

Overload List

This member supports the .NET Framework infrastructure and is not intended to be used directly from your code.

[Visual Basic] **Overloads Overrides Public Function GetStandardValuesSupported(ITypeDescriptorContext) As Boolean**

[C#] **public override bool GetStandardValues-Supported(ITypeDescriptorContext);**

[C++] **public: bool GetStandardValues-Supported(ITypeDescriptorContext*);**

[JScript] **public override function GetStandardValues-Supported(ITypeDescriptorContext) : Boolean;**

Inherited from **TypeConverter**.

[Visual Basic] **Overloads Public Function GetStandard-ValuesSupported() As Boolean**

[C#] **public bool GetStandardValuesSupported();**

[C++] **public: bool GetStandardValuesSupported();**

[JScript] **public function GetStandardValuesSupported() : Boolean;**

ImageIndexConverter.GetStandardValuesSupported Method (ITypeDescriptorContext)

This member overrides **TypeConverter.GetStandardValuesSupported**.

[Visual Basic]
```
Overrides Overloads Public Function GetStandardValuesSupported( _
   ByVal context As ITypeDescriptorContext _
) As Boolean
```
[C#]
```
public override bool GetStandardValuesSupported(
   ITypeDescriptorContext context
);
```
[C++]
```
public: bool GetStandardValuesSupported(
   ITypeDescriptorContext* context
);
```
[JScript]
```
public override function GetStandardValuesSupported(
   context : ITypeDescriptorContext
) : Boolean;
```

Requirements

Platforms: Windows 98, Windows NT 4.0, Windows Millennium Edition, Windows 2000, Windows XP Home Edition, Windows XP Professional, Windows Server 2003 family

ImageList Class

Provides methods to manage a collection of **Image** objects. This class cannot be inherited.

System.Object
  System.MarshalByRefObject
    System.ComponentModel.Component
      System.Windows.Forms.ImageList

[Visual Basic]
```
NotInheritable Public Class ImageList
   Inherits Component
```
[C#]
```
public sealed class ImageList : Component
```
[C++]
```
public __gc __sealed class ImageList : public Component
```
[JScript]
```
public class ImageList extends Component
```

Thread Safety

Any public static (**Shared** in Visual Basic) members of this type are safe for multithreaded operations. Any instance members are not guaranteed to be thread safe.

Remarks

ImageList is typically used by other controls, such as the **ListView**, **TreeView**, or **ToolBar**. You can add bitmaps, icons, or meta files to the **ImageList**, and the other controls are able to use the images as they require.

ImageList uses a handle to manage the list of images. The **Handle** is not created until certain operations, including getting the **Count**, getting the **Handle**, and calling **Draw** are performed on the image list.

Example

[Visual Basic, C#] The following code example shows selecting images, removing images and displaying images.

[Visual Basic]
```
Imports System
Imports System.Drawing
Imports System.ComponentModel
Imports System.Windows.Forms

Namespace myImageRotator

    Public Class Form1
        Inherits System.Windows.Forms.Form
        Protected components As Container
        Protected listBox1 As ListBox
        Protected label2 As Label
        Protected label3 As Label
        Protected label5 As Label
        Protected pictureBox1 As PictureBox
        Protected button1 As Button
        Protected button2 As Button
        Protected button3 As Button
        Protected button4 As Button
        Protected panel1 As Panel
        Protected imageList1 As ImageList
        Protected myGraphics As Graphics
        Protected openFileDialog1 As OpenFileDialog

        Private currentImage As Integer = 0

        Public Sub New()
            InitializeComponent()
            imageList1 = New ImageList()
            ' The default image size is 16 x 16, which sets up a larger
            ' image size.
            imageList1.ImageSize = New Size(255, 255)
            imageList1.TransparentColor = Color.White
            ' Assigns the graphics object to use in the draw options.
            myGraphics = Graphics.FromHwnd(panel1.Handle)
        End Sub

        Protected Overloads Overrides Sub Dispose(ByVal disposing ↵
As Boolean)
            If disposing Then
                If Not (components Is Nothing) Then
                    components.Dispose()
                End If
            End If
            MyBase.Dispose(disposing)
        End Sub

        Private Sub InitializeComponent()
            ' Initializations for listBox1, label2, pictureBox1,
            ' button2, button3, panel1, openFileDialog1, ↵
button4, label1,
            ' button1, and imageList1.
        End Sub

        Protected Sub button1_Click(sender As Object, e As ↵
System.EventArgs)
            displayNextImage()
        End Sub

        Protected Sub button2_Click(sender As Object, e As ↵
System.EventArgs)
            imageList1.Images.RemoveAt(listBox1.SelectedIndex)
            listBox1.Items.Remove(listBox1.SelectedIndex)
        End Sub

        Protected Sub button3_Click(sender As Object, e As ↵
System.EventArgs)
            imageList1.Images.Clear()
        End Sub

        Protected Sub button4_Click(sender As Object, e As ↵
System.EventArgs)
            openFileDialog1.Multiselect = True
            If openFileDialog1.ShowDialog() = DialogResult.OK Then
                If Not (openFileDialog1.FileNames Is Nothing) Then
                    Dim i As Integer
                    For i = 0 To openFileDialog1.FileNames.Length - 1
                        addImage(openFileDialog1.FileNames(i))
                    Next i
                Else
                    addImage(openFileDialog1.FileName)
                End If
            End If
        End Sub

        Private Sub addImage(imageToLoad As String)
            If imageToLoad <> "" Then
                imageList1.Images.Add(Image.FromFile(imageToLoad))
                listBox1.BeginUpdate()
                listBox1.Items.Add(imageToLoad)
                listBox1.EndUpdate()
            End If
        End Sub

        Sub displayNextImage()
            If imageList1.Images.Empty <> True Then
                If imageList1.Images.Count - 1 < currentImage Then
                    currentImage += 1
                Else
                    currentImage = 0
                End If
                panel1.Refresh()
                imageList1.Draw(myGraphics, 10, 10, currentImage)
                pictureBox1.Image = imageList1.Images(currentImage)
```

```
                label3.Text = "Current image is " & currentImage
                listBox1.SelectedIndex = currentImage
                label5.Text = "Image is " & listBox1.Text
            End If
        End Sub

        Public Shared Sub Main()
            Application.Run(New Form1())
        End Sub

    End Class

End Namespace
```

[C#]

```
namespace myImageRotator
{
    using System;
    using System.Drawing;
    using System.ComponentModel;
    using System.Windows.Forms;

    public class Form1 : System.Windows.Forms.Form
    {
        protected Container components;
        protected ListBox listBox1;
        protected Label label2;
        protected Label label3;
        protected Label label5;
        protected PictureBox pictureBox1;
        protected Button button1;
        protected Button button2;
        protected Button button3;
        protected Button button4;
        protected Panel panel1;
        protected ImageList imageList1;
        protected Graphics myGraphics;
        protected OpenFileDialog openFileDialog1;

        private int currentImage = 0;

        public Form1()
        {
            InitializeComponent();
            imageList1 = new ImageList () ;
            // The default image size is 16 x 16, which sets          ↵
 up a larger
            // image size.
            imageList1.ImageSize = new Size(255,255);
            imageList1.TransparentColor = Color.White;
            // Assigns the graphics object to use in the draw options.
            myGraphics = Graphics.FromHwnd(panel1.Handle);
        }

        protected override void Dispose( bool disposing )
        {
            if( disposing )
            {
                if (components != null)
                {
                    components.Dispose();
                }
            }
            base.Dispose( disposing );
        }

        private void InitializeComponent()
        {
            // Initializations for listBox1, label2, pictureBox1,
            // button2, button3, panel1, openFileDialog1,          ↵
 button4, label1,
            // button1, and imageList1.
        }

        protected void button1_Click (object sender,               ↵
System.EventArgs e)
        {
            displayNextImage();
        }

        protected void button2_Click (object sender,               ↵
 System.EventArgs e)
        {
            imageList1.Images.RemoveAt(listBox1.SelectedIndex);
            listBox1.Items.Remove(listBox1.SelectedIndex);
        }

        protected void button3_Click (object sender,               ↵
System.EventArgs e)
        {
            imageList1.Images.Clear();
        }

        protected void button4_Click (object sender,               ↵
System.EventArgs e)
        {
            openFileDialog1.Multiselect = true ;
            if(openFileDialog1.ShowDialog() == DialogResult.OK)
            {
                if (openFileDialog1.FileNames != null)
                {
                    for(int i =0 ; i <                             ↵
openFileDialog1.FileNames.Length ; i++ )
                    {
                        addImage(openFileDialog1.FileNames[i]);
                    }
                }
                else
                    addImage(openFileDialog1.FileName);
            }
        }

        private void addImage(string imageToLoad)
        {
            if (imageToLoad != "")
            {
                imageList1.Images.Add(Image.FromFile(imageToLoad));
                listBox1.BeginUpdate();
                listBox1.Items.Add(imageToLoad);
                listBox1.EndUpdate();
            }
        }

        void displayNextImage()
        {
            if(imageList1.Images.Empty != true)
            {
                if(imageList1.Images.Count-1 < currentImage)
                {
                    currentImage++;
                }
                else
                    currentImage=0;
                panel1.Refresh();
                imageList1.Draw(myGraphics,10,10,currentImage);
                pictureBox1.Image = imageList1.Images[currentImage];
                label3.Text = "Current image is " + currentImage ;
                listBox1.SelectedIndex = currentImage;
                label5.Text = "Image is " + listBox1.Text ;
            }
        }

        public static void Main(string[] args)
        {
            Application.Run(new Form1());
        }
    }
}
```

Requirements

Namespace: System.Windows.Forms

Platforms: Windows 98, Windows NT 4.0, Windows Millennium Edition, Windows 2000, Windows XP Home Edition, Windows XP Professional, Windows Server 2003 family, .NET Compact Framework - Windows CE .NET

Assembly: System.Windows.Forms (in System.Windows.Forms.dll)

ImageList Constructor

Initializes a new instance of the **ImageList** class.

Overload List

Initializes a new instance of the **ImageList** class with default values for **ColorDepth**, **ImageSize**, and **TransparentColor**.

Supported by the .NET Compact Framework.

[Visual Basic] **Public Sub New()**

[C#] **public ImageList();**

[C++] **public: ImageList();**

[JScript] **public function ImageList();**

Initializes a new instance of the **ImageList** class, associating it with a container.

[Visual Basic] **Public Sub New(IContainer)**

[C#] **public ImageList(IContainer);**

[C++] **public: ImageList(IContainer*);**

[JScript] **public function ImageList(IContainer);**

ImageList Constructor ()

Initializes a new instance of the **ImageList** class with default values for **ColorDepth**, **ImageSize**, and **TransparentColor**.

```
[Visual Basic]
Public Sub New()
[C#]
public ImageList();
[C++]
public: ImageList();
[JScript]
public function ImageList();
```

Remarks

The following table shows initial property values for an instance of **ImageList**.

Item	Description
ColorDepth	The default value is **Depth4Bit**.
ImageSize	The default is a **Size** object with a height and width of 16 by 16.
TransparentColor	The default value is **Transparent**.

Requirements

Platforms: Windows 98, Windows NT 4.0, Windows Millennium Edition, Windows 2000, Windows XP Home Edition, Windows XP Professional, Windows Server 2003 family, .NET Compact Framework - Windows CE .NET

ImageList Constructor (IContainer)

Initializes a new instance of the **ImageList** class, associating it with a container.

```
[Visual Basic]
Public Sub New( _
   ByVal container As IContainer _
)
[C#]
public ImageList(
   IContainer container
);
[C++]
public: ImageList(
   IContainer* container
);
[JScript]
public function ImageList(
   container : IContainer
);
```

Parameters

container

An object implementing **IContainer** to associate with this instance of **ImageList**.

Remarks

This constructor adds the image list to the specified container.

Requirements

Platforms: Windows 98, Windows NT 4.0, Windows Millennium Edition, Windows 2000, Windows XP Home Edition, Windows XP Professional, Windows Server 2003 family

ImageList.ColorDepth Property

Gets the color depth of the image list.

```
[Visual Basic]
Public Property ColorDepth As ColorDepth
[C#]
public ColorDepth ColorDepth {get; set;}
[C++]
public: __property ColorDepth get_ColorDepth();
public: __property void set_ColorDepth(ColorDepth);
[JScript]
public function get ColorDepth() : ColorDepth;
public function set ColorDepth(ColorDepth);
```

Property Value

The number of available colors for the image. In the .NET Framework version 1.0, the default is **Depth4Bit**. In the .NET Framework version 1.1, the default is **Depth8Bit**.

Exceptions

Exception Type	Condition
InvalidEnumArgument-Exception	Not a valid **ColorDepth** Enumeration value.

Remarks

When you set the color depth to a new value, the **Handle** for the image list is recreated.

Requirements

Platforms: Windows 98, Windows NT 4.0,
Windows Millennium Edition, Windows 2000,
Windows XP Home Edition, Windows XP Professional,
Windows Server 2003 family

ImageList.Handle Property

Gets the handle of the image list object.

```
[Visual Basic]
Public ReadOnly Property Handle As IntPtr
[C#]
public IntPtr Handle {get;}
[C++]
public: __property IntPtr get_Handle();
[JScript]
public function get Handle() : IntPtr;
```

Property Value

The handle for the image list. The default value is a null reference (**Nothing** in Visual Basic).

Remarks

This corresponds to a Win32 HIMAGELIST handle. The handle is not created until you need to use it. Getting the handle causes it to be created.

Requirements

Platforms: Windows 98, Windows NT 4.0,
Windows Millennium Edition, Windows 2000,
Windows XP Home Edition, Windows XP Professional,
Windows Server 2003 family

ImageList.HandleCreated Property

Gets a value indicating whether the underlying Win32 handle has been created.

```
[Visual Basic]
Public ReadOnly Property HandleCreated As Boolean
[C#]
public bool HandleCreated {get;}
[C++]
public: __property bool get_HandleCreated();
[JScript]
public function get HandleCreated() : Boolean;
```

Property Value

true if the **Handle** has been created; otherwise, **false**. The default is **false**.

Requirements

Platforms: Windows 98, Windows NT 4.0,
Windows Millennium Edition, Windows 2000,
Windows XP Home Edition, Windows XP Professional,
Windows Server 2003 family

ImageList.Images Property

Gets the **ImageList.ImageCollection** for this image list.

```
[Visual Basic]
Public ReadOnly Property Images As ImageList.ImageCollection
[C#]
public ImageList.ImageCollection Images {get;}
[C++]
public: __property ImageList.ImageCollection* get_Images();
[JScript]
public function get Images() : ImageList.ImageCollection;
```

Property Value

The collection of images.

Remarks

If the image collection has not yet been created, it is created when you retrieve this property.

Requirements

Platforms: Windows 98, Windows NT 4.0,
Windows Millennium Edition, Windows 2000,
Windows XP Home Edition, Windows XP Professional,
Windows Server 2003 family,
.NET Compact Framework - Windows CE .NET

ImageList.ImageSize Property

Gets or sets the size of the images in the image list.

```
[Visual Basic]
Public Property ImageSize As Size
[C#]
public Size ImageSize {get; set;}
[C++]
public: __property Size get_ImageSize();
public: __property void set_ImageSize(Size);
[JScript]
public function get ImageSize() : Size;
public function set ImageSize(Size);
```

Property Value

The **Size** that defines the height and width of the images in the list. The default height and width is 16 by 16. The maximum size is 256 by 256.

Exceptions

Exception Type	Condition
ArgumentException	The value assigned is equal to **IsEmpty**. -or- The value height or width is less than or equal to Zero. -or- The value height or width is greater than 256.

Remarks

When you set a new image size, the handle is recreated.

Requirements

Platforms: Windows 98, Windows NT 4.0, Windows Millennium Edition, Windows 2000, Windows XP Home Edition, Windows XP Professional, Windows Server 2003 family, .NET Compact Framework - Windows CE .NET

ImageList.ImageStream Property

Gets the handle to the **ImageListStreamer** associated with this image list.

```
[Visual Basic]
Public Property ImageStream As ImageListStreamer
[C#]
public ImageListStreamer ImageStream {get; set;}
[C++]
public: __property ImageListStreamer* get_ImageStream();
public: __property void set_ImageStream(ImageListStreamer*);
[JScript]
public function get ImageStream() : ImageListStreamer;
public function set ImageStream(ImageListStreamer);
```

Property Value

A null reference (**Nothing** in Visual Basic) if the image list is empty; otherwise, a handle to the **ImageListStreamer** for this **ImageList**.

Remarks

The **ImageListStreamer** is the data portion of the image list.

You can pass this handle to another instance of an **ImageList**.

Requirements

Platforms: Windows 98, Windows NT 4.0, Windows Millennium Edition, Windows 2000, Windows XP Home Edition, Windows XP Professional, Windows Server 2003 family

ImageList.TransparentColor Property

Gets or sets the color to treat as transparent.

```
[Visual Basic]
Public Property TransparentColor As Color
[C#]
public Color TransparentColor {get; set;}
[C++]
public: __property Color get_TransparentColor();
public: __property void set_TransparentColor(Color);
[JScript]
public function get TransparentColor() : Color;
public function set TransparentColor(Color);
```

Property Value

One of the **Color** values. The default is **Transparent**.

Remarks

The transparent color is not rendered when the image is drawn.

Requirements

Platforms: Windows 98, Windows NT 4.0, Windows Millennium Edition, Windows 2000, Windows XP Home Edition, Windows XP Professional, Windows Server 2003 family

ImageList.Dispose Method

Overload List

This member supports the .NET Framework infrastructure and is not intended to be used directly from your code.

Supported by the .NET Compact Framework.

[Visual Basic] **Overloads Overrides Protected Sub Dispose(Boolean)**

[C#] **protected override void Dispose(bool);**

[C++] **protected: void Dispose(bool);**

[JScript] **protected override function Dispose(Boolean);**

Inherited from **Component**.

[Visual Basic] **Overloads Public Overridable Sub Dispose() Implements IDisposable.Dispose**

[C#] **public virtual void Dispose();**

[C++] **public: virtual void Dispose();**

[JScript] **public function Dispose();**

ImageList.Dispose Method (Boolean)

This member overrides **Component.Dispose**.

```
[Visual Basic]
Overrides Overloads Protected Sub Dispose( _
   ByVal disposing As Boolean _
)
[C#]
protected override void Dispose(
   bool disposing
);
[C++]
protected: void Dispose(
   bool disposing
);
[JScript]
protected override function Dispose(
   disposing : Boolean
);
```

Requirements

Platforms: Windows 98, Windows NT 4.0, Windows Millennium Edition, Windows 2000, Windows XP Home Edition, Windows XP Professional, Windows Server 2003 family, .NET Compact Framework - Windows CE .NET

ImageList.Draw Method

Draws the indicated image.

Overload List

Draws the image indicated by the specified index on the specified **Graphics** at the given location.

[Visual Basic] **Overloads Public Sub Draw(Graphics, Point, Integer)**

[C#] **public void Draw(Graphics, Point, int);**

[C++] **public: void Draw(Graphics*, Point, int);**

[JScript] **public function Draw(Graphics, Point, int);**

Draws the image indicated by the given index on the specified **Graphics** at the specified location.

[Visual Basic] **Overloads Public Sub Draw(Graphics, Integer, Integer, Integer)**

[C#] **public void Draw(Graphics, int, int, int);**

[C++] **public: void Draw(Graphics*, int, int, int);**

[JScript] **public function Draw(Graphics, int, int, int);**

Draw the image indicated by the given index using the location, size and raster op code specified.

[Visual Basic] **Overloads Public Sub Draw(Graphics, Integer, Integer, Integer, Integer, Integer)**

[C#] **public void Draw(Graphics, int, int, int, int, int);**

[C++] **public: void Draw(Graphics*, int, int, int, int, int);**

[JScript] **public function Draw(Graphics, int, int, int, int, int);**

ImageList.Draw Method (Graphics, Point, Int32)

Draws the image indicated by the specified index on the specified **Graphics** at the given location.

```
[Visual Basic]
Overloads Public Sub Draw( _
   ByVal g As Graphics, _
   ByVal pt As Point, _
   ByVal index As Integer _
)
[C#]
public void Draw(
   Graphics g,
   Point pt,
   int index
);
[C++]
public: void Draw(
   Graphics* g,
   Point pt,
   int index
);
[JScript]
public function Draw(
   g : Graphics,
   pt : Point,
   index : int
);
```

Parameters

g
: **Graphics** object to draw into.

pt
: The location defined by a **Point** at which to draw the image.

index
: Index of the image in the **ImageList** to draw.

Exceptions

Exception Type	Condition
ArgumentException	The index is less than Zero. -or- The index is greater than or equal to the count of images in the image list.

Requirements

Platforms: Windows 98, Windows NT 4.0, Windows Millennium Edition, Windows 2000, Windows XP Home Edition, Windows XP Professional, Windows Server 2003 family

ImageList.Draw Method (Graphics, Int32, Int32, Int32)

Draws the image indicated by the given index on the specified **Graphics** at the specified location.

```
[Visual Basic]
Overloads Public Sub Draw( _
   ByVal g As Graphics, _
   ByVal x As Integer, _
   ByVal y As Integer, _
   ByVal index As Integer _
)
[C#]
public void Draw(
   Graphics g,
   int x,
   int y,
   int index
);
[C++]
public: void Draw(
   Graphics* g,
   int x,
   int y,
   int index
);
[JScript]
public function Draw(
   g : Graphics,
   x : int,
   y : int,
   index : int
);
```

Parameters

g
: **Graphics** object to draw into.

x
: Horizontal position at which to draw the image.

y
: Vertical position at which to draw the image.

index
: Index of the image in the **ImageList** to draw.

Exceptions

Exception Type	Condition
ArgumentOutOfRange-Exception	The index is less than zero. -or- The index is greater than or equal to the count of images in the image list.

Requirements

Platforms: Windows 98, Windows NT 4.0, Windows Millennium Edition, Windows 2000, Windows XP Home Edition, Windows XP Professional, Windows Server 2003 family

ImageList.Draw Method (Graphics, Int32, Int32, Int32, Int32, Int32)

Draw the image indicated by the given index using the location, size and raster op code specified.

[Visual Basic]
```
Overloads Public Sub Draw( _
   ByVal g As Graphics, _
   ByVal x As Integer, _
   ByVal y As Integer, _
   ByVal width As Integer, _
   ByVal height As Integer, _
   ByVal index As Integer _
)
```
[C#]
```
public void Draw(
   Graphics g,
   int x,
   int y,
   int width,
   int height,
   int index
);
```
[C++]
```
public: void Draw(
   Graphics* g,
   int x,
   int y,
   int width,
   int height,
   int index
);
```
[JScript]
```
public function Draw(
   g : Graphics,
   x : int,
   y : int,
   width : int,
   height : int,
   index : int
);
```

Parameters

g
: **Graphics** object to draw into.

x
: Horizontal position at which to draw the image.

y
: Vertical position at which to draw the image.

width
: Width of destination image.

height
: Height of destination image.

index
: Index of the image in the **ImageList** to draw.

Exceptions

Exception Type	Condition
ArgumentOutOfRange-Exception	The index is less than zero. -or- The index is greater than or equal to the count of images in the image list.

Remarks

The image is stretched or compressed as necessary to fit the bounds provided.

Requirements

Platforms: Windows 98, Windows NT 4.0, Windows Millennium Edition, Windows 2000, Windows XP Home Edition, Windows XP Professional, Windows Server 2003 family

ImageList.ToString Method

This member overrides **Object.ToString**.

[Visual Basic]
```
Overrides Public Function ToString() As String
```
[C#]
```
public override string ToString();
```
[C++]
```
public: String* ToString();
```
[JScript]
```
public override function ToString() : String;
```

Requirements

Platforms: Windows 98, Windows NT 4.0, Windows Millennium Edition, Windows 2000, Windows XP Home Edition, Windows XP Professional, Windows Server 2003 family, .NET Compact Framework - Windows CE .NET

ImageList.RecreateHandle Event

Occurs when the **Handle** is recreated.

[Visual Basic]
```
Public Event RecreateHandle As EventHandler
```
[C#]
```
public event EventHandler RecreateHandle;
```
[C++]
```
public: __event EventHandler* RecreateHandle;
```

[JScript] In JScript, you can handle the events defined by a class, but you cannot define your own.

Event Data

The event handler receives an argument of type **EventArgs**.

Remarks

You can use this event to do special processing when the **Handle** is created by actions such as changing the **ColorDepth** or **ImageSize**. Special processing is recommended when you have supplied the handle for the list.

When the handle is recreated, **ImageList** checks to see if the handle was created internally or if it was supplied in the constructor. If the handle was created internally, it is destroyed and new one is created. If it was supplied in the constructor, the old one is not destroyed and a new one will be created. If a new one is created, you will need to explicitly free the handle.

Requirements

Platforms: Windows 98, Windows NT 4.0, Windows Millennium Edition, Windows 2000, Windows XP Home Edition, Windows XP Professional, Windows Server 2003 family

ImageList.ImageCollection Class

Encapsulates the collection of **Image** objects in an **ImageList**.

System.Object
 System.Windows.Forms.ImageList.ImageCollection

[Visual Basic]
```
NotInheritable Public Class ImageList.ImageCollection
   Implements IList, ICollection, IEnumerable
```
[C#]
```
public sealed class ImageList.ImageCollection : IList, ICollection,
   IEnumerable
```
[C++]
```
public __gc __sealed class ImageList.ImageCollection : public
   IList, ICollection, IEnumerable
```
[JScript]
```
public class ImageList.ImageCollection implements IList,
   ICollection, IEnumerable
```

Thread Safety

Any public static (**Shared** in Visual Basic) members of this type are safe for multithreaded operations. Any instance members are not guaranteed to be thread safe.

Remarks

This is used to manage the images in the **ImageList** programmatically, providing methods to add and remove image objects.

Requirements

Namespace: System.Windows.Forms

Platforms: Windows 98, Windows NT 4.0,
Windows Millennium Edition, Windows 2000,
Windows XP Home Edition, Windows XP Professional,
Windows Server 2003 family,
.NET Compact Framework - Windows CE .NET

Assembly: System.Windows.Forms (in System.Windows.Forms.dll)

ImageList.ImageCollection.Count Property

Gets the number of images currently in the list.

[Visual Basic]
```
Public Overridable ReadOnly Property Count As Integer  Implements _
   ICollection.Count
```
[C#]
```
public virtual int Count {get;}
```
[C++]
```
public: __property virtual int get_Count();
```
[JScript]
```
public function get Count() : int;
```

Property Value

The number of images in the list. The default is zero.

Implements

ICollection.Count

Remarks

Counting the images forces the **Handle** to be created.

Requirements

Platforms: Windows 98, Windows NT 4.0,
Windows Millennium Edition, Windows 2000,
Windows XP Home Edition, Windows XP Professional,
Windows Server 2003 family,
.NET Compact Framework - Windows CE .NET

ImageList.ImageCollection.Empty Property

Gets a value indicating whether the **ImageList** has any images.

[Visual Basic]
```
Public ReadOnly Property Empty As Boolean
```
[C#]
```
public bool Empty {get;}
```
[C++]
```
public: __property bool get_Empty();
```
[JScript]
```
public function get Empty() : Boolean;
```

Property Value

true if there are no images in the list; otherwise, **false**. The default is **false**.

Remarks

You can check this property without forcing the creation of a **Handle**.

Requirements

Platforms: Windows 98, Windows NT 4.0,
Windows Millennium Edition, Windows 2000,
Windows XP Home Edition, Windows XP Professional,
Windows Server 2003 family

ImageList.ImageCollection.IsReadOnly Property

Gets a value indicating whether the list is read only.

[Visual Basic]
```
Public Overridable ReadOnly Property IsReadOnly As Boolean _
   Implements IList.IsReadOnly
```
[C#]
```
public virtual bool IsReadOnly {get;}
```
[C++]
```
public: __property virtual bool get_IsReadOnly();
```
[JScript]
```
public function get IsReadOnly() : Boolean;
```

Property Value

Always **false**.

Implements

IList.IsReadOnly

Requirements

Platforms: Windows 98, Windows NT 4.0,
Windows Millennium Edition, Windows 2000,
Windows XP Home Edition, Windows XP Professional,
Windows Server 2003 family,
.NET Compact Framework - Windows CE .NET

ImageList.ImageCollection.Item Property

Gets or sets an **Image** in an existing **ImageList**.

[C#] In C#, this property is the indexer for the **ImageList.ImageCollection** class.

```
[Visual Basic]
Public Default Property Item( _
   ByVal index As Integer _
) As Image
[C#]
public Image this[
   int index
] {get; set;}
[C++]
public: __property Image* get_Item(
   int index
);
public: __property void set_Item(
   int index,
   Image*
);
[JScript]
returnValue = ImageCollectionObject.Item(index);
ImageCollectionObject.Item(index) = returnValue;
-or-
returnValue = ImageCollectionObject(index);
ImageCollectionObject(index) = returnValue;
```

[JScript] In JScript, you can use the default indexed properties defined by a type, but you cannot explicitly define your own. However, specifying the **expando** attribute on a class automatically provides a default indexed property whose type is **Object** and whose index type is **String**.

Arguments [JScript]

index

The index of the image to get or set.

Parameters [Visual Basic, C#, C++]

index

The index of the image to get or set.

Property Value

The image in the list specified by the *index*.

Exceptions

Exception Type	Condition
ArgumentOutOfRange-Exception	The index is less than zero or greater than or equal to **Count**.
Exception	The attempt to replace the image failed.
ArgumentNull-Exception	The image to be assigned is a null reference (**Nothing** in Visual Basic) or not a **Bitmap**.

Requirements

Platforms: Windows 98, Windows NT 4.0, Windows Millennium Edition, Windows 2000, Windows XP Home Edition, Windows XP Professional, Windows Server 2003 family

ImageList.ImageCollection.System.Collections.ICollection.IsSynchronized Property

Note: This namespace, class, or member is supported only in version 1.1 of the .NET Framework.

This member supports the .NET Framework infrastructure and is not intended to be used directly from your code.

```
[Visual Basic]
Private ReadOnly Property IsSynchronized As Boolean Implements _
   ICollection.IsSynchronized
[C#]
bool ICollection.IsSynchronized {get;}
[C++]
private: __property bool
   System::Collections::ICollection::get_IsSynchronized();
[JScript]
private function get ICollection.IsSynchronized() : Boolean;
```

ImageList.ImageCollection.System.Collections.ICollection.SyncRoot Property

Note: This namespace, class, or member is supported only in version 1.1 of the .NET Framework.

This member supports the .NET Framework infrastructure and is not intended to be used directly from your code.

```
[Visual Basic]
Private ReadOnly Property SyncRoot As Object Implements _
   ICollection.SyncRoot
[C#]
object ICollection.SyncRoot {get;}
[C++]
private: __property Object*
   System::Collections::ICollection::get_SyncRoot();
[JScript]
private function get ICollection.SyncRoot() : Object;
```

ImageList.ImageCollection.System.Collections.IList.IsFixedSize Property

Note: This namespace, class, or member is supported only in version 1.1 of the .NET Framework.

This member supports the .NET Framework infrastructure and is not intended to be used directly from your code.

```
[Visual Basic]
Private ReadOnly Property IsFixedSize As Boolean Implements _
   IList.IsFixedSize
[C#]
bool IList.IsFixedSize {get;}
[C++]
private: __property bool
   System::Collections::IList::get_IsFixedSize();
[JScript]
private function get IList.IsFixedSize() : Boolean;
```

ImageList.ImageCollection.System.Collections.IList.Item Property

Note: This namespace, class, or member is supported only in version 1.1 of the .NET Framework.

[C#] In C#, this property is the indexer for the **ImageList.ImageCollection** class.

```
[Visual Basic]
Private Default Property Item( _
   ByVal index As Integer _
) As Object Implements IList.Item
[C#]
object IList.this[
   int index
] {get; set;}
[C++]
private: __property Object* System::Collections::IList::get_Item(
   int index
);
private: __property void System::Collections::IList::set_Item(
   int index,
   Object*
);
[JScript]
private function get IList.get_Item(index : int) : Object;
private function set IList.set_Item(index : int, value : Object);
-or-
private function get IList.get_Item(index : int) : Object;
private function set IList.set_Item(index : int, value : Object);
```

[JScript] In JScript, you can use the default indexed properties defined by a type, but you cannot explicitly define your own. However, specifying the **expando** attribute on a class automatically provides a default indexed property whose type is **Object** and whose index type is **String**.

Arguments [JScript]

index

Parameters [Visual Basic, C#, C++]

index

Requirements

Platforms: Windows 98, Windows NT 4.0, Windows Millennium Edition, Windows 2000, Windows XP Home Edition, Windows XP Professional, Windows Server 2003 family

ImageList.ImageCollection.Add Method

Adds the specified object to the **ImageList**.

Overload List

Adds the specified icon to the **ImageList**.

Supported by the .NET Compact Framework.

[Visual Basic] **Overloads Public Sub Add(Icon)**

[C#] **public void Add(Icon);**

[C++] **public: void Add(Icon*);**

[JScript] **public function Add(Icon);**

Adds the specified image to the **ImageList**.

Supported by the .NET Compact Framework.

[Visual Basic] **Overloads Public Sub Add(Image)**

[C#] **public void Add(Image);**

[C++] **public: void Add(Image*);**

[JScript] **public function Add(Image);**

Adds the specified image to the **ImageList**, using the specified color to generate the mask.

[Visual Basic] **Overloads Public Function Add(Image, Color) As Integer**

[C#] **public int Add(Image, Color);**

[C++] **public: int Add(Image*, Color);**

[JScript] **public function Add(Image, Color) : int;**

ImageList.ImageCollection.Add Method (Icon)

Adds the specified icon to the **ImageList**.

```
[Visual Basic]
Overloads Public Sub Add( _
   ByVal value As Icon _
)
[C#]
public void Add(
   Icon value
);
[C++]
public: void Add(
   Icon* value
);
[JScript]
public function Add(
   value : Icon
);
```

Parameters

value

An **Icon** to add to the list.

Exceptions

Exception Type	Condition
Exception	Image **Add** failed.
ArgumentNull-Exception	Image being added is a null reference (**Nothing** in Visual Basic).
ArgumentException	Image being added is not a **Bitmap**.

Remarks

The **Icon** is converted to a **Bitmap** before it is added to the list.

Requirements

Platforms: Windows 98, Windows NT 4.0, Windows Millennium Edition, Windows 2000, Windows XP Home Edition, Windows XP Professional, Windows Server 2003 family, .NET Compact Framework - Windows CE .NET

ImageList.ImageCollection.Add Method (Image)

Adds the specified image to the **ImageList**.

```
[Visual Basic]
Overloads Public Sub Add( _
   ByVal value As Image _
)
[C#]
public void Add(
   Image value
);
```

```
[C++]
public: void Add(
   Image* value
);
[JScript]
public function Add(
   value : Image
);
```

Parameters

value

A **Bitmap** of the image to add to the list.

Exceptions

Exception Type	Condition
Exception	Image **Add** failed.
ArgumentNull-Exception	Image being added is a null reference (**Nothing** in Visual Basic).
ArgumentException	Image being added is not a **Bitmap**.

Requirements

Platforms: Windows 98, Windows NT 4.0, Windows Millennium Edition, Windows 2000, Windows XP Home Edition, Windows XP Professional, Windows Server 2003 family, .NET Compact Framework - Windows CE .NET

ImageList.ImageCollection.Add Method (Image, Color)

Adds the specified image to the **ImageList**, using the specified color to generate the mask.

```
[Visual Basic]
Overloads Public Function Add( _
   ByVal value As Image, _
   ByVal transparentColor As Color _
) As Integer
[C#]
public int Add(
   Image value,
   Color transparentColor
);
[C++]
public: int Add(
   Image* value,
   Color transparentColor
);
[JScript]
public function Add(
   value : Image,
   transparentColor : Color
) : int;
```

Parameters

value

A **Bitmap** of the image to add to the list.

transparentColor

The **Color** to mask this image.

Return Value

The index of the newly added image or -1 if the the image could not be added.

Exceptions

Exception Type	Condition
ArgumentNull-Exception	Image being added is a null reference (**Nothing** in Visual Basic).
Exception	Image **Add** failed.
ArgumentException	Image being added is not a **Bitmap**.

Requirements

Platforms: Windows 98, Windows NT 4.0, Windows Millennium Edition, Windows 2000, Windows XP Home Edition, Windows XP Professional, Windows Server 2003 family

ImageList.ImageCollection.AddStrip Method

Adds an image strip to the specified image to the **ImageList**.

```
[Visual Basic]
Public Function AddStrip( _
   ByVal value As Image _
) As Integer
[C#]
public int AddStrip(
   Image value
);
[C++]
public: int AddStrip(
   Image* value
);
[JScript]
public function AddStrip(
   value : Image
) : int;
```

Parameters

value

A **Bitmap** object with the image(s) to add.

Return Value

The index of the newly added image or -1 if the the image could not be added.

Exceptions

Exception Type	Condition
ArgumentException	Image being added is a null reference (**Nothing** in Visual Basic). -or- Image being added is not a **Bitmap**.
Exception	Image **Add** failed. -or- The width of image strip being added is zero or the width is not equal to the existing image width. -or- The image strip height is not equal to existing image height.

Remarks

The number of images to add is inferred from the width of the given image.

A strip is a single image that is treated as multiple images arranged side-by-side.

Requirements

Platforms: Windows 98, Windows NT 4.0, Windows Millennium Edition, Windows 2000, Windows XP Home Edition, Windows XP Professional, Windows Server 2003 family

ImageList.ImageCollection.Clear Method

Removes all the images and masks from the **ImageList**.

[Visual Basic]
```
Public Overridable Sub Clear() Implements IList.Clear
```
[C#]
```
public virtual void Clear();
```
[C++]
```
public: virtual void Clear();
```
[JScript]
```
public function Clear();
```

Implements

IList.Clear

Requirements

Platforms: Windows 98, Windows NT 4.0, Windows Millennium Edition, Windows 2000, Windows XP Home Edition, Windows XP Professional, Windows Server 2003 family, .NET Compact Framework - Windows CE .NET

ImageList.ImageCollection.Contains Method

Not supported. The **IList.Contains** method indicates whether a specified object is contained in the list.

[Visual Basic]
```
Public Function Contains( _
   ByVal image As Image _
) As Boolean
```
[C#]
```
public bool Contains(
   Image image
);
```
[C++]
```
public: bool Contains(
   Image* image
);
```
[JScript]
```
public function Contains(
   image : Image
) : Boolean;
```

Parameters

image

The **Image** to find in the list.

Return Value

true if the image is found in the list; otherwise, **false**.

Exceptions

Exception Type	Condition
NotSupportedException	This method is not supported.

Remarks

This implementation of **IList.Contains** throws a **NotSupportedException** exception.

Requirements

Platforms: Windows 98, Windows NT 4.0, Windows Millennium Edition, Windows 2000, Windows XP Home Edition, Windows XP Professional, Windows Server 2003 family

ImageList.ImageCollection.GetEnumerator Method

Returns an enumerator that can be used to iterate through the item collection.

[Visual Basic]
```
Public Overridable Function GetEnumerator() As IEnumerator _
   Implements IEnumerable.GetEnumerator
```
[C#]
```
public virtual IEnumerator GetEnumerator();
```
[C++]
```
public: virtual IEnumerator* GetEnumerator();
```
[JScript]
```
public function GetEnumerator() : IEnumerator;
```

Return Value

An **IEnumerator** object that represents the item collection.

Implements

IEnumerable.GetEnumerator

Requirements

Platforms: Windows 98, Windows NT 4.0, Windows Millennium Edition, Windows 2000, Windows XP Home Edition, Windows XP Professional, Windows Server 2003 family, .NET Compact Framework - Windows CE .NET

ImageList.ImageCollection.ICollection.CopyTo Method

This member supports the .NET Framework infrastructure and is not intended to be used directly from your code.

[Visual Basic]
```
Private Sub CopyTo( _
   ByVal dest As Array, _
   ByVal index As Integer _
) Implements ICollection.CopyTo
```
[C#]
```
void ICollection.CopyTo(
   Array dest,
   int index
);
```
[C++]
```
private: void ICollection::CopyTo(
   Array* dest,
   int index
);
```

[JScript]
```
private function ICollection.CopyTo(
   dest : Array,
   index : int
);
```

ImageList.ImageCollection.IList.Add Method

This member supports the .NET Framework infrastructure and is not intended to be used directly from your code.

[Visual Basic]
```
Private Function Add( _
   ByVal value As Object _
) As Integer Implements IList.Add
```
[C#]
```
int IList.Add(
   object value
);
```
[C++]
```
private: int IList::Add(
   Object* value
);
```
[JScript]
```
private function IList.Add(
   value : Object
) : int;
```

ImageList.ImageCollection.IList.Contains Method

This member supports the .NET Framework infrastructure and is not intended to be used directly from your code.

[Visual Basic]
```
Private Function Contains( _
   ByVal image As Object _
) As Boolean Implements IList.Contains
```
[C#]
```
bool IList.Contains(
   object image
);
```
[C++]
```
private: bool IList::Contains(
   Object* image
);
```
[JScript]
```
private function IList.Contains(
   image : Object
) : Boolean;
```

ImageList.ImageCollection.IList.IndexOf Method

This member supports the .NET Framework infrastructure and is not intended to be used directly from your code.

[Visual Basic]
```
Private Function IndexOf( _
   ByVal image As Object _
) As Integer Implements IList.IndexOf
```
[C#]
```
int IList.IndexOf(
   object image
);
```
[C++]
```
private: int IList::IndexOf(
   Object* image
);
```
[JScript]
```
private function IList.IndexOf(
   image : Object
) : int;
```

ImageList.ImageCollection.IList.Insert Method

This member supports the .NET Framework infrastructure and is not intended to be used directly from your code.

[Visual Basic]
```
Private Sub Insert( _
   ByVal index As Integer, _
   ByVal value As Object _
) Implements IList.Insert
```
[C#]
```
void IList.Insert(
   int index,
   object value
);
```
[C++]
```
private: void IList::Insert(
   int index,
   Object* value
);
```
[JScript]
```
private function IList.Insert(
   index : int,
   value : Object
);
```

ImageList.ImageCollection.IList.Remove Method

This member supports the .NET Framework infrastructure and is not intended to be used directly from your code.

[Visual Basic]
```
Private Sub Remove( _
   ByVal image As Object _
) Implements IList.Remove
```
[C#]
```
void IList.Remove(
   object image
);
```
[C++]
```
private: void IList::Remove(
   Object* image
);
```
[JScript]
```
private function IList.Remove(
   image : Object
);
```

ImageList.ImageCollection.IndexOf Method

Not supported. The **IList.IndexOf** method returns the index of a specified object in the list.

```
[Visual Basic]
Public Function IndexOf( _
   ByVal image As Image _
) As Integer
[C#]
public int IndexOf(
   Image image
);
[C++]
public: int IndexOf(
   Image* image
);
[JScript]
public function IndexOf(
   image : Image
) : int;
```

Parameters

image

The **Image** to find in the list.

Return Value

The index of the image in the list.

Exceptions

Exception Type	Condition
NotSupportedException	This method is not supported.

Remarks

This implementation of **IList.IndexOf** throws a **NotSupported-Exception** exception.

Requirements

Platforms: Windows 98, Windows NT 4.0, Windows Millennium Edition, Windows 2000, Windows XP Home Edition, Windows XP Professional, Windows Server 2003 family

ImageList.ImageCollection.Remove Method

Not supported. The **IList.Remove** method removes a specified object from the list.

```
[Visual Basic]
Public Sub Remove( _
   ByVal image As Image _
)
[C#]
public void Remove(
   Image image
);
[C++]
public: void Remove(
   Image* image
);
[JScript]
public function Remove(
   image : Image
);
```

Parameters

image

The **Image** to remove from the list.

Exceptions

Exception Type	Condition
NotSupportedException	This method is not supported.

Remarks

This implementation of **IList.Remove** throws a **NotSupported-Exception** exception.

Requirements

Platforms: Windows 98, Windows NT 4.0, Windows Millennium Edition, Windows 2000, Windows XP Home Edition, Windows XP Professional, Windows Server 2003 family

ImageList.ImageCollection.RemoveAt Method

Removes an image from the list.

```
[Visual Basic]
Public Overridable Sub RemoveAt( _
   ByVal index As Integer _
) Implements IList.RemoveAt
[C#]
public virtual void RemoveAt(
   int index
);
[C++]
public: virtual void RemoveAt(
   int index
);
[JScript]
public function RemoveAt(
   index : int
);
```

Parameters

index

The index of the image to remove.

Implements

IList.RemoveAt

Exceptions

Exception Type	Condition
Exception	The attempt to remove the image failed.
ArgumentOutOfRange-Exception	The index value was less than zero. -or- The index value is greater than or equal to the **Count** of images.

Requirements

Platforms: Windows 98, Windows NT 4.0, Windows Millennium Edition, Windows 2000, Windows XP Home Edition, Windows XP Professional, Windows Server 2003 family, .NET Compact Framework - Windows CE .NET

ImageListStreamer Class

Provides the data portion of an **ImageList**.

System.Object
System.Windows.Forms.ImageListStreamer

```
[Visual Basic]
<Serializable>
NotInheritable Public Class ImageListStreamer
   Implements ISerializable
[C#]
[Serializable]
public sealed class ImageListStreamer : ISerializable
[C++]
[Serializable]
public __gc __sealed class ImageListStreamer : public
   ISerializable
[JScript]
public
   Serializable
class ImageListStreamer implements ISerializable
```

Thread Safety

Any public static (**Shared** in Visual Basic) members of this type are safe for multithreaded operations. Any instance members are not guaranteed to be thread safe.

Remarks

This is a sealed class, so you can not inherit from it. Also, the constructor is private. So you cannot create a new instance of it.

Requirements

Namespace: System.Windows.Forms

Platforms: Windows 98, Windows NT 4.0, Windows Millennium Edition, Windows 2000, Windows XP Home Edition, Windows XP Professional, Windows Server 2003 family

Assembly: System.Windows.Forms (in System.Windows.Forms.dll)

ImageListStreamer.GetObjectData Method

This member supports the .NET Framework infrastructure and is not intended to be used directly from your code.

```
[Visual Basic]
Public Overridable Sub GetObjectData( _
   ByVal si As SerializationInfo, _
   ByVal context As StreamingContext _
) Implements ISerializable.GetObjectData
[C#]
public virtual void GetObjectData(
   SerializationInfo si,
   StreamingContext context
);
[C++]
public: virtual void GetObjectData(
   SerializationInfo* si,
   StreamingContext context
);
[JScript]
public function GetObjectData(
   si : SerializationInfo,
   context : StreamingContext
);
```

ImeMode Enumeration

Specifies a value that determines the Input Method Editor (IME) status of an object when the object is selected.

[Visual Basic]
```
<Serializable>
<ComVisible(True)>
Public Enum ImeMode
```
[C#]
```
[Serializable]
[ComVisible(true)]
public enum ImeMode
```
[C++]
```
[Serializable]
[ComVisible(true)]
__value public enum ImeMode
```
[JScript]
```
public
   Serializable
   ComVisible(true)
enum ImeMode
```

Remarks

An Input Method Editor (IME) allows users to enter and edit Chinese, Japanese, and Korean characters. The IME is an essential component for writing Chinese, Japanese, and Korean scripts. These writing systems have more characters than can be encoded for a regular keyboard. The IMEs for these languages use sequences of base characters that describe an individual character or group of characters to allow you to enter a larger set of characters. Base characters can be component letters from Hangul syllables, phonetic components for Japanese Kanji characters, or various combinations for Chinese characters.

Members

Member name	Description
Alpha	Alphanumeric single-byte characters(SBC). This setting is valid for Korean and Japanese IME only.
AlphaFull	Alphanumeric double-byte characters. This setting is valid for Korean and Japanese IME only.
Disable	The IME is disabled. With this setting, the users cannot turn the IME on from the keyboard, and the IME floating window is hidden.
Hangul	Hangul SBC. This setting is valid for the Korean IME only.
HangulFull	Hangul DBC. This setting is valid for the Korean IME only.
Hiragana	Hiragana DBC. This setting is valid for the Japanese IME only.
Inherit	Inherits the IME mode of the parent control.
Katakana	Katakana DBC. This setting is valid for the Japanese IME only.
KatakanaHalf	Katakana SBC. This setting is valid for the Japanese IME only.
NoControl	None (Default).
Off	The IME is off. This mode indicates that the IME is off, meaning that the object behaves the same as English entry mode. This setting is valid for Japanese, Simplified Chinese, and Traditional Chinese IME only.
On	The IME is on. This value indicates that the IME is on and characters specific to Chinese or Japanese can be entered. This setting is valid for Japanese, Simplified Chinese, and Traditional Chinese IME only.

Requirements

Namespace: System.Windows.Forms

Platforms: Windows 98, Windows NT 4.0, Windows Millennium Edition, Windows 2000, Windows XP Home Edition, Windows XP Professional, Windows Server 2003 family

Assembly: System.Windows.Forms (in System.Windows.Forms.dll)

IMessageFilter Interface

Defines a message filter interface.

For a list of all members of this type, see **IMessageFilter Members**.

[Visual Basic]
```
Public Interface IMessageFilter
```
[C#]
```
public interface IMessageFilter
```
[C++]
```
public __gc __interface IMessageFilter
```
[JScript]
```
public interface IMessageFilter
```

Classes that Implement IMessageFilter

Class	Description
Splitter	Represents a splitter control that allows the user to resize docked controls.

Remarks

This interface allows an application to capture a message before it is dispatched to a control or form.

A class that implements the **IMessageFilter** interface can be added to the application's message pump to filter out a message or perform other operations before the message is dispatched to a form or control. To add the message filter to an application's message pump, use the **AddMessageFilter** method in the **Application** class.

Requirements

Namespace: System.Windows.Forms

Platforms: Windows 98, Windows NT 4.0, Windows Millennium Edition, Windows 2000, Windows XP Home Edition, Windows XP Professional, Windows Server 2003 family

Assembly: System.Windows.Forms (in System.Windows.Forms.dll)

IMessageFilter.PreFilterMessage Method

Filters out a message before it is dispatched.

[Visual Basic]
```
Function PreFilterMessage( _
   ByRef m As Message _
) As Boolean
```
[C#]
```
bool PreFilterMessage(
   ref Message m
);
```
[C++]
```
bool PreFilterMessage(
   Message* m
);
```
[JScript]
```
function PreFilterMessage(
   m : Message
) : Boolean;
```

Parameters

m

The message to be dispatched. You cannot modify this message.

Return Value

true to filter the message and prevent it from being dispatched; **false** to allow the message to continue to the next filter or control.

Remarks

Use **PreFilterMessage** to filter out a message before it is dispatched to a control or form. For example, to prevent the **Click** event of a **Button** control from being dispatched to the control, you implement the **PreFilterMessage** method and return a **true** value when the **Click** message occurs. You can also use this method to perform code work that you might need to do before the message is dispatched.

Requirements

Platforms: Windows 98, Windows NT 4.0, Windows Millennium Edition, Windows 2000, Windows XP Home Edition, Windows XP Professional, Windows Server 2003 family

InputLanguage Class

Provides methods and fields to manage the input language. This class cannot be inherited.

System.Object
  System.Windows.Forms.InputLanguage

[Visual Basic]
```
NotInheritable Public Class InputLanguage
```
[C#]
```
public sealed class InputLanguage
```
[C++]
```
public __gc __sealed class InputLanguage
```
[JScript]
```
public class InputLanguage
```

Thread Safety

Any public static (**Shared** in Visual Basic) members of this type are safe for multithreaded operations. Any instance members are not guaranteed to be thread safe.

Remarks

An input language is a culture/keyboard layout pair that determines how the physical keys on a keyboard map or plot to characters in a language.

Use the static (**Shared** in Visual Basic) methods provided to find all installed mappings of the system and to change the input language for a thread or process. Call **CurrentInputLanguage** to get the current input language. Call **DefaultInputLanguage** for the default input language. Call **InstalledInputLanguages** to get all the installed languages in this system. Once you have a list of all the installed languages, use **CurrentInputLanguage** to change the current input language to a different language.

Example

[Visual Basic, C#] The following example gets a list of installed languages. It assumes that `textBox1` has been instantiated and that `textBox1.MultiLine` has been set to **true**.

[Visual Basic]
```
Public Sub GetLanguages()
    ' Gets the list of installed languages.
    Dim lang As InputLanguage
    For Each lang In  InputLanguage.InstalledInputLanguages
        textBox1.Text &= lang.Culture.EnglishName & ControlChars.Cr
    Next lang
End Sub 'GetLanguages
```

[C#]
```
public void GetLanguages() {
    // Gets the list of installed languages.
    foreach(InputLanguage lang in InputLanguage.InstalledInputLanguages)
{
        textBox1.Text += lang.Culture.EnglishName + '\n';
    }
}
```

[Visual Basic, C#] The next example sets the default input language as the current input language. It assumes that `textBox1` has been instantiated and that `textBox1.MultiLine` has been set to **true**.

[Visual Basic]
```
Public Sub SetNewCurrentLanguage()
    ' Gets the default, and current languages.
    Dim myDefaultLanguage As InputLanguage =                         ↵
InputLanguage.DefaultInputLanguage
    Dim myCurrentLanguage As InputLanguage =                         ↵
InputLanguage.CurrentInputLanguage
    textBox1.Text = "Current input language is: " & _
        myCurrentLanguage.Culture.EnglishName & ControlChars.Cr

    textBox1.Text &= "Default input language is: " & _
        myDefaultLanguage.Culture.EnglishName & ControlChars.Cr

    ' Changes the current input language to the default, and        ↵
prints the new current language.
    InputLanguage.CurrentInputLanguage = myDefaultLanguage
    textBox1.Text &= "Current input language is now: " & _
        myDefaultLanguage.Culture.EnglishName
End Sub 'SetNewCurrentLanguage
```

[C#]
```
public void SetNewCurrentLanguage() {
    // Gets the default, and current languages.
    InputLanguage myDefaultLanguage =                                ↵
InputLanguage.DefaultInputLanguage;
    InputLanguage myCurrentLanguage =                                ↵
InputLanguage.CurrentInputLanguage;
    textBox1.Text = "Current input language is: " +                  ↵
myCurrentLanguage.Culture.EnglishName + '\n';
    textBox1.Text += "Default input language is: " +                 ↵
myDefaultLanguage.Culture.EnglishName + '\n';

    // Changes the current input language to the default, and        ↵
 prints the new current language.
    InputLanguage.CurrentInputLanguage = myDefaultLanguage;
    textBox1.Text += "Current input language is now: " +             ↵
myDefaultLanguage.Culture.EnglishName;
}
```

Requirements

Namespace: System.Windows.Forms

Platforms: Windows 98, Windows NT 4.0, Windows Millennium Edition, Windows 2000, Windows XP Home Edition, Windows XP Professional, Windows Server 2003 family

Assembly: System.Windows.Forms (in System.Windows.Forms.dll)

InputLanguage.Culture Property

Gets the culture of the current input language.

[Visual Basic]
```
Public ReadOnly Property Culture As CultureInfo
```
[C#]
```
public CultureInfo Culture {get;}
```
[C++]
```
public: __property CultureInfo* get_Culture();
```
[JScript]
```
public function get Culture() : CultureInfo;
```

Property Value

A **CultureInfo** that represents the culture of the current input language.

Example

See related example in the **System.Windows.Forms.InputLanguage** class topic.

Requirements

Platforms: Windows 98, Windows NT 4.0, Windows Millennium Edition, Windows 2000, Windows XP Home Edition, Windows XP Professional, Windows Server 2003 family

InputLanguage.CurrentInputLanguage Property

Gets or sets the input language for the current thread.

[Visual Basic]
```
Public Shared Property CurrentInputLanguage As InputLanguage
```
[C#]
```
public static InputLanguage CurrentInputLanguage {get; set;}
```
[C++]
```
public: __property static InputLanguage* get_CurrentInputLanguage();
public: __property static void
set_CurrentInputLanguage(InputLanguage*);
```
[JScript]
```
public static function get CurrentInputLanguage() : InputLanguage;
public static function set CurrentInputLanguage(InputLanguage);
```

Property Value

An **InputLanguage** that represents the input language for the current thread.

Example

See related example in the **System.Windows.Forms.InputLanguage** class topic.

Requirements

Platforms: Windows 98, Windows NT 4.0, Windows Millennium Edition, Windows 2000, Windows XP Home Edition, Windows XP Professional, Windows Server 2003 family

InputLanguage.DefaultInputLanguage Property

Gets the default input language for the system.

[Visual Basic]
```
Public Shared ReadOnly Property DefaultInputLanguage As _
   InputLanguage
```
[C#]
```
public static InputLanguage DefaultInputLanguage {get;}
```
[C++]
```
public: __property static InputLanguage* get_DefaultInputLanguage();
```
[JScript]
```
public static function get DefaultInputLanguage() : InputLanguage;
```

Property Value

An **InputLanguage** representing the default input language for the system.

Example

See related example in the **System.Windows.Forms.InputLanguage** class topic.

Requirements

Platforms: Windows 98, Windows NT 4.0, Windows Millennium Edition, Windows 2000, Windows XP Home Edition, Windows XP Professional, Windows Server 2003 family

InputLanguage.Handle Property

Gets the handle for the input language.

[Visual Basic]
```
Public ReadOnly Property Handle As IntPtr
```
[C#]
```
public IntPtr Handle {get;}
```
[C++]
```
public: __property IntPtr get_Handle();
```
[JScript]
```
public function get Handle() : IntPtr;
```

Property Value

An **IntPtr** that represents the handle of this input language.

Example

See related example in the **System.Windows.Forms.InputLanguage** class topic.

Requirements

Platforms: Windows 98, Windows NT 4.0, Windows Millennium Edition, Windows 2000, Windows XP Home Edition, Windows XP Professional, Windows Server 2003 family

InputLanguage.InstalledInputLanguages Property

Gets a list of all installed input languages.

[Visual Basic]
```
Public Shared ReadOnly Property InstalledInputLanguages As _
   InputLanguageCollection
```
[C#]
```
public static InputLanguageCollection InstalledInputLanguages
   {get;}
```
[C++]
```
public: __property static InputLanguageCollection*
   get_InstalledInputLanguages();
```
[JScript]
```
public static function get InstalledInputLanguages() :
   InputLanguageCollection;
```

Property Value

An array of **InputLanguage** objects that represent the input languages installed on the computer.

Example

See related example in the **System.Windows.Forms.InputLanguage** class topic.

Requirements

Platforms: Windows 98, Windows NT 4.0, Windows Millennium Edition, Windows 2000, Windows XP Home Edition, Windows XP Professional, Windows Server 2003 family

InputLanguage.LayoutName Property

Gets the name of the current keyboard layout as it appears in the regional settings of the operating system on the computer.

[Visual Basic]
```
Public ReadOnly Property LayoutName As String
```
[C#]
```
public string LayoutName {get;}
```
[C++]
```
public: __property String* get_LayoutName();
```
[JScript]
```
public function get LayoutName() : String;
```

Property Value

The name of the layout.

Example

See related example in the **System.Windows.Forms.InputLanguage** class topic.

Requirements

Platforms: Windows 98, Windows NT 4.0, Windows Millennium Edition, Windows 2000, Windows XP Home Edition, Windows XP Professional, Windows Server 2003 family

InputLanguage.Equals Method

Specifies whether two input languages are equal.

```
[Visual Basic]
Overrides Public Function Equals( _
   ByVal value As Object _
) As Boolean
[C#]
public override bool Equals(
   object value
);
[C++]
public: bool Equals(
   Object* value
);
[JScript]
public override function Equals(
   value : Object
) : Boolean;
```

Parameters

value
The language to test for equality.

Return Value

true if the two languages are equal; otherwise, **false**.

Requirements

Platforms: Windows 98, Windows NT 4.0, Windows Millennium Edition, Windows 2000, Windows XP Home Edition, Windows XP Professional, Windows Server 2003 family

InputLanguage.FromCulture Method

Returns the input language associated with the specified culture.

```
[Visual Basic]
Public Shared Function FromCulture( _
   ByVal culture As CultureInfo _
) As InputLanguage
[C#]
public static InputLanguage FromCulture(
   CultureInfo culture
);
[C++]
public: static InputLanguage* FromCulture(
   CultureInfo* culture
);
[JScript]
public static function FromCulture(
   culture : CultureInfo
) : InputLanguage;
```

Parameters

culture
The **CultureInfo** object that specifies the culture to convert from.

Return Value

An **InputLanguage** that represents the previously selected input language.

Example

See related example in the **System.Windows.Forms.InputLanguage** class topic.

Requirements

Platforms: Windows 98, Windows NT 4.0, Windows Millennium Edition, Windows 2000, Windows XP Home Edition, Windows XP Professional, Windows Server 2003 family

InputLanguage.GetHashCode Method

This member overrides **Object.GetHashCode**.

```
[Visual Basic]
Overrides Public Function GetHashCode() As Integer
[C#]
public override int GetHashCode();
[C++]
public: int GetHashCode();
[JScript]
public override function GetHashCode() : int;
```

Requirements

Platforms: Windows 98, Windows NT 4.0, Windows Millennium Edition, Windows 2000, Windows XP Home Edition, Windows XP Professional, Windows Server 2003 family

InputLanguageChangedEventArgs Class

Provides data for the **InputLanguageChanged** event.

System.Object
  System.EventArgs
    System.Windows.Forms.InputLanguageChangedEventArgs

[Visual Basic]
```
Public Class InputLanguageChangedEventArgs
   Inherits EventArgs
```
[C#]
```
public class InputLanguageChangedEventArgs : EventArgs
```
[C++]
```
public __gc class InputLanguageChangedEventArgs : public EventArgs
```
[JScript]
```
public class InputLanguageChangedEventArgs extends EventArgs
```

Thread Safety

Any public static (**Shared** in Visual Basic) members of this type are safe for multithreaded operations. Any instance members are not guaranteed to be thread safe.

Remarks

You can use the data from the **InputLanguageChangedEventArgs** to make decisions about whether to change Input Method Editors (IMEs) or swap right-to-left values. You can also change the **CurrentCulture** of a thread and the **CurrentUICulture** properties so that different resources get picked up.

An **InputLanguageChangedEventArgs** identifies the locale and the character set of the new input language.

The **InputLanguageChanging** event precedes the **InputLanguageChanged** event.

Example

[Visual Basic, C#] The following example creates a new **Form** and attaches an event handler to the **InputLanguageChanged** event. This event changes the **IMEmode** when the input language changes to Japanese.

[Visual Basic]
```
Imports System
Imports System.Drawing
Imports System.Collections
Imports System.ComponentModel
Imports System.Windows.Forms
Imports System.Data

Public Class Form1
   Inherits System.Windows.Forms.Form

   Dim WithEvents rtb As New RichTextBox()

   Public Sub New()
      MyBase.New()
      Me.Controls.Add(rtb)
      rtb.Dock = DockStyle.Fill
   End Sub

   Private Sub languageChange( _
      ByVal sender As Object, _
      ByVal e As InputLanguageChangedEventArgs _
   ) Handles MyBase.InputLanguageChanged

      ' If the input language is Japanese.
      ' set the initial IMEMode to Katakana.
      If e.InputLanguage.Culture.TwoLetterISOLanguageName.Equals ↵
("ja") = True Then
         rtb.ImeMode = System.Windows.Forms.ImeMode.Katakana
      End If
   End Sub

   Public Shared Sub Main()
      Application.Run(new Form1())
   End Sub

End Class
```

[C#]
```
using System;
using System.Drawing;
using System.Collections;
using System.ComponentModel;
using System.Windows.Forms;
using System.Data;

public class Form1 : System.Windows.Forms.Form
{
    RichTextBox rtb = new RichTextBox();
    public Form1()
    {
        this.Controls.Add(rtb);
        rtb.Dock = DockStyle.Fill;
        this.InputLanguageChanged += new ↵
InputLanguageChangedEventHandler(languageChange);
    }
    private void languageChange(Object sender, ↵
InputLanguageChangedEventArgs e)
    {
        // If the input language is Japanese.
        // set the initial IMEMode to Katakana.
        if
(e.InputLanguage.Culture.TwoLetterISOLanguageName.Equals("ja"))
        {
            rtb.ImeMode = System.Windows.Forms.ImeMode.Katakana;
        }
    }
    public static void Main(string[] args)
    {
        Application.Run(new Form1());
    }
}
```

Requirements

Namespace: System.Windows.Forms

Platforms: Windows 98, Windows NT 4.0, Windows Millennium Edition, Windows 2000, Windows XP Home Edition, Windows XP Professional, Windows Server 2003 family

Assembly: System.Windows.Forms (in System.Windows.Forms.dll)

InputLanguageChangedEventArgs Constructor

This member supports the .NET Framework infrastructure and is not intended to be used directly from your code.

Overload List

This member supports the .NET Framework infrastructure and is not intended to be used directly from your code.

[Visual Basic] **Public Sub New(CultureInfo, Byte)**

[C#] **public InputLanguageChangedEventArgs(CultureInfo, byte);**

[C++] **public: InputLanguageChangedEventArgs(CultureInfo*, unsigned char);**

[JScript] **public function InputLanguageChangedEventArgs(CultureInfo, Byte);**

Initializes a new instance of the **InputLanguageChangedEventArgs** class with the specified input language and character set.

[Visual Basic] **Public Sub New(InputLanguage, Byte)**

[C#] **public InputLanguageChangedEventArgs(InputLanguage, byte);**

[C++] **public: InputLanguageChangedEventArgs(InputLanguage*, unsigned char);**

[JScript] **public function InputLanguageChangedEventArgs(InputLanguage, Byte);**

InputLanguageChangedEventArgs Constructor (CultureInfo, Byte)

This member supports the .NET Framework infrastructure and is not intended to be used directly from your code.

```
[Visual Basic]
Public Sub New( _
   ByVal culture As CultureInfo, _
   ByVal charSet As Byte _
)
[C#]
public InputLanguageChangedEventArgs(
   CultureInfo culture,
   byte charSet
);
[C++]
public: InputLanguageChangedEventArgs(
   CultureInfo* culture,
   unsigned char charSet
);
[JScript]
public function InputLanguageChangedEventArgs(
   culture : CultureInfo,
   charSet : Byte
);
```

InputLanguageChangedEventArgs Constructor (InputLanguage, Byte)

Initializes a new instance of the **InputLanguageChangedEventArgs** class with the specified input language and character set.

```
[Visual Basic]
Public Sub New( _
   ByVal inputLanguage As InputLanguage, _
   ByVal charSet As Byte _
)
[C#]
public InputLanguageChangedEventArgs(
   InputLanguage inputLanguage,
   byte charSet
);
[C++]
public: InputLanguageChangedEventArgs(
   InputLanguage* inputLanguage,
   unsigned char charSet
);
[JScript]
public function InputLanguageChangedEventArgs(
   inputLanguage : InputLanguage,
   charSet : Byte
);
```

Parameters

inputLanguage

The input language.

charSet

The character set associated with the new input language.

Remarks

The input language specifies a culture/keyboard layout pair.

See the **CharSet** property for a list of valid character sets.

Requirements

Platforms: Windows 98, Windows NT 4.0, Windows Millennium Edition, Windows 2000, Windows XP Home Edition, Windows XP Professional, Windows Server 2003 family

InputLanguageChangedEventArgs.CharSet Property

Gets the character set associated with the new input language.

```
[Visual Basic]
Public ReadOnly Property CharSet As Byte
[C#]
public byte CharSet {get;}
[C++]
public: __property unsigned char get_CharSet();
[JScript]
public function get CharSet() : Byte;
```

Property Value

An 8-bit unsigned integer that corresponds to the character set, as shown in the following table.

Character Set	Value
ANSI_CHARSET	0
DEFAULT_CHARSET	1
SYMBOL_CHARSET	2
MAC_CHARSET	77
SHIFTJI_CHARSET	128
HANGEUL_CHARSET	129
HANGUL_CHARSET	129
JOHAB_CHARSET	130
GB2312_CHARSET	134
CHINESEBIG5_CHARSET	136
GREEK_CHARSET	161
TURKISH_CHARSET	162
VIETNAMESE_CHARSET	163
HEBREW_CHARSET	177
ARABIC_CHARSET	178
BALTIC_CHARSET	186

Character Set	Value
RUSSIAN_CHARSET	204
THAI_CHARSET	222
EASTEUROPE_CHARSET	238
OEM_CHARSET	255

Remarks

This property is the Win32 character set that the user switched to. On ANSI systems, this property can be used to create fonts that can display the correct character set. On Unicode systems, you typically do not need to use this property. Instead, use the **CultureInfo** class for these functionalities.

Requirements

Platforms: Windows 98, Windows NT 4.0, Windows Millennium Edition, Windows 2000, Windows XP Home Edition, Windows XP Professional, Windows Server 2003 family

InputLanguageChangedEventArgs.Culture Property

Gets the locale of the input language.

```
[Visual Basic]
Public ReadOnly Property Culture As CultureInfo
[C#]
public CultureInfo Culture {get;}
[C++]
public: __property CultureInfo* get_Culture();
[JScript]
public function get Culture() : CultureInfo;
```

Property Value

A **CultureInfo** that specifies the locale of the input language.

Remarks

The **Culture** property specifies a **CultureInfo** and defines a set of user preference information dependent on the language, sublanguage, country/region, and cultural conventions of the user.

Requirements

Platforms: Windows 98, Windows NT 4.0, Windows Millennium Edition, Windows 2000, Windows XP Home Edition, Windows XP Professional, Windows Server 2003 family

InputLanguageChangedEventArgs.InputLanguage Property

Gets a value indicating the input language.

```
[Visual Basic]
Public ReadOnly Property InputLanguage As InputLanguage
[C#]
public InputLanguage InputLanguage {get;}
[C++]
public: __property InputLanguage* get_InputLanguage();
[JScript]
public function get InputLanguage() : InputLanguage;
```

Property Value

An **InputLanguage**.

Requirements

Platforms: Windows 98, Windows NT 4.0, Windows Millennium Edition, Windows 2000, Windows XP Home Edition, Windows XP Professional, Windows Server 2003 family

InputLanguageChangedEvent-Handler Delegate

Represents the method that will handle the **InputLanguageChanged** event of a **Form**.

[Visual Basic]
```
<Serializable>
Public Delegate Sub InputLanguageChangedEventHandler( _
   ByVal sender As Object, _
   ByVal e As InputLanguageChangedEventArgs _
)
```
[C#]
```
[Serializable]
public delegate void InputLanguageChangedEventHandler(
   object sender,
   InputLanguageChangedEventArgs e
);
```
[C++]
```
[Serializable]
public __gc __delegate void InputLanguageChangedEventHandler(
   Object* sender,
   InputLanguageChangedEventArgs* e
);
```

[JScript] In JScript, you can use the delegates in the .NET Framework, but you cannot define your own.

Parameters [Visual Basic, C#, C++]

The declaration of your event handler must have the same parameters as the **InputLanguageChangedEventHandler** delegate declaration.

sender
: The source of the event.

e
: An **InputLanguageChangedEventArgs** that contains the event data.

Remarks

When you create an **InputLanguageChangedEventHandler** delegate, you identify the method that will handle the event. To associate the event with your event handler, add an instance of the delegate to the event. The event handler is called whenever the event occurs, unless you remove the delegate.

Requirements

Namespace: System.Windows.Forms

Platforms: Windows 98, Windows NT 4.0, Windows Millennium Edition, Windows 2000, Windows XP Home Edition, Windows XP Professional, Windows Server 2003 family

Assembly: System.Windows.Forms (in System.Windows.Forms.dll)

InputLanguageChangingEventArgs Class

Provides data for the **InputLanguageChanging** event.

For a list of all members of this type, see **InputLanguageChangingEventArgs Members**.

System.Object
  System.EventArgs
    System.ComponentModel.CancelEventArgs
      System.Windows.Forms.InputLanguageChangingEventArgs

[Visual Basic]
```
Public Class InputLanguageChangingEventArgs
   Inherits CancelEventArgs
```
[C#]
```
public class InputLanguageChangingEventArgs : CancelEventArgs
```
[C++]
```
public __gc class InputLanguageChangingEventArgs : public
   CancelEventArgs
```
[JScript]
```
public class InputLanguageChangingEventArgs extends CancelEventArgs
```

Thread Safety

Any public static (**Shared** in Visual Basic) members of this type are safe for multithreaded operations. Any instance members are not guaranteed to be thread safe.

Remarks

You can use the data from the **InputLanguageChangingEventArgs** to prepare to change Input Method Editors (IMEs) or swap right-to-left values. You can also change a thread's **CurrentCulture** and **CurrentUICulture** properties so that different resources get picked up. To prevent the input language from changing, set the **Cancel** property to **true**.

An **InputLanguageChangingEventArgs** identifies the requested input language and the character set of new input language. The **Culture** property identifies the locale of the requested language.

The **InputLanguageChanging** event precedes the **InputLanguageChanged** event.

Requirements

Namespace: System.Windows.Forms

Platforms: Windows 98, Windows NT 4.0, Windows Millennium Edition, Windows 2000, Windows XP Home Edition, Windows XP Professional, Windows Server 2003 family

Assembly: System.Windows.Forms (in System.Windows.Forms.dll)

InputLanguageChangingEventArgs Constructor

This member supports the .NET Framework infrastructure and is not intended to be used directly from your code.

Overload List

This member supports the .NET Framework infrastructure and is not intended to be used directly from your code.

[Visual Basic] **Public Sub New(CultureInfo, Boolean)**

[C#] **public InputLanguageChangingEventArgs(CultureInfo, bool);**

[C++] **public: InputLanguageChangingEventArgs(CultureInfo*, bool);**

[JScript] **public function InputLanguageChangingEventArgs(CultureInfo, Boolean);**

Initializes a new instance of the **InputLanguageChangingEventArgs** class with the specified input language, character set, and acceptance of a language change.

[Visual Basic] **Public Sub New(InputLanguage, Boolean)**

[C#] **public InputLanguageChangingEventArgs(InputLanguage, bool);**

[C++] **public: InputLanguageChangingEventArgs(InputLanguage*, bool);**

[JScript] **public function InputLanguageChangingEventArgs(InputLanguage, Boolean);**

InputLanguageChangingEventArgs Constructor (CultureInfo, Boolean)

This member supports the .NET Framework infrastructure and is not intended to be used directly from your code.

[Visual Basic]
```
Public Sub New( _
   ByVal culture As CultureInfo, _
   ByVal sysCharSet As Boolean _
)
```
[C#]
```
public InputLanguageChangingEventArgs(
   CultureInfo culture,
   bool sysCharSet
);
```
[C++]
```
public: InputLanguageChangingEventArgs(
   CultureInfo* culture,
   bool sysCharSet
);
```
[JScript]
```
public function InputLanguageChangingEventArgs(
   culture : CultureInfo,
   sysCharSet : Boolean
);
```

InputLanguageChangingEventArgs Constructor (InputLanguage, Boolean)

Initializes a new instance of the **InputLanguageChangingEventArgs** class with the specified input language, character set, and acceptance of a language change.

```
[Visual Basic]
Public Sub New( _
   ByVal inputLanguage As InputLanguage, _
   ByVal sysCharSet As Boolean _
)
[C#]
public InputLanguageChangingEventArgs(
   InputLanguage inputLanguage,
   bool sysCharSet
);
[C++]
public: InputLanguageChangingEventArgs(
   InputLanguage* inputLanguage,
   bool sysCharSet
);
[JScript]
public function InputLanguageChangingEventArgs(
   inputLanguage : InputLanguage,
   sysCharSet : Boolean
);
```

Parameters

inputLanguage
The requested input language.

sysCharSet
true if the system default font supports the character set required for the requested input language; otherwise, **false**.

Exceptions

Exception Type	Condition
ArgumentException	*inputLanguage* is a null reference (**Nothing** in Visual Basic).

Requirements

Platforms: Windows 98, Windows NT 4.0, Windows Millennium Edition, Windows 2000, Windows XP Home Edition, Windows XP Professional, Windows Server 2003 family

InputLanguageChangingEventArgs.Culture Property

Gets the locale of the requested input language.

```
[Visual Basic]
Public ReadOnly Property Culture As CultureInfo
[C#]
public CultureInfo Culture {get;}
[C++]
public: __property CultureInfo* get_Culture();
[JScript]
public function get Culture() : CultureInfo;
```

Property Value

A **CultureInfo** that specifies the locale of the requested input language.

Remarks

The **Culture** property specifies a **CultureInfo** that defines a set of user preference information dependent on the user's language, sublanguage, country/region, and cultural conventions.

Requirements

Platforms: Windows 98, Windows NT 4.0, Windows Millennium Edition, Windows 2000, Windows XP Home Edition, Windows XP Professional, Windows Server 2003 family

InputLanguageChangingEventArgs.InputLanguage Property

Gets a value indicating the input language.

```
[Visual Basic]
Public ReadOnly Property InputLanguage As InputLanguage
[C#]
public InputLanguage InputLanguage {get;}
[C++]
public: __property InputLanguage* get_InputLanguage();
[JScript]
public function get InputLanguage() : InputLanguage;
```

Property Value

An **InputLanguage**.

Requirements

Platforms: Windows 98, Windows NT 4.0, Windows Millennium Edition, Windows 2000, Windows XP Home Edition, Windows XP Professional, Windows Server 2003 family

InputLanguageChangingEventArgs.SysCharSet Property

Gets a value indicating whether the system default font supports the character set required for the requested input language.

```
[Visual Basic]
Public ReadOnly Property SysCharSet As Boolean
[C#]
public bool SysCharSet {get;}
[C++]
public: __property bool get_SysCharSet();
[JScript]
public function get SysCharSet() : Boolean;
```

Property Value

true if the system default font supports the character set required for the requested input language; otherwise, **false**.

Requirements

Platforms: Windows 98, Windows NT 4.0, Windows Millennium Edition, Windows 2000, Windows XP Home Edition, Windows XP Professional, Windows Server 2003 family

InputLanguageChangingEvent-Handler Delegate

Represents the method that will handle the **InputLanguage-Changing** event of a **Form**.

[Visual Basic]
```
<Serializable>
Public Delegate Sub InputLanguageChangingEventHandler( _
   ByVal sender As Object, _
   ByVal e As InputLanguageChangingEventArgs _
)
```
[C#]
```
[Serializable]
public delegate void InputLanguageChangingEventHandler(
   object sender,
   InputLanguageChangingEventArgs e
);
```
[C++]
```
[Serializable]
public __gc __delegate void InputLanguageChangingEventHandler(
   Object* sender,
   InputLanguageChangingEventArgs* e
);
```
[JScript] In JScript, you can use the delegates in the .NET Framework, but you cannot define your own.

Parameters [Visual Basic, C#, C++]

The declaration of your event handler must have the same parameters as the **InputLanguageChangingEventHandler** delegate declaration.

sender
   The source of the event.

e
   An **InputLanguageChangingEventArgs** that contains the event data.

Remarks

When you create an **InputLanguageChangingEventHandler** delegate, you identify the method that will handle the event. To associate the event with your event handler, add an instance of the delegate to the event. The event handler is called whenever the event occurs, unless you remove the delegate.

Requirements

Namespace: System.Windows.Forms

Platforms: Windows 98, Windows NT 4.0, Windows Millennium Edition, Windows 2000, Windows XP Home Edition, Windows XP Professional, Windows Server 2003 family

Assembly: System.Windows.Forms (in System.Windows.Forms.dll)

InputLanguageCollection Class

Stores **InputLanguage** objects.

For a list of all members of this type, see **InputLanguageCollection Members**.

System.Object
  System.Collections.ReadOnlyCollectionBase
    System.Windows.Forms.InputLanguageCollection

```
[Visual Basic]
Public Class InputLanguageCollection
   Inherits ReadOnlyCollectionBase
[C#]
public class InputLanguageCollection : ReadOnlyCollectionBase
[C++]
public __gc class InputLanguageCollection : public
   ReadOnlyCollectionBase
[JScript]
public class InputLanguageCollection extends ReadOnlyCollectionBase
```

Thread Safety

Any public static (**Shared** in Visual Basic) members of this type are safe for multithreaded operations. Any instance members are not guaranteed to be thread safe.

Remarks

The **InputLanguageCollection** class is used by **InputLanguage** to provide a list of the input languages installed on the system.

You cannot directly create an instance of this class.

Requirements

Namespace: System.Windows.Forms

Platforms: Windows 98, Windows NT 4.0, Windows Millennium Edition, Windows 2000, Windows XP Home Edition, Windows XP Professional, Windows Server 2003 family

Assembly: System.Windows.Forms (in System.Windows.Forms.dll)

InputLanguageCollection.Item Property

Gets the entry at the specified index of the **InputLanguageCollection**.

[C#] In C#, this property is the indexer for the **InputLanguage-Collection** class.

```
[Visual Basic]
Public Default ReadOnly Property Item( _
   ByVal index As Integer _
) As InputLanguage
[C#]
public InputLanguage this[
   int index
] {get;}
[C++]
public: __property InputLanguage* get_Item(
   int index
);
[JScript]
returnValue = InputLanguageCollectionObject.Item(index);
-or-
returnValue = InputLanguageCollectionObject(index);
```

[JScript] In JScript, you can use the default indexed properties defined by a type, but you cannot explicitly define your own. However, specifying the **expando** attribute on a class automatically provides a default indexed property whose type is **Object** and whose index type is **String**.

Arguments [JScript]

index
  The zero-based index of the entry to locate in the collection.

Parameters [Visual Basic, C#, C++]

index
  The zero-based index of the entry to locate in the collection.

Property Value

The **InputLanguage** at the specified index of the collection.

Exceptions

Exception Type	Condition
ArgumentOutOfRange-Exception	*index* is outside the valid range of indexes for the collection.

Requirements

Platforms: Windows 98, Windows NT 4.0, Windows Millennium Edition, Windows 2000, Windows XP Home Edition, Windows XP Professional, Windows Server 2003 family

InputLanguageCollection.Contains Method

Gets a value indicating whether the **InputLanguageCollection** contains the specified **InputLanguage**.

```
[Visual Basic]
Public Function Contains( _
   ByVal value As InputLanguage _
) As Boolean
[C#]
public bool Contains(
   InputLanguage value
);
[C++]
public: bool Contains(
   InputLanguage* value
);
[JScript]
public function Contains(
   value : InputLanguage
) : Boolean;
```

Parameters

value
  The **InputLanguage** to locate.

Return Value

true if the **InputLanguage** is contained in the collection; otherwise, **false**.

Requirements

Platforms: Windows 98, Windows NT 4.0, Windows Millennium Edition, Windows 2000, Windows XP Home Edition, Windows XP Professional, Windows Server 2003 family

InputLanguageCollection.CopyTo Method

Copies the **InputLanguageCollection** values to a one-dimensional **Array** at the specified index.

```
[Visual Basic]
Public Sub CopyTo( _
   ByVal array() As InputLanguage, _
   ByVal index As Integer _
)
[C#]
public void CopyTo(
   InputLanguage[] array,
   int index
);
[C++]
public: void CopyTo(
   InputLanguage* array[],
   int index
);
[JScript]
public function CopyTo(
   array : InputLanguage[],
   index : int
);
```

Parameters

array
The one-dimensional array that is the destination of the values copied from **InputLanguageCollection**.

index
The index in the *array* parameter where copying begins.

Exceptions

Exception Type	Condition
ArgumentException	*array* specifies a multidimensional array. -or- The number of elements in the **InputLanguageCollection** is greater than the available space between the *index* and the end of *array*.
ArgumentNull-Exception	*array* is a null reference (**Nothing** in Visual Basic).
ArgumentOutOfRange-Exception	*index* is less than the lower bound of *array*.

Requirements

Platforms: Windows 98, Windows NT 4.0, Windows Millennium Edition, Windows 2000, Windows XP Home Edition, Windows XP Professional, Windows Server 2003 family

InputLanguageCollection.IndexOf Method

Returns the index of an **InputLanguage** in the **InputLanguage-Collection**.

```
[Visual Basic]
Public Function IndexOf( _
   ByVal value As InputLanguage _
) As Integer
[C#]
public int IndexOf(
   InputLanguage value
);
[C++]
public: int IndexOf(
   InputLanguage* value
);
[JScript]
public function IndexOf(
   value : InputLanguage
) : int;
```

Parameters

value
The **InputLanguage** to locate.

Return Value

The index of the **InputLanguage** in **InputLanguageCollection**, if found; otherwise, -1.

Requirements

Platforms: Windows 98, Windows NT 4.0, Windows Millennium Edition, Windows 2000, Windows XP Home Edition, Windows XP Professional, Windows Server 2003 family

InvalidateEventArgs Class

Provides data for the **Invalidated** event.

System.Object
  System.EventArgs
    System.Windows.Forms.InvalidateEventArgs

```
[Visual Basic]
Public Class InvalidateEventArgs
   Inherits EventArgs
[C#]
public class InvalidateEventArgs : EventArgs
[C++]
public __gc class InvalidateEventArgs : public EventArgs
[JScript]
public class InvalidateEventArgs extends EventArgs
```

Thread Safety

Any public static (**Shared** in Visual Basic) members of this type are safe for multithreaded operations. Any instance members are not guaranteed to be thread safe.

Remarks

The **Invalidated** event occurs when a control's display is updated. An **InvalidateEventArgs** specifies the rectangle that contains the invalidated window area.

Requirements

Namespace: System.Windows.Forms

Platforms: Windows 98, Windows NT 4.0, Windows Millennium Edition, Windows 2000, Windows XP Home Edition, Windows XP Professional, Windows Server 2003 family

Assembly: System.Windows.Forms (in System.Windows.Forms.dll)

InvalidateEventArgs Constructor

Initializes a new instance of the **InvalidateEventArgs** class.

```
[Visual Basic]
Public Sub New( _
   ByVal invalidRect As Rectangle _
)
[C#]
public InvalidateEventArgs(
   Rectangle invalidRect
);
[C++]
public: InvalidateEventArgs(
   Rectangle invalidRect
);
[JScript]
public function InvalidateEventArgs(
   invalidRect : Rectangle
);
```

Parameters

invalidRect
  The **Rectangle** that contains the invalidated window area.

Requirements

Platforms: Windows 98, Windows NT 4.0, Windows Millennium Edition, Windows 2000, Windows XP Home Edition, Windows XP Professional, Windows Server 2003 family

InvalidateEventArgs.InvalidRect Property

Gets the **Rectangle** that contains the invalidated window area.

```
[Visual Basic]
Public ReadOnly Property InvalidRect As Rectangle
[C#]
public Rectangle InvalidRect {get;}
[C++]
public: __property Rectangle get_InvalidRect();
[JScript]
public function get InvalidRect() : Rectangle;
```

Property Value

The invalidated window area.

Requirements

Platforms: Windows 98, Windows NT 4.0, Windows Millennium Edition, Windows 2000, Windows XP Home Edition, Windows XP Professional, Windows Server 2003 family

InvalidateEventHandler Delegate

Represents the method that will handle the **Invalidated** event of a **Control**.

[Visual Basic]
```
<Serializable>
Public Delegate Sub InvalidateEventHandler( _
   ByVal sender As Object, _
   ByVal e As InvalidateEventArgs _
)
```
[C#]
```
[Serializable]
public delegate void InvalidateEventHandler(
   object sender,
   InvalidateEventArgs e
);
```
[C++]
```
[Serializable]
public __gc __delegate void InvalidateEventHandler(
   Object* sender,
   InvalidateEventArgs* e
);
```

[JScript] In JScript, you can use the delegates in the .NET Framework, but you cannot define your own.

Parameters [Visual Basic, C#, C++]

The declaration of your event handler must have the same parameters as the **InvalidateEventHandler** delegate declaration.

sender

The source of the event.

e

An **InvalidateEventArgs** that contains the event data.

Remarks

When you create an **InvalidateEventHandler** delegate, you identify the method that will handle the event. To associate the event with your event handler, add an instance of the delegate to the event. The event handler is called whenever the event occurs, unless you remove the delegate.

Requirements

Namespace: System.Windows.Forms

Platforms: Windows 98, Windows NT 4.0, Windows Millennium Edition, Windows 2000, Windows XP Home Edition, Windows XP Professional, Windows Server 2003 family

Assembly: System.Windows.Forms (in System.Windows.Forms.dll)

ItemActivation Enumeration

Specifies the user action that is required to activate items in a list view control and the feedback that is given as the user moves the mouse pointer over an item.

[Visual Basic]
```
<Serializable>
Public Enum ItemActivation
```
[C#]
```
[Serializable]
public enum ItemActivation
```
[C++]
```
[Serializable]
__value public enum ItemActivation
```
[JScript]
```
public
   Serializable
enum ItemActivation
```

Remarks

Use the members of this enumeration to set the value of the **Activation** property of the **ListView** control.

Members

Member name	Description
OneClick Supported by the .NET Compact Framework.	The user must single-click to activate items. The cursor changes to a hand pointer cursor, and the item text changes color as the user moves the mouse pointer over the item.
Standard Supported by the .NET Compact Framework.	The user must double-click to activate items. No feedback is given as the user moves the mouse pointer over an item.
TwoClick Supported by the .NET Compact Framework.	The user must double-click to activate items and the item text changes color as the user moves the mouse pointer over the item.

Requirements

Namespace: System.Windows.Forms

Platforms: Windows 98, Windows NT 4.0, Windows Millennium Edition, Windows 2000, Windows XP Home Edition, Windows XP Professional, Windows Server 2003 family, .NET Compact Framework - Windows CE .NET

Assembly: System.Windows.Forms (in System.Windows.Forms.dll)

ItemBoundsPortion Enumeration

Specifies a portion of the list view item from which to retrieve the bounding rectangle.

[Visual Basic]
```
<Serializable>
Public Enum ItemBoundsPortion
```
[C#]
```
[Serializable]
public enum ItemBoundsPortion
```
[C++]
```
[Serializable]
__value public enum ItemBoundsPortion
```
[JScript]
```
public
   Serializable
enum ItemBoundsPortion
```

Remarks

Use the members of this enumeration when calling the **GetItemRect** method of the **ListView** control. This enumeration is also used when calling the **GetBounds** method of the **ListViewItem** class.

Members

Member name	Description
Entire	The bounding rectangle of the entire item, including the icon, the item text, and the subitem text (if displayed), should be retrieved.
Icon	The bounding rectangle of the icon or small icon should be retrieved.
ItemOnly	The bounding rectangle of the icon or small icon and the item text should be retrieved. In all views except the details view of the **ListView**, this value specifies the same bounding rectangle as the **Entire** value. In details view, this value specifies the bounding rectangle specified by the **Entire** value without the subitems. If the **CheckBoxes** property is set to **true**, this property does not include the area of the check boxes in its bounding rectangle. To include the entire item, including the check boxes, use the **Entire** value when calling the **GetItemRect** method.
Label	The bounding rectangle of the item text should be retrieved.

Requirements

Namespace: System.Windows.Forms

Platforms: Windows 98, Windows NT 4.0, Windows Millennium Edition, Windows 2000, Windows XP Home Edition, Windows XP Professional, Windows Server 2003 family

Assembly: System.Windows.Forms (in System.Windows.Forms.dll)

ItemChangedEventArgs Class

Provides data for the **ItemChanged** event.

System.Object
  System.EventArgs
    System.Windows.Forms.ItemChangedEventArgs

[Visual Basic]
```
Public Class ItemChangedEventArgs
   Inherits EventArgs
```
[C#]
```
public class ItemChangedEventArgs : EventArgs
```
[C++]
```
public __gc class ItemChangedEventArgs : public EventArgs
```
[JScript]
```
public class ItemChangedEventArgs extends EventArgs
```

Thread Safety

Any public static (**Shared** in Visual Basic) members of this type are safe for multithreaded operations. Any instance members are not guaranteed to be thread safe.

Remarks

An **ItemChanged** event occurs whenever the item in a list is changed. For example, this event will occur when the text of the list item is changed to a new value. This event is not raised when the item is moved to a new position within the list because of a new item being added.

Requirements

Namespace: System.Windows.Forms

Platforms: Windows 98, Windows NT 4.0, Windows Millennium Edition, Windows 2000, Windows XP Home Edition, Windows XP Professional, Windows Server 2003 family, .NET Compact Framework - Windows CE .NET

Assembly: System.Windows.Forms (in System.Windows.Forms.dll)

ItemChangedEventArgs.Index Property

Indicates the position of the item being changed within the list.

[Visual Basic]
```
Public ReadOnly Property Index As Integer
```
[C#]
```
public int Index {get;}
```
[C++]
```
public: __property int get_Index();
```
[JScript]
```
public function get Index() : int;
```

Property Value

The zero-based index to the item being changed.

Requirements

Platforms: Windows 98, Windows NT 4.0, Windows Millennium Edition, Windows 2000, Windows XP Home Edition, Windows XP Professional, Windows Server 2003 family, .NET Compact Framework - Windows CE .NET

ItemChangedEventHandler Delegate

Represents the method that will handle the **ItemChanged** event of the **CurrencyManager** class.

[Visual Basic]

```
<Serializable>
Public Delegate Sub ItemChangedEventHandler( _
   ByVal sender As Object, _
   ByVal e As ItemChangedEventArgs _
)
```

[C#]

```
[Serializable]
public delegate void ItemChangedEventHandler(
   object sender,
   ItemChangedEventArgs e
);
```

[C++]

```
[Serializable]
public __gc __delegate void ItemChangedEventHandler(
   Object* sender,
   ItemChangedEventArgs* e
);
```

[JScript] In JScript, you can use the delegates in the .NET Framework, but you cannot define your own.

Parameters [Visual Basic, C#, C++]

The declaration of your event handler must have the same parameters as the **ItemChangedEventHandler** delegate declaration.

sender

The source of the event.

e

An **ItemChangedEventArgs** that contains the event data.

Remarks

When you create an **ItemChangedEventHandler** delegate, you identify the method that will handle the event. To associate the event with your event handler, add an instance of the delegate to the event. The event handler is called whenever the event occurs, unless you remove the delegate.

Requirements

Namespace: System.Windows.Forms

Platforms: Windows 98, Windows NT 4.0,
Windows Millennium Edition, Windows 2000,
Windows XP Home Edition, Windows XP Professional,
Windows Server 2003 family,
.NET Compact Framework - Windows CE .NET

Assembly: System.Windows.Forms (in System.Windows.Forms.dll)

ItemCheckEventArgs Class

Provides data for the **ItemCheck** event of the **CheckedListBox** and **ListView** controls.

For a list of all members of this type, see **ItemCheckEventArgs Members**.

System.Object
 System.EventArgs
  System.Windows.Forms.ItemCheckEventArgs

[Visual Basic]
```
<ComVisible(True)>
Public Class ItemCheckEventArgs
   Inherits EventArgs
```
[C#]
```
[ComVisible(true)]
public class ItemCheckEventArgs : EventArgs
```
[C++]
```
[ComVisible(true)]
public __gc class ItemCheckEventArgs : public EventArgs
```
[JScript]
```
public
   ComVisible(true)
class ItemCheckEventArgs extends EventArgs
```

Thread Safety

Any public static (**Shared** in Visual Basic) members of this type are safe for multithreaded operations. Any instance members are not guaranteed to be thread safe.

Remarks

The **ItemCheck** event occurs when the checked state of an item in a checked list box changes. The **ItemCheckEventArgs** class specifies the index of the item to change, the current value of the check box for the item, and the new value to set for the check box.

Requirements

Namespace: System.Windows.Forms

Platforms: Windows 98, Windows NT 4.0, Windows Millennium Edition, Windows 2000, Windows XP Home Edition, Windows XP Professional, Windows Server 2003 family, .NET Compact Framework - Windows CE .NET

Assembly: System.Windows.Forms (in System.Windows.Forms.dll)

ItemCheckEventArgs Constructor

Initializes a new instance of the **ItemCheckEventArgs** class.

[Visual Basic]
```
Public Sub New( _
   ByVal index As Integer, _
   ByVal newCheckValue As CheckState, _
   ByVal currentValue As CheckState _
)
```
[C#]
```
public ItemCheckEventArgs(
   int index,
   CheckState newCheckValue,
   CheckState currentValue
);
```
[C++]
```
public: ItemCheckEventArgs(
   int index,
   CheckState newCheckValue,
   CheckState currentValue
);
```
[JScript]
```
public function ItemCheckEventArgs(
   index : int,
   newCheckValue : CheckState,
   currentValue : CheckState
);
```

Parameters

index
  The zero-based index of the item to change.

newCheckValue
  One of the **CheckState** values that indicates whether to change the check box for the item to be checked, unchecked, or indeterminate.

currentValue
  One of the **CheckState** values that indicates whether the check box for the item is currently checked, unchecked, or indeterminate.

Requirements

Platforms: Windows 98, Windows NT 4.0, Windows Millennium Edition, Windows 2000, Windows XP Home Edition, Windows XP Professional, Windows Server 2003 family, .NET Compact Framework - Windows CE .NET

ItemCheckEventArgs.CurrentValue Property

Gets a value indicating the current state of the item's check box.

[Visual Basic]
```
Public ReadOnly Property CurrentValue As CheckState
```
[C#]
```
public CheckState CurrentValue {get;}
```
[C++]
```
public: __property CheckState get_CurrentValue();
```
[JScript]
```
public function get CurrentValue() : CheckState;
```

Property Value

One of the **CheckState** values.

Remarks

This property enables you to determine the check state of the specified item in the **CheckedListBox** before the check state change to apply is made.

Requirements

Platforms: Windows 98, Windows NT 4.0, Windows Millennium Edition, Windows 2000, Windows XP Home Edition, Windows XP Professional, Windows Server 2003 family, .NET Compact Framework - Windows CE .NET

ItemCheckEventArgs.Index Property

Gets the zero-based index of the item to change.

```
[Visual Basic]
Public ReadOnly Property Index As Integer
[C#]
public int Index {get;}
[C++]
public: __property int get_Index();
[JScript]
public function get Index() : int;
```

Property Value

The zero-based index of the item to change.

Remarks

You can use this property to determine which item's check box in the **CheckedListBox** is being changed.

Requirements

Platforms: Windows 98, Windows NT 4.0, Windows Millennium Edition, Windows 2000, Windows XP Home Edition, Windows XP Professional, Windows Server 2003 family, .NET Compact Framework - Windows CE .NET

ItemCheckEventArgs.NewValue Property

Gets or sets a value indicating whether to set the check box for the item to be checked, unchecked, or indeterminate.

```
[Visual Basic]
Public Property NewValue As CheckState
[C#]
public CheckState NewValue {get; set;}
[C++]
public: __property CheckState get_NewValue();
public: __property void set_NewValue(CheckState);
[JScript]
public function get NewValue() : CheckState;
public function set NewValue(CheckState);
```

Property Value

One of the **CheckState** values.

Remarks

This property enables you to determine the new check state for the specified item before the check state is changed by the **CheckedListBox** control. In addition to determining the new check state, you can use this property in an event handler for the **ItemCheck** event to change the state to a different check state than the one specified. For example, if the user placed a check mark next to an item in the **CheckedListBox** that you have determined should not be checked based on the state of your application, you can override the change in the check mark state by setting this property to its previous setting or to a different check state.

Requirements

Platforms: Windows 98, Windows NT 4.0, Windows Millennium Edition, Windows 2000, Windows XP Home Edition, Windows XP Professional, Windows Server 2003 family, .NET Compact Framework - Windows CE .NET

ItemCheckEventHandler Delegate

Represents the method that will handle the **ItemCheck** event of a **CheckedListBox** or **ListView** control.

[Visual Basic]
```
<Serializable>
Public Delegate Sub ItemCheckEventHandler( _
   ByVal sender As Object, _
   ByVal e As ItemCheckEventArgs _
)
```
[C#]
```
[Serializable]
public delegate void ItemCheckEventHandler(
   object sender,
   ItemCheckEventArgs e
);
```
[C++]
```
[Serializable]
public __gc __delegate void ItemCheckEventHandler(
   Object* sender,
   ItemCheckEventArgs* e
);
```

[JScript] In JScript, you can use the delegates in the .NET Framework, but you cannot define your own.

Parameters [Visual Basic, C#, C++]

The declaration of your event handler must have the same parameters as the **ItemCheckEventHandler** delegate declaration.

sender
: The source of the event.

e
: An **ItemCheckEventArgs** that contains the event data.

Remarks

When you create an **ItemCheckEventHandler** delegate, you identify the method that will handle the event. To associate the event with your event handler, add an instance of the delegate to the event. The event handler is called whenever the event occurs, unless you remove the delegate.

Requirements

Namespace: System.Windows.Forms

Platforms: Windows 98, Windows NT 4.0, Windows Millennium Edition, Windows 2000, Windows XP Home Edition, Windows XP Professional, Windows Server 2003 family, .NET Compact Framework - Windows CE .NET

Assembly: System.Windows.Forms (in System.Windows.Forms.dll)

ItemDragEventArgs Class

Provides data for the **ItemDrag** event of the **ListView** and **TreeView** controls.

System.Object
  System.EventArgs
    System.Windows.Forms.ItemDragEventArgs

```
[Visual Basic]
<ComVisible(True)>
Public Class ItemDragEventArgs
   Inherits EventArgs
[C#]
[ComVisible(true)]
public class ItemDragEventArgs : EventArgs
[C++]
[ComVisible(true)]
public __gc class ItemDragEventArgs : public EventArgs
[JScript]
public
   ComVisible(true)
class ItemDragEventArgs extends EventArgs
```

Thread Safety

Any public static (**Shared** in Visual Basic) members of this type are safe for multithreaded operations. Any instance members are not guaranteed to be thread safe.

Remarks

The **ItemDrag** event occurs when the user begins dragging an item. An **ItemDragEventArgs** object specifies which mouse button was pressed.

Requirements

Namespace: System.Windows.Forms

Platforms: Windows 98, Windows NT 4.0, Windows Millennium Edition, Windows 2000, Windows XP Home Edition, Windows XP Professional, Windows Server 2003 family

Assembly: System.Windows.Forms (in System.Windows.Forms.dll)

ItemDragEventArgs Constructor

Initializes a new instance of the **ItemDragEventArgs** class.

Overload List

Initializes a new instance of the **ItemDragEventArgs** class with a specified mouse button.

[Visual Basic] **Public Sub New(MouseButtons)**

[C#] **public ItemDragEventArgs(MouseButtons);**

[C++] **public: ItemDragEventArgs(MouseButtons);**

[JScript] **public function ItemDragEventArgs(MouseButtons);**

Initializes a new instance of the **ItemDragEventArgs** class with a specified mouse button and the item that is being dragged.

[Visual Basic] **Public Sub New(MouseButtons, Object)**

[C#] **public ItemDragEventArgs(MouseButtons, object);**

[C++] **public: ItemDragEventArgs(MouseButtons, Object*);**

[JScript] **public function ItemDragEventArgs(MouseButtons, Object);**

ItemDragEventArgs Constructor (MouseButtons)

Initializes a new instance of the **ItemDragEventArgs** class with a specified mouse button.

```
[Visual Basic]
Public Sub New( _
   ByVal button As MouseButtons _
)
[C#]
public ItemDragEventArgs(
   MouseButtons button
);
[C++]
public: ItemDragEventArgs(
   MouseButtons button
);
[JScript]
public function ItemDragEventArgs(
   button : MouseButtons
);
```

Parameters

button
One of the **MouseButtons** values that represents which mouse button was pressed.

Remarks

When this version of the constructor is used, the value of the **Item** property is automatically set to a null reference (**Nothing** in Visual Basic).

Requirements

Platforms: Windows 98, Windows NT 4.0, Windows Millennium Edition, Windows 2000, Windows XP Home Edition, Windows XP Professional, Windows Server 2003 family

ItemDragEventArgs Constructor (MouseButtons, Object)

Initializes a new instance of the **ItemDragEventArgs** class with a specified mouse button and the item that is being dragged.

```
[Visual Basic]
Public Sub New( _
   ByVal button As MouseButtons, _
   ByVal item As Object _
)
[C#]
public ItemDragEventArgs(
   MouseButtons button,
   object item
);
[C++]
public: ItemDragEventArgs(
   MouseButtons button,
   Object* item
);
[JScript]
public function ItemDragEventArgs(
   button : MouseButtons,
   item : Object
);
```

Parameters

button

One of the **MouseButtons** values that represents which mouse button was pressed.

item

The item being dragged.

Requirements

Platforms: Windows 98, Windows NT 4.0, Windows Millennium Edition, Windows 2000, Windows XP Home Edition, Windows XP Professional, Windows Server 2003 family

ItemDragEventArgs.Button Property

Gets the name of the mouse button that was clicked during the drag operation.

[Visual Basic]
```
Public ReadOnly Property Button As MouseButtons
```
[C#]
```
public MouseButtons Button {get;}
```
[C++]
```
public: __property MouseButtons get_Button();
```
[JScript]
```
public function get Button() : MouseButtons;
```

Property Value

One of the **MouseButtons** values.

Remarks

This property enables you to determine which mouse button was pressed during a drag-and-drop operation. The value of this property can be used to properly determine how the drag-and drop-operation should be performed.

Requirements

Platforms: Windows 98, Windows NT 4.0, Windows Millennium Edition, Windows 2000, Windows XP Home Edition, Windows XP Professional, Windows Server 2003 family

ItemDragEventArgs.Item Property

Gets the item that is being dragged.

[Visual Basic]
```
Public ReadOnly Property Item As Object
```
[C#]
```
public object Item {get;}
```
[C++]
```
public: __property Object* get_Item();
```
[JScript]
```
public function get Item() : Object;
```

Property Value

An object that represents the item being dragged.

Remarks

You can use this property to determine which item from the **TreeView** or **ListView** controls is being dragged from the control.

Requirements

Platforms: Windows 98, Windows NT 4.0, Windows Millennium Edition, Windows 2000, Windows XP Home Edition, Windows XP Professional, Windows Server 2003 family

ItemDragEventHandler Delegate

Represents the method that will handle the **ItemDrag** event of a **ListView** or **TreeView** control.

[Visual Basic]
```
<Serializable>
Public Delegate Sub ItemDragEventHandler( _
   ByVal sender As Object, _
   ByVal e As ItemDragEventArgs _
)
```
[C#]
```
[Serializable]
public delegate void ItemDragEventHandler(
   object sender,
   ItemDragEventArgs e
);
```
[C++]
```
[Serializable]
public __gc __delegate void ItemDragEventHandler(
   Object* sender,
   ItemDragEventArgs* e
);
```

[JScript] In JScript, you can use the delegates in the .NET Framework, but you cannot define your own.

Parameters [Visual Basic, C#, C++]

The declaration of your event handler must have the same parameters as the **ItemDragEventHandler** delegate declaration.

sender
: The source of the event.

e
: An **ItemDragEventArgs** that contains the event data.

Remarks

When you create an **ItemDragEventHandler** delegate, you identify the method that will handle the event. To associate the event with your event handler, add an instance of the delegate to the event. The event handler is called whenever the event occurs, unless you remove the delegate.

Requirements

Namespace: System.Windows.Forms

Platforms: Windows 98, Windows NT 4.0,
Windows Millennium Edition, Windows 2000,
Windows XP Home Edition, Windows XP Professional,
Windows Server 2003 family

Assembly: System.Windows.Forms (in System.Windows.Forms.dll)

IWin32Window Interface

Provides an interface to expose Win32 HWND handles.

[Visual Basic]
```
<ComVisible(True)>
<Guid("458AB8A2-A1EA-4d7b-8EBE-DEE5D3D9442C")>
<InterfaceType(ComInterfaceType.InterfaceIsIUnknown)>
Public Interface IWin32Window
```
[C#]
```
[ComVisible(true)]
[Guid("458AB8A2-A1EA-4d7b-8EBE-DEE5D3D9442C")]
[InterfaceType(ComInterfaceType.InterfaceIsIUnknown)]
public interface IWin32Window
```
[C++]
```
[ComVisible(true)]
[Guid("458AB8A2-A1EA-4d7b-8EBE-DEE5D3D9442C")]
[InterfaceType(ComInterfaceType::InterfaceIsIUnknown)]
public __gc __interface IWin32Window
```
[JScript]
```
public
   ComVisible(true)
   Guid("458AB8A2-A1EA-4d7b-8EBE-DEE5D3D9442C")
   InterfaceType(ComInterfaceType.InterfaceIsIUnknown)
interface IWin32Window
```

Classes that Implement IWin32Window

Class	Description
Control	Defines the base class for controls, which are components with visual representation.

Remarks

This interface is implemented on objects that expose Win32 HWND handles. The resultant handle can be used with Win32 API calls.

Example

[Visual Basic, C#] The following example sets the **Text** property of `label1` to the current **Handle** of `Form1`. This example assumes that you have a **Form** called `Form1` with a **Label** called `label1` on it.

[Visual Basic]
```
Public Sub New()
    InitializeComponent()

    Me.label1.Text = Me.Handle.ToString()
End Sub
```

[C#]
```
public Form1()
{
   InitializeComponent();

   this.label1.Text = this.Handle.ToString();
}
```

Requirements

Namespace: System.Windows.Forms

Platforms: Windows 98, Windows NT 4.0, Windows Millennium Edition, Windows 2000, Windows XP Home Edition, Windows XP Professional, Windows Server 2003 family

Assembly: System.Windows.Forms (in System.Windows.Forms.dll)

IWin32Window.Handle Property

Gets the handle to the window represented by the implementer.

[Visual Basic]
```
ReadOnly Property Handle As IntPtr
```
[C#]
```
IntPtr Handle {get;}
```
[C++]
```
__property IntPtr get_Handle();
```
[JScript]
```
function get Handle() : IntPtr;
```

Property Value

A handle to the window represented by the implementer.

Remarks

Depending on the implementer, the value of the **Handle** property could change during the life of the window.

Example

[Visual Basic, C#] The following example sets the **Text** property of `label1` to the current **Handle** of `Form1`. This example assumes that you have a **Form** called `Form1` with a **Label** called `label1` on it.

[Visual Basic]
```
Public Sub New()
    InitializeComponent()

    Me.label1.Text = Me.Handle.ToString()
End Sub
```

[C#]
```
public Form1()
{
   InitializeComponent();

   this.label1.Text = this.Handle.ToString();
}
```

Requirements

Platforms: Windows 98, Windows NT 4.0, Windows Millennium Edition, Windows 2000, Windows XP Home Edition, Windows XP Professional, Windows Server 2003 family

IWindowTarget Interface

This type supports the .NET Framework infrastructure and is not intended to be used directly from your code.

[Visual Basic]
```
Public Interface IWindowTarget
```
[C#]
```
public interface IWindowTarget
```
[C++]
```
public __gc __interface IWindowTarget
```
[JScript]
```
public interface IWindowTarget
```

IWindowTarget.OnHandleChange Method

This member supports the .NET Framework infrastructure and is not intended to be used directly from your code.

[Visual Basic]
```
Sub OnHandleChange( _
   ByVal newHandle As IntPtr _
)
```
[C#]
```
void OnHandleChange(
   IntPtr newHandle
);
```
[C++]
```
void OnHandleChange(
   IntPtr newHandle
);
```
[JScript]
```
function OnHandleChange(
   newHandle : IntPtr
);
```

IWindowTarget.OnMessage Method

This member supports the .NET Framework infrastructure and is not intended to be used directly from your code.

[Visual Basic]
```
Sub OnMessage( _
   ByRef m As Message _
)
```
[C#]
```
void OnMessage(
   ref Message m
);
```
[C++]
```
void OnMessage(
   Message* m
);
```
[JScript]
```
function OnMessage(
   m : Message
);
```

KeyEventArgs Class

Provides data for the **KeyDown** or **KeyUp** event.

System.Object
  System.EventArgs
    System.Windows.Forms.KeyEventArgs

```
[Visual Basic]
<ComVisible(True)>
Public Class KeyEventArgs
   Inherits EventArgs
[C#]
[ComVisible(true)]
public class KeyEventArgs : EventArgs
[C++]
[ComVisible(true)]
public __gc class KeyEventArgs : public EventArgs
[JScript]
public
   ComVisible(true)
class KeyEventArgs extends EventArgs
```

Thread Safety

Any public static (**Shared** in Visual Basic) members of this type are safe for multithreaded operations. Any instance members are not guaranteed to be thread safe.

Remarks

A **KeyEventArgs**, which specifies the key the user pressed and whether any modifier keys (CTRL, ALT, and SHIFT) were pressed at the same time, is passed with each **KeyDown** or **KeyUp** event.

The **KeyDown** event occurs when the user presses any key. The **KeyUp** event occurs when the user releases the key. Duplicate **KeyDown** events occur each time the key repeats, if the key is held down, but only one **KeyUp** event is generated when the user releases the key.

The **KeyPress** event also occurs when a key is depressed. A **KeyPressEventArgs** is passed with each **KeyPress** event, and specifies the character that was composed as a result of each key press.

Requirements

Namespace: System.Windows.Forms

Platforms: Windows 98, Windows NT 4.0, Windows Millennium Edition, Windows 2000, Windows XP Home Edition, Windows XP Professional, Windows Server 2003 family, .NET Compact Framework - Windows CE .NET

Assembly: System.Windows.Forms (in System.Windows.Forms.dll)

KeyEventArgs Constructor

Initializes a new instance of the **KeyEventArgs** class.

```
[Visual Basic]
Public Sub New( _
   ByVal keyData As Keys _
)
[C#]
public KeyEventArgs(
   Keys keyData
);
[C++]
public: KeyEventArgs(
   Keys keyData
);
[JScript]
public function KeyEventArgs(
   keyData : Keys
);
```

Parameters

keyData

A **Keys** value representing the key that was pressed, combined with any modifier flags that indicate which CTRL, SHIFT, and ALT keys were pressed at the same time. Possible values are obtained be applying the bitwise OR (|) operator to constants from the **Keys** enumeration.

Requirements

Platforms: Windows 98, Windows NT 4.0, Windows Millennium Edition, Windows 2000, Windows XP Home Edition, Windows XP Professional, Windows Server 2003 family, .NET Compact Framework - Windows CE .NET

KeyEventArgs.Alt Property

Gets a value indicating whether the ALT key was pressed.

```
[Visual Basic]
Public Overridable ReadOnly Property Alt As Boolean
[C#]
public virtual bool Alt {get;}
[C++]
public: __property virtual bool get_Alt();
[JScript]
public function get Alt() : Boolean;
```

Property Value

true if the ALT key was pressed; otherwise, **false**.

Example

```
[Visual Basic]
' This example demonstrates how to use the KeyDown event with ↵
the Help class to display
' pop-up style help to the user of the application. The example ↵
 filters for all variations
' of pressing the F1 key with a modifier key by using the ↵
KeyEventArgs properties passed
' to the event handling method.
' When the user presses any variation of F1 that includes any ↵
 keyboard modifier, the Help
' class displays a pop-up window, similar to a ToolTip, near ↵
 the control. If the user presses
' ALT + F2, a different Help pop-up is displayed with ↵
additional information. This example assumes
' that a TextBox control, named textBox1, has been added to ↵
 the form and its KeyDown
' event has been contected to this event handling method.
Private Sub textBox1_KeyDown(ByVal sender As Object, ByVal ↵
e As System.Windows.Forms.KeyEventArgs) Handles textBox1.KeyDown
    ' Determine whether the key entered is the F1 key. If ↵
it is, display Help.
    If e.KeyCode = Keys.F1 AndAlso (e.Alt OrElse e.Control ↵
OrElse e.Shift) Then
        ' Display a pop-up Help topic to assist the user.
        Help.ShowPopup(textBox1, "Enter your name.", New ↵
Point(textBox1.Bottom, textBox1.Right))
```

```
    ElseIf e.KeyCode = Keys.F2 AndAlso e.Modifiers = Keys.Alt Then
        ' Display a pop-up Help topic to provide additional
 assistance to the user.
        Help.ShowPopup(textBox1, "Enter your first name
followed by your last name. Middle name is optional.", _
            New Point(textBox1.Top, Me.textBox1.Left))
    End If
End Sub 'textBox1_KeyDown
```

[C#]

```
// This example demonstrates how to use the KeyDown event with
the Help class to display
// pop-up style help to the user of the application. The example
filters for all variations
// of pressing the F1 key with a modifier key by using the
 KeyEventArgs properties passed
// to the event handling method.
// When the user presses any variation of F1 that includes any
keyboard modifier, the Help
// class displays a pop-up window, similar to a ToolTip, near
 the control. If the user presses
// ALT + F2, a different Help pop-up is displayed with
additional information. This example assumes
// that a tTextBox control, named textBox1, has been added to the
 form and its KeyDown
// event has been contected to this event handling method.
private void textBox1_KeyDown(object sender,
System.Windows.Forms.KeyEventArgs e)
{
    // Determine whether the key entered is the F1 key. If
 it is, display Help.
    if(e.KeyCode == Keys.F1 && (e.Alt || e.Control || e.Shift))
    {
        // Display a pop-up Help topic to assist the user.
        Help.ShowPopup(textBox1, "Enter your name.", new
 Point(textBox1.Bottom, textBox1.Right));
    }
    else if(e.KeyCode == Keys.F2 && e.Modifiers == Keys.Alt)
    {
        // Display a pop-up Help topic to provide additional
 assistance to the user.
        Help.ShowPopup(textBox1, "Enter your first name followed
 by your last name. Middle name is optional.",
            new Point(textBox1.Top, this.textBox1.Left));
    }
}
```

[Visual Basic]

```
Private Sub treeView1_KeyDown(sender As Object, _
  e As KeyEventArgs) Handles treeView1.KeyDown
   ' If the 'Alt' and 'E' keys are pressed,
   ' allow the user to edit the TreeNode label.
   If e.Alt And e.KeyCode = Keys.E Then
      treeView1.LabelEdit = True
      ' If there is a TreeNode under the mose cursor, begin editing.
      Dim editNode As TreeNode = treeView1.GetNodeAt( _
        treeView1.PointToClient(Control.MousePosition))
      If Not (editNode Is Nothing) Then
         editNode.BeginEdit()
      End If
   End If
End Sub

Private Sub treeView1_AfterLabelEdit(sender As Object, _
  e As NodeLabelEditEventArgs) Handles treeView1.AfterLabelEdit
   ' Disable the ability to edit the TreeNode labels.
   treeView1.LabelEdit = False
End Sub
```

[C#]

```
private void treeView1_KeyDown(object sender, KeyEventArgs e)
{
   /* If the 'Alt' and 'E' keys are pressed,
      * allow the user to edit the TreeNode label. */
   if(e.Alt && e.KeyCode == Keys.E)
   {
      treeView1.LabelEdit = true;
      // If there is a TreeNode under the mose cursor, begin editing.
      TreeNode editNode = treeView1.GetNodeAt(
         treeView1.PointToClient(Control.MousePosition));
      if(editNode != null)
      {
         editNode.BeginEdit();
      }
   }
}

private void treeView1_AfterLabelEdit(object sender,
NodeLabelEditEventArgs e)
{
   // Disable the ability to edit the TreeNode labels.
   treeView1.LabelEdit = false;
}
```

[C++]

```
private:
    void treeView1_KeyDown(Object* /*sender*/, KeyEventArgs* e) {
        /* If the 'Alt' and 'E' keys are pressed,
         * allow the user to edit the TreeNode label. */
        if (e->Alt && e->KeyCode == Keys::E) {
            treeView1->LabelEdit = true;
            // If there is a TreeNode under the mose cursor,
begin editing.
            TreeNode* editNode = treeView1->GetNodeAt(
                treeView1->PointToClient(Control::MousePosition));
            if (editNode != 0) {
                editNode->BeginEdit();
            }
        }
    }

    void treeView1_AfterLabelEdit(Object* /*sender*/,
NodeLabelEditEventArgs* /*e*/) {
        // Disable the ability to edit the TreeNode labels.
        treeView1->LabelEdit = false;
    }
```

Requirements

Platforms: Windows 98, Windows NT 4.0, Windows Millennium Edition, Windows 2000, Windows XP Home Edition, Windows XP Professional, Windows Server 2003 family, .NET Compact Framework - Windows CE .NET

KeyEventArgs.Control Property

Gets a value indicating whether the CTRL key was pressed.

[Visual Basic]

```
Public ReadOnly Property Control As Boolean
```

[C#]

```
public bool Control {get;}
```

[C++]

```
public: __property bool get_Control();
```

[JScript]

```
public function get Control() : Boolean;
```

Property Value

true if the CTRL key was pressed; otherwise, **false**.

Example

See related example in the **System.Windows.Forms.KeyEventArgs.Alt** property topic.

Requirements

Platforms: Windows 98, Windows NT 4.0, Windows Millennium Edition, Windows 2000, Windows XP Home Edition, Windows XP Professional, Windows Server 2003 family, .NET Compact Framework - Windows CE .NET

KeyEventArgs.Handled Property

Gets or sets a value indicating whether the event was handled.

```
[Visual Basic]
Public Property Handled As Boolean
[C#]
public bool Handled {get; set;}
[C++]
public: __property bool get_Handled();
public: __property void set_Handled(bool);
[JScript]
public function get Handled() : Boolean;
public function set Handled(Boolean);
```

Property Value

true if the event was handled; otherwise, **false**.

Requirements

Platforms: Windows 98, Windows NT 4.0, Windows Millennium Edition, Windows 2000, Windows XP Home Edition, Windows XP Professional, Windows Server 2003 family, .NET Compact Framework - Windows CE .NET

KeyEventArgs.KeyCode Property

Gets the keyboard code for a **KeyDown** or **KeyUp** event.

```
[Visual Basic]
Public ReadOnly Property KeyCode As Keys
[C#]
public Keys KeyCode {get;}
[C++]
public: __property Keys get_KeyCode();
[JScript]
public function get KeyCode() : Keys;
```

Property Value

A **Keys** value that is the key code for the event.

Requirements

Platforms: Windows 98, Windows NT 4.0, Windows Millennium Edition, Windows 2000, Windows XP Home Edition, Windows XP Professional, Windows Server 2003 family, .NET Compact Framework - Windows CE .NET

KeyEventArgs.KeyData Property

Gets the key data for a **KeyDown** or **KeyUp** event.

```
[Visual Basic]
Public ReadOnly Property KeyData As Keys
[C#]
public Keys KeyData {get;}
[C++]
public: __property Keys get_KeyData();
[JScript]
public function get KeyData() : Keys;
```

Property Value

A **Keys** value representing the key code for the key that was pressed, combined with modifier flags that indicate which combination of CTRL, SHIFT, and ALT keys were pressed at the same time.

Remarks

You can use constants from **Keys** to extract information from the **KeyData** property. Use the bitwise AND operator to compare data returned by **KeyData** with constants in **Keys** to obtain information about which keys the user pressed. To determine whether a specific modifier key was pressed, use the **Control**, **Shift**, and **Alt** properties.

Requirements

Platforms: Windows 98, Windows NT 4.0, Windows Millennium Edition, Windows 2000, Windows XP Home Edition, Windows XP Professional, Windows Server 2003 family, .NET Compact Framework - Windows CE .NET

KeyEventArgs.KeyValue Property

Gets the keyboard value for a **KeyDown** or **KeyUp** event.

```
[Visual Basic]
Public ReadOnly Property KeyValue As Integer
[C#]
public int KeyValue {get;}
[C++]
public: __property int get_KeyValue();
[JScript]
public function get KeyValue() : int;
```

Property Value

The integer representation of the **KeyData** property.

Requirements

Platforms: Windows 98, Windows NT 4.0, Windows Millennium Edition, Windows 2000, Windows XP Home Edition, Windows XP Professional, Windows Server 2003 family, .NET Compact Framework - Windows CE .NET

KeyEventArgs.Modifiers Property

Gets the modifier flags for a **KeyDown** or **KeyUp** event. This indicates which combination of modifier keys (CTRL, SHIFT, and ALT) were pressed.

```
[Visual Basic]
Public ReadOnly Property Modifiers As Keys
[C#]
public Keys Modifiers {get;}
[C++]
public: __property Keys get_Modifiers();
[JScript]
public function get Modifiers() : Keys;
```

Property Value

A **Keys** value representing one or more modifier flags.

Remarks

To determine whether a specific modifier key was pressed, use the **Control**, **Shift**, and **Alt** properties. Modifier flags can be combined with bitwise OR.

Example

See related example in the **System.Windows.Forms.KeyEventArgs.Alt** property topic.

Requirements

Platforms: Windows 98, Windows NT 4.0,
Windows Millennium Edition, Windows 2000,
Windows XP Home Edition, Windows XP Professional,
Windows Server 2003 family,
.NET Compact Framework - Windows CE .NET

KeyEventArgs.Shift Property

Gets a value indicating whether the SHIFT key was pressed.

[Visual Basic]
```
Public Overridable ReadOnly Property Shift As Boolean
```
[C#]
```
public virtual bool Shift {get;}
```
[C++]
```
public: __property virtual bool get_Shift();
```
[JScript]
```
public function get Shift() : Boolean;
```

Property Value

true if the SHIFT key was pressed; otherwise, **false**.

Example

See related example in the **System.Windows.Forms.KeyEventArgs.Alt** property topic.

Requirements

Platforms: Windows 98, Windows NT 4.0,
Windows Millennium Edition, Windows 2000,
Windows XP Home Edition, Windows XP Professional,
Windows Server 2003 family,
.NET Compact Framework - Windows CE .NET

KeyEventHandler Delegate

Represents the method that will handle the **KeyUp** or **KeyDown** event of a **Control**.

[Visual Basic]
```
<Serializable>
Public Delegate Sub KeyEventHandler( _
   ByVal sender As Object, _
   ByVal e As KeyEventArgs _
)
```
[C#]
```
[Serializable]
public delegate void KeyEventHandler(
   object sender,
   KeyEventArgs e
);
```
[C++]
```
[Serializable]
public __gc __delegate void KeyEventHandler(
   Object* sender,
   KeyEventArgs* e
);
```
[JScript] In JScript, you can use the delegates in the .NET Framework, but you cannot define your own.

Parameters [Visual Basic, C#, C++]

The declaration of your event handler must have the same parameters as the **KeyEventHandler** delegate declaration.

sender

The source of the event.

e

A **KeyEventArgs** that contains the event data.

Remarks

When you create a **KeyEventHandler** delegate, you identify the method that will handle the event. To associate the event with your event handler, add an instance of the delegate to the event. The event handler is called whenever the event occurs, unless you remove the delegate.

Requirements

Namespace: System.Windows.Forms

Platforms: Windows 98, Windows NT 4.0, Windows Millennium Edition, Windows 2000, Windows XP Home Edition, Windows XP Professional, Windows Server 2003 family, .NET Compact Framework - Windows CE .NET

Assembly: System.Windows.Forms (in System.Windows.Forms.dll)

KeyPressEventArgs Class

Provides data for the **KeyPress** event.

System.Object
 System.EventArgs
  System.Windows.Forms.KeyPressEventArgs

[Visual Basic]
```
<ComVisible(True)>
Public Class KeyPressEventArgs
   Inherits EventArgs
```
[C#]
```
[ComVisible(true)]
public class KeyPressEventArgs : EventArgs
```
[C++]
```
[ComVisible(true)]
public __gc class KeyPressEventArgs : public EventArgs
```
[JScript]
```
public
   ComVisible(true)
class KeyPressEventArgs extends EventArgs
```

Thread Safety

Any public static (**Shared** in Visual Basic) members of this type are safe for multithreaded operations. Any instance members are not guaranteed to be thread safe.

Remarks

A **KeyPressEventArgs** specifies the character that is composed when the user presses a key. For example, when the user presses SHIFT + K, the **KeyChar** property returns an uppercase K.

A **KeyPress** event occurs when the user presses a key. Two events that are closely related to the **KeyPress** event are **KeyUp** and **KeyDown**. The **KeyDown** event precedes each **KeyPress** event when the user presses a key, and a **KeyUp** event occurs when the user releases a key. When the user holds down a key, duplicate **KeyDown** and **KeyPress** events occur each time the character repeats. One **KeyUp** event is generated upon release.

With each **KeyPress** event, a **KeyPressEventArgs** is passed. A **KeyEventArgs** is passed with each **KeyDown** and **KeyUp** event. A **KeyEventArgs** specifies whether any modifier keys (CTRL, SHIFT, or ALT) were pressed along with another key.

Set **Handled** to **true** to cancel the **KeyPress** event. This keeps the control from processing the key press.

.NET Compact Framework - Windows CE .NET Platform Note: The KeyPress event for combinations using the Ctrl-Shift keys is not provided. Instead, you can trap the KeyDown and KeyUp events.

Example

[Visual Basic, C#] The following example illustrates using the **KeyPressEventArgs** to count keys as they are pressed and to display the results after each key press. **Handled** is then set to true to keep the operating system from further processing the key. The example assumes a form with a **TextBox** placed on it.

[Visual Basic]
```
Public Class myKeyPressClass
    Private Shared keyPressCount As Long = 0
    Private Shared backspacePressed As Long = 0
    Private Shared returnPressed As Long = 0
    Private Shared escPressed As Long = 0
    Private textBox1 As TextBox

    Private Sub myKeyCounter(sender As Object, ex As KeyPressEventArgs)
        Select Case ex.KeyChar
            ' Counts the backspaces.
            Case ControlChars.Back
                backspacePressed = backspacePressed + 1
            ' Counts the ENTER keys.
            Case ControlChars.Lf
                returnPressed = returnPressed + 1
            ' Counts the ESC keys.
            Case Convert.ToChar(27)
                escPressed = escPressed + 1
            ' Counts all other keys.
            Case Else
                keyPressCount = keyPressCount + 1
        End Select

        textBox1.Text = backspacePressed & " backspaces pressed" & _
            ControlChars.Lf & ControlChars.Cr & escPressed & _
            " escapes pressed" & ControlChars.CrLf & returnPressed & _
            " returns pressed" & ControlChars.CrLf & keyPressCount & _
            " other keys pressed" & ControlChars.CrLf
        ex.Handled = True
    End Sub 'myKeyCounter
End Class 'myKeyPressClass
```

[C#]
```
public class myKeyPressClass
 {
     static long keyPressCount = 0 ;
     static long backspacePressed =  0;
     static long returnPressed = 0 ;
     static long escPressed = 0 ;
     private TextBox textBox1 = new TextBox();
     private void myKeyCounter(object sender, KeyPressEventArgs ex)
     {
     switch(ex.KeyChar)
     {
             // Counts the backspaces.
         case '\b':
         backspacePressed = backspacePressed + 1;
         break ;
             // Counts the ENTER keys.
         case '\r':
         returnPressed = returnPressed + 1 ;
         break ;
             // Counts the ESC keys.
         case (char)27:
         escPressed = escPressed + 1 ;
         break ;
             // Counts all other keys.
         default:
         keyPressCount = keyPressCount + 1 ;
         break;
     }

     textBox1.Text =
         backspacePressed + " backspaces pressed\r\n" +
         escPressed + " escapes pressed\r\n" +
         returnPressed + " returns pressed\r\n" +
         keyPressCount + " other keys pressed\r\n" ;
     ex.Handled = true ;
     }
 }
```

[Visual Basic, C#] You must create a new instance of this class. You must also set the event handler. You can do this in the constructor for your class.

[Visual Basic]
```
Private myKeyPressHandler As New myKeyPressClass()

Public Sub New()
   InitializeComponent()

   AddHandler textBox1.KeyPress, AddressOf ↵
myKeyPressHandler.myKeyCounter
End Sub 'New
```

[C#]
```
myKeyPressClass myKeyPressHandler = new myKeyPressClass();
public Form1()
{
     InitializeComponent();

     textBox1.KeyPress += new ↵
KeyPressEventHandler(myKeyPressHandler.myKeyCounter);
}
```

[Visual Basic, C#] When the specified event is raised in the control, the attached method is called and the application can execute code in response to the event.

Requirements

Namespace: System.Windows.Forms

Platforms: Windows 98, Windows NT 4.0, Windows Millennium Edition, Windows 2000, Windows XP Home Edition, Windows XP Professional, Windows Server 2003 family, .NET Compact Framework - Windows CE .NET

Assembly: System.Windows.Forms (in System.Windows.Forms.dll)

KeyPressEventArgs Constructor

Initializes a new instance of the **KeyPressEventArgs** class.

[Visual Basic]
```
Public Sub New( _
   ByVal keyChar As Char _
)
```
[C#]
```
public KeyPressEventArgs(
   char keyChar
);
```
[C++]
```
public: KeyPressEventArgs(
   __wchar_t keyChar
);
```
[JScript]
```
public function KeyPressEventArgs(
   keyChar : Char
);
```

Parameters

keyChar
The ASCII character corresponding to the key the user pressed.

Requirements

Platforms: Windows 98, Windows NT 4.0, Windows Millennium Edition, Windows 2000, Windows XP Home Edition, Windows XP Professional, Windows Server 2003 family, .NET Compact Framework - Windows CE .NET

KeyPressEventArgs.Handled Property

Gets or sets a value indicating whether the **KeyPress** event was handled.

[Visual Basic]
```
Public Property Handled As Boolean
```
[C#]
```
public bool Handled {get; set;}
```
[C++]
```
public: __property bool get_Handled();
public: __property void set_Handled(bool);
```
[JScript]
```
public function get Handled() : Boolean;
public function set Handled(Boolean);
```

Property Value

true if the event is handled; otherwise, **false**.

Remarks

If the event is not handled, it will be sent to the operating system for default processing. Set **Handled** to **true** to cancel the **KeyPress** event.

Example

See related example in the **System.Windows.Forms.KeyPress-EventArgs** class topic.

Requirements

Platforms: Windows 98, Windows NT 4.0, Windows Millennium Edition, Windows 2000, Windows XP Home Edition, Windows XP Professional, Windows Server 2003 family, .NET Compact Framework - Windows CE .NET

KeyPressEventArgs.KeyChar Property

Gets the character corresponding to the key pressed.

[Visual Basic]
```
Public ReadOnly Property KeyChar As Char
```
[C#]
```
public char KeyChar {get;}
```
[C++]
```
public: __property __wchar_t get_KeyChar();
```
[JScript]
```
public function get KeyChar() : Char;
```

Property Value

The ASCII character that is composed. For example, if the user presses the SHIFT + K, this property returns an uppercase K.

Example

See related example in the **System.Windows.Forms.KeyPress-EventArgs** class topic.

Requirements

Platforms: Windows 98, Windows NT 4.0, Windows Millennium Edition, Windows 2000, Windows XP Home Edition, Windows XP Professional, Windows Server 2003 family, .NET Compact Framework - Windows CE .NET

KeyPressEventHandler Delegate

Represents the method that will handle the **KeyPress** event of a **Control**.

[Visual Basic]

```
<Serializable>
Public Delegate Sub KeyPressEventHandler( _
   ByVal sender As Object, _
   ByVal e As KeyPressEventArgs _
)
```

[C#]

```
[Serializable]
public delegate void KeyPressEventHandler(
   object sender,
   KeyPressEventArgs e
);
```

[C++]

```
[Serializable]
public __gc __delegate void KeyPressEventHandler(
   Object* sender,
   KeyPressEventArgs* e
);
```

[JScript] In JScript, you can use the delegates in the .NET Framework, but you cannot define your own.

Parameters [Visual Basic, C#, C++]

The declaration of your event handler must have the same parameters as the **KeyPressEventHandler** delegate declaration.

sender

The source of the event.

e

A **KeyPressEventArgs** that contains the event data.

Remarks

Set **KeyPressEventArgs.Handled** to **true** to cancel the **KeyPress** event. This keeps the control from processing the key press.

When you create a **KeyPressEventHandler** delegate, you identify the method that will handle the event. To associate the event with your event handler, add an instance of the delegate to the event. The event handler is called whenever the event occurs, unless you remove the delegate.

Requirements

Namespace: System.Windows.Forms

Platforms: Windows 98, Windows NT 4.0, Windows Millennium Edition, Windows 2000, Windows XP Home Edition, Windows XP Professional, Windows Server 2003 family, .NET Compact Framework - Windows CE .NET

Assembly: System.Windows.Forms (in System.Windows.Forms.dll)

Keys Enumeration

Specifies key codes and modifiers.

This enumeration has a **FlagsAttribute** attribute that allows a bitwise combination of its member values.

[Visual Basic]
```
<Flags>
<Serializable>
<ComVisible(True)>
Public Enum Keys
```
[C#]
```
[Flags]
[Serializable]
[ComVisible(true)]
public enum Keys
```
[C++]
```
[Flags]
[Serializable]
[ComVisible(true)]
__value public enum Keys
```
[JScript]
```
public
   Flags
   Serializable
   ComVisible(true)
enum Keys
```

Remarks

This class contains constants to use for processing keyboard input. Keys are identified by key values, which consist of a key code and a set of modifiers combined into a single integer value. The four left digits of a key value contain the key code (which is the same as a Windows virtual key code). The four right digits of a key value contain modifier bits for the SHIFT, CONTROL, and ALT keys.

Members

Member name	Description	Value
A Supported by the .NET Compact Framework.	The A key.	65
Add Supported by the .NET Compact Framework.	The add key.	107
Alt Supported by the .NET Compact Framework.	The ALT modifier key.	262144
Apps Supported by the .NET Compact Framework.	The application key (Microsoft Natural Keyboard).	93
Attn Supported by the .NET Compact Framework.	The ATTN key.	246
B Supported by the .NET Compact Framework.	The B key.	66
Back Supported by the .NET Compact Framework.	The BACKSPACE key.	8
BrowserBack	The browser back key (Windows 2000 or later).	166
BrowserFavorites	The browser favorites key (Windows 2000 or later).	171
BrowserForward	The browser forward key (Windows 2000 or later).	167
BrowserHome	The browser home key (Windows 2000 or later).	172
BrowserRefresh	The browser refresh key (Windows 2000 or later).	168
BrowserSearch	The browser search key (Windows 2000 or later).	170
BrowserStop	The browser stop key (Windows 2000 or later).	169
C Supported by the .NET Compact Framework.	The C key.	67
Cancel Supported by the .NET Compact Framework.	The CANCEL key.	3
Capital Supported by the .NET Compact Framework.	The CAPS LOCK key.	20
CapsLock Supported by the .NET Compact Framework.	The CAPS LOCK key.	20
Clear Supported by the .NET Compact Framework.	The CLEAR key.	12
Control Supported by the .NET Compact Framework.	The CTRL modifier key.	131072
ControlKey Supported by the .NET Compact Framework.	The CTRL key.	17
Crsel Supported by the .NET Compact Framework.	The CRSEL key.	247
D Supported by the .NET Compact Framework.	The D key.	68
D0 Supported by the .NET Compact Framework.	The 0 key.	48
D1 Supported by the .NET Compact Framework.	The 1 key.	49

Member name	Description	Value
D2 Supported by the .NET Compact Framework.	The 2 key.	50
D3 Supported by the .NET Compact Framework.	The 3 key.	51
D4 Supported by the .NET Compact Framework.	The 4 key.	52
D5 Supported by the .NET Compact Framework.	The 5 key.	53
D6 Supported by the .NET Compact Framework.	The 6 key.	54
D7 Supported by the .NET Compact Framework.	The 7 key.	55
D8 Supported by the .NET Compact Framework.	The 8 key.	56
D9 Supported by the .NET Compact Framework.	The 9 key.	57
Decimal Supported by the .NET Compact Framework.	The decimal key.	110
Delete Supported by the .NET Compact Framework.	The DEL key.	46
Divide Supported by the .NET Compact Framework.	The divide key.	111
Down Supported by the .NET Compact Framework.	The DOWN ARROW key.	40
E Supported by the .NET Compact Framework.	The E key.	69
End Supported by the .NET Compact Framework.	The END key.	35
Enter Supported by the .NET Compact Framework.	The ENTER key.	13
EraseEof Supported by the .NET Compact Framework.	The ERASE EOF key.	249
Escape Supported by the .NET Compact Framework.	The ESC key.	27

Member name	Description	Value
Execute Supported by the .NET Compact Framework.	The EXECUTE key.	43
Exsel Supported by the .NET Compact Framework.	The EXSEL key.	248
F Supported by the .NET Compact Framework.	The F key.	70
F1 Supported by the .NET Compact Framework.	The F1 key.	112
F10 Supported by the .NET Compact Framework.	The F10 key.	121
F11 Supported by the .NET Compact Framework.	The F11 key.	122
F12 Supported by the .NET Compact Framework.	The F12 key.	123
F13 Supported by the .NET Compact Framework.	The F13 key.	124
F14 Supported by the .NET Compact Framework.	The F14 key.	125
F15 Supported by the .NET Compact Framework.	The F15 key.	126
F16 Supported by the .NET Compact Framework.	The F16 key.	127
F17 Supported by the .NET Compact Framework.	The F17 key.	128
F18 Supported by the .NET Compact Framework.	The F18 key.	129
F19 Supported by the .NET Compact Framework.	The F19 key.	130
F2 Supported by the .NET Compact Framework.	The F2 key.	113
F20 Supported by the .NET Compact Framework.	The F20 key.	131
F21 Supported by the .NET Compact Framework.	The F21 key.	132

Member name	Description	Value
F22 Supported by the .NET Compact Framework.	The F22 key.	133
F23 Supported by the .NET Compact Framework.	The F23 key.	134
F24 Supported by the .NET Compact Framework.	The F24 key.	135
F3 Supported by the .NET Compact Framework.	The F3 key.	114
F4 Supported by the .NET Compact Framework.	The F4 key.	115
F5 Supported by the .NET Compact Framework.	The F5 key.	116
F6 Supported by the .NET Compact Framework.	The F6 key.	117
F7 Supported by the .NET Compact Framework.	The F7 key.	118
F8 Supported by the .NET Compact Framework.	The F8 key.	119
F9 Supported by the .NET Compact Framework.	The F9 key.	120
FinalMode	The IME final mode key.	24
G Supported by the .NET Compact Framework.	The G key.	71
H Supported by the .NET Compact Framework.	The H key.	72
HanguelMode	The IME Hanguel mode key. (maintained for compatibility; use **HangulMode**)	21
HangulMode	The IME Hangul mode key.	21
HanjaMode	The IME Hanja mode key.	25
Help Supported by the .NET Compact Framework.	The HELP key.	47
Home Supported by the .NET Compact Framework.	The HOME key.	36
I Supported by the .NET Compact Framework.	The I key.	73

Member name	Description	Value
IMEAceept	The IME accept key.	30
IMEConvert	The IME convert key.	28
IMEModeChange	The IME mode change key.	31
IMENonconvert	The IME nonconvert key.	29
Insert Supported by the .NET Compact Framework.	The INS key.	45
J Supported by the .NET Compact Framework.	The J key.	74
JunjaMode	The IME Junja mode key.	23
K Supported by the .NET Compact Framework.	The K key.	75
KanaMode	The IME Kana mode key.	21
KanjiMode	The IME Kanji mode key.	25
KeyCode Supported by the .NET Compact Framework.	The bitmask to extract a key code from a key value.	65535
L Supported by the .NET Compact Framework.	The L key.	76
LaunchApplication1	The start application one key (Windows 2000 or later).	182
LaunchApplication2	The start application two key (Windows 2000 or later).	183
LaunchMail	The launch mail key (Windows 2000 or later).	180
LButton Supported by the .NET Compact Framework.	The left mouse button.	1
LControlKey Supported by the .NET Compact Framework.	The left CTRL key.	162
Left Supported by the .NET Compact Framework.	The LEFT ARROW key.	37
LineFeed Supported by the .NET Compact Framework.	The LINEFEED key.	10
LMenu Supported by the .NET Compact Framework.	The left ALT key.	164
LShiftKey Supported by the .NET Compact Framework.	The left SHIFT key.	160
LWin Supported by the .NET Compact Framework.	The left Windows logo key (Microsoft Natural Keyboard).	91

Member name	Description	Value
M Supported by the .NET Compact Framework.	The M key.	77
MButton Supported by the .NET Compact Framework.	The middle mouse button (three-button mouse).	4
MediaNextTrack	The media next track key (Windows 2000 or later).	176
MediaPlayPause	The media play pause key (Windows 2000 or later).	179
MediaPreviousTrack	The media previous track key (Windows 2000 or later).	177
MediaStop	The media Stop key (Windows 2000 or later).	178
Menu Supported by the .NET Compact Framework.	The ALT key.	18
Modifiers Supported by the .NET Compact Framework.	The bitmask to extract modifiers from a key value.	-65536
Multiply Supported by the .NET Compact Framework.	The multiply key.	106
N Supported by the .NET Compact Framework.	The N key.	78
Next Supported by the .NET Compact Framework.	The PAGE DOWN key.	34
NoName Supported by the .NET Compact Framework.	A constant reserved for future use.	252
None Supported by the .NET Compact Framework.	No key pressed.	0
NumLock Supported by the .NET Compact Framework.	The NUM LOCK key.	144
NumPad0 Supported by the .NET Compact Framework.	The 0 key on the numeric keypad.	96
NumPad1 Supported by the .NET Compact Framework.	The 1 key on the numeric keypad.	97
NumPad2 Supported by the .NET Compact Framework.	The 2 key on the numeric keypad.	98
NumPad3 Supported by the .NET Compact Framework.	The 3 key on the numeric keypad.	99

Member name	Description	Value
NumPad4 Supported by the .NET Compact Framework.	The 4 key on the numeric keypad.	100
NumPad5 Supported by the .NET Compact Framework.	The 5 key on the numeric keypad.	101
NumPad6 Supported by the .NET Compact Framework.	The 6 key on the numeric keypad.	102
NumPad7 Supported by the .NET Compact Framework.	The 7 key on the numeric keypad.	103
NumPad8 Supported by the .NET Compact Framework.	The 8 key on the numeric keypad.	104
NumPad9 Supported by the .NET Compact Framework.	The 9 key on the numeric keypad.	105
O Supported by the .NET Compact Framework.	The O key.	79
Oem8	OEM specific.	223
OemBackslash	The OEM angle bracket or backslash key on the RT 102 key keyboard (Windows 2000 or later).	226
OemClear Supported by the .NET Compact Framework.	The CLEAR key.	254
OemCloseBrackets	The OEM close bracket key on a US standard keyboard (Windows 2000 or later).	221
Oemcomma	The OEM comma key on any country/region keyboard (Windows 2000 or later).	188
OemMinus	The OEM minus key on any country/region keyboard (Windows 2000 or later).	189
OemOpenBrackets	The OEM open bracket key on a US standard keyboard (Windows 2000 or later).	219
OemPeriod	The OEM period key on any country/region keyboard (Windows 2000 or later).	190
OemPipe	The OEM pipe key on a US standard keyboard (Windows 2000 or later).	220
Oemplus	The OEM plus key on any country/region keyboard (Windows 2000 or later).	187

Member name	Description	Value
OemQuestion	The OEM question mark key on a US standard keyboard (Windows 2000 or later).	191
OemQuotes	The OEM singled/double quote key on a US standard keyboard (Windows 2000 or later).	222
OemSemicolon	The OEM semicolon key on a US standard keyboard (Windows 2000 or later).	186
Oemtilde	The OEM tilde key on a US standard keyboard (Windows 2000 or later).	192
P Supported by the .NET Compact Framework.	The P key.	80
Pa1 Supported by the .NET Compact Framework.	The PA1 key.	253
PageDown Supported by the .NET Compact Framework.	The PAGE DOWN key.	34
PageUp Supported by the .NET Compact Framework.	The PAGE UP key.	33
Pause Supported by the .NET Compact Framework.	The PAUSE key.	19
Play Supported by the .NET Compact Framework.	The PLAY key.	250
Print Supported by the .NET Compact Framework.	The PRINT key.	42
PrintScreen Supported by the .NET Compact Framework.	The PRINT SCREEN key.	44
Prior Supported by the .NET Compact Framework.	The PAGE UP key.	33
ProcessKey Supported by the .NET Compact Framework.	The PROCESS KEY key.	229
Q Supported by the .NET Compact Framework.	The Q key.	81
R Supported by the .NET Compact Framework.	The R key.	82
RButton Supported by the .NET Compact Framework.	The right mouse button.	2

Member name	Description	Value
RControlKey Supported by the .NET Compact Framework.	The right CTRL key.	163
Return Supported by the .NET Compact Framework.	The RETURN key.	13
Right Supported by the .NET Compact Framework.	The RIGHT ARROW key.	39
RMenu Supported by the .NET Compact Framework.	The right ALT key.	165
RShiftKey Supported by the .NET Compact Framework.	The right SHIFT key.	161
RWin Supported by the .NET Compact Framework.	The right Windows logo key (Microsoft Natural Keyboard).	92
S Supported by the .NET Compact Framework.	The S key.	83
Scroll Supported by the .NET Compact Framework.	The SCROLL LOCK key.	145
Select Supported by the .NET Compact Framework.	The SELECT key.	41
SelectMedia	The select media key (Windows 2000 or later).	181
Separator Supported by the .NET Compact Framework.	The separator key.	108
Shift Supported by the .NET Compact Framework.	The SHIFT modifier key.	65536
ShiftKey Supported by the .NET Compact Framework.	The SHIFT key.	16
Snapshot Supported by the .NET Compact Framework.	The PRINT SCREEN key.	44
Space Supported by the .NET Compact Framework.	The SPACEBAR key.	32
Subtract Supported by the .NET Compact Framework.	The subtract key.	109
T Supported by the .NET Compact Framework.	The T key.	84

Member name	Description	Value
Tab Supported by the .NET Compact Framework.	The TAB key.	9
U Supported by the .NET Compact Framework.	The U key.	85
Up Supported by the .NET Compact Framework.	The UP ARROW key.	38
V Supported by the .NET Compact Framework.	The V key.	86
VolumeDown	The volume down key (Windows 2000 or later).	174
VolumeMute	The volume mute key (Windows 2000 or later).	173
VolumeUp	The volume up key (Windows 2000 or later).	175
W Supported by the .NET Compact Framework.	The W key.	87
X Supported by the .NET Compact Framework.	The X key.	88
XButton1 Supported by the .NET Compact Framework.	The first x mouse button (five-button mouse).	5
XButton2 Supported by the .NET Compact Framework.	The second x mouse button (five-button mouse).	6
Y Supported by the .NET Compact Framework.	The Y key.	89
Z Supported by the .NET Compact Framework.	The Z key.	90
Zoom Supported by the .NET Compact Framework.	The ZOOM key.	251

Requirements

Namespace: System.Windows.Forms

Platforms: Windows 98, Windows NT 4.0, Windows Millennium Edition, Windows 2000, Windows XP Home Edition, Windows XP Professional, Windows Server 2003 family, .NET Compact Framework - Windows CE .NET

Assembly: System.Windows.Forms (in System.Windows.Forms.dll)

KeysConverter Class

Provides a **TypeConverter** to convert **Keys** objects to and from other representations.

System.Object
System.ComponentModel.TypeConverter
System.Windows.Forms.KeysConverter

[Visual Basic]
```
Public Class KeysConverter
   Inherits TypeConverter
   Implements IComparer
```
[C#]
```
public class KeysConverter : TypeConverter, IComparer
```
[C++]
```
public __gc class KeysConverter : public TypeConverter, IComparer
```
[JScript]
```
public class KeysConverter extends TypeConverter implements
   IComparer
```

Thread Safety

Any public static (**Shared** in Visual Basic) members of this type are safe for multithreaded operations. Any instance members are not guaranteed to be thread safe.

Requirements

Namespace: System.Windows.Forms

Platforms: Windows 98, Windows NT 4.0, Windows Millennium Edition, Windows 2000, Windows XP Home Edition, Windows XP Professional, Windows Server 2003 family

Assembly: System.Windows.Forms (in System.Windows.Forms.dll)

KeysConverter Constructor

Initializes a new instance of the **KeysConverter** class.

[Visual Basic]
```
Public Sub New()
```
[C#]
```
public KeysConverter();
```
[C++]
```
public: KeysConverter();
```
[JScript]
```
public function KeysConverter();
```

Remarks

The default constructor initializes any fields to their default values.

Requirements

Platforms: Windows 98, Windows NT 4.0, Windows Millennium Edition, Windows 2000, Windows XP Home Edition, Windows XP Professional, Windows Server 2003 family

KeysConverter.CanConvertFrom Method

Gets a value indicating whether this converter can convert an object in the Specified source type to the native type of the converter.

Overload List

This member supports the .NET Framework infrastructure and is not intended to be used directly from your code.

[Visual Basic] **Overloads Overrides Public Function CanConvertFrom(ITypeDescriptorContext, Type) As Boolean**

[C#] **public override bool CanConvertFrom(ITypeDescriptorContext, Type);**

[C++] **public: bool CanConvertFrom(ITypeDescriptorContext*, Type*);**

[JScript] **public override function CanConvertFrom(ITypeDescriptorContext, Type) : Boolean;**

Inherited from **TypeConverter**.

[Visual Basic] **Overloads Public Function CanConvertFrom(Type) As Boolean**

[C#] **public bool CanConvertFrom(Type);**

[C++] **public: bool CanConvertFrom(Type*);**

[JScript] **public function CanConvertFrom(Type) : Boolean;**

KeysConverter.CanConvertFrom Method (ITypeDescriptorContext, Type)

This member overrides **TypeConverter.CanConvertFrom**.

[Visual Basic]
```
Overrides Overloads Public Function CanConvertFrom( _
   ByVal context As ITypeDescriptorContext, _
   ByVal sourceType As Type _
) As Boolean
```
[C#]
```
public override bool CanConvertFrom(
   ITypeDescriptorContext context,
   Type sourceType
);
```
[C++]
```
public: bool CanConvertFrom(
   ITypeDescriptorContext* context,
   Type* sourceType
);
```
[JScript]
```
public override function CanConvertFrom(
   context : ITypeDescriptorContext,
   sourceType : Type
) : Boolean;
```

Requirements

Platforms: Windows 98, Windows NT 4.0, Windows Millennium Edition, Windows 2000, Windows XP Home Edition, Windows XP Professional, Windows Server 2003 family

KeysConverter.Compare Method

Compares two key values for equivalence.

```
[Visual Basic]
Public Overridable Function Compare( _
   ByVal a As Object, _
   ByVal b As Object _
) As Integer Implements IComparer.Compare
[C#]
public virtual int Compare(
   object a,
   object b
);
[C++]
public: virtual int Compare(
   Object* a,
   Object* b
);
[JScript]
public function Compare(
   a : Object,
   b : Object
) : int;
```

Parameters

a

An **Object** that represents the first key to compare.

b

An **Object** that represents the second key to compare.

Return Value

An integer indicating the relationship between the to comparands.

Value Type	Condition
A negative integer.	*a* is less than *b*.
zero	*a* equals *b*.
A positive integer.	*a* is greater than *b*.

Implements

IComparer.Compare

Remarks

This method uses **String.Compare** to compare the two objects.

Requirements

Platforms: Windows 98, Windows NT 4.0, Windows Millennium Edition, Windows 2000, Windows XP Home Edition, Windows XP Professional, Windows Server 2003 family

KeysConverter.ConvertFrom Method

Converts the specified object to the native type of the converter.

Overload List

This member supports the .NET Framework infrastructure and is not intended to be used directly from your code.

[Visual Basic] **Overloads Overrides Public Function ConvertFrom(ITypeDescriptorContext, CultureInfo, Object) As Object**

[C#] **public override object ConvertFrom(ITypeDescriptorContext, CultureInfo, object);**

[C++] **public: Object* ConvertFrom(ITypeDescriptorContext*, CultureInfo*, Object*);**

[JScript] **public override function ConvertFrom(ITypeDescriptorContext, CultureInfo, Object) : Object;**

Inherited from **TypeConverter**.

[Visual Basic] **Overloads Public Function ConvertFrom(Object) As Object**

[C#] **public object ConvertFrom(object);**

[C++] **public: Object* ConvertFrom(Object*);**

[JScript] **public function ConvertFrom(Object) : Object;**

KeysConverter.ConvertFrom Method (ITypeDescriptorContext, CultureInfo, Object)

This member overrides **TypeConverter.ConvertFrom**.

```
[Visual Basic]
Overrides Overloads Public Function ConvertFrom( _
   ByVal context As ITypeDescriptorContext, _
   ByVal culture As CultureInfo, _
   ByVal value As Object _
) As Object
[C#]
public override object ConvertFrom(
   ITypeDescriptorContext context,
   CultureInfo culture,
   object value
);
[C++]
public: Object* ConvertFrom(
   ITypeDescriptorContext* context,
   CultureInfo* culture,
   Object* value
);
[JScript]
public override function ConvertFrom(
   context : ITypeDescriptorContext,
   culture : CultureInfo,
   value : Object
) : Object;
```

Requirements

Platforms: Windows 98, Windows NT 4.0, Windows Millennium Edition, Windows 2000, Windows XP Home Edition, Windows XP Professional, Windows Server 2003 family

KeysConverter.ConvertTo Method

Converts the specified object to the specified destination type.

Overload List

This member supports the .NET Framework infrastructure and is not intended to be used directly from your code.

[Visual Basic] **Overloads Overrides Public Function ConvertTo(ITypeDescriptorContext, CultureInfo, Object, Type) As Object**

[C#] **public override object ConvertTo(ITypeDescriptorContext, CultureInfo, object, Type);**

[C++] **public: Object* ConvertTo(ITypeDescriptorContext*, CultureInfo*, Object*, Type*);**

[JScript] **public override function ConvertTo(ITypeDescriptorContext, CultureInfo, Object, Type) : Object;**

Inherited from **TypeConverter**.

[Visual Basic] **Overloads Public Function ConvertTo(Object, Type) As Object**

[C#] **public object ConvertTo(object, Type);**

[C++] **public: Object* ConvertTo(Object*, Type*);**

[JScript] **public function ConvertTo(Object, Type) : Object;**

KeysConverter.ConvertTo Method (ITypeDescriptorContext, CultureInfo, Object, Type)

This member overrides **TypeConverter.ConvertTo**.

```
[Visual Basic]
Overrides Overloads Public Function ConvertTo( _
   ByVal context As ITypeDescriptorContext, _
   ByVal culture As CultureInfo, _
   ByVal value As Object, _
   ByVal destinationType As Type _
) As Object
[C#]
public override object ConvertTo(
   ITypeDescriptorContext context,
   CultureInfo culture,
   object value,
   Type destinationType
);
[C++]
public: Object* ConvertTo(
   ITypeDescriptorContext* context,
   CultureInfo* culture,
   Object* value,
   Type* destinationType
);
[JScript]
public override function ConvertTo(
   context : ITypeDescriptorContext,
   culture : CultureInfo,
   value : Object,
   destinationType : Type
) : Object;
```

Requirements

Platforms: Windows 98, Windows NT 4.0, Windows Millennium Edition, Windows 2000, Windows XP Home Edition, Windows XP Professional, Windows Server 2003 family

KeysConverter.GetStandardValues Method

Returns a collection of standard values for the data type that this type converter is designed for.

Overload List

This member supports the .NET Framework infrastructure and is not intended to be used directly from your code.

[Visual Basic] **Overloads Overrides Public Function GetStandardValues(ITypeDescriptorContext) As StandardValuesCollection**

[C#] **public override StandardValuesCollection GetStandardValues(ITypeDescriptorContext);**

[C++] **public: StandardValuesCollection* GetStandardValues(ITypeDescriptorContext*);**

[JScript] **public override function GetStandardValues(ITypeDescriptorContext) : StandardValuesCollection;**

Inherited from **TypeConverter**.

[Visual Basic] **Overloads Public Function GetStandardValues() As ICollection**

[C#] **public ICollection GetStandardValues();**

[C++] **public: ICollection* GetStandardValues();**

[JScript] **public function GetStandardValues() : ICollection;**

KeysConverter.GetStandardValues Method (ITypeDescriptorContext)

This member overrides **TypeConverter.GetStandardValues**.

```
[Visual Basic]
Overrides Overloads Public Function GetStandardValues( _
   ByVal context As ITypeDescriptorContext _
) As StandardValuesCollection
[C#]
public override StandardValuesCollection GetStandardValues(
   ITypeDescriptorContext context
);
[C++]
public: StandardValuesCollection* GetStandardValues(
   ITypeDescriptorContext* context
);
[JScript]
public override function GetStandardValues(
   context : ITypeDescriptorContext
) : StandardValuesCollection;
```

Requirements

Platforms: Windows 98, Windows NT 4.0, Windows Millennium Edition, Windows 2000, Windows XP Home Edition, Windows XP Professional, Windows Server 2003 family

KeysConverter.GetStandardValuesExclusive Method

Overload List

This member supports the .NET Framework infrastructure and is not intended to be used directly from your code.

[Visual Basic] **Overloads Overrides Public Function GetStandardValuesExclusive(ITypeDescriptorContext) As Boolean**

[C#] **public override bool GetStandardValues-Exclusive(ITypeDescriptorContext);**

[C++] **public: bool GetStandardValues-Exclusive(ITypeDescriptorContext*);**

[JScript] **public override function GetStandardValues-Exclusive(ITypeDescriptorContext) : Boolean;**

Inherited from **TypeConverter**.

[Visual Basic] **Overloads Public Function GetStandard-ValuesExclusive() As Boolean**

[C#] **public bool GetStandardValuesExclusive();**

[C++] **public: bool GetStandardValuesExclusive();**

[JScript] **public function GetStandardValuesExclusive() : Boolean;**

KeysConverter.GetStandardValuesExclusive Method (ITypeDescriptorContext)

This member overrides **TypeConverter.GetStandardValuesExclusive**.

```
[Visual Basic]
Overrides Overloads Public Function GetStandardValuesExclusive( _
   ByVal context As ITypeDescriptorContext _
) As Boolean
[C#]
public override bool GetStandardValuesExclusive(
   ITypeDescriptorContext context
);
[C++]
public: bool GetStandardValuesExclusive(
   ITypeDescriptorContext* context
);
[JScript]
public override function GetStandardValuesExclusive(
   context : ITypeDescriptorContext
) : Boolean;
```

Requirements

Platforms: Windows 98, Windows NT 4.0, Windows Millennium Edition, Windows 2000, Windows XP Home Edition, Windows XP Professional, Windows Server 2003 family

KeysConverter.GetStandardValuesSupported Method

Gets a value indicating whether this object supports a standard set of values that can be picked from a list.

Overload List

This member supports the .NET Framework infrastructure and is not intended to be used directly from your code.

[Visual Basic] **Overloads Overrides Public Function GetStandardValuesSupported(ITypeDescriptorContext) As Boolean**

[C#] **public override bool GetStandardValues-Supported(ITypeDescriptorContext);**

[C++] **public: bool GetStandardValues-Supported(ITypeDescriptorContext*);**

[JScript] **public override function GetStandardValues-Supported(ITypeDescriptorContext) : Boolean;**

Inherited from **TypeConverter**.

[Visual Basic] **Overloads Public Function GetStandard-ValuesSupported() As Boolean**

[C#] **public bool GetStandardValuesSupported();**

[C++] **public: bool GetStandardValuesSupported();**

[JScript] **public function GetStandardValuesSupported() : Boolean;**

KeysConverter.GetStandardValuesSupported Method (ITypeDescriptorContext)

This member overrides **TypeConverter.GetStandardValuesSupported**.

```
[Visual Basic]
Overrides Overloads Public Function GetStandardValuesSupported( _
   ByVal context As ITypeDescriptorContext _
) As Boolean
[C#]
public override bool GetStandardValuesSupported(
   ITypeDescriptorContext context
);
[C++]
public: bool GetStandardValuesSupported(
   ITypeDescriptorContext* context
);
[JScript]
public override function GetStandardValuesSupported(
   context : ITypeDescriptorContext
) : Boolean;
```

Requirements

Platforms: Windows 98, Windows NT 4.0, Windows Millennium Edition, Windows 2000, Windows XP Home Edition, Windows XP Professional, Windows Server 2003 family

Label Class

Represents a standard Windows label.

System.Object
  System.MarshalByRefObject
    System.ComponentModel.Component
      System.Windows.Forms.Control
        System.Windows.Forms.Label
          System.Windows.Forms.LinkLabel

[Visual Basic]
```
Public Class Label
   Inherits Control
```
[C#]
```
public class Label : Control
```
[C++]
```
public __gc class Label : public Control
```
[JScript]
```
public class Label extends Control
```

Thread Safety

Any public static (**Shared** in Visual Basic) members of this type are safe for multithreaded operations. Any instance members are not guaranteed to be thread safe.

Remarks

Label controls are typically used to provide descriptive text for a control. For example, you can use a **Label** to add descriptive text for a **TextBox** control to inform the user about the type of data expected in the control. **Label** controls can also be used to add descriptive text to a **Form** to provide the user with helpful information. For example, you can add a **Label** to the top of a **Form** that provides instructions to the user on how to input data in the controls on the form. **Label** controls can be also used to display run time information on the status of an application. For example, you can add a **Label** control to a form to display the status of each file as a list of files is processed.

A **Label** participates in the tab order of a form, but does not receive focus (the next control in the tab order receives focus). For example, if the **UseMnemonic** property is set to **true**, and a mnemonic character (the first character after an ampersand (&)) is specified in the **Text** property of the control, when a user presses ALT+ the mnemonic key, focus moves to the next control in the tab order. This feature provides keyboard navigation for a form. In addition to displaying text, the **Label** control can also display an image using the **Image** property, or a combination of the **ImageIndex** and **ImageList** properties.

> **Note** A **Label** can be made transparent by setting its **BackColor** property to **Color.Transparent**. When you use a transparent label, use only the current device coordinate system to draw on the container, or the **Label** background might paint improperly.

Example

[Visual Basic, C#, JScript] The following example demonstrates how to create a **Label** control that has a three-dimensional border and contains an image. The image is displayed using the **ImageList** and **ImageIndex** properties. The control also has a caption with a mnemonic character specified. The example code uses the **PreferredHeight** and **PreferredWidth** properties to properly size the **Label** control. This example assumes that an **ImageList** has been created and named `imageList1` and that it has loaded two images. The example also assumes that the code is within a form that has the **System.Drawing** namespace added to its code.

[Visual Basic]
```
Public Sub CreateMyLabel()
    ' Create an instance of a Label.
    Dim label1 As New Label()

    ' Set the border to a three-dimensional border.
    label1.BorderStyle = System.Windows.Forms.BorderStyle.Fixed3D
    ' Set the ImageList to use for displaying an image.
    label1.ImageList = imageList1
    ' Use the second image in imageList1.
    label1.ImageIndex = 1
    ' Align the image to the top left corner.
    label1.ImageAlign = ContentAlignment.TopLeft

    ' Specify that the text can display mnemonic characters.
    label1.UseMnemonic = True
    ' Set the text of the control and specify a mnemonic character.
    label1.Text = "First &Name:"

    ' Set the size of the control based on the PreferredHeight ↵
and PreferredWidth values.
    label1.Size = New Size(label1.PreferredHeight, ↵
label1.PreferredWidth)

    '...Code to add the control to the form...
End Sub
```

[C#]
```
public void CreateMyLabel()
{
   // Create an instance of a Label.
   Label label1 = new Label();

   // Set the border to a three-dimensional border.
   label1.BorderStyle = System.Windows.Forms.BorderStyle.Fixed3D;
   // Set the ImageList to use for displaying an image.
   label1.ImageList = imageList1;
   // Use the second image in imageList1.
   label1.ImageIndex = 1;
   // Align the image to the top left corner.
   label1.ImageAlign = ContentAlignment.TopLeft;

   // Specify that the text can display mnemonic characters.
   label1.UseMnemonic = true;
   // Set the text of the control and specify a mnemonic character.
   label1.Text = "First &Name:";

   /* Set the size of the control based on the PreferredHeight ↵
and PreferredWidth values. */
   label1.Size = new Size (label1.PreferredHeight, ↵
label1.PreferredWidth);

   //...Code to add the control to the form...
}
```

[JScript]
```
public function CreateMyLabel()
{
   // Create an instance of a Label.
   var label1 : Label = new Label();

   // Set the border to a three-dimensional border.
   label1.BorderStyle = System.Windows.Forms.BorderStyle.Fixed3D;
   // Set the ImageList to use for displaying an image.
   label1.ImageList = imageList1;
   // Use the second image in imageList1.
   label1.ImageIndex = 1;
   // Align the image to the top left corner.
   label1.ImageAlign = ContentAlignment.TopLeft;

   // Specify that the text can display mnemonic characters.
   label1.UseMnemonic = true;
   // Set the text of the control and specify a mnemonic character.
   label1.Text = "First &Name:";
```

```
   /* Set the size of the control based on the PreferredHeight ↵
 and PreferredWidth values. */
   label1.Size = new System.Drawing.Size ↵
 (label1.PreferredHeight, label1.PreferredWidth);

   //...Code to add the control to the form...
}
```

Requirements

Namespace: System.Windows.Forms

Platforms: Windows 98, Windows NT 4.0, Windows Millennium Edition, Windows 2000, Windows XP Home Edition, Windows XP Professional, Windows Server 2003 family, .NET Compact Framework - Windows CE .NET

Assembly: System.Windows.Forms (in System.Windows.Forms.dll)

Label Constructor

Initializes a new instance of the **Label** class.

[Visual Basic]
```
Public Sub New()
```
[C#]
```
public Label();
```
[C++]
```
public: Label();
```
[JScript]
```
public function Label();
```

Remarks

By default, a label is displayed with its **AutoSize** property set to **false** and with its **BorderStyle** property set to **BorderStyle.None**.

Example

See related example in the **System.Windows.Forms.Label** class topic.

Requirements

Platforms: Windows 98, Windows NT 4.0, Windows Millennium Edition, Windows 2000, Windows XP Home Edition, Windows XP Professional, Windows Server 2003 family, .NET Compact Framework - Windows CE .NET

Label.AutoSize Property

Gets or sets a value indicating whether the control is automatically resized to display its entire contents.

[Visual Basic]
```
Public Overridable Property AutoSize As Boolean
```
[C#]
```
public virtual bool AutoSize {get; set;}
```
[C++]
```
public: __property virtual bool get_AutoSize();
public: __property virtual void set_AutoSize(bool);
```
[JScript]
```
public function get AutoSize() : Boolean;
public function set AutoSize(Boolean);
```

Property Value

true if the control adjusts its width to closely fit its contents; otherwise, **false**. The default is **false**.

Remarks

When this property is set to **true**, the control's height and width are automatically adjusted to display the entire contents of the control. This property is typically set to **true** when you use a **Label** control to display various lengths of text, such as the status of an application process. You can also use this property when the application will display text in various languages, and the size of the text might increase or decrease based on the language settings in Windows.

Requirements

Platforms: Windows 98, Windows NT 4.0, Windows Millennium Edition, Windows 2000, Windows XP Home Edition, Windows XP Professional, Windows Server 2003 family

Label.BackgroundImage Property

This member overrides **Control.BackgroundImage**.

[Visual Basic]
```
Overrides Public Property BackgroundImage As Image
```
[C#]
```
public override Image BackgroundImage {get; set;}
```
[C++]
```
public: __property Image* get_BackgroundImage();
public: __property void set_BackgroundImage(Image*);
```
[JScript]
```
public override function get BackgroundImage() : Image;
public override function set BackgroundImage(Image);
```

Requirements

Platforms: Windows 98, Windows NT 4.0, Windows Millennium Edition, Windows 2000, Windows XP Home Edition, Windows XP Professional, Windows Server 2003 family

Label.BorderStyle Property

Gets or sets the border style for the control.

[Visual Basic]
```
Public Overridable Property BorderStyle As BorderStyle
```
[C#]
```
public virtual BorderStyle BorderStyle {get; set;}
```
[C++]
```
public: __property virtual BorderStyle get_BorderStyle();
public: __property virtual void set_BorderStyle(BorderStyle);
```
[JScript]
```
public function get BorderStyle() : BorderStyle;
public function set BorderStyle(BorderStyle);
```

Property Value

One of the **BorderStyle** values. The default is **BorderStyle.None**.

Exceptions

Exception Type	Condition
InvalidEnumArgument-Exception	The value assigned is not one of the **BorderStyle** values.

Remarks

You can use this property to add a border to the control. This property is typically used to differentiate a **Label** that labels another control from a **Label** that displays the status of a process in an application.

Example

See related example in the **System.Windows.Forms.Label** class topic.

Requirements

Platforms: Windows 98, Windows NT 4.0, Windows Millennium Edition, Windows 2000, Windows XP Home Edition, Windows XP Professional, Windows Server 2003 family

Label.CreateParams Property

This member overrides **Control.CreateParams**.

```
[Visual Basic]
Overrides Protected ReadOnly Property CreateParams As CreateParams
[C#]
protected override CreateParams CreateParams {get;}
[C++]
protected: __property CreateParams* get_CreateParams();
[JScript]
protected override function get CreateParams() : CreateParams;
```

Requirements

Platforms: Windows 98, Windows NT 4.0, Windows Millennium Edition, Windows 2000, Windows XP Home Edition, Windows XP Professional, Windows Server 2003 family

Label.DefaultImeMode Property

Gets the default Input Method Editor(IME) mode supported by this control.

```
[Visual Basic]
Overrides Protected ReadOnly Property DefaultImeMode As ImeMode
[C#]
protected override ImeMode DefaultImeMode {get;}
[C++]
protected: __property ImeMode get_DefaultImeMode();
[JScript]
protected override function get DefaultImeMode() : ImeMode;
```

Property Value

One of the **ImeMode** supported by this control. The default is **Disable**.

Requirements

Platforms: Windows 98, Windows NT 4.0, Windows Millennium Edition, Windows 2000, Windows XP Home Edition, Windows XP Professional, Windows Server 2003 family

Label.DefaultSize Property

This member overrides **Control.DefaultSize**.

```
[Visual Basic]
Overrides Protected ReadOnly Property DefaultSize As Size
[C#]
protected override Size DefaultSize {get;}
[C++]
protected: __property Size get_DefaultSize();
[JScript]
protected override function get DefaultSize() : Size;
```

Requirements

Platforms: Windows 98, Windows NT 4.0, Windows Millennium Edition, Windows 2000, Windows XP Home Edition, Windows XP Professional, Windows Server 2003 family

Label.FlatStyle Property

Gets or sets the flat style appearance of the label control.

```
[Visual Basic]
Public Property FlatStyle As FlatStyle
[C#]
public FlatStyle FlatStyle {get; set;}
[C++]
public: __property FlatStyle get_FlatStyle();
public: __property void set_FlatStyle(FlatStyle);
[JScript]
public function get FlatStyle() : FlatStyle;
public function set FlatStyle(FlatStyle);
```

Property Value

One of the **FlatStyle** values. The default value is **Standard**.

Exceptions

Exception Type	Condition
InvalidEnumArgument-Exception	The value assigned is not one of the **FlatStyle** values.

Remarks

When the **FlatStyle** property is set to **FlatStyle.System**, any values assigned to the **ImageList**, **Image**, **ImageIndex**, and **ImageAlign** properties are ignored. In addition, the **TextAlign** property ignores any property values that are not vertical property settings. Horizontally aligned settings of the **TextAlign** property are aligned to the top of the control. For example, if you set the **TextAlign** property to **ContentAlignment.TopCenter**, **ContentAlignment.MiddleCenter**, or **ContentAlignment.BottomCenter**, when the **FlatStyle** property is set to **FlatStyle.System**, the text in the **Label** control will be aligned to the top and center locations within the bounds of the control.

> **Note** In version 1.1 of the .NET Framework, setting the **FlatStyle** property to **FlatStyle.System** does not cause the value of the **TextAlign** property to be ignored.

> **Note** This property has no effect in the derived class, **LinkLabel**.

Requirements

Platforms: Windows 98, Windows NT 4.0, Windows Millennium Edition, Windows 2000, Windows XP Home Edition, Windows XP Professional, Windows Server 2003 family

Label.Image Property

Gets or sets the image that is displayed on a **Label**.

```
[Visual Basic]
Public Property Image As Image
[C#]
public Image Image {get; set;}
[C++]
public: __property Image* get_Image();
public: __property void set_Image(Image*);
[JScript]
public function get Image() : Image;
public function set Image(Image);
```

Property Value

An **Image** displayed on the **Label**. The default is a null reference (**Nothing** in Visual Basic).

Remarks

The **Image** property cannot be used at the same time as the **ImageList** and **ImageIndex** properties. When the **Image** property is used to display an image, the **ImageList** and **ImageIndex** properties are automatically set to their default settings.

Example

See related example in the **System.Windows.Forms.Label** class topic.

Requirements

Platforms: Windows 98, Windows NT 4.0, Windows Millennium Edition, Windows 2000, Windows XP Home Edition, Windows XP Professional, Windows Server 2003 family

Label.ImageAlign Property

Gets or sets the alignment of an image that is displayed in the control.

```
[Visual Basic]
Public Property ImageAlign As ContentAlignment
[C#]
public ContentAlignment ImageAlign {get; set;}
[C++]
public: __property ContentAlignment get_ImageAlign();
public: __property void set_ImageAlign(ContentAlignment);
[JScript]
public function get ImageAlign() : ContentAlignment;
public function set ImageAlign(ContentAlignment);
```

Property Value

One of the **ContentAlignment** values. The default is **ContentAlignment.MiddleCenter**.

Exceptions

Exception Type	Condition
InvalidEnumArgument-Exception	The value assigned is not one of the **ContentAlignment** values.

Remarks

This property enables you to align an image within the boundaries of the **Label** control to ensure that the image is properly displayed. You can add an image to a **Label** using the **Image** property or the **ImageList** and **ImageIndex** properties. Images displayed in the control cannot be stretched or shrunk to fill the control if the control is larger or smaller than the image.

Example

See related example in the **System.Windows.Forms.Label** class topic.

Requirements

Platforms: Windows 98, Windows NT 4.0, Windows Millennium Edition, Windows 2000, Windows XP Home Edition, Windows XP Professional, Windows Server 2003 family

Label.ImageIndex Property

Gets or sets the index value of the image displayed on the **Label**.

```
[Visual Basic]
Public Property ImageIndex As Integer
[C#]
public int ImageIndex {get; set;}
[C++]
public: __property int get_ImageIndex();
public: __property void set_ImageIndex(int);
[JScript]
public function get ImageIndex() : int;
public function set ImageIndex(int);
```

Property Value

A zero-based index that represents the position in the **ImageList** control (assigned to the **ImageList** property) where the image is located. The default is -1.

Exceptions

Exception Type	Condition
ArgumentException	The value assigned is less than the lower bounds of the **ImageIndex** property.

Remarks

The **ImageIndex** and the **ImageList** properties cannot be used at the same time as the **Image** property. When the **ImageIndex** property and **ImageList** properties are used to display an image, the **Image** property is automatically set to a null reference (**Nothing** in Visual Basic).

Example

See related example in the **System.Windows.Forms.Label** class topic.

Requirements

Platforms: Windows 98, Windows NT 4.0, Windows Millennium Edition, Windows 2000, Windows XP Home Edition, Windows XP Professional, Windows Server 2003 family

Label.ImageList Property

Gets or sets the **ImageList** that contains the images to display in the **Label** control.

```
[Visual Basic]
Public Property ImageList As ImageList
[C#]
public ImageList ImageList {get; set;}
[C++]
public: __property ImageList* get_ImageList();
public: __property void set_ImageList(ImageList*);
[JScript]
public function get ImageList() : ImageList;
public function set ImageList(ImageList);
```

Property Value

An **ImageList** that stores the collection of **Image** objects. The default value is a null reference (**Nothing** in Visual Basic).

Remarks

The **ImageIndex** and the **ImageList** properties cannot be used at the same time as the **Image** property. When the **ImageIndex** property and **ImageList** properties are used to display an image, the **Image** property is set to a null reference (**Nothing** in Visual Basic).

Example

See related example in the **System.Windows.Forms.Label** class topic.

Requirements

Platforms: Windows 98, Windows NT 4.0, Windows Millennium Edition, Windows 2000, Windows XP Home Edition, Windows XP Professional, Windows Server 2003 family

Label.ImeMode Property

This member supports the .NET Framework infrastructure and is not intended to be used directly from your code.

```
[Visual Basic]
Public Shadows Property ImeMode As ImeMode
[C#]
public new ImeMode ImeMode {get; set;}
[C++]
public: __property ImeMode get_ImeMode();
public: __property void set_ImeMode(ImeMode);
[JScript]
public hide function get ImeMode() : ImeMode;
public hide function set ImeMode(ImeMode);
```

Label.PreferredHeight Property

Gets the preferred height of the control.

```
[Visual Basic]
Public Overridable ReadOnly Property PreferredHeight As Integer
[C#]
public virtual int PreferredHeight {get;}
[C++]
public: __property virtual int get_PreferredHeight();
[JScript]
public function get PreferredHeight() : int;
```

Property Value

The height of the control (in pixels), assuming a single line of text is displayed.

Remarks

This property returns the height that the control should be in order to properly display text, based on the font assigned to the control. You can use this property along with the **PreferredWidth** property to ensure that the text in the **Label** control is displayed properly. You can use the **AutoSize** property to automatically adjust the height and the width of the **Label** control, based on the text and font size.

> **Note** If the **BorderStyle** property of the **Label** control is set to **BorderStyle.None**, the value returned by **PreferredHeight** property will be larger due to the lack of borders.

Example

See related example in the **System.Windows.Forms.Label** class topic.

Requirements

Platforms: Windows 98, Windows NT 4.0, Windows Millennium Edition, Windows 2000, Windows XP Home Edition, Windows XP Professional, Windows Server 2003 family

Label.PreferredWidth Property

Gets the preferred width of the control.

```
[Visual Basic]
Public Overridable ReadOnly Property PreferredWidth As Integer
[C#]
public virtual int PreferredWidth {get;}
[C++]
public: __property virtual int get_PreferredWidth();
[JScript]
public function get PreferredWidth() : int;
```

Property Value

The width of the control (in pixels), assuming a single line of text is displayed.

Remarks

This property returns the length of the text string, but does not take line wrapping into consideration. For example, a text string that measures 300 pixels wide could be displayed as three lines in a **Label** that is only 100 pixels wide. The **PreferredWidth** property still returns 300 pixels. You can use this property, along with the **PreferredHeight** property, to ensure that the text in the **Label** control is displayed properly. You can use the **AutoSize** property to automatically adjust the height and the width of the **Label** control based on the text and font size.

Note If the **BorderStyle** property of the **Label** control is set to **BorderStyle.None**, the value returned by **PreferredWidth** property will be larger due to the lack of borders.

Example

See related example in the **System.Windows.Forms.Label** class topic.

Requirements

Platforms: Windows 98, Windows NT 4.0, Windows Millennium Edition, Windows 2000, Windows XP Home Edition, Windows XP Professional, Windows Server 2003 family

Label.RenderTransparent Property

Indicates whether the container control background is rendered on the **Label**.

```
[Visual Basic]
Protected Overridable Property RenderTransparent As Boolean
[C#]
protected virtual bool RenderTransparent {get; set;}
[C++]
protected: __property virtual bool get_RenderTransparent();
protected: __property virtual void set_RenderTransparent(bool);
[JScript]
protected function get RenderTransparent() : Boolean;
protected function set RenderTransparent(Boolean);
```

Property Value

true if the background of the **Label** control's container is rendered on the **Label**; otherwise, **false**. The default is **false**.

Remarks

Classes that inherit from Label can override this method to determine whether the derived control background will be rendered transparently on the form on which the control is drawn.

Requirements

Platforms: Windows 98, Windows NT 4.0, Windows Millennium Edition, Windows 2000, Windows XP Home Edition, Windows XP Professional, Windows Server 2003 family

Label.TabStop Property

This member supports the .NET Framework infrastructure and is not intended to be used directly from your code.

```
[Visual Basic]
Public Shadows Property TabStop As Boolean
[C#]
public new bool TabStop {get; set;}
[C++]
public: __property bool get_TabStop();
public: __property void set_TabStop(bool);
[JScript]
public hide function get TabStop() : Boolean;
public hide function set TabStop(Boolean);
```

Label.TextAlign Property

Gets or sets the alignment of text in the label.

```
[Visual Basic]
Public Overridable Property TextAlign As ContentAlignment
[C#]
public virtual ContentAlignment TextAlign {get; set;}
[C++]
public: __property virtual ContentAlignment get_TextAlign();
public: __property virtual void set_TextAlign(ContentAlignment);
[JScript]
public function get TextAlign() : ContentAlignment;
public function set TextAlign(ContentAlignment);
```

Property Value

One of the **ContentAlignment** values. The default is **TopLeft**.

Exceptions

Exception Type	Condition
InvalidEnumArgument-Exception	The value assigned is not one of the **ContentAlignment** values.

Remarks

You can use this property to align the text within a label to match the layout of controls on your form. For example, if your controls are located to the right edge of the labels, you can set the **TextAlign** property to one of the right-aligned horizontal alignments (**TopRight**, **MiddleRight**, **BottomRight**) and the text will be aligned with the right edge of the labels to align with your controls.

Requirements

Platforms: Windows 98, Windows NT 4.0, Windows Millennium Edition, Windows 2000, Windows XP Home Edition, Windows XP Professional, Windows Server 2003 family, .NET Compact Framework - Windows CE .NET

Label.UseMnemonic Property

Gets or sets a value indicating whether the control interprets an ampersand character (&) in the control's **Text** property to be an access key prefix character.

```
[Visual Basic]
Public Property UseMnemonic As Boolean
[C#]
public bool UseMnemonic {get; set;}
[C++]
public: __property bool get_UseMnemonic();
public: __property void set_UseMnemonic(bool);
[JScript]
public function get UseMnemonic() : Boolean;
public function set UseMnemonic(Boolean);
```

Property Value

true if the label doesn't display the ampersand character and underlines the character after the ampersand in its displayed text and treats the underlined character as an access key; otherwise, **false** if the ampersand character is displayed in the text of the control. The default is **true**.

Remarks

If the **UseMnemonic** property is set to **true** and a mnemonic character (a character preceded by the ampersand) is defined in the **Text** property of the **Label**, pressing ALT+ the mnemonic character sets the focus to the control that follows the **Label** in the tab order. You can use this property to provide proper keyboard navigation to the controls on your form.

Example

See related example in the **System.Windows.Forms.Label** class topic.

Requirements

Platforms: Windows 98, Windows NT 4.0, Windows Millennium Edition, Windows 2000, Windows XP Home Edition, Windows XP Professional, Windows Server 2003 family

Label.CalcImageRenderBounds Method

Determines the size and location of an image drawn within the **Label** control based on the alignment of the control.

[Visual Basic]
```
Protected Function CalcImageRenderBounds( _
   ByVal image As Image, _
   ByVal r As Rectangle, _
   ByVal align As ContentAlignment _
) As Rectangle
```
[C#]
```
protected Rectangle CalcImageRenderBounds(
   Image image,
   Rectangle r,
   ContentAlignment align
);
```
[C++]
```
protected: Rectangle CalcImageRenderBounds(
   Image* image,
   Rectangle r,
   ContentAlignment align
);
```
[JScript]
```
protected function CalcImageRenderBounds(
   image : Image,
   r : Rectangle,
   align : ContentAlignment
) : Rectangle;
```

Parameters

image
The **Image** used to determine size and location when drawn within the control.

r
A **Rectangle** that represents the area to draw the image in.

align
The alignment of content within the control.

Return Value

A **Rectangle** that represents the size and location of the specified image within the control.

Remarks

You can use this method within a derived class of **Label**, to determine the size and location of an image to draw within the **Label** control based on its location within the control. The location of the image is based on the value of the control's **ImageAlign** property.

Requirements

Platforms: Windows 98, Windows NT 4.0, Windows Millennium Edition, Windows 2000, Windows XP Home Edition, Windows XP Professional, Windows Server 2003 family

Label.CreateAccessibilityInstance Method

This member overrides **Control.CreateAccessibilityInstance**.

[Visual Basic]
```
Overrides Protected Function CreateAccessibilityInstance() As _
   AccessibleObject
```
[C#]
```
protected override AccessibleObject CreateAccessibilityInstance();
```
[C++]
```
protected: AccessibleObject* CreateAccessibilityInstance();
```
[JScript]
```
protected override function CreateAccessibilityInstance() :
   AccessibleObject;
```

Requirements

Platforms: Windows 98, Windows NT 4.0, Windows Millennium Edition, Windows 2000, Windows XP Home Edition, Windows XP Professional, Windows Server 2003 family

Label.Dispose Method

Overload List

This member supports the .NET Framework infrastructure and is not intended to be used directly from your code.

Supported by the .NET Compact Framework.

[Visual Basic] **Overloads Overrides Protected Sub Dispose(Boolean)**

[C#] **protected override void Dispose(bool);**

[C++] **protected: void Dispose(bool);**

[JScript] **protected override function Dispose(Boolean);**

Inherited from **Component**.

Supported by the .NET Compact Framework.

[Visual Basic] **Overloads Public Overridable Sub Dispose() Implements IDisposable.Dispose**

[C#] **public virtual void Dispose();**

[C++] **public: virtual void Dispose();**

[JScript] **public function Dispose();**

Label.Dispose Method (Boolean)

This member overrides **Control.Dispose**.

[Visual Basic]
```
Overrides Overloads Protected Sub Dispose( _
   ByVal disposing As Boolean _
)
```
[C#]
```
protected override void Dispose(
   bool disposing
);
```
[C++]
```
protected: void Dispose(
   bool disposing
);
```
[JScript]
```
protected override function Dispose(
   disposing : Boolean
);
```

Requirements

Platforms: Windows 98, Windows NT 4.0, Windows Millennium Edition, Windows 2000, Windows XP Home Edition, Windows XP Professional, Windows Server 2003 family, .NET Compact Framework - Windows CE .NET

Label.DrawImage Method

Draws an **Image** within the specified bounds.

[Visual Basic]
```
Protected Sub DrawImage( _
   ByVal g As Graphics, _
   ByVal image As Image, _
   ByVal r As Rectangle, _
   ByVal align As ContentAlignment _
)
```
[C#]
```
protected void DrawImage(
   Graphics g,
   Image image,
   Rectangle r,
   ContentAlignment align
);
```
[C++]
```
protected: void DrawImage(
   Graphics* g,
   Image* image,
   Rectangle r,
   ContentAlignment align
);
```
[JScript]
```
protected function DrawImage(
   g : Graphics,
   image : Image,
   r : Rectangle,
   align : ContentAlignment
);
```

Parameters

g
: The **Graphics** surface on which to draw.

image
: The **Image** to draw.

r
: The **Rectangle** bounds to draw within.

align
: The alignment of the image to draw within the **Label**.

Remarks

Notes to Inheritors: When you are creating your own control that derives from **Label**, you can use this method to draw images onto the surface of the control.

Requirements

Platforms: Windows 98, Windows NT 4.0, Windows Millennium Edition, Windows 2000, Windows XP Home Edition, Windows XP Professional, Windows Server 2003 family

Label.OnAutoSizeChanged Method

Raises the **AutoSizeChanged** event.

[Visual Basic]
```
Protected Overridable Sub OnAutoSizeChanged( _
   ByVal e As EventArgs _
)
```
[C#]
```
protected virtual void OnAutoSizeChanged(
   EventArgs e
);
```
[C++]
```
protected: virtual void OnAutoSizeChanged(
   EventArgs* e
);
```
[JScript]
```
protected function OnAutoSizeChanged(
   e : EventArgs
);
```

Parameters

e
: A **EventArgs** that contains the event data.

Remarks

Raising an event invokes the event handler through a delegate.

Notes to Inheritors: When overriding **OnAutoSizeChanged** in a derived class, be sure to call the base class's **OnAutoSizeChanged** method.

Requirements

Platforms: Windows 98, Windows NT 4.0, Windows Millennium Edition, Windows 2000, Windows XP Home Edition, Windows XP Professional, Windows Server 2003 family

Label.OnEnabledChanged Method

This member overrides **Control.OnEnabledChanged**.

```
[Visual Basic]
Overrides Protected Sub OnEnabledChanged( _
   ByVal e As EventArgs _
)
[C#]
protected override void OnEnabledChanged(
   EventArgs e
);
[C++]
protected: void OnEnabledChanged(
   EventArgs* e
);
[JScript]
protected override function OnEnabledChanged(
   e : EventArgs
);
```

Requirements

Platforms: Windows 98, Windows NT 4.0, Windows Millennium Edition, Windows 2000, Windows XP Home Edition, Windows XP Professional, Windows Server 2003 family, .NET Compact Framework - Windows CE .NET

Label.OnFontChanged Method

This member overrides **Control.OnFontChanged**.

```
[Visual Basic]
Overrides Protected Sub OnFontChanged( _
   ByVal e As EventArgs _
)
[C#]
protected override void OnFontChanged(
   EventArgs e
);
[C++]
protected: void OnFontChanged(
   EventArgs* e
);
[JScript]
protected override function OnFontChanged(
   e : EventArgs
);
```

Requirements

Platforms: Windows 98, Windows NT 4.0, Windows Millennium Edition, Windows 2000, Windows XP Home Edition, Windows XP Professional, Windows Server 2003 family

Label.OnPaint Method

This member overrides **Control.OnPaint**.

```
[Visual Basic]
Overrides Protected Sub OnPaint( _
   ByVal e As PaintEventArgs _
)
[C#]
protected override void OnPaint(
   PaintEventArgs e
);
[C++]
protected: void OnPaint(
   PaintEventArgs* e
);
[JScript]
protected override function OnPaint(
   e : PaintEventArgs
);
```

Requirements

Platforms: Windows 98, Windows NT 4.0, Windows Millennium Edition, Windows 2000, Windows XP Home Edition, Windows XP Professional, Windows Server 2003 family, .NET Compact Framework - Windows CE .NET

Label.OnParentChanged Method

This member overrides **Control.OnParentChanged**.

```
[Visual Basic]
Overrides Protected Sub OnParentChanged( _
   ByVal e As EventArgs _
)
[C#]
protected override void OnParentChanged(
   EventArgs e
);
[C++]
protected: void OnParentChanged(
   EventArgs* e
);
[JScript]
protected override function OnParentChanged(
   e : EventArgs
);
```

Requirements

Platforms: Windows 98, Windows NT 4.0, Windows Millennium Edition, Windows 2000, Windows XP Home Edition, Windows XP Professional, Windows Server 2003 family, .NET Compact Framework - Windows CE .NET

Label.OnTextAlignChanged Method

Raises the **TextAlignChanged** event.

```
[Visual Basic]
Protected Overridable Sub OnTextAlignChanged( _
   ByVal e As EventArgs _
)
[C#]
protected virtual void OnTextAlignChanged(
   EventArgs e
);
[C++]
protected: virtual void OnTextAlignChanged(
   EventArgs* e
);
```

```
[JScript]
protected function OnTextAlignChanged(
   e : EventArgs
);
```

Parameters

e

An **EventArgs** that contains the event data.

Remarks

Raising an event invokes the event handler through a delegate.

Notes to Inheritors: When overriding **OnTextAlignChanged** in a derived class, be sure to call the base class's **OnTextAlignChanged** method.

Requirements

Platforms: Windows 98, Windows NT 4.0,
Windows Millennium Edition, Windows 2000,
Windows XP Home Edition, Windows XP Professional,
Windows Server 2003 family

Label.OnTextChanged Method

This member overrides **Control.OnTextChanged**.

```
[Visual Basic]
Overrides Protected Sub OnTextChanged( _
   ByVal e As EventArgs _
)
[C#]
protected override void OnTextChanged(
   EventArgs e
);
[C++]
protected: void OnTextChanged(
   EventArgs* e
);
[JScript]
protected override function OnTextChanged(
   e : EventArgs
);
```

Requirements

Platforms: Windows 98, Windows NT 4.0,
Windows Millennium Edition, Windows 2000,
Windows XP Home Edition, Windows XP Professional,
Windows Server 2003 family,
.NET Compact Framework - Windows CE .NET

Label.OnVisibleChanged Method

This member overrides **Control.OnVisibleChanged**.

```
[Visual Basic]
Overrides Protected Sub OnVisibleChanged( _
   ByVal e As EventArgs _
)
[C#]
protected override void OnVisibleChanged(
   EventArgs e
);
[C++]
protected: void OnVisibleChanged(
   EventArgs* e
);
[JScript]
protected override function OnVisibleChanged(
   e : EventArgs
);
```

Requirements

Platforms: Windows 98, Windows NT 4.0,
Windows Millennium Edition, Windows 2000,
Windows XP Home Edition, Windows XP Professional,
Windows Server 2003 family

Label.ProcessMnemonic Method

This member overrides **Control.ProcessMnemonic**.

```
[Visual Basic]
Overrides Protected Function ProcessMnemonic( _
   ByVal charCode As Char _
) As Boolean
[C#]
protected override bool ProcessMnemonic(
   char charCode
);
[C++]
protected: bool ProcessMnemonic(
   __wchar_t charCode
);
[JScript]
protected override function ProcessMnemonic(
   charCode : Char
) : Boolean;
```

Requirements

Platforms: Windows 98, Windows NT 4.0,
Windows Millennium Edition, Windows 2000,
Windows XP Home Edition, Windows XP Professional,
Windows Server 2003 family

Label.SetBoundsCore Method

This member overrides **Control.SetBoundsCore**.

```
[Visual Basic]
Overrides Protected Sub SetBoundsCore( _
   ByVal x As Integer, _
   ByVal y As Integer, _
   ByVal width As Integer, _
   ByVal height As Integer, _
   ByVal specified As BoundsSpecified _
)
[C#]
protected override void SetBoundsCore(
   int x,
   int y,
   int width,
   int height,
   BoundsSpecified specified
);
```

[C++]
```
protected: void SetBoundsCore(
   int x,
   int y,
   int width,
   int height,
   BoundsSpecified specified
);
```
[JScript]
```
protected override function SetBoundsCore(
   x : int,
   y : int,
   width : int,
   height : int,
   specified : BoundsSpecified
);
```

Requirements

Platforms: Windows 98, Windows NT 4.0, Windows Millennium Edition, Windows 2000, Windows XP Home Edition, Windows XP Professional, Windows Server 2003 family

Label.ToString Method

This member overrides **Object.ToString**.

[Visual Basic]
```
Overrides Public Function ToString() As String
```
[C#]
```
public override string ToString();
```
[C++]
```
public: String* ToString();
```
[JScript]
```
public override function ToString() : String;
```

Requirements

Platforms: Windows 98, Windows NT 4.0, Windows Millennium Edition, Windows 2000, Windows XP Home Edition, Windows XP Professional, Windows Server 2003 family, .NET Compact Framework - Windows CE .NET

Label.WndProc Method

This member overrides **Control.WndProc**.

[Visual Basic]
```
Overrides Protected Sub WndProc( _
   ByRef m As Message _
)
```
[C#]
```
protected override void WndProc(
   ref Message m
);
```
[C++]
```
protected: void WndProc(
   Message* m
);
```
[JScript]
```
protected override function WndProc(
   m : Message
);
```

Requirements

Platforms: Windows 98, Windows NT 4.0, Windows Millennium Edition, Windows 2000, Windows XP Home Edition, Windows XP Professional, Windows Server 2003 family

Label.AutoSizeChanged Event

Occurs when the value of the **AutoSize** property has changed.

[Visual Basic]
```
Public Event AutoSizeChanged As EventHandler
```
[C#]
```
public event EventHandler AutoSizeChanged;
```
[C++]
```
public: __event EventHandler* AutoSizeChanged;
```

[JScript] In JScript, you can handle the events defined by a class, but you cannot define your own.

Event Data

The event handler receives an argument of type **EventArgs**.

Remarks

For more information about handling events, see **Consuming Events**.

Requirements

Platforms: Windows 98, Windows NT 4.0, Windows Millennium Edition, Windows 2000, Windows XP Home Edition, Windows XP Professional, Windows Server 2003 family

Label.BackgroundImageChanged Event

This member supports the .NET Framework infrastructure and is not intended to be used directly from your code.

[Visual Basic]
```
Public Shadows Event BackgroundImageChanged As EventHandler
```
[C#]
```
public new event EventHandler BackgroundImageChanged;
```
[C++]
```
public: __event EventHandler* BackgroundImageChanged;
```

[JScript] In JScript, you can handle the events defined by a class, but you cannot define your own.

Label.ImeModeChanged Event

This member supports the .NET Framework infrastructure and is not intended to be used directly from your code.

[Visual Basic]
```
Public Shadows Event ImeModeChanged As EventHandler
```
[C#]
```
public new event EventHandler ImeModeChanged;
```
[C++]
```
public: __event EventHandler* ImeModeChanged;
```

[JScript] In JScript, you can handle the events defined by a class, but you cannot define your own.

Label.KeyDown Event

This member supports the .NET Framework infrastructure and is not intended to be used directly from your code.

[Visual Basic]
```
Public Shadows Event KeyDown As KeyEventHandler
```
[C#]
```
public new event KeyEventHandler KeyDown;
```
[C++]
```
public: __event KeyEventHandler* KeyDown;
```

[JScript] In JScript, you can handle the events defined by a class, but you cannot define your own.

Label.KeyPress Event

This member supports the .NET Framework infrastructure and is not intended to be used directly from your code.

[Visual Basic]
```
Public Shadows Event KeyPress As KeyPressEventHandler
```
[C#]
```
public new event KeyPressEventHandler KeyPress;
```
[C++]
```
public: __event KeyPressEventHandler* KeyPress;
```

[JScript] In JScript, you can handle the events defined by a class, but you cannot define your own.

Label.KeyUp Event

This member supports the .NET Framework infrastructure and is not intended to be used directly from your code.

[Visual Basic]
```
Public Shadows Event KeyUp As KeyEventHandler
```
[C#]
```
public new event KeyEventHandler KeyUp;
```
[C++]
```
public: __event KeyEventHandler* KeyUp;
```

[JScript] In JScript, you can handle the events defined by a class, but you cannot define your own.

Label.TabStopChanged Event

This member supports the .NET Framework infrastructure and is not intended to be used directly from your code.

[Visual Basic]
```
Public Shadows Event TabStopChanged As EventHandler
```
[C#]
```
public new event EventHandler TabStopChanged;
```
[C++]
```
public: __event EventHandler* TabStopChanged;
```

[JScript] In JScript, you can handle the events defined by a class, but you cannot define your own.

Label.TextAlignChanged Event

Occurs when the value of the **TextAlign** property has changed.

[Visual Basic]
```
Public Event TextAlignChanged As EventHandler
```
[C#]
```
public event EventHandler TextAlignChanged;
```
[C++]
```
public: __event EventHandler* TextAlignChanged;
```

[JScript] In JScript, you can handle the events defined by a class, but you cannot define your own.

Event Data

The event handler receives an argument of type **EventArgs**.

Requirements

Platforms: Windows 98, Windows NT 4.0, Windows Millennium Edition, Windows 2000, Windows XP Home Edition, Windows XP Professional, Windows Server 2003 family

LabelEditEventArgs Class

Provides data for the **LabelEdit** event.

System.Object
  System.EventArgs
    System.Windows.Forms.LabelEditEventArgs

```
[Visual Basic]
Public Class LabelEditEventArgs
   Inherits EventArgs
[C#]
public class LabelEditEventArgs : EventArgs
[C++]
public __gc class LabelEditEventArgs : public EventArgs
[JScript]
public class LabelEditEventArgs extends EventArgs
```

Thread Safety

Any public static (**Shared** in Visual Basic) members of this type are safe for multithreaded operations. Any instance members are not guaranteed to be thread safe.

Remarks

A **LabelEditEventArgs** specifies the index and caption of a **ListViewItem** and the caption after it has been edited by the user. This class also provides the **CancelEdit** property, which enables code in an event handler for the **LabelEdit** event to cancel the changes made to the label by the user.

Requirements

Namespace: System.Windows.Forms

Platforms: Windows 98, Windows NT 4.0, Windows Millennium Edition, Windows 2000, Windows XP Home Edition, Windows XP Professional, Windows Server 2003 family

Assembly: System.Windows.Forms (in System.Windows.Forms.dll)

LabelEditEventArgs Constructor

Initializes a new instance of the **LabelEditEventArgs** class.

Overload List

Initializes a new instance of the **LabelEditEventArgs** class with the specified index to the **ListViewItem** to edit.

[Visual Basic] **Public Sub New(Integer)**

[C#] **public LabelEditEventArgs(int);**

[C++] **public: LabelEditEventArgs(int);**

[JScript] **public function LabelEditEventArgs(int);**

Initializes a new instance of the **LabelEditEventArgs** class with the specified index to the **ListViewItem** being edited and the new text for the label of the **ListViewItem**.

[Visual Basic] **Public Sub New(Integer, String)**

[C#] **public LabelEditEventArgs(int, string);**

[C++] **public: LabelEditEventArgs(int, String*);**

[JScript] **public function LabelEditEventArgs(int, String);**

LabelEditEventArgs Constructor (Int32)

Initializes a new instance of the **LabelEditEventArgs** class with the specified index to the **ListViewItem** to edit.

```
[Visual Basic]
Public Sub New( _
   ByVal item As Integer _
)
[C#]
public LabelEditEventArgs(
   int item
);
[C++]
public: LabelEditEventArgs(
   int item
);
[JScript]
public function LabelEditEventArgs(
   item : int
);
```

Parameters

item
  The zero-based index of the **ListViewItem**, containing the label to edit.

Remarks

You can use this constructor when raising the **LabelEdit** event at run time to specify a specific list item in the **ListView** to edit.

Requirements

Platforms: Windows 98, Windows NT 4.0, Windows Millennium Edition, Windows 2000, Windows XP Home Edition, Windows XP Professional, Windows Server 2003 family

LabelEditEventArgs Constructor (Int32, String)

Initializes a new instance of the **LabelEditEventArgs** class with the specified index to the **ListViewItem** being edited and the new text for the label of the **ListViewItem**.

```
[Visual Basic]
Public Sub New( _
   ByVal item As Integer, _
   ByVal label As String _
)
[C#]
public LabelEditEventArgs(
   int item,
   string label
);
[C++]
public: LabelEditEventArgs(
   int item,
   String* label
);
[JScript]
public function LabelEditEventArgs(
   item : int,
   label : String
);
```

Parameters

item

The zero-based index of the **ListViewItem**, containing the label to edit.

label

The new text assigned to the label of the **ListViewItem**.

Remarks

You can use this constructor when raising the **LabelEdit** event at run time to specify a list item in the **ListView** to edit. The constructor also enables you to specify the new text associated with the label of the **ListViewItem**.

Requirements

Platforms: Windows 98, Windows NT 4.0, Windows Millennium Edition, Windows 2000, Windows XP Home Edition, Windows XP Professional, Windows Server 2003 family

LabelEditEventArgs.CancelEdit Property

Gets or sets a value indicating whether changes made to the label of the **ListViewItem** should be canceled.

```
[Visual Basic]
Public Property CancelEdit As Boolean
[C#]
public bool CancelEdit {get; set;}
[C++]
public: __property bool get_CancelEdit();
public: __property void set_CancelEdit(bool);
[JScript]
public function get CancelEdit() : Boolean;
public function set CancelEdit(Boolean);
```

Property Value

true if the edit operation of the label for the **ListViewItem** should be canceled; otherwise **false**.

Remarks

You can use this property to cancel changes made to the label of a **ListViewItem** and revert it to its original text. Use this property to prevent an item's caption from being changed to a value that does not meet your application's requirements.

Requirements

Platforms: Windows 98, Windows NT 4.0, Windows Millennium Edition, Windows 2000, Windows XP Home Edition, Windows XP Professional, Windows Server 2003 family

LabelEditEventArgs.Item Property

Gets the zero-based index of the **ListViewItem** containing the label to edit.

```
[Visual Basic]
Public ReadOnly Property Item As Integer
[C#]
public int Item {get;}
[C++]
public: __property int get_Item();
[JScript]
public function get Item() : int;
```

Property Value

The zero-based index of the **ListViewItem**.

Requirements

Platforms: Windows 98, Windows NT 4.0, Windows Millennium Edition, Windows 2000, Windows XP Home Edition, Windows XP Professional, Windows Server 2003 family

LabelEditEventArgs.Label Property

Gets the new text assigned to the label of the **ListViewItem**.

```
[Visual Basic]
Public ReadOnly Property Label As String
[C#]
public string Label {get;}
[C++]
public: __property String* get_Label();
[JScript]
public function get Label() : String;
```

Property Value

The new text to associate with the **ListViewItem**.

Requirements

Platforms: Windows 98, Windows NT 4.0, Windows Millennium Edition, Windows 2000, Windows XP Home Edition, Windows XP Professional, Windows Server 2003 family

LabelEditEventHandler Delegate

Represents the method that handles the **LabelEdit** event of a **ListView**.

[Visual Basic]

```
<Serializable>
Public Delegate Sub LabelEditEventHandler( _
   ByVal sender As Object, _
   ByVal e As LabelEditEventArgs _
)
```

[C#]

```
[Serializable]
public delegate void LabelEditEventHandler(
   object sender,
   LabelEditEventArgs e
);
```

[C++]

```
[Serializable]
public __gc __delegate void LabelEditEventHandler(
   Object* sender,
   LabelEditEventArgs* e
);
```

[JScript] In JScript, you can use the delegates in the .NET Framework, but you cannot define your own.

Parameters [Visual Basic, C#, C++]

The declaration of your event handler must have the same parameters as the **LabelEditEventHandler** delegate declaration.

sender
: The source of the event.

e
: A **LabelEditEventArgs** that contains the event data.

Remarks

When you create a **LabelEditEventHandler** delegate, you identify the method that will handle the event. To associate the event with your event handler, add an instance of the delegate to the event. The event handler is called whenever the event occurs, unless you remove the delegate.

Requirements

Namespace: System.Windows.Forms

Platforms: Windows 98, Windows NT 4.0, Windows Millennium Edition, Windows 2000, Windows XP Home Edition, Windows XP Professional, Windows Server 2003 family

Assembly: System.Windows.Forms (in System.Windows.Forms.dll)

LayoutEventArgs Class

Provides data for the **Layout** event.

System.Object
  System.EventArgs
    System.Windows.Forms.LayoutEventArgs

[Visual Basic]
```
NotInheritable Public Class LayoutEventArgs
   Inherits EventArgs
```
[C#]
```
public sealed class LayoutEventArgs : EventArgs
```
[C++]
```
public __gc __sealed class LayoutEventArgs : public EventArgs
```
[JScript]
```
public class LayoutEventArgs extends EventArgs
```

Thread Safety

Any public static (**Shared** in Visual Basic) members of this type are safe for multithreaded operations. Any instance members are not guaranteed to be thread safe.

Remarks

Changes to a control such as resizing, showing or hiding child controls, and adding or removing child controls make it necessary for a control to layout its child controls. A **LayoutEventArgs** specifies the child control that has been changed and its affected property. For example, if a control has been made visible since the last layout operation, the **Visible** property is affected.

The **AffectedControl** and **AffectedProperty** properties are set to a null reference (**Nothing** in Visual Basic) if no values were provided when the **PerformLayout** method was called.

For more information about handling events, see **Consuming Events**.

Example

[Visual Basic]
```
Public Class Form1
    Inherits System.Windows.Forms.Form
    Private WithEvents textBox1 As System.Windows.Forms.TextBox
    Private label1 As System.Windows.Forms.Label
    Private layoutButton As System.Windows.Forms.Button
    Private components As System.ComponentModel.Container = Nothing

    Public Sub New()
        InitializeComponent()
    End Sub

    Protected Overloads Overrides Sub Dispose(ByVal disposing ↵
 As Boolean)
        If disposing Then
            If Not (components Is Nothing) Then
                components.Dispose()
            End If
        End If
        MyBase.Dispose(disposing)
    End Sub

    Private Sub InitializeComponent()
        Me.layoutButton = New System.Windows.Forms.Button()
        Me.textBox1 = New System.Windows.Forms.TextBox()
        Me.label1 = New System.Windows.Forms.Label()
        Me.SuspendLayout()
        '
        ' layoutButton
        '
        Me.layoutButton.Anchor = ↵
System.Windows.Forms.AnchorStyles.Bottom
        Me.layoutButton.Location = New System.Drawing.Point(72, 88)
        Me.layoutButton.Name = "layoutButton"
        Me.layoutButton.Size = New System.Drawing.Size(150, 23)
        Me.layoutButton.TabIndex = 0
        Me.layoutButton.Text = "Hello"
        '
        ' textBox1
        '
        Me.textBox1.Anchor = ↵
 System.Windows.Forms.AnchorStyles.Top Or ↵
System.Windows.Forms.AnchorStyles.Left Or ↵
System.Windows.Forms.AnchorStyles.Right
        Me.textBox1.Location = New System.Drawing.Point(24, 40)
        Me.textBox1.Name = "textBox1"
        Me.textBox1.Size = New System.Drawing.Size(248, 20)
        Me.textBox1.TabIndex = 1
        Me.textBox1.Text = "Hello"
        '
        ' label1
        '
        Me.label1.Location = New System.Drawing.Point(24, 16)
        Me.label1.Name = "label1"
        Me.label1.TabIndex = 2
        Me.label1.Text = "Button's Text:"
        '
        ' Form1
        '
        Me.AutoScaleBaseSize = New System.Drawing.Size(5, 13)
        Me.ClientSize = New System.Drawing.Size(292, 129)
        Me.Controls.AddRange ↵
 (New System.Windows.Forms.Control() {Me.label1, Me.textBox1, ↵
Me.layoutButton})
        Me.Name = "Form1"
        Me.Text = "Layout Sample"
        Me.ResumeLayout(False)
    End Sub

    ' This method will enforce that the form's width is the ↵
 preferred size of 300 pixels,
    ' or, the size of the button + 50 pixels, whichever is smaller.
    Private Sub Form1_Layout(ByVal sender As Object, ByVal e ↵
As System.Windows.Forms.LayoutEventArgs) Handles MyBase.Layout
        ' This event is raised once at startup with the AffectedControl
        ' and AffectedProperty proeprties on the LayoutEventArgs ↵
as null.
        ' The if statement protects against that case.
        If Not (e.AffectedControl Is Nothing) And Not ↵
 (e.AffectedProperty Is Nothing) Then
            ' Make sure the affected property is the Bounds property
            ' of the form.
            If e.AffectedProperty.ToString() = "Bounds" Then
                ' If layoutButton's width + a 50 pixel padding ↵
 is greater than the preferred
                ' size of 300 pixels, then grow the form's width.
                If Me.layoutButton.Width + 50 > 300 Then
                    Me.Width = Me.layoutButton.Width + 50
                    ' If not, keep the form's width at 300 pixels.
                Else
                    Me.Width = 300
                End If

                ' Center layoutButton on the form.
                Me.layoutButton.Left = (Me.ClientSize.Width - ↵
Me.layoutButton.Width) / 2
            End If
        End If
    End Sub

    ' This method sets the Text property of layoutButton to ↵
 the Text property
    ' of textBox1.  If the new text + a 20 pixel padding is larger than
    ' the 150 pixel preferred size, adjust layoutButton's Width ↵
property.
    Private Sub textBox1_TextChanged(ByVal sender As Object, ↵
ByVal e As System.EventArgs) Handles textBox1.TextChanged
        ' Set the Text property of layoutButton.
        Me.layoutButton.Text = Me.textBox1.Text
        ' Get the width of the text using the proper font.
        Dim textWidth As Integer = ↵
CInt(Me.CreateGraphics().MeasureString(layoutButton.Text, ↵
layoutButton.Font).Width)
```

```
        ' If the width of the text + a 20 pixel padding is
greater than the preferred size of
        ' 150 pixels, grow layoutButton's width.
        If textWidth + 20 > 150 Then
            ' Setting the size property on any control raises
            ' the Layout event for it's container.
            Me.layoutButton.Width = textWidth + 20
            ' If not, keep layoutButton's width at 150 pixels.
        Else
            Me.layoutButton.Width = 150
        End If
    End Sub
End Class
```

[C#]

```
public class Form1 : System.Windows.Forms.Form
{
   private System.Windows.Forms.TextBox textBox1;
   private System.Windows.Forms.Label label1;
   private System.Windows.Forms.Button layoutButton;
   private System.ComponentModel.Container components = null;

   public Form1()
   {
      InitializeComponent();
   }

   protected override void Dispose( bool disposing )
   {
      if( disposing )
      {
         if (components != null)
         {
            components.Dispose();
         }
      }
      base.Dispose( disposing );
   }

   private void InitializeComponent()
   {
      this.layoutButton = new System.Windows.Forms.Button();
      this.textBox1 = new System.Windows.Forms.TextBox();
      this.label1 = new System.Windows.Forms.Label();
      this.SuspendLayout();
      //
      // layoutButton
      //
      this.layoutButton.Anchor =
System.Windows.Forms.AnchorStyles.Bottom;
      this.layoutButton.Location = new System.Drawing.Point(72, 88);
      this.layoutButton.Name = "layoutButton";
      this.layoutButton.Size = new System.Drawing.Size(150, 23);
      this.layoutButton.TabIndex = 0;
      this.layoutButton.Text = "Hello";
      //
      // textBox1
      //
      this.textBox1.Anchor =
((System.Windows.Forms.AnchorStyles.Top |
System.Windows.Forms.AnchorStyles.Left)
         | System.Windows.Forms.AnchorStyles.Right);
      this.textBox1.Location = new System.Drawing.Point(24, 40);
      this.textBox1.Name = "textBox1";
      this.textBox1.Size = new System.Drawing.Size(248, 20);
      this.textBox1.TabIndex = 1;
      this.textBox1.Text = "Hello";
      this.textBox1.TextChanged += new
System.EventHandler(this.textBox1_TextChanged);
      //
      // label1
      //
      this.label1.Location = new System.Drawing.Point(24, 16);
      this.label1.Name = "label1";
      this.label1.TabIndex = 2;
      this.label1.Text = "Button\'s Text:";
      //
      // Form1
      //
      this.AutoScaleBaseSize = new System.Drawing.Size(5, 13);
      this.ClientSize = new System.Drawing.Size(292, 129);
      this.Controls.AddRange(new System.Windows.Forms.Control[] {
                                                   this.label1,
                                                   this.textBox1,
                                                   this.layoutButton});
      this.Name = "Form1";
      this.Text = "Layout Sample";
      this.Layout += new
System.Windows.Forms.LayoutEventHandler(this.Form1_Layout);
      this.ResumeLayout(false);

   }

   [STAThread]
   static void Main()
   {
      Application.Run(new Form1());
   }

   // This method will enforce that the form's width is the
preferred size of 300 pixels,
   // or, the size of the button + 50 pixels, whichever is
smaller.
   private void Form1_Layout(object sender,
System.Windows.Forms.LayoutEventArgs e)
   {
      // This event is raised once at startup with the AffectedControl
      // and AffectedProperty properties on the LayoutEventArgs
as null.
      // The if statement protects against that case.
      if ((e.AffectedControl != null) && (e.AffectedProperty != null))
      {
         // Make sure the affected property is the Bounds property
         // of the form.
         if (e.AffectedProperty.ToString() == "Bounds")
         {
            // If layoutButton's width + a 50 pixel padding
is greater than the preferred
            // size of 300 pixels, then grow the form's width.
            if ((this.layoutButton.Width + 50) > 300)
            {
               this.Width = this.layoutButton.Width + 50;
            }
               // If not, keep the form's width at 300 pixels.
            else
            {
               this.Width = 300;
            }

            // Center layoutButton on the form.
            this.layoutButton.Left = (this.ClientSize.Width -
this.layoutButton.Width) / 2;
         }
      }
   }

   // This method sets the Text property of layoutButton to the
Text property
   // of textBox1.  If the new text + a 20 pixel padding is larger than
   // the 150 pixel preferred size, adjust layoutButton's Width
property.
   private void textBox1_TextChanged(object sender, System.EventArgs e)
   {
      // Set the Text property of layoutButton.
      this.layoutButton.Text = this.textBox1.Text;
      // Get the width of the text using the proper font.
      int textWidth =
(int)this.CreateGraphics().MeasureString(layoutButton.Text,
layoutButton.Font).Width;

      // If the width of the text + a 20 pixel padding is greater
than the preferred size of
      // 150 pixels, grow layoutButton's width.
      if ((textWidth + 20) > 150)
      {
         // Setting the size property on any control raises
         // the Layout event for it's container.
         this.layoutButton.Width = textWidth + 20;
      }
         // If not, keep layoutButton's width at 150 pixels.
```

```
      else
      {
         this.layoutButton.Width = 150;
      }
   }
}
```

Requirements

Namespace: System.Windows.Forms

Platforms: Windows 98, Windows NT 4.0, Windows Millennium Edition, Windows 2000, Windows XP Home Edition, Windows XP Professional, Windows Server 2003 family

Assembly: System.Windows.Forms (in System.Windows.Forms.dll)

LayoutEventArgs Constructor

Initializes a new instance of the **LayoutEventArgs** class with the specified control and property affected.

```
[Visual Basic]
Public Sub New( _
   ByVal affectedControl As Control, _
   ByVal affectedProperty As String _
)
[C#]
public LayoutEventArgs(
   Control affectedControl,
   string affectedProperty
);
[C++]
public: LayoutEventArgs(
   Control* affectedControl,
   String* affectedProperty
);
[JScript]
public function LayoutEventArgs(
   affectedControl : Control,
   affectedProperty : String
);
```

Parameters

affectedControl
The **Control** affected by the change.

affectedProperty
The property affected by the change.

Requirements

Platforms: Windows 98, Windows NT 4.0, Windows Millennium Edition, Windows 2000, Windows XP Home Edition, Windows XP Professional, Windows Server 2003 family

LayoutEventArgs.AffectedControl Property

Gets the child control affected by the change.

```
[Visual Basic]
Public ReadOnly Property AffectedControl As Control
[C#]
public Control AffectedControl {get;}
[C++]
public: __property Control* get_AffectedControl();
[JScript]
public function get AffectedControl() : Control;
```

Property Value

The child **Control** affected by the change.

Remarks

The **AffectedControl** property is set to a null reference (**Nothing** in Visual Basic) if no value was provided when the **PerformLayout** method was called.

Example

See related example in the **System.Windows.Forms.LayoutEventArgs** class topic.

Requirements

Platforms: Windows 98, Windows NT 4.0, Windows Millennium Edition, Windows 2000, Windows XP Home Edition, Windows XP Professional, Windows Server 2003 family

LayoutEventArgs.AffectedProperty Property

Gets the property affected by the change.

```
[Visual Basic]
Public ReadOnly Property AffectedProperty As String
[C#]
public string AffectedProperty {get;}
[C++]
public: __property String* get_AffectedProperty();
[JScript]
public function get AffectedProperty() : String;
```

Property Value

The property affected by the change.

Remarks

If a child control has been made visible since the last layout operation, the **Visible** property is affected. The **AffectedProperty** property is set to a null reference (**Nothing** in Visual Basic) if no value was provided when the **PerformLayout** method was called.

Example

See related example in the **System.Windows.Forms.LayoutEventArgs** class topic.

Requirements

Platforms: Windows 98, Windows NT 4.0, Windows Millennium Edition, Windows 2000, Windows XP Home Edition, Windows XP Professional, Windows Server 2003 family

LayoutEventHandler Delegate

Represents the method that will handle the **Layout** event of a **Control**.

[Visual Basic]

```
<Serializable>
Public Delegate Sub LayoutEventHandler( _
   ByVal sender As Object, _
   ByVal e As LayoutEventArgs _
)
```

[C#]

```
[Serializable]
public delegate void LayoutEventHandler(
   object sender,
   LayoutEventArgs e
);
```

[C++]

```
[Serializable]
public __gc __delegate void LayoutEventHandler(
   Object* sender,
   LayoutEventArgs* e
);
```

[JScript] In JScript, you can use the delegates in the .NET Framework, but you cannot define your own.

Parameters [Visual Basic, C#, C++]

The declaration of your event handler must have the same parameters as the **LayoutEventHandler** delegate declaration.

sender

The source of the event.

e

A **LayoutEventArgs** that contains the event data.

Remarks

When you create a **LayoutEventArgs** delegate, you identify the method that will handle the event. To associate the event with your event handler, add an instance of the delegate to the event. The event handler is called whenever the event occurs, unless you remove the delegate.

Example

See related example in the **System.Windows.Forms.LayoutEventArgs** class topic.

Requirements

Namespace: System.Windows.Forms

Platforms: Windows 98, Windows NT 4.0, Windows Millennium Edition, Windows 2000, Windows XP Home Edition, Windows XP Professional, Windows Server 2003 family

Assembly: System.Windows.Forms (in System.Windows.Forms.dll)

LeftRightAlignment Enumeration

Specifies whether an object or text is aligned to the left or right of a reference point.

[Visual Basic]
```
<Serializable>
<ComVisible(True)>
Public Enum LeftRightAlignment
```
[C#]
```
[Serializable]
[ComVisible(true)]
public enum LeftRightAlignment
```
[C++]
```
[Serializable]
[ComVisible(true)]
__value public enum LeftRightAlignment
```
[JScript]
```
public
   Serializable
   ComVisible(true)
enum LeftRightAlignment
```

Remarks

Use the members of this enumeration to set the values of the **DropDownAlign** and **UpDownAlign** properties.

Members

Member name	Description
Left	The object or text is aligned to the left of the reference point.
Right	The object or text is aligned to the right of the reference point.

Requirements

Namespace: System.Windows.Forms

Platforms: Windows 98, Windows NT 4.0, Windows Millennium Edition, Windows 2000, Windows XP Home Edition, Windows XP Professional, Windows Server 2003 family

Assembly: System.Windows.Forms (in System.Windows.Forms.dll)

LinkArea Structure

Represents an area within a **LinkLabel** control that represents a hyperlink within the control.

System.Object
  System.ValueType
    System.Windows.Forms.LinkArea

[Visual Basic]
```
<Serializable>
Public Structure LinkArea
```
[C#]
```
[Serializable]
public struct LinkArea
```
[C++]
```
[Serializable]
public __value struct LinkArea
```

[JScript] In JScript, you can use the structures in the .NET Framework, but you cannot define your own.

Thread Safety

Any public static (**Shared** in Visual Basic) members of this type are safe for multithreaded operations. Any instance members are not guaranteed to be thread safe.

Remarks

There are two ways to add a hyperlink to the text of a **LinkLabel** control. You can access the **Add** method of the **LinkLabel.LinkCollection** class through the **Links** property of the **LinkLabel** to add multiple hyperlinks to the control's text. If you only need to add a single hyperlink to the text of the control, you can use the **LinkArea** property of the **LinkLabel**. This property accepts a **LinkArea** object that defines the location of the hyperlink within the control's text. When a hyperlink is specified using the **LinkArea** property, the link area is then added to the **LinkLabel.LinkCollection** in the same manner as adding the link using the **Add** method of the **LinkLabel.LinkCollection**.

The **Length** property specifies the number of characters within the text of the **LinkLabel** to include in the link area. The **Start** property specifies the first character in the control text to include in the hyperlink. If you want to determine whether a specific **LinkArea** object is empty, you can use the **IsEmpty** property instead of checking the values of the **Start** and **Length** properties.

Example

[Visual Basic, C#, C++] The following example demonstrates using the **LinkLabel** class, with multiple **LinkArea** sections defined, to display a label on a form. The example demonstrates setting the **AutoSize**, **LinkBehavior**, **DisabledLinkColor**, **LinkColor**, and **VisitedLinkColor** properties to customize the look of the **LinkLabel**. The first **LinkArea** is specified using the **LinkLabel.LinkArea** property. Additional links are added to the **LinkLabel** using the **LinkCollection.Add** method. The example handles the **LinkClicked** event by starting the Web browser for hyperlinks, and displaying a **MessageBox** for other links.

[Visual Basic]
```
Imports System
Imports System.Drawing
Imports System.Windows.Forms

Public NotInheritable Class Form1
    Inherits System.Windows.Forms.Form

    Friend WithEvents LinkLabel1 As System.Windows.Forms.LinkLabel

    <System.STAThread()> _
    Public Shared Sub Main()
        System.Windows.Forms.Application.Run(New Form1)
    End Sub 'Main

    Public Sub New()
        MyBase.New()

        Me.LinkLabel1 = New System.Windows.Forms.LinkLabel

        ' Configure the LinkLabel's size and location. Specify that the
        ' size should be automatically determined by the content.
        Me.linkLabel1.Location = New System.Drawing.Point(34, 56)
        Me.linkLabel1.Size = New System.Drawing.Size(224, 16)
        Me.linkLabel1.AutoSize = True

        ' Configure the appearance.
        Me.linkLabel1.DisabledLinkColor = System.Drawing.Color.Silver
        Me.linkLabel1.VisitedLinkColor = System.Drawing.Color.Blue
        Me.linkLabel1.LinkBehavior = ↵
System.Windows.Forms.LinkBehavior.HoverUnderline
        Me.linkLabel1.LinkColor = System.Drawing.Color.Navy

        Me.linkLabel1.TabIndex = 0
        Me.linkLabel1.TabStop = True

        ' Identify what the first Link is.
        Me.linkLabel1.LinkArea = New ↵
System.Windows.Forms.LinkArea(0, 8)

        ' Identify that the first link is visited already.
        Me.linkLabel1.Links(0).Visited = true

        ' Set the Text property to a string.
        Me.linkLabel1.Text = "Register Online.  Visit Microsoft. ↵
 Visit MSN."

        ' Create new links using the Add method of the ↵
LinkCollection class.
        ' Underline the appropriate words in the LinkLabel's ↵
Text property.
        ' The words 'Register', 'Microsoft', and 'MSN' will
        ' all be underlined and behave as hyperlinks.

        ' First check that the Text property is long enough ↵
to accommodate
        ' the desired hyperlinked areas.  If it's not, ↵
don't add hyperlinks.
        If Me.LinkLabel1.Text.Length >= 45 Then
            Me.LinkLabel1.Links(0).LinkData = "Register"
            Me.LinkLabel1.Links.Add(24, 9, "www.microsoft.com")
            Me.LinkLabel1.Links.Add(42, 3, "www.msn.com")
        End If

        ' Set up how the form should be displayed and adds ↵
the controls to the form.
        Me.ClientSize = New System.Drawing.Size(292, 266)
        Me.Controls.AddRange(New System.Windows.Forms.Control() ↵
{Me.LinkLabel1})
        Me.Text = "Link Label Example"
    End Sub

    Private Sub linkLabel1_LinkClicked(ByVal sender As Object, _
            ByVal e As ↵
System.Windows.Forms.LinkLabelLinkClickedEventArgs) Handles ↵
LinkLabel1.LinkClicked

        ' Determine which link was clicked within the LinkLabel.
        Me.LinkLabel1.Links ↵
(LinkLabel1.Links.IndexOf(e.Link)).Visited = True

        ' Displays the appropriate link based on the value of ↵
 the LinkData property of the Link object.
        Dim target As String = CType(e.Link.LinkData, String)
```

```
        ' If the value looks like a URL, navigate to it.
        ' Otherwise, display it in a message box.
        If (Nothing <> target) And (target.StartsWith("www")) Then
            System.Diagnostics.Process.Start(target)
        Else
            MessageBox.Show(("Item clicked: " + target))
        End If

    End Sub

End Class
```

[C#]

```
using System;
using System.Drawing;
using System.Windows.Forms;

public class Form1 : System.Windows.Forms.Form
{
    private System.Windows.Forms.LinkLabel linkLabel1;

    [STAThread]
    static void Main()
    {
        Application.Run(new Form1());
    }

    public Form1()
    {
        // Create the LinkLabel.
        this.linkLabel1 = new System.Windows.Forms.LinkLabel();

        // Configure the LinkLabel's size and location. ↵
Specify that the
        // size should be automatically determined by the content.
        this.linkLabel1.Location = new System.Drawing.Point(34, 56);
        this.linkLabel1.Size = new System.Drawing.Size(224, 16);
        this.linkLabel1.AutoSize = true;

        // Configure the appearance.
        this.linkLabel1.DisabledLinkColor = ↵
System.Drawing.Color.Silver;
        this.linkLabel1.VisitedLinkColor = System.Drawing.Color.Blue;
        this.linkLabel1.LinkBehavior = ↵
System.Windows.Forms.LinkBehavior.HoverUnderline;
        this.linkLabel1.LinkColor = System.Drawing.Color.Navy;

        this.linkLabel1.TabIndex = 0;
        this.linkLabel1.TabStop = true;

        // Add an event handler to do something when the ↵
 links are clicked.
        this.linkLabel1.LinkClicked += new ↵
System.Windows.Forms.LinkLabelLinkClickedEventHandler(this.linkLabel1_Li
nkClicked);

        // Identify what the first Link is.
        this.linkLabel1.LinkArea = new ↵
System.Windows.Forms.LinkArea(0, 8);

        // Identify that the first link is visited already.
        this.linkLabel1.Links[0].Visited = true;

        // Set the Text property to a string.
        this.linkLabel1.Text = "Register Online. ↵
Visit Microsoft.  Visit MSN.";

        // Create new links using the Add method of the ↵
 LinkCollection class.
        // Underline the appropriate words in the ↵
 LinkLabel's Text property.
        // The words 'Register', 'Microsoft', and 'MSN' will
        // all be underlined and behave as hyperlinks.

        // First check that the Text property is long ↵
enough to accommodate
        // the desired hyperlinked areas.  If it's not, ↵
 don't add hyperlinks.
        if(this.linkLabel1.Text.Length >= 45)
        {
            this.linkLabel1.Links[0].LinkData = "Register";
            this.linkLabel1.Links.Add(24, 9, "www.microsoft.com");
            this.linkLabel1.Links.Add(42, 3, "www.msn.com");
        }

        // Set up how the form should be displayed and ↵
 add the controls to the form.
        this.ClientSize = new System.Drawing.Size(292, 266);
        this.Controls.AddRange(new ↵
System.Windows.Forms.Control[] {this.linkLabel1});
        this.Text = "Link Label Example";
    }

    private void linkLabel1_LinkClicked(object sender, ↵
System.Windows.Forms.LinkLabelLinkClickedEventArgs e)
    {
        // Determine which link was clicked within the LinkLabel.
        this.linkLabel1.Links ↵
 [linkLabel1.Links.IndexOf(e.Link)].Visited = true;

        // Display the appropriate link based on the value of the
        // LinkData property of the Link object.
        string target = e.Link.LinkData as string;

        // If the value looks like a URL, navigate to it.
        // Otherwise, display it in a message box.
        if(null != target && target.StartsWith("www"))
        {
            System.Diagnostics.Process.Start(target);
        }
        else
        {
            MessageBox.Show("Item clicked: " + target);
        }
    }
}
```

[C++]

```
#using <mscorlib.dll>
#using <System.dll>
#using <System.Windows.Forms.dll>
#using <System.Drawing.dll>

using namespace System;
using namespace System::Drawing;
using namespace System::Windows::Forms;

public __gc class Form1 : public System::Windows::Forms::Form {
private:
   System::Windows::Forms::LinkLabel*  linkLabel1;
public:
   Form1() {
      // Create the LinkLabel.
      this->linkLabel1 = new System::Windows::Forms::LinkLabel();

      // Configure the LinkLabel's size and location. Specify that the
      // size should be automatically determined by the content.
      this->linkLabel1->Location =  System::Drawing::Point(34, 56);
      this->linkLabel1->Size =  System::Drawing::Size(224, 16);
      this->linkLabel1->AutoSize = true;

      // Configure the appearance.
      this->linkLabel1->DisabledLinkColor = ↵
System::Drawing::Color::Silver;
      this->linkLabel1->VisitedLinkColor = ↵
System::Drawing::Color::Blue;
      this->linkLabel1->LinkBehavior = ↵
System::Windows::Forms::LinkBehavior::HoverUnderline;
      this->linkLabel1->LinkColor = System::Drawing::Color::Navy;

      this->linkLabel1->TabIndex = 0;
      this->linkLabel1->TabStop = true;
```

```
      // Add an event handler to do something when the ↵
 links are clicked.
      this->linkLabel1->LinkClicked += new ↵
System::Windows::Forms::LinkLabelLinkClickedEventHandler ↵
 (this, linkLabel1_LinkClicked);

      // Identify what the first Link is.
      this->linkLabel1->LinkArea = ↵
System::Windows::Forms::LinkArea(0, 8);

      // Identify that the first link is visited already.
      this->linkLabel1->Links->Item[0]->Visited = true;

      // Set the Text property to a String*.
      this->linkLabel1->Text = S"Register Online. ↵
Visit Microsoft.  Visit MSN.";

      // Create new links using the Add method of the ↵
LinkCollection class.
      // Underline the appropriate words in the ↵
LinkLabel's Text property.
      // The words 'Register', 'Microsoft', and 'MSN' will
      // all be underlined and behave as hyperlinks.

      // First check that the Text property is long enough ↵
to accommodate
      // the desired hyperlinked areas.  If it's not, don't ↵
 add hyperlinks.
      if (this->linkLabel1->Text->Length >= 45) {
         this->linkLabel1->Links->Item[0]->LinkData = S"Register";
         this->linkLabel1->Links->Add(24, 9, S"www.microsoft.com");
         this->linkLabel1->Links->Add(42, 3, S"www.msn.com");
      }

      // Set up how the form should be displayed and add the ↵
 controls to the form.
      this->ClientSize =  System::Drawing::Size(292, 266);

      System::Windows::Forms::Control* temp0 [] = {this->linkLabel1};

      this->Controls->AddRange(temp0);
      this->Text = S"Link Label Example";
   }

private:
   void linkLabel1_LinkClicked(Object* sender, ↵
System::Windows::Forms::LinkLabelLinkClickedEventArgs* e) {
      // Determine which link was clicked within the LinkLabel.
      this->linkLabel1->Links->Item[linkLabel1->Links-> ↵
IndexOf(e->Link)]->Visited = true;

      // Display the appropriate link based on the value of the
      // LinkData property of the Link Object*.
      String* target = dynamic_cast<String*>(e->Link->LinkData);

      // If the value looks like a URL, navigate to it.
      // Otherwise, display it in a message box.
      if (0 != target && target->StartsWith(S"www")) {
         System::Diagnostics::Process::Start(target);
      } else {
         MessageBox::Show(S"Item clicked: {0}", target);
      }
   }
};

[STAThread]
int main() {
   Application::Run(new Form1());
}
```

Requirements

Namespace: System.Windows.Forms

Platforms: Windows 98, Windows NT 4.0, Windows Millennium Edition, Windows 2000, Windows XP Home Edition, Windows XP Professional, Windows Server 2003 family

Assembly: System.Windows.Forms (in System.Windows.Forms.dll)

LinkArea Constructor

Initializes a new instance of the **LinkArea** class.

[Visual Basic]
```
Public Sub New( _
   ByVal start As Integer, _
   ByVal length As Integer _
)
```
[C#]
```
public LinkArea(
   int start,
   int length
);
```
[C++]
```
public: LinkArea(
   int start,
   int length
);
```
[JScript]
```
public function LinkArea(
   start : int,
   length : int
);
```

Parameters

start
: The zero-based starting location of the link area within the text of the **LinkLabel**.

length
: The number of characters, after the starting character, to include in the link area.

Requirements

Platforms: Windows 98, Windows NT 4.0, Windows Millennium Edition, Windows 2000, Windows XP Home Edition, Windows XP Professional, Windows Server 2003 family

LinkArea.IsEmpty Property

Gets a value indicating whether the **LinkArea** is empty.

[Visual Basic]
```
Public ReadOnly Property IsEmpty As Boolean
```
[C#]
```
public bool IsEmpty {get;}
```
[C++]
```
public: __property bool get_IsEmpty();
```
[JScript]
```
public function get IsEmpty() : Boolean;
```

Property Value

true if the specified start and length return an empty link area; otherwise, **false**.

Remarks

You can use this property to determine whether a valid link area has been specified in this object instead of evaluating the values of the **Length** and **Start** properties.

Requirements

Platforms: Windows 98, Windows NT 4.0, Windows Millennium Edition, Windows 2000, Windows XP Home Edition, Windows XP Professional, Windows Server 2003 family

LinkArea.Length Property

Gets or sets the number of characters in the link area.

[Visual Basic]
```
Public Property Length As Integer
```
[C#]
```
public int Length {get; set;}
```
[C++]
```
public: __property int get_Length();
public: __property void set_Length(int);
```
[JScript]
```
public function get Length() : int;
public function set Length(int);
```

Property Value

The number of characters, including spaces, in the link area.

Remarks

To specify text from the **LinkLabel** to display as a link, set the **Start** property to the location in the text to start creating the link. After the **Start** property is set, set the value of the **Length** property to the number of characters, including the character position specified in the **Start** property, that you want to make the link text. For example, if you want to make the first word of the text "The quick brown fox" a link, you set the **Start** property to zero (0) and the **Length** property to three (3).

Requirements

Platforms: Windows 98, Windows NT 4.0, Windows Millennium Edition, Windows 2000, Windows XP Home Edition, Windows XP Professional, Windows Server 2003 family

LinkArea.Start Property

Gets or sets the starting location of the link area within the text of the **LinkLabel**.

[Visual Basic]
```
Public Property Start As Integer
```
[C#]
```
public int Start {get; set;}
```
[C++]
```
public: __property int get_Start();
public: __property void set_Start(int);
```
[JScript]
```
public function get Start() : int;
public function set Start(int);
```

Property Value

The location within the text of the **LinkLabel** control where the link starts.

Remarks

To specify text from the **LinkLabel** to display as a link, set the **Start** property to the location in the text to start creating the link. After the **Start** property is set, set the value of the **Length** property to the number of characters, including the character position specified in the **Start** property, that you want to make the link text. For example, if you want to make the first word of the text "The quick brown fox" a link, you set the **Start** property to zero (0) and the **Length** property to three (3).

Requirements

Platforms: Windows 98, Windows NT 4.0, Windows Millennium Edition, Windows 2000, Windows XP Home Edition, Windows XP Professional, Windows Server 2003 family

LinkArea.Equals Method

This member overrides **ValueType.Equals**.

[Visual Basic]
```
Overrides Public Function Equals( _
   ByVal o As Object _
) As Boolean
```
[C#]
```
public override bool Equals(
   object o
);
```
[C++]
```
public: bool Equals(
   Object* o
);
```
[JScript]
```
public override function Equals(
   o : Object
) : Boolean;
```

Requirements

Platforms: Windows 98, Windows NT 4.0, Windows Millennium Edition, Windows 2000, Windows XP Home Edition, Windows XP Professional, Windows Server 2003 family

LinkArea.GetHashCode Method

This member overrides **ValueType.GetHashCode**.

[Visual Basic]
```
Overrides Public Function GetHashCode() As Integer
```
[C#]
```
public override int GetHashCode();
```
[C++]
```
public: int GetHashCode();
```
[JScript]
```
public override function GetHashCode() : int;
```

Requirements

Platforms: Windows 98, Windows NT 4.0, Windows Millennium Edition, Windows 2000, Windows XP Home Edition, Windows XP Professional, Windows Server 2003 family

LinkArea.LinkAreaConverter Class

Provides a type converter to convert **LinkArea.LinkAreaConverter** objects to and from various other representations.

System.Object
  System.ComponentModel.TypeConverter
    System.Windows.Forms.LinkArea.LinkAreaConverter

[Visual Basic]
```
Public Class LinkArea.LinkAreaConverter
   Inherits TypeConverter
```
[C#]
```
public class LinkArea.LinkAreaConverter : TypeConverter
```
[C++]
```
public __gc class LinkArea.LinkAreaConverter : public TypeConverter
```
[JScript]
```
public class LinkArea.LinkAreaConverter extends TypeConverter
```

Thread Safety

Any public static (**Shared** in Visual Basic) members of this type are safe for multithreaded operations. Any instance members are not guaranteed to be thread safe.

Remarks

> **Note** You should never create an instance of a **LinkArea.LinkAreaConverter**. Instead, call the **GetConverter** method of **TypeDescriptor**. For more information, see the examples in the **TypeConverter** base class.

Requirements

Namespace: System.Windows.Forms

Platforms: Windows 98, Windows NT 4.0, Windows Millennium Edition, Windows 2000, Windows XP Home Edition, Windows XP Professional, Windows Server 2003 family

Assembly: System.Windows.Forms (in System.Windows.Forms.dll)

LinkArea.LinkAreaConverter Constructor

Initializes a new instance of the **LinkArea.LinkAreaConverter** class.

[Visual Basic]
```
Public Sub New()
```
[C#]
```
public LinkArea.LinkAreaConverter();
```
[C++]
```
public: LinkAreaConverter();
```
[JScript]
```
public function LinkArea.LinkAreaConverter();
```

Remarks

The default constructor initializes any fields to their default values.

Requirements

Platforms: Windows 98, Windows NT 4.0, Windows Millennium Edition, Windows 2000, Windows XP Home Edition, Windows XP Professional, Windows Server 2003 family

LinkArea.LinkAreaConverter.CanConvertFrom Method

Overload List

This member supports the .NET Framework infrastructure and is not intended to be used directly from your code.

[Visual Basic] **Overloads Overrides Public Function CanConvertFrom(ITypeDescriptorContext, Type) As Boolean**

[C#] **public override bool CanConvertFrom(ITypeDescriptorContext, Type);**

[C++] **public: bool CanConvertFrom(ITypeDescriptorContext*, Type*);**

[JScript] **public override function CanConvertFrom(ITypeDescriptorContext, Type) : Boolean;**

Inherited from **TypeConverter**.

[Visual Basic] **Overloads Public Function CanConvertFrom(Type) As Boolean**

[C#] **public bool CanConvertFrom(Type);**

[C++] **public: bool CanConvertFrom(Type*);**

[JScript] **public function CanConvertFrom(Type) : Boolean;**

LinkArea.LinkAreaConverter.CanConvertFrom Method (ITypeDescriptorContext, Type)

This member overrides **TypeConverter.CanConvertFrom**.

[Visual Basic]
```
Overrides Overloads Public Function CanConvertFrom( _
   ByVal context As ITypeDescriptorContext, _
   ByVal sourceType As Type _
) As Boolean
```
[C#]
```
public override bool CanConvertFrom(
   ITypeDescriptorContext context,
   Type sourceType
);
```
[C++]
```
public: bool CanConvertFrom(
   ITypeDescriptorContext* context,
   Type* sourceType
);
```
[JScript]
```
public override function CanConvertFrom(
   context : ITypeDescriptorContext,
   sourceType : Type
) : Boolean;
```

Requirements

Platforms: Windows 98, Windows NT 4.0, Windows Millennium Edition, Windows 2000, Windows XP Home Edition, Windows XP Professional, Windows Server 2003 family

LinkArea.LinkAreaConverter.CanConvertTo Method

Overload List

This member supports the .NET Framework infrastructure and is not intended to be used directly from your code.

[Visual Basic] **Overloads Overrides Public Function CanConvertTo(ITypeDescriptorContext, Type) As Boolean**

[C#] **public override bool CanConvertTo(ITypeDescriptorContext, Type);**

[C++] **public: bool CanConvertTo(ITypeDescriptorContext*, Type*);**

[JScript] **public override function CanConvertTo(ITypeDescriptorContext, Type) : Boolean;**

Inherited from **TypeConverter**.

[Visual Basic] **Overloads Public Function CanConvertTo(Type) As Boolean**

[C#] **public bool CanConvertTo(Type);**

[C++] **public: bool CanConvertTo(Type*);**

[JScript] **public function CanConvertTo(Type) : Boolean;**

LinkArea.LinkAreaConverter.CanConvertTo Method (ITypeDescriptorContext, Type)

This member overrides **TypeConverter.CanConvertTo**.

```
[Visual Basic]
Overrides Overloads Public Function CanConvertTo( _
   ByVal context As ITypeDescriptorContext, _
   ByVal destinationType As Type _
) As Boolean
[C#]
public override bool CanConvertTo(
   ITypeDescriptorContext context,
   Type destinationType
);
[C++]
public: bool CanConvertTo(
   ITypeDescriptorContext* context,
   Type* destinationType
);
[JScript]
public override function CanConvertTo(
   context : ITypeDescriptorContext,
   destinationType : Type
) : Boolean;
```

Requirements

Platforms: Windows 98, Windows NT 4.0, Windows Millennium Edition, Windows 2000, Windows XP Home Edition, Windows XP Professional, Windows Server 2003 family

LinkArea.LinkAreaConverter.ConvertFrom Method

Overload List

This member supports the .NET Framework infrastructure and is not intended to be used directly from your code.

[Visual Basic] **Overloads Overrides Public Function ConvertFrom(ITypeDescriptorContext, CultureInfo, Object) As Object**

[C#] **public override object ConvertFrom(ITypeDescriptorContext, CultureInfo, object);**

[C++] **public: Object* ConvertFrom(ITypeDescriptorContext*, CultureInfo*, Object*);**

[JScript] **public override function ConvertFrom(ITypeDescriptorContext, CultureInfo, Object) : Object;**

Inherited from **TypeConverter**.

[Visual Basic] **Overloads Public Function ConvertFrom(Object) As Object**

[C#] **public object ConvertFrom(object);**

[C++] **public: Object* ConvertFrom(Object*);**

[JScript] **public function ConvertFrom(Object) : Object;**

LinkArea.LinkAreaConverter.ConvertFrom Method (ITypeDescriptorContext, CultureInfo, Object)

This member overrides **TypeConverter.ConvertFrom**.

```
[Visual Basic]
Overrides Overloads Public Function ConvertFrom( _
   ByVal context As ITypeDescriptorContext, _
   ByVal culture As CultureInfo, _
   ByVal value As Object _
) As Object
[C#]
public override object ConvertFrom(
   ITypeDescriptorContext context,
   CultureInfo culture,
   object value
);
[C++]
public: Object* ConvertFrom(
   ITypeDescriptorContext* context,
   CultureInfo* culture,
   Object* value
);
[JScript]
public override function ConvertFrom(
   context : ITypeDescriptorContext,
   culture : CultureInfo,
   value : Object
) : Object;
```

Requirements

Platforms: Windows 98, Windows NT 4.0, Windows Millennium Edition, Windows 2000, Windows XP Home Edition, Windows XP Professional, Windows Server 2003 family

LinkArea.LinkAreaConverter.ConvertTo Method

Overload List

This member supports the .NET Framework infrastructure and is not intended to be used directly from your code.

[Visual Basic] **Overloads Overrides Public Function ConvertTo(ITypeDescriptorContext, CultureInfo, Object, Type) As Object**

[C#] **public override object ConvertTo(ITypeDescriptorContext, CultureInfo, object, Type);**

[C++] **public: Object* ConvertTo(ITypeDescriptorContext*, CultureInfo*, Object*, Type*);**

[JScript] **public override function ConvertTo(ITypeDescriptorContext, CultureInfo, Object, Type) : Object;**

Inherited from **TypeConverter**.

[Visual Basic] **Overloads Public Function ConvertTo(Object, Type) As Object**

[C#] **public object ConvertTo(object, Type);**

[C++] **public: Object* ConvertTo(Object*, Type*);**

[JScript] **public function ConvertTo(Object, Type) : Object;**

LinkArea.LinkAreaConverter.ConvertTo Method (ITypeDescriptorContext, CultureInfo, Object, Type)

This member overrides **TypeConverter.ConvertTo**.

```
[Visual Basic]
Overrides Overloads Public Function ConvertTo( _
   ByVal context As ITypeDescriptorContext, _
   ByVal culture As CultureInfo, _
   ByVal value As Object, _
   ByVal destinationType As Type _
) As Object
[C#]
public override object ConvertTo(
   ITypeDescriptorContext context,
   CultureInfo culture,
   object value,
   Type destinationType
);
[C++]
public: Object* ConvertTo(
   ITypeDescriptorContext* context,
   CultureInfo* culture,
   Object* value,
   Type* destinationType
);
[JScript]
public override function ConvertTo(
   context : ITypeDescriptorContext,
   culture : CultureInfo,
   value : Object,
   destinationType : Type
) : Object;
```

Requirements

Platforms: Windows 98, Windows NT 4.0, Windows Millennium Edition, Windows 2000, Windows XP Home Edition, Windows XP Professional, Windows Server 2003 family

LinkArea.LinkAreaConverter.CreateInstance Method

Overload List

This member supports the .NET Framework infrastructure and is not intended to be used directly from your code.

[Visual Basic] **Overloads Overrides Public Function CreateInstance(ITypeDescriptorContext, IDictionary) As Object**

[C#] **public override object CreateInstance(ITypeDescriptorContext, IDictionary);**

[C++] **public: Object* CreateInstance(ITypeDescriptorContext*, IDictionary*);**

[JScript] **public override function CreateInstance(ITypeDescriptorContext, IDictionary) : Object;**

Inherited from **TypeConverter**.

[Visual Basic] **Overloads Public Function CreateInstance(IDictionary) As Object**

[C#] **public object CreateInstance(IDictionary);**

[C++] **public: Object* CreateInstance(IDictionary*);**

[JScript] **public function CreateInstance(IDictionary) : Object;**

LinkArea.LinkAreaConverter.CreateInstance Method (ITypeDescriptorContext, IDictionary)

This member overrides **TypeConverter.CreateInstance**.

```
[Visual Basic]
Overrides Overloads Public Function CreateInstance( _
   ByVal context As ITypeDescriptorContext, _
   ByVal propertyValues As IDictionary _
) As Object
[C#]
public override object CreateInstance(
   ITypeDescriptorContext context,
   IDictionary propertyValues
);
[C++]
public: Object* CreateInstance(
   ITypeDescriptorContext* context,
   IDictionary* propertyValues
);
[JScript]
public override function CreateInstance(
   context : ITypeDescriptorContext,
   propertyValues : IDictionary
) : Object;
```

Requirements

Platforms: Windows 98, Windows NT 4.0, Windows Millennium Edition, Windows 2000, Windows XP Home Edition, Windows XP Professional, Windows Server 2003 family

LinkArea.LinkAreaConverter.GetCreateInstance Supported Method

Overload List

This member supports the .NET Framework infrastructure and is not intended to be used directly from your code.

[Visual Basic] **Overloads Overrides Public Function GetCreateInstanceSupported(ITypeDescriptorContext) As Boolean**

[C#] **public override bool GetCreateInstance-Supported(ITypeDescriptorContext);**

[C++] **public: bool GetCreateInstance-Supported(ITypeDescriptorContext*);**

[JScript] **public override function GetCreateInstance-Supported(ITypeDescriptorContext) : Boolean;**

Inherited from **TypeConverter**.

[Visual Basic] **Overloads Public Function GetCreateInstance-Supported() As Boolean**

[C#] **public bool GetCreateInstanceSupported();**

[C++] **public: bool GetCreateInstanceSupported();**

[JScript] **public function GetCreateInstanceSupported() : Boolean;**

LinkArea.LinkAreaConverter.GetCreateInstanceSupported Method (ITypeDescriptorContext)

This member overrides **TypeConverter.GetCreateInstanceSupported**.

```
[Visual Basic]
Overrides Overloads Public Function GetCreateInstanceSupported( _
   ByVal context As ITypeDescriptorContext _
) As Boolean
[C#]
public override bool GetCreateInstanceSupported(
   ITypeDescriptorContext context
);
[C++]
public: bool GetCreateInstanceSupported(
   ITypeDescriptorContext* context
);
[JScript]
public override function GetCreateInstanceSupported(
   context : ITypeDescriptorContext
) : Boolean;
```

Requirements

Platforms: Windows 98, Windows NT 4.0, Windows Millennium Edition, Windows 2000, Windows XP Home Edition, Windows XP Professional, Windows Server 2003 family

LinkArea.LinkAreaConverter.GetProperties Method

Overload List

This member supports the .NET Framework infrastructure and is not intended to be used directly from your code.

[Visual Basic] **Overloads Overrides Public Function Get-Properties(ITypeDescriptorContext, Object, Attribute()) As PropertyDescriptorCollection**

[C#] **public override PropertyDescriptorCollection Get-Properties(ITypeDescriptorContext, object, Attribute[]);**

[C++] **public: PropertyDescriptorCollection* Get-Properties(ITypeDescriptorContext*, Object*, Attribute[]);**

[JScript] **public override function GetProperties(IType-DescriptorContext, Object, Attribute[]) : PropertyDescriptorCollection;**

Inherited from **TypeConverter**.

[Visual Basic] **Overloads Public Function GetProperties(Object) As PropertyDescriptorCollection**

[C#] **public PropertyDescriptorCollection GetProperties(object);**

[C++] **public: PropertyDescriptorCollection* GetProperties(Object*);**

[JScript] **public function GetProperties(Object) : PropertyDescriptorCollection;**

Inherited from **TypeConverter**.

[Visual Basic] **Overloads Public Function Get-Properties(ITypeDescriptorContext, Object) As PropertyDescriptorCollection**

[C#] **public PropertyDescriptorCollection GetProperties(ITypeDescriptorContext, object);**

[C++] **public: PropertyDescriptorCollection* GetProperties(ITypeDescriptorContext*, Object*);**

[JScript] **public function GetProperties(IType-DescriptorContext, Object) : PropertyDescriptorCollection;**

LinkArea.LinkAreaConverter.GetProperties Method (ITypeDescriptorContext, Object, Attribute[])

This member overrides **TypeConverter.GetProperties**.

```
[Visual Basic]
Overrides Overloads Public Function GetProperties( _
   ByVal context As ITypeDescriptorContext, _
   ByVal value As Object, _
   ByVal attributes() As Attribute _
) As PropertyDescriptorCollection
[C#]
public override PropertyDescriptorCollection GetProperties(
   ITypeDescriptorContext context,
   object value,
   Attribute[] attributes
);
[C++]
public: PropertyDescriptorCollection* GetProperties(
   ITypeDescriptorContext* context,
   Object* value,
   Attribute* attributes[]
);
```

```
[JScript]
public override function GetProperties(
   context : ITypeDescriptorContext,
   value : Object,
   attributes : Attribute[]
) : PropertyDescriptorCollection;
```

Requirements

Platforms: Windows 98, Windows NT 4.0, Windows Millennium Edition, Windows 2000, Windows XP Home Edition, Windows XP Professional, Windows Server 2003 family

LinkArea.LinkAreaConverter.GetProperties-Supported Method

Overload List

This member supports the .NET Framework infrastructure and is not intended to be used directly from your code.

[Visual Basic] **Overloads Overrides Public Function Get-PropertiesSupported(ITypeDescriptorContext) As Boolean**

[C#] **public override bool GetProperties-Supported(ITypeDescriptorContext);**

[C++] **public: bool GetProperties-Supported(ITypeDescriptorContext*);**

[JScript] **public override function GetProperties-Supported(ITypeDescriptorContext) : Boolean;**

Inherited from **TypeConverter**.

[Visual Basic] **Overloads Public Function GetPropertiesSupported() As Boolean**

[C#] **public bool GetPropertiesSupported();**

[C++] **public: bool GetPropertiesSupported();**

[JScript] **public function GetPropertiesSupported() : Boolean;**

LinkArea.LinkAreaConverter.GetPropertiesSupported Method (ITypeDescriptorContext)

This member overrides **TypeConverter.GetPropertiesSupported**.

```
[Visual Basic]
Overrides Overloads Public Function GetPropertiesSupported( _
   ByVal context As ITypeDescriptorContext _
) As Boolean
[C#]
public override bool GetPropertiesSupported(
   ITypeDescriptorContext context
);
[C++]
public: bool GetPropertiesSupported(
   ITypeDescriptorContext* context
);
[JScript]
public override function GetPropertiesSupported(
   context : ITypeDescriptorContext
) : Boolean;
```

Requirements

Platforms: Windows 98, Windows NT 4.0, Windows Millennium Edition, Windows 2000, Windows XP Home Edition, Windows XP Professional, Windows Server 2003 family

LinkBehavior Enumeration

Specifies the behaviors of a link in a **LinkLabel**.

[Visual Basic]
```
<Serializable>
Public Enum LinkBehavior
```
[C#]
```
[Serializable]
public enum LinkBehavior
```
[C++]
```
[Serializable]
__value public enum LinkBehavior
```
[JScript]
```
public
   Serializable
enum LinkBehavior
```

Remarks

Use the members of this enumeration to set the value of the **LinkBehavior** property of the **LinkLabel**.

Members

Member name	Description
AlwaysUnderline	The link always displays with underlined text.
HoverUnderline	The link displays underlined text only when the mouse is hovered over the link text.
NeverUnderline	The link text is never underlined. The link can still be distinguished from other text by use of the **LinkColor** property of the **LinkLabel** control.
SystemDefault	The behavior of this setting depends on the options set using the Internet Options dialog box in Control Panel or Internet Explorer.

Requirements

Namespace: System.Windows.Forms

Platforms: Windows 98, Windows NT 4.0, Windows Millennium Edition, Windows 2000, Windows XP Home Edition, Windows XP Professional, Windows Server 2003 family

Assembly: System.Windows.Forms (in System.Windows.Forms.dll)

LinkClickedEventArgs Class

Provides data for the **LinkClicked** event.

System.Object
  System.EventArgs
    System.Windows.Forms.LinkClickedEventArgs

```
[Visual Basic]
<ComVisible(True)>
Public Class LinkClickedEventArgs
   Inherits EventArgs
[C#]
[ComVisible(true)]
public class LinkClickedEventArgs : EventArgs
[C++]
[ComVisible(true)]
public __gc class LinkClickedEventArgs : public EventArgs
[JScript]
public
   ComVisible(true)
class LinkClickedEventArgs extends EventArgs
```

Thread Safety

Any public static (**Shared** in Visual Basic) members of this type are safe for multithreaded operations. Any instance members are not guaranteed to be thread safe.

Remarks

A **LinkClickedEventArgs** specifies the text of the link that is clicked in the **RichTextBox**.

Requirements

Namespace: System.Windows.Forms

Platforms: Windows 98, Windows NT 4.0, Windows Millennium Edition, Windows 2000, Windows XP Home Edition, Windows XP Professional, Windows Server 2003 family

Assembly: System.Windows.Forms (in System.Windows.Forms.dll)

LinkClickedEventArgs Constructor

Initializes a new instance of the **LinkClickedEventArgs** class.

```
[Visual Basic]
Public Sub New( _
   ByVal linkText As String _
)
[C#]
public LinkClickedEventArgs(
   string linkText
);
[C++]
public: LinkClickedEventArgs(
   String* linkText
);
[JScript]
public function LinkClickedEventArgs(
   linkText : String
);
```

Parameters

linkText
  The text of the link that is clicked in the **RichTextBox** control.

Remarks

The text specified in the *linkText* parameter can be a URL, file path, or other data that you want specified for the link being clicked.

Requirements

Platforms: Windows 98, Windows NT 4.0, Windows Millennium Edition, Windows 2000, Windows XP Home Edition, Windows XP Professional, Windows Server 2003 family

LinkClickedEventArgs.LinkText Property

Gets the text of the link being clicked.

```
[Visual Basic]
Public ReadOnly Property LinkText As String
[C#]
public string LinkText {get;}
[C++]
public: __property String* get_LinkText();
[JScript]
public function get LinkText() : String;
```

Property Value

The text of the link that is clicked in the **RichTextBox** control.

Remarks

The text returned by this property could be a file, URL, or other data specified by the link that is clicked.

Requirements

Platforms: Windows 98, Windows NT 4.0, Windows Millennium Edition, Windows 2000, Windows XP Home Edition, Windows XP Professional, Windows Server 2003 family

LinkClickedEventHandler Delegate

Represents the method that will handle the **LinkClicked** event of a **RichTextBox**.

[Visual Basic]
```
<Serializable>
Public Delegate Sub LinkClickedEventHandler( _
   ByVal sender As Object, _
   ByVal e As LinkClickedEventArgs _
)
```
[C#]
```
[Serializable]
public delegate void LinkClickedEventHandler(
   object sender,
   LinkClickedEventArgs e
);
```
[C++]
```
[Serializable]
public __gc __delegate void LinkClickedEventHandler(
   Object* sender,
   LinkClickedEventArgs* e
);
```

[JScript] In JScript, you can use the delegates in the .NET Framework, but you cannot define your own.

Parameters [Visual Basic, C#, C++]

The declaration of your event handler must have the same parameters as the **LinkClickedEventHandler** delegate declaration.

sender

The source of the object.

e

The **LinkClickedEventArgs** that contains the event data.

Remarks

When you create a **LinkClickedEventHandler** delegate, you identify the method that will handle the event. To associate the event with your event handler, add an instance of the delegate to the event. The event handler is called whenever the event occurs, unless you remove the delegate.

Requirements

Namespace: System.Windows.Forms

Platforms: Windows 98, Windows NT 4.0, Windows Millennium Edition, Windows 2000, Windows XP Home Edition, Windows XP Professional, Windows Server 2003 family

Assembly: System.Windows.Forms (in System.Windows.Forms.dll)

LinkLabel Class

Represents a Windows label control that can display hyperlinks.

System.Object
  System.MarshalByRefObject
    System.ComponentModel.Component
      System.Windows.Forms.Control
        System.Windows.Forms.Label
          System.Windows.Forms.LinkLabel

[Visual Basic]
```
Public Class LinkLabel
   Inherits Label
   Implements IButtonControl
```
[C#]
```
public class LinkLabel : Label, IButtonControl
```
[C++]
```
public __gc class LinkLabel : public Label, IButtonControl
```
[JScript]
```
public class LinkLabel extends Label implements IButtonControl
```

Thread Safety

Any public static (**Shared** in Visual Basic) members of this type are safe for multithreaded operations. Any instance members are not guaranteed to be thread safe.

Remarks

The **LinkLabel** control is similar to a **Label** control with the exception that it can display a hyperlink. Multiple hyperlinks can be specified in the text of the control. Each hyperlink can perform a different task within an application. For example, you can use a hyperlink to display a Web site in Microsoft Internet Explorer or to load a log file associated with an application.

Each hyperlink displayed in the **LinkLabel** control is an instance of the **LinkLabel.Link** class. The **LinkLabel.Link** class defines display information, state, and location of the hyperlink. In addition, the **LinkData** property of the **LinkLabel.Link** class enables you to associate information, such as a URL to display, with the hyperlink. When a user clicks a hyperlink within the control, the **LinkClicked** event is raised, and the **LinkLabel.Link** object representing the hyperlink that was clicked is passed as part of the **LinkLabelLinkClickedEventArgs** object that is passed as a parameter to the event handler. You can use this object to obtain the **LinkLabel.Link** object associated with the hyperlink that was clicked by the user. All hyperlinks contained within the **LinkLabel** control are stored in the **LinkLabel.LinkCollection** class instance for the control.

There are two ways to add a hyperlink to the **LinkLabel** control. The quickest way is to specify a **LinkArea** object and assign it to the **LinkArea** property. This enables you to specify a single hyperlink within the text of the control. To add multiple hyperlinks, you can use the **Add** method of the **LinkLabel.LinkCollection** class by accessing the collection through the **Links** property.

When a **LinkLabel** control is created, a default hyperlink that contains all the text within the **LinkLabel** control is added to the **LinkLabel.LinkCollection**. You can override this default link by specifying a new link area with the **LinkArea** property, or specify a link using the **Add** method of the **LinkLabel.LinkCollection**. You can also remove the default hyperlink by using the **Remove** method of the **LinkLabel.LinkCollection** class.

The **LinkLabel** provides a number of properties that enable you to define the display appearance of hyperlinks in the control. The **ActiveLinkColor**, **DisabledLinkColor**, **LinkColor**, and **VisitedLinkColor** properties define the colors used when displaying a hyperlink in various states. The **LinkBehavior** property defines the display of the underline that is associated with a hyperlink.

Example

[Visual Basic, C#, C++] The following example demonstrates using the **LinkLabel** class, with multiple **LinkArea** sections defined, to display a label on a form. The example demonstrates setting the **AutoSize**, **LinkBehavior**, **DisabledLinkColor**, **LinkColor**, and **VisitedLinkColor** properties to customize the look of the **LinkLabel**. The first **LinkArea** is specified using the **LinkLabel.LinkArea** property. Additional links are added to the **LinkLabel** using the **LinkCollection.Add** method. The example handles the **LinkClicked** event by starting the Web browser for hyperlinks, and displaying a **MessageBox** for other links.

[Visual Basic]
```
Imports System
Imports System.Drawing
Imports System.Windows.Forms

Public NotInheritable Class Form1
    Inherits System.Windows.Forms.Form

    Friend WithEvents LinkLabel1 As System.Windows.Forms.LinkLabel

    <System.STAThread()> _
    Public Shared Sub Main()
        System.Windows.Forms.Application.Run(New Form1)
    End Sub 'Main

    Public Sub New()
        MyBase.New()

        Me.LinkLabel1 = New System.Windows.Forms.LinkLabel

        ' Configure the LinkLabel's size and location. Specify that the
        ' size should be automatically determined by the content.
        Me.linkLabel1.Location = New System.Drawing.Point(34, 56)
        Me.linkLabel1.Size = New System.Drawing.Size(224, 16)
        Me.linkLabel1.AutoSize = True

        ' Configure the appearance.
        Me.linkLabel1.DisabledLinkColor = System.Drawing.Color.Silver
        Me.linkLabel1.VisitedLinkColor = System.Drawing.Color.Blue
        Me.linkLabel1.LinkBehavior =                                      ↵
System.Windows.Forms.LinkBehavior.HoverUnderline
        Me.linkLabel1.LinkColor = System.Drawing.Color.Navy

        Me.linkLabel1.TabIndex = 0
        Me.linkLabel1.TabStop = True

        ' Identify what the first Link is.
        Me.linkLabel1.LinkArea = New                                      ↵
System.Windows.Forms.LinkArea(0, 8)

        ' Identify that the first link is visited already.
        Me.linkLabel1.Links(0).Visited = true

        ' Set the Text property to a string.
        Me.linkLabel1.Text = "Register Online.  Visit Microsoft.         ↵
Visit MSN."

        ' Create new links using the Add method of the                    ↵
LinkCollection class.
        ' Underline the appropriate words in the LinkLabel's              ↵
Text property.
        ' The words 'Register', 'Microsoft', and 'MSN' will
        ' all be underlined and behave as hyperlinks.

        ' First check that the Text property is long enough               ↵
to accommodate
```

```
        ' the desired hyperlinked areas.  If it's not, don't ↵
 add hyperlinks.
        If Me.LinkLabel1.Text.Length >= 45 Then
            Me.LinkLabel1.Links(0).LinkData = "Register"
            Me.LinkLabel1.Links.Add(24, 9, "www.microsoft.com")
            Me.LinkLabel1.Links.Add(42, 3, "www.msn.com")
        End If

        ' Set up how the form should be displayed and adds the ↵
 controls to the form.
        Me.ClientSize = New System.Drawing.Size(292, 266)
        Me.Controls.AddRange(New ↵
System.Windows.Forms.Control() {Me.LinkLabel1})
        Me.Text = "Link Label Example"
    End Sub

    Private Sub linkLabel1_LinkClicked(ByVal sender As Object, _
                ByVal e As ↵
System.Windows.Forms.LinkLabelLinkClickedEventArgs) ↵
Handles LinkLabel1.LinkClicked

        ' Determine which link was clicked within the LinkLabel.
        Me.LinkLabel1.Links ↵
(LinkLabel1.Links.IndexOf(e.Link)).Visited = True

        ' Displays the appropriate link based on the value ↵
 of the LinkData property of the Link object.
        Dim target As String = CType(e.Link.LinkData, String)

        ' If the value looks like a URL, navigate to it.
        ' Otherwise, display it in a message box.
        If (Nothing <> target) And (target.StartsWith("www")) ↵
 Then
            System.Diagnostics.Process.Start(target)
        Else
            MessageBox.Show(("Item clicked: " + target))
        End If

    End Sub

End Class
```

[C#]

```
using System;
using System.Drawing;
using System.Windows.Forms;

public class Form1 : System.Windows.Forms.Form
{
    private System.Windows.Forms.LinkLabel linkLabel1;

    [STAThread]
    static void Main()
    {
        Application.Run(new Form1());
    }

    public Form1()
    {
        // Create the LinkLabel.
        this.linkLabel1 = new System.Windows.Forms.LinkLabel();

        // Configure the LinkLabel's size and location. ↵
 Specify that the
        // size should be automatically determined by the content.
        this.linkLabel1.Location = new System.Drawing.Point(34, 56);
        this.linkLabel1.Size = new System.Drawing.Size(224, 16);
        this.linkLabel1.AutoSize = true;

        // Configure the appearance.
        this.linkLabel1.DisabledLinkColor = ↵
System.Drawing.Color.Silver;
        this.linkLabel1.VisitedLinkColor = System.Drawing.Color.Blue;
        this.linkLabel1.LinkBehavior = ↵
System.Windows.Forms.LinkBehavior.HoverUnderline;
        this.linkLabel1.LinkColor = System.Drawing.Color.Navy;

        this.linkLabel1.TabIndex = 0;
        this.linkLabel1.TabStop = true;

        // Add an event handler to do something when the ↵
 links are clicked.
        this.linkLabel1.LinkClicked += new ↵
System.Windows.Forms.LinkLabelLinkClickedEventHandler(this.linkLabel1_Li
nkClicked);

        // Identify what the first Link is.
        this.linkLabel1.LinkArea = new ↵
System.Windows.Forms.LinkArea(0, 8);

        // Identify that the first link is visited already.
        this.linkLabel1.Links[0].Visited = true;

        // Set the Text property to a string.
        this.linkLabel1.Text = "Register Online. ↵
 Visit Microsoft.  Visit MSN.";

        // Create new links using the Add method of the ↵
 LinkCollection class.
        // Underline the appropriate words in the ↵
LinkLabel's Text property.
        // The words 'Register', 'Microsoft', and 'MSN' will
        // all be underlined and behave as hyperlinks.

        // First check that the Text property is long ↵
 enough to accommodate
        // the desired hyperlinked areas.  If it's not, ↵
don't add hyperlinks.
        if(this.linkLabel1.Text.Length >= 45)
        {
            this.linkLabel1.Links[0].LinkData = "Register";
            this.linkLabel1.Links.Add(24, 9, "www.microsoft.com");
            this.linkLabel1.Links.Add(42, 3, "www.msn.com");
        }

        // Set up how the form should be displayed and ↵
add the controls to the form.
        this.ClientSize = new System.Drawing.Size(292, 266);
        this.Controls.AddRange(new ↵
System.Windows.Forms.Control[] {this.linkLabel1});
        this.Text = "Link Label Example";
    }

    private void linkLabel1_LinkClicked(object sender, ↵
System.Windows.Forms.LinkLabelLinkClickedEventArgs e)
    {
        // Determine which link was clicked within the LinkLabel.
        this.linkLabel1.Links ↵
[linkLabel1.Links.IndexOf(e.Link)].Visited = true;

        // Display the appropriate link based on the value of the
        // LinkData property of the Link object.
        string target = e.Link.LinkData as string;

        // If the value looks like a URL, navigate to it.
        // Otherwise, display it in a message box.
        if(null != target && target.StartsWith("www"))
        {
            System.Diagnostics.Process.Start(target);
        }
        else
        {
            MessageBox.Show("Item clicked: " + target);
        }
    }
}
```

[C++]

```
#using <mscorlib.dll>
#using <System.dll>
#using <System.Windows.Forms.dll>
#using <System.Drawing.dll>
```

```
using namespace System;
using namespace System::Drawing;
using namespace System::Windows::Forms;

public __gc class Form1 : public System::Windows::Forms::Form {
private:
   System::Windows::Forms::LinkLabel*  linkLabel1;
public:
   Form1() {
      // Create the LinkLabel.
      this->linkLabel1 = new System::Windows::Forms::LinkLabel();

      // Configure the LinkLabel's size and location. Specify that the
      // size should be automatically determined by the content.
      this->linkLabel1->Location =  System::Drawing::Point(34, 56);
      this->linkLabel1->Size =  System::Drawing::Size(224, 16);
      this->linkLabel1->AutoSize = true;

      // Configure the appearance.
      this->linkLabel1->DisabledLinkColor = ↵
System::Drawing::Color::Silver;
      this->linkLabel1->VisitedLinkColor = ↵
System::Drawing::Color::Blue;
      this->linkLabel1->LinkBehavior = ↵
System::Windows::Forms::LinkBehavior::HoverUnderline;
      this->linkLabel1->LinkColor = System::Drawing::Color::Navy;

      this->linkLabel1->TabIndex = 0;
      this->linkLabel1->TabStop = true;

      // Add an event handler to do something when the ↵
links are clicked.
      this->linkLabel1->LinkClicked += new ↵
System::Windows::Forms::LinkLabelLinkClickedEventHandler(this, ↵
linkLabel1_LinkClicked);

      // Identify what the first Link is.
      this->linkLabel1->LinkArea = ↵
System::Windows::Forms::LinkArea(0, 8);

      // Identify that the first link is visited already.
      this->linkLabel1->Links->Item[0]->Visited = true;

      // Set the Text property to a String*.
      this->linkLabel1->Text = S"Register Online. ↵
Visit Microsoft.  Visit MSN.";

      // Create new links using the Add method of ↵
the LinkCollection class.
      // Underline the appropriate words in the LinkLabel's ↵
Text property.
      // The words 'Register', 'Microsoft', and 'MSN' will
      // all be underlined and behave as hyperlinks.

      // First check that the Text property is long enough ↵
to accommodate
      // the desired hyperlinked areas.  If it's not, don't ↵
add hyperlinks.
      if (this->linkLabel1->Text->Length >= 45) {
         this->linkLabel1->Links->Item[0]->LinkData = S"Register";
         this->linkLabel1->Links->Add(24, 9, S"www.microsoft.com");
         this->linkLabel1->Links->Add(42, 3, S"www.msn.com");
      }

      // Set up how the form should be displayed and add ↵
the controls to the form.
      this->ClientSize =  System::Drawing::Size(292, 266);

      System::Windows::Forms::Control* temp0 [] = {this->linkLabel1};

      this->Controls->AddRange(temp0);
      this->Text = S"Link Label Example";
   }

private:
   void linkLabel1_LinkClicked(Object* sender, ↵
System::Windows::Forms::LinkLabelLinkClickedEventArgs* e) {
      // Determine which link was clicked within the LinkLabel.
      this->linkLabel1->Links->Item[linkLabel1->Links-> ↵
IndexOf(e->Link)]->Visited = true;

      // Display the appropriate link based on the value of the
      // LinkData property of the Link Object*.
      String* target = dynamic_cast<String*>(e->Link->LinkData);

      // If the value looks like a URL, navigate to it.
      // Otherwise, display it in a message box.
      if (0 != target && target->StartsWith(S"www")) {
         System::Diagnostics::Process::Start(target);
      } else {
         MessageBox::Show(S"Item clicked: {0}", target);
      }
   }
};

[STAThread]
int main() {
   Application::Run(new Form1());
}
```

Requirements

Namespace: System.Windows.Forms

Platforms: Windows 98, Windows NT 4.0, Windows Millennium Edition, Windows 2000, Windows XP Home Edition, Windows XP Professional, Windows Server 2003 family

Assembly: System.Windows.Forms (in System.Windows.Forms.dll)

LinkLabel Constructor

Initializes a new default instance of the **LinkLabel** class.

```
[Visual Basic]
Public Sub New()
[C#]
public LinkLabel();
[C++]
public: LinkLabel();
[JScript]
public function LinkLabel();
```

Example

See related example in the **System.Windows.Forms.LinkLabel** class topic.

Requirements

Platforms: Windows 98, Windows NT 4.0, Windows Millennium Edition, Windows 2000, Windows XP Home Edition, Windows XP Professional, Windows Server 2003 family

LinkLabel.ActiveLinkColor Property

Gets or sets the color used to display an active link.

```
[Visual Basic]
Public Property ActiveLinkColor As Color
[C#]
public Color ActiveLinkColor {get; set;}
[C++]
public: __property Color get_ActiveLinkColor();
public: __property void set_ActiveLinkColor(Color);
```

```
[JScript]
public function get ActiveLinkColor() : Color;
public function set ActiveLinkColor(Color);
```

Property Value

A **Color** that represents the color to display an active link. The default color is specified by the system, typically this color is **Color.Red**.

Remarks

An active link is a link that is in the process of being clicked. This is similar to the depressed state of a **Button** control. You can use this property to specify the color that the link is displayed in when the link is in the process of being clicked.

There are a number of colors associated with a link. The **LinkColor** specifies the color of all links displayed in the **LinkLabel** control. The **VisitedLinkColor** property enables you to specify the color of a link after it has been visited by the user. When a link is disabled, the **DisabledLinkColor** is used to display the link in a disabled state.

> **Note** When setting this property, ensure that the color you are setting the property to does not conflict with the color of the control's background or the text does not display properly. For example, if the background color of the control is **Color.Red** and this property is set to **Color.Red**, the text is not shown properly when the link is in the process of being clicked.

Requirements

Platforms: Windows 98, Windows NT 4.0, Windows Millennium Edition, Windows 2000, Windows XP Home Edition, Windows XP Professional, Windows Server 2003 family

LinkLabel.DisabledLinkColor Property

Gets or sets the color used when displaying a disabled link.

```
[Visual Basic]
Public Property DisabledLinkColor As Color
[C#]
public Color DisabledLinkColor {get; set;}
[C++]
public: __property Color get_DisabledLinkColor();
public: __property void set_DisabledLinkColor(Color);
[JScript]
public function get DisabledLinkColor() : Color;
public function set DisabledLinkColor(Color);
```

Property Value

A **Color** that represents the color when displaying a disabled link.

Remarks

This property enables you to specify the color for links that are disabled in the **LinkLabel**. Disabled links do not cause the **LinkClicked** event to be raised.

There are a number of colors associated with a link. All links in the **LinkLabel** are initially displayed with the color defined in the **LinkColor** property. The **ActiveLinkColor** property enables you to specify the color of the link when it is in the process of being clicked. The **VisitedLinkColor** property enables you to specify the color of a link after it has been visited by the user.

> **Note** When setting this property, ensure that the color you are setting the property to does not conflict with the color of the control's background or the text does not display properly. For example, if the background color of the control is **Color.Red** and this property is set to **Color.Red**, the text is not shown properly when the link is disabled.

Example

See related example in the **System.Windows.Forms.LinkLabel** class topic.

Requirements

Platforms: Windows 98, Windows NT 4.0, Windows Millennium Edition, Windows 2000, Windows XP Home Edition, Windows XP Professional, Windows Server 2003 family

LinkLabel.LinkArea Property

Gets or sets the range in the text to treat as a link.

```
[Visual Basic]
Public Property LinkArea As LinkArea
[C#]
public LinkArea LinkArea {get; set;}
[C++]
public: __property LinkArea get_LinkArea();
public: __property void set_LinkArea(LinkArea);
[JScript]
public function get LinkArea() : LinkArea;
public function set LinkArea(LinkArea);
```

Property Value

A **LinkArea** that represents the area treated as a link.

Exceptions

Exception Type	Condition
ArgumentException	The **Start** property of the **LinkArea** object is less than zero. -or- The **Length** property of the **LinkArea** object is less than zero.

Remarks

The **LinkArea** property provides a quick way to specify a single hyperlink to display in the text of the **LinkLabel** control. The **LinkArea** object provides properties that specify the starting position of the link within the text of the control and the length of text for the hyperlink. When a hyperlink is specified using the **LinkArea** property, the hyperlink is added to the **LinkLabel.LinkCollection** of the control. The **LinkArea** property converts the **LinkArea** object assigned to it to a **LinkLabel.Link** object that is stored within the collection.

To add multiple hyperlinks to the text of the control, you can use the **Links** property. The **Links** property enables you to access the properties and methods of the **LinkLabel.LinkCollection**, which stores the links specified for the control. This method of adding links to the **LinkLabel** also enables you to specify data in the **LinkData** property that is associated with the link being created. The value of the **LinkData** property can be used to store the location of a file to display or the address of a Web site.

When a **LinkLabel** control is created, a default hyperlink that contains all the text within the **LinkLabel** control is added to the **LinkLabel.LinkCollection**. You can override this default link by specifying a new link area with the **LinkArea** property, or specify a link using the **Add** method of the **LinkLabel.LinkCollection**. You can also remove the default hyperlink by using the **Remove** method of the **LinkLabel.LinkCollection** class.

Note The **LinkArea** property always returns the first item in the **LinkLabel.LinkCollection**, regardless of how the hyperlink was added to the collection.

Example

See related example in the **System.Windows.Forms.LinkLabel** class topic.

Requirements

Platforms: Windows 98, Windows NT 4.0, Windows Millennium Edition, Windows 2000, Windows XP Home Edition, Windows XP Professional, Windows Server 2003 family

LinkLabel.LinkBehavior Property

Gets or sets a value that represents the behavior of a link.

[Visual Basic]
```
Public Property LinkBehavior As LinkBehavior
```
[C#]
```
public LinkBehavior LinkBehavior {get; set;}
```
[C++]
```
public: __property LinkBehavior get_LinkBehavior();
public: __property void set_LinkBehavior(LinkBehavior);
```
[JScript]
```
public function get LinkBehavior() : LinkBehavior;
public function set LinkBehavior(LinkBehavior);
```

Property Value

One of the **LinkBehavior** values. The default is **LinkBehavior.SystemDefault**.

Remarks

This property enables you to specify the behavior of links when they are displayed in the control. For example, if you want links to be displayed with an underline only when the mouse pointer is over a link, you can set this property to **LinkBehavior.HoverUnderline**.

Example

See related example in the **System.Windows.Forms.LinkLabel** class topic.

Requirements

Platforms: Windows 98, Windows NT 4.0, Windows Millennium Edition, Windows 2000, Windows XP Home Edition, Windows XP Professional, Windows Server 2003 family

LinkLabel.LinkColor Property

Gets or sets the color used when displaying a normal link.

[Visual Basic]
```
Public Property LinkColor As Color
```
[C#]
```
public Color LinkColor {get; set;}
```
[C++]
```
public: __property Color get_LinkColor();
public: __property void set_LinkColor(Color);
```
[JScript]
```
public function get LinkColor() : Color;
public function set LinkColor(Color);
```

Property Value

A **Color** that represents the color used to displaying a normal link. The default color is specified by the system, typically this color is **Color.Blue**.

Remarks

This property enables you to specify the color that is initially displayed for all links in the **LinkLabel**.

There are a number of colors associated with a link. The **ActiveLinkColor** property enables you to specify the color of the link when it is in the process of being clicked. The **VisitedLinkColor** property enables you to specify the color of a link after it has been visited by the user. When a link is disabled, the **DisabledLinkColor** is used to display the link in a disabled state.

Note When setting this property, ensure that the color you are setting the property to does not conflict with the color of the control's background or the text does not display properly. For example, if the background color of the control is **Color.Red** and this property is set to **Color.Red**, the text of the link is not shown properly.

Example

See related example in the **System.Windows.Forms.LinkLabel** class topic.

Requirements

Platforms: Windows 98, Windows NT 4.0, Windows Millennium Edition, Windows 2000, Windows XP Home Edition, Windows XP Professional, Windows Server 2003 family

LinkLabel.Links Property

Gets the collection of links contained within the **LinkLabel**.

[Visual Basic]
```
Public ReadOnly Property Links As LinkLabel.LinkCollection
```
[C#]
```
public LinkLabel.LinkCollection Links {get;}
```
[C++]
```
public: __property LinkLabel.LinkCollection* get_Links();
```
[JScript]
```
public function get Links() : LinkLabel.LinkCollection;
```

Property Value

A **LinkLabel.LinkCollection** that represents the links contained within the **LinkLabel** control.

Remarks

A **LinkLabel** control can display any number of links within the text of the control. This property enables you to access the **LinkLabel.LinkCollection** instance associated with the **LinkLabel** that represents the collection of links displayed in the control. You can then use the members of the **LinkLabel.LinkCollection** class to add, remove, and find links in the collection. For more information on the types of tasks you can perform with the link collection, see **LinkLabel.LinkCollection**.

When a **LinkLabel** control is created, a default hyperlink that contains all the text within the **LinkLabel** control is added to the **LinkLabel.LinkCollection**. You can override this default link by specifying a new link area with the **LinkArea** property, or specify a link using the **Add** method of the **LinkLabel.LinkCollection**. You can also remove the default hyperlink by using the **Remove** method of the **LinkLabel.LinkCollection** class.

If you do not need to specify more than one link to display within the **LinkLabel**, you can use the **LinkArea** property.

Example

See related example in the **System.Windows.Forms.LinkLabel** class topic.

Requirements

Platforms: Windows 98, Windows NT 4.0, Windows Millennium Edition, Windows 2000, Windows XP Home Edition, Windows XP Professional, Windows Server 2003 family

LinkLabel.LinkVisited Property

Gets or sets a value indicating whether a link should be displayed as though it were visited.

```
[Visual Basic]
Public Property LinkVisited As Boolean
[C#]
public bool LinkVisited {get; set;}
[C++]
public: __property bool get_LinkVisited();
public: __property void set_LinkVisited(bool);
[JScript]
public function get LinkVisited() : Boolean;
public function set LinkVisited(Boolean);
```

Property Value

true if links should display as though they were visited; otherwise, **false**. The default is **false**.

Remarks

A **LinkLabel** control does not automatically denote that a link is a visited link. To display the link as a visited link, you can set the value of this property to **true** in an event handler for the **LinkClicked** event of a **LinkLabel**. A visited link is displayed using the color specified in the **VisitedLinkColor** property of the **LinkLabel** control. Once the form containing the **LinkLabel** control is closed, the all display state associated with the link is deleted. In order to retain the display state of the link, you need to store the display state of the link in a registry setting associated with your application.

> **Note** This property only affects the first link defined in the **LinkLabel** control. If you have more than one link specified in the control, use the **Visited** property of the **LinkLabel.Link** class. You can access all the links defined in the **LinkLabel** by using the **Links** property.

Requirements

Platforms: Windows 98, Windows NT 4.0, Windows Millennium Edition, Windows 2000, Windows XP Home Edition, Windows XP Professional, Windows Server 2003 family

LinkLabel.OverrideCursor Property

This member supports the .NET Framework infrastructure and is not intended to be used directly from your code.

```
[Visual Basic]
Protected Property OverrideCursor As Cursor
[C#]
protected Cursor OverrideCursor {get; set;}
[C++]
protected: __property Cursor* get_OverrideCursor();
protected: __property void set_OverrideCursor(Cursor*);
[JScript]
protected function get OverrideCursor() : Cursor;
protected function set OverrideCursor(Cursor);
```

LinkLabel.Text Property

This member overrides **Control.Text**.

```
[Visual Basic]
Overrides Public Property Text As String
[C#]
public override string Text {get; set;}
[C++]
public: __property String* get_Text();
public: __property void set_Text(String*);
[JScript]
public override function get Text() : String;
public override function set Text(String);
```

Requirements

Platforms: Windows 98, Windows NT 4.0, Windows Millennium Edition, Windows 2000, Windows XP Home Edition, Windows XP Professional, Windows Server 2003 family

LinkLabel.VisitedLinkColor Property

Gets or sets the color used when displaying a link that that has been previously visited.

```
[Visual Basic]
Public Property VisitedLinkColor As Color
[C#]
public Color VisitedLinkColor {get; set;}
[C++]
public: __property Color get_VisitedLinkColor();
public: __property void set_VisitedLinkColor(Color);
[JScript]
public function get VisitedLinkColor() : Color;
public function set VisitedLinkColor(Color);
```

Property Value

A **Color** that represents the color used to display links that have been visited. The default color is specified by the system, typically this color is **Color.Purple**.

Remarks

This property enables you to specify the color that is displayed for all links in the **LinkLabel System.Windows.Forms** that have been visited by the user.

There are a number of colors associated with a link. All links in the **LinkLabel** are initially displayed with the color defined in the **LinkColor** property. The **ActiveLinkColor** property enables you to specify the color of the link when it is in the process of being clicked. When a link is disabled, the **DisabledLinkColor** is used to display the link in a disabled state.

Note When setting this property, ensure that the color you are setting the property to does not conflict with the color of the control's background or the text does not display properly. For example, if the background color of the control is **Color.Red** and this property is set to **Color.Red**, the text is not shown properly when the link is displayed as a visited link.

Example

See related example in the **System.Windows.Forms.LinkLabel** class topic.

Requirements

Platforms: Windows 98, Windows NT 4.0, Windows Millennium Edition, Windows 2000, Windows XP Home Edition, Windows XP Professional, Windows Server 2003 family

LinkLabel.CreateAccessibilityInstance Method

This member overrides **Control.CreateAccessibilityInstance**.

```
[Visual Basic]
Overrides Protected Function CreateAccessibilityInstance() As _
   AccessibleObject
[C#]
protected override AccessibleObject CreateAccessibilityInstance();
[C++]
protected: AccessibleObject* CreateAccessibilityInstance();
[JScript]
protected override function CreateAccessibilityInstance() :
   AccessibleObject;
```

Requirements

Platforms: Windows 98, Windows NT 4.0, Windows Millennium Edition, Windows 2000, Windows XP Home Edition, Windows XP Professional, Windows Server 2003 family

LinkLabel.CreateHandle Method

This member overrides **Control.CreateHandle**.

```
[Visual Basic]
Overrides Protected Sub CreateHandle()
[C#]
protected override void CreateHandle();
[C++]
protected: void CreateHandle();
[JScript]
protected override function CreateHandle();
```

Requirements

Platforms: Windows 98, Windows NT 4.0, Windows Millennium Edition, Windows 2000, Windows XP Home Edition, Windows XP Professional, Windows Server 2003 family

LinkLabel.IButtonControl.NotifyDefault Method

This member supports the .NET Framework infrastructure and is not intended to be used directly from your code.

```
[Visual Basic]
Private Sub NotifyDefault( _
   ByVal value As Boolean _
) Implements IButtonControl.NotifyDefault
[C#]
void IButtonControl.NotifyDefault(
   bool value
);
[C++]
private: void IButtonControl::NotifyDefault(
   bool value
);
[JScript]
private function IButtonControl.NotifyDefault(
   value : Boolean
);
```

LinkLabel.IButtonControl.PerformClick Method

This member supports the .NET Framework infrastructure and is not intended to be used directly from your code.

```
[Visual Basic]
Private Sub PerformClick() Implements IButtonControl.PerformClick
[C#]
void IButtonControl.PerformClick();
[C++]
private: void IButtonControl::PerformClick();
[JScript]
private function IButtonControl.PerformClick();
```

LinkLabel.OnEnabledChanged Method

This member overrides **Control.OnEnabledChanged**.

```
[Visual Basic]
Overrides Protected Sub OnEnabledChanged( _
   ByVal e As EventArgs _
)
[C#]
protected override void OnEnabledChanged(
   EventArgs e
);
[C++]
protected: void OnEnabledChanged(
   EventArgs* e
);
[JScript]
protected override function OnEnabledChanged(
   e : EventArgs
);
```

Requirements

Platforms: Windows 98, Windows NT 4.0, Windows Millennium Edition, Windows 2000, Windows XP Home Edition, Windows XP Professional, Windows Server 2003 family

LinkLabel.OnFontChanged Method

This member overrides **Control.OnFontChanged**.

[Visual Basic]
```
Overrides Protected Sub OnFontChanged( _
   ByVal e As EventArgs _
)
```
[C#]
```
protected override void OnFontChanged(
   EventArgs e
);
```
[C++]
```
protected: void OnFontChanged(
   EventArgs* e
);
```
[JScript]
```
protected override function OnFontChanged(
   e : EventArgs
);
```

Requirements

Platforms: Windows 98, Windows NT 4.0, Windows Millennium Edition, Windows 2000, Windows XP Home Edition, Windows XP Professional, Windows Server 2003 family

LinkLabel.OnGotFocus Method

This member overrides **Control.OnGotFocus**.

[Visual Basic]
```
Overrides Protected Sub OnGotFocus( _
   ByVal e As EventArgs _
)
```
[C#]
```
protected override void OnGotFocus(
   EventArgs e
);
```
[C++]
```
protected: void OnGotFocus(
   EventArgs* e
);
```
[JScript]
```
protected override function OnGotFocus(
   e : EventArgs
);
```

Requirements

Platforms: Windows 98, Windows NT 4.0, Windows Millennium Edition, Windows 2000, Windows XP Home Edition, Windows XP Professional, Windows Server 2003 family

LinkLabel.OnKeyDown Method

This member overrides **Control.OnKeyDown**.

[Visual Basic]
```
Overrides Protected Sub OnKeyDown( _
   ByVal e As KeyEventArgs _
)
```
[C#]
```
protected override void OnKeyDown(
   KeyEventArgs e
);
```
[C++]
```
protected: void OnKeyDown(
   KeyEventArgs* e
);
```
[JScript]
```
protected override function OnKeyDown(
   e : KeyEventArgs
);
```

Requirements

Platforms: Windows 98, Windows NT 4.0, Windows Millennium Edition, Windows 2000, Windows XP Home Edition, Windows XP Professional, Windows Server 2003 family

LinkLabel.OnLinkClicked Method

Raises the **LinkClicked** event.

[Visual Basic]
```
Protected Overridable Sub OnLinkClicked( _
   ByVal e As LinkLabelLinkClickedEventArgs _
)
```
[C#]
```
protected virtual void OnLinkClicked(
   LinkLabelLinkClickedEventArgs e
);
```
[C++]
```
protected: virtual void OnLinkClicked(
   LinkLabelLinkClickedEventArgs* e
);
```
[JScript]
```
protected function OnLinkClicked(
   e : LinkLabelLinkClickedEventArgs
);
```

Parameters

e

A **LinkLabelLinkClickedEventArgs** that contains the event data.

Remarks

Raising an event invokes the event handler through a delegate.

The **OnLinkClicked** method also allows derived classes to handle the event without attaching a delegate. This is the preferred technique for handling the event in a derived class.

Notes to Inheritors: When overriding **OnLinkClicked** in a derived class, be sure to call the base class's **OnLinkClicked** method so that registered delegates receive the event.

Requirements

Platforms: Windows 98, Windows NT 4.0, Windows Millennium Edition, Windows 2000, Windows XP Home Edition, Windows XP Professional, Windows Server 2003 family

LinkLabel.OnLostFocus Method

This member overrides **Control.OnLostFocus**.

[Visual Basic]
```
Overrides Protected Sub OnLostFocus( _
   ByVal e As EventArgs _
)
```

```
[C#]
protected override void OnLostFocus(
   EventArgs e
);
[C++]
protected: void OnLostFocus(
   EventArgs* e
);
[JScript]
protected override function OnLostFocus(
   e : EventArgs
);
```

Requirements

Platforms: Windows 98, Windows NT 4.0, Windows Millennium Edition, Windows 2000, Windows XP Home Edition, Windows XP Professional, Windows Server 2003 family

LinkLabel.OnMouseDown Method

This member overrides **Control.OnMouseDown**.

```
[Visual Basic]
Overrides Protected Sub OnMouseDown( _
   ByVal e As MouseEventArgs _
)
[C#]
protected override void OnMouseDown(
   MouseEventArgs e
);
[C++]
protected: void OnMouseDown(
   MouseEventArgs* e
);
[JScript]
protected override function OnMouseDown(
   e : MouseEventArgs
);
```

Requirements

Platforms: Windows 98, Windows NT 4.0, Windows Millennium Edition, Windows 2000, Windows XP Home Edition, Windows XP Professional, Windows Server 2003 family

LinkLabel.OnMouseLeave Method

This member overrides **Control.OnMouseLeave**.

```
[Visual Basic]
Overrides Protected Sub OnMouseLeave( _
   ByVal e As EventArgs _
)
[C#]
protected override void OnMouseLeave(
   EventArgs e
);
[C++]
protected: void OnMouseLeave(
   EventArgs* e
);
[JScript]
protected override function OnMouseLeave(
   e : EventArgs
);
```

Requirements

Platforms: Windows 98, Windows NT 4.0, Windows Millennium Edition, Windows 2000, Windows XP Home Edition, Windows XP Professional, Windows Server 2003 family

LinkLabel.OnMouseMove Method

This member overrides **Control.OnMouseMove**.

```
[Visual Basic]
Overrides Protected Sub OnMouseMove( _
   ByVal e As MouseEventArgs _
)
[C#]
protected override void OnMouseMove(
   MouseEventArgs e
);
[C++]
protected: void OnMouseMove(
   MouseEventArgs* e
);
[JScript]
protected override function OnMouseMove(
   e : MouseEventArgs
);
```

Requirements

Platforms: Windows 98, Windows NT 4.0, Windows Millennium Edition, Windows 2000, Windows XP Home Edition, Windows XP Professional, Windows Server 2003 family

LinkLabel.OnMouseUp Method

This member overrides **Control.OnMouseUp**.

```
[Visual Basic]
Overrides Protected Sub OnMouseUp( _
   ByVal e As MouseEventArgs _
)
[C#]
protected override void OnMouseUp(
   MouseEventArgs e
);
[C++]
protected: void OnMouseUp(
   MouseEventArgs* e
);
[JScript]
protected override function OnMouseUp(
   e : MouseEventArgs
);
```

Requirements

Platforms: Windows 98, Windows NT 4.0, Windows Millennium Edition, Windows 2000, Windows XP Home Edition, Windows XP Professional, Windows Server 2003 family

LinkLabel.OnPaint Method

This member overrides **Control.OnPaint**.

```
[Visual Basic]
Overrides Protected Sub OnPaint( _
   ByVal e As PaintEventArgs _
)
[C#]
protected override void OnPaint(
   PaintEventArgs e
);
[C++]
protected: void OnPaint(
   PaintEventArgs* e
);
[JScript]
protected override function OnPaint(
   e : PaintEventArgs
);
```

Requirements

Platforms: Windows 98, Windows NT 4.0, Windows Millennium Edition, Windows 2000, Windows XP Home Edition, Windows XP Professional, Windows Server 2003 family

LinkLabel.OnPaintBackground Method

This member overrides **Control.OnPaintBackground**.

```
[Visual Basic]
Overrides Protected Sub OnPaintBackground( _
   ByVal e As PaintEventArgs _
)
[C#]
protected override void OnPaintBackground(
   PaintEventArgs e
);
[C++]
protected: void OnPaintBackground(
   PaintEventArgs* e
);
[JScript]
protected override function OnPaintBackground(
   e : PaintEventArgs
);
```

Requirements

Platforms: Windows 98, Windows NT 4.0, Windows Millennium Edition, Windows 2000, Windows XP Home Edition, Windows XP Professional, Windows Server 2003 family

LinkLabel.OnTextAlignChanged Method

This member overrides **Label.OnTextAlignChanged**.

```
[Visual Basic]
Overrides Protected Sub OnTextAlignChanged( _
   ByVal e As EventArgs _
)
[C#]
protected override void OnTextAlignChanged(
   EventArgs e
);
[C++]
protected: void OnTextAlignChanged(
   EventArgs* e
);
[JScript]
protected override function OnTextAlignChanged(
   e : EventArgs
);
```

Requirements

Platforms: Windows 98, Windows NT 4.0, Windows Millennium Edition, Windows 2000, Windows XP Home Edition, Windows XP Professional, Windows Server 2003 family

LinkLabel.OnTextChanged Method

This member overrides **Control.OnTextChanged**.

```
[Visual Basic]
Overrides Protected Sub OnTextChanged( _
   ByVal e As EventArgs _
)
[C#]
protected override void OnTextChanged(
   EventArgs e
);
[C++]
protected: void OnTextChanged(
   EventArgs* e
);
[JScript]
protected override function OnTextChanged(
   e : EventArgs
);
```

Requirements

Platforms: Windows 98, Windows NT 4.0, Windows Millennium Edition, Windows 2000, Windows XP Home Edition, Windows XP Professional, Windows Server 2003 family

LinkLabel.PointInLink Method

Gets the link located at the specified client coordinates.

```
[Visual Basic]
Protected Function PointInLink( _
   ByVal x As Integer, _
   ByVal y As Integer _
) As Link
[C#]
protected Link PointInLink(
   int x,
   int y
);
[C++]
protected: Link* PointInLink(
   int x,
   int y
);
```

```
[JScript]
protected function PointInLink(
   x : int,
   y : int
) : Link;
```

Parameters

x
The horizontal coordinate of the point to search for a link.

y
The vertical coordinate of the point to search for a link.

Return Value

A **LinkLabel.Link** representing the link located at the specified coordinates. If the point does not contain a link, a null reference (**Nothing** in Visual Basic) is returned.

Remarks

This method enables you to determine whether a link is located at a specific point within a **LinkLabel** control. You can use this method in an event handler for the **MouseEnter** event of the control to determine whether the mouse pointer is hovering over a link in the control. Once you have determined that the mouse pointer is over a link, you can then display additional information about the link to the user through **StatusBar** text or a **ToolTip**.

Requirements

Platforms: Windows 98, Windows NT 4.0, Windows Millennium Edition, Windows 2000, Windows XP Home Edition, Windows XP Professional, Windows Server 2003 family

LinkLabel.ProcessDialogKey Method

This member overrides **Control.ProcessDialogKey**.

```
[Visual Basic]
Overrides Protected Function ProcessDialogKey( _
   ByVal keyData As Keys _
) As Boolean
[C#]
protected override bool ProcessDialogKey(
   Keys keyData
);
[C++]
protected: bool ProcessDialogKey(
   Keys keyData
);
[JScript]
protected override function ProcessDialogKey(
   keyData : Keys
) : Boolean;
```

Requirements

Platforms: Windows 98, Windows NT 4.0, Windows Millennium Edition, Windows 2000, Windows XP Home Edition, Windows XP Professional, Windows Server 2003 family

LinkLabel.Select Method

Overload List

This member supports the .NET Framework infrastructure and is not intended to be used directly from your code.

[Visual Basic] **Overloads Overrides Protected Sub Select(Boolean, Boolean)**

[C#] **protected override void Select(bool, bool);**

[C++] **protected: void Select(bool, bool);**

[JScript] **protected override function Select(Boolean, Boolean);**

Inherited from **Control**.

[Visual Basic] **Overloads Public Sub Select()**

[C#] **public void Select();**

[C++] **public: void Select();**

[JScript] **public function Select();**

LinkLabel.Select Method (Boolean, Boolean)

This member overrides **Control.Select**.

```
[Visual Basic]
Overrides Overloads Protected Sub Select( _
   ByVal directed As Boolean, _
   ByVal forward As Boolean _
)
[C#]
protected override void Select(
   bool directed,
   bool forward
);
[C++]
protected: void Select(
   bool directed,
   bool forward
);
[JScript]
protected override function Select(
   directed : Boolean,
   forward : Boolean
);
```

Requirements

Platforms: Windows 98, Windows NT 4.0, Windows Millennium Edition, Windows 2000, Windows XP Home Edition, Windows XP Professional, Windows Server 2003 family

LinkLabel.SetBoundsCore Method

This member overrides **Control.SetBoundsCore**.

```
[Visual Basic]
Overrides Protected Sub SetBoundsCore( _
   ByVal x As Integer, _
   ByVal y As Integer, _
   ByVal width As Integer, _
   ByVal height As Integer, _
   ByVal specified As BoundsSpecified _
)
```

[C#]
```
protected override void SetBoundsCore(
   int x,
   int y,
   int width,
   int height,
   BoundsSpecified specified
);
```
[C++]
```
protected: void SetBoundsCore(
   int x,
   int y,
   int width,
   int height,
   BoundsSpecified specified
);
```
[JScript]
```
protected override function SetBoundsCore(
   x : int,
   y : int,
   width : int,
   height : int,
   specified : BoundsSpecified
);
```

Requirements

Platforms: Windows 98, Windows NT 4.0, Windows Millennium Edition, Windows 2000, Windows XP Home Edition, Windows XP Professional, Windows Server 2003 family

LinkLabel.WndProc Method

This member overrides **Control.WndProc**.

[Visual Basic]
```
Overrides Protected Sub WndProc( _
   ByRef msg As Message _
)
```
[C#]
```
protected override void WndProc(
   ref Message msg
);
```
[C++]
```
protected: void WndProc(
   Message* msg
);
```
[JScript]
```
protected override function WndProc(
   msg : Message
);
```

Requirements

Platforms: Windows 98, Windows NT 4.0, Windows Millennium Edition, Windows 2000, Windows XP Home Edition, Windows XP Professional, Windows Server 2003 family

LinkLabel.LinkClicked Event

Occurs when a link is clicked within the control.

[Visual Basic]
```
Public Event LinkClicked As LinkLabelLinkClickedEventHandler
```
[C#]
```
public event LinkLabelLinkClickedEventHandler LinkClicked;
```
[C++]
```
public: __event LinkLabelLinkClickedEventHandler* LinkClicked;
```

[JScript] In JScript, you can handle the events defined by a class, but you cannot define your own.

Event Data

The event handler receives an argument of type **LinkLabelLinkClickedEventArgs** containing data related to this event. The following **LinkLabelLinkClickedEventArgs** property provides information specific to this event.

Property	Description
Link	Gets the **LinkLabel.Link** that was clicked.

Remarks

Typically, the **LinkClicked** event is handled to perform tasks when the user clicks on a link in the control. The event handler for the **LinkClicked** event is passed an instance of the **LinkLabelLinkClickedEventArgs** class that contains a **LinkLabel.Link** object that is associated with the link that was clicked. You can use information specified in the **LinkData** property of **LinkLabel.Link** class to determine which link was clicked or what type of task to perform when the link is clicked. For example, if a **LinkLabel** control has a **LinkLabel.Link** object defined with its **LinkData** property set to the string www.microsoft.com, you can use this information in an event handler for the **LinkClicked** event to display the Web site.

Example

See related example in the **System.Windows.Forms.LinkLabel** class topic.

Requirements

Platforms: Windows 98, Windows NT 4.0, Windows Millennium Edition, Windows 2000, Windows XP Home Edition, Windows XP Professional, Windows Server 2003 family

LinkLabel.Link Class

Represents a link within a **LinkLabel** control.

System.Object
System.Windows.Forms.LinkLabel.Link

```
[Visual Basic]
Public Class LinkLabel.Link
[C#]
public class LinkLabel.Link
[C++]
public __gc class LinkLabel.Link
[JScript]
public class LinkLabel.Link
```

Thread Safety

Any public static (**Shared** in Visual Basic) members of this type are safe for multithreaded operations. Any instance members are not guaranteed to be thread safe.

Remarks

The **LinkLabel.Link** class defines the properties of a link within a **LinkLabel** control. You can use these properties to provide data to the **LinkClicked** event of the **LinkLabel** control to perform tasks when the link is clicked in the control. The **LinkData** property enables you to define information that the **LinkClicked** event can use to display a URL within Microsoft Internet Explorer or to open a file.

In addition to information related to the link, the properties of the **LinkLabel.Link** class also help define the text of the **LinkLabel.Link** and its display state. The **Start** and **Length** properties define the location and length of text from the text of the **LinkLabel** control to display as a link. The **Enabled** property allows you to display the link as a disabled link, and the **Visited** property can alert the user that they already visited the specified link in the current instance of the **LinkLabel**.

You can display multiple links in a single **LinkLabel** control. Each **LinkLabel.Link** is added into the **LinkLabel.LinkCollection** associated with the **LinkLabel** control. To obtain the collection of links defined in a **LinkLabel** control, use the **LinkLabel.Links** property.

Example

See related example in the **System.Windows.Forms.LinkLabel** class topic.

Requirements

Namespace: System.Windows.Forms

Platforms: Windows 98, Windows NT 4.0,
Windows Millennium Edition, Windows 2000,
Windows XP Home Edition, Windows XP Professional,
Windows Server 2003 family

Assembly: System.Windows.Forms (in System.Windows.Forms.dll)

LinkLabel.Link.Enabled Property

Gets or sets a value indicating whether the link is enabled.

```
[Visual Basic]
Public Property Enabled As Boolean
[C#]
public bool Enabled {get; set;}
[C++]
public: __property bool get_Enabled();
public: __property void set_Enabled(bool);
[JScript]
public function get Enabled() : Boolean;
public function set Enabled(Boolean);
```

Property Value

true if the link is enabled; otherwise, **false**.

Remarks

You can use this property to display a link in a disabled state within the **LinkLabel** control. When a link is disabled, clicking on the link does not cause the **LinkLabel** control to raise the **LinkClicked** event.

Requirements

Platforms: Windows 98, Windows NT 4.0,
Windows Millennium Edition, Windows 2000,
Windows XP Home Edition, Windows XP Professional,
Windows Server 2003 family

LinkLabel.Link.Length Property

Gets or sets the number of characters in the link text.

```
[Visual Basic]
Public Property Length As Integer
[C#]
public int Length {get; set;}
[C++]
public: __property int get_Length();
public: __property void set_Length(int);
[JScript]
public function get Length() : int;
public function set Length(int);
```

Property Value

The number of characters, including spaces, in the link text.

Remarks

To specify text from the **LinkLabel** to display as a link, set the **Start** property to the location in the text to start creating the link. After the **Start** property is set, set the value of the **Length** property to the number of characters, including the character position specified in the **Start** property, that you want to make the link text. For example, if you want to make the first word of the text "The quick brown fox" a link, you set the **Start** property to zero (0) and the **Length** property to three (3).

Requirements

Platforms: Windows 98, Windows NT 4.0,
Windows Millennium Edition, Windows 2000,
Windows XP Home Edition, Windows XP Professional,
Windows Server 2003 family

LinkLabel.Link.LinkData Property

Gets or sets the data associated with the link.

```
[Visual Basic]
Public Property LinkData As Object
[C#]
public object LinkData {get; set;}
```

[C++]
```
public: __property Object* get_LinkData();
public: __property void set_LinkData(Object*);
```
[JScript]
```
public function get LinkData() : Object;
public function set LinkData(Object);
```

Property Value

An **Object** representing the data associated with the link.

Remarks

You can use this property to supply information related to the link. The information provided by this property can be used within the **LinkClicked** event of the **LinkLabel** to provide information about the link that can be used to process the link being clicked. For example, you can specify the URL to display in Internet Explorer when the link is clicked as the value of the **LinkData** property. You can also use the **LinkData** property to identify a dialog to display when the user clicks on the link.

Example

See related example in the **System.Windows.Forms.LinkLabel** class topic.

Requirements

Platforms: Windows 98, Windows NT 4.0,
Windows Millennium Edition, Windows 2000,
Windows XP Home Edition, Windows XP Professional,
Windows Server 2003 family

LinkLabel.Link.Start Property

Gets or sets the starting location of the link within the text of the **LinkLabel**.

[Visual Basic]
```
Public Property Start As Integer
```
[C#]
```
public int Start {get; set;}
```
[C++]
```
public: __property int get_Start();
public: __property void set_Start(int);
```
[JScript]
```
public function get Start() : int;
public function set Start(int);
```

Property Value

The location within the text of the **LinkLabel** control where the link starts.

Remarks

To specify text from the **LinkLabel** to display as a link, set the **Start** property to the location in the text to start creating the link. After the **Start** property is set, set the value of the **Length** property to the number of characters, including the character position specified in the **Start** property, that you want to make the link text. For example, if you want to make the first word of the text "The quick brown fox" a link, you set the **Start** property to zero (0) and the **Length** property to three (3).

Requirements

Platforms: Windows 98, Windows NT 4.0,
Windows Millennium Edition, Windows 2000,
Windows XP Home Edition, Windows XP Professional,
Windows Server 2003 family

LinkLabel.Link.Visited Property

Gets or sets a value indicating whether the user has visited the link.

[Visual Basic]
```
Public Property Visited As Boolean
```
[C#]
```
public bool Visited {get; set;}
```
[C++]
```
public: __property bool get_Visited();
public: __property void set_Visited(bool);
```
[JScript]
```
public function get Visited() : Boolean;
public function set Visited(Boolean);
```

Property Value

true if the link has been visited; otherwise, **false**.

Remarks

A **LinkLabel** control does not automatically denote that a link is a visited link. To display the link as a visited link, you can set the value of this property to **true** in an event handler for the **LinkClicked** event of a **LinkLabel**. A visited link is displayed using the color specified in the **VisitedLinkColor** property of the **LinkLabel** control. Once the form containing the **LinkLabel** control is closed, the all display state associated with the link is deleted. In order to retain the display state of the link, you need to store the display state of the link in a registry setting associated with your application.

Note If you have only one link specified in a **LinkLabel** control, you can use the **LinkVisited** property of the **LinkLabel** to specify the link as visited. You can also use the **LinkVisited** property if you have multiple links defined, but the setting only applies to the first link defined in the control.

Example

See related example in the **System.Windows.Forms.LinkLabel** class topic.

Requirements

Platforms: Windows 98, Windows NT 4.0,
Windows Millennium Edition, Windows 2000,
Windows XP Home Edition, Windows XP Professional,
Windows Server 2003 family

LinkLabelLinkClickedEvent-Args Class

Provides data for the **LinkClicked** event.

System.Object
  System.EventArgs
    System.Windows.Forms.LinkLabelLinkClickedEventArgs

```
[Visual Basic]
<ComVisible(True)>
Public Class LinkLabelLinkClickedEventArgs
   Inherits EventArgs
[C#]
[ComVisible(true)]
public class LinkLabelLinkClickedEventArgs : EventArgs
[C++]
[ComVisible(true)]
public __gc class LinkLabelLinkClickedEventArgs : public EventArgs
[JScript]
public
   ComVisible(true)
class LinkLabelLinkClickedEventArgs extends EventArgs
```

Thread Safety

Any public static (**Shared** in Visual Basic) members of this type are safe for multithreaded operations. Any instance members are not guaranteed to be thread safe.

Example

See related example in the **System.Windows.Forms.LinkLabel** class topic.

Requirements

Namespace: System.Windows.Forms

Platforms: Windows 98, Windows NT 4.0, Windows Millennium Edition, Windows 2000, Windows XP Home Edition, Windows XP Professional, Windows Server 2003 family

Assembly: System.Windows.Forms (in System.Windows.Forms.dll)

LinkLabelLinkClickedEventArgs Constructor

Initializes a new instance of the **LinkLabelLinkClickedEventArgs** class, given the link.

```
[Visual Basic]
Public Sub New( _
   ByVal link As LinkLabel.Link _
)
[C#]
public LinkLabelLinkClickedEventArgs(
   LinkLabel.Link link
);
[C++]
public: LinkLabelLinkClickedEventArgs(
   LinkLabel.Link* link
);
[JScript]
public function LinkLabelLinkClickedEventArgs(
   link : LinkLabel.Link
);
```

Parameters

link
  The **LinkLabel.Link** that was clicked.

Requirements

Platforms: Windows 98, Windows NT 4.0, Windows Millennium Edition, Windows 2000, Windows XP Home Edition, Windows XP Professional, Windows Server 2003 family

LinkLabelLinkClickedEventArgs.Link Property

Gets the **LinkLabel.Link** that was clicked.

```
[Visual Basic]
Public ReadOnly Property Link As LinkLabel.Link
[C#]
public LinkLabel.Link Link {get;}
[C++]
public: __property LinkLabel.Link* get_Link();
[JScript]
public function get Link() : LinkLabel.Link;
```

Property Value

A link on the **LinkLabel**.

Example

See related example in the **System.Windows.Forms.LinkLabel** class topic.

Requirements

Platforms: Windows 98, Windows NT 4.0, Windows Millennium Edition, Windows 2000, Windows XP Home Edition, Windows XP Professional, Windows Server 2003 family

LinkLabelLinkClickedEvent-Handler Delegate

Represents the method that will handle the **LinkClicked** event of a **LinkLabel**.

[Visual Basic]
```
<Serializable>
Public Delegate Sub LinkLabelLinkClickedEventHandler( _
   ByVal sender As Object, _
   ByVal e As LinkLabelLinkClickedEventArgs _
)
```
[C#]
```
[Serializable]
public delegate void LinkLabelLinkClickedEventHandler(
   object sender,
   LinkLabelLinkClickedEventArgs e
);
```
[C++]
```
[Serializable]
public __gc __delegate void LinkLabelLinkClickedEventHandler(
   Object* sender,
   LinkLabelLinkClickedEventArgs* e
);
```

[JScript] In JScript, you can use the delegates in the .NET Framework, but you cannot define your own.

Parameters [Visual Basic, C#, C++]

The declaration of your event handler must have the same parameters as the **LinkLabelLinkClickedEventHandler** delegate declaration.

sender

The source of the event.

e

A **LinkLabelLinkClickedEventArgs** that contains the event data.

Remarks

When you create a **LinkLabelLinkClickedEventHandler** delegate, you identify the method that will handle the event. To associate the event with your event handler, add an instance of the delegate to the event. The event handler is called whenever the event occurs, until you remove the delegate.

Example

See related example in the **System.Windows.Forms.LinkLabel** class topic.

Requirements

Namespace: System.Windows.Forms

Platforms: Windows 98, Windows NT 4.0, Windows Millennium Edition, Windows 2000, Windows XP Home Edition, Windows XP Professional, Windows Server 2003 family

Assembly: System.Windows.Forms (in System.Windows.Forms.dll)

LinkLabel.LinkCollection Class

Represents the collection of links within a **LinkLabel** control.

System.Object
  System.Windows.Forms.LinkLabel.LinkCollection

```
[Visual Basic]
Public Class LinkLabel.LinkCollection
   Implements IList, ICollection, IEnumerable
[C#]
public class LinkLabel.LinkCollection : IList, ICollection,
   IEnumerable
[C++]
public __gc class LinkLabel.LinkCollection : public IList,
   ICollection, IEnumerable
[JScript]
public class LinkLabel.LinkCollection implements IList,
   ICollection, IEnumerable
```

Thread Safety

Any public static (**Shared** in Visual Basic) members of this type are safe for multithreaded operations. Any instance members are not guaranteed to be thread safe.

Remarks

The **LinkLabel.LinkCollection** class stores the link displayed in the **LinkLabel** control. Each item in the collection is an instance of the **LinkLabel.Link** class, which defines the information of the link.

The **Add** method provides the ability to add a single **LinkLabel.Link** object to the collection. To remove links, you can use either the **Remove** method or the **RemoveAt** method if you know where the link is located within the collection. The **Clear** method enables you to remove all links from the collection instead of using the **Remove** method to remove a single link at a time.

In addition to methods and properties for adding and removing items, the **LinkLabel.LinkCollection** also provides methods to find links within the collection. The **Contains** method enables you to determine whether a **LinkLabel.Link** is a member of the collection. Once you know that the link is located within the collection, you can use the **IndexOf** method to determine where the link is located within the collection.

Requirements

Namespace: System.Windows.Forms

Platforms: Windows 98, Windows NT 4.0, Windows Millennium Edition, Windows 2000, Windows XP Home Edition, Windows XP Professional, Windows Server 2003 family

Assembly: System.Windows.Forms (in System.Windows.Forms.dll)

LinkLabel.LinkCollection Constructor

Initializes a new instance of the **LinkLabel.LinkCollection** class.

```
[Visual Basic]
Public Sub New( _
   ByVal owner As LinkLabel _
)
[C#]
public LinkLabel.LinkCollection(
   LinkLabel owner
);
[C++]
public: LinkCollection(
   LinkLabel* owner
);
[JScript]
public function LinkLabel.LinkCollection(
   owner : LinkLabel
);
```

Parameters

owner
   The **LinkLabel** control that owns the collection.

Remarks

An instance of this class cannot be created without associating it with a **LinkLabel** control.

Requirements

Platforms: Windows 98, Windows NT 4.0, Windows Millennium Edition, Windows 2000, Windows XP Home Edition, Windows XP Professional, Windows Server 2003 family

LinkLabel.LinkCollection.Count Property

Gets the number of links in the collection.

```
[Visual Basic]
Public Overridable ReadOnly Property Count As Integer  Implements _
   ICollection.Count
[C#]
public virtual int Count {get;}
[C++]
public: __property virtual int get_Count();
[JScript]
public function get Count() : int;
```

Property Value

The number of links in the collection.

Implements

ICollection.Count

Remarks

This property enables you to determine the number of links in the **LinkLabel** control. You can then use this value when looping through the values of the collection and need to provide a number of iterations to perform the loop.

Requirements

Platforms: Windows 98, Windows NT 4.0, Windows Millennium Edition, Windows 2000, Windows XP Home Edition, Windows XP Professional, Windows Server 2003 family

LinkLabel.LinkCollection.IsReadOnly Property

Gets a value indicating whether this collection is read-only.

```
[Visual Basic]
Public Overridable ReadOnly Property IsReadOnly As Boolean _
   Implements IList.IsReadOnly
```

```
[C#]
public virtual bool IsReadOnly {get;}
[C++]
public: __property virtual bool get_IsReadOnly();
[JScript]
public function get IsReadOnly() : Boolean;
```

Property Value

true if the collection is read-only; otherwise, **false**.

Implements

IList.IsReadOnly

Remarks

This property is always **false** for this collection.

Requirements

Platforms: Windows 98, Windows NT 4.0, Windows Millennium Edition, Windows 2000, Windows XP Home Edition, Windows XP Professional, Windows Server 2003 family

LinkLabel.LinkCollection.Item Property

Gets and sets the link at the specified index within the collection.

[C#] In C#, this property is the indexer for the **LinkLabel.LinkCollection** class.

```
[Visual Basic]
Public Overridable Default Property Item( _
   ByVal index As Integer _
) As LinkLabel.Link
[C#]
public virtual LinkLabel.Link this[
   int index
] {get; set;}
[C++]
public: __property virtual LinkLabel.Link* get_Item(
   int index
);
public: __property virtual void set_Item(
   int index,
   LinkLabel.Link*
);
[JScript]
returnValue = LinkCollectionObject.Item(index);
LinkCollectionObject.Item(index) = returnValue;
-or-
returnValue = LinkCollectionObject(index);
LinkCollectionObject(index) = returnValue;
```

[JScript] In JScript, you can use the default indexed properties defined by a type, but you cannot explicitly define your own. However, specifying the **expando** attribute on a class automatically provides a default indexed property whose type is **Object** and whose index type is **String**.

Arguments [JScript]

index

The index of the link in the collection to get.

Parameters [Visual Basic, C#, C++]

index

The index of the link in the collection to get.

Property Value

An object representing the link located at the specified index within the collection.

Exceptions

Exception Type	Condition
ArgumentOutOfRange-Exception	The value of *index* is a negative value or greater than the number of items in the collection.

Remarks

You can use this method to obtain the link stored at a specific location within the collection. To determine the index of a specific item within the collection, use the **IndexOf** method.

Requirements

Platforms: Windows 98, Windows NT 4.0, Windows Millennium Edition, Windows 2000, Windows XP Home Edition, Windows XP Professional, Windows Server 2003 family

LinkLabel.LinkCollection.Add Method

Adds a link to the collection.

Overload List

Adds a link to the collection.

[Visual Basic] **Overloads Public Function Add(Integer, Integer) As Link**

[C#] **public Link Add(int, int);**

[C++] **public: Link* Add(int, int);**

[JScript] **public function Add(int, int) : Link;**

Adds a link to the collection with information to associate with the link.

[Visual Basic] **Overloads Public Function Add(Integer, Integer, Object) As Link**

[C#] **public Link Add(int, int, object);**

[C++] **public: Link* Add(int, int, Object*);**

[JScript] **public function Add(int, int, Object) : Link;**

Example

See related example in the **System.Windows.Forms.LinkLabel** class topic.

LinkLabel.LinkCollection.Add Method (Int32, Int32)

Adds a link to the collection.

```
[Visual Basic]
Overloads Public Function Add( _
   ByVal start As Integer, _
   ByVal length As Integer _
) As Link
[C#]
public Link Add(
   int start,
   int length
);
[C++]
public: Link* Add(
   int start,
   int length
);
```

```
[JScript]
public function Add(
   start : int,
   length : int
) : Link;
```

Parameters

start
: The starting character within the text of the label where the link is created.

length
: The number of characters after the starting character to include in the link text.

Return Value

A **LinkLabel.Link** object representing the link that was created and added to the collection.

Remarks

A **LinkLabel** control can display multiple links within the text of the control. The **Add** method enables you to convert text within the **LinkLabel** control to a link that can be clicked on by the user to perform tasks similar to a **Button** control. This method adds the link that is created to the **LinkLabel.LinkCollection** for the **LinkLabel**. For example, if you want to set the word "quick" in the label text, "The quick brown fox", you call this method with the *start* parameter set to the value of four (4), and the *length* parameter to five (5). The word "quick" then changes to a link and the link is added to the collection. If you want to associate information with the link, such as the URL to display or a file to open when the user clicks on the link, use the other version of the **Add** method.

> **Note** Two links cannot share the same text. If you create a link that uses text that is already used by another link, an exception is thrown.

Requirements

Platforms: Windows 98, Windows NT 4.0, Windows Millennium Edition, Windows 2000, Windows XP Home Edition, Windows XP Professional, Windows Server 2003 family

LinkLabel.LinkCollection.Add Method (Int32, Int32, Object)

Adds a link to the collection with information to associate with the link.

```
[Visual Basic]
Overloads Public Function Add( _
   ByVal start As Integer, _
   ByVal length As Integer, _
   ByVal linkData As Object _
) As Link
[C#]
public Link Add(
   int start,
   int length,
   object linkData
);
[C++]
public: Link* Add(
   int start,
   int length,
   Object* linkData
);
[JScript]
public function Add(
   start : int,
   length : int,
   linkData : Object
) : Link;
```

Parameters

start
: The starting character within the text of the label where the link is created.

length
: The number of characters after the starting character to include in the link text.

linkData
: The object containing the information to associate with the link.

Return Value

A **LinkLabel.Link** object representing the link that was created and added to the collection.

Remarks

A **LinkLabel** control can display multiple links within the text of the control. The **Add** method enables you to convert text within the **LinkLabel** control to a link that can be clicked on by the user to perform tasks similar to a **Button** control. This method adds the link that is created to the **LinkLabel.LinkCollection** for the **LinkLabel**. For example, if you want to set the word "quick" in the label text, "The quick brown fox", you call this method with the *start* parameter set to the value of four (4), and the *length* parameter to five (5). The word "quick" then changes to a link and the link is added to the collection. This version of the Add method enables you to provide additional information that can be associated with the link through the *linkData* parameter. For example, you can pass a **String** object to the *linkData* parameter that contains a URL to display when the link is clicked. You can then use this information in your handler for the **LinkClicked** event of the **LinkLabel** control to display the URL in Microsoft Internet Explorer.

> **Note** Two links cannot share the same text. If you create a link that uses text that is already used by another link, an exception is thrown.

Example

See related example in the **System.Windows.Forms.LinkLabel** class topic.

Requirements

Platforms: Windows 98, Windows NT 4.0, Windows Millennium Edition, Windows 2000, Windows XP Home Edition, Windows XP Professional, Windows Server 2003 family

LinkLabel.LinkCollection.Clear Method

Clears all links from the collection.

[Visual Basic]
```
Public Overridable Sub Clear() Implements IList.Clear
```
[C#]
```
public virtual void Clear();
```
[C++]
```
public: virtual void Clear();
```
[JScript]
```
public function Clear();
```

Implements

IList.Clear

Remarks

When you remove links from the collection, all information about the removed links is deleted. To remove a single link from the **LinkLabel**, use the **Remove** or **RemoveAt** method.

Requirements

Platforms: Windows 98, Windows NT 4.0, Windows Millennium Edition, Windows 2000, Windows XP Home Edition, Windows XP Professional, Windows Server 2003 family

LinkLabel.LinkCollection.Contains Method

Determines whether the specified link is within the collection.

[Visual Basic]
```
Public Function Contains( _
   ByVal link As LinkLabel.Link _
) As Boolean
```
[C#]
```
public bool Contains(
   LinkLabel.Link link
);
```
[C++]
```
public: bool Contains(
   LinkLabel.Link* link
);
```
[JScript]
```
public function Contains(
   link : LinkLabel.Link
) : Boolean;
```

Parameters

link

A **LinkLabel.Link** representing the link to search for in the collection.

Return Value

true if the specified link is within the collection; otherwise, **false**.

Remarks

The **Contains** method enables you to determine whether a **LinkLabel.Link** object is a member of the collection. Once you know that the link is located within the collection, you can use the **IndexOf** method to determine where the link is located within the collection.

Requirements

Platforms: Windows 98, Windows NT 4.0, Windows Millennium Edition, Windows 2000, Windows XP Home Edition, Windows XP Professional, Windows Server 2003 family

LinkLabel.LinkCollection.GetEnumerator Method

Returns an enumerator to use to iterate through the link collection.

[Visual Basic]
```
Public Overridable Function GetEnumerator() As IEnumerator _
   Implements IEnumerable.GetEnumerator
```
[C#]
```
public virtual IEnumerator GetEnumerator();
```
[C++]
```
public: virtual IEnumerator* GetEnumerator();
```
[JScript]
```
public function GetEnumerator() : IEnumerator;
```

Return Value

An **IEnumerator** object that represents the link collection.

Implements

IEnumerable.GetEnumerator

Requirements

Platforms: Windows 98, Windows NT 4.0, Windows Millennium Edition, Windows 2000, Windows XP Home Edition, Windows XP Professional, Windows Server 2003 family

LinkLabel.LinkCollection.ICollection.CopyTo Method

This member supports the .NET Framework infrastructure and is not intended to be used directly from your code.

[Visual Basic]
```
Private Sub CopyTo( _
   ByVal dest As Array, _
   ByVal index As Integer _
) Implements ICollection.CopyTo
```
[C#]
```
void ICollection.CopyTo(
   Array dest,
   int index
);
```
[C++]
```
private: void ICollection::CopyTo(
   Array* dest,
   int index
);
```
[JScript]
```
private function ICollection.CopyTo(
   dest : Array,
   index : int
);
```

LinkLabel.LinkCollection.IList.Add Method

This member supports the .NET Framework infrastructure and is not intended to be used directly from your code.

[Visual Basic]
```
Private Function Add( _
   ByVal value As Object _
) As Integer Implements IList.Add
```

```
[C#]
int IList.Add(
   object value
);
[C++]
private: int IList::Add(
   Object* value
);
[JScript]
private function IList.Add(
   value : Object
) : int;
```

LinkLabel.LinkCollection.IList.Contains Method

This member supports the .NET Framework infrastructure and is not intended to be used directly from your code.

```
[Visual Basic]
Private Function Contains( _
   ByVal link As Object _
) As Boolean Implements IList.Contains
[C#]
bool IList.Contains(
   object link
);
[C++]
private: bool IList::Contains(
   Object* link
);
[JScript]
private function IList.Contains(
   link : Object
) : Boolean;
```

LinkLabel.LinkCollection.IList.IndexOf Method

This member supports the .NET Framework infrastructure and is not intended to be used directly from your code.

```
[Visual Basic]
Private Function IndexOf( _
   ByVal link As Object _
) As Integer Implements IList.IndexOf
[C#]
int IList.IndexOf(
   object link
);
[C++]
private: int IList::IndexOf(
   Object* link
);
[JScript]
private function IList.IndexOf(
   link : Object
) : int;
```

LinkLabel.LinkCollection.IList.Insert Method

This member supports the .NET Framework infrastructure and is not intended to be used directly from your code.

```
[Visual Basic]
Private Sub Insert( _
   ByVal index As Integer, _
   ByVal value As Object _
) Implements IList.Insert
[C#]
void IList.Insert(
   int index,
   object value
);
[C++]
private: void IList::Insert(
   int index,
   Object* value
);
[JScript]
private function IList.Insert(
   index : int,
   value : Object
);
```

LinkLabel.LinkCollection.IList.Remove Method

This member supports the .NET Framework infrastructure and is not intended to be used directly from your code.

```
[Visual Basic]
Private Sub Remove( _
   ByVal value As Object _
) Implements IList.Remove
[C#]
void IList.Remove(
   object value
);
[C++]
private: void IList::Remove(
   Object* value
);
[JScript]
private function IList.Remove(
   value : Object
);
```

LinkLabel.LinkCollection.IndexOf Method

Returns the index of the specified link within the collection.

```
[Visual Basic]
Public Function IndexOf( _
   ByVal link As LinkLabel.Link _
) As Integer
[C#]
public int IndexOf(
   LinkLabel.Link link
);
[C++]
public: int IndexOf(
   LinkLabel.Link* link
);
```

```
[JScript]
public function IndexOf(
   link : LinkLabel.Link
) : int;
```

Parameters

link

A **LinkLabel.Link** representing the link to search for in the collection.

Return Value

The zero-based index where the link is located within the collection; otherwise, negative one (-1).

Remarks

The **IndexOf** method enables you to determine where a link is located within the collection. To determine if a link is located within the collection before calling this method, use the **Contains** method.

Requirements

Platforms: Windows 98, Windows NT 4.0,
Windows Millennium Edition, Windows 2000,
Windows XP Home Edition, Windows XP Professional,
Windows Server 2003 family

LinkLabel.LinkCollection.Remove Method

Removes the specified link from the collection.

```
[Visual Basic]
Public Sub Remove( _
   ByVal value As LinkLabel.Link _
)
[C#]
public void Remove(
   LinkLabel.Link value
);
[C++]
public: void Remove(
   LinkLabel.Link* value
);
[JScript]
public function Remove(
   value : LinkLabel.Link
);
```

Parameters

value

A **LinkLabel.Link** that represents the link to remove from the collection.

Remarks

When you remove a link from the collection, the indexes change for subsequent items in the collection. All information about the removed item is deleted. You can use this method to remove a specific link from the collection by specifying the actual item to remove from the collection. To specify the index of the link to remove instead of the link itself, use the **RemoveAt** method. To remove all links from the collection, use the **Clear** method.

Requirements

Platforms: Windows 98, Windows NT 4.0,
Windows Millennium Edition, Windows 2000,
Windows XP Home Edition, Windows XP Professional,
Windows Server 2003 family

LinkLabel.LinkCollection.RemoveAt Method

Removes a link at a specified location within the collection.

```
[Visual Basic]
Public Overridable Sub RemoveAt( _
   ByVal index As Integer _
) Implements IList.RemoveAt
[C#]
public virtual void RemoveAt(
   int index
);
[C++]
public: virtual void RemoveAt(
   int index
);
[JScript]
public function RemoveAt(
   index : int
);
```

Parameters

index

The zero-based index of the item to remove from the collection.

Implements

IList.RemoveAt

Exceptions

Exception Type	Condition
ArgumentOutOfRange-Exception	The value of *index* is a negative value or greater than the number of items in the collection.

Remarks

When you remove a link from the collection, the indexes change for subsequent items in the collection. All information about the deleted link is lost. You can use this method to remove a specific link from the collection by specifying the index of the link to remove from the collection. To specify the link to remove instead of the index to the link, use the **Remove** method. To remove all links from the collection, use the **Clear** method.

Requirements

Platforms: Windows 98, Windows NT 4.0,
Windows Millennium Edition, Windows 2000,
Windows XP Home Edition, Windows XP Professional,
Windows Server 2003 family

LinkState Enumeration

This type supports the .NET Framework infrastructure and is not intended to be used directly from your code.

[Visual Basic]
```
<Serializable>
Public Enum LinkState
```
[C#]
```
[Serializable]
public enum LinkState
```
[C++]
```
[Serializable]
__value public enum LinkState
```
[JScript]
```
public
   Serializable
enum LinkState
```

Members

Active

Hover

Normal

Visited

ListBindingConverter Class

Provides a type converter to convert **Binding** objects to and from various other representations.

System.Object
  System.ComponentModel.TypeConverter
    System.Windows.Forms.ListBindingConverter

```
[Visual Basic]
Public Class ListBindingConverter
   Inherits TypeConverter
[C#]
public class ListBindingConverter : TypeConverter
[C++]
public __gc class ListBindingConverter : public TypeConverter
[JScript]
public class ListBindingConverter extends TypeConverter
```

Thread Safety

Any public static (**Shared** in Visual Basic) members of this type are safe for multithreaded operations. Any instance members are not guaranteed to be thread safe.

Remarks

The **ListBindingConverter** is used to evaluate and convert a property of an object into a **Binding**.

The **TypeConverterAttribute** is applied to the **Binding** class with the type of the **ListBindingConverter** as an argument.

> **Note** You should never create an instance of a **ListBinding-Converter**. Instead, call the **GetConverter** method of **Type-Descriptor**. For more information, see the examples in the **TypeConverter** base class.

Requirements

Namespace: System.Windows.Forms

Platforms: Windows 98, Windows NT 4.0, Windows Millennium Edition, Windows 2000, Windows XP Home Edition, Windows XP Professional, Windows Server 2003 family

Assembly: System.Windows.Forms (in System.Windows.Forms.dll)

ListBindingConverter Constructor

Initializes a new instance of the **ListBindingConverter** class.

```
[Visual Basic]
Public Sub New()
[C#]
public ListBindingConverter();
[C++]
public: ListBindingConverter();
[JScript]
public function ListBindingConverter();
```

Remarks

The default constructor initializes any fields to their default values.

Requirements

Platforms: Windows 98, Windows NT 4.0, Windows Millennium Edition, Windows 2000, Windows XP Home Edition, Windows XP Professional, Windows Server 2003 family

ListBindingConverter.CanConvertTo Method

Overload List

This member supports the .NET Framework infrastructure and is not intended to be used directly from your code.

[Visual Basic] **Overloads Overrides Public Function Can-ConvertTo(ITypeDescriptorContext, Type) As Boolean**

[C#] **public override bool CanConvertTo(IType-DescriptorContext, Type);**

[C++] **public: bool CanConvertTo(IType-DescriptorContext*, Type*);**

[JScript] **public override function CanConvertTo(IType-DescriptorContext, Type) : Boolean;**

Inherited from **TypeConverter**.

[Visual Basic] **Overloads Public Function CanConvertTo(Type) As Boolean**

[C#] **public bool CanConvertTo(Type);**

[C++] **public: bool CanConvertTo(Type*);**

[JScript] **public function CanConvertTo(Type) : Boolean;**

ListBindingConverter.CanConvertTo Method (ITypeDescriptorContext, Type)

This member overrides **TypeConverter.CanConvertTo**.

```
[Visual Basic]
Overrides Overloads Public Function CanConvertTo( _
   ByVal context As ITypeDescriptorContext, _
   ByVal destinationType As Type _
) As Boolean
[C#]
public override bool CanConvertTo(
   ITypeDescriptorContext context,
   Type destinationType
);
[C++]
public: bool CanConvertTo(
   ITypeDescriptorContext* context,
   Type* destinationType
);
[JScript]
public override function CanConvertTo(
   context : ITypeDescriptorContext,
   destinationType : Type
) : Boolean;
```

Requirements

Platforms: Windows 98, Windows NT 4.0, Windows Millennium Edition, Windows 2000, Windows XP Home Edition, Windows XP Professional, Windows Server 2003 family

ListBindingConverter.ConvertTo Method

Overload List

This member supports the .NET Framework infrastructure and is not intended to be used directly from your code.

[Visual Basic] **Overloads Overrides Public Function ConvertTo(ITypeDescriptorContext, CultureInfo, Object, Type) As Object**

[C#] **public override object ConvertTo(ITypeDescriptorContext, CultureInfo, object, Type);**

[C++] **public: Object* ConvertTo(ITypeDescriptorContext*, CultureInfo*, Object*, Type*);**

[JScript] **public override function ConvertTo(ITypeDescriptorContext, CultureInfo, Object, Type) : Object;**

Inherited from **TypeConverter**.

[Visual Basic] **Overloads Public Function ConvertTo(Object, Type) As Object**

[C#] **public object ConvertTo(object, Type);**

[C++] **public: Object* ConvertTo(Object*, Type*);**

[JScript] **public function ConvertTo(Object, Type) : Object;**

ListBindingConverter.ConvertTo Method (ITypeDescriptorContext, CultureInfo, Object, Type)

This member overrides **TypeConverter.ConvertTo**.

```
[Visual Basic]
Overrides Overloads Public Function ConvertTo( _
   ByVal context As ITypeDescriptorContext, _
   ByVal culture As CultureInfo, _
   ByVal value As Object, _
   ByVal destinationType As Type _
) As Object
[C#]
public override object ConvertTo(
   ITypeDescriptorContext context,
   CultureInfo culture,
   object value,
   Type destinationType
);
[C++]
public: Object* ConvertTo(
   ITypeDescriptorContext* context,
   CultureInfo* culture,
   Object* value,
   Type* destinationType
);
[JScript]
public override function ConvertTo(
   context : ITypeDescriptorContext,
   culture : CultureInfo,
   value : Object,
   destinationType : Type
) : Object;
```

Requirements

Platforms: Windows 98, Windows NT 4.0, Windows Millennium Edition, Windows 2000, Windows XP Home Edition, Windows XP Professional, Windows Server 2003 family

ListBindingConverter.CreateInstance Method

Overload List

This member supports the .NET Framework infrastructure and is not intended to be used directly from your code.

[Visual Basic] **Overloads Overrides Public Function CreateInstance(ITypeDescriptorContext, IDictionary) As Object**

[C#] **public override object CreateInstance(ITypeDescriptorContext, IDictionary);**

[C++] **public: Object* CreateInstance(ITypeDescriptorContext*, IDictionary*);**

[JScript] **public override function CreateInstance(ITypeDescriptorContext, IDictionary) : Object;**

Inherited from **TypeConverter**.

[Visual Basic] **Overloads Public Function CreateInstance(IDictionary) As Object**

[C#] **public object CreateInstance(IDictionary);**

[C++] **public: Object* CreateInstance(IDictionary*);**

[JScript] **public function CreateInstance(IDictionary) : Object;**

ListBindingConverter.CreateInstance Method (ITypeDescriptorContext, IDictionary)

This member overrides **TypeConverter.CreateInstance**.

```
[Visual Basic]
Overrides Overloads Public Function CreateInstance( _
   ByVal context As ITypeDescriptorContext, _
   ByVal propertyValues As IDictionary _
) As Object
[C#]
public override object CreateInstance(
   ITypeDescriptorContext context,
   IDictionary propertyValues
);
[C++]
public: Object* CreateInstance(
   ITypeDescriptorContext* context,
   IDictionary* propertyValues
);
[JScript]
public override function CreateInstance(
   context : ITypeDescriptorContext,
   propertyValues : IDictionary
) : Object;
```

Requirements

Platforms: Windows 98, Windows NT 4.0, Windows Millennium Edition, Windows 2000, Windows XP Home Edition, Windows XP Professional, Windows Server 2003 family

ListBindingConverter.GetCreateInstance-Supported Method

Overload List

This member supports the .NET Framework infrastructure and is not intended to be used directly from your code.

[Visual Basic] **Overloads Overrides Public Function Get-CreateInstanceSupported(ITypeDescriptorContext) As Boolean**

[C#] **public override bool GetCreateInstance-Supported(ITypeDescriptorContext);**

[C++] **public: bool GetCreateInstance-Supported(ITypeDescriptorContext*);**

[JScript] **public override function GetCreateInstance-Supported(ITypeDescriptorContext) : Boolean;**

Inherited from **TypeConverter**.

[Visual Basic] **Overloads Public Function GetCreate-InstanceSupported() As Boolean**

[C#] **public bool GetCreateInstanceSupported();**

[C++] **public: bool GetCreateInstanceSupported();**

[JScript] **public function GetCreateInstanceSupported() : Boolean;**

ListBindingConverter.GetCreateInstanceSupported Method (ITypeDescriptorContext)

This member overrides **TypeConverter.GetCreateInstanceSupported**.

```
[Visual Basic]
Overrides Overloads Public Function GetCreateInstanceSupported( _
   ByVal context As ITypeDescriptorContext _
) As Boolean
[C#]
public override bool GetCreateInstanceSupported(
   ITypeDescriptorContext context
);
[C++]
public: bool GetCreateInstanceSupported(
   ITypeDescriptorContext* context
);
[JScript]
public override function GetCreateInstanceSupported(
   context : ITypeDescriptorContext
) : Boolean;
```

Requirements

Platforms: Windows 98, Windows NT 4.0, Windows Millennium Edition, Windows 2000, Windows XP Home Edition, Windows XP Professional, Windows Server 2003 family

ListBox Class

Represents a Windows list box control.

System.Object
  System.MarshalByRefObject
    System.ComponentModel.Component
      System.Windows.Forms.Control
        System.Windows.Forms.ListControl
          System.Windows.Forms.ListBox
            System.Windows.Forms.CheckedListBox

[Visual Basic]
```
Public Class ListBox
   Inherits ListControl
```
[C#]
```
public class ListBox : ListControl
```
[C++]
```
public __gc class ListBox : public ListControl
```
[JScript]
```
public class ListBox extends ListControl
```

Thread Safety

Any public static (**Shared** in Visual Basic) members of this type are safe for multithreaded operations. Any instance members are not guaranteed to be thread safe.

Remarks

The **ListBox** control enables you to display a list of items to the user that the user can select by clicking. A **ListBox** control can provide single or multiple selections using the **SelectionMode** property. The **ListBox** also provides the **MultiColumn** property to enable the display of items in columns instead of a straight vertical list of items. This allows the control to display more visible items and prevents the need for the user to scroll to an item.

Typically, Windows handles the task of drawing the items to display in the **ListBox**. You can use the **DrawMode** property and handle the **MeasureItem** and **DrawItem** events to provide the ability to override the automatic drawing that Windows provides and draw the items yourself. You can use owner-drawn **ListBox** controls to display variable-height items, images, or a different color or font for the text of each item in the list. The **HorizontalExtent** property, **GetItemHeight**, and **GetItemRectangle** property also provide assistance for drawing your own items.

In addition to display and selection functionality, the **ListBox** also provides features that enable you to efficiently add items to the **ListBox** and to find text within the items of the list. The **BeginUpdate** and **EndUpdate** methods enable you to add a large number of items to the **ListBox** without the control being repainted each time an item is added to the list. The **FindString** and **FindStringExact** methods enable you to search for an item in the list that contains a specific search string.

The **Items**, **SelectedItems**, and **SelectedIndices** properties provide access to the three collections that are used by the **ListBox**. The following table outlines the three collections used by the **ListBox** and their use within the control.

Collection Class	Use Within The List Box
ListBox.ObjectCollection	Contains all items contained in the **ListBox** control.
ListBox.SelectedObjectCollection	Contains a collection of the selected items which is a subset of the items contained in the **ListBox** control.
ListBox.SelectedIndexCollection	Contains a collection of the selected indexes, which is a subset of the indexes of the **ListBox.ObjectCollection**. These indexes specify items that are selected.

The following three examples illustrate the three indexed collections that the **ListBox** class supports.

The following table demonstrates an example of how the **ListBox.ObjectCollection** stores the items of the **ListBox** as well as their selection state within an example **ListBox**.

Index	Item	Selection State Within the ListBox
0	object1	Unselected
1	object2	Selected
2	object3	Unselected
3	object4	Selected
4	object5	Selected

Based on the **ListBox.ObjectCollection** demonstrated in the table above, this table demonstrates how the **ListBox.SelectedObjectCollection** would appear.

Index	Item
0	object2
1	object4
2	object5

Based on the **ListBox.ObjectCollection** demonstrated in the table above, this table demonstrates how the **ListBox.SelectedIndexCollection** would appear.

Index	Index of Item
0	1
1	3
2	4

The **Add** method of the **ListBox.ObjectCollection** class enables you to add items to the **ListBox**. The **Add** method can accept any object when adding a member to the **ListBox**. When an object is being added to the **ListBox**, the control uses the text defined in the **ToString** method of the object unless a member name within the object is specified in the **DisplayMember** property. In addition to adding items using the **Add** method of the **ListBox.ObjectCollection** class you can also add items using the **DataSource** property of the **ListControl** class.

Example

[Visual Basic, C#, JScript] The following example demonstrates how to create a **ListBox** control that displays multiple items in columns and can have more than one item selected in the control's list. The code for the example adds 50 items to the **ListBox** using the **Add** method of the **ListBox.ObjectCollection** class and then selects three items from the list using the **SetSelected** method. The code then displays values from the **ListBox.SelectedObjectCollection** collection (through the **SelectedItems** property) and the **ListBox.SelectedIndexCollection** (through the **SelectedIndices** property). This example assumes that the code is located in and called from a **Form**.

[Visual Basic]
```
Private Sub button1_Click(sender As Object, e As System.EventArgs)
    ' Create an instance of the ListBox.
    Dim listBox1 As New ListBox()
    ' Set the size and location of the ListBox.
    listBox1.Size = New System.Drawing.Size(200, 100)
    listBox1.Location = New System.Drawing.Point(10, 10)
    ' Add the ListBox to the form.
    Me.Controls.Add(listBox1)
    ' Set the ListBox to display items in multiple columns.
    listBox1.MultiColumn = True
    ' Set the selection mode to multiple and extended.
    listBox1.SelectionMode = SelectionMode.MultiExtended

    ' Shutdown the painting of the ListBox as items are added.
    listBox1.BeginUpdate()
    ' Loop through and add 50 items to the ListBox.
    Dim x As Integer
    For x = 1 To 50
        listBox1.Items.Add("Item " & x.ToString())
    Next x
    ' Allow the ListBox to repaint and display the new items.
    listBox1.EndUpdate()

    ' Select three items from the ListBox.
    listBox1.SetSelected(1, True)
    listBox1.SetSelected(3, True)
    listBox1.SetSelected(5, True)

    ' Display the second selected item in the ListBox to the console.
    System.Diagnostics.Debug.WriteLine ↵
(listBox1.SelectedItems(1).ToString())
    ' Display the index of the first selected item in the ListBox.
    System.Diagnostics.Debug.WriteLine ↵
 (listBox1.SelectedIndices(0).ToString())
End Sub
```

[C#]
```
private void button1_Click(object sender, System.EventArgs e)
{
   // Create an instance of the ListBox.
   ListBox listBox1 = new ListBox();
   // Set the size and location of the ListBox.
   listBox1.Size = new System.Drawing.Size(200, 100);
   listBox1.Location = new System.Drawing.Point(10,10);
   // Add the ListBox to the form.
   this.Controls.Add(listBox1);
   // Set the ListBox to display items in multiple columns.
   listBox1.MultiColumn = true;
   // Set the selection mode to multiple and extended.
   listBox1.SelectionMode = SelectionMode.MultiExtended;

   // Shutdown the painting of the ListBox as items are added.
   listBox1.BeginUpdate();
   // Loop through and add 50 items to the ListBox.
   for (int x = 1; x <= 50; x++)
   {
      listBox1.Items.Add("Item " + x.ToString());
   }
   // Allow the ListBox to repaint and display the new items.
   listBox1.EndUpdate();

   // Select three items from the ListBox.
   listBox1.SetSelected(1, true);
   listBox1.SetSelected(3, true);
   listBox1.SetSelected(5, true);

   // Display the second selected item in the ListBox to the console.
   System.Diagnostics.Debug.WriteLine ↵
 (listBox1.SelectedItems[1].ToString());
   // Display the index of the first selected item in the ListBox.
   System.Diagnostics.Debug.WriteLine ↵
 (listBox1.SelectedIndices[0].ToString());
}
```

[JScript]
```
private function button1_Click(sender : Object, e : System.EventArgs)
{
   // Create an instance of the ListBox.
   var listBox1 : ListBox = new ListBox();
   // Set the size and location of the ListBox.
   listBox1.Size = new System.Drawing.Size(200, 100);
   listBox1.Location = new System.Drawing.Point(10,10);
   // Add the ListBox to the form.
   this.Controls.Add(listBox1);
   // Set the ListBox to display items in multiple columns.
   listBox1.MultiColumn = true;
   // Set the selection mode to multiple and extended.
   listBox1.SelectionMode = SelectionMode.MultiExtended;

   // Shutdown the painting of the ListBox as items are added.
   listBox1.BeginUpdate();
   // Loop through and add 50 items to the ListBox.
   for (var x : int = 1; x <= 50; x++)
   {
      listBox1.Items.Add("Item " + x.ToString());
   }
   // Allow the ListBox to repaint and display the new items.
   listBox1.EndUpdate();

   // Select three items from the ListBox.
   listBox1.SetSelected(1, true);
   listBox1.SetSelected(3, true);
   listBox1.SetSelected(5, true);

   // Display the second selected item in the ListBox to the console.
   System.Diagnostics.Debug.WriteLine ↵
 (listBox1.SelectedItems[1].ToString());
   // Display the index of the first selected item in the ListBox.
   System.Diagnostics.Debug.WriteLine ↵
 (listBox1.SelectedIndices[0].ToString());
}
```

Requirements

Namespace: System.Windows.Forms

Platforms: Windows 98, Windows NT 4.0, Windows Millennium Edition, Windows 2000, Windows XP Home Edition, Windows XP Professional, Windows Server 2003 family, .NET Compact Framework - Windows CE .NET

Assembly: System.Windows.Forms (in System.Windows.Forms.dll)

ListBox Constructor

Initializes a new instance of the **ListBox** class.

[Visual Basic]
```
Public Sub New()
```
[C#]
```
public ListBox();
```
[C++]
```
public: ListBox();
```
[JScript]
```
public function ListBox();
```

Example

See related example in the **System.Windows.Forms.ListBox** class topic.

Requirements

Platforms: Windows 98, Windows NT 4.0, Windows Millennium Edition, Windows 2000, Windows XP Home Edition, Windows XP Professional, Windows Server 2003 family, .NET Compact Framework - Windows CE .NET

ListBox.DefaultItemHeight Field

Specifies the default item height for an owner-drawn **ListBox**.

```
[Visual Basic]
Public Const DefaultItemHeight As Integer
[C#]
public const int DefaultItemHeight;
[C++]
public: const int DefaultItemHeight;
[JScript]
public var DefaultItemHeight : int;
```

Requirements

Platforms: Windows 98, Windows NT 4.0, Windows Millennium Edition, Windows 2000, Windows XP Home Edition, Windows XP Professional, Windows Server 2003 family

ListBox.NoMatches Field

Specifies that no matches are found during a search.

```
[Visual Basic]
Public Const NoMatches As Integer
[C#]
public const int NoMatches;
[C++]
public: const int NoMatches;
[JScript]
public var NoMatches : int;
```

Remarks

This constant is returned by the **FindString**, **FindStringExact**, and **IndexFromPoint** methods when no matching values are found in a search.

Requirements

Platforms: Windows 98, Windows NT 4.0, Windows Millennium Edition, Windows 2000, Windows XP Home Edition, Windows XP Professional, Windows Server 2003 family

ListBox.BackColor Property

This member overrides **Control.BackColor**.

```
[Visual Basic]
Overrides Public Property BackColor As Color
[C#]
public override Color BackColor {get; set;}
[C++]
public: __property Color get_BackColor();
public: __property void set_BackColor(Color);
[JScript]
public override function get BackColor() : Color;
public override function set BackColor(Color);
```

Requirements

Platforms: Windows 98, Windows NT 4.0, Windows Millennium Edition, Windows 2000, Windows XP Home Edition, Windows XP Professional, Windows Server 2003 family

ListBox.BackgroundImage Property

This member overrides **Control.BackgroundImage**.

```
[Visual Basic]
Overrides Public Property BackgroundImage As Image
[C#]
public override Image BackgroundImage {get; set;}
[C++]
public: __property Image* get_BackgroundImage();
public: __property void set_BackgroundImage(Image*);
[JScript]
public override function get BackgroundImage() : Image;
public override function set BackgroundImage(Image);
```

Requirements

Platforms: Windows 98, Windows NT 4.0, Windows Millennium Edition, Windows 2000, Windows XP Home Edition, Windows XP Professional, Windows Server 2003 family

ListBox.BorderStyle Property

This member supports the .NET Framework infrastructure and is not intended to be used directly from your code.

```
[Visual Basic]
Public Property BorderStyle As BorderStyle
[C#]
public BorderStyle BorderStyle {get; set;}
[C++]
public: __property BorderStyle get_BorderStyle();
public: __property void set_BorderStyle(BorderStyle);
[JScript]
public function get BorderStyle() : BorderStyle;
public function set BorderStyle(BorderStyle);
```

ListBox.ColumnWidth Property

Gets or sets the width of columns in a multicolumn **ListBox**.

```
[Visual Basic]
Public Property ColumnWidth As Integer
[C#]
public int ColumnWidth {get; set;}
[C++]
public: __property int get_ColumnWidth();
public: __property void set_ColumnWidth(int);
[JScript]
public function get ColumnWidth() : int;
public function set ColumnWidth(int);
```

Property Value

The width, in pixels, of each column in the control. The default is 0.

Exceptions

Exception Type	Condition
ArgumentException	A value less than zero is assigned to the property.

Remarks

If you set the value to zero (0), a default width is assigned to each column. If the **ListBox** is a multicolumn list box, this property returns the current width of each column in the list. You can use this property to ensure that each column in a multicolumn **ListBox** can properly display its items.

Example

See related example in the **System.Windows.Forms.ListBox** class topic.

Requirements

Platforms: Windows 98, Windows NT 4.0, Windows Millennium Edition, Windows 2000, Windows XP Home Edition, Windows XP Professional, Windows Server 2003 family

ListBox.CreateParams Property

This member overrides **Control.CreateParams**.

```
[Visual Basic]
Overrides Protected ReadOnly Property CreateParams As CreateParams
[C#]
protected override CreateParams CreateParams {get;}
[C++]
protected: __property CreateParams* get_CreateParams();
[JScript]
protected override function get CreateParams() : CreateParams;
```

Requirements

Platforms: Windows 98, Windows NT 4.0, Windows Millennium Edition, Windows 2000, Windows XP Home Edition, Windows XP Professional, Windows Server 2003 family

ListBox.DefaultSize Property

This member overrides **Control.DefaultSize**.

```
[Visual Basic]
Overrides Protected ReadOnly Property DefaultSize As Size
[C#]
protected override Size DefaultSize {get;}
[C++]
protected: __property Size get_DefaultSize();
[JScript]
protected override function get DefaultSize() : Size;
```

Requirements

Platforms: Windows 98, Windows NT 4.0, Windows Millennium Edition, Windows 2000, Windows XP Home Edition, Windows XP Professional, Windows Server 2003 family

ListBox.DrawMode Property

Gets or sets the drawing mode for the control.

```
[Visual Basic]
Public Overridable Property DrawMode As DrawMode
[C#]
public virtual DrawMode DrawMode {get; set;}
[C++]
public: __property virtual DrawMode get_DrawMode();
public: __property virtual void set_DrawMode(DrawMode);
[JScript]
public function get DrawMode() : DrawMode;
public function set DrawMode(DrawMode);
```

Property Value

One of the **DrawMode** values representing the mode for drawing the items of the control. The default is **DrawMode.Normal**.

Exceptions

Exception Type	Condition
InvalidEnumArgumentException	The value assigned to the property is not a member of the **DrawMode** enumeration.
ArgumentException	A multicolumn **ListBox** cannot have a variable-sized height.

Example

See related example in the **System.Windows.Forms.ListBox** class topic.

Requirements

Platforms: Windows 98, Windows NT 4.0, Windows Millennium Edition, Windows 2000, Windows XP Home Edition, Windows XP Professional, Windows Server 2003 family

ListBox.ForeColor Property

This member overrides **Control.ForeColor**.

```
[Visual Basic]
Overrides Public Property ForeColor As Color
[C#]
public override Color ForeColor {get; set;}
[C++]
public: __property Color get_ForeColor();
public: __property void set_ForeColor(Color);
[JScript]
public override function get ForeColor() : Color;
public override function set ForeColor(Color);
```

Requirements

Platforms: Windows 98, Windows NT 4.0, Windows Millennium Edition, Windows 2000, Windows XP Home Edition, Windows XP Professional, Windows Server 2003 family

ListBox.HorizontalExtent Property

Gets or sets the width by which the horizontal scroll bar of a **ListBox** can scroll.

```
[Visual Basic]
Public Property HorizontalExtent As Integer
[C#]
public int HorizontalExtent {get; set;}
[C++]
public: __property int get_HorizontalExtent();
public: __property void set_HorizontalExtent(int);
```

[JScript]
```
public function get HorizontalExtent() : int;
public function set HorizontalExtent(int);
```

Property Value

The width, in pixels, that the horizontal scroll bar can scroll the control. The default is zero.

Remarks

This property only reports a useful value if the **HorizontalScrollbar** property is set to **true**. If the width of the **ListBox** is smaller than the value of this property, the horizontal scroll bar horizontally scrolls items in the **ListBox**. If the width of the **ListBox** is equal to or greater than this value, the horizontal scroll bar is hidden. The value of this property is not dynamically updated by the **ListBox**. This property is useful when the items of the **ListBox** are owner-drawn. For example, if the owner drawn items of the **ListBox** are 200 pixels wide, but the **ListBox** is 60 pixels wide, the **HorizontalExtent** property would need to be set to 200 in order to scroll the right edge of the items into the visible region of the control.

Example

See related example in the **System.Windows.Forms.ListBox** class topic.

Requirements

Platforms: Windows 98, Windows NT 4.0, Windows Millennium Edition, Windows 2000, Windows XP Home Edition, Windows XP Professional, Windows Server 2003 family

ListBox.HorizontalScrollbar Property

Gets or sets a value indicating whether a horizontal scroll bar is displayed in the control.

[Visual Basic]
```
Public Property HorizontalScrollbar As Boolean
```
[C#]
```
public bool HorizontalScrollbar {get; set;}
```
[C++]
```
public: __property bool get_HorizontalScrollbar();
public: __property void set_HorizontalScrollbar(bool);
```
[JScript]
```
public function get HorizontalScrollbar() : Boolean;
public function set HorizontalScrollbar(Boolean);
```

Property Value

true to display a horizontal scroll bar in the control; otherwise, **false**. The default is **false**.

Remarks

The **HorizontalScrollbar** property determines whether the **ListBox** should display a horizontal scroll bar when the width of items within the **ListBox** extend beyond the right edge of the control. When this property is set to **true**, the scroll bar is automatically displayed based on the width of items in the **ListBox**. If the **ListBox** is an owner-drawn list box, in order to properly display a horizontal scroll bar, you must set the **HorizontalExtent** property.

Example

See related example in the **System.Windows.Forms.ListBox** class topic.

Requirements

Platforms: Windows 98, Windows NT 4.0, Windows Millennium Edition, Windows 2000, Windows XP Home Edition, Windows XP Professional, Windows Server 2003 family

ListBox.IntegralHeight Property

Gets or sets a value indicating whether the control should resize to avoid showing partial items.

[Visual Basic]
```
Public Property IntegralHeight As Boolean
```
[C#]
```
public bool IntegralHeight {get; set;}
```
[C++]
```
public: __property bool get_IntegralHeight();
public: __property void set_IntegralHeight(bool);
```
[JScript]
```
public function get IntegralHeight() : Boolean;
public function set IntegralHeight(Boolean);
```

Property Value

true if the control resizes so that it does not display partial items; otherwise, **false**. The default is **true**.

Remarks

When this property is set to **true**, the control automatically resizes to ensure that an item is not partially displayed. If you want to maintain the original size of the **ListBox** based on the space requirements of your form, set this property to **false**. If the **ListBox** does not contain any items, this property has no effect.

> **Note** The integral height is based on the height of the **ListBox**, rather than the client area height. As a result, when the **IntegralHeight** property is set **true**, items can still be partially shown if scroll bars are displayed.

> **Note** If the **DrawMode** property is set to **DrawMode.OwnerDrawVariable**, this property has no effect.

Example

See related example in the **System.Windows.Forms.ListBox** class topic.

Requirements

Platforms: Windows 98, Windows NT 4.0, Windows Millennium Edition, Windows 2000, Windows XP Home Edition, Windows XP Professional, Windows Server 2003 family

ListBox.ItemHeight Property

Gets or sets the height of an item in the **ListBox**.

[Visual Basic]
```
Public Overridable Property ItemHeight As Integer
```
[C#]
```
public virtual int ItemHeight {get; set;}
```
[C++]
```
public: __property virtual int get_ItemHeight();
public: __property virtual void set_ItemHeight(int);
```
[JScript]
```
public function get ItemHeight() : int;
public function set ItemHeight(int);
```

Property Value

The height, in pixels, of an item in the control.

Remarks

When the **DrawMode** property is set to **DrawMode.OwnerDrawFixed**, all items have the same height. When the **DrawMode** property is set to **DrawMode.OwnerDrawVariable**, the **ItemHeight** property specifies the height of each item added to the **ListBox**. Because each item in an owner-drawn list can have a different height, you can use the **GetItemHeight** method to get the height of a specific item in the **ListBox**. If you use the **ItemHeight** property on a **ListBox** with items of variable height, this property returns the height of the first item in the control.

Requirements

Platforms: Windows 98, Windows NT 4.0,
Windows Millennium Edition, Windows 2000,
Windows XP Home Edition, Windows XP Professional,
Windows Server 2003 family

ListBox.Items Property

Gets the items of the **ListBox**.

```
[Visual Basic]
Public ReadOnly Property Items As ListBox.ObjectCollection
[C#]
public ListBox.ObjectCollection Items {get;}
[C++]
public: __property ListBox.ObjectCollection* get_Items();
[JScript]
public function get Items() : ListBox.ObjectCollection;
```

Property Value

An **ListBox.ObjectCollection** representing the items in the **ListBox**.

Remarks

This property enables you to obtain a reference to the list of items that are currently stored in the **ListBox**. With this reference, you can add items, remove items, and obtain a count of the items in the collection. For more information on the tasks that can be performed with the item collection, see the **ListBox.ObjectCollection** class reference topics.

You can also manipulate the items of a **ListBox** by using the **DataSource** property. If you use the **DataSource** property to add items to a **ListBox**, you can view the items in the **ListBox** using the **Items** property but you cannot add or remove items from the list using the methods of the **ListBox.ObjectCollection**.

Example

See related example in the **System.Windows.Forms.ListBox** class topic.

Requirements

Platforms: Windows 98, Windows NT 4.0,
Windows Millennium Edition, Windows 2000,
Windows XP Home Edition, Windows XP Professional,
Windows Server 2003 family,
.NET Compact Framework - Windows CE .NET

ListBox.MultiColumn Property

Gets or sets a value indicating whether the **ListBox** supports multiple columns.

```
[Visual Basic]
Public Property MultiColumn As Boolean
[C#]
public bool MultiColumn {get; set;}
[C++]
public: __property bool get_MultiColumn();
public: __property void set_MultiColumn(bool);
[JScript]
public function get MultiColumn() : Boolean;
public function set MultiColumn(Boolean);
```

Property Value

true if the list box supports multiple columns; otherwise, **false**. The default is **false**.

Exceptions

Exception Type	Condition
ArgumentException	A multicolumn **ListBox** cannot have a variable-sized height.

Remarks

A multicolumn list box places items into as many columns as are needed to make vertical scrolling unnecessary. The user can use the keyboard to navigate to columns that are not currently visible. Set the **HorizontalScrollbar** property to **true** to display a horizontal scroll bar that allows the user to scroll to columns that are not currently shown in the visible region of the **ListBox**. The value of the **ColumnWidth** property determines the width of each column.

Example

See related example in the **System.Windows.Forms.ListBox** class topic.

Requirements

Platforms: Windows 98, Windows NT 4.0,
Windows Millennium Edition, Windows 2000,
Windows XP Home Edition, Windows XP Professional,
Windows Server 2003 family

ListBox.PreferredHeight Property

Gets the combined height of all items in the **ListBox**.

```
[Visual Basic]
Public ReadOnly Property PreferredHeight As Integer
[C#]
public int PreferredHeight {get;}
[C++]
public: __property int get_PreferredHeight();
[JScript]
public function get PreferredHeight() : int;
```

Property Value

The combined height, in pixels, of all items in the control.

Remarks

This property enables you to determine the height that the **ListBox** needs to be sized to, in order to display every available item in the list and to avoid displaying vertical scroll bars. If the amount of items in the **ListBox** is large, sizing the control using the value of the **PreferredHeight** property might cause the **ListBox** to be sized outside of the client area of the form or container it is located within.

Example

See related example in the **System.Windows.Forms.ListBox** class topic.

Requirements

Platforms: Windows 98, Windows NT 4.0,
Windows Millennium Edition, Windows 2000,
Windows XP Home Edition, Windows XP Professional,
Windows Server 2003 family

ListBox.RightToLeft Property

Gets or sets a value indicating whether text displayed by the control is displayed from right to left.

[Visual Basic]
```
Overrides Public Property RightToLeft As RightToLeft
```
[C#]
```
public override RightToLeft RightToLeft {get; set;}
```
[C++]
```
public: __property RightToLeft get_RightToLeft();
public: __property void set_RightToLeft(RightToLeft);
```
[JScript]
```
public override function get RightToLeft() : RightToLeft;
public override function set RightToLeft(RightToLeft);
```

Property Value

One of the **RightToLeft** values.

Remarks

This property allows your menus to support languages that are written from right to left. When this property is set to **true**, item text is displayed from right to left instead of the default left to right method.

Windows 98, Windows Millennium Edition Platform Note: This property has no effect in Windows 98 or Windows Millennium Edition.

Requirements

Platforms: Windows 98, Windows NT 4.0,
Windows Millennium Edition, Windows 2000,
Windows XP Home Edition, Windows XP Professional,
Windows Server 2003 family

ListBox.ScrollAlwaysVisible Property

Gets or sets a value indicating whether the vertical scroll bar is shown at all times.

[Visual Basic]
```
Public Property ScrollAlwaysVisible As Boolean
```
[C#]
```
public bool ScrollAlwaysVisible {get; set;}
```
[C++]
```
public: __property bool get_ScrollAlwaysVisible();
public: __property void set_ScrollAlwaysVisible(bool);
```
[JScript]
```
public function get ScrollAlwaysVisible() : Boolean;
public function set ScrollAlwaysVisible(Boolean);
```

Property Value

true if the vertical scroll bar should always be displayed; otherwise, **false**. The default is **false**.

Remarks

The **ScrollAlwaysVisible** property indicates whether a vertical scroll bar is always displayed, even if the number of items in the **ListBox** does not require displaying the vertical scroll bar. By default, a **ListBox** only shows a vertical scroll bar when there are enough items to warrant displaying. For multicolumn list boxes, the **ScrollAlwaysVisible** property indicates that a horizontal scroll bar is displayed. A vertical scroll bar is never displayed regardless of the value of this property for a multicolumn **ListBox**.

Requirements

Platforms: Windows 98, Windows NT 4.0,
Windows Millennium Edition, Windows 2000,
Windows XP Home Edition, Windows XP Professional,
Windows Server 2003 family

ListBox.SelectedIndex Property

Gets or sets the zero-based index of the currently selected item in a **ListBox**.

[Visual Basic]
```
Overrides Public Property SelectedIndex As Integer
```
[C#]
```
public override int SelectedIndex {get; set;}
```
[C++]
```
public: __property int get_SelectedIndex();
public: __property void set_SelectedIndex(int);
```
[JScript]
```
public override function get SelectedIndex() : int;
public override function set SelectedIndex(int);
```

Property Value

A zero-based index of the currently selected item. A value of negative one (-1) is returned if no item is selected.

Remarks

For a standard **ListBox**, you can use this property to determine the index of the item that is selected in the **ListBox**. If the **SelectionMode** property of the **ListBox** is set to either **SelectionMode.MultiSimple** or **SelectionMode.MultiExtended** (which indicates a multiple-selection **ListBox**) and multiple items are selected in the list, this property can return the index to any selected item.

To retrieve a collection containing the indexes of all selected items in a multiple-selection **ListBox**, use the **SelectedIndices** property. If you want to obtain the item that is currently selected in the **ListBox**, use the **SelectedItem** property. In addition, you can use the **SelectedItems** property to obtain all the selected items in a multiple-selection **ListBox**.

Example

See related example in the **System.Windows.Forms.ListBox** class topic.

Requirements

Platforms: Windows 98, Windows NT 4.0,
Windows Millennium Edition, Windows 2000,
Windows XP Home Edition, Windows XP Professional,
Windows Server 2003 family,
.NET Compact Framework - Windows CE .NET

ListBox.SelectedIndices Property

Gets a collection that contains the zero-based indexes of all currently selected items in the **ListBox**.

[Visual Basic]
```
Public ReadOnly Property SelectedIndices As _
   ListBox.SelectedIndexCollection
```
[C#]
```
public ListBox.SelectedIndexCollection SelectedIndices {get;}
```
[C++]
```
public: __property ListBox.SelectedIndexCollection*
   get_SelectedIndices();
```
[JScript]
```
public function get SelectedIndices() :
   ListBox.SelectedIndexCollection;
```

Property Value

A **ListBox.SelectedIndexCollection** containing the indexes of the currently selected items in the control. If no items are currently selected, an empty **ListBox.SelectedIndexCollection** is returned.

Remarks

For a multiple-selection **ListBox**, this property returns a collection containing the indexes to all items that are selected in the **ListBox**. For a single-selection **ListBox**, this property returns a collection containing a single element containing the index of the only selected item in the **ListBox**. For more information on how to manipulate the items of the collection, see **ListBox.SelectedIndexCollection**.

The **ListBox** class provides a number of ways to reference selected items. Instead of using the **SelectedIndices** property to obtain the index position of the currently selected item in a single-selection **ListBox**, you can use the **SelectedIndex** property. If you want to obtain the item that is currently selected in the **ListBox**, instead of the index position of the item, use the **SelectedItem** property. In addition, you can use the **SelectedItems** property if you want to obtain all the selected items in a multiple-selection **ListBox**.

Example

See related example in the **System.Windows.Forms.ListBox** class topic.

Requirements

Platforms: Windows 98, Windows NT 4.0,
Windows Millennium Edition, Windows 2000,
Windows XP Home Edition, Windows XP Professional,
Windows Server 2003 family

ListBox.SelectedItem Property

Gets or sets the currently selected item in the **ListBox**.

[Visual Basic]
```
Public Property SelectedItem As Object
```
[C#]
```
public object SelectedItem {get; set;}
```
[C++]
```
public: __property Object* get_SelectedItem();
public: __property void set_SelectedItem(Object*);
```
[JScript]
```
public function get SelectedItem() : Object;
public function set SelectedItem(Object);
```

Property Value

An object that represents the current selection in the control.

Remarks

For a standard **ListBox**, you can use this property to determine which item is selected in the **ListBox**. If the **SelectionMode** property of the **ListBox** is set to either **SelectionMode.MultiSimple** or **SelectionMode.MultiExtended** (which indicates a multiple-selection **ListBox**) and multiple items are selected in the list, this property can return any selected item.

To retrieve a collection containing all selected items in a multiple-selection **ListBox**, use the **SelectedItems** property. If you want to obtain the index position of the currently selected item in the **ListBox**, use the **SelectedIndex** property. In addition, you can use the **SelectedIndices** property to obtain all the selected indexes in a multiple-selection **ListBox**.

Example

See related example in the **System.Windows.Forms.ListBox** class topic.

Requirements

Platforms: Windows 98, Windows NT 4.0,
Windows Millennium Edition, Windows 2000,
Windows XP Home Edition, Windows XP Professional,
Windows Server 2003 family,
.NET Compact Framework - Windows CE .NET

ListBox.SelectedItems Property

Gets a collection containing the currently selected items in the **ListBox**.

[Visual Basic]
```
Public ReadOnly Property SelectedItems As _
   ListBox.SelectedObjectCollection
```
[C#]
```
public ListBox.SelectedObjectCollection SelectedItems {get;}
```
[C++]
```
public: __property ListBox.SelectedObjectCollection*
   get_SelectedItems();
```
[JScript]
```
public function get SelectedItems() :
   ListBox.SelectedObjectCollection;
```

Property Value

A **ListBox.SelectedObjectCollection** containing the currently selected items in the control.

Remarks

For a multiple-selection **ListBox**, this property returns a collection containing all items that are selected in the **ListBox**. For a single-selection **ListBox**, this property returns a collection containing a single element containing the only selected item in the **ListBox**. For more information on how to manipulate the items of the collection, see **ListBox.SelectedObjectCollection**.

The **ListBox** class provides a number of ways to reference selected items. Instead of using the **SelectedItems** property to obtain the currently selected item in a single-selection **ListBox**, you can use the **SelectedItem** property. If you want to obtain the index position of an item that is currently selected in the **ListBox**, instead of the item itself, use the **SelectedIndex** property. In addition, you can use the **SelectedIndices** property if you want to obtain the index positions of all selected items in a multiple-selection **ListBox**.

Requirements

Platforms: Windows 98, Windows NT 4.0, Windows Millennium Edition, Windows 2000, Windows XP Home Edition, Windows XP Professional, Windows Server 2003 family

ListBox.SelectionMode Property

Gets or sets the method in which items are selected in the **ListBox**.

```
[Visual Basic]
Public Overridable Property SelectionMode As SelectionMode
[C#]
public virtual SelectionMode SelectionMode {get; set;}
[C++]
public: __property virtual SelectionMode get_SelectionMode();
public: __property virtual void set_SelectionMode(SelectionMode);
[JScript]
public function get SelectionMode() : SelectionMode;
public function set SelectionMode(SelectionMode);
```

Property Value

One of the **SelectionMode** values. The default is **SelectionMode.One**.

Remarks

The **SelectionMode** property enables you to determine how many items in the **ListBox** a user can select at one time and how the user can make multiple-selections. When the **SelectionMode** property is set to **SelectionMode.MultiExtended**, pressing SHIFT and clicking the mouse or pressing SHIFT and one of the arrow keys (UP ARROW, DOWN ARROW, LEFT ARROW, and RIGHT ARROW) extends the selection from the previously selected item to the current item. Pressing CTRL and clicking the mouse selects or deselects an item in the list. When the property is set to **SelectionMode.MultiSimple**, a mouse click or pressing the SPACEBAR selects or deselects an item in the list.

Example

See related example in the **System.Windows.Forms.ListBox** class topic.

Requirements

Platforms: Windows 98, Windows NT 4.0, Windows Millennium Edition, Windows 2000, Windows XP Home Edition, Windows XP Professional, Windows Server 2003 family

ListBox.Sorted Property

Gets or sets a value indicating whether the items in the **ListBox** are sorted alphabetically.

```
[Visual Basic]
Public Property Sorted As Boolean
[C#]
public bool Sorted {get; set;}
[C++]
public: __property bool get_Sorted();
public: __property void set_Sorted(bool);
[JScript]
public function get Sorted() : Boolean;
public function set Sorted(Boolean);
```

Property Value

true if items in the control are sorted; otherwise, **false**. The default is **false**.

Remarks

You can use this property to automatically sort items alphabetically in a **ListBox**. As items are added to a sorted **ListBox**, the items are moved to the appropriate location in the sorted list. When adding items to a **ListBox**, it is more efficient to sort the items first and then add new items.

Example

See related example in the **System.Windows.Forms.ListBox** class topic.

Requirements

Platforms: Windows 98, Windows NT 4.0, Windows Millennium Edition, Windows 2000, Windows XP Home Edition, Windows XP Professional, Windows Server 2003 family

ListBox.Text Property

Gets or searches for the text of the currently selected item in the **ListBox**.

```
[Visual Basic]
Overrides Public Property Text As String
[C#]
public override string Text {get; set;}
[C++]
public: __property String* get_Text();
public: __property void set_Text(String*);
[JScript]
public override function get Text() : String;
public override function set Text(String);
```

Property Value

The text of the currently selected item in the control.

Remarks

When the value of this property is set to a string value, the **ListBox** searches for the item within the **ListBox** that matches the specified text and selects the item. You can also use this property to determine which items are currently selected in the **ListBox**. If the **SelectionMode** property of the **ListBox** is set to **SelectionMode.MultiExtended**, this property returns the text of the first selected item. If the **SelectionMode** property of the **ListBox** is not set to **SelectionMode.None**, this property returns the text of the first selected item.

Requirements

Platforms: Windows 98, Windows NT 4.0, Windows Millennium Edition, Windows 2000, Windows XP Home Edition, Windows XP Professional, Windows Server 2003 family, .NET Compact Framework - Windows CE .NET

ListBox.TopIndex Property

Gets or sets the index of the first visible item in the **ListBox**.

```
[Visual Basic]
Public Property TopIndex As Integer
[C#]
public int TopIndex {get; set;}
```

```
[C++]
public: __property int get_TopIndex();
public: __property void set_TopIndex(int);
[JScript]
public function get TopIndex() : int;
public function set TopIndex(int);
```

Property Value

The zero-based index of the first visible item in the control.

Remarks

Initially, the item with the index position zero (0) is at the top of the visible region of the **ListBox**. If the contents of the **ListBox** have been scrolled, another item might be at the top of the control's display area. You can use this property to obtain the index within the **ListBox.ObjectCollection** for the **ListBox** of the item that is currently positioned at the top of the visible region of the control. You can also use this property to position an item in the list at the top of the visible region of the control.

Example

See related example in the **System.Windows.Forms.ListBox** class topic.

Requirements

Platforms: Windows 98, Windows NT 4.0,
Windows Millennium Edition, Windows 2000,
Windows XP Home Edition, Windows XP Professional,
Windows Server 2003 family,
.NET Compact Framework - Windows CE .NET

ListBox.UseTabStops Property

Gets or sets a value indicating whether the **ListBox** can recognize and expand tab characters when drawing its strings.

```
[Visual Basic]
Public Property UseTabStops As Boolean
[C#]
public bool UseTabStops {get; set;}
[C++]
public: __property bool get_UseTabStops();
public: __property void set_UseTabStops(bool);
[JScript]
public function get UseTabStops() : Boolean;
public function set UseTabStops(Boolean);
```

Property Value

true if the control can expand tab characters; otherwise, **false**. The default is **true**.

Example

See related example in the **System.Windows.Forms.ListBox** class topic.

Requirements

Platforms: Windows 98, Windows NT 4.0,
Windows Millennium Edition, Windows 2000,
Windows XP Home Edition, Windows XP Professional,
Windows Server 2003 family

ListBox.AddItemsCore Method

This member supports the .NET Framework infrastructure and is not intended to be used directly from your code.

```
[Visual Basic]
Protected Overridable Sub AddItemsCore( _
   ByVal value() As Object _
)
[C#]
protected virtual void AddItemsCore(
   object[] value
);
[C++]
protected: virtual void AddItemsCore(
   Object* value __gc[]
);
[JScript]
protected function AddItemsCore(
   value : Object[]
);
```

ListBox.BeginUpdate Method

Maintains performance while items are added to the **ListBox** one at a time by preventing the control from drawing until the **EndUpdate** method is called.

```
[Visual Basic]
Public Sub BeginUpdate()
[C#]
public void BeginUpdate();
[C++]
public: void BeginUpdate();
[JScript]
public function BeginUpdate();
```

Remarks

The preferred way to add multiple items to the **ListBox** is to use the **AddRange** method of the **ListBox.ObjectCollection** class (through the **Items** property of the **ListBox**). This enables you to add an array of items to the list in a single operation. However, if you want to add items one at a time using the **Add** method of the **ListBox.ObjectCollection** class, you can use the **BeginUpdate** method to prevent the control from repainting the **ListBox** each time an item is added to the list. Once you have completed the task of adding items to the list, call the **EndUpdate** method to enable the **ListBox** to repaint. This way of adding items can prevent flickered drawing of the **ListBox** when a large number of items are being added to the list.

Example

See related example in the **System.Windows.Forms.ListBox** class topic.

Requirements

Platforms: Windows 98, Windows NT 4.0,
Windows Millennium Edition, Windows 2000,
Windows XP Home Edition, Windows XP Professional,
Windows Server 2003 family

ListBox.ClearSelected Method

Unselects all items in the **ListBox**.

[Visual Basic]
```
Public Sub ClearSelected()
```
[C#]
```
public void ClearSelected();
```
[C++]
```
public: void ClearSelected();
```
[JScript]
```
public function ClearSelected();
```

Remarks

Calling this method is equivalent to setting the **SelectedIndex** property to negative one (-1). You can use this method to quickly remove unselect all items in the list.

Example

See related example in the **System.Windows.Forms.ListBox** class topic.

Requirements

Platforms: Windows 98, Windows NT 4.0, Windows Millennium Edition, Windows 2000, Windows XP Home Edition, Windows XP Professional, Windows Server 2003 family

ListBox.CreateItemCollection Method

Creates a new instance of the item collection.

[Visual Basic]
```
Protected Overridable Function CreateItemCollection() As _
   ObjectCollection
```
[C#]
```
protected virtual ObjectCollection CreateItemCollection();
```
[C++]
```
protected: virtual ObjectCollection* CreateItemCollection();
```
[JScript]
```
protected function CreateItemCollection() : ObjectCollection;
```

Return Value

A **ListBox.ObjectCollection** that represents the new item collection.

Remarks

Notes to Inheritors: You can override this in your derived classes to provide a different collection to store your items.

Requirements

Platforms: Windows 98, Windows NT 4.0, Windows Millennium Edition, Windows 2000, Windows XP Home Edition, Windows XP Professional, Windows Server 2003 family

ListBox.EndUpdate Method

Resumes painting the **ListBox** control after painting is suspended by the **BeginUpdate** method.

[Visual Basic]
```
Public Sub EndUpdate()
```
[C#]
```
public void EndUpdate();
```
[C++]
```
public: void EndUpdate();
```
[JScript]
```
public function EndUpdate();
```

Remarks

The preferred way to add items to the **ListBox** is to use the **AddRange** method of the **ListBox.ObjectCollection** class (through the **Items** property of the **ListBox**). This enables you to add an array of items to the list at one time. However, if you want to add items one at a time using the **Add** method of the **ListBox.ObjectCollection** class, you can use the **BeginUpdate** method to prevent the control from repainting the **ListBox** each time an item is added to the list. Once you have completed the task of adding items to the list, call the **EndUpdate** method to enable the **ListBox** to repaint. This way of adding items can prevent flickered drawing of the **ListBox** when a large number of items are being added to the list.

Example

See related example in the **System.Windows.Forms.ListBox** class topic.

Requirements

Platforms: Windows 98, Windows NT 4.0, Windows Millennium Edition, Windows 2000, Windows XP Home Edition, Windows XP Professional, Windows Server 2003 family

ListBox.FindString Method

Finds the first item in the **ListBox** that starts with the specified string.

Overload List

Finds the first item in the **ListBox** that starts with the specified string.

[Visual Basic] **Overloads Public Function FindString(String) As Integer**

[C#] **public int FindString(string);**

[C++] **public: int FindString(String*);**

[JScript] **public function FindString(String) : int;**

Finds the first item in the **ListBox** that starts with the specified string. The search starts at a specific starting index.

[Visual Basic] **Overloads Public Function FindString(String, Integer) As Integer**

[C#] **public int FindString(string, int);**

[C++] **public: int FindString(String*, int);**

[JScript] **public function FindString(String, int) : int;**

Example

See related example in the **System.Windows.Forms.ListBox** class topic.

ListBox.FindString Method (String)

Finds the first item in the **ListBox** that starts with the specified string.

[Visual Basic]
```
Overloads Public Function FindString( _
   ByVal s As String _
) As Integer
```
[C#]
```
public int FindString(
   string s
);
```
[C++]
```
public: int FindString(
   String* s
);
```
[JScript]
```
public function FindString(
   s : String
) : int;
```

Parameters

s

The text to search for.

Return Value

The zero-based index of the first item found; returns **ListBox.NoMatches** if no match is found.

Remarks

The search performed by this method is not case-sensitive. The search looks for words that partially match the specified search string parameter, *s*. You can use this method to search for the first item that matches the specified string. You can then perform tasks such as removing the item that contains the search text by using the **Remove** method or changing the item's text. Once you have found the specified text, if you want to search for other instances of the text in the **ListBox**, you can use the version of the **FindString** method that provides a parameter for specifying a starting index within the **ListBox**. If you want to perform a search for an exact word match instead of a partial match, use the **FindStringExact** method.

Example

See related example in the **System.Windows.Forms.ListBox** class topic.

Requirements

Platforms: Windows 98, Windows NT 4.0, Windows Millennium Edition, Windows 2000, Windows XP Home Edition, Windows XP Professional, Windows Server 2003 family

ListBox.FindString Method (String, Int32)

Finds the first item in the **ListBox** that starts with the specified string. The search starts at a specific starting index.

[Visual Basic]
```
Overloads Public Function FindString( _
   ByVal s As String, _
   ByVal startIndex As Integer _
) As Integer
```
[C#]
```
public int FindString(
   string s,
   int startIndex
);
```
[C++]
```
public: int FindString(
   String* s,
   int startIndex
);
```
[JScript]
```
public function FindString(
   s : String,
   startIndex : int
) : int;
```

Parameters

s

The text to search for.

startIndex

The zero-based index of the item before the first item to be searched. Set to negative one (-1) to search from the beginning of the control.

Return Value

The zero-based index of the first item found; returns **ListBox.NoMatches** if no match is found.

Exceptions

Exception Type	Condition
ArgumentOutOfRange-Exception	The *startIndex* parameter is less than zero or greater than or equal to the value of the **Count** property of the **ListBox.ObjectCollection** class.

Remarks

The search performed by this method is not case-sensitive. The search looks for words that partially match the specified search string parameter, *s*. You can use this method to search for the first item that matches the specified string at the specified starting index within the list of items for the **ListBox**. You can then perform tasks such as removing the item that contains the search text by using the **Remove** method or changing the item's text. This method is typically used after a call has been made using the version of this method that does not specify a starting index. Once an initial item has been found in the list, this method is typically used to find further instances of the search text by specifying the index position in the *startIndex* parameter of the item after the first found instance of the search text. If you want to perform a search for an exact word match instead of a partial match, use the **FindStringExact** method.

Note When the search reaches the bottom of the **ListBox**, it continues searching from the top of the **ListBox** back to the item specified by the *startIndex* parameter.

Example

See related example in the **System.Windows.Forms.ListBox** class topic.

Requirements

Platforms: Windows 98, Windows NT 4.0, Windows Millennium Edition, Windows 2000, Windows XP Home Edition, Windows XP Professional, Windows Server 2003 family

ListBox.FindStringExact Method

Finds the first item in the **ListBox** that exactly matches the specified string.

Overload List

Finds the first item in the **ListBox** that exactly matches the specified string.

[Visual Basic] **Overloads Public Function FindStringExact(String) As Integer**

[C#] **public int FindStringExact(string);**

[C++] **public: int FindStringExact(String*);**

[JScript] **public function FindStringExact(String) : int;**

Finds the first item in the **ListBox** that exactly matches the specified string. The search starts at a specific starting index.

[Visual Basic] **Overloads Public Function FindString-Exact(String, Integer) As Integer**

[C#] **public int FindStringExact(string, int);**

[C++] **public: int FindStringExact(String*, int);**

[JScript] **public function FindStringExact(String, int) : int;**

Example

See related example in the **System.Windows.Forms.ListBox** class topic.

ListBox.FindStringExact Method (String)

Finds the first item in the **ListBox** that exactly matches the specified string.

```
[Visual Basic]
Overloads Public Function FindStringExact( _
   ByVal s As String _
) As Integer
[C#]
public int FindStringExact(
   string s
);
[C++]
public: int FindStringExact(
   String* s
);
[JScript]
public function FindStringExact(
   s : String
) : int;
```

Parameters

s

The text to search for.

Return Value

The zero-based index of the first item found; returns **ListBox.NoMatches** if no match is found.

Remarks

The search performed by this method is not case-sensitive. The search looks for an exact match to the words specified in the search string parameter, *s*. You can use this method to search for the first item that matches the specified string. You can then perform tasks such as removing the item that contains the search text by using the **Remove** method or changing the item's text. Once you have found the specified text, if you want to search for other instances of the text in the **ListBox**, you can use the version of the **FindStringExact** method that provides a parameter for specifying a starting index within the **ListBox**. If you want to perform partial word search instead of an exact word match, use the **FindString** method.

Example

See related example in the **System.Windows.Forms.ListBox** class topic.

Requirements

Platforms: Windows 98, Windows NT 4.0, Windows Millennium Edition, Windows 2000, Windows XP Home Edition, Windows XP Professional, Windows Server 2003 family

ListBox.FindStringExact Method (String, Int32)

Finds the first item in the **ListBox** that exactly matches the specified string. The search starts at a specific starting index.

```
[Visual Basic]
Overloads Public Function FindStringExact( _
   ByVal s As String, _
   ByVal startIndex As Integer _
) As Integer
[C#]
public int FindStringExact(
   string s,
   int startIndex
);
[C++]
public: int FindStringExact(
   String* s,
   int startIndex
);
[JScript]
public function FindStringExact(
   s : String,
   startIndex : int
) : int;
```

Parameters

s

The text to search for.

startIndex

The zero-based index of the item before the first item to be searched. Set to negative one (-1) to search from the beginning of the control.

Return Value

The zero-based index of the first item found; returns **ListBox.NoMatches** if no match is found.

Exceptions

Exception Type	Condition
ArgumentOutOfRange-Exception	The *startIndex* parameter is less than zero or greater than or equal to the value of the **Count** property of the **ListBox.ObjectCollection** class.

Remarks

The search performed by this method is not case-sensitive. The search looks for words that exactly match the specified search string parameter, *s*. You can use this method to search for the first item that matches the specified string at the specified starting index within the list of items for the **ListBox**. You can then perform tasks such as removing the item that contains the search text using the **Remove** method or change the item's text. This method is typically used after a call has been made using the version of this method that does not specify a starting index. Once an initial item has been found in the list, this method is typically used to find further instances of the search text by specifying the index position in the *startIndex* parameter of the item after the first found instance of the search text. If you want to perform a partial word search instead of an exact word match, use the **FindString** method.

> **Note** When the search reaches the bottom of the **ListBox**, it continues searching from the top of the **ListBox** back to the item specified by the *startIndex* parameter.

Example

See related example in the **System.Windows.Forms.ListBox** class topic.

Requirements

Platforms: Windows 98, Windows NT 4.0, Windows Millennium Edition, Windows 2000, Windows XP Home Edition, Windows XP Professional, Windows Server 2003 family

ListBox.GetItemHeight Method

Returns the height of an item in the **ListBox**.

```
[Visual Basic]
Public Function GetItemHeight( _
   ByVal index As Integer _
) As Integer
[C#]
public int GetItemHeight(
   int index
);
[C++]
public: int GetItemHeight(
   int index
);
[JScript]
public function GetItemHeight(
   index : int
) : int;
```

Parameters

index

The zero-based index of the item to return the height for.

Return Value

The height, in pixels, of the specified item.

Exceptions

Exception Type	Condition
ArgumentOutOfRange-Exception	The specified index was outside the range valid values.

Remarks

If the **DrawMode** property is not set to **DrawMode.OwnerDrawVariable**, the value of the index parameter is ignored because all items in a standard **ListBox** are the same size. You can use this property when you are using an owner-drawn **ListBox** to determine the size of any item within the **ListBox**.

Requirements

Platforms: Windows 98, Windows NT 4.0, Windows Millennium Edition, Windows 2000, Windows XP Home Edition, Windows XP Professional, Windows Server 2003 family

ListBox.GetItemRectangle Method

Returns the bounding rectangle for an item in the **ListBox**.

```
[Visual Basic]
Public Function GetItemRectangle( _
   ByVal index As Integer _
) As Rectangle
[C#]
public Rectangle GetItemRectangle(
   int index
);
[C++]
public: Rectangle GetItemRectangle(
   int index
);
[JScript]
public function GetItemRectangle(
   index : int
) : Rectangle;
```

Parameters

index

The zero-based index of item whose bounding rectangle you want to return.

Return Value

A **Rectangle** that represents the bounding rectangle for the specified item.

Exceptions

Exception Type	Condition
ArgumentOutOfRange-Exception	The *index* parameter is less than zero or greater than or equal to the value of the **Count** property of the **ListBox.ObjectCollection** class.

Remarks

If the item specified in the *index* parameter is not visible, the rectangle returned by this method will be outside the visible portion of the control. You can use this method to determine the size and position of an item within the list. To get the height of an item, especially a variable-height owner drawn list item, you can use the **GetItemHeight** method.

Requirements

Platforms: Windows 98, Windows NT 4.0, Windows Millennium Edition, Windows 2000, Windows XP Home Edition, Windows XP Professional, Windows Server 2003 family

ListBox.GetSelected Method

Returns a value indicating whether the specified item is selected.

```
[Visual Basic]
Public Function GetSelected( _
   ByVal index As Integer _
) As Boolean
```

```
[C#]
public bool GetSelected(
   int index
);
[C++]
public: bool GetSelected(
   int index
);
[JScript]
public function GetSelected(
   index : int
) : Boolean;
```

Parameters

index

The zero-based index of the item that determines whether it is selected.

Return Value

true if the specified item is currently selected in the **ListBox**; otherwise, **false**.

Exceptions

Exception Type	Condition
ArgumentOutOfRange-Exception	The *index* parameter is less than zero or greater than or equal to the value of the **Count** property of the **ListBox.ObjectCollection** class.

Remarks

You can used this method to quickly determine whether a specified item is selected. This method is useful when a specific operation needs to be performed when a specific item in a multiple-selection **ListBox** is selected.

Example

See related example in the **System.Windows.Forms.ListBox** class topic.

Requirements

Platforms: Windows 98, Windows NT 4.0, Windows Millennium Edition, Windows 2000, Windows XP Home Edition, Windows XP Professional, Windows Server 2003 family

ListBox.IndexFromPoint Method

Returns the zero-based index of the item at the specified coordinates.

Overload List

Returns the zero-based index of the item at the specified coordinates.

[Visual Basic] **Overloads Public Function IndexFromPoint(Point) As Integer**

[C#] **public int IndexFromPoint(Point);**

[C++] **public: int IndexFromPoint(Point);**

[JScript] **public function IndexFromPoint(Point) : int;**

Returns the zero-based index of the item at the specified coordinates.

[Visual Basic] **Overloads Public Function IndexFromPoint(Integer, Integer) As Integer**

[C#] **public int IndexFromPoint(int, int);**

[C++] **public: int IndexFromPoint(int, int);**

[JScript] **public function IndexFromPoint(int, int) : int;**

Example

See related example in the **System.Windows.Forms.ListBox** class topic.

ListBox.IndexFromPoint Method (Point)

Returns the zero-based index of the item at the specified coordinates.

```
[Visual Basic]
Overloads Public Function IndexFromPoint( _
   ByVal p As Point _
) As Integer
[C#]
public int IndexFromPoint(
   Point p
);
[C++]
public: int IndexFromPoint(
   Point p
);
[JScript]
public function IndexFromPoint(
   p : Point
) : int;
```

Parameters

p

A **Point** object containing the coordinates used to obtain the item index.

Return Value

The zero-based index of the item found at the specified coordinates; returns **ListBox.NoMatches** if no match is found.

Remarks

This method enables you to determine which item is located at a specific location within the control. You can use this method to determine which item within the list is selected when a user right-clicks over the **ListBox**. The location of the cursor can be determined and passed to the *p* parameter of the **IndexFromPoint** method to determine which item the user right-clicked the mouse over. You can then display a shortcut menu to the user to provide tasks and features based on the specific item.

Example

See related example in the **System.Windows.Forms.ListBox** class topic.

Requirements

Platforms: Windows 98, Windows NT 4.0, Windows Millennium Edition, Windows 2000, Windows XP Home Edition, Windows XP Professional, Windows Server 2003 family

ListBox.IndexFromPoint Method (Int32, Int32)

Returns the zero-based index of the item at the specified coordinates.

```
[Visual Basic]
Overloads Public Function IndexFromPoint( _
   ByVal x As Integer, _
   ByVal y As Integer _
) As Integer
```

```
[C#]
public int IndexFromPoint(
   int x,
   int y
);
[C++]
public: int IndexFromPoint(
   int x,
   int y
);
[JScript]
public function IndexFromPoint(
   x : int,
   y : int
) : int;
```

Parameters

x

The x coordinate of the location to search.

y

The y coordinate of the location to search.

Return Value

The zero-based index of the item found at the specified coordinates; returns **ListBox.NoMatches** if no match is found.

Remarks

This method enables you to determine which item that is located at a specific location within the control. You can use this method to determine which item within the list is selected when a user right-clicks over the **ListBox**. The location of the cursor can be determined and passed to the *x* and *y* parameters of the **IndexFromPoint** method to determine which item the user right-clicked the mouse over. You can then display a shortcut menu to the user to provide tasks and features based on the specific item.

Example

See related example in the **System.Windows.Forms.ListBox** class topic.

Requirements

Platforms: Windows 98, Windows NT 4.0, Windows Millennium Edition, Windows 2000, Windows XP Home Edition, Windows XP Professional, Windows Server 2003 family

ListBox.OnChangeUICues Method

This member overrides **Control.OnChangeUICues**.

```
[Visual Basic]
Overrides Protected Sub OnChangeUICues( _
   ByVal e As UICuesEventArgs _
)
[C#]
protected override void OnChangeUICues(
   UICuesEventArgs e
);
[C++]
protected: void OnChangeUICues(
   UICuesEventArgs* e
);
[JScript]
protected override function OnChangeUICues(
   e : UICuesEventArgs
);
```

Requirements

Platforms: Windows 98, Windows NT 4.0, Windows Millennium Edition, Windows 2000, Windows XP Home Edition, Windows XP Professional, Windows Server 2003 family

ListBox.OnDataSourceChanged Method

This member overrides **ListControl.OnDataSourceChanged**.

```
[Visual Basic]
Overrides Protected Sub OnDataSourceChanged( _
   ByVal e As EventArgs _
)
[C#]
protected override void OnDataSourceChanged(
   EventArgs e
);
[C++]
protected: void OnDataSourceChanged(
   EventArgs* e
);
[JScript]
protected override function OnDataSourceChanged(
   e : EventArgs
);
```

Requirements

Platforms: Windows 98, Windows NT 4.0, Windows Millennium Edition, Windows 2000, Windows XP Home Edition, Windows XP Professional, Windows Server 2003 family, .NET Compact Framework - Windows CE .NET

ListBox.OnDisplayMemberChanged Method

This member overrides **ListControl.OnDisplayMemberChanged**.

```
[Visual Basic]
Overrides Protected Sub OnDisplayMemberChanged( _
   ByVal e As EventArgs _
)
[C#]
protected override void OnDisplayMemberChanged(
   EventArgs e
);
[C++]
protected: void OnDisplayMemberChanged(
   EventArgs* e
);
[JScript]
protected override function OnDisplayMemberChanged(
   e : EventArgs
);
```

Requirements

Platforms: Windows 98, Windows NT 4.0, Windows Millennium Edition, Windows 2000, Windows XP Home Edition, Windows XP Professional, Windows Server 2003 family, .NET Compact Framework - Windows CE .NET

ListBox.OnDrawItem Method

Raises the **DrawItem** event.

[Visual Basic]
```
Protected Overridable Sub OnDrawItem( _
   ByVal e As DrawItemEventArgs _
)
```
[C#]
```
protected virtual void OnDrawItem(
   DrawItemEventArgs e
);
```
[C++]
```
protected: virtual void OnDrawItem(
   DrawItemEventArgs* e
);
```
[JScript]
```
protected function OnDrawItem(
   e : DrawItemEventArgs
);
```

Parameters

e

A **DrawItemEventArgs** that contains the event data.

Remarks

Raising an event invokes the event handler through a delegate.

The **OnDrawItem** method also allows derived classes to handle the event without attaching a delegate. This is the preferred technique for handling the event in a derived class.

Notes to Inheritors: When overriding **OnDrawItem** in a derived class, be sure to call the base class's **OnDrawItem** method so that registered delegates receive the event.

Example

See related example in the **System.Windows.Forms.ListBox** class topic.

Requirements

Platforms: Windows 98, Windows NT 4.0, Windows Millennium Edition, Windows 2000, Windows XP Home Edition, Windows XP Professional, Windows Server 2003 family

ListBox.OnFontChanged Method

This member overrides **Control.OnFontChanged**.

[Visual Basic]
```
Overrides Protected Sub OnFontChanged( _
   ByVal e As EventArgs _
)
```
[C#]
```
protected override void OnFontChanged(
   EventArgs e
);
```
[C++]
```
protected: void OnFontChanged(
   EventArgs* e
);
```
[JScript]
```
protected override function OnFontChanged(
   e : EventArgs
);
```

Requirements

Platforms: Windows 98, Windows NT 4.0, Windows Millennium Edition, Windows 2000, Windows XP Home Edition, Windows XP Professional, Windows Server 2003 family

ListBox.OnHandleCreated Method

This member overrides **Control.OnHandleCreated**.

[Visual Basic]
```
Overrides Protected Sub OnHandleCreated( _
   ByVal e As EventArgs _
)
```
[C#]
```
protected override void OnHandleCreated(
   EventArgs e
);
```
[C++]
```
protected: void OnHandleCreated(
   EventArgs* e
);
```
[JScript]
```
protected override function OnHandleCreated(
   e : EventArgs
);
```

Requirements

Platforms: Windows 98, Windows NT 4.0, Windows Millennium Edition, Windows 2000, Windows XP Home Edition, Windows XP Professional, Windows Server 2003 family

ListBox.OnHandleDestroyed Method

This member overrides **Control.OnHandleDestroyed**.

[Visual Basic]
```
Overrides Protected Sub OnHandleDestroyed( _
   ByVal e As EventArgs _
)
```
[C#]
```
protected override void OnHandleDestroyed(
   EventArgs e
);
```
[C++]
```
protected: void OnHandleDestroyed(
   EventArgs* e
);
```
[JScript]
```
protected override function OnHandleDestroyed(
   e : EventArgs
);
```

Requirements

Platforms: Windows 98, Windows NT 4.0, Windows Millennium Edition, Windows 2000, Windows XP Home Edition, Windows XP Professional, Windows Server 2003 family

ListBox.OnMeasureItem Method

Raises the **MeasureItem** event.

```
[Visual Basic]
Protected Overridable Sub OnMeasureItem( _
   ByVal e As MeasureItemEventArgs _
)
[C#]
protected virtual void OnMeasureItem(
   MeasureItemEventArgs e
);
[C++]
protected: virtual void OnMeasureItem(
   MeasureItemEventArgs* e
);
[JScript]
protected function OnMeasureItem(
   e : MeasureItemEventArgs
);
```

Parameters

e

A **MeasureItemEventArgs** that contains the event data.

Remarks

Raising an event invokes the event handler through a delegate.

The **OnMeasureItem** method also allows derived classes to handle the event without attaching a delegate. This is the preferred technique for handling the event in a derived class.

Notes to Inheritors: When overriding **OnMeasureItem** in a derived class, be sure to call the base class's **OnMeasureItem** method so that registered delegates receive the event.

Requirements

Platforms: Windows 98, Windows NT 4.0, Windows Millennium Edition, Windows 2000, Windows XP Home Edition, Windows XP Professional, Windows Server 2003 family

ListBox.OnParentChanged Method

This member overrides **Control.OnParentChanged**.

```
[Visual Basic]
Overrides Protected Sub OnParentChanged( _
   ByVal e As EventArgs _
)
[C#]
protected override void OnParentChanged(
   EventArgs e
);
[C++]
protected: void OnParentChanged(
   EventArgs* e
);
[JScript]
protected override function OnParentChanged(
   e : EventArgs
);
```

Requirements

Platforms: Windows 98, Windows NT 4.0, Windows Millennium Edition, Windows 2000, Windows XP Home Edition, Windows XP Professional, Windows Server 2003 family, .NET Compact Framework - Windows CE .NET

ListBox.OnResize Method

This member overrides **Control.OnResize**.

```
[Visual Basic]
Overrides Protected Sub OnResize( _
   ByVal e As EventArgs _
)
[C#]
protected override void OnResize(
   EventArgs e
);
[C++]
protected: void OnResize(
   EventArgs* e
);
[JScript]
protected override function OnResize(
   e : EventArgs
);
```

Requirements

Platforms: Windows 98, Windows NT 4.0, Windows Millennium Edition, Windows 2000, Windows XP Home Edition, Windows XP Professional, Windows Server 2003 family, .NET Compact Framework - Windows CE .NET

ListBox.OnSelectedIndexChanged Method

This member overrides **ListControl.OnSelectedIndexChanged**.

```
[Visual Basic]
Overrides Protected Sub OnSelectedIndexChanged( _
   ByVal e As EventArgs _
)
[C#]
protected override void OnSelectedIndexChanged(
   EventArgs e
);
[C++]
protected: void OnSelectedIndexChanged(
   EventArgs* e
);
[JScript]
protected override function OnSelectedIndexChanged(
   e : EventArgs
);
```

Requirements

Platforms: Windows 98, Windows NT 4.0, Windows Millennium Edition, Windows 2000, Windows XP Home Edition, Windows XP Professional, Windows Server 2003 family, .NET Compact Framework - Windows CE .NET

ListBox.OnSelectedValueChanged Method

This member overrides **ListControl.OnSelectedValueChanged**.

```
[Visual Basic]
Overrides Protected Sub OnSelectedValueChanged( _
   ByVal e As EventArgs _
)
[C#]
protected override void OnSelectedValueChanged(
   EventArgs e
);
[C++]
protected: void OnSelectedValueChanged(
   EventArgs* e
);
[JScript]
protected override function OnSelectedValueChanged(
   e : EventArgs
);
```

Requirements

Platforms: Windows 98, Windows NT 4.0, Windows Millennium Edition, Windows 2000, Windows XP Home Edition, Windows XP Professional, Windows Server 2003 family, .NET Compact Framework - Windows CE .NET

ListBox.Refresh Method

This member overrides **Control.Refresh**.

```
[Visual Basic]
Overrides Public Sub Refresh()
[C#]
public override void Refresh();
[C++]
public: void Refresh();
[JScript]
public override function Refresh();
```

Requirements

Platforms: Windows 98, Windows NT 4.0, Windows Millennium Edition, Windows 2000, Windows XP Home Edition, Windows XP Professional, Windows Server 2003 family

ListBox.RefreshItem Method

This member overrides **ListControl.RefreshItem**.

```
[Visual Basic]
Overrides Protected Sub RefreshItem( _
   ByVal index As Integer _
)
[C#]
protected override void RefreshItem(
   int index
);
[C++]
protected: void RefreshItem(
   int index
);
[JScript]
protected override function RefreshItem(
   index : int
);
```

Requirements

Platforms: Windows 98, Windows NT 4.0, Windows Millennium Edition, Windows 2000, Windows XP Home Edition, Windows XP Professional, Windows Server 2003 family

ListBox.SetBoundsCore Method

This member overrides **Control.SetBoundsCore**.

```
[Visual Basic]
Overrides Protected Sub SetBoundsCore( _
   ByVal x As Integer, _
   ByVal y As Integer, _
   ByVal width As Integer, _
   ByVal height As Integer, _
   ByVal specified As BoundsSpecified _
)
[C#]
protected override void SetBoundsCore(
   int x,
   int y,
   int width,
   int height,
   BoundsSpecified specified
);
[C++]
protected: void SetBoundsCore(
   int x,
   int y,
   int width,
   int height,
   BoundsSpecified specified
);
[JScript]
protected override function SetBoundsCore(
   x : int,
   y : int,
   width : int,
   height : int,
   specified : BoundsSpecified
);
```

Requirements

Platforms: Windows 98, Windows NT 4.0, Windows Millennium Edition, Windows 2000, Windows XP Home Edition, Windows XP Professional, Windows Server 2003 family

ListBox.SetItemCore Method

This member supports the .NET Framework infrastructure and is not intended to be used directly from your code.

```
[Visual Basic]
Overrides Protected Sub SetItemCore( _
   ByVal index As Integer, _
   ByVal value As Object _
)
```

```
[C#]
protected override void SetItemCore(
   int index,
   object value
);
[C++]
protected: void SetItemCore(
   int index,
   Object* value
);
[JScript]
protected override function SetItemCore(
   index : int,
   value : Object
);
```

ListBox.SetItemsCore Method

This member supports the .NET Framework infrastructure and is not intended to be used directly from your code.

```
[Visual Basic]
Overrides Protected Sub SetItemsCore( _
   ByVal value As IList _
)
[C#]
protected override void SetItemsCore(
   IList value
);
[C++]
protected: void SetItemsCore(
   IList* value
);
[JScript]
protected override function SetItemsCore(
   value : IList
);
```

ListBox.SetSelected Method

Selects or clears the selection for the specified item in a **ListBox**.

```
[Visual Basic]
Public Sub SetSelected( _
   ByVal index As Integer, _
   ByVal value As Boolean _
)
[C#]
public void SetSelected(
   int index,
   bool value
);
[C++]
public: void SetSelected(
   int index,
   bool value
);
[JScript]
public function SetSelected(
   index : int,
   value : Boolean
);
```

Parameters

index

The zero-based index of the item in a **ListBox** to select or clear the selection for.

value

true to select the specified item; otherwise, **false**.

Exceptions

Exception Type	Condition
ArgumentOutOfRangeException	The specified index was outside the range of valid values.

Remarks

You can use this property to set the selection of items in a multiple-selection **ListBox**. To select an item in a single-selection **ListBox**, use the **SelectedIndex** property.

Example

See related example in the **System.Windows.Forms.ListBox** class topic.

Requirements

Platforms: Windows 98, Windows NT 4.0, Windows Millennium Edition, Windows 2000, Windows XP Home Edition, Windows XP Professional, Windows Server 2003 family

ListBox.Sort Method

Sorts the items in the **ListBox** alphabetically.

```
[Visual Basic]
Protected Overridable Sub Sort()
[C#]
protected virtual void Sort();
[C++]
protected: virtual void Sort();
[JScript]
protected function Sort();
```

Remarks

Notes to Inheritors: You can override this method in your derived class to provide your own sorting routine. When adding items to a **ListBox**, it is more efficient to sort the items first and then add new items.

Requirements

Platforms: Windows 98, Windows NT 4.0, Windows Millennium Edition, Windows 2000, Windows XP Home Edition, Windows XP Professional, Windows Server 2003 family

ListBox.ToString Method

This member overrides **Object.ToString**.

```
[Visual Basic]
Overrides Public Function ToString() As String
[C#]
public override string ToString();
[C++]
public: String* ToString();
[JScript]
public override function ToString() : String;
```

Requirements

Platforms: Windows 98, Windows NT 4.0, Windows Millennium Edition, Windows 2000, Windows XP Home Edition, Windows XP Professional, Windows Server 2003 family, .NET Compact Framework - Windows CE .NET

ListBox.WmReflectCommand Method

This member supports the .NET Framework infrastructure and is not intended to be used directly from your code.

```
[Visual Basic]
Protected Overridable Sub WmReflectCommand( _
   ByRef m As Message _
)
[C#]
protected virtual void WmReflectCommand(
   ref Message m
);
[C++]
protected: virtual void WmReflectCommand(
   Message* m
);
[JScript]
protected function WmReflectCommand(
   m : Message
);
```

ListBox.WndProc Method

This member overrides **Control.WndProc**.

```
[Visual Basic]
Overrides Protected Sub WndProc( _
   ByRef m As Message _
)
[C#]
protected override void WndProc(
   ref Message m
);
[C++]
protected: void WndProc(
   Message* m
);
[JScript]
protected override function WndProc(
   m : Message
);
```

Requirements

Platforms: Windows 98, Windows NT 4.0, Windows Millennium Edition, Windows 2000, Windows XP Home Edition, Windows XP Professional, Windows Server 2003 family

ListBox.BackgroundImageChanged Event

This member supports the .NET Framework infrastructure and is not intended to be used directly from your code.

```
[Visual Basic]
Public Shadows Event BackgroundImageChanged As EventHandler
[C#]
public new event EventHandler BackgroundImageChanged;
[C++]
public: __event EventHandler* BackgroundImageChanged;
```

[JScript] In JScript, you can handle the events defined by a class, but you cannot define your own.

ListBox.Click Event

This member supports the .NET Framework infrastructure and is not intended to be used directly from your code.

```
[Visual Basic]
Public Shadows Event Click As EventHandler
[C#]
public new event EventHandler Click;
[C++]
public: __event EventHandler* Click;
```

[JScript] In JScript, you can handle the events defined by a class, but you cannot define your own.

ListBox.DrawItem Event

Occurs when a visual aspect of an owner-drawn **ListBox** changes.

```
[Visual Basic]
Public Event DrawItem As DrawItemEventHandler
[C#]
public event DrawItemEventHandler DrawItem;
[C++]
public: __event DrawItemEventHandler* DrawItem;
```

[JScript] In JScript, you can handle the events defined by a class, but you cannot define your own.

Event Data

The event handler receives an argument of type **DrawItemEventArgs** containing data related to this event. The following **DrawItemEventArgs** properties provide information specific to this event.

Property	Description
BackColor	Gets the background color of the item that is being drawn.
Bounds	Gets the rectangle that represents the bounds of the item that is being drawn.
Font	Gets the font assigned to the item being drawn.
ForeColor	Gets the foreground color of the of the item being drawn.
Graphics	Gets the graphics surface to draw the item on.
Index	Gets the index value of the item that is being drawn.
State	Gets the state of the item being drawn.

Remarks

This event is used by an owner-drawn **ListBox**. The event is only raised when the **DrawMode** property is set to **DrawMode.OwnerDrawFixed** or **DrawMode.OwnerDrawVariable**. You can use this event to perform the tasks needed to draw items in the **ListBox**. If you have a variable-sized item (when the **DrawMode** property is set to **DrawMode.OwnerDrawVariable**), before drawing an item, the **MeasureItem** event is raised. You can create an event handler for the **MeasureItem** event to specify the size for the item that you are going to draw in your event handler for the **DrawItem** event.

Example

See related example in the **System.Windows.Forms.ListBox** class topic.

Requirements

Platforms: Windows 98, Windows NT 4.0, Windows Millennium Edition, Windows 2000, Windows XP Home Edition, Windows XP Professional, Windows Server 2003 family

ListBox.MeasureItem Event

Occurs when an owner-drawn **ListBox** is created and the sizes of the list items are determined.

```
[Visual Basic]
Public Event MeasureItem As MeasureItemEventHandler
[C#]
public event MeasureItemEventHandler MeasureItem;
[C++]
public: __event MeasureItemEventHandler* MeasureItem;
```

[JScript] In JScript, you can handle the events defined by a class, but you cannot define your own.

Event Data

The event handler receives an argument of type **MeasureItemEventArgs** containing data related to this event. The following **MeasureItemEventArgs** properties provide information specific to this event.

Property	Description
Graphics	Gets the **Graphics** object to measure against.
Index	Gets or sets the index of the item for which the height and width is needed.
ItemHeight	Gets or sets the height of the item specified by the **Index**.
ItemWidth	Gets or sets the width of the item specified by the **Index**.

Remarks

You can create an event handler for this event to specify the size an item will be made before it is drawn in the **DrawItem** event. The event is only raised when the **DrawMode** property is set **DrawMode.OwnerDrawVariable**.

Requirements

Platforms: Windows 98, Windows NT 4.0, Windows Millennium Edition, Windows 2000, Windows XP Home Edition, Windows XP Professional, Windows Server 2003 family

ListBox.Paint Event

This member supports the .NET Framework infrastructure and is not intended to be used directly from your code.

```
[Visual Basic]
Public Shadows Event Paint As PaintEventHandler
[C#]
public new event PaintEventHandler Paint;
[C++]
public: __event PaintEventHandler* Paint;
```

[JScript] In JScript, you can handle the events defined by a class, but you cannot define your own.

ListBox.SelectedIndexChanged Event

Occurs when the **SelectedIndex** property has changed.

```
[Visual Basic]
Public Event SelectedIndexChanged As EventHandler
[C#]
public event EventHandler SelectedIndexChanged;
[C++]
public: __event EventHandler* SelectedIndexChanged;
```

[JScript] In JScript, you can handle the events defined by a class, but you cannot define your own.

Event Data

The event handler receives an argument of type **EventArgs**.

Remarks

You can create an event handler for this event to determine when the selected index in the **ListBox** has been changed. This can be useful when you need to display information in other controls based on the current selection in the **ListBox**. You can use the event handler for this event to load the information in the other controls.

Example

See related example in the **System.Windows.Forms.ListBox** class topic.

Requirements

Platforms: Windows 98, Windows NT 4.0, Windows Millennium Edition, Windows 2000, Windows XP Home Edition, Windows XP Professional, Windows Server 2003 family

ListBox.TextChanged Event

This member supports the .NET Framework infrastructure and is not intended to be used directly from your code.

```
[Visual Basic]
Public Shadows Event TextChanged As EventHandler
[C#]
public new event EventHandler TextChanged;
[C++]
public: __event EventHandler* TextChanged;
```

[JScript] In JScript, you can handle the events defined by a class, but you cannot define your own.

ListBox.ObjectCollection Class

Represents the collection of items in a **ListBox**.

System.Object
  System.Windows.Forms.ListBox.ObjectCollection
    System.Windows.Forms.CheckedListBox.ObjectCollection

[Visual Basic]
```
Public Class ListBox.ObjectCollection
   Implements IList, ICollection, IEnumerable
```
[C#]
```
public class ListBox.ObjectCollection : IList, ICollection,
   IEnumerable
```
[C++]
```
public __gc class ListBox.ObjectCollection : public IList,
   ICollection, IEnumerable
```
[JScript]
```
public class ListBox.ObjectCollection implements IList,
   ICollection, IEnumerable
```

Thread Safety

Any public static (**Shared** in Visual Basic) members of this type are safe for multithreaded operations. Any instance members are not guaranteed to be thread safe.

Remarks

The **ListBox.ObjectCollection** class stores the items displayed in the **ListBox**. There are two other collections defined within the **ListBox** class that enable you to determine what items are selected within this collection. The **ListBox.SelectedObjectCollection** class provides properties and methods for determining what items are selected within the **ListBox.ObjectCollection**, while the **ListBox.SelectedIndexCollection** class enables you to determine what indexes within the **ListBox.ObjectCollection** are selected.

There are a number of ways to add items to the collection. The **Add** method provides the ability to add a single object to the collection. To add a number of objects to the collection, you create an array of items and assign it to the **AddRange** method. If you want to insert an object at a specific location within the collection, you can use the **Insert** method. To remove items, you can use either the **Remove** method or the **RemoveAt** method if you know where the item is located within the collection. The **Clear** method enables you to remove all items from the collection instead of using the **Remove** method to remove a single item at a time.

You can also manipulate the items of a **ListBox** by using the **DataSource** property. If you use the **DataSource** property to add items to a **ListBox**, you can view the items in the **ListBox** using the **Items** property but you cannot add or remove items from the list using the methods of the **ListBox.ObjectCollection**.

In addition to methods and properties for adding and removing items, the **ListBox.ObjectCollection** also provides methods to find items within the collection. The **Contains** method enables you to determine whether an object is a member of the collection. Once you know that the item is located within the collection, you can use the **IndexOf** method to determine where the item is located within the collection.

Requirements

Namespace: System.Windows.Forms

Platforms: Windows 98, Windows NT 4.0, Windows Millennium Edition, Windows 2000, Windows XP Home Edition, Windows XP Professional, Windows Server 2003 family, .NET Compact Framework - Windows CE .NET

Assembly: System.Windows.Forms (in System.Windows.Forms.dll)

ListBox.ObjectCollection Constructor

Initializes a new instance of **ListBox.ObjectCollection**.

Overload List

Initializes a new instance of **ListBox.ObjectCollection**.

[Visual Basic] **Public Sub New(ListBox)**

[C#] **public ListBox.ObjectCollection(ListBox);**

[C++] **public: ObjectCollection(ListBox*);**

[JScript] **public function ListBox.ObjectCollection(ListBox);**

Initializes a new instance of **ListBox.ObjectCollection** containing an array of objects.

[Visual Basic] **Public Sub New(ListBox, Object())**

[C#] **public ListBox.ObjectCollection(ListBox, object[]);**

[C++] **public: ObjectCollection(ListBox*, Object[]);**

[JScript] **public function ListBox.ObjectCollection(ListBox, Object[]);**

Initializes a new instance of **ListBox.ObjectCollection** based on another **ListBox.ObjectCollection**.

[Visual Basic] **Public Sub New(ListBox, ListBox.ObjectCollection)**

[C#] **public ListBox.ObjectCollection(ListBox, ListBox.ObjectCollection);**

[C++] **public: ObjectCollection(ListBox*, ListBox.ObjectCollection*);**

[JScript] **public function ListBox.ObjectCollection(ListBox, ListBox.ObjectCollection);**

ListBox.ObjectCollection Constructor (ListBox)

Initializes a new instance of **ListBox.ObjectCollection**.

[Visual Basic]
```
Public Sub New( _
   ByVal owner As ListBox _
)
```
[C#]
```
public ListBox.ObjectCollection(
   ListBox owner
);
```
[C++]
```
public: ObjectCollection(
   ListBox* owner
);
```
[JScript]
```
public function ListBox.ObjectCollection(
   owner : ListBox
);
```

Parameters

owner

The **ListBox** that owns the collection.

Remarks

You cannot create an instance of this class without associating it with a **ListBox** control.

Requirements

Platforms: Windows 98, Windows NT 4.0, Windows Millennium Edition, Windows 2000, Windows XP Home Edition, Windows XP Professional, Windows Server 2003 family

ListBox.ObjectCollection Constructor (ListBox, Object[])

Initializes a new instance of **ListBox.ObjectCollection** containing an array of objects.

```
[Visual Basic]
Public Sub New( _
   ByVal owner As ListBox, _
   ByVal value() As Object _
)
[C#]
public ListBox.ObjectCollection(
   ListBox owner,
   object[] value
);
[C++]
public: ObjectCollection(
   ListBox* owner,
   Object* value __gc[]
);
[JScript]
public function ListBox.ObjectCollection(
   owner : ListBox,
   value : Object[]
);
```

Parameters

owner

The **ListBox** that owns the collection.

value

An array of objects to add to the collection.

Remarks

You cannot create an instance of this class without associating it with a **ListBox** control.

Requirements

Platforms: Windows 98, Windows NT 4.0, Windows Millennium Edition, Windows 2000, Windows XP Home Edition, Windows XP Professional, Windows Server 2003 family

ListBox.ObjectCollection Constructor (ListBox, ListBox.ObjectCollection)

Initializes a new instance of **ListBox.ObjectCollection** based on another **ListBox.ObjectCollection**.

```
[Visual Basic]
Public Sub New( _
   ByVal owner As ListBox, _
   ByVal value As ListBox.ObjectCollection _
)
[C#]
public ListBox.ObjectCollection(
   ListBox owner,
   ListBox.ObjectCollection value
);
[C++]
public: ObjectCollection(
   ListBox* owner,
   ListBox.ObjectCollection* value
);
[JScript]
public function ListBox.ObjectCollection(
   owner : ListBox,
   value : ListBox.ObjectCollection
);
```

Parameters

owner

The **ListBox** that owns the collection.

value

A **ListBox.ObjectCollection** from which the contents are copied to this collection.

Remarks

You cannot create an instance of this class without associating it with a **ListBox** control. This version of the constructor enables you to use the items specified in an existing instance of the **ListBox.ObjectCollection** class to add items to the collection when it is created. You can use this constructor to use the items specified in another **ListBox** control with this collection.

Requirements

Platforms: Windows 98, Windows NT 4.0, Windows Millennium Edition, Windows 2000, Windows XP Home Edition, Windows XP Professional, Windows Server 2003 family

ListBox.ObjectCollection.Count Property

Gets the number of items in the collection.

```
[Visual Basic]
Public Overridable ReadOnly Property Count As Integer  Implements _
   ICollection.Count
[C#]
public virtual int Count {get;}
[C++]
public: __property virtual int get_Count();
[JScript]
public function get Count() : int;
```

Property Value

The number of items in the collection

Implements

ICollection.Count

Remarks

This property enables you to determine the number of items in the **ListBox**. You can then use this value when you are looping through the values of the collection and you need to provide a number of iterations to perform the loop.

Requirements

Platforms: Windows 98, Windows NT 4.0,
Windows Millennium Edition, Windows 2000,
Windows XP Home Edition, Windows XP Professional,
Windows Server 2003 family,
.NET Compact Framework - Windows CE .NET

ListBox.ObjectCollection.IsReadOnly Property

Gets a value indicating whether the collection is read-only.

```
[Visual Basic]
Public Overridable ReadOnly Property IsReadOnly As Boolean _
   Implements IList.IsReadOnly
[C#]
public virtual bool IsReadOnly {get;}
[C++]
public: __property virtual bool get_IsReadOnly();
[JScript]
public function get IsReadOnly() : Boolean;
```

Property Value

true if this collection is read-only; otherwise, **false**.

Implements

IList.IsReadOnly

Remarks

This property is always **false** for this collection.

Requirements

Platforms: Windows 98, Windows NT 4.0,
Windows Millennium Edition, Windows 2000,
Windows XP Home Edition, Windows XP Professional,
Windows Server 2003 family,
.NET Compact Framework - Windows CE .NET

ListBox.ObjectCollection.Item Property

Gets or sets the item at the specified index within the collection.

[C#] In C#, this property is the indexer for the **ListBox.ObjectCollection** class.

```
[Visual Basic]
Public Overridable Default Property Item( _
   ByVal index As Integer _
) As Object  Implements IList.Item
[C#]
public virtual object this[
   int index
] {get; set;}
[C++]
public: __property virtual Object* get_Item(
   int index
);
public: __property virtual void set_Item(
   int index,
   Object*
);
[JScript]
returnValue = ObjectCollectionObject.Item(index);
ObjectCollectionObject.Item(index) = returnValue;
-or-
returnValue = ObjectCollectionObject(index);
ObjectCollectionObject(index) = returnValue;
```

[JScript] In JScript, you can use the default indexed properties defined by a type, but you cannot explicitly define your own. However, specifying the **expando** attribute on a class automatically provides a default indexed property whose type is **Object** and whose index type is **String**.

Arguments [JScript]

index
The index of the item in the collection to get or set.

Parameters [Visual Basic, C#, C++]

index
The index of the item in the collection to get or set.

Property Value

An object representing the item located at the specified index within the collection.

Implements

IList.Item

Exceptions

Exception Type	Condition
ArgumentOutOfRangeException	The *index* parameter is less than zero or greater than or equal to the value of the **Count** property of the **ListBox.ObjectCollection** class.

Remarks

You can use this method to obtain the **ListBox** item stored at a specific location within the collection. To determine the index of a specific item within the collection, use the **IndexOf** method.

Requirements

Platforms: Windows 98, Windows NT 4.0,
Windows Millennium Edition, Windows 2000,
Windows XP Home Edition, Windows XP Professional,
Windows Server 2003 family

ListBox.ObjectCollection.System.Collections.ICollection.IsSynchronized Property

Note: This namespace, class, or member is supported only in version 1.1 of the .NET Framework.

This member supports the .NET Framework infrastructure and is not intended to be used directly from your code.

```
[Visual Basic]
Private ReadOnly Property IsSynchronized As Boolean Implements _
   ICollection.IsSynchronized
[C#]
bool ICollection.IsSynchronized {get;}
[C++]
private: __property bool
   System::Collections::ICollection::get_IsSynchronized();
[JScript]
private function get ICollection.IsSynchronized() : Boolean;
```

ListBox.ObjectCollection.System.Collections.ICollection.SyncRoot Property

Note: This namespace, class, or member is supported only in version 1.1 of the .NET Framework.

This member supports the .NET Framework infrastructure and is not intended to be used directly from your code.

```
[Visual Basic]
Private ReadOnly Property SyncRoot As Object Implements _
   ICollection.SyncRoot
[C#]
object ICollection.SyncRoot {get;}
[C++]
private: __property Object*
   System::Collections::ICollection::get_SyncRoot();
[JScript]
private function get ICollection.SyncRoot() : Object;
```

ListBox.ObjectCollection.System.Collections.IList.IsFixedSize Property

Note: This namespace, class, or member is supported only in version 1.1 of the .NET Framework.

This member supports the .NET Framework infrastructure and is not intended to be used directly from your code.

```
[Visual Basic]
Private ReadOnly Property IsFixedSize As Boolean Implements _
   IList.IsFixedSize
[C#]
bool IList.IsFixedSize {get;}
[C++]
private: __property bool
   System::Collections::IList::get_IsFixedSize();
[JScript]
private function get IList.IsFixedSize() : Boolean;
```

ListBox.ObjectCollection.Add Method

Adds an item to the list of items for a **ListBox**.

```
[Visual Basic]
Public Function Add( _
   ByVal item As Object _
) As Integer
[C#]
public int Add(
   object item
);
[C++]
public: int Add(
   Object* item
);
[JScript]
public function Add(
   item : Object
) : int;
```

Parameters

item
  An object representing the item to add to the collection.

Return Value

The zero-based index of the item in the collection.

Exceptions

Exception Type	Condition
SystemException	There is insufficient space available to add the new item to the list.

Remarks

If the **Sorted** property of the **ListBox** is set to **true**, the item is inserted into the list alphabetically. Otherwise, the item is inserted at the end of the list. To insert an item into the list box at a specific position, use the **Insert** method. To add a set of items to the list box in a single operation, use the **AddRange** method. If you want to use the **Add** method to add a large number of items to the list, use the **BeginUpdate** and **EndUpdate** methods to prevent the **ListBox** from repainting each time an item is added to the list until all items are added to the list. When adding items to a **ListBox**, it is more efficient to sort the items first and then add new items.

When an object is added to the collection, the **ListBox** first checks to see if the **DisplayMember** property of the **ListControl** class has the name of a member from the object specified to reference when obtaining the item text. If the **DisplayMember** property does not have a member specified, the **ListBox** then calls the **ToString** method of the object to obtain the text to display in the list.

Example

See related example in the **System.Windows.Forms.ListBox** class topic.

Requirements

Platforms: Windows 98, Windows NT 4.0,
Windows Millennium Edition, Windows 2000,
Windows XP Home Edition, Windows XP Professional,
Windows Server 2003 family,
.NET Compact Framework - Windows CE .NET

ListBox.ObjectCollection.AddRange Method

Adds a group of items to the list of items for a **ListBox**.

Overload List

Adds an array of items to the list of items for a **ListBox**.

[Visual Basic] **Overloads Public Sub AddRange(Object())**

[C#] **public void AddRange(object[]);**

[C++] **public: void AddRange(Object*[]);**

[JScript] **public function AddRange(Object[]);**

Adds the items of an existing **ListBox.ObjectCollection** to the list of items in a **ListBox**.

[Visual Basic] **Overloads Public Sub AddRange(ListBox.ObjectCollection)**

[C#] **public void AddRange(ListBox.ObjectCollection);**

[C++] **public: void AddRange(ListBox.ObjectCollection*);**

[JScript] **public function AddRange(ListBox.ObjectCollection);**

ListBox.ObjectCollection.AddRange Method (Object[])

Adds an array of items to the list of items for a **ListBox**.

```
[Visual Basic]
Overloads Public Sub AddRange( _
   ByVal items() As Object _
)
[C#]
public void AddRange(
   object[] items
);
[C++]
public: void AddRange(
   Object* items __gc[]
);
[JScript]
public function AddRange(
   items : Object[]
);
```

Parameters

items

An array of objects to add to the list.

Remarks

This method removes all existing items from the list box before inserting the new items. If the **Sorted** property of the **ListBox** is set to **true**, the items are inserted into the list alphabetically. Otherwise, the items are inserted in the order that they occur within the array. This method is typically passed an array of **String** objects, but an array of any type of object can be passed to this method. When an object is added to the collection, the **ListBox** first checks to see if the **DisplayMember** property of the **ListControl** class has the name of a member from the object specified to reference when obtaining the item text. If the **DisplayMember** property does not have a member specified, the **ListBox** then calls the **ToString** method of the object to obtain the text to display in the list. When using this method to add items to the **ListBox**, you do not need to call the **BeginUpdate** and **EndUpdate** methods to optimize performance. When adding items to a **ListBox**, it is more efficient to sort the items first and then add new items. You can use this method to add a group of items to the list or to reuse the items stored in a different **ListBox**.

Requirements

Platforms: Windows 98, Windows NT 4.0, Windows Millennium Edition, Windows 2000, Windows XP Home Edition, Windows XP Professional, Windows Server 2003 family

ListBox.ObjectCollection.AddRange Method (ListBox.ObjectCollection)

Adds the items of an existing **ListBox.ObjectCollection** to the list of items in a **ListBox**.

```
[Visual Basic]
Overloads Public Sub AddRange( _
   ByVal value As ListBox.ObjectCollection _
)
[C#]
public void AddRange(
   ListBox.ObjectCollection value
);
[C++]
public: void AddRange(
   ListBox.ObjectCollection* value
);
[JScript]
public function AddRange(
   value : ListBox.ObjectCollection
);
```

Parameters

value

A **ListBox.ObjectCollection** to load into this collection.

Remarks

This method removes all existing items from the list box before inserting the new items. If the **Sorted** property of the **ListBox** is set to **true**, the items are inserted into the list alphabetically. Otherwise, the items are inserted in the order that they occur within the array. This method is typically passed an array of **String** objects, but an array of any type of object can be passed to this method. When an object is added to the collection, the **ListBox** first checks to see if the **DisplayMember** property of the **ListControl** class has the name of a member from the object specified to reference when obtaining the item text. If the **DisplayMember** property does not have a member specified, the **ListBox** then calls the **ToString** method of the object to obtain the text to display in the list.

When using this method to add items to the **ListBox**, you do not need to call the **BeginUpdate** and **EndUpdate** methods to optimize performance. When adding items to a **ListBox**, it is more efficient to sort the items first and then add new items. You can use this method to reuse the items stored in a different **ListBox**.

Requirements

Platforms: Windows 98, Windows NT 4.0, Windows Millennium Edition, Windows 2000, Windows XP Home Edition, Windows XP Professional, Windows Server 2003 family

ListBox.ObjectCollection.Clear Method

Removes all items from the collection.

```
[Visual Basic]
Public Overridable Sub Clear() Implements IList.Clear
[C#]
public virtual void Clear();
[C++]
public: virtual void Clear();
[JScript]
public function Clear();
```

Implements

IList.Clear

Remarks

When you remove items from the list, all information about the deleted items is lost. To remove a single item from the **ListBox**, use the **Remove** or **RemoveAt** method.

Requirements

Platforms: Windows 98, Windows NT 4.0, Windows Millennium Edition, Windows 2000, Windows XP Home Edition, Windows XP Professional, Windows Server 2003 family, .NET Compact Framework - Windows CE .NET

ListBox.ObjectCollection.Contains Method

Determines whether the specified item is located within the collection.

```
[Visual Basic]
Public Overridable Function Contains( _
   ByVal value As Object _
) As Boolean Implements IList.Contains
[C#]
public virtual bool Contains(
   object value
);
[C++]
public: virtual bool Contains(
   Object* value
);
[JScript]
public function Contains(
   value : Object
) : Boolean;
```

Parameters

value

An object representing the item to locate in the collection.

Return Value

true if the item is located within the collection; otherwise, **false**.

Implements

IList.Contains

Remarks

The **Contains** method enables you to determine whether an object is a member of the collection. Once you know that the item is located within the collection, you can use the **IndexOf** method to determine where the item is located within the collection.

Requirements

Platforms: Windows 98, Windows NT 4.0,
Windows Millennium Edition, Windows 2000,
Windows XP Home Edition, Windows XP Professional,
Windows Server 2003 family,
.NET Compact Framework - Windows CE .NET

ListBox.ObjectCollection.CopyTo Method

Copies the entire collection into an existing array of objects at a specified location within the array.

```
[Visual Basic]
Public Sub CopyTo( _
   ByVal dest() As Object, _
   ByVal arrayIndex As Integer _
)
[C#]
public void CopyTo(
   object[] dest,
   int arrayIndex
);
[C++]
public: void CopyTo(
   Object* dest __gc[],
   int arrayIndex
);
[JScript]
public function CopyTo(
   dest : Object[],
   arrayIndex : int
);
```

Parameters

dest

The object array in which the items from the collection are copied to.

arrayIndex

The location within the destination array to copy the items from the collection to.

Remarks

You can use this method to combine the items from multiple collections into a single array. You can then use this array to populate the contents of another **ListBox** control using the **AddRange** method of the **ListBox.ObjectCollection** class.

Requirements

Platforms: Windows 98, Windows NT 4.0,
Windows Millennium Edition, Windows 2000,
Windows XP Home Edition, Windows XP Professional,
Windows Server 2003 family

ListBox.ObjectCollection.GetEnumerator Method

Returns an enumerator to use to iterate through the item collection.

```
[Visual Basic]
Public Overridable Function GetEnumerator() As IEnumerator _
   Implements IEnumerable.GetEnumerator
[C#]
public virtual IEnumerator GetEnumerator();
[C++]
public: virtual IEnumerator* GetEnumerator();
[JScript]
public function GetEnumerator() : IEnumerator;
```

Return Value

An **IEnumerator** object that represents the item collection.

Implements

IEnumerable.GetEnumerator

Requirements

Platforms: Windows 98, Windows NT 4.0,
Windows Millennium Edition, Windows 2000,
Windows XP Home Edition, Windows XP Professional,
Windows Server 2003 family,
.NET Compact Framework - Windows CE .NET

ListBox.ObjectCollection.ICollection.CopyTo Method

This member supports the .NET Framework infrastructure and is not intended to be used directly from your code.

```
[Visual Basic]
Private Sub CopyTo( _
   ByVal dest As Array, _
   ByVal index As Integer _
) Implements ICollection.CopyTo
```

```
[C#]
void ICollection.CopyTo(
   Array dest,
   int index
);
[C++]
private: void ICollection::CopyTo(
   Array* dest,
   int index
);
[JScript]
private function ICollection.CopyTo(
   dest : Array,
   index : int
);
```

ListBox.ObjectCollection.IList.Add Method

This member supports the .NET Framework infrastructure and is not intended to be used directly from your code.

```
[Visual Basic]
Private Function Add( _
   ByVal item As Object _
) As Integer Implements IList.Add
[C#]
int IList.Add(
   object item
);
[C++]
private: int IList::Add(
   Object* item
);
[JScript]
private function IList.Add(
   item : Object
) : int;
```

ListBox.ObjectCollection.IndexOf Method

Returns the index within the collection of the specified item.

```
[Visual Basic]
Public Overridable Function IndexOf( _
   ByVal value As Object _
) As Integer Implements IList.IndexOf
[C#]
public virtual int IndexOf(
   object value
);
[C++]
public: virtual int IndexOf(
   Object* value
);
[JScript]
public function IndexOf(
   value : Object
) : int;
```

Parameters

value

An object representing the item to locate in the collection.

Return Value

The zero-based index where the item is located within the collection; otherwise, negative one (-1).

Implements

IList.IndexOf

Exceptions

Exception Type	Condition
ArgumentNull-Exception	The *value* parameter is null.

Remarks

The **IndexOf** method enables you to determine where an item is located within the collection. To determine whether a item is located within the collection before calling this method, use the **Contains** method.

Requirements

Platforms: Windows 98, Windows NT 4.0, Windows Millennium Edition, Windows 2000, Windows XP Home Edition, Windows XP Professional, Windows Server 2003 family, .NET Compact Framework - Windows CE .NET

ListBox.ObjectCollection.Insert Method

Inserts an item into the list box at the specified index.

```
[Visual Basic]
Public Overridable Sub Insert( _
   ByVal index As Integer, _
   ByVal item As Object _
) Implements IList.Insert
[C#]
public virtual void Insert(
   int index,
   object item
);
[C++]
public: virtual void Insert(
   int index,
   Object* item
);
[JScript]
public function Insert(
   index : int,
   item : Object
);
```

Parameters

index

The zero-based index location where the item is inserted.

item

An object representing the item to insert.

Implements

IList.Insert

Exceptions

Exception Type	Condition
ArgumentOutOfRange-Exception	The *index* parameter is less than zero or greater than or equal to the value of the **Count** property of the **List-Box.ObjectCollection** class.

Remarks

This method enables you to insert an item at a specific position within the **ListBox**. If the **Sorted** property of the **ListBox** is set to true, the item is added in the correct position within the sorted list regardless of the values specified in the *index* parameter. When an object is added to the collection, the **ListBox** first checks to see if the **DisplayMember** property of the **ListControl** class has the name of a member from the object specified to reference when obtaining the item text. If the **DisplayMember** property does not have a member specified, the **ListBox** then calls the **ToString** method of the object to obtain the text to display in the list.

Requirements

Platforms: Windows 98, Windows NT 4.0,
Windows Millennium Edition, Windows 2000,
Windows XP Home Edition, Windows XP Professional,
Windows Server 2003 family,
.NET Compact Framework - Windows CE .NET

ListBox.ObjectCollection.Remove Method

Removes the specified object from the collection.

```
[Visual Basic]
Public Overridable Sub Remove( _
   ByVal value As Object _
) Implements IList.Remove
[C#]
public virtual void Remove(
   object value
);
[C++]
public: virtual void Remove(
   Object* value
);
[JScript]
public function Remove(
   value : Object
);
```

Parameters

value

An object representing the item to remove from the collection.

Implements

IList.Remove

Remarks

When you remove an item from the list, the indexes change for subsequent items in the list. All information about the removed item is deleted. You can use this method to remove a specific item from the list by specifying the actual item to remove from the list. To specify the index of the item to remove instead of the item itself, use the **RemoveAt** method. To remove all items from the list, use the **Clear** method.

Requirements

Platforms: Windows 98, Windows NT 4.0,
Windows Millennium Edition, Windows 2000,
Windows XP Home Edition, Windows XP Professional,
Windows Server 2003 family,
.NET Compact Framework - Windows CE .NET

ListBox.ObjectCollection.RemoveAt Method

Removes the item at the specified index within the collection.

```
[Visual Basic]
Public Overridable Sub RemoveAt( _
   ByVal index As Integer _
) Implements IList.RemoveAt
[C#]
public virtual void RemoveAt(
   int index
);
[C++]
public: virtual void RemoveAt(
   int index
);
[JScript]
public function RemoveAt(
   index : int
);
```

Parameters

index

The zero-based index of the item to remove.

Implements

IList.RemoveAt

Exceptions

Exception Type	Condition
ArgumentOutOfRange-Exception	The *index* parameter is less than zero or greater than or equal to the value of the **Count** property of the **ListBox.ObjectCollection** class.

Remarks

When you remove an item from the list, the indexes change for subsequent items in the list. All information about the removed item is deleted. You can use this method to remove a specific item from the list by specifying the index of the item to remove from the list. To specify the item to remove instead of the index to the item, use the **Remove** method. To remove all items from the list, use the **Clear** method.

Example

See related example in the **System.Windows.Forms.ListBox** class topic.

Requirements

Platforms: Windows 98, Windows NT 4.0,
Windows Millennium Edition, Windows 2000,
Windows XP Home Edition, Windows XP Professional,
Windows Server 2003 family,
.NET Compact Framework - Windows CE .NET

ListBox.SelectedIndex-Collection Class

Represents the collection containing the indexes to the selected items in a **ListBox**.

System.Object
  System.Windows.Forms.ListBox.SelectedIndexCollection

```
[Visual Basic]
Public Class ListBox.SelectedIndexCollection
   Implements IList, ICollection, IEnumerable
[C#]
public class ListBox.SelectedIndexCollection : IList, ICollection,
   IEnumerable
[C++]
public __gc class ListBox.SelectedIndexCollection : public IList,
   ICollection, IEnumerable
[JScript]
public class ListBox.SelectedIndexCollection implements IList,
   ICollection, IEnumerable
```

Thread Safety

Any public static (**Shared** in Visual Basic) members of this type are safe for multithreaded operations. Any instance members are not guaranteed to be thread safe.

Remarks

The **ListBox.SelectedIndexCollection** class stores the indexes to the selected items in the **ListBox**. The indexes stored in the **ListBox.SelectedIndexCollection** are index positions within the **ListBox.ObjectCollection** class. The **ListBox.ObjectCollection** class stores all items displayed in the **ListBox**.

The following table is an example of how the **ListBox.ObjectCollection** stores the items of the **ListBox** as well as their selection states within an example **ListBox**.

Index	Item	Selection State Within the ListBox
0	object1	Unselected
1	object2	Selected
2	object3	Unselected
3	object4	Selected
4	object5	Selected

Based on the **ListBox.ObjectCollection** example in the previous table, the following table demonstrates how the **ListBox.SelectedIndexCollection** would appear.

Index	Index of Selected Item in ObjectCollection
0	1
1	3
2	4

You can use the properties and methods of this class to perform a variety of tasks with the collection. The **Contains** method enables you to determine whether an index position from the **ListBox.ObjectCollection** class is a member of the selected indexes stored in the **ListBox.SelectedIndexCollection**. Once you know that the item is located within the collection, you can use the **IndexOf** method to determine where a specific index position within the **ListBox.ObjectCollection** for the **ListBox** is stored.

Example

See related example in the **System.Windows.Forms.ListBox** class topic.

Requirements

Namespace: System.Windows.Forms

Platforms: Windows 98, Windows NT 4.0, Windows Millennium Edition, Windows 2000, Windows XP Home Edition, Windows XP Professional, Windows Server 2003 family

Assembly: System.Windows.Forms (in System.Windows.Forms.dll)

ListBox.SelectedIndexCollection Constructor

Initializes a new instance of the **ListBox.SelectedIndexCollection** class.

```
[Visual Basic]
Public Sub New( _
   ByVal owner As ListBox _
)
[C#]
public ListBox.SelectedIndexCollection(
   ListBox owner
);
[C++]
public: SelectedIndexCollection(
   ListBox* owner
);
[JScript]
public function ListBox.SelectedIndexCollection(
   owner : ListBox
);
```

Parameters

owner
  A **ListBox** representing the owner of the collection.

Remarks

You cannot create an instance of this class without associating it with a **ListBox** control.

Requirements

Platforms: Windows 98, Windows NT 4.0, Windows Millennium Edition, Windows 2000, Windows XP Home Edition, Windows XP Professional, Windows Server 2003 family

ListBox.SelectedIndexCollection.Count Property

Gets the number of items in the collection.

```
[Visual Basic]
Public Overridable ReadOnly Property Count As Integer  Implements _
   ICollection.Count
[C#]
public virtual int Count {get;}
[C++]
public: __property virtual int get_Count();
[JScript]
public function get Count() : int;
```

Property Value

The number of items in the collection.

Implements

ICollection.Count

Remarks

This property enables you to determine the number of selected items in the **ListBox**. You can then use this value when looping through the values of the collection and you need to provide a number of iterations to perform the loop. Unless the **SelectionMode** property of the **ListBox** is set to **SelectionMode.MultiSimple** or **SelectionMode.MultiExtended**, this property always returns a value of zero (0) or one (1) depending on whether you have a selected item.

Example

See related example in the **System.Windows.Forms.ListBox** class topic.

Requirements

Platforms: Windows 98, Windows NT 4.0, Windows Millennium Edition, Windows 2000, Windows XP Home Edition, Windows XP Professional, Windows Server 2003 family

ListBox.SelectedIndexCollection.IsReadOnly Property

Gets a value indicating whether the collection is read-only.

```
[Visual Basic]
Public Overridable ReadOnly Property IsReadOnly As Boolean _
   Implements IList.IsReadOnly
[C#]
public virtual bool IsReadOnly {get;}
[C++]
public: __property virtual bool get_IsReadOnly();
[JScript]
public function get IsReadOnly() : Boolean;
```

Property Value

true if the collection is read-only; otherwise, **false**.

Implements

IList.IsReadOnly

Remarks

This property is always **true** for this collection. The items in this collection are modified only by the **ListBox** control.

Requirements

Platforms: Windows 98, Windows NT 4.0, Windows Millennium Edition, Windows 2000, Windows XP Home Edition, Windows XP Professional, Windows Server 2003 family

ListBox.SelectedIndexCollection.Item Property

Gets the index value at the specified index within this collection.

[C#] In C#, this property is the indexer for the **ListBox.SelectedIndexCollection** class.

```
[Visual Basic]
Public Default ReadOnly Property Item( _
   ByVal index As Integer _
) As Integer
[C#]
public int this[
   int index
] {get;}
[C++]
public: __property int get_Item(
   int index
);
[JScript]
returnValue = SelectedIndexCollectionObject.Item(index);
-or-
returnValue = SelectedIndexCollectionObject(index);
```

[JScript] In JScript, you can use the default indexed properties defined by a type, but you cannot explicitly define your own. However, specifying the **expando** attribute on a class automatically provides a default indexed property whose type is **Object** and whose index type is **String**.

Arguments [JScript]

index

The index of the item in the collection to get.

Parameters [Visual Basic, C#, C++]

index

The index of the item in the collection to get.

Property Value

The index value from the **ListBox.ObjectCollection** that is stored at the specified location.

Exceptions

Exception Type	Condition
ArgumentOutOfRangeException	The *index* parameter is less than zero or greater than or equal to the value of the **Count** property of the **ListBox.SelectedIndexCollection** class.

Remarks

This indexer enables you to get a specific selected index from the **ListBox.SelectedIndexCollection**. The index stored in the collection is an index into the **ListBox.ObjectCollection** of the **ListBox** that represents a selected item in the **ListBox**.

Requirements

Platforms: Windows 98, Windows NT 4.0, Windows Millennium Edition, Windows 2000, Windows XP Home Edition, Windows XP Professional, Windows Server 2003 family

ListBox.SelectedIndexCollection.Contains Method

Determines whether the specified index is located within the collection.

```
[Visual Basic]
Public Function Contains( _
   ByVal selectedIndex As Integer _
) As Boolean
[C#]
public bool Contains(
   int selectedIndex
);
```

```
[C++]
public: bool Contains(
   int selectedIndex
);
[JScript]
public function Contains(
   selectedIndex : int
) : Boolean;
```

Parameters

selectedIndex
The index to locate in the collection.

Return Value

true if the specified index from the **ListBox.ObjectCollection** for the **ListBox** is an item in this collection; otherwise, **false**.

Remarks

The **Contains** method enables you to determine whether an index position from the **ListBox.ObjectCollection** class is a member of the selected indexes stored in the **ListBox.SelectedIndexCollection**. You can use this to determine whether a specific item in a multiple-selection **ListBox** is selected.

Requirements

Platforms: Windows 98, Windows NT 4.0, Windows Millennium Edition, Windows 2000, Windows XP Home Edition, Windows XP Professional, Windows Server 2003 family

ListBox.SelectedIndexCollection.CopyTo Method

Copies the entire collection into an existing array at a specified location within the array.

```
[Visual Basic]
Public Overridable Sub CopyTo( _
   ByVal dest As Array, _
   ByVal index As Integer _
) Implements ICollection.CopyTo
[C#]
public virtual void CopyTo(
   Array dest,
   int index
);
[C++]
public: virtual void CopyTo(
   Array* dest,
   int index
);
[JScript]
public function CopyTo(
   dest : Array,
   index : int
);
```

Parameters

dest
The destination array.

index
The index in the destination array at which storing begins.

Implements

ICollection.CopyTo

Remarks

You can use this method to combine the selected indexes from multiple collections into a single array.

Requirements

Platforms: Windows 98, Windows NT 4.0, Windows Millennium Edition, Windows 2000, Windows XP Home Edition, Windows XP Professional, Windows Server 2003 family

ListBox.SelectedIndexCollection.GetEnumerator Method

Returns an enumerator to use to iterate through the selected indexes collection.

```
[Visual Basic]
Public Overridable Function GetEnumerator() As IEnumerator _
   Implements IEnumerable.GetEnumerator
[C#]
public virtual IEnumerator GetEnumerator();
[C++]
public: virtual IEnumerator* GetEnumerator();
[JScript]
public function GetEnumerator() : IEnumerator;
```

Return Value

An **IEnumerator** object that represents the selected indexes collection.

Implements

IEnumerable.GetEnumerator

Requirements

Platforms: Windows 98, Windows NT 4.0, Windows Millennium Edition, Windows 2000, Windows XP Home Edition, Windows XP Professional, Windows Server 2003 family

ListBox.SelectedIndexCollection.IList.Add Method

This member supports the .NET Framework infrastructure and is not intended to be used directly from your code.

```
[Visual Basic]
Private Function Add( _
   ByVal value As Object _
) As Integer Implements IList.Add
[C#]
int IList.Add(
   object value
);
[C++]
private: int IList::Add(
   Object* value
);
[JScript]
private function IList.Add(
   value : Object
) : int;
```

ListBox.SelectedIndexCollection.IList.Clear Method

This member supports the .NET Framework infrastructure and is not intended to be used directly from your code.

```
[Visual Basic]
Private Sub Clear() Implements IList.Clear
[C#]
void IList.Clear();
[C++]
private: void IList::Clear();
[JScript]
private function IList.Clear();
```

ListBox.SelectedIndexCollection.IList.Contains Method

This member supports the .NET Framework infrastructure and is not intended to be used directly from your code.

```
[Visual Basic]
Private Function Contains( _
   ByVal selectedIndex As Object _
) As Boolean Implements IList.Contains
[C#]
bool IList.Contains(
   object selectedIndex
);
[C++]
private: bool IList::Contains(
   Object* selectedIndex
);
[JScript]
private function IList.Contains(
   selectedIndex : Object
) : Boolean;
```

ListBox.SelectedIndexCollection.IList.IndexOf Method

This member supports the .NET Framework infrastructure and is not intended to be used directly from your code.

```
[Visual Basic]
Private Function IndexOf( _
   ByVal selectedIndex As Object _
) As Integer Implements IList.IndexOf
[C#]
int IList.IndexOf(
   object selectedIndex
);
[C++]
private: int IList::IndexOf(
   Object* selectedIndex
);
[JScript]
private function IList.IndexOf(
   selectedIndex : Object
) : int;
```

ListBox.SelectedIndexCollection.IList.Insert Method

This member supports the .NET Framework infrastructure and is not intended to be used directly from your code.

```
[Visual Basic]
Private Sub Insert( _
   ByVal index As Integer, _
   ByVal value As Object _
) Implements IList.Insert
[C#]
void IList.Insert(
   int index,
   object value
);
[C++]
private: void IList::Insert(
   int index,
   Object* value
);
[JScript]
private function IList.Insert(
   index : int,
   value : Object
);
```

ListBox.SelectedIndexCollection.IList.Remove Method

This member supports the .NET Framework infrastructure and is not intended to be used directly from your code.

```
[Visual Basic]
Private Sub Remove( _
   ByVal value As Object _
) Implements IList.Remove
[C#]
void IList.Remove(
   object value
);
[C++]
private: void IList::Remove(
   Object* value
);
[JScript]
private function IList.Remove(
   value : Object
);
```

ListBox.SelectedIndexCollection.IList.RemoveAt Method

This member supports the .NET Framework infrastructure and is not intended to be used directly from your code.

```
[Visual Basic]
Private Sub RemoveAt( _
   ByVal index As Integer _
) Implements IList.RemoveAt
[C#]
void IList.RemoveAt(
   int index
);
```

[C++]
```
private: void IList::RemoveAt(
   int index
);
```
[JScript]
```
private function IList.RemoveAt(
   index : int
);
```

ListBox.SelectedIndexCollection.IndexOf Method

Returns the index within the **ListBox.SelectedIndexCollection** of the specified index from the **ListBox.ObjectCollection** of the **ListBox**.

[Visual Basic]
```
Public Function IndexOf( _
   ByVal selectedIndex As Integer _
) As Integer
```
[C#]
```
public int IndexOf(
   int selectedIndex
);
```
[C++]
```
public: int IndexOf(
   int selectedIndex
);
```
[JScript]
```
public function IndexOf(
   selectedIndex : int
) : int;
```

Parameters

selectedIndex
The zero-based index from the **ListBox.ObjectCollection** to locate in this collection.

Return Value

The zero-based index in the collection where the specified index of the **ListBox.ObjectCollection** was located within the **ListBox.SelectedIndexCollection**; otherwise, negative one (-1).

Remarks

Once you know that an item is located within the collection (using the **Contains** method), you can use the **IndexOf** method to determine where a specific index position within the **ListBox.ObjectCollection** for the **ListBox** is stored within the **ListBox.SelectedIndexCollection**.

Requirements

Platforms: Windows 98, Windows NT 4.0, Windows Millennium Edition, Windows 2000, Windows XP Home Edition, Windows XP Professional, Windows Server 2003 family

ListBox.SelectedObjectCollection Class

Represents the collection of selected items in the **ListBox**.

System.Object
  System.Windows.Forms.ListBox.SelectedObjectCollection

[Visual Basic]
```
Public Class ListBox.SelectedObjectCollection
   Implements IList, ICollection, IEnumerable
```
[C#]
```
public class ListBox.SelectedObjectCollection : IList, ICollection,
   IEnumerable
```
[C++]
```
public __gc class ListBox.SelectedObjectCollection : public IList,
   ICollection, IEnumerable
```
[JScript]
```
public class ListBox.SelectedObjectCollection implements IList,
   ICollection, IEnumerable
```

Thread Safety

Any public static (**Shared** in Visual Basic) members of this type are safe for multithreaded operations. Any instance members are not guaranteed to be thread safe.

Remarks

The **ListBox.SelectedObjectCollection** class stores the selected items in the **ListBox**. The items stored in the **ListBox.SelectedObjectCollection** are items contained within the **ListBox.ObjectCollection** class. The **ListBox.ObjectCollection** class stores all items displayed in the **ListBox**.

The following table is an example of how the **ListBox.ObjectCollection** stores the items of the **ListBox** as well as their selection states within an example **ListBox**.

Index	Item	Selection State Within the ListBox
0	object1	Unselected
1	object2	Selected
2	object3	Unselected
3	object4	Selected
4	object5	Selected

Based on the **ListBox.ObjectCollection** demonstrated in the previous table, the following table demonstrates how the **ListBox.SelectedObjectCollection** would appear.

Index	Selected Item from ObjectCollection
0	object2
1	object4
2	object5

You can use the properties and methods of this class to perform a variety of tasks with the collection. The **Contains** method enables you to determine whether an item from the **ListBox.ObjectCollection** class is a member of the **ListBox.SelectedObjectCollection**. Once you know that the item is located within the collection, you can use the **IndexOf** method to determine where a specific item within the **ListBox.ObjectCollection** for the **ListBox** is stored within the **ListBox.SelectedObjectCollection**.

Requirements

Namespace: System.Windows.Forms

Platforms: Windows 98, Windows NT 4.0, Windows Millennium Edition, Windows 2000, Windows XP Home Edition, Windows XP Professional, Windows Server 2003 family

Assembly: System.Windows.Forms (in System.Windows.Forms.dll)

ListBox.SelectedObjectCollection Constructor

Initializes a new instance of the **ListBox.SelectedObjectCollection** class.

[Visual Basic]
```
Public Sub New( _
   ByVal owner As ListBox _
)
```
[C#]
```
public ListBox.SelectedObjectCollection(
   ListBox owner
);
```
[C++]
```
public: SelectedObjectCollection(
   ListBox* owner
);
```
[JScript]
```
public function ListBox.SelectedObjectCollection(
   owner : ListBox
);
```

Parameters

owner

A **ListBox** representing the owner of the collection.

Remarks

An instance of this class cannot be created without associating it with a **ListBox** control.

Requirements

Platforms: Windows 98, Windows NT 4.0, Windows Millennium Edition, Windows 2000, Windows XP Home Edition, Windows XP Professional, Windows Server 2003 family

ListBox.SelectedObjectCollection.Count Property

Gets the number of items in the collection.

[Visual Basic]
```
Public Overridable ReadOnly Property Count As Integer  Implements _
   ICollection.Count
```
[C#]
```
public virtual int Count {get;}
```
[C++]
```
public: __property virtual int get_Count();
```
[JScript]
```
public function get Count() : int;
```

Property Value

The number of items in the collection.

Implements

ICollection.Count

Remarks

This property enables you to determine the number of selected items in the **ListBox**. You can then use this value when looping through the values of the collection and you need to provide a number of iterations to perform the loop. Unless the **SelectionMode** property of the **ListBox** is set to **SelectionMode.MultiSimple** or **SelectionMode.MultiExtended**, this property always returns a value of zero (0) or one (1) depending on whether you have a selected item.

Requirements

Platforms: Windows 98, Windows NT 4.0, Windows Millennium Edition, Windows 2000, Windows XP Home Edition, Windows XP Professional, Windows Server 2003 family

ListBox.SelectedObjectCollection.IsReadOnly Property

Gets a value indicating whether the collection is read-only.

[Visual Basic]
```
Public Overridable ReadOnly Property IsReadOnly As Boolean _
   Implements IList.IsReadOnly
```
[C#]
```
public virtual bool IsReadOnly {get;}
```
[C++]
```
public: __property virtual bool get_IsReadOnly();
```
[JScript]
```
public function get IsReadOnly() : Boolean;
```

Property Value

true if the collection is read-only; otherwise, **false**.

Implements

IList.IsReadOnly

Remarks

This property is always **true** for this collection.

Requirements

Platforms: Windows 98, Windows NT 4.0, Windows Millennium Edition, Windows 2000, Windows XP Home Edition, Windows XP Professional, Windows Server 2003 family

ListBox.SelectedObjectCollection.Item Property

Gets the item at the specified index within the collection.

[C#] In C#, this property is the indexer for the **ListBox.SelectedObjectCollection** class.

[Visual Basic]
```
Public Overridable Default Property Item( _
   ByVal index As Integer _
) As Object  Implements IList.Item
```
[C#]
```
public virtual object this[
   int index
] {get; set;}
```
[C++]
```
public: __property virtual Object* get_Item(
   int index
);
public: __property virtual void set_Item(
   int index,
   Object*
);
```
[JScript]
```
returnValue = SelectedObjectCollectionObject.Item(index);
SelectedObjectCollectionObject.Item(index) = returnValue;
-or-
returnValue = SelectedObjectCollectionObject(index);
SelectedObjectCollectionObject(index) = returnValue;
```

[JScript] In JScript, you can use the default indexed properties defined by a type, but you cannot explicitly define your own. However, specifying the **expando** attribute on a class automatically provides a default indexed property whose type is **Object** and whose index type is **String**.

Arguments [JScript]

index
  The index of the item in the collection to retrieve.

Parameters [Visual Basic, C#, C++]

index
  The index of the item in the collection to retrieve.

Property Value

An object representing the item located at the specified index within the collection.

Implements

IList.Item

Exceptions

Exception Type	Condition
ArgumentOutOfRangeException	The *index* parameter is less than zero or greater than or equal to the value of the **Count** property of the **ListBox.SelectedObjectCollection** class.

Remarks

This indexer enables you to get a specific item from the **ListBox.SelectedObjectCollection**. The item stored in this collection is an item within the **ListBox.ObjectCollection** of the **ListBox** that represents a selected item in the **ListBox**.

Requirements

Platforms: Windows 98, Windows NT 4.0, Windows Millennium Edition, Windows 2000, Windows XP Home Edition, Windows XP Professional, Windows Server 2003 family

ListBox.SelectedObjectCollection.Contains Method

Determines whether the specified item is located within the collection.

[Visual Basic]
```
Public Overridable Function Contains( _
   ByVal selectedObject As Object _
) As Boolean Implements IList.Contains
```

```
[C#]
public virtual bool Contains(
   object selectedObject
);
[C++]
public: virtual bool Contains(
   Object* selectedObject
);
[JScript]
public function Contains(
   selectedObject : Object
) : Boolean;
```

Parameters

selectedObject

An object representing the item to locate in the collection.

Return Value

true if the specified item is located in the collection; otherwise, **false**.

Implements

IList.Contains

Remarks

The **Contains** method enables you to determine whether an item from the **ListBox.ObjectCollection** class is a member of the selected items stored in the **ListBox.SelectedObjectCollection**. You can use this to determine if a specific item in a multiple-selection **ListBox** is selected.

Requirements

Platforms: Windows 98, Windows NT 4.0, Windows Millennium Edition, Windows 2000, Windows XP Home Edition, Windows XP Professional, Windows Server 2003 family

ListBox.SelectedObjectCollection.CopyTo Method

Copies the entire collection into an existing array at a specified location within the array.

```
[Visual Basic]
Public Overridable Sub CopyTo( _
   ByVal dest As Array, _
   ByVal index As Integer _
) Implements ICollection.CopyTo
[C#]
public virtual void CopyTo(
   Array dest,
   int index
);
[C++]
public: virtual void CopyTo(
   Array* dest,
   int index
);
[JScript]
public function CopyTo(
   dest : Array,
   index : int
);
```

Parameters

dest

An **Array** representing the array to copy the contents of the collection to.

index

The location within the destination array to copy the items from the collection to.

Implements

ICollection.CopyTo

Remarks

You can use this method to combine the selected items from multiple collections into a single array.

Requirements

Platforms: Windows 98, Windows NT 4.0, Windows Millennium Edition, Windows 2000, Windows XP Home Edition, Windows XP Professional, Windows Server 2003 family

ListBox.SelectedObjectCollection.GetEnumerator Method

Returns an enumerator that can be used to iterate through the selected item collection.

```
[Visual Basic]
Public Overridable Function GetEnumerator() As IEnumerator _
   Implements IEnumerable.GetEnumerator
[C#]
public virtual IEnumerator GetEnumerator();
[C++]
public: virtual IEnumerator* GetEnumerator();
[JScript]
public function GetEnumerator() : IEnumerator;
```

Return Value

An **IEnumerator** object that represents the item collection.

Implements

IEnumerable.GetEnumerator

Requirements

Platforms: Windows 98, Windows NT 4.0, Windows Millennium Edition, Windows 2000, Windows XP Home Edition, Windows XP Professional, Windows Server 2003 family

ListBox.SelectedObjectCollection.IList.Add Method

This member supports the .NET Framework infrastructure and is not intended to be used directly from your code.

```
[Visual Basic]
Private Function Add( _
   ByVal value As Object _
) As Integer Implements IList.Add
[C#]
int IList.Add(
   object value
);
```

```
[C++]
private: int IList::Add(
   Object* value
);
[JScript]
private function IList.Add(
   value : Object
) : int;
```

ListBox.SelectedObjectCollection.IList.Clear Method

This member supports the .NET Framework infrastructure and is not intended to be used directly from your code.

```
[Visual Basic]
Private Sub Clear() Implements IList.Clear
[C#]
void IList.Clear();
[C++]
private: void IList::Clear();
[JScript]
private function IList.Clear();
```

ListBox.SelectedObjectCollection.IList.Insert Method

This member supports the .NET Framework infrastructure and is not intended to be used directly from your code.

```
[Visual Basic]
Private Sub Insert( _
   ByVal index As Integer, _
   ByVal value As Object _
) Implements IList.Insert
[C#]
void IList.Insert(
   int index,
   object value
);
[C++]
private: void IList::Insert(
   int index,
   Object* value
);
[JScript]
private function IList.Insert(
   index : int,
   value : Object
);
```

ListBox.SelectedObjectCollection.IList.Remove Method

This member supports the .NET Framework infrastructure and is not intended to be used directly from your code.

```
[Visual Basic]
Private Sub Remove( _
   ByVal value As Object _
) Implements IList.Remove
[C#]
void IList.Remove(
   object value
);
[C++]
private: void IList::Remove(
   Object* value
);
[JScript]
private function IList.Remove(
   value : Object
);
```

ListBox.SelectedObjectCollection.IList.RemoveAt Method

This member supports the .NET Framework infrastructure and is not intended to be used directly from your code.

```
[Visual Basic]
Private Sub RemoveAt( _
   ByVal index As Integer _
) Implements IList.RemoveAt
[C#]
void IList.RemoveAt(
   int index
);
[C++]
private: void IList::RemoveAt(
   int index
);
[JScript]
private function IList.RemoveAt(
   index : int
);
```

ListBox.SelectedObjectCollection.IndexOf Method

Returns the index within the collection of the specified item.

[Visual Basic]
```
Public Overridable Function IndexOf( _
   ByVal selectedObject As Object _
) As Integer Implements IList.IndexOf
```
[C#]
```
public virtual int IndexOf(
   object selectedObject
);
```
[C++]
```
public: virtual int IndexOf(
   Object* selectedObject
);
```
[JScript]
```
public function IndexOf(
   selectedObject : Object
) : int;
```

Parameters

selectedObject

An object representing the item to locate in the collection.

Return Value

The zero-based index of the item in the collection; otherwise, -1.

Implements

IList.IndexOf

Remarks

Once you know that an item is located within the collection (using the **Contains** method), you can use the **IndexOf** method to determine where a specific item within the **ListBox.ObjectCollection** for the **ListBox** is stored within the **ListBox.SelectedObjectCollection**.

Requirements

Platforms: Windows 98, Windows NT 4.0, Windows Millennium Edition, Windows 2000, Windows XP Home Edition, Windows XP Professional, Windows Server 2003 family

ListControl Class

Provides a common implementation of members for the **ListBox** and **ComboBox** classes.

System.Object
  System.MarshalByRefObject
    System.ComponentModel.Component
      System.Windows.Forms.Control
        System.Windows.Forms.ListControl
          System.Windows.Forms.ComboBox
          System.Windows.Forms.ListBox

[Visual Basic]
```
MustInherit Public Class ListControl
   Inherits Control
```
[C#]
```
public abstract class ListControl : Control
```
[C++]
```
public __gc __abstract class ListControl : public Control
```
[JScript]
```
public abstract class ListControl extends Control
```

Thread Safety

Any public static (**Shared** in Visual Basic) members of this type are safe for multithreaded operations. Any instance members are not guaranteed to be thread safe.

Remarks

The **ListControl** class provides implementations of common elements for the **ListBox** and **ComboBox** controls.

The following properties are of primary concern to users of a data-bound **ListBox** or **ComboBox**: **DataSource**, **DisplayMember**, **SelectedValue**, and **ValueMember** properties.

Example

[Visual Basic, C#] The following example is a complete application illustrating how you can use **DataSource**, **DisplayMember**, **ValueMember**, and **SelectedValue** members of the **ListControl** class as implemented by the **ListBox** class. The example loads an **ArrayList** and the list box. When the user selects an item in the list box, the selected value is used to return the data associated with the selected item.

[Visual Basic]
```
Imports System.Windows.Forms
Imports System.Drawing
Imports System.Collections

Public Class USState

    Private myShortName As String
    Private myLongName As String

    Public Sub New(ByVal strlongName As String, ByVal ↵
strShortName As String)
        MyBase.New()
        Me.myShortName = strShortName
        Me.myLongName = strLongName
    End Sub

    Public ReadOnly Property ShortName() As String
        Get
            Return myShortName
        End Get
    End Property

    Public ReadOnly Property LongName() As String
        Get
            Return myLongName
        End Get
    End Property

    Public Overrides Function ToString() As String
        Return Me.ShortName & " - " & Me.LongName
    End Function
End Class

Public Class ListBoxSample3
    Inherits Form
    Friend WithEvents ListBox1 As ListBox = New ListBox()
    Dim textBox1 As TextBox = New TextBox()

    <System.STAThreadAttribute()> _
    Public Shared Sub Main()
        System.Windows.Forms.Application.Run(New ListBoxSample3())
    End Sub

    Public Sub New()
        Me.AutoScaleBaseSize = New Size(5, 13)
        Me.ClientSize = New Size(292, 181)
        Me.Text = "ListBox Sample3"

        ListBox1.Location = New Point(24, 16)
        ListBox1.Name = "ListBox1"
        ListBox1.Size = New Size(232, 130)

        textBox1.Location = New Point(24, 160)
        textBox1.Name = "textBox1"
        textBox1.Size = New Size(40, 24)
        Me.Controls.AddRange(New Control() {ListBox1, textBox1})

        ' Populates the list box using DataSource.
        ' DisplayMember is used to display just the long name of ↵
each state.
        Dim USStates As New ArrayList()
        USStates.Add(New USState("Washington", "WA"))
        USStates.Add(New USState("West Virginia", "WV"))
        USStates.Add(New USState("Wisconsin", "WI"))
        USStates.Add(New USState("Wyoming", "WY"))

        ListBox1.DataSource = USStates
        ListBox1.DisplayMember = "LongName"
        ListBox1.ValueMember = "ShortName"

    End Sub

    Private Sub InitializeComponent()

    End Sub

    Private Sub ListBox1_SelectedValueChanged(ByVal ↵
sender As System.Object, ByVal e As System.EventArgs) ↵
 Handles ListBox1.SelectedValueChanged
        If ListBox1.SelectedIndex <> -1 Then
            textBox1.Text = ListBox1.SelectedValue
        End If
    End Sub
End Class
```

[C#]
```
using System;
using System.Windows.Forms ;
using System.Drawing ;
using System.Collections ;

namespace MyListControlSample
{

    public class USState
    {
        private string myShortName ;
        private string myLongName ;
```

```
        public  USState(string strLongName, string strShortName)
        {

            this.myShortName = strShortName;
            this.myLongName = strLongName;
        }

        public string ShortName
        {
            get
            {
                return myShortName;
            }
        }

        public string LongName
        {

            get
            {
                return myLongName ;
            }
        }

        public override string ToString()
        {
            return this.ShortName + " - " + this.LongName;
        }
    }

    public class ListBoxSample3:Form
    {
        private ListBox ListBox1 = new ListBox();
        private TextBox textBox1 = new TextBox() ;

        [STAThread]
        static void Main()
        {
            Application.Run(new ListBoxSample3()) ;
        }

        public ListBoxSample3()
        {

            this.AutoScaleBaseSize = new Size(5, 13) ;
            this.ClientSize = new Size(292, 181) ;
            this.Text = "ListBox Sample3" ;

            ListBox1.Location = new Point(24, 16) ;
            ListBox1.Name = "ListBox1" ;
            ListBox1.Size = new Size(232, 130) ;

            textBox1.Location = new Point(24, 160) ;
            textBox1.Name = "textBox1" ;
            textBox1.Size = new Size(240, 24) ;
            this.Controls.AddRange(new Control[] {ListBox1,                ↵
textBox1}) ;

            // Populates the list box using DataSource.
            // DisplayMember is used to display just the long              ↵
name of each state.
            ArrayList USStates = new ArrayList()    ;
            USStates.Add(new USState("Alabama", "AL"));
            USStates.Add(new USState("Washington", "WA"))  ;
            USStates.Add(new USState("West Virginia", "WV"));
            USStates.Add(new USState("Wisconsin", "WI")) ;
            USStates.Add(new USState("Wyoming", "WY"));

            ListBox1.SelectedValueChanged += new                           ↵
EventHandler(ListBox1_SelectedValueChanged);
            ListBox1.DataSource = USStates ;
            ListBox1.DisplayMember = "LongName"        ;
            ListBox1.ValueMember = "ShortName" ;
        }
        private void InitializeComponent()
        {

        }

        private void ListBox1_SelectedValueChanged(object                  ↵
sender, EventArgs e)
        {
            if (ListBox1.SelectedIndex != -1)
                textBox1.Text = ListBox1.SelectedValue.ToString();
        }
    }
}
```

Requirements

Namespace: System.Windows.Forms

Platforms: Windows 98, Windows NT 4.0, Windows Millennium Edition, Windows 2000, Windows XP Home Edition, Windows XP Professional, Windows Server 2003 family, .NET Compact Framework - Windows CE .NET

Assembly: System.Windows.Forms (in System.Windows.Forms.dll)

ListControl Constructor

Initializes a new instance of the **ListControl** class.

```
[Visual Basic]
Protected Sub New()
[C#]
protected ListControl();
[C++]
protected: ListControl();
[JScript]
protected function ListControl();
```

Remarks

This constructor is called by derived class constructors to initialize state in this type.

Requirements

Platforms: Windows 98, Windows NT 4.0, Windows Millennium Edition, Windows 2000, Windows XP Home Edition, Windows XP Professional, Windows Server 2003 family

ListControl.DataManager Property

Gets the **CurrencyManager** associated with this control.

```
[Visual Basic]
Protected ReadOnly Property DataManager As CurrencyManager
[C#]
protected CurrencyManager DataManager {get;}
[C++]
protected: __property CurrencyManager* get_DataManager();
[JScript]
protected function get DataManager() : CurrencyManager;
```

Property Value

The **CurrencyManager** associated with this control. The default is a null reference (**Nothing** in Visual Basic).

Remarks

The **DataManager** property is valid if the **DataSource** property is set. If this is not a data-bound control, the default is a null reference (**Nothing** in Visual Basic).

Requirements

Platforms: Windows 98, Windows NT 4.0,
Windows Millennium Edition, Windows 2000,
Windows XP Home Edition, Windows XP Professional,
Windows Server 2003 family,
.NET Compact Framework - Windows CE .NET

ListControl.DataSource Property

Gets or sets the data source for this **ListControl**.

```
[Visual Basic]
Public Property DataSource As Object
[C#]
public object DataSource {get; set;}
[C++]
public: __property Object* get_DataSource();
public: __property void set_DataSource(Object*);
[JScript]
public function get DataSource() : Object;
public function set DataSource(Object);
```

Property Value

An object that implements the **IList** interface, such as a **DataSet** or an **Array**. The default is a null reference (**Nothing** in Visual Basic).

Remarks

There are two ways to fill the **ComboBox** and **ListBox** controls.

For example, you can add objects to the **ComboBox** by using the **Add** method. You can also add objects to a **ComboBox** by the using the **DataSource**, **DisplayMember**, and **ValueMember** properties to fill the **ComboBox**.

When the **DataSource** property is set, a user cannot modify the items collection.

If setting the **DataSource** property causes the data source to change, the **DataSourceChanged** event is raised. If setting this property causes the data member to change, the **DisplayMemberChanged** event is raised.

When you set **DataSource** to a null reference (**Nothing** in Visual Basic), **DisplayMember** is set to an empty string ("").

Example

See related example in the **System.Windows.Forms.ListControl** class topic.

Requirements

Platforms: Windows 98, Windows NT 4.0,
Windows Millennium Edition, Windows 2000,
Windows XP Home Edition, Windows XP Professional,
Windows Server 2003 family,
.NET Compact Framework - Windows CE .NET

ListControl.DisplayMember Property

Gets or sets a string that specifies the property of the data source whose contents you want to display.

```
[Visual Basic]
Public Property DisplayMember As String
[C#]
public string DisplayMember {get; set;}
[C++]
public: __property String* get_DisplayMember();
public: __property void set_DisplayMember(String*);
[JScript]
public function get DisplayMember() : String;
public function set DisplayMember(String);
```

Property Value

A **String** specifying the name of a property of the object specified by the **DataSource** property. The default is an empty string ("").

Remarks

The controls that inherit from **ListControl** can display diverse types of objects. If the specified property does not exist on the object or the value of **DisplayMember** is an empty string (""), the results of the object's **ToString** method are displayed instead.

If the new display member cannot be set, the previous display member setting is maintained.

Example

See related example in the **System.Windows.Forms.ListControl** class topic.

Requirements

Platforms: Windows 98, Windows NT 4.0,
Windows Millennium Edition, Windows 2000,
Windows XP Home Edition, Windows XP Professional,
Windows Server 2003 family,
.NET Compact Framework - Windows CE .NET

ListControl.SelectedIndex Property

When overridden in a derived class, gets or sets the zero-based index of the currently selected item.

```
[Visual Basic]
Public MustOverride Property SelectedIndex As Integer
[C#]
public abstract int SelectedIndex {get; set;}
[C++]
public: __property virtual int get_SelectedIndex() = 0;
public: __property virtual void set_SelectedIndex(int) = 0;
[JScript]
public abstract function get SelectedIndex() : int;
public abstract function set SelectedIndex(int);
```

Property Value

A zero-based index of the currently selected item. A value of negative one (-1) is returned if no item is selected.

Requirements

Platforms: Windows 98, Windows NT 4.0,
Windows Millennium Edition, Windows 2000,
Windows XP Home Edition, Windows XP Professional,
Windows Server 2003 family,
.NET Compact Framework - Windows CE .NET

ListControl.SelectedValue Property

Gets or sets the value of the member property specified by the **ValueMember** property.

```
[Visual Basic]
Public Property SelectedValue As Object
[C#]
public object SelectedValue {get; set;}
[C++]
public: __property Object* get_SelectedValue();
public: __property void set_SelectedValue(Object*);
[JScript]
public function get SelectedValue() : Object;
public function set SelectedValue(Object);
```

Property Value

An object containing the value of the member of the data source specified by the **ValueMember** property.

Remarks

If a property is not specified in **ValueMember**, **SelectedValue** returns the results of the **ToString** method of the object.

Example

See related example in the **System.Windows.Forms.ListControl** class topic.

Requirements

Platforms: Windows 98, Windows NT 4.0, Windows Millennium Edition, Windows 2000, Windows XP Home Edition, Windows XP Professional, Windows Server 2003 family, .NET Compact Framework - Windows CE .NET

ListControl.ValueMember Property

Gets or sets a string that specifies the property of the data source from which to draw the value.

```
[Visual Basic]
Public Property ValueMember As String
[C#]
public string ValueMember {get; set;}
[C++]
public: __property String* get_ValueMember();
public: __property void set_ValueMember(String*);
[JScript]
public function get ValueMember() : String;
public function set ValueMember(String);
```

Property Value

A **String** specifying the name of a property of the object specified by the **DataSource** property. The default is an empty string ("").

Exceptions

Exception Type	Condition
Exception	The specified property cannot be found on the object specified by the **DataSource** property.

Remarks

Specify the contents of the **ValueMember** property in cases where you bind data.

You can clear the **ValueMember** property by setting the property to an empty string ("") or a null reference (**Nothing** in Visual Basic).

Setting a new **ValueMember** property raises the **ValueMemberChanged** and **SelectedValueChanged** events.

Example

See related example in the **System.Windows.Forms.ListControl** class topic.

Requirements

Platforms: Windows 98, Windows NT 4.0, Windows Millennium Edition, Windows 2000, Windows XP Home Edition, Windows XP Professional, Windows Server 2003 family, .NET Compact Framework - Windows CE .NET

ListControl.FilterItemOnProperty Method

This member supports the .NET Framework infrastructure and is not intended to be used directly from your code.

Overload List

This member supports the .NET Framework infrastructure and is not intended to be used directly from your code.

[Visual Basic] **Overloads Protected Function FilterItemOnProperty(Object) As Object**

[C#] **protected object FilterItemOnProperty(object);**

[C++] **protected: Object* FilterItemOnProperty(Object*);**

[JScript] **protected function FilterItemOnProperty(Object) : Object;**

This member supports the .NET Framework infrastructure and is not intended to be used directly from your code.

Supported by the .NET Compact Framework.

[Visual Basic] **Overloads Protected Function FilterItemOnProperty(Object, String) As Object**

[C#] **protected object FilterItemOnProperty(object, string);**

[C++] **protected: Object* FilterItemOnProperty(Object*, String*);**

[JScript] **protected function FilterItemOnProperty(Object, String) : Object;**

ListControl.FilterItemOnProperty Method (Object)

This member supports the .NET Framework infrastructure and is not intended to be used directly from your code.

```
[Visual Basic]
Overloads Protected Function FilterItemOnProperty( _
   ByVal item As Object _
) As Object
[C#]
protected object FilterItemOnProperty(
   object item
);
[C++]
protected: Object* FilterItemOnProperty(
   Object* item
);
[JScript]
protected function FilterItemOnProperty(
   item : Object
) : Object;
```

ListControl.FilterItemOnProperty Method (Object, String)

This member supports the .NET Framework infrastructure and is not intended to be used directly from your code.

```
[Visual Basic]
Overloads Protected Function FilterItemOnProperty( _
   ByVal item As Object, _
   ByVal field As String _
) As Object
[C#]
protected object FilterItemOnProperty(
   object item,
   string field
);
[C++]
protected: Object* FilterItemOnProperty(
   Object* item,
   String* field
);
[JScript]
protected function FilterItemOnProperty(
   item : Object,
   field : String
) : Object;
```

ListControl.GetItemText Method

Returns the text representation of the specified item.

```
[Visual Basic]
Public Function GetItemText( _
   ByVal item As Object _
) As String
[C#]
public string GetItemText(
   object item
);
[C++]
public: String* GetItemText(
   Object* item
);
[JScript]
public function GetItemText(
   item : Object
) : String;
```

Parameters

item

The object from which to get the contents to display.

Return Value

If the **DisplayMember** property is not specified, the value returned by **GetItemText** is the value of the item's **toString** method. Otherwise, the method returns the string value of the member specified in the **DisplayMember** property for the object specified in the *item* parameter.

Requirements

Platforms: Windows 98, Windows NT 4.0, Windows Millennium Edition, Windows 2000, Windows XP Home Edition, Windows XP Professional, Windows Server 2003 family, .NET Compact Framework - Windows CE .NET

ListControl.IsInputKey Method

This member overrides **Control.IsInputKey**.

```
[Visual Basic]
Overrides Protected Function IsInputKey( _
   ByVal keyData As Keys _
) As Boolean
[C#]
protected override bool IsInputKey(
   Keys keyData
);
[C++]
protected: bool IsInputKey(
   Keys keyData
);
[JScript]
protected override function IsInputKey(
   keyData : Keys
) : Boolean;
```

Requirements

Platforms: Windows 98, Windows NT 4.0, Windows Millennium Edition, Windows 2000, Windows XP Home Edition, Windows XP Professional, Windows Server 2003 family

ListControl.OnBindingContextChanged Method

This member overrides **Control.OnBindingContextChanged**.

```
[Visual Basic]
Overrides Protected Sub OnBindingContextChanged( _
   ByVal e As EventArgs _
)
[C#]
protected override void OnBindingContextChanged(
   EventArgs e
);
[C++]
protected: void OnBindingContextChanged(
   EventArgs* e
);
[JScript]
protected override function OnBindingContextChanged(
   e : EventArgs
);
```

Requirements

Platforms: Windows 98, Windows NT 4.0, Windows Millennium Edition, Windows 2000, Windows XP Home Edition, Windows XP Professional, Windows Server 2003 family, .NET Compact Framework - Windows CE .NET

ListControl.OnDataSourceChanged Method

Raises the **DataSourceChanged** event.

```
[Visual Basic]
Protected Overridable Sub OnDataSourceChanged( _
   ByVal e As EventArgs _
)
```

[C#]
```
protected virtual void OnDataSourceChanged(
   EventArgs e
);
```
[C++]
```
protected: virtual void OnDataSourceChanged(
   EventArgs* e
);
```
[JScript]
```
protected function OnDataSourceChanged(
   e : EventArgs
);
```

Parameters

e

An **EventArgs** that contains the event data.

Remarks

Raising an event invokes the event handler through a delegate. For more information, see **Raising an Event**.

The **OnDataSourceChanged** method also allows derived classes to handle the event without attaching a delegate. This is the preferred technique for handling the event in a derived class.

Notes to Inheritors: When overriding **OnDataSourceChanged** in a derived class, be sure to call the base class's **OnDataSource-Changed** method so that registered delegates receive the event.

Requirements

Platforms: Windows 98, Windows NT 4.0,
Windows Millennium Edition, Windows 2000,
Windows XP Home Edition, Windows XP Professional,
Windows Server 2003 family,
.NET Compact Framework - Windows CE .NET

ListControl.OnDisplayMemberChanged Method

Raises the **DisplayMemberChanged** event.

[Visual Basic]
```
Protected Overridable Sub OnDisplayMemberChanged( _
   ByVal e As EventArgs _
)
```
[C#]
```
protected virtual void OnDisplayMemberChanged(
   EventArgs e
);
```
[C++]
```
protected: virtual void OnDisplayMemberChanged(
   EventArgs* e
);
```
[JScript]
```
protected function OnDisplayMemberChanged(
   e : EventArgs
);
```

Parameters

e

An **EventArgs** that contains the event data.

Remarks

Raising an event invokes the event handler through a delegate. For more information, see **Raising an Event**.

The **OnDisplayMemberChanged** method also allows derived classes to handle the event without attaching a delegate. This is the preferred technique for handling the event in a derived class.

Notes to Inheritors: When overriding **OnDisplayMember-Changed** in a derived class, be sure to call the base class's **OnDisplayMemberChanged** method so that registered delegates receive the event.

Requirements

Platforms: Windows 98, Windows NT 4.0,
Windows Millennium Edition, Windows 2000,
Windows XP Home Edition, Windows XP Professional,
Windows Server 2003 family,
.NET Compact Framework - Windows CE .NET

ListControl.OnSelectedIndexChanged Method

Raises the **SelectedValueChanged** event.

[Visual Basic]
```
Protected Overridable Sub OnSelectedIndexChanged( _
   ByVal e As EventArgs _
)
```
[C#]
```
protected virtual void OnSelectedIndexChanged(
   EventArgs e
);
```
[C++]
```
protected: virtual void OnSelectedIndexChanged(
   EventArgs* e
);
```
[JScript]
```
protected function OnSelectedIndexChanged(
   e : EventArgs
);
```

Parameters

e

An **EventArgs** that contains the event data.

Remarks

Raising an event invokes the event handler through a delegate. For more information, see **Raising an Event**.

The **OnSelectedIndexChanged** method also allows derived classes to handle the event without attaching a delegate. This is the preferred technique for handling the event in a derived class.

Notes to Inheritors: When overriding **OnSelectedIndexChanged** in a derived class, be sure to call the base class's **OnSelectedIndex-Changed** method so that registered delegates receive the event.

Requirements

Platforms: Windows 98, Windows NT 4.0,
Windows Millennium Edition, Windows 2000,
Windows XP Home Edition, Windows XP Professional,
Windows Server 2003 family,
.NET Compact Framework - Windows CE .NET

ListControl.OnSelectedValueChanged Method

Raises the **SelectedValueChanged** event.

[Visual Basic]
```
Protected Overridable Sub OnSelectedValueChanged( _
   ByVal e As EventArgs _
)
```
[C#]
```
protected virtual void OnSelectedValueChanged(
   EventArgs e
);
```
[C++]
```
protected: virtual void OnSelectedValueChanged(
   EventArgs* e
);
```
[JScript]
```
protected function OnSelectedValueChanged(
   e : EventArgs
);
```

Parameters

e

An **EventArgs** that contains the event data.

Remarks

Raising an event invokes the event handler through a delegate. For more information, see **Raising an Event**.

The **OnSelectedValueChanged** method also allows derived classes to handle the event without attaching a delegate. This is the preferred technique for handling the event in a derived class.

Notes to Inheritors: When overriding **OnSelectedValueChanged** in a derived class, be sure to call the base class's **OnSelectedValue-Changed** method so that registered delegates receive the event.

Requirements

Platforms: Windows 98, Windows NT 4.0,
Windows Millennium Edition, Windows 2000,
Windows XP Home Edition, Windows XP Professional,
Windows Server 2003 family,
.NET Compact Framework - Windows CE .NET

ListControl.OnValueMemberChanged Method

Raises the **ValueMemberChanged** event.

[Visual Basic]
```
Protected Overridable Sub OnValueMemberChanged( _
   ByVal e As EventArgs _
)
```
[C#]
```
protected virtual void OnValueMemberChanged(
   EventArgs e
);
```
[C++]
```
protected: virtual void OnValueMemberChanged(
   EventArgs* e
);
```
[JScript]
```
protected function OnValueMemberChanged(
   e : EventArgs
);
```

Parameters

e

An **EventArgs** that contains the event data.

Remarks

Raising an event invokes the event handler through a delegate.

The **OnValueMemberChanged** method also allows derived classes to handle the event without attaching a delegate. This is the preferred technique for handling the event in a derived class.

Notes to Inheritors: When overriding **OnValueMemberChanged** in a derived class, be sure to call the base class's **OnValueMember-Changed** method so that registered delegates receive the event.

Requirements

Platforms: Windows 98, Windows NT 4.0,
Windows Millennium Edition, Windows 2000,
Windows XP Home Edition, Windows XP Professional,
Windows Server 2003 family

ListControl.RefreshItem Method

When overridden in a derived class, resynchronizes the data of the object at the specified index with the contents of the data source.

[Visual Basic]
```
Protected MustOverride Sub RefreshItem( _
   ByVal index As Integer _
)
```
[C#]
```
protected abstract void RefreshItem(
   int index
);
```
[C++]
```
protected: virtual void RefreshItem(
   int index
) = 0;
```
[JScript]
```
protected abstract function RefreshItem(
   index : int
);
```

Parameters

index

The zero-based index of the item whose data to refresh.

Requirements

Platforms: Windows 98, Windows NT 4.0,
Windows Millennium Edition, Windows 2000,
Windows XP Home Edition, Windows XP Professional,
Windows Server 2003 family

ListControl.SetItemCore Method

This member supports the .NET Framework infrastructure and is not intended to be used directly from your code.

[Visual Basic]
```
Protected Overridable Sub SetItemCore( _
   ByVal index As Integer, _
   ByVal value As Object _
)
```

```
[C#]
protected virtual void SetItemCore(
   int index,
   object value
);
[C++]
protected: virtual void SetItemCore(
   int index,
   Object* value
);
[JScript]
protected function SetItemCore(
   index : int,
   value : Object
);
```

ListControl.SetItemsCore Method

This member supports the .NET Framework infrastructure and is not intended to be used directly from your code.

```
[Visual Basic]
Protected MustOverride Sub SetItemsCore( _
   ByVal items As IList _
)
[C#]
protected abstract void SetItemsCore(
   IList items
);
[C++]
protected: virtual void SetItemsCore(
   IList* items
) = 0;
[JScript]
protected abstract function SetItemsCore(
   items : IList
);
```

ListControl.DataSourceChanged Event

Occurs when the **DataSource** changes.

```
[Visual Basic]
Public Event DataSourceChanged As EventHandler
[C#]
public event EventHandler DataSourceChanged;
[C++]
public: __event EventHandler* DataSourceChanged;
```

[JScript] In JScript, you can handle the events defined by a class, but you cannot define your own.

Event Data

The event handler receives an argument of type **EventArgs**.

Remarks

When you create a **ListControl** delegate, you identify the method that will handle the event. To associate the event with your event handler, add an instance of the delegate to the event. The event handler is called whenever the event occurs, unless you remove the delegate. For more information about event-handler delegates, see **Events and Delegates**.

Requirements

Platforms: Windows 98, Windows NT 4.0, Windows Millennium Edition, Windows 2000, Windows XP Home Edition, Windows XP Professional, Windows Server 2003 family

ListControl.DisplayMemberChanged Event

Occurs when the **DisplayMember** property changes.

```
[Visual Basic]
Public Event DisplayMemberChanged As EventHandler
[C#]
public event EventHandler DisplayMemberChanged;
[C++]
public: __event EventHandler* DisplayMemberChanged;
```

[JScript] In JScript, you can handle the events defined by a class, but you cannot define your own.

Event Data

The event handler receives an argument of type **EventArgs**.

Remarks

When you create a **ListControl** delegate, you identify the method that will handle the event. To associate the event with your event handler, add an instance of the delegate to the event. The event handler is called whenever the event occurs, unless you remove the delegate. For more information about event-handler delegates, see **Events and Delegates**.

Requirements

Platforms: Windows 98, Windows NT 4.0, Windows Millennium Edition, Windows 2000, Windows XP Home Edition, Windows XP Professional, Windows Server 2003 family

ListControl.SelectedValueChanged Event

Occurs when the **SelectedValue** property changes.

```
[Visual Basic]
Public Event SelectedValueChanged As EventHandler
[C#]
public event EventHandler SelectedValueChanged;
[C++]
public: __event EventHandler* SelectedValueChanged;
```

[JScript] In JScript, you can handle the events defined by a class, but you cannot define your own.

Event Data

The event handler receives an argument of type **EventArgs**.

Remarks

When you create a **ListControl** delegate, you identify the method that will handle the event. To associate the event with your event handler, add an instance of the delegate to the event. The event handler is called whenever the event occurs, unless you remove the delegate.

Example

See related example in the **System.Windows.Forms.ListControl** class topic.

Requirements

Platforms: Windows 98, Windows NT 4.0, Windows Millennium Edition, Windows 2000, Windows XP Home Edition, Windows XP Professional, Windows Server 2003 family

ListControl.ValueMemberChanged Event

Occurs when the **ValueMember** property changes.

[Visual Basic]
```
Public Event ValueMemberChanged As EventHandler
```
[C#]
```
public event EventHandler ValueMemberChanged;
```
[C++]
```
public: __event EventHandler* ValueMemberChanged;
```

[JScript] In JScript, you can handle the events defined by a class, but you cannot define your own.

Event Data

The event handler receives an argument of type **EventArgs**.

Remarks

When you create a **ListControl** delegate, you identify the method that will handle the event. To associate the event with your event handler, add an instance of the delegate to the event. The event handler is called whenever the event occurs, unless you remove the delegate.

Requirements

Platforms: Windows 98, Windows NT 4.0, Windows Millennium Edition, Windows 2000, Windows XP Home Edition, Windows XP Professional, Windows Server 2003 family

ListView Class

Represents a Windows list view control, which displays a collection of items that can be displayed using one of four different views.

System.Object
System.MarshalByRefObject
System.ComponentModel.Component
System.Windows.Forms.Control
System.Windows.Forms.ListView

[Visual Basic]
```
Public Class ListView
   Inherits Control
```
[C#]
```
public class ListView : Control
```
[C++]
```
public __gc class ListView : public Control
```
[JScript]
```
public class ListView extends Control
```

Thread Safety

Any public static (**Shared** in Visual Basic) members of this type are safe for multithreaded operations. Any instance members are not guaranteed to be thread safe.

Remarks

A **ListView** control allows you to display a list of items with item text and, optionally, an icon to identify the type of item. For example, the Windows Explorer list of files is similar in appearance to a **ListView** control. It displays a list of the files and folders currently selected in the tree. Each file and folder displays an icon associated with it to help identify the type of file or folder. The **ListViewItem** class represents an item within a **ListView** control. The items that are displayed in the list can be shown in one of four different views. Items can be displayed as large icons, as small icons, or as small icons in a vertical list. Items can also have subitems which contain information that is related to the parent item. The fourth view style, details view, allows you to display the item and its subitems in a grid with column headers that identify the information being displayed in a subitem. **ListView** supports single or multiple selection. The multiple selection feature lets the user select from a list of items in a way similar to a **ListBox** control. Additionally, the user can activate selected items to perform a task. For example, you could use a **ListView** control to display a list of files that the application can then open and utilize. The user can select the files to open and then double-click them to activate the items and open the files in the application. The **ListView** can also display check boxes, using the **CheckBoxes** property, to allow the user to check the items that they want to perform an action on. You can use the **ListView** control in a variety of ways. The control can be used to display information from an application, a database, or a text file. The **ListView** can also be used to obtain information from the user, such as selecting a set of files to process.

ListView provides a large number of properties that provide flexibility in appearance and behavior. The **View** property allows you to change the way in which items are displayed. The **LargeImageList**, **SmallImageList**, and **StateImageList** properties allow you to specify the **ImageList** objects that contain the images displayed for items and, in the case of the **StateImageList**, the check boxes that are displayed when the **CheckBoxes** property is set to **true**. To determine which items are checked, you can use the **CheckedItems** property to access the **ListView.CheckedListViewItemCollection** collection. The **Columns** property allows access to the **ListView.ColumnHeaderCollection**, which stores the column headers that are displayed when the **View** property of the control is set to **View.Details**. Items are added and removed from the **ListView** through the **Items** property. The **Items** property allows you to access the **ListView.ListViewItemCollection** of the control, which provides methods for manipulating the items in the control. If you want to allow the user to edit the text of an item, you can use the **LabelEdit** property. When your control contains a large number of items, it is often easier for the user to see them in a sorted list. You can use the **Sorting** property to sort the items alphabetically.

Many of the properties of the **ListView** control are used when the **View** property of the control is set to **View.Details**. The **AllowColumnReorder** property allows the user of your **ListView** control to reconfigure the order of columns at run time. The **FullRowSelect** property allows an item and its subitems to be selected instead of just the item. To display grid lines in the details view to identify the boundaries of items and subitems in the **ListView**, you can use the **GridLines** property. The **HeaderStyle** property allows you to specify the type of column headers to display.

In addition to the many properties that are available for a **ListView** control, there are methods and events that your application can use to provide additional capabilities to the **ListView**. The **BeginUpdate** and **EndUpdate** methods allow you to add many items to a **ListView** without displaying the repainting of the control each time an item is added, improving performance. If your **ListView** control is displaying items and subitems, you may want to provide functionality when the user right-clicks a subitem. To determine the item whose subitem is being clicked, you can use the **GetItemAt** method. When performing validation of the items after the user has edited them, you may want to display a specific item to the user to change. The **EnsureVisible** method can be called to ensure that the specific item is in the visible area of the control.

If the **LabelEdit** property set to **true**, you can perform tasks such as validating the text being edited before and after the text changed by creating an event handler for the **BeforeLabelEdit** and **AfterLabelEdit** events. To perform tasks such as opening a file or displaying a dialog box to edit an item displayed in a **ListView**, you can create an event handler for the **ItemActivate** event. If you allow the user to sort the items in a **ListView** when they click a column header, you can create an event handler for the **ColumnClick** event to perform the sorting. When the **CheckBoxes** property is set to **true**, you can determine when a change in an item's check state has occurred by handling the **ItemCheck** event.

Example

[Visual Basic, C#, C++] The following example creates a **ListView** control with three **ListViewItem** objects specified and three **ListViewItem.ListViewSubItem** objects specified for each item. The example also creates **ColumnHeader** objects to display the subitems in details view. Two **ImageList** objects are also created in the code example to provide images for the **ListViewItem** objects. These **ImageList** objects are added to the **LargeImageList** and **SmallImageList** properties. The example uses the following properties in creating the **ListView** control.

- **View**
- **LabelEdit**
- **AllowColumnReorder**
- **CheckBoxes**
- **FullRowSelect**
- **GridLines**
- **Sorting**

[Visual Basic, C#, C++] This example assumes that you have added the code to a **Form** and call the method created in the example from the constructor or another method on the form. The example also assumes that images named `MySmallImage1`, `MySmallImage2`, `MyLargeImage1`, and `MyLargeImage2` are located in the root directory of drive C.

[Visual Basic]

```
Private Sub CreateMyListView()
    ' Create a new ListView control.
    Dim listView1 As New ListView()
    listView1.Bounds = New Rectangle(New Point(10, 10), New ↵
 Size(300, 200))

    ' Set the view to show details.
    listView1.View = View.Details
    ' Allow the user to edit item text.
    listView1.LabelEdit = True
    ' Allow the user to rearrange columns.
    listView1.AllowColumnReorder = True
    ' Display check boxes.
    listView1.CheckBoxes = True
    ' Select the item and subitems when selection is made.
    listView1.FullRowSelect = True
    ' Display grid lines.
    listView1.GridLines = True
    ' Sort the items in the list in ascending order.
    listView1.Sorting = SortOrder.Ascending

    ' Create three items and three sets of subitems for each item.
    Dim item1 As New ListViewItem("item1", 0)
    ' Place a check mark next to the item.
    item1.Checked = True
    item1.SubItems.Add("1")
    item1.SubItems.Add("2")
    item1.SubItems.Add("3")
    Dim item2 As New ListViewItem("item2", 1)
    item2.SubItems.Add("4")
    item2.SubItems.Add("5")
    item2.SubItems.Add("6")
    Dim item3 As New ListViewItem("item3", 0)
    ' Place a check mark next to the item.
    item3.Checked = True
    item3.SubItems.Add("7")
    item3.SubItems.Add("8")
    item3.SubItems.Add("9")

    ' Create columns for the items and subitems.
    listView1.Columns.Add("Item Column", -2, HorizontalAlignment.Left)
    listView1.Columns.Add("Column 2", -2, HorizontalAlignment.Left)
    listView1.Columns.Add("Column 3", -2, HorizontalAlignment.Left)
    listView1.Columns.Add("Column 4", -2, HorizontalAlignment.Center)

    'Add the items to the ListView.
    listView1.Items.AddRange(New ListViewItem() {item1, item2, item3})

    ' Create two ImageList objects.
    Dim imageListSmall As New ImageList()
    Dim imageListLarge As New ImageList()

    ' Initialize the ImageList objects with bitmaps.
    imageListSmall.Images.Add(Bitmap.FromFile("C:\MySmallImage1.bmp"))
    imageListSmall.Images.Add(Bitmap.FromFile("C:\MySmallImage2.bmp"))
    imageListLarge.Images.Add(Bitmap.FromFile("C:\MyLargeImage1.bmp"))
    imageListLarge.Images.Add(Bitmap.FromFile("C:\MyLargeImage2.bmp"))

    'Assign the ImageList objects to the ListView.
    listView1.LargeImageList = imageListLarge
    listView1.SmallImageList = imageListSmall

    ' Add the ListView to the control collection.
    Me.Controls.Add(listView1)
End Sub 'CreateMyListView
```

[C#]

```
private void CreateMyListView()
{
    // Create a new ListView control.
    ListView listView1 = new ListView();
    listView1.Bounds = new Rectangle(new Point(10,10), new ↵
Size(300,200));

    // Set the view to show details.
    listView1.View = View.Details;
    // Allow the user to edit item text.
    listView1.LabelEdit = true;
    // Allow the user to rearrange columns.
    listView1.AllowColumnReorder = true;
    // Display check boxes.
    listView1.CheckBoxes = true;
    // Select the item and subitems when selection is made.
    listView1.FullRowSelect = true;
    // Display grid lines.
    listView1.GridLines = true;
    // Sort the items in the list in ascending order.
    listView1.Sorting = SortOrder.Ascending;

    // Create three items and three sets of subitems for each item.
    ListViewItem item1 = new ListViewItem("item1",0);
    // Place a check mark next to the item.
    item1.Checked = true;
    item1.SubItems.Add("1");
    item1.SubItems.Add("2");
    item1.SubItems.Add("3");
    ListViewItem item2 = new ListViewItem("item2",1);
    item2.SubItems.Add("4");
    item2.SubItems.Add("5");
    item2.SubItems.Add("6");
    ListViewItem item3 = new ListViewItem("item3",0);
    // Place a check mark next to the item.
    item3.Checked = true;
    item3.SubItems.Add("7");
    item3.SubItems.Add("8");
    item3.SubItems.Add("9");

    // Create columns for the items and subitems.
    listView1.Columns.Add("Item Column", -2, HorizontalAlignment.Left);
    listView1.Columns.Add("Column 2", -2, HorizontalAlignment.Left);
    listView1.Columns.Add("Column 3", -2, HorizontalAlignment.Left);
    listView1.Columns.Add("Column 4", -2, HorizontalAlignment.Center);

    //Add the items to the ListView.
            listView1.Items.AddRange(new ↵
ListViewItem[]{item1,item2,item3});

    // Create two ImageList objects.
    ImageList imageListSmall = new ImageList();
    ImageList imageListLarge = new ImageList();

    // Initialize the ImageList objects with bitmaps.
imageListSmall.Images.Add(Bitmap.FromFile("C:\\MySmallImage1.bmp"));
imageListSmall.Images.Add(Bitmap.FromFile("C:\\MySmallImage2.bmp"));
imageListLarge.Images.Add(Bitmap.FromFile("C:\\MyLargeImage1.bmp"));
imageListLarge.Images.Add(Bitmap.FromFile("C:\\MyLargeImage2.bmp"));

    //Assign the ImageList objects to the ListView.
    listView1.LargeImageList = imageListLarge;
    listView1.SmallImageList = imageListSmall;

    // Add the ListView to the control collection.
    this.Controls.Add(listView1);
}
```

[C++]

```
private:
   void CreateMyListView() {
      // Create a new ListView control.
      ListView* listView1 = new ListView();
      listView1->Bounds = Rectangle(Point(10, 10), ↵
System::Drawing::Size(300, 200));

      // Set the view to show details.
      listView1->View = View::Details;
      // Allow the user to edit item text.
      listView1->LabelEdit = true;
      // Allow the user to rearrange columns.
      listView1->AllowColumnReorder = true;
```

```
      // Display check boxes.
      listView1->CheckBoxes = true;
      // Select the item and subitems when selection is made.
      listView1->FullRowSelect = true;
      // Display grid lines.
      listView1->GridLines = true;
      // Sort the items in the list in ascending order.
      listView1->Sorting = SortOrder::Ascending;

      // Create three items and three sets of subitems for each item.
      ListViewItem* item1 = new ListViewItem(S"item1", 0);
      // Place a check mark next to the item.
      item1->Checked = true;
      item1->SubItems->Add(S"1");
      item1->SubItems->Add(S"2");
      item1->SubItems->Add(S"3");
      ListViewItem* item2 = new ListViewItem(S"item2", 1);
      item2->SubItems->Add(S"4");
      item2->SubItems->Add(S"5");
      item2->SubItems->Add(S"6");
      ListViewItem* item3 = new ListViewItem(S"item3", 0);
      // Place a check mark next to the item.
      item3->Checked = true;
      item3->SubItems->Add(S"7");
      item3->SubItems->Add(S"8");
      item3->SubItems->Add(S"9");

      // Create columns for the items and subitems.
      listView1->Columns->Add(S"Item Column", -2,                    ↵
HorizontalAlignment::Left);
      listView1->Columns->Add(S"Column 2", -2,                       ↵
HorizontalAlignment::Left);
      listView1->Columns->Add(S"Column 3", -2,                       ↵
HorizontalAlignment::Left);
      listView1->Columns->Add(S"Column 4", -2,                       ↵
HorizontalAlignment::Center);

      //Add the items to the ListView.

      ListViewItem* temp1 [] = {item1, item2, item3};

      listView1->Items->AddRange(temp1);

      // Create two ImageList objects.
      ImageList* imageListSmall = new ImageList();
      ImageList* imageListLarge = new ImageList();

      // Initialize the ImageList objects with bitmaps.
      imageListSmall->Images-                                        ↵
>Add(Bitmap::FromFile(S"C:\\MySmallImage1.bmp"));
      imageListSmall->Images-                                        ↵
>Add(Bitmap::FromFile(S"C:\\MySmallImage2.bmp"));
      imageListLarge->Images-                                        ↵
>Add(Bitmap::FromFile(S"C:\\MyLargeImage1.bmp"));
      imageListLarge->Images-                                        ↵
>Add(Bitmap::FromFile(S"C:\\MyLargeImage2.bmp"));

      //Assign the ImageList objects to the ListView.
      listView1->LargeImageList = imageListLarge;
      listView1->SmallImageList = imageListSmall;

      // Add the ListView to the control collection.
      this->Controls->Add(listView1);
   }
```

Requirements

Namespace: System.Windows.Forms

Platforms: Windows 98, Windows NT 4.0, Windows Millennium Edition, Windows 2000, Windows XP Home Edition, Windows XP Professional, Windows Server 2003 family, .NET Compact Framework - Windows CE .NET

Assembly: System.Windows.Forms (in System.Windows.Forms.dll)

ListView Constructor

Initializes a new instance of the **ListView** class.

[Visual Basic]
```
Public Sub New()
```
[C#]
```
public ListView();
```
[C++]
```
public: ListView();
```
[JScript]
```
public function ListView();
```

Example

See related example in the **System.Windows.Forms.ListView** class topic.

Requirements

Platforms: Windows 98, Windows NT 4.0, Windows Millennium Edition, Windows 2000, Windows XP Home Edition, Windows XP Professional, Windows Server 2003 family, .NET Compact Framework - Windows CE .NET

ListView.Activation Property

Gets or sets the type of action the user must take to activate an item.

[Visual Basic]
```
Public Property Activation As ItemActivation
```
[C#]
```
public ItemActivation Activation {get; set;}
```
[C++]
```
public: __property ItemActivation get_Activation();
public: __property void set_Activation(ItemActivation);
```
[JScript]
```
public function get Activation() : ItemActivation;
public function set Activation(ItemActivation);
```

Property Value

One of the **ItemActivation** values. The default is **ItemActivation.Standard**.

Exceptions

Exception Type	Condition
InvalidEnumArgumentException	The value specified is not one of the **ItemActivation** members.

Remarks

The **Activation** property allows you to specify how the user will activate an item in the **ListView** control. Activating an item in a **ListView** is different from simply selecting an item. When an item is selected, an action is typically performed in an event handler for the **ItemActivate** event. For example, when an item is activated you might open a file or display a dialog box that allows the item to be edited. Typically, an item is double-clicked by the user to activate it. If the **Activation** property is set to **ItemActivation.OneClick**, clicking the item once activates it. Setting the **Activation** property to **ItemActivation.TwoClick** is different from the standard double-click because the two clicks can have any duration between them.

Note If the **Activation** property is set to **ItemActivation.OneClick** or **ItemActivation.TwoClick**, label editing will not be allowed regardless of the value of the **LabelEdit** property.

Requirements

Platforms: Windows 98, Windows NT 4.0, Windows Millennium Edition, Windows 2000, Windows XP Home Edition, Windows XP Professional, Windows Server 2003 family, .NET Compact Framework - Windows CE .NET

ListView.Alignment Property

Gets or sets the alignment of items in the control.

```
[Visual Basic]
Public Property Alignment As ListViewAlignment
[C#]
public ListViewAlignment Alignment {get; set;}
[C++]
public: __property ListViewAlignment get_Alignment();
public: __property void set_Alignment(ListViewAlignment);
[JScript]
public function get Alignment() : ListViewAlignment;
public function set Alignment(ListViewAlignment);
```

Property Value

One of the **ListViewAlignment** values. The default is **ListViewAlignment.Top**.

Exceptions

Exception Type	Condition
InvalidEnumArgumentException	The value specified is not one of the **ListViewAlignment** values.

Remarks

The **Alignment** property only affects alignment when the **View** property is set to **View.LargeIcon** or **View.SmallIcon**.

Note This property has no effect with the **View** property is set to **View.List**.

Requirements

Platforms: Windows 98, Windows NT 4.0, Windows Millennium Edition, Windows 2000, Windows XP Home Edition, Windows XP Professional, Windows Server 2003 family

ListView.AllowColumnReorder Property

Gets or sets a value indicating whether the user can drag column headers to reorder columns in the control.

```
[Visual Basic]
Public Property AllowColumnReorder As Boolean
[C#]
public bool AllowColumnReorder {get; set;}
[C++]
public: __property bool get_AllowColumnReorder();
public: __property void set_AllowColumnReorder(bool);
[JScript]
public function get AllowColumnReorder() : Boolean;
public function set AllowColumnReorder(Boolean);
```

Property Value

true if drag-and-drop column reordering is allowed; otherwise, **false**. The default is **false**.

Remarks

Setting the value of the **AllowColumnReorder** property has no effect unless the **View** property is set to **Details**. You can use this property to allow users to reposition columns in the control at run time. When the **AllowColumnReorder** property is set to **true**, users can position the columns in the control to display the item and its subitems in a way that meets their needs within your application.

Example

See related example in the **System.Windows.Forms.ListView** class topic.

Requirements

Platforms: Windows 98, Windows NT 4.0, Windows Millennium Edition, Windows 2000, Windows XP Home Edition, Windows XP Professional, Windows Server 2003 family

ListView.AutoArrange Property

Gets or sets whether icons are automatically kept arranged.

```
[Visual Basic]
Public Property AutoArrange As Boolean
[C#]
public bool AutoArrange {get; set;}
[C++]
public: __property bool get_AutoArrange();
public: __property void set_AutoArrange(bool);
[JScript]
public function get AutoArrange() : Boolean;
public function set AutoArrange(Boolean);
```

Property Value

true if icons are automatically kept arranged and snapped to the grid; otherwise, **false**. The default is **true**.

Remarks

The **AutoArrange** property only arranges items in the **ListView** control when the **View** property is set to **View.LargeIcon** or **View.SmallIcon**. To change the alignment of items in the **ListView** control, use the **Alignment** property. You can use **AutoArrange** to ensure that all items in your **ListView** control are automatically arranged to avoid overlapping at run time.

Requirements

Platforms: Windows 98, Windows NT 4.0, Windows Millennium Edition, Windows 2000, Windows XP Home Edition, Windows XP Professional, Windows Server 2003 family

ListView.BackColor Property

This member overrides **Control.BackColor**.

```
[Visual Basic]
Overrides Public Property BackColor As Color
[C#]
public override Color BackColor {get; set;}
[C++]
public: __property Color get_BackColor();
public: __property void set_BackColor(Color);
```

[JScript]
```
public override function get BackColor() : Color;
public override function set BackColor(Color);
```

Requirements

Platforms: Windows 98, Windows NT 4.0,
Windows Millennium Edition, Windows 2000,
Windows XP Home Edition, Windows XP Professional,
Windows Server 2003 family

ListView.BackgroundImage Property

This member overrides **Control.BackgroundImage**.

[Visual Basic]
```
Overrides Public Property BackgroundImage As Image
```
[C#]
```
public override Image BackgroundImage {get; set;}
```
[C++]
```
public: __property Image* get_BackgroundImage();
public: __property void set_BackgroundImage(Image*);
```
[JScript]
```
public override function get BackgroundImage() : Image;
public override function set BackgroundImage(Image);
```

Requirements

Platforms: Windows 98, Windows NT 4.0,
Windows Millennium Edition, Windows 2000,
Windows XP Home Edition, Windows XP Professional,
Windows Server 2003 family

ListView.BorderStyle Property

Gets or sets the border style of the control.

[Visual Basic]
```
Public Property BorderStyle As BorderStyle
```
[C#]
```
public BorderStyle BorderStyle {get; set;}
```
[C++]
```
public: __property BorderStyle get_BorderStyle();
public: __property void set_BorderStyle(BorderStyle);
```
[JScript]
```
public function get BorderStyle() : BorderStyle;
public function set BorderStyle(BorderStyle);
```

Property Value

One of the **BorderStyle** values. The default is **BorderStyle.Fixed3D**.

Exceptions

Exception Type	Condition
InvalidEnumArgumentException	The value specified is not one of the **BorderStyle** values.

Remarks

You can use the **BorderStyle** property to change the border style of the **ListView** control to match the border style settings of other controls on the form. For example, if none of the other controls on your form displays a border, you can set the **BorderStyle** property of the **ListView** control to **BorderStyle.None** to match the other controls.

Requirements

Platforms: Windows 98, Windows NT 4.0,
Windows Millennium Edition, Windows 2000,
Windows XP Home Edition, Windows XP Professional,
Windows Server 2003 family

ListView.CheckBoxes Property

Gets or sets a value indicating whether a check box appears next to each item in the control.

[Visual Basic]
```
Public Property CheckBoxes As Boolean
```
[C#]
```
public bool CheckBoxes {get; set;}
```
[C++]
```
public: __property bool get_CheckBoxes();
public: __property void set_CheckBoxes(bool);
```
[JScript]
```
public function get CheckBoxes() : Boolean;
public function set CheckBoxes(Boolean);
```

Property Value

true if a check box appears next to each item in the **ListView** control; otherwise, **false**. The default is **false**.

Remarks

The **CheckBoxes** property allows you to display a check box next to each item in the list. This enables your application to display a list of items (and subitems if the **View** property is set to **View.Details**) that the user can select by clicking the check box. The **CheckBoxes** property offers a way to select multiple items in the **ListView** control without using the CTRL key. Depending on your application, using check boxes to select items rather than the standard multiple selection method may be easier for the user. Even if the **MultiSelect** property of the **ListView** control is set to false, you can still display checkboxes and provide multiple selection capabilities to the user. This feature can be useful if you do not want multiple items to be selected yet still want to allow the user to choose multiple items from the list to perform an operation within your application.

To determine when an item has been checked, create an event handler for the **ItemCheck** event. To get all the items that are checked in the **ListView**, use the **CheckedItems** property to access the **ListView.CheckedIndexCollection** for the control. To get the indexes of all items that are checked in the **ListView**, use the **CheckedIndices** property.

If an **ImageList** is specified in the **StateImageList** property, the images at index positions 0 and 1 in the **ImageList** are displayed instead of the check box. The image at index position 0 is displayed instead of the unchecked check box, and the image at index position 1 is displayed instead of the checked check box.

Example

See related example in the **System.Windows.Forms.ListView** class topic.

Requirements

Platforms: Windows 98, Windows NT 4.0,
Windows Millennium Edition, Windows 2000,
Windows XP Home Edition, Windows XP Professional,
Windows Server 2003 family,
.NET Compact Framework - Windows CE .NET

ListView.CheckedIndices Property

Gets the indexes of the currently checked items in the control.

[Visual Basic]
```
Public ReadOnly Property CheckedIndices As _
   ListView.CheckedIndexCollection
```
[C#]
```
public ListView.CheckedIndexCollection CheckedIndices {get;}
```
[C++]
```
public: __property ListView.CheckedIndexCollection*
   get_CheckedIndices();
```
[JScript]
```
public function get CheckedIndices() :
   ListView.CheckedIndexCollection;
```

Property Value

A **ListView.CheckedIndexCollection** that contains the indexes of the currently checked items. If no items are currently checked, an empty **ListView.CheckedIndexCollection** is returned.

Remarks

This property is only useful when the **CheckBoxes** property of the **ListView** control is set to **true**. The **CheckedIndices** property returns a collection containing the index positions in the **ListView.ListViewItemCollection** of all items that are checked in the control.

If you want to obtain a collection of the items that are checked in the **ListView** control, instead of the index positions of the items that are checked, use the **CheckedItems** property.

Requirements

Platforms: Windows 98, Windows NT 4.0,
Windows Millennium Edition, Windows 2000,
Windows XP Home Edition, Windows XP Professional,
Windows Server 2003 family

ListView.CheckedItems Property

Gets the currently checked items in the control.

[Visual Basic]
```
Public ReadOnly Property CheckedItems As _
   ListView.CheckedListViewItemCollection
```
[C#]
```
public ListView.CheckedListViewItemCollection CheckedItems {get;}
```
[C++]
```
public: __property ListView.CheckedListViewItemCollection*
   get_CheckedItems();
```
[JScript]
```
public function get CheckedItems() :
   ListView.CheckedListViewItemCollection;
```

Property Value

A **ListView.CheckedListViewItemCollection** that contains the currently checked items. If no items are currently checked, an empty **ListView.CheckedListViewItemCollection** is returned.

Remarks

This property is only useful when the **CheckBoxes** property of the **ListView** control is set to **true**. The **CheckedItems** property returns a collection containing all items that are checked in the control. For more information on how to manipulate the items in the collection, see **ListView.CheckedListViewItemCollection**.

If you want to obtain a collection of the index positions within the **ListView.ListViewItemCollection** of the items that are checked in the **ListView** control, instead of the items that are checked, use the **CheckedIndices** property.

Requirements

Platforms: Windows 98, Windows NT 4.0,
Windows Millennium Edition, Windows 2000,
Windows XP Home Edition, Windows XP Professional,
Windows Server 2003 family

ListView.Columns Property

Gets the collection of all column headers that appear in the control.

[Visual Basic]
```
Public ReadOnly Property Columns As ListView.ColumnHeaderCollection
```
[C#]
```
public ListView.ColumnHeaderCollection Columns {get;}
```
[C++]
```
public: __property ListView.ColumnHeaderCollection* get_Columns();
```
[JScript]
```
public function get Columns() : ListView.ColumnHeaderCollection;
```

Property Value

A **ListView.ColumnHeaderCollection** that represents the column headers that appear when the **View** property is set to **View.Details**.

Remarks

The **Columns** property returns a collection containing the **ColumnHeader** objects that are displayed in the **ListView** control. **ColumnHeader** objects define the columns that are displayed in the **ListView** control when the **View** property is set to **View.Details**. Each column is used to display subitem information for each item in the **ListView**.

> **Note** If your **ListView** control does not have any column headers specified and you set the **View** property to **View.Details**, the **ListView** control will not display any items.

Example

See related example in the **System.Windows.Forms.ListView** class topic.

Requirements

Platforms: Windows 98, Windows NT 4.0,
Windows Millennium Edition, Windows 2000,
Windows XP Home Edition, Windows XP Professional,
Windows Server 2003 family,
.NET Compact Framework - Windows CE .NET

ListView.CreateParams Property

This member overrides **Control.CreateParams**.

[Visual Basic]
```
Overrides Protected ReadOnly Property CreateParams As CreateParams
```
[C#]
```
protected override CreateParams CreateParams {get;}
```
[C++]
```
protected: __property CreateParams* get_CreateParams();
```
[JScript]
```
protected override function get CreateParams() : CreateParams;
```

Requirements

Platforms: Windows 98, Windows NT 4.0, Windows Millennium Edition, Windows 2000, Windows XP Home Edition, Windows XP Professional, Windows Server 2003 family

ListView.DefaultSize Property

This member overrides **Control.DefaultSize**.

```
[Visual Basic]
Overrides Protected ReadOnly Property DefaultSize As Size
[C#]
protected override Size DefaultSize {get;}
[C++]
protected: __property Size get_DefaultSize();
[JScript]
protected override function get DefaultSize() : Size;
```

Requirements

Platforms: Windows 98, Windows NT 4.0, Windows Millennium Edition, Windows 2000, Windows XP Home Edition, Windows XP Professional, Windows Server 2003 family

ListView.FocusedItem Property

Gets the item in the control that currently has focus.

```
[Visual Basic]
Public ReadOnly Property FocusedItem As ListViewItem
[C#]
public ListViewItem FocusedItem {get;}
[C++]
public: __property ListViewItem* get_FocusedItem();
[JScript]
public function get FocusedItem() : ListViewItem;
```

Property Value

A **ListViewItem** that represents the item that has focus. If no item has the focus in the **ListView** control, a null reference (**Nothing** in Visual Basic) is returned.

Remarks

The **FocusedItem** property returns the **ListViewItem** representing the item that is currently displaying the focus reticle for the **ListView** control. Because a **ListView** control has no directly editable areas other than the items it displays, when the **ListView** control has focus, an item within the **ListView** displays the focus reticle around its item text. Typically, the last selected item in the **ListView** control is the focused item. Although an item may be the one displaying the focus reticle, it may not actually be a selected item in the **ListView**. Use the **SelectedItems** or **SelectedIndices** properties to obtain the selected item(s) in the **ListView** control, the **FocusedItem** property is not necessarily selected. You can use the **FocusedItem** property to determine which item was last clicked in the **ListView** control, regardless of selection state.

Requirements

Platforms: Windows 98, Windows NT 4.0, Windows Millennium Edition, Windows 2000, Windows XP Home Edition, Windows XP Professional, Windows Server 2003 family, .NET Compact Framework - Windows CE .NET

ListView.ForeColor Property

This member overrides **Control.ForeColor**.

```
[Visual Basic]
Overrides Public Property ForeColor As Color
[C#]
public override Color ForeColor {get; set;}
[C++]
public: __property Color get_ForeColor();
public: __property void set_ForeColor(Color);
[JScript]
public override function get ForeColor() : Color;
public override function set ForeColor(Color);
```

Requirements

Platforms: Windows 98, Windows NT 4.0, Windows Millennium Edition, Windows 2000, Windows XP Home Edition, Windows XP Professional, Windows Server 2003 family

ListView.FullRowSelect Property

Gets or sets a value indicating whether clicking an item selects all its subitems.

```
[Visual Basic]
Public Property FullRowSelect As Boolean
[C#]
public bool FullRowSelect {get; set;}
[C++]
public: __property bool get_FullRowSelect();
public: __property void set_FullRowSelect(bool);
[JScript]
public function get FullRowSelect() : Boolean;
public function set FullRowSelect(Boolean);
```

Property Value

true if clicking an item selects the item and all its subitems; **false** if clicking an item selects only the item itself. The default is **false**.

Remarks

The **FullRowSelect** property has no effect unless the **View** property of the **ListView** control is set to **View.Details**. The **FullRowSelect** property is typically used when a **ListView** displays items with many subitems and it is important to be able to see selected items when the item text is not visible due to horizontal scrolling of the control's contents.

Example

See related example in the **System.Windows.Forms.ListView** class topic.

Requirements

Platforms: Windows 98, Windows NT 4.0, Windows Millennium Edition, Windows 2000, Windows XP Home Edition, Windows XP Professional, Windows Server 2003 family, .NET Compact Framework - Windows CE .NET

ListView.GridLines Property

Gets or sets a value indicating whether grid lines appear between the rows and columns containing the items and subitems in the control.

[Visual Basic]
```
Public Property GridLines As Boolean
```
[C#]
```
public bool GridLines {get; set;}
```
[C++]
```
public: __property bool get_GridLines();
public: __property void set_GridLines(bool);
```
[JScript]
```
public function get GridLines() : Boolean;
public function set GridLines(Boolean);
```

Property Value

true if grid lines are drawn around items and subitems; otherwise, **false**. The default is **false**.

Remarks

The **GridLines** property has no effect unless the **View** property of the **ListView** control is set to **View.Details**. The **GridLines** property allows you to display lines to identify the rows and columns that are displayed in the **ListView** control when it displays items and their subitems. The grid lines that are displayed do not provide the ability to resize rows and columns as an application such as Microsoft Excel does. Only columns can be resized, if column headers are displayed, by moving the mouse pointer to the right side of the column to resize and then clicking and dragging until the column is the size you want. The grid lines feature is used to provide the user of the control with visible boundaries around items and subitems.

Example

See related example in the **System.Windows.Forms.ListView** class topic.

Requirements

Platforms: Windows 98, Windows NT 4.0,
Windows Millennium Edition, Windows 2000,
Windows XP Home Edition, Windows XP Professional,
Windows Server 2003 family

ListView.HeaderStyle Property

Gets or sets the column header style.

[Visual Basic]
```
Public Property HeaderStyle As ColumnHeaderStyle
```
[C#]
```
public ColumnHeaderStyle HeaderStyle {get; set;}
```
[C++]
```
public: __property ColumnHeaderStyle get_HeaderStyle();
public: __property void set_HeaderStyle(ColumnHeaderStyle);
```
[JScript]
```
public function get HeaderStyle() : ColumnHeaderStyle;
public function set HeaderStyle(ColumnHeaderStyle);
```

Property Value

One of the **ColumnHeaderStyle** values. The default is **ColumnHeaderStyle.Clickable**.

Exceptions

Exception Type	Condition
InvalidEnumArgument-Exception	The value specified is not one of the **ColumnHeaderStyle** values.

Remarks

The **HeaderStyle** property allows you to specify the type of column headers to display when the **View** property of the **ListView** control is set to **View.Details** and the **ListView** control has **ColumnHeader** objects specified in the **ListView.ColumnHeaderCollection**. **ColumnHeader** objects define the columns that are displayed in the **ListView** control. Each column is used to display subitem information for each item in the **ListView**. The **HeaderStyle** property allows you to specify whether the column headers will function as clickable buttons. If the **HeaderStyle** property is set to **ColumnHeaderStyle.Button**, column headers act like buttons that users can click to carry out an action, such as sorting the items in the **ListView** control using the items in the clicked column as a key. The **HeaderStyle** property can also be set to **ColumnHeaderStyle.None** to hide all columns headers.

Requirements

Platforms: Windows 98, Windows NT 4.0,
Windows Millennium Edition, Windows 2000,
Windows XP Home Edition, Windows XP Professional,
Windows Server 2003 family,
.NET Compact Framework - Windows CE .NET

ListView.HideSelection Property

Gets or sets a value indicating whether the selected item in the control remains highlighted when the control loses focus.

[Visual Basic]
```
Public Property HideSelection As Boolean
```
[C#]
```
public bool HideSelection {get; set;}
```
[C++]
```
public: __property bool get_HideSelection();
public: __property void set_HideSelection(bool);
```
[JScript]
```
public function get HideSelection() : Boolean;
public function set HideSelection(Boolean);
```

Property Value

true if the selected item does not appear highlighted when the control loses focus; **false** if the selected item still appears highlighted when the control loses focus. The default is **true**.

Remarks

When this property is set to **false**, selected items in the **ListView** control remain highlighted in a different color than the current selection color specified by the operating system when the **ListView** control loses focus. You can use this property to keep items that are selected by the user visible when the user clicks a different control on the form or moves to a different window.

Requirements

Platforms: Windows 98, Windows NT 4.0,
Windows Millennium Edition, Windows 2000,
Windows XP Home Edition, Windows XP Professional,
Windows Server 2003 family

ListView.HoverSelection Property

Gets or sets a value indicating whether an item is automatically selected when the mouse pointer remains over the item for a few seconds.

```
[Visual Basic]
Public Property HoverSelection As Boolean
[C#]
public bool HoverSelection {get; set;}
[C++]
public: __property bool get_HoverSelection();
public: __property void set_HoverSelection(bool);
[JScript]
public function get HoverSelection() : Boolean;
public function set HoverSelection(Boolean);
```

Property Value

true if an item is automatically selected when the mouse pointer hovers over it; otherwise, **false**. The default is **false**.

Remarks

When this property is set to **true**, the user can point to an item in the **ListView** control to select the item. Multiple items can be selected (when the **MultiSelect** property is set to true) by holding down the CTRL key while pointing to each item. You can use this feature to provide an easier method for the user of your application to select items in the **ListView** control.

Requirements

Platforms: Windows 98, Windows NT 4.0,
Windows Millennium Edition, Windows 2000,
Windows XP Home Edition, Windows XP Professional,
Windows Server 2003 family

ListView.Items Property

Gets a collection containing all items in the control.

```
[Visual Basic]
Public ReadOnly Property Items As ListView.ListViewItemCollection
[C#]
public ListView.ListViewItemCollection Items {get;}
[C++]
public: __property ListView.ListViewItemCollection* get_Items();
[JScript]
public function get Items() : ListView.ListViewItemCollection;
```

Property Value

A **ListView.ListViewItemCollection** that contains all the items in the **ListView** control.

Remarks

Using the **ListView.ListViewItemCollection** returned by this property, you can add items, remove items, and obtain a count of items. For more information on the tasks that can be performed with the items in the collection, see the **ListView.ListViewItem-Collection** class reference topics.

Example

See related example in the **System.Windows.Forms.ListView** class topic.

Requirements

Platforms: Windows 98, Windows NT 4.0,
Windows Millennium Edition, Windows 2000,
Windows XP Home Edition, Windows XP Professional,
Windows Server 2003 family,
.NET Compact Framework - Windows CE .NET

ListView.LabelEdit Property

Gets or sets a value indicating whether the user can edit the labels of items in the control.

```
[Visual Basic]
Public Property LabelEdit As Boolean
[C#]
public bool LabelEdit {get; set;}
[C++]
public: __property bool get_LabelEdit();
public: __property void set_LabelEdit(bool);
[JScript]
public function get LabelEdit() : Boolean;
public function set LabelEdit(Boolean);
```

Property Value

true if the user can edit the labels of items at run time; otherwise, **false**. The default is **false**.

Remarks

When the **LabelEdit** property is set to **true**, the user is able to modify the text of an item by clicking the item text to select it and then clicking the item text again to put the label text into edit mode. The user can then modify or replace the item's text label. You can use the **BeforeLabelEdit** and **AfterLabelEdit** events to perform tasks before and after the user edits an item's text. The text of subitems cannot be modified if this property is set to **true**. To change the text of subitems, you can display a dialog box to users when they double-click a subitem in the control.

> **Note** If the **Activation** property is set to **ItemActivation.OneClick** or **ItemActivation.TwoClick**, label editing will not be allowed regardless of the value of the **LabelEdit** property.

Example

See related example in the **System.Windows.Forms.ListView** class topic.

Requirements

Platforms: Windows 98, Windows NT 4.0,
Windows Millennium Edition, Windows 2000,
Windows XP Home Edition, Windows XP Professional,
Windows Server 2003 family

ListView.LabelWrap Property

Gets or sets a value indicating whether item labels wrap when items are displayed in the control as icons.

```
[Visual Basic]
Public Property LabelWrap As Boolean
[C#]
public bool LabelWrap {get; set;}
```

```
[C++]
public: __property bool get_LabelWrap();
public: __property void set_LabelWrap(bool);
[JScript]
public function get LabelWrap() : Boolean;
public function set LabelWrap(Boolean);
```

Property Value

true if item labels wrap when items are displayed as icons; otherwise, **false**. The default is **true**.

Remarks

When the **LabelWrap** property is set to **true**, the item text is wrapped to the next line of text if needed. If the text is longer than two lines of text, the text is shortened. If the user selects the item, all the item text is displayed. If the **LabelWrap** property is set to **false**, all item text is displayed on a single line. The entire item text is displayed when the **LabelWrap** is set to **false**. This property is only used when the **View** property is set to **View.LargeIcon** or **View.SmallIcon**.

Requirements

Platforms: Windows 98, Windows NT 4.0,
Windows Millennium Edition, Windows 2000,
Windows XP Home Edition, Windows XP Professional,
Windows Server 2003 family

ListView.LargeImageList Property

Gets or sets the **ImageList** to use when displaying items as large icons in the control.

```
[Visual Basic]
Public Property LargeImageList As ImageList
[C#]
public ImageList LargeImageList {get; set;}
[C++]
public: __property ImageList* get_LargeImageList();
public: __property void set_LargeImageList(ImageList*);
[JScript]
public function get LargeImageList() : ImageList;
public function set LargeImageList(ImageList);
```

Property Value

An **ImageList** that contains the icons to use when the **View** property is set to **View.LargeIcon**. The default is a null reference (**Nothing** in Visual Basic).

Remarks

The **LargeImageList** property allows you to specify an **ImageList** object that contains icons to use when displaying items with large icons (when the **View** property is set to **View.LargeIcon**). The **ListView** control can accept any graphics format that the **ImageList** control supports when displaying icons. The **ListView** control is not limited to .ico files. Once an **ImageList** is assigned to the **LargeImageList** property, you can set the **ImageIndex** property of each **ListViewItem** in the **ListView** control to the index position of the appropriate image in the **ImageList**.

Because only one index can be specified for the **ListViewItem.ImageIndex** property, the **ImageList** objects specified in the **LargeImageList** and **SmallImageList** properties should have the same index positions for the images to display. For example, if the **ImageIndex** property of a **ListViewItem** is set to 0, the images to use for both small and large icons should be at the same index position in the **ImageList** objects specified in the **LargeImageList** and **SmallImageList** properties.

To set the **ImageList** to use when displaying items with small icons (all view modes other than **View.LargeIcon**), use the **SmallImageList** property. If you want to use images to display item state, use the **StateImageList** property.

Example

See related example in the **System.Windows.Forms.ListView** class topic.

Requirements

Platforms: Windows 98, Windows NT 4.0,
Windows Millennium Edition, Windows 2000,
Windows XP Home Edition, Windows XP Professional,
Windows Server 2003 family,
.NET Compact Framework - Windows CE .NET

ListView.ListViewItemSorter Property

Gets or sets the sorting comparer for the control.

```
[Visual Basic]
Public Property ListViewItemSorter As IComparer
[C#]
public IComparer ListViewItemSorter {get; set;}
[C++]
public: __property IComparer* get_ListViewItemSorter();
public: __property void set_ListViewItemSorter(IComparer*);
[JScript]
public function get ListViewItemSorter() : IComparer;
public function set ListViewItemSorter(IComparer);
```

Property Value

An **IComparer** that represents the sorting comparer for the control.

Remarks

The **ListViewItemSorter** property allows you to specify the object that performs the sorting of items in the **ListView**. You can use the **ListViewItemSorter** property in combination with the **Sort** method to perform custom sorting. For example, you could create a class (that implements the **IComparer** interface) to support column sorting in the **ListView** control. If an instance of the class is assigned to the **ListViewItemSorter** property and the **Sort** method is called, you can then create code in the event handler for the **ColumnClick** event to perform sorting based on the column that was clicked.

> **Note** Setting the value of the **ListViewItemSorter** property causes the **Sort** method to be called automatically.

Example

See related example in the **System.Windows.Forms.ListView** class topic.

Requirements

Platforms: Windows 98, Windows NT 4.0,
Windows Millennium Edition, Windows 2000,
Windows XP Home Edition, Windows XP Professional,
Windows Server 2003 family

ListView.MultiSelect Property

Gets or sets a value indicating whether multiple items can be selected.

```
[Visual Basic]
Public Property MultiSelect As Boolean
[C#]
public bool MultiSelect {get; set;}
[C++]
public: __property bool get_MultiSelect();
public: __property void set_MultiSelect(bool);
[JScript]
public function get MultiSelect() : Boolean;
public function set MultiSelect(Boolean);
```

Property Value

true if multiple items in the control can be selected at one time; otherwise, **false**. The default is **true**.

Remarks

When the **MultiSelect** property is set to **true**, multiple items can be selected in the **ListView** control. To select multiple items, the user must hold down the CTRL key while clicking the items to select. Consecutive items can be selected by clicking the first item to select and then, while holding down the SHIFT key, clicking the last item to select. You can use the multiselection feature to select multiple items in the **ListView** control and perform an operation on all the items selected. For example, the user could select multiple items and then right-click a selected item to display a shortcut menu that displays a set of tasks that can be performed on the selected items.

To determine which items are selected in the **ListView** control, use the **SelectedItems** property. The **SelectedItems** property allows you to access the **ListView.SelectedListViewItemCollection** that contains a list of the selected items. If you want the index positions in the **ListView.ListViewItemCollection** instead of the items, you can use the **SelectedIndices** property to access the **ListView.SelectedIndexCollection**.

If you do not want to allow multiple selections in the **ListView**, yet still want to offer the user a way for multiple items to be chosen, you can display check boxes by setting the **CheckBoxes** property to **true**.

Requirements

Platforms: Windows 98, Windows NT 4.0,
Windows Millennium Edition, Windows 2000,
Windows XP Home Edition, Windows XP Professional,
Windows Server 2003 family

ListView.Scrollable Property

Gets or sets a value indicating whether a scroll bar is added to the control when there is not enough room to display all items.

```
[Visual Basic]
Public Property Scrollable As Boolean
[C#]
public bool Scrollable {get; set;}
[C++]
public: __property bool get_Scrollable();
public: __property void set_Scrollable(bool);
[JScript]
public function get Scrollable() : Boolean;
public function set Scrollable(Boolean);
```

Property Value

true if scroll bars are added to the control when necessary to allow the user to see all the items; otherwise, **false**. The default is **true**.

Remarks

When this property is set to **true**, the **ListView** displays a vertical scrollbar to use when the number of items exceeds the size of the client area of the control. You can use this property to ensure that the user can access all items that are available in the **ListView** control.

Requirements

Platforms: Windows 98, Windows NT 4.0,
Windows Millennium Edition, Windows 2000,
Windows XP Home Edition, Windows XP Professional,
Windows Server 2003 family

ListView.SelectedIndices Property

Gets the indexes of the selected items in the control.

```
[Visual Basic]
Public ReadOnly Property SelectedIndices As _
   ListView.SelectedIndexCollection
[C#]
public ListView.SelectedIndexCollection SelectedIndices {get;}
[C++]
public: __property ListView.SelectedIndexCollection*
   get_SelectedIndices();
[JScript]
public function get SelectedIndices() :
   ListView.SelectedIndexCollection;
```

Property Value

A **ListView.SelectedIndexCollection** that contains the indexes of the selected items. If no items are currently selected, an empty **ListView.SelectedIndexCollection** is returned.

Remarks

When the **MultiSelect** property is set to **true**, this property returns a collection containing the indexes of all items that are selected in the **ListView**. For a single-selection **ListView**, this property returns a collection containing a single element containing the index of the only selected item in the **ListView**. For more information on the tasks that can be performed with the items in the collection, see **ListView.SelectedIndexCollection**.

If you want to obtain a collection of the items that are selected in the **ListView** control, instead of the index positions of the items that are selected, use the **SelectedItems** property.

Requirements

Platforms: Windows 98, Windows NT 4.0,
Windows Millennium Edition, Windows 2000,
Windows XP Home Edition, Windows XP Professional,
Windows Server 2003 family,
.NET Compact Framework - Windows CE .NET

ListView.SelectedItems Property

Gets the items that are selected in the control.

```
[Visual Basic]
Public ReadOnly Property SelectedItems As _
   ListView.SelectedListViewItemCollection
[C#]
public ListView.SelectedListViewItemCollection SelectedItems {get;}
```

[C++]
```
public: __property ListView.SelectedListViewItemCollection*
   get_SelectedItems();
```
[JScript]
```
public function get SelectedItems() :
   ListView.SelectedListViewItemCollection;
```

Property Value

A **ListView.SelectedListViewItemCollection** that contains the items that are selected in the control. If no items are currently selected, an empty **ListView.SelectedListViewItemCollection** is returned.

Remarks

When the **MultiSelect** property is set to **true**, this property returns a collection containing the items that are selected in the **ListView**. For a single-selection **ListView**, this property returns a collection containing the only selected item in the **ListView**. For more information on the tasks that can be performed with the items in the collection, see **ListView.SelectedListViewItemCollection**.

If you want to obtain a collection of the index positions within the **ListView.ListViewItemCollection** of the items that are selected in the **ListView** control, instead of the items that are selected, use the **SelectedIndices** property.

Requirements

Platforms: Windows 98, Windows NT 4.0,
Windows Millennium Edition, Windows 2000,
Windows XP Home Edition, Windows XP Professional,
Windows Server 2003 family

ListView.SmallImageList Property

Gets or sets the **ImageList** to use when displaying items as small icons in the control.

[Visual Basic]
```
Public Property SmallImageList As ImageList
```
[C#]
```
public ImageList SmallImageList {get; set;}
```
[C++]
```
public: __property ImageList* get_SmallImageList();
public: __property void set_SmallImageList(ImageList*);
```
[JScript]
```
public function get SmallImageList() : ImageList;
public function set SmallImageList(ImageList);
```

Property Value

An **ImageList** that contains the icons to use when the **View** property is set to **View.SmallIcon**. The default is a null reference (**Nothing** in Visual Basic).

Remarks

The **SmallImageList** property allows you to specify an **ImageList** object that contains icons to use when displaying items with small icons (when the **View** property is set to any value other than **View.LargeIcon**). The **ListView** control can accept any graphics format that the **ImageList** control supports when displaying icons. The **ListView** control is not limited to .ico files. Once an **ImageList** is assigned to the **SmallImageList** property, you can set the **ImageIndex** property of each **ListViewItem** in the **ListView** control to the index position of the appropriate image in the **ImageList**.

Because only one index can be specified for the **ListViewItem.ImageIndex** property, the **ImageList** objects specified in the **LargeImageList** and **SmallImageList** properties should have the same index positions for the images to display. For example, if the **ImageIndex** property of a **ListViewItem** is set to 0, the images to use for both small and large icons should be at the same index position in the **ImageList** objects specified in the **LargeImageList** and **SmallImageList** properties.

To set the **ImageList** to use when displaying items with large icons (when the **View** property is set to **View.LargeIcon**), use the **LargeImageList** property. If you want to use images to display item state, use the **StateImageList** property.

Example

See related example in the **System.Windows.Forms.ListView** class topic.

Requirements

Platforms: Windows 98, Windows NT 4.0,
Windows Millennium Edition, Windows 2000,
Windows XP Home Edition, Windows XP Professional,
Windows Server 2003 family,
.NET Compact Framework - Windows CE .NET

ListView.Sorting Property

Gets or sets the sort order for items in the control.

[Visual Basic]
```
Public Property Sorting As SortOrder
```
[C#]
```
public SortOrder Sorting {get; set;}
```
[C++]
```
public: __property SortOrder get_Sorting();
public: __property void set_Sorting(SortOrder);
```
[JScript]
```
public function get Sorting() : SortOrder;
public function set Sorting(SortOrder);
```

Property Value

One of the **SortOrder** values. The default is **SortOrder.None**.

Exceptions

Exception Type	Condition
InvalidEnumArgumentException	The value specified is not one of the **SortOrder** values.

Remarks

The **Sorting** property allows you to specify whether or not items are sorted in the **ListView** control. By default, no sorting is performed. When the **Sorting** property is set to **SortOrder.Ascending** or **SortOrder.Descending**, the items in the **ListView** are sorted automatically in ascending alphabetical order (when the property is set to **SortOrder.Ascending**) or descending alphabetical order (when the property is set to **SortOrder.Descending**). You can use this property to automatically sort items that are displayed in your **ListView** control to make it easier for users to find items when a large number of items are available.

If you want to perform your own item sorting instead of using the **Sorting** property, use the **ListViewItemSorter** property in combination with the **Sort** method.

Example

See related example in the **System.Windows.Forms.ListView** class topic.

Requirements

Platforms: Windows 98, Windows NT 4.0,
Windows Millennium Edition, Windows 2000,
Windows XP Home Edition, Windows XP Professional,
Windows Server 2003 family

ListView.StateImageList Property

Gets or sets the **ImageList** associated with application-defined states in the control.

```
[Visual Basic]
Public Property StateImageList As ImageList
[C#]
public ImageList StateImageList {get; set;}
[C++]
public: __property ImageList* get_StateImageList();
public: __property void set_StateImageList(ImageList*);
[JScript]
public function get StateImageList() : ImageList;
public function set StateImageList(ImageList);
```

Property Value

An **ImageList** that contains a set of state images that can be used to indicate an application-defined state of an item. The default is a null reference (**Nothing** in Visual Basic).

Remarks

The **StateImageList** property allows you to specify an **ImageList** that contains images to use to represent an application-specific state of an item in a **ListView** control. State images are displayed to the left of an icon for the item. You can use state images, such as checked and unchecked check boxes, to indicate application-defined item states. State images are visible in all views of the **ListView** control.

If an **ImageList** is specified in the **StateImageList** property and the **CheckBoxes** property is set to **true**, the images at index positions 0 and 1 in the **ImageList** are displayed instead of the check box. The image at index position 0 is displayed instead of the unchecked check box, and the image at index position 1 is displayed instead of the checked check box.

Requirements

Platforms: Windows 98, Windows NT 4.0,
Windows Millennium Edition, Windows 2000,
Windows XP Home Edition, Windows XP Professional,
Windows Server 2003 family

ListView.Text Property

This member overrides **Control.Text**.

```
[Visual Basic]
Overrides Public Property Text As String
[C#]
public override string Text {get; set;}
[C++]
public: __property String* get_Text();
public: __property void set_Text(String*);
[JScript]
public override function get Text() : String;
public override function set Text(String);
```

Requirements

Platforms: Windows 98, Windows NT 4.0,
Windows Millennium Edition, Windows 2000,
Windows XP Home Edition, Windows XP Professional,
Windows Server 2003 family

ListView.TopItem Property

Gets the first visible item in the control.

```
[Visual Basic]
Public ReadOnly Property TopItem As ListViewItem
[C#]
public ListViewItem TopItem {get;}
[C++]
public: __property ListViewItem* get_TopItem();
[JScript]
public function get TopItem() : ListViewItem;
```

Property Value

A **ListViewItem** that represents the first visible item in the control.

Remarks

Initially, the item with the index position of zero (0) is at the top of the **ListView** control. If the **ListView** control contents are scrolled, a different item can be at the top of the control. You can use this property to determine which item is visible at the top of the **ListView** control. To position a specific item in the visible region of the control, use the **EnsureVisible** method.

Requirements

Platforms: Windows 98, Windows NT 4.0,
Windows Millennium Edition, Windows 2000,
Windows XP Home Edition, Windows XP Professional,
Windows Server 2003 family

ListView.View Property

Gets or sets how items are displayed in the control.

```
[Visual Basic]
Public Property View As View
[C#]
public View View {get; set;}
[C++]
public: __property View get_View();
public: __property void set_View(View);
[JScript]
public function get View() : View;
public function set View(View);
```

Property Value

One of the **View** values. The default is **View.LargeIcon**.

Exceptions

Exception Type	Condition
InvalidEnumArgumentException	The value specified is not one of the **View** values.

Remarks

The **View** property allows you to specify the type of display the **ListView** control uses to display items. You can set the **View** property to display each item with large or small icons or display items in a vertical list. The richest option is the details view, which allows you to view not only the items but any subitems specified for each item. Each item is displayed in a grid, with each item listed vertically and the subitems for each item displayed in a column, with column headers. The details view is a perfect way to display database information to a user.

Most of the properties in the **ListView** control affect how the different views behave or are displayed. Some properties that affect the views of the items are only useful when the **View** property is set to a specific value, while others are useful in all views. For example, properties such as **GridLines** and **FullRowSelect** are only useful when the **View** property is set to **View.Details**, while the **MultiSelect** and **CheckBoxes** properties are useful in all views.

You can use the **View** property to provide different views of data in your application, or to lock a specific view to utilize that view's benefits. For example, the **View** property is often set to **View.Details** because the details view provides a number of viewing options not available in the other views.

> **Note** If your **ListView** control does not have any column headers specified and you set the **View** property to **View.Details**, the **ListView** control will not display any items.

Example

See related example in the **System.Windows.Forms.ListView** class topic.

Requirements

Platforms: Windows 98, Windows NT 4.0,
Windows Millennium Edition, Windows 2000,
Windows XP Home Edition, Windows XP Professional,
Windows Server 2003 family,
.NET Compact Framework - Windows CE .NET

ListView.ArrangeIcons Method

Arranges items in the control when they are displayed as icons.

Overload List

Arranges items in the control when they are displayed as icons based on the value of the **Alignment** property.

[Visual Basic] **Overloads Public Sub ArrangeIcons()**

[C#] **public void ArrangeIcons();**

[C++] **public: void ArrangeIcons();**

[JScript] **public function ArrangeIcons();**

Arranges items in the control when they are displayed as icons with a specified alignment setting.

[Visual Basic] **Overloads Public Sub ArrangeIcons(ListViewAlignment)**

[C#] **public void ArrangeIcons(ListViewAlignment);**

[C++] **public: void ArrangeIcons(ListViewAlignment);**

[JScript] **public function ArrangeIcons(ListViewAlignment);**

ListView.ArrangeIcons Method ()

Arranges items in the control when they are displayed as icons based on the value of the **Alignment** property.

```
[Visual Basic]
Overloads Public Sub ArrangeIcons()
[C#]
public void ArrangeIcons();
[C++]
public: void ArrangeIcons();
[JScript]
public function ArrangeIcons();
```

Remarks

The **ArrangeIcons** method is only useful when the **View** property is set to **View.LargeIcon** or **View.SmallIcon**. Calling this version of the **ArrangeIcons** method arranges the items using the default alignment setting (**ListViewAlignment.Default**). To cause the items to be aligned based on a value that is different than that of the **Alignment** property, use the other version of the **ArrangeIcons** method.

Requirements

Platforms: Windows 98, Windows NT 4.0,
Windows Millennium Edition, Windows 2000,
Windows XP Home Edition, Windows XP Professional,
Windows Server 2003 family

ListView.ArrangeIcons Method (ListViewAlignment)

Arranges items in the control when they are displayed as icons with a specified alignment setting.

```
[Visual Basic]
Overloads Public Sub ArrangeIcons( _
   ByVal value As ListViewAlignment _
)
[C#]
public void ArrangeIcons(
   ListViewAlignment value
);
[C++]
public: void ArrangeIcons(
   ListViewAlignment value
);
[JScript]
public function ArrangeIcons(
   value : ListViewAlignment
);
```

Parameters

value

One of the **ListViewAlignment** values.

Exceptions

Exception Type	Condition
ArgumentException	The value specified in the *value* parameter is not a member of the **ListViewAlignment** enumeration.

Remarks

The **ArrangeIcons** method is only useful when the **View** property is set to **View.LargeIcon** or **View.SmallIcon**. This version of the **ArrangeIcons** method arranges the icons in the **ListView** based on the **ListViewAlignment** value specified in the *value* parameter. Calling this method does not change the value of the **Alignment** property of the control. This method is used to arrange icons on the control using a different value than that of the **Alignment** property. To cause the items to be aligned based on the value of the **Alignment** property, use the other version of the **ArrangeIcons** method.

Requirements

Platforms: Windows 98, Windows NT 4.0,
Windows Millennium Edition, Windows 2000,
Windows XP Home Edition, Windows XP Professional,
Windows Server 2003 family

ListView.BeginUpdate Method

Prevents the control from drawing until the **EndUpdate** method is called.

```
[Visual Basic]
Public Sub BeginUpdate()
[C#]
public void BeginUpdate();
[C++]
public: void BeginUpdate();
[JScript]
public function BeginUpdate();
```

Remarks

The preferred way to add multiple items to a **ListView** is to use the **AddRange** method of the **ListView.ListViewItemCollection** (accessed through the **Items** property of the **ListView**). This enables you to add an array of items to the list in a single operation. However, if you want to add items one at a time using the **Add** method of the **ListView.ListViewItemCollection** class, you can use the **BeginUpdate** method to prevent the control from repainting the **ListView** each time an item is added. Once you have completed the task of adding items to the control, call the **EndUpdate** method to enable the **ListView** to repaint. This way of adding items can prevent flickered drawing of the **ListView** when a large number of items are being added to the control.

Requirements

Platforms: Windows 98, Windows NT 4.0,
Windows Millennium Edition, Windows 2000,
Windows XP Home Edition, Windows XP Professional,
Windows Server 2003 family,
.NET Compact Framework - Windows CE .NET

ListView.Clear Method

Removes all items and columns from the control.

```
[Visual Basic]
Public Sub Clear()
[C#]
public void Clear();
[C++]
public: void Clear();
[JScript]
public function Clear();
```

Remarks

You can use this method to remove all items and columns from the **ListView** control without having to call the individual **Clear** methods from the **ListView.ColumnHeaderCollection** and **ListView.ListViewItemCollection** classes.

Requirements

Platforms: Windows 98, Windows NT 4.0,
Windows Millennium Edition, Windows 2000,
Windows XP Home Edition, Windows XP Professional,
Windows Server 2003 family,
.NET Compact Framework - Windows CE .NET

ListView.CreateHandle Method

This member overrides **Control.CreateHandle**.

```
[Visual Basic]
Overrides Protected Sub CreateHandle()
[C#]
protected override void CreateHandle();
[C++]
protected: void CreateHandle();
[JScript]
protected override function CreateHandle();
```

Requirements

Platforms: Windows 98, Windows NT 4.0,
Windows Millennium Edition, Windows 2000,
Windows XP Home Edition, Windows XP Professional,
Windows Server 2003 family

ListView.Dispose Method

Overload List

This member supports the .NET Framework infrastructure and is not intended to be used directly from your code.

Supported by the .NET Compact Framework.

[Visual Basic] **Overloads Overrides Protected Sub Dispose(Boolean)**

[C#] **protected override void Dispose(bool);**

[C++] **protected: void Dispose(bool);**

[JScript] **protected override function Dispose(Boolean);**

Inherited from **Component**.

Supported by the .NET Compact Framework.

[Visual Basic] **Overloads Public Overridable Sub Dispose() Implements IDisposable.Dispose**

[C#] **public virtual void Dispose();**

[C++] **public: virtual void Dispose();**

[JScript] **public function Dispose();**

ListView.Dispose Method (Boolean)

This member overrides **Control.Dispose**.

```
[Visual Basic]
Overrides Overloads Protected Sub Dispose( _
   ByVal disposing As Boolean _
)
```

```
[C#]
protected override void Dispose(
   bool disposing
);
[C++]
protected: void Dispose(
   bool disposing
);
[JScript]
protected override function Dispose(
   disposing : Boolean
);
```

Requirements

Platforms: Windows 98, Windows NT 4.0,
Windows Millennium Edition, Windows 2000,
Windows XP Home Edition, Windows XP Professional,
Windows Server 2003 family,
.NET Compact Framework - Windows CE .NET

ListView.EndUpdate Method

Resumes drawing of the list view control after drawing is suspended by the **BeginUpdate** method.

```
[Visual Basic]
Public Sub EndUpdate()
[C#]
public void EndUpdate();
[C++]
public: void EndUpdate();
[JScript]
public function EndUpdate();
```

Remarks

The preferred way to add multiple items to a **ListView** is to use the **AddRange** method of the **ListView.ListViewItemCollection** (accessed through the **Items** property of the **ListView**). This enables you to add an array of items to the list in a single operation. However, if you want to add items one at a time using the **Add** method of the **ListView.ListViewItemCollection** class, you can use the **BeginUpdate** method to prevent the control from repainting the **ListView** each time an item is added. Once you have completed the task of adding items to the control, call the **EndUpdate** method to enable the **ListView** to repaint. This way of adding items can prevent flickered drawing of the **ListView** when a large number of items are being added to the control.

Requirements

Platforms: Windows 98, Windows NT 4.0,
Windows Millennium Edition, Windows 2000,
Windows XP Home Edition, Windows XP Professional,
Windows Server 2003 family,
.NET Compact Framework - Windows CE .NET

ListView.EnsureVisible Method

Ensures that the specified item is visible within the control, scrolling the contents of the control if necessary.

```
[Visual Basic]
Public Sub EnsureVisible( _
   ByVal index As Integer _
)
[C#]
public void EnsureVisible(
   int index
);
[C++]
public: void EnsureVisible(
   int index
);
[JScript]
public function EnsureVisible(
   index : int
);
```

Parameters

index
: The zero-based index of the item to scroll into view.

Remarks

You can use this method to ensure that a specific item is visible within the **ListView** control. When performing validation on the items in a **ListView**, you can call the **EnsureVisible** method to ensure that an item that failed validation is displayed in the **ListView** control to allow the user to perform changes on the item. If the item that you want to ensure is visible is located above the viewable region of the **ListView** control, calling the **EnsureVisible** method will scroll the contents of the control until it is the first item in the viewable area of the control. If the item is below the viewable region of the **ListView** control, calling the **EnsureVisible** method will scroll the contents of the **ListView** control until the item is the last item in the viewable area of the control.

To determine if an item is located at the top of the display area of a **ListView** control, use the **TopItem** property.

Requirements

Platforms: Windows 98, Windows NT 4.0,
Windows Millennium Edition, Windows 2000,
Windows XP Home Edition, Windows XP Professional,
Windows Server 2003 family,
.NET Compact Framework - Windows CE .NET

ListView.GetItemAt Method

Retrieves the item at the specified location.

```
[Visual Basic]
Public Function GetItemAt( _
   ByVal x As Integer, _
   ByVal y As Integer _
) As ListViewItem
[C#]
public ListViewItem GetItemAt(
   int x,
   int y
);
[C++]
public: ListViewItem* GetItemAt(
   int x,
   int y
);
[JScript]
public function GetItemAt(
   x : int,
   y : int
) : ListViewItem;
```

Parameters

x

The x-coordinate of the location to search for an item (expressed in client coordinates).

y

The y-coordinate of the location to search for an item (expressed in client coordinates).

Return Value

A **ListViewItem** that represents the item at the specified position. If there is no item at the specified location, the method returns a null reference (**Nothing** in Visual Basic).

Remarks

The **GetItemAt** method enables you to determine which item is located at a specific location within the client region of the **ListView** control. You can use this method when the user clicks or right-clicks a subitem (when the **View** property is set to **View.Details**) and you want to determine which item owns the subitem that was clicked based on the mouse coordinates at the time the user clicked the mouse.

Requirements

Platforms: Windows 98, Windows NT 4.0, Windows Millennium Edition, Windows 2000, Windows XP Home Edition, Windows XP Professional, Windows Server 2003 family

ListView.GetItemRect Method

Retrieves the bounding rectangle for an item within the control.

Overload List

Retrieves the bounding rectangle for a specific item within the list view control.

[Visual Basic] **Overloads Public Function GetItemRect(Integer) As Rectangle**

[C#] **public Rectangle GetItemRect(int);**

[C++] **public: Rectangle GetItemRect(int);**

[JScript] **public function GetItemRect(int) : Rectangle;**

Retrieves the specified portion of the bounding rectangle for a specific item within the list view control.

[Visual Basic] **Overloads Public Function GetItemRect(Integer, ItemBoundsPortion) As Rectangle**

[C#] **public Rectangle GetItemRect(int, ItemBoundsPortion);**

[C++] **public: Rectangle GetItemRect(int, ItemBoundsPortion);**

[JScript] **public function GetItemRect(int, ItemBoundsPortion) : Rectangle;**

ListView.GetItemRect Method (Int32)

Retrieves the bounding rectangle for a specific item within the list view control.

```
[Visual Basic]
Overloads Public Function GetItemRect( _
   ByVal index As Integer _
) As Rectangle
[C#]
public Rectangle GetItemRect(
   int index
);
[C++]
public: Rectangle GetItemRect(
   int index
);
[JScript]
public function GetItemRect(
   index : int
) : Rectangle;
```

Parameters

index

The zero-based index of the item within the **ListView.ListViewItemCollection** whose bounding rectangle you want to return.

Return Value

A **Rectangle** that represents the bounding rectangle of the specified **ListViewItem**.

Remarks

The bounding rectangle returned by this version of the **GetItemRect** method represents the entire item, including the icon, item text, and subitem text. To specify a specific portion of the item's bounding rectangle, use the other version of the **GetItemRect** method.

Requirements

Platforms: Windows 98, Windows NT 4.0, Windows Millennium Edition, Windows 2000, Windows XP Home Edition, Windows XP Professional, Windows Server 2003 family

ListView.GetItemRect Method (Int32, ItemBoundsPortion)

Retrieves the specified portion of the bounding rectangle for a specific item within the list view control.

```
[Visual Basic]
Overloads Public Function GetItemRect( _
   ByVal index As Integer, _
   ByVal portion As ItemBoundsPortion _
) As Rectangle
[C#]
public Rectangle GetItemRect(
   int index,
   ItemBoundsPortion portion
);
[C++]
public: Rectangle GetItemRect(
   int index,
   ItemBoundsPortion portion
);
[JScript]
public function GetItemRect(
   index : int,
   portion : ItemBoundsPortion
) : Rectangle;
```

Parameters

index

The zero-based index of the item within the **ListView.ListViewItemCollection** whose bounding rectangle you want to return.

portion

One of the **ItemBoundsPortion** values that represents a portion of the **ListViewItem** for which to retrieve the bounding rectangle.

Return Value

A **Rectangle** that represents the bounding rectangle for the specified portion of the specified **ListViewItem**.

Remarks

The bounding rectangle returned by this version of the **GetItemRect** method represents only the section of the item specified in the *portion* parameter. To return the bounding rectangle of the entire item, use the other version of the **GetItemRect** method.

Requirements

Platforms: Windows 98, Windows NT 4.0, Windows Millennium Edition, Windows 2000, Windows XP Home Edition, Windows XP Professional, Windows Server 2003 family

ListView.IsInputKey Method

This member overrides **Control.IsInputKey**.

```
[Visual Basic]
Overrides Protected Function IsInputKey( _
   ByVal keyData As Keys _
) As Boolean
[C#]
protected override bool IsInputKey(
   Keys keyData
);
[C++]
protected: bool IsInputKey(
   Keys keyData
);
[JScript]
protected override function IsInputKey(
   keyData : Keys
) : Boolean;
```

Requirements

Platforms: Windows 98, Windows NT 4.0, Windows Millennium Edition, Windows 2000, Windows XP Home Edition, Windows XP Professional, Windows Server 2003 family

ListView.OnAfterLabelEdit Method

Raises the **AfterLabelEdit** event.

```
[Visual Basic]
Protected Overridable Sub OnAfterLabelEdit( _
   ByVal e As LabelEditEventArgs _
)
[C#]
protected virtual void OnAfterLabelEdit(
   LabelEditEventArgs e
);
[C++]
protected: virtual void OnAfterLabelEdit(
   LabelEditEventArgs* e
);
[JScript]
protected function OnAfterLabelEdit(
   e : LabelEditEventArgs
);
```

Parameters

e

A **LabelEditEventArgs** that contains the event data.

Remarks

Raising an event invokes the event handler through a delegate.

The **OnAfterLabelEdit** method also allows derived classes to handle the event without attaching a delegate. This is the preferred technique for handling the event in a derived class.

Notes to Inheritors: When overriding **OnAfterLabelEdit** in a derived class, be sure to call the base class's **OnAfterLabelEdit** method so that registered delegates receive the event.

Example

See related example in the **System.Windows.Forms.ListView** class topic.

Requirements

Platforms: Windows 98, Windows NT 4.0, Windows Millennium Edition, Windows 2000, Windows XP Home Edition, Windows XP Professional, Windows Server 2003 family

ListView.OnBeforeLabelEdit Method

Raises the **BeforeLabelEdit** event.

```
[Visual Basic]
Protected Overridable Sub OnBeforeLabelEdit( _
   ByVal e As LabelEditEventArgs _
)
[C#]
protected virtual void OnBeforeLabelEdit(
   LabelEditEventArgs e
);
[C++]
protected: virtual void OnBeforeLabelEdit(
   LabelEditEventArgs* e
);
[JScript]
protected function OnBeforeLabelEdit(
   e : LabelEditEventArgs
);
```

Parameters

e

A **LabelEditEventArgs** that contains the event data.

Remarks

Raising an event invokes the event handler through a delegate.

The **OnBeforeLabelEdit** method also allows derived classes to handle the event without attaching a delegate. This is the preferred technique for handling the event in a derived class.

Notes to Inheritors: When overriding **OnBeforeLabelEdit** in a derived class, be sure to call the base class's **OnBeforeLabelEdit** method so that registered delegates receive the event.

Requirements

Platforms: Windows 98, Windows NT 4.0, Windows Millennium Edition, Windows 2000, Windows XP Home Edition, Windows XP Professional, Windows Server 2003 family

ListView.OnColumnClick Method

Raises the **ColumnClick** event.

```
[Visual Basic]
Protected Overridable Sub OnColumnClick( _
   ByVal e As ColumnClickEventArgs _
)
[C#]
protected virtual void OnColumnClick(
   ColumnClickEventArgs e
);
[C++]
protected: virtual void OnColumnClick(
   ColumnClickEventArgs* e
);
[JScript]
protected function OnColumnClick(
   e : ColumnClickEventArgs
);
```

Parameters

e

A **ColumnClickEventArgs** that contains the event data.

Remarks

Raising an event invokes the event handler through a delegate.

The **OnColumnClick** method also allows derived classes to handle the event without attaching a delegate. This is the preferred technique for handling the event in a derived class.

Notes to Inheritors: When overriding **OnColumnClick** in a derived class, be sure to call the base class's **OnColumnClick** method so that registered delegates receive the event.

Example

See related example in the **System.Windows.Forms.ListView** class topic.

Requirements

Platforms: Windows 98, Windows NT 4.0, Windows Millennium Edition, Windows 2000, Windows XP Home Edition, Windows XP Professional, Windows Server 2003 family, .NET Compact Framework - Windows CE .NET

ListView.OnEnabledChanged Method

This member overrides **Control.OnEnabledChanged**.

```
[Visual Basic]
Overrides Protected Sub OnEnabledChanged( _
   ByVal e As EventArgs _
)
[C#]
protected override void OnEnabledChanged(
   EventArgs e
);
[C++]
protected: void OnEnabledChanged(
   EventArgs* e
);
[JScript]
protected override function OnEnabledChanged(
   e : EventArgs
);
```

Requirements

Platforms: Windows 98, Windows NT 4.0, Windows Millennium Edition, Windows 2000, Windows XP Home Edition, Windows XP Professional, Windows Server 2003 family, .NET Compact Framework - Windows CE .NET

ListView.OnFontChanged Method

This member overrides **Control.OnFontChanged**.

```
[Visual Basic]
Overrides Protected Sub OnFontChanged( _
   ByVal e As EventArgs _
)
[C#]
protected override void OnFontChanged(
   EventArgs e
);
[C++]
protected: void OnFontChanged(
   EventArgs* e
);
[JScript]
protected override function OnFontChanged(
   e : EventArgs
);
```

Requirements

Platforms: Windows 98, Windows NT 4.0, Windows Millennium Edition, Windows 2000, Windows XP Home Edition, Windows XP Professional, Windows Server 2003 family

ListView.OnHandleCreated Method

This member overrides **Control.OnHandleCreated**.

```
[Visual Basic]
Overrides Protected Sub OnHandleCreated( _
   ByVal e As EventArgs _
)
[C#]
protected override void OnHandleCreated(
   EventArgs e
);
[C++]
protected: void OnHandleCreated(
   EventArgs* e
);
```

```
[JScript]
protected override function OnHandleCreated(
   e : EventArgs
);
```

Requirements

Platforms: Windows 98, Windows NT 4.0, Windows Millennium Edition, Windows 2000, Windows XP Home Edition, Windows XP Professional, Windows Server 2003 family

ListView.OnHandleDestroyed Method

This member overrides **Control.OnHandleDestroyed**.

```
[Visual Basic]
Overrides Protected Sub OnHandleDestroyed( _
   ByVal e As EventArgs _
)
[C#]
protected override void OnHandleDestroyed(
   EventArgs e
);
[C++]
protected: void OnHandleDestroyed(
   EventArgs* e
);
[JScript]
protected override function OnHandleDestroyed(
   e : EventArgs
);
```

Requirements

Platforms: Windows 98, Windows NT 4.0, Windows Millennium Edition, Windows 2000, Windows XP Home Edition, Windows XP Professional, Windows Server 2003 family

ListView.OnItemActivate Method

Raises the **ItemActivate** event.

```
[Visual Basic]
Protected Overridable Sub OnItemActivate( _
   ByVal e As EventArgs _
)
[C#]
protected virtual void OnItemActivate(
   EventArgs e
);
[C++]
protected: virtual void OnItemActivate(
   EventArgs* e
);
[JScript]
protected function OnItemActivate(
   e : EventArgs
);
```

Parameters

e

An **EventArgs** that contains the event data.

Remarks

Raising an event invokes the event handler through a delegate.

The **OnItemActivate** method also allows derived classes to handle the event without attaching a delegate. This is the preferred technique for handling the event in a derived class.

Notes to Inheritors: When overriding **OnItemActivate** in a derived class, be sure to call the base class's **OnItemActivate** method so that registered delegates receive the event.

Requirements

Platforms: Windows 98, Windows NT 4.0, Windows Millennium Edition, Windows 2000, Windows XP Home Edition, Windows XP Professional, Windows Server 2003 family, .NET Compact Framework - Windows CE .NET

ListView.OnItemCheck Method

Raises the **ItemCheck** event.

```
[Visual Basic]
Protected Overridable Sub OnItemCheck( _
   ByVal ice As ItemCheckEventArgs _
)
[C#]
protected virtual void OnItemCheck(
   ItemCheckEventArgs ice
);
[C++]
protected: virtual void OnItemCheck(
   ItemCheckEventArgs* ice
);
[JScript]
protected function OnItemCheck(
   ice : ItemCheckEventArgs
);
```

Parameters

ice

An **ItemCheckEventArgs** that contains the event data.

Remarks

Raising an event invokes the event handler through a delegate.

The **OnItemCheck** method also allows derived classes to handle the event without attaching a delegate. This is the preferred technique for handling the event in a derived class.

Notes to Inheritors: When overriding **OnItemCheck** in a derived class, be sure to call the base class's **OnItemCheck** method so that registered delegates receive the event.

Requirements

Platforms: Windows 98, Windows NT 4.0, Windows Millennium Edition, Windows 2000, Windows XP Home Edition, Windows XP Professional, Windows Server 2003 family, .NET Compact Framework - Windows CE .NET

ListView.OnItemDrag Method

Raises the **ItemDrag** event.

```
[Visual Basic]
Protected Overridable Sub OnItemDrag( _
   ByVal e As ItemDragEventArgs _
)
```

[C#]
```
protected virtual void OnItemDrag(
   ItemDragEventArgs e
);
```
[C++]
```
protected: virtual void OnItemDrag(
   ItemDragEventArgs* e
);
```
[JScript]
```
protected function OnItemDrag(
   e : ItemDragEventArgs
);
```

Parameters

e

An **ItemDragEventArgs** that contains the event data.

Remarks

Raising an event invokes the event handler through a delegate.

The **OnItemDrag** method also allows derived classes to handle the event without attaching a delegate. This is the preferred technique for handling the event in a derived class.

Notes to Inheritors: When overriding **OnItemDrag** in a derived class, be sure to call the base class's **OnItemDrag** method so that registered delegates receive the event.

Requirements

Platforms: Windows 98, Windows NT 4.0, Windows Millennium Edition, Windows 2000, Windows XP Home Edition, Windows XP Professional, Windows Server 2003 family

ListView.OnSelectedIndexChanged Method

Raises the **SelectedIndexChanged** event.

[Visual Basic]
```
Protected Overridable Sub OnSelectedIndexChanged( _
   ByVal e As EventArgs _
)
```
[C#]
```
protected virtual void OnSelectedIndexChanged(
   EventArgs e
);
```
[C++]
```
protected: virtual void OnSelectedIndexChanged(
   EventArgs* e
);
```
[JScript]
```
protected function OnSelectedIndexChanged(
   e : EventArgs
);
```

Parameters

e

An **EventArgs** that contains the event data.

Remarks

Raising an event invokes the event handler through a delegate.

The **OnSelectedIndexChanged** method also allows derived classes to handle the event without attaching a delegate. This is the preferred technique for handling the event in a derived class.

Notes to Inheritors: When overriding **OnSelectedIndexChanged** in a derived class, be sure to call the base class's **OnSelected-IndexChanged** method so that registered delegates receive the event.

Requirements

Platforms: Windows 98, Windows NT 4.0, Windows Millennium Edition, Windows 2000, Windows XP Home Edition, Windows XP Professional, Windows Server 2003 family, .NET Compact Framework - Windows CE .NET

ListView.OnSystemColorsChanged Method

This member overrides **Control.OnSystemColorsChanged**.

[Visual Basic]
```
Overrides Protected Sub OnSystemColorsChanged( _
   ByVal e As EventArgs _
)
```
[C#]
```
protected override void OnSystemColorsChanged(
   EventArgs e
);
```
[C++]
```
protected: void OnSystemColorsChanged(
   EventArgs* e
);
```
[JScript]
```
protected override function OnSystemColorsChanged(
   e : EventArgs
);
```

Requirements

Platforms: Windows 98, Windows NT 4.0, Windows Millennium Edition, Windows 2000, Windows XP Home Edition, Windows XP Professional, Windows Server 2003 family

ListView.RealizeProperties Method

This member supports the .NET Framework infrastructure and is not intended to be used directly from your code.

[Visual Basic]
```
Protected Sub RealizeProperties()
```
[C#]
```
protected void RealizeProperties();
```
[C++]
```
protected: void RealizeProperties();
```
[JScript]
```
protected function RealizeProperties();
```

ListView.Sort Method

Sorts the items of the list view.

[Visual Basic]
```
Public Sub Sort()
```
[C#]
```
public void Sort();
```
[C++]
```
public: void Sort();
```
[JScript]
```
public function Sort();
```

Remarks

Typically items are sorted using the **Sorting** property, which sorts items based on the item text. If you want to sort the items in the **ListView** based on subitem text, you would use the **Sort** method. The **Sort** method uses the **IComparer** specified in the **ListViewItemSorter** property to perform a manual sort of the items in the **ListView**. See the example for more information on performing manual sorting of items.

Example

See related example in the **System.Windows.Forms.ListView** class topic.

Requirements

Platforms: Windows 98, Windows NT 4.0, Windows Millennium Edition, Windows 2000, Windows XP Home Edition, Windows XP Professional, Windows Server 2003 family

ListView.ToString Method

This member overrides **Object.ToString**.

[Visual Basic]
```
Overrides Public Function ToString() As String
```
[C#]
```
public override string ToString();
```
[C++]
```
public: String* ToString();
```
[JScript]
```
public override function ToString() : String;
```

Requirements

Platforms: Windows 98, Windows NT 4.0, Windows Millennium Edition, Windows 2000, Windows XP Home Edition, Windows XP Professional, Windows Server 2003 family, .NET Compact Framework - Windows CE .NET

ListView.UpdateExtendedStyles Method

Updates the extended styles applied to the list view control.

[Visual Basic]
```
Protected Sub UpdateExtendedStyles()
```
[C#]
```
protected void UpdateExtendedStyles();
```
[C++]
```
protected: void UpdateExtendedStyles();
```
[JScript]
```
protected function UpdateExtendedStyles();
```

Remarks

You can use the **UpdateExtendedStyles** method in your derived class to override the extended styles used by the **ListView** control. If you override this method, you should ensure that the extended styles that are set by the properties on the **ListView** control are utilized in your derived version of the control.

The following are the properties that apply an extended style to the **ListView** control.

- **Activation**
- **AllowColumnReorder**
- **CheckBoxes**
- **FullRowSelect**
- **GridLines**
- **HoverSelection**

Requirements

Platforms: Windows 98, Windows NT 4.0, Windows Millennium Edition, Windows 2000, Windows XP Home Edition, Windows XP Professional, Windows Server 2003 family

ListView.WndProc Method

This member overrides **Control.WndProc**.

[Visual Basic]
```
Overrides Protected Sub WndProc( _
   ByRef m As Message _
)
```
[C#]
```
protected override void WndProc(
   ref Message m
);
```
[C++]
```
protected: void WndProc(
   Message* m
);
```
[JScript]
```
protected override function WndProc(
   m : Message
);
```

Requirements

Platforms: Windows 98, Windows NT 4.0, Windows Millennium Edition, Windows 2000, Windows XP Home Edition, Windows XP Professional, Windows Server 2003 family

ListView.AfterLabelEdit Event

Occurs when the label for an item is edited by the user.

[Visual Basic]
```
Public Event AfterLabelEdit As LabelEditEventHandler
```
[C#]
```
public event LabelEditEventHandler AfterLabelEdit;
```
[C++]
```
public: __event LabelEditEventHandler* AfterLabelEdit;
```

[JScript] In JScript, you can handle the events defined by a class, but you cannot define your own.

Event Data

The event handler receives an argument of type **LabelEditEventArgs** containing data related to this event. The following **LabelEditEventArgs** properties provide information specific to this event.

Property	Description
CancelEdit	Gets or sets a value indicating whether changes made to the label of the **ListViewItem** should be canceled.
Item	Gets the zero-based index of the **ListViewItem** containing the label to edit.
Label	Gets the new text assigned to the label of the **ListViewItem**.

Remarks

The **AfterLabelEdit** event occurs when the user finishes modifying the text for an item. The new string that the user types for the item is passed to the event, and the event handler can reject the change. If the event handler rejects the change, the text reverts to the text as it was before the user began editing the item. In order for the **AfterLabelEdit** event to be raised, the **LabelEdit** property of the **ListView** control must be set to **true**. You can create an event handler for the **BeforeLabelEdit** event to perform tasks before the user edits the text of an item.

Example

See related example in the **System.Windows.Forms.ListView** class topic.

Requirements

Platforms: Windows 98, Windows NT 4.0,
Windows Millennium Edition, Windows 2000,
Windows XP Home Edition, Windows XP Professional,
Windows Server 2003 family

ListView.BackgroundImageChanged Event

This member supports the .NET Framework infrastructure and is not intended to be used directly from your code.

[Visual Basic]
```
Public Shadows Event BackgroundImageChanged As EventHandler
```
[C#]
```
public new event EventHandler BackgroundImageChanged;
```
[C++]
```
public: __event EventHandler* BackgroundImageChanged;
```

[JScript] In JScript, you can handle the events defined by a class, but you cannot define your own.

ListView.BeforeLabelEdit Event

Occurs when the user starts editing the label of an item.

[Visual Basic]
```
Public Event BeforeLabelEdit As LabelEditEventHandler
```
[C#]
```
public event LabelEditEventHandler BeforeLabelEdit;
```
[C++]
```
public: __event LabelEditEventHandler* BeforeLabelEdit;
```

[JScript] In JScript, you can handle the events defined by a class, but you cannot define your own.

Event Data

The event handler receives an argument of type **LabelEditEventArgs** containing data related to this event. The following **LabelEditEventArgs** properties provide information specific to this event.

Property	Description
CancelEdit	Gets or sets a value indicating whether changes made to the label of the **ListViewItem** should be canceled.
Item	Gets the zero-based index of the **ListViewItem** containing the label to edit.
Label	Gets the new text assigned to the label of the **ListViewItem**.

Remarks

The **BeforeLabelEdit** event occurs when the user begins modifying the text for an item. If the event handler cancels this event, the user cannot edit the text. You can use this event to prevent the user from editing specific items in the **ListView** control. If the **LabelEdit** property of the **ListView** control is set to **false**, the **BeforeLabelEdit** event is not raised; all user attempts to edit item labels are automatically rejected.

Requirements

Platforms: Windows 98, Windows NT 4.0,
Windows Millennium Edition, Windows 2000,
Windows XP Home Edition, Windows XP Professional,
Windows Server 2003 family

ListView.ColumnClick Event

Occurs when the user clicks a column header within the list view control.

[Visual Basic]
```
Public Event ColumnClick As ColumnClickEventHandler
```
[C#]
```
public event ColumnClickEventHandler ColumnClick;
```
[C++]
```
public: __event ColumnClickEventHandler* ColumnClick;
```

[JScript] In JScript, you can handle the events defined by a class, but you cannot define your own.

Event Data

The event handler receives an argument of type **ColumnClickEventArgs** containing data related to this event. The following **ColumnClickEventArgs** property provides information specific to this event.

Property	Description
Column	Gets the zero-based index of the column that is clicked.

Remarks

The **ColumnClick** event occurs when the user clicks one of the column headers in a details view of the items in a **ListView** control (when the **View** property is set to **View.Details**). The **ColumnClick** event it typically handled to sort the items in the **ListView** using the clicked column as the column to sort by.

Example

See related example in the **System.Windows.Forms.ListView** class topic.

Requirements

Platforms: Windows 98, Windows NT 4.0,
Windows Millennium Edition, Windows 2000,
Windows XP Home Edition, Windows XP Professional,
Windows Server 2003 family

ListView.ItemActivate Event

Occurs when an item is activated.

[Visual Basic]
```
Public Event ItemActivate As EventHandler
```
[C#]
```
public event EventHandler ItemActivate;
```
[C++]
```
public: __event EventHandler* ItemActivate;
```

[JScript] In JScript, you can handle the events defined by a class, but you cannot define your own.

Event Data

The event handler receives an argument of type **EventArgs**.

Remarks

The **ItemActivate** event occurs when the user activates one or more items in the **ListView** control. The user can activate an item with either a single-click or double-click, depending on the value of the **Activation** property, or with the keyboard. From within the event handler for the **ItemActivate** event, you can reference the **SelectedItems** or **SelectedIndices** properties to access the collection of items selected in the **ListView** to determine which items are being activated.

Requirements

Platforms: Windows 98, Windows NT 4.0, Windows Millennium Edition, Windows 2000, Windows XP Home Edition, Windows XP Professional, Windows Server 2003 family

ListView.ItemCheck Event

Occurs when the check state of an item changes.

[Visual Basic]
```
Public Event ItemCheck As ItemCheckEventHandler
```
[C#]
```
public event ItemCheckEventHandler ItemCheck;
```
[C++]
```
public: __event ItemCheckEventHandler* ItemCheck;
```

[JScript] In JScript, you can handle the events defined by a class, but you cannot define your own.

Event Data

The event handler receives an argument of type **ItemCheckEventArgs** containing data related to this event. The following **ItemCheckEventArgs** properties provide information specific to this event.

Property	Description
CurrentValue	Gets a value indicating the current state of the item's check box.
Index	Gets the zero-based index of the item to change.
NewValue	Gets or sets a value indicating whether to set the check box for the item to be checked, unchecked, or indeterminate.

Remarks

The **ItemCheck** event occurs when the check state of an item changes. The **CheckBoxes** property must be set to true in order for check boxes to be displayed next to each item in the **ListView** control. You can create an event handler for the **ItemCheck** event to perform tasks such as changing the state of an item's icon or another application-specific task each time an item is checked in the **ListView** control.

> **Note** If the **Visible** property of the **ListView** control is set to **false** at the time the control is created, the **ItemCheck** event is not raised. Once the control is visible, the event is raised regardless of the state of the **Visible** property.

Requirements

Platforms: Windows 98, Windows NT 4.0, Windows Millennium Edition, Windows 2000, Windows XP Home Edition, Windows XP Professional, Windows Server 2003 family

ListView.ItemDrag Event

Occurs when the user begins dragging an item.

[Visual Basic]
```
Public Event ItemDrag As ItemDragEventHandler
```
[C#]
```
public event ItemDragEventHandler ItemDrag;
```
[C++]
```
public: __event ItemDragEventHandler* ItemDrag;
```

[JScript] In JScript, you can handle the events defined by a class, but you cannot define your own.

Event Data

The event handler receives an argument of type **ItemDragEventArgs** containing data related to this event. The following **ItemDragEventArgs** properties provide information specific to this event.

Property	Description
Button	Gets the name of the mouse button that was clicked during the drag operation.
Item	Gets the item that is being dragged.

Remarks

The **ItemDrag** event occurs when the user begins dragging an item. Typically the event handler for the **ItemDrag** event performs the task of dragging by calling the **Control.DoDragDrop** method. You can use this event to perform the tasks necessary to drag items into and out of your application's **ListView** control.

Requirements

Platforms: Windows 98, Windows NT 4.0, Windows Millennium Edition, Windows 2000, Windows XP Home Edition, Windows XP Professional, Windows Server 2003 family

ListView.Paint Event

This member supports the .NET Framework infrastructure and is not intended to be used directly from your code.

[Visual Basic]
```
Public Shadows Event Paint As PaintEventHandler
```
[C#]
```
public new event PaintEventHandler Paint;
```
[C++]
```
public: __event PaintEventHandler* Paint;
```

[JScript] In JScript, you can handle the events defined by a class, but you cannot define your own.

ListView.SelectedIndexChanged Event

Occurs when the index of the selected item in the list view control changes.

[Visual Basic]
```
Public Event SelectedIndexChanged As EventHandler
```
[C#]
```
public event EventHandler SelectedIndexChanged;
```
[C++]
```
public: __event EventHandler* SelectedIndexChanged;
```

[JScript] In JScript, you can handle the events defined by a class, but you cannot define your own.

Event Data

The event handler receives an argument of type **EventArgs**.

Remarks

The **SelectedIndexChanged** event occurs in single selection **ListView** controls, whenever there is a change to the index position of the selected item. In a multiple selection **ListView** control, this event occurs whenever an item is removed or added to the list of selected items. To determine which items are selected in the **ListView** control, use the **SelectedItems** property to access the **ListView.SelectedListViewItemCollection**. You can create an event handler for this event to perform tasks whenever there is a change to the selected items in the **ListView** control.

Requirements

Platforms: Windows 98, Windows NT 4.0, Windows Millennium Edition, Windows 2000, Windows XP Home Edition, Windows XP Professional, Windows Server 2003 family

ListView.TextChanged Event

This member supports the .NET Framework infrastructure and is not intended to be used directly from your code.

[Visual Basic]
```
Public Shadows Event TextChanged As EventHandler
```
[C#]
```
public new event EventHandler TextChanged;
```
[C++]
```
public: __event EventHandler* TextChanged;
```

[JScript] In JScript, you can handle the events defined by a class, but you cannot define your own.

ListViewAlignment Enumeration

Specifies how items align in the **ListView**.

[Visual Basic]

```
<Serializable>
Public Enum ListViewAlignment
```

[C#]

```
[Serializable]
public enum ListViewAlignment
```

[C++]

```
[Serializable]
__value public enum ListViewAlignment
```

[JScript]

```
public
   Serializable
enum ListViewAlignment
```

Remarks

Use the members of this enumeration to set the value of the **Alignment** property and the **ArrangeIcons** method of the **ListView** control.

Members

Member name	Description
Default	When the user moves an item, it remains where it is dropped.
Left	Items are aligned to the left of the **ListView** control.
SnapToGrid	Items are aligned to an invisible grid in the control. When the user moves an item, it moves to the closest juncture in the grid.
Top	Items are aligned to the top of the **ListView** control.

Requirements

Namespace: System.Windows.Forms

Platforms: Windows 98, Windows NT 4.0, Windows Millennium Edition, Windows 2000, Windows XP Home Edition, Windows XP Professional, Windows Server 2003 family

Assembly: System.Windows.Forms (in System.Windows.Forms.dll)

ListView.CheckedIndex-Collection Class

Represents the collection containing the indexes to the checked items in a list view control.

System.Object
 System.Windows.Forms.ListView.CheckedIndexCollection

```
[Visual Basic]
Public Class ListView.CheckedIndexCollection
   Implements IList, ICollection, IEnumerable
[C#]
public class ListView.CheckedIndexCollection : IList, ICollection,
   IEnumerable
[C++]
public __gc class ListView.CheckedIndexCollection : public IList,
   ICollection, IEnumerable
[JScript]
public class ListView.CheckedIndexCollection implements IList,
   ICollection, IEnumerable
```

Thread Safety

Any public static (**Shared** in Visual Basic) members of this type are safe for multithreaded operations. Any instance members are not guaranteed to be thread safe.

Remarks

A **ListView.CheckedIndexCollection** stores the indexes to the checked items in a **ListView** control. Items can only be checked if the **CheckBoxes** property of the **ListView** control is set to **true**. The indexes stored in the **ListView.CheckedIndexCollection** are index positions within the **ListView.ListViewItemCollection**. The **ListView.ListViewItemCollection** stores all items displayed in the **ListView** control.

The following table is an example of how the **ListView.ListViewItemCollection** stores the items of the **ListView** as well as their checked states in an example **ListView** control.

Index	Item	Checked state in the ListView
0	Item1	Unchecked
1	Item2	Checked
2	Item3	Unchecked
3	Item4	Checked
4	Item5	Checked

Based on the **ListView.ListViewItemCollection** example in the previous table, the following table demonstrates how the **ListView.CheckedIndexCollection** would appear.

Index	Index of checked item in ListViewItemCollection
0	1
1	3
2	4

You can use the properties and methods of this class to perform a variety of tasks with the collection. The **Contains** method enables you to determine whether an index position from the **ListView.ListViewItemCollection** is one of the indexes stored in the **ListView.CheckedIndexCollection**. Once you know that the item is in the collection, you can use the **IndexOf** method to determine the position of the index in the **ListView.CheckedIndexCollection**.

Requirements

Namespace: System.Windows.Forms

Platforms: Windows 98, Windows NT 4.0, Windows Millennium Edition, Windows 2000, Windows XP Home Edition, Windows XP Professional, Windows Server 2003 family

Assembly: System.Windows.Forms (in System.Windows.Forms.dll)

ListView.CheckedIndexCollection Constructor

Initializes a new instance of the **ListView.CheckedIndexCollection** class.

```
[Visual Basic]
Public Sub New( _
   ByVal owner As ListView _
)
[C#]
public ListView.CheckedIndexCollection(
   ListView owner
);
[C++]
public: CheckedIndexCollection(
   ListView* owner
);
[JScript]
public function ListView.CheckedIndexCollection(
   owner : ListView
);
```

Parameters

owner
  A **ListView** control that owns the collection.

Remarks

You cannot create an instance of this class without associating it with a **ListView** control.

Requirements

Platforms: Windows 98, Windows NT 4.0, Windows Millennium Edition, Windows 2000, Windows XP Home Edition, Windows XP Professional, Windows Server 2003 family

ListView.CheckedIndexCollection.Count Property

Gets the number of items in the collection.

```
[Visual Basic]
Public Overridable ReadOnly Property Count As Integer  Implements _
   ICollection.Count
[C#]
public virtual int Count {get;}
[C++]
public: __property virtual int get_Count();
[JScript]
public function get Count() : int;
```

Property Value

The number of items in the collection.

Implements

ICollection.Count

Remarks

This property enables you to determine the number of checked items in the **ListView**. You can then use this value when looping through the values of the collection and you need to provide a number of iterations to perform the loop.

Requirements

Platforms: Windows 98, Windows NT 4.0, Windows Millennium Edition, Windows 2000, Windows XP Home Edition, Windows XP Professional, Windows Server 2003 family

ListView.CheckedIndexCollection.IsReadOnly Property

Gets a value indicating whether the collection is read-only.

```
[Visual Basic]
Public Overridable ReadOnly Property IsReadOnly As Boolean _
   Implements IList.IsReadOnly
[C#]
public virtual bool IsReadOnly {get;}
[C++]
public: __property virtual bool get_IsReadOnly();
[JScript]
public function get IsReadOnly() : Boolean;
```

Property Value

true if the collection is read-only; otherwise, **false**.

Implements

IList.IsReadOnly

Remarks

This property is always **true** for this collection. The items in the collection can only be modified by the **ListView** control.

Requirements

Platforms: Windows 98, Windows NT 4.0, Windows Millennium Edition, Windows 2000, Windows XP Home Edition, Windows XP Professional, Windows Server 2003 family

ListView.CheckedIndexCollection.Item Property

Gets the index value at the specified index within the collection.

[C#] In C#, this property is the indexer for the **ListView.CheckedIndexCollection** class.

```
[Visual Basic]
Public Default ReadOnly Property Item( _
   ByVal index As Integer _
) As Integer
[C#]
public int this[
   int index
] {get;}
[C++]
public: __property int get_Item(
   int index
);
[JScript]
returnValue = CheckedIndexCollectionObject.Item(index);
-or-
returnValue = CheckedIndexCollectionObject(index);
```

[JScript] In JScript, you can use the default indexed properties defined by a type, but you cannot explicitly define your own. However, specifying the **expando** attribute on a class automatically provides a default indexed property whose type is **Object** and whose index type is **String**.

Arguments [JScript]

index
The index of the item in the collection to retrieve.

Parameters [Visual Basic, C#, C++]

index
The index of the item in the collection to retrieve.

Property Value

The index value from the **ListView.ListViewItemCollection** that is stored at the specified location.

Exceptions

Exception Type	Condition
ArgumentOutOfRange-Exception	The *index* parameter is less than zero or greater than or equal to the value of the **Count** property of **ListView.CheckedIndexCollection**.

Remarks

This indexer enables you to get a specific index from the **ListView.CheckedIndexCollection**. The index stored in the collection is an index into the **ListView.ListViewItemCollection** of the **ListView** that represents a checked item in the **ListView**.

Requirements

Platforms: Windows 98, Windows NT 4.0, Windows Millennium Edition, Windows 2000, Windows XP Home Edition, Windows XP Professional, Windows Server 2003 family

ListView.CheckedIndexCollection.Contains Method

Determines whether the specified index is located in the collection.

```
[Visual Basic]
Public Function Contains( _
   ByVal checkedIndex As Integer _
) As Boolean
[C#]
public bool Contains(
   int checkedIndex
);
[C++]
public: bool Contains(
   int checkedIndex
);
[JScript]
public function Contains(
   checkedIndex : int
) : Boolean;
```

Parameters

checkedIndex

The index to locate in the collection.

Return Value

true if the specified index from the **ListView.ListViewItemCollection** for the **ListView** is an item in the collection; otherwise, **false**.

Remarks

The **Contains** method enables you to determine whether an index position from the **ListView.ListViewItemCollection** is one of the checked indexes stored in the **ListView.CheckedIndexCollection**. Once you know that an item is in the checked index collection, you can use the **IndexOf** method to determine the position of the index in the **ListView.CheckedIndexCollection**.

Requirements

Platforms: Windows 98, Windows NT 4.0, Windows Millennium Edition, Windows 2000, Windows XP Home Edition, Windows XP Professional, Windows Server 2003 family

ListView.CheckedIndexCollection.GetEnumerator Method

Returns an enumerator that can be used to iterate through the checked index collection.

```
[Visual Basic]
Public Overridable Function GetEnumerator() As IEnumerator _
   Implements IEnumerable.GetEnumerator
[C#]
public virtual IEnumerator GetEnumerator();
[C++]
public: virtual IEnumerator* GetEnumerator();
[JScript]
public function GetEnumerator() : IEnumerator;
```

Return Value

An **IEnumerator** that represents the checked index collection.

Implements

IEnumerable.GetEnumerator

Requirements

Platforms: Windows 98, Windows NT 4.0, Windows Millennium Edition, Windows 2000, Windows XP Home Edition, Windows XP Professional, Windows Server 2003 family

ListView.CheckedIndexCollection.ICollection.CopyTo Method

This member supports the .NET Framework infrastructure and is not intended to be used directly from your code.

```
[Visual Basic]
Private Sub CopyTo( _
   ByVal dest As Array, _
   ByVal index As Integer _
) Implements ICollection.CopyTo
[C#]
void ICollection.CopyTo(
   Array dest,
   int index
);
[C++]
private: void ICollection::CopyTo(
   Array* dest,
   int index
);
[JScript]
private function ICollection.CopyTo(
   dest : Array,
   index : int
);
```

ListView.CheckedIndexCollection.IList.Add Method

This member supports the .NET Framework infrastructure and is not intended to be used directly from your code.

```
[Visual Basic]
Private Function Add( _
   ByVal value As Object _
) As Integer Implements IList.Add
[C#]
int IList.Add(
   object value
);
[C++]
private: int IList::Add(
   Object* value
);
[JScript]
private function IList.Add(
   value : Object
) : int;
```

ListView.CheckedIndexCollection.IList.Clear Method

This member supports the .NET Framework infrastructure and is not intended to be used directly from your code.

```
[Visual Basic]
Private Sub Clear() Implements IList.Clear
[C#]
void IList.Clear();
[C++]
private: void IList::Clear();
[JScript]
private function IList.Clear();
```

ListView.CheckedIndexCollection.IList.Contains Method

This member supports the .NET Framework infrastructure and is not intended to be used directly from your code.

```
[Visual Basic]
Private Function Contains( _
   ByVal checkedIndex As Object _
) As Boolean Implements IList.Contains
[C#]
bool IList.Contains(
   object checkedIndex
);
```

```
[C++]
private: bool IList::Contains(
   Object* checkedIndex
);
[JScript]
private function IList.Contains(
   checkedIndex : Object
) : Boolean;
```

ListView.CheckedIndexCollection.IList.IndexOf Method

This member supports the .NET Framework infrastructure and is not intended to be used directly from your code.

```
[Visual Basic]
Private Function IndexOf( _
   ByVal checkedIndex As Object _
) As Integer Implements IList.IndexOf
[C#]
int IList.IndexOf(
   object checkedIndex
);
[C++]
private: int IList::IndexOf(
   Object* checkedIndex
);
[JScript]
private function IList.IndexOf(
   checkedIndex : Object
) : int;
```

ListView.CheckedIndexCollection.IList.Insert Method

This member supports the .NET Framework infrastructure and is not intended to be used directly from your code.

```
[Visual Basic]
Private Sub Insert( _
   ByVal index As Integer, _
   ByVal value As Object _
) Implements IList.Insert
[C#]
void IList.Insert(
   int index,
   object value
);
[C++]
private: void IList::Insert(
   int index,
   Object* value
);
[JScript]
private function IList.Insert(
   index : int,
   value : Object
);
```

ListView.CheckedIndexCollection.IList.Remove Method

This member supports the .NET Framework infrastructure and is not intended to be used directly from your code.

```
[Visual Basic]
Private Sub Remove( _
   ByVal value As Object _
) Implements IList.Remove
[C#]
void IList.Remove(
   object value
);
[C++]
private: void IList::Remove(
   Object* value
);
[JScript]
private function IList.Remove(
   value : Object
);
```

ListView.CheckedIndexCollection.IList.RemoveAt Method

This member supports the .NET Framework infrastructure and is not intended to be used directly from your code.

```
[Visual Basic]
Private Sub RemoveAt( _
   ByVal index As Integer _
) Implements IList.RemoveAt
[C#]
void IList.RemoveAt(
   int index
);
[C++]
private: void IList::RemoveAt(
   int index
);
[JScript]
private function IList.RemoveAt(
   index : int
);
```

ListView.CheckedIndexCollection.IndexOf Method

Returns the index within the **System.Windows.Forms.ListView.CheckedIndexCollection** of the specified index from the **ListView.ListViewItemCollection** of the list view control.

```
[Visual Basic]
Public Function IndexOf( _
   ByVal checkedIndex As Integer _
) As Integer
[C#]
public int IndexOf(
   int checkedIndex
);
```

```
[C++]
public: int IndexOf(
   int checkedIndex
);
[JScript]
public function IndexOf(
   checkedIndex : int
) : int;
```

Parameters

checkedIndex

The zero-based index from the **ListView.ListViewItem-Collection** to locate in the collection.

Return Value

The zero-based index in the collection where the specified index of the **ListView.ListViewItemCollection** is located within the **ListView.CheckedIndexCollection**. If the index is not located in the collection, the return value is negative one (-1).

Remarks

Once you know that an item is in the checked index collection (using the **Contains** method), you can use the **IndexOf** method to determine the position of the index in the **ListView.Checked-IndexCollection**.

Requirements

Platforms: Windows 98, Windows NT 4.0, Windows Millennium Edition, Windows 2000, Windows XP Home Edition, Windows XP Professional, Windows Server 2003 family

ListView.CheckedListView-ItemCollection Class

Represents the collection of checked items in a list view control.

System.Object
  System.Windows.Forms.ListView.CheckedListViewItem-Collection

```
[Visual Basic]
Public Class ListView.CheckedListViewItemCollection
   Implements IList, ICollection, IEnumerable
[C#]
public class ListView.CheckedListViewItemCollection : IList,
   ICollection, IEnumerable
[C++]
public __gc class ListView.CheckedListViewItemCollection : public
   IList, ICollection, IEnumerable
[JScript]
public class ListView.CheckedListViewItemCollection implements
   IList, ICollection, IEnumerable
```

Thread Safety

Any public static (**Shared** in Visual Basic) members of this type are safe for multithreaded operations. Any instance members are not guaranteed to be thread safe.

Remarks

A **ListView.CheckedListViewItemCollection** stores the checked items in a **ListView** control. Items can only be checked if the **CheckBoxes** property of the **ListView** control is set to **true**. The items stored in the **ListView.CheckedListViewItemCollection** are items contained in the **ListView.ListViewItemCollection**. The **ListView.ListViewItemCollection** class stores all items displayed in the **ListView** control.

The following table is an example of how the **ListView.ListView-ItemCollection** stores the items of the **ListView** as well as their selection states in an example **ListView** control.

Index	Item	Checked state in the ListView
0	Iem1	Unchecked
1	Item2	Checked
2	Item3	Unchecked
3	Item4	Checked
4	Item5	Checked

Based on the **ListView.ListViewItemCollection** example in the previous table, the following table demonstrates how the **ListView.CheckedListViewItemCollection** would appear.

Index	Checked Item In ListViewItemCollection
0	Item2
1	Item4
2	Item5

You can use the properties and methods of this class to perform a variety of tasks with the collection. The **Contains** method enables you to determine whether an item from the **ListView.ListViewItem-Collection** class is a member of the **ListView.CheckedListView-ItemCollection**. Once you know that the item is in the collection, you can use the **IndexOf** method to determine the position of the item in the **ListView.CheckedListViewItemCollection**.

Requirements

Namespace: System.Windows.Forms

Platforms: Windows 98, Windows NT 4.0, Windows Millennium Edition, Windows 2000, Windows XP Home Edition, Windows XP Professional, Windows Server 2003 family

Assembly: System.Windows.Forms (in System.Windows.Forms.dll)

ListView.CheckedListViewItemCollection Constructor

Initializes a new instance of the **ListView.CheckedListViewItemCollection** class.

```
[Visual Basic]
Public Sub New( _
   ByVal owner As ListView _
)
[C#]
public ListView.CheckedListViewItemCollection(
   ListView owner
);
[C++]
public: CheckedListViewItemCollection(
   ListView* owner
);
[JScript]
public function ListView.CheckedListViewItemCollection(
   owner : ListView
);
```

Parameters

owner
    The **ListView** control that owns the collection.

Remarks

You cannot create an instance of this class without associating it with a **ListView** control.

Requirements

Platforms: Windows 98, Windows NT 4.0, Windows Millennium Edition, Windows 2000, Windows XP Home Edition, Windows XP Professional, Windows Server 2003 family

ListView.CheckedListViewItemCollection.Count Property

Gets the number of items in the collection.

```
[Visual Basic]
Public Overridable ReadOnly Property Count As Integer  Implements _
   ICollection.Count
[C#]
public virtual int Count {get;}
[C++]
public: __property virtual int get_Count();
[JScript]
public function get Count() : int;
```

Property Value

The number of items in the collection.

Implements

ICollection.Count

Remarks

This property enables you to determine the number of checked items in the **ListView** control. You can then use this value when looping through the values of the collection and you need to provide a number of iterations to perform the loop.

Requirements

Platforms: Windows 98, Windows NT 4.0, Windows Millennium Edition, Windows 2000, Windows XP Home Edition, Windows XP Professional, Windows Server 2003 family

ListView.CheckedListViewItemCollection.IsReadOnly Property

Gets a value indicating whether the collection is read-only.

```
[Visual Basic]
Public Overridable ReadOnly Property IsReadOnly As Boolean _
   Implements IList.IsReadOnly
[C#]
public virtual bool IsReadOnly {get;}
[C++]
public: __property virtual bool get_IsReadOnly();
[JScript]
public function get IsReadOnly() : Boolean;
```

Property Value

true if the collection is read-only; otherwise, **false**.

Implements

IList.IsReadOnly

Remarks

This property is always **true** for this collection. The items in the collection can only be modified by the **ListView** control.

Requirements

Platforms: Windows 98, Windows NT 4.0, Windows Millennium Edition, Windows 2000, Windows XP Home Edition, Windows XP Professional, Windows Server 2003 family

ListView.CheckedListViewItemCollection.Item Property

Gets the item at the specified index within the collection.

[C#] In C#, this property is the indexer for the **ListView.CheckedListViewItemCollection** class.

```
[Visual Basic]
Public Default ReadOnly Property Item( _
   ByVal index As Integer _
) As ListViewItem
[C#]
public ListViewItem this[
   int index
] {get;}
[C++]
public: __property ListViewItem* get_Item(
   int index
);
[JScript]
returnValue = CheckedListViewItemCollectionObject.Item(index);
-or-
returnValue = CheckedListViewItemCollectionObject(index);
```

[JScript] In JScript, you can use the default indexed properties defined by a type, but you cannot explicitly define your own. However, specifying the **expando** attribute on a class automatically provides a default indexed property whose type is **Object** and whose index type is **String**.

Arguments [JScript]

index

The index of the item in the collection to retrieve.

Parameters [Visual Basic, C#, C++]

index

The index of the item in the collection to retrieve.

Property Value

A **ListViewItem** representing the item located at the specified index within the collection.

Exceptions

Exception Type	Condition
ArgumentOutOfRangeException	The *index* parameter is less than zero or greater than or equal to the value of the **Count** property of **ListView.CheckedListViewItemCollection**.

Remarks

This indexer enables you to get a specific item from the **ListView.CheckedListViewItemCollection**. The item stored in this collection is an item in the **ListView.ListViewItemCollection** of the **ListView** that represents a checked item in the **ListView**.

Requirements

Platforms: Windows 98, Windows NT 4.0, Windows Millennium Edition, Windows 2000, Windows XP Home Edition, Windows XP Professional, Windows Server 2003 family

ListView.CheckedListViewItemCollection.Contains Method

Determines whether the specified item is located in the collection.

```
[Visual Basic]
Public Function Contains( _
   ByVal item As ListViewItem _
) As Boolean
[C#]
public bool Contains(
   ListViewItem item
);
[C++]
public: bool Contains(
   ListViewItem* item
);
```

```
[JScript]
public function Contains(
   item : ListViewItem
) : Boolean;
```

Parameters

item

A **ListViewItem** representing the item to locate in the collection.

Return Value

true if the specified item is located in the collection; otherwise, **false**.

Remarks

The **Contains** method enables you to determine whether an item from the **ListView.ListViewItemCollection** is a one of the checked items stored in the **ListView.CheckedListViewItemCollection**. Once you know that an item is in the checked item collection, you can use the **CheckedListViewItemCollection.IndexOf** method to determine the position of the item in the **ListView.CheckedListViewItemCollection**.

Requirements

Platforms: Windows 98, Windows NT 4.0, Windows Millennium Edition, Windows 2000, Windows XP Home Edition, Windows XP Professional, Windows Server 2003 family

ListView.CheckedListViewItemCollection.CopyTo Method

Copies the entire collection into an existing array at a specified location within the array.

```
[Visual Basic]
Public Overridable Sub CopyTo( _
   ByVal dest As Array, _
   ByVal index As Integer _
) Implements ICollection.CopyTo
[C#]
public virtual void CopyTo(
   Array dest,
   int index
);
[C++]
public: virtual void CopyTo(
   Array* dest,
   int index
);
[JScript]
public function CopyTo(
   dest : Array,
   index : int
);
```

Parameters

dest

An **Array** representing the array to copy the contents of the collection to.

index

The location within the destination array to copy the items from the collection to.

Implements

ICollection.CopyTo

Remarks

You can use this method to combine the checked items from multiple collections into a single array.

Requirements

Platforms: Windows 98, Windows NT 4.0, Windows Millennium Edition, Windows 2000, Windows XP Home Edition, Windows XP Professional, Windows Server 2003 family

ListView.CheckedListViewItemCollection.GetEnumerator Method

Returns an enumerator that can be used to iterate through the checked item collection.

```
[Visual Basic]
Public Overridable Function GetEnumerator() As IEnumerator _
   Implements IEnumerable.GetEnumerator
[C#]
public virtual IEnumerator GetEnumerator();
[C++]
public: virtual IEnumerator* GetEnumerator();
[JScript]
public function GetEnumerator() : IEnumerator;
```

Return Value

An **IEnumerator** object that represents the checked item collection.

Implements

IEnumerable.GetEnumerator

Requirements

Platforms: Windows 98, Windows NT 4.0, Windows Millennium Edition, Windows 2000, Windows XP Home Edition, Windows XP Professional, Windows Server 2003 family

ListView.CheckedListViewItemCollection.IList.Add Method

This member supports the .NET Framework infrastructure and is not intended to be used directly from your code.

```
[Visual Basic]
Private Function Add( _
   ByVal value As Object _
) As Integer Implements IList.Add
[C#]
int IList.Add(
   object value
);
[C++]
private: int IList::Add(
   Object* value
);
[JScript]
private function IList.Add(
   value : Object
) : int;
```

ListView.CheckedListViewItemCollection.IList.Clear Method

This member supports the .NET Framework infrastructure and is not intended to be used directly from your code.

[Visual Basic]
```
Private Sub Clear() Implements IList.Clear
```
[C#]
```
void IList.Clear();
```
[C++]
```
private: void IList::Clear();
```
[JScript]
```
private function IList.Clear();
```

ListView.CheckedListViewItemCollection.IList.Contains Method

This member supports the .NET Framework infrastructure and is not intended to be used directly from your code.

[Visual Basic]
```
Private Function Contains( _
   ByVal item As Object _
) As Boolean Implements IList.Contains
```
[C#]
```
bool IList.Contains(
   object item
);
```
[C++]
```
private: bool IList::Contains(
   Object* item
);
```
[JScript]
```
private function IList.Contains(
   item : Object
) : Boolean;
```

ListView.CheckedListViewItemCollection.IList.IndexOf Method

This member supports the .NET Framework infrastructure and is not intended to be used directly from your code.

[Visual Basic]
```
Private Function IndexOf( _
   ByVal item As Object _
) As Integer Implements IList.IndexOf
```
[C#]
```
int IList.IndexOf(
   object item
);
```
[C++]
```
private: int IList::IndexOf(
   Object* item
);
```
[JScript]
```
private function IList.IndexOf(
   item : Object
) : int;
```

ListView.CheckedListViewItemCollection.IList.Insert Method

This member supports the .NET Framework infrastructure and is not intended to be used directly from your code.

[Visual Basic]
```
Private Sub Insert( _
   ByVal index As Integer, _
   ByVal value As Object _
) Implements IList.Insert
```
[C#]
```
void IList.Insert(
   int index,
   object value
);
```
[C++]
```
private: void IList::Insert(
   int index,
   Object* value
);
```
[JScript]
```
private function IList.Insert(
   index : int,
   value : Object
);
```

ListView.CheckedListViewItemCollection.IList.Remove Method

This member supports the .NET Framework infrastructure and is not intended to be used directly from your code.

[Visual Basic]
```
Private Sub Remove( _
   ByVal value As Object _
) Implements IList.Remove
```
[C#]
```
void IList.Remove(
   object value
);
```
[C++]
```
private: void IList::Remove(
   Object* value
);
```
[JScript]
```
private function IList.Remove(
   value : Object
);
```

ListView.CheckedListViewItemCollection.IList.RemoveAt Method

This member supports the .NET Framework infrastructure and is not intended to be used directly from your code.

[Visual Basic]
```
Private Sub RemoveAt( _
   ByVal index As Integer _
) Implements IList.RemoveAt
```
[C#]
```
void IList.RemoveAt(
   int index
);
```
[C++]
```
private: void IList::RemoveAt(
   int index
);
```
[JScript]
```
private function IList.RemoveAt(
   index : int
);
```

ListView.CheckedListViewItemCollection.IndexOf Method

Returns the index within the collection of the specified item.

[Visual Basic]
```
Public Function IndexOf( _
   ByVal item As ListViewItem _
) As Integer
```
[C#]
```
public int IndexOf(
   ListViewItem item
);
```
[C++]
```
public: int IndexOf(
   ListViewItem* item
);
```
[JScript]
```
public function IndexOf(
   item : ListViewItem
) : int;
```

Parameters

item

A **ListViewItem** representing the item to locate in the collection.

Return Value

The zero-based index of the item in the collection; otherwise, -1.

Remarks

Once you know that an item is located within the collection (using the **Contains** method), you can use the **IndexOf** method to determine where a specific item within the **ListView.ListViewItemCollection** for the **ListView** is stored within the **ListView.CheckedListViewItemCollection**.

Requirements

Platforms: Windows 98, Windows NT 4.0, Windows Millennium Edition, Windows 2000, Windows XP Home Edition, Windows XP Professional, Windows Server 2003 family

ListView.ColumnHeader-Collection Class

Represents the collection of column headers in a **ListView** control.

System.Object
  System.Windows.Forms.ListView.ColumnHeaderCollection

[Visual Basic]
```
Public Class ListView.ColumnHeaderCollection
   Implements IList, ICollection, IEnumerable
```
[C#]
```
public class ListView.ColumnHeaderCollection : IList, ICollection,
   IEnumerable
```
[C++]
```
public __gc class ListView.ColumnHeaderCollection : public IList,
   ICollection, IEnumerable
```
[JScript]
```
public class ListView.ColumnHeaderCollection implements IList,
   ICollection, IEnumerable
```

Thread Safety

Any public static (**Shared** in Visual Basic) members of this type are safe for multithreaded operations. Any instance members are not guaranteed to be thread safe.

Remarks

A **ListView.ColumnHeaderCollection** class stores the column headers that are displayed in the **ListView** control when the **View** property is set to **View.Details**. The **ListView.ColumnHeader-Collection** stores **ColumnHeader** objects that define the text to display for a column as well as how the column header is displayed in the **ListView** control when displaying columns. When a **ListView** displays columns, the items and their subitems are displayed in their own columns. To specify which columns subitem data is displayed under, see the **ListViewItem.ListViewSubItemCollection** class.

There are a number of ways to add column headers to the collection. The **Add** method adds a single column header to the collection. To add a number of column headers to the collection, you create an array of **ColumnHeader** objects and pass it to the **AddRange** method. If you want to insert a column header at a specific location in the collection, you can use the **Insert** method. To remove column headers, you can use either the **Remove** method or the **RemoveAt** method if you know where the column header is located in the collection. The **Clear** method allows you to remove all column headers from the collection instead of using the **Remove** method to remove a single column header at a time.

In addition to methods and properties for adding and removing column headers, the **ListView.ColumnHeaderCollection** also provides methods to find column headers in the collection. The **Contains** method enables you to determine whether a column header is a member of the collection. Once you know that the column header is located in the collection, you can use the **IndexOf** method to determine where the column header is located in the collection.

Example

See related example in the **System.Windows.Forms.ListView** class topic.

Requirements

Namespace: System.Windows.Forms

Platforms: Windows 98, Windows NT 4.0, Windows Millennium Edition, Windows 2000, Windows XP Home Edition, Windows XP Professional, Windows Server 2003 family, .NET Compact Framework - Windows CE .NET

Assembly: System.Windows.Forms (in System.Windows.Forms.dll)

ListView.ColumnHeaderCollection Constructor

Initializes a new instance of the **ListView.ColumnHeaderCollection** class.

[Visual Basic]
```
Public Sub New( _
   ByVal owner As ListView _
)
```
[C#]
```
public ListView.ColumnHeaderCollection(
   ListView owner
);
```
[C++]
```
public: ColumnHeaderCollection(
   ListView* owner
);
```
[JScript]
```
public function ListView.ColumnHeaderCollection(
   owner : ListView
);
```

Parameters

owner
  The **ListView** control that owns this collection.

Remarks

You cannot create an instance of this class without associating it with a **ListView** control.

Requirements

Platforms: Windows 98, Windows NT 4.0, Windows Millennium Edition, Windows 2000, Windows XP Home Edition, Windows XP Professional, Windows Server 2003 family

ListView.ColumnHeaderCollection.Count Property

Gets the number of items in the collection.

[Visual Basic]
```
Public Overridable ReadOnly Property Count As Integer  Implements _
   ICollection.Count
```
[C#]
```
public virtual int Count {get;}
```
[C++]
```
public: __property virtual int get_Count();
```
[JScript]
```
public function get Count() : int;
```

Property Value

The number of items in the collection.

Implements

ICollection.Count

Remarks

This property enables you to determine the number of columns that are displayed in the **ListView** when the **View** property is set to **View.Details**. You can then use this value when you are looping through the values of the collection and you need to provide a number of iterations to perform the loop.

Requirements

Platforms: Windows 98, Windows NT 4.0,
Windows Millennium Edition, Windows 2000,
Windows XP Home Edition, Windows XP Professional,
Windows Server 2003 family,
.NET Compact Framework - Windows CE .NET

ListView.ColumnHeaderCollection.IsReadOnly Property

Gets a value indicating whether the collection is read-only.

```
[Visual Basic]
Public Overridable ReadOnly Property IsReadOnly As Boolean _
   Implements IList.IsReadOnly
[C#]
public virtual bool IsReadOnly {get;}
[C++]
public: __property virtual bool get_IsReadOnly();
[JScript]
public function get IsReadOnly() : Boolean;
```

Property Value

true if the collection is read-only; otherwise, **false**.

Implements

IList.IsReadOnly

Remarks

This property is always **false** for this collection.

Requirements

Platforms: Windows 98, Windows NT 4.0,
Windows Millennium Edition, Windows 2000,
Windows XP Home Edition, Windows XP Professional,
Windows Server 2003 family,
.NET Compact Framework - Windows CE .NET

ListView.ColumnHeaderCollection.Item Property

Gets or sets the column header at the specified index within the collection.

[C#] In C#, this property is the indexer for the **ListView.ColumnHeaderCollection** class.

```
[Visual Basic]
Public Overridable Default ReadOnly Property Item( _
   ByVal index As Integer _
) As ColumnHeader
[C#]
public virtual ColumnHeader this[
   int index
] {get;}
[C++]
public: __property virtual ColumnHeader* get_Item(
   int index
);
[JScript]
returnValue = ColumnHeaderCollectionObject.Item(index);
-or-
returnValue = ColumnHeaderCollectionObject(index);
```

[JScript] In JScript, you can use the default indexed properties defined by a type, but you cannot explicitly define your own. However, specifying the **expando** attribute on a class automatically provides a default indexed property whose type is **Object** and whose index type is **String**.

Arguments [JScript]

index

The index of the column header in the collection to get or set.

Parameters [Visual Basic, C#, C++]

index

The index of the column header in the collection to get or set.

Property Value

A **ColumnHeader** representing the column header located at the specified index within the collection.

Exceptions

Exception Type	Condition
ArgumentOutOfRange-Exception	The *index* parameter is less than zero or greater than or equal to the value of the **Count** property of the **List-View.ColumnHeaderCollection**.

Remarks

You can use this method to obtain the **ColumnHeader** stored at a specific location in the collection. To determine the index of a specific column header in the collection, use the **IndexOf** method.

Requirements

Platforms: Windows 98, Windows NT 4.0,
Windows Millennium Edition, Windows 2000,
Windows XP Home Edition, Windows XP Professional,
Windows Server 2003 family

ListView.ColumnHeaderCollection.System.Collections.ICollection.IsSynchronized Property

Note: This namespace, class, or member is supported only in version 1.1 of the .NET Framework.

This member supports the .NET Framework infrastructure and is not intended to be used directly from your code.

```
[Visual Basic]
Private ReadOnly Property IsSynchronized As Boolean Implements _
   ICollection.IsSynchronized
[C#]
bool ICollection.IsSynchronized {get;}
[C++]
private: __property bool
   System::Collections::ICollection::get_IsSynchronized();
[JScript]
private function get ICollection.IsSynchronized() : Boolean;
```

ListView.ColumnHeaderCollection.System.Collections.ICollection.SyncRoot Property

Note: This namespace, class, or member is supported only in version 1.1 of the .NET Framework.

This member supports the .NET Framework infrastructure and is not intended to be used directly from your code.

```
[Visual Basic]
Private ReadOnly Property SyncRoot As Object Implements _
   ICollection.SyncRoot
[C#]
object ICollection.SyncRoot {get;}
[C++]
private: __property Object*
   System::Collections::ICollection::get_SyncRoot();
[JScript]
private function get ICollection.SyncRoot() : Object;
```

ListView.ColumnHeaderCollection.System.Collections.IList.IsFixedSize Property

Note: This namespace, class, or member is supported only in version 1.1 of the .NET Framework.

This member supports the .NET Framework infrastructure and is not intended to be used directly from your code.

```
[Visual Basic]
Private ReadOnly Property IsFixedSize As Boolean Implements _
   IList.IsFixedSize
[C#]
bool IList.IsFixedSize {get;}
[C++]
private: __property bool
   System::Collections::IList::get_IsFixedSize();
[JScript]
private function get IList.IsFixedSize() : Boolean;
```

ListView.ColumnHeaderCollection.System.Collections.IList.Item Property

Note: This namespace, class, or member is supported only in version 1.1 of the .NET Framework.

[C#] In C#, this property is the indexer for the **ListView.ColumnHeaderCollection** class.

```
[Visual Basic]
Private Default Property Item( _
   ByVal index As Integer _
) As Object Implements IList.Item
[C#]
object IList.this[
   int index
] {get; set;}
[C++]
private: __property Object* System::Collections::IList::get_Item(
   int index
);
private: __property void System::Collections::IList::set_Item(
   int index,
   Object*
);
[JScript]
private function get IList.get_Item(index : int) : Object;
private function set IList.set_Item(index : int, value : Object);
-or-
private function get IList.get_Item(index : int) : Object;
private function set IList.set_Item(index : int, value : Object);
```

[JScript] In JScript, you can use the default indexed properties defined by a type, but you cannot explicitly define your own. However, specifying the **expando** attribute on a class automatically provides a default indexed property whose type is **Object** and whose index type is **String**.

Arguments [JScript]

index

Parameters [Visual Basic, C#, C++]

index

Requirements

Platforms: Windows 98, Windows NT 4.0, Windows Millennium Edition, Windows 2000, Windows XP Home Edition, Windows XP Professional, Windows Server 2003 family

ListView.ColumnHeaderCollection.Add Method

Adds a column header to the collection.

Overload List

Adds an existing **ColumnHeader** to the collection.

Supported by the .NET Compact Framework.

[Visual Basic] **Overloads Public Overridable Function Add(ColumnHeader) As Integer**

[C#] **public virtual int Add(ColumnHeader);**

[C++] **public: virtual int Add(ColumnHeader*);**

[JScript] **public function Add(ColumnHeader) : int;**

Adds a column header to the collection with specified text, width, and alignment settings.

Supported by the .NET Compact Framework.

[Visual Basic] **Overloads Public Overridable Function Add(String, Integer, HorizontalAlignment) As ColumnHeader**

[C#] **public virtual ColumnHeader Add(string, int, HorizontalAlignment);**

[C++] **public: virtual ColumnHeader* Add(String*, int, HorizontalAlignment);**

[JScript] **public function Add(String, int, HorizontalAlignment) : ColumnHeader;**

Example

See related example in the **System.Windows.Forms.ListView** class topic.

ListView.ColumnHeaderCollection.Add Method (ColumnHeader)

Adds an existing **ColumnHeader** to the collection.

```
[Visual Basic]
Overloads Public Overridable Function Add( _
   ByVal value As ColumnHeader _
) As Integer
```

[C#]
```
public virtual int Add(
   ColumnHeader value
);
```
[C++]
```
public: virtual int Add(
   ColumnHeader* value
);
```
[JScript]
```
public function Add(
   value : ColumnHeader
) : int;
```

Parameters

value
The **ColumnHeader** to add to the collection.

Return Value

The zero-based index into the collection where the item was added.

Remarks

You can use this version of the **Add** method to add an existing **ColumnHeader** to the collection. If you want to create a new **ColumnHeader** at the time you add it to the collection, you can use the other version of the **Add** method.

When column headers are added, they are added to the end of the collection. To insert a column header into the collection at a specific position, use the **Insert** method. To add a set of column headers to the collection in a single operation, use the **AddRange** method.

Example

See related example in the **System.Windows.Forms.ListView** class topic.

Requirements

Platforms: Windows 98, Windows NT 4.0,
Windows Millennium Edition, Windows 2000,
Windows XP Home Edition, Windows XP Professional,
Windows Server 2003 family,
.NET Compact Framework - Windows CE .NET

ListView.ColumnHeaderCollection.Add Method (String, Int32, HorizontalAlignment)

Adds a column header to the collection with specified text, width, and alignment settings.

[Visual Basic]
```
Overloads Public Overridable Function Add( _
   ByVal str As String, _
   ByVal width As Integer, _
   ByVal textAlign As HorizontalAlignment _
) As ColumnHeader
```
[C#]
```
public virtual ColumnHeader Add(
   string str,
   int width,
   HorizontalAlignment textAlign
);
```
[C++]
```
public: virtual ColumnHeader* Add(
   String* str,
   int width,
   HorizontalAlignment textAlign
);
```
[JScript]
```
public function Add(
   str : String,
   width : int,
   textAlign : HorizontalAlignment
) : ColumnHeader;
```

Parameters

str
The text to display in the column header.

width
The initial width of the column header. Set to -1 to autosize the column header to the size of the largest subitem text in the column or -2 to autosize the column header to the size of the text of the column header.

textAlign
One of the **HorizontalAlignment** values.

Return Value

The **ColumnHeader** that was created and added to the collection.

Remarks

You can use this version of the **Add** method to create a new **ColumnHeader** to add to the collection. The text of the new **ColumnHeader** added to the control is based on the *text* parameter. This version of the **Add** method also allows you to specify the width of the column and the alignment of text in the column header. If you have an existing **ColumnHeader** that you want to add to the collection, use the version of the **Add** method that accepts a **ColumnHeader** as its parameter.

When column headers are added, they are added to the end of the collection. To insert a column header into the collection at a specific position, use the **Insert** method. To add a set of column headers to the collection in a single operation, use the **AddRange** method.

Example

See related example in the **System.Windows.Forms.ListView** class topic.

Requirements

Platforms: Windows 98, Windows NT 4.0,
Windows Millennium Edition, Windows 2000,
Windows XP Home Edition, Windows XP Professional,
Windows Server 2003 family,
.NET Compact Framework - Windows CE .NET

ListView.ColumnHeaderCollection.AddRange Method

Adds an array of column headers to the collection.

[Visual Basic]
```
Public Overridable Sub AddRange( _
   ByVal values() As ColumnHeader _
)
```
[C#]
```
public virtual void AddRange(
   ColumnHeader[] values
);
```
[C++]
```
public: virtual void AddRange(
   ColumnHeader* values[]
);
```

```
[JScript]
public function AddRange(
   values : ColumnHeader[]
);
```

Parameters

values

An array of **ColumnHeader** objects to add to the collection.

Remarks

This method removes all existing column headers from the collection before inserting new items. You can use this method to reuse the column headers used in a different **ListView** control. If you want to add a single **ColumnHeader**, use the **Add** method. You can also use the **Insert** method if you want to add a single **ColumnHeader** at a specific position in the collection.

Requirements

Platforms: Windows 98, Windows NT 4.0, Windows Millennium Edition, Windows 2000, Windows XP Home Edition, Windows XP Professional, Windows Server 2003 family

ListView.ColumnHeaderCollection.Clear Method

Removes all column headers from the collection.

```
[Visual Basic]
Public Overridable Sub Clear() Implements IList.Clear
[C#]
public virtual void Clear();
[C++]
public: virtual void Clear();
[JScript]
public function Clear();
```

Implements

IList.Clear

Remarks

When you remove column headers from the collection, all information about the deleted column headers is lost. To remove a single column header from the collection use the **Remove** or **RemoveAt** method.

Requirements

Platforms: Windows 98, Windows NT 4.0, Windows Millennium Edition, Windows 2000, Windows XP Home Edition, Windows XP Professional, Windows Server 2003 family, .NET Compact Framework - Windows CE .NET

ListView.ColumnHeaderCollection.Contains Method

Determines whether the specified column header is located in the collection.

```
[Visual Basic]
Public Function Contains( _
   ByVal value As ColumnHeader _
) As Boolean
[C#]
public bool Contains(
   ColumnHeader value
);
[C++]
public: bool Contains(
   ColumnHeader* value
);
[JScript]
public function Contains(
   value : ColumnHeader
) : Boolean;
```

Parameters

value

A **ColumnHeader** representing the column header to locate in the collection.

Return Value

true if the column header is contained in the collection; otherwise, **false**.

Remarks

The **Contains** method enables you to determine whether a **ColumnHeader** is a member of the collection. Once you know that the column header is in the collection, you can use the **IndexOf** method to determine the position of the column header in the collection.

Requirements

Platforms: Windows 98, Windows NT 4.0, Windows Millennium Edition, Windows 2000, Windows XP Home Edition, Windows XP Professional, Windows Server 2003 family, .NET Compact Framework - Windows CE .NET

ListView.ColumnHeaderCollection.GetEnumerator Method

Returns an enumerator to use to iterate through the column header collection.

```
[Visual Basic]
Public Overridable Function GetEnumerator() As IEnumerator _
   Implements IEnumerable.GetEnumerator
[C#]
public virtual IEnumerator GetEnumerator();
[C++]
public: virtual IEnumerator* GetEnumerator();
[JScript]
public function GetEnumerator() : IEnumerator;
```

Return Value

An **IEnumerator** that represents the column header collection.

Implements

IEnumerable.GetEnumerator

Requirements

Platforms: Windows 98, Windows NT 4.0, Windows Millennium Edition, Windows 2000, Windows XP Home Edition, Windows XP Professional, Windows Server 2003 family, .NET Compact Framework - Windows CE .NET

ListView.ColumnHeaderCollection.ICollection.CopyTo Method

This member supports the .NET Framework infrastructure and is not intended to be used directly from your code.

```
[Visual Basic]
Private Sub CopyTo( _
   ByVal dest As Array, _
   ByVal index As Integer _
) Implements ICollection.CopyTo
[C#]
void ICollection.CopyTo(
   Array dest,
   int index
);
[C++]
private: void ICollection::CopyTo(
   Array* dest,
   int index
);
[JScript]
private function ICollection.CopyTo(
   dest : Array,
   index : int
);
```

ListView.ColumnHeaderCollection.IList.Add Method

This member supports the .NET Framework infrastructure and is not intended to be used directly from your code.

```
[Visual Basic]
Private Function Add( _
   ByVal value As Object _
) As Integer Implements IList.Add
[C#]
int IList.Add(
   object value
);
[C++]
private: int IList::Add(
   Object* value
);
[JScript]
private function IList.Add(
   value : Object
) : int;
```

ListView.ColumnHeaderCollection.IList.Contains Method

This member supports the .NET Framework infrastructure and is not intended to be used directly from your code.

```
[Visual Basic]
Private Function Contains( _
   ByVal value As Object _
) As Boolean Implements IList.Contains
[C#]
bool IList.Contains(
   object value
);
[C++]
private: bool IList::Contains(
   Object* value
);
[JScript]
private function IList.Contains(
   value : Object
) : Boolean;
```

ListView.ColumnHeaderCollection.IList.IndexOf Method

This member supports the .NET Framework infrastructure and is not intended to be used directly from your code.

```
[Visual Basic]
Private Function IndexOf( _
   ByVal value As Object _
) As Integer Implements IList.IndexOf
[C#]
int IList.IndexOf(
   object value
);
[C++]
private: int IList::IndexOf(
   Object* value
);
[JScript]
private function IList.IndexOf(
   value : Object
) : int;
```

ListView.ColumnHeaderCollection.IList.Insert Method

This member supports the .NET Framework infrastructure and is not intended to be used directly from your code.

```
[Visual Basic]
Private Sub Insert( _
   ByVal index As Integer, _
   ByVal value As Object _
) Implements IList.Insert
[C#]
void IList.Insert(
   int index,
   object value
);
[C++]
private: void IList::Insert(
   int index,
   Object* value
);
[JScript]
private function IList.Insert(
   index : int,
   value : Object
);
```

ListView.ColumnHeaderCollection.IList.Remove Method

This member supports the .NET Framework infrastructure and is not intended to be used directly from your code.

```
[Visual Basic]
Private Sub Remove( _
   ByVal value As Object _
) Implements IList.Remove
[C#]
void IList.Remove(
   object value
);
[C++]
private: void IList::Remove(
   Object* value
);
[JScript]
private function IList.Remove(
   value : Object
);
```

ListView.ColumnHeaderCollection.IndexOf Method

Returns the index within the collection of the specified column header.

```
[Visual Basic]
Public Function IndexOf( _
   ByVal value As ColumnHeader _
) As Integer
[C#]
public int IndexOf(
   ColumnHeader value
);
[C++]
public: int IndexOf(
   ColumnHeader* value
);
[JScript]
public function IndexOf(
   value : ColumnHeader
) : int;
```

Parameters

value

A **ColumnHeader** representing the column header to locate in the collection.

Return Value

The zero-based index of the column header's location in the collection. If the column header is not located in the collection, the return value is negative one (-1).

Remarks

The **IndexOf** method enables you to determine the position of a column header in the collection. To determine whether a column header is contained in the collection before calling this method, use the **Contains** method.

Requirements

Platforms: Windows 98, Windows NT 4.0, Windows Millennium Edition, Windows 2000, Windows XP Home Edition, Windows XP Professional, Windows Server 2003 family, .NET Compact Framework - Windows CE .NET

ListView.ColumnHeaderCollection.Insert Method

Inserts a column header into the collection at the specified index.

Overload List

Inserts an existing column header into the collection at the specified index.

Supported by the .NET Compact Framework.

[Visual Basic] **Overloads Public Sub Insert(Integer, ColumnHeader)**

[C#] **public void Insert(int, ColumnHeader);**

[C++] **public: void Insert(int, ColumnHeader*);**

[JScript] **public function Insert(int, ColumnHeader);**

Creates a new column header and inserts it into the collection at the specified index.

[Visual Basic] **Overloads Public Sub Insert(Integer, String, Integer, HorizontalAlignment)**

[C#] **public void Insert(int, string, int, HorizontalAlignment);**

[C++] **public: void Insert(int, String*, int, HorizontalAlignment);**

[JScript] **public function Insert(int, String, int, HorizontalAlignment);**

ListView.ColumnHeaderCollection.Insert Method (Int32, ColumnHeader)

Inserts an existing column header into the collection at the specified index.

```
[Visual Basic]
Overloads Public Sub Insert( _
   ByVal index As Integer, _
   ByVal value As ColumnHeader _
)
[C#]
public void Insert(
   int index,
   ColumnHeader value
);
[C++]
public: void Insert(
   int index,
   ColumnHeader* value
);
[JScript]
public function Insert(
   index : int,
   value : ColumnHeader
);
```

Parameters

index

The zero-based index location where the column header is inserted.

value

The **ColumnHeader** to insert into the collection.

Exceptions

Exception Type	Condition
ArgumentOutOfRange-Exception	The *index* parameter is less than zero or greater than or equal to the value of the **Count** property of the **List-View.ColumnHeaderCollection**.

Remarks

This version of the **Insert** method enables you to insert an existing **ColumnHeader** at a specific position in the **ListView.Column-HeaderCollection**.

If you want to create a new **ColumnHeader** and insert it at a specific position in the collection, use the other version of the **Insert** method. To add a column header without specifying a specific position in the collection, use the **Add** method. If you want to add an array of column headers to the collection, use the **AddRange** method.

Requirements

Platforms: Windows 98, Windows NT 4.0,
Windows Millennium Edition, Windows 2000,
Windows XP Home Edition, Windows XP Professional,
Windows Server 2003 family,
.NET Compact Framework - Windows CE .NET

ListView.ColumnHeaderCollection.Insert Method (Int32, String, Int32, HorizontalAlignment)

Creates a new column header and inserts it into the collection at the specified index.

```
[Visual Basic]
Overloads Public Sub Insert( _
   ByVal index As Integer, _
   ByVal str As String, _
   ByVal width As Integer, _
   ByVal textAlign As HorizontalAlignment _
)
[C#]
public void Insert(
   int index,
   string str,
   int width,
   HorizontalAlignment textAlign
);
[C++]
public: void Insert(
   int index,
   String* str,
   int width,
   HorizontalAlignment textAlign
);
[JScript]
public function Insert(
   index : int,
   str : String,
   width : int,
   textAlign : HorizontalAlignment
);
```

Parameters

index
The zero-based index location where the column header is inserted.

str
The text to display in the column header.

width
The initial width of the column header. Set to -1 to autosize the column header to the size of the largest subitem text in the column or -2 to autosize the column header to the size of the text of the column header.

textAlign
One of the **HorizontalAlignment** values.

Exceptions

Exception Type	Condition
ArgumentOutOfRange-Exception	The *index* parameter is less than zero or greater than or equal to the value of the **Count** property of the **List-View.ColumnHeaderCollection**.

Remarks

This version of the **Insert** method enables you to create a new **ColumnHeader** with specific column header text, width, and text alignment setting and insert it at a specific position in the **List-View.ColumnHeaderCollection**. You can use this method if you want to insert a new column header into an existing collection of column headers. If you want to use an existing **ColumnHeader** object and insert it at a specific position in the collection, use the other version of the **Insert** method. To add a column header without specifying a specific position in the collection, use the **Add** method. If you want to add an array of column headers to the collection, use the **AddRange** method.

Requirements

Platforms: Windows 98, Windows NT 4.0,
Windows Millennium Edition, Windows 2000,
Windows XP Home Edition, Windows XP Professional,
Windows Server 2003 family

ListView.ColumnHeaderCollection.Remove Method

Removes the specified column header from the collection.

```
[Visual Basic]
Public Overridable Sub Remove( _
   ByVal column As ColumnHeader _
)
[C#]
public virtual void Remove(
   ColumnHeader column
);
[C++]
public: virtual void Remove(
   ColumnHeader* column
);
[JScript]
public function Remove(
   column : ColumnHeader
);
```

Parameters

column

A **ColumnHeader** representing the column header to remove from the collection.

Remarks

When you remove a column header from the collection, the indexes change for subsequent column headers in the collection. All information about the removed column header is deleted. You can use this method to remove a specific column header from the collection by specifying the actual **ColumnHeader** to remove. To specify the index of the column header to remove instead of the column header itself, use the **RemoveAt** method. To remove all column headers from the collection, use the **Clear** method.

Requirements

Platforms: Windows 98, Windows NT 4.0, Windows Millennium Edition, Windows 2000, Windows XP Home Edition, Windows XP Professional, Windows Server 2003 family, .NET Compact Framework - Windows CE .NET

ListView.ColumnHeaderCollection.RemoveAt Method

Removes the column header at the specified index within the collection.

```
[Visual Basic]
Public Overridable Sub RemoveAt( _
   ByVal index As Integer _
) Implements IList.RemoveAt
[C#]
public virtual void RemoveAt(
   int index
);
[C++]
public: virtual void RemoveAt(
   int index
);
[JScript]
public function RemoveAt(
   index : int
);
```

Parameters

index

The zero-based index of the column header to remove.

Implements

IList.RemoveAt

Exceptions

Exception Type	Condition
ArgumentOutOfRangeException	The *index* parameter is less than zero or greater than or equal to the value of the **Count** property of the **ListView.ColumnHeaderCollection**.

Remarks

When you remove a column header from the collection, the indexes change for subsequent column headers in the collection. All information about the removed column header is deleted. You can use this method to remove a specific column header from the collection by specifying the index of the column header to remove from the collection. To specify the column header to remove instead of the index to the column header, use the **Remove** method. To remove all column headers from the collection, use the **Clear** method.

Requirements

Platforms: Windows 98, Windows NT 4.0, Windows Millennium Edition, Windows 2000, Windows XP Home Edition, Windows XP Professional, Windows Server 2003 family, .NET Compact Framework - Windows CE .NET

ListViewItem Class

Represents an item in a **ListView** control.

System.Object
  System.Windows.Forms.ListViewItem

```
[Visual Basic]
<Serializable>
Public Class ListViewItem
   Implements ICloneable, ISerializable
[C#]
[Serializable]
public class ListViewItem : ICloneable, ISerializable
[C++]
[Serializable]
public __gc class ListViewItem : public ICloneable, ISerializable
[JScript]
public
   Serializable
class ListViewItem implements ICloneable, ISerializable
```

Thread Safety

Any public static (**Shared** in Visual Basic) members of this type are safe for multithreaded operations. Any instance members are not guaranteed to be thread safe.

Remarks

The **ListView** control is similar to a **ListBox** in that it displays a list of items. The main difference is that the ListView control provides a number of different ways items can be viewed by the user. The **ListViewItem** class defines the appearance, behavior, and data associated with an item that is displayed in the **ListView** control. **ListViewItem** objects can be displayed in the **ListView** control in one of four different views. Items can be displayed as large or small icons or as small icons in a vertical list. Items can also have subitems that contain information that is related to the parent item. The fourth view style, details view, allows you to display the item and its subitems in a grid with column headers that can be used to identify the information being displayed in a subitem.

Most of the properties of the **ListViewItem** class provide ways to change the display of the item in the **ListView** control it is associated with. The **BackColor**, **ForeColor**, and **Font** properties allow you to change how the text of the item is displayed in the **ListView** control. The **ImageIndex** property allows you to specify the image to load from the **ImageList** that is assigned to the **ListView** control (by setting the **LargeImageList** or **SmallImage-List** properties of the **ListView**). Items can display check boxes in order to obtain item choices from the user in a way similar to a **CheckedListBox** control. You can use the **Checked** property to determine if an item is checked or to check or uncheck the item at run time. Items can display any number of subitems when the **View** property of the associated **ListView** control is set to **View.Details** and columns are defined in the **ListView.ColumnHeaderCollection** of the **ListView** control. You can add subitems to an item by calling the **Add** method of the **ListViewItem.ListViewSubItemCollection**. The **SubItems** property allows you to gain access to the **ListView-Item.ListViewSubItemCollection** class and its members.

Some of the properties and methods of the **ListViewItem** class are item-specific versions of properties and methods in the **ListView** control. For example, the **EnsureVisible** method is similar to the **ListView** version of the method, but the **ListViewItem** version only affects the current item.

The **ListViewItem** class also provides methods that are not versions of **ListView** methods. The **BeginEdit** method places the item's text into edit mode so the user can change the item's text (when the **LabelEdit** property of the **ListView** control is set to **true**). The **Clone** method allows you to create copies of existing **ListViewItem** objects to reuse in other **ListView** controls.

Example

See related example in the **System.Windows.Forms.ListView** class topic.

Requirements

Namespace: System.Windows.Forms

Platforms: Windows 98, Windows NT 4.0, Windows Millennium Edition, Windows 2000, Windows XP Home Edition, Windows XP Professional, Windows Server 2003 family, .NET Compact Framework - Windows CE .NET

Assembly: System.Windows.Forms (in System.Windows.Forms.dll)

ListViewItem Constructor

Initializes a new instance of the **ListViewItem** class.

Overload List

Initializes a new instance of the **ListViewItem** class with default values.

Supported by the .NET Compact Framework.

[Visual Basic] **Public Sub New()**

[C#] **public ListViewItem();**

[C++] **public: ListViewItem();**

[JScript] **public function ListViewItem();**

Initializes a new instance of the **ListViewItem** class with specified item text.

Supported by the .NET Compact Framework.

[Visual Basic] **Public Sub New(String)**

[C#] **public ListViewItem(string);**

[C++] **public: ListViewItem(String*);**

[JScript] **public function ListViewItem(String);**

Initializes a new instance of the **ListViewItem** class with an array of strings representing subitems.

Supported by the .NET Compact Framework.

[Visual Basic] **Public Sub New(String())**

[C#] **public ListViewItem(string[]);**

[C++] **public: ListViewItem(String*[]);**

[JScript] **public function ListViewItem(String[]);**

Initializes a new instance of the **ListViewItem** class with an array of **ListViewItem.ListViewSubItem** objects and the image index position of the item's icon.

[Visual Basic] **Public Sub New(ListView-Item.ListViewSubItem(), Integer)**

[C#] **public ListViewItem(ListViewItem.ListViewSubItem[], int);**

[C++] **public: ListViewItem(ListView-Item.ListViewSubItem*[], int);**

[JScript] **public function ListViewItem(ListView-Item.ListViewSubItem[], int);**

Initializes a new instance of the **ListViewItem** class with specified item text and the image index position of the item's icon.

[Visual Basic] **Public Sub New(String, Integer)**

[C#] **public ListViewItem(string, int);**

[C++] **public: ListViewItem(String*, int);**

[JScript] **public function ListViewItem(String, int);**

Initializes a new instance of the **ListViewItem** class with an array of strings representing subitems and the image index position of the item's icon.

[Visual Basic] **Public Sub New(String(), Integer)**

[C#] **public ListViewItem(string[], int);**

[C++] **public: ListViewItem(String*[], int);**

[JScript] **public function ListViewItem(String[], int);**

Initializes a new instance of the **ListViewItem** class with an array of strings representing subitems, the image index position of the item's icon, and the foreground color, background color, and font of the item.

[Visual Basic] **Public Sub New(String(), Integer, Color, Color, Font)**

[C#] **public ListViewItem(string[], int, Color, Color, Font);**

[C++] **public: ListViewItem(String*[], int, Color, Color, Font*);**

[JScript] **public function ListViewItem(String[], int, Color, Color, Font);**

Example

See related example in the **System.Windows.Forms.ListView** class topic.

ListViewItem Constructor ()

Initializes a new instance of the **ListViewItem** class with default values.

```
[Visual Basic]
Public Sub New()
[C#]
public ListViewItem();
[C++]
public: ListViewItem();
[JScript]
public function ListViewItem();
```

Example

See related example in the **System.Windows.Forms.ListView** class topic.

Requirements

Platforms: Windows 98, Windows NT 4.0, Windows Millennium Edition, Windows 2000, Windows XP Home Edition, Windows XP Professional, Windows Server 2003 family, .NET Compact Framework - Windows CE .NET

ListViewItem Constructor (String)

Initializes a new instance of the **ListViewItem** class with specified item text.

```
[Visual Basic]
Public Sub New( _
   ByVal text As String _
)
[C#]
public ListViewItem(
   string text
);
[C++]
public: ListViewItem(
   String* text
);
[JScript]
public function ListViewItem(
   text : String
);
```

Parameters

text

The text to display for the item.

Requirements

Platforms: Windows 98, Windows NT 4.0, Windows Millennium Edition, Windows 2000, Windows XP Home Edition, Windows XP Professional, Windows Server 2003 family, .NET Compact Framework - Windows CE .NET

ListViewItem Constructor (String[])

Initializes a new instance of the **ListViewItem** class with an array of strings representing subitems.

```
[Visual Basic]
Public Sub New( _
   ByVal items() As String _
)
[C#]
public ListViewItem(
   string[] items
);
[C++]
public: ListViewItem(
   String* items __gc[]
);
[JScript]
public function ListViewItem(
   items : String[]
);
```

Parameters

items

An array of strings that represent the subitems of the new item.

Requirements

Platforms: Windows 98, Windows NT 4.0, Windows Millennium Edition, Windows 2000, Windows XP Home Edition, Windows XP Professional, Windows Server 2003 family, .NET Compact Framework - Windows CE .NET

ListViewItem Constructor (ListViewItem.ListViewSubItem[], Int32)

Initializes a new instance of the **ListViewItem** class with an array of **ListViewItem.ListViewSubItem** objects and the image index position of the item's icon.

```
[Visual Basic]
Public Sub New( _
   ByVal subItems() As ListViewItem.ListViewSubItem, _
   ByVal imageIndex As Integer _
)
[C#]
public ListViewItem(
   ListViewItem.ListViewSubItem[] subItems,
   int imageIndex
);
[C++]
public: ListViewItem(
   ListViewItem.ListViewSubItem* subItems[],
   int imageIndex
);
[JScript]
public function ListViewItem(
   subItems : ListViewItem.ListViewSubItem[],
   imageIndex : int
);
```

Parameters

subItems
An array of **ListViewItem.ListViewSubItem** objects that represent the subitems of the item.

imageIndex
The zero-based index of the image within the **ImageList** associated with the **ListView** control that contains the item.

Remarks

This version of the constructor allows you to reuse the subitems from another item.

Requirements

Platforms: Windows 98, Windows NT 4.0, Windows Millennium Edition, Windows 2000, Windows XP Home Edition, Windows XP Professional, Windows Server 2003 family

ListViewItem Constructor (String, Int32)

Initializes a new instance of the **ListViewItem** class with specified item text and the image index position of the item's icon.

```
[Visual Basic]
Public Sub New( _
   ByVal text As String, _
   ByVal imageIndex As Integer _
)
[C#]
public ListViewItem(
   string text,
   int imageIndex
);
[C++]
public: ListViewItem(
   String* text,
   int imageIndex
);
[JScript]
public function ListViewItem(
   text : String,
   imageIndex : int
);
```

Parameters

text
The text to display for the item.

imageIndex
The zero-based index of the image within the **ImageList** associated with the **ListView** control that contains the item.

Requirements

Platforms: Windows 98, Windows NT 4.0, Windows Millennium Edition, Windows 2000, Windows XP Home Edition, Windows XP Professional, Windows Server 2003 family

ListViewItem Constructor (String[], Int32)

Initializes a new instance of the **ListViewItem** class with an array of strings representing subitems and the image index position of the item's icon.

```
[Visual Basic]
Public Sub New( _
   ByVal items() As String, _
   ByVal imageIndex As Integer _
)
[C#]
public ListViewItem(
   string[] items,
   int imageIndex
);
[C++]
public: ListViewItem(
   String* items __gc[],
   int imageIndex
);
[JScript]
public function ListViewItem(
   items : String[],
   imageIndex : int
);
```

Parameters

items
An array of strings that represent the subitems of the new item.

imageIndex
The zero-based index of the image within the **ImageList** associated with the **ListView** control that contains the item.

Requirements

Platforms: Windows 98, Windows NT 4.0, Windows Millennium Edition, Windows 2000, Windows XP Home Edition, Windows XP Professional, Windows Server 2003 family

ListViewItem Constructor (String[], Int32, Color, Color, Font)

Initializes a new instance of the **ListViewItem** class with an array of strings representing subitems, the image index position of the item's icon, and the foreground color, background color, and font of the item.

```
[Visual Basic]
Public Sub New( _
   ByVal items() As String, _
   ByVal imageIndex As Integer, _
   ByVal foreColor As Color, _
   ByVal backColor As Color, _
   ByVal font As Font _
)
[C#]
public ListViewItem(
   string[] items,
   int imageIndex,
   Color foreColor,
   Color backColor,
   Font font
);
[C++]
public: ListViewItem(
   String* items __gc[],
   int imageIndex,
   Color foreColor,
   Color backColor,
   Font* font
);
[JScript]
public function ListViewItem(
   items : String[],
   imageIndex : int,
   foreColor : Color,
   backColor : Color,
   font : Font
);
```

Parameters

items
: An array of strings that represent the subitems of the new item.

imageIndex
: The zero-based index of the image within the **ImageList** associated with the **ListView** control that contains the item.

foreColor
: A **Color** that represents the foreground color of the item.

backColor
: A **Color** that represents the background color of the item.

font
: A **Font** that represents the typeface to display the item's text in.

Example

See related example in the **System.Windows.Forms.ListView** class topic.

Requirements

Platforms: Windows 98, Windows NT 4.0, Windows Millennium Edition, Windows 2000, Windows XP Home Edition, Windows XP Professional, Windows Server 2003 family

ListViewItem.BackColor Property

Gets or sets the background color of the item's text.

```
[Visual Basic]
Public Property BackColor As Color
[C#]
public Color BackColor {get; set;}
[C++]
public: __property Color get_BackColor();
public: __property void set_BackColor(Color);
[JScript]
public function get BackColor() : Color;
public function set BackColor(Color);
```

Property Value

A **Color** that represents the background color of the item's text.

Remarks

You can use the **BackColor** property to change the color displayed behind the item text. This property can be used if you want to use different background and foreground color combinations (using the **ForeColor** property to set the foreground color) to differentiate one item from another. For example, you could set the **BackColor** property to **Color.Red** to identify items that have failed validation or are missing subitem information.

If you want to use the same background color for all subitems of an item, set the **UseItemStyleForSubItems** property to **true**. This will cause the colors and fonts specified for the item to be used for all subitem text.

Requirements

Platforms: Windows 98, Windows NT 4.0, Windows Millennium Edition, Windows 2000, Windows XP Home Edition, Windows XP Professional, Windows Server 2003 family

ListViewItem.Bounds Property

Gets the bounding rectangle of the item, including subitems.

```
[Visual Basic]
Public ReadOnly Property Bounds As Rectangle
[C#]
public Rectangle Bounds {get;}
[C++]
public: __property Rectangle get_Bounds();
[JScript]
public function get Bounds() : Rectangle;
```

Property Value

A **Rectangle** that represents the bounding rectangle of the item.

Remarks

You can use this method to obtain the bounding rectangle of an entire item. If you want to obtain the bounding rectangle for a portion of the entire item, use the **GetBounds** method. The **ListView** class provides a **GetItemRect** method that allows you to get the bounding rectangle of any item located within the control.

Requirements

Platforms: Windows 98, Windows NT 4.0, Windows Millennium Edition, Windows 2000, Windows XP Home Edition, Windows XP Professional, Windows Server 2003 family

ListViewItem.Checked Property

Gets or sets a value indicating whether the item is checked.

```
[Visual Basic]
Public Property Checked As Boolean
[C#]
public bool Checked {get; set;}
[C++]
public: __property bool get_Checked();
public: __property void set_Checked(bool);
[JScript]
public function get Checked() : Boolean;
public function set Checked(Boolean);
```

Property Value

true if the item is checked; otherwise, **false**. The default is **false**.

Remarks

This property is only useful if the **CheckBoxes** property of the **ListView** control the item is contained in is set to **true**. You can use this property to determine if the item has been checked by the user or through code at run time. To determine all the items that are checked in a **ListView** control, you can use the **CheckedItems** property. To take action when an item has been checked, you can create an event handler for the **ItemCheck** property of the **ListView** control.

Example

See related example in the **System.Windows.Forms.ListView** class topic.

Requirements

Platforms: Windows 98, Windows NT 4.0,
Windows Millennium Edition, Windows 2000,
Windows XP Home Edition, Windows XP Professional,
Windows Server 2003 family,
.NET Compact Framework - Windows CE .NET

ListViewItem.Focused Property

Gets or sets a value indicating whether the item has focus within the list view control.

```
[Visual Basic]
Public Property Focused As Boolean
[C#]
public bool Focused {get; set;}
[C++]
public: __property bool get_Focused();
public: __property void set_Focused(bool);
[JScript]
public function get Focused() : Boolean;
public function set Focused(Boolean);
```

Property Value

true if the item has focus; otherwise, **false**.

Remarks

Because a **ListView** control has no directly editable areas, except items it displays, when the **ListView** control has focus, an item within the **ListView** displays the focus reticle around its item text. Typically, the last selected item in the **ListView** control is the focused item. Although an item can be the one displaying the focus reticle, it might not actually be a selected item in the **ListView**. You can use this property to determine if the item is currently the focused item in the **ListView** control that contains it. If the **ListViewItem** is not associated with a **ListView** control, then this property will return **false**.

The **ListView** control provides a property called **FocusedItem** that allows you to determine which **ListViewItem** in the **ListView** has the focus.

Requirements

Platforms: Windows 98, Windows NT 4.0,
Windows Millennium Edition, Windows 2000,
Windows XP Home Edition, Windows XP Professional,
Windows Server 2003 family,
.NET Compact Framework - Windows CE .NET

ListViewItem.Font Property

Gets or sets the font of the text displayed by the item.

```
[Visual Basic]
Public Property Font As Font
[C#]
public Font Font {get; set;}
[C++]
public: __property Font* get_Font();
public: __property void set_Font(Font*);
[JScript]
public function get Font() : Font;
public function set Font(Font);
```

Property Value

The **Font** to apply to the text displayed by the control. The default is the value of the **DefaultFont** property if the **ListViewItem** is not associated with a **ListView** control; otherwise the font specified in the **Font** property for the **ListView** control is used.

Remarks

You can use this method to change the typeface styles applied to the text of the item. Because a **Font** is immutable (you cannot adjust any of its properties), you can only assign the **Font** property a new **Font**. However, you can base the new font on the existing font.

[Visual Basic, C#]] The following is an example of how to adjust the existing font to make it bold:

```
[C#]
listViewItem1.Font = new Font(listViewItem1.Font,
   listViewItem1.Font.Style | FontStyle.Bold);
```

```
[Visual Basic]
ListViewItem1.Font = New Font(ListViewItem1.Font, _
   ListViewItem1.Font.Style Or FontStyle.Bold)
```

Requirements

Platforms: Windows 98, Windows NT 4.0,
Windows Millennium Edition, Windows 2000,
Windows XP Home Edition, Windows XP Professional,
Windows Server 2003 family

ListViewItem.ForeColor Property

Gets or sets the foreground color of the item's text.

```
[Visual Basic]
Public Property ForeColor As Color
[C#]
public Color ForeColor {get; set;}
```

[C++]
```
public: __property Color get_ForeColor();
public: __property void set_ForeColor(Color);
```
[JScript]
```
public function get ForeColor() : Color;
public function set ForeColor(Color);
```

Property Value

A **Color** that represents the foreground color of the item's text.

Remarks

You can use the **ForeColor** property to change the color of the item text. This property can be used if you want to use different background and foreground color combinations (using the **BackColor** property to set the background color) to differentiate one item from another. For example, you could set the **ForeColor** property to **Color.Red** to identify items that have a negative number associated with them or have failed item validation.

If you want to use the same foreground color for all subitems of an item, set the **UseItemStyleForSubItems** property to **true**. This will cause the colors and fonts specified for the item to be used for all subitem text.

Requirements

Platforms: Windows 98, Windows NT 4.0,
Windows Millennium Edition, Windows 2000,
Windows XP Home Edition, Windows XP Professional,
Windows Server 2003 family

ListViewItem.ImageIndex Property

Gets or sets the index of the image that is displayed for the item.

[Visual Basic]
```
Public Property ImageIndex As Integer
```
[C#]
```
public int ImageIndex {get; set;}
```
[C++]
```
public: __property int get_ImageIndex();
public: __property void set_ImageIndex(int);
```
[JScript]
```
public function get ImageIndex() : int;
public function set ImageIndex(int);
```

Property Value

The zero-based index of the image in the **ImageList** that is displayed for the item. The default is -1.

Exceptions

Exception Type	Condition
ArgumentException	The value specified is less than -1.

Remarks

The value of this property depends on the value of the **ImageList** property. Depending on the current value of the **View** property of the **ListView** control associated with the item, the **ImageList** used by the item could be one specified in the **LargeImageList** property or the **SmallImageList** property of the **ListView** control. If the **View** property is set to **View.LargeIcons**, the **ImageList** specified in the **LargeImageList** property is used; otherwise the **ImageList** specified in the **SmallImageList** property is used. It is recommended that the images defined in the **ImageList** specified in the **SmallImageList** have the same index positions as the images in the **ImageList** specified in the **LargeImageList** property. If the index positions are the same for both **ImageList** controls, you can set a single index value for the **ImageIndex** property and the appropriate image will be displayed regardless of the value of the **View** property of the **ListView** control.

Requirements

Platforms: Windows 98, Windows NT 4.0,
Windows Millennium Edition, Windows 2000,
Windows XP Home Edition, Windows XP Professional,
Windows Server 2003 family,
.NET Compact Framework - Windows CE .NET

ListViewItem.ImageList Property

Gets the **ImageList** that contains the image displayed with the item.

[Visual Basic]
```
Public ReadOnly Property ImageList As ImageList
```
[C#]
```
public ImageList ImageList {get;}
```
[C++]
```
public: __property ImageList* get_ImageList();
```
[JScript]
```
public function get ImageList() : ImageList;
```

Property Value

The **ImageList** used by the **ListView** control that contains the image displayed with the item.

Remarks

Depending on the current value of the **View** property of the **ListView** control associated with the item, the **ImageList** used by the item could be one specified in the **LargeImageList** property or the **SmallImageList** property of the **ListView** control. If the **View** property is set to **View.LargeIcons**, the **ImageList** specified in the **LargeImageList** property is used; otherwise the **ImageList** specified in the **SmallImageList** property is used. You can use this property to determine which **ImageList** control is providing the image for the item. To determine the index position in the **ImageList** that contains the image to display for the item, use the **ImageIndex** property.

Requirements

Platforms: Windows 98, Windows NT 4.0,
Windows Millennium Edition, Windows 2000,
Windows XP Home Edition, Windows XP Professional,
Windows Server 2003 family

ListViewItem.Index Property

Gets the zero-based index of the item within the list view control.

[Visual Basic]
```
Public ReadOnly Property Index As Integer
```
[C#]
```
public int Index {get;}
```
[C++]
```
public: __property int get_Index();
```
[JScript]
```
public function get Index() : int;
```

Property Value

The zero-based index of the item within the **ListView** control's **ListView.ListViewItemCollection**. If the item is not associated with a **ListView** control, this property returns -1.

Remarks

You can use this property to determine if the item is associated with a **ListView** control as well as to determine its position within the **ListView.ListViewItemCollection** of the **ListView**.

Requirements

Platforms: Windows 98, Windows NT 4.0, Windows Millennium Edition, Windows 2000, Windows XP Home Edition, Windows XP Professional, Windows Server 2003 family, .NET Compact Framework - Windows CE .NET

ListViewItem.ListView Property

Gets the **ListView** control that contains the item.

```
[Visual Basic]
Public ReadOnly Property ListView As ListView
[C#]
public ListView ListView {get;}
[C++]
public: __property ListView* get_ListView();
[JScript]
public function get ListView() : ListView;
```

Property Value

A **ListView** that contains the **ListViewItem**.

Remarks

You can use this property to access the **ListView** control that owns the **ListViewItem**.

Requirements

Platforms: Windows 98, Windows NT 4.0, Windows Millennium Edition, Windows 2000, Windows XP Home Edition, Windows XP Professional, Windows Server 2003 family, .NET Compact Framework - Windows CE .NET

ListViewItem.Selected Property

Gets or sets a value indicating whether the item is selected.

```
[Visual Basic]
Public Property Selected As Boolean
[C#]
public bool Selected {get; set;}
[C++]
public: __property bool get_Selected();
public: __property void set_Selected(bool);
[JScript]
public function get Selected() : Boolean;
public function set Selected(Boolean);
```

Property Value

true if the item is selected; otherwise, **false**.

Remarks

If the **MultiSelect** property of the **ListView** control the item is contained in is set to **true**, setting the value of this property adds or removes the item from the set of selected items; if the **MultiSelect** property is set to **false**, setting the value of this property to select an item automatically cancels the selection for any other items in the **ListView** control. You can use this property to determine if an item is selected or to select an item at run time. You can access all items that are selected in a **ListView** control by using the **ListView.SelectedItems** property.

Requirements

Platforms: Windows 98, Windows NT 4.0, Windows Millennium Edition, Windows 2000, Windows XP Home Edition, Windows XP Professional, Windows Server 2003 family, .NET Compact Framework - Windows CE .NET

ListViewItem.StateImageIndex Property

Gets or sets the index of the state image (an image such as a checked or cleared check box that indicates the state of the item) that is displayed for the item.

```
[Visual Basic]
Public Property StateImageIndex As Integer
[C#]
public int StateImageIndex {get; set;}
[C++]
public: __property int get_StateImageIndex();
public: __property void set_StateImageIndex(int);
[JScript]
public function get StateImageIndex() : int;
public function set StateImageIndex(int);
```

Property Value

The zero-based index of the state image in the **ImageList** that is displayed for the item.

Exceptions

Exception Type	Condition
ArgumentOutOfRange-Exception	The value specified for this property is less than -1. -or- The value specified for this property is greater than 14.

Remarks

This property allows you to specify the index into the **ImageList** assigned to the **StateImageList** property of the associated **ListView** control, where the state images to display to the left of the item are stored. Typically the state image is a checked or cleared check box or an image that is intended to represent checked or unchecked states for the item. If no value is specified for the **StateImageList** property, the **ListView** control displays a default checked or cleared check box when the **CheckBoxes** property of the control is set to **true**.

> **Note** Although the **ImageList** specified in the **StateImageList** property can contain any number of images, and the **State-ImageIndex** property can be set to any value lower than 14, only the images at index positions 0 and 1 are displayed as state images.

Requirements

Platforms: Windows 98, Windows NT 4.0,
Windows Millennium Edition, Windows 2000,
Windows XP Home Edition, Windows XP Professional,
Windows Server 2003 family

ListViewItem.SubItems Property

Gets a collection containing all subitems of the item.

```
[Visual Basic]
Public ReadOnly Property SubItems As _
   ListViewItem.ListViewSubItemCollection
[C#]
public ListViewItem.ListViewSubItemCollection SubItems {get;}
[C++]
public: __property ListViewItem.ListViewSubItemCollection*
   get_SubItems();
[JScript]
public function get SubItems() :
   ListViewItem.ListViewSubItemCollection;
```

Property Value

A **ListViewItem.ListViewSubItemCollection** that contains the subitems.

Remarks

Using the **ListViewItem.ListViewSubItemCollection**, you can add subitems, remove subitems, and obtain a count of subitems. For more information on the tasks that can be performed with the subitems in the collection, see the **ListViewItem.ListViewSubItemCollection** class reference topics.

> **Note** The first subitem in the **ListViewItem.ListViewSubItemCollection** is always the item that owns the subitems. Care should be taken when performing operations on subitems in the collection to reference index position 1 instead of 0 to make changes to the first subitem.

Example

See related example in the **System.Windows.Forms.ListView** class topic.

Requirements

Platforms: Windows 98, Windows NT 4.0,
Windows Millennium Edition, Windows 2000,
Windows XP Home Edition, Windows XP Professional,
Windows Server 2003 family,
.NET Compact Framework - Windows CE .NET

ListViewItem.Tag Property

Gets or sets an object that contains data to associate with the item.

```
[Visual Basic]
Public Property Tag As Object
[C#]
public object Tag {get; set;}
[C++]
public: __property Object* get_Tag();
public: __property void set_Tag(Object*);
[JScript]
public function get Tag() : Object;
public function set Tag(Object);
```

Property Value

An object that contains information that is associated with the item.

Remarks

The **Tag** property can be used to store any object that you want to associate with an item. Although you can store any item, the **Tag** property is typically used to store string information about the item such as a unique identifier or the index position of the item's data in a database.

Requirements

Platforms: Windows 98, Windows NT 4.0,
Windows Millennium Edition, Windows 2000,
Windows XP Home Edition, Windows XP Professional,
Windows Server 2003 family

ListViewItem.Text Property

Gets or sets the text of the item.

```
[Visual Basic]
Public Property Text As String
[C#]
public string Text {get; set;}
[C++]
public: __property String* get_Text();
public: __property void set_Text(String*);
[JScript]
public function get Text() : String;
public function set Text(String);
```

Property Value

The text to display for the item.

Remarks

The **Text** property allows you to change the text displayed for the item. You can use the **BackColor**, **ForeColor**, and **Font** properties to specify how the text is displayed. The **ListView** class provides the **LabelWrap** property that determines whether text wraps to the next line or is displayed on a single line.

Requirements

Platforms: Windows 98, Windows NT 4.0,
Windows Millennium Edition, Windows 2000,
Windows XP Home Edition, Windows XP Professional,
Windows Server 2003 family,
.NET Compact Framework - Windows CE .NET

ListViewItem.UseItemStyleForSubItems Property

Gets or sets a value indicating whether the **Font**, **ForeColor**, and **BackColor** properties for the item are used for all its subitems.

```
[Visual Basic]
Public Property UseItemStyleForSubItems As Boolean
[C#]
public bool UseItemStyleForSubItems {get; set;}
[C++]
public: __property bool get_UseItemStyleForSubItems();
public: __property void set_UseItemStyleForSubItems(bool);
[JScript]
public function get UseItemStyleForSubItems() : Boolean;
public function set UseItemStyleForSubItems(Boolean);
```

Property Value

true if all subitems use the font, foreground color, and background color settings of the item; otherwise, **false**. The default is **true**.

Remarks

If you do not want to have a uniform background color, foreground color, and font used for all items and subitems in your **ListView** control, you can set this property to **false**. When this property is set to true, any changes made to the subitem's **ListViewSubItem.Font**, **ListViewSubItem.ForeColor**, and **ListViewSubItem.BackColor** properties are ignored, and the values of the item are used instead. You can use this property if you need to specify a different text color, background color, or font to be used for a subitem to highlight the item when subitems are displayed in the **ListView** control.

Requirements

Platforms: Windows 98, Windows NT 4.0, Windows Millennium Edition, Windows 2000, Windows XP Home Edition, Windows XP Professional, Windows Server 2003 family

ListViewItem.BeginEdit Method

Places the item text into edit mode.

```
[Visual Basic]
Public Sub BeginEdit()
[C#]
public void BeginEdit();
[C++]
public: void BeginEdit();
[JScript]
public function BeginEdit();
```

Exceptions

Exception Type	Condition
InvalidOperation-Exception	The **LabelEdit** property of the associated **ListView** control is not set to **true**.

Remarks

This property is only effective if the **LabelEdit** property of the **ListView** control that contains the item is set to **true**. You can use this method at run time to force the item's text to display in edit mode. For example, if you are validating the item text edited by the user, and an item fails validation, you could select the item in the **ListView** control and call the **BeginEdit** method to force the user to change the text that failed validation.

Requirements

Platforms: Windows 98, Windows NT 4.0, Windows Millennium Edition, Windows 2000, Windows XP Home Edition, Windows XP Professional, Windows Server 2003 family

ListViewItem.Clone Method

Creates an identical copy of the item.

```
[Visual Basic]
Public Overridable Function Clone() As Object Implements _
   ICloneable.Clone
[C#]
public virtual object Clone();
[C++]
public: virtual Object* Clone();
[JScript]
public function Clone() : Object;
```

Return Value

An object that represents an item that has the same text, image, and subitems associated with it as the cloned item.

Implements

ICloneable.Clone

Remarks

You can use this method to create a new instance of the **ListViewItem** class based on an existing item. Even the subitems of the item being cloned are specified for the new version. This feature is useful if you want to reuse a **ListViewItem** in more than one **ListView** control.

Requirements

Platforms: Windows 98, Windows NT 4.0, Windows Millennium Edition, Windows 2000, Windows XP Home Edition, Windows XP Professional, Windows Server 2003 family

ListViewItem.Deserialize Method

Deserializes the item.

```
[Visual Basic]
Protected Overridable Sub Deserialize( _
   ByVal info As SerializationInfo, _
   ByVal context As StreamingContext _
)
[C#]
protected virtual void Deserialize(
   SerializationInfo info,
   StreamingContext context
);
[C++]
protected: virtual void Deserialize(
   SerializationInfo* info,
   StreamingContext context
);
[JScript]
protected function Deserialize(
   info : SerializationInfo,
   context : StreamingContext
);
```

Parameters

info

A **SerializationInfo** that holds the data needed to deserialize the item.

context

A **StreamingContext** that represents the source and destination of the stream being deserialized.

Remarks

Notes to Inheritors: This method should be overridden if you are going to serialize and deserialize your derived version of this class and your derived class contains state information you want to be serialized and deserialized. You must call the base class implementation of this method in order to ensure that your items are serialized and deserialized properly.

Requirements

Platforms: Windows 98, Windows NT 4.0, Windows Millennium Edition, Windows 2000, Windows XP Home Edition, Windows XP Professional, Windows Server 2003 family

ListViewItem.EnsureVisible Method

Ensures that the item is visible within the control, scrolling the contents of the control if necessary.

```
[Visual Basic]
Public Overridable Sub EnsureVisible()
[C#]
public virtual void EnsureVisible();
[C++]
public: virtual void EnsureVisible();
[JScript]
public function EnsureVisible();
```

Remarks

You can use this method to ensure that the item is visible within the **ListView** control. This method can be used when performing validation on the item. You can call the **EnsureVisible** method to ensure that the item is displayed in the **ListView** control, if it failed validation, to allow the user to perform changes on the item.

This method is similar to the **EnsureVisible** method of the **ListView** control.

Requirements

Platforms: Windows 98, Windows NT 4.0, Windows Millennium Edition, Windows 2000, Windows XP Home Edition, Windows XP Professional, Windows Server 2003 family

ListViewItem.GetBounds Method

Retrieves the specified portion of the bounding rectangle for the item.

```
[Visual Basic]
Public Function GetBounds( _
   ByVal portion As ItemBoundsPortion _
) As Rectangle
[C#]
public Rectangle GetBounds(
   ItemBoundsPortion portion
);
[C++]
public: Rectangle GetBounds(
   ItemBoundsPortion portion
);
[JScript]
public function GetBounds(
   portion : ItemBoundsPortion
) : Rectangle;
```

Parameters

portion

One of the **ItemBoundsPortion** values that represents a portion of the item for which to retrieve the bounding rectangle.

Return Value

A **Rectangle** that represents the bounding rectangle for the specified portion of the item.

Remarks

The bounding rectangle returned by the **GetBounds** method represents only the section of the item specified in the *portion* parameter. You can also call the **GetItemRect** methods of the **ListView** class to obtain the bounding rectangle of any item in a **ListView** control.

Requirements

Platforms: Windows 98, Windows NT 4.0, Windows Millennium Edition, Windows 2000, Windows XP Home Edition, Windows XP Professional, Windows Server 2003 family

ListViewItem.ISerializable.GetObjectData Method

This member supports the .NET Framework infrastructure and is not intended to be used directly from your code.

```
[Visual Basic]
Private Sub GetObjectData( _
   ByVal info As SerializationInfo, _
   ByVal context As StreamingContext _
) Implements ISerializable.GetObjectData
[C#]
void ISerializable.GetObjectData(
   SerializationInfo info,
   StreamingContext context
);
[C++]
private: void ISerializable::GetObjectData(
   SerializationInfo* info,
   StreamingContext context
);
[JScript]
private function ISerializable.GetObjectData(
   info : SerializationInfo,
   context : StreamingContext
);
```

ListViewItem.Remove Method

Removes the item from its associated list view control.

```
[Visual Basic]
Public Overridable Sub Remove()
[C#]
public virtual void Remove();
[C++]
public: virtual void Remove();
[JScript]
public function Remove();
```

Remarks

This method is similar in function to the **Remove** method of the **ListView.ListViewItemCollection** in the ListView control that contains the item. You can use this method to remove an item from its **ListView** control. This feature can be useful if you want to move the item to a different **ListView** control or need to remove the item based on a request from the user to remove the item from within your application.

Requirements

Platforms: Windows 98, Windows NT 4.0, Windows Millennium Edition, Windows 2000, Windows XP Home Edition, Windows XP Professional, Windows Server 2003 family

ListViewItem.Serialize Method

Serializes the item.

```
[Visual Basic]
Protected Overridable Sub Serialize( _
   ByVal info As SerializationInfo, _
   ByVal context As StreamingContext _
)
[C#]
protected virtual void Serialize(
   SerializationInfo info,
   StreamingContext context
);
[C++]
protected: virtual void Serialize(
   SerializationInfo* info,
   StreamingContext context
);
[JScript]
protected function Serialize(
   info : SerializationInfo,
   context : StreamingContext
);
```

Parameters

info
  A **SerializationInfo** that holds the data needed to serialize the item.

context
  A **StreamingContext** that represents the source and destination of the stream being serialized.

Remarks

Notes to Inheritors: This method should be overridden if you are going to serialize and deserialize your derived version of this class and your derived class contains state information you want to be serialized and deserialized. You must call the base class implementation of this method in order to ensure that your items are serialized and deserialized properly.

Requirements

Platforms: Windows 98, Windows NT 4.0, Windows Millennium Edition, Windows 2000, Windows XP Home Edition, Windows XP Professional, Windows Server 2003 family

ListViewItem.ToString Method

This member overrides **Object.ToString**.

```
[Visual Basic]
Overrides Public Function ToString() As String
[C#]
public override string ToString();
[C++]
public: String* ToString();
[JScript]
public override function ToString() : String;
```

Requirements

Platforms: Windows 98, Windows NT 4.0, Windows Millennium Edition, Windows 2000, Windows XP Home Edition, Windows XP Professional, Windows Server 2003 family, .NET Compact Framework - Windows CE .NET

ListViewItemConverter Class

Provides a type converter to convert **ListViewItem** objects to and from various other representations.

System.Object
System.ComponentModel.TypeConverter
System.ComponentModel.ExpandableObjectConverter
System.Windows.Forms.ListViewItemConverter

[Visual Basic]
```
Public Class ListViewItemConverter
   Inherits ExpandableObjectConverter
```
[C#]
```
public class ListViewItemConverter : ExpandableObjectConverter
```
[C++]
```
public __gc class ListViewItemConverter : public
   ExpandableObjectConverter
```
[JScript]
```
public class ListViewItemConverter extends
   ExpandableObjectConverter
```

Thread Safety

Any public static (**Shared** in Visual Basic) members of this type are safe for multithreaded operations. Any instance members are not guaranteed to be thread safe.

Remarks

For more information about type converters, see the **TypeConverter** base class and **Implementing a Type Converter**.

> **Note** You should never create an instance of a **ListViewItem-Converter**. Instead, call the **GetConverter** method of **Type-Descriptor**. For more information, see the examples in the **TypeConverter** base class.

Requirements

Namespace: System.Windows.Forms

Platforms: Windows 98, Windows NT 4.0, Windows Millennium Edition, Windows 2000, Windows XP Home Edition, Windows XP Professional, Windows Server 2003 family

Assembly: System.Windows.Forms (in System.Windows.Forms.dll)

ListViewItemConverter Constructor

Initializes a new instance of the **ListViewItemConverter** class.

[Visual Basic]
```
Public Sub New()
```
[C#]
```
public ListViewItemConverter();
```
[C++]
```
public: ListViewItemConverter();
```
[JScript]
```
public function ListViewItemConverter();
```

Remarks

The default constructor initializes any fields to their default values.

Requirements

Platforms: Windows 98, Windows NT 4.0, Windows Millennium Edition, Windows 2000, Windows XP Home Edition, Windows XP Professional, Windows Server 2003 family

ListViewItemConverter.CanConvertTo Method

Overload List

This member supports the .NET Framework infrastructure and is not intended to be used directly from your code.

[Visual Basic] **Overloads Overrides Public Function CanConvertTo(ITypeDescriptorContext, Type) As Boolean**

[C#] **public override bool CanConvertTo(ITypeDescriptorContext, Type);**

[C++] **public: bool CanConvertTo(ITypeDescriptorContext*, Type*);**

[JScript] **public override function CanConvertTo(ITypeDescriptorContext, Type) : Boolean;**

Inherited from **TypeConverter**.

[Visual Basic] **Overloads Public Function CanConvertTo(Type) As Boolean**

[C#] **public bool CanConvertTo(Type);**

[C++] **public: bool CanConvertTo(Type*);**

[JScript] **public function CanConvertTo(Type) : Boolean;**

ListViewItemConverter.CanConvertTo Method (ITypeDescriptorContext, Type)

This member overrides **TypeConverter.CanConvertTo**.

[Visual Basic]
```
Overrides Overloads Public Function CanConvertTo( _
   ByVal context As ITypeDescriptorContext, _
   ByVal destinationType As Type _
) As Boolean
```
[C#]
```
public override bool CanConvertTo(
   ITypeDescriptorContext context,
   Type destinationType
);
```
[C++]
```
public: bool CanConvertTo(
   ITypeDescriptorContext* context,
   Type* destinationType
);
```
[JScript]
```
public override function CanConvertTo(
   context : ITypeDescriptorContext,
   destinationType : Type
) : Boolean;
```

Requirements

Platforms: Windows 98, Windows NT 4.0, Windows Millennium Edition, Windows 2000, Windows XP Home Edition, Windows XP Professional, Windows Server 2003 family

ListViewItemConverter.ConvertTo Method

Overload List

This member supports the .NET Framework infrastructure and is not intended to be used directly from your code.

[Visual Basic] **Overloads Overrides Public Function ConvertTo(ITypeDescriptorContext, CultureInfo, Object, Type) As Object**

[C#] **public override object ConvertTo(ITypeDescriptorContext, CultureInfo, object, Type);**

[C++] **public: Object* ConvertTo(ITypeDescriptorContext*, CultureInfo*, Object*, Type*);**

[JScript] **public override function ConvertTo(ITypeDescriptorContext, CultureInfo, Object, Type) : Object;**

Inherited from **TypeConverter**.

[Visual Basic] **Overloads Public Function ConvertTo(Object, Type) As Object**

[C#] **public object ConvertTo(object, Type);**

[C++] **public: Object* ConvertTo(Object*, Type*);**

[JScript] **public function ConvertTo(Object, Type) : Object;**

ListViewItemConverter.ConvertTo Method (ITypeDescriptorContext, CultureInfo, Object, Type)

This member overrides **TypeConverter.ConvertTo**.

[Visual Basic]
```
Overrides Overloads Public Function ConvertTo( _
   ByVal context As ITypeDescriptorContext, _
   ByVal culture As CultureInfo, _
   ByVal value As Object, _
   ByVal destinationType As Type _
) As Object
```
[C#]
```
public override object ConvertTo(
   ITypeDescriptorContext context,
   CultureInfo culture,
   object value,
   Type destinationType
);
```
[C++]
```
public: Object* ConvertTo(
   ITypeDescriptorContext* context,
   CultureInfo* culture,
   Object* value,
   Type* destinationType
);
```
[JScript]
```
public override function ConvertTo(
   context : ITypeDescriptorContext,
   culture : CultureInfo,
   value : Object,
   destinationType : Type
) : Object;
```

Requirements

Platforms: Windows 98, Windows NT 4.0, Windows Millennium Edition, Windows 2000, Windows XP Home Edition, Windows XP Professional, Windows Server 2003 family

ListViewItem.ListViewSubItem Class

Represents a subitem of a **ListViewItem**.

System.Object
  System.Windows.Forms.ListViewItem.ListViewSubItem

```
[Visual Basic]
<Serializable>
Public Class ListViewItem.ListViewSubItem
[C#]
[Serializable]
public class ListViewItem.ListViewSubItem
[C++]
[Serializable]
public __gc class ListViewItem.ListViewSubItem
[JScript]
public
   Serializable
class ListViewItem.ListViewSubItem
```

Thread Safety

Any public static (**Shared** in Visual Basic) members of this type are safe for multithreaded operations. Any instance members are not guaranteed to be thread safe.

Remarks

A **ListView** control displays a list of items that are defined by the **ListViewItem** class. Each **ListViewItem** can store subitem objects that are defined by the **ListViewItem.ListViewSubItem** class. Subitems are displayed when the **View** property of the **ListView** control is set to **View.Details**. Typically, subitems contain information that is related to their parent item. For example, if a **ListView** control displays items that represent orders, each item could display the order number. Subitems could be added to each item to display information such as the product ordered, the quantity of items ordered, and the total price of the items ordered. Unlike **ListViewItem** objects, **ListViewItem.ListViewSubItem** objects cannot be edited directly by the user (the user can edit **ListViewItem** objects if the **LabelEdit** property of the **ListView** control is set to **true**).

Because subitems cannot be directly edited by the user and do not display images, properties are limited to those that affect the style of the subitem text when it is displayed in the **ListView** control. If the **UseItemStyleForSubItems** property of the **ListView** that contains the subitems is set to **false**, you can use the **Font**, **BackColor**, and **ForeColor** properties to change the styles applied to the text display. Typically, the styles of the item and the subitems are the same in a **ListView** control, but if you want to change the style of a specific **ListViewItem.ListViewSubItem** to highlight it, you can use these properties on the items you want to display differently.

Example

See related example in the **System.Windows.Forms.ListView** class topic.

Requirements

Namespace: System.Windows.Forms

Platforms: Windows 98, Windows NT 4.0, Windows Millennium Edition, Windows 2000, Windows XP Home Edition, Windows XP Professional, Windows Server 2003 family, .NET Compact Framework - Windows CE .NET

Assembly: System.Windows.Forms (in System.Windows.Forms.dll)

ListViewItem.ListViewSubItem Constructor

Initializes a new instance of the **ListViewItem.ListViewSubItem** class.

Overload List

Initializes a new instance of the **ListViewItem.ListViewSubItem** class with default values.

Supported by the .NET Compact Framework.

[Visual Basic] **Public Sub New()**

[C#] **public ListViewItem.ListViewSubItem();**

[C++] **public: ListViewSubItem();**

[JScript] **public function ListViewItem.ListViewSubItem();**

Initializes a new instance of the **ListViewItem.ListViewSubItem** class with a specified owner and text.

[Visual Basic] **Public Sub New(ListViewItem, String)**

[C#] **public ListViewItem.ListViewSubItem(ListViewItem, string);**

[C++] **public: ListViewSubItem(ListViewItem*, String*);**

[JScript] **public function ListViewItem.ListViewSubItem(ListViewItem, String);**

Initializes a new instance of the **ListViewItem.ListViewSubItem** class with a specified owner, text, foreground color, background color, and font values.

[Visual Basic] **Public Sub New(ListViewItem, String, Color, Color, Font)**

[C#] **public ListViewItem.ListViewSubItem(ListViewItem, string, Color, Color, Font);**

[C++] **public: ListViewSubItem(ListViewItem*, String*, Color, Color, Font*);**

[JScript] **public function ListViewItem.ListViewSubItem(ListViewItem, String, Color, Color, Font);**

ListViewItem.ListViewSubItem Constructor ()

Initializes a new instance of the **ListViewItem.ListViewSubItem** class with default values.

```
[Visual Basic]
Public Sub New()
[C#]
public ListViewItem.ListViewSubItem();
[C++]
public: ListViewSubItem();
[JScript]
public function ListViewItem.ListViewSubItem();
```

Requirements

Platforms: Windows 98, Windows NT 4.0, Windows Millennium Edition, Windows 2000, Windows XP Home Edition, Windows XP Professional, Windows Server 2003 family, .NET Compact Framework - Windows CE .NET

ListViewItem.ListViewSubItem Constructor (ListViewItem, String)

Initializes a new instance of the **ListViewItem.ListViewSubItem** class with a specified owner and text.

```
[Visual Basic]
Public Sub New( _
   ByVal owner As ListViewItem, _
   ByVal text As String _
)
[C#]
public ListViewItem.ListViewSubItem(
   ListViewItem owner,
   string text
);
[C++]
public: ListViewSubItem(
   ListViewItem* owner,
   String* text
);
[JScript]
public function ListViewItem.ListViewSubItem(
   owner : ListViewItem,
   text : String
);
```

Parameters

owner
A **ListViewItem** that represents the item that owns the subitem.

text
The text to display for the subitem.

Requirements

Platforms: Windows 98, Windows NT 4.0, Windows Millennium Edition, Windows 2000, Windows XP Home Edition, Windows XP Professional, Windows Server 2003 family

ListViewItem.ListViewSubItem Constructor (ListViewItem, String, Color, Color, Font)

Initializes a new instance of the **ListViewItem.ListViewSubItem** class with a specified owner, text, foreground color, background color, and font values.

```
[Visual Basic]
Public Sub New( _
   ByVal owner As ListViewItem, _
   ByVal text As String, _
   ByVal foreColor As Color, _
   ByVal backColor As Color, _
   ByVal font As Font _
)
[C#]
public ListViewItem.ListViewSubItem(
   ListViewItem owner,
   string text,
   Color foreColor,
   Color backColor,
   Font font
);
[C++]
public: ListViewSubItem(
   ListViewItem* owner,
   String* text,
   Color foreColor,
   Color backColor,
   Font* font
);
[JScript]
public function ListViewItem.ListViewSubItem(
   owner : ListViewItem,
   text : String,
   foreColor : Color,
   backColor : Color,
   font : Font
);
```

Parameters

owner
A **ListViewItem** that represents the item that owns the subitem.

text
The text to display for the subitem.

foreColor
A **Color** that represents the foreground color of the subitem.

backColor
A **Color** that represents the background color of the subitem.

font
A **Font** that represents the typeface to display the subitem's text in.

Requirements

Platforms: Windows 98, Windows NT 4.0, Windows Millennium Edition, Windows 2000, Windows XP Home Edition, Windows XP Professional, Windows Server 2003 family

ListViewItem.ListViewSubItem.BackColor Property

Gets or sets the background color of the subitem's text.

```
[Visual Basic]
Public Property BackColor As Color
[C#]
public Color BackColor {get; set;}
[C++]
public: __property Color get_BackColor();
public: __property void set_BackColor(Color);
[JScript]
public function get BackColor() : Color;
public function set BackColor(Color);
```

Property Value

A **Color** that represents the background color of the subitem's text.

Remarks

You can use the **BackColor** property to change the color displayed behind the subitem text. This property can be used if you want to use different background and foreground color combinations (using the **ForeColor** property to set the foreground color) to differentiate one subitem from another. For example, you could set the **BackColor** property to **Color.Red** to identify subitems that display a negative value.

If the **UseItemStyleForSubItems** property of the **ListViewItem** that owns the subitem is set to **true**, setting this property has no effect.

Requirements

Platforms: Windows 98, Windows NT 4.0,
Windows Millennium Edition, Windows 2000,
Windows XP Home Edition, Windows XP Professional,
Windows Server 2003 family

ListViewItem.ListViewSubItem.Font Property

Gets or sets the font of the text displayed by the subitem.

```
[Visual Basic]
Public Property Font As Font
[C#]
public Font Font {get; set;}
[C++]
public: __property Font* get_Font();
public: __property void set_Font(Font*);
[JScript]
public function get Font() : Font;
public function set Font(Font);
```

Property Value

The **Font** to apply to the text displayed by the control.

Remarks

You can use this method to change the typeface styles applied to the text of the subitem. If the **UseItemStyleForSubItems** property of the **ListViewItem** is set to **true**, changing this property will have no effect. Because the **Font** is immutable (meaning that you cannot adjust any of its properties), you can only assign the **Font** property a new **Font**. However, you can base the new font on the existing font.

[Visual Basic, C#]] The following is an example of how to adjust the existing font to make it bold:

```
[C#]
listViewItem1.SubItems[1].Font = new
Font(listViewItem1.SubItems[1].Font,
   listViewItem1.SubItems[1].Font.Style | FontStyle.Bold);
```

```
[Visual Basic]
ListViewItem1.SubItems[1].Font = New
Font(ListViewItem1.SubItems[1].Font, _
   ListViewItem1.SubItems[1].Font.Style Or FontStyle.Bold)
```

If the **UseItemStyleForSubItems** property of the **ListViewItem** that owns the subitem is set to **true**, setting this property has no effect.

Requirements

Platforms: Windows 98, Windows NT 4.0,
Windows Millennium Edition, Windows 2000,
Windows XP Home Edition, Windows XP Professional,
Windows Server 2003 family

ListViewItem.ListViewSubItem.ForeColor Property

Gets or sets the foreground color of the subitem's text.

```
[Visual Basic]
Public Property ForeColor As Color
[C#]
public Color ForeColor {get; set;}
[C++]
public: __property Color get_ForeColor();
public: __property void set_ForeColor(Color);
[JScript]
public function get ForeColor() : Color;
public function set ForeColor(Color);
```

Property Value

A **Color** that represents the foreground color of the subitem's text.

Remarks

You can use the **ForeColor** property to change the color of the subitem text. This property can be used if you want to use different background and foreground color combinations (using the **BackColor** property to set the background color) to differentiate one item from another. For example, you could set the **ForeColor** property to **Color.Red** to identify items that have a negative number associated with them.

If the **UseItemStyleForSubItems** property of the **ListViewItem** that owns the subitem is set to **true**, setting this property has no effect.

Requirements

Platforms: Windows 98, Windows NT 4.0,
Windows Millennium Edition, Windows 2000,
Windows XP Home Edition, Windows XP Professional,
Windows Server 2003 family

ListViewItem.ListViewSubItem.Text Property

Gets or sets the text of the subitem.

```
[Visual Basic]
Public Property Text As String
[C#]
public string Text {get; set;}
[C++]
public: __property String* get_Text();
public: __property void set_Text(String*);
[JScript]
public function get Text() : String;
public function set Text(String);
```

Property Value

The text to display for the subitem.

Remarks

The **Text** property allows you to determine the text displayed for the subitem. You can use the **BackColor**, **ForeColor**, and **Font** properties to specify how the text is displayed.

Requirements

Platforms: Windows 98, Windows NT 4.0,
Windows Millennium Edition, Windows 2000,
Windows XP Home Edition, Windows XP Professional,
Windows Server 2003 family,
.NET Compact Framework - Windows CE .NET

ListViewItem.ListViewSubItem.ResetStyle Method

Resets the styles applied to the subitem.

[Visual Basic]
```
Public Sub ResetStyle()
```
[C#]
```
public void ResetStyle();
```
[C++]
```
public: void ResetStyle();
```
[JScript]
```
public function ResetStyle();
```

Remarks

You can use this method to reset the font, background color, and foreground color settings applied to the subitem. When the styles are reset, the subitem is displayed using the default font, background color, and foreground color settings.

Requirements

Platforms: Windows 98, Windows NT 4.0, Windows Millennium Edition, Windows 2000, Windows XP Home Edition, Windows XP Professional, Windows Server 2003 family

ListViewItem.ListViewSubItem.ToString Method

This member overrides **Object.ToString**.

[Visual Basic]
```
Overrides Public Function ToString() As String
```
[C#]
```
public override string ToString();
```
[C++]
```
public: String* ToString();
```
[JScript]
```
public override function ToString() : String;
```

Requirements

Platforms: Windows 98, Windows NT 4.0, Windows Millennium Edition, Windows 2000, Windows XP Home Edition, Windows XP Professional, Windows Server 2003 family, .NET Compact Framework - Windows CE .NET

ListViewItem.ListViewSubItem Collection Class

Represents a collection of **ListViewItem.ListViewSubItem** objects stored in a **ListViewItem**.

System.Object
  System.Windows.Forms.ListViewItem.ListViewSubItem-Collection

[Visual Basic]
```
Public Class ListViewItem.ListViewSubItemCollection
   Implements IList, ICollection, IEnumerable
```
[C#]
```
public class ListViewItem.ListViewSubItemCollection : IList,
   ICollection, IEnumerable
```
[C++]
```
public __gc class ListViewItem.ListViewSubItemCollection : public
   IList, ICollection, IEnumerable
```
[JScript]
```
public class ListViewItem.ListViewSubItemCollection implements
   IList, ICollection, IEnumerable
```

Thread Safety

Any public static (**Shared** in Visual Basic) members of this type are safe for multithreaded operations. Any instance members are not guaranteed to be thread safe.

Remarks

A **ListViewItem.ListViewSubItemCollection** stores **ListViewItem.ListViewSubItem** objects that represent subitems of a parent **ListViewItem** in the **ListView** control. Subitems are only displayed in a **ListView** control when columns are specified in the **Columns** property of the **ListView** control and when the **View** property of the **ListView** control is set to **View.Details**. The order of subitems in the **ListViewItem.ListViewSubItemCollection** determines the columns the subitems are displayed in in the **ListView** control.

There are a number of ways to add subitems to the collection. The **Add** method adds a single **ListViewItem.ListViewSubItem** to the collection. To add a number of subitems to the collection, you create an array of **ListViewItem.ListViewSubItem** objects and pass it to the **AddRange** method. If you want to insert a subitem at a specific location in the collection, you can use the **Insert** method. To remove subitems, you can use either the **Remove** method or the **RemoveAt** method if you know where the subitem is located in the collection. The **Clear** method enables you to remove all subitems from the collection instead of using the **Remove** method to remove a single subitem at a time.

In addition to methods and properties for adding and removing subitems, the **ListViewItem.ListViewSubItemCollection** also provides methods to find subitems in the collection. The **Contains** method enables you to determine whether a **ListViewItem.ListViewSubItem** is a member of the collection. Once you know that the subitem is located in the collection, you can use the **IndexOf** method to determine where the subitem is located in the collection.

Requirements

Namespace: System.Windows.Forms

Platforms: Windows 98, Windows NT 4.0, Windows Millennium Edition, Windows 2000, Windows XP Home Edition, Windows XP Professional, Windows Server 2003 family, .NET Compact Framework - Windows CE .NET

Assembly: System.Windows.Forms (in System.Windows.Forms.dll)

ListViewItem.ListViewSubItemCollection Constructor

Initializes a new instance of the **ListViewItem.ListViewSubItemCollection** class.

[Visual Basic]
```
Public Sub New( _
   ByVal owner As ListViewItem _
)
```
[C#]
```
public ListViewItem.ListViewSubItemCollection(
   ListViewItem owner
);
```
[C++]
```
public: ListViewSubItemCollection(
   ListViewItem* owner
);
```
[JScript]
```
public function ListViewItem.ListViewSubItemCollection(
   owner : ListViewItem
);
```

Parameters

owner
  The **ListViewItem** that owns the collection.

Remarks

You cannot create an instance of this class without associating it with a **ListViewItem**.

Requirements

Platforms: Windows 98, Windows NT 4.0, Windows Millennium Edition, Windows 2000, Windows XP Home Edition, Windows XP Professional, Windows Server 2003 family

ListViewItem.ListViewSubItemCollection.Count Property

Gets the number of subitems in the collection.

[Visual Basic]
```
Public Overridable ReadOnly Property Count As Integer  Implements _
   ICollection.Count
```
[C#]
```
public virtual int Count {get;}
```
[C++]
```
public: __property virtual int get_Count();
```
[JScript]
```
public function get Count() : int;
```

Property Value

The number of subitems in the collection.

Implements

ICollection.Count

Remarks

This property enables you to determine the number of subitems that are defined for a **ListViewItem**. You can then use this value when you are looping through the values of the collection and you need to provide a number of iterations to perform the loop.

Requirements

Platforms: Windows 98, Windows NT 4.0, Windows Millennium Edition, Windows 2000, Windows XP Home Edition, Windows XP Professional, Windows Server 2003 family, .NET Compact Framework - Windows CE .NET

ListViewItem.ListViewSubItemCollection.IsReadOnly Property

Gets a value indicating whether the collection is read-only.

[Visual Basic]
```
Public Overridable ReadOnly Property IsReadOnly As Boolean _
   Implements IList.IsReadOnly
```
[C#]
```
public virtual bool IsReadOnly {get;}
```
[C++]
```
public: __property virtual bool get_IsReadOnly();
```
[JScript]
```
public function get IsReadOnly() : Boolean;
```

Property Value

true if the collection is read-only; otherwise, **false**.

Implements

IList.IsReadOnly

Remarks

This property is always **false** for this collection.

Requirements

Platforms: Windows 98, Windows NT 4.0, Windows Millennium Edition, Windows 2000, Windows XP Home Edition, Windows XP Professional, Windows Server 2003 family, .NET Compact Framework - Windows CE .NET

ListViewItem.ListViewSubItemCollection.Item Property

Gets or sets the subitem at the specified index within the collection.

[C#] In C#, this property is the indexer for the **ListViewItem.ListViewSubItemCollection** class.

[Visual Basic]
```
Public Default Property Item( _
   ByVal index As Integer _
) As ListViewItem.ListViewSubItem
```
[C#]
```
public ListViewItem.ListViewSubItem this[
   int index
] {get; set;}
```
[C++]
```
public: __property ListViewItem.ListViewSubItem* get_Item(
   int index
);
public: __property void set_Item(
   int index,
   ListViewItem.ListViewSubItem*
);
```
[JScript]
```
returnValue = ListViewSubItemCollectionObject.Item(index);
ListViewSubItemCollectionObject.Item(index) = returnValue;
-or-
returnValue = ListViewSubItemCollectionObject(index);
ListViewSubItemCollectionObject(index) = returnValue;
```

[JScript] In JScript, you can use the default indexed properties defined by a type, but you cannot explicitly define your own. However, specifying the **expando** attribute on a class automatically provides a default indexed property whose type is **Object** and whose index type is **String**.

Arguments [JScript]

index
 The index of the item in the collection to retrieve.

Parameters [Visual Basic, C#, C++]

index
 The index of the item in the collection to retrieve.

Property Value

A **ListViewItem.ListViewSubItem** representing the subitem located at the specified index within the collection.

Exceptions

Exception Type	Condition
ArgumentOutOfRange-Exception	The *index* parameter is less than zero or greater than or equal to the value of the **Count** property of the **ListView-Item.ListViewSubItemCollection**.

Remarks

You can use this method to obtain the **ListViewItem.ListView-SubItem** stored at a specific location in the collection. To determine the index of a specific item in the collection, use the **IndexOf** method.

Requirements

Platforms: Windows 98, Windows NT 4.0, Windows Millennium Edition, Windows 2000, Windows XP Home Edition, Windows XP Professional, Windows Server 2003 family

ListViewItem.ListViewSubItemCollection.System.Collections.ICollection.IsSynchronized Property

Note: This namespace, class, or member is supported only in version 1.1 of the .NET Framework.

This member supports the .NET Framework infrastructure and is not intended to be used directly from your code.

[Visual Basic]
```
Private ReadOnly Property IsSynchronized As Boolean Implements _
   ICollection.IsSynchronized
```

[C#]
```
bool ICollection.IsSynchronized {get;}
```
[C++]
```
private: __property bool
   System::Collections::ICollection::get_IsSynchronized();
```
[JScript]
```
private function get ICollection.IsSynchronized() : Boolean;
```

ListViewItem.ListViewSubItemCollection.System.Collections.ICollection.SyncRoot Property

Note: This namespace, class, or member is supported only in version 1.1 of the .NET Framework.

This member supports the .NET Framework infrastructure and is not intended to be used directly from your code.

[Visual Basic]
```
Private ReadOnly Property SyncRoot As Object Implements _
   ICollection.SyncRoot
```
[C#]
```
object ICollection.SyncRoot {get;}
```
[C++]
```
private: __property Object*
   System::Collections::ICollection::get_SyncRoot();
```
[JScript]
```
private function get ICollection.SyncRoot() : Object;
```

ListViewItem.ListViewSubItemCollection.System.Collections.IList.IsFixedSize Property

Note: This namespace, class, or member is supported only in version 1.1 of the .NET Framework.

This member supports the .NET Framework infrastructure and is not intended to be used directly from your code.

[Visual Basic]
```
Private ReadOnly Property IsFixedSize As Boolean Implements _
   IList.IsFixedSize
```
[C#]
```
bool IList.IsFixedSize {get;}
```
[C++]
```
private: __property bool
   System::Collections::IList::get_IsFixedSize();
```
[JScript]
```
private function get IList.IsFixedSize() : Boolean;
```

ListViewItem.ListViewSubItemCollection.System.Collections.IList.Item Property

Note: This namespace, class, or member is supported only in version 1.1 of the .NET Framework.

[C#] In C#, this property is the indexer for the **ListViewItem.ListViewSubItemCollection** class.

[Visual Basic]
```
Private Default Property Item( _
   ByVal index As Integer _
) As Object Implements IList.Item
```
[C#]
```
object IList.this[
   int index
] {get; set;}
```
[C++]
```
private: __property Object* System::Collections::IList::get_Item(
   int index
);
private: __property void System::Collections::IList::set_Item(
   int index,
   Object*
);
```
[JScript]
```
private function get IList.get_Item(index : int) : Object;
private function set IList.set_Item(index : int, value : Object);
-or-
private function get IList.get_Item(index : int) : Object;
private function set IList.set_Item(index : int, value : Object);
```

[JScript] In JScript, you can use the default indexed properties defined by a type, but you cannot explicitly define your own. However, specifying the **expando** attribute on a class automatically provides a default indexed property whose type is **Object** and whose index type is **String**.

Arguments [JScript]

index

Parameters [Visual Basic, C#, C++]

index

Requirements

Platforms: Windows 98, Windows NT 4.0, Windows Millennium Edition, Windows 2000, Windows XP Home Edition, Windows XP Professional, Windows Server 2003 family

ListViewItem.ListViewSubItemCollection.Add Method

Adds a subitem to the collection of subitems.

Overload List

Adds an existing **ListViewItem.ListViewSubItem** to the collection.

Supported by the .NET Compact Framework.

[Visual Basic] **Overloads Public Function Add(ListViewItem.ListViewSubItem) As ListViewSubItem**

[C#] **public ListViewSubItem Add(ListViewItem.ListViewSubItem);**

[C++] **public: ListViewSubItem* Add(ListViewItem.ListViewSubItem*);**

[JScript] **public function Add(ListViewItem.ListViewSubItem) : ListViewSubItem;**

Adds a subitem to the collection with specified text.

Supported by the .NET Compact Framework.

[Visual Basic] **Overloads Public Function Add(String) As ListViewSubItem**

[C#] **public ListViewSubItem Add(string);**

[C++] **public: ListViewSubItem* Add(String*);**

[JScript] **public function Add(String) : ListViewSubItem;**

Adds a subitem to the collection with specified text, foreground color, background color, and font settings.

[Visual Basic] **Overloads Public Function Add(String, Color, Color, Font) As ListViewSubItem**

[C#] **public ListViewSubItem Add(string, Color, Color, Font);**

[C++] **public: ListViewSubItem* Add(String*, Color, Color, Font*);**

[JScript] **public function Add(String, Color, Color, Font) : ListViewSubItem;**

Example

See related example in the **System.Windows.Forms.ListView** class topic.

ListViewItem.ListViewSubItemCollection.Add Method (ListViewItem.ListViewSubItem)

Adds an existing **ListViewItem.ListViewSubItem** to the collection.

[Visual Basic]
```
Overloads Public Function Add( _
   ByVal item As ListViewItem.ListViewSubItem _
) As ListViewSubItem
```
[C#]
```
public ListViewSubItem Add(
   ListViewItem.ListViewSubItem item
);
```
[C++]
```
public: ListViewSubItem* Add(
   ListViewItem.ListViewSubItem* item
);
```
[JScript]
```
public function Add(
   item : ListViewItem.ListViewSubItem
) : ListViewSubItem;
```

Parameters

item

The **ListViewItem.ListViewSubItem** to add to the collection.

Return Value

The **ListViewItem.ListViewSubItem** that was added to the collection.

Remarks

You can use this version of the **Add** method to add an existing **ListViewItem.ListViewSubItem** to the collection. This method is typically used to reuse existing subitems from other **ListViewItem** objects. Items that are added to the collection are inserted at the end of the list. To insert an item into the collection at a specific position, use the **Insert** method. If you want to add an array of existing **ListViewItem.ListViewSubItem** objects, you can use the version of the **AddRange** method that accepts an array of **ListViewItem.ListViewSubItem** objects as a parameter.

Requirements

Platforms: Windows 98, Windows NT 4.0, Windows Millennium Edition, Windows 2000, Windows XP Home Edition, Windows XP Professional, Windows Server 2003 family, .NET Compact Framework - Windows CE .NET

ListViewItem.ListViewSubItemCollection.Add Method (String)

Adds a subitem to the collection with specified text.

[Visual Basic]
```
Overloads Public Function Add( _
   ByVal text As String _
) As ListViewSubItem
```
[C#]
```
public ListViewSubItem Add(
   string text
);
```
[C++]
```
public: ListViewSubItem* Add(
   String* text
);
```
[JScript]
```
public function Add(
   text : String
) : ListViewSubItem;
```

Parameters

text

The text to display for the subitem.

Return Value

The **ListViewItem.ListViewSubItem** that was added to the collection.

Remarks

This version of the **Add** method allows you to add a subitem to the collection by specifying the text of the subitem. When this method is called, a new **ListViewItem.ListViewSubItem** is created with the specified text. You can then use the **ListViewItem.ListViewSubItem** that is returned by this method to set properties and call methods to manipulate the subitem. If you already have an existing **ListViewItem.ListViewSubItem** that you want to add to the collection, you can use the version of the **Add** method that accepts a **ListViewItem.ListViewSubItem** as a parameter, or use the **Insert** method if you want to add the subitem at a specific position within the collection.

Example

See related example in the **System.Windows.Forms.ListView** class topic.

Requirements

Platforms: Windows 98, Windows NT 4.0, Windows Millennium Edition, Windows 2000, Windows XP Home Edition, Windows XP Professional, Windows Server 2003 family, .NET Compact Framework - Windows CE .NET

ListViewItem.ListViewSubItemCollection.Add Method (String, Color, Color, Font)

Adds a subitem to the collection with specified text, foreground color, background color, and font settings.

[Visual Basic]
```
Overloads Public Function Add( _
   ByVal text As String, _
   ByVal foreColor As Color, _
   ByVal backColor As Color, _
   ByVal font As Font _
) As ListViewSubItem
```

[C#]
```
public ListViewSubItem Add(
   string text,
   Color foreColor,
   Color backColor,
   Font font
);
```
[C++]
```
public: ListViewSubItem* Add(
   String* text,
   Color foreColor,
   Color backColor,
   Font* font
);
```
[JScript]
```
public function Add(
   text : String,
   foreColor : Color,
   backColor : Color,
   font : Font
) : ListViewSubItem;
```

Parameters

text
: The text to display for the subitem.

foreColor
: A **Color** that represents the foreground color of the subitem.

backColor
: A **Color** that represents the background color of the subitem.

font
: A **Font** that represents the typeface to display the subitem's text in.

Return Value

The **ListViewItem.ListViewSubItem** that was added to the collection.

Remarks

This version of the **Add** method allows you to add a subitem to the collection by specifying the text of the subitem. In addition, this version of the Add method allows you to specify the initial foreground color, background color, and font of the subitem text. When this method is called, a new **ListViewItem.ListViewSubItem** is created with the specified text. You can then use the **ListViewItem.ListViewSubItem** that is returned by this method to set properties and call methods to manipulate the subitem. If you already have an existing **ListViewItem.ListViewSubItem** that you want to add to the collection, you can use the version of the **Add** method that accepts a **ListViewItem.ListViewSubItem** as a parameter, or use the **Insert** method if you want to add the subitem at a specific position in the collection.

Requirements

Platforms: Windows 98, Windows NT 4.0, Windows Millennium Edition, Windows 2000, Windows XP Home Edition, Windows XP Professional, Windows Server 2003 family

ListViewItem.ListViewSubItemCollection.AddRange Method

Adds an array of subitems to the collection.

Overload List

Adds an array of **ListViewItem.ListViewSubItem** objects to the collection.

[Visual Basic] **Overloads Public Sub AddRange(ListViewItem.ListViewSubItem())**

[C#] **public void AddRange(ListViewItem.ListViewSubItem[]);**

[C++] **public: void AddRange(ListViewItem.ListViewSubItem*[]);**

[JScript] **public function AddRange(ListViewItem.ListViewSubItem[]);**

Creates new subitems based on an array and adds them to the collection.

[Visual Basic] **Overloads Public Sub AddRange(String())**

[C#] **public void AddRange(string[]);**

[C++] **public: void AddRange(String*[]);**

[JScript] **public function AddRange(String[]);**

Creates new subitems based on an array and adds them to the collection with specified foreground color, background color, and font.

[Visual Basic] **Overloads Public Sub AddRange(String(), Color, Color, Font)**

[C#] **public void AddRange(string[], Color, Color, Font);**

[C++] **public: void AddRange(String*[], Color, Color, Font*);**

[JScript] **public function AddRange(String[], Color, Color, Font);**

ListViewItem.ListViewSubItemCollection.AddRange Method (ListViewItem.ListViewSubItem[])

Adds an array of **ListViewItem.ListViewSubItem** objects to the collection.

[Visual Basic]
```
Overloads Public Sub AddRange( _
   ByVal items() As ListViewItem.ListViewSubItem _
)
```
[C#]
```
public void AddRange(
   ListViewItem.ListViewSubItem[] items
);
```
[C++]
```
public: void AddRange(
   ListViewItem.ListViewSubItem* items[]
);
```
[JScript]
```
public function AddRange(
   items : ListViewItem.ListViewSubItem[]
);
```

Parameters

items
: An array of **ListViewItem.ListViewSubItem** objects to add to the collection.

Remarks

This method removes all existing subitems from the parent **ListViewItem** before inserting the new items. You can use this method to reuse the subitems stored in a different **ListViewItem**. If you want to add a single **ListViewItem.ListViewSubItem** object, use the **Add** method. You can also use the **Insert** method if you want to add a single **ListViewItem.ListViewSubItem** at a specific position in the collection.

Requirements

Platforms: Windows 98, Windows NT 4.0, Windows Millennium Edition, Windows 2000, Windows XP Home Edition, Windows XP Professional, Windows Server 2003 family

ListViewItem.ListViewSubItemCollection.AddRange Method (String[])

Creates new subitems based on an array and adds them to the collection.

```
[Visual Basic]
Overloads Public Sub AddRange( _
   ByVal items() As String _
)
[C#]
public void AddRange(
   string[] items
);
[C++]
public: void AddRange(
   String* items __gc[]
);
[JScript]
public function AddRange(
   items : String[]
);
```

Parameters

items

An array of strings representing the text of each subitem to add to the collection.

Remarks

This method removes all existing subitems from the parent **ListViewItem** before inserting the new items. You can use this version of the **AddRange** method to add an array of strings to the collection, where each string in the collection represents the text of a new subitem. You can use the other version of the **AddRange** method that accepts an array of strings as a parameter to specify the foreground color, background color, and font for each item being added. If you want to reuse existing **ListViewItem.ListViewSubItem** objects and add them to the collection, you can use the version of the **AddRange** method that accepts an array of **ListViewItem.ListViewSubItem** objects as a parameter.

If you want to add a single **ListViewItem.ListViewSubItem**, use the **Add** method. You can also use the **Insert** method if you want to add a single **ListViewItem.ListViewSubItem** at a specific position in the collection.

Requirements

Platforms: Windows 98, Windows NT 4.0, Windows Millennium Edition, Windows 2000, Windows XP Home Edition, Windows XP Professional, Windows Server 2003 family

ListViewItem.ListViewSubItemCollection.AddRange Method (String[], Color, Color, Font)

Creates new subitems based on an array and adds them to the collection with specified foreground color, background color, and font.

```
[Visual Basic]
Overloads Public Sub AddRange( _
   ByVal items() As String, _
   ByVal foreColor As Color, _
   ByVal backColor As Color, _
   ByVal font As Font _
)
[C#]
public void AddRange(
   string[] items,
   Color foreColor,
   Color backColor,
   Font font
);
[C++]
public: void AddRange(
   String* items __gc[],
   Color foreColor,
   Color backColor,
   Font* font
);
[JScript]
public function AddRange(
   items : String[],
   foreColor : Color,
   backColor : Color,
   font : Font
);
```

Parameters

items

An array of strings representing the text of each subitem to add to the collection.

foreColor

A **Color** that represents the foreground color of the subitem.

backColor

A **Color** that represents the background color of the subitem.

font

A **Font** that represents the typeface to display the subitem's text in.

Remarks

This method removes all existing subitems from the parent **ListViewItem** before inserting the new items. You can use this version of the **AddRange** method to add an array of strings to the collection, where each string in the collection represents the text of a new subitem. In addition, this version of the **AddRange** method allows you to specify the foreground color, background color, and font for each subitem. You can use the other version of the **AddRange** method that accepts an array of strings as a parameter if you do not want to specify foreground color, background color, and font settings for each subitem. If you want to reuse existing **ListViewItem.ListViewSubItem** objects and add them to the collection, you can use the version of the **AddRange** method that accepts an array of **ListViewItem.ListViewSubItem** objects as a parameter.

If you want to add a single **ListViewItem.ListViewSubItem**, use the **Add** method. You can also use the **Insert** method if you want to add a single **ListViewItem.ListViewSubItem** at a specific position in the collection.

Requirements

Platforms: Windows 98, Windows NT 4.0, Windows Millennium Edition, Windows 2000, Windows XP Home Edition, Windows XP Professional, Windows Server 2003 family

ListViewItem.ListViewSubItemCollection.Clear Method

Removes all subitems from the collection.

[Visual Basic]
```
Public Overridable Sub Clear() Implements IList.Clear
```
[C#]
```
public virtual void Clear();
```
[C++]
```
public: virtual void Clear();
```
[JScript]
```
public function Clear();
```

Implements

IList.Clear

Remarks

When you remove subitems from the collection, all information about the deleted subitems is lost. To remove a single subitem from the collection use the **Remove** or **RemoveAt** method.

Requirements

Platforms: Windows 98, Windows NT 4.0, Windows Millennium Edition, Windows 2000, Windows XP Home Edition, Windows XP Professional, Windows Server 2003 family, .NET Compact Framework - Windows CE .NET

ListViewItem.ListViewSubItemCollection.Contains Method

Determines whether the specified subitem is located in the collection.

[Visual Basic]
```
Public Function Contains( _
   ByVal subItem As ListViewItem.ListViewSubItem _
) As Boolean
```
[C#]
```
public bool Contains(
   ListViewItem.ListViewSubItem subItem
);
```
[C++]
```
public: bool Contains(
   ListViewItem.ListViewSubItem* subItem
);
```
[JScript]
```
public function Contains(
   subItem : ListViewItem.ListViewSubItem
) : Boolean;
```

Parameters

subItem
: A **ListViewItem.ListViewSubItem** representing the subitem to locate in the collection.

Return Value

true if the subitem is contained in the collection; otherwise, **false**.

Remarks

The **Contains** method enables you to determine whether a **ListViewItem.ListViewSubItem** is a member of the collection. Once you know that the subitem is in the collection, you can use the **IndexOf** method to determine the position of the subitem in the collection.

Requirements

Platforms: Windows 98, Windows NT 4.0, Windows Millennium Edition, Windows 2000, Windows XP Home Edition, Windows XP Professional, Windows Server 2003 family, .NET Compact Framework - Windows CE .NET

ListViewItem.ListViewSubItemCollection.GetEnumerator Method

Returns an enumerator to use to iterate through the subitem collection.

[Visual Basic]
```
Public Overridable Function GetEnumerator() As IEnumerator _
   Implements IEnumerable.GetEnumerator
```
[C#]
```
public virtual IEnumerator GetEnumerator();
```
[C++]
```
public: virtual IEnumerator* GetEnumerator();
```
[JScript]
```
public function GetEnumerator() : IEnumerator;
```

Return Value

An **IEnumerator** that represents the subitem collection.

Implements

IEnumerable.GetEnumerator

Requirements

Platforms: Windows 98, Windows NT 4.0, Windows Millennium Edition, Windows 2000, Windows XP Home Edition, Windows XP Professional, Windows Server 2003 family, .NET Compact Framework - Windows CE .NET

ListViewItem.ListViewSubItemCollection.ICollection.CopyTo Method

This member supports the .NET Framework infrastructure and is not intended to be used directly from your code.

[Visual Basic]
```
Private Sub CopyTo( _
   ByVal dest As Array, _
   ByVal index As Integer _
) Implements ICollection.CopyTo
```
[C#]
```
void ICollection.CopyTo(
   Array dest,
   int index
);
```
[C++]
```
private: void ICollection::CopyTo(
   Array* dest,
   int index
);
```
[JScript]
```
private function ICollection.CopyTo(
   dest : Array,
   index : int
);
```

ListViewItem.ListViewSubItemCollection.IList.Add Method

This member supports the .NET Framework infrastructure and is not intended to be used directly from your code.

[Visual Basic]
```
Private Function Add( _
   ByVal item As Object _
) As Integer Implements IList.Add
```
[C#]
```
int IList.Add(
   object item
);
```
[C++]
```
private: int IList::Add(
   Object* item
);
```
[JScript]
```
private function IList.Add(
   item : Object
) : int;
```

ListViewItem.ListViewSubItemCollection.IList.Contains Method

This member supports the .NET Framework infrastructure and is not intended to be used directly from your code.

[Visual Basic]
```
Private Function Contains( _
   ByVal subItem As Object _
) As Boolean Implements IList.Contains
```
[C#]
```
bool IList.Contains(
   object subItem
);
```
[C++]
```
private: bool IList::Contains(
   Object* subItem
);
```
[JScript]
```
private function IList.Contains(
   subItem : Object
) : Boolean;
```

ListViewItem.ListViewSubItemCollection.IList.IndexOf Method

This member supports the .NET Framework infrastructure and is not intended to be used directly from your code.

[Visual Basic]
```
Private Function IndexOf( _
   ByVal subItem As Object _
) As Integer Implements IList.IndexOf
```
[C#]
```
int IList.IndexOf(
   object subItem
);
```
[C++]
```
private: int IList::IndexOf(
   Object* subItem
);
```
[JScript]
```
private function IList.IndexOf(
   subItem : Object
) : int;
```

ListViewItem.ListViewSubItemCollection.IList.Insert Method

This member supports the .NET Framework infrastructure and is not intended to be used directly from your code.

[Visual Basic]
```
Private Sub Insert( _
   ByVal index As Integer, _
   ByVal item As Object _
) Implements IList.Insert
```
[C#]
```
void IList.Insert(
   int index,
   object item
);
```
[C++]
```
private: void IList::Insert(
   int index,
   Object* item
);
```
[JScript]
```
private function IList.Insert(
   index : int,
   item : Object
);
```

ListViewItem.ListViewSubItemCollection.IList.Remove Method

This member supports the .NET Framework infrastructure and is not intended to be used directly from your code.

```
[Visual Basic]
Private Sub Remove( _
   ByVal item As Object _
) Implements IList.Remove
[C#]
void IList.Remove(
   object item
);
[C++]
private: void IList::Remove(
   Object* item
);
[JScript]
private function IList.Remove(
   item : Object
);
```

ListViewItem.ListViewSubItemCollection.IndexOf Method

Returns the index within the collection of the specified subitem.

```
[Visual Basic]
Public Function IndexOf( _
   ByVal subItem As ListViewItem.ListViewSubItem _
) As Integer
[C#]
public int IndexOf(
   ListViewItem.ListViewSubItem subItem
);
[C++]
public: int IndexOf(
   ListViewItem.ListViewSubItem* subItem
);
[JScript]
public function IndexOf(
   subItem : ListViewItem.ListViewSubItem
) : int;
```

Parameters

subItem

A **ListViewItem.ListViewSubItem** representing the subitem to locate in the collection.

Return Value

The zero-based index of the subitem's location in the collection. If the subitem is not located in the collection, the return value is negative one (-1).

Remarks

The **IndexOf** method enables you to determine the position of a subitem in the collection. To determine whether a subitem is contained in the collection before calling this method, use the **Contains** method.

Requirements

Platforms: Windows 98, Windows NT 4.0, Windows Millennium Edition, Windows 2000, Windows XP Home Edition, Windows XP Professional, Windows Server 2003 family, .NET Compact Framework - Windows CE .NET

ListViewItem.ListViewSubItemCollection.Insert Method

Inserts a subitem into the collection at the specified index.

```
[Visual Basic]
Public Sub Insert( _
   ByVal index As Integer, _
   ByVal item As ListViewItem.ListViewSubItem _
)
[C#]
public void Insert(
   int index,
   ListViewItem.ListViewSubItem item
);
[C++]
public: void Insert(
   int index,
   ListViewItem.ListViewSubItem* item
);
[JScript]
public function Insert(
   index : int,
   item : ListViewItem.ListViewSubItem
);
```

Parameters

index

The zero-based index location where the item is inserted.

item

A **ListViewItem.ListViewSubItem** representing the subitem to insert into the collection.

Exceptions

Exception Type	Condition
ArgumentOutOfRange-Exception	The *index* parameter is less than zero or greater than or equal to the value of the **Count** property of the **ListView-Item.ListViewSubItemCollection**.

Remarks

This method allows you to insert a subitem at a specific position in the **ListViewItem.ListViewSubItemCollection**. To add a subitem without specifying a specific position, use the **Add** method. If you want to add an array of subitems to the collection, use the **Add-Range** method. You can use this method if you want to insert a new subitem into an existing collection of subitems.

Requirements

Platforms: Windows 98, Windows NT 4.0, Windows Millennium Edition, Windows 2000, Windows XP Home Edition, Windows XP Professional, Windows Server 2003 family, .NET Compact Framework - Windows CE .NET

ListViewItem.ListViewSubItemCollection.Remove Method

Removes the specified **ListViewItem.ListViewSubItem** from the collection.

[Visual Basic]
```
Public Sub Remove( _
   ByVal item As ListViewItem.ListViewSubItem _
)
```
[C#]
```
public void Remove(
   ListViewItem.ListViewSubItem item
);
```
[C++]
```
public: void Remove(
   ListViewItem.ListViewSubItem* item
);
```
[JScript]
```
public function Remove(
   item : ListViewItem.ListViewSubItem
);
```

Parameters

item

A **ListViewItem.ListViewSubItem** representing the item to remove from the collection.

Remarks

When you remove a subitem from the collection, the indexes change for subsequent subitems in the collection. All information about the removed subitem is deleted. You can use this method to remove a specific subitem from the collection by specifying the actual subitem to remove from the collection. To specify the index of the subitem to remove instead of the subitem itself, use the **RemoveAt** method. To remove all subitems from the collection, use the **Clear** method.

Requirements

Platforms: Windows 98, Windows NT 4.0, Windows Millennium Edition, Windows 2000, Windows XP Home Edition, Windows XP Professional, Windows Server 2003 family, .NET Compact Framework - Windows CE .NET

ListViewItem.ListViewSubItemCollection.RemoveAt Method

Removes the subitem at the specified index within the collection.

[Visual Basic]
```
Public Overridable Sub RemoveAt( _
   ByVal index As Integer _
) Implements IList.RemoveAt
```
[C#]
```
public virtual void RemoveAt(
   int index
);
```
[C++]
```
public: virtual void RemoveAt(
   int index
);
```
[JScript]
```
public function RemoveAt(
   index : int
);
```

Parameters

index

The zero-based index of the subitem to remove.

Implements

IList.RemoveAt

Exceptions

Exception Type	Condition
ArgumentOutOfRange-Exception	The *index* parameter is less than zero or greater than or equal to the value of the **Count** property of the **ListView-Item.ListViewSubItemCollection**.

Remarks

When you remove a subitem from the collection, the indexes change for subsequent subitems in the collection. All information about the removed subitem is deleted. You can use this method to remove a specific subitem from the collection by specifying the index of the subitem to remove from the collection. To specify the subitem to remove instead of the index to the subitem, use the **Remove** method. To remove all subitems from the collection, use the **Clear** method.

Requirements

Platforms: Windows 98, Windows NT 4.0, Windows Millennium Edition, Windows 2000, Windows XP Home Edition, Windows XP Professional, Windows Server 2003 family, .NET Compact Framework - Windows CE .NET

ListView.ListViewItem-Collection Class

Represents the collection of items in a **ListView** control.

System.Object
  System.Windows.Forms.ListView.ListViewItemCollection

[Visual Basic]
```
Public Class ListView.ListViewItemCollection
   Implements IList, ICollection, IEnumerable
```
[C#]
```
public class ListView.ListViewItemCollection : IList, ICollection,
   IEnumerable
```
[C++]
```
public __gc class ListView.ListViewItemCollection : public IList,
   ICollection, IEnumerable
```
[JScript]
```
public class ListView.ListViewItemCollection implements IList,
   ICollection, IEnumerable
```

Thread Safety

Any public static (**Shared** in Visual Basic) members of this type are safe for multithreaded operations. Any instance members are not guaranteed to be thread safe.

Remarks

A **ListView.ListViewItemCollection** stores the items displayed in the **ListView** control. There are two other collections defined within the **ListView** class that enable you to determine what items are selected within this collection. The **ListView.SelectedListView-ItemCollection** class provides properties and methods for determining what items are selected in the **ListView.ListViewItem-Collection**, while the **ListView.SelectedIndexCollection** class enables you to determine what indexes within the **ListView.List-ViewItemCollection** are selected. In addition to selection collection classes there are also two classes that enable you to determine what items are checked (when the **CheckBoxes** property of the **ListView** control is set to **true**) within this collection.

There are a number of ways to add items to the collection. The **Add** method adds a single item to the collection. To add a number of items to the collection, you create an array of items and pass it to the **AddRange** method. If you want to insert an item at a specific location in the collection, you can use the **Insert** method. To remove items, you can use either the **Remove** method or the **RemoveAt** method if you know where the item is located in the collection. The **Clear** method enables you to remove all items from the collection instead of using the **Remove** method to remove a single item at a time.

In addition to methods and properties for adding and removing items, the **ListView.ListViewItemCollection** also provides methods to find items in the collection. The **Contains** method enables you to determine whether an item is a member of the collection. Once you know that the item is located in the collection, you can use the **IndexOf** method to determine where the item is located in the collection.

Requirements

Namespace: System.Windows.Forms

Platforms: Windows 98, Windows NT 4.0, Windows Millennium Edition, Windows 2000, Windows XP Home Edition, Windows XP Professional, Windows Server 2003 family, .NET Compact Framework - Windows CE .NET

Assembly: System.Windows.Forms (in System.Windows.Forms.dll)

ListView.ListViewItemCollection Constructor

Initializes a new instance of the **ListView.ListViewItemCollection** class.

[Visual Basic]
```
Public Sub New( _
   ByVal owner As ListView _
)
```
[C#]
```
public ListView.ListViewItemCollection(
   ListView owner
);
```
[C++]
```
public: ListViewItemCollection(
   ListView* owner
);
```
[JScript]
```
public function ListView.ListViewItemCollection(
   owner : ListView
);
```

Parameters

owner
  The **ListView** that owns the collection.

Remarks

You cannot create an instance of this class without associating it with a **ListView** control.

Requirements

Platforms: Windows 98, Windows NT 4.0, Windows Millennium Edition, Windows 2000, Windows XP Home Edition, Windows XP Professional, Windows Server 2003 family

ListView.ListViewItemCollection.Count Property

Gets the number of items in the collection.

[Visual Basic]
```
Public Overridable ReadOnly Property Count As Integer  Implements _
   ICollection.Count
```
[C#]
```
public virtual int Count {get;}
```
[C++]
```
public: __property virtual int get_Count();
```
[JScript]
```
public function get Count() : int;
```

Property Value

The number of items in the collection.

Implements

ICollection.Count

Remarks

This property enables you to determine the number of items in the **ListView**. You can then use this value when you are looping through the values of the collection and you need to provide a number of iterations to perform the loop.

Requirements

Platforms: Windows 98, Windows NT 4.0, Windows Millennium Edition, Windows 2000, Windows XP Home Edition, Windows XP Professional, Windows Server 2003 family, .NET Compact Framework - Windows CE .NET

ListView.ListViewItemCollection.IsReadOnly Property

Gets a value indicating whether the collection is read-only.

```
[Visual Basic]
Public Overridable ReadOnly Property IsReadOnly As Boolean _
   Implements IList.IsReadOnly
[C#]
public virtual bool IsReadOnly {get;}
[C++]
public: __property virtual bool get_IsReadOnly();
[JScript]
public function get IsReadOnly() : Boolean;
```

Property Value

true if the collection is read-only; otherwise, **false**.

Implements

IList.IsReadOnly

Remarks

This property is always **false** for this collection.

Requirements

Platforms: Windows 98, Windows NT 4.0, Windows Millennium Edition, Windows 2000, Windows XP Home Edition, Windows XP Professional, Windows Server 2003 family, .NET Compact Framework - Windows CE .NET

ListView.ListViewItemCollection.Item Property

Gets or sets the item at the specified index within the collection.

[C#] In C#, this property is the indexer for the **ListView.ListViewItemCollection** class.

```
[Visual Basic]
Public Overridable Default Property Item( _
   ByVal displayIndex As Integer _
) As ListViewItem
[C#]
public virtual ListViewItem this[
   int displayIndex
] {get; set;}
[C++]
public: __property virtual ListViewItem* get_Item(
   int displayIndex
);
public: __property virtual void set_Item(
   int displayIndex,
   ListViewItem*
);
[JScript]
returnValue = ListViewItemCollectionObject.Item(displayIndex);
ListViewItemCollectionObject.Item(displayIndex) = returnValue;
-or-
returnValue = ListViewItemCollectionObject(displayIndex);
ListViewItemCollectionObject(displayIndex) = returnValue;
```

[JScript] In JScript, you can use the default indexed properties defined by a type, but you cannot explicitly define your own. However, specifying the **expando** attribute on a class automatically provides a default indexed property whose type is **Object** and whose index type is **String**.

Arguments [JScript]

displayIndex
  The index of the item in the collection to get or set.

Parameters [Visual Basic, C#, C++]

displayIndex
  The index of the item in the collection to get or set.

Property Value

A **ListViewItem** representing the item located at the specified index within the collection.

Exceptions

Exception Type	Condition
ArgumentOutOfRange-Exception	The *index* parameter is less than zero or greater than or equal to the value of the **Count** property of the **ListView.ListViewItemCollection**.

Remarks

You can use this method to obtain the **ListViewItem** stored at a specific location in the collection. To determine the index of a specific item in the collection, use the **IndexOf** method.

Requirements

Platforms: Windows 98, Windows NT 4.0, Windows Millennium Edition, Windows 2000, Windows XP Home Edition, Windows XP Professional, Windows Server 2003 family

ListView.ListViewItemCollection.System.Collections.ICollection.IsSynchronized Property

Note: This namespace, class, or member is supported only in version 1.1 of the .NET Framework

This member supports the .NET Framework infrastructure and is not intended to be used directly from your code.

```
[Visual Basic]
Private ReadOnly Property IsSynchronized As Boolean Implements _
   ICollection.IsSynchronized
[C#]
bool ICollection.IsSynchronized {get;}
```

```
[C++]
private: __property bool
   System::Collections::ICollection::get_IsSynchronized();
[JScript]
private function get ICollection.IsSynchronized() : Boolean;
```

ListView.ListViewItemCollection.System.Collections.ICollection.SyncRoot Property

Note: This namespace, class, or member is supported only in version 1.1 of the .NET Framework

This member supports the .NET Framework infrastructure and is not intended to be used directly from your code.

```
[Visual Basic]
Private ReadOnly Property SyncRoot As Object Implements _
   ICollection.SyncRoot
[C#]
object ICollection.SyncRoot {get;}
[C++]
private: __property Object*
   System::Collections::ICollection::get_SyncRoot();
[JScript]
private function get ICollection.SyncRoot() : Object;
```

ListView.ListViewItemCollection.System.Collections.IList.IsFixedSize Property

Note: This namespace, class, or member is supported only in version 1.1 of the .NET Framework

This member supports the .NET Framework infrastructure and is not intended to be used directly from your code.

```
[Visual Basic]
Private ReadOnly Property IsFixedSize As Boolean Implements _
   IList.IsFixedSize
[C#]
bool IList.IsFixedSize {get;}
[C++]
private: __property bool
   System::Collections::IList::get_IsFixedSize();
[JScript]
private function get IList.IsFixedSize() : Boolean;
```

ListView.ListViewItemCollection.System.Collections.IList.Item Property

Note: This namespace, class, or member is supported only in version 1.1 of the .NET Framework

[C#] In C#, this property is the indexer for the **ListView.ListViewItemCollection** class.

```
[Visual Basic]
Private Default Property Item( _
   ByVal index As Integer _
) As Object Implements IList.Item
[C#]
object IList.this[
   int index
] {get; set;}
[C++]
private: __property Object* System::Collections::IList::get_Item(
   int index
);
private: __property void System::Collections::IList::set_Item(
   int index,
   Object*
);
[JScript]
private function get IList.get_Item(index : int) : Object;
private function set IList.set_Item(index : int, value : Object);
-or-
private function get IList.get_Item(index : int) : Object;
private function set IList.set_Item(index : int, value : Object);
```

[JScript] In JScript, you can use the default indexed properties defined by a type, but you cannot explicitly define your own. However, specifying the **expando** attribute on a class automatically provides a default indexed property whose type is **Object** and whose index type is **String**.

Arguments [JScript]

index

Parameters [Visual Basic, C#, C++]

index

Requirements

Platforms: Windows 98, Windows NT 4.0, Windows Millennium Edition, Windows 2000, Windows XP Home Edition, Windows XP Professional, Windows Server 2003 family

ListView.ListViewItemCollection.Add Method

Adds an item to the collection of items.

Overload List

Adds an existing **ListViewItem** object to the collection.

Supported by the .NET Compact Framework.

[Visual Basic] **Overloads Public Overridable Function Add(ListViewItem) As ListViewItem**

[C#] **public virtual ListViewItem Add(ListViewItem);**

[C++] **public: virtual ListViewItem* Add(ListViewItem*);**

[JScript] **public function Add(ListViewItem) : ListViewItem;**

Adds an item to the collection with the specified text.

[Visual Basic] **Overloads Public Overridable Function Add(String) As ListViewItem**

[C#] **public virtual ListViewItem Add(string);**

[C++] **public: virtual ListViewItem* Add(String*);**

[JScript] **public function Add(String) : ListViewItem;**

Adds an item to the collection with the specified text and image.

[Visual Basic] **Overloads Public Overridable Function Add(String, Integer) As ListViewItem**

[C#] **public virtual ListViewItem Add(string, int);**

[C++] **public: virtual ListViewItem* Add(String*, int);**

[JScript] **public function Add(String, int) : ListViewItem;**

ListView.ListViewItemCollection.Add Method (ListViewItem)

Adds an existing **ListViewItem** object to the collection.

```
[Visual Basic]
Overloads Public Overridable Function Add( _
   ByVal value As ListViewItem _
) As ListViewItem
[C#]
public virtual ListViewItem Add(
   ListViewItem value
);
[C++]
public: virtual ListViewItem* Add(
   ListViewItem* value
);
[JScript]
public function Add(
   value : ListViewItem
) : ListViewItem;
```

Parameters

value

The **ListViewItem** to add to the collection.

Return Value

The **ListViewItem** that was added to the collection.

Remarks

You can use this version of the **Add** method to add an existing **ListViewItem** to the collection. This version of the **Add** method is typically used to reuse items from other **ListView** controls or if the **ListViewItem** was created manually before adding it to the collection. If you want to create a new **ListViewItem** instead of using an existing item, use the other versions of the **Add** method.

If the **Sorting** property of the **ListView** is set to **true**, the item is inserted into the list alphabetically. Otherwise, the item is inserted at the end of the list. To insert an item into the **ListView** at a specific position, use the **Insert** method. To add a set of items to the control in a single operation, use the **AddRange** method. If you want to use the **Add** method to add a large number of items to the control, use the **BeginUpdate** and **EndUpdate** methods to prevent the **ListView** from repainting until all items are added. When adding items to a **ListView**, it is more efficient to sort the items first and then add new items.

Requirements

Platforms: Windows 98, Windows NT 4.0, Windows Millennium Edition, Windows 2000, Windows XP Home Edition, Windows XP Professional, Windows Server 2003 family, .NET Compact Framework - Windows CE .NET

ListView.ListViewItemCollection.Add Method (String)

Adds an item to the collection with the specified text.

```
[Visual Basic]
Overloads Public Overridable Function Add( _
   ByVal text As String _
) As ListViewItem
[C#]
public virtual ListViewItem Add(
   string text
);
[C++]
public: virtual ListViewItem* Add(
   String* text
);
[JScript]
public function Add(
   text : String
) : ListViewItem;
```

Parameters

text

The text to display for the item.

Return Value

The **ListViewItem** that was added to the collection.

Remarks

You can use this version of the **Add** method to create a new **ListViewItem** to add to the **ListView** control. The text of the new **ListViewItem** added to the control is based on the *text* parameter. If you want to specify an image for the item, use the version of the **Add** method that accepts an image index as a parameter. If you have an existing **ListViewItem** that you want to add to the collection, use the version of the **Add** method that accepts a **ListViewItem** as its parameter.

If the **Sorting** property of the **ListView** is set to **true**, the item is inserted into the list alphabetically. Otherwise, the item is inserted at the end of the list. To insert an item into the **ListView** at a specific position, use the **Insert** method. To add a set of items to the control in a single operation, use the **AddRange** method. If you want to use the **Add** method to add a large number of items to the control, use the **BeginUpdate** and **EndUpdate** methods to prevent the **ListView** from repainting until all items are added. When adding items to a **ListView**, it is more efficient to sort the items first and then add new items.

Requirements

Platforms: Windows 98, Windows NT 4.0, Windows Millennium Edition, Windows 2000, Windows XP Home Edition, Windows XP Professional, Windows Server 2003 family

ListView.ListViewItemCollection.Add Method (String, Int32)

Adds an item to the collection with the specified text and image.

```
[Visual Basic]
Overloads Public Overridable Function Add( _
   ByVal text As String, _
   ByVal imageIndex As Integer _
) As ListViewItem
[C#]
public virtual ListViewItem Add(
   string text,
   int imageIndex
);
[C++]
public: virtual ListViewItem* Add(
   String* text,
   int imageIndex
);
[JScript]
public function Add(
   text : String,
   imageIndex : int
) : ListViewItem;
```

Parameters

text

The text of the item.

imageIndex

The index of the image to display for the item.

Return Value

The **ListViewItem** that was added to the collection.

Remarks

You can use this version of the **Add** method to create a new **ListViewItem** to add to the **ListView** control. The text of the new **ListViewItem** added to the control is based on the *text* parameter. You can also specify an image to use for the item by passing an index into the **ImageList** assigned to the **ListView.LargeImageList** and **ListView.SmallImageList** properties (typically these two properties use the same index positions for related images to display) to the *imageIndex* parameter. If you do not want to specify an image index for the item, use the version of the **Add** method that only accepts a string as a parameter. If you have an existing **ListViewItem** that you want to add to the collection, use the version of the **Add** method that accepts a **ListViewItem** as its parameter.

If the **Sorting** property of the **ListView** is set to **true**, the item is inserted into the list alphabetically. Otherwise, the item is inserted at the end of the list. To insert an item into the **ListView** at a specific position, use the **Insert** method. To add a set of items to the control in a single operation, use the **AddRange** method. If you want to use the **Add** method to add a large number of items to the control, use the **BeginUpdate** and **EndUpdate** methods to prevent the **ListView** from repainting until all items are added. When adding items to a **ListView**, it is more efficient to sort the items first and then add new items.

Requirements

Platforms: Windows 98, Windows NT 4.0,
Windows Millennium Edition, Windows 2000,
Windows XP Home Edition, Windows XP Professional,
Windows Server 2003 family

ListView.ListViewItemCollection.AddRange Method

Adds an array of **ListViewItem** objects to the collection.

```
[Visual Basic]
Public Sub AddRange( _
   ByVal values() As ListViewItem _
)
[C#]
public void AddRange(
   ListViewItem[] values
);
[C++]
public: void AddRange(
   ListViewItem* values[]
);
[JScript]
public function AddRange(
   values : ListViewItem[]
);
```

Parameters

values

An array of **ListViewItem** objects to add to the collection.

Remarks

This method removes all existing items from the **ListView** control before inserting the new items. You can use this method to reuse items from a different **ListView** control. If you want to add a single **ListViewItem**, use the **Add** method. You can also use the **Insert** method if you want to add a single **ListViewItem** at a specific position in the collection.

Example

See related example in the **System.Windows.Forms.ListView** class topic.

Requirements

Platforms: Windows 98, Windows NT 4.0,
Windows Millennium Edition, Windows 2000,
Windows XP Home Edition, Windows XP Professional,
Windows Server 2003 family

ListView.ListViewItemCollection.Clear Method

Removes all items from the collection.

```
[Visual Basic]
Public Overridable Sub Clear() Implements IList.Clear
[C#]
public virtual void Clear();
[C++]
public: virtual void Clear();
[JScript]
public function Clear();
```

Implements

IList.Clear

Remarks

When you remove items from the collection, all information about the deleted items is lost. To remove a single item from the collection use the **Remove** or **RemoveAt** method.

Requirements

Platforms: Windows 98, Windows NT 4.0,
Windows Millennium Edition, Windows 2000,
Windows XP Home Edition, Windows XP Professional,
Windows Server 2003 family,
.NET Compact Framework - Windows CE .NET

ListView.ListViewItemCollection.Contains Method

Determines whether the specified item is located in the collection.

```
[Visual Basic]
Public Function Contains( _
   ByVal item As ListViewItem _
) As Boolean
[C#]
public bool Contains(
   ListViewItem item
);
```

```
[C++]
public: bool Contains(
   ListViewItem* item
);
[JScript]
public function Contains(
   item : ListViewItem
) : Boolean;
```

Parameters

item

A **ListViewItem** representing the item to locate in the collection.

Return Value

true if the item is contained in the collection; otherwise, **false**.

Remarks

The **Contains** method enables you to determine whether a **ListViewItem** is a member of the collection. Once you know that the item is the collection, you can use the **IndexOf** method to determine the position of the item in the collection.

Requirements

Platforms: Windows 98, Windows NT 4.0, Windows Millennium Edition, Windows 2000, Windows XP Home Edition, Windows XP Professional, Windows Server 2003 family, .NET Compact Framework - Windows CE .NET

ListView.ListViewItemCollection.CopyTo Method

Copies the entire collection into an existing array at a specified location within the array.

```
[Visual Basic]
Public Overridable Sub CopyTo( _
   ByVal dest As Array, _
   ByVal index As Integer _
) Implements ICollection.CopyTo
[C#]
public virtual void CopyTo(
   Array dest,
   int index
);
[C++]
public: virtual void CopyTo(
   Array* dest,
   int index
);
[JScript]
public function CopyTo(
   dest : Array,
   index : int
);
```

Parameters

dest

An **Array** representing the array to copy the contents of the collection to.

index

The location within the destination array to copy the items from the collection to.

Implements

ICollection.CopyTo

Remarks

You can use this method to combine the selected items from multiple collections into a single array.

Requirements

Platforms: Windows 98, Windows NT 4.0, Windows Millennium Edition, Windows 2000, Windows XP Home Edition, Windows XP Professional, Windows Server 2003 family, .NET Compact Framework - Windows CE .NET

ListView.ListViewItemCollection.GetEnumerator Method

Returns an enumerator to use to iterate through the item collection.

```
[Visual Basic]
Public Overridable Function GetEnumerator() As IEnumerator _
   Implements IEnumerable.GetEnumerator
[C#]
public virtual IEnumerator GetEnumerator();
[C++]
public: virtual IEnumerator* GetEnumerator();
[JScript]
public function GetEnumerator() : IEnumerator;
```

Return Value

An **IEnumerator** that represents the item collection.

Implements

IEnumerable.GetEnumerator

Requirements

Platforms: Windows 98, Windows NT 4.0, Windows Millennium Edition, Windows 2000, Windows XP Home Edition, Windows XP Professional, Windows Server 2003 family, .NET Compact Framework - Windows CE .NET

ListView.ListViewItemCollection.IList.Add Method

This member supports the .NET Framework infrastructure and is not intended to be used directly from your code.

```
[Visual Basic]
Private Function Add( _
   ByVal item As Object _
) As Integer Implements IList.Add
[C#]
int IList.Add(
   object item
);
[C++]
private: int IList::Add(
   Object* item
);
[JScript]
private function IList.Add(
   item : Object
) : int;
```

ListView.ListViewItemCollection.IList.Contains Method

This member supports the .NET Framework infrastructure and is not intended to be used directly from your code.

```
[Visual Basic]
Private Function Contains( _
   ByVal item As Object _
) As Boolean Implements IList.Contains
[C#]
bool IList.Contains(
   object item
);
[C++]
private: bool IList::Contains(
   Object* item
);
[JScript]
private function IList.Contains(
   item : Object
) : Boolean;
```

ListView.ListViewItemCollection.IList.IndexOf Method

This member supports the .NET Framework infrastructure and is not intended to be used directly from your code.

```
[Visual Basic]
Private Function IndexOf( _
   ByVal item As Object _
) As Integer Implements IList.IndexOf
[C#]
int IList.IndexOf(
   object item
);
[C++]
private: int IList::IndexOf(
   Object* item
);
[JScript]
private function IList.IndexOf(
   item : Object
) : int;
```

ListView.ListViewItemCollection.IList.Insert Method

This member supports the .NET Framework infrastructure and is not intended to be used directly from your code.

```
[Visual Basic]
Private Sub Insert( _
   ByVal index As Integer, _
   ByVal item As Object _
) Implements IList.Insert
[C#]
void IList.Insert(
   int index,
   object item
);
[C++]
private: void IList::Insert(
   int index,
   Object* item
);
[JScript]
private function IList.Insert(
   index : int,
   item : Object
);
```

ListView.ListViewItemCollection.IList.Remove Method

This member supports the .NET Framework infrastructure and is not intended to be used directly from your code.

```
[Visual Basic]
Private Sub Remove( _
   ByVal item As Object _
) Implements IList.Remove
[C#]
void IList.Remove(
   object item
);
[C++]
private: void IList::Remove(
   Object* item
);
[JScript]
private function IList.Remove(
   item : Object
);
```

ListView.ListViewItemCollection.IndexOf Method

Returns the index within the collection of the specified item.

```
[Visual Basic]
Public Function IndexOf( _
   ByVal item As ListViewItem _
) As Integer
[C#]
public int IndexOf(
   ListViewItem item
);
[C++]
public: int IndexOf(
   ListViewItem* item
);
[JScript]
public function IndexOf(
   item : ListViewItem
) : int;
```

Parameters

item

A **ListViewItem** representing the item to locate in the collection.

Return Value

The zero-based index of the item's location in the collection. If the item is not located in the collection, the return value is negative one (-1).

Remarks

The **IndexOf** method enables you to determine the position of an item in the collection. To determine whether an item is contained in the collection before calling this method, use the **Contains** method.

Requirements

Platforms: Windows 98, Windows NT 4.0,
Windows Millennium Edition, Windows 2000,
Windows XP Home Edition, Windows XP Professional,
Windows Server 2003 family,
.NET Compact Framework - Windows CE .NET

ListView.ListViewItemCollection.Insert Method

Inserts an item into the collection at the specified index.

Overload List

Inserts an existing **ListViewItem** into the collection at the specified index.

Supported by the .NET Compact Framework.

[Visual Basic] **Overloads Public Function Insert(Integer, ListViewItem) As ListViewItem**

[C#] **public ListViewItem Insert(int, ListViewItem);**

[C++] **public: ListViewItem* Insert(int, ListViewItem*);**

[JScript] **public function Insert(int, ListViewItem) : ListViewItem;**

Creates a new item and inserts it into the collection at the specified index.

[Visual Basic] **Overloads Public Function Insert(Integer, String) As ListViewItem**

[C#] **public ListViewItem Insert(int, string);**

[C++] **public: ListViewItem* Insert(int, String*);**

[JScript] **public function Insert(int, String) : ListViewItem;**

Creates a new item with the specified image index and inserts it into the collection at the specified index.

[Visual Basic] **Overloads Public Function Insert(Integer, String, Integer) As ListViewItem**

[C#] **public ListViewItem Insert(int, string, int);**

[C++] **public: ListViewItem* Insert(int, String*, int);**

[JScript] **public function Insert(int, String, int) : ListViewItem;**

ListView.ListViewItemCollection.Insert Method (Int32, ListViewItem)

Inserts an existing **ListViewItem** into the collection at the specified index.

```
[Visual Basic]
Overloads Public Function Insert( _
   ByVal index As Integer, _
   ByVal item As ListViewItem _
) As ListViewItem
[C#]
public ListViewItem Insert(
   int index,
   ListViewItem item
);
[C++]
public: ListViewItem* Insert(
   int index,
   ListViewItem* item
);
[JScript]
public function Insert(
   index : int,
   item : ListViewItem
) : ListViewItem;
```

Parameters

index
The zero-based index location where the item is inserted.

item
The **ListViewItem** that represents the item to insert.

Return Value

The **ListViewItem** that was inserted into the collection.

Exceptions

Exception Type	Condition
ArgumentOutOfRange-Exception	The *index* parameter is less than zero or greater than or equal to the value of the **Count** property of the **List-View.ListViewItemCollection**.

Remarks

This version of the **Insert** method allows you to insert an existing **ListViewItem** at a specific position in the **ListView.ListView-ItemCollection**.

To add an item without specifying a specific position in the collection to add the item, use the **Add** method. If you want to add an array of items to the collection, use the **AddRange** method. You can use this method if you want to insert a new item into an existing collection of items.

Requirements

Platforms: Windows 98, Windows NT 4.0,
Windows Millennium Edition, Windows 2000,
Windows XP Home Edition, Windows XP Professional,
Windows Server 2003 family,
.NET Compact Framework - Windows CE .NET

ListView.ListViewItemCollection.Insert Method (Int32, String)

Creates a new item and inserts it into the collection at the specified index.

```
[Visual Basic]
Overloads Public Function Insert( _
   ByVal index As Integer, _
   ByVal text As String _
) As ListViewItem
[C#]
public ListViewItem Insert(
   int index,
   string text
);
```

[C++]
```
public: ListViewItem* Insert(
   int index,
   String* text
);
```
[JScript]
```
public function Insert(
   index : int,
   text : String
) : ListViewItem;
```

Parameters

index
The zero-based index location where the item is inserted.

text
The text to display for the item.

Return Value

The **ListViewItem** that was inserted into the collection.

Exceptions

Exception Type	Condition
ArgumentOutOfRange-Exception	The *index* parameter is less than zero or greater than or equal to the value of the **Count** property of the **ListView.ListViewItemCollection**.

Remarks

This version of the **Insert** method allows you to insert a new item at a specific position in the **ListView.ListViewItemCollection**. The text specified in the *text* parameter is used to create a new **ListViewItem** that is then inserted into the **ListView.ListViewItemCollection** at the specified location.

To add an item without specifying a specific position in the collection, use the **Add** method. If you want to add an array of items to the collection, use the **AddRange** method. You can use this method if you want to insert a new item into an existing collection of items.

Requirements

Platforms: Windows 98, Windows NT 4.0, Windows Millennium Edition, Windows 2000, Windows XP Home Edition, Windows XP Professional, Windows Server 2003 family

ListView.ListViewItemCollection.Insert Method (Int32, String, Int32)

Creates a new item with the specified image index and inserts it into the collection at the specified index.

[Visual Basic]
```
Overloads Public Function Insert( _
   ByVal index As Integer, _
   ByVal text As String, _
   ByVal imageIndex As Integer _
) As ListViewItem
```
[C#]
```
public ListViewItem Insert(
   int index,
   string text,
   int imageIndex
);
```
[C++]
```
public: ListViewItem* Insert(
   int index,
   String* text,
   int imageIndex
);
```
[JScript]
```
public function Insert(
   index : int,
   text : String,
   imageIndex : int
) : ListViewItem;
```

Parameters

index
The zero-based index location where the item is inserted.

text
The text to display for the item.

imageIndex
The index of the image to display for the item.

Return Value

The **ListViewItem** that was inserted into the collection.

Exceptions

Exception Type	Condition
ArgumentOutOfRange-Exception	The *index* parameter is less than zero or greater than or equal to the value of the **Count** property of the **ListView.ListViewItemCollection**.

Remarks

This version of the **Insert** method allows you to insert a new item at a specific position in the **ListView.ListViewItemCollection**. The text specified in the *text* parameter is used to create a new **ListViewItem** that is then inserted into the **ListView.ListViewItemCollection** at the specified location. You can also use this version of the **Insert** method to specify an image to display for the item by passing an index into the **ImageList** assigned to the **ListView.LargeImageList** and **ListView.SmallImageList** properties (typically these two properties use the same index positions for related images to display) to the *imageIndex* parameter. If you do not want to specify an image index for the item, use the other version of the **Insert** method that accepts a string as a parameter.

To add an item without specifying a specific position in the collection, use the **Add** method. If you want to add an array of items to the collection, use the **AddRange** method.

Requirements

Platforms: Windows 98, Windows NT 4.0, Windows Millennium Edition, Windows 2000, Windows XP Home Edition, Windows XP Professional, Windows Server 2003 family

ListView.ListViewItemCollection.Remove Method

Removes the specified item from the collection.

[Visual Basic]
```
Public Overridable Sub Remove( _
   ByVal item As ListViewItem _
)
```

```
[C#]
public virtual void Remove(
   ListViewItem item
);
[C++]
public: virtual void Remove(
   ListViewItem* item
);
[JScript]
public function Remove(
   item : ListViewItem
);
```

Parameters

item

A **ListViewItem** representing the item to remove from the collection.

Exceptions

Exception Type	Condition
ArgumentException	The **ListViewItem** assigned to the *item* parameter is a null reference (**Nothing** in Visual Basic).

Remarks

When you remove an item from the collection, the indexes change for subsequent items in the collection. All information about the removed item is deleted. You can use this method to remove a specific item from the collection by specifying the actual item to remove. To specify the index of the item to remove instead of the item itself, use the **RemoveAt** method. To remove all items from the collection, use the **Clear** method.

Requirements

Platforms: Windows 98, Windows NT 4.0, Windows Millennium Edition, Windows 2000, Windows XP Home Edition, Windows XP Professional, Windows Server 2003 family, .NET Compact Framework - Windows CE .NET

ListView.ListViewItemCollection.RemoveAt Method

Removes the item at the specified index within the collection.

```
[Visual Basic]
Public Overridable Sub RemoveAt( _
   ByVal index As Integer _
) Implements IList.RemoveAt
[C#]
public virtual void RemoveAt(
   int index
);
[C++]
public: virtual void RemoveAt(
   int index
);
[JScript]
public function RemoveAt(
   index : int
);
```

Parameters

index

The zero-based index of the item to remove.

Implements

IList.RemoveAt

Exceptions

Exception Type	Condition
ArgumentOutOfRange-Exception	The *index* parameter is less than zero or greater than or equal to the value of the **Count** property of the **List-View.ListViewItemCollection**.

Remarks

When you remove an item from the collection, the indexes change for subsequent items in the collection. All information about the removed item is deleted. You can use this method to remove a specific item from the collection by specifying the index of the item to remove from the collection. To specify the item to remove instead of the index to the item, use the **Remove** method. To remove all items from the collection, use the **Clear** method.

Requirements

Platforms: Windows 98, Windows NT 4.0, Windows Millennium Edition, Windows 2000, Windows XP Home Edition, Windows XP Professional, Windows Server 2003 family, .NET Compact Framework - Windows CE .NET

ListView.SelectedIndexCollection Class

Represents the collection containing the indexes to the selected items in a list view control.

System.Object
System.Windows.Forms.ListView.SelectedIndexCollection

[Visual Basic]
```
Public Class ListView.SelectedIndexCollection
   Implements IList, ICollection, IEnumerable
```
[C#]
```
public class ListView.SelectedIndexCollection : IList, ICollection,
   IEnumerable
```
[C++]
```
public __gc class ListView.SelectedIndexCollection : public IList,
   ICollection, IEnumerable
```
[JScript]
```
public class ListView.SelectedIndexCollection implements IList,
   ICollection, IEnumerable
```

Thread Safety

Any public static (**Shared** in Visual Basic) members of this type are safe for multithreaded operations. Any instance members are not guaranteed to be thread safe.

Remarks

A **ListView.SelectedIndexCollection** stores the indexes to the selected items in a **ListView** control. The indexes stored in the **ListView.SelectedIndexCollection** are index positions within the **ListView.ListViewItemCollection**. The **ListView.ListViewItem-Collection** stores all items displayed in the **ListView** control.

The following table is an example of how the **ListView.ListView-ItemCollection** stores the items of the **ListView** as well as their selection states in an example **ListView**.

Index	Item	Selection state in the ListView
0	Item1	Unselected
1	Item2	Selected
2	Item3	Unselected
3	Item4	Selected
4	Item5	Selected

Based on the **ListView.ListViewItemCollection** example in the previous table, the following table demonstrates how the **ListView.SelectedIndexCollection** would appear.

Index	Index of Selected Item in ListViewItemCollection
0	1
1	3
2	4

You can use the properties and methods of this class to perform a variety of tasks with the collection. The **Contains** method enables you to determine whether an index position from the **ListView.List-ViewItemCollection** is one of the indexes stored in the **List-View.SelectedIndexCollection**. Once you know that the item is in the collection, you can use the **IndexOf** method to the position of the index in the **ListView.SelectedIndexCollection**.

Requirements

Namespace: System.Windows.Forms

Platforms: Windows 98, Windows NT 4.0, Windows Millennium Edition, Windows 2000, Windows XP Home Edition, Windows XP Professional, Windows Server 2003 family, .NET Compact Framework - Windows CE .NET

Assembly: System.Windows.Forms (in System.Windows.Forms.dll)

ListView.SelectedIndexCollection Constructor

Initializes a new instance of the **ListView.SelectedIndexCollection** class.

[Visual Basic]
```
Public Sub New( _
   ByVal owner As ListView _
)
```
[C#]
```
public ListView.SelectedIndexCollection(
   ListView owner
);
```
[C++]
```
public: SelectedIndexCollection(
   ListView* owner
);
```
[JScript]
```
public function ListView.SelectedIndexCollection(
   owner : ListView
);
```

Parameters

owner

A **ListView** control that owns the collection.

Remarks

You cannot create an instance of this class without associating it with a **ListView** control.

Requirements

Platforms: Windows 98, Windows NT 4.0, Windows Millennium Edition, Windows 2000, Windows XP Home Edition, Windows XP Professional, Windows Server 2003 family, .NET Compact Framework - Windows CE .NET

ListView.SelectedIndexCollection.Count Property

Gets the number of items in the collection.

[Visual Basic]
```
Public Overridable ReadOnly Property Count As Integer Implements _
   ICollection.Count
```
[C#]
```
public virtual int Count {get;}
```
[C++]
```
public: __property virtual int get_Count();
```
[JScript]
```
public function get Count() : int;
```

Property Value

The number of items in the collection.

Implements

ICollection.Count

Remarks

This property enables you to determine the number of selected items in the **ListView**. You can then use this value when looping through the values of the collection and you need to provide a number of iterations to perform the loop. If the **MultiSelect** property of the **ListView** is set to **false**, this property returns a value of either zero (0) or one (1) depending on whether an item is selected.

Requirements

Platforms: Windows 98, Windows NT 4.0, Windows Millennium Edition, Windows 2000, Windows XP Home Edition, Windows XP Professional, Windows Server 2003 family, .NET Compact Framework - Windows CE .NET

ListView.SelectedIndexCollection.IsReadOnly Property

Gets a value indicating whether the collection is read-only.

[Visual Basic]
```
Public Overridable ReadOnly Property IsReadOnly As Boolean _
   Implements IList.IsReadOnly
```
[C#]
```
public virtual bool IsReadOnly {get;}
```
[C++]
```
public: __property virtual bool get_IsReadOnly();
```
[JScript]
```
public function get IsReadOnly() : Boolean;
```

Property Value

true if the collection is read-only; otherwise, **false**.

Implements

IList.IsReadOnly

Remarks

This property is always **true** for this collection. The items in the collection can only be modified by the **ListView** control.

Requirements

Platforms: Windows 98, Windows NT 4.0, Windows Millennium Edition, Windows 2000, Windows XP Home Edition, Windows XP Professional, Windows Server 2003 family, .NET Compact Framework - Windows CE .NET

ListView.SelectedIndexCollection.Item Property

Gets the index value at the specified index within the collection.

[C#] In C#, this property is the indexer for the **ListView.SelectedIndexCollection** class.

[Visual Basic]
```
Public Default ReadOnly Property Item( _
   ByVal index As Integer _
) As Integer
```
[C#]
```
public int this[
   int index
] {get;}
```
[C++]
```
public: __property int get_Item(
   int index
);
```
[JScript]
```
returnValue = SelectedIndexCollectionObject.Item(index);
-or-
returnValue = SelectedIndexCollectionObject(index);
```

[JScript] In JScript, you can use the default indexed properties defined by a type, but you cannot explicitly define your own. However, specifying the **expando** attribute on a class automatically provides a default indexed property whose type is **Object** and whose index type is **String**.

Arguments [JScript]

index
: The index of the item in the collection to retrieve.

Parameters [Visual Basic, C#, C++]

index
: The index of the item in the collection to retrieve.

Property Value

The index value from the **ListView.ListViewItemCollection** that is stored at the specified location.

Exceptions

Exception Type	Condition
ArgumentOutOfRange-Exception	The *index* parameter is less than zero or greater than or equal to the value of the **Count** property of the **List-View.SelectedIndexCollection**.

Remarks

This indexer enables you to get a specific selected index from the **ListView.SelectedIndexCollection**. The index stored in the collection is an index into the **ListView.ListViewItemCollection** of the **ListView** that represents a selected item in the **ListView**.

Requirements

Platforms: Windows 98, Windows NT 4.0, Windows Millennium Edition, Windows 2000, Windows XP Home Edition, Windows XP Professional, Windows Server 2003 family

ListView.SelectedIndexCollection.System.Collections.ICollection.IsSynchronized Property

Note: This namespace, class, or member is supported only in version 1.1 of the .NET Framework.

This member supports the .NET Framework infrastructure and is not intended to be used directly from your code.

[Visual Basic]
```
Private ReadOnly Property IsSynchronized As Boolean Implements _
   ICollection.IsSynchronized
```
[C#]
```
bool ICollection.IsSynchronized {get;}
```

```
[C++]
private: __property bool
   System::Collections::ICollection::get_IsSynchronized();
[JScript]
private function get ICollection.IsSynchronized() : Boolean;
```

ListView.SelectedIndexCollection.System.Collections.ICollection.SyncRoot Property

Note: This namespace, class, or member is supported only in version 1.1 of the .NET Framework.

This member supports the .NET Framework infrastructure and is not intended to be used directly from your code.

```
[Visual Basic]
Private ReadOnly Property SyncRoot As Object Implements _
   ICollection.SyncRoot
[C#]
object ICollection.SyncRoot {get;}
[C++]
private: __property Object*
   System::Collections::ICollection::get_SyncRoot();
[JScript]
private function get ICollection.SyncRoot() : Object;
```

ListView.SelectedIndexCollection.System.Collections.IList.IsFixedSize Property

Note: This namespace, class, or member is supported only in version 1.1 of the .NET Framework.

This member supports the .NET Framework infrastructure and is not intended to be used directly from your code.

```
[Visual Basic]
Private ReadOnly Property IsFixedSize As Boolean Implements _
   IList.IsFixedSize
[C#]
bool IList.IsFixedSize {get;}
[C++]
private: __property bool
   System::Collections::IList::get_IsFixedSize();
[JScript]
private function get IList.IsFixedSize() : Boolean;
```

ListView.SelectedIndexCollection.System.Collections.IList.Item Property

Note: This namespace, class, or member is supported only in version 1.1 of the .NET Framework.

[C#] In C#, this property is the indexer for the **ListView.SelectedIndexCollection** class.

```
[Visual Basic]
Private Default Property Item( _
   ByVal index As Integer _
) As Object Implements IList.Item
[C#]
object IList.this[
   int index
] {get; set;}
[C++]
private: __property Object* System::Collections::IList::get_Item(
   int index
);
private: __property void System::Collections::IList::set_Item(
   int index,
   Object*
);
[JScript]
private function get IList.get_Item(index : int) : Object;
private function set IList.set_Item(index : int, value : Object);
-or-
private function get IList.get_Item(index : int) : Object;
private function set IList.set_Item(index : int, value : Object);
```

[JScript] In JScript, you can use the default indexed properties defined by a type, but you cannot explicitly define your own. However, specifying the **expando** attribute on a class automatically provides a default indexed property whose type is **Object** and whose index type is **String**.

Arguments [JScript]

index

Parameters [Visual Basic, C#, C++]

index

Requirements

Platforms: Windows 98, Windows NT 4.0, Windows Millennium Edition, Windows 2000, Windows XP Home Edition, Windows XP Professional, Windows Server 2003 family

ListView.SelectedIndexCollection.Contains Method

Determines whether the specified index is located in the collection.

```
[Visual Basic]
Public Function Contains( _
   ByVal selectedIndex As Integer _
) As Boolean
[C#]
public bool Contains(
   int selectedIndex
);
[C++]
public: bool Contains(
   int selectedIndex
);
[JScript]
public function Contains(
   selectedIndex : int
) : Boolean;
```

Parameters

selectedIndex

The index to locate in the collection.

Return Value

true if the specified index from the **ListView.ListViewItemCollection** for the **ListView** is an item in the collection; otherwise, **false**.

Remarks

The **Contains** method enables you to determine whether an index position from the **ListView.ListViewItemCollection** is one of the selected indexes stored in **ListView.SelectedIndexCollection**. Once you know that an item is in the selected index collection, you can use the **IndexOf** method to determine the position of the index in the **ListView.SelectedIndexCollection**.

Requirements

Platforms: Windows 98, Windows NT 4.0, Windows Millennium Edition, Windows 2000, Windows XP Home Edition, Windows XP Professional, Windows Server 2003 family, .NET Compact Framework - Windows CE .NET

ListView.SelectedIndexCollection.CopyTo Method

Copies the entire collection into an existing array at a specified location within the array.

```
[Visual Basic]
Public Overridable Sub CopyTo( _
   ByVal dest As Array, _
   ByVal index As Integer _
) Implements ICollection.CopyTo
[C#]
public virtual void CopyTo(
   Array dest,
   int index
);
[C++]
public: virtual void CopyTo(
   Array* dest,
   int index
);
[JScript]
public function CopyTo(
   dest : Array,
   index : int
);
```

Parameters

dest
: An **Array** representing the array to copy the contents of the collection to.The destination array.

index
: The location within the destination array to copy the items from the collection to.

Implements

ICollection.CopyTo

Remarks

You can use this method to combine the selected indexes from multiple collections into a single array.

Requirements

Platforms: Windows 98, Windows NT 4.0, Windows Millennium Edition, Windows 2000, Windows XP Home Edition, Windows XP Professional, Windows Server 2003 family, .NET Compact Framework - Windows CE .NET

ListView.SelectedIndexCollection.GetEnumerator Method

Returns an enumerator that can be used to iterate through the selected index collection.

```
[Visual Basic]
Public Overridable Function GetEnumerator() As IEnumerator _
   Implements IEnumerable.GetEnumerator
[C#]
public virtual IEnumerator GetEnumerator();
[C++]
public: virtual IEnumerator* GetEnumerator();
[JScript]
public function GetEnumerator() : IEnumerator;
```

Return Value

An **IEnumerator** that represents the selected indexes collection.

Implements

IEnumerable.GetEnumerator

Requirements

Platforms: Windows 98, Windows NT 4.0, Windows Millennium Edition, Windows 2000, Windows XP Home Edition, Windows XP Professional, Windows Server 2003 family, .NET Compact Framework - Windows CE .NET

ListView.SelectedIndexCollection.IList.Add Method

This member supports the .NET Framework infrastructure and is not intended to be used directly from your code.

```
[Visual Basic]
Private Function Add( _
   ByVal value As Object _
) As Integer Implements IList.Add
[C#]
int IList.Add(
   object value
);
[C++]
private: int IList::Add(
   Object* value
);
[JScript]
private function IList.Add(
   value : Object
) : int;
```

ListView.SelectedIndexCollection.IList.Clear Method

This member supports the .NET Framework infrastructure and is not intended to be used directly from your code.

```
[Visual Basic]
Private Sub Clear() Implements IList.Clear
[C#]
void IList.Clear();
[C++]
private: void IList::Clear();
[JScript]
private function IList.Clear();
```

ListView.SelectedIndexCollection.IList.Contains Method

This member supports the .NET Framework infrastructure and is not intended to be used directly from your code.

```
[Visual Basic]
Private Function Contains( _
   ByVal selectedIndex As Object _
) As Boolean Implements IList.Contains
[C#]
bool IList.Contains(
   object selectedIndex
);
[C++]
private: bool IList::Contains(
   Object* selectedIndex
);
[JScript]
private function IList.Contains(
   selectedIndex : Object
) : Boolean;
```

ListView.SelectedIndexCollection.IList.IndexOf Method

This member supports the .NET Framework infrastructure and is not intended to be used directly from your code.

```
[Visual Basic]
Private Function IndexOf( _
   ByVal selectedIndex As Object _
) As Integer Implements IList.IndexOf
[C#]
int IList.IndexOf(
   object selectedIndex
);
[C++]
private: int IList::IndexOf(
   Object* selectedIndex
);
[JScript]
private function IList.IndexOf(
   selectedIndex : Object
) : int;
```

ListView.SelectedIndexCollection.IList.Insert Method

This member supports the .NET Framework infrastructure and is not intended to be used directly from your code.

```
[Visual Basic]
Private Sub Insert( _
   ByVal index As Integer, _
   ByVal value As Object _
) Implements IList.Insert
[C#]
void IList.Insert(
   int index,
   object value
);
[C++]
private: void IList::Insert(
   int index,
   Object* value
);
[JScript]
private function IList.Insert(
   index : int,
   value : Object
);
```

ListView.SelectedIndexCollection.IList.Remove Method

This member supports the .NET Framework infrastructure and is not intended to be used directly from your code.

```
[Visual Basic]
Private Sub Remove( _
   ByVal value As Object _
) Implements IList.Remove
[C#]
void IList.Remove(
   object value
);
[C++]
private: void IList::Remove(
   Object* value
);
[JScript]
private function IList.Remove(
   value : Object
);
```

ListView.SelectedIndexCollection.IList.RemoveAt Method

This member supports the .NET Framework infrastructure and is not intended to be used directly from your code.

```
[Visual Basic]
Private Sub RemoveAt( _
   ByVal index As Integer _
) Implements IList.RemoveAt
[C#]
void IList.RemoveAt(
   int index
);
[C++]
private: void IList::RemoveAt(
   int index
);
[JScript]
private function IList.RemoveAt(
   index : int
);
```

ListView.SelectedIndexCollection.IndexOf Method

Returns the index within the **ListView.SelectedIndexCollection** of the specified index from the **ListView.ListViewItemCollection** of the list view control.

[Visual Basic]
```
Public Function IndexOf( _
   ByVal selectedIndex As Integer _
) As Integer
```
[C#]
```
public int IndexOf(
   int selectedIndex
);
```
[C++]
```
public: int IndexOf(
   int selectedIndex
);
```
[JScript]
```
public function IndexOf(
   selectedIndex : int
) : int;
```

Parameters

selectedIndex
The zero-based index from the **ListView.ListViewItemCollection** to locate in the collection.

Return Value

The zero-based index in the collection where the specified index of the **ListView.ListViewItemCollection** is located within the **ListView.SelectedIndexCollection**. If the index is not located in the collection, the return value is negative one (-1).

Remarks

Once you know that an item is in the selected index collection (using the **Contains** method), you can use the **IndexOf** method to determine the position of the index in the **ListView.SelectedIndexCollection**.

Requirements

Platforms: Windows 98, Windows NT 4.0, Windows Millennium Edition, Windows 2000, Windows XP Home Edition, Windows XP Professional, Windows Server 2003 family, .NET Compact Framework - Windows CE .NET

ListView.SelectedListViewItem Collection Class

Represents the collection of selected items in a list view control.

System.Object
  System.Windows.Forms.ListView.SelectedListViewItem-Collection

```
[Visual Basic]
Public Class ListView.SelectedListViewItemCollection
   Implements IList, ICollection, IEnumerable
[C#]
public class ListView.SelectedListViewItemCollection : IList,
   ICollection, IEnumerable
[C++]
public __gc class ListView.SelectedListViewItemCollection : public
   IList, ICollection, IEnumerable
[JScript]
public class ListView.SelectedListViewItemCollection implements
   IList, ICollection, IEnumerable
```

Thread Safety

Any public static (**Shared** in Visual Basic) members of this type are safe for multithreaded operations. Any instance members are not guaranteed to be thread safe.

Remarks

A **ListView.SelectedListViewItemCollection** stores the selected items in a **ListView** control. The items stored in the **ListView.SelectedListViewItemCollection** are items contained in the **ListView.ListViewItemCollection**. The **ListView.ListViewItem-Collection** stores all items displayed in the **ListView**.

The following table is an example of how the **ListView.ListViewItemCollection** stores the items of the **ListView** as well as their selection states in an example **ListView** control.

Index	Item	Selection state in the ListView
0	Item1	Unselected
1	Item2	Selected
2	Item3	Unselected
3	Item4	Selected
4	Item5	Selected

Based on the **ListView.ListViewItemCollection** example in the previous table, the following table demonstrates how the **ListView.SelectedListViewItemCollection** would appear.

Index	Selected item in the ListViewItemCollection
0	Item2
1	Item4
2	Item5

You can use the properties and methods of this class to perform a variety of tasks with the collection. The **Contains** method enables you to determine whether an item from the **ListView.ListViewItemCollection** class is a member of the **ListView.SelectedListViewItemCollection**. Once you know that the item is in the collection, you can use the **IndexOf** method to determine the position of the item in the **ListView.SelectedListViewItemCollection**.

Requirements

Namespace: System.Windows.Forms

Platforms: Windows 98, Windows NT 4.0, Windows Millennium Edition, Windows 2000, Windows XP Home Edition, Windows XP Professional, Windows Server 2003 family

Assembly: System.Windows.Forms (in System.Windows.Forms.dll)

ListView.SelectedListViewItemCollection Constructor

Initializes a new instance of the **ListView.SelectedListViewItemCollection** class.

```
[Visual Basic]
Public Sub New( _
   ByVal owner As ListView _
)
[C#]
public ListView.SelectedListViewItemCollection(
   ListView owner
);
[C++]
public: SelectedListViewItemCollection(
   ListView* owner
);
[JScript]
public function ListView.SelectedListViewItemCollection(
   owner : ListView
);
```

Parameters

owner
  The **ListView** control that owns the collection.

Remarks

You cannot create an instance of this class without associating it with a **ListView** control.

Requirements

Platforms: Windows 98, Windows NT 4.0, Windows Millennium Edition, Windows 2000, Windows XP Home Edition, Windows XP Professional, Windows Server 2003 family

ListView.SelectedListViewItemCollection.Count Property

Gets the number of items in the collection.

```
[Visual Basic]
Public Overridable ReadOnly Property Count As Integer  Implements _
   ICollection.Count
[C#]
public virtual int Count {get;}
[C++]
public: __property virtual int get_Count();
[JScript]
public function get Count() : int;
```

Property Value

The number of items in the collection.

Implements

ICollection.Count

Remarks

This property enables you to determine the number of selected items in the **ListView** control. You can then use this value when looping through the values of the collection and you need to provide a number of iterations to perform the loop. Unless the **MultiSelect** property of the **ListView** is set to **true**, this property always returns a value of zero (0) or one (1) depending on whether you have a selected item.

Requirements

Platforms: Windows 98, Windows NT 4.0, Windows Millennium Edition, Windows 2000, Windows XP Home Edition, Windows XP Professional, Windows Server 2003 family

ListView.SelectedListViewItemCollection.IsReadOnly Property

Gets a value indicating whether the collection is read-only.

```
[Visual Basic]
Public Overridable ReadOnly Property IsReadOnly As Boolean _
   Implements IList.IsReadOnly
[C#]
public virtual bool IsReadOnly {get;}
[C++]
public: __property virtual bool get_IsReadOnly();
[JScript]
public function get IsReadOnly() : Boolean;
```

Property Value

true if the collection is read-only; otherwise, **false**.

Implements

IList.IsReadOnly

Remarks

This property is always **true** for this collection. The items in the collection can only be modified by the **ListView** control.

Requirements

Platforms: Windows 98, Windows NT 4.0, Windows Millennium Edition, Windows 2000, Windows XP Home Edition, Windows XP Professional, Windows Server 2003 family

ListView.SelectedListViewItemCollection.Item Property

Gets the item at the specified index within the collection.

[C#] In C#, this property is the indexer for the **ListView.SelectedListViewItemCollection** class.

```
[Visual Basic]
Public Default ReadOnly Property Item( _
   ByVal index As Integer _
) As ListViewItem
[C#]
public ListViewItem this[
   int index
] {get;}
[C++]
public: __property ListViewItem* get_Item(
   int index
);
[JScript]
returnValue = SelectedListViewItemCollectionObject.Item(index);
-or-
returnValue = SelectedListViewItemCollectionObject(index);
```

[JScript] In JScript, you can use the default indexed properties defined by a type, but you cannot explicitly define your own. However, specifying the **expando** attribute on a class automatically provides a default indexed property whose type is **Object** and whose index type is **String**.

Arguments [JScript]

index

The index of the item in the collection to retrieve.

Parameters [Visual Basic, C#, C++]

index

The index of the item in the collection to retrieve.

Property Value

A **ListViewItem** representing the item located at the specified index within the collection.

Exceptions

Exception Type	Condition
ArgumentOutOfRange-Exception	The *index* parameter is less than zero or greater than or equal to the value of the **Count** property of the **ListView.SelectedListViewItem-Collection**.

Remarks

This indexer enables you to get a specific item from the **List-View.SelectedListViewItemCollection**. The item stored in the collection is an item in the **ListView.ListViewItemCollection** of the **ListView** that represents a selected item in the **ListView**.

Requirements

Platforms: Windows 98, Windows NT 4.0, Windows Millennium Edition, Windows 2000, Windows XP Home Edition, Windows XP Professional, Windows Server 2003 family

ListView.SelectedListViewItemCollection.Clear Method

Removes all items from the collection.

```
[Visual Basic]
Public Overridable Sub Clear() Implements IList.Clear
[C#]
public virtual void Clear();
[C++]
public: virtual void Clear();
[JScript]
public function Clear();
```

Implements

IList.Clear

Remarks

This method allows you to clear all selections from the **ListView** control.

Requirements

Platforms: Windows 98, Windows NT 4.0,
Windows Millennium Edition, Windows 2000,
Windows XP Home Edition, Windows XP Professional,
Windows Server 2003 family

ListView.SelectedListViewItemCollection.Contains Method

Determines whether the specified item is located in the collection.

```
[Visual Basic]
Public Function Contains( _
   ByVal item As ListViewItem _
) As Boolean
[C#]
public bool Contains(
   ListViewItem item
);
[C++]
public: bool Contains(
   ListViewItem* item
);
[JScript]
public function Contains(
   item : ListViewItem
) : Boolean;
```

Parameters

item

A **ListViewItem** representing the item to locate in the collection.

Return Value

true if the specified item is located in the collection; otherwise, **false**.

Remarks

The **Contains** method enables you to determine whether an item from the **ListView.ListViewItemCollection** class is one of the selected items stored in the **ListView.SelectedListViewItem-Collection**. Once you know that the item is in the selected item collection, you can use the **IndexOf** method to determine the position of the item in the **ListView.SelectedListViewItemCollection**.

Requirements

Platforms: Windows 98, Windows NT 4.0,
Windows Millennium Edition, Windows 2000,
Windows XP Home Edition, Windows XP Professional,
Windows Server 2003 family

ListView.SelectedListViewItemCollection.CopyTo Method

Copies the entire collection into an existing array at a specified location within the array.

```
[Visual Basic]
Public Overridable Sub CopyTo( _
   ByVal dest As Array, _
   ByVal index As Integer _
) Implements ICollection.CopyTo
[C#]
public virtual void CopyTo(
   Array dest,
   int index
);
[C++]
public: virtual void CopyTo(
   Array* dest,
   int index
);
[JScript]
public function CopyTo(
   dest : Array,
   index : int
);
```

Parameters

dest

An **Array** representing the array to copy the contents of the collection to.

index

The location within the destination array to copy the items from the collection to.

Implements

ICollection.CopyTo

Remarks

You can use this method to combine the selected items from multiple collections into a single array.

Requirements

Platforms: Windows 98, Windows NT 4.0,
Windows Millennium Edition, Windows 2000,
Windows XP Home Edition, Windows XP Professional,
Windows Server 2003 family

ListView.SelectedListViewItemCollection.Get-Enumerator Method

Returns an enumerator that can be used to iterate through the selected item collection.

```
[Visual Basic]
Public Overridable Function GetEnumerator() As IEnumerator _
   Implements IEnumerable.GetEnumerator
[C#]
public virtual IEnumerator GetEnumerator();
[C++]
public: virtual IEnumerator* GetEnumerator();
[JScript]
public function GetEnumerator() : IEnumerator;
```

Return Value

An **IEnumerator** that represents the collection of selected items.

Implements

IEnumerable.GetEnumerator

Requirements

Platforms: Windows 98, Windows NT 4.0, Windows Millennium Edition, Windows 2000, Windows XP Home Edition, Windows XP Professional, Windows Server 2003 family

ListView.SelectedListViewItemCollection.IList.Add Method

This member supports the .NET Framework infrastructure and is not intended to be used directly from your code.

```
[Visual Basic]
Private Function Add( _
   ByVal value As Object _
) As Integer Implements IList.Add
[C#]
int IList.Add(
   object value
);
[C++]
private: int IList::Add(
   Object* value
);
[JScript]
private function IList.Add(
   value : Object
) : int;
```

ListView.SelectedListViewItemCollection.IList.Contains Method

This member supports the .NET Framework infrastructure and is not intended to be used directly from your code.

```
[Visual Basic]
Private Function Contains( _
   ByVal item As Object _
) As Boolean Implements IList.Contains
[C#]
bool IList.Contains(
   object item
);
[C++]
private: bool IList::Contains(
   Object* item
);
[JScript]
private function IList.Contains(
   item : Object
) : Boolean;
```

ListView.SelectedListViewItemCollection.IList.IndexOf Method

This member supports the .NET Framework infrastructure and is not intended to be used directly from your code.

```
[Visual Basic]
Private Function IndexOf( _
   ByVal item As Object _
) As Integer Implements IList.IndexOf
[C#]
int IList.IndexOf(
   object item
);
[C++]
private: int IList::IndexOf(
   Object* item
);
[JScript]
private function IList.IndexOf(
   item : Object
) : int;
```

ListView.SelectedListViewItemCollection.IList.Insert Method

This member supports the .NET Framework infrastructure and is not intended to be used directly from your code.

```
[Visual Basic]
Private Sub Insert( _
   ByVal index As Integer, _
   ByVal value As Object _
) Implements IList.Insert
[C#]
void IList.Insert(
   int index,
   object value
);
[C++]
private: void IList::Insert(
   int index,
   Object* value
);
[JScript]
private function IList.Insert(
   index : int,
   value : Object
);
```

ListView.SelectedListViewItemCollection.IList.Remove Method

This member supports the .NET Framework infrastructure and is not intended to be used directly from your code.

```
[Visual Basic]
Private Sub Remove( _
   ByVal value As Object _
) Implements IList.Remove
[C#]
void IList.Remove(
   object value
);
```

```
[C++]
private: void IList::Remove(
   Object* value
);
[JScript]
private function IList.Remove(
   value : Object
);
```

ListView.SelectedListViewItemCollection.IList.RemoveAt Method

This member supports the .NET Framework infrastructure and is not intended to be used directly from your code.

```
[Visual Basic]
Private Sub RemoveAt( _
   ByVal index As Integer _
) Implements IList.RemoveAt
[C#]
void IList.RemoveAt(
   int index
);
[C++]
private: void IList::RemoveAt(
   int index
);
[JScript]
private function IList.RemoveAt(
   index : int
);
```

ListView.SelectedListViewItemCollection.IndexOf Method

Returns the index within the collection of the specified item.

```
[Visual Basic]
Public Function IndexOf( _
   ByVal item As ListViewItem _
) As Integer
[C#]
public int IndexOf(
   ListViewItem item
);
[C++]
public: int IndexOf(
   ListViewItem* item
);
[JScript]
public function IndexOf(
   item : ListViewItem
) : int;
```

Parameters

item

A **ListViewItem** representing the item to locate in the collection.

Return Value

The zero-based index of the item in the collection. If the item is not located in the collection, the return value is negative one (-1).

Remarks

Once you know that an item is in the selected item collection (using the **Contains** method), you can use the **IndexOf** method to determine the position of the item in the **ListView.SelectedListViewItemCollection**.

Requirements

Platforms: Windows 98, Windows NT 4.0, Windows Millennium Edition, Windows 2000, Windows XP Home Edition, Windows XP Professional, Windows Server 2003 family

MainMenu Class

Represents the menu structure of a form.

System.Object
  System.MarshalByRefObject
    System.ComponentModel.Component
      System.Windows.Forms.Menu
        System.Windows.Forms.MainMenu

[Visual Basic]
```
Public Class MainMenu
   Inherits Menu
```
[C#]
```
public class MainMenu : Menu
```
[C++]
```
public __gc class MainMenu : public Menu
```
[JScript]
```
public class MainMenu extends Menu
```

Thread Safety

Any public static (**Shared** in Visual Basic) members of this type are safe for multithreaded operations. Any instance members are not guaranteed to be thread safe.

Remarks

The **MainMenu** control represents the container for the menu structure of a form. A menu is composed of **MenuItem** objects that represent the individual menu commands in the menu structure. Each **MenuItem** can be a command for your application or a parent menu for other submenu items. To bind the **MainMenu** to the **Form** that will display it, assign the **MainMenu** to the **Menu** property of the **Form**.

For applications that will have support for multiple languages, you can use the **RightToLeft** property to display the text of the menu from right to left to support languages such as Arabic, which read from right to left.

You can create different **MainMenu** objects to represent different menu strutures for your form. If you want to reuse the menu structure contained in a specific **MainMenu**, you can use its **CloneMenu** method to create a copy. Once you have a copy of the menu structure, you can make the appropriate modifications for your new menu structure.

Example

[Visual Basic, C#] The following example creates a **MainMenu**, assigns two **MenuItem** objects to the **MainMenu** and binds it to a form. This example assumes that you have a **Form** created that is named `Form1`.

[Visual Basic]
```
Public Sub CreateMyMainMenu()
    ' Create an empty MainMenu.
    Dim mainMenu1 As New MainMenu()

    Dim menuItem1 As New MenuItem()
    Dim menuItem2 As New MenuItem()

    menuItem1.Text = "File"
    menuItem2.Text = "Edit"
    ' Add two MenuItem objects to the MainMenu.
    mainMenu1.MenuItems.Add(menuItem1)
    mainMenu1.MenuItems.Add(menuItem2)

    ' Bind the MainMenu to Form1.
    Menu = mainMenu1
End Sub
```

[C#]
```
public void CreateMyMainMenu()
{
   // Create an empty MainMenu.
   MainMenu mainMenu1 = new MainMenu();

   MenuItem menuItem1 = new MenuItem();
   MenuItem menuItem2 = new MenuItem();

   menuItem1.Text = "File";
   menuItem2.Text = "Edit";
   // Add two MenuItem objects to the MainMenu.
   mainMenu1.MenuItems.Add(menuItem1);
   mainMenu1.MenuItems.Add(menuItem2);

   // Bind the MainMenu to Form1.
   Menu = mainMenu1;
}
```

Requirements

Namespace: System.Windows.Forms

Platforms: Windows 98, Windows NT 4.0, Windows Millennium Edition, Windows 2000, Windows XP Home Edition, Windows XP Professional, Windows Server 2003 family, .NET Compact Framework - Windows CE .NET

Assembly: System.Windows.Forms (in System.Windows.Forms.dll)

MainMenu Constructor

Initializes a new instance of the **MainMenu** class.

Overload List

Initializes a new instance of the **MainMenu** class without any specified menu items.

Supported by the .NET Compact Framework.

[Visual Basic] **Public Sub New()**

[C#] **public MainMenu();**

[C++] **public: MainMenu();**

[JScript] **public function MainMenu();**

Initializes a new instance of the **MainMenu** with a specified set of **MenuItem** objects.

[Visual Basic] **Public Sub New(MenuItem())**

[C#] **public MainMenu(MenuItem[]);**

[C++] **public: MainMenu(MenuItem*[]);**

[JScript] **public function MainMenu(MenuItem[]);**

Example

See related example in the **System.Windows.Forms.MainMenu** class topic.

MainMenu Constructor ()

Initializes a new instance of the **MainMenu** class without any specified menu items.

[Visual Basic]
```
Public Sub New()
```
[C#]
```
public MainMenu();
```
[C++]
```
public: MainMenu();
```
[JScript]
```
public function MainMenu();
```

Remarks

This version of the constructor creates a **MainMenu** without any specified **MenuItem** objects. To add menu items to the control use the other version of this constructor that accepts an array of **MenuItem** objects as its parameter or use the **Add** method of the **MenuItems** property.

Example

See related example in the **System.Windows.Forms.MainMenu** class topic.

Requirements

Platforms: Windows 98, Windows NT 4.0, Windows Millennium Edition, Windows 2000, Windows XP Home Edition, Windows XP Professional, Windows Server 2003 family, .NET Compact Framework - Windows CE .NET

MainMenu Constructor (MenuItem[])

Initializes a new instance of the **MainMenu** with a specified set of **MenuItem** objects.

```
[Visual Basic]
Public Sub New( _
   ByVal items() As MenuItem _
)
[C#]
public MainMenu(
   MenuItem[] items
);
[C++]
public: MainMenu(
   MenuItem* items[]
);
[JScript]
public function MainMenu(
   items : MenuItem[]
);
```

Parameters

items

An array of **MenuItem** objects that will be added to the **MainMenu**.

Remarks

You can use this constructor to assign an array of **MenuItem** objects to the **MainMenu** at the time of its creation. After the **MainMenu** has been created you can add additional **MenuItem** objects to the **MainMenu** using the **Add** method of the **MenuItems** property.

Example

See related example in the **System.Windows.Forms.MainMenu** class topic.

Requirements

Platforms: Windows 98, Windows NT 4.0, Windows Millennium Edition, Windows 2000, Windows XP Home Edition, Windows XP Professional, Windows Server 2003 family

MainMenu.RightToLeft Property

Gets or sets whether the text displayed by the control is displayed from right to left.

```
[Visual Basic]
Public Overridable Property RightToLeft As RightToLeft
[C#]
public virtual RightToLeft RightToLeft {get; set;}
[C++]
public: __property virtual RightToLeft get_RightToLeft();
public: __property virtual void set_RightToLeft(RightToLeft);
[JScript]
public function get RightToLeft() : RightToLeft;
public function set RightToLeft(RightToLeft);
```

Property Value

One of the **RightToLeft** values.

Exceptions

Exception Type	Condition
InvalidEnumArgument-Exception	The value assigned to the property is not a valid member of the **RightToLeft** enumeration.

Remarks

This property allows your menus to support languages that are written from right to left. When this property is set to **RightTo-Left.Yes**, the menu item text will be displayed from right to left instead of the default left to right method.

> **Note** For more information about how enabling right-to-left alignment affects Windows Forms controls, see the **RightTo-Left** property.

Example

See related example in the **System.Windows.Forms.MainMenu** class topic.

Requirements

Platforms: Windows 98, Windows NT 4.0, Windows Millennium Edition, Windows 2000, Windows XP Home Edition, Windows XP Professional, Windows Server 2003 family

MainMenu.CloneMenu Method

Creates a copy of the menu object.

Overload List

Creates a new **MainMenu** that is a duplicate of the current **MainMenu**.

[Visual Basic] **Overloads Public Overridable Function CloneMenu() As MainMenu**

[C#] **public virtual MainMenu CloneMenu();**

[C++] **public: virtual MainMenu* CloneMenu();**

[JScript] **public function CloneMenu() : MainMenu;**

Inherited from **Menu**.

[Visual Basic] **Overloads Protected Sub CloneMenu(Menu)**

[C#] **protected void CloneMenu(Menu);**

[C++] **protected: void CloneMenu(Menu*);**

[JScript] **protected function CloneMenu(Menu);**

Example

See related example in the **System.Windows.Forms.MainMenu** class topic.

MainMenu.CloneMenu Method ()

Creates a new **MainMenu** that is a duplicate of the current **MainMenu**.

[Visual Basic]
```
Overloads Public Overridable Function CloneMenu() As MainMenu
```
[C#]
```
public virtual MainMenu CloneMenu();
```
[C++]
```
public: virtual MainMenu* CloneMenu();
```
[JScript]
```
public function CloneMenu() : MainMenu;
```

Return Value

A **MainMenu** that represents the cloned menu.

Remarks

You can use this method to create a copy of the menu structure stored in a **MainMenu**. You can use this method to reuse the menu structure stored in a **MainMenu** as the foundation for a new **MainMenu**. For example, if you want to create a menu structure that has the same menu items as an existing **MainMenu** but will also have additional **MenuItem** objects added to it, you can use the **CloneMenu** method to create a copy of the original **MainMenu** and then add the new **MenuItem** objects to the cloned **MainMenu**.

Example

See related example in the **System.Windows.Forms.MainMenu** class topic.

Requirements

Platforms: Windows 98, Windows NT 4.0, Windows Millennium Edition, Windows 2000, Windows XP Home Edition, Windows XP Professional, Windows Server 2003 family

MainMenu.CreateMenuHandle Method

This member supports the .NET Framework infrastructure and is not intended to be used directly from your code.

[Visual Basic]
```
Overrides Protected Function CreateMenuHandle() As IntPtr
```
[C#]
```
protected override IntPtr CreateMenuHandle();
```
[C++]
```
protected: IntPtr CreateMenuHandle();
```
[JScript]
```
protected override function CreateMenuHandle() : IntPtr;
```

MainMenu.Dispose Method

Overload List

This member supports the .NET Framework infrastructure and is not intended to be used directly from your code.

Supported by the .NET Compact Framework.

[Visual Basic] **Overloads Overrides Protected Sub Dispose(Boolean)**

[C#] **protected override void Dispose(bool);**

[C++] **protected: void Dispose(bool);**

[JScript] **protected override function Dispose(Boolean);**

Inherited from **Component**.

[Visual Basic] **Overloads Public Overridable Sub Dispose() Implements IDisposable.Dispose**

[C#] **public virtual void Dispose();**

[C++] **public: virtual void Dispose();**

[JScript] **public function Dispose();**

MainMenu.Dispose Method (Boolean)

This member overrides **Component.Dispose**.

[Visual Basic]
```
Overrides Overloads Protected Sub Dispose( _
   ByVal disposing As Boolean _
)
```
[C#]
```
protected override void Dispose(
   bool disposing
);
```
[C++]
```
protected: void Dispose(
   bool disposing
);
```
[JScript]
```
protected override function Dispose(
   disposing : Boolean
);
```

Requirements

Platforms: Windows 98, Windows NT 4.0, Windows Millennium Edition, Windows 2000, Windows XP Home Edition, Windows XP Professional, Windows Server 2003 family, .NET Compact Framework - Windows CE .NET

MainMenu.GetForm Method

Gets the **Form** that contains this control.

[Visual Basic]
```
Public Function GetForm() As Form
```
[C#]
```
public Form GetForm();
```
[C++]
```
public: Form* GetForm();
```
[JScript]
```
public function GetForm() : Form;
```

Return Value

A **Form** that is the container for this control. Returns a null reference (**Nothing** in Visual Basic) if the **MainMenu** is not currently hosted on a form.

Remarks

This property enables you to determine if a specific **MainMenu** is parented to a form. The property is typically used when multiple **MainMenu** objects are being used on a form and you need to determine which one is currently being used by a form.

Example

See related example in the **System.Windows.Forms.MainMenu** class topic.

Requirements

Platforms: Windows 98, Windows NT 4.0,
Windows Millennium Edition, Windows 2000,
Windows XP Home Edition, Windows XP Professional,
Windows Server 2003 family

MainMenu.ToString Method

This member overrides **Object.ToString**.

```
[Visual Basic]
Overrides Public Function ToString() As String
[C#]
public override string ToString();
[C++]
public: String* ToString();
[JScript]
public override function ToString() : String;
```

Requirements

Platforms: Windows 98, Windows NT 4.0,
Windows Millennium Edition, Windows 2000,
Windows XP Home Edition, Windows XP Professional,
Windows Server 2003 family,
.NET Compact Framework - Windows CE .NET

MdiClient Class

This type supports the .NET Framework infrastructure and is not intended to be used directly from your code.

```
[Visual Basic]
NotInheritable Public Class MdiClient
   Inherits Control
[C#]
public sealed class MdiClient : Control
[C++]
public __gc __sealed class MdiClient : public Control
[JScript]
public class MdiClient extends Control
```

MdiClient Constructor

This member supports the .NET Framework infrastructure and is not intended to be used directly from your code.

```
[Visual Basic]
Public Sub New()
[C#]
public MdiClient();
[C++]
public: MdiClient();
[JScript]
public function MdiClient();
```

MdiClient.BackgroundImage Property

This member supports the .NET Framework infrastructure and is not intended to be used directly from your code.

```
[Visual Basic]
Overrides Public Property BackgroundImage As Image
[C#]
public override Image BackgroundImage {get; set;}
[C++]
public: __property Image* get_BackgroundImage();
public: __property void set_BackgroundImage(Image*);
[JScript]
public override function get BackgroundImage() : Image;
public override function set BackgroundImage(Image);
```

MdiClient.CreateParams Property

This member overrides **Control.CreateParams**.

```
[Visual Basic]
Overrides Protected ReadOnly Property CreateParams As CreateParams
[C#]
protected override CreateParams CreateParams {get;}
[C++]
protected: __property CreateParams* get_CreateParams();
[JScript]
protected override function get CreateParams() : CreateParams;
```

Requirements

Platforms: Windows 98, Windows NT 4.0, Windows Millennium Edition, Windows 2000, Windows XP Home Edition, Windows XP Professional, Windows Server 2003 family

MdiClient.MdiChildren Property

This member supports the .NET Framework infrastructure and is not intended to be used directly from your code.

```
[Visual Basic]
Public ReadOnly Property MdiChildren As Form ()
[C#]
public Form[] MdiChildren {get;}
[C++]
public: __property Form* get_MdiChildren();
[JScript]
public function get MdiChildren() : Form[];
```

MdiClient.CreateControlsInstance Method

This member supports the .NET Framework infrastructure and is not intended to be used directly from your code.

```
[Visual Basic]
Overrides Protected Function CreateControlsInstance() As _
   ControlCollection
[C#]
protected override ControlCollection CreateControlsInstance();
[C++]
protected: ControlCollection* CreateControlsInstance();
[JScript]
protected override function CreateControlsInstance() :
   ControlCollection;
```

MdiClient.LayoutMdi Method

This member supports the .NET Framework infrastructure and is not intended to be used directly from your code.

```
[Visual Basic]
Public Sub LayoutMdi( _
   ByVal value As MdiLayout _
)
[C#]
public void LayoutMdi(
   MdiLayout value
);
[C++]
public: void LayoutMdi(
   MdiLayout value
);
[JScript]
public function LayoutMdi(
   value : MdiLayout
);
```

MdiClient.OnResize Method

This member overrides **Control.OnResize**.

```
[Visual Basic]
Overrides Protected Sub OnResize( _
   ByVal e As EventArgs _
)
[C#]
protected override void OnResize(
   EventArgs e
);
```

[C++]
```
protected: void OnResize(
   EventArgs* e
);
```
[JScript]
```
protected override function OnResize(
   e : EventArgs
);
```

Requirements

Platforms: Windows 98, Windows NT 4.0, Windows Millennium Edition, Windows 2000, Windows XP Home Edition, Windows XP Professional, Windows Server 2003 family

MdiClient.ScaleCore Method

This member supports the .NET Framework infrastructure and is not intended to be used directly from your code.

[Visual Basic]
```
Overrides Protected Sub ScaleCore( _
   ByVal dx As Single, _
   ByVal dy As Single _
)
```
[C#]
```
protected override void ScaleCore(
   float dx,
   float dy
);
```
[C++]
```
protected: void ScaleCore(
   float dx,
   float dy
);
```
[JScript]
```
protected override function ScaleCore(
   dx : float,
   dy : float
);
```

MdiClient.SetBoundsCore Method

This member supports the .NET Framework infrastructure and is not intended to be used directly from your code.

[Visual Basic]
```
Overrides Protected Sub SetBoundsCore( _
   ByVal x As Integer, _
   ByVal y As Integer, _
   ByVal width As Integer, _
   ByVal height As Integer, _
   ByVal specified As BoundsSpecified _
)
```
[C#]
```
protected override void SetBoundsCore(
   int x,
   int y,
   int width,
   int height,
   BoundsSpecified specified
);
```
[C++]
```
protected: void SetBoundsCore(
   int x,
   int y,
   int width,
   int height,
   BoundsSpecified specified
);
```
[JScript]
```
protected override function SetBoundsCore(
   x : int,
   y : int,
   width : int,
   height : int,
   specified : BoundsSpecified
);
```

MdiClient.WndProc Method

This member overrides **Control.WndProc**.

[Visual Basic]
```
Overrides Protected Sub WndProc( _
   ByRef m As Message _
)
```
[C#]
```
protected override void WndProc(
   ref Message m
);
```
[C++]
```
protected: void WndProc(
   Message* m
);
```
[JScript]
```
protected override function WndProc(
   m : Message
);
```

Requirements

Platforms: Windows 98, Windows NT 4.0, Windows Millennium Edition, Windows 2000, Windows XP Home Edition, Windows XP Professional, Windows Server 2003 family

MdiClient.ControlCollection Class

This type supports the .NET Framework infrastructure and is not intended to be used directly from your code.

```
[Visual Basic]
Public Class MdiClient.ControlCollection
   Inherits Control.ControlCollection
[C#]
public class MdiClient.ControlCollection :
   Control.ControlCollection
[C++]
public __gc class MdiClient.ControlCollection : public
   Control.ControlCollection
[JScript]
public class MdiClient.ControlCollection extends
   Control.ControlCollection
```

MdiClient.ControlCollection Constructor

This member supports the .NET Framework infrastructure and is not intended to be used directly from your code.

```
[Visual Basic]
Public Sub New( _
   ByVal owner As MdiClient _
)
[C#]
public MdiClient.ControlCollection(
   MdiClient owner
);
[C++]
public: ControlCollection(
   MdiClient* owner
);
[JScript]
public function MdiClient.ControlCollection(
   owner : MdiClient
);
```

MdiClient.ControlCollection.Add Method

This member supports the .NET Framework infrastructure and is not intended to be used directly from your code.

```
[Visual Basic]
Overrides Public Sub Add( _
   ByVal value As Control _
)
[C#]
public override void Add(
   Control value
);
[C++]
public: void Add(
   Control* value
);
[JScript]
public override function Add(
   value : Control
);
```

MdiClient.ControlCollection.Remove Method

This member supports the .NET Framework infrastructure and is not intended to be used directly from your code.

```
[Visual Basic]
Overrides Public Sub Remove( _
   ByVal value As Control _
)
[C#]
public override void Remove(
   Control value
);
[C++]
public: void Remove(
   Control* value
);
[JScript]
public override function Remove(
   value : Control
);
```

MdiLayout Enumeration

Specifies the layout of multiple document interface (MDI) child windows in an MDI parent window.

```
[Visual Basic]
<Serializable>
Public Enum MdiLayout
[C#]
[Serializable]
public enum MdiLayout
[C++]
[Serializable]
__value public enum MdiLayout
[JScript]
public
   Serializable
enum MdiLayout
```

Remarks

Use the members of this enumeration when calling the **LayoutMdi** method of the **Form** class.

Members

Member name	Description
ArrangeIcons	All MDI child icons are arranged within the client region of the MDI parent form.
Cascade	All MDI child windows are cascaded within the client region of the MDI parent form.
TileHorizontal	All MDI child windows are tiled horizontally within the client region of the MDI parent form.
TileVertical	All MDI child windows are tiled vertically within the client region of the MDI parent form.

Requirements

Namespace: System.Windows.Forms

Platforms: Windows 98, Windows NT 4.0, Windows Millennium Edition, Windows 2000, Windows XP Home Edition, Windows XP Professional, Windows Server 2003 family

Assembly: System.Windows.Forms (in System.Windows.Forms.dll)

MeasureItemEventArgs Class

Provides data for the **MeasureItem** event of the **ListBox**, **ComboBox**, **CheckedListBox**, and **MenuItem** controls.

System.Object
  System.EventArgs
    System.Windows.Forms.MeasureItemEventArgs

[Visual Basic]
```
Public Class MeasureItemEventArgs
   Inherits EventArgs
```
[C#]
```
public class MeasureItemEventArgs : EventArgs
```
[C++]
```
public __gc class MeasureItemEventArgs : public EventArgs
```
[JScript]
```
public class MeasureItemEventArgs extends EventArgs
```

Thread Safety

Any public static (**Shared** in Visual Basic) members of this type are safe for multithreaded operations. Any instance members are not guaranteed to be thread safe.

Remarks

This event is sent when the **OwnerDraw** property of **ListBox**, **ComboBox**, **CheckedListBox**, or **MenuItem** is set to **true**. It is used to tell the drawing function how to size an item.

For information about the event model, see **Events and Delegates**.

Example

[Visual Basic]
```
Public Class Form1
   Inherits System.Windows.Forms.Form
   Private WithEvents listBox1 As System.Windows.Forms.ListBox
   Private components As System.ComponentModel.Container = Nothing

   Private FontSize As Single = 12.0F

   '
   ' This sample displays a ListBox that contains a list of ↵
all the fonts
   ' installed on the system and draws each item in its ↵
respective font.
   '
   Public Sub New()
      InitializeComponent()

      ' Populate control with the fonts installed on the system.
      Dim families As FontFamily() = FontFamily.Families

      Dim family As FontFamily
      For Each family In families
         Dim style As FontStyle = FontStyle.Regular

         ' Monotype Corsiva is only available in italic
         If family.Name = "Monotype Corsiva" Then
            style = style Or FontStyle.Italic
         End If

         listBox1.Items.Add(New ListBoxFontItem(New Font ↵
(family.Name, FontSize, style, GraphicsUnit.Point)))
      Next family
   End Sub

   Protected Overloads Overrides Sub Dispose(ByVal disposing ↵
As Boolean)
      If disposing Then
         If Not (components Is Nothing) Then
            components.Dispose()
         End If
         If Not (foreColorBrush Is Nothing) Then
            foreColorBrush.Dispose()
         End If
      End If

      MyBase.Dispose(disposing)
   End Sub

   Private Sub InitializeComponent()
      Me.listBox1 = New System.Windows.Forms.ListBox()
      Me.SuspendLayout()
      '
      ' listBox1
      '
      Me.listBox1.DrawMode = ↵
System.Windows.Forms.DrawMode.OwnerDrawVariable
      Me.listBox1.Location = New System.Drawing.Point(16, 48)
      Me.listBox1.Name = "listBox1"
      Me.listBox1.SelectionMode = ↵
System.Windows.Forms.SelectionMode.MultiExtended
      Me.listBox1.Size = New System.Drawing.Size(256, 134)
      Me.listBox1.TabIndex = 0
      '
      ' Form1
      '
      Me.AutoScaleBaseSize = New System.Drawing.Size(5, 13)
      Me.ClientSize = New System.Drawing.Size(292, 273)
      Me.Controls.AddRange(New ↵
System.Windows.Forms.Control() {Me.listBox1})
      Me.Name = "Form1"
      Me.Text = "Form1"
      Me.ResumeLayout(False)
   End Sub

   <STAThread()> Shared Sub Main()
      Application.Run(New Form1())
   End Sub

   Private Sub listBox1_MeasureItem(ByVal sender As Object, ↵
ByVal e As System.Windows.Forms.MeasureItemEventArgs) Handles ↵
listBox1.MeasureItem
      Dim font As Font = CType(listBox1.Items(e.Index), ↵
ListBoxFontItem).Font
      Dim stringSize As SizeF = e.Graphics.MeasureString ↵
(font.Name, font)

      ' Set the height and width of the item
      e.ItemHeight = CInt(stringSize.Height)
      e.ItemWidth = CInt(stringSize.Width)
   End Sub

   ' For efficiency, cache the brush used for drawing.
   Private foreColorBrush As SolidBrush

   Private Sub listBox1_DrawItem(ByVal sender As Object, ↵
ByVal e As System.Windows.Forms.DrawItemEventArgs) Handles ↵
listBox1.DrawItem
      Dim brush As Brush

      ' Create the brush using the ForeColor specified by ↵
the DrawItemEventArgs
      If foreColorBrush Is Nothing Then
         foreColorBrush = New SolidBrush(e.ForeColor)
      Else
         If Not foreColorBrush.Color.Equals(e.ForeColor) Then
            ' The control's ForeColor has changed, so dispose ↵
of the cached brush and
            ' create a new one.
            foreColorBrush.Dispose()
            foreColorBrush = New SolidBrush(e.ForeColor)
         End If
      End If

      ' Select the appropriate brush depending on if the ↵
item is selected.
      ' Since State can be a combinateion (bit-flag) of ↵
enum values, you can't use
      ' "==" to compare them.
      If (e.State And DrawItemState.Selected) = ↵
DrawItemState.Selected Then
```

```
         brush = SystemBrushes.HighlightText
      Else
         brush = foreColorBrush
      End If

      ' Perform the painting.
      Dim font As Font = CType(listBox1.Items(e.Index), ↵
ListBoxFontItem).Font
      e.DrawBackground()
      e.Graphics.DrawString(font.Name, font, brush, ↵
e.Bounds.X, e.Bounds.Y)
      e.DrawFocusRectangle()
   End Sub

   '
   ' A wrapper class for use with storing Fonts in a ListBox. ↵
 Since ListBox uses the
   ' ToString() of its items for the text it displays, this ↵
class is needed to return
   ' the name of the font, rather than its ToString() value.
   '
   Public Class ListBoxFontItem
      Public Font As Font

      Public Sub New(ByVal f As Font)
         Font = f
      End Sub

      Public Overrides Function ToString() As String
         Return Font.Name
      End Function
   End Class
End Class
```

[C#]

```
public class Form1 : System.Windows.Forms.Form
{
   private System.Windows.Forms.ListBox listBox1;
   private System.ComponentModel.Container components = null;

   protected override void Dispose(bool disposing)
   {
      if( disposing )
      {
         if ( components != null )
            components.Dispose();

         if ( foreColorBrush != null )
            foreColorBrush.Dispose();
      }
      base.Dispose(disposing);
   }

     #region Windows Form Designer generated code
   /// <summary>
   /// Required method for Designer support - do not modify
   /// the contents of this method with the code editor.
   /// </summary>
   private void InitializeComponent()
   {
      this.listBox1 = new System.Windows.Forms.ListBox();
      this.SuspendLayout();
      //
      // listBox1
      //
      this.listBox1.DrawMode = ↵
System.Windows.Forms.DrawMode.OwnerDrawVariable;
      this.listBox1.Location = new System.Drawing.Point(16, 48);
      this.listBox1.Name = "listBox1";
      this.listBox1.SelectionMode = ↵
System.Windows.Forms.SelectionMode.MultiExtended;
      this.listBox1.Size = new System.Drawing.Size(256, 134);
      this.listBox1.TabIndex = 0;
      this.listBox1.MeasureItem += new ↵
System.Windows.Forms.MeasureItemEventHandler(this.listBox1_MeasureItem);
      this.listBox1.DrawItem += new ↵
System.Windows.Forms.DrawItemEventHandler(this.listBox1_DrawItem);
      //
      // Form1
      //
      this.AutoScaleBaseSize = new System.Drawing.Size(5, 13);
      this.ClientSize = new System.Drawing.Size(292, 273);
      this.Controls.AddRange(new System.Windows.Forms.Control[] {
                                                   this.listBox1});
      this.Name = "Form1";
      this.Text = "Form1";
      this.ResumeLayout(false);

   }
     #endregion

   [STAThread]
   static void Main()
   {
      Application.Run(new Form1());
   }

   private void listBox1_MeasureItem(object sender, ↵
System.Windows.Forms.MeasureItemEventArgs e)
   {
      Font font = ((ListBoxFontItem)listBox1.Items[e.Index]).Font;
      SizeF stringSize = e.Graphics.MeasureString(font.Name, font);

      // Set the height and width of the item
      e.ItemHeight = (int)stringSize.Height;
      e.ItemWidth = (int)stringSize.Width;
   }

   // For efficiency, cache the brush to use for drawing.
   private SolidBrush foreColorBrush;

   private void listBox1_DrawItem(object sender, ↵
System.Windows.Forms.DrawItemEventArgs e)
   {
      Brush brush;

      // Create the brush using the ForeColor specified by ↵
 the DrawItemEventArgs
      if ( foreColorBrush == null )
         foreColorBrush = new SolidBrush(e.ForeColor);
      else if ( foreColorBrush.Color != e.ForeColor )
      {
         // The control's ForeColor has changed, so dispose ↵
 of the cached brush and
         // create a new one.
         foreColorBrush.Dispose();
         foreColorBrush = new SolidBrush(e.ForeColor);
      }

      // Select the appropriate brush depending on if the ↵
item is selected.
      // Since State can be a combinateion (bit-flag) of ↵
enum values, you can't use
      // "==" to compare them.
      if ( (e.State & DrawItemState.Selected) == ↵
DrawItemState.Selected )
         brush = SystemBrushes.HighlightText;
      else
         brush = foreColorBrush;

      // Perform the painting.
      Font font = ((ListBoxFontItem)listBox1.Items[e.Index]) ↵
.Font;
      e.DrawBackground();
      e.Graphics.DrawString(font.Name, font, brush, e.Bounds);
      e.DrawFocusRectangle();
   }

   /// <summary>
   /// A wrapper class for use with storing Fonts in a ListBox. ↵
 Since ListBox uses the
   /// ToString() of its items for the text it displays, this ↵
class is needed to return
   /// the name of the font, rather than its ToString() value.
   /// </summary>
   public class ListBoxFontItem
   {
      public Font Font;
```

```
      public ListBoxFontItem(Font f)
      {
         Font = f;
      }

      public override string ToString()
      {
         return Font.Name;
      }
   }
}
```

Requirements

Namespace: System.Windows.Forms

Platforms: Windows 98, Windows NT 4.0, Windows Millennium Edition, Windows 2000, Windows XP Home Edition, Windows XP Professional, Windows Server 2003 family

Assembly: System.Windows.Forms (in System.Windows.Forms.dll)

MeasureItemEventArgs Constructor

Initializes a new instance of the **MeasureItemEventArgs** class.

Overload List

Initializes a new instance of the **MeasureItemEventArgs** class.

[Visual Basic] **Public Sub New(Graphics, Integer)**

[C#] **public MeasureItemEventArgs(Graphics, int);**

[C++] **public: MeasureItemEventArgs(Graphics*, int);**

[JScript] **public function MeasureItemEventArgs(Graphics, int);**

Initializes a new instance of the **MeasureItemEventArgs** class providing a parameter for the item height.

[Visual Basic] **Public Sub New(Graphics, Integer, Integer)**

[C#] **public MeasureItemEventArgs(Graphics, int, int);**

[C++] **public: MeasureItemEventArgs(Graphics*, int, int);**

[JScript] **public function MeasureItemEventArgs(Graphics, int, int);**

MeasureItemEventArgs Constructor (Graphics, Int32)

Initializes a new instance of the **MeasureItemEventArgs** class.

[Visual Basic]

```
Public Sub New( _
   ByVal graphics As Graphics, _
   ByVal index As Integer _
)
```

[C#]

```
public MeasureItemEventArgs(
   Graphics graphics,
   int index
);
```

[C++]

```
public: MeasureItemEventArgs(
   Graphics* graphics,
   int index
);
```

[JScript]

```
public function MeasureItemEventArgs(
   graphics : Graphics,
   index : int
);
```

Parameters

graphics

The **Graphics** object being written to.

index

The index of the item for which you need the height or width.

Requirements

Platforms: Windows 98, Windows NT 4.0, Windows Millennium Edition, Windows 2000, Windows XP Home Edition, Windows XP Professional, Windows Server 2003 family

MeasureItemEventArgs Constructor (Graphics, Int32, Int32)

Initializes a new instance of the **MeasureItemEventArgs** class providing a parameter for the item height.

[Visual Basic]

```
Public Sub New( _
   ByVal graphics As Graphics, _
   ByVal index As Integer, _
   ByVal itemHeight As Integer _
)
```

[C#]

```
public MeasureItemEventArgs(
   Graphics graphics,
   int index,
   int itemHeight
);
```

[C++]

```
public: MeasureItemEventArgs(
   Graphics* graphics,
   int index,
   int itemHeight
);
```

[JScript]

```
public function MeasureItemEventArgs(
   graphics : Graphics,
   index : int,
   itemHeight : int
);
```

Parameters

graphics

The **Graphics** object being written to.

index

The index of the item for which you need the height or width.

itemHeight

The height of the item to measure relative to the *graphics* object.

Requirements

Platforms: Windows 98, Windows NT 4.0, Windows Millennium Edition, Windows 2000, Windows XP Home Edition, Windows XP Professional, Windows Server 2003 family

MeasureItemEventArgs.Graphics Property

Gets the **Graphics** object to measure against.

```
[Visual Basic]
Public ReadOnly Property Graphics As Graphics
[C#]
public Graphics Graphics {get;}
[C++]
public: __property Graphics* get_Graphics();
[JScript]
public function get Graphics() : Graphics;
```

Property Value

The **Graphics** object to use to determine the scale of the item you are drawing.

Remarks

You use a **Graphics** object to determine the scale to use when setting the **ItemHeight** and **ItemWidth**. Different types of graphics objects can have different scales, such as the difference in measurement scale between a monitor screen and a printer.

Example

See related example in the **System.Windows.Forms.MeasureItemEventArgs** class topic.

Requirements

Platforms: Windows 98, Windows NT 4.0, Windows Millennium Edition, Windows 2000, Windows XP Home Edition, Windows XP Professional, Windows Server 2003 family

MeasureItemEventArgs.Index Property

Gets or sets the index of the item for which the height and width is needed.

```
[Visual Basic]
Public ReadOnly Property Index As Integer
[C#]
public int Index {get;}
[C++]
public: __property int get_Index();
[JScript]
public function get Index() : int;
```

Property Value

The index of the item to be measured.

Example

See related example in the **System.Windows.Forms.MeasureItemEventArgs** class topic.

Requirements

Platforms: Windows 98, Windows NT 4.0, Windows Millennium Edition, Windows 2000, Windows XP Home Edition, Windows XP Professional, Windows Server 2003 family

MeasureItemEventArgs.ItemHeight Property

Gets or sets the height of the item specified by the **Index**.

```
[Visual Basic]
Public Property ItemHeight As Integer
[C#]
public int ItemHeight {get; set;}
[C++]
public: __property int get_ItemHeight();
public: __property void set_ItemHeight(int);
[JScript]
public function get ItemHeight() : int;
public function set ItemHeight(int);
```

Property Value

The height of the item measured.

Example

See related example in the **System.Windows.Forms.MeasureItemEventArgs** class topic.

Requirements

Platforms: Windows 98, Windows NT 4.0, Windows Millennium Edition, Windows 2000, Windows XP Home Edition, Windows XP Professional, Windows Server 2003 family

MeasureItemEventArgs.ItemWidth Property

Gets or sets the width of the item specified by the **Index**.

```
[Visual Basic]
Public Property ItemWidth As Integer
[C#]
public int ItemWidth {get; set;}
[C++]
public: __property int get_ItemWidth();
public: __property void set_ItemWidth(int);
[JScript]
public function get ItemWidth() : int;
public function set ItemWidth(int);
```

Property Value

The width of the item measured.

Remarks

This member is only used by **MenuItem**. You use this property to ensure the menu is at least as wide as the widest menu item in the menu list.

Example

See related example in the **System.Windows.Forms.MeasureItemEventArgs** class topic.

Requirements

Platforms: Windows 98, Windows NT 4.0, Windows Millennium Edition, Windows 2000, Windows XP Home Edition, Windows XP Professional, Windows Server 2003 family

MeasureItemEventHandler Delegate

Represents the method that will handle the **MeasureItem** event of the **ListBox**, **ComboBox**, **CheckedListBox**, or **MenuItem** controls.

[Visual Basic]
```
<Serializable>
Public Delegate Sub MeasureItemEventHandler( _
   ByVal sender As Object, _
   ByVal e As MeasureItemEventArgs _
)
```
[C#]
```
[Serializable]
public delegate void MeasureItemEventHandler(
   object sender,
   MeasureItemEventArgs e
);
```
[C++]
```
[Serializable]
public __gc __delegate void MeasureItemEventHandler(
   Object* sender,
   MeasureItemEventArgs* e
);
```

[JScript] In JScript, you can use the delegates in the .NET Framework, but you cannot define your own.

Parameters [Visual Basic, C#, C++]

The declaration of your event handler must have the same parameters as the **MeasureItemEventHandler** delegate declaration.

sender
: The source of the event.

e
: A **MeasureItemEventArgs** that contains the event data.

Remarks

When you create a **MeasureItemEventHandler** delegate, you identify the method that will handle the event. To associate the event with your event handler, add an instance of the delegate to the event. The event handler is called whenever the event occurs, unless you remove the delegate.

Example

See related example in the **System.Windows.Forms.MeasureItemEventArgs** class topic.

Requirements

Namespace: System.Windows.Forms

Platforms: Windows 98, Windows NT 4.0, Windows Millennium Edition, Windows 2000, Windows XP Home Edition, Windows XP Professional, Windows Server 2003 family

Assembly: System.Windows.Forms (in System.Windows.Forms.dll)

Menu Class

Represents the base functionality for all menus.

System.Object
  System.MarshalByRefObject
    System.ComponentModel.Component
      System.Windows.Forms.Menu
        System.Windows.Forms.ContextMenu
        System.Windows.Forms.MainMenu
        System.Windows.Forms.MenuItem

[Visual Basic]
```
MustInherit Public Class Menu
   Inherits Component
```
[C#]
```
public abstract class Menu : Component
```
[C++]
```
public __gc __abstract class Menu : public Component
```
[JScript]
```
public abstract class Menu extends Component
```

Thread Safety

Any public static (**Shared** in Visual Basic) members of this type are safe for multithreaded operations. Any instance members are not guaranteed to be thread safe.

Remarks

This class is the base class for the **MainMenu**, **MenuItem**, and **ContextMenu** classes. You cannot create an instance of this class. The menus for an application consist of **MenuItem** objects. These can contain other **MenuItem** objects, representing submenu items. The **MenuItem** objects can be stored in a **MainMenu** for display as an entire menu structure for a form or a **ContextMenu** that is used to display shortcut menus. This class provides functionality that is common for all the menu classes.

Unlike many base classes, the **Menu** class uses its derived classes to define many of its properties. If you are using your menu in a Multiple Document Interface (MDI) application, you can use the **MdiListItem** property to specify a **MenuItem** that displays a list of open MDI child forms in your application. The **MenuItems** property contains a list of **MenuItem** objects stored in the menu class. For a **MainMenu** or **ContextMenu**, this property contains all the **MenuItem** objects that are displayed. For a **MenuItem**, the **MenuItems** property represents the submenu items associated with it.

In addition to the properties that are provided for all the derived menu classes, the **Menu** class also provides methods, such as **CloneMenu** and **MergeMenu**, that enable you to create new menus from existing menus, and also merge two menu structures together.

The **Menu** class also defines the nested class **Menu.MenuItemCollection**. This class defines the collection of **MenuItem** objects used by the **MenuItems** property. You can use the methods of the **Menu.MenuItemCollection** class to add and remove menu items from a **MainMenu**, **ContextMenu**, or **MenuItem**.

Example

[Visual Basic, C#] The following example uses the derived class, **MenuItem**, to create a menu structure for a form. The example code adds a **MenuItem** to represent the top-level menu item, adds a submenu item to it for selecting a font size, and then adds two submenu items to that menu item that represent large and small font choices in an application. The example assumes that there is a **MainMenu** object named `mainMenu1` and four **MenuItem** objects named `menuItem1`, `menuItem2`, `menuItem3`, and `menuItem4`.

[Visual Basic]
```
Public Sub CreateMyMenu()
    ' Set the caption for the top-level menu item.
    menuItem1.Text = "Edit"
    ' Set the caption for the first submenu.
    menuItem2.Text = "Font Size"
    ' Set the caption for menuItem2's first submenu.
    menuItem3.Text = "Small"
    ' Set the checked property to true since this is the default value.
    menuItem3.Checked = True
    ' Define a shortcut key combination for the menu item.
    menuItem3.Shortcut = Shortcut.CtrlS
    ' Set the caption of the second sub menu item of menuItem2.
    menuItem4.Text = "Large"
    ' Define a shortcut key combination for the menu item.
    menuItem4.Shortcut = Shortcut.CtrlL
    ' Set the index of the menu item so it is placed below the        ↲
first submenu item.
    menuItem4.Index = 1
    ' Add menuItem3 and menuItem4 to menuItem2's list of menu items.
    menuItem2.MenuItems.Add(menuItem3)
    menuItem2.MenuItems.Add(menuItem4)
    ' Add menuItem2 to menuItem1's list of menu items.
    menuItem1.MenuItems.Add(menuItem2)
    ' Add menuItem1 to the MainMenu for displaying.
    mainMenu1.MenuItems.Add(menuItem1)
End Sub
```

[C#]
```
public void CreateMyMenu()
    {
    // Set the caption for the top-level menu item.
    menuItem1.Text = "Edit";
    // Set the caption for the first submenu.
    menuItem2.Text = "Font Size";
    // Set the caption for menuItem2's first submenu.
    menuItem3.Text = "Small";
    // Set the checked property to true since this is the            ↲
default value.
    menuItem3.Checked = true;
    // Define a shortcut key combination for the menu item.
    menuItem3.Shortcut = Shortcut.CtrlS;
    // Set the caption of the second sub menu item of menuItem2.
    menuItem4.Text = "Large";
    // Define a shortcut key combination for the menu item.
    menuItem4.Shortcut = Shortcut.CtrlL;
    // Set the index of the menu item so it is placed below the      ↲
first submenu item.
    menuItem4.Index = 1;
    // Add menuItem3 and menuItem4 to menuItem2's list of menu items.
    menuItem2.MenuItems.Add(menuItem3);
    menuItem2.MenuItems.Add(menuItem4);
    // Add menuItem2 to menuItem1's list of menu items.
    menuItem1.MenuItems.Add(menuItem2);
    // Add menuItem1 to the MainMenu for displaying.
    mainMenu1.MenuItems.Add(menuItem1);
    }
```

Requirements

Namespace: System.Windows.Forms

Platforms: Windows 98, Windows NT 4.0,
Windows Millennium Edition, Windows 2000,
Windows XP Home Edition, Windows XP Professional,
Windows Server 2003 family,
.NET Compact Framework - Windows CE .NET

Assembly: System.Windows.Forms (in System.Windows.Forms.dll)

Menu Constructor

This member supports the .NET Framework infrastructure and is not intended to be used directly from your code.

```
[Visual Basic]
Protected Sub New( _
   ByVal items() As MenuItem _
)
[C#]
protected Menu(
   MenuItem[] items
);
[C++]
protected: Menu(
   MenuItem* items[]
);
[JScript]
protected function Menu(
   items : MenuItem[]
);
```

Menu.FindHandle Field

This member supports the .NET Framework infrastructure and is not intended to be used directly from your code.

```
[Visual Basic]
Public Const FindHandle As Integer
[C#]
public const int FindHandle;
[C++]
public: const int FindHandle;
[JScript]
public var FindHandle : int;
```

Menu.FindShortcut Field

This member supports the .NET Framework infrastructure and is not intended to be used directly from your code.

```
[Visual Basic]
Public Const FindShortcut As Integer
[C#]
public const int FindShortcut;
[C++]
public: const int FindShortcut;
[JScript]
public var FindShortcut : int;
```

Menu.Handle Property

Gets a value representing the window handle for the menu.

```
[Visual Basic]
Public ReadOnly Property Handle As IntPtr
[C#]
public IntPtr Handle {get;}
[C++]
public: __property IntPtr get_Handle();
[JScript]
public function get Handle() : IntPtr;
```

Property Value

The window handle of the menu.

Remarks

You can use this property to obtain the handle to the menu to perform special operations to the menu outside of the functionality provided by this class or its derived classes.

Requirements

Platforms: Windows 98, Windows NT 4.0, Windows Millennium Edition, Windows 2000, Windows XP Home Edition, Windows XP Professional, Windows Server 2003 family

Menu.IsParent Property

Gets a value indicating whether this menu contains any menu items. This property is read-only.

```
[Visual Basic]
Public Overridable ReadOnly Property IsParent As Boolean
[C#]
public virtual bool IsParent {get;}
[C++]
public: __property virtual bool get_IsParent();
[JScript]
public function get IsParent() : Boolean;
```

Property Value

true if this menu contains **MenuItem** objects; otherwise, **false**. The default is **false**.

Remarks

You can use this method to determine whether any **MenuItem** objects are assigned to this menu. This is equivalent to checking for a null reference (**Nothing** in Visual Basic) in the **MenuItems** property.

Example

See related example in the **System.Windows.Forms.Menu** class topic.

Requirements

Platforms: Windows 98, Windows NT 4.0, Windows Millennium Edition, Windows 2000, Windows XP Home Edition, Windows XP Professional, Windows Server 2003 family

Menu.MdiListItem Property

Gets a value indicating the **MenuItem** that is used to display a list of Multiple Document Interface (MDI) child forms.

```
[Visual Basic]
Public ReadOnly Property MdiListItem As MenuItem
[C#]
public MenuItem MdiListItem {get;}
[C++]
public: __property MenuItem* get_MdiListItem();
[JScript]
public function get MdiListItem() : MenuItem;
```

Property Value

A **MenuItem** that represents the menu item displaying a list of MDI child forms that are open in the application.

Remarks

You can use this property to determine whether a **MenuItem** has been specified to display the list of open child windows in an MDI application. To use a specific **MenuItem** as an MDI list, set the **MdiList** property in the **MenuItem** to be used.

Requirements

Platforms: Windows 98, Windows NT 4.0, Windows Millennium Edition, Windows 2000, Windows XP Home Edition, Windows XP Professional, Windows Server 2003 family

Menu.MenuItems Property

Gets a value indicating the collection of **MenuItem** objects associated with the menu.

[Visual Basic]
```
Public ReadOnly Property MenuItems As Menu.MenuItemCollection
```
[C#]
```
public Menu.MenuItemCollection MenuItems {get;}
```
[C++]
```
public: __property Menu.MenuItemCollection* get_MenuItems();
```
[JScript]
```
public function get MenuItems() : Menu.MenuItemCollection;
```

Property Value

A **System.Windows.Forms.Menu.MenuItemCollection** that represents the list of **MenuItem** objects stored in the menu.

Remarks

You can use this property to obtain a reference to the list of menu items that are currently stored in the menu. For **MainMenu** and **ContextMenu** objects, the **MenuItems** property contains the entire menu structure in the control. For the **MenuItem** class, the **MenuItems** property contains the list of submenu items associated with the **MenuItem**. With the reference to the collection of menu items for the menu (provided by this property), you can add and remove menu items, determine the total number of menu items, and clear the list of menu items from the collection.

Example

See related example in the **System.Windows.Forms.Menu** class topic.

Requirements

Platforms: Windows 98, Windows NT 4.0, Windows Millennium Edition, Windows 2000, Windows XP Home Edition, Windows XP Professional, Windows Server 2003 family, .NET Compact Framework - Windows CE .NET

Menu.CloneMenu Method

Copies the **Menu** that is passed as a parameter to the current **Menu**.

[Visual Basic]
```
Protected Sub CloneMenu( _
   ByVal menuSrc As Menu _
)
```
[C#]
```
protected void CloneMenu(
   Menu menuSrc
);
```
[C++]
```
protected: void CloneMenu(
   Menu* menuSrc
);
```
[JScript]
```
protected function CloneMenu(
   menuSrc : Menu
);
```

Parameters

menuSrc

The **Menu** to copy.

Remarks

This method copies the entire list of **MenuItem** objects (stored in the **Menu** passed in to *menuSrc*) into the current menu. You can use this method in your derived class to clone **MenuItem** objects. They can then be reused by other classes that derive from **Menu**, such as **MainMenu**, **ContextMenu**, and **MenuItem**.

Example

See related example in the **System.Windows.Forms.Menu** class topic.

Requirements

Platforms: Windows 98, Windows NT 4.0, Windows Millennium Edition, Windows 2000, Windows XP Home Edition, Windows XP Professional, Windows Server 2003 family

Menu.CreateMenuHandle Method

This member supports the .NET Framework infrastructure and is not intended to be used directly from your code.

[Visual Basic]
```
Protected Overridable Function CreateMenuHandle() As IntPtr
```
[C#]
```
protected virtual IntPtr CreateMenuHandle();
```
[C++]
```
protected: virtual IntPtr CreateMenuHandle();
```
[JScript]
```
protected function CreateMenuHandle() : IntPtr;
```

Menu.Dispose Method

Overload List

This member supports the .NET Framework infrastructure and is not intended to be used directly from your code.

Supported by the .NET Compact Framework.

[Visual Basic] **Overloads Overrides Protected Sub Dispose(Boolean)**

[C#] **protected override void Dispose(bool);**

[C++] **protected: void Dispose(bool);**

[JScript] **protected override function Dispose(Boolean);**

Inherited from **Component**.

[Visual Basic] **Overloads Public Overridable Sub Dispose() Implements IDisposable.Dispose**

[C#] **public virtual void Dispose();**

[C++] **public: virtual void Dispose();**

[JScript] **public function Dispose();**

Menu.Dispose Method (Boolean)

This member overrides **Component.Dispose**.

```
[Visual Basic]
Overrides Overloads Protected Sub Dispose( _
   ByVal disposing As Boolean _
)
[C#]
protected override void Dispose(
   bool disposing
);
[C++]
protected: void Dispose(
   bool disposing
);
[JScript]
protected override function Dispose(
   disposing : Boolean
);
```

Requirements

Platforms: Windows 98, Windows NT 4.0, Windows Millennium Edition, Windows 2000, Windows XP Home Edition, Windows XP Professional, Windows Server 2003 family, .NET Compact Framework - Windows CE .NET

Menu.FindMenuItem Method

This member supports the .NET Framework infrastructure and is not intended to be used directly from your code.

```
[Visual Basic]
Public Function FindMenuItem( _
   ByVal type As Integer, _
   ByVal value As IntPtr _
) As MenuItem
[C#]
public MenuItem FindMenuItem(
   int type,
   IntPtr value
);
[C++]
public: MenuItem* FindMenuItem(
   int type,
   IntPtr value
);
[JScript]
public function FindMenuItem(
   type : int,
   value : IntPtr
) : MenuItem;
```

Menu.FindMergePosition Method

This member supports the .NET Framework infrastructure and is not intended to be used directly from your code.

```
[Visual Basic]
Protected Function FindMergePosition( _
   ByVal mergeOrder As Integer _
) As Integer
[C#]
protected int FindMergePosition(
   int mergeOrder
);
[C++]
protected: int FindMergePosition(
   int mergeOrder
);
[JScript]
protected function FindMergePosition(
   mergeOrder : int
) : int;
```

Menu.GetContextMenu Method

Gets the **ContextMenu** that contains this menu.

```
[Visual Basic]
Public Function GetContextMenu() As ContextMenu
[C#]
public ContextMenu GetContextMenu();
[C++]
public: ContextMenu* GetContextMenu();
[JScript]
public function GetContextMenu() : ContextMenu;
```

Return Value

The **ContextMenu** that contains this menu. The default is a null reference (**Nothing** in Visual Basic).

Remarks

This method allows you to obtain a reference to the **ContextMenu** that this menu is contained in. This property returns a null reference (**Nothing** in Visual Basic) if the menu is not contained in a **ContextMenu**. This can occur if the menu is contained in a **MenuItem** or **MainMenu**, or if the menu is not contained in any menu. You can use this property to determine whether a menu is currently being used, and also to determine where.

Example

See related example in the **System.Windows.Forms.Menu** class topic.

Requirements

Platforms: Windows 98, Windows NT 4.0, Windows Millennium Edition, Windows 2000, Windows XP Home Edition, Windows XP Professional, Windows Server 2003 family

Menu.GetMainMenu Method

Gets the **MainMenu** that contains this menu.

```
[Visual Basic]
Public Function GetMainMenu() As MainMenu
[C#]
public MainMenu GetMainMenu();
[C++]
public: MainMenu* GetMainMenu();
```

```
[JScript]
public function GetMainMenu() : MainMenu;
```

Return Value

The **MainMenu** that contains this menu.

Remarks

This method allows you to obtain a reference to the **MainMenu** this menu is currently located in. This property returns a null reference (**Nothing** in Visual Basic) if the menu is not contained in a **MainMenu**. This can occur if the menu is contained in a **MenuItem** or **ContextMenu**, or if the menu is not contained in any menu. You can use this property to determine whether a menu is currently being used, and also to determine where.

Example

See related example in the **System.Windows.Forms.Menu** class topic.

Requirements

Platforms: Windows 98, Windows NT 4.0, Windows Millennium Edition, Windows 2000, Windows XP Home Edition, Windows XP Professional, Windows Server 2003 family

Menu.MergeMenu Method

Merges the **MenuItem** objects of one menu with the current menu.

```
[Visual Basic]
Public Overridable Sub MergeMenu( _
   ByVal menuSrc As Menu _
)
[C#]
public virtual void MergeMenu(
   Menu menuSrc
);
[C++]
public: virtual void MergeMenu(
   Menu* menuSrc
);
[JScript]
public function MergeMenu(
   menuSrc : Menu
);
```

Parameters

menuSrc
: The **Menu** whose menu items are merged with the menu items of the current menu.

Exceptions

Exception Type	Condition
Exception	The menu was merged with itself.

Remarks

This method merges **MenuItem** objects from one menu with the current menu. **MenuItem** objects are merged according to the values of the **MenuItem.MergeType** and **MenuItem.MergeOrder** properties.

Menu merging is typically done to merge the menus of a Multiple Document Interface (MDI) parent form with those of its active MDI child form. This is performed automatically by the .NET Framework common language runtime. For example, if an MDI parent form contains a set of menus for handling files and your MDI child form also has file-related menu items, the menu sets will automatically merge into a single file menu set when the child form is displayed in the MDI parent form.

You can use the **MergeMenu** method if you are merging two menu structures that are not part of an MDI application. This implementation can be called by the **MainMenu** or **ContextMenu** classes to merge two or more objects that derive from **Menu**.

To merge two **MenuItem** objects use the **MenuItem.MergeMenu** method.

Example

See related example in the **System.Windows.Forms.Menu** class topic.

Requirements

Platforms: Windows 98, Windows NT 4.0, Windows Millennium Edition, Windows 2000, Windows XP Home Edition, Windows XP Professional, Windows Server 2003 family

Menu.ProcessCmdKey Method

This member supports the .NET Framework infrastructure and is not intended to be used directly from your code.

```
[Visual Basic]
Protected Friend Overridable Function ProcessCmdKey( _
   ByRef msg As Message, _
   ByVal keyData As Keys _
) As Boolean
[C#]
protected internal virtual bool ProcessCmdKey(
   ref Message msg,
   Keys keyData
);
[C++]
protected public: virtual bool ProcessCmdKey(
   Message* msg,
   Keys keyData
);
[JScript]
protected internal function ProcessCmdKey(
   msg : Message,
   keyData : Keys
) : Boolean;
```

Menu.ToString Method

This member overrides **Object.ToString**.

```
[Visual Basic]
Overrides Public Function ToString() As String
[C#]
public override string ToString();
[C++]
public: String* ToString();
[JScript]
public override function ToString() : String;
```

Requirements

Platforms: Windows 98, Windows NT 4.0, Windows Millennium Edition, Windows 2000, Windows XP Home Edition, Windows XP Professional, Windows Server 2003 family, .NET Compact Framework - Windows CE .NET

MenuGlyph Enumeration

Specifies the image to draw when drawing a menu with the **ControlPaint.DrawMenuGlyph** method.

[Visual Basic]
```
<Serializable>
Public Enum MenuGlyph
```
[C#]
```
[Serializable]
public enum MenuGlyph
```
[C++]
```
[Serializable]
__value public enum MenuGlyph
```
[JScript]
```
public
   Serializable
enum MenuGlyph
```

Remarks

The values of this enumeration are used in the **DrawMenuGlyph** method of the **ControlPaint** class. These values represent the different types of symbols that can be drawn on a menu item.

Members

Member name	Description
Arrow	Draws a submenu arrow.
Bullet	Draws a menu bullet.
Checkmark	Draws a menu check mark.
Max	This member supports the .NET Framework infrastructure and is not intended to be used directly from your code.
Min	This member supports the .NET Framework infrastructure and is not intended to be used directly from your code.

Requirements

Namespace: System.Windows.Forms

Platforms: Windows 98, Windows NT 4.0, Windows Millennium Edition, Windows 2000, Windows XP Home Edition, Windows XP Professional, Windows Server 2003 family

Assembly: System.Windows.Forms (in System.Windows.Forms.dll)

MenuItem Class

Represents an individual item that is displayed within a **MainMenu** or **ContextMenu**.

System.Object
  System.MarshalByRefObject
    System.ComponentModel.Component
      System.Windows.Forms.Menu
        System.Windows.Forms.MenuItem

```
[Visual Basic]
Public Class MenuItem
   Inherits Menu
[C#]
public class MenuItem : Menu
[C++]
public __gc class MenuItem : public Menu
[JScript]
public class MenuItem extends Menu
```

Thread Safety

Any public static (**Shared** in Visual Basic) members of this type are safe for multithreaded operations. Any instance members are not guaranteed to be thread safe.

Remarks

In order for a **MenuItem** to be displayed, you must add it to a **MainMenu** or **ContextMenu**. To create submenus, you can add **MenuItem** objects to the **MenuItems** property of the parent **MenuItem**.

The **MenuItem** class provides properties that enable you to configure the appearance and functionality of a menu item. To display a check mark next to a menu item, use the **Checked** property. You can use this feature to identify a menu item that is selected in a list of mutually exclusive menu items. For example, if you have a set of menu items for setting the color of text in a **TextBox** control, you can use the **Checked** property to identify which color is currently selected. The **Shortcut** property can be used to define a keyboard combination that can be pressed to select the menu item.

For **MenuItem** objects displayed in a Multiple Document Interface (MDI) application, you can use the **MergeMenu** method to merge the menus of an MDI parent for with that of its child forms to create a consolidated menu structure. Because a **MenuItem** cannot be reused in multiple locations at the same time, such as in a **MainMenu** and a **ContextMenu**, you can use the **CloneMenu** method to create a copy of a **MenuItem** for use in another location.

The **Popup** event enables you to perform tasks before a menu is displayed. For example, you can create an event handler for this event to display or hide menu items based on the state of your code. The **Select** event enables you to perform tasks such as providing detailed help for your application's menu items when the user places the mouse cursor over a menu item.

Example

See related example in the **System.Windows.Forms.Menu** class topic.

Requirements

Namespace: System.Windows.Forms

Platforms: Windows 98, Windows NT 4.0, Windows Millennium Edition, Windows 2000, Windows XP Home Edition, Windows XP Professional, Windows Server 2003 family, .NET Compact Framework - Windows CE .NET

Assembly: System.Windows.Forms (in System.Windows.Forms.dll)

MenuItem Constructor

Initializes a new instance of the **MenuItem** class.

Overload List

Initializes a **MenuItem** with a blank caption.

Supported by the .NET Compact Framework.

[Visual Basic] **Public Sub New()**

[C#] **public MenuItem();**

[C++] **public: MenuItem();**

[JScript] **public function MenuItem();**

Initializes a new instance of the **MenuItem** class with a specified caption for the menu item.

[Visual Basic] **Public Sub New(String)**

[C#] **public MenuItem(string);**

[C++] **public: MenuItem(String*);**

[JScript] **public function MenuItem(String);**

Initializes a new instance of the class with a specified caption and event handler for the **Click** event of the menu item.

[Visual Basic] **Public Sub New(String, EventHandler)**

[C#] **public MenuItem(string, EventHandler);**

[C++] **public: MenuItem(String*, EventHandler*);**

[JScript] **public function MenuItem(String, EventHandler);**

Initializes a new instance of the class with a specified caption and an array of submenu items defined for the menu item.

[Visual Basic] **Public Sub New(String, MenuItem())**

[C#] **public MenuItem(string, MenuItem[]);**

[C++] **public: MenuItem(String*, MenuItem[]);**

[JScript] **public function MenuItem(String, MenuItem[]);**

Initializes a new instance of the class with a specified caption, event handler, and associated shortcut key for the menu item.

[Visual Basic] **Public Sub New(String, EventHandler, Shortcut)**

[C#] **public MenuItem(string, EventHandler, Shortcut);**

[C++] **public: MenuItem(String*, EventHandler*, Shortcut);**

[JScript] **public function MenuItem(String, EventHandler, Shortcut);**

Initializes a new instance of the **MenuItem** class with a specified caption; defined event-handlers for the **Click**, **Select** and **Popup** events; a shortcut key; a merge type; and order specified for the menu item.

[Visual Basic] **Public Sub New(MenuMerge, Integer, Shortcut, String, EventHandler, EventHandler, EventHandler, MenuItem())**

[C#] **public MenuItem(MenuMerge, int, Shortcut, string, EventHandler, EventHandler, EventHandler, MenuItem[]);**

[C++] **public: MenuItem(MenuMerge, int, Shortcut, String*, EventHandler*, EventHandler*, EventHandler*, MenuItem[]);**

[JScript] **public function MenuItem(MenuMerge, int, Shortcut, String, EventHandler, EventHandler, EventHandler, MenuItem[]);**

Example

See related example in the **System.Windows.Forms.Menu** class topic.

MenuItem Constructor ()

Initializes a **MenuItem** with a blank caption.

```
[Visual Basic]
Public Sub New()
[C#]
public MenuItem();
[C++]
public: MenuItem();
[JScript]
public function MenuItem();
```

Remarks

Once you have created a blank **MenuItem** using this constructor, you can use the properties and methods of the **MenuItem** class to specify the appearance and behavior of your **MenuItem**.

Example

See related example in the **System.Windows.Forms.Menu** class topic.

Requirements

Platforms: Windows 98, Windows NT 4.0,
Windows Millennium Edition, Windows 2000,
Windows XP Home Edition, Windows XP Professional,
Windows Server 2003 family,
.NET Compact Framework - Windows CE .NET

MenuItem Constructor (String)

Initializes a new instance of the **MenuItem** class with a specified caption for the menu item.

```
[Visual Basic]
Public Sub New( _
   ByVal text As String _
)
[C#]
public MenuItem(
   string text
);
[C++]
public: MenuItem(
   String* text
);
[JScript]
public function MenuItem(
   text : String
);
```

Parameters

text

The caption for the menu item.

Remarks

When you specify a caption for your menu item with the *text* parameter, you can also specify an access key by placing an '&' character before the character to be used as the access key. For example, to specify the "F" in "File" as an access key, you would specify the caption for the menu item as "&File". You can use this feature to provide keyboard navigation for your menus.

Example

See related example in the **System.Windows.Forms.Menu** class topic.

Requirements

Platforms: Windows 98, Windows NT 4.0,
Windows Millennium Edition, Windows 2000,
Windows XP Home Edition, Windows XP Professional,
Windows Server 2003 family

MenuItem Constructor (String, EventHandler)

Initializes a new instance of the class with a specified caption and event handler for the **Click** event of the menu item.

```
[Visual Basic]
Public Sub New( _
   ByVal text As String, _
   ByVal onClick As EventHandler _
)
[C#]
public MenuItem(
   string text,
   EventHandler onClick
);
[C++]
public: MenuItem(
   String* text,
   EventHandler* onClick
);
[JScript]
public function MenuItem(
   text : String,
   onClick : EventHandler
);
```

Parameters

text

The caption for the menu item.

onClick

The **EventHandler** that handles the **Click** event for this menu item.

Remarks

When you specify a caption for your menu item with the *text* parameter, you can also specify an access key by placing an '&' before the character to be used as the access key. For example, to specify the "F" in "File" as an access key, you would specify the caption for the menu item as "&File". You can use this feature to provide keyboard navigation for your menus.

In addition, you can use this constructor to specify a delegate that will handle the **Click** event for the menu item being created. The **EventHandler** that you pass to this constructor must be configured to call an event handler that can handle the **Click** event. For more information on handling events, see **Events and Delegates**.

Example

See related example in the **System.Windows.Forms.Menu** class topic.

Requirements

Platforms: Windows 98, Windows NT 4.0,
Windows Millennium Edition, Windows 2000,
Windows XP Home Edition, Windows XP Professional,
Windows Server 2003 family

MenuItem Constructor (String, MenuItem[])

Initializes a new instance of the class with a specified caption and an array of submenu items defined for the menu item.

```
[Visual Basic]
Public Sub New( _
   ByVal text As String, _
   ByVal items() As MenuItem _
)
[C#]
public MenuItem(
   string text,
   MenuItem[] items
);
[C++]
public: MenuItem(
   String* text,
   MenuItem* items[]
);
[JScript]
public function MenuItem(
   text : String,
   items : MenuItem[]
);
```

Parameters

text

The caption for the menu item.

items

An array of **MenuItem** objects that contains the submenu items for this menu item.

Remarks

When you specify a caption for your menu item with the *text* parameter, you can also specify an access key by placing an '&' before the character to be used as the access key. For example, to specify the "F" in "File" as an access key, you would specify the caption for the menu item as "&File". You can use this feature to provide keyboard navigation for your menus.

The *items* parameter enables you to assign an array of menu items to define a submenu of this menu item. Each item in the array can also have an array of menu items assigned to it. This enables you to create complete menu structures and assign them to the constructor for the menu item.

Example

See related example in the **System.Windows.Forms.Menu** class topic.

Requirements

Platforms: Windows 98, Windows NT 4.0, Windows Millennium Edition, Windows 2000, Windows XP Home Edition, Windows XP Professional, Windows Server 2003 family

MenuItem Constructor (String, EventHandler, Shortcut)

Initializes a new instance of the class with a specified caption, event handler, and associated shortcut key for the menu item.

```
[Visual Basic]
Public Sub New( _
   ByVal text As String, _
   ByVal onClick As EventHandler, _
   ByVal shortcut As Shortcut _
)
[C#]
public MenuItem(
   string text,
   EventHandler onClick,
   Shortcut shortcut
);
[C++]
public: MenuItem(
   String* text,
   EventHandler* onClick,
   Shortcut shortcut
);
[JScript]
public function MenuItem(
   text : String,
   onClick : EventHandler,
   shortcut : Shortcut
);
```

Parameters

text

The caption for the menu item.

onClick

The **EventHandler** that handles the **Click** event for this menu item.

shortcut

One of the **Shortcut** values.

Remarks

When you specify a caption for your menu item with the *text* parameter, you can also specify an access key by placing an '&' before the character to be used as the access key. For example, to specify the "F" in "File" as an access key, you would specify the caption for the menu item as "&File". You can use this feature to provide keyboard navigation for your menus. This constructor also enables you to specify a shortcut key in addition to an access key to provide keyboard navigation. Shortcut keys allow you to specify a combination of keys that can be used to activate the menu item.

In addition, you can use this constructor to specify a delegate that will handle the **Click** event for the menu item being created. The **EventHandler** that you pass to this constructor must be configured to call an event handler that can handle the **Click** event.

Example

See related example in the **System.Windows.Forms.Menu** class topic.

Requirements

Platforms: Windows 98, Windows NT 4.0, Windows Millennium Edition, Windows 2000, Windows XP Home Edition, Windows XP Professional, Windows Server 2003 family

MenuItem Constructor (MenuMerge, Int32, Shortcut, String, EventHandler, EventHandler, EventHandler, MenuItem[])

Initializes a new instance of the **MenuItem** class with a specified caption; defined event-handlers for the **Click**, **Select** and **Popup** events; a shortcut key; a merge type; and order specified for the menu item.

[Visual Basic]
```
Public Sub New( _
   ByVal mergeType As MenuMerge, _
   ByVal mergeOrder As Integer, _
   ByVal shortcut As Shortcut, _
   ByVal text As String, _
   ByVal onClick As EventHandler, _
   ByVal onPopup As EventHandler, _
   ByVal onSelect As EventHandler, _
   ByVal items() As MenuItem _
)
```
[C#]
```
public MenuItem(
   MenuMerge mergeType,
   int mergeOrder,
   Shortcut shortcut,
   string text,
   EventHandler onClick,
   EventHandler onPopup,
   EventHandler onSelect,
   MenuItem[] items
);
```
[C++]
```
public: MenuItem(
   MenuMerge mergeType,
   int mergeOrder,
   Shortcut shortcut,
   String* text,
   EventHandler* onClick,
   EventHandler* onPopup,
   EventHandler* onSelect,
   MenuItem* items[]
);
```
[JScript]
```
public function MenuItem(
   mergeType : MenuMerge,
   mergeOrder : int,
   shortcut : Shortcut,
   text : String,
   onClick : EventHandler,
   onPopup : EventHandler,
   onSelect : EventHandler,
   items : MenuItem[]
);
```

Parameters

mergeType
One of the **MenuMerge** values.

mergeOrder
The relative position that this menu item will assume in a merged menu.

shortcut
One of the **Shortcut** values.

text
The caption for the menu item.

onClick
The **EventHandler** that handles the **Click** event for this menu item.

onPopup
The **EventHandler** that handles the **Popup** event for this menu item.

onSelect
The **EventHandler** that handles the **Select** event for this menu item.

items
An array of **MenuItem** objects that contains the submenu items for this menu item.

Remarks

When you specify a caption for your menu item with the *text* parameter, you can also specify an access key by placing an '&' before the character to be used as the access key. For example, to specify the "F" in "File" as an access key, you would specify the caption for the menu item as "&File". You can use this feature to provide keyboard navigation for your menus.

The *items* parameter enables you to assign an array of menu items to define a submenu of this menu item. Each item in the array can also have an array of menu items assigned to it. This enables you to create complete menu structures and assign them to the constructor for the menu item.

The *mergeType* and *mergeOrder* parameters allow you to determine how this menu item will behave when the menu item is merged with another menu. Depending on the value you specify for the *mergeType* parameter, you can either add, remove, replace, or merge the menu item and its submenu items with the menu that it is merging with. The *mergeOrder* parameter determines where the menu item being created will be positioned when the menu is merged.

In addition, you can use this constructor to create a **MenuItem** and have it connected to an event handler in your code that will process the click of the menu item. The **EventHandler** that you pass into this constructor should be configured to call an event handler that can handle the **Click** event. By using this constructor version, you can also connect the **Popup** and **Select** events to determine when this menu item is selected. You can use these events for tasks such as determining whether or not to display a check mark next to submenu items or to enable or disable menu items based on the state of the application. The **Select** and **Click** events are raised only for **MenuItem** objects that are not parent menu items.

Example

See related example in the **System.Windows.Forms.Menu** class topic.

Requirements

Platforms: Windows 98, Windows NT 4.0,
Windows Millennium Edition, Windows 2000,
Windows XP Home Edition, Windows XP Professional,
Windows Server 2003 family

MenuItem.BarBreak Property

Gets or sets a value indicating whether the **MenuItem** is placed on a new line (for a menu item added to a **MainMenu** object) or in a new column (for a submenu item or menu item displayed in a **ContextMenu**).

```
[Visual Basic]
Public Property BarBreak As Boolean
[C#]
public bool BarBreak {get; set;}
[C++]
public: __property bool get_BarBreak();
public: __property void set_BarBreak(bool);
[JScript]
public function get BarBreak() : Boolean;
public function set BarBreak(Boolean);
```

Property Value

true to place the menu item on a new line or in a new column; **false** to leave the menu item in its default placement. The default is **false**.

Remarks

You can use the **BarBreak** property to create a menu where each menu item is placed next to each other horizontally instead of in a vertical list. You can also use this property to create a menu bar that contains multiple rows of top-level menu items.

This property differs from the **Break** property in that a bar is displayed on the left edge of each menu item that has the **Break** property set to **true**. The bar is only displayed when the menu item is not a top-level menu item.

Example

See related example in the **System.Windows.Forms.Menu** class topic.

Requirements

Platforms: Windows 98, Windows NT 4.0,
Windows Millennium Edition, Windows 2000,
Windows XP Home Edition, Windows XP Professional,
Windows Server 2003 family

MenuItem.Break Property

Gets or sets a value indicating whether the item is placed on a new line (for a menu item added to a **MainMenu** object) or in a new column (for a menu item or submenu item displayed in a **ContextMenu**).

```
[Visual Basic]
Public Property Break As Boolean
[C#]
public bool Break {get; set;}
[C++]
public: __property bool get_Break();
public: __property void set_Break(bool);
[JScript]
public function get Break() : Boolean;
public function set Break(Boolean);
```

Property Value

true to place the menu item on a new line or in a new column; **false** to leave the menu item in its default placement. The default is **false**.

Remarks

You can use the **Break** property to create a menu where each menu is placed next to each other horizontally instead of in a vertical list. You can also use this property to create a menu bar that contains multiple rows of top-level menu items.

Example

See related example in the **System.Windows.Forms.Menu** class topic.

Requirements

Platforms: Windows 98, Windows NT 4.0,
Windows Millennium Edition, Windows 2000,
Windows XP Home Edition, Windows XP Professional,
Windows Server 2003 family

MenuItem.Checked Property

Gets or sets a value indicating whether a check mark appears next to the text of the menu item.

```
[Visual Basic]
Public Property Checked As Boolean
[C#]
public bool Checked {get; set;}
[C++]
public: __property bool get_Checked();
public: __property void set_Checked(bool);
[JScript]
public function get Checked() : Boolean;
public function set Checked(Boolean);
```

Property Value

true if the menu item to place a check mark next to the menu item; otherwise, **false**. The default is **false**.

Remarks

You can use the **Checked** property in combination with other menu items in a menu to provide state for an application. For example, you can place a check mark on a menu item in a group of items to identify the size of the font to be displayed for the text in an application. You can also use the **Checked** property to identify the selected menu item in a group of mutually exclusive menu items.

> **Note** This property cannot be set to **true** for top-level menu items.

Example

See related example in the **System.Windows.Forms.Menu** class topic.

Requirements

Platforms: Windows 98, Windows NT 4.0,
Windows Millennium Edition, Windows 2000,
Windows XP Home Edition, Windows XP Professional,
Windows Server 2003 family,
.NET Compact Framework - Windows CE .NET

MenuItem.DefaultItem Property

Gets or sets a value indicating whether the menu item is the default menu item.

```
[Visual Basic]
Public Property DefaultItem As Boolean
[C#]
public bool DefaultItem {get; set;}
[C++]
public: __property bool get_DefaultItem();
public: __property void set_DefaultItem(bool);
```

```
[JScript]
public function get DefaultItem() : Boolean;
public function set DefaultItem(Boolean);
```

Property Value

true if the menu item is the default item in a menu; otherwise, **false**. The default is **false**.

Remarks

The default menu item for a menu is boldfaced. When the user double-clicks a submenu that contains a default item, the default item is selected, and the submenu is closed. You can use the **DefaultItem** property to indicate, the default action that is expected in a menu or shortcut menu.

Example

See related example in the **System.Windows.Forms.Menu** class topic.

Requirements

Platforms: Windows 98, Windows NT 4.0, Windows Millennium Edition, Windows 2000, Windows XP Home Edition, Windows XP Professional, Windows Server 2003 family

MenuItem.Enabled Property

Gets or sets a value indicating whether the menu item is enabled.

```
[Visual Basic]
Public Property Enabled As Boolean
[C#]
public bool Enabled {get; set;}
[C++]
public: __property bool get_Enabled();
public: __property void set_Enabled(bool);
[JScript]
public function get Enabled() : Boolean;
public function set Enabled(Boolean);
```

Property Value

true if the menu item is enabled; otherwise, **false**. The default is **true**.

Remarks

A **MenuItem** that is disabled is displayed in a gray color to indicate its state. When a parent menu item is disabled, all submenu items are not displayed.

Example

See related example in the **System.Windows.Forms.Menu** class topic.

Requirements

Platforms: Windows 98, Windows NT 4.0, Windows Millennium Edition, Windows 2000, Windows XP Home Edition, Windows XP Professional, Windows Server 2003 family, .NET Compact Framework - Windows CE .NET

MenuItem.Index Property

Gets or sets a value indicating the position of the menu item in its parent menu.

```
[Visual Basic]
Public Property Index As Integer
[C#]
public int Index {get; set;}
[C++]
public: __property int get_Index();
public: __property void set_Index(int);
[JScript]
public function get Index() : int;
public function set Index(int);
```

Property Value

The zero-based index representing the position of the menu item in its parent menu.

Remarks

This property provides the indexed position of a menu item in the menu item collection of its parent menu. You can use this property to reposition a menu item to a different location within its menu. You can also use this property when creating a **MenuItem** to specify its position in a menu structure at the time of creation.

Example

See related example in the **System.Windows.Forms.Menu** class topic.

Requirements

Platforms: Windows 98, Windows NT 4.0, Windows Millennium Edition, Windows 2000, Windows XP Home Edition, Windows XP Professional, Windows Server 2003 family

MenuItem.IsParent Property

Gets a value indicating whether the menu item contains child menu items.

```
[Visual Basic]
Overrides Public ReadOnly Property IsParent As Boolean
[C#]
public override bool IsParent {get;}
[C++]
public: __property bool get_IsParent();
[JScript]
public override function get IsParent() : Boolean;
```

Property Value

true if the menu item contains child menu items; **false** if the menu is a standalone menu item.

Remarks

You can use this property with the **Parent** property to navigate in code through an entire menu structure.

Example

See related example in the **System.Windows.Forms.Menu** class topic.

Requirements

Platforms: Windows 98, Windows NT 4.0, Windows Millennium Edition, Windows 2000, Windows XP Home Edition, Windows XP Professional, Windows Server 2003 family

MenuItem.MdiList Property

Gets or sets a value indicating whether the menu item will be populated with a list of the Multiple Document Interface (MDI) child windows that are displayed within the associated form.

[Visual Basic]
```
Public Property MdiList As Boolean
```
[C#]
```
public bool MdiList {get; set;}
```
[C++]
```
public: __property bool get_MdiList();
public: __property void set_MdiList(bool);
```
[JScript]
```
public function get MdiList() : Boolean;
public function set MdiList(Boolean);
```

Property Value

true to display a list of the MDI child windows in this menu item; otherwise, **false**. The default is **false**.

Remarks

When a menu item is selected to display an MDI child window list, the list is displayed as a submenu of the menu item. Only forms that are defined as MDI child forms are displayed in the window list. Only nine child windows can be displayed at a time. If there are more than nine child windows displayed, a "More Windows..." menu item is displayed at the end of the window list. Clicking this menu item displays a dialog box with a complete list of the child windows that are currently active.

Example

See related example in the **System.Windows.Forms.Menu** class topic.

Requirements

Platforms: Windows 98, Windows NT 4.0, Windows Millennium Edition, Windows 2000, Windows XP Home Edition, Windows XP Professional, Windows Server 2003 family

MenuItem.MenuID Property

Gets a value indicating the Windows identifier for this menu item.

[Visual Basic]
```
Protected ReadOnly Property MenuID As Integer
```
[C#]
```
protected int MenuID {get;}
```
[C++]
```
protected: __property int get_MenuID();
```
[JScript]
```
protected function get MenuID() : int;
```

Property Value

The Windows identifier for this menu item.

Requirements

Platforms: Windows 98, Windows NT 4.0, Windows Millennium Edition, Windows 2000, Windows XP Home Edition, Windows XP Professional, Windows Server 2003 family

MenuItem.MergeOrder Property

Gets or sets a value indicating the relative position of the menu item when it is merged with another.

[Visual Basic]
```
Public Property MergeOrder As Integer
```
[C#]
```
public int MergeOrder {get; set;}
```
[C++]
```
public: __property int get_MergeOrder();
public: __property void set_MergeOrder(int);
```
[JScript]
```
public function get MergeOrder() : int;
public function set MergeOrder(int);
```

Property Value

A zero-based index representing the merge order position for this menu item. The default is 0.

Remarks

The merge order of a menu item specifies the relative position that this menu item will assume if the menu structure that the **MenuItem** is contained in is merged with another.

Requirements

Platforms: Windows 98, Windows NT 4.0, Windows Millennium Edition, Windows 2000, Windows XP Home Edition, Windows XP Professional, Windows Server 2003 family

MenuItem.MergeType Property

Gets or sets a value indicating the behavior of this menu item when its menu is merged with another.

[Visual Basic]
```
Public Property MergeType As MenuMerge
```
[C#]
```
public MenuMerge MergeType {get; set;}
```
[C++]
```
public: __property MenuMerge get_MergeType();
public: __property void set_MergeType(MenuMerge);
```
[JScript]
```
public function get MergeType() : MenuMerge;
public function set MergeType(MenuMerge);
```

Property Value

A **MenuMerge** value that represents the menu item's merge type.

Remarks

The merge type of a menu item indicates how the menu item behaves when it has the same merge order as another menu item being merged. You can use merged menus to create a consolidated menu based on two or more existing menus.

Example

See related example in the **System.Windows.Forms.Menu** class topic.

Requirements

Platforms: Windows 98, Windows NT 4.0, Windows Millennium Edition, Windows 2000, Windows XP Home Edition, Windows XP Professional, Windows Server 2003 family

MenuItem.Mnemonic Property

Gets a value indicating the mnemonic character that is associated with this menu item.

```
[Visual Basic]
Public ReadOnly Property Mnemonic As Char
[C#]
public char Mnemonic {get;}
[C++]
public: __property __wchar_t get_Mnemonic();
[JScript]
public function get Mnemonic() : Char;
```

Property Value

A character that represents the mnemonic character associated with this menu item. Returns the character '0' if no mnemonic character is specified in the text of the **MenuItem**.

Remarks

The mnemonic character is the first character after a ampersand chracter in the text of the **MenuItem**. This property will not return a mnemonic if two ampersand characters are placed together as the ampersands are used to display an ampersand in the text of the **MenuItem** instead of defining a mnemonic character.

Requirements

Platforms: Windows 98, Windows NT 4.0, Windows Millennium Edition, Windows 2000, Windows XP Home Edition, Windows XP Professional, Windows Server 2003 family

MenuItem.OwnerDraw Property

Gets or sets a value indicating whether the code that you provide draws the menu item or Windows draws the menu item.

```
[Visual Basic]
Public Property OwnerDraw As Boolean
[C#]
public bool OwnerDraw {get; set;}
[C++]
public: __property bool get_OwnerDraw();
public: __property void set_OwnerDraw(bool);
[JScript]
public function get OwnerDraw() : Boolean;
public function set OwnerDraw(Boolean);
```

Property Value

true if the menu item is to be drawn using code; **false** if the menu item is to be drawn by Windows. The default is **false**.

Remarks

When the **OwnerDraw** property is set to **true**, you need to handle all drawing of the menu item. You can use this capability to create your own special menu displays.

Requirements

Platforms: Windows 98, Windows NT 4.0, Windows Millennium Edition, Windows 2000, Windows XP Home Edition, Windows XP Professional, Windows Server 2003 family

MenuItem.Parent Property

Gets a value indicating the menu that contains this menu item.

```
[Visual Basic]
Public ReadOnly Property Parent As Menu
[C#]
public Menu Parent {get;}
[C++]
public: __property Menu* get_Parent();
[JScript]
public function get Parent() : Menu;
```

Property Value

A **Menu** that represents the menu that contains this menu item.

Remarks

You can use this property to obtain the **Menu** object for a submenu. You can cast the **Menu** object returned by this property to a **MenuItem** object to manipulate it.

Example

See related example in the **System.Windows.Forms.Menu** class topic.

Requirements

Platforms: Windows 98, Windows NT 4.0, Windows Millennium Edition, Windows 2000, Windows XP Home Edition, Windows XP Professional, Windows Server 2003 family, .NET Compact Framework - Windows CE .NET

MenuItem.RadioCheck Property

Gets or sets a value indicating whether the **MenuItem**, if checked, displays a radio-button instead of a check mark.

```
[Visual Basic]
Public Property RadioCheck As Boolean
[C#]
public bool RadioCheck {get; set;}
[C++]
public: __property bool get_RadioCheck();
public: __property void set_RadioCheck(bool);
[JScript]
public function get RadioCheck() : Boolean;
public function set RadioCheck(Boolean);
```

Property Value

true if a radio-button is to be used instead of a check mark; **false** if the standard check mark is to be displayed when the menu item is checked. The default is **false**.

Remarks

Check marks do not necessarily imply a mutually exclusive state for a group of menu items. You can use this property to indicate to the user that the check mark of a menu item is mutually exclusive.

Example

See related example in the **System.Windows.Forms.Menu** class topic.

Requirements

Platforms: Windows 98, Windows NT 4.0, Windows Millennium Edition, Windows 2000, Windows XP Home Edition, Windows XP Professional, Windows Server 2003 family

MenuItem.Shortcut Property

Gets or sets a value indicating the shortcut key associated with the menu item.

```
[Visual Basic]
Public Property Shortcut As Shortcut
[C#]
public Shortcut Shortcut {get; set;}
[C++]
public: __property Shortcut get_Shortcut();
public: __property void set_Shortcut(Shortcut);
[JScript]
public function get Shortcut() : Shortcut;
public function set Shortcut(Shortcut);
```

Property Value

One of the **Shortcut** values. The default is **Shortcut.None**.

Remarks

Shortcut keys provide a method for users to activate frequently used menu items in your menu system and to provide keyboard access to your application for those users who do not have access to a mouse or other pointer device.

Example

See related example in the **System.Windows.Forms.Menu** class topic.

Requirements

Platforms: Windows 98, Windows NT 4.0,
Windows Millennium Edition, Windows 2000,
Windows XP Home Edition, Windows XP Professional,
Windows Server 2003 family

MenuItem.ShowShortcut Property

Gets or sets a value indicating whether the shortcut key that is associated with the menu item is displayed next to the menu item caption.

```
[Visual Basic]
Public Property ShowShortcut As Boolean
[C#]
public bool ShowShortcut {get; set;}
[C++]
public: __property bool get_ShowShortcut();
public: __property void set_ShowShortcut(bool);
[JScript]
public function get ShowShortcut() : Boolean;
public function set ShowShortcut(Boolean);
```

Property Value

true if the shortcut key combination is displayed next to the menu item caption; **false** if the shortcut key combination is not to be displayed. The default is **true**.

Remarks

You can use this property to provide the option for users to hide shortcuts from menus to conserve menu space or to hide a shortcut key from being displayed.

Example

See related example in the **System.Windows.Forms.Menu** class topic.

Requirements

Platforms: Windows 98, Windows NT 4.0,
Windows Millennium Edition, Windows 2000,
Windows XP Home Edition, Windows XP Professional,
Windows Server 2003 family

MenuItem.Text Property

Gets or sets a value indicating the caption of the menu item.

```
[Visual Basic]
Public Property Text As String
[C#]
public string Text {get; set;}
[C++]
public: __property String* get_Text();
public: __property void set_Text(String*);
[JScript]
public function get Text() : String;
public function set Text(String);
```

Property Value

The text caption of the menu item.

Remarks

When you specify a caption for your menu item with the *text* parameter, you can also specify an access key by placing an '&' before the character to be used as the access key. For example, to specify the "F" in "File" as an access key, you would specify the caption for the menu item as "&File". You can use this feature to provide keyboard navigation for your menus.

Example

See related example in the **System.Windows.Forms.Menu** class topic.

Requirements

Platforms: Windows 98, Windows NT 4.0,
Windows Millennium Edition, Windows 2000,
Windows XP Home Edition, Windows XP Professional,
Windows Server 2003 family,
.NET Compact Framework - Windows CE .NET

MenuItem.Visible Property

Gets or sets a value indicating whether the menu item is visible.

```
[Visual Basic]
Public Property Visible As Boolean
[C#]
public bool Visible {get; set;}
[C++]
public: __property bool get_Visible();
public: __property void set_Visible(bool);
[JScript]
public function get Visible() : Boolean;
public function set Visible(Boolean);
```

Property Value

true if the menu item will be made visible on the menu; otherwise, **false**. The default is **true**.

Remarks

You can use this property to modify a menu structure without having to merge menus or disable menus. For example, if you want to hide a complete section of functionality from the menus for your application, you can hide them from the user by setting this property to **false**.

Example

See related example in the **System.Windows.Forms.Menu** class topic.

Requirements

Platforms: Windows 98, Windows NT 4.0, Windows Millennium Edition, Windows 2000, Windows XP Home Edition, Windows XP Professional, Windows Server 2003 family

MenuItem.CloneMenu Method

Creates a copy of a **MenuItem**.

Overload List

Creates a copy of the current **MenuItem**.

[Visual Basic] **Overloads Public Overridable Function CloneMenu() As MenuItem**

[C#] **public virtual MenuItem CloneMenu();**

[C++] **public: virtual MenuItem* CloneMenu();**

[JScript] **public function CloneMenu() : MenuItem;**

Creates a copy of the specified **MenuItem**.

[Visual Basic] **Overloads Protected Sub CloneMenu(MenuItem)**

[C#] **protected void CloneMenu(MenuItem);**

[C++] **protected: void CloneMenu(MenuItem*);**

[JScript] **protected function CloneMenu(MenuItem);**

Inherited from **Menu**.

[Visual Basic] **Overloads Protected Sub CloneMenu(Menu)**

[C#] **protected void CloneMenu(Menu);**

[C++] **protected: void CloneMenu(Menu*);**

[JScript] **protected function CloneMenu(Menu);**

Example

See related example in the **System.Windows.Forms.Menu** class topic.

MenuItem.CloneMenu Method ()

Creates a copy of the current **MenuItem**.

```
[Visual Basic]
Overloads Public Overridable Function CloneMenu() As MenuItem
[C#]
public virtual MenuItem CloneMenu();
[C++]
public: virtual MenuItem* CloneMenu();
[JScript]
public function CloneMenu() : MenuItem;
```

Return Value

A **MenuItem** that represents the duplicated menu item.

Remarks

MenuItem objects cannot be used in more than one place unless you obtain a copy of the **MenuItem**. You can call this method to create a copy of this menu item for use in a **ContextMenu**, **MainMenu**, or other **MenuItem** within your application. When a menu item is cloned, any event handlers specified in the original menu item will continue to function in the cloned version of the menu item. For example, if you created a **MenuItem** and connected its **Click** event to an event handler. When the menu item is cloned, the cloned menu item will call the same event handler.

Example

See related example in the **System.Windows.Forms.Menu** class topic.

Requirements

Platforms: Windows 98, Windows NT 4.0, Windows Millennium Edition, Windows 2000, Windows XP Home Edition, Windows XP Professional, Windows Server 2003 family

MenuItem.CloneMenu Method (MenuItem)

Creates a copy of the specified **MenuItem**.

```
[Visual Basic]
Overloads Protected Sub CloneMenu( _
   ByVal itemSrc As MenuItem _
)
[C#]
protected void CloneMenu(
   MenuItem itemSrc
);
[C++]
protected: void CloneMenu(
   MenuItem* itemSrc
);
[JScript]
protected function CloneMenu(
   itemSrc : MenuItem
);
```

Parameters

itemSrc

The **MenuItem** that represents the menu item to copy.

Return Value

A **MenuItem** that represents the duplicated menu item.

Remarks

Call this method to create copies of menu items that you have already created for use in a shortcut menu or another menu structure within your application. This version of **CloneMenu** allows you to specify a specific **MenuItem** to copy instead of the menu item that is calling the method. You can use this method to initialize a new **MenuItem** object with a copy of another **MenuItem**. When a menu item is cloned, any event handlers specified in the original menu item will continue to function in the cloned version of the menu item. For example, if you created a **MenuItem** and connected its **Click** event to an event handler. When the menu item is cloned, the cloned menu item will call the same event handler.

Example

See related example in the **System.Windows.Forms.Menu** class topic.

Requirements

Platforms: Windows 98, Windows NT 4.0, Windows Millennium Edition, Windows 2000, Windows XP Home Edition, Windows XP Professional, Windows Server 2003 family

MenuItem.Dispose Method

Overload List

This member supports the .NET Framework infrastructure and is not intended to be used directly from your code.

Supported by the .NET Compact Framework.

[Visual Basic] **Overloads Overrides Protected Sub Dispose(Boolean)**

[C#] **protected override void Dispose(bool);**

[C++] **protected: void Dispose(bool);**

[JScript] **protected override function Dispose(Boolean);**

Inherited from **Component**.

[Visual Basic] **Overloads Public Overridable Sub Dispose() Implements IDisposable.Dispose**

[C#] **public virtual void Dispose();**

[C++] **public: virtual void Dispose();**

[JScript] **public function Dispose();**

MenuItem.Dispose Method (Boolean)

This member overrides **Component.Dispose**.

[Visual Basic]
```
Overrides Overloads Protected Sub Dispose( _
   ByVal disposing As Boolean _
)
```
[C#]
```
protected override void Dispose(
   bool disposing
);
```
[C++]
```
protected: void Dispose(
   bool disposing
);
```
[JScript]
```
protected override function Dispose(
   disposing : Boolean
);
```

Requirements

Platforms: Windows 98, Windows NT 4.0, Windows Millennium Edition, Windows 2000, Windows XP Home Edition, Windows XP Professional, Windows Server 2003 family, .NET Compact Framework - Windows CE .NET

MenuItem.MergeMenu Method

Merges this **MenuItem** with another **MenuItem**.

Overload List

Merges this **MenuItem** with another **MenuItem** and returns the resulting merged **MenuItem**.

[Visual Basic] **Overloads Public Overridable Function MergeMenu() As MenuItem**

[C#] **public virtual MenuItem MergeMenu();**

[C++] **public: virtual MenuItem* MergeMenu();**

[JScript] **public function MergeMenu() : MenuItem;**

Merges another menu item with this menu item.

[Visual Basic] **Overloads Public Sub MergeMenu(MenuItem)**

[C#] **public void MergeMenu(MenuItem);**

[C++] **public: void MergeMenu(MenuItem*);**

[JScript] **public function MergeMenu(MenuItem);**

Inherited from **Menu**.

[Visual Basic] **Overloads Public Overridable Sub MergeMenu(Menu)**

[C#] **public virtual void MergeMenu(Menu);**

[C++] **public: virtual void MergeMenu(Menu*);**

[JScript] **public function MergeMenu(Menu);**

Example

See related example in the **System.Windows.Forms.Menu** class topic.

MenuItem.MergeMenu Method ()

Merges this **MenuItem** with another **MenuItem** and returns the resulting merged **MenuItem**.

[Visual Basic]
```
Overloads Public Overridable Function MergeMenu() As MenuItem
```
[C#]
```
public virtual MenuItem MergeMenu();
```
[C++]
```
public: virtual MenuItem* MergeMenu();
```
[JScript]
```
public function MergeMenu() : MenuItem;
```

Return Value

A **MenuItem** that represents the merged menu item.

Remarks

When you call this version of **MergeMenu**, the **MenuItem** returned is a copy of the current menu item that can be merged with another menu item without affecting the functionality of the current item. This version of the **MergeMenu** method is similar to calling the **CloneMenu** method that contains no parameters.

Requirements

Platforms: Windows 98, Windows NT 4.0, Windows Millennium Edition, Windows 2000, Windows XP Home Edition, Windows XP Professional, Windows Server 2003 family

MenuItem.MergeMenu Method (MenuItem)

Merges another menu item with this menu item.

[Visual Basic]
```
Overloads Public Sub MergeMenu( _
   ByVal itemSrc As MenuItem _
)
```
[C#]
```
public void MergeMenu(
   MenuItem itemSrc
);
```

```
[C++]
public: void MergeMenu(
   MenuItem* itemSrc
);
[JScript]
public function MergeMenu(
   itemSrc : MenuItem
);
```

Parameters

itemSrc

A **MenuItem** that specifies the menu item to merge with this one.

Remarks

Menu items are merged according to the value of the menu item's **MergeType** and **MergeOrder** properties. This version of the **MergeMenu** method enables you to merge two **MenuItem** objects (and their submenus) into a single menu. Menu merging is handled automatically when a Multiple Document Interface(MDI) parent form and a child both have menus. You can use this version of the method to merge two **MenuItem** objects (and their submenu items) located in a **MainMenu** control into a single menu within a **ContextMenu**. For example, you can call this version of the **MergeMenu** method to merge the menu items of a File and Edit menu into a single **MenuItem** that can then be added to and displayed by a **ContextMenu**.

Example

See related example in the **System.Windows.Forms.Menu** class topic.

Requirements

Platforms: Windows 98, Windows NT 4.0, Windows Millennium Edition, Windows 2000, Windows XP Home Edition, Windows XP Professional, Windows Server 2003 family

MenuItem.OnClick Method

Raises the **Click** event.

```
[Visual Basic]
Protected Overridable Sub OnClick( _
   ByVal e As EventArgs _
)
[C#]
protected virtual void OnClick(
   EventArgs e
);
[C++]
protected: virtual void OnClick(
   EventArgs* e
);
[JScript]
protected function OnClick(
   e : EventArgs
);
```

Parameters

e

An **EventArgs** that contains the event data.

Remarks

Raising an event invokes the event handler through a delegate. For more information, see **Raising an Event**.

Notes to Inheritors: When overriding **OnClick** in a derived class, be sure to call the base class's **OnClick** method.

Example

See related example in the **System.Windows.Forms.Menu** class topic.

Requirements

Platforms: Windows 98, Windows NT 4.0, Windows Millennium Edition, Windows 2000, Windows XP Home Edition, Windows XP Professional, Windows Server 2003 family

MenuItem.OnDrawItem Method

Raises the **DrawItem** event.

```
[Visual Basic]
Protected Overridable Sub OnDrawItem( _
   ByVal e As DrawItemEventArgs _
)
[C#]
protected virtual void OnDrawItem(
   DrawItemEventArgs e
);
[C++]
protected: virtual void OnDrawItem(
   DrawItemEventArgs* e
);
[JScript]
protected function OnDrawItem(
   e : DrawItemEventArgs
);
```

Parameters

e

A **DrawItemEventArgs** that contains the event data.

Remarks

Raising an event invokes the event handler through a delegate.

Notes to Inheritors: When overriding **OnDrawItem** in a derived class, be sure to call the base class's **OnDrawItem** method.

Requirements

Platforms: Windows 98, Windows NT 4.0, Windows Millennium Edition, Windows 2000, Windows XP Home Edition, Windows XP Professional, Windows Server 2003 family

MenuItem.OnInitMenuPopup Method

This member supports the .NET Framework infrastructure and is not intended to be used directly from your code.

```
[Visual Basic]
Protected Overridable Sub OnInitMenuPopup( _
   ByVal e As EventArgs _
)
[C#]
protected virtual void OnInitMenuPopup(
   EventArgs e
);
[C++]
protected: virtual void OnInitMenuPopup(
   EventArgs* e
);
```

```
[JScript]
protected function OnInitMenuPopup(
   e : EventArgs
);
```

MenuItem.OnMeasureItem Method

Raises the **MeasureItem** event.

```
[Visual Basic]
Protected Overridable Sub OnMeasureItem( _
   ByVal e As MeasureItemEventArgs _
)
[C#]
protected virtual void OnMeasureItem(
   MeasureItemEventArgs e
);
[C++]
protected: virtual void OnMeasureItem(
   MeasureItemEventArgs* e
);
[JScript]
protected function OnMeasureItem(
   e : MeasureItemEventArgs
);
```

Parameters

e

A **MeasureItemEventArgs** that contains the event data.

Remarks

Raising an event invokes the event handler through a delegate.

Notes to Inheritors: When overriding **OnMeasureItem** in a derived class, be sure to call the base class's **OnMeasureItem** method.

Requirements

Platforms: Windows 98, Windows NT 4.0,
Windows Millennium Edition, Windows 2000,
Windows XP Home Edition, Windows XP Professional,
Windows Server 2003 family

MenuItem.OnPopup Method

Raises the **Popup** event.

```
[Visual Basic]
Protected Overridable Sub OnPopup( _
   ByVal e As EventArgs _
)
[C#]
protected virtual void OnPopup(
   EventArgs e
);
[C++]
protected: virtual void OnPopup(
   EventArgs* e
);
[JScript]
protected function OnPopup(
   e : EventArgs
);
```

Parameters

e

An **EventArgs** that contains the event data.

Remarks

Raising an event invokes the event handler through a delegate.

Notes to Inheritors: When overriding in a derived class, be sure to call the base class's **OnPopup** method.

Example

See related example in the **System.Windows.Forms.Menu** class topic.

Requirements

Platforms: Windows 98, Windows NT 4.0,
Windows Millennium Edition, Windows 2000,
Windows XP Home Edition, Windows XP Professional,
Windows Server 2003 family

MenuItem.OnSelect Method

Raises the **Select** event.

```
[Visual Basic]
Protected Overridable Sub OnSelect( _
   ByVal e As EventArgs _
)
[C#]
protected virtual void OnSelect(
   EventArgs e
);
[C++]
protected: virtual void OnSelect(
   EventArgs* e
);
[JScript]
protected function OnSelect(
   e : EventArgs
);
```

Parameters

e

An **EventArgs** that contains the event data.

Remarks

Raising an event invokes the event handler through a delegate.

Notes to Inheritors: When overriding **OnSelect** in a derived class, be sure to call the base class's **OnSelect** method.

Example

See related example in the **System.Windows.Forms.Menu** class topic.

Requirements

Platforms: Windows 98, Windows NT 4.0,
Windows Millennium Edition, Windows 2000,
Windows XP Home Edition, Windows XP Professional,
Windows Server 2003 family

MenuItem.PerformClick Method

Generates a **Click** event for the **MenuItem**, simulating a click by a user.

```
[Visual Basic]
Public Sub PerformClick()
[C#]
public void PerformClick();
```

```
[C++]
public: void PerformClick();
[JScript]
public function PerformClick();
```

Remarks

You can use this menu to activate a menu item through code without passing any event information. For example, if you want to activate a menu item based on an action that occurs in your application, you can call the **PerformClick** method for that **MenuItem**.

Example

See related example in the **System.Windows.Forms.Menu** class topic.

Requirements

Platforms: Windows 98, Windows NT 4.0, Windows Millennium Edition, Windows 2000, Windows XP Home Edition, Windows XP Professional, Windows Server 2003 family

MenuItem.PerformSelect Method

Raises the **Select** event for this menu item.

```
[Visual Basic]
Public Overridable Sub PerformSelect()
[C#]
public virtual void PerformSelect();
[C++]
public: virtual void PerformSelect();
[JScript]
public function PerformSelect();
```

Remarks

This method allows you to raise the **Select** event without passing any event information to the event handler.

Example

See related example in the **System.Windows.Forms.Menu** class topic.

Requirements

Platforms: Windows 98, Windows NT 4.0, Windows Millennium Edition, Windows 2000, Windows XP Home Edition, Windows XP Professional, Windows Server 2003 family

MenuItem.ToString Method

This member overrides **Object.ToString**.

```
[Visual Basic]
Overrides Public Function ToString() As String
[C#]
public override string ToString();
[C++]
public: String* ToString();
[JScript]
public override function ToString() : String;
```

Requirements

Platforms: Windows 98, Windows NT 4.0, Windows Millennium Edition, Windows 2000, Windows XP Home Edition, Windows XP Professional, Windows Server 2003 family, .NET Compact Framework - Windows CE .NET

MenuItem.Click Event

Occurs when the menu item is clicked or selected using a shortcut key or access key defined for the menu item.

```
[Visual Basic]
Public Event Click As EventHandler
[C#]
public event EventHandler Click;
[C++]
public: __event EventHandler* Click;
```

[JScript] In JScript, you can handle the events defined by a class, but you cannot define your own.

Event Data

The event handler receives an argument of type **EventArgs**.

Remarks

The **Click** event occurs when this **MenuItem** is clicked by the user. This event also occurs if the user selects the menu item using the keyboard and presses the Enter key. It can also occur if an access key or shortcut key is pressed that is associated with the **MenuItem**.

> **Note** If the **MenuItems** property for the **MenuItem** contains any items, this event is not raised. This event is not raised for parent menu items.

Example

See related example in the **System.Windows.Forms.Menu** class topic.

Requirements

Platforms: Windows 98, Windows NT 4.0, Windows Millennium Edition, Windows 2000, Windows XP Home Edition, Windows XP Professional, Windows Server 2003 family

MenuItem.DrawItem Event

Occurs when the **OwnerDraw** property of a menu item is set to **true** and a request is made to draw the menu item.

```
[Visual Basic]
Public Event DrawItem As DrawItemEventHandler
[C#]
public event DrawItemEventHandler DrawItem;
[C++]
public: __event DrawItemEventHandler* DrawItem;
```

[JScript] In JScript, you can handle the events defined by a class, but you cannot define your own.

Event Data

The event handler receives an argument of type **DrawItemEventArgs** containing data related to this event. The following **DrawItemEventArgs** properties provide information specific to this event.

Property	Description
BackColor	Gets the background color of the item that is being drawn.
Bounds	Gets the rectangle that represents the bounds of the item that is being drawn.
Font	Gets the font assigned to the item being drawn.
ForeColor	Gets the foreground color of the of the item being drawn.
Graphics	Gets the graphics surface to draw the item on.

Property	Description
Index	Gets the index value of the item that is being drawn.
State	Gets the state of the item being drawn.

Remarks

The **DrawItemEventArgs** argument passed to a **DrawItem** event handler provides a **Graphics** object that enables you to perform drawing and other graphical operations on the surface of the menu item. You can use this event handler to create custom menus that meet the needs of your application.

Example

See related example in the **System.Windows.Forms.Menu** class topic.

Requirements

Platforms: Windows 98, Windows NT 4.0,
Windows Millennium Edition, Windows 2000,
Windows XP Home Edition, Windows XP Professional,
Windows Server 2003 family

MenuItem.MeasureItem Event

Occurs when the menu needs to know the size of a menu item before drawing it.

```
[Visual Basic]
Public Event MeasureItem As MeasureItemEventHandler
[C#]
public event MeasureItemEventHandler MeasureItem;
[C++]
public: __event MeasureItemEventHandler* MeasureItem;
```

[JScript] In JScript, you can handle the events defined by a class, but you cannot define your own.

Event Data

The event handler receives an argument of type **MeasureItemEventArgs** containing data related to this event. The following **MeasureItemEventArgs** properties provide information specific to this event.

Property	Description
Graphics	Gets the **Graphics** object to measure against.
Index	Gets or sets the index of the item for which the height and width is needed.
ItemHeight	Gets or sets the height of the item specified by the **Index**.
ItemWidth	Gets or sets the width of the item specified by the **Index**.

Remarks

In order for this event to be raised, you must have the **OwnerDraw** property of the menu item set to **true**. This event is raised before owner drawn menus are drawn to allow for the size of the menu item to be drawn to be specified. For more information about handling events, see **Consuming Events**.

Requirements

Platforms: Windows 98, Windows NT 4.0,
Windows Millennium Edition, Windows 2000,
Windows XP Home Edition, Windows XP Professional,
Windows Server 2003 family

MenuItem.Popup Event

Occurs before a menu item's list of menu items is displayed.

```
[Visual Basic]
Public Event Popup As EventHandler
[C#]
public event EventHandler Popup;
[C++]
public: __event EventHandler* Popup;
```

[JScript] In JScript, you can handle the events defined by a class, but you cannot define your own.

Event Data

The event handler receives an argument of type **EventArgs**.

Remarks

This event only occurs when a menu item has submenu items to display. You can use this event handler to add, remove, enable, disable, check, or uncheck menu items based on the state of your application before they are displayed.

Example

See related example in the **System.Windows.Forms.Menu** class topic.

Requirements

Platforms: Windows 98, Windows NT 4.0,
Windows Millennium Edition, Windows 2000,
Windows XP Home Edition, Windows XP Professional,
Windows Server 2003 family

MenuItem.Select Event

Occurs when the user places the cursor over a menu item.

```
[Visual Basic]
Public Event Select As EventHandler
[C#]
public event EventHandler Select;
[C++]
public: __event EventHandler* Select;
```

[JScript] In JScript, you can handle the events defined by a class, but you cannot define your own.

Event Data

The event handler receives an argument of type **EventArgs**.

Remarks

This event is typically raised when the user places the mouse cursor over the menu item. The event can also be raised when the user highlights a menu item using the keyboard by scrolling to the menu item with the arrow keys. You can use this event to display a detailed help string pertaining to this menu item in an application's status bar.

> **Note** If the **MenuItems** property for the **MenuItem** contains any items, this event is not raised. This event is not raised for parent menu items.

Example

See related example in the **System.Windows.Forms.Menu** class topic.

Requirements

Platforms: Windows 98, Windows NT 4.0,
Windows Millennium Edition, Windows 2000,
Windows XP Home Edition, Windows XP Professional,
Windows Server 2003 family

Menu.MenuItemCollection Class

Represents a collection of **MenuItem** objects.

System.Object
  System.Windows.Forms.Menu.MenuItemCollection

```
[Visual Basic]
Public Class Menu.MenuItemCollection
   Implements IList, ICollection, IEnumerable
[C#]
public class Menu.MenuItemCollection : IList, ICollection,
   IEnumerable
[C++]
public __gc class Menu.MenuItemCollection : public IList,
   ICollection, IEnumerable
[JScript]
public class Menu.MenuItemCollection implements IList, ICollection,
   IEnumerable
```

Thread Safety

Any public static (**Shared** in Visual Basic) members of this type are safe for multithreaded operations. Any instance members are not guaranteed to be thread safe.

Remarks

This class represents the collection of **MenuItem** objects stored in a **MainMenu**, **ContextMenu**, or **MenuItem**. For the **MainMenu** and **ContextMenu** classes, this collection represents the entire menu structure for the control. For the **MenuItem** class, this collection represents the list of submenu items associated with the **MenuItem**.

The **Add** and **Remove** methods enable you to add and remove individual menu items from the collection. You can also use the **Clear** method to remove all the menu items from the collection.

Requirements

Namespace: System.Windows.Forms

Platforms: Windows 98, Windows NT 4.0,
Windows Millennium Edition, Windows 2000,
Windows XP Home Edition, Windows XP Professional,
Windows Server 2003 family,
.NET Compact Framework - Windows CE .NET

Assembly: System.Windows.Forms (in System.Windows.Forms.dll)

Menu.MenuItemCollection Constructor

Initializes a new instance of the **Menu.MenuItemCollection** class.

```
[Visual Basic]
Public Sub New( _
   ByVal owner As Menu _
)
[C#]
public Menu.MenuItemCollection(
   Menu owner
);
[C++]
public: MenuItemCollection(
   Menu* owner
);
[JScript]
public function Menu.MenuItemCollection(
   owner : Menu
);
```

Parameters

owner
The **Menu** that owns this collection.

Remarks

This class requires that you associate the collection with a class that derives from **Menu**, such as the **MainMenu**, **ContextMenu**, or **MenuItem** class. Since you must specify a menu that is associated with this collection, you cannot create multiple menu item collections and associate them with a menu as needed. In order to switch the menu items associated with a menu, you must clear the collection of items and add the menu items to display to the collection.

Requirements

Platforms: Windows 98, Windows NT 4.0,
Windows Millennium Edition, Windows 2000,
Windows XP Home Edition, Windows XP Professional,
Windows Server 2003 family

Menu.MenuItemCollection.Count Property

Gets a value indicating the total number of **MenuItem** objects in the collection.

```
[Visual Basic]
Public Overridable ReadOnly Property Count As Integer  Implements _
   ICollection.Count
[C#]
public virtual int Count {get;}
[C++]
public: __property virtual int get_Count();
[JScript]
public function get Count() : int;
```

Property Value

The number of **MenuItem** objects in the collection.

Implements

ICollection.Count

Remarks

The **Count** property holds the number of **MenuItem** objects assigned to the collection. You can use the **Count** property value as the upper bounds of a loop to iterate through a collection. Keep in mind, the index value of a collection is a zero-based index, so you must subtract one from the looping variable. If you do not account for this, you will exceed the upper bounds of the collection and throw an exception.

Example

See related example in the **System.Windows.Forms.Menu** class topic.

Requirements

Platforms: Windows 98, Windows NT 4.0,
Windows Millennium Edition, Windows 2000,
Windows XP Home Edition, Windows XP Professional,
Windows Server 2003 family,
.NET Compact Framework - Windows CE .NET

Menu.MenuItemCollection.IsReadOnly Property

This member supports the .NET Framework infrastructure and is not intended to be used directly from your code.

```
[Visual Basic]
Public Overridable ReadOnly Property IsReadOnly As Boolean _
   Implements IList.IsReadOnly
[C#]
public virtual bool IsReadOnly {get;}
[C++]
public: __property virtual bool get_IsReadOnly();
[JScript]
public function get IsReadOnly() : Boolean;
```

Menu.MenuItemCollection.Item Property

Retrieves the **MenuItem** at the specified indexed location in the collection.

[C#] In C#, this property is the indexer for the **Menu.MenuItem-Collection** class.

```
[Visual Basic]
Public Overridable Default ReadOnly Property Item( _
   ByVal index As Integer _
) As MenuItem
[C#]
public virtual MenuItem this[
   int index
] {get;}
[C++]
public: __property virtual MenuItem* get_Item(
   int index
);
[JScript]
returnValue = MenuItemCollectionObject.Item(index);
-or-
returnValue = MenuItemCollectionObject(index);
```

[JScript] In JScript, you can use the default indexed properties defined by a type, but you cannot explicitly define your own. However, specifying the **expando** attribute on a class automatically provides a default indexed property whose type is **Object** and whose index type is **String**.

Arguments [JScript]

index

The indexed location of the **MenuItem** in the collection.

Parameters [Visual Basic, C#, C++]

index

The indexed location of the **MenuItem** in the collection.

Property Value

The **MenuItem** at the specified location.

Exceptions

Exception Type	Condition
ArgumentException	The *value* parameter is a null reference (**Nothing** in Visual Basic). or The *index* parameter is less than zero. or The *index* parameter is greater than the number of menu items in the collection, and the collection of menu items is not a null reference (**Nothing**).

Remarks

To assign **MenuItem** objects to a specific location, or to retrieve them from the **Menu.MenuItemCollection**, you can reference the collection object with a specific index value. The index value of the **Menu.MenuItemCollection** is a zero-based index.

Requirements

Platforms: Windows 98, Windows NT 4.0, Windows Millennium Edition, Windows 2000, Windows XP Home Edition, Windows XP Professional, Windows Server 2003 family

Menu.MenuItemCollection.System.Collections.ICollection.IsSynchronized Property

Note: This namespace, class, or member is supported only in version 1.1 of the .NET Framework.

This member supports the .NET Framework infrastructure and is not intended to be used directly from your code.

```
[Visual Basic]
Private ReadOnly Property IsSynchronized As Boolean Implements _
   ICollection.IsSynchronized
[C#]
bool ICollection.IsSynchronized {get;}
[C++]
private: __property bool
   System::Collections::ICollection::get_IsSynchronized();
[JScript]
private function get ICollection.IsSynchronized() : Boolean;
```

Menu.MenuItemCollection.System.Collections.ICollection.SyncRoot Property

Note: This namespace, class, or member is supported only in version 1.1 of the .NET Framework.

This member supports the .NET Framework infrastructure and is not intended to be used directly from your code.

```
[Visual Basic]
Private ReadOnly Property SyncRoot As Object Implements _
   ICollection.SyncRoot
[C#]
object ICollection.SyncRoot {get;}
[C++]
private: __property Object*
   System::Collections::ICollection::get_SyncRoot();
[JScript]
private function get ICollection.SyncRoot() : Object;
```

Menu.MenuItemCollection.System.Collections.IList.IsFixedSize Property

Note: This namespace, class, or member is supported only in version 1.1 of the .NET Framework.

This member supports the .NET Framework infrastructure and is not intended to be used directly from your code.

```
[Visual Basic]
Private ReadOnly Property IsFixedSize As Boolean Implements _
   IList.IsFixedSize
[C#]
bool IList.IsFixedSize {get;}
[C++]
private: __property bool
   System::Collections::IList::get_IsFixedSize();
[JScript]
private function get IList.IsFixedSize() : Boolean;
```

Menu.MenuItemCollection.System.Collections.IList.Item Property

Note: This namespace, class, or member is supported only in version 1.1 of the .NET Framework.

[C#] In C#, this property is the indexer for the **Menu.MenuItemCollection** class.

```
[Visual Basic]
Private Default Property Item( _
   ByVal index As Integer _
) As Object Implements IList.Item
[C#]
object IList.this[
   int index
] {get; set;}
[C++]
private: __property Object* System::Collections::IList::get_Item(
   int index
);
private: __property void System::Collections::IList::set_Item(
   int index,
   Object*
);
[JScript]
private function get IList.get_Item(index : int) : Object;
private function set IList.set_Item(index : int, value : Object);
-or-
private function get IList.get_Item(index : int) : Object;
private function set IList.set_Item(index : int, value : Object);
```

[JScript] In JScript, you can use the default indexed properties defined by a type, but you cannot explicitly define your own. However, specifying the **expando** attribute on a class automatically provides a default indexed property whose type is **Object** and whose index type is **String**.

Arguments [JScript]

index

Parameters [Visual Basic, C#, C++]

index

Requirements

Platforms: Windows 98, Windows NT 4.0, Windows Millennium Edition, Windows 2000, Windows XP Home Edition, Windows XP Professional, Windows Server 2003 family

Menu.MenuItemCollection.Add Method

Adds a new **MenuItem** to the collection.

Overload List

Adds a previously created **MenuItem** to the end of the current menu.

Supported by the .NET Compact Framework.

[Visual Basic] **Overloads Public Overridable Function Add(MenuItem) As Integer**

[C#] **public virtual int Add(MenuItem);**

[C++] **public: virtual int Add(MenuItem*);**

[JScript] **public function Add(MenuItem) : int;**

Adds a new **MenuItem**, to the end of the current menu, with a specified caption.

[Visual Basic] **Overloads Public Overridable Function Add(String) As MenuItem**

[C#] **public virtual MenuItem Add(string);**

[C++] **public: virtual MenuItem* Add(String*);**

[JScript] **public function Add(String) : MenuItem;**

Adds a previously created **MenuItem** at the specified index within the menu item collection.

[Visual Basic] **Overloads Public Overridable Function Add(Integer, MenuItem) As Integer**

[C#] **public virtual int Add(int, MenuItem);**

[C++] **public: virtual int Add(int, MenuItem*);**

[JScript] **public function Add(int, MenuItem) : int;**

Adds a new **MenuItem** to the end of the current menu with a specified caption and a specified event handler for the **Click** event.

[Visual Basic] **Overloads Public Overridable Function Add(String, EventHandler) As MenuItem**

[C#] **public virtual MenuItem Add(string, EventHandler);**

[C++] **public: virtual MenuItem* Add(String*, EventHandler*);**

[JScript] **public function Add(String, EventHandler) : MenuItem;**

Adds a new **MenuItem** to the end of this menu with the specified caption, **Click** event handler, and items.

[Visual Basic] **Overloads Public Overridable Function Add(String, MenuItem()) As MenuItem**

[C#] **public virtual MenuItem Add(string, MenuItem[]);**

[C++] **public: virtual MenuItem* Add(String*, MenuItem[]);**

[JScript] **public function Add(String, MenuItem[]) : MenuItem;**

Example

See related example in the **System.Windows.Forms.Menu** class topic.

Menu.MenuItemCollection.Add Method (MenuItem)

Adds a previously created **MenuItem** to the end of the current menu.

[Visual Basic]
```
Overloads Public Overridable Function Add( _
   ByVal item As MenuItem _
) As Integer
```
[C#]
```
public virtual int Add(
   MenuItem item
);
```
[C++]
```
public: virtual int Add(
   MenuItem* item
);
```
[JScript]
```
public function Add(
   item : MenuItem
) : int;
```

Parameters

item
The **MenuItem** to add.

Return Value

The zero-based index where the item is stored in the collection.

Remarks

A **MenuItem** can only be contained in one menu at a time, and cannot be added more than once to the same menu. To reuse a **MenuItem** in more than one menu, use the **CloneMenu** method of the **MenuItem** class. To remove a **MenuItem** that you have previously added, use the **Remove** method.

This version of the **Add** method allows you to add previously created **MenuItem** objects to the end of the menu item collection.

Example

See related example in the **System.Windows.Forms.Menu** class topic.

Requirements

Platforms: Windows 98, Windows NT 4.0,
Windows Millennium Edition, Windows 2000,
Windows XP Home Edition, Windows XP Professional,
Windows Server 2003 family,
.NET Compact Framework - Windows CE .NET

Menu.MenuItemCollection.Add Method (String)

Adds a new **MenuItem**, to the end of the current menu, with a specified caption.

[Visual Basic]
```
Overloads Public Overridable Function Add( _
   ByVal caption As String _
) As MenuItem
```
[C#]
```
public virtual MenuItem Add(
   string caption
);
```
[C++]
```
public: virtual MenuItem* Add(
   String* caption
);
```
[JScript]
```
public function Add(
   caption : String
) : MenuItem;
```

Parameters

caption
The caption of the menu item.

Return Value

A **MenuItem** that represents the menu item being added to the collection.

Remarks

A **MenuItem** can only be contained in one menu at a time, and cannot be added more than once to the same menu. To reuse a **MenuItem** in more than one menu, use the **CloneMenu** method of the **MenuItem** class. To remove a **MenuItem** that you have previously added, use the **Remove** method.

Example

See related example in the **System.Windows.Forms.Menu** class topic.

Requirements

Platforms: Windows 98, Windows NT 4.0,
Windows Millennium Edition, Windows 2000,
Windows XP Home Edition, Windows XP Professional,
Windows Server 2003 family

Menu.MenuItemCollection.Add Method (Int32, MenuItem)

Adds a previously created **MenuItem** at the specified index within the menu item collection.

[Visual Basic]
```
Overloads Public Overridable Function Add( _
   ByVal index As Integer, _
   ByVal item As MenuItem _
) As Integer
```
[C#]
```
public virtual int Add(
   int index,
   MenuItem item
);
```
[C++]
```
public: virtual int Add(
   int index,
   MenuItem* item
);
```
[JScript]
```
public function Add(
   index : int,
   item : MenuItem
) : int;
```

Parameters

index
The position to add the new item.

item
The **MenuItem** to add.

Return Value

The zero-based index where the item is stored in the collection.

Exceptions

Exception Type	Condition
Exception	The **MenuItem** being added is already in use.
ArgumentException	The index supplied in the *index* parameter is larger than the size of the collection.

Remarks

A **MenuItem** can only be contained in one menu at a time, and cannot be added more than once to the same menu. To reuse a **MenuItem** in more than one menu, use the **CloneMenu** method of the **MenuItem** class. To remove a **MenuItem** that you have previously added, use the **Remove** method.

This version of the **Add** method allows you to add previously created **MenuItem** objects to a specific index location within the collection. Any **MenuItem** currently located at that index, and all **MenuItem** objects after that index, are moved to the next lowest index in the collection.

Example

See related example in the **System.Windows.Forms.Menu** class topic.

Requirements

Platforms: Windows 98, Windows NT 4.0,
Windows Millennium Edition, Windows 2000,
Windows XP Home Edition, Windows XP Professional,
Windows Server 2003 family

Menu.MenuItemCollection.Add Method (String, EventHandler)

Adds a new **MenuItem** to the end of the current menu with a specified caption and a specified event handler for the **Click** event.

```
[Visual Basic]
Overloads Public Overridable Function Add( _
   ByVal caption As String, _
   ByVal onClick As EventHandler _
) As MenuItem
[C#]
public virtual MenuItem Add(
   string caption,
   EventHandler onClick
);
[C++]
public: virtual MenuItem* Add(
   String* caption,
   EventHandler* onClick
);
[JScript]
public function Add(
   caption : String,
   onClick : EventHandler
) : MenuItem;
```

Parameters

caption
: The caption of the menu item.

onClick
: An **EventHandler** that represents the event handler that is called when the item is clicked by the user or when a user, presses an accelerator or shortcut key for the menu item.

Return Value

A **MenuItem** that represents the menu item being added to the collection.

Remarks

A **MenuItem** can only be contained in one menu at a time, and cannot be added more than once to the same menu. To reuse a **MenuItem** in more than one menu, use the **CloneMenu** method of the **MenuItem** class. To remove a **MenuItem** that you have previously added, use the **Remove** method.

This version of the **Add** method allows you to specify a caption for the menu item and a delegate to handle the **Click** event. You can use this version of the **Add** method if your application already has an event handler to handle the **Click** event.

> **Note** The **Click** event is not raised for a **MenuItem** that contains submenu items.

Example

See related example in the **System.Windows.Forms.Menu** class topic.

Requirements

Platforms: Windows 98, Windows NT 4.0,
Windows Millennium Edition, Windows 2000,
Windows XP Home Edition, Windows XP Professional,
Windows Server 2003 family

Menu.MenuItemCollection.Add Method (String, MenuItem[])

Adds a new **MenuItem** to the end of this menu with the specified caption, **Click** event handler, and items.

```
[Visual Basic]
Overloads Public Overridable Function Add( _
   ByVal caption As String, _
   ByVal items() As MenuItem _
) As MenuItem
[C#]
public virtual MenuItem Add(
   string caption,
   MenuItem[] items
);
[C++]
public: virtual MenuItem* Add(
   String* caption,
   MenuItem* items[]
);
[JScript]
public function Add(
   caption : String,
   items : MenuItem[]
) : MenuItem;
```

Parameters

caption

The caption of the menu item.

items

An array of **MenuItem** objects that this **MenuItem** will contain.

Return Value

A **MenuItem** that represents the menu item being added to the collection.

Remarks

A **MenuItem** can only be contained in one menu at a time, and cannot be added more than once to the same menu. To reuse a **MenuItem** in more than one menu, use the **CloneMenu** method of the **MenuItem** class. To remove a **MenuItem** that you have previously added, use the **Remove** method.

This version of the **Add** method allows you to specify a caption for the menu item and a delegate that will handle its **Click** event. You can use this version of the **Add** method if your application already has an event handler to handle the **Click** event. This version of the method also allows you to specify an array of previously created **MenuItem** objects that you want to add to the collection. You can use this feature to reuse existing **MenuItem** objects that have been cloned using the **CloneMenu** method. If the *items* parameter is not empty or a null reference (**Nothing** in Visual Basic), the **MenuItem** being added to the collection will contain submenu items.

> **Note** The **Click** event is not raised for a **MenuItem** that contains submenu items.

Requirements

Platforms: Windows 98, Windows NT 4.0,
Windows Millennium Edition, Windows 2000,
Windows XP Home Edition, Windows XP Professional,
Windows Server 2003 family

Menu.MenuItemCollection.AddRange Method

Adds an array of previously created **MenuItem** objects to the collection.

```
[Visual Basic]
Public Overridable Sub AddRange( _
   ByVal items() As MenuItem _
)
[C#]
public virtual void AddRange(
   MenuItem[] items
);
[C++]
public: virtual void AddRange(
   MenuItem* items[]
);
[JScript]
public function AddRange(
   items : MenuItem[]
);
```

Parameters

items

An array of **MenuItem** objects representing the menu items to add to the collection.

Remarks

You can use method to quickly add a group of previouly created **MenuItem** objects to the collection instead of manually adding each **MenuItem** to the collection using the **Add** method. If the collection already contains **MenuItem** objects, calling this method will add the new **MenuItem** objects to the end of the collection.

Example

See related example in the **System.Windows.Forms.Menu** class topic.

Requirements

Platforms: Windows 98, Windows NT 4.0,
Windows Millennium Edition, Windows 2000,
Windows XP Home Edition, Windows XP Professional,
Windows Server 2003 family

Menu.MenuItemCollection.Clear Method

Removes all **MenuItem** objects from the menu item collection.

```
[Visual Basic]
Public Overridable Sub Clear() Implements IList.Clear
[C#]
public virtual void Clear();
[C++]
public: virtual void Clear();
[JScript]
public function Clear();
```

Implements

IList.Clear

Remarks

You can use this method to clear the entire collection of menu items from a menu. To remove an individual menu item from the collection, use the **Remove** method. To add new **MenuItem** objects to the collection, use the **Add** method.

Example

See related example in the **System.Windows.Forms.Menu** class topic.

Requirements

Platforms: Windows 98, Windows NT 4.0,
Windows Millennium Edition, Windows 2000,
Windows XP Home Edition, Windows XP Professional,
Windows Server 2003 family,
.NET Compact Framework - Windows CE .NET

Menu.MenuItemCollection.Contains Method

Determines if the specified **MenuItem** is a member of the collection.

```
[Visual Basic]
Public Function Contains( _
   ByVal value As MenuItem _
) As Boolean
[C#]
public bool Contains(
   MenuItem value
);
```

```
[C++]
public: bool Contains(
   MenuItem* value
);
[JScript]
public function Contains(
   value : MenuItem
) : Boolean;
```

Parameters

value
: The **MenuItem** to locate in the collection.

Return Value

true if the **MenuItem** is a member of the collection; otherwise, **false**.

Remarks

This method enables you to determine whether a **MenuItem** is member of the collection before attempting to perform operations on the **MenuItem**. You can use this method to confirm that a **MenuItem** has been added to or is still a member of the collection.

Example

See related example in the **System.Windows.Forms.Menu** class topic.

Requirements

Platforms: Windows 98, Windows NT 4.0,
Windows Millennium Edition, Windows 2000,
Windows XP Home Edition, Windows XP Professional,
Windows Server 2003 family,
.NET Compact Framework - Windows CE .NET

Menu.MenuItemCollection.CopyTo Method

Copies the entire collection into an existing array at a specified location within the array.

```
[Visual Basic]
Public Overridable Sub CopyTo( _
   ByVal dest As Array, _
   ByVal index As Integer _
) Implements ICollection.CopyTo
[C#]
public virtual void CopyTo(
   Array dest,
   int index
);
[C++]
public: virtual void CopyTo(
   Array* dest,
   int index
);
[JScript]
public function CopyTo(
   dest : Array,
   index : int
);
```

Parameters

dest
: The destination array.

index
: The index in the destination array at which storing begins.

Implements

ICollection.CopyTo

Remarks

You can use this method to combine **MenuItem** objects from multiple collections into a single array. This feature enables you to easily combine two or more sets of menu items for use in a **ContextMenu** or **MainMenu**.

Example

See related example in the **System.Windows.Forms.Menu** class topic.

Requirements

Platforms: Windows 98, Windows NT 4.0,
Windows Millennium Edition, Windows 2000,
Windows XP Home Edition, Windows XP Professional,
Windows Server 2003 family,
.NET Compact Framework - Windows CE .NET

Menu.MenuItemCollection.GetEnumerator Method

Returns an enumerator that can be used to iterate through the menu item collection.

```
[Visual Basic]
Public Overridable Function GetEnumerator() As IEnumerator _
   Implements IEnumerable.GetEnumerator
[C#]
public virtual IEnumerator GetEnumerator();
[C++]
public: virtual IEnumerator* GetEnumerator();
[JScript]
public function GetEnumerator() : IEnumerator;
```

Return Value

An **IEnumerator** object that represents the menu item collection.

Implements

IEnumerable.GetEnumerator

Requirements

Platforms: Windows 98, Windows NT 4.0,
Windows Millennium Edition, Windows 2000,
Windows XP Home Edition, Windows XP Professional,
Windows Server 2003 family,
.NET Compact Framework - Windows CE .NET

Menu.MenuItemCollection.IList.Add Method

This member supports the .NET Framework infrastructure and is not intended to be used directly from your code.

```
[Visual Basic]
Private Function Add( _
   ByVal value As Object _
) As Integer Implements IList.Add
[C#]
int IList.Add(
   object value
);
[C++]
private: int IList::Add(
```

```
[Visual Basic]
   Object* value
);
[JScript]
private function IList.Add(
   value : Object
) : int;
```

Menu.MenuItemCollection.IList.Contains Method

This member supports the .NET Framework infrastructure and is not intended to be used directly from your code.

```
[Visual Basic]
Private Function Contains( _
   ByVal value As Object _
) As Boolean Implements IList.Contains
[C#]
bool IList.Contains(
   object value
);
[C++]
private: bool IList::Contains(
   Object* value
);
[JScript]
private function IList.Contains(
   value : Object
) : Boolean;
```

Menu.MenuItemCollection.IList.IndexOf Method

This member supports the .NET Framework infrastructure and is not intended to be used directly from your code.

```
[Visual Basic]
Private Function IndexOf( _
   ByVal value As Object _
) As Integer Implements IList.IndexOf
[C#]
int IList.IndexOf(
   object value
);
[C++]
private: int IList::IndexOf(
   Object* value
);
[JScript]
private function IList.IndexOf(
   value : Object
) : int;
```

Menu.MenuItemCollection.IList.Insert Method

This member supports the .NET Framework infrastructure and is not intended to be used directly from your code.

```
[Visual Basic]
Private Sub Insert( _
   ByVal index As Integer, _
   ByVal value As Object _
) Implements IList.Insert
[C#]
void IList.Insert(
   int index,
   object value
);
[C++]
private: void IList::Insert(
   int index,
   Object* value
);
[JScript]
private function IList.Insert(
   index : int,
   value : Object
);
```

Menu.MenuItemCollection.IList.Remove Method

This member supports the .NET Framework infrastructure and is not intended to be used directly from your code.

```
[Visual Basic]
Private Sub Remove( _
   ByVal value As Object _
) Implements IList.Remove
[C#]
void IList.Remove(
   object value
);
[C++]
private: void IList::Remove(
   Object* value
);
[JScript]
private function IList.Remove(
   value : Object
);
```

Menu.MenuItemCollection.IndexOf Method

Retrieves the index of a specific item in the collection.

```
[Visual Basic]
Public Function IndexOf( _
   ByVal value As MenuItem _
) As Integer
[C#]
public int IndexOf(
   MenuItem value
);
[C++]
public: int IndexOf(
   MenuItem* value
);
[JScript]
public function IndexOf(
   value : MenuItem
) : int;
```

Parameters

value

The **MenuItem** to locate in the collection.

Return Value

The zero-based index of the item found in the collection; otherwise, -1.

Example

See related example in the **System.Windows.Forms.Menu** class topic.

Requirements

Platforms: Windows 98, Windows NT 4.0,
Windows Millennium Edition, Windows 2000,
Windows XP Home Edition, Windows XP Professional,
Windows Server 2003 family,
.NET Compact Framework - Windows CE .NET

Menu.MenuItemCollection.Remove Method

Removes the specified **MenuItem** from the menu item collection.

[Visual Basic]
```
Public Overridable Sub Remove( _
   ByVal item As MenuItem _
)
```
[C#]
```
public virtual void Remove(
   MenuItem item
);
```
[C++]
```
public: virtual void Remove(
   MenuItem* item
);
```
[JScript]
```
public function Remove(
   item : MenuItem
);
```

Parameters

item

The **MenuItem** to remove.

Remarks

When a **MenuItem** is removed from the menu item collection, all subsequent menu items are moved up one position in the collection. You can use this version of the **Remove** to remove a specific **MenuItem** from the collection using a reference to the **MenuItem** to be removed. If you do not have a reference to the **MenuItem** that you want to remove, you can use the other version of this method that accepts, as a parameter, an index corresponding to the **MenuItem** to be removed.

Example

See related example in the **System.Windows.Forms.Menu** class topic.

Requirements

Platforms: Windows 98, Windows NT 4.0,
Windows Millennium Edition, Windows 2000,
Windows XP Home Edition, Windows XP Professional,
Windows Server 2003 family,
.NET Compact Framework - Windows CE .NET

Menu.MenuItemCollection.RemoveAt Method

Removes a **MenuItem** from the menu item collection at a specified index.

[Visual Basic]
```
Public Overridable Sub RemoveAt( _
   ByVal index As Integer _
) Implements IList.RemoveAt
```
[C#]
```
public virtual void RemoveAt(
   int index
);
```
[C++]
```
public: virtual void RemoveAt(
   int index
);
```
[JScript]
```
public function RemoveAt(
   index : int
);
```

Parameters

index

The index of the **MenuItem** to remove.

Implements

IList.RemoveAt

Remarks

When a **MenuItem** is removed from the menu item collection, all subsequent menu items are moved up one position in the collection.

Example

See related example in the **System.Windows.Forms.Menu** class topic.

Requirements

Platforms: Windows 98, Windows NT 4.0,
Windows Millennium Edition, Windows 2000,
Windows XP Home Edition, Windows XP Professional,
Windows Server 2003 family,
.NET Compact Framework - Windows CE .NET

MenuMerge Enumeration

Specifies the behavior of a **MenuItem** when it is merged with items in another menu.

[Visual Basic]

```
<Serializable>
Public Enum MenuMerge
```

[C#]

```
[Serializable]
public enum MenuMerge
```

[C++]

```
[Serializable]
__value public enum MenuMerge
```

[JScript]

```
public
   Serializable
enum MenuMerge
```

Remarks

Use the members of this enumeration to set the value of the **MergeType** property of the **MenuItem**.

Members

Member name	Description
Add	The **MenuItem** is added to the collection of existing **MenuItem** objects in a merged menu.
MergeItems	All submenu items of this **MenuItem** are merged with those of existing **MenuItem** objects at the same position in a merged menu.
Remove	The **MenuItem** is not included in a merged menu.
Replace	The **MenuItem** replaces an existing **MenuItem** at the same position in a merged menu.

Example

See related example in the **System.Windows.Forms.Menu** class topic.

Requirements

Namespace: System.Windows.Forms

Platforms: Windows 98, Windows NT 4.0, Windows Millennium Edition, Windows 2000, Windows XP Home Edition, Windows XP Professional, Windows Server 2003 family

Assembly: System.Windows.Forms (in System.Windows.Forms.dll)

Message Structure

Implements a Windows message.

System.Object
  System.ValueType
    System.Windows.Forms.Message

[Visual Basic]
```
Public Structure Message
```
[C#]
```
public struct Message
```
[C++]
```
public __value struct Message
```

[JScript] In JScript, you can use the structures in the .NET Framework, but you cannot define your own.

Thread Safety

Any public static (**Shared** in Visual Basic) members of this type are safe for multithreaded operations. Any instance members are not guaranteed to be thread safe.

Remarks

The **Message** structure wraps messages that Windows sends. You can use this structure to wrap a message and assign it to the window procedure to be dispatched. You can also use this structure to get information about a message the system sends to your application or controls.

You cannot create the **Message** structure directly. To create a **Message** structure, use the **Create** method. To make creating **Message** structures more efficient, the **Message** structure uses its pool of existing **Message** structures instead of instantiating a new one, if possible. However, if a **Message** structure is not available in the pool, a new structure is instantiated.

Example

[Visual Basic, C#, C++] The following example demonstrates overriding the **WndProc** method to handle operating system messages identified in the **Message** structure. The WM_ACTIVATEAPP operating system message is handled in this example to know when another application is becoming active. Refer to the Platform SDK documentation reference located in the MSDN Library to understand the available **Message.Msg**, **Message.LParam**, and **Message.WParam** values. Actual constant values can be found in the windows.h header file included in the Platform SDK (Core SDK section) download, which is also available on MSDN.

[Visual Basic]
```
Imports System
Imports System.Drawing
Imports System.Windows.Forms

Namespace csTempWindowsApplication1

    Public Class Form1
        Inherits System.Windows.Forms.Form

        ' Constant value was found in the "windows.h" header file.
        Private Const WM_ACTIVATEAPP As Integer = &H1C
        Private appActive As Boolean = True

        <STAThread()> _
        Shared Sub Main()
            Application.Run(New Form1())
        End Sub 'Main

        Public Sub New()
            MyBase.New()

            Me.Size = New System.Drawing.Size(300, 300)
            Me.Text = "Form1"
            Me.Font = New System.Drawing.Font("Microsoft Sans ↵
 Serif", 18.0!, System.Drawing.FontStyle.Bold, ↵
System.Drawing.GraphicsUnit.Point, CType(0, Byte))
        End Sub

        Protected Overrides Sub OnPaint(ByVal e As PaintEventArgs)

            ' Paint a string in different styles depending on ↵
 whether the
            ' application is active.
            If (appActive) Then
                e.Graphics.FillRectangle ↵
 (SystemBrushes.ActiveCaption, 20, 20, 260, 50)
                e.Graphics.DrawString("Application is active", ↵
 Me.Font, SystemBrushes.ActiveCaptionText, 20, 20)
            Else
                e.Graphics.FillRectangle ↵
 (SystemBrushes.InactiveCaption, 20, 20, 260, 50)
                e.Graphics.DrawString("Application is ↵
Inactive", Me.Font, SystemBrushes.ActiveCaptionText, 20, 20)
            End If
        End Sub
    <System.Security.Permissions.PermissionSetAttribute ↵
 (System.Security.Permissions.SecurityAction.Demand, ↵
Name:="FullTrust")> _
        Protected Overrides Sub WndProc(ByRef m As Message)
            ' Listen for operating system messages
            Select Case (m.Msg)
                ' The WM_ACTIVATEAPP message occurs when the ↵
application
                ' becomes the active application or becomes inactive.
            Case WM_ACTIVATEAPP

                    ' The WParam value identifies what is occurring.
                    appActive = (m.WParam.ToInt32() <> 0)

                    ' Invalidate to get new text painted.
                    Me.Invalidate()

            End Select
            MyBase.WndProc(m)
        End Sub
    End Class
End Namespace
```

[C#]
```
using System;
using System.Drawing;
using System.Windows.Forms;

namespace csTempWindowsApplication1
{
    public class Form1 : System.Windows.Forms.Form
    {
        // Constant value was found in the "windows.h" header file.
        private const int WM_ACTIVATEAPP = 0x001C;
        private bool appActive = true;

        [STAThread]
        static void Main()
        {
            Application.Run(new Form1());
        }

        public Form1()
        {
            this.Size = new System.Drawing.Size(300,300);
            this.Text = "Form1";
            this.Font = new System.Drawing.Font ↵
 ("Microsoft Sans Serif", 18F, ↵
 System.Drawing.FontStyle.Bold, ↵
```

```
System.Drawing.GraphicsUnit.Point, ((System.Byte)(0)));
        }

        protected override void OnPaint(PaintEventArgs e)
        {
            // Paint a string in different styles depending on         ↵
 whether the
            // application is active.
            if (appActive)
            {

e.Graphics.FillRectangle(SystemBrushes.ActiveCaption,20,20,260,50);
                e.Graphics.DrawString("Application is active",         ↵
this.Font, SystemBrushes.ActiveCaptionText, 20,20);
            }
            else
            {

e.Graphics.FillRectangle(SystemBrushes.InactiveCaption,20,20,260,50);
                e.Graphics.DrawString("Application is Inactive",       ↵
this.Font, SystemBrushes.ActiveCaptionText, 20,20);
            }
        }

    [System.Security.Permissions.PermissionSet                         ↵
 (System.Security.Permissions.SecurityAction.Demand, Name="FullTrust")]
        protected override void WndProc(ref Message m)
        {
            // Listen for operating system messages.
            switch (m.Msg)
            {
                // The WM_ACTIVATEAPP message occurs when the          ↵
application
                // becomes the active application or becomes inactive.
                case WM_ACTIVATEAPP:

                    // The WParam value identifies what is occurring.
                    appActive = (((int)m.WParam != 0));

                    // Invalidate to get new text painted.
                    this.Invalidate();

                    break;
            }
            base.WndProc(ref m);
        }
    }
}
```

[C++]

```
using namespace System;
using namespace System::Drawing;
using namespace System::Windows::Forms;

namespace csTempWindowsApplication1 {
public __gc class Form1 : public System::Windows::Forms::Form {

private:
    // Constant value was found in the S"windows.h" header file.
    const static Int32  WM_ACTIVATEAPP = 0x001C;

    Boolean appActive;

public:
    Form1() {
        appActive = true;
        this->Size = System::Drawing::Size(300, 300);
        this->Text = S"Form1";
        this->Font = new System::Drawing::Font(S"Microsoft Sans Serif",
            18.0F, System::Drawing::FontStyle::Bold,
            System::Drawing::GraphicsUnit::Point, ((System::Byte)(0)));
    }

protected:
    void OnPaint(PaintEventArgs* e) {
        // Paint a String* in different styles depending on whether the
        // application is active.
        if (appActive) {
            e->Graphics->FillRectangle(SystemBrushes::ActiveCaption,
                20, 20, 260, 50);
            e->Graphics->DrawString(S"Application is active",
                this->Font, SystemBrushes::ActiveCaptionText, 20, 20);
        } else {
            e->Graphics->FillRectangle(SystemBrushes::InactiveCaption,
                20, 20, 260, 50);
            e->Graphics->DrawString(S"Application is Inactive",
                this->Font, SystemBrushes::ActiveCaptionText, 20, 20);
        }
    }

[System::Security::Permissions::PermissionSet                          ↵
 (System::Security::Permissions::SecurityAction::Demand,               ↵
Name="FullTrust")]
    void WndProc(Message* m) {
        // Listen for operating system messages.
        switch (m->Msg) {
            // The WM_ACTIVATEAPP message occurs when the application
            // becomes the active application or becomes inactive.
                case WM_ACTIVATEAPP:

                    // The WParam value identifies what is occurring.
                    appActive = (((int)m->WParam != 0));

                    // Invalidate to get new text painted.
                    this->Invalidate();

                    break;
        }
        Form::WndProc(m);
    }
};
}

[STAThread]
int main() {
    Application::Run(new csTempWindowsApplication1::Form1());
}
```

Requirements

Namespace: System.Windows.Forms

Platforms: Windows 98, Windows NT 4.0, Windows Millennium Edition, Windows 2000, Windows XP Home Edition, Windows XP Professional, Windows Server 2003 family

Assembly: System.Windows.Forms (in System.Windows.Forms.dll)

Message.HWnd Property

Gets or sets the window handle of the message.

[Visual Basic]

```
Public Property HWnd As IntPtr
```

[C#]

```
public IntPtr HWnd {get; set;}
```

[C++]

```
public: __property IntPtr get_HWnd();
public: __property void set_HWnd(IntPtr);
```

[JScript]

```
public function get HWnd() : IntPtr;
public function set HWnd(IntPtr);
```

Property Value

The window handle of the message.

Requirements

Platforms: Windows 98, Windows NT 4.0, Windows Millennium Edition, Windows 2000, Windows XP Home Edition, Windows XP Professional, Windows Server 2003 family

Message.LParam Property

Specifies the **LParam** field of the message.

```
[Visual Basic]
Public Property LParam As IntPtr
[C#]
public IntPtr LParam {get; set;}
[C++]
public: __property IntPtr get_LParam();
public: __property void set_LParam(IntPtr);
[JScript]
public function get LParam() : IntPtr;
public function set LParam(IntPtr);
```

Property Value

The **LParam** field of the message.

Remarks

The value of this field depends on the message. Use the **LParam** field to get information that is important for handling the message. **LParam** is typically used to store an object if it is needed by the message. Use the **GetLParam** method to retrieve and convert information from the **LParam** field into an object.

Requirements

Platforms: Windows 98, Windows NT 4.0, Windows Millennium Edition, Windows 2000, Windows XP Home Edition, Windows XP Professional, Windows Server 2003 family

Message.Msg Property

Gets or sets the ID number for the message.

```
[Visual Basic]
Public Property Msg As Integer
[C#]
public int Msg {get; set;}
[C++]
public: __property int get_Msg();
public: __property void set_Msg(int);
[JScript]
public function get Msg() : int;
public function set Msg(int);
```

Property Value

The ID number for the message.

Example

See related example in the **System.Windows.Forms.Message** structure topic.

Requirements

Platforms: Windows 98, Windows NT 4.0, Windows Millennium Edition, Windows 2000, Windows XP Home Edition, Windows XP Professional, Windows Server 2003 family

Message.Result Property

Specifies the value that is returned to Windows in response to handling the message.

```
[Visual Basic]
Public Property Result As IntPtr
[C#]
public IntPtr Result {get; set;}
[C++]
public: __property IntPtr get_Result();
public: __property void set_Result(IntPtr);
[JScript]
public function get Result() : IntPtr;
public function set Result(IntPtr);
```

Property Value

The return value of the message.

Requirements

Platforms: Windows 98, Windows NT 4.0, Windows Millennium Edition, Windows 2000, Windows XP Home Edition, Windows XP Professional, Windows Server 2003 family

Message.WParam Property

Gets or sets the **WParam** field of the message.

```
[Visual Basic]
Public Property WParam As IntPtr
[C#]
public IntPtr WParam {get; set;}
[C++]
public: __property IntPtr get_WParam();
public: __property void set_WParam(IntPtr);
[JScript]
public function get WParam() : IntPtr;
public function set WParam(IntPtr);
```

Property Value

The **WParam** field of the message.

Remarks

The value of this field depends on the message. Use the **WParam** field to get information that is important to handling the message. This field is typically used to store small pieces of information, such as flags.

Example

See related example in the **System.Windows.Forms.Message** structure topic.

Requirements

Platforms: Windows 98, Windows NT 4.0, Windows Millennium Edition, Windows 2000, Windows XP Home Edition, Windows XP Professional, Windows Server 2003 family

Message.Create Method

Creates a new **Message** structure.

[Visual Basic]
```
Public Shared Function Create( _
   ByVal hWnd As IntPtr, _
   ByVal msg As Integer, _
   ByVal wparam As IntPtr, _
   ByVal lparam As IntPtr _
) As Message
```
[C#]
```
public static Message Create(
   IntPtr hWnd,
   int msg,
   IntPtr wparam,
   IntPtr lparam
);
```
[C++]
```
public: static Message Create(
   IntPtr hWnd,
   int msg,
   IntPtr wparam,
   IntPtr lparam
);
```
[JScript]
```
public static function Create(
   hWnd : IntPtr,
   msg : int,
   wparam : IntPtr,
   lparam : IntPtr
) : Message;
```

Parameters

hWnd
The window handle that the message is for.

msg
The message ID.

wparam
The message wparam field.

lparam
The message lparam field.

Return Value

A **Message** structure that represents the message that was created.

Remarks

Use the **Create** method to create a **Message** structure to wrap a message sent by Windows.

Requirements

Platforms: Windows 98, Windows NT 4.0, Windows Millennium Edition, Windows 2000, Windows XP Home Edition, Windows XP Professional, Windows Server 2003 family

Message.Equals Method

This member overrides **ValueType.Equals**.

[Visual Basic]
```
Overrides Public Function Equals( _
   ByVal o As Object _
) As Boolean
```
[C#]
```
public override bool Equals(
   object o
);
```
[C++]
```
public: bool Equals(
   Object* o
);
```
[JScript]
```
public override function Equals(
   o : Object
) : Boolean;
```

Requirements

Platforms: Windows 98, Windows NT 4.0, Windows Millennium Edition, Windows 2000, Windows XP Home Edition, Windows XP Professional, Windows Server 2003 family

Message.GetHashCode Method

This member overrides **ValueType.GetHashCode**.

[Visual Basic]
```
Overrides Public Function GetHashCode() As Integer
```
[C#]
```
public override int GetHashCode();
```
[C++]
```
public: int GetHashCode();
```
[JScript]
```
public override function GetHashCode() : int;
```

Requirements

Platforms: Windows 98, Windows NT 4.0, Windows Millennium Edition, Windows 2000, Windows XP Home Edition, Windows XP Professional, Windows Server 2003 family

Message.GetLParam Method

Gets the **LParam** value, and converts the value to an object.

[Visual Basic]
```
Public Function GetLParam( _
   ByVal cls As Type _
) As Object
```
[C#]
```
public object GetLParam(
   Type cls
);
```
[C++]
```
public: Object* GetLParam(
   Type* cls
);
```
[JScript]
```
public function GetLParam(
   cls : Type
) : Object;
```

Parameters

cls
The type to use to create an instance. This type must be declared as a structure type.

Return Value

An **Object** that represents an instance of the class specified by the *cls* parameter, with the data from the **LParam** field of the message.

Remarks

Use the **GetLParam** method to retrieve information from the **LParam** field of a message and convert it to an object. You can use this method to access objects passed in a message.

Requirements

Platforms: Windows 98, Windows NT 4.0, Windows Millennium Edition, Windows 2000, Windows XP Home Edition, Windows XP Professional, Windows Server 2003 family

Message.ToString Method

This member overrides **ValueType.ToString**.

```
[Visual Basic]
Overrides Public Function ToString() As String
[C#]
public override string ToString();
[C++]
public: String* ToString();
[JScript]
public override function ToString() : String;
```

Requirements

Platforms: Windows 98, Windows NT 4.0, Windows Millennium Edition, Windows 2000, Windows XP Home Edition, Windows XP Professional, Windows Server 2003 family

MessageBox Class

Displays a message box that can contain text, buttons, and symbols that inform and instruct the user.

System.Object
System.Windows.Forms.MessageBox

[Visual Basic]
```
Public Class MessageBox
```
[C#]
```
public class MessageBox
```
[C++]
```
public __gc class MessageBox
```
[JScript]
```
public class MessageBox
```

Thread Safety

Any public static (**Shared** in Visual Basic) members of this type are safe for multithreaded operations. Any instance members are not guaranteed to be thread safe.

Remarks

You cannot create a new instance of the **MessageBox** class. To display a message box, call the static (**Shared** in Visual Basic) method **MessageBox.Show**. The title, message, buttons, and icons displayed in the message box are determined by parameters that you pass to this method.

Example

[Visual Basic, C#] The following example shows how to use a **MessageBox** to inform the user of a missing entry in a **TextBox**. This example assumes that the method is called from an existing form with a **Button** and a **TextBox** on it.

[Visual Basic]
```
Protected Sub button1_Click(sender As Object, e As System.EventArgs)
    If textBox1.Text = "" Then
        MessageBox.Show("You must enter a name.", "Name Entry Error", _
           MessageBoxButtons.OK, MessageBoxIcon.Exclamation)
    Else
        ' Code to act on the data entered would go here.
    End If
End Sub
```

[C#]
```
protected void button1_Click(object sender, System.EventArgs e) {
   if(textBox1.Text == "") {
      MessageBox.Show("You must enter a name.", "Name Entry Error",
         MessageBoxButtons.OK, MessageBoxIcon.Exclamation);
   }
   else {
      // Code to act on the data entered would go here.
   }
}
```

Requirements

Namespace: System.Windows.Forms

Platforms: Windows 98, Windows NT 4.0,
Windows Millennium Edition, Windows 2000,
Windows XP Home Edition, Windows XP Professional,
Windows Server 2003 family,
.NET Compact Framework - Windows CE .NET

Assembly: System.Windows.Forms (in System.Windows.Forms.dll)

MessageBox.Show Method

Displays a message box.

Overload List

Displays a message box with specified text.

Supported by the .NET Compact Framework.

[Visual Basic] **Overloads Public Shared Function Show(String) As DialogResult**

[C#] **public static DialogResult Show(string);**

[C++] **public: static DialogResult Show(String*);**

[JScript] **public static function Show(String) : DialogResult;**

Displays a message box in front of the specified object and with the specified text.

[Visual Basic] **Overloads Public Shared Function Show(IWin32Window, String) As DialogResult**

[C#] **public static DialogResult Show(IWin32Window, string);**

[C++] **public: static DialogResult Show(IWin32Window*, String*);**

[JScript] **public static function Show(IWin32Window, String) : DialogResult;**

Displays a message box with specified text and caption.

Supported by the .NET Compact Framework.

[Visual Basic] **Overloads Public Shared Function Show(String, String) As DialogResult**

[C#] **public static DialogResult Show(string, string);**

[C++] **public: static DialogResult Show(String*, String*);**

[JScript] **public static function Show(String, String) : DialogResult;**

Displays a message box in front of the specified object and with the specified text and caption.

[Visual Basic] **Overloads Public Shared Function Show(IWin32Window, String, String) As DialogResult**

[C#] **public static DialogResult Show(IWin32Window, string, string);**

[C++] **public: static DialogResult Show(IWin32Window*, String*, String*);**

[JScript] **public static function Show(IWin32Window, String, String) : DialogResult;**

Displays a message box with specified text, caption, and buttons.

[Visual Basic] **Overloads Public Shared Function Show(String, String, MessageBoxButtons) As DialogResult**

[C#] **public static DialogResult Show(string, string, MessageBoxButtons);**

[C++] **public: static DialogResult Show(String*, String*, MessageBoxButtons);**

[JScript] **public static function Show(String, String, MessageBoxButtons) : DialogResult;**

Displays a message box in front of the specified object and with the specified text, caption, and buttons.

[Visual Basic] **Overloads Public Shared Function Show(IWin32Window, String, String, MessageBoxButtons) As DialogResult**

[C#] **public static DialogResult Show(IWin32Window, string, string, MessageBoxButtons);**

[C++] **public: static DialogResult Show(IWin32Window*, String*, String*, MessageBoxButtons);**

[JScript] **public static function Show(IWin32Window, String, String, MessageBoxButtons) : DialogResult;**

Displays a message box with specified text, caption, buttons, and icon.

[Visual Basic] **Overloads Public Shared Function Show(String, String, MessageBoxButtons, MessageBoxIcon) As DialogResult**

[C#] **public static DialogResult Show(string, string, MessageBoxButtons, MessageBoxIcon);**

[C++] **public: static DialogResult Show(String*, String*, MessageBoxButtons, MessageBoxIcon);**

[JScript] **public static function Show(String, String, MessageBoxButtons, MessageBoxIcon) : DialogResult;**

Displays a message box in front of the specified object and with the specified text, caption, buttons, and icon.

[Visual Basic] **Overloads Public Shared Function Show(IWin32Window, String, String, MessageBoxButtons, MessageBoxIcon) As DialogResult**

[C#] **public static DialogResult Show(IWin32Window, string, string, MessageBoxButtons, MessageBoxIcon);**

[C++] **public: static DialogResult Show(IWin32Window*, String*, String*, MessageBoxButtons, MessageBoxIcon);**

[JScript] **public static function Show(IWin32Window, String, String, MessageBoxButtons, MessageBoxIcon) : DialogResult;**

Displays a message box with the specified text, caption, buttons, icon, and default button.

Supported by the .NET Compact Framework.

[Visual Basic] **Overloads Public Shared Function Show(String, String, MessageBoxButtons, MessageBoxIcon, MessageBoxDefaultButton) As DialogResult**

[C#] **public static DialogResult Show(string, string, MessageBoxButtons, MessageBoxIcon, MessageBoxDefaultButton);**

[C++] **public: static DialogResult Show(String*, String*, MessageBoxButtons, MessageBoxIcon, MessageBoxDefaultButton);**

[JScript] **public static function Show(String, String, MessageBoxButtons, MessageBoxIcon, MessageBoxDefaultButton) : DialogResult;**

Displays a message box in front of the specified object and with the specified text, caption, buttons, icon, and default button.

[Visual Basic] **Overloads Public Shared Function Show(IWin32Window, String, String, MessageBoxButtons, MessageBoxIcon, MessageBoxDefaultButton) As DialogResult**

[C#] **public static DialogResult Show(IWin32Window, string, string, MessageBoxButtons, MessageBoxIcon, MessageBoxDefaultButton);**

[C++] **public: static DialogResult Show(IWin32Window*, String*, String*, MessageBoxButtons, MessageBoxIcon, MessageBoxDefaultButton);**

[JScript] **public static function Show(IWin32Window, String, String, MessageBoxButtons, MessageBoxIcon, MessageBoxDefaultButton) : DialogResult;**

Displays a message box with the specified text, caption, buttons, icon, default button, and options.

[Visual Basic] **Overloads Public Shared Function Show(String, String, MessageBoxButtons, MessageBoxIcon, MessageBoxDefaultButton, MessageBoxOptions) As DialogResult**

[C#] **public static DialogResult Show(string, string, MessageBoxButtons, MessageBoxIcon, MessageBoxDefaultButton, MessageBoxOptions);**

[C++] **public: static DialogResult Show(String*, String*, MessageBoxButtons, MessageBoxIcon, MessageBoxDefaultButton, MessageBoxOptions);**

[JScript] **public static function Show(String, String, MessageBoxButtons, MessageBoxIcon, MessageBox-DefaultButton, MessageBoxOptions) : DialogResult;**

Displays a message box in front of the specified object and with the specified text, caption, buttons, icon, default button, and options.

[Visual Basic] **Overloads Public Shared Function Show(IWin32Window, String, String, MessageBoxButtons, MessageBoxIcon, MessageBoxDefaultButton, MessageBoxOptions) As DialogResult**

[C#] **public static DialogResult Show(IWin32Window, string, string, MessageBoxButtons, MessageBoxIcon, MessageBoxDefaultButton, MessageBoxOptions);**

[C++] **public: static DialogResult Show(IWin32Window*, String*, String*, MessageBoxButtons, MessageBoxIcon, MessageBoxDefaultButton, MessageBoxOptions);**

[JScript] **public static function Show(IWin32Window, String, String, MessageBoxButtons, MessageBoxIcon, MessageBox-DefaultButton, MessageBoxOptions) : DialogResult;**

Example

[Visual Basic, C#, C++] The following example demonstrates how to display a **MessageBox** with the options supported by this overload of **Show**. After verifying that a string variable, `ServerName`, is empty, the example displays a **MessageBox**, offering the user the option to cancel the operation. If the **Show** method's return value evaluates to **Yes**, the form that displayed the **MessageBox** is closed.

> [Visual Basic, C#, C++] **Note** This example shows how to use one of the overloaded versions of **Show**. For other examples that might be available, see the individual overload topics.

[Visual Basic]
```
Private Sub ValidateUserEntry2()

    ' Checks the value of the text.

    If ServerName.Text.Length = 0 Then

        ' Initializes variables to pass to the MessageBox.Show method.

        Dim Message As String = "You did not enter a server ↵
 name. Cancel this operation?"
        Dim Caption As String = "No Server Name Specified"
        Dim Buttons As Integer = MessageBoxButtons.YesNo

        Dim Result As DialogResult

        'Displays a MessageBox using the Question icon and ↵
 specifying the No button as the default.

        Result = MessageBox.Show(Me, Message, Caption, ↵
MessageBoxButtons.YesNo, _
            MessageBoxIcon.Question, ↵
MessageBoxDefaultButton.Button1, MessageBoxOptions.RightAlign)

        ' Gets the result of the MessageBox display.

        If Result = DialogResult.Yes Then

            ' Closes the parent form.

            Me.Close()

        End If

    End If

End Sub
```

[C#]
```
    private void validateUserEntry2()
    {

        // Checks the value of the text.

        if(serverName.Text.Length == 0)
        {

            // Initializes the variables to pass to the ↵
 MessageBox.Show method.

            string message = "You did not enter a server name. ↵
 Cancel this operation?";
            string caption = "No Server Name Specified";
            MessageBoxButtons buttons = MessageBoxButtons.YesNo;
            DialogResult result;

            // Displays the MessageBox.

            result = MessageBox.Show(this, message, caption, buttons,
                MessageBoxIcon.Question, ↵
MessageBoxDefaultButton.Button1,
                MessageBoxOptions.RightAlign);

            if(result == DialogResult.Yes)
            {

                // Closes the parent form.

                this.Close();

            }

        }

    }
```

[C++]
```
private:
    void validateUserEntry2() {
        // Checks the value of the text.
        if (serverName->Text->Length == 0) {

            // Initializes the variables to pass to the ↵
MessageBox::Show method.
            String* message = S"You did not enter a server name. ↵
 Cancel this operation?";
            String* caption = S"No Server Name Specified";
            MessageBoxButtons buttons = MessageBoxButtons::YesNo;
            System::Windows::Forms::DialogResult result;

            // Displays the MessageBox.
            result = MessageBox::Show(this, message, caption, buttons,
                MessageBoxIcon::Question, ↵
MessageBoxDefaultButton::Button1,
                MessageBoxOptions::RightAlign);

            if (result == DialogResult::Yes) {
                // Closes the parent form.
                this->Close();
            }
        }
    }
```

MessageBox.Show Method (String)

Displays a message box with specified text.

[Visual Basic]
```
Overloads Public Shared Function Show( _
   ByVal text As String _
) As DialogResult
```
[C#]
```
public static DialogResult Show(
   string text
);
```
[C++]
```
public: static DialogResult Show(
   String* text
);
```
[JScript]
```
public static function Show(
   text : String
) : DialogResult;
```

Parameters

text

The text to display in the message box.

Return Value

One of the **DialogResult** values.

Remarks

By default, the message box displays an **OK** button. The message box does not contain a caption in the title.

Requirements

Platforms: Windows 98, Windows NT 4.0, Windows Millennium Edition, Windows 2000, Windows XP Home Edition, Windows XP Professional, Windows Server 2003 family, .NET Compact Framework - Windows CE .NET

.NET Framework Security:

- **UIPermission** for safe subwindows to set this property. Associated enumeration: **UIPermissionWindow.SafeSubWindows**

MessageBox.Show Method (IWin32Window, String)

Displays a message box in front of the specified object and with the specified text.

```
[Visual Basic]
Overloads Public Shared Function Show( _
   ByVal owner As IWin32Window, _
   ByVal text As String _
) As DialogResult
[C#]
public static DialogResult Show(
   IWin32Window owner,
   string text
);
[C++]
public: static DialogResult Show(
   IWin32Window* owner,
   String* text
);
[JScript]
public static function Show(
   owner : IWin32Window,
   text : String
) : DialogResult;
```

Parameters

owner
  The **IWin32Window** the message box will display in front of.

text
  The text to display in the message box.

Return Value

One of the **DialogResult** values.

Remarks

You can use the *owner* parameter to specify a particular object, which implements the **IWin32Window** interface, to place the message box in front of. A message box is a modal dialog, which means no input (keyboard or mouse click) can occur except to objects on the modal form. The program must hide or close a modal form (typically in response to some user action) before input to another form can occur.

By default, the message box displays an **OK** button. The message box does not contain a caption in the title.

Requirements

Platforms: Windows 98, Windows NT 4.0, Windows Millennium Edition, Windows 2000, Windows XP Home Edition, Windows XP Professional, Windows Server 2003 family

.NET Framework Security:

- **UIPermission** for safe subwindows to call this method. Associated enumeration: **UIPermissionWindow.SafeSubWindows**

MessageBox.Show Method (String, String)

Displays a message box with specified text and caption.

```
[Visual Basic]
Overloads Public Shared Function Show( _
   ByVal text As String, _
   ByVal caption As String _
) As DialogResult
[C#]
public static DialogResult Show(
   string text,
   string caption
);
[C++]
public: static DialogResult Show(
   String* text,
   String* caption
);
[JScript]
public static function Show(
   text : String,
   caption : String
) : DialogResult;
```

Parameters

text
  The text to display in the message box.

caption
  The text to display in the title bar of the message box.

Return Value

One of the **DialogResult** values.

Remarks

By default, the message box displays an **OK** button.

Requirements

Platforms: Windows 98, Windows NT 4.0, Windows Millennium Edition, Windows 2000, Windows XP Home Edition, Windows XP Professional, Windows Server 2003 family, .NET Compact Framework - Windows CE .NET

.NET Framework Security:

- **UIPermission** for safe subwindows to call this method. Associated enumeration: **UIPermissionWindow.SafeSubWindows**

MessageBox.Show Method (IWin32Window, String, String)

Displays a message box in front of the specified object and with the specified text and caption.

```
[Visual Basic]
Overloads Public Shared Function Show( _
   ByVal owner As IWin32Window, _
   ByVal text As String, _
   ByVal caption As String _
) As DialogResult
[C#]
public static DialogResult Show(
   IWin32Window owner,
   string text,
   string caption
);
[C++]
public: static DialogResult Show(
   IWin32Window* owner,
   String* text,
   String* caption
);
```

```
[JScript]
public static function Show(
   owner : IWin32Window,
   text : String,
   caption : String
) : DialogResult;
```

Parameters

owner
: The **IWin32Window** the message box will display in front of.

text
: The text to display in the message box.

caption
: The text to display in the title bar of the message box.

Return Value

One of the **DialogResult** values.

Remarks

You can use the *owner* parameter to specify a particular object, which implements the **IWin32Window** interface, to place the message box in front of. A message box is a modal dialog, which means no input (keyboard or mouse click) can occur except to objects on the modal form. The program must hide or close a modal form (typically in response to some user action) before input to another form can occur.

By default, the message box displays an **OK** button.

Requirements

Platforms: Windows 98, Windows NT 4.0, Windows Millennium Edition, Windows 2000, Windows XP Home Edition, Windows XP Professional, Windows Server 2003 family

.NET Framework Security:

- **UIPermission** for safe subwindows to call this method. Associated enumeration: **UIPermissionWindow.SafeSubWindows**

MessageBox.Show Method (String, String, MessageBoxButtons)

Displays a message box with specified text, caption, and buttons.

```
[Visual Basic]
Overloads Public Shared Function Show( _
   ByVal text As String, _
   ByVal caption As String, _
   ByVal buttons As MessageBoxButtons _
) As DialogResult
[C#]
public static DialogResult Show(
   string text,
   string caption,
   MessageBoxButtons buttons
);
[C++]
public: static DialogResult Show(
   String* text,
   String* caption,
   MessageBoxButtons buttons
);
[JScript]
public static function Show(
   text : String,
   caption : String,
   buttons : MessageBoxButtons
) : DialogResult;
```

Parameters

text
: The text to display in the message box.

caption
: The text to display in the title bar of the message box.

buttons
: One of the **MessageBoxButtons** values that specifies which buttons to display in the message box.

Return Value

One of the **DialogResult** values.

Exceptions

Exception Type	Condition
InvalidEnumArgumentException	The *buttons* parameter specified is not a member of **MessageBoxButtons**.
InvalidOperationException	An attempt was made to display the **MessageBox** in a process that is not running in User Interactive mode. This is specified by the **SystemInformation.UserInteractive** property.

Remarks

You can have a maximum of three buttons on the message box.

Example

[Visual Basic, C#, C++] The following example demonstrates how to display a **MessageBox** with the options supported by this overload of **Show**. After verifying that a string variable, `ServerName`, is empty, the example displays a **MessageBox**, offering the user the option to cancel the operation. If the **Show** method's return value evaluates to **Yes**, the form that displayed the **MessageBox** is closed.

```
[Visual Basic]
Private Sub ValidateUserEntry()

    ' Checks the value of the text.

    If ServerName.Text.Length = 0 Then

        ' Initializes variables to pass to the MessageBox.Show method.

        Dim Message As String = "You did not enter a server ↵
name. Cancel this operation?"
        Dim Caption As String = "No Server Name Specified"
        Dim Buttons As MessageBoxButtons = MessageBoxButtons.YesNo

        Dim Result As DialogResult

        'Displays the MessageBox

        Result = MessageBox.Show(Me, Message, Caption, Buttons)

        ' Gets the result of the MessageBox display.

        If Result = DialogResult.Yes Then

            ' Closes the parent form.

            Me.Close()

        End If
```

```
    End If

End Sub
```

[C#]

```
    private void validateUserEntry()
    {

        // Checks the value of the text.

        if(serverName.Text.Length == 0)
        {

            // Initializes the variables to pass to the ↵
MessageBox.Show method.

            string message = "You did not enter a server name. ↵
 Cancel this operation?";
            string caption = "No Server Name Specified";
            MessageBoxButtons buttons = MessageBoxButtons.YesNo;
            DialogResult result;

            // Displays the MessageBox.

            result = MessageBox.Show(this, message, caption, buttons);

            if(result == DialogResult.Yes)
            {

                // Closes the parent form.

                this.Close();

            }

        }

    }
```

[C++]

```
private:
    void validateUserEntry() {
        // Checks the value of the text.
        if (serverName->Text->Length == 0) {

            // Initializes the variables to pass to the ↵
MessageBox::Show method.
            String* message = S"You did not enter a server name. ↵
Cancel this operation?";
            String* caption = S"No Server Name Specified";
            MessageBoxButtons buttons = MessageBoxButtons::YesNo;
            System::Windows::Forms::DialogResult result;

            // Displays the MessageBox.
            result = MessageBox::Show(this, message, caption, buttons);

            if (result == DialogResult::Yes) {
                // Closes the parent form.
                this->Close();
            }
        }
    }
```

Requirements

Platforms: Windows 98, Windows NT 4.0, Windows Millennium Edition, Windows 2000, Windows XP Home Edition, Windows XP Professional, Windows Server 2003 family

.NET Framework Security:

- **UIPermission** for safe subwindows to call this method. Associated enumeration: **UIPermissionWindow.SafeSubWindows**

MessageBox.Show Method (IWin32Window, String, String, MessageBoxButtons)

Displays a message box in front of the specified object and with the specified text, caption, and buttons.

[Visual Basic]

```
Overloads Public Shared Function Show( _
   ByVal owner As IWin32Window, _
   ByVal text As String, _
   ByVal caption As String, _
   ByVal buttons As MessageBoxButtons _
) As DialogResult
```

[C#]

```
public static DialogResult Show(
   IWin32Window owner,
   string text,
   string caption,
   MessageBoxButtons buttons
);
```

[C++]

```
public: static DialogResult Show(
   IWin32Window* owner,
   String* text,
   String* caption,
   MessageBoxButtons buttons
);
```

[JScript]

```
public static function Show(
   owner : IWin32Window,
   text : String,
   caption : String,
   buttons : MessageBoxButtons
) : DialogResult;
```

Parameters

owner
: The **IWin32Window** the message box will display in front of.

text
: The text to display in the message box.

caption
: The text to display in the title bar of the message box.

buttons
: One of the **MessageBoxButtons** values that specifies which buttons to display in the message box.

Return Value

One of the **DialogResult** values.

Exceptions

Exception Type	Condition
InvalidEnumArgumentException	*buttons* is not a member of **MessageBoxButtons**.
InvalidOperationException	An attempt was made to display the **MessageBox** in a process that is not running in User Interactive mode. This is specified by the **SystemInformation.UserInteractive** property.

Remarks

You can use the *owner* parameter to specify a particular object, which implements the **IWin32Window** interface, to place the message box in front of. A message box is a modal dialog, which means no input (keyboard or mouse click) can occur except to objects on the modal form. The program must hide or close a modal form (typically in response to some user action) before input to another form can occur.

You can have a maximum of three buttons on the message box.

Example

[Visual Basic, C#, C++] The following example demonstrates how to display a **MessageBox** with the options supported by this overload of **Show**. After verifying that a string variable, `ServerName`, is empty, the example displays a **MessageBox**, offering the user the option to cancel the operation. If the **Show** method's return value evaluates to **Yes**, the form that displayed the **MessageBox** is closed.

[Visual Basic]

```
Private Sub ValidateUserEntry5()

    ' Checks the value of the text.

    If ServerName.Text.Length = 0 Then

        ' Initializes variables to pass to the MessageBox.Show method.

        Dim Message As String = "You did not enter a server
 name. Cancel this operation?"
        Dim Caption As String = "No Server Name Specified"
        Dim Buttons As Integer = MessageBoxButtons.YesNo

        Dim Result As DialogResult

        'Displays a MessageBox using the Question icon and
specifying the No button as the default.

        Result = MessageBox.Show(Me, Message, Caption,
MessageBoxButtons.YesNo)

        ' Gets the result of the MessageBox display.

        If Result = DialogResult.Yes Then

            ' Closes the parent form.

            Me.Close()

        End If

    End If

End Sub
```

[C#]

```
private void validateUserEntry5()
{

    // Checks the value of the text.

    if(serverName.Text.Length == 0)
    {

        // Initializes the variables to pass to the
 MessageBox.Show method.

        string message = "You did not enter a server name.
Cancel this operation?";
        string caption = "No Server Name Specified";
        MessageBoxButtons buttons = MessageBoxButtons.YesNo;
        DialogResult result;

        // Displays the MessageBox.

        result = MessageBox.Show(this, message, caption, buttons);

        if(result == DialogResult.Yes)
        {

            // Closes the parent form.

            this.Close();

        }

    }

}
```

[C++]

```
private:
    void validateUserEntry5() {
        // Checks the value of the text.
        if (serverName->Text->Length == 0) {

            // Initializes the variables to pass to the
MessageBox::Show method.
            String* message = S"You did not enter a server name.
Cancel this operation?";
            String* caption = S"No Server Name Specified";
            MessageBoxButtons buttons = MessageBoxButtons::YesNo;
            System::Windows::Forms::DialogResult result;

            // Displays the MessageBox.
            result = MessageBox::Show(this, message, caption, buttons);

            if (result == DialogResult::Yes) {
                // Closes the parent form.
                this->Close();
            }
        }
    }
```

Requirements

Platforms: Windows 98, Windows NT 4.0, Windows Millennium Edition, Windows 2000, Windows XP Home Edition, Windows XP Professional, Windows Server 2003 family

.NET Framework Security:

- **UIPermission** for safe subwindows to call this method. Associated enumeration: **UIPermissionWindow.SafeSubWindows**

MessageBox.Show Method (String, String, MessageBoxButtons, MessageBoxIcon)

Displays a message box with specified text, caption, buttons, and icon.

[Visual Basic]

```
Overloads Public Shared Function Show( _
   ByVal text As String, _
   ByVal caption As String, _
   ByVal buttons As MessageBoxButtons, _
   ByVal icon As MessageBoxIcon _
) As DialogResult
```

[C#]

```
public static DialogResult Show(
   string text,
   string caption,
   MessageBoxButtons buttons,
   MessageBoxIcon icon
);
```

```
[C++]
public: static DialogResult Show(
   String* text,
   String* caption,
   MessageBoxButtons buttons,
   MessageBoxIcon icon
);
[JScript]
public static function Show(
   text : String,
   caption : String,
   buttons : MessageBoxButtons,
   icon : MessageBoxIcon
) : DialogResult;
```

Parameters

text
The text to display in the message box.

caption
The text to display in the title bar of the message box.

buttons
One of the **MessageBoxButtons** values that specifies which buttons to display in the message box.

icon
One of the **MessageBoxIcon** values that specifies which icon to display in the message box.

Return Value

One of the **DialogResult** values.

Exceptions

Exception Type	Condition
InvalidEnumArgument-Exception	The *buttons* parameter specified is not a member of **MessageBoxButtons**. -or- The *icon* parameter specified is not a member of **MessageBoxIcon**.
InvalidOperation-Exception	An attempt was made to display the **MessageBox** in a process that is not running in User Interactive mode. This is specified by the **SystemInformation.UserInteractive** property.

Remarks

You can have a maximum of three buttons on the message box.

Requirements

Platforms: Windows 98, Windows NT 4.0, Windows Millennium Edition, Windows 2000, Windows XP Home Edition, Windows XP Professional, Windows Server 2003 family

.NET Framework Security:

- **UIPermission** for safe subwindows to call this method. Associated enumeration: **UIPermissionWindow.SafeSubWindows**

MessageBox.Show Method (IWin32Window, String, String, MessageBoxButtons, MessageBoxIcon)

Displays a message box in front of the specified object and with the specified text, caption, buttons, and icon.

```
[Visual Basic]
Overloads Public Shared Function Show( _
   ByVal owner As IWin32Window, _
   ByVal text As String, _
   ByVal caption As String, _
   ByVal buttons As MessageBoxButtons, _
   ByVal icon As MessageBoxIcon _
) As DialogResult
[C#]
public static DialogResult Show(
   IWin32Window owner,
   string text,
   string caption,
   MessageBoxButtons buttons,
   MessageBoxIcon icon
);
[C++]
public: static DialogResult Show(
   IWin32Window* owner,
   String* text,
   String* caption,
   MessageBoxButtons buttons,
   MessageBoxIcon icon
);
[JScript]
public static function Show(
   owner : IWin32Window,
   text : String,
   caption : String,
   buttons : MessageBoxButtons,
   icon : MessageBoxIcon
) : DialogResult;
```

Parameters

owner
The **IWin32Window** the message box will display in front of.

text
The text to display in the message box.

caption
The text to display in the title bar of the message box.

buttons
One of the **MessageBoxButtons** values that specifies which buttons to display in the message box.

icon
One of the **MessageBoxIcon** values that specifies which icon to display in the message box.

Return Value

One of the **DialogResult** values.

Exceptions

Exception Type	Condition
InvalidEnumArgument-Exception	*buttons* is not a member of **MessageBoxButtons**. -or- *icon* is not a member of **MessageBoxIcon**.
InvalidOperation-Exception	An attempt was made to display the **MessageBox** in a process that is not running in User Interactive mode. This is specified by the **SystemInformation.UserInteractive** property.

Remarks

You can use the *owner* parameter to specify a particular object, Which implements the **IWin32Window** interface, to place the message box in front of. A message box is a modal dialog, which means no input (keyboard or mouse click) can occur except to objects on the modal form. The program must hide or close a modal form (typically in response to some user action) before input to another form can occur.

You can have a maximum of three buttons on the message box.

Example

See related example in the **System.Windows.Forms.MessageBox.Show** method topic.

Requirements

Platforms: Windows 98, Windows NT 4.0, Windows Millennium Edition, Windows 2000, Windows XP Home Edition, Windows XP Professional, Windows Server 2003 family

.NET Framework Security:

- **UIPermission** for safe subwindows to call this method. Associated enumeration: **UIPermissionWindow.SafeSubWindows**

MessageBox.Show Method (String, String, MessageBoxButtons, MessageBoxIcon, MessageBoxDefaultButton)

Displays a message box with the specified text, caption, buttons, icon, and default button.

[Visual Basic]
```
Overloads Public Shared Function Show( _
   ByVal text As String, _
   ByVal caption As String, _
   ByVal buttons As MessageBoxButtons, _
   ByVal icon As MessageBoxIcon, _
   ByVal defaultButton As MessageBoxDefaultButton _
) As DialogResult
```
[C#]
```
public static DialogResult Show(
   string text,
   string caption,
   MessageBoxButtons buttons,
   MessageBoxIcon icon,
   MessageBoxDefaultButton defaultButton
);
```
[C++]
```
public: static DialogResult Show(
   String* text,
   String* caption,
   MessageBoxButtons buttons,
   MessageBoxIcon icon,
   MessageBoxDefaultButton defaultButton
);
```
[JScript]
```
public static function Show(
   text : String,
   caption : String,
   buttons : MessageBoxButtons,
   icon : MessageBoxIcon,
   defaultButton : MessageBoxDefaultButton
) : DialogResult;
```

Parameters

text
: The text to display in the message box.

caption
: The text to display in the title bar of the message box.

buttons
: One of the **MessageBoxButtons** values that specifies which buttons to display in the message box.

icon
: One of the **MessageBoxIcon** values that specifies which icon to display in the message box.

defaultButton
: One of the **MessageBoxDefaultButton** values that specifies the default button for the message box.

Return Value

One of the **DialogResult** values.

Exceptions

Exception Type	Condition
InvalidEnumArgument-Exception	*buttons* is not a member of **MessageBoxButtons**. -or- *icon* is not a member of **MessageBoxIcon**. -or- *defaultButton* is not a member of **MessageBoxDefaultButton**.
InvalidOperation-Exception	An attempt was made to display the **MessageBox** in a process that is not running in User Interactive mode. This is specified by the **SystemInformation.UserInteractive** property.

Remarks

You can have a maximum of three buttons on the message box.

Example

See related example in the **System.Windows.Forms.MessageBox.Show** method topic.

Requirements

Platforms: Windows 98, Windows NT 4.0, Windows Millennium Edition, Windows 2000, Windows XP Home Edition, Windows XP Professional, Windows Server 2003 family, .NET Compact Framework - Windows CE .NET

.NET Framework Security:

- **UIPermission** for safe subwindows to call this method. Associated enumeration: **UIPermissionWindow.SafeSubWindows**

MessageBox.Show Method (IWin32Window, String, String, MessageBoxButtons, MessageBoxIcon, MessageBoxDefaultButton)

Displays a message box in front of the specified object and with the specified text, caption, buttons, icon, and default button.

```
[Visual Basic]
Overloads Public Shared Function Show( _
   ByVal owner As IWin32Window, _
   ByVal text As String, _
   ByVal caption As String, _
   ByVal buttons As MessageBoxButtons, _
   ByVal icon As MessageBoxIcon, _
   ByVal defaultButton As MessageBoxDefaultButton _
) As DialogResult
[C#]
public static DialogResult Show(
   IWin32Window owner,
   string text,
   string caption,
   MessageBoxButtons buttons,
   MessageBoxIcon icon,
   MessageBoxDefaultButton defaultButton
);
[C++]
public: static DialogResult Show(
   IWin32Window* owner,
   String* text,
   String* caption,
   MessageBoxButtons buttons,
   MessageBoxIcon icon,
   MessageBoxDefaultButton defaultButton
);
[JScript]
public static function Show(
   owner : IWin32Window,
   text : String,
   caption : String,
   buttons : MessageBoxButtons,
   icon : MessageBoxIcon,
   defaultButton : MessageBoxDefaultButton
) : DialogResult;
```

Parameters

owner
The **IWin32Window** the message box will display in front of.

text
The text to display in the message box.

caption
The text to display in the title bar of the message box.

buttons
One of the **MessageBoxButtons** values that specifies which buttons to display in the message box.

icon
One of the **MessageBoxIcon** values that specifies which icon to display in the message box.

defaultButton
One of the **MessageBoxDefaultButton** values that specifies the default button for the message box.

Return Value

One of the **DialogResult** values.

Exceptions

Exception Type	Condition
InvalidEnumArgumentException	*buttons* is not a member of **MessageBoxButtons**. -or- *icon* is not a member of **MessageBoxIcon**. -or- *defaultButton* is not a member of **MessageBoxDefaultButton**.
InvalidOperationException	An attempt was made to display the **MessageBox** in a process that is not running in User Interactive mode. This is specified by the **SystemInformation.UserInteractive** property.

Remarks

You can use the *owner* parameter to specify a particular object, which implements the **IWin32Window** interface, to place the message box in front of. A message box is a modal dialog, which means no input (keyboard or mouse click) can occur except to objects on the modal form. The program must hide or close a modal form (typically in response to some user action) before input to another form can occur.

You can have a maximum of three buttons on the message box.

Example

See related example in the **System.Windows.Forms.MessageBox.Show** method topic.

Requirements

Platforms: Windows 98, Windows NT 4.0, Windows Millennium Edition, Windows 2000, Windows XP Home Edition, Windows XP Professional, Windows Server 2003 family

.NET Framework Security:

- **UIPermission** for safe subwindows to call this method. Associated enumeration: **UIPermissionWindow.SafeSubWindows**

MessageBox.Show Method (String, String, MessageBoxButtons, MessageBoxIcon, MessageBoxDefaultButton, MessageBoxOptions)

Displays a message box with the specified text, caption, buttons, icon, default button, and options.

[Visual Basic]
```
Overloads Public Shared Function Show( _
   ByVal text As String, _
   ByVal caption As String, _
   ByVal buttons As MessageBoxButtons, _
   ByVal icon As MessageBoxIcon, _
   ByVal defaultButton As MessageBoxDefaultButton, _
   ByVal options As MessageBoxOptions _
) As DialogResult
```
[C#]
```
public static DialogResult Show(
   string text,
   string caption,
   MessageBoxButtons buttons,
   MessageBoxIcon icon,
   MessageBoxDefaultButton defaultButton,
   MessageBoxOptions options
);
```
[C++]
```
public: static DialogResult Show(
   String* text,
   String* caption,
   MessageBoxButtons buttons,
   MessageBoxIcon icon,
   MessageBoxDefaultButton defaultButton,
   MessageBoxOptions options
);
```
[JScript]
```
public static function Show(
   text : String,
   caption : String,
   buttons : MessageBoxButtons,
   icon : MessageBoxIcon,
   defaultButton : MessageBoxDefaultButton,
   options : MessageBoxOptions
) : DialogResult;
```

Parameters

text

The text to display in the message box.

caption

The text to display in the title bar of the message box.

buttons

One of the **MessageBoxButtons** values that specifies which buttons to display in the message box.

icon

One of the **MessageBoxIcon** values that specifies which icon to display in the message box.

defaultButton

One of the **MessageBoxDefaultButton** values that specifies the default button for the message box.

options

One of the **MessageBoxOptions** values that specifies which display and association options will be used for the message box.

Return Value

One of the **DialogResult** values.

Exceptions

Exception Type	Condition
InvalidEnumArgument-Exception	*buttons* is not a member of **MessageBoxButtons**. -or- *icon* is not a member of **MessageBoxIcon**. -or- The *defaultButton* specified is not a member of **MessageBox-DefaultButton**.
InvalidOperation-Exception	An attempt was made to display the **MessageBox** in a process that is not running in User Interactive mode. This is specified by the **SystemInforma-tion.UserInteractive** property.
ArgumentException	*options* specified both **Default-DesktopOnly** and **Service-Notification**. -or- *buttons* specified an invalid combination of **MessageBoxButtons**.

Remarks

You can have a maximum of three buttons on the message box.

Example

See related example in the **System.Windows.Forms.Message-Box.Show** method topic.

Requirements

Platforms: Windows 98, Windows NT 4.0, Windows Millennium Edition, Windows 2000, Windows XP Home Edition, Windows XP Professional, Windows Server 2003 family

.NET Framework Security:

- **UIPermission** for safe subwindows to call this method. Associated enumeration: **UIPermissionWindow.Safe-SubWindows**

MessageBox.Show Method (IWin32Window, String, String, MessageBoxButtons, MessageBoxIcon, MessageBoxDefaultButton, MessageBoxOptions)

Displays a message box in front of the specified object and with the specified text, caption, buttons, icon, default button, and options.

[Visual Basic]
```
Overloads Public Shared Function Show( _
   ByVal owner As IWin32Window, _
   ByVal text As String, _
   ByVal caption As String, _
   ByVal buttons As MessageBoxButtons, _
   ByVal icon As MessageBoxIcon, _
   ByVal defaultButton As MessageBoxDefaultButton, _
   ByVal options As MessageBoxOptions _
) As DialogResult
```

[C#]
```
public static DialogResult Show(
   IWin32Window owner,
   string text,
   string caption,
   MessageBoxButtons buttons,
   MessageBoxIcon icon,
   MessageBoxDefaultButton defaultButton,
   MessageBoxOptions options
);
```
[C++]
```
public: static DialogResult Show(
   IWin32Window* owner,
   String* text,
   String* caption,
   MessageBoxButtons buttons,
   MessageBoxIcon icon,
   MessageBoxDefaultButton defaultButton,
   MessageBoxOptions options
);
```
[JScript]
```
public static function Show(
   owner : IWin32Window,
   text : String,
   caption : String,
   buttons : MessageBoxButtons,
   icon : MessageBoxIcon,
   defaultButton : MessageBoxDefaultButton,
   options : MessageBoxOptions
) : DialogResult;
```

Parameters

owner
: The **IWin32Window** the message box will display in front of.

text
: The text to display in the message box.

caption
: The text to display in the title bar of the message box.

buttons
: One of the **MessageBoxButtons** values that specifies which buttons to display in the message box.

icon
: One of the **MessageBoxIcon** values that specifies which icon to display in the message box.

defaultButton
: One of the **MessageBoxDefaultButton** values the specifies the default button for the message box.

options
: One of the **MessageBoxOptions** values that specifies which display and association options will be used for the message box.

Return Value

One of the **DialogResult** values.

Exceptions

Exception Type	Condition
InvalidEnumArgumentException	*buttons* is not a member of **MessageBoxButtons**. -or- *icon* is not a member of **MessageBoxIcon**. -or- *defaultButton* is not a member of **MessageBoxDefaultButton**.
InvalidOperationException	An attempt was made to display the **MessageBox** in a process that is not running in User Interactive mode. This is specified by the **SystemInformation.UserInteractive** property.
ArgumentException	*options* specified both **DefaultDesktopOnly** and **ServiceNotification**. -or- *options* specified **DefaultDesktopOnly** or **ServiceNotification** and specified a value in the *owner* parameter. These two options should be used only if you invoke the version of this method that does not take an *owner* parameter. -or- *buttons* specified an invalid combination of **MessageBoxButtons**.

Remarks

You can use the *owner* parameter to specify a particular object, which implements the **IWin32Window** interface, to place the message box in front of. A message box is a modal dialog, which means no input (keyboard or mouse click) can occur except to objects on the modal form. The program must hide or close a modal form (typically in response to some user action) before input to another form can occur.

You can have a maximum of three buttons on the message box.

Example

See related example in the **System.Windows.Forms.MessageBox.Show** method topic.

Requirements

Platforms: Windows 98, Windows NT 4.0, Windows Millennium Edition, Windows 2000, Windows XP Home Edition, Windows XP Professional, Windows Server 2003 family

.NET Framework Security:

- **UIPermission** for safe subwindows to call this method. Associated enumeration: **UIPermissionWindow.SafeSubWindows**

MessageBoxButtons Enumeration

Specifies constants defining which buttons to display on a **MessageBox**.

[Visual Basic]
```
<Serializable>
Public Enum MessageBoxButtons
```
[C#]
```
[Serializable]
public enum MessageBoxButtons
```
[C++]
```
[Serializable]
__value public enum MessageBoxButtons
```
[JScript]
```
public
   Serializable
enum MessageBoxButtons
```

Remarks

This enumeration is used by the **MessageBox** class.

Members

Member name	Description
AbortRetryIgnore Supported by the .NET Compact Framework.	The message box contains **Abort**, **Retry**, and **Ignore** buttons.
OK Supported by the .NET Compact Framework.	The message box contains an **OK** button.
OKCancel Supported by the .NET Compact Framework.	The message box contains **OK** and **Cancel** buttons.
RetryCancel Supported by the .NET Compact Framework.	The message box contains **Retry** and **Cancel** buttons.
YesNo Supported by the .NET Compact Framework.	The message box contains **Yes** and **No** buttons.
YesNoCancel Supported by the .NET Compact Framework.	The message box contains **Yes**, **No**, and **Cancel** buttons.

Example

[Visual Basic]
```
Protected Sub button1_Click(sender As Object, e As System.EventArgs)
    If textBox1.Text = "" Then
        MessageBox.Show("You must enter a name.", "Name Entry Error", _
           MessageBoxButtons.OK, MessageBoxIcon.Exclamation)
    Else
        ' Code to act on the data entered would go here.
    End If
End Sub
```

[C#]
```
protected void button1_Click(object sender, System.EventArgs e) {
   if(textBox1.Text == "") {
      MessageBox.Show("You must enter a name.", "Name Entry Error",
         MessageBoxButtons.OK, MessageBoxIcon.Exclamation);
   }
   else {
      // Code to act on the data entered would go here.
   }
}
```

Requirements

Namespace: System.Windows.Forms

Platforms: Windows 98, Windows NT 4.0, Windows Millennium Edition, Windows 2000, Windows XP Home Edition, Windows XP Professional, Windows Server 2003 family, .NET Compact Framework - Windows CE .NET

Assembly: System.Windows.Forms (in System.Windows.Forms.dll)

MessageBoxDefaultButton Enumeration

Specifies constants defining the default button on a **MessageBox**.

[Visual Basic]
```
<Serializable>
Public Enum MessageBoxDefaultButton
```
[C#]
```
[Serializable]
public enum MessageBoxDefaultButton
```
[C++]
```
[Serializable]
__value public enum MessageBoxDefaultButton
```
[JScript]
```
public
   Serializable
enum MessageBoxDefaultButton
```

Remarks

This enumeration is used by the **MessageBox** class.

Members

Member name	Description
Button1 Supported by the .NET Compact Framework.	The first button on the message box is the default button.
Button2 Supported by the .NET Compact Framework.	The second button on the message box is the default button.
Button3 Supported by the .NET Compact Framework.	The third button on the message box is the default button.

Example

[Visual Basic]
```
Private Sub ValidateUserEntry2()

    ' Checks the value of the text.

    If ServerName.Text.Length = 0 Then

        ' Initializes variables to pass to the MessageBox.Show method.

        Dim Message As String = "You did not enter a server
 name. Cancel this operation?"
        Dim Caption As String = "No Server Name Specified"
        Dim Buttons As Integer = MessageBoxButtons.YesNo

        Dim Result As DialogResult

        'Displays a MessageBox using the Question icon and
specifying the No button as the default.

        Result = MessageBox.Show(Me, Message, Caption,
MessageBoxButtons.YesNo, _
            MessageBoxIcon.Question,
MessageBoxDefaultButton.Button1, MessageBoxOptions.RightAlign)

        ' Gets the result of the MessageBox display.

        If Result = DialogResult.Yes Then

            ' Closes the parent form.

            Me.Close()

        End If

    End If

End Sub
```

[C#]
```
    private void validateUserEntry2()
    {

        // Checks the value of the text.

        if(serverName.Text.Length == 0)
        {

            // Initializes the variables to pass to the
MessageBox.Show method.

            string message = "You did not enter a server name.
 Cancel this operation?";
            string caption = "No Server Name Specified";
            MessageBoxButtons buttons = MessageBoxButtons.YesNo;
            DialogResult result;

            // Displays the MessageBox.

            result = MessageBox.Show(this, message, caption, buttons,
                MessageBoxIcon.Question,
MessageBoxDefaultButton.Button1,
                MessageBoxOptions.RightAlign);

            if(result == DialogResult.Yes)
            {

                // Closes the parent form.

                this.Close();

            }

        }

    }
```

[C++]
```
private:
    void validateUserEntry2() {
        // Checks the value of the text.
        if (serverName->Text->Length == 0) {

            // Initializes the variables to pass to the
MessageBox::Show method.
            String* message = S"You did not enter a server name.
Cancel this operation?";
            String* caption = S"No Server Name Specified";
            MessageBoxButtons buttons = MessageBoxButtons::YesNo;
            System::Windows::Forms::DialogResult result;

            // Displays the MessageBox.
            result = MessageBox::Show(this, message, caption, buttons,
                MessageBoxIcon::Question,
MessageBoxDefaultButton::Button1,
                MessageBoxOptions::RightAlign);

            if (result == DialogResult::Yes) {
                // Closes the parent form.
                this->Close();
            }
        }
    }
```

Requirements

Namespace: System.Windows.Forms

Platforms: Windows 98, Windows NT 4.0, Windows Millennium Edition, Windows 2000, Windows XP Home Edition, Windows XP Professional, Windows Server 2003 family, .NET Compact Framework - Windows CE .NET

Assembly: System.Windows.Forms (in System.Windows.Forms.dll)

MessageBoxIcon Enumeration

Specifies constants defining which information to display.

[Visual Basic]
```
<Serializable>
Public Enum MessageBoxIcon
```
[C#]
```
[Serializable]
public enum MessageBoxIcon
```
[C++]
```
[Serializable]
__value public enum MessageBoxIcon
```
[JScript]
```
public
   Serializable
enum MessageBoxIcon
```

Remarks

This enumeration is used by the **MessageBox** class. The description of each member of this enumeration contains a typical representation of the symbol. The actual graphic displayed is a function of the operating system constants. In current implementations there are four unique symbols with multiple values assigned to them.

Members

Member name	Description
Asterisk Supported by the .NET Compact Framework.	The message box contains a symbol consisting of a lowercase letter i in a circle.
Error	The message box contains a symbol consisting of white X in a circle with a red background.
Exclamation Supported by the .NET Compact Framework.	The message box contains a symbol consisting of an exclamation point in a triangle with a yellow background.
Hand Supported by the .NET Compact Framework.	The message box contains a symbol consisting of a white X in a circle with a red background.
Information	The message box contains a symbol consisting of a lowercase letter i in a circle.
None Supported by the .NET Compact Framework.	The message box contain no symbols.
Question Supported by the .NET Compact Framework.	The message box contains a symbol consisting of a question mark in a circle.
Stop	The message box contains a symbol consisting of white X in a circle with a red background.
Warning	The message box contains a symbol consisting of an exclamation point in a triangle with a yellow background.

Example

[Visual Basic]
```
Protected Sub button1_Click(sender As Object, e As System.EventArgs)
    If textBox1.Text = "" Then
        MessageBox.Show("You must enter a name.", "Name Entry Error", _
           MessageBoxButtons.OK, MessageBoxIcon.Exclamation)
    Else
        ' Code to act on the data entered would go here.
    End If
End Sub
```

[C#]
```
protected void button1_Click(object sender, System.EventArgs e) {
   if(textBox1.Text == "") {
      MessageBox.Show("You must enter a name.", "Name Entry Error",
         MessageBoxButtons.OK, MessageBoxIcon.Exclamation);
   }
   else {
      // Code to act on the data entered would go here.
   }
}
```

Requirements

Namespace: System.Windows.Forms

Platforms: Windows 98, Windows NT 4.0, Windows Millennium Edition, Windows 2000, Windows XP Home Edition, Windows XP Professional, Windows Server 2003 family, .NET Compact Framework - Windows CE .NET

Assembly: System.Windows.Forms (in System.Windows.Forms.dll)

MessageBoxOptions Enumeration

Specifies options on a **MessageBox**.

This enumeration has a **FlagsAttribute** attribute that allows a bitwise combination of its member values.

```
[Visual Basic]
<Flags>
<Serializable>
Public Enum MessageBoxOptions
[C#]
[Flags]
[Serializable]
public enum MessageBoxOptions
[C++]
[Flags]
[Serializable]
__value public enum MessageBoxOptions
[JScript]
public
   Flags
   Serializable
enum MessageBoxOptions
```

Remarks

This enumeration is used by the **MessageBox** class.

Members

Member name	Description	Value
DefaultDesktopOnly	The message box is displayed on the active desktop. This constant is the same as **ServiceNotification** except that the system displays the message box only on the default desktop of the interactive window station.	131072
RightAlign	The message box text is right-aligned.	524288
RtlReading	Specifies that the message box text is displayed with right to left reading order.	1048576
ServiceNotification	The message box is displayed on the active desktop. The caller is a service notifying the user of an event. The function displays a message box on the current active desktop, even if there is no user logged on to the computer.	2097152

Example

```
[Visual Basic]
Private Sub ValidateUserEntry2()

    ' Checks the value of the text.

    If ServerName.Text.Length = 0 Then

        ' Initializes variables to pass to the MessageBox.Show method.

        Dim Message As String = "You did not enter a server
name. Cancel this operation?"
        Dim Caption As String = "No Server Name Specified"
        Dim Buttons As Integer = MessageBoxButtons.YesNo

        Dim Result As DialogResult

        'Displays a MessageBox using the Question icon and
 specifying the No button as the default.

        Result = MessageBox.Show(Me, Message, Caption,
MessageBoxButtons.YesNo, _
            MessageBoxIcon.Question,
 MessageBoxDefaultButton.Button1, MessageBoxOptions.RightAlign)

        ' Gets the result of the MessageBox display.

        If Result = DialogResult.Yes Then

            ' Closes the parent form.

            Me.Close()

        End If

    End If

End Sub
```

```
[C#]
    private void validateUserEntry2()
    {

        // Checks the value of the text.

        if(serverName.Text.Length == 0)
        {

            // Initializes the variables to pass to the
MessageBox.Show method.

            string message = "You did not enter a server name.
 Cancel this operation?";
            string caption = "No Server Name Specified";
            MessageBoxButtons buttons = MessageBoxButtons.YesNo;
            DialogResult result;

            // Displays the MessageBox.

            result = MessageBox.Show(this, message, caption, buttons,
                MessageBoxIcon.Question,
MessageBoxDefaultButton.Button1,
                MessageBoxOptions.RightAlign);

            if(result == DialogResult.Yes)
            {

                // Closes the parent form.

                this.Close();

            }

        }

    }
```

[C++]
```
private:
    void validateUserEntry2() {
        // Checks the value of the text.
        if (serverName->Text->Length == 0) {

            // Initializes the variables to pass to the            ↵
MessageBox::Show method.
            String* message = S"You did not enter a server name.    ↵
 Cancel this operation?";
            String* caption = S"No Server Name Specified";
            MessageBoxButtons buttons = MessageBoxButtons::YesNo;
            System::Windows::Forms::DialogResult result;

            // Displays the MessageBox.
            result = MessageBox::Show(this, message, caption, buttons,
                MessageBoxIcon::Question,                            ↵
MessageBoxDefaultButton::Button1,
                MessageBoxOptions::RightAlign);

            if (result == DialogResult::Yes) {
                // Closes the parent form.
                this->Close();
            }
        }
    }
```

Requirements

Namespace: System.Windows.Forms

Platforms: Windows 98, Windows NT 4.0, Windows Millennium Edition, Windows 2000, Windows XP Home Edition, Windows XP Professional, Windows Server 2003 family

Assembly: System.Windows.Forms (in System.Windows.Forms.dll)

MethodInvoker Delegate

Represents the method that handles the **Invoke** event for a method.

[Visual Basic]
```
<Serializable>
Public Delegate Sub MethodInvoker()
```
[C#]
```
[Serializable]
public delegate void MethodInvoker();
```
[C++]
```
[Serializable]
public __gc __delegate void MethodInvoker();
```

[JScript] In JScript, you can use the delegates in the .NET Framework, but you cannot define your own.

Parameters [Visual Basic, C#, C++]

The declaration of your callback method must have the same parameters as the **MethodInvoker** delegate declaration.

Remarks

MethodInvoker provides a simple delegate that is used to invoke a method with a void parameter list. This delegate can be used when making calls to a control's invoke method, or when you need a simple delegate but don't want to define one yourself.

When you create a **MethodInvoker** delegate, you identify the method that will handle the event. To associate the event with your event handler, add an instance of the delegate to the event. The event handler is called whenever the event occurs, unless you remove the delegate.

Requirements

Namespace: System.Windows.Forms

Platforms: Windows 98, Windows NT 4.0, Windows Millennium Edition, Windows 2000, Windows XP Home Edition, Windows XP Professional, Windows Server 2003 family

Assembly: System.Windows.Forms (in System.Windows.Forms.dll)

MonthCalendar Class

Represents a standard Windows month calendar control.

System.Object
  System.MarshalByRefObject
    System.ComponentModel.Component
      System.Windows.Forms.Control
        System.Windows.Forms.MonthCalendar

[Visual Basic]
```
Public Class MonthCalendar
   Inherits Control
```
[C#]
```
public class MonthCalendar : Control
```
[C++]
```
public __gc class MonthCalendar : public Control
```
[JScript]
```
public class MonthCalendar extends Control
```

Thread Safety

Any public static (**Shared** in Visual Basic) members of this type are safe for multithreaded operations. Any instance members are not guaranteed to be thread safe.

Remarks

The **MonthCalendar** control allows the user to select a date and time using a visual display. You can limit the date and times that can be selected by setting the **MinDate** and **MaxDate** properties.

You can change the look of the calendar portion of the control by setting the **ForeColor**, **Font**, **TitleBackColor**, **TitleForeColor**, **TrailingForeColor**, and **BackColor** properties.

You might consider using a **DateTimePicker** control instead of a **MonthCalendar**, if you need custom date formatting and a selection limited to just one date. Using the **DateTimePicker** eliminates much of the need for validating date/time values.

For more information on month calendar controls, see the Month Calendar controls topic under Windows Common Controls, under User Interface Services, in the Platform SDK documentation in the MSDN library.

Example

[Visual Basic, C#, C++] The following example displays a form containing a **MonthCalendar** control that displays one calendar year. The example demonstrates setting properties like **BackColor**, **ForeColor**, **TitleBackColor**, **TitleForeColor**, **Calendar-Dimensions**, and **TrailingForeColor** to customize the look of the calendar control. Other properties like **AnnuallyBoldedDates**, **BoldedDates**, and **MonthlyBoldedDates** are set to customize which dates are bolded. The example also sets properties to change the calendar format, including **FirstDayOfWeek**, **MaxDate**, **MinDate**, and **MaxSelectionCount**. The **DateSelected** and **DateChanged** events are also handled and their status displayed on the form.

[Visual Basic]
```
Imports System
Imports System.Drawing
Imports System.Windows.Forms

Public NotInheritable Class Form1
    Inherits System.Windows.Forms.Form

    Friend WithEvents MonthCalendar1 As
System.Windows.Forms.MonthCalendar
    Friend WithEvents TextBox1 As System.Windows.Forms.TextBox

    <System.STAThread()> _
    Public Shared Sub Main()
        System.Windows.Forms.Application.Run(New Form1)
    End Sub 'Main

    Public Sub New()
        MyBase.New()

        Me.TextBox1 = New System.Windows.Forms.TextBox
        Me.TextBox1.BorderStyle =                                      ↵
System.Windows.Forms.BorderStyle.FixedSingle
        Me.TextBox1.Location = New System.Drawing.Point(48, 488)
        Me.TextBox1.Multiline = True
        Me.TextBox1.ReadOnly = True
        Me.TextBox1.Size = New System.Drawing.Size(824, 32)

        ' Create the calendar.
        Me.MonthCalendar1 = New System.Windows.Forms.MonthCalendar

        ' Set the calendar location.
        Me.MonthCalendar1.Location = New System.Drawing.Point(47, 16)

        ' Change the color.
        Me.MonthCalendar1.BackColor = System.Drawing.SystemColors.Info
        Me.MonthCalendar1.ForeColor = System.Drawing.Color.FromArgb( _
                                CType(192, System.Byte),               ↵
CType(0, System.Byte), CType(192, System.Byte))
        Me.MonthCalendar1.TitleBackColor = System.Drawing.Color.Purple
        Me.MonthCalendar1.TitleForeColor = System.Drawing.Color.Yellow
        Me.MonthCalendar1.TrailingForeColor =                          ↵
System.Drawing.Color.FromArgb( _
                                CType(192, System.Byte),               ↵
CType(192, System.Byte), CType(0, System.Byte))

        ' Add dates to the AnnuallyBoldedDates array.
        Me.MonthCalendar1.AnnuallyBoldedDates = New System.DateTime() _
                    {New System.DateTime(2002, 4, 20, 0, 0, 0, 0), _
                     New System.DateTime(2002, 4, 28, 0, 0, 0, 0), _
                     New System.DateTime(2002, 5, 5, 0, 0, 0, 0), _
                     New System.DateTime(2002, 7, 4, 0, 0, 0, 0), _
                     New System.DateTime(2002, 12, 15, 0, 0, 0, 0), _
                     New System.DateTime(2002, 12, 18, 0, 0, 0, 0)}

        ' Add dates to BoldedDates array.
        Me.MonthCalendar1.BoldedDates = New System.DateTime()          ↵
{New System.DateTime(2002, 9, 26, 0, 0, 0, 0)}

        ' Add dates to MonthlyBoldedDates array.
        Me.MonthCalendar1.MonthlyBoldedDates = New System.DateTime() _
                    {New System.DateTime(2002, 1, 15, 0, 0, 0, 0), _
                     New System.DateTime(2002, 1, 30, 0, 0, 0, 0)}

        ' Configure the calendar to display 3 rows by 4 columns        ↵
of months.
        Me.MonthCalendar1.CalendarDimensions = New                     ↵
System.Drawing.Size(4, 3)

        ' Set the week to begin on Monday.
        Me.MonthCalendar1.FirstDayOfWeek =                             ↵
System.Windows.Forms.Day.Monday

        ' Sets the maximum visible date on the calendar to 12/31/2010.
        Me.MonthCalendar1.MaxDate = New System.DateTime(2010,          ↵
12, 31, 0, 0, 0, 0)

        ' Set the minimum visible date on the calendar to 12/31/2010.
        Me.MonthCalendar1.MinDate = New System.DateTime(1999, 1,       ↵
1, 0, 0, 0, 0)

        ' Only allow 21 days to be selected at the same time.
        Me.MonthCalendar1.MaxSelectionCount = 21

        ' Set the calendar to move one month at a time when            ↵
navigating using the arrows.
        Me.MonthCalendar1.ScrollChange = 1
```

```
        ' Do not show the "Today" banner.
        Me.MonthCalendar1.ShowToday = False

        ' Do not circle today's date.
        Me.MonthCalendar1.ShowTodayCircle = False

        ' Show the week numbers to the left of each week.
        Me.MonthCalendar1.ShowWeekNumbers = True

        ' Set up how the form should be displayed and add ↵
the controls to the form.
        Me.ClientSize = New System.Drawing.Size(920, 566)
        Me.Controls.AddRange(New ↵
System.Windows.Forms.Control() {Me.TextBox1, Me.MonthCalendar1})
        Me.Text = "Month Calendar Example"

    End Sub

    Private Sub monthCalendar1_DateSelected(ByVal sender As Object, _
                ByVal e As ↵
System.Windows.Forms.DateRangeEventArgs) Handles ↵
MonthCalendar1.DateSelected

        ' Show the start and end dates in the text box.
        Me.TextBox1.Text = "Date Selected: Start = " + _
            e.Start.ToShortDateString() + " : End = " + ↵
e.End.ToShortDateString()
    End Sub

    Private Sub monthCalendar1_DateChanged(ByVal sender As Object, _
                ByVal e As ↵
System.Windows.Forms.DateRangeEventArgs) Handles ↵
MonthCalendar1.DateChanged

        ' Show the start and end dates in the text box.
        Me.TextBox1.Text = "Date Changed: Start = " + _
            e.Start.ToShortDateString() + " : End = " + ↵
e.End.ToShortDateString()
    End Sub
End Class
```

[C#]

```
using System;
using System.Drawing;
using System.Windows.Forms;

public class Form1 : System.Windows.Forms.Form
{
    private System.Windows.Forms.MonthCalendar monthCalendar1;
    private System.Windows.Forms.TextBox textBox1;

    [STAThread]
    static void Main()
    {
        Application.Run(new Form1());
    }

    public Form1()
    {
        this.textBox1 = new System.Windows.Forms.TextBox();
        this.textBox1.BorderStyle = ↵
System.Windows.Forms.BorderStyle.FixedSingle;
        this.textBox1.Location = new System.Drawing.Point(48, 488);
        this.textBox1.Multiline = true;
        this.textBox1.ReadOnly = true;
        this.textBox1.Size = new System.Drawing.Size(824, 32);

        // Create the calendar.
        this.monthCalendar1 = new System.Windows.Forms.MonthCalendar();

        // Set the calendar location.
        this.monthCalendar1.Location = new ↵
System.Drawing.Point(47, 16);

        // Change the color.
        this.monthCalendar1.BackColor = ↵
System.Drawing.SystemColors.Info;
        this.monthCalendar1.ForeColor = System.Drawing.Color.FromArgb(
                            ((System.Byte)(192)), ↵
((System.Byte)(0)), ((System.Byte)(192)));
        this.monthCalendar1.TitleBackColor = ↵
System.Drawing.Color.Purple;
        this.monthCalendar1.TitleForeColor = ↵
System.Drawing.Color.Yellow;
        this.monthCalendar1.TrailingForeColor = ↵
System.Drawing.Color.FromArgb(
                            ((System.Byte)(192)), ↵
((System.Byte)(192)), ((System.Byte)(0)));

        // Add dates to the AnnuallyBoldedDates array.
        this.monthCalendar1.AnnuallyBoldedDates =
            new System.DateTime[] { new System.DateTime(2002, ↵
4, 20, 0, 0, 0, 0),
                                    new System.DateTime(2002, ↵
4, 28, 0, 0, 0, 0),
                                    new System.DateTime(2002, ↵
5, 5, 0, 0, 0, 0),
                                    new System.DateTime(2002, ↵
7, 4, 0, 0, 0, 0),
                                    new System.DateTime(2002, ↵
12, 15, 0, 0, 0, 0),
                                    new System.DateTime(2002, ↵
12, 18, 0, 0, 0, 0)};

        // Add dates to BoldedDates array.
        this.monthCalendar1.BoldedDates = new System.DateTime[] ↵
{new System.DateTime(2002, 9, 26, 0, 0, 0, 0)};

        // Add dates to MonthlyBoldedDates array.
        this.monthCalendar1.MonthlyBoldedDates =
           new System.DateTime[] {new System.DateTime(2002, ↵
1, 15, 0, 0, 0, 0),
                                  new System.DateTime(2002, ↵
1, 30, 0, 0, 0, 0)};

        // Configure the calendar to display 3 rows by 4 ↵
columns of months.
        this.monthCalendar1.CalendarDimensions = new ↵
System.Drawing.Size(4, 3);

        // Set week to begin on Monday.
        this.monthCalendar1.FirstDayOfWeek = ↵
System.Windows.Forms.Day.Monday;

        // Set the maximum visible date on the calendar to 12/31/2010.
        this.monthCalendar1.MaxDate = new System.DateTime(2010, ↵
12, 31, 0, 0, 0, 0);

        // Set the minimum visible date on calendar to 12/31/2010.
        this.monthCalendar1.MinDate = new System.DateTime(1999, ↵
1, 1, 0, 0, 0, 0);

        // Only allow 21 days to be selected at the same time.
        this.monthCalendar1.MaxSelectionCount = 21;

        // Set the calendar to move one month at a time when ↵
navigating using the arrows.
        this.monthCalendar1.ScrollChange = 1;

        // Do not show the "Today" banner.
        this.monthCalendar1.ShowToday = false;

        // Do not circle today's date.
        this.monthCalendar1.ShowTodayCircle = false;

        // Show the week numbers to the left of each week.
        this.monthCalendar1.ShowWeekNumbers = true;

        // Add event handlers for the DateSelected and ↵
DateChanged events
        this.monthCalendar1.DateSelected += new ↵
System.Windows.Forms.DateRangeEventHandler ↵
```

```
 (this.monthCalendar1_DateSelected);
        this.monthCalendar1.DateChanged += new                         ↵
System.Windows.Forms.DateRangeEventHandler                             ↵
 (this.monthCalendar1_DateChanged);

        // Set up how the form should be displayed and add            ↵
the controls to the form.
        this.ClientSize = new System.Drawing.Size(920, 566);
        this.Controls.AddRange(new                                     ↵
System.Windows.Forms.Control[] {this.textBox1, this.monthCalendar1});
        this.Text = "Month Calendar Example";
    }

    private void monthCalendar1_DateSelected(object sender,            ↵
System.Windows.Forms.DateRangeEventArgs e)
    {
        // Show the start and end dates in the text box.
        this.textBox1.Text = "Date Selected: Start = " +
            e.Start.ToShortDateString() + " : End = " +                ↵
e.End.ToShortDateString();
    }

    private void monthCalendar1_DateChanged(object sender,             ↵
System.Windows.Forms.DateRangeEventArgs e)
    {
        // Show the start and end dates in the text box.
        this.textBox1.Text = "Date Changed: Start =  " +
            e.Start.ToShortDateString() + " : End = " +                ↵
e.End.ToShortDateString();
    }
}
```

[C++]

```
#using <mscorlib.dll>
#using <System.dll>
#using <System.Windows.Forms.dll>
#using <System.Drawing.dll>

using namespace System;
using namespace System::Drawing;
using namespace System::Windows::Forms;

public __gc class Form1 : public System::Windows::Forms::Form {
private:
   System::Windows::Forms::MonthCalendar*  monthCalendar1;
   System::Windows::Forms::TextBox*  textBox1;
public:
   Form1() {
      this->textBox1 = new System::Windows::Forms::TextBox();
      this->textBox1->BorderStyle =                                    ↵
System::Windows::Forms::BorderStyle::FixedSingle;
      this->textBox1->Location =  System::Drawing::Point(48, 488);
      this->textBox1->Multiline = true;
      this->textBox1->ReadOnly = true;
      this->textBox1->Size =  System::Drawing::Size(824, 32);

      // Create the calendar.
      this->monthCalendar1 = new                                       ↵
System::Windows::Forms::MonthCalendar();

      // Set the calendar location.
      this->monthCalendar1->Location =  System::Drawing::Point(47, 16);

      // Change the color.
      this->monthCalendar1->BackColor =                                ↵
System::Drawing::SystemColors::Info;
      this->monthCalendar1->ForeColor =                                ↵
System::Drawing::Color::FromArgb(((System::Byte)(192)),                ↵
 ((System::Byte)(0)), ((System::Byte)(192)));
      this->monthCalendar1->TitleBackColor =                           ↵
System::Drawing::Color::Purple;
      this->monthCalendar1->TitleForeColor =                           ↵
System::Drawing::Color::Yellow;
      this->monthCalendar1->TrailingForeColor =                        ↵
System::Drawing::Color::FromArgb(((System::Byte)(192)),                ↵
 ((System::Byte)(192)), ((System::Byte)(0)));

      // Add dates to the AnnuallyBoldedDates array.

      System::DateTime temp1 [] = {System::DateTime(2002,              ↵
4, 20, 0, 0, 0, 0),
          System::DateTime(2002, 4, 28, 0, 0, 0, 0),
          System::DateTime(2002, 5, 5, 0, 0, 0, 0),
          System::DateTime(2002, 7, 4, 0, 0, 0, 0),
          System::DateTime(2002, 12, 15, 0, 0, 0, 0),
          System::DateTime(2002, 12, 18, 0, 0, 0, 0)};

      this->monthCalendar1->AnnuallyBoldedDates = temp1;

      // Add dates to BoldedDates array.

      System::DateTime temp2 [] = {System::DateTime(2002,              ↵
 9, 26, 0, 0, 0, 0)};

      this->monthCalendar1->BoldedDates = temp2;

      // Add dates to MonthlyBoldedDates array.

      System::DateTime temp5 [] = {System::DateTime(2002,              ↵
 1, 15, 0, 0, 0, 0),
          System::DateTime(2002, 1, 30, 0, 0, 0, 0)};

      this->monthCalendar1->MonthlyBoldedDates = temp5;

      // Configure the calendar to display 3 rows by 4                 ↵
columns of months.
      this->monthCalendar1->CalendarDimensions =                       ↵
System::Drawing::Size(4, 3);

      // Set week to begin on Monday.
      this->monthCalendar1->FirstDayOfWeek =                           ↵
System::Windows::Forms::Day::Monday;

      // Set the maximum visible date on the calendar to 12/31/2010.
      this->monthCalendar1->MaxDate = System::DateTime(2010,           ↵
 12, 31, 0, 0, 0, 0);

      // Set the minimum visible date on calendar to 12/31/2010.
      this->monthCalendar1->MinDate = System::DateTime(1999,           ↵
1, 1, 0, 0, 0, 0);

      // Only allow 21 days to be selected at the same time.
      this->monthCalendar1->MaxSelectionCount = 21;

      // Set the calendar to move one month at a time when             ↵
navigating using the arrows.
      this->monthCalendar1->ScrollChange = 1;

      // Do not show the S"Today" banner.
      this->monthCalendar1->ShowToday = false;

      // Do not circle today's date.
      this->monthCalendar1->ShowTodayCircle = false;

      // Show the week numbers to the left of each week.
      this->monthCalendar1->ShowWeekNumbers = true;

      // Add event handlers for the DateSelected and                   ↵
DateChanged events
      this->monthCalendar1->DateSelected += new                        ↵
System::Windows::Forms::DateRangeEventHandler(this,                    ↵
monthCalendar1_DateSelected);
      this->monthCalendar1->DateChanged += new                         ↵
System::Windows::Forms::DateRangeEventHandler(this,
monthCalendar1_DateChanged);

      // Set up how the form should be displayed and add              ↵
the controls to the form.
      this->ClientSize =  System::Drawing::Size(920, 566);

      System::Windows::Forms::Control* temp0 [] =                      ↵
{this->textBox1, this->monthCalendar1};
```

```
      this->Controls->AddRange(temp0);
      this->Text = S"Month Calendar Example";
   }

private:
   void monthCalendar1_DateSelected(Object* sender,                    ↵
System::Windows::Forms::DateRangeEventArgs* e) {
      // Show the start and end dates in the text box.
      this->textBox1->Text = String::Format( S"Date Selected:          ↵
 Start = {0} : End = {1}", e->Start.ToShortDateString(), e-            ↵
>End.ToShortDateString() );
   }

private:
   void monthCalendar1_DateChanged(Object* sender,                     ↵
System::Windows::Forms::DateRangeEventArgs* e) {
      // Show the start and end dates in the text box.
      this->textBox1->Text = String::Format( S"Date Changed:           ↵
 Start = {0} : End = {1}", e->Start.ToShortDateString(), e-            ↵
>End.ToShortDateString() );
   }
};

[STAThread]
int main() {
   Application::Run(new Form1());
}
```

Requirements

Namespace: System.Windows.Forms

Platforms: Windows 98, Windows NT 4.0, Windows Millennium Edition, Windows 2000, Windows XP Home Edition, Windows XP Professional, Windows Server 2003 family

Assembly: System.Windows.Forms (in System.Windows.Forms.dll)

MonthCalendar Constructor

Initializes a new instance of the **MonthCalendar** class.

[Visual Basic]
```
Public Sub New()
```
[C#]
```
public MonthCalendar();
```
[C++]
```
public: MonthCalendar();
```
[JScript]
```
public function MonthCalendar();
```

Remarks

Creates a new **MonthCalendar**.

The following table shows initial property values for an instance of **MonthCalendar**.

Item	Description
SelectionStart	Today's date.
SelectionEnd	Today's date.

Example

See related example in the **System.Windows.Forms.MonthCalendar** class topic.

Requirements

Platforms: Windows 98, Windows NT 4.0, Windows Millennium Edition, Windows 2000, Windows XP Home Edition, Windows XP Professional, Windows Server 2003 family

MonthCalendar.AnnuallyBoldedDates Property

Gets or sets the array of **DateTime** objects that determines which annual days are displayed in bold.

[Visual Basic]
```
Public Property AnnuallyBoldedDates As DateTime ()
```
[C#]
```
public DateTime[] AnnuallyBoldedDates {get; set;}
```
[C++]
```
public: __property DateTime get_AnnuallyBoldedDates();
public: __property void set_AnnuallyBoldedDates(DateTime[]);
```
[JScript]
```
public function get AnnuallyBoldedDates() : DateTime[];
public function set AnnuallyBoldedDates(DateTime[]);
```

Property Value

An array of **DateTime** objects.

Remarks

Using this property, you can assign an array of annually bolded dates. When you assign an array of dates, the existing dates are first cleared.

Example

See related example in the **System.Windows.Forms.MonthCalendar** class topic.

Requirements

Platforms: Windows 98, Windows NT 4.0, Windows Millennium Edition, Windows 2000, Windows XP Home Edition, Windows XP Professional, Windows Server 2003 family

MonthCalendar.BackColor Property

This member overrides **Control.BackColor**.

[Visual Basic]
```
Overrides Public Property BackColor As Color
```
[C#]
```
public override Color BackColor {get; set;}
```
[C++]
```
public: __property Color get_BackColor();
public: __property void set_BackColor(Color);
```
[JScript]
```
public override function get BackColor() : Color;
public override function set BackColor(Color);
```

Requirements

Platforms: Windows 98, Windows NT 4.0, Windows Millennium Edition, Windows 2000, Windows XP Home Edition, Windows XP Professional, Windows Server 2003 family

MonthCalendar.BackgroundImage Property

This member overrides **Control.BackgroundImage**.

[Visual Basic]
```
Overrides Public Property BackgroundImage As Image
```
[C#]
```
public override Image BackgroundImage {get; set;}
```
[C++]
```
public: __property Image* get_BackgroundImage();
public: __property void set_BackgroundImage(Image*);
```
[JScript]
```
public override function get BackgroundImage() : Image;
public override function set BackgroundImage(Image);
```

Requirements

Platforms: Windows 98, Windows NT 4.0, Windows Millennium Edition, Windows 2000, Windows XP Home Edition, Windows XP Professional, Windows Server 2003 family

MonthCalendar.BoldedDates Property

Gets or sets the array of **DateTime** objects that determines which nonrecurring dates are displayed in bold.

[Visual Basic]
```
Public Property BoldedDates As DateTime ()
```
[C#]
```
public DateTime[] BoldedDates {get; set;}
```
[C++]
```
public: __property DateTime get_BoldedDates();
public: __property void set_BoldedDates(DateTime[]);
```
[JScript]
```
public function get BoldedDates() : DateTime[];
public function set BoldedDates(DateTime[]);
```

Property Value

The array of bolded dates.

Remarks

Using this property, you can assign an array of bolded dates. When you assign an array of dates, the existing dates are first cleared.

Example

See related example in the **System.Windows.Forms.MonthCalendar** class topic.

Requirements

Platforms: Windows 98, Windows NT 4.0, Windows Millennium Edition, Windows 2000, Windows XP Home Edition, Windows XP Professional, Windows Server 2003 family

MonthCalendar.CalendarDimensions Property

Gets or sets the number of columns and rows of months displayed.

[Visual Basic]
```
Public Property CalendarDimensions As Size
```
[C#]
```
public Size CalendarDimensions {get; set;}
```
[C++]
```
public: __property Size get_CalendarDimensions();
public: __property void set_CalendarDimensions(Size);
```
[JScript]
```
public function get CalendarDimensions() : Size;
public function set CalendarDimensions(Size);
```

Property Value

A **Size** with the number of columns and rows to use to display the calendar.

Remarks

Only one calendar year is displayed at a time, and the maximum number of months that can be displayed is 12. Valid combinations of columns and rows make a maximum product of 12; for values greater than 12, the display is modified on a best-fit basis.

Example

See related example in the **System.Windows.Forms.MonthCalendar** class topic.

Requirements

Platforms: Windows 98, Windows NT 4.0, Windows Millennium Edition, Windows 2000, Windows XP Home Edition, Windows XP Professional, Windows Server 2003 family

MonthCalendar.CreateParams Property

This member overrides **Control.CreateParams**.

[Visual Basic]
```
Overrides Protected ReadOnly Property CreateParams As CreateParams
```
[C#]
```
protected override CreateParams CreateParams {get;}
```
[C++]
```
protected: __property CreateParams* get_CreateParams();
```
[JScript]
```
protected override function get CreateParams() : CreateParams;
```

Requirements

Platforms: Windows 98, Windows NT 4.0, Windows Millennium Edition, Windows 2000, Windows XP Home Edition, Windows XP Professional, Windows Server 2003 family

MonthCalendar.DefaultImeMode Property

Gets a value indicating the input method editor for the **MonthCalendar**.

[Visual Basic]
```
Overrides Protected ReadOnly Property DefaultImeMode As ImeMode
```
[C#]
```
protected override ImeMode DefaultImeMode {get;}
```
[C++]
```
protected: __property ImeMode get_DefaultImeMode();
```
[JScript]
```
protected override function get DefaultImeMode() : ImeMode;
```

Property Value

As implemented for this object, always **ImeMode.Disable**.

Requirements

Platforms: Windows 98, Windows NT 4.0, Windows Millennium Edition, Windows 2000, Windows XP Home Edition, Windows XP Professional, Windows Server 2003 family

MonthCalendar.DefaultSize Property

Gets the default size of the calendar.

```
[Visual Basic]
Overrides Protected ReadOnly Property DefaultSize As Size
[C#]
protected override Size DefaultSize {get;}
[C++]
protected: __property Size get_DefaultSize();
[JScript]
protected override function get DefaultSize() : Size;
```

Property Value

A **Size** specifying the height and width of the control in pixels.

Remarks

The **DefaultSize** property includes the area necessary to display the "Today:" date display at the bottom of the calendar.

Requirements

Platforms: Windows 98, Windows NT 4.0, Windows Millennium Edition, Windows 2000, Windows XP Home Edition, Windows XP Professional, Windows Server 2003 family

MonthCalendar.FirstDayOfWeek Property

Gets or sets the first day of the week as displayed in the month calendar.

```
[Visual Basic]
Public Property FirstDayOfWeek As Day
[C#]
public Day FirstDayOfWeek {get; set;}
[C++]
public: __property Day get_FirstDayOfWeek();
public: __property void set_FirstDayOfWeek(Day);
[JScript]
public function get FirstDayOfWeek() : Day;
public function set FirstDayOfWeek(Day);
```

Property Value

One of the **Day** values. The default is **Day.Default**.

Exceptions

Exception Type	Condition
InvalidEnumArgument-Exception	The assigned is not one of the **Day** enumeration members.

Example

See related example in the **System.Windows.Forms.Month-Calendar** class topic.

Requirements

Platforms: Windows 98, Windows NT 4.0, Windows Millennium Edition, Windows 2000, Windows XP Home Edition, Windows XP Professional, Windows Server 2003 family

MonthCalendar.ForeColor Property

This member overrides **Control.ForeColor**.

```
[Visual Basic]
Overrides Public Property ForeColor As Color
[C#]
public override Color ForeColor {get; set;}
[C++]
public: __property Color get_ForeColor();
public: __property void set_ForeColor(Color);
[JScript]
public override function get ForeColor() : Color;
public override function set ForeColor(Color);
```

Requirements

Platforms: Windows 98, Windows NT 4.0, Windows Millennium Edition, Windows 2000, Windows XP Home Edition, Windows XP Professional, Windows Server 2003 family

MonthCalendar.ImeMode Property

This member supports the .NET Framework infrastructure and is not intended to be used directly from your code.

```
[Visual Basic]
Public Shadows Property ImeMode As ImeMode
[C#]
public new ImeMode ImeMode {get; set;}
[C++]
public: __property ImeMode get_ImeMode();
public: __property void set_ImeMode(ImeMode);
[JScript]
public hide function get ImeMode() : ImeMode;
public hide function set ImeMode(ImeMode);
```

MonthCalendar.MaxDate Property

Gets or sets the maximum allowable date.

```
[Visual Basic]
Public Property MaxDate As DateTime
[C#]
public DateTime MaxDate {get; set;}
[C++]
public: __property DateTime get_MaxDate();
public: __property void set_MaxDate(DateTime);
[JScript]
public function get MaxDate() : DateTime;
public function set MaxDate(DateTime);
```

Property Value

A **DateTime** representing the maximum allowable date. The default is 12/31/9998.

Exceptions

Exception Type	Condition
ArgumentException	The value is less than the **MinDate**.

Example

See related example in the **System.Windows.Forms.MonthCalendar** class topic.

Requirements

Platforms: Windows 98, Windows NT 4.0, Windows Millennium Edition, Windows 2000, Windows XP Home Edition, Windows XP Professional, Windows Server 2003 family

MonthCalendar.MaxSelectionCount Property

Gets or sets the maximum number of days that can be selected in a month calendar control.

```
[Visual Basic]
Public Property MaxSelectionCount As Integer
[C#]
public int MaxSelectionCount {get; set;}
[C++]
public: __property int get_MaxSelectionCount();
public: __property void set_MaxSelectionCount(int);
[JScript]
public function get MaxSelectionCount() : int;
public function set MaxSelectionCount(int);
```

Property Value

The maximum number of days that you can select. The default is seven.

Exceptions

Exception Type	Condition
ArgumentException	The value is less than one. -or- The **MaxSelectionCount** cannot be set.

Remarks

Setting this property does not affect the current selection range.

It is important to remember that **MaxSelectionCount** represents the number of days in the selection, not the difference between **SelectionStart** and **SelectionEnd**. For example, if **MaxSelectionCount** is seven (the default), then **SelectionStart** and **SelectionEnd** can be no more than six days apart.

Example

See related example in the **System.Windows.Forms.MonthCalendar** class topic.

Requirements

Platforms: Windows 98, Windows NT 4.0, Windows Millennium Edition, Windows 2000, Windows XP Home Edition, Windows XP Professional, Windows Server 2003 family

MonthCalendar.MinDate Property

Gets or sets the minimum allowable date.

```
[Visual Basic]
Public Property MinDate As DateTime
[C#]
public DateTime MinDate {get; set;}
[C++]
public: __property DateTime get_MinDate();
public: __property void set_MinDate(DateTime);
[JScript]
public function get MinDate() : DateTime;
public function set MinDate(DateTime);
```

Property Value

A **DateTime** representing the minimum allowable date. The default is 01/01/1753.

Exceptions

Exception Type	Condition
ArgumentException	The date set is greater than the **MaxDate**.
ArgumentException	The date set is earlier than 01/01/1753.

Example

See related example in the **System.Windows.Forms.MonthCalendar** class topic.

Requirements

Platforms: Windows 98, Windows NT 4.0, Windows Millennium Edition, Windows 2000, Windows XP Home Edition, Windows XP Professional, Windows Server 2003 family

MonthCalendar.MonthlyBoldedDates Property

Gets or sets the array of **DateTime** objects that determine which monthly days to bold.

```
[Visual Basic]
Public Property MonthlyBoldedDates As DateTime ()
[C#]
public DateTime[] MonthlyBoldedDates {get; set;}
[C++]
public: __property DateTime get_MonthlyBoldedDates();
public: __property void set_MonthlyBoldedDates(DateTime[]);
[JScript]
public function get MonthlyBoldedDates() : DateTime[];
public function set MonthlyBoldedDates(DateTime[]);
```

Property Value

An array of **DateTime** objects.

Remarks

Using this property, you assign an array of monthly bolded dates. When you assign an array of dates, any preexisting dates are cleared.

Example

See related example in the **System.Windows.Forms.MonthCalendar** class topic.

Requirements

Platforms: Windows 98, Windows NT 4.0, Windows Millennium Edition, Windows 2000, Windows XP Home Edition, Windows XP Professional, Windows Server 2003 family

MonthCalendar.ScrollChange Property

Gets or sets the scroll rate for a month calendar control.

```
[Visual Basic]
Public Property ScrollChange As Integer
[C#]
public int ScrollChange {get; set;}
[C++]
public: __property int get_ScrollChange();
public: __property void set_ScrollChange(int);
[JScript]
public function get ScrollChange() : int;
public function set ScrollChange(int);
```

Property Value

A positive number representing the current scroll rate in number of months moved. The default is the number of months currently displayed. The maximum is 20,000.

Exceptions

Exception Type	Condition
ArgumentException	The value is less than zero. -or- The value is greater than 20,000.

Remarks

The scroll rate is the number of months that the control moves its display when the user clicks a scroll button. If this value is zero, the number of months is reset to the default, which is the number of months displayed in the control. The maximum value is 20,000.

Example

See related example in the **System.Windows.Forms.MonthCalendar** class topic.

Requirements

Platforms: Windows 98, Windows NT 4.0, Windows Millennium Edition, Windows 2000, Windows XP Home Edition, Windows XP Professional, Windows Server 2003 family

MonthCalendar.SelectionEnd Property

Gets or sets the end date of the selected range of dates.

```
[Visual Basic]
Public Property SelectionEnd As DateTime
[C#]
public DateTime SelectionEnd {get; set;}
[C++]
public: __property DateTime get_SelectionEnd();
public: __property void set_SelectionEnd(DateTime);
[JScript]
public function get SelectionEnd() : DateTime;
public function set SelectionEnd(DateTime);
```

Property Value

A **DateTime** indicating the last date in the selection range.

Exceptions

Exception Type	Condition
ArgumentException	The date value is less than the **MinDate** value. -or- The date value is greater than the **MaxDate** value.

Remarks

If you set **SelectionEnd** to a date that is earlier than the current **SelectionStart**, then **SelectionStart** is automatically set equal to **SelectionEnd**.

If you set a date in **SelectionEnd** that causes the selection to exceed the number of days specified by the **MaxSelectionCount** property, the value of **SelectionStart** is adjusted: **SelectionStart** is automatically set so that the number of days selected is equal to **MaxSelectionCount**.

Note **MaxSelectionCount** represents the number of days in the selection, not the difference between **SelectionStart** and **SelectionEnd**. For example, if **MaxSelectionCount** is seven (the default), then **SelectionStart** and **SelectionEnd** can be no more than six days apart.

Requirements

Platforms: Windows 98, Windows NT 4.0, Windows Millennium Edition, Windows 2000, Windows XP Home Edition, Windows XP Professional, Windows Server 2003 family

MonthCalendar.SelectionRange Property

Gets or sets the selected range of dates for a month calendar control.

```
[Visual Basic]
Public Property SelectionRange As SelectionRange
[C#]
public SelectionRange SelectionRange {get; set;}
[C++]
public: __property SelectionRange* get_SelectionRange();
public: __property void set_SelectionRange(SelectionRange*);
[JScript]
public function get SelectionRange() : SelectionRange;
public function set SelectionRange(SelectionRange);
```

Property Value

A **SelectionRange** with the start and end dates of the selected range.

Exceptions

Exception Type	Condition
ArgumentException	The **Start** property value of the assigned **SelectionRange** is less than the minimum date allowable for a month calendar control. -or- The **Start** property value of the assigned **SelectionRange** is greater than the maximum allowable date for a month calendar control. -or- The **End** property value of the assigned **SelectionRange** is less than the minimum date allowable for a month calendar control. -or- The **End** property value of the assigned **SelectionRange** is greater than the maximum allowable date for a month calendar control.

Remarks

Setting this property is functionally equivalent to using the **SetSelectionRange** method. You can set the start and end dates separately by setting either **SelectionStart** or **SelectionEnd**.

If the **Start** property value of the **SelectionRange** is greater than its **End** property value, the dates are swapped; the **End** property value becomes the starting date, and **Start** property value becomes the end date.

Note Scrolling the calendar display with the navigation buttons when a range is selected can cause unexpected results. For example, the date range is not preserved. If you have a single month displayed with a range of 04/01/2001 to 04/10/2001, scrolling the calendar to March changes the selected range as follows: 03/01/2001 to 03/10/2001. If you have multiple months displayed, such as March and April with a selected range of 04/01/2001 to 04/10/2001, scrolling the calendar back (to January and February) changes the selected range as follows: 01/01/2001 to 01/10/2001.

Requirements

Platforms: Windows 98, Windows NT 4.0, Windows Millennium Edition, Windows 2000, Windows XP Home Edition, Windows XP Professional, Windows Server 2003 family

MonthCalendar.SelectionStart Property

Gets or sets the start date of the selected range of dates.

```
[Visual Basic]
Public Property SelectionStart As DateTime
[C#]
public DateTime SelectionStart {get; set;}
[C++]
public: __property DateTime get_SelectionStart();
public: __property void set_SelectionStart(DateTime);
[JScript]
public function get SelectionStart() : DateTime;
public function set SelectionStart(DateTime);
```

Property Value

A **DateTime** indicating the first date in the selection range.

Exceptions

Exception Type	Condition
ArgumentException	The date value is less than **MinDate**. -or- The date value is greater than **MaxDate**.

Remarks

If you set **SelectionStart** to a date that is later than the current **SelectionEnd**, then **SelectionEnd** is automatically set equal to **SelectionStart**.

If you set a date in **SelectionStart** that causes the selection to exceed the number of days specified by the **MaxSelectionCount** property, the value of **SelectionEnd** is adjusted: **SelectionEnd** is automatically set so that the number of days selected is equal to **MaxSelectionCount**.

Note **MaxSelectionCount** represents the number of days in the selection, not the difference between **SelectionStart** and **SelectionEnd**. For example, if **MaxSelectionCount** is seven (the default), then **SelectionStart** and **SelectionEnd** can be no more than six days apart.

Requirements

Platforms: Windows 98, Windows NT 4.0, Windows Millennium Edition, Windows 2000, Windows XP Home Edition, Windows XP Professional, Windows Server 2003 family

MonthCalendar.ShowToday Property

Gets or sets a value indicating whether the date represented by the **TodayDate** property is displayed at the bottom of the control.

```
[Visual Basic]
Public Property ShowToday As Boolean
[C#]
public bool ShowToday {get; set;}
[C++]
public: __property bool get_ShowToday();
public: __property void set_ShowToday(bool);
[JScript]
public function get ShowToday() : Boolean;
public function set ShowToday(Boolean);
```

Property Value

true if today's date is displayed; otherwise, **false**. The default is **true**.

Remarks

The date is displayed in the format specified by the system settings for the short date format.

Example

See related example in the **System.Windows.Forms.Month-Calendar** class topic.

Requirements

Platforms: Windows 98, Windows NT 4.0, Windows Millennium Edition, Windows 2000, Windows XP Home Edition, Windows XP Professional, Windows Server 2003 family

MonthCalendar.ShowTodayCircle Property

Gets or sets a value indicating whether today's date is circled.

```
[Visual Basic]
Public Property ShowTodayCircle As Boolean
[C#]
public bool ShowTodayCircle {get; set;}
[C++]
public: __property bool get_ShowTodayCircle();
public: __property void set_ShowTodayCircle(bool);
[JScript]
public function get ShowTodayCircle() : Boolean;
public function set ShowTodayCircle(Boolean);
```

Property Value

true if today's date is circled; otherwise, **false**. The default is **true**.

Example

See related example in the **System.Windows.Forms.Month-Calendar** class topic.

Requirements

Platforms: Windows 98, Windows NT 4.0, Windows Millennium Edition, Windows 2000, Windows XP Home Edition, Windows XP Professional, Windows Server 2003 family

MonthCalendar.ShowWeekNumbers Property

Gets or sets a value indicating whether the month calendar control displays week numbers (1-52) to the left of each row of days.

```
[Visual Basic]
Public Property ShowWeekNumbers As Boolean
[C#]
public bool ShowWeekNumbers {get; set;}
[C++]
public: __property bool get_ShowWeekNumbers();
public: __property void set_ShowWeekNumbers(bool);
[JScript]
public function get ShowWeekNumbers() : Boolean;
public function set ShowWeekNumbers(Boolean);
```

Property Value

true if the week numbers are displayed; otherwise, **false**. The default is **false**.

Example

See related example in the **System.Windows.Forms.MonthCalendar** class topic.

Requirements

Platforms: Windows 98, Windows NT 4.0, Windows Millennium Edition, Windows 2000, Windows XP Home Edition, Windows XP Professional, Windows Server 2003 family

MonthCalendar.SingleMonthSize Property

Gets the minimum size to display one month of the calendar.

```
[Visual Basic]
Public ReadOnly Property SingleMonthSize As Size
[C#]
public Size SingleMonthSize {get;}
[C++]
public: __property Size get_SingleMonthSize();
[JScript]
public function get SingleMonthSize() : Size;
```

Property Value

The size, in pixels, necessary to fully display one month in the calendar.

Exceptions

Exception Type	Condition
InvalidOperationException	The dimensions cannot be retrieved.

Remarks

The size information is presented in the form of **Width** and **Height** members, representing the minimum width and height required to display one month in the control. The minimum required window size for a month calendar control depends on the currently selected font.

Requirements

Platforms: Windows 98, Windows NT 4.0, Windows Millennium Edition, Windows 2000, Windows XP Home Edition, Windows XP Professional, Windows Server 2003 family

MonthCalendar.Text Property

This member overrides **Control.Text**.

```
[Visual Basic]
Overrides Public Property Text As String
[C#]
public override string Text {get; set;}
[C++]
public: __property String* get_Text();
public: __property void set_Text(String*);
[JScript]
public override function get Text() : String;
public override function set Text(String);
```

Requirements

Platforms: Windows 98, Windows NT 4.0, Windows Millennium Edition, Windows 2000, Windows XP Home Edition, Windows XP Professional, Windows Server 2003 family

MonthCalendar.TitleBackColor Property

Gets or sets a value indicating the background color of the title area of the calendar.

```
[Visual Basic]
Public Property TitleBackColor As Color
[C#]
public Color TitleBackColor {get; set;}
[C++]
public: __property Color get_TitleBackColor();
public: __property void set_TitleBackColor(Color);
[JScript]
public function get TitleBackColor() : Color;
public function set TitleBackColor(Color);
```

Property Value

One of the **Color** values. The default is the system color for active captions.

Exceptions

Exception Type	Condition
ArgumentException	The value is not one of the valid **Color** values.

Remarks

The font color of the days-of-the-week text depends on the **TitleBackColor** property. Setting the **TitleBackColor** equal to the **BackColor** for the main display area of the calendar causes the days-of-the-week text to become unreadable.

Example

See related example in the **System.Windows.Forms.MonthCalendar** class topic.

Requirements

Platforms: Windows 98, Windows NT 4.0, Windows Millennium Edition, Windows 2000, Windows XP Home Edition, Windows XP Professional, Windows Server 2003 family

MonthCalendar.TitleForeColor Property

Gets or sets a value indicating the foreground color of the title area of the calendar.

[Visual Basic]
```
Public Property TitleForeColor As Color
```
[C#]
```
public Color TitleForeColor {get; set;}
```
[C++]
```
public: __property Color get_TitleForeColor();
public: __property void set_TitleForeColor(Color);
```
[JScript]
```
public function get TitleForeColor() : Color;
public function set TitleForeColor(Color);
```

Property Value

One of the **Color** values. The default is the system color for active caption text.

Exceptions

Exception Type	Condition
ArgumentException	The value is not one of the valid **Color** values.

Example

See related example in the **System.Windows.Forms.Month-Calendar** class topic.

Requirements

Platforms: Windows 98, Windows NT 4.0, Windows Millennium Edition, Windows 2000, Windows XP Home Edition, Windows XP Professional, Windows Server 2003 family

MonthCalendar.TodayDate Property

Gets or sets the value that is used by **MonthCalendar** as today's date.

[Visual Basic]
```
Public Property TodayDate As DateTime
```
[C#]
```
public DateTime TodayDate {get; set;}
```
[C++]
```
public: __property DateTime get_TodayDate();
public: __property void set_TodayDate(DateTime);
```
[JScript]
```
public function get TodayDate() : DateTime;
public function set TodayDate(DateTime);
```

Property Value

A **DateTime** representing today's date. The default value is the current system date.

Remarks

By default, the **TodayDate** property returns the current system date, and the **TodayDateSet** property is **false**. Setting the **TodayDate** property sets the **TodayDateSet** property to **true** and, from that point, the value returned by the **TodayDate** property is the one the user sets.

Requirements

Platforms: Windows 98, Windows NT 4.0, Windows Millennium Edition, Windows 2000, Windows XP Home Edition, Windows XP Professional, Windows Server 2003 family

MonthCalendar.TodayDateSet Property

Gets a value indicating whether the **TodayDate** property has been explicitly set.

[Visual Basic]
```
Public ReadOnly Property TodayDateSet As Boolean
```
[C#]
```
public bool TodayDateSet {get;}
```
[C++]
```
public: __property bool get_TodayDateSet();
```
[JScript]
```
public function get TodayDateSet() : Boolean;
```

Property Value

true if the value for the **TodayDate** property has been explicitly set; otherwise, **false**. The default is **false**.

Requirements

Platforms: Windows 98, Windows NT 4.0, Windows Millennium Edition, Windows 2000, Windows XP Home Edition, Windows XP Professional, Windows Server 2003 family

MonthCalendar.TrailingForeColor Property

Gets or sets a value indicating the color of days in months that are not fully displayed in the control.

[Visual Basic]
```
Public Property TrailingForeColor As Color
```
[C#]
```
public Color TrailingForeColor {get; set;}
```
[C++]
```
public: __property Color get_TrailingForeColor();
public: __property void set_TrailingForeColor(Color);
```
[JScript]
```
public function get TrailingForeColor() : Color;
public function set TrailingForeColor(Color);
```

Property Value

One of the **Color** values. The default is **Color.Gray**.

Exceptions

Exception Type	Condition
ArgumentException	The value is not one of the valid **Color** values.

Remarks

When the calendar is displayed, some dates precede and some follow the months that are fully displayed. Using the **TrailingForeColor** property, you can modify the color of the text in which those dates are displayed.

Example

See related example in the **System.Windows.Forms.Month-Calendar** class topic.

Requirements

Platforms: Windows 98, Windows NT 4.0, Windows Millennium Edition, Windows 2000, Windows XP Home Edition, Windows XP Professional, Windows Server 2003 family

MonthCalendar.AddAnnuallyBoldedDate Method

Adds a day that is displayed in bold on an annual basis in the month calendar.

[Visual Basic]
```
Public Sub AddAnnuallyBoldedDate( _
   ByVal date As DateTime _
)
```
[C#]
```
public void AddAnnuallyBoldedDate(
   DateTime date
);
```
[C++]
```
public: void AddAnnuallyBoldedDate(
   DateTime date
);
```
[JScript]
```
public function AddAnnuallyBoldedDate(
   date : DateTime
);
```

Parameters

date
The date to be displayed in bold.

Remarks

You must call **UpdateBoldedDates** afterwards to update the display.

To add multiple dates in a single assignment, you can assign an array of **DateTime** objects to the **AnnuallyBoldedDates** property.

Requirements

Platforms: Windows 98, Windows NT 4.0,
Windows Millennium Edition, Windows 2000,
Windows XP Home Edition, Windows XP Professional,
Windows Server 2003 family

MonthCalendar.AddBoldedDate Method

Adds a day to be displayed in bold in the month calendar.

[Visual Basic]
```
Public Sub AddBoldedDate( _
   ByVal date As DateTime _
)
```
[C#]
```
public void AddBoldedDate(
   DateTime date
);
```
[C++]
```
public: void AddBoldedDate(
   DateTime date
);
```
[JScript]
```
public function AddBoldedDate(
   date : DateTime
);
```

Parameters

date
The date to be displayed in bold.

Remarks

You must call **UpdateBoldedDates** afterwards to update the display.

To add multiple dates in a single assignment, you can assign an array of **DateTime** objects to the **BoldedDates** property.

Example

See related example in the **System.Windows.Forms.MonthCalendar** class topic.

Requirements

Platforms: Windows 98, Windows NT 4.0,
Windows Millennium Edition, Windows 2000,
Windows XP Home Edition, Windows XP Professional,
Windows Server 2003 family

MonthCalendar.AddMonthlyBoldedDate Method

Adds a day that is displayed in bold on a monthly basis in the month calendar.

[Visual Basic]
```
Public Sub AddMonthlyBoldedDate( _
   ByVal date As DateTime _
)
```
[C#]
```
public void AddMonthlyBoldedDate(
   DateTime date
);
```
[C++]
```
public: void AddMonthlyBoldedDate(
   DateTime date
);
```
[JScript]
```
public function AddMonthlyBoldedDate(
   date : DateTime
);
```

Parameters

date
The date to be displayed in bold.

Remarks

You must call **UpdateBoldedDates** afterwards to update the display.

To add multiple dates in a single assignment, you can assign an array of **DateTime** objects to the **MonthlyBoldedDates** property.

Requirements

Platforms: Windows 98, Windows NT 4.0,
Windows Millennium Edition, Windows 2000,
Windows XP Home Edition, Windows XP Professional,
Windows Server 2003 family

MonthCalendar.CreateHandle Method

This member overrides **Control.CreateHandle**.

[Visual Basic]
```
Overrides Protected Sub CreateHandle()
```
[C#]
```
protected override void CreateHandle();
```
[C++]
```
protected: void CreateHandle();
```
[JScript]
```
protected override function CreateHandle();
```

Requirements

Platforms: Windows 98, Windows NT 4.0, Windows Millennium Edition, Windows 2000, Windows XP Home Edition, Windows XP Professional, Windows Server 2003 family

MonthCalendar.Dispose Method

Overload List

This member supports the .NET Framework infrastructure and is not intended to be used directly from your code.

[Visual Basic] **Overloads Overrides Protected Sub Dispose(Boolean)**

[C#] **protected override void Dispose(bool);**

[C++] **protected: void Dispose(bool);**

[JScript] **protected override function Dispose(Boolean);**

Inherited from **Component**.

[Visual Basic] **Overloads Public Overridable Sub Dispose() Implements IDisposable.Dispose**

[C#] **public virtual void Dispose();**

[C++] **public: virtual void Dispose();**

[JScript] **public function Dispose();**

MonthCalendar.Dispose Method (Boolean)

This member overrides **Control.Dispose**.

```
[Visual Basic]
Overrides Overloads Protected Sub Dispose( _
   ByVal disposing As Boolean _
)
[C#]
protected override void Dispose(
   bool disposing
);
[C++]
protected: void Dispose(
   bool disposing
);
[JScript]
protected override function Dispose(
   disposing : Boolean
);
```

Requirements

Platforms: Windows 98, Windows NT 4.0, Windows Millennium Edition, Windows 2000, Windows XP Home Edition, Windows XP Professional, Windows Server 2003 family

MonthCalendar.GetDisplayRange Method

Retrieves date information that represents the low and high limits of the displayed dates of the control.

```
[Visual Basic]
Public Function GetDisplayRange( _
   ByVal visible As Boolean _
) As SelectionRange
[C#]
public SelectionRange GetDisplayRange(
   bool visible
);
[C++]
public: SelectionRange* GetDisplayRange(
   bool visible
);
[JScript]
public function GetDisplayRange(
   visible : Boolean
) : SelectionRange;
```

Parameters

visible

true to retrieve only the dates that are fully contained in displayed months; otherwise, **false**.

Return Value

The begin and end dates of the displayed calendar.

Remarks

The **GetDisplayRange** method returns a **SelectionRange** that contains the begin and end dates displayed in the current view of the control. You can modify the returned range based on the value you specify for the *visible* parameter. By specifying **false**, you can retrieve all dates displayed on the control; specifying **true** retrieves only those dates that are part of fully displayed months.

Requirements

Platforms: Windows 98, Windows NT 4.0, Windows Millennium Edition, Windows 2000, Windows XP Home Edition, Windows XP Professional, Windows Server 2003 family

MonthCalendar.HitTest Method

Determines which element of the calendar is at a specified location.

Overload List

Returns an object with information on which portion of a month calendar control is at a location specified by **Point**.

[Visual Basic] **Overloads Public Function HitTest(Point) As HitTestInfo**

[C#] **public HitTestInfo HitTest(Point);**

[C++] **public: HitTestInfo* HitTest(Point);**

[JScript] **public function HitTest(Point) : HitTestInfo;**

Returns **MonthCalendar.HitTestInfo** with information on which portion of a month calendar control is at a specified x and y location.

[Visual Basic] **Overloads Public Function HitTest(Integer, Integer) As HitTestInfo**

[C#] **public HitTestInfo HitTest(int, int);**

[C++] **public: HitTestInfo* HitTest(int, int);**

[JScript] **public function HitTest(int, int) : HitTestInfo;**

MonthCalendar.HitTest Method (Point)

Returns an object with information on which portion of a month calendar control is at a location specified by **Point**.

```
[Visual Basic]
Overloads Public Function HitTest( _
   ByVal point As Point _
) As HitTestInfo
[C#]
public HitTestInfo HitTest(
   Point point
);
[C++]
public: HitTestInfo* HitTest(
   Point point
);
[JScript]
public function HitTest(
   point : Point
) : HitTestInfo;
```

Parameters

point
: A **Point** containing the **X** and **Y** coordinates of the point to be hit-tested.

Return Value

A **MonthCalendar.HitTestInfo** that contains information about the specified point on the **MonthCalendar**.

Requirements

Platforms: Windows 98, Windows NT 4.0, Windows Millennium Edition, Windows 2000, Windows XP Home Edition, Windows XP Professional, Windows Server 2003 family

MonthCalendar.HitTest Method (Int32, Int32)

Returns **MonthCalendar.HitTestInfo** with information on which portion of a month calendar control is at a specified x and y location.

```
[Visual Basic]
Overloads Public Function HitTest( _
   ByVal x As Integer, _
   ByVal y As Integer _
) As HitTestInfo
[C#]
public HitTestInfo HitTest(
   int x,
   int y
);
[C++]
public: HitTestInfo* HitTest(
   int x,
   int y
);
[JScript]
public function HitTest(
   x : int,
   y : int
) : HitTestInfo;
```

Parameters

x
: The **X** coordinate of the point to be hit-tested.

y
: The **Y** coordinate of the point to be hit-tested.

Return Value

A **MonthCalendar.HitTestInfo** that contains information about the specified point on the **MonthCalendar**.

Requirements

Platforms: Windows 98, Windows NT 4.0, Windows Millennium Edition, Windows 2000, Windows XP Home Edition, Windows XP Professional, Windows Server 2003 family

MonthCalendar.IsInputKey Method

This member overrides **Control.IsInputKey**.

```
[Visual Basic]
Overrides Protected Function IsInputKey( _
   ByVal keyData As Keys _
) As Boolean
[C#]
protected override bool IsInputKey(
   Keys keyData
);
[C++]
protected: bool IsInputKey(
   Keys keyData
);
[JScript]
protected override function IsInputKey(
   keyData : Keys
) : Boolean;
```

Requirements

Platforms: Windows 98, Windows NT 4.0, Windows Millennium Edition, Windows 2000, Windows XP Home Edition, Windows XP Professional, Windows Server 2003 family

MonthCalendar.OnBackColorChanged Method

This member overrides **Control.OnBackColorChanged**.

```
[Visual Basic]
Overrides Protected Sub OnBackColorChanged( _
   ByVal e As EventArgs _
)
[C#]
protected override void OnBackColorChanged(
   EventArgs e
);
[C++]
protected: void OnBackColorChanged(
   EventArgs* e
);
[JScript]
protected override function OnBackColorChanged(
   e : EventArgs
);
```

Requirements

Platforms: Windows 98, Windows NT 4.0, Windows Millennium Edition, Windows 2000, Windows XP Home Edition, Windows XP Professional, Windows Server 2003 family

MonthCalendar.OnDateChanged Method

Raises the **DateChanged** event.

```
[Visual Basic]
Protected Overridable Sub OnDateChanged( _
   ByVal drevent As DateRangeEventArgs _
)
[C#]
protected virtual void OnDateChanged(
   DateRangeEventArgs drevent
);
[C++]
protected: virtual void OnDateChanged(
   DateRangeEventArgs* drevent
);
[JScript]
protected function OnDateChanged(
   drevent : DateRangeEventArgs
);
```

Parameters

drevent
A **DateRangeEventArgs** that contains the event data.

Remarks

Raising an event invokes the event handler through a delegate.

The **OnDateChanged** method allows derived classes to handle the event without attaching a delegate. This is the preferred technique for handling the event in a derived class.

Notes to Inheritors: When overriding **OnDateChanged** in a derived class, be sure to call the base class's **OnDateChanged** method so that registered delegates receive the event.

Requirements

Platforms: Windows 98, Windows NT 4.0, Windows Millennium Edition, Windows 2000, Windows XP Home Edition, Windows XP Professional, Windows Server 2003 family

MonthCalendar.OnDateSelected Method

Raises the **DateSelected** event.

```
[Visual Basic]
Protected Overridable Sub OnDateSelected( _
   ByVal drevent As DateRangeEventArgs _
)
[C#]
protected virtual void OnDateSelected(
   DateRangeEventArgs drevent
);
[C++]
protected: virtual void OnDateSelected(
   DateRangeEventArgs* drevent
);
[JScript]
protected function OnDateSelected(
   drevent : DateRangeEventArgs
);
```

Parameters

drevent
A **DateRangeEventArgs** that contains the event data.

Remarks

Raising an event invokes the event handler through a delegate.

The **OnDateSelected** method also allows derived classes to handle the event without attaching a delegate. This is the preferred technique for handling the event in a derived class.

Notes to Inheritors: When overriding **OnDateSelected** in a derived class, be sure to call the base class's **OnDateSelected** method so that registered delegates receive the event.

Requirements

Platforms: Windows 98, Windows NT 4.0, Windows Millennium Edition, Windows 2000, Windows XP Home Edition, Windows XP Professional, Windows Server 2003 family

MonthCalendar.OnFontChanged Method

Raises the **FontChanged** event.

```
[Visual Basic]
Overrides Protected Sub OnFontChanged( _
   ByVal e As EventArgs _
)
[C#]
protected override void OnFontChanged(
   EventArgs e
);
[C++]
protected: void OnFontChanged(
   EventArgs* e
);
[JScript]
protected override function OnFontChanged(
   e : EventArgs
);
```

Parameters

e
An **EventArgs** that contains the event data.

Remarks

The **OnFontChanged** method resizes the control based on the new font size. This can cause the calendar to overlap other controls on the form if the potential sizing issues have not been taken into account.

Raising an event invokes the event handler through a delegate.

The **OnFontChanged** method also allows derived classes to handle the event without attaching a delegate. This is the preferred technique for handling the event in a derived class.

Notes to Inheritors: When overriding **OnFontChanged** in a derived class, be sure to call the base class's **OnFontChanged** method so that registered delegates receive the event.

Requirements

Platforms: Windows 98, Windows NT 4.0, Windows Millennium Edition, Windows 2000, Windows XP Home Edition, Windows XP Professional, Windows Server 2003 family

MonthCalendar.OnForeColorChanged Method

This member overrides **Control.OnForeColorChanged**.

```
[Visual Basic]
Overrides Protected Sub OnForeColorChanged( _
   ByVal e As EventArgs _
)
[C#]
protected override void OnForeColorChanged(
   EventArgs e
);
[C++]
protected: void OnForeColorChanged(
   EventArgs* e
);
[JScript]
protected override function OnForeColorChanged(
   e : EventArgs
);
```

Requirements

Platforms: Windows 98, Windows NT 4.0, Windows Millennium Edition, Windows 2000, Windows XP Home Edition, Windows XP Professional, Windows Server 2003 family

MonthCalendar.OnHandleCreated Method

This member overrides **Control.OnHandleCreated**.

```
[Visual Basic]
Overrides Protected Sub OnHandleCreated( _
   ByVal e As EventArgs _
)
[C#]
protected override void OnHandleCreated(
   EventArgs e
);
[C++]
protected: void OnHandleCreated(
   EventArgs* e
);
[JScript]
protected override function OnHandleCreated(
   e : EventArgs
);
```

Requirements

Platforms: Windows 98, Windows NT 4.0, Windows Millennium Edition, Windows 2000, Windows XP Home Edition, Windows XP Professional, Windows Server 2003 family

MonthCalendar.RemoveAllAnnuallyBoldedDates Method

Removes all the annually bolded dates.

```
[Visual Basic]
Public Sub RemoveAllAnnuallyBoldedDates()
[C#]
public void RemoveAllAnnuallyBoldedDates();
[C++]
public: void RemoveAllAnnuallyBoldedDates();
[JScript]
public function RemoveAllAnnuallyBoldedDates();
```

Remarks

This method clears all dates from the **AnnuallyBoldedDates** array. To remove a single date from the bolded dates, use the **RemoveAnnuallyBoldedDate** method.

You must call **UpdateBoldedDates** to ensure that the display is updated to reflect the removal.

Requirements

Platforms: Windows 98, Windows NT 4.0, Windows Millennium Edition, Windows 2000, Windows XP Home Edition, Windows XP Professional, Windows Server 2003 family

MonthCalendar.RemoveAllBoldedDates Method

Removes all the nonrecurring bolded dates.

```
[Visual Basic]
Public Sub RemoveAllBoldedDates()
[C#]
public void RemoveAllBoldedDates();
[C++]
public: void RemoveAllBoldedDates();
[JScript]
public function RemoveAllBoldedDates();
```

Remarks

This method clears the **BoldedDates** array. To remove a single date from the bolded dates, use the **RemoveBoldedDate** method.

You must call **UpdateBoldedDates** to ensure that the display is updated to reflect the removal.

Example

```
[Visual Basic]
Private Sub button3_Click(ByVal sender As Object, ByVal e ↵
 As System.EventArgs)
   monthCalendar1.RemoveAllBoldedDates()
   monthCalendar1.UpdateBoldedDates()
   listBox1.Items.Clear()
   button3.Enabled = False
End Sub 'button3_Click

[C#]
private void button3_Click(object sender, System.EventArgs e)
{
    monthCalendar1.RemoveAllBoldedDates();
    monthCalendar1.UpdateBoldedDates();
    listBox1.Items.Clear();
    button3.Enabled = false ;
}
```

Requirements

Platforms: Windows 98, Windows NT 4.0, Windows Millennium Edition, Windows 2000, Windows XP Home Edition, Windows XP Professional, Windows Server 2003 family

MonthCalendar.RemoveAllMonthlyBoldedDates Method

Removes all the monthly bolded dates.

```
[Visual Basic]
Public Sub RemoveAllMonthlyBoldedDates()
[C#]
public void RemoveAllMonthlyBoldedDates();
[C++]
public: void RemoveAllMonthlyBoldedDates();
[JScript]
public function RemoveAllMonthlyBoldedDates();
```

Remarks

This method clears the **MonthlyBoldedDates** array. To remove a single date from the bolded dates, use the **RemoveMonthlyBoldedDate** method.

You must call **UpdateBoldedDates** to ensure that the display is updated to reflect the removal.

Requirements

Platforms: Windows 98, Windows NT 4.0, Windows Millennium Edition, Windows 2000, Windows XP Home Edition, Windows XP Professional, Windows Server 2003 family

MonthCalendar.RemoveAnnuallyBoldedDate Method

Removes the specified date from the list of annually bolded dates.

```
[Visual Basic]
Public Sub RemoveAnnuallyBoldedDate( _
   ByVal date As DateTime _
)
[C#]
public void RemoveAnnuallyBoldedDate(
   DateTime date
);
[C++]
public: void RemoveAnnuallyBoldedDate(
   DateTime date
);
[JScript]
public function RemoveAnnuallyBoldedDate(
   date : DateTime
);
```

Parameters

date

The date to remove from the date list.

Remarks

If the specified date occurs more than once in the date list, then only the first date is removed. When comparing dates, only the day and month are used. You must call **UpdateBoldedDates** to ensure that the display is updated to reflect the removal.

Requirements

Platforms: Windows 98, Windows NT 4.0, Windows Millennium Edition, Windows 2000, Windows XP Home Edition, Windows XP Professional, Windows Server 2003 family

MonthCalendar.RemoveBoldedDate Method

Removes the specified date from the list of nonrecurring bolded dates.

```
[Visual Basic]
Public Sub RemoveBoldedDate( _
   ByVal date As DateTime _
)
[C#]
public void RemoveBoldedDate(
   DateTime date
);
[C++]
public: void RemoveBoldedDate(
   DateTime date
);
[JScript]
public function RemoveBoldedDate(
   date : DateTime
);
```

Parameters

date

The date to remove from the date list.

Remarks

If the specified date occurs more than once in the date list, then only the first date is removed. You must call **UpdateBoldedDates** to ensure that the display is updated to reflect the removal.

Example

[Visual Basic, C#] The following example uses the **RemoveBoldedDate** method to remove a specified date from the list of bolded dates. This example assumes that a **MonthCalendar** control, named `monthCalendar1`, has been added to a **Form** and that this method is placed within the form and called from it.

```
[Visual Basic]
Private Sub button2_Click(ByVal sender As Object, ByVal ↵
 e As System.EventArgs)
   monthCalendar1.RemoveBoldedDate(DateTime.Parse ↵
 (listBox1.SelectedItem.ToString().Substring(0, ↵
listBox1.SelectedItem.ToString().IndexOf(" "))))
   monthCalendar1.UpdateBoldedDates()
   listBox1.Items.RemoveAt(listBox1.SelectedIndex)
   If listBox1.Items.Count = 0 Then
      button3.Enabled = False
   End If
End Sub 'button2_Click
```

```
[C#]
private void button2_Click(object sender, System.EventArgs e)
{
   monthCalendar1.RemoveBoldedDate(DateTime.Parse ↵
 (listBox1.SelectedItem.ToString().Substring ↵
 (0,listBox1.SelectedItem.ToString().IndexOf(" "))));
   monthCalendar1.UpdateBoldedDates();
   listBox1.Items.RemoveAt(listBox1.SelectedIndex);
   if(listBox1.Items.Count == 0)
      button3.Enabled = false;
}
```

Requirements

Platforms: Windows 98, Windows NT 4.0, Windows Millennium Edition, Windows 2000, Windows XP Home Edition, Windows XP Professional, Windows Server 2003 family

MonthCalendar.RemoveMonthlyBoldedDate Method

Removes the specified date from the list of monthly bolded dates.

```
[Visual Basic]
Public Sub RemoveMonthlyBoldedDate( _
   ByVal date As DateTime _
)
[C#]
public void RemoveMonthlyBoldedDate(
   DateTime date
);
[C++]
public: void RemoveMonthlyBoldedDate(
   DateTime date
);
[JScript]
public function RemoveMonthlyBoldedDate(
   date : DateTime
);
```

Parameters

date

The date to remove from the date list.

Remarks

If the specified date occurs more than once in the date list, then only the first date is removed. When comparing dates, only the day and month are used. You must call **UpdateBoldedDates** to ensure that the display is updated to reflect the removal.

Requirements

Platforms: Windows 98, Windows NT 4.0, Windows Millennium Edition, Windows 2000, Windows XP Home Edition, Windows XP Professional, Windows Server 2003 family

MonthCalendar.SetBoundsCore Method

This member overrides **Control.SetBoundsCore**.

```
[Visual Basic]
Overrides Protected Sub SetBoundsCore( _
   ByVal x As Integer, _
   ByVal y As Integer, _
   ByVal width As Integer, _
   ByVal height As Integer, _
   ByVal specified As BoundsSpecified _
)
[C#]
protected override void SetBoundsCore(
   int x,
   int y,
   int width,
   int height,
   BoundsSpecified specified
);
[C++]
protected: void SetBoundsCore(
   int x,
   int y,
   int width,
   int height,
   BoundsSpecified specified
);
[JScript]
protected override function SetBoundsCore(
   x : int,
   y : int,
   width : int,
   height : int,
   specified : BoundsSpecified
);
```

Requirements

Platforms: Windows 98, Windows NT 4.0, Windows Millennium Edition, Windows 2000, Windows XP Home Edition, Windows XP Professional, Windows Server 2003 family

MonthCalendar.SetCalendarDimensions Method

Sets the number of columns and rows of months to display.

```
[Visual Basic]
Public Sub SetCalendarDimensions( _
   ByVal x As Integer, _
   ByVal y As Integer _
)
[C#]
public void SetCalendarDimensions(
   int x,
   int y
);
[C++]
public: void SetCalendarDimensions(
   int x,
   int y
);
[JScript]
public function SetCalendarDimensions(
   x : int,
   y : int
);
```

Parameters

x

The number of columns.

y

The number of rows.

Exceptions

Exception Type	Condition
ArgumentException	The *x* parameter or the *y* parameter is less than zero.

Remarks

The maximum number of months that you can display is 12, restricted to one calendar year. The product of the *x* and *y* parameters should be 12 or less. For values of *x* and *y* that have a product of more than 12, the greater of the *x* and *y* values will be iteratively reduced until the product is 12 or less.

Requirements

Platforms: Windows 98, Windows NT 4.0, Windows Millennium Edition, Windows 2000, Windows XP Home Edition, Windows XP Professional, Windows Server 2003 family

MonthCalendar.SetDate Method

Sets a date as the current selected date.

```
[Visual Basic]
Public Sub SetDate( _
   ByVal date As DateTime _
)
[C#]
public void SetDate(
   DateTime date
);
[C++]
public: void SetDate(
   DateTime date
);
[JScript]
public function SetDate(
   date : DateTime
);
```

Parameters

date

The date to be selected.

Exceptions

Exception Type	Condition
ArgumentException	The value is less than the minimum allowable date. -or- The value is greater than the maximum allowable date.

Remarks

This method sets the **SelectionStart** and the **SelectionEnd** properties to the specified date. This method is the functional equivalent of setting the selection range to a single day through the **SetSelectionRange** method or the **SelectionRange** property.

Requirements

Platforms: Windows 98, Windows NT 4.0, Windows Millennium Edition, Windows 2000, Windows XP Home Edition, Windows XP Professional, Windows Server 2003 family

MonthCalendar.SetSelectionRange Method

Sets the selected dates in a month calendar control to the specified date range.

```
[Visual Basic]
Public Sub SetSelectionRange( _
   ByVal date1 As DateTime, _
   ByVal date2 As DateTime _
)
[C#]
public void SetSelectionRange(
   DateTime date1,
   DateTime date2
);
[C++]
public: void SetSelectionRange(
   DateTime date1,
   DateTime date2
);
[JScript]
public function SetSelectionRange(
   date1 : DateTime,
   date2 : DateTime
);
```

Parameters

date1

The beginning date of the selection range.

date2

The end date of the selection range.

Exceptions

Exception Type	Condition
ArgumentException	The *date1* parameter value is less than the minimum date allowable for a month calendar control. -or- The *date1* value is greater than the maximum allowable date for a month calendar control. -or- The *date2* parameter value is less than the minimum date allowable for a month calendar control. -or- The *date2* value is greater than the maximum allowable date for a month calendar control.

Remarks

Using this method is functionally equivalent to setting the **SelectionRange** property. You can set the start and end dates separately by setting either **SelectionStart** or **SelectionEnd**.

If you set the *date1* parameter greater than the *date2* parameter, the dates are exchanged; *date2* becomes the start date, and *date1* becomes the end date.

Note Scrolling the calendar display with the navigation buttons when a range is selected can cause unexpected results. For example, the date range is not preserved. If you have a single month displayed with a range of 04/01/2001 to 04/10/2001, scrolling the calendar back changes the selected range as follows: 03/01/2001 to 03/10/2001. If you have multiple months displayed, such as March and April with a selected range of 04/01/2001 to 04/10/2001, scrolling the calendar back changes the selected range as follows: 01/01/2001 to 01/10/2001.

Requirements

Platforms: Windows 98, Windows NT 4.0, Windows Millennium Edition, Windows 2000, Windows XP Home Edition, Windows XP Professional, Windows Server 2003 family

MonthCalendar.ToString Method

This member overrides **Object.ToString**.

```
[Visual Basic]
Overrides Public Function ToString() As String
[C#]
public override string ToString();
[C++]
public: String* ToString();
[JScript]
public override function ToString() : String;
```

Requirements

Platforms: Windows 98, Windows NT 4.0, Windows Millennium Edition, Windows 2000, Windows XP Home Edition, Windows XP Professional, Windows Server 2003 family

MonthCalendar.UpdateBoldedDates Method

Repaints the bolded dates to reflect the dates set in the lists of bolded dates.

```
[Visual Basic]
Public Sub UpdateBoldedDates()
[C#]
public void UpdateBoldedDates();
[C++]
public: void UpdateBoldedDates();
[JScript]
public function UpdateBoldedDates();
```

Remarks

Use the **UpdateBoldedDates** method to reflect changes made to **AnnuallyBoldedDates**, **MonthlyBoldedDates**, or **BoldedDates**, either directly by modifying elements of the array or by using the add or remove methods provided to modify the date lists.

Requirements

Platforms: Windows 98, Windows NT 4.0, Windows Millennium Edition, Windows 2000, Windows XP Home Edition, Windows XP Professional, Windows Server 2003 family

MonthCalendar.WndProc Method

This member overrides **Control.WndProc**.

```
[Visual Basic]
Overrides Protected Sub WndProc( _
   ByRef m As Message _
)
[C#]
protected override void WndProc(
   ref Message m
);
[C++]
protected: void WndProc(
   Message* m
);
[JScript]
protected override function WndProc(
   m : Message
);
```

Requirements

Platforms: Windows 98, Windows NT 4.0, Windows Millennium Edition, Windows 2000, Windows XP Home Edition, Windows XP Professional, Windows Server 2003 family

MonthCalendar.BackgroundImageChanged Event

This member supports the .NET Framework infrastructure and is not intended to be used directly from your code.

```
[Visual Basic]
Public Shadows Event BackgroundImageChanged As EventHandler
[C#]
public new event EventHandler BackgroundImageChanged;
[C++]
public: __event EventHandler* BackgroundImageChanged;
```

[JScript] In JScript, you can handle the events defined by a class, but you cannot define your own.

MonthCalendar.Click Event

This member supports the .NET Framework infrastructure and is not intended to be used directly from your code.

```
[Visual Basic]
Public Shadows Event Click As EventHandler
[C#]
public new event EventHandler Click;
[C++]
public: __event EventHandler* Click;
```

[JScript] In JScript, you can handle the events defined by a class, but you cannot define your own.

MonthCalendar.DateChanged Event

Occurs when the date selected in the **MonthCalendar** changes.

```
[Visual Basic]
Public Event DateChanged As DateRangeEventHandler
[C#]
public event DateRangeEventHandler DateChanged;
```

```
[C++]
public: __event DateRangeEventHandler* DateChanged;
```

[JScript] In JScript, you can handle the events defined by a class, but you cannot define your own.

Event Data

The event handler receives an argument of type **DateRangeEventArgs** containing data related to this event. The following **DateRangeEventArgs** properties provide information specific to this event.

Property	Description
End	Gets the last date/time value in the range that the user has selected.
Start	Gets the first date/time value in the range that the user has selected.

Remarks

The **DateChanged** event occurs during any date selection, whether by mouse, keyboard, or code. The **DateSelected** event is similar, but it occurs only at the end of a date selection made using the mouse.

When you create a **DateChanged** delegate, you identify the method that will handle the event. To associate the event with your event handler, add an instance of the delegate to the event. The event handler is called whenever the event occurs, unless you remove the delegate.

Example

See related example in the **System.Windows.Forms.Month** class topic.

Requirements

Platforms: Windows 98, Windows NT 4.0,
Windows Millennium Edition, Windows 2000,
Windows XP Home Edition, Windows XP Professional,
Windows Server 2003 family

MonthCalendar.DateSelected Event

Occurs when the user makes an explicit date selection using the mouse.

```
[Visual Basic]
Public Event DateSelected As DateRangeEventHandler
[C#]
public event DateRangeEventHandler DateSelected;
[C++]
public: __event DateRangeEventHandler* DateSelected;
```

[JScript] In JScript, you can handle the events defined by a class, but you cannot define your own.

Event Data

The event handler receives an argument of type **DateRangeEventArgs** containing data related to this event. The following **DateRangeEventArgs** properties provide information specific to this event.

Property	Description
End	Gets the last date/time value in the range that the user has selected.
Start	Gets the first date/time value in the range that the user has selected.

Remarks

This event is similar to **DateChanged**, but it occurs at the end of a date selection made using the mouse. The **DateChanged** event occurs during any date selection, whether by mouse, keyboard, or code.

When you create a **DateSelected** delegate, you identify the method that will handle the event. To associate the event with your event handler, add an instance of the delegate to the event. The event handler is called whenever the event occurs, unless you remove the delegate.

Example

For more information about event-handler delegates, see **Events and Delegates**.

Requirements

Platforms: Windows 98, Windows NT 4.0,
Windows Millennium Edition, Windows 2000,
Windows XP Home Edition, Windows XP Professional,
Windows Server 2003 family

MonthCalendar.DoubleClick Event

This member supports the .NET Framework infrastructure and is not intended to be used directly from your code.

```
[Visual Basic]
Public Shadows Event DoubleClick As EventHandler
[C#]
public new event EventHandler DoubleClick;
[C++]
public: __event EventHandler* DoubleClick;
```

[JScript] In JScript, you can handle the events defined by a class, but you cannot define your own.

MonthCalendar.ImeModeChanged Event

This member supports the .NET Framework infrastructure and is not intended to be used directly from your code.

```
[Visual Basic]
Public Shadows Event ImeModeChanged As EventHandler
[C#]
public new event EventHandler ImeModeChanged;
[C++]
public: __event EventHandler* ImeModeChanged;
```

[JScript] In JScript, you can handle the events defined by a class, but you cannot define your own.

MonthCalendar.Paint Event

This member supports the .NET Framework infrastructure and is not intended to be used directly from your code.

```
[Visual Basic]
Public Shadows Event Paint As PaintEventHandler
[C#]
public new event PaintEventHandler Paint;
[C++]
public: __event PaintEventHandler* Paint;
```

[JScript] In JScript, you can handle the events defined by a class, but you cannot define your own.

MonthCalendar.TextChanged Event

This member supports the .NET Framework infrastructure and is not intended to be used directly from your code.

[Visual Basic]
```
Public Shadows Event TextChanged As EventHandler
```
[C#]
```
public new event EventHandler TextChanged;
```
[C++]
```
public: __event EventHandler* TextChanged;
```

[JScript] In JScript, you can handle the events defined by a class, but you cannot define your own.

MonthCalendar.HitArea Enumeration

Defines constants that represent areas in a **MonthCalendar** control.

[Visual Basic]
```
<Serializable>
Public Enum MonthCalendar.HitArea
```
[C#]
```
[Serializable]
public enum MonthCalendar.HitArea
```
[C++]
```
[Serializable]
__value public enum MonthCalendar.HitArea
```
[JScript]
```
public
   Serializable
enum MonthCalendar.HitArea
```

Remarks

This enumeration includes specific areas of the **MonthCalendar** control as its enumerated values. The **HitArea** member of **MonthCalendar.HitTestInfo** is one of these enumerated values, and indicates which portion of a month calendar is under a specified point.

Members

Member name	Description
CalendarBackground	The specified point is part of the calendar's background.
Date	The specified point is on a date within the calendar. The **Time** property of **MonthCalendar.HitTestInfo** is set to the date at the specified point.
DayOfWeek	The specified point is over a day abbreviation ("Fri", for example). The **Time** property of **MonthCalendar.HitTestInfo** is set to the corresponding date on the top row.
NextMonthButton	The specified point is over the button at the upper-right corner of the control. If the user clicks here, the month calendar scrolls its display to the next month or set of months.
NextMonthDate	The specified point is over a date from the next month (partially displayed at the end of the currently displayed month). If the user clicks here, the month calendar scrolls its display to the next month or set of months.
Nowhere	The specified point is either not on the month calendar control, or it is in an inactive portion of the control.
PrevMonthButton	The specified point is over the button at the upper-left corner of the control. If the user clicks here, the month calendar scrolls its display to the previous month or set of months.
PrevMonthDate	The specified point is over a date from the previous month (partially displayed at the end of the currently displayed month). If the user clicks here, the month calendar scrolls its display to the previous month or set of months.
TitleBackground	The specified point is over the background of a month's title.
TitleMonth	The specified point is in a month's title bar, over a month name.
TitleYear	The specified point is in a month's title bar, over the year value.
TodayLink	The specified point is on the today link at the bottom of the month calendar control.
WeekNumbers	The specified point is over a week number. This occurs only if the **ShowWeekNumbers** property of **MonthCalendar** is enabled. The **Time** property of **MonthCalendar.HitTestInfo** is set to the corresponding date in the leftmost column.

Requirements

Namespace: System.Windows.Forms

Platforms: Windows 98, Windows NT 4.0, Windows Millennium Edition, Windows 2000, Windows XP Home Edition, Windows XP Professional, Windows Server 2003 family

Assembly: System.Windows.Forms (in System.Windows.Forms.dll)

MonthCalendar.HitTestInfo Class

Contains information about an area of a **MonthCalendar** control. This class cannot be inherited.

System.Object
  System.Windows.Forms.MonthCalendar.HitTestInfo

[Visual Basic]
```
NotInheritable Public Class MonthCalendar.HitTestInfo
```
[C#]
```
public sealed class MonthCalendar.HitTestInfo
```
[C++]
```
public __gc __sealed class MonthCalendar.HitTestInfo
```
[JScript]
```
public class MonthCalendar.HitTestInfo
```

Thread Safety

Any public static (**Shared** in Visual Basic) members of this type are safe for multithreaded operations. Any instance members are not guaranteed to be thread safe.

Remarks

MonthCalendar.HitTestInfo objects are returned by **MonthCalendar** controls in response to the **HitTest** method.

> **CAUTION** **MonthCalendar.HitTestInfo** is for informational purposes only; you should not construct these objects and cannot modify any of the members.

Requirements

Namespace: System.Windows.Forms

Platforms: Windows 98, Windows NT 4.0, Windows Millennium Edition, Windows 2000, Windows XP Home Edition, Windows XP Professional, Windows Server 2003 family

Assembly: System.Windows.Forms (in System.Windows.Forms.dll)

MonthCalendar.HitTestInfo.HitArea Property

Gets the **MonthCalendar.HitArea** that represents the area of the calendar evaluated by the hit-test operation.

[Visual Basic]
```
Public ReadOnly Property HitArea As MonthCalendar.HitArea
```
[C#]
```
public MonthCalendar.HitArea HitArea {get;}
```
[C++]
```
public: __property MonthCalendar.HitArea get_HitArea();
```
[JScript]
```
public function get HitArea() : MonthCalendar.HitArea;
```

Property Value

One of the **MonthCalendar.HitArea** values. The default is **HitArea.Nowhere**.

Requirements

Platforms: Windows 98, Windows NT 4.0, Windows Millennium Edition, Windows 2000, Windows XP Home Edition, Windows XP Professional, Windows Server 2003 family

MonthCalendar.HitTestInfo.Point Property

Gets the point that was hit-tested.

[Visual Basic]
```
Public ReadOnly Property Point As Point
```
[C#]
```
public Point Point {get;}
```
[C++]
```
public: __property Point get_Point();
```
[JScript]
```
public function get Point() : Point;
```

Property Value

A **Point** containing the **X** and **Y** values tested.

Requirements

Platforms: Windows 98, Windows NT 4.0, Windows Millennium Edition, Windows 2000, Windows XP Home Edition, Windows XP Professional, Windows Server 2003 family

MonthCalendar.HitTestInfo.Time Property

Gets the time information specific to the location that was hit-tested.

[Visual Basic]
```
Public ReadOnly Property Time As DateTime
```
[C#]
```
public DateTime Time {get;}
```
[C++]
```
public: __property DateTime get_Time();
```
[JScript]
```
public function get Time() : DateTime;
```

Property Value

A **DateTime**.

Remarks

The **Time** property contains a valid date when the **MonthCalendar.HitArea** property is set to **Date** or **WeekNumbers**.

Requirements

Platforms: Windows 98, Windows NT 4.0, Windows Millennium Edition, Windows 2000, Windows XP Home Edition, Windows XP Professional, Windows Server 2003 family

MouseButtons Enumeration

Specifies constants that define which mouse button was pressed.

This enumeration has a **FlagsAttribute** attribute that allows a bitwise combination of its member values.

[Visual Basic]
```
<Flags>
<Serializable>
<ComVisible(True)>
Public Enum MouseButtons
```
[C#]
```
[Flags]
[Serializable]
[ComVisible(true)]
public enum MouseButtons
```
[C++]
```
[Flags]
[Serializable]
[ComVisible(true)]
__value public enum MouseButtons
```
[JScript]
```
public
   Flags
   Serializable
   ComVisible(true)
enum MouseButtons
```

Remarks

This enumeration is used by many classes, including **AxHost**, **Control**, **DataGrid**, **Form**, **RadioButton**, **Splitter**, **StatusBar**, and **UpDownBase**.

Members

Member name	Description	Value
Left Supported by the .NET Compact Framework.	The left mouse button was pressed.	1048576
Middle	The middle mouse button was pressed.	4194304
None Supported by the .NET Compact Framework.	No mouse button was pressed.	0
Right Supported by the .NET Compact Framework.	The right mouse button was pressed.	2097152
XButton1	The first XButton was pressed. With Windows 2000, Microsoft is introducing support for the Microsoft IntelliMouse Explorer, which is a mouse with five buttons. The two new mouse buttons (XBUTTON1 and XBUTTON2) provide backward/forward navigation.	8388608
XButton2	The second XButton was pressed. With Windows 2000, Microsoft is introducing support for the Microsoft IntelliMouse Explorer, which is a mouse with five buttons. The two new mouse buttons (XBUTTON1 and XBUTTON2) provide backward/forward navigation.	16777216

Example

[Visual Basic, C#, C++] The following example demonstrates how to use the **GetCharFromPosition** method to obtain a character from the contents of a **RichTextBox** given its control coordinates. The example code uses coordinates located in the **MouseEventArgs** object passed as a parameter to the event handler to determine the location in the control to obtain the character. The character is then displayed in a **MessageBox** if it is not a space character. This example assumes that a **RichTextBox** control named `richTextBox1` has been created and that the example code is connected to the **MouseDown** event of the **RichTextBox**.

[Visual Basic]
```
Private Sub richTextBox1_MouseDown(ByVal sender As Object, ByVal      ↵
 e As System.Windows.Forms.MouseEventArgs) Handles
richTextBox1.MouseDown
    ' Determine which mouse button is clicked.
    If e.Button = MouseButtons.Left Then
        ' Obtain the character at which the mouse cursor was clicked.
        Dim tempChar As Char = richTextBox1.GetCharFromPosition        ↵
 (New Point(e.X, e.Y))
        ' Determine whether the character is an empty space.
        If tempChar <> " " Then
            ' Display the character in a message box.
            MessageBox.Show(("The character at the specified          ↵
 position is " + tempChar + "."))
        End If
    End If
End Sub
```

[C#]
```
private void richTextBox1_MouseDown(object sender,                    ↵
System.Windows.Forms.MouseEventArgs e)
{
    // Determine which mouse button is clicked.
    if(e.Button == MouseButtons.Left)
    {
        // Obtain the character at which the mouse cursor             ↵
was clicked at.
        char tempChar = richTextBox1.GetCharFromPosition              ↵
 (new Point(e.X, e.Y));
        // Determine whether the character is an empty space.
        if (tempChar.ToString() != " ")
            // Display the character in a message box.
            MessageBox.Show("The character at the specified           ↵
position is " + tempChar + ".");

    }
}
```

[Visual Basic, C#, C++] The following example demonstrates using different mouse events to draw the path of the mouse on a **Panel**. A line segment is added to the **GraphicsPath** for each **MouseMove** and **MouseDown** events that occur. To update the graphics, the **Invalidate** method is called for the **Panel** on each **MouseDown** and **MouseUp** event. In addition, the graphic path is scrolled up or down when the **MouseWheel** event occurs. Additional mouse events, like **MouseHover**, are identified on screen as well. Also displayed on the screen is additional information about the mouse from the **SystemInformation** class.

[Visual Basic]

```
Imports System
Imports System.Drawing
Imports System.Windows.Forms

Namespace MouseEvent
    ' Summary description for Form1.
    Public NotInheritable Class Form1
        Inherits System.Windows.Forms.Form

        Friend WithEvents panel1 As System.Windows.Forms.Panel
        Private label1 As System.Windows.Forms.Label
        Private label2 As System.Windows.Forms.Label
        Private label3 As System.Windows.Forms.Label
        Private label4 As System.Windows.Forms.Label
        Private label5 As System.Windows.Forms.Label
        Private label6 As System.Windows.Forms.Label
        Private label7 As System.Windows.Forms.Label
        Private label8 As System.Windows.Forms.Label
        Private label9 As System.Windows.Forms.Label
        Friend WithEvents clearButton As System.Windows.Forms.Button
        Private mousePath As System.Drawing.Drawing2D.GraphicsPath
        Private groupBox1 As System.Windows.Forms.GroupBox

        Private fontSize As Integer = 20

        <System.STAThread()> _
        Public Shared Sub Main()
            System.Windows.Forms.Application.Run(New Form1())
        End Sub 'Main

        Public Sub New()

            mousePath = New System.Drawing.Drawing2D.GraphicsPath()

            Me.panel1 = New System.Windows.Forms.Panel()
            Me.label1 = New System.Windows.Forms.Label()
            Me.clearButton = New System.Windows.Forms.Button()
            Me.label2 = New System.Windows.Forms.Label()
            Me.label3 = New System.Windows.Forms.Label()
            Me.label4 = New System.Windows.Forms.Label()
            Me.label5 = New System.Windows.Forms.Label()
            Me.label6 = New System.Windows.Forms.Label()
            Me.label7 = New System.Windows.Forms.Label()
            Me.label8 = New System.Windows.Forms.Label()
            Me.label9 = New System.Windows.Forms.Label()
            Me.groupBox1 = New System.Windows.Forms.GroupBox()

            ' Mouse Events Label
            Me.label1.Location = New System.Drawing.Point(24, 504)
            Me.label1.Size = New System.Drawing.Size(392, 23)
            ' DoubleClickSize Label
            Me.label2.AutoSize = True
            Me.label2.Location = New System.Drawing.Point(24, 48)
            Me.label2.Size = New System.Drawing.Size(35, 13)
            ' DoubleClickTime Label
            Me.label3.AutoSize = True
            Me.label3.Location = New System.Drawing.Point(24, 72)
            Me.label3.Size = New System.Drawing.Size(35, 13)
            ' MousePresent Label
            Me.label4.AutoSize = True
            Me.label4.Location = New System.Drawing.Point(24, 96)
            Me.label4.Size = New System.Drawing.Size(35, 13)
            ' MouseButtons Label
            Me.label5.AutoSize = True
            Me.label5.Location = New System.Drawing.Point(24, 120)
            Me.label5.Size = New System.Drawing.Size(35, 13)
            ' MouseButtonsSwapped Label
            Me.label6.AutoSize = True
            Me.label6.Location = New System.Drawing.Point(320, 48)
            Me.label6.Size = New System.Drawing.Size(35, 13)
            ' MouseWheelPresent Label
            Me.label7.AutoSize = True
            Me.label7.Location = New System.Drawing.Point(320, 72)
            Me.label7.Size = New System.Drawing.Size(35, 13)
            ' MouseWheelScrollLines Label
            Me.label8.AutoSize = True
            Me.label8.Location = New System.Drawing.Point(320, 96)
            Me.label8.Size = New System.Drawing.Size(35, 13)
            ' NativeMouseWheelSupport Label
            Me.label9.AutoSize = True
            Me.label9.Location = New System.Drawing.Point(320, 120)
            Me.label9.Size = New System.Drawing.Size(35, 13)

            ' Mouse Panel
            Me.panel1.Anchor =                                          ↵
System.Windows.Forms.AnchorStyles.Top Or _
                                System.Windows.Forms.AnchorStyles.Left
Or _
                                System.Windows.Forms.AnchorStyles.Right
            Me.panel1.BackColor =                                       ↵
System.Drawing.SystemColors.ControlDark
            Me.panel1.Location = New System.Drawing.Point(16, 160)
            Me.panel1.Size = New System.Drawing.Size(664, 320)

            ' Clear Button
            Me.clearButton.Anchor =                                     ↵
System.Windows.Forms.AnchorStyles.Top Or _
                                System.Windows.Forms.AnchorStyles.Right
            Me.clearButton.Location = New                               ↵
System.Drawing.Point(592, 504)
            Me.clearButton.TabIndex = 1
            Me.clearButton.Text = "Clear"

            ' GroupBox
            Me.groupBox1.Anchor =                                       ↵
System.Windows.Forms.AnchorStyles.Top Or _
                                                                        ↵
System.Windows.Forms.AnchorStyles.Left Or _
                                                                        ↵
System.Windows.Forms.AnchorStyles.Right
            Me.groupBox1.Location = New System.Drawing.Point(16, 24)
            Me.groupBox1.Size = New System.Drawing.Size(664, 128)
            Me.groupBox1.Text =                                         ↵
"System.Windows.Forms.SystemInformation"

            ' Set up how the form should be displayed and               ↵
 add the controls to the form.
            Me.ClientSize = New System.Drawing.Size(696, 534)
            Me.Controls.AddRange(New                                    ↵
System.Windows.Forms.Control() {Me.label9, _
                                Me.label8, Me.label7, Me.label6,        ↵
 Me.label5, Me.label4, _
                                Me.label3, Me.label2,                   ↵
Me.clearButton, Me.panel1, Me.label1, Me.groupBox1})

            Me.Text = "Mouse Event Example"

            ' Display information about the system mouse.
            label2.Text = "SystemInformation.DoubleClickSize:           ↵
 " + SystemInformation.DoubleClickSize.ToString()
            label3.Text = "SystemInformation.DoubleClickTime:           ↵
 " + SystemInformation.DoubleClickTime.ToString()
            label4.Text = "SystemInformation.MousePresent:              ↵
 " + SystemInformation.MousePresent.ToString()
            label5.Text = "SystemInformation.MouseButtons:              ↵
 " + SystemInformation.MouseButtons.ToString()
            label6.Text =                                               ↵
"SystemInformation.MouseButtonsSwapped: " +                             ↵
SystemInformation.MouseButtonsSwapped.ToString()
            label7.Text = "SystemInformation.MouseWheelPresent:         ↵
 " + SystemInformation.MouseWheelPresent.ToString()
            label8.Text =                                               ↵
"SystemInformation.MouseWheelScrollLines: " +                           ↵
SystemInformation.MouseWheelScrollLines.ToString()
            label9.Text =                                               ↵
"SystemInformation.NativeMouseWheelSupport: " +                         ↵
SystemInformation.NativeMouseWheelSupport.ToString()
        End Sub 'New

        Private Sub panel1_MouseDown(sender As Object, e As             ↵
System.Windows.Forms.MouseEventArgs) Handles panel1.MouseDown
            ' Update the mouse path with the mouse information
            Dim mouseDownLocation As New Point(e.X, e.Y)
```

```
            Dim eventString As String = Nothing
            Select Case e.Button
                Case MouseButtons.Left
                    eventString = "L"
                Case MouseButtons.Right
                    eventString = "R"
                Case MouseButtons.Middle
                    eventString = "M"
                Case MouseButtons.XButton1
                    eventString = "X1"
                Case MouseButtons.XButton2
                    eventString = "X2"
                Case MouseButtons.None:
                    eventString = Nothing
            End Select

            If Not (eventString Is Nothing) Then
              mousePath.AddString(eventString, FontFamily.GenericSerif, ↵
CInt(FontStyle.Bold), fontSize, ↵
mouseDownLocation, StringFormat.GenericDefault)
            Else
                mousePath.AddLine(mouseDownLocation, mouseDownLocation)
            End If

            panel1.Focus()
            panel1.Invalidate()
        End Sub

        Private Sub panel1_MouseEnter(sender As Object, e As ↵
System.EventArgs) Handles panel1.MouseEnter
            ' Update the mouse event label to indicate the ↵
MouseEnter event occurred.
            label1.Text = sender.GetType().ToString() + ": MouseEnter"
        End Sub

        Private Sub panel1_MouseHover(sender As Object, e As ↵
System.EventArgs) Handles panel1.MouseHover
            ' Update the mouse event label to indicate the ↵
MouseHover event occurred.
            label1.Text = sender.GetType().ToString() + ": MouseHover"
        End Sub

        Private Sub panel1_MouseLeave(sender As Object, e As ↵
System.EventArgs) Handles panel1.MouseLeave
            ' Update the mouse event label to indicate the ↵
 MouseLeave event occurred.
            label1.Text = sender.GetType().ToString() + ": MouseLeave"
        End Sub

        Private Sub panel1_MouseMove(sender As Object, e As ↵
System.Windows.Forms.MouseEventArgs) Handles panel1.MouseMove
            ' Update the mouse path that is drawn onto the Panel.
            Dim mouseX As Integer = e.X
            Dim mouseY As Integer = e.Y

            mousePath.AddLine(mouseX, mouseY, mouseX, mouseY)
        End Sub
        Private Sub panel1_MouseWheel(sender As Object, e As ↵
System.Windows.Forms.MouseEventArgs) Handles panel1.MouseWheel
            ' Update the drawing based upon the mouse wheel scrolling.
            Dim numberOfTextLinesToMove As Integer = e.Delta * ↵
SystemInformation.MouseWheelScrollLines / 120 ' WHEEL_DATA
            Dim numberOfPixelsToMove As Integer = ↵
numberOfTextLinesToMove * fontSize

            If numberOfPixelsToMove <> 0 Then
                Dim translateMatrix As New ↵
System.Drawing.Drawing2D.Matrix()
                translateMatrix.Translate(0, numberOfPixelsToMove)
                mousePath.Transform(translateMatrix)
            End If

            panel1.Invalidate()
        End Sub
        Private Sub panel1_MouseUp(sender As Object, e As ↵
System.Windows.Forms.MouseEventArgs) Handles panel1.MouseUp
            Dim mouseUpLocation = New System.Drawing.Point(e.X, e.Y)

            ' Show the number of clicks in the path graphic.
            Dim numberOfClicks As Integer = e.Clicks
            mousePath.AddString("     " + numberOfClicks.ToString(), _
                                FontFamily.GenericSerif, ↵
CInt(FontStyle.Bold), _
                                fontSize, mouseUpLocation, ↵
StringFormat.GenericDefault)

            panel1.Invalidate()
        End Sub

        Private Sub panel1_Paint(sender As Object, e As ↵
System.Windows.Forms.PaintEventArgs) Handles panel1.Paint
            ' Perform the painting of the Panel.
            e.Graphics.DrawPath(System.Drawing.Pens.DarkRed, mousePath)
        End Sub

        Private Sub clearButton_Click(sender As Object, e As ↵
System.EventArgs) Handles clearButton.Click
            ' Clear the Panel display.
            mousePath.Dispose()
            mousePath = New System.Drawing.Drawing2D.GraphicsPath()
            panel1.Invalidate()
        End Sub

    End Class 'Form1
End Namespace
```

[C#]

```
using System;
using System.Drawing;
using System.Windows.Forms;

namespace MouseEvent
{
    public class Form1 : System.Windows.Forms.Form
    {
        private System.Windows.Forms.Panel panel1;
        private System.Windows.Forms.Label label1;
        private System.Windows.Forms.Label label2;
        private System.Windows.Forms.Label label3;
        private System.Windows.Forms.Label label4;
        private System.Windows.Forms.Label label5;
        private System.Windows.Forms.Label label6;
        private System.Windows.Forms.Label label7;
        private System.Windows.Forms.Label label8;
        private System.Windows.Forms.Label label9;
        private System.Windows.Forms.Button clearButton;
        private System.Drawing.Drawing2D.GraphicsPath mousePath;
        private System.Windows.Forms.GroupBox groupBox1;

        private int fontSize = 20;

        [STAThread]
        static void Main()
        {
            Application.Run(new Form1());
        }

        public Form1()
        {
            mousePath = new System.Drawing.Drawing2D.GraphicsPath();

            this.panel1 = new System.Windows.Forms.Panel();
            this.label1 = new System.Windows.Forms.Label();
            this.clearButton = new System.Windows.Forms.Button();
            this.label2 = new System.Windows.Forms.Label();
            this.label3 = new System.Windows.Forms.Label();
            this.label4 = new System.Windows.Forms.Label();
            this.label5 = new System.Windows.Forms.Label();
            this.label6 = new System.Windows.Forms.Label();
            this.label7 = new System.Windows.Forms.Label();
            this.label8 = new System.Windows.Forms.Label();
            this.label9 = new System.Windows.Forms.Label();
            this.groupBox1 = new System.Windows.Forms.GroupBox();

            // Mouse Events Label
            this.label1.Location = new System.Drawing.Point(24, 504);
            this.label1.Size = new System.Drawing.Size(392, 23);
            // DoubleClickSize Label
            this.label2.AutoSize = true;
            this.label2.Location = new System.Drawing.Point(24, 48);
```

```
            this.label2.Size = new System.Drawing.Size(35, 13);
            // DoubleClickTime Label
            this.label3.AutoSize = true;
            this.label3.Location = new System.Drawing.Point(24, 72);
            this.label3.Size = new System.Drawing.Size(35, 13);
            // MousePresent Label
            this.label4.AutoSize = true;
            this.label4.Location = new System.Drawing.Point(24, 96);
            this.label4.Size = new System.Drawing.Size(35, 13);
            // MouseButtons Label
            this.label5.AutoSize = true;
            this.label5.Location = new System.Drawing.Point(24, 120);
            this.label5.Size = new System.Drawing.Size(35, 13);
            // MouseButtonsSwapped Label
            this.label6.AutoSize = true;
            this.label6.Location = new System.Drawing.Point(320, 48);
            this.label6.Size = new System.Drawing.Size(35, 13);
            // MouseWheelPresent Label
            this.label7.AutoSize = true;
            this.label7.Location = new System.Drawing.Point(320, 72);
            this.label7.Size = new System.Drawing.Size(35, 13);
            // MouseWheelScrollLines Label
            this.label8.AutoSize = true;
            this.label8.Location = new System.Drawing.Point(320, 96);
            this.label8.Size = new System.Drawing.Size(35, 13);
            // NativeMouseWheelSupport Label
            this.label9.AutoSize = true;
            this.label9.Location = new System.Drawing.Point(320, 120);
            this.label9.Size = new System.Drawing.Size(35, 13);

            // Mouse Panel
            this.panel1.Anchor =                                          ↵
 ((System.Windows.Forms.AnchorStyles.Top |                                 ↵
System.Windows.Forms.AnchorStyles.Left)
                | System.Windows.Forms.AnchorStyles.Right);
            this.panel1.BackColor =                                       ↵
System.Drawing.SystemColors.ControlDark;
            this.panel1.Location = new System.Drawing.Point(16, 160);
            this.panel1.Size = new System.Drawing.Size(664, 320);
            this.panel1.MouseUp += new                                    ↵
System.Windows.Forms.MouseEventHandler(this.panel1_MouseUp);
            this.panel1.Paint += new                                      ↵
System.Windows.Forms.PaintEventHandler(this.panel1_Paint);
            this.panel1.MouseEnter += new                                 ↵
System.EventHandler(this.panel1_MouseEnter);
            this.panel1.MouseHover += new                                 ↵
System.EventHandler(this.panel1_MouseHover);
            this.panel1.MouseMove += new                                  ↵
System.Windows.Forms.MouseEventHandler(this.panel1_MouseMove);
            this.panel1.MouseLeave += new                                 ↵
System.EventHandler(this.panel1_MouseLeave);
            this.panel1.MouseDown += new                                  ↵
System.Windows.Forms.MouseEventHandler(this.panel1_MouseDown);
            this.panel1.MouseWheel += new                                 ↵
System.Windows.Forms.MouseEventHandler(this.panel1_MouseWheel);

            // Clear Button
            this.clearButton.Anchor =                                     ↵
 (System.Windows.Forms.AnchorStyles.Top |                                  ↵
System.Windows.Forms.AnchorStyles.Right);
            this.clearButton.Location = new                               ↵
System.Drawing.Point(592, 504);
            this.clearButton.TabIndex = 1;
            this.clearButton.Text = "Clear";
            this.clearButton.Click += new                                 ↵
System.EventHandler(this.clearButton_Click);

            // GroupBox
            this.groupBox1.Anchor =                                       ↵
 ((System.Windows.Forms.AnchorStyles.Top |                                 ↵
System.Windows.Forms.AnchorStyles.Left)
                | System.Windows.Forms.AnchorStyles.Right);
            this.groupBox1.Location = new System.Drawing.Point(16, 24);
            this.groupBox1.Size = new System.Drawing.Size(664, 128);
            this.groupBox1.Text =                                         ↵
"System.Windows.Forms.SystemInformation";

            // Set up how the form should be displayed                    ↵
and add the controls to the form.
            this.ClientSize = new System.Drawing.Size(696, 534);
            this.Controls.AddRange(new System.Windows.Forms.Control[] {    ↵

this.label9,this.label8,this.label7,this.label6,                           ↵

this.label5,this.label4,this.label3,this.label2,                           ↵

this.clearButton,this.panel1,this.label1,this.groupBox1});
            this.Text = "Mouse Event Example";

            // Displays information about the system mouse.
            label2.Text = "SystemInformation.DoubleClickSize:             ↵
 " + SystemInformation.DoubleClickSize.ToString();
            label3.Text = "SystemInformation.DoubleClickTime:             ↵
 " + SystemInformation.DoubleClickTime.ToString();
            label4.Text = "SystemInformation.MousePresent:                ↵
" + SystemInformation.MousePresent.ToString();
            label5.Text = "SystemInformation.MouseButtons:                ↵
 " + SystemInformation.MouseButtons.ToString();
            label6.Text =                                                 ↵
"SystemInformation.MouseButtonsSwapped: " +                                ↵
SystemInformation.MouseButtonsSwapped.ToString();
            label7.Text =                                                 ↵
"SystemInformation.MouseWheelPresent: " +                                  ↵
SystemInformation.MouseWheelPresent.ToString();
            label8.Text =                                                 ↵
"SystemInformation.MouseWheelScrollLines: " +                              ↵
SystemInformation.MouseWheelScrollLines.ToString();
            label9.Text =                                                 ↵
"SystemInformation.NativeMouseWheelSupport: " +                            ↵
SystemInformation.NativeMouseWheelSupport.ToString();

        }

        private void panel1_MouseDown(object sender,                      ↵
 System.Windows.Forms.MouseEventArgs e)
        {
            // Update the mouse path with the mouse information
            Point mouseDownLocation = new Point(e.X, e.Y);

            string eventString = null;
            switch (e.Button) {
                case MouseButtons.Left:
                    eventString = "L";
                    break;
                case MouseButtons.Right:
                    eventString = "R";
                    break;
                case MouseButtons.Middle:
                    eventString = "M";
                    break;
                case MouseButtons.XButton1:
                    eventString = "X1";
                    break;
                case MouseButtons.XButton2:
                    eventString = "X2";
                    break;
                case MouseButtons.None:
                default:
                    break;
            }

            if (eventString != null)
            {
                mousePath.AddString(eventString,                          ↵
FontFamily.GenericSerif, (int)FontStyle.Bold, fontSize,                    ↵
mouseDownLocation, StringFormat.GenericDefault);
            }
            else
            {
                mousePath.AddLine(mouseDownLocation,mouseDownLocation);
            }
            panel1.Focus();
            panel1.Invalidate();
        }

        private void panel1_MouseEnter(object sender,                     ↵
System.EventArgs e)
        {
            // Update the mouse event label to indicate the              ↵
MouseEnter event occurred.
```

```
            label1.Text = sender.GetType().ToString() + ": MouseEnter";
        }

        private void panel1_MouseHover(object sender,                ↵
System.EventArgs e)
        {
            // Update the mouse event label to indicate the          ↵
MouseHover event occurred.
            label1.Text = sender.GetType().ToString() + ": MouseHover";
        }

        private void panel1_MouseLeave(object sender,                ↵
System.EventArgs e)
        {
            // Update the mouse event label to indicate the          ↵
MouseLeave event occurred.
            label1.Text = sender.GetType().ToString() + ": MouseLeave";
        }

        private void panel1_MouseMove(object sender,                 ↵
System.Windows.Forms.MouseEventArgs e)
        {
            // Update the mouse path that is drawn onto the Panel.
            int mouseX = e.X;
            int mouseY = e.Y;

            mousePath.AddLine(mouseX,mouseY,mouseX,mouseY);
        }

        private void panel1_MouseWheel(object sender,                ↵
System.Windows.Forms.MouseEventArgs e)
        {
            // Update the drawing based upon the mouse wheel scrolling.

            int numberOfTextLinesToMove = e.Delta *                  ↵
SystemInformation.MouseWheelScrollLines / 120;
            int numberOfPixelsToMove = numberOfTextLinesToMove *     ↵
fontSize;

            if (numberOfPixelsToMove != 0) {
                System.Drawing.Drawing2D.Matrix translateMatrix      ↵
 = new  System.Drawing.Drawing2D.Matrix();
                translateMatrix.Translate(0, numberOfPixelsToMove);
                mousePath.Transform(translateMatrix);
            }
            panel1.Invalidate();
        }
        private void panel1_MouseUp(object sender,                   ↵
System.Windows.Forms.MouseEventArgs e)
        {
            Point mouseUpLocation = new System.Drawing.Point(e.X, e.Y);

            // Show the number of clicks in the path graphic.
            int numberOfClicks = e.Clicks;
            mousePath.AddString("    " + numberOfClicks.ToString(),
                        FontFamily.GenericSerif, (int)FontStyle.Bold,
                        fontSize, mouseUpLocation,                   ↵
StringFormat.GenericDefault);

            panel1.Invalidate();
        }

        private void panel1_Paint(object sender,                     ↵
System.Windows.Forms.PaintEventArgs e)
        {
            // Perform the painting of the Panel.
            e.Graphics.DrawPath(System.Drawing.Pens.DarkRed,         ↵
mousePath);
        }

        private void clearButton_Click(object sender,                ↵
System.EventArgs e)
        {
            // Clear the Panel display.
            mousePath.Dispose();
            mousePath = new System.Drawing.Drawing2D.GraphicsPath();
            panel1.Invalidate();
        }
    }
}
```

[C++]

```
#using <mscorlib.dll>
#using <System.dll>
#using <System.Windows.Forms.dll>
#using <System.Drawing.dll>

using namespace System;
using namespace System::Drawing;
using namespace System::Windows::Forms;

namespace MouseEvent {
public __gc class Form1 : public System::Windows::Forms::Form {
private:
   System::Windows::Forms::Panel*  panel1;
   System::Windows::Forms::Label*  label1;
   System::Windows::Forms::Label*  label2;
   System::Windows::Forms::Label*  label3;
   System::Windows::Forms::Label*  label4;
   System::Windows::Forms::Label*  label5;
   System::Windows::Forms::Label*  label6;
   System::Windows::Forms::Label*  label7;
   System::Windows::Forms::Label*  label8;
   System::Windows::Forms::Label*  label9;
   System::Windows::Forms::Button*  clearButton;
   System::Drawing::Drawing2D::GraphicsPath*  mousePath;
   System::Windows::Forms::GroupBox*  groupBox1;

   int  fontSize;
public:
   Form1() {
      fontSize = 20;
      mousePath = new System::Drawing::Drawing2D::GraphicsPath();
      this->panel1 = new System::Windows::Forms::Panel();
      this->label1 = new System::Windows::Forms::Label();
      this->clearButton = new System::Windows::Forms::Button();
      this->label2 = new System::Windows::Forms::Label();
      this->label3 = new System::Windows::Forms::Label();
      this->label4 = new System::Windows::Forms::Label();
      this->label5 = new System::Windows::Forms::Label();
      this->label6 = new System::Windows::Forms::Label();
      this->label7 = new System::Windows::Forms::Label();
      this->label8 = new System::Windows::Forms::Label();
      this->label9 = new System::Windows::Forms::Label();
      this->groupBox1 = new System::Windows::Forms::GroupBox();

      // Mouse Events Label
      this->label1->Location = System::Drawing::Point(24, 504);
      this->label1->Size =  System::Drawing::Size(392, 23);
      // DoubleClickSize Label
      this->label2->AutoSize = true;
      this->label2->Location =  System::Drawing::Point(24, 48);
      this->label2->Size =  System::Drawing::Size(35, 13);
      // DoubleClickTime Label
      this->label3->AutoSize = true;
      this->label3->Location =  System::Drawing::Point(24, 72);
      this->label3->Size =  System::Drawing::Size(35, 13);
      // MousePresent Label
      this->label4->AutoSize = true;
      this->label4->Location =  System::Drawing::Point(24, 96);
      this->label4->Size =  System::Drawing::Size(35, 13);
      // MouseButtons Label
      this->label5->AutoSize = true;
      this->label5->Location =  System::Drawing::Point(24, 120);
      this->label5->Size =  System::Drawing::Size(35, 13);
      // MouseButtonsSwapped Label
      this->label6->AutoSize = true;
      this->label6->Location =  System::Drawing::Point(320, 48);
      this->label6->Size =  System::Drawing::Size(35, 13);
      // MouseWheelPresent Label
      this->label7->AutoSize = true;
      this->label7->Location =  System::Drawing::Point(320, 72);
      this->label7->Size =  System::Drawing::Size(35, 13);
      // MouseWheelScrollLines Label
      this->label8->AutoSize = true;
      this->label8->Location =  System::Drawing::Point(320, 96);
      this->label8->Size =  System::Drawing::Size(35, 13);
      // NativeMouseWheelSupport Label
      this->label9->AutoSize = true;
      this->label9->Location =  System::Drawing::Point(320, 120);
      this->label9->Size =  System::Drawing::Size(35, 13);
```

```
      // Mouse Panel
      this->panel1->Anchor =                                            ↵
static_cast<System::Windows::Forms::AnchorStyles>                       ↵
 (System::Windows::Forms::AnchorStyles::Top |                           ↵
System::Windows::Forms::AnchorStyles::Left
         | System::Windows::Forms::AnchorStyles::Right);
      this->panel1->BackColor =                                         ↵
System::Drawing::SystemColors::ControlDark;
      this->panel1->Location =  System::Drawing::Point(16, 160);
      this->panel1->Size =  System::Drawing::Size(664, 320);
      this->panel1->MouseUp += new                                      ↵
System::Windows::Forms::MouseEventHandler(this, panel1_MouseUp);
      this->panel1->Paint += new                                        ↵
System::Windows::Forms::PaintEventHandler(this, panel1_Paint);
      this->panel1->MouseEnter += new System::EventHandler              ↵
 (this, panel1_MouseEnter);
      this->panel1->MouseHover += new System::EventHandler              ↵
 (this, panel1_MouseHover);
      this->panel1->MouseMove += new                                    ↵
System::Windows::Forms::MouseEventHandler(this, panel1_MouseMove);
      this->panel1->MouseLeave += new System::EventHandler              ↵
 (this, panel1_MouseLeave);
      this->panel1->MouseDown += new                                    ↵
System::Windows::Forms::MouseEventHandler(this, panel1_MouseDown);
      this->panel1->MouseWheel += new                                   ↵
System::Windows::Forms::MouseEventHandler(this, panel1_MouseWheel);

      // Clear Button
      this->clearButton->Anchor =                                       ↵
static_cast<System::Windows::Forms::AnchorStyles>                       ↵
 (System::Windows::Forms::AnchorStyles::Top |                           ↵
System::Windows::Forms::AnchorStyles::Right);
      this->clearButton->Location =  System::Drawing::Point(592, 504);
      this->clearButton->TabIndex = 1;
      this->clearButton->Text = S"Clear";
      this->clearButton->Click += new System::EventHandler(this,        ↵
clearButton_Click);

      // GroupBox
      this->groupBox1->Anchor =                                         ↵
static_cast<System::Windows::Forms::AnchorStyles>                       ↵
 (System::Windows::Forms::AnchorStyles::Top |                           ↵
System::Windows::Forms::AnchorStyles::Left
         | System::Windows::Forms::AnchorStyles::Right);
      this->groupBox1->Location =  System::Drawing::Point(16, 24);
      this->groupBox1->Size =  System::Drawing::Size(664, 128);
      this->groupBox1->Text =                                           ↵
S"System::Windows::Forms::SystemInformation";

      // Set up how the form should be displayed and add the            ↵
controls to the form.
      this->ClientSize =  System::Drawing::Size(696, 534);

      System::Windows::Forms::Control* temp0 [] = {this->label9,        ↵
 this->label8, this->label7, this->label6,
         this->label5, this->label4, this->label3, this->label2,
         this->clearButton, this->panel1, this->label1, this-           ↵
>groupBox1};

      this->Controls->AddRange(temp0);
      this->Text = S"Mouse Event Example";

      // Displays information about the system mouse.
      label2->Text = S"SystemInformation::DoubleClickSize:              ↵
 {0}", SystemInformation::DoubleClickSize;
      label3->Text = S"SystemInformation::DoubleClickTime:              ↵
 {0}", SystemInformation::DoubleClickTime;
      label4->Text = S"SystemInformation::MousePresent:                 ↵
 {0}", SystemInformation::MousePresent;
      label5->Text = S"SystemInformation::MouseButtons:                 ↵
 {0}", SystemInformation::MouseButtons;
      label6->Text = S"SystemInformation::MouseButtonsSwapped:          ↵
 {0}", SystemInformation::MouseButtonsSwapped;
      label7->Text = S"SystemInformation::MouseWheelPresent:            ↵
{0}", SystemInformation::MouseWheelPresent;
      label8->Text = S"SystemInformation::MouseWheelScrollLines:        ↵
{0}", SystemInformation::MouseWheelScrollLines;
      label9->Text =                                                    ↵
S"SystemInformation::NativeMouseWheelSupport: {0}",                     ↵
SystemInformation::NativeMouseWheelSupport;
   }

private:
   void panel1_MouseDown(Object* sender,                                ↵
System::Windows::Forms::MouseEventArgs* e) {
      // Update the mouse path with the mouse information
      Point mouseDownLocation =  Point(e->X, e->Y);

      String* eventString = 0;
      switch (e->Button) {
      case MouseButtons::Left:
         eventString = S"L";
         break;
      case MouseButtons::Right:
         eventString = S"R";
         break;
      case MouseButtons::Middle:
         eventString = S"M";
         break;
      case MouseButtons::XButton1:
         eventString = S"X1";
         break;
      case MouseButtons::XButton2:
         eventString = S"X2";
         break;
      case MouseButtons::None:
      default:
         break;
      }

      if (eventString != 0) {
         mousePath->AddString(eventString,                              ↵
FontFamily::GenericSerif, (int)FontStyle::Bold, (float)fontSize,        ↵
mouseDownLocation, StringFormat::GenericDefault);
      } else {
         mousePath->AddLine(mouseDownLocation, mouseDownLocation);
      }
      panel1->Focus();
      panel1->Invalidate();
   }

   void panel1_MouseEnter(Object* sender, System::EventArgs* e) {
      // Update the mouse event label to indicate the MouseEnter        ↵
 event occurred.
      label1->Text = String::Concat( sender->GetType(), S":             ↵
MouseEnter" );
   }

   void panel1_MouseHover(Object* sender, System::EventArgs* e) {
      // Update the mouse event label to indicate the MouseHover        ↵
 event occurred.
      label1->Text = String::Concat( sender->GetType(), S":             ↵
MouseHover" );
   }

   void panel1_MouseLeave(Object* sender, System::EventArgs* e) {
      // Update the mouse event label to indicate the MouseLeave        ↵
event occurred.
      label1->Text = String::Concat( sender->GetType(), S":             ↵
MouseLeave" );
   }

   void panel1_MouseMove(Object* sender,                                ↵
System::Windows::Forms::MouseEventArgs* e) {
      // Update the mouse path that is drawn onto the Panel.
      int mouseX = e->X;
      int mouseY = e->Y;

      mousePath->AddLine(mouseX, mouseY, mouseX, mouseY);
   }

   void panel1_MouseWheel(Object* sender,                               ↵
System::Windows::Forms::MouseEventArgs* e) {
      // Update the drawing based upon the mouse wheel scrolling.

      int numberOfTextLinesToMove = e->Delta *                          ↵
SystemInformation::MouseWheelScrollLines / 120;
      int numberOfPixelsToMove = numberOfTextLinesToMove * fontSize;
```

```
      if (numberOfPixelsToMove != 0) {
         System::Drawing::Drawing2D::Matrix* translateMatrix =      ↵
 new System::Drawing::Drawing2D::Matrix();
         translateMatrix->Translate(0, (float)numberOfPixelsToMove);
         mousePath->Transform(translateMatrix);
      }
      panel1->Invalidate();
   }
   void panel1_MouseUp(Object* sender,                              ↵
System::Windows::Forms::MouseEventArgs* e) {
      Point mouseUpLocation =  System::Drawing::Point(e->X, e->Y);

      // Show the number of clicks in the path graphic.
      int numberOfClicks = e->Clicks;
      mousePath->AddString(String::Format( S"   {0}",                ↵
__box(numberOfClicks)),
         FontFamily::GenericSerif, (int)FontStyle::Bold,
         (float)fontSize, mouseUpLocation,                          ↵
StringFormat::GenericDefault);

      panel1->Invalidate();
   }

   void panel1_Paint(Object* sender,                                ↵
System::Windows::Forms::PaintEventArgs* e) {
      // Perform the painting of the Panel.
      e->Graphics->DrawPath(System::Drawing::Pens::DarkRed, mousePath);
   }

   void clearButton_Click(Object* sender, System::EventArgs* e) {
      // Clear the Panel display.
      mousePath->Dispose();
      mousePath = new System::Drawing::Drawing2D::GraphicsPath();
      panel1->Invalidate();
   }
};
}

[STAThread]
int main() {
   Application::Run(new MouseEvent::Form1());
}
```

Requirements

Namespace: System.Windows.Forms

Platforms: Windows 98, Windows NT 4.0,
Windows Millennium Edition, Windows 2000,
Windows XP Home Edition, Windows XP Professional,
Windows Server 2003 family,
.NET Compact Framework - Windows CE .NET

Assembly: System.Windows.Forms (in System.Windows.Forms.dll)

MouseEventArgs Class

Provides data for the **MouseUp**, **MouseDown**, and **MouseMove** events.

System.Object
  System.EventArgs
    System.Windows.Forms.MouseEventArgs
      System.Windows.Forms.StatusBarPanelClickEventArgs

```
[Visual Basic]
<ComVisible(True)>
Public Class MouseEventArgs
   Inherits EventArgs
[C#]
[ComVisible(true)]
public class MouseEventArgs : EventArgs
[C++]
[ComVisible(true)]
public __gc class MouseEventArgs : public EventArgs
[JScript]
public
   ComVisible(true)
class MouseEventArgs extends EventArgs
```

Thread Safety

Any public static (**Shared** in Visual Basic) members of this type are safe for multithreaded operations. Any instance members are not guaranteed to be thread safe.

Remarks

The **MouseDown** event occurs when the user presses the mouse button while the pointer is over a control. The **MouseUp** event occurs when the user releases the mouse button while the pointer remains over the control. The **MouseMove** event occurs when the user moves the mouse pointer over a control. A **MouseEventArgs** specifies which mouse button is pressed, how many times the mouse button was pressed and released, the coordinates of the mouse, and the amount the mouse wheel moved.

These three events exist for the **Control**, **AxHost**, and **NotifyIcon** classes.

Example

See related example in the **System.Windows.Forms.MouseButtons** enumeration topic.

Requirements

Namespace: System.Windows.Forms

Platforms: Windows 98, Windows NT 4.0, Windows Millennium Edition, Windows 2000, Windows XP Home Edition, Windows XP Professional, Windows Server 2003 family, .NET Compact Framework - Windows CE .NET

Assembly: System.Windows.Forms (in System.Windows.Forms.dll)

MouseEventArgs Constructor

Initializes a new instance of the **MouseEventArgs** class.

```
[Visual Basic]
Public Sub New( _
   ByVal button As MouseButtons, _
   ByVal clicks As Integer, _
   ByVal x As Integer, _
   ByVal y As Integer, _
   ByVal delta As Integer _
)
[C#]
public MouseEventArgs(
   MouseButtons button,
   int clicks,
   int x,
   int y,
   int delta
);
[C++]
public: MouseEventArgs(
   MouseButtons button,
   int clicks,
   int x,
   int y,
   int delta
);
[JScript]
public function MouseEventArgs(
   button : MouseButtons,
   clicks : int,
   x : int,
   y : int,
   delta : int
);
```

Parameters

button
  One of the **MouseButtons** values indicating which mouse button was pressed.

clicks
  The number of times a mouse button was pressed.

x
  The x-coordinate of a mouse click, in pixels.

y
  The y-coordinate of a mouse click, in pixels.

delta
  A signed count of the number of detents the wheel has rotated.

Requirements

Platforms: Windows 98, Windows NT 4.0, Windows Millennium Edition, Windows 2000, Windows XP Home Edition, Windows XP Professional, Windows Server 2003 family, .NET Compact Framework - Windows CE .NET

MouseEventArgs.Button Property

Gets which mouse button was pressed.

[Visual Basic]
```
Public ReadOnly Property Button As MouseButtons
```
[C#]
```
public MouseButtons Button {get;}
```
[C++]
```
public: __property MouseButtons get_Button();
```
[JScript]
```
public function get Button() : MouseButtons;
```

Property Value

One of the **MouseButtons** values.

Example

See related example in the **System.Windows.Forms.MouseButtons** enumeration topic.

Requirements

Platforms: Windows 98, Windows NT 4.0,
Windows Millennium Edition, Windows 2000,
Windows XP Home Edition, Windows XP Professional,
Windows Server 2003 family,
.NET Compact Framework - Windows CE .NET

MouseEventArgs.Clicks Property

Gets the number of times the mouse button was pressed and released.

[Visual Basic]
```
Public ReadOnly Property Clicks As Integer
```
[C#]
```
public int Clicks {get;}
```
[C++]
```
public: __property int get_Clicks();
```
[JScript]
```
public function get Clicks() : int;
```

Property Value

The number of times the mouse button was pressed and released.

Example

See related example in the **System.Windows.Forms.MouseButtons** enumeration topic.

Requirements

Platforms: Windows 98, Windows NT 4.0,
Windows Millennium Edition, Windows 2000,
Windows XP Home Edition, Windows XP Professional,
Windows Server 2003 family

MouseEventArgs.Delta Property

Gets a signed count of the number of detents the mouse wheel has rotated. A detent is one notch of the mouse wheel.

[Visual Basic]
```
Public ReadOnly Property Delta As Integer
```
[C#]
```
public int Delta {get;}
```
[C++]
```
public: __property int get_Delta();
```
[JScript]
```
public function get Delta() : int;
```

Property Value

A signed count of the number of detents the mouse wheel has rotated.

Remarks

The mouse wheel combines the features of a wheel and a mouse button. The wheel has discrete, evenly-spaced notches. When you rotate the wheel, a wheel message is sent as each notch is encountered. One wheel notch, a detent, is defined by the windows constant WHEEL_DELTA, which is 120. A positive value indicates that the wheel was rotated forward, away from the user; a negative value indicates that the wheel was rotated backward, toward the user.

Currently, a value of 120 is the standard for one detent. If higher resolution mice are introduced, the definition of WHEEL_DATA might become smaller. Most applications should check for a positive or negative value rather than an aggregate total.

Example

See related example in the **System.Windows.Forms.MouseButtons** enumeration topic.

Requirements

Platforms: Windows 98, Windows NT 4.0,
Windows Millennium Edition, Windows 2000,
Windows XP Home Edition, Windows XP Professional,
Windows Server 2003 family

MouseEventArgs.X Property

Gets the x-coordinate of the mouse.

[Visual Basic]
```
Public ReadOnly Property X As Integer
```
[C#]
```
public int X {get;}
```
[C++]
```
public: __property int get_X();
```
[JScript]
```
public function get X() : int;
```

Property Value

The x-coordinate of the mouse, in pixels.

Remarks

The mouse coordinates are based on the client area of the form.

Example

See related example in the **System.Windows.Forms.MouseButtons** enumeration topic.

Requirements

Platforms: Windows 98, Windows NT 4.0,
Windows Millennium Edition, Windows 2000,
Windows XP Home Edition, Windows XP Professional,
Windows Server 2003 family,
.NET Compact Framework - Windows CE .NET

MouseEventArgs.Y Property

Gets the y-coordinate of the mouse.

[Visual Basic]
```
Public ReadOnly Property Y As Integer
```
[C#]
```
public int Y {get;}
```
[C++]
```
public: __property int get_Y();
```
[JScript]
```
public function get Y() : int;
```

Property Value

The y-coordinate of the mouse, in pixels.

Remarks

The mouse coordinates are based on the client area of the form.

Example

See related example in the **System.Windows.Forms.MouseButtons** enumeration topic.

Requirements

Platforms: Windows 98, Windows NT 4.0,
Windows Millennium Edition, Windows 2000,
Windows XP Home Edition, Windows XP Professional,
Windows Server 2003 family,
.NET Compact Framework - Windows CE .NET

MouseEventHandler Delegate

Represents the method that will handle the **MouseDown**, **MouseUp**, or **MouseMove** event of a form, control, or other component.

[Visual Basic]
```
<Serializable>
Public Delegate Sub MouseEventHandler( _
   ByVal sender As Object, _
   ByVal e As MouseEventArgs _
)
```
[C#]
```
[Serializable]
public delegate void MouseEventHandler(
   object sender,
   MouseEventArgs e
);
```
[C++]
```
[Serializable]
public __gc __delegate void MouseEventHandler(
   Object* sender,
   MouseEventArgs* e
);
```

[JScript] In JScript, you can use the delegates in the .NET Framework, but you cannot define your own.

Parameters [Visual Basic, C#, C++]

The declaration of your event handler must have the same parameters as the **MouseEventHandler** delegate declaration.

sender
The source of the event.

e
A **MouseEventArgs** that contains the event data.

Remarks

When you create a **MouseEventHandler** delegate, you identify the method that will handle the event. To associate the event with your event handler, add an instance of the delegate to the event. The event handler is called whenever the event occurs, unless you remove the delegate.

Example

See related example in the **System.Windows.Forms.MouseButtons** enumeration topic.

Requirements

Namespace: System.Windows.Forms

Platforms: Windows 98, Windows NT 4.0, Windows Millennium Edition, Windows 2000, Windows XP Home Edition, Windows XP Professional, Windows Server 2003 family, .NET Compact Framework - Windows CE .NET

Assembly: System.Windows.Forms (in System.Windows.Forms.dll)

NativeWindow Class

Provides a low-level encapsulation of a window handle and a window procedure.

System.Object
System.MarshalByRefObject
System.Windows.Forms.NativeWindow

[Visual Basic]
```
Public Class NativeWindow
   Inherits MarshalByRefObject
```
[C#]
```
public class NativeWindow : MarshalByRefObject
```
[C++]
```
public __gc class NativeWindow : public MarshalByRefObject
```
[JScript]
```
public class NativeWindow extends MarshalByRefObject
```

Thread Safety

Any public static (**Shared** in Visual Basic) members of this type are safe for multithreaded operations. Any instance members are not guaranteed to be thread safe.

Remarks

This class automatically manages window class creation and registration.

A window is not eligible for garbage collection when it is associated with a window handle. To ensure proper garbage collection, handles must either be destroyed manually using **DestroyHandle** or released using **ReleaseHandle**.

The **NativeWindow** class provides the following procedure and methods to manage handles: **Handle**, **CreateHandle**, **AssignHandle**, **DestroyHandle**, and **ReleaseHandle**.

Example

[Visual Basic, C#, C++] The following example demonstrates intercepting operating system window messages in a window procedure, and creating a window with a specific operating system window class name. The example create two classes that inherit from **NativeWindow** that accomplish this.

[Visual Basic, C#, C++] The `MyNativeWindowListener` class hooks into the window procedure of the form passed into the constructor, and overrides the **WndProc** method to intercept the `WM_ACTIVATEAPP` window message. The class demonstrates the usage of the **AssignHandle** and **ReleaseHandle** methods to identify the window handle the **NativeWindow** will use. The handle is assign based upon the **Control.HandleCreated** and **Control.HandleDestroyed** events. When the `WM_ACTIVATEAPP` window message is received, the class calls the `form1 ApplicationActivated` method.

[Visual Basic, C#, C++] The `MyNativeWindow` class creates a new window with the **ClassName** set to `BUTTON`. The class demonstrates using the **CreateHandle** method and overriding the **WndProc** method to intercept window messages that are received.

[Visual Basic]
```
Imports System
Imports System.Drawing
Imports System.Windows.Forms
Imports System.Runtime.InteropServices

' Summary description for Form1.
Public Class Form1
    Inherits System.Windows.Forms.Form
    Private nwl As MyNativeWindowListener
    Private nw As MyNativeWindow

    Friend Sub ApplicationActived(ByVal ApplicationActivated As ↵
Boolean)
        ' The application has been activated or deactivated
        System.Diagnostics.Debug.WriteLine("Application Active = ↵
" + ApplicationActivated.ToString())
    End Sub

    Public Sub New()
        MyBase.New()

        Me.Size = New System.Drawing.Size(300, 300)
        Me.Text = "Form1"

        nwl = New MyNativeWindowListener(Me)
        nw = New MyNativeWindow(Me)

    End Sub

End Class

' NativeWindow class to listen to operating system messages.
Public Class MyNativeWindowListener
    Inherits NativeWindow

    ' Constant value was found in the "windows.h" header file.
    Private Const WM_ACTIVATEAPP As Integer = &H1C

    Private parent As Form1

    Public Sub New(ByVal parent As Form1)

        AddHandler parent.HandleCreated, AddressOf Me.OnHandleCreated
        AddHandler parent.HandleDestroyed, AddressOf ↵
Me.OnHandleDestroyed
        Me.parent = parent
    End Sub

    ' Listen for the control's window creation and hook into it.
    Private Sub OnHandleCreated(ByVal sender As Object, ↵
ByVal e As EventArgs)
        ' Window is now created, assign handle to NativeWindow.
        AssignHandle(CType(sender, Form).Handle)
    End Sub

    Private Sub OnHandleDestroyed(ByVal sender As Object, ↵
 ByVal e As EventArgs)
        ' Window was destroyed, release hook.
        ReleaseHandle()
    End Sub

<System.Security.Permissions.PermissionSetAttribute ↵
 (System.Security.Permissions.SecurityAction.Demand, ↵
Name:="FullTrust")> _
    Protected Overrides Sub WndProc(ByRef m As Message)
        ' Listen for operating system messages

        Select Case (m.Msg)
            Case WM_ACTIVATEAPP

                ' Notify the form that this message was received.
                ' Application is activated or deactivated,
                ' based upon the WParam parameter.
                parent.ApplicationActived(m.WParam.ToInt32() <> 0)

        End Select

        MyBase.WndProc(m)
    End Sub
End Class

' MyNativeWindow class to create a window given a class name.
Public Class MyNativeWindow
    Inherits NativeWindow
```

```
    ' Constant values were found in the "windows.h" header file.
    Private Const WS_CHILD As Integer = &H40000000, _
                 WS_VISIBLE As Integer = &H10000000, _
                 WM_ACTIVATEAPP As Integer = &H1C

    private windowHandle as integer

    Public Sub New(ByVal parent As Form)

        Dim cp As CreateParams = New CreateParams()

        ' Fill in the CreateParams details.
        cp.Caption = "Click here"
        cp.ClassName = "Button"

        ' Set the position on the form
        cp.X = 100
        cp.Y = 100
        cp.Height = 100
        cp.Width = 100

        ' Specify the form as the parent.
        cp.Parent = parent.Handle

        ' Create as a child of the specified parent
        cp.Style = WS_CHILD Or WS_VISIBLE

        ' Create the actual window
        Me.CreateHandle(cp)
    End Sub

    ' Listen to when the handle changes to keep the variable in sync
 <System.Security.Permissions.PermissionSetAttribute ↵
 (System.Security.Permissions.SecurityAction.Demand, ↵
Name:="FullTrust")> _
Protected Overrides Sub OnHandleChange()
        windowHandle = Me.Handle.ToInt32()
    End Sub

<System.Security.Permissions.PermissionSetAttribute ↵
 (System.Security.Permissions.SecurityAction.Demand, ↵
Name:="FullTrust")> _
    Protected Overrides Sub WndProc(ByRef m As Message)
        ' Listen for messages that are sent to the button ↵
window. Some messages are sent
        ' to the parent window instead of the button's window.

        Select Case (m.Msg)
            Case WM_ACTIVATEAPP
                ' Do something here in response to messages
        End Select

        MyBase.WndProc(m)
    End Sub

End Class
```

[C#]

```
using System;
using System.Drawing;
using System.Windows.Forms;
using System.Runtime.InteropServices;

namespace NativeWindowApplication
{

    // Summary description for Form1.
    public class Form1 : System.Windows.Forms.Form
    {
        private MyNativeWindowListener nwl;
        private MyNativeWindow nw;

        internal void ApplicationActived(bool ApplicationActivated){
            // The application has been activated or deactivated
            System.Diagnostics.Debug.WriteLine ↵
("Application Active = " + ApplicationActivated.ToString());
        }

        public Form1()
        {
            this.Size = new System.Drawing.Size(300,300);
            this.Text = "Form1";

            nwl = new MyNativeWindowListener(this);
            nw = new MyNativeWindow(this);

        }

        // The main entry point for the application.
        [STAThread]
        static void Main()
        {
            Application.Run(new Form1());
        }
    }

    // NativeWindow class to listen to operating system messages.
    public class MyNativeWindowListener: NativeWindow{

        // Constant value was found in the "windows.h" header file.
        private const int WM_ACTIVATEAPP = 0x001C;

        private Form1 parent;

        public MyNativeWindowListener(Form1 parent){

            parent.HandleCreated += new ↵
EventHandler(this.OnHandleCreated);
            parent.HandleDestroyed+= new ↵
EventHandler(this.OnHandleDestroyed);
            this.parent = parent;
        }

        // Listen for the control's window creation and ↵
 then hook into it.
        internal void OnHandleCreated(object sender, EventArgs e){
            // Window is now created, assign handle to NativeWindow.
            AssignHandle(((Form1)sender).Handle);
        }
        internal void OnHandleDestroyed(object sender, EventArgs e) {
            // Window was destroyed, release hook.
            ReleaseHandle();
        }
    [System.Security.Permissions.PermissionSet ↵
 (System.Security.Permissions.SecurityAction.Demand, Name="FullTrust")]
        protected override void WndProc(ref Message m){
            // Listen for operating system messages

            switch (m.Msg){
                case WM_ACTIVATEAPP:

                    // Notify the form that this message was received.
                    // Application is activated or deactivated,
                    // based upon the WParam parameter.
                    parent.ApplicationActived(((int)m.WParam != 0));

                    break;
            }
            base.WndProc(ref m);
        }
    }

    // MyNativeWindow class to create a window given a class name.
    public class MyNativeWindow: NativeWindow{

        // Constant values were found in the "windows.h" header file.
        private const int WS_CHILD = 0x40000000,
                          WS_VISIBLE = 0x10000000,
                          WM_ACTIVATEAPP = 0x001C;

        private int windowHandle ;
```

```
        public MyNativeWindow(Form parent){

            CreateParams cp = new CreateParams();

            // Fill in the CreateParams details.
            cp.Caption = "Click here";
            cp.ClassName = "Button";

            // Set the position on the form
            cp.X = 100;
            cp.Y = 100;
            cp.Height = 100;
            cp.Width = 100;

            // Specify the form as the parent.
            cp.Parent = parent.Handle;

            // Create as a child of the specified parent
            cp.Style = WS_CHILD | WS_VISIBLE;

            // Create the actual window
            this.CreateHandle(cp);
        }

        // Listen to when the handle changes to keep the                ↵
variable in sync
        [System.Security.Permissions.PermissionSet                      ↵
 (System.Security.Permissions.SecurityAction.Demand, Name="FullTrust")]
        protected override void OnHandleChange(){
            windowHandle  = (int)this.Handle;
        }

    [System.Security.Permissions.PermissionSet                          ↵
 (System.Security.Permissions.SecurityAction.Demand, Name="FullTrust")]
        protected override void WndProc(ref Message m){
            // Listen for messages that are sent to the button          ↵
window. Some messages are sent
            // to the parent window instead of the button's window.

            switch (m.Msg){
                case WM_ACTIVATEAPP:
                    // Do something here in response to messages
                    break;
            }
            base.WndProc(ref m);
        }
    }
}
```

[C++]

```
using namespace System;
using namespace System::Drawing;
using namespace System::Windows::Forms;
using namespace System::Runtime::InteropServices;

namespace NativeWindowApplication {

__gc class MyNativeWindowListener;
__gc class MyNativeWindow;

    // Summary description for Form1.
__gc class Form1 : public System::Windows::Forms::Form {
private:
    MyNativeWindowListener*  nwl;
    MyNativeWindow*  nw;

public private:
    void ApplicationActived(bool ApplicationActivated) {
        // The application has been activated or deactivated
        System::Diagnostics::Debug::WriteLine                           ↵
 (S"Application Active = {0}", ApplicationActivated.ToString());
    }

public:
    Form1();
};

// NativeWindow class to listen to operating system messages.
__gc class MyNativeWindowListener : public NativeWindow {

    // Constant value was found in the S"windows.h" header file.
private:
    const static int  WM_ACTIVATEAPP = 0x001C;
    Form1*  parent;

public:
    MyNativeWindowListener(Form1* parent) {
        parent->HandleCreated += new EventHandler(this,                 ↵
OnHandleCreated);
        parent->HandleDestroyed += new EventHandler(this,               ↵
OnHandleDestroyed);
        this->parent = parent;
    }

public private:
    // Listen for the control's window creation and then hook into it.
    void OnHandleCreated(Object* sender, EventArgs* /*e*/) {
        // Window is now created, assign handle to NativeWindow.
        AssignHandle((dynamic_cast<Form1*>(sender))->Handle);
    }
    void OnHandleDestroyed(Object* /*sender*/, EventArgs* /*e*/) {
        // Window was destroyed, release hook.
        ReleaseHandle();
    }

protected:
    [System::Security::Permissions::PermissionSet                       ↵
 (System::Security::Permissions::SecurityAction::Demand,                ↵
Name="FullTrust")]
    void WndProc(Message* m) {
        // Listen for operating system messages

        switch (m->Msg) {
                case WM_ACTIVATEAPP:

                    // Notify the form that this message was received.
                    // Application is activated or deactivated,
                    // based upon the WParam parameter.
                    parent->ApplicationActived(((int)m->WParam != 0));

                    break;
        }
        NativeWindow::WndProc(m);

    }
};

// MyNativeWindow class to create a window given a class name.
__gc class MyNativeWindow : public NativeWindow {

    // Constant values were found in the S"windows.h" header file.
private:
    const static int  WS_CHILD = 0x40000000,
        WS_VISIBLE = 0x10000000,
        WM_ACTIVATEAPP = 0x001C;

    int windowHandle;

public:
    MyNativeWindow(Form* parent) {

        CreateParams* cp = new CreateParams();

        // Fill in the CreateParams details.
        cp->Caption = S"Click here";
        cp->ClassName = S"Button";

        // Set the position on the form
        cp->X = 100;
        cp->Y = 100;
        cp->Height = 100;
        cp->Width = 100;
```

```
        // Specify the form as the parent.
        cp->Parent = parent->Handle;

        // Create as a child of the specified parent
        cp->Style = WS_CHILD | WS_VISIBLE;

        // Create the actual window
        this->CreateHandle(cp);
    }

protected:
    // Listen to when the handle changes to keep the variable in sync
    [System::Security::Permissions::PermissionSet                        ↵
 (System::Security::Permissions::SecurityAction::Demand,               ↵
Name="FullTrust")]
    void OnHandleChange() {
        windowHandle  = (int)this->Handle;
    }

    [System::Security::Permissions::PermissionSet                        ↵
 (System::Security::Permissions::SecurityAction::Demand,               ↵
Name="FullTrust")]
    void WndProc(Message* m) {
        // Listen for messages that are sent to the button              ↵
 window. Some messages are sent
        // to the parent window instead of the button's window.

        switch (m->Msg) {
                case WM_ACTIVATEAPP:
                    // Do something here in response to messages
                    break;
        }
        NativeWindow::WndProc(m);
    }
};

Form1::Form1() {
    this->Size = System::Drawing::Size(300, 300);
    this->Text = S"Form1";
    nwl = new MyNativeWindowListener(this);
    nw = new MyNativeWindow(this);
}

}

// The main entry point for the application.
[STAThread]
int main() {
    Application::Run(new NativeWindowApplication::Form1());
}
```

Requirements

Namespace: System.Windows.Forms

Platforms: Windows 98, Windows NT 4.0, Windows Millennium Edition, Windows 2000, Windows XP Home Edition, Windows XP Professional, Windows Server 2003 family

Assembly: System.Windows.Forms (in System.Windows.Forms.dll)

.NET Framework Security:

- **SecurityPermission** for inheriting classes to call unmanaged code. Associated enumeration: **SecurityPermissionFlag.UnmanagedCode**
- **SecurityPermission** for the immediate caller to call unmanaged code. Associated enumeration: **SecurityPermissionFlag.UnmanagedCode**

NativeWindow Constructor

Initializes a new instance of the **NativeWindow** class.

[Visual Basic]
```
Public Sub New()
```
[C#]
```
public NativeWindow();
```
[C++]
```
public: NativeWindow();
```
[JScript]
```
public function NativeWindow();
```

Remarks

The default constructor initializes any fields to their default values.

Requirements

Platforms: Windows 98, Windows NT 4.0, Windows Millennium Edition, Windows 2000, Windows XP Home Edition, Windows XP Professional, Windows Server 2003 family

NativeWindow.Handle Property

Gets the handle for this window.

[Visual Basic]
```
Public ReadOnly Property Handle As IntPtr
```
[C#]
```
public IntPtr Handle {get;}
```
[C++]
```
public: __property IntPtr get_Handle();
```
[JScript]
```
public function get Handle() : IntPtr;
```

Property Value

The handle for this window. Returns 0 if no handle is associated with the window.

Remarks

Use this method when calling Windows API methods that require a handle for a window or control.

Example

See related example in the **System.Windows.Forms.Native.Window** class topic.

Requirements

Platforms: Windows 98, Windows NT 4.0, Windows Millennium Edition, Windows 2000, Windows XP Home Edition, Windows XP Professional, Windows Server 2003 family

NativeWindow.AssignHandle Method

Assigns a handle to this window.

[Visual Basic]
```
Public Sub AssignHandle( _
   ByVal handle As IntPtr _
)
```
[C#]
```
public void AssignHandle(
   IntPtr handle
);
```

```
[C++]
public: void AssignHandle(
   IntPtr handle
);
[JScript]
public function AssignHandle(
   handle : IntPtr
);
```

Parameters

handle

The handle to assign to this window.

Exceptions

Exception Type	Condition
Exception	This window already has a handle.

Remarks

WndProc intercepts window messages sent to the *handle* parameter. Use **ReleaseHandle** to reset the handle's window procedure to the default window procedure.

The **AssignHandle** method calls the **OnHandleChange** method to indicate that the value of the **Handle** property has changed.

> **Note** The handle to assign cannot be in a different application process.

Example

See related example in the **System.Windows.Forms.Native.Window** class topic.

Requirements

Platforms: Windows 98, Windows NT 4.0, Windows Millennium Edition, Windows 2000, Windows XP Home Edition, Windows XP Professional, Windows Server 2003 family

NativeWindow.CreateHandle Method

Creates a window and its handle with the specified creation parameters.

```
[Visual Basic]
Public Overridable Sub CreateHandle( _
   ByVal cp As CreateParams _
)
[C#]
public virtual void CreateHandle(
   CreateParams cp
);
[C++]
public: virtual void CreateHandle(
   CreateParams* cp
);
[JScript]
public function CreateHandle(
   cp : CreateParams
);
```

Parameters

cp

A **CreateParams** that specifies the creation parameters for this window.

Exceptions

Exception Type	Condition
Win32Exception	The native Win32 API could not create the window.

Remarks

The *cp* parameter specifies the values that are passed to the native Win32 **CreateWindowEx** API method to create a window and its handle.

When the **ClassName** field is not a null reference (**Nothing** in Visual Basic), the newly created window handle inherits from the specified class. For example, if **ClassName** is set to BUTTON, the newly created window is based on the Win32 BUTTON window class. The **param** field of the **ClassName** object must either be a null reference (**Nothing**) or reference an instance of a class that was declared as a structure.

This code is an excerpt from the example shown in the **NativeWindow** class overview. Some code is not shown for the purpose of brevity. See **NativeWindow** for the whole code listing.

> **Note** The class name provided is registered with the operating system.

Example

See related example in the **System.Windows.Forms.Native.Window** class topic.

Requirements

Platforms: Windows 98, Windows NT 4.0, Windows Millennium Edition, Windows 2000, Windows XP Home Edition, Windows XP Professional, Windows Server 2003 family

.NET Framework Security:

- **UIPermission** for safe subwindows to call this method. Associated enumeration: **UIPermissionWindow.SafeSubWindows**
- **UIPermission** to create a top-level window. This permission is only demanded if the window style is not a child or if the window does not have a parent. Associated enumeration: **UIPermissionWindow.SafeTopLevelWindows**

NativeWindow.DefWndProc Method

Invokes the default window procedure associated with this window. It is an error to call this method when the **Handle** property is 0.

```
[Visual Basic]
Public Sub DefWndProc( _
   ByRef m As Message _
)
[C#]
public void DefWndProc(
   ref Message m
);
[C++]
public: void DefWndProc(
   Message* m
);
[JScript]
public function DefWndProc(
   m : Message
);
```

Parameters

m

The message that is currently being processed.

Remarks

Typically, you only call the **DefWndProc** method when you are intercepting window messages and would like the default window procedure to handle the message. **DefWndProc** should not be called to send a window message to the window; call the Win32 **SendMessage** API instead.

Requirements

Platforms: Windows 98, Windows NT 4.0, Windows Millennium Edition, Windows 2000, Windows XP Home Edition, Windows XP Professional, Windows Server 2003 family

NativeWindow.DestroyHandle Method

Destroys the window and its handle.

[Visual Basic]
```
Public Overridable Sub DestroyHandle()
```
[C#]
```
public virtual void DestroyHandle();
```
[C++]
```
public: virtual void DestroyHandle();
```
[JScript]
```
public function DestroyHandle();
```

Remarks

This method destroys the window associated with the **Handle**, sets the **Handle** property to 0, and calls the **OnHandleChange** method to reflect the change. Typically, you only call **DestroyHandle** when you are done with the native window.

> **Note** The **NativeWindow** class automatically will destroy the associated window and release its resources in response to a WM_DESTROY message.

Requirements

Platforms: Windows 98, Windows NT 4.0, Windows Millennium Edition, Windows 2000, Windows XP Home Edition, Windows XP Professional, Windows Server 2003 family

NativeWindow.Finalize Method

Releases the resources associated with this window.

[C#] In C#, finalizers are expressed using destructor syntax.

[C++] In C++, finalizers are expressed using destructor syntax.

[Visual Basic]
```
Overrides Protected Sub Finalize()
```
[C#]
```
~NativeWindow();
```
[C++]
```
~NativeWindow();
```
[JScript]
```
protected override function Finalize();
```

Requirements

Platforms: Windows 98, Windows NT 4.0, Windows Millennium Edition, Windows 2000, Windows XP Home Edition, Windows XP Professional, Windows Server 2003 family

NativeWindow.FromHandle Method

Retrieves the window associated with the specified handle.

[Visual Basic]
```
Public Shared Function FromHandle( _
   ByVal handle As IntPtr _
) As NativeWindow
```
[C#]
```
public static NativeWindow FromHandle(
   IntPtr handle
);
```
[C++]
```
public: static NativeWindow* FromHandle(
   IntPtr handle
);
```
[JScript]
```
public static function FromHandle(
   handle : IntPtr
) : NativeWindow;
```

Parameters

handle

A handle to a window.

Return Value

The **NativeWindow** associated with the specified handle. This method returns a null reference (**Nothing** in Visual Basic) when the handle does not have an associated window.

Remarks

If you receive a handle from another method, use this method to retrieve the window associated with the handle. The handle must already be owned by another **NativeWindow** in the current process, otherwise a null reference (**Nothing** in Visual Basic) is returned.

Requirements

Platforms: Windows 98, Windows NT 4.0, Windows Millennium Edition, Windows 2000, Windows XP Home Edition, Windows XP Professional, Windows Server 2003 family

NativeWindow.OnHandleChange Method

Specifies a notification method that is called when the handle for a window is changed.

[Visual Basic]
```
Protected Overridable Sub OnHandleChange()
```
[C#]
```
protected virtual void OnHandleChange();
```
[C++]
```
protected: virtual void OnHandleChange();
```
[JScript]
```
protected function OnHandleChange();
```

Remarks

This method is invoked when the value of the **Handle** property has changed.

Notes to Inheritors: Override this method to track changes that are made to the window handle.

Example

See related example in the **System.Windows.Forms.Native.Window** class topic.

Requirements

Platforms: Windows 98, Windows NT 4.0, Windows Millennium Edition, Windows 2000, Windows XP Home Edition, Windows XP Professional, Windows Server 2003 family

NativeWindow.OnThreadException Method

When overridden in a derived class, manages an unhandled thread exception.

```
[Visual Basic]
Protected Overridable Sub OnThreadException( _
   ByVal e As Exception _
)
[C#]
protected virtual void OnThreadException(
   Exception e
);
[C++]
protected: virtual void OnThreadException(
   Exception* e
);
[JScript]
protected function OnThreadException(
   e : Exception
);
```

Parameters

e

An **Exception** that specifies the unhandled thread exception.

Remarks

Typically, **OnThreadException** handles thread exceptions.

Requirements

Platforms: Windows 98, Windows NT 4.0, Windows Millennium Edition, Windows 2000, Windows XP Home Edition, Windows XP Professional, Windows Server 2003 family

NativeWindow.ReleaseHandle Method

Releases the handle associated with this window.

```
[Visual Basic]
Public Overridable Sub ReleaseHandle()
[C#]
public virtual void ReleaseHandle();
[C++]
public: virtual void ReleaseHandle();
[JScript]
public function ReleaseHandle();
```

Remarks

This method does not destroy the window handle. Instead, it sets the handle's window procedure to the default window procedure. It sets the **Handle** property to 0 and calls **OnHandleChange** to reflect the change.

A window automatically calls this method if it receives a native Win32 WM_NCDESTROY message, indicating that Windows has destroyed the handle.

Example

See related example in the **System.Windows.Forms.Native.Window** class topic.

Requirements

Platforms: Windows 98, Windows NT 4.0, Windows Millennium Edition, Windows 2000, Windows XP Home Edition, Windows XP Professional, Windows Server 2003 family

NativeWindow.WndProc Method

Invokes the default window procedure associated with this window.

```
[Visual Basic]
Protected Overridable Sub WndProc( _
   ByRef m As Message _
)
[C#]
protected virtual void WndProc(
   ref Message m
);
[C++]
protected: virtual void WndProc(
   Message* m
);
[JScript]
protected function WndProc(
   m : Message
);
```

Parameters

m

A **Message** that is associated with the current Windows message.

Remarks

This method is called when a window message is sent to the handle of the window.

Notes to Inheritors: Override this method to implement specific message processing. Call **base.WndProc** for unhandled messages.

Example

See related example in the **System.Windows.Forms.Native.Window** class topic.

Requirements

Platforms: Windows 98, Windows NT 4.0, Windows Millennium Edition, Windows 2000, Windows XP Home Edition, Windows XP Professional, Windows Server 2003 family

NavigateEventArgs Class

Provides data for the **Navigate** event.

System.Object
  System.EventArgs
    System.Windows.Forms.NavigateEventArgs

[Visual Basic]
```
<ComVisible(True)>
Public Class NavigateEventArgs
   Inherits EventArgs
```
[C#]
```
[ComVisible(true)]
public class NavigateEventArgs : EventArgs
```
[C++]
```
[ComVisible(true)]
public __gc class NavigateEventArgs : public EventArgs
```
[JScript]
```
public
   ComVisible(true)
class NavigateEventArgs extends EventArgs
```

Thread Safety

Any public static (**Shared** in Visual Basic) members of this type are safe for multithreaded operations. Any instance members are not guaranteed to be thread safe.

Requirements

Namespace: System.Windows.Forms

Platforms: Windows 98, Windows NT 4.0, Windows Millennium Edition, Windows 2000, Windows XP Home Edition, Windows XP Professional, Windows Server 2003 family

Assembly: System.Windows.Forms (in System.Windows.Forms.dll)

NavigateEventArgs Constructor

Initializes a new instance of the **NavigateEventArgs** class.

[Visual Basic]
```
Public Sub New( _
   ByVal isForward As Boolean _
)
```
[C#]
```
public NavigateEventArgs(
   bool isForward
);
```
[C++]
```
public: NavigateEventArgs(
   bool isForward
);
```
[JScript]
```
public function NavigateEventArgs(
   isForward : Boolean
);
```

Parameters

isForward
  true to navigate in a forward direction; otherwise, **false**.

Remarks

The *isForward* parameter value is assigned to the **Forward** property.

Requirements

Platforms: Windows 98, Windows NT 4.0, Windows Millennium Edition, Windows 2000, Windows XP Home Edition, Windows XP Professional, Windows Server 2003 family

NavigateEventArgs.Forward Property

Gets a value indicating whether to navigate in a forward direction.

[Visual Basic]
```
Public ReadOnly Property Forward As Boolean
```
[C#]
```
public bool Forward {get;}
```
[C++]
```
public: __property bool get_Forward();
```
[JScript]
```
public function get Forward() : Boolean;
```

Property Value

true if the navigation is in a forward direction; otherwise, **false**.

Requirements

Platforms: Windows 98, Windows NT 4.0, Windows Millennium Edition, Windows 2000, Windows XP Home Edition, Windows XP Professional, Windows Server 2003 family

NavigateEventHandler Delegate

Represents the method that will handle the **NavigateEventArgs** event of a **DataGrid**.

[Visual Basic]

```
<Serializable>
Public Delegate Sub NavigateEventHandler( _
   ByVal sender As Object, _
   ByVal ne As NavigateEventArgs _
)
```

[C#]

```
[Serializable]
public delegate void NavigateEventHandler(
   object sender,
   NavigateEventArgs ne
);
```

[C++]

```
[Serializable]
public __gc __delegate void NavigateEventHandler(
   Object* sender,
   NavigateEventArgs* ne
);
```

[JScript] In JScript, you can use the delegates in the .NET Framework, but you cannot define your own.

Parameters [Visual Basic, C#, C++]

The declaration of your event handler must have the same parameters as the **NavigateEventHandler** delegate declaration.

sender
   The source of the event.

ne
   A **NavigateEventArgs** that contains the event data.

Remarks

When you create a **NavigateEventArgs** delegate, you identify the method that will handle the event. To associate the event with your event handler, add an instance of the delegate to the event. The event handler is called whenever the event occurs, unless you remove the delegate.

Requirements

Namespace: System.Windows.Forms

Platforms: Windows 98, Windows NT 4.0, Windows Millennium Edition, Windows 2000, Windows XP Home Edition, Windows XP Professional, Windows Server 2003 family

Assembly: System.Windows.Forms (in System.Windows.Forms.dll)

NodeLabelEditEventArgs Class

Provides data for the **BeforeLabelEdit** and **AfterLabelEdit** events.

System.Object
  System.EventArgs
    System.Windows.Forms.NodeLabelEditEventArgs

[Visual Basic]
```
Public Class NodeLabelEditEventArgs
   Inherits EventArgs
```
[C#]
```
public class NodeLabelEditEventArgs : EventArgs
```
[C++]
```
public __gc class NodeLabelEditEventArgs : public EventArgs
```
[JScript]
```
public class NodeLabelEditEventArgs extends EventArgs
```

Thread Safety

Any public static (**Shared** in Visual Basic) members of this type are safe for multithreaded operations. Any instance members are not guaranteed to be thread safe.

Remarks

The **AfterLabelEdit** event occurs when the user finishes editing the text for a tree node. The **BeforeLabelEdit** event occurs when the user begins editing the text for a tree node. A **NodeLabelEditEventArgs** object specifies the new text to associate with the tree node, the tree node that contains the label to edit, and whether the edit operation has been canceled.

For more information about handling events, see **Consuming Events**.

Example

[Visual Basic, C#] The following example allows the user to edit nonroot tree nodes by using a **ContextMenu**. When the user right clicks the mouse, the **TreeNode** at that position is determined and stored in a variable named `mySelectedNode`. If a nonroot tree node was selected, it is put into an editable state, allowing the user to edit the node label. After the user stops editing the tree node label, the new label text is evaluated and saved. For this example, several characters are considered not valid in the label text. If one of the invalid characters is in the label string, or the string is empty, the user is notified of the error and the label is returned to its previous text.

[Visual Basic]
```
' Get the tree node under the mouse pointer and
' save it in the mySelectedNode variable.
Private Sub treeView1_MouseDown(sender As Object, _
  e As System.Windows.Forms.MouseEventArgs)

   mySelectedNode = treeView1.GetNodeAt(e.X, e.Y)
End Sub

Private Sub menuItem1_Click(sender As Object, e As System.EventArgs)
   If Not (mySelectedNode Is Nothing) And _
     Not (mySelectedNode.Parent Is Nothing) Then
      treeView1.SelectedNode = mySelectedNode
      treeView1.LabelEdit = True
      If Not mySelectedNode.IsEditing Then
         mySelectedNode.BeginEdit()
      End If
   Else
      MessageBox.Show("No tree node selected or selected node is
 a root node." & _
         Microsoft.VisualBasic.ControlChars.Cr & _
         "Editing of root nodes is not allowed.", "Invalid selection")
   End If
End Sub

Private Sub treeView1_AfterLabelEdit(sender As Object, _
  e As System.Windows.Forms.NodeLabelEditEventArgs)
   If Not (e.Label Is Nothing) Then
      If e.Label.Length > 0 Then
         If e.Label.IndexOfAny(New Char() {"@"c, "."c, ","c,
"!"c}) = -1 Then
            ' Stop editing without canceling the label change.
            e.Node.EndEdit(False)
         Else
            ' Cancel the label edit action, inform the user, and
            ' place the node in edit mode again.
            e.CancelEdit = True
            MessageBox.Show("Invalid tree node label." & _
              Microsoft.VisualBasic.ControlChars.Cr & _
              "The invalid characters are: '@','.', ',', '!'", _
              "Node Label Edit")
            e.Node.BeginEdit()
         End If
      Else
         ' Cancel the label edit action, inform the user, and
         ' place the node in edit mode again.
         e.CancelEdit = True
         MessageBox.Show("Invalid tree node label." & _
           Microsoft.VisualBasic.ControlChars.Cr & _
           "The label cannot be blank", "Node Label Edit")
           e.Node.BeginEdit()
      End If
         Me.treeView1.LabelEdit = False
   End If
End Sub
```

[C#]
```
/* Get the tree node under the mouse pointer and
   save it in the mySelectedNode variable. */
private void treeView1_MouseDown(object sender,
  System.Windows.Forms.MouseEventArgs e)
{
   mySelectedNode = treeView1.GetNodeAt(e.X, e.Y);
}

private void menuItem1_Click(object sender, System.EventArgs e)
{
   if (mySelectedNode != null && mySelectedNode.Parent != null)
   {
      treeView1.SelectedNode = mySelectedNode;
      treeView1.LabelEdit = true;
      if(!mySelectedNode.IsEditing)
      {
         mySelectedNode.BeginEdit();
      }
   }
   else
   {
      MessageBox.Show("No tree node selected or selected node
is a root node.\n" +
         "Editing of root nodes is not allowed.", "Invalid selection");
   }
}

private void treeView1_AfterLabelEdit(object sender,
         System.Windows.Forms.NodeLabelEditEventArgs e)
{
   if (e.Label != null)
   {
     if(e.Label.Length > 0)
     {
        if (e.Label.IndexOfAny(new char[]{'@', '.', ',', '!'}) == -1)
        {
           // Stop editing without canceling the label change.
           e.Node.EndEdit(false);
```

```
      }
      else
      {
         /* Cancel the label edit action, inform the user, and
            place the node in edit mode again. */
         e.CancelEdit = true;
         MessageBox.Show("Invalid tree node label.\n" +
            "The invalid characters are: '@','.', ',', '!'",
            "Node Label Edit");
         e.Node.BeginEdit();
      }
   }
   else
   {
      /* Cancel the label edit action, inform the user, and
         place the node in edit mode again. */
      e.CancelEdit = true;
      MessageBox.Show("Invalid tree node label.\nThe label      ↵
cannot be blank",
         "Node Label Edit");
      e.Node.BeginEdit();
   }
   this.treeView1.LabelEdit = false;
  }
}
```

Requirements

Namespace: System.Windows.Forms

Platforms: Windows 98, Windows NT 4.0, Windows Millennium Edition, Windows 2000, Windows XP Home Edition, Windows XP Professional, Windows Server 2003 family

Assembly: System.Windows.Forms (in System.Windows.Forms.dll)

NodeLabelEditEventArgs Constructor

Initializes a new instance of the **NodeLabelEditEventArgs** class.

Overload List

Initializes a new instance of the **NodeLabelEditEventArgs** class for the specified **TreeNode**.

[Visual Basic] **Public Sub New(TreeNode)**

[C#] **public NodeLabelEditEventArgs(TreeNode);**

[C++] **public: NodeLabelEditEventArgs(TreeNode*);**

[JScript] **public function NodeLabelEditEventArgs(TreeNode);**

Initializes a new instance of the **NodeLabelEditEventArgs** class for the specified **TreeNode** and the specified text with which to update the tree node label.

[Visual Basic] **Public Sub New(TreeNode, String)**

[C#] **public NodeLabelEditEventArgs(TreeNode, string);**

[C++] **public: NodeLabelEditEventArgs(TreeNode*, String*);**

[JScript] **public function NodeLabelEditEventArgs(TreeNode, String);**

NodeLabelEditEventArgs Constructor (TreeNode)

Initializes a new instance of the **NodeLabelEditEventArgs** class for the specified **TreeNode**.

```
[Visual Basic]
Public Sub New( _
   ByVal node As TreeNode _
)
[C#]
public NodeLabelEditEventArgs(
   TreeNode node
);
[C++]
public: NodeLabelEditEventArgs(
   TreeNode* node
);
[JScript]
public function NodeLabelEditEventArgs(
   node : TreeNode
);
```

Parameters

node
The tree node containing the text to edit.

Remarks

The **Node** property is assigned the *node* parameter value.

Requirements

Platforms: Windows 98, Windows NT 4.0, Windows Millennium Edition, Windows 2000, Windows XP Home Edition, Windows XP Professional, Windows Server 2003 family

NodeLabelEditEventArgs Constructor (TreeNode, String)

Initializes a new instance of the **NodeLabelEditEventArgs** class for the specified **TreeNode** and the specified text with which to update the tree node label.

```
[Visual Basic]
Public Sub New( _
   ByVal node As TreeNode, _
   ByVal label As String _
)
[C#]
public NodeLabelEditEventArgs(
   TreeNode node,
   string label
);
[C++]
public: NodeLabelEditEventArgs(
   TreeNode* node,
   String* label
);
[JScript]
public function NodeLabelEditEventArgs(
   node : TreeNode,
   label : String
);
```

Parameters

node

The tree node containing the text to edit.

label

The new text to associate with the tree node.

Remarks

The **Node** property is assigned the *node* parameter value, and the **Label** property is assigned the *label* parameter value.

Requirements

Platforms: Windows 98, Windows NT 4.0, Windows Millennium Edition, Windows 2000, Windows XP Home Edition, Windows XP Professional, Windows Server 2003 family

NodeLabelEditEventArgs.CancelEdit Property

Gets or sets a value indicating whether the edit has been canceled.

```
[Visual Basic]
Public Property CancelEdit As Boolean
[C#]
public bool CancelEdit {get; set;}
[C++]
public: __property bool get_CancelEdit();
public: __property void set_CancelEdit(bool);
[JScript]
public function get CancelEdit() : Boolean;
public function set CancelEdit(Boolean);
```

Property Value

true if the edit has been canceled; otherwise, **false**.

Example

See related example in the **System.Windows.Forms.NodeLabelEditEventArgs** class topic.

Requirements

Platforms: Windows 98, Windows NT 4.0, Windows Millennium Edition, Windows 2000, Windows XP Home Edition, Windows XP Professional, Windows Server 2003 family

NodeLabelEditEventArgs.Label Property

Gets the new text to associate with the tree node.

```
[Visual Basic]
Public ReadOnly Property Label As String
[C#]
public string Label {get;}
[C++]
public: __property String* get_Label();
[JScript]
public function get Label() : String;
```

Property Value

The string value that represents the **TreeNode** label.

Example

See related example in the **System.Windows.Forms.NodeLabelEditEventArgs** class topic.

Requirements

Platforms: Windows 98, Windows NT 4.0, Windows Millennium Edition, Windows 2000, Windows XP Home Edition, Windows XP Professional, Windows Server 2003 family

NodeLabelEditEventArgs.Node Property

Gets the tree node containing the text to edit.

```
[Visual Basic]
Public ReadOnly Property Node As TreeNode
[C#]
public TreeNode Node {get;}
[C++]
public: __property TreeNode* get_Node();
[JScript]
public function get Node() : TreeNode;
```

Property Value

A **TreeNode** that represents the tree node containing the text to edit.

Example

See related example in the **System.Windows.Forms.NodeLabelEditEventArgs** class topic.

Requirements

Platforms: Windows 98, Windows NT 4.0, Windows Millennium Edition, Windows 2000, Windows XP Home Edition, Windows XP Professional, Windows Server 2003 family

NodeLabelEditEventHandler Delegate

Represents the method that will handle the **BeforeLabelEdit** and **AfterLabelEdit** events of a **TreeView** control.

[Visual Basic]
```
<Serializable>
Public Delegate Sub NodeLabelEditEventHandler( _
   ByVal sender As Object, _
   ByVal e As NodeLabelEditEventArgs _
)
```
[C#]
```
[Serializable]
public delegate void NodeLabelEditEventHandler(
   object sender,
   NodeLabelEditEventArgs e
);
```
[C++]
```
[Serializable]
public __gc __delegate void NodeLabelEditEventHandler(
   Object* sender,
   NodeLabelEditEventArgs* e
);
```

[JScript] In JScript, you can use the delegates in the .NET Framework, but you cannot define your own.

Parameters [Visual Basic, C#, C++]

The declaration of your event handler must have the same parameters as the **NodeLabelEditEventHandler** delegate declaration.

sender
: The source of the event.

e
: A **NodeLabelEditEventArgs** that contains the event data.

Remarks

When you create a **NodeLabelEditEventArgs** delegate, you identify the method that will handle the event. To associate the event with your event handler, add an instance of the delegate to the event. The event handler is called whenever the event occurs, unless you remove the delegate.

Requirements

Namespace: System.Windows.Forms

Platforms: Windows 98, Windows NT 4.0, Windows Millennium Edition, Windows 2000, Windows XP Home Edition, Windows XP Professional, Windows Server 2003 family

Assembly: System.Windows.Forms (in System.Windows.Forms.dll)

NotifyIcon Class

Specifies a component that creates an icon in the status area. This class cannot be inherited.

System.Object
  System.MarshalByRefObject
    System.ComponentModel.Component
      System.Windows.Forms.NotifyIcon

[Visual Basic]
```
NotInheritable Public Class NotifyIcon
   Inherits Component
```
[C#]
```
public sealed class NotifyIcon : Component
```
[C++]
```
public __gc __sealed class NotifyIcon : public Component
```
[JScript]
```
public class NotifyIcon extends Component
```

Thread Safety

Any public static (**Shared** in Visual Basic) members of this type are safe for multithreaded operations. Any instance members are not guaranteed to be thread safe.

Remarks

Icons in the status area are short cuts to processes that are running in the background of a computer, such as a virus protection program or a volume control. These processes do not come with their own user interfaces. The **NotifyIcon** class provides a way to program in this functionality. The **Icon** property defines the icon that appears in the status area. Pop-up menus for an icon are addressed with the **ContextMenu** property. The **Text** property assigns ToolTip text. In order for the icon to show up in the status area, the **Visible** property must be set to **true**.

Example

[Visual Basic, C#, C++] The following example demonstrates using the **NotifyIcon** class to display an icon for an application in the notification area. The example demonstrates setting the **Icon**, **ContextMenu**, **Text** and **Visible** properties and handling the **DoubleClick** event. A **ContextMenu** with a **Exit** item on it is assigned to the **NotifyIcon.ContextMenu** property that allows the user to close the application. When the NotifyIcon. **DoubleClick** event occurs, the application form is activated by calling the **Form.Activate** method.

[Visual Basic]
```
Imports System
Imports System.Drawing
Imports System.Windows.Forms

Public NotInheritable Class Form1
    Inherits System.Windows.Forms.Form

    Private contextMenu1 As System.Windows.Forms.ContextMenu
    Friend WithEvents menuItem1 As System.Windows.Forms.MenuItem
    Friend WithEvents notifyIcon1 As System.Windows.Forms.NotifyIcon
    Private components As System.ComponentModel.IContainer

    <System.STAThread()> _
    Public Shared Sub Main()
        System.Windows.Forms.Application.Run(New Form1)
    End Sub 'Main

    Public Sub New()

        Me.components = New System.ComponentModel.Container
        Me.contextMenu1 = New System.Windows.Forms.ContextMenu
        Me.menuItem1 = New System.Windows.Forms.MenuItem

        ' Initialize contextMenu1
        Me.contextMenu1.MenuItems.AddRange(New System.Windows.Forms.MenuItem() _
                            {Me.menuItem1})

        ' Initialize menuItem1
        Me.menuItem1.Index = 0
        Me.menuItem1.Text = "E&xit"

        ' Set up how the form should be displayed.
        Me.AutoScaleBaseSize = New System.Drawing.Size(5, 13)
        Me.ClientSize = New System.Drawing.Size(292, 266)
        Me.Text = "Notify Icon Example"

        ' Create the NotifyIcon.
        Me.notifyIcon1 = New System.Windows.Forms.NotifyIcon(Me.components)

        ' The Icon property sets the icon that will appear
        ' in the systray for this application.
        notifyIcon1.Icon = New Icon("appicon.ico")

        ' The ContextMenu property sets the menu that will
        ' appear when the systray icon is right clicked.
        notifyIcon1.ContextMenu = Me.contextMenu1

        ' The Text property sets the text that will be displayed,
        ' in a tooltip, when the mouse hovers over the systray icon.
        notifyIcon1.Text = "Form1 (NotifyIcon example)"
        notifyIcon1.Visible = True
    End Sub 'New

    Protected Overloads Overrides Sub Dispose(ByVal disposing As Boolean)
        ' Clean up any components being used.
        If disposing Then
            If Not (components Is Nothing) Then
                components.Dispose()
            End If
        End If
        MyBase.Dispose(disposing)
    End Sub 'Dispose

    Private Sub notifyIcon1_DoubleClick(Sender as object, e as EventArgs) handles notifyIcon1.DoubleClick
        ' Show the form when the user double clicks on the notify icon.

        ' Set the WindowState to normal if the form is minimized.
        if (me.WindowState = FormWindowState.Minimized) then _
            me.WindowState = FormWindowState.Normal

        ' Activate the form.
        me.Activate()
    end sub

    Private Sub menuItem1_Click(Sender as object, e as EventArgs) handles menuItem1.Click
        ' Close the form, which closes the application.
        me.Close()
    end sub

End Class 'Form1
```

[C#]
```
using System;
using System.Drawing;
using System.Windows.Forms;

public class Form1 : System.Windows.Forms.Form
{
    private System.Windows.Forms.NotifyIcon notifyIcon1;
```

```
    private System.Windows.Forms.ContextMenu contextMenu1;
    private System.Windows.Forms.MenuItem menuItem1;
    private System.ComponentModel.IContainer components;

    [STAThread]
    static void Main()
    {
        Application.Run(new Form1());
    }

    public Form1()
    {
        this.components = new System.ComponentModel.Container();
        this.contextMenu1 = new System.Windows.Forms.ContextMenu();
        this.menuItem1 = new System.Windows.Forms.MenuItem();

        // Initialize contextMenu1
        this.contextMenu1.MenuItems.AddRange(
                    new System.Windows.Forms.MenuItem[]                    ↵
{this.menuItem1});

        // Initialize menuItem1
        this.menuItem1.Index = 0;
        this.menuItem1.Text = "E&xit";
        this.menuItem1.Click += new
System.EventHandler(this.menuItem1_Click);

        // Set up how the form should be displayed.
        this.ClientSize = new System.Drawing.Size(292, 266);
        this.Text = "Notify Icon Example";

        // Create the NotifyIcon.
        this.notifyIcon1 = new                                              ↵
System.Windows.Forms.NotifyIcon(this.components);

        // The Icon property sets the icon that will appear
        // in the systray for this application.
        notifyIcon1.Icon = new Icon("appicon.ico");

        // The ContextMenu property sets the menu that will
        // appear when the systray icon is right clicked.
        notifyIcon1.ContextMenu = this.contextMenu1;

        // The Text property sets the text that will be displayed,
        // in a tooltip, when the mouse hovers over the systray icon.
        notifyIcon1.Text = "Form1 (NotifyIcon example)";
        notifyIcon1.Visible = true;

        // Handle the DoubleClick event to activate the form.
        notifyIcon1.DoubleClick += new                                      ↵
System.EventHandler(this.notifyIcon1_DoubleClick);

    }

    protected override void Dispose( bool disposing )
    {
        // Clean up any components being used.
        if( disposing )
            if (components != null)
                components.Dispose();

        base.Dispose( disposing );
    }

    private void notifyIcon1_DoubleClick(object Sender, EventArgs e)
    {
        // Show the form when the user double clicks on the                  ↵
notify icon.

        // Set the WindowState to normal if the form is minimized.
        if (this.WindowState == FormWindowState.Minimized)
            this.WindowState = FormWindowState.Normal;

        // Activate the form.
        this.Activate();
    }

    private void menuItem1_Click(object Sender, EventArgs e) {
        // Close the form, which closes the application.
        this.Close();
    }
}
```

[C++]

```
#using <mscorlib.dll>
#using <System.dll>
#using <System.Windows.Forms.dll>
#using <System.Drawing.dll>

using namespace System;
using namespace System::Drawing;
using namespace System::Windows::Forms;

public __gc class Form1 : public System::Windows::Forms::Form {
private:
   System::Windows::Forms::NotifyIcon*  notifyIcon1;
   System::Windows::Forms::ContextMenu*  contextMenu1;
   System::Windows::Forms::MenuItem*  menuItem1;
   System::ComponentModel::IContainer*  components;

public:
   Form1() {
      this->components = new System::ComponentModel::Container();
      this->contextMenu1 = new System::Windows::Forms::ContextMenu();
      this->menuItem1 = new System::Windows::Forms::MenuItem();

      // Initialize contextMenu1

      System::Windows::Forms::MenuItem* temp0 [] = {this->menuItem1};

      this->contextMenu1->MenuItems->AddRange(temp0);

      // Initialize menuItem1
      this->menuItem1->Index = 0;
      this->menuItem1->Text = S"E&xit";
      this->menuItem1->Click += new System::EventHandler(this,             ↵
menuItem1_Click);

      // Set up how the form should be displayed.
      this->ClientSize =  System::Drawing::Size(292, 266);
      this->Text = S"Notify Icon Example";

      // Create the NotifyIcon.
      this->notifyIcon1 = new                                              ↵
System::Windows::Forms::NotifyIcon(this->components);

      // The Icon property sets the icon that will appear
      // in the systray for this application.
      notifyIcon1->Icon = new System::Drawing::Icon(S"appicon.ico");

      // The ContextMenu property sets the menu that will
      // appear when the systray icon is right clicked.
      notifyIcon1->ContextMenu = this->contextMenu1;

      // The Text property sets the text that will be displayed,
      // in a tooltip, when the mouse hovers over the systray icon.
      notifyIcon1->Text = S"Form1 (NotifyIcon example)";
      notifyIcon1->Visible = true;

      // Handle the DoubleClick event to activate the form.
      notifyIcon1->DoubleClick += new System::EventHandler                 ↵
 (this, notifyIcon1_DoubleClick);

   }

protected:
   void Dispose(bool disposing) {
      // Clean up any components being used.
```

```
      if (disposing)
         if (components != 0)
            components->Dispose();

      Form::Dispose(disposing);
   }

private:
   void notifyIcon1_DoubleClick(Object* Sender, EventArgs* e) {
      // Show the form when the user double clicks on the notify icon.

      // Set the WindowState to normal if the form is minimized.
      if (this->WindowState == FormWindowState::Minimized)
         this->WindowState = FormWindowState::Normal;

      // Activate the form.
      this->Activate();
   }

private:
   void menuItem1_Click(Object* Sender, EventArgs* e) {
      // Close the form, which closes the application.
      this->Close();
   }
};

[STAThread]
int main() {
   Application::Run(new Form1());
}
```

Requirements

Namespace: System.Windows.Forms

Platforms: Windows 98, Windows NT 4.0, Windows Millennium Edition, Windows 2000, Windows XP Home Edition, Windows XP Professional, Windows Server 2003 family

Assembly: System.Windows.Forms (in System.Windows.Forms.dll)

.NET Framework Security:

- **UIPermission** to create the **NotifyIcon** component. Associated enumeration: **UIPermissionWindow.AllWindows**

NotifyIcon Constructor

Initializes a new instance of the **NotifyIcon** class.

Overload List

Initializes a new instance of the **NotifyIcon** class.

[Visual Basic] **Public Sub New()**

[C#] **public NotifyIcon();**

[C++] **public: NotifyIcon();**

[JScript] **public function NotifyIcon();**

Initializes a new instance of the **NotifyIcon** class with the specified container.

[Visual Basic] **Public Sub New(IContainer)**

[C#] **public NotifyIcon(IContainer);**

[C++] **public: NotifyIcon(IContainer*);**

[JScript] **public function NotifyIcon(IContainer);**

Example

See related example in the **System.Windows.Forms.NotifyIcon** class topic.

NotifyIcon Constructor ()

Initializes a new instance of the **NotifyIcon** class.

[Visual Basic]
```
Public Sub New()
```
[C#]
```
public NotifyIcon();
```
[C++]
```
public: NotifyIcon();
```
[JScript]
```
public function NotifyIcon();
```

Remarks

When a new **NotifyIcon** is created, the **Visible** property is set to **false.** You must set the **Visible** property to **true** in order to use the **NotifyIcon** you created. This instance will exist until its container releases it to garbage collection.

Requirements

Platforms: Windows 98, Windows NT 4.0, Windows Millennium Edition, Windows 2000, Windows XP Home Edition, Windows XP Professional, Windows Server 2003 family

NotifyIcon Constructor (IContainer)

Initializes a new instance of the **NotifyIcon** class with the specified container.

[Visual Basic]
```
Public Sub New( _
   ByVal container As IContainer _
)
```
[C#]
```
public NotifyIcon(
   IContainer container
);
```
[C++]
```
public: NotifyIcon(
   IContainer* container
);
```
[JScript]
```
public function NotifyIcon(
   container : IContainer
);
```

Parameters

container

An **IContainer** that represents the container for the **NotifyIcon** control.

Remarks

When a new **NotifyIcon** is created, the **Visible** property is set to **false.** You must set the **Visible** property to **true** in order to use the **NotifyIcon** you created. This instance will exist until its container releases it to garbage collection.

Example

See related example in the **System.Windows.Forms.NotifyIcon** class topic.

Requirements

Platforms: Windows 98, Windows NT 4.0, Windows Millennium Edition, Windows 2000, Windows XP Home Edition, Windows XP Professional, Windows Server 2003 family

NotifyIcon.ContextMenu Property

Gets or sets the shortcut menu for the icon.

```
[Visual Basic]
Public Property ContextMenu As ContextMenu
[C#]
public ContextMenu ContextMenu {get; set;}
[C++]
public: __property ContextMenu* get_ContextMenu();
public: __property void set_ContextMenu(ContextMenu*);
[JScript]
public function get ContextMenu() : ContextMenu;
public function set ContextMenu(ContextMenu);
```

Property Value

The **ContextMenu** for the icon. The default value is a null reference (**Nothing** in Visual Basic).

Remarks

The menu is shown when a right-mouse click is performed on an icon in the status notification area of the taskbar. Shortcut menus also are known as pop-up menus.

Example

See related example in the **System.Windows.Forms.NotifyIcon** class topic.

Requirements

Platforms: Windows 98, Windows NT 4.0, Windows Millennium Edition, Windows 2000, Windows XP Home Edition, Windows XP Professional, Windows Server 2003 family

NotifyIcon.Icon Property

Gets or sets the current icon.

```
[Visual Basic]
Public Property Icon As Icon
[C#]
public Icon Icon {get; set;}
[C++]
public: __property Icon* get_Icon();
public: __property void set_Icon(Icon*);
[JScript]
public function get Icon() : Icon;
public function set Icon(Icon);
```

Property Value

The **Icon** displayed by the **NotifyIcon** component. The default value is a null reference (**Nothing** in Visual Basic).

Example

See related example in the **System.Windows.Forms.NotifyIcon** class topic.

Requirements

Platforms: Windows 98, Windows NT 4.0, Windows Millennium Edition, Windows 2000, Windows XP Home Edition, Windows XP Professional, Windows Server 2003 family

NotifyIcon.Text Property

Gets or sets the ToolTip text displayed when the mouse hovers over a status area icon.

```
[Visual Basic]
Public Property Text As String
[C#]
public string Text {get; set;}
[C++]
public: __property String* get_Text();
public: __property void set_Text(String*);
[JScript]
public function get Text() : String;
public function set Text(String);
```

Property Value

The ToolTip text displayed when the mouse hovers over a status area icon.

Exceptions

Exception Type	Condition
ArgumentException	ToolTip text must be less than 64 characters long.

Remarks

If the text is a null reference (**Nothing** in Visual Basic), no ToolTip is displayed.

Example

See related example in the **System.Windows.Forms.NotifyIcon** class topic.

Requirements

Platforms: Windows 98, Windows NT 4.0, Windows Millennium Edition, Windows 2000, Windows XP Home Edition, Windows XP Professional, Windows Server 2003 family

NotifyIcon.Visible Property

Gets or sets a value indicating whether the icon is visible in the status notification area of the taskbar.

```
[Visual Basic]
Public Property Visible As Boolean
[C#]
public bool Visible {get; set;}
[C++]
public: __property bool get_Visible();
public: __property void set_Visible(bool);
[JScript]
public function get Visible() : Boolean;
public function set Visible(Boolean);
```

Property Value

true if the icon is visible in the status area; otherwise, **false**. The default value is **false**.

Remarks

Since the default value is **false**, in order for the icon to show up in the status area, you must set the **Visible** property to **true**.

Example

See related example in the **System.Windows.Forms.NotifyIcon** class topic.

Requirements

Platforms: Windows 98, Windows NT 4.0, Windows Millennium Edition, Windows 2000, Windows XP Home Edition, Windows XP Professional, Windows Server 2003 family

NotifyIcon.Dispose Method

Overload List

This member supports the .NET Framework infrastructure and is not intended to be used directly from your code.

[Visual Basic] **Overloads Overrides Protected Sub Dispose(Boolean)**

[C#] **protected override void Dispose(bool);**

[C++] **protected: void Dispose(bool);**

[JScript] **protected override function Dispose(Boolean);**

Inherited from **Component**.

[Visual Basic] **Overloads Public Overridable Sub Dispose() Implements IDisposable.Dispose**

[C#] **public virtual void Dispose();**

[C++] **public: virtual void Dispose();**

[JScript] **public function Dispose();**

NotifyIcon.Dispose Method (Boolean)

This member overrides **Component.Dispose**.

[Visual Basic]
```
Overrides Overloads Protected Sub Dispose( _
   ByVal disposing As Boolean _
)
```
[C#]
```
protected override void Dispose(
   bool disposing
);
```
[C++]
```
protected: void Dispose(
   bool disposing
);
```
[JScript]
```
protected override function Dispose(
   disposing : Boolean
);
```

Requirements

Platforms: Windows 98, Windows NT 4.0, Windows Millennium Edition, Windows 2000, Windows XP Home Edition, Windows XP Professional, Windows Server 2003 family

NotifyIcon.Click Event

Occurs when the user clicks the icon in the status area.

[Visual Basic]
```
Public Event Click As EventHandler
```
[C#]
```
public event EventHandler Click;
```
[C++]
```
public: __event EventHandler* Click;
```

[JScript] In JScript, you can handle the events defined by a class, but you cannot define your own.

Event Data

The event handler receives an argument of type **EventArgs**.

Requirements

Platforms: Windows 98, Windows NT 4.0, Windows Millennium Edition, Windows 2000, Windows XP Home Edition, Windows XP Professional, Windows Server 2003 family

NotifyIcon.DoubleClick Event

Occurs when the user double-clicks the icon in the status notification area of the taskbar.

[Visual Basic]
```
Public Event DoubleClick As EventHandler
```
[C#]
```
public event EventHandler DoubleClick;
```
[C++]
```
public: __event EventHandler* DoubleClick;
```

[JScript] In JScript, you can handle the events defined by a class, but you cannot define your own.

Event Data

The event handler receives an argument of type **EventArgs**.

Example

See related example in the **System.Windows.Forms.NotifyIcon** class topic.

Requirements

Platforms: Windows 98, Windows NT 4.0, Windows Millennium Edition, Windows 2000, Windows XP Home Edition, Windows XP Professional, Windows Server 2003 family

NotifyIcon.MouseDown Event

Occurs when the user presses the mouse button while the pointer is over the icon in the status notification area of the taskbar.

[Visual Basic]
```
Public Event MouseDown As MouseEventHandler
```
[C#]
```
public event MouseEventHandler MouseDown;
```
[C++]
```
public: __event MouseEventHandler* MouseDown;
```

[JScript] In JScript, you can handle the events defined by a class, but you cannot define your own.

Event Data

The event handler receives an argument of type **MouseEventArgs** containing data related to this event. The following **MouseEventArgs** properties provide information specific to this event.

Property	Description
Button	Gets which mouse button was pressed.
Clicks	Gets the number of times the mouse button was pressed and released.
Delta	Gets a signed count of the number of detents the mouse wheel has rotated. A detent is one notch of the mouse wheel.
X	Gets the x-coordinate of the mouse.
Y	Gets the y-coordinate of the mouse.

Requirements

Platforms: Windows 98, Windows NT 4.0, Windows Millennium Edition, Windows 2000, Windows XP Home Edition, Windows XP Professional, Windows Server 2003 family

NotifyIcon.MouseMove Event

Occurs when the user moves the mouse while the pointer is over the icon in the status notification area of the taskbar.

[Visual Basic]
```
Public Event MouseMove As MouseEventHandler
```
[C#]
```
public event MouseEventHandler MouseMove;
```
[C++]
```
public: __event MouseEventHandler* MouseMove;
```

[JScript] In JScript, you can handle the events defined by a class, but you cannot define your own.

Event Data

The event handler receives an argument of type **MouseEventArgs** containing data related to this event. The following **MouseEventArgs** properties provide information specific to this event.

Property	Description
Button	Gets which mouse button was pressed.
Clicks	Gets the number of times the mouse button was pressed and released.
Delta	Gets a signed count of the number of detents the mouse wheel has rotated. A detent is one notch of the mouse wheel.
X	Gets the x-coordinate of the mouse.
Y	Gets the y-coordinate of the mouse.

Requirements

Platforms: Windows 98, Windows NT 4.0, Windows Millennium Edition, Windows 2000, Windows XP Home Edition, Windows XP Professional, Windows Server 2003 family

NotifyIcon.MouseUp Event

Occurs when the user releases the mouse button while the pointer is over the icon in the status notification area of the taskbar.

[Visual Basic]
```
Public Event MouseUp As MouseEventHandler
```
[C#]
```
public event MouseEventHandler MouseUp;
```
[C++]
```
public: __event MouseEventHandler* MouseUp;
```

[JScript] In JScript, you can handle the events defined by a class, but you cannot define your own.

Event Data

The event handler receives an argument of type **MouseEventArgs** containing data related to this event. The following **MouseEventArgs** properties provide information specific to this event.

Property	Description
Button	Gets which mouse button was pressed.
Clicks	Gets the number of times the mouse button was pressed and released.
Delta	Gets a signed count of the number of detents the mouse wheel has rotated. A detent is one notch of the mouse wheel.
X	Gets the x-coordinate of the mouse.
Y	Gets the y-coordinate of the mouse.

Requirements

Platforms: Windows 98, Windows NT 4.0, Windows Millennium Edition, Windows 2000, Windows XP Home Edition, Windows XP Professional, Windows Server 2003 family

NumericUpDown Class

Represents a Windows up-down control that displays numeric values.

System.Object
  System.MarshalByRefObject
    System.ComponentModel.Component
      System.Windows.Forms.Control
        System.Windows.Forms.ScrollableControl
          System.Windows.Forms.ContainerControl
            System.Windows.Forms.UpDownBase
              System.Windows.Forms.NumericUpDown

[Visual Basic]
```
Public Class NumericUpDown
   Inherits UpDownBase
   Implements ISupportInitialize
```
[C#]
```
public class NumericUpDown : UpDownBase, ISupportInitialize
```
[C++]
```
public __gc class NumericUpDown : public UpDownBase,
   ISupportInitialize
```
[JScript]
```
public class NumericUpDown extends UpDownBase implements
   ISupportInitialize
```

Thread Safety

Any public static (**Shared** in Visual Basic) members of this type are safe for multithreaded operations. Any instance members are not guaranteed to be thread safe.

Remarks

A **NumericUpDown** control contains a single numeric value that can be incremented or decremented by clicking the up or down buttons of the control. The user can also enter in a value, unless the **ReadOnly** property is set to **true**.

The numeric display can be formatted by setting the **DecimalPlaces**, **Hexadecimal**, or **ThousandsSeparator** properties. To display hexadecimal values in the control, set the **Hexadecimal** property to **true**. To display a thousands separator in decimal numbers when appropriate, set the **ThousandsSeparator** property to **true**. To specify the number of digits displayed after the decimal symbol, set the **DecimalPlaces** property to the number of decimal places to display.

To specify the allowable range of values for the control, set the **Minimum** and **Maximum** properties. Set the **Increment** value to specify the value to be incremented or decremented to the **Value** property when the user clicks the up or down arrow buttons.

When the **UpButton** or **DownButton** methods are called, either in code or by the click of the up or down buttons, the new value is validated and the control is updated with the new value in the appropriate format. Specifically, if **UserEdit** is set to **true**, **ParseEditText** is called prior to validating or updating the value. The value is then verified to be between the **Minimum** and **Maximum** values and the **UpdateEditText** method is called.

Example

[Visual Basic, C#, JScript] The following example creates and initializes a **NumericUpDown** control, sets some of its common properties, and allows the user to change some of these properties at run time. This code assumes three **CheckBox** controls have been placed on a form and handlers for their **Click** events have been instantiated. The **DecimalPlaces**, **ThousandsSeparator** and **Hexadecimal** properties are set on the **Click** event of each check box.

[Visual Basic]
```
Public Sub InstantiateMyNumericUpDown()
    ' Create and initialize a NumericUpDown control.
    numericUpDown1 = New NumericUpDown()

    ' Dock the control to the top of the form.
    numericUpDown1.Dock = System.Windows.Forms.DockStyle.Top

    ' Set the Minimum, Maximum, and initial Value.
    numericUpDown1.Value = 5
    numericUpDown1.Maximum = 2500
    numericUpDown1.Minimum = - 100

    ' Add the NumericUpDown to the Form.
    Controls.Add(numericUpDown1)
End Sub

' Check box to toggle decimal places to be displayed.
Private Sub checkBox1_Click(sender As Object, e As EventArgs)
    ' If DecimalPlaces is greater than 0, set them to 0 and round the
    ' current Value; otherwise, set DecimalPlaces to 2 and change the
    ' Increment to 0.25.
    If numericUpDown1.DecimalPlaces > 0 Then
        numericUpDown1.DecimalPlaces = 0
        numericUpDown1.Value = Decimal.Round(numericUpDown1.Value, 0)
    Else
        numericUpDown1.DecimalPlaces = 2
        numericUpDown1.Increment = 0.25D
    End If
End Sub

' Check box to toggle thousands separators to be displayed.
Private Sub checkBox2_Click(sender As Object, e As EventArgs)
    ' If ThousandsSeparator is true, set it to false;
    ' otherwise, set it to true.
    If numericUpDown1.ThousandsSeparator Then
        numericUpDown1.ThousandsSeparator = False
    Else
        numericUpDown1.ThousandsSeparator = True
    End If
End Sub

' Check box to toggle hexadecimal to be displayed.
Private Sub checkBox3_Click(sender As Object, e As EventArgs)
    ' If Hexadecimal is true, set it to false;
    ' otherwise, set it to true.
    If numericUpDown1.Hexadecimal Then
        numericUpDown1.Hexadecimal = False
    Else
        numericUpDown1.Hexadecimal = True
    End If
End Sub
```

[C#]
```
public void InstantiateMyNumericUpDown()
{
   // Create and initialize a NumericUpDown control.
   numericUpDown1 = new NumericUpDown();

   // Dock the control to the top of the form.
   numericUpDown1.Dock = System.Windows.Forms.DockStyle.Top;

   // Set the Minimum, Maximum, and initial Value.
   numericUpDown1.Value = 5;
   numericUpDown1.Maximum = 2500;
   numericUpDown1.Minimum = -100;

   // Add the NumericUpDown to the Form.
   Controls.Add(numericUpDown1);
}

// Check box to toggle decimal places to be displayed.
private void checkBox1_Click(Object sender,
                             EventArgs e)
{
   /* If DecimalPlaces is greater than 0, set them to 0 and round the
```

```
      current Value; otherwise, set DecimalPlaces to 2 and change the
      Increment to 0.25. */
   if (numericUpDown1.DecimalPlaces > 0)
   {
      numericUpDown1.DecimalPlaces = 0;
      numericUpDown1.Value = Decimal.Round(numericUpDown1.Value, 0);
   }
   else
   {
      numericUpDown1.DecimalPlaces = 2;
      numericUpDown1.Increment = 0.25M;
   }
}

// Check box to toggle thousands separators to be displayed.
private void checkBox2_Click(Object sender,
                             EventArgs e)
{
   /* If ThousandsSeparator is true, set it to false;
      otherwise, set it to true. */
   if (numericUpDown1.ThousandsSeparator)
   {
      numericUpDown1.ThousandsSeparator = false;
   }
   else
   {
      numericUpDown1.ThousandsSeparator = true;
   }
}

// Check box to toggle hexadecimal to be displayed.
private void checkBox3_Click(Object sender,
                             EventArgs e)
{
   /* If Hexadecimal is true, set it to false;
      otherwise, set it to true. */
   if (numericUpDown1.Hexadecimal)
   {
      numericUpDown1.Hexadecimal = false;
   }
   else
   {
      numericUpDown1.Hexadecimal = true;
   }
}
```

[JScript]

```
function InstantiateMyNumericUpDown(){
  // Create and initialize a NumericUpDown control.
  numericUpDown1 = new NumericUpDown()

  // Dock the control to the top of the form.
  numericUpDown1.Dock = System.Windows.Forms.DockStyle.Top

  // Set the Minimum, Maximum, and initial Value.
  numericUpDown1.Value = 5
  numericUpDown1.Maximum = 2500
  numericUpDown1.Minimum = - 100

  // Add the NumericUpDown to the Form.
  Controls.Add(numericUpDown1)
}

// Check box to toggle decimal places to be displayed.
function checkBox1_Click(sender : Object, e : EventArgs){
  // If DecimalPlaces is greater than 0, set them to 0 and round the
  // current Value; otherwise, set DecimalPlaces to 2 and change the
  // Increment to 0.25.
  if(numericUpDown1.DecimalPlaces > 0){
    numericUpDown1.DecimalPlaces = 0
    numericUpDown1.Value = Decimal.Round(numericUpDown1.Value, 0)
  }else{
    numericUpDown1.DecimalPlaces = 2
    numericUpDown1.Increment = 0.25
  }
}

// Check box to toggle thousands separators to be displayed.
function checkBox2_Click(sender : Object, e : EventArgs){
  // If ThousandsSeparator is true, set it to false;
  // otherwise, set it to true.
  numericUpDown1.ThousandsSeparator = !numericUpDown1.ThousandsSeparator
}

// Check box to toggle hexadecimal to be displayed.
function checkBox3_Click(sender : Object, e : EventArgs){
  // If Hexadecimal is true, set it to false;
  // otherwise, set it to true.
  numericUpDown1.Hexadecimal = !numericUpDown1.Hexadecimal
}
```

Requirements

Namespace: System.Windows.Forms

Platforms: Windows 98, Windows NT 4.0, Windows Millennium Edition, Windows 2000, Windows XP Home Edition, Windows XP Professional, Windows Server 2003 family, .NET Compact Framework - Windows CE .NET

Assembly: System.Windows.Forms (in System.Windows.Forms.dll)

NumericUpDown Constructor

Initializes a new instance of the **NumericUpDown** class.

[Visual Basic]
```
Public Sub New()
```
[C#]
```
public NumericUpDown();
```
[C++]
```
public: NumericUpDown();
```
[JScript]
```
public function NumericUpDown();
```

Example

See related example in the **System.Windows.Forms.NumericUpDown** class topic.

Requirements

Platforms: Windows 98, Windows NT 4.0, Windows Millennium Edition, Windows 2000, Windows XP Home Edition, Windows XP Professional, Windows Server 2003 family, .NET Compact Framework - Windows CE .NET

NumericUpDown.DecimalPlaces Property

Gets or sets the number of decimal places to display in the up-down control.

[Visual Basic]
```
Public Property DecimalPlaces As Integer
```
[C#]
```
public int DecimalPlaces {get; set;}
```
[C++]
```
public: __property int get_DecimalPlaces();
public: __property void set_DecimalPlaces(int);
```
[JScript]
```
public function get DecimalPlaces() : int;
public function set DecimalPlaces(int);
```

Property Value

The number of decimal places to display in the up-down control. The default value is zero.

Exceptions

Exception Type	Condition
ArgumentException	The value assigned is less than 0. -or- The value assigned is greater than 99.

Remarks

When the **DecimalPlaces** property is set, the **UpdateEditText** method is called to update the up-down control's display to the new format.

The appropriate decimal symbol is determined by the regional settings of the user's operating system.

Example

See related example in the **System.Windows.Forms.NumericUp-Down** class topic.

Requirements

Platforms: Windows 98, Windows NT 4.0,
Windows Millennium Edition, Windows 2000,
Windows XP Home Edition, Windows XP Professional,
Windows Server 2003 family

NumericUpDown.Hexadecimal Property

Gets or sets a value indicating whether the up-down control should display the value it contains in hexadecimal format.

```
[Visual Basic]
Public Property Hexadecimal As Boolean
[C#]
public bool Hexadecimal {get; set;}
[C++]
public: __property bool get_Hexadecimal();
public: __property void set_Hexadecimal(bool);
[JScript]
public function get Hexadecimal() : Boolean;
public function set Hexadecimal(Boolean);
```

Property Value

true if the up-down control should display its value in hexadecimal format; otherwise, **false**. The default value is **false**.

Remarks

When the **Hexadecimal** property is set, the **UpdateEditText** method is called to update the up-down control's display to the new format.

Example

See related example in the **System.Windows.Forms.NumericUp-Down** class topic.

Requirements

Platforms: Windows 98, Windows NT 4.0,
Windows Millennium Edition, Windows 2000,
Windows XP Home Edition, Windows XP Professional,
Windows Server 2003 family

NumericUpDown.Increment Property

Gets or sets the value to increment or decrement the up-down control when the up or down buttons are clicked.

```
[Visual Basic]
Public Property Increment As Decimal
[C#]
public decimal Increment {get; set;}
[C++]
public: __property Decimal get_Increment();
public: __property void set_Increment(Decimal);
[JScript]
public function get Increment() : Decimal;
public function set Increment(Decimal);
```

Property Value

The value to increment or decrement the **Value** property when the up or down buttons are clicked on the up-down control. The default value is 1.

Exceptions

Exception Type	Condition
ArgumentException	The assigned value is not a positive number.

Remarks

Clicking the up button causes the **Value** property to increment by the amount specified by the **Increment** property and approach the **Maximum** property. Clicking the down button causes the **Value** property to be decremented by the amount specified by the **Increment** property and approach the **Minimum** property.

Example

See related example in the **System.Windows.Forms.NumericUp-Down** class topic.

Requirements

Platforms: Windows 98, Windows NT 4.0,
Windows Millennium Edition, Windows 2000,
Windows XP Home Edition, Windows XP Professional,
Windows Server 2003 family,
.NET Compact Framework - Windows CE .NET

NumericUpDown.Maximum Property

Gets or sets the maximum value for the up-down control.

```
[Visual Basic]
Public Property Maximum As Decimal
[C#]
public decimal Maximum {get; set;}
[C++]
public: __property Decimal get_Maximum();
public: __property void set_Maximum(Decimal);
[JScript]
public function get Maximum() : Decimal;
public function set Maximum(Decimal);
```

Property Value

The maximum value for the up-down control. The default value is 100.

Remarks

When the **Maximum** property is set, the **Minimum** property is evaluated and the **UpdateEditText** method is called. If the **Minimum** property is greater than the new **Maximum** property, the **Minimum** property value is set equal to the **Maximum** value. If the current **Value** is greater than the new **Maximum** value. the **Value** property value is set equal to the **Maximum** value.

Example

See related example in the **System.Windows.Forms.NumericUp-Down** class topic.

Requirements

Platforms: Windows 98, Windows NT 4.0, Windows Millennium Edition, Windows 2000, Windows XP Home Edition, Windows XP Professional, Windows Server 2003 family, .NET Compact Framework - Windows CE .NET

NumericUpDown.Minimum Property

Gets or sets the minimum allowed value for the up-down control.

[Visual Basic]
```
Public Property Minimum As Decimal
```
[C#]
```
public decimal Minimum {get; set;}
```
[C++]
```
public: __property Decimal get_Minimum();
public: __property void set_Minimum(Decimal);
```
[JScript]
```
public function get Minimum() : Decimal;
public function set Minimum(Decimal);
```

Property Value

The minimum allowed value for the up-down control. The default value is 0.

Remarks

When the **Minimum** property is set, the **Maximum** property is evaluated and the **UpdateEditText** method is called. If the new **Minimum** property value is greater than the **Maximum** property value, the **Maximum** value is set equal to the **Minimum** value. If the **Value** is less than the new **Minimum** value, the **Value** property is also set equal to the **Minimum** value.

Example

See related example in the **System.Windows.Forms.NumericUp-Down** class topic.

Requirements

Platforms: Windows 98, Windows NT 4.0, Windows Millennium Edition, Windows 2000, Windows XP Home Edition, Windows XP Professional, Windows Server 2003 family, .NET Compact Framework - Windows CE .NET

NumericUpDown.Text Property

This member overrides **UpDownBase.Text**.

[Visual Basic]
```
Overrides Public Property Text As String
```
[C#]
```
public override string Text {get; set;}
```
[C++]
```
public: __property String* get_Text();
public: __property void set_Text(String*);
```
[JScript]
```
public override function get Text() : String;
public override function set Text(String);
```

Requirements

Platforms: Windows 98, Windows NT 4.0, Windows Millennium Edition, Windows 2000, Windows XP Home Edition, Windows XP Professional, Windows Server 2003 family, .NET Compact Framework - Windows CE .NET

NumericUpDown.ThousandsSeparator Property

Gets or sets a value indicating whether a thousands separator is displayed in the up-down control when appropriate.

[Visual Basic]
```
Public Property ThousandsSeparator As Boolean
```
[C#]
```
public bool ThousandsSeparator {get; set;}
```
[C++]
```
public: __property bool get_ThousandsSeparator();
public: __property void set_ThousandsSeparator(bool);
```
[JScript]
```
public function get ThousandsSeparator() : Boolean;
public function set ThousandsSeparator(Boolean);
```

Property Value

true if a thousands separator is displayed in the up-down control when appropriate; otherwise, **false**. The default value is **false**.

Remarks

When the **ThousandsSeparator** property is set, the **UpdateEditText** method is called to update the up-down control's display to the new format.

The appropriate thousands separator is determined by the regional settings of the user's operating system.

Example

See related example in the **System.Windows.Forms.NumericUp-Down** class topic.

Requirements

Platforms: Windows 98, Windows NT 4.0, Windows Millennium Edition, Windows 2000, Windows XP Home Edition, Windows XP Professional, Windows Server 2003 family

NumericUpDown.Value Property

Gets or sets the value assigned to the up-down control.

[Visual Basic]
```
Public Property Value As Decimal
```
[C#]
```
public decimal Value {get; set;}
```
[C++]
```
public: __property Decimal get_Value();
public: __property void set_Value(Decimal);
```
[JScript]
```
public function get Value() : Decimal;
public function set Value(Decimal);
```

Property Value

The numeric value of the **NumericUpDown** control.

Exceptions

Exception Type	Condition
ArgumentException	The assigned value is less than the **Minimum** property value. -or- The assigned value is greater than the **Maximum** property value.

Remarks

When the **Value** property is set, the new value is validated to be between the **Minimum** and **Maximum** values. Following this, the **UpdateEditText** method is called to update the up-down control's display with the new value in the appropriate format.

Example

See related example in the **System.Windows.Forms.NumericUpDown** class topic.

Requirements

Platforms: Windows 98, Windows NT 4.0, Windows Millennium Edition, Windows 2000, Windows XP Home Edition, Windows XP Professional, Windows Server 2003 family, .NET Compact Framework - Windows CE .NET

NumericUpDown.BeginInit Method

This member supports the .NET Framework infrastructure and is not intended to be used directly from your code.

```
[Visual Basic]
Public Overridable Sub BeginInit() Implements _
   ISupportInitialize.BeginInit
[C#]
public virtual void BeginInit();
[C++]
public: virtual void BeginInit();
[JScript]
public function BeginInit();
```

NumericUpDown.CreateAccessibilityInstance Method

This member overrides **Control.CreateAccessibilityInstance**.

```
[Visual Basic]
Overrides Protected Function CreateAccessibilityInstance() As _
   AccessibleObject
[C#]
protected override AccessibleObject CreateAccessibilityInstance();
[C++]
protected: AccessibleObject* CreateAccessibilityInstance();
[JScript]
protected override function CreateAccessibilityInstance() :
   AccessibleObject;
```

Requirements

Platforms: Windows 98, Windows NT 4.0, Windows Millennium Edition, Windows 2000, Windows XP Home Edition, Windows XP Professional, Windows Server 2003 family

NumericUpDown.DownButton Method

Decrements the value of the up-down control.

```
[Visual Basic]
Overrides Public Sub DownButton()
[C#]
public override void DownButton();
[C++]
public: void DownButton();
[JScript]
public override function DownButton();
```

Remarks

When the **DownButton** method is called, either in code or by the click of the down button, the new value is validated and the control updated with the new value in the appropriate format. Specifically, if **UserEdit** is set to **true**, **ParseEditText** is called prior to validating or updating the value. The value is then validated to be between the **Minimum** and **Maximum** values and the **UpdateEditText** method is called.

Requirements

Platforms: Windows 98, Windows NT 4.0, Windows Millennium Edition, Windows 2000, Windows XP Home Edition, Windows XP Professional, Windows Server 2003 family

NumericUpDown.EndInit Method

This member supports the .NET Framework infrastructure and is not intended to be used directly from your code.

```
[Visual Basic]
Public Overridable Sub EndInit() Implements _
   ISupportInitialize.EndInit
[C#]
public virtual void EndInit();
[C++]
public: virtual void EndInit();
[JScript]
public function EndInit();
```

NumericUpDown.OnTextBoxKeyPress Method

This member overrides **UpDownBase.OnTextBoxKeyPress**.

```
[Visual Basic]
Overrides Protected Sub OnTextBoxKeyPress( _
   ByVal source As Object, _
   ByVal e As KeyPressEventArgs _
)
[C#]
protected override void OnTextBoxKeyPress(
   object source,
   KeyPressEventArgs e
);
[C++]
protected: void OnTextBoxKeyPress(
   Object* source,
   KeyPressEventArgs* e
);
```

[JScript]
```
protected override function OnTextBoxKeyPress(
   source : Object,
   e : KeyPressEventArgs
);
```

Requirements

Platforms: Windows 98, Windows NT 4.0, Windows Millennium Edition, Windows 2000, Windows XP Home Edition, Windows XP Professional, Windows Server 2003 family

NumericUpDown.OnValueChanged Method

Raises the **ValueChanged** event.

[Visual Basic]
```
Protected Overridable Sub OnValueChanged( _
   ByVal e As EventArgs _
)
```
[C#]
```
protected virtual void OnValueChanged(
   EventArgs e
);
```
[C++]
```
protected: virtual void OnValueChanged(
   EventArgs* e
);
```
[JScript]
```
protected function OnValueChanged(
   e : EventArgs
);
```

Parameters

e

An **EventArgs** that contains the event data.

Remarks

Raising an event invokes the event handler through a delegate.

The **OnValueChanged** method also allows derived classes to handle the event without attaching a delegate. This is the preferred technique for handling the event in a derived class.

Notes to Inheritors: When overriding **OnValueChanged** in a derived class, be sure to call the base class's **OnValueChanged** method so that registered delegates receive the event.

Requirements

Platforms: Windows 98, Windows NT 4.0, Windows Millennium Edition, Windows 2000, Windows XP Home Edition, Windows XP Professional, Windows Server 2003 family, .NET Compact Framework - Windows CE .NET

NumericUpDown.ParseEditText Method

Converts the text displayed in the up-down control to a numeric value and evaluates it.

[Visual Basic]
```
Protected Sub ParseEditText()
```
[C#]
```
protected void ParseEditText();
```
[C++]
```
protected: void ParseEditText();
```
[JScript]
```
protected function ParseEditText();
```

Remarks

If **UserEdit** is set to **true**, the text displayed is converted to a numeric value so it can be validated to be between the **Minimum** and **Maximum** property values.

Requirements

Platforms: Windows 98, Windows NT 4.0, Windows Millennium Edition, Windows 2000, Windows XP Home Edition, Windows XP Professional, Windows Server 2003 family

NumericUpDown.ToString Method

This member overrides **Object.ToString**.

[Visual Basic]
```
Overrides Public Function ToString() As String
```
[C#]
```
public override string ToString();
```
[C++]
```
public: String* ToString();
```
[JScript]
```
public override function ToString() : String;
```

Requirements

Platforms: Windows 98, Windows NT 4.0, Windows Millennium Edition, Windows 2000, Windows XP Home Edition, Windows XP Professional, Windows Server 2003 family, .NET Compact Framework - Windows CE .NET

NumericUpDown.UpButton Method

Increments the value of the up-down control.

[Visual Basic]
```
Overrides Public Sub UpButton()
```
[C#]
```
public override void UpButton();
```
[C++]
```
public: void UpButton();
```
[JScript]
```
public override function UpButton();
```

Remarks

When the **UpButton** method is called, either in code or by the click of the up button, the new value is validated and the control is updated with the new value in the appropriate format. Specifically, if **UserEdit** is set to **true**, **ParseEditText** is called prior to validating or updating the value. The value is then validated to be between the **Minimum** and **Maximum** values and the **UpdateEditText** method is called.

Requirements

Platforms: Windows 98, Windows NT 4.0, Windows Millennium Edition, Windows 2000, Windows XP Home Edition, Windows XP Professional, Windows Server 2003 family

NumericUpDown.UpdateEditText Method

Displays the current value of the up-down control in the appropriate format.

[Visual Basic]
```
Overrides Protected Sub UpdateEditText()
```
[C#]
```
protected override void UpdateEditText();
```
[C++]
```
protected: void UpdateEditText();
```
[JScript]
```
protected override function UpdateEditText();
```

Remarks

If the up-down control is not being initialized, the current value is validated to be between the **Minimum** and **Maximum** values and is converted to the correct format for display in the control.

Requirements

Platforms: Windows 98, Windows NT 4.0, Windows Millennium Edition, Windows 2000, Windows XP Home Edition, Windows XP Professional, Windows Server 2003 family

NumericUpDown.ValidateEditText Method

Validates and updates the text displayed in the up-down control.

[Visual Basic]
```
Overrides Protected Sub ValidateEditText()
```
[C#]
```
protected override void ValidateEditText();
```
[C++]
```
protected: void ValidateEditText();
```
[JScript]
```
protected override function ValidateEditText();
```

Remarks

The **ValidateEditText** method calls the **ParseEditText** and **UpdateEditText** methods to validate and update the display of the up-down control.

Requirements

Platforms: Windows 98, Windows NT 4.0, Windows Millennium Edition, Windows 2000, Windows XP Home Edition, Windows XP Professional, Windows Server 2003 family

NumericUpDown.TextChanged Event

This member supports the .NET Framework infrastructure and is not intended to be used directly from your code.

[Visual Basic]
```
Public Shadows Event TextChanged As EventHandler
```
[C#]
```
public new event EventHandler TextChanged;
```
[C++]
```
public: __event EventHandler* TextChanged;
```

[JScript] In JScript, you can handle the events defined by a class, but you cannot define your own.

NumericUpDown.ValueChanged Event

Occurs when the **Value** property has been changed in some way.

[Visual Basic]
```
Public Event ValueChanged As EventHandler
```
[C#]
```
public event EventHandler ValueChanged;
```
[C++]
```
public: __event EventHandler* ValueChanged;
```

[JScript] In JScript, you can handle the events defined by a class, but you cannot define your own.

Event Data

The event handler receives an argument of type **EventArgs**.

Remarks

For the **OnValueChanged** event to occur, the **Value** property can be changed in code, by the user typing in a new value, or by clicking the up or down button.

Requirements

Platforms: Windows 98, Windows NT 4.0, Windows Millennium Edition, Windows 2000, Windows XP Home Edition, Windows XP Professional, Windows Server 2003 family

OpacityConverter Class

Provides a type converter to convert opacity values to and from a string.

System.Object
  System.ComponentModel.TypeConverter
    System.Windows.Forms.OpacityConverter

```
[Visual Basic]
Public Class OpacityConverter
   Inherits TypeConverter
[C#]
public class OpacityConverter : TypeConverter
[C++]
public __gc class OpacityConverter : public TypeConverter
[JScript]
public class OpacityConverter extends TypeConverter
```

Thread Safety

Any public static (**Shared** in Visual Basic) members of this type are safe for multithreaded operations. Any instance members are not guaranteed to be thread safe.

Remarks

For more information about type converters, see the **TypeConverter** base class and **Implementing a Type Converter**.

> **Note** Typically, you do not directly create an instance of an **OpacityConverter**. Instead, call the **GetConverter** method of **TypeDescriptor**. For more information, see the examples in the **TypeConverter** base class.

Requirements

Namespace: System.Windows.Forms

Platforms: Windows 98, Windows NT 4.0, Windows Millennium Edition, Windows 2000, Windows XP Home Edition, Windows XP Professional, Windows Server 2003 family

Assembly: System.Windows.Forms (in System.Windows.Forms.dll)

OpacityConverter Constructor

Initializes a new instance of the **OpacityConverter** class.

```
[Visual Basic]
Public Sub New()
[C#]
public OpacityConverter();
[C++]
public: OpacityConverter();
[JScript]
public function OpacityConverter();
```

Remarks

The default constructor initializes any fields to their default values.

Requirements

Platforms: Windows 98, Windows NT 4.0, Windows Millennium Edition, Windows 2000, Windows XP Home Edition, Windows XP Professional, Windows Server 2003 family

OpacityConverter.CanConvertFrom Method

Returns whether this converter can convert an object in the given source type to the native type of the converter.

Overload List

This member supports the .NET Framework infrastructure and is not intended to be used directly from your code.

[Visual Basic] **Overloads Overrides Public Function CanConvertFrom(ITypeDescriptorContext, Type) As Boolean**

[C#] **public override bool CanConvertFrom(ITypeDescriptorContext, Type);**

[C++] **public: bool CanConvertFrom(ITypeDescriptorContext*, Type*);**

[JScript] **public override function CanConvertFrom(ITypeDescriptorContext, Type) : Boolean;**

Inherited from **TypeConverter**.

[Visual Basic] **Overloads Public Function CanConvertFrom(Type) As Boolean**

[C#] **public bool CanConvertFrom(Type);**

[C++] **public: bool CanConvertFrom(Type*);**

[JScript] **public function CanConvertFrom(Type) : Boolean;**

OpacityConverter.CanConvertFrom Method (ITypeDescriptorContext, Type)

This member overrides **TypeConverter.CanConvertFrom**.

```
[Visual Basic]
Overrides Overloads Public Function CanConvertFrom( _
   ByVal context As ITypeDescriptorContext, _
   ByVal sourceType As Type _
) As Boolean
[C#]
public override bool CanConvertFrom(
   ITypeDescriptorContext context,
   Type sourceType
);
[C++]
public: bool CanConvertFrom(
   ITypeDescriptorContext* context,
   Type* sourceType
);
[JScript]
public override function CanConvertFrom(
   context : ITypeDescriptorContext,
   sourceType : Type
) : Boolean;
```

Requirements

Platforms: Windows 98, Windows NT 4.0, Windows Millennium Edition, Windows 2000, Windows XP Home Edition, Windows XP Professional, Windows Server 2003 family

OpacityConverter.ConvertFrom Method

Converts the given value to the native type of the converter.

Overload List

This member supports the .NET Framework infrastructure and is not intended to be used directly from your code.

[Visual Basic] **Overloads Overrides Public Function ConvertFrom(ITypeDescriptorContext, CultureInfo, Object) As Object**

[C#] **public override object ConvertFrom(ITypeDescriptorContext, CultureInfo, object);**

[C++] **public: Object* ConvertFrom(ITypeDescriptorContext*, CultureInfo*, Object*);**

[JScript] **public override function ConvertFrom(ITypeDescriptorContext, CultureInfo, Object) : Object;**

Inherited from **TypeConverter**.

[Visual Basic] **Overloads Public Function ConvertFrom(Object) As Object**

[C#] **public object ConvertFrom(object);**

[C++] **public: Object* ConvertFrom(Object*);**

[JScript] **public function ConvertFrom(Object) : Object;**

OpacityConverter.ConvertFrom Method (ITypeDescriptorContext, CultureInfo, Object)

This member overrides **TypeConverter.ConvertFrom**.

```
[Visual Basic]
Overrides Overloads Public Function ConvertFrom( _
   ByVal context As ITypeDescriptorContext, _
   ByVal culture As CultureInfo, _
   ByVal value As Object _
) As Object
[C#]
public override object ConvertFrom(
   ITypeDescriptorContext context,
   CultureInfo culture,
   object value
);
[C++]
public: Object* ConvertFrom(
   ITypeDescriptorContext* context,
   CultureInfo* culture,
   Object* value
);
[JScript]
public override function ConvertFrom(
   context : ITypeDescriptorContext,
   culture : CultureInfo,
   value : Object
) : Object;
```

Requirements

Platforms: Windows 98, Windows NT 4.0, Windows Millennium Edition, Windows 2000, Windows XP Home Edition, Windows XP Professional, Windows Server 2003 family

OpacityConverter.ConvertTo Method

Converts the given value object to the specified destination type.

Overload List

This member supports the .NET Framework infrastructure and is not intended to be used directly from your code.

[Visual Basic] **Overloads Overrides Public Function ConvertTo(ITypeDescriptorContext, CultureInfo, Object, Type) As Object**

[C#] **public override object ConvertTo(ITypeDescriptorContext, CultureInfo, object, Type);**

[C++] **public: Object* ConvertTo(ITypeDescriptorContext*, CultureInfo*, Object*, Type*);**

[JScript] **public override function ConvertTo(ITypeDescriptorContext, CultureInfo, Object, Type) : Object;**

Inherited from **TypeConverter**.

[Visual Basic] **Overloads Public Function ConvertTo(Object, Type) As Object**

[C#] **public object ConvertTo(object, Type);**

[C++] **public: Object* ConvertTo(Object*, Type*);**

[JScript] **public function ConvertTo(Object, Type) : Object;**

OpacityConverter.ConvertTo Method (ITypeDescriptorContext, CultureInfo, Object, Type)

This member overrides **TypeConverter.ConvertTo**.

```
[Visual Basic]
Overrides Overloads Public Function ConvertTo( _
   ByVal context As ITypeDescriptorContext, _
   ByVal culture As CultureInfo, _
   ByVal value As Object, _
   ByVal destinationType As Type _
) As Object
[C#]
public override object ConvertTo(
   ITypeDescriptorContext context,
   CultureInfo culture,
   object value,
   Type destinationType
);
[C++]
public: Object* ConvertTo(
   ITypeDescriptorContext* context,
   CultureInfo* culture,
   Object* value,
   Type* destinationType
);
[JScript]
public override function ConvertTo(
   context : ITypeDescriptorContext,
   culture : CultureInfo,
   value : Object,
   destinationType : Type
) : Object;
```

Requirements

Platforms: Windows 98, Windows NT 4.0, Windows Millennium Edition, Windows 2000, Windows XP Home Edition, Windows XP Professional, Windows Server 2003 family

OpenFileDialog Class

Represents a common dialog box that displays the control that allows the user to open a file. This class cannot be inherited.

System.Object
  System.MarshalByRefObject
    System.ComponentModel.Component
      System.Windows.Forms.CommonDialog
        System.Windows.Forms.FileDialog
          System.Windows.Forms.OpenFileDialog

[Visual Basic]
```
NotInheritable Public Class OpenFileDialog
   Inherits FileDialog
```
[C#]
```
public sealed class OpenFileDialog : FileDialog
```
[C++]
```
public __gc __sealed class OpenFileDialog : public FileDialog
```
[JScript]
```
public class OpenFileDialog extends FileDialog
```

Thread Safety

Any public static (**Shared** in Visual Basic) members of this type are safe for multithreaded operations. Any instance members are not guaranteed to be thread safe.

Remarks

This class allows you to check whether a file exists and to open it. The **ShowReadOnly** property determines whether a read-only check box appears in the dialog box. The **ReadOnlyChecked** property indicates whether the read-only check box is checked.

Most of the functionality for this class is found in the **FileDialog** class.

Example

[Visual Basic, C#] The following example creates an **OpenFileDialog**, sets several properties, and displays the dialog box using the **CommonDialog.ShowDialog** method. The example assumes a form with a **Button** placed on it and the **System.IO** namespace added to it.

[Visual Basic]
```
Protected Sub button1_Click(sender As Object, e As System.EventArgs)
    Dim myStream As Stream
    Dim openFileDialog1 As New OpenFileDialog()

    openFileDialog1.InitialDirectory = "c:\"
    openFileDialog1.Filter = "txt files (*.txt)|*.txt|All ↵
files (*.*)|*.*"
    openFileDialog1.FilterIndex = 2
    openFileDialog1.RestoreDirectory = True

    If openFileDialog1.ShowDialog() = DialogResult.OK Then
        myStream = openFileDialog1.OpenFile()
        If Not (myStream Is Nothing) Then
            ' Insert code to read the stream here.
            myStream.Close()
        End If
    End If
End Sub
```

[C#]
```
protected void button1_Click(object sender, System.EventArgs e)
{
    Stream myStream;
    OpenFileDialog openFileDialog1 = new OpenFileDialog();

    openFileDialog1.InitialDirectory = "c:\\" ;
    openFileDialog1.Filter = "txt files (*.txt)|*.txt|All ↵
files (*.*)|*.*" ;
    openFileDialog1.FilterIndex = 2 ;
    openFileDialog1.RestoreDirectory = true ;

    if(openFileDialog1.ShowDialog() == DialogResult.OK)
    {
        if((myStream = openFileDialog1.OpenFile())!= null)
        {
            // Insert code to read the stream here.
            myStream.Close();
        }
    }
}
```

Requirements

Namespace: System.Windows.Forms

Platforms: Windows 98, Windows NT 4.0, Windows Millennium Edition, Windows 2000, Windows XP Home Edition, Windows XP Professional, Windows Server 2003 family, .NET Compact Framework - Windows CE .NET

Assembly: System.Windows.Forms (in System.Windows.Forms.dll)

OpenFileDialog Constructor

Initializes a new instance of the **OpenFileDialog** class.

[Visual Basic]
```
Public Sub New()
```
[C#]
```
public OpenFileDialog();
```
[C++]
```
public: OpenFileDialog();
```
[JScript]
```
public function OpenFileDialog();
```

Remarks

The default constructor initializes any fields to their default values.

Requirements

Platforms: Windows 98, Windows NT 4.0, Windows Millennium Edition, Windows 2000, Windows XP Home Edition, Windows XP Professional, Windows Server 2003 family, .NET Compact Framework - Windows CE .NET

OpenFileDialog.CheckFileExists Property

Gets or sets a value indicating whether the dialog box displays a warning if the user specifies a file name that does not exist.

[Visual Basic]
```
Overrides Public Property CheckFileExists As Boolean
```
[C#]
```
public override bool CheckFileExists {get; set;}
```
[C++]
```
public: __property bool get_CheckFileExists();
public: __property void set_CheckFileExists(bool);
```
[JScript]
```
public override function get CheckFileExists() : Boolean;
public override function set CheckFileExists(Boolean);
```

Property Value

true if the dialog box displays a warning when the user specifies a file name that does not exist; otherwise, **false**. The default value is **true**.

Requirements

Platforms: Windows 98, Windows NT 4.0, Windows Millennium Edition, Windows 2000, Windows XP Home Edition, Windows XP Professional, Windows Server 2003 family

OpenFileDialog.Multiselect Property

Gets or sets a value indicating whether the dialog box allows multiple files to be selected.

[Visual Basic]
```
Public Property Multiselect As Boolean
```
[C#]
```
public bool Multiselect {get; set;}
```
[C++]
```
public: __property bool get_Multiselect();
public: __property void set_Multiselect(bool);
```
[JScript]
```
public function get Multiselect() : Boolean;
public function set Multiselect(Boolean);
```

Property Value

true if the dialog box allows multiple files to be selected together or concurrently; otherwise, **false**. The default value is **false**.

Remarks

Use **FileNames** to access the full list of selected file names.

Requirements

Platforms: Windows 98, Windows NT 4.0, Windows Millennium Edition, Windows 2000, Windows XP Home Edition, Windows XP Professional, Windows Server 2003 family

OpenFileDialog.ReadOnlyChecked Property

Gets or sets a value indicating whether the read-only check box is selected.

[Visual Basic]
```
Public Property ReadOnlyChecked As Boolean
```
[C#]
```
public bool ReadOnlyChecked {get; set;}
```
[C++]
```
public: __property bool get_ReadOnlyChecked();
public: __property void set_ReadOnlyChecked(bool);
```
[JScript]
```
public function get ReadOnlyChecked() : Boolean;
public function set ReadOnlyChecked(Boolean);
```

Property Value

true if the read-only check box is selected; otherwise, **false**. The default value is **false**.

Remarks

The **ReadOnlyChecked** state does not affect the read/write mode that **OpenFileDialog.OpenFile** uses to open a file selected in the dialog box. **OpenFile** will always open the file in read-only mode.

The **ShowReadOnly** property must be set before in order for the read-only check box to appear in the dialog box.

Example

[Visual Basic, C#, C++] The following example demonstrates the use of the **ReadOnlyChecked** property. This example displays the **OpenFileDialog** box with the **ShowReadOnly** property set to **true**. If the user clicks the option to open the file in read-only mode, the **ReadOnlyChecked** property evaluates to **true**, and the **OpenFile** method is used to open the file. Otherwise, the **FileStream** class is used to open the file in read/write mode.

[Visual Basic]
```
    Private Function OpenFile() As FileStream

        ' Displays an OpenFileDialog and shows the read/only files.

        Dim DlgOpenFile As New OpenFileDialog()
        DlgOpenFile.ShowReadOnly = True
        Dim Fs As FileStream

        If DlgOpenFile.ShowDialog() = DialogResult.OK Then

            ' If ReadOnlyChecked is true, uses the OpenFile method to
            ' open the file with read/only access.

            If DlgOpenFile.ReadOnlyChecked = True Then

                Return DlgOpenFile.OpenFile()

                ' Otherwise, opens the file with read/write access.

            Else

                Dim Path As String = DlgOpenFile.FileName
                Return New FileStream(Path, System.IO.FileMode.Open, _
                        System.IO.FileAccess.ReadWrite)

            End If

        End If

    End Function
```

[C#]
```
private FileStream OpenFile()
{
    // Displays an OpenFileDialog and shows the read/only files.

    OpenFileDialog dlgOpenFile = new OpenFileDialog();
    dlgOpenFile.ShowReadOnly = true;

    if(dlgOpenFile.ShowDialog() == DialogResult.OK)
    {

        // If ReadOnlyChecked is true, uses the OpenFile method to
        // open the file with read/only access.

        if(dlgOpenFile.ReadOnlyChecked == true)
        {
            return (FileStream)dlgOpenFile.OpenFile();

        }

        // Otherwise, opens the file with read/write access.

        else
        {
```

```
            string path = dlgOpenFile.FileName;
            return new FileStream(path, System.IO.FileMode.Open,
                    System.IO.FileAccess.ReadWrite);
        }

    }

    return null;

}
```

[C++]

```
private:
    FileStream* OpenFile() {
        // Displays an OpenFileDialog and shows the read/only files.

        OpenFileDialog* dlgOpenFile = new OpenFileDialog();
        dlgOpenFile->ShowReadOnly = true;

        if (dlgOpenFile->ShowDialog() == DialogResult::OK) {
            // If ReadOnlyChecked is true, uses the OpenFile method to
            // open the file with read/only access.
            if (dlgOpenFile->ReadOnlyChecked == true) {
                return dynamic_cast<FileStream*>(dlgOpenFile-          ↵
>OpenFile());
            }

            // Otherwise, opens the file with read/write access.
            else {
                String* path = dlgOpenFile->FileName;
                return new FileStream(path, System::IO::FileMode::Open,
                    System::IO::FileAccess::ReadWrite);
            }
        }
        return 0;
    }
```

Requirements

Platforms: Windows 98, Windows NT 4.0, Windows Millennium Edition, Windows 2000, Windows XP Home Edition, Windows XP Professional, Windows Server 2003 family

OpenFileDialog.ShowReadOnly Property

Gets or sets a value indicating whether the dialog box contains a read-only check box.

[Visual Basic]

```
Public Property ShowReadOnly As Boolean
```

[C#]

```
public bool ShowReadOnly {get; set;}
```

[C++]

```
public: __property bool get_ShowReadOnly();
public: __property void set_ShowReadOnly(bool);
```

[JScript]

```
public function get ShowReadOnly() : Boolean;
public function set ShowReadOnly(Boolean);
```

Property Value

true if the dialog box contains a read-only check box; otherwise, **false**. The default value is **false**.

Example

[Visual Basic, C#, C++] The following example demonstrates the use of the **ShowReadOnly** property. This example displays the **OpenFileDialog** box with the **ShowReadOnly** property set to **true**. If the user clicks the option to open the file in read-only mode, the **OpenFile** method is used to open the file. Otherwise, the **FileStream** class is used to open the file in read/write mode.

[Visual Basic]

```
    Private Function OpenFile() As FileStream

        ' Displays an OpenFileDialog and shows the read/only files.

        Dim DlgOpenFile As New OpenFileDialog()
        DlgOpenFile.ShowReadOnly = True
        Dim Fs As FileStream

        If DlgOpenFile.ShowDialog() = DialogResult.OK Then

            ' If ReadOnlyChecked is true, uses the OpenFile method to
            ' open the file with read/only access.

            If DlgOpenFile.ReadOnlyChecked = True Then

                Return DlgOpenFile.OpenFile()

                ' Otherwise, opens the file with read/write access.

            Else

                Dim Path As String = DlgOpenFile.FileName
                Return New FileStream(Path, System.IO.FileMode.Open, _
                        System.IO.FileAccess.ReadWrite)

            End If

        End If

    End Function
```

[C#]

```
private FileStream OpenFile()
{
    // Displays an OpenFileDialog and shows the read/only files.

    OpenFileDialog dlgOpenFile = new OpenFileDialog();
    dlgOpenFile.ShowReadOnly = true;

    if(dlgOpenFile.ShowDialog() == DialogResult.OK)
    {

        // If ReadOnlyChecked is true, uses the OpenFile method to
        // open the file with read/only access.

        if(dlgOpenFile.ReadOnlyChecked == true)
        {
            return (FileStream)dlgOpenFile.OpenFile();

        }

        // Otherwise, opens the file with read/write access.

        else
        {
            string path = dlgOpenFile.FileName;
            return new FileStream(path, System.IO.FileMode.Open,
                    System.IO.FileAccess.ReadWrite);
        }

    }

    return null;

}
```

[C++]

```
private:
    FileStream* OpenFile() {
        // Displays an OpenFileDialog and shows the read/only files.

        OpenFileDialog* dlgOpenFile = new OpenFileDialog();
        dlgOpenFile->ShowReadOnly = true;
```

```
        if (dlgOpenFile->ShowDialog() == DialogResult::OK) {
            // If ReadOnlyChecked is true, uses the OpenFile method to
            // open the file with read/only access.
            if (dlgOpenFile->ReadOnlyChecked == true) {
                return dynamic_cast<FileStream*>(dlgOpenFile-        ↵
>OpenFile());
            }

            // Otherwise, opens the file with read/write access.
            else {
                String* path = dlgOpenFile->FileName;
                return new FileStream(path, System::IO::FileMode::Open,
                    System::IO::FileAccess::ReadWrite);
            }
        }
        return 0;
    }
```

Requirements

Platforms: Windows 98, Windows NT 4.0, Windows Millennium Edition, Windows 2000, Windows XP Home Edition, Windows XP Professional, Windows Server 2003 family

OpenFileDialog.OpenFile Method

Opens the file selected by the user, with read-only permission. The file is specified by the **FileName** property.

[Visual Basic]
```
Public Function OpenFile() As Stream
```
[C#]
```
public Stream OpenFile();
```
[C++]
```
public: Stream* OpenFile();
```
[JScript]
```
public function OpenFile() : Stream;
```

Return Value

A **Stream** that specifies the read-only file selected by the user.

Exceptions

Exception Type	Condition
ArgumentNull-Exception	The file name is a null reference (**Nothing** in Visual Basic).

Remarks

The **OpenFile** method is used to provide a facility to quickly open a file from the dialog box. The file is opened in read-only mode for security purposes. To open a file in read/write mode, you must use another method such as **FileStream**.

Example

[Visual Basic, C#, C++] The following example demonstrates how to use the **OpenFile** method. This example display an **OpenFile-Dialog** with the **ShowReadOnly** property set to **true**. If the user clicks the option to open the file in read-only mode, the **OpenFile** method is used to open the file. Otherwise, the **FileStream** class is used to open the file in read/write mode.

[Visual Basic]
```
    Private Function OpenFile() As FileStream

        ' Displays an OpenFileDialog and shows the read/only files.

        Dim DlgOpenFile As New OpenFileDialog()
        DlgOpenFile.ShowReadOnly = True
        Dim Fs As FileStream

        If DlgOpenFile.ShowDialog() = DialogResult.OK Then

            ' If ReadOnlyChecked is true, uses the OpenFile method to
            ' open the file with read/only access.

            If DlgOpenFile.ReadOnlyChecked = True Then

                Return DlgOpenFile.OpenFile()

                ' Otherwise, opens the file with read/write access.

            Else

                Dim Path As String = DlgOpenFile.FileName
                Return New FileStream(Path, System.IO.FileMode.Open, _
                        System.IO.FileAccess.ReadWrite)

            End If

        End If

    End Function
```

[C#]
```
private FileStream OpenFile()
{
    // Displays an OpenFileDialog and shows the read/only files.

    OpenFileDialog dlgOpenFile = new OpenFileDialog();
    dlgOpenFile.ShowReadOnly = true;

    if(dlgOpenFile.ShowDialog() == DialogResult.OK)
    {

        // If ReadOnlyChecked is true, uses the OpenFile method to
        // open the file with read/only access.

        if(dlgOpenFile.ReadOnlyChecked == true)
        {
            return (FileStream)dlgOpenFile.OpenFile();

        }

        // Otherwise, opens the file with read/write access.

        else
        {
            string path = dlgOpenFile.FileName;
            return new FileStream(path, System.IO.FileMode.Open,
                    System.IO.FileAccess.ReadWrite);
        }

    }

    return null;

}
```

[C++]
```
private:
    FileStream* OpenFile() {
        // Displays an OpenFileDialog and shows the read/only files.

        OpenFileDialog* dlgOpenFile = new OpenFileDialog();
        dlgOpenFile->ShowReadOnly = true;
```

```
        if (dlgOpenFile->ShowDialog() == DialogResult::OK) {
            // If ReadOnlyChecked is true, uses the OpenFile method to
            // open the file with read/only access.
            if (dlgOpenFile->ReadOnlyChecked == true) {
                return dynamic_cast<FileStream*>(dlgOpenFile-          ↵
>OpenFile());
            }

            // Otherwise, opens the file with read/write access.
            else {
                String* path = dlgOpenFile->FileName;
                return new FileStream(path, System::IO::FileMode::Open,
                    System::IO::FileAccess::ReadWrite);
            }
        }
        return 0;
    }
```

Requirements

Platforms: Windows 98, Windows NT 4.0, Windows Millennium Edition, Windows 2000, Windows XP Home Edition, Windows XP Professional, Windows Server 2003 family

.NET Framework Security:

- **FileDialogPermission** to open a file. Associated enumeration: **FileDialogPermissionAccess.Open**.

OpenFileDialog.Reset Method

This member overrides **FileDialog.Reset**.

[Visual Basic]
```
Overrides Public Sub Reset()
```
[C#]
```
public override void Reset();
```
[C++]
```
public: void Reset();
```
[JScript]
```
public override function Reset();
```

Requirements

Platforms: Windows 98, Windows NT 4.0, Windows Millennium Edition, Windows 2000, Windows XP Home Edition, Windows XP Professional, Windows Server 2003 family

Orientation Enumeration

Specifies the orientation of controls or elements of controls.

[Visual Basic]
```
<Serializable>
Public Enum Orientation
```
[C#]
```
[Serializable]
public enum Orientation
```
[C++]
```
[Serializable]
__value public enum Orientation
```
[JScript]
```
public
   Serializable
enum Orientation
```

Remarks

This enumeration is used by members such as **TrackBar.Orientation**.

Members

Member name	Description
Horizontal Supported by the .NET Compact Framework.	The control or element is oriented horizontally.
Vertical Supported by the .NET Compact Framework.	The control or element is oriented vertically.

Requirements

Namespace: System.Windows.Forms

Platforms: Windows 98, Windows NT 4.0, Windows Millennium Edition, Windows 2000, Windows XP Home Edition, Windows XP Professional, Windows Server 2003 family, .NET Compact Framework - Windows CE .NET

Assembly: System.Windows.Forms (in System.Windows.Forms.dll)

OSFeature Class

Provides operating-system specific feature queries.

System.Object
 System.Windows.Forms.FeatureSupport
  System.Windows.Forms.OSFeature

[Visual Basic]
```
Public Class OSFeature
   Inherits FeatureSupport
```
[C#]
```
public class OSFeature : FeatureSupport
```
[C++]
```
public __gc class OSFeature : public FeatureSupport
```
[JScript]
```
public class OSFeature extends FeatureSupport
```

Thread Safety

Any public static (**Shared** in Visual Basic) members of this type are safe for multithreaded operations. Any instance members are not guaranteed to be thread safe.

Remarks

Use the static (**Shared** in Visual Basic) instance of this class provided in the **Feature** property to query for operating system features. You cannot create an instance of this class.

To determine the version of a feature, call the **GetVersionPresent** method. To determine if a feature or a specific version is present, call the **IsPresent** method and specify the feature to look for with the feature identifiers provided in this class.

Example

[Visual Basic, C#] The following example uses **OSFeature** to query the operating system to determine if the **LayeredWindows** feature is installed. The example presents two different ways of checking to see whether the feature is present. In the first method, `myVersion` is checked to see if it is a null reference (**Nothing** in Visual Basic). If the version is a null reference (**Nothing**), the feature is not installed. In the second method, the example calls the base class method **IsPresent** to see if the feature is installed. The results are displayed in a text box.

[Visual Basic, C#] This code assumes `textBox1` has been created and placed on a form.

[Visual Basic]
```
Private Sub LayeredWindows()
    ' Gets the version of the layered windows feature.
    Dim myVersion As Version = _
       OSFeature.Feature.GetVersionPresent(OSFeature.LayeredWindows)

    ' Prints whether the feature is available.
    If Not (myVersion Is Nothing) Then
        textBox1.Text = "Layered windows feature is installed." & _
           ControlChars.CrLf
    Else
        textBox1.Text = "Layered windows feature is not installed." & _
           ControlChars.CrLf
    End If
    'This is an alternate way to check whether a feature is present.
    If OSFeature.Feature.IsPresent(OSFeature.LayeredWindows) Then
        textBox1.Text &= "Again, layered windows feature is installed."
    Else
        textBox1.Text &= "Again, layered windows feature is not        ↵
installed."
    End If
End Sub
```

[C#]
```
private void LayeredWindows() {
   // Gets the version of the layered windows feature.
   Version myVersion =
OSFeature.Feature.GetVersionPresent(OSFeature.LayeredWindows);

   // Prints whether the feature is available.
   if (myVersion != null)
      textBox1.Text = "Layered windows feature is installed." + '\n';
   else
      textBox1.Text = "Layered windows feature is not installed.       ↵
" + '\n';

   // This is an alternate way to check whether a feature is present.
   if (OSFeature.Feature.IsPresent(OSFeature.LayeredWindows))
      textBox1.Text += "Again, layered windows feature is installed.";
   else
      textBox1.Text += "Again, layered windows feature is not          ↵
installed.";
}
```

Requirements

Namespace: System.Windows.Forms

Platforms: Windows 98, Windows NT 4.0, Windows Millennium Edition, Windows 2000, Windows XP Home Edition, Windows XP Professional, Windows Server 2003 family

Assembly: System.Windows.Forms (in System.Windows.Forms.dll)

OSFeature Constructor

This member supports the .NET Framework infrastructure and is not intended to be used directly from your code.

[Visual Basic]
```
Protected Sub New()
```
[C#]
```
protected OSFeature();
```
[C++]
```
protected: OSFeature();
```
[JScript]
```
protected function OSFeature();
```

OSFeature.LayeredWindows Field

Represents the layered, top-level windows feature. This field is read-only.

[Visual Basic]
```
Public Shared ReadOnly LayeredWindows As Object
```
[C#]
```
public static readonly object LayeredWindows;
```
[C++]
```
public: static Object* LayeredWindows;
```
[JScript]
```
public static var LayeredWindows : Object;
```

Remarks

Layered windows are available only in Windows 2000. A layered window can be made transparent or translucent by the operating system.

To determine if the layered windows feature is installed, use the **Feature** property to call the base class method **IsPresent** with **OSFeature.LayeredWindows** as the feature to look for.

Alternatively, you can check to see if the feature is installed by calling the **GetVersionPresent** method of **Feature** with **OSFeature.LayeredWindows** as the feature to find.

Example

[Visual Basic, C#] The following example determines whether the current system supports layered windows. The base class method **IsPresent** is called with **OSFeature.LayeredWindows** as the feature to look for. The result is displayed in a text box. This code assumes `textBox1` has been instantiated and placed on a form.

[Visual Basic]
```
Private Sub LayeredWindows()
    ' Gets the version of the layered windows feature.
    Dim myVersion As Version = _
       OSFeature.Feature.GetVersionPresent(OSFeature.LayeredWindows)

    ' Prints whether the feature is available.
    If OSFeature.Feature.IsPresent(OSFeature.LayeredWindows) Then
        textBox1.Text = "Layered windows feature is installed."
    Else
        textBox1.Text = "Layered windows feature is not installed."
    End If
End Sub
```

[C#]
```
private void LayeredWindows() {
   // Gets the version of the layered windows feature.
   Version myVersion =
       OSFeature.Feature.GetVersionPresent(OSFeature.LayeredWindows);

   // Prints whether the feature is available.
   if (OSFeature.Feature.IsPresent(OSFeature.LayeredWindows))
      textBox1.Text = "Layered windows feature is installed.";
   else
      textBox1.Text = "Layered windows feature is not installed.";
}
```

Requirements

Platforms: Windows 98, Windows NT 4.0, Windows Millennium Edition, Windows 2000, Windows XP Home Edition, Windows XP Professional, Windows Server 2003 family

OSFeature.Themes Field

Represents the operating system themes feature. This field is read-only.

[Visual Basic]
```
Public Shared ReadOnly Themes As Object
```
[C#]
```
public static readonly object Themes;
```
[C++]
```
public: static Object* Themes;
```
[JScript]
```
public static var Themes : Object;
```

Requirements

Platforms: Windows 98, Windows NT 4.0, Windows Millennium Edition, Windows 2000, Windows XP Home Edition, Windows XP Professional, Windows Server 2003 family

OSFeature.Feature Property

Represents the static (**Shared** in Visual Basic) instance of the **OSFeature** class to use for feature queries. This property is read-only.

[Visual Basic]
```
Public Shared ReadOnly Property Feature As OSFeature
```
[C#]
```
public static OSFeature Feature {get;}
```
[C++]
```
public: __property static OSFeature* get_Feature();
```
[JScript]
```
public static function get Feature() : OSFeature;
```

Property Value

An **OSFeature**.

Remarks

Use this static (**Shared** in Visual Basic) property to query for operating system features. You cannot create an instance of this class.

To determine the version of a feature, call the **GetVersionPresent** method. To determine if a feature or a specific version is present, call the **IsPresent** method and specify the feature to look for with the feature identifiers provided in this class.

Example

[Visual Basic, C#] The following example queries **OSFeature** for the **LayeredWindows** feature. The version is checked to see if it is a null reference (**Nothing** in Visual Basic), to determine whether the feature is present. The result is displayed in a text box. This code assumes `textBox1` has been created and placed on a form.

[Visual Basic]
```
Private Sub LayeredWindows()
    ' Gets the version of the layered windows feature.
    Dim myVersion As Version = _
       OSFeature.Feature.GetVersionPresent(OSFeature.LayeredWindows)

    ' Prints whether the feature is available.
    If Not (myVersion Is Nothing) Then
        textBox1.Text = "Layered windows feature is installed." & _
           ControlChars.CrLf
    Else
        textBox1.Text = "Layered windows feature is not installed." & _
           ControlChars.CrLf
    End If
End Sub
```

[C#]
```
private void LayeredWindows() {
   // Gets the version of the layered windows feature.
   Version myVersion =
       OSFeature.Feature.GetVersionPresent(OSFeature.LayeredWindows);

   // Prints whether the feature is available.
   if (myVersion != null)
      textBox1.Text = "Layered windows feature is installed.\n";
   else
      textBox1.Text = "Layered windows feature is not installed.\n";
}
```

Requirements

Platforms: Windows 98, Windows NT 4.0, Windows Millennium Edition, Windows 2000, Windows XP Home Edition, Windows XP Professional, Windows Server 2003 family

OSFeature.GetVersionPresent Method

Retrieves the version of the specified feature currently available on the system.

[Visual Basic]
```
Overrides Public Function GetVersionPresent( _
   ByVal feature As Object _
) As Version Implements IFeatureSupport.GetVersionPresent
```
[C#]
```
public override Version GetVersionPresent(
   object feature
);
```
[C++]
```
public: Version* GetVersionPresent(
   Object* feature
);
```
[JScript]
```
public override function GetVersionPresent(
   feature : Object
) : Version;
```

Parameters

feature
The feature whose version is requested.

Return Value

A **Version** representing the version of the specified operating system feature currently available on the system; or a null reference (**Nothing** in Visual Basic) if the feature cannot be found.

Implements

IFeatureSupport.GetVersionPresent

Remarks

Use the **Feature** property, the static (**Shared** in Visual Basic) instance of **OSFeature** provided in this class, to query for the version number of a feature.

Example

[Visual Basic, C#] The following example queries **OSFeature** for the **LayeredWindows** feature. The version is checked to see if it is a null reference (**Nothing** in Visual Basic), to determine whether the feature is present. The result is displayed in a text box. This code assumes `textBox1` has been created and placed on a form.

[Visual Basic]
```
Private Sub LayeredWindows()
    ' Gets the version of the layered windows feature.
    Dim myVersion As Version = _
       OSFeature.Feature.GetVersionPresent(OSFeature.LayeredWindows)

    ' Prints whether the feature is available.
    If Not (myVersion Is Nothing) Then
        textBox1.Text = "Layered windows feature is installed." & _
           ControlChars.CrLf
    Else
        textBox1.Text = "Layered windows feature is not installed." & _
           ControlChars.CrLf
    End If
End Sub
```

[C#]
```
private void LayeredWindows() {
   // Gets the version of the layered windows feature.
   Version myVersion =
       OSFeature.Feature.GetVersionPresent(OSFeature.LayeredWindows);

   // Prints whether the feature is available.
   if (myVersion != null)
      textBox1.Text = "Layered windows feature is installed.\n";
   else
      textBox1.Text = "Layered windows feature is not installed.\n";
}
```

Requirements

Platforms: Windows 98, Windows NT 4.0, Windows Millennium Edition, Windows 2000, Windows XP Home Edition, Windows XP Professional, Windows Server 2003 family

OwnerDrawPropertyBag Class

This type supports the .NET Framework infrastructure and is not intended to be used directly from your code.

```
[Visual Basic]
<Serializable>
Public Class OwnerDrawPropertyBag
   Inherits MarshalByRefObject
   Implements ISerializable
[C#]
[Serializable]
public class OwnerDrawPropertyBag : MarshalByRefObject,
   ISerializable
[C++]
[Serializable]
public __gc class OwnerDrawPropertyBag : public
   MarshalByRefObject, ISerializable
[JScript]
public
   Serializable
class OwnerDrawPropertyBag extends MarshalByRefObject
   implements ISerializable
```

OwnerDrawPropertyBag.BackColor Property

This member supports the .NET Framework infrastructure and is not intended to be used directly from your code.

```
[Visual Basic]
Public Property BackColor As Color
[C#]
public Color BackColor {get; set;}
[C++]
public: __property Color get_BackColor();
public: __property void set_BackColor(Color);
[JScript]
public function get BackColor() : Color;
public function set BackColor(Color);
```

OwnerDrawPropertyBag.Font Property

This member supports the .NET Framework infrastructure and is not intended to be used directly from your code.

```
[Visual Basic]
Public Property Font As Font
[C#]
public Font Font {get; set;}
[C++]
public: __property Font* get_Font();
public: __property void set_Font(Font*);
[JScript]
public function get Font() : Font;
public function set Font(Font);
```

OwnerDrawPropertyBag.ForeColor Property

This member supports the .NET Framework infrastructure and is not intended to be used directly from your code.

```
[Visual Basic]
Public Property ForeColor As Color
[C#]
public Color ForeColor {get; set;}
[C++]
public: __property Color get_ForeColor();
public: __property void set_ForeColor(Color);
[JScript]
public function get ForeColor() : Color;
public function set ForeColor(Color);
```

OwnerDrawPropertyBag.Copy Method

This member supports the .NET Framework infrastructure and is not intended to be used directly from your code.

```
[Visual Basic]
Public Shared Function Copy( _
   ByVal value As OwnerDrawPropertyBag _
) As OwnerDrawPropertyBag
[C#]
public static OwnerDrawPropertyBag Copy(
   OwnerDrawPropertyBag value
);
[C++]
public: static OwnerDrawPropertyBag* Copy(
   OwnerDrawPropertyBag* value
);
[JScript]
public static function Copy(
   value : OwnerDrawPropertyBag
) : OwnerDrawPropertyBag;
```

OwnerDrawPropertyBag.IsEmpty Method

This member supports the .NET Framework infrastructure and is not intended to be used directly from your code.

```
[Visual Basic]
Public Overridable Function IsEmpty() As Boolean
[C#]
public virtual bool IsEmpty();
[C++]
public: virtual bool IsEmpty();
[JScript]
public function IsEmpty() : Boolean;
```

OwnerDrawPropertyBag.ISerializable.GetObjectData Method

This member supports the .NET Framework infrastructure and is not intended to be used directly from your code.

[Visual Basic]
```
Private Sub GetObjectData( _
   ByVal si As SerializationInfo, _
   ByVal context As StreamingContext _
) Implements ISerializable.GetObjectData
```
[C#]
```
void ISerializable.GetObjectData(
   SerializationInfo si,
   StreamingContext context
);
```
[C++]
```
private: void ISerializable::GetObjectData(
   SerializationInfo* si,
   StreamingContext context
);
```
[JScript]
```
private function ISerializable.GetObjectData(
   si : SerializationInfo,
   context : StreamingContext
);
```

PageSetupDialog Class

Represents a dialog box that allows users to manipulate page settings, including margins and paper orientation.

System.Object
  System.MarshalByRefObject
    System.ComponentModel.Component
      System.Windows.Forms.CommonDialog
        System.Windows.Forms.PageSetupDialog

```
[Visual Basic]
NotInheritable Public Class PageSetupDialog
   Inherits CommonDialog
[C#]
public sealed class PageSetupDialog : CommonDialog
[C++]
public __gc __sealed class PageSetupDialog : public CommonDialog
[JScript]
public class PageSetupDialog extends CommonDialog
```

Thread Safety

Any public static (**Shared** in Visual Basic) members of this type are safe for multithreaded operations. Any instance members are not guaranteed to be thread safe.

Remarks

The **PageSetupDialog** dialog box modifies the **PageSettings** and **PrinterSettings** information for a given **Document**. The user can enable sections of the dialog box to manipulate printing, margins, and paper orientation, size, and source and to show help and network buttons. **MinMargins** defines the minimum margins a user can select.

When you create an instance of **PageSetupDialog**, the read/write properties are set to initial values. For a list of these values, see the **PageSetupDialog** constructor.

Requirements

Namespace: System.Windows.Forms

Platforms: Windows 98, Windows NT 4.0, Windows Millennium Edition, Windows 2000, Windows XP Home Edition, Windows XP Professional, Windows Server 2003 family

Assembly: System.Windows.Forms (in System.Windows.Forms.dll)

PageSetupDialog Constructor

Initializes a new instance of the **PageSetupDialog** class.

```
[Visual Basic]
Public Sub New()
[C#]
public PageSetupDialog();
[C++]
public: PageSetupDialog();
[JScript]
public function PageSetupDialog();
```

Remarks

When an instance of **PageSetupDialog** is created, the following properties are initialized to the specified values.

Property	Initial Value
AllowMargins	**true**
AllowOrientation	**true**
AllowPaper	**true**
AllowPrinter	**true**
Document	A null reference (**Nothing** in Visual Basic)
MinMargins	A null reference (**Nothing**)
PageSettings	A null reference (**Nothing**)
PrinterSettings	A null reference (**Nothing**)
ShowHelp	**false**
ShowNetwork	**true**

You can change the value for any of these properties through a separate call to the property.

Requirements

Platforms: Windows 98, Windows NT 4.0, Windows Millennium Edition, Windows 2000, Windows XP Home Edition, Windows XP Professional, Windows Server 2003 family

PageSetupDialog.AllowMargins Property

Gets or sets a value indicating whether the margins section of the dialog box is enabled.

```
[Visual Basic]
Public Property AllowMargins As Boolean
[C#]
public bool AllowMargins {get; set;}
[C++]
public: __property bool get_AllowMargins();
public: __property void set_AllowMargins(bool);
[JScript]
public function get AllowMargins() : Boolean;
public function set AllowMargins(Boolean);
```

Property Value

true if the margins section of the dialog box is enabled; otherwise, **false**. The default is **true**.

Requirements

Platforms: Windows 98, Windows NT 4.0, Windows Millennium Edition, Windows 2000, Windows XP Home Edition, Windows XP Professional, Windows Server 2003 family

PageSetupDialog.AllowOrientation Property

Gets or sets a value indicating whether the orientation section of the dialog box (landscape vs. portrait) is enabled.

```
[Visual Basic]
Public Property AllowOrientation As Boolean
[C#]
public bool AllowOrientation {get; set;}
[C++]
public: __property bool get_AllowOrientation();
public: __property void set_AllowOrientation(bool);
[JScript]
public function get AllowOrientation() : Boolean;
public function set AllowOrientation(Boolean);
```

Property Value

true if the orientation section of the dialog box is enabled; otherwise, **false**. The default is **true**.

Requirements

Platforms: Windows 98, Windows NT 4.0, Windows Millennium Edition, Windows 2000, Windows XP Home Edition, Windows XP Professional, Windows Server 2003 family

PageSetupDialog.AllowPaper Property

Gets or sets a value indicating whether the paper section of the dialog box (paper size and paper source) is enabled.

```
[Visual Basic]
Public Property AllowPaper As Boolean
[C#]
public bool AllowPaper {get; set;}
[C++]
public: __property bool get_AllowPaper();
public: __property void set_AllowPaper(bool);
[JScript]
public function get AllowPaper() : Boolean;
public function set AllowPaper(Boolean);
```

Property Value

true if the paper section of the dialog box is enabled; otherwise, **false**. The default is **true**.

Requirements

Platforms: Windows 98, Windows NT 4.0, Windows Millennium Edition, Windows 2000, Windows XP Home Edition, Windows XP Professional, Windows Server 2003 family

PageSetupDialog.AllowPrinter Property

Gets or sets a value indicating whether the Printer button is enabled.

```
[Visual Basic]
Public Property AllowPrinter As Boolean
[C#]
public bool AllowPrinter {get; set;}
[C++]
public: __property bool get_AllowPrinter();
public: __property void set_AllowPrinter(bool);
[JScript]
public function get AllowPrinter() : Boolean;
public function set AllowPrinter(Boolean);
```

Property Value

true if the Printer button is enabled; otherwise, **false**. The default is **true**.

Requirements

Platforms: Windows 98, Windows NT 4.0, Windows Millennium Edition, Windows 2000, Windows XP Home Edition, Windows XP Professional, Windows Server 2003 family

PageSetupDialog.Document Property

Gets or sets a value indicating the **PrintDocument** to get page settings from.

```
[Visual Basic]
Public Property Document As PrintDocument
[C#]
public PrintDocument Document {get; set;}
[C++]
public: __property PrintDocument* get_Document();
public: __property void set_Document(PrintDocument*);
[JScript]
public function get Document() : PrintDocument;
public function set Document(PrintDocument);
```

Property Value

The **PrintDocument** to get page settings from. The default is a null reference (**Nothing** in Visual Basic).

Requirements

Platforms: Windows 98, Windows NT 4.0, Windows Millennium Edition, Windows 2000, Windows XP Home Edition, Windows XP Professional, Windows Server 2003 family

PageSetupDialog.MinMargins Property

Gets or sets a value indicating the minimum margins the user is allowed to select, in hundredths of an inch.

```
[Visual Basic]
Public Property MinMargins As Margins
[C#]
public Margins MinMargins {get; set;}
[C++]
public: __property Margins* get_MinMargins();
public: __property void set_MinMargins(Margins*);
[JScript]
public function get MinMargins() : Margins;
public function set MinMargins(Margins);
```

Property Value

The minimum margins the user is allowed to select, in hundredths of an inch. The default is a null reference (**Nothing** in Visual Basic).

Requirements

Platforms: Windows 98, Windows NT 4.0, Windows Millennium Edition, Windows 2000, Windows XP Home Edition, Windows XP Professional, Windows Server 2003 family

PageSetupDialog.PageSettings Property

Gets or sets a value indicating the page settings to modify.

```
[Visual Basic]
Public Property PageSettings As PageSettings
[C#]
public PageSettings PageSettings {get; set;}
[C++]
public: __property PageSettings* get_PageSettings();
public: __property void set_PageSettings(PageSettings*);
[JScript]
public function get PageSettings() : PageSettings;
public function set PageSettings(PageSettings);
```

Property Value

The **PageSettings** to modify. The default is a null reference (**Nothing** in Visual Basic).

Requirements

Platforms: Windows 98, Windows NT 4.0, Windows Millennium Edition, Windows 2000, Windows XP Home Edition, Windows XP Professional, Windows Server 2003 family

PageSetupDialog.PrinterSettings Property

Gets or sets the printer settings that are modified when the user clicks the Printer button in the dialog.

```
[Visual Basic]
Public Property PrinterSettings As PrinterSettings
[C#]
public PrinterSettings PrinterSettings {get; set;}
[C++]
public: __property PrinterSettings* get_PrinterSettings();
public: __property void set_PrinterSettings(PrinterSettings*);
[JScript]
public function get PrinterSettings() : PrinterSettings;
public function set PrinterSettings(PrinterSettings);
```

Property Value

The **PrinterSettings** to modify when the user clicks the Printer button. The default is a null reference (**Nothing** in Visual Basic).

Requirements

Platforms: Windows 98, Windows NT 4.0, Windows Millennium Edition, Windows 2000, Windows XP Home Edition, Windows XP Professional, Windows Server 2003 family

PageSetupDialog.ShowHelp Property

Gets or sets a value indicating whether the Help button is visible.

```
[Visual Basic]
Public Property ShowHelp As Boolean
[C#]
public bool ShowHelp {get; set;}
[C++]
public: __property bool get_ShowHelp();
public: __property void set_ShowHelp(bool);
[JScript]
public function get ShowHelp() : Boolean;
public function set ShowHelp(Boolean);
```

Property Value

true if the Help button is visible; otherwise, **false**. The default is **false**.

Requirements

Platforms: Windows 98, Windows NT 4.0, Windows Millennium Edition, Windows 2000, Windows XP Home Edition, Windows XP Professional, Windows Server 2003 family

PageSetupDialog.ShowNetwork Property

Gets or sets a value indicating whether the Network button is visible.

```
[Visual Basic]
Public Property ShowNetwork As Boolean
[C#]
public bool ShowNetwork {get; set;}
[C++]
public: __property bool get_ShowNetwork();
public: __property void set_ShowNetwork(bool);
[JScript]
public function get ShowNetwork() : Boolean;
public function set ShowNetwork(Boolean);
```

Property Value

true if the Network button is visible; otherwise, **false**. The default is **true**.

Requirements

Platforms: Windows 98, Windows NT 4.0, Windows Millennium Edition, Windows 2000, Windows XP Home Edition, Windows XP Professional, Windows Server 2003 family

PageSetupDialog.Reset Method

Resets all options to their default values.

```
[Visual Basic]
Overrides Public Sub Reset()
[C#]
public override void Reset();
[C++]
public: void Reset();
[JScript]
public override function Reset();
```

Requirements

Platforms: Windows 98, Windows NT 4.0, Windows Millennium Edition, Windows 2000, Windows XP Home Edition, Windows XP Professional, Windows Server 2003 family

PageSetupDialog.RunDialog Method

This member overrides **CommonDialog.RunDialog**.

```
[Visual Basic]
Overrides Protected Function RunDialog( _
   ByVal hwndOwner As IntPtr _
) As Boolean
[C#]
protected override bool RunDialog(
   IntPtr hwndOwner
);
[C++]
protected: bool RunDialog(
   IntPtr hwndOwner
);
[JScript]
protected override function RunDialog(
   hwndOwner : IntPtr
) : Boolean;
```

Requirements

Platforms: Windows 98, Windows NT 4.0, Windows Millennium Edition, Windows 2000, Windows XP Home Edition, Windows XP Professional, Windows Server 2003 family

PaintEventArgs Class

Provides data for the **Paint** event.

For a list of all members of this type, see **PaintEventArgs Members**.

System.Object
  System.EventArgs
    System.Windows.Forms.PaintEventArgs

[Visual Basic]
```
Public Class PaintEventArgs
   Inherits EventArgs
   Implements IDisposable
```
[C#]
```
public class PaintEventArgs : EventArgs, IDisposable
```
[C++]
```
public __gc class PaintEventArgs : public EventArgs, IDisposable
```
[JScript]
```
public class PaintEventArgs extends EventArgs implements
   IDisposable
```

Thread Safety

Any public static (**Shared** in Visual Basic) members of this type are safe for multithreaded operations. Any instance members are not guaranteed to be thread safe.

Remarks

The **Paint** event occurs when a control is redrawn. A **PaintEventArgs** specifies the **Graphics** to use to paint the control and the **ClipRectangle** in which to paint.

For information about the event model, see **Events and Delegates**.

Example

[Visual Basic, C#] The following example demonstrates handling the **Paint** event and using the **PaintEventArgs** class to draw rectangles on the form. The **MouseDown** and **MouseUp** events are handled to determine the size of the rectangle. The example also demonstrates the **Invalidate** method to invalidate the area of the rectangle, causing it to be redrawn.

[Visual Basic]
```
Dim RcDraw As Rectangle
Dim PenWidth As Integer = 5

Private Sub Form1_MouseDown(ByVal sender As Object, ByVal ┘
e As System.Windows.Forms.MouseEventArgs) Handles MyBase.MouseDown

    ' Determine the initial rectangle coordinates...

    RcDraw.X = e.X
    RcDraw.Y = e.Y

End Sub

Private Sub Form1_MouseUp(ByVal sender As Object, ByVal ┘
 e As System.Windows.Forms.MouseEventArgs) Handles MyBase.MouseUp

    ' Determine the width and height of the rectangle...

    If e.X < RcDraw.X Then
        RcDraw.Width = RcDraw.X - e.X
        RcDraw.X = e.X
    Else
        RcDraw.Width = e.X - RcDraw.X
    End If

    If e.Y < RcDraw.Y Then
        RcDraw.Height = RcDraw.Y - e.Y
        RcDraw.Y = e.Y
    Else
        RcDraw.Height = e.Y - RcDraw.Y
    End If

    ' Force a repaint of the region occupied by the rectangle...

    Me.Invalidate(RcDraw)

End Sub

Private Sub Form1_Paint(ByVal sender As Object, ByVal e ┘
 As System.Windows.Forms.PaintEventArgs) Handles MyBase.Paint

    ' Draw the rectangle...

    e.Graphics.DrawRectangle(New Pen(Color.Blue, PenWidth), RcDraw)

End Sub
```

[C#]
```
        private Rectangle RcDraw;
        private float PenWidth = 5;

        private void Form1_MouseDown(object sender, ┘
System.Windows.Forms.MouseEventArgs e)
        {

            // Determine the initial rectangle coordinates...

            RcDraw.X = e.X;
            RcDraw.Y = e.Y;

        }

        private void Form1_MouseUp(object sender, ┘
System.Windows.Forms.MouseEventArgs e)
        {

            // Determine the width and height of the rectangle...

            if(e.X < RcDraw.X)
            {
                RcDraw.Width = RcDraw.X - e.X;
                RcDraw.X = e.X;
            }
            else
            {
                RcDraw.Width = e.X - RcDraw.X;
            }

            if(e.Y < RcDraw.Y)
            {
                RcDraw.Height = RcDraw.Y - e.Y;
                RcDraw.Y = e.Y;
            }
            else
            {
                RcDraw.Height = e.Y - RcDraw.Y;
            }

            // Force a repaint of the region occupied by the ┘
rectangle...

            this.Invalidate(RcDraw);

        }

        private void Form1_Paint(object sender, ┘
System.Windows.Forms.PaintEventArgs e)
        {

            // Draw the rectangle...
```

```
        e.Graphics.DrawRectangle(new Pen(Color.Blue, ↵
 PenWidth), RcDraw);

        }
```

[Visual Basic]

```
' This example creates a PictureBox control on the form ↵
and draws to it.
' This example assumes that the Form_Load event handling ↵
 method is connected
' to the Load event of the form.
Private pictureBox1 As New PictureBox()

Private Sub Form1_Load(ByVal sender As Object, ByVal e As ↵
System.EventArgs) Handles MyBase.Load
    ' Dock the PictureBox to the form and set its background to white.
    pictureBox1.Dock = DockStyle.Fill
    pictureBox1.BackColor = Color.White
    ' Connect the Paint event of the PictureBox to the event ↵
 handling method.
    AddHandler pictureBox1.Paint, AddressOf Me.pictureBox1_Paint

    ' Add the PictureBox control to the Form.
    Me.Controls.Add(pictureBox1)
End Sub 'Form1_Load

Private Sub pictureBox1_Paint(ByVal sender As Object, ↵
ByVal e As System.Windows.Forms.PaintEventArgs)
    ' Create a local version of the graphics object for the PictureBox.
    Dim g As Graphics = e.Graphics

    ' Draw a string on the PictureBox.
    g.DrawString("This is a diagonal line drawn on the control", _
        New Font("Arial", 10), Brushes.Red, New PointF(30.0F, 30.0F))
    ' Draw a line in the PictureBox.
    g.DrawLine(System.Drawing.Pens.Red, pictureBox1.Left, _
        pictureBox1.Top, pictureBox1.Right, pictureBox1.Bottom)
End Sub 'pictureBox1_Paint
```

[C#]

```
// This example creates a PictureBox control on the form ↵
and draws to it.
// This example assumes that the Form_Load event handling method is
// connected to the Load event of the form.

private PictureBox pictureBox1 = new PictureBox();
private void Form1_Load(object sender, System.EventArgs e)
{
    // Dock the PictureBox to the form and set its background to white.
    pictureBox1.Dock = DockStyle.Fill;
    pictureBox1.BackColor = Color.White;
    // Connect the Paint event of the PictureBox to the event ↵
 handling method.
    pictureBox1.Paint += new ↵
System.Windows.Forms.PaintEventHandler(this.pictureBox1_Paint);

    // Add the PictureBox control to the Form.
    this.Controls.Add(pictureBox1);
}

private void pictureBox1_Paint(object sender, ↵
System.Windows.Forms.PaintEventArgs e)
{
    // Create a local version of the graphics object ↵
 for the PictureBox.
    Graphics g = e.Graphics;

    // Draw a string on the PictureBox.
    g.DrawString("This is a diagonal line drawn on the control",
        new Font("Arial",10), System.Drawing.Brushes.Blue, ↵
new Point(30,30));
    // Draw a line in the PictureBox.
    g.DrawLine(System.Drawing.Pens.Red, pictureBox1.Left, ↵
pictureBox1.Top,
        pictureBox1.Right, pictureBox1.Bottom);
}
```

Requirements

Namespace: System.Windows.Forms

Platforms: Windows 98, Windows NT 4.0, Windows Millennium Edition, Windows 2000, Windows XP Home Edition, Windows XP Professional, Windows Server 2003 family, .NET Compact Framework - Windows CE .NET

Assembly: System.Windows.Forms (in System.Windows.Forms.dll)

PaintEventArgs Constructor

Initializes a new instance of the **PaintEventArgs** class with the specified graphics and clipping rectangle.

[Visual Basic]

```
Public Sub New( _
   ByVal graphics As Graphics, _
   ByVal clipRect As Rectangle _
)
```

[C#]

```
public PaintEventArgs(
   Graphics graphics,
   Rectangle clipRect
);
```

[C++]

```
public: PaintEventArgs(
   Graphics* graphics,
   Rectangle clipRect
);
```

[JScript]

```
public function PaintEventArgs(
   graphics : Graphics,
   clipRect : Rectangle
);
```

Parameters

graphics

The **Graphics** used to paint the item.

clipRect

The **Rectangle** that represents the rectangle in which to paint.

Remarks

The **Graphics** identified by the *graphics* parameter is disposed when the **PaintEventArgs** is disposed.

Example

See related example in the **System.Windows.Forms.PaintEventArgs** class topic.

Requirements

Platforms: Windows 98, Windows NT 4.0, Windows Millennium Edition, Windows 2000, Windows XP Home Edition, Windows XP Professional, Windows Server 2003 family, .NET Compact Framework - Windows CE .NET

PaintEventArgs.ClipRectangle Property

Gets the rectangle in which to paint.

```
[Visual Basic]
Public ReadOnly Property ClipRectangle As Rectangle
[C#]
public Rectangle ClipRectangle {get;}
[C++]
public: __property Rectangle get_ClipRectangle();
[JScript]
public function get ClipRectangle() : Rectangle;
```

Property Value

The **Rectangle** in which to paint.

Requirements

Platforms: Windows 98, Windows NT 4.0, Windows Millennium Edition, Windows 2000, Windows XP Home Edition, Windows XP Professional, Windows Server 2003 family, .NET Compact Framework - Windows CE .NET

PaintEventArgs.Graphics Property

Gets the graphics used to paint.

```
[Visual Basic]
Public ReadOnly Property Graphics As Graphics
[C#]
public Graphics Graphics {get;}
[C++]
public: __property Graphics* get_Graphics();
[JScript]
public function get Graphics() : Graphics;
```

Property Value

The **Graphics** object used to paint. The **Graphics** object provides methods for drawing objects on the display device.

Example

See related example in the **System.Windows.Forms.PaintEventArgs** class topic.

Requirements

Platforms: Windows 98, Windows NT 4.0, Windows Millennium Edition, Windows 2000, Windows XP Home Edition, Windows XP Professional, Windows Server 2003 family, .NET Compact Framework - Windows CE .NET

PaintEventArgs.Dispose Method

Releases the resources used by the **PaintEventArgs**.

Overload List

Releases all resources used by the **PaintEventArgs**.

[Visual Basic] **Overloads Public Overridable Sub Dispose() Implements IDisposable.Dispose**

[C#] **public virtual void Dispose();**

[C++] **public: virtual void Dispose();**

[JScript] **public function Dispose();**

Releases the unmanaged resources used by the **PaintEventArgs** and optionally releases the managed resources.

[Visual Basic] **Overloads Protected Overridable Sub Dispose(Boolean)**

[C#] **protected virtual void Dispose(bool);**

[C++] **protected: virtual void Dispose(bool);**

[JScript] **protected function Dispose(Boolean);**

PaintEventArgs.Dispose Method ()

Releases all resources used by the **PaintEventArgs**.

```
[Visual Basic]
Overloads Public Overridable Sub Dispose() Implements _
   IDisposable.Dispose
[C#]
public virtual void Dispose();
[C++]
public: virtual void Dispose();
[JScript]
public function Dispose();
```

Implements

IDisposable.Dispose

Remarks

Call **Dispose** when you are finished using the **PaintEventArgs**. The dispose method leaves the **PaintEventArgs** in an unusable state. After calling **Dispose** you must release all references to the **PaintEventArgs** so the garbage collector can reclaim the memory that the **PaintEventArgs** was occupying. **Dispose** also disposes the associated **Graphics**.

Requirements

Platforms: Windows 98, Windows NT 4.0, Windows Millennium Edition, Windows 2000, Windows XP Home Edition, Windows XP Professional, Windows Server 2003 family

PaintEventArgs.Dispose Method (Boolean)

Releases the unmanaged resources used by the **PaintEventArgs** and optionally releases the managed resources.

```
[Visual Basic]
Overloads Protected Overridable Sub Dispose( _
   ByVal disposing As Boolean _
)
[C#]
protected virtual void Dispose(
   bool disposing
);
[C++]
protected: virtual void Dispose(
   bool disposing
);
[JScript]
protected function Dispose(
   disposing : Boolean
);
```

Parameters

disposing

true to release both managed and unmanaged resources; **false** to release only unmanaged resources.

Remarks

This method is called by the public **Dispose()** method and the **Finalize** method. **Dispose()** invokes the protected **Dispose(Boolean)** method with the *disposing* parameter set to **true**. **Finalize()** invokes **Dispose(Boolean)** with *disposing* set to **false**.

When the *disposing* parameter is **true**, this method releases all resources held by any managed objects that this **PaintEventArgs** references. This method invokes the **Dispose()** method of each referenced object.

Notes to Inheritors: **Dispose** can be called multiple times by other objects. When overriding **Dispose(Boolean)**, be careful not to reference objects that have been previously disposed of in an earlier call to **Dispose**.

Requirements

Platforms: Windows 98, Windows NT 4.0,
Windows Millennium Edition, Windows 2000,
Windows XP Home Edition, Windows XP Professional,
Windows Server 2003 family

PaintEventArgs.Finalize Method

This member overrides **Object.Finalize**.

[Visual Basic]
```
Overrides Protected Sub Finalize()
```
[C#]
```
~PaintEventArgs();
```
[C++]
```
~PaintEventArgs();
```
[JScript]
```
protected override function Finalize();
```

Requirements

Platforms: Windows 98, Windows NT 4.0,
Windows Millennium Edition, Windows 2000,
Windows XP Home Edition, Windows XP Professional,
Windows Server 2003 family,
.NET Compact Framework - Windows CE .NET

PaintEventHandler Delegate

Represents the method that will handle the **Paint** event of a **Control**.

[Visual Basic]
```
<Serializable>
Public Delegate Sub PaintEventHandler( _
   ByVal sender As Object, _
   ByVal e As PaintEventArgs _
)
```
[C#]
```
[Serializable]
public delegate void PaintEventHandler(
   object sender,
   PaintEventArgs e
);
```
[C++]
```
[Serializable]
public __gc __delegate void PaintEventHandler(
   Object* sender,
   PaintEventArgs* e
);
```

[JScript] In JScript, you can use the delegates in the .NET Framework, but you cannot define your own.

Parameters [Visual Basic, C#, C++]

The declaration of your event handler must have the same parameters as the **PaintEventHandler** delegate declaration.

sender

The source of the event.

e

A **PaintEventArgs** that contains the event data.

Remarks

When you create a **PaintEventHandler** delegate, you identify the method that will handle the event. To associate the event with your event handler, add an instance of the delegate to the event. The event handler is called whenever the event occurs, unless you remove the delegate.

Example

[Visual Basic]
```
' This example creates a PictureBox control on the form and ↵
draws to it.
' This example assumes that the Form_Load event handling method ↵
is connected
' to the Load event of the form.
Private pictureBox1 As New PictureBox()

Private Sub Form1_Load(ByVal sender As Object, ByVal e As ↵
System.EventArgs) Handles MyBase.Load
    ' Dock the PictureBox to the form and set its background to white.
    pictureBox1.Dock = DockStyle.Fill
    pictureBox1.BackColor = Color.White
    ' Connect the Paint event of the PictureBox to the event ↵
handling method.
    AddHandler pictureBox1.Paint, AddressOf Me.pictureBox1_Paint

    ' Add the PictureBox control to the Form.
    Me.Controls.Add(pictureBox1)
End Sub 'Form1_Load

Private Sub pictureBox1_Paint(ByVal sender As Object, ByVal ↵
e As System.Windows.Forms.PaintEventArgs)
    ' Create a local version of the graphics object for the PictureBox.
    Dim g As Graphics = e.Graphics
    ' Draw a string on the PictureBox.
    g.DrawString("This is a diagonal line drawn on the control", _
        New Font("Arial", 10), Brushes.Red, New PointF(30.0F, 30.0F))
    ' Draw a line in the PictureBox.
    g.DrawLine(System.Drawing.Pens.Red, pictureBox1.Left, _
        pictureBox1.Top, pictureBox1.Right, pictureBox1.Bottom)
End Sub 'pictureBox1_Paint
```

[C#]
```
// This example creates a PictureBox control on the form and ↵
 draws to it.
// This example assumes that the Form_Load event handling method is
// connected to the Load event of the form.

private PictureBox pictureBox1 = new PictureBox();
private void Form1_Load(object sender, System.EventArgs e)
{
    // Dock the PictureBox to the form and set its background to white.
    pictureBox1.Dock = DockStyle.Fill;
    pictureBox1.BackColor = Color.White;
    // Connect the Paint event of the PictureBox to the event ↵
handling method.
    pictureBox1.Paint += new ↵
System.Windows.Forms.PaintEventHandler(this.pictureBox1_Paint);

    // Add the PictureBox control to the Form.
    this.Controls.Add(pictureBox1);
}

private void pictureBox1_Paint(object sender, ↵
System.Windows.Forms.PaintEventArgs e)
{
    // Create a local version of the graphics object ↵
for the PictureBox.
    Graphics g = e.Graphics;

    // Draw a string on the PictureBox.
    g.DrawString("This is a diagonal line drawn on the control",
        new Font("Arial",10), System.Drawing.Brushes.Blue, ↵
 new Point(30,30));
    // Draw a line in the PictureBox.
    g.DrawLine(System.Drawing.Pens.Red, pictureBox1.Left, ↵
pictureBox1.Top,
        pictureBox1.Right, pictureBox1.Bottom);
}
```

Requirements

Namespace: System.Windows.Forms

Platforms: Windows 98, Windows NT 4.0, Windows Millennium Edition, Windows 2000, Windows XP Home Edition, Windows XP Professional, Windows Server 2003 family, .NET Compact Framework - Windows CE .NET

Assembly: System.Windows.Forms (in System.Windows.Forms.dll)

Panel Class

Represents a Windows **Panel** control.

System.Object
  System.MarshalByRefObject
    System.ComponentModel.Component
      System.Windows.Forms.Control
        System.Windows.Forms.ScrollableControl
          System.Windows.Forms.Panel
            System.Windows.Forms.Design.ComponentEditorPage
            System.Windows.Forms.TabPage

[Visual Basic]
```
Public Class Panel
   Inherits ScrollableControl
```
[C#]
```
public class Panel : ScrollableControl
```
[C++]
```
public __gc class Panel : public ScrollableControl
```
[JScript]
```
public class Panel extends ScrollableControl
```

Thread Safety

Any public static (**Shared** in Visual Basic) members of this type are safe for multithreaded operations. Any instance members are not guaranteed to be thread safe.

Remarks

A **Panel** is a control that contains other controls. You can use a **Panel** to group collections of controls such as a group of **RadioButton** controls. As with other container controls such as the **GroupBox** control, if the **Panel** control's **Enabled** property is set to **false**, the controls contained within the **Panel** will also be disabled.

The **Panel** control is displayed by default without any borders. You can provide a standard or three-dimensional border using the **BorderStyle** property to distinguish the area of the panel from other areas on the form. Because the **Panel** control derives from the **ScrollableControl** class, you can use the **AutoScroll** property to enable scroll bars in the **Panel** control. When the **AutoScroll** property is set to **true**, any controls located within the **Panel** (but outside of its visible region), can be scrolled to with the scroll bars provided.

Example

[Visual Basic, C#] The following example creates a **Panel** control and adds a **Label** and a **TextBox** to the **Panel**. The **Panel** control is displayed with a three-dimensional border to distinguish where the **Panel** control is located in relation to other objects on the form. This example assumes that the method defined in this example is called from within an existing form and that the **System.Drawing** namespace has been added to the source code for the form.

[Visual Basic]
```
Public Sub CreateMyPanel()
    Dim panel1 As New Panel()
    Dim textBox1 As New TextBox()
    Dim label1 As New Label()

    ' Initialize the Panel control.
    panel1.Location = New Point(56, 72)
    panel1.Size = New Size(264, 152)
    ' Set the Borderstyle for the Panel to three-dimensional.
    panel1.BorderStyle = System.Windows.Forms.BorderStyle.Fixed3D

    ' Initialize the Label and TextBox controls.
    label1.Location = New Point(16, 16)
    label1.Text = "label1"
    label1.Size = New Size(104, 16)
    textBox1.Location = New Point(16, 32)
    textBox1.Text = ""
    textBox1.Size = New Size(152, 20)

    ' Add the Panel control to the form.
    Me.Controls.Add(panel1)
    ' Add the Label and TextBox controls to the Panel.
    panel1.Controls.Add(label1)
    panel1.Controls.Add(textBox1)
End Sub
```

[C#]
```
public void CreateMyPanel()
{
   Panel panel1 = new Panel();
   TextBox textBox1 = new TextBox();
   Label label1 = new Label();

   // Initialize the Panel control.
   panel1.Location = new Point(56,72);
   panel1.Size = new Size(264, 152);
   // Set the Borderstyle for the Panel to three-dimensional.
   panel1.BorderStyle = System.Windows.Forms.BorderStyle.Fixed3D;

   // Initialize the Label and TextBox controls.
   label1.Location = new Point(16,16);
   label1.Text = "label1";
   label1.Size = new Size(104, 16);
   textBox1.Location = new Point(16,32);
   textBox1.Text = "";
   textBox1.Size = new Size(152, 20);

   // Add the Panel control to the form.
   this.Controls.Add(panel1);
   // Add the Label and TextBox controls to the Panel.
   panel1.Controls.Add(label1);
   panel1.Controls.Add(textBox1);
}
```

Requirements

Namespace: System.Windows.Forms

Platforms: Windows 98, Windows NT 4.0, Windows Millennium Edition, Windows 2000, Windows XP Home Edition, Windows XP Professional, Windows Server 2003 family, .NET Compact Framework - Windows CE .NET

Assembly: System.Windows.Forms (in System.Windows.Forms.dll)

Panel Constructor

Initializes a new instance of the **Panel** class.

[Visual Basic]
```
Public Sub New()
```
[C#]
```
public Panel();
```
[C++]
```
public: Panel();
```
[JScript]
```
public function Panel();
```

Requirements

Platforms: Windows 98, Windows NT 4.0, Windows Millennium Edition, Windows 2000, Windows XP Home Edition, Windows XP Professional, Windows Server 2003 family, .NET Compact Framework - Windows CE .NET

Panel.BorderStyle Property

Indicates the border style for the control.

```
[Visual Basic]
Public Property BorderStyle As BorderStyle
[C#]
public BorderStyle BorderStyle {get; set;}
[C++]
public: __property BorderStyle get_BorderStyle();
public: __property void set_BorderStyle(BorderStyle);
[JScript]
public function get BorderStyle() : BorderStyle;
public function set BorderStyle(BorderStyle);
```

Property Value

One of the **BorderStyle** values. The default is **BorderStyle.None**.

Remarks

By default, the **Panel** control is displayed without a border. You can use this property to distinguish the boundaries of the **Panel** control from other areas on the form.

Example

[Visual Basic, C#] The following example creates a **Panel** control with a three-dimensional border.

```
[Visual Basic]
Public Sub CreateMyPanel()
    Dim panel1 As New Panel()

    ' Initialize the Panel control.
    panel1.Location = New Point(56, 72)
    panel1.Size = New Size(264, 152)
    ' Set the Borderstyle for the Panel to three-dimensional.
    panel1.BorderStyle = System.Windows.Forms.BorderStyle.Fixed3D
End Sub
```

```
[C#]
public void CreateMyPanel()
{
   Panel panel1 = new Panel();

   // Initialize the Panel control.
   panel1.Location = new Point(56,72);
   panel1.Size = new Size(264, 152);
   // Set the Borderstyle for the Panel to three-dimensional.
   panel1.BorderStyle = System.Windows.Forms.BorderStyle.Fixed3D;
}
```

Requirements

Platforms: Windows 98, Windows NT 4.0, Windows Millennium Edition, Windows 2000, Windows XP Home Edition, Windows XP Professional, Windows Server 2003 family

Panel.CreateParams Property

This member overrides **Control.CreateParams**.

```
[Visual Basic]
Overrides Protected ReadOnly Property CreateParams As CreateParams
[C#]
protected override CreateParams CreateParams {get;}
[C++]
protected: __property CreateParams* get_CreateParams();
[JScript]
protected override function get CreateParams() : CreateParams;
```

Requirements

Platforms: Windows 98, Windows NT 4.0, Windows Millennium Edition, Windows 2000, Windows XP Home Edition, Windows XP Professional, Windows Server 2003 family

Panel.DefaultSize Property

This member overrides **Control.DefaultSize**.

```
[Visual Basic]
Overrides Protected ReadOnly Property DefaultSize As Size
[C#]
protected override Size DefaultSize {get;}
[C++]
protected: __property Size get_DefaultSize();
[JScript]
protected override function get DefaultSize() : Size;
```

Requirements

Platforms: Windows 98, Windows NT 4.0, Windows Millennium Edition, Windows 2000, Windows XP Home Edition, Windows XP Professional, Windows Server 2003 family

Panel.TabStop Property

Gets or sets a value indicating whether the user can give the focus to this control using the TAB key.

```
[Visual Basic]
Public Shadows Property TabStop As Boolean
[C#]
public new bool TabStop {get; set;}
[C++]
public: __property bool get_TabStop();
public: __property void set_TabStop(bool);
[JScript]
public hide function get TabStop() : Boolean;
public hide function set TabStop(Boolean);
```

Property Value

true if the user can give the focus to the control using the TAB key; otherwise, **false**. The default is **false**.

Remarks

When the user presses the TAB key, the input focus is set to the next control in the tab order. Controls with the **TabStop** property value of **false** are not included in the collection of controls in the tab order. The tab order can be manipulated by setting the control's **TabIndex** property value.

> **Note** The **TabStop** property has no effect on the **Panel** control as it is a container object.

Requirements

Platforms: Windows 98, Windows NT 4.0, Windows Millennium Edition, Windows 2000, Windows XP Home Edition, Windows XP Professional, Windows Server 2003 family

Panel.Text Property

This member overrides **Control.Text**.

```
[Visual Basic]
Overrides Public Property Text As String
[C#]
public override string Text {get; set;}
[C++]
public: __property String* get_Text();
public: __property void set_Text(String*);
[JScript]
public override function get Text() : String;
public override function set Text(String);
```

Requirements

Platforms: Windows 98, Windows NT 4.0, Windows Millennium Edition, Windows 2000, Windows XP Home Edition, Windows XP Professional, Windows Server 2003 family

Panel.OnResize Method

This member overrides **Control.OnResize**.

```
[Visual Basic]
Overrides Protected Sub OnResize( _
   ByVal eventargs As EventArgs _
)
[C#]
protected override void OnResize(
   EventArgs eventargs
);
[C++]
protected: void OnResize(
   EventArgs* eventargs
);
[JScript]
protected override function OnResize(
   eventargs : EventArgs
);
```

Requirements

Platforms: Windows 98, Windows NT 4.0, Windows Millennium Edition, Windows 2000, Windows XP Home Edition, Windows XP Professional, Windows Server 2003 family, .NET Compact Framework - Windows CE .NET

Panel.ToString Method

This member overrides **Object.ToString**.

```
[Visual Basic]
Overrides Public Function ToString() As String
[C#]
public override string ToString();
[C++]
public: String* ToString();
[JScript]
public override function ToString() : String;
```

Requirements

Platforms: Windows 98, Windows NT 4.0, Windows Millennium Edition, Windows 2000, Windows XP Home Edition, Windows XP Professional, Windows Server 2003 family, .NET Compact Framework - Windows CE .NET

Panel.KeyDown Event

This member supports the .NET Framework infrastructure and is not intended to be used directly from your code.

```
[Visual Basic]
Public Shadows Event KeyDown As KeyEventHandler
[C#]
public new event KeyEventHandler KeyDown;
[C++]
public: __event KeyEventHandler* KeyDown;
```

[JScript] In JScript, you can handle the events defined by a class, but you cannot define your own.

Panel.KeyPress Event

This member supports the .NET Framework infrastructure and is not intended to be used directly from your code.

```
[Visual Basic]
Public Shadows Event KeyPress As KeyPressEventHandler
[C#]
public new event KeyPressEventHandler KeyPress;
[C++]
public: __event KeyPressEventHandler* KeyPress;
```

[JScript] In JScript, you can handle the events defined by a class, but you cannot define your own.

Panel.KeyUp Event

This member supports the .NET Framework infrastructure and is not intended to be used directly from your code.

```
[Visual Basic]
Public Shadows Event KeyUp As KeyEventHandler
[C#]
public new event KeyEventHandler KeyUp;
[C++]
public: __event KeyEventHandler* KeyUp;
```

[JScript] In JScript, you can handle the events defined by a class, but you cannot define your own.

Panel.TextChanged Event

This member supports the .NET Framework infrastructure and is not intended to be used directly from your code.

```
[Visual Basic]
Public Shadows Event TextChanged As EventHandler
[C#]
public new event EventHandler TextChanged;
[C++]
public: __event EventHandler* TextChanged;
```

[JScript] In JScript, you can handle the events defined by a class, but you cannot define your own.

PictureBox Class

Represents a Windows picture box control for displaying an image.

System.Object
  System.MarshalByRefObject
    System.ComponentModel.Component
      System.Windows.Forms.Control
        System.Windows.Forms.PictureBox

[Visual Basic]
```
Public Class PictureBox
   Inherits Control
```
[C#]
```
public class PictureBox : Control
```
[C++]
```
public __gc class PictureBox : public Control
```
[JScript]
```
public class PictureBox extends Control
```

Thread Safety

Any public static (**Shared** in Visual Basic) members of this type are safe for multithreaded operations. Any instance members are not guaranteed to be thread safe.

Remarks

Typically the **PictureBox** is used to display graphics from a bitmap, metafile, icon, JPEG, GIF or PNG file.

Set the **Image** property to the **Image** you want to display, either at design time or at run time. Clipping and positioning of the image in the display area is controlled by the **SizeMode** property which is set to values in the **PictureBoxSizeMode** enumeration. You can change the size of the display area at run time with the **ClientSize** property.

The **PictureBox** control is displayed by default without any borders. You can provide a standard or three-dimensional border using the **BorderStyle** property to distinguish the picture box from the rest of the form, even if it contains no image.

Example

[Visual Basic, C#] The following example illustrates how you can set an image and resize the display area of the picture box. This example assumes that ShowMyImage is called from within an existing form, and that the **System.Drawing** namespace has been added to the source code for your form.

[Visual Basic]
```
Private MyImage As Bitmap

Public Sub ShowMyImage(fileToDisplay As String, xSize As Integer, _
                       ySize As Integer)
    ' Sets up an image object to be displayed.
    If Not (MyImage Is Nothing) Then
        MyImage.Dispose()
    End If

    ' Stretches the image to fit the pictureBox.
    pictureBox1.SizeMode = PictureBoxSizeMode.StretchImage
    MyImage = New Bitmap(fileToDisplay)
    pictureBox1.ClientSize = New Size(xSize, ySize)
    pictureBox1.Image = CType(MyImage, Image)
End Sub
```

[C#]
```
private Bitmap MyImage ;
public void ShowMyImage(String fileToDisplay, int xSize, int ySize)
{
   // Sets up an image object to be displayed.
   if (MyImage != null)
   {
      MyImage.Dispose();
   }

   // Stretches the image to fit the pictureBox.
   pictureBox1.SizeMode = PictureBoxSizeMode.StretchImage ;
   MyImage = new Bitmap(fileToDisplay);
   pictureBox1.ClientSize = new Size(xSize, ySize);
   pictureBox1.Image = (Image) MyImage ;
}
```

Requirements

Namespace: System.Windows.Forms

Platforms: Windows 98, Windows NT 4.0, Windows Millennium Edition, Windows 2000, Windows XP Home Edition, Windows XP Professional, Windows Server 2003 family, .NET Compact Framework - Windows CE .NET

Assembly: System.Windows.Forms (in System.Windows.Forms.dll)

PictureBox Constructor

Initializes a new instance of the **PictureBox** class.

[Visual Basic]
```
Public Sub New()
```
[C#]
```
public PictureBox();
```
[C++]
```
public: PictureBox();
```
[JScript]
```
public function PictureBox();
```

Remarks

The following table shows initial property values for an instance of **PictureBox**.

Item	Description
Image	A null reference (**Nothing** in Visual Basic)
SizeMode	**PictureBoxSizeMode.Normal**

Requirements

Platforms: Windows 98, Windows NT 4.0, Windows Millennium Edition, Windows 2000, Windows XP Home Edition, Windows XP Professional, Windows Server 2003 family, .NET Compact Framework - Windows CE .NET

PictureBox.AllowDrop Property

This member overrides **Control.AllowDrop**.

[Visual Basic]
```
Overrides Public Property AllowDrop As Boolean
```
[C#]
```
public override bool AllowDrop {get; set;}
```
[C++]
```
public: __property bool get_AllowDrop();
public: __property void set_AllowDrop(bool);
```
[JScript]
```
public override function get AllowDrop() : Boolean;
public override function set AllowDrop(Boolean);
```

Requirements

Platforms: Windows 98, Windows NT 4.0, Windows Millennium Edition, Windows 2000, Windows XP Home Edition, Windows XP Professional, Windows Server 2003 family

PictureBox.BorderStyle Property

Indicates the border style for the control.

```
[Visual Basic]
Public Property BorderStyle As BorderStyle
[C#]
public BorderStyle BorderStyle {get; set;}
[C++]
public: __property BorderStyle get_BorderStyle();
public: __property void set_BorderStyle(BorderStyle);
[JScript]
public function get BorderStyle() : BorderStyle;
public function set BorderStyle(BorderStyle);
```

Property Value

One of the **BorderStyle** enumeration values. The default is **None**.

Exceptions

Exception Type	Condition
InvalidEnumArgument-Exception	The value assigned is not one of the **BorderStyle** values.

Remarks

You can specify this property at design time or run time.

Requirements

Platforms: Windows 98, Windows NT 4.0, Windows Millennium Edition, Windows 2000, Windows XP Home Edition, Windows XP Professional, Windows Server 2003 family

PictureBox.CausesValidation Property

This member supports the .NET Framework infrastructure and is not intended to be used directly from your code.

```
[Visual Basic]
Public Shadows Property CausesValidation As Boolean
[C#]
public new bool CausesValidation {get; set;}
[C++]
public: __property bool get_CausesValidation();
public: __property void set_CausesValidation(bool);
[JScript]
public hide function get CausesValidation() : Boolean;
public hide function set CausesValidation(Boolean);
```

PictureBox.CreateParams Property

This member overrides **Control.CreateParams**.

```
[Visual Basic]
Overrides Protected ReadOnly Property CreateParams As CreateParams
[C#]
protected override CreateParams CreateParams {get;}
[C++]
protected: __property CreateParams* get_CreateParams();
[JScript]
protected override function get CreateParams() : CreateParams;
```

Requirements

Platforms: Windows 98, Windows NT 4.0, Windows Millennium Edition, Windows 2000, Windows XP Home Edition, Windows XP Professional, Windows Server 2003 family

PictureBox.DefaultImeMode Property

Gets a value indicating the mode for Input Method Editor (IME) for the **PictureBox**.

```
[Visual Basic]
Overrides Protected ReadOnly Property DefaultImeMode As ImeMode
[C#]
protected override ImeMode DefaultImeMode {get;}
[C++]
protected: __property ImeMode get_DefaultImeMode();
[JScript]
protected override function get DefaultImeMode() : ImeMode;
```

Property Value

Always **ImeMode.Disable**.

Requirements

Platforms: Windows 98, Windows NT 4.0, Windows Millennium Edition, Windows 2000, Windows XP Home Edition, Windows XP Professional, Windows Server 2003 family

PictureBox.DefaultSize Property

This member overrides **Control.DefaultSize**.

```
[Visual Basic]
Overrides Protected ReadOnly Property DefaultSize As Size
[C#]
protected override Size DefaultSize {get;}
[C++]
protected: __property Size get_DefaultSize();
[JScript]
protected override function get DefaultSize() : Size;
```

Requirements

Platforms: Windows 98, Windows NT 4.0, Windows Millennium Edition, Windows 2000, Windows XP Home Edition, Windows XP Professional, Windows Server 2003 family

PictureBox.Font Property

This member overrides **Control.Font**.

```
[Visual Basic]
Overrides Public Property Font As Font
[C#]
public override Font Font {get; set;}
[C++]
public: __property Font* get_Font();
public: __property void set_Font(Font*);
```

```
[JScript]
public override function get Font() : Font;
public override function set Font(Font);
```

Requirements

Platforms: Windows 98, Windows NT 4.0, Windows Millennium Edition, Windows 2000, Windows XP Home Edition, Windows XP Professional, Windows Server 2003 family

PictureBox.ForeColor Property

This member overrides **Control.ForeColor**.

```
[Visual Basic]
Overrides Public Property ForeColor As Color
[C#]
public override Color ForeColor {get; set;}
[C++]
public: __property Color get_ForeColor();
public: __property void set_ForeColor(Color);
[JScript]
public override function get ForeColor() : Color;
public override function set ForeColor(Color);
```

Requirements

Platforms: Windows 98, Windows NT 4.0, Windows Millennium Edition, Windows 2000, Windows XP Home Edition, Windows XP Professional, Windows Server 2003 family

PictureBox.Image Property

Gets or sets the image that the **PictureBox** displays.

```
[Visual Basic]
Public Property Image As Image
[C#]
public Image Image {get; set;}
[C++]
public: __property Image* get_Image();
public: __property void set_Image(Image*);
[JScript]
public function get Image() : Image;
public function set Image(Image);
```

Property Value

The **Image** object to display.

Remarks

The **Image** property is set to the **Image** to display. You can do this either at design time or at run time.

Requirements

Platforms: Windows 98, Windows NT 4.0, Windows Millennium Edition, Windows 2000, Windows XP Home Edition, Windows XP Professional, Windows Server 2003 family, .NET Compact Framework - Windows CE .NET

PictureBox.ImeMode Property

This member supports the .NET Framework infrastructure and is not intended to be used directly from your code.

```
[Visual Basic]
Public Shadows Property ImeMode As ImeMode
[C#]
public new ImeMode ImeMode {get; set;}
[C++]
public: __property ImeMode get_ImeMode();
public: __property void set_ImeMode(ImeMode);
[JScript]
public hide function get ImeMode() : ImeMode;
public hide function set ImeMode(ImeMode);
```

PictureBox.RightToLeft Property

This member overrides **Control.RightToLeft**.

```
[Visual Basic]
Overrides Public Property RightToLeft As RightToLeft
[C#]
public override RightToLeft RightToLeft {get; set;}
[C++]
public: __property RightToLeft get_RightToLeft();
public: __property void set_RightToLeft(RightToLeft);
[JScript]
public override function get RightToLeft() : RightToLeft;
public override function set RightToLeft(RightToLeft);
```

Requirements

Platforms: Windows 98, Windows NT 4.0, Windows Millennium Edition, Windows 2000, Windows XP Home Edition, Windows XP Professional, Windows Server 2003 family

PictureBox.SizeMode Property

Indicates how the image is displayed.

```
[Visual Basic]
Public Property SizeMode As PictureBoxSizeMode
[C#]
public PictureBoxSizeMode SizeMode {get; set;}
[C++]
public: __property PictureBoxSizeMode get_SizeMode();
public: __property void set_SizeMode(PictureBoxSizeMode);
[JScript]
public function get SizeMode() : PictureBoxSizeMode;
public function set SizeMode(PictureBoxSizeMode);
```

Property Value

One of the **PictureBoxSizeMode** values. The default is **Normal**.

Exceptions

Exception Type	Condition
InvalidEnumArgumentException	The value assigned is not one of the **PictureBoxSizeMode** values.

Remarks

Valid values for this property are taken from the **PictureBoxSizeMode** enumeration. By default, in **PictureBoxSizeMode.Normal** mode, the **Image** is placed in the upper left corner of the **PictureBox**, and any part of the image too big for the **PictureBox** is clipped. Using the **PictureBoxSizeMode.StretchImage** value causes the image to stretch to fit the **PictureBox**.

Using the **PictureBoxSizeMode.AutoSize** value causes the control to resize to always fit the image. Using the **PictureBoxSizeMode.CenterImage** value causes the image to be centered in the client area.

Requirements

Platforms: Windows 98, Windows NT 4.0, Windows Millennium Edition, Windows 2000, Windows XP Home Edition, Windows XP Professional, Windows Server 2003 family, .NET Compact Framework - Windows CE .NET

PictureBox.TabIndex Property

This member supports the .NET Framework infrastructure and is not intended to be used directly from your code.

```
[Visual Basic]
Public Shadows Property TabIndex As Integer
[C#]
public new int TabIndex {get; set;}
[C++]
public: __property int get_TabIndex();
public: __property void set_TabIndex(int);
[JScript]
public hide function get TabIndex() : int;
public hide function set TabIndex(int);
```

PictureBox.TabStop Property

This member supports the .NET Framework infrastructure and is not intended to be used directly from your code.

```
[Visual Basic]
Public Shadows Property TabStop As Boolean
[C#]
public new bool TabStop {get; set;}
[C++]
public: __property bool get_TabStop();
public: __property void set_TabStop(bool);
[JScript]
public hide function get TabStop() : Boolean;
public hide function set TabStop(Boolean);
```

PictureBox.Text Property

This member overrides **Control.Text**.

```
[Visual Basic]
Overrides Public Property Text As String
[C#]
public override string Text {get; set;}
[C++]
public: __property String* get_Text();
public: __property void set_Text(String*);
[JScript]
public override function get Text() : String;
public override function set Text(String);
```

Requirements

Platforms: Windows 98, Windows NT 4.0, Windows Millennium Edition, Windows 2000, Windows XP Home Edition, Windows XP Professional, Windows Server 2003 family

PictureBox.Dispose Method

Overload List

This member supports the .NET Framework infrastructure and is not intended to be used directly from your code.

Supported by the .NET Compact Framework.

[Visual Basic] **Overloads Overrides Protected Sub Dispose(Boolean)**

[C#] **protected override void Dispose(bool);**

[C++] **protected: void Dispose(bool);**

[JScript] **protected override function Dispose(Boolean);**

Inherited from **Component**.

Supported by the .NET Compact Framework.

[Visual Basic] **Overloads Public Overridable Sub Dispose() Implements IDisposable.Dispose**

[C#] **public virtual void Dispose();**

[C++] **public: virtual void Dispose();**

[JScript] **public function Dispose();**

PictureBox.Dispose Method (Boolean)

This member overrides **Control.Dispose**.

```
[Visual Basic]
Overrides Overloads Protected Sub Dispose( _
   ByVal disposing As Boolean _
)
[C#]
protected override void Dispose(
   bool disposing
);
[C++]
protected: void Dispose(
   bool disposing
);
[JScript]
protected override function Dispose(
   disposing : Boolean
);
```

Requirements

Platforms: Windows 98, Windows NT 4.0, Windows Millennium Edition, Windows 2000, Windows XP Home Edition, Windows XP Professional, Windows Server 2003 family, .NET Compact Framework - Windows CE .NET

PictureBox.OnEnabledChanged Method

This member overrides **Control.OnEnabledChanged**.

```
[Visual Basic]
Overrides Protected Sub OnEnabledChanged( _
   ByVal e As EventArgs _
)
[C#]
protected override void OnEnabledChanged(
   EventArgs e
);
[C++]
protected: void OnEnabledChanged(
   EventArgs* e
);
[JScript]
protected override function OnEnabledChanged(
   e : EventArgs
);
```

Requirements

Platforms: Windows 98, Windows NT 4.0, Windows Millennium Edition, Windows 2000, Windows XP Home Edition, Windows XP Professional, Windows Server 2003 family, .NET Compact Framework - Windows CE .NET

PictureBox.OnPaint Method

This member overrides **Control.OnPaint**.

```
[Visual Basic]
Overrides Protected Sub OnPaint( _
   ByVal pe As PaintEventArgs _
)
[C#]
protected override void OnPaint(
   PaintEventArgs pe
);
[C++]
protected: void OnPaint(
   PaintEventArgs* pe
);
[JScript]
protected override function OnPaint(
   pe : PaintEventArgs
);
```

Requirements

Platforms: Windows 98, Windows NT 4.0, Windows Millennium Edition, Windows 2000, Windows XP Home Edition, Windows XP Professional, Windows Server 2003 family, .NET Compact Framework - Windows CE .NET

PictureBox.OnParentChanged Method

This member overrides **Control.OnParentChanged**.

```
[Visual Basic]
Overrides Protected Sub OnParentChanged( _
   ByVal e As EventArgs _
)
[C#]
protected override void OnParentChanged(
   EventArgs e
);
[C++]
protected: void OnParentChanged(
   EventArgs* e
);
[JScript]
protected override function OnParentChanged(
   e : EventArgs
);
```

Requirements

Platforms: Windows 98, Windows NT 4.0, Windows Millennium Edition, Windows 2000, Windows XP Home Edition, Windows XP Professional, Windows Server 2003 family, .NET Compact Framework - Windows CE .NET

PictureBox.OnResize Method

This member overrides **Control.OnResize**.

```
[Visual Basic]
Overrides Protected Sub OnResize( _
   ByVal e As EventArgs _
)
[C#]
protected override void OnResize(
   EventArgs e
);
[C++]
protected: void OnResize(
   EventArgs* e
);
[JScript]
protected override function OnResize(
   e : EventArgs
);
```

Requirements

Platforms: Windows 98, Windows NT 4.0, Windows Millennium Edition, Windows 2000, Windows XP Home Edition, Windows XP Professional, Windows Server 2003 family, .NET Compact Framework - Windows CE .NET

PictureBox.OnSizeModeChanged Method

Raises the **SizeModeChanged** event.

```
[Visual Basic]
Protected Overridable Sub OnSizeModeChanged( _
   ByVal e As EventArgs _
)
[C#]
protected virtual void OnSizeModeChanged(
   EventArgs e
);
[C++]
protected: virtual void OnSizeModeChanged(
   EventArgs* e
);
```

[JScript]
```
protected function OnSizeModeChanged(
   e : EventArgs
);
```

Parameters

e

An **EventArgs** that contains the event data.

Remarks

Raising an event invokes the event handler through a delegate. For more information, see **Raising an Event**.

The **OnSizeModeChanged** method also allows derived classes to handle the event without attaching a delegate. This is the preferred technique for handling the event in a derived class.

Notes to Inheritors: When overriding **OnSizeModeChanged** in a derived class, be sure to call the base class's **OnSizeModeChanged** method so that registered delegates receive the event.

Requirements

Platforms: Windows 98, Windows NT 4.0, Windows Millennium Edition, Windows 2000, Windows XP Home Edition, Windows XP Professional, Windows Server 2003 family

PictureBox.OnVisibleChanged Method

This member overrides **Control.OnVisibleChanged**.

[Visual Basic]
```
Overrides Protected Sub OnVisibleChanged( _
   ByVal e As EventArgs _
)
```
[C#]
```
protected override void OnVisibleChanged(
   EventArgs e
);
```
[C++]
```
protected: void OnVisibleChanged(
   EventArgs* e
);
```
[JScript]
```
protected override function OnVisibleChanged(
   e : EventArgs
);
```

Requirements

Platforms: Windows 98, Windows NT 4.0, Windows Millennium Edition, Windows 2000, Windows XP Home Edition, Windows XP Professional, Windows Server 2003 family

PictureBox.SetBoundsCore Method

This member overrides **Control.SetBoundsCore**.

[Visual Basic]
```
Overrides Protected Sub SetBoundsCore( _
   ByVal x As Integer, _
   ByVal y As Integer, _
   ByVal width As Integer, _
   ByVal height As Integer, _
   ByVal specified As BoundsSpecified _
)
```
[C#]
```
protected override void SetBoundsCore(
   int x,
   int y,
   int width,
   int height,
   BoundsSpecified specified
);
```
[C++]
```
protected: void SetBoundsCore(
   int x,
   int y,
   int width,
   int height,
   BoundsSpecified specified
);
```
[JScript]
```
protected override function SetBoundsCore(
   x : int,
   y : int,
   width : int,
   height : int,
   specified : BoundsSpecified
);
```

Requirements

Platforms: Windows 98, Windows NT 4.0, Windows Millennium Edition, Windows 2000, Windows XP Home Edition, Windows XP Professional, Windows Server 2003 family

PictureBox.ToString Method

This member overrides **Object.ToString**.

[Visual Basic]
```
Overrides Public Function ToString() As String
```
[C#]
```
public override string ToString();
```
[C++]
```
public: String* ToString();
```
[JScript]
```
public override function ToString() : String;
```

Requirements

Platforms: Windows 98, Windows NT 4.0, Windows Millennium Edition, Windows 2000, Windows XP Home Edition, Windows XP Professional, Windows Server 2003 family, .NET Compact Framework - Windows CE .NET

PictureBox.CausesValidationChanged Event

This member supports the .NET Framework infrastructure and is not intended to be used directly from your code.

[Visual Basic]
```
Public Shadows Event CausesValidationChanged As EventHandler
```
[C#]
```
public new event EventHandler CausesValidationChanged;
```
[C++]
```
public: __event EventHandler* CausesValidationChanged;
```

[JScript] In JScript, you can handle the events defined by a class, but you cannot define your own.

PictureBox.Enter Event

This member supports the .NET Framework infrastructure and is not intended to be used directly from your code.

[Visual Basic]
```
Public Shadows Event Enter As EventHandler
```
[C#]
```
public new event EventHandler Enter;
```
[C++]
```
public: __event EventHandler* Enter;
```

[JScript] In JScript, you can handle the events defined by a class, but you cannot define your own.

PictureBox.FontChanged Event

This member supports the .NET Framework infrastructure and is not intended to be used directly from your code.

[Visual Basic]
```
Public Shadows Event FontChanged As EventHandler
```
[C#]
```
public new event EventHandler FontChanged;
```
[C++]
```
public: __event EventHandler* FontChanged;
```

[JScript] In JScript, you can handle the events defined by a class, but you cannot define your own.

PictureBox.ForeColorChanged Event

This member supports the .NET Framework infrastructure and is not intended to be used directly from your code.

[Visual Basic]
```
Public Shadows Event ForeColorChanged As EventHandler
```
[C#]
```
public new event EventHandler ForeColorChanged;
```
[C++]
```
public: __event EventHandler* ForeColorChanged;
```

[JScript] In JScript, you can handle the events defined by a class, but you cannot define your own.

PictureBox.ImeModeChanged Event

This member supports the .NET Framework infrastructure and is not intended to be used directly from your code.

[Visual Basic]
```
Public Shadows Event ImeModeChanged As EventHandler
```
[C#]
```
public new event EventHandler ImeModeChanged;
```
[C++]
```
public: __event EventHandler* ImeModeChanged;
```

[JScript] In JScript, you can handle the events defined by a class, but you cannot define your own.

PictureBox.KeyDown Event

This member supports the .NET Framework infrastructure and is not intended to be used directly from your code.

[Visual Basic]
```
Public Shadows Event KeyDown As KeyEventHandler
```
[C#]
```
public new event KeyEventHandler KeyDown;
```
[C++]
```
public: __event KeyEventHandler* KeyDown;
```

[JScript] In JScript, you can handle the events defined by a class, but you cannot define your own.

PictureBox.KeyPress Event

This member supports the .NET Framework infrastructure and is not intended to be used directly from your code.

[Visual Basic]
```
Public Shadows Event KeyPress As KeyPressEventHandler
```
[C#]
```
public new event KeyPressEventHandler KeyPress;
```
[C++]
```
public: __event KeyPressEventHandler* KeyPress;
```

[JScript] In JScript, you can handle the events defined by a class, but you cannot define your own.

PictureBox.KeyUp Event

This member supports the .NET Framework infrastructure and is not intended to be used directly from your code.

[Visual Basic]
```
Public Shadows Event KeyUp As KeyEventHandler
```
[C#]
```
public new event KeyEventHandler KeyUp;
```
[C++]
```
public: __event KeyEventHandler* KeyUp;
```

[JScript] In JScript, you can handle the events defined by a class, but you cannot define your own.

PictureBox.Leave Event

This member supports the .NET Framework infrastructure and is not intended to be used directly from your code.

[Visual Basic]
```
Public Shadows Event Leave As EventHandler
```
[C#]
```
public new event EventHandler Leave;
```
[C++]
```
public: __event EventHandler* Leave;
```

[JScript] In JScript, you can handle the events defined by a class, but you cannot define your own.

PictureBox.RightToLeftChanged Event

This member supports the .NET Framework infrastructure and is not intended to be used directly from your code.

[Visual Basic]
```
Public Shadows Event RightToLeftChanged As EventHandler
```
[C#]
```
public new event EventHandler RightToLeftChanged;
```
[C++]
```
public: __event EventHandler* RightToLeftChanged;
```

[JScript] In JScript, you can handle the events defined by a class, but you cannot define your own.

PictureBox.SizeModeChanged Event

Occurs when **SizeMode** changes.

[Visual Basic]
```
Public Event SizeModeChanged As EventHandler
```
[C#]
```
public event EventHandler SizeModeChanged;
```
[C++]
```
public: __event EventHandler* SizeModeChanged;
```

[JScript] In JScript, you can handle the events defined by a class, but you cannot define your own.

Event Data

The event handler receives an argument of type **EventArgs**.

Remarks

For more information about handling events, see **Consuming Events**.

Requirements

Platforms: Windows 98, Windows NT 4.0, Windows Millennium Edition, Windows 2000, Windows XP Home Edition, Windows XP Professional, Windows Server 2003 family

PictureBox.TabIndexChanged Event

This member supports the .NET Framework infrastructure and is not intended to be used directly from your code.

[Visual Basic]
```
Public Shadows Event TabIndexChanged As EventHandler
```
[C#]
```
public new event EventHandler TabIndexChanged;
```
[C++]
```
public: __event EventHandler* TabIndexChanged;
```

[JScript] In JScript, you can handle the events defined by a class, but you cannot define your own.

PictureBox.TabStopChanged Event

This member supports the .NET Framework infrastructure and is not intended to be used directly from your code.

[Visual Basic]
```
Public Shadows Event TabStopChanged As EventHandler
```
[C#]
```
public new event EventHandler TabStopChanged;
```
[C++]
```
public: __event EventHandler* TabStopChanged;
```

[JScript] In JScript, you can handle the events defined by a class, but you cannot define your own.

PictureBox.TextChanged Event

This member supports the .NET Framework infrastructure and is not intended to be used directly from your code.

[Visual Basic]
```
Public Shadows Event TextChanged As EventHandler
```
[C#]
```
public new event EventHandler TextChanged;
```
[C++]
```
public: __event EventHandler* TextChanged;
```

[JScript] In JScript, you can handle the events defined by a class, but you cannot define your own.

PictureBoxSizeMode Enumeration

Specifies how an image is positioned within a **PictureBox**.

[Visual Basic]
```
<Serializable>
Public Enum PictureBoxSizeMode
```
[C#]
```
[Serializable]
public enum PictureBoxSizeMode
```
[C++]
```
[Serializable]
__value public enum PictureBoxSizeMode
```
[JScript]
```
public
   Serializable
enum PictureBoxSizeMode
```

Remarks

Use the members of this enumeration to set the value of the **SizeMode** property of the **PictureBox**.

Members

Member name	Description
AutoSize	The **PictureBox** is sized equal to the size of the image that it contains.
CenterImage Supported by the .NET Compact Framework.	The image is displayed in the center if the **PictureBox** is larger than the image. If the image is larger than the **PictureBox**, the picture is placed in the center of the **PictureBox** and the outside edges are clipped.
Normal Supported by the .NET Compact Framework.	The image is placed in the upper-left corner of the **PictureBox**. The image is clipped if it is larger than the **PictureBox** it is contained in.
StretchImage Supported by the .NET Compact Framework.	The image within the **PictureBox** is stretched or shrunk to fit the size of the **PictureBox**.

Requirements

Namespace: System.Windows.Forms

Platforms: Windows 98, Windows NT 4.0, Windows Millennium Edition, Windows 2000, Windows XP Home Edition, Windows XP Professional, Windows Server 2003 family, .NET Compact Framework - Windows CE .NET

Assembly: System.Windows.Forms (in System.Windows.Forms.dll)

PrintControllerWithStatus-Dialog Class

Controls how a document is printed.

System.Object
  System.Drawing.Printing.PrintController
    System.Windows.Forms.PrintControllerWithStatusDialog

[Visual Basic]
```
Public Class PrintControllerWithStatusDialog
   Inherits PrintController
```
[C#]
```
public class PrintControllerWithStatusDialog : PrintController
```
[C++]
```
public __gc class PrintControllerWithStatusDialog : public
   PrintController
```
[JScript]
```
public class PrintControllerWithStatusDialog extends
   PrintController
```

Thread Safety

Any public static (**Shared** in Visual Basic) members of this type are safe for multithreaded operations. Any instance members are not guaranteed to be thread safe.

Remarks

This class implements a **PrintController** and adds a status dialog. A print controller specifies how a **PrintDocument** is printed.

For a list of initial property values for an instance of **PrintControllerWithStatusDialog**, see the **PrintControllerWithStatusDialog** constructor.

Example

[Visual Basic, C#] The following example shows how to create a new **PrintController** and assign it to the **PrintController** property. The example assumes that you have added the **System.Drawing.Printing** namespace to the class and that you have created a new instance of a **PrintDocument** as `myDocumentPrinter`.

[Visual Basic]
```
Sub myPrint()
    If useMyPrintController = True Then
        myDocumentPrinter.PrintController = New                ↵
myControllerImplementation()
        If wantsStatusDialog = True Then
            myDocumentPrinter.PrintController = _
                New                                            ↵
PrintControllerWithStatusDialog(myDocumentPrinter.PrintController)
        End If
    End If
    myDocumentPrinter.Print()
End Sub
```

[C#]
```
void myPrint() {
   if (useMyPrintController==true) {
      myDocumentPrinter.PrintController = new                  ↵
myControllerImplementation();
      if (wantsStatusDialog==true) {
         myDocumentPrinter.PrintController =
            new
PrintControllerWithStatusDialog(myDocumentPrinter.PrintController);
      }
   }
   myDocumentPrinter.Print();
}
```

Requirements

Namespace: System.Windows.Forms

Platforms: Windows 98, Windows NT 4.0, Windows Millennium Edition, Windows 2000, Windows XP Home Edition, Windows XP Professional, Windows Server 2003 family

Assembly: System.Windows.Forms (in System.Windows.Forms.dll)

PrintControllerWithStatusDialog Constructor

Initializes a new instance of the **PrintControllerWithStatusDialog** class.

Overload List

Initializes a new instance of the **PrintControllerWithStatusDialog** class, wrapping the supplied **PrintController**.

[Visual Basic] **Public Sub New(PrintController)**

[C#] **public PrintControllerWithStatusDialog(PrintController);**

[C++] **public: PrintControllerWithStatusDialog(PrintController*);**

[JScript] **public function PrintControllerWithStatusDialog(PrintController);**

Initializes a new instance of the **PrintControllerWithStatusDialog** class, wrapping the supplied **PrintController** and specifying a title for the dialog.

[Visual Basic] **Public Sub New(PrintController, String)**

[C#] **public PrintControllerWithStatusDialog(PrintController, string);**

[C++] **public: PrintControllerWithStatusDialog(PrintController*, String*);**

[JScript] **public function PrintControllerWithStatusDialog(PrintController, String);**

PrintControllerWithStatusDialog Constructor (PrintController)

Initializes a new instance of the **PrintControllerWithStatusDialog** class, wrapping the supplied **PrintController**.

[Visual Basic]
```
Public Sub New( _
   ByVal underlyingController As PrintController _
)
```
[C#]
```
public PrintControllerWithStatusDialog(
   PrintController underlyingController
);
```
[C++]
```
public: PrintControllerWithStatusDialog(
   PrintController* underlyingController
);
```
[JScript]
```
public function PrintControllerWithStatusDialog(
   underlyingController : PrintController
);
```

Parameters

underlyingController
A **PrintController** to encapsulate.

Requirements

Platforms: Windows 98, Windows NT 4.0, Windows Millennium Edition, Windows 2000, Windows XP Home Edition, Windows XP Professional, Windows Server 2003 family

PrintControllerWithStatusDialog Constructor (PrintController, String)

Initializes a new instance of the **PrintControllerWithStatusDialog** class, wrapping the supplied **PrintController** and specifying a title for the dialog.

```
[Visual Basic]
Public Sub New( _
   ByVal underlyingController As PrintController, _
   ByVal dialogTitle As String _
)
[C#]
public PrintControllerWithStatusDialog(
   PrintController underlyingController,
   string dialogTitle
);
[C++]
public: PrintControllerWithStatusDialog(
   PrintController* underlyingController,
   String* dialogTitle
);
[JScript]
public function PrintControllerWithStatusDialog(
   underlyingController : PrintController,
   dialogTitle : String
);
```

Parameters

underlyingController
A **PrintController** to encapsulate.

dialogTitle
A **String** containing a title for the status dialog.

Requirements

Platforms: Windows 98, Windows NT 4.0, Windows Millennium Edition, Windows 2000, Windows XP Home Edition, Windows XP Professional, Windows Server 2003 family

PrintControllerWithStatusDialog.OnEndPage Method

This member overrides **PrintController.OnEndPage**.

```
[Visual Basic]
Overrides Public Sub OnEndPage( _
   ByVal document As PrintDocument, _
   ByVal e As PrintPageEventArgs _
)
[C#]
public override void OnEndPage(
   PrintDocument document,
   PrintPageEventArgs e
);
[C++]
public: void OnEndPage(
   PrintDocument* document,
   PrintPageEventArgs* e
);
[JScript]
public override function OnEndPage(
   document : PrintDocument,
   e : PrintPageEventArgs
);
```

Requirements

Platforms: Windows 98, Windows NT 4.0, Windows Millennium Edition, Windows 2000, Windows XP Home Edition, Windows XP Professional, Windows Server 2003 family

PrintControllerWithStatusDialog.OnEndPrint Method

This member overrides **PrintController.OnEndPrint**.

```
[Visual Basic]
Overrides Public Sub OnEndPrint( _
   ByVal document As PrintDocument, _
   ByVal e As PrintEventArgs _
)
[C#]
public override void OnEndPrint(
   PrintDocument document,
   PrintEventArgs e
);
[C++]
public: void OnEndPrint(
   PrintDocument* document,
   PrintEventArgs* e
);
[JScript]
public override function OnEndPrint(
   document : PrintDocument,
   e : PrintEventArgs
);
```

Requirements

Platforms: Windows 98, Windows NT 4.0, Windows Millennium Edition, Windows 2000, Windows XP Home Edition, Windows XP Professional, Windows Server 2003 family

PrintControllerWithStatusDialog.OnStartPage Method

This member overrides **PrintController.OnStartPage**.

[Visual Basic]
```
Overrides Public Function OnStartPage( _
   ByVal document As PrintDocument, _
   ByVal e As PrintPageEventArgs _
) As Graphics
```
[C#]
```
public override Graphics OnStartPage(
   PrintDocument document,
   PrintPageEventArgs e
);
```
[C++]
```
public: Graphics* OnStartPage(
   PrintDocument* document,
   PrintPageEventArgs* e
);
```
[JScript]
```
public override function OnStartPage(
   document : PrintDocument,
   e : PrintPageEventArgs
) : Graphics;
```

Requirements

Platforms: Windows 98, Windows NT 4.0, Windows Millennium Edition, Windows 2000, Windows XP Home Edition, Windows XP Professional, Windows Server 2003 family

PrintControllerWithStatusDialog.OnStartPrint Method

This member overrides **PrintController.OnStartPrint**.

[Visual Basic]
```
Overrides Public Sub OnStartPrint( _
   ByVal document As PrintDocument, _
   ByVal e As PrintEventArgs _
)
```
[C#]
```
public override void OnStartPrint(
   PrintDocument document,
   PrintEventArgs e
);
```
[C++]
```
public: void OnStartPrint(
   PrintDocument* document,
   PrintEventArgs* e
);
```
[JScript]
```
public override function OnStartPrint(
   document : PrintDocument,
   e : PrintEventArgs
);
```

Requirements

Platforms: Windows 98, Windows NT 4.0, Windows Millennium Edition, Windows 2000, Windows XP Home Edition, Windows XP Professional, Windows Server 2003 family

PrintDialog Class

Allows users to select a printer and choose which portions of the document to print.

System.Object
  System.MarshalByRefObject
    System.ComponentModel.Component
      System.Windows.Forms.CommonDialog
        System.Windows.Forms.PrintDialog

```
[Visual Basic]
NotInheritable Public Class PrintDialog
   Inherits CommonDialog
[C#]
public sealed class PrintDialog : CommonDialog
[C++]
public __gc __sealed class PrintDialog : public CommonDialog
[JScript]
public class PrintDialog extends CommonDialog
```

Thread Safety

Any public static (**Shared** in Visual Basic) members of this type are safe for multithreaded operations. Any instance members are not guaranteed to be thread safe.

Remarks

When you create an instance of **PrintDialog**, the read/write properties are set to initial values. For a list of these values, see the **PrintDialog** constructor.

Requirements

Namespace: System.Windows.Forms

Platforms: Windows 98, Windows NT 4.0, Windows Millennium Edition, Windows 2000, Windows XP Home Edition, Windows XP Professional, Windows Server 2003 family

Assembly: System.Windows.Forms (in System.Windows.Forms.dll)

PrintDialog Constructor

Initializes a new instance of the **PrintDialog** class.

```
[Visual Basic]
Public Sub New()
[C#]
public PrintDialog();
[C++]
public: PrintDialog();
[JScript]
public function PrintDialog();
```

Remarks

When you create an instance of **PrintDialog**, the following read/write properties are set to initial values.

Property	Initial Value
AllowSomePages	**false**
AllowPrintToFile	**true**
AllowSelection	**false**
Document	A null reference (**Nothing** in Visual Basic)
PrinterSettings	**false**
PrintToFile	A null reference (**Nothing**)
ShowHelp	**false**
ShowNetwork	**true**

You can change the value for any of these properties through a separate call to the property.

Requirements

Platforms: Windows 98, Windows NT 4.0, Windows Millennium Edition, Windows 2000, Windows XP Home Edition, Windows XP Professional, Windows Server 2003 family

PrintDialog.AllowPrintToFile Property

Gets or sets a value indicating whether the Print to file check box is enabled.

```
[Visual Basic]
Public Property AllowPrintToFile As Boolean
[C#]
public bool AllowPrintToFile {get; set;}
[C++]
public: __property bool get_AllowPrintToFile();
public: __property void set_AllowPrintToFile(bool);
[JScript]
public function get AllowPrintToFile() : Boolean;
public function set AllowPrintToFile(Boolean);
```

Property Value

true if the Print to file check box is enabled; otherwise, **false**. The default is **true**.

Requirements

Platforms: Windows 98, Windows NT 4.0, Windows Millennium Edition, Windows 2000, Windows XP Home Edition, Windows XP Professional, Windows Server 2003 family

PrintDialog.AllowSelection Property

Gets or sets a value indicating whether the From... To... Page option button is enabled.

```
[Visual Basic]
Public Property AllowSelection As Boolean
[C#]
public bool AllowSelection {get; set;}
[C++]
public: __property bool get_AllowSelection();
public: __property void set_AllowSelection(bool);
[JScript]
public function get AllowSelection() : Boolean;
public function set AllowSelection(Boolean);
```

Property Value

true if the From... To... Page option button is enabled; otherwise, **false**. The default is **true**.

Requirements

Platforms: Windows 98, Windows NT 4.0, Windows Millennium Edition, Windows 2000, Windows XP Home Edition, Windows XP Professional, Windows Server 2003 family

PrintDialog.AllowSomePages Property

Gets or sets a value indicating whether the Pages option button is enabled.

```
[Visual Basic]
Public Property AllowSomePages As Boolean
[C#]
public bool AllowSomePages {get; set;}
[C++]
public: __property bool get_AllowSomePages();
public: __property void set_AllowSomePages(bool);
[JScript]
public function get AllowSomePages() : Boolean;
public function set AllowSomePages(Boolean);
```

Property Value

true if the Pages option button is enabled; otherwise, **false**. The default is **false**.

Requirements

Platforms: Windows 98, Windows NT 4.0, Windows Millennium Edition, Windows 2000, Windows XP Home Edition, Windows XP Professional, Windows Server 2003 family

PrintDialog.Document Property

Gets or sets a value indicating the **PrintDocument** used to obtain **PrinterSettings**.

```
[Visual Basic]
Public Property Document As PrintDocument
[C#]
public PrintDocument Document {get; set;}
[C++]
public: __property PrintDocument* get_Document();
public: __property void set_Document(PrintDocument*);
[JScript]
public function get Document() : PrintDocument;
public function set Document(PrintDocument);
```

Property Value

The **PrintDocument** used to obtain **PrinterSettings**. The default is a null reference (**Nothing** in Visual Basic).

Requirements

Platforms: Windows 98, Windows NT 4.0, Windows Millennium Edition, Windows 2000, Windows XP Home Edition, Windows XP Professional, Windows Server 2003 family

PrintDialog.PrinterSettings Property

Gets or sets the printer settings the dialog box modifies.

```
[Visual Basic]
Public Property PrinterSettings As PrinterSettings
[C#]
public PrinterSettings PrinterSettings {get; set;}
[C++]
public: __property PrinterSettings* get_PrinterSettings();
public: __property void set_PrinterSettings(PrinterSettings*);
[JScript]
public function get PrinterSettings() : PrinterSettings;
public function set PrinterSettings(PrinterSettings);
```

Property Value

The **PrinterSettings** the dialog box modifies.

Requirements

Platforms: Windows 98, Windows NT 4.0, Windows Millennium Edition, Windows 2000, Windows XP Home Edition, Windows XP Professional, Windows Server 2003 family

PrintDialog.PrintToFile Property

Gets or sets a value indicating whether the Print to file check box is checked.

```
[Visual Basic]
Public Property PrintToFile As Boolean
[C#]
public bool PrintToFile {get; set;}
[C++]
public: __property bool get_PrintToFile();
public: __property void set_PrintToFile(bool);
[JScript]
public function get PrintToFile() : Boolean;
public function set PrintToFile(Boolean);
```

Property Value

true if the Print to file check box is checked; otherwise, **false**. The default is **false**.

Requirements

Platforms: Windows 98, Windows NT 4.0, Windows Millennium Edition, Windows 2000, Windows XP Home Edition, Windows XP Professional, Windows Server 2003 family

PrintDialog.ShowHelp Property

Gets or sets a value indicating whether the Help button is displayed.

```
[Visual Basic]
Public Property ShowHelp As Boolean
[C#]
public bool ShowHelp {get; set;}
[C++]
public: __property bool get_ShowHelp();
public: __property void set_ShowHelp(bool);
[JScript]
public function get ShowHelp() : Boolean;
public function set ShowHelp(Boolean);
```

Property Value

true if the Help button is displayed; otherwise, **false**. The default is **false**.

Requirements

Platforms: Windows 98, Windows NT 4.0, Windows Millennium Edition, Windows 2000, Windows XP Home Edition, Windows XP Professional, Windows Server 2003 family

PrintDialog.ShowNetwork Property

Gets or sets a value indicating whether the Network button is displayed.

```
[Visual Basic]
Public Property ShowNetwork As Boolean
[C#]
public bool ShowNetwork {get; set;}
[C++]
public: __property bool get_ShowNetwork();
public: __property void set_ShowNetwork(bool);
[JScript]
public function get ShowNetwork() : Boolean;
public function set ShowNetwork(Boolean);
```

Property Value

true if the Network button is displayed; otherwise, **false**. The default is **true**.

Requirements

Platforms: Windows 98, Windows NT 4.0, Windows Millennium Edition, Windows 2000, Windows XP Home Edition, Windows XP Professional, Windows Server 2003 family

PrintDialog.Reset Method

Resets all options, the last selected printer, and the page settings to their default values.

```
[Visual Basic]
Overrides Public Sub Reset()
[C#]
public override void Reset();
[C++]
public: void Reset();
[JScript]
public override function Reset();
```

Requirements

Platforms: Windows 98, Windows NT 4.0, Windows Millennium Edition, Windows 2000, Windows XP Home Edition, Windows XP Professional, Windows Server 2003 family

PrintDialog.RunDialog Method

This member overrides **CommonDialog.RunDialog**.

```
[Visual Basic]
Overrides Protected Function RunDialog( _
   ByVal hwndOwner As IntPtr _
) As Boolean
[C#]
protected override bool RunDialog(
   IntPtr hwndOwner
);
[C++]
protected: bool RunDialog(
   IntPtr hwndOwner
);
[JScript]
protected override function RunDialog(
   hwndOwner : IntPtr
) : Boolean;
```

Requirements

Platforms: Windows 98, Windows NT 4.0, Windows Millennium Edition, Windows 2000, Windows XP Home Edition, Windows XP Professional, Windows Server 2003 family

PrintPreviewControl Class

Represents the raw "preview" part of print previewing, without any dialog boxes or buttons. Most **PrintPreviewControl** objects are found on **PrintPreviewDialog** objects, but they do not have to be.

System.Object
  System.MarshalByRefObject
    System.ComponentModel.Component
      System.Windows.Forms.Control
        System.Windows.Forms.PrintPreviewControl

[Visual Basic]
```
Public Class PrintPreviewControl
   Inherits Control
```
[C#]
```
public class PrintPreviewControl : Control
```
[C++]
```
public __gc class PrintPreviewControl : public Control
```
[JScript]
```
public class PrintPreviewControl extends Control
```

Thread Safety

Any public static (**Shared** in Visual Basic) members of this type are safe for multithreaded operations. Any instance members are not guaranteed to be thread safe.

Remarks

When you create an instance of the **PrintPreviewControl** class, some of the read/write properties are set to initial values. For a list of these values, see the **PrintPreviewControl** contructor.

Requirements

Namespace: System.Windows.Forms

Platforms: Windows 98, Windows NT 4.0, Windows Millennium Edition, Windows 2000, Windows XP Home Edition, Windows XP Professional, Windows Server 2003 family

Assembly: System.Windows.Forms (in System.Windows.Forms.dll)

PrintPreviewControl Constructor

Initializes a new instance of the **PrintPreviewControl** class.

[Visual Basic]
```
Public Sub New()
```
[C#]
```
public PrintPreviewControl();
```
[C++]
```
public: PrintPreviewControl();
```
[JScript]
```
public function PrintPreviewControl();
```

Remarks

When you create an instance of the **PrintPreviewControl** class, the following read/write properties are initialized.

Property	Default Value
AutoZoom	**true**
Document	A null reference (**Nothing** in Visual Basic)
Columns	1
Rows	0
StartPage	0

You can change the value for any of these properties through a separate call to the property.

Requirements

Platforms: Windows 98, Windows NT 4.0, Windows Millennium Edition, Windows 2000, Windows XP Home Edition, Windows XP Professional, Windows Server 2003 family

PrintPreviewControl.AutoZoom Property

Gets or sets a value indicating whether resizing the control or changing the number of pages shown automatically adjusts the **Zoom** property.

[Visual Basic]
```
Public Property AutoZoom As Boolean
```
[C#]
```
public bool AutoZoom {get; set;}
```
[C++]
```
public: __property bool get_AutoZoom();
public: __property void set_AutoZoom(bool);
```
[JScript]
```
public function get AutoZoom() : Boolean;
public function set AutoZoom(Boolean);
```

Property Value

true if the changing the control size or number of pages adjusts the **Zoom** property; otherwise, false. The default is **true**.

Requirements

Platforms: Windows 98, Windows NT 4.0, Windows Millennium Edition, Windows 2000, Windows XP Home Edition, Windows XP Professional, Windows Server 2003 family

PrintPreviewControl.Columns Property

Gets or sets the number of pages displayed horizontally across the screen.

[Visual Basic]
```
Public Property Columns As Integer
```
[C#]
```
public int Columns {get; set;}
```
[C++]
```
public: __property int get_Columns();
public: __property void set_Columns(int);
```
[JScript]
```
public function get Columns() : int;
public function set Columns(int);
```

Property Value

The number of pages displayed horizontally across the screen. The default is one.

Requirements

Platforms: Windows 98, Windows NT 4.0, Windows Millennium Edition, Windows 2000, Windows XP Home Edition, Windows XP Professional, Windows Server 2003 family

PrintPreviewControl.CreateParams Property

This member overrides **Control.CreateParams**.

[Visual Basic]
```
Overrides Protected ReadOnly Property CreateParams As CreateParams
```
[C#]
```
protected override CreateParams CreateParams {get;}
```
[C++]
```
protected: __property CreateParams* get_CreateParams();
```
[JScript]
```
protected override function get CreateParams() : CreateParams;
```

Requirements

Platforms: Windows 98, Windows NT 4.0, Windows Millennium Edition, Windows 2000, Windows XP Home Edition, Windows XP Professional, Windows Server 2003 family

PrintPreviewControl.Document Property

Gets or sets a value indicating the document to preview.

[Visual Basic]
```
Public Property Document As PrintDocument
```
[C#]
```
public PrintDocument Document {get; set;}
```
[C++]
```
public: __property PrintDocument* get_Document();
public: __property void set_Document(PrintDocument*);
```
[JScript]
```
public function get Document() : PrintDocument;
public function set Document(PrintDocument);
```

Property Value

The **PrintDocument** representing the document to preview.

Requirements

Platforms: Windows 98, Windows NT 4.0, Windows Millennium Edition, Windows 2000, Windows XP Home Edition, Windows XP Professional, Windows Server 2003 family

PrintPreviewControl.Rows Property

Gets or sets the number of pages displayed vertically down the screen.

[Visual Basic]
```
Public Property Rows As Integer
```
[C#]
```
public int Rows {get; set;}
```
[C++]
```
public: __property int get_Rows();
public: __property void set_Rows(int);
```
[JScript]
```
public function get Rows() : int;
public function set Rows(int);
```

Property Value

The number of pages displayed vertically down the screen. The default is 0.

Requirements

Platforms: Windows 98, Windows NT 4.0, Windows Millennium Edition, Windows 2000, Windows XP Home Edition, Windows XP Professional, Windows Server 2003 family

PrintPreviewControl.StartPage Property

Gets or sets the page number of the upper left page.

[Visual Basic]
```
Public Property StartPage As Integer
```
[C#]
```
public int StartPage {get; set;}
```
[C++]
```
public: __property int get_StartPage();
public: __property void set_StartPage(int);
```
[JScript]
```
public function get StartPage() : int;
public function set StartPage(int);
```

Property Value

The page number of the upper left page. The default is 0.

Requirements

Platforms: Windows 98, Windows NT 4.0, Windows Millennium Edition, Windows 2000, Windows XP Home Edition, Windows XP Professional, Windows Server 2003 family

PrintPreviewControl.Text Property

This member overrides **Control.Text**.

[Visual Basic]
```
Overrides Public Property Text As String
```
[C#]
```
public override string Text {get; set;}
```
[C++]
```
public: __property String* get_Text();
public: __property void set_Text(String*);
```
[JScript]
```
public override function get Text() : String;
public override function set Text(String);
```

Requirements

Platforms: Windows 98, Windows NT 4.0, Windows Millennium Edition, Windows 2000, Windows XP Home Edition, Windows XP Professional, Windows Server 2003 family

PrintPreviewControl.UseAntiAlias Property

Gets or sets a value indicating whether printing uses the anti-aliasing features of the operating system.

[Visual Basic]
```
Public Property UseAntiAlias As Boolean
```
[C#]
```
public bool UseAntiAlias {get; set;}
```
[C++]
```
public: __property bool get_UseAntiAlias();
public: __property void set_UseAntiAlias(bool);
```

```
[JScript]
public function get UseAntiAlias() : Boolean;
public function set UseAntiAlias(Boolean);
```

Property Value

true if anti-aliasing is used; otherwise, **false**.

Remarks

Anti-aliasing removes jagged lines when fonts are rendered.

Requirements

Platforms: Windows 98, Windows NT 4.0, Windows Millennium Edition, Windows 2000, Windows XP Home Edition, Windows XP Professional, Windows Server 2003 family

PrintPreviewControl.Zoom Property

Gets or sets a value indicating how large the pages will appear.

```
[Visual Basic]
Public Property Zoom As Double
[C#]
public double Zoom {get; set;}
[C++]
public: __property double get_Zoom();
public: __property void set_Zoom(double);
[JScript]
public function get Zoom() : double;
public function set Zoom(double);
```

Property Value

How large the pages will appear. The value 1.0 is full size.

Exceptions

Exception Type	Condition
ArgumentException	The value is less than 0.

Requirements

Platforms: Windows 98, Windows NT 4.0, Windows Millennium Edition, Windows 2000, Windows XP Home Edition, Windows XP Professional, Windows Server 2003 family

PrintPreviewControl.InvalidatePreview Method

Refreshes the preview of the document.

```
[Visual Basic]
Public Sub InvalidatePreview()
[C#]
public void InvalidatePreview();
[C++]
public: void InvalidatePreview();
[JScript]
public function InvalidatePreview();
```

Remarks

Call this method if the document appearance has changed.

Requirements

Platforms: Windows 98, Windows NT 4.0, Windows Millennium Edition, Windows 2000, Windows XP Home Edition, Windows XP Professional, Windows Server 2003 family

PrintPreviewControl.OnPaint Method

This member overrides **Control.OnPaint**.

```
[Visual Basic]
Overrides Protected Sub OnPaint( _
   ByVal pevent As PaintEventArgs _
)
[C#]
protected override void OnPaint(
   PaintEventArgs pevent
);
[C++]
protected: void OnPaint(
   PaintEventArgs* pevent
);
[JScript]
protected override function OnPaint(
   pevent : PaintEventArgs
);
```

Requirements

Platforms: Windows 98, Windows NT 4.0, Windows Millennium Edition, Windows 2000, Windows XP Home Edition, Windows XP Professional, Windows Server 2003 family

PrintPreviewControl.OnResize Method

This member overrides **Control.OnResize**.

```
[Visual Basic]
Overrides Protected Sub OnResize( _
   ByVal eventargs As EventArgs _
)
[C#]
protected override void OnResize(
   EventArgs eventargs
);
[C++]
protected: void OnResize(
   EventArgs* eventargs
);
[JScript]
protected override function OnResize(
   eventargs : EventArgs
);
```

Requirements

Platforms: Windows 98, Windows NT 4.0, Windows Millennium Edition, Windows 2000, Windows XP Home Edition, Windows XP Professional, Windows Server 2003 family

PrintPreviewControl.OnStartPageChanged Method

Raises the **StartPageChanged** event.

```
[Visual Basic]
Protected Overridable Sub OnStartPageChanged( _
   ByVal e As EventArgs _
)
```

```
[C#]
protected virtual void OnStartPageChanged(
   EventArgs e
);
[C++]
protected: virtual void OnStartPageChanged(
   EventArgs* e
);
[JScript]
protected function OnStartPageChanged(
   e : EventArgs
);
```

Parameters

e

An **EventArgs** that contains the event data.

Remarks

Raising an event invokes the event handler through a delegate. For more information, see **Raising an Event**.

The **OnStartPageChanged** method also allows derived classes to handle the event without attaching a delegate. This is the preferred technique for handling the event in a derived class.

Notes to Inheritors: When overriding **OnStartPageChanged** in a derived class, be sure to call the base class's **OnStartPageChanged** method so that registered delegates receive the event.

Requirements

Platforms: Windows 98, Windows NT 4.0, Windows Millennium Edition, Windows 2000, Windows XP Home Edition, Windows XP Professional, Windows Server 2003 family

PrintPreviewControl.ResetBackColor Method

This member overrides **Control.ResetBackColor**.

```
[Visual Basic]
Overrides Public Sub ResetBackColor()
[C#]
public override void ResetBackColor();
[C++]
public: void ResetBackColor();
[JScript]
public override function ResetBackColor();
```

Requirements

Platforms: Windows 98, Windows NT 4.0, Windows Millennium Edition, Windows 2000, Windows XP Home Edition, Windows XP Professional, Windows Server 2003 family

PrintPreviewControl.ResetForeColor Method

This member overrides **Control.ResetForeColor**.

```
[Visual Basic]
Overrides Public Sub ResetForeColor()
[C#]
public override void ResetForeColor();
[C++]
public: void ResetForeColor();
[JScript]
public override function ResetForeColor();
```

Requirements

Platforms: Windows 98, Windows NT 4.0, Windows Millennium Edition, Windows 2000, Windows XP Home Edition, Windows XP Professional, Windows Server 2003 family

PrintPreviewControl.WndProc Method

This member overrides **Control.WndProc**.

```
[Visual Basic]
Overrides Protected Sub WndProc( _
   ByRef m As Message _
)
[C#]
protected override void WndProc(
   ref Message m
);
[C++]
protected: void WndProc(
   Message* m
);
[JScript]
protected override function WndProc(
   m : Message
);
```

Requirements

Platforms: Windows 98, Windows NT 4.0, Windows Millennium Edition, Windows 2000, Windows XP Home Edition, Windows XP Professional, Windows Server 2003 family

PrintPreviewControl.StartPageChanged Event

Occurs when the start page changes.

```
[Visual Basic]
Public Event StartPageChanged As EventHandler
[C#]
public event EventHandler StartPageChanged;
[C++]
public: __event EventHandler* StartPageChanged;
```

[JScript] In JScript, you can handle the events defined by a class, but you cannot define your own.

Event Data

The event handler receives an argument of type **EventArgs**.

Remarks

For more information about handling events, see **Consuming Events**.

Requirements

Platforms: Windows 98, Windows NT 4.0, Windows Millennium Edition, Windows 2000, Windows XP Home Edition, Windows XP Professional, Windows Server 2003 family

PrintPreviewControl.TextChanged Event

This member supports the .NET Framework infrastructure and is not intended to be used directly from your code.

[Visual Basic]
```
Public Shadows Event TextChanged As EventHandler
```
[C#]
```
public new event EventHandler TextChanged;
```
[C++]
```
public: __event EventHandler* TextChanged;
```

[JScript] In JScript, you can handle the events defined by a class, but you cannot define your own.

PrintPreviewDialog Class

Represents a dialog box form that contains a **PrintPreviewControl**.

System.Object
  System.MarshalByRefObject
    System.ComponentModel.Component
      System.Windows.Forms.Control
        System.Windows.Forms.ScrollableControl
          System.Windows.Forms.ContainerControl
            System.Windows.Forms.Form
              System.Windows.Forms.PrintPreviewDialog

```
[Visual Basic]
Public Class PrintPreviewDialog
   Inherits Form
[C#]
public class PrintPreviewDialog : Form
[C++]
public __gc class PrintPreviewDialog : public Form
[JScript]
public class PrintPreviewDialog extends Form
```

Thread Safety

Any public static (**Shared** in Visual Basic) members of this type are safe for multithreaded operations. Any instance members are not guaranteed to be thread safe.

Remarks

When you create an instance of **PrintPreviewDialog**, some of the read/write properties are set to initial values. For a list of these, see the **PrintPreviewDialog** constructor.

Requirements

Namespace: System.Windows.Forms

Platforms: Windows 98, Windows NT 4.0, Windows Millennium Edition, Windows 2000, Windows XP Home Edition, Windows XP Professional, Windows Server 2003 family

Assembly: System.Windows.Forms (in System.Windows.Forms.dll)

PrintPreviewDialog Constructor

Initializes a new instance of the **PrintPreviewDialog** class.

```
[Visual Basic]
Public Sub New()
[C#]
public PrintPreviewDialog();
[C++]
public: PrintPreviewDialog();
[JScript]
public function PrintPreviewDialog();
```

Remarks

When you create an instance of **PrintPreviewDialog**, the **Document** property is initialized to a null reference (**Nothing** in Visual Basic). You can change the value for this property at run time.

Requirements

Platforms: Windows 98, Windows NT 4.0, Windows Millennium Edition, Windows 2000, Windows XP Home Edition, Windows XP Professional, Windows Server 2003 family

PrintPreviewDialog.AcceptButton Property

This member supports the .NET Framework infrastructure and is not intended to be used directly from your code.

```
[Visual Basic]
Public Shadows Property AcceptButton As IButtonControl
[C#]
public new IButtonControl AcceptButton {get; set;}
[C++]
public: __property IButtonControl* get_AcceptButton();
public: __property void set_AcceptButton(IButtonControl*);
[JScript]
public hide function get AcceptButton() : IButtonControl;
public hide function set AcceptButton(IButtonControl);
```

PrintPreviewDialog.AccessibleDescription Property

This member supports the .NET Framework infrastructure and is not intended to be used directly from your code.

```
[Visual Basic]
Public Shadows Property AccessibleDescription As String
[C#]
public new string AccessibleDescription {get; set;}
[C++]
public: __property String* get_AccessibleDescription();
public: __property void set_AccessibleDescription(String*);
[JScript]
public hide function get AccessibleDescription() : String;
public hide function set AccessibleDescription(String);
```

PrintPreviewDialog.AccessibleName Property

This member supports the .NET Framework infrastructure and is not intended to be used directly from your code.

```
[Visual Basic]
Public Shadows Property AccessibleName As String
[C#]
public new string AccessibleName {get; set;}
[C++]
public: __property String* get_AccessibleName();
public: __property void set_AccessibleName(String*);
[JScript]
public hide function get AccessibleName() : String;
public hide function set AccessibleName(String);
```

PrintPreviewDialog.AccessibleRole Property

This member supports the .NET Framework infrastructure and is not intended to be used directly from your code.

```
[Visual Basic]
Public Shadows Property AccessibleRole As AccessibleRole
[C#]
public new AccessibleRole AccessibleRole {get; set;}
[C++]
public: __property AccessibleRole get_AccessibleRole();
public: __property void set_AccessibleRole(AccessibleRole);
[JScript]
public hide function get AccessibleRole() : AccessibleRole;
public hide function set AccessibleRole(AccessibleRole);
```

PrintPreviewDialog.AllowDrop Property

This member overrides **Control.AllowDrop**.

[Visual Basic]
```
Overrides Public Property AllowDrop As Boolean
```
[C#]
```
public override bool AllowDrop {get; set;}
```
[C++]
```
public: __property bool get_AllowDrop();
public: __property void set_AllowDrop(bool);
```
[JScript]
```
public override function get AllowDrop() : Boolean;
public override function set AllowDrop(Boolean);
```

Requirements

Platforms: Windows 98, Windows NT 4.0, Windows Millennium Edition, Windows 2000, Windows XP Home Edition, Windows XP Professional, Windows Server 2003 family

PrintPreviewDialog.Anchor Property

This member overrides **Control.Anchor**.

[Visual Basic]
```
Overrides Public Property Anchor As AnchorStyles
```
[C#]
```
public override AnchorStyles Anchor {get; set;}
```
[C++]
```
public: __property AnchorStyles get_Anchor();
public: __property void set_Anchor(AnchorStyles);
```
[JScript]
```
public override function get Anchor() : AnchorStyles;
public override function set Anchor(AnchorStyles);
```

Requirements

Platforms: Windows 98, Windows NT 4.0, Windows Millennium Edition, Windows 2000, Windows XP Home Edition, Windows XP Professional, Windows Server 2003 family

PrintPreviewDialog.AutoScale Property

This member supports the .NET Framework infrastructure and is not intended to be used directly from your code.

[Visual Basic]
```
Public Shadows Property AutoScale As Boolean
```
[C#]
```
public new bool AutoScale {get; set;}
```
[C++]
```
public: __property bool get_AutoScale();
public: __property void set_AutoScale(bool);
```
[JScript]
```
public hide function get AutoScale() : Boolean;
public hide function set AutoScale(Boolean);
```

PrintPreviewDialog.AutoScaleBaseSize Property

This member overrides **Form.AutoScaleBaseSize**.

[Visual Basic]
```
Overrides Public Property AutoScaleBaseSize As Size
```
[C#]
```
public override Size AutoScaleBaseSize {get; set;}
```
[C++]
```
public: __property Size get_AutoScaleBaseSize();
public: __property void set_AutoScaleBaseSize(Size);
```
[JScript]
```
public override function get AutoScaleBaseSize() : Size;
public override function set AutoScaleBaseSize(Size);
```

Requirements

Platforms: Windows 98, Windows NT 4.0, Windows Millennium Edition, Windows 2000, Windows XP Home Edition, Windows XP Professional, Windows Server 2003 family

PrintPreviewDialog.AutoScroll Property

This member overrides **Form.AutoScroll**.

[Visual Basic]
```
Overrides Public Property AutoScroll As Boolean
```
[C#]
```
public override bool AutoScroll {get; set;}
```
[C++]
```
public: __property bool get_AutoScroll();
public: __property void set_AutoScroll(bool);
```
[JScript]
```
public override function get AutoScroll() : Boolean;
public override function set AutoScroll(Boolean);
```

Requirements

Platforms: Windows 98, Windows NT 4.0, Windows Millennium Edition, Windows 2000, Windows XP Home Edition, Windows XP Professional, Windows Server 2003 family

PrintPreviewDialog.AutoScrollMargin Property

This member supports the .NET Framework infrastructure and is not intended to be used directly from your code.

[Visual Basic]
```
Public Shadows Property AutoScrollMargin As Size
```
[C#]
```
public new Size AutoScrollMargin {get; set;}
```
[C++]
```
public: __property Size get_AutoScrollMargin();
public: __property void set_AutoScrollMargin(Size);
```
[JScript]
```
public hide function get AutoScrollMargin() : Size;
public hide function set AutoScrollMargin(Size);
```

PrintPreviewDialog.AutoScrollMinSize Property

This member supports the .NET Framework infrastructure and is not intended to be used directly from your code.

[Visual Basic]
```
Public Shadows Property AutoScrollMinSize As Size
```
[C#]
```
public new Size AutoScrollMinSize {get; set;}
```
[C++]
```
public: __property Size get_AutoScrollMinSize();
public: __property void set_AutoScrollMinSize(Size);
```
[JScript]
```
public hide function get AutoScrollMinSize() : Size;
public hide function set AutoScrollMinSize(Size);
```

PrintPreviewDialog.BackColor Property

This member overrides **Control.BackColor**.

[Visual Basic]
```
Overrides Public Property BackColor As Color
```
[C#]
```
public override Color BackColor {get; set;}
```
[C++]
```
public: __property Color get_BackColor();
public: __property void set_BackColor(Color);
```
[JScript]
```
public override function get BackColor() : Color;
public override function set BackColor(Color);
```

Requirements

Platforms: Windows 98, Windows NT 4.0, Windows Millennium Edition, Windows 2000, Windows XP Home Edition, Windows XP Professional, Windows Server 2003 family

PrintPreviewDialog.BackgroundImage Property

This member overrides **Control.BackgroundImage**.

[Visual Basic]
```
Overrides Public Property BackgroundImage As Image
```
[C#]
```
public override Image BackgroundImage {get; set;}
```
[C++]
```
public: __property Image* get_BackgroundImage();
public: __property void set_BackgroundImage(Image*);
```
[JScript]
```
public override function get BackgroundImage() : Image;
public override function set BackgroundImage(Image);
```

Requirements

Platforms: Windows 98, Windows NT 4.0, Windows Millennium Edition, Windows 2000, Windows XP Home Edition, Windows XP Professional, Windows Server 2003 family

PrintPreviewDialog.CancelButton Property

This member supports the .NET Framework infrastructure and is not intended to be used directly from your code.

[Visual Basic]
```
Public Shadows Property CancelButton As IButtonControl
```
[C#]
```
public new IButtonControl CancelButton {get; set;}
```
[C++]
```
public: __property IButtonControl* get_CancelButton();
public: __property void set_CancelButton(IButtonControl*);
```
[JScript]
```
public hide function get CancelButton() : IButtonControl;
public hide function set CancelButton(IButtonControl);
```

PrintPreviewDialog.CausesValidation Property

This member supports the .NET Framework infrastructure and is not intended to be used directly from your code.

[Visual Basic]
```
Public Shadows Property CausesValidation As Boolean
```
[C#]
```
public new bool CausesValidation {get; set;}
```
[C++]
```
public: __property bool get_CausesValidation();
public: __property void set_CausesValidation(bool);
```
[JScript]
```
public hide function get CausesValidation() : Boolean;
public hide function set CausesValidation(Boolean);
```

PrintPreviewDialog.ContextMenu Property

This member overrides **Control.ContextMenu**.

[Visual Basic]
```
Overrides Public Property ContextMenu As ContextMenu
```
[C#]
```
public override ContextMenu ContextMenu {get; set;}
```
[C++]
```
public: __property ContextMenu* get_ContextMenu();
public: __property void set_ContextMenu(ContextMenu*);
```
[JScript]
```
public override function get ContextMenu() : ContextMenu;
public override function set ContextMenu(ContextMenu);
```

Requirements

Platforms: Windows 98, Windows NT 4.0, Windows Millennium Edition, Windows 2000, Windows XP Home Edition, Windows XP Professional, Windows Server 2003 family

PrintPreviewDialog.ControlBox Property

This member supports the .NET Framework infrastructure and is not intended to be used directly from your code.

[Visual Basic]
```
Public Shadows Property ControlBox As Boolean
```
[C#]
```
public new bool ControlBox {get; set;}
```
[C++]
```
public: __property bool get_ControlBox();
public: __property void set_ControlBox(bool);
```
[JScript]
```
public hide function get ControlBox() : Boolean;
public hide function set ControlBox(Boolean);
```

PrintPreviewDialog.Cursor Property

This member overrides **Control.Cursor**.

[Visual Basic]
```
Overrides Public Property Cursor As Cursor
```
[C#]
```
public override Cursor Cursor {get; set;}
```
[C++]
```
public: __property Cursor* get_Cursor();
public: __property void set_Cursor(Cursor*);
```
[JScript]
```
public override function get Cursor() : Cursor;
public override function set Cursor(Cursor);
```

Requirements

Platforms: Windows 98, Windows NT 4.0, Windows Millennium Edition, Windows 2000, Windows XP Home Edition, Windows XP Professional, Windows Server 2003 family

PrintPreviewDialog.DataBindings Property

This member supports the .NET Framework infrastructure and is not intended to be used directly from your code.

```
[Visual Basic]
Public Shadows ReadOnly Property DataBindings As _
   ControlBindingsCollection
[C#]
public new ControlBindingsCollection DataBindings {get;}
[C++]
public: __property ControlBindingsCollection* get_DataBindings();
[JScript]
public hide function get DataBindings() : ControlBindingsCollection;
```

PrintPreviewDialog.Dock Property

This member overrides **Control.Dock**.

```
[Visual Basic]
Overrides Public Property Dock As DockStyle
[C#]
public override DockStyle Dock {get; set;}
[C++]
public: __property DockStyle get_Dock();
public: __property void set_Dock(DockStyle);
[JScript]
public override function get Dock() : DockStyle;
public override function set Dock(DockStyle);
```

Requirements

Platforms: Windows 98, Windows NT 4.0, Windows Millennium Edition, Windows 2000, Windows XP Home Edition, Windows XP Professional, Windows Server 2003 family

PrintPreviewDialog.DockPadding Property

This member supports the .NET Framework infrastructure and is not intended to be used directly from your code.

```
[Visual Basic]
Public Shadows ReadOnly Property DockPadding As _
   ScrollableControl.DockPaddingEdges
[C#]
public new ScrollableControl.DockPaddingEdges DockPadding {get;}
[C++]
public: __property ScrollableControl.DockPaddingEdges*
   get_DockPadding();
[JScript]
public hide function get DockPadding() :
   ScrollableControl.DockPaddingEdges;
```

PrintPreviewDialog.Document Property

Gets or sets the document to preview.

```
[Visual Basic]
Public Property Document As PrintDocument
[C#]
public PrintDocument Document {get; set;}
[C++]
public: __property PrintDocument* get_Document();
public: __property void set_Document(PrintDocument*);
[JScript]
public function get Document() : PrintDocument;
public function set Document(PrintDocument);
```

Property Value

The **PrintDocument** representing the document to preview.

Remarks

This property is equivalent to **PrintPreviewControl.Document**.

Requirements

Platforms: Windows 98, Windows NT 4.0, Windows Millennium Edition, Windows 2000, Windows XP Home Edition, Windows XP Professional, Windows Server 2003 family

PrintPreviewDialog.Enabled Property

This member supports the .NET Framework infrastructure and is not intended to be used directly from your code.

```
[Visual Basic]
Public Shadows Property Enabled As Boolean
[C#]
public new bool Enabled {get; set;}
[C++]
public: __property bool get_Enabled();
public: __property void set_Enabled(bool);
[JScript]
public hide function get Enabled() : Boolean;
public hide function set Enabled(Boolean);
```

PrintPreviewDialog.Font Property

This member overrides **Control.Font**.

```
[Visual Basic]
Overrides Public Property Font As Font
[C#]
public override Font Font {get; set;}
[C++]
public: __property Font* get_Font();
public: __property void set_Font(Font*);
[JScript]
public override function get Font() : Font;
public override function set Font(Font);
```

Requirements

Platforms: Windows 98, Windows NT 4.0, Windows Millennium Edition, Windows 2000, Windows XP Home Edition, Windows XP Professional, Windows Server 2003 family

PrintPreviewDialog.ForeColor Property

This member overrides **Control.ForeColor**.

[Visual Basic]
```
Overrides Public Property ForeColor As Color
```
[C#]
```
public override Color ForeColor {get; set;}
```
[C++]
```
public: __property Color get_ForeColor();
public: __property void set_ForeColor(Color);
```
[JScript]
```
public override function get ForeColor() : Color;
public override function set ForeColor(Color);
```

Requirements

Platforms: Windows 98, Windows NT 4.0, Windows Millennium Edition, Windows 2000, Windows XP Home Edition, Windows XP Professional, Windows Server 2003 family

PrintPreviewDialog.FormBorderStyle Property

This member supports the .NET Framework infrastructure and is not intended to be used directly from your code.

[Visual Basic]
```
Public Shadows Property FormBorderStyle As FormBorderStyle
```
[C#]
```
public new FormBorderStyle FormBorderStyle {get; set;}
```
[C++]
```
public: __property FormBorderStyle get_FormBorderStyle();
public: __property void set_FormBorderStyle(FormBorderStyle);
```
[JScript]
```
public hide function get FormBorderStyle() : FormBorderStyle;
public hide function set FormBorderStyle(FormBorderStyle);
```

PrintPreviewDialog.HelpButton Property

This member supports the .NET Framework infrastructure and is not intended to be used directly from your code.

[Visual Basic]
```
Public Shadows Property HelpButton As Boolean
```
[C#]
```
public new bool HelpButton {get; set;}
```
[C++]
```
public: __property bool get_HelpButton();
public: __property void set_HelpButton(bool);
```
[JScript]
```
public hide function get HelpButton() : Boolean;
public hide function set HelpButton(Boolean);
```

PrintPreviewDialog.Icon Property

This member supports the .NET Framework infrastructure and is not intended to be used directly from your code.

[Visual Basic]
```
Public Shadows Property Icon As Icon
```
[C#]
```
public new Icon Icon {get; set;}
```
[C++]
```
public: __property Icon* get_Icon();
public: __property void set_Icon(Icon*);
```
[JScript]
```
public hide function get Icon() : Icon;
public hide function set Icon(Icon);
```

PrintPreviewDialog.ImeMode Property

This member supports the .NET Framework infrastructure and is not intended to be used directly from your code.

[Visual Basic]
```
Public Shadows Property ImeMode As ImeMode
```
[C#]
```
public new ImeMode ImeMode {get; set;}
```
[C++]
```
public: __property ImeMode get_ImeMode();
public: __property void set_ImeMode(ImeMode);
```
[JScript]
```
public hide function get ImeMode() : ImeMode;
public hide function set ImeMode(ImeMode);
```

PrintPreviewDialog.IsMdiContainer Property

This member supports the .NET Framework infrastructure and is not intended to be used directly from your code.

[Visual Basic]
```
Public Shadows Property IsMdiContainer As Boolean
```
[C#]
```
public new bool IsMdiContainer {get; set;}
```
[C++]
```
public: __property bool get_IsMdiContainer();
public: __property void set_IsMdiContainer(bool);
```
[JScript]
```
public hide function get IsMdiContainer() : Boolean;
public hide function set IsMdiContainer(Boolean);
```

PrintPreviewDialog.KeyPreview Property

This member supports the .NET Framework infrastructure and is not intended to be used directly from your code.

[Visual Basic]
```
Public Shadows Property KeyPreview As Boolean
```
[C#]
```
public new bool KeyPreview {get; set;}
```
[C++]
```
public: __property bool get_KeyPreview();
public: __property void set_KeyPreview(bool);
```
[JScript]
```
public hide function get KeyPreview() : Boolean;
public hide function set KeyPreview(Boolean);
```

PrintPreviewDialog.Location Property

This member supports the .NET Framework infrastructure and is not intended to be used directly from your code.

[Visual Basic]
```
Public Shadows Property Location As Point
```
[C#]
```
public new Point Location {get; set;}
```
[C++]
```
public: __property Point get_Location();
public: __property void set_Location(Point);
```

[JScript]
```
public hide function get Location() : Point;
public hide function set Location(Point);
```

PrintPreviewDialog.MaximizeBox Property

This member supports the .NET Framework infrastructure and is not intended to be used directly from your code.

[Visual Basic]
```
Public Shadows Property MaximizeBox As Boolean
```
[C#]
```
public new bool MaximizeBox {get; set;}
```
[C++]
```
public: __property bool get_MaximizeBox();
public: __property void set_MaximizeBox(bool);
```
[JScript]
```
public hide function get MaximizeBox() : Boolean;
public hide function set MaximizeBox(Boolean);
```

PrintPreviewDialog.MaximumSize Property

This member supports the .NET Framework infrastructure and is not intended to be used directly from your code.

[Visual Basic]
```
Public Shadows Property MaximumSize As Size
```
[C#]
```
public new Size MaximumSize {get; set;}
```
[C++]
```
public: __property Size get_MaximumSize();
public: __property void set_MaximumSize(Size);
```
[JScript]
```
public hide function get MaximumSize() : Size;
public hide function set MaximumSize(Size);
```

PrintPreviewDialog.Menu Property

This member supports the .NET Framework infrastructure and is not intended to be used directly from your code.

[Visual Basic]
```
Public Shadows Property Menu As MainMenu
```
[C#]
```
public new MainMenu Menu {get; set;}
```
[C++]
```
public: __property MainMenu* get_Menu();
public: __property void set_Menu(MainMenu*);
```
[JScript]
```
public hide function get Menu() : MainMenu;
public hide function set Menu(MainMenu);
```

PrintPreviewDialog.MinimizeBox Property

This member supports the .NET Framework infrastructure and is not intended to be used directly from your code.

[Visual Basic]
```
Public Shadows Property MinimizeBox As Boolean
```
[C#]
```
public new bool MinimizeBox {get; set;}
```
[C++]
```
public: __property bool get_MinimizeBox();
public: __property void set_MinimizeBox(bool);
```
[JScript]
```
public hide function get MinimizeBox() : Boolean;
public hide function set MinimizeBox(Boolean);
```

PrintPreviewDialog.MinimumSize Property

This member supports the .NET Framework infrastructure and is not intended to be used directly from your code.

[Visual Basic]
```
Public Shadows Property MinimumSize As Size
```
[C#]
```
public new Size MinimumSize {get; set;}
```
[C++]
```
public: __property Size get_MinimumSize();
public: __property void set_MinimumSize(Size);
```
[JScript]
```
public hide function get MinimumSize() : Size;
public hide function set MinimumSize(Size);
```

PrintPreviewDialog.Opacity Property

This member supports the .NET Framework infrastructure and is not intended to be used directly from your code.

[Visual Basic]
```
Public Shadows Property Opacity As Double
```
[C#]
```
public new double Opacity {get; set;}
```
[C++]
```
public: __property double get_Opacity();
public: __property void set_Opacity(double);
```
[JScript]
```
public hide function get Opacity() : double;
public hide function set Opacity(double);
```

PrintPreviewDialog.PrintPreviewControl Property

This member supports the .NET Framework infrastructure and is not intended to be used directly from your code.

[Visual Basic]
```
Public ReadOnly Property PrintPreviewControl As PrintPreviewControl
```
[C#]
```
public PrintPreviewControl PrintPreviewControl {get;}
```
[C++]
```
public: __property PrintPreviewControl* get_PrintPreviewControl();
```
[JScript]
```
public function get PrintPreviewControl() : PrintPreviewControl;
```

PrintPreviewDialog.RightToLeft Property

This member overrides **Control.RightToLeft**.

[Visual Basic]
```
Overrides Public Property RightToLeft As RightToLeft
```
[C#]
```
public override RightToLeft RightToLeft {get; set;}
```
[C++]
```
public: __property RightToLeft get_RightToLeft();
public: __property void set_RightToLeft(RightToLeft);
```

[JScript]
```
public override function get RightToLeft() : RightToLeft;
public override function set RightToLeft(RightToLeft);
```

Requirements

Platforms: Windows 98, Windows NT 4.0, Windows Millennium Edition, Windows 2000, Windows XP Home Edition, Windows XP Professional, Windows Server 2003 family

PrintPreviewDialog.ShowInTaskbar Property

This member supports the .NET Framework infrastructure and is not intended to be used directly from your code.

[Visual Basic]
```
Public Shadows Property ShowInTaskbar As Boolean
```
[C#]
```
public new bool ShowInTaskbar {get; set;}
```
[C++]
```
public: __property bool get_ShowInTaskbar();
public: __property void set_ShowInTaskbar(bool);
```
[JScript]
```
public hide function get ShowInTaskbar() : Boolean;
public hide function set ShowInTaskbar(Boolean);
```

PrintPreviewDialog.Size Property

This member supports the .NET Framework infrastructure and is not intended to be used directly from your code.

[Visual Basic]
```
Public Shadows Property Size As Size
```
[C#]
```
public new Size Size {get; set;}
```
[C++]
```
public: __property Size get_Size();
public: __property void set_Size(Size);
```
[JScript]
```
public hide function get Size() : Size;
public hide function set Size(Size);
```

PrintPreviewDialog.SizeGripStyle Property

This member supports the .NET Framework infrastructure and is not intended to be used directly from your code.

[Visual Basic]
```
Public Shadows Property SizeGripStyle As SizeGripStyle
```
[C#]
```
public new SizeGripStyle SizeGripStyle {get; set;}
```
[C++]
```
public: __property SizeGripStyle get_SizeGripStyle();
public: __property void set_SizeGripStyle(SizeGripStyle);
```
[JScript]
```
public hide function get SizeGripStyle() : SizeGripStyle;
public hide function set SizeGripStyle(SizeGripStyle);
```

PrintPreviewDialog.StartPosition Property

This member supports the .NET Framework infrastructure and is not intended to be used directly from your code.

[Visual Basic]
```
Public Shadows Property StartPosition As FormStartPosition
```
[C#]
```
public new FormStartPosition StartPosition {get; set;}
```
[C++]
```
public: __property FormStartPosition get_StartPosition();
public: __property void set_StartPosition(FormStartPosition);
```
[JScript]
```
public hide function get StartPosition() : FormStartPosition;
public hide function set StartPosition(FormStartPosition);
```

PrintPreviewDialog.TabStop Property

This member supports the .NET Framework infrastructure and is not intended to be used directly from your code.

[Visual Basic]
```
Public Shadows Property TabStop As Boolean
```
[C#]
```
public new bool TabStop {get; set;}
```
[C++]
```
public: __property bool get_TabStop();
public: __property void set_TabStop(bool);
```
[JScript]
```
public hide function get TabStop() : Boolean;
public hide function set TabStop(Boolean);
```

PrintPreviewDialog.Tag Property

This member supports the .NET Framework infrastructure and is not intended to be used directly from your code.

[Visual Basic]
```
Public Shadows Property Tag As Object
```
[C#]
```
public new object Tag {get; set;}
```
[C++]
```
public: __property Object* get_Tag();
public: __property void set_Tag(Object*);
```
[JScript]
```
public hide function get Tag() : Object;
public hide function set Tag(Object);
```

PrintPreviewDialog.Text Property

This member overrides **Control.Text**.

[Visual Basic]
```
Overrides Public Property Text As String
```
[C#]
```
public override string Text {get; set;}
```
[C++]
```
public: __property String* get_Text();
public: __property void set_Text(String*);
```
[JScript]
```
public override function get Text() : String;
public override function set Text(String);
```

Requirements

Platforms: Windows 98, Windows NT 4.0, Windows Millennium Edition, Windows 2000, Windows XP Home Edition, Windows XP Professional, Windows Server 2003 family

PrintPreviewDialog.TopMost Property

This member supports the .NET Framework infrastructure and is not intended to be used directly from your code.

```
[Visual Basic]
Public Shadows Property TopMost As Boolean
[C#]
public new bool TopMost {get; set;}
[C++]
public: __property bool get_TopMost();
public: __property void set_TopMost(bool);
[JScript]
public hide function get TopMost() : Boolean;
public hide function set TopMost(Boolean);
```

PrintPreviewDialog.TransparencyKey Property

This member supports the .NET Framework infrastructure and is not intended to be used directly from your code.

```
[Visual Basic]
Public Shadows Property TransparencyKey As Color
[C#]
public new Color TransparencyKey {get; set;}
[C++]
public: __property Color get_TransparencyKey();
public: __property void set_TransparencyKey(Color);
[JScript]
public hide function get TransparencyKey() : Color;
public hide function set TransparencyKey(Color);
```

PrintPreviewDialog.UseAntiAlias Property

Gets or sets a value indicating whether printing uses the anti-aliasing features of the operating system.

```
[Visual Basic]
Public Property UseAntiAlias As Boolean
[C#]
public bool UseAntiAlias {get; set;}
[C++]
public: __property bool get_UseAntiAlias();
public: __property void set_UseAntiAlias(bool);
[JScript]
public function get UseAntiAlias() : Boolean;
public function set UseAntiAlias(Boolean);
```

Property Value

true if anti-aliasing is used; otherwise, **false**.

Remarks

Anti-aliasing removes jagged lines when fonts are rendered.

Requirements

Platforms: Windows 98, Windows NT 4.0, Windows Millennium Edition, Windows 2000, Windows XP Home Edition, Windows XP Professional, Windows Server 2003 family

PrintPreviewDialog.Visible Property

This member supports the .NET Framework infrastructure and is not intended to be used directly from your code.

```
[Visual Basic]
Public Shadows Property Visible As Boolean
[C#]
public new bool Visible {get; set;}
[C++]
public: __property bool get_Visible();
public: __property void set_Visible(bool);
[JScript]
public hide function get Visible() : Boolean;
public hide function set Visible(Boolean);
```

PrintPreviewDialog.WindowState Property

This member supports the .NET Framework infrastructure and is not intended to be used directly from your code.

```
[Visual Basic]
Public Shadows Property WindowState As FormWindowState
[C#]
public new FormWindowState WindowState {get; set;}
[C++]
public: __property FormWindowState get_WindowState();
public: __property void set_WindowState(FormWindowState);
[JScript]
public hide function get WindowState() : FormWindowState;
public hide function set WindowState(FormWindowState);
```

PrintPreviewDialog.CreateHandle Method

Creates the handle for the form that encapsulates the **PrintPreviewDialog**.

```
[Visual Basic]
Overrides Protected Sub CreateHandle()
[C#]
protected override void CreateHandle();
[C++]
protected: void CreateHandle();
[JScript]
protected override function CreateHandle();
```

Exceptions

Exception Type	Condition
InvalidPrinterException	The printer settings in **Document** are not valid.

Remarks

For more information on **PrintPreviewDialog.CreateHandle** see the **Control.CreateHandle** method.

Requirements

Platforms: Windows 98, Windows NT 4.0, Windows Millennium Edition, Windows 2000, Windows XP Home Edition, Windows XP Professional, Windows Server 2003 family

PrintPreviewDialog.OnClosing Method

This member overrides **Form.OnClosing**.

```
[Visual Basic]
Overrides Protected Sub OnClosing( _
   ByVal e As CancelEventArgs _
)
```

```
[C#]
protected override void OnClosing(
   CancelEventArgs e
);
[C++]
protected: void OnClosing(
   CancelEventArgs* e
);
[JScript]
protected override function OnClosing(
   e : CancelEventArgs
);
```

Requirements

Platforms: Windows 98, Windows NT 4.0, Windows Millennium Edition, Windows 2000, Windows XP Home Edition, Windows XP Professional, Windows Server 2003 family

PrintPreviewDialog.BackColorChanged Event

This member supports the .NET Framework infrastructure and is not intended to be used directly from your code.

```
[Visual Basic]
Public Shadows Event BackColorChanged As EventHandler
[C#]
public new event EventHandler BackColorChanged;
[C++]
public: __event EventHandler* BackColorChanged;
```

[JScript] In JScript, you can handle the events defined by a class, but you cannot define your own.

PrintPreviewDialog.BackgroundImageChanged Event

This member supports the .NET Framework infrastructure and is not intended to be used directly from your code.

```
[Visual Basic]
Public Shadows Event BackgroundImageChanged As EventHandler
[C#]
public new event EventHandler BackgroundImageChanged;
[C++]
public: __event EventHandler* BackgroundImageChanged;
```

[JScript] In JScript, you can handle the events defined by a class, but you cannot define your own.

PrintPreviewDialog.CausesValidationChanged Event

This member supports the .NET Framework infrastructure and is not intended to be used directly from your code.

```
[Visual Basic]
Public Shadows Event CausesValidationChanged As EventHandler
[C#]
public new event EventHandler CausesValidationChanged;
[C++]
public: __event EventHandler* CausesValidationChanged;
```

[JScript] In JScript, you can handle the events defined by a class, but you cannot define your own.

PrintPreviewDialog.ContextMenuChanged Event

This member supports the .NET Framework infrastructure and is not intended to be used directly from your code.

```
[Visual Basic]
Public Shadows Event ContextMenuChanged As EventHandler
[C#]
public new event EventHandler ContextMenuChanged;
[C++]
public: __event EventHandler* ContextMenuChanged;
```

[JScript] In JScript, you can handle the events defined by a class, but you cannot define your own.

PrintPreviewDialog.CursorChanged Event

This member supports the .NET Framework infrastructure and is not intended to be used directly from your code.

```
[Visual Basic]
Public Shadows Event CursorChanged As EventHandler
[C#]
public new event EventHandler CursorChanged;
[C++]
public: __event EventHandler* CursorChanged;
```

[JScript] In JScript, you can handle the events defined by a class, but you cannot define your own.

PrintPreviewDialog.DockChanged Event

This member supports the .NET Framework infrastructure and is not intended to be used directly from your code.

```
[Visual Basic]
Public Shadows Event DockChanged As EventHandler
[C#]
public new event EventHandler DockChanged;
[C++]
public: __event EventHandler* DockChanged;
```

[JScript] In JScript, you can handle the events defined by a class, but you cannot define your own.

PrintPreviewDialog.EnabledChanged Event

This member supports the .NET Framework infrastructure and is not intended to be used directly from your code.

```
[Visual Basic]
Public Shadows Event EnabledChanged As EventHandler
[C#]
public new event EventHandler EnabledChanged;
[C++]
public: __event EventHandler* EnabledChanged;
```

[JScript] In JScript, you can handle the events defined by a class, but you cannot define your own.

PrintPreviewDialog.FontChanged Event

This member supports the .NET Framework infrastructure and is not intended to be used directly from your code.

[Visual Basic]
```
Public Shadows Event FontChanged As EventHandler
```
[C#]
```
public new event EventHandler FontChanged;
```
[C++]
```
public: __event EventHandler* FontChanged;
```

[JScript] In JScript, you can handle the events defined by a class, but you cannot define your own.

PrintPreviewDialog.ForeColorChanged Event

This member supports the .NET Framework infrastructure and is not intended to be used directly from your code.

[Visual Basic]
```
Public Shadows Event ForeColorChanged As EventHandler
```
[C#]
```
public new event EventHandler ForeColorChanged;
```
[C++]
```
public: __event EventHandler* ForeColorChanged;
```

[JScript] In JScript, you can handle the events defined by a class, but you cannot define your own.

PrintPreviewDialog.ImeModeChanged Event

This member supports the .NET Framework infrastructure and is not intended to be used directly from your code.

[Visual Basic]
```
Public Shadows Event ImeModeChanged As EventHandler
```
[C#]
```
public new event EventHandler ImeModeChanged;
```
[C++]
```
public: __event EventHandler* ImeModeChanged;
```

[JScript] In JScript, you can handle the events defined by a class, but you cannot define your own.

PrintPreviewDialog.LocationChanged Event

This member supports the .NET Framework infrastructure and is not intended to be used directly from your code.

[Visual Basic]
```
Public Shadows Event LocationChanged As EventHandler
```
[C#]
```
public new event EventHandler LocationChanged;
```
[C++]
```
public: __event EventHandler* LocationChanged;
```

[JScript] In JScript, you can handle the events defined by a class, but you cannot define your own.

PrintPreviewDialog.MaximumSizeChanged Event

This member supports the .NET Framework infrastructure and is not intended to be used directly from your code.

[Visual Basic]
```
Public Shadows Event MaximumSizeChanged As EventHandler
```
[C#]
```
public new event EventHandler MaximumSizeChanged;
```
[C++]
```
public: __event EventHandler* MaximumSizeChanged;
```

[JScript] In JScript, you can handle the events defined by a class, but you cannot define your own.

PrintPreviewDialog.MinimumSizeChanged Event

This member supports the .NET Framework infrastructure and is not intended to be used directly from your code.

[Visual Basic]
```
Public Shadows Event MinimumSizeChanged As EventHandler
```
[C#]
```
public new event EventHandler MinimumSizeChanged;
```
[C++]
```
public: __event EventHandler* MinimumSizeChanged;
```

[JScript] In JScript, you can handle the events defined by a class, but you cannot define your own.

PrintPreviewDialog.RightToLeftChanged Event

This member supports the .NET Framework infrastructure and is not intended to be used directly from your code.

[Visual Basic]
```
Public Shadows Event RightToLeftChanged As EventHandler
```
[C#]
```
public new event EventHandler RightToLeftChanged;
```
[C++]
```
public: __event EventHandler* RightToLeftChanged;
```

[JScript] In JScript, you can handle the events defined by a class, but you cannot define your own.

PrintPreviewDialog.SizeChanged Event

This member supports the .NET Framework infrastructure and is not intended to be used directly from your code.

[Visual Basic]
```
Public Shadows Event SizeChanged As EventHandler
```
[C#]
```
public new event EventHandler SizeChanged;
```
[C++]
```
public: __event EventHandler* SizeChanged;
```

[JScript] In JScript, you can handle the events defined by a class, but you cannot define your own.

PrintPreviewDialog.TabStopChanged Event

This member supports the .NET Framework infrastructure and is not intended to be used directly from your code.

[Visual Basic]
```
Public Shadows Event TabStopChanged As EventHandler
```
[C#]
```
public new event EventHandler TabStopChanged;
```
[C++]
```
public: __event EventHandler* TabStopChanged;
```

[JScript] In JScript, you can handle the events defined by a class, but you cannot define your own.

PrintPreviewDialog.TextChanged Event

This member supports the .NET Framework infrastructure and is not intended to be used directly from your code.

[Visual Basic]
```
Public Shadows Event TextChanged As EventHandler
```
[C#]
```
public new event EventHandler TextChanged;
```
[C++]
```
public: __event EventHandler* TextChanged;
```

[JScript] In JScript, you can handle the events defined by a class, but you cannot define your own.

PrintPreviewDialog.VisibleChanged Event

This member supports the .NET Framework infrastructure and is not intended to be used directly from your code.

[Visual Basic]
```
Public Shadows Event VisibleChanged As EventHandler
```
[C#]
```
public new event EventHandler VisibleChanged;
```
[C++]
```
public: __event EventHandler* VisibleChanged;
```

[JScript] In JScript, you can handle the events defined by a class, but you cannot define your own.

ProgressBar Class

Represents a Windows progress bar control.

System.Object
  System.MarshalByRefObject
    System.ComponentModel.Component
      System.Windows.Forms.Control
        System.Windows.Forms.ProgressBar

[Visual Basic]
```
NotInheritable Public Class ProgressBar
   Inherits Control
```
[C#]
```
public sealed class ProgressBar : Control
```
[C++]
```
public __gc __sealed class ProgressBar : public Control
```
[JScript]
```
public class ProgressBar extends Control
```

Thread Safety

Any public static (**Shared** in Visual Basic) members of this type are safe for multithreaded operations. Any instance members are not guaranteed to be thread safe.

Remarks

A **ProgressBar** control visually indicates the progress of a lengthy operation. The **ProgressBar** control displays a bar that fills in from left to right with the system highlight color as an operation progresses. The **ProgressBar** control is typically used when an application performs tasks such as copying files or printing documents. Users of an application might consider an application unresponsive if there is no visual cue. By using the **ProgressBar** in your application, you alert the user that the application is performing a lengthy task and that the application is still responding.

The **Maximum** and **Minimum** properties define the range of values to represent the progress of a task. The **Minimum** property is typically set to a value of zero, and the **Maximum** property is typically set to a value indicating the completion of a task. For example, to properly display the progress when copying a group of files, the **Maximum** property could be set to the total number of files to be copied. The **Value** property represents the progress that the application has made toward completing the operation. Because the bar displayed in the control is a collection of blocks, the value displayed by the **ProgressBar** only approximates the **Value** property's current value. Based on the size of the **ProgressBar**, the **Value** property determines when to display the next block.

There are a number of ways to modify the value displayed by the **ProgressBar** other than changing the **Value** property directly. You can use the **Step** property to specify a specific value to increment the **Value** property by, and then call the **PerformStep** method to increment the value. To vary the increment value, you can use the **Increment** method and specify a value with which to increment the **Value** property.

Example

[Visual Basic, C#] The following example uses a **ProgressBar** control to display the progress of a file copy operation. The example uses the **Minimum** and **Maximum** properties to specify a range for the **ProgressBar** that is equivalent to the number of files to copy. The code also uses the **Step** property with the **PerformStep** method to increment the value of the **ProgressBar** as a file is copied. This example assumes that you have a **ProgressBar** control created called `pBar1` that is created within a **Form** and that there is a method created called `CopyFile` (that returns a Boolean value indicating the file copy operation was completed successfully) that performs the file copy operation. The code also assumes that an array of strings containing the files to copy is created and passed to the `CopyWithProgress` method defined in the example and that the method is called from another method or event in the **Form**.

[Visual Basic]
```
Private Sub CopyWithProgress(ByVal ParamArray filenames As String())
    ' Display the ProgressBar control.
    pBar1.Visible = True
    ' Set Minimum to 1 to represent the first file being copied.
    pBar1.Minimum = 1
    ' Set Maximum to the total number of files to copy.
    pBar1.Maximum = filenames.Length
    ' Set the initial value of the ProgressBar.
    pBar1.Value = 1
    ' Set the Step property to a value of 1 to represent each           ↵
 file being copied.
    pBar1.Step = 1

    ' Loop through all files to copy.
    Dim x As Integer
    for x = 1 To filenames.Length - 1
        ' Copy the file and increment the ProgressBar if successful.
        If CopyFile(filenames(x - 1)) = True Then
            ' Perform the increment on the ProgressBar.
            pBar1.PerformStep()
        End If
    Next x
End Sub
```

[C#]
```
private void CopyWithProgress(string[] filenames)
{
    // Display the ProgressBar control.
    pBar1.Visible = true;
    // Set Minimum to 1 to represent the first file being copied.
    pBar1.Minimum = 1;
    // Set Maximum to the total number of files to copy.
    pBar1.Maximum = filenames.Length;
    // Set the initial value of the ProgressBar.
    pBar1.Value = 1;
    // Set the Step property to a value of 1 to represent each           ↵
 file being copied.
    pBar1.Step = 1;

    // Loop through all files to copy.
    for (int x = 1; x <= filenames.Length; x++)
    {
        // Copy the file and increment the ProgressBar if successful.
        if(CopyFile(filenames[x-1]) == true)
        {
            // Perform the increment on the ProgressBar.
            pBar1.PerformStep();
        }
    }
}
```

Requirements

Namespace: System.Windows.Forms

Platforms: Windows 98, Windows NT 4.0, Windows Millennium Edition, Windows 2000, Windows XP Home Edition, Windows XP Professional, Windows Server 2003 family, .NET Compact Framework - Windows CE .NET

Assembly: System.Windows.Forms (in System.Windows.Forms.dll)

ProgressBar Constructor

Initializes a new instance of the **ProgressBar** class.

```
[Visual Basic]
Public Sub New()
[C#]
public ProgressBar();
[C++]
public: ProgressBar();
[JScript]
public function ProgressBar();
```

Remarks

By default, the **Minimum** property is set to 0, the **Maximum** property is set to 100, and the **Step** property is set to 10.

Requirements

Platforms: Windows 98, Windows NT 4.0, Windows Millennium Edition, Windows 2000, Windows XP Home Edition, Windows XP Professional, Windows Server 2003 family, .NET Compact Framework - Windows CE .NET

ProgressBar.AllowDrop Property

This member overrides **Control.AllowDrop**.

```
[Visual Basic]
Overrides Public Property AllowDrop As Boolean
[C#]
public override bool AllowDrop {get; set;}
[C++]
public: __property bool get_AllowDrop();
public: __property void set_AllowDrop(bool);
[JScript]
public override function get AllowDrop() : Boolean;
public override function set AllowDrop(Boolean);
```

Requirements

Platforms: Windows 98, Windows NT 4.0, Windows Millennium Edition, Windows 2000, Windows XP Home Edition, Windows XP Professional, Windows Server 2003 family

ProgressBar.BackColor Property

This member overrides **Control.BackColor**.

```
[Visual Basic]
Overrides Public Property BackColor As Color
[C#]
public override Color BackColor {get; set;}
[C++]
public: __property Color get_BackColor();
public: __property void set_BackColor(Color);
[JScript]
public override function get BackColor() : Color;
public override function set BackColor(Color);
```

Requirements

Platforms: Windows 98, Windows NT 4.0, Windows Millennium Edition, Windows 2000, Windows XP Home Edition, Windows XP Professional, Windows Server 2003 family

ProgressBar.BackgroundImage Property

This member overrides **Control.BackgroundImage**.

```
[Visual Basic]
Overrides Public Property BackgroundImage As Image
[C#]
public override Image BackgroundImage {get; set;}
[C++]
public: __property Image* get_BackgroundImage();
public: __property void set_BackgroundImage(Image*);
[JScript]
public override function get BackgroundImage() : Image;
public override function set BackgroundImage(Image);
```

Requirements

Platforms: Windows 98, Windows NT 4.0, Windows Millennium Edition, Windows 2000, Windows XP Home Edition, Windows XP Professional, Windows Server 2003 family

ProgressBar.CausesValidation Property

This member supports the .NET Framework infrastructure and is not intended to be used directly from your code.

```
[Visual Basic]
Public Shadows Property CausesValidation As Boolean
[C#]
public new bool CausesValidation {get; set;}
[C++]
public: __property bool get_CausesValidation();
public: __property void set_CausesValidation(bool);
[JScript]
public hide function get CausesValidation() : Boolean;
public hide function set CausesValidation(Boolean);
```

ProgressBar.CreateParams Property

This member overrides **Control.CreateParams**.

```
[Visual Basic]
Overrides Protected ReadOnly Property CreateParams As CreateParams
[C#]
protected override CreateParams CreateParams {get;}
[C++]
protected: __property CreateParams* get_CreateParams();
[JScript]
protected override function get CreateParams() : CreateParams;
```

Requirements

Platforms: Windows 98, Windows NT 4.0, Windows Millennium Edition, Windows 2000, Windows XP Home Edition, Windows XP Professional, Windows Server 2003 family

ProgressBar.DefaultImeMode Property

This member overrides **Control.DefaultImeMode**.

```
[Visual Basic]
Overrides Protected ReadOnly Property DefaultImeMode As ImeMode
[C#]
protected override ImeMode DefaultImeMode {get;}
```

```
[C++]
protected: __property ImeMode get_DefaultImeMode();
[JScript]
protected override function get DefaultImeMode() : ImeMode;
```

Requirements

Platforms: Windows 98, Windows NT 4.0, Windows Millennium Edition, Windows 2000, Windows XP Home Edition, Windows XP Professional, Windows Server 2003 family

ProgressBar.DefaultSize Property

This member overrides **Control.DefaultSize**.

```
[Visual Basic]
Overrides Protected ReadOnly Property DefaultSize As Size
[C#]
protected override Size DefaultSize {get;}
[C++]
protected: __property Size get_DefaultSize();
[JScript]
protected override function get DefaultSize() : Size;
```

Requirements

Platforms: Windows 98, Windows NT 4.0, Windows Millennium Edition, Windows 2000, Windows XP Home Edition, Windows XP Professional, Windows Server 2003 family

ProgressBar.Font Property

This member overrides **Control.Font**.

```
[Visual Basic]
Overrides Public Property Font As Font
[C#]
public override Font Font {get; set;}
[C++]
public: __property Font* get_Font();
public: __property void set_Font(Font*);
[JScript]
public override function get Font() : Font;
public override function set Font(Font);
```

Requirements

Platforms: Windows 98, Windows NT 4.0, Windows Millennium Edition, Windows 2000, Windows XP Home Edition, Windows XP Professional, Windows Server 2003 family

ProgressBar.ForeColor Property

This member overrides **Control.ForeColor**.

```
[Visual Basic]
Overrides Public Property ForeColor As Color
[C#]
public override Color ForeColor {get; set;}
[C++]
public: __property Color get_ForeColor();
public: __property void set_ForeColor(Color);
[JScript]
public override function get ForeColor() : Color;
public override function set ForeColor(Color);
```

Requirements

Platforms: Windows 98, Windows NT 4.0, Windows Millennium Edition, Windows 2000, Windows XP Home Edition, Windows XP Professional, Windows Server 2003 family

ProgressBar.ImeMode Property

This member supports the .NET Framework infrastructure and is not intended to be used directly from your code.

```
[Visual Basic]
Public Shadows Property ImeMode As ImeMode
[C#]
public new ImeMode ImeMode {get; set;}
[C++]
public: __property ImeMode get_ImeMode();
public: __property void set_ImeMode(ImeMode);
[JScript]
public hide function get ImeMode() : ImeMode;
public hide function set ImeMode(ImeMode);
```

ProgressBar.Maximum Property

Gets or sets the maximum value of the range of the control.

```
[Visual Basic]
Public Property Maximum As Integer
[C#]
public int Maximum {get; set;}
[C++]
public: __property int get_Maximum();
public: __property void set_Maximum(int);
[JScript]
public function get Maximum() : int;
public function set Maximum(int);
```

Property Value

The maximum value of the range. The default is 100.

Exceptions

Exception Type	Condition
ArgumentException	The value specified is less than zero.

Remarks

This property specifies the upper limit of the **Value** property. When the value of the **Maximum** property is changed, the **ProgressBar** control is redrawn to reflect the new range of the control. When the value of the **Value** property is equal to the value of the **Maximum** property, the progress bar is completely filled.

You can use this property to specify a value that the **Value** property must be set to (by setting the **Value** property or using the **Increment** or **PerformStep** methods) to indicate that an operation is complete. For example, you can set the value of the **Maximum** property to the total number of files in a file copy operation. Each time a file is copied, the **Value** property can be increased by one until the total number of files is copied. At that point the progress bar would be completely filled.

Example

[Visual Basic, C#] The following example uses a **ProgressBar** control to display the progress of a file copy operation. The example uses the **Minimum** and **Maximum** properties to specify a range for the **ProgressBar** that is equivalent to the number of files to copy. The code also uses the **Step** property with the **PerformStep** method to increment the value of the **ProgressBar** as a file is copied. This example assumes that you have a **ProgressBar** control created called `pBar1` that is created within a **Form** and that there is a method created called `CopyFile` (that returns a Boolean value indicating the file copy operation was completed successfully) that performs the file copy operation. The code also assumes that an array of strings containing the files to copy is created and passed to the `CopyWithProgress` method defined in the example and that the method is called from another method or event in the **Form**.

[Visual Basic]
```
Private Sub CopyWithProgress(ByVal ParamArray filenames As String())
    ' Display the ProgressBar control.
    pBar1.Visible = True
    ' Set Minimum to 1 to represent the first file being copied.
    pBar1.Minimum = 1
    ' Set Maximum to the total number of files to copy.
    pBar1.Maximum = filenames.Length
    ' Set the initial value of the ProgressBar.
    pBar1.Value = 1
    ' Set the Step property to a value of 1 to represent each
file being copied.
    pBar1.Step = 1

    ' Loop through all files to copy.
    Dim x As Integer
    for x = 1 To filenames.Length - 1
        ' Copy the file and increment the ProgressBar if successful.
        If CopyFile(filenames(x - 1)) = True Then
            ' Perform the increment on the ProgressBar.
            pBar1.PerformStep()
        End If
    Next x
End Sub
```

[C#]
```
private void CopyWithProgress(string[] filenames)
{
    // Display the ProgressBar control.
    pBar1.Visible = true;
    // Set Minimum to 1 to represent the first file being copied.
    pBar1.Minimum = 1;
    // Set Maximum to the total number of files to copy.
    pBar1.Maximum = filenames.Length;
    // Set the initial value of the ProgressBar.
    pBar1.Value = 1;
    // Set the Step property to a value of 1 to represent
 each file being copied.
    pBar1.Step = 1;

    // Loop through all files to copy.
    for (int x = 1; x <= filenames.Length; x++)
    {
        // Copy the file and increment the ProgressBar if successful.
        if(CopyFile(filenames[x-1]) == true)
        {
            // Perform the increment on the ProgressBar.
            pBar1.PerformStep();
        }
    }
}
```

Requirements

Platforms: Windows 98, Windows NT 4.0, Windows Millennium Edition, Windows 2000, Windows XP Home Edition, Windows XP Professional, Windows Server 2003 family, .NET Compact Framework - Windows CE .NET

ProgressBar.Minimum Property

Gets or sets the minimum value of the range of the control.

[Visual Basic]
```
Public Property Minimum As Integer
```
[C#]
```
public int Minimum {get; set;}
```
[C++]
```
public: __property int get_Minimum();
public: __property void set_Minimum(int);
```
[JScript]
```
public function get Minimum() : int;
public function set Minimum(int);
```

Property Value

The minimum value of the range. The default is 0.

Exceptions

Exception Type	Condition
ArgumentException	The value specified for the property is less than zero.

Remarks

This property specifies the lower limit of the **Value** property. When the value of the **Minimum** property is changed, the **ProgressBar** control is redrawn to reflect the new range of the control. When the value of the **Value** property is equal to the value of the **Minimum** property, the progress bar is empty. To change the value of the progress bar, use the **Step** property with the **PerformStep** method, use the **Increment** method, or set the value of the **Value** property directly.

Example

[Visual Basic, C#] The following example uses a **ProgressBar** control to display the progress of a file copy operation. The example uses the **Minimum** and **Maximum** properties to specify a range for the **ProgressBar** that is equivalent to the number of files to copy. The code also uses the **Step** property with the **PerformStep** method to increment the value of the **ProgressBar** as a file is copied. This example assumes that you have a **ProgressBar** control created called `pBar1` that is created within a **Form** and that there is a method created called `CopyFile` (that returns a Boolean value indicating the file copy operation was completed successfully) that performs the file copy operation. The code also assumes that an array of strings containing the files to copy is created and passed to the `CopyWithProgress` method defined in the example and that the method is called from another method or event in the **Form**.

[Visual Basic]
```
Private Sub CopyWithProgress(ByVal ParamArray filenames As String())
    ' Display the ProgressBar control.
    pBar1.Visible = True
    ' Set Minimum to 1 to represent the first file being copied.
    pBar1.Minimum = 1
    ' Set Maximum to the total number of files to copy.
    pBar1.Maximum = filenames.Length
    ' Set the initial value of the ProgressBar.
    pBar1.Value = 1
    ' Set the Step property to a value of 1 to represent each
file being copied.
    pBar1.Step = 1

    ' Loop through all files to copy.
    Dim x As Integer
    for x = 1 To filenames.Length - 1
        ' Copy the file and increment the ProgressBar if successful.
```

```
        If CopyFile(filenames(x - 1)) = True Then
            ' Perform the increment on the ProgressBar.
            pBar1.PerformStep()
        End If
    Next x
End Sub
```

[C#]

```
private void CopyWithProgress(string[] filenames)
{
    // Display the ProgressBar control.
    pBar1.Visible = true;
    // Set Minimum to 1 to represent the first file being copied.
    pBar1.Minimum = 1;
    // Set Maximum to the total number of files to copy.
    pBar1.Maximum = filenames.Length;
    // Set the initial value of the ProgressBar.
    pBar1.Value = 1;
    // Set the Step property to a value of 1 to represent each ↵
file being copied.
    pBar1.Step = 1;

    // Loop through all files to copy.
    for (int x = 1; x <= filenames.Length; x++)
    {
        // Copy the file and increment the ProgressBar if successful.
        if(CopyFile(filenames[x-1]) == true)
        {
            // Perform the increment on the ProgressBar.
            pBar1.PerformStep();
        }
    }
}
```

Requirements

Platforms: Windows 98, Windows NT 4.0, Windows Millennium Edition, Windows 2000, Windows XP Home Edition, Windows XP Professional, Windows Server 2003 family, .NET Compact Framework - Windows CE .NET

ProgressBar.RightToLeft Property

This member overrides **Control.RightToLeft**.

[Visual Basic]

```
Overrides Public Property RightToLeft As RightToLeft
```

[C#]

```
public override RightToLeft RightToLeft {get; set;}
```

[C++]

```
public: __property RightToLeft get_RightToLeft();
public: __property void set_RightToLeft(RightToLeft);
```

[JScript]

```
public override function get RightToLeft() : RightToLeft;
public override function set RightToLeft(RightToLeft);
```

Requirements

Platforms: Windows 98, Windows NT 4.0, Windows Millennium Edition, Windows 2000, Windows XP Home Edition, Windows XP Professional, Windows Server 2003 family

ProgressBar.Step Property

Gets or sets the amount by which a call to the **PerformStep** method increases the current position of the progress bar.

[Visual Basic]

```
Public Property Step As Integer
```

[C#]

```
public int Step {get; set;}
```

[C++]

```
public: __property int get_Step();
public: __property void set_Step(int);
```

[JScript]

```
public function get Step() : int;
public function set Step(int);
```

Property Value

The amount by which to increment the progress bar with each call to the **PerformStep** method. The default is 10.

Remarks

You can use the **Step** property to specify the amount that each completed task in an operation changes the value of the progress bar. For example, if you are copying a group of files, you might want to set the value of the **Step** property to 1 and the value of the **Maximum** property to the total number of files to copy. When each file is copied, you can call the **PerformStep** method to increment the progress bar by the value of the **Step** property. If you want to have more flexible control of the value of the progress bar, you can use the **Increment** method or set the value of the **Value** property directly.

Example

[Visual Basic, C#] The following example uses a **ProgressBar** control to display the progress of a file copy operation. The example uses the **Minimum** and **Maximum** properties to specify a range for the **ProgressBar** that is equivalent to the number of files to copy. The code also uses the **Step** property with the **PerformStep** method to increment the value of the **ProgressBar** as a file is copied. This example assumes that you have a **ProgressBar** control created called `pBar1` that is created within a **Form** and that there is a method created called `CopyFile` (that returns a Boolean value indicating the file copy operation was completed successfully) that performs the file copy operation. The code also assumes that an array of strings containing the files to copy is created and passed to the `CopyWithProgress` method defined in the example and that the method is called from another method or event in the **Form**.

[Visual Basic]

```
Private Sub CopyWithProgress(ByVal ParamArray filenames As String())
    ' Display the ProgressBar control.
    pBar1.Visible = True
    ' Set Minimum to 1 to represent the first file being copied.
    pBar1.Minimum = 1
    ' Set Maximum to the total number of files to copy.
    pBar1.Maximum = filenames.Length
    ' Set the initial value of the ProgressBar.
    pBar1.Value = 1
    ' Set the Step property to a value of 1 to represent each ↵
file being copied.
    pBar1.Step = 1

    ' Loop through all files to copy.
    Dim x As Integer
    for x = 1 To filenames.Length - 1
        ' Copy the file and increment the ProgressBar if successful.
        If CopyFile(filenames(x - 1)) = True Then
            ' Perform the increment on the ProgressBar.
            pBar1.PerformStep()
        End If
    Next x
End Sub
```

[C#]

```
private void CopyWithProgress(string[] filenames)
{
```

```
    // Display the ProgressBar control.
    pBar1.Visible = true;
    // Set Minimum to 1 to represent the first file being copied.
    pBar1.Minimum = 1;
    // Set Maximum to the total number of files to copy.
    pBar1.Maximum = filenames.Length;
    // Set the initial value of the ProgressBar.
    pBar1.Value = 1;
    // Set the Step property to a value of 1 to represent each        ↵
file being copied.
    pBar1.Step = 1;

    // Loop through all files to copy.
    for (int x = 1; x <= filenames.Length; x++)
    {
        // Copy the file and increment the ProgressBar if successful.
        if(CopyFile(filenames[x-1]) == true)
        {
            // Perform the increment on the ProgressBar.
            pBar1.PerformStep();
        }
    }
}
```

Requirements

Platforms: Windows 98, Windows NT 4.0, Windows Millennium Edition, Windows 2000, Windows XP Home Edition, Windows XP Professional, Windows Server 2003 family

ProgressBar.TabStop Property

This member supports the .NET Framework infrastructure and is not intended to be used directly from your code.

[Visual Basic]
```
Public Shadows Property TabStop As Boolean
```
[C#]
```
public new bool TabStop {get; set;}
```
[C++]
```
public: __property bool get_TabStop();
public: __property void set_TabStop(bool);
```
[JScript]
```
public hide function get TabStop() : Boolean;
public hide function set TabStop(Boolean);
```

ProgressBar.Text Property

This member overrides **Control.Text**.

[Visual Basic]
```
Overrides Public Property Text As String
```
[C#]
```
public override string Text {get; set;}
```
[C++]
```
public: __property String* get_Text();
public: __property void set_Text(String*);
```
[JScript]
```
public override function get Text() : String;
public override function set Text(String);
```

Requirements

Platforms: Windows 98, Windows NT 4.0, Windows Millennium Edition, Windows 2000, Windows XP Home Edition, Windows XP Professional, Windows Server 2003 family

ProgressBar.Value Property

Gets or sets the current position of the progress bar.

[Visual Basic]
```
Public Property Value As Integer
```
[C#]
```
public int Value {get; set;}
```
[C++]
```
public: __property int get_Value();
public: __property void set_Value(int);
```
[JScript]
```
public function get Value() : int;
public function set Value(int);
```

Property Value

The position within the range of the progress bar. The default is 0.

Exceptions

Exception Type	Condition
ArgumentException	The value specified is greater than the value of the **Maximum** property. -or- The value specified is less than the value of the **Minimum** property.

Remarks

The minimum and maximum values of the **Value** property are specified by the **Minimum** and **Maximum** properties. This property enables you to increment or decrement the value of the progress bar directly. To perform consistent increases in the value of the **ProgressBar** control you can use the **Step** property with the **PerformStep** method. To increase the progress bar value by varying amounts, use the **Increment** method.

Example

[Visual Basic, C#] The following example demonstrates how to use the **Increment** method and the **Value** property to increment the value of a **ProgressBar** in the **Tick** event of a **Timer**. The example also displays the Value property in a **StatusBarPanel** object to provide a textual representation of the **ProgressBar**. This example assumes that you have a **ProgressBar** control, named `progressBar1`, and a **StatusBar** control that contains a **StatusBarPanel**, named `statusBarPanel1`. The **Timer** object, named time, must be added to the form as a member.

[Visual Basic]
```
Private time As New Timer()

' Call this method from the constructor of the form.
Private Sub InitializeMyTimer()
   ' Set the interval for the timer.
   time.Interval = 250
   ' Connect the Tick event of the timer to its event handler.
   AddHandler time.Tick, AddressOf IncreaseProgressBar
   ' Start the timer.
   time.Start()
End Sub

Private Sub IncreaseProgressBar(ByVal sender As Object, ByVal        ↵
 e As EventArgs)
   ' Increment the value of the ProgressBar a value of one each time.
   ProgressBar1.Increment(1)
   ' Display the textual value of the ProgressBar in the        ↵
StatusBar control's first panel.
   statusBarPanel1.Text = ProgressBar1.Value.ToString() + "% Completed"
   ' Determine if we have completed by comparing the value of        ↵
the Value property to the Maximum value.
```

```
   If ProgressBar1.Value = ProgressBar1.Maximum Then
      ' Stop the timer.
      time.Stop()
   End If
End Sub
```

[C#]

```
private Timer time = new Timer();

// Call this method from the constructor of the form.
private void InitializeMyTimer()
{
   // Set the interval for the timer.
   time.Interval = 250;
   // Connect the Tick event of the timer to its event handler.
   time.Tick += new EventHandler(IncreaseProgressBar);
   // Start the timer.
   time.Start();
}

private void IncreaseProgressBar(object sender, EventArgs e)
{
   // Increment the value of the ProgressBar a value of one each time.
   progressBar1.Increment(1);
   // Display the textual value of the ProgressBar in the ↵
StatusBar control's first panel.
   statusBarPanel1.Text = progressBar1.Value.ToString() + "% ↵
Completed";
   // Determine if we have completed by comparing the value ↵
of the Value property to the Maximum value.
   if (progressBar1.Value == progressBar1.Maximum)
      // Stop the timer.
      time.Stop();
}
```

Requirements

Platforms: Windows 98, Windows NT 4.0, Windows Millennium Edition, Windows 2000, Windows XP Home Edition, Windows XP Professional, Windows Server 2003 family, .NET Compact Framework - Windows CE .NET

ProgressBar.CreateHandle Method

This member overrides **Control.CreateHandle**.

[Visual Basic]

```
Overrides Protected Sub CreateHandle()
```

[C#]

```
protected override void CreateHandle();
```

[C++]

```
protected: void CreateHandle();
```

[JScript]

```
protected override function CreateHandle();
```

Requirements

Platforms: Windows 98, Windows NT 4.0, Windows Millennium Edition, Windows 2000, Windows XP Home Edition, Windows XP Professional, Windows Server 2003 family

ProgressBar.Increment Method

Advances the current position of the progress bar by the specified amount.

[Visual Basic]

```
Public Sub Increment( _
   ByVal value As Integer _
)
```

[C#]

```
public void Increment(
   int value
);
```

[C++]

```
public: void Increment(
   int value
);
```

[JScript]

```
public function Increment(
   value : int
);
```

Parameters

value

The amount by which to increment the progress bar's current position.

Remarks

The **Increment** method enables you to increment the value of the progress bar by a specific amount. This method of incrementing the progress bar is similar to using the **Step** property with the **PerformStep** method. The **Value** property specifies the current position of the **ProgressBar**. If, after calling the **Increment** method, the **Value** property is greater than the value of the **Maximum** property, the **Value** property remains at the value of the **Maximum** property. If, after calling the **Increment** method with a negative value specified in the *value* parameter, the **Value** property is less than the value of the **Minimum** property, the **Value** property remains at the value of the **Minimum** property.

Example

[Visual Basic, C#] The following example demonstrates how to use the **Increment** method and the **Value** property to increment the value of a **ProgressBar** in the **Tick** event of a **Timer**. The example also displays the Value property in a **StatusBarPanel** object to provide a textual representation of the **ProgressBar**. This example assumes that you have a **ProgressBar** control, named `progressBar1`, and a **StatusBar** control that contains a **StatusBarPanel**, named `statusBarPanel1`. The **Timer** object, named time, must be added to the form as a member.

[Visual Basic]

```
Private time As New Timer()

' Call this method from the constructor of the form.
Private Sub InitializeMyTimer()
   ' Set the interval for the timer.
   time.Interval = 250
   ' Connect the Tick event of the timer to its event handler.
   AddHandler time.Tick, AddressOf IncreaseProgressBar
   ' Start the timer.
   time.Start()
End Sub

Private Sub IncreaseProgressBar(ByVal sender As Object, ByVal ↵
 e As EventArgs)
   ' Increment the value of the ProgressBar a value of one each time.
   ProgressBar1.Increment(1)
   ' Display the textual value of the ProgressBar in the ↵
 StatusBar control's first panel.
   statusBarPanel1.Text = ProgressBar1.Value.ToString() + "% Completed"
   ' Determine if we have completed by comparing the value of the ↵
 Value property to the Maximum value.
   If ProgressBar1.Value = ProgressBar1.Maximum Then
      ' Stop the timer.
      time.Stop()
```

```
   End If
End Sub
```

[C#]

```
private Timer time = new Timer();

// Call this method from the constructor of the form.
private void InitializeMyTimer()
{
   // Set the interval for the timer.
   time.Interval = 250;
   // Connect the Tick event of the timer to its event handler.
   time.Tick += new EventHandler(IncreaseProgressBar);
   // Start the timer.
   time.Start();
}

private void IncreaseProgressBar(object sender, EventArgs e)
{
   // Increment the value of the ProgressBar a value of one each time.
   progressBar1.Increment(1);
   // Display the textual value of the ProgressBar in the           ↵
StatusBar control's first panel.
   statusBarPanel1.Text = progressBar1.Value.ToString() + "%        ↵
Completed";
   // Determine if we have completed by comparing the value of      ↵
 the Value property to the Maximum value.
   if (progressBar1.Value == progressBar1.Maximum)
      // Stop the timer.
      time.Stop();
}
```

Requirements

Platforms: Windows 98, Windows NT 4.0, Windows Millennium Edition, Windows 2000, Windows XP Home Edition, Windows XP Professional, Windows Server 2003 family

ProgressBar.OnHandleCreated Method

This member overrides **Control.OnHandleCreated**.

[Visual Basic]

```
Overrides Protected Sub OnHandleCreated( _
   ByVal e As EventArgs _
)
```

[C#]

```
protected override void OnHandleCreated(
   EventArgs e
);
```

[C++]

```
protected: void OnHandleCreated(
   EventArgs* e
);
```

[JScript]

```
protected override function OnHandleCreated(
   e : EventArgs
);
```

Requirements

Platforms: Windows 98, Windows NT 4.0, Windows Millennium Edition, Windows 2000, Windows XP Home Edition, Windows XP Professional, Windows Server 2003 family

ProgressBar.PerformStep Method

Advances the current position of the progress bar by the amount of the **Step** property.

[Visual Basic]

```
Public Sub PerformStep()
```

[C#]

```
public void PerformStep();
```

[C++]

```
public: void PerformStep();
```

[JScript]

```
public function PerformStep();
```

Remarks

The **PerformStep** method increments the value of the progress bar by the amount specified by the **Step** property. You can use the **Step** property to specify the amount that each completed task in an operation changes the value of the progress bar. For example, if you are copying a group of files, you might want to set the value of the **Step** property to 1 and the value of the **Maximum** property to the total number of files to copy. When each file is copied, you can call the **PerformStep** method to increment the progress bar by the value of the **Step** property. If you want to have more flexible control of the value of the progress bar, you can use the **Increment** method or set the value of the **Value** property directly.

The **Value** property specifies the current position of the **ProgressBar**. If, after calling the **PerformStep** method, the **Value** property is greater than the value of the **Maximum** property, the **Value** property remains at the value of the **Maximum** property. If, after calling the **PerformStep** method with a negative value specified in the *value* parameter, the **Value** property is less than the value of the **Minimum** property, the **Value** property remains at the value of the **Minimum** property.

Example

[Visual Basic, C#] The following example uses a **ProgressBar** control to display the progress of a file copy operation. The example uses the **Minimum** and **Maximum** properties to specify a range for the **ProgressBar** that is equivalent to the number of files to copy. The code also uses the **Step** property with the **PerformStep** method to increment the value of the **ProgressBar** as a file is copied. This example assumes that you have a **ProgressBar** control created called `pBar1` that is created within a **Form** and that there is a method created called `CopyFile` (that returns a Boolean value indicating the file copy operation was completed successfully) that performs the file copy operation. The code also assumes that an array of strings containing the files to copy is created and passed to the `CopyWithProgress` method defined in the example and that the method is called from another method or event in the **Form**.

[Visual Basic]

```
Private Sub CopyWithProgress(ByVal ParamArray filenames As String())
    ' Display the ProgressBar control.
    pBar1.Visible = True
    ' Set Minimum to 1 to represent the first file being copied.
    pBar1.Minimum = 1
    ' Set Maximum to the total number of files to copy.
    pBar1.Maximum = filenames.Length
    ' Set the initial value of the ProgressBar.
    pBar1.Value = 1
    ' Set the Step property to a value of 1 to represent          ↵
 each file being copied.
    pBar1.Step = 1
```

```
    ' Loop through all files to copy.
    Dim x As Integer
    for x = 1 To filenames.Length - 1
        ' Copy the file and increment the ProgressBar if successful.
        If CopyFile(filenames(x - 1)) = True Then
            ' Perform the increment on the ProgressBar.
            pBar1.PerformStep()
        End If
    Next x
End Sub
```

[C#]

```
private void CopyWithProgress(string[] filenames)
{
    // Display the ProgressBar control.
    pBar1.Visible = true;
    // Set Minimum to 1 to represent the first file being copied.
    pBar1.Minimum = 1;
    // Set Maximum to the total number of files to copy.
    pBar1.Maximum = filenames.Length;
    // Set the initial value of the ProgressBar.
    pBar1.Value = 1;
    // Set the Step property to a value of 1 to represent                ↵
each file being copied.
    pBar1.Step = 1;

    // Loop through all files to copy.
    for (int x = 1; x <= filenames.Length; x++)
    {
        // Copy the file and increment the ProgressBar if successful.
        if(CopyFile(filenames[x-1]) == true)
        {
            // Perform the increment on the ProgressBar.
            pBar1.PerformStep();
        }
    }
}
```

Requirements

Platforms: Windows 98, Windows NT 4.0, Windows Millennium Edition, Windows 2000, Windows XP Home Edition, Windows XP Professional, Windows Server 2003 family

ProgressBar.ToString Method

This member overrides **Object.ToString**.

[Visual Basic]
```
Overrides Public Function ToString() As String
```
[C#]
```
public override string ToString();
```
[C++]
```
public: String* ToString();
```
[JScript]
```
public override function ToString() : String;
```

Requirements

Platforms: Windows 98, Windows NT 4.0, Windows Millennium Edition, Windows 2000, Windows XP Home Edition, Windows XP Professional, Windows Server 2003 family, .NET Compact Framework - Windows CE .NET

ProgressBar.BackColorChanged Event

This member supports the .NET Framework infrastructure and is not intended to be used directly from your code.

[Visual Basic]
```
Public Shadows Event BackColorChanged As EventHandler
```
[C#]
```
public new event EventHandler BackColorChanged;
```
[C++]
```
public: __event EventHandler* BackColorChanged;
```

[JScript] In JScript, you can handle the events defined by a class, but you cannot define your own.

ProgressBar.BackgroundImageChanged Event

This member supports the .NET Framework infrastructure and is not intended to be used directly from your code.

[Visual Basic]
```
Public Shadows Event BackgroundImageChanged As EventHandler
```
[C#]
```
public new event EventHandler BackgroundImageChanged;
```
[C++]
```
public: __event EventHandler* BackgroundImageChanged;
```

[JScript] In JScript, you can handle the events defined by a class, but you cannot define your own.

ProgressBar.CausesValidationChanged Event

This member supports the .NET Framework infrastructure and is not intended to be used directly from your code.

[Visual Basic]
```
Public Shadows Event CausesValidationChanged As EventHandler
```
[C#]
```
public new event EventHandler CausesValidationChanged;
```
[C++]
```
public: __event EventHandler* CausesValidationChanged;
```

[JScript] In JScript, you can handle the events defined by a class, but you cannot define your own.

ProgressBar.DoubleClick Event

This member supports the .NET Framework infrastructure and is not intended to be used directly from your code.

[Visual Basic]
```
Public Shadows Event DoubleClick As EventHandler
```
[C#]
```
public new event EventHandler DoubleClick;
```
[C++]
```
public: __event EventHandler* DoubleClick;
```

[JScript] In JScript, you can handle the events defined by a class, but you cannot define your own.

ProgressBar.Enter Event

This member supports the .NET Framework infrastructure and is not intended to be used directly from your code.

[Visual Basic]
```
Public Shadows Event Enter As EventHandler
```
[C#]
```
public new event EventHandler Enter;
```
[C++]
```
public: __event EventHandler* Enter;
```

[JScript] In JScript, you can handle the events defined by a class, but you cannot define your own.

ProgressBar.FontChanged Event

This member supports the .NET Framework infrastructure and is not intended to be used directly from your code.

[Visual Basic]
```
Public Shadows Event FontChanged As EventHandler
```
[C#]
```
public new event EventHandler FontChanged;
```
[C++]
```
public: __event EventHandler* FontChanged;
```

[JScript] In JScript, you can handle the events defined by a class, but you cannot define your own.

ProgressBar.ForeColorChanged Event

This member supports the .NET Framework infrastructure and is not intended to be used directly from your code.

[Visual Basic]
```
Public Shadows Event ForeColorChanged As EventHandler
```
[C#]
```
public new event EventHandler ForeColorChanged;
```
[C++]
```
public: __event EventHandler* ForeColorChanged;
```

[JScript] In JScript, you can handle the events defined by a class, but you cannot define your own.

ProgressBar.ImeModeChanged Event

This member supports the .NET Framework infrastructure and is not intended to be used directly from your code.

[Visual Basic]
```
Public Shadows Event ImeModeChanged As EventHandler
```
[C#]
```
public new event EventHandler ImeModeChanged;
```
[C++]
```
public: __event EventHandler* ImeModeChanged;
```

[JScript] In JScript, you can handle the events defined by a class, but you cannot define your own.

ProgressBar.KeyDown Event

This member supports the .NET Framework infrastructure and is not intended to be used directly from your code.

[Visual Basic]
```
Public Shadows Event KeyDown As KeyEventHandler
```
[C#]
```
public new event KeyEventHandler KeyDown;
```
[C++]
```
public: __event KeyEventHandler* KeyDown;
```

[JScript] In JScript, you can handle the events defined by a class, but you cannot define your own.

ProgressBar.KeyPress Event

This member supports the .NET Framework infrastructure and is not intended to be used directly from your code.

[Visual Basic]
```
Public Shadows Event KeyPress As KeyPressEventHandler
```
[C#]
```
public new event KeyPressEventHandler KeyPress;
```
[C++]
```
public: __event KeyPressEventHandler* KeyPress;
```

[JScript] In JScript, you can handle the events defined by a class, but you cannot define your own.

ProgressBar.KeyUp Event

This member supports the .NET Framework infrastructure and is not intended to be used directly from your code.

[Visual Basic]
```
Public Shadows Event KeyUp As KeyEventHandler
```
[C#]
```
public new event KeyEventHandler KeyUp;
```
[C++]
```
public: __event KeyEventHandler* KeyUp;
```

[JScript] In JScript, you can handle the events defined by a class, but you cannot define your own.

ProgressBar.Leave Event

This member supports the .NET Framework infrastructure and is not intended to be used directly from your code.

[Visual Basic]
```
Public Shadows Event Leave As EventHandler
```
[C#]
```
public new event EventHandler Leave;
```
[C++]
```
public: __event EventHandler* Leave;
```

[JScript] In JScript, you can handle the events defined by a class, but you cannot define your own.

ProgressBar.Paint Event

This member supports the .NET Framework infrastructure and is not intended to be used directly from your code.

[Visual Basic]
```
Public Shadows Event Paint As PaintEventHandler
```
[C#]
```
public new event PaintEventHandler Paint;
```
[C++]
```
public: __event PaintEventHandler* Paint;
```

[JScript] In JScript, you can handle the events defined by a class, but you cannot define your own.

ProgressBar.RightToLeftChanged Event

This member supports the .NET Framework infrastructure and is not intended to be used directly from your code.

[Visual Basic]
```
Public Shadows Event RightToLeftChanged As EventHandler
```
[C#]
```
public new event EventHandler RightToLeftChanged;
```
[C++]
```
public: __event EventHandler* RightToLeftChanged;
```

[JScript] In JScript, you can handle the events defined by a class, but you cannot define your own.

ProgressBar.TabStopChanged Event

This member supports the .NET Framework infrastructure and is not intended to be used directly from your code.

[Visual Basic]
```
Public Shadows Event TabStopChanged As EventHandler
```
[C#]
```
public new event EventHandler TabStopChanged;
```
[C++]
```
public: __event EventHandler* TabStopChanged;
```

[JScript] In JScript, you can handle the events defined by a class, but you cannot define your own.

ProgressBar.TextChanged Event

This member supports the .NET Framework infrastructure and is not intended to be used directly from your code.

[Visual Basic]
```
Public Shadows Event TextChanged As EventHandler
```
[C#]
```
public new event EventHandler TextChanged;
```
[C++]
```
public: __event EventHandler* TextChanged;
```

[JScript] In JScript, you can handle the events defined by a class, but you cannot define your own.

PropertyGrid Class

Provides a user interface for browsing the properties of an object.

System.Object
  System.MarshalByRefObject
    System.ComponentModel.Component
      System.Windows.Forms.Control
        System.Windows.Forms.ScrollableControl
          System.Windows.Forms.ContainerControl
            System.Windows.Forms.PropertyGrid

[Visual Basic]
```
Public Class PropertyGrid
   Inherits ContainerControl
```
[C#]
```
public class PropertyGrid : ContainerControl
```
[C++]
```
public __gc class PropertyGrid : public ContainerControl
```
[JScript]
```
public class PropertyGrid extends ContainerControl
```

Thread Safety

Any public static (**Shared** in Visual Basic) members of this type are safe for multithreaded operations. Any instance members are not guaranteed to be thread safe.

Remarks

To use the property grid, you create a new instance of the **PropertyGrid** class on a parent control and set **SelectedObject** to the object to display the properties for.

The information displayed in the grid is a snapshot of the properties at the time the object is assigned. If a property value of the object specified by the **SelectedObject** is changed in code at run time, the new value is not displayed until an action is taken in the grid that causes the grid to refresh.

The property tabs within the property grid appear as buttons on the toolbar at the top of the **PropertyGrid**, and can vary in scope as defined in the **PropertyTabScope** enumeration.

The **PropertyGrid** control is not initially presented in the toolbox in the development environment. You can add a property grid to the toolbox, which allows you to drag and drop a **PropertyGrid** object onto your form. You can also define an instance of **PropertyGrid** by adding the appropriate code in your source code.

Example

[Visual Basic, C#] The following example illustrates creating a property grid and setting its location on a form. This example assumes a form of with a **TextBox** on it.

[Visual Basic]
```
Public Sub New()

    ' The initial constructor code goes here.

    Dim propertyGrid1 As New PropertyGrid()
    propertyGrid1.CommandsVisibleIfAvailable = True
    propertyGrid1.Location = New Point(10, 20)
    propertyGrid1.Size = New System.Drawing.Size(400, 300)
    propertyGrid1.TabIndex = 1
    propertyGrid1.Text = "Property Grid"

    Me.Controls.Add(propertyGrid1)

    propertyGrid1.SelectedObject = textBox1
End Sub
```

[C#]
```
public Form1() {

   // The initial constructor code goes here.

   PropertyGrid propertyGrid1 = new PropertyGrid();
   propertyGrid1.CommandsVisibleIfAvailable = true;
   propertyGrid1.Location = new Point(10, 20);
   propertyGrid1.Size = new System.Drawing.Size(400, 300);
   propertyGrid1.TabIndex = 1;
   propertyGrid1.Text = "Property Grid";

   this.Controls.Add(propertyGrid1);

   propertyGrid1.SelectedObject = textBox1;
}
```

Requirements

Namespace: System.Windows.Forms

Platforms: Windows 98, Windows NT 4.0, Windows Millennium Edition, Windows 2000, Windows XP Home Edition, Windows XP Professional, Windows Server 2003 family

Assembly: System.Windows.Forms (in System.Windows.Forms.dll)

PropertyGrid Constructor

Initializes a new instance of the **PropertyGrid** class.

[Visual Basic]
```
Public Sub New()
```
[C#]
```
public PropertyGrid();
```
[C++]
```
public: PropertyGrid();
```
[JScript]
```
public function PropertyGrid();
```

Remarks

To populate the grid, you must set the **SelectedObject** property.

Requirements

Platforms: Windows 98, Windows NT 4.0, Windows Millennium Edition, Windows 2000, Windows XP Home Edition, Windows XP Professional, Windows Server 2003 family

PropertyGrid.AutoScroll Property

This member overrides **ScrollableControl.AutoScroll**.

[Visual Basic]
```
Overrides Public Property AutoScroll As Boolean
```
[C#]
```
public override bool AutoScroll {get; set;}
```
[C++]
```
public: __property bool get_AutoScroll();
public: __property void set_AutoScroll(bool);
```
[JScript]
```
public override function get AutoScroll() : Boolean;
public override function set AutoScroll(Boolean);
```

Requirements

Platforms: Windows 98, Windows NT 4.0, Windows Millennium Edition, Windows 2000, Windows XP Home Edition, Windows XP Professional, Windows Server 2003 family

PropertyGrid.BackColor Property

This member overrides **Control.BackColor**.

```
[Visual Basic]
Overrides Public Property BackColor As Color
[C#]
public override Color BackColor {get; set;}
[C++]
public: __property Color get_BackColor();
public: __property void set_BackColor(Color);
[JScript]
public override function get BackColor() : Color;
public override function set BackColor(Color);
```

Requirements

Platforms: Windows 98, Windows NT 4.0, Windows Millennium Edition, Windows 2000, Windows XP Home Edition, Windows XP Professional, Windows Server 2003 family

PropertyGrid.BackgroundImage Property

This member overrides **Control.BackgroundImage**.

```
[Visual Basic]
Overrides Public Property BackgroundImage As Image
[C#]
public override Image BackgroundImage {get; set;}
[C++]
public: __property Image* get_BackgroundImage();
public: __property void set_BackgroundImage(Image*);
[JScript]
public override function get BackgroundImage() : Image;
public override function set BackgroundImage(Image);
```

Requirements

Platforms: Windows 98, Windows NT 4.0, Windows Millennium Edition, Windows 2000, Windows XP Home Edition, Windows XP Professional, Windows Server 2003 family

PropertyGrid.BrowsableAttributes Property

Gets or sets the browsable attributes associated with the object that the property grid is attached to.

```
[Visual Basic]
Public Property BrowsableAttributes As AttributeCollection
[C#]
public AttributeCollection BrowsableAttributes {get; set;}
[C++]
public: __property AttributeCollection* get_BrowsableAttributes();
public: __property void set_BrowsableAttributes(AttributeCollection*);
[JScript]
public function get BrowsableAttributes() : AttributeCollection;
public function set BrowsableAttributes(AttributeCollection);
```

Property Value

The collection of browsable attributes associated with the object.

Remarks

Only properties with attributes matching the values specified are displayed in the **PropertyGrid**. The default is an **AttributeCollection** containing only **BrowsableAttribute.Yes**.

Assigning an attribute collection that is empty or is a null reference (**Nothing** in Visual Basic) causes a new **AttributeCollection** to be created with **BrowsableAttribute.Yes** set.

Requirements

Platforms: Windows 98, Windows NT 4.0, Windows Millennium Edition, Windows 2000, Windows XP Home Edition, Windows XP Professional, Windows Server 2003 family

PropertyGrid.CanShowCommands Property

Gets a value indicating whether the commands pane can be made visible for the currently selected objects.

```
[Visual Basic]
Public Overridable ReadOnly Property CanShowCommands As Boolean
[C#]
public virtual bool CanShowCommands {get;}
[C++]
public: __property virtual bool get_CanShowCommands();
[JScript]
public function get CanShowCommands() : Boolean;
```

Property Value

true if the commands pane can be made visible; otherwise, **false**.

Remarks

This property is **true** if **CommandsVisibleIfAvailable** is **true** and the object has commands available.

Requirements

Platforms: Windows 98, Windows NT 4.0, Windows Millennium Edition, Windows 2000, Windows XP Home Edition, Windows XP Professional, Windows Server 2003 family

PropertyGrid.CommandsBackColor Property

Gets or sets the background color of the hot commands region.

```
[Visual Basic]
Public Property CommandsBackColor As Color
[C#]
public Color CommandsBackColor {get; set;}
[C++]
public: __property Color get_CommandsBackColor();
public: __property void set_CommandsBackColor(Color);
[JScript]
public function get CommandsBackColor() : Color;
public function set CommandsBackColor(Color);
```

Property Value

One of the **Color** values. The default is the default system color for controls.

Requirements

Platforms: Windows 98, Windows NT 4.0, Windows Millennium Edition, Windows 2000, Windows XP Home Edition, Windows XP Professional, Windows Server 2003 family

PropertyGrid.CommandsForeColor Property

Gets or sets the foreground color for the hot commands region.

```
[Visual Basic]
Public Property CommandsForeColor As Color
[C#]
public Color CommandsForeColor {get; set;}
[C++]
public: __property Color get_CommandsForeColor();
public: __property void set_CommandsForeColor(Color);
[JScript]
public function get CommandsForeColor() : Color;
public function set CommandsForeColor(Color);
```

Property Value

One of the **Color** values. The default is the default system color for control text.

Requirements

Platforms: Windows 98, Windows NT 4.0, Windows Millennium Edition, Windows 2000, Windows XP Home Edition, Windows XP Professional, Windows Server 2003 family

PropertyGrid.CommandsVisible Property

Gets a value indicating whether the commands pane is visible.

```
[Visual Basic]
Public Overridable ReadOnly Property CommandsVisible As Boolean
[C#]
public virtual bool CommandsVisible {get;}
[C++]
public: __property virtual bool get_CommandsVisible();
[JScript]
public function get CommandsVisible() : Boolean;
```

Property Value

true if the commands pane is visible; otherwise, **false**. The default is **false**.

Remarks

This property is true if the selected object has commands available and the **CommandsVisibleIfAvailable** property is **true**.

Requirements

Platforms: Windows 98, Windows NT 4.0, Windows Millennium Edition, Windows 2000, Windows XP Home Edition, Windows XP Professional, Windows Server 2003 family

PropertyGrid.CommandsVisibleIfAvailable Property

Gets or sets a value indicating whether the commands pane is visible for objects that expose verbs.

```
[Visual Basic]
Public Overridable Property CommandsVisibleIfAvailable As Boolean
[C#]
public virtual bool CommandsVisibleIfAvailable {get; set;}
[C++]
public: __property virtual bool get_CommandsVisibleIfAvailable();
public: __property virtual void set_CommandsVisibleIfAvailable(bool);
[JScript]
public function get CommandsVisibleIfAvailable() : Boolean;
public function set CommandsVisibleIfAvailable(Boolean);
```

Property Value

true if the commands pane is visible; otherwise, **false**. The default is **false**.

Requirements

Platforms: Windows 98, Windows NT 4.0, Windows Millennium Edition, Windows 2000, Windows XP Home Edition, Windows XP Professional, Windows Server 2003 family

PropertyGrid.ContextMenuDefaultLocation Property

Gets the default location for the shortcut menu.

```
[Visual Basic]
Public ReadOnly Property ContextMenuDefaultLocation As Point
[C#]
public Point ContextMenuDefaultLocation {get;}
[C++]
public: __property Point get_ContextMenuDefaultLocation();
[JScript]
public function get ContextMenuDefaultLocation() : Point;
```

Property Value

The default location for the shortcut menu if the command is invoked. Typically, this is centered over the selected property.

Remarks

The shortcut menu location is the center of the active property label in the grid. You can use this information to position the shortcut menu when the menu is invoked using the keyboard.

Requirements

Platforms: Windows 98, Windows NT 4.0, Windows Millennium Edition, Windows 2000, Windows XP Home Edition, Windows XP Professional, Windows Server 2003 family

PropertyGrid.Controls Property

This member supports the .NET Framework infrastructure and is not intended to be used directly from your code.

```
[Visual Basic]
Public Shadows ReadOnly Property Controls As _
   Control.ControlCollection
[C#]
public new Control.ControlCollection Controls {get;}
[C++]
public: __property Control.ControlCollection* get_Controls();
[JScript]
public hide function get Controls() : Control.ControlCollection;
```

PropertyGrid.DefaultSize Property

This member overrides **Control.DefaultSize**.

[Visual Basic]
```
Overrides Protected ReadOnly Property DefaultSize As Size
```
[C#]
```
protected override Size DefaultSize {get;}
```
[C++]
```
protected: __property Size get_DefaultSize();
```
[JScript]
```
protected override function get DefaultSize() : Size;
```

Requirements

Platforms: Windows 98, Windows NT 4.0, Windows Millennium Edition, Windows 2000, Windows XP Home Edition, Windows XP Professional, Windows Server 2003 family

PropertyGrid.DefaultTabType Property

Gets the type of the default tab.

[Visual Basic]
```
Protected Overridable ReadOnly Property DefaultTabType As Type
```
[C#]
```
protected virtual Type DefaultTabType {get;}
```
[C++]
```
protected: __property virtual Type* get_DefaultTabType();
```
[JScript]
```
protected function get DefaultTabType() : Type;
```

Property Value

A **Type** representing the default tab.

Remarks

The default implementation of this property returns **PropertyTab**. Override this property to specify a modified version of the **PropertyTab**.

Requirements

Platforms: Windows 98, Windows NT 4.0, Windows Millennium Edition, Windows 2000, Windows XP Home Edition, Windows XP Professional, Windows Server 2003 family

PropertyGrid.DrawFlatToolbar Property

This member supports the .NET Framework infrastructure and is not intended to be used directly from your code.

[Visual Basic]
```
Protected Property DrawFlatToolbar As Boolean
```
[C#]
```
protected bool DrawFlatToolbar {get; set;}
```
[C++]
```
protected: __property bool get_DrawFlatToolbar();
protected: __property void set_DrawFlatToolbar(bool);
```
[JScript]
```
protected function get DrawFlatToolbar() : Boolean;
protected function set DrawFlatToolbar(Boolean);
```

PropertyGrid.ForeColor Property

This member overrides **Control.ForeColor**.

[Visual Basic]
```
Overrides Public Property ForeColor As Color
```
[C#]
```
public override Color ForeColor {get; set;}
```
[C++]
```
public: __property Color get_ForeColor();
public: __property void set_ForeColor(Color);
```
[JScript]
```
public override function get ForeColor() : Color;
public override function set ForeColor(Color);
```

Requirements

Platforms: Windows 98, Windows NT 4.0, Windows Millennium Edition, Windows 2000, Windows XP Home Edition, Windows XP Professional, Windows Server 2003 family

PropertyGrid.HelpBackColor Property

Gets or sets the background color for the Help region.

[Visual Basic]
```
Public Property HelpBackColor As Color
```
[C#]
```
public Color HelpBackColor {get; set;}
```
[C++]
```
public: __property Color get_HelpBackColor();
public: __property void set_HelpBackColor(Color);
```
[JScript]
```
public function get HelpBackColor() : Color;
public function set HelpBackColor(Color);
```

Property Value

One of the **Color** values. The default is the default system color for controls.

Requirements

Platforms: Windows 98, Windows NT 4.0, Windows Millennium Edition, Windows 2000, Windows XP Home Edition, Windows XP Professional, Windows Server 2003 family

PropertyGrid.HelpForeColor Property

Gets or sets the foreground color for the Help region.

[Visual Basic]
```
Public Property HelpForeColor As Color
```
[C#]
```
public Color HelpForeColor {get; set;}
```
[C++]
```
public: __property Color get_HelpForeColor();
public: __property void set_HelpForeColor(Color);
```
[JScript]
```
public function get HelpForeColor() : Color;
public function set HelpForeColor(Color);
```

Property Value

One of the **Color** values. The default is the default system color for control text.

Requirements

Platforms: Windows 98, Windows NT 4.0,
Windows Millennium Edition, Windows 2000,
Windows XP Home Edition, Windows XP Professional,
Windows Server 2003 family

PropertyGrid.HelpVisible Property

Gets or sets a value indicating whether the Help text is visible.

```
[Visual Basic]
Public Overridable Property HelpVisible As Boolean
[C#]
public virtual bool HelpVisible {get; set;}
[C++]
public: __property virtual bool get_HelpVisible();
public: __property virtual void set_HelpVisible(bool);
[JScript]
public function get HelpVisible() : Boolean;
public function set HelpVisible(Boolean);
```

Property Value

true if the help text is visible; otherwise, **false**. The default is **true**.

Remarks

This method allows the display of any available help text associated with the selected property in the grid.

Requirements

Platforms: Windows 98, Windows NT 4.0,
Windows Millennium Edition, Windows 2000,
Windows XP Home Edition, Windows XP Professional,
Windows Server 2003 family

PropertyGrid.LargeButtons Property

Gets or sets a value indicating whether buttons appear in standard size or in large size.

```
[Visual Basic]
Public Property LargeButtons As Boolean
[C#]
public bool LargeButtons {get; set;}
[C++]
public: __property bool get_LargeButtons();
public: __property void set_LargeButtons(bool);
[JScript]
public function get LargeButtons() : Boolean;
public function set LargeButtons(Boolean);
```

Property Value

true if buttons on the control appear large; otherwise, **false**. The default is **false**.

Remarks

You can use this property to enhance accessibility. Large buttons are 32 by 32 pixels rather than the standard 16 by 16 pixels.

Requirements

Platforms: Windows 98, Windows NT 4.0,
Windows Millennium Edition, Windows 2000,
Windows XP Home Edition, Windows XP Professional,
Windows Server 2003 family

PropertyGrid.LineColor Property

Gets or sets the color of the gridlines and borders.

```
[Visual Basic]
Public Property LineColor As Color
[C#]
public Color LineColor {get; set;}
[C++]
public: __property Color get_LineColor();
public: __property void set_LineColor(Color);
[JScript]
public function get LineColor() : Color;
public function set LineColor(Color);
```

Property Value

One of the **Color** values. The default is the default system color for scroll bars.

Requirements

Platforms: Windows 98, Windows NT 4.0,
Windows Millennium Edition, Windows 2000,
Windows XP Home Edition, Windows XP Professional,
Windows Server 2003 family

PropertyGrid.PropertySort Property

Gets or sets the type of sorting the **PropertyGrid** uses to display properties.

```
[Visual Basic]
Public Property PropertySort As PropertySort
[C#]
public PropertySort PropertySort {get; set;}
[C++]
public: __property PropertySort get_PropertySort();
public: __property void set_PropertySort(PropertySort);
[JScript]
public function get PropertySort() : PropertySort;
public function set PropertySort(PropertySort);
```

Property Value

One of the **PropertySort** values. The default is **PropertySort.Categorized** or **PropertySort.Alphabetical**.

Remarks

When you set the **PropertySort** property, the appearance of the property sort buttons on the grid changes to reflect the current state of the property. Setting **PropertySort** to **PropertySort.NoSort** causes the properties to be displayed in the order they were retrieved.

Requirements

Platforms: Windows 98, Windows NT 4.0,
Windows Millennium Edition, Windows 2000,
Windows XP Home Edition, Windows XP Professional,
Windows Server 2003 family

PropertyGrid.PropertyTabs Property

Gets the collection of property tabs that are displayed in the grid.

```
[Visual Basic]
Public ReadOnly Property PropertyTabs As _
   PropertyGrid.PropertyTabCollection
[C#]
public PropertyGrid.PropertyTabCollection PropertyTabs {get;}
```

```
[C++]
public: __property PropertyGrid.PropertyTabCollection*
   get_PropertyTabs();
[JScript]
public function get PropertyTabs() :
   PropertyGrid.PropertyTabCollection;
```

Property Value

A **PropertyGrid.PropertyTabCollection** containing the collection of **PropertyTab** objects being displayed by the **PropertyGrid**.

Remarks

All property tabs derive from the **PropertyTab** class.

Requirements

Platforms: Windows 98, Windows NT 4.0, Windows Millennium Edition, Windows 2000, Windows XP Home Edition, Windows XP Professional, Windows Server 2003 family

PropertyGrid.SelectedGridItem Property

Gets or sets the selected grid item.

```
[Visual Basic]
Public Property SelectedGridItem As GridItem
[C#]
public GridItem SelectedGridItem {get; set;}
[C++]
public: __property GridItem* get_SelectedGridItem();
public: __property void set_SelectedGridItem(GridItem*);
[JScript]
public function get SelectedGridItem() : GridItem;
public function set SelectedGridItem(GridItem);
```

Property Value

The currently selected row in the property grid.

Remarks

Each **GridItem** corresponds to a property of the **SelectedObject**.

You can use the returned **GridItem** object to view type information, the **PropertyDescriptor**, the parent, and the children of the selected object.

Requirements

Platforms: Windows 98, Windows NT 4.0, Windows Millennium Edition, Windows 2000, Windows XP Home Edition, Windows XP Professional, Windows Server 2003 family

PropertyGrid.SelectedObject Property

Gets or sets the object for which the grid displays properties.

```
[Visual Basic]
Public Property SelectedObject As Object
[C#]
public object SelectedObject {get; set;}
[C++]
public: __property Object* get_SelectedObject();
public: __property void set_SelectedObject(Object*);
[JScript]
public function get SelectedObject() : Object;
public function set SelectedObject(Object);
```

Property Value

The first object in the object list. If there is no currently selected object the return is a null reference (**Nothing** in Visual Basic).

Remarks

The **SelectedObject** property sets a single object into the grid to be browsed. If multiple objects are being browsed, this property returns the first one in the list. If no objects are selected, a null reference (**Nothing** in Visual Basic) is returned.

Requirements

Platforms: Windows 98, Windows NT 4.0, Windows Millennium Edition, Windows 2000, Windows XP Home Edition, Windows XP Professional, Windows Server 2003 family

PropertyGrid.SelectedObjects Property

Gets or sets the currently selected objects.

```
[Visual Basic]
Public Property SelectedObjects As Object ()
[C#]
public object[] SelectedObjects {get; set;}
[C++]
public: __property Object* get_SelectedObjects();
public: __property void set_SelectedObjects(Object* __gc[]);
[JScript]
public function get SelectedObjects() : Object[];
public function set SelectedObjects(Object[]);
```

Property Value

An array of type **Object**. The default is an empty array.

Exceptions

Exception Type	Condition
ArgumentException	One of the items in the array of objects had a null reference (**Nothing** in Visual Basic) value.

Remarks

The **PropertyGrid** only displays the properties that are common to all the objects that are in the array. Assigning an array to the **SelectedObjects** replaces the reference to any **SelectedObject** you might might make.

Requirements

Platforms: Windows 98, Windows NT 4.0, Windows Millennium Edition, Windows 2000, Windows XP Home Edition, Windows XP Professional, Windows Server 2003 family

PropertyGrid.SelectedTab Property

Gets the currently selected property tab.

```
[Visual Basic]
Public ReadOnly Property SelectedTab As PropertyTab
[C#]
public PropertyTab SelectedTab {get;}
[C++]
public: __property PropertyTab* get_SelectedTab();
[JScript]
public function get SelectedTab() : PropertyTab;
```

Property Value

The **PropertyTab** that is providing the selected view.

Remarks

All property tabs derive from the **PropertyTab** class.

Requirements

Platforms: Windows 98, Windows NT 4.0, Windows Millennium Edition, Windows 2000, Windows XP Home Edition, Windows XP Professional, Windows Server 2003 family

PropertyGrid.ShowFocusCues Property

This member overrides **Control.ShowFocusCues**.

```
[Visual Basic]
Overrides Protected ReadOnly Property ShowFocusCues As Boolean
[C#]
protected override bool ShowFocusCues {get;}
[C++]
protected: __property bool get_ShowFocusCues();
[JScript]
protected override function get ShowFocusCues() : Boolean;
```

Requirements

Platforms: Windows 98, Windows NT 4.0, Windows Millennium Edition, Windows 2000, Windows XP Home Edition, Windows XP Professional, Windows Server 2003 family

PropertyGrid.Site Property

This member overrides **Control.Site**.

```
[Visual Basic]
Overrides Public Property Site As ISite  Implements IComponent.Site
[C#]
public override ISite Site {get; set;}
[C++]
public: __property ISite* get_Site();
public: __property void set_Site(ISite*);
[JScript]
public override function get Site() : ISite;
public override function set Site(ISite);
```

Requirements

Platforms: Windows 98, Windows NT 4.0, Windows Millennium Edition, Windows 2000, Windows XP Home Edition, Windows XP Professional, Windows Server 2003 family

PropertyGrid.ToolbarVisible Property

Gets or sets a value indicating whether the toolbar is visible.

```
[Visual Basic]
Public Overridable Property ToolbarVisible As Boolean
[C#]
public virtual bool ToolbarVisible {get; set;}
[C++]
public: __property virtual bool get_ToolbarVisible();
public: __property virtual void set_ToolbarVisible(bool);
[JScript]
public function get ToolbarVisible() : Boolean;
public function set ToolbarVisible(Boolean);
```

Property Value

true if the toolbar is visible; otherwise, **false**. The default is **true**.

Requirements

Platforms: Windows 98, Windows NT 4.0, Windows Millennium Edition, Windows 2000, Windows XP Home Edition, Windows XP Professional, Windows Server 2003 family

PropertyGrid.ViewBackColor Property

Gets or sets a value indicating the background color in the grid.

```
[Visual Basic]
Public Property ViewBackColor As Color
[C#]
public Color ViewBackColor {get; set;}
[C++]
public: __property Color get_ViewBackColor();
public: __property void set_ViewBackColor(Color);
[JScript]
public function get ViewBackColor() : Color;
public function set ViewBackColor(Color);
```

Property Value

One of the **Color** values. The default is the default system color for windows.

Requirements

Platforms: Windows 98, Windows NT 4.0, Windows Millennium Edition, Windows 2000, Windows XP Home Edition, Windows XP Professional, Windows Server 2003 family

PropertyGrid.ViewForeColor Property

Gets or sets a value indicating the color of the text in the grid.

```
[Visual Basic]
Public Property ViewForeColor As Color
[C#]
public Color ViewForeColor {get; set;}
[C++]
public: __property Color get_ViewForeColor();
public: __property void set_ViewForeColor(Color);
[JScript]
public function get ViewForeColor() : Color;
public function set ViewForeColor(Color);
```

Property Value

One of the **Color** values. The default is current system color for text in windows.

Requirements

Platforms: Windows 98, Windows NT 4.0, Windows Millennium Edition, Windows 2000, Windows XP Home Edition, Windows XP Professional, Windows Server 2003 family

PropertyGrid.CollapseAllGridItems Method

Collapses all the categories in the **PropertyGrid**.

```
[Visual Basic]
Public Sub CollapseAllGridItems()
[C#]
public void CollapseAllGridItems();
[C++]
public: void CollapseAllGridItems();
[JScript]
public function CollapseAllGridItems();
```

Remarks

The method collapses the categories in the grid. Those categories that have grid items in the category have a plus sign (+) displayed next to that category.

Requirements

Platforms: Windows 98, Windows NT 4.0, Windows Millennium Edition, Windows 2000, Windows XP Home Edition, Windows XP Professional, Windows Server 2003 family

PropertyGrid.CreatePropertyTab Method

When overridden in a derived class, allows for the creation of a **PropertyTab**.

```
[Visual Basic]
Protected Overridable Function CreatePropertyTab( _
   ByVal tabType As Type _
) As PropertyTab
[C#]
protected virtual PropertyTab CreatePropertyTab(
   Type tabType
);
[C++]
protected: virtual PropertyTab* CreatePropertyTab(
   Type* tabType
);
[JScript]
protected function CreatePropertyTab(
   tabType : Type
) : PropertyTab;
```

Parameters

tabType

The type of tab to create.

Return Value

The newly created property tab. Returns a null reference (**Nothing** in Visual Basic) in its default implementation.

Remarks

See **PropertyTab** for more information on creating property tabs.

Requirements

Platforms: Windows 98, Windows NT 4.0, Windows Millennium Edition, Windows 2000, Windows XP Home Edition, Windows XP Professional, Windows Server 2003 family

PropertyGrid.Dispose Method

Overload List

This member supports the .NET Framework infrastructure and is not intended to be used directly from your code.

[Visual Basic] **Overloads Overrides Protected Sub Dispose(Boolean)**

[C#] **protected override void Dispose(bool);**

[C++] **protected: void Dispose(bool);**

[JScript] **protected override function Dispose(Boolean);**

Inherited from **Component**.

[Visual Basic] **Overloads Public Overridable Sub Dispose() Implements IDisposable.Dispose**

[C#] **public virtual void Dispose();**

[C++] **public: virtual void Dispose();**

[JScript] **public function Dispose();**

PropertyGrid.Dispose Method (Boolean)

This member overrides **Control.Dispose**.

```
[Visual Basic]
Overrides Overloads Protected Sub Dispose( _
   ByVal disposing As Boolean _
)
[C#]
protected override void Dispose(
   bool disposing
);
[C++]
protected: void Dispose(
   bool disposing
);
[JScript]
protected override function Dispose(
   disposing : Boolean
);
```

Requirements

Platforms: Windows 98, Windows NT 4.0, Windows Millennium Edition, Windows 2000, Windows XP Home Edition, Windows XP Professional, Windows Server 2003 family

PropertyGrid.ExpandAllGridItems Method

Expands all the categories in the **PropertyGrid**.

```
[Visual Basic]
Public Sub ExpandAllGridItems()
[C#]
public void ExpandAllGridItems();
[C++]
public: void ExpandAllGridItems();
[JScript]
public function ExpandAllGridItems();
```

Requirements

Platforms: Windows 98, Windows NT 4.0, Windows Millennium Edition, Windows 2000, Windows XP Home Edition, Windows XP Professional, Windows Server 2003 family

PropertyGrid.IComPropertyBrowser.DropDownDone Method

This member supports the .NET Framework infrastructure and is not intended to be used directly from your code.

[Visual Basic]
```
Private Sub DropDownDone() Implements _
   IComPropertyBrowser.DropDownDone
```
[C#]
```
void IComPropertyBrowser.DropDownDone();
```
[C++]
```
private: void IComPropertyBrowser::DropDownDone();
```
[JScript]
```
private function IComPropertyBrowser.DropDownDone();
```

PropertyGrid.IComPropertyBrowser.EnsurePendingChangesCommitted Method

This member supports the .NET Framework infrastructure and is not intended to be used directly from your code.

[Visual Basic]
```
Private Function EnsurePendingChangesCommitted() As Boolean _
   Implements IComPropertyBrowser.EnsurePendingChangesCommitted
```
[C#]
```
bool IComPropertyBrowser.EnsurePendingChangesCommitted();
```
[C++]
```
private: bool IComPropertyBrowser::EnsurePendingChangesCommitted();
```
[JScript]
```
private function
   IComPropertyBrowser.EnsurePendingChangesCommitted()
   : Boolean;
```

PropertyGrid.IComPropertyBrowser.HandleF4 Method

This member supports the .NET Framework infrastructure and is not intended to be used directly from your code.

[Visual Basic]
```
Private Sub HandleF4() Implements IComPropertyBrowser.HandleF4
```
[C#]
```
void IComPropertyBrowser.HandleF4();
```
[C++]
```
private: void IComPropertyBrowser::HandleF4();
```
[JScript]
```
private function IComPropertyBrowser.HandleF4();
```

PropertyGrid.IComPropertyBrowser.LoadState Method

This member supports the .NET Framework infrastructure and is not intended to be used directly from your code.

[Visual Basic]
```
Private Sub LoadState( _
   ByVal optRoot As RegistryKey _
) Implements IComPropertyBrowser.LoadState
```
[C#]
```
void IComPropertyBrowser.LoadState(
   RegistryKey optRoot
);
```
[C++]
```
private: void IComPropertyBrowser::LoadState(
   RegistryKey* optRoot
);
```
[JScript]
```
private function IComPropertyBrowser.LoadState(
   optRoot : RegistryKey
);
```

PropertyGrid.IComPropertyBrowser.SaveState Method

This member supports the .NET Framework infrastructure and is not intended to be used directly from your code.

[Visual Basic]
```
Private Sub SaveState( _
   ByVal optRoot As RegistryKey _
) Implements IComPropertyBrowser.SaveState
```
[C#]
```
void IComPropertyBrowser.SaveState(
   RegistryKey optRoot
);
```
[C++]
```
private: void IComPropertyBrowser::SaveState(
   RegistryKey* optRoot
);
```
[JScript]
```
private function IComPropertyBrowser.SaveState(
   optRoot : RegistryKey
);
```

PropertyGrid.OnComComponentNameChanged Method

This member supports the .NET Framework infrastructure and is not intended to be used directly from your code.

[Visual Basic]
```
Protected Sub OnComComponentNameChanged( _
   ByVal e As ComponentRenameEventArgs _
)
```
[C#]
```
protected void OnComComponentNameChanged(
   ComponentRenameEventArgs e
);
```
[C++]
```
protected: void OnComComponentNameChanged(
   ComponentRenameEventArgs* e
);
```
[JScript]
```
protected function OnComComponentNameChanged(
   e : ComponentRenameEventArgs
);
```

PropertyGrid.OnFontChanged Method

This member overrides **Control.OnFontChanged**.

[Visual Basic]
```
Overrides Protected Sub OnFontChanged( _
   ByVal e As EventArgs _
)
```

```
[C#]
protected override void OnFontChanged(
   EventArgs e
);
[C++]
protected: void OnFontChanged(
   EventArgs* e
);
[JScript]
protected override function OnFontChanged(
   e : EventArgs
);
```

Requirements

Platforms: Windows 98, Windows NT 4.0, Windows Millennium Edition, Windows 2000, Windows XP Home Edition, Windows XP Professional, Windows Server 2003 family

PropertyGrid.OnGotFocus Method

This member overrides **Control.OnGotFocus**.

```
[Visual Basic]
Overrides Protected Sub OnGotFocus( _
   ByVal e As EventArgs _
)
[C#]
protected override void OnGotFocus(
   EventArgs e
);
[C++]
protected: void OnGotFocus(
   EventArgs* e
);
[JScript]
protected override function OnGotFocus(
   e : EventArgs
);
```

Requirements

Platforms: Windows 98, Windows NT 4.0, Windows Millennium Edition, Windows 2000, Windows XP Home Edition, Windows XP Professional, Windows Server 2003 family

PropertyGrid.OnHandleCreated Method

This member overrides **Control.OnHandleCreated**.

```
[Visual Basic]
Overrides Protected Sub OnHandleCreated( _
   ByVal e As EventArgs _
)
[C#]
protected override void OnHandleCreated(
   EventArgs e
);
[C++]
protected: void OnHandleCreated(
   EventArgs* e
);
[JScript]
protected override function OnHandleCreated(
   e : EventArgs
);
```

Requirements

Platforms: Windows 98, Windows NT 4.0, Windows Millennium Edition, Windows 2000, Windows XP Home Edition, Windows XP Professional, Windows Server 2003 family

PropertyGrid.OnHandleDestroyed Method

This member overrides **Control.OnHandleDestroyed**.

```
[Visual Basic]
Overrides Protected Sub OnHandleDestroyed( _
   ByVal e As EventArgs _
)
[C#]
protected override void OnHandleDestroyed(
   EventArgs e
);
[C++]
protected: void OnHandleDestroyed(
   EventArgs* e
);
[JScript]
protected override function OnHandleDestroyed(
   e : EventArgs
);
```

Requirements

Platforms: Windows 98, Windows NT 4.0, Windows Millennium Edition, Windows 2000, Windows XP Home Edition, Windows XP Professional, Windows Server 2003 family

PropertyGrid.OnMouseDown Method

Raises the **MouseDown** event.

```
[Visual Basic]
Overrides Protected Sub OnMouseDown( _
   ByVal me As MouseEventArgs _
)
[C#]
protected override void OnMouseDown(
   MouseEventArgs me
);
[C++]
protected: void OnMouseDown(
   MouseEventArgs* me
);
[JScript]
protected override function OnMouseDown(
   me : MouseEventArgs
);
```

Parameters

me

A **MouseEventArgs** that contains the event data.

Remarks

Raising an event invokes the event handler through a delegate. For more information, see **Raising an Event**.

The **OnMouseDown** method also allows derived classes to handle the event without attaching a delegate. This is the preferred technique for handling the event in a derived class.

Notes to Inheritors: When overriding **OnMouseDown** in a derived class, be sure to call the base class's **OnMouseDown** method so that registered delegates receive the event.

Requirements

Platforms: Windows 98, Windows NT 4.0, Windows Millennium Edition, Windows 2000, Windows XP Home Edition, Windows XP Professional, Windows Server 2003 family

PropertyGrid.OnMouseMove Method

Raises the **MouseMove** event.

```
[Visual Basic]
Overrides Protected Sub OnMouseMove( _
   ByVal me As MouseEventArgs _
)
[C#]
protected override void OnMouseMove(
   MouseEventArgs me
);
[C++]
protected: void OnMouseMove(
   MouseEventArgs* me
);
[JScript]
protected override function OnMouseMove(
   me : MouseEventArgs
);
```

Parameters

me

A **MouseEventArgs** that contains the event data.

Remarks

Raising an event invokes the event handler through a delegate. For more information, see **Raising an Event**.

The **OnMouseMove** method also allows derived classes to handle the event without attaching a delegate. This is the preferred technique for handling the event in a derived class.

Notes to Inheritors: When overriding **OnMouseMove** in a derived class, be sure to call the base class's **OnMouseMove** method so that registered delegates receive the event.

Requirements

Platforms: Windows 98, Windows NT 4.0, Windows Millennium Edition, Windows 2000, Windows XP Home Edition, Windows XP Professional, Windows Server 2003 family

PropertyGrid.OnMouseUp Method

Raises the **MouseUp** event.

```
[Visual Basic]
Overrides Protected Sub OnMouseUp( _
   ByVal me As MouseEventArgs _
)
[C#]
protected override void OnMouseUp(
   MouseEventArgs me
);
[C++]
protected: void OnMouseUp(
   MouseEventArgs* me
);
[JScript]
protected override function OnMouseUp(
   me : MouseEventArgs
);
```

Parameters

me

A **MouseEventArgs** that contains the event data.

Remarks

Raising an event invokes the event handler through a delegate. For more information, see **Raising an Event**.

The **OnMouseUp** method also allows derived classes to handle the event without attaching a delegate. This is the preferred technique for handling the event in a derived class.

Notes to Inheritors: When overriding **OnMouseUp** in a derived class, be sure to call the base class's **OnMouseUp** method so that registered delegates receive the event.

Requirements

Platforms: Windows 98, Windows NT 4.0, Windows Millennium Edition, Windows 2000, Windows XP Home Edition, Windows XP Professional, Windows Server 2003 family

PropertyGrid.OnNotifyPropertyValueUIItems-Changed Method

This member supports the .NET Framework infrastructure and is not intended to be used directly from your code.

```
[Visual Basic]
Protected Sub OnNotifyPropertyValueUIItemsChanged( _
   ByVal sender As Object, _
   ByVal e As EventArgs _
)
[C#]
protected void OnNotifyPropertyValueUIItemsChanged(
   object sender,
   EventArgs e
);
[C++]
protected: void OnNotifyPropertyValueUIItemsChanged(
   Object* sender,
   EventArgs* e
);
[JScript]
protected function OnNotifyPropertyValueUIItemsChanged(
   sender : Object,
   e : EventArgs
);
```

PropertyGrid.OnPaint Method

This member overrides **Control.OnPaint**.

```
[Visual Basic]
Overrides Protected Sub OnPaint( _
   ByVal pevent As PaintEventArgs _
)
[C#]
protected override void OnPaint(
   PaintEventArgs pevent
);
[C++]
protected: void OnPaint(
   PaintEventArgs* pevent
);
[JScript]
protected override function OnPaint(
   pevent : PaintEventArgs
);
```

Requirements

Platforms: Windows 98, Windows NT 4.0, Windows Millennium Edition, Windows 2000, Windows XP Home Edition, Windows XP Professional, Windows Server 2003 family

PropertyGrid.OnPropertyTabChanged Method

Raises the **PropertyTabChanged** event.

```
[Visual Basic]
Protected Overridable Sub OnPropertyTabChanged( _
   ByVal e As PropertyTabChangedEventArgs _
)
[C#]
protected virtual void OnPropertyTabChanged(
   PropertyTabChangedEventArgs e
);
[C++]
protected: virtual void OnPropertyTabChanged(
   PropertyTabChangedEventArgs* e
);
[JScript]
protected function OnPropertyTabChanged(
   e : PropertyTabChangedEventArgs
);
```

Parameters

e

A **PropertyTabChangedEventArgs** that contains the event data.

Remarks

Raising an event invokes the event handler through a delegate. For more information, see **Raising an Event**.

The **OnPropertyTabChanged** method also allows derived classes to handle the event without attaching a delegate. This is the preferred technique for handling the event in a derived class.

Notes to Inheritors: When overriding **OnPropertyTabChanged** in a derived class, be sure to call the base class's **OnPropertyTabChanged** method so that registered delegates receive the event.

Requirements

Platforms: Windows 98, Windows NT 4.0, Windows Millennium Edition, Windows 2000, Windows XP Home Edition, Windows XP Professional, Windows Server 2003 family

PropertyGrid.OnPropertyValueChanged Method

Raises the **PropertyValueChanged** event.

```
[Visual Basic]
Protected Overridable Sub OnPropertyValueChanged( _
   ByVal e As PropertyValueChangedEventArgs _
)
[C#]
protected virtual void OnPropertyValueChanged(
   PropertyValueChangedEventArgs e
);
[C++]
protected: virtual void OnPropertyValueChanged(
   PropertyValueChangedEventArgs* e
);
[JScript]
protected function OnPropertyValueChanged(
   e : PropertyValueChangedEventArgs
);
```

Parameters

e

A **PropertyValueChangedEventArgs** that contains the event data.

Remarks

Raising an event invokes the event handler through a delegate. For more information, see **Raising an Event**.

The **OnPropertyValueChanged** method also allows derived classes to handle the event without attaching a delegate. This is the preferred technique for handling the event in a derived class.

Notes to Inheritors: When overriding **OnPropertyValueChanged** in a derived class, be sure to call the base class's **OnPropertyValueChanged** method so that registered delegates receive the event.

Requirements

Platforms: Windows 98, Windows NT 4.0, Windows Millennium Edition, Windows 2000, Windows XP Home Edition, Windows XP Professional, Windows Server 2003 family

PropertyGrid.OnResize Method

This member overrides **Control.OnResize**.

```
[Visual Basic]
Overrides Protected Sub OnResize( _
   ByVal e As EventArgs _
)
[C#]
protected override void OnResize(
   EventArgs e
);
```

```
[C++]
protected: void OnResize(
   EventArgs* e
);
[JScript]
protected override function OnResize(
   e : EventArgs
);
```

Requirements

Platforms: Windows 98, Windows NT 4.0, Windows Millennium Edition, Windows 2000, Windows XP Home Edition, Windows XP Professional, Windows Server 2003 family

PropertyGrid.OnSelectedGridItemChanged Method

Raises the **SelectedGridItemChanged** event.

```
[Visual Basic]
Protected Overridable Sub OnSelectedGridItemChanged( _
   ByVal e As SelectedGridItemChangedEventArgs _
)
[C#]
protected virtual void OnSelectedGridItemChanged(
   SelectedGridItemChangedEventArgs e
);
[C++]
protected: virtual void OnSelectedGridItemChanged(
   SelectedGridItemChangedEventArgs* e
);
[JScript]
protected function OnSelectedGridItemChanged(
   e : SelectedGridItemChangedEventArgs
);
```

Parameters

e

A **SelectedGridItemChangedEventArgs** that contains the event data.

Remarks

Raising an event invokes the event handler through a delegate. For more information, see **Raising an Event**.

The **OnSelectedGridItemChanged** method also allows derived classes to handle the event without attaching a delegate. This is the preferred technique for handling the event in a derived class.

Notes to Inheritors: When overriding **OnSelectedGridItem-Changed** in a derived class, be sure to call the base class's **OnSelectedGridItemChanged** method so that registered delegates receive the event.

Requirements

Platforms: Windows 98, Windows NT 4.0, Windows Millennium Edition, Windows 2000, Windows XP Home Edition, Windows XP Professional, Windows Server 2003 family

PropertyGrid.OnSelectedObjectsChanged Method

Raises the **SelectedObjectsChanged** event.

```
[Visual Basic]
Protected Overridable Sub OnSelectedObjectsChanged( _
   ByVal e As EventArgs _
)
[C#]
protected virtual void OnSelectedObjectsChanged(
   EventArgs e
);
[C++]
protected: virtual void OnSelectedObjectsChanged(
   EventArgs* e
);
[JScript]
protected function OnSelectedObjectsChanged(
   e : EventArgs
);
```

Parameters

e

An **EventArgs** that contains the event data.

Remarks

Raising an event invokes the event handler through a delegate. For more information, see **Raising an Event**.

The **OnSelectedObjectsChanged** method also allows derived classes to handle the event without attaching a delegate. This is the preferred technique for handling the event in a derived class.

Notes to Inheritors: When overriding **OnSelectedObjects-Changed** in a derived class, be sure to call the base class's **OnSelectedObjectsChanged** method so that registered delegates receive the event.

Requirements

Platforms: Windows 98, Windows NT 4.0, Windows Millennium Edition, Windows 2000, Windows XP Home Edition, Windows XP Professional, Windows Server 2003 family

PropertyGrid.OnSystemColorsChanged Method

This member overrides **Control.OnSystemColorsChanged**.

```
[Visual Basic]
Overrides Protected Sub OnSystemColorsChanged( _
   ByVal e As EventArgs _
)
[C#]
protected override void OnSystemColorsChanged(
   EventArgs e
);
[C++]
protected: void OnSystemColorsChanged(
   EventArgs* e
);
[JScript]
protected override function OnSystemColorsChanged(
   e : EventArgs
);
```

Requirements

Platforms: Windows 98, Windows NT 4.0, Windows Millennium Edition, Windows 2000, Windows XP Home Edition, Windows XP Professional, Windows Server 2003 family

PropertyGrid.OnVisibleChanged Method

This member overrides **Control.OnVisibleChanged**.

```
[Visual Basic]
Overrides Protected Sub OnVisibleChanged( _
   ByVal e As EventArgs _
)
[C#]
protected override void OnVisibleChanged(
   EventArgs e
);
[C++]
protected: void OnVisibleChanged(
   EventArgs* e
);
[JScript]
protected override function OnVisibleChanged(
   e : EventArgs
);
```

Requirements

Platforms: Windows 98, Windows NT 4.0, Windows Millennium Edition, Windows 2000, Windows XP Home Edition, Windows XP Professional, Windows Server 2003 family

PropertyGrid.ProcessDialogKey Method

This member overrides **Control.ProcessDialogKey**.

```
[Visual Basic]
Overrides Protected Function ProcessDialogKey( _
   ByVal keyData As Keys _
) As Boolean
[C#]
protected override bool ProcessDialogKey(
   Keys keyData
);
[C++]
protected: bool ProcessDialogKey(
   Keys keyData
);
[JScript]
protected override function ProcessDialogKey(
   keyData : Keys
) : Boolean;
```

Requirements

Platforms: Windows 98, Windows NT 4.0, Windows Millennium Edition, Windows 2000, Windows XP Home Edition, Windows XP Professional, Windows Server 2003 family

PropertyGrid.Refresh Method

This member overrides **Control.Refresh**.

```
[Visual Basic]
Overrides Public Sub Refresh()
[C#]
public override void Refresh();
[C++]
public: void Refresh();
[JScript]
public override function Refresh();
```

Requirements

Platforms: Windows 98, Windows NT 4.0, Windows Millennium Edition, Windows 2000, Windows XP Home Edition, Windows XP Professional, Windows Server 2003 family

PropertyGrid.RefreshTabs Method

Refreshes the property tabs of the specified scope.

```
[Visual Basic]
Public Sub RefreshTabs( _
   ByVal tabScope As PropertyTabScope _
)
[C#]
public void RefreshTabs(
   PropertyTabScope tabScope
);
[C++]
public: void RefreshTabs(
   PropertyTabScope tabScope
);
[JScript]
public function RefreshTabs(
   tabScope : PropertyTabScope
);
```

Parameters

tabScope

Either **PropertyTabScope.Component** or **PropertyTabScope.Document**.

Exceptions

Exception Type	Condition
ArgumentException	The *tabScope* parameter is not **PropertyTabScope.Component** or **PropertyTabScope.Document**.

Remarks

The **RefreshTabs** method first deletes the property tabs of the specified scope, it then requires the objects and documents to rebuild the tabs.

Requirements

Platforms: Windows 98, Windows NT 4.0, Windows Millennium Edition, Windows 2000, Windows XP Home Edition, Windows XP Professional, Windows Server 2003 family

PropertyGrid.ResetSelectedProperty Method

Resets the selected property to its default value.

[Visual Basic]
```
Public Sub ResetSelectedProperty()
```
[C#]
```
public void ResetSelectedProperty();
```
[C++]
```
public: void ResetSelectedProperty();
```
[JScript]
```
public function ResetSelectedProperty();
```

Remarks

Typically, the **ResetSelectedProperty** method is invoked by right clicking on the property. This method discards changes and attempts to reset the property to its default value.

Requirements

Platforms: Windows 98, Windows NT 4.0, Windows Millennium Edition, Windows 2000, Windows XP Home Edition, Windows XP Professional, Windows Server 2003 family

PropertyGrid.ScaleCore Method

This member overrides **Control.ScaleCore**.

[Visual Basic]
```
Overrides Protected Sub ScaleCore( _
   ByVal dx As Single, _
   ByVal dy As Single _
)
```
[C#]
```
protected override void ScaleCore(
   float dx,
   float dy
);
```
[C++]
```
protected: void ScaleCore(
   float dx,
   float dy
);
```
[JScript]
```
protected override function ScaleCore(
   dx : float,
   dy : float
);
```

Requirements

Platforms: Windows 98, Windows NT 4.0, Windows Millennium Edition, Windows 2000, Windows XP Home Edition, Windows XP Professional, Windows Server 2003 family

PropertyGrid.ShowEventsButton Method

This member supports the .NET Framework infrastructure and is not intended to be used directly from your code.

[Visual Basic]
```
Protected Sub ShowEventsButton( _
   ByVal value As Boolean _
)
```
[C#]
```
protected void ShowEventsButton(
   bool value
);
```
[C++]
```
protected: void ShowEventsButton(
   bool value
);
```
[JScript]
```
protected function ShowEventsButton(
   value : Boolean
);
```

PropertyGrid.WndProc Method

This member overrides **Control.WndProc**.

[Visual Basic]
```
Overrides Protected Sub WndProc( _
   ByRef m As Message _
)
```
[C#]
```
protected override void WndProc(
   ref Message m
);
```
[C++]
```
protected: void WndProc(
   Message* m
);
```
[JScript]
```
protected override function WndProc(
   m : Message
);
```

Requirements

Platforms: Windows 98, Windows NT 4.0, Windows Millennium Edition, Windows 2000, Windows XP Home Edition, Windows XP Professional, Windows Server 2003 family

PropertyGrid.BackgroundImageChanged Event

This member supports the .NET Framework infrastructure and is not intended to be used directly from your code.

[Visual Basic]
```
Public Shadows Event BackgroundImageChanged As EventHandler
```
[C#]
```
public new event EventHandler BackgroundImageChanged;
```
[C++]
```
public: __event EventHandler* BackgroundImageChanged;
```

[JScript] In JScript, you can handle the events defined by a class, but you cannot define your own.

PropertyGrid.ForeColorChanged Event

This member supports the .NET Framework infrastructure and is not intended to be used directly from your code.

[Visual Basic]
```
Public Shadows Event ForeColorChanged As EventHandler
```
[C#]
```
public new event EventHandler ForeColorChanged;
```

[C++]
```
public: __event EventHandler* ForeColorChanged;
```

[JScript] In JScript, you can handle the events defined by a class, but you cannot define your own.

PropertyGrid.PropertySortChanged Event

Occurs when the sort mode is changed.

[Visual Basic]
```
Public Event PropertySortChanged As EventHandler
```
[C#]
```
public event EventHandler PropertySortChanged;
```
[C++]
```
public: __event EventHandler* PropertySortChanged;
```

[JScript] In JScript, you can handle the events defined by a class, but you cannot define your own.

Event Data

The event handler receives an argument of type **EventArgs**.

Remarks

For more information about handling events, see **Consuming Events**.

Requirements

Platforms: Windows 98, Windows NT 4.0, Windows Millennium Edition, Windows 2000, Windows XP Home Edition, Windows XP Professional, Windows Server 2003 family

PropertyGrid.PropertyTabChanged Event

Occurs when a property tab changes.

[Visual Basic]
```
Public Event PropertyTabChanged As PropertyTabChangedEventHandler
```
[C#]
```
public event PropertyTabChangedEventHandler PropertyTabChanged;
```
[C++]
```
public: __event PropertyTabChangedEventHandler* PropertyTabChanged;
```

[JScript] In JScript, you can handle the events defined by a class, but you cannot define your own.

Event Data

The event handler receives an argument of type **PropertyTabChangedEventArgs** containing data related to this event. The following **PropertyTabChangedEventArgs** properties provide information specific to this event.

Property	Description
NewTab	Gets the new **PropertyTab** selected.
OldTab	Gets the old **PropertyTab** selected.

Remarks

For more information about handling events, see **Consuming Events**.

Requirements

Platforms: Windows 98, Windows NT 4.0, Windows Millennium Edition, Windows 2000, Windows XP Home Edition, Windows XP Professional, Windows Server 2003 family

PropertyGrid.PropertyValueChanged Event

Occurs when a property value changes.

[Visual Basic]
```
Public Event PropertyValueChanged As _
   PropertyValueChangedEventHandler
```
[C#]
```
public event PropertyValueChangedEventHandler PropertyValueChanged;
```
[C++]
```
public: __event PropertyValueChangedEventHandler*
   PropertyValueChanged;
```

[JScript] In JScript, you can handle the events defined by a class, but you cannot define your own.

Event Data

The event handler receives an argument of type **PropertyValueChangedEventArgs** containing data related to this event. The following **PropertyValueChangedEventArgs** properties provide information specific to this event.

Property	Description
ChangedItem	Gets the **GridItem** that was changed.
OldValue	The value of the grid item before it was changed.

Remarks

For more information about handling events, see **Consuming Events**.

Requirements

Platforms: Windows 98, Windows NT 4.0, Windows Millennium Edition, Windows 2000, Windows XP Home Edition, Windows XP Professional, Windows Server 2003 family

PropertyGrid.SelectedGridItemChanged Event

Occurs when the selected **GridItem** is changed.

[Visual Basic]
```
Public Event SelectedGridItemChanged As _
   SelectedGridItemChangedEventHandler
```
[C#]
```
public event SelectedGridItemChangedEventHandler
   SelectedGridItemChanged;
```
[C++]
```
public: __event SelectedGridItemChangedEventHandler*
   SelectedGridItemChanged;
```

[JScript] In JScript, you can handle the events defined by a class, but you cannot define your own.

Event Data

The event handler receives an argument of type **SelectedGridItemChangedEventArgs** containing data related to this event. The following **SelectedGridItemChangedEventArgs** properties provide information specific to this event.

Property	Description
NewSelection	Gets the newly selected **GridItem** object.
OldSelection	Gets the previously selected **GridItem** object.

Remarks

For more information about handling events, see **Consuming Events**.

Requirements

Platforms: Windows 98, Windows NT 4.0, Windows Millennium Edition, Windows 2000, Windows XP Home Edition, Windows XP Professional, Windows Server 2003 family

PropertyGrid.SelectedObjectsChanged Event

Occurs when the objects selected by the **SelectedObjects** property have changed.

[Visual Basic]
```
Public Event SelectedObjectsChanged As EventHandler
```
[C#]
```
public event EventHandler SelectedObjectsChanged;
```
[C++]
```
public: __event EventHandler* SelectedObjectsChanged;
```

[JScript] In JScript, you can handle the events defined by a class, but you cannot define your own.

Event Data

The event handler receives an argument of type **EventArgs**.

Remarks

For more information about handling events, see **Consuming Events**.

Requirements

Platforms: Windows 98, Windows NT 4.0, Windows Millennium Edition, Windows 2000, Windows XP Home Edition, Windows XP Professional, Windows Server 2003 family

PropertyGrid.PropertyTab-Collection Class

Contains a collection of **PropertyTab** objects.

System.Object
  System.Windows.Forms.PropertyGrid.PropertyTabCollection

```
[Visual Basic]
Public Class PropertyGrid.PropertyTabCollection
   Implements ICollection, IEnumerable
[C#]
public class PropertyGrid.PropertyTabCollection : ICollection,
   IEnumerable
[C++]
public __gc class PropertyGrid.PropertyTabCollection : public
   ICollection, IEnumerable
[JScript]
public class PropertyGrid.PropertyTabCollection implements
   ICollection, IEnumerable
```

Thread Safety

Any public static (**Shared** in Visual Basic) members of this type are safe for multithreaded operations. Any instance members are not guaranteed to be thread safe.

Requirements

Namespace: System.Windows.Forms

Platforms: Windows 98, Windows NT 4.0, Windows Millennium Edition, Windows 2000, Windows XP Home Edition, Windows XP Professional, Windows Server 2003 family

Assembly: System.Windows.Forms (in System.Windows.Forms.dll)

PropertyGrid.PropertyTabCollection.Count Property

Gets the number of property tabs in the collection.

```
[Visual Basic]
Public Overridable ReadOnly Property Count As Integer  Implements _
   ICollection.Count
[C#]
public virtual int Count {get;}
[C++]
public: __property virtual int get_Count();
[JScript]
public function get Count() : int;
```

Property Value

The number of property tabs in the collection.

Implements

ICollection.Count

Requirements

Platforms: Windows 98, Windows NT 4.0, Windows Millennium Edition, Windows 2000, Windows XP Home Edition, Windows XP Professional, Windows Server 2003 family

PropertyGrid.PropertyTabCollection.Item Property

Gets the **PropertyTab** at the specified index.

[C#] In C#, this property is the indexer for the **PropertyGrid.PropertyTabCollection** class.

```
[Visual Basic]
Public Default ReadOnly Property Item( _
   ByVal index As Integer _
) As PropertyTab
[C#]
public PropertyTab this[
   int index
] {get;}
[C++]
public: __property PropertyTab* get_Item(
   int index
);
[JScript]
returnValue = PropertyTabCollectionObject.Item(index);
-or-
returnValue = PropertyTabCollectionObject(index);
```

[JScript] In JScript, you can use the default indexed properties defined by a type, but you cannot explicitly define your own. However, specifying the **expando** attribute on a class automatically provides a default indexed property whose type is **Object** and whose index type is **String**.

Arguments [JScript]

index
  The index of the **PropertyTab** to return.

Parameters [Visual Basic, C#, C++]

index
  The index of the **PropertyTab** to return.

Property Value

The **PropertyTab** at the specified index.

Requirements

Platforms: Windows 98, Windows NT 4.0, Windows Millennium Edition, Windows 2000, Windows XP Home Edition, Windows XP Professional, Windows Server 2003 family

PropertyGrid.PropertyTabCollection.AddTabType Method

Adds a property tab to the collection.

Overload List

Adds a property tab of the specified type to the collection.

  [Visual Basic] **Overloads Public Sub AddTabType(Type)**
  [C#] **public void AddTabType(Type);**
  [C++] **public: void AddTabType(Type*);**
  [JScript] **public function AddTabType(Type);**

Adds a property tab of the specified type and with the specified scope to the collection.

[Visual Basic] **Overloads Public Sub AddTabType(Type, PropertyTabScope)**

[C#] **public void AddTabType(Type, PropertyTabScope);**

[C++] **public: void AddTabType(Type*, PropertyTabScope);**

[JScript] **public function AddTabType(Type, PropertyTabScope);**

PropertyGrid.PropertyTabCollection.AddTabType Method (Type)

Adds a property tab of the specified type to the collection.

```
[Visual Basic]
Overloads Public Sub AddTabType( _
   ByVal propertyTabType As Type _
)
[C#]
public void AddTabType(
   Type propertyTabType
);
[C++]
public: void AddTabType(
   Type* propertyTabType
);
[JScript]
public function AddTabType(
   propertyTabType : Type
);
```

Parameters

propertyTabType
The property tab type to add to the grid.

Remarks

The property tab is added to the collection with a scope of **PropertyTabScope.Global**.

Requirements

Platforms: Windows 98, Windows NT 4.0, Windows Millennium Edition, Windows 2000, Windows XP Home Edition, Windows XP Professional, Windows Server 2003 family

PropertyGrid.PropertyTabCollection.AddTabType Method (Type, PropertyTabScope)

Adds a property tab of the specified type and with the specified scope to the collection.

```
[Visual Basic]
Overloads Public Sub AddTabType( _
   ByVal propertyTabType As Type, _
   ByVal tabScope As PropertyTabScope _
)
[C#]
public void AddTabType(
   Type propertyTabType,
   PropertyTabScope tabScope
);
[C++]
public: void AddTabType(
   Type* propertyTabType,
   PropertyTabScope tabScope
);
[JScript]
public function AddTabType(
   propertyTabType : Type,
   tabScope : PropertyTabScope
);
```

Parameters

propertyTabType
The property tab type to add to the grid.

tabScope
One of the **PropertyTabScope** values.

Requirements

Platforms: Windows 98, Windows NT 4.0, Windows Millennium Edition, Windows 2000, Windows XP Home Edition, Windows XP Professional, Windows Server 2003 family

PropertyGrid.PropertyTabCollection.Clear Method

Removes all the property tabs of the specified scope from the collection.

```
[Visual Basic]
Public Sub Clear( _
   ByVal tabScope As PropertyTabScope _
)
[C#]
public void Clear(
   PropertyTabScope tabScope
);
[C++]
public: void Clear(
   PropertyTabScope tabScope
);
[JScript]
public function Clear(
   tabScope : PropertyTabScope
);
```

Parameters

tabScope
The scope of the tabs to clear.

Exceptions

Exception Type	Condition
ArgumentException	The assigned value of the *tabScope* parameter is less than **Property-TabScope.Document**.

Remarks

This method clears the tabs of the specified scope or smaller. The *tabScope* parameter must be **PropertyTabScope.Component** or **PropertyTabScope.Document**.

Requirements

Platforms: Windows 98, Windows NT 4.0, Windows Millennium Edition, Windows 2000, Windows XP Home Edition, Windows XP Professional, Windows Server 2003 family

PropertyGrid.PropertyTabCollection.GetEnumerator Method

Returns an enumeration of all the property tabs in the collection.

```
[Visual Basic]
Public Overridable Function GetEnumerator() As IEnumerator _
   Implements IEnumerable.GetEnumerator
[C#]
public virtual IEnumerator GetEnumerator();
[C++]
public: virtual IEnumerator* GetEnumerator();
[JScript]
public function GetEnumerator() : IEnumerator;
```

Return Value

An **IEnumerator** for the **System.Windows.Forms.PropertyGrid.PropertyTabCollection**.

Implements

IEnumerable.GetEnumerator

Remarks

This method creates an enumerator that contains a snapshot of the collection. You can change the collection by changing the enumerator; however, multiple enumerators can simultaneously access the same collection. Changing the collection (either directly or through another enumerator) can cause **Current** or **MoveNext** to throw an exception.

Two enumerators created from the same collection at the same time can contain different snapshots. Removing objects from the enumerator also removes them from the collection.

Requirements

Platforms: Windows 98, Windows NT 4.0, Windows Millennium Edition, Windows 2000, Windows XP Home Edition, Windows XP Professional, Windows Server 2003 family

PropertyGrid.PropertyTabCollection.ICollection.CopyTo Method

This member supports the .NET Framework infrastructure and is not intended to be used directly from your code.

```
[Visual Basic]
Private Sub CopyTo( _
   ByVal dest As Array, _
   ByVal index As Integer _
) Implements ICollection.CopyTo
[C#]
void ICollection.CopyTo(
   Array dest,
   int index
);
[C++]
private: void ICollection::CopyTo(
   Array* dest,
   int index
);
[JScript]
private function ICollection.CopyTo(
   dest : Array,
   index : int
);
```

PropertyGrid.PropertyTabCollection.RemoveTabType Method

Removes the specified tab type from the collection.

```
[Visual Basic]
Public Sub RemoveTabType( _
   ByVal propertyTabType As Type _
)
[C#]
public void RemoveTabType(
   Type propertyTabType
);
[C++]
public: void RemoveTabType(
   Type* propertyTabType
);
[JScript]
public function RemoveTabType(
   propertyTabType : Type
);
```

Parameters

propertyTabType

The tab type to remove from the collection.

Remarks

Removing the tab from the collection removes it from the property grid.

Requirements

Platforms: Windows 98, Windows NT 4.0, Windows Millennium Edition, Windows 2000, Windows XP Home Edition, Windows XP Professional, Windows Server 2003 family

PropertyManager Class

Maintains a **Binding** between an object's property and a data-bound control property.

System.Object
  System.Windows.Forms.BindingManagerBase
    System.Windows.Forms.PropertyManager

[Visual Basic]
```
Public Class PropertyManager
   Inherits BindingManagerBase
```
[C#]
```
public class PropertyManager : BindingManagerBase
```
[C++]
```
public __gc class PropertyManager : public BindingManagerBase
```
[JScript]
```
public class PropertyManager extends BindingManagerBase
```

Thread Safety

Any public static (**Shared** in Visual Basic) members of this type are safe for multithreaded operations. Any instance members are not guaranteed to be thread safe.

Remarks

The **PropertyManager** inherits from the **BindingManagerBase**, and it is used to maintain the current property of an object, rather than the property of a current object in a list. For this reason, trying to set the **Position** or **Count** property for a **PropertyManager** has no effect. Similarly, the **AddNew** and **RemoveAt** methods are not supported because there is no underlying list of data to add to or delete from.

Requirements

Namespace: System.Windows.Forms

Platforms: Windows 98, Windows NT 4.0, Windows Millennium Edition, Windows 2000, Windows XP Home Edition, Windows XP Professional, Windows Server 2003 family, .NET Compact Framework - Windows CE .NET

Assembly: System.Windows.Forms (in System.Windows.Forms.dll)

PropertyManager Constructor

Initializes a new instance of the **PropertyManager** class.

[Visual Basic]
```
Public Sub New()
```
[C#]
```
public PropertyManager();
```
[C++]
```
public: PropertyManager();
```
[JScript]
```
public function PropertyManager();
```

Requirements

Platforms: Windows 98, Windows NT 4.0, Windows Millennium Edition, Windows 2000, Windows XP Home Edition, Windows XP Professional, Windows Server 2003 family

PropertyManager.Count Property

This member overrides **BindingManagerBase.Count**.

[Visual Basic]
```
Overrides Public ReadOnly Property Count As Integer
```
[C#]
```
public override int Count {get;}
```
[C++]
```
public: __property int get_Count();
```
[JScript]
```
public override function get Count() : int;
```

Requirements

Platforms: Windows 98, Windows NT 4.0, Windows Millennium Edition, Windows 2000, Windows XP Home Edition, Windows XP Professional, Windows Server 2003 family, .NET Compact Framework - Windows CE .NET

PropertyManager.Current Property

Gets the object to which the data-bound property belongs.

[Visual Basic]
```
Overrides Public ReadOnly Property Current As Object
```
[C#]
```
public override object Current {get;}
```
[C++]
```
public: __property Object* get_Current();
```
[JScript]
```
public override function get Current() : Object;
```

Property Value

An Object that represents the object to which the property belongs.

Remarks

The **Current** property returns the data source of a data-bound relationship.

Requirements

Platforms: Windows 98, Windows NT 4.0, Windows Millennium Edition, Windows 2000, Windows XP Home Edition, Windows XP Professional, Windows Server 2003 family, .NET Compact Framework - Windows CE .NET

PropertyManager.Position Property

This member overrides **BindingManagerBase.Position**.

[Visual Basic]
```
Overrides Public Property Position As Integer
```
[C#]
```
public override int Position {get; set;}
```
[C++]
```
public: __property int get_Position();
public: __property void set_Position(int);
```
[JScript]
```
public override function get Position() : int;
public override function set Position(int);
```

Requirements

Platforms: Windows 98, Windows NT 4.0, Windows Millennium Edition, Windows 2000, Windows XP Home Edition, Windows XP Professional, Windows Server 2003 family, .NET Compact Framework - Windows CE .NET

PropertyManager.AddNew Method

This member overrides **BindingManagerBase.AddNew**.

```
[Visual Basic]
Overrides Public Sub AddNew()
[C#]
public override void AddNew();
[C++]
public: void AddNew();
[JScript]
public override function AddNew();
```

Requirements

Platforms: Windows 98, Windows NT 4.0, Windows Millennium Edition, Windows 2000, Windows XP Home Edition, Windows XP Professional, Windows Server 2003 family, .NET Compact Framework - Windows CE .NET

PropertyManager.CancelCurrentEdit Method

This member overrides **BindingManagerBase.CancelCurrentEdit**.

```
[Visual Basic]
Overrides Public Sub CancelCurrentEdit()
[C#]
public override void CancelCurrentEdit();
[C++]
public: void CancelCurrentEdit();
[JScript]
public override function CancelCurrentEdit();
```

Requirements

Platforms: Windows 98, Windows NT 4.0, Windows Millennium Edition, Windows 2000, Windows XP Home Edition, Windows XP Professional, Windows Server 2003 family, .NET Compact Framework - Windows CE .NET

PropertyManager.EndCurrentEdit Method

This member overrides **BindingManagerBase.EndCurrentEdit**.

```
[Visual Basic]
Overrides Public Sub EndCurrentEdit()
[C#]
public override void EndCurrentEdit();
[C++]
public: void EndCurrentEdit();
[JScript]
public override function EndCurrentEdit();
```

Requirements

Platforms: Windows 98, Windows NT 4.0, Windows Millennium Edition, Windows 2000, Windows XP Home Edition, Windows XP Professional, Windows Server 2003 family, .NET Compact Framework - Windows CE .NET

PropertyManager.GetItemProperties Method

This member supports the .NET Framework infrastructure and is not intended to be used directly from your code.

Overload List

This member overrides **BindingManagerBase.GetItemProperties**.

Supported by the .NET Compact Framework.

[Visual Basic] **Overloads Overrides Public Function GetItemProperties() As PropertyDescriptorCollection**

[C#] **public override PropertyDescriptorCollection GetItemProperties();**

[C++] **public: PropertyDescriptorCollection* GetItemProperties();**

[JScript] **public override function GetItemProperties() : PropertyDescriptorCollection;**

Inherited from **BindingManagerBase**.

[Visual Basic] **Overloads Protected Friend Overridable Function GetItemProperties(ArrayList, ArrayList) As PropertyDescriptorCollection**

[C#] **protected internal virtual PropertyDescriptorCollection GetItemProperties(ArrayList, ArrayList);**

[C++] **protected public: virtual PropertyDescriptorCollection* GetItemProperties(ArrayList*, ArrayList*);**

[JScript] **protected internal function GetItemProperties(ArrayList, ArrayList) : PropertyDescriptorCollection;**

Inherited from **BindingManagerBase**.

Supported by the .NET Compact Framework.

[Visual Basic] **Overloads Protected Overridable Function GetItemProperties(Type, Integer, ArrayList, ArrayList) As PropertyDescriptorCollection**

[C#] **protected virtual PropertyDescriptorCollection GetItemProperties(Type, int, ArrayList, ArrayList);**

[C++] **protected: virtual PropertyDescriptorCollection* GetItemProperties(Type*, int, ArrayList*, ArrayList*);**

[JScript] **protected function GetItemProperties(Type, int, ArrayList, ArrayList) : PropertyDescriptorCollection;**

PropertyManager.GetItemProperties Method ()

This member overrides **BindingManagerBase.GetItemProperties**.

```
[Visual Basic]
Overrides Overloads Public Function GetItemProperties() As _
   PropertyDescriptorCollection
[C#]
public override PropertyDescriptorCollection GetItemProperties();
[C++]
public: PropertyDescriptorCollection* GetItemProperties();
[JScript]
public override function GetItemProperties() :
   PropertyDescriptorCollection;
```

Requirements

Platforms: Windows 98, Windows NT 4.0, Windows Millennium Edition, Windows 2000, Windows XP Home Edition, Windows XP Professional, Windows Server 2003 family, .NET Compact Framework - Windows CE .NET

PropertyManager.GetListName Method

This member overrides **BindingManagerBase.GetListName**.

```
[Visual Basic]
Protected Friend Overrides Function GetListName( _
   ByVal listAccessors As ArrayList _
) As String
[C#]
protected internal override string GetListName(
   ArrayList listAccessors
);
[C++]
protected public: String* GetListName(
   ArrayList* listAccessors
);
[JScript]
protected internal override function GetListName(
   listAccessors : ArrayList
) : String;
```

Requirements

Platforms: Windows 98, Windows NT 4.0, Windows Millennium Edition, Windows 2000, Windows XP Home Edition, Windows XP Professional, Windows Server 2003 family

PropertyManager.OnCurrentChanged Method

This member overrides **BindingManagerBase.OnCurrentChanged**.

```
[Visual Basic]
Protected Friend Overrides Sub OnCurrentChanged( _
   ByVal ea As EventArgs _
)
[C#]
protected internal override void OnCurrentChanged(
   EventArgs ea
);
[C++]
protected public: void OnCurrentChanged(
   EventArgs* ea
);
[JScript]
protected internal override function OnCurrentChanged(
   ea : EventArgs
);
```

Requirements

Platforms: Windows 98, Windows NT 4.0, Windows Millennium Edition, Windows 2000, Windows XP Home Edition, Windows XP Professional, Windows Server 2003 family

PropertyManager.RemoveAt Method

This member overrides **BindingManagerBase.RemoveAt**.

```
[Visual Basic]
Overrides Public Sub RemoveAt( _
   ByVal index As Integer _
)
[C#]
public override void RemoveAt(
   int index
);
[C++]
public: void RemoveAt(
   int index
);
[JScript]
public override function RemoveAt(
   index : int
);
```

Requirements

Platforms: Windows 98, Windows NT 4.0, Windows Millennium Edition, Windows 2000, Windows XP Home Edition, Windows XP Professional, Windows Server 2003 family, .NET Compact Framework - Windows CE .NET

PropertyManager.ResumeBinding Method

This member overrides **BindingManagerBase.ResumeBinding**.

```
[Visual Basic]
Overrides Public Sub ResumeBinding()
[C#]
public override void ResumeBinding();
[C++]
public: void ResumeBinding();
[JScript]
public override function ResumeBinding();
```

Requirements

Platforms: Windows 98, Windows NT 4.0, Windows Millennium Edition, Windows 2000, Windows XP Home Edition, Windows XP Professional, Windows Server 2003 family

PropertyManager.SuspendBinding Method

This member overrides **BindingManagerBase.SuspendBinding**.

```
[Visual Basic]
Overrides Public Sub SuspendBinding()
[C#]
public override void SuspendBinding();
[C++]
public: void SuspendBinding();
[JScript]
public override function SuspendBinding();
```

Requirements

Platforms: Windows 98, Windows NT 4.0, Windows Millennium Edition, Windows 2000, Windows XP Home Edition, Windows XP Professional, Windows Server 2003 family

PropertyManager.UpdateIsBinding Method

This member overrides **BindingManagerBase.UpdateIsBinding**.

```
[Visual Basic]
Overrides Protected Sub UpdateIsBinding()
[C#]
protected override void UpdateIsBinding();
[C++]
protected: void UpdateIsBinding();
[JScript]
protected override function UpdateIsBinding();
```

Requirements

Platforms: Windows 98, Windows NT 4.0, Windows Millennium Edition, Windows 2000, Windows XP Home Edition, Windows XP Professional, Windows Server 2003 family, .NET Compact Framework - Windows CE .NET

PropertySort Enumeration

Specifies how properties are sorted in the **PropertyGrid**.

[Visual Basic]
```
<Serializable>
<ComVisible(True)>
Public Enum PropertySort
```
[C#]
```
[Serializable]
[ComVisible(true)]
public enum PropertySort
```
[C++]
```
[Serializable]
[ComVisible(true)]
__value public enum PropertySort
```
[JScript]
```
public
   Serializable
   ComVisible(true)
enum PropertySort
```

Remarks

Use the members of this enumeration to set the value of the **PropertySort** property of the **PropertyGrid**.

Members

Member name	Description
Alphabetical	Properties are sorted in an alphabetical list.
Categorized	Properties are displayed according to their category in a group. The categories are defined by the properties themselves.
Categorized-Alphabetical	Properties are displayed according to their category in a group. The properties are further sorted alphabetically within the group. The categories are defined by the properties themselves.
NoSort	Properties are displayed in the order in which they are retrieved from the **TypeDescriptor**.

Requirements

Namespace: System.Windows.Forms

Platforms: Windows 98, Windows NT 4.0, Windows Millennium Edition, Windows 2000, Windows XP Home Edition, Windows XP Professional, Windows Server 2003 family

Assembly: System.Windows.Forms (in System.Windows.Forms.dll)

PropertyTabChangedEventArgs Class

Provides data for the **PropertyTabChanged** event of a **PropertyGrid**.

System.Object
  System.EventArgs
    System.Windows.Forms.PropertyTabChangedEventArgs

```
[Visual Basic]
<ComVisible(True)>
Public Class PropertyTabChangedEventArgs
   Inherits EventArgs
[C#]
[ComVisible(true)]
public class PropertyTabChangedEventArgs : EventArgs
[C++]
[ComVisible(true)]
public __gc class PropertyTabChangedEventArgs : public EventArgs
[JScript]
public
   ComVisible(true)
class PropertyTabChangedEventArgs extends EventArgs
```

Thread Safety

Any public static (**Shared** in Visual Basic) members of this type are safe for multithreaded operations. Any instance members are not guaranteed to be thread safe.

Remarks

The **PropertyTabChanged** event occurs when the user selects a new property tab in the **PropertyGrid**.

A **PropertyTabChangedEventArgs** provides data on the old tab and new tab being selected.

Requirements

Namespace: System.Windows.Forms

Platforms: Windows 98, Windows NT 4.0, Windows Millennium Edition, Windows 2000, Windows XP Home Edition, Windows XP Professional, Windows Server 2003 family

Assembly: System.Windows.Forms (in System.Windows.Forms.dll)

PropertyTabChangedEventArgs Constructor

Initializes a new instance of the **PropertyTabChangedEventArgs** class.

```
[Visual Basic]
Public Sub New( _
   ByVal oldTab As PropertyTab, _
   ByVal newTab As PropertyTab _
)
[C#]
public PropertyTabChangedEventArgs(
   PropertyTab oldTab,
   PropertyTab newTab
);
[C++]
public: PropertyTabChangedEventArgs(
   PropertyTab* oldTab,
   PropertyTab* newTab
);
[JScript]
public function PropertyTabChangedEventArgs(
   oldTab : PropertyTab,
   newTab : PropertyTab
);
```

Parameters

oldTab
  The Previously selected property tab.

newTab
  The newly selected property tab.

Requirements

Platforms: Windows 98, Windows NT 4.0, Windows Millennium Edition, Windows 2000, Windows XP Home Edition, Windows XP Professional, Windows Server 2003 family

PropertyTabChangedEventArgs.NewTab Property

Gets the new **PropertyTab** selected.

```
[Visual Basic]
Public ReadOnly Property NewTab As PropertyTab
[C#]
public PropertyTab NewTab {get;}
[C++]
public: __property PropertyTab* get_NewTab();
[JScript]
public function get NewTab() : PropertyTab;
```

Property Value

The newly selected **PropertyTab**.

Requirements

Platforms: Windows 98, Windows NT 4.0, Windows Millennium Edition, Windows 2000, Windows XP Home Edition, Windows XP Professional, Windows Server 2003 family

PropertyTabChangedEventArgs.OldTab Property

Gets the old **PropertyTab** selected.

```
[Visual Basic]
Public ReadOnly Property OldTab As PropertyTab
[C#]
public PropertyTab OldTab {get;}
[C++]
public: __property PropertyTab* get_OldTab();
[JScript]
public function get OldTab() : PropertyTab;
```

Property Value

The old **PropertyTab** that was selected.

Requirements

Platforms: Windows 98, Windows NT 4.0, Windows Millennium Edition, Windows 2000, Windows XP Home Edition, Windows XP Professional, Windows Server 2003 family

PropertyTabChangedEvent-Handler Delegate

Represents the method that will handle the **PropertyTabChanged** event of a **PropertyGrid**.

[Visual Basic]
```
<Serializable>
Public Delegate Sub PropertyTabChangedEventHandler( _
   ByVal s As Object, _
   ByVal e As PropertyTabChangedEventArgs _
)
```
[C#]
```
[Serializable]
public delegate void PropertyTabChangedEventHandler(
   object s,
   PropertyTabChangedEventArgs e
);
```
[C++]
```
[Serializable]
public __gc __delegate void PropertyTabChangedEventHandler(
   Object* s,
   PropertyTabChangedEventArgs* e
);
```

[JScript] In JScript, you can use the delegates in the .NET Framework, but you cannot define your own.

Parameters [Visual Basic, C#, C++]

The declaration of your event handler must have the same parameters as the **PropertyTabChangedEventHandler** delegate declaration.

s

The source of the event.

e

A **PropertyTabChangedEventArgs** that contains the event data.

Remarks

When you create a **PropertyTabChangedEventHandler** delegate, you identify the method that will handle the event. To associate the event with your event handler, add an instance of the delegate to the event. The event handler is called whenever the event occurs, unless you remove the delegate.

For more information about event handler delegates, see **Events and Delegates**.

Requirements

Namespace: System.Windows.Forms

Platforms: Windows 98, Windows NT 4.0, Windows Millennium Edition, Windows 2000, Windows XP Home Edition, Windows XP Professional, Windows Server 2003 family

Assembly: System.Windows.Forms (in System.Windows.Forms.dll)

PropertyValueChangedEvent-Args Class

Provides data for the **PropertyValueChanged** event of a **PropertyGrid**.

System.Object
  System.EventArgs
    System.Windows.Forms.PropertyValueChangedEventArgs

```
[Visual Basic]
<ComVisible(True)>
Public Class PropertyValueChangedEventArgs
   Inherits EventArgs
[C#]
[ComVisible(true)]
public class PropertyValueChangedEventArgs : EventArgs
[C++]
[ComVisible(true)]
public __gc class PropertyValueChangedEventArgs : public EventArgs
[JScript]
public
   ComVisible(true)
class PropertyValueChangedEventArgs extends EventArgs
```

Thread Safety

Any public static (**Shared** in Visual Basic) members of this type are safe for multithreaded operations. Any instance members are not guaranteed to be thread safe.

Remarks

The **PropertyValueChanged** event occurs when the user changes the value of a property, which is specified as a **GridItem**, in a **PropertyGrid**.

For more information about handling events, see **Consuming Events**.

Requirements

Namespace: System.Windows.Forms

Platforms: Windows 98, Windows NT 4.0, Windows Millennium Edition, Windows 2000, Windows XP Home Edition, Windows XP Professional, Windows Server 2003 family

Assembly: System.Windows.Forms (in System.Windows.Forms.dll)

PropertyValueChangedEventArgs Constructor

Initializes a new instance of the **PropertyValueChangedEventArgs** class.

```
[Visual Basic]
Public Sub New( _
   ByVal changedItem As GridItem, _
   ByVal oldValue As Object _
)
[C#]
public PropertyValueChangedEventArgs(
   GridItem changedItem,
   object oldValue
);
[C++]
public: PropertyValueChangedEventArgs(
   GridItem* changedItem,
   Object* oldValue
);
[JScript]
public function PropertyValueChangedEventArgs(
   changedItem : GridItem,
   oldValue : Object
);
```

Parameters

changedItem
  The item in the grid that changed.
oldValue
  The old property value.

Requirements

Platforms: Windows 98, Windows NT 4.0, Windows Millennium Edition, Windows 2000, Windows XP Home Edition, Windows XP Professional, Windows Server 2003 family

PropertyValueChangedEventArgs.ChangedItem Property

Gets the **GridItem** that was changed.

```
[Visual Basic]
Public ReadOnly Property ChangedItem As GridItem
[C#]
public GridItem ChangedItem {get;}
[C++]
public: __property GridItem* get_ChangedItem();
[JScript]
public function get ChangedItem() : GridItem;
```

Property Value

A **GridItem** in the **PropertyGrid**.

Requirements

Platforms: Windows 98, Windows NT 4.0, Windows Millennium Edition, Windows 2000, Windows XP Home Edition, Windows XP Professional, Windows Server 2003 family

PropertyValueChangedEventArgs.OldValue Property

The value of the grid item before it was changed.

```
[Visual Basic]
Public ReadOnly Property OldValue As Object
[C#]
public object OldValue {get;}
[C++]
public: __property Object* get_OldValue();
[JScript]
public function get OldValue() : Object;
```

Property Value

A object representing the old value of the property.

Remarks

This property provides you with the value of the property as it was before the change was applied. You can find the new value by querying the property grid with the specified **ChangedItem**.

Requirements

Platforms: Windows 98, Windows NT 4.0,
Windows Millennium Edition, Windows 2000,
Windows XP Home Edition, Windows XP Professional,
Windows Server 2003 family

PropertyValueChangedEvent-Handler Delegate

The event handler class that is invoked when a property in the grid is modified by the user.

[Visual Basic]
```
<Serializable>
Public Delegate Sub PropertyValueChangedEventHandler( _
   ByVal s As Object, _
   ByVal e As PropertyValueChangedEventArgs _
)
```
[C#]
```
[Serializable]
public delegate void PropertyValueChangedEventHandler(
   object s,
   PropertyValueChangedEventArgs e
);
```
[C++]
```
[Serializable]
public __gc __delegate void PropertyValueChangedEventHandler(
   Object* s,
   PropertyValueChangedEventArgs* e
);
```

[JScript] In JScript, you can use the delegates in the .NET Framework, but you cannot define your own.

Parameters [Visual Basic, C#, C++]

The declaration of your event handler must have the same parameters as the **PropertyValueChangedEventHandler** delegate declaration.

s

The source of the event.

e

A **PropertyValueChangedEventArgs** that contains the event data.

Requirements

Namespace: System.Windows.Forms

Platforms: Windows 98, Windows NT 4.0, Windows Millennium Edition, Windows 2000, Windows XP Home Edition, Windows XP Professional, Windows Server 2003 family

Assembly: System.Windows.Forms (in System.Windows.Forms.dll)

QueryAccessibilityHelpEvent-Args Class

Provides data for the **QueryAccessibilityHelp** event.

System.Object
  System.EventArgs
    System.Windows.Forms.QueryAccessibilityHelpEventArgs

[Visual Basic]
```
<ComVisible(True)>
Public Class QueryAccessibilityHelpEventArgs
   Inherits EventArgs
```
[C#]
```
[ComVisible(true)]
public class QueryAccessibilityHelpEventArgs : EventArgs
```
[C++]
```
[ComVisible(true)]
public __gc class QueryAccessibilityHelpEventArgs : public
   EventArgs
```
[JScript]
```
public
   ComVisible(true)
class QueryAccessibilityHelpEventArgs extends EventArgs
```

Thread Safety

Any public static (**Shared** in Visual Basic) members of this type are safe for multithreaded operations. Any instance members are not guaranteed to be thread safe.

Remarks

The **Control** class exposes a public **QueryAccessibilityHelp** event. You can use the properties of the **QueryAccessibilityHelpEventArgs** class to return custom help for a particular control to an accessible client, such as a screen reader. When you handle the **QueryAccessibilityHelp** event, you must set the values of the **HelpNamespace**, **HelpKeyword**, and **HelpString** properties to appropriate values.

> **Note** The **HelpKeyword** property should be a string representation of a numeric Help topic ID.

Example

[Visual Basic, C#, C++] The following example demonstrates the creation of an accessibility-aware chart control, using the **AccessibleObject** and **Control.ControlAccessibleObject** classes to expose accessible information. The control plots two curves along with a legend. The `ChartControlAccessibleObject` class, which derives from **ControlAccessibleObject**, is used in the **CreateAccessibilityInstance** method to provide custom accessible information for the chart control. Since the chart legend is not an actual **Control**-based control, but instead is drawn by the chart control, it does not any built-in accessible information. Because of this, the `ChartControlAccessibleObject` class overrides the **GetChild** method to return the `CurveLegendAccessibleObject` that represents accessible information for each part of the legend. When an accessible-aware application uses this control, the control can provide the necessary accessible information.

[Visual Basic, C#, C++] This code excerpt demonstrates using the **QueryAccessibilityHelpEventArgs** class with the **QueryAccessibilityHelp** event. See the **AccessibleObject** class overview for the complete code example.

[Visual Basic]
```
' Handle the QueryAccessibilityHelp event.
Private Sub ChartControl_QueryAccessibilityHelp(sender As Object, _
                 e As                                                  ↵
System.Windows.Forms.QueryAccessibilityHelpEventArgs) Handles          ↵
MyBase.QueryAccessibilityHelp
    e.HelpString = "Displays chart data"
End Sub
```

[C#]
```
// Handles the QueryAccessibilityHelp event.
private void ChartControl_QueryAccessibilityHelp(object sender,

System.Windows.Forms.QueryAccessibilityHelpEventArgs e)
{
    e.HelpString = "Displays chart data";
}
```

[C++]
```
// Handles the QueryAccessibilityHelp event.
private:
void ChartControl_QueryAccessibilityHelp(Object* sender,
   System::Windows::Forms::QueryAccessibilityHelpEventArgs* e) {
      e->HelpString = S"Displays chart data";
   }
```

Requirements

Namespace: System.Windows.Forms

Platforms: Windows 98, Windows NT 4.0, Windows Millennium Edition, Windows 2000, Windows XP Home Edition, Windows XP Professional, Windows Server 2003 family

Assembly: System.Windows.Forms (in System.Windows.Forms.dll)

QueryAccessibilityHelpEventArgs Constructor

Initializes a new instance of the **QueryAccessibilityHelpEventArgs** class.

Overload List

Initializes a new instance of the **QueryAccessibilityHelpEventArgs** class.

[Visual Basic] **Public Sub New()**

[C#] **public QueryAccessibilityHelpEventArgs();**

[C++] **public: QueryAccessibilityHelpEventArgs();**

[JScript] **public function QueryAccessibilityHelpEventArgs();**

Initializes a new instance of the **QueryAccessibilityHelpEventArgs** class.

[Visual Basic] **Public Sub New(String, String, String)**

[C#] **public QueryAccessibilityHelpEventArgs(string, string, string);**

[C++] **public: QueryAccessibilityHelpEventArgs(String*, String*, String*);**

[JScript] **public function QueryAccessibilityHelpEventArgs(String, String, String);**

QueryAccessibilityHelpEventArgs Constructor ()

Initializes a new instance of the **QueryAccessibilityHelpEventArgs** class.

```
[Visual Basic]
Public Sub New()
[C#]
public QueryAccessibilityHelpEventArgs();
[C++]
public: QueryAccessibilityHelpEventArgs();
[JScript]
public function QueryAccessibilityHelpEventArgs();
```

Requirements

Platforms: Windows 98, Windows NT 4.0, Windows Millennium Edition, Windows 2000, Windows XP Home Edition, Windows XP Professional, Windows Server 2003 family

QueryAccessibilityHelpEventArgs Constructor (String, String, String)

Initializes a new instance of the **QueryAccessibilityHelpEventArgs** class.

```
[Visual Basic]
Public Sub New( _
   ByVal helpNamespace As String, _
   ByVal helpString As String, _
   ByVal helpKeyword As String _
)
[C#]
public QueryAccessibilityHelpEventArgs(
   string helpNamespace,
   string helpString,
   string helpKeyword
);
[C++]
public: QueryAccessibilityHelpEventArgs(
   String* helpNamespace,
   String* helpString,
   String* helpKeyword
);
[JScript]
public function QueryAccessibilityHelpEventArgs(
   helpNamespace : String,
   helpString : String,
   helpKeyword : String
);
```

Parameters

helpNamespace
: The file containing Help for the **AccessibleObject**.

helpString
: The string defining what Help to get for the **AccessibleObject**.

helpKeyword
: The keyword to associate with the Help request for the **AccessibleObject**.

Requirements

Platforms: Windows 98, Windows NT 4.0, Windows Millennium Edition, Windows 2000, Windows XP Home Edition, Windows XP Professional, Windows Server 2003 family

QueryAccessibilityHelpEventArgs.HelpKeyword Property

Gets or sets the Help keyword for the specified control.

```
[Visual Basic]
Public Property HelpKeyword As String
[C#]
public string HelpKeyword {get; set;}
[C++]
public: __property String* get_HelpKeyword();
public: __property void set_HelpKeyword(String*);
[JScript]
public function get HelpKeyword() : String;
public function set HelpKeyword(String);
```

Property Value

The Help topic associated with the **AccessibleObject** that was queried.

Requirements

Platforms: Windows 98, Windows NT 4.0, Windows Millennium Edition, Windows 2000, Windows XP Home Edition, Windows XP Professional, Windows Server 2003 family

QueryAccessibilityHelpEventArgs.HelpNamespace Property

Gets or sets a value specifying the name of the Help file.

```
[Visual Basic]
Public Property HelpNamespace As String
[C#]
public string HelpNamespace {get; set;}
[C++]
public: __property String* get_HelpNamespace();
public: __property void set_HelpNamespace(String*);
[JScript]
public function get HelpNamespace() : String;
public function set HelpNamespace(String);
```

Property Value

The name of the Help file. This name can be in the form C:\path\sample.chm or/folder/file.htm.

Requirements

Platforms: Windows 98, Windows NT 4.0, Windows Millennium Edition, Windows 2000, Windows XP Home Edition, Windows XP Professional, Windows Server 2003 family

QueryAccessibilityHelpEventArgs.HelpString Property

Gets or sets the string defining what Help to get for the **AccessibleObject**.

```
[Visual Basic]
Public Property HelpString As String
[C#]
public string HelpString {get; set;}
```

[C++]
```
public: __property String* get_HelpString();
public: __property void set_HelpString(String*);
```
[JScript]
```
public function get HelpString() : String;
public function set HelpString(String);
```

Property Value

The Help to retrieve for the accessible object.

Example

[Visual Basic, C#, C++] The following example demonstrates the creation of an accessibility-aware chart control, using the **AccessibleObject** and **Control.ControlAccessibleObject** classes to expose accessible information. The control plots two curves along with a legend. The `ChartControlAccessibleObject` class, which derives from **ControlAccessibleObject**, is used in the **CreateAccessibilityInstance** method to provide custom accessible information for the chart control. Since the chart legend is not an actual **Control**-based control, but instead is drawn by the chart control, it does not any built-in accessible information. Because of this, the `ChartControlAccessibleObject` class overrides the **GetChild** method to return the `CurveLegendAccessibleObject` that represents accessible information for each part of the legend. When an accessible-aware application uses this control, the control can provide the necessary accessible information.

[Visual Basic, C#, C++] This code excerpt demonstrates using the **QueryAccessibilityHelpEventArgs** class with the **QueryAccessibilityHelp** event. See the **AccessibleObject** class overview for the complete code example.

[Visual Basic]
```
' Overridden to return the custom AccessibleObject
' for the entire chart.
Protected Overrides Function CreateAccessibilityInstance()          ↵
As AccessibleObject
    Return New ChartControlAccessibleObject(Me)
End Function
```

[C#]
```
// Overridden to return the custom AccessibleObject
// for the entire chart.
protected override AccessibleObject CreateAccessibilityInstance()
{
    return new ChartControlAccessibleObject(this);
}
```

[C++]
```
// Overridden to return the custom AccessibleObject
// for the entire chart.
protected:
AccessibleObject* CreateAccessibilityInstance() {
   return new ChartControlAccessibleObject(this);
}
```

Requirements

Platforms: Windows 98, Windows NT 4.0, Windows Millennium Edition, Windows 2000, Windows XP Home Edition, Windows XP Professional, Windows Server 2003 family

QueryAccessibilityHelpEvent-Handler Delegate

Represents the method that will handle the **QueryAccessibilityHelp** event of a control.

[Visual Basic]
```
<Serializable>
Public Delegate Sub QueryAccessibilityHelpEventHandler( _
   ByVal sender As Object, _
   ByVal e As QueryAccessibilityHelpEventArgs _
)
```
[C#]
```
[Serializable]
public delegate void QueryAccessibilityHelpEventHandler(
   object sender,
   QueryAccessibilityHelpEventArgs e
);
```
[C++]
```
[Serializable]
public __gc __delegate void QueryAccessibilityHelpEventHandler(
   Object* sender,
   QueryAccessibilityHelpEventArgs* e
);
```

[JScript] In JScript, you can use the delegates in the .NET Framework, but you cannot define your own.

Parameters [Visual Basic, C#, C++]

The declaration of your event handler must have the same parameters as the **QueryAccessibilityHelpEventHandler** delegate declaration.

Remarks

When you create a **QueryAccessibilityHelpEventHandler** delegate, you identify the method that will handle the event. To associate the event with your event handler, add an instance of the delegate to the event. The event handler is called whenever the event occurs, unless you remove the delegate.

Example

[Visual Basic, C#, C++] The following example demonstrates the creation of an accessibility-aware chart control, using the **AccessibleObject** and **Control.ControlAccessibleObject** classes to expose accessible information. The control plots two curves along with a legend. The `ChartControlAccessibleObject` class, which derives from **ControlAccessibleObject**, is used in the **CreateAccessibilityInstance** method to provide custom accessible information for the chart control. Since the chart legend is not an actual **Control**-based control, but instead is drawn by the chart control, it does not any built-in accessible information. Because of this, the `ChartControlAccessibleObject` class overrides the **GetChild** method to return the `CurveLegendAccessibleObject` that represents accessible information for each part of the legend. When an accessible-aware application uses this control, the control can provide the necessary accessible information.

[Visual Basic, C#, C++] This code excerpt demonstrates using the **QueryAccessibilityHelpEventHandler** delegate with the **QueryAccessibilityHelp** event. See the **AccessibleObject** class overview for the complete code example.

[Visual Basic]
```
' Overridden to return the custom AccessibleObject
' for the entire chart.
Protected Overrides Function CreateAccessibilityInstance() As ↵
AccessibleObject
    Return New ChartControlAccessibleObject(Me)
End Function
```

[C#]
```
// Overridden to return the custom AccessibleObject
// for the entire chart.
protected override AccessibleObject CreateAccessibilityInstance()
{
    return new ChartControlAccessibleObject(this);
}
```

[C++]
```
// Overridden to return the custom AccessibleObject
// for the entire chart.
protected:
AccessibleObject* CreateAccessibilityInstance() {
   return new ChartControlAccessibleObject(this);
}
```

Requirements

Namespace: System.Windows.Forms

Platforms: Windows 98, Windows NT 4.0, Windows Millennium Edition, Windows 2000, Windows XP Home Edition, Windows XP Professional, Windows Server 2003 family

Assembly: System.Windows.Forms (in System.Windows.Forms.dll)

QueryContinueDragEventArgs Class

Provides data for the **QueryContinueDrag** event.

System.Object
  System.EventArgs
    System.Windows.Forms.QueryContinueDragEventArgs

[Visual Basic]
```
<ComVisible(True)>
Public Class QueryContinueDragEventArgs
   Inherits EventArgs
```
[C#]
```
[ComVisible(true)]
public class QueryContinueDragEventArgs : EventArgs
```
[C++]
```
[ComVisible(true)]
public __gc class QueryContinueDragEventArgs : public EventArgs
```
[JScript]
```
public
   ComVisible(true)
class QueryContinueDragEventArgs extends EventArgs
```

Thread Safety

Any public static (**Shared** in Visual Basic) members of this type are safe for multithreaded operations. Any instance members are not guaranteed to be thread safe.

Remarks

The **QueryContinueDrag** event occurs during a drag-and-drop operation and allows the drag source to determine whether the drag-and-drop operation should be canceled. A **QueryContinueDrag-EventArgs** specifies whether and how the drag-and-drop operation should proceed, whether any modifier keys are pressed, and whether the user has pressed the ESC key.

By default, the **QueryContinueDrag** event sets **Action** to **Drag-Action.Cancel** if the ESC key was pressed and sets **Action** to **Drag-Action.Drop** if the left, middle, or right mouse button is pressed.

Example

[Visual Basic, C#, C++] The following example demonstrates a drag-and-drop operation between two **ListBox** controls. The example calls the **DoDragDrop** method when the drag action starts. The drag action starts if the mouse has moved more than **System-Information.DragSize** from the mouse location during the **Mouse-Down** event. The **IndexFromPoint** method is used to determine the index of the item to drag during the **MouseDown** event.

[Visual Basic, C#, C++] The example also demonstrates using custom cursors for the drag-and-drop operation. The example assumes that two cursor files, `3dwarro.cur` and `3dwno.cur`, exist in the application directory, for the custom drag and no-drop cursors, respectively. The custom cursors will be used if the `UseCustomCursors-Check` **CheckBox** is checked. The custom cursors are set in the **GiveFeedback** event handler.

[Visual Basic, C#, C++] The keyboard state is evaluated in the **DragOver** event handler for the right **ListBox**, to determine what the drag operation will be based upon state of the SHIFT, CTRL, ALT, or CTRL+ALT keys. The location in the **ListBox** where the drop would occur is also determined during the **DragOver** event. If the data to drop is not a **String**, then the **DragEventArgs.Effect** is set to **DragDropEffects.None**. Finally, the status of the drop is displayed in the `DropLocationLabel` **Label**.

[Visual Basic, C#, C++] The data to drop for the right **ListBox** is determined in the **DragDrop** event handler and the **String** value is added at the appropriate place in the **ListBox**. If the drag operation moves outside the bounds of the form, then the drag-and-drop operation is canceled in the **QueryContinueDrag** event handler.

[Visual Basic, C#, C++] This code excerpt demonstrates using the **QueryContinueDragEventArgs** class with the **System.Windows.Forms.Control.QueryContinueDragEvent** event. See the **DoDragDrop** method for the complete code example.

[Visual Basic]
```
Private Sub ListDragSource_QueryContinueDrag(ByVal sender As ↵
 Object, ByVal e As QueryContinueDragEventArgs) Handles
ListDragSource.QueryContinueDrag
    ' Cancel the drag if the mouse moves off the form.
    Dim lb as ListBox = CType(sender, System.Windows.Forms.ListBox)

    If Not (lb is nothing) Then

        Dim f as Form = lb.FindForm()

        ' Cancel the drag if the mouse moves off the form. The ↵
screenOffset
        ' takes into account any desktop bands that may be at ↵
the top or left
        ' side of the screen.
        If (((Control.MousePosition.X - screenOffset.X) < ↵
f.DesktopBounds.Left) Or _
            ((Control.MousePosition.X - screenOffset.X) > ↵
f.DesktopBounds.Right) Or _
            ((Control.MousePosition.Y - screenOffset.Y) < ↵
f.DesktopBounds.Top) Or _
            ((Control.MousePosition.Y - screenOffset.Y) > ↵
f.DesktopBounds.Bottom)) Then

            e.Action = DragAction.Cancel
        End If
    End if
End Sub
```

[C#]
```
private void ListDragSource_QueryContinueDrag(object sender, ↵
System.Windows.Forms.QueryContinueDragEventArgs e) {
    // Cancel the drag if the mouse moves off the form.
    ListBox lb = sender as ListBox;

    if (lb != null) {

        Form f = lb.FindForm();

        // Cancel the drag if the mouse moves off the form. The ↵
screenOffset
        // takes into account any desktop bands that may be at ↵
the top or left
        // side of the screen.
        if (((Control.MousePosition.X - screenOffset.X) < ↵
f.DesktopBounds.Left) ||
            ((Control.MousePosition.X - screenOffset.X) > ↵
f.DesktopBounds.Right) ||
            ((Control.MousePosition.Y - screenOffset.Y) < ↵
f.DesktopBounds.Top) ||
            ((Control.MousePosition.Y - screenOffset.Y) > ↵
f.DesktopBounds.Bottom)) {

            e.Action = DragAction.Cancel;
        }
    }
}
```

[C++]
```
private:
    void ListDragSource_QueryContinueDrag(Object* sender,
        System::Windows::Forms::QueryContinueDragEventArgs* e) {
        // Cancel the drag if the mouse moves off the form.
        ListBox* lb = dynamic_cast<ListBox*>(sender);

        if (lb != 0) {

            Form* f = lb->FindForm();

            // Cancel the drag if the mouse moves off the form.        ↵
 The screenOffset
            // takes into account any desktop bands that may be        ↵
at the top or left
            // side of the screen.
            if (((Control::MousePosition.X - screenOffset.X) < f-        ↵
>DesktopBounds.Left) ||
                ((Control::MousePosition.X - screenOffset.X) > f-        ↵
>DesktopBounds.Right) ||
                ((Control::MousePosition.Y - screenOffset.Y) < f-        ↵
>DesktopBounds.Top) ||
                ((Control::MousePosition.Y - screenOffset.Y) > f-        ↵
>DesktopBounds.Bottom)) {

                    e->Action = DragAction::Cancel;
                }
        }
    }
```

Requirements

Namespace: System.Windows.Forms

Platforms: Windows 98, Windows NT 4.0, Windows Millennium Edition, Windows 2000, Windows XP Home Edition, Windows XP Professional, Windows Server 2003 family

Assembly: System.Windows.Forms (in System.Windows.Forms.dll)

QueryContinueDragEventArgs Constructor

Initializes a new instance of the **QueryContinueDragEventArgs** class.

[Visual Basic]
```
Public Sub New( _
   ByVal keyState As Integer, _
   ByVal escapePressed As Boolean, _
   ByVal action As DragAction _
)
```
[C#]
```
public QueryContinueDragEventArgs(
   int keyState,
   bool escapePressed,
   DragAction action
);
```
[C++]
```
public: QueryContinueDragEventArgs(
   int keyState,
   bool escapePressed,
   DragAction action
);
```
[JScript]
```
public function QueryContinueDragEventArgs(
   keyState : int,
   escapePressed : Boolean,
   action : DragAction
);
```

Parameters

keyState
    The current state of the SHIFT, CTRL, and ALT keys.

escapePressed
    true if the ESC key was pressed; otherwise, **false**.

action
    A **DragAction** value.

Requirements

Platforms: Windows 98, Windows NT 4.0, Windows Millennium Edition, Windows 2000, Windows XP Home Edition, Windows XP Professional, Windows Server 2003 family

QueryContinueDragEventArgs.Action Property

Gets or sets the status of a drag-and-drop operation.

[Visual Basic]
```
Public Property Action As DragAction
```
[C#]
```
public DragAction Action {get; set;}
```
[C++]
```
public: __property DragAction get_Action();
public: __property void set_Action(DragAction);
```
[JScript]
```
public function get Action() : DragAction;
public function set Action(DragAction);
```

Property Value

A **DragAction** value.

Remarks

By default, the **QueryContinueDrag** event sets **Action** to **DragAction.Cancel** if the ESC key was pressed and sets **Action** to **DragAction.Drop** if the left, middle, or right mouse button is pressed.

Example

[Visual Basic, C#, C++] The following example demonstrates a drag-and-drop operation between two **ListBox** controls. The example calls the **DoDragDrop** method when the drag action starts. The drag action starts if the mouse has moved more than **SystemInformation.DragSize** from the mouse location during the **MouseDown** event. The **IndexFromPoint** method is used to determine the index of the item to drag during the **MouseDown** event.

[Visual Basic, C#, C++] The example also demonstrates using custom cursors for the drag-and-drop operation. The example assumes that two cursor files, `3dwarro.cur` and `3dwno.cur`, exist in the application directory, for the custom drag and no-drop cursors, respectively. The custom cursors will be used if the `UseCustomCursorsCheck` **CheckBox** is checked. The custom cursors are set in the **GiveFeedback** event handler.

[Visual Basic, C#, C++] The keyboard state is evaluated in the **DragOver** event handler for the right **ListBox**, to determine what the drag operation will be based upon state of the SHIFT, CTRL, ALT, or CTRL+ALT keys. The location in the **ListBox** where the drop would occur is also determined during the **DragOver** event. If the data to drop is not a **String**, then the **DragEventArgs.Effect** is set to **DragDropEffects.None**. Finally, the status of the drop is displayed in the `DropLocationLabel` **Label**.

[Visual Basic, C#, C++] The data to drop for the right **ListBox** is determined in the **DragDrop** event handler and the **String** value is added at the appropriate place in the **ListBox**. If the drag operation moves outside the bounds of the form, then the drag-and-drop operation is canceled in the **QueryContinueDrag** event handler.

[Visual Basic, C#, C++] This code excerpt demonstrates using the **QueryContinueDragEventArgs** class with the **System.Windows.Forms.Control.QueryContinueDragEvent** event. See the **DoDragDrop** method for the complete code example.

[Visual Basic]
```
Private Sub ListDragSource_QueryContinueDrag(ByVal sender As ↵
Object, ByVal e As QueryContinueDragEventArgs) Handles
ListDragSource.QueryContinueDrag
    ' Cancel the drag if the mouse moves off the form.
    Dim lb as ListBox = CType(sender, System.Windows.Forms.ListBox)

    If Not (lb is nothing) Then

        Dim f as Form = lb.FindForm()

        ' Cancel the drag if the mouse moves off the form. The ↵
screenOffset
        ' takes into account any desktop bands that may be at ↵
the top or left
        ' side of the screen.
        If (((Control.MousePosition.X - screenOffset.X) < ↵
f.DesktopBounds.Left) Or _
            ((Control.MousePosition.X - screenOffset.X) > ↵
f.DesktopBounds.Right) Or _
            ((Control.MousePosition.Y - screenOffset.Y) < ↵
f.DesktopBounds.Top) Or _
            ((Control.MousePosition.Y - screenOffset.Y) > ↵
f.DesktopBounds.Bottom)) Then

            e.Action = DragAction.Cancel
        End If
    End if
End Sub
```

[C#]
```
private void ListDragSource_QueryContinueDrag(object sender, ↵
System.Windows.Forms.QueryContinueDragEventArgs e) {
    // Cancel the drag if the mouse moves off the form.
    ListBox lb = sender as ListBox;

    if (lb != null) {

        Form f = lb.FindForm();

        // Cancel the drag if the mouse moves off the form. ↵
 The screenOffset
        // takes into account any desktop bands that may be ↵
at the top or left
        // side of the screen.
        if (((Control.MousePosition.X - screenOffset.X) < ↵
f.DesktopBounds.Left) ||
            ((Control.MousePosition.X - screenOffset.X) > ↵
f.DesktopBounds.Right) ||
            ((Control.MousePosition.Y - screenOffset.Y) < ↵
f.DesktopBounds.Top) ||
            ((Control.MousePosition.Y - screenOffset.Y) > ↵
f.DesktopBounds.Bottom)) {

            e.Action = DragAction.Cancel;
        }
    }
}
```

[C++]
```
private:
    void ListDragSource_QueryContinueDrag(Object* sender,
        System::Windows::Forms::QueryContinueDragEventArgs* e) {
        // Cancel the drag if the mouse moves off the form.
        ListBox* lb = dynamic_cast<ListBox*>(sender);

        if (lb != 0) {

            Form* f = lb->FindForm();

            // Cancel the drag if the mouse moves off the form. ↵
The screenOffset
            // takes into account any desktop bands that may be ↵
 at the top or left
            // side of the screen.
            if (((Control::MousePosition.X - screenOffset.X) < f- ↵
>DesktopBounds.Left) ||
                ((Control::MousePosition.X - screenOffset.X) > f- ↵
>DesktopBounds.Right) ||
                ((Control::MousePosition.Y - screenOffset.Y) < f- ↵
>DesktopBounds.Top) ||
                ((Control::MousePosition.Y - screenOffset.Y) > f- ↵
>DesktopBounds.Bottom)) {

                    e->Action = DragAction::Cancel;
                }
        }
    }
```

Requirements

Platforms: Windows 98, Windows NT 4.0, Windows Millennium Edition, Windows 2000, Windows XP Home Edition, Windows XP Professional, Windows Server 2003 family

QueryContinueDragEventArgs.EscapePressed Property

Gets whether the user pressed the ESC key.

[Visual Basic]
```
Public ReadOnly Property EscapePressed As Boolean
```
[C#]
```
public bool EscapePressed {get;}
```
[C++]
```
public: __property bool get_EscapePressed();
```
[JScript]
```
public function get EscapePressed() : Boolean;
```

Property Value

true if the ESC key was pressed; otherwise, **false**.

Remarks

By default, the **QueryContinueDrag** event sets **Action** to **DragAction.Cancel** if **EscapePressed** is true.

Requirements

Platforms: Windows 98, Windows NT 4.0, Windows Millennium Edition, Windows 2000, Windows XP Home Edition, Windows XP Professional, Windows Server 2003 family

QueryContinueDragEventArgs.KeyState Property

Gets the current state of the SHIFT, CTRL, and ALT keys.

[Visual Basic]
```
Public ReadOnly Property KeyState As Integer
```
[C#]
```
public int KeyState {get;}
```
[C++]
```
public: __property int get_KeyState();
```
[JScript]
```
public function get KeyState() : int;
```

Property Value

The current state of the SHIFT, CTRL, and ALT keys.

Remarks

The bits that are set in the **KeyState** property identify the keys or mouse buttons that were pressed during the operation. For example, if the left mouse button is pressed, the first bit in the **KeyState** property is set. You can use the bitwise **AND** operator to test for a given key state.

The following table lists the bits that are set for a specified event.

Bit	Key
1	The left mouse button.
2	The right mouse button.
4	The SHIFT key.
8	The CTL key.
16	The middle mouse button.
32	The ALT key.

By default, the **QueryContinueDrag** event sets **Action** to **DragAction.Drop** if **KeyState** indicates that the left, middle, or right mouse button is pressed.

Requirements

Platforms: Windows 98, Windows NT 4.0, Windows Millennium Edition, Windows 2000, Windows XP Home Edition, Windows XP Professional, Windows Server 2003 family

QueryContinueDragEvent-Handler Delegate

Represents the method that will handle the **QueryContinueDrag** event of a **Control**.

[Visual Basic]
```
<Serializable>
Public Delegate Sub QueryContinueDragEventHandler( _
   ByVal sender As Object, _
   ByVal e As QueryContinueDragEventArgs _
)
```
[C#]
```
[Serializable]
public delegate void QueryContinueDragEventHandler(
   object sender,
   QueryContinueDragEventArgs e
);
```
[C++]
```
[Serializable]
public __gc __delegate void QueryContinueDragEventHandler(
   Object* sender,
   QueryContinueDragEventArgs* e
);
```

[JScript] In JScript, you can use the delegates in the .NET Framework, but you cannot define your own.

Parameters [Visual Basic, C#, C++]

The declaration of your event handler must have the same parameters as the **QueryContinueDragEventHandler** delegate declaration.

sender
The source of an event.

e
A **QueryContinueDragEventArgs** that contains the event data.

Remarks

When you create a **QueryContinueDragEventHandler** delegate, you identify the method that will handle the event. To associate the event with your event handler, add an instance of the delegate to the event. The event handler is called whenever the event occurs, unless you remove the delegate.

Example

[Visual Basic, C#, C++] The following example demonstrates a drag-and-drop operation between two **ListBox** controls. The example calls the **DoDragDrop** method when the drag action starts. The drag action starts if the mouse has moved more than **SystemInformation.DragSize** from the mouse location during the **MouseDown** event. The **IndexFromPoint** method is used to determine the index of the item to drag during the **MouseDown** event.

[Visual Basic, C#, C++] The example also demonstrates using custom cursors for the drag-and-drop operation. The example assumes that two cursor files, `3dwarro.cur` and `3dwno.cur`, exist in the application directory, for the custom drag and no-drop cursors, respectively. The custom cursors will be used if the `UseCustomCursorsCheck` **CheckBox** is checked. The custom cursors are set in the **GiveFeedback** event handler.

[Visual Basic, C#, C++] The keyboard state is evaluated in the **DragOver** event handler for the right **ListBox**, to determine what the drag operation will be based upon state of the SHIFT, CTRL, ALT, or CTRL+ALT keys. The location in the **ListBox** where the drop would occur is also determined during the **DragOver** event. If the data to drop is not a **String**, then the **DragEventArgs.Effect** is set to **DragDropEffects.None**. Finally, the status of the drop is displayed in the `DropLocationLabel` **Label**.

[Visual Basic, C#, C++] The data to drop for the right **ListBox** is determined in the **DragDrop** event handler and the **String** value is added at the appropriate place in the **ListBox**. If the drag operation moves outside the bounds of the form, then the drag-and-drop operation is canceled in the **QueryContinueDrag** event handler.

[Visual Basic, C#, C++] This code excerpt demonstrates using the **QueryContinueDragEventHandler** delegate with the **QueryContinueDrag** event. See the **DoDragDrop** method for the complete code example.

[Visual Basic]
```
Private Sub ListDragSource_QueryContinueDrag(ByVal sender As ↵
Object, ByVal e As QueryContinueDragEventArgs) Handles
ListDragSource.QueryContinueDrag
    ' Cancel the drag if the mouse moves off the form.
    Dim lb as ListBox = CType(sender, System.Windows.Forms.ListBox)

    If Not (lb is nothing) Then

        Dim f as Form = lb.FindForm()

        ' Cancel the drag if the mouse moves off the form. The ↵
screenOffset
        ' takes into account any desktop bands that may be at ↵
the top or left
        ' side of the screen.
        If (((Control.MousePosition.X - screenOffset.X) < ↵
f.DesktopBounds.Left) Or _
            ((Control.MousePosition.X - screenOffset.X) > ↵
f.DesktopBounds.Right) Or _
            ((Control.MousePosition.Y - screenOffset.Y) < ↵
f.DesktopBounds.Top) Or _
            ((Control.MousePosition.Y - screenOffset.Y) > ↵
f.DesktopBounds.Bottom)) Then

            e.Action = DragAction.Cancel
        End If
    End if
End Sub
```

[C#]
```
private void ListDragSource_QueryContinueDrag(object sender, ↵
System.Windows.Forms.QueryContinueDragEventArgs e) {
    // Cancel the drag if the mouse moves off the form.
    ListBox lb = sender as ListBox;

    if (lb != null) {

        Form f = lb.FindForm();

        // Cancel the drag if the mouse moves off the form. ↵
The screenOffset
        // takes into account any desktop bands that may be at ↵
 the top or left
        // side of the screen.
        if (((Control.MousePosition.X - screenOffset.X) < ↵
f.DesktopBounds.Left) ||
            ((Control.MousePosition.X - screenOffset.X) > ↵
f.DesktopBounds.Right) ||
            ((Control.MousePosition.Y - screenOffset.Y) < ↵
f.DesktopBounds.Top) ||
            ((Control.MousePosition.Y - screenOffset.Y) > ↵
f.DesktopBounds.Bottom)) {
```

```
            e.Action = DragAction.Cancel;
        }
    }
}
```

[C++]

```
private:
    void ListDragSource_QueryContinueDrag(Object* sender,
        System::Windows::Forms::QueryContinueDragEventArgs* e) {
        // Cancel the drag if the mouse moves off the form.
        ListBox* lb = dynamic_cast<ListBox*>(sender);

        if (lb != 0) {

            Form* f = lb->FindForm();

            // Cancel the drag if the mouse moves off the form.        ↵
The screenOffset
            // takes into account any desktop bands that may be        ↵
at the top or left
            // side of the screen.
            if (((Control::MousePosition.X - screenOffset.X) < f-     ↵
>DesktopBounds.Left) ||
                ((Control::MousePosition.X - screenOffset.X) > f-     ↵
>DesktopBounds.Right) ||
                ((Control::MousePosition.Y - screenOffset.Y) < f-     ↵
>DesktopBounds.Top) ||
                ((Control::MousePosition.Y - screenOffset.Y) > f-     ↵
>DesktopBounds.Bottom)) {

                    e->Action = DragAction::Cancel;
                }
        }
    }
```

Requirements

Namespace: System.Windows.Forms

Platforms: Windows 98, Windows NT 4.0,
Windows Millennium Edition, Windows 2000,
Windows XP Home Edition, Windows XP Professional,
Windows Server 2003 family

Assembly: System.Windows.Forms (in System.Windows.Forms.dll)

RadioButton Class

Represents a Windows radio button.

System.Object
  System.MarshalByRefObject
    System.ComponentModel.Component
      System.Windows.Forms.Control
        System.Windows.Forms.ButtonBase
          System.Windows.Forms.RadioButton

[Visual Basic]
```
Public Class RadioButton
   Inherits ButtonBase
```
[C#]
```
public class RadioButton : ButtonBase
```
[C++]
```
public __gc class RadioButton : public ButtonBase
```
[JScript]
```
public class RadioButton extends ButtonBase
```

Thread Safety

Any public static (**Shared** in Visual Basic) members of this type are safe for multithreaded operations. Any instance members are not guaranteed to be thread safe.

Remarks

The **RadioButton** control can display text, an **Image**, or both.

When the user selects one radio button within a group, the others clear automatically. All **RadioButton** controls in a given container, such as a **Form**, constitute a group. To create multiple groups on one form, place each group in its own container, such as a **GroupBox** or **Panel** control.

RadioButton and **CheckBox** controls have a similar function: they offer choices a user can select or clear. The difference is that multiple **CheckBox** controls can be selected at the same time, but radio buttons are mutually exclusive.

Use the **Checked** property to get or set the state of a **RadioButton**. The radio button's appearance can be altered to appear as a toggle-style button or as a standard radio button by setting the **Appearance** property.

Note The radio button is sometimes referred to as an option button.

Example

[Visual Basic, C#, C++] The following example creates and initializes a **RadioButton**, gives it the appearance of a toggle button, sets its **AutoCheck** property to **false**, and adds it to a **Form**.

[Visual Basic]
```
Private Sub InitializeMyRadioButton()
    ' Create and initialize a new RadioButton.
    Dim radioButton1 As New RadioButton()

    ' Make the radio button control appear as a toggle button.
    radioButton1.Appearance = Appearance.Button

    ' Turn off the update of the display on the click of the control.
    radioButton1.AutoCheck = False

    ' Add the radio button to the form.
    Controls.Add(radioButton1)
End Sub
```

[C#]
```
private void InitializeMyRadioButton()
{
   // Create and initialize a new RadioButton.
   RadioButton radioButton1 = new RadioButton();

   // Make the radio button control appear as a toggle button.
   radioButton1.Appearance = Appearance.Button;

   // Turn off the update of the display on the click of the control.
   radioButton1.AutoCheck = false;

   // Add the radio button to the form.
   Controls.Add(radioButton1);
}
```

[C++]
```
private:
    void InitializeMyRadioButton() {
        // Create and initialize a new RadioButton.
        RadioButton __gc *radioButton1 = new RadioButton();

        // Make the radio button control appear as a toggle button.
        radioButton1->Appearance = Appearance::Button;

        // Turn off the update of the display on the click of          ↵
the control.
        radioButton1->AutoCheck = false;

        // Add the radio button to the form.
        Controls->Add(radioButton1);
    };
```

Requirements

Namespace: System.Windows.Forms

Platforms: Windows 98, Windows NT 4.0, Windows Millennium Edition, Windows 2000, Windows XP Home Edition, Windows XP Professional, Windows Server 2003 family, .NET Compact Framework - Windows CE .NET

Assembly: System.Windows.Forms (in System.Windows.Forms.dll)

RadioButton Constructor

Initializes a new instance of the **RadioButton** class.

[Visual Basic]
```
Public Sub New()
```
[C#]
```
public RadioButton();
```
[C++]
```
public: RadioButton();
```
[JScript]
```
public function RadioButton();
```

Remarks

The default view of the **RadioButton** has its text aligned to the right of the button and the **AutoCheck** property is set to **true**.

Example

[Visual Basic, C#, C++] The following example creates and initializes a **RadioButton**, gives it the appearance of a toggle button, sets its **AutoCheck** property to **false**, and adds it to a **Form**.

[Visual Basic]
```
Private Sub InitializeMyRadioButton()
    ' Create and initialize a new RadioButton.
    Dim radioButton1 As New RadioButton()

    ' Make the radio button control appear as a toggle button.
    radioButton1.Appearance = Appearance.Button

    ' Turn off the update of the display on the click of the control.
    radioButton1.AutoCheck = False

    ' Add the radio button to the form.
    Controls.Add(radioButton1)
End Sub
```

[C#]
```
private void InitializeMyRadioButton()
{
   // Create and initialize a new RadioButton.
   RadioButton radioButton1 = new RadioButton();

   // Make the radio button control appear as a toggle button.
   radioButton1.Appearance = Appearance.Button;

   // Turn off the update of the display on the click of the control.
   radioButton1.AutoCheck = false;

   // Add the radio button to the form.
   Controls.Add(radioButton1);
}
```

[C++]
```
private:
    void InitializeMyRadioButton() {
        // Create and initialize a new RadioButton.
        RadioButton __gc *radioButton1 = new RadioButton();

        // Make the radio button control appear as a toggle button.
        radioButton1->Appearance = Appearance::Button;

        // Turn off the update of the display on the click        ↵
of the control.
        radioButton1->AutoCheck = false;

        // Add the radio button to the form.
        Controls->Add(radioButton1);
    };
```

Requirements

Platforms: Windows 98, Windows NT 4.0, Windows Millennium Edition, Windows 2000, Windows XP Home Edition, Windows XP Professional, Windows Server 2003 family, .NET Compact Framework - Windows CE .NET

RadioButton.Appearance Property

Gets or set the value that determines the appearance of the radio button control.

[Visual Basic]
```
Public Property Appearance As Appearance
```
[C#]
```
public Appearance Appearance {get; set;}
```
[C++]
```
public: __property Appearance get_Appearance();
public: __property void set_Appearance(Appearance);
```
[JScript]
```
public function get Appearance() : Appearance;
public function set Appearance(Appearance);
```

Property Value

One of the **Appearance** values. The default value is **Normal**.

Exceptions

Exception Type	Condition
InvalidEnumArgumentException	The assigned value is not one of the **Appearance** values.

Remarks

If the **Appearance** value is set to **Normal**, then the **RadioButton** control is drawn with a circular check box. If the value is set to **Appearance.Button**, then the **RadioButton** control is drawn as a button that can be toggled to an up or down state. Either type can display text, an image, or both.

Example

[Visual Basic, C#, C++] The following example creates and initializes a **RadioButton**, gives it the appearance of a toggle button, sets its **AutoCheck** property to **false**, and adds it to a **Form**.

[Visual Basic]
```
Private Sub InitializeMyRadioButton()
    ' Create and initialize a new RadioButton.
    Dim radioButton1 As New RadioButton()

    ' Make the radio button control appear as a toggle button.
    radioButton1.Appearance = Appearance.Button

    ' Turn off the update of the display on the click of the control.
    radioButton1.AutoCheck = False

    ' Add the radio button to the form.
    Controls.Add(radioButton1)
End Sub
```

[C#]
```
private void InitializeMyRadioButton()
{
   // Create and initialize a new RadioButton.
   RadioButton radioButton1 = new RadioButton();

   // Make the radio button control appear as a toggle button.
   radioButton1.Appearance = Appearance.Button;

   // Turn off the update of the display on the click of the control.
   radioButton1.AutoCheck = false;

   // Add the radio button to the form.
   Controls.Add(radioButton1);
}
```

[C++]
```
private:
    void InitializeMyRadioButton() {
        // Create and initialize a new RadioButton.
        RadioButton __gc *radioButton1 = new RadioButton();

        // Make the radio button control appear as a toggle button.
        radioButton1->Appearance = Appearance::Button;

        // Turn off the update of the display on the click of        ↵
the control.
        radioButton1->AutoCheck = false;

        // Add the radio button to the form.
        Controls->Add(radioButton1);
    };
```

Requirements

Platforms: Windows 98, Windows NT 4.0, Windows Millennium Edition, Windows 2000, Windows XP Home Edition, Windows XP Professional, Windows Server 2003 family

RadioButton.AutoCheck Property

Gets or sets a value indicating whether the **Checked** value and the appearance of the control automatically change when the control is clicked.

[Visual Basic]
```
Public Property AutoCheck As Boolean
```
[C#]
```
public bool AutoCheck {get; set;}
```
[C++]
```
public: __property bool get_AutoCheck();
public: __property void set_AutoCheck(bool);
```
[JScript]
```
public function get AutoCheck() : Boolean;
public function set AutoCheck(Boolean);
```

Property Value

true if the **Checked** value and the appearance of the control automatically change on the **Click** event; otherwise, **false**. The default value is **true**.

Remarks

If the **Checked** value is set to **false**, the radio button portion of the control must be checked in code in the **Click** event handler. In addition, if the **RadioButton** is part of a **RadioButton** control group, this property ensures that only one of the controls is checked at a given time.

If the **AutoCheck** property is set to **false**, a group of **RadioButton** controls will not act as a mutually exclusive group and the **Checked** property must be updated in code.

Example

[Visual Basic, C#, C++] The following example creates and initializes a **RadioButton**, gives it the appearance of a toggle button, sets its **AutoCheck** property to **false**, and adds it to a **Form**.

[Visual Basic]
```
Private Sub InitializeMyRadioButton()
    ' Create and initialize a new RadioButton.
    Dim radioButton1 As New RadioButton()

    ' Make the radio button control appear as a toggle button.
    radioButton1.Appearance = Appearance.Button

    ' Turn off the update of the display on the click of the control.
    radioButton1.AutoCheck = False

    ' Add the radio button to the form.
    Controls.Add(radioButton1)
End Sub
```

[C#]
```
private void InitializeMyRadioButton()
{
   // Create and initialize a new RadioButton.
   RadioButton radioButton1 = new RadioButton();

   // Make the radio button control appear as a toggle button.
   radioButton1.Appearance = Appearance.Button;

   // Turn off the update of the display on the click of the control.
   radioButton1.AutoCheck = false;

   // Add the radio button to the form.
   Controls.Add(radioButton1);
}
```

[C++]
```
private:
    void InitializeMyRadioButton() {
        // Create and initialize a new RadioButton.
        RadioButton __gc *radioButton1 = new RadioButton();

        // Make the radio button control appear as a toggle button.
        radioButton1->Appearance = Appearance::Button;

        // Turn off the update of the display on the click of         ↵
the control.
        radioButton1->AutoCheck = false;

        // Add the radio button to the form.
        Controls->Add(radioButton1);
    };
```

Requirements

Platforms: Windows 98, Windows NT 4.0, Windows Millennium Edition, Windows 2000, Windows XP Home Edition, Windows XP Professional, Windows Server 2003 family

RadioButton.CheckAlign Property

Gets or sets the location of the check box portion of the radio button control.

[Visual Basic]
```
Public Property CheckAlign As ContentAlignment
```
[C#]
```
public ContentAlignment CheckAlign {get; set;}
```
[C++]
```
public: __property ContentAlignment get_CheckAlign();
public: __property void set_CheckAlign(ContentAlignment);
```
[JScript]
```
public function get CheckAlign() : ContentAlignment;
public function set CheckAlign(ContentAlignment);
```

Property Value

One of the valid **ContentAlignment** values. The default value is **MiddleLeft**.

Exceptions

Exception Type	Condition
InvalidEnumArgument-Exception	The assigned value is not one of the **ContentAlignment** values.

Example

[Visual Basic, C#, C++] The following example demonstrates how the **CheckAlign** property can be changed at run time. The check box portion of a radio button control is moved to the right or left of the text when the **Checked** value changes. This code assumes that a **RadioButton** control has been instantiated on a form and that a reference to the **System.Drawing** namespace has been included.

[Visual Basic]
```
Private Sub radioButton1_CheckedChanged(sender As Object, e ↵
As EventArgs)
    ' Change the check box position to be opposite its ↵
current position.
    If radioButton1.CheckAlign = ContentAlignment.MiddleLeft Then
        radioButton1.CheckAlign = ContentAlignment.MiddleRight
    Else
        radioButton1.CheckAlign = ContentAlignment.MiddleLeft
    End If
End Sub
```

[C#]
```
private void radioButton1_CheckedChanged(Object sender,
                                          EventArgs e)
{
   // Change the check box position to be opposite its current ↵
 position.
   if (radioButton1.CheckAlign == ContentAlignment.MiddleLeft)
   {
      radioButton1.CheckAlign = ContentAlignment.MiddleRight;
   }
   else
   {
      radioButton1.CheckAlign = ContentAlignment.MiddleLeft;
   }
}
```

[C++]
```
private: System::Void radioButton1_CheckedChanged ↵
 (System::Object *  sender, System::EventArgs *  e)
{
    // Change the check box position to be opposite its ↵
current position.
    if (radioButton1->CheckAlign == ContentAlignment::MiddleLeft)
    {
       radioButton1->CheckAlign = ContentAlignment::MiddleRight;
    }
    else
    {
       radioButton1->CheckAlign = ContentAlignment::MiddleLeft;
    }
 }

};
```

Requirements

Platforms: Windows 98, Windows NT 4.0, Windows Millennium Edition, Windows 2000, Windows XP Home Edition, Windows XP Professional, Windows Server 2003 family

RadioButton.Checked Property

Gets or sets a value indicating whether the control is checked.

[Visual Basic]
```
Public Property Checked As Boolean
```
[C#]
```
public bool Checked {get; set;}
```
[C++]
```
public: __property bool get_Checked();
public: __property void set_Checked(bool);
```
[JScript]
```
public function get Checked() : Boolean;
public function set Checked(Boolean);
```

Property Value

true if the check box is checked; otherwise, **false**.

Example

[Visual Basic, C#, C++] The following example evaluates a **ListBox** selection and the **Checked** property of a **RadioButton**. When a specified item is selected from the list box, the **PerformClick** method of another **RadioButton** is called. This code assumes that two **RadioButton** controls and a **ListBox** have been instantiated on a form.

[Visual Basic]
```
Private Sub ClickMyRadioButton()
    ' If Item1 is selected and radioButton2
    ' is checked, click radioButton1.
    If (listBox1.Text = "Item1") And radioButton2.Checked Then
        radioButton1.PerformClick()
    End If
End Sub
```

[C#]
```
private void ClickMyRadioButton()
{
   // If Item1 is selected and radioButton2
   // is checked, click radioButton1.
   if (listBox1.Text == "Item1" && radioButton2.Checked)
   {
      radioButton1.PerformClick();
   }
}
```

[C++]
```
private:
    void ClickMyRadioButton() {
   // If Item1 is selected and radioButton2
    // is checked, click radioButton1.
    if (listBox1->Text == "Item1" && radioButton2->Checked)
    {
       radioButton1->PerformClick();
    }
}
```

Requirements

Platforms: Windows 98, Windows NT 4.0, Windows Millennium Edition, Windows 2000, Windows XP Home Edition, Windows XP Professional, Windows Server 2003 family, .NET Compact Framework - Windows CE .NET

RadioButton.CreateParams Property

This member overrides **Control.CreateParams**.

[Visual Basic]
```
Overrides Protected ReadOnly Property CreateParams As CreateParams
```
[C#]
```
protected override CreateParams CreateParams {get;}
```
[C++]
```
protected: __property CreateParams* get_CreateParams();
```
[JScript]
```
protected override function get CreateParams() : CreateParams;
```

Requirements

Platforms: Windows 98, Windows NT 4.0, Windows Millennium Edition, Windows 2000, Windows XP Home Edition, Windows XP Professional, Windows Server 2003 family

RadioButton.DefaultSize Property

This member overrides **Control.DefaultSize**.

[Visual Basic]
```
Overrides Protected ReadOnly Property DefaultSize As Size
```
[C#]
```
protected override Size DefaultSize {get;}
```
[C++]
```
protected: __property Size get_DefaultSize();
```
[JScript]
```
protected override function get DefaultSize() : Size;
```

Requirements

Platforms: Windows 98, Windows NT 4.0, Windows Millennium Edition, Windows 2000, Windows XP Home Edition, Windows XP Professional, Windows Server 2003 family

RadioButton.TabStop Property

This member supports the .NET Framework infrastructure and is not intended to be used directly from your code.

[Visual Basic]
```
Public Shadows Property TabStop As Boolean
```
[C#]
```
public new bool TabStop {get; set;}
```
[C++]
```
public: __property bool get_TabStop();
public: __property void set_TabStop(bool);
```
[JScript]
```
public hide function get TabStop() : Boolean;
public hide function set TabStop(Boolean);
```

RadioButton.TextAlign Property

This member overrides **ButtonBase.TextAlign**.

[Visual Basic]
```
Overrides Public Property TextAlign As ContentAlignment
```
[C#]
```
public override ContentAlignment TextAlign {get; set;}
```
[C++]
```
public: __property ContentAlignment get_TextAlign();
public: __property void set_TextAlign(ContentAlignment);
```
[JScript]
```
public override function get TextAlign() : ContentAlignment;
public override function set TextAlign(ContentAlignment);
```

Requirements

Platforms: Windows 98, Windows NT 4.0, Windows Millennium Edition, Windows 2000, Windows XP Home Edition, Windows XP Professional, Windows Server 2003 family

RadioButton.CreateAccessibilityInstance Method

This member overrides **Control.CreateAccessibilityInstance**.

[Visual Basic]
```
Overrides Protected Function CreateAccessibilityInstance() As _
   AccessibleObject
```
[C#]
```
protected override AccessibleObject CreateAccessibilityInstance();
```
[C++]
```
protected: AccessibleObject* CreateAccessibilityInstance();
```
[JScript]
```
protected override function CreateAccessibilityInstance() :
   AccessibleObject;
```

Requirements

Platforms: Windows 98, Windows NT 4.0, Windows Millennium Edition, Windows 2000, Windows XP Home Edition, Windows XP Professional, Windows Server 2003 family

RadioButton.OnCheckedChanged Method

Raises the **CheckedChanged** event.

[Visual Basic]
```
Protected Overridable Sub OnCheckedChanged( _
   ByVal e As EventArgs _
)
```
[C#]
```
protected virtual void OnCheckedChanged(
   EventArgs e
);
```
[C++]
```
protected: virtual void OnCheckedChanged(
   EventArgs* e
);
```
[JScript]
```
protected function OnCheckedChanged(
   e : EventArgs
);
```

Parameters

e

An **EventArgs** that contains the event data.

Remarks

Raising an event invokes the event handler through a delegate. For more information, see **Raising an Event**.

The **OnCheckedChanged** method also allows derived classes to handle the event without attaching a delegate. This is the preferred technique for handling the event in a derived class.

Notes to Inheritors: When overriding **OnCheckedChanged** in a derived class, be sure to call the base class's **OnCheckedChanged** method so that registered delegates receive the event.

Example

[Visual Basic, C#, C++] The following example demonstrates how the **CheckAlign** property can be changed at run time. The check box portion of a radio button control is moved to the right or left of the text when the **Checked** value changes. This code assumes that a **RadioButton** control has been instantiated on a form and that a reference to the **System.Drawing** namespace has been included.

[Visual Basic]
```
Private Sub radioButton1_CheckedChanged(sender As Object, e As
EventArgs)
    ' Change the check box position to
    ' be the opposite its current position.
    If radioButton1.CheckAlign = ContentAlignment.MiddleLeft Then
        radioButton1.CheckAlign = ContentAlignment.MiddleRight
```

```
    Else
        radioButton1.CheckAlign = ContentAlignment.MiddleLeft
    End If
End Sub
```

[C#]
```
private void radioButton1_CheckedChanged(Object sender,
                                        EventArgs e)
{
   /* Change the check box position to
   be the opposite its current position.*/
   if (radioButton1.CheckAlign == ContentAlignment.MiddleLeft)
   {
      radioButton1.CheckAlign = ContentAlignment.MiddleRight;
   }
   else
   {
      radioButton1.CheckAlign = ContentAlignment.MiddleLeft;
   }
}
```

[C++]
```
private: System::Void radioButton1_CheckedChanged                    ↵
 (System::Object *  sender, System::EventArgs *  e)
{
    // Change the check box position to be opposite its               ↵
current position.
    if (radioButton1->CheckAlign == ContentAlignment::MiddleLeft)
    {
       radioButton1->CheckAlign = ContentAlignment::MiddleRight;
    }
    else
    {
       radioButton1->CheckAlign = ContentAlignment::MiddleLeft;
    }
 }

};
```

Requirements

Platforms: Windows 98, Windows NT 4.0,
Windows Millennium Edition, Windows 2000,
Windows XP Home Edition, Windows XP Professional,
Windows Server 2003 family,
.NET Compact Framework - Windows CE .NET

RadioButton.OnClick Method

This member overrides **Control.OnClick**.

[Visual Basic]
```
Overrides Protected Sub OnClick( _
   ByVal e As EventArgs _
)
```
[C#]
```
protected override void OnClick(
   EventArgs e
);
```
[C++]
```
protected: void OnClick(
   EventArgs* e
);
```
[JScript]
```
protected override function OnClick(
   e : EventArgs
);
```

Requirements

Platforms: Windows 98, Windows NT 4.0,
Windows Millennium Edition, Windows 2000,
Windows XP Home Edition, Windows XP Professional,
Windows Server 2003 family,
.NET Compact Framework - Windows CE .NET

RadioButton.OnEnter Method

This member overrides **Control.OnEnter**.

[Visual Basic]
```
Overrides Protected Sub OnEnter( _
   ByVal e As EventArgs _
)
```
[C#]
```
protected override void OnEnter(
   EventArgs e
);
```
[C++]
```
protected: void OnEnter(
   EventArgs* e
);
```
[JScript]
```
protected override function OnEnter(
   e : EventArgs
);
```

Requirements

Platforms: Windows 98, Windows NT 4.0,
Windows Millennium Edition, Windows 2000,
Windows XP Home Edition, Windows XP Professional,
Windows Server 2003 family

RadioButton.OnHandleCreated Method

This member overrides **Control.OnHandleCreated**.

[Visual Basic]
```
Overrides Protected Sub OnHandleCreated( _
   ByVal e As EventArgs _
)
```
[C#]
```
protected override void OnHandleCreated(
   EventArgs e
);
```
[C++]
```
protected: void OnHandleCreated(
   EventArgs* e
);
```
[JScript]
```
protected override function OnHandleCreated(
   e : EventArgs
);
```

Requirements

Platforms: Windows 98, Windows NT 4.0,
Windows Millennium Edition, Windows 2000,
Windows XP Home Edition, Windows XP Professional,
Windows Server 2003 family

RadioButton.OnMouseUp Method

This member overrides **Control.OnMouseUp**.

```
[Visual Basic]
Overrides Protected Sub OnMouseUp( _
   ByVal mevent As MouseEventArgs _
)
[C#]
protected override void OnMouseUp(
   MouseEventArgs mevent
);
[C++]
protected: void OnMouseUp(
   MouseEventArgs* mevent
);
[JScript]
protected override function OnMouseUp(
   mevent : MouseEventArgs
);
```

Requirements

Platforms: Windows 98, Windows NT 4.0, Windows Millennium Edition, Windows 2000, Windows XP Home Edition, Windows XP Professional, Windows Server 2003 family, .NET Compact Framework - Windows CE .NET

RadioButton.PerformClick Method

Generates a **Click** event for the button, simulating a click by a user.

```
[Visual Basic]
Public Sub PerformClick()
[C#]
public void PerformClick();
[C++]
public: void PerformClick();
[JScript]
public function PerformClick();
```

Example

[Visual Basic, C#, C++] The following example evaluates a **ListBox** selection and the **Checked** property of a **RadioButton**. When a specified item is selected from the list box, the **PerformClick** method of another **RadioButton** is called. This code assumes that two **RadioButton** controls and a **ListBox** have been instantiated on a form.

```
[Visual Basic]
Private Sub ClickMyRadioButton()
    ' If Item1 is selected and radioButton2
    ' is checked, click radioButton1.
    If (listBox1.Text = "Item1") And radioButton2.Checked Then
        radioButton1.PerformClick()
    End If
End Sub

[C#]
private void ClickMyRadioButton()
{
   // If Item1 is selected and radioButton2
   // is checked, click radioButton1.
   if (listBox1.Text == "Item1" && radioButton2.Checked)
   {
      radioButton1.PerformClick();
   }
}

[C++]
private:
   void ClickMyRadioButton() {
   // If Item1 is selected and radioButton2
    // is checked, click radioButton1.
    if (listBox1->Text == "Item1" && radioButton2->Checked)
    {
       radioButton1->PerformClick();
    }
}
```

Requirements

Platforms: Windows 98, Windows NT 4.0, Windows Millennium Edition, Windows 2000, Windows XP Home Edition, Windows XP Professional, Windows Server 2003 family

RadioButton.ProcessMnemonic Method

This member overrides **Control.ProcessMnemonic**.

```
[Visual Basic]
Overrides Protected Function ProcessMnemonic( _
   ByVal charCode As Char _
) As Boolean
[C#]
protected override bool ProcessMnemonic(
   char charCode
);
[C++]
protected: bool ProcessMnemonic(
   __wchar_t charCode
);
[JScript]
protected override function ProcessMnemonic(
   charCode : Char
) : Boolean;
```

Requirements

Platforms: Windows 98, Windows NT 4.0, Windows Millennium Edition, Windows 2000, Windows XP Home Edition, Windows XP Professional, Windows Server 2003 family

RadioButton.ToString Method

This member overrides **Object.ToString**.

```
[Visual Basic]
Overrides Public Function ToString() As String
[C#]
public override string ToString();
[C++]
public: String* ToString();
[JScript]
public override function ToString() : String;
```

Requirements

Platforms: Windows 98, Windows NT 4.0, Windows Millennium Edition, Windows 2000, Windows XP Home Edition, Windows XP Professional, Windows Server 2003 family, .NET Compact Framework - Windows CE .NET

RadioButton.AppearanceChanged Event

Occurs when the **Appearance** property value changes.

```
[Visual Basic]
Public Event AppearanceChanged As EventHandler
[C#]
public event EventHandler AppearanceChanged;
[C++]
public: __event EventHandler* AppearanceChanged;
```

[JScript] In JScript, you can handle the events defined by a class, but you cannot define your own.

Event Data

The event handler receives an argument of type **EventArgs**.

Remarks

For more information about handling events, see **Consuming Events**.

Requirements

Platforms: Windows 98, Windows NT 4.0, Windows Millennium Edition, Windows 2000, Windows XP Home Edition, Windows XP Professional, Windows Server 2003 family

RadioButton.CheckedChanged Event

Occurs when the value of the **Checked** property changes.

```
[Visual Basic]
Public Event CheckedChanged As EventHandler
[C#]
public event EventHandler CheckedChanged;
[C++]
public: __event EventHandler* CheckedChanged;
```

[JScript] In JScript, you can handle the events defined by a class, but you cannot define your own.

Event Data

The event handler receives an argument of type **EventArgs**.

Remarks

For more information about handling events, see **Consuming Events**.

Example

[Visual Basic, C#, C++] The following example demonstrates how the **CheckAlign** property can be changed at run time. The check box portion of a radio button control is moved to the right or left of the text when the **Checked** value changes. This code assumes that a **RadioButton** control has been instantiated on a form and that a reference to the **System.Drawing** namespace has been included.

```
[Visual Basic]
Private Sub radioButton1_CheckedChanged(sender As Object, ↵
e As EventArgs)
    ' Change the check box position to be opposite its ↵
current position.
    If radioButton1.CheckAlign = ContentAlignment.MiddleLeft Then
        radioButton1.CheckAlign = ContentAlignment.MiddleRight
    Else
        radioButton1.CheckAlign = ContentAlignment.MiddleLeft
    End If
End Sub
```

```
[C#]
private void radioButton1_CheckedChanged(Object sender,
                                          EventArgs e)
{
   // Change the check box position to be opposite its ↵
current position.
   if (radioButton1.CheckAlign == ContentAlignment.MiddleLeft)
   {
      radioButton1.CheckAlign = ContentAlignment.MiddleRight;
   }
   else
   {
      radioButton1.CheckAlign = ContentAlignment.MiddleLeft;
   }
}
```

```
[C++]
private: System::Void radioButton1_CheckedChanged ↵
 (System::Object *  sender, System::EventArgs *  e)
{
    // Change the check box position to be opposite its ↵
current position.
    if (radioButton1->CheckAlign == ContentAlignment::MiddleLeft)
    {
       radioButton1->CheckAlign = ContentAlignment::MiddleRight;
    }
    else
    {
       radioButton1->CheckAlign = ContentAlignment::MiddleLeft;
    }
 }

};
```

Requirements

Platforms: Windows 98, Windows NT 4.0, Windows Millennium Edition, Windows 2000, Windows XP Home Edition, Windows XP Professional, Windows Server 2003 family

RadioButton.DoubleClick Event

This member supports the .NET Framework infrastructure and is not intended to be used directly from your code.

```
[Visual Basic]
Public Shadows Event DoubleClick As EventHandler
[C#]
public new event EventHandler DoubleClick;
[C++]
public: __event EventHandler* DoubleClick;
```

[JScript] In JScript, you can handle the events defined by a class, but you cannot define your own.

RadioButton.RadioButton-AccessibleObject Class

This type supports the .NET Framework infrastructure and is not intended to be used directly from your code.

```
[Visual Basic]
<ComVisible(True)>
Public Class RadioButton.RadioButtonAccessibleObject
   Inherits Control.ControlAccessibleObject
[C#]
[ComVisible(true)]
public class RadioButton.RadioButtonAccessibleObject :
   Control.ControlAccessibleObject
[C++]
[ComVisible(true)]
public __gc class RadioButton.RadioButtonAccessibleObject : public
   Control.ControlAccessibleObject
[JScript]
public
   ComVisible(true)
class RadioButton.RadioButtonAccessibleObject extends
   Control.ControlAccessibleObject
```

Requirements

Platforms: Windows 98, Windows NT 4.0, Windows Millennium Edition, Windows 2000, Windows XP Home Edition, Windows XP Professional, Windows Server 2003 family

RadioButton.RadioButtonAccessible-Object Constructor

This member supports the .NET Framework infrastructure and is not intended to be used directly from your code.

```
[Visual Basic]
Public Sub New( _
   ByVal owner As RadioButton _
)
[C#]
public RadioButton.RadioButtonAccessibleObject(
   RadioButton owner
);
[C++]
public: RadioButtonAccessibleObject(
   RadioButton* owner
);
[JScript]
public function RadioButton.RadioButtonAccessibleObject(
   owner : RadioButton
);
```

RadioButton.RadioButtonAccessible-Object.DefaultAction Property

This member overrides **AccessibleObject.DefaultAction**.

```
[Visual Basic]
Overrides Public ReadOnly Property DefaultAction As String
[C#]
public override string DefaultAction {get;}
[C++]
public: __property String* get_DefaultAction();
[JScript]
public override function get DefaultAction() : String;
```

Requirements

Platforms: Windows 98, Windows NT 4.0, Windows Millennium Edition, Windows 2000, Windows XP Home Edition, Windows XP Professional, Windows Server 2003 family

RadioButton.RadioButtonAccessible-Object.Role Property

This member overrides **AccessibleObject.Role**.

```
[Visual Basic]
Overrides Public ReadOnly Property Role As AccessibleRole
[C#]
public override AccessibleRole Role {get;}
[C++]
public: __property AccessibleRole get_Role();
[JScript]
public override function get Role() : AccessibleRole;
```

Requirements

Platforms: Windows 98, Windows NT 4.0, Windows Millennium Edition, Windows 2000, Windows XP Home Edition, Windows XP Professional, Windows Server 2003 family

RadioButton.RadioButtonAccessible-Object.State Property

This member overrides **AccessibleObject.State**.

```
[Visual Basic]
Overrides Public ReadOnly Property State As AccessibleStates
[C#]
public override AccessibleStates State {get;}
[C++]
public: __property AccessibleStates get_State();
[JScript]
public override function get State() : AccessibleStates;
```

Requirements

Platforms: Windows 98, Windows NT 4.0, Windows Millennium Edition, Windows 2000, Windows XP Home Edition, Windows XP Professional, Windows Server 2003 family

RadioButton.RadioButtonAccessible-Object.DoDefaultAction Method

This member overrides **AccessibleObject.DoDefaultAction**.

```
[Visual Basic]
Overrides Public Sub DoDefaultAction()
[C#]
public override void DoDefaultAction();
[C++]
public: void DoDefaultAction();
[JScript]
public override function DoDefaultAction();
```

Requirements

Platforms: Windows 98, Windows NT 4.0, Windows Millennium Edition, Windows 2000, Windows XP Home Edition, Windows XP Professional, Windows Server 2003 family

RichTextBox Class

Represents a Windows rich text box control.

System.Object
  System.MarshalByRefObject
    System.ComponentModel.Component
      System.Windows.Forms.Control
        System.Windows.Forms.TextBoxBase
          System.Windows.Forms.RichTextBox

[Visual Basic]
```
Public Class RichTextBox
   Inherits TextBoxBase
```
[C#]
```
public class RichTextBox : TextBoxBase
```
[C++]
```
public __gc class RichTextBox : public TextBoxBase
```
[JScript]
```
public class RichTextBox extends TextBoxBase
```

Thread Safety

Any public static (**Shared** in Visual Basic) members of this type are safe for multithreaded operations. Any instance members are not guaranteed to be thread safe.

Remarks

The **RichTextBox** control allows the user to enter and edit text while also providing more advanced formatting features than the standard **TextBox** control. Text can be assigned directly to the control, or can be loaded from a Rich Text Format (RTF) or plain text file. The text within the control can be assigned character and paragraph formatting.

The **RichTextBox** control provides a number of properties you can use to apply formatting to any portion of text within the control. To change the formatting of text, it must first be selected. Only selected text can be assigned character and paragraph formatting. Once a setting has been made to a selected section of text, all text entered after the selection is also formatted with the same settings until a setting change is made or a different section of the control's document is selected. The **SelectionFont** property enables you to make text bold or italic. You can also use this property to change the size and typeface of the text. The **SelectionColor** property enables you to change the color of the text. To create bulleted lists you can use the **SelectionBullet** property. You can also adjust paragraph formatting by setting the **SelectionIndent**, **SelectionRightIndent**, and **SelectionHangingIndent** properties.

The **RichTextBox** control provides methods that provide functionality for opening and saving files. The **LoadFile** method enables you to load an existing RTF or ASCII text file into the control. You can also load data from an already opened data stream. The **SaveFile** enables you to save a file to RTF or ASCII text. Similar to the **LoadFile** method, you can also use the **SaveFile** method to save to an open data stream. The **RichTextBox** control also provides features for finding strings of text. The **Find** method is overloaded to find both strings of text as well as specific characters within the text of the control.

You can also initialize the **RichTextBox** control to data stored in memory. For example, you can initialize the **Rtf** property to a string that contains the text to display, including the RTF codes that determine how the text should be formatted.

If the text within the control contains links, such as a link to a Web site, you can use the **DetectUrls** property to display the link appropriately in the control's text. You can then handle the **LinkClicked** event to perform the tasks associated with the link. The **SelectionProtected** property enables you to protect text within the control from manipulation by the user. With protected text in your control, you can handle the **Protected** event to determine when the user has attempted to modify protected text to either alert the user that the text is protected or to provide the user with a standard form of manipulating the protected text.

Applications that already use **TextBox** controls can easily be adapted to make use of **RichTextBox** controls. However, the **RichTextBox** control does not have the same 64K character capacity limit of the **TextBox** control. The **RichTextBox** is typically used to provide text manipulation and display features similar to word processing applications such as Microsoft Word.

Example

[Visual Basic, C#] The following example creates a **RichTextBox** control that loads an RTF file into the control and searches for the first instance of the word "Text". The code then changes the font style, font size, and font color of the selected text and saves the changes back to the original file. The example code finishes by adding the control to its **Form**. This example assumes that the method created in the example code is added to a **Form** class and called from the constructor of the form. The example also assumes that an RTF file is created, in the root of the C drive, containing the word "Text".

[Visual Basic]
```
Public Sub CreateMyRichTextBox()
    Dim richTextBox1 As New RichTextBox()
    richTextBox1.Dock = DockStyle.Fill


    richTextBox1.LoadFile("C:\MyDocument.rtf")
    richTextBox1.Find("Text", RichTextBoxFinds.MatchCase)

    richTextBox1.SelectionFont = New Font("Verdana", 12,           ↵
FontStyle.Bold)
    richTextBox1.SelectionColor = Color.Red

    richTextBox1.SaveFile("C:\MyDocument.rtf",                     ↵
RichTextBoxStreamType.RichText)

    Me.Controls.Add(richTextBox1)
End Sub
```

[C#]
```
public void CreateMyRichTextBox()
{
    RichTextBox richTextBox1 = new RichTextBox();
    richTextBox1.Dock = DockStyle.Fill;

    richTextBox1.LoadFile("C:\\MyDocument.rtf");
    richTextBox1.Find("Text", RichTextBoxFinds.MatchCase);

    richTextBox1.SelectionFont = new Font("Verdana",               ↵
12, FontStyle.Bold);
    richTextBox1.SelectionColor = Color.Red;

    richTextBox1.SaveFile("C:\\MyDocument.rtf",                    ↵
RichTextBoxStreamType.RichText);

    this.Controls.Add(richTextBox1);
}
```

Requirements

Namespace: System.Windows.Forms

Platforms: Windows 98, Windows NT 4.0, Windows Millennium Edition, Windows 2000, Windows XP Home Edition, Windows XP Professional, Windows Server 2003 family

Assembly: System.Windows.Forms (in System.Windows.Forms.dll)

RichTextBox Constructor

Initializes a new instance of the **RichTextBox** class.

```
[Visual Basic]
Public Sub New()
[C#]
public RichTextBox();
[C++]
public: RichTextBox();
[JScript]
public function RichTextBox();
```

Remarks

By default, the **Multiline** property of the control is set to **true**.

Example

See related example in the **System.Windows.Forms.RichTextBox** class topic.

Requirements

Platforms: Windows 98, Windows NT 4.0, Windows Millennium Edition, Windows 2000, Windows XP Home Edition, Windows XP Professional, Windows Server 2003 family

RichTextBox.AllowDrop Property

Gets or sets a value indicating whether the control will allow drag-and-drop operations.

```
[Visual Basic]
Overrides Public Property AllowDrop As Boolean
[C#]
public override bool AllowDrop {get; set;}
[C++]
public: __property bool get_AllowDrop();
public: __property void set_AllowDrop(bool);
[JScript]
public override function get AllowDrop() : Boolean;
public override function set AllowDrop(Boolean);
```

Property Value

true if drag-and-drop is allowed in the control; otherwise, **false**.

Example

See related example in the **System.Windows.Forms.RichTextBox** class topic.

Requirements

Platforms: Windows 98, Windows NT 4.0, Windows Millennium Edition, Windows 2000, Windows XP Home Edition, Windows XP Professional, Windows Server 2003 family

RichTextBox.AutoSize Property

Gets or sets a value indicating whether the size of the **RichTextBox** automatically adjusts when the font assigned to the control is changed.

```
[Visual Basic]
Overrides Public Property AutoSize As Boolean
[C#]
public override bool AutoSize {get; set;}
[C++]
public: __property bool get_AutoSize();
public: __property void set_AutoSize(bool);
[JScript]
public override function get AutoSize() : Boolean;
public override function set AutoSize(Boolean);
```

Property Value

true if the size of the control automatically adjusts when the font is changed; otherwise **false**. The default is **false**.

Remarks

When this property is set to **true**, the **RichTextBox** resizes its height based on the size of the font assigned to the control. You can use this property to ensure that the user can read text assigned to the control regardless of the font.

Requirements

Platforms: Windows 98, Windows NT 4.0, Windows Millennium Edition, Windows 2000, Windows XP Home Edition, Windows XP Professional, Windows Server 2003 family

RichTextBox.AutoWordSelection Property

Gets or sets a value indicating whether automatic word selection is enabled.

```
[Visual Basic]
Public Property AutoWordSelection As Boolean
[C#]
public bool AutoWordSelection {get; set;}
[C++]
public: __property bool get_AutoWordSelection();
public: __property void set_AutoWordSelection(bool);
[JScript]
public function get AutoWordSelection() : Boolean;
public function set AutoWordSelection(Boolean);
```

Property Value

true if automatic word selection is enabled; otherwise, **false**. The default is **false**.

Remarks

If this property is set to **true**, selecting any part of the text in the control results in the selection of the entire word. For example, if **AutoWordSelection** is set to **true**, the user can double-click on any part of a word in the control and the entire word is selected automatically.

Example

See related example in the **System.Windows.Forms.RichTextBox** class topic.

Requirements

Platforms: Windows 98, Windows NT 4.0, Windows Millennium Edition, Windows 2000, Windows XP Home Edition, Windows XP Professional, Windows Server 2003 family

RichTextBox.BackgroundImage Property

This member overrides **Control.BackgroundImage**.

```
[Visual Basic]
Overrides Public Property BackgroundImage As Image
[C#]
public override Image BackgroundImage {get; set;}
[C++]
public: __property Image* get_BackgroundImage();
public: __property void set_BackgroundImage(Image*);
[JScript]
public override function get BackgroundImage() : Image;
public override function set BackgroundImage(Image);
```

Requirements

Platforms: Windows 98, Windows NT 4.0, Windows Millennium Edition, Windows 2000, Windows XP Home Edition, Windows XP Professional, Windows Server 2003 family

RichTextBox.BulletIndent Property

Gets or sets the indentation used in the **RichTextBox** control when the bullet style is applied to the text.

```
[Visual Basic]
Public Property BulletIndent As Integer
[C#]
public int BulletIndent {get; set;}
[C++]
public: __property int get_BulletIndent();
public: __property void set_BulletIndent(int);
[JScript]
public function get BulletIndent() : int;
public function set BulletIndent(int);
```

Property Value

The number of pixels inserted as the indentation after a bullet. The default is zero.

Exceptions

Exception Type	Condition
ArgumentException	The specified intentation was less than zero.

Remarks

To apply the bullet style to a paragraph of text, set the **SelectionBullet** property to **true** and then set the **BulletIndent** property to the number of pixels that the text should be indented. The paragraph will have the bullet style applied to it with the specified amount of indentation after the bullet. This property only affects the current paragraph within the control's text and the currently selected bullet in a list of bulleted items. To apply a different indentation level to an entire list of bulleted items, all the text of the bulleted items must be selected before setting the **BulletIndent** property.

Example

See related example in the **System.Windows.Forms.RichTextBox** class topic.

Requirements

Platforms: Windows 98, Windows NT 4.0, Windows Millennium Edition, Windows 2000, Windows XP Home Edition, Windows XP Professional, Windows Server 2003 family

RichTextBox.CanRedo Property

Gets a value indicating whether there are actions that have occurred within the **RichTextBox** that can be reapplied.

```
[Visual Basic]
Public ReadOnly Property CanRedo As Boolean
[C#]
public bool CanRedo {get;}
[C++]
public: __property bool get_CanRedo();
[JScript]
public function get CanRedo() : Boolean;
```

Property Value

true if there are operations that have been undone that can be reapplied to the content of the control; otherwise, **false**.

Remarks

You can use this property to determine whether the last operation undone in the **RichTextBox** can be reapplied using the **Redo** method.

Example

See related example in the **System.Windows.Forms.RichTextBox** class topic.

Requirements

Platforms: Windows 98, Windows NT 4.0, Windows Millennium Edition, Windows 2000, Windows XP Home Edition, Windows XP Professional, Windows Server 2003 family

RichTextBox.CreateParams Property

This member overrides **Control.CreateParams**.

```
[Visual Basic]
Overrides Protected ReadOnly Property CreateParams As CreateParams
[C#]
protected override CreateParams CreateParams {get;}
[C++]
protected: __property CreateParams* get_CreateParams();
[JScript]
protected override function get CreateParams() : CreateParams;
```

Requirements

Platforms: Windows 98, Windows NT 4.0, Windows Millennium Edition, Windows 2000, Windows XP Home Edition, Windows XP Professional, Windows Server 2003 family

RichTextBox.DefaultSize Property

This member overrides **Control.DefaultSize**.

[Visual Basic]
```
Overrides Protected ReadOnly Property DefaultSize As Size
```
[C#]
```
protected override Size DefaultSize {get;}
```
[C++]
```
protected: __property Size get_DefaultSize();
```
[JScript]
```
protected override function get DefaultSize() : Size;
```

Requirements

Platforms: Windows 98, Windows NT 4.0, Windows Millennium Edition, Windows 2000, Windows XP Home Edition, Windows XP Professional, Windows Server 2003 family

RichTextBox.DetectUrls Property

Gets or sets a value indicating whether or not the **RichTextBox** will automatically format a Uniform Resource Locator (URL) when it is typed into the control.

[Visual Basic]
```
Public Property DetectUrls As Boolean
```
[C#]
```
public bool DetectUrls {get; set;}
```
[C++]
```
public: __property bool get_DetectUrls();
public: __property void set_DetectUrls(bool);
```
[JScript]
```
public function get DetectUrls() : Boolean;
public function set DetectUrls(Boolean);
```

Property Value

true if the **RichTextBox** will automatically format URLs that are typed into the control as a link; otherwise, **false**. The default is **true**.

Remarks

If this property is set to **true**, any text entered into the control that is determined by the **RichTextBox** to be a URL is automatically formatted as a link. You can create an event handler for the **LinkClicked** event to handle all links clicked in the control. The **LinkClickedEventArgs** that is provided to the event handler for the **LinkClicked** event provides data that enables you to determine which link was clicked in the control in order to process the link.

Example

See related example in the **System.Windows.Forms.RichTextBox** class topic.

Requirements

Platforms: Windows 98, Windows NT 4.0, Windows Millennium Edition, Windows 2000, Windows XP Home Edition, Windows XP Professional, Windows Server 2003 family

RichTextBox.Font Property

This member overrides **Control.Font**.

[Visual Basic]
```
Overrides Public Property Font As Font
```
[C#]
```
public override Font Font {get; set;}
```
[C++]
```
public: __property Font* get_Font();
public: __property void set_Font(Font*);
```
[JScript]
```
public override function get Font() : Font;
public override function set Font(Font);
```

Requirements

Platforms: Windows 98, Windows NT 4.0, Windows Millennium Edition, Windows 2000, Windows XP Home Edition, Windows XP Professional, Windows Server 2003 family

RichTextBox.ForeColor Property

This member overrides **TextBoxBase.ForeColor**.

[Visual Basic]
```
Overrides Public Property ForeColor As Color
```
[C#]
```
public override Color ForeColor {get; set;}
```
[C++]
```
public: __property Color get_ForeColor();
public: __property void set_ForeColor(Color);
```
[JScript]
```
public override function get ForeColor() : Color;
public override function set ForeColor(Color);
```

Requirements

Platforms: Windows 98, Windows NT 4.0, Windows Millennium Edition, Windows 2000, Windows XP Home Edition, Windows XP Professional, Windows Server 2003 family

RichTextBox.MaxLength Property

Gets or sets the maximum number of characters the user can type or paste into the rich text box control.

[Visual Basic]
```
Overrides Public Property MaxLength As Integer
```
[C#]
```
public override int MaxLength {get; set;}
```
[C++]
```
public: __property int get_MaxLength();
public: __property void set_MaxLength(int);
```
[JScript]
```
public override function get MaxLength() : int;
public override function set MaxLength(int);
```

Property Value

The number of characters that can be entered into the control. The default is **MaxValue**.

Exceptions

Exception Type	Condition
ArgumentException	The value assigned to the property is less than 0.

Remarks

When this property is set to 0, the maximum length of the text that can be entered in the control is 64 KB of characters. This property is typically used when the **RichTextBox** is used to display a single line of Rich Text Format (RTF) text. You can use this property to restrict the length of text entered in the control for values such as postal codes and telephone numbers, or to restrict the length of text entered when the data is to be entered in a database. You can limit the text entered into the control to the maximum length of the corresponding field in the database.

> **Note** In code, you can set the value of the **Text** property to a value that has a length greater than the value specified by the **MaxLength** property. This property only affects text entered into the control at run time.

Example

See related example in the **System.Windows.Forms.RichTextBox** class topic.

Requirements

Platforms: Windows 98, Windows NT 4.0, Windows Millennium Edition, Windows 2000, Windows XP Home Edition, Windows XP Professional, Windows Server 2003 family

RichTextBox.Multiline Property

This member overrides **TextBoxBase.Multiline**.

```
[Visual Basic]
Overrides Public Property Multiline As Boolean
[C#]
public override bool Multiline {get; set;}
[C++]
public: __property bool get_Multiline();
public: __property void set_Multiline(bool);
[JScript]
public override function get Multiline() : Boolean;
public override function set Multiline(Boolean);
```

Requirements

Platforms: Windows 98, Windows NT 4.0, Windows Millennium Edition, Windows 2000, Windows XP Home Edition, Windows XP Professional, Windows Server 2003 family

RichTextBox.RedoActionName Property

Gets the name of the action that can be reapplied to the control when the **Redo** method is called.

```
[Visual Basic]
Public ReadOnly Property RedoActionName As String
[C#]
public string RedoActionName {get;}
[C++]
public: __property String* get_RedoActionName();
[JScript]
public function get RedoActionName() : String;
```

Property Value

A string that represents the name of the action that will be performed when a call to the **Redo** method is made.

Remarks

If this property returns an empty string (""), there is no operation available to reapply to the control. You can use this method to determine the last action undone in the **RichTextBox** control that can then be reapplied to the control when a call to the **Redo** method is made. You can determine whether there are any operations to be reapplied to the control by using the **CanRedo** property.

Example

See related example in the **System.Windows.Forms.RichTextBox** class topic.

Requirements

Platforms: Windows 98, Windows NT 4.0, Windows Millennium Edition, Windows 2000, Windows XP Home Edition, Windows XP Professional, Windows Server 2003 family

RichTextBox.RightMargin Property

Gets or sets the size of a single line of text within the **RichTextBox** control.

```
[Visual Basic]
Public Property RightMargin As Integer
[C#]
public int RightMargin {get; set;}
[C++]
public: __property int get_RightMargin();
public: __property void set_RightMargin(int);
[JScript]
public function get RightMargin() : int;
public function set RightMargin(int);
```

Property Value

The size, in pixels, of a single line of text in the control. The default is zero.

Exceptions

Exception Type	Condition
ArgumentException	The specified value was less than zero.

Remarks

When a value greater than zero is entered into the control, a nonvisible margin is placed in the control at the specified number of pixels from the left side of the control. Any text that is entered that extends beyond this margin is placed on the next line of text in the control. This property affects all text currently entered into the control as well as any additional text entered into the control after the property is set. You can use this property to specify a maximum line width for all text entered into a **RichTextBox** control.

Example

See related example in the **System.Windows.Forms.RichTextBox** class topic.

Requirements

Platforms: Windows 98, Windows NT 4.0, Windows Millennium Edition, Windows 2000, Windows XP Home Edition, Windows XP Professional, Windows Server 2003 family

RichTextBox.Rtf Property

Gets or sets the text of the **RichTextBox** control, including all Rich Text Format (RTF) codes.

```
[Visual Basic]
Public Property Rtf As String
[C#]
public string Rtf {get; set;}
[C++]
public: __property String* get_Rtf();
public: __property void set_Rtf(String*);
[JScript]
public function get Rtf() : String;
public function set Rtf(String);
```

Property Value

The text of the control in RTF format.

Remarks

You can use this property to place RTF formatted text into the control for display or to extract the text of the control with the specified RTF formatting defined in the text of the control. This property is typically used when you are assigning RTF text from another RTF source, such as Microsoft Word or Windows WordPad, to the control.

Requirements

Platforms: Windows 98, Windows NT 4.0, Windows Millennium Edition, Windows 2000, Windows XP Home Edition, Windows XP Professional, Windows Server 2003 family

RichTextBox.ScrollBars Property

Gets or sets the type of scroll bars to display in the **RichTextBox** control.

```
[Visual Basic]
Public Property ScrollBars As RichTextBoxScrollBars
[C#]
public RichTextBoxScrollBars ScrollBars {get; set;}
[C++]
public: __property RichTextBoxScrollBars get_ScrollBars();
public: __property void set_ScrollBars(RichTextBoxScrollBars);
[JScript]
public function get ScrollBars() : RichTextBoxScrollBars;
public function set ScrollBars(RichTextBoxScrollBars);
```

Property Value

One of the **RichTextBoxScrollBars** values. The default is **RichTextBoxScrollBars.Both**.

Exceptions

Exception Type	Condition
InvalidEnumArgument-Exception	The specified value is not defined in the **RichTextBoxScrollBars** enumeration.

Remarks

This property enables you to provide horizontal and vertical scroll bars to the user of the **RichTextBox** control to enable scrolling text within the control that is outside of the physical dimensions of the control. You can also use this property to remove scroll bars from the control to restrict scrolling the contents of the control.

Note Horizontal scroll bars will not be shown if the **WordWrap** is **true**, regardless of the value of the **ScrollBars** property.

Requirements

Platforms: Windows 98, Windows NT 4.0, Windows Millennium Edition, Windows 2000, Windows XP Home Edition, Windows XP Professional, Windows Server 2003 family

RichTextBox.SelectedRtf Property

Gets or sets the currently selected Rich Text Format (RTF) formatted text in the control.

```
[Visual Basic]
Public Property SelectedRtf As String
[C#]
public string SelectedRtf {get; set;}
[C++]
public: __property String* get_SelectedRtf();
public: __property void set_SelectedRtf(String*);
[JScript]
public function get SelectedRtf() : String;
public function set SelectedRtf(String);
```

Property Value

The selected RTF text in the control.

Remarks

This property enables you to obtain the selected text in the control, including the RTF formatting codes. You can use this property to copy text from your control, complete with formatting, and paste the text in other applications that accept RTF formatted text, such as Microsoft Word and Windows WordPad. To get the selected text, without RTF formatting codes, use the **SelectedText** property.

If no text is currently selected, the text specified in this property is inserted at the insertion point. If text is selected, any text assigned to this property replaces the selected text.

Requirements

Platforms: Windows 98, Windows NT 4.0, Windows Millennium Edition, Windows 2000, Windows XP Home Edition, Windows XP Professional, Windows Server 2003 family

RichTextBox.SelectedText Property

Gets or sets the selected text within the **RichTextBox**.

```
[Visual Basic]
Overrides Public Property SelectedText As String
[C#]
public override string SelectedText {get; set;}
[C++]
public: __property String* get_SelectedText();
public: __property void set_SelectedText(String*);
[JScript]
public override function get SelectedText() : String;
public override function set SelectedText(String);
```

Property Value

A string that represents the selected text in the control.

Example

See related example in the **System.Windows.Forms.RichTextBox** class topic.

Requirements

Platforms: Windows 98, Windows NT 4.0, Windows Millennium Edition, Windows 2000, Windows XP Home Edition, Windows XP Professional, Windows Server 2003 family

RichTextBox.SelectionAlignment Property

Gets or sets the alignment to apply to the current selection or insertion point.

```
[Visual Basic]
Public Property SelectionAlignment As HorizontalAlignment
[C#]
public HorizontalAlignment SelectionAlignment {get; set;}
[C++]
public: __property HorizontalAlignment get_SelectionAlignment();
public: __property void set_SelectionAlignment(HorizontalAlignment);
[JScript]
public function get SelectionAlignment() : HorizontalAlignment;
public function set SelectionAlignment(HorizontalAlignment);
```

Property Value

One of the **HorizontalAlignment** values.

Exceptions

Exception Type	Condition
InvalidEnumArgument-Exception	The specified value is not one of the values defined in the **HorizontalAlignment** class.

Remarks

If no paragraph is selected in the control, setting this property applies the alignment setting to the paragraph in which the insertion point appears as well as to paragraphs created after the paragraph that has the alignment property setting. For example, if there are two paragraphs in a **RichTextBox** control and the insertion point is located within the second paragraph. If you set the **Selection-Alignment** property to **HorizontalAlignment.Center**, the paragraph at the insertion point will be centered within the control. If a third paragraph is created after the second paragraph, it also is aligned to the center of the control.

If a selection is made within the control when the property is set, all paragraphs selected are aligned based on this property setting. You can use this property to align the paragraphs in a document being created in the **RichTextBox**. For example, if you want all paragraphs in a document to be centered, you can select all the paragraphs in the control and set the **SelectionAlignment** property to **HorizontalAlignment.Center**.

> **Note** **SelectionAlignment** returns **SelectionAlignment.Left** when the text selection contains multiple paragraphs with mixed alignment.

Example

See related example in the **System.Windows.Forms.RichTextBox** class topic.

Requirements

Platforms: Windows 98, Windows NT 4.0, Windows Millennium Edition, Windows 2000, Windows XP Home Edition, Windows XP Professional, Windows Server 2003 family

RichTextBox.SelectionBullet Property

Gets or sets a value indicating whether the bullet style is applied to the current selection or insertion point.

```
[Visual Basic]
Public Property SelectionBullet As Boolean
[C#]
public bool SelectionBullet {get; set;}
[C++]
public: __property bool get_SelectionBullet();
public: __property void set_SelectionBullet(bool);
[JScript]
public function get SelectionBullet() : Boolean;
public function set SelectionBullet(Boolean);
```

Property Value

true if the current selection or insertion point has the bullet style applied; otherwise, **false**.

Remarks

If no text is selected, the bullet style is applied to the current insertion point and to all paragraphs that the user enters after the insertion point. The bullet style is applied to the text of the control until the insertion point is moved or when the user presses the Enter key on an empty bullet item.

If text is selected within the control when this property is set, all paragraphs within the selected text are converted into bulleted items in the bulleted list. You can use this property to create bulleted lists within the documents you create in the **RichTextBox** control.

The **BulletIndent** property enables you to specify the amount of indentation to apply between the bullet and the bulleted item's text.

Example

See related example in the **System.Windows.Forms.RichTextBox** class topic.

Requirements

Platforms: Windows 98, Windows NT 4.0, Windows Millennium Edition, Windows 2000, Windows XP Home Edition, Windows XP Professional, Windows Server 2003 family

RichTextBox.SelectionCharOffset Property

Gets or sets whether text in the control appears on the baseline, as a superscript, or as a subscript below the baseline.

```
[Visual Basic]
Public Property SelectionCharOffset As Integer
[C#]
public int SelectionCharOffset {get; set;}
[C++]
public: __property int get_SelectionCharOffset();
public: __property void set_SelectionCharOffset(int);
[JScript]
public function get SelectionCharOffset() : int;
public function set SelectionCharOffset(int);
```

Property Value

A number that specifies the character offset.

Exceptions

Exception Type	Condition
ArgumentException	The specified value was less than -2000 or greater than 2000.

Remarks

The value of this property must be between -2000 and 2000.

If this property is set to zero, the text appears on the baseline. If it is a positive number, the number specifies the number of pixels by which to raise the text selection above the baseline. If it is a negative number, this number specifies the number of pixels by which to subscript the text selection. You can use this property to specify text as superscript or subscript.

If no text is selected, the offset is applied to the current insertion point and to all text that the user types after the insertion point. The character offset applies until the property is changed to a different value or until the insertion point is moved to a different section within the control.

If text is selected within the control, the selected text and any text entered after the text selection will have the value of this property applied to it. You can use this property to create superscript and subscript text for such applications as mathematical expressions.

Example

See related example in the **System.Windows.Forms.RichTextBox** class topic.

Requirements

Platforms: Windows 98, Windows NT 4.0, Windows Millennium Edition, Windows 2000, Windows XP Home Edition, Windows XP Professional, Windows Server 2003 family

RichTextBox.SelectionColor Property

Gets or sets the text color of the current text selection or insertion point.

```
[Visual Basic]
Public Property SelectionColor As Color
[C#]
public Color SelectionColor {get; set;}
[C++]
public: __property Color get_SelectionColor();
public: __property void set_SelectionColor(Color);
[JScript]
public function get SelectionColor() : Color;
public function set SelectionColor(Color);
```

Property Value

A **Color** that represents the color to apply to the current text selection or to text entered after the insertion point.

Remarks

If the current text selection has more than one color specified, this property returns **Color.Empty**. If no text is currently selected, the text color specified in this property is applied to the current insertion point and to all text that is typed into the control after the insertion point. The text color setting applies until the property is changed to a different color or until the insertion point is moved to a different section within the control.

If text is selected within the control, the selected text and any text entered after the text selection will have the value of this property applied to it. You can use this property to change the color of text in the **RichTextBox**.

To make text bold in the control, use the **SelectionFont** property to assign a new font that has the bold font style specified.

Example

See related example in the **System.Windows.Forms.RichTextBox** class topic.

Requirements

Platforms: Windows 98, Windows NT 4.0, Windows Millennium Edition, Windows 2000, Windows XP Home Edition, Windows XP Professional, Windows Server 2003 family

RichTextBox.SelectionFont Property

Gets or sets the font of the current text selection or insertion point.

```
[Visual Basic]
Public Property SelectionFont As Font
[C#]
public Font SelectionFont {get; set;}
[C++]
public: __property Font* get_SelectionFont();
public: __property void set_SelectionFont(Font*);
[JScript]
public function get SelectionFont() : Font;
public function set SelectionFont(Font);
```

Property Value

A **Font** that represents the font to apply to the current text selection or to text entered after the insertion point.

Remarks

If the current text selection has more than one font specified, this property is a null reference (**Nothing** in Visual Basic). If no text is currently selected, the font specified in this property is applied to the current insertion point and to all text that is typed into the control after the insertion point. The font setting applies until the property is changed to a different font or until the insertion point is moved to a different section within the control.

If text is selected within the control, the selected text and any text entered after the text selection will have the value of this property applied to it. You can use this property to change the font style of text in the **RichTextBox**. You can make the text in the control bold, italic, and underlined. You can also change the size of the text and the font applied to the text.

To change the color of the text in the control, use the **SelectionColor** property.

Example

See related example in the **System.Windows.Forms.RichTextBox** class topic.

Requirements

Platforms: Windows 98, Windows NT 4.0, Windows Millennium Edition, Windows 2000, Windows XP Home Edition, Windows XP Professional, Windows Server 2003 family

RichTextBox.SelectionHangingIndent Property

Gets or sets the distance between the left edge of the first line of text in the selected paragraph and the left edge of subsequent lines in the same paragraph.

```
[Visual Basic]
Public Property SelectionHangingIndent As Integer
[C#]
public int SelectionHangingIndent {get; set;}
[C++]
public: __property int get_SelectionHangingIndent();
public: __property void set_SelectionHangingIndent(int);
[JScript]
public function get SelectionHangingIndent() : int;
public function set SelectionHangingIndent(int);
```

Property Value

The distance, in pixels, for the hanging indent applied to the current text selection or the insertion point.

Remarks

If no text is currently selected, the hanging indent is applied to the paragraph in which the insertion point appears and to all text that is typed into the control after the insertion point. The hanging indent setting applies until the property is changed to a different value or until the insertion point is moved to a different paragraph within the control.

If text is selected within the control, the selected text and any text entered after the text selection will have the value of this property applied to it. You can use this property to apply a hanging indent to your paragraphs.

To set the indention of the first line of a paragraph selection, use the **SelectionIndent** property.

Example

See related example in the **System.Windows.Forms.RichTextBox** class topic.

Requirements

Platforms: Windows 98, Windows NT 4.0, Windows Millennium Edition, Windows 2000, Windows XP Home Edition, Windows XP Professional, Windows Server 2003 family

RichTextBox.SelectionIndent Property

Gets or sets the distance in pixels between the left edge of the **RichTextBox** and the left edge of the current text selection or text added after the insertion point.

```
[Visual Basic]
Public Property SelectionIndent As Integer
[C#]
public int SelectionIndent {get; set;}
[C++]
public: __property int get_SelectionIndent();
public: __property void set_SelectionIndent(int);
[JScript]
public function get SelectionIndent() : int;
public function set SelectionIndent(int);
```

Property Value

The current distance, in pixels, of the indentation applied to the left of the current text selection or the insertion point.

Remarks

If no text is currently selected, the indentation setting is applied to the paragraph in which the insertion point appears and to all text that is typed into the control after the insertion point. The indentation setting applies until the property is changed to a different value or until the insertion point is moved to a different paragraph within the control.

If text is selected within the control, the selected text and any text entered after the text selection will have the value of this property applied to it. You can use this property to indent paragraphs contained in document of the **RichTextBox**. You can use this property in conjunction with the **SelectionRightIndent** to create paragraphs displayed in paragraphs.

To create a hanging indent for paragraphs in the control, use the **SelectionHangingIndent** property.

Example

See related example in the **System.Windows.Forms.RichTextBox** class topic.

Requirements

Platforms: Windows 98, Windows NT 4.0, Windows Millennium Edition, Windows 2000, Windows XP Home Edition, Windows XP Professional, Windows Server 2003 family

RichTextBox.SelectionLength Property

Gets or sets the number of characters selected in control.

```
[Visual Basic]
Overrides Public Property SelectionLength As Integer
[C#]
public override int SelectionLength {get; set;}
[C++]
public: __property int get_SelectionLength();
public: __property void set_SelectionLength(int);
[JScript]
public override function get SelectionLength() : int;
public override function set SelectionLength(int);
```

Property Value

The number of characters selected in the text box.

Remarks

You can use this property to determine if any characters are currently selected in the text box control before performing operations on the selected text. You can also use this property to determine the total number of characters (including spaces) that are selected when performing single character tasks in a **for** loop.

Example

See related example in the **System.Windows.Forms.RichTextBox** class topic.

Requirements

Platforms: Windows 98, Windows NT 4.0, Windows Millennium Edition, Windows 2000, Windows XP Home Edition, Windows XP Professional, Windows Server 2003 family

RichTextBox.SelectionProtected Property

Gets or sets a value indicating whether the current text selection is protected.

```
[Visual Basic]
Public Property SelectionProtected As Boolean
[C#]
public bool SelectionProtected {get; set;}
[C++]
public: __property bool get_SelectionProtected();
public: __property void set_SelectionProtected(bool);
[JScript]
public function get SelectionProtected() : Boolean;
public function set SelectionProtected(Boolean);
```

Property Value

true if the current text selection is protected; otherwise, **false**. The default is **false**.

Remarks

If no text is currently selected, the protection setting is applied to the paragraph in which the insertion point appears and to all text that is typed into the control after the insertion point. The protection setting applies until the property is changed to a different value or until the insertion point is moved to a different paragraph within the control.

If text is selected within the control, the selected text and any text entered after the text selection will have the value of this property applied to it. You can use this property to prevent the user from modifying sections of text within the control.

If this property is set to **true**, the **Protected** event is raised when the user attempts to change the current text selection.

> **Note** This property will return **true** only if the entire selection within the control contains protected content.

Example

See related example in the **System.Windows.Forms.RichTextBox** class topic.

Requirements

Platforms: Windows 98, Windows NT 4.0, Windows Millennium Edition, Windows 2000, Windows XP Home Edition, Windows XP Professional, Windows Server 2003 family

RichTextBox.SelectionRightIndent Property

The distance (in pixels) between the right edge of the RichTextBox control and the right edge of the text that is selected or added at the current insertion point.

```
[Visual Basic]
Public Property SelectionRightIndent As Integer
[C#]
public int SelectionRightIndent {get; set;}
[C++]
public: __property int get_SelectionRightIndent();
public: __property void set_SelectionRightIndent(int);
[JScript]
public function get SelectionRightIndent() : int;
public function set SelectionRightIndent(int);
```

Property Value

The indentation space, in pixels, at the right of the current selection or insertion point.

Remarks

If no text is currently selected, the indentation setting is applied to the paragraph in which the insertion point appears and to all text that is typed into the control after the insertion point. The indentation setting applies until the property is changed to a different value or until the insertion point is moved to a different paragraph within the control.

If text is selected within the control, the selected text and any text entered after the text selection will have the value of this property applied to it. You can use this property to indent paragraphs contained in document of the **RichTextBox**. You can use this property in conjunction with the **SelectionIndent** to create paragraphs displayed in paragraphs.

To create a hanging indent for paragraphs in the control, use the **SelectionHangingIndent** property.

Example

See related example in the **System.Windows.Forms.RichTextBox** class topic.

Requirements

Platforms: Windows 98, Windows NT 4.0, Windows Millennium Edition, Windows 2000, Windows XP Home Edition, Windows XP Professional, Windows Server 2003 family

RichTextBox.SelectionTabs Property

Gets or sets the absolute tab stop positions in a **RichTextBox** control.

```
[Visual Basic]
Public Property SelectionTabs As Integer ()
[C#]
public int[] SelectionTabs {get; set;}
[C++]
public: __property int get_SelectionTabs();
public: __property void set_SelectionTabs(int __gc[]);
[JScript]
public function get SelectionTabs() : int[];
public function set SelectionTabs(int[]);
```

Property Value

An array in which each member specifies a tab offset, in pixels.

Exceptions

Exception Type	Condition
ArgumentException	The specified value is less than 0 or greater than 32.

Remarks

This property enables you to obtain an array that contains the spacing for each tab in the current text selection within the **RichTextBox** control. You can then use this property to adjust the size of each tab within the text selection. For example, if you want to adjust the tab space within the document, you can select the entire document and obtain the list of tab spaces using the **SelectionTabs** property. You can then adjust them to new values and reassign them to this property.

Requirements

Platforms: Windows 98, Windows NT 4.0, Windows Millennium Edition, Windows 2000, Windows XP Home Edition, Windows XP Professional, Windows Server 2003 family

RichTextBox.SelectionType Property

Gets the selection type within the control.

```
[Visual Basic]
Public ReadOnly Property SelectionType As RichTextBoxSelectionTypes
[C#]
public RichTextBoxSelectionTypes SelectionType {get;}
[C++]
public: __property RichTextBoxSelectionTypes get_SelectionType();
[JScript]
public function get SelectionType() : RichTextBoxSelectionTypes;
```

Property Value

A bitwise combination of the **RichTextBoxSelectionTypes** values.

Remarks

You can use this property to determine the type of data that is currently selected in the control in order to handle the selection properly when performing tasks within the control on the current selection. The property can represent any combination of values from the **RichTextBoxSelectionTypes** enumeration representing the many types of objects in the current selection.

Requirements

Platforms: Windows 98, Windows NT 4.0, Windows Millennium Edition, Windows 2000, Windows XP Home Edition, Windows XP Professional, Windows Server 2003 family

RichTextBox.ShowSelectionMargin Property

Gets or sets a value indicating whether a selection margin is displayed in the **RichTextBox**.

```
[Visual Basic]
Public Property ShowSelectionMargin As Boolean
[C#]
public bool ShowSelectionMargin {get; set;}
[C++]
public: __property bool get_ShowSelectionMargin();
public: __property void set_ShowSelectionMargin(bool);
[JScript]
public function get ShowSelectionMargin() : Boolean;
public function set ShowSelectionMargin(Boolean);
```

Property Value

true if a selection margin is enabled in the control; otherwise, **false**. The default is **false**.

Remarks

You can use this property to enable the user to easily select lines of text in the **RichTextBox**. The selection margin is added to the left side of the **RichTextBox**. This margin makes it easier for the user to select text starting on the left side of the control. The user can click in the selection margin to select a single line of text or double-click to select the entire paragraph that the line double-clicked is contained within.

Note If the **ShowSelectionMargin** property is set to **true**, setting the **ScrollBars** property to **RichTextBoxScrollBars.Horizontal**, **RichTextBoxScrollBars.Vertical**, or **RichTextBoxScrollBars.Both** will not cause scroll bars to be displayed. In order to display scroll bars while the **ShowSelectionMargin** property is set to **true**, set the **ScrollBars** property to **RichTextBoxScrollBars.ForcedHorizontal**, **RichTextBoxScrollBars.ForcedVertical**, or **RichTextBoxScrollBars.ForcedBoth**.

Requirements

Platforms: Windows 98, Windows NT 4.0, Windows Millennium Edition, Windows 2000, Windows XP Home Edition, Windows XP Professional, Windows Server 2003 family

RichTextBox.Text Property

Gets or sets the current text in the rich text box.

```
[Visual Basic]
Overrides Public Property Text As String
[C#]
public override string Text {get; set;}
[C++]
public: __property String* get_Text();
public: __property void set_Text(String*);
[JScript]
public override function get Text() : String;
public override function set Text(String);
```

Property Value

The text displayed in the control.

Remarks

To display multiple lines of text in a **RichTextBox**, set the **Multiline** property to **true**. To read or set the text of a multiline text box, use the **Lines** property. The **Text** property does not return any information about the formatting applied to the contents of the **RichTextBox**. To get the Rich Text Formatting (RTF) codes, use the **Rtf** property. The amount of text that can be entered in the **RichTextBox** control is limited only by available system memory.

Requirements

Platforms: Windows 98, Windows NT 4.0, Windows Millennium Edition, Windows 2000, Windows XP Home Edition, Windows XP Professional, Windows Server 2003 family

RichTextBox.TextLength Property

This member overrides **TextBoxBase.TextLength**.

```
[Visual Basic]
Overrides Public ReadOnly Property TextLength As Integer
[C#]
public override int TextLength {get;}
[C++]
public: __property int get_TextLength();
[JScript]
public override function get TextLength() : int;
```

Requirements

Platforms: Windows 98, Windows NT 4.0, Windows Millennium Edition, Windows 2000, Windows XP Home Edition, Windows XP Professional, Windows Server 2003 family

RichTextBox.UndoActionName Property

Gets the name of the action that can be undone in the control when the **Undo** method is called.

```
[Visual Basic]
Public ReadOnly Property UndoActionName As String
[C#]
public string UndoActionName {get;}
[C++]
public: __property String* get_UndoActionName();
[JScript]
public function get UndoActionName() : String;
```

Property Value

The text name of the action that can be undone.

Remarks

This property enables you to determine the last action that was done within the control that can be undone. You can use this property to limit the operations available to be undone by the user of the control.

Requirements

Platforms: Windows 98, Windows NT 4.0, Windows Millennium Edition, Windows 2000, Windows XP Home Edition, Windows XP Professional, Windows Server 2003 family

RichTextBox.ZoomFactor Property

Gets or sets the current zoom level of the **RichTextBox**.

```
[Visual Basic]
Public Property ZoomFactor As Single
[C#]
public float ZoomFactor {get; set;}
[C++]
public: __property float get_ZoomFactor();
public: __property void set_ZoomFactor(float);
[JScript]
public function get ZoomFactor() : float;
public function set ZoomFactor(float);
```

Property Value

The factor by which the contents of the control is zoomed.

Exceptions

Exception Type	Condition
ArgumentException	The specified zoom factor did not fall within the permissible range.

Remarks

The value of this property can be between 0.64 and 64.0. A value of 1.0 indicates that no zoom is applied to the control. The zoom feature performs optimally when the document contains TrueType fonts. When a font that is not TrueType is used within the document of the control, the **ZoomFactor** property will use the nearest whole number value. You can use this property to enable the user of the **RichTextBox** control to zoom into sections of the documentation that are too small to view or to condense the view to enable more of the document to be viewed on screen.

Example

See related example in the **System.Windows.Forms.RichTextBox** class topic.

Requirements

Platforms: Windows 98, Windows NT 4.0, Windows Millennium Edition, Windows 2000, Windows XP Home Edition, Windows XP Professional, Windows Server 2003 family

RichTextBox.CanPaste Method

Determines whether you can paste information from the Clipboard in the specified data format.

```
[Visual Basic]
Public Function CanPaste( _
   ByVal clipFormat As DataFormats.Format _
) As Boolean
[C#]
public bool CanPaste(
   DataFormats.Format clipFormat
);
[C++]
public: bool CanPaste(
   DataFormats.Format* clipFormat
);
[JScript]
public function CanPaste(
   clipFormat : DataFormats.Format
) : Boolean;
```

Parameters

clipFormat

One of the **System.Windows.Forms.DataFormats.Format** values.

Return Value

true if you can paste data from the Clipboard in the specified data format; otherwise, **false**.

Remarks

You can use this method to determine whether the current contents of the Clipboard are in a specified Clipboard data format before allowing the user to paste the information into the **RichTextBox** control. For example, you could create an event handler for a **Popup** event of a paste command **MenuItem** and use this method to determine whether the paste **MenuItem** should be enabled based on the type of data in the Clipboard.

Example

See related example in the **System.Windows.Forms.RichTextBox** class topic.

Requirements

Platforms: Windows 98, Windows NT 4.0, Windows Millennium Edition, Windows 2000, Windows XP Home Edition, Windows XP Professional, Windows Server 2003 family

RichTextBox.CreateRichEditOleCallback Method

Creates an **IRichEditOleCallback** compatible object for handling RichEdit callback operations.

[Visual Basic]
```
Protected Overridable Function CreateRichEditOleCallback() As Object
```
[C#]
```
protected virtual object CreateRichEditOleCallback();
```
[C++]
```
protected: virtual Object* CreateRichEditOleCallback();
```
[JScript]
```
protected function CreateRichEditOleCallback() : Object;
```

Return Value

An object that implements the **IRichEditOleCallback** interface.

Remarks

Notes to Inheritors: You can override this method in your derived class to allow access to the underlying RichEdit features. If you override this method, all drag-and-drop events will not be raised. You will have to provide your own support for drag-and-drop as a result. For more information on the **IRichEditOleCallback** interface, refer to the MSDN documentation in the Platform SDK reference.

Requirements

Platforms: Windows 98, Windows NT 4.0, Windows Millennium Edition, Windows 2000, Windows XP Home Edition, Windows XP Professional, Windows Server 2003 family

RichTextBox.Find Method

Searches for text within the contents of the **RichTextBox**.

Overload List

Searches the text of a **RichTextBox** control for the first instance of a character from a list of characters.

[Visual Basic] **Overloads Public Function Find(Char()) As Integer**

[C#] **public int Find(char[]);**

[C++] **public: int Find(__wchar_t __gc[]);**

[JScript] **public function Find(Char[]) : int;**

Searches the text in a **RichTextBox** control for a string.

[Visual Basic] **Overloads Public Function Find(String) As Integer**

[C#] **public int Find(string);**

[C++] **public: int Find(String*);**

[JScript] **public function Find(String) : int;**

Searches the text of a **RichTextBox** control, at a specific starting point, for the first instance of a character from a list of characters.

[Visual Basic] **Overloads Public Function Find(Char(), Integer) As Integer**

[C#] **public int Find(char[], int);**

[C++] **public: int Find(__wchar_t __gc[], int);**

[JScript] **public function Find(Char[], int) : int;**

Searches the text in a **RichTextBox** control for a string with specific options applied to the search.

[Visual Basic] **Overloads Public Function Find(String, RichTextBoxFinds) As Integer**

[C#] **public int Find(string, RichTextBoxFinds);**

[C++] **public: int Find(String*, RichTextBoxFinds);**

[JScript] **public function Find(String, RichTextBoxFinds) : int;**

Searches a range of text in a **RichTextBox** control for the first instance of a character from a list of characters.

[Visual Basic] **Overloads Public Function Find(Char(), Integer, Integer) As Integer**

[C#] **public int Find(char[], int, int);**

[C++] **public: int Find(__wchar_t __gc[], int, int);**

[JScript] **public function Find(Char[], int, int) : int;**

Searches the text in a **RichTextBox** control for a string at a specific location within the control and with specific options applied to the search.

[Visual Basic] **Overloads Public Function Find(String, Integer, RichTextBoxFinds) As Integer**

[C#] **public int Find(string, int, RichTextBoxFinds);**

[C++] **public: int Find(String*, int, RichTextBoxFinds);**

[JScript] **public function Find(String, int, RichTextBoxFinds) : int;**

Searches the text in a **RichTextBox** control for a string within a range of text within the control and with specific options applied to the search.

[Visual Basic] **Overloads Public Function Find(String, Integer, Integer, RichTextBoxFinds) As Integer**

[C#] **public int Find(string, int, int, RichTextBoxFinds);**

[C++] **public: int Find(String*, int, int, RichTextBoxFinds);**

[JScript] **public function Find(String, int, int, RichTextBoxFinds) : int;**

Example

See related example in the **System.Windows.Forms.RichTextBox** class topic.

RichTextBox.Find Method (Char[])

Searches the text of a **RichTextBox** control for the first instance of a character from a list of characters.

[Visual Basic]
```
Overloads Public Function Find( _
   ByVal characterSet() As Char _
) As Integer
```
[C#]
```
public int Find(
   char[] characterSet
);
```
[C++]
```
public: int Find(
   __wchar_t characterSet __gc[]
);
```
[JScript]
```
public function Find(
   characterSet : Char[]
) : int;
```

Parameters

characterSet

The array of characters to search for.

Return Value

The location within the control where the search characters were found or a negative one (-1) if the search characters are not found or an empty search character set is specified in the *char* parameter.

Remarks

This version of the **Find** method searches for the first instance of a character from a list of characters specified in the *characterSet* parameter and returns the location of the character. For example, you pass an array of characters containing the character 'Q'. If the control contained the text "The Quick Brown Fox", the **Find** method would return the value of four. An upper case character and a lower case character are considered different values in the search.

If the property returns a negative value, the characters being searched for were not found within the contents of the control. You can use this method to search for a group of characters within the control. This version of the **Find** method assumes that the entire document contained in the control is searched for the characters. If a character from the character list provided in the method's *characterSet* parameter is found, the value returned by this method is a zero-based index of the character's position in the control. A space is considered a character by the method when determining the location of a character.

Example

See related example in the **System.Windows.Forms.RichTextBox** class topic.

Requirements

Platforms: Windows 98, Windows NT 4.0, Windows Millennium Edition, Windows 2000, Windows XP Home Edition, Windows XP Professional, Windows Server 2003 family

RichTextBox.Find Method (String)

Searches the text in a **RichTextBox** control for a string.

```
[Visual Basic]
Overloads Public Function Find( _
   ByVal str As String _
) As Integer
[C#]
public int Find(
   string str
);
[C++]
public: int Find(
   String* str
);
[JScript]
public function Find(
   str : String
) : int;
```

Parameters

str

The text to locate in the control.

Return Value

The location within the control where the search text was found or a negative one (-1) if the search string is not found or an empty search string is specified in the *str* parameter.

Remarks

The **Find** method searches for the text specified in the *str* parameter and returns the location of the first character within the control. If the property returns a negative value, the text string being searched for was not found within the contents of the control. You can use this method to create search functionality that can be provided to the user of the control. You can also use this method to search for text to be replaced with a specific format. For example, if the user entered dates into the control, you could use the **Find** method to search for all dates in the document and replace them with the appropriate format before using the **SaveFile** method of the control.

> **Note** The **Find** methods that accept a **string** as a parameter cannot find text that is contained on more than one line of text within the **RichTextBox**. Performing such a search will return a value of negative one (-1).

Example

See related example in the **System.Windows.Forms.RichTextBox** class topic.

Requirements

Platforms: Windows 98, Windows NT 4.0, Windows Millennium Edition, Windows 2000, Windows XP Home Edition, Windows XP Professional, Windows Server 2003 family

RichTextBox.Find Method (Char[], Int32)

Searches the text of a **RichTextBox** control, at a specific starting point, for the first instance of a character from a list of characters.

```
[Visual Basic]
Overloads Public Function Find( _
   ByVal characterSet() As Char, _
   ByVal start As Integer _
) As Integer
[C#]
public int Find(
   char[] characterSet,
   int start
);
[C++]
public: int Find(
   __wchar_t characterSet __gc[],
   int start
);
[JScript]
public function Find(
   characterSet : Char[],
   start : int
) : int;
```

Parameters

characterSet

The array of characters to search for.

start

The location within the control's text at which to begin searching.

Return Value

The location within the control where the search characters are found.

Remarks

This version of the **Find** method searches for the first instance of a character from a list of characters specified in the *characterSet* parameter and returns the location the character. For example, you pass an array of characters containing the character 'Q'. If the control contained the text "The Quick Brown Fox", the **Find** method would return the value of four. An upper case character and a lower case character are considered different values in the search.

If the property returns a negative value, the characters being searched for were not found within the contents of the control. You can use this method to search for a group of characters within the control. If a character from the character list provided in the method's *characterSet* parameter is found, the value returned by this method is a zero-based index of the character's position in the control. A space is considered a character by the method when determining the location of a character.

This version of the **Find** method enables you to search for a character set from a specified start position within the text of the control by specifying a value for the *start* parameter. A value of zero indicates that the search should start from the beginning of the control's document. You can use this version of the **Find** method to narrow your search to avoid text that you already know does not contain the specified characters you are searching for or are not important in your search.

Example

See related example in the **System.Windows.Forms.RichTextBox** class topic.

Requirements

Platforms: Windows 98, Windows NT 4.0, Windows Millennium Edition, Windows 2000, Windows XP Home Edition, Windows XP Professional, Windows Server 2003 family

RichTextBox.Find Method (String, RichTextBoxFinds)

Searches the text in a **RichTextBox** control for a string with specific options applied to the search.

```
[Visual Basic]
Overloads Public Function Find( _
   ByVal str As String, _
   ByVal options As RichTextBoxFinds _
) As Integer
[C#]
public int Find(
   string str,
   RichTextBoxFinds options
);
[C++]
public: int Find(
   String* str,
   RichTextBoxFinds options
);
[JScript]
public function Find(
   str : String,
   options : RichTextBoxFinds
) : int;
```

Parameters

str

The text to locate in the control.

options

A bitwise combination of the **RichTextBoxFinds** values.

Return Value

The location within the control where the search text was found.

Remarks

The **Find** method searches for the text specified in the *str* parameter and returns the location of the first character within the control. If the property returns a negative value, the text string being searched for was not found within the contents of the control. You can use this method to create search functionality that can be provided to the user of the control. You can also use this method to search for text to be replaced with a specific format. For example, if the user entered dates into the control, you can use the **Find** method to search for all dates in the document and replace them with the appropriate format before using the **SaveFile** method of the control.

With this version of the **Find** method, you can specify options that enable you to expand or narrow your search. You can specify options that enable you to match the casing of the search word or to search for entire words instead of partial words. By specifying the **RichTextBoxFinds.Reverse** enumeration in the *options* parameter, you can search for text from the bottom of the document to the top instead of the default top to bottom search method.

> **Note** The **Find** methods that accept a **string** as a parameter cannot find text that is contained on more than one line of text within the **RichTextBox**. Performing such a search will return a value of negative one (-1).

Example

See related example in the **System.Windows.Forms.RichTextBox** class topic.

Requirements

Platforms: Windows 98, Windows NT 4.0, Windows Millennium Edition, Windows 2000, Windows XP Home Edition, Windows XP Professional, Windows Server 2003 family

RichTextBox.Find Method (Char[], Int32, Int32)

Searches a range of text in a **RichTextBox** control for the first instance of a character from a list of characters.

```
[Visual Basic]
Overloads Public Function Find( _
   ByVal characterSet() As Char, _
   ByVal start As Integer, _
   ByVal end As Integer _
) As Integer
[C#]
public int Find(
   char[] characterSet,
   int start,
   int end
);
[C++]
public: int Find(
   __wchar_t characterSet __gc[],
   int start,
   int end
);
```

[JScript]
```
public function Find(
   characterSet : Char[],
   start : int,
   end : int
) : int;
```

Parameters

characterSet
The array of characters to search for.

start
The location within the control's text at which to begin searching.

end
The location within the control's text at which to end searching.

Return Value

The location within the control where the search characters are found.

Exceptions

Exception Type	Condition
ArgumentNull-Exception	*characterSet* is null.
ArgumentException	*start* is less than 0 or greater than the length of the text in the control.

Remarks

This version of the **Find** method searches for the first instance of a character from a list of characters specified in the *characterSet* parameter and returns the location of the character. For example, you pass an array of characters containing the character 'Q'. If the control contained the text "The Quick Brown Fox", the **Find** method would return the value of four. An upper case character and a lower case character are considered different values in the search.

If the property returns a negative value, the characters being searched for were not found within the contents of the control. You can use this method to search for a group of characters within the control. If a character from the character list provided in the method's *characterSet* parameter is found, the value returned by this method is a zero based index of the character's position in the control. A space is considered a character by the method when determining the location of a character.

This version of the **Find** method enables you to search for a character set from a range of text in the control by specifying a value for the *start* and *end* parameters. A value of zero for the *start* parameter indicates that the search should start from the beginning of the control's document. A -1 value for the *end* parameter indicates that the search should end at the end of the text within the control. You can use this version of the **Find** method to narrow your search to a specific range of text within the control to avoid searching areas of the document that are not important to the needs of your application.

Requirements

Platforms: Windows 98, Windows NT 4.0, Windows Millennium Edition, Windows 2000, Windows XP Home Edition, Windows XP Professional, Windows Server 2003 family

RichTextBox.Find Method (String, Int32, RichTextBoxFinds)

Searches the text in a **RichTextBox** control for a string at a specific location within the control and with specific options applied to the search.

[Visual Basic]
```
Overloads Public Function Find( _
   ByVal str As String, _
   ByVal start As Integer, _
   ByVal options As RichTextBoxFinds _
) As Integer
```
[C#]
```
public int Find(
   string str,
   int start,
   RichTextBoxFinds options
);
```
[C++]
```
public: int Find(
   String* str,
   int start,
   RichTextBoxFinds options
);
```
[JScript]
```
public function Find(
   str : String,
   start : int,
   options : RichTextBoxFinds
) : int;
```

Parameters

str
The text to locate in the control.

start
The location within the control's text at which to begin searching.

options
A bitwise combination of the **RichTextBoxFinds** values.

Return Value

The location within the control where the search text was found.

Remarks

The **Find** method searches for the text specified in the *str* parameter and returns the location of the first character of the search string within the control. If the property returns a negative value, the text string being searched for was not found within the contents of the control. You can use this method to create search functionality that can be provided to the user of the control. You can also use this method to search for text to be replaced with a specific format. For example, if the user entered dates into the control, you could use the **Find** method to search for all dates in the document and replace them with the appropriate format before using the **SaveFile** method of the control.

With this version of the **Find** method, you can specify options that enable you to expand or narrow your search. You can specify options that enable you to match the casing of the search word or to search for entire words instead of partial words. By specifying the **RichTextBoxFinds.Reverse** enumeration in the *options* parameter, you can search for text from the bottom of the document to the top instead of the default top to bottom search method. This version of the **Find** method also enables you to narrow the search for text by selecting a specific starting position within the control's text. This feature can enable you to avoid text that might have already been searched or where the specific text you are searching for is known not to exist. When the **RichTextBoxFinds.Reverse** value is specified in the *options* parameter, the value of the *start* parameter indicates the position where the reverse search will end since the search will start at the bottom of the document when using this version of the **Find** method.

> **Note** The **Find** methods that accept a **string** as a parameter cannot find text that is contained on more than one line of text within the **RichTextBox**. Performing such a search will return a value of negative one (-1).

Example

See related example in the **System.Windows.Forms.RichTextBox** class topic.

Requirements

Platforms: Windows 98, Windows NT 4.0, Windows Millennium Edition, Windows 2000, Windows XP Home Edition, Windows XP Professional, Windows Server 2003 family

RichTextBox.Find Method (String, Int32, Int32, RichTextBoxFinds)

Searches the text in a **RichTextBox** control for a string within a range of text within the control and with specific options applied to the search.

```
[Visual Basic]
Overloads Public Function Find( _
   ByVal str As String, _
   ByVal start As Integer, _
   ByVal end As Integer, _
   ByVal options As RichTextBoxFinds _
) As Integer
[C#]
public int Find(
   string str,
   int start,
   int end,
   RichTextBoxFinds options
);
[C++]
public: int Find(
   String* str,
   int start,
   int end,
   RichTextBoxFinds options
);
[JScript]
public function Find(
   str : String,
   start : int,
   end : int,
   options : RichTextBoxFinds
) : int;
```

Parameters

str

The text to locate in the control.

start

The location within the control's text at which to begin searching.

end

The location within the control's text at which to end searching. This value must be equal to negative one (-1) or greater than or equal to the *start* parameter.

options

A bitwise combination of the **RichTextBoxFinds** values.

Return Value

The location within the control where the search text was found.

Exceptions

Exception Type	Condition
ArgumentNull-Exception	The *str* parameter was a null reference (**Nothing** in Visual Basic).
ArgumentException	The *start* parameter was less than zero.
ArgumentException	The *end* parameter was less the *start* parameter.

Remarks

The **Find** method searches for the text specified in the *str* parameter and returns the location of the first character of the search string within the control. If the property returns a negative value, the text string being searched for was not found within the contents of the control. You can use this method to create search functionality that can be provided to the user of the control. You can also use this method to search for text to be replaced with a specific format. For example, if the user entered dates into the control, you can use the **Find** method to search for all dates in the document and replace them with the appropriate format before using the **SaveFile** method of the control.

With this version of the **Find** method, you can specify options that enable you to expand or narrow your search. You can specify options that enable you to match the casing of the search word or to search for entire words instead of partial words. By specifying the **RichTextBoxFinds.Reverse** enumeration in the *options* parameter, you can search for text from the bottom of the document to the top instead of the default top to bottom search method. This version of the **Find** method also enables you to narrow the search for text by selecting a specific start and end position within the control's text. This feature can enable you to limit the search range to a specific section of the control's text. If a value of negative one (-1) is assigned to the *end* parameter, the method will search until the end of the text in the **RichTextBox** for normal searches. For reverse searches, a value of negative one (-1) assigned to the *end* parameter indicates that text will be searched from the end of text (bottom) to the position defined by *start* parameter . When the *start* and *end* parameters are provided the same value the entire control is searched for normal searches. For a reverse search, the entire control is searched but the search begins at the bottom of the document and searches to the top of the document.

> **Note** The **Find** methods that accept a **string** as a parameter cannot find text that is contained on more than one line of text within the **RichTextBox**. Performing such a search will return a value of negative one (-1).

Example

See related example in the **System.Windows.Forms.RichTextBox** class topic.

Requirements

Platforms: Windows 98, Windows NT 4.0, Windows Millennium Edition, Windows 2000, Windows XP Home Edition, Windows XP Professional, Windows Server 2003 family

RichTextBox.GetCharFromPosition Method

Gets the character that is closest to the specified location within the control.

[Visual Basic]
```
Public Function GetCharFromPosition( _
   ByVal pt As Point _
) As Char
```
[C#]
```
public char GetCharFromPosition(
   Point pt
);
```
[C++]
```
public: __wchar_t GetCharFromPosition(
   Point pt
);
```
[JScript]
```
public function GetCharFromPosition(
   pt : Point
) : Char;
```

Parameters

pt
The location from which to seek the nearest character.

Return Value

The character at the specified location.

Remarks

If the location specified in the *pt* parameter is outside the client area of the control, the first character of the string closest to the point specified in *pt* is returned. You can use this method to determine which characters are located near a specific point within the control. You can then use this value to perform operations on the text at that location.

> **Note** If the specified location in the *pt* parameter is located on the right side of the client area of the control, the last character of the string closest to the point specified in *pt* is returned.

Example

See related example in the **System.Windows.Forms.RichTextBox** class topic.

Requirements

Platforms: Windows 98, Windows NT 4.0, Windows Millennium Edition, Windows 2000, Windows XP Home Edition, Windows XP Professional, Windows Server 2003 family

RichTextBox.GetCharIndexFromPosition Method

Gets the index of the character nearest to the specified location.

[Visual Basic]
```
Public Function GetCharIndexFromPosition( _
   ByVal pt As Point _
) As Integer
```
[C#]
```
public int GetCharIndexFromPosition(
   Point pt
);
```
[C++]
```
public: int GetCharIndexFromPosition(
   Point pt
);
```
[JScript]
```
public function GetCharIndexFromPosition(
   pt : Point
) : int;
```

Parameters

pt
The location to search.

Return Value

The zero-based character index at the specified location.

Remarks

This method returns the character index that is closest to the position specified in the *pt* parameter. The character index is a zero-based index of text in the control, including spaces. You can use this method to determine where in the text the user has the mouse over by passing the mouse coordinates to this method. This can be useful if you want to perform tasks when the user hovers the mouse pointer over a word in the text of the control.

Example

See related example in the **System.Windows.Forms.RichTextBox** class topic.

Requirements

Platforms: Windows 98, Windows NT 4.0, Windows Millennium Edition, Windows 2000, Windows XP Home Edition, Windows XP Professional, Windows Server 2003 family

RichTextBox.GetLineFromCharIndex Method

Gets the line number from the specified character position within the text of the **RichTextBox** control.

[Visual Basic]
```
Public Function GetLineFromCharIndex( _
   ByVal index As Integer _
) As Integer
```
[C#]
```
public int GetLineFromCharIndex(
   int index
);
```
[C++]
```
public: int GetLineFromCharIndex(
   int index
);
```
[JScript]
```
public function GetLineFromCharIndex(
   index : int
) : int;
```

Parameters

index
The character index position to search.

Return Value

The zero-based line number where the character index is located in.

Remarks

This method enables you to determine the line number based on the character index specified in the *index* parameter of the method. The first line of text in the control returns the value zero. The **GetLineFromCharIndex** method returns the physical line number where the indexed character is located within the control. For example, if a portion of the first logical line of text in the control wraps to the next line, the **GetLineFromCharIndex** method returns 1 if the character at the specified character index has wrapped to the second physical line. If **WordWrap** is set to **false**, no portion of the line wraps to the next, and the method returns 0 for the specified character index. You can use this method to determine which line a specific character index is located within. For example, after calling the **Find** method to search for text, you can obtain the character index to where the search results are found. You can call this method with the character index returned by the **Find** method to determine which line the word was found.

> **Note** If the character index specified in the *index* parameter is beyond the available number of lines contained within the control, the last line number is returned.

Requirements

Platforms: Windows 98, Windows NT 4.0,
Windows Millennium Edition, Windows 2000,
Windows XP Home Edition, Windows XP Professional,
Windows Server 2003 family

RichTextBox.GetPositionFromCharIndex Method

Gets the location within the control at the specified character index.

[Visual Basic]
```
Public Function GetPositionFromCharIndex( _
   ByVal index As Integer _
) As Point
```
[C#]
```
public Point GetPositionFromCharIndex(
   int index
);
```
[C++]
```
public: Point GetPositionFromCharIndex(
   int index
);
```
[JScript]
```
public function GetPositionFromCharIndex(
   index : int
) : Point;
```

Parameters

index
The index of the character for which to retrieve the location.

Return Value

The location of the specified character.

Remarks

This method enables you to determine where in the control a specific character index is located. You can use this method for such tasks as displaying shortcut menu items or help information for a word in the control. For example, if you wanted to display a menu of options to the user when the user right clicks on a word in the control, you can use this method to determine the position of the word to properly display a **ContextMenu** control.

Requirements

Platforms: Windows 98, Windows NT 4.0,
Windows Millennium Edition, Windows 2000,
Windows XP Home Edition, Windows XP Professional,
Windows Server 2003 family

RichTextBox.LoadFile Method

Loads the contents of a file into the **RichTextBox** control.

Overload List

Loads a Rich Text Format (RTF) or standard ASCII text file into the **RichTextBox** control.

[Visual Basic] **Overloads Public Sub LoadFile(String)**

[C#] **public void LoadFile(string);**

[C++] **public: void LoadFile(String*);**

[JScript] **public function LoadFile(String);**

Loads the contents of an existing data stream into the **RichTextBox** control.

[Visual Basic] **Overloads Public Sub LoadFile(Stream, RichTextBoxStreamType)**

[C#] **public void LoadFile(Stream, RichTextBoxStreamType);**

[C++] **public: void LoadFile(Stream*, RichTextBoxStreamType);**

[JScript] **public function LoadFile(Stream, RichTextBoxStreamType);**

Loads a specific type of file into the **RichTextBox** control.

[Visual Basic] **Overloads Public Sub LoadFile(String, RichTextBoxStreamType)**

[C#] **public void LoadFile(string, RichTextBoxStreamType);**

[C++] **public: void LoadFile(String*, RichTextBoxStreamType);**

[JScript] **public function LoadFile(String, RichTextBoxStreamType);**

Example

See related example in the **System.Windows.Forms.RichTextBox** class topic.

RichTextBox.LoadFile Method (String)

Loads a Rich Text Format (RTF) or standard ASCII text file into the **RichTextBox** control.

[Visual Basic]
```
Overloads Public Sub LoadFile( _
   ByVal path As String _
)
```
[C#]
```
public void LoadFile(
   string path
);
```
[C++]
```
public: void LoadFile(
   String* path
);
```

```
[JScript]
public function LoadFile(
   path : String
);
```

Parameters

path
The name and location of the file to load into the control.

Exceptions

Exception Type	Condition
IOException	Occurs when there is an error in loading the file into the control.

Remarks

When loading a file with the **LoadFile** method, the contents of the file being loaded replace the entire contents of the **RichTextBox** control. This will cause the values of the **Text** and **Rtf** properties to change. You can use this method to load a previously created text or RTF document into the control for manipulation. If you want to save the file, you can use the **SaveFile** method.

Note With this version of the **LoadFile** method, if the file being loaded is not an RTF document, an exception will occur. To load a different type of file such as an ASCII text file, use the other versions of this method that accept a value from the **RichTextBoxStreamType** enumeration as a parameter.

Note The **LoadFile** method will not open a file until a handle is created for the **RichTextBox**. Ensure that the control's handle is created before calling the **LoadFile** method.

Example

See related example in the **System.Windows.Forms.RichTextBox** class topic.

Requirements

Platforms: Windows 98, Windows NT 4.0, Windows Millennium Edition, Windows 2000, Windows XP Home Edition, Windows XP Professional, Windows Server 2003 family

.NET Framework Security:

- **FileIOPermission** for opening a file. Associated enumeration: **System.Security.Permissions.FileIoPermissionAccess.Read**.

RichTextBox.LoadFile Method (Stream, RichTextBoxStreamType)

Loads the contents of an existing data stream into the **RichTextBox** control.

```
[Visual Basic]
Overloads Public Sub LoadFile( _
   ByVal data As Stream, _
   ByVal fileType As RichTextBoxStreamType _
)
[C#]
public void LoadFile(
   Stream data,
   RichTextBoxStreamType fileType
);
[C++]
public: void LoadFile(
   Stream* data,
   RichTextBoxStreamType fileType
);
[JScript]
public function LoadFile(
   data : Stream,
   fileType : RichTextBoxStreamType
);
```

Parameters

data
A stream of data to load into the **RichTextBox** control.

fileType
One of the **RichTextBoxStreamType** values.

Exceptions

Exception Type	Condition
ArgumentException	An invalid file type is specified in the *fileType* parameter.
IOException	An error in loading the file into the control.

Remarks

You can use this version of the **LoadFile** method to load the **RichTextBox** with data from an existing stream of data. The data that is loaded into the control replaces the entire contents of the **RichTextBox** control. This will cause the values of the **Text** and **Rtf** properties to change. You can use this method to load a file that has been previously opened into a data stream into the control for manipulation. If you want to save contents of the control back into the stream, you can use the **SaveFile** method that accepts a **Stream** object as a parameter.

This version of the **LoadFile** method also enables you to specify the type of data that is being loaded into the control. This feature enables you to use data streams that contain data other than Rich Text Format (RTF) documents into the control.

Note The **LoadFile** method will not open a file until a handle is created for the **RichTextBox**. Ensure that the control's handle is created before calling the **LoadFile** method.

Requirements

Platforms: Windows 98, Windows NT 4.0, Windows Millennium Edition, Windows 2000, Windows XP Home Edition, Windows XP Professional, Windows Server 2003 family

RichTextBox.LoadFile Method (String, RichTextBoxStreamType)

Loads a specific type of file into the **RichTextBox** control.

```
[Visual Basic]
Overloads Public Sub LoadFile( _
   ByVal path As String, _
   ByVal fileType As RichTextBoxStreamType _
)
[C#]
public void LoadFile(
   string path,
   RichTextBoxStreamType fileType
);
```

```
[C++]
public: void LoadFile(
   String* path,
   RichTextBoxStreamType fileType
);
[JScript]
public function LoadFile(
   path : String,
   fileType : RichTextBoxStreamType
);
```

Parameters

path

The name and location of the file to load into the control.

fileType

One of the **RichTextBoxStreamType** values.

Exceptions

Exception Type	Condition
ArgumentException	An invalid file type is specified in the *fileType* parameter.
IOException	An error in loading the file into the control.

Remarks

When loading a file with the **LoadFile** method, the contents of the file being loaded replace the entire contents of the **RichTextBox** control. This will cause the values of the **Text** and **Rtf** properties to change. You can use this method to load a previously created text or Rich Text Format (RTF) document into the control for manipulation. If you want to save the file, you can use the **SaveFile** method.

You can use this version of the **LoadFile** method to specify the file type of the file being loaded. This feature enables you to load files other than RTF documents into the control.

> **Note** The **LoadFile** method will not open a file until a handle is created for the **RichTextBox**. Ensure that the control's handle is created before calling the **LoadFile** method.

Example

See related example in the **System.Windows.Forms.RichTextBox** class topic.

Requirements

Platforms: Windows 98, Windows NT 4.0, Windows Millennium Edition, Windows 2000, Windows XP Home Edition, Windows XP Professional, Windows Server 2003 family

.NET Framework Security:

- **FileIOPermission** for opening a file. Associated enumeration: **System.Security.Permissions.FileIoPermissionAccess.Read**.

RichTextBox.OnBackColorChanged Method

This member overrides **Control.OnBackColorChanged**.

```
[Visual Basic]
Overrides Protected Sub OnBackColorChanged( _
   ByVal e As EventArgs _
)
[C#]
protected override void OnBackColorChanged(
   EventArgs e
);
[C++]
protected: void OnBackColorChanged(
   EventArgs* e
);
[JScript]
protected override function OnBackColorChanged(
   e : EventArgs
);
```

Requirements

Platforms: Windows 98, Windows NT 4.0, Windows Millennium Edition, Windows 2000, Windows XP Home Edition, Windows XP Professional, Windows Server 2003 family

RichTextBox.OnContentsResized Method

Raises the **ContentsResized** event.

```
[Visual Basic]
Protected Overridable Sub OnContentsResized( _
   ByVal e As ContentsResizedEventArgs _
)
[C#]
protected virtual void OnContentsResized(
   ContentsResizedEventArgs e
);
[C++]
protected: virtual void OnContentsResized(
   ContentsResizedEventArgs* e
);
[JScript]
protected function OnContentsResized(
   e : ContentsResizedEventArgs
);
```

Parameters

e

A **ContentsResizedEventArgs** that contains the event data.

Remarks

Raising an event invokes the event handler through a delegate.

The **OnContentsResized** method also allows derived classes to handle the event without attaching a delegate. This is the preferred technique for handling the event in a derived class.

Notes to Inheritors: When overriding **OnContentsResized** in a derived class, be sure to call the base class's **OnContentsResized** method so that registered delegates receive the event.

Requirements

Platforms: Windows 98, Windows NT 4.0, Windows Millennium Edition, Windows 2000, Windows XP Home Edition, Windows XP Professional, Windows Server 2003 family

RichTextBox.OnContextMenuChanged Method

This member overrides **Control.OnContextMenuChanged**.

```
[Visual Basic]
Overrides Protected Sub OnContextMenuChanged( _
   ByVal e As EventArgs _
)
```

```
[C#]
protected override void OnContextMenuChanged(
   EventArgs e
);
[C++]
protected: void OnContextMenuChanged(
   EventArgs* e
);
[JScript]
protected override function OnContextMenuChanged(
   e : EventArgs
);
```

Requirements

Platforms: Windows 98, Windows NT 4.0, Windows Millennium Edition, Windows 2000, Windows XP Home Edition, Windows XP Professional, Windows Server 2003 family

RichTextBox.OnHandleCreated Method

This member overrides **Control.OnHandleCreated**.

```
[Visual Basic]
Overrides Protected Sub OnHandleCreated( _
   ByVal e As EventArgs _
)
[C#]
protected override void OnHandleCreated(
   EventArgs e
);
[C++]
protected: void OnHandleCreated(
   EventArgs* e
);
[JScript]
protected override function OnHandleCreated(
   e : EventArgs
);
```

Requirements

Platforms: Windows 98, Windows NT 4.0, Windows Millennium Edition, Windows 2000, Windows XP Home Edition, Windows XP Professional, Windows Server 2003 family

RichTextBox.OnHandleDestroyed Method

This member overrides **Control.OnHandleDestroyed**.

```
[Visual Basic]
Overrides Protected Sub OnHandleDestroyed( _
   ByVal e As EventArgs _
)
[C#]
protected override void OnHandleDestroyed(
   EventArgs e
);
[C++]
protected: void OnHandleDestroyed(
   EventArgs* e
);
[JScript]
protected override function OnHandleDestroyed(
   e : EventArgs
);
```

Requirements

Platforms: Windows 98, Windows NT 4.0, Windows Millennium Edition, Windows 2000, Windows XP Home Edition, Windows XP Professional, Windows Server 2003 family

RichTextBox.OnHScroll Method

Raises the **HScroll** event.

```
[Visual Basic]
Protected Overridable Sub OnHScroll( _
   ByVal e As EventArgs _
)
[C#]
protected virtual void OnHScroll(
   EventArgs e
);
[C++]
protected: virtual void OnHScroll(
   EventArgs* e
);
[JScript]
protected function OnHScroll(
   e : EventArgs
);
```

Parameters

e

An **EventArgs** that contains the event data.

Remarks

Raising an event invokes the event handler through a delegate.

The **OnHScroll** method also allows derived classes to handle the event without attaching a delegate. This is the preferred technique for handling the event in a derived class.

Notes to Inheritors: When overriding **OnHScroll** in a derived class, be sure to call the base class's **OnHScroll** method so that registered delegates receive the event.

Requirements

Platforms: Windows 98, Windows NT 4.0, Windows Millennium Edition, Windows 2000, Windows XP Home Edition, Windows XP Professional, Windows Server 2003 family

RichTextBox.OnImeChange Method

Raises the **ImeChange** event.

```
[Visual Basic]
Protected Overridable Sub OnImeChange( _
   ByVal e As EventArgs _
)
[C#]
protected virtual void OnImeChange(
   EventArgs e
);
```

[C++]
```
protected: virtual void OnImeChange(
   EventArgs* e
);
```
[JScript]
```
protected function OnImeChange(
   e : EventArgs
);
```

Parameters

e

An **EventArgs** that contains the event data.

Remarks

Raising an event invokes the event handler through a delegate.

The **OnImeChange** method also allows derived classes to handle the event without attaching a delegate. This is the preferred technique for handling the event in a derived class.

Notes to Inheritors: When overriding **OnImeChange** in a derived class, be sure to call the base class's **OnImeChange** method so that registered delegates receive the event.

Requirements

Platforms: Windows 98, Windows NT 4.0, Windows Millennium Edition, Windows 2000, Windows XP Home Edition, Windows XP Professional, Windows Server 2003 family

RichTextBox.OnLinkClicked Method

Raises the **LinkClicked** event.

[Visual Basic]
```
Protected Overridable Sub OnLinkClicked( _
   ByVal e As LinkClickedEventArgs _
)
```
[C#]
```
protected virtual void OnLinkClicked(
   LinkClickedEventArgs e
);
```
[C++]
```
protected: virtual void OnLinkClicked(
   LinkClickedEventArgs* e
);
```
[JScript]
```
protected function OnLinkClicked(
   e : LinkClickedEventArgs
);
```

Parameters

e

A **LinkClickedEventArgs** that contains the event data.

Remarks

Raising an event invokes the event handler through a delegate.

The **OnLinkClicked** method also allows derived classes to handle the event without attaching a delegate. This is the preferred technique for handling the event in a derived class.

Notes to Inheritors: When overriding **OnLinkClicked** in a derived class, be sure to call the base class's **OnLinkClicked** method so that registered delegates receive the event.

Requirements

Platforms: Windows 98, Windows NT 4.0, Windows Millennium Edition, Windows 2000, Windows XP Home Edition, Windows XP Professional, Windows Server 2003 family

RichTextBox.OnProtected Method

Raises the **Protected** event.

[Visual Basic]
```
Protected Overridable Sub OnProtected( _
   ByVal e As EventArgs _
)
```
[C#]
```
protected virtual void OnProtected(
   EventArgs e
);
```
[C++]
```
protected: virtual void OnProtected(
   EventArgs* e
);
```
[JScript]
```
protected function OnProtected(
   e : EventArgs
);
```

Parameters

e

An **EventArgs** that contains the event data.

Remarks

Raising an event invokes the event handler through a delegate.

The **OnProtected** method also allows derived classes to handle the event without attaching a delegate. This is the preferred technique for handling the event in a derived class.

Notes to Inheritors: When overriding **OnProtected** in a derived class, be sure to call the base class's **OnProtected** method so that registered delegates receive the event.

Requirements

Platforms: Windows 98, Windows NT 4.0, Windows Millennium Edition, Windows 2000, Windows XP Home Edition, Windows XP Professional, Windows Server 2003 family

RichTextBox.OnRightToLeftChanged Method

This member overrides **Control.OnRightToLeftChanged**.

[Visual Basic]
```
Overrides Protected Sub OnRightToLeftChanged( _
   ByVal e As EventArgs _
)
```
[C#]
```
protected override void OnRightToLeftChanged(
   EventArgs e
);
```
[C++]
```
protected: void OnRightToLeftChanged(
   EventArgs* e
);
```

[JScript]
```
protected override function OnRightToLeftChanged(
   e : EventArgs
);
```

Requirements

Platforms: Windows 98, Windows NT 4.0, Windows Millennium Edition, Windows 2000, Windows XP Home Edition, Windows XP Professional, Windows Server 2003 family

RichTextBox.OnSelectionChanged Method

Raises the **SelectionChanged** event.

[Visual Basic]
```
Protected Overridable Sub OnSelectionChanged( _
   ByVal e As EventArgs _
)
```
[C#]
```
protected virtual void OnSelectionChanged(
   EventArgs e
);
```
[C++]
```
protected: virtual void OnSelectionChanged(
   EventArgs* e
);
```
[JScript]
```
protected function OnSelectionChanged(
   e : EventArgs
);
```

Parameters

e

An **EventArgs** that contains the event data.

Remarks

Raising an event invokes the event handler through a delegate.

The **OnSelectionChanged** method also allows derived classes to handle the event without attaching a delegate. This is the preferred technique for handling the event in a derived class.

Notes to Inheritors: When overriding **OnSelectionChanged** in a derived class, be sure to call the base class's **OnSelectionChanged** method so that registered delegates receive the event.

Requirements

Platforms: Windows 98, Windows NT 4.0, Windows Millennium Edition, Windows 2000, Windows XP Home Edition, Windows XP Professional, Windows Server 2003 family

RichTextBox.OnSystemColorsChanged Method

This member overrides **Control.OnSystemColorsChanged**.

[Visual Basic]
```
Overrides Protected Sub OnSystemColorsChanged( _
   ByVal e As EventArgs _
)
```
[C#]
```
protected override void OnSystemColorsChanged(
   EventArgs e
);
```
[C++]
```
protected: void OnSystemColorsChanged(
   EventArgs* e
);
```
[JScript]
```
protected override function OnSystemColorsChanged(
   e : EventArgs
);
```

Requirements

Platforms: Windows 98, Windows NT 4.0, Windows Millennium Edition, Windows 2000, Windows XP Home Edition, Windows XP Professional, Windows Server 2003 family

RichTextBox.OnTextChanged Method

This member overrides **Control.OnTextChanged**.

[Visual Basic]
```
Overrides Protected Sub OnTextChanged( _
   ByVal e As EventArgs _
)
```
[C#]
```
protected override void OnTextChanged(
   EventArgs e
);
```
[C++]
```
protected: void OnTextChanged(
   EventArgs* e
);
```
[JScript]
```
protected override function OnTextChanged(
   e : EventArgs
);
```

Requirements

Platforms: Windows 98, Windows NT 4.0, Windows Millennium Edition, Windows 2000, Windows XP Home Edition, Windows XP Professional, Windows Server 2003 family

RichTextBox.OnVScroll Method

Raises the **VScroll** event.

[Visual Basic]
```
Protected Overridable Sub OnVScroll( _
   ByVal e As EventArgs _
)
```
[C#]
```
protected virtual void OnVScroll(
   EventArgs e
);
```
[C++]
```
protected: virtual void OnVScroll(
   EventArgs* e
);
```
[JScript]
```
protected function OnVScroll(
   e : EventArgs
);
```

Parameters

e

An **EventArgs** that contains the event data.

Remarks

Raising an event invokes the event handler through a delegate.

The **OnVScroll** method also allows derived classes to handle the event without attaching a delegate. This is the preferred technique for handling the event in a derived class.

Notes to Inheritors: When overriding **OnVScroll** in a derived class, be sure to call the base class's **OnVScroll** method so that registered delegates receive the event.

Requirements

Platforms: Windows 98, Windows NT 4.0, Windows Millennium Edition, Windows 2000, Windows XP Home Edition, Windows XP Professional, Windows Server 2003 family

RichTextBox.Paste Method

Pastes the contents of the Clipboard into the control.

Overload List

Pastes the contents of the Clipboard in the specified Clipboard format.

[Visual Basic] **Overloads Public Sub Paste(DataFormats.Format)**

[C#] **public void Paste(DataFormats.Format);**

[C++] **public: void Paste(DataFormats.Format*);**

[JScript] **public function Paste(DataFormats.Format);**

Inherited from **TextBoxBase**.

[Visual Basic] **Overloads Public Sub Paste()**

[C#] **public void Paste();**

[C++] **public: void Paste();**

[JScript] **public function Paste();**

Example

See related example in the **System.Windows.Forms.RichTextBox** class topic.

RichTextBox.Paste Method (DataFormats.Format)

Pastes the contents of the Clipboard in the specified Clipboard format.

```
[Visual Basic]
Overloads Public Sub Paste( _
   ByVal clipFormat As DataFormats.Format _
)
[C#]
public void Paste(
   DataFormats.Format clipFormat
);
[C++]
public: void Paste(
   DataFormats.Format* clipFormat
);
[JScript]
public function Paste(
   clipFormat : DataFormats.Format
);
```

Parameters

clipFormat

The Clipboard format in which the data should be obtained from the Clipboard.

Remarks

You can use this method to paste data from the clipboard into the control. This version of the **Paste** method is different from the **TextBoxBase.Paste** method as it allows you to paste only text in a specified Clipboard format. You can use the **CanPaste** method to determine whether the data within the Clipboard is in the specified Clipboard format. You can then call this version of the **Paste** method to ensure that the paste operation is made with the appropriate data format.

Example

See related example in the **System.Windows.Forms.RichTextBox** class topic.

Requirements

Platforms: Windows 98, Windows NT 4.0, Windows Millennium Edition, Windows 2000, Windows XP Home Edition, Windows XP Professional, Windows Server 2003 family

.NET Framework Security:

- **UIPermission** for reading from the Clipboard. Associated enumeration: **UIPermissionClipboard.AllClipboard**.

RichTextBox.Redo Method

Reapplies the last operation that was undone in the control.

```
[Visual Basic]
Public Sub Redo()
[C#]
public void Redo();
[C++]
public: void Redo();
[JScript]
public function Redo();
```

Remarks

You can then use the **Redo** method to reapply the last undo operation to the control. The **CanRedo** method enables you to determine whether the last operation the user has undone can be reapplied to the control.

Example

See related example in the **System.Windows.Forms.RichTextBox** class topic.

Requirements

Platforms: Windows 98, Windows NT 4.0, Windows Millennium Edition, Windows 2000, Windows XP Home Edition, Windows XP Professional, Windows Server 2003 family

RichTextBox.SaveFile Method

Saves the contents of the **RichTextBox** to a file.

Overload List

Saves the contents of the **RichTextBox** to a Rich Text Format (RTF) file.

[Visual Basic] **Overloads Public Sub SaveFile(String)**

[C#] **public void SaveFile(string);**

[C++] **public: void SaveFile(String*);**

[JScript] **public function SaveFile(String);**

Saves the contents of a **RichTextBox** control to an open data stream.

[Visual Basic] **Overloads Public Sub SaveFile(Stream, RichTextBoxStreamType)**

[C#] **public void SaveFile(Stream, RichTextBoxStreamType);**

[C++] **public: void SaveFile(Stream*, RichTextBoxStreamType);**

[JScript] **public function SaveFile(Stream, RichTextBoxStreamType);**

Saves the contents of the **RichTextBox** to a specific type of file.

[Visual Basic] **Overloads Public Sub SaveFile(String, RichTextBoxStreamType)**

[C#] **public void SaveFile(string, RichTextBoxStreamType);**

[C++] **public: void SaveFile(String*, RichTextBoxStreamType);**

[JScript] **public function SaveFile(String, RichTextBoxStreamType);**

Example

See related example in the **System.Windows.Forms.RichTextBox** class topic.

RichTextBox.SaveFile Method (String)

Saves the contents of the **RichTextBox** to a Rich Text Format (RTF) file.

```
[Visual Basic]
Overloads Public Sub SaveFile( _
   ByVal path As String _
)
[C#]
public void SaveFile(
   string path
);
[C++]
public: void SaveFile(
   String* path
);
[JScript]
public function SaveFile(
   path : String
);
```

Parameters

path
The name and location of the file to save.

Exceptions

Exception Type	Condition
IOException	An error occurs in saving the contents of the control to a file.

Remarks

The **SaveFile** method enables you to save the entire contents of the control to an RTF file that can be used by other programs such as Microsoft Word and Windows WordPad. If the file name that is passed to the *path* parameter already exists at the specified directory, the file will be overwritten without notice. You can use the **LoadFile** method to load the contents of a file into the **RichTextBox**.

Note To save the contents of the control to a different type of file format such as ASCII text, use the other versions of this method that accept a value from the **RichTextBoxStreamType** enumeration as a parameter.

Example

See related example in the **System.Windows.Forms.RichTextBox** class topic.

Requirements

Platforms: Windows 98, Windows NT 4.0, Windows Millennium Edition, Windows 2000, Windows XP Home Edition, Windows XP Professional, Windows Server 2003 family

RichTextBox.SaveFile Method (Stream, RichTextBoxStreamType)

Saves the contents of a **RichTextBox** control to an open data stream.

```
[Visual Basic]
Overloads Public Sub SaveFile( _
   ByVal data As Stream, _
   ByVal fileType As RichTextBoxStreamType _
)
[C#]
public void SaveFile(
   Stream data,
   RichTextBoxStreamType fileType
);
[C++]
public: void SaveFile(
   Stream* data,
   RichTextBoxStreamType fileType
);
[JScript]
public function SaveFile(
   data : Stream,
   fileType : RichTextBoxStreamType
);
```

Parameters

data
The data stream that contains the file to save to.

fileType
One of the **RichTextBoxStreamType** values.

Exceptions

Exception Type	Condition
ArgumentException	An invalid file type is specified in the *fileType* parameter.
IOException	An error occurs in saving the contents of the control to a file.

Remarks

This version of the **SaveFile** method enables you to save the entire contents of the control to the data stream that is already opened. The data stream can then save the information to a file. You can use the **LoadFile** method to load the contents of a file into the **RichTextBox**.

This version of the **SaveFile** method also enables you to specify a data format of the information that will be sent to the **Stream** object.

Requirements

Platforms: Windows 98, Windows NT 4.0, Windows Millennium Edition, Windows 2000, Windows XP Home Edition, Windows XP Professional, Windows Server 2003 family

.NET Framework Security:

- **FileIOPermission** for creating or modifying a file. Associated enumeration: **System.Security.Permissions.FileIoPermissionAccess.Write**.

RichTextBox.SaveFile Method (String, RichTextBoxStreamType)

Saves the contents of the **RichTextBox** to a specific type of file.

```
[Visual Basic]
Overloads Public Sub SaveFile( _
   ByVal path As String, _
   ByVal fileType As RichTextBoxStreamType _
)
[C#]
public void SaveFile(
   string path,
   RichTextBoxStreamType fileType
);
[C++]
public: void SaveFile(
   String* path,
   RichTextBoxStreamType fileType
);
[JScript]
public function SaveFile(
   path : String,
   fileType : RichTextBoxStreamType
);
```

Parameters

path

The name and location of the file to save.

fileType

One of the **RichTextBoxStreamType** values.

Exceptions

Exception Type	Condition
ArgumentException	An invalid file type is specified in the *fileType* parameter.
IOException	An error occurs in saving the contents of the control to a file.

Remarks

The **SaveFile** method enables you to save the entire contents of the control to an RTF file that can be used by other programs such as Microsoft Word and Windows WordPad. If the file name that is passed to the *path* parameter already exists at the specified directory, the file will be overwritten without notice. You can use the **LoadFile** method to load the contents of a file into the **RichTextBox**.

This version of the **SaveFile** method enables you to specify a file type to save the contents of the control to. You can use this feature to ensure that the file is saved in the proper format based on the contents of the control. For example, if your document has no differences in font style or coloring, you can save the file as an ASCII text file by setting the *fileType* parameter to **RichTextBoxStreamType.PlainText**.

Example

See related example in the **System.Windows.Forms.RichTextBox** class topic.

Requirements

Platforms: Windows 98, Windows NT 4.0, Windows Millennium Edition, Windows 2000, Windows XP Home Edition, Windows XP Professional, Windows Server 2003 family

.NET Framework Security:

- **FileIOPermission** for creating or modifying a file. Associated enumeration: **System.Security.Permissions.FileIoPermissionAccess.Write**.

RichTextBox.WndProc Method

This member overrides **Control.WndProc**.

```
[Visual Basic]
Overrides Protected Sub WndProc( _
   ByRef m As Message _
)
[C#]
protected override void WndProc(
   ref Message m
);
[C++]
protected: void WndProc(
   Message* m
);
[JScript]
protected override function WndProc(
   m : Message
);
```

Requirements

Platforms: Windows 98, Windows NT 4.0, Windows Millennium Edition, Windows 2000, Windows XP Home Edition, Windows XP Professional, Windows Server 2003 family

RichTextBox.BackgroundImageChanged Event

This member supports the .NET Framework infrastructure and is not intended to be used directly from your code.

```
[Visual Basic]
Public Shadows Event BackgroundImageChanged As EventHandler
[C#]
public new event EventHandler BackgroundImageChanged;
[C++]
public: __event EventHandler* BackgroundImageChanged;
```

[JScript] In JScript, you can handle the events defined by a class, but you cannot define your own.

RichTextBox.ContentsResized Event

Occurs when contents within the control are resized.

```
[Visual Basic]
Public Event ContentsResized As ContentsResizedEventHandler
[C#]
public event ContentsResizedEventHandler ContentsResized;
[C++]
public: __event ContentsResizedEventHandler* ContentsResized;
```

[JScript] In JScript, you can handle the events defined by a class, but you cannot define your own.

Event Data

The event handler receives an argument of type **ContentsResized-EventArgs** containing data related to this event. The following **ContentsResizedEventArgs** property provides information specific to this event.

Property	Description
NewRectangle	Represents the requested size of the **RichTextBox** control.

Requirements

Platforms: Windows 98, Windows NT 4.0, Windows Millennium Edition, Windows 2000, Windows XP Home Edition, Windows XP Professional, Windows Server 2003 family

RichTextBox.DoubleClick Event

This member supports the .NET Framework infrastructure and is not intended to be used directly from your code.

```
[Visual Basic]
Public Shadows Event DoubleClick As EventHandler
[C#]
public new event EventHandler DoubleClick;
[C++]
public: __event EventHandler* DoubleClick;
```

[JScript] In JScript, you can handle the events defined by a class, but you cannot define your own.

RichTextBox.DragDrop Event

This member supports the .NET Framework infrastructure and is not intended to be used directly from your code.

```
[Visual Basic]
Public Shadows Event DragDrop As DragEventHandler
[C#]
public new event DragEventHandler DragDrop;
[C++]
public: __event DragEventHandler* DragDrop;
```

[JScript] In JScript, you can handle the events defined by a class, but you cannot define your own.

RichTextBox.DragEnter Event

This member supports the .NET Framework infrastructure and is not intended to be used directly from your code.

```
[Visual Basic]
Public Shadows Event DragEnter As DragEventHandler
[C#]
public new event DragEventHandler DragEnter;
[C++]
public: __event DragEventHandler* DragEnter;
```

[JScript] In JScript, you can handle the events defined by a class, but you cannot define your own.

RichTextBox.DragLeave Event

This member supports the .NET Framework infrastructure and is not intended to be used directly from your code.

```
[Visual Basic]
Public Shadows Event DragLeave As EventHandler
[C#]
public new event EventHandler DragLeave;
[C++]
public: __event EventHandler* DragLeave;
```

[JScript] In JScript, you can handle the events defined by a class, but you cannot define your own.

RichTextBox.DragOver Event

This member supports the .NET Framework infrastructure and is not intended to be used directly from your code.

```
[Visual Basic]
Public Shadows Event DragOver As DragEventHandler
[C#]
public new event DragEventHandler DragOver;
[C++]
public: __event DragEventHandler* DragOver;
```

[JScript] In JScript, you can handle the events defined by a class, but you cannot define your own.

RichTextBox.GiveFeedback Event

This member supports the .NET Framework infrastructure and is not intended to be used directly from your code.

```
[Visual Basic]
Public Shadows Event GiveFeedback As GiveFeedbackEventHandler
[C#]
public new event GiveFeedbackEventHandler GiveFeedback;
[C++]
public: __event GiveFeedbackEventHandler* GiveFeedback;
```

[JScript] In JScript, you can handle the events defined by a class, but you cannot define your own.

RichTextBox.HScroll Event

Occurs when the user clicks the horizontal scroll bar of the control.

[Visual Basic]
```
Public Event HScroll As EventHandler
```
[C#]
```
public event EventHandler HScroll;
```
[C++]
```
public: __event EventHandler* HScroll;
```

[JScript] In JScript, you can handle the events defined by a class, but you cannot define your own.

Event Data

The event handler receives an argument of type **EventArgs**.

Remarks

For more information about handling events, see **Consuming Events**.

Requirements

Platforms: Windows 98, Windows NT 4.0, Windows Millennium Edition, Windows 2000, Windows XP Home Edition, Windows XP Professional, Windows Server 2003 family

RichTextBox.ImeChange Event

Occurs when the user switches input methods on an Asian version of the Windows operating system.

[Visual Basic]
```
Public Event ImeChange As EventHandler
```
[C#]
```
public event EventHandler ImeChange;
```
[C++]
```
public: __event EventHandler* ImeChange;
```

[JScript] In JScript, you can handle the events defined by a class, but you cannot define your own.

Event Data

The event handler receives an argument of type **EventArgs**.

Remarks

For more information about handling events, see **Consuming Events**.

Requirements

Platforms: Windows 98, Windows NT 4.0, Windows Millennium Edition, Windows 2000, Windows XP Home Edition, Windows XP Professional, Windows Server 2003 family

RichTextBox.LinkClicked Event

Occurs when the user clicks on a link within the text of the control.

[Visual Basic]
```
Public Event LinkClicked As LinkClickedEventHandler
```
[C#]
```
public event LinkClickedEventHandler LinkClicked;
```
[C++]
```
public: __event LinkClickedEventHandler* LinkClicked;
```

[JScript] In JScript, you can handle the events defined by a class, but you cannot define your own.

Event Data

The event handler receives an argument of type **LinkClickedEventArgs** containing data related to this event. The following **LinkClickedEventArgs** property provides information specific to this event.

Property	Description
LinkText	Gets the text of the link being clicked.

Remarks

You can create an event handler for this event to process a link that has been clicked within the control. Using the information provided to the event handler, you can determine which link was clicked in the document.

Example

See related example in the **System.Windows.Forms.RichTextBox** class topic.

Requirements

Platforms: Windows 98, Windows NT 4.0, Windows Millennium Edition, Windows 2000, Windows XP Home Edition, Windows XP Professional, Windows Server 2003 family

RichTextBox.Protected Event

Occurs when the user attempts to modify protected text in the control.

[Visual Basic]
```
Public Event Protected As EventHandler
```
[C#]
```
public event EventHandler Protected;
```
[C++]
```
public: __event EventHandler* Protected;
```

[JScript] In JScript, you can handle the events defined by a class, but you cannot define your own.

Event Data

The event handler receives an argument of type **EventArgs**.

Remarks

You can create an event handler for this event in your applications to determine when the user has attempted to modify text that has been marked as protected in the control. The event handler can be used to notify the user that the text the user is attempting to modify is protected or to display a dialog box that enables the user to make appropriate changes to the text. For example, if the protected area is a date, you can display a dialog box that enables the user to choose a date which can then be applied to the text of the control.

Requirements

Platforms: Windows 98, Windows NT 4.0, Windows Millennium Edition, Windows 2000, Windows XP Home Edition, Windows XP Professional, Windows Server 2003 family

RichTextBox.QueryContinueDrag Event

This member supports the .NET Framework infrastructure and is not intended to be used directly from your code.

[Visual Basic]
```
Public Shadows Event QueryContinueDrag As _
   QueryContinueDragEventHandler
```
[C#]
```
public new event QueryContinueDragEventHandler QueryContinueDrag;
```
[C++]
```
public: __event QueryContinueDragEventHandler* QueryContinueDrag;
```

[JScript] In JScript, you can handle the events defined by a class, but you cannot define your own.

RichTextBox.SelectionChanged Event

Occurs when the selection of text within the control has changed.

[Visual Basic]
```
Public Event SelectionChanged As EventHandler
```
[C#]
```
public event EventHandler SelectionChanged;
```
[C++]
```
public: __event EventHandler* SelectionChanged;
```

[JScript] In JScript, you can handle the events defined by a class, but you cannot define your own.

Event Data

The event handler receives an argument of type **EventArgs**.

Remarks

You can create an event handler for this event to determine when the user has changed text selection within the control. An event handler for this event can be used to keep text selected until the user has completed a task within the application.

Requirements

Platforms: Windows 98, Windows NT 4.0, Windows Millennium Edition, Windows 2000, Windows XP Home Edition, Windows XP Professional, Windows Server 2003 family

RichTextBox.VScroll Event

Occurs when the user clicks the vertical scroll bars of the control.

[Visual Basic]
```
Public Event VScroll As EventHandler
```
[C#]
```
public event EventHandler VScroll;
```
[C++]
```
public: __event EventHandler* VScroll;
```

[JScript] In JScript, you can handle the events defined by a class, but you cannot define your own.

Event Data

The event handler receives an argument of type **EventArgs**.

Requirements

Platforms: Windows 98, Windows NT 4.0, Windows Millennium Edition, Windows 2000, Windows XP Home Edition, Windows XP Professional, Windows Server 2003 family

RichTextBoxFinds Enumeration

Specifies how a text search is carried out in a **RichTextBox** control.

This enumeration has a **FlagsAttribute** attribute that allows a bitwise combination of its member values.

[Visual Basic]
```
<Flags>
<Serializable>
Public Enum RichTextBoxFinds
```
[C#]
```
[Flags]
[Serializable]
public enum RichTextBoxFinds
```
[C++]
```
[Flags]
[Serializable]
__value public enum RichTextBoxFinds
```
[JScript]
```
public
   Flags
   Serializable
enum RichTextBoxFinds
```

Remarks

An application locates text in the **RichTextBox** control by calling the **Find** method of the **RichTextBox** control. This enumeration enables you to specify how the search is performed when the **Find** method is called. You can combine one or more values from this enumeration to specify more than one search option when calling the **Find** method.

Members

Member name	Description	Value
MatchCase	Locate only instances of the search text that have the exact casing.	4
NoHighlight	The search text, if found, should not be highlighted.	8
None	Locate all instances of the search text, whether the instances found in the search are whole words or not.	0
Reverse	The search starts at the end of the control's document and searches to the beginning of the document.	16
WholeWord	Locate only instances of the search text that are whole words.	2

Example

[Visual Basic, C#] The following example searches the entire contents of a **RichTextBox** for the first instance of a search string passed into the text parameter of the method. The search starting location is specified by the start parameter of the method. If the search string is found in the **RichTextBox**, the method returns the index location of the first character of the found text and highlights the found text; otherwise, it returns a value of -1. The example also specifies options in the search to match the case of the specified search string. The example assumes that this method is placed in the class of a **Form** that contains a **RichTextBox** named `richTextBox1`. You can use this example when performing a "Find Next" type operation once the first instance of search text has been found to find other instances of the text.

[Visual Basic]
```
Public Function FindMyText(text As String, start As Integer) As Integer
    ' Initialize the return value to false by default.
    Dim returnValue As Integer = - 1

    ' Ensure that a search string has been specified and a valid ↵
start point.
    If text.Length > 0 And start >= 0 Then
        ' Obtain the location of the search string in richTextBox1.
        Dim indexToText As Integer = richTextBox1.Find(text, start, _
            RichTextBoxFinds.MatchCase)
        ' Determine whether the text was found in richTextBox1.
        If indexToText >= 0 Then
            returnValue = indexToText
        End If
    End If

    Return returnValue
End Function
```

[C#]
```
public int FindMyText(string text, int start)
{
   // Initialize the return value to false by default.
   int returnValue = -1;

   // Ensure that a search string has been specified and a valid ↵
start point.
   if (text.Length > 0 && start >= 0)
   {
      // Obtain the location of the search string in richTextBox1.
      int indexToText = richTextBox1.Find(text, start, ↵
RichTextBoxFinds.MatchCase);
      // Determine whether the text was found in richTextBox1.
      if(indexToText >= 0)
      {
         returnValue = indexToText;
      }
   }

   return returnValue;
}
```

Requirements

Namespace: System.Windows.Forms

Platforms: Windows 98, Windows NT 4.0, Windows Millennium Edition, Windows 2000, Windows XP Home Edition, Windows XP Professional, Windows Server 2003 family

Assembly: System.Windows.Forms (in System.Windows.Forms.dll)

RichTextBoxScrollBars Enumeration

Specifies the type of scroll bars to display in a **RichTextBox** control.

[Visual Basic]
```
<Serializable>
Public Enum RichTextBoxScrollBars
```
[C#]
```
[Serializable]
public enum RichTextBoxScrollBars
```
[C++]
```
[Serializable]
__value public enum RichTextBoxScrollBars
```
[JScript]
```
public
   Serializable
enum RichTextBoxScrollBars
```

Remarks

Use the members of this enumeration to set the value of the **ScrollBars** property of the **RichTextBox** control.

Members

Member name	Description
Both	Display both a horizontal and a vertical scroll bar when needed.
ForcedBoth	Always display both a horizontal and a vertical scroll bar.
ForcedHorizontal	Always display a horizontal scroll bar.
ForcedVertical	Always display a vertical scroll bar.
Horizontal	Display a horizontal scroll bar only when text is longer than the width of the control.
None	No scroll bars are displayed.
Vertical	Display a vertical scroll bar only when text is longer than the height of the control.

Requirements

Namespace: System.Windows.Forms

Platforms: Windows 98, Windows NT 4.0, Windows Millennium Edition, Windows 2000, Windows XP Home Edition, Windows XP Professional, Windows Server 2003 family

Assembly: System.Windows.Forms (in System.Windows.Forms.dll)

RichTextBoxSelectionAttribute Enumeration

This type supports the .NET Framework infrastructure and is not intended to be used directly from your code.

[Visual Basic]
```
<Serializable>
Public Enum RichTextBoxSelectionAttribute
```
[C#]
```
[Serializable]
public enum RichTextBoxSelectionAttribute
```
[C++]
```
[Serializable]
__value public enum RichTextBoxSelectionAttribute
```
[JScript]
```
public
   Serializable
enum RichTextBoxSelectionAttribute
```

Members

All

Mixed

None

RichTextBoxSelectionTypes Enumeration

Specifies the type of selection in a **RichTextBox** control.

This enumeration has a **FlagsAttribute** attribute that allows a bitwise combination of its member values.

[Visual Basic]
```
<Flags>
<Serializable>
Public Enum RichTextBoxSelectionTypes
```
[C#]
```
[Flags]
[Serializable]
public enum RichTextBoxSelectionTypes
```
[C++]
```
[Flags]
[Serializable]
__value public enum RichTextBoxSelectionTypes
```
[JScript]
```
public
   Flags
   Serializable
enum RichTextBoxSelectionTypes
```

Remarks

Use the members of this enumeration to determine the value of the **SelectionType** property of the **RichTextBox** class. The **RichTextBox.SelectionType** property can return any combination of values from this enumeration.

Members

Member name	Description	Value
Empty	No text is selected in the current selection.	0
MultiChar	More than one character is selected.	4
MultiObject	More than one Object Linking and Embedding (OLE) object is selected.	8
Object	At least one Object Linking and Embedding (OLE) object is selected.	2
Text	The current selection contains only text.	1

Requirements

Namespace: System.Windows.Forms

Platforms: Windows 98, Windows NT 4.0, Windows Millennium Edition, Windows 2000, Windows XP Home Edition, Windows XP Professional, Windows Server 2003 family

Assembly: System.Windows.Forms (in System.Windows.Forms.dll)

RichTextBoxStreamType Enumeration

Specifies the types of input and output streams used to load and save data in the **RichTextBox** control.

[Visual Basic]
```
<Serializable>
Public Enum RichTextBoxStreamType
```
[C#]
```
[Serializable]
public enum RichTextBoxStreamType
```
[C++]
```
[Serializable]
__value public enum RichTextBoxStreamType
```
[JScript]
```
public
   Serializable
enum RichTextBoxStreamType
```

Remarks

Use the members of this enumeration when calling the **LoadFile** and **SaveFile** methods of the **RichTextBox** control.

Members

Member name	Description
PlainText	A plain text stream that includes spaces in places of Object Linking and Embedding (OLE) objects.
RichNoOleObjs	A Rich Text Format (RTF) stream with spaces in place of OLE objects. This value is only valid for use with the **SaveFile** method of the **RichTextBox** control.
RichText	A Rich Text Format (RTF) stream.
TextTextOleObjs	A plain text stream with a textual representation of OLE objects. This value is only valid for use with the **SaveFile** method of the **RichTextBox** control.
UnicodePlainText	A text stream that contains spaces in place of Object Linking and Embedding (OLE) objects. The text is encoded in Unicode.

Example

[Visual Basic, C#] The following example saves the contents of the **RichTextBox** into an ASCII text file. The example uses the **SaveFileDialog** class to display a dialog to request the path and file name from the user. The code then saves the contents of the control to that file. The example uses this version of the **SaveFile** method to specify that the file be saved as an ASCII text file instead of the standard Rich Text Format. This example assumes that the code is placed in a **Form** class that has a **RichTextBox** control named `richTextBox1`.

[Visual Basic]
```
Public Sub SaveMyFile()
    ' Create a SaveFileDialog to request a path and file name to ↵
save to.
    Dim saveFile1 As New SaveFileDialog()

    ' Initialize the SaveFileDialog to specify the RTF extension ↵
for the file.
    saveFile1.DefaultExt = "*.rtf"
    saveFile1.Filter = "RTF Files|*.rtf"

    ' Determine if the user selected a file name from the ↵
saveFileDialog.
    If (saveFile1.ShowDialog() = ↵
System.Windows.Forms.DialogResult.OK) _
        And (saveFile1.FileName.Length) > 0 Then

        ' Save the contents of the RichTextBox into the file.
        richTextBox1.SaveFile(saveFile1.FileName, _
            RichTextBoxStreamType.PlainText)
    End If
End Sub
```

[C#]
```
public void SaveMyFile()
{
   // Create a SaveFileDialog to request a path and file name ↵
 to save to.
   SaveFileDialog saveFile1 = new SaveFileDialog();

   // Initialize the SaveFileDialog to specify the RTF extension ↵
 for the file.
   saveFile1.DefaultExt = "*.rtf";
   saveFile1.Filter = "RTF Files|*.rtf";

   // Determine if the user selected a file name from the ↵
saveFileDialog.
   if(saveFile1.ShowDialog() == System.Windows.Forms.DialogResult.OK &&
      saveFile1.FileName.Length > 0)
   {
      // Save the contents of the RichTextBox into the file.
      richTextBox1.SaveFile(saveFile1.FileName, ↵
RichTextBoxStreamType.PlainText);
   }
}
```

Requirements

Namespace: System.Windows.Forms

Platforms: Windows 98, Windows NT 4.0, Windows Millennium Edition, Windows 2000, Windows XP Home Edition, Windows XP Professional, Windows Server 2003 family

Assembly: System.Windows.Forms (in System.Windows.Forms.dll)

RichTextBoxWordPunctuations Enumeration

This type supports the .NET Framework infrastructure and is not intended to be used directly from your code.

[Visual Basic]
```
<Serializable>
Public Enum RichTextBoxWordPunctuations
```
[C#]
```
[Serializable]
public enum RichTextBoxWordPunctuations
```
[C++]
```
[Serializable]
__value public enum RichTextBoxWordPunctuations
```
[JScript]
```
public
   Serializable
enum RichTextBoxWordPunctuations
```

Members

All

Custom

Level1

Level2

RightToLeft Enumeration

Specifies a value indicating whether the text appears from right to left, such as when using Hebrew or Arabic fonts.

[Visual Basic]
```
<Serializable>
Public Enum RightToLeft
```
[C#]
```
[Serializable]
public enum RightToLeft
```
[C++]
```
[Serializable]
__value public enum RightToLeft
```
[JScript]
```
public
   Serializable
enum RightToLeft
```

Remarks

This enumeration is used by **ContextMenu**, **MainMenu**, **ProgressBar**, **Regex** and **Control**.When you retrieve the value of the **RightToLeft** property from **ContextMenu**, **MainMenu**, and **ProgressBar** you will get the value of **RightToLeft** you assigned. In contrast, if you are deriving your own class from **Control**, and you assign a value of **Inherit** to the **RightToLeft** property, the value returned will be the setting of the **RightToLeft** property of the parent control. If there is no parent control, it will return a value of **No**. Otherwise, it will return a value of **Yes** or **No**, depending on the value that you assigned to the **RightToLeft** property of your derived class.

> **Note** For more information about how enabling right-to-left alignment affects Windows Forms controls, see the **Control.RightToLeft** property.

Members

Member name	Description
Inherit	The direction the text read is inherited from the parent control.
No	The text reads from left to right. This is the default.
Yes	The text reads from right to left.

Requirements

Namespace: System.Windows.Forms

Platforms: Windows 98, Windows NT 4.0, Windows Millennium Edition, Windows 2000, Windows XP Home Edition, Windows XP Professional, Windows Server 2003 family

Assembly: System.Windows.Forms (in System.Windows.Forms.dll)

SaveFileDialog Class

Represents a common dialog box that allows the user to specify options for saving a file. This class cannot be inherited.

System.Object
  System.MarshalByRefObject
    System.ComponentModel.Component
      System.Windows.Forms.CommonDialog
        System.Windows.Forms.FileDialog
          System.Windows.Forms.SaveFileDialog

[Visual Basic]
```
NotInheritable Public Class SaveFileDialog
   Inherits FileDialog
```
[C#]
```
public sealed class SaveFileDialog : FileDialog
```
[C++]
```
public __gc __sealed class SaveFileDialog : public FileDialog
```
[JScript]
```
public class SaveFileDialog extends FileDialog
```

Thread Safety

Any public static (**Shared** in Visual Basic) members of this type are safe for multithreaded operations. Any instance members are not guaranteed to be thread safe.

Remarks

This class allows you to open and overwrite an existing file or create a new file.

Most of the functionality for this class is found in the **FileDialog** class.

.NET Compact Framework - Windows CE .NET Platform Note: On the Pocket PC, if you do not specify a file name extension, the control appends the extension of the selected type from the dialog box. On Windows CE .NET, the control does not append an extension.

All platforms support the FilterIndex property which returns the index of the selected extension filter.

Example

[Visual Basic, C#] The following example illustrates creating a **SaveFileDialog**, setting members, calling the dialog box using the **ShowDialog** method, and opening the selected file. The example assumes a form with a button placed on it.

[Visual Basic]
```
Protected Sub button1_Click(sender As Object, e As System.EventArgs)
    Dim myStream As Stream
    Dim saveFileDialog1 As New SaveFileDialog()

    saveFileDialog1.Filter = "txt files (*.txt)|*.txt|All files
(*.*)|*.*"
    saveFileDialog1.FilterIndex = 2
    saveFileDialog1.RestoreDirectory = True

    If saveFileDialog1.ShowDialog() = DialogResult.OK Then
        myStream = saveFileDialog1.OpenFile()
        If Not (myStream Is Nothing) Then
            ' Code to write the stream goes here.
            myStream.Close()
        End If
    End If
End Sub
```

[C#]
```
protected void button1_Click(object sender, System.EventArgs e)
 {
     Stream myStream ;
     SaveFileDialog saveFileDialog1 = new SaveFileDialog();

     saveFileDialog1.Filter = "txt files (*.txt)|*.txt|All
files (*.*)|*.*"  ;
     saveFileDialog1.FilterIndex = 2 ;
     saveFileDialog1.RestoreDirectory = true ;

     if(saveFileDialog1.ShowDialog() == DialogResult.OK)
     {
         if((myStream = saveFileDialog1.OpenFile()) != null)
         {
             // Code to write the stream goes here.
             myStream.Close();
         }
     }
 }
```

Requirements

Namespace: System.Windows.Forms

Platforms: Windows 98, Windows NT 4.0, Windows Millennium Edition, Windows 2000, Windows XP Home Edition, Windows XP Professional, Windows Server 2003 family, .NET Compact Framework - Windows CE .NET

Assembly: System.Windows.Forms (in System.Windows.Forms.dll)

SaveFileDialog Constructor

[To be supplied.]

[Visual Basic]
```
Public Sub New()
```
[C#]
```
public SaveFileDialog();
```
[C++]
```
public: SaveFileDialog();
```
[JScript]
```
public function SaveFileDialog();
```

Requirements

Platforms: Windows 98, Windows NT 4.0, Windows Millennium Edition, Windows 2000, Windows XP Home Edition, Windows XP Professional, Windows Server 2003 family, .NET Compact Framework - Windows CE .NET

SaveFileDialog.CreatePrompt Property

Gets or sets a value indicating whether the dialog box prompts the user for permission to create a file if the user specifies a file that does not exist.

[Visual Basic]
```
Public Property CreatePrompt As Boolean
```
[C#]
```
public bool CreatePrompt {get; set;}
```
[C++]
```
public: __property bool get_CreatePrompt();
public: __property void set_CreatePrompt(bool);
```
[JScript]
```
public function get CreatePrompt() : Boolean;
public function set CreatePrompt(Boolean);
```

Property Value

true if the dialog box prompts the user before creating a file if the user specifies a file name that does not exist; **false** if the dialog box automatically creates the new file without prompting the user for permission. The default value is **false**.

Requirements

Platforms: Windows 98, Windows NT 4.0,
Windows Millennium Edition, Windows 2000,
Windows XP Home Edition, Windows XP Professional,
Windows Server 2003 family

.NET Framework Security:

- **FileIOPermission** to set the property. Associated enumeration: **PermissionState.Unrestricted**.

SaveFileDialog.OverwritePrompt Property

Gets or sets a value indicating whether the **Save As** dialog box displays a warning if the user specifies a file name that already exists.

[Visual Basic]
```
Public Property OverwritePrompt As Boolean
```
[C#]
```
public bool OverwritePrompt {get; set;}
```
[C++]
```
public: __property bool get_OverwritePrompt();
public: __property void set_OverwritePrompt(bool);
```
[JScript]
```
public function get OverwritePrompt() : Boolean;
public function set OverwritePrompt(Boolean);
```

Property Value

true if the dialog box prompts the user before overwriting an existing file if the user specifies a file name that already exists; **false** if the dialog box automatically overwrites the existing file without prompting the user for permission. The default value is **true**.

Requirements

Platforms: Windows 98, Windows NT 4.0,
Windows Millennium Edition, Windows 2000,
Windows XP Home Edition, Windows XP Professional,
Windows Server 2003 family

.NET Framework Security:

- **FileIOPermission** to set the property. Associated enumeration: **PermissionState.Unrestricted**.

SaveFileDialog.OpenFile Method

Opens the file with read/write permission selected by the user.

[Visual Basic]
```
Public Function OpenFile() As Stream
```
[C#]
```
public Stream OpenFile();
```
[C++]
```
public: Stream* OpenFile();
```
[JScript]
```
public function OpenFile() : Stream;
```

Return Value

The read/write file selected by the user.

Remarks

CAUTION For security purposes, this method creates a new file with the selected name and opens it with read/write permissions. This can cause unintentional loss of data if you select an existing file to save to. To save data to an existing file while retaining existing data, use the **File** class to open the file using the file name returned in the **FileName** property.

Example

[Visual Basic, C#] The following example illustrates creating a **SaveFileDialog**, setting members, calling the dialog box using the **ShowDialog** method, and opening the selected file. The example assumes a form with a button placed on it.

[Visual Basic]
```
Protected Sub button1_Click(sender As Object, e As System.EventArgs)
    Dim myStream As Stream
    Dim saveFileDialog1 As New SaveFileDialog()

    saveFileDialog1.Filter = "txt files (*.txt)|*.txt|All ↵
 files (*.*)|*.*"
    saveFileDialog1.FilterIndex = 2
    saveFileDialog1.RestoreDirectory = True

    If saveFileDialog1.ShowDialog() = DialogResult.OK Then
        myStream = saveFileDialog1.OpenFile()
        If Not (myStream Is Nothing) Then
            ' Code to write the stream goes here.
            myStream.Close()
        End If
    End If
End Sub
```

[C#]
```
protected void button1_Click(object sender, System.EventArgs e)
 {
     Stream myStream ;
     SaveFileDialog saveFileDialog1 = new SaveFileDialog();

     saveFileDialog1.Filter = "txt files (*.txt)|*.txt|All ↵
files (*.*)|*.*"  ;
     saveFileDialog1.FilterIndex = 2 ;
     saveFileDialog1.RestoreDirectory = true ;

     if(saveFileDialog1.ShowDialog() == DialogResult.OK)
     {
         if((myStream = saveFileDialog1.OpenFile()) != null)
         {
             // Code to write the stream goes here.
             myStream.Close();
         }
     }
 }
```

Requirements

Platforms: Windows 98, Windows NT 4.0,
Windows Millennium Edition, Windows 2000,
Windows XP Home Edition, Windows XP Professional,
Windows Server 2003 family

.NET Framework Security:

- **FileDialogPermission** to save a file. Associated enumeration: **FileDialogPermissionAccess.Save**.

SaveFileDialog.Reset Method

This member overrides **FileDialog.Reset**.

[Visual Basic]
```
Overrides Public Sub Reset()
```
[C#]
```
public override void Reset();
```
[C++]
```
public: void Reset();
```
[JScript]
```
public override function Reset();
```

Requirements

Platforms: Windows 98, Windows NT 4.0, Windows Millennium Edition, Windows 2000, Windows XP Home Edition, Windows XP Professional, Windows Server 2003 family

Screen Class

Represents a display device or multiple display devices on a single system.

System.Object
  System.Windows.Forms.Screen

[Visual Basic]
```
Public Class Screen
```
[C#]
```
public class Screen
```
[C++]
```
public __gc class Screen
```
[JScript]
```
public class Screen
```

Thread Safety

Any public static (**Shared** in Visual Basic) members of this type are safe for multithreaded operations. Any instance members are not guaranteed to be thread safe.

Remarks

The constructor for this object is not public, so you cannot explicitly create a **Screen** object. The object is created when you call its public methods.

Example

[Visual Basic, C#, C++] The following example shows how to use various methods and properties of the **Screen** class. The example calls the **AllScreens** property to retrieve an array of all the screens connected to the system. For each returned **Screen**, the example adds the device name, bounds, type, working area, and primary screen to a **ListBox**.

[Visual Basic]
```
Private Sub Button1_Click(ByVal sender As System.Object, ByVal ↵
e As System.EventArgs) Handles BtnGetScreenInfo.Click

    Dim Index As Integer
    Dim UpperBound As Integer

    ' Gets an array of all the screens connected to the system.

    Dim Screens() As System.Windows.Forms.Screen = _
        System.Windows.Forms.Screen.AllScreens
    UpperBound = Screens.GetUpperBound(0)

    For Index = 0 To UpperBound

        ' For each screen, add the screen properties to a list box.

        ListBox1.Items.Add("Device Name: " + Screens(Index).DeviceName)
        ListBox1.Items.Add("Bounds: " + ↵
Screens(Index).Bounds.ToString())
        ListBox1.Items.Add("Type: " + ↵
Screens(Index).GetType().ToString())
        ListBox1.Items.Add("Working Area: " + ↵
Screens(Index).WorkingArea.ToString())
        ListBox1.Items.Add("Primary Screen: " + ↵
Screens(Index).Primary.ToString())

    Next

End Sub
```

[C#]
```
private void button1_Click(object sender, System.EventArgs e)
{
    int index;
    int upperBound;

    // Gets an array of all the screens connected to the system.

    Screen [] screens = Screen.AllScreens;
    upperBound = screens.GetUpperBound(0);

    for(index = 0; index <= upperBound; index++)
    {

        // For each screen, add the screen properties to a list box.

        listBox1.Items.Add("Device Name: " + ↵
screens[index].DeviceName);
        listBox1.Items.Add("Bounds: " + ↵
screens[index].Bounds.ToString());
        listBox1.Items.Add("Type: " + ↵
screens[index].GetType().ToString());
        listBox1.Items.Add("Working Area: " + ↵
screens[index].WorkingArea.ToString());
        listBox1.Items.Add("Primary Screen: " + ↵
screens[index].Primary.ToString());

    }

}
```

[C++]
```
private:
    void button1_Click(Object* /*sender*/, System::EventArgs* /*e*/) {
        int index;
        int upperBound;

        // Gets an array of all the screens connected to the system.

        Screen* screens[] = Screen::AllScreens;
        upperBound = screens->GetUpperBound(0);

        for (index = 0; index <= upperBound; index++) {

            // For each screen, add the screen properties to a ↵
list box.

            listBox1->Items->Add(String::Concat(
                S"Device Name: ", screens[index]->DeviceName));
            listBox1->Items->Add(String::Concat(
                S"Bounds: ", __box( screens[index]->Bounds)));
            listBox1->Items->Add(String::Concat(
                S"Type: ", screens->Item[index]->GetType()));
            listBox1->Items->Add(String::Concat(
                S"Working Area: ", __box( screens[index]- ↵
>WorkingArea)));
            listBox1->Items->Add(String::Concat(
                S"Primary Screen: ", __box( screens[index]->Primary)));
        }

    }
```

Requirements

Namespace: System.Windows.Forms

Platforms: Windows 98, Windows NT 4.0, Windows Millennium Edition, Windows 2000, Windows XP Home Edition, Windows XP Professional, Windows Server 2003 family, .NET Compact Framework - Windows CE .NET

Assembly: System.Windows.Forms (in System.Windows.Forms.dll)

Screen.AllScreens Property

Gets an array of all displays on the system.

```
[Visual Basic]
Public Shared ReadOnly Property AllScreens As Screen ()
[C#]
public static Screen[] AllScreens {get;}
[C++]
public: __property static Screen* get_AllScreens();
[JScript]
public static function get AllScreens() : Screen[];
```

Property Value

An array of type **Screen**, containing all displays on the system.

Requirements

Platforms: Windows 98, Windows NT 4.0, Windows Millennium Edition, Windows 2000, Windows XP Home Edition, Windows XP Professional, Windows Server 2003 family

Screen.Bounds Property

Gets the bounds of the display.

```
[Visual Basic]
Public ReadOnly Property Bounds As Rectangle
[C#]
public Rectangle Bounds {get;}
[C++]
public: __property Rectangle get_Bounds();
[JScript]
public function get Bounds() : Rectangle;
```

Property Value

A **Rectangle**, representing the bounds of the display.

Requirements

Platforms: Windows 98, Windows NT 4.0, Windows Millennium Edition, Windows 2000, Windows XP Home Edition, Windows XP Professional, Windows Server 2003 family, .NET Compact Framework - Windows CE .NET

Screen.DeviceName Property

Gets the device name associated with a display.

```
[Visual Basic]
Public ReadOnly Property DeviceName As String
[C#]
public string DeviceName {get;}
[C++]
public: __property String* get_DeviceName();
[JScript]
public function get DeviceName() : String;
```

Property Value

The device name associated with a display.

Requirements

Platforms: Windows 98, Windows NT 4.0, Windows Millennium Edition, Windows 2000, Windows XP Home Edition, Windows XP Professional, Windows Server 2003 family

Screen.Primary Property

Gets a value indicating whether a particular display is the primary device.

```
[Visual Basic]
Public ReadOnly Property Primary As Boolean
[C#]
public bool Primary {get;}
[C++]
public: __property bool get_Primary();
[JScript]
public function get Primary() : Boolean;
```

Property Value

true if this display is primary; otherwise, **false**.

Requirements

Platforms: Windows 98, Windows NT 4.0, Windows Millennium Edition, Windows 2000, Windows XP Home Edition, Windows XP Professional, Windows Server 2003 family

Screen.PrimaryScreen Property

Gets the primary display.

```
[Visual Basic]
Public Shared ReadOnly Property PrimaryScreen As Screen
[C#]
public static Screen PrimaryScreen {get;}
[C++]
public: __property static Screen* get_PrimaryScreen();
[JScript]
public static function get PrimaryScreen() : Screen;
```

Property Value

The primary display.

Remarks

For a single display system, the primary display is the only display.

Requirements

Platforms: Windows 98, Windows NT 4.0, Windows Millennium Edition, Windows 2000, Windows XP Home Edition, Windows XP Professional, Windows Server 2003 family, .NET Compact Framework - Windows CE .NET

Screen.WorkingArea Property

Gets the working area of the display. The working area is the desktop area of the display, excluding taskbars, docked windows, and docked tool bars.

```
[Visual Basic]
Public ReadOnly Property WorkingArea As Rectangle
[C#]
public Rectangle WorkingArea {get;}
[C++]
public: __property Rectangle get_WorkingArea();
[JScript]
public function get WorkingArea() : Rectangle;
```

Property Value

A **Rectangle**, representing the working area of the display.

Remarks

The working area is the desktop area of the display, excluding taskbars, docked windows, and docked tool bars.

Requirements

Platforms: Windows 98, Windows NT 4.0, Windows Millennium Edition, Windows 2000, Windows XP Home Edition, Windows XP Professional, Windows Server 2003 family, .NET Compact Framework - Windows CE .NET

Screen.Equals Method

Gets or sets a value indicating whether the specified object is equal to this **Screen**.

[Visual Basic]
```
Overrides Public Function Equals( _
   ByVal obj As Object _
) As Boolean
```
[C#]
```
public override bool Equals(
   object obj
);
```
[C++]
```
public: bool Equals(
   Object* obj
);
```
[JScript]
```
public override function Equals(
   obj : Object
) : Boolean;
```

Parameters

obj

The object to compare to this **Screen**.

Return Value

true if the specified object is equal to this **Screen**; otherwise, **false**.

Requirements

Platforms: Windows 98, Windows NT 4.0, Windows Millennium Edition, Windows 2000, Windows XP Home Edition, Windows XP Professional, Windows Server 2003 family, .NET Compact Framework - Windows CE .NET

Screen.FromControl Method

Retrieves a **Screen** for the display that contains the largest portion of the specified control.

[Visual Basic]
```
Public Shared Function FromControl( _
   ByVal control As Control _
) As Screen
```
[C#]
```
public static Screen FromControl(
   Control control
);
```
[C++]
```
public: static Screen* FromControl(
   Control* control
);
```
[JScript]
```
public static function FromControl(
   control : Control
) : Screen;
```

Parameters

control

A **Control** for which to retrieve a **Screen**.

Return Value

A **Screen** for the display that contains the largest region of the specified control. In multiple display environments where no display contains the control, the display closest to the specified control is returned.

Requirements

Platforms: Windows 98, Windows NT 4.0, Windows Millennium Edition, Windows 2000, Windows XP Home Edition, Windows XP Professional, Windows Server 2003 family

Screen.FromHandle Method

Retrieves a **Screen** for the display that contains the largest portion of the object referred to by the specified handle.

[Visual Basic]
```
Public Shared Function FromHandle( _
   ByVal hwnd As IntPtr _
) As Screen
```
[C#]
```
public static Screen FromHandle(
   IntPtr hwnd
);
```
[C++]
```
public: static Screen* FromHandle(
   IntPtr hwnd
);
```
[JScript]
```
public static function FromHandle(
   hwnd : IntPtr
) : Screen;
```

Parameters

hwnd

The window handle for which to retrieve the **Screen**.

Return Value

A **Screen** for the display that contains the largest region of the object. In multiple display environments where no display contains any portion of the specified window, the display closest to the object is returned.

Requirements

Platforms: Windows 98, Windows NT 4.0, Windows Millennium Edition, Windows 2000, Windows XP Home Edition, Windows XP Professional, Windows Server 2003 family

.NET Framework Security:

- **SecurityPermission** to get an object from a Win32 Handle. Associated enumeration: **SecurityPermissionFlag.UnmanagedCode**

Screen.FromPoint Method

Retrieves a **Screen** for the display that contains the specified point.

[Visual Basic]
```
Public Shared Function FromPoint( _
   ByVal point As Point _
) As Screen
```
[C#]
```
public static Screen FromPoint(
   Point point
);
```
[C++]
```
public: static Screen* FromPoint(
   Point point
);
```
[JScript]
```
public static function FromPoint(
   point : Point
) : Screen;
```

Parameters

point

A **Point** that specifies the location for which to retrieve a **Screen**.

Return Value

A **Screen** for the display that contains the point. In multiple display environments where no display contains the point, the display closest to the specified point is returned.

Example

[Visual Basic, C#, C++] The following example shows how to use the **FromPoint** method. This example creates a **Point** referencing the **X** and **Y** coordinates passed by a **MouseEventArgs**, and then uses the **FromPoint** method to determine if the point clicked is on the primary screen.

[Visual Basic]
```
Private Sub Form1_MouseDown(ByVal sender As Object, ByVal ↵
 e As System.Windows.Forms.MouseEventArgs) Handles MyBase.MouseDown
    Dim p As New System.Drawing.Point(e.X, e.Y)
    Dim s As System.Windows.Forms.Screen = Screen.FromPoint(p)

    If s.Primary = True Then
        MessageBox.Show("You clicked the primary screen")
    Else
        MessageBox.Show("This isn't the primary screen")
    End If
End Sub
```

[C#]
```
private void Form1_MouseDown(object sender, ↵
System.Windows.Forms.MouseEventArgs e)
{
    Point p = new Point(e.X, e.Y);
    Screen s = Screen.FromPoint(p);

if (s.Primary)
{
    MessageBox.Show("You clicked the primary screen");
}
else
{
    MessageBox.Show("This isn't the primary screen");
}
```

[C++]
```
private:
    void Form1_MouseDown(Object* /*sender*/,
        System::Windows::Forms::MouseEventArgs* e) {
        Point p = Point(e->X, e->Y);
        Screen* s = Screen::FromPoint(p);

        if (s->Primary) {
            MessageBox::Show(S"You clicked the primary screen");
        } else {
            MessageBox::Show(S"This isn't the primary screen");
        }
```

Requirements

Platforms: Windows 98, Windows NT 4.0, Windows Millennium Edition, Windows 2000, Windows XP Home Edition, Windows XP Professional, Windows Server 2003 family

Screen.FromRectangle Method

Retrieves a **Screen** for the display that contains the largest portion of the rectangle.

[Visual Basic]
```
Public Shared Function FromRectangle( _
   ByVal rect As Rectangle _
) As Screen
```
[C#]
```
public static Screen FromRectangle(
   Rectangle rect
);
```
[C++]
```
public: static Screen* FromRectangle(
   Rectangle rect
);
```
[JScript]
```
public static function FromRectangle(
   rect : Rectangle
) : Screen;
```

Parameters

rect

A **Rectangle** that specifies the area for which to retrieve the display.

Return Value

A **Screen** for the display that contains the largest region of the specified rectangle. In multiple display environments where no display contains the rectangle, the display closest to the rectangle is returned.

Requirements

Platforms: Windows 98, Windows NT 4.0, Windows Millennium Edition, Windows 2000, Windows XP Home Edition, Windows XP Professional, Windows Server 2003 family

Screen.GetBounds Method

Retrieves the bounds of the display.

Overload List

Retrieves the bounds of the display that contains the largest portion of the specified control.

[Visual Basic] **Overloads Public Shared Function GetBounds(Control) As Rectangle**

[C#] **public static Rectangle GetBounds(Control);**

[C++] **public: static Rectangle GetBounds(Control*);**

[JScript] **public static function GetBounds(Control) : Rectangle;**

Retrieves the bounds of the display that contains the specified point.

[Visual Basic] **Overloads Public Shared Function GetBounds(Point) As Rectangle**

[C#] **public static Rectangle GetBounds(Point);**

[C++] **public: static Rectangle GetBounds(Point);**

[JScript] **public static function GetBounds(Point) : Rectangle;**

Retrieves the bounds of the display that contains the largest portion of the specified rectangle.

[Visual Basic] **Overloads Public Shared Function GetBounds(Rectangle) As Rectangle**

[C#] **public static Rectangle GetBounds(Rectangle);**

[C++] **public: static Rectangle GetBounds(Rectangle);**

[JScript] **public static function GetBounds(Rectangle) : Rectangle;**

Screen.GetBounds Method (Control)

Retrieves the bounds of the display that contains the largest portion of the specified control.

```
[Visual Basic]
Overloads Public Shared Function GetBounds( _
   ByVal ctl As Control _
) As Rectangle
[C#]
public static Rectangle GetBounds(
   Control ctl
);
[C++]
public: static Rectangle GetBounds(
   Control* ctl
);
[JScript]
public static function GetBounds(
   ctl : Control
) : Rectangle;
```

Parameters

ctl

The **Control** for which to retrieve the display bounds.

Return Value

A **Rectangle** that specifies the bounds of the display that contains the specified control. In multiple display environments where no display contains the specified control, the display closest to the control is returned.

Requirements

Platforms: Windows 98, Windows NT 4.0, Windows Millennium Edition, Windows 2000, Windows XP Home Edition, Windows XP Professional, Windows Server 2003 family

Screen.GetBounds Method (Point)

Retrieves the bounds of the display that contains the specified point.

```
[Visual Basic]
Overloads Public Shared Function GetBounds( _
   ByVal pt As Point _
) As Rectangle
[C#]
public static Rectangle GetBounds(
   Point pt
);
[C++]
public: static Rectangle GetBounds(
   Point pt
);
[JScript]
public static function GetBounds(
   pt : Point
) : Rectangle;
```

Parameters

pt

A **Point** that specifies the coordinates for which to retrieve the display bounds.

Return Value

A **Rectangle** that specifies the bounds of the display that contains the specified point. In multiple display environments where no display contains the specified point, the display closest to the point is returned.

Requirements

Platforms: Windows 98, Windows NT 4.0, Windows Millennium Edition, Windows 2000, Windows XP Home Edition, Windows XP Professional, Windows Server 2003 family

Screen.GetBounds Method (Rectangle)

Retrieves the bounds of the display that contains the largest portion of the specified rectangle.

```
[Visual Basic]
Overloads Public Shared Function GetBounds( _
   ByVal rect As Rectangle _
) As Rectangle
[C#]
public static Rectangle GetBounds(
   Rectangle rect
);
[C++]
public: static Rectangle GetBounds(
   Rectangle rect
);
[JScript]
public static function GetBounds(
   rect : Rectangle
) : Rectangle;
```

Parameters

rect

A **Rectangle** that specifies the area for which to retrieve the display bounds.

Return Value

A **Rectangle** that specifies the bounds of the display that contains the specified rectangle. In multiple display environments where no monitor contains the specified rectangle, the monitor closest to the rectangle is returned.

Requirements

Platforms: Windows 98, Windows NT 4.0, Windows Millennium Edition, Windows 2000, Windows XP Home Edition, Windows XP Professional, Windows Server 2003 family

Screen.GetHashCode Method

This member overrides **Object.GetHashCode**.

[Visual Basic]
```
Overrides Public Function GetHashCode() As Integer
```
[C#]
```
public override int GetHashCode();
```
[C++]
```
public: int GetHashCode();
```
[JScript]
```
public override function GetHashCode() : int;
```

Requirements

Platforms: Windows 98, Windows NT 4.0, Windows Millennium Edition, Windows 2000, Windows XP Home Edition, Windows XP Professional, Windows Server 2003 family, .NET Compact Framework - Windows CE .NET

Screen.GetWorkingArea Method

Retrieves the working area of a display.

Overload List

Retrieves the working area for the display that contains the largest region of the specified control. The working area is the desktop area of the display, excluding taskbars, docked windows, and docked tool bars.

[Visual Basic] **Overloads Public Shared Function GetWorkingArea(Control) As Rectangle**

[C#] **public static Rectangle GetWorkingArea(Control);**

[C++] **public: static Rectangle GetWorkingArea(Control*);**

[JScript] **public static function GetWorkingArea(Control) : Rectangle;**

Retrieves the working area closest to the specified point. The working area is the desktop area of the display, excluding taskbars, docked windows, and docked tool bars.

[Visual Basic] **Overloads Public Shared Function GetWorkingArea(Point) As Rectangle**

[C#] **public static Rectangle GetWorkingArea(Point);**

[C++] **public: static Rectangle GetWorkingArea(Point);**

[JScript] **public static function GetWorkingArea(Point) : Rectangle;**

Retrieves the working area for the display that contains the largest portion of the specified rectangle. The working area is the desktop area of the display, excluding taskbars, docked windows, and docked tool bars.

[Visual Basic] **Overloads Public Shared Function GetWorkingArea(Rectangle) As Rectangle**

[C#] **public static Rectangle GetWorkingArea(Rectangle);**

[C++] **public: static Rectangle GetWorkingArea(Rectangle);**

[JScript] **public static function GetWorkingArea(Rectangle) : Rectangle;**

Screen.GetWorkingArea Method (Control)

Retrieves the working area for the display that contains the largest region of the specified control. The working area is the desktop area of the display, excluding taskbars, docked windows, and docked tool bars.

[Visual Basic]
```
Overloads Public Shared Function GetWorkingArea( _
   ByVal ctl As Control _
) As Rectangle
```
[C#]
```
public static Rectangle GetWorkingArea(
   Control ctl
);
```
[C++]
```
public: static Rectangle GetWorkingArea(
   Control* ctl
);
```
[JScript]
```
public static function GetWorkingArea(
   ctl : Control
) : Rectangle;
```

Parameters

ctl

The **Control** for which to retrieve the working area.

Return Value

A **Rectangle** that specifies the working area. In multiple display environments where no display contains the specified control, the display closest to the control is returned.

Requirements

Platforms: Windows 98, Windows NT 4.0, Windows Millennium Edition, Windows 2000, Windows XP Home Edition, Windows XP Professional, Windows Server 2003 family

Screen.GetWorkingArea Method (Point)

Retrieves the working area closest to the specified point. The working area is the desktop area of the display, excluding taskbars, docked windows, and docked tool bars.

[Visual Basic]
```
Overloads Public Shared Function GetWorkingArea( _
   ByVal pt As Point _
) As Rectangle
```
[C#]
```
public static Rectangle GetWorkingArea(
   Point pt
);
```
[C++]
```
public: static Rectangle GetWorkingArea(
   Point pt
);
```
[JScript]
```
public static function GetWorkingArea(
   pt : Point
) : Rectangle;
```

Parameters

pt

A **Point** that specifies the coordinates for which to retrieve the working area.

Return Value

A **Rectangle** that specifies the working area. In multiple display environments where no display contains the specified point, the display closest to the point is returned.

Requirements

Platforms: Windows 98, Windows NT 4.0, Windows Millennium Edition, Windows 2000, Windows XP Home Edition, Windows XP Professional, Windows Server 2003 family

Screen.GetWorkingArea Method (Rectangle)

Retrieves the working area for the display that contains the largest portion of the specified rectangle. The working area is the desktop area of the display, excluding taskbars, docked windows, and docked tool bars.

```
[Visual Basic]
Overloads Public Shared Function GetWorkingArea( _
   ByVal rect As Rectangle _
) As Rectangle
[C#]
public static Rectangle GetWorkingArea(
   Rectangle rect
);
[C++]
public: static Rectangle GetWorkingArea(
   Rectangle rect
);
[JScript]
public static function GetWorkingArea(
   rect : Rectangle
) : Rectangle;
```

Parameters

rect
The **Rectangle** that specifies the area for which to retrieve the working area.

Return Value

A **Rectangle** that specifies the working area. In multiple display environments where no display contains the specified rectangle, the display closest to the rectangle is returned.

Requirements

Platforms: Windows 98, Windows NT 4.0, Windows Millennium Edition, Windows 2000, Windows XP Home Edition, Windows XP Professional, Windows Server 2003 family

Screen.ToString Method

This member overrides **Object.ToString**.

```
[Visual Basic]
Overrides Public Function ToString() As String
[C#]
public override string ToString();
[C++]
public: String* ToString();
[JScript]
public override function ToString() : String;
```

Requirements

Platforms: Windows 98, Windows NT 4.0, Windows Millennium Edition, Windows 2000, Windows XP Home Edition, Windows XP Professional, Windows Server 2003 family, .NET Compact Framework - Windows CE .NET

ScrollableControl Class

Defines a base class for controls that support auto-scrolling behavior.

System.Object
  System.MarshalByRefObject
    System.ComponentModel.Component
      System.Windows.Forms.Control
        System.Windows.Forms.ScrollableControl
          System.Windows.Forms.ContainerControl
          System.Windows.Forms.Design.ComponentTray
          System.Windows.Forms.Panel

```
[Visual Basic]
Public Class ScrollableControl
   Inherits Control
[C#]
public class ScrollableControl : Control
[C++]
public __gc class ScrollableControl : public Control
[JScript]
public class ScrollableControl extends Control
```

Thread Safety

Any public static (**Shared** in Visual Basic) members of this type are safe for multithreaded operations. Any instance members are not guaranteed to be thread safe.

Remarks

You do not typically use this class directly. The **ContainerControl** and **Panel** classes inherit from this class.

The **ScrollableControl** class acts as a base class for controls that require the ability to scroll. To allow a control to display scroll bars as needed, set the **AutoScroll** property to **true** and set the **AutoScrollMinSize** property to the desired size. When the control is sized smaller than the specified minimum size, or a child control is located outside the bounds of the control, the appropriate scroll bars are displayed.

To manually override which scroll bars are visible, set the **VScroll** and **HScroll** properties. If either property is set to **false**, the corresponding scroll bar will not be visible, even if the **AutoScroll** property is set to **true**.

When adding controls to a scrollable control the x-coordinate and y-coordinate of the **AutoScrollPosition** must be added to or subtracted as an offset from the corresponding coordinates of the **Control.Location** property of the control being added. To add a control above or to the left of the scroll position, the offset must be added to the desired location. Alternatively, to add a control below or to the right of the scroll position, the offset must be subtracted.

Requirements

Namespace: System.Windows.Forms

Platforms: Windows 98, Windows NT 4.0, Windows Millennium Edition, Windows 2000, Windows XP Home Edition, Windows XP Professional, Windows Server 2003 family, .NET Compact Framework - Windows CE .NET

Assembly: System.Windows.Forms (in System.Windows.Forms.dll)

ScrollableControl Constructor

Initializes a new instance of the **ScrollableControl** class.

```
[Visual Basic]
Public Sub New()
[C#]
public ScrollableControl();
[C++]
public: ScrollableControl();
[JScript]
public function ScrollableControl();
```

Requirements

Platforms: Windows 98, Windows NT 4.0, Windows Millennium Edition, Windows 2000, Windows XP Home Edition, Windows XP Professional, Windows Server 2003 family, .NET Compact Framework - Windows CE .NET

ScrollableControl.ScrollStateAutoScrolling Field

This member supports the .NET Framework infrastructure and is not intended to be used directly from your code.

```
[Visual Basic]
Protected Const ScrollStateAutoScrolling As Integer
[C#]
protected const int ScrollStateAutoScrolling;
[C++]
protected: const int ScrollStateAutoScrolling;
[JScript]
protected var ScrollStateAutoScrolling : int;
```

ScrollableControl.ScrollStateFullDrag Field

This member supports the .NET Framework infrastructure and is not intended to be used directly from your code.

```
[Visual Basic]
Protected Const ScrollStateFullDrag As Integer
[C#]
protected const int ScrollStateFullDrag;
[C++]
protected: const int ScrollStateFullDrag;
[JScript]
protected var ScrollStateFullDrag : int;
```

ScrollableControl.ScrollStateHScrollVisible Field

This member supports the .NET Framework infrastructure and is not intended to be used directly from your code.

```
[Visual Basic]
Protected Const ScrollStateHScrollVisible As Integer
[C#]
protected const int ScrollStateHScrollVisible;
[C++]
protected: const int ScrollStateHScrollVisible;
[JScript]
protected var ScrollStateHScrollVisible : int;
```

ScrollableControl.ScrollStateUserHasScrolled Field

This member supports the .NET Framework infrastructure and is not intended to be used directly from your code.

```
[Visual Basic]
Protected Const ScrollStateUserHasScrolled As Integer
[C#]
protected const int ScrollStateUserHasScrolled;
[C++]
protected: const int ScrollStateUserHasScrolled;
[JScript]
protected var ScrollStateUserHasScrolled : int;
```

ScrollableControl.ScrollStateVScrollVisible Field

This member supports the .NET Framework infrastructure and is not intended to be used directly from your code.

```
[Visual Basic]
Protected Const ScrollStateVScrollVisible As Integer
[C#]
protected const int ScrollStateVScrollVisible;
[C++]
protected: const int ScrollStateVScrollVisible;
[JScript]
protected var ScrollStateVScrollVisible : int;
```

ScrollableControl.AutoScroll Property

Gets or sets a value indicating whether the container will allow the user to scroll to any controls placed outside of its visible boundaries.

```
[Visual Basic]
Public Overridable Property AutoScroll As Boolean
[C#]
public virtual bool AutoScroll {get; set;}
[C++]
public: __property virtual bool get_AutoScroll();
public: __property virtual void set_AutoScroll(bool);
[JScript]
public function get AutoScroll() : Boolean;
public function set AutoScroll(Boolean);
```

Property Value

true if the container allows auto-scrolling; otherwise, **false**. The default value is **false**.

Remarks

When **true**, this property allows the container to have a virtual size that is larger than its visible boundaries.

Example

[Visual Basic, C#] The following example uses the derived class, **Panel**. The example evaluates the location of a text box and changes the appearance and behavior of its parent container, the panel control. This example assumes a **Panel** control, **TextBox**, and **Button** have been instantiated. Place the text box on the panel so that it overlaps at least one of the panel's edges. Call this subprocedure on the click of a button to see the difference in the panel's behavior and appearance.

```
[Visual Basic]
Private Sub SetAutoScrollMargins()
    ' If the text box is outside the panel's bounds,
    ' turn on auto-scrolling and set the margin.
    If (text1.Location.X > panel1.Location.X) Or _
        (text1.Location.Y > panel1.Location.Y) Then
        panel1.AutoScroll = True
        ' If the AutoScrollMargin is set to less
        ' than (5,5), set it to 5,5.
        If (panel1.AutoScrollMargin.Width < 5) Or _
            (panel1.AutoScrollMargin.Height < 5) Then

            panel1.SetAutoScrollMargin(5, 5)
        End If
    End If
End Sub
```

```
[C#]
private void SetAutoScrollMargins()
 {
    /* If the text box is outside the panel's bounds,
       turn on auto-scrolling and set the margin. */
    if (text1.Location.X > panel1.Location.X ||
       text1.Location.Y > panel1.Location.Y)
    {
       panel1.AutoScroll = true;
       /* If the AutoScrollMargin is set to less
          than (5,5), set it to 5,5. */
       if( panel1.AutoScrollMargin.Width < 5 ||
          panel1.AutoScrollMargin.Height < 5)
       {
          panel1.SetAutoScrollMargin(5, 5);
       }
    }
 }
```

Requirements

Platforms: Windows 98, Windows NT 4.0, Windows Millennium Edition, Windows 2000, Windows XP Home Edition, Windows XP Professional, Windows Server 2003 family

ScrollableControl.AutoScrollMargin Property

Gets or sets the size of the auto-scroll margin.

```
[Visual Basic]
Public Property AutoScrollMargin As Size
[C#]
public Size AutoScrollMargin {get; set;}
[C++]
public: __property Size get_AutoScrollMargin();
public: __property void set_AutoScrollMargin(Size);
[JScript]
public function get AutoScrollMargin() : Size;
public function set AutoScrollMargin(Size);
```

Property Value

A **Size** object that represents the height and width of the auto-scroll margin in pixels.

Exceptions

Exception Type	Condition
ArgumentException	The **Height** or **Width** value assigned is less than 0.

Remarks

The auto-scroll margin is the distance between any child controls and the edges of the scrollable parent control. The **AutoScrollMargin** size is added to the size of any child controls contained in the scrollable control to determine whether or not scroll bars are needed. The **AutoScrollMargin** property is evaluated when the parent scrollable control is resized or the individual child controls are brought into view, and is used to determine if scroll bars need to be displayed. Docked controls are excluded from the calculations that determine if scroll bars need to be displayed.

> **Note** If a docked control's **Dock** property is set to **DockStyle.Fill**, the control fills the parent scrollable control and the docked control is ignored when using the **AutoScrollMargin** to determine whether scroll bars are needed.

If the distance from the edge of a child control to the parent scrollable control is less than the value assigned to the **AutoScrollMargin** property and the **AutoScroll** property is set to **true**, the appropriate scroll bar is displayed.

> **Note** It is advisable, when docking controls within a scrollable control, to add a child scrollable control such as a **Panel** to contain any other controls that might require scrolling. The child **Panel** control should be added to the scrollable control and its **Dock** property set to **DockStyle.Fill** and its **AutoScroll** property set to **true**. The **AutoScroll** property of the parent scrollable control should be set to **false**.

Example

[Visual Basic, C#] The following example uses the derived class, **Panel**. The example evaluates the location of a text box and changes the appearance and behavior of its parent container, the panel control. This example assumes a **Panel** control, **TextBox**, and **Button** have been instantiated. Place the text box on the panel so that it overlaps at least one of the panel's edges. Call this subprocedure on the click of a button to see the difference in the panel's behavior and appearance.

[Visual Basic]
```
Private Sub SetAutoScrollMargins()
    ' If the text box is outside the panel's bounds,
    ' turn on auto-scrolling and set the margin.
    If (text1.Location.X > panel1.Location.X) Or _
        (text1.Location.Y > panel1.Location.Y) Then
        panel1.AutoScroll = True
        ' If the AutoScrollMargin is set to less
        ' than (5,5), set it to 5,5.
        If (panel1.AutoScrollMargin.Width < 5) Or _
            (panel1.AutoScrollMargin.Height < 5) Then

            panel1.SetAutoScrollMargin(5, 5)
        End If
    End If
End Sub
```

[C#]
```
private void SetAutoScrollMargins()
 {
    /* If the text box is outside the panel's bounds,
       turn on auto-scrolling and set the margin. */
    if (text1.Location.X > panel1.Location.X ||
       text1.Location.Y > panel1.Location.Y)
    {
       panel1.AutoScroll = true;
       /* If the AutoScrollMargin is set to less
          than (5,5), set it to 5,5. */
       if( panel1.AutoScrollMargin.Width < 5 ||
          panel1.AutoScrollMargin.Height < 5)
       {
          panel1.SetAutoScrollMargin(5, 5);
       }
    }
 }
```

Requirements

Platforms: Windows 98, Windows NT 4.0, Windows Millennium Edition, Windows 2000, Windows XP Home Edition, Windows XP Professional, Windows Server 2003 family

ScrollableControl.AutoScrollMinSize Property

Gets or sets the minimum size of the auto-scroll.

[Visual Basic]
```
Public Property AutoScrollMinSize As Size
```
[C#]
```
public Size AutoScrollMinSize {get; set;}
```
[C++]
```
public: __property Size get_AutoScrollMinSize();
public: __property void set_AutoScrollMinSize(Size);
```
[JScript]
```
public function get AutoScrollMinSize() : Size;
public function set AutoScrollMinSize(Size);
```

Property Value

A **Size** object that represents the minimum height and width of the scrollbars in pixels.

Remarks

The **AutoScrollMinSize** property is used to manage the screen size allocated to the automatic scroll bars.

Requirements

Platforms: Windows 98, Windows NT 4.0, Windows Millennium Edition, Windows 2000, Windows XP Home Edition, Windows XP Professional, Windows Server 2003 family

ScrollableControl.AutoScrollPosition Property

Gets or sets the location of the auto-scroll position.

[Visual Basic]
```
Public Property AutoScrollPosition As Point
```
[C#]
```
public Point AutoScrollPosition {get; set;}
```
[C++]
```
public: __property Point get_AutoScrollPosition();
public: __property void set_AutoScrollPosition(Point);
```
[JScript]
```
public function get AutoScrollPosition() : Point;
public function set AutoScrollPosition(Point);
```

Property Value

A **Point** object that represents the auto-scroll position in pixels.

Remarks

The **AutoScrollPosition** property is used to adjust the position of controls contained on the scrollable control.

When adding controls to a scrollable control the x-coordinate and y-coordinate of the **AutoScrollPosition** must be added to or subtracted as an offset from the corresponding coordinates of the **Control.Location** property of the control being added. To add a control above or to the left of the scroll position, the offset must be added to the desired location. Alternatively, to add a control below or to the right of the scroll position, the offset must be subtracted.

> **Note** **AutoScrollPosition** represents the location of the scrollable control's display rectangle. The **X** and **Y** coordinate values retrieved are negative if the control has scrolled away from its starting position (0,0). However, when setting this property, you must assign positive **X** and **Y** values to scroll away from the starting position and negative values to move toward it.

Example

[Visual Basic, C#, C++] The following example uses the **Scrollable-Control** derived class **Panel** and adds a button to the upper left corner of the scrollable area. The example allows for the offset determined by the **AutoScrollPosition**. This example assumes you have a **Form** that contains a **Panel** with a **Button** on it. To enable auto-scrolling, you should place the button outside of the client area of the **Panel**.

[Visual Basic]
```
Private Sub button1_Click(sender As Object, _
   e As EventArgs) Handles button1.Click
   ' Add a button to top left corner of the
   ' scrollable area, allowing for the offset.
   panel1.AutoScroll = True
   Dim myButton As New Button()
   myButton.Location = New Point( _
      0 + panel1.AutoScrollPosition.X, _
      0 + panel1.AutoScrollPosition.Y)
   panel1.Controls.Add(myButton)
End Sub
```

[C#]
```
private void button1_Click(object sender, EventArgs e)
{
   /* Add a button to top left corner of the
    * scrollable area, allowing for the offset. */
   panel1.AutoScroll = true;
   Button myButton = new Button();
   myButton.Location = new Point(
      0 + panel1.AutoScrollPosition.X,
      0 + panel1.AutoScrollPosition.Y);
   panel1.Controls.Add(myButton);
}
```

[C++]
```
private:
   void button1_Click(Object* sender, EventArgs* e) {
      /* Add a button to top left corner of the
      * scrollable area, allowing for the offset. */
      panel1->AutoScroll = true;
      Button* myButton = new Button();
      myButton->Location =  Point(
         0 + panel1->AutoScrollPosition.X,
         0 + panel1->AutoScrollPosition.Y);
      panel1->Controls->Add(myButton);
   }
```

Requirements

Platforms: Windows 98, Windows NT 4.0, Windows Millennium Edition, Windows 2000, Windows XP Home Edition, Windows XP Professional, Windows Server 2003 family

ScrollableControl.CreateParams Property

This member overrides **Control.CreateParams**.

[Visual Basic]
```
Overrides Protected ReadOnly Property CreateParams As CreateParams
```
[C#]
```
protected override CreateParams CreateParams {get;}
```
[C++]
```
protected: __property CreateParams* get_CreateParams();
```
[JScript]
```
protected override function get CreateParams() : CreateParams;
```

Requirements

Platforms: Windows 98, Windows NT 4.0, Windows Millennium Edition, Windows 2000, Windows XP Home Edition, Windows XP Professional, Windows Server 2003 family

ScrollableControl.DisplayRectangle Property

This member overrides **Control.DisplayRectangle**.

[Visual Basic]
```
Overrides Public ReadOnly Property DisplayRectangle As Rectangle
```
[C#]
```
public override Rectangle DisplayRectangle {get;}
```
[C++]
```
public: __property Rectangle get_DisplayRectangle();
```
[JScript]
```
public override function get DisplayRectangle() : Rectangle;
```

Requirements

Platforms: Windows 98, Windows NT 4.0, Windows Millennium Edition, Windows 2000, Windows XP Home Edition, Windows XP Professional, Windows Server 2003 family

ScrollableControl.DockPadding Property

Gets the dock padding settings for all edges of the control.

[Visual Basic]
```
Public ReadOnly Property DockPadding As _
   ScrollableControl.DockPaddingEdges
```
[C#]
```
public ScrollableControl.DockPaddingEdges DockPadding {get;}
```
[C++]
```
public: __property ScrollableControl.DockPaddingEdges*
   get_DockPadding();
```
[JScript]
```
public function get DockPadding() :
   ScrollableControl.DockPaddingEdges;
```

Property Value

A **ScrollableControl.DockPaddingEdges** object that represents the padding for all the edges of a docked control.

Remarks

This property controls the border inside of this control for docked components.

Example

[Visual Basic, C#] The following example uses the derived class, **Panel**. The example docks a button in a panel control and cycles through the **ScrollableControl.DockPaddingEdges** properties, setting each individually on the click of the button. This code assumes a **Panel** control and a **Button** have been instantiated on a form, and a class level member variable named `myCounter` has been declared as a 32-bit signed integer. This code should be called on the **Click** event of the button.

[Visual Basic]
```
Private Sub SetDockPadding()
    ' Dock the button in the panel.
    button1.Dock = System.Windows.Forms.DockStyle.Fill

    ' Reset the counter if it is greater than 5.
    If myCounter > 5 Then
        myCounter = 0
    End If

    ' Set the appropriate DockPadding and display
    ' which one was set on the button face.
    Select Case myCounter
        Case 0
            panel1.DockPadding.All = 0
            button1.Text = "Start"
        Case 1
            panel1.DockPadding.Top = 10
            button1.Text = "Top"
        Case 2
            panel1.DockPadding.Bottom = 10
            button1.Text = "Bottom"
        Case 3
            panel1.DockPadding.Left = 10
            button1.Text = "Left"
        Case 4
            panel1.DockPadding.Right = 10
            button1.Text = "Right"
        Case 5
            panel1.DockPadding.All = 20
            button1.Text = "All"
    End Select

    ' Increment the counter.
    myCounter += 1
End Sub
```

[C#]
```
private void SetDockPadding()
 {
    // Dock the button in the panel.
    button1.Dock = System.Windows.Forms.DockStyle.Fill;

    // Reset the counter if it is greater than 5.
    if (myCounter > 5)
    {
       myCounter = 0;
    }

    // Set the appropriate DockPadding and display
    // which one was set on the button face.
    switch (myCounter)
    {
       case 0:
          panel1.DockPadding.All = 0;
          button1.Text = "Start";
          break;
       case 1:
          panel1.DockPadding.Top = 10;
          button1.Text = "Top";
          break;
       case 2:
          panel1.DockPadding.Bottom = 10;
          button1.Text = "Bottom";
          break;
       case 3:
          panel1.DockPadding.Left = 10;
          button1.Text = "Left";
          break;
       case 4:
          panel1.DockPadding.Right = 10;
          button1.Text = "Right";
          break;
       case 5:
          panel1.DockPadding.All = 20;
          button1.Text = "All";
          break;
    }

    // Increment the counter.
    myCounter += 1;
 }
```

Requirements

Platforms: Windows 98, Windows NT 4.0, Windows Millennium Edition, Windows 2000, Windows XP Home Edition, Windows XP Professional, Windows Server 2003 family

ScrollableControl.HScroll Property

Gets or sets a value indicating whether the horizontal scroll bar is visible.

[Visual Basic]
```
Protected Property HScroll As Boolean
```
[C#]
```
protected bool HScroll {get; set;}
```
[C++]
```
protected: __property bool get_HScroll();
protected: __property void set_HScroll(bool);
```
[JScript]
```
protected function get HScroll() : Boolean;
protected function set HScroll(Boolean);
```

Property Value

true if the horizontal scroll bar is visible; otherwise, **false**.

Requirements

Platforms: Windows 98, Windows NT 4.0, Windows Millennium Edition, Windows 2000, Windows XP Home Edition, Windows XP Professional, Windows Server 2003 family

ScrollableControl.VScroll Property

Gets or sets a value indicating whether the vertical scroll bar is visible.

[Visual Basic]
```
Protected Property VScroll As Boolean
```
[C#]
```
protected bool VScroll {get; set;}
```
[C++]
```
protected: __property bool get_VScroll();
protected: __property void set_VScroll(bool);
```

[JScript]
```
protected function get VScroll() : Boolean;
protected function set VScroll(Boolean);
```

Property Value

true if the vertical scroll bar is visible; otherwise, **false**.

Requirements

Platforms: Windows 98, Windows NT 4.0, Windows Millennium Edition, Windows 2000, Windows XP Home Edition, Windows XP Professional, Windows Server 2003 family

ScrollableControl.AdjustFormScrollbars Method

This member supports the .NET Framework infrastructure and is not intended to be used directly from your code.

[Visual Basic]
```
Protected Overridable Sub AdjustFormScrollbars( _
   ByVal displayScrollbars As Boolean _
)
```
[C#]
```
protected virtual void AdjustFormScrollbars(
   bool displayScrollbars
);
```
[C++]
```
protected: virtual void AdjustFormScrollbars(
   bool displayScrollbars
);
```
[JScript]
```
protected function AdjustFormScrollbars(
   displayScrollbars : Boolean
);
```

ScrollableControl.GetScrollState Method

This member supports the .NET Framework infrastructure and is not intended to be used directly from your code.

[Visual Basic]
```
Protected Function GetScrollState( _
   ByVal bit As Integer _
) As Boolean
```
[C#]
```
protected bool GetScrollState(
   int bit
);
```
[C++]
```
protected: bool GetScrollState(
   int bit
);
```
[JScript]
```
protected function GetScrollState(
   bit : int
) : Boolean;
```

ScrollableControl.OnLayout Method

This member overrides **Control.OnLayout**.

[Visual Basic]
```
Overrides Protected Sub OnLayout( _
   ByVal levent As LayoutEventArgs _
)
```
[C#]
```
protected override void OnLayout(
   LayoutEventArgs levent
);
```
[C++]
```
protected: void OnLayout(
   LayoutEventArgs* levent
);
```
[JScript]
```
protected override function OnLayout(
   levent : LayoutEventArgs
);
```

Requirements

Platforms: Windows 98, Windows NT 4.0, Windows Millennium Edition, Windows 2000, Windows XP Home Edition, Windows XP Professional, Windows Server 2003 family

ScrollableControl.OnMouseWheel Method

This member overrides **Control.OnMouseWheel**.

[Visual Basic]
```
Overrides Protected Sub OnMouseWheel( _
   ByVal e As MouseEventArgs _
)
```
[C#]
```
protected override void OnMouseWheel(
   MouseEventArgs e
);
```
[C++]
```
protected: void OnMouseWheel(
   MouseEventArgs* e
);
```
[JScript]
```
protected override function OnMouseWheel(
   e : MouseEventArgs
);
```

Requirements

Platforms: Windows 98, Windows NT 4.0, Windows Millennium Edition, Windows 2000, Windows XP Home Edition, Windows XP Professional, Windows Server 2003 family

ScrollableControl.OnVisibleChanged Method

This member overrides **Control.OnVisibleChanged**.

[Visual Basic]
```
Overrides Protected Sub OnVisibleChanged( _
   ByVal e As EventArgs _
)
```
[C#]
```
protected override void OnVisibleChanged(
   EventArgs e
);
```
[C++]
```
protected: void OnVisibleChanged(
   EventArgs* e
);
```

```
[JScript]
protected override function OnVisibleChanged(
   e : EventArgs
);
```

Requirements

Platforms: Windows 98, Windows NT 4.0, Windows Millennium Edition, Windows 2000, Windows XP Home Edition, Windows XP Professional, Windows Server 2003 family

ScrollableControl.ScaleCore Method

This member overrides **Control.ScaleCore**.

```
[Visual Basic]
Overrides Protected Sub ScaleCore( _
   ByVal dx As Single, _
   ByVal dy As Single _
)
[C#]
protected override void ScaleCore(
   float dx,
   float dy
);
[C++]
protected: void ScaleCore(
   float dx,
   float dy
);
[JScript]
protected override function ScaleCore(
   dx : float,
   dy : float
);
```

Requirements

Platforms: Windows 98, Windows NT 4.0, Windows Millennium Edition, Windows 2000, Windows XP Home Edition, Windows XP Professional, Windows Server 2003 family

ScrollableControl.ScrollControlIntoView Method

This member supports the .NET Framework infrastructure and is not intended to be used directly from your code.

```
[Visual Basic]
Public Sub ScrollControlIntoView( _
   ByVal activeControl As Control _
)
[C#]
public void ScrollControlIntoView(
   Control activeControl
);
[C++]
public: void ScrollControlIntoView(
   Control* activeControl
);
[JScript]
public function ScrollControlIntoView(
   activeControl : Control
);
```

ScrollableControl.SetAutoScrollMargin Method

Sets the size of the auto-scroll margins.

```
[Visual Basic]
Public Sub SetAutoScrollMargin( _
   ByVal x As Integer, _
   ByVal y As Integer _
)
[C#]
public void SetAutoScrollMargin(
   int x,
   int y
);
[C++]
public: void SetAutoScrollMargin(
   int x,
   int y
);
[JScript]
public function SetAutoScrollMargin(
   x : int,
   y : int
);
```

Parameters

x

The **Width** value.

y

The **Height** value.

Remarks

The margin sets the width and height of the border around each control. This margin is used to determine when scroll bars are needed on the container and where to scroll to when a control is selected.

> **Note** If a negative number is passed in as the *x* or *y* values, the value will be reset to zero.

Example

[Visual Basic, C#] The following example uses the derived class, **Panel**. The example evaluates the location of a text box and changes the appearance and behavior of its parent container, the panel control. This example assumes a **Panel** control, **TextBox**, and **Button** have been instantiated. Place the box on the panel so that it overlaps at least one of the panel's edges. Call this subprocedure on the click of a button to see the difference in the panel's behavior and appearance.

```
[Visual Basic]
Private Sub MySub()
    ' If the text box is outside the panel's bounds,
    ' turn on auto-scrolling and set the margin.
    If (text1.Location.X > panel1.Location.X) Or _
        (text1.Location.Y > panel1.Location.Y) Then

        panel1.AutoScroll = True
        ' If the AutoScrollMargin is set to
        ' less than (5,5), set it to 5,5.
        If (panel1.AutoScrollMargin.Width < 5) Or _
            (panel1.AutoScrollMargin.Height < 5) Then

            panel1.SetAutoScrollMargin(5, 5)
        End If
    End If
End Sub
```

[C#]
```
private void MySub()
 {
    /* If the text box is outside the panel's bounds,
       turn on auto-scrolling and set the margin. */
    if (text1.Location.X > panel1.Location.X ||
     text1.Location.Y > panel1.Location.Y)
    {
       panel1.AutoScroll = true;
       /* If the AutoScrollMargin is set to
          less than (5,5), set it to 5,5. */
       if(panel1.AutoScrollMargin.Width < 5 ||
        panel1.AutoScrollMargin.Height < 5)
       {
          panel1.SetAutoScrollMargin(5, 5);
       }
    }
 }
```

Requirements

Platforms: Windows 98, Windows NT 4.0, Windows Millennium Edition, Windows 2000, Windows XP Home Edition, Windows XP Professional, Windows Server 2003 family

ScrollableControl.SetDisplayRectLocation Method

This member supports the .NET Framework infrastructure and is not intended to be used directly from your code.

[Visual Basic]
```
Protected Sub SetDisplayRectLocation( _
   ByVal x As Integer, _
   ByVal y As Integer _
)
```
[C#]
```
protected void SetDisplayRectLocation(
   int x,
   int y
);
```
[C++]
```
protected: void SetDisplayRectLocation(
   int x,
   int y
);
```
[JScript]
```
protected function SetDisplayRectLocation(
   x : int,
   y : int
);
```

ScrollableControl.SetScrollState Method

This member supports the .NET Framework infrastructure and is not intended to be used directly from your code.

[Visual Basic]
```
Protected Sub SetScrollState( _
   ByVal bit As Integer, _
   ByVal value As Boolean _
)
```
[C#]
```
protected void SetScrollState(
   int bit,
   bool value
);
```
[C++]
```
protected: void SetScrollState(
   int bit,
   bool value
);
```
[JScript]
```
protected function SetScrollState(
   bit : int,
   value : Boolean
);
```

ScrollableControl.WndProc Method

This member overrides **Control.WndProc**.

[Visual Basic]
```
Overrides Protected Sub WndProc( _
   ByRef m As Message _
)
```
[C#]
```
protected override void WndProc(
   ref Message m
);
```
[C++]
```
protected: void WndProc(
   Message* m
);
```
[JScript]
```
protected override function WndProc(
   m : Message
);
```

Requirements

Platforms: Windows 98, Windows NT 4.0, Windows Millennium Edition, Windows 2000, Windows XP Home Edition, Windows XP Professional, Windows Server 2003 family

ScrollableControl.DockPaddingEdges Class

Determines the border padding for docked controls.

System.Object
  System.Windows.Forms.ScrollableControl.DockPaddingEdges

[Visual Basic]
```
Public Class ScrollableControl.DockPaddingEdges
   Implements ICloneable
```
[C#]
```
public class ScrollableControl.DockPaddingEdges : ICloneable
```
[C++]
```
public __gc class ScrollableControl.DockPaddingEdges : public
   ICloneable
```
[JScript]
```
public class ScrollableControl.DockPaddingEdges implements
   ICloneable
```

Thread Safety

Any public static (**Shared** in Visual Basic) members of this type are safe for multithreaded operations. Any instance members are not guaranteed to be thread safe.

Remarks

The **ScrollableControl.DockPaddingEdges** class creates a margin on a given edge or all edges of a docked control. You can set the width of this margin for each individual edge by setting the following properties: **Bottom**, **Top**, **Left**, **Right**. Alternatively, you can set all the edges to the same width simultaneously by setting the **All** property. If the size of the control is too large for its container, the control will be resized to fit in the container, minus the specified margin width.

Example

[Visual Basic, C#] The following example uses the derived class, **Panel**. The example docks a button in a panel control and cycles through the **ScrollableControl.DockPaddingEdges** properties, setting each individually on the click of the button. This code assumes a **Panel** control and a **Button** have been instantiated on a form, and a class-level member variable named `myCounter` has been declared as a 32-bit signed integer. This code should be called on the **Click** event of the button.

[Visual Basic]
```
Private Sub SetDockPadding()
    ' Dock the button in the panel.
    button1.Dock = System.Windows.Forms.DockStyle.Fill

    ' Reset the counter if it is greater than 5.
    If myCounter > 5 Then
        myCounter = 0
    End If

    ' Set the appropriate DockPadding and display
    ' which one was set on the button face.
    Select Case myCounter
        Case 0
            panel1.DockPadding.All = 0
            button1.Text = "Start"
        Case 1
            panel1.DockPadding.Top = 10
            button1.Text = "Top"
        Case 2
            panel1.DockPadding.Bottom = 10
            button1.Text = "Bottom"
        Case 3
            panel1.DockPadding.Left = 10
            button1.Text = "Left"
        Case 4
            panel1.DockPadding.Right = 10
            button1.Text = "Right"
        Case 5
            panel1.DockPadding.All = 20
            button1.Text = "All"
    End Select

    ' Increment the counter.
    myCounter += 1
End Sub
```

[C#]
```
private void SetDockPadding()
 {
    // Dock the button in the panel.
    button1.Dock = System.Windows.Forms.DockStyle.Fill;

    // Reset the counter if it is greater than 5.
    if (myCounter > 5)
    {
       myCounter = 0;
    }

    /* Set the appropriate DockPadding and display
       which one was set on the button face. */
    switch (myCounter)
    {
       case 0:
          panel1.DockPadding.All = 0;
          button1.Text = "Start";
          break;
       case 1:
          panel1.DockPadding.Top = 10;
          button1.Text = "Top";
          break;
       case 2:
          panel1.DockPadding.Bottom = 10;
          button1.Text = "Bottom";
          break;
       case 3:
          panel1.DockPadding.Left = 10;
          button1.Text = "Left";
          break;
       case 4:
          panel1.DockPadding.Right = 10;
          button1.Text = "Right";
          break;
       case 5:
          panel1.DockPadding.All = 20;
          button1.Text = "All";
          break;
    }

    // Increment the counter.
    myCounter += 1;
 }
```

Requirements

Namespace: System.Windows.Forms

Platforms: Windows 98, Windows NT 4.0, Windows Millennium Edition, Windows 2000, Windows XP Home Edition, Windows XP Professional, Windows Server 2003 family

Assembly: System.Windows.Forms (in System.Windows.Forms.dll)

ScrollableControl.DockPaddingEdges.All Property

Gets or sets the padding width for all edges of a docked control.

[Visual Basic]
```
Public Property All As Integer
```
[C#]
```
public int All {get; set;}
```
[C++]
```
public: __property int get_All();
public: __property void set_All(int);
```
[JScript]
```
public function get All() : int;
public function set All(int);
```

Property Value

The padding width in pixels.

Remarks

The padding width assigned to this property is applied to all edges of the docked control.

Example

See related example in the **System.Windows.Forms.Scrollable-ControlDockPaddingEdges** class topic.

Requirements

Platforms: Windows 98, Windows NT 4.0, Windows Millennium Edition, Windows 2000, Windows XP Home Edition, Windows XP Professional, Windows Server 2003 family

ScrollableControl.DockPaddingEdges.Bottom Property

Gets or sets the padding width for the bottom edge of a docked control.

[Visual Basic]
```
Public Property Bottom As Integer
```
[C#]
```
public int Bottom {get; set;}
```
[C++]
```
public: __property int get_Bottom();
public: __property void set_Bottom(int);
```
[JScript]
```
public function get Bottom() : int;
public function set Bottom(int);
```

Property Value

The padding width in pixels.

Remarks

The padding width assigned to this property is applied only to the bottom edge of the docked control.

Example

See related example in the **System.Windows.Forms.Scrollable-ControlDockPaddingEdges** class topic.

Requirements

Platforms: Windows 98, Windows NT 4.0, Windows Millennium Edition, Windows 2000, Windows XP Home Edition, Windows XP Professional, Windows Server 2003 family

ScrollableControl.DockPaddingEdges.Left Property

Gets or sets the padding width for the left edge of a docked control.

[Visual Basic]
```
Public Property Left As Integer
```
[C#]
```
public int Left {get; set;}
```
[C++]
```
public: __property int get_Left();
public: __property void set_Left(int);
```
[JScript]
```
public function get Left() : int;
public function set Left(int);
```

Property Value

The padding width in pixels.

Remarks

The padding width assigned to this property is applied only to the left edge of the docked control.

Example

See related example in the **System.Windows.Forms.Scrollable-ControlDockPaddingEdges** class topic.

Requirements

Platforms: Windows 98, Windows NT 4.0, Windows Millennium Edition, Windows 2000, Windows XP Home Edition, Windows XP Professional, Windows Server 2003 family

ScrollableControl.DockPaddingEdges.Right Property

Gets or sets the padding width for the right edge of a docked control.

[Visual Basic]
```
Public Property Right As Integer
```
[C#]
```
public int Right {get; set;}
```
[C++]
```
public: __property int get_Right();
public: __property void set_Right(int);
```
[JScript]
```
public function get Right() : int;
public function set Right(int);
```

Property Value

The padding width in pixels.

Remarks

The padding width assigned to this property is applied only to the right edge of the docked control.

Example

See related example in the **System.Windows.Forms.Scrollable-ControlDockPaddingEdges** class topic.

Requirements

Platforms: Windows 98, Windows NT 4.0, Windows Millennium Edition, Windows 2000, Windows XP Home Edition, Windows XP Professional, Windows Server 2003 family

ScrollableControl.DockPaddingEdges.Top Property

Gets or sets the padding width for the top edge of a docked control.

```
[Visual Basic]
Public Property Top As Integer
[C#]
public int Top {get; set;}
[C++]
public: __property int get_Top();
public: __property void set_Top(int);
[JScript]
public function get Top() : int;
public function set Top(int);
```

Property Value

The padding width in pixels.

Remarks

The padding width assigned to this property is applied only to the top edge of the docked control.

Example

See related example in the **System.Windows.Forms.Scrollable-ControlDockPaddingEdges** class topic.

Requirements

Platforms: Windows 98, Windows NT 4.0, Windows Millennium Edition, Windows 2000, Windows XP Home Edition, Windows XP Professional, Windows Server 2003 family

ScrollableControl.DockPaddingEdges.Equals Method

This member overrides **Object.Equals**.

```
[Visual Basic]
Overrides Public Function Equals( _
   ByVal other As Object _
) As Boolean
[C#]
public override bool Equals(
   object other
);
[C++]
public: bool Equals(
   Object* other
);
[JScript]
public override function Equals(
   other : Object
) : Boolean;
```

Requirements

Platforms: Windows 98, Windows NT 4.0, Windows Millennium Edition, Windows 2000, Windows XP Home Edition, Windows XP Professional, Windows Server 2003 family

ScrollableControl.DockPaddingEdges.GetHashCode Method

This member overrides **Object.GetHashCode**.

```
[Visual Basic]
Overrides Public Function GetHashCode() As Integer
[C#]
public override int GetHashCode();
[C++]
public: int GetHashCode();
[JScript]
public override function GetHashCode() : int;
```

Requirements

Platforms: Windows 98, Windows NT 4.0, Windows Millennium Edition, Windows 2000, Windows XP Home Edition, Windows XP Professional, Windows Server 2003 family

ScrollableControl.DockPadding-Edges.ICloneable.Clone Method

This member supports the .NET Framework infrastructure and is not intended to be used directly from your code.

```
[Visual Basic]
Private Function Clone() As Object Implements ICloneable.Clone
[C#]
object ICloneable.Clone();
[C++]
private: Object* ICloneable::Clone();
[JScript]
private function ICloneable.Clone() : Object;
```

ScrollableControl.DockPaddingEdges.ToString Method

This member overrides **Object.ToString**.

```
[Visual Basic]
Overrides Public Function ToString() As String
[C#]
public override string ToString();
[C++]
public: String* ToString();
[JScript]
public override function ToString() : String;
```

Requirements

Platforms: Windows 98, Windows NT 4.0, Windows Millennium Edition, Windows 2000, Windows XP Home Edition, Windows XP Professional, Windows Server 2003 family

ScrollableControl.DockPaddingEdgesConverter Class

This type supports the .NET Framework infrastructure and is not intended to be used directly from your code.

[Visual Basic]
```
Public Class ScrollableControl.DockPaddingEdgesConverter
   Inherits TypeConverter
```
[C#]
```
public class ScrollableControl.DockPaddingEdgesConverter :
   TypeConverter
```
[C++]
```
public __gc class ScrollableControl.DockPaddingEdgesConverter :
   public TypeConverter
```
[JScript]
```
public class ScrollableControl.DockPaddingEdgesConverter extends
   TypeConverter
```

ScrollableControl.DockPaddingEdgesConverter Constructor

This member supports the .NET Framework infrastructure and is not intended to be used directly from your code.

[Visual Basic]
```
Public Sub New()
```
[C#]
```
public ScrollableControl.DockPaddingEdgesConverter();
```
[C++]
```
public: DockPaddingEdgesConverter();
```
[JScript]
```
public function ScrollableControl.DockPaddingEdgesConverter();
```

ScrollableControl.DockPaddingEdgesConverter.GetProperties Method

This member supports the .NET Framework infrastructure and is not intended to be used directly from your code.

Overload List

This member overrides **TypeConverter.GetProperties**.

[Visual Basic] **Overloads Overrides Public Function GetProperties(ITypeDescriptorContext, Object, Attribute()) As PropertyDescriptorCollection**

[C#] **public override PropertyDescriptorCollection GetProperties(ITypeDescriptorContext, object, Attribute[]);**

[C++] **public: PropertyDescriptorCollection* GetProperties(ITypeDescriptorContext*, Object*, Attribute[]);**

[JScript] **public override function GetProperties(ITypeDescriptorContext, Object, Attribute[]) : PropertyDescriptorCollection;**

This member supports the .NET Framework infrastructure and is not intended to be used directly from your code.

[Visual Basic] **Overloads Public Function GetProperties(Object) As PropertyDescriptorCollection**

[C#] **public PropertyDescriptorCollection GetProperties(object);**

[C++] **public: PropertyDescriptorCollection* GetProperties(Object*);**

[JScript] **public function GetProperties(Object) : PropertyDescriptorCollection;**

This member supports the .NET Framework infrastructure and is not intended to be used directly from your code.

[Visual Basic] **Overloads Public Function GetProperties(ITypeDescriptorContext, Object) As PropertyDescriptorCollection**

[C#] **public PropertyDescriptorCollection GetProperties(ITypeDescriptorContext, object);**

[C++] **public: PropertyDescriptorCollection* GetProperties(ITypeDescriptorContext*, Object*);**

[JScript] **public function GetProperties(ITypeDescriptorContext, Object) : PropertyDescriptorCollection;**

ScrollableControl.DockPaddingEdgesConverter.GetProperties Method (ITypeDescriptorContext, Object, Attribute[])

This member overrides **TypeConverter.GetProperties**.

[Visual Basic]
```
Overrides Overloads Public Function GetProperties( _
   ByVal context As ITypeDescriptorContext, _
   ByVal value As Object, _
   ByVal attributes() As Attribute _
) As PropertyDescriptorCollection
```
[C#]
```
public override PropertyDescriptorCollection GetProperties(
   ITypeDescriptorContext context,
   object value,
   Attribute[] attributes
);
```
[C++]
```
public: PropertyDescriptorCollection* GetProperties(
   ITypeDescriptorContext* context,
   Object* value,
   Attribute* attributes[]
);
```
[JScript]
```
public override function GetProperties(
   context : ITypeDescriptorContext,
   value : Object,
   attributes : Attribute[]
) : PropertyDescriptorCollection;
```

Requirements

Platforms: Windows 98, Windows NT 4.0, Windows Millennium Edition, Windows 2000, Windows XP Home Edition, Windows XP Professional, Windows Server 2003 family

ScrollableControl.DockPaddingEdgesConverter.GetPropertiesSupported Method

This member supports the .NET Framework infrastructure and is not intended to be used directly from your code.

Overload List

This member overrides **TypeConverter.GetPropertiesSupported**.

[Visual Basic] **Overloads Overrides Public Function GetPropertiesSupported(ITypeDescriptorContext) As Boolean**

[C#] **public override bool GetPropertiesSupported(ITypeDescriptorContext);**

[C++] **public: bool GetPropertiesSupported(ITypeDescriptorContext*);**

[JScript] **public override function GetPropertiesSupported(ITypeDescriptorContext) : Boolean;**

This member supports the .NET Framework infrastructure and is not intended to be used directly from your code.

[Visual Basic] **Overloads Public Function GetPropertiesSupported() As Boolean**

[C#] **public bool GetPropertiesSupported();**

[C++] **public: bool GetPropertiesSupported();**

[JScript] **public function GetPropertiesSupported() : Boolean;**

ScrollableControl.DockPaddingEdgesConverter.GetPropertiesSupported Method (ITypeDescriptorContext)

This member overrides **TypeConverter.GetPropertiesSupported**.

[Visual Basic]
```
Overrides Overloads Public Function GetPropertiesSupported( _
   ByVal context As ITypeDescriptorContext _
) As Boolean
```
[C#]
```
public override bool GetPropertiesSupported(
   ITypeDescriptorContext context
);
```
[C++]
```
public: bool GetPropertiesSupported(
   ITypeDescriptorContext* context
);
```
[JScript]
```
public override function GetPropertiesSupported(
   context : ITypeDescriptorContext
) : Boolean;
```

Requirements

Platforms: Windows 98, Windows NT 4.0, Windows Millennium Edition, Windows 2000, Windows XP Home Edition, Windows XP Professional, Windows Server 2003 family

ScrollBar Class

Implements the basic functionality of a scroll bar control.

System.Object
  System.MarshalByRefObject
    System.ComponentModel.Component
      System.Windows.Forms.Control
        System.Windows.Forms.ScrollBar
          System.Windows.Forms.HScrollBar
          System.Windows.Forms.VScrollBar

[Visual Basic]
```
MustInherit Public Class ScrollBar
   Inherits Control
```
[C#]
```
public abstract class ScrollBar : Control
```
[C++]
```
public __gc __abstract class ScrollBar : public Control
```
[JScript]
```
public abstract class ScrollBar extends Control
```

Thread Safety

Any public static (**Shared** in Visual Basic) members of this type are safe for multithreaded operations. Any instance members are not guaranteed to be thread safe.

Remarks

You typically do not inherit directly from **ScrollBar**. To create your own scroll bar class, inherit from the **VScrollBar** or **HScrollBar** class.

To adjust the value range of the scroll bar control, set the **Minimum** and **Maximum** properties. To adjust the distance the scroll box moves, set the **SmallChange** and **LargeChange** properties. To adjust the starting point of the scroll box, set the **Value** property when the control is initially displayed.

> **Note** The scroll box is sometimes referred to as the scroll thumb.

Example

[Visual Basic, C#, JScript] The following example adds horizontal and vertical scroll bars to a **PictureBox** control, and loads an **Image** into the picture box on the **DoubleClick** event of the control. At any time you can double-click the picture box and load a new image. If the image is larger than the control, the scroll bars will be displayed so you can scroll to view the remainder of the image. The example assumes that a **PictureBox**, with a **VScrollBar** and **HScrollBar** docked to two of its edges, has been created on a **Form**. It also assumes a refernce to the the **System.Drawing** namespace has been added. Make sure the `HandleScroll` method is set as the **Scroll** event handler delegate for both the **VScrollBar** and **HScrollBar**. For additional code that can extend this example, see the **LargeChange**, **SmallChange**, **Maximum**, **Minimum** or **Value** members. You might consider setting the properties of your scroll bar based on the properties of its parent control. For instance, you can add a method to the example that sets the **Maximum** value equal to the **Height** or **Width** of the **Image** assigned to the **PictureBox**. Set the **LargeChange** value equal to the height or width of the **PictureBox** (with the height or width of the scroll bar subtracted). This prevents the user from scrolling past the edge of the image, and the **LargeChange** will only move the image's viewable area the same distance as the area displayed in the picture box.

[Visual Basic]
```
Private Sub pictureBox1_DoubleClick(sender As [Object], e As ↵
EventArgs) _
  Handles pictureBox1.DoubleClick
   ' Open the dialog box so the user can select a new image.
   If openFileDialog1.ShowDialog() <> DialogResult.Cancel Then
      ' Display the image in the PictureBox.
      pictureBox1.Image = Image.FromFile(openFileDialog1.FileName)
      Me.DisplayScrollBars()
      Me.SetScrollBarValues()
   End If
End Sub

Private Sub Form1_Resize(ByVal sender As Object, ByVal e ↵
As System.EventArgs) Handles MyBase.Resize
   ' If the PictureBox has an image, see if it needs
   ' scrollbars and refresh the image.
   If Not (pictureBox1.Image Is Nothing) Then
      Me.DisplayScrollBars()
      Me.SetScrollBarValues()
      Me.Refresh()
   End If
End Sub

Public Sub DisplayScrollBars()
   ' If the image is wider than the PictureBox, show the HScrollBar.
   If pictureBox1.Width > pictureBox1.Image.Width - _
     Me.vScrollBar1.Width Then
      hScrollBar1.Visible = False
   Else
      hScrollBar1.Visible = True
   End If

   ' If the image is taller than the PictureBox, show the VScrollBar.
   If pictureBox1.Height > pictureBox1.Image.Height - _
     Me.hScrollBar1.Height Then
      vScrollBar1.Visible = False
   Else
      vScrollBar1.Visible = True
   End If
End Sub

Private Sub HandleScroll(sender As [Object], se As ScrollEventArgs) _
  Handles vScrollBar1.Scroll, hScrollBar1.Scroll
   ' Create a graphics object and draw a portion
   ' of the image in the PictureBox.
   Dim g As Graphics = pictureBox1.CreateGraphics()

   g.DrawImage(pictureBox1.Image, New Rectangle(0, 0, ↵
pictureBox1.Right - vScrollBar1.Width, _
     pictureBox1.Bottom - hScrollBar1.Height), _
     New Rectangle(hScrollBar1.Value, vScrollBar1.Value, ↵
pictureBox1.Right - vScrollBar1.Width, _
     pictureBox1.Bottom - hScrollBar1.Height), GraphicsUnit.Pixel)

   pictureBox1.Update()
End Sub

Public Sub SetScrollBarValues()
   ' Set the Maximum, Minimum, LargeChange and SmallChange properties.
   Me.vScrollBar1.Minimum = 0
   Me.hScrollBar1.Minimum = 0

   ' If the offset does not make the Maximum less than zero, ↵
set its value.
   If Me.pictureBox1.Image.Size.Width - ↵
pictureBox1.ClientSize.Width > 0 Then
      Me.hScrollBar1.Maximum = Me.pictureBox1.Image.Size.Width - _
        pictureBox1.ClientSize.Width
   End If
   ' If the VScrollBar is visible, adjust the Maximum of the
   ' HScrollBar to account for the width of the VScrollBar.
   If Me.vScrollBar1.Visible Then
      Me.hScrollBar1.Maximum += Me.vScrollBar1.Width
   End If
   Me.hScrollBar1.LargeChange = Me.hScrollBar1.Maximum / 10
```

```
   Me.hScrollBar1.SmallChange = Me.hScrollBar1.Maximum / 20
   ' Adjust the Maximum value to make the raw Maximum value           ↵
attainable by user interaction.
   Me.hScrollBar1.Maximum += Me.hScrollBar1.LargeChange

   ' If the offset does not make the Maximum less than zero,          ↵
 set its value.
   If Me.pictureBox1.Image.Size.Height -                              ↵
pictureBox1.ClientSize.Height > 0 Then
      Me.vScrollBar1.Maximum = Me.pictureBox1.Image.Size.Height - _
        pictureBox1.ClientSize.Height
   End If
   ' If the HScrollBar is visible, adjust the Maximum of the
   ' VSCrollBar to account for the width of the HScrollBar.
   If Me.hScrollBar1.Visible Then
      Me.vScrollBar1.Maximum += Me.hScrollBar1.Height
   End If
   Me.vScrollBar1.LargeChange = Me.vScrollBar1.Maximum / 10
   Me.vScrollBar1.SmallChange = Me.vScrollBar1.Maximum / 20
   ' Adjust the Maximum value to make the raw Maximum value           ↵
attainable by user interaction.
   Me.vScrollBar1.Maximum += Me.vScrollBar1.LargeChange
End Sub
```

[C#]

```
private void pictureBox1_DoubleClick (Object sender, EventArgs e)
{
   // Open the dialog box so the user can select a new image.
   if(openFileDialog1.ShowDialog() != DialogResult.Cancel)
   {
      // Display the image in the PictureBox.
      pictureBox1.Image = Image.FromFile(openFileDialog1.FileName);
      this.DisplayScrollBars();
      this.SetScrollBarValues();
   }
}

protected void Form1_Resize (Object sender, EventArgs e)
{
   /* If the PictureBox has an image, see if it needs
      scrollbars and refresh the image. */
   if(pictureBox1.Image != null)
   {
      this.DisplayScrollBars();
      this.SetScrollBarValues();
      this.Refresh();
   }
}

public void DisplayScrollBars()
{
   // If the image is wider than the PictureBox, show the HScrollBar.
   if (pictureBox1.Width > pictureBox1.Image.Width -                  ↵
this.vScrollBar1.Width)
   {
      hScrollBar1.Visible = false;
   }
   else
   {
      hScrollBar1.Visible = true;
   }

   // If the image is taller than the PictureBox, show the VScrollBar.
   if (pictureBox1.Height > pictureBox1.Image.Height -                ↵
this.hScrollBar1.Height)
   {
      vScrollBar1.Visible = false;
   }
   else
   {
      vScrollBar1.Visible = true;
   }
}

private void HandleScroll(Object sender, ScrollEventArgs se)
{
   /* Create a graphics object and draw a portion
      of the image in the PictureBox. */
   Graphics g = pictureBox1.CreateGraphics();

   g.DrawImage(pictureBox1.Image,
     new Rectangle(0, 0, pictureBox1.Right - vScrollBar1.Width,
     pictureBox1.Bottom - hScrollBar1.Height),
     new Rectangle(hScrollBar1.Value, vScrollBar1.Value,
     pictureBox1.Right - vScrollBar1.Width,
     pictureBox1.Bottom - hScrollBar1.Height),
     GraphicsUnit.Pixel);

     pictureBox1.Update();
}

public void SetScrollBarValues()
{
   // Set the Maximum, Minimum, LargeChange and SmallChange properties.
   this.vScrollBar1.Minimum = 0;
   this.hScrollBar1.Minimum = 0;
   // If the offset does not make the Maximum less than zero,         ↵
set its value.
   if( (this.pictureBox1.Image.Size.Width -                           ↵
pictureBox1.ClientSize.Width) > 0)
   {
      this.hScrollBar1.Maximum =                                      ↵
this.pictureBox1.Image.Size.Width - pictureBox1.ClientSize.Width;
   }
   /* If the VScrollBar is visible, adjust the Maximum of the
      HSCrollBar to account for the width of the VScrollBar. */
   if(this.vScrollBar1.Visible)
   {
      this.hScrollBar1.Maximum += this.vScrollBar1.Width;
   }
   this.hScrollBar1.LargeChange = this.hScrollBar1.Maximum / 10;
   this.hScrollBar1.SmallChange = this.hScrollBar1.Maximum / 20;
   // Adjust the Maximum value to make the raw Maximum value          ↵
attainable by user interaction.
   this.hScrollBar1.Maximum += this.hScrollBar1.LargeChange;

   // If the offset does not make the Maximum less than zero,         ↵
 set its value.
   if( (this.pictureBox1.Image.Size.Height -                          ↵
pictureBox1.ClientSize.Height) > 0)
   {
      this.vScrollBar1.Maximum =                                      ↵
this.pictureBox1.Image.Size.Height - pictureBox1.ClientSize.Height;
   }
   /* If the HScrollBar is visible, adjust the Maximum of the
      VSCrollBar to account for the width of the HScrollBar.*/
   if(this.hScrollBar1.Visible)
   {
      this.vScrollBar1.Maximum += this.hScrollBar1.Height;
   }
   this.vScrollBar1.LargeChange = this.vScrollBar1.Maximum / 10;
   this.vScrollBar1.SmallChange = this.vScrollBar1.Maximum / 20;
   // Adjust the Maximum value to make the raw Maximum value          ↵
attainable by user interaction.
   this.vScrollBar1.Maximum += this.vScrollBar1.LargeChange;
}
```

[JScript]

```
private function pictureBox1_DoubleClick (sender : Object,
                                         e : EventArgs)
 {
    // Open the dialog so the user can select a new image.
    if(openFileDialog1.ShowDialog() !=                                ↵
System.Windows.Forms.DialogResult.Cancel)
    {
       // Display the image in the PictureBox.
       pictureBox1.Image = Image.FromFile(openFileDialog1.FileName);
       this.DisplayScrollBars();
       this.SetScrollBarValues();
    }
 }
```

```
private function Form1_Resize (sender : Object,
                              e : EventArgs)
{
   /* If the PictureBox has an image, see if it needs
      scrollbars and refresh the image. */
   if(pictureBox1.Image != null)
   {
      this.SetScrollBarValues();
      this.DisplayScrollBars();
      this.Refresh();
   }
}

public function DisplayScrollBars()
{
   // If the image is wider than the PictureBox, show the HScrollBar.
   if (pictureBox1.Width > pictureBox1.Image.Width -                ↵
this.vScrollBar1.Width)
   {
      hScrollBar1.Visible = false;
   }
   else
   {
      hScrollBar1.Visible = true;
   }

   // If the image is taller than the PictureBox, show the VScrollBar.
      if (pictureBox1.Height > pictureBox1.Image.Height -             ↵
this.hScrollBar1.Height)
   {
      vScrollBar1.Visible = false;
   }
   else
   {
      vScrollBar1.Visible = true;
   }
}

private function HandleScroll(sender : Object,
                             se : ScrollEventArgs)
{
   /* Create a graphics object and draw a portion
      of the image in the PictureBox. */
   Graphics g = pictureBox1.CreateGraphics();

   g.DrawImage(pictureBox1.Image,
     new Rectangle(0, 0, pictureBox1.Right - vScrollBar1.Width,
     pictureBox1.Bottom - hScrollBar1.Height),
     new Rectangle(hScrollBar1.Value, vScrollBar1.Value,
     pictureBox1.Right - vScrollBar1.Width,
     pictureBox1.Bottom - hScrollBar1.Height),
     GraphicsUnit.Pixel);

     pictureBox1.Update();
}

public function SetScrollBarValues() {
   // Set the Maximum, Minimum, LargeChange and SmallChange properties.
   this.vScrollBar1.Minimum = 0;
   this.hScrollBar1.Minimum = 0;
   // If the offset does not make the Maximum less than zero,        ↵
set its value.
   if( (this.pictureBox1.Image.Size.Width -                          ↵
pictureBox1.ClientSize.Width) > 0)
   {
      this.hScrollBar1.Maximum =                                     ↵
this.pictureBox1.Image.Size.Width - pictureBox1.ClientSize.Width;
   }
   /* If the VScrollBar is visible, adjust the Maximum of the
      HSCrollBar to account for the width of the VScrollBar. */
   if(this.vScrollBar1.Visible)
   {
      this.hScrollBar1.Maximum += this.vScrollBar1.Width;
   }
   this.hScrollBar1.LargeChange = this.hScrollBar1.Maximum / 10;
   this.hScrollBar1.SmallChange = this.hScrollBar1.Maximum / 20;
   // Adjust the Maximum value to make the raw Maximum value         ↵
attainable by user interaction.
   this.hScrollBar1.Maximum += this.hScrollBar1.LargeChange;

   // If the offset does not make the Maximum less than zero,        ↵
set its value.
   if( (this.pictureBox1.Image.Size.Height -                         ↵
pictureBox1.ClientSize.Height) > 0)
   {
      this.vScrollBar1.Maximum =                                     ↵
this.pictureBox1.Image.Size.Height - pictureBox1.ClientSize.Height;
   }
   /* If the HScrollBar is visible, adjust the Maximum of the
      VSCrollBar to account for the width of the HScrollBar.*/
   if(this.hScrollBar1.Visible)
   {
      this.vScrollBar1.Maximum += this.hScrollBar1.Height;
   }
   this.vScrollBar1.LargeChange = this.vScrollBar1.Maximum / 10;
   this.vScrollBar1.SmallChange = this.vScrollBar1.Maximum / 20;
   // Adjust the Maximum value to make the raw Maximum value         ↵
attainable by user interaction.
   this.vScrollBar1.Maximum += this.vScrollBar1.LargeChange;
}
```

Requirements

Namespace: System.Windows.Forms

Platforms: Windows 98, Windows NT 4.0, Windows Millennium Edition, Windows 2000, Windows XP Home Edition, Windows XP Professional, Windows Server 2003 family, .NET Compact Framework - Windows CE .NET

Assembly: System.Windows.Forms (in System.Windows.Forms.dll)

ScrollBar Constructor

Initializes a new instance of the **ScrollBar** class.

[Visual Basic]
```
Public Sub New()
```
[C#]
```
public ScrollBar();
```
[C++]
```
public: ScrollBar();
```
[JScript]
```
public function ScrollBar();
```

Remarks

By default, the **TabStop** property is set to **false** when a new instance of a **ScrollBar** is created.

Requirements

Platforms: Windows 98, Windows NT 4.0, Windows Millennium Edition, Windows 2000, Windows XP Home Edition, Windows XP Professional, Windows Server 2003 family

ScrollBar.BackColor Property

This member overrides **Control.BackColor**.

[Visual Basic]
```
Overrides Public Property BackColor As Color
```
[C#]
```
public override Color BackColor {get; set;}
```

[C++]
```
public: __property Color get_BackColor();
public: __property void set_BackColor(Color);
```
[JScript]
```
public override function get BackColor() : Color;
public override function set BackColor(Color);
```

Requirements

Platforms: Windows 98, Windows NT 4.0, Windows Millennium Edition, Windows 2000, Windows XP Home Edition, Windows XP Professional, Windows Server 2003 family

ScrollBar.BackgroundImage Property

This member overrides **Control.BackgroundImage**.

[Visual Basic]
```
Overrides Public Property BackgroundImage As Image
```
[C#]
```
public override Image BackgroundImage {get; set;}
```
[C++]
```
public: __property Image* get_BackgroundImage();
public: __property void set_BackgroundImage(Image*);
```
[JScript]
```
public override function get BackgroundImage() : Image;
public override function set BackgroundImage(Image);
```

Requirements

Platforms: Windows 98, Windows NT 4.0, Windows Millennium Edition, Windows 2000, Windows XP Home Edition, Windows XP Professional, Windows Server 2003 family

ScrollBar.CreateParams Property

This member overrides **Control.CreateParams**.

[Visual Basic]
```
Overrides Protected ReadOnly Property CreateParams As CreateParams
```
[C#]
```
protected override CreateParams CreateParams {get;}
```
[C++]
```
protected: __property CreateParams* get_CreateParams();
```
[JScript]
```
protected override function get CreateParams() : CreateParams;
```

Requirements

Platforms: Windows 98, Windows NT 4.0, Windows Millennium Edition, Windows 2000, Windows XP Home Edition, Windows XP Professional, Windows Server 2003 family

ScrollBar.DefaultImeMode Property

Gets the default Input Method Editor (IME) mode supported by this control.

[Visual Basic]
```
Overrides Protected ReadOnly Property DefaultImeMode As ImeMode
```
[C#]
```
protected override ImeMode DefaultImeMode {get;}
```
[C++]
```
protected: __property ImeMode get_DefaultImeMode();
```
[JScript]
```
protected override function get DefaultImeMode() : ImeMode;
```

Property Value

One of the **ImeMode** values.

Remarks

As implemented in the **ScrollBar** class, this property always returns the **ImeMode.Disable** value.

Requirements

Platforms: Windows 98, Windows NT 4.0, Windows Millennium Edition, Windows 2000, Windows XP Home Edition, Windows XP Professional, Windows Server 2003 family

ScrollBar.Font Property

This member overrides **Control.Font**.

[Visual Basic]
```
Overrides Public Property Font As Font
```
[C#]
```
public override Font Font {get; set;}
```
[C++]
```
public: __property Font* get_Font();
public: __property void set_Font(Font*);
```
[JScript]
```
public override function get Font() : Font;
public override function set Font(Font);
```

Requirements

Platforms: Windows 98, Windows NT 4.0, Windows Millennium Edition, Windows 2000, Windows XP Home Edition, Windows XP Professional, Windows Server 2003 family

ScrollBar.ForeColor Property

This member overrides **Control.ForeColor**.

[Visual Basic]
```
Overrides Public Property ForeColor As Color
```
[C#]
```
public override Color ForeColor {get; set;}
```
[C++]
```
public: __property Color get_ForeColor();
public: __property void set_ForeColor(Color);
```
[JScript]
```
public override function get ForeColor() : Color;
public override function set ForeColor(Color);
```

Requirements

Platforms: Windows 98, Windows NT 4.0, Windows Millennium Edition, Windows 2000, Windows XP Home Edition, Windows XP Professional, Windows Server 2003 family

ScrollBar.ImeMode Property

Gets or sets the Input Method Editor (IME) mode supported by this control.

[Visual Basic]
```
Public Shadows Property ImeMode As ImeMode
```

```
[C#]
public new ImeMode ImeMode {get; set;}
[C++]
public: __property ImeMode get_ImeMode();
public: __property void set_ImeMode(ImeMode);
[JScript]
public hide function get ImeMode() : ImeMode;
public hide function set ImeMode(ImeMode);
```

Property Value

One of the **ImeMode** values.

Requirements

Platforms: Windows 98, Windows NT 4.0,
Windows Millennium Edition, Windows 2000,
Windows XP Home Edition, Windows XP Professional,
Windows Server 2003 family

ScrollBar.LargeChange Property

Gets or sets a value to be added to or subtracted from the **Value** property when the scroll box is moved a large distance.

```
[Visual Basic]
Public Property LargeChange As Integer
[C#]
public int LargeChange {get; set;}
[C++]
public: __property int get_LargeChange();
public: __property void set_LargeChange(int);
[JScript]
public function get LargeChange() : int;
public function set LargeChange(int);
```

Property Value

A numeric value. The default value is 10.

Exceptions

Exception Type	Condition
ArgumentException	The assigned value is less than 0.

Remarks

When the user presses the PAGE UP or PAGE DOWN key or clicks in the scroll bar track on either side of the scroll box, the **Value** property changes according to the value set in the **LargeChange** property.

You might consider setting the **LargeChange** value to a percentage of the **Height** (for a vertically oriented scroll bar) or **Width** (for a horizontally oriented scroll bar) values. This keeps the distance your scroll bar moves in proportion to its size.

Example

See related example in the **System.Windows.Forms.ScrollBar** class topic.

Requirements

Platforms: Windows 98, Windows NT 4.0,
Windows Millennium Edition, Windows 2000,
Windows XP Home Edition, Windows XP Professional,
Windows Server 2003 family,
.NET Compact Framework - Windows CE .NET

ScrollBar.Maximum Property

Gets or sets the upper limit of values of the scrollable range.

```
[Visual Basic]
Public Property Maximum As Integer
[C#]
public int Maximum {get; set;}
[C++]
public: __property int get_Maximum();
public: __property void set_Maximum(int);
[JScript]
public function get Maximum() : int;
public function set Maximum(int);
```

Property Value

A numeric value. The default value is 100.

Remarks

You might consider adjusting the **Maximum** property dynamically to match the size of the scroll bar's parent in proportion to pixel size or to the number of rows or lines displayed.

> **Note** The value of a scroll bar cannot reach its maximum value through user interaction at run time. The maximum value that can be reached is equal to the **Maximum** property value minus the **LargeChange** property value plus one. The maximum value can only be reached programmatically.

Example

See related example in the **System.Windows.Forms.ScrollBar** class topic.

Requirements

Platforms: Windows 98, Windows NT 4.0,
Windows Millennium Edition, Windows 2000,
Windows XP Home Edition, Windows XP Professional,
Windows Server 2003 family,
.NET Compact Framework - Windows CE .NET

ScrollBar.Minimum Property

Gets or sets the lower limit of values of the scrollable range.

```
[Visual Basic]
Public Property Minimum As Integer
[C#]
public int Minimum {get; set;}
[C++]
public: __property int get_Minimum();
public: __property void set_Minimum(int);
[JScript]
public function get Minimum() : int;
public function set Minimum(int);
```

Property Value

A numeric value. The default value is 0.

Example

See related example in the **System.Windows.Forms.ScrollBar** class topic.

Requirements

Platforms: Windows 98, Windows NT 4.0, Windows Millennium Edition, Windows 2000, Windows XP Home Edition, Windows XP Professional, Windows Server 2003 family, .NET Compact Framework - Windows CE .NET

ScrollBar.SmallChange Property

Gets or sets the value to be added to or subtracted from the **Value** property when the scroll box is moved a small distance.

```
[Visual Basic]
Public Property SmallChange As Integer
[C#]
public int SmallChange {get; set;}
[C++]
public: __property int get_SmallChange();
public: __property void set_SmallChange(int);
[JScript]
public function get SmallChange() : int;
public function set SmallChange(int);
```

Property Value

A numeric value. The default value is 1.

Exceptions

Exception Type	Condition
ArgumentException	The assigned value is less than 0.

Remarks

When the user presses one of the arrow keys or clicks one of the scroll bar buttons, the **Value** property changes according to the value set in the **SmallChange** property.

You might consider setting the **SmallChange** value to a percentage of the **Height** (for a vertically oriented scroll bar) or **Width** (for a horizontally oriented scroll bar) values. This keeps the distance your scroll bar moves in proportion to its size.

Example

See related example in the **System.Windows.Forms.ScrollBar** class topic.

Requirements

Platforms: Windows 98, Windows NT 4.0, Windows Millennium Edition, Windows 2000, Windows XP Home Edition, Windows XP Professional, Windows Server 2003 family, .NET Compact Framework - Windows CE .NET

ScrollBar.TabStop Property

This member supports the .NET Framework infrastructure and is not intended to be used directly from your code.

```
[Visual Basic]
Public Shadows Property TabStop As Boolean
[C#]
public new bool TabStop {get; set;}
[C++]
public: __property bool get_TabStop();
public: __property void set_TabStop(bool);
[JScript]
public hide function get TabStop() : Boolean;
public hide function set TabStop(Boolean);
```

ScrollBar.Text Property

This member overrides **Control.Text**.

```
[Visual Basic]
Overrides Public Property Text As String
[C#]
public override string Text {get; set;}
[C++]
public: __property String* get_Text();
public: __property void set_Text(String*);
[JScript]
public override function get Text() : String;
public override function set Text(String);
```

Requirements

Platforms: Windows 98, Windows NT 4.0, Windows Millennium Edition, Windows 2000, Windows XP Home Edition, Windows XP Professional, Windows Server 2003 family

ScrollBar.Value Property

Gets or sets a numeric value that represents the current position of the scroll box on the scroll bar control.

```
[Visual Basic]
Public Property Value As Integer
[C#]
public int Value {get; set;}
[C++]
public: __property int get_Value();
public: __property void set_Value(int);
[JScript]
public function get Value() : int;
public function set Value(int);
```

Property Value

A numeric value that is within the **Minimum** and **Maximum** range. The default value is 0.

Exceptions

Exception Type	Condition
ArgumentException	The assigned value is less than the **Minimum** property value. -or- The assigned value is greater than the **Maximum** property value.

Example

See related example in the **System.Windows.Forms.ScrollBar** class topic.

Requirements

Platforms: Windows 98, Windows NT 4.0, Windows Millennium Edition, Windows 2000, Windows XP Home Edition, Windows XP Professional, Windows Server 2003 family, .NET Compact Framework - Windows CE .NET

ScrollBar.OnEnabledChanged Method

This member overrides **Control.OnEnabledChanged**.

[Visual Basic]
```
Overrides Protected Sub OnEnabledChanged( _
   ByVal e As EventArgs _
)
```
[C#]
```
protected override void OnEnabledChanged(
   EventArgs e
);
```
[C++]
```
protected: void OnEnabledChanged(
   EventArgs* e
);
```
[JScript]
```
protected override function OnEnabledChanged(
   e : EventArgs
);
```

Requirements

Platforms: Windows 98, Windows NT 4.0, Windows Millennium Edition, Windows 2000, Windows XP Home Edition, Windows XP Professional, Windows Server 2003 family, .NET Compact Framework - Windows CE .NET

ScrollBar.OnHandleCreated Method

This member overrides **Control.OnHandleCreated**.

[Visual Basic]
```
Overrides Protected Sub OnHandleCreated( _
   ByVal e As EventArgs _
)
```
[C#]
```
protected override void OnHandleCreated(
   EventArgs e
);
```
[C++]
```
protected: void OnHandleCreated(
   EventArgs* e
);
```
[JScript]
```
protected override function OnHandleCreated(
   e : EventArgs
);
```

Requirements

Platforms: Windows 98, Windows NT 4.0, Windows Millennium Edition, Windows 2000, Windows XP Home Edition, Windows XP Professional, Windows Server 2003 family

ScrollBar.OnScroll Method

Raises the **Scroll** event.

[Visual Basic]
```
Protected Overridable Sub OnScroll( _
   ByVal se As ScrollEventArgs _
)
```
[C#]
```
protected virtual void OnScroll(
   ScrollEventArgs se
);
```
[C++]
```
protected: virtual void OnScroll(
   ScrollEventArgs* se
);
```
[JScript]
```
protected function OnScroll(
   se : ScrollEventArgs
);
```

Parameters

se

A **ScrollEventArgs** that contains the event data.

Remarks

Raising an event invokes the event handler through a delegate. For more information, see **Raising an Event**.

The **OnScroll** method also allows derived classes to handle the event without attaching a delegate. This is the preferred technique for handling the event in a derived class.

Notes to Inheritors: When overriding **OnScroll** in a derived class, be sure to call the base class's **OnScroll** method so that registered delegates receive the event.

Example

See related example in the **System.Windows.Forms.ScrollBar** class topic.

Requirements

Platforms: Windows 98, Windows NT 4.0, Windows Millennium Edition, Windows 2000, Windows XP Home Edition, Windows XP Professional, Windows Server 2003 family

ScrollBar.OnValueChanged Method

Raises the **ValueChanged** event.

[Visual Basic]
```
Protected Overridable Sub OnValueChanged( _
   ByVal e As EventArgs _
)
```
[C#]
```
protected virtual void OnValueChanged(
   EventArgs e
);
```
[C++]
```
protected: virtual void OnValueChanged(
   EventArgs* e
);
```
[JScript]
```
protected function OnValueChanged(
   e : EventArgs
);
```

Parameters

e

An **EventArgs** that contains the event data.

Remarks

Raising an event invokes the event handler through a delegate.

The **OnValueChanged** method also allows derived classes to handle the event without attaching a delegate. This is the preferred technique for handling the event in a derived class.

Notes to Inheritors: When overriding **OnValueChanged** in a derived class, be sure to call the base class's **OnValueChanged** method so that registered delegates receive the event.

Example

See related example in the **System.Windows.Forms.ScrollBar** class topic.

Requirements

Platforms: Windows 98, Windows NT 4.0, Windows Millennium Edition, Windows 2000, Windows XP Home Edition, Windows XP Professional, Windows Server 2003 family, .NET Compact Framework - Windows CE .NET

ScrollBar.ToString Method

This member overrides **Object.ToString**.

[Visual Basic]
```
Overrides Public Function ToString() As String
```
[C#]
```
public override string ToString();
```
[C++]
```
public: String* ToString();
```
[JScript]
```
public override function ToString() : String;
```

Requirements

Platforms: Windows 98, Windows NT 4.0, Windows Millennium Edition, Windows 2000, Windows XP Home Edition, Windows XP Professional, Windows Server 2003 family, .NET Compact Framework - Windows CE .NET

ScrollBar.UpdateScrollInfo Method

This member supports the .NET Framework infrastructure and is not intended to be used directly from your code.

[Visual Basic]
```
Protected Sub UpdateScrollInfo()
```
[C#]
```
protected void UpdateScrollInfo();
```
[C++]
```
protected: void UpdateScrollInfo();
```
[JScript]
```
protected function UpdateScrollInfo();
```

ScrollBar.WndProc Method

This member overrides **Control.WndProc**.

[Visual Basic]
```
Overrides Protected Sub WndProc( _
   ByRef m As Message _
)
```
[C#]
```
protected override void WndProc(
   ref Message m
);
```
[C++]
```
protected: void WndProc(
   Message* m
);
```
[JScript]
```
protected override function WndProc(
   m : Message
);
```

Requirements

Platforms: Windows 98, Windows NT 4.0, Windows Millennium Edition, Windows 2000, Windows XP Home Edition, Windows XP Professional, Windows Server 2003 family

ScrollBar.BackColorChanged Event

This member supports the .NET Framework infrastructure and is not intended to be used directly from your code.

[Visual Basic]
```
Public Shadows Event BackColorChanged As EventHandler
```
[C#]
```
public new event EventHandler BackColorChanged;
```
[C++]
```
public: __event EventHandler* BackColorChanged;
```

[JScript] In JScript, you can handle the events defined by a class, but you cannot define your own.

ScrollBar.BackgroundImageChanged Event

This member supports the .NET Framework infrastructure and is not intended to be used directly from your code.

[Visual Basic]
```
Public Shadows Event BackgroundImageChanged As EventHandler
```
[C#]
```
public new event EventHandler BackgroundImageChanged;
```
[C++]
```
public: __event EventHandler* BackgroundImageChanged;
```

[JScript] In JScript, you can handle the events defined by a class, but you cannot define your own.

ScrollBar.Click Event

This member supports the .NET Framework infrastructure and is not intended to be used directly from your code.

[Visual Basic]
```
Public Shadows Event Click As EventHandler
```
[C#]
```
public new event EventHandler Click;
```
[C++]
```
public: __event EventHandler* Click;
```

[JScript] In JScript, you can handle the events defined by a class, but you cannot define your own.

ScrollBar.DoubleClick Event

This member supports the .NET Framework infrastructure and is not intended to be used directly from your code.

[Visual Basic]
```
Public Shadows Event DoubleClick As EventHandler
```
[C#]
```
public new event EventHandler DoubleClick;
```
[C++]
```
public: __event EventHandler* DoubleClick;
```

[JScript] In JScript, you can handle the events defined by a class, but you cannot define your own.

ScrollBar.FontChanged Event

This member supports the .NET Framework infrastructure and is not intended to be used directly from your code.

[Visual Basic]
```
Public Shadows Event FontChanged As EventHandler
```
[C#]
```
public new event EventHandler FontChanged;
```
[C++]
```
public: __event EventHandler* FontChanged;
```

[JScript] In JScript, you can handle the events defined by a class, but you cannot define your own.

ScrollBar.ForeColorChanged Event

This member supports the .NET Framework infrastructure and is not intended to be used directly from your code.

[Visual Basic]
```
Public Shadows Event ForeColorChanged As EventHandler
```
[C#]
```
public new event EventHandler ForeColorChanged;
```
[C++]
```
public: __event EventHandler* ForeColorChanged;
```

[JScript] In JScript, you can handle the events defined by a class, but you cannot define your own.

ScrollBar.ImeModeChanged Event

This member supports the .NET Framework infrastructure and is not intended to be used directly from your code.

[Visual Basic]
```
Public Shadows Event ImeModeChanged As EventHandler
```
[C#]
```
public new event EventHandler ImeModeChanged;
```
[C++]
```
public: __event EventHandler* ImeModeChanged;
```

[JScript] In JScript, you can handle the events defined by a class, but you cannot define your own.

ScrollBar.MouseDown Event

This member supports the .NET Framework infrastructure and is not intended to be used directly from your code.

[Visual Basic]
```
Public Shadows Event MouseDown As MouseEventHandler
```
[C#]
```
public new event MouseEventHandler MouseDown;
```
[C++]
```
public: __event MouseEventHandler* MouseDown;
```

[JScript] In JScript, you can handle the events defined by a class, but you cannot define your own.

ScrollBar.MouseMove Event

This member supports the .NET Framework infrastructure and is not intended to be used directly from your code.

[Visual Basic]
```
Public Shadows Event MouseMove As MouseEventHandler
```
[C#]
```
public new event MouseEventHandler MouseMove;
```
[C++]
```
public: __event MouseEventHandler* MouseMove;
```

[JScript] In JScript, you can handle the events defined by a class, but you cannot define your own.

ScrollBar.MouseUp Event

This member supports the .NET Framework infrastructure and is not intended to be used directly from your code.

[Visual Basic]
```
Public Shadows Event MouseUp As MouseEventHandler
```
[C#]
```
public new event MouseEventHandler MouseUp;
```
[C++]
```
public: __event MouseEventHandler* MouseUp;
```

[JScript] In JScript, you can handle the events defined by a class, but you cannot define your own.

ScrollBar.Paint Event

This member supports the .NET Framework infrastructure and is not intended to be used directly from your code.

[Visual Basic]
```
Public Shadows Event Paint As PaintEventHandler
```
[C#]
```
public new event PaintEventHandler Paint;
```
[C++]
```
public: __event PaintEventHandler* Paint;
```

[JScript] In JScript, you can handle the events defined by a class, but you cannot define your own.

ScrollBar.Scroll Event

Occurs when the scroll box has been moved by either a mouse or keyboard action.

[Visual Basic]
```
Public Event Scroll As ScrollEventHandler
```
[C#]
```
public event ScrollEventHandler Scroll;
```
[C++]
```
public: __event ScrollEventHandler* Scroll;
```

[JScript] In JScript, you can handle the events defined by a class, but you cannot define your own.

Event Data

The event handler receives an argument of type **ScrollEventArgs** containing data related to this event. The following **ScrollEventArgs** properties provide information specific to this event.

Property	Description
NewValue	Gets or sets the new **Value** of the scroll bar.
Type	Gets the type of scroll event that occurred.

Example

See related example in the **System.Windows.Forms.ScrollBar** class topic.

Requirements

Platforms: Windows 98, Windows NT 4.0, Windows Millennium Edition, Windows 2000, Windows XP Home Edition, Windows XP Professional, Windows Server 2003 family

ScrollBar.TextChanged Event

This member supports the .NET Framework infrastructure and is not intended to be used directly from your code.

[Visual Basic]
```
Public Shadows Event TextChanged As EventHandler
```
[C#]
```
public new event EventHandler TextChanged;
```
[C++]
```
public: __event EventHandler* TextChanged;
```

[JScript] In JScript, you can handle the events defined by a class, but you cannot define your own.

ScrollBar.ValueChanged Event

Occurs when the **Value** property has changed, either by a **Scroll** event or programmatically.

[Visual Basic]
```
Public Event ValueChanged As EventHandler
```
[C#]
```
public event EventHandler ValueChanged;
```
[C++]
```
public: __event EventHandler* ValueChanged;
```

[JScript] In JScript, you can handle the events defined by a class, but you cannot define your own.

Event Data

The event handler receives an argument of type **EventArgs**.

Example

See related example in the **System.Windows.Forms.ScrollBar** class topic.

Requirements

Platforms: Windows 98, Windows NT 4.0, Windows Millennium Edition, Windows 2000, Windows XP Home Edition, Windows XP Professional, Windows Server 2003 family

ScrollBars Enumeration

Specifies which scroll bars will be visible on a control.

[Visual Basic]
```
<Serializable>
Public Enum ScrollBars
```
[C#]
```
[Serializable]
public enum ScrollBars
```
[C++]
```
[Serializable]
__value public enum ScrollBars
```
[JScript]
```
public
   Serializable
enum ScrollBars
```

Remarks

This enumeration is used by **TextBox.ScrollBars**.

Not all controls support scroll bars. Use this enumeration to specify which scroll bars will be visible on a control, either under some or all circumstances.

Members

Member name	Description
Both Supported by the .NET Compact Framework.	Both horizontal and vertical scroll bars are shown.
Horizontal Supported by the .NET Compact Framework.	Only horizontal scroll bars are shown.
None Supported by the .NET Compact Framework.	No scroll bars are shown.
Vertical Supported by the .NET Compact Framework.	Only vertical scroll bars are shown.

Requirements

Namespace: System.Windows.Forms

Platforms: Windows 98, Windows NT 4.0, Windows Millennium Edition, Windows 2000, Windows XP Home Edition, Windows XP Professional, Windows Server 2003 family, .NET Compact Framework - Windows CE .NET

Assembly: System.Windows.Forms (in System.Windows.Forms.dll)

ScrollButton Enumeration

Specifies the type of scroll arrow to draw on a scroll bar.

[Visual Basic]
```
<Serializable>
Public Enum ScrollButton
```
[C#]
```
[Serializable]
public enum ScrollButton
```
[C++]
```
[Serializable]
__value public enum ScrollButton
```
[JScript]
```
public
   Serializable
enum ScrollButton
```

Remarks

This enumeration is used by **ControlPaint.DrawScrollButton**.

Members

Member name	Description
Down	A down-scroll arrow.
Left	A left-scroll arrow.
Max	A maximum-scroll arrow.
Min	A minimum-scroll arrow.
Right	A right-scroll arrow.
Up	An up-scroll arrow.

Requirements

Namespace: System.Windows.Forms

Platforms: Windows 98, Windows NT 4.0, Windows Millennium Edition, Windows 2000, Windows XP Home Edition, Windows XP Professional, Windows Server 2003 family

Assembly: System.Windows.Forms (in System.Windows.Forms.dll)

ScrollEventArgs Class

Provides data for the **Scroll** event.

System.Object
  System.EventArgs
    System.Windows.Forms.ScrollEventArgs

[Visual Basic]
```
<ComVisible(True)>
Public Class ScrollEventArgs
   Inherits EventArgs
```
[C#]
```
[ComVisible(true)]
public class ScrollEventArgs : EventArgs
```
[C++]
```
[ComVisible(true)]
public __gc class ScrollEventArgs : public EventArgs
```
[JScript]
```
public
   ComVisible(true)
class ScrollEventArgs extends EventArgs
```

Thread Safety

Any public static (**Shared** in Visual Basic) members of this type are safe for multithreaded operations. Any instance members are not guaranteed to be thread safe.

Remarks

The **Scroll** event occurs when the user changes the value of the scroll bar. This event can result from a variety of actions, such as clicking a scroll bar arrow, pressing the UP ARROW or DOWN ARROW, or dragging the scroll box. The **ScrollEventArgs** specifies the type of scroll event that occurred and the new value of the scroll bar.

Example

[Visual Basic]
```
Private Sub AddMyScrollEventHandlers()
    ' Create and initialize a VScrollBar.
    Dim vScrollBar1 As New VScrollBar()

    ' Add event handlers for the OnScroll and OnValueChanged events.
    AddHandler vScrollBar1.Scroll, AddressOf Me.vScrollBar1_Scroll
    AddHandler vScrollBar1.ValueChanged, AddressOf
Me.vScrollBar1_ValueChanged
End Sub

' Create the ValueChanged event handler.
Private Sub vScrollBar1_ValueChanged(sender As Object, e As EventArgs)
    ' Display the new value in the label.
    label1.Text = "vScrollBar Value:(OnValueChanged Event) " & _
        vScrollBar1.Value.ToString()
End Sub

' Create the Scroll event handler.
Private Sub vScrollBar1_Scroll(sender As Object, e As ScrollEventArgs)
    ' Display the new value in the label.
    label1.Text = "VScrollBar Value:(OnScroll Event) " & _
        e.NewValue.ToString()
End Sub

Private Sub button1_Click(sender As Object, e As EventArgs)
    ' Add 40 to the Value property if it will not exceed the          ↵
 Maximum value.
    If vScrollBar1.Value + 40 < vScrollBar1.Maximum Then
        vScrollBar1.Value = vScrollBar1.Value + 40
    End If
End Sub
```

[C#]
```
private void AddMyScrollEventHandlers()
 {
    // Create and initialize a VScrollBar.
    VScrollBar vScrollBar1 = new VScrollBar();

    // Add event handlers for the OnScroll and OnValueChanged events.
    vScrollBar1.Scroll += new ScrollEventHandler(
       this.vScrollBar1_Scroll);
    vScrollBar1.ValueChanged += new EventHandler(
       this.vScrollBar1_ValueChanged);
 }

 // Create the ValueChanged event handler.
 private void vScrollBar1_ValueChanged(Object sender,
                                       EventArgs e)
 {
     // Display the new value in the label.
     label1.Text = "vScrollBar Value:(OnValueChanged Event)          ↵
 " + vScrollBar1.Value.ToString();
 }

 // Create the Scroll event handler.
 private void vScrollBar1_Scroll(Object sender,
                                 ScrollEventArgs e)
 {
     // Display the new value in the label.
     label1.Text = "VScrollBar Value:(OnScroll Event)          ↵
" + e.NewValue.ToString();
 }

 private void button1_Click(Object sender,
                            EventArgs e)
 {
    // Add 40 to the Value property if it will not exceed          ↵
the Maximum value.
    if (vScrollBar1.Value + 40 < vScrollBar1.Maximum)
    {
        vScrollBar1.Value = vScrollBar1.Value + 40;
    }
 }
```

Requirements

Namespace: System.Windows.Forms

Platforms: Windows 98, Windows NT 4.0, Windows Millennium Edition, Windows 2000, Windows XP Home Edition, Windows XP Professional, Windows Server 2003 family

Assembly: System.Windows.Forms (in System.Windows.Forms.dll)

ScrollEventArgs Constructor

Initializes a new instance of the **ScrollEventArgs** class.

[Visual Basic]
```
Public Sub New( _
   ByVal type As ScrollEventType, _
   ByVal newValue As Integer _
)
```
[C#]
```
public ScrollEventArgs(
   ScrollEventType type,
   int newValue
);
```
[C++]
```
public: ScrollEventArgs(
   ScrollEventType type,
   int newValue
);
```
[JScript]
```
public function ScrollEventArgs(
```

```
[Visual Basic]
   type : ScrollEventType,
   newValue : int
);
```

Parameters

type
One of the **ScrollEventType** values.

newValue
The new value for the scroll bar.

Requirements

Platforms: Windows 98, Windows NT 4.0, Windows Millennium Edition, Windows 2000, Windows XP Home Edition, Windows XP Professional, Windows Server 2003 family

ScrollEventArgs.NewValue Property

Gets or sets the new **Value** of the scroll bar.

```
[Visual Basic]
Public Property NewValue As Integer
[C#]
public int NewValue {get; set;}
[C++]
public: __property int get_NewValue();
public: __property void set_NewValue(int);
[JScript]
public function get NewValue() : int;
public function set NewValue(int);
```

Property Value

The numeric value that the **Value** property will be changed to.

Example

```
[Visual Basic]
Private Sub AddMyScrollEventHandlers()
    ' Create and initialize a VScrollBar.
    Dim vScrollBar1 As New VScrollBar()

    ' Add event handlers for the OnScroll and OnValueChanged events.
    AddHandler vScrollBar1.Scroll, AddressOf Me.vScrollBar1_Scroll
    AddHandler vScrollBar1.ValueChanged, AddressOf
Me.vScrollBar1_ValueChanged
End Sub

' Create the ValueChanged event handler.
Private Sub vScrollBar1_ValueChanged(sender As Object, e As EventArgs)
    ' Display the new value in the label.
    label1.Text = "vScrollBar Value:(OnValueChanged Event) " & _
        vScrollBar1.Value.ToString()
End Sub

' Create the Scroll event handler.
Private Sub vScrollBar1_Scroll(sender As Object, e As ScrollEventArgs)
    ' Display the new value in the label.
    label1.Text = "VScrollBar Value:(OnScroll Event) " & _
        e.NewValue.ToString()
End Sub

Private Sub button1_Click(sender As Object, e As EventArgs)
    ' Add 40 to the Value property if it will not exceed the        ↵
Maximum value.
    If vScrollBar1.Value + 40 < vScrollBar1.Maximum Then
        vScrollBar1.Value = vScrollBar1.Value + 40
    End If
End Sub
```

```
[C#]
private void AddMyScrollEventHandlers()
{
   // Create and initialize a VScrollBar.
   VScrollBar vScrollBar1 = new VScrollBar();

   // Add event handlers for the OnScroll and OnValueChanged events.
   vScrollBar1.Scroll += new ScrollEventHandler(
      this.vScrollBar1_Scroll);
   vScrollBar1.ValueChanged += new EventHandler(
      this.vScrollBar1_ValueChanged);
}

// Create the ValueChanged event handler.
private void vScrollBar1_ValueChanged(Object sender,
                                      EventArgs e)
{
    // Display the new value in the label.
    label1.Text = "vScrollBar Value:(OnValueChanged Event)        ↵
" + vScrollBar1.Value.ToString();
}

// Create the Scroll event handler.
private void vScrollBar1_Scroll(Object sender,
                                ScrollEventArgs e)
{
    // Display the new value in the label.
    label1.Text = "VScrollBar Value:(OnScroll Event) " +        ↵
e.NewValue.ToString();
}

private void button1_Click(Object sender,
                           EventArgs e)
{
   // Add 40 to the Value property if it will not exceed the        ↵
Maximum value.
   if (vScrollBar1.Value + 40 < vScrollBar1.Maximum)
   {
       vScrollBar1.Value = vScrollBar1.Value + 40;
   }
}
```

Requirements

Platforms: Windows 98, Windows NT 4.0, Windows Millennium Edition, Windows 2000, Windows XP Home Edition, Windows XP Professional, Windows Server 2003 family

ScrollEventArgs.Type Property

Gets the type of scroll event that occurred.

```
[Visual Basic]
Public ReadOnly Property Type As ScrollEventType
[C#]
public ScrollEventType Type {get;}
[C++]
public: __property ScrollEventType get_Type();
[JScript]
public function get Type() : ScrollEventType;
```

Property Value

One of the **ScrollEventType** values.

Requirements

Platforms: Windows 98, Windows NT 4.0, Windows Millennium Edition, Windows 2000, Windows XP Home Edition, Windows XP Professional, Windows Server 2003 family

ScrollEventHandler Delegate

Represents the method that handles the **Scroll** event of a **ScrollBar**, **TrackBar**, or **DataGrid**.

[Visual Basic]

```
<Serializable>
Public Delegate Sub ScrollEventHandler( _
   ByVal sender As Object, _
   ByVal e As ScrollEventArgs _
)
```

[C#]

```
[Serializable]
public delegate void ScrollEventHandler(
   object sender,
   ScrollEventArgs e
);
```

[C++]

```
[Serializable]
public __gc __delegate void ScrollEventHandler(
   Object* sender,
   ScrollEventArgs* e
);
```

[JScript] In JScript, you can use the delegates in the .NET Framework, but you cannot define your own.

Parameters [Visual Basic, C#, C++]

The declaration of your event handler must have the same parameters as the **ScrollEventHandler** delegate declaration.

sender

The source of the event.

e

A **ScrollEventArgs** that contains the event data.

Remarks

When you create a **ScrollEventArgs** delegate, you identify the method that will handle the event. To associate the event with your event handler, add an instance of the delegate to the event. The event handler is called whenever the event occurs, unless you remove the delegate.

Example

[Visual Basic]

```
Private Sub AddMyScrollEventHandlers()
    ' Create and initialize a VScrollBar.
    Dim vScrollBar1 As New VScrollBar()

    ' Add event handlers for the OnScroll and OnValueChanged events.
    AddHandler vScrollBar1.Scroll, AddressOf Me.vScrollBar1_Scroll
    AddHandler vScrollBar1.ValueChanged, AddressOf
Me.vScrollBar1_ValueChanged
End Sub

' Create the ValueChanged event handler.
Private Sub vScrollBar1_ValueChanged(sender As Object, e As EventArgs)
    ' Display the new value in the label.
    label1.Text = "vScrollBar Value:(OnValueChanged Event) " & _
        vScrollBar1.Value.ToString()
End Sub

' Create the Scroll event handler.
Private Sub vScrollBar1_Scroll(sender As Object, e As ScrollEventArgs)
    ' Display the new value in the label.
    label1.Text = "VScrollBar Value:(OnScroll Event) " & _
        e.NewValue.ToString()
End Sub

Private Sub button1_Click(sender As Object, e As EventArgs)
    ' Add 40 to the Value property if it will not exceed the <;RD>
Maximum value.
    If vScrollBar1.Value + 40 < vScrollBar1.Maximum Then
        vScrollBar1.Value = vScrollBar1.Value + 40
    End If
End Sub
```

[C#]

```
private void AddMyScrollEventHandlers()
 {
    // Create and initialize a VScrollBar.
    VScrollBar vScrollBar1 = new VScrollBar();

    // Add event handlers for the OnScroll and OnValueChanged events.
    vScrollBar1.Scroll += new ScrollEventHandler(
       this.vScrollBar1_Scroll);
    vScrollBar1.ValueChanged += new EventHandler(
       this.vScrollBar1_ValueChanged);
 }

 // Create the ValueChanged event handler.
 private void vScrollBar1_ValueChanged(Object sender,
                                       EventArgs e)
 {
     // Display the new value in the label.
     label1.Text = "vScrollBar Value:(OnValueChanged Event) <;RD>
" + vScrollBar1.Value.ToString();
 }

 // Create the Scroll event handler.
 private void vScrollBar1_Scroll(Object sender,
                                 ScrollEventArgs e)
 {
     // Display the new value in the label.
     label1.Text = "VScrollBar Value:(OnScroll Event) " + <;RD>
e.NewValue.ToString();
 }

 private void button1_Click(Object sender,
                            EventArgs e)
 {
    // Add 40 to the Value property if it will not exceed the<;RD>
Maximum value.
    if (vScrollBar1.Value + 40 < vScrollBar1.Maximum)
    {
        vScrollBar1.Value = vScrollBar1.Value + 40;
    }
 }
```

Requirements

Namespace: System.Windows.Forms

Platforms: Windows 98, Windows NT 4.0, Windows Millennium Edition, Windows 2000, Windows XP Home Edition, Windows XP Professional, Windows Server 2003 family

Assembly: System.Windows.Forms (in System.Windows.Forms.dll)

ScrollEventType Enumeration

Specifies the type of action used to raise the **Scroll** event.

[Visual Basic]
```
<Serializable>
<ComVisible(True)>
Public Enum ScrollEventType
```
[C#]
```
[Serializable]
[ComVisible(true)]
public enum ScrollEventType
```
[C++]
```
[Serializable]
[ComVisible(true)]
__value public enum ScrollEventType
```
[JScript]
```
public
   Serializable
   ComVisible(true)
enum ScrollEventType
```

Remarks

This enumeration is used by **ScrollEventArgs.Type**.

Members

Member name	Description
EndScroll	The scroll box has stopped moving.
First	The scroll box was moved to the **Minimum** position.
LargeDecrement	The scroll box moved a large distance. The user clicked the scroll bar to the left(horizontal) or above(vertical) the scroll box, or pressed the PAGE UP key.
LargeIncrement	The scroll box moved a large distance. The user clicked the scroll bar to the right(horizontal) or below(vertical) the scroll box, or pressed the PAGE DOWN key.
Last	The scroll box was moved to the **Maximum** position.
SmallDecrement	The scroll box was moved a small distance. The user clicked the left(horizontal) or top(vertical) scroll arrow, or pressed the UP ARROW key.
SmallIncrement	The scroll box was moved a small distance. The user clicked the right(horizontal) or bottom(vertical) scroll arrow, or pressed the DOWN ARROW key.
ThumbPosition	The scroll box was moved.
ThumbTrack	The scroll box is currently being moved.

Requirements

Namespace: System.Windows.Forms

Platforms: Windows 98, Windows NT 4.0, Windows Millennium Edition, Windows 2000, Windows XP Home Edition, Windows XP Professional, Windows Server 2003 family

Assembly: System.Windows.Forms (in System.Windows.Forms.dll)

SecurityIDType Enumeration

This type supports the .NET Framework infrastructure and is not intended to be used directly from your code.

[Visual Basic]
```
<Serializable>
Public Enum SecurityIDType
```
[C#]
```
[Serializable]
public enum SecurityIDType
```
[C++]
```
[Serializable]
__value public enum SecurityIDType
```
[JScript]
```
public
   Serializable
enum SecurityIDType
```

Members

Alias

Computer

DeletedAccount

Domain

Group

Invalid

Unknown

User

WellKnownGroup

SelectedGridItemChanged-EventArgs Class

Provides data for the **SelectedGridItemChanged** event of the **PropertyGrid** control.

System.Object
  System.EventArgs
    System.Windows.Forms.SelectedGridItemChangedEvent-Args

[Visual Basic]
```
Public Class SelectedGridItemChangedEventArgs
   Inherits EventArgs
```
[C#]
```
public class SelectedGridItemChangedEventArgs : EventArgs
```
[C++]
```
public __gc class SelectedGridItemChangedEventArgs : public
   EventArgs
```
[JScript]
```
public class SelectedGridItemChangedEventArgs extends EventArgs
```

Thread Safety

Any public static (**Shared** in Visual Basic) members of this type are safe for multithreaded operations. Any instance members are not guaranteed to be thread safe.

Remarks

The **SelectedGridItemChanged** event occurs when the user changes the **GridItem** that is selected in a **PropertyGrid**.

Requirements

Namespace: System.Windows.Forms

Platforms: Windows 98, Windows NT 4.0, Windows Millennium Edition, Windows 2000, Windows XP Home Edition, Windows XP Professional, Windows Server 2003 family

Assembly: System.Windows.Forms (in System.Windows.Forms.dll)

SelectedGridItemChangedEventArgs Constructor

Initializes a new instance of the **SelectedGridItemChangedEventArgs** class.

[Visual Basic]
```
Public Sub New( _
   ByVal oldSel As GridItem, _
   ByVal newSel As GridItem _
)
```
[C#]
```
public SelectedGridItemChangedEventArgs(
   GridItem oldSel,
   GridItem newSel
);
```
[C++]
```
public: SelectedGridItemChangedEventArgs(
   GridItem* oldSel,
   GridItem* newSel
);
```
[JScript]
```
public function SelectedGridItemChangedEventArgs(
   oldSel : GridItem,
   newSel : GridItem
);
```

Parameters

oldSel
   The previously selected grid item.

newSel
   The newly selected grid item.

Requirements

Platforms: Windows 98, Windows NT 4.0, Windows Millennium Edition, Windows 2000, Windows XP Home Edition, Windows XP Professional, Windows Server 2003 family

SelectedGridItemChangedEventArgs.New-Selection Property

Gets the newly selected **GridItem** object.

[Visual Basic]
```
Public ReadOnly Property NewSelection As GridItem
```
[C#]
```
public GridItem NewSelection {get;}
```
[C++]
```
public: __property GridItem* get_NewSelection();
```
[JScript]
```
public function get NewSelection() : GridItem;
```

Property Value

The new **GridItem**.

Requirements

Platforms: Windows 98, Windows NT 4.0, Windows Millennium Edition, Windows 2000, Windows XP Home Edition, Windows XP Professional, Windows Server 2003 family

SelectedGridItemChangedEventArgs.Old-Selection Property

Gets the previously selected **GridItem** object.

[Visual Basic]
```
Public ReadOnly Property OldSelection As GridItem
```
[C#]
```
public GridItem OldSelection {get;}
```
[C++]
```
public: __property GridItem* get_OldSelection();
```
[JScript]
```
public function get OldSelection() : GridItem;
```

Property Value

The old **GridItem**. This can be a null reference (**Nothing** in Visual Basic).

Requirements

Platforms: Windows 98, Windows NT 4.0, Windows Millennium Edition, Windows 2000, Windows XP Home Edition, Windows XP Professional, Windows Server 2003 family

SelectedGridItemChanged-EventHandler Delegate

Represents the method that will handle the **SelectedGridItemChanged** event of a **PropertyGrid**.

[Visual Basic]
```
<Serializable>
Public Delegate Sub SelectedGridItemChangedEventHandler( _
   ByVal sender As Object, _
   ByVal e As SelectedGridItemChangedEventArgs _
)
```
[C#]
```
[Serializable]
public delegate void SelectedGridItemChangedEventHandler(
   object sender,
   SelectedGridItemChangedEventArgs e
);
```
[C++]
```
[Serializable]
public __gc __delegate void SelectedGridItemChangedEventHandler(
   Object* sender,
   SelectedGridItemChangedEventArgs* e
);
```

[JScript] In JScript, you can use the delegates in the .NET Framework, but you cannot define your own.

Parameters [Visual Basic, C#, C++]

The declaration of your event handler must have the same parameters as the **SelectedGridItemChangedEventHandler** delegate declaration.

sender

The source of the event.

e

A **SelectedGridItemChangedEventArgs** that contains the event data.

Remarks

When you create a **SelectedGridItemChangedEventHandler** delegate, you identify the method that will handle the event. To associate the event with your event handler, add an instance of the delegate to the event. The event handler is called whenever the event occurs, unless you remove the delegate.

Requirements

Namespace: System.Windows.Forms

Platforms: Windows 98, Windows NT 4.0, Windows Millennium Edition, Windows 2000, Windows XP Home Edition, Windows XP Professional, Windows Server 2003 family

Assembly: System.Windows.Forms (in System.Windows.Forms.dll)

SelectionMode Enumeration

Specifies the selection behavior of a list box.

[Visual Basic]
```
<Serializable>
<ComVisible(True)>
Public Enum SelectionMode
```
[C#]
```
[Serializable]
[ComVisible(true)]
public enum SelectionMode
```
[C++]
```
[Serializable]
[ComVisible(true)]
__value public enum SelectionMode
```
[JScript]
```
public
   Serializable
   ComVisible(true)
enum SelectionMode
```

Remarks

This enumeration is used by classes such as **ListBox** and **CheckedListBox**.

Members

Member name	Description
MultiExtended	Multiple items can be selected, and the user can use the SHIFT, CTRL, and arrow keys to make selections
MultiSimple	Multiple items can be selected.
None	No items can be selected.
One	Only one item can be selected.

Example

[Visual Basic, C#] The following example demonstrates how to use the **GetSelected** method to determine which items in a **ListBox** are selected in order to select the items that are not selected and deselect the items that are selected. The example also demonstrates using the **SelectionMode** property to enable a **ListBox** to have more than one selected item and uses the **Sorted** property to demonstrate how to sort items in a **ListBox** automatically. This example assumes that a **ListBox**, named `listBox1`, has been added to a form and that the `InitializeMyListBox` method defined in the example is called from the **Load** event of the form.

[Visual Basic]
```
Private Sub InitializeMyListBox()
   ' Add items to the ListBox.
   listBox1.Items.Add("A")
   listBox1.Items.Add("C")
   listBox1.Items.Add("E")
   listBox1.Items.Add("F")
   listBox1.Items.Add("G")
   listBox1.Items.Add("D")
   listBox1.Items.Add("B")

   ' Sort all items added previously.
   listBox1.Sorted = True

   ' Set the SelectionMode to select multiple items.
   listBox1.SelectionMode = SelectionMode.MultiExtended

   ' Select three initial items from the list.
   listBox1.SetSelected(0, True)
   listBox1.SetSelected(2, True)
   listBox1.SetSelected(4, True)

   ' Force the ListBox to scroll back to the top of the list.
   listBox1.TopIndex = 0
End Sub

Private Sub InvertMySelection()

   Dim x As Integer
   ' Loop through all items the ListBox.
   For x = 0 To listBox1.Items.Count - 1

      ' Determine if the item is selected.
      If listBox1.GetSelected(x) = True Then
         ' Deselect all items that are selected.
         listBox1.SetSelected(x, False)
      Else
         ' Select all items that are not selected.
         listBox1.SetSelected(x, True)
      End If
   Next x
   ' Force the ListBox to scroll back to the top of the list.
   listBox1.TopIndex = 0
End Sub
```

[C#]
```
private void InitializeMyListBox()
{
   // Add items to the ListBox.
   listBox1.Items.Add("A");
   listBox1.Items.Add("C");
   listBox1.Items.Add("E");
   listBox1.Items.Add("F");
   listBox1.Items.Add("G");
   listBox1.Items.Add("D");
   listBox1.Items.Add("B");

   // Sort all items added previously.
   listBox1.Sorted = true;

   // Set the SelectionMode to select multiple items.
   listBox1.SelectionMode = SelectionMode.MultiExtended;

   // Select three initial items from the list.
   listBox1.SetSelected(0,true);
   listBox1.SetSelected(2,true);
   listBox1.SetSelected(4,true);

   // Force the ListBox to scroll back to the top of the list.
   listBox1.TopIndex=0;
}

private void InvertMySelection()
{
   // Loop through all items the ListBox.
   for (int x = 0; x < listBox1.Items.Count; x++)
   {
      // Determine if the item is selected.
      if(listBox1.GetSelected(x) == true)
         // Deselect all items that are selected.
         listBox1.SetSelected(x,false);
      else
         // Select all items that are not selected.
         listBox1.SetSelected(x,true);
   }
   // Force the ListBox to scroll back to the top of the list.
   listBox1.TopIndex=0;
}
```

Requirements

Namespace: System.Windows.Forms

Platforms: Windows 98, Windows NT 4.0, Windows Millennium Edition, Windows 2000, Windows XP Home Edition, Windows XP Professional, Windows Server 2003 family

Assembly: System.Windows.Forms (in System.Windows.Forms.dll)

SelectionRange Class

Represents a date selection range in a month calendar control.

System.Object
  System.Windows.Forms.SelectionRange

[Visual Basic]
```
NotInheritable Public Class SelectionRange
```
[C#]
```
public sealed class SelectionRange
```
[C++]
```
public __gc __sealed class SelectionRange
```
[JScript]
```
public class SelectionRange
```

Thread Safety

Any public static (**Shared** in Visual Basic) members of this type are safe for multithreaded operations. Any instance members are not guaranteed to be thread safe.

Remarks

The **SelectionRange** is the date or dates selected and highlighted on the **MonthCalendar** control. If only one date is selected, the **Start** and **End** property values will be equal. The **SelectionRange** can be changed by the user clicking a date while dragging the mouse pointer across the desired dates, or you can set the range in code. For example, you might want to have the user enter a date range into two **TextBox** controls or two **DateTimePicker** controls and set the **SelectionRange** based on those dates.

Example

[Visual Basic, C#] The following example sets the **SelectionRange** property of a **MonthCalendar** control based on two dates entered into two **TextBox** controls when a **Button** is clicked. This code assumes new instances of a **MonthCalendar** control, two **TextBox** controls, and a **Button** have been created on a **Form**. You might consider adding code to validate the **Text** assigned to the text boxes to verify that they contain valid dates.

[Visual Basic]
```
Private Sub button1_Click(sender As Object, e As EventArgs)
   ' Set the SelectionRange with start and end dates from text boxes.
   Try
      monthCalendar1.SelectionRange = New SelectionRange( _
        DateTime.Parse(textBox1.Text), _
        DateTime.Parse(textBox2.Text))
   Catch ex As Exception
      MessageBox.Show(ex.Message)
   End Try
End Sub
```

[C#]
```
private void button1_Click(object sender,
                           EventArgs e)
{
   // Set the SelectionRange with start and end dates from text boxes.
   try
   {
      monthCalendar1.SelectionRange = new SelectionRange(
        DateTime.Parse(textBox1.Text),
        DateTime.Parse(textBox2.Text));
   }
   catch(Exception ex)
   {
      MessageBox.Show(ex.Message);
   }
}
```

Requirements

Namespace: System.Windows.Forms

Platforms: Windows 98, Windows NT 4.0, Windows Millennium Edition, Windows 2000, Windows XP Home Edition, Windows XP Professional, Windows Server 2003 family

Assembly: System.Windows.Forms (in System.Windows.Forms.dll)

SelectionRange Constructor

Initializes a new instance of the **SelectionRange** class.

Overload List

Initializes a new instance of the **SelectionRange** class.

[Visual Basic] **Public Sub New()**

[C#] **public SelectionRange();**

[C++] **public: SelectionRange();**

[JScript] **public function SelectionRange();**

Initializes a new instance of the **SelectionRange** class with the specified selection range.

[Visual Basic] **Public Sub New(SelectionRange)**

[C#] **public SelectionRange(SelectionRange);**

[C++] **public: SelectionRange(SelectionRange*);**

[JScript] **public function SelectionRange(SelectionRange);**

Initializes a new instance of the **SelectionRange** class with the specified beginning and ending dates.

[Visual Basic] **Public Sub New(DateTime, DateTime)**

[C#] **public SelectionRange(DateTime, DateTime);**

[C++] **public: SelectionRange(DateTime, DateTime);**

[JScript] **public function SelectionRange(DateTime, DateTime);**

Example

[Visual Basic, C#] The following example sets the **SelectionRange** property of a **MonthCalendar** control based on two dates entered into two **TextBox** controls when a **Button** is clicked. This code assumes new instances of a **MonthCalendar** control, two **TextBox** controls, and a **Button** have been created on a **Form**. You might consider adding code to validate the **Text** assigned to the text boxes to verify that they contain valid dates.

> [Visual Basic, C#] **Note** This example shows how to use one of the overloaded versions of the **SelectionRange** constructor. For other examples that might be available, see the individual overload topics.

[Visual Basic]
```
Private Sub button1_Click(sender As Object, e As EventArgs)
   ' Set the SelectionRange with start and end dates from text boxes.
   Try
      monthCalendar1.SelectionRange = New SelectionRange( _
        DateTime.Parse(textBox1.Text), _
        DateTime.Parse(textBox2.Text))
   Catch ex As Exception
      MessageBox.Show(ex.Message)
   End Try
End Sub
```

[C#]
```
private void button1_Click(object sender,
                           EventArgs e)
{
   // Set the SelectionRange with start and end dates from text boxes.
   try
   {
      monthCalendar1.SelectionRange = new SelectionRange(
        DateTime.Parse(textBox1.Text),
        DateTime.Parse(textBox2.Text));
   }
   catch(Exception ex)
   {
      MessageBox.Show(ex.Message);
   }
}
```

SelectionRange Constructor ()

Initializes a new instance of the **SelectionRange** class.

[Visual Basic]
```
Public Sub New()
```
[C#]
```
public SelectionRange();
```
[C++]
```
public: SelectionRange();
```
[JScript]
```
public function SelectionRange();
```

Remarks

The **Start** and **End** values are set to a null reference (**Nothing** in Visual Basic) when this constructor is used.

Example

[Visual Basic, C#, C++] The following example creates a **SelectionRange** object, sets its **Start** and **End** properties, and assigns the **SelectionRange** object to the **SelectionRange** property of the **MonthCalendar** control. When the **DateChanged** event is raised, the **Start** and **End** property values are displayed in the text boxes. This example assumes that you have a **Form** with two **TextBox** controls, a **Button**, and a **MonthCalendar** control.

[Visual Basic]
```
Private Sub button1_Click(sender As Object, _
  e As EventArgs) Handles button1.Click
   ' Create a SelectionRange object and set its Start and ↵
End properties.
   Dim sr As New SelectionRange()
   sr.Start = DateTime.Parse(Me.textBox1.Text)
   sr.End = DateTime.Parse(Me.textBox2.Text)
   ' Assign the SelectionRange object to the
   ' SelectionRange property of the MonthCalendar control.
   Me.monthCalendar1.SelectionRange = sr
End Sub

Private Sub monthCalendar1_DateChanged(sender As Object, _
  e As DateRangeEventArgs) Handles monthCalendar1.DateChanged
   ' Display the Start and End property values of
   ' the SelectionRange object in the text boxes.
   Me.textBox1.Text = ↵
monthCalendar1.SelectionRange.Start.Date.ToShortDateString()
   Me.textBox2.Text = ↵
monthCalendar1.SelectionRange.End.Date.ToShortDateString()
End Sub
```

[C#]
```
private void button1_Click(object sender, System.EventArgs e)
{
   // Create a SelectionRange object and set its Start and ↵
End properties.
   SelectionRange sr = new SelectionRange();
   sr.Start = DateTime.Parse(this.textBox1.Text);
   sr.End = DateTime.Parse(this.textBox2.Text);
   /* Assign the SelectionRange object to the
      SelectionRange property of the MonthCalendar control. */
   this.monthCalendar1.SelectionRange = sr;
}

private void monthCalendar1_DateChanged(object sender, ↵
DateRangeEventArgs e)
{
   /* Display the Start and End property values of
      the SelectionRange object in the text boxes. */
   this.textBox1.Text =
     monthCalendar1.SelectionRange.Start.Date.ToShortDateString();
   this.textBox2.Text =
     monthCalendar1.SelectionRange.End.Date.ToShortDateString();
}
```

[C++]
```
void button1_Click(Object* sender, System::EventArgs* e) {
   // Create a SelectionRange Object* and set its Start and ↵
 End properties.
   SelectionRange* sr = new SelectionRange();
   sr->Start = DateTime::Parse(this->textBox1->Text);
   sr->End = DateTime::Parse(this->textBox2->Text);
   /* Assign the SelectionRange Object* to the
   SelectionRange property of the MonthCalendar control. */
   this->monthCalendar1->SelectionRange = sr;
}

void monthCalendar1_DateChanged(Object* sender, ↵
DateRangeEventArgs* e) {
   /* Display the Start and End property values of
   the SelectionRange Object* in the text boxes. */
   this->textBox1->Text =
      monthCalendar1->SelectionRange->Start.Date.ToShortDateString();
   this->textBox2->Text =
      monthCalendar1->SelectionRange->End.Date.ToShortDateString();
}
```

Requirements

Platforms: Windows 98, Windows NT 4.0, Windows Millennium Edition, Windows 2000, Windows XP Home Edition, Windows XP Professional, Windows Server 2003 family

SelectionRange Constructor (SelectionRange)

Initializes a new instance of the **SelectionRange** class with the specified selection range.

[Visual Basic]
```
Public Sub New( _
   ByVal range As SelectionRange _
)
```
[C#]
```
public SelectionRange(
   SelectionRange range
);
```
[C++]
```
public: SelectionRange(
   SelectionRange* range
);
```
[JScript]
```
public function SelectionRange(
   range : SelectionRange
);
```

Parameters

range

The existing **SelectionRange**.

Remarks

The **Start** and **End** property values are assigned the **Start** and **End** property values of the assigned **SelectionRange** object.

Example

[Visual Basic, C#, C++] The following example creates a **SelectionRange** object, sets its **Start** and **End** properties, and assigns the **SelectionRange** object to the **SelectionRange** property of the **MonthCalendar** control. When the **DateChanged** event is raised, the **Start** and **End** property values are displayed in the text boxes. This example assumes that you have a **Form** with two **TextBox** controls, a **Button**, and a **MonthCalendar** control.

[Visual Basic]

```
Private Sub button1_Click(sender As Object, _
  e As EventArgs) Handles button1.Click
    ' Create a SelectionRange object and set its Start and ↵
End properties.
    Dim sr As New SelectionRange()
    sr.Start = DateTime.Parse(Me.textBox1.Text)
    sr.End = DateTime.Parse(Me.textBox2.Text)
    ' Assign the SelectionRange object to the
    ' SelectionRange property of the MonthCalendar control.
    Me.monthCalendar1.SelectionRange = sr
End Sub

Private Sub monthCalendar1_DateChanged(sender As Object, _
  e As DateRangeEventArgs) Handles monthCalendar1.DateChanged
    ' Display the Start and End property values of
    ' the SelectionRange object in the text boxes.
    Me.textBox1.Text = ↵
monthCalendar1.SelectionRange.Start.Date.ToShortDateString()
    Me.textBox2.Text = ↵
monthCalendar1.SelectionRange.End.Date.ToShortDateString()
End Sub
```

[C#]

```
private void button1_Click(object sender, System.EventArgs e)
{
    // Create a SelectionRange object and set its Start and ↵
End properties.
    SelectionRange sr = new SelectionRange();
    sr.Start = DateTime.Parse(this.textBox1.Text);
    sr.End = DateTime.Parse(this.textBox2.Text);
    /* Assign the SelectionRange object to the
       SelectionRange property of the MonthCalendar control. */
    this.monthCalendar1.SelectionRange = sr;
}

private void monthCalendar1_DateChanged(object sender, ↵
DateRangeEventArgs e)
{
    /* Display the Start and End property values of
       the SelectionRange object in the text boxes. */
    this.textBox1.Text =
      monthCalendar1.SelectionRange.Start.Date.ToShortDateString();
    this.textBox2.Text =
      monthCalendar1.SelectionRange.End.Date.ToShortDateString();
}
```

[C++]

```
void button1_Click(Object* sender, System::EventArgs* e) {
    // Create a SelectionRange Object* and set its Start and ↵
 End properties.
    SelectionRange* sr = new SelectionRange();
    sr->Start = DateTime::Parse(this->textBox1->Text);
    sr->End = DateTime::Parse(this->textBox2->Text);
    /* Assign the SelectionRange Object* to the
    SelectionRange property of the MonthCalendar control. */
    this->monthCalendar1->SelectionRange = sr;
}

void monthCalendar1_DateChanged(Object* sender, ↵
DateRangeEventArgs* e) {
    /* Display the Start and End property values of
    the SelectionRange Object* in the text boxes. */
    this->textBox1->Text =
       monthCalendar1->SelectionRange->Start.Date.ToShortDateString();
    this->textBox2->Text =
       monthCalendar1->SelectionRange->End.Date.ToShortDateString();
}
```

Requirements

Platforms: Windows 98, Windows NT 4.0, Windows Millennium Edition, Windows 2000, Windows XP Home Edition, Windows XP Professional, Windows Server 2003 family

SelectionRange Constructor (DateTime, DateTime)

Initializes a new instance of the **SelectionRange** class with the specified beginning and ending dates.

[Visual Basic]

```
Public Sub New( _
   ByVal lower As DateTime, _
   ByVal upper As DateTime _
)
```

[C#]

```
public SelectionRange(
   DateTime lower,
   DateTime upper
);
```

[C++]

```
public: SelectionRange(
   DateTime lower,
   DateTime upper
);
```

[JScript]

```
public function SelectionRange(
   lower : DateTime,
   upper : DateTime
);
```

Parameters

lower

The starting date in the **SelectionRange**.

upper

The ending date in the **SelectionRange**.

Remarks

> **Note** If the *lower* **DateTime** value is greater than the *upper* **DateTime** value, the *lower* value will be assigned to the **End** property instead of the **Start** property.

Example

[Visual Basic, C#] The following example sets the **SelectionRange** property of a **MonthCalendar** control based on two dates entered into two **TextBox** controls when a **Button** is clicked. This code assumes new instances of a **MonthCalendar** control, two **TextBox** controls, and a **Button** have been created on a **Form**. You might consider adding code to validate the **Text** assigned to the text boxes to verify that they contain valid dates.

[Visual Basic]
```
Private Sub button1_Click(sender As Object, e As EventArgs)
   ' Set the SelectionRange with start and end dates from text boxes.
   Try
      monthCalendar1.SelectionRange = New SelectionRange( _
        DateTime.Parse(textBox1.Text), _
        DateTime.Parse(textBox2.Text))
   Catch ex As Exception
      MessageBox.Show(ex.Message)
   End Try
End Sub
```

[C#]
```
private void button1_Click(object sender,
                           EventArgs e)
{
   // Set the SelectionRange with start and end dates from text boxes.
   try
   {
      monthCalendar1.SelectionRange = new SelectionRange(
        DateTime.Parse(textBox1.Text),
        DateTime.Parse(textBox2.Text));
   }
   catch(Exception ex)
   {
      MessageBox.Show(ex.Message);
   }
}
```

Requirements

Platforms: Windows 98, Windows NT 4.0, Windows Millennium Edition, Windows 2000, Windows XP Home Edition, Windows XP Professional, Windows Server 2003 family

SelectionRange.End Property

Gets or sets the ending date and time of the selection range.

[Visual Basic]
```
Public Property End As DateTime
```
[C#]
```
public DateTime End {get; set;}
```
[C++]
```
public: __property DateTime get_End();
public: __property void set_End(DateTime);
```
[JScript]
```
public function get End() : DateTime;
public function set End(DateTime);
```

Property Value

The ending **DateTime** value of the range.

Example

[Visual Basic, C#, C++] The following example creates a **SelectionRange** object, sets its **Start** and **End** properties, and assigns the **SelectionRange** object to the **SelectionRange** property of the **MonthCalendar** control. When the **DateChanged** event is raised, the **Start** and **End** property values are displayed in the text boxes. This example assumes that you have a **Form** with two **TextBox** controls, a **Button**, and a **MonthCalendar** control.

[Visual Basic]
```
Private Sub button1_Click(sender As Object, _
  e As EventArgs) Handles button1.Click
   ' Create a SelectionRange object and set its Start and End properties.
   Dim sr As New SelectionRange()
   sr.Start = DateTime.Parse(Me.textBox1.Text)
   sr.End = DateTime.Parse(Me.textBox2.Text)
   ' Assign the SelectionRange object to the
   ' SelectionRange property of the MonthCalendar control.
   Me.monthCalendar1.SelectionRange = sr
End Sub

Private Sub monthCalendar1_DateChanged(sender As Object, _
  e As DateRangeEventArgs) Handles monthCalendar1.DateChanged
   ' Display the Start and End property values of
   ' the SelectionRange object in the text boxes.
   Me.textBox1.Text =                                              ↵
monthCalendar1.SelectionRange.Start.Date.ToShortDateString()
   Me.textBox2.Text =                                              ↵
monthCalendar1.SelectionRange.End.Date.ToShortDateString()
End Sub
```

[C#]
```
private void button1_Click(object sender, System.EventArgs e)
{
   // Create a SelectionRange object and set its Start and End
properties.
   SelectionRange sr = new SelectionRange();
   sr.Start = DateTime.Parse(this.textBox1.Text);
   sr.End = DateTime.Parse(this.textBox2.Text);
   /* Assign the SelectionRange object to the
      SelectionRange property of the MonthCalendar control. */
   this.monthCalendar1.SelectionRange = sr;
}

private void monthCalendar1_DateChanged(object sender,              ↵
DateRangeEventArgs e)
{
   /* Display the Start and End property values of
      the SelectionRange object in the text boxes. */
   this.textBox1.Text =
     monthCalendar1.SelectionRange.Start.Date.ToShortDateString();
   this.textBox2.Text =
     monthCalendar1.SelectionRange.End.Date.ToShortDateString();
}
```

[C++]
```
void button1_Click(Object* sender, System::EventArgs* e) {
   // Create a SelectionRange Object* and set its Start and          ↵
End properties.
   SelectionRange* sr = new SelectionRange();
   sr->Start = DateTime::Parse(this->textBox1->Text);
   sr->End = DateTime::Parse(this->textBox2->Text);
   /* Assign the SelectionRange Object* to the
   SelectionRange property of the MonthCalendar control. */
   this->monthCalendar1->SelectionRange = sr;
}

void monthCalendar1_DateChanged(Object* sender,                      ↵
DateRangeEventArgs* e) {
   /* Display the Start and End property values of
   the SelectionRange Object* in the text boxes. */
   this->textBox1->Text =
      monthCalendar1->SelectionRange->Start.Date.ToShortDateString();
   this->textBox2->Text =
      monthCalendar1->SelectionRange->End.Date.ToShortDateString();
}
```

Requirements

Platforms: Windows 98, Windows NT 4.0, Windows Millennium Edition, Windows 2000, Windows XP Home Edition, Windows XP Professional, Windows Server 2003 family

SelectionRange.Start Property

Gets or sets the starting date and time of the selection range.

[Visual Basic]
```
Public Property Start As DateTime
```
[C#]
```
public DateTime Start {get; set;}
```
[C++]
```
public: __property DateTime get_Start();
public: __property void set_Start(DateTime);
```
[JScript]
```
public function get Start() : DateTime;
public function set Start(DateTime);
```

Property Value

The starting **DateTime** value of the range.

Example

[Visual Basic, C#, C++] The following example creates a **SelectionRange** object, sets its **Start** and **End** properties, and assigns the **SelectionRange** object to the **SelectionRange** property of the **MonthCalendar** control. When the **DateChanged** event is raised, the **Start** and **End** property values are displayed in the text boxes. This example assumes that you have a **Form** with two **TextBox** controls, a **Button**, and a **MonthCalendar** control.

[Visual Basic]
```
Private Sub button1_Click(sender As Object, _
  e As EventArgs) Handles button1.Click
   ' Create a SelectionRange object and set its Start and
 End properties.
   Dim sr As New SelectionRange()
   sr.Start = DateTime.Parse(Me.textBox1.Text)
   sr.End = DateTime.Parse(Me.textBox2.Text)
   ' Assign the SelectionRange object to the
   ' SelectionRange property of the MonthCalendar control.
   Me.monthCalendar1.SelectionRange = sr
End Sub

Private Sub monthCalendar1_DateChanged(sender As Object, _
  e As DateRangeEventArgs) Handles monthCalendar1.DateChanged
   ' Display the Start and End property values of
   ' the SelectionRange object in the text boxes.
   Me.textBox1.Text =
monthCalendar1.SelectionRange.Start.Date.ToShortDateString()
   Me.textBox2.Text =
monthCalendar1.SelectionRange.End.Date.ToShortDateString()
End Sub
```

[C#]
```
private void button1_Click(object sender, System.EventArgs e)
{
   // Create a SelectionRange object and set its Start and
 End properties.
   SelectionRange sr = new SelectionRange();
   sr.Start = DateTime.Parse(this.textBox1.Text);
   sr.End = DateTime.Parse(this.textBox2.Text);
   /* Assign the SelectionRange object to the
      SelectionRange property of the MonthCalendar control. */
   this.monthCalendar1.SelectionRange = sr;
}

private void monthCalendar1_DateChanged(object sender,
DateRangeEventArgs e)
{
   /* Display the Start and End property values of
      the SelectionRange object in the text boxes. */
   this.textBox1.Text =
     monthCalendar1.SelectionRange.Start.Date.ToShortDateString();
   this.textBox2.Text =
      monthCalendar1.SelectionRange.End.Date.ToShortDateString();
}
```

[C++]
```
void button1_Click(Object* sender, System::EventArgs* e) {
   // Create a SelectionRange Object* and set its Start
 and End properties.
   SelectionRange* sr = new SelectionRange();
   sr->Start = DateTime::Parse(this->textBox1->Text);
   sr->End = DateTime::Parse(this->textBox2->Text);
   /* Assign the SelectionRange Object* to the
   SelectionRange property of the MonthCalendar control. */
   this->monthCalendar1->SelectionRange = sr;
}

void monthCalendar1_DateChanged(Object* sender,
DateRangeEventArgs* e) {
   /* Display the Start and End property values of
   the SelectionRange Object* in the text boxes. */
   this->textBox1->Text =
      monthCalendar1->SelectionRange->Start.Date.ToShortDateString();
   this->textBox2->Text =
      monthCalendar1->SelectionRange->End.Date.ToShortDateString();
}
```

Requirements

Platforms: Windows 98, Windows NT 4.0, Windows Millennium Edition, Windows 2000, Windows XP Home Edition, Windows XP Professional, Windows Server 2003 family

SelectionRange.ToString Method

This member overrides **Object.ToString**.

[Visual Basic]
```
Overrides Public Function ToString() As String
```
[C#]
```
public override string ToString();
```
[C++]
```
public: String* ToString();
```
[JScript]
```
public override function ToString() : String;
```

Requirements

Platforms: Windows 98, Windows NT 4.0, Windows Millennium Edition, Windows 2000, Windows XP Home Edition, Windows XP Professional, Windows Server 2003 family

SelectionRangeConverter Class

Provides a type converter to convert **SelectionRange** objects to and from various other representations.

System.Object
  System.ComponentModel.TypeConverter
    System.Windows.Forms.SelectionRangeConverter

[Visual Basic]
```
Public Class SelectionRangeConverter
   Inherits TypeConverter
```
[C#]
```
public class SelectionRangeConverter : TypeConverter
```
[C++]
```
public __gc class SelectionRangeConverter : public TypeConverter
```
[JScript]
```
public class SelectionRangeConverter extends TypeConverter
```

Thread Safety

Any public static (**Shared** in Visual Basic) members of this type are safe for multithreaded operations. Any instance members are not guaranteed to be thread safe.

Remarks

> **Note** You should never create a **SelectionRangeConverter**. Instead, call the **GetConverter** method of **TypeDescriptor**. For more information, see the examples in the **TypeConverter** base class.

Requirements

Namespace: System.Windows.Forms

Platforms: Windows 98, Windows NT 4.0, Windows Millennium Edition, Windows 2000, Windows XP Home Edition, Windows XP Professional, Windows Server 2003 family

Assembly: System.Windows.Forms (in System.Windows.Forms.dll)

SelectionRangeConverter Constructor

Initializes a new instance of the **SelectionRangeConverter** class.

[Visual Basic]
```
Public Sub New()
```
[C#]
```
public SelectionRangeConverter();
```
[C++]
```
public: SelectionRangeConverter();
```
[JScript]
```
public function SelectionRangeConverter();
```

Remarks

The default constructor initializes any fields to their default values.

Requirements

Platforms: Windows 98, Windows NT 4.0, Windows Millennium Edition, Windows 2000, Windows XP Home Edition, Windows XP Professional, Windows Server 2003 family

SelectionRangeConverter.CanConvertFrom Method

Overload List

This member supports the .NET Framework infrastructure and is not intended to be used directly from your code.

[Visual Basic] **Overloads Overrides Public Function CanConvertFrom(ITypeDescriptorContext, Type) As Boolean**

[C#] **public override bool CanConvertFrom(ITypeDescriptorContext, Type);**

[C++] **public: bool CanConvertFrom(ITypeDescriptorContext*, Type*);**

[JScript] **public override function CanConvertFrom(ITypeDescriptorContext, Type) : Boolean;**

Inherited from **TypeConverter**.

[Visual Basic] **Overloads Public Function CanConvertFrom(Type) As Boolean**

[C#] **public bool CanConvertFrom(Type);**

[C++] **public: bool CanConvertFrom(Type*);**

[JScript] **public function CanConvertFrom(Type) : Boolean;**

SelectionRangeConverter.CanConvertFrom Method (ITypeDescriptorContext, Type)

This member overrides **TypeConverter.CanConvertFrom**.

[Visual Basic]
```
Overrides Overloads Public Function CanConvertFrom( _
   ByVal context As ITypeDescriptorContext, _
   ByVal sourceType As Type _
) As Boolean
```
[C#]
```
public override bool CanConvertFrom(
   ITypeDescriptorContext context,
   Type sourceType
);
```
[C++]
```
public: bool CanConvertFrom(
   ITypeDescriptorContext* context,
   Type* sourceType
);
```
[JScript]
```
public override function CanConvertFrom(
   context : ITypeDescriptorContext,
   sourceType : Type
) : Boolean;
```

Requirements

Platforms: Windows 98, Windows NT 4.0, Windows Millennium Edition, Windows 2000, Windows XP Home Edition, Windows XP Professional, Windows Server 2003 family

SelectionRangeConverter.CanConvertTo Method

Overload List

This member supports the .NET Framework infrastructure and is not intended to be used directly from your code.

[Visual Basic] **Overloads Overrides Public Function CanConvertTo(ITypeDescriptorContext, Type) As Boolean**

[C#] **public override bool CanConvertTo(ITypeDescriptorContext, Type);**

[C++] **public: bool CanConvertTo(ITypeDescriptorContext*, Type*);**

[JScript] **public override function CanConvertTo(ITypeDescriptorContext, Type) : Boolean;**

Inherited from **TypeConverter**.

[Visual Basic] **Overloads Public Function CanConvertTo(Type) As Boolean**

[C#] **public bool CanConvertTo(Type);**

[C++] **public: bool CanConvertTo(Type*);**

[JScript] **public function CanConvertTo(Type) : Boolean;**

SelectionRangeConverter.CanConvertTo Method (ITypeDescriptorContext, Type)

This member overrides **TypeConverter.CanConvertTo**.

[Visual Basic]
```
Overrides Overloads Public Function CanConvertTo( _
   ByVal context As ITypeDescriptorContext, _
   ByVal destinationType As Type _
) As Boolean
```
[C#]
```
public override bool CanConvertTo(
   ITypeDescriptorContext context,
   Type destinationType
);
```
[C++]
```
public: bool CanConvertTo(
   ITypeDescriptorContext* context,
   Type* destinationType
);
```
[JScript]
```
public override function CanConvertTo(
   context : ITypeDescriptorContext,
   destinationType : Type
) : Boolean;
```

Requirements

Platforms: Windows 98, Windows NT 4.0, Windows Millennium Edition, Windows 2000, Windows XP Home Edition, Windows XP Professional, Windows Server 2003 family

SelectionRangeConverter.ConvertFrom Method

Overload List

This member supports the .NET Framework infrastructure and is not intended to be used directly from your code.

[Visual Basic] **Overloads Overrides Public Function ConvertFrom(ITypeDescriptorContext, CultureInfo, Object) As Object**

[C#] **public override object ConvertFrom(ITypeDescriptorContext, CultureInfo, object);**

[C++] **public: Object* ConvertFrom(ITypeDescriptorContext*, CultureInfo*, Object*);**

[JScript] **public override function ConvertFrom(ITypeDescriptorContext, CultureInfo, Object) : Object;**

Inherited from **TypeConverter**.

[Visual Basic] **Overloads Public Function ConvertFrom(Object) As Object**

[C#] **public object ConvertFrom(object);**

[C++] **public: Object* ConvertFrom(Object*);**

[JScript] **public function ConvertFrom(Object) : Object;**

SelectionRangeConverter.ConvertFrom Method (ITypeDescriptorContext, CultureInfo, Object)

This member overrides **TypeConverter.ConvertFrom**.

[Visual Basic]
```
Overrides Overloads Public Function ConvertFrom( _
   ByVal context As ITypeDescriptorContext, _
   ByVal culture As CultureInfo, _
   ByVal value As Object _
) As Object
```
[C#]
```
public override object ConvertFrom(
   ITypeDescriptorContext context,
   CultureInfo culture,
   object value
);
```
[C++]
```
public: Object* ConvertFrom(
   ITypeDescriptorContext* context,
   CultureInfo* culture,
   Object* value
);
```
[JScript]
```
public override function ConvertFrom(
   context : ITypeDescriptorContext,
   culture : CultureInfo,
   value : Object
) : Object;
```

Requirements

Platforms: Windows 98, Windows NT 4.0, Windows Millennium Edition, Windows 2000, Windows XP Home Edition, Windows XP Professional, Windows Server 2003 family

SelectionRangeConverter.ConvertTo Method

Overload List

This member supports the .NET Framework infrastructure and is not intended to be used directly from your code.

[Visual Basic] **Overloads Overrides Public Function ConvertTo(ITypeDescriptorContext, CultureInfo, Object, Type) As Object**

[C#] **public override object ConvertTo(ITypeDescriptorContext, CultureInfo, object, Type);**

[C++] **public: Object* ConvertTo(ITypeDescriptorContext*, CultureInfo*, Object*, Type*);**

[JScript] **public override function ConvertTo(ITypeDescriptorContext, CultureInfo, Object, Type) : Object;**

Inherited from **TypeConverter**.

[Visual Basic] **Overloads Public Function ConvertTo(Object, Type) As Object**

[C#] **public object ConvertTo(object, Type);**

[C++] **public: Object* ConvertTo(Object*, Type*);**

[JScript] **public function ConvertTo(Object, Type) : Object;**

SelectionRangeConverter.ConvertTo Method (ITypeDescriptorContext, CultureInfo, Object, Type)

This member overrides **TypeConverter.ConvertTo**.

```
[Visual Basic]
Overrides Overloads Public Function ConvertTo( _
   ByVal context As ITypeDescriptorContext, _
   ByVal culture As CultureInfo, _
   ByVal value As Object, _
   ByVal destinationType As Type _
) As Object
[C#]
public override object ConvertTo(
   ITypeDescriptorContext context,
   CultureInfo culture,
   object value,
   Type destinationType
);
[C++]
public: Object* ConvertTo(
   ITypeDescriptorContext* context,
   CultureInfo* culture,
   Object* value,
   Type* destinationType
);
[JScript]
public override function ConvertTo(
   context : ITypeDescriptorContext,
   culture : CultureInfo,
   value : Object,
   destinationType : Type
) : Object;
```

Requirements

Platforms: Windows 98, Windows NT 4.0, Windows Millennium Edition, Windows 2000, Windows XP Home Edition, Windows XP Professional, Windows Server 2003 family

SelectionRangeConverter.CreateInstance Method

Overload List

This member supports the .NET Framework infrastructure and is not intended to be used directly from your code.

[Visual Basic] **Overloads Overrides Public Function CreateInstance(ITypeDescriptorContext, IDictionary) As Object**

[C#] **public override object CreateInstance(ITypeDescriptorContext, IDictionary);**

[C++] **public: Object* CreateInstance(ITypeDescriptorContext*, IDictionary*);**

[JScript] **public override function CreateInstance(ITypeDescriptorContext, IDictionary) : Object;**

Inherited from **TypeConverter**.

[Visual Basic] **Overloads Public Function CreateInstance(IDictionary) As Object**

[C#] **public object CreateInstance(IDictionary);**

[C++] **public: Object* CreateInstance(IDictionary*);**

[JScript] **public function CreateInstance(IDictionary) : Object;**

SelectionRangeConverter.CreateInstance Method (ITypeDescriptorContext, IDictionary)

This member overrides **TypeConverter.CreateInstance**.

```
[Visual Basic]
Overrides Overloads Public Function CreateInstance( _
   ByVal context As ITypeDescriptorContext, _
   ByVal propertyValues As IDictionary _
) As Object
[C#]
public override object CreateInstance(
   ITypeDescriptorContext context,
   IDictionary propertyValues
);
[C++]
public: Object* CreateInstance(
   ITypeDescriptorContext* context,
   IDictionary* propertyValues
);
[JScript]
public override function CreateInstance(
   context : ITypeDescriptorContext,
   propertyValues : IDictionary
) : Object;
```

Requirements

Platforms: Windows 98, Windows NT 4.0, Windows Millennium Edition, Windows 2000, Windows XP Home Edition, Windows XP Professional, Windows Server 2003 family

SelectionRangeConverter.GetCreateInstance-Supported Method

Overload List

This member supports the .NET Framework infrastructure and is not intended to be used directly from your code.

[Visual Basic] **Overloads Overrides Public Function GetCreateInstanceSupported(ITypeDescriptorContext) As Boolean**

[C#] **public override bool GetCreateInstance-Supported(ITypeDescriptorContext);**

[C++] **public: bool GetCreateInstance-Supported(ITypeDescriptorContext*);**

[JScript] **public override function GetCreateInstance-Supported(ITypeDescriptorContext) : Boolean;**

Inherited from **TypeConverter**.

[Visual Basic] **Overloads Public Function GetCreateInstance-Supported() As Boolean**

[C#] **public bool GetCreateInstanceSupported();**

[C++] **public: bool GetCreateInstanceSupported();**

[JScript] **public function GetCreateInstanceSupported() : Boolean;**

SelectionRangeConverter.GetCreateInstanceSupported Method (ITypeDescriptorContext)

This member overrides **TypeConverter.GetCreateInstanceSupported**.

```
[Visual Basic]
Overrides Overloads Public Function GetCreateInstanceSupported( _
   ByVal context As ITypeDescriptorContext _
) As Boolean
[C#]
public override bool GetCreateInstanceSupported(
   ITypeDescriptorContext context
);
[C++]
public: bool GetCreateInstanceSupported(
   ITypeDescriptorContext* context
);
[JScript]
public override function GetCreateInstanceSupported(
   context : ITypeDescriptorContext
) : Boolean;
```

Requirements

Platforms: Windows 98, Windows NT 4.0, Windows Millennium Edition, Windows 2000, Windows XP Home Edition, Windows XP Professional, Windows Server 2003 family

SelectionRangeConverter.GetProperties Method

Overload List

This member supports the .NET Framework infrastructure and is not intended to be used directly from your code.

[Visual Basic] **Overloads Overrides Public Function GetProperties(ITypeDescriptorContext, Object, Attribute()) As PropertyDescriptorCollection**

[C#] **public override PropertyDescriptorCollection GetProperties(ITypeDescriptorContext, object, Attribute[]);**

[C++] **public: PropertyDescriptorCollection* Get-Properties(ITypeDescriptorContext*, Object*, Attribute[]);**

[JScript] **public override function GetProperties(IType-DescriptorContext, Object, Attribute[]) : PropertyDescriptorCollection;**

Inherited from **TypeConverter**.

[Visual Basic] **Overloads Public Function Get-Properties(Object) As PropertyDescriptorCollection**

[C#] **public PropertyDescriptorCollection GetProperties(object);**

[C++] **public: PropertyDescriptorCollection* GetProperties(Object*);**

[JScript] **public function GetProperties(Object) : PropertyDescriptorCollection;**

Inherited from **TypeConverter**.

[Visual Basic] **Overloads Public Function Get-Properties(ITypeDescriptorContext, Object) As PropertyDescriptorCollection**

[C#] **public PropertyDescriptorCollection GetProperties(ITypeDescriptorContext, object);**

[C++] **public: PropertyDescriptorCollection* GetProperties(ITypeDescriptorContext*, Object*);**

[JScript] **public function GetProperties(IType-DescriptorContext, Object) : PropertyDescriptorCollection;**

SelectionRangeConverter.GetProperties Method (ITypeDescriptorContext, Object, Attribute[])

This member overrides **TypeConverter.GetProperties**.

```
[Visual Basic]
Overrides Overloads Public Function GetProperties( _
   ByVal context As ITypeDescriptorContext, _
   ByVal value As Object, _
   ByVal attributes() As Attribute _
) As PropertyDescriptorCollection
[C#]
public override PropertyDescriptorCollection GetProperties(
   ITypeDescriptorContext context,
   object value,
   Attribute[] attributes
);
[C++]
public: PropertyDescriptorCollection* GetProperties(
   ITypeDescriptorContext* context,
   Object* value,
   Attribute* attributes[]
);
```

```
[JScript]
public override function GetProperties(
   context : ITypeDescriptorContext,
   value : Object,
   attributes : Attribute[]
) : PropertyDescriptorCollection;
```

Requirements

Platforms: Windows 98, Windows NT 4.0, Windows Millennium Edition, Windows 2000, Windows XP Home Edition, Windows XP Professional, Windows Server 2003 family

SelectionRangeConverter.GetPropertiesSupported Method

Overload List

This member supports the .NET Framework infrastructure and is not intended to be used directly from your code.

[Visual Basic] **Overloads Overrides Public Function GetPropertiesSupported(ITypeDescriptorContext) As Boolean**

[C#] **public override bool GetPropertiesSupported(ITypeDescriptorContext);**

[C++] **public: bool GetPropertiesSupported(ITypeDescriptorContext*);**

[JScript] **public override function GetPropertiesSupported(ITypeDescriptorContext) : Boolean;**

Inherited from **TypeConverter**.

[Visual Basic] **Overloads Public Function GetPropertiesSupported() As Boolean**

[C#] **public bool GetPropertiesSupported();**

[C++] **public: bool GetPropertiesSupported();**

[JScript] **public function GetPropertiesSupported() : Boolean;**

SelectionRangeConverter.GetPropertiesSupported Method (ITypeDescriptorContext)

This member overrides **TypeConverter.GetPropertiesSupported**.

```
[Visual Basic]
Overrides Overloads Public Function GetPropertiesSupported( _
   ByVal context As ITypeDescriptorContext _
) As Boolean
[C#]
public override bool GetPropertiesSupported(
   ITypeDescriptorContext context
);
[C++]
public: bool GetPropertiesSupported(
   ITypeDescriptorContext* context
);
[JScript]
public override function GetPropertiesSupported(
   context : ITypeDescriptorContext
) : Boolean;
```

Requirements

Platforms: Windows 98, Windows NT 4.0, Windows Millennium Edition, Windows 2000, Windows XP Home Edition, Windows XP Professional, Windows Server 2003 family

SendKeys Class

Provides methods for sending keystrokes to an application.

System.Object
  System.Windows.Forms.SendKeys

[Visual Basic]
```
Public Class SendKeys
```
[C#]
```
public class SendKeys
```
[C++]
```
public __gc class SendKeys
```
[JScript]
```
public class SendKeys
```

Thread Safety

Any public static (**Shared** in Visual Basic) members of this type are safe for multithreaded operations. Any instance members are not guaranteed to be thread safe.

Remarks

Use **SendKeys** to send keystrokes and keystroke combinations to the active application. This class cannot be instantiated. To send a keystroke to a class and immediately continue with the flow of your program, use **Send**. To wait for any processes started by the keystroke, use **SendWait**.

Each key is represented by one or more characters. To specify a single keyboard character, use the character itself. For example, to represent the letter A, pass in the string "A" to the method. To represent more than one character, append each additional character to the one preceding it. To represent the letters A, B, and C, specify the parameter as "ABC".

The plus sign (+), caret (^), percent sign (%), tilde (~), and parentheses () have special meanings to **SendKeys**. To specify one of these characters, enclose it within braces ({}). For example, to specify the plus sign, use "{+}". To specify brace characters, use "{{}" and "{}}". Brackets ([ ]) have no special meaning to **SendKeys**, but you must enclose them in braces. In other applications, brackets do have a special meaning that might be significant when dynamic data exchange (DDE) occurs.

To specify characters that aren't displayed when you press a key, such as ENTER or TAB, and keys that represent actions rather than characters, use the codes in the following table.

Key	Code
BACKSPACE	{BACKSPACE}, {BS}, or {BKSP}
BREAK	{BREAK}
CAPS LOCK	{CAPSLOCK}
DEL or DELETE	{DELETE} or {DEL}
DOWN ARROW	{DOWN}
END	{END}
ENTER	{ENTER}or ~
ESC	{ESC}
HELP	{HELP}
HOME	{HOME}
INS or INSERT	{INSERT} or {INS}
LEFT ARROW	{LEFT}
NUM LOCK	{NUMLOCK}
PAGE DOWN	{PGDN}
PAGE UP	{PGUP}
PRINT SCREEN	{PRTSC} (reserved for future use)
RIGHT ARROW	{RIGHT}
SCROLL LOCK	{SCROLLLOCK}
TAB	{TAB}
UP ARROW	{UP}
F1	{F1}
F2	{F2}
F3	{F3}
F4	{F4}
F5	{F5}
F6	{F6}
F7	{F7}
F8	{F8}
F9	{F9}
F10	{F10}
F11	{F11}
F12	{F12}
F13	{F13}
F14	{F14}
F15	{F15}
F16	{F16}
Keypad add	{ADD}
Keypad subtract	{SUBTRACT}
Keypad multiply	{MULTIPLY}
Keypad divide	{DIVIDE}

To specify keys combined with any combination of the SHIFT, CTRL, and ALT keys, precede the key code with one or more of the following codes.

Key	Code
SHIFT	+
CTRL	^
ALT	%

To specify that any combination of SHIFT, CTRL, and ALT should be held down while several other keys are pressed, enclose the code for those keys in parentheses. For example, to specify to hold down SHIFT while E and C are pressed, use "+(EC)". To specify to hold down SHIFT while E is pressed, followed by C without SHIFT, use "+EC".

To specify repeating keys, use the form {key number}. You must put a space between key and number. For example, {LEFT 42} means press the LEFT ARROW key 42 times; {h 10} means press H 10 times.

> **Note** Because there is no managed method to activate another application, you can either use this class within the current application or use native Windows methods, such as **FindWindow** and **SetForegroundWindow**, to force focus on other applications.

Requirements

Namespace: System.Windows.Forms

Platforms: Windows 98, Windows NT 4.0, Windows Millennium Edition, Windows 2000, Windows XP Home Edition, Windows XP Professional, Windows Server 2003 family

Assembly: System.Windows.Forms (in System.Windows.Forms.dll)

SendKeys.Flush Method

Processes all the Windows messages currently in the message queue.

```
[Visual Basic]
Public Shared Sub Flush()
[C#]
public static void Flush();
[C++]
public: static void Flush();
[JScript]
public static function Flush();
```

Remarks

Use **Flush** to wait for the application to process keystrokes and other operating system messages that are in the message queue. This is equivalent to calling **Application.DoEvents** until there are no more keys to process.

> **Note** Because there is no managed method to activate another application, you can either use this class within the current application or use native Windows methods, such as **FindWindow** and **SetForegroundWindow**, to force focus on other applications.

Requirements

Platforms: Windows 98, Windows NT 4.0, Windows Millennium Edition, Windows 2000, Windows XP Home Edition, Windows XP Professional, Windows Server 2003 family

SendKeys.Send Method

Sends keystrokes to the active application.

```
[Visual Basic]
Public Shared Sub Send( _
   ByVal keys As String _
)
[C#]
public static void Send(
   string keys
);
[C++]
public: static void Send(
   String* keys
);
[JScript]
public static function Send(
   keys : String
);
```

Parameters

keys

The string of keystrokes to send.

Remarks

Each key is represented by one or more characters. To specify a single keyboard character, use the character itself. For example, to represent the letter A, pass in the string "A" to the method. To represent more than one character, append each additional character to the one preceding it. To represent the letters A, B, and C, specify the parameter as "ABC".

The plus sign (+), caret (^), percent sign (%), tilde (~), and parentheses () have special meanings to **SendKeys**. To specify one of these characters, enclose it within braces ({}). For example, to specify the plus sign, use "{+}". To specify brace characters, use "{{}" and "{}}". Brackets ([ ]) have no special meaning to **SendKeys**, but you must enclose them in braces. In other applications, brackets do have a special meaning that might be significant when dynamic data exchange (DDE) occurs.

To specify characters that aren't displayed when you press a key, such as ENTER or TAB, and keys that represent actions rather than characters, use the codes in the following table.

Key	Code
BACKSPACE	{BACKSPACE}, {BS}, or {BKSP}
BREAK	{BREAK}
CAPS LOCK	{CAPSLOCK}
DEL or DELETE	{DELETE} or {DEL}
DOWN ARROW	{DOWN}
END	{END}
ENTER	{ENTER}or ~
ESC	{ESC}
HELP	{HELP}
HOME	{HOME}
INS or INSERT	{INSERT} or {INS}
LEFT ARROW	{LEFT}
NUM LOCK	{NUMLOCK}
PAGE DOWN	{PGDN}
PAGE UP	{PGUP}
PRINT SCREEN	{PRTSC} (reserved for future use)
RIGHT ARROW	{RIGHT}
SCROLL LOCK	{SCROLLLOCK}
TAB	{TAB}
UP ARROW	{UP}
F1	{F1}
F2	{F2}
F3	{F3}
F4	{F4}
F5	{F5}
F6	{F6}
F7	{F7}
F8	{F8}
F9	{F9}
F10	{F10}
F11	{F11}

Key	Code
F12	{F12}
F13	{F13}
F14	{F14}
F15	{F15}
F16	{F16}
Keypad add	{ADD}
Keypad subtract	{SUBTRACT}
Keypad multiply	{MULTIPLY}
Keypad divide	{DIVIDE}

To specify keys combined with any combination of the SHIFT, CTRL, and ALT keys, precede the key code with one or more of the following codes.

Key	Code
SHIFT	+
CTRL	^
ALT	%

To specify that any combination of SHIFT, CTRL, and ALT should be held down while several other keys are pressed, enclose the code for those keys in parentheses. For example, to specify to hold down SHIFT while E and C are pressed, use "+(EC)". To specify to hold down SHIFT while E is pressed, followed by C without SHIFT, use "+EC".

To specify repeating keys, use the form {key number}. You must put a space between key and number. For example, {LEFT 42} means press the LEFT ARROW key 42 times; {h 10} means press H 10 times.

> **Note** Because there is no managed method to activate another application, you can either use this class within the current application or use native Windows methods, such as **Find-Window** and **SetForegroundWindow**, to force focus on other applications.

Requirements

Platforms: Windows 98, Windows NT 4.0, Windows Millennium Edition, Windows 2000, Windows XP Home Edition, Windows XP Professional, Windows Server 2003 family

.NET Framework Security:

- **SecurityPermission** for unmanaged code to call this method. Associated enumeration: **SecurityPermissionFlag.UnmanagedCode**

SendKeys.SendWait Method

Sends the given keys to the active application, and then waits for the messages to be processed.

```
[Visual Basic]
Public Shared Sub SendWait( _
   ByVal keys As String _
)
[C#]
public static void SendWait(
   string keys
);
[C++]
public: static void SendWait(
   String* keys
);
[JScript]
public static function SendWait(
   keys : String
);
```

Parameters

keys
The string of keystrokes to send.

Remarks

Use **SendWait** to send keystrokes or combinations of keystrokes to the active application and wait for the keystroke messages to be processed. You can use this method to send keystrokes to an application and wait for any processes that are started by the keystrokes to be completed. This can be important if the other application must finish before your application can continue.

> **Note** Because there is no managed method to activate another application, you can either use this class within the current application or use native Windows methods, such as **Find-Window** and **SetForegroundWindow**, to force focus on other applications.

Requirements

Platforms: Windows 98, Windows NT 4.0, Windows Millennium Edition, Windows 2000, Windows XP Home Edition, Windows XP Professional, Windows Server 2003 family

.NET Framework Security:

- **SecurityPermission** for unmanaged code to call this method. Associated enumeration: **SecurityPermission-Flag.UnmanagedCode**

Shortcut Enumeration

Specifies shortcut keys that can be used by menu items.

[Visual Basic]
```
<Serializable>
<ComVisible(True)>
Public Enum Shortcut
```
[C#]
```
[Serializable]
[ComVisible(true)]
public enum Shortcut
```
[C++]
```
[Serializable]
[ComVisible(true)]
__value public enum Shortcut
```
[JScript]
```
public
   Serializable
   ComVisible(true)
enum Shortcut
```

Remarks

Use the members of this enumeration to set the value of the **Shortcut** property of the **MenuItem** class.

Members

Member name	Description
Alt0	The shortcut keys ALT+0.
Alt1	The shortcut keys ALT+1.
Alt2	The shortcut keys ALT+2.
Alt3	The shortcut keys ALT+3.
Alt4	The shortcut keys ALT+4.
Alt5	The shortcut keys ALT+5.
Alt6	The shortcut keys ALT+6.
Alt7	The shortcut keys ALT+7.
Alt8	The shortcut keys ALT+8.
Alt9	The shortcut keys ALT+9.
AltBksp	The shortcut keys ALT+BACKSPACE.
AltF1	The shortcut keys ALT+F1.
AltF10	The shortcut keys ALT+F10.
AltF11	The shortcut keys ALT+F11.
AltF12	The shortcut keys ALT+F12.
AltF2	The shortcut keys ALT+F2.
AltF3	The shortcut keys ALT+F3.
AltF4	The shortcut keys ALT+F4.
AltF5	The shortcut keys ALT+F5.
AltF6	The shortcut keys ALT+F6.
AltF7	The shortcut keys ALT+F7.
AltF8	The shortcut keys ALT+F8.
AltF9	The shortcut keys ALT+F9.
Ctrl0	The shortcut keys CTRL+0.
Ctrl1	The shortcut keys CTRL+1.
Ctrl2	The shortcut keys CTRL+2.
Ctrl3	The shortcut keys CTRL+3.
Ctrl4	The shortcut keys CTRL+4.
Ctrl5	The shortcut keys CTRL+5.
Ctrl6	The shortcut keys CTRL+6.
Ctrl7	The shortcut keys CTRL+7.
Ctrl8	The shortcut keys CTRL+8.
Ctrl9	The shortcut keys CTRL+9.
CtrlA	The shortcut keys CTRL+A.
CtrlB	The shortcut keys CTRL+B.
CtrlC	The shortcut keys CTRL+C.
CtrlD	The shortcut keys CTRL+D.
CtrlDel	The shortcut keys CTRL+DELETE.
CtrlE	The shortcut keys CTRL+E.
CtrlF	The shortcut keys CTRL+F.
CtrlF1	The shortcut keys CTRL+F1.
CtrlF10	The shortcut keys CTRL+F10.
CtrlF11	The shortcut keys CTRL+F11.
CtrlF12	The shortcut keys CTRL+F12.
CtrlF2	The shortcut keys CTRL+F2.
CtrlF3	The shortcut keys CTRL+F3.
CtrlF4	The shortcut keys CTRL+F4.
CtrlF5	The shortcut keys CTRL+F5.
CtrlF6	The shortcut keys CTRL+F6.
CtrlF7	The shortcut keys CTRL+F7.
CtrlF8	The shortcut keys CTRL+F8.
CtrlF9	The shortcut keys CTRL+F9.
CtrlG	The shortcut keys CTRL+G.
CtrlH	The shortcut keys CTRL+H.
CtrlI	The shortcut keys CTRL+I.
CtrlIns	The shortcut keys CTRL+INSERT.
CtrlJ	The shortcut keys CTRL+J.
CtrlK	The shortcut keys CTRL+K.
CtrlL	The shortcut keys CTRL+L.
CtrlM	The shortcut keys CTRL+M.
CtrlN	The shortcut keys CTRL+N.
CtrlO	The shortcut keys CTRL+O.
CtrlP	The shortcut keys CTRL+P.
CtrlQ	The shortcut keys CTRL+Q.
CtrlR	The shortcut keys CTRL+R.
CtrlS	The shortcut keys CTRL+S.
CtrlShift0	The shortcut keys CTRL+SHIFT+0.
CtrlShift1	The shortcut keys CTRL+SHIFT+1.
CtrlShift2	The shortcut keys CTRL+SHIFT+2.
CtrlShift3	The shortcut keys CTRL+SHIFT+3.
CtrlShift4	The shortcut keys CTRL+SHIFT+4.
CtrlShift5	The shortcut keys CTRL+SHIFT+5.
CtrlShift6	The shortcut keys CTRL+SHIFT+6.
CtrlShift7	The shortcut keys CTRL+SHIFT+7.
CtrlShift8	The shortcut keys CTRL+SHIFT+8.
CtrlShift9	The shortcut keys CTRL+SHIFT+9.
CtrlShiftA	The shortcut keys CTRL+SHIFT+A.

Member name	Description
CtrlShiftB	The shortcut keys CTRL+SHIFT+B.
CtrlShiftC	The shortcut keys CTRL+SHIFT+C.
CtrlShiftD	The shortcut keys CTRL+SHIFT+D.
CtrlShiftE	The shortcut keys CTRL+SHIFT+E.
CtrlShiftF	The shortcut keys CTRL+SHIFT+F.
CtrlShiftF1	The shortcut keys CTRL+SHIFT+F1.
CtrlShiftF10	The shortcut keys CTRL+SHIFT+F10.
CtrlShiftF11	The shortcut keys CTRL+SHIFT+F11.
CtrlShiftF12	The shortcut keys CTRL+SHIFT+F12.
CtrlShiftF2	The shortcut keys CTRL+SHIFT+F2.
CtrlShiftF3	The shortcut keys CTRL+SHIFT+F3.
CtrlShiftF4	The shortcut keys CTRL+SHIFT+F4.
CtrlShiftF5	The shortcut keys CTRL+SHIFT+F5.
CtrlShiftF6	The shortcut keys CTRL+SHIFT+F6.
CtrlShiftF7	The shortcut keys CTRL+SHIFT+F7.
CtrlShiftF8	The shortcut keys CTRL+SHIFT+F8.
CtrlShiftF9	The shortcut keys CTRL+SHIFT+F9.
CtrlShiftG	The shortcut keys CTRL+SHIFT+G.
CtrlShiftH	The shortcut keys CTRL+SHIFT+H.
CtrlShiftI	The shortcut keys CTRL+SHIFT+I.
CtrlShiftJ	The shortcut keys CTRL+SHIFT+J.
CtrlShiftK	The shortcut keys CTRL+SHIFT+K.
CtrlShiftL	The shortcut keys CTRL+SHIFT+L.
CtrlShiftM	The shortcut keys CTRL+SHIFT+M.
CtrlShiftN	The shortcut keys CTRL+SHIFT+N.
CtrlShiftO	The shortcut keys CTRL+SHIFT+O.
CtrlShiftP	The shortcut keys CTRL+SHIFT+P.
CtrlShiftQ	The shortcut keys CTRL+SHIFT+Q.
CtrlShiftR	The shortcut keys CTRL+SHIFT+R.
CtrlShiftS	The shortcut keys CTRL+SHIFT+S.
CtrlShiftT	The shortcut keys CTRL+SHIFT+T.
CtrlShiftU	The shortcut keys CTRL+SHIFT+U.
CtrlShiftV	The shortcut keys CTRL+SHIFT+V.
CtrlShiftW	The shortcut keys CTRL+SHIFT+W.
CtrlShiftX	The shortcut keys CTRL+SHIFT+X.
CtrlShiftY	The shortcut keys CTRL+SHIFT+Y.
CtrlShiftZ	The shortcut keys CTRL+SHIFT+Z.
CtrlT	The shortcut keys CTRL+T.
CtrlU	The shortcut keys CTRL+U
CtrlV	The shortcut keys CTRL+V.
CtrlW	The shortcut keys CTRL+W.
CtrlX	The shortcut keys CTRL+X.
CtrlY	The shortcut keys CTRL+Y.
CtrlZ	The shortcut keys CTRL+Z.
Del	The shortcut key DELETE.
F1	The shortcut key F1.
F10	The shortcut key F10.
F11	The shortcut key F11.
F12	The shortcut key F12.
F2	The shortcut key F2.
F3	The shortcut key F3.
F4	The shortcut key F4.
F5	The shortcut key F5.
F6	The shortcut key F6.
F7	The shortcut key F7.
F8	The shortcut key F8.
F9	The shortcut key F9.
Ins	The shortcut key INSERT.
None	No shortcut key is associated with the menu item.
ShiftDel	The shortcut keys SHIFT+DELETE.
ShiftF1	The shortcut keys SHIFT+F1.
ShiftF10	The shortcut keys SHIFT+F10.
ShiftF11	The shortcut keys SHIFT+F11.
ShiftF12	The shortcut keys SHIFT+F12.
ShiftF2	The shortcut keys SHIFT+F2.
ShiftF3	The shortcut keys SHIFT+F3.
ShiftF4	The shortcut keys SHIFT+F4.
ShiftF5	The shortcut keys SHIFT+F5.
ShiftF6	The shortcut keys SHIFT+F6.
ShiftF7	The shortcut keys SHIFT+F7.
ShiftF8	The shortcut keys SHIFT+F8.
ShiftF9	The shortcut keys SHIFT+F9.
ShiftIns	The shortcut keys SHIFT+INSERT.

Requirements

Namespace: System.Windows.Forms

Platforms: Windows 98, Windows NT 4.0, Windows Millennium Edition, Windows 2000, Windows XP Home Edition, Windows XP Professional, Windows Server 2003 family

Assembly: System.Windows.Forms (in System.Windows.Forms.dll)

SizeGripStyle Enumeration

Specifies the style of the sizing grip on a **Form**.

[Visual Basic]
```
<Serializable>
Public Enum SizeGripStyle
```
[C#]
```
[Serializable]
public enum SizeGripStyle
```
[C++]
```
[Serializable]
__value public enum SizeGripStyle
```
[JScript]
```
public
   Serializable
enum SizeGripStyle
```

Remarks

Use the members of this enumeration to set the value of the **SizeGripStyle** property of the **Form**.

Members

Member name	Description
Auto	The sizing grip is automatically displayed when needed.
Hide	The sizing grip is hidden.
Show	The sizing grip is always shown on the form.

Requirements

Namespace: System.Windows.Forms

Platforms: Windows 98, Windows NT 4.0, Windows Millennium Edition, Windows 2000, Windows XP Home Edition, Windows XP Professional, Windows Server 2003 family

Assembly: System.Windows.Forms (in System.Windows.Forms.dll)

SortOrder Enumeration

Specifies how items in a list are sorted.

[Visual Basic]

```
<Serializable>
Public Enum SortOrder
```

[C#]

```
[Serializable]
public enum SortOrder
```

[C++]

```
[Serializable]
__value public enum SortOrder
```

[JScript]

```
public
   Serializable
enum SortOrder
```

Remarks

Use the members of this enumeration to set the value of the **Sorting** property of the **ListView** control.

Members

Member name	Description
Ascending	The items are sorted in ascending order.
Descending	The items are sorted in descending order.
None	The items are not sorted.

Requirements

Namespace: System.Windows.Forms

Platforms: Windows 98, Windows NT 4.0, Windows Millennium Edition, Windows 2000, Windows XP Home Edition, Windows XP Professional, Windows Server 2003 family

Assembly: System.Windows.Forms (in System.Windows.Forms.dll)

Splitter Class

Represents a splitter control that allows the user to resize docked controls.

System.Object
 System.MarshalByRefObject
  System.ComponentModel.Component
   System.Windows.Forms.Control
    System.Windows.Forms.Splitter

[Visual Basic]
```
Public Class Splitter
   Inherits Control
   Implements IMessageFilter
```
[C#]
```
public class Splitter : Control, IMessageFilter
```
[C++]
```
public __gc class Splitter : public Control, IMessageFilter
```
[JScript]
```
public class Splitter extends Control implements IMessageFilter
```

Thread Safety

Any public static (**Shared** in Visual Basic) members of this type are safe for multithreaded operations. Any instance members are not guaranteed to be thread safe.

Remarks

The **Splitter** control enables you to resize controls that are docked to the edges of the **Splitter** control at run time. When the user passes the mouse pointer over the **Splitter** control, the cursor changes to indicate that the controls docked to the **Splitter** control can be resized. The **Splitter** control enables the user to resize the docked control that is immediately before it in the docking order. Therefore, to enable the user to resize a docked control, dock the control you want the user to be able to resize to an edge of a container, and then dock a splitter to the same side of that container. For example, to create a window similar to Windows Explorer, add a **TreeView** control to a form and set its **Dock** property to **DockStyle.Left**. Add a **Splitter** control to the form and set its **Dock** property to **DockStyle.Left** as well. To complete the form layout, add a **ListView** control and set its **Dock** property to **DockStyle.Fill** to have the **ListView** occupy the remaining space on the form. At run time, the user can then resize the width of the **TreeView** control (as well as the **ListView** control) by moving the **Splitter** control.

To ensure that the **Splitter** control does not resize controls docked to a size that is too small to be useful to the user, you use the **MinExtra** and **MinSize** properties. The **MinExtra** and **MinSize** properties determine the minimum size that controls docked to the left and right (or top and bottom if a horizontal **Splitter** control) can be sized to. If the other controls on your form that the **Splitter** control is docked to display a specific style of border, you can use the **BorderStyle** property to match the border style of the controls that are docked to it.

You might find it desirable to set a maximum size limit on controls that the **Splitter** control is docked to. The **SplitterMoved** and **SplitterMoving** events enable you to determine when the user is resizing a docked control. You can use the **SplitPosition** property in an event handler for the **SplitterMoved** or **SplitterMoving** events to determine the size of the control that the **Splitter** control is docked to and set the **SplitPosition** property to a different value to limit the docked control's width to a specified maximum width (or height if a horizontally aligned **Splitter** control).

Note Resizing a control using the **Splitter** control can only be done using the mouse. It is not possible to access the **Splitter** control using the keyboard.

Example

[Visual Basic, C#] The following example uses a **Splitter** control in combination with **TreeView** and **ListView** controls to create a window similar to Windows Explorer. To identify the **TreeView** and **ListView** controls, nodes and items are added to both controls. The example uses the **MinExtra** and **MinSize** properties of the **Splitter** to prevent the **TreeView** or **ListView** control from being sized too small or too large. This example assumes that the method created in this example is defined within a **Form** and that the method is called from the constructor of the **Form**.

[Visual Basic]
```
Private Sub CreateMySplitControls()
   ' Create TreeView, ListView, and Splitter controls.
   Dim treeView1 As New TreeView()
   Dim listView1 As New ListView()
   Dim splitter1 As New Splitter()

   ' Set the TreeView control to dock to the left side of the form.
   treeView1.Dock = DockStyle.Left
   ' Set the Splitter to dock to the left side of the TreeView control.
   splitter1.Dock = DockStyle.Left
   ' Set the minimum size the ListView control can be sized to.
     splitter1.MinExtra = 100
   ' Set the minimum size the TreeView control can be sized to.
     splitter1.MinSize = 75
   ' Set the ListView control to fill the remaining space on the form.
     listView1.Dock = DockStyle.Fill

     ' Add a TreeView and a ListView item to identify the ↵
controls on the form.
     treeView1.Nodes.Add("TreeView Node")
     listView1.Items.Add("ListView Item")

   ' Add the controls in reverse order to the form to ensure ↵
proper location.
   Me.Controls.AddRange(New Control() {listView1, splitter1, ↵
treeView1})
End Sub 'CreateMySplitControls
```

[C#]
```
private void CreateMySplitControls()
{
    // Create TreeView, ListView, and Splitter controls.
    TreeView treeView1 = new TreeView();
    ListView listView1 = new ListView();
    Splitter splitter1 = new Splitter();

    // Set the TreeView control to dock to the left side of the form.
    treeView1.Dock = DockStyle.Left;
    // Set the Splitter to dock to the left side of the ↵
TreeView control.
    splitter1.Dock = DockStyle.Left;
    // Set the minimum size the ListView control can be sized to.
    splitter1.MinExtra = 100;
    // Set the minimum size the TreeView control can be sized to.
    splitter1.MinSize = 75;
    // Set the ListView control to fill the remaining space on ↵
 the form.
    listView1.Dock = DockStyle.Fill;
    // Add a TreeView and a ListView item to identify the ↵
 controls on the form.
    treeView1.Nodes.Add("TreeView Node");
    listView1.Items.Add("ListView Item");

    // Add the controls in reverse order to the form to ↵
 ensure proper location.
    this.Controls.AddRange(new Control[]{listView1, ↵
 splitter1, treeView1});
}
```

Requirements

Namespace: System.Windows.Forms

Platforms: Windows 98, Windows NT 4.0, Windows Millennium Edition, Windows 2000, Windows XP Home Edition, Windows XP Professional, Windows Server 2003 family

Assembly: System.Windows.Forms (in System.Windows.Forms.dll)

Splitter Constructor

Initializes a new instance of the **Splitter** class.

```
[Visual Basic]
Public Sub New()
[C#]
public Splitter();
[C++]
public: Splitter();
[JScript]
public function Splitter();
```

Remarks

By default, the **MinSize** and **MinExtra** properties are set to 25. The **Dock** property is set to **DockStyle.Left** by default.

Example

See related example in the **System.Windows.Forms.Splitter** class topic.

Requirements

Platforms: Windows 98, Windows NT 4.0, Windows Millennium Edition, Windows 2000, Windows XP Home Edition, Windows XP Professional, Windows Server 2003 family

Splitter.AllowDrop Property

This member overrides **Control.AllowDrop**.

```
[Visual Basic]
Overrides Public Property AllowDrop As Boolean
[C#]
public override bool AllowDrop {get; set;}
[C++]
public: __property bool get_AllowDrop();
public: __property void set_AllowDrop(bool);
[JScript]
public override function get AllowDrop() : Boolean;
public override function set AllowDrop(Boolean);
```

Requirements

Platforms: Windows 98, Windows NT 4.0, Windows Millennium Edition, Windows 2000, Windows XP Home Edition, Windows XP Professional, Windows Server 2003 family

Splitter.Anchor Property

This member overrides **Control.Anchor**.

```
[Visual Basic]
Overrides Public Property Anchor As AnchorStyles
[C#]
public override AnchorStyles Anchor {get; set;}
[C++]
public: __property AnchorStyles get_Anchor();
public: __property void set_Anchor(AnchorStyles);
[JScript]
public override function get Anchor() : AnchorStyles;
public override function set Anchor(AnchorStyles);
```

Requirements

Platforms: Windows 98, Windows NT 4.0, Windows Millennium Edition, Windows 2000, Windows XP Home Edition, Windows XP Professional, Windows Server 2003 family

Splitter.BackgroundImage Property

This member overrides **Control.BackgroundImage**.

```
[Visual Basic]
Overrides Public Property BackgroundImage As Image
[C#]
public override Image BackgroundImage {get; set;}
[C++]
public: __property Image* get_BackgroundImage();
public: __property void set_BackgroundImage(Image*);
[JScript]
public override function get BackgroundImage() : Image;
public override function set BackgroundImage(Image);
```

Requirements

Platforms: Windows 98, Windows NT 4.0, Windows Millennium Edition, Windows 2000, Windows XP Home Edition, Windows XP Professional, Windows Server 2003 family

Splitter.BorderStyle Property

Gets or sets the style of border for the control.

```
[Visual Basic]
Public Property BorderStyle As BorderStyle
[C#]
public BorderStyle BorderStyle {get; set;}
[C++]
public: __property BorderStyle get_BorderStyle();
public: __property void set_BorderStyle(BorderStyle);
[JScript]
public function get BorderStyle() : BorderStyle;
public function set BorderStyle(BorderStyle);
```

Property Value

One of the **BorderStyle** values. The default is **BorderStyle.None**.

Exceptions

Exception Type	Condition
InvalidEnumArgument-Exception	The value of the property is not one of the **BorderStyle** values.

Remarks

This property is typically used when the controls the **Splitter** control is docked to are displayed with a specific border style and it is desirable for the **Splitter** control to match their display style. For example, if you have a **TreeView** and a **ListView** control that the **Splitter** control will be docked to that you want to display without any borders, you can set the **BorderStyle** property to **BorderStyle.None**.

Requirements

Platforms: Windows 98, Windows NT 4.0, Windows Millennium Edition, Windows 2000, Windows XP Home Edition, Windows XP Professional, Windows Server 2003 family

Splitter.CreateParams Property

This member overrides **Control.CreateParams**.

```
[Visual Basic]
Overrides Protected ReadOnly Property CreateParams As CreateParams
[C#]
protected override CreateParams CreateParams {get;}
[C++]
protected: __property CreateParams* get_CreateParams();
[JScript]
protected override function get CreateParams() : CreateParams;
```

Requirements

Platforms: Windows 98, Windows NT 4.0, Windows Millennium Edition, Windows 2000, Windows XP Home Edition, Windows XP Professional, Windows Server 2003 family

Splitter.DefaultImeMode Property

This member overrides **Control.DefaultImeMode**.

```
[Visual Basic]
Overrides Protected ReadOnly Property DefaultImeMode As ImeMode
[C#]
protected override ImeMode DefaultImeMode {get;}
[C++]
protected: __property ImeMode get_DefaultImeMode();
[JScript]
protected override function get DefaultImeMode() : ImeMode;
```

Requirements

Platforms: Windows 98, Windows NT 4.0, Windows Millennium Edition, Windows 2000, Windows XP Home Edition, Windows XP Professional, Windows Server 2003 family

Splitter.DefaultSize Property

This member overrides **Control.DefaultSize**.

```
[Visual Basic]
Overrides Protected ReadOnly Property DefaultSize As Size
[C#]
protected override Size DefaultSize {get;}
[C++]
protected: __property Size get_DefaultSize();
[JScript]
protected override function get DefaultSize() : Size;
```

Requirements

Platforms: Windows 98, Windows NT 4.0, Windows Millennium Edition, Windows 2000, Windows XP Home Edition, Windows XP Professional, Windows Server 2003 family

Splitter.Dock Property

This member overrides **Control.Dock**.

```
[Visual Basic]
Overrides Public Property Dock As DockStyle
[C#]
public override DockStyle Dock {get; set;}
[C++]
public: __property DockStyle get_Dock();
public: __property void set_Dock(DockStyle);
[JScript]
public override function get Dock() : DockStyle;
public override function set Dock(DockStyle);
```

Requirements

Platforms: Windows 98, Windows NT 4.0, Windows Millennium Edition, Windows 2000, Windows XP Home Edition, Windows XP Professional, Windows Server 2003 family

Splitter.Font Property

This member overrides **Control.Font**.

```
[Visual Basic]
Overrides Public Property Font As Font
[C#]
public override Font Font {get; set;}
[C++]
public: __property Font* get_Font();
public: __property void set_Font(Font*);
[JScript]
public override function get Font() : Font;
public override function set Font(Font);
```

Requirements

Platforms: Windows 98, Windows NT 4.0, Windows Millennium Edition, Windows 2000, Windows XP Home Edition, Windows XP Professional, Windows Server 2003 family

Splitter.ForeColor Property

This member overrides **Control.ForeColor**.

```
[Visual Basic]
Overrides Public Property ForeColor As Color
[C#]
public override Color ForeColor {get; set;}
[C++]
public: __property Color get_ForeColor();
public: __property void set_ForeColor(Color);
[JScript]
public override function get ForeColor() : Color;
public override function set ForeColor(Color);
```

Requirements

Platforms: Windows 98, Windows NT 4.0, Windows Millennium Edition, Windows 2000, Windows XP Home Edition, Windows XP Professional, Windows Server 2003 family

Splitter.ImeMode Property

This member supports the .NET Framework infrastructure and is not intended to be used directly from your code.

```
[Visual Basic]
Public Shadows Property ImeMode As ImeMode
[C#]
public new ImeMode ImeMode {get; set;}
[C++]
public: __property ImeMode get_ImeMode();
public: __property void set_ImeMode(ImeMode);
[JScript]
public hide function get ImeMode() : ImeMode;
public hide function set ImeMode(ImeMode);
```

Splitter.MinExtra Property

Gets or sets the minimum distance that must remain between the splitter control and the edge of the opposite side of the container (or the closest control docked to that side).

```
[Visual Basic]
Public Property MinExtra As Integer
[C#]
public int MinExtra {get; set;}
[C++]
public: __property int get_MinExtra();
public: __property void set_MinExtra(int);
[JScript]
public function get MinExtra() : int;
public function set MinExtra(int);
```

Property Value

The minimum distance, in pixels, between the **Splitter** control and the edge of the opposite side of the container (or the closest control docked to that side). The default is 25.

Remarks

For a horizontal **Splitter** control (a **Splitter** control docked to the top or bottom of a container), the minimum height of the area of the container reserved for undocked controls is this value minus the height of the **Splitter** control. For a vertical **Splitter** control (a **Splitter** control docked to the left or right of a container), the minimum width of the area of the container reserved for undocked controls is this value minus the width of the **Splitter** control. The user cannot move the splitter past the limit specified by this property.

> **Note** If the **MinExtra** property is set to a negative value, the property value is reset to 0.

Example

See related example in the **System.Windows.Forms.Splitter** class topic.

Requirements

Platforms: Windows 98, Windows NT 4.0, Windows Millennium Edition, Windows 2000, Windows XP Home Edition, Windows XP Professional, Windows Server 2003 family

Splitter.MinSize Property

Gets or sets the minimum distance that must remain between the splitter control and the container edge that the control is docked to.

```
[Visual Basic]
Public Property MinSize As Integer
[C#]
public int MinSize {get; set;}
[C++]
public: __property int get_MinSize();
public: __property void set_MinSize(int);
[JScript]
public function get MinSize() : int;
public function set MinSize(int);
```

Property Value

The minimum distance, in pixels, between the **Splitter** control and the container edge that the control is docked to. The default is 25.

Remarks

For a horizontal **Splitter** control (a **Splitter** control docked to the top or bottom of a container), this value is the minimum height of the resizable control. For a vertical **Splitter** control (a **Splitter** control docked to the left or right of a container), this value is the minimum width of the resizable control. The user cannot move the splitter past the limit specified by this property.

> **Note** If the **MinSize** property is set to a negative value, the property value is reset to 0.

Example

See related example in the **System.Windows.Forms.Splitter** class topic.

Requirements

Platforms: Windows 98, Windows NT 4.0, Windows Millennium Edition, Windows 2000, Windows XP Home Edition, Windows XP Professional, Windows Server 2003 family

Splitter.SplitPosition Property

Gets or sets the distance between the splitter control and the container edge that the control is docked to.

```
[Visual Basic]
Public Property SplitPosition As Integer
[C#]
public int SplitPosition {get; set;}
[C++]
public: __property int get_SplitPosition();
public: __property void set_SplitPosition(int);
[JScript]
public function get SplitPosition() : int;
public function set SplitPosition(int);
```

Property Value

The distance, in pixels, between the **Splitter** control and the container edge that the control is docked to. If the **Splitter** control is not bound to a control, the value is -1.

Remarks

For a horizontal **Splitter** control (a **Splitter** control docked to the top or bottom of a container), this value is the height of the resizable control. For a vertical **Splitter** control (a **Splitter** control docked to the left or right of a container), this value is the width of the resizable control. You can use the **SplitPosition** property in an event handler for the **SplitterMoved** or **SplitterMoving** events to determine the size of the control that the **Splitter** control is docked to and limit its width to a specified maximum width (or height if a horizontally docked **Splitter** control).

Requirements

Platforms: Windows 98, Windows NT 4.0, Windows Millennium Edition, Windows 2000, Windows XP Home Edition, Windows XP Professional, Windows Server 2003 family

Splitter.TabStop Property

This member supports the .NET Framework infrastructure and is not intended to be used directly from your code.

```
[Visual Basic]
Public Shadows Property TabStop As Boolean
[C#]
public new bool TabStop {get; set;}
[C++]
public: __property bool get_TabStop();
public: __property void set_TabStop(bool);
[JScript]
public hide function get TabStop() : Boolean;
public hide function set TabStop(Boolean);
```

Splitter.Text Property

This member overrides **Control.Text**.

```
[Visual Basic]
Overrides Public Property Text As String
[C#]
public override string Text {get; set;}
[C++]
public: __property String* get_Text();
public: __property void set_Text(String*);
[JScript]
public override function get Text() : String;
public override function set Text(String);
```

Requirements

Platforms: Windows 98, Windows NT 4.0, Windows Millennium Edition, Windows 2000, Windows XP Home Edition, Windows XP Professional, Windows Server 2003 family

Splitter.OnKeyDown Method

This member overrides **Control.OnKeyDown**.

```
[Visual Basic]
Overrides Protected Sub OnKeyDown( _
   ByVal e As KeyEventArgs _
)
[C#]
protected override void OnKeyDown(
   KeyEventArgs e
);
[C++]
protected: void OnKeyDown(
   KeyEventArgs* e
);
[JScript]
protected override function OnKeyDown(
   e : KeyEventArgs
);
```

Requirements

Platforms: Windows 98, Windows NT 4.0, Windows Millennium Edition, Windows 2000, Windows XP Home Edition, Windows XP Professional, Windows Server 2003 family

Splitter.OnMouseDown Method

This member overrides **Control.OnMouseDown**.

```
[Visual Basic]
Overrides Protected Sub OnMouseDown( _
   ByVal e As MouseEventArgs _
)
[C#]
protected override void OnMouseDown(
   MouseEventArgs e
);
[C++]
protected: void OnMouseDown(
   MouseEventArgs* e
);
[JScript]
protected override function OnMouseDown(
   e : MouseEventArgs
);
```

Requirements

Platforms: Windows 98, Windows NT 4.0, Windows Millennium Edition, Windows 2000, Windows XP Home Edition, Windows XP Professional, Windows Server 2003 family

Splitter.OnMouseMove Method

This member overrides **Control.OnMouseMove**.

```
[Visual Basic]
Overrides Protected Sub OnMouseMove( _
   ByVal e As MouseEventArgs _
)
[C#]
protected override void OnMouseMove(
   MouseEventArgs e
);
```

```
[C++]
protected: void OnMouseMove(
   MouseEventArgs* e
);
[JScript]
protected override function OnMouseMove(
   e : MouseEventArgs
);
```

Requirements

Platforms: Windows 98, Windows NT 4.0, Windows Millennium Edition, Windows 2000, Windows XP Home Edition, Windows XP Professional, Windows Server 2003 family

Splitter.OnMouseUp Method

This member overrides **Control.OnMouseUp**.

```
[Visual Basic]
Overrides Protected Sub OnMouseUp( _
   ByVal e As MouseEventArgs _
)
[C#]
protected override void OnMouseUp(
   MouseEventArgs e
);
[C++]
protected: void OnMouseUp(
   MouseEventArgs* e
);
[JScript]
protected override function OnMouseUp(
   e : MouseEventArgs
);
```

Requirements

Platforms: Windows 98, Windows NT 4.0, Windows Millennium Edition, Windows 2000, Windows XP Home Edition, Windows XP Professional, Windows Server 2003 family

Splitter.OnSplitterMoved Method

Raises the **SplitterMoved** event.

```
[Visual Basic]
Protected Overridable Sub OnSplitterMoved( _
   ByVal sevent As SplitterEventArgs _
)
[C#]
protected virtual void OnSplitterMoved(
   SplitterEventArgs sevent
);
[C++]
protected: virtual void OnSplitterMoved(
   SplitterEventArgs* sevent
);
[JScript]
protected function OnSplitterMoved(
   sevent : SplitterEventArgs
);
```

Parameters

sevent

A **SplitterEventArgs** that contains the event data.

Remarks

Raising an event invokes the event handler through a delegate.

The **OnSplitterMoved** method also allows derived classes to handle the event without attaching a delegate. This is the preferred technique for handling the event in a derived class.

Notes to Inheritors: When overriding **OnSplitterMoved** in a derived class, be sure to call the base class's **OnSplitterMoved** method so that registered delegates receive the event.

Requirements

Platforms: Windows 98, Windows NT 4.0, Windows Millennium Edition, Windows 2000, Windows XP Home Edition, Windows XP Professional, Windows Server 2003 family

Splitter.OnSplitterMoving Method

Raises the **SplitterMoving** event.

```
[Visual Basic]
Protected Overridable Sub OnSplitterMoving( _
   ByVal sevent As SplitterEventArgs _
)
[C#]
protected virtual void OnSplitterMoving(
   SplitterEventArgs sevent
);
[C++]
protected: virtual void OnSplitterMoving(
   SplitterEventArgs* sevent
);
[JScript]
protected function OnSplitterMoving(
   sevent : SplitterEventArgs
);
```

Parameters

sevent

A **SplitterEventArgs** that contains the event data.

Remarks

Raising an event invokes the event handler through a delegate.

The **OnSplitterMoving** method also allows derived classes to handle the event without attaching a delegate. This is the preferred technique for handling the event in a derived class.

Notes to Inheritors: When overriding **OnSplitterMoving** in a derived class, be sure to call the base class's **OnSplitterMoving** method so that registered delegates receive the event.

Requirements

Platforms: Windows 98, Windows NT 4.0, Windows Millennium Edition, Windows 2000, Windows XP Home Edition, Windows XP Professional, Windows Server 2003 family

Splitter.PreFilterMessage Method

This member supports the .NET Framework infrastructure and is not intended to be used directly from your code.

```
[Visual Basic]
Public Overridable Function PreFilterMessage( _
   ByRef m As Message _
) As Boolean Implements IMessageFilter.PreFilterMessage
[C#]
public virtual bool PreFilterMessage(
   ref Message m
);
[C++]
public: virtual bool PreFilterMessage(
   Message* m
);
[JScript]
public function PreFilterMessage(
   m : Message
) : Boolean;
```

Splitter.SetBoundsCore Method

This member overrides **Control.SetBoundsCore**.

```
[Visual Basic]
Overrides Protected Sub SetBoundsCore( _
   ByVal x As Integer, _
   ByVal y As Integer, _
   ByVal width As Integer, _
   ByVal height As Integer, _
   ByVal specified As BoundsSpecified _
)
[C#]
protected override void SetBoundsCore(
   int x,
   int y,
   int width,
   int height,
   BoundsSpecified specified
);
[C++]
protected: void SetBoundsCore(
   int x,
   int y,
   int width,
   int height,
   BoundsSpecified specified
);
[JScript]
protected override function SetBoundsCore(
   x : int,
   y : int,
   width : int,
   height : int,
   specified : BoundsSpecified
);
```

Requirements

Platforms: Windows 98, Windows NT 4.0, Windows Millennium Edition, Windows 2000, Windows XP Home Edition, Windows XP Professional, Windows Server 2003 family

Splitter.ToString Method

This member overrides **Object.ToString**.

```
[Visual Basic]
Overrides Public Function ToString() As String
[C#]
public override string ToString();
[C++]
public: String* ToString();
[JScript]
public override function ToString() : String;
```

Requirements

Platforms: Windows 98, Windows NT 4.0, Windows Millennium Edition, Windows 2000, Windows XP Home Edition, Windows XP Professional, Windows Server 2003 family

Splitter.BackgroundImageChanged Event

This member supports the .NET Framework infrastructure and is not intended to be used directly from your code.

```
[Visual Basic]
Public Shadows Event BackgroundImageChanged As EventHandler
[C#]
public new event EventHandler BackgroundImageChanged;
[C++]
public: __event EventHandler* BackgroundImageChanged;
```

[JScript] In JScript, you can handle the events defined by a class, but you cannot define your own.

Splitter.Enter Event

This member supports the .NET Framework infrastructure and is not intended to be used directly from your code.

```
[Visual Basic]
Public Shadows Event Enter As EventHandler
[C#]
public new event EventHandler Enter;
[C++]
public: __event EventHandler* Enter;
```

[JScript] In JScript, you can handle the events defined by a class, but you cannot define your own.

Splitter.FontChanged Event

This member supports the .NET Framework infrastructure and is not intended to be used directly from your code.

```
[Visual Basic]
Public Shadows Event FontChanged As EventHandler
[C#]
public new event EventHandler FontChanged;
[C++]
public: __event EventHandler* FontChanged;
```

[JScript] In JScript, you can handle the events defined by a class, but you cannot define your own.

Splitter.ForeColorChanged Event

This member supports the .NET Framework infrastructure and is not intended to be used directly from your code.

[Visual Basic]
```
Public Shadows Event ForeColorChanged As EventHandler
```
[C#]
```
public new event EventHandler ForeColorChanged;
```
[C++]
```
public: __event EventHandler* ForeColorChanged;
```

[JScript] In JScript, you can handle the events defined by a class, but you cannot define your own.

Splitter.ImeModeChanged Event

This member supports the .NET Framework infrastructure and is not intended to be used directly from your code.

[Visual Basic]
```
Public Shadows Event ImeModeChanged As EventHandler
```
[C#]
```
public new event EventHandler ImeModeChanged;
```
[C++]
```
public: __event EventHandler* ImeModeChanged;
```

[JScript] In JScript, you can handle the events defined by a class, but you cannot define your own.

Splitter.KeyDown Event

This member supports the .NET Framework infrastructure and is not intended to be used directly from your code.

[Visual Basic]
```
Public Shadows Event KeyDown As KeyEventHandler
```
[C#]
```
public new event KeyEventHandler KeyDown;
```
[C++]
```
public: __event KeyEventHandler* KeyDown;
```

[JScript] In JScript, you can handle the events defined by a class, but you cannot define your own.

Splitter.KeyPress Event

This member supports the .NET Framework infrastructure and is not intended to be used directly from your code.

[Visual Basic]
```
Public Shadows Event KeyPress As KeyPressEventHandler
```
[C#]
```
public new event KeyPressEventHandler KeyPress;
```
[C++]
```
public: __event KeyPressEventHandler* KeyPress;
```

[JScript] In JScript, you can handle the events defined by a class, but you cannot define your own.

Splitter.KeyUp Event

This member supports the .NET Framework infrastructure and is not intended to be used directly from your code.

[Visual Basic]
```
Public Shadows Event KeyUp As KeyEventHandler
```
[C#]
```
public new event KeyEventHandler KeyUp;
```
[C++]
```
public: __event KeyEventHandler* KeyUp;
```

[JScript] In JScript, you can handle the events defined by a class, but you cannot define your own.

Splitter.Leave Event

This member supports the .NET Framework infrastructure and is not intended to be used directly from your code.

[Visual Basic]
```
Public Shadows Event Leave As EventHandler
```
[C#]
```
public new event EventHandler Leave;
```
[C++]
```
public: __event EventHandler* Leave;
```

[JScript] In JScript, you can handle the events defined by a class, but you cannot define your own.

Splitter.SplitterMoved Event

Occurs when the splitter control is moved.

[Visual Basic]
```
Public Event SplitterMoved As SplitterEventHandler
```
[C#]
```
public event SplitterEventHandler SplitterMoved;
```
[C++]
```
public: __event SplitterEventHandler* SplitterMoved;
```

[JScript] In JScript, you can handle the events defined by a class, but you cannot define your own.

Event Data

The event handler receives an argument of type **SplitterEventArgs** containing data related to this event. The following **SplitterEventArgs** properties provide information specific to this event.

Property	Description
SplitX	Gets or sets the x-coordinate of the upper-left corner of the **Splitter** (in client coordinates).
SplitY	Gets or sets the y-coordinate of the upper-left corner of the **Splitter** (in client coordinates).
X	Gets the x-coordinate of the mouse pointer (in client coordinates).
Y	Gets the y-coordinate of the mouse pointer (in client coordinates).

Remarks

You can create an event handler for the **SplitterMoved** event to perform resize validation in your application. For example, if a **Splitter** control is docked to the edges of a **TreeView** control and a **ListView** control, you can write code in the **SplitterMoved** event to determine if the minimum and/or maximum size for the **TreeView** and **ListView** controls has been exceeded and resize the controls to their minimum or maximum size.

For more information about handling events, see **Consuming Events**.

Requirements

Platforms: Windows 98, Windows NT 4.0,
Windows Millennium Edition, Windows 2000,
Windows XP Home Edition, Windows XP Professional,
Windows Server 2003 family

Splitter.SplitterMoving Event

Occurs when the splitter control is in the process of moving.

```
[Visual Basic]
Public Event SplitterMoving As SplitterEventHandler
[C#]
public event SplitterEventHandler SplitterMoving;
[C++]
public: __event SplitterEventHandler* SplitterMoving;
```

[JScript] In JScript, you can handle the events defined by a class, but you cannot define your own.

Event Data

The event handler receives an argument of type **SplitterEventArgs** containing data related to this event. The following **SplitterEventArgs** properties provide information specific to this event.

Property	Description
SplitX	Gets or sets the x-coordinate of the upper-left corner of the **Splitter** (in client coordinates).
SplitY	Gets or sets the y-coordinate of the upper-left corner of the **Splitter** (in client coordinates).
X	Gets the x-coordinate of the mouse pointer (in client coordinates).
Y	Gets the y-coordinate of the mouse pointer (in client coordinates).

Remarks

You can create an event handler for the **SplitterMoving** event to perform resize validation in your application. For example, if a **Splitter** control is docked to the edges of a **TreeView** control and a **ListView** control, you can write code in the **SplitterMoved** event to determine if the minimum and/or maximum size for the **TreeView** and **ListView** controls has been exceeded and restrict the resizing of the controls to their minimum or maximum size.

For more information about handling events, see **Consuming Events**.

Requirements

Platforms: Windows 98, Windows NT 4.0,
Windows Millennium Edition, Windows 2000,
Windows XP Home Edition, Windows XP Professional,
Windows Server 2003 family

Splitter.TabStopChanged Event

This member supports the .NET Framework infrastructure and is not intended to be used directly from your code.

```
[Visual Basic]
Public Shadows Event TabStopChanged As EventHandler
[C#]
public new event EventHandler TabStopChanged;
[C++]
public: __event EventHandler* TabStopChanged;
```

[JScript] In JScript, you can handle the events defined by a class, but you cannot define your own.

Splitter.TextChanged Event

This member supports the .NET Framework infrastructure and is not intended to be used directly from your code.

```
[Visual Basic]
Public Shadows Event TextChanged As EventHandler
[C#]
public new event EventHandler TextChanged;
[C++]
public: __event EventHandler* TextChanged;
```

[JScript] In JScript, you can handle the events defined by a class, but you cannot define your own.

SplitterEventArgs Class

Provides data for **SplitterMoving** and the **SplitterMoved** events.

System.Object
  System.EventArgs
    System.Windows.Forms.SplitterEventArgs

```
[Visual Basic]
<ComVisible(True)>
Public Class SplitterEventArgs
   Inherits EventArgs
[C#]
[ComVisible(true)]
public class SplitterEventArgs : EventArgs
[C++]
[ComVisible(true)]
public __gc class SplitterEventArgs : public EventArgs
[JScript]
public
   ComVisible(true)
class SplitterEventArgs extends EventArgs
```

Thread Safety

Any public static (**Shared** in Visual Basic) members of this type are safe for multithreaded operations. Any instance members are not guaranteed to be thread safe.

Remarks

The **SplitterMoving** event occurs when the user is moving the **Splitter** control. The **SplitterMoved** event occurs when the user finishes moving the **Splitter** control. The **SplitterEventArgs** class specifies the position of the mouse pointer and the position of the upper-left corner of the **Splitter** control.

Requirements

Namespace: System.Windows.Forms

Platforms: Windows 98, Windows NT 4.0, Windows Millennium Edition, Windows 2000, Windows XP Home Edition, Windows XP Professional, Windows Server 2003 family

Assembly: System.Windows.Forms (in System.Windows.Forms.dll)

SplitterEventArgs Constructor

Initializes an instance of the **SplitterEventArgs** class with the specified coordinates of the mouse pointer and the coordinates of the upper-left corner of the **Splitter** control.

```
[Visual Basic]
Public Sub New( _
   ByVal x As Integer, _
   ByVal y As Integer, _
   ByVal splitX As Integer, _
   ByVal splitY As Integer _
)
[C#]
public SplitterEventArgs(
   int x,
   int y,
   int splitX,
   int splitY
);
[C++]
public: SplitterEventArgs(
   int x,
   int y,
   int splitX,
   int splitY
);
[JScript]
public function SplitterEventArgs(
   x : int,
   y : int,
   splitX : int,
   splitY : int
);
```

Parameters

x
   The x-coordinate of the mouse pointer (in client coordinates).

y
   The y-coordinate of the mouse pointer (in client coordinates).

splitX
   The x-coordinate of the upper-left corner of the **Splitter** (in client coordinates).

splitY
   The y-coordinate of the upper-left corner of the **Splitter** (in client coordinates).

Requirements

Platforms: Windows 98, Windows NT 4.0, Windows Millennium Edition, Windows 2000, Windows XP Home Edition, Windows XP Professional, Windows Server 2003 family

SplitterEventArgs.SplitX Property

Gets or sets the x-coordinate of the upper-left corner of the **Splitter** (in client coordinates).

```
[Visual Basic]
Public Property SplitX As Integer
[C#]
public int SplitX {get; set;}
[C++]
public: __property int get_SplitX();
public: __property void set_SplitX(int);
[JScript]
public function get SplitX() : int;
public function set SplitX(int);
```

Property Value

The x-coordinate of the upper-left corner of the control.

Remarks

You can use this property along with the **SplitY** property of this class to determine the position of the **Splitter** control when the **SplitterMoving** and **SplitterMoved** events are raised.

Requirements

Platforms: Windows 98, Windows NT 4.0, Windows Millennium Edition, Windows 2000, Windows XP Home Edition, Windows XP Professional, Windows Server 2003 family

SplitterEventArgs.SplitY Property

Gets or sets the y-coordinate of the upper-left corner of the **Splitter** (in client coordinates).

[Visual Basic]
```
Public Property SplitY As Integer
```
[C#]
```
public int SplitY {get; set;}
```
[C++]
```
public: __property int get_SplitY();
public: __property void set_SplitY(int);
```
[JScript]
```
public function get SplitY() : int;
public function set SplitY(int);
```

Property Value

The y-coordinate of the upper-left corner of the control.

Remarks

You can use this property along with the **SplitX** property of this class to determine the position of the **Splitter** control when the **SplitterMoving** and **SplitterMoved** events are raised.

Requirements

Platforms: Windows 98, Windows NT 4.0, Windows Millennium Edition, Windows 2000, Windows XP Home Edition, Windows XP Professional, Windows Server 2003 family

SplitterEventArgs.X Property

Gets the x-coordinate of the mouse pointer (in client coordinates).

[Visual Basic]
```
Public ReadOnly Property X As Integer
```
[C#]
```
public int X {get;}
```
[C++]
```
public: __property int get_X();
```
[JScript]
```
public function get X() : int;
```

Property Value

The x-coordinate of the mouse pointer.

Remarks

You can use this property along with the **Y** property of this class to determine the current location of the mouse pointer when the **SplitterMoving** and **SplitterMoved** events are raised.

Requirements

Platforms: Windows 98, Windows NT 4.0, Windows Millennium Edition, Windows 2000, Windows XP Home Edition, Windows XP Professional, Windows Server 2003 family

SplitterEventArgs.Y Property

Gets the y-coordinate of the mouse pointer (in client coordinates).

[Visual Basic]
```
Public ReadOnly Property Y As Integer
```
[C#]
```
public int Y {get;}
```
[C++]
```
public: __property int get_Y();
```
[JScript]
```
public function get Y() : int;
```

Property Value

The y-coordinate of the mouse pointer.

Remarks

You can use this property along with the **X** property of this class to determine the current location of the mouse pointer when the **SplitterMoving** and **SplitterMoved** events are raised.

Requirements

Platforms: Windows 98, Windows NT 4.0, Windows Millennium Edition, Windows 2000, Windows XP Home Edition, Windows XP Professional, Windows Server 2003 family

SplitterEventHandler Delegate

Represents the method that will handle the **SplitterMoving** and **SplitterMoved** events of a **Splitter**.

[Visual Basic]
```
<Serializable>
Public Delegate Sub SplitterEventHandler( _
   ByVal sender As Object, _
   ByVal e As SplitterEventArgs _
)
```
[C#]
```
[Serializable]
public delegate void SplitterEventHandler(
   object sender,
   SplitterEventArgs e
);
```
[C++]
```
[Serializable]
public __gc __delegate void SplitterEventHandler(
   Object* sender,
   SplitterEventArgs* e
);
```

[JScript] In JScript, you can use the delegates in the .NET Framework, but you cannot define your own.

Parameters [Visual Basic, C#, C++]

The declaration of your event handler must have the same parameters as the **SplitterEventHandler** delegate declaration.

sender
  The source of the event.

e
  A **SplitterEventArgs** that contains the event data.

Remarks

When you create a(n) **SplitterEventHandler** delegate, you identify the method that will handle the event. To associate the event with your event handler, add an instance of the delegate to the event. The event handler is called whenever the event occurs, unless you remove the delegate.

Requirements

Namespace: System.Windows.Forms

Platforms: Windows 98, Windows NT 4.0,
Windows Millennium Edition, Windows 2000,
Windows XP Home Edition, Windows XP Professional,
Windows Server 2003 family

Assembly: System.Windows.Forms (in System.Windows.Forms.dll)

StatusBar Class

Represents a Windows status bar control.

System.Object
System.MarshalByRefObject
System.ComponentModel.Component
System.Windows.Forms.Control
System.Windows.Forms.StatusBar

[Visual Basic]
```
Public Class StatusBar
   Inherits Control
```
[C#]
```
public class StatusBar : Control
```
[C++]
```
public __gc class StatusBar : public Control
```
[JScript]
```
public class StatusBar extends Control
```

Thread Safety

Any public static (**Shared** in Visual Basic) members of this type are safe for multithreaded operations. Any instance members are not guaranteed to be thread safe.

Remarks

Typically a **StatusBar** control consists of **StatusBarPanel** objects, each of which displays text and/or an icon. You can also provide owner-drawn panels to provide custom panels such as a progress bar or a series of images that displays the state of your application. A **StatusBar** control typically displays information about an object being viewed on a **Form**, the object's components, or contextual information that relates to that object's operation within your application.

The **StatusBar** control provides properties that enable you to customize the appearance of the control. If the **StatusBar** is displayed on a form that can be resized, you can use the **SizingGrip** property to display a sizing grip in the lower-right corner of the form to indicate to users that the form can be resized. The **ShowPanels** property enables you to display panels within your **StatusBar** or to display only the value of the **Text** property of the control.

The default **StatusBar** has no panels. To add panels to a **StatusBar** you can use the **Add** method of the **StatusBar.StatusBarPanel-Collection** class that is accessible through the **Panels** property of the control. You can also use the **StatusBar.StatusBarPanelCollection** object provided through the **Panels** property to remove panels from the control and access a specific **StatusBarPanel** object to manipulate the panel.

If you want to determine when a **StatusBarPanel** object within a **StatusBar** control is clicked, you can create an event handler for the **PanelClick** event. To perform owner-draw operations on a panel, you can create an event handler for the **DrawItem** event. The event data passed to the event handler provides information on the panel to draw and a **Graphics** object to use to perform drawing tasks.

When you create an instance of **StatusBar**, the read/write properties are set to initial values. For a list of these values, see the **StatusBar** constructor.

Example

[Visual Basic, C#] The following example creates a **StatusBar** control on a form and adds two **StatusBarPanel** objects. One of the **StatusBarPanel** objects, named `panel1`, displays status text for an application. The second **StatusBarPanel** object, named `panel2`, displays the current date and uses the **ToolTipText** property of the **StatusBarPanel** class to display the current time. The example uses the **ShowPanels** property to ensure that the panels are displayed instead of a standard panel, and it uses and the **Panels** property to access the **Add** method of the **StatusBar.StatusBarPanel-Collection** to add the panels to the **StatusBar**. The example also uses the **AutoSize**, **BorderStyle**, **ToolTipText**, and **Text** properties to initialize the **StatusBarPanel** objects. This example assumes that the method defined in the example is defined and called from the constructor of a **Form**.

[Visual Basic]
```
Private Sub CreateMyStatusBar()
   ' Create a StatusBar control.
   Dim statusBar1 As New StatusBar()
   ' Create two StatusBarPanel objects to display in the StatusBar.
   Dim panel1 As New StatusBarPanel()
   Dim panel2 As New StatusBarPanel()

   ' Display the first panel with a sunken border style.
   panel1.BorderStyle = StatusBarPanelBorderStyle.Sunken
   ' Initialize the text of the panel.
   panel1.Text = "Ready..."
   ' Set the AutoSize property to use all remaining space on        ↵
 the StatusBar.
   panel1.AutoSize = StatusBarPanelAutoSize.Spring
   ' Display the second panel with a raised border style.
   panel2.BorderStyle = StatusBarPanelBorderStyle.Raised
   ' Create ToolTip text that displays the current time.
   panel2.ToolTipText = System.DateTime.Now.ToShortTimeString()
   ' Set the text of the panel to the current date.
   panel2.Text = System.DateTime.Today.ToLongDateString()
   ' Set the AutoSize property to size the panel to the size of        ↵
the contents.
   panel2.AutoSize = StatusBarPanelAutoSize.Contents

   ' Display panels in the StatusBar control.
   statusBar1.ShowPanels = True

   ' Add both panels to the StatusBarPanelCollection of the StatusBar.
   statusBar1.Panels.Add(panel1)
   statusBar1.Panels.Add(panel2)

   ' Add the StatusBar to the form.
   Me.Controls.Add(statusBar1)
End Sub
```

[C#]
```
private void CreateMyStatusBar()
{
    // Create a StatusBar control.
    StatusBar statusBar1 = new StatusBar();
    // Create two StatusBarPanel objects to display in the StatusBar.
    StatusBarPanel panel1 = new StatusBarPanel();
    StatusBarPanel panel2 = new StatusBarPanel();

    // Display the first panel with a sunken border style.
    panel1.BorderStyle = StatusBarPanelBorderStyle.Sunken;
    // Initialize the text of the panel.
    panel1.Text = "Ready...";
    // Set the AutoSize property to use all remaining space on        ↵
 the StatusBar.
    panel1.AutoSize = StatusBarPanelAutoSize.Spring;
    // Display the second panel with a raised border style.
    panel2.BorderStyle = StatusBarPanelBorderStyle.Raised;
    // Create ToolTip text that displays the current time.
    panel2.ToolTipText = System.DateTime.Now.ToShortTimeString();
    // Set the text of the panel to the current date.
    panel2.Text = System.DateTime.Today.ToLongDateString();
    // Set the AutoSize property to size the panel to the size        ↵
 of the contents.
    panel2.AutoSize = StatusBarPanelAutoSize.Contents;
```

```
    // Display panels in the StatusBar control.
    statusBar1.ShowPanels = true;

    // Add both panels to the StatusBarPanelCollection of ↵
the StatusBar.
    statusBar1.Panels.Add(panel1);
    statusBar1.Panels.Add(panel2);

    // Add the StatusBar to the form.
    this.Controls.Add(statusBar1);
}
```

Requirements

Namespace: System.Windows.Forms

Platforms: Windows 98, Windows NT 4.0, Windows Millennium Edition, Windows 2000, Windows XP Home Edition, Windows XP Professional, Windows Server 2003 family, .NET Compact Framework - Windows CE .NET

Assembly: System.Windows.Forms (in System.Windows.Forms.dll)

StatusBar Constructor

Initializes a new instance of the **StatusBar** class.

[Visual Basic]
```
Public Sub New()
```
[C#]
```
public StatusBar();
```
[C++]
```
public: StatusBar();
```
[JScript]
```
public function StatusBar();
```

Remarks

The default **StatusBar** has no panels.

When you create an instance of **StatusBar**, the following read/write properties are set to initial values.

Property	Initial Value
Dock	**DockStyle.Bottom**
ShowPanels	**false**
SizingGrip	**true**

You can change the value for any of these properties through a separate call to the property.

Requirements

Platforms: Windows 98, Windows NT 4.0, Windows Millennium Edition, Windows 2000, Windows XP Home Edition, Windows XP Professional, Windows Server 2003 family, .NET Compact Framework - Windows CE .NET

StatusBar.BackColor Property

This member overrides **Control.BackColor**.

[Visual Basic]
```
Overrides Public Property BackColor As Color
```
[C#]
```
public override Color BackColor {get; set;}
```
[C++]
```
public: __property Color get_BackColor();
public: __property void set_BackColor(Color);
```
[JScript]
```
public override function get BackColor() : Color;
public override function set BackColor(Color);
```

Requirements

Platforms: Windows 98, Windows NT 4.0, Windows Millennium Edition, Windows 2000, Windows XP Home Edition, Windows XP Professional, Windows Server 2003 family

StatusBar.BackgroundImage Property

This member overrides **Control.BackgroundImage**.

[Visual Basic]
```
Overrides Public Property BackgroundImage As Image
```
[C#]
```
public override Image BackgroundImage {get; set;}
```
[C++]
```
public: __property Image* get_BackgroundImage();
public: __property void set_BackgroundImage(Image*);
```
[JScript]
```
public override function get BackgroundImage() : Image;
public override function set BackgroundImage(Image);
```

Requirements

Platforms: Windows 98, Windows NT 4.0, Windows Millennium Edition, Windows 2000, Windows XP Home Edition, Windows XP Professional, Windows Server 2003 family

StatusBar.CreateParams Property

This member overrides **Control.CreateParams**.

[Visual Basic]
```
Overrides Protected ReadOnly Property CreateParams As CreateParams
```
[C#]
```
protected override CreateParams CreateParams {get;}
```
[C++]
```
protected: __property CreateParams* get_CreateParams();
```
[JScript]
```
protected override function get CreateParams() : CreateParams;
```

Requirements

Platforms: Windows 98, Windows NT 4.0, Windows Millennium Edition, Windows 2000, Windows XP Home Edition, Windows XP Professional, Windows Server 2003 family

StatusBar.DefaultImeMode Property

This member overrides **Control.DefaultImeMode**.

[Visual Basic]
```
Overrides Protected ReadOnly Property DefaultImeMode As ImeMode
```
[C#]
```
protected override ImeMode DefaultImeMode {get;}
```
[C++]
```
protected: __property ImeMode get_DefaultImeMode();
```
[JScript]
```
protected override function get DefaultImeMode() : ImeMode;
```

Requirements

Platforms: Windows 98, Windows NT 4.0, Windows Millennium Edition, Windows 2000, Windows XP Home Edition, Windows XP Professional, Windows Server 2003 family

StatusBar.DefaultSize Property

This member overrides **Control.DefaultSize**.

```
[Visual Basic]
Overrides Protected ReadOnly Property DefaultSize As Size
[C#]
protected override Size DefaultSize {get;}
[C++]
protected: __property Size get_DefaultSize();
[JScript]
protected override function get DefaultSize() : Size;
```

Requirements

Platforms: Windows 98, Windows NT 4.0, Windows Millennium Edition, Windows 2000, Windows XP Home Edition, Windows XP Professional, Windows Server 2003 family

StatusBar.Dock Property

This member overrides **Control.Dock**.

```
[Visual Basic]
Overrides Public Property Dock As DockStyle
[C#]
public override DockStyle Dock {get; set;}
[C++]
public: __property DockStyle get_Dock();
public: __property void set_Dock(DockStyle);
[JScript]
public override function get Dock() : DockStyle;
public override function set Dock(DockStyle);
```

Requirements

Platforms: Windows 98, Windows NT 4.0, Windows Millennium Edition, Windows 2000, Windows XP Home Edition, Windows XP Professional, Windows Server 2003 family

StatusBar.Font Property

This member overrides **Control.Font**.

```
[Visual Basic]
Overrides Public Property Font As Font
[C#]
public override Font Font {get; set;}
[C++]
public: __property Font* get_Font();
public: __property void set_Font(Font*);
[JScript]
public override function get Font() : Font;
public override function set Font(Font);
```

Requirements

Platforms: Windows 98, Windows NT 4.0, Windows Millennium Edition, Windows 2000, Windows XP Home Edition, Windows XP Professional, Windows Server 2003 family, .NET Compact Framework - Windows CE .NET

StatusBar.ForeColor Property

This member overrides **Control.ForeColor**.

```
[Visual Basic]
Overrides Public Property ForeColor As Color
[C#]
public override Color ForeColor {get; set;}
[C++]
public: __property Color get_ForeColor();
public: __property void set_ForeColor(Color);
[JScript]
public override function get ForeColor() : Color;
public override function set ForeColor(Color);
```

Requirements

Platforms: Windows 98, Windows NT 4.0, Windows Millennium Edition, Windows 2000, Windows XP Home Edition, Windows XP Professional, Windows Server 2003 family

StatusBar.ImeMode Property

This member supports the .NET Framework infrastructure and is not intended to be used directly from your code.

```
[Visual Basic]
Public Shadows Property ImeMode As ImeMode
[C#]
public new ImeMode ImeMode {get; set;}
[C++]
public: __property ImeMode get_ImeMode();
public: __property void set_ImeMode(ImeMode);
[JScript]
public hide function get ImeMode() : ImeMode;
public hide function set ImeMode(ImeMode);
```

StatusBar.Panels Property

Gets the collection of **StatusBar** panels contained within the control.

```
[Visual Basic]
Public ReadOnly Property Panels As _
   StatusBar.StatusBarPanelCollection
[C#]
public StatusBar.StatusBarPanelCollection Panels {get;}
[C++]
public: __property StatusBar.StatusBarPanelCollection* get_Panels();
[JScript]
public function get Panels() : StatusBar.StatusBarPanelCollection;
```

Property Value

A **StatusBar.StatusBarPanelCollection** containing the **StatusBarPanel** objects of the **StatusBar** control.

Remarks

The **StatusBar** control can display a number of panels to provide information to the user of your application. For example, a panel could display the current time or the progress of a file download. Each panel displayed by the **StatusBar** control is an instance of the **StatusBarPanel** class. The **Panels** property enables you to obtain a reference to the collection of **StatusBarPanel** objects that are currently stored in the **StatusBar** control. With this reference, you can add panels, remove panels, access a specific panel within the collection, and obtain a count of the panels in the **StatusBar** control. For more information on the tasks that can be performed with the panel collection, see the **StatusBar.StatusBarPanelCollection** class reference topics.

Example

See related example in the **System.Windows.Forms.StatusBar** class topic.

Requirements

Platforms: Windows 98, Windows NT 4.0, Windows Millennium Edition, Windows 2000, Windows XP Home Edition, Windows XP Professional, Windows Server 2003 family

StatusBar.ShowPanels Property

Gets or sets a value indicating whether any panels that have been added to the control are displayed.

```
[Visual Basic]
Public Property ShowPanels As Boolean
[C#]
public bool ShowPanels {get; set;}
[C++]
public: __property bool get_ShowPanels();
public: __property void set_ShowPanels(bool);
[JScript]
public function get ShowPanels() : Boolean;
public function set ShowPanels(Boolean);
```

Property Value

true if panels are displayed; otherwise, **false**. The default is **false**.

Remarks

By default, the **StatusBar** control displays the value of its **Text** property without any panels. When ShowPanels is set to **true**, any **StatusBarPanel** objects specified in the **StatusBar** control are displayed. No panels are initially created when you create an instance of the **StatusBar** class. You can add panels to a **StatusBar** control by using the **Add** method of the **StatusBar.StatusBarPanelCollection** class. This collection class can be accessed through the **Panels** property of **StatusBar**.

Example

See related example in the **System.Windows.Forms.StatusBar** class topic.

Requirements

Platforms: Windows 98, Windows NT 4.0, Windows Millennium Edition, Windows 2000, Windows XP Home Edition, Windows XP Professional, Windows Server 2003 family

StatusBar.SizingGrip Property

Gets or sets a value indicating whether a sizing grip is displayed in the lower-right corner of the control.

```
[Visual Basic]
Public Property SizingGrip As Boolean
[C#]
public bool SizingGrip {get; set;}
[C++]
public: __property bool get_SizingGrip();
public: __property void set_SizingGrip(bool);
[JScript]
public function get SizingGrip() : Boolean;
public function set SizingGrip(Boolean);
```

Property Value

true if a sizing grip is displayed; otherwise, **false**. The default is **true**.

Remarks

You can use this property to display a sizing grip to provide an indication to the user when a form is resizable. If the **FormBorderStyle** property of your **Form** is set to a border style that is not resizable, such as **FormBorderStyle.Fixed3D** or **FormBorderStyle.Dialog**, you should set the **SizingGrip** property to **false** to prevent the user from thinking that the form can be resized.

Requirements

Platforms: Windows 98, Windows NT 4.0, Windows Millennium Edition, Windows 2000, Windows XP Home Edition, Windows XP Professional, Windows Server 2003 family

StatusBar.TabStop Property

This member supports the .NET Framework infrastructure and is not intended to be used directly from your code.

```
[Visual Basic]
Public Shadows Property TabStop As Boolean
[C#]
public new bool TabStop {get; set;}
[C++]
public: __property bool get_TabStop();
public: __property void set_TabStop(bool);
[JScript]
public hide function get TabStop() : Boolean;
public hide function set TabStop(Boolean);
```

StatusBar.Text Property

This member overrides **Control.Text**.

```
[Visual Basic]
Overrides Public Property Text As String
[C#]
public override string Text {get; set;}
[C++]
public: __property String* get_Text();
public: __property void set_Text(String*);
[JScript]
public override function get Text() : String;
public override function set Text(String);
```

Requirements

Platforms: Windows 98, Windows NT 4.0, Windows Millennium Edition, Windows 2000, Windows XP Home Edition, Windows XP Professional, Windows Server 2003 family, .NET Compact Framework - Windows CE .NET

StatusBar.CreateHandle Method

This member overrides **Control.CreateHandle**.

```
[Visual Basic]
Overrides Protected Sub CreateHandle()
[C#]
protected override void CreateHandle();
[C++]
protected: void CreateHandle();
[JScript]
protected override function CreateHandle();
```

Requirements

Platforms: Windows 98, Windows NT 4.0, Windows Millennium Edition, Windows 2000, Windows XP Home Edition, Windows XP Professional, Windows Server 2003 family

StatusBar.Dispose Method

Overload List

This member supports the .NET Framework infrastructure and is not intended to be used directly from your code.

Supported by the .NET Compact Framework.

[Visual Basic] **Overloads Overrides Protected Sub Dispose(Boolean)**

[C#] **protected override void Dispose(bool);**

[C++] **protected: void Dispose(bool);**

[JScript] **protected override function Dispose(Boolean);**

Inherited from **Component**.

Supported by the .NET Compact Framework.

[Visual Basic] **Overloads Public Overridable Sub Dispose() Implements IDisposable.Dispose**

[C#] **public virtual void Dispose();**

[C++] **public: virtual void Dispose();**

[JScript] **public function Dispose();**

StatusBar.Dispose Method (Boolean)

This member overrides **Control.Dispose**.

```
[Visual Basic]
Overrides Overloads Protected Sub Dispose( _
   ByVal disposing As Boolean _
)
[C#]
protected override void Dispose(
   bool disposing
);
[C++]
protected: void Dispose(
   bool disposing
);
[JScript]
protected override function Dispose(
   disposing : Boolean
);
```

Requirements

Platforms: Windows 98, Windows NT 4.0, Windows Millennium Edition, Windows 2000, Windows XP Home Edition, Windows XP Professional, Windows Server 2003 family, .NET Compact Framework - Windows CE .NET

StatusBar.OnDrawItem Method

Raises the **OnDrawItem** event.

```
[Visual Basic]
Protected Overridable Sub OnDrawItem( _
   ByVal sbdievent As StatusBarDrawItemEventArgs _
)
[C#]
protected virtual void OnDrawItem(
   StatusBarDrawItemEventArgs sbdievent
);
[C++]
protected: virtual void OnDrawItem(
   StatusBarDrawItemEventArgs* sbdievent
);
[JScript]
protected function OnDrawItem(
   sbdievent : StatusBarDrawItemEventArgs
);
```

Parameters

sbdievent

A **StatusBarDrawItemEventArgs** that contains the event data.

Remarks

Raising an event invokes the event handler through a delegate. For more information, see **Raising an Event**.

The **OnDrawItem** method also allows derived classes to handle the event without attaching a delegate. This is the preferred technique for handling the event in a derived class.

Notes to Inheritors: When overriding **OnDrawItem** in a derived class, be sure to call the base class's **OnDrawItem** method so that registered delegates receive the event.

Example

See related example in the **System.Windows.Forms.StatusBar** class topic.

Requirements

Platforms: Windows 98, Windows NT 4.0, Windows Millennium Edition, Windows 2000, Windows XP Home Edition, Windows XP Professional, Windows Server 2003 family

StatusBar.OnHandleCreated Method

This member overrides **Control.OnHandleCreated**.

```
[Visual Basic]
Overrides Protected Sub OnHandleCreated( _
   ByVal e As EventArgs _
)
```

```
[C#]
protected override void OnHandleCreated(
   EventArgs e
);
[C++]
protected: void OnHandleCreated(
   EventArgs* e
);
[JScript]
protected override function OnHandleCreated(
   e : EventArgs
);
```

Requirements

Platforms: Windows 98, Windows NT 4.0, Windows Millennium Edition, Windows 2000, Windows XP Home Edition, Windows XP Professional, Windows Server 2003 family

StatusBar.OnHandleDestroyed Method

This member overrides **Control.OnHandleDestroyed**.

```
[Visual Basic]
Overrides Protected Sub OnHandleDestroyed( _
   ByVal e As EventArgs _
)
[C#]
protected override void OnHandleDestroyed(
   EventArgs e
);
[C++]
protected: void OnHandleDestroyed(
   EventArgs* e
);
[JScript]
protected override function OnHandleDestroyed(
   e : EventArgs
);
```

Requirements

Platforms: Windows 98, Windows NT 4.0, Windows Millennium Edition, Windows 2000, Windows XP Home Edition, Windows XP Professional, Windows Server 2003 family

StatusBar.OnLayout Method

This member overrides **Control.OnLayout**.

```
[Visual Basic]
Overrides Protected Sub OnLayout( _
   ByVal levent As LayoutEventArgs _
)
[C#]
protected override void OnLayout(
   LayoutEventArgs levent
);
[C++]
protected: void OnLayout(
   LayoutEventArgs* levent
);
[JScript]
protected override function OnLayout(
   levent : LayoutEventArgs
);
```

Requirements

Platforms: Windows 98, Windows NT 4.0, Windows Millennium Edition, Windows 2000, Windows XP Home Edition, Windows XP Professional, Windows Server 2003 family

StatusBar.OnMouseDown Method

This member overrides **Control.OnMouseDown**.

```
[Visual Basic]
Overrides Protected Sub OnMouseDown( _
   ByVal e As MouseEventArgs _
)
[C#]
protected override void OnMouseDown(
   MouseEventArgs e
);
[C++]
protected: void OnMouseDown(
   MouseEventArgs* e
);
[JScript]
protected override function OnMouseDown(
   e : MouseEventArgs
);
```

Requirements

Platforms: Windows 98, Windows NT 4.0, Windows Millennium Edition, Windows 2000, Windows XP Home Edition, Windows XP Professional, Windows Server 2003 family, .NET Compact Framework - Windows CE .NET

StatusBar.OnPanelClick Method

Raises the **OnPanelClick** event.

```
[Visual Basic]
Protected Overridable Sub OnPanelClick( _
   ByVal e As StatusBarPanelClickEventArgs _
)
[C#]
protected virtual void OnPanelClick(
   StatusBarPanelClickEventArgs e
);
[C++]
protected: virtual void OnPanelClick(
   StatusBarPanelClickEventArgs* e
);
[JScript]
protected function OnPanelClick(
   e : StatusBarPanelClickEventArgs
);
```

Parameters

e

A **StatusBarPanelClickEventArgs** that contains the event data.

Remarks

Raising an event invokes the event handler through a delegate. For more information, see **Raising an Event**.

The **OnPanelClick** method also allows derived classes to handle the event without attaching a delegate. This is the preferred technique for handling the event in a derived class.

Notes to Inheritors: When overriding **OnPanelClick** in a derived class, be sure to call the base class's **OnPanelClick** method so that registered delegates receive the event.

Requirements

Platforms: Windows 98, Windows NT 4.0, Windows Millennium Edition, Windows 2000, Windows XP Home Edition, Windows XP Professional, Windows Server 2003 family

StatusBar.OnResize Method

This member overrides **Control.OnResize**.

```
[Visual Basic]
Overrides Protected Sub OnResize( _
   ByVal e As EventArgs _
)
[C#]
protected override void OnResize(
   EventArgs e
);
[C++]
protected: void OnResize(
   EventArgs* e
);
[JScript]
protected override function OnResize(
   e : EventArgs
);
```

Requirements

Platforms: Windows 98, Windows NT 4.0, Windows Millennium Edition, Windows 2000, Windows XP Home Edition, Windows XP Professional, Windows Server 2003 family, .NET Compact Framework - Windows CE .NET

StatusBar.ToString Method

This member overrides **Object.ToString**.

```
[Visual Basic]
Overrides Public Function ToString() As String
[C#]
public override string ToString();
[C++]
public: String* ToString();
[JScript]
public override function ToString() : String;
```

Requirements

Platforms: Windows 98, Windows NT 4.0, Windows Millennium Edition, Windows 2000, Windows XP Home Edition, Windows XP Professional, Windows Server 2003 family, .NET Compact Framework - Windows CE .NET

StatusBar.WndProc Method

This member overrides **Control.WndProc**.

```
[Visual Basic]
Overrides Protected Sub WndProc( _
   ByRef m As Message _
)
[C#]
protected override void WndProc(
   ref Message m
);
[C++]
protected: void WndProc(
   Message* m
);
[JScript]
protected override function WndProc(
   m : Message
);
```

Requirements

Platforms: Windows 98, Windows NT 4.0, Windows Millennium Edition, Windows 2000, Windows XP Home Edition, Windows XP Professional, Windows Server 2003 family

StatusBar.BackColorChanged Event

This member supports the .NET Framework infrastructure and is not intended to be used directly from your code.

```
[Visual Basic]
Public Shadows Event BackColorChanged As EventHandler
[C#]
public new event EventHandler BackColorChanged;
[C++]
public: __event EventHandler* BackColorChanged;
```

[JScript] In JScript, you can handle the events defined by a class, but you cannot define your own.

StatusBar.BackgroundImageChanged Event

This member supports the .NET Framework infrastructure and is not intended to be used directly from your code.

```
[Visual Basic]
Public Shadows Event BackgroundImageChanged As EventHandler
[C#]
public new event EventHandler BackgroundImageChanged;
[C++]
public: __event EventHandler* BackgroundImageChanged;
```

[JScript] In JScript, you can handle the events defined by a class, but you cannot define your own.

StatusBar.DrawItem Event

Occurs when a visual aspect of an owner-drawn status bar control changes.

[Visual Basic]
```
Public Event DrawItem As StatusBarDrawItemEventHandler
```
[C#]
```
public event StatusBarDrawItemEventHandler DrawItem;
```
[C++]
```
public: __event StatusBarDrawItemEventHandler* DrawItem;
```

[JScript] In JScript, you can handle the events defined by a class, but you cannot define your own.

Event Data

The event handler receives an argument of type **StatusBarDrawItemEventArgs** containing data related to this event. The following **StatusBarDrawItemEventArgs** properties provide information specific to this event.

Property	Description
BackColor (inherited from **DrawItemEventArgs**)	Gets the background color of the item that is being drawn.
Bounds (inherited from **DrawItemEventArgs**)	Gets the rectangle that represents the bounds of the item that is being drawn.
Font (inherited from **DrawItemEventArgs**)	Gets the font assigned to the item being drawn.
ForeColor (inherited from **DrawItemEventArgs**)	Gets the foreground color of the of the item being drawn.
Graphics (inherited from **DrawItemEventArgs**)	Gets the graphics surface to draw the item on.
Index (inherited from **DrawItemEventArgs**)	Gets the index value of the item that is being drawn.
Panel	Gets the **StatusBarPanel** to draw.
State (inherited from **DrawItemEventArgs**)	Gets the state of the item being drawn.

Remarks

You can use this event to perform drawing operations in an owner-drawn **StatusBar** control. For example, if you display an owner-drawn **StatusBarPanel** that displays a progress bar, you can use this event to perform the drawing of the progress bar on the panel. The data provided to the event through the **StatusBarDrawItemEventArgs** object passed as a parameter to the event handler enables you to determine the panel that needs to be drawn and the **Graphics** to use to draw to the panel. This event is only raised when the **StatusBarPanel.Style** property of a **StatusBarPanel** in a **StatusBar** control is set to **OwnerDraw**.

Example

See related example in the **System.Windows.Forms.StatusBar** class topic.

Requirements

Platforms: Windows 98, Windows NT 4.0, Windows Millennium Edition, Windows 2000, Windows XP Home Edition, Windows XP Professional, Windows Server 2003 family

StatusBar.ForeColorChanged Event

This member supports the .NET Framework infrastructure and is not intended to be used directly from your code.

[Visual Basic]
```
Public Shadows Event ForeColorChanged As EventHandler
```
[C#]
```
public new event EventHandler ForeColorChanged;
```
[C++]
```
public: __event EventHandler* ForeColorChanged;
```

[JScript] In JScript, you can handle the events defined by a class, but you cannot define your own.

StatusBar.ImeModeChanged Event

This member supports the .NET Framework infrastructure and is not intended to be used directly from your code.

[Visual Basic]
```
Public Shadows Event ImeModeChanged As EventHandler
```
[C#]
```
public new event EventHandler ImeModeChanged;
```
[C++]
```
public: __event EventHandler* ImeModeChanged;
```

[JScript] In JScript, you can handle the events defined by a class, but you cannot define your own.

StatusBar.Paint Event

This member supports the .NET Framework infrastructure and is not intended to be used directly from your code.

[Visual Basic]
```
Public Shadows Event Paint As PaintEventHandler
```
[C#]
```
public new event PaintEventHandler Paint;
```
[C++]
```
public: __event PaintEventHandler* Paint;
```

[JScript] In JScript, you can handle the events defined by a class, but you cannot define your own.

StatusBar.PanelClick Event

Occurs when a **StatusBarPanel** object on a **StatusBar** control is clicked.

[Visual Basic]
```
Public Event PanelClick As StatusBarPanelClickEventHandler
```
[C#]
```
public event StatusBarPanelClickEventHandler PanelClick;
```
[C++]
```
public: __event StatusBarPanelClickEventHandler* PanelClick;
```

[JScript] In JScript, you can handle the events defined by a class, but you cannot define your own.

Event Data

The event handler receives an argument of type **StatusBarPanelClickEventArgs** containing data related to this event. The following **StatusBarPanelClickEventArgs** properties provide information specific to this event.

Property	Description
Button (inherited from **MouseEventArgs**)	Gets which mouse button was pressed.
Clicks (inherited from **MouseEventArgs**)	Gets the number of times the mouse button was pressed and released.
Delta (inherited from **MouseEventArgs**)	Gets a signed count of the number of detents the mouse wheel has rotated. A detent is one notch of the mouse wheel.
StatusBarPanel	Gets the **StatusBarPanel** to draw.
X (inherited from **MouseEventArgs**)	Gets the x-coordinate of the mouse.
Y (inherited from **MouseEventArgs**)	Gets the y-coordinate of the mouse.

Remarks

You can use this event to perform tasks when a panel within a **StatusBar** control is clicked. The data provided to the event through the **StatusBarPanelClickEventArgs** object passed as a parameter to the event handler enables you to determine the **StatusBarPanel** object that was clicked by the user in order to perform tasks on the selected panel.

Requirements

Platforms: Windows 98, Windows NT 4.0,
Windows Millennium Edition, Windows 2000,
Windows XP Home Edition, Windows XP Professional,
Windows Server 2003 family

StatusBarDrawItemEventArgs Class

Provides data for the **DrawItem** event.

System.Object
  System.EventArgs
    System.Windows.Forms.DrawItemEventArgs
      System.Windows.Forms.StatusBarDrawItemEventArgs

```
[Visual Basic]
Public Class StatusBarDrawItemEventArgs
   Inherits DrawItemEventArgs
[C#]
public class StatusBarDrawItemEventArgs : DrawItemEventArgs
[C++]
public __gc class StatusBarDrawItemEventArgs : public
   DrawItemEventArgs
[JScript]
public class StatusBarDrawItemEventArgs extends DrawItemEventArgs
```

Thread Safety

Any public static (**Shared** in Visual Basic) members of this type are safe for multithreaded operations. Any instance members are not guaranteed to be thread safe.

Remarks

The **DrawItem** event occurs when a visual aspect of an owner-drawn **StatusBarPanel** changes. A **StatusBarDrawItemEventArgs** specifies the **Graphics** object to use to draw the panel, the **Rectangle** object in which to draw the panel, the panel identification number, state information about the panel, and the panel to draw. You can use the data provided by this class in an event handler for the **DrawItem** event to create custom-drawn panels in your application's **StatusBar** control.

Requirements

Namespace: System.Windows.Forms

Platforms: Windows 98, Windows NT 4.0, Windows Millennium Edition, Windows 2000, Windows XP Home Edition, Windows XP Professional, Windows Server 2003 family

Assembly: System.Windows.Forms (in System.Windows.Forms.dll)

StatusBarDrawItemEventArgs Constructor

Initializes a new instance of the **StatusBarDrawItemEventArgs** class.

Overload List

Initializes a new instance of the **StatusBarDrawItemEventArgs** class without specifying a background and foreground color for the **StatusBarPanel**.

[Visual Basic] **Public Sub New(Graphics, Font, Rectangle, Integer, DrawItemState, StatusBarPanel)**

[C#] **public StatusBarDrawItemEventArgs(Graphics, Font, Rectangle, int, DrawItemState, StatusBarPanel);**

[C++] **public: StatusBarDrawItemEventArgs(Graphics*, Font*, Rectangle, int, DrawItemState, StatusBarPanel*);**

[JScript] **public function StatusBarDrawItemEventArgs(Graphics, Font, Rectangle, int, DrawItemState, StatusBarPanel);**

Initializes a new instance of the **StatusBarDrawItemEventArgs** class with a specified background and foreground color for the **StatusBarPanel**.

[Visual Basic] **Public Sub New(Graphics, Font, Rectangle, Integer, DrawItemState, StatusBarPanel, Color, Color)**

[C#] **public StatusBarDrawItemEventArgs(Graphics, Font, Rectangle, int, DrawItemState, StatusBarPanel, Color, Color);**

[C++] **public: StatusBarDrawItemEventArgs(Graphics*, Font*, Rectangle, int, DrawItemState, StatusBarPanel*, Color, Color);**

[JScript] **public function StatusBarDrawItemEventArgs(Graphics, Font, Rectangle, int, DrawItemState, StatusBarPanel, Color, Color);**

StatusBarDrawItemEventArgs Constructor (Graphics, Font, Rectangle, Int32, DrawItemState, StatusBarPanel)

Initializes a new instance of the **StatusBarDrawItemEventArgs** class without specifying a background and foreground color for the **StatusBarPanel**.

```
[Visual Basic]
Public Sub New( _
   ByVal g As Graphics, _
   ByVal font As Font, _
   ByVal r As Rectangle, _
   ByVal itemId As Integer, _
   ByVal itemState As DrawItemState, _
   ByVal panel As StatusBarPanel _
)
[C#]
public StatusBarDrawItemEventArgs(
   Graphics g,
   Font font,
   Rectangle r,
   int itemId,
   DrawItemState itemState,
   StatusBarPanel panel
);
[C++]
public: StatusBarDrawItemEventArgs(
   Graphics* g,
   Font* font,
   Rectangle r,
   int itemId,
   DrawItemState itemState,
   StatusBarPanel* panel
);
[JScript]
public function StatusBarDrawItemEventArgs(
   g : Graphics,
   font : Font,
   r : Rectangle,
   itemId : int,
   itemState : DrawItemState,
   panel : StatusBarPanel
);
```

Parameters

g
The **Graphics** object to use to draw the **StatusBarPanel**.

font
The **Font** used to render text.

r
The **Rectangle** that represents the client area of the **StatusBarPanel**.

itemId
The zero-based index of the panel in the **StatusBar.StatusBarPanelCollection** of the **StatusBar** control.

itemState
One of the **DrawItemState** values that represents state information about the **StatusBarPanel**.

panel
A **StatusBarPanel** that represents the panel to draw.

Requirements

Platforms: Windows 98, Windows NT 4.0, Windows Millennium Edition, Windows 2000, Windows XP Home Edition, Windows XP Professional, Windows Server 2003 family

StatusBarDrawItemEventArgs Constructor (Graphics, Font, Rectangle, Int32, DrawItemState, StatusBarPanel, Color, Color)

Note: This namespace, class, or member is supported only in version 1.1 of the .NET Framework.

Initializes a new instance of the **StatusBarDrawItemEventArgs** class with a specified background and foreground color for the **StatusBarPanel**.

[Visual Basic]
```
Public Sub New( _
   ByVal g As Graphics, _
   ByVal font As Font, _
   ByVal r As Rectangle, _
   ByVal itemId As Integer, _
   ByVal itemState As DrawItemState, _
   ByVal panel As StatusBarPanel, _
   ByVal foreColor As Color, _
   ByVal backColor As Color _
)
```
[C#]
```
public StatusBarDrawItemEventArgs(
   Graphics g,
   Font font,
   Rectangle r,
   int itemId,
   DrawItemState itemState,
   StatusBarPanel panel,
   Color foreColor,
   Color backColor
);
```
[C++]
```
public: StatusBarDrawItemEventArgs(
   Graphics* g,
   Font* font,
   Rectangle r,
   int itemId,
   DrawItemState itemState,
   StatusBarPanel* panel,
   Color foreColor,
   Color backColor
);
```
[JScript]
```
public function StatusBarDrawItemEventArgs(
   g : Graphics,
   font : Font,
   r : Rectangle,
   itemId : int,
   itemState : DrawItemState,
   panel : StatusBarPanel,
   foreColor : Color,
   backColor : Color
);
```

Parameters

g
The **Graphics** object to use to draw the **StatusBarPanel**.

font
The **Font** used to render text.

r
The **Rectangle** that represents the client area of the **StatusBarPanel**.

itemId
The zero-based index of the panel in the **StatusBar.StatusBarPanelCollection** of the **StatusBar** control.

itemState
One of the **DrawItemState** values that represents state information about the **StatusBarPanel**.

panel
A **StatusBarPanel** that represents the panel to draw.

foreColor
One of the **System.Drawing.Color** values that represents the foreground color of the panel to draw.

backColor
One of the **System.Drawing.Color** values that represents the background color of the panel to draw.

Requirements

Platforms: Windows 98, Windows NT 4.0, Windows Millennium Edition, Windows 2000, Windows XP Home Edition, Windows XP Professional, Windows Server 2003 family

StatusBarDrawItemEventArgs.Panel Property

Gets the **StatusBarPanel** to draw.

[Visual Basic]
```
Public ReadOnly Property Panel As StatusBarPanel
```
[C#]
```
public StatusBarPanel Panel {get;}
```
[C++]
```
public: __property StatusBarPanel* get_Panel();
```
[JScript]
```
public function get Panel() : StatusBarPanel;
```

Property Value

The **StatusBarPanel** object to draw.

Remarks

The **Panel** property enables you to obtain the **StatusBarPanel** object that needs to be drawn. You can use this information within the event handler for the **DrawItem** event of a **StatusBar** control to perform drawing tasks on the **StatusBarPanel**.

Requirements

Platforms: Windows 98, Windows NT 4.0, Windows Millennium Edition, Windows 2000, Windows XP Home Edition, Windows XP Professional, Windows Server 2003 family

StatusBarDrawItemEvent-Handler Delegate

Represents the method that will handle the **DrawItem** event of a **StatusBar**.

[Visual Basic]
```
<Serializable>
Public Delegate Sub StatusBarDrawItemEventHandler( _
   ByVal sender As Object, _
   ByVal sbdevent As StatusBarDrawItemEventArgs _
)
```
[C#]
```
[Serializable]
public delegate void StatusBarDrawItemEventHandler(
   object sender,
   StatusBarDrawItemEventArgs sbdevent
);
```
[C++]
```
[Serializable]
public __gc __delegate void StatusBarDrawItemEventHandler(
   Object* sender,
   StatusBarDrawItemEventArgs* sbdevent
);
```
[JScript] In JScript, you can use the delegates in the .NET Framework, but you cannot define your own.

Parameters [Visual Basic, C#, C++]

The declaration of your event handler must have the same parameters as the **StatusBarDrawItemEventHandler** delegate declaration.

sender
  The source of the event.

sbdevent
  A **StatusBarDrawItemEventArgs** that contains the event data.

Remarks

When you create a **StatusBarDrawItemEventHandler** delegate, you identify the method that will handle the event. To associate the event with your event handler, add an instance of the delegate to the event. The event handler is called whenever the event occurs, unless you remove the delegate.

Requirements

Namespace: System.Windows.Forms

Platforms: Windows 98, Windows NT 4.0, Windows Millennium Edition, Windows 2000, Windows XP Home Edition, Windows XP Professional, Windows Server 2003 family

Assembly: System.Windows.Forms (in System.Windows.Forms.dll)

StatusBarPanel Class

Represents a panel in a **StatusBar** control.

System.Object
  System.MarshalByRefObject
    System.ComponentModel.Component
      System.Windows.Forms.StatusBarPanel

[Visual Basic]
```
Public Class StatusBarPanel
   Inherits Component
   Implements ISupportInitialize
```
[C#]
```
public class StatusBarPanel : Component, ISupportInitialize
```
[C++]
```
public __gc class StatusBarPanel : public Component,
   ISupportInitialize
```
[JScript]
```
public class StatusBarPanel extends Component implements
   ISupportInitialize
```

Thread Safety

Any public static (**Shared** in Visual Basic) members of this type are safe for multithreaded operations. Any instance members are not guaranteed to be thread safe.

Remarks

A **StatusBarPanel** object represents an individual panel in the **StatusBar.StatusBarPanelCollection** of a **StatusBar** control. A **StatusBarPanel** object can contain text and/or an icon that can be used to reflect the status of an application. Use the **StatusBar.StatusBarPanelCollection**, accessible through the **StatusBar.Panels** property of a **StatusBar** control, to retrieve, add, or remove an individual **StatusBarPanel** object.

The **StatusBarPanel** object provides properties that enable you to modify the display behavior of a panel within a **StatusBar** control. You can use the **Icon** property to display an icon within a panel. This property can be used to provide a graphical representation of state in an application. The **Alignment** property enables you to specify how text and/or an icon is aligned within the panel. To ensure that your panel is sized properly to fit the text of the panel, you can use the **AutoSize** property to autosize the panel to fit the text of the panel or to fill the remaining space within the **StatusBar** control. The **MinWidth** property enables you to specify a minimum width for the panel to ensure that it does not get smaller than the data it is intended to display.

The **StatusBar** control is typically used to display help information or state information about your application. Often, it is important to display additional information about data that is presented in a panel. You can use the **ToolTipText** property to display information whenever the user hovers the cursor over a panel.

Although the **StatusBar** control is typically used to display textual information, you can also provide your own type of display to a **StatusBarPanel**. The **Style** property enables you to specify how the **StatusBarPanel** will be drawn. By default, the Style property is used to display the value of the **Text** property (and an icon if specified in the **Icon** property). If the property is set to **StatusBarPanelStyle.OwnerDraw**, you can draw your own information into the panel. You can use this feature to draw a progress bar or an animated icon in the panel.

When you create an instance of **StatusBarPanel**, the read/write properties are set to initial values. For a list of these values, see the **StatusBarPanel** constructor.

Example

[Visual Basic, C#] The following example creates a **StatusBar** control on a form and adds two **StatusBarPanel** objects. One of the **StatusBarPanel** objects, named `panel1`, displays status text for an application. The second **StatusBarPanel** object, named `panel2`, displays the current date and uses the **ToolTipText** property of the **StatusBarPanel** class to display the current time. The example uses the **ShowPanels** property to ensure that the panels are displayed instead of a standard panel, and it uses the **Panels** property to access the **Add** method of the **StatusBar.StatusBarPanelCollection** to add the panels to the **StatusBar**. The example also uses the **AutoSize**, **BorderStyle**, **ToolTipText**, and **Text** properties to initialize the **StatusBarPanel** objects. This example assumes that the method defined in the example is defined and called from the constructor of a **Form**.

[Visual Basic]
```
Private Sub CreateMyStatusBar()
   ' Create a StatusBar control.
   Dim statusBar1 As New StatusBar()
   ' Create two StatusBarPanel objects to display in the StatusBar.
   Dim panel1 As New StatusBarPanel()
   Dim panel2 As New StatusBarPanel()

   ' Display the first panel with a sunken border style.
   panel1.BorderStyle = StatusBarPanelBorderStyle.Sunken
   ' Initialize the text of the panel.
   panel1.Text = "Ready..."
   ' Set the AutoSize property to use all remaining space on ↵
 the StatusBar.
   panel1.AutoSize = StatusBarPanelAutoSize.Spring
   ' Display the second panel with a raised border style.
   panel2.BorderStyle = StatusBarPanelBorderStyle.Raised
   ' Create ToolTip text that displays the current time.
   panel2.ToolTipText = System.DateTime.Now.ToShortTimeString()
   ' Set the text of the panel to the current date.
   panel2.Text = System.DateTime.Today.ToLongDateString()
   ' Set the AutoSize property to size the panel to the size ↵
of the contents.
   panel2.AutoSize = StatusBarPanelAutoSize.Contents

   ' Display panels in the StatusBar control.
   statusBar1.ShowPanels = True

   ' Add both panels to the StatusBarPanelCollection of the StatusBar.
   statusBar1.Panels.Add(panel1)
   statusBar1.Panels.Add(panel2)

   ' Add the StatusBar to the form.
   Me.Controls.Add(statusBar1)
End Sub
```

[C#]
```
private void CreateMyStatusBar()
{
    // Create a StatusBar control.
    StatusBar statusBar1 = new StatusBar();
    // Create two StatusBarPanel objects to display in the StatusBar.
    StatusBarPanel panel1 = new StatusBarPanel();
    StatusBarPanel panel2 = new StatusBarPanel();

    // Display the first panel with a sunken border style.
    panel1.BorderStyle = StatusBarPanelBorderStyle.Sunken;
    // Initialize the text of the panel.
    panel1.Text = "Ready...";
    // Set the AutoSize property to use all remaining space on ↵
 the StatusBar.
    panel1.AutoSize = StatusBarPanelAutoSize.Spring;
```

```
        // Display the second panel with a raised border style.
        panel2.BorderStyle = StatusBarPanelBorderStyle.Raised;
        // Create ToolTip text that displays the current time.
        panel2.ToolTipText = System.DateTime.Now.ToShortTimeString();
        // Set the text of the panel to the current date.
        panel2.Text = System.DateTime.Today.ToLongDateString();
        // Set the AutoSize property to size the panel to the size ↵
    of the contents.
        panel2.AutoSize = StatusBarPanelAutoSize.Contents;

        // Display panels in the StatusBar control.
        statusBar1.ShowPanels = true;

        // Add both panels to the StatusBarPanelCollection of ↵
the StatusBar.
        statusBar1.Panels.Add(panel1);
        statusBar1.Panels.Add(panel2);

        // Add the StatusBar to the form.
        this.Controls.Add(statusBar1);
}
```

Requirements

Namespace: System.Windows.Forms

Platforms: Windows 98, Windows NT 4.0, Windows Millennium Edition, Windows 2000, Windows XP Home Edition, Windows XP Professional, Windows Server 2003 family

Assembly: System.Windows.Forms (in System.Windows.Forms.dll)

StatusBarPanel Constructor

Initializes a new instance of the **StatusBarPanel** class.

[Visual Basic]
```
Public Sub New()
```
[C#]
```
public StatusBarPanel();
```
[C++]
```
public: StatusBarPanel();
```
[JScript]
```
public function StatusBarPanel();
```

Remarks

When you create an instance of **StatusBarPanel**, the following read/write properties are set to initial values.

Property	Initial Value
Alignment	**HorizontalAlignment.Left**
AutoSize	**StatusBarPanelAutoSize.None**
BorderStyle	**StatusBarPanelBorderStyle.Sunken**
Icon	A null reference (**Nothing** in Visual Basic)
MinWidth	10
Style	**StatusBarPanelStyle.Text**
Text	A zero-length string.
ToolTipText	A zero-length string.
Width	100

You can change the value for any of these properties through a separate call to the property.

Example

See related example in the **System.Windows.Forms.StatusBarPanel** class topic.

Requirements

Platforms: Windows 98, Windows NT 4.0, Windows Millennium Edition, Windows 2000, Windows XP Home Edition, Windows XP Professional, Windows Server 2003 family

StatusBarPanel.Alignment Property

Gets or sets the alignment of text and icons within the status bar panel.

[Visual Basic]
```
Public Property Alignment As HorizontalAlignment
```
[C#]
```
public HorizontalAlignment Alignment {get; set;}
```
[C++]
```
public: __property HorizontalAlignment get_Alignment();
public: __property void set_Alignment(HorizontalAlignment);
```
[JScript]
```
public function get Alignment() : HorizontalAlignment;
public function set Alignment(HorizontalAlignment);
```

Property Value

One of the **HorizontalAlignment** values. The default is **HorizontalAlignment.Left**.

Exceptions

Exception Type	Condition
InvalidEnumArgumentException	The value assigned to the property is not a member of the **HorizontalAlignment** enumeration.

Remarks

You can use this property to horizontally align the text and/or the icon assigned to the **Icon** property within the borders of the panel. Text and icons can be aligned to the left, right, or center of the **StatusBarPanel**. There is no way to independently position an icon within the **StatusBarPanel**. For example, you cannot position an icon to the left side of the **StatusBarPanel** while aligning the text on the right side. The icon is always positioned to the left side of the text regardless of how the text is aligned.

Requirements

Platforms: Windows 98, Windows NT 4.0, Windows Millennium Edition, Windows 2000, Windows XP Home Edition, Windows XP Professional, Windows Server 2003 family

StatusBarPanel.AutoSize Property

Gets or sets a value indicating whether the status bar panel is autosized.

[Visual Basic]
```
Public Property AutoSize As StatusBarPanelAutoSize
```
[C#]
```
public StatusBarPanelAutoSize AutoSize {get; set;}
```
[C++]
```
public: __property StatusBarPanelAutoSize get_AutoSize();
public: __property void set_AutoSize(StatusBarPanelAutoSize);
```
[JScript]
```
public function get AutoSize() : StatusBarPanelAutoSize;
public function set AutoSize(StatusBarPanelAutoSize);
```

Property Value

One of the **StatusBarPanelAutoSize** values. The default is **StatusBarPanelAutoSize.None**.

Exceptions

Exception Type	Condition
InvalidEnumArgument-Exception	The value assigned to the property is not a member of the **StatusBarPanelAutoSize** enumeration.

Remarks

StatusBarPanel objects set to **StatusBarPanelAutoSize.Contents** have precedence over those panels set to the **StatusBarPanel-AutoSize.Spring** value. For example, a **StatusBarPanel** that has its **AutoSize** property set to **StatusBarPanelAutoSize.Spring** is shortened if a **StatusBarPanel** object with the **AutoSize** property set to **StatusBarPanelAutoSize.Contents** requires that space. You can use this property to ensure that the contents of a **StatusBarPanel** are properly displayed is a **StatusBar** control that contains more than one panel. For example, you might want a panel containing text to adjust automatically to the amount of text it is displaying (**StatusBarPanelAutoSize.Contents**), while another panel on the **StatusBar** that displays an owner-drawn progress bar would need to be a fixed size (**StatusBarPanelAutoSize.None**).

Example

See related example in the **System.Windows.Forms.StatusBar-Panel** class topic.

Requirements

Platforms: Windows 98, Windows NT 4.0, Windows Millennium Edition, Windows 2000, Windows XP Home Edition, Windows XP Professional, Windows Server 2003 family

StatusBarPanel.BorderStyle Property

Gets or sets the border style of the status bar panel.

```
[Visual Basic]
Public Property BorderStyle As StatusBarPanelBorderStyle
[C#]
public StatusBarPanelBorderStyle BorderStyle {get; set;}
[C++]
public: __property StatusBarPanelBorderStyle get_BorderStyle();
public: __property void set_BorderStyle(StatusBarPanelBorderStyle);
[JScript]
public function get BorderStyle() : StatusBarPanelBorderStyle;
public function set BorderStyle(StatusBarPanelBorderStyle);
```

Property Value

One of the **StatusBarPanelBorderStyle** values. The default is **Sunken**.

Exceptions

Exception Type	Condition
InvalidEnumArgument-Exception	The value assigned to the property is not a member of the **StatusBar-PanelBorderStyle** enumeration.

Remarks

You can use this property to differentiate a panel from other panels in a **StatusBar** control.

Example

See related example in the **System.Windows.Forms.StatusBar-Panel** class topic.

Requirements

Platforms: Windows 98, Windows NT 4.0, Windows Millennium Edition, Windows 2000, Windows XP Home Edition, Windows XP Professional, Windows Server 2003 family

StatusBarPanel.Icon Property

Gets or sets the icon to display within the status bar panel.

```
[Visual Basic]
Public Property Icon As Icon
[C#]
public Icon Icon {get; set;}
[C++]
public: __property Icon* get_Icon();
public: __property void set_Icon(Icon*);
[JScript]
public function get Icon() : Icon;
public function set Icon(Icon);
```

Property Value

An **Icon** that represents the icon to display in the panel.

Remarks

You can use this property to display an icon that represents the state of your application or a process within your application. For example, you can display an icon in a **StatusBarPanel** to indicate whether a file save operation is in progress or complete.

> **Note** There is no way to independently position an icon within the **StatusBarPanel**. For example, you cannot position an icon to the left side of the **StatusBarPanel** while aligning the text on the right side using the **Alignment** property. The icon is always positioned to the left side of the panel's text regardless of how the text is aligned.

Requirements

Platforms: Windows 98, Windows NT 4.0, Windows Millennium Edition, Windows 2000, Windows XP Home Edition, Windows XP Professional, Windows Server 2003 family

StatusBarPanel.MinWidth Property

Gets or sets the minimum allowed width of the status bar panel within the **StatusBar** control.

```
[Visual Basic]
Public Property MinWidth As Integer
[C#]
public int MinWidth {get; set;}
[C++]
public: __property int get_MinWidth();
public: __property void set_MinWidth(int);
[JScript]
public function get MinWidth() : int;
public function set MinWidth(int);
```

Property Value

The minimum width (in pixels) of the **StatusBarPanel**.

Exceptions

Exception Type	Condition
ArgumentException	A value less than zero is assigned to the property.

Remarks

The **MinWidth** property is used when the **AutoSize** property is set to **StatusBarPanelAutoSize.Contents** or **StatusBarPanelAutoSize.Spring**, to prevent the **StatusBarPanel** from autosizing to a width that is too small. When the **AutoSize** property is set to **StatusBarPanelAutoSize.None**, the **MinWidth** property is automatically set to the same value as the **Width** property.

Requirements

Platforms: Windows 98, Windows NT 4.0, Windows Millennium Edition, Windows 2000, Windows XP Home Edition, Windows XP Professional, Windows Server 2003 family

StatusBarPanel.Parent Property

Gets the **StatusBar** control that hosts the status bar panel.

```
[Visual Basic]
Public ReadOnly Property Parent As StatusBar
[C#]
public StatusBar Parent {get;}
[C++]
public: __property StatusBar* get_Parent();
[JScript]
public function get Parent() : StatusBar;
```

Property Value

The **StatusBar** object that contains the panel.

Remarks

You can use this property to determine the **StatusBar** control that a **StatusBarPanel** object is contained within. **StatusBarPanel** objects are added to a **StatusBar** control by calling the **Add** method of the **StatusBar.StatusBarPanelCollection** class. The **StatusBar.StatusBarPanelCollection** of a **StatusBar** control is accessible through the **Panels** property.

Requirements

Platforms: Windows 98, Windows NT 4.0, Windows Millennium Edition, Windows 2000, Windows XP Home Edition, Windows XP Professional, Windows Server 2003 family

StatusBarPanel.Style Property

Gets or sets the style of the status bar panel.

```
[Visual Basic]
Public Property Style As StatusBarPanelStyle
[C#]
public StatusBarPanelStyle Style {get; set;}
[C++]
public: __property StatusBarPanelStyle get_Style();
public: __property void set_Style(StatusBarPanelStyle);
[JScript]
public function get Style() : StatusBarPanelStyle;
public function set Style(StatusBarPanelStyle);
```

Property Value

One of the **StatusBarPanelStyle** values. The default is **StatusBarPanelStyle.Text**.

Exceptions

Exception Type	Condition
InvalidEnumArgumentException	The value assigned to the property is not a member of the **StatusBarPanelStyle** enumeration.

Remarks

You can use this property to indicate whether a **StatusBarPanel** displays text or whether the panel is managed as an owner-drawn **StatusBarPanel**. To determine when a **StatusBarPanel** object needs to be drawn, create an event handler for the **DrawItem** event of the **StatusBar** control. The **StatusBarDrawItemEventArgs** object passed as a parameter to an event handler of the **DrawItem** event enables you to determine which panel needs to be drawn. The **StatusBarDrawItemEventArgs** also provides a **Graphics** object you can use to perform drawing tasks on the **StatusBarPanel**.

Requirements

Platforms: Windows 98, Windows NT 4.0, Windows Millennium Edition, Windows 2000, Windows XP Home Edition, Windows XP Professional, Windows Server 2003 family

StatusBarPanel.Text Property

Gets or sets the text of the status bar panel.

```
[Visual Basic]
Public Property Text As String
[C#]
public string Text {get; set;}
[C++]
public: __property String* get_Text();
public: __property void set_Text(String*);
[JScript]
public function get Text() : String;
public function set Text(String);
```

Property Value

The text displayed in the panel.

Remarks

This property represents the text that is displayed when the **Style** property is set to **StatusBarPanelStyle.Text**. You can use this property to display information about your application in a **StatusBar** control. For example, you can use the **Text** property to display help information when the user moves the mouse over a menu or to display the name and location of a file that is opened in an application. To align the text within a **StatusBarPanel**, use the **Alignment** property.

Example

See related example in the **System.Windows.Forms.StatusBarPanel** class topic.

Requirements

Platforms: Windows 98, Windows NT 4.0, Windows Millennium Edition, Windows 2000, Windows XP Home Edition, Windows XP Professional, Windows Server 2003 family

StatusBarPanel.ToolTipText Property

Gets or sets ToolTip text associated with the status bar panel.

```
[Visual Basic]
Public Property ToolTipText As String
[C#]
public string ToolTipText {get; set;}
[C++]
public: __property String* get_ToolTipText();
public: __property void set_ToolTipText(String*);
[JScript]
public function get ToolTipText() : String;
public function set ToolTipText(String);
```

Property Value

The ToolTip text for the panel.

Remarks

You can use this property to display additional information in a ToolTip when the user hovers the mouse over a **StatusBarPanel**. For example, you can display a ToolTip that provides data transfer speed for a **StatusBarPanel** that displays the status of a file transfer.

To display ToolTips for other controls in your application, use the **ToolTip** control.

Example

See related example in the **System.Windows.Forms.StatusBarPanel** class topic.

Requirements

Platforms: Windows 98, Windows NT 4.0, Windows Millennium Edition, Windows 2000, Windows XP Home Edition, Windows XP Professional, Windows Server 2003 family

StatusBarPanel.Width Property

Gets or sets the width of the status bar panel within the **StatusBar** control.

```
[Visual Basic]
Public Property Width As Integer
[C#]
public int Width {get; set;}
[C++]
public: __property int get_Width();
public: __property void set_Width(int);
[JScript]
public function get Width() : int;
public function set Width(int);
```

Property Value

The width (in pixels) of the **StatusBarPanel**.

Exceptions

Exception Type	Condition
ArgumentException	The width specified is less than the value of the **MinWidth** property.

Remarks

The **Width** property always reflects the actual width of a **StatusBarPanel** and cannot be smaller than the **MinWidth** property. To autosize the width of the **StatusBarPanel** to the contents of the **StatusBarPanel**, you can use the **AutoSize** property.

Requirements

Platforms: Windows 98, Windows NT 4.0, Windows Millennium Edition, Windows 2000, Windows XP Home Edition, Windows XP Professional, Windows Server 2003 family

StatusBarPanel.BeginInit Method

This member supports the .NET Framework infrastructure and is not intended to be used directly from your code.

```
[Visual Basic]
Public Overridable Sub BeginInit() Implements _
   ISupportInitialize.BeginInit
[C#]
public virtual void BeginInit();
[C++]
public: virtual void BeginInit();
[JScript]
public function BeginInit();
```

StatusBarPanel.Dispose Method

Overload List

This member supports the .NET Framework infrastructure and is not intended to be used directly from your code.

[Visual Basic] **Overloads Overrides Protected Sub Dispose(Boolean)**

[C#] **protected override void Dispose(bool);**

[C++] **protected: void Dispose(bool);**

[JScript] **protected override function Dispose(Boolean);**

Inherited from **Component**.

[Visual Basic] **Overloads Public Overridable Sub Dispose() Implements IDisposable.Dispose**

[C#] **public virtual void Dispose();**

[C++] **public: virtual void Dispose();**

[JScript] **public function Dispose();**

StatusBarPanel.Dispose Method (Boolean)

This member overrides **Component.Dispose**.

```
[Visual Basic]
Overrides Overloads Protected Sub Dispose( _
   ByVal disposing As Boolean _
)
[C#]
protected override void Dispose(
   bool disposing
);
[C++]
protected: void Dispose(
   bool disposing
);
[JScript]
protected override function Dispose(
   disposing : Boolean
);
```

Requirements

Platforms: Windows 98, Windows NT 4.0, Windows Millennium Edition, Windows 2000, Windows XP Home Edition, Windows XP Professional, Windows Server 2003 family

StatusBarPanel.EndInit Method

This member supports the .NET Framework infrastructure and is not intended to be used directly from your code.

```
[Visual Basic]
Public Overridable Sub EndInit() Implements _
   ISupportInitialize.EndInit
[C#]
public virtual void EndInit();
[C++]
public: virtual void EndInit();
[JScript]
public function EndInit();
```

StatusBarPanel.ToString Method

This member overrides **Object.ToString**.

```
[Visual Basic]
Overrides Public Function ToString() As String
[C#]
public override string ToString();
[C++]
public: String* ToString();
[JScript]
public override function ToString() : String;
```

Requirements

Platforms: Windows 98, Windows NT 4.0, Windows Millennium Edition, Windows 2000, Windows XP Home Edition, Windows XP Professional, Windows Server 2003 family

StatusBarPanelAutoSize Enumeration

Specifies how a **StatusBarPanel** on a **StatusBar** control behaves when the control resizes.

[Visual Basic]
```
<Serializable>
Public Enum StatusBarPanelAutoSize
```
[C#]
```
[Serializable]
public enum StatusBarPanelAutoSize
```
[C++]
```
[Serializable]
__value public enum StatusBarPanelAutoSize
```
[JScript]
```
public
   Serializable
enum StatusBarPanelAutoSize
```

Remarks

This enumeration is used by the **StatusBarPanel.AutoSize** property. The **AutoSize** property specifies how a **StatusBarPanel** is autosized on a **StatusBar** control.

Members

Member name	Description
Contents	The width of the **StatusBarPanel** is determined by its contents.
None	The **StatusBarPanel** does not change size when the **StatusBar** control resizes.
Spring	The **StatusBarPanel** shares the available space on the **StatusBar** (the space not taken up by other panels whose **AutoSize** property is set to **StatusBarPanelAutoSize.None** or **StatusBarPanelAutoSize.Contents**) with other panels that have their **AutoSize** property set to **StatusBarPanelAutoSize.Spring**.

Requirements

Namespace: System.Windows.Forms

Platforms: Windows 98, Windows NT 4.0, Windows Millennium Edition, Windows 2000, Windows XP Home Edition, Windows XP Professional, Windows Server 2003 family

Assembly: System.Windows.Forms (in System.Windows.Forms.dll)

StatusBarPanelBorderStyle Enumeration

Specifies the appearance of the border for a **StatusBarPanel** on a **StatusBar** control.

[Visual Basic]
```
<Serializable>
Public Enum StatusBarPanelBorderStyle
```
[C#]
```
[Serializable]
public enum StatusBarPanelBorderStyle
```
[C++]
```
[Serializable]
__value public enum StatusBarPanelBorderStyle
```
[JScript]
```
public
   Serializable
enum StatusBarPanelBorderStyle
```

Remarks

This enumeration is used by the **BorderStyle** property of the **StatusBarPanel** class. The **BorderStyle** property enables you to specify the style of border to display on a **StatusBarPanel** within a **StatusBar**.

Members

Member name	Description
None	No border is displayed.
Raised	The **StatusBarPanel** is displayed with a three-dimensional raised border.
Sunken	The **StatusBarPanel** is displayed with a three-dimensional sunken border.

Requirements

Namespace: System.Windows.Forms

Platforms: Windows 98, Windows NT 4.0, Windows Millennium Edition, Windows 2000, Windows XP Home Edition, Windows XP Professional, Windows Server 2003 family

Assembly: System.Windows.Forms (in System.Windows.Forms.dll)

StatusBarPanelClick-EventArgs Class

Provides data for the **PanelClick** event.

System.Object
  System.EventArgs
    System.Windows.Forms.MouseEventArgs
      System.Windows.Forms.StatusBarPanelClickEventArgs

[Visual Basic]
```
Public Class StatusBarPanelClickEventArgs
   Inherits MouseEventArgs
```
[C#]
```
public class StatusBarPanelClickEventArgs : MouseEventArgs
```
[C++]
```
public __gc class StatusBarPanelClickEventArgs : public
   MouseEventArgs
```
[JScript]
```
public class StatusBarPanelClickEventArgs extends MouseEventArgs
```

Thread Safety

Any public static (**Shared** in Visual Basic) members of this type are safe for multithreaded operations. Any instance members are not guaranteed to be thread safe.

Remarks

The **PanelClick** event occurs when the user clicks a panel on the **StatusBar**. A **StatusBarPanelClickEventArgs** specifies which **StatusBarPanel** was clicked, the mouse button that was pressed, how many times it was pressed, and the coordinates of the mouse click at the time the **StatusBarPanel** was clicked. You can use the data provided by this class in an event handler for the **PanelClick** event to perform tasks related to the **StatusBarPanel** being clicked. For example, if a **StatusBarPanel** is used to display the time, you could create an event handler for the **PanelClick** event and use data provided by this class to display a dialog box that allows you to modify the date and time on the system.

Requirements

Namespace: System.Windows.Forms

Platforms: Windows 98, Windows NT 4.0, Windows Millennium Edition, Windows 2000, Windows XP Home Edition, Windows XP Professional, Windows Server 2003 family

Assembly: System.Windows.Forms (in System.Windows.Forms.dll)

StatusBarPanelClickEventArgs Constructor

Initializes a new instance of the **StatusBarPanelClickEventArgs** class.

[Visual Basic]
```
Public Sub New( _
   ByVal statusBarPanel As StatusBarPanel, _
   ByVal button As MouseButtons, _
   ByVal clicks As Integer, _
   ByVal x As Integer, _
   ByVal y As Integer _
)
```
[C#]
```
public StatusBarPanelClickEventArgs(
   StatusBarPanel statusBarPanel,
   MouseButtons button,
   int clicks,
   int x,
   int y
);
```
[C++]
```
public: StatusBarPanelClickEventArgs(
   StatusBarPanel* statusBarPanel,
   MouseButtons button,
   int clicks,
   int x,
   int y
);
```
[JScript]
```
public function StatusBarPanelClickEventArgs(
   statusBarPanel : StatusBarPanel,
   button : MouseButtons,
   clicks : int,
   x : int,
   y : int
);
```

Parameters

statusBarPanel
  The **StatusBarPanel** that represents the panel that was clicked.

button
  One of the **MouseButtons** values that represents the mouse buttons that were clicked while over the **StatusBarPanel**.

clicks
  The number of times that the mouse button was clicked.

x
  The x-coordinate of the mouse click.

y
  The y-coordinate of the mouse click.

Requirements

Platforms: Windows 98, Windows NT 4.0, Windows Millennium Edition, Windows 2000, Windows XP Home Edition, Windows XP Professional, Windows Server 2003 family

StatusBarPanelClickEventArgs.StatusBarPanel Property

Gets the **StatusBarPanel** to draw.

[Visual Basic]
```
Public ReadOnly Property StatusBarPanel As StatusBarPanel
```
[C#]
```
public StatusBarPanel StatusBarPanel {get;}
```
[C++]
```
public: __property StatusBarPanel* get_StatusBarPanel();
```
[JScript]
```
public function get StatusBarPanel() : StatusBarPanel;
```

Property Value

The **StatusBarPanel** to draw.

Remarks

The **StatusBarPanel** property enables you to obtain the **StatusBar-Panel** that was clicked. You can use this within the event handler for the **PanelClick** event of a **StatusBar** control to perform tasks such as displaying custom dialog boxes when a **StatusBarPanel** within a **StatusBar** control is clicked.

Requirements

Platforms: Windows 98, Windows NT 4.0, Windows Millennium Edition, Windows 2000, Windows XP Home Edition, Windows XP Professional, Windows Server 2003 family

StatusBarPanelClickEvent-Handler Delegate

Represents the method that will handle the **PanelClick** event of a **StatusBar**.

[Visual Basic]
```
<Serializable>
Public Delegate Sub StatusBarPanelClickEventHandler( _
   ByVal sender As Object, _
   ByVal e As StatusBarPanelClickEventArgs _
)
```
[C#]
```
[Serializable]
public delegate void StatusBarPanelClickEventHandler(
   object sender,
   StatusBarPanelClickEventArgs e
);
```
[C++]
```
[Serializable]
public __gc __delegate void StatusBarPanelClickEventHandler(
   Object* sender,
   StatusBarPanelClickEventArgs* e
);
```

[JScript] In JScript, you can use the delegates in the .NET Framework, but you cannot define your own.

Parameters [Visual Basic, C#, C++]

The declaration of your event handler must have the same parameters as the **StatusBarPanelClickEventHandler** delegate declaration.

sender

The source of the event.

e

A **StatusBarPanelClickEventArgs** that contains the event data.

Remarks

When you create a **StatusBarPanelClickEventHandler** delegate, you identify the method that will handle the event. To associate the event with your event handler, add an instance of the delegate to the event. The event handler is called whenever the event occurs, unless you remove the delegate.

Requirements

Namespace: System.Windows.Forms

Platforms: Windows 98, Windows NT 4.0,
Windows Millennium Edition, Windows 2000,
Windows XP Home Edition, Windows XP Professional,
Windows Server 2003 family

Assembly: System.Windows.Forms (in System.Windows.Forms.dll)

StatusBarPanelStyle Enumeration

Specifies whether a **StatusBarPanel** object on a **StatusBar** control is owner-drawn or system-drawn.

[Visual Basic]

```
<Serializable>
Public Enum StatusBarPanelStyle
```

[C#]

```
[Serializable]
public enum StatusBarPanelStyle
```

[C++]

```
[Serializable]
__value public enum StatusBarPanelStyle
```

[JScript]

```
public
   Serializable
enum StatusBarPanelStyle
```

Remarks

Use the members of this enumeration to set the value of the **Style** property of the **StatusBarPanel** class. The Style property determines the way in which the **StatusBarPanel** will be displayed. **StatusBarPanel** objects can display simple text or be owner-drawn. Owner-drawn **StatusBarPanel** objects support displaying images or a different font from the rest of the **StatusBarPanel** objects on a **StatusBar** control, while system-drawn **StatusBarPanel** objects are used to display only text (or text and an icon if an icon is specified in the **Icon** property of the **StatusBarPanel**). To perform the owner-draw operations on an owner-drawn **StatusBarPanel**, use the **DrawItem** event of the **StatusBar** control.

Members

Member name	Description
OwnerDraw	The **StatusBarPanel** is drawn by the owner.
Text	The **StatusBarPanel** displays text in the standard font.

Requirements

Namespace: System.Windows.Forms

Platforms: Windows 98, Windows NT 4.0, Windows Millennium Edition, Windows 2000, Windows XP Home Edition, Windows XP Professional, Windows Server 2003 family

Assembly: System.Windows.Forms (in System.Windows.Forms.dll)

StatusBar.StatusBarPanel-Collection Class

Represents the collection of panels in a **StatusBar** control.

System.Object
  System.Windows.Forms.StatusBar.StatusBarPanelCollection

[Visual Basic]
```
Public Class StatusBar.StatusBarPanelCollection
   Implements IList, ICollection, IEnumerable
```
[C#]
```
public class StatusBar.StatusBarPanelCollection : IList,
   ICollection, IEnumerable
```
[C++]
```
public __gc class StatusBar.StatusBarPanelCollection : public
   IList, ICollection, IEnumerable
```
[JScript]
```
public class StatusBar.StatusBarPanelCollection implements IList,
   ICollection, IEnumerable
```

Thread Safety

Any public static (**Shared** in Visual Basic) members of this type are safe for multithreaded operations. Any instance members are not guaranteed to be thread safe.

Remarks

The **StatusBar.StatusBarPanelCollection** class stores the panels displayed in the **StatusBar**. Each object in the collection is an instance of the StatusBarPanel class which defines the display characteristics and behaviors of a panel displayed in a **StatusBar**.

There are a number of ways to add panels to the collection. The **Add** method provides the ability to add a single panel to the collection. To add a number of panels to the collection, you create an array of **StatusBarPanel** objects and assign it to the **AddRange** method. If you want to insert a panel at a specific location within the collection, you can use the **Insert** method. To remove panels, you can use either the **Remove** method or the **RemoveAt** method if you know where the panel is located within the collection. The **Clear** method enables you to remove all panels from the collection instead of using the **Remove** method to remove a single panel at a time.

In addition to methods and properties for adding and removing panels, the **StatusBar.StatusBarPanelCollection** also provides methods to find panels within the collection. The **Contains** method enables you to determine whether a panel is a member of the collection. Once you know that the panel is located within the collection, you can use the **IndexOf** method to determine where the panel is located within the collection.

Example

[Visual Basic, C#] The following example creates a **StatusBar** control on a form and adds two **StatusBarPanel** objects. One of the **StatusBarPanel** objects, named `panel1`, displays status text for an application. The second **StatusBarPanel** object, named `panel2`, displays the current date and uses the **ToolTipText** property of the **StatusBarPanel** class to display the current time. The example uses the **ShowPanels** property to ensure that the panels are displayed instead of a standard panel, and it uses and the **Panels** property to access the **Add** method of the **StatusBar.StatusBarPanel-Collection** to add the panels to the **StatusBar**. The example also uses the **AutoSize**, **BorderStyle**, **ToolTipText**, and **Text** properties to initialize the **StatusBarPanel** objects. This example assumes that the method defined in the example is defined and called from the constructor of a **Form**.

[Visual Basic]
```
Private Sub CreateMyStatusBar()
   ' Create a StatusBar control.
   Dim statusBar1 As New StatusBar()
   ' Create two StatusBarPanel objects to display in the StatusBar.
   Dim panel1 As New StatusBarPanel()
   Dim panel2 As New StatusBarPanel()

   ' Display the first panel with a sunken border style.
   panel1.BorderStyle = StatusBarPanelBorderStyle.Sunken
   ' Initialize the text of the panel.
   panel1.Text = "Ready..."
   ' Set the AutoSize property to use all remaining space on
the StatusBar.
   panel1.AutoSize = StatusBarPanelAutoSize.Spring
   ' Display the second panel with a raised border style.
   panel2.BorderStyle = StatusBarPanelBorderStyle.Raised
   ' Create ToolTip text that displays the current time.
   panel2.ToolTipText = System.DateTime.Now.ToShortTimeString()
   ' Set the text of the panel to the current date.
   panel2.Text = System.DateTime.Today.ToLongDateString()
   ' Set the AutoSize property to size the panel to the size
of the contents.
   panel2.AutoSize = StatusBarPanelAutoSize.Contents

   ' Display panels in the StatusBar control.
   statusBar1.ShowPanels = True

   ' Add both panels to the StatusBarPanelCollection of the StatusBar.
   statusBar1.Panels.Add(panel1)
   statusBar1.Panels.Add(panel2)

   ' Add the StatusBar to the form.
   Me.Controls.Add(statusBar1)
End Sub
```

[C#]
```
private void CreateMyStatusBar()
{
   // Create a StatusBar control.
   StatusBar statusBar1 = new StatusBar();
   // Create two StatusBarPanel objects to display in the StatusBar.
   StatusBarPanel panel1 = new StatusBarPanel();
   StatusBarPanel panel2 = new StatusBarPanel();

   // Display the first panel with a sunken border style.
   panel1.BorderStyle = StatusBarPanelBorderStyle.Sunken;
   // Initialize the text of the panel.
   panel1.Text = "Ready...";
   // Set the AutoSize property to use all remaining space
on the StatusBar.
   panel1.AutoSize = StatusBarPanelAutoSize.Spring;
   // Display the second panel with a raised border style.
   panel2.BorderStyle = StatusBarPanelBorderStyle.Raised;
   // Create ToolTip text that displays the current time.
   panel2.ToolTipText = System.DateTime.Now.ToShortTimeString();
   // Set the text of the panel to the current date.
   panel2.Text = System.DateTime.Today.ToLongDateString();
   // Set the AutoSize property to size the panel to the size
of the contents.
   panel2.AutoSize = StatusBarPanelAutoSize.Contents;

   // Display panels in the StatusBar control.
   statusBar1.ShowPanels = true;

   // Add both panels to the StatusBarPanelCollection of
the StatusBar.
   statusBar1.Panels.Add(panel1);
   statusBar1.Panels.Add(panel2);

   // Add the StatusBar to the form.
   this.Controls.Add(statusBar1);
}
```

Requirements

Namespace: System.Windows.Forms

Platforms: Windows 98, Windows NT 4.0, Windows Millennium Edition, Windows 2000, Windows XP Home Edition, Windows XP Professional, Windows Server 2003 family

Assembly: System.Windows.Forms (in System.Windows.Forms.dll)

StatusBar.StatusBarPanelCollection Constructor

Initializes a new instance of the **StatusBar.StatusBarPanelCollection** class.

```
[Visual Basic]
Public Sub New( _
   ByVal owner As StatusBar _
)
[C#]
public StatusBar.StatusBarPanelCollection(
   StatusBar owner
);
[C++]
public: StatusBarPanelCollection(
   StatusBar* owner
);
[JScript]
public function StatusBar.StatusBarPanelCollection(
   owner : StatusBar
);
```

Parameters

owner

The **StatusBar** control that contains this collection.

Remarks

You cannot create an instance of this class without associating it with a **StatusBar** control.

Requirements

Platforms: Windows 98, Windows NT 4.0, Windows Millennium Edition, Windows 2000, Windows XP Home Edition, Windows XP Professional, Windows Server 2003 family

StatusBar.StatusBarPanelCollection.Count Property

Gets the number of items in the collection.

```
[Visual Basic]
Public Overridable ReadOnly Property Count As Integer  Implements _
   ICollection.Count
[C#]
public virtual int Count {get;}
[C++]
public: __property virtual int get_Count();
[JScript]
public function get Count() : int;
```

Property Value

The number of **StatusBarPanel** objects in the collection.

Implements

ICollection.Count

Remarks

This property enables you to determine the number of panels in the **StatusBar**. You can then use this value when you are looping through the values of the collection and you need to provide a number of iterations to perform the loop.

Requirements

Platforms: Windows 98, Windows NT 4.0, Windows Millennium Edition, Windows 2000, Windows XP Home Edition, Windows XP Professional, Windows Server 2003 family

StatusBar.StatusBarPanelCollection.IsReadOnly Property

Gets a value indicating whether this collection is read-only.

```
[Visual Basic]
Public Overridable ReadOnly Property IsReadOnly As Boolean  _
   Implements IList.IsReadOnly
[C#]
public virtual bool IsReadOnly {get;}
[C++]
public: __property virtual bool get_IsReadOnly();
[JScript]
public function get IsReadOnly() : Boolean;
```

Property Value

true if this collection is read-only; otherwise, **false**.

Implements

IList.IsReadOnly

Remarks

This property is always **false** for this collection.

Requirements

Platforms: Windows 98, Windows NT 4.0, Windows Millennium Edition, Windows 2000, Windows XP Home Edition, Windows XP Professional, Windows Server 2003 family

StatusBar.StatusBarPanelCollection.Item Property

Gets or sets the **StatusBarPanel** at the specified index.

[C#] In C#, this property is the indexer for the **StatusBar.StatusBarPanelCollection** class.

```
[Visual Basic]
Public Overridable Default Property Item( _
   ByVal index As Integer _
) As StatusBarPanel
[C#]
public virtual StatusBarPanel this[
   int index
] {get; set;}
```

[C++]
```
public: __property virtual StatusBarPanel* get_Item(
   int index
);
public: __property virtual void set_Item(
   int index,
   StatusBarPanel*
);
```
[JScript]
```
returnValue = StatusBarPanelCollectionObject.Item(index);
StatusBarPanelCollectionObject.Item(index) = returnValue;
-or-
returnValue = StatusBarPanelCollectionObject(index);
StatusBarPanelCollectionObject(index) = returnValue;
```

[JScript] In JScript, you can use the default indexed properties defined by a type, but you cannot explicitly define your own. However, specifying the **expando** attribute on a class automatically provides a default indexed property whose type is **Object** and whose index type is **String**.

Arguments [JScript]

index

The index of the panel in the collection to get or set.

Parameters [Visual Basic, C#, C++]

index

The index of the panel in the collection to get or set.

Property Value

A **StatusBarPanel** representing the panel located at the specified index within the collection.

Exceptions

Exception Type	Condition
ArgumentOutOfRange-Exception	The *index* parameter is less than zero or greater than or equal to the value of the **Count** property of the **Status-Bar.StatusBarPanelCollection** class.
ArgumentNull-Exception	The **StatusBarPanel** assigned to the collection was null.

Remarks

You can use this method to obtain the **StatusBarPanel** stored at a specific location within the collection. To determine the index of a specific panel within the collection, use the **IndexOf** method.

Requirements

Platforms: Windows 98, Windows NT 4.0, Windows Millennium Edition, Windows 2000, Windows XP Home Edition, Windows XP Professional, Windows Server 2003 family

StatusBar.StatusBarPanelCollection.Add Method

Adds a **StatusBarPanel** to the collection.

Overload List

Adds a **StatusBarPanel** to the collection.

[Visual Basic] **Overloads Public Overridable Function Add(StatusBarPanel) As Integer**

[C#] **public virtual int Add(StatusBarPanel);**

[C++] **public: virtual int Add(StatusBarPanel*);**

[JScript] **public function Add(StatusBarPanel) : int;**

Adds a **StatusBarPanel** with the specified text to the collection.

[Visual Basic] **Overloads Public Overridable Function Add(String) As StatusBarPanel**

[C#] **public virtual StatusBarPanel Add(string);**

[C++] **public: virtual StatusBarPanel* Add(String*);**

[JScript] **public function Add(String) : StatusBarPanel;**

Example

See related example in the **System.Windows.Forms.Status-Bar.StatusBarPanelCollection** class topic.

StatusBar.StatusBarPanelCollection.Add Method (StatusBarPanel)

Adds a **StatusBarPanel** to the collection.

[Visual Basic]
```
Overloads Public Overridable Function Add( _
   ByVal value As StatusBarPanel _
) As Integer
```
[C#]
```
public virtual int Add(
   StatusBarPanel value
);
```
[C++]
```
public: virtual int Add(
   StatusBarPanel* value
);
```
[JScript]
```
public function Add(
   value : StatusBarPanel
) : int;
```

Parameters

value

A **StatusBarPanel** that represents the panel to add to the collection.

Return Value

The zero-based index of the item in the collection.

Exceptions

Exception Type	Condition
ArgumentNull-Exception	The **StatusBarPanel** being added to the collection was null.
ArgumentException	The parent of the **StatusBarPanel** specified in the *value* parameter is not null.

Remarks

You can add panels to a **StatusBar** control to display more than one type of information. This version of the **Add** method adds the **StatusBarPanel** object specified in the *value* parameter to the collection. The order in which panels are located in the **Status-Bar.StatusBarPanelCollection** represents the order that panels are displayed within the **StatusBar** control. Panels are displayed from left to right starting with the first panel in the collection. The **RightToLeft** property of the **StatusBar** control does not change the order in which panels are displayed in the **StatusBar**. To insert a panel at a specific position in the collection, use the **Insert** method. To add a set of panels to the collection in a single operation, use the **AddRange** method.

Example

See related example in the **System.Windows.Forms.StatusBar.StatusBarPanelCollection** class topic.

Requirements

Platforms: Windows 98, Windows NT 4.0, Windows Millennium Edition, Windows 2000, Windows XP Home Edition, Windows XP Professional, Windows Server 2003 family

StatusBar.StatusBarPanelCollection.Add Method (String)

Adds a **StatusBarPanel** with the specified text to the collection.

[Visual Basic]
```
Overloads Public Overridable Function Add( _
   ByVal text As String _
) As StatusBarPanel
```
[C#]
```
public virtual StatusBarPanel Add(
   string text
);
```
[C++]
```
public: virtual StatusBarPanel* Add(
   String* text
);
```
[JScript]
```
public function Add(
   text : String
) : StatusBarPanel;
```

Parameters

text
The text for the **StatusBarPanel** that is being added.

Return Value

A **StatusBarPanel** that represents the panel that was added to the collection.

Remarks

You can add panels to a **StatusBar** control to display more than one type of information. This version of the **Add** method creates a new **StatusBarPanel** object with the text specified in the *text* parameter and adds it to collection. The order in which panels are located in the **StatusBar.StatusBarPanelCollection** represents the order that panels are displayed within the **StatusBar** control. Panels are displayed from left to right starting with the first panel in the collection. The **RightToLeft** property of the **StatusBar** control does not change the order in which panels are displayed in the **StatusBar**. To insert a panel at a specific position in the collection, use the **Insert** method. To add a set of panels to the collection in a single operation, use the **AddRange** method.

Requirements

Platforms: Windows 98, Windows NT 4.0, Windows Millennium Edition, Windows 2000, Windows XP Home Edition, Windows XP Professional, Windows Server 2003 family

StatusBar.StatusBarPanelCollection.AddRange Method

Adds an array of **StatusBarPanel** objects to the collection.

[Visual Basic]
```
Public Overridable Sub AddRange( _
   ByVal panels() As StatusBarPanel _
)
```
[C#]
```
public virtual void AddRange(
   StatusBarPanel[] panels
);
```
[C++]
```
public: virtual void AddRange(
   StatusBarPanel* panels[]
);
```
[JScript]
```
public function AddRange(
   panels : StatusBarPanel[]
);
```

Parameters

panels
An array of **StatusBarPanel** objects to add.

Exceptions

Exception Type	Condition
ArgumentNull-Exception	The array of **StatusBarPanel** objects being added to the collection was null.

Remarks

You can add panels to a **StatusBar** control to display more than one type of information. The **AddRange** method adds an array of **StatusBarPanel** objects specified in the *panels* parameter to the collection. All existing panels in the collection are removed from the collection before inserting new panels. The order in which panels are located in the **StatusBar.StatusBarPanelCollection** represents the order that panels are displayed within the **StatusBar** control. Panels are displayed from left to right starting with the first panel in the collection. The **RightToLeft** property of the **StatusBar** control does not change the order in which panels are displayed in the **StatusBar**. To add a single **StatusBarPanel** object to the collection, use the **Add** method. To insert a panel at a specific position in the **StatusBar** control (and in this collection), use the **Insert** method.

Requirements

Platforms: Windows 98, Windows NT 4.0, Windows Millennium Edition, Windows 2000, Windows XP Home Edition, Windows XP Professional, Windows Server 2003 family

StatusBar.StatusBarPanelCollection.Clear Method

Removes all items from the collection.

[Visual Basic]
```
Public Overridable Sub Clear() Implements IList.Clear
```
[C#]
```
public virtual void Clear();
```
[C++]
```
public: virtual void Clear();
```
[JScript]
```
public function Clear();
```

Implements

IList.Clear

Remarks

When you remove panels from the collection, all information about the deleted panels is lost. To remove a single panel from the **StatusBar**, use the **Remove** or **RemoveAt** method.

Requirements

Platforms: Windows 98, Windows NT 4.0,
Windows Millennium Edition, Windows 2000,
Windows XP Home Edition, Windows XP Professional,
Windows Server 2003 family

StatusBar.StatusBarPanelCollection.Contains Method

Determines whether the specified panel is located within the collection.

```
[Visual Basic]
Public Function Contains( _
   ByVal panel As StatusBarPanel _
) As Boolean
[C#]
public bool Contains(
   StatusBarPanel panel
);
[C++]
public: bool Contains(
   StatusBarPanel* panel
);
[JScript]
public function Contains(
   panel : StatusBarPanel
) : Boolean;
```

Parameters

panel

The **StatusBarPanel** to locate in the collection.

Return Value

true if the panel is located within the collection; otherwise, **false**.

Remarks

The **Contains** method enables you to determine whether a panel is a member of the collection. Once you know that the item is located within the collection, you can use the **IndexOf** method to determine where the panel is located within the collection.

Requirements

Platforms: Windows 98, Windows NT 4.0,
Windows Millennium Edition, Windows 2000,
Windows XP Home Edition, Windows XP Professional,
Windows Server 2003 family

StatusBar.StatusBarPanelCollection.GetEnumerator Method

Returns an enumerator to use to iterate through the item collection.

```
[Visual Basic]
Public Overridable Function GetEnumerator() As IEnumerator _
   Implements IEnumerable.GetEnumerator
[C#]
public virtual IEnumerator GetEnumerator();
[C++]
public: virtual IEnumerator* GetEnumerator();
[JScript]
public function GetEnumerator() : IEnumerator;
```

Return Value

An **IEnumerator** object that represents the item collection.

Implements

IEnumerable.GetEnumerator

Requirements

Platforms: Windows 98, Windows NT 4.0,
Windows Millennium Edition, Windows 2000,
Windows XP Home Edition, Windows XP Professional,
Windows Server 2003 family

StatusBar.StatusBarPanelCollection.ICollection.CopyTo Method

This member supports the .NET Framework infrastructure and is not intended to be used directly from your code.

```
[Visual Basic]
Private Sub CopyTo( _
   ByVal dest As Array, _
   ByVal index As Integer _
) Implements ICollection.CopyTo
[C#]
void ICollection.CopyTo(
   Array dest,
   int index
);
[C++]
private: void ICollection::CopyTo(
   Array* dest,
   int index
);
[JScript]
private function ICollection.CopyTo(
   dest : Array,
   index : int
);
```

StatusBar.StatusBarPanelCollection.IList.Add Method

This member supports the .NET Framework infrastructure and is not intended to be used directly from your code.

```
[Visual Basic]
Private Function Add( _
   ByVal value As Object _
) As Integer Implements IList.Add
[C#]
int IList.Add(
   object value
);
[C++]
private: int IList::Add(
   Object* value
);
```

```
[JScript]
private function IList.Add(
   value : Object
) : int;
```

StatusBar.StatusBarPanelCollection.IList.Contains Method

This member supports the .NET Framework infrastructure and is not intended to be used directly from your code.

```
[Visual Basic]
Private Function Contains( _
   ByVal panel As Object _
) As Boolean Implements IList.Contains
[C#]
bool IList.Contains(
   object panel
);
[C++]
private: bool IList::Contains(
   Object* panel
);
[JScript]
private function IList.Contains(
   panel : Object
) : Boolean;
```

StatusBar.StatusBarPanelCollection.IList.IndexOf Method

This member supports the .NET Framework infrastructure and is not intended to be used directly from your code.

```
[Visual Basic]
Private Function IndexOf( _
   ByVal panel As Object _
) As Integer Implements IList.IndexOf
[C#]
int IList.IndexOf(
   object panel
);
[C++]
private: int IList::IndexOf(
   Object* panel
);
[JScript]
private function IList.IndexOf(
   panel : Object
) : int;
```

StatusBar.StatusBarPanelCollection.IList.Insert Method

This member supports the .NET Framework infrastructure and is not intended to be used directly from your code.

```
[Visual Basic]
Private Sub Insert( _
   ByVal index As Integer, _
   ByVal value As Object _
) Implements IList.Insert
[C#]
void IList.Insert(
   int index,
   object value
);
[C++]
private: void IList::Insert(
   int index,
   Object* value
);
[JScript]
private function IList.Insert(
   index : int,
   value : Object
);
```

StatusBar.StatusBarPanelCollection.IList.Remove Method

This member supports the .NET Framework infrastructure and is not intended to be used directly from your code.

```
[Visual Basic]
Private Sub Remove( _
   ByVal value As Object _
) Implements IList.Remove
[C#]
void IList.Remove(
   object value
);
[C++]
private: void IList::Remove(
   Object* value
);
[JScript]
private function IList.Remove(
   value : Object
);
```

StatusBar.StatusBarPanelCollection.IndexOf Method

Returns the index within the collection of the specified panel.

```
[Visual Basic]
Public Function IndexOf( _
   ByVal panel As StatusBarPanel _
) As Integer
[C#]
public int IndexOf(
   StatusBarPanel panel
);
[C++]
public: int IndexOf(
   StatusBarPanel* panel
);
[JScript]
public function IndexOf(
   panel : StatusBarPanel
) : int;
```

Parameters

panel

The **StatusBarPanel** object to locate in the collection.

Return Value

The zero-based index where the panel is located within the collection; otherwise, negative one (-1).

Remarks

The **IndexOf** method enables you to determine where a panel is located within the collection. To determine whether an item is located within the collection before calling this method, use the **Contains** method.

Requirements

Platforms: Windows 98, Windows NT 4.0, Windows Millennium Edition, Windows 2000, Windows XP Home Edition, Windows XP Professional, Windows Server 2003 family

StatusBar.StatusBarPanelCollection.Insert Method

Inserts the specified **StatusBarPanel** into the collection at the specified index.

[Visual Basic]
```
Public Overridable Sub Insert( _
   ByVal index As Integer, _
   ByVal value As StatusBarPanel _
)
```
[C#]
```
public virtual void Insert(
   int index,
   StatusBarPanel value
);
```
[C++]
```
public: virtual void Insert(
   int index,
   StatusBarPanel* value
);
```
[JScript]
```
public function Insert(
   index : int,
   value : StatusBarPanel
);
```

Parameters

index

The zero-based index location where the panel is inserted.

value

A **StatusBarPanel** representing the panel to insert.

Exceptions

Exception Type	Condition
ArgumentNull-Exception	The *value* parameter is a null reference (**Nothing** in Visual Basic).
ArgumentException	The *value* parameter's parent is not a null reference (**Nothing** in Visual Basic).
ArgumentOutOfRange-Exception	The *index* parameter is less than zero or greater than the value of the **Count** property of the **StatusBar.StatusBar-PanelCollection** class.
InvalidEnumArgument-Exception	The **AutoSize** property of the *value* parameter's panel is not a valid **StatusBarPanelAutoSize** value.

Remarks

You can add panels to a **StatusBar** control to display more than one type of information. The **Insert** method enables you to create a new **StatusBarPanel** object and insert it at a specific location within the collection. The order in which panels are located in the **Status-Bar.StatusBarPanelCollection** represents the order that panels are displayed within the **StatusBar** control. Panels are displayed from left to right starting with the first panel in the collection. The **Right-ToLeft** property of the **StatusBar** control does not change the order in which panels are displayed in the **StatusBar**. To add a panel to the end of the collection, use the **Add** method. To add a set of panels to the collection in a single operation, use the **AddRange** method.

Requirements

Platforms: Windows 98, Windows NT 4.0, Windows Millennium Edition, Windows 2000, Windows XP Home Edition, Windows XP Professional, Windows Server 2003 family

StatusBar.StatusBarPanelCollection.Remove Method

Removes the specified **StatusBarPanel** from the collection.

[Visual Basic]
```
Public Overridable Sub Remove( _
   ByVal value As StatusBarPanel _
)
```
[C#]
```
public virtual void Remove(
   StatusBarPanel value
);
```
[C++]
```
public: virtual void Remove(
   StatusBarPanel* value
);
```
[JScript]
```
public function Remove(
   value : StatusBarPanel
);
```

Parameters

value

The **StatusBarPanel** representing the panel to remove from the collection.

Exceptions

Exception Type	Condition
ArgumentNull-Exception	The **StatusBarPanel** assigned to the *value* parameter is null.

Remarks

When you remove a panel from the list, the indexes change for subsequent items in the collection. All information about the removed panel is deleted. You can use this method to remove a specific panel from the **StatusBar** by specifying the actual **StatusBarPanel** to remove from the collection. To specify the index of the panel to remove instead of the panel itself, use the **RemoveAt** method. To remove all panels from the collection, use the **Clear** method.

Requirements

Platforms: Windows 98, Windows NT 4.0, Windows Millennium Edition, Windows 2000, Windows XP Home Edition, Windows XP Professional, Windows Server 2003 family

StatusBar.StatusBarPanelCollection.RemoveAt Method

Removes the **StatusBarPanel** located at the specified index within the collection.

```
[Visual Basic]
Public Overridable Sub RemoveAt( _
   ByVal index As Integer _
) Implements IList.RemoveAt
[C#]
public virtual void RemoveAt(
   int index
);
[C++]
public: virtual void RemoveAt(
   int index
);
[JScript]
public function RemoveAt(
   index : int
);
```

Parameters

index
  The zero-based index of the item to remove.

Implements

IList.RemoveAt

Exceptions

Exception Type	Condition
ArgumentOutOfRange-Exception	The *index* parameter is less than zero or greater than or equal to the value of the **Count** property of the **StatusBar.StatusBarPanelCollection** class.

Remarks

When you remove a panel from the collection, the indexes change for subsequent panels in the collection. All information about the removed panel is deleted. You can use this method to remove a specific panel from the list by specifying the index of the panel to remove from the collection. To specify the panel to remove instead of the index to the panel, use the **Remove** method. To remove all panels from the **StatusBar** control, use the **Clear** method.

Requirements

Platforms: Windows 98, Windows NT 4.0, Windows Millennium Edition, Windows 2000, Windows XP Home Edition, Windows XP Professional, Windows Server 2003 family

StructFormat Enumeration

This type supports the .NET Framework infrastructure and is not intended to be used directly from your code.

[Visual Basic]
```
<Serializable>
Public Enum StructFormat
```
[C#]
```
[Serializable]
public enum StructFormat
```
[C++]
```
[Serializable]
__value public enum StructFormat
```
[JScript]
```
public
   Serializable
enum StructFormat
```

Members

Ansi

Auto

Unicode

SystemInformation Class

Provides information about the operating system.

System.Object
  System.Windows.Forms.SystemInformation

[Visual Basic]
```
Public Class SystemInformation
```
[C#]
```
public class SystemInformation
```
[C++]
```
public __gc class SystemInformation
```
[JScript]
```
public class SystemInformation
```

Thread Safety

Any public static (**Shared** in Visual Basic) members of this type are safe for multithreaded operations. Any instance members are not guaranteed to be thread safe.

Remarks

SystemInformation provides static (**Shared** in Visual Basic) methods and properties that can be used to get information such as Windows display element sizes, operating system settings, network availability, and the capabilities of hardware installed on the system. This class cannot be instantiated.

Example

[Visual Basic, C#, C++] The following example demonstrates reading system information via the **SystemInformation** class and adds the information to a **ListBox** on the form.

[Visual Basic]
```
Imports System
Imports System.Drawing
Imports System.Windows.Forms

Public NotInheritable Class Form1
    Inherits System.Windows.Forms.Form

    Friend WithEvents BtnGetScreenInfo As System.Windows.Forms.Button
    Friend WithEvents ListBox1 As System.Windows.Forms.ListBox

    <System.STAThread()> _
    Public Shared Sub Main()
        System.Windows.Forms.Application.Run(New Form1())
    End Sub 'Main

    Public Sub New()
        MyBase.New()

        Me.BtnGetScreenInfo = New System.Windows.Forms.Button
        Me.ListBox1 = New System.Windows.Forms.ListBox

        ' Get System Information Button
        Me.BtnGetScreenInfo.Location = New System.Drawing.Point(16, 16)
        Me.BtnGetScreenInfo.Size = New System.Drawing.Size(256, 48)
        Me.BtnGetScreenInfo.TabIndex = 0
        Me.BtnGetScreenInfo.Text = "Get System Information"

        ' System Information ListBox
        Me.ListBox1.Location = New System.Drawing.Point(16, 72)
        Me.ListBox1.Size = New System.Drawing.Size(256, 186)
        Me.ListBox1.TabIndex = 1

        ' Form1
        Me.ClientSize = New System.Drawing.Size(292, 317)
        Me.Controls.AddRange(New                                        ↵
System.Windows.Forms.Control() {Me.ListBox1, Me.BtnGetScreenInfo})
        Me.Text = "System Information Example"

    End Sub

    Private Sub Button1_Click(ByVal sender As System.Object,            ↵
ByVal e As System.EventArgs) Handles BtnGetScreenInfo.Click
        ' Get System Information for the current machine.
        ListBox1.Items.Add("ComputerName : " +                          ↵
SystemInformation.ComputerName)
        ListBox1.Items.Add("Network  : " +                              ↵
SystemInformation.Network.ToString())
        ListBox1.Items.Add("UserDomainName  : " +                       ↵
SystemInformation.UserDomainName)
        ListBox1.Items.Add("UserName   : " +                            ↵
SystemInformation.UserName)
        ListBox1.Items.Add("BootMode : " +                              ↵
SystemInformation.BootMode.ToString())
        ListBox1.Items.Add("MenuFont : " +                              ↵
SystemInformation.MenuFont.ToString())
        ListBox1.Items.Add("MonitorCount : " +                          ↵
SystemInformation.MonitorCount.ToString())
        ListBox1.Items.Add("MonitorsSameDisplayFormat :                 ↵
" + SystemInformation.MonitorsSameDisplayFormat.ToString())
        ListBox1.Items.Add("ArrangeDirection: " +                       ↵
SystemInformation.ArrangeDirection.ToString())
        ListBox1.Items.Add("MousePresent : " +                          ↵
SystemInformation.MousePresent.ToString())
        ListBox1.Items.Add("MouseButtonsSwapped    : " +                ↵
SystemInformation.MouseButtonsSwapped.ToString())
        ListBox1.Items.Add("UserInteractive    : " +                    ↵
SystemInformation.UserInteractive.ToString())
        ListBox1.Items.Add("VirtualScreen: " +                          ↵
SystemInformation.VirtualScreen.ToString())
    End Sub
End Class
```

[C#]
```
using System;
using System.Drawing;
using System.Windows.Forms;

namespace Screen_Example_cs
{
    public class Form1 : System.Windows.Forms.Form
    {
        private System.Windows.Forms.Button button1;
        private System.Windows.Forms.ListBox listBox1;

        [STAThread]
        static void Main()
        {
            Application.Run(new Form1());
        }

        public Form1()
        {
            this.button1 = new System.Windows.Forms.Button();
            this.listBox1 = new System.Windows.Forms.ListBox();

            // Get System Information Button
            this.button1.Location = new System.Drawing.Point(56, 16);
            this.button1.Size = new System.Drawing.Size(168, 23);
            this.button1.TabIndex = 0;
            this.button1.Text = "Get System Information";
            this.button1.Click += new
 System.EventHandler(this.button1_Click);

            // System Information ListBox
            this.listBox1.Location = new System.Drawing.Point(8, 48);
            this.listBox1.Size = new System.Drawing.Size(280, 186);
            this.listBox1.TabIndex = 1;

            // Form1
            this.ClientSize = new System.Drawing.Size(292, 273);
            this.Controls.AddRange(new System.Windows.Forms.Control[] {
                                         this.listBox1, this.button1});
            this.Text = "System Information Example";
        }
        private void button1_Click(object sender, System.EventArgs e)
```

```
        {
            // Get system information for the current machine.
            listBox1.Items.Add("ComputerName : " + ↵
SystemInformation.ComputerName );
            listBox1.Items.Add("Network  : " + ↵
SystemInformation.Network  );
            listBox1.Items.Add("UserDomainName  : " + ↵
SystemInformation.UserDomainName  );
            listBox1.Items.Add("UserName   : " + ↵
SystemInformation.UserName   );
            listBox1.Items.Add("BootMode : " + ↵
SystemInformation.BootMode );
            listBox1.Items.Add("MenuFont : " + ↵
SystemInformation.MenuFont );
            listBox1.Items.Add("MonitorCount : " + ↵
SystemInformation.MonitorCount );
            listBox1.Items.Add("MonitorsSameDisplayFormat ↵
 : " + SystemInformation.MonitorsSameDisplayFormat.ToString() );
            listBox1.Items.Add("ArrangeDirection: " + ↵
SystemInformation.ArrangeDirection);
            listBox1.Items.Add("MousePresent : " + ↵
SystemInformation.MousePresent );
            listBox1.Items.Add("MouseButtonsSwapped    : ↵
 " + SystemInformation.MouseButtonsSwapped    );
            listBox1.Items.Add("UserInteractive    : " + ↵
SystemInformation.UserInteractive    );
            listBox1.Items.Add("VirtualScreen: " + ↵
SystemInformation.VirtualScreen );
        }
    }
}
```

[C++]

```
#using <mscorlib.dll>
#using <System.dll>
#using <System.Windows.Forms.dll>
#using <System.Drawing.dll>

using namespace System;
using namespace System::Drawing;
using namespace System::Windows::Forms;

namespace Screen_Example_cs {
public __gc class Form1 : public System::Windows::Forms::Form {
private:
   System::Windows::Forms::Button*  button1;
   System::Windows::Forms::ListBox*  listBox1;
public:
   Form1() {
      this->button1 = new System::Windows::Forms::Button();
      this->listBox1 = new System::Windows::Forms::ListBox();

      // Get System Information Button
      this->button1->Location =  System::Drawing::Point(56, 16);
      this->button1->Size =  System::Drawing::Size(168, 23);
      this->button1->TabIndex = 0;
      this->button1->Text = S"Get System Information";
      this->button1->Click += new System::EventHandler(this, ↵
button1_Click);

      // System Information ListBox
      this->listBox1->Location =  System::Drawing::Point(8, 48);
      this->listBox1->Size =  System::Drawing::Size(280, 186);
      this->listBox1->TabIndex = 1;

      // Form1
      this->ClientSize =  System::Drawing::Size(292, 273);

      System::Windows::Forms::Control* temp0 [] = ↵
{this->listBox1, this->button1};

      this->Controls->AddRange(temp0);
      this->Text = S"System Information Example";
   }
private:
   void button1_Click(Object* sender, System::EventArgs* e) {
      // Get system information for the current machine.
      listBox1->Items->Add(String::Format(S"ComputerName : ↵
{0}", SystemInformation::ComputerName));
      listBox1->Items->Add(String::Format(S"Network  : {0}", ↵
__box(SystemInformation::Network)));
      listBox1->Items->Add(String::Format(S"UserDomainName  : ↵
{0}", SystemInformation::UserDomainName));
      listBox1->Items->Add(String::Format(S"UserName   : {0}", ↵
SystemInformation::UserName));
      listBox1->Items->Add(String::Format(S"BootMode : {0}", ↵
__box(SystemInformation::BootMode)));
      listBox1->Items->Add(String::Format(S"MenuFont : {0}", ↵
SystemInformation::MenuFont));
      listBox1->Items->Add(String::Format(S"MonitorCount : {0}", ↵
__box(SystemInformation::MonitorCount)));
      listBox1->Items->Add(String::Format ↵
 (S"MonitorsSameDisplayFormat : {0}", ↵
__box(SystemInformation::MonitorsSameDisplayFormat)));
      listBox1->Items->Add(String::Format(S"ArrangeDirection: ↵
{0}", __box(SystemInformation::ArrangeDirection)));
      listBox1->Items->Add(String::Format(S"MousePresent : ↵
{0}", __box(SystemInformation::MousePresent)));
      listBox1->Items->Add(String::Format(S"MouseButtonsSwapped ↵
  : {0}", __box(SystemInformation::MouseButtonsSwapped)));
      listBox1->Items->Add(String::Format(S"UserInteractive ↵
: {0}", __box(SystemInformation::UserInteractive)));
      listBox1->Items->Add(String::Format(S"VirtualScreen: {0}", ↵
__box(SystemInformation::VirtualScreen)));
   }
};
}

[STAThread]
int main() {
   Application::Run(new Screen_Example_cs::Form1());
}
```

Requirements

Namespace: System.Windows.Forms

Platforms: Windows 98, Windows NT 4.0, Windows Millennium Edition, Windows 2000, Windows XP Home Edition, Windows XP Professional, Windows Server 2003 family, .NET Compact Framework - Windows CE .NET

Assembly: System.Windows.Forms (in System.Windows.Forms.dll)

SystemInformation.ArrangeDirection Property

Gets flags specifying how the operating system arranges minimized windows.

[Visual Basic]

```
Public Shared ReadOnly Property ArrangeDirection As _
   ArrangeDirection
```

[C#]

```
public static ArrangeDirection ArrangeDirection {get;}
```

[C++]

```
public: __property static ArrangeDirection get_ArrangeDirection();
```

[JScript]

```
public static function get ArrangeDirection() : ArrangeDirection;
```

Property Value

An **ArrangeDirection** that is a Boolean combination of **ArrangeStartingPosition** and **ArrangeDirection** values of the operating system.

Example

See related example in the **System.Windows.Forms.System-Information** class topic.

Requirements

Platforms: Windows 98, Windows NT 4.0,
Windows Millennium Edition, Windows 2000,
Windows XP Home Edition, Windows XP Professional,
Windows Server 2003 family

SystemInformation.ArrangeStartingPosition Property

Gets flags specifying how the operating system arranges minimized windows.

[Visual Basic]
```
Public Shared ReadOnly Property ArrangeStartingPosition As _
   ArrangeStartingPosition
```
[C#]
```
public static ArrangeStartingPosition ArrangeStartingPosition
   {get;}
```
[C++]
```
public: __property static ArrangeStartingPosition
   get_ArrangeStartingPosition();
```
[JScript]
```
public static function get ArrangeStartingPosition() :
   ArrangeStartingPosition;
```

Property Value

An **ArrangeStartingPosition** that is a Boolean combination of **ArrangeStartingPosition** and **ArrangeDirection** values of the operating system.

Remarks

The value is a combination of one starting position value and one direction value.

Requirements

Platforms: Windows 98, Windows NT 4.0,
Windows Millennium Edition, Windows 2000,
Windows XP Home Edition, Windows XP Professional,
Windows Server 2003 family

SystemInformation.BootMode Property

Gets a value that specifies how the system was started.

[Visual Basic]
```
Public Shared ReadOnly Property BootMode As BootMode
```
[C#]
```
public static BootMode BootMode {get;}
```
[C++]
```
public: __property static BootMode get_BootMode();
```
[JScript]
```
public static function get BootMode() : BootMode;
```

Property Value

One of the **BootMode** values that specifies how the system was started.

Remarks

Use **BootMode** to determine how the user started the system. For applications running on Windows 98, you can use this property to determine whether the operating system is in fail-safe mode. Your application uses this information to operate appropriately when it accesses system services and hardware.

The value returned can be one of the following values:

- **Normal**: The computer started in the standard mode.
- **FailSafe**: The computer started with only the basic files and drivers.
- **FailSafeWithNetwork**: The computer started with the basic files, drivers, and services and drivers necessary to start networking.

> **Note** Fail-safe boot (also called SafeBoot) bypasses the user's startup files.

Example

See related example in the **System.Windows.Forms.System-Information** class topic.

Requirements

Platforms: Windows 98, Windows NT 4.0,
Windows Millennium Edition, Windows 2000,
Windows XP Home Edition, Windows XP Professional,
Windows Server 2003 family

.NET Framework Security:

- **EnvironmentPermission** to get the value of this property. Associated enumeration: **PermissionState.Unrestricted**

SystemInformation.Border3DSize Property

Gets the dimensions, in pixels, of a three-dimensional (3-D) border.

[Visual Basic]
```
Public Shared ReadOnly Property Border3DSize As Size
```
[C#]
```
public static Size Border3DSize {get;}
```
[C++]
```
public: __property static Size get_Border3DSize();
```
[JScript]
```
public static function get Border3DSize() : Size;
```

Property Value

A **Size** that specifies the dimensions of a 3-D border in pixels.

Remarks

Border3DSize is the three-dimensional counterpart of the **BorderSize**. Use this property when creating a control that has a 3-D border to determine the proper sizing of the border.

Requirements

Platforms: Windows 98, Windows NT 4.0,
Windows Millennium Edition, Windows 2000,
Windows XP Home Edition, Windows XP Professional,
Windows Server 2003 family

SystemInformation.BorderSize Property

Gets the width and height, in pixels, of a window border.

```
[Visual Basic]
Public Shared ReadOnly Property BorderSize As Size
[C#]
public static Size BorderSize {get;}
[C++]
public: __property static Size get_BorderSize();
[JScript]
public static function get BorderSize() : Size;
```

Property Value

A **Size** that specifies the width and height of a window border in pixels.

Remarks

The **BorderSize** property is the non-three-dimensional counterpart of the **Border3DSize** property. Use this property when creating a control that has a border to determine the proper sizing of the border.

Requirements

Platforms: Windows 98, Windows NT 4.0, Windows Millennium Edition, Windows 2000, Windows XP Home Edition, Windows XP Professional, Windows Server 2003 family

SystemInformation.CaptionButtonSize Property

Gets the dimensions, in pixels, of a caption bar or title bar button.

```
[Visual Basic]
Public Shared ReadOnly Property CaptionButtonSize As Size
[C#]
public static Size CaptionButtonSize {get;}
[C++]
public: __property static Size get_CaptionButtonSize();
[JScript]
public static function get CaptionButtonSize() : Size;
```

Property Value

A **Size** that specifies the dimensions of a caption bar button in pixels.

Remarks

Use **CaptionButtonSize** to get the dimensions of a button in the caption bar of window, to place additional caption buttons in the caption of a window, and to ensure the button is properly sized.

Requirements

Platforms: Windows 98, Windows NT 4.0, Windows Millennium Edition, Windows 2000, Windows XP Home Edition, Windows XP Professional, Windows Server 2003 family

SystemInformation.CaptionHeight Property

Gets the height, in pixels, of the normal caption area of a window.

```
[Visual Basic]
Public Shared ReadOnly Property CaptionHeight As Integer
[C#]
public static int CaptionHeight {get;}
[C++]
public: __property static int get_CaptionHeight();
[JScript]
public static function get CaptionHeight() : int;
```

Property Value

The height of the normal caption area of a window in pixels.

Remarks

Use **CaptionHeight** to determine the size of the standard window caption. You can also perform special display operations or add a caption button to the caption of a window.

Requirements

Platforms: Windows 98, Windows NT 4.0, Windows Millennium Edition, Windows 2000, Windows XP Home Edition, Windows XP Professional, Windows Server 2003 family

SystemInformation.ComputerName Property

Gets the computer name of the current system.

```
[Visual Basic]
Public Shared ReadOnly Property ComputerName As String
[C#]
public static string ComputerName {get;}
[C++]
public: __property static String* get_ComputerName();
[JScript]
public static function get ComputerName() : String;
```

Property Value

The name of this computer.

Remarks

Use **ComputerName** to determine the name of the computer as it is displayed to other users on a network. This name is established at system startup, when it is initialized from the registry.

Example

See related example in the **System.Windows.Forms.SystemInformation** class topic.

Requirements

Platforms: Windows 98, Windows NT 4.0, Windows Millennium Edition, Windows 2000, Windows XP Home Edition, Windows XP Professional, Windows Server 2003 family

.NET Framework Security:

- **EnvironmentPermission** to get the value of this property. Associated enumeration: **PermissionState.Unrestricted**

SystemInformation.CursorSize Property

Gets the dimensions, in pixels, of a cursor.

```
[Visual Basic]
Public Shared ReadOnly Property CursorSize As Size
[C#]
public static Size CursorSize {get;}
[C++]
public: __property static Size get_CursorSize();
[JScript]
public static function get CursorSize() : Size;
```

Property Value

A **Size** that specifies the dimensions of a cursor in pixels.

Remarks

The system cannot create cursors of other sizes.

Requirements

Platforms: Windows 98, Windows NT 4.0,
Windows Millennium Edition, Windows 2000,
Windows XP Home Edition, Windows XP Professional,
Windows Server 2003 family

SystemInformation.DbcsEnabled Property

Gets a value indicating whether the operating system is capable of handling double-byte character set (DBCS) characters.

```
[Visual Basic]
Public Shared ReadOnly Property DbcsEnabled As Boolean
[C#]
public static bool DbcsEnabled {get;}
[C++]
public: __property static bool get_DbcsEnabled();
[JScript]
public static function get DbcsEnabled() : Boolean;
```

Property Value

true if the operating system supports DBCS; otherwise, **false**.

Remarks

Use **DbcsEnabled** to determine whether the operating system on which your application is running supports DBCS. Although an operating system can support DBCS, this does not mean that the user runs a culture that uses DBCS.

Requirements

Platforms: Windows 98, Windows NT 4.0,
Windows Millennium Edition, Windows 2000,
Windows XP Home Edition, Windows XP Professional,
Windows Server 2003 family

SystemInformation.DebugOS Property

Gets a value indicating whether the debugging version of USER.EXE is installed.

```
[Visual Basic]
Public Shared ReadOnly Property DebugOS As Boolean
[C#]
public static bool DebugOS {get;}
[C++]
public: __property static bool get_DebugOS();
[JScript]
public static function get DebugOS() : Boolean;
```

Property Value

true if the debugging version of USER.EXE is installed; otherwise, **false**.

Requirements

Platforms: Windows 98, Windows NT 4.0,
Windows Millennium Edition, Windows 2000,
Windows XP Home Edition, Windows XP Professional,
Windows Server 2003 family

.NET Framework Security:

- **EnvironmentPermission** to get the value of this property. Associated enumeration: **PermissionState.Unrestricted**

SystemInformation.DoubleClickSize Property

Gets the dimensions, in pixels, of the area within which the user must click for the operating system to consider the two clicks a double-click.

```
[Visual Basic]
Public Shared ReadOnly Property DoubleClickSize As Size
[C#]
public static Size DoubleClickSize {get;}
[C++]
public: __property static Size get_DoubleClickSize();
[JScript]
public static function get DoubleClickSize() : Size;
```

Property Value

A **Size** that specifies the dimensions, in pixels, of the area within which the user must click for the operating system to consider the two clicks a double-click.

Remarks

The rectangle is centered around the first click.

Use **DoubleClickSize** to determine the height and width of the rectangle that Windows uses to determine whether the second click in a double-click sequence is in a valid location. The second click must occur within this rectangle for the operating system to consider the two clicks to be a double-click. The two clicks must also occur within a specified time range. See **DoubleClickTime**.

Requirements

Platforms: Windows 98, Windows NT 4.0,
Windows Millennium Edition, Windows 2000,
Windows XP Home Edition, Windows XP Professional,
Windows Server 2003 family

SystemInformation.DoubleClickTime Property

Gets the maximum number of milliseconds allowed between mouse clicks for a double-click to be valid.

```
[Visual Basic]
Public Shared ReadOnly Property DoubleClickTime As Integer
[C#]
public static int DoubleClickTime {get;}
[C++]
public: __property static int get_DoubleClickTime();
[JScript]
public static function get DoubleClickTime() : int;
```

Property Value

The maximum number of milliseconds allowed between mouse clicks for a double-click to be valid.

Remarks

A double-click is a series of two clicks of the mouse button, the second occurring within a specified length of time after the first. The double-click time is the maximum number of milliseconds that can occur between the first and second click of a double-click. For a double-click to be registered, it must also be within the same region. To determine this region, use **DoubleClickSize**.

Requirements

Platforms: Windows 98, Windows NT 4.0,
Windows Millennium Edition, Windows 2000,
Windows XP Home Edition, Windows XP Professional,
Windows Server 2003 family,
.NET Compact Framework - Windows CE .NET

SystemInformation.DragFullWindows Property

Gets a value indicating whether the user has enabled full window drag.

[Visual Basic]
```
Public Shared ReadOnly Property DragFullWindows As Boolean
```
[C#]
```
public static bool DragFullWindows {get;}
```
[C++]
```
public: __property static bool get_DragFullWindows();
```
[JScript]
```
public static function get DragFullWindows() : Boolean;
```

Property Value

true if the user has enabled full window drag; otherwise, **false**.

Remarks

When this property is **true**, the contents of windows are displayed when moving and sizing.

Requirements

Platforms: Windows 98, Windows NT 4.0, Windows Millennium Edition, Windows 2000, Windows XP Home Edition, Windows XP Professional, Windows Server 2003 family

SystemInformation.DragSize Property

Gets the dimensions, in pixels, of the rectangle that a drag operation must extend to be considered a drag operation. The rectangle is centered on a drag point.

[Visual Basic]
```
Public Shared ReadOnly Property DragSize As Size
```
[C#]
```
public static Size DragSize {get;}
```
[C++]
```
public: __property static Size get_DragSize();
```
[JScript]
```
public static function get DragSize() : Size;
```

Property Value

A **Size** that specifies the rectangle, in pixels, that a drag operation must extend to be considered a drag operation.

Remarks

Use **DragSize** to determine the size of the rectangle that Windows uses as a boundary before starting a drag operation. This rectangle allows limited movement before a drag operation begins, enabling the user to click and release the mouse button easily without unintentionally starting a drag operation.

Requirements

Platforms: Windows 98, Windows NT 4.0, Windows Millennium Edition, Windows 2000, Windows XP Home Edition, Windows XP Professional, Windows Server 2003 family

SystemInformation.FixedFrameBorderSize Property

Gets the thickness, in pixels, of the border for a window that has a caption and is not resizable.

[Visual Basic]
```
Public Shared ReadOnly Property FixedFrameBorderSize As Size
```
[C#]
```
public static Size FixedFrameBorderSize {get;}
```
[C++]
```
public: __property static Size get_FixedFrameBorderSize();
```
[JScript]
```
public static function get FixedFrameBorderSize() : Size;
```

Property Value

A **Size** that specifies the size, in pixels, of a fixed sized window border.

Requirements

Platforms: Windows 98, Windows NT 4.0, Windows Millennium Edition, Windows 2000, Windows XP Home Edition, Windows XP Professional, Windows Server 2003 family

SystemInformation.FrameBorderSize Property

Gets the thickness, in pixels, of the border for a window that can be resized.

[Visual Basic]
```
Public Shared ReadOnly Property FrameBorderSize As Size
```
[C#]
```
public static Size FrameBorderSize {get;}
```
[C++]
```
public: __property static Size get_FrameBorderSize();
```
[JScript]
```
public static function get FrameBorderSize() : Size;
```

Property Value

A **Size** that specifies the thickness, in pixels, of the border for a window that can be resized.

Requirements

Platforms: Windows 98, Windows NT 4.0, Windows Millennium Edition, Windows 2000, Windows XP Home Edition, Windows XP Professional, Windows Server 2003 family

SystemInformation.HighContrast Property

Gets a value indicating whether the user has selected to run in high-contrast mode.

[Visual Basic]
```
Public Shared ReadOnly Property HighContrast As Boolean
```
[C#]
```
public static bool HighContrast {get;}
```
[C++]
```
public: __property static bool get_HighContrast();
```
[JScript]
```
public static function get HighContrast() : Boolean;
```

Property Value

true if the user has enabled high-contrast mode; otherwise, **false**.

Requirements

Platforms: Windows 98, Windows NT 4.0, Windows Millennium Edition, Windows 2000, Windows XP Home Edition, Windows XP Professional, Windows Server 2003 family

SystemInformation.HorizontalScrollBarArrowWidth Property

Gets the width, in pixels, of the arrow bitmap on the horizontal scroll bar.

[Visual Basic]
```
Public Shared ReadOnly Property HorizontalScrollBarArrowWidth As _
   Integer
```
[C#]
```
public static int HorizontalScrollBarArrowWidth {get;}
```
[C++]
```
public: __property static int get_HorizontalScrollBarArrowWidth();
```
[JScript]
```
public static function get HorizontalScrollBarArrowWidth() : int;
```

Property Value

The width, in pixels, of a horizontal scroll bar arrow.

Requirements

Platforms: Windows 98, Windows NT 4.0, Windows Millennium Edition, Windows 2000, Windows XP Home Edition, Windows XP Professional, Windows Server 2003 family

SystemInformation.HorizontalScrollBarHeight Property

Gets the height, in pixels, of the horizontal scroll bar.

[Visual Basic]
```
Public Shared ReadOnly Property HorizontalScrollBarHeight As _
   Integer
```
[C#]
```
public static int HorizontalScrollBarHeight {get;}
```
[C++]
```
public: __property static int get_HorizontalScrollBarHeight();
```
[JScript]
```
public static function get HorizontalScrollBarHeight() : int;
```

Property Value

The height, in pixels, of a horizontal scroll bar.

Requirements

Platforms: Windows 98, Windows NT 4.0, Windows Millennium Edition, Windows 2000, Windows XP Home Edition, Windows XP Professional, Windows Server 2003 family

SystemInformation.HorizontalScrollBarThumbWidth Property

Gets the width, in pixels, of the scroll box in a horizontal scroll bar.

[Visual Basic]
```
Public Shared ReadOnly Property HorizontalScrollBarThumbWidth As _
   Integer
```
[C#]
```
public static int HorizontalScrollBarThumbWidth {get;}
```
[C++]
```
public: __property static int get_HorizontalScrollBarThumbWidth();
```
[JScript]
```
public static function get HorizontalScrollBarThumbWidth() : int;
```

Property Value

The width, in pixels, of the scroll box in a horizontal scroll bar.

Remarks

Use **HorizontalScrollBarThumbWidth** to determine the width of the scroll box used to indicate scroll bar position and to drag the scroll bar to a new position. The scroll box is also called the thumb.

Requirements

Platforms: Windows 98, Windows NT 4.0, Windows Millennium Edition, Windows 2000, Windows XP Home Edition, Windows XP Professional, Windows Server 2003 family

SystemInformation.IconSize Property

Gets the default dimensions, in pixels, of an icon.

[Visual Basic]
```
Public Shared ReadOnly Property IconSize As Size
```
[C#]
```
public static Size IconSize {get;}
```
[C++]
```
public: __property static Size get_IconSize();
```
[JScript]
```
public static function get IconSize() : Size;
```

Property Value

A **Size** that specifies the default dimensions of an icon in pixels.

Remarks

Use **IconSize** to determine the Windows default icon size. This property determines whether the size of icons displayed in your applications are consistent with icons displayed in Windows.

The icon size returned by this property represents the icon size for large icons.

Requirements

Platforms: Windows 98, Windows NT 4.0, Windows Millennium Edition, Windows 2000, Windows XP Home Edition, Windows XP Professional, Windows Server 2003 family

SystemInformation.IconSpacingSize Property

Gets the dimensions, in pixels, of the grid used to arrange icons in a large-icon view.

[Visual Basic]
```
Public Shared ReadOnly Property IconSpacingSize As Size
```
[C#]
```
public static Size IconSpacingSize {get;}
```
[C++]
```
public: __property static Size get_IconSpacingSize();
```
[JScript]
```
public static function get IconSpacingSize() : Size;
```

Property Value

A **Size** that specifies the dimensions, in pixels, of the grid used to arrange icons in a large-icon view.

Remarks

Use **IconSpacingSize** to determine the grid that each icon fits into when you arrange them. This value is always greater than or equal to **IconSize**.

Requirements

Platforms: Windows 98, Windows NT 4.0, Windows Millennium Edition, Windows 2000, Windows XP Home Edition, Windows XP Professional, Windows Server 2003 family

SystemInformation.KanjiWindowHeight Property

Gets the height, in pixels, of the Kanji window at the bottom of the screen for double-byte character set (DBCS) versions of Windows.

[Visual Basic]
```
Public Shared ReadOnly Property KanjiWindowHeight As Integer
```
[C#]
```
public static int KanjiWindowHeight {get;}
```
[C++]
```
public: __property static int get_KanjiWindowHeight();
```
[JScript]
```
public static function get KanjiWindowHeight() : int;
```

Property Value

The height of the Kanji window in pixels.

Remarks

Use **KanjiWindowHeight** to determine the height of the Kanji window on operating systems that support DBCS. To determine whether the operating system supports DBCS, use the **DbcsEnabled** property.

Requirements

Platforms: Windows 98, Windows NT 4.0, Windows Millennium Edition, Windows 2000, Windows XP Home Edition, Windows XP Professional, Windows Server 2003 family

SystemInformation.MaxWindowTrackSize Property

Gets the default maximum dimensions, in pixels, of a window that has a caption and sizing borders.

[Visual Basic]
```
Public Shared ReadOnly Property MaxWindowTrackSize As Size
```
[C#]
```
public static Size MaxWindowTrackSize {get;}
```
[C++]
```
public: __property static Size get_MaxWindowTrackSize();
```
[JScript]
```
public static function get MaxWindowTrackSize() : Size;
```

Property Value

A **Size** that specifies the maximum size to which a window can be sized.

Remarks

The value returned by **MaxWindowTrackSize** refers to dimensions of the entire desktop. The user cannot drag the window frame to a size larger than these dimensions. A **Form** can override this value by overriding the **MaximumSize** property.

Requirements

Platforms: Windows 98, Windows NT 4.0, Windows Millennium Edition, Windows 2000, Windows XP Home Edition, Windows XP Professional, Windows Server 2003 family

SystemInformation.MenuButtonSize Property

Gets the dimensions, in pixels, of menu bar buttons.

[Visual Basic]
```
Public Shared ReadOnly Property MenuButtonSize As Size
```
[C#]
```
public static Size MenuButtonSize {get;}
```
[C++]
```
public: __property static Size get_MenuButtonSize();
```
[JScript]
```
public static function get MenuButtonSize() : Size;
```

Property Value

A **Size** that specifies the dimensions, in pixels, of menu-bar buttons.

Remarks

Use this property to determine the size of a menu button, such as the child window close buttons used in a multiple-document-interface application. The dimensions of a menu button can be similar to the dimensions returned for caption buttons using **ToolWindowCaptionButtonSize**.

Requirements

Platforms: Windows 98, Windows NT 4.0, Windows Millennium Edition, Windows 2000, Windows XP Home Edition, Windows XP Professional, Windows Server 2003 family

SystemInformation.MenuCheckSize Property

Gets the dimensions, in pixels, of the default size of a menu check mark.

[Visual Basic]
```
Public Shared ReadOnly Property MenuCheckSize As Size
```
[C#]
```
public static Size MenuCheckSize {get;}
```
[C++]
```
public: __property static Size get_MenuCheckSize();
```
[JScript]
```
public static function get MenuCheckSize() : Size;
```

Property Value

A **Size** that specifies the default size of a menu check mark in pixels.

Remarks

Use **MenuCheckSize** to determine the size of the image used by Windows to display a check mark next to a selected menu item.

Requirements

Platforms: Windows 98, Windows NT 4.0, Windows Millennium Edition, Windows 2000, Windows XP Home Edition, Windows XP Professional, Windows Server 2003 family

SystemInformation.MenuFont Property

Gets the operating system font for menus.

[Visual Basic]
```
Public Shared ReadOnly Property MenuFont As Font
```
[C#]
```
public static Font MenuFont {get;}
```
[C++]
```
public: __property static Font* get_MenuFont();
```
[JScript]
```
public static function get MenuFont() : Font;
```

Property Value

The operating system **Font** for menus.

Example

See related example in the **System.Windows.Forms.SystemInformation** class topic.

Requirements

Platforms: Windows 98, Windows NT 4.0, Windows Millennium Edition, Windows 2000, Windows XP Home Edition, Windows XP Professional, Windows Server 2003 family

SystemInformation.MenuHeight Property

Gets the height of one line of a menu in pixels.

[Visual Basic]
```
Public Shared ReadOnly Property MenuHeight As Integer
```
[C#]
```
public static int MenuHeight {get;}
```
[C++]
```
public: __property static int get_MenuHeight();
```
[JScript]
```
public static function get MenuHeight() : int;
```

Property Value

The height of one line of a menu in pixels.

Remarks

Use **MenuHeight** to determine the height that is currently defined by Windows for a menu bar.

Requirements

Platforms: Windows 98, Windows NT 4.0, Windows Millennium Edition, Windows 2000, Windows XP Home Edition, Windows XP Professional, Windows Server 2003 family, .NET Compact Framework - Windows CE .NET

SystemInformation.MidEastEnabled Property

Gets a value indicating whether the operating system is enabled for Hebrew and Arabic languages.

[Visual Basic]
```
Public Shared ReadOnly Property MidEastEnabled As Boolean
```
[C#]
```
public static bool MidEastEnabled {get;}
```
[C++]
```
public: __property static bool get_MidEastEnabled();
```
[JScript]
```
public static function get MidEastEnabled() : Boolean;
```

Property Value

true if the operating system is enabled for Hebrew or Arabic; otherwise, **false**.

Requirements

Platforms: Windows 98, Windows NT 4.0, Windows Millennium Edition, Windows 2000, Windows XP Home Edition, Windows XP Professional, Windows Server 2003 family

SystemInformation.MinimizedWindowSize Property

Gets the dimensions, in pixels, of a normal minimized window.

[Visual Basic]
```
Public Shared ReadOnly Property MinimizedWindowSize As Size
```
[C#]
```
public static Size MinimizedWindowSize {get;}
```
[C++]
```
public: __property static Size get_MinimizedWindowSize();
```
[JScript]
```
public static function get MinimizedWindowSize() : Size;
```

Property Value

A **Size** that specifies the dimensions of a normal minimized window.

Requirements

Platforms: Windows 98, Windows NT 4.0, Windows Millennium Edition, Windows 2000, Windows XP Home Edition, Windows XP Professional, Windows Server 2003 family

SystemInformation.MinimizedWindowSpacingSize Property

Gets the dimensions, in pixels, of the grid into which minimized windows are placed.

[Visual Basic]
```
Public Shared ReadOnly Property MinimizedWindowSpacingSize As Size
```
[C#]
```
public static Size MinimizedWindowSpacingSize {get;}
```
[C++]
```
public: __property static Size get_MinimizedWindowSpacingSize();
```
[JScript]
```
public static function get MinimizedWindowSpacingSize() : Size;
```

Property Value

A **Size** that specifies the grid into which minimized windows are placed.

Remarks

Use **MinimizedWindowSpacingSize** to determine the rectangle to which a minimized window is sized when arranged. The value of this property is always greater than or equal to the value of the **MinimumWindowSize** property.

Requirements

Platforms: Windows 98, Windows NT 4.0, Windows Millennium Edition, Windows 2000, Windows XP Home Edition, Windows XP Professional, Windows Server 2003 family

SystemInformation.MinimumWindowSize Property

Gets the minimum allowable dimensions, in pixels, of a window.

[Visual Basic]
```
Public Shared ReadOnly Property MinimumWindowSize As Size
```
[C#]
```
public static Size MinimumWindowSize {get;}
```
[C++]
```
public: __property static Size get_MinimumWindowSize();
```
[JScript]
```
public static function get MinimumWindowSize() : Size;
```

Property Value

A **Size** that specifies the minimum allowable dimensions of a window in pixels.

Remarks

Use **MinimumWindowSize** to determine the dimensions specified by Windows as the minimum size for a window. You can use this property to limit the resizing of the windows of your application to a size larger than the dimension returned by this property.

Requirements

Platforms: Windows 98, Windows NT 4.0, Windows Millennium Edition, Windows 2000, Windows XP Home Edition, Windows XP Professional, Windows Server 2003 family

SystemInformation.MinWindowTrackSize Property

Gets the default minimum tracking dimensions, in pixels, of the operating system for a window.

[Visual Basic]
```
Public Shared ReadOnly Property MinWindowTrackSize As Size
```
[C#]
```
public static Size MinWindowTrackSize {get;}
```
[C++]
```
public: __property static Size get_MinWindowTrackSize();
```
[JScript]
```
public static function get MinWindowTrackSize() : Size;
```

Property Value

A **Size** that specifies default minimum tracking dimensions of the operating system for a window, in pixels.

Remarks

The user cannot drag the window frame to a size smaller than these dimensions. A Form can override these values by overriding the **MinimumSize**.

Requirements

Platforms: Windows 98, Windows NT 4.0, Windows Millennium Edition, Windows 2000, Windows XP Home Edition, Windows XP Professional, Windows Server 2003 family

SystemInformation.MonitorCount Property

Gets the number of display monitors on the desktop.

[Visual Basic]
```
Public Shared ReadOnly Property MonitorCount As Integer
```
[C#]
```
public static int MonitorCount {get;}
```
[C++]
```
public: __property static int get_MonitorCount();
```
[JScript]
```
public static function get MonitorCount() : int;
```

Property Value

The number of monitors that make up the desktop.

Remarks

This property returns a value greater than one only if multiple monitors are currently connected to the operating system.

Example

See related example in the **System.Windows.Forms.SystemInformation** class topic.

Requirements

Platforms: Windows 98, Windows NT 4.0, Windows Millennium Edition, Windows 2000, Windows XP Home Edition, Windows XP Professional, Windows Server 2003 family

SystemInformation.MonitorsSameDisplayFormat Property

Gets a value indicating whether all the display monitors have the same color format.

[Visual Basic]
```
Public Shared ReadOnly Property MonitorsSameDisplayFormat As _
   Boolean
```
[C#]
```
public static bool MonitorsSameDisplayFormat {get;}
```
[C++]
```
public: __property static bool get_MonitorsSameDisplayFormat();
```
[JScript]
```
public static function get MonitorsSameDisplayFormat() : Boolean;
```

Property Value

true if all monitors have the same color format; otherwise, **false**.

Remarks

Use **MonitorsSameDisplayFormat** to determine whether all monitors currently connected to the system have the same color format. For example, the RGB values can be encoded with a different number of bits, or those bits can be located in different places in a pixel's color value.

> **Note** Two displays can have the same bit depth but different color formats.

Example

See related example in the **System.Windows.Forms.SystemInformation** class topic.

Requirements

Platforms: Windows 98, Windows NT 4.0, Windows Millennium Edition, Windows 2000, Windows XP Home Edition, Windows XP Professional, Windows Server 2003 family

SystemInformation.MouseButtons Property

Gets the number of buttons on the mouse.

[Visual Basic]
```
Public Shared ReadOnly Property MouseButtons As Integer
```
[C#]
```
public static int MouseButtons {get;}
```
[C++]
```
public: __property static int get_MouseButtons();
```
[JScript]
```
public static function get MouseButtons() : int;
```

Property Value

The number of buttons on the mouse, or zero if no mouse is installed.

Remarks

Use **MouseButtons** to determine the number of mouse buttons that your application can support. You can also use **MouseButtons** to provide additional functionality if more than two buttons are available.

Requirements

Platforms: Windows 98, Windows NT 4.0,
Windows Millennium Edition, Windows 2000,
Windows XP Home Edition, Windows XP Professional,
Windows Server 2003 family

SystemInformation.MouseButtonsSwapped Property

Gets a value indicating whether the functions of the left and right mouse buttons have been swapped.

[Visual Basic]
```
Public Shared ReadOnly Property MouseButtonsSwapped As Boolean
```
[C#]
```
public static bool MouseButtonsSwapped {get;}
```
[C++]
```
public: __property static bool get_MouseButtonsSwapped();
```
[JScript]
```
public static function get MouseButtonsSwapped() : Boolean;
```

Property Value

true if the functions of the left and right mouse buttons are swapped; otherwise, **false**.

Remarks

Use **MouseButtonsSwapped** to determine whether the left and right mouse buttons have opposite usage. This property determines how the system responds to mouse button clicks and other mouse button events.

Example

See related example in the **System.Windows.Forms.SystemInformation** class topic.

Requirements

Platforms: Windows 98, Windows NT 4.0,
Windows Millennium Edition, Windows 2000,
Windows XP Home Edition, Windows XP Professional,
Windows Server 2003 family

SystemInformation.MousePresent Property

Gets a value indicating whether a mouse is installed.

[Visual Basic]
```
Public Shared ReadOnly Property MousePresent As Boolean
```
[C#]
```
public static bool MousePresent {get;}
```
[C++]
```
public: __property static bool get_MousePresent();
```
[JScript]
```
public static function get MousePresent() : Boolean;
```

Property Value

true if a mouse is installed; otherwise, **false**.

Example

See related example in the **System.Windows.Forms.SystemInformation** class topic.

Requirements

Platforms: Windows 98, Windows NT 4.0,
Windows Millennium Edition, Windows 2000,
Windows XP Home Edition, Windows XP Professional,
Windows Server 2003 family

SystemInformation.MouseWheelPresent Property

Gets a value indicating whether a mouse with a mouse wheel is installed.

[Visual Basic]
```
Public Shared ReadOnly Property MouseWheelPresent As Boolean
```
[C#]
```
public static bool MouseWheelPresent {get;}
```
[C++]
```
public: __property static bool get_MouseWheelPresent();
```
[JScript]
```
public static function get MouseWheelPresent() : Boolean;
```

Property Value

true if a mouse with a mouse wheel is installed; otherwise, **false**.

Remarks

Use this property to determine whether to process code that requires a mouse wheel.

Requirements

Platforms: Windows 98, Windows NT 4.0,
Windows Millennium Edition, Windows 2000,
Windows XP Home Edition, Windows XP Professional,
Windows Server 2003 family

SystemInformation.MouseWheelScrollLines Property

Gets the number of lines to scroll when the mouse wheel is rotated.

[Visual Basic]
```
Public Shared ReadOnly Property MouseWheelScrollLines As Integer
```
[C#]
```
public static int MouseWheelScrollLines {get;}
```
[C++]
```
public: __property static int get_MouseWheelScrollLines();
```

[JScript]
```
public static function get MouseWheelScrollLines() : int;
```

Property Value

The number of lines to scroll.

Remarks

Use this property to determine how many lines to increase or decrease in a control that has a scroll bar.

Requirements

Platforms: Windows 98, Windows NT 4.0, Windows Millennium Edition, Windows 2000, Windows XP Home Edition, Windows XP Professional, Windows Server 2003 family

SystemInformation.NativeMouseWheelSupport Property

Gets a value indicating whether the operating system natively supports a mouse wheel.

[Visual Basic]
```
Public Shared ReadOnly Property NativeMouseWheelSupport As Boolean
```
[C#]
```
public static bool NativeMouseWheelSupport {get;}
```
[C++]
```
public: __property static bool get_NativeMouseWheelSupport();
```
[JScript]
```
public static function get NativeMouseWheelSupport() : Boolean;
```

Property Value

true if the operating system natively supports a mouse wheel; otherwise, **false**.

Remarks

Mouse wheel operations that occur through a **Control** object work even if the operating system does not natively support the wheel.

Requirements

Platforms: Windows 98, Windows NT 4.0, Windows Millennium Edition, Windows 2000, Windows XP Home Edition, Windows XP Professional, Windows Server 2003 family

SystemInformation.Network Property

Gets a value indicating whether this computer is connected to a network.

[Visual Basic]
```
Public Shared ReadOnly Property Network As Boolean
```
[C#]
```
public static bool Network {get;}
```
[C++]
```
public: __property static bool get_Network();
```
[JScript]
```
public static function get Network() : Boolean;
```

Property Value

true if a network connection is present; otherwise, **false**.

Remarks

Use **Network** to determine whether a network is available before performing network-oriented operations.

Example

See related example in the **System.Windows.Forms.SystemInformation** class topic.

Requirements

Platforms: Windows 98, Windows NT 4.0, Windows Millennium Edition, Windows 2000, Windows XP Home Edition, Windows XP Professional, Windows Server 2003 family

SystemInformation.PenWindows Property

Gets a value indicating whether the Microsoft Windows for Pen Computing extensions are installed.

[Visual Basic]
```
Public Shared ReadOnly Property PenWindows As Boolean
```
[C#]
```
public static bool PenWindows {get;}
```
[C++]
```
public: __property static bool get_PenWindows();
```
[JScript]
```
public static function get PenWindows() : Boolean;
```

Property Value

true if the Windows for Pen Computing extensions are installed; **false** if Windows for Pen Computing extensions are not installed.

Requirements

Platforms: Windows 98, Windows NT 4.0, Windows Millennium Edition, Windows 2000, Windows XP Home Edition, Windows XP Professional, Windows Server 2003 family

SystemInformation.PrimaryMonitorMaximizedWindowSize Property

Gets the default dimensions, in pixels, of a maximized window on the primary monitor.

[Visual Basic]
```
Public Shared ReadOnly Property PrimaryMonitorMaximizedWindowSize _
   As Size
```
[C#]
```
public static Size PrimaryMonitorMaximizedWindowSize {get;}
```
[C++]
```
public: __property static Size
   get_PrimaryMonitorMaximizedWindowSize();
```
[JScript]
```
public static function get PrimaryMonitorMaximizedWindowSize() :
   Size;
```

Property Value

A **Size** that specifies the dimensions of a maximized window on the primary monitor.

Requirements

Platforms: Windows 98, Windows NT 4.0, Windows Millennium Edition, Windows 2000, Windows XP Home Edition, Windows XP Professional, Windows Server 2003 family

SystemInformation.PrimaryMonitorSize Property

Gets the dimensions, in pixels, of the primary display monitor.

[Visual Basic]
```
Public Shared ReadOnly Property PrimaryMonitorSize As Size
```
[C#]
```
public static Size PrimaryMonitorSize {get;}
```
[C++]
```
public: __property static Size get_PrimaryMonitorSize();
```
[JScript]
```
public static function get PrimaryMonitorSize() : Size;
```

Property Value

A **Size** that specifies the dimensions of the primary monitor in pixels.

Requirements

Platforms: Windows 98, Windows NT 4.0, Windows Millennium Edition, Windows 2000, Windows XP Home Edition, Windows XP Professional, Windows Server 2003 family

SystemInformation.RightAlignedMenus Property

Gets a value indicating whether drop-down menus are right-aligned with the corresponding menu-bar item.

[Visual Basic]
```
Public Shared ReadOnly Property RightAlignedMenus As Boolean
```
[C#]
```
public static bool RightAlignedMenus {get;}
```
[C++]
```
public: __property static bool get_RightAlignedMenus();
```
[JScript]
```
public static function get RightAlignedMenus() : Boolean;
```

Property Value

true if drop-down menus are right-aligned with the corresponding menu-bar item; **false** if the menus are left-aligned.

Requirements

Platforms: Windows 98, Windows NT 4.0, Windows Millennium Edition, Windows 2000, Windows XP Home Edition, Windows XP Professional, Windows Server 2003 family

SystemInformation.Secure Property

Gets a value indicating whether security is present on this operating system.

[Visual Basic]
```
Public Shared ReadOnly Property Secure As Boolean
```
[C#]
```
public static bool Secure {get;}
```
[C++]
```
public: __property static bool get_Secure();
```
[JScript]
```
public static function get Secure() : Boolean;
```

Property Value

true if security is present; otherwise, **false**.

Remarks

Secure allows you to determine whether a Security Manager is available from the operating system. Windows NT and Windows 2000 provide a Security Manager to determine access to the operating system registry and to the file system. Windows 98 does not provide a Security Manager.

Requirements

Platforms: Windows 98, Windows NT 4.0, Windows Millennium Edition, Windows 2000, Windows XP Home Edition, Windows XP Professional, Windows Server 2003 family

.NET Framework Security:

- **EnvironmentPermission** to get the value of this property. Associated enumeration: **PermissionState.Unrestricted**

SystemInformation.ShowSounds Property

Gets a value indicating whether the user requires an application to present information in visual form in situations when it would present the information in audible form.

[Visual Basic]
```
Public Shared ReadOnly Property ShowSounds As Boolean
```
[C#]
```
public static bool ShowSounds {get;}
```
[C++]
```
public: __property static bool get_ShowSounds();
```
[JScript]
```
public static function get ShowSounds() : Boolean;
```

Property Value

true if the application can visually show audible output; **false** if the application can freely use audio.

Remarks

Use **ShowSounds** to determine whether the application can play sounds and other audio outputs or whether the audio needs to be visually shown. This property can help provide accessibility to your application.

Requirements

Platforms: Windows 98, Windows NT 4.0, Windows Millennium Edition, Windows 2000, Windows XP Home Edition, Windows XP Professional, Windows Server 2003 family

SystemInformation.SmallIconSize Property

Gets the recommended dimensions, in pixels, of a small icon.

[Visual Basic]
```
Public Shared ReadOnly Property SmallIconSize As Size
```
[C#]
```
public static Size SmallIconSize {get;}
```
[C++]
```
public: __property static Size get_SmallIconSize();
```
[JScript]
```
public static function get SmallIconSize() : Size;
```

Property Value

A **Size** that specifies the dimensions of a small icon in pixels.

Remarks

Use **SmallIconSize** to determine the size of small icons in Windows. Small icons typically appear in window captions and in the Small Icon view in Windows Explorer.

Requirements

Platforms: Windows 98, Windows NT 4.0, Windows Millennium Edition, Windows 2000, Windows XP Home Edition, Windows XP Professional, Windows Server 2003 family

SystemInformation.ToolWindowCaptionButtonSize Property

Gets the dimensions, in pixels, of small caption buttons.

```
[Visual Basic]
Public Shared ReadOnly Property ToolWindowCaptionButtonSize As Size
[C#]
public static Size ToolWindowCaptionButtonSize {get;}
[C++]
public: __property static Size get_ToolWindowCaptionButtonSize();
[JScript]
public static function get ToolWindowCaptionButtonSize() : Size;
```

Property Value

A **Size** that specifies the dimensions of small caption buttons in pixels.

Remarks

Small captions are used in floating tool windows. Use **ToolWindowCaptionButtonSize** to get the dimensions of the buttons placed in the caption of a tool window. You can use this property when adding your own custom buttons to the caption in a tool window.

Requirements

Platforms: Windows 98, Windows NT 4.0, Windows Millennium Edition, Windows 2000, Windows XP Home Edition, Windows XP Professional, Windows Server 2003 family

SystemInformation.ToolWindowCaptionHeight Property

Gets the height, in pixels, of a small caption.

```
[Visual Basic]
Public Shared ReadOnly Property ToolWindowCaptionHeight As Integer
[C#]
public static int ToolWindowCaptionHeight {get;}
[C++]
public: __property static int get_ToolWindowCaptionHeight();
[JScript]
public static function get ToolWindowCaptionHeight() : int;
```

Property Value

The height of a small caption in pixels.

Remarks

Small captions are used in floating tool windows. Use **ToolWindowCaptionHeight** to determine the height of a tool window caption in Windows. This property can assist in manipulating the caption area of a tool window.

Requirements

Platforms: Windows 98, Windows NT 4.0, Windows Millennium Edition, Windows 2000, Windows XP Home Edition, Windows XP Professional, Windows Server 2003 family

SystemInformation.UserDomainName Property

Gets the name of the user domain.

```
[Visual Basic]
Public Shared ReadOnly Property UserDomainName As String
[C#]
public static string UserDomainName {get;}
[C++]
public: __property static String* get_UserDomainName();
[JScript]
public static function get UserDomainName() : String;
```

Property Value

The name of the user domain. If a local user account exists with the same name as the user name, this property gets the computer name.

Example

See related example in the **System.Windows.Forms.SystemInformation** class topic.

Requirements

Platforms: Windows 98, Windows NT 4.0, Windows Millennium Edition, Windows 2000, Windows XP Home Edition, Windows XP Professional, Windows Server 2003 family

.NET Framework Security:

- **EnvironmentPermission** to get the value of this property. Associated enumeration: **PermissionState.Unrestricted**

SystemInformation.UserInteractive Property

Gets a value indicating whether the current process is running in user-interactive mode.

```
[Visual Basic]
Public Shared ReadOnly Property UserInteractive As Boolean
[C#]
public static bool UserInteractive {get;}
[C++]
public: __property static bool get_UserInteractive();
[JScript]
public static function get UserInteractive() : Boolean;
```

Property Value

true if the current process is running in user-interactive mode; otherwise, **false**.

Remarks

This property is **false** only when running as a service process or from inside a Web application. When **UserInteractive** is **false**, do not display any modal dialogs or message boxes, as there is no GUI for the user to interact with.

Example

See related example in the **System.Windows.Forms.SystemInformation** class topic.

Requirements

Platforms: Windows 98, Windows NT 4.0, Windows Millennium Edition, Windows 2000, Windows XP Home Edition, Windows XP Professional, Windows Server 2003 family

SystemInformation.UserName Property

Gets the user name for the current thread (the name of the user currently logged on to the operating system).

```
[Visual Basic]
Public Shared ReadOnly Property UserName As String
[C#]
public static string UserName {get;}
[C++]
public: __property static String* get_UserName();
[JScript]
public static function get UserName() : String;
```

Property Value

The name of the user currently logged on to the operating system.

Example

See related example in the **System.Windows.Forms.SystemInformation** class topic.

Requirements

Platforms: Windows 98, Windows NT 4.0, Windows Millennium Edition, Windows 2000, Windows XP Home Edition, Windows XP Professional, Windows Server 2003 family

.NET Framework Security:

- **EnvironmentPermission** to get the value of this property. Associated enumeration: **PermissionState.Unrestricted**

SystemInformation.VerticalScrollBarArrowHeight Property

Gets the height, in pixels, of the arrow bitmap on the vertical scroll bar.

```
[Visual Basic]
Public Shared ReadOnly Property VerticalScrollBarArrowHeight As _
   Integer
[C#]
public static int VerticalScrollBarArrowHeight {get;}
[C++]
public: __property static int get_VerticalScrollBarArrowHeight();
[JScript]
public static function get VerticalScrollBarArrowHeight() : int;
```

Property Value

The height of a vertical scroll bar arrow.

Requirements

Platforms: Windows 98, Windows NT 4.0, Windows Millennium Edition, Windows 2000, Windows XP Home Edition, Windows XP Professional, Windows Server 2003 family

SystemInformation.VerticalScrollBarThumbHeight Property

Gets the height, in pixels, of the scroll box in a vertical scroll bar.

```
[Visual Basic]
Public Shared ReadOnly Property VerticalScrollBarThumbHeight As _
   Integer
[C#]
public static int VerticalScrollBarThumbHeight {get;}
[C++]
public: __property static int get_VerticalScrollBarThumbHeight();
[JScript]
public static function get VerticalScrollBarThumbHeight() : int;
```

Property Value

The height of the scroll box in a vertical scroll bar in pixels.

Remarks

Use **VerticalScrollBarThumbHeight** to determine the height of the box used to indicate scroll bar position and to drag the scroll bar to a new position. The scroll box is also called the thumb.

Requirements

Platforms: Windows 98, Windows NT 4.0, Windows Millennium Edition, Windows 2000, Windows XP Home Edition, Windows XP Professional, Windows Server 2003 family

SystemInformation.VerticalScrollBarWidth Property

Gets the width, in pixels, of the vertical scroll bar.

```
[Visual Basic]
Public Shared ReadOnly Property VerticalScrollBarWidth As Integer
[C#]
public static int VerticalScrollBarWidth {get;}
[C++]
public: __property static int get_VerticalScrollBarWidth();
[JScript]
public static function get VerticalScrollBarWidth() : int;
```

Property Value

The width of a vertical scroll bar in pixels.

Requirements

Platforms: Windows 98, Windows NT 4.0, Windows Millennium Edition, Windows 2000, Windows XP Home Edition, Windows XP Professional, Windows Server 2003 family

SystemInformation.VirtualScreen Property

Gets the bounds of the virtual screen.

[Visual Basic]
```
Public Shared ReadOnly Property VirtualScreen As Rectangle
```
[C#]
```
public static Rectangle VirtualScreen {get;}
```
[C++]
```
public: __property static Rectangle get_VirtualScreen();
```
[JScript]
```
public static function get VirtualScreen() : Rectangle;
```

Property Value

A **Rectangle** that specifies the bounding rectangle of the entire virtual screen.

Remarks

Use **VirtualScreen** to determine the bounds of the entire desktop on a multi-monitor system. You can then determine the maximum visual space available on a system that has multiple monitors installed.

> **Note** The left and top coordinates of the rectangle can be nonzero or negative.

Example

See related example in the **System.Windows.Forms.SystemInformation** class topic.

Requirements

Platforms: Windows 98, Windows NT 4.0,
Windows Millennium Edition, Windows 2000,
Windows XP Home Edition, Windows XP Professional,
Windows Server 2003 family

SystemInformation.WorkingArea Property

Gets the size, in pixels, of the working area.

[Visual Basic]
```
Public Shared ReadOnly Property WorkingArea As Rectangle
```
[C#]
```
public static Rectangle WorkingArea {get;}
```
[C++]
```
public: __property static Rectangle get_WorkingArea();
```
[JScript]
```
public static function get WorkingArea() : Rectangle;
```

Property Value

A **Rectangle** that represents the size of the working area in pixels.

Remarks

Use **WorkingArea** to determine the bounds of the screen that can be used by applications. The working area is the portion of the screen not hidden by the operating system tray and other top-level windows that are docked to the Windows desktop.

Requirements

Platforms: Windows 98, Windows NT 4.0,
Windows Millennium Edition, Windows 2000,
Windows XP Home Edition, Windows XP Professional,
Windows Server 2003 family

TabAlignment Enumeration

Specifies the locations of the tabs in a tab control.

[Visual Basic]

```
<Serializable>
Public Enum TabAlignment
```

[C#]

```
[Serializable]
public enum TabAlignment
```

[C++]

```
[Serializable]
__value public enum TabAlignment
```

[JScript]

```
public
   Serializable
enum TabAlignment
```

Remarks

This enumeration is used by members such as **TabControl.Alignment**.

Members

Member name	Description
Bottom	The tabs are located across the bottom of the control.
Left	The tabs are located along the left edge of the control.
Right	The tabs are located along the right edge of the control.
Top	The tabs are located across the top of the control.

Requirements

Namespace: System.Windows.Forms

Platforms: Windows 98, Windows NT 4.0, Windows Millennium Edition, Windows 2000, Windows XP Home Edition, Windows XP Professional, Windows Server 2003 family

Assembly: System.Windows.Forms (in System.Windows.Forms.dll)

TabAppearance Enumeration

Specifies the appearance of the tabs in a tab control.

[Visual Basic]
```
<Serializable>
Public Enum TabAppearance
```
[C#]
```
[Serializable]
public enum TabAppearance
```
[C++]
```
[Serializable]
__value public enum TabAppearance
```
[JScript]
```
public
   Serializable
enum TabAppearance
```

Remarks

This enumeration is used by members such as **TabControl.Appearance**.

Members

Member name	Description
Buttons	The tabs have the appearance of three-dimensional buttons.
FlatButtons	The tabs have the appearance of flat buttons.
Normal	The tabs have the standard appearance of tabs.

Requirements

Namespace: System.Windows.Forms

Platforms: Windows 98, Windows NT 4.0, Windows Millennium Edition, Windows 2000, Windows XP Home Edition, Windows XP Professional, Windows Server 2003 family

Assembly: System.Windows.Forms (in System.Windows.Forms.dll)

TabControl Class

Manages a related set of tab pages.

System.Object
System.MarshalByRefObject
System.ComponentModel.Component
System.Windows.Forms.Control
System.Windows.Forms.TabControl

[Visual Basic]
```
Public Class TabControl
   Inherits Control
```
[C#]
```
public class TabControl : Control
```
[C++]
```
public __gc class TabControl : public Control
```
[JScript]
```
public class TabControl extends Control
```

Thread Safety

Any public static (**Shared** in Visual Basic) members of this type are safe for multithreaded operations. Any instance members are not guaranteed to be thread safe.

Remarks

A **TabControl** contains tab pages, which are represented by **TabPage** objects that you add through the **Controls** property.

> **Note** The following events are not raised for the **TabControl** class unless there is at least one **TabPage** in the **TabControl.TabPages** collection: **Control.Click**, **Control.DoubleClick**, **Control.MouseDown**, **Control.MouseUp**, **Control.MouseHover**, **Control.MouseEnter**, **Control.MouseLeave** and **Control.MouseMove**. If there is at least one **TabPage** in the collection, and the user interacts with the tab control's header (where the **TabPage** names appear), the **TabControl** raises the appropriate event. However, if the user interaction is within the **ClientRectangle** of the tab page, the **TabPage** raises the appropriate event.

Example

[Visual Basic, C#] The following example uses the Visual Studio .NET Windows Forms Designer to create a **TabControl** with three tab pages. Each tab page contains several controls.

[Visual Basic]
```
Public Class Form1
    Inherits System.Windows.Forms.Form
    ' Required designer variable.
    Private components As System.ComponentModel.Container

    ' Declares variables.
    Private tab3RadioButton2 As System.Windows.Forms.RadioButton
    Private tab3RadioButton1 As System.Windows.Forms.RadioButton
    Private tab2CheckBox3 As System.Windows.Forms.CheckBox
    Private tab2CheckBox2 As System.Windows.Forms.CheckBox
    Private tab2CheckBox1 As System.Windows.Forms.CheckBox
    Private tab1Label1 As System.Windows.Forms.Label
    Private WithEvents tab1Button1 As System.Windows.Forms.Button
    Private tabPage3 As System.Windows.Forms.TabPage
    Private tabPage2 As System.Windows.Forms.TabPage
    Private tabPage1 As System.Windows.Forms.TabPage
    Private tabControl1 As System.Windows.Forms.TabControl

    Public Sub New()
        ' This call is required for Windows Form Designer support.
        InitializeComponent()
    End Sub

    ' This method is required for Designer support.
    Private Sub InitializeComponent()
        Me.components = New System.ComponentModel.Container()
        Me.tabPage1 = New System.Windows.Forms.TabPage()
        Me.tab2CheckBox3 = New System.Windows.Forms.CheckBox()
        Me.tab3RadioButton2 = New System.Windows.Forms.RadioButton()
        Me.tabControl1 = New System.Windows.Forms.TabControl()
        Me.tab2CheckBox2 = New System.Windows.Forms.CheckBox()
        Me.tab2CheckBox1 = New System.Windows.Forms.CheckBox()
        Me.tab3RadioButton1 = New System.Windows.Forms.RadioButton()
        Me.tab1Label1 = New System.Windows.Forms.Label()
        Me.tabPage3 = New System.Windows.Forms.TabPage()
        Me.tabPage2 = New System.Windows.Forms.TabPage()
        Me.tab1Button1 = New System.Windows.Forms.Button()

        tabPage1.Text = "tabPage1"
        tabPage1.Size = New System.Drawing.Size(256, 214)
        tabPage1.TabIndex = 0
        tab2CheckBox3.Location = New System.Drawing.Point(32, 136)
        tab2CheckBox3.Text = "checkBox3"
        tab2CheckBox3.Size = New System.Drawing.Size(176, 32)
        tab2CheckBox3.TabIndex = 2
        tab2CheckBox3.Visible = True
        tab3RadioButton2.Location = New System.Drawing.Point(40, 72)
        tab3RadioButton2.Text = "radioButton2"
        tab3RadioButton2.Size = New System.Drawing.Size(152, 24)
        tab3RadioButton2.TabIndex = 1
        tab3RadioButton2.Visible = True
        tabControl1.Location = New System.Drawing.Point(16, 16)
        tabControl1.Size = New System.Drawing.Size(264, 240)
        tabControl1.SelectedIndex = 0
        tabControl1.TabIndex = 0
        tab2CheckBox2.Location = New System.Drawing.Point(32, 80)
        tab2CheckBox2.Text = "checkBox2"
        tab2CheckBox2.Size = New System.Drawing.Size(176, 32)
        tab2CheckBox2.TabIndex = 1
        tab2CheckBox2.Visible = True
        tab2CheckBox1.Location = New System.Drawing.Point(32, 24)
        tab2CheckBox1.Text = "checkBox1"
        tab2CheckBox1.Size = New System.Drawing.Size(176, 32)
        tab2CheckBox1.TabIndex = 0
        tab3RadioButton1.Location = New System.Drawing.Point(40, 32)
        tab3RadioButton1.Text = "radioButton1"
        tab3RadioButton1.Size = New System.Drawing.Size(152, 24)
        tab3RadioButton1.TabIndex = 0
        tab1Label1.Location = New System.Drawing.Point(16, 24)
        tab1Label1.Text = "label1"
        tab1Label1.Size = New System.Drawing.Size(224, 96)
        tab1Label1.TabIndex = 1
        tabPage3.Text = "tabPage3"
        tabPage3.Size = New System.Drawing.Size(256, 214)
        tabPage3.TabIndex = 2
        tabPage2.Text = "tabPage2"
        tabPage2.Size = New System.Drawing.Size(256, 214)
        tabPage2.TabIndex = 1
        tab1Button1.Location = New System.Drawing.Point(88, 144)
        tab1Button1.Size = New System.Drawing.Size(80, 40)
        tab1Button1.TabIndex = 0
        tab1Button1.Text = "button1"
        Me.Text = "Form1"
        Me.AutoScaleBaseSize = New System.Drawing.Size(5, 13)

        ' Adds controls to the second tab page.
        tabPage2.Controls.Add(Me.tab2CheckBox3)
        tabPage2.Controls.Add(Me.tab2CheckBox2)
        tabPage2.Controls.Add(Me.tab2CheckBox1)
        ' Adds controls to the third tab page.
        tabPage3.Controls.Add(Me.tab3RadioButton2)
        tabPage3.Controls.Add(Me.tab3RadioButton1)
        ' Adds controls to the first tab page.
        tabPage1.Controls.Add(Me.tab1Label1)
        tabPage1.Controls.Add(Me.tab1Button1)
        ' Adds the TabControl to the form.
```

```
        Me.Controls.Add(tabControl1)
        ' Adds the tab pages to the TabControl.
        tabControl1.Controls.Add(Me.tabPage1)
        tabControl1.Controls.Add(Me.tabPage2)
        tabControl1.Controls.Add(Me.tabPage3)
    End Sub

    Private Sub tab1Button1_Click(sender As Object, e As ↵
System.EventArgs) _
        Handles tab1Button1.Click

        ' Inserts the code that should run when the button is clicked.
    End Sub

    Public Shared Sub Main()
        Application.Run(New Form1())
    End Sub

End Class
```

[C#]

```
public class Form1 : System.Windows.Forms.Form
{
    // Required designer variable.
    private System.ComponentModel.Container components;

    // Declare variables.
    private System.Windows.Forms.RadioButton tab3RadioButton2;
    private System.Windows.Forms.RadioButton tab3RadioButton1;
    private System.Windows.Forms.CheckBox tab2CheckBox3;
    private System.Windows.Forms.CheckBox tab2CheckBox2;
    private System.Windows.Forms.CheckBox tab2CheckBox1;
    private System.Windows.Forms.Label tab1Label1;
    private System.Windows.Forms.Button tab1Button1;
    private System.Windows.Forms.TabPage tabPage3;
    private System.Windows.Forms.TabPage tabPage2;
    private System.Windows.Forms.TabPage tabPage1;
    private System.Windows.Forms.TabControl tabControl1;

    public Form1()
    {
        // This call is required for Windows Form Designer support.
        InitializeComponent();
    }

    // This method is required for Designer support.
    private void InitializeComponent()
    {
        this.components = new System.ComponentModel.Container();
        this.tabPage1 = new System.Windows.Forms.TabPage();
        this.tab2CheckBox3 = new System.Windows.Forms.CheckBox();
        this.tab3RadioButton2 = new System.Windows.Forms.RadioButton();
        this.tabControl1 = new System.Windows.Forms.TabControl();
        this.tab2CheckBox2 = new System.Windows.Forms.CheckBox();
        this.tab2CheckBox1 = new System.Windows.Forms.CheckBox();
        this.tab3RadioButton1 = new System.Windows.Forms.RadioButton();
        this.tab1Label1 = new System.Windows.Forms.Label();
        this.tabPage3 = new System.Windows.Forms.TabPage();
        this.tabPage2 = new System.Windows.Forms.TabPage();
        this.tab1Button1 = new System.Windows.Forms.Button();

        tabPage1.Text = "tabPage1";
        tabPage1.Size = new System.Drawing.Size(256, 214);
        tabPage1.TabIndex = 0;
        tab2CheckBox3.Location = new System.Drawing.Point(32, 136);
        tab2CheckBox3.Text = "checkBox3";
        tab2CheckBox3.Size = new System.Drawing.Size(176, 32);
        tab2CheckBox3.TabIndex = 2;
        tab2CheckBox3.Visible = true;
        tab3RadioButton2.Location = new System.Drawing.Point(40, 72);
        tab3RadioButton2.Text = "radioButton2";
        tab3RadioButton2.Size = new System.Drawing.Size(152, 24);
        tab3RadioButton2.TabIndex = 1;
        tab3RadioButton2.Visible = true;
        tabControl1.Location = new System.Drawing.Point(16, 16);
        tabControl1.Size = new System.Drawing.Size(264, 240);
        tabControl1.SelectedIndex = 0;
        tabControl1.TabIndex = 0;
        tab2CheckBox2.Location = new System.Drawing.Point(32, 80);
        tab2CheckBox2.Text = "checkBox2";
        tab2CheckBox2.Size = new System.Drawing.Size(176, 32);
        tab2CheckBox2.TabIndex = 1;
        tab2CheckBox2.Visible = true;
        tab2CheckBox1.Location = new System.Drawing.Point(32, 24);
        tab2CheckBox1.Text = "checkBox1";
        tab2CheckBox1.Size = new System.Drawing.Size(176, 32);
        tab2CheckBox1.TabIndex = 0;
        tab3RadioButton1.Location = new System.Drawing.Point(40, 32);
        tab3RadioButton1.Text = "radioButton1";
        tab3RadioButton1.Size = new System.Drawing.Size(152, 24);
        tab3RadioButton1.TabIndex = 0;
        tab1Label1.Location = new System.Drawing.Point(16, 24);
        tab1Label1.Text = "label1";
        tab1Label1.Size = new System.Drawing.Size(224, 96);
        tab1Label1.TabIndex = 1;
        tabPage3.Text = "tabPage3";
        tabPage3.Size = new System.Drawing.Size(256, 214);
        tabPage3.TabIndex = 2;
        tabPage2.Text = "tabPage2";
        tabPage2.Size = new System.Drawing.Size(256, 214);
        tabPage2.TabIndex = 1;
        tab1Button1.Location = new System.Drawing.Point(88, 144);
        tab1Button1.Size = new System.Drawing.Size(80, 40);
        tab1Button1.TabIndex = 0;
        tab1Button1.Text = "button1";
        tab1Button1.Click += new
           System.EventHandler(this.tab1Button1_Click);
        this.Text = "Form1";
        this.AutoScaleBaseSize = new System.Drawing.Size(5, 13);

        // Adds controls to the second tab page.
        tabPage2.Controls.Add(this.tab2CheckBox3);
        tabPage2.Controls.Add(this.tab2CheckBox2);
        tabPage2.Controls.Add(this.tab2CheckBox1);
        // Adds controls to the third tab page.
        tabPage3.Controls.Add(this.tab3RadioButton2);
        tabPage3.Controls.Add(this.tab3RadioButton1);
        // Adds controls to the first tab page.
        tabPage1.Controls.Add(this.tab1Label1);
        tabPage1.Controls.Add(this.tab1Button1);
        // Adds the TabControl to the form.
        this.Controls.Add(this.tabControl1);
        // Adds the tab pages to the TabControl.
        tabControl1.Controls.Add(this.tabPage1);
        tabControl1.Controls.Add(this.tabPage2);
        tabControl1.Controls.Add(this.tabPage3);
    }

    private void tab1Button1_Click (object sender, System.EventArgs e)
    {
        // Inserts the code that should run when the button is clicked.
    }

    public static void Main(string[] args)
    {
        Application.Run(new Form1());
    }
}
```

Requirements

Namespace: System.Windows.Forms

Platforms: Windows 98, Windows NT 4.0, Windows Millennium Edition, Windows 2000, Windows XP Home Edition, Windows XP Professional, Windows Server 2003 family, .NET Compact Framework - Windows CE .NET

Assembly: System.Windows.Forms (in System.Windows.Forms.dll)

TabControl Constructor

Initializes a new instance of the **TabControl** class.

```
[Visual Basic]
Public Sub New()
[C#]
public TabControl();
[C++]
public: TabControl();
[JScript]
public function TabControl();
```

Example

See related example in **System.Windows.Forms.TabControl** class topic.

Requirements

Platforms: Windows 98, Windows NT 4.0, Windows Millennium Edition, Windows 2000, Windows XP Home Edition, Windows XP Professional, Windows Server 2003 family, .NET Compact Framework - Windows CE .NET

TabControl.Alignment Property

Gets or sets the area of the control (for example, along the top) where the tabs are aligned.

```
[Visual Basic]
Public Property Alignment As TabAlignment
[C#]
public TabAlignment Alignment {get; set;}
[C++]
public: __property TabAlignment get_Alignment();
public: __property void set_Alignment(TabAlignment);
[JScript]
public function get Alignment() : TabAlignment;
public function set Alignment(TabAlignment);
```

Property Value

One of the **TabAlignment** values. The default is **Top**.

Exceptions

Exception Type	Condition
InvalidEnumArgument-Exception	The property value is not a valid **TabAlignment** value.

Remarks

When the **Alignment** property is set to **Left** or **Right**, the **Multiline** property is automatically set to **true**.

When you set the **Appearance** property to **FlatButtons**, it only appears as such when the **Alignment** property is set to **Top**. Otherwise, the **Appearance** property displays as if set to the **Buttons** value.

> **Note** When you set the **Appearance** property to **Buttons**, you must also set the **Alignment** property to **Top** so that the buttons display correctly.

Example

See related example in **System.Windows.Forms.TabControl** class topic.

Requirements

Platforms: Windows 98, Windows NT 4.0, Windows Millennium Edition, Windows 2000, Windows XP Home Edition, Windows XP Professional, Windows Server 2003 family

TabControl.Appearance Property

Gets or sets the visual appearance of the control's tabs.

```
[Visual Basic]
Public Property Appearance As TabAppearance
[C#]
public TabAppearance Appearance {get; set;}
[C++]
public: __property TabAppearance get_Appearance();
public: __property void set_Appearance(TabAppearance);
[JScript]
public function get Appearance() : TabAppearance;
public function set Appearance(TabAppearance);
```

Property Value

One of the **TabAppearance** values. The default is **Normal**.

Exceptions

Exception Type	Condition
InvalidEnumArgument-Exception	The property value is not a valid **TabAppearance** value.

Remarks

When you set the **Appearance** property to **FlatButtons**, it only appears as such when the **Alignment** property is set to **Top**. Otherwise, the **Appearance** property appears as if set to the **Buttons** value.

> **Note** When you set the **Appearance** property to **Buttons**, you must also set the **Alignment** property to **Top** so that the buttons display correctly.

Example

See related example in **System.Windows.Forms.TabControl** class topic.

Requirements

Platforms: Windows 98, Windows NT 4.0, Windows Millennium Edition, Windows 2000, Windows XP Home Edition, Windows XP Professional, Windows Server 2003 family

TabControl.BackColor Property

This member overrides **Control.BackColor**.

```
[Visual Basic]
Overrides Public Property BackColor As Color
[C#]
public override Color BackColor {get; set;}
[C++]
public: __property Color get_BackColor();
public: __property void set_BackColor(Color);
[JScript]
public override function get BackColor() : Color;
public override function set BackColor(Color);
```

Requirements

Platforms: Windows 98, Windows NT 4.0, Windows Millennium Edition, Windows 2000, Windows XP Home Edition, Windows XP Professional, Windows Server 2003 family

TabControl.BackgroundImage Property

This member overrides **Control.BackgroundImage**.

```
[Visual Basic]
Overrides Public Property BackgroundImage As Image
[C#]
public override Image BackgroundImage {get; set;}
[C++]
public: __property Image* get_BackgroundImage();
public: __property void set_BackgroundImage(Image*);
[JScript]
public override function get BackgroundImage() : Image;
public override function set BackgroundImage(Image);
```

Requirements

Platforms: Windows 98, Windows NT 4.0, Windows Millennium Edition, Windows 2000, Windows XP Home Edition, Windows XP Professional, Windows Server 2003 family

TabControl.CreateParams Property

This member overrides **Control.CreateParams**.

```
[Visual Basic]
Overrides Protected ReadOnly Property CreateParams As CreateParams
[C#]
protected override CreateParams CreateParams {get;}
[C++]
protected: __property CreateParams* get_CreateParams();
[JScript]
protected override function get CreateParams() : CreateParams;
```

Requirements

Platforms: Windows 98, Windows NT 4.0, Windows Millennium Edition, Windows 2000, Windows XP Home Edition, Windows XP Professional, Windows Server 2003 family

TabControl.DefaultSize Property

This member overrides **Control.DefaultSize**.

```
[Visual Basic]
Overrides Protected ReadOnly Property DefaultSize As Size
[C#]
protected override Size DefaultSize {get;}
[C++]
protected: __property Size get_DefaultSize();
[JScript]
protected override function get DefaultSize() : Size;
```

Requirements

Platforms: Windows 98, Windows NT 4.0, Windows Millennium Edition, Windows 2000, Windows XP Home Edition, Windows XP Professional, Windows Server 2003 family

TabControl.DisplayRectangle Property

Gets the display area of the control's tab pages.

```
[Visual Basic]
Overrides Public ReadOnly Property DisplayRectangle As Rectangle
[C#]
public override Rectangle DisplayRectangle {get;}
[C++]
public: __property Rectangle get_DisplayRectangle();
[JScript]
public override function get DisplayRectangle() : Rectangle;
```

Property Value

A **Rectangle** that represents the display area of the tab pages.

Example

See related example in **System.Windows.Forms.TabControl** class topic.

Requirements

Platforms: Windows 98, Windows NT 4.0, Windows Millennium Edition, Windows 2000, Windows XP Home Edition, Windows XP Professional, Windows Server 2003 family

TabControl.DrawMode Property

Gets or sets the way that the control's tab pages are drawn.

```
[Visual Basic]
Public Property DrawMode As TabDrawMode
[C#]
public TabDrawMode DrawMode {get; set;}
[C++]
public: __property TabDrawMode get_DrawMode();
public: __property void set_DrawMode(TabDrawMode);
[JScript]
public function get DrawMode() : TabDrawMode;
public function set DrawMode(TabDrawMode);
```

Property Value

One of the **TabDrawMode** values. The default is **Normal**.

Exceptions

Exception Type	Condition
InvalidEnumArgument-Exception	The property value is not a valid **TabDrawMode** value.

Remarks

Tab pages can be drawn by the control or by the user of the control. The **DrawMode** property allows users of the control to customize the way that the tab control is drawn.

Example

See related example in **System.Windows.Forms.TabControl** class topic.

Requirements

Platforms: Windows 98, Windows NT 4.0, Windows Millennium Edition, Windows 2000, Windows XP Home Edition, Windows XP Professional, Windows Server 2003 family

TabControl.ForeColor Property

This member overrides **Control.ForeColor**.

[Visual Basic]
```
Overrides Public Property ForeColor As Color
```
[C#]
```
public override Color ForeColor {get; set;}
```
[C++]
```
public: __property Color get_ForeColor();
public: __property void set_ForeColor(Color);
```
[JScript]
```
public override function get ForeColor() : Color;
public override function set ForeColor(Color);
```

Requirements

Platforms: Windows 98, Windows NT 4.0, Windows Millennium Edition, Windows 2000, Windows XP Home Edition, Windows XP Professional, Windows Server 2003 family

TabControl.HotTrack Property

Gets or sets a value indicating whether the control's tabs change in appearance when the mouse passes over them.

[Visual Basic]
```
Public Property HotTrack As Boolean
```
[C#]
```
public bool HotTrack {get; set;}
```
[C++]
```
public: __property bool get_HotTrack();
public: __property void set_HotTrack(bool);
```
[JScript]
```
public function get HotTrack() : Boolean;
public function set HotTrack(Boolean);
```

Property Value

true if the tabs change in appearance when the mouse passes over them; otherwise, **false**. The default is **false**.

Remarks

The color that the tab changes to when the mouse is over it is determined by the local computer's system colors. To change the system colors, use Control Panel.

Example

See related example in **System.Windows.Forms.TabControl** class topic.

Requirements

Platforms: Windows 98, Windows NT 4.0, Windows Millennium Edition, Windows 2000, Windows XP Home Edition, Windows XP Professional, Windows Server 2003 family

TabControl.ImageList Property

Gets or sets the images to display on the control's tabs.

[Visual Basic]
```
Public Property ImageList As ImageList
```
[C#]
```
public ImageList ImageList {get; set;}
```
[C++]
```
public: __property ImageList* get_ImageList();
public: __property void set_ImageList(ImageList*);
```
[JScript]
```
public function get ImageList() : ImageList;
public function set ImageList(ImageList);
```

Property Value

An **ImageList** that specifies the images to display on the tabs.

Remarks

To display an image on a tab, set the **ImageIndex** property of that **TabPage**. The **ImageIndex** acts as the index into the **ImageList**.

Example

See related example in **System.Windows.Forms.TabControl** class topic.

Requirements

Platforms: Windows 98, Windows NT 4.0, Windows Millennium Edition, Windows 2000, Windows XP Home Edition, Windows XP Professional, Windows Server 2003 family

TabControl.ItemSize Property

Gets or sets the size of the control's tabs.

[Visual Basic]
```
Public Property ItemSize As Size
```
[C#]
```
public Size ItemSize {get; set;}
```
[C++]
```
public: __property Size get_ItemSize();
public: __property void set_ItemSize(Size);
```
[JScript]
```
public function get ItemSize() : Size;
public function set ItemSize(Size);
```

Property Value

A **Size** that represents the size of the tabs. The default automatically sizes the tabs to fit the icons and labels on the tabs.

Exceptions

Exception Type	Condition
ArgumentException	The width or height of the **Size** is less than 0.

Remarks

To change the **Width** property of the **ItemSize** property, the **SizeMode** property must be set to **Fixed**.

Example

See related example in **System.Windows.Forms.TabControl** class topic.

Requirements

Platforms: Windows 98, Windows NT 4.0, Windows Millennium Edition, Windows 2000, Windows XP Home Edition, Windows XP Professional, Windows Server 2003 family

TabControl.Multiline Property

Gets or sets a value indicating whether more than one row of tabs can be displayed.

```
[Visual Basic]
Public Property Multiline As Boolean
[C#]
public bool Multiline {get; set;}
[C++]
public: __property bool get_Multiline();
public: __property void set_Multiline(bool);
[JScript]
public function get Multiline() : Boolean;
public function set Multiline(Boolean);
```

Property Value

true if more than one row of tabs can be displayed; otherwise, **false**. The default is **false**.

Remarks

If **Multiline** is **false**, only one row of tabs is displayed, even if all the tabs do not fit in the available space. In that case, however, arrows are displayed that allow the user to navigate to the undisplayed tabs.

If the **Multiline** property is changed to **false** while the **Alignment** property is set to **Left** or **Right**, the **Alignment** property is automatically reset to **Top**.

Example

See related example in **System.Windows.Forms.TabControl** class topic.

Requirements

Platforms: Windows 98, Windows NT 4.0,
Windows Millennium Edition, Windows 2000,
Windows XP Home Edition, Windows XP Professional,
Windows Server 2003 family

TabControl.Padding Property

Gets or sets the amount of space around each item on the control's tab pages.

```
[Visual Basic]
Public Property Padding As Point
[C#]
public Point Padding {get; set;}
[C++]
public: __property Point get_Padding();
public: __property void set_Padding(Point);
[JScript]
public function get Padding() : Point;
public function set Padding(Point);
```

Property Value

A **Point** that specifies the amount of space to pad each item with. The default is (6,3).

Exceptions

Exception Type	Condition
ArgumentException	The width or height of the **Point** is less than 0.

Example

See related example in **System.Windows.Forms.TabControl** class topic.

Requirements

Platforms: Windows 98, Windows NT 4.0,
Windows Millennium Edition, Windows 2000,
Windows XP Home Edition, Windows XP Professional,
Windows Server 2003 family

TabControl.RowCount Property

Gets the number of rows that are currently being displayed in the control's tab strip.

```
[Visual Basic]
Public ReadOnly Property RowCount As Integer
[C#]
public int RowCount {get;}
[C++]
public: __property int get_RowCount();
[JScript]
public function get RowCount() : int;
```

Property Value

The number of rows that are currently being displayed in the tab strip.

Remarks

Use the **RowCount** property when the **Multiline** property is **true** and you want to know the number of rows that the tabs occupy.

Example

See related example in **System.Windows.Forms.TabControl** class topic.

Requirements

Platforms: Windows 98, Windows NT 4.0,
Windows Millennium Edition, Windows 2000,
Windows XP Home Edition, Windows XP Professional,
Windows Server 2003 family

TabControl.SelectedIndex Property

Gets or sets the index of the currently-selected tab page.

```
[Visual Basic]
Public Property SelectedIndex As Integer
[C#]
public int SelectedIndex {get; set;}
[C++]
public: __property int get_SelectedIndex();
public: __property void set_SelectedIndex(int);
[JScript]
public function get SelectedIndex() : int;
public function set SelectedIndex(int);
```

Property Value

The 0-based index of the currently-selected tab page. The default is -1, which is also the value if no tab page is selected.

Exceptions

Exception Type	Condition
ArgumentException	The value is less than -1.

Example

See related example in **System.Windows.Forms.TabControl** class topic.

Requirements

Platforms: Windows 98, Windows NT 4.0, Windows Millennium Edition, Windows 2000, Windows XP Home Edition, Windows XP Professional, Windows Server 2003 family, .NET Compact Framework - Windows CE .NET

TabControl.SelectedTab Property

Gets or sets the currently-selected tab page.

```
[Visual Basic]
Public Property SelectedTab As TabPage
[C#]
public TabPage SelectedTab {get; set;}
[C++]
public: __property TabPage* get_SelectedTab();
public: __property void set_SelectedTab(TabPage*);
[JScript]
public function get SelectedTab() : TabPage;
public function set SelectedTab(TabPage);
```

Property Value

A **TabPage** that represents the selected tab page. If no tab page is selected, the value is a null reference (**Nothing** in Visual Basic).

Remarks

The selection to the given tab, provided it equals a tab in the list.

Example

See related example in **System.Windows.Forms.TabControl** class topic.

Requirements

Platforms: Windows 98, Windows NT 4.0, Windows Millennium Edition, Windows 2000, Windows XP Home Edition, Windows XP Professional, Windows Server 2003 family

TabControl.ShowToolTips Property

Gets or sets a value indicating whether a tab's ToolTip is shown when the mouse passes over the tab.

```
[Visual Basic]
Public Property ShowToolTips As Boolean
[C#]
public bool ShowToolTips {get; set;}
[C++]
public: __property bool get_ShowToolTips();
public: __property void set_ShowToolTips(bool);
[JScript]
public function get ShowToolTips() : Boolean;
public function set ShowToolTips(Boolean);
```

Property Value

true if ToolTips are shown for the tabs that have them; otherwise, **false**. The default is **false**.

Remarks

To create a ToolTip for a tab, set the **ToolTipText** property of the **TabPage**.

Example

See related example in **System.Windows.Forms.TabControl** class topic.

Requirements

Platforms: Windows 98, Windows NT 4.0, Windows Millennium Edition, Windows 2000, Windows XP Home Edition, Windows XP Professional, Windows Server 2003 family

TabControl.SizeMode Property

Gets or sets the way that the control's tabs are sized.

```
[Visual Basic]
Public Property SizeMode As TabSizeMode
[C#]
public TabSizeMode SizeMode {get; set;}
[C++]
public: __property TabSizeMode get_SizeMode();
public: __property void set_SizeMode(TabSizeMode);
[JScript]
public function get SizeMode() : TabSizeMode;
public function set SizeMode(TabSizeMode);
```

Property Value

One of the **TabSizeMode** values. The default is **Normal**.

Exceptions

Exception Type	Condition
InvalidEnumArgument-Exception	The property value is not a valid **TabSizeMode** value.

Example

See related example in **System.Windows.Forms.TabControl** class topic.

Requirements

Platforms: Windows 98, Windows NT 4.0, Windows Millennium Edition, Windows 2000, Windows XP Home Edition, Windows XP Professional, Windows Server 2003 family

TabControl.TabCount Property

Gets the number of tabs in the tab strip.

```
[Visual Basic]
Public ReadOnly Property TabCount As Integer
[C#]
public int TabCount {get;}
[C++]
public: __property int get_TabCount();
[JScript]
public function get TabCount() : int;
```

Property Value

The number of tabs in the tab strip.

Example

See related example in **System.Windows.Forms.TabControl** class topic.

Requirements

Platforms: Windows 98, Windows NT 4.0, Windows Millennium Edition, Windows 2000, Windows XP Home Edition, Windows XP Professional, Windows Server 2003 family

TabControl.TabPages Property

Gets the collection of tab pages in this tab control.

```
[Visual Basic]
Public ReadOnly Property TabPages As TabControl.TabPageCollection
[C#]
public TabControl.TabPageCollection TabPages {get;}
[C++]
public: __property TabControl.TabPageCollection* get_TabPages();
[JScript]
public function get TabPages() : TabControl.TabPageCollection;
```

Property Value

A **TabControl.TabPageCollection** that contains the **TabPage** objects in this **TabControl**.

Example

See related example in **System.Windows.Forms.TabControl** class topic.

Requirements

Platforms: Windows 98, Windows NT 4.0, Windows Millennium Edition, Windows 2000, Windows XP Home Edition, Windows XP Professional, Windows Server 2003 family, .NET Compact Framework - Windows CE .NET

TabControl.Text Property

This member overrides **Control.Text**.

```
[Visual Basic]
Overrides Public Property Text As String
[C#]
public override string Text {get; set;}
[C++]
public: __property String* get_Text();
public: __property void set_Text(String*);
[JScript]
public override function get Text() : String;
public override function set Text(String);
```

Requirements

Platforms: Windows 98, Windows NT 4.0, Windows Millennium Edition, Windows 2000, Windows XP Home Edition, Windows XP Professional, Windows Server 2003 family

TabControl.CreateControlsInstance Method

This member overrides **Control.CreateControlsInstance**.

```
[Visual Basic]
Overrides Protected Function CreateControlsInstance() As _
   ControlCollection
[C#]
protected override ControlCollection CreateControlsInstance();
[C++]
protected: ControlCollection* CreateControlsInstance();
[JScript]
protected override function CreateControlsInstance() :
   ControlCollection;
```

Requirements

Platforms: Windows 98, Windows NT 4.0, Windows Millennium Edition, Windows 2000, Windows XP Home Edition, Windows XP Professional, Windows Server 2003 family

TabControl.CreateHandle Method

This member overrides **Control.CreateHandle**.

```
[Visual Basic]
Overrides Protected Sub CreateHandle()
[C#]
protected override void CreateHandle();
[C++]
protected: void CreateHandle();
[JScript]
protected override function CreateHandle();
```

Requirements

Platforms: Windows 98, Windows NT 4.0, Windows Millennium Edition, Windows 2000, Windows XP Home Edition, Windows XP Professional, Windows Server 2003 family

TabControl.Dispose Method

Overload List

This member supports the .NET Framework infrastructure and is not intended to be used directly from your code.

Supported by the .NET Compact Framework.

[Visual Basic] **Overloads Overrides Protected Sub Dispose(Boolean)**

[C#] **protected override void Dispose(bool);**

[C++] **protected: void Dispose(bool);**

[JScript] **protected override function Dispose(Boolean);**

Inherited from **Component**.

Supported by the .NET Compact Framework.

[Visual Basic] **Overloads Public Overridable Sub Dispose() Implements IDisposable.Dispose**

[C#] **public virtual void Dispose();**

[C++] **public: virtual void Dispose();**

[JScript] **public function Dispose();**

TabControl.Dispose Method (Boolean)

This member overrides **Control.Dispose**.

```
[Visual Basic]
Overrides Overloads Protected Sub Dispose( _
   ByVal disposing As Boolean _
)
[C#]
protected override void Dispose(
   bool disposing
);
[C++]
protected: void Dispose(
   bool disposing
);
[JScript]
protected override function Dispose(
   disposing : Boolean
);
```

Requirements

Platforms: Windows 98, Windows NT 4.0, Windows Millennium Edition, Windows 2000, Windows XP Home Edition, Windows XP Professional, Windows Server 2003 family, .NET Compact Framework - Windows CE .NET

TabControl.GetControl Method

This member supports the .NET Framework infrastructure and is not intended to be used directly from your code.

```
[Visual Basic]
Public Function GetControl( _
   ByVal index As Integer _
) As Control
[C#]
public Control GetControl(
   int index
);
[C++]
public: Control* GetControl(
   int index
);
[JScript]
public function GetControl(
   index : int
) : Control;
```

TabControl.GetItems Method

This member supports the .NET Framework infrastructure and is not intended to be used directly from your code.

Overload List

This member supports the .NET Framework infrastructure and is not intended to be used directly from your code.

[Visual Basic] **Overloads Protected Overridable Function GetItems() As Object()**

[C#] **protected virtual object[] GetItems();**

[C++] **protected: virtual Object* GetItems() __gc[];**

[JScript] **protected function GetItems() : Object[];**

This member supports the .NET Framework infrastructure and is not intended to be used directly from your code.

[Visual Basic] **Overloads Protected Overridable Function GetItems(Type) As Object()**

[C#] **protected virtual object[] GetItems(Type);**

[C++] **protected: virtual Object* GetItems(Type*) __gc[];**

[JScript] **protected function GetItems(Type) : Object[];**

TabControl.GetItems Method ()

This member supports the .NET Framework infrastructure and is not intended to be used directly from your code.

```
[Visual Basic]
Overloads Protected Overridable Function GetItems() As Object()
[C#]
protected virtual object[] GetItems();
[C++]
protected: virtual Object* GetItems() __gc[];
[JScript]
protected function GetItems() : Object[];
```

TabControl.GetItems Method (Type)

This member supports the .NET Framework infrastructure and is not intended to be used directly from your code.

```
[Visual Basic]
Overloads Protected Overridable Function GetItems( _
   ByVal baseType As Type _
) As Object()
[C#]
protected virtual object[] GetItems(
   Type baseType
);
[C++]
protected: virtual Object* GetItems(
   Type* baseType
) __gc[];
[JScript]
protected function GetItems(
   baseType : Type
) : Object[];
```

TabControl.GetTabRect Method

Returns the bounding rectangle for a specified tab in this tab control.

```
[Visual Basic]
Public Function GetTabRect( _
   ByVal index As Integer _
) As Rectangle
[C#]
public Rectangle GetTabRect(
   int index
);
[C++]
public: Rectangle GetTabRect(
   int index
);
[JScript]
public function GetTabRect(
   index : int
) : Rectangle;
```

Parameters

index

The 0-based index of the tab you want.

Return Value

A **Rectangle** that represents the bounds of the specified tab.

Exceptions

Exception Type	Condition
ArgumentOutOfRange-Exception	The index is less than zero. -or- The index is greater than or equal to **Count**.

Example

See related example in **System.Windows.Forms.TabControl** class topic.

Requirements

Platforms: Windows 98, Windows NT 4.0, Windows Millennium Edition, Windows 2000, Windows XP Home Edition, Windows XP Professional, Windows Server 2003 family

TabControl.GetToolTipText Method

This member supports the .NET Framework infrastructure and is not intended to be used directly from your code.

[Visual Basic]
```
Protected Function GetToolTipText( _
   ByVal item As Object _
) As String
```
[C#]
```
protected string GetToolTipText(
   object item
);
```
[C++]
```
protected: String* GetToolTipText(
   Object* item
);
```
[JScript]
```
protected function GetToolTipText(
   item : Object
) : String;
```

TabControl.IsInputKey Method

Determines whether the specified key is a regular input key or a special key that requires preprocessing.

[Visual Basic]
```
Overrides Protected Function IsInputKey( _
   ByVal keyData As Keys _
) As Boolean
```
[C#]
```
protected override bool IsInputKey(
   Keys keyData
);
```
[C++]
```
protected: bool IsInputKey(
   Keys keyData
);
```
[JScript]
```
protected override function IsInputKey(
   keyData : Keys
) : Boolean;
```

Parameters

keyData

One of the **Keys** values.

Return Value

true if the specified key is a regular input key; otherwise, **false**.

Remarks

Call this method during window-message preprocessing to determine whether the specified key is a regular input key that should be sent directly to the tab control or a special key (such as PAGE UP and PAGE DOWN) that should preprocessed. In the latter case, send the key to the control only if it is not consumed by the preprocessing phase.

Requirements

Platforms: Windows 98, Windows NT 4.0, Windows Millennium Edition, Windows 2000, Windows XP Home Edition, Windows XP Professional, Windows Server 2003 family

TabControl.OnDrawItem Method

Raises the **DrawItem** event.

[Visual Basic]
```
Protected Overridable Sub OnDrawItem( _
   ByVal e As DrawItemEventArgs _
)
```
[C#]
```
protected virtual void OnDrawItem(
   DrawItemEventArgs e
);
```
[C++]
```
protected: virtual void OnDrawItem(
   DrawItemEventArgs* e
);
```
[JScript]
```
protected function OnDrawItem(
   e : DrawItemEventArgs
);
```

Parameters

e

A **DrawItemEventArgs** that contains the event data.

Remarks

Raising an event invokes the event handler through a delegate.

The **OnDrawItem** method also allows derived classes to handle the event without attaching a delegate. This is the preferred technique for handling the event in a derived class.

Notes to Inheritors: When overriding **OnDrawItem** in a derived class, be sure to call the base class's **OnDrawItem** method so that registered delegates receive the event.

Requirements

Platforms: Windows 98, Windows NT 4.0, Windows Millennium Edition, Windows 2000, Windows XP Home Edition, Windows XP Professional, Windows Server 2003 family

TabControl.OnFontChanged Method

Raises the **FontChanged** event.

```
[Visual Basic]
Overrides Protected Sub OnFontChanged( _
   ByVal e As EventArgs _
)
[C#]
protected override void OnFontChanged(
   EventArgs e
);
[C++]
protected: void OnFontChanged(
   EventArgs* e
);
[JScript]
protected override function OnFontChanged(
   e : EventArgs
);
```

Parameters

e

An **EventArgs** that contains the event data.

Remarks

Raising an event invokes the event handler through a delegate.

The **OnFontChanged** method also allows derived classes to handle the event without attaching a delegate. This is the preferred technique for handling the event in a derived class.

Notes to Inheritors: When overriding **OnFontChanged** in a derived class, be sure to call the base class's **OnFontChanged** method so that registered delegates receive the event.

Requirements

Platforms: Windows 98, Windows NT 4.0, Windows Millennium Edition, Windows 2000, Windows XP Home Edition, Windows XP Professional, Windows Server 2003 family

TabControl.OnHandleCreated Method

This member overrides **Control.OnHandleCreated**.

```
[Visual Basic]
Overrides Protected Sub OnHandleCreated( _
   ByVal e As EventArgs _
)
[C#]
protected override void OnHandleCreated(
   EventArgs e
);
[C++]
protected: void OnHandleCreated(
   EventArgs* e
);
[JScript]
protected override function OnHandleCreated(
   e : EventArgs
);
```

Requirements

Platforms: Windows 98, Windows NT 4.0, Windows Millennium Edition, Windows 2000, Windows XP Home Edition, Windows XP Professional, Windows Server 2003 family

TabControl.OnHandleDestroyed Method

Raises the **Control.HandleDestroyed** event.

```
[Visual Basic]
Overrides Protected Sub OnHandleDestroyed( _
   ByVal e As EventArgs _
)
[C#]
protected override void OnHandleDestroyed(
   EventArgs e
);
[C++]
protected: void OnHandleDestroyed(
   EventArgs* e
);
[JScript]
protected override function OnHandleDestroyed(
   e : EventArgs
);
```

Parameters

e

An **EventArgs** that contains the event data.

Remarks

Raising an event invokes the event handler through a delegate.

The **OnHandleDestroyed** method also allows derived classes to handle the event without attaching a delegate. This is the preferred technique for handling the event in a derived class.

Notes to Inheritors: When overriding **OnHandleDestroyed** in a derived class, be sure to call the base class's **OnHandleDestroyed** method so that registered delegates receive the event.

Requirements

Platforms: Windows 98, Windows NT 4.0, Windows Millennium Edition, Windows 2000, Windows XP Home Edition, Windows XP Professional, Windows Server 2003 family

TabControl.OnKeyDown Method

This member overrides **Control.OnKeyDown**.

```
[Visual Basic]
Overrides Protected Sub OnKeyDown( _
   ByVal ke As KeyEventArgs _
)
[C#]
protected override void OnKeyDown(
   KeyEventArgs ke
);
[C++]
protected: void OnKeyDown(
   KeyEventArgs* ke
);
[JScript]
protected override function OnKeyDown(
   ke : KeyEventArgs
);
```

Requirements

Platforms: Windows 98, Windows NT 4.0,
Windows Millennium Edition, Windows 2000,
Windows XP Home Edition, Windows XP Professional,
Windows Server 2003 family,
.NET Compact Framework - Windows CE .NET

TabControl.OnResize Method

This member overrides **Control.OnResize**.

[Visual Basic]
```
Overrides Protected Sub OnResize( _
   ByVal e As EventArgs _
)
```
[C#]
```
protected override void OnResize(
   EventArgs e
);
```
[C++]
```
protected: void OnResize(
   EventArgs* e
);
```
[JScript]
```
protected override function OnResize(
   e : EventArgs
);
```

Requirements

Platforms: Windows 98, Windows NT 4.0,
Windows Millennium Edition, Windows 2000,
Windows XP Home Edition, Windows XP Professional,
Windows Server 2003 family,
.NET Compact Framework - Windows CE .NET

TabControl.OnSelectedIndexChanged Method

Raises the **SelectedIndexChanged** event.

[Visual Basic]
```
Protected Overridable Sub OnSelectedIndexChanged( _
   ByVal e As EventArgs _
)
```
[C#]
```
protected virtual void OnSelectedIndexChanged(
   EventArgs e
);
```
[C++]
```
protected: virtual void OnSelectedIndexChanged(
   EventArgs* e
);
```
[JScript]
```
protected function OnSelectedIndexChanged(
   e : EventArgs
);
```

Parameters

e

An **EventArgs** that contains the event data.

Remarks

Raising an event invokes the event handler through a delegate.

The **OnSelectedIndexChanged** method also allows derived classes to handle the event without attaching a delegate. This is the preferred technique for handling the event in a derived class.

Notes to Inheritors: When overriding **OnSelectedIndexChanged** in a derived class, be sure to call the base class's **OnSelectedIndexChanged** method so that registered delegates receive the event.

Requirements

Platforms: Windows 98, Windows NT 4.0,
Windows Millennium Edition, Windows 2000,
Windows XP Home Edition, Windows XP Professional,
Windows Server 2003 family,
.NET Compact Framework - Windows CE .NET

TabControl.OnStyleChanged Method

This member overrides **Control.OnStyleChanged**.

[Visual Basic]
```
Overrides Protected Sub OnStyleChanged( _
   ByVal e As EventArgs _
)
```
[C#]
```
protected override void OnStyleChanged(
   EventArgs e
);
```
[C++]
```
protected: void OnStyleChanged(
   EventArgs* e
);
```
[JScript]
```
protected override function OnStyleChanged(
   e : EventArgs
);
```

Requirements

Platforms: Windows 98, Windows NT 4.0,
Windows Millennium Edition, Windows 2000,
Windows XP Home Edition, Windows XP Professional,
Windows Server 2003 family

TabControl.ProcessKeyPreview Method

This member overrides **Control.ProcessKeyPreview**.

[Visual Basic]
```
Overrides Protected Function ProcessKeyPreview( _
   ByRef m As Message _
) As Boolean
```
[C#]
```
protected override bool ProcessKeyPreview(
   ref Message m
);
```
[C++]
```
protected: bool ProcessKeyPreview(
   Message* m
);
```
[JScript]
```
protected override function ProcessKeyPreview(
   m : Message
) : Boolean;
```

Requirements

Platforms: Windows 98, Windows NT 4.0, Windows Millennium Edition, Windows 2000, Windows XP Home Edition, Windows XP Professional, Windows Server 2003 family

TabControl.RemoveAll Method

Removes all the tab pages and additional controls from this tab control.

```
[Visual Basic]
Protected Sub RemoveAll()
[C#]
protected void RemoveAll();
[C++]
protected: void RemoveAll();
[JScript]
protected function RemoveAll();
```

Remarks

All controls are removed through the Controls property.

Requirements

Platforms: Windows 98, Windows NT 4.0, Windows Millennium Edition, Windows 2000, Windows XP Home Edition, Windows XP Professional, Windows Server 2003 family

TabControl.ToString Method

This member overrides **Object.ToString**.

```
[Visual Basic]
Overrides Public Function ToString() As String
[C#]
public override string ToString();
[C++]
public: String* ToString();
[JScript]
public override function ToString() : String;
```

Requirements

Platforms: Windows 98, Windows NT 4.0, Windows Millennium Edition, Windows 2000, Windows XP Home Edition, Windows XP Professional, Windows Server 2003 family, .NET Compact Framework - Windows CE .NET

TabControl.UpdateTabSelection Method

This member supports the .NET Framework infrastructure and is not intended to be used directly from your code.

```
[Visual Basic]
Protected Sub UpdateTabSelection( _
   ByVal uiselected As Boolean _
)
[C#]
protected void UpdateTabSelection(
   bool uiselected
);
[C++]
protected: void UpdateTabSelection(
   bool uiselected
);
[JScript]
protected function UpdateTabSelection(
   uiselected : Boolean
);
```

TabControl.WndProc Method

This member overrides **Control.WndProc**.

```
[Visual Basic]
Overrides Protected Sub WndProc( _
   ByRef m As Message _
)
[C#]
protected override void WndProc(
   ref Message m
);
[C++]
protected: void WndProc(
   Message* m
);
[JScript]
protected override function WndProc(
   m : Message
);
```

Requirements

Platforms: Windows 98, Windows NT 4.0, Windows Millennium Edition, Windows 2000, Windows XP Home Edition, Windows XP Professional, Windows Server 2003 family

TabControl.BackColorChanged Event

This member supports the .NET Framework infrastructure and is not intended to be used directly from your code.

```
[Visual Basic]
Public Shadows Event BackColorChanged As EventHandler
[C#]
public new event EventHandler BackColorChanged;
[C++]
public: __event EventHandler* BackColorChanged;
```

[JScript] In JScript, you can handle the events defined by a class, but you cannot define your own.

TabControl.BackgroundImageChanged Event

This member supports the .NET Framework infrastructure and is not intended to be used directly from your code.

```
[Visual Basic]
Public Shadows Event BackgroundImageChanged As EventHandler
[C#]
public new event EventHandler BackgroundImageChanged;
[C++]
public: __event EventHandler* BackgroundImageChanged;
```

[JScript] In JScript, you can handle the events defined by a class, but you cannot define your own.

TabControl.DrawItem Event

Occurs when the tabs are drawn, if the **DrawMode** property is set to **OwnerDrawFixed**.

[Visual Basic]
```
Public Event DrawItem As DrawItemEventHandler
```
[C#]
```
public event DrawItemEventHandler DrawItem;
```
[C++]
```
public: __event DrawItemEventHandler* DrawItem;
```

[JScript] In JScript, you can handle the events defined by a class, but you cannot define your own.

Event Data

The event handler receives an argument of type **DrawItemEventArgs** containing data related to this event. The following **DrawItemEventArgs** properties provide information specific to this event.

Property	Description
BackColor	Gets the background color of the item that is being drawn.
Bounds	Gets the rectangle that represents the bounds of the item that is being drawn.
Font	Gets the font assigned to the item being drawn.
ForeColor	Gets the foreground color of the of the item being drawn.
Graphics	Gets the graphics surface to draw the item on.
Index	Gets the index value of the item that is being drawn.
State	Gets the state of the item being drawn.

Example

See related example in **System.Windows.Forms.TabControl** class topic.

Requirements

Platforms: Windows 98, Windows NT 4.0, Windows Millennium Edition, Windows 2000, Windows XP Home Edition, Windows XP Professional, Windows Server 2003 family

TabControl.ForeColorChanged Event

This member supports the .NET Framework infrastructure and is not intended to be used directly from your code.

[Visual Basic]
```
Public Shadows Event ForeColorChanged As EventHandler
```
[C#]
```
public new event EventHandler ForeColorChanged;
```
[C++]
```
public: __event EventHandler* ForeColorChanged;
```

[JScript] In JScript, you can handle the events defined by a class, but you cannot define your own.

TabControl.Paint Event

This member supports the .NET Framework infrastructure and is not intended to be used directly from your code.

[Visual Basic]
```
Public Shadows Event Paint As PaintEventHandler
```
[C#]
```
public new event PaintEventHandler Paint;
```
[C++]
```
public: __event PaintEventHandler* Paint;
```

[JScript] In JScript, you can handle the events defined by a class, but you cannot define your own.

TabControl.SelectedIndexChanged Event

Occurs when the **SelectedIndex** property is changed.

[Visual Basic]
```
Public Event SelectedIndexChanged As EventHandler
```
[C#]
```
public event EventHandler SelectedIndexChanged;
```
[C++]
```
public: __event EventHandler* SelectedIndexChanged;
```

[JScript] In JScript, you can handle the events defined by a class, but you cannot define your own.

Event Data

The event handler receives an argument of type **EventArgs**.

Requirements

Platforms: Windows 98, Windows NT 4.0, Windows Millennium Edition, Windows 2000, Windows XP Home Edition, Windows XP Professional, Windows Server 2003 family

TabControl.TextChanged Event

This member supports the .NET Framework infrastructure and is not intended to be used directly from your code.

[Visual Basic]
```
Public Shadows Event TextChanged As EventHandler
```
[C#]
```
public new event EventHandler TextChanged;
```
[C++]
```
public: __event EventHandler* TextChanged;
```

[JScript] In JScript, you can handle the events defined by a class, but you cannot define your own.

TabControl.ControlCollection Class

Contains a collection of **Control** objects.

System.Object
  System.Windows.Forms.Control.ControlCollection
    System.Windows.Forms.TabControl.ControlCollection

```
[Visual Basic]
Public Class TabControl.ControlCollection
   Inherits Control.ControlCollection
[C#]
public class TabControl.ControlCollection :
   Control.ControlCollection
[C++]
public __gc class TabControl.ControlCollection : public
   Control.ControlCollection
[JScript]
public class TabControl.ControlCollection extends
   Control.ControlCollection
```

Thread Safety

Any public static (**Shared** in Visual Basic) members of this type are safe for multithreaded operations. Any instance members are not guaranteed to be thread safe.

Requirements

Namespace: System.Windows.Forms

Platforms: Windows 98, Windows NT 4.0, Windows Millennium Edition, Windows 2000, Windows XP Home Edition, Windows XP Professional, Windows Server 2003 family

Assembly: System.Windows.Forms (in System.Windows.Forms.dll)

TabControl.ControlCollection Constructor

This member supports the .NET Framework infrastructure and is not intended to be used directly from your code.

```
[Visual Basic]
Public Sub New( _
   ByVal owner As TabControl _
)
[C#]
public TabControl.ControlCollection(
   TabControl owner
);
[C++]
public: ControlCollection(
   TabControl* owner
);
[JScript]
public function TabControl.ControlCollection(
   owner : TabControl
);
```

TabControl.ControlCollection.Add Method

Adds a **Control** to the collection.

```
[Visual Basic]
Overrides Public Sub Add( _
   ByVal value As Control _
)
[C#]
public override void Add(
   Control value
);
[C++]
public: void Add(
   Control* value
);
[JScript]
public override function Add(
   value : Control
);
```

Parameters

value
  The **Control** to add.

Exceptions

Exception Type	Condition
Exception	The specified **Control** is a **TabPage**.

Remarks

You cannot add a **TabPage** to a **TabPage**.

Requirements

Platforms: Windows 98, Windows NT 4.0, Windows Millennium Edition, Windows 2000, Windows XP Home Edition, Windows XP Professional, Windows Server 2003 family

TabControl.ControlCollection.Remove Method

Removes a **Control** from the collection.

```
[Visual Basic]
Overrides Public Sub Remove( _
   ByVal value As Control _
)
[C#]
public override void Remove(
   Control value
);
[C++]
public: void Remove(
   Control* value
);
[JScript]
public override function Remove(
   value : Control
);
```

Parameters

value
  The **Control** to remove.

Requirements

Platforms: Windows 98, Windows NT 4.0, Windows Millennium Edition, Windows 2000, Windows XP Home Edition, Windows XP Professional, Windows Server 2003 family

TabControl.TabPageCollection Class

Contains a collection of **TabPage** objects.

System.Object
  System.Windows.Forms.TabControl.TabPageCollection

[Visual Basic]
```
Public Class TabControl.TabPageCollection
   Implements IList, ICollection, IEnumerable
```
[C#]
```
public class TabControl.TabPageCollection : IList, ICollection,
   IEnumerable
```
[C++]
```
public __gc class TabControl.TabPageCollection : public IList,
   ICollection, IEnumerable
```
[JScript]
```
public class TabControl.TabPageCollection implements IList,
   ICollection, IEnumerable
```

Thread Safety

Any public static (**Shared** in Visual Basic) members of this type are safe for multithreaded operations. Any instance members are not guaranteed to be thread safe.

Requirements

Namespace: System.Windows.Forms

Platforms: Windows 98, Windows NT 4.0, Windows Millennium Edition, Windows 2000, Windows XP Home Edition, Windows XP Professional, Windows Server 2003 family, .NET Compact Framework - Windows CE .NET

Assembly: System.Windows.Forms (in System.Windows.Forms.dll)

TabControl.TabPageCollection Constructor

Initializes a new instance of the **TabControl.TabPageCollection** class.

[Visual Basic]
```
Public Sub New( _
   ByVal owner As TabControl _
)
```
[C#]
```
public TabControl.TabPageCollection(
   TabControl owner
);
```
[C++]
```
public: TabPageCollection(
   TabControl* owner
);
```
[JScript]
```
public function TabControl.TabPageCollection(
   owner : TabControl
);
```

Parameters

owner
  The **TabControl** that this collection belongs to.

Exceptions

Exception Type	Condition
ArgumentNull-Exception	The specified **TabControl** is a null reference (**Nothing** in Visual Basic).

Requirements

Platforms: Windows 98, Windows NT 4.0, Windows Millennium Edition, Windows 2000, Windows XP Home Edition, Windows XP Professional, Windows Server 2003 family, .NET Compact Framework - Windows CE .NET

TabControl.TabPageCollection.Count Property

Gets the number of tab pages in the collection.

[Visual Basic]
```
Public Overridable ReadOnly Property Count As Integer  Implements _
   ICollection.Count
```
[C#]
```
public virtual int Count {get;}
```
[C++]
```
public: __property virtual int get_Count();
```
[JScript]
```
public function get Count() : int;
```

Property Value

The number of tab pages in the collection.

Implements

ICollection.Count

Example

[Visual Basic, C#, C++] The following example creates a **TabControl** with three **TabPage**. The **Count** property gets the number of **TabPage** objects in the `tabControl1` controls collection.

[Visual Basic, C#, C++] Use the **System.Drawing** and **System.Windows.Forms** namespaces for this example.

[Visual Basic]
```
Imports System.Drawing
Imports System.Windows.Forms

Public Class Form1
    Inherits Form
    Private tabControl1 As TabControl
    Private tabPage1 As TabPage
    Private tabPage2 As TabPage
    Private tabPage3 As TabPage
    Private label1 As Label

    Public Sub New()
        Me.tabControl1 = New TabControl()
        Me.tabPage1 = New TabPage()
        Me.tabPage2 = New TabPage()
        Me.tabPage3 = New TabPage()
        Me.label1 = New Label()

        Me.tabControl1.TabPages.AddRange(New TabPage()                    ↵
{tabPage1, tabPage2, tabPage3})
        Me.tabControl1.Location = New Point(25, 75)
        Me.tabControl1.Size = New Size(250, 200)

        ' Gets the number of TabPage objects in the                       ↵
tabControl1 controls collection.
        Dim tabCount As Integer =                                         ↵
tabControl1.TabPages.Count
```

```
        Me.label1.Location = New Point(25, 25)
        Me.label1.Size = New Size(250, 25)
        Me.label1.Text = "The TabControl below has " +                ↵
tabCount.ToString() + _
            " TabPage objects in its controls collection."

        Me.ClientSize = New Size(300, 300)
        Me.Controls.AddRange(New Control() {tabControl1, label1})
    End Sub

    Shared Sub Main()
        Application.Run(New Form1())
    End Sub
End Class
```

[C#]

```
using System.Drawing;
using System.Windows.Forms;

public class Form1 : Form
{
    private TabControl tabControl1;
    private TabPage tabPage1;
    private TabPage tabPage2;
    private TabPage tabPage3;
    private Label label1;

    public Form1()
    {
        this.tabControl1 = new TabControl();
        this.tabPage1 = new TabPage();
        this.tabPage2 = new TabPage();
        this.tabPage3 = new TabPage();
        this.label1 = new Label();

        this.tabControl1.TabPages.AddRange(new TabPage[] {
            tabPage1, tabPage2, tabPage3});

        this.tabControl1.Location = new Point(25, 75);
        this.tabControl1.Size = new Size(250, 200);

        // Gets the number of TabPage objects in the                ↵
tabControl1 controls collection.
        int tabCount = tabControl1.TabPages.Count;

        this.label1.Location = new Point(25, 25);
        this.label1.Size = new Size(250, 25);
        this.label1.Text = "The TabControl below has " +              ↵
tabCount.ToString() +
            " TabPage objects in its controls collection.";

        this.ClientSize = new Size(300, 300);
        this.Controls.AddRange(new Control[] {tabControl1, label1});
    }

    static void Main()
    {
        Application.Run(new Form1());
    }
}
```

[C++]

```
using namespace System::Drawing;
using namespace System::Windows::Forms;

public __gc class Form1 : public Form {
private:
    TabControl*  tabControl1;
    TabPage*  tabPage1;
    TabPage*  tabPage2;
    TabPage*  tabPage3;
    Label*  label1;

public:
    Form1() {
        this->tabControl1 = new TabControl();
        this->tabPage1 = new TabPage();
        this->tabPage2 = new TabPage();
        this->tabPage3 = new TabPage();
        this->label1 = new Label();

        TabPage* tabPages[] = {tabPage1, tabPage2, tabPage3};
        this->tabControl1->TabPages->AddRange(tabPages);
        this->tabControl1->Location = Point(25, 75);
        this->tabControl1->Size = System::Drawing::Size(250, 200);

        // Gets the number of TabPage objects in the                ↵
tabControl1 controls collection.
        int tabCount = tabControl1->TabPages->Count;

        this->label1->Location = Point(25, 25);
        this->label1->Size = System::Drawing::Size(250, 25);
        this->label1->Text = System::String::Concat(
            S"The TabControl below has ", __box(tabCount),
            S" TabPage objects in its controls collection.");
        this->ClientSize = System::Drawing::Size(300, 300);
        Control* formControls[] = {tabControl1, label1};
        this->Controls->AddRange(formControls);
    }
};

int main() {
    Application::Run(new Form1());
}
```

Requirements

Platforms: Windows 98, Windows NT 4.0, Windows Millennium Edition, Windows 2000, Windows XP Home Edition, Windows XP Professional, Windows Server 2003 family, .NET Compact Framework - Windows CE .NET

TabControl.TabPageCollection.IsReadOnly Property

Gets a value indicating whether the collection is read-only.

[Visual Basic]

```
Public Overridable ReadOnly Property IsReadOnly As Boolean _
   Implements IList.IsReadOnly
```

[C#]

```
public virtual bool IsReadOnly {get;}
```

[C++]

```
public: __property virtual bool get_IsReadOnly();
```

[JScript]

```
public function get IsReadOnly() : Boolean;
```

Property Value

This property always returns **false**.

Implements

IList.IsReadOnly

Example

See related example in the **System.Windows.Forms.TabControl.TabPageCollection** class topic.

Requirements

Platforms: Windows 98, Windows NT 4.0, Windows Millennium Edition, Windows 2000, Windows XP Home Edition, Windows XP Professional, Windows Server 2003 family

TabControl.TabPageCollection.Item Property

Gets or sets a **TabPage** in the collection.

[C#] In C#, this property is the indexer for the **TabControl.TabPageCollection** class.

```
[Visual Basic]
Public Overridable Default Property Item( _
   ByVal index As Integer _
) As TabPage
[C#]
public virtual TabPage this[
   int index
] {get; set;}
[C++]
public: __property virtual TabPage* get_Item(
   int index
);
public: __property virtual void set_Item(
   int index,
   TabPage*
);
[JScript]
returnValue = TabPageCollectionObject.Item(index);
TabPageCollectionObject.Item(index) = returnValue;
-or-
returnValue = TabPageCollectionObject(index);
TabPageCollectionObject(index) = returnValue;
```

[JScript] In JScript, you can use the default indexed properties defined by a type, but you cannot explicitly define your own. However, specifying the **expando** attribute on a class automatically provides a default indexed property whose type is **Object** and whose index type is **String**.

Arguments [JScript]

index

The 0-based index of the tab page to get or set.

Parameters [Visual Basic, C#, C++]

index

The 0-based index of the tab page to get or set.

Property Value

The **TabPage** at the specified index.

Exceptions

Exception Type	Condition
ArgumentException	The value is not a **TabPage**.

Requirements

Platforms: Windows 98, Windows NT 4.0, Windows Millennium Edition, Windows 2000, Windows XP Home Edition, Windows XP Professional, Windows Server 2003 family

TabControl.TabPageCollection.System.Collections.ICollection.Count Property

Note: This namespace, class, or member is supported only in version 1.1 of the .NET Framework.

```
[Visual Basic]
Private ReadOnly Property Count As Integer Implements _
   ICollection.Count
[C#]
int ICollection.Count {get;}
[C++]
private: __property int
   System::Collections::ICollection::get_Count();
[JScript]
private function get ICollection.Count() : int;
```

Requirements

Platforms: Windows 98, Windows NT 4.0, Windows Millennium Edition, Windows 2000, Windows XP Home Edition, Windows XP Professional, Windows Server 2003 family

TabControl.TabPageCollection.System.Collections.ICollection.IsSynchronized Property

Note: This namespace, class, or member is supported only in version 1.1 of the .NET Framework.

This member supports the .NET Framework infrastructure and is not intended to be used directly from your code.

```
[Visual Basic]
Private ReadOnly Property IsSynchronized As Boolean Implements _
   ICollection.IsSynchronized
[C#]
bool ICollection.IsSynchronized {get;}
[C++]
private: __property bool
   System::Collections::ICollection::get_IsSynchronized();
[JScript]
private function get ICollection.IsSynchronized() : Boolean;
```

TabControl.TabPageCollection.System.Collections.ICollection.SyncRoot Property

Note: This namespace, class, or member is supported only in version 1.1 of the .NET Framework.

This member supports the .NET Framework infrastructure and is not intended to be used directly from your code.

```
[Visual Basic]
Private ReadOnly Property SyncRoot As Object Implements _
   ICollection.SyncRoot
[C#]
object ICollection.SyncRoot {get;}
[C++]
private: __property Object*
   System::Collections::ICollection::get_SyncRoot();
[JScript]
private function get ICollection.SyncRoot() : Object;
```

TabControl.TabPageCollection.System.Collections.IList.IsFixedSize Property

Note: This namespace, class, or member is supported only in version 1.1 of the .NET Framework.

This member supports the .NET Framework infrastructure and is not intended to be used directly from your code.

```
[Visual Basic]
Private ReadOnly Property IsFixedSize As Boolean Implements _
   IList.IsFixedSize
[C#]
bool IList.IsFixedSize {get;}
[C++]
private: __property bool
   System::Collections::IList::get_IsFixedSize();
[JScript]
private function get IList.IsFixedSize() : Boolean;
```

TabControl.TabPageCollection.System.Collections.IList.IsReadOnly Property

Note: This namespace, class, or member is supported only in version 1.1 of the .NET Framework.

```
[Visual Basic]
Private ReadOnly Property IsReadOnly As Boolean Implements _
   IList.IsReadOnly
[C#]
bool IList.IsReadOnly {get;}
[C++]
private: __property bool
   System::Collections::IList::get_IsReadOnly();
[JScript]
private function get IList.IsReadOnly() : Boolean;
```

Requirements

Platforms: Windows 98, Windows NT 4.0, Windows Millennium Edition, Windows 2000, Windows XP Home Edition, Windows XP Professional, Windows Server 2003 family

TabControl.TabPageCollection.System.Collections.IList.Item Property

Note: This namespace, class, or member is supported only in version 1.1 of the .NET Framework.

[C#] In C#, this property is the indexer for the **TabControl.TabPageCollection** class.

```
[Visual Basic]
Private Default Property Item( _
   ByVal index As Integer _
) As Object Implements IList.Item
[C#]
object IList.this[
   int index
] {get; set;}
[C++]
private: __property Object* System::Collections::IList::get_Item(
   int index
);
private: __property void System::Collections::IList::set_Item(
   int index,
   Object*
);
[JScript]
private function get IList.get_Item(index : int) : Object;
private function set IList.set_Item(index : int, value : Object);
-or-
private function get IList.get_Item(index : int) : Object;
private function set IList.set_Item(index : int, value : Object);
```

[JScript] In JScript, you can use the default indexed properties defined by a type, but you cannot explicitly define your own. However, specifying the **expando** attribute on a class automatically provides a default indexed property whose type is **Object** and whose index type is **String**.

Arguments [JScript]

index

Parameters [Visual Basic, C#, C++]

index

Requirements

Platforms: Windows 98, Windows NT 4.0, Windows Millennium Edition, Windows 2000, Windows XP Home Edition, Windows XP Professional, Windows Server 2003 family

TabControl.TabPageCollection.Add Method

Adds a **TabPage** to the collection.

```
[Visual Basic]
Public Sub Add( _
   ByVal value As TabPage _
)
[C#]
public void Add(
   TabPage value
);
[C++]
public: void Add(
   TabPage* value
);
[JScript]
public function Add(
   value : TabPage
);
```

Parameters

value

The **TabPage** to add.

Exceptions

Exception Type	Condition
ArgumentNullException	The specified *value* is a null reference (**Nothing** in Visual Basic).
ArgumentException	The specified object is not a **TabPage**.

Example

See related example in the **System.Windows.Forms.TabControl.TabPageCollection** class topic.

Requirements

Platforms: Windows 98, Windows NT 4.0, Windows Millennium Edition, Windows 2000, Windows XP Home Edition, Windows XP Professional, Windows Server 2003 family, .NET Compact Framework - Windows CE .NET

TabControl.TabPageCollection.AddRange Method

Adds a set of tab pages to the collection.

```
[Visual Basic]
Public Sub AddRange( _
   ByVal pages() As TabPage _
)
[C#]
public void AddRange(
   TabPage[] pages
);
[C++]
public: void AddRange(
   TabPage* pages[]
);
[JScript]
public function AddRange(
   pages : TabPage[]
);
```

Parameters

pages
An array of type **TabPage** that contains the tab pages to add.

Exceptions

Exception Type	Condition
ArgumentNull-Exception	The value of pages equals null.

Example

See related example in the **System.Windows.Forms.TabControl.TabPageCollection** class topic.

Requirements

Platforms: Windows 98, Windows NT 4.0, Windows Millennium Edition, Windows 2000, Windows XP Home Edition, Windows XP Professional, Windows Server 2003 family

TabControl.TabPageCollection.Clear Method

Removes all the tab pages from the collection.

```
[Visual Basic]
Public Overridable Sub Clear() Implements IList.Clear
[C#]
public virtual void Clear();
[C++]
public: virtual void Clear();
[JScript]
public function Clear();
```

Implements

IList.Clear

Example

See related example in the **System.Windows.Forms.TabControl.TabPageCollection** class topic.

Requirements

Platforms: Windows 98, Windows NT 4.0, Windows Millennium Edition, Windows 2000, Windows XP Home Edition, Windows XP Professional, Windows Server 2003 family, .NET Compact Framework - Windows CE .NET

TabControl.TabPageCollection.Contains Method

Determines whether a specified tab page is in the collection.

```
[Visual Basic]
Public Function Contains( _
   ByVal page As TabPage _
) As Boolean
[C#]
public bool Contains(
   TabPage page
);
[C++]
public: bool Contains(
   TabPage* page
);
[JScript]
public function Contains(
   page : TabPage
) : Boolean;
```

Parameters

page
The **TabPage** to locate in the collection.

Return Value

true if the specified **TabPage** is in the collection; otherwise, **false**.

Exceptions

Exception Type	Condition
ArgumentNull-Exception	The value of *page* is a null reference (**Nothing** in Visual Basic).

Example

See related example in the **System.Windows.Forms.TabControl.TabPageCollection** class topic.

Requirements

Platforms: Windows 98, Windows NT 4.0, Windows Millennium Edition, Windows 2000, Windows XP Home Edition, Windows XP Professional, Windows Server 2003 family, .NET Compact Framework - Windows CE .NET

TabControl.TabPageCollection.GetEnumerator Method

Returns an enumeration of all the tab pages in the collection.

[Visual Basic]
```
Public Overridable Function GetEnumerator() As IEnumerator _
   Implements IEnumerable.GetEnumerator
```
[C#]
```
public virtual IEnumerator GetEnumerator();
```
[C++]
```
public: virtual IEnumerator* GetEnumerator();
```
[JScript]
```
public function GetEnumerator() : IEnumerator;
```

Return Value

An **IEnumerator** for the **TabControl.TabPageCollection**.

Implements

IEnumerable.GetEnumerator

Remarks

This method creates an enumerator that contains a snapshot of the collection. You can change the collection by changing the enumerator; however, multiple enumerators can simultaneously access the same collection. Changing the collection (either directly or through another enumerator) can thus cause **Current** or **MoveNext** to throw an exception.

Two enumerators created from the same collection at the same time can contain different snapshots.

Removing objects from the enumerator also removes them from the collection.

Requirements

Platforms: Windows 98, Windows NT 4.0,
Windows Millennium Edition, Windows 2000,
Windows XP Home Edition, Windows XP Professional,
Windows Server 2003 family,
.NET Compact Framework - Windows CE .NET

TabControl.TabPageCollection.ICollection.CopyTo Method

This member supports the .NET Framework infrastructure and is not intended to be used directly from your code.

[Visual Basic]
```
Private Sub CopyTo( _
   ByVal dest As Array, _
   ByVal index As Integer _
) Implements ICollection.CopyTo
```
[C#]
```
void ICollection.CopyTo(
   Array dest,
   int index
);
```
[C++]
```
private: void ICollection::CopyTo(
   Array* dest,
   int index
);
```
[JScript]
```
private function ICollection.CopyTo(
   dest : Array,
   index : int
);
```

TabControl.TabPageCollection.IList.Add Method

This member supports the .NET Framework infrastructure and is not intended to be used directly from your code.

[Visual Basic]
```
Private Function Add( _
   ByVal value As Object _
) As Integer Implements IList.Add
```
[C#]
```
int IList.Add(
   object value
);
```
[C++]
```
private: int IList::Add(
   Object* value
);
```
[JScript]
```
private function IList.Add(
   value : Object
) : int;
```

TabControl.TabPageCollection.IList.Contains Method

This member supports the .NET Framework infrastructure and is not intended to be used directly from your code.

[Visual Basic]
```
Private Function Contains( _
   ByVal page As Object _
) As Boolean Implements IList.Contains
```
[C#]
```
bool IList.Contains(
   object page
);
```
[C++]
```
private: bool IList::Contains(
   Object* page
);
```
[JScript]
```
private function IList.Contains(
   page : Object
) : Boolean;
```

TabControl.TabPageCollection.IList.IndexOf Method

This member supports the .NET Framework infrastructure and is not intended to be used directly from your code.

[Visual Basic]
```
Private Function IndexOf( _
   ByVal page As Object _
) As Integer Implements IList.IndexOf
```
[C#]
```
int IList.IndexOf(
   object page
);
```
[C++]
```
private: int IList::IndexOf(
   Object* page
);
```

```
[JScript]
private function IList.IndexOf(
   page : Object
) : int;
```

TabControl.TabPageCollection.IList.Insert Method

This member supports the .NET Framework infrastructure and is not intended to be used directly from your code.

```
[Visual Basic]
Private Sub Insert( _
   ByVal index As Integer, _
   ByVal value As Object _
) Implements IList.Insert
[C#]
void IList.Insert(
   int index,
   object value
);
[C++]
private: void IList::Insert(
   int index,
   Object* value
);
[JScript]
private function IList.Insert(
   index : int,
   value : Object
);
```

TabControl.TabPageCollection.IList.Remove Method

This member supports the .NET Framework infrastructure and is not intended to be used directly from your code.

```
[Visual Basic]
Private Sub Remove( _
   ByVal value As Object _
) Implements IList.Remove
[C#]
void IList.Remove(
   object value
);
[C++]
private: void IList::Remove(
   Object* value
);
[JScript]
private function IList.Remove(
   value : Object
);
```

TabControl.TabPageCollection.IndexOf Method

Returns the index of the specified tab page in the collection.

```
[Visual Basic]
Public Function IndexOf( _
   ByVal page As TabPage _
) As Integer
[C#]
public int IndexOf(
   TabPage page
);
[C++]
public: int IndexOf(
   TabPage* page
);
[JScript]
public function IndexOf(
   page : TabPage
) : int;
```

Parameters

page
The **TabPage** to locate in the collection.

Return Value

The 0-based index of the tab page; -1 if it cannot be found.

Exceptions

Exception Type	Condition
ArgumentNull-Exception	The value of *page* is a null reference (**Nothing** in Visual Basic).

Example

See related example in the **System.Windows.Forms.TabControl.TabPageCollection** class topic.

Requirements

Platforms: Windows 98, Windows NT 4.0, Windows Millennium Edition, Windows 2000, Windows XP Home Edition, Windows XP Professional, Windows Server 2003 family, .NET Compact Framework - Windows CE .NET

TabControl.TabPageCollection.Remove Method

Removes a **TabPage** from the collection.

```
[Visual Basic]
Public Sub Remove( _
   ByVal value As TabPage _
)
[C#]
public void Remove(
   TabPage value
);
[C++]
public: void Remove(
   TabPage* value
);
[JScript]
public function Remove(
   value : TabPage
);
```

Parameters

value
The **TabPage** to remove.

Exceptions

Exception Type	Condition
ArgumentNull-Exception	The *value* parameter is a null reference (**Nothing** in Visual Basic).

Example

See related example in the **System.Windows.Forms.Tab-Control.TabPageCollection** class topic.

Requirements

Platforms: Windows 98, Windows NT 4.0, Windows Millennium Edition, Windows 2000, Windows XP Home Edition, Windows XP Professional, Windows Server 2003 family

TabControl.TabPageCollection.RemoveAt Method

Removes the tab page at the specified index from the collection.

```
[Visual Basic]
Public Overridable Sub RemoveAt( _
   ByVal index As Integer _
) Implements IList.RemoveAt
[C#]
public virtual void RemoveAt(
   int index
);
[C++]
public: virtual void RemoveAt(
   int index
);
[JScript]
public function RemoveAt(
   index : int
);
```

Parameters

index
: The 0-based index of the **TabPage** to remove.

Implements

IList.RemoveAt

Example

See related example in the **System.Windows.Forms.Tab-Control.TabPageCollection** class topic.

Requirements

Platforms: Windows 98, Windows NT 4.0, Windows Millennium Edition, Windows 2000, Windows XP Home Edition, Windows XP Professional, Windows Server 2003 family, .NET Compact Framework - Windows CE .NET

TabDrawMode Enumeration

Specifies whether the tabs in a tab control are owner-drawn (drawn by the parent window), or drawn by the operating system.

[Visual Basic]
```
<Serializable>
Public Enum TabDrawMode
```
[C#]
```
[Serializable]
public enum TabDrawMode
```
[C++]
```
[Serializable]
__value public enum TabDrawMode
```
[JScript]
```
public
   Serializable
enum TabDrawMode
```

Remarks

This enumeration is used by members such as **TabControl.DrawMode**.

The **TabControl** class and its derived classes support owner-draw functionality, but only one type, in which you can draw the tabs individually.

Members

Member name	Description
Normal	The tabs are drawn by the operating system, and are of the same size.
OwnerDrawFixed	The tabs are drawn by the parent window, and are of the same size.

Requirements

Namespace: System.Windows.Forms

Platforms: Windows 98, Windows NT 4.0, Windows Millennium Edition, Windows 2000, Windows XP Home Edition, Windows XP Professional, Windows Server 2003 family

Assembly: System.Windows.Forms (in System.Windows.Forms.dll)

TabPage Class

Represents a single tab page in a **TabControl**.

System.Object
  System.MarshalByRefObject
    System.ComponentModel.Component
      System.Windows.Forms.Control
        System.Windows.Forms.ScrollableControl
          System.Windows.Forms.Panel
            System.Windows.Forms.TabPage

[Visual Basic]
```
Public Class TabPage
   Inherits Panel
```
[C#]
```
public class TabPage : Panel
```
[C++]
```
public __gc class TabPage : public Panel
```
[JScript]
```
public class TabPage extends Panel
```

Thread Safety

Any public static (**Shared** in Visual Basic) members of this type are safe for multithreaded operations. Any instance members are not guaranteed to be thread safe.

Remarks

For more information about how this control responds to the **Focus** and **Select** methods, see the following **Control** members: **CanFocus**, **CanSelect**, **Focused**, **ContainsFocus**, **Focus**, **Select**.

Example

[Visual Basic, C#, C++] The following example creates a **TabControl** with one **TabPage**.

[Visual Basic, C#, C++] Use the **System.Drawing** and **System.Windows.Forms** namespaces for this example.

[Visual Basic]
```
Imports System.Drawing
Imports System.Windows.Forms

Public Class Form1
    Inherits Form
    Private tabControl1 As TabControl

    ' Declares tabPage1 as a TabPage type.
    Private tabPage1 As System.Windows.Forms.TabPage

    Private Sub MyTabs()
        Me.tabControl1 = New TabControl()

        ' Invokes the TabPage() constructor to create the tabPage1.
        Me.tabPage1 = New System.Windows.Forms.TabPage()

        Me.tabControl1.Controls.AddRange(New Control() {Me.tabPage1})
        Me.tabControl1.Location = New Point(25, 25)
        Me.tabControl1.Size = New Size(250, 250)

        Me.ClientSize = New Size(300, 300)
        Me.Controls.AddRange(New Control() {Me.tabControl1})
    End Sub

    Public Sub New()
        MyTabs()
    End Sub

    Shared Sub Main()
        Application.Run(New Form1())
    End Sub
End Class
```

[C#]
```
using System.Drawing;
using System.Windows.Forms;

public class Form1 : Form
{
    private TabControl tabControl1;

    // Declares tabPage1 as a TabPage type.
    private System.Windows.Forms.TabPage tabPage1;

    private void MyTabs()
    {
        this.tabControl1 = new TabControl();

        // Invokes the TabPage() constructor to create the tabPage1.
        this.tabPage1 = new System.Windows.Forms.TabPage();

        this.tabControl1.Controls.AddRange(new Control[] {
            this.tabPage1});
        this.tabControl1.Location = new Point(25, 25);
        this.tabControl1.Size = new Size(250, 250);

        this.ClientSize = new Size(300, 300);
        this.Controls.AddRange(new Control[] {
            this.tabControl1});
    }

    public Form1()
    {
        MyTabs();
    }

    static void Main()
    {
        Application.Run(new Form1());
    }
}
```

[C++]
```
using namespace System::Drawing;
using namespace System::Windows::Forms;

public __gc class Form1 : public Form {
private:
    TabControl*  tabControl1;

    // Declares tabPage1 as a TabPage type.
    System::Windows::Forms::TabPage*  tabPage1;

    void MyTabs() {
        this->tabControl1 = new TabControl();

        // Invokes the TabPage() constructor to create the tabPage1.
        this->tabPage1 = new System::Windows::Forms::TabPage();

        Control* tabControls[] = {this->tabPage1};
        this->tabControl1->Controls->AddRange(tabControls);
        this->tabControl1->Location = Point(25, 25);
        this->tabControl1->Size = System::Drawing::Size(250, 250);
        this->ClientSize = System::Drawing::Size(300, 300);
        Control* formControls[] = {this->tabControl1};
        this->Controls->AddRange(formControls);
    }

public:
    Form1() {
        MyTabs();
    }
};

int main() {
    Application::Run(new Form1());
}
```

Requirements

Namespace: System.Windows.Forms

Platforms: Windows 98, Windows NT 4.0,
Windows Millennium Edition, Windows 2000,
Windows XP Home Edition, Windows XP Professional,
Windows Server 2003 family,
.NET Compact Framework - Windows CE .NET

Assembly: System.Windows.Forms (in System.Windows.Forms.dll)

TabPage Constructor

Initializes a new instance of the **TabPage** class.

Overload List

Initializes a new instance of the **TabPage** class.

Supported by the .NET Compact Framework.

[Visual Basic] **Public Sub New()**

[C#] **public TabPage();**

[C++] **public: TabPage();**

[JScript] **public function TabPage();**

Initializes a new instance of the **TabPage** class, specifies the text for the tab.

[Visual Basic] **Public Sub New(String)**

[C#] **public TabPage(string);**

[C++] **public: TabPage(String*);**

[JScript] **public function TabPage(String);**

Example

See related example in the **System.Windows.Forms.TabPage** class topic.

TabPage Constructor ()

Initializes a new instance of the **TabPage** class.

```
[Visual Basic]
Public Sub New()
[C#]
public TabPage();
[C++]
public: TabPage();
[JScript]
public function TabPage();
```

Example

See related example in the **System.Windows.Forms.TabPage** class topic.

Requirements

Platforms: Windows 98, Windows NT 4.0,
Windows Millennium Edition, Windows 2000,
Windows XP Home Edition, Windows XP Professional,
Windows Server 2003 family,
.NET Compact Framework - Windows CE .NET

TabPage Constructor (String)

Initializes a new instance of the **TabPage** class, specifies the text for the tab.

```
[Visual Basic]
Public Sub New( _
   ByVal text As String _
)
[C#]
public TabPage(
   string text
);
[C++]
public: TabPage(
   String* text
);
[JScript]
public function TabPage(
   text : String
);
```

Parameters

text

The text for the tab.

Remarks

The **Text** property is set to the value of the *text* parameter.

Example

See related example in the **System.Windows.Forms.TabPage** class topic.

Requirements

Platforms: Windows 98, Windows NT 4.0,
Windows Millennium Edition, Windows 2000,
Windows XP Home Edition, Windows XP Professional,
Windows Server 2003 family

TabPage.Anchor Property

This member overrides **Control.Anchor**.

```
[Visual Basic]
Overrides Public Property Anchor As AnchorStyles
[C#]
public override AnchorStyles Anchor {get; set;}
[C++]
public: __property AnchorStyles get_Anchor();
public: __property void set_Anchor(AnchorStyles);
[JScript]
public override function get Anchor() : AnchorStyles;
public override function set Anchor(AnchorStyles);
```

Requirements

Platforms: Windows 98, Windows NT 4.0,
Windows Millennium Edition, Windows 2000,
Windows XP Home Edition, Windows XP Professional,
Windows Server 2003 family

TabPage.Dock Property

This member overrides **Control.Dock**.

```
[Visual Basic]
Overrides Public Property Dock As DockStyle
[C#]
public override DockStyle Dock {get; set;}
[C++]
public: __property DockStyle get_Dock();
public: __property void set_Dock(DockStyle);
[JScript]
public override function get Dock() : DockStyle;
public override function set Dock(DockStyle);
```

Requirements

Platforms: Windows 98, Windows NT 4.0, Windows Millennium Edition, Windows 2000, Windows XP Home Edition, Windows XP Professional, Windows Server 2003 family

TabPage.Enabled Property

This member supports the .NET Framework infrastructure and is not intended to be used directly from your code.

```
[Visual Basic]
Public Shadows Property Enabled As Boolean
[C#]
public new bool Enabled {get; set;}
[C++]
public: __property bool get_Enabled();
public: __property void set_Enabled(bool);
[JScript]
public hide function get Enabled() : Boolean;
public hide function set Enabled(Boolean);
```

TabPage.ImageIndex Property

Gets or sets the index to the image displayed on this tab.

```
[Visual Basic]
Public Property ImageIndex As Integer
[C#]
public int ImageIndex {get; set;}
[C++]
public: __property int get_ImageIndex();
public: __property void set_ImageIndex(int);
[JScript]
public function get ImageIndex() : int;
public function set ImageIndex(int);
```

Property Value

The zero-based index to the image in the **TabControl.ImageList** that appears on the tab. The default is -1, which signifies no image.

Exceptions

Exception Type	Condition
ArgumentException	The **ImageIndex** value is less than -1.

Remarks

The **ImageIndex** points to an image in the associated **ImageList** of the **TabControl**.

Example

See related example in the **System.Windows.Forms.TabPage** class topic.

Requirements

Platforms: Windows 98, Windows NT 4.0, Windows Millennium Edition, Windows 2000, Windows XP Home Edition, Windows XP Professional, Windows Server 2003 family

TabPage.TabIndex Property

This member supports the .NET Framework infrastructure and is not intended to be used directly from your code.

```
[Visual Basic]
Public Shadows Property TabIndex As Integer
[C#]
public new int TabIndex {get; set;}
[C++]
public: __property int get_TabIndex();
public: __property void set_TabIndex(int);
[JScript]
public hide function get TabIndex() : int;
public hide function set TabIndex(int);
```

TabPage.TabStop Property

This member supports the .NET Framework infrastructure and is not intended to be used directly from your code.

```
[Visual Basic]
Public Shadows Property TabStop As Boolean
[C#]
public new bool TabStop {get; set;}
[C++]
public: __property bool get_TabStop();
public: __property void set_TabStop(bool);
[JScript]
public hide function get TabStop() : Boolean;
public hide function set TabStop(Boolean);
```

TabPage.Text Property

Gets or sets the text to display on the tab.

```
[Visual Basic]
Overrides Public Property Text As String
[C#]
public override string Text {get; set;}
[C++]
public: __property String* get_Text();
public: __property void set_Text(String*);
[JScript]
public override function get Text() : String;
public override function set Text(String);
```

Property Value

The text to display on the tab.

Example

See related example in the **System.Windows.Forms.TabPage** class topic.

Requirements

Platforms: Windows 98, Windows NT 4.0, Windows Millennium Edition, Windows 2000, Windows XP Home Edition, Windows XP Professional, Windows Server 2003 family, .NET Compact Framework - Windows CE .NET

TabPage.ToolTipText Property

Gets or sets the ToolTip text for this tab.

```
[Visual Basic]
Public Property ToolTipText As String
[C#]
public string ToolTipText {get; set;}
[C++]
public: __property String* get_ToolTipText();
public: __property void set_ToolTipText(String*);
[JScript]
public function get ToolTipText() : String;
public function set ToolTipText(String);
```

Property Value

The ToolTip text for this tab.

Remarks

This tab page belongs to a **TabControl**. The ToolTip text appears when the user moves the mouse over the tab - if the **ShowToolTips** property of the **TabControl** is **true**. For more information on ToolTips, see the **ToolTip** class.

Example

See related example in the **System.Windows.Forms.TabPage** class topic.

Requirements

Platforms: Windows 98, Windows NT 4.0, Windows Millennium Edition, Windows 2000, Windows XP Home Edition, Windows XP Professional, Windows Server 2003 family

TabPage.Visible Property

This member supports the .NET Framework infrastructure and is not intended to be used directly from your code.

```
[Visual Basic]
Public Shadows Property Visible As Boolean
[C#]
public new bool Visible {get; set;}
[C++]
public: __property bool get_Visible();
public: __property void set_Visible(bool);
[JScript]
public hide function get Visible() : Boolean;
public hide function set Visible(Boolean);
```

TabPage.CreateControlsInstance Method

This member overrides **Control.CreateControlsInstance**.

```
[Visual Basic]
Overrides Protected Function CreateControlsInstance() As _
   ControlCollection
[C#]
protected override ControlCollection CreateControlsInstance();
[C++]
protected: ControlCollection* CreateControlsInstance();
[JScript]
protected override function CreateControlsInstance() :
   ControlCollection;
```

Requirements

Platforms: Windows 98, Windows NT 4.0, Windows Millennium Edition, Windows 2000, Windows XP Home Edition, Windows XP Professional, Windows Server 2003 family

TabPage.GetTabPageOfComponent Method

Retrieves the tab page that contains the specified object.

```
[Visual Basic]
Public Shared Function GetTabPageOfComponent( _
   ByVal comp As Object _
) As TabPage
[C#]
public static TabPage GetTabPageOfComponent(
   object comp
);
[C++]
public: static TabPage* GetTabPageOfComponent(
   Object* comp
);
[JScript]
public static function GetTabPageOfComponent(
   comp : Object
) : TabPage;
```

Parameters

comp
   The object to look for.

Return Value

The **TabPage** that contains the specified object, or a null reference (**Nothing** in Visual Basic) if the object cannot be found.

Example

See related example in the **System.Windows.Forms.TabPage** class topic.

Requirements

Platforms: Windows 98, Windows NT 4.0, Windows Millennium Edition, Windows 2000, Windows XP Home Edition, Windows XP Professional, Windows Server 2003 family

TabPage.SetBoundsCore Method

This member overrides **Control.SetBoundsCore**.

```
[Visual Basic]
Overrides Protected Sub SetBoundsCore( _
   ByVal x As Integer, _
   ByVal y As Integer, _
   ByVal width As Integer, _
   ByVal height As Integer, _
   ByVal specified As BoundsSpecified _
)
```

```
[C#]
protected override void SetBoundsCore(
   int x,
   int y,
   int width,
   int height,
   BoundsSpecified specified
);
[C++]
protected: void SetBoundsCore(
   int x,
   int y,
   int width,
   int height,
   BoundsSpecified specified
);
[JScript]
protected override function SetBoundsCore(
   x : int,
   y : int,
   width : int,
   height : int,
   specified : BoundsSpecified
);
```

Requirements

Platforms: Windows 98, Windows NT 4.0, Windows Millennium Edition, Windows 2000, Windows XP Home Edition, Windows XP Professional, Windows Server 2003 family

TabPage.ToString Method

Returns a string containing the value of the **Text** property.

```
[Visual Basic]
Overrides Public Function ToString() As String
[C#]
public override string ToString();
[C++]
public: String* ToString();
[JScript]
public override function ToString() : String;
```

Return Value

A string containing the value of the **Text** property.

Example

See related example in the **System.Windows.Forms.TabPage** class topic.

Requirements

Platforms: Windows 98, Windows NT 4.0, Windows Millennium Edition, Windows 2000, Windows XP Home Edition, Windows XP Professional, Windows Server 2003 family, .NET Compact Framework - Windows CE .NET

TabPage.DockChanged Event

This member supports the .NET Framework infrastructure and is not intended to be used directly from your code.

```
[Visual Basic]
Public Shadows Event DockChanged As EventHandler
[C#]
public new event EventHandler DockChanged;
[C++]
public: __event EventHandler* DockChanged;
```

[JScript] In JScript, you can handle the events defined by a class, but you cannot define your own.

TabPage.EnabledChanged Event

This member supports the .NET Framework infrastructure and is not intended to be used directly from your code.

```
[Visual Basic]
Public Shadows Event EnabledChanged As EventHandler
[C#]
public new event EventHandler EnabledChanged;
[C++]
public: __event EventHandler* EnabledChanged;
```

[JScript] In JScript, you can handle the events defined by a class, but you cannot define your own.

TabPage.TabIndexChanged Event

This member supports the .NET Framework infrastructure and is not intended to be used directly from your code.

```
[Visual Basic]
Public Shadows Event TabIndexChanged As EventHandler
[C#]
public new event EventHandler TabIndexChanged;
[C++]
public: __event EventHandler* TabIndexChanged;
```

[JScript] In JScript, you can handle the events defined by a class, but you cannot define your own.

TabPage.TabStopChanged Event

This member supports the .NET Framework infrastructure and is not intended to be used directly from your code.

```
[Visual Basic]
Public Shadows Event TabStopChanged As EventHandler
[C#]
public new event EventHandler TabStopChanged;
[C++]
public: __event EventHandler* TabStopChanged;
```

[JScript] In JScript, you can handle the events defined by a class, but you cannot define your own.

TabPage.VisibleChanged Event

This member supports the .NET Framework infrastructure and is not intended to be used directly from your code.

```
[Visual Basic]
Public Shadows Event VisibleChanged As EventHandler
[C#]
public new event EventHandler VisibleChanged;
[C++]
public: __event EventHandler* VisibleChanged;
```

[JScript] In JScript, you can handle the events defined by a class, but you cannot define your own.

TabPage.TabPageControl-Collection Class

Contains the collection of controls that the **TabPage** uses.

System.Object
 System.Windows.Forms.Control.ControlCollection
  System.Windows.Forms.TabPage.TabPageControlCollection

```
[Visual Basic]
Public Class TabPage.TabPageControlCollection
   Inherits Control.ControlCollection
[C#]
public class TabPage.TabPageControlCollection :
   Control.ControlCollection
[C++]
public __gc class TabPage.TabPageControlCollection : public
   Control.ControlCollection
[JScript]
public class TabPage.TabPageControlCollection extends
   Control.ControlCollection
```

Thread Safety

Any public static (**Shared** in Visual Basic) members of this type are safe for multithreaded operations. Any instance members are not guaranteed to be thread safe.

Requirements

Namespace: System.Windows.Forms

Platforms: Windows 98, Windows NT 4.0, Windows Millennium Edition, Windows 2000, Windows XP Home Edition, Windows XP Professional, Windows Server 2003 family

Assembly: System.Windows.Forms (in System.Windows.Forms.dll)

TabPage.TabPageControlCollection Constructor

This member supports the .NET Framework infrastructure and is not intended to be used directly from your code.

```
[Visual Basic]
Public Sub New( _
   ByVal owner As TabPage _
)
[C#]
public TabPage.TabPageControlCollection(
   TabPage owner
);
[C++]
public: TabPageControlCollection(
   TabPage* owner
);
[JScript]
public function TabPage.TabPageControlCollection(
   owner : TabPage
);
```

TabPage.TabPageControlCollection.Add Method

Adds a control to the collection.

```
[Visual Basic]
Overrides Public Sub Add( _
   ByVal value As Control _
)
[C#]
public override void Add(
   Control value
);
[C++]
public: void Add(
   Control* value
);
[JScript]
public override function Add(
   value : Control
);
```

Parameters

value

The control to add.

Exceptions

Exception Type	Condition
ArgumentException	The specified control is a **TabPage**.

Remarks

The specified control is added to the end of the collection. If the control is already a child of another control, it is removed from the other control.

Example

[Visual Basic, C#, C++] The following example creates a **Tab-Control** with one **TabPage**. This example uses the **Add** method to add a single control, `button1`, to the `tabPage1`. Notice the **Controls** property is used to get the `tabPage1` controls collection to add controls to the collection.

[Visual Basic, C#, C++] Use the **System.Drawing** and **System.Windows.Forms** namespaces for this example.

[Visual Basic]
```
Imports System.Drawing
Imports System.Windows.Forms

Public Class Form1
    Inherits Form
    Private tabControl1 As TabControl
    Private tabPage1 As TabPage
    Private button1 As Button

    Public Sub New()
        Me.tabControl1 = New TabControl()
        Me.tabPage1 = New TabPage()
        Me.button1 = New Button()

        Me.tabControl1.TabPages.Add(tabPage1)
        Me.tabControl1.Location = New Point(25, 25)
        Me.tabControl1.Size = New Size(250, 250)

        ' Gets the controls collection for tabPage1.
        ' Adds button1 to this collection.
        Me.tabPage1.Controls.Add(button1)

        Me.button1.Text = "button1"
        Me.button1.Location = New Point(25, 25)
```

```
        Me.ClientSize = New Size(300, 300)
        Me.Controls.Add(tabControl1)
    End Sub

    Shared Sub Main()
        Application.Run(New Form1())
    End Sub
End Class
```

[C#]

```
using System.Drawing;
using System.Windows.Forms;

public class Form1 : Form
{
    private TabControl tabControl1;
    private TabPage tabPage1;
    private Button button1;

    public Form1()
    {
        this.tabControl1 = new TabControl();
        this.tabPage1 = new TabPage();
        this.button1 = new Button();

        this.tabControl1.TabPages.Add(tabPage1);
        this.tabControl1.Location = new Point(25, 25);
        this.tabControl1.Size = new Size(250, 250);

        // Gets the controls collection for tabPage1.
        // Adds button1 to this collection.
        this.tabPage1.Controls.Add(button1);

        this.button1.Text = "button1";
        this.button1.Location = new Point(25, 25);

        this.ClientSize = new Size(300, 300);
        this.Controls.Add(tabControl1);
    }

    static void Main()
    {
        Application.Run(new Form1());
    }
}
```

[C++]

```
using namespace System::Drawing;
using namespace System::Windows::Forms;

public __gc class Form1 : public Form {
private:
    TabControl*  tabControl1;
    TabPage*  tabPage1;
    Button*  button1;

public:
    Form1() {
        this->tabControl1 = new TabControl();
        this->tabPage1 = new TabPage();
        this->button1 = new Button();

        this->tabControl1->TabPages->Add(tabPage1);
        this->tabControl1->Location = Point(25, 25);
        this->tabControl1->Size = System::Drawing::Size(250, 250);

        // Gets the controls collection for tabPage1.
        // Adds button1 to this collection.
        this->tabPage1->Controls->Add(button1);

        this->button1->Text = S"button1";
        this->button1->Location = Point(25, 25);
        this->ClientSize = System::Drawing::Size(300, 300);
        this->Controls->Add(tabControl1);
    }
};

int main() {
    Application::Run(new Form1());
}
```

Requirements

Platforms: Windows 98, Windows NT 4.0, Windows Millennium Edition, Windows 2000, Windows XP Home Edition, Windows XP Professional, Windows Server 2003 family

TabSizeMode Enumeration

Specifies how tabs in a tab control are sized.

[Visual Basic]
```
<Serializable>
Public Enum TabSizeMode
```
[C#]
```
[Serializable]
public enum TabSizeMode
```
[C++]
```
[Serializable]
__value public enum TabSizeMode
```
[JScript]
```
public
   Serializable
enum TabSizeMode
```

Remarks

This enumeration is used by members such as **TabControl.SizeMode**.

Members

Member name	Description
FillToRight	The width of each tab is sized so that each row of tabs fills the entire width of the container control. This is only applicable to tab controls with more than one row.
Fixed	All tabs in a control are the same width.
Normal	The width of each tab is sized to accommodate what is displayed on the tab, and the size of tabs in a row are not adjusted to fill the entire width of the container control.

Requirements

Namespace: System.Windows.Forms

Platforms: Windows 98, Windows NT 4.0, Windows Millennium Edition, Windows 2000, Windows XP Home Edition, Windows XP Professional, Windows Server 2003 family

Assembly: System.Windows.Forms (in System.Windows.Forms.dll)

TextBox Class

Represents a Windows text box control.

System.Object
  System.MarshalByRefObject
    System.ComponentModel.Component
      System.Windows.Forms.Control
        System.Windows.Forms.TextBoxBase
          System.Windows.Forms.TextBox
            System.Windows.Forms.DataGridTextBox

[Visual Basic]
```
Public Class TextBox
   Inherits TextBoxBase
```
[C#]
```
public class TextBox : TextBoxBase
```
[C++]
```
public __gc class TextBox : public TextBoxBase
```
[JScript]
```
public class TextBox extends TextBoxBase
```

Thread Safety

Any public static (**Shared** in Visual Basic) members of this type are safe for multithreaded operations. Any instance members are not guaranteed to be thread safe.

Remarks

The **TextBox** control allows the user to enter text in an application. This control has additional functionality that is not found in the standard Windows text box control, including multiline editing and password character masking.

Typically, a **TextBox** control is used to display, or accept as input, a single line of text. You can use the **Multiline** and **ScrollBars** properties to enable multiple lines of text to be displayed or entered. Set the **AcceptsTab** and **AcceptsReturn** properties to **true** to allow greater text manipulation in a multiline **TextBox** control.

You can limit the amount of text entered into a **TextBox** control by setting the **MaxLength** property to a specific number of characters. **TextBox** controls can also be used to accept passwords and other sensitive information. You can use the **PasswordChar** property to mask characters entered in a single-line version of the control.

To restrict text from being entered in a **TextBox** control, you can create an event handler for the **KeyDown** event in order to validate each character entered in the control. You can also restrict all entry of data in a **TextBox** control by setting the **ReadOnly** property to **true**.

> **Note** Most of the functionality of the **TextBox** control is inherited from the **TextBoxBase** class.

.NET Compact Framework - Windows CE .NET Platform Note: In Pocket PC applications, tabs in a single-line **TextBox** display as brackets, but display normally when **Multiline** is set to **true**.

Example

The following example creates a multiline **TextBox** control with vertical scroll bars. This example uses the **AcceptsTab**, **AcceptsReturn**, and **WordWrap** properties to make the multiline text box control useful for creating text documents.

[Visual Basic]
```
Private Sub CreateMyMultilineTextBox()
    ' Create an instance of a TextBox control.
    Dim textBox1 As New TextBox()

    ' Set the Multiline property to true.
    textBox1.Multiline = True
    ' Add vertical scroll bars to the TextBox control.
    textBox1.ScrollBars = ScrollBars.Vertical
    ' Allow the RETURN key to be entered in the TextBox control.
    textBox1.AcceptsReturn = True
    ' Allow the TAB key to be entered in the TextBox control.
    textBox1.AcceptsTab = True
    ' Set WordWrap to True to allow text to wrap to the next line.
    textBox1.WordWrap = True
    ' Set the default text of the control.
    textBox1.Text = "Welcome!"
End Sub
```

[C#]
```
private void CreateMyMultilineTextBox()
 {
    // Create an instance of a TextBox control.
    TextBox textBox1 = new TextBox();

    // Set the Multiline property to true.
    textBox1.Multiline = true;
    // Add vertical scroll bars to the TextBox control.
    textBox1.ScrollBars = ScrollBars.Vertical;
    // Allow the RETURN key to be entered in the TextBox control.
    textBox1.AcceptsReturn = true;
    // Allow the TAB key to be entered in the TextBox control.
    textBox1.AcceptsTab = true;
    // Set WordWrap to True to allow text to wrap to the next line.
    textBox1.WordWrap = true;
    // Set the default text of the control.
    textBox1.Text = "Welcome!";
 }
```

[C++]
```
private:
    void CreateMyMultilineTextBox() {
        // Create an instance of a TextBox control
        TextBox __gc *textBox1 = new TextBox();

        // Set the Multiline property to true.
        textBox1->Multiline = true;
        // Add vertical scroll bars to the TextBox control.
        textBox1->ScrollBars = ScrollBars::Vertical;
        // Allow the RETURN key to be entered in the TextBox control.
        textBox1->AcceptsReturn = true;
        // Allow the TAB key to be entered in the TextBox control.
        textBox1->AcceptsTab = true;
        // Set WordWrap to True to allow text to wrap to the next line.
        textBox1->WordWrap = true;
        // Set the default text of the control.
        textBox1->Text = S"Welcome!";
    };
```

[JScript]
```
private function CreateMyMultilineTextBox()
 {
    // Create an instance of a TextBox control
    textBox1 = new TextBox();

    // Set the Multiline property to true.
    textBox1.Multiline = true;
    // Add vertical scroll bars to the TextBox control.
    textBox1.ScrollBars = ScrollBars.Vertical;
    // Allow the RETURN key to be entered in the TextBox control.
    textBox1.AcceptsReturn = true;
    // Allow the TAB key to be entered in the TextBox control.
    textBox1.AcceptsTab = true;
    // Set WordWrap to True to allow text to wrap to the next line.
    textBox1.WordWrap = true;
    // Set the default text of the control.
    textBox1.Text = "Welcome!";
 }
```

Requirements

Namespace: System.Windows.Forms

Platforms: Windows 98, Windows NT 4.0, Windows Millennium Edition, Windows 2000, Windows XP Home Edition, Windows XP Professional, Windows Server 2003 family, .NET Compact Framework - Windows CE .NET

Assembly: System.Windows.Forms (in System.Windows.Forms.dll)

TextBox Constructor

Initializes a new instance of the **TextBox** class.

[Visual Basic]
```
Public Sub New()
```
[C#]
```
public TextBox();
```
[C++]
```
public: TextBox();
```
[JScript]
```
public function TextBox();
```

Remarks

The parent container control defines the color and font settings for the **TextBox**.

Example

See related example in the **System.Windows.Forms.TextBox** class topic.

Requirements

Platforms: Windows 98, Windows NT 4.0, Windows Millennium Edition, Windows 2000, Windows XP Home Edition, Windows XP Professional, Windows Server 2003 family, .NET Compact Framework - Windows CE .NET

TextBox.AcceptsReturn Property

Gets or sets a value indicating whether pressing ENTER in a multiline **TextBox** control creates a new line of text in the control or activates the default button for the form.

[Visual Basic]
```
Public Property AcceptsReturn As Boolean
```
[C#]
```
public bool AcceptsReturn {get; set;}
```
[C++]
```
public: __property bool get_AcceptsReturn();
public: __property void set_AcceptsReturn(bool);
```
[JScript]
```
public function get AcceptsReturn() : Boolean;
public function set AcceptsReturn(Boolean);
```

Property Value

true if the ENTER key creates a new line of text in a multiline version of the control; **false** if the ENTER key activates the default button for the form. The default is **false**.

Remarks

If the value of this property is **false**, the user must press CTRL+ENTER to create a new line in a multiline **TextBox** control. If there is no default button for the form, then the ENTER key will always create a new line of text in the control, no matter what the value of this property.

.NET Compact Framework - Windows CE .NET Platform Note: Although you can set **AcceptsReturn** to **false**, it always operates as **true**. If you want the ENTER key to activate a particular button, you can derive a class from **TextBox** and provide event handling code for ENTER when the **KeyPress** event occurs.

Example

See related example in the **System.Windows.Forms.TextBox** class topic.

Requirements

Platforms: Windows 98, Windows NT 4.0, Windows Millennium Edition, Windows 2000, Windows XP Home Edition, Windows XP Professional, Windows Server 2003 family, .NET Compact Framework - Windows CE .NET

TextBox.CharacterCasing Property

Gets or sets whether the **TextBox** control modifies the case of characters as they are typed.

[Visual Basic]
```
Public Property CharacterCasing As CharacterCasing
```
[C#]
```
public CharacterCasing CharacterCasing {get; set;}
```
[C++]
```
public: __property CharacterCasing get_CharacterCasing();
public: __property void set_CharacterCasing(CharacterCasing);
```
[JScript]
```
public function get CharacterCasing() : CharacterCasing;
public function set CharacterCasing(CharacterCasing);
```

Property Value

One of the **CharacterCasing** enumeration values that specifies whether the **TextBox** control modifies the case of characters. The default is **CharacterCasing.Normal**.

Exceptions

Exception Type	Condition
InvalidEnumArgumentException	A value that is not within the range of valid values for the enumeration was assigned to the property.

Remarks

You can use the **CharacterCasing** property to change the case of characters as required by your application. For example, you could change the case of all characters entered in a **TextBox** control used for password entry to uppercase or lowercase to enforce a policy for passwords.

Example

See related example in the **System.Windows.Forms.TextBox** class topic.

Requirements

Platforms: Windows 98, Windows NT 4.0, Windows Millennium Edition, Windows 2000, Windows XP Home Edition, Windows XP Professional, Windows Server 2003 family

TextBox.CreateParams Property

This member overrides **Control.CreateParams**.

```
[Visual Basic]
Overrides Protected ReadOnly Property CreateParams As CreateParams
[C#]
protected override CreateParams CreateParams {get;}
[C++]
protected: __property CreateParams* get_CreateParams();
[JScript]
protected override function get CreateParams() : CreateParams;
```

Requirements

Platforms: Windows 98, Windows NT 4.0, Windows Millennium Edition, Windows 2000, Windows XP Home Edition, Windows XP Professional, Windows Server 2003 family

TextBox.DefaultImeMode Property

This member overrides **Control.DefaultImeMode**.

```
[Visual Basic]
Overrides Protected ReadOnly Property DefaultImeMode As ImeMode
[C#]
protected override ImeMode DefaultImeMode {get;}
[C++]
protected: __property ImeMode get_DefaultImeMode();
[JScript]
protected override function get DefaultImeMode() : ImeMode;
```

Requirements

Platforms: Windows 98, Windows NT 4.0, Windows Millennium Edition, Windows 2000, Windows XP Home Edition, Windows XP Professional, Windows Server 2003 family

TextBox.PasswordChar Property

Gets or sets the character used to mask characters of a password in a single-line **TextBox** control.

```
[Visual Basic]
Public Property PasswordChar As Char
[C#]
public char PasswordChar {get; set;}
[C++]
public: __property __wchar_t get_PasswordChar();
public: __property void set_PasswordChar(__wchar_t);
[JScript]
public function get PasswordChar() : Char;
public function set PasswordChar(Char);
```

Property Value

The character used to mask characters entered in a single-line **TextBox** control. Set the value of this property to 0 (character value) if you do not want the control to mask characters as they are typed. Equals 0 (character value) by default.

Remarks

If the **Multiline** property is set to **true**, setting the **PasswordChar** property has no visual effect. When the **PasswordChar** property is set to **true**, cut, copy, and paste actions in the control using the keyboard are not allowed, regardless of whether the **Multiline** property is set to **true** or **false**.

Example

See related example in the **System.Windows.Forms.TextBox** class topic.

Requirements

Platforms: Windows 98, Windows NT 4.0, Windows Millennium Edition, Windows 2000, Windows XP Home Edition, Windows XP Professional, Windows Server 2003 family, .NET Compact Framework - Windows CE .NET

TextBox.ScrollBars Property

Gets or sets which scroll bars should appear in a multiline **TextBox** control.

```
[Visual Basic]
Public Property ScrollBars As ScrollBars
[C#]
public ScrollBars ScrollBars {get; set;}
[C++]
public: __property ScrollBars get_ScrollBars();
public: __property void set_ScrollBars(ScrollBars);
[JScript]
public function get ScrollBars() : ScrollBars;
public function set ScrollBars(ScrollBars);
```

Property Value

On of the **ScrollBars** enumeration values that indicates whether a multiline **TextBox** control appears with no scroll bars, a horizontal scroll bar, a vertical scroll bar, or both. The default is **ScrollBars.None**.

Exceptions

Exception Type	Condition
InvalidEnumArgument-Exception	A value that is not within the range of valid values for the enumeration was assigned to the property.

Remarks

Horizontal scroll bars will not be shown if the **WordWrap** property is set to **true**, regardless of the value of the **ScrollBars** property.

Example

See related example in the **System.Windows.Forms.TextBox** class topic.

Requirements

Platforms: Windows 98, Windows NT 4.0, Windows Millennium Edition, Windows 2000, Windows XP Home Edition, Windows XP Professional, Windows Server 2003 family, .NET Compact Framework - Windows CE .NET

TextBox.SelectionLength Property

This member overrides **TextBoxBase.SelectionLength**.

```
[Visual Basic]
Overrides Public Property SelectionLength As Integer
[C#]
public override int SelectionLength {get; set;}
[C++]
public: __property int get_SelectionLength();
public: __property void set_SelectionLength(int);
```

```
[JScript]
public override function get SelectionLength() : int;
public override function set SelectionLength(int);
```

Requirements

Platforms: Windows 98, Windows NT 4.0, Windows Millennium Edition, Windows 2000, Windows XP Home Edition, Windows XP Professional, Windows Server 2003 family, .NET Compact Framework - Windows CE .NET

TextBox.Text Property

This member overrides **TextBoxBase.Text**.

```
[Visual Basic]
Overrides Public Property Text As String
[C#]
public override string Text {get; set;}
[C++]
public: __property String* get_Text();
public: __property void set_Text(String*);
[JScript]
public override function get Text() : String;
public override function set Text(String);
```

Requirements

Platforms: Windows 98, Windows NT 4.0, Windows Millennium Edition, Windows 2000, Windows XP Home Edition, Windows XP Professional, Windows Server 2003 family, .NET Compact Framework - Windows CE .NET

TextBox.TextAlign Property

Gets or sets how text is aligned in a **TextBox** control.

```
[Visual Basic]
Public Property TextAlign As HorizontalAlignment
[C#]
public HorizontalAlignment TextAlign {get; set;}
[C++]
public: __property HorizontalAlignment get_TextAlign();
public: __property void set_TextAlign(HorizontalAlignment);
[JScript]
public function get TextAlign() : HorizontalAlignment;
public function set TextAlign(HorizontalAlignment);
```

Property Value

One of the **HorizontalAlignment** enumeration values that specifies how text is aligned in the control. The default is **HorizontalAlignment.Left**.

Exceptions

Exception Type	Condition
InvalidEnumArgument-Exception	A value that is not within the range of valid values for the enumeration was assigned to the property.

Remarks

You can use this property to align the text within a **TextBox** to match the layout of text on your form. For example, if your controls are all located on the right side of the form, you can set the **TextAlign** property to **HorizontalAlignment.Right**, and the text will be aligned with the right side of the control instead of the default left alignment.

.NET Compact Framework - Windows CE .NET Platform Note: In Pocket PC applications, a single-line **TextBox** supports only left alignment. A multiline **TextBox** can be aligned on the left, right, or center.

Example

See related example in the **System.Windows.Forms.TextBox** class topic.

Requirements

Platforms: Windows 98, Windows NT 4.0, Windows Millennium Edition, Windows 2000, Windows XP Home Edition, Windows XP Professional, Windows Server 2003 family, .NET Compact Framework - Windows CE .NET

TextBox.IsInputKey Method

This member overrides **Control.IsInputKey**.

```
[Visual Basic]
Overrides Protected Function IsInputKey( _
   ByVal keyData As Keys _
) As Boolean
[C#]
protected override bool IsInputKey(
   Keys keyData
);
[C++]
protected: bool IsInputKey(
   Keys keyData
);
[JScript]
protected override function IsInputKey(
   keyData : Keys
) : Boolean;
```

Requirements

Platforms: Windows 98, Windows NT 4.0, Windows Millennium Edition, Windows 2000, Windows XP Home Edition, Windows XP Professional, Windows Server 2003 family

TextBox.OnGotFocus Method

This member overrides **Control.OnGotFocus**.

```
[Visual Basic]
Overrides Protected Sub OnGotFocus( _
   ByVal e As EventArgs _
)
[C#]
protected override void OnGotFocus(
   EventArgs e
);
[C++]
protected: void OnGotFocus(
   EventArgs* e
);
```

```
[JScript]
protected override function OnGotFocus(
   e : EventArgs
);
```

Requirements

Platforms: Windows 98, Windows NT 4.0, Windows Millennium Edition, Windows 2000, Windows XP Home Edition, Windows XP Professional, Windows Server 2003 family, .NET Compact Framework - Windows CE .NET

TextBox.OnHandleCreated Method

This member overrides **Control.OnHandleCreated**.

```
[Visual Basic]
Overrides Protected Sub OnHandleCreated( _
   ByVal e As EventArgs _
)
[C#]
protected override void OnHandleCreated(
   EventArgs e
);
[C++]
protected: void OnHandleCreated(
   EventArgs* e
);
[JScript]
protected override function OnHandleCreated(
   e : EventArgs
);
```

Requirements

Platforms: Windows 98, Windows NT 4.0, Windows Millennium Edition, Windows 2000, Windows XP Home Edition, Windows XP Professional, Windows Server 2003 family

TextBox.OnMouseUp Method

This member overrides **Control.OnMouseUp**.

```
[Visual Basic]
Overrides Protected Sub OnMouseUp( _
   ByVal mevent As MouseEventArgs _
)
[C#]
protected override void OnMouseUp(
   MouseEventArgs mevent
);
[C++]
protected: void OnMouseUp(
   MouseEventArgs* mevent
);
[JScript]
protected override function OnMouseUp(
   mevent : MouseEventArgs
);
```

Requirements

Platforms: Windows 98, Windows NT 4.0, Windows Millennium Edition, Windows 2000, Windows XP Home Edition, Windows XP Professional, Windows Server 2003 family, .NET Compact Framework - Windows CE .NET

TextBox.OnTextAlignChanged Method

Raises the **TextAlignChanged** event.

```
[Visual Basic]
Protected Overridable Sub OnTextAlignChanged( _
   ByVal e As EventArgs _
)
[C#]
protected virtual void OnTextAlignChanged(
   EventArgs e
);
[C++]
protected: virtual void OnTextAlignChanged(
   EventArgs* e
);
[JScript]
protected function OnTextAlignChanged(
   e : EventArgs
);
```

Parameters

e

An **EventArgs** that contains the event data.

Remarks

Raising an event invokes the event handler through a delegate. For more information, see **Raising an Event**.

The **OnTextAlignChanged** method also allows derived classes to handle the event without attaching a delegate. This is the preferred technique for handling the event in a derived class.

Notes to Inheritors: When overriding **OnTextAlignChanged** in a derived class, be sure to call the base class's **OnTextAlignChanged** method so that registered delegates receive the event.

Requirements

Platforms: Windows 98, Windows NT 4.0, Windows Millennium Edition, Windows 2000, Windows XP Home Edition, Windows XP Professional, Windows Server 2003 family

TextBox.WndProc Method

This member overrides **Control.WndProc**.

```
[Visual Basic]
Overrides Protected Sub WndProc( _
   ByRef m As Message _
)
[C#]
protected override void WndProc(
   ref Message m
);
```

```
[C++]
protected: void WndProc(
   Message* m
);
[JScript]
protected override function WndProc(
   m : Message
);
```

Requirements

Platforms: Windows 98, Windows NT 4.0, Windows Millennium Edition, Windows 2000, Windows XP Home Edition, Windows XP Professional, Windows Server 2003 family

TextBox.TextAlignChanged Event

Occurs when the value of the **TextAlign** property has changed.

```
[Visual Basic]
Public Event TextAlignChanged As EventHandler
[C#]
public event EventHandler TextAlignChanged;
[C++]
public: __event EventHandler* TextAlignChanged;
```

[JScript] In JScript, you can handle the events defined by a class, but you cannot define your own.

Event Data

The event handler receives an argument of type **EventArgs**.

Remarks

For more information about handling events, see **Consuming Events**.

Requirements

Platforms: Windows 98, Windows NT 4.0, Windows Millennium Edition, Windows 2000, Windows XP Home Edition, Windows XP Professional, Windows Server 2003 family

TextBoxBase Class

Implements the basic functionality required by text controls.

System.Object
System.MarshalByRefObject
System.ComponentModel.Component
System.Windows.Forms.Control
System.Windows.Forms.TextBoxBase
System.Windows.Forms.RichTextBox
System.Windows.Forms.TextBox

[Visual Basic]
```
MustInherit Public Class TextBoxBase
   Inherits Control
```
[C#]
```
public abstract class TextBoxBase : Control
```
[C++]
```
public __gc __abstract class TextBoxBase : public Control
```
[JScript]
```
public abstract class TextBoxBase extends Control
```

Thread Safety

Any public static (**Shared** in Visual Basic) members of this type are safe for multithreaded operations. Any instance members are not guaranteed to be thread safe.

Remarks

This class implements the core features of text manipulation controls, such as **TextBox** and **RichTextBox**. These include text selection, Clipboard functionality, multiline text control support, and many events.

Notes to Inheritors: You do not typically inherit from **TextBox-Base**. To create your own text control class, inherit from **TextBox** or **RichTextBox**.

Example

[Visual Basic, C#] The following example uses **TextBox**, a derived class, to create a multiline **TextBox** control with vertical scroll bars. This example also uses the **AcceptsTab**, **AcceptsReturn**, and **WordWrap** properties to make the multiline text box control useful for creating text documents.

[Visual Basic]
```
Public Sub CreateMyMultilineTextBox()
    ' Create an instance of a TextBox control.
    Dim textBox1 As New TextBox()

    ' Set the Multiline property to true.
    textBox1.Multiline = True
    ' Add vertical scroll bars to the TextBox control.
    textBox1.ScrollBars = ScrollBars.Vertical
    ' Allow the RETURN key in the TextBox control.
    textBox1.AcceptsReturn = True
    ' Allow the TAB key to be entered in the TextBox control.
    textBox1.AcceptsTab = True
    ' Set WordWrap to true to allow text to wrap to the next line.
    textBox1.WordWrap = True
    ' Set the default text of the control.
    textBox1.Text = "Welcome!"
End Sub
```

[C#]
```
public void CreateMyMultilineTextBox()
{
    // Create an instance of a TextBox control.
    TextBox textBox1 = new TextBox();

    // Set the Multiline property to true.
    textBox1.Multiline = true;
    // Add vertical scroll bars to the TextBox control.
    textBox1.ScrollBars = ScrollBars.Vertical;
    // Allow the RETURN key in the TextBox control.
    textBox1.AcceptsReturn = true;
    // Allow the TAB key to be entered in the TextBox control.
    textBox1.AcceptsTab = true;
    // Set WordWrap to true to allow text to wrap to the next line.
    textBox1.WordWrap = true;
    // Set the default text of the control.
    textBox1.Text = "Welcome!";
}
```

Requirements

Namespace: System.Windows.Forms

Platforms: Windows 98, Windows NT 4.0, Windows Millennium Edition, Windows 2000, Windows XP Home Edition, Windows XP Professional, Windows Server 2003 family, .NET Compact Framework - Windows CE .NET

Assembly: System.Windows.Forms (in System.Windows.Forms.dll)

TextBoxBase.AcceptsTab Property

Gets or sets a value indicating whether pressing the TAB key in a multiline text box control types a TAB character in the control instead of moving the focus to the next control in the tab order.

[Visual Basic]
```
Public Property AcceptsTab As Boolean
```
[C#]
```
public bool AcceptsTab {get; set;}
```
[C++]
```
public: __property bool get_AcceptsTab();
public: __property void set_AcceptsTab(bool);
```
[JScript]
```
public function get AcceptsTab() : Boolean;
public function set AcceptsTab(Boolean);
```

Property Value

true if users can enter tabs in a multiline text box using the TAB key; **false** if pressing the TAB key moves the focus. The default is **false**.

Remarks

If the **AcceptsTab** property is set to **true**, the user must press CTRL+TAB to move the focus to the next control in the tab order.

Example

See related example in the **System.Windows.Forms.TextBoxBase** class topic.

Requirements

Platforms: Windows 98, Windows NT 4.0, Windows Millennium Edition, Windows 2000, Windows XP Home Edition, Windows XP Professional, Windows Server 2003 family, .NET Compact Framework - Windows CE .NET

TextBoxBase.AutoSize Property

Gets or sets a value indicating whether the height of the control automatically adjusts when the font assigned to the control is changed.

```
[Visual Basic]
Public Overridable Property AutoSize As Boolean
[C#]
public virtual bool AutoSize {get; set;}
[C++]
public: __property virtual bool get_AutoSize();
public: __property virtual void set_AutoSize(bool);
[JScript]
public function get AutoSize() : Boolean;
public function set AutoSize(Boolean);
```

Property Value

true if the height of the control automatically adjusts when the font is changed; otherwise, **false**. The default is **true**.

Remarks

Multiline text box controls ignore this property setting. When this property is set to **true**, the text box control resizes its height based on the size of the font assigned to the control. You can use this property to ensure that the user can read text assigned to a single-line version of the control regardless of the font.

Requirements

Platforms: Windows 98, Windows NT 4.0, Windows Millennium Edition, Windows 2000, Windows XP Home Edition, Windows XP Professional, Windows Server 2003 family

TextBoxBase.BackColor Property

Gets or sets the background color of the control.

```
[Visual Basic]
Overrides Public Property BackColor As Color
[C#]
public override Color BackColor {get; set;}
[C++]
public: __property Color get_BackColor();
public: __property void set_BackColor(Color);
[JScript]
public override function get BackColor() : Color;
public override function set BackColor(Color);
```

Property Value

A **Color** that represents the background of the control.

Remarks

You can use the **BackColor** property to change the background color of the text control to blend into the color scheme of your forms.

To change the color of the text within the control, use the **ForeColor** property. When setting the **BackColor** property of your text control, ensure that the color you choose does not cause the text of the control to disappear. For example, if the **BackColor** and **ForeColor** properties are both set to **Color.Black**, the text within your textbox control will not be visible.

Requirements

Platforms: Windows 98, Windows NT 4.0, Windows Millennium Edition, Windows 2000, Windows XP Home Edition, Windows XP Professional, Windows Server 2003 family, .NET Compact Framework - Windows CE .NET

TextBoxBase.BackgroundImage Property

This member overrides **Control.BackgroundImage**.

```
[Visual Basic]
Overrides Public Property BackgroundImage As Image
[C#]
public override Image BackgroundImage {get; set;}
[C++]
public: __property Image* get_BackgroundImage();
public: __property void set_BackgroundImage(Image*);
[JScript]
public override function get BackgroundImage() : Image;
public override function set BackgroundImage(Image);
```

Requirements

Platforms: Windows 98, Windows NT 4.0, Windows Millennium Edition, Windows 2000, Windows XP Home Edition, Windows XP Professional, Windows Server 2003 family

TextBoxBase.BorderStyle Property

Gets or sets the border type of the text box control.

```
[Visual Basic]
Public Property BorderStyle As BorderStyle
[C#]
public BorderStyle BorderStyle {get; set;}
[C++]
public: __property BorderStyle get_BorderStyle();
public: __property void set_BorderStyle(BorderStyle);
[JScript]
public function get BorderStyle() : BorderStyle;
public function set BorderStyle(BorderStyle);
```

Property Value

A **BorderStyle** that represents the border type of the text box control. The default is **Fixed3D**.

Exceptions

Exception Type	Condition
InvalidEnumArgumentException	A value that is not within the range of valid values for the enumeration was assigned to the property.

Remarks

You can use the **BorderStyle** property to create borderless and flat style controls, in addition to the default three-dimensional control.

Note The derived class, **RichTextBox**, does not support the **BorderStyle.FixedSingle** style. This style will cause the borderstyle to use the **BorderStyle.Fixed3D** style instead.

Example

See related example in the **System.Windows.Forms.TextBoxBase** class topic.

Requirements

Platforms: Windows 98, Windows NT 4.0, Windows Millennium Edition, Windows 2000, Windows XP Home Edition, Windows XP Professional, Windows Server 2003 family

TextBoxBase.CanUndo Property

Gets a value indicating whether the user can undo the previous operation in a text box control.

[Visual Basic]
```
Public ReadOnly Property CanUndo As Boolean
```
[C#]
```
public bool CanUndo {get;}
```
[C++]
```
public: __property bool get_CanUndo();
```
[JScript]
```
public function get CanUndo() : Boolean;
```

Property Value

true if the user can undo the previous operation performed in a text box control; otherwise, **false**.

Remarks

If this method returns **true**, you can call the **Undo** method to undo the last operation in a text box. You can use this method in the **Popup** event of a **MenuItem**, or in code that manages the state of buttons on a **ToolBar** to enable or disable the ability to undo the previous operation in a text box control.

Example

See related example in the **System.Windows.Forms.TextBoxBase** class topic.

Requirements

Platforms: Windows 98, Windows NT 4.0, Windows Millennium Edition, Windows 2000, Windows XP Home Edition, Windows XP Professional, Windows Server 2003 family

TextBoxBase.CreateParams Property

This member overrides **Control.CreateParams**.

[Visual Basic]
```
Overrides Protected ReadOnly Property CreateParams As CreateParams
```
[C#]
```
protected override CreateParams CreateParams {get;}
```
[C++]
```
protected: __property CreateParams* get_CreateParams();
```
[JScript]
```
protected override function get CreateParams() : CreateParams;
```

Requirements

Platforms: Windows 98, Windows NT 4.0, Windows Millennium Edition, Windows 2000, Windows XP Home Edition, Windows XP Professional, Windows Server 2003 family

TextBoxBase.DefaultSize Property

This member overrides **Control.DefaultSize**.

[Visual Basic]
```
Overrides Protected ReadOnly Property DefaultSize As Size
```
[C#]
```
protected override Size DefaultSize {get;}
```
[C++]
```
protected: __property Size get_DefaultSize();
```
[JScript]
```
protected override function get DefaultSize() : Size;
```

Requirements

Platforms: Windows 98, Windows NT 4.0, Windows Millennium Edition, Windows 2000, Windows XP Home Edition, Windows XP Professional, Windows Server 2003 family

TextBoxBase.ForeColor Property

Gets or sets the foreground color of the control.

[Visual Basic]
```
Overrides Public Property ForeColor As Color
```
[C#]
```
public override Color ForeColor {get; set;}
```
[C++]
```
public: __property Color get_ForeColor();
public: __property void set_ForeColor(Color);
```
[JScript]
```
public override function get ForeColor() : Color;
public override function set ForeColor(Color);
```

Property Value

A **Color** that represents the control's foreground color.

Remarks

You can use the **ForeColor** property to change the color of the text within the control to match the text of other controls on your form. You can also use this property to highlight a specific text box that contains an invalid value.

To change the background color of the control, use the **BackColor** property. When setting the **ForeColor** property of your text control, ensure that the color you choose does not cause the text of the control to disappear. For example, if the **ForeColor** and **BackColor** properties are both set to **Color.Black**, the text within your textbox control will not be visible.

Requirements

Platforms: Windows 98, Windows NT 4.0, Windows Millennium Edition, Windows 2000, Windows XP Home Edition, Windows XP Professional, Windows Server 2003 family, .NET Compact Framework - Windows CE .NET

TextBoxBase.HideSelection Property

Gets or sets a value indicating whether the selected text in the text box control remains highlighted when the control loses focus.

[Visual Basic]
```
Public Property HideSelection As Boolean
```
[C#]
```
public bool HideSelection {get; set;}
```

```
[C++]
public: __property bool get_HideSelection();
public: __property void set_HideSelection(bool);
[JScript]
public function get HideSelection() : Boolean;
public function set HideSelection(Boolean);
```

Property Value

true if the selected text does not appear highlighted when the text box control loses focus; **false**, if the selected text remains highlighted when the text box control loses focus. The default is **true**.

Remarks

You can use this property to keep text highlighted in a text box control while another form or a dialog box has focus, such as a spelling checker dialog box.

Requirements

Platforms: Windows 98, Windows NT 4.0, Windows Millennium Edition, Windows 2000, Windows XP Home Edition, Windows XP Professional, Windows Server 2003 family

TextBoxBase.Lines Property

Gets or sets the lines of text in a text box control.

```
[Visual Basic]
Public Property Lines As String ()
[C#]
public string[] Lines {get; set;}
[C++]
public: __property String* get_Lines();
public: __property void set_Lines(String* __gc[]);
[JScript]
public function get Lines() : String[];
public function set Lines(String[]);
```

Property Value

An array of strings that contains the text in a text box control.

Remarks

Each element in the array becomes a line of text in the text box control. If the **Multiline** property of the text box control is set to **true** and a newline character appears in the text, the text following the newline character is added to a new element in the array and displayed on a separate line.

Example

See related example in the **System.Windows.Forms.TextBoxBase** class topic.

Requirements

Platforms: Windows 98, Windows NT 4.0, Windows Millennium Edition, Windows 2000, Windows XP Home Edition, Windows XP Professional, Windows Server 2003 family

TextBoxBase.MaxLength Property

Gets or sets the maximum number of characters the user can type or paste into the text box control.

```
[Visual Basic]
Public Overridable Property MaxLength As Integer
[C#]
public virtual int MaxLength {get; set;}
[C++]
public: __property virtual int get_MaxLength();
public: __property virtual void set_MaxLength(int);
[JScript]
public function get MaxLength() : int;
public function set MaxLength(int);
```

Property Value

The number of characters that can be entered into the control. The default is 32767.

Exceptions

Exception Type	Condition
ArgumentException	The value assigned to the property is less than 0.

Remarks

You can use this property to restrict the length of text entered in the control for values such as postal codes and telephone numbers, or to restrict the length of text entered when the data is to be entered in a database. You can limit the text entered into the control to the maximum length of the corresponding field in the database.

> **Note** In code, you can set the value of the **Text** property to a value that has a length greater than the value specified by the **MaxLength** property. This property only affects text entered into the control at run time.

Windows NT 4.0, Windows 2000, Windows Server 2003 family Platform Note: For single line text box controls, if the **MaxLength** property is set to 0, the maximum number of characters the user can enter is 2147483646 or an amount based on available memory, whichever is smaller. For multiline text box controls, the maximum number of characters the user can enter is 4294967295 or an amount based on available memory, whichever is smaller.

Windows 95, Windows 98, Windows 98 Second Edition, Windows Millennium Edition Platform Note: For single line text box controls, if the **MaxLength** property is set to 0, the maximum number of characters the user can enter is 32,766 or an amount based on available memory, whichever is smaller. For multiline text box controls, the maximum number of characters the user can enter is 65,535 or an amount based on available memory, whichever is smaller.

Example

See related example in the **System.Windows.Forms.TextBoxBase** class topic.

Requirements

Platforms: Windows 98, Windows NT 4.0, Windows Millennium Edition, Windows 2000, Windows XP Home Edition, Windows XP Professional, Windows Server 2003 family, .NET Compact Framework - Windows CE .NET

TextBoxBase.Modified Property

Gets or sets a value that indicates that the text box control has been modified by the user since the control was created or its contents were last set.

```
[Visual Basic]
Public Property Modified As Boolean
```

```
[C#]
public bool Modified {get; set;}
[C++]
public: __property bool get_Modified();
public: __property void set_Modified(bool);
[JScript]
public function get Modified() : Boolean;
public function set Modified(Boolean);
```

Property Value

true if the control's contents have been modified; otherwise, **false**. The default is **false**.

Remarks

You can use this property to determine if the user has modified the contents of the text box control. You can also set this property in code to indicate that changes were made to the text box control by the application. This property can be used by validation and data-saving methods to determine if changes were made in a text box control so the changed contents can be validated or saved.

Example

See related example in the **System.Windows.Forms.TextBoxBase** class topic.

Requirements

Platforms: Windows 98, Windows NT 4.0, Windows Millennium Edition, Windows 2000, Windows XP Home Edition, Windows XP Professional, Windows Server 2003 family, .NET Compact Framework - Windows CE .NET

TextBoxBase.Multiline Property

Gets or sets a value indicating whether this is a multiline text box control.

```
[Visual Basic]
Public Overridable Property Multiline As Boolean
[C#]
public virtual bool Multiline {get; set;}
[C++]
public: __property virtual bool get_Multiline();
public: __property virtual void set_Multiline(bool);
[JScript]
public function get Multiline() : Boolean;
public function set Multiline(Boolean);
```

Property Value

true if the control is a multiline text box control; otherwise, **false**.

Remarks

A multiline text box allows you to display more than one line of text in the control. If the **WordWrap** property is set to **true**, text entered into the multiline text box is wrapped to the next line in the control. If the **WordWrap** property is set to **false**, text entered into the multiline text box control will be displayed on the same line until a newline character is entered.

You can add scroll bars to a text box using the **ScrollBars** property to display horizontal and/or vertical scroll bars. This allows the user to scroll through the text that extends beyond the dimensions of the control.

Note This property is set to **false** by default for all derived classes, with the exception of the **RichTextBox** control.

Example

See related example in the **System.Windows.Forms.TextBoxBase** class topic.

Requirements

Platforms: Windows 98, Windows NT 4.0, Windows Millennium Edition, Windows 2000, Windows XP Home Edition, Windows XP Professional, Windows Server 2003 family, .NET Compact Framework - Windows CE .NET

TextBoxBase.PreferredHeight Property

Gets the preferred height for a single-line text box.

```
[Visual Basic]
Public ReadOnly Property PreferredHeight As Integer
[C#]
public int PreferredHeight {get;}
[C++]
public: __property int get_PreferredHeight();
[JScript]
public function get PreferredHeight() : int;
```

Property Value

The preferred height of a single-line text box.

Remarks

The size returned by this property is based on the font height and border style of the text box. You can use this property to determine the appropriate size of the text box to ensure that text is properly displayed in the control. The value returned by this property is in pixels.

Example

See related example in the **System.Windows.Forms.TextBoxBase** class topic.

Requirements

Platforms: Windows 98, Windows NT 4.0, Windows Millennium Edition, Windows 2000, Windows XP Home Edition, Windows XP Professional, Windows Server 2003 family

TextBoxBase.ReadOnly Property

Gets or sets a value indicating whether text in the text box is read-only.

```
[Visual Basic]
Public Property ReadOnly As Boolean
[C#]
public bool ReadOnly {get; set;}
[C++]
public: __property bool get_ReadOnly();
public: __property void set_ReadOnly(bool);
[JScript]
public function get ReadOnly() : Boolean;
public function set ReadOnly(Boolean);
```

Property Value

true if the text box is read-only; otherwise, **false**. The default is **false**.

Remarks

When this property is set to **true**, the contents of the control cannot be changed by the user at runtime. With this property set to **true**, you can still set the value of the **Text** property in code. You can use this feature instead of disabling the control with the **Enabled** property to allow the contents to be copied.

Requirements

Platforms: Windows 98, Windows NT 4.0,
Windows Millennium Edition, Windows 2000,
Windows XP Home Edition, Windows XP Professional,
Windows Server 2003 family,
.NET Compact Framework - Windows CE .NET

TextBoxBase.SelectedText Property

Gets or sets a value indicating the currently selected text in the control.

```
[Visual Basic]
Public Overridable Property SelectedText As String
[C#]
public virtual string SelectedText {get; set;}
[C++]
public: __property virtual String* get_SelectedText();
public: __property virtual void set_SelectedText(String*);
[JScript]
public function get SelectedText() : String;
public function set SelectedText(String);
```

Property Value

A string that represents the currently selected text in the text box.

Remarks

You can assign text to this property to change the text currently selected in the text box. If no text is currently selected in the text box, this property returns a zero-length string.

Example

See related example in the **System.Windows.Forms.TextBoxBase** class topic.

Requirements

Platforms: Windows 98, Windows NT 4.0,
Windows Millennium Edition, Windows 2000,
Windows XP Home Edition, Windows XP Professional,
Windows Server 2003 family,
.NET Compact Framework - Windows CE .NET

TextBoxBase.SelectionLength Property

Gets or sets the number of characters selected in the text box.

```
[Visual Basic]
Public Overridable Property SelectionLength As Integer
[C#]
public virtual int SelectionLength {get; set;}
[C++]
public: __property virtual int get_SelectionLength();
public: __property virtual void set_SelectionLength(int);
[JScript]
public function get SelectionLength() : int;
public function set SelectionLength(int);
```

Property Value

The number of characters selected in the text box.

Exceptions

Exception Type	Condition
ArgumentException	The value assigned to the property is less than zero.

Remarks

You can use this property to determine if any characters are currently selected in the text box control before performing operations on the selected text. When the value of the **SelectionLength** property is set to a value that is larger than the number of characters within the text of the control, the value of the **SelectionLength** property is set to the entire length of text within the control minus the value of the **SelectionStart** property (if any value is specified for the **SelectionStart** property).

> **Note** You can programmatically move the caret within the text box by setting the **SelectionStart** to the position within the text box where you want the caret to move to and set the **SelectionLength** property to a value of zero (0). The text box must have focus in order for the caret to be moved.

Example

See related example in the **System.Windows.Forms.TextBoxBase** class topic.

Requirements

Platforms: Windows 98, Windows NT 4.0,
Windows Millennium Edition, Windows 2000,
Windows XP Home Edition, Windows XP Professional,
Windows Server 2003 family,
.NET Compact Framework - Windows CE .NET

TextBoxBase.SelectionStart Property

Gets or sets the starting point of text selected in the text box.

```
[Visual Basic]
Public Property SelectionStart As Integer
[C#]
public int SelectionStart {get; set;}
[C++]
public: __property int get_SelectionStart();
public: __property void set_SelectionStart(int);
[JScript]
public function get SelectionStart() : int;
public function set SelectionStart(int);
```

Property Value

The starting position of text selected in the text box.

Exceptions

Exception Type	Condition
ArgumentException	The value assigned to the property is less than zero.

Remarks

If no text is selected in the control, this property indicates the insertion point for new text. If you set this property to a location beyond the length of the text in the control, the selection start position will be placed after the last character. When text is selected in the text box control, changing this property might decrease the value of the **SelectionLength** property. If the remaining text in the control after the position indicated by the **SelectionStart** property is less than the value of the **SelectionLength** property, the value of the **SelectionLength** property is automatically decreased. The value of the **SelectionStart** property never causes an increase in the **SelectionLength** property.

> **Note** You can programmatically move the caret within the text box by setting the **SelectionStart** to the position within the text box where you want the caret to move to and set the **SelectionLength** property to a value of zero (0). The text box must have focus in order for the caret to be moved.

Example

See related example in the **System.Windows.Forms.TextBoxBase** class topic.

Requirements

Platforms: Windows 98, Windows NT 4.0, Windows Millennium Edition, Windows 2000, Windows XP Home Edition, Windows XP Professional, Windows Server 2003 family, .NET Compact Framework - Windows CE .NET

TextBoxBase.Text Property

Gets or sets the current text in the text box.

```
[Visual Basic]
Overrides Public Property Text As String
[C#]
public override string Text {get; set;}
[C++]
public: __property String* get_Text();
public: __property void set_Text(String*);
[JScript]
public override function get Text() : String;
public override function set Text(String);
```

Property Value

The text displayed in the control.

Remarks

To display multiple lines of text in a text box, set the **Multiline** property to **true**. To read or set the text of a multiline text box, use the **Lines** property. The amount of text that can be entered in the **RichTextBox** control is limited only by available system memory.

Windows 98, Windows Millennium Edition Platform Note: The amount of text that can be stored in the **Text** property is limited to 65KB of memory for the **TextBox** control.

Windows NT 4.0, Windows 2000, Windows Server 2003 family Platform Note: The amount of text that can be stored in the **Text** property is limited to the amount available system memory.

Example

See related example in the **System.Windows.Forms.TextBoxBase** class topic.

Requirements

Platforms: Windows 98, Windows NT 4.0, Windows Millennium Edition, Windows 2000, Windows XP Home Edition, Windows XP Professional, Windows Server 2003 family, .NET Compact Framework - Windows CE .NET

TextBoxBase.TextLength Property

Gets the length of text in the control.

```
[Visual Basic]
Public Overridable ReadOnly Property TextLength As Integer
[C#]
public virtual int TextLength {get;}
[C++]
public: __property virtual int get_TextLength();
[JScript]
public function get TextLength() : int;
```

Property Value

The number of characters contained in the text of the control.

Remarks

You can use this property to determine the number of characters in a string for tasks such as searching for specific strings of text within the text of the control, where knowledge of the total number of characters is needed.

Example

See related example in the **System.Windows.Forms.TextBoxBase** class topic.

Requirements

Platforms: Windows 98, Windows NT 4.0, Windows Millennium Edition, Windows 2000, Windows XP Home Edition, Windows XP Professional, Windows Server 2003 family, .NET Compact Framework - Windows CE .NET

TextBoxBase.WordWrap Property

Indicates whether a multiline text box control automatically wraps words to the beginning of the next line when necessary.

```
[Visual Basic]
Public Property WordWrap As Boolean
[C#]
public bool WordWrap {get; set;}
[C++]
public: __property bool get_WordWrap();
public: __property void set_WordWrap(bool);
[JScript]
public function get WordWrap() : Boolean;
public function set WordWrap(Boolean);
```

Property Value

true if the multiline text box control wraps words; **false** if the text box control automatically scrolls horizontally when the user types past the right edge of the control. The default is **true**.

Remarks

If this property is set to **true**, horizontal scroll bars are not displayed regardless of the **ScrollBars** property setting.

Note In the derived class, **TextBox**, text within the control will always wrap regardless of the property setting of this property unless the **TextAlign** property is set to **HorizontalAlignment.Left**.

Example

See related example in the **System.Windows.Forms.TextBoxBase** class topic.

Requirements

Platforms: Windows 98, Windows NT 4.0, Windows Millennium Edition, Windows 2000, Windows XP Home Edition, Windows XP Professional, Windows Server 2003 family, .NET Compact Framework - Windows CE .NET

TextBoxBase.AppendText Method

Appends text to the current text of text box.

```
[Visual Basic]
Public Sub AppendText( _
   ByVal text As String _
)
[C#]
public void AppendText(
   string text
);
[C++]
public: void AppendText(
   String* text
);
[JScript]
public function AppendText(
   text : String
);
```

Parameters

text

The text to append to the current contents of the text box.

Remarks

You can use this method to add text to the existing text in the control instead of using the concatenation operator (+) to concatenate text to the **Text** property.

Example

See related example in the **System.Windows.Forms.TextBoxBase** class topic.

Requirements

Platforms: Windows 98, Windows NT 4.0, Windows Millennium Edition, Windows 2000, Windows XP Home Edition, Windows XP Professional, Windows Server 2003 family

TextBoxBase.Clear Method

Clears all text from the text box control.

```
[Visual Basic]
Public Sub Clear()
[C#]
public void Clear();
[C++]
public: void Clear();
[JScript]
public function Clear();
```

Remarks

You can use this method to clear the contents of the control instead of assigning the **Text** property an empty string.

Example

See related example in the **System.Windows.Forms.TextBoxBase** class topic.

Requirements

Platforms: Windows 98, Windows NT 4.0, Windows Millennium Edition, Windows 2000, Windows XP Home Edition, Windows XP Professional, Windows Server 2003 family

TextBoxBase.ClearUndo Method

Clears information about the most recent operation from the undo buffer of the text box.

```
[Visual Basic]
Public Sub ClearUndo()
[C#]
public void ClearUndo();
[C++]
public: void ClearUndo();
[JScript]
public function ClearUndo();
```

Remarks

You can use this method to prevent an undo operation from repeating, based on the state of your application.

Example

See related example in the **System.Windows.Forms.TextBoxBase** class topic.

Requirements

Platforms: Windows 98, Windows NT 4.0, Windows Millennium Edition, Windows 2000, Windows XP Home Edition, Windows XP Professional, Windows Server 2003 family

TextBoxBase.Copy Method

Copies the current selection in the text box to the Clipboard.

```
[Visual Basic]
Public Sub Copy()
[C#]
public void Copy();
[C++]
public: void Copy();
[JScript]
public function Copy();
```

Remarks

You can use this method, instead of using the **Clipboard** class, to copy text in the text box and place it in the Clipboard.

Example

See related example in the **System.Windows.Forms.TextBoxBase** class topic.

Requirements

Platforms: Windows 98, Windows NT 4.0, Windows Millennium Edition, Windows 2000, Windows XP Home Edition, Windows XP Professional, Windows Server 2003 family

TextBoxBase.CreateHandle Method

This member overrides **Control.CreateHandle**.

```
[Visual Basic]
Overrides Protected Sub CreateHandle()
[C#]
protected override void CreateHandle();
[C++]
protected: void CreateHandle();
[JScript]
protected override function CreateHandle();
```

Requirements

Platforms: Windows 98, Windows NT 4.0, Windows Millennium Edition, Windows 2000, Windows XP Home Edition, Windows XP Professional, Windows Server 2003 family

TextBoxBase.Cut Method

Moves the current selection in the text box to the Clipboard.

```
[Visual Basic]
Public Sub Cut()
[C#]
public void Cut();
[C++]
public: void Cut();
[JScript]
public function Cut();
```

Remarks

This method will only cut text from the text box if text is selected in the control. You can use this method, instead of using the **Clipboard** class, to copy text in the text box and move it to the Clipboard.

Example

See related example in the **System.Windows.Forms.TextBoxBase** class topic.

Requirements

Platforms: Windows 98, Windows NT 4.0, Windows Millennium Edition, Windows 2000, Windows XP Home Edition, Windows XP Professional, Windows Server 2003 family

TextBoxBase.IsInputKey Method

This member overrides **Control.IsInputKey**.

```
[Visual Basic]
Overrides Protected Function IsInputKey( _
   ByVal keyData As Keys _
) As Boolean
[C#]
protected override bool IsInputKey(
   Keys keyData
);
[C++]
protected: bool IsInputKey(
   Keys keyData
);
[JScript]
protected override function IsInputKey(
   keyData : Keys
) : Boolean;
```

Requirements

Platforms: Windows 98, Windows NT 4.0, Windows Millennium Edition, Windows 2000, Windows XP Home Edition, Windows XP Professional, Windows Server 2003 family

TextBoxBase.OnAcceptsTabChanged Method

Raises the **AcceptsTabChanged** event.

```
[Visual Basic]
Protected Overridable Sub OnAcceptsTabChanged( _
   ByVal e As EventArgs _
)
[C#]
protected virtual void OnAcceptsTabChanged(
   EventArgs e
);
[C++]
protected: virtual void OnAcceptsTabChanged(
   EventArgs* e
);
[JScript]
protected function OnAcceptsTabChanged(
   e : EventArgs
);
```

Parameters

e

An **EventArgs** that contains the event data.

Remarks

Raising an event invokes the event handler through a delegate. For more information, see **Raising an Event**.

The **OnAcceptsTabChanged** method also allows derived classes to handle the event without attaching a delegate. This is the preferred technique for handling the event in a derived class.

Notes to Inheritors: When overriding **OnAcceptsTabChanged** in a derived class, be sure to call the base class's **OnAcceptsTabChanged** method so that registered delegates receive the event.

Requirements

Platforms: Windows 98, Windows NT 4.0, Windows Millennium Edition, Windows 2000, Windows XP Home Edition, Windows XP Professional, Windows Server 2003 family

TextBoxBase.OnAutoSizeChanged Method

Raises the **AutoSizeChanged** event.

```
[Visual Basic]
Protected Overridable Sub OnAutoSizeChanged( _
   ByVal e As EventArgs _
)
[C#]
protected virtual void OnAutoSizeChanged(
   EventArgs e
);
[C++]
protected: virtual void OnAutoSizeChanged(
   EventArgs* e
);
[JScript]
protected function OnAutoSizeChanged(
   e : EventArgs
);
```

Parameters

e

An **EventArgs** that contains the event data.

Remarks

Raising an event invokes the event handler through a delegate. For more information, see **Raising an Event**.

The **OnAutoSizeChanged** method also allows derived classes to handle the event without attaching a delegate. This is the preferred technique for handling the event in a derived class.

Notes to Inheritors: When overriding **OnAutoSizeChanged** in a derived class, be sure to call the base class's **OnAutoSizeChanged** method so that registered delegates receive the event.

Requirements

Platforms: Windows 98, Windows NT 4.0, Windows Millennium Edition, Windows 2000, Windows XP Home Edition, Windows XP Professional, Windows Server 2003 family

TextBoxBase.OnBorderStyleChanged Method

Raises the **BorderStyleChanged** event.

```
[Visual Basic]
Protected Overridable Sub OnBorderStyleChanged( _
   ByVal e As EventArgs _
)
[C#]
protected virtual void OnBorderStyleChanged(
   EventArgs e
);
[C++]
protected: virtual void OnBorderStyleChanged(
   EventArgs* e
);
[JScript]
protected function OnBorderStyleChanged(
   e : EventArgs
);
```

Parameters

e

An **EventArgs** that contains the event data.

Remarks

Raising an event invokes the event handler through a delegate. For more information, see **Raising an Event**.

The **OnBorderStyleChanged** method also allows derived classes to handle the event without attaching a delegate. This is the preferred technique for handling the event in a derived class.

Notes to Inheritors: When overriding **OnBorderStyleChanged** in a derived class, be sure to call the base class's **OnBorderStyleChanged** method so that registered delegates receive the event.

Requirements

Platforms: Windows 98, Windows NT 4.0, Windows Millennium Edition, Windows 2000, Windows XP Home Edition, Windows XP Professional, Windows Server 2003 family

TextBoxBase.OnFontChanged Method

This member overrides **Control.OnFontChanged**.

```
[Visual Basic]
Overrides Protected Sub OnFontChanged( _
   ByVal e As EventArgs _
)
[C#]
protected override void OnFontChanged(
   EventArgs e
);
[C++]
protected: void OnFontChanged(
   EventArgs* e
);
[JScript]
protected override function OnFontChanged(
   e : EventArgs
);
```

Requirements

Platforms: Windows 98, Windows NT 4.0, Windows Millennium Edition, Windows 2000, Windows XP Home Edition, Windows XP Professional, Windows Server 2003 family

TextBoxBase.OnHandleCreated Method

This member overrides **Control.OnHandleCreated**.

```
[Visual Basic]
Overrides Protected Sub OnHandleCreated( _
   ByVal e As EventArgs _
)
[C#]
protected override void OnHandleCreated(
   EventArgs e
);
[C++]
protected: void OnHandleCreated(
   EventArgs* e
);
```

```
[JScript]
protected override function OnHandleCreated(
   e : EventArgs
);
```

Requirements

Platforms: Windows 98, Windows NT 4.0, Windows Millennium Edition, Windows 2000, Windows XP Home Edition, Windows XP Professional, Windows Server 2003 family

TextBoxBase.OnHandleDestroyed Method

This member overrides **Control.OnHandleDestroyed**.

```
[Visual Basic]
Overrides Protected Sub OnHandleDestroyed( _
   ByVal e As EventArgs _
)
[C#]
protected override void OnHandleDestroyed(
   EventArgs e
);
[C++]
protected: void OnHandleDestroyed(
   EventArgs* e
);
[JScript]
protected override function OnHandleDestroyed(
   e : EventArgs
);
```

Requirements

Platforms: Windows 98, Windows NT 4.0, Windows Millennium Edition, Windows 2000, Windows XP Home Edition, Windows XP Professional, Windows Server 2003 family

TextBoxBase.OnHideSelectionChanged Method

Raise the **HideSelectionChanged** event.

```
[Visual Basic]
Protected Overridable Sub OnHideSelectionChanged( _
   ByVal e As EventArgs _
)
[C#]
protected virtual void OnHideSelectionChanged(
   EventArgs e
);
[C++]
protected: virtual void OnHideSelectionChanged(
   EventArgs* e
);
[JScript]
protected function OnHideSelectionChanged(
   e : EventArgs
);
```

Parameters

e

An **EventArgs** that contains the event data.

Remarks

Raising an event invokes the event handler through a delegate.

The **OnHideSelectionChanged** method also allows derived classes to handle the event without attaching a delegate. This is the preferred technique for handling the event in a derived class.

Notes to Inheritors: When overriding **OnHideSelectionChanged** in a derived class, be sure to call the base class's **OnHideSelectionChanged** method so that registered delegates receive the event.

Requirements

Platforms: Windows 98, Windows NT 4.0, Windows Millennium Edition, Windows 2000, Windows XP Home Edition, Windows XP Professional, Windows Server 2003 family

TextBoxBase.OnModifiedChanged Method

Raises the **ModifiedChanged** event.

```
[Visual Basic]
Protected Overridable Sub OnModifiedChanged( _
   ByVal e As EventArgs _
)
[C#]
protected virtual void OnModifiedChanged(
   EventArgs e
);
[C++]
protected: virtual void OnModifiedChanged(
   EventArgs* e
);
[JScript]
protected function OnModifiedChanged(
   e : EventArgs
);
```

Parameters

e

An **EventArgs** that contains the event data.

Remarks

Raising an event invokes the event handler through a delegate.

The **OnModifiedChanged** method also allows derived classes to handle the event without attaching a delegate. This is the preferred technique for handling the event in a derived class.

Notes to Inheritors: When overriding **OnModifiedChanged** in a derived class, be sure to call the base class's **OnModifiedChanged** method so that registered delegates receive the event.

Requirements

Platforms: Windows 98, Windows NT 4.0, Windows Millennium Edition, Windows 2000, Windows XP Home Edition, Windows XP Professional, Windows Server 2003 family

TextBoxBase.OnMultilineChanged Method

Raises the **MultilineChanged** event.

```
[Visual Basic]
Protected Overridable Sub OnMultilineChanged( _
   ByVal e As EventArgs _
)
```

[C#]
```
protected virtual void OnMultilineChanged(
   EventArgs e
);
```
[C++]
```
protected: virtual void OnMultilineChanged(
   EventArgs* e
);
```
[JScript]
```
protected function OnMultilineChanged(
   e : EventArgs
);
```

Parameters

e

An **EventArgs** that contains the event data.

Remarks

Raising an event invokes the event handler through a delegate.

The **OnMultilineChanged** method also allows derived classes to handle the event without attaching a delegate. This is the preferred technique for handling the event in a derived class.

Notes to Inheritors: When overriding **OnMultilineChanged** in a derived class, be sure to call the base class's **OnMultilineChanged** method so that registered delegates receive the event.

Requirements

Platforms: Windows 98, Windows NT 4.0, Windows Millennium Edition, Windows 2000, Windows XP Home Edition, Windows XP Professional, Windows Server 2003 family

TextBoxBase.OnReadOnlyChanged Method

Raises the **ReadOnlyChanged** event.

[Visual Basic]
```
Protected Overridable Sub OnReadOnlyChanged( _
   ByVal e As EventArgs _
)
```
[C#]
```
protected virtual void OnReadOnlyChanged(
   EventArgs e
);
```
[C++]
```
protected: virtual void OnReadOnlyChanged(
   EventArgs* e
);
```
[JScript]
```
protected function OnReadOnlyChanged(
   e : EventArgs
);
```

Parameters

e

An **EventArgs** that contains the event data.

Remarks

Raising an event invokes the event handler through a delegate.

The **OnReadOnlyChanged** method also allows derived classes to handle the event without attaching a delegate. This is the preferred technique for handling the event in a derived class.

Notes to Inheritors: When overriding **OnReadOnlyChanged** in a derived class, be sure to call the base class's **OnReadOnlyChanged** method so that registered delegates receive the event.

Requirements

Platforms: Windows 98, Windows NT 4.0, Windows Millennium Edition, Windows 2000, Windows XP Home Edition, Windows XP Professional, Windows Server 2003 family

TextBoxBase.Paste Method

Replaces the current selection in the text box with the contents of the Clipboard.

[Visual Basic]
```
Public Sub Paste()
```
[C#]
```
public void Paste();
```
[C++]
```
public: void Paste();
```
[JScript]
```
public function Paste();
```

Remarks

The **Paste** method will only paste text into the control if text is currently stored in the Clipboard. Once your application exits, any content stored in the Clipboard is removed.

Example

See related example in the **System.Windows.Forms.TextBoxBase** class topic.

Requirements

Platforms: Windows 98, Windows NT 4.0, Windows Millennium Edition, Windows 2000, Windows XP Home Edition, Windows XP Professional, Windows Server 2003 family

.NET Framework Security:

- **UIPermission** for reading from the Clipboard. Associated enumeration: **UIPermissionClipboard.AllClipboard**.

TextBoxBase.ProcessDialogKey Method

This member overrides **Control.ProcessDialogKey**.

[Visual Basic]
```
Overrides Protected Function ProcessDialogKey( _
   ByVal keyData As Keys _
) As Boolean
```
[C#]
```
protected override bool ProcessDialogKey(
   Keys keyData
);
```
[C++]
```
protected: bool ProcessDialogKey(
   Keys keyData
);
```
[JScript]
```
protected override function ProcessDialogKey(
   keyData : Keys
) : Boolean;
```

Requirements

Platforms: Windows 98, Windows NT 4.0, Windows Millennium Edition, Windows 2000, Windows XP Home Edition, Windows XP Professional, Windows Server 2003 family

TextBoxBase.ScrollToCaret Method

Scrolls the contents of the control to the current caret position.

```
[Visual Basic]
Public Sub ScrollToCaret()
[C#]
public void ScrollToCaret();
[C++]
public: void ScrollToCaret();
[JScript]
public function ScrollToCaret();
```

Remarks

This method enables you to scroll the contents of the control until the caret is within the visibile region of the control. If the caret is positioned below the visible region of the control, the **ScrollToCaret** method will scroll the contents of the control until the caret is visible at the bottom of the control. If the caret is positioned above the visible region of the control, this method scrolls the contents of the control until the caret is visible at the top of the control. You can use this method in a multiline text box to ensure that the current text entry point is within the visible region of the control.

> **Note** This method has no effect if the control does not have focus or if the caret is already positioned in the visible region of the control.

Requirements

Platforms: Windows 98, Windows NT 4.0, Windows Millennium Edition, Windows 2000, Windows XP Home Edition, Windows XP Professional, Windows Server 2003 family, .NET Compact Framework - Windows CE .NET

TextBoxBase.Select Method

Selects text within the control.

Overload List

Selects a range of text in the text box.

Supported by the .NET Compact Framework.

[Visual Basic] **Overloads Public Sub Select(Integer, Integer)**

[C#] **public void Select(int, int);**

[C++] **public: void Select(int, int);**

[JScript] **public function Select(int, int);**

Inherited from **Control**.

[Visual Basic] **Overloads Public Sub Select()**

[C#] **public void Select();**

[C++] **public: void Select();**

[JScript] **public function Select();**

Inherited from **Control**.

[Visual Basic] **Overloads Protected Overridable Sub Select(Boolean, Boolean)**

[C#] **protected virtual void Select(bool, bool);**

[C++] **protected: virtual void Select(bool, bool);**

[JScript] **protected function Select(Boolean, Boolean);**

Example

See related example in the **System.Windows.Forms.TextBoxBase** class topic.

TextBoxBase.Select Method (Int32, Int32)

Selects a range of text in the text box.

```
[Visual Basic]
Overloads Public Sub Select( _
   ByVal start As Integer, _
   ByVal length As Integer _
)
[C#]
public void Select(
   int start,
   int length
);
[C++]
public: void Select(
   int start,
   int length
);
[JScript]
public function Select(
   start : int,
   length : int
);
```

Parameters

start
: The position of the first character in the current text selection within the text box.

length
: The number of characters to select.

Exceptions

Exception Type	Condition
ArgumentException	The value assigned to either the *start* parameter or the *length* parameter is less than zero.

Remarks

If you want to set the start position to the first character in the control's text, set the *start* parameter to 0. You can use this method to select a substring of text, such as when searching through the text of the control and replacing information.

> **Note** You can programmatically move the caret within the text box by setting the *start* parameter to the position within the text box where you want the caret to move to and set the *length* parameter to a value of zero (0). The text box must have focus in order for the caret to be moved.

Example

See related example in the **System.Windows.Forms.TextBoxBase** class topic.

Requirements

Platforms: Windows 98, Windows NT 4.0, Windows Millennium Edition, Windows 2000, Windows XP Home Edition, Windows XP Professional, Windows Server 2003 family, .NET Compact Framework - Windows CE .NET

TextBoxBase.SelectAll Method

Selects all text in the text box.

```
[Visual Basic]
Public Sub SelectAll()
[C#]
public void SelectAll();
[C++]
public: void SelectAll();
[JScript]
public function SelectAll();
```

Remarks

This method enables you to select all text within the control. You can use this method inconjunction with the **Cut** method, which requires text to be selected in the control, to cut the entire contents of the control and paste them into the Clipboard.

Example

See related example in the **System.Windows.Forms.TextBoxBase** class topic.

Requirements

Platforms: Windows 98, Windows NT 4.0, Windows Millennium Edition, Windows 2000, Windows XP Home Edition, Windows XP Professional, Windows Server 2003 family, .NET Compact Framework - Windows CE .NET

TextBoxBase.SetBoundsCore Method

This member overrides **Control.SetBoundsCore**.

```
[Visual Basic]
Overrides Protected Sub SetBoundsCore( _
   ByVal x As Integer, _
   ByVal y As Integer, _
   ByVal width As Integer, _
   ByVal height As Integer, _
   ByVal specified As BoundsSpecified _
)
[C#]
protected override void SetBoundsCore(
   int x,
   int y,
   int width,
   int height,
   BoundsSpecified specified
);
[C++]
protected: void SetBoundsCore(
   int x,
   int y,
   int width,
   int height,
   BoundsSpecified specified
);
[JScript]
protected override function SetBoundsCore(
   x : int,
   y : int,
   width : int,
   height : int,
   specified : BoundsSpecified
);
```

Requirements

Platforms: Windows 98, Windows NT 4.0, Windows Millennium Edition, Windows 2000, Windows XP Home Edition, Windows XP Professional, Windows Server 2003 family

TextBoxBase.ToString Method

This member overrides **Object.ToString**.

```
[Visual Basic]
Overrides Public Function ToString() As String
[C#]
public override string ToString();
[C++]
public: String* ToString();
[JScript]
public override function ToString() : String;
```

Requirements

Platforms: Windows 98, Windows NT 4.0, Windows Millennium Edition, Windows 2000, Windows XP Home Edition, Windows XP Professional, Windows Server 2003 family, .NET Compact Framework - Windows CE .NET

TextBoxBase.Undo Method

Undoes the last edit operation in the text box.

```
[Visual Basic]
Public Sub Undo()
[C#]
public void Undo();
[C++]
public: void Undo();
[JScript]
public function Undo();
```

Remarks

This method will undo the last clipboard or text change operation performed in the text box control if the **CanUndo** property returns **true**.

Example

See related example in the **System.Windows.Forms.TextBoxBase** class topic.

Requirements

Platforms: Windows 98, Windows NT 4.0, Windows Millennium Edition, Windows 2000, Windows XP Home Edition, Windows XP Professional, Windows Server 2003 family

TextBoxBase.WndProc Method

This member overrides **Control.WndProc**.

```
[Visual Basic]
Overrides Protected Sub WndProc( _
   ByRef m As Message _
)
[C#]
protected override void WndProc(
   ref Message m
);
[C++]
protected: void WndProc(
   Message* m
);
[JScript]
protected override function WndProc(
   m : Message
);
```

Requirements

Platforms: Windows 98, Windows NT 4.0, Windows Millennium Edition, Windows 2000, Windows XP Home Edition, Windows XP Professional, Windows Server 2003 family

TextBoxBase.AcceptsTabChanged Event

Occurs when the value of the **AcceptsTab** property has changed.

```
[Visual Basic]
Public Event AcceptsTabChanged As EventHandler
[C#]
public event EventHandler AcceptsTabChanged;
[C++]
public: __event EventHandler* AcceptsTabChanged;
```

[JScript] In JScript, you can handle the events defined by a class, but you cannot define your own.

Event Data

The event handler receives an argument of type **EventArgs**.

Requirements

Platforms: Windows 98, Windows NT 4.0, Windows Millennium Edition, Windows 2000, Windows XP Home Edition, Windows XP Professional, Windows Server 2003 family

TextBoxBase.AutoSizeChanged Event

Occurs when the value of the **AutoSize** property has changed.

```
[Visual Basic]
Public Event AutoSizeChanged As EventHandler
[C#]
public event EventHandler AutoSizeChanged;
[C++]
public: __event EventHandler* AutoSizeChanged;
```

[JScript] In JScript, you can handle the events defined by a class, but you cannot define your own.

Event Data

The event handler receives an argument of type **EventArgs**.

Requirements

Platforms: Windows 98, Windows NT 4.0, Windows Millennium Edition, Windows 2000, Windows XP Home Edition, Windows XP Professional, Windows Server 2003 family

TextBoxBase.BackgroundImageChanged Event

This member supports the .NET Framework infrastructure and is not intended to be used directly from your code.

```
[Visual Basic]
Public Shadows Event BackgroundImageChanged As EventHandler
[C#]
public new event EventHandler BackgroundImageChanged;
[C++]
public: __event EventHandler* BackgroundImageChanged;
```

[JScript] In JScript, you can handle the events defined by a class, but you cannot define your own.

TextBoxBase.BorderStyleChanged Event

Occurs when the value of the **BorderStyle** property has changed.

```
[Visual Basic]
Public Event BorderStyleChanged As EventHandler
[C#]
public event EventHandler BorderStyleChanged;
[C++]
public: __event EventHandler* BorderStyleChanged;
```

[JScript] In JScript, you can handle the events defined by a class, but you cannot define your own.

Event Data

The event handler receives an argument of type **EventArgs**.

Requirements

Platforms: Windows 98, Windows NT 4.0, Windows Millennium Edition, Windows 2000, Windows XP Home Edition, Windows XP Professional, Windows Server 2003 family

TextBoxBase.Click Event

Occurs when the text box is clicked.

[Visual Basic]
```
Public Shadows Event Click As EventHandler
```
[C#]
```
public new event EventHandler Click;
```
[C++]
```
public: __event EventHandler* Click;
```

[JScript] In JScript, you can handle the events defined by a class, but you cannot define your own.

Event Data

The event handler receives an argument of type **EventArgs**.

Requirements

Platforms: Windows 98, Windows NT 4.0, Windows Millennium Edition, Windows 2000, Windows XP Home Edition, Windows XP Professional, Windows Server 2003 family

TextBoxBase.HideSelectionChanged Event

Occurs when the value of the **HideSelection** property has changed.

[Visual Basic]
```
Public Event HideSelectionChanged As EventHandler
```
[C#]
```
public event EventHandler HideSelectionChanged;
```
[C++]
```
public: __event EventHandler* HideSelectionChanged;
```

[JScript] In JScript, you can handle the events defined by a class, but you cannot define your own.

Event Data

The event handler receives an argument of type **EventArgs**.

Requirements

Platforms: Windows 98, Windows NT 4.0, Windows Millennium Edition, Windows 2000, Windows XP Home Edition, Windows XP Professional, Windows Server 2003 family

TextBoxBase.ModifiedChanged Event

Occurs when the value of the **Modified** property has changed.

[Visual Basic]
```
Public Event ModifiedChanged As EventHandler
```
[C#]
```
public event EventHandler ModifiedChanged;
```
[C++]
```
public: __event EventHandler* ModifiedChanged;
```

[JScript] In JScript, you can handle the events defined by a class, but you cannot define your own.

Event Data

The event handler receives an argument of type **EventArgs**.

Requirements

Platforms: Windows 98, Windows NT 4.0, Windows Millennium Edition, Windows 2000, Windows XP Home Edition, Windows XP Professional, Windows Server 2003 family

TextBoxBase.MultilineChanged Event

Occurs when the value of the **Multiline** property has changed.

[Visual Basic]
```
Public Event MultilineChanged As EventHandler
```
[C#]
```
public event EventHandler MultilineChanged;
```
[C++]
```
public: __event EventHandler* MultilineChanged;
```

[JScript] In JScript, you can handle the events defined by a class, but you cannot define your own.

Event Data

The event handler receives an argument of type **EventArgs**.

Requirements

Platforms: Windows 98, Windows NT 4.0, Windows Millennium Edition, Windows 2000, Windows XP Home Edition, Windows XP Professional, Windows Server 2003 family

TextBoxBase.Paint Event

This member supports the .NET Framework infrastructure and is not intended to be used directly from your code.

[Visual Basic]
```
Public Shadows Event Paint As PaintEventHandler
```
[C#]
```
public new event PaintEventHandler Paint;
```
[C++]
```
public: __event PaintEventHandler* Paint;
```

[JScript] In JScript, you can handle the events defined by a class, but you cannot define your own.

TextBoxBase.ReadOnlyChanged Event

Occurs when the value of the **ReadOnly** property has changed.

[Visual Basic]
```
Public Event ReadOnlyChanged As EventHandler
```
[C#]
```
public event EventHandler ReadOnlyChanged;
```
[C++]
```
public: __event EventHandler* ReadOnlyChanged;
```

[JScript] In JScript, you can handle the events defined by a class, but you cannot define your own.

Event Data

The event handler receives an argument of type **EventArgs**.

Requirements

Platforms: Windows 98, Windows NT 4.0, Windows Millennium Edition, Windows 2000, Windows XP Home Edition, Windows XP Professional, Windows Server 2003 family

ThreadExceptionDialog Class

This type supports the .NET Framework infrastructure and is not intended to be used directly from your code.

[Visual Basic]
```
Public Class ThreadExceptionDialog
   Inherits Form
```
[C#]
```
public class ThreadExceptionDialog : Form
```
[C++]
```
public __gc class ThreadExceptionDialog : public Form
```
[JScript]
```
public class ThreadExceptionDialog extends Form
```

ThreadExceptionDialog Constructor

This member supports the .NET Framework infrastructure and is not intended to be used directly from your code.

[Visual Basic]
```
Public Sub New( _
   ByVal t As Exception _
)
```
[C#]
```
public ThreadExceptionDialog(
   Exception t
);
```
[C++]
```
public: ThreadExceptionDialog(
   Exception* t
);
```
[JScript]
```
public function ThreadExceptionDialog(
   t : Exception
);
```

TickStyle Enumeration

Specifies the location of tick marks in a **TrackBar** control.

[Visual Basic]
```
<Serializable>
Public Enum TickStyle
```
[C#]
```
[Serializable]
public enum TickStyle
```
[C++]
```
[Serializable]
__value public enum TickStyle
```
[JScript]
```
public
   Serializable
enum TickStyle
```

Remarks

Use the members of this enumeration to set the value of the **TickStyle** property of the **TrackBar** control.

Members

Member name	Description
Both	Tick marks are located on both sides of the control.
BottomRight	Tick marks are located on the bottom of a horizontal control or on the right side of a vertical control.
None	No tick marks appear in the control.
TopLeft	Tick marks are located on the top of a horizontal control or on the left of a vertical control.

Requirements

Namespace: System.Windows.Forms

Platforms: Windows 98, Windows NT 4.0, Windows Millennium Edition, Windows 2000, Windows XP Home Edition, Windows XP Professional, Windows Server 2003 family

Assembly: System.Windows.Forms (in System.Windows.Forms.dll)

Timer Class

Implements a timer that raises an event at user-defined intervals. This timer is optimized for use in Windows Forms applications and must be used in a window.

System.Object
  System.MarshalByRefObject
    System.ComponentModel.Component
      System.Windows.Forms.Timer

[Visual Basic]
```
Public Class Timer
   Inherits Component
```
[C#]
```
public class Timer : Component
```
[C++]
```
public __gc class Timer : public Component
```
[JScript]
```
public class Timer extends Component
```

Thread Safety

Any public static (**Shared** in Visual Basic) members of this type are safe for multithreaded operations. Any instance members are not guaranteed to be thread safe.

Remarks

A **Timer** is used to raise an event at user-defined intervals. This Windows timer is designed for a single-threaded environment where UI threads are used to perform processing. It requires that the user code have a UI message pump available and always operate from the same thread, or marshal the call onto another thread.

When using this timer, use the **Tick** event to perform a polling operation or to display a splash screen for a specified amount of time. Whenever the **Enabled** property is set to **true** and the **Interval** property is greater than zero, the **Tick** event is raised at intervals based on the **Interval** property setting.

This class provides methods to set the interval, and to start and stop the timer.

Example

[Visual Basic, C#] The following example implements a simple interval timer, which sets off an alarm every five seconds. When the alarm occurs, a **MessageBox** displays a count of the number of times the alarm has activated and asks the user whether the timer should continue running.

[Visual Basic]
```
Public Class Class1
    Private Shared myTimer As New System.Windows.Forms.Timer()
    Private Shared alarmCounter As Integer = 1
    Private Shared exitFlag As Boolean = False

    ' This is the method to run when the timer is raised.
    Private Shared Sub TimerEventProcessor(myObject As Object, _
                                           myEventArgs As EventArgs)
        myTimer.Stop()

        ' Displays a message box asking whether to continue           ↵
running the timer.
        If MessageBox.Show("Continue running?", "Count is: " &        ↵
alarmCounter, _
                           MessageBoxButtons.YesNo) =                 ↵
DialogResult.Yes Then
            ' Restarts the timer and increments the counter.
            alarmCounter += 1
            myTimer.Enabled = True
        Else
            ' Stops the timer.
            exitFlag = True
        End If
    End Sub

    Public Shared Sub Main()
        ' Adds the event and the event handler for the method that will
        ' process the timer event to the timer.
        AddHandler myTimer.Tick, AddressOf TimerEventProcessor

        ' Sets the timer interval to 5 seconds.
        myTimer.Interval = 5000
        myTimer.Start()

        ' Runs the timer, and raises the event.
        While exitFlag = False
            ' Processes all the events in the queue.
            Application.DoEvents()
        End While

    End Sub

End Class
```

[C#]
```
public class Class1 {
    static System.Windows.Forms.Timer myTimer = new                  ↵
System.Windows.Forms.Timer();
    static int alarmCounter = 1;
    static bool exitFlag = false;

    // This is the method to run when the timer is raised.
    private static void TimerEventProcessor(Object myObject,
                                            EventArgs myEventArgs) {
       myTimer.Stop();

       // Displays a message box asking whether to continue            ↵
running the timer.
       if(MessageBox.Show("Continue running?", "Count is: " +          ↵
alarmCounter,
          MessageBoxButtons.YesNo) == DialogResult.Yes) {
          // Restarts the timer and increments the counter.
          alarmCounter +=1;
          myTimer.Enabled = true;
       }
       else {
          // Stops the timer.
          exitFlag = true;
       }
    }

    public static int Main() {
       /* Adds the event and the event handler for the method that will
          process the timer event to the timer. */
       myTimer.Tick += new EventHandler(TimerEventProcessor);

       // Sets the timer interval to 5 seconds.
       myTimer.Interval = 5000;
       myTimer.Start();

       // Runs the timer, and raises the event.
       while(exitFlag == false) {
          // Processes all the events in the queue.
          Application.DoEvents();
       }
    return 0;
    }
 }
```

Requirements

Namespace: System.Windows.Forms

Platforms: Windows 98, Windows NT 4.0, Windows Millennium Edition, Windows 2000, Windows XP Home Edition, Windows XP Professional, Windows Server 2003 family, .NET Compact Framework - Windows CE .NET

Assembly: System.Windows.Forms (in System.Windows.Forms.dll)

Timer Constructor

Initializes a new instance of the **Timer** class.

Overload List

Initializes a new instance of the **Timer** class.

Supported by the .NET Compact Framework.

[Visual Basic] **Public Sub New()**

[C#] **public Timer();**

[C++] **public: Timer();**

[JScript] **public function Timer();**

Initializes a new instance of the **Timer** class with the specified container.

[Visual Basic] **Public Sub New(IContainer)**

[C#] **public Timer(IContainer);**

[C++] **public: Timer(IContainer*);**

[JScript] **public function Timer(IContainer);**

Timer Constructor ()

Initializes a new instance of the **Timer** class.

```
[Visual Basic]
Public Sub New()
[C#]
public Timer();
[C++]
public: Timer();
[JScript]
public function Timer();
```

Remarks

When a new timer is created, it is disabled; that is, **Enabled** is set to **false**. To enable the timer, call the **Start** method or set **Enabled** to **true**.

If the timer is disabled and the timer is out of scope, the timer will be disposed when garbage collection occurs. If the timer is enabled, even if it is out of scope, it is not subject to garbage collection.

Requirements

Platforms: Windows 98, Windows NT 4.0, Windows Millennium Edition, Windows 2000, Windows XP Home Edition, Windows XP Professional, Windows Server 2003 family, .NET Compact Framework - Windows CE .NET

Timer Constructor (IContainer)

Initializes a new instance of the **Timer** class with the specified container.

```
[Visual Basic]
Public Sub New( _
   ByVal container As IContainer _
)
[C#]
public Timer(
   IContainer container
);
[C++]
public: Timer(
   IContainer* container
);
[JScript]
public function Timer(
   container : IContainer
);
```

Parameters

container

An **IContainer** that represents the container for the timer.

Remarks

When a new timer is created, it is disabled; that is, **Enabled** is set to **false**. To enable the timer, call the **Start** method or set **Enabled** to **true**.

This instance will exist until its container releases it to garbage collection.

Requirements

Platforms: Windows 98, Windows NT 4.0, Windows Millennium Edition, Windows 2000, Windows XP Home Edition, Windows XP Professional, Windows Server 2003 family

Timer.Enabled Property

Gets or sets whether the timer is running.

```
[Visual Basic]
Public Overridable Property Enabled As Boolean
[C#]
public virtual bool Enabled {get; set;}
[C++]
public: __property virtual bool get_Enabled();
public: __property virtual void set_Enabled(bool);
[JScript]
public function get Enabled() : Boolean;
public function set Enabled(Boolean);
```

Property Value

true if the timer is currently enabled; otherwise, **false**. The default is **false**.

Remarks

The timer is not subject to garbage collection when the value is **true**.

Example

See related example in the **System.Windows.Forms.Timer** class topic.

Requirements

Platforms: Windows 98, Windows NT 4.0, Windows Millennium Edition, Windows 2000, Windows XP Home Edition, Windows XP Professional, Windows Server 2003 family, .NET Compact Framework - Windows CE .NET

Timer.Interval Property

Gets or sets the time, in milliseconds, between timer ticks.

```
[Visual Basic]
Public Property Interval As Integer
[C#]
public int Interval {get; set;}
[C++]
public: __property int get_Interval();
public: __property void set_Interval(int);
```

```
[JScript]
public function get Interval() : int;
public function set Interval(int);
```

Property Value

The number of milliseconds between each timer tick. The value is not less than one.

Remarks

To get the number of seconds in the interval, divide this number by 1,000.

Example

See related example in the **System.Windows.Forms.Timer** class topic.

Requirements

Platforms: Windows 98, Windows NT 4.0,
Windows Millennium Edition, Windows 2000,
Windows XP Home Edition, Windows XP Professional,
Windows Server 2003 family,
.NET Compact Framework - Windows CE .NET

Timer.Dispose Method

Overload List

This member supports the .NET Framework infrastructure and is not intended to be used directly from your code.

Supported by the .NET Compact Framework.

[Visual Basic] **Overloads Overrides Protected Sub Dispose(Boolean)**

[C#] **protected override void Dispose(bool);**

[C++] **protected: void Dispose(bool);**

[JScript] **protected override function Dispose(Boolean);**

Inherited from **Component**.

Supported by the .NET Compact Framework.

[Visual Basic] **Overloads Public Overridable Sub Dispose() Implements IDisposable.Dispose**

[C#] **public virtual void Dispose();**

[C++] **public: virtual void Dispose();**

[JScript] **public function Dispose();**

Timer.Dispose Method (Boolean)

This member overrides **Component.Dispose**.

```
[Visual Basic]
Overrides Overloads Protected Sub Dispose( _
   ByVal disposing As Boolean _
)
[C#]
protected override void Dispose(
   bool disposing
);
[C++]
protected: void Dispose(
   bool disposing
);
[JScript]
protected override function Dispose(
   disposing : Boolean
);
```

Requirements

Platforms: Windows 98, Windows NT 4.0,
Windows Millennium Edition, Windows 2000,
Windows XP Home Edition, Windows XP Professional,
Windows Server 2003 family,
.NET Compact Framework - Windows CE .NET

Timer.OnTick Method

Raises the **Tick** event.

```
[Visual Basic]
Protected Overridable Sub OnTick( _
   ByVal e As EventArgs _
)
[C#]
protected virtual void OnTick(
   EventArgs e
);
[C++]
protected: virtual void OnTick(
   EventArgs* e
);
[JScript]
protected function OnTick(
   e : EventArgs
);
```

Parameters

e

An **EventArgs** that contains the event data. This is always **Empty**.

Remarks

This method is called for each timer tick. It calls any methods that are added through **Tick**. If you are inheriting from **Timer**, you can override this method.

Raising an event invokes the event handler through a delegate.

Notes to Inheritors: When overriding **OnTick** in a derived class, be sure to call the base class's **OnTick** method.

Requirements

Platforms: Windows 98, Windows NT 4.0,
Windows Millennium Edition, Windows 2000,
Windows XP Home Edition, Windows XP Professional,
Windows Server 2003 family

Timer.Start Method

Starts the timer.

```
[Visual Basic]
Public Sub Start()
[C#]
public void Start();
[C++]
public: void Start();
[JScript]
public function Start();
```

Remarks

You can also start the timer by setting the **Enabled** property to **true**.

Example

See related example in the **System.Windows.Forms.Timer** class topic.

Requirements

Platforms: Windows 98, Windows NT 4.0, Windows Millennium Edition, Windows 2000, Windows XP Home Edition, Windows XP Professional, Windows Server 2003 family

Timer.Stop Method

Stops the timer.

```
[Visual Basic]
Public Sub Stop()
[C#]
public void Stop();
[C++]
public: void Stop();
[JScript]
public function Stop();
```

Remarks

You can also stop the timer by setting the **Enabled** property to **false**. A timer that is disabled is subject to garbage collection.

Example

See related example in the **System.Windows.Forms.Timer** class topic.

Requirements

Platforms: Windows 98, Windows NT 4.0, Windows Millennium Edition, Windows 2000, Windows XP Home Edition, Windows XP Professional, Windows Server 2003 family

Timer.ToString Method

This member overrides **Object.ToString**.

```
[Visual Basic]
Overrides Public Function ToString() As String
[C#]
public override string ToString();
[C++]
public: String* ToString();
[JScript]
public override function ToString() : String;
```

Requirements

Platforms: Windows 98, Windows NT 4.0, Windows Millennium Edition, Windows 2000, Windows XP Home Edition, Windows XP Professional, Windows Server 2003 family, .NET Compact Framework - Windows CE .NET

Timer.Tick Event

Occurs when the specified timer interval has elapsed and the timer is enabled.

```
[Visual Basic]
Public Event Tick As EventHandler
[C#]
public event EventHandler Tick;
[C++]
public: __event EventHandler* Tick;
```

[JScript] In JScript, you can handle the events defined by a class, but you cannot define your own.

Event Data

The event handler receives an argument of type **EventArgs**.

Example

See related example in the **System.Windows.Forms.Timer** class topic.

Requirements

Platforms: Windows 98, Windows NT 4.0, Windows Millennium Edition, Windows 2000, Windows XP Home Edition, Windows XP Professional, Windows Server 2003 family

ToolBar Class

Represents a Windows toolbar.

System.Object
 System.MarshalByRefObject
  System.ComponentModel.Component
   System.Windows.Forms.Control
    System.Windows.Forms.ToolBar

[Visual Basic]
```
Public Class ToolBar
   Inherits Control
```
[C#]
```
public class ToolBar : Control
```
[C++]
```
public __gc class ToolBar : public Control
```
[JScript]
```
public class ToolBar extends Control
```

Thread Safety

Any public static (**Shared** in Visual Basic) members of this type are safe for multithreaded operations. Any instance members are not guaranteed to be thread safe.

Remarks

ToolBar controls are used to display **ToolBarButton** controls that can appear as a standard button, a toggle-style button, or a drop-down style button. You can assign images to the buttons by creating an **ImageList**, assigning it to the **ImageList** property of the toolbar, and assigning the image index value to the **ImageIndex** property each **ToolBarButton**. You can then assign text to be displayed underneath or to the right of the image by setting the **Text** property of the **ToolBarButton**.

Set the **Appearance** property of the toolbar to **Flat** to give the toolbar and its buttons a flat appearance. As the mouse pointer moves over the buttons, their appearance changes to three-dimensional. Toolbar buttons can be divided into logical groups by using separators. A separator is a toolbar button with the **Style** property set to **ToolBarButtonStyle.Separator**. Button separators appear as lines rather than spaces between the buttons when the toolbar has a flat appearance. If the **Appearance** property is set to **Normal**, the toolbar buttons appear raised and three-dimensional.

If the **ButtonSize** is not set, a **Size** object is computed within the class to set it by default. The computed size will accommodate the largest image and text assigned to the **ToolBarButton** controls.

To create a collection of **ToolBarButton** controls to display on the **ToolBar**, add the buttons individually by using the **Add** or **Insert** methods of the **Buttons** property.

.NET Compact Framework - Windows CE .NET Platform Note: In Pocket PC applications, adding a **ToolBar** to any control besides a **Form** is not supported, for example, to a **Panel**.

Example

[Visual Basic, C#] The following example creates a **ToolBar** and three **ToolBarButton** controls. The toolbar buttons are assigned to the button collection, the collection is assigned to the toolbar, and the toolbar is added to the form. On the **ButtonClick** event of the toolbar, the **Button** property of the **ToolBarButtonClickEventArgs** is evaluated, and the appropriate dialog box opened. This code assumes that a **Form**, an **OpenFileDialog**, a **SaveFileDialog**, and a **PrintDialog** have been created.

[Visual Basic]
```
Public Sub InitializeMyToolBar()
    ' Create and initialize the ToolBar and ToolBarButton controls.
    Dim toolBar1 As New ToolBar()
    Dim toolBarButton1 As New ToolBarButton()
    Dim toolBarButton2 As New ToolBarButton()
    Dim toolBarButton3 As New ToolBarButton()

    ' Set the Text properties of the ToolBarButton controls.
    toolBarButton1.Text = "Open"
    toolBarButton2.Text = "Save"
    toolBarButton3.Text = "Print"

    ' Add the ToolBarButton controls to the ToolBar.
    toolBar1.Buttons.Add(toolBarButton1)
    toolBar1.Buttons.Add(toolBarButton2)
    toolBar1.Buttons.Add(toolBarButton3)

    ' Add the event-handler delegate.
    AddHandler toolBar1.ButtonClick, AddressOf Me.toolBar1_ButtonClick

    ' Add the ToolBar to the Form.
    Controls.Add(toolBar1)
End Sub

Protected Sub toolBar1_ButtonClick(sender As Object, _
    e As ToolBarButtonClickEventArgs)

    ' Evaluate the Button property to determine which button ↵
was clicked.
    Select Case toolBar1.Buttons.IndexOf(e.Button)
        Case 0
            openFileDialog1.ShowDialog()
            ' Insert code to open the file.
        Case 1
            saveFileDialog1.ShowDialog()
            ' Insert code to save the file.
        Case 2
            printDialog1.ShowDialog()
            ' Insert code to print the file.
    End Select
End Sub
```

[C#]
```
public void InitializeMyToolBar()
 {
    // Create and initialize the ToolBar and ToolBarButton controls.
    toolBar1 = new ToolBar();
    ToolBarButton toolBarButton1 = new ToolBarButton();
    ToolBarButton toolBarButton2 = new ToolBarButton();
    ToolBarButton toolBarButton3 = new ToolBarButton();

    // Set the Text properties of the ToolBarButton controls.
    toolBarButton1.Text = "Open";
    toolBarButton2.Text = "Save";
    toolBarButton3.Text = "Print";

    // Add the ToolBarButton controls to the ToolBar.
    toolBar1.Buttons.Add(toolBarButton1);
    toolBar1.Buttons.Add(toolBarButton2);
    toolBar1.Buttons.Add(toolBarButton3);

    // Add the event-handler delegate.
    toolBar1.ButtonClick += new ToolBarButtonClickEventHandler (
       this.toolBar1_ButtonClick);

    // Add the ToolBar to the Form.
    Controls.Add(toolBar1);
 }

 protected void toolBar1_ButtonClick (
                        Object sender,
                        ToolBarButtonClickEventArgs e)
 {
   // Evaluate the Button property to determine which ↵
```

```
button was clicked.
   switch(toolBar1.Buttons.IndexOf(e.Button))
   {
      case 0:
         openFileDialog1.ShowDialog();
         // Insert code to open the file.
         break;
      case 1:
         saveFileDialog1.ShowDialog();
         // Insert code to save the file.
         break;
      case 2:
         printDialog1.ShowDialog();
         // Insert code to print the file.
         break;
   }
}
```

Requirements

Namespace: System.Windows.Forms

Platforms: Windows 98, Windows NT 4.0, Windows Millennium Edition, Windows 2000, Windows XP Home Edition, Windows XP Professional, Windows Server 2003 family, .NET Compact Framework - Windows CE .NET

Assembly: System.Windows.Forms (in System.Windows.Forms.dll)

ToolBar Constructor

Initializes a new instance of the **ToolBar** class.

[Visual Basic]
```
Public Sub New()
```
[C#]
```
public ToolBar();
```
[C++]
```
public: ToolBar();
```
[JScript]
```
public function ToolBar();
```

Remarks

A newly created toolbar control is empty; add **ToolBarButton** controls by setting the **Buttons** property.

Example

See related example in the **System.Windows.Forms.ToolBar** class topic.

Requirements

Platforms: Windows 98, Windows NT 4.0, Windows Millennium Edition, Windows 2000, Windows XP Home Edition, Windows XP Professional, Windows Server 2003 family, .NET Compact Framework - Windows CE .NET

ToolBar.Appearance Property

Gets or set the value that determines the appearance of a toolbar control and its buttons.

[Visual Basic]
```
Public Property Appearance As ToolBarAppearance
```
[C#]
```
public ToolBarAppearance Appearance {get; set;}
```
[C++]
```
public: __property ToolBarAppearance get_Appearance();
public: __property void set_Appearance(ToolBarAppearance);
```
[JScript]
```
public function get Appearance() : ToolBarAppearance;
public function set Appearance(ToolBarAppearance);
```

Property Value

One of the **ToolBarAppearance** values. The default is **ToolBarAppearance.Normal**.

Exceptions

Exception Type	Condition
InvalidEnumArgumentException	The assigned value is not one of the **ToolBarAppearance** values.

Remarks

The **Appearance** property affects the appearance of the buttons assigned to the toolbar. When the appearance is set to **ToolBarAppearance.Normal**, the toolbar's buttons appear three-dimensional and raised. Set the **Appearance** property of the toolbar to **ToolBarAppearance.Flat** to give the toolbar's buttons a flat appearance. As the mouse pointer moves over the flat buttons, they appear raised and three-dimensional. Separators on a **ToolBar** with the **Appearance** property set to **Flat** appear as etched lines rather than spaces between the raised buttons. The flat style buttons give your application a more Web-like look.

Example

See related example in the **System.Windows.Forms.ToolBar** class topic.

Requirements

Platforms: Windows 98, Windows NT 4.0, Windows Millennium Edition, Windows 2000, Windows XP Home Edition, Windows XP Professional, Windows Server 2003 family

ToolBar.AutoSize Property

Gets or sets a value indicating whether the toolbar adjusts its size automatically, based on the size of the buttons and the dock style.

[Visual Basic]
```
Public Property AutoSize As Boolean
```
[C#]
```
public bool AutoSize {get; set;}
```
[C++]
```
public: __property bool get_AutoSize();
public: __property void set_AutoSize(bool);
```
[JScript]
```
public function get AutoSize() : Boolean;
public function set AutoSize(Boolean);
```

Property Value

true if the toolbar adjusts its size automatically, based on the size of the buttons and dock style; otherwise, **false**. The default is **true**.

Remarks

When **AutoSize** is set to **true**, the **ToolBar** control sizes itself to accommodate the toolbar buttons, based upon the button size, the number of **ToolBarButton** objects it contains, and the **DockStyle** of the toolbar.

Example

See related example in the **System.Windows.Forms.ToolBar** class topic.

Requirements

Platforms: Windows 98, Windows NT 4.0, Windows Millennium Edition, Windows 2000, Windows XP Home Edition, Windows XP Professional, Windows Server 2003 family

ToolBar.BackColor Property

This member overrides **Control.BackColor**.

```
[Visual Basic]
Overrides Public Property BackColor As Color
[C#]
public override Color BackColor {get; set;}
[C++]
public: __property Color get_BackColor();
public: __property void set_BackColor(Color);
[JScript]
public override function get BackColor() : Color;
public override function set BackColor(Color);
```

Requirements

Platforms: Windows 98, Windows NT 4.0, Windows Millennium Edition, Windows 2000, Windows XP Home Edition, Windows XP Professional, Windows Server 2003 family

ToolBar.BackgroundImage Property

This member overrides **Control.BackgroundImage**.

```
[Visual Basic]
Overrides Public Property BackgroundImage As Image
[C#]
public override Image BackgroundImage {get; set;}
[C++]
public: __property Image* get_BackgroundImage();
public: __property void set_BackgroundImage(Image*);
[JScript]
public override function get BackgroundImage() : Image;
public override function set BackgroundImage(Image);
```

Requirements

Platforms: Windows 98, Windows NT 4.0, Windows Millennium Edition, Windows 2000, Windows XP Home Edition, Windows XP Professional, Windows Server 2003 family

ToolBar.BorderStyle Property

Gets or sets the border style of the toolbar control.

```
[Visual Basic]
Public Property BorderStyle As BorderStyle
[C#]
public BorderStyle BorderStyle {get; set;}
[C++]
public: __property BorderStyle get_BorderStyle();
public: __property void set_BorderStyle(BorderStyle);
[JScript]
public function get BorderStyle() : BorderStyle;
public function set BorderStyle(BorderStyle);
```

Property Value

One of the **BorderStyle** values. The default is **BorderStyle.None**.

Exceptions

Exception Type	Condition
InvalidEnumArgument-Exception	The assigned value is not one of the **BorderStyle** values.

Remarks

The **ToolBar** can take on a sunken, three-dimensional appearance when the **BorderStyle** property is set to **BorderStyle.Fixed3D**. To display a flat thin border around the toolbar control, set the **BorderStyle** property to **BorderStyle.FixedSingle**.

Example

See related example in the **System.Windows.Forms.ToolBar** class topic.

Requirements

Platforms: Windows 98, Windows NT 4.0, Windows Millennium Edition, Windows 2000, Windows XP Home Edition, Windows XP Professional, Windows Server 2003 family

ToolBar.Buttons Property

Gets the collection of **ToolBarButton** controls assigned to the toolbar control.

```
[Visual Basic]
Public ReadOnly Property Buttons As ToolBar.ToolBarButtonCollection
[C#]
public ToolBar.ToolBarButtonCollection Buttons {get;}
[C++]
public: __property ToolBar.ToolBarButtonCollection* get_Buttons();
[JScript]
public function get Buttons() : ToolBar.ToolBarButtonCollection;
```

Property Value

A **ToolBar.ToolBarButtonCollection** that contains a collection of **ToolBarButton** controls.

Remarks

The **Buttons** property is a zero-based indexed collection used to hold all the **ToolBarButton** controls assigned to the toolbar. Since the property is read-only, it can not be assigned a collection of toolbar buttons directly. Toolbar buttons can be added or removed by using the methods inherited from the **ToolBar.ToolBarButton-Collection** class. Use the **Add** method to add individual buttons and the **Remove** method to delete a button. Call the **Clear** method to remove all the buttons from the collection.

Example

See related example in the **System.Windows.Forms.ToolBar** class topic.

Requirements

Platforms: Windows 98, Windows NT 4.0, Windows Millennium Edition, Windows 2000, Windows XP Home Edition, Windows XP Professional, Windows Server 2003 family, .NET Compact Framework - Windows CE .NET

ToolBar.ButtonSize Property

Gets or sets the size of the buttons on the toolbar control.

```
[Visual Basic]
Public Property ButtonSize As Size
[C#]
public Size ButtonSize {get; set;}
[C++]
public: __property Size get_ButtonSize();
public: __property void set_ButtonSize(Size);
[JScript]
public function get ButtonSize() : Size;
public function set ButtonSize(Size);
```

Property Value

A **Size** object that represents the size of the **ToolBarButton** controls on the toolbar. The default size has a width of 24 pixels and a height of 22 pixels, or large enough to accommodate the **Image** and text, whichever is greater.

Exceptions

Exception Type	Condition
ArgumentException	The **Width** or **Height** property of the **Size** object is less than 0.

Remarks

If the **ButtonSize** is not set, it is set to its default. Alternatively, a **Size** is computed to accommodate the largest **Image** and text assigned to the **ToolBarButton** controls.

Example

See related example in the **System.Windows.Forms.ToolBar** class topic.

Requirements

Platforms: Windows 98, Windows NT 4.0, Windows Millennium Edition, Windows 2000, Windows XP Home Edition, Windows XP Professional, Windows Server 2003 family

ToolBar.CreateParams Property

This member overrides **Control.CreateParams**.

```
[Visual Basic]
Overrides Protected ReadOnly Property CreateParams As CreateParams
[C#]
protected override CreateParams CreateParams {get;}
[C++]
protected: __property CreateParams* get_CreateParams();
[JScript]
protected override function get CreateParams() : CreateParams;
```

Requirements

Platforms: Windows 98, Windows NT 4.0, Windows Millennium Edition, Windows 2000, Windows XP Home Edition, Windows XP Professional, Windows Server 2003 family

ToolBar.DefaultImeMode Property

Gets the default Input Method Editor (IME) mode supported by this control.

```
[Visual Basic]
Overrides Protected ReadOnly Property DefaultImeMode As ImeMode
[C#]
protected override ImeMode DefaultImeMode {get;}
[C++]
protected: __property ImeMode get_DefaultImeMode();
[JScript]
protected override function get DefaultImeMode() : ImeMode;
```

Property Value

One of the **ImeMode** values.

Remarks

As implemented in the **ToolBar** class, this property always returns the **ImeMode.Disable** value.

Requirements

Platforms: Windows 98, Windows NT 4.0, Windows Millennium Edition, Windows 2000, Windows XP Home Edition, Windows XP Professional, Windows Server 2003 family

ToolBar.DefaultSize Property

This member overrides **Control.DefaultSize**.

```
[Visual Basic]
Overrides Protected ReadOnly Property DefaultSize As Size
[C#]
protected override Size DefaultSize {get;}
[C++]
protected: __property Size get_DefaultSize();
[JScript]
protected override function get DefaultSize() : Size;
```

Requirements

Platforms: Windows 98, Windows NT 4.0, Windows Millennium Edition, Windows 2000, Windows XP Home Edition, Windows XP Professional, Windows Server 2003 family

ToolBar.Divider Property

Gets or sets a value indicating whether the toolbar displays a divider.

```
[Visual Basic]
Public Property Divider As Boolean
[C#]
public bool Divider {get; set;}
[C++]
public: __property bool get_Divider();
public: __property void set_Divider(bool);
[JScript]
public function get Divider() : Boolean;
public function set Divider(Boolean);
```

Property Value

true if the toolbar displays a divider; otherwise, **false**. The default is **true**.

Remarks

Dividers are displayed to help distinguish the toolbar from adjacent controls, such as menus. A divider is displayed as a raised edge along the top of the **ToolBar** control.

Example

See related example in the **System.Windows.Forms.ToolBar** class topic.

Requirements

Platforms: Windows 98, Windows NT 4.0, Windows Millennium Edition, Windows 2000, Windows XP Home Edition, Windows XP Professional, Windows Server 2003 family

ToolBar.Dock Property

This member overrides **Control.Dock**.

```
[Visual Basic]
Overrides Public Property Dock As DockStyle
[C#]
public override DockStyle Dock {get; set;}
[C++]
public: __property DockStyle get_Dock();
public: __property void set_Dock(DockStyle);
[JScript]
public override function get Dock() : DockStyle;
public override function set Dock(DockStyle);
```

Requirements

Platforms: Windows 98, Windows NT 4.0, Windows Millennium Edition, Windows 2000, Windows XP Home Edition, Windows XP Professional, Windows Server 2003 family

ToolBar.DropDownArrows Property

Gets or sets a value indicating whether drop-down buttons on a toolbar display down arrows.

```
[Visual Basic]
Public Property DropDownArrows As Boolean
[C#]
public bool DropDownArrows {get; set;}
[C++]
public: __property bool get_DropDownArrows();
public: __property void set_DropDownArrows(bool);
[JScript]
public function get DropDownArrows() : Boolean;
public function set DropDownArrows(Boolean);
```

Property Value

true if drop-down toolbar buttons display down arrows; otherwise, **false**. The default is **false**.

Remarks

When **DropDownArrows** is set to **false**, no down arrows display on drop-down style toolbar buttons. When the user clicks the drop-down button on the toolbar, the menu drops down for selection. When the drop-down arrow is displayed, the user must press the down arrow to display the menu.

Example

See related example in the **System.Windows.Forms.ToolBar** class topic.

Requirements

Platforms: Windows 98, Windows NT 4.0, Windows Millennium Edition, Windows 2000, Windows XP Home Edition, Windows XP Professional, Windows Server 2003 family

ToolBar.ForeColor Property

This member overrides **Control.ForeColor**.

```
[Visual Basic]
Overrides Public Property ForeColor As Color
[C#]
public override Color ForeColor {get; set;}
[C++]
public: __property Color get_ForeColor();
public: __property void set_ForeColor(Color);
[JScript]
public override function get ForeColor() : Color;
public override function set ForeColor(Color);
```

Requirements

Platforms: Windows 98, Windows NT 4.0, Windows Millennium Edition, Windows 2000, Windows XP Home Edition, Windows XP Professional, Windows Server 2003 family

ToolBar.ImageList Property

Gets or sets the collection of images available to the toolbar button controls.

```
[Visual Basic]
Public Property ImageList As ImageList
[C#]
public ImageList ImageList {get; set;}
[C++]
public: __property ImageList* get_ImageList();
public: __property void set_ImageList(ImageList*);
[JScript]
public function get ImageList() : ImageList;
public function set ImageList(ImageList);
```

Property Value

An **ImageList** that contains images available to the **ToolBarButton** controls. The default is a null reference (**Nothing** in Visual Basic).

Remarks

If you create an **ImageList** and assign it to the **ImageList** property, you can assign an image from the collection to the **ToolBarButton** controls by assigning the image's index value to the **ImageIndex** property of the toolbar button.

Example

See related example in the **System.Windows.Forms.ToolBar** class topic.

Requirements

Platforms: Windows 98, Windows NT 4.0, Windows Millennium Edition, Windows 2000, Windows XP Home Edition, Windows XP Professional, Windows Server 2003 family, .NET Compact Framework - Windows CE .NET

ToolBar.ImageSize Property

Gets the size of the images in the image list assigned to the toolbar.

```
[Visual Basic]
Public ReadOnly Property ImageSize As Size
[C#]
public Size ImageSize {get;}
[C++]
public: __property Size get_ImageSize();
[JScript]
public function get ImageSize() : Size;
```

Property Value

A **Size** that represents the size of the images (in the **ImageList**) assigned to the **ToolBar**.

Requirements

Platforms: Windows 98, Windows NT 4.0, Windows Millennium Edition, Windows 2000, Windows XP Home Edition, Windows XP Professional, Windows Server 2003 family

ToolBar.ImeMode Property

Gets or sets the Input Method Editor (IME) mode supported by this control.

```
[Visual Basic]
Public Shadows Property ImeMode As ImeMode
[C#]
public new ImeMode ImeMode {get; set;}
[C++]
public: __property ImeMode get_ImeMode();
public: __property void set_ImeMode(ImeMode);
[JScript]
public hide function get ImeMode() : ImeMode;
public hide function set ImeMode(ImeMode);
```

Property Value

One of the **ImeMode** values.

Requirements

Platforms: Windows 98, Windows NT 4.0, Windows Millennium Edition, Windows 2000, Windows XP Home Edition, Windows XP Professional, Windows Server 2003 family

ToolBar.RightToLeft Property

This member overrides **Control.RightToLeft**.

```
[Visual Basic]
Overrides Public Property RightToLeft As RightToLeft
[C#]
public override RightToLeft RightToLeft {get; set;}
[C++]
public: __property RightToLeft get_RightToLeft();
public: __property void set_RightToLeft(RightToLeft);
[JScript]
public override function get RightToLeft() : RightToLeft;
public override function set RightToLeft(RightToLeft);
```

Requirements

Platforms: Windows 98, Windows NT 4.0, Windows Millennium Edition, Windows 2000, Windows XP Home Edition, Windows XP Professional, Windows Server 2003 family

ToolBar.ShowToolTips Property

Gets or sets a value indicating whether the toolbar displays a ToolTip for each button.

```
[Visual Basic]
Public Property ShowToolTips As Boolean
[C#]
public bool ShowToolTips {get; set;}
[C++]
public: __property bool get_ShowToolTips();
public: __property void set_ShowToolTips(bool);
[JScript]
public function get ShowToolTips() : Boolean;
public function set ShowToolTips(Boolean);
```

Property Value

true if the toolbar display a ToolTip for each button; otherwise, **false**. The default is **false**.

Remarks

To set the text displayed by the ToolTip, set the **ToolTipText** property of each **ToolBarButton** on the **ToolBar**. To cause the ToolTip to display as the user moves the mouse pointer over the toolbar button, set the **ShowToolTips** property to **true**.

Example

See related example in the **System.Windows.Forms.ToolBar** class topic.

Requirements

Platforms: Windows 98, Windows NT 4.0, Windows Millennium Edition, Windows 2000, Windows XP Home Edition, Windows XP Professional, Windows Server 2003 family

ToolBar.TabStop Property

This member supports the .NET Framework infrastructure and is not intended to be used directly from your code.

```
[Visual Basic]
Public Shadows Property TabStop As Boolean
[C#]
public new bool TabStop {get; set;}
[C++]
public: __property bool get_TabStop();
public: __property void set_TabStop(bool);
[JScript]
public hide function get TabStop() : Boolean;
public hide function set TabStop(Boolean);
```

ToolBar.Text Property

This member overrides **Control.Text**.

```
[Visual Basic]
Overrides Public Property Text As String
[C#]
public override string Text {get; set;}
[C++]
public: __property String* get_Text();
public: __property void set_Text(String*);
[JScript]
public override function get Text() : String;
public override function set Text(String);
```

Requirements

Platforms: Windows 98, Windows NT 4.0, Windows Millennium Edition, Windows 2000, Windows XP Home Edition, Windows XP Professional, Windows Server 2003 family

ToolBar.TextAlign Property

Gets or sets the alignment of text in relation to each image displayed on the toolbar button controls.

```
[Visual Basic]
Public Property TextAlign As ToolBarTextAlign
[C#]
public ToolBarTextAlign TextAlign {get; set;}
[C++]
public: __property ToolBarTextAlign get_TextAlign();
public: __property void set_TextAlign(ToolBarTextAlign);
[JScript]
public function get TextAlign() : ToolBarTextAlign;
public function set TextAlign(ToolBarTextAlign);
```

Property Value

One of the **ToolBarTextAlign** values. The default is **ToolBarTextAlign.Underneath**.

Exceptions

Exception Type	Condition
InvalidEnumArgument-Exception	The assigned value is not one of the **ToolBarTextAlign** values.

Remarks

The **Text** can be aligned underneath or to the right of the image displayed on the **ToolBarButton** controls.

Example

See related example in the **System.Windows.Forms.ToolBar** class topic.

Requirements

Platforms: Windows 98, Windows NT 4.0, Windows Millennium Edition, Windows 2000, Windows XP Home Edition, Windows XP Professional, Windows Server 2003 family

ToolBar.Wrappable Property

Gets or sets a value indicating whether the toolbar buttons wrap to the next line if the toolbar becomes too small to display all the buttons on the same line.

```
[Visual Basic]
Public Property Wrappable As Boolean
[C#]
public bool Wrappable {get; set;}
[C++]
public: __property bool get_Wrappable();
public: __property void set_Wrappable(bool);
[JScript]
public function get Wrappable() : Boolean;
public function set Wrappable(Boolean);
```

Property Value

true if the toolbar buttons wrap to another line if the toolbar becomes too small to display all the buttons on the same line; otherwise, **false**. The default value is **true**.

Remarks

Toolbar buttons can be divided into logical groups by using separators. A separator is a toolbar button with the **Style** property set to **ToolBarButtonStyle.Separator**. If the **Wrappable** property is set to **true** and the toolbar becomes too small to display all the buttons on the same line, the toolbar is broken into additional lines, with the breaks occurring at the separators. This ensures that button groups stay together. Toolbar buttons that are not in a group can be separated when the toolbar wraps. The toolbar can become too small to display all its buttons on the same line if its parent **Form** is resized.

Example

See related example in the **System.Windows.Forms.ToolBar** class topic.

Requirements

Platforms: Windows 98, Windows NT 4.0, Windows Millennium Edition, Windows 2000, Windows XP Home Edition, Windows XP Professional, Windows Server 2003 family

ToolBar.CreateHandle Method

This member overrides **Control.CreateHandle**.

```
[Visual Basic]
Overrides Protected Sub CreateHandle()
[C#]
protected override void CreateHandle();
[C++]
protected: void CreateHandle();
[JScript]
protected override function CreateHandle();
```

Requirements

Platforms: Windows 98, Windows NT 4.0, Windows Millennium Edition, Windows 2000, Windows XP Home Edition, Windows XP Professional, Windows Server 2003 family

ToolBar.Dispose Method

Overload List

This member supports the .NET Framework infrastructure and is not intended to be used directly from your code.

Supported by the .NET Compact Framework.

[Visual Basic] **Overloads Overrides Protected Sub Dispose(Boolean)**

[C#] **protected override void Dispose(bool);**

[C++] **protected: void Dispose(bool);**

[JScript] **protected override function Dispose(Boolean);**

Inherited from **Component**.

Supported by the .NET Compact Framework.

[Visual Basic] **Overloads Public Overridable Sub Dispose() Implements IDisposable.Dispose**

[C#] **public virtual void Dispose();**

[C++] **public: virtual void Dispose();**

[JScript] **public function Dispose();**

ToolBar.Dispose Method (Boolean)

This member overrides **Control.Dispose**.

[Visual Basic]
```
Overrides Overloads Protected Sub Dispose( _
   ByVal disposing As Boolean _
)
```
[C#]
```
protected override void Dispose(
   bool disposing
);
```
[C++]
```
protected: void Dispose(
   bool disposing
);
```
[JScript]
```
protected override function Dispose(
   disposing : Boolean
);
```

Requirements

Platforms: Windows 98, Windows NT 4.0, Windows Millennium Edition, Windows 2000, Windows XP Home Edition, Windows XP Professional, Windows Server 2003 family, .NET Compact Framework - Windows CE .NET

ToolBar.OnButtonClick Method

Raises the **ButtonClick** event.

[Visual Basic]
```
Protected Overridable Sub OnButtonClick( _
   ByVal e As ToolBarButtonClickEventArgs _
)
```
[C#]
```
protected virtual void OnButtonClick(
   ToolBarButtonClickEventArgs e
);
```
[C++]
```
protected: virtual void OnButtonClick(
   ToolBarButtonClickEventArgs* e
);
```
[JScript]
```
protected function OnButtonClick(
   e : ToolBarButtonClickEventArgs
);
```

Parameters

e

A **ToolBarButtonClickEventArgs** that contains the event data.

Remarks

Raising an event invokes the event handler through a delegate. For more information, see **Raising an Event**.

The **OnButtonClick** method also allows derived classes to handle the event without attaching a delegate. This is the preferred technique for handling the event in a derived class.

Notes to Inheritors: When overriding **OnButtonClick** in a derived class, be sure to call the base class's **OnButtonClick** method so that registered delegates receive the event.

Requirements

Platforms: Windows 98, Windows NT 4.0, Windows Millennium Edition, Windows 2000, Windows XP Home Edition, Windows XP Professional, Windows Server 2003 family

ToolBar.OnButtonDropDown Method

Raises the **ButtonDropDown** event.

[Visual Basic]
```
Protected Overridable Sub OnButtonDropDown( _
   ByVal e As ToolBarButtonClickEventArgs _
)
```
[C#]
```
protected virtual void OnButtonDropDown(
   ToolBarButtonClickEventArgs e
);
```
[C++]
```
protected: virtual void OnButtonDropDown(
   ToolBarButtonClickEventArgs* e
);
```
[JScript]
```
protected function OnButtonDropDown(
   e : ToolBarButtonClickEventArgs
);
```

Parameters

e

A **ToolBarButtonClickEventArgs** that contains the event data.

Remarks

Raising an event invokes the event handler through a delegate.

The **OnButtonDropDown** method also allows derived classes to handle the event without attaching a delegate. This is the preferred technique for handling the event in a derived class.

Notes to Inheritors: When overriding **OnButtonDropDown** in a derived class, be sure to call the base class's **OnButtonDropDown** method so that registered delegates receive the event.

Requirements

Platforms: Windows 98, Windows NT 4.0, Windows Millennium Edition, Windows 2000, Windows XP Home Edition, Windows XP Professional, Windows Server 2003 family

ToolBar.OnFontChanged Method

This member overrides **Control.OnFontChanged**.

```
[Visual Basic]
Overrides Protected Sub OnFontChanged( _
   ByVal e As EventArgs _
)
[C#]
protected override void OnFontChanged(
   EventArgs e
);
[C++]
protected: void OnFontChanged(
   EventArgs* e
);
[JScript]
protected override function OnFontChanged(
   e : EventArgs
);
```

Requirements

Platforms: Windows 98, Windows NT 4.0, Windows Millennium Edition, Windows 2000, Windows XP Home Edition, Windows XP Professional, Windows Server 2003 family

ToolBar.OnHandleCreated Method

This member overrides **Control.OnHandleCreated**.

```
[Visual Basic]
Overrides Protected Sub OnHandleCreated( _
   ByVal e As EventArgs _
)
[C#]
protected override void OnHandleCreated(
   EventArgs e
);
[C++]
protected: void OnHandleCreated(
   EventArgs* e
);
[JScript]
protected override function OnHandleCreated(
   e : EventArgs
);
```

Requirements

Platforms: Windows 98, Windows NT 4.0, Windows Millennium Edition, Windows 2000, Windows XP Home Edition, Windows XP Professional, Windows Server 2003 family

ToolBar.OnResize Method

This member overrides **Control.OnResize**.

```
[Visual Basic]
Overrides Protected Sub OnResize( _
   ByVal e As EventArgs _
)
[C#]
protected override void OnResize(
   EventArgs e
);
[C++]
protected: void OnResize(
   EventArgs* e
);
[JScript]
protected override function OnResize(
   e : EventArgs
);
```

Requirements

Platforms: Windows 98, Windows NT 4.0, Windows Millennium Edition, Windows 2000, Windows XP Home Edition, Windows XP Professional, Windows Server 2003 family, .NET Compact Framework - Windows CE .NET

ToolBar.SetBoundsCore Method

This member overrides **Control.SetBoundsCore**.

```
[Visual Basic]
Overrides Protected Sub SetBoundsCore( _
   ByVal x As Integer, _
   ByVal y As Integer, _
   ByVal width As Integer, _
   ByVal height As Integer, _
   ByVal specified As BoundsSpecified _
)
[C#]
protected override void SetBoundsCore(
   int x,
   int y,
   int width,
   int height,
   BoundsSpecified specified
);
[C++]
protected: void SetBoundsCore(
   int x,
   int y,
   int width,
   int height,
   BoundsSpecified specified
);
[JScript]
protected override function SetBoundsCore(
   x : int,
   y : int,
   width : int,
   height : int,
   specified : BoundsSpecified
);
```

Requirements

Platforms: Windows 98, Windows NT 4.0, Windows Millennium Edition, Windows 2000, Windows XP Home Edition, Windows XP Professional, Windows Server 2003 family

ToolBar.ToString Method

This member overrides **Object.ToString**.

[Visual Basic]
```
Overrides Public Function ToString() As String
```
[C#]
```
public override string ToString();
```
[C++]
```
public: String* ToString();
```
[JScript]
```
public override function ToString() : String;
```

Requirements

Platforms: Windows 98, Windows NT 4.0, Windows Millennium Edition, Windows 2000, Windows XP Home Edition, Windows XP Professional, Windows Server 2003 family, .NET Compact Framework - Windows CE .NET

ToolBar.WndProc Method

This member overrides **Control.WndProc**.

[Visual Basic]
```
Overrides Protected Sub WndProc( _
   ByRef m As Message _
)
```
[C#]
```
protected override void WndProc(
   ref Message m
);
```
[C++]
```
protected: void WndProc(
   Message* m
);
```
[JScript]
```
protected override function WndProc(
   m : Message
);
```

Requirements

Platforms: Windows 98, Windows NT 4.0, Windows Millennium Edition, Windows 2000, Windows XP Home Edition, Windows XP Professional, Windows Server 2003 family

ToolBar.BackColorChanged Event

This member supports the .NET Framework infrastructure and is not intended to be used directly from your code.

[Visual Basic]
```
Public Shadows Event BackColorChanged As EventHandler
```
[C#]
```
public new event EventHandler BackColorChanged;
```
[C++]
```
public: __event EventHandler* BackColorChanged;
```

[JScript] In JScript, you can handle the events defined by a class, but you cannot define your own.

ToolBar.BackgroundImageChanged Event

This member supports the .NET Framework infrastructure and is not intended to be used directly from your code.

[Visual Basic]
```
Public Shadows Event BackgroundImageChanged As EventHandler
```
[C#]
```
public new event EventHandler BackgroundImageChanged;
```
[C++]
```
public: __event EventHandler* BackgroundImageChanged;
```

[JScript] In JScript, you can handle the events defined by a class, but you cannot define your own.

ToolBar.ButtonClick Event

Occurs when a **ToolBarButton** on the **ToolBar** is clicked.

[Visual Basic]
```
Public Event ButtonClick As ToolBarButtonClickEventHandler
```
[C#]
```
public event ToolBarButtonClickEventHandler ButtonClick;
```
[C++]
```
public: __event ToolBarButtonClickEventHandler* ButtonClick;
```

[JScript] In JScript, you can handle the events defined by a class, but you cannot define your own.

Event Data

The event handler receives an argument of type **ToolBarButton-ClickEventArgs** containing data related to this event. The following **ToolBarButtonClickEventArgs** property provides information specific to this event.

Property	Description
Button	Gets or sets the **ToolBarButton** that was clicked.

Remarks

Example

See related example in the **System.Windows.Forms.ToolBar** class topic.

Requirements

Platforms: Windows 98, Windows NT 4.0, Windows Millennium Edition, Windows 2000, Windows XP Home Edition, Windows XP Professional, Windows Server 2003 family

ToolBar.ButtonDropDown Event

Occurs when a drop-down style **ToolBarButton** or its down arrow is clicked.

[Visual Basic]
```
Public Event ButtonDropDown As ToolBarButtonClickEventHandler
```
[C#]
```
public event ToolBarButtonClickEventHandler ButtonDropDown;
```
[C++]
```
public: __event ToolBarButtonClickEventHandler* ButtonDropDown;
```

[JScript] In JScript, you can handle the events defined by a class, but you cannot define your own.

Event Data

The event handler receives an argument of type **ToolBarButton-ClickEventArgs** containing data related to this event. The following **ToolBarButtonClickEventArgs** property provides information specific to this event.

Property	Description
Button	Gets or sets the **ToolBarButton** that was clicked.

Example

See related example in the **System.Windows.Forms.ToolBar** class topic.

Requirements

Platforms: Windows 98, Windows NT 4.0, Windows Millennium Edition, Windows 2000, Windows XP Home Edition, Windows XP Professional, Windows Server 2003 family

ToolBar.ForeColorChanged Event

This member supports the .NET Framework infrastructure and is not intended to be used directly from your code.

[Visual Basic]
```
Public Shadows Event ForeColorChanged As EventHandler
```
[C#]
```
public new event EventHandler ForeColorChanged;
```
[C++]
```
public: __event EventHandler* ForeColorChanged;
```

[JScript] In JScript, you can handle the events defined by a class, but you cannot define your own.

ToolBar.ImeModeChanged Event

This member supports the .NET Framework infrastructure and is not intended to be used directly from your code.

[Visual Basic]
```
Public Shadows Event ImeModeChanged As EventHandler
```
[C#]
```
public new event EventHandler ImeModeChanged;
```
[C++]
```
public: __event EventHandler* ImeModeChanged;
```

[JScript] In JScript, you can handle the events defined by a class, but you cannot define your own.

ToolBar.Paint Event

This member supports the .NET Framework infrastructure and is not intended to be used directly from your code.

[Visual Basic]
```
Public Shadows Event Paint As PaintEventHandler
```
[C#]
```
public new event PaintEventHandler Paint;
```
[C++]
```
public: __event PaintEventHandler* Paint;
```

[JScript] In JScript, you can handle the events defined by a class, but you cannot define your own.

ToolBar.RightToLeftChanged Event

This member supports the .NET Framework infrastructure and is not intended to be used directly from your code.

[Visual Basic]
```
Public Shadows Event RightToLeftChanged As EventHandler
```
[C#]
```
public new event EventHandler RightToLeftChanged;
```
[C++]
```
public: __event EventHandler* RightToLeftChanged;
```

[JScript] In JScript, you can handle the events defined by a class, but you cannot define your own.

ToolBar.TextChanged Event

This member supports the .NET Framework infrastructure and is not intended to be used directly from your code.

[Visual Basic]
```
Public Shadows Event TextChanged As EventHandler
```
[C#]
```
public new event EventHandler TextChanged;
```
[C++]
```
public: __event EventHandler* TextChanged;
```

[JScript] In JScript, you can handle the events defined by a class, but you cannot define your own.

ToolBarAppearance Enumeration

Specifies the type of toolbar to display.

[Visual Basic]
```
<Serializable>
Public Enum ToolBarAppearance
```
[C#]
```
[Serializable]
public enum ToolBarAppearance
```
[C++]
```
[Serializable]
__value public enum ToolBarAppearance
```
[JScript]
```
public
   Serializable
enum ToolBarAppearance
```

Remarks

This enumeration is used by members such as **ToolBar.Appearance**.

Set the **Appearance** property of the toolbar to **ToolBarAppearance.Flat** to give the toolbar and its buttons a flat appearance. As the mouse pointer moves over the buttons, their appearance changes to three-dimensional. Button separators appear as lines rather than spaces between the buttons when the toolbar has a flat appearance.

Members

Member name	Description
Flat	The toolbar and buttons appear flat, but the buttons change to three-dimensional as the mouse pointer moves over them.
Normal	The toolbar and buttons appear as standard three-dimensional controls.

Example

[Visual Basic, C#, C++] The following example creates a **ToolBar** control, sets some of its common properties, and adds it to a **Form**. Delegates are also added to the **ButtonClick** and **ButtonDropDown** events. This example assumes a **ToolBar** named `toolBar1` and an **ImageList** named `imageList1` have been declared.

[Visual Basic]
```
Private Sub AddToolBar()
   ' Add a toolbar and set some of its properties.
   toolBar1 = New ToolBar()
   toolBar1.Appearance = System.Windows.Forms.ToolBarAppearance.Flat
   toolBar1.BorderStyle = System.Windows.Forms.BorderStyle.None
   toolBar1.Buttons.Add(Me.toolBarButton1)
   toolBar1.ButtonSize = New System.Drawing.Size(24, 24)
   toolBar1.Divider = True
   toolBar1.DropDownArrows = True
   toolBar1.ImageList = Me.imageList1
   toolBar1.ShowToolTips = True
   toolBar1.Size = New System.Drawing.Size(292, 25)
   toolBar1.TabIndex = 0
   toolBar1.TextAlign = System.Windows.Forms.ToolBarTextAlign.Right
   toolBar1.Wrappable = False

   ' Add handlers for the ButtonClick and ButtonDropDown events.
   AddHandler toolBar1.ButtonDropDown, AddressOf ↵
toolBar1_ButtonDropDown
   AddHandler toolBar1.ButtonClick, AddressOf toolBar1_ButtonClicked

   ' Add the toolbar to the form.
   Me.Controls.Add(toolBar1)
End Sub
```

[C#]
```
private void AddToolBar()
{
   // Add a toolbar and set some of its properties.
   toolBar1 = new ToolBar();
   toolBar1.Appearance = System.Windows.Forms.ToolBarAppearance.Flat;
   toolBar1.BorderStyle = System.Windows.Forms.BorderStyle.None;
   toolBar1.Buttons.Add(this.toolBarButton1);
   toolBar1.ButtonSize = new System.Drawing.Size(24, 24);
   toolBar1.Divider = true;
   toolBar1.DropDownArrows = true;
   toolBar1.ImageList = this.imageList1;
   toolBar1.ShowToolTips = true;
   toolBar1.Size = new System.Drawing.Size(292, 25);
   toolBar1.TabIndex = 0;
   toolBar1.TextAlign = System.Windows.Forms.ToolBarTextAlign.Right;
   toolBar1.Wrappable = false;

   // Add handlers for the ButtonClick and ButtonDropDown events.
   toolBar1.ButtonDropDown +=
     new ToolBarButtonClickEventHandler(toolBar1_ButtonDropDown);
   toolBar1.ButtonClick +=
     new ToolBarButtonClickEventHandler(toolBar1_ButtonClicked);

   // Add the toolbar to the form.
   this.Controls.Add(toolBar1);
}
```

[C++]
```
private:
    void AddToolBar() {
        // Add a toolbar and set some of its properties.
        toolBar1 = new ToolBar();
        toolBar1->Appearance =                                          ↵
System::Windows::Forms::ToolBarAppearance::Flat;
        toolBar1->BorderStyle =                                         ↵
System::Windows::Forms::BorderStyle::None;
        toolBar1->Buttons->Add(this->toolBarButton1);
        toolBar1->ButtonSize = System::Drawing::Size(24, 24);
        toolBar1->Divider = true;
        toolBar1->DropDownArrows = true;
        toolBar1->ImageList = this->imageList1;
        toolBar1->ShowToolTips = true;
        toolBar1->Size = System::Drawing::Size(292, 25);
        toolBar1->TabIndex = 0;
        toolBar1->TextAlign =                                           ↵
System::Windows::Forms::ToolBarTextAlign::Right;
        toolBar1->Wrappable = false;

        // Add handlers for the ButtonClick and ButtonDropDown events.
        toolBar1->ButtonDropDown += new                                 ↵
ToolBarButtonClickEventHandler(this, toolBar1_ButtonDropDown);
        toolBar1->ButtonClick += new                                    ↵
ToolBarButtonClickEventHandler(this, toolBar1_ButtonClicked);

        // Add the toolbar to the form.
        this->Controls->Add(toolBar1);
    }
```

Requirements

Namespace: System.Windows.Forms

Platforms: Windows 98, Windows NT 4.0, Windows Millennium Edition, Windows 2000, Windows XP Home Edition, Windows XP Professional, Windows Server 2003 family

Assembly: System.Windows.Forms (in System.Windows.Forms.dll)

ToolBarButton Class

Represents a Windows toolbar button.

System.Object
  System.MarshalByRefObject
    System.ComponentModel.Component
      System.Windows.Forms.ToolBarButton

[Visual Basic]
```
Public Class ToolBarButton
   Inherits Component
```
[C#]
```
public class ToolBarButton : Component
```
[C++]
```
public __gc class ToolBarButton : public Component
```
[JScript]
```
public class ToolBarButton extends Component
```

Thread Safety

Any public static (**Shared** in Visual Basic) members of this type are safe for multithreaded operations. Any instance members are not guaranteed to be thread safe.

Remarks

ToolBarButton controls are parented by **ToolBar** controls. Common properties to set once the toolbar button has been created are **Text** and **ImageIndex**. Set the **Text** property of the buttonto display text beneath or to the right of the image. To assign images to the buttons by creating an **ImageList**, assigning it to the **ImageList** property of the toolbar; then assign the image index value to the **ImageIndex** property of the button.

To change the appearance of the toolbar buttons assigned to the toolbar, set the **Appearance** property of the parent toolbar control. The **ToolBarAppearance.Flat** appearance give the buttons a flat appearance. As the mouse pointer moves over the buttons, their appearance changes to three-dimensional. Button separators appear as lines rather than spaces between the buttons when the buttons have a flat appearance. If the **Appearance** property is set to **ToolBarAppearance.Normal**, the buttons appear raised and three-dimensional, and the separators appear as a gap between the buttons.

You can assign a **ContextMenu** to a button if the **Style** property is set to **ToolBarButtonStyle.DropDown**. When the button is clicked, the assigned menu is displayed.

To create a collection of **ToolBarButton** controls to display on a **ToolBar**, add the buttons individually by using the **Add** method of the **Buttons** property. Alternatively, you can add several toolbar buttons using the **AddRange** method.

Example

[Visual Basic, C#] The following example creates a **ToolBar** and three **ToolBarButton** controls. The toolbar buttons are assigned to the button collection, the collection is assigned to the toolbar, and the toolbar is added to the form. On the **ButtonClick** event of the toolbar, the **Button** property of the **ToolBarButtonClickEventArgs** is evaluated and the appropriate dialog box opened. This code assumes that a **Form**, an **OpenFileDialog**, a **SaveFileDialog**, and a **PrintDialog** have all been created.

[Visual Basic]
```
Public Sub InitializeMyToolBar()
    ' Create and initialize the ToolBar and ToolBarButton controls.
    Dim toolBar1 As New ToolBar()
    Dim toolBarButton1 As New ToolBarButton()
    Dim toolBarButton2 As New ToolBarButton()
    Dim toolBarButton3 As New ToolBarButton()

    ' Set the Text properties of the ToolBarButton controls.
    toolBarButton1.Text = "Open"
    toolBarButton2.Text = "Save"
    toolBarButton3.Text = "Print"

    ' Add the ToolBarButton controls to the ToolBar.
    toolBar1.Buttons.Add(toolBarButton1)
    toolBar1.Buttons.Add(toolBarButton2)
    toolBar1.Buttons.Add(toolBarButton3)

    ' Add the event-handler delegate.
    AddHandler toolBar1.ButtonClick, AddressOf Me.toolBar1_ButtonClick

    ' Add the ToolBar to the Form.
    Controls.Add(toolBar1)
End Sub

Protected Sub toolBar1_ButtonClick(sender As Object, _
    e As ToolBarButtonClickEventArgs)

    ' Evaluate the Button property to determine which button ↵
was clicked.
    Select Case toolBar1.Buttons.IndexOf(e.Button)
        Case 0
            openFileDialog1.ShowDialog()
            ' Insert code to open the file.
        Case 1
            saveFileDialog1.ShowDialog()
            ' Insert code to save the file.
        Case 2
            printDialog1.ShowDialog()
            ' Insert code to print the file.
    End Select
End Sub
```

[C#]
```
public void InitializeMyToolBar()
 {
    // Create and initialize the ToolBar and ToolBarButton controls.
    toolBar1 = new ToolBar();
    ToolBarButton toolBarButton1 = new ToolBarButton();
    ToolBarButton toolBarButton2 = new ToolBarButton();
    ToolBarButton toolBarButton3 = new ToolBarButton();

    // Set the Text properties of the ToolBarButton controls.
    toolBarButton1.Text = "Open";
    toolBarButton2.Text = "Save";
    toolBarButton3.Text = "Print";

    // Add the ToolBarButton controls to the ToolBar.
    toolBar1.Buttons.Add(toolBarButton1);
    toolBar1.Buttons.Add(toolBarButton2);
    toolBar1.Buttons.Add(toolBarButton3);

    // Add the event-handler delegate.
    toolBar1.ButtonClick += new ToolBarButtonClickEventHandler (
       this.toolBar1_ButtonClick);

    // Add the ToolBar to the Form.
    Controls.Add(toolBar1);
 }

 protected void toolBar1_ButtonClick (
                         Object sender,
                         ToolBarButtonClickEventArgs e)
 {
   // Evaluate the Button property to determine which ↵
button was clicked.
   switch(toolBar1.Buttons.IndexOf(e.Button))
   {
      case 0:
         openFileDialog1.ShowDialog();
```

```
            // Insert code to open the file.
            break;
        case 1:
            saveFileDialog1.ShowDialog();
            // Insert code to save the file.
            break;
        case 2:
            printDialog1.ShowDialog();
            // Insert code to print the file.
            break;
    }
}
```

Requirements

Namespace: System.Windows.Forms

Platforms: Windows 98, Windows NT 4.0, Windows Millennium Edition, Windows 2000, Windows XP Home Edition, Windows XP Professional, Windows Server 2003 family, .NET Compact Framework - Windows CE .NET

Assembly: System.Windows.Forms (in System.Windows.Forms.dll)

ToolBarButton Constructor

Initializes a new instance of the **ToolBarButton** class.

Overload List

Initializes a new instance of the **ToolBarButton** class.

Supported by the .NET Compact Framework.

[Visual Basic] **Public Sub New()**

[C#] **public ToolBarButton();**

[C++] **public: ToolBarButton();**

[JScript] **public function ToolBarButton();**

Initializes a new instance of the **ToolBarButton** class and displays the assigned text on the button.

[Visual Basic] **Public Sub New(String)**

[C#] **public ToolBarButton(string);**

[C++] **public: ToolBarButton(String*);**

[JScript] **public function ToolBarButton(String);**

Example

See related example in the **System.Windows.Forms.ToolBarButton** class topic.

ToolBarButton Constructor ()

Initializes a new instance of the **ToolBarButton** class.

```
[Visual Basic]
Public Sub New()
[C#]
public ToolBarButton();
[C++]
public: ToolBarButton();
[JScript]
public function ToolBarButton();
```

Remarks

A newly created **ToolBarButton** has no default **Text** or **Image** assigned to it. The button's default style is **ToolBarButtonStyle.PushButton**.

Example

See related example in the **System.Windows.Forms.ToolBarButton** class topic.

Requirements

Platforms: Windows 98, Windows NT 4.0, Windows Millennium Edition, Windows 2000, Windows XP Home Edition, Windows XP Professional, Windows Server 2003 family, .NET Compact Framework - Windows CE .NET

ToolBarButton Constructor (String)

Initializes a new instance of the **ToolBarButton** class and displays the assigned text on the button.

```
[Visual Basic]
Public Sub New( _
   ByVal text As String _
)
[C#]
public ToolBarButton(
   string text
);
[C++]
public: ToolBarButton(
   String* text
);
[JScript]
public function ToolBarButton(
   text : String
);
```

Parameters

text

The text to display on the new **ToolBarButton**.

Remarks

The newly created **ToolBarButton** has no **Image** assigned to it. The button's default style is **PushButton**. The *text* parameter is assigned to the **Text** property and is displayed on the new toolbar button control.

Example

See related example in the **System.Windows.Forms.ToolBarButton** class topic.

Requirements

Platforms: Windows 98, Windows NT 4.0, Windows Millennium Edition, Windows 2000, Windows XP Home Edition, Windows XP Professional, Windows Server 2003 family

ToolBarButton.DropDownMenu Property

Gets or sets the menu to be displayed in the drop-down toolbar button.

```
[Visual Basic]
Public Property DropDownMenu As Menu
[C#]
public Menu DropDownMenu {get; set;}
[C++]
public: __property Menu* get_DropDownMenu();
public: __property void set_DropDownMenu(Menu*);
[JScript]
public function get DropDownMenu() : Menu;
public function set DropDownMenu(Menu);
```

Property Value

A **ContextMenu** to be displayed in the drop-down toolbar button. The default is a null reference (**Nothing** in Visual Basic).

Exceptions

Exception Type	Condition
ArgumentException	The assigned object is not a **ContextMenu**.

Remarks

You can specify a **ContextMenu** to be displayed when the drop-down button is clicked. This property is not used unless the **Style** property value is set to **ToolBarButtonStyle.DropDownButton**.

> **Note** Although the **DropDownMenu** property is defined as a **Menu** type, you must assign it a **ContextMenu** for it to display properly. If you are creating your own **MenuItem** derived class you must assign that object to a **ContextMenu** and assign the **ContextMenu** to the **DropDownMenu** property.

Example

See related example in the **System.Windows.Forms.ToolBar-Button** class topic.

Requirements

Platforms: Windows 98, Windows NT 4.0,
Windows Millennium Edition, Windows 2000,
Windows XP Home Edition, Windows XP Professional,
Windows Server 2003 family,
.NET Compact Framework - Windows CE .NET

ToolBarButton.Enabled Property

Gets or sets a value indicating whether the button is enabled.

```
[Visual Basic]
Public Property Enabled As Boolean
[C#]
public bool Enabled {get; set;}
[C++]
public: __property bool get_Enabled();
public: __property void set_Enabled(bool);
[JScript]
public function get Enabled() : Boolean;
public function set Enabled(Boolean);
```

Property Value

true if the button is enabled; otherwise, **false**. The default is **true**.

Remarks

When the **Enabled** property is set to **false**, the toolbar button cannot be clicked, and the button's appearance changes. The **Image** and **Text** assigned to the button appear grayed out. If the image or text has multiple colors, they display in a monochromatic gray.

Requirements

Platforms: Windows 98, Windows NT 4.0,
Windows Millennium Edition, Windows 2000,
Windows XP Home Edition, Windows XP Professional,
Windows Server 2003 family,
.NET Compact Framework - Windows CE .NET

ToolBarButton.ImageIndex Property

Gets or sets the index value of the image assigned to the button.

```
[Visual Basic]
Public Property ImageIndex As Integer
[C#]
public int ImageIndex {get; set;}
[C++]
public: __property int get_ImageIndex();
public: __property void set_ImageIndex(int);
[JScript]
public function get ImageIndex() : int;
public function set ImageIndex(int);
```

Property Value

The index value of the **Image** assigned to the toolbar button. The default is -1.

Exceptions

Exception Type	Condition
ArgumentException	The assigned value is less than -1.

Remarks

The **ImageIndex** value references the indexed value of the images in an **ImageList** assigned to the parent **ToolBar** control.

Example

See related example in the **System.Windows.Forms.ToolBar-Button** class topic.

Requirements

Platforms: Windows 98, Windows NT 4.0,
Windows Millennium Edition, Windows 2000,
Windows XP Home Edition, Windows XP Professional,
Windows Server 2003 family,
.NET Compact Framework - Windows CE .NET

ToolBarButton.Parent Property

Gets the toolbar control that the toolbar button is assigned to.

```
[Visual Basic]
Public ReadOnly Property Parent As ToolBar
[C#]
public ToolBar Parent {get;}
[C++]
public: __property ToolBar* get_Parent();
[JScript]
public function get Parent() : ToolBar;
```

Property Value

The **ToolBar** control that the **ToolBarButton** is assigned to.

Requirements

Platforms: Windows 98, Windows NT 4.0,
Windows Millennium Edition, Windows 2000,
Windows XP Home Edition, Windows XP Professional,
Windows Server 2003 family

ToolBarButton.PartialPush Property

Gets or sets a value indicating whether a toggle-style toolbar button is partially pushed.

[Visual Basic]
```
Public Property PartialPush As Boolean
```
[C#]
```
public bool PartialPush {get; set;}
```
[C++]
```
public: __property bool get_PartialPush();
public: __property void set_PartialPush(bool);
```
[JScript]
```
public function get PartialPush() : Boolean;
public function set PartialPush(Boolean);
```

Property Value

true if a toggle-style toolbar button is partially pushed; otherwise, **false**. The default is **false**.

Remarks

When **PartialPush** is set to **true**, the toolbar button appears to have its face grayed. This appearance is different from the dimmed appearance when the **Enabled** property is set to **false** since the partial-push appearance gives a haze to the entire button face. This property has no effect unless the **ToolBarButtonStyle** is set to **ToggleButton**.

Requirements

Platforms: Windows 98, Windows NT 4.0,
Windows Millennium Edition, Windows 2000,
Windows XP Home Edition, Windows XP Professional,
Windows Server 2003 family

ToolBarButton.Pushed Property

Gets or sets a value indicating whether a toggle-style toolbar button is currently in the pushed state.

[Visual Basic]
```
Public Property Pushed As Boolean
```
[C#]
```
public bool Pushed {get; set;}
```
[C++]
```
public: __property bool get_Pushed();
public: __property void set_Pushed(bool);
```
[JScript]
```
public function get Pushed() : Boolean;
public function set Pushed(Boolean);
```

Property Value

true if a toggle-style toolbar button is currently in the pushed state; otherwise, **false**. The default is **false**.

Remarks

When **Pushed** is set to **true**, the toolbar button appears sunken or inset relative to the other buttons. This property has no effect unless the **ToolBarButtonStyle** is set to **ToggleButton**.

Requirements

Platforms: Windows 98, Windows NT 4.0,
Windows Millennium Edition, Windows 2000,
Windows XP Home Edition, Windows XP Professional,
Windows Server 2003 family,
.NET Compact Framework - Windows CE .NET

ToolBarButton.Rectangle Property

Gets the bounding rectangle for a toolbar button.

[Visual Basic]
```
Public ReadOnly Property Rectangle As Rectangle
```
[C#]
```
public Rectangle Rectangle {get;}
```
[C++]
```
public: __property Rectangle get_Rectangle();
```
[JScript]
```
public function get Rectangle() : Rectangle;
```

Property Value

The bounding **Rectangle** for a toolbar button.

Remarks

If the **ToolBar** and the current button are both **Visible**, then this property retrieves the bounding rectangle the button is currently contained in.

Requirements

Platforms: Windows 98, Windows NT 4.0,
Windows Millennium Edition, Windows 2000,
Windows XP Home Edition, Windows XP Professional,
Windows Server 2003 family

ToolBarButton.Style Property

Gets or sets the style of the toolbar button.

[Visual Basic]
```
Public Property Style As ToolBarButtonStyle
```
[C#]
```
public ToolBarButtonStyle Style {get; set;}
```
[C++]
```
public: __property ToolBarButtonStyle get_Style();
public: __property void set_Style(ToolBarButtonStyle);
```
[JScript]
```
public function get Style() : ToolBarButtonStyle;
public function set Style(ToolBarButtonStyle);
```

Property Value

One of the **ToolBarButtonStyle** values. The default is **ToolBarButtonStyle.PushButton**.

Exceptions

Exception Type	Condition
InvalidEnumArgument-Exception	The assigned value is not one of the **ToolBarButtonStyle** values.

Remarks

If the button **Style** is set to **DropDownButton** you can specify a **MenuItem** to be displayed when the drop-down button is pressed. If the style is set to **ToolBarButtonStyle.Separator**, the toolbar button appears as a button separator and not as a button. The **ToolBarButtonStyle.ToggleButton** style causes the toolbar button to act like a toggle button; it can be in an on or off state.

Example

See related example in the **System.Windows.Forms.ToolBar-Button** class topic.

Requirements

Platforms: Windows 98, Windows NT 4.0,
Windows Millennium Edition, Windows 2000,
Windows XP Home Edition, Windows XP Professional,
Windows Server 2003 family,
.NET Compact Framework - Windows CE .NET

ToolBarButton.Tag Property

Gets or sets the object that contains data about the toolbar button.

```
[Visual Basic]
Public Property Tag As Object
[C#]
public object Tag {get; set;}
[C++]
public: __property Object* get_Tag();
public: __property void set_Tag(Object*);
[JScript]
public function get Tag() : Object;
public function set Tag(Object);
```

Property Value

An **Object** that contains data about the toolbar button. The default is a null reference (**Nothing** in Visual Basic).

Remarks

Retrieves or assigns the data currently associated with the toolbar button. Any **Object** derived type can be assigned to this property. If this property is being set through the Windows Forms designer, only text can be assigned.

Requirements

Platforms: Windows 98, Windows NT 4.0,
Windows Millennium Edition, Windows 2000,
Windows XP Home Edition, Windows XP Professional,
Windows Server 2003 family

ToolBarButton.Text Property

Gets or sets the text displayed on the toolbar button.

```
[Visual Basic]
Public Property Text As String
[C#]
public string Text {get; set;}
[C++]
public: __property String* get_Text();
public: __property void set_Text(String*);
[JScript]
public function get Text() : String;
public function set Text(String);
```

Property Value

The text displayed on the toolbar button. The default is an empty string ("").

Remarks

The default the Text property value is an empty string ("") unless you created the control with the **ToolBar** constructor that accepts the text string as a parameter. The orientation of the text on the toolbar button is determined by the **TextAlign** property of the button's parent **ToolBar**, which can be set to one of the **ToolBarTextAlign** enumeration values. The orientation is in relation to the image assigned to the button. If no image is assigned to the button, there will be space left for one on the surface of the toolbar button.

Example

See related example in the **System.Windows.Forms.ToolBar-Button** class topic.

Requirements

Platforms: Windows 98, Windows NT 4.0,
Windows Millennium Edition, Windows 2000,
Windows XP Home Edition, Windows XP Professional,
Windows Server 2003 family

ToolBarButton.ToolTipText Property

Gets or sets the text that appears as a ToolTip for a control.

```
[Visual Basic]
Public Property ToolTipText As String
[C#]
public string ToolTipText {get; set;}
[C++]
public: __property String* get_ToolTipText();
public: __property void set_ToolTipText(String*);
[JScript]
public function get ToolTipText() : String;
public function set ToolTipText(String);
```

Property Value

The text that is displayed when the mouse pointer moves over the toolbar button. The default is an empty string ("").

Remarks

To enable the display of the ToolTip text when the mouse pointer is moved over the button, set the **ShowToolTips** property of the button's parent **ToolBar** to **true**.

Example

See related example in the **System.Windows.Forms.ToolBar-Button** class topic.

Requirements

Platforms: Windows 98, Windows NT 4.0,
Windows Millennium Edition, Windows 2000,
Windows XP Home Edition, Windows XP Professional,
Windows Server 2003 family

ToolBarButton.Visible Property

Gets or sets a value indicating whether the toolbar button is visible.

[Visual Basic]
```
Public Property Visible As Boolean
```
[C#]
```
public bool Visible {get; set;}
```
[C++]
```
public: __property bool get_Visible();
public: __property void set_Visible(bool);
```
[JScript]
```
public function get Visible() : Boolean;
public function set Visible(Boolean);
```

Property Value

true if the toolbar button is visible; otherwise, **false**. The default is **true**.

Remarks

If the toolbar button is not visible, it will not be displayed on the toolbar, and therefore cannot receive user input.

Requirements

Platforms: Windows 98, Windows NT 4.0, Windows Millennium Edition, Windows 2000, Windows XP Home Edition, Windows XP Professional, Windows Server 2003 family, .NET Compact Framework - Windows CE .NET

ToolBarButton.Dispose Method

Overload List

This member supports the .NET Framework infrastructure and is not intended to be used directly from your code.

Supported by the .NET Compact Framework.

[Visual Basic] **Overloads Overrides Protected Sub Dispose(Boolean)**

[C#] **protected override void Dispose(bool);**

[C++] **protected: void Dispose(bool);**

[JScript] **protected override function Dispose(Boolean);**

Inherited from **Component**.

[Visual Basic] **Overloads Public Overridable Sub Dispose() Implements IDisposable.Dispose**

[C#] **public virtual void Dispose();**

[C++] **public: virtual void Dispose();**

[JScript] **public function Dispose();**

ToolBarButton.Dispose Method (Boolean)

This member overrides **Component.Dispose**.

[Visual Basic]
```
Overrides Overloads Protected Sub Dispose( _
   ByVal disposing As Boolean _
)
```
[C#]
```
protected override void Dispose(
   bool disposing
);
```
[C++]
```
protected: void Dispose(
   bool disposing
);
```
[JScript]
```
protected override function Dispose(
   disposing : Boolean
);
```

Requirements

Platforms: Windows 98, Windows NT 4.0, Windows Millennium Edition, Windows 2000, Windows XP Home Edition, Windows XP Professional, Windows Server 2003 family, .NET Compact Framework - Windows CE .NET

ToolBarButton.ToString Method

This member overrides **Object.ToString**.

[Visual Basic]
```
Overrides Public Function ToString() As String
```
[C#]
```
public override string ToString();
```
[C++]
```
public: String* ToString();
```
[JScript]
```
public override function ToString() : String;
```

Requirements

Platforms: Windows 98, Windows NT 4.0, Windows Millennium Edition, Windows 2000, Windows XP Home Edition, Windows XP Professional, Windows Server 2003 family, .NET Compact Framework - Windows CE .NET

ToolBarButtonClickEventArgs Class

Provides data for the **ButtonClick** event.

System.Object
  System.EventArgs
    System.Windows.Forms.ToolBarButtonClickEventArgs

[Visual Basic]
```
Public Class ToolBarButtonClickEventArgs
   Inherits EventArgs
```
[C#]
```
public class ToolBarButtonClickEventArgs : EventArgs
```
[C++]
```
public __gc class ToolBarButtonClickEventArgs : public EventArgs
```
[JScript]
```
public class ToolBarButtonClickEventArgs extends EventArgs
```

Thread Safety

Any public static (**Shared** in Visual Basic) members of this type are safe for multithreaded operations. Any instance members are not guaranteed to be thread safe.

Remarks

The event occurs whenever the user clicks on a button on a **ToolBar** control. The **Button** property contains the **ToolBarButton** wiith the information about the button that was clicked.

Example

[Visual Basic, C#] The following example instantiates a **ToolBar** and three **ToolBarButton** controls. The toolbar buttons are assigned to the button collection, the collection is assigned to the toolbar, and the toolbar is added to the form. On the **ButtonClick** event of the toolbar, the **Button** property of the **ToolBarButtonClickEventArgs** is evaluated, and the appropriate dialog opened. This code assumes that a **Form**, an **OpenFileDialog**, a **SaveFileDialog**, and a **PrintDialog** have been instantiated.

[Visual Basic]
```
Public Sub InitializeMyToolBar()
    ' Create and initialize the ToolBar and ToolBarButton controls.
    Dim toolBar1 As New ToolBar()
    Dim toolBarButton1 As New ToolBarButton()
    Dim toolBarButton2 As New ToolBarButton()
    Dim toolBarButton3 As New ToolBarButton()

    ' Set the Text properties of the ToolBarButton controls.
    toolBarButton1.Text = "Open"
    toolBarButton2.Text = "Save"
    toolBarButton3.Text = "Print"

    ' Add the ToolBarButton controls to the ToolBar.
    toolBar1.Buttons.Add(toolBarButton1)
    toolBar1.Buttons.Add(toolBarButton2)
    toolBar1.Buttons.Add(toolBarButton3)

    ' Add the event-handler delegate.
    AddHandler toolBar1.ButtonClick, AddressOf Me.toolBar1_ButtonClick

    ' Add the ToolBar to the Form.
    Controls.Add(toolBar1)
End Sub

Protected Sub toolBar1_ButtonClick(sender As Object, _
    e As ToolBarButtonClickEventArgs)

    ' Evaluate the Button property to determine which button
 was clicked.
    Select Case toolBar1.Buttons.IndexOf(e.Button)
        Case 0
            openFileDialog1.ShowDialog()
            ' Insert code to open the file.
        Case 1
            saveFileDialog1.ShowDialog()
            ' Insert code to save the file.
        Case 2
            printDialog1.ShowDialog()
            ' Insert code to print the file.
    End Select
End Sub
```

[C#]
```
public void InitializeMyToolBar()
 {
    // Create and initialize the ToolBar and ToolBarButton controls.
    toolBar1 = new ToolBar();
    ToolBarButton toolBarButton1 = new ToolBarButton();
    ToolBarButton toolBarButton2 = new ToolBarButton();
    ToolBarButton toolBarButton3 = new ToolBarButton();

    // Set the Text properties of the ToolBarButton controls.
    toolBarButton1.Text = "Open";
    toolBarButton2.Text = "Save";
    toolBarButton3.Text = "Print";

    // Add the ToolBarButton controls to the ToolBar.
    toolBar1.Buttons.Add(toolBarButton1);
    toolBar1.Buttons.Add(toolBarButton2);
    toolBar1.Buttons.Add(toolBarButton3);

    // Add the event-handler delegate.
    toolBar1.ButtonClick += new ToolBarButtonClickEventHandler (
       this.toolBar1_ButtonClick);

    // Add the ToolBar to the Form.
    Controls.Add(toolBar1);
 }

 protected void toolBar1_ButtonClick (
                         Object sender,
                         ToolBarButtonClickEventArgs e)
 {
   // Evaluate the Button property to determine which button
 was clicked.
   switch(toolBar1.Buttons.IndexOf(e.Button))
   {
      case 0:
         openFileDialog1.ShowDialog();
         // Insert code to open the file.
         break;
      case 1:
         saveFileDialog1.ShowDialog();
         // Insert code to save the file.
         break;
      case 2:
         printDialog1.ShowDialog();
         // Insert code to print the file.
         break;
    }
 }
```

Requirements

Namespace: System.Windows.Forms

Platforms: Windows 98, Windows NT 4.0, Windows Millennium Edition, Windows 2000, Windows XP Home Edition, Windows XP Professional, Windows Server 2003 family, .NET Compact Framework - Windows CE .NET

Assembly: System.Windows.Forms (in System.Windows.Forms.dll)

ToolBarButtonClickEventArgs Constructor

Initializes a new instance of the **ToolBarButtonClickEventArgs** class.

```
[Visual Basic]
Public Sub New( _
   ByVal button As ToolBarButton _
)
[C#]
public ToolBarButtonClickEventArgs(
   ToolBarButton button
);
[C++]
public: ToolBarButtonClickEventArgs(
   ToolBarButton* button
);
[JScript]
public function ToolBarButtonClickEventArgs(
   button : ToolBarButton
);
```

Parameters

button

The **ToolBarButton** that was clicked.

Remarks

The **Button** property is set equal to the *button* parameter.

Requirements

Platforms: Windows 98, Windows NT 4.0, Windows Millennium Edition, Windows 2000, Windows XP Home Edition, Windows XP Professional, Windows Server 2003 family, .NET Compact Framework - Windows CE .NET

ToolBarButtonClickEventArgs.Button Property

Gets or sets the **ToolBarButton** that was clicked.

```
[Visual Basic]
Public Property Button As ToolBarButton
[C#]
public ToolBarButton Button {get; set;}
[C++]
public: __property ToolBarButton* get_Button();
public: __property void set_Button(ToolBarButton*);
[JScript]
public function get Button() : ToolBarButton;
public function set Button(ToolBarButton);
```

Property Value

The **ToolBarButton** that was clicked.

Remarks

The **Button** property is initially set equal to the *button* parameter of the **ToolBarButtonClickEventArgs** constructor.

Example

[Visual Basic, C#] The following example instantiates a **ToolBar** and three **ToolBarButton** controls. The toolbar buttons are assigned to the button collection, the collection is assigned to the toolbar, and the toolbar is added to the form. On the **ButtonClick** event of the toolbar, the **Button** property of the **ToolBarButtonClickEventArgs** is evaluated, and the appropriate dialog opened. This code assumes that a **Form**, an **OpenFileDialog**, a **SaveFileDialog**, and a **PrintDialog** have been instantiated.

```
[Visual Basic]
Public Sub InitializeMyToolBar()
    ' Create and initialize the ToolBar and ToolBarButton controls.
    Dim toolBar1 As New ToolBar()
    Dim toolBarButton1 As New ToolBarButton()
    Dim toolBarButton2 As New ToolBarButton()
    Dim toolBarButton3 As New ToolBarButton()

    ' Set the Text properties of the ToolBarButton controls.
    toolBarButton1.Text = "Open"
    toolBarButton2.Text = "Save"
    toolBarButton3.Text = "Print"

    ' Add the ToolBarButton controls to the ToolBar.
    toolBar1.Buttons.Add(toolBarButton1)
    toolBar1.Buttons.Add(toolBarButton2)
    toolBar1.Buttons.Add(toolBarButton3)

    ' Add the event-handler delegate.
    AddHandler toolBar1.ButtonClick, AddressOf Me.toolBar1_ButtonClick

    ' Add the ToolBar to the Form.
    Controls.Add(toolBar1)
End Sub

Protected Sub toolBar1_ButtonClick(sender As Object, _
    e As ToolBarButtonClickEventArgs)

    ' Evaluate the Button property to determine which button
 was clicked.
    Select Case toolBar1.Buttons.IndexOf(e.Button)
        Case 0
            openFileDialog1.ShowDialog()
            ' Insert code to open the file.
        Case 1
            saveFileDialog1.ShowDialog()
            ' Insert code to save the file.
        Case 2
            printDialog1.ShowDialog()
            ' Insert code to print the file.
    End Select
End Sub
```

```
[C#]
public void InitializeMyToolBar()
 {
    // Create and initialize the ToolBar and ToolBarButton controls.
    toolBar1 = new ToolBar();
    ToolBarButton toolBarButton1 = new ToolBarButton();
    ToolBarButton toolBarButton2 = new ToolBarButton();
    ToolBarButton toolBarButton3 = new ToolBarButton();

    // Set the Text properties of the ToolBarButton controls.
    toolBarButton1.Text = "Open";
    toolBarButton2.Text = "Save";
    toolBarButton3.Text = "Print";

    // Add the ToolBarButton controls to the ToolBar.
    toolBar1.Buttons.Add(toolBarButton1);
    toolBar1.Buttons.Add(toolBarButton2);
    toolBar1.Buttons.Add(toolBarButton3);
```

```
   // Add the event-handler delegate.
   toolBar1.ButtonClick += new ToolBarButtonClickEventHandler (
      this.toolBar1_ButtonClick);

   // Add the ToolBar to the Form.
   Controls.Add(toolBar1);
}

protected void toolBar1_ButtonClick (
                        Object sender,
                        ToolBarButtonClickEventArgs e)
{
  // Evaluate the Button property to determine which button        ↵
was clicked.
  switch(toolBar1.Buttons.IndexOf(e.Button))
  {
     case 0:
        openFileDialog1.ShowDialog();
        // Insert code to open the file.
        break;
     case 1:
        saveFileDialog1.ShowDialog();
        // Insert code to save the file.
        break;
     case 2:
        printDialog1.ShowDialog();
        // Insert code to print the file.
        break;
   }
}
```

Requirements

Platforms: Windows 98, Windows NT 4.0,
Windows Millennium Edition, Windows 2000,
Windows XP Home Edition, Windows XP Professional,
Windows Server 2003 family,
.NET Compact Framework - Windows CE .NET

ToolBarButtonClickEvent-Handler Delegate

Represents the method that will handle the **ButtonClick** event of a **ToolBar**.

[Visual Basic]
```
<Serializable>
Public Delegate Sub ToolBarButtonClickEventHandler( _
   ByVal sender As Object, _
   ByVal e As ToolBarButtonClickEventArgs _
)
```
[C#]
```
[Serializable]
public delegate void ToolBarButtonClickEventHandler(
   object sender,
   ToolBarButtonClickEventArgs e
);
```
[C++]
```
[Serializable]
public __gc __delegate void ToolBarButtonClickEventHandler(
   Object* sender,
   ToolBarButtonClickEventArgs* e
);
```

[JScript] In JScript, you can use the delegates in the .NET Framework, but you cannot define your own.

Parameters [Visual Basic, C#, C++]

The declaration of your event handler must have the same parameters as the **ToolBarButtonClickEventHandler** delegate declaration.

sender
: The source of the event.

e
: A **ToolBarButtonClickEventArgs** that contains the event data.

Remarks

When you create a **ToolBarButtonClickEventHandler** delegate, you identify the method that will handle the event. To associate the event with your event handler, add an instance of the delegate to the event. The event handler is called whenever the event occurs, unless you remove the delegate. For more information about handling events with delegates, see **Events and Delegates**.

Example

[Visual Basic, C#] The following example instantiates a **ToolBar** and three **ToolBarButton** controls. The toolbar buttons are assigned to the button collection, the collection is assigned to the toolbar, and the toolbar is added to the form. On the **ButtonClick** event of the toolbar, the **Button** property of the **ToolBarButtonClickEventArgs** is evaluated, and the appropriate dialog opened. This code assumes that a **Form**, an **OpenFileDialog**, a **SaveFileDialog**, and a **PrintDialog** have been instantiated.

[Visual Basic]
```
Public Sub InitializeMyToolBar()
    ' Create and initialize the ToolBar and ToolBarButton controls.
    Dim toolBar1 As New ToolBar()
    Dim toolBarButton1 As New ToolBarButton()
    Dim toolBarButton2 As New ToolBarButton()
    Dim toolBarButton3 As New ToolBarButton()

    ' Set the Text properties of the ToolBarButton controls.
    toolBarButton1.Text = "Open"
    toolBarButton2.Text = "Save"
    toolBarButton3.Text = "Print"

    ' Add the ToolBarButton controls to the ToolBar.
    toolBar1.Buttons.Add(toolBarButton1)
    toolBar1.Buttons.Add(toolBarButton2)
    toolBar1.Buttons.Add(toolBarButton3)

    ' Add the event-handler delegate.
    AddHandler toolBar1.ButtonClick, AddressOf Me.toolBar1_ButtonClick

    ' Add the ToolBar to the Form.
    Controls.Add(toolBar1)
End Sub

Protected Sub toolBar1_ButtonClick(sender As Object, _
    e As ToolBarButtonClickEventArgs)

    ' Evaluate the Button property to determine which button ↵
was clicked.
    Select Case toolBar1.Buttons.IndexOf(e.Button)
        Case 0
            openFileDialog1.ShowDialog()
            ' Insert code to open the file.
        Case 1
            saveFileDialog1.ShowDialog()
            ' Insert code to save the file.
        Case 2
            printDialog1.ShowDialog()
            ' Insert code to print the file.
    End Select
End Sub
```

[C#]
```
public void InitializeMyToolBar()
 {
    // Create and initialize the ToolBar and ToolBarButton controls.
    toolBar1 = new ToolBar();
    ToolBarButton toolBarButton1 = new ToolBarButton();
    ToolBarButton toolBarButton2 = new ToolBarButton();
    ToolBarButton toolBarButton3 = new ToolBarButton();

    // Set the Text properties of the ToolBarButton controls.
    toolBarButton1.Text = "Open";
    toolBarButton2.Text = "Save";
    toolBarButton3.Text = "Print";

    // Add the ToolBarButton controls to the ToolBar.
    toolBar1.Buttons.Add(toolBarButton1);
    toolBar1.Buttons.Add(toolBarButton2);
    toolBar1.Buttons.Add(toolBarButton3);

    // Add the event-handler delegate.
    toolBar1.ButtonClick += new ToolBarButtonClickEventHandler (
       this.toolBar1_ButtonClick);

    // Add the ToolBar to the Form.
    Controls.Add(toolBar1);
 }

 protected void toolBar1_ButtonClick (
                         Object sender,
                         ToolBarButtonClickEventArgs e)
 {
   // Evaluate the Button property to determine which ↵
 button was clicked.
   switch(toolBar1.Buttons.IndexOf(e.Button))
   {
      case 0:
         openFileDialog1.ShowDialog();
         // Insert code to open the file.
         break;
      case 1:
```

```
            saveFileDialog1.ShowDialog();
            // Insert code to save the file.
            break;
        case 2:
            printDialog1.ShowDialog();
            // Insert code to print the file.
            break;
    }
}
```

Requirements

Namespace: System.Windows.Forms

Platforms: Windows 98, Windows NT 4.0,
Windows Millennium Edition, Windows 2000,
Windows XP Home Edition, Windows XP Professional,
Windows Server 2003 family,
.NET Compact Framework - Windows CE .NET

Assembly: System.Windows.Forms (in System.Windows.Forms.dll)

ToolBarButtonStyle Enumeration

Specifies the button style within a toolbar.

[Visual Basic]
```
<Serializable>
Public Enum ToolBarButtonStyle
```
[C#]
```
[Serializable]
public enum ToolBarButtonStyle
```
[C++]
```
[Serializable]
__value public enum ToolBarButtonStyle
```
[JScript]
```
public
   Serializable
enum ToolBarButtonStyle
```

Remarks

This enumeration is used by members such as **ToolBarButton.Style**.

The toolbar button appearance is determined by the **Appearance** property of the toolbar. Setting the **Appearance** property to **Flat** will give the toolbar and its buttons a flat appearance. As the mouse pointer moves over the buttons, they take on a three-dimensional appearance. Also, when the toolbar has a flat appearance, button separators appear as a line rather than as a space between the buttons.

Members

Member name	Description
DropDownButton Supported by the .NET Compact Framework.	A drop-down control that displays a menu or other window when clicked.
PushButton Supported by the .NET Compact Framework.	A standard, three-dimensional button.
Separator Supported by the .NET Compact Framework.	A space or line between toolbar buttons. The appearance depends on the value of the **Appearance** property.
ToggleButton Supported by the .NET Compact Framework.	A toggle button that appears sunken when clicked and retains the sunken appearance until clicked again.

Example

[Visual Basic, C#] The following example instantiates a **ToolBar** and three **ToolBarButton** controls, assigns the buttons to the toolbar, and sets some of the buttons' common properties. This code assumes a **MenuItem**, **ImageList**, **ToolTip** and a **Form** have been instantiated and the **ImageList** has at least one **Image** assigned to it.

[Visual Basic]
```
Public Sub InitializeMyToolBar()
    ' Create the ToolBar, ToolBarButton controls, and menus.
    Dim toolBarButton1 As New ToolBarButton("Open")
    Dim toolBarButton2 As New ToolBarButton()
    Dim toolBarButton3 As New ToolBarButton()
    Dim toolBar1 As New ToolBar()
Dim menuItem1 As New MenuItem("Print")
Dim contextMenu1 As New ContextMenu(New MenuItem(){menuItem1})

    ' Add the ToolBarButton controls to the ToolBar.
    toolBar1.Buttons.Add(toolBarButton1)
    toolBar1.Buttons.Add(toolBarButton2)
    toolBar1.Buttons.Add(toolBarButton3)

    ' Assign an ImageList to the ToolBar and show ToolTips.
    toolBar1.ImageList = imageList1
    toolBar1.ShowToolTips = True

    ' Assign ImageIndex, ContextMenu, Text, ToolTip, and
    ' Style properties of the ToolBarButton controls.
    toolBarButton2.Style = ToolBarButtonStyle.Separator
    toolBarButton3.Text = "Print"
    toolBarButton3.Style = ToolBarButtonStyle.DropDownButton
    toolBarButton3.ToolTipText = "Print"
    toolBarButton3.ImageIndex = 0
    toolBarButton3.DropDownMenu = contextMenu1

    ' Add the ToolBar to a form.
    Controls.Add(toolBar1)
End Sub
```

[C#]
```
public void InitializeMyToolBar()
 {
    // Create the ToolBar, ToolBarButton controls, and menus.
    ToolBarButton toolBarButton1 = new ToolBarButton("Open");
    ToolBarButton toolBarButton2 = new ToolBarButton();
    ToolBarButton toolBarButton3 = new ToolBarButton();
    ToolBar toolBar1 = new ToolBar();
    MenuItem menuItem1 = new MenuItem("Print");
    ContextMenu contextMenu1 = new ContextMenu(new
MenuItem[]{menuItem1});

    // Add the ToolBarButton controls to the ToolBar.
    toolBar1.Buttons.Add(toolBarButton1);
    toolBar1.Buttons.Add(toolBarButton2);
    toolBar1.Buttons.Add(toolBarButton3);

    // Assign an ImageList to the ToolBar and show ToolTips.
    toolBar1.ImageList = imageList1;
    toolBar1.ShowToolTips = true;

    /* Assign ImageIndex, ContextMenu, Text, ToolTip, and
       Style properties of the ToolBarButton controls. */
    toolBarButton2.Style = ToolBarButtonStyle.Separator;
    toolBarButton3.Text = "Print";
    toolBarButton3.Style = ToolBarButtonStyle.DropDownButton;
    toolBarButton3.ToolTipText = "Print";
    toolBarButton3.ImageIndex = 0;
    toolBarButton3.DropDownMenu = contextMenu1;

    // Add the ToolBar to a form.
    Controls.Add(toolBar1);
 }
```

Requirements

Namespace: System.Windows.Forms

Platforms: Windows 98, Windows NT 4.0, Windows Millennium Edition, Windows 2000, Windows XP Home Edition, Windows XP Professional, Windows Server 2003 family, .NET Compact Framework - Windows CE .NET

Assembly: System.Windows.Forms (in System.Windows.Forms.dll)

ToolBarTextAlign Enumeration

Specifies the alignment of text on the toolbar button control.

[Visual Basic]
```
<Serializable>
Public Enum ToolBarTextAlign
```
[C#]
```
[Serializable]
public enum ToolBarTextAlign
```
[C++]
```
[Serializable]
__value public enum ToolBarTextAlign
```
[JScript]
```
public
   Serializable
enum ToolBarTextAlign
```

Remarks

This enumeration is used by members such as **ToolBar.TextAlign**.

Room is reserved for an image to be displayed on toolbar buttons. The alignment of text is in relation to the image displayed on the toolbar button. If no image is assigned to the button, the reserved space will appear to the left, or above the text displayed.

Members

Member name	Description
Right	The text is aligned to the right of the toolbar button image.
Underneath	The text is aligned underneath the toolbar button image.

Example

[Visual Basic, C#, C++] The following example creates a **ToolBar** control, sets some of its common properties, and adds it to a **Form**. Delegates are also added to the **ButtonClick** and **ButtonDropDown** events. This example assumes a **ToolBar** named `toolBar1` and an **ImageList** named `imageList1` have been declared.

[Visual Basic]
```
Private Sub AddToolBar()
   ' Add a toolbar and set some of its properties.
   toolBar1 = New ToolBar()
   toolBar1.Appearance = System.Windows.Forms.ToolBarAppearance.Flat
   toolBar1.BorderStyle = System.Windows.Forms.BorderStyle.None
   toolBar1.Buttons.Add(Me.toolBarButton1)
   toolBar1.ButtonSize = New System.Drawing.Size(24, 24)
   toolBar1.Divider = True
   toolBar1.DropDownArrows = True
   toolBar1.ImageList = Me.imageList1
   toolBar1.ShowToolTips = True
   toolBar1.Size = New System.Drawing.Size(292, 25)
   toolBar1.TabIndex = 0
   toolBar1.TextAlign = System.Windows.Forms.ToolBarTextAlign.Right
   toolBar1.Wrappable = False

   ' Add handlers for the ButtonClick and ButtonDropDown events.
   AddHandler toolBar1.ButtonDropDown, AddressOf ↵
toolBar1_ButtonDropDown
   AddHandler toolBar1.ButtonClick, AddressOf toolBar1_ButtonClicked

   ' Add the toolbar to the form.
   Me.Controls.Add(toolBar1)
End Sub
```

[C#]
```
private void AddToolBar()
{
   // Add a toolbar and set some of its properties.
   toolBar1 = new ToolBar();
   toolBar1.Appearance = System.Windows.Forms.ToolBarAppearance.Flat;
   toolBar1.BorderStyle = System.Windows.Forms.BorderStyle.None;
   toolBar1.Buttons.Add(this.toolBarButton1);
   toolBar1.ButtonSize = new System.Drawing.Size(24, 24);
   toolBar1.Divider = true;
   toolBar1.DropDownArrows = true;
   toolBar1.ImageList = this.imageList1;
   toolBar1.ShowToolTips = true;
   toolBar1.Size = new System.Drawing.Size(292, 25);
   toolBar1.TabIndex = 0;
   toolBar1.TextAlign = System.Windows.Forms.ToolBarTextAlign.Right;
   toolBar1.Wrappable = false;

   // Add handlers for the ButtonClick and ButtonDropDown events.
   toolBar1.ButtonDropDown +=
     new ToolBarButtonClickEventHandler(toolBar1_ButtonDropDown);
   toolBar1.ButtonClick +=
     new ToolBarButtonClickEventHandler(toolBar1_ButtonClicked);

   // Add the toolbar to the form.
   this.Controls.Add(toolBar1);
}
```

[C++]
```
private:
    void AddToolBar() {
        // Add a toolbar and set some of its properties.
        toolBar1 = new ToolBar();
        toolBar1->Appearance = ↵
System::Windows::Forms::ToolBarAppearance::Flat;
        toolBar1->BorderStyle = ↵
System::Windows::Forms::BorderStyle::None;
        toolBar1->Buttons->Add(this->toolBarButton1);
        toolBar1->ButtonSize = System::Drawing::Size(24, 24);
        toolBar1->Divider = true;
        toolBar1->DropDownArrows = true;
        toolBar1->ImageList = this->imageList1;
        toolBar1->ShowToolTips = true;
        toolBar1->Size = System::Drawing::Size(292, 25);
        toolBar1->TabIndex = 0;
        toolBar1->TextAlign = ↵
System::Windows::Forms::ToolBarTextAlign::Right;
        toolBar1->Wrappable = false;

        // Add handlers for the ButtonClick and ButtonDropDown events.
        toolBar1->ButtonDropDown += new ↵
ToolBarButtonClickEventHandler(this, toolBar1_ButtonDropDown);
        toolBar1->ButtonClick += new ↵
ToolBarButtonClickEventHandler(this, toolBar1_ButtonClicked);

        // Add the toolbar to the form.
        this->Controls->Add(toolBar1);
    }
```

Requirements

Namespace: System.Windows.Forms

Platforms: Windows 98, Windows NT 4.0, Windows Millennium Edition, Windows 2000, Windows XP Home Edition, Windows XP Professional, Windows Server 2003 family

Assembly: System.Windows.Forms (in System.Windows.Forms.dll)

ToolBar.ToolBarButton-Collection Class

Encapsulates a collection of **ToolBarButton** controls for use by the **ToolBar** class.

System.Object
  System.Windows.Forms.ToolBar.ToolBarButtonCollection

[Visual Basic]
```
Public Class ToolBar.ToolBarButtonCollection
   Implements IList, ICollection, IEnumerable
```
[C#]
```
public class ToolBar.ToolBarButtonCollection : IList, ICollection,
   IEnumerable
```
[C++]
```
public __gc class ToolBar.ToolBarButtonCollection : public IList,
   ICollection, IEnumerable
```
[JScript]
```
public class ToolBar.ToolBarButtonCollection implements IList,
   ICollection, IEnumerable
```

Thread Safety

Any public static (**Shared** in Visual Basic) members of this type are safe for multithreaded operations. Any instance members are not guaranteed to be thread safe.

Remarks

The **ToolBar.ToolBarButtonCollection** is a zero-based indexed collection used by the **ToolBar** class to hold all the **ToolBarButton** controls assigned to the toolbar. Use the **Add** method to add individual buttons and the **Remove** method to delete them. Call the **Clear** method to remove all the buttons from the collection.

Example

See related example in the **System.Windows.Forms.ToolBar** class topic.

Requirements

Namespace: System.Windows.Forms

Platforms: Windows 98, Windows NT 4.0,
Windows Millennium Edition, Windows 2000,
Windows XP Home Edition, Windows XP Professional,
Windows Server 2003 family,
.NET Compact Framework - Windows CE .NET

Assembly: System.Windows.Forms (in System.Windows.Forms.dll)

ToolBar.ToolBarButtonCollection Constructor

Initializes a new instance of the **ToolBar.ToolBarButtonCollection** class and assigns it to the specified toolbar.

[Visual Basic]
```
Public Sub New( _
   ByVal owner As ToolBar _
)
```
[C#]
```
public ToolBar.ToolBarButtonCollection(
   ToolBar owner
);
```
[C++]
```
public: ToolBarButtonCollection(
   ToolBar* owner
);
```
[JScript]
```
public function ToolBar.ToolBarButtonCollection(
   owner : ToolBar
);
```

Parameters

owner
  The **ToolBar** that is the parent of the collection of **ToolBarButton** controls.

Remarks

You do not typically create a **ToolBar.ToolBarButtonCollection** and explicitly call its constructor. By referencing the **Buttons** property of the **ToolBar** control, a **ToolBar.ToolBarButton-Collection** is created. You can then gain access to its properties and methods, and assign **ToolBarButton** controls to the collection.

Requirements

Platforms: Windows 98, Windows NT 4.0,
Windows Millennium Edition, Windows 2000,
Windows XP Home Edition, Windows XP Professional,
Windows Server 2003 family

ToolBar.ToolBarButtonCollection.Count Property

Gets the number of buttons in the toolbar button collection.

[Visual Basic]
```
Public Overridable ReadOnly Property Count As Integer  Implements _
   ICollection.Count
```
[C#]
```
public virtual int Count {get;}
```
[C++]
```
public: __property virtual int get_Count();
```
[JScript]
```
public function get Count() : int;
```

Property Value

The number of the **ToolBarButton** controls assigned to the toolbar.

Implements

ICollection.Count

Remarks

The **Count** property holds the actual number of **ToolBarButton** controls assigned to the collection. It is common to use the **Count** property value as the upper bounds of a loop to iterate through a collection. The index value of a collection is a zero-based index, so you must subtract one from the looping variable otherwise you will exceed the upper bounds of the collection and throw an exception.

Example

See related example in the **System.Windows.Forms.ToolBar** class topic.

Requirements

Platforms: Windows 98, Windows NT 4.0,
Windows Millennium Edition, Windows 2000,
Windows XP Home Edition, Windows XP Professional,
Windows Server 2003 family,
.NET Compact Framework - Windows CE .NET

ToolBar.ToolBarButtonCollection.IsReadOnly Property

Gets a value indicating whether the collection is read-only.

```
[Visual Basic]
Public Overridable ReadOnly Property IsReadOnly As Boolean _
   Implements IList.IsReadOnly
[C#]
public virtual bool IsReadOnly {get;}
[C++]
public: __property virtual bool get_IsReadOnly();
[JScript]
public function get IsReadOnly() : Boolean;
```

Property Value

true if the collection is read-only; otherwise, **false**. The default is **false**.

Implements

IList.IsReadOnly

Example

See related example in the **System.Windows.Forms.ToolBar** class topic.

Requirements

Platforms: Windows 98, Windows NT 4.0,
Windows Millennium Edition, Windows 2000,
Windows XP Home Edition, Windows XP Professional,
Windows Server 2003 family,
.NET Compact Framework - Windows CE .NET

ToolBar.ToolBarButtonCollection.Item Property

Gets or sets the toolbar button at the specified indexed location in the toolbar button collection.

[C#] In C#, this property is the indexer for the **ToolBar.ToolBarButtonCollection** class.

```
[Visual Basic]
Public Overridable Default Property Item( _
   ByVal index As Integer _
) As ToolBarButton
[C#]
public virtual ToolBarButton this[
   int index
] {get; set;}
[C++]
public: __property virtual ToolBarButton* get_Item(
   int index
);
public: __property virtual void set_Item(
   int index,
   ToolBarButton*
);
[JScript]
returnValue = ToolBarButtonCollectionObject.Item(index);
ToolBarButtonCollectionObject.Item(index) = returnValue;
-or-
returnValue = ToolBarButtonCollectionObject(index);
ToolBarButtonCollectionObject(index) = returnValue;
```

[JScript] In JScript, you can use the default indexed properties defined by a type, but you cannot explicitly define your own. However, specifying the **expando** attribute on a class automatically provides a default indexed property whose type is **Object** and whose index type is **String**.

Arguments [JScript]

index
The indexed location of the **ToolBarButton** in the collection.

Parameters [Visual Basic, C#, C++]

index
The indexed location of the **ToolBarButton** in the collection.

Property Value

A **ToolBarButton** that represents the toolbar button at the specified indexed location.

Exceptions

Exception Type	Condition
ArgumentNull-Exception	The *index* value is a null reference (**Nothing** in Visual Basic).
ArgumentOutOfRange-Exception	The *index* value is less than zero. -or- The *index* value is greater than the number of buttons in the collection, and the collection of buttons is not a null reference (**Nothing** in Visual Basic).

Remarks

To assign **ToolBarButton** controls to a specific location, or to retrieve them from the **ToolBar.ToolBarButtonCollection**, you can reference the collection object with a specific index value. The index value of the **ToolBar.ToolBarButtonCollection** is a zero-based index.

Example

See related example in the **System.Windows.Forms.ToolBar** class topic.

Requirements

Platforms: Windows 98, Windows NT 4.0,
Windows Millennium Edition, Windows 2000,
Windows XP Home Edition, Windows XP Professional,
Windows Server 2003 family

ToolBar.ToolBarButtonCollection.System.Collections.ICollection.IsSynchronized Property

Note: This namespace, class, or member is supported only in version 1.1 of the .NET Framework.

This member supports the .NET Framework infrastructure and is not intended to be used directly from your code.

```
[Visual Basic]
Private ReadOnly Property IsSynchronized As Boolean Implements _
   ICollection.IsSynchronized
[C#]
bool ICollection.IsSynchronized {get;}
[C++]
private: __property bool
   System::Collections::ICollection::get_IsSynchronized();
[JScript]
private function get ICollection.IsSynchronized() : Boolean;
```

ToolBar.ToolBarButtonCollection.System.Collections.ICollection.SyncRoot Property

Note: This namespace, class, or member is supported only in version 1.1 of the .NET Framework.

This member supports the .NET Framework infrastructure and is not intended to be used directly from your code.

```
[Visual Basic]
Private ReadOnly Property SyncRoot As Object Implements _
   ICollection.SyncRoot
[C#]
object ICollection.SyncRoot {get;}
[C++]
private: __property Object*
   System::Collections::ICollection::get_SyncRoot();
[JScript]
private function get ICollection.SyncRoot() : Object;
```

ToolBar.ToolBarButtonCollection.System.Collections.IList.IsFixedSize Property

Note: This namespace, class, or member is supported only in version 1.1 of the .NET Framework.

This member supports the .NET Framework infrastructure and is not intended to be used directly from your code.

```
[Visual Basic]
Private ReadOnly Property IsFixedSize As Boolean Implements _
   IList.IsFixedSize
[C#]
bool IList.IsFixedSize {get;}
[C++]
private: __property bool
   System::Collections::IList::get_IsFixedSize();
[JScript]
private function get IList.IsFixedSize() : Boolean;
```

ToolBar.ToolBarButtonCollection.System.Collections.IList.Item Property

Note: This namespace, class, or member is supported only in version 1.1 of the .NET Framework.

This member supports the .NET Framework infrastructure and is not intended to be used directly from your code.

```
[Visual Basic]
Private Default Property Item( _
   ByVal index As Integer _
) As Object Implements IList.Item
[C#]
object IList.this[
   int index
] {get; set;}
[C++]
private: __property Object* System::Collections::IList::get_Item(
   int index
);
private: __property void System::Collections::IList::set_Item(
   int index,
   Object*
);
[JScript]
private function get IList.get_Item(index : int) : Object;
private function set IList.set_Item(index : int, value : Object);
-or-
private function get IList.get_Item(index : int) : Object;
private function set IList.set_Item(index : int, value : Object);
```

[JScript] In JScript, you can use the default indexed properties defined by a type, but you cannot explicitly define your own. However, specifying the **expando** attribute on a class automatically provides a default indexed property whose type is **Object** and whose index type is **String**.

ToolBar.ToolBarButtonCollection.Add Method

Adds a new toolbar button to the end of the toolbar button collection.

Overload List

Adds a new toolbar button to the end of the toolbar button collection with the specified **ToolBarButton.Text** property value.

[Visual Basic] **Overloads Public Function Add(String) As Integer**

[C#] **public int Add(string);**

[C++] **public: int Add(String*);**

[JScript] **public function Add(String) : int;**

Adds a the specified toolbar button to the end of the toolbar button collection.

Supported by the .NET Compact Framework.

[Visual Basic] **Overloads Public Function Add(ToolBarButton) As Integer**

[C#] **public int Add(ToolBarButton);**

[C++] **public: int Add(ToolBarButton*);**

[JScript] **public function Add(ToolBarButton) : int;**

Example

See related example in the **System.Windows.Forms.ToolBar** class topic.

ToolBar.ToolBarButtonCollection.Add Method (String)

Adds a new toolbar button to the end of the toolbar button collection with the specified **ToolBarButton.Text** property value.

```
[Visual Basic]
Overloads Public Function Add( _
   ByVal text As String _
) As Integer
[C#]
public int Add(
   string text
);
[C++]
public: int Add(
   String* text
);
[JScript]
public function Add(
   text : String
) : int;
```

Parameters

text

The text to display on the new **ToolBarButton**.

Return Value

The zero-based index value of the **ToolBarButton** added to the collection.

Remarks

You can also add new **ToolBarButton** objects to the collection by using the **AddRange** or **Insert** methods, or the other version of the **Add** method.

To remove a **ToolBarButton** that you have previously added, use the **Remove**, **RemoveAt** or **Clear** methods.

Example

See related example in the **System.Windows.Forms.ToolBar** class topic.

Requirements

Platforms: Windows 98, Windows NT 4.0,
Windows Millennium Edition, Windows 2000,
Windows XP Home Edition, Windows XP Professional,
Windows Server 2003 family

ToolBar.ToolBarButtonCollection.Add Method (ToolBarButton)

Adds a the specified toolbar button to the end of the toolbar button collection.

```
[Visual Basic]
Overloads Public Function Add( _
   ByVal button As ToolBarButton _
) As Integer
[C#]
public int Add(
   ToolBarButton button
);
[C++]
public: int Add(
   ToolBarButton* button
);
[JScript]
public function Add(
   button : ToolBarButton
) : int;
```

Parameters

button

The **ToolBarButton** to be added after all existing buttons.

Return Value

The zero-based index value of the **ToolBarButton** added to the collection.

Remarks

You can also add new **ToolBarButton** objects to the collection by using the **AddRange** or **Insert** methods, or the other version of the **Add** method.

To remove a **ToolBarButton** that you have previously added, use the **Remove**, **RemoveAt** or **Clear** methods.

Example

See related example in the **System.Windows.Forms.ToolBar** class topic.

Requirements

Platforms: Windows 98, Windows NT 4.0,
Windows Millennium Edition, Windows 2000,
Windows XP Home Edition, Windows XP Professional,
Windows Server 2003 family,
.NET Compact Framework - Windows CE .NET

ToolBar.ToolBarButtonCollection.AddRange Method

Adds a collection of toolbar buttons to this toolbar button collection.

```
[Visual Basic]
Public Sub AddRange( _
   ByVal buttons() As ToolBarButton _
)
[C#]
public void AddRange(
   ToolBarButton[] buttons
);
[C++]
public: void AddRange(
   ToolBarButton* buttons[]
);
[JScript]
public function AddRange(
   buttons : ToolBarButton[]
);
```

Parameters

buttons

The collection of **ToolBarButton** controls to add to this **ToolBar.ToolBarButtonCollection** contained in an array.

Remarks

The **ToolBarButton** objects contained in the *nodes* array are appended to the end of the collection.

You can use method to quickly add a group of previouly created **ToolBarButton** objects to the collection instead of manually adding each **ToolBarButton** to the collection using the **Add** method.

To remove a **ToolBarButton** that you have previously added, use the **Remove**, **RemoveAt** or **Clear** methods.

Example

See related example in the **System.Windows.Forms.ToolBar** class topic.

Requirements

Platforms: Windows 98, Windows NT 4.0,
Windows Millennium Edition, Windows 2000,
Windows XP Home Edition, Windows XP Professional,
Windows Server 2003 family

ToolBar.ToolBarButtonCollection.Clear Method

Removes all buttons from the toolbar button collection.

```
[Visual Basic]
Public Overridable Sub Clear() Implements IList.Clear
[C#]
public virtual void Clear();
```

```
[C++]
public: virtual void Clear();
[JScript]
public function Clear();
```

Implements

IList.Clear

Remarks

The **Clear** method iterates through the collection and removes all toolbar buttons assigned to the **ToolBar.ToolBarButtonCollection**.

To remove an individual toolbar button from the collection, use the **Remove** or **RemoveAt** methods.

To add new **ToolBarButton** objects to the collection, use the **Add**, **AddRange** or **Insert** methods.

Example

See related example in the **System.Windows.Forms.ToolBar** class topic.

Requirements

Platforms: Windows 98, Windows NT 4.0,
Windows Millennium Edition, Windows 2000,
Windows XP Home Edition, Windows XP Professional,
Windows Server 2003 family,
.NET Compact Framework - Windows CE .NET

ToolBar.ToolBarButtonCollection.Contains Method

Determines if the specified toolbar button is a member of the collection.

```
[Visual Basic]
Public Function Contains( _
   ByVal button As ToolBarButton _
) As Boolean
[C#]
public bool Contains(
   ToolBarButton button
);
[C++]
public: bool Contains(
   ToolBarButton* button
);
[JScript]
public function Contains(
   button : ToolBarButton
) : Boolean;
```

Parameters

button

The **ToolBarButton** to locate in the collection.

Return Value

true if the **ToolBarButton** is a member of the collection; otherwise, **false**.

Remarks

This method enables you to determine whether a **ToolBarButton** is member of the collection before attempting to perform operations on the **ToolBarButton**. You can use this method to confirm that a **ToolBarButton** has been added to or is still a member of the collection.

Example

See related example in the **System.Windows.Forms.ToolBar** class topic.

Requirements

Platforms: Windows 98, Windows NT 4.0,
Windows Millennium Edition, Windows 2000,
Windows XP Home Edition, Windows XP Professional,
Windows Server 2003 family,
.NET Compact Framework - Windows CE .NET

ToolBar.ToolBarButtonCollection.GetEnumerator Method

Returns an enumerator that can be used to iterate through the toolbar button collection.

```
[Visual Basic]
Public Overridable Function GetEnumerator() As IEnumerator _
   Implements IEnumerable.GetEnumerator
[C#]
public virtual IEnumerator GetEnumerator();
[C++]
public: virtual IEnumerator* GetEnumerator();
[JScript]
public function GetEnumerator() : IEnumerator;
```

Return Value

An **IEnumerator** object that represents the tree node collection.

Implements

IEnumerable.GetEnumerator

Example

See related example in the **System.Windows.Forms.ToolBar** class topic.

Requirements

Platforms: Windows 98, Windows NT 4.0,
Windows Millennium Edition, Windows 2000,
Windows XP Home Edition, Windows XP Professional,
Windows Server 2003 family,
.NET Compact Framework - Windows CE .NET

ToolBar.ToolBarButtonCollection.ICollection.CopyTo Method

This member supports the .NET Framework infrastructure and is not intended to be used directly from your code.

```
[Visual Basic]
Private Sub CopyTo( _
   ByVal dest As Array, _
   ByVal index As Integer _
) Implements ICollection.CopyTo
[C#]
void ICollection.CopyTo(
   Array dest,
   int index
);
[C++]
private: void ICollection::CopyTo(
   Array* dest,
   int index
);
```

[JScript]
```
private function ICollection.CopyTo(
   dest : Array,
   index : int
);
```

ToolBar.ToolBarButtonCollection.IList.Add Method

This member supports the .NET Framework infrastructure and is not intended to be used directly from your code.

[Visual Basic]
```
Private Function Add( _
   ByVal button As Object _
) As Integer Implements IList.Add
```
[C#]
```
int IList.Add(
   object button
);
```
[C++]
```
private: int IList::Add(
   Object* button
);
```
[JScript]
```
private function IList.Add(
   button : Object
) : int;
```

ToolBar.ToolBarButtonCollection.IList.Contains Method

This member supports the .NET Framework infrastructure and is not intended to be used directly from your code.

[Visual Basic]
```
Private Function Contains( _
   ByVal button As Object _
) As Boolean Implements IList.Contains
```
[C#]
```
bool IList.Contains(
   object button
);
```
[C++]
```
private: bool IList::Contains(
   Object* button
);
```
[JScript]
```
private function IList.Contains(
   button : Object
) : Boolean;
```

ToolBar.ToolBarButtonCollection.IList.IndexOf Method

This member supports the .NET Framework infrastructure and is not intended to be used directly from your code.

[Visual Basic]
```
Private Function IndexOf( _
   ByVal button As Object _
) As Integer Implements IList.IndexOf
```
[C#]
```
int IList.IndexOf(
   object button
);
```
[C++]
```
private: int IList::IndexOf(
   Object* button
);
```
[JScript]
```
private function IList.IndexOf(
   button : Object
) : int;
```

ToolBar.ToolBarButtonCollection.IList.Insert Method

This member supports the .NET Framework infrastructure and is not intended to be used directly from your code.

[Visual Basic]
```
Private Sub Insert( _
   ByVal index As Integer, _
   ByVal button As Object _
) Implements IList.Insert
```
[C#]
```
void IList.Insert(
   int index,
   object button
);
```
[C++]
```
private: void IList::Insert(
   int index,
   Object* button
);
```
[JScript]
```
private function IList.Insert(
   index : int,
   button : Object
);
```

ToolBar.ToolBarButtonCollection.IList.Remove Method

This member supports the .NET Framework infrastructure and is not intended to be used directly from your code.

[Visual Basic]
```
Private Sub Remove( _
   ByVal button As Object _
) Implements IList.Remove
```
[C#]
```
void IList.Remove(
   object button
);
```
[C++]
```
private: void IList::Remove(
   Object* button
);
```
[JScript]
```
private function IList.Remove(
   button : Object
);
```

ToolBar.ToolBarButtonCollection.IndexOf Method

Retrieves the index of the specified toolbar button in the collection.

```
[Visual Basic]
Public Function IndexOf( _
   ByVal button As ToolBarButton _
) As Integer
[C#]
public int IndexOf(
   ToolBarButton button
);
[C++]
public: int IndexOf(
   ToolBarButton* button
);
[JScript]
public function IndexOf(
   button : ToolBarButton
) : int;
```

Parameters

button

The **ToolBarButton** to locate in the collection.

Return Value

The zero-based index of the item found in the collection; otherwise, -1.

Remarks

This method gives you easy access to the index value of the **ToolBarButton** in the collection. The index value allows you to easily determine which **ToolBarButton** was clicked on the **ToolBar**. The **ToolBarButton** clicked can be determined by evaluating the **IndexOf** value of the **ToolBarButtonClickEventArgs.Button** property.

Example

See related example in the **System.Windows.Forms.ToolBar** class topic.

Requirements

Platforms: Windows 98, Windows NT 4.0, Windows Millennium Edition, Windows 2000, Windows XP Home Edition, Windows XP Professional, Windows Server 2003 family, .NET Compact Framework - Windows CE .NET

ToolBar.ToolBarButtonCollection.Insert Method

Inserts an existing toolbar button in the toolbar button collection at the specified location.

```
[Visual Basic]
Public Sub Insert( _
   ByVal index As Integer, _
   ByVal button As ToolBarButton _
)
[C#]
public void Insert(
   int index,
   ToolBarButton button
);
[C++]
public: void Insert(
   int index,
   ToolBarButton* button
);
[JScript]
public function Insert(
   index : int,
   button : ToolBarButton
);
```

Parameters

index

The indexed location within the collection to insert the toolbar button.

button

The **ToolBarButton** to insert.

Remarks

You can also add new **ToolBarButton** objects to the collection by using the **Add** or **AddRange** methods.

To remove a **ToolBarButton** that you have previously added, use the **Remove**, **RemoveAt** or **Clear** methods.

Example

[Visual Basic, C#, C++] The following example removes an existing **ToolBarButton** from a **ToolBar** control if it exists and adds and inserts four new **ToolBarButton** objects to the **ToolBar**. This example assumes you have a **Form** with a **ToolBar** control on it. See related example in the **System.Windows.Forms.ToolBar** class topic.

Requirements

Platforms: Windows 98, Windows NT 4.0, Windows Millennium Edition, Windows 2000, Windows XP Home Edition, Windows XP Professional, Windows Server 2003 family, .NET Compact Framework - Windows CE .NET

ToolBar.ToolBarButtonCollection.Remove Method

Removes a given button from the toolbar button collection.

```
[Visual Basic]
Public Sub Remove( _
   ByVal button As ToolBarButton _
)
[C#]
public void Remove(
   ToolBarButton button
);
[C++]
public: void Remove(
   ToolBarButton* button
);
[JScript]
public function Remove(
   button : ToolBarButton
);
```

Parameters

button

The **ToolBarButton** to remove from the collection.

Remarks

To remove toolbar buttons from the collection, use the **RemoveAt**, or **Clear** methods.

To add new **ToolBarButton** objects to the collection, use the **Add**, **AddRange** or **Insert** methods.

Example

See related example in the **System.Windows.Forms.ToolBar** class topic.

Requirements

Platforms: Windows 98, Windows NT 4.0, Windows Millennium Edition, Windows 2000, Windows XP Home Edition, Windows XP Professional, Windows Server 2003 family, .NET Compact Framework - Windows CE .NET

ToolBar.ToolBarButtonCollection.RemoveAt Method

Removes a given button from the toolbar button collection.

```
[Visual Basic]
Public Overridable Sub RemoveAt( _
   ByVal index As Integer _
) Implements IList.RemoveAt
[C#]
public virtual void RemoveAt(
   int index
);
[C++]
public: virtual void RemoveAt(
   int index
);
[JScript]
public function RemoveAt(
   index : int
);
```

Parameters

index

The indexed location of the **ToolBarButton** in the collection.

Implements

IList.RemoveAt

Exceptions

Exception Type	Condition
ArgumentOutOfRange-Exception	The *index* value is less than 0, or it is greater than the number of buttons in the collection.

Remarks

The **Remove** method removes the **ToolBarButton** at the specified location in the **ToolBar.ToolBarButtonCollection**. If you want to remove all **ToolBarButton** controls from the collection, use the **Clear** method.

Example

See related example in the **System.Windows.Forms.ToolBar** class topic.

Requirements

Platforms: Windows 98, Windows NT 4.0, Windows Millennium Edition, Windows 2000, Windows XP Home Edition, Windows XP Professional, Windows Server 2003 family, .NET Compact Framework - Windows CE .NET

ToolTip Class

Represents a small rectangular pop-up window that displays a brief description of a control's purpose when the mouse hovers over the control.

System.Object
  System.MarshalByRefObject
    System.ComponentModel.Component
      System.Windows.Forms.ToolTip

[Visual Basic]
```
NotInheritable Public Class ToolTip
   Inherits Component
   Implements IExtenderProvider
```
[C#]
```
public sealed class ToolTip : Component, IExtenderProvider
```
[C++]
```
public __gc __sealed class ToolTip : public Component,
   IExtenderProvider
```
[JScript]
```
public class ToolTip extends Component implements IExtenderProvider
```

Thread Safety

Any public static (**Shared** in Visual Basic) members of this type are safe for multithreaded operations. Any instance members are not guaranteed to be thread safe.

Remarks

The **ToolTip** class allows you to provide help to users when they place the mouse cursor over a control. The **ToolTip** class is typically used to alert users to the intended use of a control. For example, you could specify ToolTip text for a **TextBox** control that accepts a name, specifying the format of the name to typed into the control. In addition to providing help, you can also use the **ToolTip** class to provide run time status information. For example, you could use the **ToolTip** class to display connection speed and line quality data when the user moves the mouse cursor over a **PictureBox** control that displays Internet connection status.

The **ToolTip** class provides properties that enable you to modify how long and how quickly a ToolTip window is displayed. The **AutoPopDelay** determines how long a ToolTip window is displayed; the **InitialDelay** and **ReshowDelay** properties determine the delay before a ToolTip window is displayed. To set all these properties to a consistent pattern, you can use the **AutomaticDelay** property. This value is then used to calculate and set the values of the other delay properties. To enable a control's ToolTip text to be displayed regardless of whether the **Form** or container the control is contained within is enabled, you can use the **ShowAlways** property. If you want to disable all ToolTip text from being displayed in your application, you can use the **Active** property.

The **ToolTip** class can be used in any container. To specify a specific container to use the **ToolTip** class within, use the **ToolTip** constructor. In order for ToolTip text to be displayed when the user moves the mouse cursor over a control, the ToolTip text to be displayed must be associated with the control within an instance of the **ToolTip** class. To associate ToolTip text with a control, use the **SetToolTip** method. The **SetToolTip** method can be called more than once for the same control to change the text that is associated with the control. If you want to get the text that is associated with a control, use the **GetToolTip** method. To remove all ToolTip text associations with an instance of the **ToolTip** class, use the **RemoveAll** method.

Note ToolTip text is not displayed for controls that are disabled.

Example

[Visual Basic, C#] The following example creates an instance of the **ToolTip** class and associates it with the **Form** the instance is created within. The code then initializes the delay properties **AutoPopDelay**, **InitialDelay**, and **ReshowDelay**. In addition the instance of the **ToolTip** class sets the **ShowAlways** property to **true** to enable ToolTip text to always be display regardless of whether the form is active. Finally, the example associates ToolTip text with two controls on a form, a **Button** and a **CheckBox**. This example assumes that the method defined in the example is located within a **Form** that contains a **Button** control named `button1` and a **CheckBox** control named `checkBox1` and that the method is called from the constructor of the **Form**.

[Visual Basic]
```
' This example assumes that the Form_Load event handling method
' is connected to the Load event of the form.
Private Sub Form1_Load(sender As Object, e As System.EventArgs)     ↵
 Handles MyBase.Load
   ' Create the ToolTip and associate with the Form container.
   Dim toolTip1 As New ToolTip()

   ' Set up the delays for the ToolTip.
   toolTip1.AutoPopDelay = 5000
   toolTip1.InitialDelay = 1000
   toolTip1.ReshowDelay = 500
   ' Force the ToolTip text to be displayed whether or not the     ↵
 form is active.
   toolTip1.ShowAlways = True

   ' Set up the ToolTip text for the Button and Checkbox.
   toolTip1.SetToolTip(Me.button1, "My button1")
   toolTip1.SetToolTip(Me.checkBox1, "My checkBox1")
End Sub
```

[C#]
```
// This example assumes that the Form_Load event handling method
// is connected to the Load event of the form.
private void Form1_Load(object sender, System.EventArgs e)
{
   // Create the ToolTip and associate with the Form container.
   ToolTip toolTip1 = new ToolTip();

   // Set up the delays for the ToolTip.
   toolTip1.AutoPopDelay = 5000;
   toolTip1.InitialDelay = 1000;
   toolTip1.ReshowDelay = 500;
   // Force the ToolTip text to be displayed whether or not the     ↵
form is active.
   toolTip1.ShowAlways = true;

   // Set up the ToolTip text for the Button and Checkbox.
   toolTip1.SetToolTip(this.button1, "My button1");
   toolTip1.SetToolTip(this.checkBox1, "My checkBox1");
}
```

Requirements

Namespace: System.Windows.Forms

Platforms: Windows 98, Windows NT 4.0, Windows Millennium Edition, Windows 2000, Windows XP Home Edition, Windows XP Professional, Windows Server 2003 family

Assembly: System.Windows.Forms (in System.Windows.Forms.dll)

ToolTip Constructor

Initializes a new instance of the **ToolTip** class.

Overload List

Initializes a new instance of the **ToolTip** without a specified container.

[Visual Basic] **Public Sub New()**

[C#] **public ToolTip();**

[C++] **public: ToolTip();**

[JScript] **public function ToolTip();**

Initializes a new instance of the **ToolTip** class with a specified container.

[Visual Basic] **Public Sub New(IContainer)**

[C#] **public ToolTip(IContainer);**

[C++] **public: ToolTip(IContainer*);**

[JScript] **public function ToolTip(IContainer);**

Example

See related example in the **System.Windows.Forms.ToolTip** class topic.

ToolTip Constructor ()

Initializes a new instance of the **ToolTip** without a specified container.

```
[Visual Basic]
Public Sub New()
[C#]
public ToolTip();
[C++]
public: ToolTip();
[JScript]
public function ToolTip();
```

Remarks

This constructor associates the **ToolTip** class with the container that is creating the instance of the control.

Requirements

Platforms: Windows 98, Windows NT 4.0, Windows Millennium Edition, Windows 2000, Windows XP Home Edition, Windows XP Professional, Windows Server 2003 family

ToolTip Constructor (IContainer)

Initializes a new instance of the **ToolTip** class with a specified container.

```
[Visual Basic]
Public Sub New( _
   ByVal cont As IContainer _
)
[C#]
public ToolTip(
   IContainer cont
);
[C++]
public: ToolTip(
   IContainer* cont
);
[JScript]
public function ToolTip(
   cont : IContainer
);
```

Parameters

cont

An **IContainer** that represents the container of the **ToolTip**.

Remarks

This constructor enables you to associate a **ToolTip** with any container.

Example

See related example in the **System.Windows.Forms.ToolTip** class topic.

Requirements

Platforms: Windows 98, Windows NT 4.0, Windows Millennium Edition, Windows 2000, Windows XP Home Edition, Windows XP Professional, Windows Server 2003 family

ToolTip.Active Property

Gets or sets a value indicating whether the ToolTip is currently active.

```
[Visual Basic]
Public Property Active As Boolean
[C#]
public bool Active {get; set;}
[C++]
public: __property bool get_Active();
public: __property void set_Active(bool);
[JScript]
public function get Active() : Boolean;
public function set Active(Boolean);
```

Property Value

true if the ToolTip is currently active; otherwise, **false**. The default is **true**.

Remarks

This property allows you to enable or disable the display of ToolTip text for all controls that have text specified in this particular **ToolTip**. More than one **ToolTip** can be created and assigned to a form; setting the **Active** property to **false** only affects the specified **ToolTip**. You can allow users to set the value of this property in a form that provides application options to provide the ability for the user to enable or disable the display of ToolTips in your application.

Requirements

Platforms: Windows 98, Windows NT 4.0, Windows Millennium Edition, Windows 2000, Windows XP Home Edition, Windows XP Professional, Windows Server 2003 family

ToolTip.AutomaticDelay Property

Gets or sets the automatic delay for the ToolTip.

```
[Visual Basic]
Public Property AutomaticDelay As Integer
[C#]
public int AutomaticDelay {get; set;}
```

```
[C++]
public: __property int get_AutomaticDelay();
public: __property void set_AutomaticDelay(int);
[JScript]
public function get AutomaticDelay() : int;
public function set AutomaticDelay(int);
```

Property Value

The automatic delay (in milliseconds). The default is 500.

Remarks

The **AutomaticDelay** property enables you to set a single delay value which is then used to set the values of the **AutoPopDelay**, **InitialDelay**, and **ReshowDelay** properties. Each time the **AutomaticDelay** property is set, the following values are set by default.

Property	Default Value
AutoPopDelay	10 times the **AutomaticDelay** property value.
InitialDelay	Equal to the **AutomaticDelay** property value.
ReshowDelay	1/5 of the **AutomaticDelay** property value.

These properties can also be set independently once the **AutomaticDelay** property has been set. For more information, see the **AutoPopDelay**, **InitialDelay**, and **ReshowDelay** properties. This property is typically used to provide a consistent delay pattern for your ToolTip windows.

Requirements

Platforms: Windows 98, Windows NT 4.0, Windows Millennium Edition, Windows 2000, Windows XP Home Edition, Windows XP Professional, Windows Server 2003 family

ToolTip.AutoPopDelay Property

Gets or sets the period of time the ToolTip remains visible if the mouse pointer is stationary within a control with specified ToolTip text.

```
[Visual Basic]
Public Property AutoPopDelay As Integer
[C#]
public int AutoPopDelay {get; set;}
[C++]
public: __property int get_AutoPopDelay();
public: __property void set_AutoPopDelay(int);
[JScript]
public function get AutoPopDelay() : int;
public function set AutoPopDelay(int);
```

Property Value

The period of time (in milliseconds) that the **ToolTip** remains visible when the mouse pointer is stationary within a control. The default value is 5000.

Remarks

This property enables you to shorten or lengthen the time that the **ToolTip** window is displayed when the mouse pointer is over a control. For example, if you display extensive help in a ToolTip window, you can increase the value of this property to ensure that the user has sufficient time to read the text.

If you want to have a consistent delay pattern for your ToolTip windows, you can set the **AutomaticDelay** property. The **AutomaticDelay** property sets the **AutoPopDelay**, **ReshowDelay**, and **InitialDelay** properties to initial values based on a single value. Every time the **AutomaticDelay** property is set, the **AutoPopDelay** property is set to 10 times the **AutomaticDelay** property value. Once the **AutomaticDelay** property is set, you can independently set the **AutoPopDelay** property, overriding the default value.

Example

See related example in the **System.Windows.Forms.ToolTip** class topic.

Requirements

Platforms: Windows 98, Windows NT 4.0, Windows Millennium Edition, Windows 2000, Windows XP Home Edition, Windows XP Professional, Windows Server 2003 family

ToolTip.InitialDelay Property

Gets or sets the time that passes before the ToolTip appears.

```
[Visual Basic]
Public Property InitialDelay As Integer
[C#]
public int InitialDelay {get; set;}
[C++]
public: __property int get_InitialDelay();
public: __property void set_InitialDelay(int);
[JScript]
public function get InitialDelay() : int;
public function set InitialDelay(int);
```

Property Value

The period of time (in milliseconds) that the mouse pointer must remain stationary within a control before the ToolTip window is displayed.

Remarks

This property enables you to shorten or lengthen the time that the **ToolTip** waits before displaying a ToolTip window. If the value of the **InitialDelay** property is set to a value that is too long in duration, the user of your application might not know that your application provides ToolTip help. You can use this property to ensure that the user has ToolTips displayed quickly by shortening the time specified.

If you want to have a consistent delay pattern for your ToolTip windows, you can set the **AutomaticDelay** property. The **AutomaticDelay** property sets the **AutoPopDelay**, **ReshowDelay**, and **InitialDelay** properties to initial values based on a single time value. Every time the **AutomaticDelay** property is set, the **InitialDelay** property is set to the same value as the **AutomaticDelay** property. Once the **AutomaticDelay** property is set, you can independently set the **InitialDelay** property, overriding the default value.

Example

See related example in the **System.Windows.Forms.ToolTip** class topic.

Requirements

Platforms: Windows 98, Windows NT 4.0, Windows Millennium Edition, Windows 2000, Windows XP Home Edition, Windows XP Professional, Windows Server 2003 family

ToolTip.ReshowDelay Property

Gets or sets the length of time that must transpire before subsequent ToolTip windows appear as the mouse pointer moves from one control to another.

```
[Visual Basic]
Public Property ReshowDelay As Integer
[C#]
public int ReshowDelay {get; set;}
[C++]
public: __property int get_ReshowDelay();
public: __property void set_ReshowDelay(int);
[JScript]
public function get ReshowDelay() : int;
public function set ReshowDelay(int);
```

Property Value

The length of time (in milliseconds) that it takes subsequent ToolTip windows to appear.

Remarks

This property enables you to shorten or lengthen the time that the **ToolTip** waits before displaying a ToolTip window after a previous ToolTip window is displayed. The first time a ToolTip window is displayed the value of the **InitialDelay** property is used to determine the delay to apply before initially showing the ToolTip window. When a ToolTip window is currently being displayed and the user moves the cursor to another control that displays a ToolTip window, the value of the **ReshowDelay** property is used before showing the ToolTip for the new control. The ToolTip window from the previous control must still be displayed in order for the delay specified in the **ReshowDelay** property to be used; otherwise the **InitialDelay** property value is used.

If you want to have a consistent delay pattern for ToolTip windows, you can set the **AutomaticDelay** property. The **AutomaticDelay** property sets the **AutoPopDelay**, **ReshowDelay**, and **InitialDelay** properties to initial values based on a single time value. Every time the **AutomaticDelay** property is set, the **ReshowDelay** property is set to 1/5 of the **AutomaticDelay** property value. Once the **AutomaticDelay** property is set, you can independently set the **ReshowDelay** property, overriding the default value.

Example

See related example in the **System.Windows.Forms.ToolTip** class topic.

Requirements

Platforms: Windows 98, Windows NT 4.0,
Windows Millennium Edition, Windows 2000,
Windows XP Home Edition, Windows XP Professional,
Windows Server 2003 family

ToolTip.ShowAlways Property

Gets or sets a value indicating whether a ToolTip window is displayed even when its parent control is not active.

```
[Visual Basic]
Public Property ShowAlways As Boolean
[C#]
public bool ShowAlways {get; set;}
[C++]
public: __property bool get_ShowAlways();
public: __property void set_ShowAlways(bool);
[JScript]
public function get ShowAlways() : Boolean;
public function set ShowAlways(Boolean);
```

Property Value

true if the ToolTip is always displayed; otherwise, **false**. The default is **false**.

Remarks

This property enables you to display a ToolTip window even when the container of the **ToolTip** is not active. You can use this feature in a modeless window application to enable ToolTip windows to be displayed regardless of which modeless window is active. This feature is also useful when creating a control using the **UserControl** that contains a number of controls within it that display ToolTip windows. Since the **UserControl** is often not the active window on a form, setting this property to **true** enables the controls within the **UserControl** to display ToolTip windows at any time.

Example

See related example in the **System.Windows.Forms.ToolTip** class topic.

Requirements

Platforms: Windows 98, Windows NT 4.0,
Windows Millennium Edition, Windows 2000,
Windows XP Home Edition, Windows XP Professional,
Windows Server 2003 family

ToolTip.CanExtend Method

This member supports the .NET Framework infrastructure and is not intended to be used directly from your code.

```
[Visual Basic]
Public Overridable Function CanExtend( _
   ByVal target As Object _
) As Boolean Implements IExtenderProvider.CanExtend
[C#]
public virtual bool CanExtend(
   object target
);
[C++]
public: virtual bool CanExtend(
   Object* target
);
[JScript]
public function CanExtend(
   target : Object
) : Boolean;
```

ToolTip.Dispose Method

Overload List

This member supports the .NET Framework infrastructure and is not intended to be used directly from your code.

[Visual Basic] **Overloads Overrides Protected Sub Dispose(Boolean)**

[C#] **protected override void Dispose(bool);**

[C++] **protected: void Dispose(bool);**

[JScript] **protected override function Dispose(Boolean);**

Inherited from **Component**.

[Visual Basic] **Overloads Public Overridable Sub Dispose() Implements IDisposable.Dispose**

[C#] **public virtual void Dispose();**

[C++] **public: virtual void Dispose();**

[JScript] **public function Dispose();**

ToolTip.Dispose Method (Boolean)

This member overrides **Component.Dispose**.

[Visual Basic]
```
Overrides Overloads Protected Sub Dispose( _
   ByVal disposing As Boolean _
)
```
[C#]
```
protected override void Dispose(
   bool disposing
);
```
[C++]
```
protected: void Dispose(
   bool disposing
);
```
[JScript]
```
protected override function Dispose(
   disposing : Boolean
);
```

Requirements

Platforms: Windows 98, Windows NT 4.0, Windows Millennium Edition, Windows 2000, Windows XP Home Edition, Windows XP Professional, Windows Server 2003 family

ToolTip.Finalize Method

Releases the unmanaged resources and performs other cleanup operations before the **Cursor** is reclaimed by garbage collection.

[C#] In C#, finalizers are expressed using destructor syntax.

[C++] In C++, finalizers are expressed using destructor syntax.

[Visual Basic]
```
Overrides Protected Sub Finalize()
```
[C#]
```
~ToolTip();
```
[C++]
```
~ToolTip();
```
[JScript]
```
protected override function Finalize();
```

Remarks

This method overrides **Object.Finalize**. Application code should not call this method; an object's **Finalize** method is automatically invoked during garbage collection, unless finalization by the garbage collector has been disabled by a call to the **GC.SuppressFinalize** method. For more information, see **Finalize Methods and Destructors**, **Cleaning Up Unmanaged Resources**, and **Overriding the Finalize Method**.

Requirements

Platforms: Windows 98, Windows NT 4.0, Windows Millennium Edition, Windows 2000, Windows XP Home Edition, Windows XP Professional, Windows Server 2003 family

ToolTip.GetToolTip Method

Retrieves the ToolTip text associated with the specified control.

[Visual Basic]
```
Public Function GetToolTip( _
   ByVal control As Control _
) As String
```
[C#]
```
public string GetToolTip(
   Control control
);
```
[C++]
```
public: String* GetToolTip(
   Control* control
);
```
[JScript]
```
public function GetToolTip(
   control : Control
) : String;
```

Parameters

control

The **Control** for which to retrieve the **ToolTip** text.

Return Value

The ToolTip text for the specified control.

Remarks

This method enables you to retrieve the ToolTip text for any control. If the ToolTip text changes dynamically in an application, you can use this method to find out what text is displayed at any point, depending on the state of the application. To change the text that a control is displaying, use the **SetToolTip** method.

Requirements

Platforms: Windows 98, Windows NT 4.0, Windows Millennium Edition, Windows 2000, Windows XP Home Edition, Windows XP Professional, Windows Server 2003 family

ToolTip.RemoveAll Method

Removes all ToolTip text currently associated with the ToolTip control.

[Visual Basic]
```
Public Sub RemoveAll()
```
[C#]
```
public void RemoveAll();
```
[C++]
```
public: void RemoveAll();
```
[JScript]
```
public function RemoveAll();
```

Remarks

You can use this method to remove all ToolTip text that is associated with the **ToolTip** control. To disable the display of text instead of removing all ToolTip text from the **ToolTip** control, use the **Active** property.

Requirements

Platforms: Windows 98, Windows NT 4.0, Windows Millennium Edition, Windows 2000, Windows XP Home Edition, Windows XP Professional, Windows Server 2003 family

ToolTip.SetToolTip Method

Associates ToolTip text with the specified control.

[Visual Basic]
```
Public Sub SetToolTip( _
   ByVal control As Control, _
   ByVal caption As String _
)
```
[C#]
```
public void SetToolTip(
   Control control,
   string caption
);
```
[C++]
```
public: void SetToolTip(
   Control* control,
   String* caption
);
```
[JScript]
```
public function SetToolTip(
   control : Control,
   caption : String
);
```

Parameters

control
: The **Control** to associate the ToolTip text with.

caption
: The ToolTip text to display when the mouse cursor is over the control.

Remarks

In addition to specifying the ToolTip text to display for a control, you can also use this method to modify the ToolTip text for a control. Calling the **SetToolTip** method more than once for a given control does not specify multiple ToolTip text to display for a control but instead changes the current ToolTip text for the control. To determine the ToolTip text that is associated with a control at run time, you can use the **GetToolTip** method.

Example

See related example in the **System.Windows.Forms.ToolTip** class topic.

Requirements

Platforms: Windows 98, Windows NT 4.0, Windows Millennium Edition, Windows 2000, Windows XP Home Edition, Windows XP Professional, Windows Server 2003 family

ToolTip.ToString Method

This member overrides **Object.ToString**.

[Visual Basic]
```
Overrides Public Function ToString() As String
```
[C#]
```
public override string ToString();
```
[C++]
```
public: String* ToString();
```
[JScript]
```
public override function ToString() : String;
```

Requirements

Platforms: Windows 98, Windows NT 4.0, Windows Millennium Edition, Windows 2000, Windows XP Home Edition, Windows XP Professional, Windows Server 2003 family

TrackBar Class

Represents a standard Windows track bar.

System.Object
 System.MarshalByRefObject
  System.ComponentModel.Component
   System.Windows.Forms.Control
    System.Windows.Forms.TrackBar

[Visual Basic]
```
Public Class TrackBar
   Inherits Control
   Implements ISupportInitialize
```
[C#]
```
public class TrackBar : Control, ISupportInitialize
```
[C++]
```
public __gc class TrackBar : public Control, ISupportInitialize
```
[JScript]
```
public class TrackBar extends Control implements ISupportInitialize
```

Thread Safety

Any public static (**Shared** in Visual Basic) members of this type are safe for multithreaded operations. Any instance members are not guaranteed to be thread safe.

Remarks

The **TrackBar** is a scrollable control similar to the **ScrollBar** control. You can configure ranges through which the value of the **Value** property of a track bar scrolls by setting the **Minimum** property to specify the lower end of the range and the **Maximum** property to specify the upper end of the range.

The **LargeChange** property defines the increment to add or subtract from the **Value** property when clicks occur on either side of the slider. The track bar can be displayed horizontally or vertically.

You can use this control to input numeric data obtained through the **Value** property. You can display this numeric data in a control or use it in code.

Example

[Visual Basic, C#, C++] The following example displays a form containing a **TrackBar** control and a **TextBox** control. The example demonstrates setting the **Maximum**, **TickFrequency**, **LargeChange**, and **SmallChange** properties and handling the **Scroll** event. The **TextBox** contents are updated to the **Value** property value when the **Scroll** event occurs.

[Visual Basic]
```
Imports System
Imports System.Drawing
Imports System.Windows.Forms

Public Class Form1
    Inherits System.Windows.Forms.Form

    Private WithEvents trackBar1 As System.Windows.Forms.TrackBar
    Private textBox1 As System.Windows.Forms.TextBox

    <System.STAThread()> _
    Public Shared Sub Main()
        System.Windows.Forms.Application.Run(New Form1)
    End Sub 'Main

    Public Sub New()
        Me.textBox1 = New System.Windows.Forms.TextBox
        Me.trackBar1 = New System.Windows.Forms.TrackBar

        ' TextBox for TrackBar.Value update.
        Me.textBox1.Location = New System.Drawing.Point(240, 16)
        Me.textBox1.Size = New System.Drawing.Size(48, 20)

        ' Set up how the form should be displayed and add the ↵
 controls to the form.
        Me.ClientSize = New System.Drawing.Size(296, 62)
        Me.Controls.AddRange(New ↵
System.Windows.Forms.Control() {Me.textBox1, Me.trackBar1})
        Me.Text = "TrackBar Example"

        ' Set up the TrackBar.
        Me.trackBar1.Location = New System.Drawing.Point(8, 8)
        Me.trackBar1.Size = New System.Drawing.Size(224, 45)

        ' The Maximum property sets the value of the track bar when
        ' the slider is all the way to the right.
        trackBar1.Maximum = 30

        ' The TickFrequency property establishes how many positions
        ' are between each tick-mark.
        trackBar1.TickFrequency = 5

        ' The LargeChange property sets how many positions to move
        ' if the bar is clicked on either side of the slider.
        trackBar1.LargeChange = 3

        ' The SmallChange property sets how many positions to move
        ' if the keyboard arrows are used to move the slider.
        trackBar1.SmallChange = 2
    End Sub 'New

    Private Sub trackBar1_Scroll(ByVal sender As Object, _
                ByVal e As System.EventArgs) Handles trackBar1.Scroll

        ' Display the trackbar value in the text box.
        textBox1.Text = trackBar1.Value
    End Sub

End Class 'Form1
```

[C#]
```
using System;
using System.Drawing;
using System.Windows.Forms;

public class Form1 : System.Windows.Forms.Form
{
    private System.Windows.Forms.TrackBar trackBar1;
    private System.Windows.Forms.TextBox textBox1;

    [STAThread]
    static void Main()
    {
        Application.Run(new Form1());
    }

    public Form1()
    {
        this.textBox1 = new System.Windows.Forms.TextBox();
        this.trackBar1 = new System.Windows.Forms.TrackBar();

        // TextBox for TrackBar.Value update.
        this.textBox1.Location = new System.Drawing.Point(240, 16);
        this.textBox1.Size = new System.Drawing.Size(48, 20);

        // Set up how the form should be displayed and add the ↵
controls to the form.
        this.ClientSize = new System.Drawing.Size(296, 62);
        this.Controls.AddRange(new ↵
System.Windows.Forms.Control[] {this.textBox1,this.trackBar1});
        this.Text = "TrackBar Example";

        // Set up the TrackBar.
        this.trackBar1.Location = new System.Drawing.Point(8, 8);
```

```
        this.trackBar1.Size = new System.Drawing.Size(224, 45);
        this.trackBar1.Scroll += new
System.EventHandler(this.trackBar1_Scroll);

        // The Maximum property sets the value of the track bar when
        // the slider is all the way to the right.
        trackBar1.Maximum = 30;

        // The TickFrequency property establishes how many positions
        // are between each tick-mark.
        trackBar1.TickFrequency = 5;

        // The LargeChange property sets how many positions to move
        // if the bar is clicked on either side of the slider.
        trackBar1.LargeChange = 3;

        // The SmallChange property sets how many positions to move
        // if the keyboard arrows are used to move the slider.
        trackBar1.SmallChange = 2;
    }

    private void trackBar1_Scroll(object sender, System.EventArgs e)
    {
        // Display the trackbar value in the text box.
        textBox1.Text = "" + trackBar1.Value;
    }
}
```

[C++]

```
using namespace System;
using namespace System::Drawing;
using namespace System::Windows::Forms;

public __gc class Form1 : public System::Windows::Forms::Form {
private:
    System::Windows::Forms::TrackBar*  trackBar1;
    System::Windows::Forms::TextBox*  textBox1;

public:
    Form1() {
        this->textBox1 = new System::Windows::Forms::TextBox();
        this->trackBar1 = new System::Windows::Forms::TrackBar();

        // TextBox for TrackBar::Value update.
        this->textBox1->Location = System::Drawing::Point(240, 16);
        this->textBox1->Size = System::Drawing::Size(48, 20);

        // Set up how the form should be displayed and add the
controls to the form.
        this->ClientSize = System::Drawing::Size(296, 62);
        System::Windows::Forms::Control* formControls[] = {
            this->textBox1, this->trackBar1};
        this->Controls->AddRange(formControls);
        this->Text = S"TrackBar Example";

        // Set up the TrackBar.
        this->trackBar1->Location = System::Drawing::Point(8, 8);
        this->trackBar1->Size = System::Drawing::Size(224, 45);
        this->trackBar1->Scroll += new
            System::EventHandler(this, trackBar1_Scroll);

        // The Maximum property sets the value of the track bar when
        // the slider is all the way to the right.
        trackBar1->Maximum = 30;

        // The TickFrequency property establishes how many positions
        // are between each tick-mark.
        trackBar1->TickFrequency = 5;

        // The LargeChange property sets how many positions to move
        // if the bar is clicked on either side of the slider.
        trackBar1->LargeChange = 3;

        // The SmallChange property sets how many positions to move
        // if the keyboard arrows are used to move the slider.
        trackBar1->SmallChange = 2;
    }

private:
    void trackBar1_Scroll(Object* sender, System::EventArgs* e) {
        // Display the trackbar value in the text box.
        textBox1->Text = String::Concat(S"", __box(trackBar1->Value));
    }
};

[STAThread]
int main() {
    Application::Run(new Form1());
}
```

Requirements

Namespace: System.Windows.Forms

Platforms: Windows 98, Windows NT 4.0, Windows Millennium Edition, Windows 2000, Windows XP Home Edition, Windows XP Professional, Windows Server 2003 family, .NET Compact Framework - Windows CE .NET

Assembly: System.Windows.Forms (in System.Windows.Forms.dll)

TrackBar Constructor

Initializes a new instance of the **TrackBar** class.

[Visual Basic]
```
Public Sub New()
```
[C#]
```
public TrackBar();
```
[C++]
```
public: TrackBar();
```
[JScript]
```
public function TrackBar();
```

Remarks

The **TrackBar** is created with a default horizontal orientation and a range of 0 to 10, with a tick mark shown for every value.

Requirements

Platforms: Windows 98, Windows NT 4.0, Windows Millennium Edition, Windows 2000, Windows XP Home Edition, Windows XP Professional, Windows Server 2003 family, .NET Compact Framework - Windows CE .NET

TrackBar.AutoSize Property

Gets or sets a value indicating whether the height or width of the track bar is being automatically sized.

[Visual Basic]
```
Public Property AutoSize As Boolean
```
[C#]
```
public bool AutoSize {get; set;}
```
[C++]
```
public: __property bool get_AutoSize();
public: __property void set_AutoSize(bool);
```
[JScript]
```
public function get AutoSize() : Boolean;
public function set AutoSize(Boolean);
```

Property Value

true if the track bar is being automatically sized; otherwise, **false**. The default is **true**.

Remarks

You can set the **AutoSize** property to **true** to cause the track bar to adjust either its height or width, depending on orientation, to ensure that the control uses only the required amount of space.

Requirements

Platforms: Windows 98, Windows NT 4.0, Windows Millennium Edition, Windows 2000, Windows XP Home Edition, Windows XP Professional, Windows Server 2003 family

TrackBar.BackgroundImage Property

This member overrides **Control.BackgroundImage**.

```
[Visual Basic]
Overrides Public Property BackgroundImage As Image
[C#]
public override Image BackgroundImage {get; set;}
[C++]
public: __property Image* get_BackgroundImage();
public: __property void set_BackgroundImage(Image*);
[JScript]
public override function get BackgroundImage() : Image;
public override function set BackgroundImage(Image);
```

Requirements

Platforms: Windows 98, Windows NT 4.0, Windows Millennium Edition, Windows 2000, Windows XP Home Edition, Windows XP Professional, Windows Server 2003 family

TrackBar.CreateParams Property

This member overrides **Control.CreateParams**.

```
[Visual Basic]
Overrides Protected ReadOnly Property CreateParams As CreateParams
[C#]
protected override CreateParams CreateParams {get;}
[C++]
protected: __property CreateParams* get_CreateParams();
[JScript]
protected override function get CreateParams() : CreateParams;
```

Requirements

Platforms: Windows 98, Windows NT 4.0, Windows Millennium Edition, Windows 2000, Windows XP Home Edition, Windows XP Professional, Windows Server 2003 family

TrackBar.DefaultImeMode Property

This member overrides **Control.DefaultImeMode**.

```
[Visual Basic]
Overrides Protected ReadOnly Property DefaultImeMode As ImeMode
[C#]
protected override ImeMode DefaultImeMode {get;}
[C++]
protected: __property ImeMode get_DefaultImeMode();
[JScript]
protected override function get DefaultImeMode() : ImeMode;
```

Requirements

Platforms: Windows 98, Windows NT 4.0, Windows Millennium Edition, Windows 2000, Windows XP Home Edition, Windows XP Professional, Windows Server 2003 family

TrackBar.DefaultSize Property

This member overrides **Control.DefaultSize**.

```
[Visual Basic]
Overrides Protected ReadOnly Property DefaultSize As Size
[C#]
protected override Size DefaultSize {get;}
[C++]
protected: __property Size get_DefaultSize();
[JScript]
protected override function get DefaultSize() : Size;
```

Requirements

Platforms: Windows 98, Windows NT 4.0, Windows Millennium Edition, Windows 2000, Windows XP Home Edition, Windows XP Professional, Windows Server 2003 family

TrackBar.Font Property

This member overrides **Control.Font**.

```
[Visual Basic]
Overrides Public Property Font As Font
[C#]
public override Font Font {get; set;}
[C++]
public: __property Font* get_Font();
public: __property void set_Font(Font*);
[JScript]
public override function get Font() : Font;
public override function set Font(Font);
```

Requirements

Platforms: Windows 98, Windows NT 4.0, Windows Millennium Edition, Windows 2000, Windows XP Home Edition, Windows XP Professional, Windows Server 2003 family

TrackBar.ForeColor Property

This member overrides **Control.ForeColor**.

```
[Visual Basic]
Overrides Public Property ForeColor As Color
[C#]
public override Color ForeColor {get; set;}
[C++]
public: __property Color get_ForeColor();
public: __property void set_ForeColor(Color);
[JScript]
public override function get ForeColor() : Color;
public override function set ForeColor(Color);
```

Requirements

Platforms: Windows 98, Windows NT 4.0, Windows Millennium Edition, Windows 2000, Windows XP Home Edition, Windows XP Professional, Windows Server 2003 family

TrackBar.ImeMode Property

This member supports the .NET Framework infrastructure and is not intended to be used directly from your code.

```
[Visual Basic]
Public Shadows Property ImeMode As ImeMode
[C#]
public new ImeMode ImeMode {get; set;}
[C++]
public: __property ImeMode get_ImeMode();
public: __property void set_ImeMode(ImeMode);
[JScript]
public hide function get ImeMode() : ImeMode;
public hide function set ImeMode(ImeMode);
```

TrackBar.LargeChange Property

Gets or sets a value to be added to or subtracted from the **Value** property when the slider is moved a large distance.

```
[Visual Basic]
Public Property LargeChange As Integer
[C#]
public int LargeChange {get; set;}
[C++]
public: __property int get_LargeChange();
public: __property void set_LargeChange(int);
[JScript]
public function get LargeChange() : int;
public function set LargeChange(int);
```

Property Value

A numeric value. The default value is 5.

Exceptions

Exception Type	Condition
Exception	The assigned value is less than 0.

Remarks

When the user presses the PAGE UP or PAGE DOWN key or clicks the track bar on either side of the slider, the **Value** property changes according to the value set in the **LargeChange** property. You might consider setting the **LargeChange** value to a percentage of the **Height** (for a vertically oriented track bar) or **Width** (for a horizontally oriented track bar) values. This keeps the distance your track bar moves proportionate to its size.

Example

See related example in the **System.Windows.Forms.TrackBar** class topic.

Requirements

Platforms: Windows 98, Windows NT 4.0, Windows Millennium Edition, Windows 2000, Windows XP Home Edition, Windows XP Professional, Windows Server 2003 family, .NET Compact Framework - Windows CE .NET

TrackBar.Maximum Property

Gets or sets the upper limit of the range this **TrackBar** is working with.

```
[Visual Basic]
Public Property Maximum As Integer
[C#]
public int Maximum {get; set;}
[C++]
public: __property int get_Maximum();
public: __property void set_Maximum(int);
[JScript]
public function get Maximum() : int;
public function set Maximum(int);
```

Property Value

The maximum value for the **TrackBar**. The default value is 10.

Remarks

You can use the **SetRange** method to set both the **Maximum** and **Minimum** properties at the same time.

Example

See related example in the **System.Windows.Forms.TrackBar** class topic.

Requirements

Platforms: Windows 98, Windows NT 4.0, Windows Millennium Edition, Windows 2000, Windows XP Home Edition, Windows XP Professional, Windows Server 2003 family, .NET Compact Framework - Windows CE .NET

TrackBar.Minimum Property

Gets or sets the lower limit of the range this **TrackBar** is working with.

```
[Visual Basic]
Public Property Minimum As Integer
[C#]
public int Minimum {get; set;}
[C++]
public: __property int get_Minimum();
public: __property void set_Minimum(int);
[JScript]
public function get Minimum() : int;
public function set Minimum(int);
```

Property Value

The minimum value for the **TrackBar**. The default value is 0.

Remarks

You can use the **SetRange** method to set both the **Maximum** and **Minimum** properties at the same time.

Requirements

Platforms: Windows 98, Windows NT 4.0, Windows Millennium Edition, Windows 2000, Windows XP Home Edition, Windows XP Professional, Windows Server 2003 family, .NET Compact Framework - Windows CE .NET

TrackBar.Orientation Property

Gets or sets a value indicating the horizontal or vertical orientation of the track bar.

```
[Visual Basic]
Public Property Orientation As Orientation
[C#]
public Orientation Orientation {get; set;}
[C++]
public: __property Orientation get_Orientation();
public: __property void set_Orientation(Orientation);
[JScript]
public function get Orientation() : Orientation;
public function set Orientation(Orientation);
```

Property Value

One of the **Orientation** values.

Exceptions

Exception Type	Condition
InvalidEnumArgumentException	The assigned value is not one of the **Orientation** values.

Remarks

When the **Orientation** property is set to **Orientation.Horizontal**, the slider moves from left to right as the **Value** increases. When the **Orientation** property is set to **Orientation.Vertical**, the slider moves from bottom to top as the **Value** increases.

Example

See related example in the **System.Windows.Forms.TrackBar** class topic.

Requirements

Platforms: Windows 98, Windows NT 4.0,
Windows Millennium Edition, Windows 2000,
Windows XP Home Edition, Windows XP Professional,
Windows Server 2003 family,
.NET Compact Framework - Windows CE .NET

TrackBar.SmallChange Property

Gets or sets the value added to or subtracted from the **Value** property when the slider is moved a small distance.

```
[Visual Basic]
Public Property SmallChange As Integer
[C#]
public int SmallChange {get; set;}
[C++]
public: __property int get_SmallChange();
public: __property void set_SmallChange(int);
[JScript]
public function get SmallChange() : int;
public function set SmallChange(int);
```

Property Value

A numeric value. The default value is 1.

Exceptions

Exception Type	Condition
Exception	The assigned value is less than 0.

Remarks

When the user presses one of the arrow keys, the **Value** property changes according to the value set in the **SmallChange** property.

You might consider setting the value of **SmallChange** to a percentage of the value of the **Height** (for a vertically oriented track bar) or **Width** (for a horizontally oriented track bar) properties. This sets the distance your track bar moves proportionate to its size.

Example

See related example in the **System.Windows.Forms.TrackBar** class topic.

Requirements

Platforms: Windows 98, Windows NT 4.0,
Windows Millennium Edition, Windows 2000,
Windows XP Home Edition, Windows XP Professional,
Windows Server 2003 family,
.NET Compact Framework - Windows CE .NET

TrackBar.Text Property

This member overrides **Control.Text**.

```
[Visual Basic]
Overrides Public Property Text As String
[C#]
public override string Text {get; set;}
[C++]
public: __property String* get_Text();
public: __property void set_Text(String*);
[JScript]
public override function get Text() : String;
public override function set Text(String);
```

Requirements

Platforms: Windows 98, Windows NT 4.0,
Windows Millennium Edition, Windows 2000,
Windows XP Home Edition, Windows XP Professional,
Windows Server 2003 family

TrackBar.TickFrequency Property

Gets or sets a value that specifies the delta between ticks drawn on the control.

```
[Visual Basic]
Public Property TickFrequency As Integer
[C#]
public int TickFrequency {get; set;}
[C++]
public: __property int get_TickFrequency();
public: __property void set_TickFrequency(int);
[JScript]
public function get TickFrequency() : int;
public function set TickFrequency(int);
```

Property Value

The numeric value representing the delta between ticks. The default is 1.

Remarks

For a **TrackBar** with a large range of values between the **Minimum** and the **Maximum**, it might be impractical to draw all the ticks for values on the control. For example, if you have a control with a range of 100, passing in a value of five here causes the control to draw 20 ticks. In this case, each tick represents five units in the range of values.

Example

See related example in the **System.Windows.Forms.TrackBar** class topic.

Requirements

Platforms: Windows 98, Windows NT 4.0,
Windows Millennium Edition, Windows 2000,
Windows XP Home Edition, Windows XP Professional,
Windows Server 2003 family,
.NET Compact Framework - Windows CE .NET

TrackBar.TickStyle Property

Gets or sets a value indicating how to display the tick marks on the track bar.

```
[Visual Basic]
Public Property TickStyle As TickStyle
[C#]
public TickStyle TickStyle {get; set;}
[C++]
public: __property TickStyle get_TickStyle();
public: __property void set_TickStyle(TickStyle);
[JScript]
public function get TickStyle() : TickStyle;
public function set TickStyle(TickStyle);
```

Property Value

One of the **TickStyle** values. The default is **TickStyle.BottomRight**.

Exceptions

Exception Type	Condition
InvalidEnumArgument-Exception	The assigned value is not one of the valid **TickStyle** values.

Remarks

You can use the **TickStyle** property to modify the manner in which the tick marks are displayed on the track bar.

Requirements

Platforms: Windows 98, Windows NT 4.0,
Windows Millennium Edition, Windows 2000,
Windows XP Home Edition, Windows XP Professional,
Windows Server 2003 family

TrackBar.Value Property

Gets or sets a numeric value that represents the current position of the slider on the track bar.

```
[Visual Basic]
Public Property Value As Integer
[C#]
public int Value {get; set;}
[C++]
public: __property int get_Value();
public: __property void set_Value(int);
[JScript]
public function get Value() : int;
public function set Value(int);
```

Property Value

A numeric value that is within the **Minimum** and **Maximum** range. The default value is 0.

Exceptions

Exception Type	Condition
ArgumentException	The assigned value is less than the value of **Minimum**. -or- The assigned value is greater than the value of **Maximum**.

Remarks

The **Value** property contains the number that represents the current position of the slider on the track bar.

Example

See related example in the **System.Windows.Forms.TrackBar** class topic.

Requirements

Platforms: Windows 98, Windows NT 4.0,
Windows Millennium Edition, Windows 2000,
Windows XP Home Edition, Windows XP Professional,
Windows Server 2003 family,
.NET Compact Framework - Windows CE .NET

TrackBar.BeginInit Method

This member supports the .NET Framework infrastructure and is not intended to be used directly from your code.

```
[Visual Basic]
Public Overridable Sub BeginInit() Implements _
   ISupportInitialize.BeginInit
[C#]
public virtual void BeginInit();
[C++]
public: virtual void BeginInit();
[JScript]
public function BeginInit();
```

TrackBar.CreateHandle Method

This member overrides **Control.CreateHandle**.

```
[Visual Basic]
Overrides Protected Sub CreateHandle()
[C#]
protected override void CreateHandle();
[C++]
protected: void CreateHandle();
[JScript]
protected override function CreateHandle();
```

Requirements

Platforms: Windows 98, Windows NT 4.0, Windows Millennium Edition, Windows 2000, Windows XP Home Edition, Windows XP Professional, Windows Server 2003 family

TrackBar.EndInit Method

This member supports the .NET Framework infrastructure and is not intended to be used directly from your code.

[Visual Basic]
```
Public Overridable Sub EndInit() Implements _
   ISupportInitialize.EndInit
```
[C#]
```
public virtual void EndInit();
```
[C++]
```
public: virtual void EndInit();
```
[JScript]
```
public function EndInit();
```

TrackBar.IsInputKey Method

This member overrides **Control.IsInputKey**.

[Visual Basic]
```
Overrides Protected Function IsInputKey( _
   ByVal keyData As Keys _
) As Boolean
```
[C#]
```
protected override bool IsInputKey(
   Keys keyData
);
```
[C++]
```
protected: bool IsInputKey(
   Keys keyData
);
```
[JScript]
```
protected override function IsInputKey(
   keyData : Keys
) : Boolean;
```

Requirements

Platforms: Windows 98, Windows NT 4.0, Windows Millennium Edition, Windows 2000, Windows XP Home Edition, Windows XP Professional, Windows Server 2003 family

TrackBar.OnBackColorChanged Method

This member overrides **Control.OnBackColorChanged**.

[Visual Basic]
```
Overrides Protected Sub OnBackColorChanged( _
   ByVal e As EventArgs _
)
```
[C#]
```
protected override void OnBackColorChanged(
   EventArgs e
);
```
[C++]
```
protected: void OnBackColorChanged(
   EventArgs* e
);
```
[JScript]
```
protected override function OnBackColorChanged(
   e : EventArgs
);
```

Requirements

Platforms: Windows 98, Windows NT 4.0, Windows Millennium Edition, Windows 2000, Windows XP Home Edition, Windows XP Professional, Windows Server 2003 family

TrackBar.OnHandleCreated Method

This member overrides **Control.OnHandleCreated**.

[Visual Basic]
```
Overrides Protected Sub OnHandleCreated( _
   ByVal e As EventArgs _
)
```
[C#]
```
protected override void OnHandleCreated(
   EventArgs e
);
```
[C++]
```
protected: void OnHandleCreated(
   EventArgs* e
);
```
[JScript]
```
protected override function OnHandleCreated(
   e : EventArgs
);
```

Requirements

Platforms: Windows 98, Windows NT 4.0, Windows Millennium Edition, Windows 2000, Windows XP Home Edition, Windows XP Professional, Windows Server 2003 family

TrackBar.OnMouseWheel Method

This member overrides **Control.OnMouseWheel**.

[Visual Basic]
```
Overrides Protected Sub OnMouseWheel( _
   ByVal e As MouseEventArgs _
)
```
[C#]
```
protected override void OnMouseWheel(
   MouseEventArgs e
);
```
[C++]
```
protected: void OnMouseWheel(
   MouseEventArgs* e
);
```
[JScript]
```
protected override function OnMouseWheel(
   e : MouseEventArgs
);
```

Requirements

Platforms: Windows 98, Windows NT 4.0, Windows Millennium Edition, Windows 2000, Windows XP Home Edition, Windows XP Professional, Windows Server 2003 family

TrackBar.OnScroll Method

Raises the **Scroll** event.

```
[Visual Basic]
Protected Overridable Sub OnScroll( _
   ByVal e As EventArgs _
)
[C#]
protected virtual void OnScroll(
   EventArgs e
);
[C++]
protected: virtual void OnScroll(
   EventArgs* e
);
[JScript]
protected function OnScroll(
   e : EventArgs
);
```

Parameters

e

An **EventArgs** that contains the event data.

Remarks

You can use the **OnScroll** event to update other controls as the position of the slider changes.

Raising an event invokes the event handler through a delegate. For more information, see **Raising an Event**.

The **OnScroll** method also allows derived classes to handle the event without attaching a delegate. This is the preferred technique for handling the event in a derived class.

Notes to Inheritors: When overriding **OnScroll** in a derived class, be sure to call the **OnScroll** method of the base class so that registered delegates receive the event.

Requirements

Platforms: Windows 98, Windows NT 4.0, Windows Millennium Edition, Windows 2000, Windows XP Home Edition, Windows XP Professional, Windows Server 2003 family

TrackBar.OnValueChanged Method

This member supports the .NET Framework infrastructure and is not intended to be used directly from your code.

```
[Visual Basic]
Protected Overridable Sub OnValueChanged( _
   ByVal e As EventArgs _
)
[C#]
protected virtual void OnValueChanged(
   EventArgs e
);
[C++]
protected: virtual void OnValueChanged(
   EventArgs* e
);
[JScript]
protected function OnValueChanged(
   e : EventArgs
);
```

TrackBar.SetBoundsCore Method

This member overrides **Control.SetBoundsCore**.

```
[Visual Basic]
Overrides Protected Sub SetBoundsCore( _
   ByVal x As Integer, _
   ByVal y As Integer, _
   ByVal width As Integer, _
   ByVal height As Integer, _
   ByVal specified As BoundsSpecified _
)
[C#]
protected override void SetBoundsCore(
   int x,
   int y,
   int width,
   int height,
   BoundsSpecified specified
);
[C++]
protected: void SetBoundsCore(
   int x,
   int y,
   int width,
   int height,
   BoundsSpecified specified
);
[JScript]
protected override function SetBoundsCore(
   x : int,
   y : int,
   width : int,
   height : int,
   specified : BoundsSpecified
);
```

Requirements

Platforms: Windows 98, Windows NT 4.0, Windows Millennium Edition, Windows 2000, Windows XP Home Edition, Windows XP Professional, Windows Server 2003 family

TrackBar.SetRange Method

Sets the minimum and maximum values for a **TrackBar**.

```
[Visual Basic]
Public Sub SetRange( _
   ByVal minValue As Integer, _
   ByVal maxValue As Integer _
)
[C#]
public void SetRange(
   int minValue,
   int maxValue
);
[C++]
public: void SetRange(
   int minValue,
   int maxValue
);
```

```
[JScript]
public function SetRange(
   minValue : int,
   maxValue : int
);
```

Parameters

minValue
The lower limit of the range of the track bar.

maxValue
The upper limit of the range of the track bar.

Remarks

You can use this method to set the entire range for the **TrackBar** at the same time. To set the minimum or maximum values individually, use the **Minimum** and **Maximum** properties. If the *minValue* parameter is greater than the *maxValue* parameter, *maxValue* is set equal to *minValue*.

Requirements

Platforms: Windows 98, Windows NT 4.0, Windows Millennium Edition, Windows 2000, Windows XP Home Edition, Windows XP Professional, Windows Server 2003 family

TrackBar.ToString Method

This member overrides **Object.ToString**.

```
[Visual Basic]
Overrides Public Function ToString() As String
[C#]
public override string ToString();
[C++]
public: String* ToString();
[JScript]
public override function ToString() : String;
```

Requirements

Platforms: Windows 98, Windows NT 4.0, Windows Millennium Edition, Windows 2000, Windows XP Home Edition, Windows XP Professional, Windows Server 2003 family, .NET Compact Framework - Windows CE .NET

TrackBar.WndProc Method

This member overrides **Control.WndProc**.

```
[Visual Basic]
Overrides Protected Sub WndProc( _
   ByRef m As Message _
)
[C#]
protected override void WndProc(
   ref Message m
);
[C++]
protected: void WndProc(
   Message* m
);
[JScript]
protected override function WndProc(
   m : Message
);
```

Requirements

Platforms: Windows 98, Windows NT 4.0, Windows Millennium Edition, Windows 2000, Windows XP Home Edition, Windows XP Professional, Windows Server 2003 family

TrackBar.BackgroundImageChanged Event

This member supports the .NET Framework infrastructure and is not intended to be used directly from your code.

```
[Visual Basic]
Public Shadows Event BackgroundImageChanged As EventHandler
[C#]
public new event EventHandler BackgroundImageChanged;
[C++]
public: __event EventHandler* BackgroundImageChanged;
```

[JScript] In JScript, you can handle the events defined by a class, but you cannot define your own.

TrackBar.Click Event

This member supports the .NET Framework infrastructure and is not intended to be used directly from your code.

```
[Visual Basic]
Public Shadows Event Click As EventHandler
[C#]
public new event EventHandler Click;
[C++]
public: __event EventHandler* Click;
```

[JScript] In JScript, you can handle the events defined by a class, but you cannot define your own.

TrackBar.DoubleClick Event

This member supports the .NET Framework infrastructure and is not intended to be used directly from your code.

```
[Visual Basic]
Public Shadows Event DoubleClick As EventHandler
[C#]
public new event EventHandler DoubleClick;
[C++]
public: __event EventHandler* DoubleClick;
```

[JScript] In JScript, you can handle the events defined by a class, but you cannot define your own.

TrackBar.FontChanged Event

This member supports the .NET Framework infrastructure and is not intended to be used directly from your code.

```
[Visual Basic]
Public Shadows Event FontChanged As EventHandler
[C#]
public new event EventHandler FontChanged;
[C++]
public: __event EventHandler* FontChanged;
```

[JScript] In JScript, you can handle the events defined by a class, but you cannot define your own.

TrackBar.ForeColorChanged Event

This member supports the .NET Framework infrastructure and is not intended to be used directly from your code.

[Visual Basic]
```
Public Shadows Event ForeColorChanged As EventHandler
```
[C#]
```
public new event EventHandler ForeColorChanged;
```
[C++]
```
public: __event EventHandler* ForeColorChanged;
```

[JScript] In JScript, you can handle the events defined by a class, but you cannot define your own.

TrackBar.ImeModeChanged Event

This member supports the .NET Framework infrastructure and is not intended to be used directly from your code.

[Visual Basic]
```
Public Shadows Event ImeModeChanged As EventHandler
```
[C#]
```
public new event EventHandler ImeModeChanged;
```
[C++]
```
public: __event EventHandler* ImeModeChanged;
```

[JScript] In JScript, you can handle the events defined by a class, but you cannot define your own.

TrackBar.Paint Event

This member supports the .NET Framework infrastructure and is not intended to be used directly from your code.

[Visual Basic]
```
Public Shadows Event Paint As PaintEventHandler
```
[C#]
```
public new event PaintEventHandler Paint;
```
[C++]
```
public: __event PaintEventHandler* Paint;
```

[JScript] In JScript, you can handle the events defined by a class, but you cannot define your own.

TrackBar.Scroll Event

Occurs when either a mouse or keyboard action moves the slider.

[Visual Basic]
```
Public Event Scroll As EventHandler
```
[C#]
```
public event EventHandler Scroll;
```
[C++]
```
public: __event EventHandler* Scroll;
```

[JScript] In JScript, you can handle the events defined by a class, but you cannot define your own.

Event Data

The event handler receives an argument of type **EventArgs**.

Remarks

When you create a **Scroll** delegate, you identify the method that will handle the event. To associate the event with your event handler, add an instance of the delegate to the event. The event handler is called whenever the event occurs, unless you remove the delegate.

Example

See related example in the **System.Windows.Forms.TrackBar** class topic.

Requirements

Platforms: Windows 98, Windows NT 4.0, Windows Millennium Edition, Windows 2000, Windows XP Home Edition, Windows XP Professional, Windows Server 2003 family

TrackBar.TextChanged Event

This member supports the .NET Framework infrastructure and is not intended to be used directly from your code.

[Visual Basic]
```
Public Shadows Event TextChanged As EventHandler
```
[C#]
```
public new event EventHandler TextChanged;
```
[C++]
```
public: __event EventHandler* TextChanged;
```

[JScript] In JScript, you can handle the events defined by a class, but you cannot define your own.

TrackBar.ValueChanged Event

Occurs when the **Value** property of a track bar changes, either by movement of the slider or by manipulation in code.

[Visual Basic]
```
Public Event ValueChanged As EventHandler
```
[C#]
```
public event EventHandler ValueChanged;
```
[C++]
```
public: __event EventHandler* ValueChanged;
```

[JScript] In JScript, you can handle the events defined by a class, but you cannot define your own.

Event Data

The event handler receives an argument of type **EventArgs**.

Remarks

You can use this event to update other controls when the value represented in the track bar changes.

When you create a **TrackBar** delegate, you identify the method that will handle the event. To associate the event with your event handler, add an instance of the delegate to the event. The event handler is called whenever the event occurs, unless you remove the delegate.

Requirements

Platforms: Windows 98, Windows NT 4.0, Windows Millennium Edition, Windows 2000, Windows XP Home Edition, Windows XP Professional, Windows Server 2003 family

TreeNode Class

Represents a node of a **TreeView**.

System.Object
  System.MarshalByRefObject
    System.Windows.Forms.TreeNode

[Visual Basic]
```
<Serializable>
Public Class TreeNode
   Inherits MarshalByRefObject
   Implements ICloneable, ISerializable
```
[C#]
```
[Serializable]
public class TreeNode : MarshalByRefObject, ICloneable,
   ISerializable
```
[C++]
```
[Serializable]
public __gc class TreeNode : public MarshalByRefObject,
   ICloneable, ISerializable
```
[JScript]
```
public
   Serializable
class TreeNode extends MarshalByRefObject implements
   ICloneable, ISerializable
```

Thread Safety

Any public static (**Shared** in Visual Basic) members of this type are safe for multithreaded operations. Any instance members are not guaranteed to be thread safe.

Remarks

The **Nodes** collection holds all the child **TreeNode** objects assigned to the current **TreeNode**. You can add, remove, or clone a **TreeNode**; when doing so, all child tree nodes are added, removed, or cloned. Each **TreeNode** can contain a collection of other **TreeNode** objects. This can make it difficult to determine where you are in the **TreeView** when iterating through the collection. To determine your location in a tree structure, use the **FullPath** property. The **FullPath** string can be parsed using the **PathSeparator** string value to determine where a **TreeNode** label begins and ends.

The **TreeNode** label is set by setting the **Text** property explicitly. The alternative is to create the tree node using one of the **TreeNode** constructors that has a string parameter that represents the **Text** property. The label is displayed next to the **TreeNode** image, if one is displayed.

To display images next to the tree nodes, assign an **ImageList** to the **ImageList** property of the parent **TreeView** control and assign an **Image** by referencing its index value in the **ImageList** property. Set the **ImageIndex** property to the index value of the **Image** you want to display when the **TreeNode** is in an unselected state. Likewise, set the **SelectedImageIndex** property to the index value of the **Image** you want to display when the **TreeNode** is selected.

Selecting specific tree nodes and iterating through the **Nodes** collection can be achieved by using the following property values: **FirstNode**, **LastNode**, **NextNode**, **PrevNode**, **NextVisibleNode**, **PrevVisibleNode**. Assign the **TreeNode** object returned by one of aforementioned properties to the **TreeView.SelectedNode** property to select that tree node in the **TreeView** control.

Tree nodes can be expanded to display the next level of child tree nodes. The user can expand the **TreeNode** by pressing the plus (+) button next to the **TreeNode**, if one is displayed, or you can expand the **TreeNode** by calling the **Expand** method. To expand all child tree node levels in the **Nodes** collection, call the **ExpandAll** method. You can collapse the child **TreeNode** level by calling the **Collapse** method, or the user can press the minus (-) button next to the **TreeNode**, if one is displayed. You can also call the **Toggle** method to alternate the **TreeNode** between the expanded and collapsed states.

Tree nodes can optionally display a check box. To display the check boxes, set the **CheckBoxes** property of the **TreeView** to **true**. The **Checked** property is set to **true** for tree nodes that are in a checked state.

Example

[Visual Basic, C#, C++] The following example displays customer information in a **TreeView** control. The root tree nodes display customer names, and the child tree nodes display the order numbers assigned to each customer. In this example, 1,000 customers are displayed with 15 orders each. The repainting of the **TreeView** is suppressed by using the **BeginUpdate** and **EndUpdate** methods, and a wait **Cursor** is displayed while the **TreeView** creates and paints the **TreeNode** objects. This example assumes you have a Customer object that can hold a collection of Order objects. It also assumes that you have created an instance of a **TreeView** control on a **Form**.

[Visual Basic]
```
' Create a new ArrayList to hold the Customer objects.
Private customerArray As New ArrayList()

Private Sub FillMyTreeView()
   ' Add customers to the ArrayList of Customer objects.
   Dim x As Integer
   For x = 0 To 999
      customerArray.Add(New Customer("Customer" + x.ToString()))
   Next x

   ' Add orders to each Customer object in the ArrayList.
   Dim customer1 As Customer
   For Each customer1 In customerArray
      Dim y As Integer
      For y = 0 To 14
         customer1.CustomerOrders.Add(New Order("Order" + ↵
y.ToString()))
      Next y
   Next customer1

   ' Display a wait cursor while the TreeNodes are being created.
   Cursor.Current = New Cursor("MyWait.cur")

   ' Suppress repainting the TreeView until all the objects ↵
 have been created.
   treeView1.BeginUpdate()

   ' Clear the TreeView each time the method is called.
   treeView1.Nodes.Clear()

   ' Add a root TreeNode for each Customer object in the ArrayList.
   Dim customer2 As Customer
   For Each customer2 In customerArray
      treeView1.Nodes.Add(New TreeNode(customer2.CustomerName))

      ' Add a child TreeNode for each Order object in the ↵
current Customer object.
      Dim order1 As Order
      For Each order1 In customer2.CustomerOrders
         treeView1.Nodes(customerArray.IndexOf(customer2)).Nodes.Add( _
   New TreeNode(customer2.CustomerName + "." + order1.OrderID))
      Next order1
   Next customer2
```

```
   ' Reset the cursor to the default for all controls.
   Cursor.Current = System.Windows.Forms.Cursors.Default

   ' Begin repainting the TreeView.
   treeView1.EndUpdate()
End Sub 'FillMyTreeView
```

[C#]

```
// Create a new ArrayList to hold the Customer objects.
private ArrayList customerArray = new ArrayList();

private void FillMyTreeView()
{
   // Add customers to the ArrayList of Customer objects.
   for(int x=0; x<1000; x++)
   {
      customerArray.Add(new Customer("Customer" + x.ToString()));
   }

   // Add orders to each Customer object in the ArrayList.
   foreach(Customer customer1 in customerArray)
   {
      for(int y=0; y<15; y++)
      {
         customer1.CustomerOrders.Add(new Order("Order" + ↵
y.ToString()));
      }
   }

   // Display a wait cursor while the TreeNodes are being created.
   Cursor.Current = new Cursor("MyWait.cur");

   // Suppress repainting the TreeView until all the objects ↵
 have been created.
   treeView1.BeginUpdate();

   // Clear the TreeView each time the method is called.
   treeView1.Nodes.Clear();

   // Add a root TreeNode for each Customer object in the ArrayList.
   foreach(Customer customer2 in customerArray)
   {
      treeView1.Nodes.Add(new TreeNode(customer2.CustomerName));

      // Add a child treenode for each Order object in the ↵
 current Customer object.
      foreach(Order order1 in customer2.CustomerOrders)
      {
         treeView1.Nodes[customerArray.IndexOf(customer2)].Nodes.Add(
           new TreeNode(customer2.CustomerName + "." + ↵
order1.OrderID));
      }
   }

   // Reset the cursor to the default for all controls.
   Cursor.Current = Cursors.Default;

   // Begin repainting the TreeView.
   treeView1.EndUpdate();
}
```

[C++]

```
void FillMyTreeView() {
    // Add customers to the ArrayList of Customer objects.
    for (int x=0; x<1000; x++) {
        customerArray->Add(new Customer(String::Concat ↵
 (S"Customer ", __box(x))));
    }

    // Add orders to each Customer object in the ArrayList.
    IEnumerator* myEnum = customerArray->GetEnumerator();
    while (myEnum->MoveNext()) {
        Customer* customer1 = __try_cast<Customer*>(myEnum->Current);
        for (int y=0; y<15; y++) {
            customer1->CustomerOrders->Add(new ↵
Order(String::Concat(S"Order ", __box(y))));
        }
    }

    // Display a wait cursor while the TreeNodes are being created.
    Cursor::Current = new System::Windows::Forms::Cursor(S"MyWait.cur");

    // Suppress repainting the TreeView until all the objects ↵
 have been created.
    treeView1->BeginUpdate();

    // Clear the TreeView each time the method is called.
    treeView1->Nodes->Clear();

    // Add a root TreeNode for each Customer object in the ArrayList.
    while (myEnum->MoveNext()) {
        Customer* customer2 = __try_cast<Customer*>(myEnum->Current);

        treeView1->Nodes->Add(new TreeNode(customer2->CustomerName));

        // Add a child treenode for each Order object in the ↵
 current Customer object.
        IEnumerator* myEnum = customer2->CustomerOrders- ↵
>GetEnumerator();
        while (myEnum->MoveNext()) {
            Order* order1 = __try_cast<Order*>(myEnum->Current);

            treeView1->Nodes->Item[customerArray->IndexOf ↵
 (customer2)]->Nodes->Add(
                new TreeNode(String::Concat(customer2-> ↵
CustomerName, S".", order1->OrderID)));
        }
    }

    // Reset the cursor to the default for all controls.
    Cursor::Current = Cursors::Default;

    // Begin repainting the TreeView.
    treeView1->EndUpdate();
}
```

Requirements

Namespace: System.Windows.Forms

Platforms: Windows 98, Windows NT 4.0, Windows Millennium Edition, Windows 2000, Windows XP Home Edition, Windows XP Professional, Windows Server 2003 family, .NET Compact Framework - Windows CE .NET

Assembly: System.Windows.Forms (in System.Windows.Forms.dll)

TreeNode Constructor

Initializes a new instance of the **TreeNode** class.

Overload List

Initializes a new instance of the **TreeNode** class.

Supported by the .NET Compact Framework.

[Visual Basic] **Public Sub New()**

[C#] **public TreeNode();**

[C++] **public: TreeNode();**

[JScript] **public function TreeNode();**

Initializes a new instance of the **TreeNode** class with the specified label text.

Supported by the .NET Compact Framework.

[Visual Basic] **Public Sub New(String)**

[C#] **public TreeNode(string);**

[C++] **public: TreeNode(String*);**

[JScript] **public function TreeNode(String);**

Initializes a new instance of the **TreeNode** class with the specified label text and child tree nodes.

[Visual Basic] **Public Sub New(String, TreeNode())**

[C#] **public TreeNode(string, TreeNode[]);**

[C++] **public: TreeNode(String*, TreeNode[]);**

[JScript] **public function TreeNode(String, TreeNode[]);**

Initializes a new instance of the **TreeNode** class with the specified label text and images to display when the tree node is in a selected and unselected state.

[Visual Basic] **Public Sub New(String, Integer, Integer)**

[C#] **public TreeNode(string, int, int);**

[C++] **public: TreeNode(String*, int, int);**

[JScript] **public function TreeNode(String, int, int);**

Initializes a new instance of the **TreeNode** class with the specified label text, child tree nodes, and images to display when the tree node is in a selected and unselected state.

[Visual Basic] **Public Sub New(String, Integer, Integer, TreeNode())**

[C#] **public TreeNode(string, int, int, TreeNode[]);**

[C++] **public: TreeNode(String*, int, int, TreeNode[]);**

[JScript] **public function TreeNode(String, int, int, TreeNode[]);**

Example

See related example in the **System.Windows.Forms.TreeNode** class topic.

TreeNode Constructor ()

Initializes a new instance of the **TreeNode** class.

```
[Visual Basic]
Public Sub New()
[C#]
public TreeNode();
[C++]
public: TreeNode();
[JScript]
public function TreeNode();
```

Example

See related example in the **System.Windows.Forms.TreeNode** class topic.

Requirements

Platforms: Windows 98, Windows NT 4.0, Windows Millennium Edition, Windows 2000, Windows XP Home Edition, Windows XP Professional, Windows Server 2003 family, .NET Compact Framework - Windows CE .NET

TreeNode Constructor (String)

Initializes a new instance of the **TreeNode** class with the specified label text.

```
[Visual Basic]
Public Sub New( _
   ByVal text As String _
)
[C#]
public TreeNode(
   string text
);
[C++]
public: TreeNode(
   String* text
);
[JScript]
public function TreeNode(
   text : String
);
```

Parameters

text

The label **Text** of the new tree node.

Remarks

The *text* parameter value is assigned to the node's **Text** property and becomes the tree node label.

Example

See related example in the **System.Windows.Forms.TreeNode** class topic.

Requirements

Platforms: Windows 98, Windows NT 4.0, Windows Millennium Edition, Windows 2000, Windows XP Home Edition, Windows XP Professional, Windows Server 2003 family, .NET Compact Framework - Windows CE .NET

TreeNode Constructor (String, TreeNode[])

Initializes a new instance of the **TreeNode** class with the specified label text and child tree nodes.

```
[Visual Basic]
Public Sub New( _
   ByVal text As String, _
   ByVal children() As TreeNode _
)
[C#]
public TreeNode(
   string text,
   TreeNode[] children
);
[C++]
public: TreeNode(
   String* text,
   TreeNode* children[]
);
[JScript]
public function TreeNode(
   text : String,
   children : TreeNode[]
);
```

Parameters

text
  The label **Text** of the new tree node.

children
  An array of child **TreeNode** objects.

Remarks

The *text* parameter value is assigned to the node's **Text** property and becomes the tree node label. The tree nodes contained in the *children* array are added to the **TreeNodeCollection** stored in the **Nodes** property.

Example

See related example in the **System.Windows.Forms.TreeNode** class topic.

Requirements

Platforms: Windows 98, Windows NT 4.0, Windows Millennium Edition, Windows 2000, Windows XP Home Edition, Windows XP Professional, Windows Server 2003 family

TreeNode Constructor (String, Int32, Int32)

Initializes a new instance of the **TreeNode** class with the specified label text and images to display when the tree node is in a selected and unselected state.

```
[Visual Basic]
Public Sub New( _
   ByVal text As String, _
   ByVal imageIndex As Integer, _
   ByVal selectedImageIndex As Integer _
)
[C#]
public TreeNode(
   string text,
   int imageIndex,
   int selectedImageIndex
);
[C++]
public: TreeNode(
   String* text,
   int imageIndex,
   int selectedImageIndex
);
[JScript]
public function TreeNode(
   text : String,
   imageIndex : int,
   selectedImageIndex : int
);
```

Parameters

text
  The label **Text** of the new tree node.

imageIndex
  The index value of **Image** to display when the tree node is unselected.

selectedImageIndex
  The index value of **Image** to display when the tree node is selected.

Remarks

The *text* parameter value is assigned to the node's **Text** property and becomes the tree node label. The *imageIndex* and *selectedImageIndex* values are the index values of an **Image** stored in the **ImageList** assigned to the **TreeView.ImageList** property. The image referenced in the *imageIndex* property is displayed when the tree node is not selected. Likewise, the image referenced in the *selectedImageIndex* property is displayed when the tree node is in a selected state.

Example

See related example in the **System.Windows.Forms.TreeNode** class topic.

Requirements

Platforms: Windows 98, Windows NT 4.0, Windows Millennium Edition, Windows 2000, Windows XP Home Edition, Windows XP Professional, Windows Server 2003 family

TreeNode Constructor (String, Int32, Int32, TreeNode[])

Initializes a new instance of the **TreeNode** class with the specified label text, child tree nodes, and images to display when the tree node is in a selected and unselected state.

```
[Visual Basic]
Public Sub New( _
   ByVal text As String, _
   ByVal imageIndex As Integer, _
   ByVal selectedImageIndex As Integer, _
   ByVal children() As TreeNode _
)
[C#]
public TreeNode(
   string text,
   int imageIndex,
   int selectedImageIndex,
   TreeNode[] children
);
[C++]
public: TreeNode(
   String* text,
   int imageIndex,
   int selectedImageIndex,
   TreeNode* children[]
);
[JScript]
public function TreeNode(
   text : String,
   imageIndex : int,
   selectedImageIndex : int,
   children : TreeNode[]
);
```

Parameters

text

The label **Text** of the new tree node.

imageIndex

The index value of **Image** to display when the tree node is unselected.

selectedImageIndex

The index value of **Image** to display when the tree node is selected.

children

An array of child **TreeNode** objects.

Remarks

The *text* parameter value is assigned to the node's **Text** property and becomes the tree node label. The *imageIndex* and *selectedImageIndex* values are the index values of an **Image** stored in the **ImageList** assigned to the **TreeView.ImageList** property. The image referenced in the *imageIndex* parameter is displayed when the tree node is not selected. Likewise, the image referenced in the *selectedImageIndex* parameter is displayed when the tree node is in a selected state. The tree nodes contained in the *children* array are added to the **TreeNodeCollection** stored in the **Nodes** property.

Example

See related example in the **System.Windows.Forms.TreeNode** class topic.

Requirements

Platforms: Windows 98, Windows NT 4.0, Windows Millennium Edition, Windows 2000, Windows XP Home Edition, Windows XP Professional, Windows Server 2003 family

TreeNode.BackColor Property

Gets or sets the background color of the tree node.

```
[Visual Basic]
Public Property BackColor As Color
[C#]
public Color BackColor {get; set;}
[C++]
public: __property Color get_BackColor();
public: __property void set_BackColor(Color);
[JScript]
public function get BackColor() : Color;
public function set BackColor(Color);
```

Property Value

The background **Color** of the tree node.

Remarks

If the **BackColor** property is set to a null reference (**Nothing** in Visual Basic), the **Color** used is the **BackColor** property value of the **TreeView** control that the tree node is assigned to.

Example

See related example in the **System.Windows.Forms.TreeNode** class topic.

Requirements

Platforms: Windows 98, Windows NT 4.0, Windows Millennium Edition, Windows 2000, Windows XP Home Edition, Windows XP Professional, Windows Server 2003 family

TreeNode.Bounds Property

Gets the bounds of the tree node.

```
[Visual Basic]
Public ReadOnly Property Bounds As Rectangle
[C#]
public Rectangle Bounds {get;}
[C++]
public: __property Rectangle get_Bounds();
[JScript]
public function get Bounds() : Rectangle;
```

Property Value

The **Rectangle** that represents the bounds of the tree node.

Remarks

The coordinates are relative to the upper left corner of the **TreeView** control.

Example

See related example in the **System.Windows.Forms.TreeNode** class topic.

Requirements

Platforms: Windows 98, Windows NT 4.0, Windows Millennium Edition, Windows 2000, Windows XP Home Edition, Windows XP Professional, Windows Server 2003 family

TreeNode.Checked Property

Gets or sets a value indicating whether the tree node is in a checked state.

```
[Visual Basic]
Public Property Checked As Boolean
[C#]
public bool Checked {get; set;}
[C++]
public: __property bool get_Checked();
public: __property void set_Checked(bool);
[JScript]
public function get Checked() : Boolean;
public function set Checked(Boolean);
```

Property Value

true if the tree node is in a checked state; otherwise, **false**.

Example

See related example in the **System.Windows.Forms.TreeNode** class topic.

Requirements

Platforms: Windows 98, Windows NT 4.0, Windows Millennium Edition, Windows 2000, Windows XP Home Edition, Windows XP Professional, Windows Server 2003 family, .NET Compact Framework - Windows CE .NET

TreeNode.FirstNode Property

Gets the first child tree node in the tree node collection.

```
[Visual Basic]
Public ReadOnly Property FirstNode As TreeNode
```

```
[C#]
public TreeNode FirstNode {get;}
[C++]
public: __property TreeNode* get_FirstNode();
[JScript]
public function get FirstNode() : TreeNode;
```

Property Value

The first child **TreeNode** in the **Nodes** collection.

Remarks

The **FirstNode** is the first child **TreeNode** in the **TreeNodeCollection** stored in the **Nodes** property of the current tree node. If the **TreeNode** has no child tree node, the **FirstNode** property returns a null reference (**Nothing** in Visual Basic).

Example

See related example in the **System.Windows.Forms.TreeNode** class topic.

Requirements

Platforms: Windows 98, Windows NT 4.0, Windows Millennium Edition, Windows 2000, Windows XP Home Edition, Windows XP Professional, Windows Server 2003 family

TreeNode.ForeColor Property

Gets or sets the foreground color of the tree node.

```
[Visual Basic]
Public Property ForeColor As Color
[C#]
public Color ForeColor {get; set;}
[C++]
public: __property Color get_ForeColor();
public: __property void set_ForeColor(Color);
[JScript]
public function get ForeColor() : Color;
public function set ForeColor(Color);
```

Property Value

The foreground **Color** of the tree node.

Remarks

If a null reference (**Nothing** in Visual Basic), the **Color** used is the **ForeColor** property value of the **TreeView** control that the tree node is assigned to.

Example

See related example in the **System.Windows.Forms.TreeNode** class topic.

Requirements

Platforms: Windows 98, Windows NT 4.0, Windows Millennium Edition, Windows 2000, Windows XP Home Edition, Windows XP Professional, Windows Server 2003 family

TreeNode.FullPath Property

Gets the path from the root tree node to the current tree node.

```
[Visual Basic]
Public ReadOnly Property FullPath As String
[C#]
public string FullPath {get;}
[C++]
public: __property String* get_FullPath();
[JScript]
public function get FullPath() : String;
```

Property Value

The path from the root tree node to the current tree node.

Remarks

The path consists of the labels of all the tree nodes that must be navigated to get to this tree node, starting at the root tree node. The node labels are separated by the delimiter character specified in the **PathSeparator** property of the **TreeView** control that contains this node. For example, if the delimiter character of the tree view control named "Location" is set to the backslash character, (\), the **FullPath** property value is "Country\Region\State".

Example

See related example in the **System.Windows.Forms.TreeNode** class topic.

Requirements

Platforms: Windows 98, Windows NT 4.0, Windows Millennium Edition, Windows 2000, Windows XP Home Edition, Windows XP Professional, Windows Server 2003 family, .NET Compact Framework - Windows CE .NET

TreeNode.Handle Property

Gets the handle of the tree node.

```
[Visual Basic]
Public ReadOnly Property Handle As IntPtr
[C#]
public IntPtr Handle {get;}
[C++]
public: __property IntPtr get_Handle();
[JScript]
public function get Handle() : IntPtr;
```

Property Value

The tree node handle.

Remarks

If a handle is not already created when the **Handle** property is referenced, it is created.

Example

See related example in the **System.Windows.Forms.TreeNode** class topic.

Requirements

Platforms: Windows 98, Windows NT 4.0, Windows Millennium Edition, Windows 2000, Windows XP Home Edition, Windows XP Professional, Windows Server 2003 family

TreeNode.ImageIndex Property

Gets or sets the image list index value of the image displayed when the tree node is in the unselected state.

```
[Visual Basic]
Public Property ImageIndex As Integer
[C#]
public int ImageIndex {get; set;}
```

```
[C++]
public: __property int get_ImageIndex();
public: __property void set_ImageIndex(int);
[JScript]
public function get ImageIndex() : int;
public function set ImageIndex(int);
```

Property Value

A zero-based index value that represents the image position in the assigned **ImageList**.

Remarks

The **ImageIndex** value is the index value of an **Image** stored in the **ImageList** assigned to the **TreeView.ImageList** property.

> **Note** The default value of the **ImageIndex** property is the same as the **ImageIndex** property of the **TreeView** control that the **TreeNode** is assigned to.

Example

See related example in the **System.Windows.Forms.TreeNode** class topic.

Requirements

Platforms: Windows 98, Windows NT 4.0,
Windows Millennium Edition, Windows 2000,
Windows XP Home Edition, Windows XP Professional,
Windows Server 2003 family,
.NET Compact Framework - Windows CE .NET

TreeNode.Index Property

Gets the position of the tree node in the tree node collection.

```
[Visual Basic]
Public ReadOnly Property Index As Integer
[C#]
public int Index {get;}
[C++]
public: __property int get_Index();
[JScript]
public function get Index() : int;
```

Property Value

A zero-based index value that represents the position of the tree node in the **Nodes** collection.

Example

See related example in the **System.Windows.Forms.TreeNode** class topic.

Requirements

Platforms: Windows 98, Windows NT 4.0,
Windows Millennium Edition, Windows 2000,
Windows XP Home Edition, Windows XP Professional,
Windows Server 2003 family,
.NET Compact Framework - Windows CE .NET

TreeNode.IsEditing Property

Gets a value indicating whether the tree node is in an editable state.

```
[Visual Basic]
Public ReadOnly Property IsEditing As Boolean
[C#]
public bool IsEditing {get;}
[C++]
public: __property bool get_IsEditing();
[JScript]
public function get IsEditing() : Boolean;
```

Property Value

true if the tree node is in editable state; otherwise, **false**.

Example

See related example in the **System.Windows.Forms.TreeNode** class topic.

Requirements

Platforms: Windows 98, Windows NT 4.0,
Windows Millennium Edition, Windows 2000,
Windows XP Home Edition, Windows XP Professional,
Windows Server 2003 family

TreeNode.IsExpanded Property

Gets a value indicating whether the tree node is in the expanded state.

```
[Visual Basic]
Public ReadOnly Property IsExpanded As Boolean
[C#]
public bool IsExpanded {get;}
[C++]
public: __property bool get_IsExpanded();
[JScript]
public function get IsExpanded() : Boolean;
```

Property Value

true if the tree node is in the expanded state; otherwise, **false**.

Example

See related example in the **System.Windows.Forms.TreeNode** class topic.

Requirements

Platforms: Windows 98, Windows NT 4.0,
Windows Millennium Edition, Windows 2000,
Windows XP Home Edition, Windows XP Professional,
Windows Server 2003 family,
.NET Compact Framework - Windows CE .NET

TreeNode.IsSelected Property

Gets a value indicating whether the tree node is in the selected state.

```
[Visual Basic]
Public ReadOnly Property IsSelected As Boolean
[C#]
public bool IsSelected {get;}
[C++]
public: __property bool get_IsSelected();
[JScript]
public function get IsSelected() : Boolean;
```

Property Value

true if the tree node is in the selected state; otherwise, **false**.

Example

See related example in the **System.Windows.Forms.TreeNode** class topic.

Requirements

Platforms: Windows 98, Windows NT 4.0, Windows Millennium Edition, Windows 2000, Windows XP Home Edition, Windows XP Professional, Windows Server 2003 family, .NET Compact Framework - Windows CE .NET

TreeNode.IsVisible Property

Gets a value indicating whether the tree node is visible.

```
[Visual Basic]
Public ReadOnly Property IsVisible As Boolean
[C#]
public bool IsVisible {get;}
[C++]
public: __property bool get_IsVisible();
[JScript]
public function get IsVisible() : Boolean;
```

Property Value

true if the tree node is visible; otherwise, **false**.

Example

See related example in the **System.Windows.Forms.TreeNode** class topic.

Requirements

Platforms: Windows 98, Windows NT 4.0, Windows Millennium Edition, Windows 2000, Windows XP Home Edition, Windows XP Professional, Windows Server 2003 family

TreeNode.LastNode Property

Gets the last child tree node.

```
[Visual Basic]
Public ReadOnly Property LastNode As TreeNode
[C#]
public TreeNode LastNode {get;}
[C++]
public: __property TreeNode* get_LastNode();
[JScript]
public function get LastNode() : TreeNode;
```

Property Value

A **TreeNode** that represents the last child tree node.

Remarks

The **LastNode** is the last child **TreeNode** in the **TreeNode-Collection** stored in the **Nodes** property of the current tree node. If the **TreeNode** has no child tree node, the **LastNode** property returns a null reference (**Nothing** in Visual Basic).

Example

See related example in the **System.Windows.Forms.TreeNode** class topic.

Requirements

Platforms: Windows 98, Windows NT 4.0, Windows Millennium Edition, Windows 2000, Windows XP Home Edition, Windows XP Professional, Windows Server 2003 family

TreeNode.NextNode Property

Gets the next sibling tree node.

```
[Visual Basic]
Public ReadOnly Property NextNode As TreeNode
[C#]
public TreeNode NextNode {get;}
[C++]
public: __property TreeNode* get_NextNode();
[JScript]
public function get NextNode() : TreeNode;
```

Property Value

A **TreeNode** that represents the next sibling tree node.

Remarks

The **NextNode** is the next sibling **TreeNode** in the **TreeNode-Collection** stored in the **Nodes** property of the tree node's parent **TreeNode**. If there is no next tree node, the **NextNode** property returns a null reference (**Nothing** in Visual Basic).

Example

See related example in the **System.Windows.Forms.TreeNode** class topic.

Requirements

Platforms: Windows 98, Windows NT 4.0, Windows Millennium Edition, Windows 2000, Windows XP Home Edition, Windows XP Professional, Windows Server 2003 family

TreeNode.NextVisibleNode Property

Gets the next visible tree node.

```
[Visual Basic]
Public ReadOnly Property NextVisibleNode As TreeNode
[C#]
public TreeNode NextVisibleNode {get;}
[C++]
public: __property TreeNode* get_NextVisibleNode();
[JScript]
public function get NextVisibleNode() : TreeNode;
```

Property Value

A **TreeNode** that represents the next visible tree node.

Remarks

The **NextVisibleNode** can be a child, sibling, or a tree node from another branch. If there is no next tree node, the **NextVisibleNode** property returns a null reference (**Nothing** in Visual Basic).

Example

See related example in the **System.Windows.Forms.TreeNode** class topic.

Requirements

Platforms: Windows 98, Windows NT 4.0, Windows Millennium Edition, Windows 2000, Windows XP Home Edition, Windows XP Professional, Windows Server 2003 family

TreeNode.NodeFont Property

Gets or sets the font used to display the text on the tree node's label.

```
[Visual Basic]
Public Property NodeFont As Font
[C#]
public Font NodeFont {get; set;}
[C++]
public: __property Font* get_NodeFont();
public: __property void set_NodeFont(Font*);
[JScript]
public function get NodeFont() : Font;
public function set NodeFont(Font);
```

Property Value

The **Font** used to display the text on the tree node's label.

Remarks

If a null reference (**Nothing** in Visual Basic), the **Font** used is the **Font** property value of the **TreeView** control that this node is attached to.

> **Note** If the node font is larger than the **Font** property value set in the **TreeView** control, the tree node label text is clipped.

Example

See related example in the **System.Windows.Forms.TreeNode** class topic.

Requirements

Platforms: Windows 98, Windows NT 4.0, Windows Millennium Edition, Windows 2000, Windows XP Home Edition, Windows XP Professional, Windows Server 2003 family

TreeNode.Nodes Property

Gets the collection of **TreeNode** objects assigned to the current tree node.

```
[Visual Basic]
Public ReadOnly Property Nodes As TreeNodeCollection
[C#]
public TreeNodeCollection Nodes {get;}
[C++]
public: __property TreeNodeCollection* get_Nodes();
[JScript]
public function get Nodes() : TreeNodeCollection;
```

Property Value

A **TreeNodeCollection** that represents the tree nodes assigned to the current tree node.

Remarks

The **Nodes** property can hold a collection of other **TreeNode** objects. Each of the tree node in the collection has a **Nodes** property that can contain its own **TreeNodeCollection**. This nesting of tree nodes can make it difficult to navigate a tree structure. The **FullPath** property makes it easier to determine your location in a tree.

Example

See related example in the **System.Windows.Forms.TreeNode** class topic.

Requirements

Platforms: Windows 98, Windows NT 4.0, Windows Millennium Edition, Windows 2000, Windows XP Home Edition, Windows XP Professional, Windows Server 2003 family, .NET Compact Framework - Windows CE .NET

TreeNode.Parent Property

Gets the parent tree node of the current tree node.

```
[Visual Basic]
Public ReadOnly Property Parent As TreeNode
[C#]
public TreeNode Parent {get;}
[C++]
public: __property TreeNode* get_Parent();
[JScript]
public function get Parent() : TreeNode;
```

Property Value

A **TreeNode** that represents the parent of the current tree node.

Remarks

If the tree node is at the root level, the **Parent** property returns a null reference (**Nothing** in Visual Basic).

Example

See related example in the **System.Windows.Forms.TreeNode** class topic.

Requirements

Platforms: Windows 98, Windows NT 4.0, Windows Millennium Edition, Windows 2000, Windows XP Home Edition, Windows XP Professional, Windows Server 2003 family, .NET Compact Framework - Windows CE .NET

TreeNode.PrevNode Property

Gets the previous sibling tree node.

```
[Visual Basic]
Public ReadOnly Property PrevNode As TreeNode
[C#]
public TreeNode PrevNode {get;}
[C++]
public: __property TreeNode* get_PrevNode();
[JScript]
public function get PrevNode() : TreeNode;
```

Property Value

A **TreeNode** that represents the previous sibling tree node.

Remarks

The **PrevNode** is the previous sibling **TreeNode** in the **TreeNodeCollection** stored in the **Nodes** property of the tree node's parent **TreeNode**. If there is no previous tree node, the **PrevNode** property returns a null reference (**Nothing** in Visual Basic).

Example

See related example in the **System.Windows.Forms.TreeNode** class topic.

Requirements

Platforms: Windows 98, Windows NT 4.0, Windows Millennium Edition, Windows 2000, Windows XP Home Edition, Windows XP Professional, Windows Server 2003 family

TreeNode.PrevVisibleNode Property

Gets the previous visible tree node.

```
[Visual Basic]
Public ReadOnly Property PrevVisibleNode As TreeNode
[C#]
public TreeNode PrevVisibleNode {get;}
[C++]
public: __property TreeNode* get_PrevVisibleNode();
[JScript]
public function get PrevVisibleNode() : TreeNode;
```

Property Value

A **TreeNode** that represents the previous visible tree node.

Remarks

The **PrevVisibleNode** can be a child, sibling, or a tree node from another branch. If there is no previous tree node, the **PrevVisibleNode** property returns a null reference (**Nothing** in Visual Basic).

Example

See related example in the **System.Windows.Forms.TreeNode** class topic.

Requirements

Platforms: Windows 98, Windows NT 4.0, Windows Millennium Edition, Windows 2000, Windows XP Home Edition, Windows XP Professional, Windows Server 2003 family

TreeNode.SelectedImageIndex Property

Gets or sets the image list index value of the image that is displayed when the tree node is in the selected state.

```
[Visual Basic]
Public Property SelectedImageIndex As Integer
[C#]
public int SelectedImageIndex {get; set;}
[C++]
public: __property int get_SelectedImageIndex();
public: __property void set_SelectedImageIndex(int);
[JScript]
public function get SelectedImageIndex() : int;
public function set SelectedImageIndex(int);
```

Property Value

A zero-based index value that represents the image position in an **ImageList**.

Remarks

The **SelectedImageIndex** value is the index value of an **Image** stored in the **ImageList** assigned to the **TreeView.ImageList** property.

Note The default value of the **SelectedImageIndex** property is the same as the **SelectedImageIndex** property of the **TreeView** control that the **TreeNode** is assigned to.

Example

See related example in the **System.Windows.Forms.TreeNode** class topic.

Requirements

Platforms: Windows 98, Windows NT 4.0, Windows Millennium Edition, Windows 2000, Windows XP Home Edition, Windows XP Professional, Windows Server 2003 family, .NET Compact Framework - Windows CE .NET

TreeNode.Tag Property

Gets or sets the object that contains data about the tree node.

```
[Visual Basic]
Public Property Tag As Object
[C#]
public object Tag {get; set;}
[C++]
public: __property Object* get_Tag();
public: __property void set_Tag(Object*);
[JScript]
public function get Tag() : Object;
public function set Tag(Object);
```

Property Value

An **Object** that contains data about the tree node. The default is a null reference (**Nothing** in Visual Basic).

Remarks

Any **Object** derived type can be assigned to this property. If this property is being set through the Windows Forms designer, only text can be assigned.

Example

See related example in the **System.Windows.Forms.TreeNode** class topic.

Requirements

Platforms: Windows 98, Windows NT 4.0, Windows Millennium Edition, Windows 2000, Windows XP Home Edition, Windows XP Professional, Windows Server 2003 family, .NET Compact Framework - Windows CE .NET

TreeNode.Text Property

Gets or sets the text displayed in the label of the tree node.

```
[Visual Basic]
Public Property Text As String
[C#]
public string Text {get; set;}
[C++]
public: __property String* get_Text();
public: __property void set_Text(String*);
[JScript]
public function get Text() : String;
public function set Text(String);
```

Property Value

The text displayed in the label of the tree node.

Remarks

This property cannot be set by the user if the **LabelEdit** property of the parent **TreeView** is set to **false**. The alternative to setting this property explicitly is to create the tree node using one of the **TreeNode** constructors that has a string parameter that represents the **Text** property. The label is displayed next to the **TreeNode** image, if one is displayed.

Example

See related example in the **System.Windows.Forms.TreeNode** class topic.

Requirements

Platforms: Windows 98, Windows NT 4.0, Windows Millennium Edition, Windows 2000, Windows XP Home Edition, Windows XP Professional, Windows Server 2003 family, .NET Compact Framework - Windows CE .NET

TreeNode.TreeView Property

Gets the parent tree view that the tree node is assigned to.

[Visual Basic]
```
Public ReadOnly Property TreeView As TreeView
```
[C#]
```
public TreeView TreeView {get;}
```
[C++]
```
public: __property TreeView* get_TreeView();
```
[JScript]
```
public function get TreeView() : TreeView;
```

Property Value

A **TreeView** that represents the parent tree view that the tree node is assigned to.

Example

See related example in the **System.Windows.Forms.TreeNode** class topic.

Requirements

Platforms: Windows 98, Windows NT 4.0, Windows Millennium Edition, Windows 2000, Windows XP Home Edition, Windows XP Professional, Windows Server 2003 family, .NET Compact Framework - Windows CE .NET

TreeNode.BeginEdit Method

Initiates the editing of the tree node label.

[Visual Basic]
```
Public Sub BeginEdit()
```
[C#]
```
public void BeginEdit();
```
[C++]
```
public: void BeginEdit();
```
[JScript]
```
public function BeginEdit();
```

Exceptions

Exception Type	Condition
Exception	**TreeView.LabelEdit** is set to **false**.

Remarks

A common place to use this method is to call it on the **Click** event of a **MenuItem** or **ContextMenu**.

> **Note** This method only works if the **LabelEdit** property of the **TreeView** is set to **true**. If **LabelEdit** is set to **false**, an exception is thrown and the tree node will not be put into an editable state.

Example

See related example in the **System.Windows.Forms.TreeNode** class topic.

Requirements

Platforms: Windows 98, Windows NT 4.0, Windows Millennium Edition, Windows 2000, Windows XP Home Edition, Windows XP Professional, Windows Server 2003 family

TreeNode.Clone Method

Copies the tree node and the entire subtree rooted at this tree node.

[Visual Basic]
```
Public Overridable Function Clone() As Object Implements _
   ICloneable.Clone
```
[C#]
```
public virtual object Clone();
```
[C++]
```
public: virtual Object* Clone();
```
[JScript]
```
public function Clone() : Object;
```

Return Value

The **Object** that represents the cloned **TreeNode** object.

Implements

ICloneable.Clone

Remarks

The tree structure from the tree node being cloned and below is copied. Any child tree nodes assigned to the **TreeNode** being cloned is included in the new tree node and subtree.

Example

See related example in the **System.Windows.Forms.TreeNode** class topic.

Requirements

Platforms: Windows 98, Windows NT 4.0, Windows Millennium Edition, Windows 2000, Windows XP Home Edition, Windows XP Professional, Windows Server 2003 family

TreeNode.Collapse Method

Collapses the tree node.

[Visual Basic]
```
Public Sub Collapse()
```
[C#]
```
public void Collapse();
```

```
[C++]
public: void Collapse();
[JScript]
public function Collapse();
```

Remarks

The **Collapse** method only collapses the current **TreeNode**; child tree nodes are not collapsed.

> **Note** The state of a **TreeNode** is persisted. For example, if the next level of child nodes was not collapsed previously, when the **Expand** method is called, the child nodes appear in their previously expanded state.

Example

See related example in the **System.Windows.Forms.TreeNode** class topic.

Requirements

Platforms: Windows 98, Windows NT 4.0, Windows Millennium Edition, Windows 2000, Windows XP Home Edition, Windows XP Professional, Windows Server 2003 family, .NET Compact Framework - Windows CE .NET

TreeNode.EndEdit Method

Ends the editing of the tree node label.

```
[Visual Basic]
Public Sub EndEdit( _
   ByVal cancel As Boolean _
)
[C#]
public void EndEdit(
   bool cancel
);
[C++]
public: void EndEdit(
   bool cancel
);
[JScript]
public function EndEdit(
   cancel : Boolean
);
```

Parameters

cancel

true if the editing of the tree node label text was canceled without being saved; otherwise, **false**.

Example

See related example in the **System.Windows.Forms.TreeNode** class topic.

Requirements

Platforms: Windows 98, Windows NT 4.0, Windows Millennium Edition, Windows 2000, Windows XP Home Edition, Windows XP Professional, Windows Server 2003 family

TreeNode.EnsureVisible Method

Ensures that the tree node is visible, expanding tree nodes and scrolling the tree view control as necessary.

```
[Visual Basic]
Public Sub EnsureVisible()
[C#]
public void EnsureVisible();
[C++]
public: void EnsureVisible();
[JScript]
public function EnsureVisible();
```

Remarks

When the **EnsureVisible** method is called, the tree is expanded and scrolled to ensure that the current tree node is visible in the **TreeView**. This method is useful if you are selecting a tree node in code based on certain criteria. By calling this method after selecting the node, it ensures that the user can see and interact with the selected node.

Example

See related example in the **System.Windows.Forms.TreeNode** class topic.

Requirements

Platforms: Windows 98, Windows NT 4.0, Windows Millennium Edition, Windows 2000, Windows XP Home Edition, Windows XP Professional, Windows Server 2003 family

TreeNode.Expand Method

Expands the tree node.

```
[Visual Basic]
Public Sub Expand()
[C#]
public void Expand();
[C++]
public: void Expand();
[JScript]
public function Expand();
```

Remarks

The **Expand** method expands the current **TreeNode** down to the next level of nodes.

> **Note** The state of a **TreeNode** is persisted. For example, if the next level of child nodes was not collapsed previously, when the **Expand** method is called, the child nodes appear in their previously expanded state.

Example

See related example in the **System.Windows.Forms.TreeNode** class topic.

Requirements

Platforms: Windows 98, Windows NT 4.0, Windows Millennium Edition, Windows 2000, Windows XP Home Edition, Windows XP Professional, Windows Server 2003 family, .NET Compact Framework - Windows CE .NET

TreeNode.ExpandAll Method

Expands all the child tree nodes.

```
[Visual Basic]
Public Sub ExpandAll()
[C#]
public void ExpandAll();
[C++]
public: void ExpandAll();
[JScript]
public function ExpandAll();
```

Remarks

The **ExpandAll** method expands all the child tree nodes assigned to the **Nodes** collection.

> **Note** The state of a **TreeNode** is persisted. For example, if the next level of child nodes was not collapsed previously, when the **Expand** method is called, the child nodes appear in their previously expanded state.

Example

See related example in the **System.Windows.Forms.TreeNode** class topic.

Requirements

Platforms: Windows 98, Windows NT 4.0,
Windows Millennium Edition, Windows 2000,
Windows XP Home Edition, Windows XP Professional,
Windows Server 2003 family,
.NET Compact Framework - Windows CE .NET

TreeNode.FromHandle Method

Returns the tree node with the specified handle and assigned to the specified tree view control.

```
[Visual Basic]
Public Shared Function FromHandle( _
   ByVal tree As TreeView, _
   ByVal handle As IntPtr _
) As TreeNode
[C#]
public static TreeNode FromHandle(
   TreeView tree,
   IntPtr handle
);
[C++]
public: static TreeNode* FromHandle(
   TreeView* tree,
   IntPtr handle
);
[JScript]
public static function FromHandle(
   tree : TreeView,
   handle : IntPtr
) : TreeNode;
```

Parameters

tree
The **TreeView** that contains the tree node.

handle
The handle of the tree node.

Return Value

A **TreeNode** that represents the tree node assigned to the specified **TreeView** control with the specified handle.

Example

See related example in the **System.Windows.Forms.TreeNode** class topic.

Requirements

Platforms: Windows 98, Windows NT 4.0,
Windows Millennium Edition, Windows 2000,
Windows XP Home Edition, Windows XP Professional,
Windows Server 2003 family

TreeNode.GetNodeCount Method

Returns the number of child tree nodes.

```
[Visual Basic]
Public Function GetNodeCount( _
   ByVal includeSubTrees As Boolean _
) As Integer
[C#]
public int GetNodeCount(
   bool includeSubTrees
);
[C++]
public: int GetNodeCount(
   bool includeSubTrees
);
[JScript]
public function GetNodeCount(
   includeSubTrees : Boolean
) : int;
```

Parameters

includeSubTrees
true if the resulting count includes all tree nodes indirectly rooted at this tree node; otherwise, **false**.

Return Value

The number of child tree nodes assigned to the **Nodes** collection.

Example

See related example in the **System.Windows.Forms.TreeNode** class topic.

Requirements

Platforms: Windows 98, Windows NT 4.0,
Windows Millennium Edition, Windows 2000,
Windows XP Home Edition, Windows XP Professional,
Windows Server 2003 family,
.NET Compact Framework - Windows CE .NET

TreeNode.ISerializable.GetObjectData Method

This member supports the .NET Framework infrastructure and is not intended to be used directly from your code.

```
[Visual Basic]
Private Sub GetObjectData( _
   ByVal si As SerializationInfo, _
   ByVal context As StreamingContext _
) Implements ISerializable.GetObjectData
```

[C#]
```
void ISerializable.GetObjectData(
   SerializationInfo si,
   StreamingContext context
);
```
[C++]
```
private: void ISerializable::GetObjectData(
   SerializationInfo* si,
   StreamingContext context
);
```
[JScript]
```
private function ISerializable.GetObjectData(
   si : SerializationInfo,
   context : StreamingContext
);
```

TreeNode.Remove Method

Removes the current tree node from the tree view control.

[Visual Basic]
```
Public Sub Remove()
```
[C#]
```
public void Remove();
```
[C++]
```
public: void Remove();
```
[JScript]
```
public function Remove();
```

Remarks

When the **Remove** method is called, the tree node and any child tree nodes assigned to the **TreeNode** are removed from the **TreeView**. The removed child nodes are removed from the **TreeView**, but are still attached to this tree node.

Example

See related example in the **System.Windows.Forms.TreeNode** class topic.

Requirements

Platforms: Windows 98, Windows NT 4.0, Windows Millennium Edition, Windows 2000, Windows XP Home Edition, Windows XP Professional, Windows Server 2003 family, .NET Compact Framework - Windows CE .NET

TreeNode.Toggle Method

Toggles the tree node to either the expanded or collapsed state.

[Visual Basic]
```
Public Sub Toggle()
```
[C#]
```
public void Toggle();
```
[C++]
```
public: void Toggle();
```
[JScript]
```
public function Toggle();
```

Remarks

The tree node is toggled to the state opposite its current state, either expanded or collapsed.

Note The state of a **TreeNode** is persisted. For example, if the next level of child nodes was not collapsed previously, when the **Expand** method is called, the child nodes appear in their previously expanded state.

Example

See related example in the **System.Windows.Forms.TreeNode** class topic.

Requirements

Platforms: Windows 98, Windows NT 4.0, Windows Millennium Edition, Windows 2000, Windows XP Home Edition, Windows XP Professional, Windows Server 2003 family, .NET Compact Framework - Windows CE .NET

TreeNode.ToString Method

This member overrides **Object.ToString**.

[Visual Basic]
```
Overrides Public Function ToString() As String
```
[C#]
```
public override string ToString();
```
[C++]
```
public: String* ToString();
```
[JScript]
```
public override function ToString() : String;
```

Requirements

Platforms: Windows 98, Windows NT 4.0, Windows Millennium Edition, Windows 2000, Windows XP Home Edition, Windows XP Professional, Windows Server 2003 family, .NET Compact Framework - Windows CE .NET

TreeNodeCollection Class

Represents a collection of **TreeNode** objects.

System.Object
 System.Windows.Forms.TreeNodeCollection

[Visual Basic]
```
Public Class TreeNodeCollection
   Implements IList, ICollection, IEnumerable
```
[C#]
```
public class TreeNodeCollection : IList, ICollection, IEnumerable
```
[C++]
```
public __gc class TreeNodeCollection : public IList, ICollection,
   IEnumerable
```
[JScript]
```
public class TreeNodeCollection implements IList, ICollection,
   IEnumerable
```

Thread Safety

Any public static (**Shared** in Visual Basic) members of this type are safe for multithreaded operations. Any instance members are not guaranteed to be thread safe.

Remarks

The **Add**, **Remove**, and **RemoveAt** methods enable you to add and remove individual tree nodes from the collection. You can also use the **AddRange** or **Clear** methods to add or remove all the tree nodes from the collection.

Example

See related example in the **System.Windows.Forms.TreeNode** class topic.

Requirements

Namespace: System.Windows.Forms

Platforms: Windows 98, Windows NT 4.0,
Windows Millennium Edition, Windows 2000,
Windows XP Home Edition, Windows XP Professional,
Windows Server 2003 family,
.NET Compact Framework - Windows CE .NET

Assembly: System.Windows.Forms (in System.Windows.Forms.dll)

TreeNodeCollection.Count Property

Gets the total number of **TreeNode** objects in the collection.

[Visual Basic]
```
Public Overridable ReadOnly Property Count As Integer  Implements _
   ICollection.Count
```
[C#]
```
public virtual int Count {get;}
```
[C++]
```
public: __property virtual int get_Count();
```
[JScript]
```
public function get Count() : int;
```

Property Value

The total number of **TreeNode** objects in the collection.

Implements

ICollection.Count

Remarks

The **Count** property holds the number of **TreeNode** objects assigned to the collection. You can use the **Count** property value as the upper bounds of a loop to iterate through a collection.

> **Note** Because the index value of a collection is a zero-based index, you must subtract one from the looping variable. If you do not account for this, you will exceed the upper bounds of the collection and throw an **IndexOutOfRangeException** exception.

Example

See related example in the **System.Windows.Forms.TreeNode** class topic.

Requirements

Platforms: Windows 98, Windows NT 4.0,
Windows Millennium Edition, Windows 2000,
Windows XP Home Edition, Windows XP Professional,
Windows Server 2003 family,
.NET Compact Framework - Windows CE .NET

TreeNodeCollection.IsReadOnly Property

Gets a value indicating whether the collection is read-only.

[Visual Basic]
```
Public Overridable ReadOnly Property IsReadOnly As Boolean _
   Implements IList.IsReadOnly
```
[C#]
```
public virtual bool IsReadOnly {get;}
```
[C++]
```
public: __property virtual bool get_IsReadOnly();
```
[JScript]
```
public function get IsReadOnly() : Boolean;
```

Property Value

true if the collection is read-only; otherwise, **false**. The default is **false**.

Implements

IList.IsReadOnly

Example

See related example in the **System.Windows.Forms.TreeNode** class topic.

Requirements

Platforms: Windows 98, Windows NT 4.0,
Windows Millennium Edition, Windows 2000,
Windows XP Home Edition, Windows XP Professional,
Windows Server 2003 family,
.NET Compact Framework - Windows CE .NET

TreeNodeCollection.Item Property

Indicates the **TreeNode** at the specified indexed location in the collection.

[C#] In C#, this property is the indexer for the **TreeNodeCollection** class.

[Visual Basic]
```
Public Overridable Default Property Item( _
   ByVal index As Integer _
) As TreeNode
```

[C#]
```
public virtual TreeNode this[
   int index
] {get; set;}
```
[C++]
```
public: __property virtual TreeNode* get_Item(
   int index
);
public: __property virtual void set_Item(
   int index,
   TreeNode*
);
```
[JScript]
```
returnValue = TreeNodeCollectionObject.Item(index);
TreeNodeCollectionObject.Item(index) = returnValue;
-or-
returnValue = TreeNodeCollectionObject(index);
TreeNodeCollectionObject(index) = returnValue;
```

[JScript] In JScript, you can use the default indexed properties defined by a type, but you cannot explicitly define your own. However, specifying the **expando** attribute on a class automatically provides a default indexed property whose type is **Object** and whose index type is **String**.

Arguments [JScript]

index
The indexed location of the **TreeNode** in the collection.

Parameters [Visual Basic, C#, C++]

index
The indexed location of the **TreeNode** in the collection.

Property Value

The **TreeNode** at the specified indexed location in the collection.

Exceptions

Exception Type	Condition
ArgumentOutOfRange-Exception	The *index* value is less than zero or is greater than the number of tree nodes in the collection.

Remarks

To assign **TreeNode** objects to a specific location, or to retrieve them from the **TreeNodeCollection**, you can reference the collection object with a specific index value. The index value of the **TreeNode-Collection** is a zero-based index.

Example

See related example in the **System.Windows.Forms.TreeNode** class topic.

Requirements

Platforms: Windows 98, Windows NT 4.0, Windows Millennium Edition, Windows 2000, Windows XP Home Edition, Windows XP Professional, Windows Server 2003 family

TreeNodeCollection.System.Collections.ICollection.IsSynchronized Property

Note: This namespace, class, or member is supported only in version 1.1 of the .NET Framework.

This member supports the .NET Framework infrastructure and is not intended to be used directly from your code.

[Visual Basic]
```
Private ReadOnly Property IsSynchronized As Boolean Implements _
   ICollection.IsSynchronized
```
[C#]
```
bool ICollection.IsSynchronized {get;}
```
[C++]
```
private: __property bool
   System::Collections::ICollection::get_IsSynchronized();
```
[JScript]
```
private function get ICollection.IsSynchronized() : Boolean;
```

TreeNodeCollection.System.Collections.ICollection.SyncRoot Property

Note: This namespace, class, or member is supported only in version 1.1 of the .NET Framework.

This member supports the .NET Framework infrastructure and is not intended to be used directly from your code.

[Visual Basic]
```
Private ReadOnly Property SyncRoot As Object Implements _
   ICollection.SyncRoot
```
[C#]
```
object ICollection.SyncRoot {get;}
```
[C++]
```
private: __property Object*
   System::Collections::ICollection::get_SyncRoot();
```
[JScript]
```
private function get ICollection.SyncRoot() : Object;
```

TreeNodeCollection.System.Collections.IList.IsFixedSize Property

Note: This namespace, class, or member is supported only in version 1.1 of the .NET Framework.

This member supports the .NET Framework infrastructure and is not intended to be used directly from your code.

[Visual Basic]
```
Private ReadOnly Property IsFixedSize As Boolean Implements _
   IList.IsFixedSize
```
[C#]
```
bool IList.IsFixedSize {get;}
```
[C++]
```
private: __property bool
   System::Collections::IList::get_IsFixedSize();
```
[JScript]
```
private function get IList.IsFixedSize() : Boolean;
```

TreeNodeCollection.System.Collections.IList.Item Property

Note: This namespace, class, or member is supported only in version 1.1 of the .NET Framework.

[C#] In C#, this property is the indexer for the **TreeNodeCollection** class.

```
[Visual Basic]
Private Default Property Item( _
   ByVal index As Integer _
) As Object Implements IList.Item
[C#]
object IList.this[
   int index
] {get; set;}
[C++]
private: __property Object* System::Collections::IList::get_Item(
   int index
);
private: __property void System::Collections::IList::set_Item(
   int index,
   Object*
);
[JScript]
private function get IList.get_Item(index : int) : Object;
private function set IList.set_Item(index : int, value : Object);
-or-
private function get IList.get_Item(index : int) : Object;
private function set IList.set_Item(index : int, value : Object);
```

[JScript] In JScript, you can use the default indexed properties defined by a type, but you cannot explicitly define your own. However, specifying the **expando** attribute on a class automatically provides a default indexed property whose type is **Object** and whose index type is **String**.

Arguments [JScript]

index

Parameters [Visual Basic, C#, C++]

index

Requirements

Platforms: Windows 98, Windows NT 4.0, Windows Millennium Edition, Windows 2000, Windows XP Home Edition, Windows XP Professional, Windows Server 2003 family

TreeNodeCollection.Add Method

Adds a new tree node to the collection.

Overload List

Adds a new tree node to the end of the current tree node collection with the specified label text.

Supported by the .NET Compact Framework.

[Visual Basic] **Overloads Public Overridable Function Add(String) As TreeNode**

[C#] **public virtual TreeNode Add(string);**

[C++] **public: virtual TreeNode* Add(String*);**

[JScript] **public function Add(String) : TreeNode;**

Adds a previously created tree node to the end of the tree node collection.

Supported by the .NET Compact Framework.

[Visual Basic] **Overloads Public Overridable Function Add(TreeNode) As Integer**

[C#] **public virtual int Add(TreeNode);**

[C++] **public: virtual int Add(TreeNode*);**

[JScript] **public function Add(TreeNode) : int;**

Example

See related example in the **System.Windows.Forms.TreeNode** class topic.

TreeNodeCollection.Add Method (String)

Adds a new tree node to the end of the current tree node collection with the specified label text.

```
[Visual Basic]
Overloads Public Overridable Function Add( _
   ByVal text As String _
) As TreeNode
[C#]
public virtual TreeNode Add(
   string text
);
[C++]
public: virtual TreeNode* Add(
   String* text
);
[JScript]
public function Add(
   text : String
) : TreeNode;
```

Parameters

text

The label text displayed by the **TreeNode**.

Return Value

A **TreeNode** that represents the tree node being added to the collection.

Remarks

You can also add new **TreeNode** objects to the collection by using the **AddRange** or **Insert** methods.

To remove a **TreeNode** that you previously added, use the **Remove**, **RemoveAt** or **Clear** methods.

Example

See related example in the **System.Windows.Forms.TreeNode** class topic.

Requirements

Platforms: Windows 98, Windows NT 4.0, Windows Millennium Edition, Windows 2000, Windows XP Home Edition, Windows XP Professional, Windows Server 2003 family, .NET Compact Framework - Windows CE .NET

TreeNodeCollection.Add Method (TreeNode)

Adds a previously created tree node to the end of the tree node collection.

```
[Visual Basic]
Overloads Public Overridable Function Add( _
   ByVal node As TreeNode _
) As Integer
[C#]
public virtual int Add(
   TreeNode node
);
[C++]
public: virtual int Add(
   TreeNode* node
);
[JScript]
public function Add(
   node : TreeNode
) : int;
```

Parameters

node

The **TreeNode** to add to the collection.

Return Value

The zero-based index value of the **TreeNode** added to the tree node collection.

Exceptions

Exception Type	Condition
Exception	The *node* is currently assigned to another **TreeView** control.

Remarks

This version of the **Add** method allows you to add previously created **TreeNode** objects to the end of the tree node collection.

You can also add new **TreeNode** objects to the collection by using the **AddRange** or **Insert** methods.

To remove a **TreeNode** that you previously added, use the **Remove**, **RemoveAt** or **Clear** methods.

> **Note** A **TreeNode** object can only be assigned to one **TreeView** control at a time. To add the tree node to a new tree view control, you must remove it from the other tree view first, or clone it.

Example

See related example in the **System.Windows.Forms.TreeNode** class topic.

Requirements

Platforms: Windows 98, Windows NT 4.0,
Windows Millennium Edition, Windows 2000,
Windows XP Home Edition, Windows XP Professional,
Windows Server 2003 family,
.NET Compact Framework - Windows CE .NET

TreeNodeCollection.AddRange Method

Adds an array of previously created tree nodes to the collection.

```
[Visual Basic]
Public Overridable Sub AddRange( _
   ByVal nodes() As TreeNode _
)
[C#]
public virtual void AddRange(
   TreeNode[] nodes
);
[C++]
public: virtual void AddRange(
   TreeNode* nodes[]
);
[JScript]
public function AddRange(
   nodes : TreeNode[]
);
```

Parameters

nodes

An array of **TreeNode** objects representing the tree nodes to add to the collection.

Remarks

The **TreeNode** objects contained in the *nodes* array are appended to the end of the collection.

You can use the **AddRange** method to quickly add a group of previously created **TreeNode** objects to the collection instead of manually adding each **TreeNode** to the collection using the **Add** method.

To remove a **TreeNode** that you previously added, use the **Remove**, **RemoveAt** or **Clear** methods.

Example

See related example in the **System.Windows.Forms.TreeNode** class topic.

Requirements

Platforms: Windows 98, Windows NT 4.0,
Windows Millennium Edition, Windows 2000,
Windows XP Home Edition, Windows XP Professional,
Windows Server 2003 family,
.NET Compact Framework - Windows CE .NET

TreeNodeCollection.Clear Method

Removes all tree nodes from the collection.

```
[Visual Basic]
Public Overridable Sub Clear() Implements IList.Clear
[C#]
public virtual void Clear();
[C++]
public: virtual void Clear();
[JScript]
public function Clear();
```

Implements

IList.Clear

Remarks

You can use this method to clear the entire collection of tree nodes from a tree view.

To remove an individual tree node from the collection, use the **Remove** or **RemoveAt** methods.

To add new **TreeNode** objects to the collection, use the **Add**, **AddRange** or **Insert** methods.

Example

See related example in the **System.Windows.Forms.TreeNode** class topic.

Requirements

Platforms: Windows 98, Windows NT 4.0, Windows Millennium Edition, Windows 2000, Windows XP Home Edition, Windows XP Professional, Windows Server 2003 family, .NET Compact Framework - Windows CE .NET

TreeNodeCollection.Contains Method

Determines whether the specified tree node is a member of the collection.

```
[Visual Basic]
Public Function Contains( _
   ByVal node As TreeNode _
) As Boolean
[C#]
public bool Contains(
   TreeNode node
);
[C++]
public: bool Contains(
   TreeNode* node
);
[JScript]
public function Contains(
   node : TreeNode
) : Boolean;
```

Parameters

node

The **TreeNode** to locate in the collection.

Return Value

true if the **TreeNode** is a member of the collection; otherwise, **false**.

Remarks

This method enables you to determine whether a **TreeNode** is a member of the collection before attempting to perform operations on the **TreeNode**. You can use this method to confirm that a **TreeNode** has been added to or is still a member of the collection.

Example

See related example in the **System.Windows.Forms.TreeNode** class topic.

Requirements

Platforms: Windows 98, Windows NT 4.0, Windows Millennium Edition, Windows 2000, Windows XP Home Edition, Windows XP Professional, Windows Server 2003 family, .NET Compact Framework - Windows CE .NET

TreeNodeCollection.CopyTo Method

Copies the entire collection into an existing array at a specified location within the array.

```
[Visual Basic]
Public Overridable Sub CopyTo( _
   ByVal dest As Array, _
   ByVal index As Integer _
) Implements ICollection.CopyTo
[C#]
public virtual void CopyTo(
   Array dest,
   int index
);
[C++]
public: virtual void CopyTo(
   Array* dest,
   int index
);
[JScript]
public function CopyTo(
   dest : Array,
   index : int
);
```

Parameters

dest

The destination array.

index

The index in the destination array at which storing begins.

Implements

ICollection.CopyTo

Example

See related example in the **System.Windows.Forms.TreeNode** class topic.

Requirements

Platforms: Windows 98, Windows NT 4.0, Windows Millennium Edition, Windows 2000, Windows XP Home Edition, Windows XP Professional, Windows Server 2003 family, .NET Compact Framework - Windows CE .NET

TreeNodeCollection.GetEnumerator Method

Returns an enumerator that can be used to iterate through the tree node collection.

```
[Visual Basic]
Public Overridable Function GetEnumerator() As IEnumerator _
   Implements IEnumerable.GetEnumerator
[C#]
public virtual IEnumerator GetEnumerator();
[C++]
public: virtual IEnumerator* GetEnumerator();
[JScript]
public function GetEnumerator() : IEnumerator;
```

Return Value

An **IEnumerator** object that represents the tree node collection.

Implements

IEnumerable.GetEnumerator

Example

See related example in the **System.Windows.Forms.TreeNode** class topic.

Requirements

Platforms: Windows 98, Windows NT 4.0, Windows Millennium Edition, Windows 2000, Windows XP Home Edition, Windows XP Professional, Windows Server 2003 family, .NET Compact Framework - Windows CE .NET

TreeNodeCollection.IList.Add Method

This member supports the .NET Framework infrastructure and is not intended to be used directly from your code.

```
[Visual Basic]
Private Function Add( _
   ByVal node As Object _
) As Integer Implements IList.Add
[C#]
int IList.Add(
   object node
);
[C++]
private: int IList::Add(
   Object* node
);
[JScript]
private function IList.Add(
   node : Object
) : int;
```

TreeNodeCollection.IList.Contains Method

This member supports the .NET Framework infrastructure and is not intended to be used directly from your code.

```
[Visual Basic]
Private Function Contains( _
   ByVal node As Object _
) As Boolean Implements IList.Contains
[C#]
bool IList.Contains(
   object node
);
[C++]
private: bool IList::Contains(
   Object* node
);
[JScript]
private function IList.Contains(
   node : Object
) : Boolean;
```

TreeNodeCollection.IList.IndexOf Method

This member supports the .NET Framework infrastructure and is not intended to be used directly from your code.

```
[Visual Basic]
Private Function IndexOf( _
   ByVal node As Object _
) As Integer Implements IList.IndexOf
[C#]
int IList.IndexOf(
   object node
);
[C++]
private: int IList::IndexOf(
   Object* node
);
[JScript]
private function IList.IndexOf(
   node : Object
) : int;
```

TreeNodeCollection.IList.Insert Method

This member supports the .NET Framework infrastructure and is not intended to be used directly from your code.

```
[Visual Basic]
Private Sub Insert( _
   ByVal index As Integer, _
   ByVal node As Object _
) Implements IList.Insert
[C#]
void IList.Insert(
   int index,
   object node
);
[C++]
private: void IList::Insert(
   int index,
   Object* node
);
[JScript]
private function IList.Insert(
   index : int,
   node : Object
);
```

TreeNodeCollection.IList.Remove Method

This member supports the .NET Framework infrastructure and is not intended to be used directly from your code.

```
[Visual Basic]
Private Sub Remove( _
   ByVal node As Object _
) Implements IList.Remove
[C#]
void IList.Remove(
   object node
);
[C++]
private: void IList::Remove(
   Object* node
);
```

```
[JScript]
private function IList.Remove(
   node : Object
);
```

TreeNodeCollection.IndexOf Method

Returns the index of the specified tree node in the collection.

```
[Visual Basic]
Public Function IndexOf( _
   ByVal node As TreeNode _
) As Integer
[C#]
public int IndexOf(
   TreeNode node
);
[C++]
public: int IndexOf(
   TreeNode* node
);
[JScript]
public function IndexOf(
   node : TreeNode
) : int;
```

Parameters

node

The **TreeNode** to locate in the collection.

Return Value

The zero-based index of the item found in the tree node collection; otherwise, -1.

Example

See related example in the **System.Windows.Forms.TreeNode** class topic.

Requirements

Platforms: Windows 98, Windows NT 4.0, Windows Millennium Edition, Windows 2000, Windows XP Home Edition, Windows XP Professional, Windows Server 2003 family, .NET Compact Framework - Windows CE .NET

TreeNodeCollection.Insert Method

Inserts an existing tree node in the tree node collection at the specified location.

```
[Visual Basic]
Public Overridable Sub Insert( _
   ByVal index As Integer, _
   ByVal node As TreeNode _
)
[C#]
public virtual void Insert(
   int index,
   TreeNode node
);
[C++]
public: virtual void Insert(
   int index,
   TreeNode* node
);
[JScript]
public function Insert(
   index : int,
   node : TreeNode
);
```

Parameters

index

The indexed location within the collection to insert the tree node.

node

The **TreeNode** to insert into the collection.

Exceptions

Exception Type	Condition
ArgumentException	The *node* is currently assigned to another **TreeView** control.

Remarks

If the **TreeView.Sorted** property is set to **true**, the *index* parameter value is ignored. The **TreeNode** is inserted into the tree view and the **TreeView** resorted.

You can also add new **TreeNode** objects to the collection by using the **Add** or **AddRange** methods.

To remove a **TreeNode** that you previously added, use the **Remove**, **RemoveAt** or **Clear** methods.

Note A **TreeNode** object can only be assigned to one **TreeView** control at a time. To add the tree node to a new tree view control, you must remove it from the other tree view first, or clone it.

Example

See related example in the **System.Windows.Forms.TreeNode** class topic.

Requirements

Platforms: Windows 98, Windows NT 4.0, Windows Millennium Edition, Windows 2000, Windows XP Home Edition, Windows XP Professional, Windows Server 2003 family, .NET Compact Framework - Windows CE .NET

TreeNodeCollection.Remove Method

Removes the specified tree node from the tree node collection.

```
[Visual Basic]
Public Sub Remove( _
   ByVal node As TreeNode _
)
[C#]
public void Remove(
   TreeNode node
);
[C++]
public: void Remove(
   TreeNode* node
);
[JScript]
public function Remove(
   node : TreeNode
);
```

Parameters

node

The **TreeNode** to remove.

Remarks

When a **TreeNode** is removed from the tree node collection, all subsequent tree nodes are moved up one position in the collection.

You can also remove a **TreeNode** that you previously added by using the **RemoveAt** or **Clear** methods.

To add new **TreeNode** objects to the collection, use the **Add**, **AddRange**, or **Insert** methods.

Example

See related example in the **System.Windows.Forms.TreeNode** class topic.

Requirements

Platforms: Windows 98, Windows NT 4.0, Windows Millennium Edition, Windows 2000, Windows XP Home Edition, Windows XP Professional, Windows Server 2003 family, .NET Compact Framework - Windows CE .NET

TreeNodeCollection.RemoveAt Method

Removes a tree node from the tree node collection at a specified index.

```
[Visual Basic]
Public Overridable Sub RemoveAt( _
   ByVal index As Integer _
) Implements IList.RemoveAt
[C#]
public virtual void RemoveAt(
   int index
);
[C++]
public: virtual void RemoveAt(
   int index
);
[JScript]
public function RemoveAt(
   index : int
);
```

Parameters

index

The index of the **TreeNode** to remove.

Implements

IList.RemoveAt

Remarks

When a **TreeNode** is removed from the tree node collection, all subsequent tree nodes are moved up one position in the collection.

You can also remove a **TreeNode** that you previously added by using the **Remove** or **Clear** methods.

To add new **TreeNode** objects to the collection, use the **Add**, **AddRange**, or **Insert** methods.

Example

See related example in the **System.Windows.Forms.TreeNode** class topic.

Requirements

Platforms: Windows 98, Windows NT 4.0, Windows Millennium Edition, Windows 2000, Windows XP Home Edition, Windows XP Professional, Windows Server 2003 family, .NET Compact Framework - Windows CE .NET

TreeNodeConverter Class

Provides a type converter to convert **TreeNode** objects to and from various other representations.

System.Object
  System.ComponentModel.TypeConverter
    System.Windows.Forms.TreeNodeConverter

```
[Visual Basic]
Public Class TreeNodeConverter
   Inherits TypeConverter
[C#]
public class TreeNodeConverter : TypeConverter
[C++]
public __gc class TreeNodeConverter : public TypeConverter
[JScript]
public class TreeNodeConverter extends TypeConverter
```

Thread Safety

Any public static (**Shared** in Visual Basic) members of this type are safe for multithreaded operations. Any instance members are not guaranteed to be thread safe.

Remarks

For more information about type converters, see the **TypeConverter** base class and **Implementing a Type Converter**.

> **Note** You should never create an instance of a **TreeNodeConverter**. Instead, call the **GetConverter** method of **TypeDescriptor**. For more information, see the examples in the **TypeConverter** base class.

Requirements

Namespace: System.Windows.Forms

Platforms: Windows 98, Windows NT 4.0, Windows Millennium Edition, Windows 2000, Windows XP Home Edition, Windows XP Professional, Windows Server 2003 family

Assembly: System.Windows.Forms (in System.Windows.Forms.dll)

TreeNodeConverter Constructor

Initializes a new instance of the **TreeNodeConverter** class.

```
[Visual Basic]
Public Sub New()
[C#]
public TreeNodeConverter();
[C++]
public: TreeNodeConverter();
[JScript]
public function TreeNodeConverter();
```

Remarks

The default constructor initializes any fields to their default values.

Requirements

Platforms: Windows 98, Windows NT 4.0, Windows Millennium Edition, Windows 2000, Windows XP Home Edition, Windows XP Professional, Windows Server 2003 family

TreeNodeConverter.CanConvertTo Method

Overload List

This member supports the .NET Framework infrastructure and is not intended to be used directly from your code.

[Visual Basic] **Overloads Overrides Public Function CanConvertTo(ITypeDescriptorContext, Type) As Boolean**

[C#] **public override bool CanConvertTo(ITypeDescriptorContext, Type);**

[C++] **public: bool CanConvertTo(ITypeDescriptorContext*, Type*);**

[JScript] **public override function CanConvertTo(ITypeDescriptorContext, Type) : Boolean;**

Inherited from **TypeConverter**.

[Visual Basic] **Overloads Public Function CanConvertTo(Type) As Boolean**

[C#] **public bool CanConvertTo(Type);**

[C++] **public: bool CanConvertTo(Type*);**

[JScript] **public function CanConvertTo(Type) : Boolean;**

TreeNodeConverter.CanConvertTo Method (ITypeDescriptorContext, Type)

This member overrides **TypeConverter.CanConvertTo**.

```
[Visual Basic]
Overrides Overloads Public Function CanConvertTo( _
   ByVal context As ITypeDescriptorContext, _
   ByVal destinationType As Type _
) As Boolean
[C#]
public override bool CanConvertTo(
   ITypeDescriptorContext context,
   Type destinationType
);
[C++]
public: bool CanConvertTo(
   ITypeDescriptorContext* context,
   Type* destinationType
);
[JScript]
public override function CanConvertTo(
   context : ITypeDescriptorContext,
   destinationType : Type
) : Boolean;
```

Requirements

Platforms: Windows 98, Windows NT 4.0, Windows Millennium Edition, Windows 2000, Windows XP Home Edition, Windows XP Professional, Windows Server 2003 family

TreeNodeConverter.ConvertTo Method

Overload List

This member supports the .NET Framework infrastructure and is not intended to be used directly from your code.

[Visual Basic] **Overloads Overrides Public Function ConvertTo(ITypeDescriptorContext, CultureInfo, Object, Type) As Object**

[C#] **public override object ConvertTo(ITypeDescriptorContext, CultureInfo, object, Type);**

[C++] **public: Object* ConvertTo(ITypeDescriptorContext*, CultureInfo*, Object*, Type*);**

[JScript] **public override function ConvertTo(ITypeDescriptorContext, CultureInfo, Object, Type) : Object;**

Inherited from **TypeConverter**.

[Visual Basic] **Overloads Public Function ConvertTo(Object, Type) As Object**

[C#] **public object ConvertTo(object, Type);**

[C++] **public: Object* ConvertTo(Object*, Type*);**

[JScript] **public function ConvertTo(Object, Type) : Object;**

TreeNodeConverter.ConvertTo Method (ITypeDescriptorContext, CultureInfo, Object, Type)

This member overrides **TypeConverter.ConvertTo**.

[Visual Basic]
```
Overrides Overloads Public Function ConvertTo( _
   ByVal context As ITypeDescriptorContext, _
   ByVal culture As CultureInfo, _
   ByVal value As Object, _
   ByVal destinationType As Type _
) As Object
```
[C#]
```
public override object ConvertTo(
   ITypeDescriptorContext context,
   CultureInfo culture,
   object value,
   Type destinationType
);
```
[C++]
```
public: Object* ConvertTo(
   ITypeDescriptorContext* context,
   CultureInfo* culture,
   Object* value,
   Type* destinationType
);
```
[JScript]
```
public override function ConvertTo(
   context : ITypeDescriptorContext,
   culture : CultureInfo,
   value : Object,
   destinationType : Type
) : Object;
```

Requirements

Platforms: Windows 98, Windows NT 4.0, Windows Millennium Edition, Windows 2000, Windows XP Home Edition, Windows XP Professional, Windows Server 2003 family

TreeView Class

Displays a hierarchical collection of labeled items, each represented by a **TreeNode**.

System.Object
  System.MarshalByRefObject
    System.ComponentModel.Component
      System.Windows.Forms.Control
        System.Windows.Forms.TreeView

[Visual Basic]
```
Public Class TreeView
   Inherits Control
```
[C#]
```
public class TreeView : Control
```
[C++]
```
public __gc class TreeView : public Control
```
[JScript]
```
public class TreeView extends Control
```

Thread Safety

Any public static (**Shared** in Visual Basic) members of this type are safe for multithreaded operations. Any instance members are not guaranteed to be thread safe.

Remarks

The **Nodes** collection holds all the **TreeNode** objects that are assigned to the **TreeView** control. The tree nodes in this collection are referred to as the root tree nodes. Any tree node that is subsequently added to a root tree node is referred to as a child node. Because each **TreeNode** can contain a collection of other **TreeNode** objects, you might find it difficult to determine your location in the tree structure when you iterate through the collection. You can parse the **TreeNode.FullPath** string by using the **PathSeparator** string value to determine where a **TreeNode** label begins and ends.

You can display images next to the tree nodes by assigning an **ImageList** object to the **ImageList** property, and referencing the index value of an **Image** in the **ImageList** to assign that **Image**. Set the **ImageIndex** property to the index value of the **Image** that you want to display when a tree node is not selected. Likewise, set the **SelectedImageIndex** property to the index value of the **Image** that you want to display when a tree node is selected. The images referenced by the **ImageIndex** and **SelectedImageIndex** property values are the default images displayed by all the tree nodes that are assigned to the **Nodes** collection. Each tree node can override the default images by setting the **TreeNode.ImageIndex** and **TreeNode.SelectedImageIndex** properties.

Tree nodes can be expanded to display the next level of child tree nodes. The user can expand the **TreeNode** by clicking the plus-sign (+) button, if one is displayed next to the **TreeNode**, or you can expand the **TreeNode** by calling the **TreeNode.Expand** method. To expand all the child tree node levels in the **Nodes** collection, call the **ExpandAll** method. You can collapse the child **TreeNode** level by calling the **TreeNode.Collapse** method, or the user can press the minus-sign (-) button, if one is displayed next to the **TreeNode**. You can also call the **TreeNode.Toggle** method to alternate between the expanded and collapsed states.

Tree nodes can optionally display check boxes. To display the check boxes, set the **CheckBoxes** property of the **TreeView** to **true**. The **Checked** property is set to **true** for tree nodes that are in a checked state.

> **Note** Setting the **TreeNode.Checked** property from within the **BeforeCheck** or **AfterCheck** event causes the event to be raised multiple times and can result in unexpected behavior. For example, you might set the **Checked** property in the event handler when you are recursively updating the child nodes, so the user does not have to expand and check each one individually. To prevent the event from being raised multiple times, add logic to your event handler that only executes your recursive code if the **Action** property of the **TreeViewEventArgs** is not set to **TreeViewAction.Unknown**. For an example of how to do this, see the Example section of the **AfterCheck** or **BeforeCheck** events.

You can change the appearance of the **TreeView** control by setting some of its display and style properties. Setting **ShowPlusMinus** to **true** displays a plus-sign or minus-sign button next to each **TreeNode** object that can be expanded or collapsed, respectively. Setting the **ShowRootLines** property to **true** causes the **TreeView** to display lines that join all the root tree nodes together. You can display lines that connect child tree nodes to their root node by setting the **ShowLines** property to **true**. Setting the **HotTracking** property to **true** changes the appearance of the tree node labels as the mouse pointer passes over them. When hot-tracked, the tree node labels take on the appearance of a hyperlink.

> **Note** When setting the **CheckBoxes**, **Scrollable**, **ImageIndex**, and **SelectedImageIndex** properties at run time, the **TreeView** handle is recreated (see **Control.RecreateHandle**) to update the control's appearance. This causes all tree nodes to be collapsed, with the exception of the selected **TreeNode**.

Example

[Visual Basic, C#, C++] The following example displays customer information in a **TreeView** control. The root tree nodes display customer names, and the child tree nodes display the order numbers assigned to each customer. In this example, 1,000 customers are displayed with 15 orders each. The repainting of the **TreeView** is suppressed by using the **BeginUpdate** and **EndUpdate** methods, and a wait **Cursor** is displayed while the **TreeView** creates and paints the **TreeNode** objects. This example assumes you have a `Customer` object that can hold a collection of `Order` objects. It also assumes that you have a cursor file named `MyWait.cur` in the application directory and that you have created an instance of a **TreeView** control on a **Form**.

[Visual Basic]
```
' Create a new ArrayList to hold the Customer objects.
Private customerArray As New ArrayList()

Private Sub FillMyTreeView()
   ' Add customers to the ArrayList of Customer objects.
   Dim x As Integer
   For x = 0 To 999
      customerArray.Add(New Customer("Customer" + x.ToString()))
   Next x

   ' Add orders to each Customer object in the ArrayList.
   Dim customer1 As Customer
   For Each customer1 In customerArray
      Dim y As Integer
      For y = 0 To 14
         customer1.CustomerOrders.Add(New Order("Order" +        ↵
y.ToString()))
      Next y
   Next customer1
```

```
   ' Display a wait cursor while the TreeNodes are being created.
   Cursor.Current = New Cursor("MyWait.cur")

   ' Suppress repainting the TreeView until all the objects ↵
have been created.
   treeView1.BeginUpdate()

   ' Clear the TreeView each time the method is called.
   treeView1.Nodes.Clear()

   ' Add a root TreeNode for each Customer object in the ArrayList.
   Dim customer2 As Customer
   For Each customer2 In customerArray
      treeView1.Nodes.Add(New TreeNode(customer2.CustomerName))

      ' Add a child TreeNode for each Order object in the ↵
current Customer object.
      Dim order1 As Order
      For Each order1 In customer2.CustomerOrders
         treeView1.Nodes(customerArray.IndexOf(customer2)).Nodes.Add( _
    New TreeNode(customer2.CustomerName + "." + order1.OrderID))
      Next order1
   Next customer2

   ' Reset the cursor to the default for all controls.
   Cursor.Current = System.Windows.Forms.Cursors.Default

   ' Begin repainting the TreeView.
   treeView1.EndUpdate()
End Sub 'FillMyTreeView
```

[C#]

```
// Create a new ArrayList to hold the Customer objects.
private ArrayList customerArray = new ArrayList();

private void FillMyTreeView()
{
   // Add customers to the ArrayList of Customer objects.
   for(int x=0; x<1000; x++)
   {
      customerArray.Add(new Customer("Customer" + x.ToString()));
   }

   // Add orders to each Customer object in the ArrayList.
   foreach(Customer customer1 in customerArray)
   {
      for(int y=0; y<15; y++)
      {
         customer1.CustomerOrders.Add(new Order("Order" + ↵
y.ToString()));
      }
   }

   // Display a wait cursor while the TreeNodes are being created.
   Cursor.Current = new Cursor("MyWait.cur");

   // Suppress repainting the TreeView until all the objects ↵
have been created.
   treeView1.BeginUpdate();

   // Clear the TreeView each time the method is called.
   treeView1.Nodes.Clear();

   // Add a root TreeNode for each Customer object in the ArrayList.
   foreach(Customer customer2 in customerArray)
   {
      treeView1.Nodes.Add(new TreeNode(customer2.CustomerName));

      // Add a child treenode for each Order object in the ↵
 current Customer object.
      foreach(Order order1 in customer2.CustomerOrders)
      {
         treeView1.Nodes[customerArray.IndexOf(customer2)].Nodes.Add(
           new TreeNode(customer2.CustomerName + "." + ↵
order1.OrderID));
      }
   }

   // Reset the cursor to the default for all controls.
   Cursor.Current = Cursors.Default;

   // Begin repainting the TreeView.
   treeView1.EndUpdate();
}
```

[C++]

```
void FillMyTreeView() {
    // Add customers to the ArrayList of Customer objects.
    for (int x=0; x<1000; x++) {
        customerArray->Add(new Customer(String::Concat ↵
 (S"Customer ", __box(x))));
    }

    // Add orders to each Customer object in the ArrayList.
    IEnumerator* myEnum = customerArray->GetEnumerator();
    while (myEnum->MoveNext()) {
        Customer* customer1 = __try_cast<Customer*>(myEnum->Current);

        for (int y=0; y<15; y++) {
            customer1->CustomerOrders->Add(new ↵
Order(String::Concat(S"Order ", __box(y))));
        }
    }

    // Display a wait cursor while the TreeNodes are being created.
    Cursor::Current = new ↵
System::Windows::Forms::Cursor(S"MyWait.cur");

    // Suppress repainting the TreeView until all the objects ↵
 have been created.
    treeView1->BeginUpdate();

    // Clear the TreeView each time the method is called.
    treeView1->Nodes->Clear();

    // Add a root TreeNode for each Customer object in the ArrayList.
    while (myEnum->MoveNext()) {
        Customer* customer2 = __try_cast<Customer*>(myEnum->Current);

        treeView1->Nodes->Add(new TreeNode(customer2->CustomerName));

        // Add a child treenode for each Order object in the ↵
 current Customer object.
        IEnumerator* myEnum = customer2->CustomerOrders- ↵
>GetEnumerator();
        while (myEnum->MoveNext()) {
            Order* order1 = __try_cast<Order*>(myEnum->Current);

            treeView1->Nodes->Item[customerArray-> ↵
IndexOf(customer2)]->Nodes->Add(
                new TreeNode(String::Concat(customer2-> ↵
CustomerName, S".", order1->OrderID)));
        }
    }

    // Reset the cursor to the default for all controls.
    Cursor::Current = Cursors::Default;

    // Begin repainting the TreeView.
    treeView1->EndUpdate();
}
```

Requirements

Namespace: System.Windows.Forms

Platforms: Windows 98, Windows NT 4.0, Windows Millennium Edition, Windows 2000, Windows XP Home Edition, Windows XP Professional, Windows Server 2003 family, .NET Compact Framework - Windows CE .NET

Assembly: System.Windows.Forms (in System.Windows.Forms.dll)

TreeView Constructor

Initializes a new instance of the **TreeView** class.

```
[Visual Basic]
Public Sub New()
[C#]
public TreeView();
[C++]
public: TreeView();
[JScript]
public function TreeView();
```

Requirements

Platforms: Windows 98, Windows NT 4.0, Windows Millennium Edition, Windows 2000, Windows XP Home Edition, Windows XP Professional, Windows Server 2003 family, .NET Compact Framework - Windows CE .NET

TreeView.BackColor Property

This member overrides **Control.BackColor**.

```
[Visual Basic]
Overrides Public Property BackColor As Color
[C#]
public override Color BackColor {get; set;}
[C++]
public: __property Color get_BackColor();
public: __property void set_BackColor(Color);
[JScript]
public override function get BackColor() : Color;
public override function set BackColor(Color);
```

Requirements

Platforms: Windows 98, Windows NT 4.0, Windows Millennium Edition, Windows 2000, Windows XP Home Edition, Windows XP Professional, Windows Server 2003 family

TreeView.BackgroundImage Property

This member overrides **Control.BackgroundImage**.

```
[Visual Basic]
Overrides Public Property BackgroundImage As Image
[C#]
public override Image BackgroundImage {get; set;}
[C++]
public: __property Image* get_BackgroundImage();
public: __property void set_BackgroundImage(Image*);
[JScript]
public override function get BackgroundImage() : Image;
public override function set BackgroundImage(Image);
```

Requirements

Platforms: Windows 98, Windows NT 4.0, Windows Millennium Edition, Windows 2000, Windows XP Home Edition, Windows XP Professional, Windows Server 2003 family

TreeView.BorderStyle Property

Gets or sets the border style of the tree view control.

```
[Visual Basic]
Public Property BorderStyle As BorderStyle
[C#]
public BorderStyle BorderStyle {get; set;}
[C++]
public: __property BorderStyle get_BorderStyle();
public: __property void set_BorderStyle(BorderStyle);
[JScript]
public function get BorderStyle() : BorderStyle;
public function set BorderStyle(BorderStyle);
```

Property Value

One of the **BorderStyle** values. The default is **Fixed3D**.

Exceptions

Exception Type	Condition
InvalidEnumArgument-Exception	The assigned value is not one of the **BorderStyle** values.

Remarks

When the **BorderStyle** property is set to **Fixed3D**, the **TreeView** has a sunken, three-dimensional appearance. To display a flat, thin border around the **TreeView** control, set the **BorderStyle** property to **FixedSingle**.

Requirements

Platforms: Windows 98, Windows NT 4.0, Windows Millennium Edition, Windows 2000, Windows XP Home Edition, Windows XP Professional, Windows Server 2003 family

TreeView.CheckBoxes Property

Gets or sets a value indicating whether check boxes are displayed next to the tree nodes in the tree view control.

```
[Visual Basic]
Public Property CheckBoxes As Boolean
[C#]
public bool CheckBoxes {get; set;}
[C++]
public: __property bool get_CheckBoxes();
public: __property void set_CheckBoxes(bool);
[JScript]
public function get CheckBoxes() : Boolean;
public function set CheckBoxes(Boolean);
```

Property Value

true if a check box is displayed next to each tree node in the tree view control; otherwise, **false**. The default is **false**.

Remarks

A check box is displayed to the left of both the tree node label and tree node **Image**, if any. Check boxes allow the user to select more than one tree node at a time.

> **Note** When setting the **CheckBoxes** property at run time, the **TreeView** handle is recreated (see **Control.RecreateHandle**) to update the control's appearance. This causes all tree nodes to be collapsed, with the exception of the selected **TreeNode**.

Requirements

Platforms: Windows 98, Windows NT 4.0,
Windows Millennium Edition, Windows 2000,
Windows XP Home Edition, Windows XP Professional,
Windows Server 2003 family,
.NET Compact Framework - Windows CE .NET

TreeView.CreateParams Property

This member overrides **Control.CreateParams**.

```
[Visual Basic]
Overrides Protected ReadOnly Property CreateParams As CreateParams
[C#]
protected override CreateParams CreateParams {get;}
[C++]
protected: __property CreateParams* get_CreateParams();
[JScript]
protected override function get CreateParams() : CreateParams;
```

Requirements

Platforms: Windows 98, Windows NT 4.0,
Windows Millennium Edition, Windows 2000,
Windows XP Home Edition, Windows XP Professional,
Windows Server 2003 family

TreeView.DefaultSize Property

This member overrides **Control.DefaultSize**.

```
[Visual Basic]
Overrides Protected ReadOnly Property DefaultSize As Size
[C#]
protected override Size DefaultSize {get;}
[C++]
protected: __property Size get_DefaultSize();
[JScript]
protected override function get DefaultSize() : Size;
```

Requirements

Platforms: Windows 98, Windows NT 4.0,
Windows Millennium Edition, Windows 2000,
Windows XP Home Edition, Windows XP Professional,
Windows Server 2003 family

TreeView.ForeColor Property

This member overrides **Control.ForeColor**.

```
[Visual Basic]
Overrides Public Property ForeColor As Color
[C#]
public override Color ForeColor {get; set;}
[C++]
public: __property Color get_ForeColor();
public: __property void set_ForeColor(Color);
[JScript]
public override function get ForeColor() : Color;
public override function set ForeColor(Color);
```

Requirements

Platforms: Windows 98, Windows NT 4.0,
Windows Millennium Edition, Windows 2000,
Windows XP Home Edition, Windows XP Professional,
Windows Server 2003 family

TreeView.FullRowSelect Property

Gets or sets a value indicating whether the selection highlight spans the width of the tree view control.

```
[Visual Basic]
Public Property FullRowSelect As Boolean
[C#]
public bool FullRowSelect {get; set;}
[C++]
public: __property bool get_FullRowSelect();
public: __property void set_FullRowSelect(bool);
[JScript]
public function get FullRowSelect() : Boolean;
public function set FullRowSelect(Boolean);
```

Property Value

true if the selection highlight spans the width of the tree view control; otherwise, **false**. The default is **false**.

Remarks

When **FullRowSelect** is **true**, a selection highlight spans the entire width of the tree view, display rather than the width of just the tree node label. The **FullRowSelect** property is ignored if **ShowLines** is set to **true**.

Requirements

Platforms: Windows 98, Windows NT 4.0,
Windows Millennium Edition, Windows 2000,
Windows XP Home Edition, Windows XP Professional,
Windows Server 2003 family

TreeView.HideSelection Property

Gets or sets a value indicating whether the selected tree node remains highlighted even when the tree view has lost the focus.

```
[Visual Basic]
Public Property HideSelection As Boolean
[C#]
public bool HideSelection {get; set;}
[C++]
public: __property bool get_HideSelection();
public: __property void set_HideSelection(bool);
[JScript]
public function get HideSelection() : Boolean;
public function set HideSelection(Boolean);
```

Property Value

true if the selected tree node is not highlighted when the tree view has lost the focus; otherwise, **false**. The default is **true**.

Requirements

Platforms: Windows 98, Windows NT 4.0,
Windows Millennium Edition, Windows 2000,
Windows XP Home Edition, Windows XP Professional,
Windows Server 2003 family

TreeView.HotTracking Property

Gets or sets a value indicating whether a tree node label takes on the appearance of a hyperlink as the mouse pointer passes over it.

```
[Visual Basic]
Public Property HotTracking As Boolean
```

```
[C#]
public bool HotTracking {get; set;}
[C++]
public: __property bool get_HotTracking();
public: __property void set_HotTracking(bool);
[JScript]
public function get HotTracking() : Boolean;
public function set HotTracking(Boolean);
```

Property Value

true if a tree node label takes on the appearance of a hyperlink as the mouse pointer passes over it; otherwise, **false**. The default is **false**.

Remarks

If the **CheckBoxes** property is set to **true**, the **HotTracking** property has no effect.

> **Note** When the **HotTracking** property is set to **true**, each tree node label takes on the appearance of a hyperlink as the mouse pointer passes over it. The **Underline** font style is applied to the **Font** and the **ForeColor** is set to blue to make the label appear as a link. The appearance is not controlled by the internet settings of the user's operating system.

Requirements

Platforms: Windows 98, Windows NT 4.0, Windows Millennium Edition, Windows 2000, Windows XP Home Edition, Windows XP Professional, Windows Server 2003 family

TreeView.ImageIndex Property

Gets or sets the image-list index value of the default image that is displayed by the tree nodes.

```
[Visual Basic]
Public Property ImageIndex As Integer
[C#]
public int ImageIndex {get; set;}
[C++]
public: __property int get_ImageIndex();
public: __property void set_ImageIndex(int);
[JScript]
public function get ImageIndex() : int;
public function set ImageIndex(int);
```

Property Value

A zero-based index, that represents the position of an **Image** in an **ImageList**. The default is zero.

Remarks

The **ImageIndex** value is the index of an **Image** stored in the **ImageList** object assigned to the **ImageList** property.

> **Note** When setting the **ImageIndex** property at run time, the **TreeView** handle is recreated (see **Control.RecreateHandle**) to update the control's appearance. This causes all tree nodes to be collapsed, with the exception of the selected **TreeNode**.

Example

See related example in the **System.Windows.Forms.TreeView** class topic.

Requirements

Platforms: Windows 98, Windows NT 4.0, Windows Millennium Edition, Windows 2000, Windows XP Home Edition, Windows XP Professional, Windows Server 2003 family, .NET Compact Framework - Windows CE .NET

TreeView.ImageList Property

Gets or sets the **ImageList** that contains the **Image** objects used by the tree nodes.

```
[Visual Basic]
Public Property ImageList As ImageList
[C#]
public ImageList ImageList {get; set;}
[C++]
public: __property ImageList* get_ImageList();
public: __property void set_ImageList(ImageList*);
[JScript]
public function get ImageList() : ImageList;
public function set ImageList(ImageList);
```

Property Value

The **ImageList** that contains the **Image** objects used by the tree nodes. The default value is a null reference (**Nothing** in Visual Basic).

Remarks

If the **ImageList** property value is anything other than a null reference (**Nothing** in Visual Basic), all the tree nodes display the first **Image** stored in the **ImageList**.

Example

See related example in the **System.Windows.Forms.TreeView** class topic.

Requirements

Platforms: Windows 98, Windows NT 4.0, Windows Millennium Edition, Windows 2000, Windows XP Home Edition, Windows XP Professional, Windows Server 2003 family, .NET Compact Framework - Windows CE .NET

TreeView.Indent Property

Gets or sets the distance to indent each of the child tree node levels.

```
[Visual Basic]
Public Property Indent As Integer
[C#]
public int Indent {get; set;}
[C++]
public: __property int get_Indent();
public: __property void set_Indent(int);
[JScript]
public function get Indent() : int;
public function set Indent(int);
```

Property Value

The distance, in pixels, to indent each of the child tree node levels.

Exceptions

Exception Type	Condition
ArgumentException	The assigned value is less than 0. -or- The assigned value is greater than 32,000.

Requirements

Platforms: Windows 98, Windows NT 4.0, Windows Millennium Edition, Windows 2000, Windows XP Home Edition, Windows XP Professional, Windows Server 2003 family, .NET Compact Framework - Windows CE .NET

TreeView.ItemHeight Property

Gets or sets the height of each tree node in the tree view control.

```
[Visual Basic]
Public Property ItemHeight As Integer
[C#]
public int ItemHeight {get; set;}
[C++]
public: __property int get_ItemHeight();
public: __property void set_ItemHeight(int);
[JScript]
public function get ItemHeight() : int;
public function set ItemHeight(int);
```

Property Value

The height, in pixels, of each tree node in the tree view.

Exceptions

Exception Type	Condition
ArgumentException	The assigned value is less than one. -or- The assigned value is greater than the **MaxValue** value.

Example

See related example in the **System.Windows.Forms.TreeView** class topic.

Requirements

Platforms: Windows 98, Windows NT 4.0, Windows Millennium Edition, Windows 2000, Windows XP Home Edition, Windows XP Professional, Windows Server 2003 family

TreeView.LabelEdit Property

Gets or sets a value indicating whether the label text of the tree nodes can be edited.

```
[Visual Basic]
Public Property LabelEdit As Boolean
[C#]
public bool LabelEdit {get; set;}
[C++]
public: __property bool get_LabelEdit();
public: __property void set_LabelEdit(bool);
[JScript]
public function get LabelEdit() : Boolean;
public function set LabelEdit(Boolean);
```

Property Value

true if the label text of the tree nodes can be edited; otherwise, **false**. The default is **false**.

Remarks

The **BeginEdit** method works only if the **LabelEdit** property is **true**. If **LabelEdit** is **false** when you attempt to edit the label, an exception will be thrown and the tree node will not be put in to an editable state.

Example

See related example in the **System.Windows.Forms.TreeView** class topic.

Requirements

Platforms: Windows 98, Windows NT 4.0, Windows Millennium Edition, Windows 2000, Windows XP Home Edition, Windows XP Professional, Windows Server 2003 family

TreeView.Nodes Property

Gets the collection of tree nodes that are assigned to the tree view control.

```
[Visual Basic]
Public ReadOnly Property Nodes As TreeNodeCollection
[C#]
public TreeNodeCollection Nodes {get;}
[C++]
public: __property TreeNodeCollection* get_Nodes();
[JScript]
public function get Nodes() : TreeNodeCollection;
```

Property Value

A **TreeNodeCollection** that represents the tree nodes assigned to the tree view control.

Remarks

The **Nodes** property holds a collection of **TreeNode** objects, each of which has a **Nodes** property that can contain its own **TreeNodeCollection**. This nesting of tree nodes can make it difficult to navigate a tree structure, but the **FullPath** property makes it easier to determine your location within the tree structure.

Example

See related example in the **System.Windows.Forms.TreeView** class topic.

Requirements

Platforms: Windows 98, Windows NT 4.0, Windows Millennium Edition, Windows 2000, Windows XP Home Edition, Windows XP Professional, Windows Server 2003 family, .NET Compact Framework - Windows CE .NET

TreeView.PathSeparator Property

Gets or sets the delimiter string that the tree node path uses.

```
[Visual Basic]
Public Property PathSeparator As String
[C#]
public string PathSeparator {get; set;}
```

[C++]
```
public: __property String* get_PathSeparator();
public: __property void set_PathSeparator(String*);
```
[JScript]
```
public function get PathSeparator() : String;
public function set PathSeparator(String);
```

Property Value

The delimiter string that the tree node **TreeNode.FullPath** property uses. The default is the backslash character (\).

Remarks

The tree node path consists of a set of tree node labels separated by the **PathSeparator** delimiter strings. The labels range from the root tree node to the tree node that you want.

Example

See related example in the **System.Windows.Forms.TreeView** class topic.

Requirements

Platforms: Windows 98, Windows NT 4.0,
Windows Millennium Edition, Windows 2000,
Windows XP Home Edition, Windows XP Professional,
Windows Server 2003 family,
.NET Compact Framework - Windows CE .NET

TreeView.Scrollable Property

Gets or sets a value indicating whether the tree view control displays scroll bars when they are needed.

[Visual Basic]
```
Public Property Scrollable As Boolean
```
[C#]
```
public bool Scrollable {get; set;}
```
[C++]
```
public: __property bool get_Scrollable();
public: __property void set_Scrollable(bool);
```
[JScript]
```
public function get Scrollable() : Boolean;
public function set Scrollable(Boolean);
```

Property Value

true if the tree view control displays scroll bars when they are needed; otherwise, **false**. The default is **true**.

Remarks

If this property is set to **true**, scroll bars are displayed on the **TreeView** when any **TreeNode** object is located outside the control's client region.

> **Note** When setting the **Scrollable** property at run time, the **TreeView** handle is recreated (see **Control.RecreateHandle**) to update the control's appearance. This causes all tree nodes to be collapsed, with the exception of the selected **TreeNode**.

Requirements

Platforms: Windows 98, Windows NT 4.0,
Windows Millennium Edition, Windows 2000,
Windows XP Home Edition, Windows XP Professional,
Windows Server 2003 family

TreeView.SelectedImageIndex Property

Gets or sets the image list index value of the image that is displayed when a tree node is selected.

[Visual Basic]
```
Public Property SelectedImageIndex As Integer
```
[C#]
```
public int SelectedImageIndex {get; set;}
```
[C++]
```
public: __property int get_SelectedImageIndex();
public: __property void set_SelectedImageIndex(int);
```
[JScript]
```
public function get SelectedImageIndex() : int;
public function set SelectedImageIndex(int);
```

Property Value

A zero-based index value that represents the position of an **Image** in an **ImageList**.

Exceptions

Exception Type	Condition
ArgumentException	The index assigned value is less than zero.

Remarks

The **SelectedImageIndex** value is the index of an **Image** stored in the **ImageList** object assigned to the **ImageList** property.

> **Note** When setting the **SelectedImageIndex** property at run time, the **TreeView** handle is recreated (see **Control.Recreate-Handle**) to update the control's appearance. This causes all tree nodes to be collapsed, with the exception of the selected **TreeNode**.

Example

See related example in the **System.Windows.Forms.TreeView** class topic.

Requirements

Platforms: Windows 98, Windows NT 4.0,
Windows Millennium Edition, Windows 2000,
Windows XP Home Edition, Windows XP Professional,
Windows Server 2003 family,
.NET Compact Framework - Windows CE .NET

TreeView.SelectedNode Property

Gets or sets the tree node that is currently selected in the tree view control.

[Visual Basic]
```
Public Property SelectedNode As TreeNode
```
[C#]
```
public TreeNode SelectedNode {get; set;}
```
[C++]
```
public: __property TreeNode* get_SelectedNode();
public: __property void set_SelectedNode(TreeNode*);
```
[JScript]
```
public function get SelectedNode() : TreeNode;
public function set SelectedNode(TreeNode);
```

Property Value

The **TreeNode** that is currently selected in the tree view control.

Remarks

If no **TreeNode** is currently selected, the **SelectedNode** property is a null reference (**Nothing** in Visual Basic).

Example

See related example in the **System.Windows.Forms.TreeView** class topic.

Requirements

Platforms: Windows 98, Windows NT 4.0, Windows Millennium Edition, Windows 2000, Windows XP Home Edition, Windows XP Professional, Windows Server 2003 family, .NET Compact Framework - Windows CE .NET

TreeView.ShowLines Property

Gets or sets a value indicating whether lines are drawn between tree nodes in the tree view control.

```
[Visual Basic]
Public Property ShowLines As Boolean
[C#]
public bool ShowLines {get; set;}
[C++]
public: __property bool get_ShowLines();
public: __property void set_ShowLines(bool);
[JScript]
public function get ShowLines() : Boolean;
public function set ShowLines(Boolean);
```

Property Value

true if lines are drawn between tree nodes in the tree view control; otherwise, **false**. The default is **true**.

Remarks

If **ShowLines** is set to **true**, the **FullRowSelect** property is ignored.

Requirements

Platforms: Windows 98, Windows NT 4.0, Windows Millennium Edition, Windows 2000, Windows XP Home Edition, Windows XP Professional, Windows Server 2003 family, .NET Compact Framework - Windows CE .NET

TreeView.ShowPlusMinus Property

Gets or sets a value indicating whether plus-sign (+) and minus-sign (-) buttons are displayed next to tree nodes that contain child tree nodes.

```
[Visual Basic]
Public Property ShowPlusMinus As Boolean
[C#]
public bool ShowPlusMinus {get; set;}
[C++]
public: __property bool get_ShowPlusMinus();
public: __property void set_ShowPlusMinus(bool);
[JScript]
public function get ShowPlusMinus() : Boolean;
public function set ShowPlusMinus(Boolean);
```

Property Value

true if plus-sign and minus-sign buttons are displayed next to tree nodes that contain child tree nodes; otherwise, **false**. The default is **true**.

Remarks

The plus-sign and minus-sign buttons appear next to the root tree nodes only if the **ShowRootLines** property is **true**. If the plus-sign and minus-sign buttons are not displayed, no visual cue exists to indicate that the tree node contains child tree nodes and is expandable. The user then must double-click a tree node to determine whether it contains child tree nodes, to expand it, or to collapse it.

Requirements

Platforms: Windows 98, Windows NT 4.0, Windows Millennium Edition, Windows 2000, Windows XP Home Edition, Windows XP Professional, Windows Server 2003 family, .NET Compact Framework - Windows CE .NET

TreeView.ShowRootLines Property

Gets or sets a value indicating whether lines are drawn between the tree nodes that are at the root of the tree view.

```
[Visual Basic]
Public Property ShowRootLines As Boolean
[C#]
public bool ShowRootLines {get; set;}
[C++]
public: __property bool get_ShowRootLines();
public: __property void set_ShowRootLines(bool);
[JScript]
public function get ShowRootLines() : Boolean;
public function set ShowRootLines(Boolean);
```

Property Value

true if lines are drawn between the tree nodes that are at the root of the tree view; otherwise, **false**. The default is **true**.

Remarks

If the **ShowRootLines** property is **false**, the plus-sign and minus-sign buttons will not appear next to the root tree nodes, and the **ShowPlusMinus** property will have no effect.

Requirements

Platforms: Windows 98, Windows NT 4.0, Windows Millennium Edition, Windows 2000, Windows XP Home Edition, Windows XP Professional, Windows Server 2003 family, .NET Compact Framework - Windows CE .NET

TreeView.Sorted Property

Gets or sets a value indicating whether the tree nodes in the tree view are sorted.

```
[Visual Basic]
Public Property Sorted As Boolean
[C#]
public bool Sorted {get; set;}
[C++]
public: __property bool get_Sorted();
public: __property void set_Sorted(bool);
```

```
[JScript]
public function get Sorted() : Boolean;
public function set Sorted(Boolean);
```

Property Value

true if the tree nodes in the tree view are sorted; otherwise, **false**. The default is **false**.

Remarks

When **Sorted** is set to **true**, the **TreeNode** objects are sorted in alphabetical order.

Requirements

Platforms: Windows 98, Windows NT 4.0,
Windows Millennium Edition, Windows 2000,
Windows XP Home Edition, Windows XP Professional,
Windows Server 2003 family

TreeView.Text Property

This member overrides **Control.Text**.

```
[Visual Basic]
Overrides Public Property Text As String
[C#]
public override string Text {get; set;}
[C++]
public: __property String* get_Text();
public: __property void set_Text(String*);
[JScript]
public override function get Text() : String;
public override function set Text(String);
```

Requirements

Platforms: Windows 98, Windows NT 4.0,
Windows Millennium Edition, Windows 2000,
Windows XP Home Edition, Windows XP Professional,
Windows Server 2003 family

TreeView.TopNode Property

Gets the first fully-visible tree node in the tree view control.

```
[Visual Basic]
Public ReadOnly Property TopNode As TreeNode
[C#]
public TreeNode TopNode {get;}
[C++]
public: __property TreeNode* get_TopNode();
[JScript]
public function get TopNode() : TreeNode;
```

Property Value

A **TreeNode** that represents the first fully-visible tree node in the tree view control.

Remarks

Initially, the **TopNode** returns the first root tree node, which is located at the top of the **TreeView**. However, if the user has scrolled the contents, another tree node might be at the top.

Requirements

Platforms: Windows 98, Windows NT 4.0,
Windows Millennium Edition, Windows 2000,
Windows XP Home Edition, Windows XP Professional,
Windows Server 2003 family

TreeView.VisibleCount Property

Gets the number of tree nodes that can be fully visible in the tree view control.

```
[Visual Basic]
Public ReadOnly Property VisibleCount As Integer
[C#]
public int VisibleCount {get;}
[C++]
public: __property int get_VisibleCount();
[JScript]
public function get VisibleCount() : int;
```

Property Value

The number of **TreeNode** items that can be fully visible in the **TreeView** control.

Remarks

The **VisibleCount** value can be greater than the number of tree nodes in the tree view. The value is calculated by dividing the height of the client window by the height of a tree node item. The result is the total number of **TreeNode** objects that the **TreeView** is capable of displaying within its current dimensions.

Requirements

Platforms: Windows 98, Windows NT 4.0,
Windows Millennium Edition, Windows 2000,
Windows XP Home Edition, Windows XP Professional,
Windows Server 2003 family

TreeView.BeginUpdate Method

Disables any redrawing of the tree view.

```
[Visual Basic]
Public Sub BeginUpdate()
[C#]
public void BeginUpdate();
[C++]
public: void BeginUpdate();
[JScript]
public function BeginUpdate();
```

Remarks

To maintain performance while items are added one at a time to the **TreeView**, call the **BeginUpdate** method. The **BeginUpdate** method prevents the control from painting until the **EndUpdate** method is called.

The preferred way to add items to a tree view control is to use the **AddRange** method to add an array of tree node items to a tree view. However, if you want to add items one at a time, use the **BeginUpdate** method to prevent the **TreeView** control from painting during the add operations. To allow control the control to resume painting, call the **EndUpdate** method when all the tree nodes have been added to the tree view.

Example

See related example in the **System.Windows.Forms.TreeView** class topic.

Requirements

Platforms: Windows 98, Windows NT 4.0,
Windows Millennium Edition, Windows 2000,
Windows XP Home Edition, Windows XP Professional,
Windows Server 2003 family,
.NET Compact Framework - Windows CE .NET

TreeView.CollapseAll Method

Collapses all the tree nodes.

```
[Visual Basic]
Public Sub CollapseAll()
[C#]
public void CollapseAll();
[C++]
public: void CollapseAll();
[JScript]
public function CollapseAll();
```

Remarks

The **CollapseAll** method collapses all the **TreeNode** objects, including all the child tree nodes, that are in the **TreeView** control.

> **Note** The state of a **TreeNode** persists. For example, suppose that you call the **Expand** method for a root tree node. If the child tree nodes were not previously collapsed, they will appear in their previously-expanded state. Calling the **CollapseAll** method ensures that all the tree nodes appear in the collapsed state.

Requirements

Platforms: Windows 98, Windows NT 4.0, Windows Millennium Edition, Windows 2000, Windows XP Home Edition, Windows XP Professional, Windows Server 2003 family, .NET Compact Framework - Windows CE .NET

TreeView.CreateHandle Method

This member overrides **Control.CreateHandle**.

```
[Visual Basic]
Overrides Protected Sub CreateHandle()
[C#]
protected override void CreateHandle();
[C++]
protected: void CreateHandle();
[JScript]
protected override function CreateHandle();
```

Requirements

Platforms: Windows 98, Windows NT 4.0, Windows Millennium Edition, Windows 2000, Windows XP Home Edition, Windows XP Professional, Windows Server 2003 family

TreeView.Dispose Method

Overload List

This member supports the .NET Framework infrastructure and is not intended to be used directly from your code.

Supported by the .NET Compact Framework.

[Visual Basic] **Overloads Overrides Protected Sub Dispose(Boolean)**

[C#] **protected override void Dispose(bool);**

[C++] **protected: void Dispose(bool);**

[JScript] **protected override function Dispose(Boolean);**

Inherited from **Component**.

Supported by the .NET Compact Framework.

[Visual Basic] **Overloads Public Overridable Sub Dispose() Implements IDisposable.Dispose**

[C#] **public virtual void Dispose();**

[C++] **public: virtual void Dispose();**

[JScript] **public function Dispose();**

TreeView.Dispose Method (Boolean)

This member overrides **Control.Dispose**.

```
[Visual Basic]
Overrides Overloads Protected Sub Dispose( _
   ByVal disposing As Boolean _
)
[C#]
protected override void Dispose(
   bool disposing
);
[C++]
protected: void Dispose(
   bool disposing
);
[JScript]
protected override function Dispose(
   disposing : Boolean
);
```

Requirements

Platforms: Windows 98, Windows NT 4.0, Windows Millennium Edition, Windows 2000, Windows XP Home Edition, Windows XP Professional, Windows Server 2003 family, .NET Compact Framework - Windows CE .NET

TreeView.EndUpdate Method

Enables the redrawing of the tree view.

```
[Visual Basic]
Public Sub EndUpdate()
[C#]
public void EndUpdate();
[C++]
public: void EndUpdate();
[JScript]
public function EndUpdate();
```

Remarks

To maintain performance while items are added one at a time to the **TreeView**, call the **BeginUpdate** method. The **BeginUpdate** method prevents the control from painting until the **EndUpdate** method is called.

The preferred way to add items to a tree view control is to use the **AddRange** method to add an array of tree node items to a tree view. However, if you want to add items one at a time, use the **BeginUpdate** method to prevent the **TreeView** control from painting during the add operations. To allow control the control to resume painting, call the **EndUpdate** method when all the tree nodes have been added to the tree view.

Example

See related example in the **System.Windows.Forms.TreeView** class topic.

Requirements

Platforms: Windows 98, Windows NT 4.0, Windows Millennium Edition, Windows 2000, Windows XP Home Edition, Windows XP Professional, Windows Server 2003 family, .NET Compact Framework - Windows CE .NET

TreeView.ExpandAll Method

Expands all the tree nodes.

```
[Visual Basic]
Public Sub ExpandAll()
[C#]
public void ExpandAll();
[C++]
public: void ExpandAll();
[JScript]
public function ExpandAll();
```

Remarks

The **ExpandAll** method expands all the **TreeNode** objects, including all the child tree nodes, that are in the **TreeView** control.

> **Note** The state of a **TreeNode** persists. For example, suppose that you call the **ExpandAll** method, then the individual root tree nodes are collapsed. The child tree nodes have not been collapsed, and will appear in their previously-expanded state when the root tree nodes are expanded again. Calling the **CollapseAll** method ensures that all the tree nodes appear in the collapsed state.

Example

See related example in the **System.Windows.Forms.TreeView** class topic.

Requirements

Platforms: Windows 98, Windows NT 4.0, Windows Millennium Edition, Windows 2000, Windows XP Home Edition, Windows XP Professional, Windows Server 2003 family, .NET Compact Framework - Windows CE .NET

TreeView.GetItemRenderStyles Method

This member supports the .NET Framework infrastructure and is not intended to be used directly from your code.

```
[Visual Basic]
Protected Function GetItemRenderStyles( _
   ByVal node As TreeNode, _
   ByVal state As Integer _
) As OwnerDrawPropertyBag
[C#]
protected OwnerDrawPropertyBag GetItemRenderStyles(
   TreeNode node,
   int state
);
[C++]
protected: OwnerDrawPropertyBag* GetItemRenderStyles(
   TreeNode* node,
   int state
);
[JScript]
protected function GetItemRenderStyles(
   node : TreeNode,
   state : int
) : OwnerDrawPropertyBag;
```

TreeView.GetNodeAt Method

Retrieves the tree node that is at the specified location.

Overload List

Retrieves the tree node that is at the specified point.

[Visual Basic] **Overloads Public Function GetNodeAt(Point) As TreeNode**

[C#] **public TreeNode GetNodeAt(Point);**

[C++] **public: TreeNode* GetNodeAt(Point);**

[JScript] **public function GetNodeAt(Point) : TreeNode;**

Retrieves the tree node at the point with the specified coordinates.

[Visual Basic] **Overloads Public Function GetNodeAt(Integer, Integer) As TreeNode**

[C#] **public TreeNode GetNodeAt(int, int);**

[C++] **public: TreeNode* GetNodeAt(int, int);**

[JScript] **public function GetNodeAt(int, int) : TreeNode;**

Example

See related example in the **System.Windows.Forms.TreeView** class topic.

TreeView.GetNodeAt Method (Point)

Retrieves the tree node that is at the specified point.

```
[Visual Basic]
Overloads Public Function GetNodeAt( _
   ByVal pt As Point _
) As TreeNode
[C#]
public TreeNode GetNodeAt(
   Point pt
);
[C++]
public: TreeNode* GetNodeAt(
   Point pt
);
[JScript]
public function GetNodeAt(
   pt : Point
) : TreeNode;
```

Parameters

pt

The **Point** to evaluate and retrieve the node from.

Return Value

The **TreeNode** at the specified point, in tree view coordinates.

Remarks

You can pass the **MouseEventArgs.X** and **MouseEventArgs.Y** coordinates of the **MouseDown** event as the **X** and **Y** values of a new **Point** object.

Requirements

Platforms: Windows 98, Windows NT 4.0, Windows Millennium Edition, Windows 2000, Windows XP Home Edition, Windows XP Professional, Windows Server 2003 family

TreeView.GetNodeAt Method (Int32, Int32)

Retrieves the tree node at the point with the specified coordinates.

```
[Visual Basic]
Overloads Public Function GetNodeAt( _
   ByVal x As Integer, _
   ByVal y As Integer _
) As TreeNode
[C#]
public TreeNode GetNodeAt(
   int x,
   int y
);
[C++]
public: TreeNode* GetNodeAt(
   int x,
   int y
);
[JScript]
public function GetNodeAt(
   x : int,
   y : int
) : TreeNode;
```

Parameters

x
The **X** position to evaluate and retrieve the node from.

y
The **Y** position to evaluate and retrieve the node from.

Return Value

The **TreeNode** at the specified location, in tree view coordinates.

Remarks

You can pass the **MouseEventArgs.X** and **MouseEventArgs.Y** coordinates of the **MouseDown** event as the *x* and *y* parameters.

Example

See related example in the **System.Windows.Forms.TreeView** class topic.

Requirements

Platforms: Windows 98, Windows NT 4.0, Windows Millennium Edition, Windows 2000, Windows XP Home Edition, Windows XP Professional, Windows Server 2003 family

TreeView.GetNodeCount Method

Retrieves the number of tree nodes, optionally including those in all subtrees, assigned to the tree view control.

```
[Visual Basic]
Public Function GetNodeCount( _
   ByVal includeSubTrees As Boolean _
) As Integer
[C#]
public int GetNodeCount(
   bool includeSubTrees
);
[C++]
public: int GetNodeCount(
   bool includeSubTrees
);
[JScript]
public function GetNodeCount(
   includeSubTrees : Boolean
) : int;
```

Parameters

includeSubTrees
true to count the **TreeNode** items that the subtrees contain; otherwise, **false**.

Return Value

The number of tree nodes, optionally including those in all subtrees, assigned to the tree view control.

Remarks

If *includeSubTrees* is **true**, the result is the number of all the tree nodes in the entire tree structure.

Example

See related example in the **System.Windows.Forms.TreeView** class topic.

Requirements

Platforms: Windows 98, Windows NT 4.0, Windows Millennium Edition, Windows 2000, Windows XP Home Edition, Windows XP Professional, Windows Server 2003 family, .NET Compact Framework - Windows CE .NET

TreeView.IsInputKey Method

This member overrides **Control.IsInputKey**.

```
[Visual Basic]
Overrides Protected Function IsInputKey( _
   ByVal keyData As Keys _
) As Boolean
[C#]
protected override bool IsInputKey(
   Keys keyData
);
[C++]
protected: bool IsInputKey(
   Keys keyData
);
[JScript]
protected override function IsInputKey(
   keyData : Keys
) : Boolean;
```

Requirements

Platforms: Windows 98, Windows NT 4.0, Windows Millennium Edition, Windows 2000, Windows XP Home Edition, Windows XP Professional, Windows Server 2003 family

TreeView.OnAfterCheck Method

Raises the **AfterCheck** event.

```
[Visual Basic]
Protected Overridable Sub OnAfterCheck( _
   ByVal e As TreeViewEventArgs _
)
[C#]
protected virtual void OnAfterCheck(
   TreeViewEventArgs e
);
[C++]
protected: virtual void OnAfterCheck(
   TreeViewEventArgs* e
);
[JScript]
protected function OnAfterCheck(
   e : TreeViewEventArgs
);
```

Parameters

e

A **TreeViewEventArgs** that contains the event data.

Remarks

Raising an event invokes the event handler through a delegate.

The **OnAfterCheck** method also allows derived classes to handle the event without attaching a delegate. This is the preferred technique for handling the event in a derived class.

Notes to Inheritors: When overriding **OnAfterCheck** in a derived class, be sure to call the base class's **OnAfterCheck** method so that registered delegates receive the event.

Requirements

Platforms: Windows 98, Windows NT 4.0, Windows Millennium Edition, Windows 2000, Windows XP Home Edition, Windows XP Professional, Windows Server 2003 family, .NET Compact Framework - Windows CE .NET

TreeView.OnAfterCollapse Method

Raises the **AfterCollapse** event.

```
[Visual Basic]
Protected Overridable Sub OnAfterCollapse( _
   ByVal e As TreeViewEventArgs _
)
[C#]
protected virtual void OnAfterCollapse(
   TreeViewEventArgs e
);
[C++]
protected: virtual void OnAfterCollapse(
   TreeViewEventArgs* e
);
[Visual Basic]
[JScript]
protected function OnAfterCollapse(
   e : TreeViewEventArgs
);
```

Parameters

e

A **TreeViewEventArgs** that contains the event data.

Remarks

Raising an event invokes the event handler through a delegate.

The **OnAfterCollapse** method also allows derived classes to handle the event without attaching a delegate. This is the preferred technique for handling the event in a derived class.

Notes to Inheritors: When overriding **OnAfterCollapse** in a derived class, be sure to call the base class's **OnAfterCollapse** method so that registered delegates receive the event.

Requirements

Platforms: Windows 98, Windows NT 4.0, Windows Millennium Edition, Windows 2000, Windows XP Home Edition, Windows XP Professional, Windows Server 2003 family

TreeView.OnAfterExpand Method

Raises the **AfterExpand** event.

```
[Visual Basic]
Protected Overridable Sub OnAfterExpand( _
   ByVal e As TreeViewEventArgs _
)
[C#]
protected virtual void OnAfterExpand(
   TreeViewEventArgs e
);
[C++]
protected: virtual void OnAfterExpand(
   TreeViewEventArgs* e
);
[JScript]
protected function OnAfterExpand(
   e : TreeViewEventArgs
);
```

Parameters

e

A **TreeViewEventArgs** that contains the event data.

Remarks

Raising an event invokes the event handler through a delegate.

The **OnAfterExpand** method also allows derived classes to handle the event without attaching a delegate. This is the preferred technique for handling the event in a derived class.

Notes to Inheritors: When overriding **OnAfterExpand** in a derived class, be sure to call the base class's **OnAfterExpand** method so that registered delegates receive the event.

Requirements

Platforms: Windows 98, Windows NT 4.0, Windows Millennium Edition, Windows 2000, Windows XP Home Edition, Windows XP Professional, Windows Server 2003 family

TreeView.OnAfterLabelEdit Method

Raises the **AfterLabelEdit** event.

```
[Visual Basic]
Protected Overridable Sub OnAfterLabelEdit( _
   ByVal e As NodeLabelEditEventArgs _
)
[C#]
protected virtual void OnAfterLabelEdit(
   NodeLabelEditEventArgs e
);
[C++]
protected: virtual void OnAfterLabelEdit(
   NodeLabelEditEventArgs* e
);
[JScript]
protected function OnAfterLabelEdit(
   e : NodeLabelEditEventArgs
);
```

Parameters

e

A **NodeLabelEditEventArgs** that contains the event data.

Remarks

Raising an event invokes the event handler through a delegate.

The **OnAfterLabelEdit** method also allows derived classes to handle the event without attaching a delegate. This is the preferred technique for handling the event in a derived class.

Notes to Inheritors: When overriding **OnAfterLabelEdit** in a derived class, be sure to call the base class's **OnAfterLabelEdit** method so that registered delegates receive the event.

Requirements

Platforms: Windows 98, Windows NT 4.0,
Windows Millennium Edition, Windows 2000,
Windows XP Home Edition, Windows XP Professional,
Windows Server 2003 family

TreeView.OnAfterSelect Method

Raises the **AfterSelect** event.

```
[Visual Basic]
Protected Overridable Sub OnAfterSelect( _
   ByVal e As TreeViewEventArgs _
)
[C#]
protected virtual void OnAfterSelect(
   TreeViewEventArgs e
);
[C++]
protected: virtual void OnAfterSelect(
   TreeViewEventArgs* e
);
[JScript]
protected function OnAfterSelect(
   e : TreeViewEventArgs
);
```

Parameters

e

A **TreeViewEventArgs** that contains the event data.

Remarks

Raising an event invokes the event handler through a delegate.

The **OnAfterSelect** method also allows derived classes to handle the event without attaching a delegate. This is the preferred technique for handling the event in a derived class.

Notes to Inheritors: When overriding **OnAfterSelect** in a derived class, be sure to call the base class's **OnAfterSelect** method so that registered delegates receive the event.

Requirements

Platforms: Windows 98, Windows NT 4.0,
Windows Millennium Edition, Windows 2000,
Windows XP Home Edition, Windows XP Professional,
Windows Server 2003 family,
.NET Compact Framework - Windows CE .NET

TreeView.OnBeforeCheck Method

Raises the **BeforeCheck** event.

```
[Visual Basic]
Protected Overridable Sub OnBeforeCheck( _
   ByVal e As TreeViewCancelEventArgs _
)
[C#]
protected virtual void OnBeforeCheck(
   TreeViewCancelEventArgs e
);
[C++]
protected: virtual void OnBeforeCheck(
   TreeViewCancelEventArgs* e
);
[JScript]
protected function OnBeforeCheck(
   e : TreeViewCancelEventArgs
);
```

Parameters

e

A **TreeViewCancelEventArgs** that contains the event data.

Remarks

Raising an event invokes the event handler through a delegate.

The **OnBeforeCheck** method also allows derived classes to handle the event without attaching a delegate. This is the preferred technique for handling the event in a derived class.

Notes to Inheritors: When overriding **OnBeforeCheck** in a derived class, be sure to call the base class's **OnBeforeCheck** method so that registered delegates receive the event.

Requirements

Platforms: Windows 98, Windows NT 4.0,
Windows Millennium Edition, Windows 2000,
Windows XP Home Edition, Windows XP Professional,
Windows Server 2003 family

TreeView.OnBeforeCollapse Method

Raises the **BeforeCollapse** event.

```
[Visual Basic]
Protected Overridable Sub OnBeforeCollapse( _
   ByVal e As TreeViewCancelEventArgs _
)
```

[C#]
```
protected virtual void OnBeforeCollapse(
   TreeViewCancelEventArgs e
);
```
[C++]
```
protected: virtual void OnBeforeCollapse(
   TreeViewCancelEventArgs* e
);
```
[JScript]
```
protected function OnBeforeCollapse(
   e : TreeViewCancelEventArgs
);
```

Parameters

e

A **TreeViewCancelEventArgs** that contains the event data.

Remarks

Raising an event invokes the event handler through a delegate.

The **OnBeforeCollapse** method also allows derived classes to handle the event without attaching a delegate. This is the preferred technique for handling the event in a derived class.

Notes to Inheritors: When overriding **OnBeforeCollapse** in a derived class, be sure to call the base class's **OnBeforeCollapse** method so that registered delegates receive the event.

Requirements

Platforms: Windows 98, Windows NT 4.0, Windows Millennium Edition, Windows 2000, Windows XP Home Edition, Windows XP Professional, Windows Server 2003 family

TreeView.OnBeforeExpand Method

Raises the **BeforeExpand** event.

[Visual Basic]
```
Protected Overridable Sub OnBeforeExpand( _
   ByVal e As TreeViewCancelEventArgs _
)
```
[C#]
```
protected virtual void OnBeforeExpand(
   TreeViewCancelEventArgs e
);
```
[C++]
```
protected: virtual void OnBeforeExpand(
   TreeViewCancelEventArgs* e
);
```
[JScript]
```
protected function OnBeforeExpand(
   e : TreeViewCancelEventArgs
);
```

Parameters

e

A **TreeViewCancelEventArgs** that contains the event data.

Remarks

Raising an event invokes the event handler through a delegate.

The **OnBeforeExpand** method also allows derived classes to handle the event without attaching a delegate. This is the preferred technique for handling the event in a derived class.

Notes to Inheritors: When overriding **OnBeforeExpand** in a derived class, be sure to call the base class's **OnBeforeExpand** method so that registered delegates receive the event.

Requirements

Platforms: Windows 98, Windows NT 4.0, Windows Millennium Edition, Windows 2000, Windows XP Home Edition, Windows XP Professional, Windows Server 2003 family, .NET Compact Framework - Windows CE .NET

TreeView.OnBeforeLabelEdit Method

Raises the **BeforeLabelEdit** event.

[Visual Basic]
```
Protected Overridable Sub OnBeforeLabelEdit( _
   ByVal e As NodeLabelEditEventArgs _
)
```
[C#]
```
protected virtual void OnBeforeLabelEdit(
   NodeLabelEditEventArgs e
);
```
[C++]
```
protected: virtual void OnBeforeLabelEdit(
   NodeLabelEditEventArgs* e
);
```
[JScript]
```
protected function OnBeforeLabelEdit(
   e : NodeLabelEditEventArgs
);
```

Parameters

e

A **NodeLabelEditEventArgs** that contains the event data.

Remarks

Raising an event invokes the event handler through a delegate.

The **OnBeforeLabelEdit** method also allows derived classes to handle the event without attaching a delegate. This is the preferred technique for handling the event in a derived class.

Notes to Inheritors: When overriding **OnBeforeLabelEdit** in a derived class, be sure to call the base class's **OnBeforeLabelEdit** method so that registered delegates receive the event.

Requirements

Platforms: Windows 98, Windows NT 4.0, Windows Millennium Edition, Windows 2000, Windows XP Home Edition, Windows XP Professional, Windows Server 2003 family

TreeView.OnBeforeSelect Method

Raises the **BeforeSelect** event.

[Visual Basic]
```
Protected Overridable Sub OnBeforeSelect( _
   ByVal e As TreeViewCancelEventArgs _
)
```
[C#]
```
protected virtual void OnBeforeSelect(
   TreeViewCancelEventArgs e
);
```

```
[C++]
protected: virtual void OnBeforeSelect(
   TreeViewCancelEventArgs* e
);
[JScript]
protected function OnBeforeSelect(
   e : TreeViewCancelEventArgs
);
```

Parameters

e

A **TreeViewCancelEventArgs** that contains the event data.

Remarks

Raising an event invokes the event handler through a delegate.

The **OnBeforeSelect** method also allows derived classes to handle the event without attaching a delegate. This is the preferred technique for handling the event in a derived class.

Notes to Inheritors: When overriding **OnBeforeSelect** in a derived class, be sure to call the base class's **OnBeforeSelect** method so that registered delegates receive the event.

Requirements

Platforms: Windows 98, Windows NT 4.0, Windows Millennium Edition, Windows 2000, Windows XP Home Edition, Windows XP Professional, Windows Server 2003 family

TreeView.OnHandleCreated Method

This member overrides **Control.OnHandleCreated**.

```
[Visual Basic]
Overrides Protected Sub OnHandleCreated( _
   ByVal e As EventArgs _
)
[C#]
protected override void OnHandleCreated(
   EventArgs e
);
[C++]
protected: void OnHandleCreated(
   EventArgs* e
);
[JScript]
protected override function OnHandleCreated(
   e : EventArgs
);
```

Requirements

Platforms: Windows 98, Windows NT 4.0, Windows Millennium Edition, Windows 2000, Windows XP Home Edition, Windows XP Professional, Windows Server 2003 family

TreeView.OnHandleDestroyed Method

This member overrides **Control.OnHandleDestroyed**.

```
[Visual Basic]
Overrides Protected Sub OnHandleDestroyed( _
   ByVal e As EventArgs _
)
[C#]
protected override void OnHandleDestroyed(
   EventArgs e
);
[C++]
protected: void OnHandleDestroyed(
   EventArgs* e
);
[JScript]
protected override function OnHandleDestroyed(
   e : EventArgs
);
```

Requirements

Platforms: Windows 98, Windows NT 4.0, Windows Millennium Edition, Windows 2000, Windows XP Home Edition, Windows XP Professional, Windows Server 2003 family

TreeView.OnItemDrag Method

Raises the **ItemDrag** event.

```
[Visual Basic]
Protected Overridable Sub OnItemDrag( _
   ByVal e As ItemDragEventArgs _
)
[C#]
protected virtual void OnItemDrag(
   ItemDragEventArgs e
);
[C++]
protected: virtual void OnItemDrag(
   ItemDragEventArgs* e
);
[JScript]
protected function OnItemDrag(
   e : ItemDragEventArgs
);
```

Parameters

e

An **ItemDragEventArgs** that contains the event data.

Remarks

Raising an event invokes the event handler through a delegate.

The **OnItemDrag** method also allows derived classes to handle the event without attaching a delegate. This is the preferred technique for handling the event in a derived class.

Notes to Inheritors: When overriding **OnItemDrag** in a derived class, be sure to call the base class's **OnItemDrag** method so that registered delegates receive the event.

Requirements

Platforms: Windows 98, Windows NT 4.0, Windows Millennium Edition, Windows 2000, Windows XP Home Edition, Windows XP Professional, Windows Server 2003 family

TreeView.OnKeyDown Method

This member overrides **Control.OnKeyDown**.

```
[Visual Basic]
Overrides Protected Sub OnKeyDown( _
   ByVal e As KeyEventArgs _
)
[C#]
protected override void OnKeyDown(
   KeyEventArgs e
);
[C++]
protected: void OnKeyDown(
   KeyEventArgs* e
);
[JScript]
protected override function OnKeyDown(
   e : KeyEventArgs
);
```

Requirements

Platforms: Windows 98, Windows NT 4.0, Windows Millennium Edition, Windows 2000, Windows XP Home Edition, Windows XP Professional, Windows Server 2003 family, .NET Compact Framework - Windows CE .NET

TreeView.OnKeyPress Method

This member overrides **Control.OnKeyPress**.

```
[Visual Basic]
Overrides Protected Sub OnKeyPress( _
   ByVal e As KeyPressEventArgs _
)
[C#]
protected override void OnKeyPress(
   KeyPressEventArgs e
);
[C++]
protected: void OnKeyPress(
   KeyPressEventArgs* e
);
[JScript]
protected override function OnKeyPress(
   e : KeyPressEventArgs
);
```

Requirements

Platforms: Windows 98, Windows NT 4.0, Windows Millennium Edition, Windows 2000, Windows XP Home Edition, Windows XP Professional, Windows Server 2003 family, .NET Compact Framework - Windows CE .NET

TreeView.OnKeyUp Method

This member overrides **Control.OnKeyUp**.

```
[Visual Basic]
Overrides Protected Sub OnKeyUp( _
   ByVal e As KeyEventArgs _
)
[C#]
protected override void OnKeyUp(
   KeyEventArgs e
);
[C++]
protected: void OnKeyUp(
   KeyEventArgs* e
);
[JScript]
protected override function OnKeyUp(
   e : KeyEventArgs
);
```

Requirements

Platforms: Windows 98, Windows NT 4.0, Windows Millennium Edition, Windows 2000, Windows XP Home Edition, Windows XP Professional, Windows Server 2003 family, .NET Compact Framework - Windows CE .NET

TreeView.ToString Method

This member overrides **Object.ToString**.

```
[Visual Basic]
Overrides Public Function ToString() As String
[C#]
public override string ToString();
[C++]
public: String* ToString();
[JScript]
public override function ToString() : String;
```

Requirements

Platforms: Windows 98, Windows NT 4.0, Windows Millennium Edition, Windows 2000, Windows XP Home Edition, Windows XP Professional, Windows Server 2003 family, .NET Compact Framework - Windows CE .NET

TreeView.WndProc Method

This member overrides **Control.WndProc**.

```
[Visual Basic]
Overrides Protected Sub WndProc( _
   ByRef m As Message _
)
[C#]
protected override void WndProc(
   ref Message m
);
[C++]
protected: void WndProc(
   Message* m
);
[JScript]
protected override function WndProc(
   m : Message
);
```

Requirements

Platforms: Windows 98, Windows NT 4.0, Windows Millennium Edition, Windows 2000, Windows XP Home Edition, Windows XP Professional, Windows Server 2003 family

TreeView.AfterCheck Event

Occurs after the tree node check box is checked.

```
[Visual Basic]
Public Event AfterCheck As TreeViewEventHandler
[C#]
public event TreeViewEventHandler AfterCheck;
[C++]
public: __event TreeViewEventHandler* AfterCheck;
```

[JScript] In JScript, you can handle the events defined by a class, but you cannot define your own.

Event Data

The event handler receives an argument of type **TreeViewEventArgs** containing data related to this event. The following **TreeViewEventArgs** properties provide information specific to this event.

Property	Description
Action	Gets the type of action that raised the event.
Node	Gets the tree node that has been checked, expanded, collapsed, or selected.

Remarks

> **Note** Setting the **TreeNode.Checked** property from within the **BeforeCheck** or **AfterCheck** event causes the event to be raised multiple times and can result in unexpected behavior. For example, you might set the **Checked** property in the event handler when you are recursively updating the child nodes, so the user does not have to expand and check each one individually. To prevent the event from being raised multiple times, add logic to your event handler that only executes your recursive code if the **Action** property of the **TreeViewEventArgs** is not set to **TreeViewAction.Unknown**.

Example

See related example in the **System.Windows.Forms.TreeView** class topic.

Requirements

Platforms: Windows 98, Windows NT 4.0, Windows Millennium Edition, Windows 2000, Windows XP Home Edition, Windows XP Professional, Windows Server 2003 family

TreeView.AfterCollapse Event

Occurs after the tree node is collapsed.

```
[Visual Basic]
Public Event AfterCollapse As TreeViewEventHandler
[C#]
public event TreeViewEventHandler AfterCollapse;
[C++]
public: __event TreeViewEventHandler* AfterCollapse;
```

[JScript] In JScript, you can handle the events defined by a class, but you cannot define your own.

Event Data

The event handler receives an argument of type **TreeViewEventArgs** containing data related to this event. The following **TreeViewEventArgs** properties provide information specific to this event.

Property	Description
Action	Gets the type of action that raised the event.
Node	Gets the tree node that has been checked, expanded, collapsed, or selected.

Example

See related example in the **System.Windows.Forms.TreeView** class topic.

Requirements

Platforms: Windows 98, Windows NT 4.0, Windows Millennium Edition, Windows 2000, Windows XP Home Edition, Windows XP Professional, Windows Server 2003 family

TreeView.AfterExpand Event

Occurs after the tree node is expanded.

```
[Visual Basic]
Public Event AfterExpand As TreeViewEventHandler
[C#]
public event TreeViewEventHandler AfterExpand;
[C++]
public: __event TreeViewEventHandler* AfterExpand;
```

[JScript] In JScript, you can handle the events defined by a class, but you cannot define your own.

Event Data

The event handler receives an argument of type **TreeViewEventArgs** containing data related to this event. The following **TreeViewEventArgs** properties provide information specific to this event.

Property	Description
Action	Gets the type of action that raised the event.
Node	Gets the tree node that has been checked, expanded, collapsed, or selected.

Requirements

Platforms: Windows 98, Windows NT 4.0, Windows Millennium Edition, Windows 2000, Windows XP Home Edition, Windows XP Professional, Windows Server 2003 family

TreeView.AfterLabelEdit Event

Occurs after the tree node label text is edited.

[Visual Basic]
```
Public Event AfterLabelEdit As NodeLabelEditEventHandler
```
[C#]
```
public event NodeLabelEditEventHandler AfterLabelEdit;
```
[C++]
```
public: __event NodeLabelEditEventHandler* AfterLabelEdit;
```

[JScript] In JScript, you can handle the events defined by a class, but you cannot define your own.

Event Data

The event handler receives an argument of type **NodeLabelEditEventArgs** containing data related to this event. The following **NodeLabelEditEventArgs** properties provide information specific to this event.

Property	Description
CancelEdit	Gets or sets a value indicating whether the edit has been canceled.
Label	Gets the new text to associate with the tree node.
Node	Gets the tree node containing the text to edit.

Example

See related example in the **System.Windows.Forms.TreeView** class topic.

Requirements

Platforms: Windows 98, Windows NT 4.0, Windows Millennium Edition, Windows 2000, Windows XP Home Edition, Windows XP Professional, Windows Server 2003 family

TreeView.AfterSelect Event

Occurs after the tree node is selected.

[Visual Basic]
```
Public Event AfterSelect As TreeViewEventHandler
```
[C#]
```
public event TreeViewEventHandler AfterSelect;
```
[C++]
```
public: __event TreeViewEventHandler* AfterSelect;
```

[JScript] In JScript, you can handle the events defined by a class, but you cannot define your own.

Event Data

The event handler receives an argument of type **TreeViewEventArgs** containing data related to this event. The following **TreeViewEventArgs** properties provide information specific to this event.

Property	Description
Action	Gets the type of action that raised the event.
Node	Gets the tree node that has been checked, expanded, collapsed, or selected.

Requirements

Platforms: Windows 98, Windows NT 4.0, Windows Millennium Edition, Windows 2000, Windows XP Home Edition, Windows XP Professional, Windows Server 2003 family

TreeView.BackgroundImageChanged Event

This member supports the .NET Framework infrastructure and is not intended to be used directly from your code.

[Visual Basic]
```
Public Shadows Event BackgroundImageChanged As EventHandler
```
[C#]
```
public new event EventHandler BackgroundImageChanged;
```
[C++]
```
public: __event EventHandler* BackgroundImageChanged;
```

[JScript] In JScript, you can handle the events defined by a class, but you cannot define your own.

TreeView.BeforeCheck Event

Occurs before the tree node check box is checked.

[Visual Basic]
```
Public Event BeforeCheck As TreeViewCancelEventHandler
```
[C#]
```
public event TreeViewCancelEventHandler BeforeCheck;
```
[C++]
```
public: __event TreeViewCancelEventHandler* BeforeCheck;
```

[JScript] In JScript, you can handle the events defined by a class, but you cannot define your own.

Event Data

The event handler receives an argument of type **TreeViewCancelEventArgs** containing data related to this event. The following **TreeViewCancelEventArgs** properties provide information specific to this event.

Property	Description
Action	Gets the type of **TreeViewAction** that raised the event.
Cancel (inherited from **CancelEventArgs**)	Gets or sets a value indicating whether the event should be canceled.
Node	Gets the tree node to be checked, expanded, collapsed, or selected.

Remarks

Note Setting the **TreeNode.Checked** property from within the **BeforeCheck** or **AfterCheck** event causes the event to be raised multiple times and can result in unexpected behavior. For example, you might set the **Checked** property in the event handler when you are recursively updating the child nodes, so the user does not have to expand and check each one individually. To prevent the event from being raised multiple times, add logic to your event handler that only executes your recursive code if the **Action** property of the **TreeViewEventArgs** is not set to **TreeViewAction.Unknown**.

Example

See related example in the **System.Windows.Forms.TreeView** class topic.

Requirements

Platforms: Windows 98, Windows NT 4.0, Windows Millennium Edition, Windows 2000, Windows XP Home Edition, Windows XP Professional, Windows Server 2003 family

TreeView.BeforeCollapse Event

Occurs before the tree node is collapsed.

```
[Visual Basic]
Public Event BeforeCollapse As TreeViewCancelEventHandler
[C#]
public event TreeViewCancelEventHandler BeforeCollapse;
[C++]
public: __event TreeViewCancelEventHandler* BeforeCollapse;
```

[JScript] In JScript, you can handle the events defined by a class, but you cannot define your own.

Event Data

The event handler receives an argument of type **TreeViewCancel-EventArgs** containing data related to this event. The following **TreeViewCancelEventArgs** properties provide information specific to this event.

Property	Description
Action	Gets the type of **TreeViewAction** that raised the event.
Cancel (inherited from **CancelEventArgs**)	Gets or sets a value indicating whether the event should be canceled.
Node	Gets the tree node to be checked, expanded, collapsed, or selected.

Requirements

Platforms: Windows 98, Windows NT 4.0, Windows Millennium Edition, Windows 2000, Windows XP Home Edition, Windows XP Professional, Windows Server 2003 family

TreeView.BeforeExpand Event

Occurs before the tree node is expanded.

```
[Visual Basic]
Public Event BeforeExpand As TreeViewCancelEventHandler
[C#]
public event TreeViewCancelEventHandler BeforeExpand;
[C++]
public: __event TreeViewCancelEventHandler* BeforeExpand;
```

[JScript] In JScript, you can handle the events defined by a class, but you cannot define your own.

Event Data

The event handler receives an argument of type **TreeViewCancel-EventArgs** containing data related to this event. The following **TreeViewCancelEventArgs** properties provide information specific to this event.

Property	Description
Action	Gets the type of **TreeViewAction** that raised the event.
Cancel (inherited from **CancelEventArgs**)	Gets or sets a value indicating whether the event should be canceled.
Node	Gets the tree node to be checked, expanded, collapsed, or selected.

Requirements

Platforms: Windows 98, Windows NT 4.0, Windows Millennium Edition, Windows 2000, Windows XP Home Edition, Windows XP Professional, Windows Server 2003 family

TreeView.BeforeLabelEdit Event

Occurs before the tree node label text is edited.

```
[Visual Basic]
Public Event BeforeLabelEdit As NodeLabelEditEventHandler
[C#]
public event NodeLabelEditEventHandler BeforeLabelEdit;
[C++]
public: __event NodeLabelEditEventHandler* BeforeLabelEdit;
```

[JScript] In JScript, you can handle the events defined by a class, but you cannot define your own.

Event Data

The event handler receives an argument of type **NodeLabelEdit-EventArgs** containing data related to this event. The following **NodeLabelEditEventArgs** properties provide information specific to this event.

Property	Description
CancelEdit	Gets or sets a value indicating whether the edit has been canceled.
Label	Gets the new text to associate with the tree node.
Node	Gets the tree node containing the text to edit.

Requirements

Platforms: Windows 98, Windows NT 4.0, Windows Millennium Edition, Windows 2000, Windows XP Home Edition, Windows XP Professional, Windows Server 2003 family

TreeView.BeforeSelect Event

Occurs before the tree node is selected.

```
[Visual Basic]
Public Event BeforeSelect As TreeViewCancelEventHandler
[C#]
public event TreeViewCancelEventHandler BeforeSelect;
[C++]
public: __event TreeViewCancelEventHandler* BeforeSelect;
```

[JScript] In JScript, you can handle the events defined by a class, but you cannot define your own.

Event Data

The event handler receives an argument of type **TreeViewCancelEventArgs** containing data related to this event. The following **TreeViewCancelEventArgs** properties provide information specific to this event.

Property	Description
Action	Gets the type of **TreeViewAction** that raised the event.
Cancel (inherited from **CancelEventArgs**)	Gets or sets a value indicating whether the event should be canceled.
Node	Gets the tree node to be checked, expanded, collapsed, or selected.

Requirements

Platforms: Windows 98, Windows NT 4.0, Windows Millennium Edition, Windows 2000, Windows XP Home Edition, Windows XP Professional, Windows Server 2003 family

TreeView.ItemDrag Event

Occurs when an item is dragged into the tree view control.

```
[Visual Basic]
Public Event ItemDrag As ItemDragEventHandler
[C#]
public event ItemDragEventHandler ItemDrag;
[C++]
public: __event ItemDragEventHandler* ItemDrag;
```

[JScript] In JScript, you can handle the events defined by a class, but you cannot define your own.

Event Data

The event handler receives an argument of type **ItemDragEventArgs** containing data related to this event. The following **ItemDragEventArgs** properties provide information specific to this event.

Property	Description
Button	Gets the name of the mouse button that was clicked during the drag operation.
Item	Gets the item that is being dragged.

Requirements

Platforms: Windows 98, Windows NT 4.0, Windows Millennium Edition, Windows 2000, Windows XP Home Edition, Windows XP Professional, Windows Server 2003 family

TreeView.Paint Event

This member supports the .NET Framework infrastructure and is not intended to be used directly from your code.

```
[Visual Basic]
Public Shadows Event Paint As PaintEventHandler
[C#]
public new event PaintEventHandler Paint;
[C++]
public: __event PaintEventHandler* Paint;
```

[JScript] In JScript, you can handle the events defined by a class, but you cannot define your own.

TreeView.TextChanged Event

This member supports the .NET Framework infrastructure and is not intended to be used directly from your code.

```
[Visual Basic]
Public Shadows Event TextChanged As EventHandler
[C#]
public new event EventHandler TextChanged;
[C++]
public: __event EventHandler* TextChanged;
```

[JScript] In JScript, you can handle the events defined by a class, but you cannot define your own.

TreeViewAction Enumeration

Specifies the action that raised a **TreeViewEventArgs** event.

[Visual Basic]
```
<Serializable>
Public Enum TreeViewAction
```
[C#]
```
[Serializable]
public enum TreeViewAction
```
[C++]
```
[Serializable]
__value public enum TreeViewAction
```
[JScript]
```
public
   Serializable
enum TreeViewAction
```

Remarks

This enumeration is used by members such as the **TreeViewEventArgs** constructor.

Members

Member name	Description
ByKeyboard Supported by the .NET Compact Framework.	The event was caused by a keystroke.
ByMouse Supported by the .NET Compact Framework.	The event was caused by a mouse operation.
Collapse Supported by the .NET Compact Framework.	The event was caused by the **TreeNode** collapsing.
Expand Supported by the .NET Compact Framework.	The event was caused by the **TreeNode** expanding.
Unknown Supported by the .NET Compact Framework.	The action that caused the event is unknown.

Requirements

Namespace: System.Windows.Forms

Platforms: Windows 98, Windows NT 4.0, Windows Millennium Edition, Windows 2000, Windows XP Home Edition, Windows XP Professional, Windows Server 2003 family, .NET Compact Framework - Windows CE .NET

Assembly: System.Windows.Forms (in System.Windows.Forms.dll)

TreeViewCancelEventArgs Class

Provides data for the **BeforeCheck**, **BeforeCollapse**, **BeforeExpand**, or **BeforeSelect** events of a **TreeView** control.

For a list of all members of this type, see **TreeViewCancelEventArgs Members**.

System.Object
  System.EventArgs
    System.ComponentModel.CancelEventArgs
      System.Windows.Forms.TreeViewCancelEventArgs

```
[Visual Basic]
Public Class TreeViewCancelEventArgs
   Inherits CancelEventArgs
[C#]
public class TreeViewCancelEventArgs : CancelEventArgs
[C++]
public __gc class TreeViewCancelEventArgs : public CancelEventArgs
[JScript]
public class TreeViewCancelEventArgs extends CancelEventArgs
```

Thread Safety

Any public static (**Shared** in Visual Basic) members of this type are safe for multithreaded operations. Any instance members are not guaranteed to be thread safe.

Requirements

Namespace: System.Windows.Forms

Platforms: Windows 98, Windows NT 4.0, Windows Millennium Edition, Windows 2000, Windows XP Home Edition, Windows XP Professional, Windows Server 2003 family, .NET Compact Framework - Windows CE .NET

Assembly: System.Windows.Forms (in System.Windows.Forms.dll)

TreeViewCancelEventArgs Constructor

Initializes a new instance of the **TreeViewCancelEventArgs** class with the specified tree node, a value specifying whether the event is to be canceled, and the type of tree view action that raised the event.

```
[Visual Basic]
Public Sub New( _
   ByVal node As TreeNode, _
   ByVal cancel As Boolean, _
   ByVal action As TreeViewAction _
)
[C#]
public TreeViewCancelEventArgs(
   TreeNode node,
   bool cancel,
   TreeViewAction action
);
[C++]
public: TreeViewCancelEventArgs(
   TreeNode* node,
   bool cancel,
   TreeViewAction action
);
[JScript]
public function TreeViewCancelEventArgs(
   node : TreeNode,
   cancel : Boolean,
   action : TreeViewAction
);
```

Parameters

node
  The **TreeNode** that the event is responding to.

cancel
  true to cancel the event; otherwise, **false**.

action
  The type of **TreeViewAction** that raised the event.

Requirements

Platforms: Windows 98, Windows NT 4.0, Windows Millennium Edition, Windows 2000, Windows XP Home Edition, Windows XP Professional, Windows Server 2003 family, .NET Compact Framework - Windows CE .NET

TreeViewCancelEventArgs.Action Property

Gets the type of **TreeViewAction** that raised the event.

```
[Visual Basic]
Public ReadOnly Property Action As TreeViewAction
[C#]
public TreeViewAction Action {get;}
[C++]
public: __property TreeViewAction get_Action();
[JScript]
public function get Action() : TreeViewAction;
```

Property Value

One of the **TreeViewAction** values.

Requirements

Platforms: Windows 98, Windows NT 4.0, Windows Millennium Edition, Windows 2000, Windows XP Home Edition, Windows XP Professional, Windows Server 2003 family, .NET Compact Framework - Windows CE .NET

TreeViewCancelEventArgs.Node Property

Gets the tree node to be checked, expanded, collapsed, or selected.

```
[Visual Basic]
Public ReadOnly Property Node As TreeNode
[C#]
public TreeNode Node {get;}
[C++]
public: __property TreeNode* get_Node();
[JScript]
public function get Node() : TreeNode;
```

Property Value

The **TreeNode** to be checked, expanded, collapsed, or selected.

Requirements

Platforms: Windows 98, Windows NT 4.0, Windows Millennium Edition, Windows 2000, Windows XP Home Edition, Windows XP Professional, Windows Server 2003 family, .NET Compact Framework - Windows CE .NET

TreeViewCancelEventHandler Delegate

Represents the method that will handle the **BeforeCheck**, **BeforeCollapse**, **BeforeExpand**, or **BeforeSelect** event of a **TreeView**.

[Visual Basic]
```
<Serializable>
Public Delegate Sub TreeViewCancelEventHandler( _
   ByVal sender As Object, _
   ByVal e As TreeViewCancelEventArgs _
)
```
[C#]
```
[Serializable]
public delegate void TreeViewCancelEventHandler(
   object sender,
   TreeViewCancelEventArgs e
);
```
[C++]
```
[Serializable]
public __gc __delegate void TreeViewCancelEventHandler(
   Object* sender,
   TreeViewCancelEventArgs* e
);
```

[JScript] In JScript, you can use the delegates in the .NET Framework, but you cannot define your own.

Parameters [Visual Basic, C#, C++]

The declaration of your event handler must have the same parameters as the **TreeViewCancelEventHandler** delegate declaration.

sender

The source of the event.

e

A **TreeViewCancelEventArgs** that contains the event data.

Remarks

When you create a **TreeViewCancelEventArgs** delegate, you identify the method that will handle the event. To associate the event with your event handler, add an instance of the delegate to the event. The event handler is called whenever the event occurs, unless you remove the delegate.

Requirements

Namespace: System.Windows.Forms

Platforms: Windows 98, Windows NT 4.0, Windows Millennium Edition, Windows 2000, Windows XP Home Edition, Windows XP Professional, Windows Server 2003 family, .NET Compact Framework - Windows CE .NET

Assembly: System.Windows.Forms (in System.Windows.Forms.dll)

TreeViewEventArgs Class

Provides data for the **AfterCheck**, **AfterCollapse**, **AfterExpand**, or **AfterSelect** events of a **TreeView** control.

System.Object
  System.EventArgs
    System.Windows.Forms.TreeViewEventArgs

[Visual Basic]
```
Public Class TreeViewEventArgs
   Inherits EventArgs
```
[C#]
```
public class TreeViewEventArgs : EventArgs
```
[C++]
```
public __gc class TreeViewEventArgs : public EventArgs
```
[JScript]
```
public class TreeViewEventArgs extends EventArgs
```

Thread Safety

Any public static (**Shared** in Visual Basic) members of this type are safe for multithreaded operations. Any instance members are not guaranteed to be thread safe.

Requirements

Namespace: System.Windows.Forms

Platforms: Windows 98, Windows NT 4.0, Windows Millennium Edition, Windows 2000, Windows XP Home Edition, Windows XP Professional, Windows Server 2003 family, .NET Compact Framework - Windows CE .NET

Assembly: System.Windows.Forms (in System.Windows.Forms.dll)

TreeViewEventArgs Constructor

Initializes a new instance of the **TreeViewEventArgs** class.

Overload List

Initializes a new instance of the **TreeViewEventArgs** class for the specified tree node.

[Visual Basic] **Public Sub New(TreeNode)**

[C#] **public TreeViewEventArgs(TreeNode);**

[C++] **public: TreeViewEventArgs(TreeNode*);**

[JScript] **public function TreeViewEventArgs(TreeNode);**

Initializes a new instance of the **TreeViewEventArgs** class for the specified tree node and with the specified type of action that raised the event.

Supported by the .NET Compact Framework.

[Visual Basic] **Public Sub New(TreeNode, TreeViewAction)**

[C#] **public TreeViewEventArgs(TreeNode, TreeViewAction);**

[C++] **public: TreeViewEventArgs(TreeNode*, TreeViewAction);**

[JScript] **public function TreeViewEventArgs(TreeNode, TreeViewAction);**

TreeViewEventArgs Constructor (TreeNode)

Initializes a new instance of the **TreeViewEventArgs** class for the specified tree node.

[Visual Basic]
```
Public Sub New( _
   ByVal node As TreeNode _
)
```
[C#]
```
public TreeViewEventArgs(
   TreeNode node
);
```
[C++]
```
public: TreeViewEventArgs(
   TreeNode* node
);
```
[JScript]
```
public function TreeViewEventArgs(
   node : TreeNode
);
```

Parameters

node
  The **TreeNode** that the event is responding to.

Requirements

Platforms: Windows 98, Windows NT 4.0, Windows Millennium Edition, Windows 2000, Windows XP Home Edition, Windows XP Professional, Windows Server 2003 family

TreeViewEventArgs Constructor (TreeNode, TreeViewAction)

Initializes a new instance of the **TreeViewEventArgs** class for the specified tree node and with the specified type of action that raised the event.

[Visual Basic]
```
Public Sub New( _
   ByVal node As TreeNode, _
   ByVal action As TreeViewAction _
)
```
[C#]
```
public TreeViewEventArgs(
   TreeNode node,
   TreeViewAction action
);
```
[C++]
```
public: TreeViewEventArgs(
   TreeNode* node,
   TreeViewAction action
);
```
[JScript]
```
public function TreeViewEventArgs(
   node : TreeNode,
   action : TreeViewAction
);
```

Parameters

node

The **TreeNode** that the event is responding to.

action

The type of **TreeViewAction** that raised the event.

Requirements

Platforms: Windows 98, Windows NT 4.0, Windows Millennium Edition, Windows 2000, Windows XP Home Edition, Windows XP Professional, Windows Server 2003 family, .NET Compact Framework - Windows CE .NET

TreeViewEventArgs.Action Property

Gets the type of action that raised the event.

```
[Visual Basic]
Public ReadOnly Property Action As TreeViewAction
[C#]
public TreeViewAction Action {get;}
[C++]
public: __property TreeViewAction get_Action();
[JScript]
public function get Action() : TreeViewAction;
```

Property Value

The type of **TreeViewAction** that raised the event.

Requirements

Platforms: Windows 98, Windows NT 4.0, Windows Millennium Edition, Windows 2000, Windows XP Home Edition, Windows XP Professional, Windows Server 2003 family, .NET Compact Framework - Windows CE .NET

TreeViewEventArgs.Node Property

Gets the tree node that has been checked, expanded, collapsed, or selected.

```
[Visual Basic]
Public ReadOnly Property Node As TreeNode
[C#]
public TreeNode Node {get;}
[C++]
public: __property TreeNode* get_Node();
[JScript]
public function get Node() : TreeNode;
```

Property Value

The **TreeNode** that has been checked, expanded, collapsed, or selected.

Requirements

Platforms: Windows 98, Windows NT 4.0, Windows Millennium Edition, Windows 2000, Windows XP Home Edition, Windows XP Professional, Windows Server 2003 family, .NET Compact Framework - Windows CE .NET

TreeViewEventHandler Delegate

Represents the method that will handle the **AfterCheck**, **After-Collapse**, **AfterExpand**, or **AfterSelect** event of a **TreeView**.

[Visual Basic]
```
<Serializable>
Public Delegate Sub TreeViewEventHandler( _
   ByVal sender As Object, _
   ByVal e As TreeViewEventArgs _
)
```
[C#]
```
[Serializable]
public delegate void TreeViewEventHandler(
   object sender,
   TreeViewEventArgs e
);
```
[C++]
```
[Serializable]
public __gc __delegate void TreeViewEventHandler(
   Object* sender,
   TreeViewEventArgs* e
);
```
[JScript] In JScript, you can use the delegates in the .NET Framework, but you cannot define your own.

Parameters [Visual Basic, C#, C++]

The declaration of your event handler must have the same parameters as the **TreeViewEventHandler** delegate declaration.

sender

The source of the event.

e

A **TreeViewEventArgs** that contains the event data.

Remarks

When you create a **TreeViewEventArgs** delegate, you identify the method that will handle the event. To associate the event with your event handler, add an instance of the delegate to the event. The event handler is called whenever the event occurs, unless you remove the delegate.

Requirements

Namespace: System.Windows.Forms

Platforms: Windows 98, Windows NT 4.0, Windows Millennium Edition, Windows 2000, Windows XP Home Edition, Windows XP Professional, Windows Server 2003 family, .NET Compact Framework - Windows CE .NET

Assembly: System.Windows.Forms (in System.Windows.Forms.dll)

TreeViewImageIndexConverter Class

Provides a type converter to convert data for an image index to and from one data type to another for use by the **TreeView** control.

System.Object
System.ComponentModel.TypeConverter
System.ComponentModel.BaseNumberConverter
System.ComponentModel.Int32Converter
System.Windows.Forms.ImageIndexConverter
System.Windows.Forms.TreeViewImageIndex-Converter

```
[Visual Basic]
Public Class TreeViewImageIndexConverter
   Inherits ImageIndexConverter
[C#]
public class TreeViewImageIndexConverter : ImageIndexConverter
[C++]
public __gc class TreeViewImageIndexConverter : public
   ImageIndexConverter
[JScript]
public class TreeViewImageIndexConverter extends
   ImageIndexConverter
```

Thread Safety

Any public static (**Shared** in Visual Basic) members of this type are safe for multithreaded operations. Any instance members are not guaranteed to be thread safe.

Remarks

Note Typically, you do not directly create an instance of a **TreeViewImageIndexConverter**. Instead, call the **GetConverter** method of **TypeDescriptor**. For more information, see the examples in the **TypeConverter** base class.

Requirements

Namespace: System.Windows.Forms

Platforms: Windows 98, Windows NT 4.0, Windows Millennium Edition, Windows 2000, Windows XP Home Edition, Windows XP Professional, Windows Server 2003 family

Assembly: System.Windows.Forms (in System.Windows.Forms.dll)

TreeViewImageIndexConverter Constructor

Initializes a new instance of the **TreeViewImageIndexConverter** class.

```
[Visual Basic]
Public Sub New()
[C#]
public TreeViewImageIndexConverter();
[C++]
public: TreeViewImageIndexConverter();
[JScript]
public function TreeViewImageIndexConverter();
```

Remarks

The default constructor initializes any fields to their default values.

Requirements

Platforms: Windows 98, Windows NT 4.0, Windows Millennium Edition, Windows 2000, Windows XP Home Edition, Windows XP Professional, Windows Server 2003 family

TreeViewImageIndexConverter.IncludeNoneAsStandardValue Property

Gets a value indicating whether a **none** or a null reference (**Nothing** in Visual Basic) value is valid in the **TypeConverter.StandardValuesCollection** collection.

```
[Visual Basic]
Overrides Protected ReadOnly Property IncludeNoneAsStandardValue As _
   _
   Boolean
[C#]
protected override bool IncludeNoneAsStandardValue {get;}
[C++]
protected: __property bool get_IncludeNoneAsStandardValue();
[JScript]
protected override function get IncludeNoneAsStandardValue() :
   Boolean;
```

Property Value

true if a **none** or a null reference (**Nothing** in Visual Basic) value is valid in the standard values collection; otherwise, **false**.

Remarks

As implemented in this class, this property always returns **false**.

Requirements

Platforms: Windows 98, Windows NT 4.0, Windows Millennium Edition, Windows 2000, Windows XP Home Edition, Windows XP Professional, Windows Server 2003 family

UICues Enumeration

Specifies the state of the user interface.

This enumeration has a **FlagsAttribute** attribute that allows a bitwise combination of its member values.

[Visual Basic]
```
<Flags>
<Serializable>
Public Enum UICues
```
[C#]
```
[Flags]
[Serializable]
public enum UICues
```
[C++]
```
[Flags]
[Serializable]
__value public enum UICues
```
[JScript]
```
public
   Flags
   Serializable
enum UICues
```

Remarks

This enumeration is used by members such as the **UICuesEventArgs** constructor.

This enumeration is used to specify which user interface cues will be displayed or changed. For example, when the user presses the ALT key, the keyboard shortcuts on the menu are displayed by underlining the appropriate character. The bitwise combination of **UICues** for this example would be **ShowKeyboard** and **ChangeKeyboard**.

Members

Member name	Description	Value
Changed	The state of the focus cues and keyboard cues has changed.	12
ChangeFocus	The state of the focus cues has changed.	4
ChangeKeyboard	The state of the keyboard cues has changed.	8
None	No change was made.	0
ShowFocus	Focus rectangles are displayed after the change.	1
ShowKeyboard	Keyboard cues are underlined after the change.	2
Shown	Focus rectangles are displayed and keyboard cues are underlined after the change.	3

Requirements

Namespace: System.Windows.Forms

Platforms: Windows 98, Windows NT 4.0, Windows Millennium Edition, Windows 2000, Windows XP Home Edition, Windows XP Professional, Windows Server 2003 family

Assembly: System.Windows.Forms (in System.Windows.Forms.dll)

UICuesEventArgs Class

Provides data for the **ChangeUICues** event.

System.Object
  System.EventArgs
    System.Windows.Forms.UICuesEventArgs

```
[Visual Basic]
Public Class UICuesEventArgs
   Inherits EventArgs
[C#]
public class UICuesEventArgs : EventArgs
[C++]
public __gc class UICuesEventArgs : public EventArgs
[JScript]
public class UICuesEventArgs extends EventArgs
```

Thread Safety

Any public static (**Shared** in Visual Basic) members of this type are safe for multithreaded operations. Any instance members are not guaranteed to be thread safe.

Remarks

A **UICuesEventArgs** specifies which user interface feature changed and its new value.

The **ChangeUICues** event occurs when the user interface changes by showing or hiding focus indicators or keyboard cues. This is usually when the user presses the TAB, ALT, or F10 keys.

Requirements

Namespace: System.Windows.Forms

Platforms: Windows 98, Windows NT 4.0, Windows Millennium Edition, Windows 2000, Windows XP Home Edition, Windows XP Professional, Windows Server 2003 family

Assembly: System.Windows.Forms (in System.Windows.Forms.dll)

UICuesEventArgs Constructor

Initializes a new instance of the **UICuesEventArgs** class with the specified **UICues**.

```
[Visual Basic]
Public Sub New( _
   ByVal uicues As UICues _
)
[C#]
public UICuesEventArgs(
   UICues uicues
);
[C++]
public: UICuesEventArgs(
   UICues uicues
);
[JScript]
public function UICuesEventArgs(
   uicues : UICues
);
```

Parameters

uicues
  A bitwise combination of the **UICues** values.

Requirements

Platforms: Windows 98, Windows NT 4.0, Windows Millennium Edition, Windows 2000, Windows XP Home Edition, Windows XP Professional, Windows Server 2003 family

UICuesEventArgs.Changed Property

Gets the bitwise combination of the **UICues** values.

```
[Visual Basic]
Public ReadOnly Property Changed As UICues
[C#]
public UICues Changed {get;}
[C++]
public: __property UICues get_Changed();
[JScript]
public function get Changed() : UICues;
```

Property Value

A bitwise combination of the **UICues** values. The default is **Changed**.

Requirements

Platforms: Windows 98, Windows NT 4.0, Windows Millennium Edition, Windows 2000, Windows XP Home Edition, Windows XP Professional, Windows Server 2003 family

UICuesEventArgs.ChangeFocus Property

Gets a value indicating whether the state of the focus cues has changed.

```
[Visual Basic]
Public ReadOnly Property ChangeFocus As Boolean
[C#]
public bool ChangeFocus {get;}
[C++]
public: __property bool get_ChangeFocus();
[JScript]
public function get ChangeFocus() : Boolean;
```

Property Value

true if the state of the focus cues has changed; otherwise, **false**.

Requirements

Platforms: Windows 98, Windows NT 4.0, Windows Millennium Edition, Windows 2000, Windows XP Home Edition, Windows XP Professional, Windows Server 2003 family

UICuesEventArgs.ChangeKeyboard Property

Gets a value indicating whether the state of the keyboard cues has changed.

```
[Visual Basic]
Public ReadOnly Property ChangeKeyboard As Boolean
[C#]
public bool ChangeKeyboard {get;}
[C++]
public: __property bool get_ChangeKeyboard();
[JScript]
public function get ChangeKeyboard() : Boolean;
```

Property Value

true if the state of the keyboard cues has changed; otherwise, **false**.

Requirements

Platforms: Windows 98, Windows NT 4.0,
Windows Millennium Edition, Windows 2000,
Windows XP Home Edition, Windows XP Professional,
Windows Server 2003 family

UICuesEventArgs.ShowFocus Property

Gets a value indicating whether focus rectangles are shown after the change.

```
[Visual Basic]
Public ReadOnly Property ShowFocus As Boolean
[C#]
public bool ShowFocus {get;}
[C++]
public: __property bool get_ShowFocus();
[JScript]
public function get ShowFocus() : Boolean;
```

Property Value

true if focus rectangles are shown after the change; otherwise, **false**.

Requirements

Platforms: Windows 98, Windows NT 4.0,
Windows Millennium Edition, Windows 2000,
Windows XP Home Edition, Windows XP Professional,
Windows Server 2003 family

UICuesEventArgs.ShowKeyboard Property

Gets a value indicating whether keyboard cues are underlined after the change.

```
[Visual Basic]
Public ReadOnly Property ShowKeyboard As Boolean
[C#]
public bool ShowKeyboard {get;}
[C++]
public: __property bool get_ShowKeyboard();
[JScript]
public function get ShowKeyboard() : Boolean;
```

Property Value

true if keyboard cues are underlined after the change; otherwise, **false**.

Requirements

Platforms: Windows 98, Windows NT 4.0,
Windows Millennium Edition, Windows 2000,
Windows XP Home Edition, Windows XP Professional,
Windows Server 2003 family

UICuesEventHandler Delegate

Represents a method that will handle the **ChangeUICues** event of a **Control**.

[Visual Basic]

```
<Serializable>
Public Delegate Sub UICuesEventHandler( _
   ByVal sender As Object, _
   ByVal e As UICuesEventArgs _
)
```

[C#]

```
[Serializable]
public delegate void UICuesEventHandler(
   object sender,
   UICuesEventArgs e
);
```

[C++]

```
[Serializable]
public __gc __delegate void UICuesEventHandler(
   Object* sender,
   UICuesEventArgs* e
);
```

[JScript] In JScript, you can use the delegates in the .NET Framework, but you cannot define your own.

Parameters [Visual Basic, C#, C++]

The declaration of your event handler must have the same parameters as the **UICuesEventHandler** delegate declaration.

sender

The source of the event.

e

A **UICuesEventArgs** that contains the event data.

Remarks

When you create a **UICuesEventHandler** delegate, you identify the method that will handle the event. To associate the event with your event handler, add an instance of the delegate to the event. The event handler is called whenever the event occurs, unless you remove the delegate.

Requirements

Namespace: System.Windows.Forms

Platforms: Windows 98, Windows NT 4.0, Windows Millennium Edition, Windows 2000, Windows XP Home Edition, Windows XP Professional, Windows Server 2003 family

Assembly: System.Windows.Forms (in System.Windows.Forms.dll)

UpDownBase Class

Implements the basic functionality required by an up-down control.

System.Object
 System.MarshalByRefObject
  System.ComponentModel.Component
   System.Windows.Forms.Control
    System.Windows.Forms.ScrollableControl
     System.Windows.Forms.ContainerControl
      System.Windows.Forms.UpDownBase
       System.Windows.Forms.DomainUpDown
       System.Windows.Forms.NumericUpDown

[Visual Basic]
```
MustInherit Public Class UpDownBase
   Inherits ContainerControl
```
[C#]
```
public abstract class UpDownBase : ContainerControl
```
[C++]
```
public __gc __abstract class UpDownBase : public ContainerControl
```
[JScript]
```
public abstract class UpDownBase extends ContainerControl
```

Thread Safety

Any public static (**Shared** in Visual Basic) members of this type are safe for multithreaded operations. Any instance members are not guaranteed to be thread safe.

Remarks

The up-down control consists of a text box and a small vertical scroll bar, commonly referred to as a spinner control. The **UpDownBase** class links the two controls and allows the user to change the display in the text box by clicking the up or down buttons or by entering the appropriate type of value directly into the text box. Use the up-down control in cases where you want to limit the list of values a user can select, similar to a list box or combo box. Depending upon the type of list you want to display, the advantage to using an up-down control is that it allows you to quickly set a range of valid values, rather than adding items one at a time. Implementing an up-down control requires less data validation than a text box, as you can limit the data type when you derive a class from **UpDownBase**. An example of this is the **NumericUpDown** class, which limits the values to the numeric type and uses a **Minimum** and **Maximum** property to validate the data.

To allow the user to use the arrow keys to change the contents of the up-down control, set the **InterceptArrowKeys** property to **true**. To restrict the user to values you specify, set the **ReadOnly** property to **true**. To control the alignment of text in the up-down control, set the **TextAlign** property. To set the alignment of the up and down buttons in relation to the text box portion of the control, set the **UpDownAlign** property to either **LeftRightAlignment.Left** or **LeftRightAlignment.Right**.

The **UpButton** and **DownButton** methods, when overridden, handle the clicking of the up or down buttons. When overridden, the methods **ValidateEditText** and **UpdateEditText** validate the value (either selected or entered) and update the text displayed in the up-down control. If the value fails validation, use the **Select** method to select the invalid text. This allows the user to quickly correct the text by simply typing in a new value without having to manually select or delete the existing text.

Notes to Inheritors: When you inherit from **UpDownBase**, you must override the following members: **DownButton**, **UpButton**, **UpdateEditText**, **ValidateEditText**.

Example

[Visual Basic, C#] The following example uses the derived class, **NumericUpDown**, and sets some of its properties derived from **UpDownBase**. This code assumes you have a **NumericUpDown** control, two **ComboBox** controls, and three **CheckBox** controls created on a form. Label the **ComboBox** controls: BorderStyle and TextAlign. Label the **CheckBox** controls: InterceptArrowKeys, ReadOnly, and UpDownAlign - Left. The code allows you to change the property values at run time and see how each affects the appearance and behavior of the up-down control. Add the following items to the combo box labled BorderStyle: None, Fixed3D, and FixedSingle items. Add the following items to the combo box labled TextAlign: Left, Right, and Center items.

[Visual Basic]
```
Private Sub comboBox1_SelectedIndexChanged(sender As Object, e As
EventArgs)
    ' Set the BorderStyle property.
    Select Case comboBox1.Text
        Case "Fixed3D"
            numericUpDown1.BorderStyle =
System.Windows.Forms.BorderStyle.Fixed3D
        Case "None"
            numericUpDown1.BorderStyle =
System.Windows.Forms.BorderStyle.None
        Case "FixedSingle"
            numericUpDown1.BorderStyle =
System.Windows.Forms.BorderStyle.FixedSingle
    End Select
End Sub

Private Sub comboBox2_SelectedIndexChanged(sender As Object, e As
EventArgs)
    ' Set the TextAlign property.
    Select Case comboBox2.Text
        Case "Right"
            numericUpDown1.TextAlign = HorizontalAlignment.Right
        Case "Left"
            numericUpDown1.TextAlign = HorizontalAlignment.Left
        Case "Center"
            numericUpDown1.TextAlign = HorizontalAlignment.Center
    End Select
End Sub

Private Sub checkBox1_Click(sender As Object, e As EventArgs)
    ' Evaluate and toggle the ReadOnly property.
    If numericUpDown1.ReadOnly Then
        numericUpDown1.ReadOnly = False
    Else
        numericUpDown1.ReadOnly = True
    End If
End Sub

Private Sub checkBox2_Click(sender As Object, e As EventArgs)
    ' Evaluate and toggle the InterceptArrowKeys property.
    If numericUpDown1.InterceptArrowKeys Then
        numericUpDown1.InterceptArrowKeys = False
    Else
        numericUpDown1.InterceptArrowKeys = True
    End If
End Sub

Private Sub checkBox3_Click(sender As Object, e As EventArgs)
    ' Evaluate and toggle the UpDownAlign property.
    If numericUpDown1.UpDownAlign = LeftRightAlignment.Left Then
        numericUpDown1.UpDownAlign = LeftRightAlignment.Right
    Else
        numericUpDown1.UpDownAlign = LeftRightAlignment.Left
```

```
    End If
End Sub
```

[C#]

```
private void comboBox1_SelectedIndexChanged(Object sender,
                                            EventArgs e)
 {
     // Set the BorderStyle property.
    switch(comboBox1.Text)
    {
        case "Fixed3D":
            numericUpDown1.BorderStyle =
System.Windows.Forms.BorderStyle.Fixed3D;
            break;
        case "None":
            numericUpDown1.BorderStyle =
System.Windows.Forms.BorderStyle.None;
            break;
        case "FixedSingle":
            numericUpDown1.BorderStyle =
System.Windows.Forms.BorderStyle.FixedSingle;
            break;
    }
 }

 private void comboBox2_SelectedIndexChanged(Object sender,
                                            EventArgs e)
 {
     // Set the TextAlign property.
    switch (comboBox2.Text)
    {
        case "Right":
            numericUpDown1.TextAlign = HorizontalAlignment.Right;
            break;
        case "Left":
            numericUpDown1.TextAlign = HorizontalAlignment.Left;
            break;
        case "Center":
            numericUpDown1.TextAlign = HorizontalAlignment.Center;
            break;
    }
 }

 private void checkBox1_Click(Object sender,
                              EventArgs e)
 {
     // Evaluate and toggle the ReadOnly property.
    if (numericUpDown1.ReadOnly)
    {
        numericUpDown1.ReadOnly = false;
    }
    else
    {
        numericUpDown1.ReadOnly = true;
    }
 }

 private void checkBox2_Click(Object sender,
                              EventArgs e)
 {
     // Evaluate and toggle the InterceptArrowKeys property.
    if (numericUpDown1.InterceptArrowKeys)
    {
        numericUpDown1.InterceptArrowKeys = false;
    }
    else
    {
        numericUpDown1.InterceptArrowKeys = true;
    }
 }

 private void checkBox3_Click(Object sender,
                              EventArgs e)
 {
     // Evaluate and toggle the UpDownAlign property.
    if (numericUpDown1.UpDownAlign == LeftRightAlignment.Left)
    {
        numericUpDown1.UpDownAlign = LeftRightAlignment.Right;
    }
    else
    {
        numericUpDown1.UpDownAlign = LeftRightAlignment.Left;
    }
 }
```

[C++, JScript] No example is available for C++ or JScript. To view a Visual Basic or C# example, click the Language Filter button <IMG SRC="filter1a.gif" ALT="Language Filter" BORDER=0> in the upper-left corner of the page.

Requirements

Namespace: System.Windows.Forms

Platforms: Windows 98, Windows NT 4.0, Windows Millennium Edition, Windows 2000, Windows XP Home Edition, Windows XP Professional, Windows Server 2003 family, .NET Compact Framework - Windows CE .NET

Assembly: System.Windows.Forms (in System.Windows.Forms.dll)

UpDownBase Constructor

Initializes a new instance of the **UpDownBase** class.

[Visual Basic]
```
Public Sub New()
```
[C#]
```
public UpDownBase();
```
[C++]
```
public: UpDownBase();
```
[JScript]
```
public function UpDownBase();
```

Requirements

Platforms: Windows 98, Windows NT 4.0, Windows Millennium Edition, Windows 2000, Windows XP Home Edition, Windows XP Professional, Windows Server 2003 family

UpDownBase.AutoScroll Property

This member overrides **ScrollableControl.AutoScroll**.

[Visual Basic]
```
Overrides Public Property AutoScroll As Boolean
```
[C#]
```
public override bool AutoScroll {get; set;}
```
[C++]
```
public: __property bool get_AutoScroll();
public: __property void set_AutoScroll(bool);
```
[JScript]
```
public override function get AutoScroll() : Boolean;
public override function set AutoScroll(Boolean);
```

Requirements

Platforms: Windows 98, Windows NT 4.0, Windows Millennium Edition, Windows 2000, Windows XP Home Edition, Windows XP Professional, Windows Server 2003 family

UpDownBase.AutoScrollMargin Property

This member supports the .NET Framework infrastructure and is not intended to be used directly from your code.

[Visual Basic]
```
Public Shadows Property AutoScrollMargin As Size
```
[C#]
```
public new Size AutoScrollMargin {get; set;}
```
[C++]
```
public: __property Size get_AutoScrollMargin();
public: __property void set_AutoScrollMargin(Size);
```
[JScript]
```
public hide function get AutoScrollMargin() : Size;
public hide function set AutoScrollMargin(Size);
```

UpDownBase.AutoScrollMinSize Property

This member supports the .NET Framework infrastructure and is not intended to be used directly from your code.

[Visual Basic]
```
Public Shadows Property AutoScrollMinSize As Size
```
[C#]
```
public new Size AutoScrollMinSize {get; set;}
```
[C++]
```
public: __property Size get_AutoScrollMinSize();
public: __property void set_AutoScrollMinSize(Size);
```
[JScript]
```
public hide function get AutoScrollMinSize() : Size;
public hide function set AutoScrollMinSize(Size);
```

UpDownBase.BackColor Property

This member overrides **Control.BackColor**.

[Visual Basic]
```
Overrides Public Property BackColor As Color
```
[C#]
```
public override Color BackColor {get; set;}
```
[C++]
```
public: __property Color get_BackColor();
public: __property void set_BackColor(Color);
```
[JScript]
```
public override function get BackColor() : Color;
public override function set BackColor(Color);
```

Requirements

Platforms: Windows 98, Windows NT 4.0, Windows Millennium Edition, Windows 2000, Windows XP Home Edition, Windows XP Professional, Windows Server 2003 family, .NET Compact Framework - Windows CE .NET

UpDownBase.BackgroundImage Property

This member overrides **Control.BackgroundImage**.

[Visual Basic]
```
Overrides Public Property BackgroundImage As Image
```
[C#]
```
public override Image BackgroundImage {get; set;}
```
[C++]
```
public: __property Image* get_BackgroundImage();
public: __property void set_BackgroundImage(Image*);
```
[JScript]
```
public override function get BackgroundImage() : Image;
public override function set BackgroundImage(Image);
```

Requirements

Platforms: Windows 98, Windows NT 4.0, Windows Millennium Edition, Windows 2000, Windows XP Home Edition, Windows XP Professional, Windows Server 2003 family

UpDownBase.BorderStyle Property

Gets or sets the border style for the up-down control.

[Visual Basic]
```
Public Property BorderStyle As BorderStyle
```
[C#]
```
public BorderStyle BorderStyle {get; set;}
```
[C++]
```
public: __property BorderStyle get_BorderStyle();
public: __property void set_BorderStyle(BorderStyle);
```
[JScript]
```
public function get BorderStyle() : BorderStyle;
public function set BorderStyle(BorderStyle);
```

Property Value

One of the **BorderStyle** values. The default value is **Fixed3D**.

Exceptions

Exception Type	Condition
InvalidEnumArgumentException	The value assigned is not one of the **BorderStyle** values.

Remarks

You can use the **BorderStyle** property to create borderless and flat controls in addition to the default three-dimensional control.

Example

[Visual Basic, C#] The following example uses the derived class, **NumericUpDown**, and sets some of its properties derived from **UpDownBase**. This code assumes you have a **NumericUpDown** control, two **ComboBox** controls, and three **CheckBox** controls created on a form. Label the **ComboBox** controls: BorderStyle and TextAlign. Label the **CheckBox** controls: InterceptArrowKeys, ReadOnly, and UpDownAlign - Left. The code allows you to change the property values at run time and see how each affects the appearance and behavior of the up-down control. Add the following items to the combo box labled BorderStyle: None, Fixed3D, and FixedSingle items. Add the following items to the combo box labled TextAlign: Left, Right, and Center items.

[Visual Basic]
```
Private Sub comboBox1_SelectedIndexChanged(sender As Object, e ↵
 As EventArgs)
    ' Set the BorderStyle property.
    Select Case comboBox1.Text
        Case "Fixed3D"
            numericUpDown1.BorderStyle = ↵
System.Windows.Forms.BorderStyle.Fixed3D
        Case "None"
            numericUpDown1.BorderStyle = ↵
System.Windows.Forms.BorderStyle.None
        Case "FixedSingle"
            numericUpDown1.BorderStyle = ↵
System.Windows.Forms.BorderStyle.FixedSingle
```

```
    End Select
End Sub

Private Sub comboBox2_SelectedIndexChanged(sender As Object, ↵
 e As EventArgs)
    ' Set the TextAlign property.
    Select Case comboBox2.Text
        Case "Right"
            numericUpDown1.TextAlign = HorizontalAlignment.Right
        Case "Left"
            numericUpDown1.TextAlign = HorizontalAlignment.Left
        Case "Center"
            numericUpDown1.TextAlign = HorizontalAlignment.Center
    End Select
End Sub

Private Sub checkBox1_Click(sender As Object, e As EventArgs)
    ' Evaluate and toggle the ReadOnly property.
    If numericUpDown1.ReadOnly Then
        numericUpDown1.ReadOnly = False
    Else
        numericUpDown1.ReadOnly = True
    End If
End Sub

Private Sub checkBox2_Click(sender As Object, e As EventArgs)
    ' Evaluate and toggle the InterceptArrowKeys property.
    If numericUpDown1.InterceptArrowKeys Then
        numericUpDown1.InterceptArrowKeys = False
    Else
        numericUpDown1.InterceptArrowKeys = True
    End If
End Sub

Private Sub checkBox3_Click(sender As Object, e As EventArgs)
    ' Evaluate and toggle the UpDownAlign property.
    If numericUpDown1.UpDownAlign = LeftRightAlignment.Left Then
        numericUpDown1.UpDownAlign = LeftRightAlignment.Right
    Else
        numericUpDown1.UpDownAlign = LeftRightAlignment.Left
    End If
End Sub
```

[C#]

```
private void comboBox1_SelectedIndexChanged(Object sender,
                                             EventArgs e)
 {
     // Set the BorderStyle property.
    switch(comboBox1.Text)
    {
        case "Fixed3D":
            numericUpDown1.BorderStyle = ↵
System.Windows.Forms.BorderStyle.Fixed3D;
            break;
        case "None":
            numericUpDown1.BorderStyle = ↵
System.Windows.Forms.BorderStyle.None;
            break;
        case "FixedSingle":
            numericUpDown1.BorderStyle = ↵
System.Windows.Forms.BorderStyle.FixedSingle;
            break;
    }
 }

 private void comboBox2_SelectedIndexChanged(Object sender,
                                             EventArgs e)
 {
     // Set the TextAlign property.
    switch (comboBox2.Text)
    {
        case "Right":
            numericUpDown1.TextAlign = HorizontalAlignment.Right;
            break;
        case "Left":
            numericUpDown1.TextAlign = HorizontalAlignment.Left;
            break;
        case "Center":
            numericUpDown1.TextAlign = HorizontalAlignment.Center;
            break;
    }
}

private void checkBox1_Click(Object sender,
                             EventArgs e)
{
     // Evaluate and toggle the ReadOnly property.
    if (numericUpDown1.ReadOnly)
    {
        numericUpDown1.ReadOnly = false;
    }
    else
    {
        numericUpDown1.ReadOnly = true;
    }
}

private void checkBox2_Click(Object sender,
                             EventArgs e)
{
     // Evaluate and toggle the InterceptArrowKeys property.
    if (numericUpDown1.InterceptArrowKeys)
    {
        numericUpDown1.InterceptArrowKeys = false;
    }
    else
    {
        numericUpDown1.InterceptArrowKeys = true;
    }
}

private void checkBox3_Click(Object sender,
                             EventArgs e)
{
     // Evaluate and toggle the UpDownAlign property.
    if (numericUpDown1.UpDownAlign == LeftRightAlignment.Left)
    {
        numericUpDown1.UpDownAlign = LeftRightAlignment.Right;
    }
    else
    {
        numericUpDown1.UpDownAlign = LeftRightAlignment.Left;
    }
}
```

Requirements

Platforms: Windows 98, Windows NT 4.0, Windows Millennium Edition, Windows 2000, Windows XP Home Edition, Windows XP Professional, Windows Server 2003 family

UpDownBase.ChangingText Property

Gets or sets a value indicating whether the text property is being changed internally by its parent class.

[Visual Basic]

```
Protected Property ChangingText As Boolean
```

[C#]

```
protected bool ChangingText {get; set;}
```

[C++]

```
protected: __property bool get_ChangingText();
protected: __property void set_ChangingText(bool);
```

[JScript]

```
protected function get ChangingText() : Boolean;
protected function set ChangingText(Boolean);
```

Property Value

true if the **Text** property is being changed internally by the **UpDownBase** class; otherwise, **false**.

Remarks

The **ChangingText** property acts as a flag for the **UpDownBase** class. This property is used by derived classes to indicate when the class is changing the current **Text** property internally. If this property is set to **false**, the control assumes that the user is changing the **Text** property, and will set the **UserEdit** property to **true**.

Requirements

Platforms: Windows 98, Windows NT 4.0, Windows Millennium Edition, Windows 2000, Windows XP Home Edition, Windows XP Professional, Windows Server 2003 family

UpDownBase.ContextMenu Property

This member overrides **Control.ContextMenu**.

```
[Visual Basic]
Overrides Public Property ContextMenu As ContextMenu
[C#]
public override ContextMenu ContextMenu {get; set;}
[C++]
public: __property ContextMenu* get_ContextMenu();
public: __property void set_ContextMenu(ContextMenu*);
[JScript]
public override function get ContextMenu() : ContextMenu;
public override function set ContextMenu(ContextMenu);
```

Requirements

Platforms: Windows 98, Windows NT 4.0, Windows Millennium Edition, Windows 2000, Windows XP Home Edition, Windows XP Professional, Windows Server 2003 family, .NET Compact Framework - Windows CE .NET

UpDownBase.CreateParams Property

This member overrides **Control.CreateParams**.

```
[Visual Basic]
Overrides Protected ReadOnly Property CreateParams As CreateParams
[C#]
protected override CreateParams CreateParams {get;}
[C++]
protected: __property CreateParams* get_CreateParams();
[JScript]
protected override function get CreateParams() : CreateParams;
```

Requirements

Platforms: Windows 98, Windows NT 4.0, Windows Millennium Edition, Windows 2000, Windows XP Home Edition, Windows XP Professional, Windows Server 2003 family

UpDownBase.DefaultSize Property

This member overrides **Control.DefaultSize**.

```
[Visual Basic]
Overrides Protected ReadOnly Property DefaultSize As Size
[C#]
protected override Size DefaultSize {get;}
[C++]
protected: __property Size get_DefaultSize();
[JScript]
protected override function get DefaultSize() : Size;
```

Requirements

Platforms: Windows 98, Windows NT 4.0, Windows Millennium Edition, Windows 2000, Windows XP Home Edition, Windows XP Professional, Windows Server 2003 family

UpDownBase.DockPadding Property

This member supports the .NET Framework infrastructure and is not intended to be used directly from your code.

```
[Visual Basic]
Public Shadows ReadOnly Property DockPadding As _
   ScrollableControl.DockPaddingEdges
[C#]
public new ScrollableControl.DockPaddingEdges DockPadding {get;}
[C++]
public: __property ScrollableControl.DockPaddingEdges*
   get_DockPadding();
[JScript]
public hide function get DockPadding() :
   ScrollableControl.DockPaddingEdges;
```

UpDownBase.Focused Property

This member overrides **Control.Focused**.

```
[Visual Basic]
Overrides Public ReadOnly Property Focused As Boolean
[C#]
public override bool Focused {get;}
[C++]
public: __property bool get_Focused();
[JScript]
public override function get Focused() : Boolean;
```

Requirements

Platforms: Windows 98, Windows NT 4.0, Windows Millennium Edition, Windows 2000, Windows XP Home Edition, Windows XP Professional, Windows Server 2003 family, .NET Compact Framework - Windows CE .NET

UpDownBase.ForeColor Property

This member overrides **Control.ForeColor**.

```
[Visual Basic]
Overrides Public Property ForeColor As Color
[C#]
public override Color ForeColor {get; set;}
[C++]
public: __property Color get_ForeColor();
public: __property void set_ForeColor(Color);
[JScript]
public override function get ForeColor() : Color;
public override function set ForeColor(Color);
```

Requirements

Platforms: Windows 98, Windows NT 4.0, Windows Millennium Edition, Windows 2000, Windows XP Home Edition, Windows XP Professional, Windows Server 2003 family, .NET Compact Framework - Windows CE .NET

UpDownBase.InterceptArrowKeys Property

Gets or sets a value indicating whether the user can use the UP ARROW and DOWN ARROW keys to select values.

```
[Visual Basic]
Public Property InterceptArrowKeys As Boolean
[C#]
public bool InterceptArrowKeys {get; set;}
[C++]
public: __property bool get_InterceptArrowKeys();
public: __property void set_InterceptArrowKeys(bool);
[JScript]
public function get InterceptArrowKeys() : Boolean;
public function set InterceptArrowKeys(Boolean);
```

Property Value

true if the control allows the use of the UP ARROW and DOWN ARROW keys to select values; otherwise, **false**. The default value is **true**.

Remarks

If **InterceptArrowKeys** is set to **true** and the up-down control has focus, the user can use the UP ARROW and DOWN ARROW keys to select values.

Example

See related example in the **System.Windows.Forms.UpDownBase** class topic.

Requirements

Platforms: Windows 98, Windows NT 4.0, Windows Millennium Edition, Windows 2000, Windows XP Home Edition, Windows XP Professional, Windows Server 2003 family

UpDownBase.PreferredHeight Property

Gets the height of the up-down control.

```
[Visual Basic]
Public ReadOnly Property PreferredHeight As Integer
[C#]
public int PreferredHeight {get;}
[C++]
public: __property int get_PreferredHeight();
[JScript]
public function get PreferredHeight() : int;
```

Property Value

The height of the up-down control in pixels.

Remarks

The **PreferredHeight** property value is based on the **PreferredHeight** property of the text box portion of the control and is adjusted for the style of border.

Example

See related example in the **System.Windows.Forms.UpDownBase** class topic.

Requirements

Platforms: Windows 98, Windows NT 4.0, Windows Millennium Edition, Windows 2000, Windows XP Home Edition, Windows XP Professional, Windows Server 2003 family

UpDownBase.ReadOnly Property

Gets or sets a value indicating whether the text can be changed by the use of the up or down buttons only.

```
[Visual Basic]
Public Property ReadOnly As Boolean
[C#]
public bool ReadOnly {get; set;}
[C++]
public: __property bool get_ReadOnly();
public: __property void set_ReadOnly(bool);
[JScript]
public function get ReadOnly() : Boolean;
public function set ReadOnly(Boolean);
```

Property Value

true if the text can be changed by the use of the up or down buttons only; otherwise, **false**. The default value is **false**.

Remarks

By setting the **ReadOnly** property to **true**, you will eliminate the need for much validation of the **Text** property. The user will be restricted to the use of the up and down buttons to change the **Text** values. It will only allow them to select values you specify.

> **Note** In the derived class **DomainUpDown**, the behavior described is slightly different. When **ReadOnly** is set to **true** and a key is pressed, the control selects the first item in the collection where the first character matches the key pressed.

Example

See related example in the **System.Windows.Forms.UpDownBase** class topic.

Requirements

Platforms: Windows 98, Windows NT 4.0, Windows Millennium Edition, Windows 2000, Windows XP Home Edition, Windows XP Professional, Windows Server 2003 family, .NET Compact Framework - Windows CE .NET

UpDownBase.Text Property

Gets or sets the text displayed in the up-down control.

```
[Visual Basic]
Overrides Public Property Text As String
[C#]
public override string Text {get; set;}
[C++]
public: __property String* get_Text();
public: __property void set_Text(String*);
[JScript]
public override function get Text() : String;
public override function set Text(String);
```

Property Value

The string value displayed in the up-down control.

Remarks

The **UpdateEditText** method is called if the **Text** property is set while the **UserEdit** property is set to **true**. The **ValidateEditText** method is called if the **Text** property is set while the **UserEdit** property is set to **false**.

Example

See related example in the **System.Windows.Forms.UpDownBase** class topic.

Requirements

Platforms: Windows 98, Windows NT 4.0, Windows Millennium Edition, Windows 2000, Windows XP Home Edition, Windows XP Professional, Windows Server 2003 family, .NET Compact Framework - Windows CE .NET

UpDownBase.TextAlign Property

Gets or sets the alignment of the text in the up-down control.

```
[Visual Basic]
Public Property TextAlign As HorizontalAlignment
[C#]
public HorizontalAlignment TextAlign {get; set;}
[C++]
public: __property HorizontalAlignment get_TextAlign();
public: __property void set_TextAlign(HorizontalAlignment);
[JScript]
public function get TextAlign() : HorizontalAlignment;
public function set TextAlign(HorizontalAlignment);
```

Property Value

One of the **HorizontalAlignment** values. The default value is **Left**.

Exceptions

Exception Type	Condition
InvalidEnumArgument-Exception	The value assigned is not one of the **HorizontalAlignment** values.

Example

See related example in the **System.Windows.Forms.UpDownBase** class topic.

Requirements

Platforms: Windows 98, Windows NT 4.0, Windows Millennium Edition, Windows 2000, Windows XP Home Edition, Windows XP Professional, Windows Server 2003 family

UpDownBase.UpDownAlign Property

Gets or sets the alignment of the up and down buttons on the up-down control.

```
[Visual Basic]
Public Property UpDownAlign As LeftRightAlignment
[C#]
public LeftRightAlignment UpDownAlign {get; set;}
[C++]
public: __property LeftRightAlignment get_UpDownAlign();
public: __property void set_UpDownAlign(LeftRightAlignment);
[JScript]
public function get UpDownAlign() : LeftRightAlignment;
public function set UpDownAlign(LeftRightAlignment);
```

Property Value

One of the **LeftRightAlignment** values. The default value is **Right**.

Exceptions

Exception Type	Condition
InvalidEnumArgument-Exception	The value assigned is not one of the **LeftRightAlignment** values.

Example

See related example in the **System.Windows.Forms.UpDownBase** class topic.

Requirements

Platforms: Windows 98, Windows NT 4.0, Windows Millennium Edition, Windows 2000, Windows XP Home Edition, Windows XP Professional, Windows Server 2003 family

UpDownBase.UserEdit Property

Gets or sets a value indicating whether a value has been entered by the user.

```
[Visual Basic]
Protected Property UserEdit As Boolean
[C#]
protected bool UserEdit {get; set;}
[C++]
protected: __property bool get_UserEdit();
protected: __property void set_UserEdit(bool);
[JScript]
protected function get UserEdit() : Boolean;
protected function set UserEdit(Boolean);
```

Property Value

true if the user has changed the **Text** property; otherwise, **false**.

Remarks

If the **Text** property is set while the **UserEdit** property is set to **true**, the **UpdateEditText** method is called. If the **Text** property is set while the **UserEdit** property is set to **false**, **ValidateEditText** is called.

Requirements

Platforms: Windows 98, Windows NT 4.0, Windows Millennium Edition, Windows 2000, Windows XP Home Edition, Windows XP Professional, Windows Server 2003 family

UpDownBase.Dispose Method

Overload List

This member supports the .NET Framework infrastructure and is not intended to be used directly from your code.

Supported by the .NET Compact Framework.

[Visual Basic] **Overloads Overrides Protected Sub Dispose(Boolean)**

[C#] **protected override void Dispose(bool);**

[C++] **protected: void Dispose(bool);**

[JScript] **protected override function Dispose(Boolean);**

Inherited from **Component**.

Supported by the .NET Compact Framework.

[Visual Basic] **Overloads Public Overridable Sub Dispose() Implements IDisposable.Dispose**

[C#] **public virtual void Dispose();**

[C++] **public: virtual void Dispose();**

[JScript] **public function Dispose();**

UpDownBase.Dispose Method (Boolean)

This member overrides **Control.Dispose**.

```
[Visual Basic]
Overrides Overloads Protected Sub Dispose( _
   ByVal disposing As Boolean _
)
[C#]
protected override void Dispose(
   bool disposing
);
[C++]
protected: void Dispose(
   bool disposing
);
[JScript]
protected override function Dispose(
   disposing : Boolean
);
```

Requirements

Platforms: Windows 98, Windows NT 4.0, Windows Millennium Edition, Windows 2000, Windows XP Home Edition, Windows XP Professional, Windows Server 2003 family, .NET Compact Framework - Windows CE .NET

UpDownBase.DownButton Method

When overridden in a derived class, handles the clicking of the down button on the up-down control.

```
[Visual Basic]
Public MustOverride Sub DownButton()
[C#]
public abstract void DownButton();
[C++]
public: virtual void DownButton() = 0;
[JScript]
public abstract function DownButton();
```

Remarks

Notes to Inheritors: When overriding this method in a derived class, be sure to call the **UpdateEditText** method.

Requirements

Platforms: Windows 98, Windows NT 4.0, Windows Millennium Edition, Windows 2000, Windows XP Home Edition, Windows XP Professional, Windows Server 2003 family

UpDownBase.OnChanged Method

This member supports the .NET Framework infrastructure and is not intended to be used directly from your code.

```
[Visual Basic]
Protected Overridable Sub OnChanged( _
   ByVal source As Object, _
   ByVal e As EventArgs _
)
[C#]
protected virtual void OnChanged(
   object source,
   EventArgs e
);
[C++]
protected: virtual void OnChanged(
   Object* source,
   EventArgs* e
);
[JScript]
protected function OnChanged(
   source : Object,
   e : EventArgs
);
```

UpDownBase.OnFontChanged Method

This member overrides **Control.OnFontChanged**.

```
[Visual Basic]
Overrides Protected Sub OnFontChanged( _
   ByVal e As EventArgs _
)
[C#]
protected override void OnFontChanged(
   EventArgs e
);
[C++]
protected: void OnFontChanged(
   EventArgs* e
);
[JScript]
protected override function OnFontChanged(
   e : EventArgs
);
```

Requirements

Platforms: Windows 98, Windows NT 4.0, Windows Millennium Edition, Windows 2000, Windows XP Home Edition, Windows XP Professional, Windows Server 2003 family

UpDownBase.OnHandleCreated Method

This member overrides **Control.OnHandleCreated**.

```
[Visual Basic]
Overrides Protected Sub OnHandleCreated( _
   ByVal e As EventArgs _
)
[C#]
protected override void OnHandleCreated(
   EventArgs e
);
```

```
[C++]
protected: void OnHandleCreated(
   EventArgs* e
);
[JScript]
protected override function OnHandleCreated(
   e : EventArgs
);
```

Requirements

Platforms: Windows 98, Windows NT 4.0, Windows Millennium Edition, Windows 2000, Windows XP Home Edition, Windows XP Professional, Windows Server 2003 family

UpDownBase.OnLayout Method

This member overrides **Control.OnLayout**.

```
[Visual Basic]
Overrides Protected Sub OnLayout( _
   ByVal e As LayoutEventArgs _
)
[C#]
protected override void OnLayout(
   LayoutEventArgs e
);
[C++]
protected: void OnLayout(
   LayoutEventArgs* e
);
[JScript]
protected override function OnLayout(
   e : LayoutEventArgs
);
```

Requirements

Platforms: Windows 98, Windows NT 4.0, Windows Millennium Edition, Windows 2000, Windows XP Home Edition, Windows XP Professional, Windows Server 2003 family

UpDownBase.OnMouseWheel Method

Raises the **MouseWheel** event.

```
[Visual Basic]
Overrides Protected Sub OnMouseWheel( _
   ByVal e As MouseEventArgs _
)
[C#]
protected override void OnMouseWheel(
   MouseEventArgs e
);
[C++]
protected: void OnMouseWheel(
   MouseEventArgs* e
);
[JScript]
protected override function OnMouseWheel(
   e : MouseEventArgs
);
```

Parameters

e

A **MouseEventArgs** that contains the event data.

Remarks

If the up-down control has focus when this event occurs, the direction the mouse wheel scrolled is determined and either the **UpButton** or **DownButton** method is called.

Raising an event invokes the event handler through a delegate.

The **OnTextBoxTextChanged** method also allows derived classes to handle the event without attaching a delegate. This is the preferred technique for handling the event in a derived class.

Notes to Inheritors: When overriding **OnTextBoxTextChanged** in a derived class, be sure to call the base class's **OnTextBoxTextChanged** method so that registered delegates receive the event.

Requirements

Platforms: Windows 98, Windows NT 4.0, Windows Millennium Edition, Windows 2000, Windows XP Home Edition, Windows XP Professional, Windows Server 2003 family

UpDownBase.OnTextBoxKeyDown Method

Raises the **KeyDown** event.

```
[Visual Basic]
Protected Overridable Sub OnTextBoxKeyDown( _
   ByVal source As Object, _
   ByVal e As KeyEventArgs _
)
[C#]
protected virtual void OnTextBoxKeyDown(
   object source,
   KeyEventArgs e
);
[C++]
protected: virtual void OnTextBoxKeyDown(
   Object* source,
   KeyEventArgs* e
);
[JScript]
protected function OnTextBoxKeyDown(
   source : Object,
   e : KeyEventArgs
);
```

Parameters

source

The source of the event.

e

A **KeyEventArgs** that contains the event data.

Remarks

If the **InterceptArrowKeys** property is set to **true** and the key being pressed is the UP ARROW key, the **UpButton** method is called. Likewise, if the key being pressed is the DOWN ARROW key, the **DownButton** method is called.

Raising an event invokes the event handler through a delegate.

The **OnTextBoxKeyDown** method also allows derived classes to handle the event without attaching a delegate. This is the preferred technique for handling the event in a derived class.

Notes to Inheritors: When overriding **OnTextBoxKeyDown** in a derived class, be sure to call the base class's **OnTextBoxKeyDown** method so that registered delegates receive the event.

Requirements

Platforms: Windows 98, Windows NT 4.0, Windows Millennium Edition, Windows 2000, Windows XP Home Edition, Windows XP Professional, Windows Server 2003 family

UpDownBase.OnTextBoxKeyPress Method

Raises the **KeyPress** event.

[Visual Basic]
```
Protected Overridable Sub OnTextBoxKeyPress( _
   ByVal source As Object, _
   ByVal e As KeyPressEventArgs _
)
```
[C#]
```
protected virtual void OnTextBoxKeyPress(
   object source,
   KeyPressEventArgs e
);
```
[C++]
```
protected: virtual void OnTextBoxKeyPress(
   Object* source,
   KeyPressEventArgs* e
);
```
[JScript]
```
protected function OnTextBoxKeyPress(
   source : Object,
   e : KeyPressEventArgs
);
```

Parameters

source

The source of the event.

e

A **KeyPressEventArgs** that contains the event data.

Remarks

Raising an event invokes the event handler through a delegate.

The **OnTextBoxKeyPress** method also allows derived classes to handle the event without attaching a delegate. This is the preferred technique for handling the event in a derived class.

Notes to Inheritors: When overriding **OnTextBoxKeyPress** in a derived class, be sure to call the base class's **OnTextBoxKeyPress** method so that registered delegates receive the event.

Requirements

Platforms: Windows 98, Windows NT 4.0, Windows Millennium Edition, Windows 2000, Windows XP Home Edition, Windows XP Professional, Windows Server 2003 family

UpDownBase.OnTextBoxLostFocus Method

Raises the **LostFocus** event.

[Visual Basic]
```
Protected Overridable Sub OnTextBoxLostFocus( _
   ByVal source As Object, _
   ByVal e As EventArgs _
)
```
[C#]
```
protected virtual void OnTextBoxLostFocus(
   object source,
   EventArgs e
);
```
[C++]
```
protected: virtual void OnTextBoxLostFocus(
   Object* source,
   EventArgs* e
);
```
[JScript]
```
protected function OnTextBoxLostFocus(
   source : Object,
   e : EventArgs
);
```

Parameters

source

The source of the event.

e

An **EventArgs** that contains the event data.

Remarks

Validates the text in the text box portion of the control when the up-down control loses focus.

Raising an event invokes the event handler through a delegate.

The **OnTextBoxLostFocus** method also allows derived classes to handle the event without attaching a delegate. This is the preferred technique for handling the event in a derived class.

Notes to Inheritors: When overriding **OnTextBoxLostFocus** in a derived class, be sure to call the base class's **OnTextBoxLostFocus** method so that registered delegates receive the event.

Requirements

Platforms: Windows 98, Windows NT 4.0, Windows Millennium Edition, Windows 2000, Windows XP Home Edition, Windows XP Professional, Windows Server 2003 family

UpDownBase.OnTextBoxResize Method

Raises the **Resize** event.

[Visual Basic]
```
Protected Overridable Sub OnTextBoxResize( _
   ByVal source As Object, _
   ByVal e As EventArgs _
)
```
[C#]
```
protected virtual void OnTextBoxResize(
   object source,
   EventArgs e
);
```

[C++]
```
protected: virtual void OnTextBoxResize(
   Object* source,
   EventArgs* e
);
```
[JScript]
```
protected function OnTextBoxResize(
   source : Object,
   e : EventArgs
);
```

Parameters

source

The source of the event.

e

An **EventArgs** that contains the event data.

Remarks

Adjusts the size of the up-down control when the text box portion of the control is resized.

Raising an event invokes the event handler through a delegate.

The **OnTextBoxResize** method also allows derived classes to handle the event without attaching a delegate. This is the preferred technique for handling the event in a derived class.

Notes to Inheritors: When overriding **OnTextBoxResize** in a derived class, be sure to call the base class's **OnTextBoxResize** method so that registered delegates receive the event.

Requirements

Platforms: Windows 98, Windows NT 4.0, Windows Millennium Edition, Windows 2000, Windows XP Home Edition, Windows XP Professional, Windows Server 2003 family

UpDownBase.OnTextBoxTextChanged Method

Raises the **TextChanged** event.

[Visual Basic]
```
Protected Overridable Sub OnTextBoxTextChanged( _
   ByVal source As Object, _
   ByVal e As EventArgs _
)
```
[C#]
```
protected virtual void OnTextBoxTextChanged(
   object source,
   EventArgs e
);
```
[C++]
```
protected: virtual void OnTextBoxTextChanged(
   Object* source,
   EventArgs* e
);
```
[JScript]
```
protected function OnTextBoxTextChanged(
   source : Object,
   e : EventArgs
);
```

Parameters

source

The source of the event.

e

An **EventArgs** that contains the event data.

Remarks

Raising an event invokes the event handler through a delegate.

The **OnTextBoxTextChanged** method also allows derived classes to handle the event without attaching a delegate. This is the preferred technique for handling the event in a derived class.

Notes to Inheritors: When overriding **OnTextBoxTextChanged** in a derived class, be sure to call the base class's **OnTextBoxTextChanged** method so that registered delegates receive the event.

Requirements

Platforms: Windows 98, Windows NT 4.0, Windows Millennium Edition, Windows 2000, Windows XP Home Edition, Windows XP Professional, Windows Server 2003 family

UpDownBase.Select Method

Selects a range of text in the up-down control.

Overload List

Selects a range of text in the up-down control specifying the starting position and number of characters to select.

[Visual Basic] **Overloads Public Sub Select(Integer, Integer)**

[C#] **public void Select(int, int);**

[C++] **public: void Select(int, int);**

[JScript] **public function Select(int, int);**

Inherited from **Control**.

[Visual Basic] **Overloads Public Sub Select()**

[C#] **public void Select();**

[C++] **public: void Select();**

[JScript] **public function Select();**

Inherited from **Control**.

[Visual Basic] **Overloads Protected Overridable Sub Select(Boolean, Boolean)**

[C#] **protected virtual void Select(bool, bool);**

[C++] **protected: virtual void Select(bool, bool);**

[JScript] **protected function Select(Boolean, Boolean);**

Example

See related example in the **System.Windows.Forms.UpDownBase** class topic.

UpDownBase.Select Method (Int32, Int32)

Selects a range of text in the up-down control specifying the starting position and number of characters to select.

[Visual Basic]
```
Overloads Public Sub Select( _
   ByVal start As Integer, _
   ByVal length As Integer _
)
```
[C#]
```
public void Select(
   int start,
   int length
);
```

[C++]
```
public: void Select(
   int start,
   int length
);
```
[JScript]
```
public function Select(
   start : int,
   length : int
);
```
Parameters

start
  The position of the first character to be selected.

length
  The total number of characters to be selected.

Remarks

The **Select** method can be used when the up-down control gets focus, or when the **Text** property fails data validation. When adding the validation code for the **ValidateEditText** method in a derived class, call the **Select** method when validation fails.

Example

See related example in the **System.Windows.Forms.UpDownBase** class topic.

Requirements

Platforms: Windows 98, Windows NT 4.0, Windows Millennium Edition, Windows 2000, Windows XP Home Edition, Windows XP Professional, Windows Server 2003 family

UpDownBase.SetBoundsCore Method

This member overrides **Control.SetBoundsCore**.

[Visual Basic]
```
Overrides Protected Sub SetBoundsCore( _
   ByVal x As Integer, _
   ByVal y As Integer, _
   ByVal width As Integer, _
   ByVal height As Integer, _
   ByVal specified As BoundsSpecified _
)
```
[C#]
```
protected override void SetBoundsCore(
   int x,
   int y,
   int width,
   int height,
   BoundsSpecified specified
);
```
[C++]
```
protected: void SetBoundsCore(
   int x,
   int y,
   int width,
   int height,
   BoundsSpecified specified
);
```
[JScript]
```
protected override function SetBoundsCore(
   x : int,
   y : int,
   width : int,
   height : int,
   specified : BoundsSpecified
);
```
Requirements

Platforms: Windows 98, Windows NT 4.0, Windows Millennium Edition, Windows 2000, Windows XP Home Edition, Windows XP Professional, Windows Server 2003 family

UpDownBase.UpButton Method

When overridden in a derived class, handles the clicking of the up button on the up-down control.

[Visual Basic]
```
Public MustOverride Sub UpButton()
```
[C#]
```
public abstract void UpButton();
```
[C++]
```
public: virtual void UpButton() = 0;
```
[JScript]
```
public abstract function UpButton();
```
Remarks

Notes to Inheritors: When overriding this method in a derived class, be sure to call the **UpdateEditText** method.

Requirements

Platforms: Windows 98, Windows NT 4.0, Windows Millennium Edition, Windows 2000, Windows XP Home Edition, Windows XP Professional, Windows Server 2003 family

UpDownBase.UpdateEditText Method

When overridden in a derived class, updates the text displayed in the up-down control.

[Visual Basic]
```
Protected MustOverride Sub UpdateEditText()
```
[C#]
```
protected abstract void UpdateEditText();
```
[C++]
```
protected: virtual void UpdateEditText() = 0;
```
[JScript]
```
protected abstract function UpdateEditText();
```
Remarks

Notes to Inheritors: When overriding this method in a derived class, be sure to update the **Text** property of the up-down control.

Requirements

Platforms: Windows 98, Windows NT 4.0, Windows Millennium Edition, Windows 2000, Windows XP Home Edition, Windows XP Professional, Windows Server 2003 family

UpDownBase.ValidateEditText Method

When overridden in a derived class, validates the text displayed in the up-down control.

```
[Visual Basic]
Protected Overridable Sub ValidateEditText()
[C#]
protected virtual void ValidateEditText();
[C++]
protected: virtual void ValidateEditText();
[JScript]
protected function ValidateEditText();
```

Remarks

Some examples of validation include comparing the text entered to the data type set in your derived class, comparing it to a list of values, or verifying it to be within a range of values.

Notes to Inheritors: When overriding this method in a derived class, be sure to add code in this method to validate the text property of the up-down control. This method will be called if the **UserEdit** property is set to **false** when the **Text** property is set.

Requirements

Platforms: Windows 98, Windows NT 4.0, Windows Millennium Edition, Windows 2000, Windows XP Home Edition, Windows XP Professional, Windows Server 2003 family

UpDownBase.WndProc Method

This member overrides **Control.WndProc**.

```
[Visual Basic]
Overrides Protected Sub WndProc( _
   ByRef m As Message _
)
[C#]
protected override void WndProc(
   ref Message m
);
[C++]
protected: void WndProc(
   Message* m
);
[JScript]
protected override function WndProc(
   m : Message
);
```

Requirements

Platforms: Windows 98, Windows NT 4.0, Windows Millennium Edition, Windows 2000, Windows XP Home Edition, Windows XP Professional, Windows Server 2003 family

UpDownBase.BackgroundImageChanged Event

This member supports the .NET Framework infrastructure and is not intended to be used directly from your code.

```
[Visual Basic]
Public Shadows Event BackgroundImageChanged As EventHandler
[C#]
public new event EventHandler BackgroundImageChanged;
[C++]
public: __event EventHandler* BackgroundImageChanged;
```

[JScript] In JScript, you can handle the events defined by a class, but you cannot define your own.

UpDownBase.MouseEnter Event

This member supports the .NET Framework infrastructure and is not intended to be used directly from your code.

```
[Visual Basic]
Public Shadows Event MouseEnter As EventHandler
[C#]
public new event EventHandler MouseEnter;
[C++]
public: __event EventHandler* MouseEnter;
```

[JScript] In JScript, you can handle the events defined by a class, but you cannot define your own.

UpDownBase.MouseHover Event

This member supports the .NET Framework infrastructure and is not intended to be used directly from your code.

```
[Visual Basic]
Public Shadows Event MouseHover As EventHandler
[C#]
public new event EventHandler MouseHover;
[C++]
public: __event EventHandler* MouseHover;
```

[JScript] In JScript, you can handle the events defined by a class, but you cannot define your own.

UpDownBase.MouseLeave Event

This member supports the .NET Framework infrastructure and is not intended to be used directly from your code.

```
[Visual Basic]
Public Shadows Event MouseLeave As EventHandler
[C#]
public new event EventHandler MouseLeave;
[C++]
public: __event EventHandler* MouseLeave;
```

[JScript] In JScript, you can handle the events defined by a class, but you cannot define your own.

UpDownBase.MouseMove Event

This member supports the .NET Framework infrastructure and is not intended to be used directly from your code.

```
[Visual Basic]
Public Shadows Event MouseMove As MouseEventHandler
[C#]
public new event MouseEventHandler MouseMove;
[C++]
public: __event MouseEventHandler* MouseMove;
```

[JScript] In JScript, you can handle the events defined by a class, but you cannot define your own.

UpDownEventArgs Class

This type supports the .NET Framework infrastructure and is not intended to be used directly from your code.

[Visual Basic]
```
Public Class UpDownEventArgs
   Inherits EventArgs
```
[C#]
```
public class UpDownEventArgs : EventArgs
```
[C++]
```
public __gc class UpDownEventArgs : public EventArgs
```
[JScript]
```
public class UpDownEventArgs extends EventArgs
```

UpDownEventArgs Constructor

This member supports the .NET Framework infrastructure and is not intended to be used directly from your code.

[Visual Basic]
```
Public Sub New( _
   ByVal buttonPushed As Integer _
)
```
[C#]
```
public UpDownEventArgs(
   int buttonPushed
);
```
[C++]
```
public: UpDownEventArgs(
   int buttonPushed
);
```
[JScript]
```
public function UpDownEventArgs(
   buttonPushed : int
);
```

UpDownEventArgs.ButtonID Property

This member supports the .NET Framework infrastructure and is not intended to be used directly from your code.

[Visual Basic]
```
Public ReadOnly Property ButtonID As Integer
```
[C#]
```
public int ButtonID {get;}
```
[C++]
```
public: __property int get_ButtonID();
```
[JScript]
```
public function get ButtonID() : int;
```

UpDownEventHandler Delegate

This type supports the .NET Framework infrastructure and is not intended to be used directly from your code.

[Visual Basic]
```
<Serializable>
Public Delegate Sub UpDownEventHandler( _
   ByVal source As Object, _
   ByVal e As UpDownEventArgs _
)
```
[C#]
```
[Serializable]
public delegate void UpDownEventHandler(
   object source,
   UpDownEventArgs e
);
```
[C++]
```
[Serializable]
public __gc __delegate void UpDownEventHandler(
   Object* source,
   UpDownEventArgs* e
);
```

[JScript] In JScript, you can use the delegates in the .NET Framework, but you cannot define your own.

UserControl Class

Provides an empty control that can be used to create other controls.

System.Object
  System.MarshalByRefObject
    System.ComponentModel.Component
      System.Windows.Forms.Control
        System.Windows.Forms.ScrollableControl
          System.Windows.Forms.ContainerControl
            System.Windows.Forms.UserControl

[Visual Basic]
```
Public Class UserControl
   Inherits ContainerControl
```
[C#]
```
public class UserControl : ContainerControl
```
[C++]
```
public __gc class UserControl : public ContainerControl
```
[JScript]
```
public class UserControl extends ContainerControl
```

Thread Safety

Any public static (**Shared** in Visual Basic) members of this type are safe for multithreaded operations. Any instance members are not guaranteed to be thread safe.

Remarks

By extending **ContainerControl**, **UserControl** inherits all the standard positioning and mnemonic-handling code that is necessary in a user control.

The **UserControl** gives you the ability to create controls that can be used in multiple places within an application or organization. You can include all the code needed for validation of common data you ask the user to input; some examples of this are e-mail addresses (see Example section), telephone numbers, and postal codes. Another efficient use of the user control is to simply preload a **ComboBox** or **ListBox** with static items you commonly use in almost every application; some examples of this are countries/regions, cities, states, and office locations.

Note You might consider creating a namespace that contains several classes of user controls and compiling it into one DLL. This DLL can be referenced and distributed with the application or all applications within an organization. This gives you the ability to reference the user control in many applications and save time laying out and coding the contained elements of the user control. A user control also gives you consistency within or across applications; for example, all address information input blocks will all have the same appearance and behavior. Consistency gives your application a more polished and professional appearance.

Example

[Visual Basic, C#] The following example creates a **UserControl** that can be reused in multiple applications to get user information. This example adds several **Label** controls, **TextBox** controls and an **ErrorProvider** object to the **UserControl** to gather the user's information. Additionally, the user's e-mail address is validated in the **Validating** event of the **TextBox** and the **ErrorProvider** object is used to give the user feedback if the data fails validation. The code is intended to be compiled into a DLL for reference in other applications.

[Visual Basic]
```
Imports System
Imports System.Windows.Forms
Imports System.Drawing
Imports System.ComponentModel
Imports Microsoft.VisualBasic

Namespace UserControls

   Public Class MyCustomerInfoUserControl
      Inherits System.Windows.Forms.UserControl

      ' Create the controls.
      Private errorProvider1 As System.Windows.Forms.ErrorProvider
      Private textName As System.Windows.Forms.TextBox
      Private textAddress As System.Windows.Forms.TextBox
      Private textCity As System.Windows.Forms.TextBox
      Private textStateProvince As System.Windows.Forms.TextBox
      Private textPostal As System.Windows.Forms.TextBox
      Private textCountryRegion As System.Windows.Forms.TextBox
      Private WithEvents textEmail As System.Windows.Forms.TextBox
      Private labelName As System.Windows.Forms.Label
      Private labelAddress As System.Windows.Forms.Label
      Private labelCityStateProvincePostal As System.Windows.Forms.Label
      Private labelCountryRegion As System.Windows.Forms.Label
      Private labelEmail As System.Windows.Forms.Label
      Private components As System.ComponentModel.IContainer

      ' Define the constructor.
      Public Sub New()
         InitializeComponent()
      End Sub

      ' Initialize the control elements.
      Public Sub InitializeComponent()
         ' Initialize the controls.
         components = New System.ComponentModel.Container()
         errorProvider1 = New System.Windows.Forms.ErrorProvider()
         textName = New System.Windows.Forms.TextBox()
         textAddress = New System.Windows.Forms.TextBox()
         textCity = New System.Windows.Forms.TextBox()
         textStateProvince = New System.Windows.Forms.TextBox()
         textPostal = New System.Windows.Forms.TextBox()
         textCountryRegion = New System.Windows.Forms.TextBox()
         textEmail = New System.Windows.Forms.TextBox()
         labelName = New System.Windows.Forms.Label()
         labelAddress = New System.Windows.Forms.Label()
         labelCityStateProvincePostal = New                          ↵
System.Windows.Forms.Label()
         labelCountryRegion = New System.Windows.Forms.Label()
         labelEmail = New System.Windows.Forms.Label()

         ' Set the tab order, text alignment, size, and              ↵
location of the controls.
         textName.Location = New System.Drawing.Point(120, 8)
         textName.Size = New System.Drawing.Size(232, 20)
         textName.TabIndex = 0

         textAddress.Location = New System.Drawing.Point(120, 32)
         textAddress.Size = New System.Drawing.Size(232, 20)
         textAddress.TabIndex = 1

         textCity.Location = New System.Drawing.Point(120, 56)
         textCity.Size = New System.Drawing.Size(96, 20)
         textCity.TabIndex = 2

         textStateProvince.Location = New System.Drawing.Point(216, 56)
         textStateProvince.Size = New System.Drawing.Size(56, 20)
         textStateProvince.TabIndex = 3

         textPostal.Location = New System.Drawing.Point(272, 56)
         textPostal.Size = New System.Drawing.Size(80, 20)
         textPostal.TabIndex = 4

         textCountryRegion.Location = New System.Drawing.Point(120, 80)
         textCountryRegion.Size = New System.Drawing.Size(232, 20)
         textCountryRegion.TabIndex = 5
```

```
        textEmail.Location = New System.Drawing.Point(120, 104)
        textEmail.Size = New System.Drawing.Size(232, 20)
        textEmail.TabIndex = 6

        labelName.Location = New System.Drawing.Point(8, 8)
        labelName.Size = New System.Drawing.Size(112, 23)
        labelName.Text = "Name:"
        labelName.TextAlign =                                           ↵
System.Drawing.ContentAlignment.MiddleRight

        labelAddress.Location = New System.Drawing.Point(8, 32)
        labelAddress.Size = New System.Drawing.Size(112, 23)
        labelAddress.Text = "Address:"
        labelAddress.TextAlign =                                        ↵
System.Drawing.ContentAlignment.MiddleRight

        labelCityStateProvincePostal.Location = New                     ↵
System.Drawing.Point(8, 56)
        labelCityStateProvincePostal.Size = New                         ↵
System.Drawing.Size(112, 23)
        labelCityStateProvincePostal.Text = "City, St/Prov. Postal:"
        labelCityStateProvincePostal.TextAlign =                        ↵
System.Drawing.ContentAlignment.MiddleRight

        labelCountryRegion.Location = New System.Drawing.Point(8, 80)
        labelCountryRegion.Size = New System.Drawing.Size(112, 23)
        labelCountryRegion.Text = "Country/Region:"
        labelCountryRegion.TextAlign =                                  ↵
System.Drawing.ContentAlignment.MiddleRight

        labelEmail.Location = New System.Drawing.Point(8, 104)
        labelEmail.Size = New System.Drawing.Size(112, 23)
        labelEmail.Text = "email:"
        labelEmail.TextAlign =                                          ↵
System.Drawing.ContentAlignment.MiddleRight

        ' Add the controls to the user control.
        Controls.AddRange(New                                           ↵
System.Windows.Forms.Control() {labelName, _
          labelAddress, labelCityStateProvincePostal,                   ↵
labelCountryRegion, _
          labelEmail, textName, textAddress, textCity,                  ↵
textStateProvince, _
          textPostal, textCountryRegion, textEmail})

        ' Size the user control.
        Size = New System.Drawing.Size(375, 150)
     End Sub

     Private Sub MyValidatingCode()
        ' Confirm there is text in the control.
        If textEmail.Text.Length = 0 Then
           Throw New Exception("Email address is a required field")
        Else
           ' Confirm that there is a "." and an "@" in the               ↵
 e-mail address.
           If textEmail.Text.IndexOf(".") = - 1 Or                      ↵
textEmail.Text.IndexOf("@") = - 1 Then
              Throw New Exception("Email address must be                ↵
valid e-mail address format." + _
                Microsoft.VisualBasic.ControlChars.Cr +                 ↵
"For example 'someone@example.com'")
           End If
        End If
     End Sub

     ' Validate the data input by the user into textEmail.
     Private Sub textEmail_Validating(sender As Object, _
                                      e As                              ↵
System.ComponentModel.CancelEventArgs) Handles textEmail.Validating
        Try
           MyValidatingCode()

        Catch ex As Exception
           ' Cancel the event and select the text to be                 ↵
 corrected by the user.
           e.Cancel = True
           textEmail.Select(0, textEmail.Text.Length)

           ' Set the ErrorProvider error with the text to display.
           Me.errorProvider1.SetError(textEmail, ex.Message)
        End Try
     End Sub

     Private Sub textEmail_Validated(sender As Object, _
                                     e As System.EventArgs)             ↵
 Handles textEmail.Validated
        ' If all conditions have been met, clear the error              ↵
 provider of errors.
        errorProvider1.SetError(textEmail, "")
     End Sub

  End Class
End Namespace
```

[C#]

```
using System;
using System.Windows.Forms;
using System.Drawing;
using System.ComponentModel;

namespace UserControls
{
   public class MyCustomerInfoUserControl :                             ↵
System.Windows.Forms.UserControl
   {
      // Create the controls.
      private System.Windows.Forms.ErrorProvider errorProvider1;
      private System.Windows.Forms.TextBox textName;
      private System.Windows.Forms.TextBox textAddress;
      private System.Windows.Forms.TextBox textCity;
      private System.Windows.Forms.TextBox textStateProvince;
      private System.Windows.Forms.TextBox textPostal;
      private System.Windows.Forms.TextBox textCountryRegion;
      private System.Windows.Forms.TextBox textEmail;
      private System.Windows.Forms.Label labelName;
      private System.Windows.Forms.Label labelAddress;
      private System.Windows.Forms.Label labelCityStateProvincePostal;
      private System.Windows.Forms.Label labelCountryRegion;
      private System.Windows.Forms.Label labelEmail;
      private System.ComponentModel.IContainer components;

      // Define the constructor.
      public MyCustomerInfoUserControl()
      {
         InitializeComponent();
      }

      // Initialize the control elements.
      public void InitializeComponent()
      {
         // Initialize the controls.
         components = new System.ComponentModel.Container();
         errorProvider1 = new System.Windows.Forms.ErrorProvider();
         textName = new System.Windows.Forms.TextBox();
         textAddress = new System.Windows.Forms.TextBox();
         textCity = new System.Windows.Forms.TextBox();
         textStateProvince = new System.Windows.Forms.TextBox();
         textPostal = new System.Windows.Forms.TextBox();
         textCountryRegion = new System.Windows.Forms.TextBox();
         textEmail = new System.Windows.Forms.TextBox();
         labelName = new System.Windows.Forms.Label();
         labelAddress = new System.Windows.Forms.Label();
         labelCityStateProvincePostal = new                             ↵
System.Windows.Forms.Label();
         labelCountryRegion = new System.Windows.Forms.Label();
         labelEmail = new System.Windows.Forms.Label();

         // Set the tab order, text alignment, size, and                ↵
location of the controls.
         textName.Location = new System.Drawing.Point(120, 8);
         textName.Size = new System.Drawing.Size(232, 20);
         textName.TabIndex = 0;
```

```
         textAddress.Location = new System.Drawing.Point(120, 32);
         textAddress.Size = new System.Drawing.Size(232, 20);
         textAddress.TabIndex = 1;

         textCity.Location = new System.Drawing.Point(120, 56);
         textCity.Size = new System.Drawing.Size(96, 20);
         textCity.TabIndex = 2;

         textStateProvince.Location = new                              ↵
System.Drawing.Point(216, 56);
         textStateProvince.Size = new                                  ↵
System.Drawing.Size(56, 20);
         textStateProvince.TabIndex = 3;

         textPostal.Location = new System.Drawing.Point(272, 56);
         textPostal.Size = new System.Drawing.Size(80, 20);
         textPostal.TabIndex = 4;

         textCountryRegion.Location = new                              ↵
System.Drawing.Point(120, 80);
         textCountryRegion.Size = new System.Drawing.Size(232, 20);
         textCountryRegion.TabIndex = 5;

         textEmail.Location = new System.Drawing.Point(120, 104);
         textEmail.Size = new System.Drawing.Size(232, 20);
         textEmail.TabIndex = 6;

         labelName.Location = new System.Drawing.Point(8, 8);
         labelName.Size = new System.Drawing.Size(112, 23);
         labelName.Text = "Name:";
         labelName.TextAlign =                                         ↵
System.Drawing.ContentAlignment.MiddleRight;

         labelAddress.Location = new System.Drawing.Point(8, 32);
         labelAddress.Size = new System.Drawing.Size(112, 23);
         labelAddress.Text = "Address:";
         labelAddress.TextAlign =                                      ↵
System.Drawing.ContentAlignment.MiddleRight;

         labelCityStateProvincePostal.Location = new                   ↵
System.Drawing.Point(8, 56);
         labelCityStateProvincePostal.Size = new                       ↵
System.Drawing.Size(112, 23);
         labelCityStateProvincePostal.Text = "City, St/Prov. Postal:";
         labelCityStateProvincePostal.TextAlign =                      ↵
System.Drawing.ContentAlignment.MiddleRight;

         labelCountryRegion.Location = new System.Drawing.Point(8, 80);
         labelCountryRegion.Size = new System.Drawing.Size(112, 23);
         labelCountryRegion.Text = "Country/Region:";
         labelCountryRegion.TextAlign =                                ↵
System.Drawing.ContentAlignment.MiddleRight;

         labelEmail.Location = new System.Drawing.Point(8, 104);
         labelEmail.Size = new System.Drawing.Size(112, 23);
         labelEmail.Text = "email:";
         labelEmail.TextAlign =                                        ↵
System.Drawing.ContentAlignment.MiddleRight;

         // Add the Validating and Validated handlers for textEmail.
         textEmail.Validating += new                                   ↵
System.ComponentModel.CancelEventHandler(textEmail_Validating);
         textEmail.Validated += new                                    ↵
System.EventHandler(textEmail_Validated);

         // Add the controls to the user control.
         Controls.AddRange(new System.Windows.Forms.Control[]
         {
            labelName,
            labelAddress,
            labelCityStateProvincePostal,
            labelCountryRegion,
            labelEmail,
            textName,
            textAddress,
            textCity,
            textStateProvince,
            textPostal,
            textCountryRegion,
            textEmail
         });

         // Size the user control.
         Size = new System.Drawing.Size(375, 150);
      }

      private void MyValidatingCode()
      {
         // Confirm there is text in the control.
         if (textEmail.Text.Length == 0)
         {
            throw new Exception("Email address is a required field.");
         }
         // Confirm that there is a "." and an "@" in                  ↵
the e-mail address.
         else if(textEmail.Text.IndexOf(".") == -1 ||                  ↵
textEmail.Text.IndexOf("@") == -1)
         {
            throw new Exception("Email address must be                 ↵
valid e-mail address format." +
             "\nFor example: 'someone@example.com'");
         }
      }

      // Validate the data input by the user into textEmail.
      private void textEmail_Validating(object sender,                 ↵
System.ComponentModel.CancelEventArgs e)
      {
         try
         {
            MyValidatingCode();
         }

         catch(Exception ex)
         {
            // Cancel the event and select the text to be              ↵
corrected by the user.
            e.Cancel = true;
            textEmail.Select(0, textEmail.Text.Length);

            // Set the ErrorProvider error with the text to display.
            this.errorProvider1.SetError(textEmail,ex.Message);
          }
      }

      private void textEmail_Validated(Object sender,                  ↵
System.EventArgs e)
      {
         //If all conditions have been met, clear the                  ↵
error provider of errors.
         errorProvider1.SetError(textEmail, "");
      }

   } // End Class
} // End Namespace
```

Requirements

Namespace: System.Windows.Forms

Platforms: Windows 98, Windows NT 4.0, Windows Millennium Edition, Windows 2000, Windows XP Home Edition, Windows XP Professional, Windows Server 2003 family

Assembly: System.Windows.Forms (in System.Windows.Forms.dll)

UserControl Constructor

Initializes a new instance of the **UserControl** class.

[Visual Basic]
```
Public Sub New()
```
[C#]
```
public UserControl();
```
[C++]
```
public: UserControl();
```
[JScript]
```
public function UserControl();
```

Remarks

You do not typically create an instance of **UserControl**. To create your own user control class, inherit from the **UserControl** class.

Example

See related example in the **System.Windows.Forms.UserControl** class topic.

Requirements

Platforms: Windows 98, Windows NT 4.0, Windows Millennium Edition, Windows 2000, Windows XP Home Edition, Windows XP Professional, Windows Server 2003 family

UserControl.DefaultSize Property

This member overrides **Control.DefaultSize**.

[Visual Basic]
```
Overrides Protected ReadOnly Property DefaultSize As Size
```
[C#]
```
protected override Size DefaultSize {get;}
```
[C++]
```
protected: __property Size get_DefaultSize();
```
[JScript]
```
protected override function get DefaultSize() : Size;
```

Requirements

Platforms: Windows 98, Windows NT 4.0, Windows Millennium Edition, Windows 2000, Windows XP Home Edition, Windows XP Professional, Windows Server 2003 family

UserControl.Text Property

This member overrides **Control.Text**.

[Visual Basic]
```
Overrides Public Property Text As String
```
[C#]
```
public override string Text {get; set;}
```
[C++]
```
public: __property String* get_Text();
public: __property void set_Text(String*);
```
[JScript]
```
public override function get Text() : String;
public override function set Text(String);
```

Requirements

Platforms: Windows 98, Windows NT 4.0, Windows Millennium Edition, Windows 2000, Windows XP Home Edition, Windows XP Professional, Windows Server 2003 family

UserControl.OnCreateControl Method

This member overrides **Control.OnCreateControl**.

[Visual Basic]
```
Overrides Protected Sub OnCreateControl()
```
[C#]
```
protected override void OnCreateControl();
```
[C++]
```
protected: void OnCreateControl();
```
[JScript]
```
protected override function OnCreateControl();
```

Requirements

Platforms: Windows 98, Windows NT 4.0, Windows Millennium Edition, Windows 2000, Windows XP Home Edition, Windows XP Professional, Windows Server 2003 family

UserControl.OnLoad Method

Raises the **Load** event.

[Visual Basic]
```
Protected Overridable Sub OnLoad( _
   ByVal e As EventArgs _
)
```
[C#]
```
protected virtual void OnLoad(
   EventArgs e
);
```
[C++]
```
protected: virtual void OnLoad(
   EventArgs* e
);
```
[JScript]
```
protected function OnLoad(
   e : EventArgs
);
```

Parameters

e

An **EventArgs** that contains the event data.

Remarks

The **Load** event occurs after the control is created, but before the control becomes visible for the first time.

Raising an event invokes the event handler through a delegate.

The **OnLoad** method also allows derived classes to handle the event without attaching a delegate. This is the preferred technique for handling the event in a derived class.

Notes to Inheritors: When overriding **OnLoad** in a derived class, be sure to call the base class's **OnLoad** method so that registered delegates receive the event.

Requirements

Platforms: Windows 98, Windows NT 4.0, Windows Millennium Edition, Windows 2000, Windows XP Home Edition, Windows XP Professional, Windows Server 2003 family

UserControl.OnMouseDown Method

This member overrides **Control.OnMouseDown**.

[Visual Basic]
```
Overrides Protected Sub OnMouseDown( _
   ByVal e As MouseEventArgs _
)
```
[C#]
```
protected override void OnMouseDown(
   MouseEventArgs e
);
```
[C++]
```
protected: void OnMouseDown(
   MouseEventArgs* e
);
```
[JScript]
```
protected override function OnMouseDown(
   e : MouseEventArgs
);
```

Requirements

Platforms: Windows 98, Windows NT 4.0, Windows Millennium Edition, Windows 2000, Windows XP Home Edition, Windows XP Professional, Windows Server 2003 family

UserControl.WndProc Method

This member overrides **Control.WndProc**.

[Visual Basic]
```
Overrides Protected Sub WndProc( _
   ByRef m As Message _
)
```
[C#]
```
protected override void WndProc(
   ref Message m
);
```
[C++]
```
protected: void WndProc(
   Message* m
);
```
[JScript]
```
protected override function WndProc(
   m : Message
);
```

Requirements

Platforms: Windows 98, Windows NT 4.0, Windows Millennium Edition, Windows 2000, Windows XP Home Edition, Windows XP Professional, Windows Server 2003 family

UserControl.Load Event

Occurs before the control becomes visible for the first time.

[Visual Basic]
```
Public Event Load As EventHandler
```
[C#]
```
public event EventHandler Load;
```
[C++]
```
public: __event EventHandler* Load;
```

[JScript] In JScript, you can handle the events defined by a class, but you cannot define your own.

Event Data

The event handler receives an argument of type **EventArgs**.

Remarks

You can use this event to perform tasks such as allocating resources used by the control.

Requirements

Platforms: Windows 98, Windows NT 4.0, Windows Millennium Edition, Windows 2000, Windows XP Home Edition, Windows XP Professional, Windows Server 2003 family

UserControl.TextChanged Event

This member supports the .NET Framework infrastructure and is not intended to be used directly from your code.

[Visual Basic]
```
Public Shadows Event TextChanged As EventHandler
```
[C#]
```
public new event EventHandler TextChanged;
```
[C++]
```
public: __event EventHandler* TextChanged;
```

[JScript] In JScript, you can handle the events defined by a class, but you cannot define your own.

View Enumeration

Specifies how list items are displayed in a **ListView** control.

[Visual Basic]
```
<Serializable>
Public Enum View
```
[C#]
```
[Serializable]
public enum View
```
[C++]
```
[Serializable]
__value public enum View
```
[JScript]
```
public
   Serializable
enum View
```

Remarks

Use the members of this enumeration to set the value of the **View** property of the **ListView** control.

Members

Member name	Description
Details Supported by the .NET Compact Framework.	Each item appears on a separate line with further information about each item arranged in columns. The left most column contains a small icon and label, and subsequent columns contain sub items as specified by the application. A column displays a header which can display a caption for the column. The user can resize each column at runtime.
LargeIcon Supported by the .NET Compact Framework.	Each item appears as a full-sized icon with a label below it.
List Supported by the .NET Compact Framework.	Each item appears as a small icon with a label to its right. Items are arranged in columns with no column headers.
SmallIcon Supported by the .NET Compact Framework.	Each item appears as a small icon with a label to its right.

Requirements

Namespace: System.Windows.Forms

Platforms: Windows 98, Windows NT 4.0, Windows Millennium Edition, Windows 2000, Windows XP Home Edition, Windows XP Professional, Windows Server 2003 family, .NET Compact Framework - Windows CE .NET

Assembly: System.Windows.Forms (in System.Windows.Forms.dll)

VScrollBar Class

Represents a standard Windows vertical scroll bar.

System.Object
  System.MarshalByRefObject
    System.ComponentModel.Component
      System.Windows.Forms.Control
        System.Windows.Forms.ScrollBar
          System.Windows.Forms.VScrollBar

[Visual Basic]
```
Public Class VScrollBar
   Inherits ScrollBar
```
[C#]
```
public class VScrollBar : ScrollBar
```
[C++]
```
public __gc class VScrollBar : public ScrollBar
```
[JScript]
```
public class VScrollBar extends ScrollBar
```

Thread Safety

Any public static (**Shared** in Visual Basic) members of this type are safe for multithreaded operations. Any instance members are not guaranteed to be thread safe.

Remarks

Most controls that need scroll bars already provide them and do not require this control. This is true of a multiline **TextBox** control, a **ListBox**, and a **ComboBox**, for example.

You can use this control to implement scrolling in containers that do not provide their own scroll bars such as a **PictureBox** or for user input of numeric data. The numeric data can be displayed in a control or used in code. The **Minimum** and **Maximum** properties determine the range of values the user can select. The **LargeChange** property determines the effect of clicking within the scroll bar but outside the scroll box. The **SmallChange** property determines the effect of clicking the scroll arrows at each end of the control.

Example

[Visual Basic, C#] The following example creates and initializes a **VScrollBar** and adds it to a **Form**.

[Visual Basic]
```
Private Sub InitializeMyScrollBar()
    ' Create and initialize a VScrollBar.
    Dim vScrollBar1 As New VScrollBar()

    ' Dock the scroll bar to the right side of the form.
    vScrollBar1.Dock = DockStyle.Right

    ' Add the scroll bar to the form.
    Controls.Add(vScrollBar1)
End Sub
```

[C#]
```
private void InitializeMyScrollBar()
 {
    // Create and initialize a VScrollBar.
    VScrollBar vScrollBar1 = new VScrollBar();

    // Dock the scroll bar to the right side of the form.
    vScrollBar1.Dock = DockStyle.Right;

    // Add the scroll bar to the form.
    Controls.Add(vScrollBar1);
 }
```

Requirements

Namespace: System.Windows.Forms

Platforms: Windows 98, Windows NT 4.0, Windows Millennium Edition, Windows 2000, Windows XP Home Edition, Windows XP Professional, Windows Server 2003 family, .NET Compact Framework - Windows CE .NET

Assembly: System.Windows.Forms (in System.Windows.Forms.dll)

VScrollBar Constructor

Initializes a new instance of the **VScrollBar** class.

[Visual Basic]
```
Public Sub New()
```
[C#]
```
public VScrollBar();
```
[C++]
```
public: VScrollBar();
```
[JScript]
```
public function VScrollBar();
```

Remarks

The default constructor initializes any fields to their default values.

Requirements

Platforms: Windows 98, Windows NT 4.0, Windows Millennium Edition, Windows 2000, Windows XP Home Edition, Windows XP Professional, Windows Server 2003 family, .NET Compact Framework - Windows CE .NET

VScrollBar.CreateParams Property

This member overrides **Control.CreateParams**.

[Visual Basic]
```
Overrides Protected ReadOnly Property CreateParams As CreateParams
```
[C#]
```
protected override CreateParams CreateParams {get;}
```
[C++]
```
protected: __property CreateParams* get_CreateParams();
```
[JScript]
```
protected override function get CreateParams() : CreateParams;
```

Requirements

Platforms: Windows 98, Windows NT 4.0, Windows Millennium Edition, Windows 2000, Windows XP Home Edition, Windows XP Professional, Windows Server 2003 family

VScrollBar.DefaultSize Property

This member overrides **Control.DefaultSize**.

[Visual Basic]
```
Overrides Protected ReadOnly Property DefaultSize As Size
```
[C#]
```
protected override Size DefaultSize {get;}
```
[C++]
```
protected: __property Size get_DefaultSize();
```
[JScript]
```
protected override function get DefaultSize() : Size;
```

Requirements

Platforms: Windows 98, Windows NT 4.0, Windows Millennium Edition, Windows 2000, Windows XP Home Edition, Windows XP Professional, Windows Server 2003 family

VScrollBar.RightToLeft Property

This member overrides **Control.RightToLeft**.

[Visual Basic]
```
Overrides Public Property RightToLeft As RightToLeft
```
[C#]
```
public override RightToLeft RightToLeft {get; set;}
```
[C++]
```
public: __property RightToLeft get_RightToLeft();
public: __property void set_RightToLeft(RightToLeft);
```
[JScript]
```
public override function get RightToLeft() : RightToLeft;
public override function set RightToLeft(RightToLeft);
```

Requirements

Platforms: Windows 98, Windows NT 4.0, Windows Millennium Edition, Windows 2000, Windows XP Home Edition, Windows XP Professional, Windows Server 2003 family

VScrollBar.RightToLeftChanged Event

This member supports the .NET Framework infrastructure and is not intended to be used directly from your code.

[Visual Basic]
```
Public Shadows Event RightToLeftChanged As EventHandler
```
[C#]
```
public new event EventHandler RightToLeftChanged;
```
[C++]
```
public: __event EventHandler* RightToLeftChanged;
```

[JScript] In JScript, you can handle the events defined by a class, but you cannot define your own.

System.Windows.Forms.Design Namespace

The **System.Windows.Forms.Design** namespace contains classes that support design-time configuration and behavior for Windows Forms components. These classes consist of: Designer classes that provide support for Windows Forms components, a set of design time services, UITypeEditor classes for configuring certain types of properties, and classes for importing ActiveX controls.

AnchorEditor Class

Provides a user interface for configuring an **Anchor** property.

System.Object
  System.Drawing.Design.UITypeEditor
    System.Windows.Forms.Design.AnchorEditor

[Visual Basic]
```
NotInheritable Public Class AnchorEditor
   Inherits UITypeEditor
```
[C#]
```
public sealed class AnchorEditor : UITypeEditor
```
[C++]
```
public __gc __sealed class AnchorEditor : public UITypeEditor
```
[JScript]
```
public class AnchorEditor extends UITypeEditor
```

Thread Safety

Any public static (**Shared** in Visual Basic) members of this type are safe for multithreaded operations. Any instance members are not guaranteed to be thread safe.

Remarks

The **AnchorEditor** provides a design-time user interface for configuring an **Anchor** property. An **Anchor** property is typically used to determine which sides of the container a control is bound to. This class provides a drop-down graphical control that allows the user to specify which sides of the container to anchor the control to.

Example

[Visual Basic]
```
<EditorAttribute(GetType                                       ↵
(System.Windows.Forms.Design.AnchorEditor),                    ↵
 GetType(System.Drawing.Design.UITypeEditor))> _
Public Property testAnchor() As System.Windows.Forms.AnchorStyles
   Get
      Return anchor
   End Get
   Set
      anchor = value
   End Set
End Property
Private anchor As AnchorStyles
```

[C#]
```
[EditorAttribute(typeof                                        ↵
 (System.Windows.Forms.Design.AnchorEditor),                   ↵
typeof(System.Drawing.Design.UITypeEditor))]
public System.Windows.Forms.AnchorStyles testAnchor
{
    get
    {
        return anchor;
    }
    set
    {
        anchor = value;
    }
}
private AnchorStyles anchor;
```

[C++]
```
public:
    [EditorAttribute(__typeof                                  ↵
 (System::Windows::Forms::Design::AnchorEditor),
        __typeof(System::Drawing::Design::UITypeEditor))]
    __property System::Windows::Forms::AnchorStyles get_testAnchor() {
        return anchor;
    }

[EditorAttribute(__typeof(System::Windows::Forms::Design::AnchorEditor),
        __typeof(System::Drawing::Design::UITypeEditor))]
    __property void set_testAnchor                             ↵
 (System::Windows::Forms::AnchorStyles value) {
        anchor = value;
    }
private:
    AnchorStyles  anchor;
```

Requirements

Namespace: System.Windows.Forms.Design

Platforms: Windows 98, Windows NT 4.0, Windows Millennium Edition, Windows 2000, Windows XP Home Edition, Windows XP Professional, Windows Server 2003 family

Assembly: System.Design (in System.Design.dll)

AnchorEditor Constructor

Initializes a new instance of the **AnchorEditor** class.

[Visual Basic]
```
Public Sub New()
```
[C#]
```
public AnchorEditor();
```
[C++]
```
public: AnchorEditor();
```
[JScript]
```
public function AnchorEditor();
```

Remarks

The default constructor initializes any fields to their default values.

Requirements

Platforms: Windows 98, Windows NT 4.0, Windows Millennium Edition, Windows 2000, Windows XP Home Edition, Windows XP Professional, Windows Server 2003 family

.NET Framework Security:

- Full trust for the immediate caller. This member cannot be used by partially trusted code.

AnchorEditor.EditValue Method

Edits the value of the specified object.

Overload List

Edits the value of the specified object using the specified service provider and context.

[Visual Basic] **Overloads Overrides Public Function EditValue(ITypeDescriptorContext, IServiceProvider, Object) As Object**

[C#] **public override object EditValue(ITypeDescriptor-Context, IServiceProvider, object);**

[C++] **public: Object* EditValue(ITypeDescriptorContext*, IServiceProvider*, Object*);**

[JScript] **public override function EditValue(IType-DescriptorContext, IServiceProvider, Object) : Object;**

Inherited from **UITypeEditor**.

[Visual Basic] **Overloads Public Function EditValue(IServiceProvider, Object) As Object**

[C#] **public object EditValue(IServiceProvider, object);**

[C++] **public: Object* EditValue(IServiceProvider*, Object*);**

[JScript] **public function EditValue(IServiceProvider, Object) : Object;**

AnchorEditor.EditValue Method (ITypeDescriptorContext, IServiceProvider, Object)

Edits the value of the specified object using the specified service provider and context.

```
[Visual Basic]
Overrides Overloads Public Function EditValue( _
   ByVal context As ITypeDescriptorContext, _
   ByVal provider As IServiceProvider, _
   ByVal value As Object _
) As Object
[C#]
public override object EditValue(
   ITypeDescriptorContext context,
   IServiceProvider provider,
   object value
);
[C++]
public: Object* EditValue(
   ITypeDescriptorContext* context,
   IServiceProvider* provider,
   Object* value
);
[JScript]
public override function EditValue(
   context : ITypeDescriptorContext,
   provider : IServiceProvider,
   value : Object
) : Object;
```

Parameters

context

An **ITypeDescriptorContext** that can be used to gain additional context information.

provider

An **IServiceProvider** through which editing services may be obtained.

value

An instance of the value being edited.

Return Value

The new value of the object. If the value of the object hasn't changed, this should return the same object it was passed.

Remarks

A service provider is provided so that any required editing services can be obtained.

Requirements

Platforms: Windows 98, Windows NT 4.0, Windows Millennium Edition, Windows 2000, Windows XP Home Edition, Windows XP Professional, Windows Server 2003 family

.NET Framework Security:

- Full trust for the immediate caller. This member cannot be used by partially trusted code.

AnchorEditor.GetEditStyle Method

Gets the editor style used by the **EditValue** method.

Overload List

Gets the editor style used by the **EditValue** method.

[Visual Basic] **Overloads Overrides Public Function GetEdit-Style(ITypeDescriptorContext) As UITypeEditorEditStyle**

[C#] **public override UITypeEditorEditStyle GetEdit-Style(ITypeDescriptorContext);**

[C++] **public: UITypeEditorEditStyle GetEdit-Style(ITypeDescriptorContext*);**

[JScript] **public override function GetEdit-Style(ITypeDescriptorContext) : UITypeEditorEditStyle;**

Inherited from **UITypeEditor**.

[Visual Basic] **Overloads Public Function GetEditStyle() As UITypeEditorEditStyle**

[C#] **public UITypeEditorEditStyle GetEditStyle();**

[C++] **public: UITypeEditorEditStyle GetEditStyle();**

[JScript] **public function GetEditStyle() : UITypeEditorEditStyle;**

AnchorEditor.GetEditStyle Method (ITypeDescriptorContext)

Gets the editor style used by the **EditValue** method.

[Visual Basic]
```
Overrides Overloads Public Function GetEditStyle( _
   ByVal context As ITypeDescriptorContext _
) As UITypeEditorEditStyle
```
[C#]
```
public override UITypeEditorEditStyle GetEditStyle(
   ITypeDescriptorContext context
);
```
[C++]
```
public: UITypeEditorEditStyle GetEditStyle(
   ITypeDescriptorContext* context
);
```
[JScript]
```
public override function GetEditStyle(
   context : ITypeDescriptorContext
) : UITypeEditorEditStyle;
```

Parameters

context
An **ITypeDescriptorContext** that can be used to gain additional context information.

Return Value

One of the **UITypeEditorEditStyle** values indicating the provided editing style. If the method is not supported, this method will return **None**.

Requirements

Platforms: Windows 98, Windows NT 4.0, Windows Millennium Edition, Windows 2000, Windows XP Home Edition, Windows XP Professional, Windows Server 2003 family

.NET Framework Security:

- Full trust for the immediate caller. This member cannot be used by partially trusted code.

AxImporter Class

Imports ActiveX controls and generates a wrapper that can be accessed by a designer.

System.Object
  System.Windows.Forms.Design.AxImporter

[Visual Basic]
```
Public Class AxImporter
```
[C#]
```
public class AxImporter
```
[C++]
```
public __gc class AxImporter
```
[JScript]
```
public class AxImporter
```

Thread Safety

Any public static (**Shared** in Visual Basic) members of this type are safe for multithreaded operations. Any instance members are not guaranteed to be thread safe.

Remarks

To generate an ActiveX wrapper for an ActiveX control, first create or obtain an instance of the **AxImporter** class. The **AxImporter** constructor accepts an **AxImporter.Options** object, which sets options for the importer, such as the filename for the wrapper .dll to generate and the output directory to generate the wrapper to. To generate the ActiveX wrapper, call the appropriate Generate method. To generate from a file, call **GenerateFromFile**. To generate from a type library, call **GenerateFromTypeLibrary**. The string that is returned will consist of an assembly qualified name (example: "Namespace.Type,Assembly") for the type an ActiveX wrapper was generated for. The wrapper for the ActiveX control will be generated in the .dll file specified in the **outputName** property of the **AxImporter.Options** passed to the **AxImporter** constructor. The type can be loaded or queried using **System.Reflection** and treated as an ordinary managed type. You can also call the **GetOcx** method of the type to retrieve a COM interface to the object, if the object supports this.

Requirements

Namespace: System.Windows.Forms.Design

Platforms: Windows 98, Windows NT 4.0, Windows Millennium Edition, Windows 2000, Windows XP Home Edition, Windows XP Professional, Windows Server 2003 family

Assembly: System.Design (in System.Design.dll)

AxImporter Constructor

Initializes a new instance of the **AxImporter** class.

[Visual Basic]
```
Public Sub New( _
   ByVal options As AxImporter.Options _
)
```
[C#]
```
public AxImporter(
   AxImporter.Options options
);
```
[C++]
```
public: AxImporter(
   AxImporter.Options* options
);
```
[JScript]
```
public function AxImporter(
   options : AxImporter.Options
);
```

Parameters

options
  An **AxImporter.Options** that indicates the options for the ActiveX control importer to use.

Requirements

Platforms: Windows 98, Windows NT 4.0, Windows Millennium Edition, Windows 2000, Windows XP Home Edition, Windows XP Professional, Windows Server 2003 family

.NET Framework Security:

- Full trust for the immediate caller. This member cannot be used by partially trusted code.

AxImporter.GeneratedAssemblies Property

Gets the names of the assemblies that are generated for the control.

[Visual Basic]
```
Public ReadOnly Property GeneratedAssemblies As String ()
```
[C#]
```
public string[] GeneratedAssemblies {get;}
```
[C++]
```
public: __property String* get_GeneratedAssemblies();
```
[JScript]
```
public function get GeneratedAssemblies() : String[];
```

Property Value

An array of names of the generated assemblies, or an empty string array if no assemblies have been generated.

Requirements

Platforms: Windows 98, Windows NT 4.0, Windows Millennium Edition, Windows 2000, Windows XP Home Edition, Windows XP Professional, Windows Server 2003 family

.NET Framework Security:

- Full trust for the immediate caller. This member cannot be used by partially trusted code.

AxImporter.GeneratedSources Property

Gets the names of the source files that were generated.

[Visual Basic]
```
Public ReadOnly Property GeneratedSources As String ()
```
[C#]
```
public string[] GeneratedSources {get;}
```
[C++]
```
public: __property String* get_GeneratedSources();
```
[JScript]
```
public function get GeneratedSources() : String[];
```

Property Value

An array of file names of the generated source files, or a null reference (**Nothing** in Visual Basic) if none exist.

Requirements

Platforms: Windows 98, Windows NT 4.0, Windows Millennium Edition, Windows 2000, Windows XP Home Edition, Windows XP Professional, Windows Server 2003 family

.NET Framework Security:

- Full trust for the immediate caller. This member cannot be used by partially trusted code.

AxImporter.GeneratedTypeLibAttributes Property

Gets the attributes for the generated type library.

```
[Visual Basic]
Public ReadOnly Property GeneratedTypeLibAttributes As TYPELIBATTR _
   ()
[C#]
public TYPELIBATTR[] GeneratedTypeLibAttributes {get;}
[C++]
public: __property TYPELIBATTR get_GeneratedTypeLibAttributes();
[JScript]
public function get GeneratedTypeLibAttributes() : TYPELIBATTR[];
```

Property Value

An array of type **TYPELIBATTR** that indicates the attributes for the generated type library.

Requirements

Platforms: Windows 98, Windows NT 4.0, Windows Millennium Edition, Windows 2000, Windows XP Home Edition, Windows XP Professional, Windows Server 2003 family

.NET Framework Security:

- Full trust for the immediate caller. This member cannot be used by partially trusted code.

AxImporter.GenerateFromFile Method

Generates a wrapper for an ActiveX control for use in the design-time environment.

```
[Visual Basic]
Public Function GenerateFromFile( _
   ByVal file As FileInfo _
) As String
[C#]
public string GenerateFromFile(
   FileInfo file
);
[C++]
public: String* GenerateFromFile(
   FileInfo* file
);
[JScript]
public function GenerateFromFile(
   file : FileInfo
) : String;
```

Parameters

file

A **FileInfo** indicating the file that contains the control.

Return Value

An assembly qualified name for the type of ActiveX control for which a wrapper was generated.

Requirements

Platforms: Windows 98, Windows NT 4.0, Windows Millennium Edition, Windows 2000, Windows XP Home Edition, Windows XP Professional, Windows Server 2003 family

.NET Framework Security:

- Full trust for the immediate caller. This member cannot be used by partially trusted code.

AxImporter.GenerateFromTypeLibrary Method

Generates a wrapper for an ActiveX control for use in the design-time environment.

Overload List

Generates a wrapper for an ActiveX control for use in the design-time environment.

[Visual Basic] **Overloads Public Function GenerateFromTypeLibrary(UCOMITypeLib) As String**

[C#] **public string GenerateFromTypeLibrary(UCOMITypeLib);**

[C++] **public: String* GenerateFromTypeLibrary(UCOMITypeLib*);**

[JScript] **public function GenerateFromTypeLibrary(UCOMITypeLib) : String;**

Generates a wrapper for an ActiveX control for use in the design-time environment.

[Visual Basic] **Overloads Public Function GenerateFromTypeLibrary(UCOMITypeLib, Guid) As String**

[C#] **public string GenerateFromTypeLibrary(UCOMITypeLib, Guid);**

[C++] **public: String* GenerateFromTypeLibrary(UCOMITypeLib*, Guid);**

[JScript] **public function GenerateFromTypeLibrary(UCOMITypeLib, Guid) : String;**

AxImporter.GenerateFromTypeLibrary Method (UCOMITypeLib)

Generates a wrapper for an ActiveX control for use in the design-time environment.

```
[Visual Basic]
Overloads Public Function GenerateFromTypeLibrary( _
   ByVal typeLib As UCOMITypeLib _
) As String
[C#]
public string GenerateFromTypeLibrary(
   UCOMITypeLib typeLib
);
[C++]
public: String* GenerateFromTypeLibrary(
   UCOMITypeLib* typeLib
);
```

[JScript]
```
public function GenerateFromTypeLibrary(
   typeLib : UCOMITypeLib
) : String;
```

Parameters

typeLib

A **UCOMITypeLib** that indicates the type library to generate the control from.

Return Value

An assembly qualified name for the type of ActiveX control for which a wrapper was generated.

Requirements

Platforms: Windows 98, Windows NT 4.0, Windows Millennium Edition, Windows 2000, Windows XP Home Edition, Windows XP Professional, Windows Server 2003 family

.NET Framework Security:

- Full trust for the immediate caller. This member cannot be used by partially trusted code.

AxImporter.GenerateFromTypeLibrary Method (UCOMITypeLib, Guid)

Generates a wrapper for an ActiveX control for use in the design-time environment.

[Visual Basic]
```
Overloads Public Function GenerateFromTypeLibrary( _
   ByVal typeLib As UCOMITypeLib, _
   ByVal clsid As Guid _
) As String
```
[C#]
```
public string GenerateFromTypeLibrary(
   UCOMITypeLib typeLib,
   Guid clsid
);
```
[C++]
```
public: String* GenerateFromTypeLibrary(
   UCOMITypeLib* typeLib,
   Guid clsid
);
```
[JScript]
```
public function GenerateFromTypeLibrary(
   typeLib : UCOMITypeLib,
   clsid : Guid
) : String;
```

Parameters

typeLib

A **UCOMITypeLib** that indicates the type library to generate the control from.

clsid

The **Guid** for the control wrapper.

Return Value

An assembly qualified name for the type of ActiveX control for which a wrapper was generated.

Requirements

Platforms: Windows 98, Windows NT 4.0, Windows Millennium Edition, Windows 2000, Windows XP Home Edition, Windows XP Professional, Windows Server 2003 family

.NET Framework Security:

- Full trust for the immediate caller. This member cannot be used by partially trusted code.

AxImporter.GetFileOfTypeLib Method

Gets the path and file name to the specified type library.

[Visual Basic]
```
Public Shared Function GetFileOfTypeLib( _
   ByRef tlibattr As TYPELIBATTR _
) As String
```
[C#]
```
public static string GetFileOfTypeLib(
   ref TYPELIBATTR tlibattr
);
```
[C++]
```
public: static String* GetFileOfTypeLib(
   TYPELIBATTR* tlibattr
);
```
[JScript]
```
public static function GetFileOfTypeLib(
   tlibattr : TYPELIBATTR
) : String;
```

Parameters

tlibattr

A **TYPELIBATTR** that indicates the type library to retrieve the file name of.

Return Value

The path and file name to the specified type library, or a null reference (**Nothing** in Visual Basic) if the library could not be located.

Requirements

Platforms: Windows 98, Windows NT 4.0, Windows Millennium Edition, Windows 2000, Windows XP Home Edition, Windows XP Professional, Windows Server 2003 family

.NET Framework Security:

- Full trust for the immediate caller. This member cannot be used by partially trusted code.

AxImporter.IReference-Resolver Interface

Provides methods to resolve references to ActiveX libraries, COM type libraries or assemblies, or managed assemblies.

```
[Visual Basic]
Public Interface AxImporter.IReferenceResolver
[C#]
public interface AxImporter.IReferenceResolver
[C++]
public __gc __interface AxImporter.IReferenceResolver
[JScript]
public interface AxImporter.IReferenceResolver
```

Requirements

Namespace: System.Windows.Forms.Design

Platforms: Windows 98, Windows NT 4.0, Windows Millennium Edition, Windows 2000, Windows XP Home Edition, Windows XP Professional, Windows Server 2003 family

Assembly: System.Design (in System.Design.dll)

AxImporter.IReferenceResolver.ResolveActiveX-Reference Method

Resolves a reference to the specified type library that contains an ActiveX control.

```
[Visual Basic]
Function ResolveActiveXReference( _
   ByVal typeLib As UCOMITypeLib _
) As String
[C#]
string ResolveActiveXReference(
   UCOMITypeLib typeLib
);
[C++]
String* ResolveActiveXReference(
   UCOMITypeLib* typeLib
);
[JScript]
function ResolveActiveXReference(
   typeLib : UCOMITypeLib
) : String;
```

Parameters

typeLib

A **UCOMITypeLib** to resolve a reference to.

Return Value

A fully qualified path to an assembly.

Requirements

Platforms: Windows 98, Windows NT 4.0, Windows Millennium Edition, Windows 2000, Windows XP Home Edition, Windows XP Professional, Windows Server 2003 family

.NET Framework Security:

- Full trust for the immediate caller. This member cannot be used by partially trusted code.

AxImporter.IReferenceResolver.ResolveCom-Reference Method

Resolves a reference to the specified type library.

Overload List

Resolves a reference to the specified assembly that contains a COM component.

[Visual Basic] **Overloads Function ResolveComReference(AssemblyName) As String**

[C#] **string ResolveComReference(AssemblyName);**

[C++] **String* ResolveComReference(AssemblyName*);**

[JScript] **function ResolveComReference(AssemblyName) : String;**

Resolves a reference to the specified type library that contains an COM component.

[Visual Basic] **Overloads Function ResolveComReference(UCOMITypeLib) As String**

[C#] **string ResolveComReference(UCOMITypeLib);**

[C++] **String* ResolveComReference(UCOMITypeLib*);**

[JScript] **function ResolveComReference(UCOMITypeLib) : String;**

AxImporter.IReferenceResolver.ResolveComReference Method (AssemblyName)

Resolves a reference to the specified assembly that contains a COM component.

```
[Visual Basic]
Function ResolveComReference( _
   ByVal name As AssemblyName _
) As String
[C#]
string ResolveComReference(
   AssemblyName name
);
[C++]
String* ResolveComReference(
   AssemblyName* name
);
[JScript]
function ResolveComReference(
   name : AssemblyName
) : String;
```

Parameters

name

An **AssemblyName** that indicates the assembly to resolve a reference to.

Return Value

A fully qualified path to an assembly.

Requirements

Platforms: Windows 98, Windows NT 4.0, Windows Millennium Edition, Windows 2000, Windows XP Home Edition, Windows XP Professional, Windows Server 2003 family

.NET Framework Security:

- Full trust for the immediate caller. This member cannot be used by partially trusted code.

AxImporter.IReferenceResolver.ResolveComReference Method (UCOMITypeLib)

Resolves a reference to the specified type library that contains an COM component.

[Visual Basic]
```
Function ResolveComReference( _
   ByVal typeLib As UCOMITypeLib _
) As String
```
[C#]
```
string ResolveComReference(
   UCOMITypeLib typeLib
);
```
[C++]
```
String* ResolveComReference(
   UCOMITypeLib* typeLib
);
```
[JScript]
```
function ResolveComReference(
   typeLib : UCOMITypeLib
) : String;
```

Parameters

typeLib

A **UCOMITypeLib** to resolve a reference to.

Return Value

A fully qualified path to an assembly.

Requirements

Platforms: Windows 98, Windows NT 4.0, Windows Millennium Edition, Windows 2000, Windows XP Home Edition, Windows XP Professional, Windows Server 2003 family

.NET Framework Security:

- Full trust for the immediate caller. This member cannot be used by partially trusted code.

AxImporter.IReferenceResolver.Resolve-ManagedReference Method

Resolves a reference to the specified assembly.

[Visual Basic]
```
Function ResolveManagedReference( _
   ByVal assemName As String _
) As String
```
[C#]
```
string ResolveManagedReference(
   string assemName
);
```
[C++]
```
String* ResolveManagedReference(
   String* assemName
);
```
[JScript]
```
function ResolveManagedReference(
   assemName : String
) : String;
```

Parameters

assemName

The name of the assembly to resolve a reference to.

Return Value

A fully qualified path to an assembly.

Requirements

Platforms: Windows 98, Windows NT 4.0, Windows Millennium Edition, Windows 2000, Windows XP Home Edition, Windows XP Professional, Windows Server 2003 family

.NET Framework Security:

- Full trust for the immediate caller. This member cannot be used by partially trusted code.

AxImporter.Options Class

Represents a set of options for an **AxImporter**.

System.Object
System.Windows.Forms.Design.AxImporter.Options

[Visual Basic]
```
NotInheritable Public Class AxImporter.Options
```
[C#]
```
public sealed class AxImporter.Options
```
[C++]
```
public __gc __sealed class AxImporter.Options
```
[JScript]
```
public class AxImporter.Options
```

Thread Safety

Any public static (**Shared** in Visual Basic) members of this type are safe for multithreaded operations. Any instance members are not guaranteed to be thread safe.

Requirements

Namespace: System.Windows.Forms.Design

Platforms: Windows 98, Windows NT 4.0, Windows Millennium Edition, Windows 2000, Windows XP Home Edition, Windows XP Professional, Windows Server 2003 family

Assembly: System.Design (in System.Design.dll)

AxImporter.Options Constructor

Initializes a new instance of the **AxImporter.Options** class.

[Visual Basic]
```
Public Sub New()
```
[C#]
```
public AxImporter.Options();
```
[C++]
```
public: Options();
```
[JScript]
```
public function AxImporter.Options();
```

Remarks

The default constructor initializes any fields to their default values.

Requirements

Platforms: Windows 98, Windows NT 4.0, Windows Millennium Edition, Windows 2000, Windows XP Home Edition, Windows XP Professional, Windows Server 2003 family

.NET Framework Security:

- Full trust for the immediate caller. This member cannot be used by partially trusted code.

AxImporter.Options.delaySign Field

Specifies whether the generated assembly is strongly named and will be signed later.

[Visual Basic]
```
Public delaySign As Boolean
```
[C#]
```
public bool delaySign;
```
[C++]
```
public: bool delaySign;
```
[JScript]
```
public var delaySign : Boolean;
```

Remarks

By default, this field is set to **false**.

Requirements

Platforms: Windows 98, Windows NT 4.0, Windows Millennium Edition, Windows 2000, Windows XP Home Edition, Windows XP Professional, Windows Server 2003 family

AxImporter.Options.genSources Field

Specifies whether sources for the type library wrapper should be generated.

[Visual Basic]
```
Public genSources As Boolean
```
[C#]
```
public bool genSources;
```
[C++]
```
public: bool genSources;
```
[JScript]
```
public var genSources : Boolean;
```

Remarks

By default, this field is set to **false**.

Requirements

Platforms: Windows 98, Windows NT 4.0, Windows Millennium Edition, Windows 2000, Windows XP Home Edition, Windows XP Professional, Windows Server 2003 family

AxImporter.Options.keyContainer Field

Specifies the path to the file that contains the strong name key container for the generated assemblies.

[Visual Basic]
```
Public keyContainer As String
```
[C#]
```
public string keyContainer;
```
[C++]
```
public: String* keyContainer;
```
[JScript]
```
public var keyContainer : String;
```

Remarks

By default, this field is set to a null reference (**Nothing** in Visual Basic).

Requirements

Platforms: Windows 98, Windows NT 4.0, Windows Millennium Edition, Windows 2000, Windows XP Home Edition, Windows XP Professional, Windows Server 2003 family

AxImporter.Options.keyFile Field

Specifies the path to the file that contains the strong name key for the generated assemblies.

```
[Visual Basic]
Public keyFile As String
[C#]
public string keyFile;
[C++]
public: String* keyFile;
[JScript]
public var keyFile : String;
```

Remarks

By default, this field is set to a null reference (**Nothing** in Visual Basic).

Requirements

Platforms: Windows 98, Windows NT 4.0, Windows Millennium Edition, Windows 2000, Windows XP Home Edition, Windows XP Professional, Windows Server 2003 family

AxImporter.Options.keyPair Field

Specifies the strong name used for the generated assemblies.

```
[Visual Basic]
Public keyPair As StrongNameKeyPair
[C#]
public StrongNameKeyPair keyPair;
[C++]
public: StrongNameKeyPair* keyPair;
[JScript]
public var keyPair : StrongNameKeyPair;
```

Remarks

By default, this field is set to a null reference (**Nothing** in Visual Basic).

Requirements

Platforms: Windows 98, Windows NT 4.0, Windows Millennium Edition, Windows 2000, Windows XP Home Edition, Windows XP Professional, Windows Server 2003 family

AxImporter.Options.noLogo Field

Indicates whether the ActiveX importer tool logo will be displayed when the control is imported.

```
[Visual Basic]
Public noLogo As Boolean
[C#]
public bool noLogo;
[C++]
public: bool noLogo;
[JScript]
public var noLogo : Boolean;
```

Remarks

By default, this field is set to **false**.

Requirements

Platforms: Windows 98, Windows NT 4.0, Windows Millennium Edition, Windows 2000, Windows XP Home Edition, Windows XP Professional, Windows Server 2003 family

AxImporter.Options.outputDirectory Field

Specifies the path to the directory that the generated assemblies will be created in.

```
[Visual Basic]
Public outputDirectory As String
[C#]
public string outputDirectory;
[C++]
public: String* outputDirectory;
[JScript]
public var outputDirectory : String;
```

Remarks

By default, this field is set to a null reference (**Nothing** in Visual Basic).

Requirements

Platforms: Windows 98, Windows NT 4.0, Windows Millennium Edition, Windows 2000, Windows XP Home Edition, Windows XP Professional, Windows Server 2003 family

AxImporter.Options.outputName Field

Specifies the filename to generate the ActiveX control wrapper to.

```
[Visual Basic]
Public outputName As String
[C#]
public string outputName;
[C++]
public: String* outputName;
[JScript]
public var outputName : String;
```

Remarks

By default, this field is set to a null reference (**Nothing** in Visual Basic). If this field is a null reference (**Nothing**), the file name will be a concatenation of "Ax" + the type library name from the assembly + ".dll".

Requirements

Platforms: Windows 98, Windows NT 4.0, Windows Millennium Edition, Windows 2000, Windows XP Home Edition, Windows XP Professional, Windows Server 2003 family

AxImporter.Options.overwriteRCW Field

Specifies whether to overwrite existing files when generating assemblies.

[Visual Basic]
```
Public overwriteRCW As Boolean
```
[C#]
```
public bool overwriteRCW;
```
[C++]
```
public: bool overwriteRCW;
```
[JScript]
```
public var overwriteRCW : Boolean;
```

Remarks

By default, this field is set to **false**.

Requirements

Platforms: Windows 98, Windows NT 4.0,
Windows Millennium Edition, Windows 2000,
Windows XP Home Edition, Windows XP Professional,
Windows Server 2003 family

AxImporter.Options.publicKey Field

Specifies the public key used to sign the generated assemblies.

[Visual Basic]
```
Public publicKey() As Byte
```
[C#]
```
public byte[] publicKey;
```
[C++]
```
public: unsigned char publicKey __gc[];
```
[JScript]
```
public var publicKey : Byte[];
```

Remarks

By default, this field is set to a null reference (**Nothing** in Visual Basic).

Requirements

Platforms: Windows 98, Windows NT 4.0,
Windows Millennium Edition, Windows 2000,
Windows XP Home Edition, Windows XP Professional,
Windows Server 2003 family

AxImporter.Options.references Field

Specifies the **AxImporter.IReferenceResolver** to use to resolve types and references when generating assemblies.

[Visual Basic]
```
Public references As AxImporter.IReferenceResolver
```
[C#]
```
public AxImporter.IReferenceResolver references;
```
[C++]
```
public: AxImporter.IReferenceResolver* references;
```
[JScript]
```
public var references : AxImporter.IReferenceResolver;
```

Remarks

By default, this field is set to a null reference (**Nothing** in Visual Basic).

Requirements

Platforms: Windows 98, Windows NT 4.0,
Windows Millennium Edition, Windows 2000,
Windows XP Home Edition, Windows XP Professional,
Windows Server 2003 family

AxImporter.Options.silentMode Field

Specifies whether to compile in silent mode, which generates less displayed information at compile time.

[Visual Basic]
```
Public silentMode As Boolean
```
[C#]
```
public bool silentMode;
```
[C++]
```
public: bool silentMode;
```
[JScript]
```
public var silentMode : Boolean;
```

Remarks

By default, this field is set to **false**.

Requirements

Platforms: Windows 98, Windows NT 4.0,
Windows Millennium Edition, Windows 2000,
Windows XP Home Edition, Windows XP Professional,
Windows Server 2003 family

AxImporter.Options.verboseMode Field

Specifies whether to compile in verbose mode, which generates more displayed information at compile time.

[Visual Basic]
```
Public verboseMode As Boolean
```
[C#]
```
public bool verboseMode;
```
[C++]
```
public: bool verboseMode;
```
[JScript]
```
public var verboseMode : Boolean;
```

Remarks

By default, this field is set to **false**.

Requirements

Platforms: Windows 98, Windows NT 4.0,
Windows Millennium Edition, Windows 2000,
Windows XP Home Edition, Windows XP Professional,
Windows Server 2003 family

AxParameterData Class

This type supports the .NET Framework infrastructure and is not intended to be used directly from your code.

```
[Visual Basic]
Public Class AxParameterData
[C#]
public class AxParameterData
[C++]
public __gc class AxParameterData
[JScript]
public class AxParameterData
```

AxParameterData Constructor

This member supports the .NET Framework infrastructure and is not intended to be used directly from your code.

Overload List

This member supports the .NET Framework infrastructure and is not intended to be used directly from your code.

[Visual Basic] **Public Sub New(ParameterInfo)**

[C#] **public AxParameterData(ParameterInfo);**

[C++] **public: AxParameterData(ParameterInfo*);**

[JScript] **public function AxParameterData(ParameterInfo);**

This member supports the .NET Framework infrastructure and is not intended to be used directly from your code.

[Visual Basic] **Public Sub New(ParameterInfo, Boolean)**

[C#] **public AxParameterData(ParameterInfo, bool);**

[C++] **public: AxParameterData(ParameterInfo*, bool);**

[JScript] **public function AxParameterData(ParameterInfo, Boolean);**

This member supports the .NET Framework infrastructure and is not intended to be used directly from your code.

[Visual Basic] **Public Sub New(String, String)**

[C#] **public AxParameterData(string, string);**

[C++] **public: AxParameterData(String*, String*);**

[JScript] **public function AxParameterData(String, String);**

This member supports the .NET Framework infrastructure and is not intended to be used directly from your code.

[Visual Basic] **Public Sub New(String, Type)**

[C#] **public AxParameterData(string, Type);**

[C++] **public: AxParameterData(String*, Type*);**

[JScript] **public function AxParameterData(String, Type);**

AxParameterData Constructor (ParameterInfo)

This member supports the .NET Framework infrastructure and is not intended to be used directly from your code.

```
[Visual Basic]
Public Sub New( _
   ByVal info As ParameterInfo _
)
[C#]
public AxParameterData(
   ParameterInfo info
);
[C++]
public: AxParameterData(
   ParameterInfo* info
);
[JScript]
public function AxParameterData(
   info : ParameterInfo
);
```

AxParameterData Constructor (ParameterInfo, Boolean)

This member supports the .NET Framework infrastructure and is not intended to be used directly from your code.

```
[Visual Basic]
Public Sub New( _
   ByVal info As ParameterInfo, _
   ByVal ignoreByRefs As Boolean _
)
[C#]
public AxParameterData(
   ParameterInfo info,
   bool ignoreByRefs
);
[C++]
public: AxParameterData(
   ParameterInfo* info,
   bool ignoreByRefs
);
[JScript]
public function AxParameterData(
   info : ParameterInfo,
   ignoreByRefs : Boolean
);
```

AxParameterData Constructor (String, String)

This member supports the .NET Framework infrastructure and is not intended to be used directly from your code.

```
[Visual Basic]
Public Sub New( _
   ByVal inname As String, _
   ByVal typeName As String _
)
[C#]
public AxParameterData(
   string inname,
   string typeName
);
[C++]
public: AxParameterData(
   String* inname,
   String* typeName
);
[JScript]
public function AxParameterData(
   inname : String,
   typeName : String
);
```

AxParameterData Constructor (String, Type)

This member supports the .NET Framework infrastructure and is not intended to be used directly from your code.

```
[Visual Basic]
Public Sub New( _
   ByVal inname As String, _
   ByVal type As Type _
)
[C#]
public AxParameterData(
   string inname,
   Type type
);
[C++]
public: AxParameterData(
   String* inname,
   Type* type
);
[JScript]
public function AxParameterData(
   inname : String,
   type : Type
);
```

AxParameterData.Direction Property

This member supports the .NET Framework infrastructure and is not intended to be used directly from your code.

```
[Visual Basic]
Public ReadOnly Property Direction As FieldDirection
[C#]
public FieldDirection Direction {get;}
[C++]
public: __property FieldDirection get_Direction();
[JScript]
public function get Direction() : FieldDirection;
```

AxParameterData.IsByRef Property

This member supports the .NET Framework infrastructure and is not intended to be used directly from your code.

```
[Visual Basic]
Public ReadOnly Property IsByRef As Boolean
[C#]
public bool IsByRef {get;}
[C++]
public: __property bool get_IsByRef();
[JScript]
public function get IsByRef() : Boolean;
```

AxParameterData.IsIn Property

This member supports the .NET Framework infrastructure and is not intended to be used directly from your code.

```
[Visual Basic]
Public ReadOnly Property IsIn As Boolean
[C#]
public bool IsIn {get;}
[C++]
public: __property bool get_IsIn();
[JScript]
public function get IsIn() : Boolean;
```

AxParameterData.IsOptional Property

This member supports the .NET Framework infrastructure and is not intended to be used directly from your code.

```
[Visual Basic]
Public ReadOnly Property IsOptional As Boolean
[C#]
public bool IsOptional {get;}
[C++]
public: __property bool get_IsOptional();
[JScript]
public function get IsOptional() : Boolean;
```

AxParameterData.IsOut Property

This member supports the .NET Framework infrastructure and is not intended to be used directly from your code.

```
[Visual Basic]
Public ReadOnly Property IsOut As Boolean
[C#]
public bool IsOut {get;}
[C++]
public: __property bool get_IsOut();
[JScript]
public function get IsOut() : Boolean;
```

AxParameterData.Name Property

This member supports the .NET Framework infrastructure and is not intended to be used directly from your code.

```
[Visual Basic]
Public Property Name As String
[C#]
public string Name {get; set;}
[C++]
public: __property String* get_Name();
public: __property void set_Name(String*);
[JScript]
public function get Name() : String;
public function set Name(String);
```

AxParameterData.ParameterType Property

This member supports the .NET Framework infrastructure and is not intended to be used directly from your code.

```
[Visual Basic]
Public ReadOnly Property ParameterType As Type
[C#]
public Type ParameterType {get;}
[C++]
public: __property Type* get_ParameterType();
[JScript]
public function get ParameterType() : Type;
```

AxParameterData.TypeName Property

This member supports the .NET Framework infrastructure and is not intended to be used directly from your code.

[Visual Basic]
```
Public ReadOnly Property TypeName As String
```
[C#]
```
public string TypeName {get;}
```
[C++]
```
public: __property String* get_TypeName();
```
[JScript]
```
public function get TypeName() : String;
```

AxParameterData.Convert Method

This member supports the .NET Framework infrastructure and is not intended to be used directly from your code.

Overload List

This member supports the .NET Framework infrastructure and is not intended to be used directly from your code.

[Visual Basic] **Overloads Public Shared Function Convert(ParameterInfo()) As AxParameterData()**

[C#] **public static AxParameterData[] Convert(ParameterInfo[]);**

[C++] **public: static AxParameterData* Convert(ParameterInfo*[]) [];**

[JScript] **public static function Convert(ParameterInfo[]) : AxParameterData[];**

This member supports the .NET Framework infrastructure and is not intended to be used directly from your code.

[Visual Basic] **Overloads Public Shared Function Convert(ParameterInfo(), Boolean) As AxParameterData()**

[C#] **public static AxParameterData[] Convert(ParameterInfo[], bool);**

[C++] **public: static AxParameterData* Convert(ParameterInfo*[], bool) [];**

[JScript] **public static function Convert(ParameterInfo[], Boolean) : AxParameterData[];**

AxParameterData.Convert Method (ParameterInfo[])

This member supports the .NET Framework infrastructure and is not intended to be used directly from your code.

[Visual Basic]
```
Overloads Public Shared Function Convert( _
   ByVal infos() As ParameterInfo _
) As AxParameterData()
```
[C#]
```
public static AxParameterData[] Convert(
   ParameterInfo[] infos
);
```
[C++]
```
public: static AxParameterData* Convert(
   ParameterInfo* infos[]
) [];
```
[JScript]
```
public static function Convert(
   infos : ParameterInfo[]
) : AxParameterData[];
```

AxParameterData.Convert Method (ParameterInfo[], Boolean)

This member supports the .NET Framework infrastructure and is not intended to be used directly from your code.

[Visual Basic]
```
Overloads Public Shared Function Convert( _
   ByVal infos() As ParameterInfo, _
   ByVal ignoreByRefs As Boolean _
) As AxParameterData()
```
[C#]
```
public static AxParameterData[] Convert(
   ParameterInfo[] infos,
   bool ignoreByRefs
);
```
[C++]
```
public: static AxParameterData* Convert(
   ParameterInfo* infos[],
   bool ignoreByRefs
) [];
```
[JScript]
```
public static function Convert(
   infos : ParameterInfo[],
   ignoreByRefs : Boolean
) : AxParameterData[];
```

AxWrapperGen Class

This type supports the .NET Framework infrastructure and is not intended to be used directly from your code.

[Visual Basic]
```
Public Class AxWrapperGen
```
[C#]
```
public class AxWrapperGen
```
[C++]
```
public __gc class AxWrapperGen
```
[JScript]
```
public class AxWrapperGen
```

AxWrapperGen Constructor

This member supports the .NET Framework infrastructure and is not intended to be used directly from your code.

[Visual Basic]
```
Public Sub New( _
   ByVal axType As Type _
)
```
[C#]
```
public AxWrapperGen(
   Type axType
);
```
[C++]
```
public: AxWrapperGen(
   Type* axType
);
```
[JScript]
```
public function AxWrapperGen(
   axType : Type
);
```

AxWrapperGen.GeneratedSources Field

This member supports the .NET Framework infrastructure and is not intended to be used directly from your code.

[Visual Basic]
```
Public Shared GeneratedSources As ArrayList
```
[C#]
```
public static ArrayList GeneratedSources;
```
[C++]
```
public: static ArrayList* GeneratedSources;
```
[JScript]
```
public static var GeneratedSources : ArrayList;
```

ComponentDocument-Designer Class

Base designer class for extending the design mode behavior of a root design document that supports nested components.

System.Object
  System.ComponentModel.Design.ComponentDesigner
    System.Windows.Forms.Design.ComponentDocument-Designer

```
[Visual Basic]
Public Class ComponentDocumentDesigner
   Inherits ComponentDesigner
   Implements IRootDesigner, IToolboxUser, _
   ITypeDescriptorFilterService
[C#]
public class ComponentDocumentDesigner : ComponentDesigner,
   IRootDesigner, IToolboxUser, ITypeDescriptorFilterService
[C++]
public __gc class ComponentDocumentDesigner : public
   ComponentDesigner, IRootDesigner, IToolboxUser,
   ITypeDescriptorFilterService
[JScript]
public class ComponentDocumentDesigner extends ComponentDesigner
   implements IRootDesigner, IToolboxUser,
   ITypeDescriptorFilterService
```

Thread Safety

Any public static (**Shared** in Visual Basic) members of this type are safe for multithreaded operations. Any instance members are not guaranteed to be thread safe.

Remarks

ComponentDocumentDesigner provides a base class for designers of root design documents that support nested components. In addition to the methods and functionality inherited from the **ComponentDesigner** class, **ComponentDocumentDesigner** implements the **IRootDesigner** interface to provide a root-level design mode view for the associated component, and any nested components.

> **Note** The root-level design mode view for a **Form** or **Control** is typically provided by a built-in root designer. A custom **IRootDesigner** implementation is required to provide a view for other types of root components in design mode.

You can associate a designer with a type using a **DesignerAttribute**.

Requirements

Namespace: System.Windows.Forms.Design

Platforms: Windows 98, Windows NT 4.0,
Windows Millennium Edition, Windows 2000,
Windows XP Home Edition, Windows XP Professional,
Windows Server 2003 family

Assembly: System.Design (in System.Design.dll)

ComponentDocumentDesigner Constructor

Initializes a new instance of the **ComponentDocumentDesigner** class.

```
[Visual Basic]
Public Sub New()
[C#]
public ComponentDocumentDesigner();
[C++]
public: ComponentDocumentDesigner();
[JScript]
public function ComponentDocumentDesigner();
```

Remarks

The default constructor initializes any fields to their default values.

Requirements

Platforms: Windows 98, Windows NT 4.0,
Windows Millennium Edition, Windows 2000,
Windows XP Home Edition, Windows XP Professional,
Windows Server 2003 family

.NET Framework Security:

- Full trust for the immediate caller. This member cannot be used by partially trusted code.

ComponentDocumentDesigner.Control Property

Gets the control for the designer.

```
[Visual Basic]
Public ReadOnly Property Control As Control
[C#]
public Control Control {get;}
[C++]
public: __property Control* get_Control();
[JScript]
public function get Control() : Control;
```

Property Value

The **Control** the designer is editing.

Requirements

Platforms: Windows 98, Windows NT 4.0,
Windows Millennium Edition, Windows 2000,
Windows XP Home Edition, Windows XP Professional,
Windows Server 2003 family

.NET Framework Security:

- Full trust for the immediate caller. This member cannot be used by partially trusted code.

ComponentDocumentDesigner.TrayAutoArrange Property

Gets or sets a value indicating whether the component tray for the designer is in auto-arrange mode.

```
[Visual Basic]
Public Property TrayAutoArrange As Boolean
[C#]
public bool TrayAutoArrange {get; set;}
```

```
[C++]
public: __property bool get_TrayAutoArrange();
public: __property void set_TrayAutoArrange(bool);
[JScript]
public function get TrayAutoArrange() : Boolean;
public function set TrayAutoArrange(Boolean);
```

Property Value

true if the component tray for the designer is in auto-arrange mode; otherwise, **false**.

Requirements

Platforms: Windows 98, Windows NT 4.0,
Windows Millennium Edition, Windows 2000,
Windows XP Home Edition, Windows XP Professional,
Windows Server 2003 family

.NET Framework Security:

- Full trust for the immediate caller. This member cannot be used by partially trusted code.

ComponentDocumentDesigner.TrayLargeIcon Property

Gets or sets a value indicating whether the component tray for the designer is in large icon mode.

```
[Visual Basic]
Public Property TrayLargeIcon As Boolean
[C#]
public bool TrayLargeIcon {get; set;}
[C++]
public: __property bool get_TrayLargeIcon();
public: __property void set_TrayLargeIcon(bool);
[JScript]
public function get TrayLargeIcon() : Boolean;
public function set TrayLargeIcon(Boolean);
```

Property Value

true if the component tray for the designer is in large icon mode; otherwise, **false**.

Requirements

Platforms: Windows 98, Windows NT 4.0,
Windows Millennium Edition, Windows 2000,
Windows XP Home Edition, Windows XP Professional,
Windows Server 2003 family

.NET Framework Security:

- Full trust for the immediate caller. This member cannot be used by partially trusted code.

ComponentDocumentDesigner.Dispose Method

Releases the unmanaged resources used by the **ComponentDocumentDesigner** and optionally releases the managed resources.

Overload List

Releases the unmanaged resources used by the **ComponentDocumentDesigner** and optionally releases the managed resources.

[Visual Basic] **Overloads Overrides Protected Sub Dispose(Boolean)**

[C#] **protected override void Dispose(bool);**

[C++] **protected: void Dispose(bool);**

[JScript] **protected override function Dispose(Boolean);**

Inherited from **ComponentDesigner**.

[Visual Basic] **Overloads Public Overridable Sub Dispose() Implements IDisposable.Dispose**

[C#] **public virtual void Dispose();**

[C++] **public: virtual void Dispose();**

[JScript] **public function Dispose();**

ComponentDocumentDesigner.Dispose Method (Boolean)

Releases the unmanaged resources used by the **ComponentDocumentDesigner** and optionally releases the managed resources.

```
[Visual Basic]
Overrides Overloads Protected Sub Dispose( _
   ByVal disposing As Boolean _
)
[C#]
protected override void Dispose(
   bool disposing
);
[C++]
protected: void Dispose(
   bool disposing
);
[JScript]
protected override function Dispose(
   disposing : Boolean
);
```

Parameters

disposing
: **true** to release both managed and unmanaged resources; **false** to release only unmanaged resources.

Remarks

This method is called by the public **Dispose()** method and the **Finalize** method. **Dispose()** invokes the protected **Dispose(Boolean)** method with the *disposing* parameter set to **true**. **Finalize** invokes **Dispose** with *disposing* set to **false**.

When the *disposing* parameter is **true**, this method releases all resources held by any managed objects that this **ComponentDocumentDesigner** references. This method invokes the **Dispose()** method of each referenced object.

Notes to Inheritors: **Dispose** can be called multiple times by other objects. When overriding **Dispose(Boolean)**, be careful not to reference objects that have been previously disposed in an earlier call to **Dispose**.

Requirements

Platforms: Windows 98, Windows NT 4.0,
Windows Millennium Edition, Windows 2000,
Windows XP Home Edition, Windows XP Professional,
Windows Server 2003 family

.NET Framework Security:

- Full trust for the immediate caller. This member cannot be used by partially trusted code.

ComponentDocumentDesigner.GetToolSupported Method

Gets a value indicating whether the specified tool is supported by the designer.

```
[Visual Basic]
Protected Overridable Function GetToolSupported( _
   ByVal tool As ToolboxItem _
) As Boolean
[C#]
protected virtual bool GetToolSupported(
   ToolboxItem tool
);
[C++]
protected: virtual bool GetToolSupported(
   ToolboxItem* tool
);
[JScript]
protected function GetToolSupported(
   tool : ToolboxItem
) : Boolean;
```

Parameters

tool

The **ToolboxItem** to test for toolbox support.

Return Value

true if the tool should be enabled on the toolbox; **false** if the document designer doesn't know how to use the tool.

Remarks

If a tool is supported, it will be enabled in the toolbox when the designer regains focus. Otherwise, it will be disabled. Once a tool is marked as enabled or disabled it cannot be queried again.

Requirements

Platforms: Windows 98, Windows NT 4.0, Windows Millennium Edition, Windows 2000, Windows XP Home Edition, Windows XP Professional, Windows Server 2003 family

.NET Framework Security:

- Full trust for the immediate caller. This member cannot be used by partially trusted code.

ComponentDocumentDesigner.Initialize Method

Initializes the designer with the specified component.

```
[Visual Basic]
Overrides Public Sub Initialize( _
   ByVal component As IComponent _
) Implements IDesigner.Initialize
[C#]
public override void Initialize(
   IComponent component
);
[C++]
public: void Initialize(
   IComponent* component
);
[JScript]
public override function Initialize(
   component : IComponent
);
```

Parameters

component

The **IComponent** to associate with the designer.

Implements

IDesigner.Initialize

Remarks

Notes to Inheritors: The designer can access the component's site and request services from it in this method.

Requirements

Platforms: Windows 98, Windows NT 4.0, Windows Millennium Edition, Windows 2000, Windows XP Home Edition, Windows XP Professional, Windows Server 2003 family

.NET Framework Security:

- Full trust for the immediate caller. This member cannot be used by partially trusted code.

ComponentDocumentDesigner.IRootDesigner.GetView Method

This member supports the .NET Framework infrastructure and is not intended to be used directly from your code.

```
[Visual Basic]
Private Function GetView( _
   ByVal technology As ViewTechnology _
) As Object Implements IRootDesigner.GetView
[C#]
object IRootDesigner.GetView(
   ViewTechnology technology
);
[C++]
private: Object* IRootDesigner::GetView(
   ViewTechnology technology
);
[JScript]
private function IRootDesigner.GetView(
   technology : ViewTechnology
) : Object;
```

ComponentDocumentDesigner.IToolboxUser.GetToolSupported Method

This member supports the .NET Framework infrastructure and is not intended to be used directly from your code.

```
[Visual Basic]
Private Function GetToolSupported( _
   ByVal tool As ToolboxItem _
) As Boolean Implements IToolboxUser.GetToolSupported
[C#]
bool IToolboxUser.GetToolSupported(
   ToolboxItem tool
);
[C++]
private: bool IToolboxUser::GetToolSupported(
   ToolboxItem* tool
);
```

[JScript]
```
private function IToolboxUser.GetToolSupported(
   tool : ToolboxItem
) : Boolean;
```

ComponentDocumentDesigner.IToolboxUser.ToolPicked Method

This member supports the .NET Framework infrastructure and is not intended to be used directly from your code.

[Visual Basic]
```
Private Sub ToolPicked( _
   ByVal tool As ToolboxItem _
) Implements IToolboxUser.ToolPicked
```
[C#]
```
void IToolboxUser.ToolPicked(
   ToolboxItem tool
);
```
[C++]
```
private: void IToolboxUser::ToolPicked(
   ToolboxItem* tool
);
```
[JScript]
```
private function IToolboxUser.ToolPicked(
   tool : ToolboxItem
);
```

ComponentDocumentDesigner.ITypeDescriptorFilterService.FilterAttributes Method

This member supports the .NET Framework infrastructure and is not intended to be used directly from your code.

[Visual Basic]
```
Private Function FilterAttributes( _
   ByVal component As IComponent, _
   ByVal attributes As IDictionary _
) As Boolean Implements ITypeDescriptorFilterService.FilterAttributes
```
[C#]
```
bool ITypeDescriptorFilterService.FilterAttributes(
   IComponent component,
   IDictionary attributes
);
```
[C++]
```
private: bool ITypeDescriptorFilterService::FilterAttributes(
   IComponent* component,
   IDictionary* attributes
);
```
[JScript]
```
private function ITypeDescriptorFilterService.FilterAttributes(
   component : IComponent,
   attributes : IDictionary
) : Boolean;
```

ComponentDocumentDesigner.ITypeDescriptorFilterService.FilterEvents Method

This member supports the .NET Framework infrastructure and is not intended to be used directly from your code.

[Visual Basic]
```
Private Function FilterEvents( _
   ByVal component As IComponent, _
   ByVal events As IDictionary _
) As Boolean Implements ITypeDescriptorFilterService.FilterEvents
```
[C#]
```
bool ITypeDescriptorFilterService.FilterEvents(
   IComponent component,
   IDictionary events
);
```
[C++]
```
private: bool ITypeDescriptorFilterService::FilterEvents(
   IComponent* component,
   IDictionary* events
);
```
[JScript]
```
private function ITypeDescriptorFilterService.FilterEvents(
   component : IComponent,
   events : IDictionary
) : Boolean;
```

ComponentDocumentDesigner.ITypeDescriptorFilterService.FilterProperties Method

This member supports the .NET Framework infrastructure and is not intended to be used directly from your code.

[Visual Basic]
```
Private Function FilterProperties( _
   ByVal component As IComponent, _
   ByVal properties As IDictionary _
) As Boolean Implements ITypeDescriptorFilterService.FilterProperties
```
[C#]
```
bool ITypeDescriptorFilterService.FilterProperties(
   IComponent component,
   IDictionary properties
);
```
[C++]
```
private: bool ITypeDescriptorFilterService::FilterProperties(
   IComponent* component,
   IDictionary* properties
);
```
[JScript]
```
private function ITypeDescriptorFilterService.FilterProperties(
   component : IComponent,
   properties : IDictionary
) : Boolean;
```

ComponentDocumentDesigner.PreFilter-Properties Method

Adjusts the set of properties the component will expose through a **TypeDescriptor**.

[Visual Basic]
```
Overrides Protected Sub PreFilterProperties( _
   ByVal properties As IDictionary _
)
```
[C#]
```
protected override void PreFilterProperties(
   IDictionary properties
);
```
[C++]
```
protected: void PreFilterProperties(
   IDictionary* properties
);
```
[JScript]
```
protected override function PreFilterProperties(
   properties : IDictionary
);
```

Parameters

properties

An **IDictionary** that contains the properties for the class of the component.

Remarks

This **IDesignerFilter** interface method override adds a non-browsable, design-time only **boolean** property named "TrayLargeIcon" to this designer's component at design time. This property is used by the component tray.

Requirements

Platforms: Windows 98, Windows NT 4.0, Windows Millennium Edition, Windows 2000, Windows XP Home Edition, Windows XP Professional, Windows Server 2003 family

.NET Framework Security:

- Full trust for the immediate caller. This member cannot be used by partially trusted code.

ComponentEditorForm Class

Provides a user interface for a **WindowsFormsComponentEditor**.

System.Object
  System.MarshalByRefObject
    System.ComponentModel.Component
      System.Windows.Forms.Control
        System.Windows.Forms.ScrollableControl
          System.Windows.Forms.ContainerControl
            System.Windows.Forms.Form
              System.Windows.Forms.Design.ComponentEditorForm

```
[Visual Basic]
Public Class ComponentEditorForm
   Inherits Form
[C#]
public class ComponentEditorForm : Form
[C++]
public __gc class ComponentEditorForm : public Form
[JScript]
public class ComponentEditorForm extends Form
```

Thread Safety

Any public static (**Shared** in Visual Basic) members of this type are safe for multithreaded operations. Any instance members are not guaranteed to be thread safe.

Remarks

A **ComponentEditorForm** shows a view of available component editor pages along with a user interface for selection.

Requirements

Namespace: System.Windows.Forms.Design

Platforms: Windows 98, Windows NT 4.0, Windows Millennium Edition, Windows 2000, Windows XP Home Edition, Windows XP Professional, Windows Server 2003 family

Assembly: System.Windows.Forms (in System.Windows.Forms.dll)

ComponentEditorForm Constructor

Initializes a new instance of the **ComponentEditorForm** class.

```
[Visual Basic]
Public Sub New( _
   ByVal component As Object, _
   ByVal pageTypes() As Type _
)
[C#]
public ComponentEditorForm(
   object component,
   Type[] pageTypes
);
[C++]
public: ComponentEditorForm(
   Object* component,
   Type* pageTypes[]
);
[JScript]
public function ComponentEditorForm(
   component : Object,
   pageTypes : Type[]
);
```

Parameters

component
  The component to be edited.

pageTypes
  The set of **ComponentEditorPage** objects to be shown in the form.

Requirements

Platforms: Windows 98, Windows NT 4.0, Windows Millennium Edition, Windows 2000, Windows XP Home Edition, Windows XP Professional, Windows Server 2003 family

ComponentEditorForm.OnActivated Method

This member overrides **Form.OnActivated**.

```
[Visual Basic]
Overrides Protected Sub OnActivated( _
   ByVal e As EventArgs _
)
[C#]
protected override void OnActivated(
   EventArgs e
);
[C++]
protected: void OnActivated(
   EventArgs* e
);
[JScript]
protected override function OnActivated(
   e : EventArgs
);
```

Requirements

Platforms: Windows 98, Windows NT 4.0, Windows Millennium Edition, Windows 2000, Windows XP Home Edition, Windows XP Professional, Windows Server 2003 family

ComponentEditorForm.OnHelpRequested Method

This member overrides **Control.OnHelpRequested**.

```
[Visual Basic]
Overrides Protected Sub OnHelpRequested( _
   ByVal e As HelpEventArgs _
)
[C#]
protected override void OnHelpRequested(
   HelpEventArgs e
);
[C++]
protected: void OnHelpRequested(
   HelpEventArgs* e
);
```

```
[JScript]
protected override function OnHelpRequested(
   e : HelpEventArgs
);
```

Requirements

Platforms: Windows 98, Windows NT 4.0, Windows Millennium Edition, Windows 2000, Windows XP Home Edition, Windows XP Professional, Windows Server 2003 family

ComponentEditorForm.OnSelChangeSelector Method

This member supports the .NET Framework infrastructure and is not intended to be used directly from your code.

```
[Visual Basic]
Protected Overridable Sub OnSelChangeSelector( _
   ByVal source As Object, _
   ByVal e As TreeViewEventArgs _
)
[C#]
protected virtual void OnSelChangeSelector(
   object source,
   TreeViewEventArgs e
);
[C++]
protected: virtual void OnSelChangeSelector(
   Object* source,
   TreeViewEventArgs* e
);
[JScript]
protected function OnSelChangeSelector(
   source : Object,
   e : TreeViewEventArgs
);
```

ComponentEditorForm.PreProcessMessage Method

Provides a method to override in order to pre-process input messages before they are dispatched.

```
[Visual Basic]
Overrides Public Function PreProcessMessage( _
   ByRef msg As Message _
) As Boolean
[C#]
public override bool PreProcessMessage(
   ref Message msg
);
[C++]
public: bool PreProcessMessage(
   Message* msg
);
[JScript]
public override function PreProcessMessage(
   msg : Message
) : Boolean;
```

Parameters

msg
A **Message** that specifies the message to pre-process.

Return Value

true if the specified message is for a component editor page; otherwise, **false**.

Remarks

PreProcessMessage is called by the application's message loop to pre-process input messages before they are dispatched.

Requirements

Platforms: Windows 98, Windows NT 4.0, Windows Millennium Edition, Windows 2000, Windows XP Home Edition, Windows XP Professional, Windows Server 2003 family

ComponentEditorForm.ShowForm Method

Shows the form. The form will have no owner window.

Overload List

Shows the form. The form will have no owner window.

[Visual Basic] **Overloads Public Overridable Function ShowForm() As DialogResult**

[C#] **public virtual DialogResult ShowForm();**

[C++] **public: virtual DialogResult ShowForm();**

[JScript] **public function ShowForm() : DialogResult;**

Shows the specified page of the specified form. The form will have no owner window.

[Visual Basic] **Overloads Public Overridable Function ShowForm(Integer) As DialogResult**

[C#] **public virtual DialogResult ShowForm(int);**

[C++] **public: virtual DialogResult ShowForm(int);**

[JScript] **public function ShowForm(int) : DialogResult;**

Shows the form with the specified owner.

[Visual Basic] **Overloads Public Overridable Function ShowForm(IWin32Window) As DialogResult**

[C#] **public virtual DialogResult ShowForm(IWin32Window);**

[C++] **public: virtual DialogResult ShowForm(IWin32Window*);**

[JScript] **public function ShowForm(IWin32Window) : DialogResult;**

Shows the form and the specified page with the specified owner.

[Visual Basic] **Overloads Public Overridable Function ShowForm(IWin32Window, Integer) As DialogResult**

[C#] **public virtual DialogResult ShowForm(IWin32Window, int);**

[C++] **public: virtual DialogResult ShowForm(IWin32Window*, int);**

[JScript] **public function ShowForm(IWin32Window, int) : DialogResult;**

ComponentEditorForm.ShowForm Method ()

Shows the form. The form will have no owner window.

```
[Visual Basic]
Overloads Public Overridable Function ShowForm() As DialogResult
[C#]
public virtual DialogResult ShowForm();
[C++]
public: virtual DialogResult ShowForm();
[JScript]
public function ShowForm() : DialogResult;
```

Return Value

One of the **DialogResult** values indicating the result code returned from the dialog box.

Requirements

Platforms: Windows 98, Windows NT 4.0, Windows Millennium Edition, Windows 2000, Windows XP Home Edition, Windows XP Professional, Windows Server 2003 family

ComponentEditorForm.ShowForm Method (Int32)

Shows the specified page of the specified form. The form will have no owner window.

```
[Visual Basic]
Overloads Public Overridable Function ShowForm( _
   ByVal page As Integer _
) As DialogResult
[C#]
public virtual DialogResult ShowForm(
   int page
);
[C++]
public: virtual DialogResult ShowForm(
   int page
);
[JScript]
public function ShowForm(
   page : int
) : DialogResult;
```

Parameters

page

The index of the page to show.

Return Value

One of the **DialogResult** values indicating the result code returned from the dialog box.

Requirements

Platforms: Windows 98, Windows NT 4.0, Windows Millennium Edition, Windows 2000, Windows XP Home Edition, Windows XP Professional, Windows Server 2003 family

ComponentEditorForm.ShowForm Method (IWin32Window)

Shows the form with the specified owner.

```
[Visual Basic]
Overloads Public Overridable Function ShowForm( _
   ByVal owner As IWin32Window _
) As DialogResult
[C#]
public virtual DialogResult ShowForm(
   IWin32Window owner
);
[C++]
public: virtual DialogResult ShowForm(
   IWin32Window* owner
);
[JScript]
public function ShowForm(
   owner : IWin32Window
) : DialogResult;
```

Parameters

owner

The **IWin32Window** to own the dialog.

Return Value

One of the **DialogResult** values indicating the result code returned from the dialog box.

Requirements

Platforms: Windows 98, Windows NT 4.0, Windows Millennium Edition, Windows 2000, Windows XP Home Edition, Windows XP Professional, Windows Server 2003 family

ComponentEditorForm.ShowForm Method (IWin32Window, Int32)

Shows the form and the specified page with the specified owner.

```
[Visual Basic]
Overloads Public Overridable Function ShowForm( _
   ByVal owner As IWin32Window, _
   ByVal page As Integer _
) As DialogResult
[C#]
public virtual DialogResult ShowForm(
   IWin32Window owner,
   int page
);
[C++]
public: virtual DialogResult ShowForm(
   IWin32Window* owner,
   int page
);
[JScript]
public function ShowForm(
   owner : IWin32Window,
   page : int
) : DialogResult;
```

Parameters

owner

The **IWin32Window** to own the dialog.

page

The index of the page to show.

Return Value

One of the **DialogResult** values indicating the result code returned from the dialog box.

Requirements

Platforms: Windows 98, Windows NT 4.0, Windows Millennium Edition, Windows 2000, Windows XP Home Edition, Windows XP Professional, Windows Server 2003 family

ComponentEditorPage Class

Provides a base implementation for a **ComponentEditorPage**.

System.Object
  System.MarshalByRefObject
    System.ComponentModel.Component
      System.Windows.Forms.Control
        System.Windows.Forms.ScrollableControl
          System.Windows.Forms.Panel
            System.Windows.Forms.Design.ComponentEditorPage

```
[Visual Basic]
MustInherit Public Class ComponentEditorPage
   Inherits Panel
[C#]
public abstract class ComponentEditorPage : Panel
[C++]
public __gc __abstract class ComponentEditorPage : public Panel
[JScript]
public abstract class ComponentEditorPage extends Panel
```

Thread Safety

Any public static (**Shared** in Visual Basic) members of this type are safe for multithreaded operations. Any instance members are not guaranteed to be thread safe.

Remarks

ComponentEditorPage is a complete implementation for a component editor page that consists of an empty window. You can extend this page to add your own controls. **ComponentEditorPage** is used by a **ComponentEditorForm** of a **WindowsForms-ComponentEditor**.

Requirements

Namespace: System.Windows.Forms.Design

Platforms: Windows 98, Windows NT 4.0, Windows Millennium Edition, Windows 2000, Windows XP Home Edition, Windows XP Professional, Windows Server 2003 family

Assembly: System.Windows.Forms (in System.Windows.Forms.dll)

ComponentEditorPage Constructor

Initializes a new instance of the **ComponentEditorPage** class.

```
[Visual Basic]
Public Sub New()
[C#]
public ComponentEditorPage();
[C++]
public: ComponentEditorPage();
[JScript]
public function ComponentEditorPage();
```

Requirements

Platforms: Windows 98, Windows NT 4.0, Windows Millennium Edition, Windows 2000, Windows XP Home Edition, Windows XP Professional, Windows Server 2003 family

ComponentEditorPage.CommitOnDeactivate Property

Specifies whether the editor should apply its changes before it is deactivated.

```
[Visual Basic]
Public Property CommitOnDeactivate As Boolean
[C#]
public bool CommitOnDeactivate {get; set;}
[C++]
public: __property bool get_CommitOnDeactivate();
public: __property void set_CommitOnDeactivate(bool);
[JScript]
public function get CommitOnDeactivate() : Boolean;
public function set CommitOnDeactivate(Boolean);
```

Property Value

true if the editor should apply its changes; otherwise, **false**.

Remarks

The standard implementation returns **false**.

Requirements

Platforms: Windows 98, Windows NT 4.0, Windows Millennium Edition, Windows 2000, Windows XP Home Edition, Windows XP Professional, Windows Server 2003 family

ComponentEditorPage.Component Property

Gets or sets the component to edit.

```
[Visual Basic]
Protected Property Component As IComponent
[C#]
protected IComponent Component {get; set;}
[C++]
protected: __property IComponent* get_Component();
protected: __property void set_Component(IComponent*);
[JScript]
protected function get Component() : IComponent;
protected function set Component(IComponent);
```

Property Value

The **IComponent** this page allows you to edit.

Requirements

Platforms: Windows 98, Windows NT 4.0, Windows Millennium Edition, Windows 2000, Windows XP Home Edition, Windows XP Professional, Windows Server 2003 family

ComponentEditorPage.CreateParams Property

Gets the creation parameters for the control.

```
[Visual Basic]
Overrides Protected ReadOnly Property CreateParams As CreateParams
[C#]
protected override CreateParams CreateParams {get;}
[C++]
protected: __property CreateParams* get_CreateParams();
[JScript]
protected override function get CreateParams() : CreateParams;
```

Property Value

A **CreateParams** that indicates the creation parameters for the control.

Requirements

Platforms: Windows 98, Windows NT 4.0, Windows Millennium Edition, Windows 2000, Windows XP Home Edition, Windows XP Professional, Windows Server 2003 family

ComponentEditorPage.FirstActivate Property

Gets or sets a value indicating whether the page is being activated for the first time.

```
[Visual Basic]
Protected Property FirstActivate As Boolean
[C#]
protected bool FirstActivate {get; set;}
[C++]
protected: __property bool get_FirstActivate();
protected: __property void set_FirstActivate(bool);
[JScript]
protected function get FirstActivate() : Boolean;
protected function set FirstActivate(Boolean);
```

Property Value

true if the page has not previously been activated; otherwise, **false**.

Requirements

Platforms: Windows 98, Windows NT 4.0, Windows Millennium Edition, Windows 2000, Windows XP Home Edition, Windows XP Professional, Windows Server 2003 family

ComponentEditorPage.Icon Property

Gets or sets the icon for the page.

```
[Visual Basic]
Public Property Icon As Icon
[C#]
public Icon Icon {get; set;}
[C++]
public: __property Icon* get_Icon();
public: __property void set_Icon(Icon*);
[JScript]
public function get Icon() : Icon;
public function set Icon(Icon);
```

Property Value

An **Icon** used to represent the page.

Requirements

Platforms: Windows 98, Windows NT 4.0, Windows Millennium Edition, Windows 2000, Windows XP Home Edition, Windows XP Professional, Windows Server 2003 family

ComponentEditorPage.Loading Property

Indicates how many load dependencies remain until loading has been completed.

```
[Visual Basic]
Protected Property Loading As Integer
[C#]
protected int Loading {get; set;}
[C++]
protected: __property int get_Loading();
protected: __property void set_Loading(int);
[JScript]
protected function get Loading() : int;
protected function set Loading(int);
```

Property Value

The number of remaining load dependencies.

Remarks

This property is used to track the number of loading stages remaining. For each process needed to completely load the document, this counter is incremented before loading begins, and decremented when each loading process completes.

Requirements

Platforms: Windows 98, Windows NT 4.0, Windows Millennium Edition, Windows 2000, Windows XP Home Edition, Windows XP Professional, Windows Server 2003 family

ComponentEditorPage.LoadRequired Property

Gets or sets a value indicating whether a component must be loaded before editing can occur.

```
[Visual Basic]
Protected Property LoadRequired As Boolean
[C#]
protected bool LoadRequired {get; set;}
[C++]
protected: __property bool get_LoadRequired();
protected: __property void set_LoadRequired(bool);
[JScript]
protected function get LoadRequired() : Boolean;
protected function set LoadRequired(Boolean);
```

Property Value

true if a component must be loaded before editing can occur; otherwise, **false**.

Requirements

Platforms: Windows 98, Windows NT 4.0, Windows Millennium Edition, Windows 2000, Windows XP Home Edition, Windows XP Professional, Windows Server 2003 family

ComponentEditorPage.PageSite Property

This member supports the .NET Framework infrastructure and is not intended to be used directly from your code.

[Visual Basic]
```
Protected Property PageSite As IComponentEditorPageSite
```
[C#]
```
protected IComponentEditorPageSite PageSite {get; set;}
```
[C++]
```
protected: __property IComponentEditorPageSite* get_PageSite();
protected: __property void set_PageSite(IComponentEditorPageSite*);
```
[JScript]
```
protected function get PageSite() : IComponentEditorPageSite;
protected function set PageSite(IComponentEditorPageSite);
```

ComponentEditorPage.Title Property

Gets the title of the page.

[Visual Basic]
```
Public Overridable ReadOnly Property Title As String
```
[C#]
```
public virtual string Title {get;}
```
[C++]
```
public: __property virtual String* get_Title();
```
[JScript]
```
public function get Title() : String;
```

Property Value

The title of the page.

Remarks

The caller may use this to show the name of this editor before it's actually activated.

Requirements

Platforms: Windows 98, Windows NT 4.0, Windows Millennium Edition, Windows 2000, Windows XP Home Edition, Windows XP Professional, Windows Server 2003 family

ComponentEditorPage.Activate Method

Activates and displays the page.

[Visual Basic]
```
Public Overridable Sub Activate()
```
[C#]
```
public virtual void Activate();
```
[C++]
```
public: virtual void Activate();
```
[JScript]
```
public function Activate();
```

Requirements

Platforms: Windows 98, Windows NT 4.0, Windows Millennium Edition, Windows 2000, Windows XP Home Edition, Windows XP Professional, Windows Server 2003 family

ComponentEditorPage.ApplyChanges Method

Applies changes to all the components being edited.

[Visual Basic]
```
Public Overridable Sub ApplyChanges()
```
[C#]
```
public virtual void ApplyChanges();
```
[C++]
```
public: virtual void ApplyChanges();
```
[JScript]
```
public function ApplyChanges();
```

Requirements

Platforms: Windows 98, Windows NT 4.0, Windows Millennium Edition, Windows 2000, Windows XP Home Edition, Windows XP Professional, Windows Server 2003 family

ComponentEditorPage.Deactivate Method

Deactivates and hides the page.

[Visual Basic]
```
Public Overridable Sub Deactivate()
```
[C#]
```
public virtual void Deactivate();
```
[C++]
```
public: virtual void Deactivate();
```
[JScript]
```
public function Deactivate();
```

Requirements

Platforms: Windows 98, Windows NT 4.0, Windows Millennium Edition, Windows 2000, Windows XP Home Edition, Windows XP Professional, Windows Server 2003 family

ComponentEditorPage.EnterLoadingMode Method

Increments the loading counter.

[Visual Basic]
```
Protected Sub EnterLoadingMode()
```
[C#]
```
protected void EnterLoadingMode();
```
[C++]
```
protected: void EnterLoadingMode();
```
[JScript]
```
protected function EnterLoadingMode();
```

Remarks

Each procedure that performs loading or initialization should first call **EnterLoadingMode** to indicate that it will load something before the editor can display the loaded editor page. When a loading procedure that called **EnterLoadingMode** completes, it should call **ExitLoadingMode** to indicate that its part of the load process is completed.

The **Loading** property is used as a counter to determine when loading has completed. A page is in loading mode if the value of the **Loading** property is non-zero.

Requirements

Platforms: Windows 98, Windows NT 4.0, Windows Millennium Edition, Windows 2000, Windows XP Home Edition, Windows XP Professional, Windows Server 2003 family

ComponentEditorPage.ExitLoadingMode Method

Decrements the loading counter.

[Visual Basic]
```
Protected Sub ExitLoadingMode()
```
[C#]
```
protected void ExitLoadingMode();
```
[C++]
```
protected: void ExitLoadingMode();
```
[JScript]
```
protected function ExitLoadingMode();
```

Remarks

Each procedure that performs loading or initialization should first call **EnterLoadingMode** to indicate that it will load something before the editor can display the loaded editor page. When a loading procedure that called **EnterLoadingMode** completes, it should call **ExitLoadingMode** to indicate that its part of the load process is completed.

The **Loading** property is used as a counter to determine when loading has completed. A page is in loading mode if the value of the **Loading** property is non-zero.

Requirements

Platforms: Windows 98, Windows NT 4.0, Windows Millennium Edition, Windows 2000, Windows XP Home Edition, Windows XP Professional, Windows Server 2003 family

ComponentEditorPage.GetControl Method

Gets the control that represents the window for this page.

[Visual Basic]
```
Public Overridable Function GetControl() As Control
```
[C#]
```
public virtual Control GetControl();
```
[C++]
```
public: virtual Control* GetControl();
```
[JScript]
```
public function GetControl() : Control;
```

Return Value

The **Control** that represents the window for this page.

Requirements

Platforms: Windows 98, Windows NT 4.0, Windows Millennium Edition, Windows 2000, Windows XP Home Edition, Windows XP Professional, Windows Server 2003 family

ComponentEditorPage.GetSelectedComponent Method

Gets the component that is to be edited.

[Visual Basic]
```
Protected Function GetSelectedComponent() As IComponent
```
[C#]
```
protected IComponent GetSelectedComponent();
```
[C++]
```
protected: IComponent* GetSelectedComponent();
```
[JScript]
```
protected function GetSelectedComponent() : IComponent;
```

Return Value

The **IComponent** that is being edited.

Requirements

Platforms: Windows 98, Windows NT 4.0, Windows Millennium Edition, Windows 2000, Windows XP Home Edition, Windows XP Professional, Windows Server 2003 family

ComponentEditorPage.IsFirstActivate Method

Gets a value indicating whether the page is being activated for the first time.

[Visual Basic]
```
Protected Function IsFirstActivate() As Boolean
```
[C#]
```
protected bool IsFirstActivate();
```
[C++]
```
protected: bool IsFirstActivate();
```
[JScript]
```
protected function IsFirstActivate() : Boolean;
```

Return Value

true if this is the first time the page is being activated; otherwise, **false**.

Requirements

Platforms: Windows 98, Windows NT 4.0, Windows Millennium Edition, Windows 2000, Windows XP Home Edition, Windows XP Professional, Windows Server 2003 family

ComponentEditorPage.IsLoading Method

Gets a value indicating whether the page is being loaded.

[Visual Basic]
```
Protected Function IsLoading() As Boolean
```
[C#]
```
protected bool IsLoading();
```
[C++]
```
protected: bool IsLoading();
```
[JScript]
```
protected function IsLoading() : Boolean;
```

Return Value

true if the page is being loaded; otherwise, **false**.

Requirements

Platforms: Windows 98, Windows NT 4.0, Windows Millennium Edition, Windows 2000, Windows XP Home Edition, Windows XP Professional, Windows Server 2003 family

ComponentEditorPage.IsPageMessage Method

Processes messages that could be handled by the page.

[Visual Basic]
```
Public Overridable Function IsPageMessage( _
   ByRef msg As Message _
) As Boolean
```
[C#]
```
public virtual bool IsPageMessage(
   ref Message msg
);
```
[C++]
```
public: virtual bool IsPageMessage(
   Message* msg
);
```
[JScript]
```
public function IsPageMessage(
   msg : Message
) : Boolean;
```

Parameters

msg
The Message to process.

Return Value

true if the page processed the message; otherwise, **false**.

Remarks

Gives the page a chance to process messages before the caller uses them. If this returns **true**, the message will be consumed. Otherwise, the caller will continue to process the message.

Requirements

Platforms: Windows 98, Windows NT 4.0, Windows Millennium Edition, Windows 2000, Windows XP Home Edition, Windows XP Professional, Windows Server 2003 family

ComponentEditorPage.LoadComponent Method

Loads the component into the page UI.

[Visual Basic]
```
Protected MustOverride Sub LoadComponent()
```
[C#]
```
protected abstract void LoadComponent();
```
[C++]
```
protected: virtual void LoadComponent() = 0;
```
[JScript]
```
protected abstract function LoadComponent();
```

Remarks

Notes to Inheritors: Each page must override this method and implement its own custom behavior.

Requirements

Platforms: Windows 98, Windows NT 4.0, Windows Millennium Edition, Windows 2000, Windows XP Home Edition, Windows XP Professional, Windows Server 2003 family

ComponentEditorPage.OnApplyComplete Method

Called when the page and any sibling pages have applied their changes.

[Visual Basic]
```
Public Overridable Sub OnApplyComplete()
```
[C#]
```
public virtual void OnApplyComplete();
```
[C++]
```
public: virtual void OnApplyComplete();
```
[JScript]
```
public function OnApplyComplete();
```

Requirements

Platforms: Windows 98, Windows NT 4.0, Windows Millennium Edition, Windows 2000, Windows XP Home Edition, Windows XP Professional, Windows Server 2003 family

ComponentEditorPage.ReloadComponent Method

Reloads the component for the page.

[Visual Basic]
```
Protected Overridable Sub ReloadComponent()
```
[C#]
```
protected virtual void ReloadComponent();
```
[C++]
```
protected: virtual void ReloadComponent();
```
[JScript]
```
protected function ReloadComponent();
```

Remarks

This method is called when the current component may have changed elsewhere and needs to be reloaded into the UI.

Requirements

Platforms: Windows 98, Windows NT 4.0, Windows Millennium Edition, Windows 2000, Windows XP Home Edition, Windows XP Professional, Windows Server 2003 family

ComponentEditorPage.SaveComponent Method

Saves the component from the page UI.

[Visual Basic]
```
Protected MustOverride Sub SaveComponent()
```
[C#]
```
protected abstract void SaveComponent();
```
[C++]
```
protected: virtual void SaveComponent() = 0;
```
[JScript]
```
protected abstract function SaveComponent();
```

Remarks

Notes to Inheritors: Each page must override this method and implement its own custom behavior.

Requirements

Platforms: Windows 98, Windows NT 4.0, Windows Millennium Edition, Windows 2000, Windows XP Home Edition, Windows XP Professional, Windows Server 2003 family

ComponentEditorPage.SetComponent Method

Sets the component to be edited.

```
[Visual Basic]
Public Overridable Sub SetComponent( _
   ByVal component As IComponent _
)
[C#]
public virtual void SetComponent(
   IComponent component
);
[C++]
public: virtual void SetComponent(
   IComponent* component
);
[JScript]
public function SetComponent(
   component : IComponent
);
```

Parameters

component

The **IComponent** to be edited.

Requirements

Platforms: Windows 98, Windows NT 4.0, Windows Millennium Edition, Windows 2000, Windows XP Home Edition, Windows XP Professional, Windows Server 2003 family

ComponentEditorPage.SetDirty Method

Sets the page as changed since the last load or save.

```
[Visual Basic]
Protected Overridable Sub SetDirty()
[C#]
protected virtual void SetDirty();
[C++]
protected: virtual void SetDirty();
[JScript]
protected function SetDirty();
```

Requirements

Platforms: Windows 98, Windows NT 4.0, Windows Millennium Edition, Windows 2000, Windows XP Home Edition, Windows XP Professional, Windows Server 2003 family

ComponentEditorPage.SetSite Method

This member supports the .NET Framework infrastructure and is not intended to be used directly from your code.

```
[Visual Basic]
Public Overridable Sub SetSite( _
   ByVal site As IComponentEditorPageSite _
)
[C#]
public virtual void SetSite(
   IComponentEditorPageSite site
);
[C++]
public: virtual void SetSite(
   IComponentEditorPageSite* site
);
[JScript]
public function SetSite(
   site : IComponentEditorPageSite
);
```

ComponentEditorPage.ShowHelp Method

Shows help information if the page supports help information.

```
[Visual Basic]
Public Overridable Sub ShowHelp()
[C#]
public virtual void ShowHelp();
[C++]
public: virtual void ShowHelp();
[JScript]
public function ShowHelp();
```

Remarks

This is only called if **SupportsHelp** returns **true**. The Help system calls **ShowHelp** to provide help for the page. **ShowHelp** is usually called in response to F1 or when the Help button is clicked to allow the page to bring up its associated Help topic.

Requirements

Platforms: Windows 98, Windows NT 4.0, Windows Millennium Edition, Windows 2000, Windows XP Home Edition, Windows XP Professional, Windows Server 2003 family

ComponentEditorPage.SupportsHelp Method

Gets a value indicating whether the editor supports Help.

```
[Visual Basic]
Public Overridable Function SupportsHelp() As Boolean
[C#]
public virtual bool SupportsHelp();
[C++]
public: virtual bool SupportsHelp();
[JScript]
public function SupportsHelp() : Boolean;
```

Return Value

true if the editor supports Help; otherwise, **false**. The default implementation returns **false**.

Requirements

Platforms: Windows 98, Windows NT 4.0, Windows Millennium Edition, Windows 2000, Windows XP Home Edition, Windows XP Professional, Windows Server 2003 family

ComponentTray Class

Provides behavior for the component tray of the form designer. The component tray represents components that do not otherwise provide a visible surface at design time and provides a way for users to access and set the properties of those components.

System.Object
  System.MarshalByRefObject
    System.ComponentModel.Component
      System.Windows.Forms.Control
        System.Windows.Forms.ScrollableControl
          System.Windows.Forms.Design.ComponentTray

```
[Visual Basic]
Public Class ComponentTray
   Inherits ScrollableControl
   Implements IExtenderProvider
[C#]
public class ComponentTray : ScrollableControl, IExtenderProvider
[C++]
public __gc class ComponentTray : public ScrollableControl,
   IExtenderProvider
[JScript]
public class ComponentTray extends ScrollableControl implements
   IExtenderProvider
```

Thread Safety

Any public static (**Shared** in Visual Basic) members of this type are safe for multithreaded operations. Any instance members are not guaranteed to be thread safe.

Remarks

Some types of components, such as a **Timer**, may not have a user interface that can be viewed at design time. These components are usually represented by icons that are shown in the component tray.

The component tray is a rectangular region displayed at the bottom of the design view window while in design view mode, once it is active. The component tray becomes active in design view after a component that is displayed in the component tray has been added to or is part of the current document.

Requirements

Namespace: System.Windows.Forms.Design

Platforms: Windows 98, Windows NT 4.0, Windows Millennium Edition, Windows 2000, Windows XP Home Edition, Windows XP Professional, Windows Server 2003 family

Assembly: System.Design (in System.Design.dll)

ComponentTray Constructor

Initializes a new instance of the **ComponentTray** class using the specified designer and service provider.

```
[Visual Basic]
Public Sub New( _
   ByVal mainDesigner As IDesigner, _
   ByVal serviceProvider As IServiceProvider _
)
[C#]
public ComponentTray(
   IDesigner mainDesigner,
   IServiceProvider serviceProvider
);
[C++]
public: ComponentTray(
   IDesigner* mainDesigner,
   IServiceProvider* serviceProvider
);
[JScript]
public function ComponentTray(
   mainDesigner : IDesigner,
   serviceProvider : IServiceProvider
);
```

Parameters

mainDesigner
: The **IDesigner** that is the main or document designer for the current project.

serviceProvider
: An **IServiceProvider** that can be used to obtain design-time services.

Remarks

The component tray monitors component additions and removals and displays appropriate user interface objects to represent the components it contains.

Requirements

Platforms: Windows 98, Windows NT 4.0, Windows Millennium Edition, Windows 2000, Windows XP Home Edition, Windows XP Professional, Windows Server 2003 family

.NET Framework Security:

- Full trust for the immediate caller. This member cannot be used by partially trusted code.

ComponentTray.AutoArrange Property

Gets or sets a value indicating whether the tray items are automatically aligned.

```
[Visual Basic]
Public Property AutoArrange As Boolean
[C#]
public bool AutoArrange {get; set;}
[C++]
public: __property bool get_AutoArrange();
public: __property void set_AutoArrange(bool);
[JScript]
public function get AutoArrange() : Boolean;
public function set AutoArrange(Boolean);
```

Property Value

true if the tray items are automatically arranged; otherwise, **false**.

Requirements

Platforms: Windows 98, Windows NT 4.0, Windows Millennium Edition, Windows 2000, Windows XP Home Edition, Windows XP Professional, Windows Server 2003 family

.NET Framework Security:

- Full trust for the immediate caller. This member cannot be used by partially trusted code.

ComponentTray.ComponentCount Property

Gets the number of components contained in the tray.

```
[Visual Basic]
Public ReadOnly Property ComponentCount As Integer
[C#]
public int ComponentCount {get;}
[C++]
public: __property int get_ComponentCount();
[JScript]
public function get ComponentCount() : int;
```

Property Value

The number of components in the tray.

Requirements

Platforms: Windows 98, Windows NT 4.0, Windows Millennium Edition, Windows 2000, Windows XP Home Edition, Windows XP Professional, Windows Server 2003 family

.NET Framework Security:

- Full trust for the immediate caller. This member cannot be used by partially trusted code.

ComponentTray.ShowLargeIcons Property

Gets or sets a value indicating whether the tray displays a large icon to represent each component in the tray.

```
[Visual Basic]
Public Property ShowLargeIcons As Boolean
[C#]
public bool ShowLargeIcons {get; set;}
[C++]
public: __property bool get_ShowLargeIcons();
public: __property void set_ShowLargeIcons(bool);
[JScript]
public function get ShowLargeIcons() : Boolean;
public function set ShowLargeIcons(Boolean);
```

Property Value

true if large icons are displayed; otherwise, **false**.

Requirements

Platforms: Windows 98, Windows NT 4.0, Windows Millennium Edition, Windows 2000, Windows XP Home Edition, Windows XP Professional, Windows Server 2003 family

.NET Framework Security:

- Full trust for the immediate caller. This member cannot be used by partially trusted code.

ComponentTray.AddComponent Method

Adds a component to the tray.

```
[Visual Basic]
Public Overridable Sub AddComponent( _
   ByVal component As IComponent _
)
[C#]
public virtual void AddComponent(
   IComponent component
);
[C++]
public: virtual void AddComponent(
   IComponent* component
);
[JScript]
public function AddComponent(
   component : IComponent
);
```

Parameters

component

The **IComponent** to add to the tray.

Requirements

Platforms: Windows 98, Windows NT 4.0, Windows Millennium Edition, Windows 2000, Windows XP Home Edition, Windows XP Professional, Windows Server 2003 family

.NET Framework Security:

- Full trust for the immediate caller. This member cannot be used by partially trusted code.

ComponentTray.CanCreateComponentFromTool Method

Gets a value indicating whether the specified tool can be used to create a new component.

```
[Visual Basic]
Protected Overridable Function CanCreateComponentFromTool( _
   ByVal tool As ToolboxItem _
) As Boolean
[C#]
protected virtual bool CanCreateComponentFromTool(
   ToolboxItem tool
);
[C++]
protected: virtual bool CanCreateComponentFromTool(
   ToolboxItem* tool
);
[JScript]
protected function CanCreateComponentFromTool(
   tool : ToolboxItem
) : Boolean;
```

Parameters

tool

The **ToolboxItem** to test.

Return Value

true if the specified tool can be used to create a component; otherwise, **false**.

Requirements

Platforms: Windows 98, Windows NT 4.0, Windows Millennium Edition, Windows 2000, Windows XP Home Edition, Windows XP Professional, Windows Server 2003 family

.NET Framework Security:

- Full trust for the immediate caller. This member cannot be used by partially trusted code.

ComponentTray.CanDisplayComponent Method

Gets a value indicating whether the specified component can be displayed.

```
[Visual Basic]
Protected Overridable Function CanDisplayComponent( _
   ByVal component As IComponent _
) As Boolean
[C#]
protected virtual bool CanDisplayComponent(
   IComponent component
);
[C++]
protected: virtual bool CanDisplayComponent(
   IComponent* component
);
[JScript]
protected function CanDisplayComponent(
   component : IComponent
) : Boolean;
```

Parameters

component

The **IComponent** to test.

Return Value

true if the component can be displayed; otherwise, **false**.

Remarks

This method tests the specified component for the existence of a **DesignTimeVisibleAttribute**, which indicates whether the component has a user interface that can be displayed.

Requirements

Platforms: Windows 98, Windows NT 4.0, Windows Millennium Edition, Windows 2000, Windows XP Home Edition, Windows XP Professional, Windows Server 2003 family

.NET Framework Security:

- Full trust for the immediate caller. This member cannot be used by partially trusted code.

ComponentTray.CreateComponentFromTool Method

Creates a component from the specified toolbox item, adds the component to the current document, and displays a representation for the component in the component tray.

```
[Visual Basic]
Public Sub CreateComponentFromTool( _
   ByVal tool As ToolboxItem _
)
[C#]
public void CreateComponentFromTool(
   ToolboxItem tool
);
[C++]
public: void CreateComponentFromTool(
   ToolboxItem* tool
);
[JScript]
public function CreateComponentFromTool(
   tool : ToolboxItem
);
```

Parameters

tool

The **ToolboxItem** to create a component from.

Remarks

This method checks the item for an appropriate **DesignTimeVisibleAttribute** before attempting to create the component and add it to the component tray.

Requirements

Platforms: Windows 98, Windows NT 4.0, Windows Millennium Edition, Windows 2000, Windows XP Home Edition, Windows XP Professional, Windows Server 2003 family

.NET Framework Security:

- Full trust for the immediate caller. This member cannot be used by partially trusted code.

ComponentTray.DisplayError Method

Displays an error message to the user with information about the specified exception.

```
[Visual Basic]
Protected Sub DisplayError( _
   ByVal e As Exception _
)
[C#]
protected void DisplayError(
   Exception e
);
[C++]
protected: void DisplayError(
   Exception* e
);
[JScript]
protected function DisplayError(
   e : Exception
);
```

Parameters

e

The exception about which to display information.

Requirements

Platforms: Windows 98, Windows NT 4.0, Windows Millennium Edition, Windows 2000, Windows XP Home Edition, Windows XP Professional, Windows Server 2003 family

.NET Framework Security:

- Full trust for the immediate caller. This member cannot be used by partially trusted code.

ComponentTray.Dispose Method

Releases the unmanaged resources used by the **ComponentTray** and optionally releases the managed resources.

Overload List

Releases the unmanaged resources used by the **ComponentTray** and optionally releases the managed resources.

[Visual Basic] **Overloads Overrides Protected Sub Dispose(Boolean)**

[C#] **protected override void Dispose(bool);**

[C++] **protected: void Dispose(bool);**

[JScript] **protected override function Dispose(Boolean);**

Inherited from **Component**.

[Visual Basic] **Overloads Public Overridable Sub Dispose() Implements IDisposable.Dispose**

[C#] **public virtual void Dispose();**

[C++] **public: virtual void Dispose();**

[JScript] **public function Dispose();**

ComponentTray.Dispose Method (Boolean)

Releases the unmanaged resources used by the **ComponentTray** and optionally releases the managed resources.

[Visual Basic]
```
Overrides Overloads Protected Sub Dispose( _
   ByVal disposing As Boolean _
)
```
[C#]
```
protected override void Dispose(
   bool disposing
);
```
[C++]
```
protected: void Dispose(
   bool disposing
);
```
[JScript]
```
protected override function Dispose(
   disposing : Boolean
);
```

Parameters

disposing

true to release both managed and unmanaged resources; **false** to release only unmanaged resources.

Remarks

This method is called by the public **Dispose()** method and the **Finalize** method. **Dispose()** invokes the protected **Dispose(Boolean)** method with the *disposing* parameter set to **true**. **Finalize** invokes **Dispose** with *disposing* set to **false**.

When the *disposing* parameter is **true**, this method releases all resources held by any managed objects that this **ComponentTray** references. This method invokes the **Dispose()** method of each referenced object.

Notes to Inheritors: **Dispose** can be called multiple times by other objects. When overriding **Dispose(Boolean)**, be careful not to reference objects that have been previously disposed in an earlier call to **Dispose**.

Requirements

Platforms: Windows 98, Windows NT 4.0, Windows Millennium Edition, Windows 2000, Windows XP Home Edition, Windows XP Professional, Windows Server 2003 family

.NET Framework Security:

- Full trust for the immediate caller. This member cannot be used by partially trusted code.

ComponentTray.GetLocation Method

Gets the location of the specified component, relative to the upper-left corner of the component tray.

[Visual Basic]
```
Public Function GetLocation( _
   ByVal receiver As IComponent _
) As Point
```
[C#]
```
public Point GetLocation(
   IComponent receiver
);
```
[C++]
```
public: Point GetLocation(
   IComponent* receiver
);
```
[JScript]
```
public function GetLocation(
   receiver : IComponent
) : Point;
```

Parameters

receiver

The **IComponent** to retrieve the location of.

Return Value

A **Point** indicating the coordinates of the specified component, or an empty **Point** if the specified component could not be found in the component tray. An empty **Point** has an **IsEmpty** property equal to **true** and typically has **X** and **Y** properties that are each equal to zero.

Remarks

GetLocation is an accessor method for the location extender property that is added to each component in the component tray.

Requirements

Platforms: Windows 98, Windows NT 4.0, Windows Millennium Edition, Windows 2000, Windows XP Home Edition, Windows XP Professional, Windows Server 2003 family

.NET Framework Security:

- Full trust for the immediate caller. This member cannot be used by partially trusted code.

ComponentTray.GetService Method

Gets the requested service type.

[Visual Basic]
```
Overrides Protected Function GetService( _
   ByVal serviceType As Type _
) As Object
```
[C#]
```
protected override object GetService(
   Type serviceType
);
```
[C++]
```
protected: Object* GetService(
   Type* serviceType
);
```
[JScript]
```
protected override function GetService(
   serviceType : Type
) : Object;
```

Parameters

serviceType
  The type of the service to retrieve.

Return Value

An instance of the requested service, or a null reference (**Nothing** in Visual Basic) if the service could not be found.

Requirements

Platforms: Windows 98, Windows NT 4.0, Windows Millennium Edition, Windows 2000, Windows XP Home Edition, Windows XP Professional, Windows Server 2003 family

.NET Framework Security:

- Full trust for the immediate caller. This member cannot be used by partially trusted code.

ComponentTray.IExtenderProvider.CanExtend Method

This member supports the .NET Framework infrastructure and is not intended to be used directly from your code.

[Visual Basic]
```
Private Function CanExtend( _
   ByVal component As Object _
) As Boolean Implements IExtenderProvider.CanExtend
```
[C#]
```
bool IExtenderProvider.CanExtend(
   object component
);
```
[C++]
```
private: bool IExtenderProvider::CanExtend(
   Object* component
);
```
[JScript]
```
private function IExtenderProvider.CanExtend(
   component : Object
) : Boolean;
```

ComponentTray.OnDoubleClick Method

Called when the mouse is double clicked over the component tray.

[Visual Basic]
```
Overrides Protected Sub OnDoubleClick( _
   ByVal e As EventArgs _
)
```
[C#]
```
protected override void OnDoubleClick(
   EventArgs e
);
```
[C++]
```
protected: void OnDoubleClick(
   EventArgs* e
);
```
[JScript]
```
protected override function OnDoubleClick(
   e : EventArgs
);
```

Parameters

e
  An **EventArgs** that provides data for the event.

Requirements

Platforms: Windows 98, Windows NT 4.0, Windows Millennium Edition, Windows 2000, Windows XP Home Edition, Windows XP Professional, Windows Server 2003 family

.NET Framework Security:

- Full trust for the immediate caller. This member cannot be used by partially trusted code.

ComponentTray.OnDragDrop Method

Called when an object that has been dragged is dropped on the component tray.

[Visual Basic]
```
Overrides Protected Sub OnDragDrop( _
   ByVal de As DragEventArgs _
)
```
[C#]
```
protected override void OnDragDrop(
   DragEventArgs de
);
```
[C++]
```
protected: void OnDragDrop(
   DragEventArgs* de
);
```
[JScript]
```
protected override function OnDragDrop(
   de : DragEventArgs
);
```

Parameters

de
  A **DragEventArgs** that provides data for the event.

Requirements

Platforms: Windows 98, Windows NT 4.0, Windows Millennium Edition, Windows 2000, Windows XP Home Edition, Windows XP Professional, Windows Server 2003 family

.NET Framework Security:

- Full trust for the immediate caller. This member cannot be used by partially trusted code.

ComponentTray.OnDragEnter Method

Called when an object is dragged over, and has entered the area over, the component tray.

```
[Visual Basic]
Overrides Protected Sub OnDragEnter( _
   ByVal de As DragEventArgs _
)
[C#]
protected override void OnDragEnter(
   DragEventArgs de
);
[C++]
protected: void OnDragEnter(
   DragEventArgs* de
);
[JScript]
protected override function OnDragEnter(
   de : DragEventArgs
);
```

Parameters

de

A **DragEventArgs** that provides data for the event.

Requirements

Platforms: Windows 98, Windows NT 4.0, Windows Millennium Edition, Windows 2000, Windows XP Home Edition, Windows XP Professional, Windows Server 2003 family

.NET Framework Security:

- Full trust for the immediate caller. This member cannot be used by partially trusted code.

ComponentTray.OnDragLeave Method

Called when an object is dragged out of the area over the component tray.

```
[Visual Basic]
Overrides Protected Sub OnDragLeave( _
   ByVal e As EventArgs _
)
[C#]
protected override void OnDragLeave(
   EventArgs e
);
[C++]
protected: void OnDragLeave(
   EventArgs* e
);
[JScript]
protected override function OnDragLeave(
   e : EventArgs
);
```

Parameters

e

An **EventArgs** that provides data for the event.

Requirements

Platforms: Windows 98, Windows NT 4.0, Windows Millennium Edition, Windows 2000, Windows XP Home Edition, Windows XP Professional, Windows Server 2003 family

.NET Framework Security:

- Full trust for the immediate caller. This member cannot be used by partially trusted code.

ComponentTray.OnDragOver Method

Called when an object is dragged over the component tray.

```
[Visual Basic]
Overrides Protected Sub OnDragOver( _
   ByVal de As DragEventArgs _
)
[C#]
protected override void OnDragOver(
   DragEventArgs de
);
[C++]
protected: void OnDragOver(
   DragEventArgs* de
);
[JScript]
protected override function OnDragOver(
   de : DragEventArgs
);
```

Parameters

de

A **DragEventArgs** that provides data for the event.

Requirements

Platforms: Windows 98, Windows NT 4.0, Windows Millennium Edition, Windows 2000, Windows XP Home Edition, Windows XP Professional, Windows Server 2003 family

.NET Framework Security:

- Full trust for the immediate caller. This member cannot be used by partially trusted code.

ComponentTray.OnGiveFeedback Method

Called during an OLE drag and drop operation to provide an opportunity for the component tray to give feedback to the user about the results of dropping the object at a specific point.

```
[Visual Basic]
Overrides Protected Sub OnGiveFeedback( _
   ByVal gfevent As GiveFeedbackEventArgs _
)
```

[C#]
```
protected override void OnGiveFeedback(
   GiveFeedbackEventArgs gfevent
);
```
[C++]
```
protected: void OnGiveFeedback(
   GiveFeedbackEventArgs* gfevent
);
```
[JScript]
```
protected override function OnGiveFeedback(
   gfevent : GiveFeedbackEventArgs
);
```

Parameters

gfevent

A **GiveFeedbackEventArgs** that provides data for the event.

Remarks

Notes to Inheritors: When overriding **OnGiveFeedback** in a derived class, be sure to call the base class's **OnGiveFeedback** method so that registered delegates receive the event.

Requirements

Platforms: Windows 98, Windows NT 4.0, Windows Millennium Edition, Windows 2000, Windows XP Home Edition, Windows XP Professional, Windows Server 2003 family

.NET Framework Security:

- Full trust for the immediate caller. This member cannot be used by partially trusted code.

ComponentTray.OnLayout Method

This member overrides **Control.OnLayout**.

[Visual Basic]
```
Overrides Protected Sub OnLayout( _
   ByVal levent As LayoutEventArgs _
)
```
[C#]
```
protected override void OnLayout(
   LayoutEventArgs levent
);
```
[C++]
```
protected: void OnLayout(
   LayoutEventArgs* levent
);
```
[JScript]
```
protected override function OnLayout(
   levent : LayoutEventArgs
);
```

Requirements

Platforms: Windows 98, Windows NT 4.0, Windows Millennium Edition, Windows 2000, Windows XP Home Edition, Windows XP Professional, Windows Server 2003 family

.NET Framework Security:

- Full trust for the immediate caller. This member cannot be used by partially trusted code.

ComponentTray.OnLostCapture Method

Called when a mouse drag selection operation is canceled.

[Visual Basic]
```
Protected Overridable Sub OnLostCapture()
```
[C#]
```
protected virtual void OnLostCapture();
```
[C++]
```
protected: virtual void OnLostCapture();
```
[JScript]
```
protected function OnLostCapture();
```

Requirements

Platforms: Windows 98, Windows NT 4.0, Windows Millennium Edition, Windows 2000, Windows XP Home Edition, Windows XP Professional, Windows Server 2003 family

.NET Framework Security:

- Full trust for the immediate caller. This member cannot be used by partially trusted code.

ComponentTray.OnMouseDown Method

Called when the mouse button is pressed.

[Visual Basic]
```
Overrides Protected Sub OnMouseDown( _
   ByVal e As MouseEventArgs _
)
```
[C#]
```
protected override void OnMouseDown(
   MouseEventArgs e
);
```
[C++]
```
protected: void OnMouseDown(
   MouseEventArgs* e
);
```
[JScript]
```
protected override function OnMouseDown(
   e : MouseEventArgs
);
```

Parameters

e

A **MouseEventArgs** that provides data for the event.

Remarks

Notes to Inheritors: When overriding **OnMouseDown** in a derived class, be sure to call the base class's **OnMouseDown** method so that registered delegates receive the event.

Requirements

Platforms: Windows 98, Windows NT 4.0, Windows Millennium Edition, Windows 2000, Windows XP Home Edition, Windows XP Professional, Windows Server 2003 family

.NET Framework Security:

- Full trust for the immediate caller. This member cannot be used by partially trusted code.

ComponentTray.OnMouseMove Method

Called when the mouse cursor position has changed.

```
[Visual Basic]
Overrides Protected Sub OnMouseMove( _
   ByVal e As MouseEventArgs _
)
[C#]
protected override void OnMouseMove(
   MouseEventArgs e
);
[C++]
protected: void OnMouseMove(
   MouseEventArgs* e
);
[JScript]
protected override function OnMouseMove(
   e : MouseEventArgs
);
```

Parameters

e

A **MouseEventArgs** that provides data for the event.

Remarks

Notes to Inheritors: When overriding **OnMouseMove** in a derived class, be sure to call the base class's **OnMouseMove** method so that registered delegates receive the event.

Requirements

Platforms: Windows 98, Windows NT 4.0, Windows Millennium Edition, Windows 2000, Windows XP Home Edition, Windows XP Professional, Windows Server 2003 family

.NET Framework Security:

- Full trust for the immediate caller. This member cannot be used by partially trusted code.

ComponentTray.OnMouseUp Method

Called when the mouse button has been released.

```
[Visual Basic]
Overrides Protected Sub OnMouseUp( _
   ByVal e As MouseEventArgs _
)
[C#]
protected override void OnMouseUp(
   MouseEventArgs e
);
[C++]
protected: void OnMouseUp(
   MouseEventArgs* e
);
[JScript]
protected override function OnMouseUp(
   e : MouseEventArgs
);
```

Parameters

e

A **MouseEventArgs** that provides data for the event.

Remarks

Notes to Inheritors: When overriding **OnMouseUp** in a derived class, be sure to call the base class's **OnMouseUp** method so that registered delegates receive the event.

Requirements

Platforms: Windows 98, Windows NT 4.0, Windows Millennium Edition, Windows 2000, Windows XP Home Edition, Windows XP Professional, Windows Server 2003 family

.NET Framework Security:

- Full trust for the immediate caller. This member cannot be used by partially trusted code.

ComponentTray.OnPaint Method

Called when the view for the component tray should be refreshed.

```
[Visual Basic]
Overrides Protected Sub OnPaint( _
   ByVal pe As PaintEventArgs _
)
[C#]
protected override void OnPaint(
   PaintEventArgs pe
);
[C++]
protected: void OnPaint(
   PaintEventArgs* pe
);
[JScript]
protected override function OnPaint(
   pe : PaintEventArgs
);
```

Parameters

pe

A **PaintEventArgs** that provides data for the event.

Requirements

Platforms: Windows 98, Windows NT 4.0, Windows Millennium Edition, Windows 2000, Windows XP Home Edition, Windows XP Professional, Windows Server 2003 family

.NET Framework Security:

- Full trust for the immediate caller. This member cannot be used by partially trusted code.

ComponentTray.OnSetCursor Method

Called to set the mouse cursor.

```
[Visual Basic]
Protected Overridable Sub OnSetCursor()
[C#]
protected virtual void OnSetCursor();
[C++]
protected: virtual void OnSetCursor();
[JScript]
protected function OnSetCursor();
```

Remarks

Notes to Inheritors: You can override this method to set your own mouse cursor.

Requirements

Platforms: Windows 98, Windows NT 4.0, Windows Millennium Edition, Windows 2000, Windows XP Home Edition, Windows XP Professional, Windows Server 2003 family

.NET Framework Security:

- Full trust for the immediate caller. This member cannot be used by partially trusted code.

ComponentTray.RemoveComponent Method

Removes the specified component from the tray.

```
[Visual Basic]
Public Overridable Sub RemoveComponent( _
   ByVal component As IComponent _
)
[C#]
public virtual void RemoveComponent(
   IComponent component
);
[C++]
public: virtual void RemoveComponent(
   IComponent* component
);
[JScript]
public function RemoveComponent(
   component : IComponent
);
```

Parameters

component
The **IComponent** to remove from the tray.

Requirements

Platforms: Windows 98, Windows NT 4.0, Windows Millennium Edition, Windows 2000, Windows XP Home Edition, Windows XP Professional, Windows Server 2003 family

.NET Framework Security:

- Full trust for the immediate caller. This member cannot be used by partially trusted code.

ComponentTray.SetLocation Method

Sets the location of the specified component to the specified location.

```
[Visual Basic]
Public Sub SetLocation( _
   ByVal receiver As IComponent, _
   ByVal location As Point _
)
[C#]
public void SetLocation(
   IComponent receiver,
   Point location
);
[C++]
public: void SetLocation(
   IComponent* receiver,
   Point location
);
[JScript]
public function SetLocation(
   receiver : IComponent,
   location : Point
);
```

Parameters

receiver
The **IComponent** to set the location of.

location
A **Point** indicating the new location for the specified component.

Requirements

Platforms: Windows 98, Windows NT 4.0, Windows Millennium Edition, Windows 2000, Windows XP Home Edition, Windows XP Professional, Windows Server 2003 family

.NET Framework Security:

- Full trust for the immediate caller. This member cannot be used by partially trusted code.

ComponentTray.WndProc Method

Processes Windows messages.

```
[Visual Basic]
Overrides Protected Sub WndProc( _
   ByRef m As Message _
)
[C#]
protected override void WndProc(
   ref Message m
);
[C++]
protected: void WndProc(
   Message* m
);
[JScript]
protected override function WndProc(
   m : Message
);
```

Parameters

m
The **Message** to process.

Requirements

Platforms: Windows 98, Windows NT 4.0, Windows Millennium Edition, Windows 2000, Windows XP Home Edition, Windows XP Professional, Windows Server 2003 family

.NET Framework Security:

- Full trust for the immediate caller. This member cannot be used by partially trusted code.

ControlDesigner Class

Base designer class for extending the design mode behavior of a **Control**.

System.Object
  System.ComponentModel.Design.ComponentDesigner
    System.Windows.Forms.Design.ControlDesigner
      System.Windows.Forms.Design.ParentControlDesigner

[Visual Basic]
```
Public Class ControlDesigner
   Inherits ComponentDesigner
```
[C#]
```
public class ControlDesigner : ComponentDesigner
```
[C++]
```
public __gc class ControlDesigner : public ComponentDesigner
```
[JScript]
```
public class ControlDesigner extends ComponentDesigner
```

Thread Safety

Any public static (**Shared** in Visual Basic) members of this type are safe for multithreaded operations. Any instance members are not guaranteed to be thread safe.

Remarks

ControlDesigner provides a base class for designers of components that derive from **Control**. In addition to the methods and functionality inherited from the **ComponentDesigner** class, **ControlDesigner** provides additional methods to support extending and altering the behavior of an associated **Control** at design time.

You can associate a designer with a type using a **DesignerAttribute**. For an overview of customizing design time behavior, see **Enhancing Design-Time Support**.

Example

[Visual Basic, C#, C++] The following example **ControlDesigner** implementation demonstrates handling **MouseEnter** and **MouseLeave** events, drawing on a control from designer code, and using part of the **IDesignerFilter** interface to add a property for the control at design time. The following sample code contains a designer and a sample user control associated with the designer. To build this sample, compile the sample into a class library, add a reference to the library to a Windows Forms project, add the control to the Toolbox, and add an instance of the control to your form. When you point to the control, the inner outline of the perimeter of the control is highlighted, and the color used to draw the outline corresponds to the `OutlineColor` property that the designer has added to the properties listed for the control.

[Visual Basic]
```
Imports System
Imports System.ComponentModel
Imports System.ComponentModel.Design
Imports System.Collections
Imports System.Drawing
Imports System.Windows.Forms
Imports System.Windows.Forms.Design

Namespace ControlDesignerExample

    ' ExampleControlDesigner is an example control designer that
    ' demonstrates basic functions of a ControlDesigner.
    Public Class TestControlDesigner
        Inherits System.Windows.Forms.Design.ControlDesigner

        ' This boolean state reflects whether the mouse is over ↵
the control.
        Private mouseover As Boolean = False
        ' This color is a private field for the OutlineColor property.
        Private lineColor As Color = Color.White

        ' This color is used to outline the control when the mouse is
        ' over the control.
        Public Property OutlineColor() As Color
            Get
                Return lineColor
            End Get
            Set(ByVal Value As Color)
                lineColor = Value
            End Set
        End Property

        Public Sub New()
        End Sub

        ' Sets a value and refreshes the control's display when the
        ' mouse position enters the area of the control.
        Protected Overrides Sub OnMouseEnter()
            Me.mouseover = True
            Me.Control.Refresh()
        End Sub

        ' Sets a value and refreshes the control's display when the
        ' mouse position enters the area of the control.
        Protected Overrides Sub OnMouseLeave()
            Me.mouseover = False
            Me.Control.Refresh()
        End Sub

        ' Draws an outline around the control when the mouse is
        ' over the control.
        Protected Overrides Sub OnPaintAdornments(ByVal ↵
pe As System.Windows.Forms.PaintEventArgs)
            If Me.mouseover Then
                pe.Graphics.DrawRectangle(New Pen(New ↵
SolidBrush(Me.lineColor), 6), 0, 0, Me.Control.Size.Width, ↵
Me.Control.Size.Height)
            End If
        End Sub

        ' Adds a property to this designer's control at design time
        ' that indicates the outline color to use.
        Protected Overrides Sub PreFilterProperties(ByVal ↵
properties As System.Collections.IDictionary)
            properties.Add("OutlineColor", ↵
TypeDescriptor.CreateProperty(GetType(TestControlDesigner), ↵
"OutlineColor", GetType(System.Drawing.Color), Nothing))
        End Sub
    End Class

    ' This example control demonstrates the ExampleControlDesigner.
    <DesignerAttribute(GetType(TestControlDesigner))> _
     Public Class TestControl
        Inherits System.Windows.Forms.UserControl
        Private components As System.ComponentModel.Container = Nothing

        Public Sub New()
            components = New System.ComponentModel.Container()
        End Sub

        Protected Overloads Sub Dispose(ByVal disposing As Boolean)
            If disposing Then
                If Not (components Is Nothing) Then
                    components.Dispose()
                End If
            End If
            MyBase.Dispose(disposing)
        End Sub
    End Class

End Namespace
```

[C#]
```
using System;
using System.ComponentModel;
using System.ComponentModel.Design;
using System.Collections;
using System.Drawing;
using System.Windows.Forms;
using System.Windows.Forms.Design;

namespace ControlDesignerExample
{
    // ExampleControlDesigner is an example control designer that
    // demonstrates basic functions of a ControlDesigner.
    public class ExampleControlDesigner  :                              ↵
System.Windows.Forms.Design.ControlDesigner
    {
        // This boolean state reflects whether the mouse is              ↵
over the control.
        private bool mouseover = false;
        // This color is a private field for the OutlineColor property.
        private Color lineColor = Color.White;

        // This color is used to outline the control when the mouse is
        // over the control.
        public Color OutlineColor
        {
            get
            {
                return lineColor;
            }
            set
            {
                lineColor = value;
            }
        }

        public ExampleControlDesigner()
        {
        }

        // Sets a value and refreshes the control's display when the
        // mouse position enters the area of the control.
        protected override void OnMouseEnter()
        {
            this.mouseover = true;
            this.Control.Refresh();
        }

        // Sets a value and refreshes the control's display when the
        // mouse position enters the area of the control.
        protected override void OnMouseLeave()
        {
            this.mouseover = false;
            this.Control.Refresh();
        }

        // Draws an outline around the control when the mouse is
        // over the control.
        protected override void
OnPaintAdornments(System.Windows.Forms.PaintEventArgs pe)
        {
            if(this.mouseover)
                pe.Graphics.DrawRectangle(new Pen(new                   ↵
SolidBrush(this.lineColor), 6), 0, 0,                                   ↵
this.Control.Size.Width, this.Control.Size.Height);
        }

        // Adds a property to this designer's control at design time
        // that indicates the outline color to use.
        protected override void
PreFilterProperties(System.Collections.IDictionary properties)
        {
            properties.Add("OutlineColor",                              ↵
TypeDescriptor.CreateProperty(typeof(ExampleControlDesigner),           ↵
"OutlineColor", typeof(System.Drawing.Color), null));
        }
    }

    // This example control demonstrates the ExampleControlDesigner.
    [DesignerAttribute(typeof(ExampleControlDesigner))]
    public class ExampleControl : System.Windows.Forms.UserControl
    {
        private System.ComponentModel.Container components = null;

        public ExampleControl()
        {
            components = new System.ComponentModel.Container();
        }

        protected override void Dispose( bool disposing )
        {
            if( disposing )
            {
                if( components != null )
                components.Dispose();
            }
            base.Dispose( disposing );
        }
    }
}
```

[C++]
```
using namespace System;
using namespace System::ComponentModel;
using namespace System::ComponentModel::Design;
using namespace System::Collections;
using namespace System::Drawing;
using namespace System::Windows::Forms;
using namespace System::Windows::Forms::Design;

namespace ControlDesignerExample {
public __gc class TestControlDesigner : public                          ↵
System::Windows::Forms::Design::ControlDesigner {
private:
    bool mouseover;
    Color lineColor;

public:
    __property Color get_OutlineColor() {
        return lineColor;
    }

    __property void    set_OutlineColor(Color value) {
        lineColor = value;
    }

    TestControlDesigner() {
        mouseover = false;
        lineColor = Color::White;
    }

protected:
    void OnMouseEnter() {
        this->mouseover = true;
        this->Control->Refresh();
    }

    void OnMouseLeave() {
        this->mouseover = false;
        this->Control->Refresh();
    }

    void OnPaintAdornments                                              ↵
  (System::Windows::Forms::PaintEventArgs* pe) {
        if (this->mouseover)
            pe->Graphics->DrawRectangle(new Pen                         ↵
  (new SolidBrush(this->lineColor), 6),
            0, 0, this->Control->Size.Width, this->                     ↵
 Control->Size.Height);
    }
```

```
protected:
    void PreFilterProperties                                          ↵
 (System::Collections::IDictionary* properties) {
        properties->Add(S"OutlineColor",                              ↵
TypeDescriptor::CreateProperty(__typeof(TestControlDesigner),
            S"OutlineColor", __typeof(System::Drawing::Color), 0));
    }
};

[DesignerAttribute(__typeof(TestControlDesigner))]
public __gc class TestControl : public                                ↵
System::Windows::Forms::UserControl {
private:
    System::ComponentModel::Container* components;

public:
    TestControl() {
        components = new System::ComponentModel::Container();
    }

protected:
    void Dispose(Boolean disposing) {
        if (disposing && components)
        {
            components->Dispose();
        }
        UserControl::Dispose(disposing);
    }
};
}
```

Requirements

Namespace: System.Windows.Forms.Design

Platforms: Windows 98, Windows NT 4.0, Windows Millennium Edition, Windows 2000, Windows XP Home Edition, Windows XP Professional, Windows Server 2003 family

Assembly: System.Design (in System.Design.dll)

ControlDesigner Constructor

Initializes a new instance of the **ControlDesigner** class.

[Visual Basic]
```
Public Sub New()
```
[C#]
```
public ControlDesigner();
```
[C++]
```
public: ControlDesigner();
```
[JScript]
```
public function ControlDesigner();
```

Remarks

The default constructor initializes any fields to their default values.

Requirements

Platforms: Windows 98, Windows NT 4.0, Windows Millennium Edition, Windows 2000, Windows XP Home Edition, Windows XP Professional, Windows Server 2003 family

.NET Framework Security:

- Full trust for the immediate caller. This member cannot be used by partially trusted code.

ControlDesigner.accessibilityObj Field

Specifies the accessibility object for the designer.

[Visual Basic]
```
Protected accessibilityObj As AccessibleObject
```
[C#]
```
protected AccessibleObject accessibilityObj;
```
[C++]
```
protected: AccessibleObject* accessibilityObj;
```
[JScript]
```
protected var accessibilityObj : AccessibleObject;
```

Remarks

The default value is a null reference (**Nothing** in Visual Basic).

Requirements

Platforms: Windows 98, Windows NT 4.0, Windows Millennium Edition, Windows 2000, Windows XP Home Edition, Windows XP Professional, Windows Server 2003 family

ControlDesigner.InvalidPoint Field

Defines a local **Point** object that represents the values of an invalid **Point** object.

[Visual Basic]
```
Protected Shared ReadOnly InvalidPoint As Point
```
[C#]
```
protected static readonly Point InvalidPoint;
```
[C++]
```
protected: static Point InvalidPoint;
```
[JScript]
```
protected static var InvalidPoint : Point;
```

Remarks

InvalidPoint has an **X** and **Y** property set to the minimum value for the integer data type.

Requirements

Platforms: Windows 98, Windows NT 4.0, Windows Millennium Edition, Windows 2000, Windows XP Home Edition, Windows XP Professional, Windows Server 2003 family

ControlDesigner.AccessibilityObject Property

Gets the **AccessibleObject** assigned to the control.

[Visual Basic]
```
Public Overridable ReadOnly Property AccessibilityObject As _
   AccessibleObject
```
[C#]
```
public virtual AccessibleObject AccessibilityObject {get;}
```
[C++]
```
public: __property virtual AccessibleObject*
   get_AccessibilityObject();
```
[JScript]
```
public function get AccessibilityObject() : AccessibleObject;
```

Property Value

The **AccessibleObject** assigned to the control.

Remarks

For more information about accessible objects, see the Active Accessibility section of the MSDN Library.

Requirements

Platforms: Windows 98, Windows NT 4.0, Windows Millennium Edition, Windows 2000, Windows XP Home Edition, Windows XP Professional, Windows Server 2003 family

.NET Framework Security:

- Full trust for the immediate caller. This member cannot be used by partially trusted code.

ControlDesigner.AssociatedComponents Property

Gets the collection of components associated with the component managed by the designer.

```
[Visual Basic]
Overrides Public ReadOnly Property AssociatedComponents As _
   ICollection
[C#]
public override ICollection AssociatedComponents {get;}
[C++]
public: __property ICollection* get_AssociatedComponents();
[JScript]
public override function get AssociatedComponents() : ICollection;
```

Property Value

The components that are associated with the component managed by the designer.

Remarks

This property indicates any components to copy or move along with the component managed by the designer during a copy, drag or move operation.

If this collection contains references to other components in the current design mode document, those components will be copied along with the component managed by the designer during a copy operation.

When the component managed by the designer is selected, this collection is filled with any nested controls. This collection can also include other components, such as the buttons of a toolbar.

Requirements

Platforms: Windows 98, Windows NT 4.0, Windows Millennium Edition, Windows 2000, Windows XP Home Edition, Windows XP Professional, Windows Server 2003 family

.NET Framework Security:

- Full trust for the immediate caller. This member cannot be used by partially trusted code.

ControlDesigner.Control Property

Gets the control that the designer is designing.

```
[Visual Basic]
Public Overridable ReadOnly Property Control As Control
[C#]
public virtual Control Control {get;}
[C++]
public: __property virtual Control* get_Control();
[JScript]
public function get Control() : Control;
```

Property Value

The control that the designer is designing.

Requirements

Platforms: Windows 98, Windows NT 4.0, Windows Millennium Edition, Windows 2000, Windows XP Home Edition, Windows XP Professional, Windows Server 2003 family

.NET Framework Security:

- Full trust for the immediate caller. This member cannot be used by partially trusted code.

ControlDesigner.EnableDragRect Property

Gets a value indicating whether drag rectangles can be drawn on this designer component.

```
[Visual Basic]
Protected Overridable ReadOnly Property EnableDragRect As Boolean
[C#]
protected virtual bool EnableDragRect {get;}
[C++]
protected: __property virtual bool get_EnableDragRect();
[JScript]
protected function get EnableDragRect() : Boolean;
```

Property Value

true if drag rectangles can be drawn; otherwise, **false**.

Requirements

Platforms: Windows 98, Windows NT 4.0, Windows Millennium Edition, Windows 2000, Windows XP Home Edition, Windows XP Professional, Windows Server 2003 family

.NET Framework Security:

- Full trust for the immediate caller. This member cannot be used by partially trusted code.

ControlDesigner.SelectionRules Property

Gets the selection rules that indicate the movement capabilities of a component.

```
[Visual Basic]
Public Overridable ReadOnly Property SelectionRules As _
   SelectionRules
[C#]
public virtual SelectionRules SelectionRules {get;}
[C++]
public: __property virtual SelectionRules get_SelectionRules();
[JScript]
public function get SelectionRules() : SelectionRules;
```

Property Value

A bitwise combination of **SelectionRules** values.

Remarks

If no designer provides rules for a component, the component will not get any UI services.

Requirements

Platforms: Windows 98, Windows NT 4.0, Windows Millennium Edition, Windows 2000, Windows XP Home Edition, Windows XP Professional, Windows Server 2003 family

.NET Framework Security:

- Full trust for the immediate caller. This member cannot be used by partially trusted code.

ControlDesigner.BaseWndProc Method

Processes Windows messages.

```
[Visual Basic]
Protected Sub BaseWndProc( _
   ByRef m As Message _
)
[C#]
protected void BaseWndProc(
   ref Message m
);
[C++]
protected: void BaseWndProc(
   Message* m
);
[JScript]
protected function BaseWndProc(
   m : Message
);
```

Parameters

m

The **Message** to process.

Remarks

This method causes the message to be processed by Windows, skipping the control. This is useful if you want to block the message from getting to the control, but you do not want to block it from getting to Windows itself because it can cause other messages to be generated.

Requirements

Platforms: Windows 98, Windows NT 4.0, Windows Millennium Edition, Windows 2000, Windows XP Home Edition, Windows XP Professional, Windows Server 2003 family

.NET Framework Security:

- Full trust for the immediate caller. This member cannot be used by partially trusted code.

ControlDesigner.CanBeParentedTo Method

Indicates if this designer's control can be parented by the control of the specified designer.

```
[Visual Basic]
Public Overridable Function CanBeParentedTo( _
   ByVal parentDesigner As IDesigner _
) As Boolean
[C#]
public virtual bool CanBeParentedTo(
   IDesigner parentDesigner
);
[C++]
public: virtual bool CanBeParentedTo(
   IDesigner* parentDesigner
);
[JScript]
public function CanBeParentedTo(
   parentDesigner : IDesigner
) : Boolean;
```

Parameters

parentDesigner

The **IDesigner** that manages the control to check.

Return Value

true if the control managed by the specified designer can parent the control managed by this designer; otherwise, **false**.

Remarks

This method is useful for testing whether a control can be parented by a particular type of parent. For example, **TabPage** controls can only be parented by **TabControl** controls.

Requirements

Platforms: Windows 98, Windows NT 4.0, Windows Millennium Edition, Windows 2000, Windows XP Home Edition, Windows XP Professional, Windows Server 2003 family

.NET Framework Security:

- Full trust for the immediate caller. This member cannot be used by partially trusted code.

ControlDesigner.DefWndProc Method

Provides default processing for Windows messages.

```
[Visual Basic]
Protected Sub DefWndProc( _
   ByRef m As Message _
)
[C#]
protected void DefWndProc(
   ref Message m
);
[C++]
protected: void DefWndProc(
   Message* m
);
[JScript]
protected function DefWndProc(
   m : Message
);
```

Parameters

m

The **Message** to process.

Remarks

This method causes the message to be processed by the control, rather than by the designer.

Requirements

Platforms: Windows 98, Windows NT 4.0, Windows Millennium Edition, Windows 2000, Windows XP Home Edition, Windows XP Professional, Windows Server 2003 family

.NET Framework Security:

- Full trust for the immediate caller. This member cannot be used by partially trusted code.

ControlDesigner.DisplayError Method

Displays information about the specified exception to the user.

```
[Visual Basic]
Protected Sub DisplayError( _
   ByVal e As Exception _
)
[C#]
protected void DisplayError(
   Exception e
);
[C++]
protected: void DisplayError(
   Exception* e
);
[JScript]
protected function DisplayError(
   e : Exception
);
```

Parameters

e

The **Exception** to display.

Requirements

Platforms: Windows 98, Windows NT 4.0, Windows Millennium Edition, Windows 2000, Windows XP Home Edition, Windows XP Professional, Windows Server 2003 family

.NET Framework Security:

- Full trust for the immediate caller. This member cannot be used by partially trusted code.

ControlDesigner.Dispose Method

Releases the unmanaged resources used by the **ControlDesigner** and optionally releases the managed resources.

Overload List

Releases the unmanaged resources used by the **ControlDesigner** and optionally releases the managed resources.

[Visual Basic] **Overloads Overrides Protected Sub Dispose(Boolean)**

[C#] **protected override void Dispose(bool);**

[C++] **protected: void Dispose(bool);**

[JScript] **protected override function Dispose(Boolean);**

Inherited from **ComponentDesigner**.

[Visual Basic] **Overloads Public Overridable Sub Dispose() Implements IDisposable.Dispose**

[C#] **public virtual void Dispose();**

[C++] **public: virtual void Dispose();**

[JScript] **public function Dispose();**

ControlDesigner.Dispose Method (Boolean)

Releases the unmanaged resources used by the **ControlDesigner** and optionally releases the managed resources.

```
[Visual Basic]
Overrides Overloads Protected Sub Dispose( _
   ByVal disposing As Boolean _
)
[C#]
protected override void Dispose(
   bool disposing
);
[C++]
protected: void Dispose(
   bool disposing
);
[JScript]
protected override function Dispose(
   disposing : Boolean
);
```

Parameters

disposing

true to release both managed and unmanaged resources; **false** to release only unmanaged resources.

Remarks

This method is called by the public **Dispose()** method and the **Finalize** method. **Dispose()** invokes the protected **Dispose(Boolean)** method with the *disposing* parameter set to **true**. **Finalize** invokes **Dispose** with *disposing* set to **false**.

When the *disposing* parameter is **true**, this method releases all resources held by any managed objects that this **ControlDesigner** references. This method invokes the **Dispose()** method of each referenced object.

Notes to Inheritors: **Dispose** can be called multiple times by other objects. When overriding **Dispose(Boolean)**, be careful not to reference objects that have been previously disposed in an earlier call to **Dispose**.

Requirements

Platforms: Windows 98, Windows NT 4.0, Windows Millennium Edition, Windows 2000, Windows XP Home Edition, Windows XP Professional, Windows Server 2003 family

.NET Framework Security:

- Full trust for the immediate caller. This member cannot be used by partially trusted code.

ControlDesigner.EnableDragDrop Method

Enables or disables drag-and-drop support for the control being designed.

```
[Visual Basic]
Protected Sub EnableDragDrop( _
   ByVal value As Boolean _
)
[C#]
protected void EnableDragDrop(
   bool value
);
[C++]
protected: void EnableDragDrop(
   bool value
);
[JScript]
protected function EnableDragDrop(
   value : Boolean
);
```

Parameters

value

true to enable drag-and-drop support for the control; **false** if the control should not have drag-and-drop support. The default is **false**.

Remarks

The default value of **false** prevents a control from having children dragged onto it at design time. To allow a control to parent other controls at design time, associate it with a designer that derives from **ParentControlDesigner**.

Requirements

Platforms: Windows 98, Windows NT 4.0, Windows Millennium Edition, Windows 2000, Windows XP Home Edition, Windows XP Professional, Windows Server 2003 family

.NET Framework Security:

- Full trust for the immediate caller. This member cannot be used by partially trusted code.

ControlDesigner.GetHitTest Method

Indicates whether a mouse click at the specified point should be handled by the control.

```
[Visual Basic]
Protected Overridable Function GetHitTest( _
   ByVal point As Point _
) As Boolean
[C#]
protected virtual bool GetHitTest(
   Point point
);
[C++]
protected: virtual bool GetHitTest(
   Point point
);
[JScript]
protected function GetHitTest(
   point : Point
) : Boolean;
```

Parameters

point

A **Point** indicating the position at which the mouse was clicked, in screen coordinates.

Return Value

true if a click at the specified point is to be handled by the control; otherwise, **false**.

Remarks

The **GetHitTest** method determines whether a click at the specified point should be passed to the control, while the control is in design mode. You can override and implement this method to enable your control to receive clicks in the design-time environment.

> **Note** You can pass a point in screen coordinates to the **PointToClient** method of the **Control** class to obtain the coordinates of the point relative to the upper-left corner of the control.

Requirements

Platforms: Windows 98, Windows NT 4.0, Windows Millennium Edition, Windows 2000, Windows XP Home Edition, Windows XP Professional, Windows Server 2003 family

.NET Framework Security:

- Full trust for the immediate caller. This member cannot be used by partially trusted code.

ControlDesigner.HookChildControls Method

Routes messages from the child controls of the specified control to the designer.

```
[Visual Basic]
Protected Sub HookChildControls( _
   ByVal firstChild As Control _
)
[C#]
protected void HookChildControls(
   Control firstChild
);
[C++]
protected: void HookChildControls(
   Control* firstChild
);
[JScript]
protected function HookChildControls(
   firstChild : Control
);
```

Parameters

firstChild

The first child **Control** to process. This method may recursively call itself for children of the control.

Requirements

Platforms: Windows 98, Windows NT 4.0, Windows Millennium Edition, Windows 2000, Windows XP Home Edition, Windows XP Professional, Windows Server 2003 family

.NET Framework Security:

- Full trust for the immediate caller. This member cannot be used by partially trusted code.

ControlDesigner.Initialize Method

Initializes the designer with the specified component.

```
[Visual Basic]
Overrides Public Sub Initialize( _
   ByVal component As IComponent _
) Implements IDesigner.Initialize
[C#]
public override void Initialize(
   IComponent component
);
[C++]
public: void Initialize(
   IComponent* component
);
[JScript]
public override function Initialize(
   component : IComponent
);
```

Parameters

component

The **IComponent** to associate the designer with. This component must always be an instance of, or derive from, **Control**.

Implements

IDesigner.Initialize

Remarks

This method is called by the designer host to initialize the designer.

Requirements

Platforms: Windows 98, Windows NT 4.0, Windows Millennium Edition, Windows 2000, Windows XP Home Edition, Windows XP Professional, Windows Server 2003 family

.NET Framework Security:

- Full trust for the immediate caller. This member cannot be used by partially trusted code.

ControlDesigner.InitializeNonDefault Method

Initializes properties of the control to any non-default values.

```
[Visual Basic]
Overrides Public Sub InitializeNonDefault()
[C#]
public override void InitializeNonDefault();
[C++]
public: void InitializeNonDefault();
[JScript]
public override function InitializeNonDefault();
```

Remarks

This method is called when a control is initialized from a state other than its default initialization state. This occurs, for instance, when it is pasted on a design surface from another location.

This method can be implemented to perform checking for valid object references, and to establish correct siting or references, after a component has been re-sited. This method is called after the **Initialize** method.

Requirements

Platforms: Windows 98, Windows NT 4.0, Windows Millennium Edition, Windows 2000, Windows XP Home Edition, Windows XP Professional, Windows Server 2003 family

.NET Framework Security:

- Full trust for the immediate caller. This member cannot be used by partially trusted code.

ControlDesigner.OnContextMenu Method

Shows the context menu and provides an opportunity to perform additional processing when the context menu is about to be displayed.

```
[Visual Basic]
Protected Overridable Sub OnContextMenu( _
   ByVal x As Integer, _
   ByVal y As Integer _
)
[C#]
protected virtual void OnContextMenu(
   int x,
   int y
);
[C++]
protected: virtual void OnContextMenu(
   int x,
   int y
);
[JScript]
protected function OnContextMenu(
   x : int,
   y : int
);
```

Parameters

x

The x coordinate at which to display the context menu.

y

The y coordinate at which to display the context menu.

Requirements

Platforms: Windows 98, Windows NT 4.0, Windows Millennium Edition, Windows 2000, Windows XP Home Edition, Windows XP Professional, Windows Server 2003 family

.NET Framework Security:

- Full trust for the immediate caller. This member cannot be used by partially trusted code.

ControlDesigner.OnCreateHandle Method

Provides an opportunity to perform additional processing immediately after the control handle has been created.

```
[Visual Basic]
Protected Overridable Sub OnCreateHandle()
[C#]
protected virtual void OnCreateHandle();
[C++]
protected: virtual void OnCreateHandle();
```

```
[JScript]
protected function OnCreateHandle();
```

Requirements

Platforms: Windows 98, Windows NT 4.0, Windows Millennium Edition, Windows 2000, Windows XP Home Edition, Windows XP Professional, Windows Server 2003 family

.NET Framework Security:

- Full trust for the immediate caller. This member cannot be used by partially trusted code.

ControlDesigner.OnDragDrop Method

Called when a drag-and-drop object is dropped onto the control designer view.

```
[Visual Basic]
Protected Overridable Sub OnDragDrop( _
   ByVal de As DragEventArgs _
)
[C#]
protected virtual void OnDragDrop(
   DragEventArgs de
);
[C++]
protected: virtual void OnDragDrop(
   DragEventArgs* de
);
[JScript]
protected function OnDragDrop(
   de : DragEventArgs
);
```

Parameters

de

A **DragEventArgs** that provides data for the event.

Requirements

Platforms: Windows 98, Windows NT 4.0, Windows Millennium Edition, Windows 2000, Windows XP Home Edition, Windows XP Professional, Windows Server 2003 family

.NET Framework Security:

- Full trust for the immediate caller. This member cannot be used by partially trusted code.

ControlDesigner.OnDragEnter Method

Called when a drag-and-drop operation enters the control designer view.

```
[Visual Basic]
Protected Overridable Sub OnDragEnter( _
   ByVal de As DragEventArgs _
)
[C#]
protected virtual void OnDragEnter(
   DragEventArgs de
);
[C++]
protected: virtual void OnDragEnter(
   DragEventArgs* de
);
[JScript]
protected function OnDragEnter(
   de : DragEventArgs
);
```

Parameters

de

A **DragEventArgs** that provides data for the event.

Requirements

Platforms: Windows 98, Windows NT 4.0, Windows Millennium Edition, Windows 2000, Windows XP Home Edition, Windows XP Professional, Windows Server 2003 family

.NET Framework Security:

- Full trust for the immediate caller. This member cannot be used by partially trusted code.

ControlDesigner.OnDragLeave Method

Called when a drag-and-drop operation leaves the control designer view.

```
[Visual Basic]
Protected Overridable Sub OnDragLeave( _
   ByVal e As EventArgs _
)
[C#]
protected virtual void OnDragLeave(
   EventArgs e
);
[C++]
protected: virtual void OnDragLeave(
   EventArgs* e
);
[JScript]
protected function OnDragLeave(
   e : EventArgs
);
```

Parameters

e

An **EventArgs** that provides data for the event.

Requirements

Platforms: Windows 98, Windows NT 4.0, Windows Millennium Edition, Windows 2000, Windows XP Home Edition, Windows XP Professional, Windows Server 2003 family

.NET Framework Security:

- Full trust for the immediate caller. This member cannot be used by partially trusted code.

ControlDesigner.OnDragOver Method

Called when a drag-and-drop object is dragged over the control designer view.

```
[Visual Basic]
Protected Overridable Sub OnDragOver( _
   ByVal de As DragEventArgs _
)
[C#]
protected virtual void OnDragOver(
   DragEventArgs de
);
[C++]
protected: virtual void OnDragOver(
   DragEventArgs* de
);
[JScript]
protected function OnDragOver(
   de : DragEventArgs
);
```

Parameters

de

A **DragEventArgs** that provides data for the event.

Requirements

Platforms: Windows 98, Windows NT 4.0, Windows Millennium Edition, Windows 2000, Windows XP Home Edition, Windows XP Professional, Windows Server 2003 family

.NET Framework Security:

- Full trust for the immediate caller. This member cannot be used by partially trusted code.

ControlDesigner.OnGiveFeedback Method

Called when a drag-and-drop operation is in progress to provide visual cues based on the location of the mouse while a drag operation is in progress.

```
[Visual Basic]
Protected Overridable Sub OnGiveFeedback( _
   ByVal e As GiveFeedbackEventArgs _
)
[C#]
protected virtual void OnGiveFeedback(
   GiveFeedbackEventArgs e
);
[C++]
protected: virtual void OnGiveFeedback(
   GiveFeedbackEventArgs* e
);
[JScript]
protected function OnGiveFeedback(
   e : GiveFeedbackEventArgs
);
```

Parameters

e

A **GiveFeedbackEventArgs** that provides data for the event.

Remarks

The designer host calls this method when an OLE drag event occurs.

Requirements

Platforms: Windows 98, Windows NT 4.0, Windows Millennium Edition, Windows 2000, Windows XP Home Edition, Windows XP Professional, Windows Server 2003 family

.NET Framework Security:

- Full trust for the immediate caller. This member cannot be used by partially trusted code.

ControlDesigner.OnMouseDragBegin Method

Called in response to the left mouse button being pressed and held while over the component.

```
[Visual Basic]
Protected Overridable Sub OnMouseDragBegin( _
   ByVal x As Integer, _
   ByVal y As Integer _
)
[C#]
protected virtual void OnMouseDragBegin(
   int x,
   int y
);
[C++]
protected: virtual void OnMouseDragBegin(
   int x,
   int y
);
[JScript]
protected function OnMouseDragBegin(
   x : int,
   y : int
);
```

Parameters

x

The x position of the mouse in screen coordinates.

y

The y position of the mouse in screen coordinates.

Remarks

This method is called at the start of a drag-and-drop operation.

> **Note** You can pass a point in screen coordinates to the **PointToClient** method of the **Control** class to obtain the coordinates of the point relative to the upper-left corner of the control.

Requirements

Platforms: Windows 98, Windows NT 4.0, Windows Millennium Edition, Windows 2000, Windows XP Home Edition, Windows XP Professional, Windows Server 2003 family

.NET Framework Security:

- Full trust for the immediate caller. This member cannot be used by partially trusted code.

ControlDesigner.OnMouseDragEnd Method

Called at the end of a drag-and-drop operation to complete or cancel the operation.

[Visual Basic]
```
Protected Overridable Sub OnMouseDragEnd( _
   ByVal cancel As Boolean _
)
```
[C#]
```
protected virtual void OnMouseDragEnd(
   bool cancel
);
```
[C++]
```
protected: virtual void OnMouseDragEnd(
   bool cancel
);
```
[JScript]
```
protected function OnMouseDragEnd(
   cancel : Boolean
);
```

Parameters

cancel

true to cancel the drag; **false** to commit it.

Requirements

Platforms: Windows 98, Windows NT 4.0, Windows Millennium Edition, Windows 2000, Windows XP Home Edition, Windows XP Professional, Windows Server 2003 family

.NET Framework Security:

- Full trust for the immediate caller. This member cannot be used by partially trusted code.

ControlDesigner.OnMouseDragMove Method

Called for each movement of the mouse during a drag-and-drop operation.

[Visual Basic]
```
Protected Overridable Sub OnMouseDragMove( _
   ByVal x As Integer, _
   ByVal y As Integer _
)
```
[C#]
```
protected virtual void OnMouseDragMove(
   int x,
   int y
);
```
[C++]
```
protected: virtual void OnMouseDragMove(
   int x,
   int y
);
```
[JScript]
```
protected function OnMouseDragMove(
   x : int,
   y : int
);
```

Parameters

x

The x position of the mouse in screen coordinates.

y

The y position of the mouse in screen coordinates.

Remarks

Note You can pass a point in screen coordinates to the **PointToClient** method of the **Control** class to obtain the coordinates of the point relative to the upper-left corner of the control.

Requirements

Platforms: Windows 98, Windows NT 4.0, Windows Millennium Edition, Windows 2000, Windows XP Home Edition, Windows XP Professional, Windows Server 2003 family

.NET Framework Security:

- Full trust for the immediate caller. This member cannot be used by partially trusted code.

ControlDesigner.OnMouseEnter Method

Called when the mouse first enters the control.

[Visual Basic]
```
Protected Overridable Sub OnMouseEnter()
```
[C#]
```
protected virtual void OnMouseEnter();
```
[C++]
```
protected: virtual void OnMouseEnter();
```
[JScript]
```
protected function OnMouseEnter();
```

Requirements

Platforms: Windows 98, Windows NT 4.0, Windows Millennium Edition, Windows 2000, Windows XP Home Edition, Windows XP Professional, Windows Server 2003 family

.NET Framework Security:

- Full trust for the immediate caller. This member cannot be used by partially trusted code.

ControlDesigner.OnMouseHover Method

Called after the mouse hovers over the control.

[Visual Basic]
```
Protected Overridable Sub OnMouseHover()
```
[C#]
```
protected virtual void OnMouseHover();
```
[C++]
```
protected: virtual void OnMouseHover();
```
[JScript]
```
protected function OnMouseHover();
```

Requirements

Platforms: Windows 98, Windows NT 4.0, Windows Millennium Edition, Windows 2000, Windows XP Home Edition, Windows XP Professional, Windows Server 2003 family

.NET Framework Security:

- Full trust for the immediate caller. This member cannot be used by partially trusted code.

ControlDesigner.OnMouseLeave Method

Called when the mouse first enters the control.

```
[Visual Basic]
Protected Overridable Sub OnMouseLeave()
[C#]
protected virtual void OnMouseLeave();
[C++]
protected: virtual void OnMouseLeave();
[JScript]
protected function OnMouseLeave();
```

Requirements

Platforms: Windows 98, Windows NT 4.0, Windows Millennium Edition, Windows 2000, Windows XP Home Edition, Windows XP Professional, Windows Server 2003 family

.NET Framework Security:

- Full trust for the immediate caller. This member cannot be used by partially trusted code.

ControlDesigner.OnPaintAdornments Method

Called when the control that the designer is managing has painted its surface so the designer can paint any additional adornments on top of the control.

```
[Visual Basic]
Protected Overridable Sub OnPaintAdornments( _
   ByVal pe As PaintEventArgs _
)
[C#]
protected virtual void OnPaintAdornments(
   PaintEventArgs pe
);
[C++]
protected: virtual void OnPaintAdornments(
   PaintEventArgs* pe
);
[JScript]
protected function OnPaintAdornments(
   pe : PaintEventArgs
);
```

Parameters

pe

A **PaintEventArgs** the designer can use to draw on the control.

Requirements

Platforms: Windows 98, Windows NT 4.0, Windows Millennium Edition, Windows 2000, Windows XP Home Edition, Windows XP Professional, Windows Server 2003 family

.NET Framework Security:

- Full trust for the immediate caller. This member cannot be used by partially trusted code.

ControlDesigner.OnSetComponentDefaults Method

Called when the designer is initialized, so the designer can set default values for properties of the component.

```
[Visual Basic]
Overrides Public Sub OnSetComponentDefaults()
[C#]
public override void OnSetComponentDefaults();
[C++]
public: void OnSetComponentDefaults();
[JScript]
public override function OnSetComponentDefaults();
```

Remarks

This method allows the designer to provide some meaningful default values for the component. The default implementation of this method sets the component's **Text** property to its name, if the property field is of type string.

Requirements

Platforms: Windows 98, Windows NT 4.0, Windows Millennium Edition, Windows 2000, Windows XP Home Edition, Windows XP Professional, Windows Server 2003 family

.NET Framework Security:

- Full trust for the immediate caller. This member cannot be used by partially trusted code.

ControlDesigner.OnSetCursor Method

Called each time the cursor needs to be set.

```
[Visual Basic]
Protected Overridable Sub OnSetCursor()
[C#]
protected virtual void OnSetCursor();
[C++]
protected: virtual void OnSetCursor();
[JScript]
protected function OnSetCursor();
```

Remarks

This method handles redirection and handling of the set cursor event. If the toolbox service has a tool selected, this method will allow the toolbox service to set the cursor. If the selection UI service has a locked selection, or if there is no location property on the control, the default arrow cursor will be set. If a user is dragging a component, the crosshair cursor will be set. Otherwise, a four headed arrow cursor will be set to indicate that the component can be clicked and moved.

Requirements

Platforms: Windows 98, Windows NT 4.0, Windows Millennium Edition, Windows 2000, Windows XP Home Edition, Windows XP Professional, Windows Server 2003 family

.NET Framework Security:

- Full trust for the immediate caller. This member cannot be used by partially trusted code.

ControlDesigner.PreFilterProperties Method

Adjusts the set of properties the component exposes through a **TypeDescriptor**.

[Visual Basic]
```
Overrides Protected Sub PreFilterProperties( _
   ByVal properties As IDictionary _
)
```
[C#]
```
protected override void PreFilterProperties(
   IDictionary properties
);
```
[C++]
```
protected: void PreFilterProperties(
   IDictionary* properties
);
```
[JScript]
```
protected override function PreFilterProperties(
   properties : IDictionary
);
```

Parameters

properties

An **IDictionary** containing the properties for the class of the component.

Remarks

This **IDesignerFilter** interface method override adds a set of properties to this designer's component at design time. This method adds the following browsable properties: "Visible", "Enabled", "ContextMenu", "AllowDrop", "Location", "Name", "Controls", and "Locked".

Requirements

Platforms: Windows 98, Windows NT 4.0, Windows Millennium Edition, Windows 2000, Windows XP Home Edition, Windows XP Professional, Windows Server 2003 family

.NET Framework Security:

- Full trust for the immediate caller. This member cannot be used by partially trusted code.

ControlDesigner.UnhookChildControls Method

Routes messages for the children of the specified control to each control rather than to a parent designer.

[Visual Basic]
```
Protected Sub UnhookChildControls( _
   ByVal firstChild As Control _
)
```
[C#]
```
protected void UnhookChildControls(
   Control firstChild
);
```
[C++]
```
protected: void UnhookChildControls(
   Control* firstChild
);
```
[JScript]
```
protected function UnhookChildControls(
   firstChild : Control
);
```

Parameters

firstChild

The first child **Control** to process. This method may recursively call itself for children of the control.

Requirements

Platforms: Windows 98, Windows NT 4.0, Windows Millennium Edition, Windows 2000, Windows XP Home Edition, Windows XP Professional, Windows Server 2003 family

.NET Framework Security:

- Full trust for the immediate caller. This member cannot be used by partially trusted code.

ControlDesigner.WndProc Method

Processes Windows messages and optionally routes them to the control.

[Visual Basic]
```
Protected Overridable Sub WndProc( _
   ByRef m As Message _
)
```
[C#]
```
protected virtual void WndProc(
   ref Message m
);
```
[C++]
```
protected: virtual void WndProc(
   Message* m
);
```
[JScript]
```
protected function WndProc(
   m : Message
);
```

Parameters

m

The **Message** to process.

Remarks

This method is called for each message the control would normally receive. This allows the designer to preprocess messages before optionally routing them to the control.

To send the message to the control, call the **WndProc** method of the control and pass the **Message** as a parameter. Optionally, you can alter or create a new **Message** to pass to the control's method.

Requirements

Platforms: Windows 98, Windows NT 4.0, Windows Millennium Edition, Windows 2000, Windows XP Home Edition, Windows XP Professional, Windows Server 2003 family

.NET Framework Security:

- Full trust for the immediate caller. This member cannot be used by partially trusted code.

ControlDesigner.Control-DesignerAccessibleObject Class

Provides an **AccessibleObject** for **ControlDesigner**.

System.Object
  System.MarshalByRefObject
    System.Windows.Forms.AccessibleObject
      System.Windows.Forms.Design.ControlDesigner.Control-DesignerAccessibleObject

```
[Visual Basic]
<ComVisible(True)>
Public Class ControlDesigner.ControlDesignerAccessibleObject
   Inherits AccessibleObject
[C#]
[ComVisible(true)]
public class ControlDesigner.ControlDesignerAccessibleObject :
   AccessibleObject
[C++]
[ComVisible(true)]
public __gc class ControlDesigner.ControlDesignerAccessibleObject
   : public AccessibleObject
[JScript]
public
   ComVisible(true)
class ControlDesigner.ControlDesignerAccessibleObject
   extends AccessibleObject
```

Thread Safety

Any public static (**Shared** in Visual Basic) members of this type are safe for multithreaded operations. Any instance members are not guaranteed to be thread safe.

Requirements

Namespace: System.Windows.Forms.Design

Platforms: Windows 98, Windows NT 4.0, Windows Millennium Edition, Windows 2000, Windows XP Home Edition, Windows XP Professional, Windows Server 2003 family

Assembly: System.Design (in System.Design.dll)

ControlDesigner.ControlDesigner-AccessibleObject Constructor

Initializes a new instance of the **ControlDesigner.ControlDesignerAccessibleObject** class using the specified designer and control.

```
[Visual Basic]
Public Sub New( _
   ByVal designer As ControlDesigner, _
   ByVal control As Control _
)
[C#]
public ControlDesigner.ControlDesignerAccessibleObject(
   ControlDesigner designer,
   Control control
);
[C++]
public: ControlDesignerAccessibleObject(
   ControlDesigner* designer,
   Control* control
);
[JScript]
public function ControlDesigner.ControlDesignerAccessibleObject(
   designer : ControlDesigner,
   control : Control
);
```

Parameters

designer
    The **ControlDesigner** for the accessible object.

control
    The **Control** for the accessible object.

Requirements

Platforms: Windows 98, Windows NT 4.0, Windows Millennium Edition, Windows 2000, Windows XP Home Edition, Windows XP Professional, Windows Server 2003 family

.NET Framework Security:

- Full trust for the immediate caller. This member cannot be used by partially trusted code.

ControlDesigner.ControlDesignerAccessible-Object.Bounds Property

This member overrides **AccessibleObject.Bounds**.

```
[Visual Basic]
Overrides Public ReadOnly Property Bounds As Rectangle
[C#]
public override Rectangle Bounds {get;}
[C++]
public: __property Rectangle get_Bounds();
[JScript]
public override function get Bounds() : Rectangle;
```

Requirements

Platforms: Windows 98, Windows NT 4.0, Windows Millennium Edition, Windows 2000, Windows XP Home Edition, Windows XP Professional, Windows Server 2003 family

.NET Framework Security:

- Full trust for the immediate caller. This member cannot be used by partially trusted code.

ControlDesigner.ControlDesignerAccessible-Object.DefaultAction Property

This member overrides **AccessibleObject.DefaultAction**.

```
[Visual Basic]
Overrides Public ReadOnly Property DefaultAction As String
[C#]
public override string DefaultAction {get;}
[C++]
public: __property String* get_DefaultAction();
[JScript]
public override function get DefaultAction() : String;
```

Requirements

Platforms: Windows 98, Windows NT 4.0, Windows Millennium Edition, Windows 2000, Windows XP Home Edition, Windows XP Professional, Windows Server 2003 family

.NET Framework Security:

- Full trust for the immediate caller. This member cannot be used by partially trusted code.

ControlDesigner.ControlDesignerAccessibleObject.Description Property

This member overrides **AccessibleObject.Description**.

```
[Visual Basic]
Overrides Public ReadOnly Property Description As String
[C#]
public override string Description {get;}
[C++]
public: __property String* get_Description();
[JScript]
public override function get Description() : String;
```

Requirements

Platforms: Windows 98, Windows NT 4.0, Windows Millennium Edition, Windows 2000, Windows XP Home Edition, Windows XP Professional, Windows Server 2003 family

.NET Framework Security:

- Full trust for the immediate caller. This member cannot be used by partially trusted code.

ControlDesigner.ControlDesignerAccessibleObject.Name Property

This member overrides **AccessibleObject.Name**.

```
[Visual Basic]
Overrides Public ReadOnly Property Name As String
[C#]
public override string Name {get;}
[C++]
public: __property String* get_Name();
[JScript]
public override function get Name() : String;
```

Requirements

Platforms: Windows 98, Windows NT 4.0, Windows Millennium Edition, Windows 2000, Windows XP Home Edition, Windows XP Professional, Windows Server 2003 family

.NET Framework Security:

- Full trust for the immediate caller. This member cannot be used by partially trusted code.

ControlDesigner.ControlDesignerAccessibleObject.Parent Property

This member overrides **AccessibleObject.Parent**.

```
[Visual Basic]
Overrides Public ReadOnly Property Parent As AccessibleObject
[C#]
public override AccessibleObject Parent {get;}
[C++]
public: __property AccessibleObject* get_Parent();
[JScript]
public override function get Parent() : AccessibleObject;
```

Requirements

Platforms: Windows 98, Windows NT 4.0, Windows Millennium Edition, Windows 2000, Windows XP Home Edition, Windows XP Professional, Windows Server 2003 family

.NET Framework Security:

- Full trust for the immediate caller. This member cannot be used by partially trusted code.

ControlDesigner.ControlDesignerAccessibleObject.Role Property

This member overrides **AccessibleObject.Role**.

```
[Visual Basic]
Overrides Public ReadOnly Property Role As AccessibleRole
[C#]
public override AccessibleRole Role {get;}
[C++]
public: __property AccessibleRole get_Role();
[JScript]
public override function get Role() : AccessibleRole;
```

Requirements

Platforms: Windows 98, Windows NT 4.0, Windows Millennium Edition, Windows 2000, Windows XP Home Edition, Windows XP Professional, Windows Server 2003 family

.NET Framework Security:

- Full trust for the immediate caller. This member cannot be used by partially trusted code.

ControlDesigner.ControlDesignerAccessibleObject.State Property

This member overrides **AccessibleObject.State**.

```
[Visual Basic]
Overrides Public ReadOnly Property State As AccessibleStates
[C#]
public override AccessibleStates State {get;}
[C++]
public: __property AccessibleStates get_State();
[JScript]
public override function get State() : AccessibleStates;
```

Requirements

Platforms: Windows 98, Windows NT 4.0, Windows Millennium Edition, Windows 2000, Windows XP Home Edition, Windows XP Professional, Windows Server 2003 family

.NET Framework Security:

- Full trust for the immediate caller. This member cannot be used by partially trusted code.

ControlDesigner.ControlDesignerAccessibleObject.Value Property

This member overrides **AccessibleObject.Value**.

```
[Visual Basic]
Overrides Public ReadOnly Property Value As String
[C#]
public override string Value {get;}
[C++]
public: __property String* get_Value();
[JScript]
public override function get Value() : String;
```

Requirements

Platforms: Windows 98, Windows NT 4.0, Windows Millennium Edition, Windows 2000, Windows XP Home Edition, Windows XP Professional, Windows Server 2003 family

.NET Framework Security:

- Full trust for the immediate caller. This member cannot be used by partially trusted code.

ControlDesigner.ControlDesignerAccessibleObject.GetChild Method

This member overrides **AccessibleObject.GetChild**.

```
[Visual Basic]
Overrides Public Function GetChild( _
   ByVal index As Integer _
) As AccessibleObject
[C#]
public override AccessibleObject GetChild(
   int index
);
[C++]
public: AccessibleObject* GetChild(
   int index
);
[JScript]
public override function GetChild(
   index : int
) : AccessibleObject;
```

Requirements

Platforms: Windows 98, Windows NT 4.0, Windows Millennium Edition, Windows 2000, Windows XP Home Edition, Windows XP Professional, Windows Server 2003 family

.NET Framework Security:

- Full trust for the immediate caller. This member cannot be used by partially trusted code.

ControlDesigner.ControlDesignerAccessibleObject.GetChildCount Method

This member overrides **AccessibleObject.GetChildCount**.

```
[Visual Basic]
Overrides Public Function GetChildCount() As Integer
[C#]
public override int GetChildCount();
[C++]
public: int GetChildCount();
[JScript]
public override function GetChildCount() : int;
```

Requirements

Platforms: Windows 98, Windows NT 4.0, Windows Millennium Edition, Windows 2000, Windows XP Home Edition, Windows XP Professional, Windows Server 2003 family

.NET Framework Security:

- Full trust for the immediate caller. This member cannot be used by partially trusted code.

ControlDesigner.ControlDesignerAccessibleObject.GetFocused Method

This member overrides **AccessibleObject.GetFocused**.

```
[Visual Basic]
Overrides Public Function GetFocused() As AccessibleObject
[C#]
public override AccessibleObject GetFocused();
[C++]
public: AccessibleObject* GetFocused();
[JScript]
public override function GetFocused() : AccessibleObject;
```

Requirements

Platforms: Windows 98, Windows NT 4.0, Windows Millennium Edition, Windows 2000, Windows XP Home Edition, Windows XP Professional, Windows Server 2003 family

.NET Framework Security:

- Full trust for the immediate caller. This member cannot be used by partially trusted code.

ControlDesigner.ControlDesignerAccessibleObject.GetSelected Method

This member overrides **AccessibleObject.GetSelected**.

```
[Visual Basic]
Overrides Public Function GetSelected() As AccessibleObject
[C#]
public override AccessibleObject GetSelected();
[C++]
public: AccessibleObject* GetSelected();
[JScript]
public override function GetSelected() : AccessibleObject;
```

Requirements

Platforms: Windows 98, Windows NT 4.0, Windows Millennium Edition, Windows 2000, Windows XP Home Edition, Windows XP Professional, Windows Server 2003 family

.NET Framework Security:

- Full trust for the immediate caller. This member cannot be used by partially trusted code.

ControlDesigner.ControlDesignerAccessible-Object.HitTest Method

This member overrides **AccessibleObject.HitTest**.

[Visual Basic]
```
Overrides Public Function HitTest( _
   ByVal x As Integer, _
   ByVal y As Integer _
) As AccessibleObject
```
[C#]
```
public override AccessibleObject HitTest(
   int x,
   int y
);
```
[C++]
```
public: AccessibleObject* HitTest(
   int x,
   int y
);
```
[JScript]
```
public override function HitTest(
   x : int,
   y : int
) : AccessibleObject;
```

Requirements

Platforms: Windows 98, Windows NT 4.0, Windows Millennium Edition, Windows 2000, Windows XP Home Edition, Windows XP Professional, Windows Server 2003 family

.NET Framework Security:

- Full trust for the immediate caller. This member cannot be used by partially trusted code.

DockEditor Class

This type supports the .NET Framework infrastructure and is not intended to be used directly from your code.

[Visual Basic]
```
NotInheritable Public Class DockEditor
   Inherits UITypeEditor
```
[C#]
```
public sealed class DockEditor : UITypeEditor
```
[C++]
```
public __gc __sealed class DockEditor : public UITypeEditor
```
[JScript]
```
public class DockEditor extends UITypeEditor
```

DockEditor Constructor

This member supports the .NET Framework infrastructure and is not intended to be used directly from your code.

[Visual Basic]
```
Public Sub New()
```
[C#]
```
public DockEditor();
```
[C++]
```
public: DockEditor();
```
[JScript]
```
public function DockEditor();
```

DockEditor.EditValue Method

This member supports the .NET Framework infrastructure and is not intended to be used directly from your code.

Overload List

This member supports the .NET Framework infrastructure and is not intended to be used directly from your code.

[Visual Basic] **Overloads Overrides Public Function EditValue(ITypeDescriptorContext, IServiceProvider, Object) As Object**

[C#] **public override object EditValue(ITypeDescriptor-Context, IServiceProvider, object);**

[C++] **public: Object* EditValue(ITypeDescriptorContext*, IServiceProvider*, Object*);**

[JScript] **public override function EditValue(IType-DescriptorContext, IServiceProvider, Object) : Object;**

This member supports the .NET Framework infrastructure and is not intended to be used directly from your code.

[Visual Basic] **Overloads Public Function EditValue(IServiceProvider, Object) As Object**

[C#] **public object EditValue(IServiceProvider, object);**

[C++] **public: Object* EditValue(IServiceProvider*, Object*);**

[JScript] **public function EditValue(IServiceProvider, Object) : Object;**

DockEditor.EditValue Method (ITypeDescriptorContext, IServiceProvider, Object)

This member supports the .NET Framework infrastructure and is not intended to be used directly from your code.

[Visual Basic]
```
Overrides Overloads Public Function EditValue( _
   ByVal context As ITypeDescriptorContext, _
   ByVal provider As IServiceProvider, _
   ByVal value As Object _
) As Object
```
[C#]
```
public override object EditValue(
   ITypeDescriptorContext context,
   IServiceProvider provider,
   object value
);
```
[C++]
```
public: Object* EditValue(
   ITypeDescriptorContext* context,
   IServiceProvider* provider,
   Object* value
);
```
[JScript]
```
public override function EditValue(
   context : ITypeDescriptorContext,
   provider : IServiceProvider,
   value : Object
) : Object;
```

DockEditor.GetEditStyle Method

This member supports the .NET Framework infrastructure and is not intended to be used directly from your code.

Overload List

This member supports the .NET Framework infrastructure and is not intended to be used directly from your code.

[Visual Basic] **Overloads Overrides Public Function GetEdit-Style(ITypeDescriptorContext) As UITypeEditorEditStyle**

[C#] **public override UITypeEditorEditStyle GetEdit-Style(ITypeDescriptorContext);**

[C++] **public: UITypeEditorEditStyle GetEdit-Style(ITypeDescriptorContext*);**

[JScript] **public override function GetEdit-Style(ITypeDescriptorContext) : UITypeEditorEditStyle;**

This member supports the .NET Framework infrastructure and is not intended to be used directly from your code.

[Visual Basic] **Overloads Public Function GetEditStyle() As UITypeEditorEditStyle**

[C#] **public UITypeEditorEditStyle GetEditStyle();**

[C++] **public: UITypeEditorEditStyle GetEditStyle();**

[JScript] **public function GetEditStyle() : UITypeEditorEditStyle;**

DockEditor.GetEditStyle Method (ITypeDescriptorContext)

This member supports the .NET Framework infrastructure and is not intended to be used directly from your code.

[Visual Basic]
```
Overrides Overloads Public Function GetEditStyle( _
   ByVal context As ITypeDescriptorContext _
) As UITypeEditorEditStyle
```
[C#]
```
public override UITypeEditorEditStyle GetEditStyle(
   ITypeDescriptorContext context
);
```
[C++]
```
public: UITypeEditorEditStyle GetEditStyle(
   ITypeDescriptorContext* context
);
```
[JScript]
```
public override function GetEditStyle(
   context : ITypeDescriptorContext
) : UITypeEditorEditStyle;
```

DocumentDesigner Class

Base designer class for extending the design mode behavior of, and providing a root-level design mode view for, a **Control** that supports nested controls and should receive scroll messages.

System.Object
System.ComponentModel.Design.ComponentDesigner
System.Windows.Forms.Design.ControlDesigner
System.Windows.Forms.Design.ParentControlDesigner
System.Windows.Forms.Design.ScrollableControl-Designer
System.Windows.Forms.Design.DocumentDesigner

```
[Visual Basic]
Public Class DocumentDesigner
   Inherits ScrollableControlDesigner
   Implements IRootDesigner, IToolboxUser
[C#]
public class DocumentDesigner : ScrollableControlDesigner,
   IRootDesigner, IToolboxUser
[C++]
public __gc class DocumentDesigner : public
   ScrollableControlDesigner, IRootDesigner, IToolboxUser
[JScript]
public class DocumentDesigner extends ScrollableControlDesigner
   implements IRootDesigner, IToolboxUser
```

Thread Safety

Any public static (**Shared** in Visual Basic) members of this type are safe for multithreaded operations. Any instance members are not guaranteed to be thread safe.

Remarks

This designer is a root designer, meaning that it provides the root-level design mode view for the associated document when it is viewed in design mode.

You can associate a designer with a type using a **DesignerAttribute**. For an overview of customizing design time behavior, see **Enhancing Design-Time Support**.

Requirements

Namespace: System.Windows.Forms.Design

Platforms: Windows 98, Windows NT 4.0, Windows Millennium Edition, Windows 2000, Windows XP Home Edition, Windows XP Professional, Windows Server 2003 family

Assembly: System.Design (in System.Design.dll)

DocumentDesigner Constructor

Initializes a new instance of the **DocumentDesigner** class.

```
[Visual Basic]
Public Sub New()
[C#]
public DocumentDesigner();
[C++]
public: DocumentDesigner();
[JScript]
public function DocumentDesigner();
```

Remarks

The default constructor initializes any fields to their default values.

Requirements

Platforms: Windows 98, Windows NT 4.0, Windows Millennium Edition, Windows 2000, Windows XP Home Edition, Windows XP Professional, Windows Server 2003 family

.NET Framework Security:

- Full trust for the immediate caller. This member cannot be used by partially trusted code.

DocumentDesigner.menuEditorService Field

This member supports the .NET Framework infrastructure and is not intended to be used directly from your code.

```
[Visual Basic]
Protected menuEditorService As IMenuEditorService
[C#]
protected IMenuEditorService menuEditorService;
[C++]
protected: IMenuEditorService* menuEditorService;
[JScript]
protected var menuEditorService : IMenuEditorService;
```

DocumentDesigner.SelectionRules Property

Gets the **SelectionRules** for the designer.

```
[Visual Basic]
Overrides Public ReadOnly Property SelectionRules As SelectionRules
[C#]
public override SelectionRules SelectionRules {get;}
[C++]
public: __property SelectionRules get_SelectionRules();
[JScript]
public override function get SelectionRules() : SelectionRules;
```

Property Value

A bitwise combination of **SelectionRules** values.

Remarks

This method returns a **SelectionRules** that prevents the document from being resized.

Requirements

Platforms: Windows 98, Windows NT 4.0, Windows Millennium Edition, Windows 2000, Windows XP Home Edition, Windows XP Professional, Windows Server 2003 family

.NET Framework Security:

- Full trust for the immediate caller. This member cannot be used by partially trusted code.

DocumentDesigner.Dispose Method

Releases the unmanaged resources used by the **DocumentDesigner** and optionally releases the managed resources.

Overload List

Releases the unmanaged resources used by the **DocumentDesigner** and optionally releases the managed resources.

[Visual Basic] **Overloads Overrides Protected Sub Dispose(Boolean)**

[C#] **protected override void Dispose(bool);**

[C++] **protected: void Dispose(bool);**

[JScript] **protected override function Dispose(Boolean);**

Inherited from **ComponentDesigner**.

[Visual Basic] **Overloads Public Overridable Sub Dispose() Implements IDisposable.Dispose**

[C#] **public virtual void Dispose();**

[C++] **public: virtual void Dispose();**

[JScript] **public function Dispose();**

DocumentDesigner.Dispose Method (Boolean)

Releases the unmanaged resources used by the **DocumentDesigner** and optionally releases the managed resources.

```
[Visual Basic]
Overrides Overloads Protected Sub Dispose( _
   ByVal disposing As Boolean _
)
[C#]
protected override void Dispose(
   bool disposing
);
[C++]
protected: void Dispose(
   bool disposing
);
[JScript]
protected override function Dispose(
   disposing : Boolean
);
```

Parameters

disposing

true to release both managed and unmanaged resources; **false** to release only unmanaged resources.

Remarks

This method is called by the public **Dispose()** method and the **Finalize** method. **Dispose()** invokes the protected **Dispose(Boolean)** method with the *disposing* parameter set to **true**. **Finalize** invokes **Dispose** with *disposing* set to **false**.

When the *disposing* parameter is **true**, this method releases all resources held by any managed objects that this **DocumentDesigner** references. This method invokes the **Dispose()** method of each referenced object.

Notes to Inheritors: **Dispose** can be called multiple times by other objects. When overriding **Dispose(Boolean)**, be careful not to reference objects that have been previously disposed in an earlier call to **Dispose**.

Requirements

Platforms: Windows 98, Windows NT 4.0, Windows Millennium Edition, Windows 2000, Windows XP Home Edition, Windows XP Professional, Windows Server 2003 family

.NET Framework Security:

- Full trust for the immediate caller. This member cannot be used by partially trusted code.

DocumentDesigner.EnsureMenuEditorService Method

Checks for the existence of a menu editor service and creates one if one does not already exist.

```
[Visual Basic]
Protected Overridable Sub EnsureMenuEditorService( _
   ByVal c As IComponent _
)
[C#]
protected virtual void EnsureMenuEditorService(
   IComponent c
);
[C++]
protected: virtual void EnsureMenuEditorService(
   IComponent* c
);
[JScript]
protected function EnsureMenuEditorService(
   c : IComponent
);
```

Parameters

c

The **IComponent** to ensure has a context menu service.

Requirements

Platforms: Windows 98, Windows NT 4.0, Windows Millennium Edition, Windows 2000, Windows XP Home Edition, Windows XP Professional, Windows Server 2003 family

.NET Framework Security:

- Full trust for the immediate caller. This member cannot be used by partially trusted code.

DocumentDesigner.GetToolSupported Method

Indicates whether the specified tool is supported by the designer.

```
[Visual Basic]
Protected Overridable Function GetToolSupported( _
   ByVal tool As ToolboxItem _
) As Boolean
[C#]
protected virtual bool GetToolSupported(
   ToolboxItem tool
);
[C++]
protected: virtual bool GetToolSupported(
   ToolboxItem* tool
);
```

```
[JScript]
protected function GetToolSupported(
   tool : ToolboxItem
) : Boolean;
```

Parameters

tool

The **ToolboxItem** to test for toolbox support.

Return Value

true if the tool should be enabled on the toolbox; **false** if the document designer doesn't know how to use the tool.

Remarks

If a tool is supported, it will be enabled in the toolbox when the designer receives focus. Otherwise, it will be disabled. Once a tool is marked as enabled or disabled it can not be queried again.

Requirements

Platforms: Windows 98, Windows NT 4.0, Windows Millennium Edition, Windows 2000, Windows XP Home Edition, Windows XP Professional, Windows Server 2003 family

.NET Framework Security:

- Full trust for the immediate caller. This member cannot be used by partially trusted code.

DocumentDesigner.Initialize Method

Initializes the designer with the specified component.

```
[Visual Basic]
Overrides Public Sub Initialize( _
   ByVal component As IComponent _
) Implements IDesigner.Initialize
[C#]
public override void Initialize(
   IComponent component
);
[C++]
public: void Initialize(
   IComponent* component
);
[JScript]
public override function Initialize(
   component : IComponent
);
```

Parameters

component

The **IComponent** to associate with the designer.

Implements

IDesigner.Initialize

Remarks

Notes to Inheritors: The designer can access the component's site and request services from it in this method.

Requirements

Platforms: Windows 98, Windows NT 4.0, Windows Millennium Edition, Windows 2000, Windows XP Home Edition, Windows XP Professional, Windows Server 2003 family

.NET Framework Security:

- Full trust for the immediate caller. This member cannot be used by partially trusted code.

DocumentDesigner.IRootDesigner.GetView Method

This member supports the .NET Framework infrastructure and is not intended to be used directly from your code.

```
[Visual Basic]
Private Function GetView( _
   ByVal technology As ViewTechnology _
) As Object Implements IRootDesigner.GetView
[C#]
object IRootDesigner.GetView(
   ViewTechnology technology
);
[C++]
private: Object* IRootDesigner::GetView(
   ViewTechnology technology
);
[JScript]
private function IRootDesigner.GetView(
   technology : ViewTechnology
) : Object;
```

DocumentDesigner.IToolboxUser.GetToolSupported Method

This member supports the .NET Framework infrastructure and is not intended to be used directly from your code.

```
[Visual Basic]
Private Function GetToolSupported( _
   ByVal tool As ToolboxItem _
) As Boolean Implements IToolboxUser.GetToolSupported
[C#]
bool IToolboxUser.GetToolSupported(
   ToolboxItem tool
);
[C++]
private: bool IToolboxUser::GetToolSupported(
   ToolboxItem* tool
);
[JScript]
private function IToolboxUser.GetToolSupported(
   tool : ToolboxItem
) : Boolean;
```

DocumentDesigner.IToolboxUser.ToolPicked Method

This member supports the .NET Framework infrastructure and is not intended to be used directly from your code.

```
[Visual Basic]
Private Sub ToolPicked( _
   ByVal tool As ToolboxItem _
) Implements IToolboxUser.ToolPicked
```

[C#]
```
void IToolboxUser.ToolPicked(
   ToolboxItem tool
);
```
[C++]
```
private: void IToolboxUser::ToolPicked(
   ToolboxItem* tool
);
```
[JScript]
```
private function IToolboxUser.ToolPicked(
   tool : ToolboxItem
);
```

DocumentDesigner.OnContextMenu Method

Called when the context menu should be displayed.

[Visual Basic]
```
Overrides Protected Sub OnContextMenu( _
   ByVal x As Integer, _
   ByVal y As Integer _
)
```
[C#]
```
protected override void OnContextMenu(
   int x,
   int y
);
```
[C++]
```
protected: void OnContextMenu(
   int x,
   int y
);
```
[JScript]
```
protected override function OnContextMenu(
   x : int,
   y : int
);
```

Parameters

x

The horizontal screen coordinate to display the context menu at.

y

The vertical screen coordinate to display the context menu at.

Remarks

This method displays the context menu of the document designer.

Requirements

Platforms: Windows 98, Windows NT 4.0, Windows Millennium Edition, Windows 2000, Windows XP Home Edition, Windows XP Professional, Windows Server 2003 family

.NET Framework Security:

- Full trust for the immediate caller. This member cannot be used by partially trusted code.

DocumentDesigner.OnCreateHandle Method

Called immediately after the handle for the designer has been created.

[Visual Basic]
```
Overrides Protected Sub OnCreateHandle()
```
[C#]
```
protected override void OnCreateHandle();
```
[C++]
```
protected: void OnCreateHandle();
```
[JScript]
```
protected override function OnCreateHandle();
```

Requirements

Platforms: Windows 98, Windows NT 4.0, Windows Millennium Edition, Windows 2000, Windows XP Home Edition, Windows XP Professional, Windows Server 2003 family

.NET Framework Security:

- Full trust for the immediate caller. This member cannot be used by partially trusted code.

DocumentDesigner.PreFilterProperties Method

Adjusts the set of properties the component exposes through a **TypeDescriptor**.

[Visual Basic]
```
Overrides Protected Sub PreFilterProperties( _
   ByVal properties As IDictionary _
)
```
[C#]
```
protected override void PreFilterProperties(
   IDictionary properties
);
```
[C++]
```
protected: void PreFilterProperties(
   IDictionary* properties
);
```
[JScript]
```
protected override function PreFilterProperties(
   properties : IDictionary
);
```

Parameters

properties

An **IDictionary** that contains the properties for the class of the component.

Remarks

This **IDesignerFilter** interface method override adds a set of properties to this designer's component at design time. This method adds the following browsable properties: "Location", and "BackColor".

Requirements

Platforms: Windows 98, Windows NT 4.0, Windows Millennium Edition, Windows 2000, Windows XP Home Edition, Windows XP Professional, Windows Server 2003 family

.NET Framework Security:

- Full trust for the immediate caller. This member cannot be used by partially trusted code.

DocumentDesigner.ToolPicked Method

Handles the behavior that occurs when a user double-clicks a toolbox item.

[Visual Basic]
```
Protected Overridable Sub ToolPicked( _
   ByVal tool As ToolboxItem _
)
```
[C#]
```
protected virtual void ToolPicked(
   ToolboxItem tool
);
```
[C++]
```
protected: virtual void ToolPicked(
   ToolboxItem* tool
);
```
[JScript]
```
protected function ToolPicked(
   tool : ToolboxItem
);
```

Parameters

tool
The **ToolboxItem** to create a component for.

Remarks

This method creates a component for the specified tool.

Requirements

Platforms: Windows 98, Windows NT 4.0, Windows Millennium Edition, Windows 2000, Windows XP Home Edition, Windows XP Professional, Windows Server 2003 family

.NET Framework Security:

- Full trust for the immediate caller. This member cannot be used by partially trusted code.

DocumentDesigner.WndProc Method

Processes Windows messages.

[Visual Basic]
```
Overrides Protected Sub WndProc( _
   ByRef m As Message _
)
```
[C#]
```
protected override void WndProc(
   ref Message m
);
```
[C++]
```
protected: void WndProc(
   Message* m
);
```
[JScript]
```
protected override function WndProc(
   m : Message
);
```

Parameters

m
The **Message** to process.

Requirements

Platforms: Windows 98, Windows NT 4.0, Windows Millennium Edition, Windows 2000, Windows XP Home Edition, Windows XP Professional, Windows Server 2003 family

.NET Framework Security:

- Full trust for the immediate caller. This member cannot be used by partially trusted code.

EventHandlerService Class

This type supports the .NET Framework infrastructure and is not intended to be used directly from your code.

[Visual Basic]
```
NotInheritable Public Class EventHandlerService
```
[C#]
```
public sealed class EventHandlerService
```
[C++]
```
public __gc __sealed class EventHandlerService
```
[JScript]
```
public class EventHandlerService
```

EventHandlerService Constructor

This member supports the .NET Framework infrastructure and is not intended to be used directly from your code.

[Visual Basic]
```
Public Sub New( _
   ByVal focusWnd As Control _
)
```
[C#]
```
public EventHandlerService(
   Control focusWnd
);
```
[C++]
```
public: EventHandlerService(
   Control* focusWnd
);
```
[JScript]
```
public function EventHandlerService(
   focusWnd : Control
);
```

EventHandlerService.FocusWindow Property

This member supports the .NET Framework infrastructure and is not intended to be used directly from your code.

[Visual Basic]
```
Public Overridable ReadOnly Property FocusWindow As Control
```
[C#]
```
public virtual Control FocusWindow {get;}
```
[C++]
```
public: __property virtual Control* get_FocusWindow();
```
[JScript]
```
public function get FocusWindow() : Control;
```

EventHandlerService.GetHandler Method

This member supports the .NET Framework infrastructure and is not intended to be used directly from your code.

[Visual Basic]
```
Public Overridable Function GetHandler( _
   ByVal handlerType As Type _
) As Object
```
[C#]
```
public virtual object GetHandler(
   Type handlerType
);
```
[C++]
```
public: virtual Object* GetHandler(
   Type* handlerType
);
```
[JScript]
```
public function GetHandler(
   handlerType : Type
) : Object;
```

EventHandlerService.PopHandler Method

This member supports the .NET Framework infrastructure and is not intended to be used directly from your code.

[Visual Basic]
```
Public Overridable Sub PopHandler( _
   ByVal handler As Object _
)
```
[C#]
```
public virtual void PopHandler(
   object handler
);
```
[C++]
```
public: virtual void PopHandler(
   Object* handler
);
```
[JScript]
```
public function PopHandler(
   handler : Object
);
```

EventHandlerService.PushHandler Method

This member supports the .NET Framework infrastructure and is not intended to be used directly from your code.

[Visual Basic]
```
Public Overridable Sub PushHandler( _
   ByVal handler As Object _
)
```
[C#]
```
public virtual void PushHandler(
   object handler
);
```
[C++]
```
public: virtual void PushHandler(
   Object* handler
);
```
[JScript]
```
public function PushHandler(
   handler : Object
);
```

EventHandlerService.EventHandlerChanged Event

This member supports the .NET Framework infrastructure and is not intended to be used directly from your code.

[Visual Basic]
```
Public Overridable Event EventHandlerChanged As EventHandler
```
[C#]
```
public virtual event EventHandler EventHandlerChanged;
```
[C++]
```
public: virtual __event EventHandler* EventHandlerChanged;
```
[JScript] In JScript, you can handle the events defined by a class, but you cannot define your own.

EventsTab Class

Provides a **PropertyTab** that can display events for selection and linking.

System.Object
  System.Windows.Forms.Design.PropertyTab
    System.Windows.Forms.Design.EventsTab

[Visual Basic]
```
Public Class EventsTab
   Inherits PropertyTab
```
[C#]
```
public class EventsTab : PropertyTab
```
[C++]
```
public __gc class EventsTab : public PropertyTab
```
[JScript]
```
public class EventsTab extends PropertyTab
```

Thread Safety

Any public static (**Shared** in Visual Basic) members of this type are safe for multithreaded operations. Any instance members are not guaranteed to be thread safe.

Requirements

Namespace: System.Windows.Forms.Design

Platforms: Windows 98, Windows NT 4.0, Windows Millennium Edition, Windows 2000, Windows XP Home Edition, Windows XP Professional, Windows Server 2003 family

Assembly: System.Windows.Forms (in System.Windows.Forms.dll)

EventsTab Constructor

Initializes a new instance of the **EventsTab** class.

[Visual Basic]
```
Public Sub New( _
   ByVal sp As IServiceProvider _
)
```
[C#]
```
public EventsTab(
   IServiceProvider sp
);
```
[C++]
```
public: EventsTab(
   IServiceProvider* sp
);
```
[JScript]
```
public function EventsTab(
   sp : IServiceProvider
);
```

Parameters

sp
  An **IServiceProvider** to use.

Requirements

Platforms: Windows 98, Windows NT 4.0, Windows Millennium Edition, Windows 2000, Windows XP Home Edition, Windows XP Professional, Windows Server 2003 family

EventsTab.HelpKeyword Property

Gets the Help keyword for the tab.

[Visual Basic]
```
Overrides Public ReadOnly Property HelpKeyword As String
```
[C#]
```
public override string HelpKeyword {get;}
```
[C++]
```
public: __property String* get_HelpKeyword();
```
[JScript]
```
public override function get HelpKeyword() : String;
```

Property Value

The Help keyword for the tab.

Requirements

Platforms: Windows 98, Windows NT 4.0, Windows Millennium Edition, Windows 2000, Windows XP Home Edition, Windows XP Professional, Windows Server 2003 family

EventsTab.TabName Property

Gets the name of the tab.

[Visual Basic]
```
Overrides Public ReadOnly Property TabName As String
```
[C#]
```
public override string TabName {get;}
```
[C++]
```
public: __property String* get_TabName();
```
[JScript]
```
public override function get TabName() : String;
```

Property Value

The name of the tab.

Requirements

Platforms: Windows 98, Windows NT 4.0, Windows Millennium Edition, Windows 2000, Windows XP Home Edition, Windows XP Professional, Windows Server 2003 family

EventsTab.CanExtend Method

Gets a value indicating whether the specified object can be extended.

[Visual Basic]
```
Overrides Public Function CanExtend( _
   ByVal extendee As Object _
) As Boolean Implements IExtenderProvider.CanExtend
```
[C#]
```
public override bool CanExtend(
   object extendee
);
```
[C++]
```
public: bool CanExtend(
   Object* extendee
);
```
[JScript]
```
public override function CanExtend(
   extendee : Object
) : Boolean;
```

Parameters

extendee

The object to test for extensibility.

Return Value

true if the specified object can be extended; otherwise, **false**.

Implements

IExtenderProvider.CanExtend

Requirements

Platforms: Windows 98, Windows NT 4.0, Windows Millennium Edition, Windows 2000, Windows XP Home Edition, Windows XP Professional, Windows Server 2003 family

EventsTab.GetDefaultProperty Method

Gets the default property from the specified object.

```
[Visual Basic]
Overrides Public Function GetDefaultProperty( _
   ByVal obj As Object _
) As PropertyDescriptor
[C#]
public override PropertyDescriptor GetDefaultProperty(
   object obj
);
[C++]
public: PropertyDescriptor* GetDefaultProperty(
   Object* obj
);
[JScript]
public override function GetDefaultProperty(
   obj : Object
) : PropertyDescriptor;
```

Parameters

obj

The object to retrieve the default property of.

Return Value

A **PropertyDescriptor** indicating the default property.

Requirements

Platforms: Windows 98, Windows NT 4.0, Windows Millennium Edition, Windows 2000, Windows XP Home Edition, Windows XP Professional, Windows Server 2003 family

EventsTab.GetProperties Method

Gets all the properties of the event tab.

Overload List

Gets all the properties of the event tab that match the specified attributes.

[Visual Basic] **Overloads Overrides Public Function GetProperties(Object, Attribute()) As PropertyDescriptorCollection**

[C#] **public override PropertyDescriptorCollection GetProperties(object, Attribute[]);**

[C++] **public: PropertyDescriptorCollection* GetProperties(Object*, Attribute[]);**

[JScript] **public override function GetProperties(Object, Attribute[]) : PropertyDescriptorCollection;**

Gets all the properties of the event tab that match the specified attributes and context.

[Visual Basic] **Overloads Overrides Public Function GetProperties(ITypeDescriptorContext, Object, Attribute()) As PropertyDescriptorCollection**

[C#] **public override PropertyDescriptorCollection GetProperties(ITypeDescriptorContext, object, Attribute[]);**

[C++] **public: PropertyDescriptorCollection* GetProperties(ITypeDescriptorContext*, Object*, Attribute[]);**

[JScript] **public override function GetProperties(ITypeDescriptorContext, Object, Attribute[]) : PropertyDescriptorCollection;**

Inherited from **PropertyTab**.

[Visual Basic] **Overloads Public Overridable Function GetProperties(Object) As PropertyDescriptorCollection**

[C#] **public virtual PropertyDescriptorCollection GetProperties(object);**

[C++] **public: virtual PropertyDescriptorCollection* GetProperties(Object*);**

[JScript] **public function GetProperties(Object) : PropertyDescriptorCollection;**

EventsTab.GetProperties Method (Object, Attribute[])

Gets all the properties of the event tab that match the specified attributes.

```
[Visual Basic]
Overrides Overloads Public Function GetProperties( _
   ByVal component As Object, _
   ByVal attributes() As Attribute _
) As PropertyDescriptorCollection
[C#]
public override PropertyDescriptorCollection GetProperties(
   object component,
   Attribute[] attributes
);
[C++]
public: PropertyDescriptorCollection* GetProperties(
   Object* component,
   Attribute* attributes[]
);
[JScript]
public override function GetProperties(
   component : Object,
   attributes : Attribute[]
) : PropertyDescriptorCollection;
```

Parameters

component

The component to retrieve the properties of.

attributes

An array of **Attribute** that indicates the attributes of the event properties to retrieve.

Return Value

A **PropertyDescriptorCollection** that contains the properties. This will be an empty **PropertyDescriptorCollection** if the component does not implement an event service.

Remarks

The event tab properties are determined from the event properties returned from a component's event service.

Requirements

Platforms: Windows 98, Windows NT 4.0,
Windows Millennium Edition, Windows 2000,
Windows XP Home Edition, Windows XP Professional,
Windows Server 2003 family

EventsTab.GetProperties Method (ITypeDescriptorContext, Object, Attribute[])

Gets all the properties of the event tab that match the specified attributes and context.

[Visual Basic]
```
Overrides Overloads Public Function GetProperties( _
   ByVal context As ITypeDescriptorContext, _
   ByVal component As Object, _
   ByVal attributes() As Attribute _
) As PropertyDescriptorCollection
```
[C#]
```
public override PropertyDescriptorCollection GetProperties(
   ITypeDescriptorContext context,
   object component,
   Attribute[] attributes
);
```
[C++]
```
public: PropertyDescriptorCollection* GetProperties(
   ITypeDescriptorContext* context,
   Object* component,
   Attribute* attributes[]
);
```
[JScript]
```
public override function GetProperties(
   context : ITypeDescriptorContext,
   component : Object,
   attributes : Attribute[]
) : PropertyDescriptorCollection;
```

Parameters

context
  An **ITypeDescriptorContext** that can be used to gain context information.

component
  The component to retrieve the properties of.

attributes
  An array of type **Attribute** that indicates the attributes of the event properties to retrieve.

Return Value

A **PropertyDescriptorCollection** that contains the properties. This will be an empty **PropertyDescriptorCollection** if the component does not implement an event service.

Requirements

Platforms: Windows 98, Windows NT 4.0,
Windows Millennium Edition, Windows 2000,
Windows XP Home Edition, Windows XP Professional,
Windows Server 2003 family

FileNameEditor Class

Provides a user interface for selecting a file name.

System.Object
  System.Drawing.Design.UITypeEditor
    System.Windows.Forms.Design.FileNameEditor

[Visual Basic]
```
Public Class FileNameEditor
   Inherits UITypeEditor
```
[C#]
```
public class FileNameEditor : UITypeEditor
```
[C++]
```
public __gc class FileNameEditor : public UITypeEditor
```
[JScript]
```
public class FileNameEditor extends UITypeEditor
```

Thread Safety

Any public static (**Shared** in Visual Basic) members of this type are safe for multithreaded operations. Any instance members are not guaranteed to be thread safe.

Remarks

FileNameEditor provides a file selection dialog box for file name selection and editing.

Notes to Inheritors: You may inherit from this class to provide your own title for the dialog and your own file list filter extensions.

Example

[Visual Basic]
```
<EditorAttribute(GetType                                              ↵
(System.Windows.Forms.Design.FileNameEditor),                         ↵
GetType(System.Drawing.Design.UITypeEditor))> _
Public Property testFilename() As String
   Get
      Return filename
   End Get
   Set
      filename = value
   End Set
End Property
Private filename As String
```

[C#]
```
[EditorAttribute(typeof                                               ↵
 (System.Windows.Forms.Design.FileNameEditor),                        ↵
typeof(System.Drawing.Design.UITypeEditor))]
public string testFilename
{
    get
    {
        return filename;
    }
    set
    {
        filename = value;
    }
}
private string filename;
```

[C++]
```
public:
    [EditorAttribute(__typeof                                         ↵
 (System::Windows::Forms::Design::FileNameEditor),
        __typeof(System::Drawing::Design::UITypeEditor))]
    __property String* get_testFilename() {
        return filename;
    }
    [EditorAttribute(__typeof                                         ↵
 (System::Windows::Forms::Design::FileNameEditor),
        __typeof(System::Drawing::Design::UITypeEditor))]
    __property void set_testFilename(String* value) {
        filename = value;
    }
private:
    String*  filename;
```

Requirements

Namespace: System.Windows.Forms.Design

Platforms: Windows 98, Windows NT 4.0, Windows Millennium Edition, Windows 2000, Windows XP Home Edition, Windows XP Professional, Windows Server 2003 family

Assembly: System.Design (in System.Design.dll)

FileNameEditor Constructor

Initializes a new instance of the **FileNameEditor** class.

[Visual Basic]
```
Public Sub New()
```
[C#]
```
public FileNameEditor();
```
[C++]
```
public: FileNameEditor();
```
[JScript]
```
public function FileNameEditor();
```

Remarks

The default constructor initializes any fields to their default values.

Requirements

Platforms: Windows 98, Windows NT 4.0, Windows Millennium Edition, Windows 2000, Windows XP Home Edition, Windows XP Professional, Windows Server 2003 family

.NET Framework Security:

- Full trust for the immediate caller. This member cannot be used by partially trusted code.

FileNameEditor.EditValue Method

Edits the specified object using the editor style provided by the **GetEditStyle** method.

Overload List

Edits the specified object using the editor style provided by the **GetEditStyle** method.

[Visual Basic] **Overloads Overrides Public Function EditValue(ITypeDescriptorContext, IServiceProvider, Object) As Object**

[C#] **public override object EditValue(ITypeDescriptor-Context, IServiceProvider, object);**

[C++] **public: Object* EditValue(ITypeDescriptorContext*, IServiceProvider*, Object*);**

[JScript] **public override function EditValue(IType-DescriptorContext, IServiceProvider, Object) : Object;**

Inherited from **UITypeEditor**.

[Visual Basic] **Overloads Public Function EditValue(IServiceProvider, Object) As Object**

[C#] **public object EditValue(IServiceProvider, object);**

[C++] **public: Object* EditValue(IServiceProvider*, Object*);**

[JScript] **public function EditValue(IServiceProvider, Object) : Object;**

FileNameEditor.EditValue Method (ITypeDescriptorContext, IServiceProvider, Object)

Edits the specified object using the editor style provided by the **GetEditStyle** method.

```
[Visual Basic]
Overrides Overloads Public Function EditValue( _
   ByVal context As ITypeDescriptorContext, _
   ByVal provider As IServiceProvider, _
   ByVal value As Object _
) As Object
[C#]
public override object EditValue(
   ITypeDescriptorContext context,
   IServiceProvider provider,
   object value
);
[C++]
public: Object* EditValue(
   ITypeDescriptorContext* context,
   IServiceProvider* provider,
   Object* value
);
[JScript]
public override function EditValue(
   context : ITypeDescriptorContext,
   provider : IServiceProvider,
   value : Object
) : Object;
```

Parameters

context
An **ITypeDescriptorContext** that can be used to gain additional context information.

provider
A service provider object through which editing services may be obtained.

value
An instance of the value being edited.

Return Value

The new value of the object. If the value of the object hasn't changed, this should return the same object it was passed.

Remarks

A service provider is provided so that any required editing services can be obtained.

Requirements

Platforms: Windows 98, Windows NT 4.0, Windows Millennium Edition, Windows 2000, Windows XP Home Edition, Windows XP Professional, Windows Server 2003 family

.NET Framework Security:

- Full trust for the immediate caller. This member cannot be used by partially trusted code.

FileNameEditor.GetEditStyle Method

Gets the editing style used by the **EditValue** method.

Overload List

Gets the editing style used by the **EditValue** method.

[Visual Basic] **Overloads Overrides Public Function GetEditStyle(ITypeDescriptorContext) As UITypeEditorEditStyle**

[C#] **public override UITypeEditorEditStyle GetEditStyle(ITypeDescriptorContext);**

[C++] **public: UITypeEditorEditStyle GetEditStyle(ITypeDescriptorContext*);**

[JScript] **public override function GetEditStyle(ITypeDescriptorContext) : UITypeEditorEditStyle;**

Inherited from **UITypeEditor**.

[Visual Basic] **Overloads Public Function GetEditStyle() As UITypeEditorEditStyle**

[C#] **public UITypeEditorEditStyle GetEditStyle();**

[C++] **public: UITypeEditorEditStyle GetEditStyle();**

[JScript] **public function GetEditStyle() : UITypeEditorEditStyle;**

FileNameEditor.GetEditStyle Method (ITypeDescriptorContext)

Gets the editing style used by the **EditValue** method.

```
[Visual Basic]
Overrides Overloads Public Function GetEditStyle( _
   ByVal context As ITypeDescriptorContext _
) As UITypeEditorEditStyle
[C#]
public override UITypeEditorEditStyle GetEditStyle(
   ITypeDescriptorContext context
);
[C++]
public: UITypeEditorEditStyle GetEditStyle(
   ITypeDescriptorContext* context
);
[JScript]
public override function GetEditStyle(
   context : ITypeDescriptorContext
) : UITypeEditorEditStyle;
```

Parameters

context
An **ITypeDescriptorContext** that can be used to gain additional context information.

Return Value

One of the **UITypeEditorEditStyle** values indicating the provided editing style.

Remarks

If the **EditValue** method is not supported, this method will return **None**.

Requirements

Platforms: Windows 98, Windows NT 4.0,
Windows Millennium Edition, Windows 2000,
Windows XP Home Edition, Windows XP Professional,
Windows Server 2003 family

.NET Framework Security:

- Full trust for the immediate caller. This member cannot be used by partially trusted code.

FileNameEditor.InitializeDialog Method

Initializes the open file dialog when it is created.

[Visual Basic]
```
Protected Overridable Sub InitializeDialog( _
   ByVal openFileDialog As OpenFileDialog _
)
```
[C#]
```
protected virtual void InitializeDialog(
   OpenFileDialog openFileDialog
);
```
[C++]
```
protected: virtual void InitializeDialog(
   OpenFileDialog* openFileDialog
);
```
[JScript]
```
protected function InitializeDialog(
   openFileDialog : OpenFileDialog
);
```

Parameters

openFileDialog

The **OpenFileDialog** to use to select a file name.

Remarks

This method configures the dialog box with a generic file filter and title.

Notes to Implementers: You can override this method to customize the initialization of the dialog.

Requirements

Platforms: Windows 98, Windows NT 4.0,
Windows Millennium Edition, Windows 2000,
Windows XP Home Edition, Windows XP Professional,
Windows Server 2003 family

.NET Framework Security:

- Full trust for the immediate caller. This member cannot be used by partially trusted code.

FolderNameEditor Class

This type supports the .NET Framework infrastructure and is not intended to be used directly from your code.

```
[Visual Basic]
Public Class FolderNameEditor
   Inherits UITypeEditor
[C#]
public class FolderNameEditor : UITypeEditor
[C++]
public __gc class FolderNameEditor : public UITypeEditor
[JScript]
public class FolderNameEditor extends UITypeEditor
```

FolderNameEditor Constructor

This member supports the .NET Framework infrastructure and is not intended to be used directly from your code.

```
[Visual Basic]
Public Sub New()
[C#]
public FolderNameEditor();
[C++]
public: FolderNameEditor();
[JScript]
public function FolderNameEditor();
```

FolderNameEditor.EditValue Method

This member supports the .NET Framework infrastructure and is not intended to be used directly from your code.

Overload List

This member overrides **UITypeEditor.EditValue**.

[Visual Basic] **Overloads Overrides Public Function EditValue(ITypeDescriptorContext, IServiceProvider, Object) As Object**

[C#] **public override object EditValue(ITypeDescriptorContext, IServiceProvider, object);**

[C++] **public: Object* EditValue(ITypeDescriptorContext*, IServiceProvider*, Object*);**

[JScript] **public override function EditValue(ITypeDescriptorContext, IServiceProvider, Object) : Object;**

This member supports the .NET Framework infrastructure and is not intended to be used directly from your code.

[Visual Basic] **Overloads Public Function EditValue(IServiceProvider, Object) As Object**

[C#] **public object EditValue(IServiceProvider, object);**

[C++] **public: Object* EditValue(IServiceProvider*, Object*);**

[JScript] **public function EditValue(IServiceProvider, Object) : Object;**

FolderNameEditor.EditValue Method (ITypeDescriptorContext, IServiceProvider, Object)

This member overrides **UITypeEditor.EditValue**.

```
[Visual Basic]
Overrides Overloads Public Function EditValue( _
   ByVal context As ITypeDescriptorContext, _
   ByVal provider As IServiceProvider, _
   ByVal value As Object _
) As Object
[C#]
public override object EditValue(
   ITypeDescriptorContext context,
   IServiceProvider provider,
   object value
);
[C++]
public: Object* EditValue(
   ITypeDescriptorContext* context,
   IServiceProvider* provider,
   Object* value
);
[JScript]
public override function EditValue(
   context : ITypeDescriptorContext,
   provider : IServiceProvider,
   value : Object
) : Object;
```

Requirements

Platforms: Windows 98, Windows NT 4.0, Windows Millennium Edition, Windows 2000, Windows XP Home Edition, Windows XP Professional, Windows Server 2003 family

.NET Framework Security:

- Full trust for the immediate caller. This member cannot be used by partially trusted code. For more information, see **Using Libraries From Partially Trusted Code**

FolderNameEditor.GetEditStyle Method

This member supports the .NET Framework infrastructure and is not intended to be used directly from your code.

Overload List

This member overrides **UITypeEditor.GetEditStyle**.

[Visual Basic] **Overloads Overrides Public Function GetEditStyle(ITypeDescriptorContext) As UITypeEditorEditStyle**

[C#] **public override UITypeEditorEditStyle GetEditStyle(ITypeDescriptorContext);**

[C++] **public: UITypeEditorEditStyle GetEditStyle(ITypeDescriptorContext*);**

[JScript] **public override function GetEditStyle(ITypeDescriptorContext) : UITypeEditorEditStyle;**

This member supports the .NET Framework infrastructure and is not intended to be used directly from your code.

[Visual Basic] **Overloads Public Function GetEditStyle() As UITypeEditorEditStyle**

[C#] **public UITypeEditorEditStyle GetEditStyle();**

[C++] **public: UITypeEditorEditStyle GetEditStyle();**

[JScript] **public function GetEditStyle() : UITypeEditorEditStyle;**

FolderNameEditor.GetEditStyle Method (ITypeDescriptorContext)

This member overrides **UITypeEditor.GetEditStyle**.

[Visual Basic]
```
Overrides Overloads Public Function GetEditStyle( _
   ByVal context As ITypeDescriptorContext _
) As UITypeEditorEditStyle
```
[C#]
```
public override UITypeEditorEditStyle GetEditStyle(
   ITypeDescriptorContext context
);
```
[C++]
```
public: UITypeEditorEditStyle GetEditStyle(
   ITypeDescriptorContext* context
);
```
[JScript]
```
public override function GetEditStyle(
   context : ITypeDescriptorContext
) : UITypeEditorEditStyle;
```

Requirements

Platforms: Windows 98, Windows NT 4.0, Windows Millennium Edition, Windows 2000, Windows XP Home Edition, Windows XP Professional, Windows Server 2003 family

.NET Framework Security:

- Full trust for the immediate caller. This member cannot be used by partially trusted code. For more information, see **Using Libraries From Partially Trusted Code**

FolderNameEditor.InitializeDialog Method

This member supports the .NET Framework infrastructure and is not intended to be used directly from your code.

[Visual Basic]
```
Protected Overridable Sub InitializeDialog( _
   ByVal folderBrowser As FolderNameEditor.FolderBrowser _
)
```
[C#]
```
protected virtual void InitializeDialog(
   FolderNameEditor.FolderBrowser folderBrowser
);
```
[C++]
```
protected: virtual void InitializeDialog(
   FolderNameEditor.FolderBrowser* folderBrowser
);
```
[JScript]
```
protected function InitializeDialog(
   folderBrowser : FolderNameEditor.FolderBrowser
);
```

FolderNameEditor.Folder-Browser Class

This type supports the .NET Framework infrastructure and is not intended to be used directly from your code.

```
[Visual Basic]
NotInheritable Protected Class FolderNameEditor.FolderBrowser
   Inherits Component
[C#]
protected sealed class FolderNameEditor.FolderBrowser : Component
[C++]
protected __gc __sealed class FolderNameEditor.FolderBrowser :
   public Component
[JScript]
protected class FolderNameEditor.FolderBrowser extends Component
```

FolderNameEditor.FolderBrowser Constructor

This member supports the .NET Framework infrastructure and is not intended to be used directly from your code.

```
[Visual Basic]
Public Sub New()
[C#]
public FolderNameEditor.FolderBrowser();
[C++]
public: FolderBrowser();
[JScript]
public function FolderNameEditor.FolderBrowser();
```

FolderNameEditor.FolderBrowser.Description Property

This member supports the .NET Framework infrastructure and is not intended to be used directly from your code.

```
[Visual Basic]
Public Property Description As String
[C#]
public string Description {get; set;}
[C++]
public: __property String* get_Description();
public: __property void set_Description(String*);
[JScript]
public function get Description() : String;
public function set Description(String);
```

FolderNameEditor.FolderBrowser.DirectoryPath Property

This member supports the .NET Framework infrastructure and is not intended to be used directly from your code.

```
[Visual Basic]
Public ReadOnly Property DirectoryPath As String
[C#]
public string DirectoryPath {get;}
[C++]
public: __property String* get_DirectoryPath();
[JScript]
public function get DirectoryPath() : String;
```

FolderNameEditor.FolderBrowser.StartLocation Property

This member supports the .NET Framework infrastructure and is not intended to be used directly from your code.

```
[Visual Basic]
Public Property StartLocation As _
   FolderNameEditor.FolderBrowserFolder
[C#]
public FolderNameEditor.FolderBrowserFolder StartLocation {get;
   set;}
[C++]
public: __property FolderNameEditor.FolderBrowserFolder
get_StartLocation();
public: __property void
set_StartLocation(FolderNameEditor.FolderBrowserFolder);
[JScript]
public function get StartLocation() :
FolderNameEditor.FolderBrowserFolder;
public function set
StartLocation(FolderNameEditor.FolderBrowserFolder);
```

FolderNameEditor.FolderBrowser.Style Property

This member supports the .NET Framework infrastructure and is not intended to be used directly from your code.

```
[Visual Basic]
Public Property Style As FolderNameEditor.FolderBrowserStyles
[C#]
public FolderNameEditor.FolderBrowserStyles Style {get; set;}
[C++]
public: __property FolderNameEditor.FolderBrowserStyles get_Style();
public: __property void
set_Style(FolderNameEditor.FolderBrowserStyles);
[JScript]
public function get Style() : FolderNameEditor.FolderBrowserStyles;
public function set Style(FolderNameEditor.FolderBrowserStyles);
```

FolderNameEditor.FolderBrowser.ShowDialog Method

This member supports the .NET Framework infrastructure and is not intended to be used directly from your code.

Overload List

This member supports the .NET Framework infrastructure and is not intended to be used directly from your code.

[Visual Basic] **Overloads Public Function ShowDialog() As DialogResult**

[C#] **public DialogResult ShowDialog();**

[C++] **public: DialogResult ShowDialog();**

[JScript] **public function ShowDialog() : DialogResult;**

This member supports the .NET Framework infrastructure and is not intended to be used directly from your code.

[Visual Basic] **Overloads Public Function ShowDialog(IWin32Window) As DialogResult**

[C#] **public DialogResult ShowDialog(IWin32Window);**

[C++] **public: DialogResult ShowDialog(IWin32Window*);**

[JScript] **public function ShowDialog(IWin32Window) : DialogResult;**

FolderNameEditor.FolderBrowser.ShowDialog Method ()

This member supports the .NET Framework infrastructure and is not intended to be used directly from your code.

[Visual Basic]
```
Overloads Public Function ShowDialog() As DialogResult
```
[C#]
```
public DialogResult ShowDialog();
```
[C++]
```
public: DialogResult ShowDialog();
```
[JScript]
```
public function ShowDialog() : DialogResult;
```

FolderNameEditor.FolderBrowser.ShowDialog Method (IWin32Window)

This member supports the .NET Framework infrastructure and is not intended to be used directly from your code.

[Visual Basic]
```
Overloads Public Function ShowDialog( _
   ByVal owner As IWin32Window _
) As DialogResult
```
[C#]
```
public DialogResult ShowDialog(
   IWin32Window owner
);
```
[C++]
```
public: DialogResult ShowDialog(
   IWin32Window* owner
);
```
[JScript]
```
public function ShowDialog(
   owner : IWin32Window
) : DialogResult;
```

FolderNameEditor.Folder-BrowserFolder Enumeration

This type supports the .NET Framework infrastructure and is not intended to be used directly from your code.

[Visual Basic]
```
<Serializable>
Protected Enum FolderNameEditor.FolderBrowserFolder
```
[C#]
```
[Serializable]
protected enum FolderNameEditor.FolderBrowserFolder
```
[C++]
```
[Serializable]
__value protected enum FolderNameEditor.FolderBrowserFolder
```
[JScript]
```
protected
   Serializable
enum FolderNameEditor.FolderBrowserFolder
```

Members

Desktop

Favorites

MyComputer

MyDocuments

MyPictures

NetAndDialUpConnections

NetworkNeighborhood

Printers

Recent

SendTo

StartMenu

Templates

FolderNameEditor.FolderBrowserStyles Enumeration

This type supports the .NET Framework infrastructure and is not intended to be used directly from your code.

```
[Visual Basic]
<Flags>
<Serializable>
Protected Enum FolderNameEditor.FolderBrowserStyles
[C#]
[Flags]
[Serializable]
protected enum FolderNameEditor.FolderBrowserStyles
[C++]
[Flags]
[Serializable]
__value protected enum FolderNameEditor.FolderBrowserStyles
[JScript]
protected
   Flags
   Serializable
enum FolderNameEditor.FolderBrowserStyles
```

Members

BrowseForComputer

BrowseForEverything

BrowseForPrinter

RestrictToDomain

RestrictToFilesystem

RestrictToSubfolders

ShowTextBox

IMenuEditorService Interface

This type supports the .NET Framework infrastructure and is not intended to be used directly from your code.

```
[Visual Basic]
Public Interface IMenuEditorService
[C#]
public interface IMenuEditorService
[C++]
public __gc __interface IMenuEditorService
[JScript]
public interface IMenuEditorService
```

IMenuEditorService.GetMenu Method

This member supports the .NET Framework infrastructure and is not intended to be used directly from your code.

```
[Visual Basic]
Function GetMenu() As Menu
[C#]
Menu GetMenu();
[C++]
Menu* GetMenu();
[JScript]
function GetMenu() : Menu;
```

IMenuEditorService.IsActive Method

This member supports the .NET Framework infrastructure and is not intended to be used directly from your code.

```
[Visual Basic]
Function IsActive() As Boolean
[C#]
bool IsActive();
[C++]
bool IsActive();
[JScript]
function IsActive() : Boolean;
```

IMenuEditorService.MessageFilter Method

This member supports the .NET Framework infrastructure and is not intended to be used directly from your code.

```
[Visual Basic]
Function MessageFilter( _
   ByRef m As Message _
) As Boolean
[C#]
bool MessageFilter(
   ref Message m
);
[C++]
bool MessageFilter(
   Message* m
);
[JScript]
function MessageFilter(
   m : Message
) : Boolean;
```

IMenuEditorService.SetMenu Method

This member supports the .NET Framework infrastructure and is not intended to be used directly from your code.

```
[Visual Basic]
Sub SetMenu( _
   ByVal menu As Menu _
)
[C#]
void SetMenu(
   Menu menu
);
[C++]
void SetMenu(
   Menu* menu
);
[JScript]
function SetMenu(
   menu : Menu
);
```

IMenuEditorService.SetSelection Method

This member supports the .NET Framework infrastructure and is not intended to be used directly from your code.

```
[Visual Basic]
Sub SetSelection( _
   ByVal item As MenuItem _
)
[C#]
void SetSelection(
   MenuItem item
);
[C++]
void SetSelection(
   MenuItem* item
);
[JScript]
function SetSelection(
   item : MenuItem
);
```

IUIService Interface

Enables interaction with the user interface of the development environment object that is hosting the designer.

[Visual Basic]
```
<Guid("06A9C74B-5E32-4561-BE73-381B37869F4F")>
Public Interface IUIService
```
[C#]
```
[Guid("06A9C74B-5E32-4561-BE73-381B37869F4F")]
public interface IUIService
```
[C++]
```
[Guid("06A9C74B-5E32-4561-BE73-381B37869F4F")]
public __gc __interface IUIService
```
[JScript]
```
public
   Guid("06A9C74B-5E32-4561-BE73-381B37869F4F")
interface IUIService
```

Remarks

IUIService can display error messages, show dialog boxes, and get ambient properties of the host, such as the font for dialogs and color schemes, through the **Styles** dictionary property.

Example

[Visual Basic]
```
Imports System
Imports System.ComponentModel
Imports System.ComponentModel.Design
Imports System.Drawing
Imports System.Windows.Forms
Imports System.Windows.Forms.Design

' This designer provides a set of designer verb shortcut menu commands
' that call methods of the IUIService.
Public Class IUIServiceTestDesigner
   Inherits System.Windows.Forms.Design.ControlDesigner

   Public Sub New()
    End Sub

    ' Provides a set of designer verb menu commands that call
    ' IUIService methods.
    Public Overrides ReadOnly Property Verbs() As                  ↵
System.ComponentModel.Design.DesignerVerbCollection
        Get
            Return New DesignerVerbCollection(New DesignerVerb() { _
                New DesignerVerb("Show a test message box using     ↵
the IUIService", _
                New EventHandler(AddressOf Me.showTestMessage)), _
                New DesignerVerb("Show a test error message using the
IUIService", _
                New EventHandler(AddressOf Me.showErrorMessage)), _
                New DesignerVerb("Show an example Form using        ↵
the IUIService", _
                New EventHandler(AddressOf Me.showDialog)), _
                New DesignerVerb("Show the Task List tool window    ↵
 using the IUIService", _
                New EventHandler(AddressOf Me.showToolWindow))})
        End Get
    End Property

    ' Displays a message box with message text, caption text
    ' and buttons of a particular MessageBoxButtons style.
    Private Sub showTestMessage(ByVal sender As Object, ByVal e      ↵
 As EventArgs)
        Dim UIservice As IUIService = CType(Me.GetService( _
            GetType(System.Windows.Forms.Design.IUIService)),        ↵
IUIService)
        If Not (UIservice Is Nothing) Then
            UIservice.ShowMessage("Test message", "Test caption", _
                System.Windows.Forms.MessageBoxButtons.AbortRetryIgnore)
        End If
    End Sub

    ' Displays an error message box that displays the message
    ' contained within a specified exception.
    Private Sub showErrorMessage(ByVal sender As Object, ByVal       ↵
 e As EventArgs)
        Dim UIservice As IUIService = CType(Me.GetService( _
            GetType(System.Windows.Forms.Design.IUIService)),        ↵
IUIService)
        If Not (UIservice Is Nothing) Then
            UIservice.ShowError(New Exception( _
                "This is a message in a test exception,              ↵
displayed by the IUIService", _
                New ArgumentException("Test inner exception")))
        End If
    End Sub

    ' Displays an example Windows Form using the
    ' IUIService.ShowDialog method.
    Private Sub showDialog(ByVal sender As Object, ByVal e           ↵
As EventArgs)
        Dim UIservice As IUIService = CType(Me.GetService( _
            GetType(System.Windows.Forms.Design.IUIService)),        ↵
IUIService)
        If Not (UIservice Is Nothing) Then
            UIservice.ShowDialog(New ExampleForm())
        End If
    End Sub

    ' Displays a standard tool window using the
    ' IUIService.ShowToolWindow method.
    Private Sub showToolWindow(ByVal sender As Object, ByVal         ↵
 e As EventArgs)
        Dim UIservice As IUIService = CType(Me.GetService( _
            GetType(System.Windows.Forms.Design.IUIService)),        ↵
IUIService)
        If Not (UIservice Is Nothing) Then
            UIservice.ShowToolWindow(StandardToolWindows.TaskList)
        End If
    End Sub

End Class

' Provides an example Form class used by the
' IUIServiceTestDesigner.showDialog method.
Friend Class ExampleForm
    Inherits System.Windows.Forms.Form

    Public Sub New()
        Me.Text = "Example Form"
        Dim okButton As New System.Windows.Forms.Button()
        okButton.Location = New Point(Me.Width - 70, Me.Height - 70)
        okButton.Size = New Size(50, 20)
        okButton.Anchor = AnchorStyles.Right Or AnchorStyles.Bottom
        okButton.DialogResult = DialogResult.OK
        okButton.Text = "OK"
        Me.Controls.Add(okButton)
    End Sub
End Class

' This control is associated with the IUIServiceTestDesigner,
' and can be sited in design mode to use the sample.
<DesignerAttribute(GetType(IUIServiceTestDesigner),                 ↵
GetType(IDesigner))> _
Public Class IUIServiceExampleControl
    Inherits UserControl

    Public Sub New()
        Me.BackColor = Color.Beige
        Me.Width = 255
        Me.Height = 60
    End Sub
```

```
    Protected Overrides Sub OnPaint(ByVal e As                          ↵
System.Windows.Forms.PaintEventArgs)
        If Me.DesignMode Then
            e.Graphics.DrawString("Right-click this control             ↵
 to display a list of the", _
                New Font("Arial", 9), Brushes.Black, 5, 6)
            e.Graphics.DrawString("designer verb menu commands          ↵
 provided", _
                New Font("Arial", 9), Brushes.Black, 5, 20)
            e.Graphics.DrawString("by the IUIServiceTestDesigner.", _
                New Font("Arial", 9), Brushes.Black, 5, 34)
        End If
    End Sub
End Class
```

[C#]

```
using System;
using System.ComponentModel;
using System.ComponentModel.Design;
using System.Drawing;
using System.Windows.Forms;
using System.Windows.Forms.Design;

// This designer provides a set of designer verb shortcut menu commands
// that call methods of the IUIService.
public class IUIServiceTestDesigner :                                   ↵
System.Windows.Forms.Design.ControlDesigner
{
    public IUIServiceTestDesigner()
    {
    }

    // Provides a set of designer verb menu commands that call
    // IUIService methods.
    public override                                                     ↵
 System.ComponentModel.Design.DesignerVerbCollection Verbs
    {
        get
        {
            return new DesignerVerbCollection( new DesignerVerb[]
            {
                new DesignerVerb(
                    "Show a test message box using the IUIService",
                     new EventHandler(this.showTestMessage)),
                new DesignerVerb(
                    "Show a test error message using the IUIService",
                     new EventHandler(this.showErrorMessage)),
                new DesignerVerb(
                    "Show an example Form using the IUIService",
                     new EventHandler(this.showDialog)),
                new DesignerVerb(
                    "Show the Task List tool window using the           ↵
 IUIService",
                     new EventHandler(this.showToolWindow))
            });
        }
    }

    // Displays a message box with message text, caption text
    // and buttons of a particular MessageBoxButtons style.
    private void showTestMessage(object sender, EventArgs e)
    {
        IUIService UIservice = (IUIService)this.GetService(
            typeof( System.Windows.Forms.Design.IUIService ) );
        if( UIservice != null )
            UIservice.ShowMessage("Test message", "Test caption",
               System.Windows.Forms.MessageBoxButtons.AbortRetryIgnore);
    }

    // Displays an error message box that displays the message
    // contained in a specified exception.
    private void showErrorMessage(object sender, EventArgs e)
    {
        IUIService UIservice = (IUIService)this.GetService(
            typeof( System.Windows.Forms.Design.IUIService ) );
        if( UIservice != null )
            UIservice.ShowError( new Exception(
                "This is a message in a test exception, " +
                "displayed by the IUIService",
                 new ArgumentException("Test inner exception")));
    }

    // Displays an example Windows Form using the
    // IUIService.ShowDialog method.
    private void showDialog(object sender, EventArgs e)
    {
        IUIService UIservice = (IUIService)this.GetService(
            typeof( System.Windows.Forms.Design.IUIService ) );
        if( UIservice != null )
            UIservice.ShowDialog(new ExampleForm());
    }

    // Displays a standard tool window using the
    // IUIService.ShowToolWindow method.
    private void showToolWindow(object sender, EventArgs e)
    {
        IUIService UIservice = (IUIService)this.GetService(
            typeof( System.Windows.Forms.Design.IUIService ) );
        if( UIservice != null )
            UIservice.ShowToolWindow(StandardToolWindows.TaskList);
    }
}

// Provides an example Form class used by the
// IUIServiceTestDesigner.showDialog method.
internal class ExampleForm : System.Windows.Forms.Form
{
    public ExampleForm()
    {
        this.Text = "Example Form";
        System.Windows.Forms.Button okButton = new                      ↵
System.Windows.Forms.Button();
        okButton.Location = new Point(this.Width-70, this.Height-70);
        okButton.Size = new Size(50, 20);
        okButton.Anchor = AnchorStyles.Right | AnchorStyles.Bottom;
        okButton.DialogResult = DialogResult.OK;
        okButton.Text = "OK";
        this.Controls.Add( okButton );
    }
}

// This control is associated with the IUIServiceTestDesigner,
// and can be sited in design mode to use the sample.
[DesignerAttribute(typeof(IUIServiceTestDesigner), typeof(IDesigner))]
public class IUIServiceExampleControl : UserControl
{
    public IUIServiceExampleControl()
    {
        this.BackColor = Color.Beige;
        this.Width = 255;
        this.Height = 60;
    }

    protected override void OnPaint                                     ↵
 (System.Windows.Forms.PaintEventArgs e)
    {
        if( this.DesignMode )
        {
            e.Graphics.DrawString(
                "Right-click this control to display a list of the",
                 new Font("Arial", 9), Brushes.Black, 5, 6);
            e.Graphics.DrawString(
                "designer verb menu commands provided",
                 new Font("Arial", 9), Brushes.Black, 5, 20);
            e.Graphics.DrawString(
                "by the IUIServiceTestDesigner.",
                 new Font("Arial", 9), Brushes.Black, 5, 34);
        }
    }
}
```

[C++]
```
#using <mscorlib.dll>
#using <System.dll>
#using <System.Windows.Forms.dll>
#using <System.Drawing.dll>
#using <System.Design.dll>

using namespace System;
using namespace System::ComponentModel;
using namespace System::ComponentModel::Design;
using namespace System::Drawing;
using namespace System::Windows::Forms;
using namespace System::Windows::Forms::Design;

// Provides an example Form class used by the
// IUIServiceTestDesigner::showDialog method.
__gc class ExampleForm : public System::Windows::Forms::Form {
public:
   ExampleForm() {
      this->Text = S"Example Form";
      System::Windows::Forms::Button* okButton = new ↲
System::Windows::Forms::Button();
      okButton->Location = Point(this->Width-70, this->Height-70);
      okButton->Size = System::Drawing::Size(50, 20);
      okButton->Anchor = static_cast<AnchorStyles> ↲
 (AnchorStyles::Right | AnchorStyles::Bottom);
      okButton->DialogResult = DialogResult::OK;
      okButton->Text = S"OK";
      this->Controls->Add(okButton);
   }
};

// This designer provides a set of designer verb shortcut menu commands
// that call methods of the IUIService.
public __gc class IUIServiceTestDesigner : public ↲
System::Windows::Forms::Design::ControlDesigner {
public:
   IUIServiceTestDesigner() {
   }

   // Provides a set of designer verb menu commands that call ↲
IUIService methods.
   __property ↲
System::ComponentModel::Design::DesignerVerbCollection* get_Verbs() {
      DesignerVerb* temp0 [] = {
         new DesignerVerb(S"Show a test message box using the ↲
IUIService", new EventHandler(this, showTestMessage)),
            new DesignerVerb(S"Show a test error message using ↲
 the IUIService", new EventHandler(this, showErrorMessage)),
            new DesignerVerb(S"Show an example Form using the ↲
IUIService", new EventHandler(this, showDialog)),
            new DesignerVerb(S"Show the Task List tool window ↲
using the IUIService", new EventHandler(this, showToolWindow))
      };
      return new DesignerVerbCollection(temp0);
   }

private:
   // Displays a message box with message text, caption text
   // and buttons of a particular MessageBoxButtons style.
   void showTestMessage(Object* sender, EventArgs* e) {
      IUIService* UIservice = dynamic_cast<IUIService*>(this-
>GetService(__typeof(System::Windows::Forms::Design::IUIService)));
      if (UIservice != 0)
         UIservice->ShowMessage(S"Test message", S"Test ↲
caption", System::Windows::Forms::MessageBoxButtons::AbortRetryIgnore);
   }

   // Displays an error message box that displays the message
   // contained within a specified exception.
   void showErrorMessage(Object* sender, EventArgs* e) {
      IUIService* UIservice = dynamic_cast<IUIService*>(this- ↲
>GetService(__typeof(System::Windows::Forms::Design::IUIService)));
      if (UIservice != 0)
         UIservice->ShowError(new Exception(S"This is a message ↲
 in a test exception, displayed by the IUIService", new ↲
ArgumentException(S"Test inner exception")));
   }

   // Displays an example Windows Form using the
   // IUIService::ShowDialog method.
   void showDialog(Object* sender, EventArgs* e) {
      IUIService* UIservice = dynamic_cast<IUIService*>(this-
>GetService(__typeof(System::Windows::Forms::Design::IUIService)));
      if (UIservice != 0)
         UIservice->ShowDialog(new ExampleForm());
   }

   // Displays a standard tool window window using the
   // IUIService::ShowToolWindow method.
   void showToolWindow(Object* sender, EventArgs* e) {
      IUIService* UIservice = dynamic_cast<IUIService*>(this- ↲
>GetService(__typeof(System::Windows::Forms::Design::IUIService)));
      if (UIservice != 0)
         UIservice->ShowToolWindow(StandardToolWindows::TaskList);
   }
};

// This control is associated with the IUIServiceTestDesigner,
// and can be sited in design mode to use the sample.
[DesignerAttribute(__typeof(IUIServiceTestDesigner), ↲
__typeof(IDesigner))]
__gc class IUIServiceExampleControl : public UserControl {
public:
   IUIServiceExampleControl() {
      this->BackColor = Color::Beige;
      this->Width = 255;
      this->Height = 60;
   }

protected:
   void OnPaint(System::Windows::Forms::PaintEventArgs* e) {
      if (this->DesignMode) {
         e->Graphics->DrawString(S"Right-click this control ↲
to display a list of the", new System::Drawing::Font(S"Arial", ↲
 9), Brushes::Black, 5, 6);
         e->Graphics->DrawString(S"designer verb menu commands provided",
new System::Drawing::Font(S"Arial", 9), ↲
 Brushes::Black, 5, 20);
         e->Graphics->DrawString(S"by the ↲
IUIServiceTestDesigner.", new System::Drawing::Font ↲
 (S"Arial", 9), Brushes::Black, 5, 34);
      }
   }
};
```

Requirements

Namespace: System.Windows.Forms.Design

Platforms: Windows 98, Windows NT 4.0, Windows Millennium Edition, Windows 2000, Windows XP Home Edition, Windows XP Professional, Windows Server 2003 family

Assembly: System.Windows.Forms (in System.Windows.Forms.dll)

IUIService.Styles Property

Gets the collection of styles that are specific to the host's environment.

[Visual Basic]
```
ReadOnly Property Styles As IDictionary
```
[C#]
```
IDictionary Styles {get;}
```
[C++]
```
__property IDictionary* get_Styles();
```
[JScript]
```
function get Styles() : IDictionary;
```

Property Value

An **IDictionary** containing style settings.

Remarks

The dictionary can provide information from the host environment. At a minimum, this consists of the font that should be used for standard UI text, and the color to use for highlighting. These required styles are "DialogFont" and "HighlightColor".

The values for these styles may be retrieved by using the style as a key for the dictionary, accessing the dictionary using the key as an indexer. For example: (object implementing IUIService).Styles[(style name string in quotes)].

Example

[Visual Basic, C#, C++] The following example gets the dialog font from the host environment:

[Visual Basic]

```
' The specified IDesigner implements IUIService.
Function GetFont(designer As IDesigner) As Font
    Dim hostfont As Font

    ' Gets the dialog box font from the host environment.
    hostfont = CType(CType(designer, IUIService).Styles ↵
("DialogFont"), Font)

    Return hostfont
End Function
```

[C#]

```
// The specified IDesigner implements IUIService.
Font GetFont(IDesigner designer)
{
      Font        hostfont;

      // Gets the dialog box font from the host environment.
      hostfont = (Font)((IUIService)designer).Styles["DialogFont"];

      return hostfont;
}
```

[C++]

```
// The specified IDesigner implements IUIService.
System::Drawing::Font* GetFont(IDesigner* designer) {
    System::Drawing::Font* hostfont;

    // Gets the dialog box font from the host environment.
    hostfont = dynamic_cast<System::Drawing::Font*>( ↵
dynamic_cast<IUIService*>(designer)->Styles->Item[S"DialogFont"] );

    return hostfont;
}
```

Requirements

Platforms: Windows 98, Windows NT 4.0, Windows Millennium Edition, Windows 2000, Windows XP Home Edition, Windows XP Professional, Windows Server 2003 family

IUIService.CanShowComponentEditor Method

Indicates whether the component can display a **ComponentEditorForm**.

[Visual Basic]

```
Function CanShowComponentEditor( _
   ByVal component As Object _
) As Boolean
```

[C#]

```
bool CanShowComponentEditor(
   object component
);
```

[C++]

```
bool CanShowComponentEditor(
   Object* component
);
```

[JScript]

```
function CanShowComponentEditor(
   component : Object
) : Boolean;
```

Parameters

component

The component to check for support for displaying a **ComponentEditorForm**.

Return Value

true if the specified component can display a component editor form; otherwise, **false**.

Remarks

Component editors can display a component editor form that is similar to a property page from COM.

This method checks to determine whether the specified component has a **ComponentEditor** that can display a **ComponentEditorForm**.

Requirements

Platforms: Windows 98, Windows NT 4.0, Windows Millennium Edition, Windows 2000, Windows XP Home Edition, Windows XP Professional, Windows Server 2003 family

IUIService.GetDialogOwnerWindow Method

Gets the window that should be used as the owner when showing dialogs.

[Visual Basic]

```
Function GetDialogOwnerWindow() As IWin32Window
```

[C#]

```
IWin32Window GetDialogOwnerWindow();
```

[C++]

```
IWin32Window* GetDialogOwnerWindow();
```

[JScript]

```
function GetDialogOwnerWindow() : IWin32Window;
```

Return Value

An **IWin32Window** that indicates the window to own any child dialog boxes.

Remarks

Some dialog boxes are parented to an owner application and are not visible in the task list. This method returns an **IWin32Window** that indicates the window that should be the owner for dialog boxes of this sort that are spawned from an integrated development environment.

Requirements

Platforms: Windows 98, Windows NT 4.0, Windows Millennium Edition, Windows 2000, Windows XP Home Edition, Windows XP Professional, Windows Server 2003 family

IUIService.SetUIDirty Method

Sets a flag indicating the UI has changed.

```
[Visual Basic]
Sub SetUIDirty()
[C#]
void SetUIDirty();
[C++]
void SetUIDirty();
[JScript]
function SetUIDirty();
```

Remarks

This method indicates that the UI has been changed and should be refreshed. It is important to indicate the need for a refresh whenever a toolbar or menu item's status changes. Most development environments cache the status of these elements for speed, and need to know when they need to be updated. This method is called, for example, after objects have been selected within designer view to enable the cut and copy menu items.

Requirements

Platforms: Windows 98, Windows NT 4.0,
Windows Millennium Edition, Windows 2000,
Windows XP Home Edition, Windows XP Professional,
Windows Server 2003 family

IUIService.ShowComponentEditor Method

Attempts to display a **ComponentEditorForm** for a component.

```
[Visual Basic]
Function ShowComponentEditor( _
   ByVal component As Object, _
   ByVal parent As IWin32Window _
) As Boolean
[C#]
bool ShowComponentEditor(
   object component,
   IWin32Window parent
);
[C++]
bool ShowComponentEditor(
   Object* component,
   IWin32Window* parent
);
[JScript]
function ShowComponentEditor(
   component : Object,
   parent : IWin32Window
) : Boolean;
```

Parameters

component

The component for which to display a **ComponentEditorForm**.

parent

The **IWin32Window** to parent any dialogs to.

Return Value

true if the attempt is successful; otherwise, **false**.

Exceptions

Exception Type	Condition
ArgumentException	The component does not support component editors.

Remarks

A **ComponentEditorForm** is similar to a property page from COM.

If the component does not support component editors, an **ArgumentException** is thrown. To avoid this, be sure to call **CanShowComponentEditor** first.

Requirements

Platforms: Windows 98, Windows NT 4.0,
Windows Millennium Edition, Windows 2000,
Windows XP Home Edition, Windows XP Professional,
Windows Server 2003 family

IUIService.ShowDialog Method

Attempts to display the specified form in a dialog box.

```
[Visual Basic]
Function ShowDialog( _
   ByVal form As Form _
) As DialogResult
[C#]
DialogResult ShowDialog(
   Form form
);
[C++]
DialogResult ShowDialog(
   Form* form
);
[JScript]
function ShowDialog(
   form : Form
) : DialogResult;
```

Parameters

form

The **Form** to display.

Return Value

One of the **DialogResult** values indicating the result code returned by the dialog box.

Example

```
[Visual Basic]
Dim UIservice As IUIService = CType(Me.GetService( _
   GetType(System.Windows.Forms.Design.IUIService)), IUIService)
If Not (UIservice Is Nothing) Then
   UIservice.ShowDialog(New ExampleForm())
End If

[C#]
IUIService UIservice = (IUIService)this.GetService(
   typeof( System.Windows.Forms.Design.IUIService ) );
if( UIservice != null )
   UIservice.ShowDialog(new ExampleForm());

[C++]
IUIService* UIservice = dynamic_cast<IUIService*>(this-    ↵
>GetService(__typeof(System::Windows::Forms::Design::IUIService)));
if (UIservice != 0)
  UIservice->ShowDialog(new ExampleForm());
```

Requirements

Platforms: Windows 98, Windows NT 4.0, Windows Millennium Edition, Windows 2000, Windows XP Home Edition, Windows XP Professional, Windows Server 2003 family

IUIService.ShowError Method

Displays the specified error message in a message box.

Overload List

Displays the specified exception and information about the exception in a message box.

[Visual Basic] **Overloads Sub ShowError(Exception)**

[C#] **void ShowError(Exception);**

[C++] **void ShowError(Exception*);**

[JScript] **function ShowError(Exception);**

Displays the specified error message in a message box.

[Visual Basic] **Overloads Sub ShowError(String)**

[C#] **void ShowError(string);**

[C++] **void ShowError(String*);**

[JScript] **function ShowError(String);**

Displays the specified exception and information about the exception in a message box.

[Visual Basic] **Overloads Sub ShowError(Exception, String)**

[C#] **void ShowError(Exception, string);**

[C++] **void ShowError(Exception*, String*);**

[JScript] **function ShowError(Exception, String);**

Example

[Visual Basic, C#, C++] **Note** This example shows how to use one of the overloaded versions of **ShowError**. For other examples that might be available, see the individual overload topics.

[Visual Basic]
```
Dim UIservice As IUIService = CType(Me.GetService( _
    GetType(System.Windows.Forms.Design.IUIService)), IUIService)
If Not (UIservice Is Nothing) Then
    UIservice.ShowError(New Exception( _
        "This is a message in a test exception, displayed by          ↵
 the IUIService", _
        New ArgumentException("Test inner exception")))
End If
```

[C#]
```
IUIService UIservice = (IUIService)this.GetService(
    typeof( System.Windows.Forms.Design.IUIService ) );
if( UIservice != null )
    UIservice.ShowError( new Exception(
        "This is a message in a test exception, " +
        "displayed by the IUIService",
         new ArgumentException("Test inner exception")));
```

[C++]
```
IUIService* UIservice = dynamic_cast<IUIService*>(this-            ↵
>GetService(__typeof(System::Windows::Forms::Design::IUIService)));
if (UIservice != 0)
   UIservice->ShowError(new Exception(S"This is a message in a     ↵
 test exception, displayed by the IUIService", new                 ↵
ArgumentException(S"Test inner exception")));
```

IUIService.ShowError Method (Exception)

Displays the specified exception and information about the exception in a message box.

[Visual Basic]
```
Sub ShowError( _
   ByVal ex As Exception _
)
```
[C#]
```
void ShowError(
   Exception ex
);
```
[C++]
```
void ShowError(
   Exception* ex
);
```
[JScript]
```
function ShowError(
   ex : Exception
);
```

Parameters

ex
  The **Exception** to display.

Remarks

Using this method allows the message box display to be properly integrated with the development environment.

Requirements

Platforms: Windows 98, Windows NT 4.0, Windows Millennium Edition, Windows 2000, Windows XP Home Edition, Windows XP Professional, Windows Server 2003 family

IUIService.ShowError Method (String)

Displays the specified error message in a message box.

[Visual Basic]
```
Sub ShowError( _
   ByVal message As String _
)
```
[C#]
```
void ShowError(
   string message
);
```
[C++]
```
void ShowError(
   String* message
);
```
[JScript]
```
function ShowError(
   message : String
);
```

Parameters

message
  The error message to display.

Remarks

Using this method allows the message box display to be properly integrated with the development environment.

Requirements

Platforms: Windows 98, Windows NT 4.0, Windows Millennium Edition, Windows 2000, Windows XP Home Edition, Windows XP Professional, Windows Server 2003 family

IUIService.ShowError Method (Exception, String)

Displays the specified exception and information about the exception in a message box.

```
[Visual Basic]
Sub ShowError( _
   ByVal ex As Exception, _
   ByVal message As String _
)
[C#]
void ShowError(
   Exception ex,
   string message
);
[C++]
void ShowError(
   Exception* ex,
   String* message
);
[JScript]
function ShowError(
   ex : Exception,
   message : String
);
```

Parameters

ex

The **Exception** to display.

message

A message to display that provides information about the exception.

Remarks

Using this method allows the message box display to be properly integrated with the development environment.

Example

[Visual Basic]

```
Dim UIservice As IUIService = CType(Me.GetService( _
    GetType(System.Windows.Forms.Design.IUIService)), IUIService)
If Not (UIservice Is Nothing) Then
    UIservice.ShowError(New Exception( _
        "This is a message in a test exception, displayed
 by the IUIService", _
        New ArgumentException("Test inner exception")))
End If
```

[C#]

```
IUIService UIservice = (IUIService)this.GetService(
    typeof( System.Windows.Forms.Design.IUIService ) );
if( UIservice != null )
    UIservice.ShowError( new Exception(
        "This is a message in a test exception, " +
        "displayed by the IUIService",
         new ArgumentException("Test inner exception")));
```

[C++]

```
IUIService* UIservice = dynamic_cast<IUIService*>(this-
>GetService(__typeof(System::Windows::Forms::Design::IUIService)));
if (UIservice != 0)
   UIservice->ShowError(new Exception(S"This is a message in
a test exception, displayed by the IUIService", new
ArgumentException(S"Test inner exception")));
```

Requirements

Platforms: Windows 98, Windows NT 4.0, Windows Millennium Edition, Windows 2000, Windows XP Home Edition, Windows XP Professional, Windows Server 2003 family

IUIService.ShowMessage Method

Displays the specified message in a message box.

Overload List

Displays the specified message in a message box.

[Visual Basic] **Overloads Sub ShowMessage(String)**

[C#] **void ShowMessage(string);**

[C++] **void ShowMessage(String*);**

[JScript] **function ShowMessage(String);**

Displays the specified message in a message box with the specified caption.

[Visual Basic] **Overloads Sub ShowMessage(String, String)**

[C#] **void ShowMessage(string, string);**

[C++] **void ShowMessage(String*, String*);**

[JScript] **function ShowMessage(String, String);**

Displays the specified message in a message box with the specified caption and buttons to place on the dialog box.

[Visual Basic] **Overloads Function ShowMessage(String, String, MessageBoxButtons) As DialogResult**

[C#] **DialogResult ShowMessage(string, string, MessageBoxButtons);**

[C++] **DialogResult ShowMessage(String*, String*, MessageBoxButtons);**

[JScript] **function ShowMessage(String, String, MessageBoxButtons) : DialogResult;**

Example

[Visual Basic, C#, C++] **Note** This example shows how to use one of the overloaded versions of **ShowMessage**. For other examples that might be available, see the individual overload topics.

[Visual Basic]

```
Dim UIservice As IUIService = CType(Me.GetService( _
    GetType(System.Windows.Forms.Design.IUIService)), IUIService)
If Not (UIservice Is Nothing) Then
    UIservice.ShowMessage("Test message", "Test caption", _
        System.Windows.Forms.MessageBoxButtons.AbortRetryIgnore)
End If
```

[C#]

```
IUIService UIservice = (IUIService)this.GetService(
    typeof( System.Windows.Forms.Design.IUIService ) );
if( UIservice != null )
    UIservice.ShowMessage("Test message", "Test caption",
        System.Windows.Forms.MessageBoxButtons.AbortRetryIgnore);
```

[C++]
```
IUIService* UIservice = dynamic_cast<IUIService*>(this-
>GetService(__typeof(System::Windows::Forms::Design::IUIService)));
if (UIservice != 0)
   UIservice->ShowMessage(S"Test message", S"Test caption",
System::Windows::Forms::MessageBoxButtons::AbortRetryIgnore);
```

IUIService.ShowMessage Method (String)

Displays the specified message in a message box.

[Visual Basic]
```
Sub ShowMessage( _
   ByVal message As String _
)
```
[C#]
```
void ShowMessage(
   string message
);
```
[C++]
```
void ShowMessage(
   String* message
);
```
[JScript]
```
function ShowMessage(
   message : String
);
```

Parameters

message
The message to display

Remarks

This method ensures that the display of the message box is properly integrated with the development environment.

Example

[Visual Basic]
```
Dim UIservice As IUIService = CType(Me.GetService( _
    GetType(System.Windows.Forms.Design.IUIService)), IUIService)
If Not (UIservice Is Nothing) Then
    UIservice.ShowMessage("Test message", "Test caption", _
        System.Windows.Forms.MessageBoxButtons.AbortRetryIgnore)
End If
```

[C#]
```
IUIService UIservice = (IUIService)this.GetService(
    typeof( System.Windows.Forms.Design.IUIService ) );
if( UIservice != null )
    UIservice.ShowMessage("Test message", "Test caption",
        System.Windows.Forms.MessageBoxButtons.AbortRetryIgnore);
```

[C++]
```
IUIService* UIservice = dynamic_cast<IUIService*>(this-
>GetService(__typeof(System::Windows::Forms::Design::IUIService)));
if (UIservice != 0)
   UIservice->ShowMessage(S"Test message", S"Test caption",
System::Windows::Forms::MessageBoxButtons::AbortRetryIgnore);
```

Requirements

Platforms: Windows 98, Windows NT 4.0, Windows Millennium Edition, Windows 2000, Windows XP Home Edition, Windows XP Professional, Windows Server 2003 family

IUIService.ShowMessage Method (String, String)

Displays the specified message in a message box with the specified caption.

[Visual Basic]
```
Sub ShowMessage( _
   ByVal message As String, _
   ByVal caption As String _
)
```
[C#]
```
void ShowMessage(
   string message,
   string caption
);
```
[C++]
```
void ShowMessage(
   String* message,
   String* caption
);
```
[JScript]
```
function ShowMessage(
   message : String,
   caption : String
);
```

Parameters

message
The message to display.

caption
The caption for the message box.

Remarks

This method ensures that the display of the message box is properly integrated with the development environment.

Example

[Visual Basic]
```
Dim UIservice As IUIService = CType(Me.GetService( _
    GetType(System.Windows.Forms.Design.IUIService)), IUIService)
If Not (UIservice Is Nothing) Then
    UIservice.ShowMessage("Test message", "Test caption", _
        System.Windows.Forms.MessageBoxButtons.AbortRetryIgnore)
End If
```

[C#]
```
IUIService UIservice = (IUIService)this.GetService(
    typeof( System.Windows.Forms.Design.IUIService ) );
if( UIservice != null )
    UIservice.ShowMessage("Test message", "Test caption",
        System.Windows.Forms.MessageBoxButtons.AbortRetryIgnore);
```

[C++]
```
IUIService* UIservice = dynamic_cast<IUIService*>(this-
>GetService(__typeof(System::Windows::Forms::Design::IUIService)));
if (UIservice != 0)
   UIservice->ShowMessage(S"Test message", S"Test caption",
System::Windows::Forms::MessageBoxButtons::AbortRetryIgnore);
```

Requirements

Platforms: Windows 98, Windows NT 4.0, Windows Millennium Edition, Windows 2000, Windows XP Home Edition, Windows XP Professional, Windows Server 2003 family

IUIService.ShowMessage Method (String, String, MessageBoxButtons)

Displays the specified message in a message box with the specified caption and buttons to place on the dialog box.

[Visual Basic]
```
Function ShowMessage( _
   ByVal message As String, _
   ByVal caption As String, _
   ByVal buttons As MessageBoxButtons _
) As DialogResult
```
[C#]
```
DialogResult ShowMessage(
   string message,
   string caption,
   MessageBoxButtons buttons
);
```
[C++]
```
DialogResult ShowMessage(
   String* message,
   String* caption,
   MessageBoxButtons buttons
);
```
[JScript]
```
function ShowMessage(
   message : String,
   caption : String,
   buttons : MessageBoxButtons
) : DialogResult;
```

Parameters

message
The message to display.

caption
The caption for the dialog box.

buttons
One of the **MessageBoxButtons** values: **OK**, **OKCancel**, **YesNo**, or **YesNoCancel**.

Return Value

One of the **DialogResult** values indicating the result code returned by the dialog box.

Remarks

This method ensures that the display of the message box is properly integrated with the development environment.

Example

[Visual Basic]
```
Dim UIservice As IUIService = CType(Me.GetService( _
    GetType(System.Windows.Forms.Design.IUIService)), IUIService)
If Not (UIservice Is Nothing) Then
    UIservice.ShowMessage("Test message", "Test caption", _
        System.Windows.Forms.MessageBoxButtons.AbortRetryIgnore)
End If
```
[C#]
```
IUIService UIservice = (IUIService)this.GetService(
    typeof( System.Windows.Forms.Design.IUIService ) );
if( UIservice != null )
    UIservice.ShowMessage("Test message", "Test caption",
        System.Windows.Forms.MessageBoxButtons.AbortRetryIgnore);
```
[C++]
```
IUIService* UIservice = dynamic_cast<IUIService*>(this- ↵
>GetService(__typeof(System::Windows::Forms::Design::IUIService)));
if (UIservice != 0)
   UIservice->ShowMessage(S"Test message", S"Test caption", ↵
System::Windows::Forms::MessageBoxButtons::AbortRetryIgnore);
```

Requirements

Platforms: Windows 98, Windows NT 4.0, Windows Millennium Edition, Windows 2000, Windows XP Home Edition, Windows XP Professional, Windows Server 2003 family

IUIService.ShowToolWindow Method

Displays the specified tool window.

[Visual Basic]
```
Function ShowToolWindow( _
   ByVal toolWindow As Guid _
) As Boolean
```
[C#]
```
bool ShowToolWindow(
   Guid toolWindow
);
```
[C++]
```
bool ShowToolWindow(
   Guid toolWindow
);
```
[JScript]
```
function ShowToolWindow(
   toolWindow : Guid
) : Boolean;
```

Parameters

toolWindow
A **Guid** identifier for the tool window. This can be a custom **Guid** or one of the predefined values from **StandardToolWindows**.

Return Value

true if the tool window was successfully shown; **false** if it couldn't be shown or found.

Example

[Visual Basic]
```
Dim UIservice As IUIService = CType(Me.GetService( _
    GetType(System.Windows.Forms.Design.IUIService)), IUIService)
If Not (UIservice Is Nothing) Then
    UIservice.ShowToolWindow(StandardToolWindows.TaskList)
End If
```
[C#]
```
IUIService UIservice = (IUIService)this.GetService(
    typeof( System.Windows.Forms.Design.IUIService ) );
if( UIservice != null )
    UIservice.ShowToolWindow(StandardToolWindows.TaskList);
```
[C++]
```
IUIService* UIservice = dynamic_cast<IUIService*>(this- ↵
>GetService(__typeof(System::Windows::Forms::Design::IUIService)));
if (UIservice != 0)
   UIservice->ShowToolWindow(StandardToolWindows::TaskList);
```

Requirements

Platforms: Windows 98, Windows NT 4.0, Windows Millennium Edition, Windows 2000, Windows XP Home Edition, Windows XP Professional, Windows Server 2003 family

IWindowsFormsEditorService Interface

Provides an interface for UITypeEditors to display Windows Forms or to display a control in a drop down area from a property grid control in design mode.

[Visual Basic]
```
Public Interface IWindowsFormsEditorService
```
[C#]
```
public interface IWindowsFormsEditorService
```
[C++]
```
public __gc __interface IWindowsFormsEditorService
```
[JScript]
```
public interface IWindowsFormsEditorService
```

Remarks

The **IWindowsFormsEditorService** is only available through the **GetService** method of the **PropertyGrid** control.

This service is typically used to display a form from the **EditValue** method of a **UITypeEditor**. When a **PropertyGrid** invokes the **EditValue** method of a **UITypeEditor** to provide a user interface for editing the value of a property, the **EditValue** method is passed a reference to an **IServiceProvider** that can typically provide an instance of the **IWindowsFormsEditorService**. The methods of this service can be used to display dialog boxes and forms, or to show a **Control** within a drop down container that is shown on top of the property grid near the area of the value field whose value is being edited.

Example

[Visual Basic, C#, C++] The following example provides an example **UITypeEditor** that uses an **IWindowsFormsEditorService** to display a **Form** for user input.

[Visual Basic]
```
Imports System
Imports System.ComponentModel
Imports System.ComponentModel.Design
Imports System.Drawing
Imports System.Drawing.Design
Imports System.Windows.Forms
Imports System.Windows.Forms.Design

' Example UITypeEditor that uses the IWindowsFormsEditorService
' to display a Form.
<System.Security.Permissions.PermissionSetAttribute ↵
(System.Security.Permissions.SecurityAction.Demand, ↵
 Name:="FullTrust")> Public Class TestDialogEditor
   Inherits System.Drawing.Design.UITypeEditor

   Public Sub New()
    End Sub

    Public Overloads Overrides Function GetEditStyle ↵
 (ByVal context As System.ComponentModel.ITypeDescriptorContext) ↵
 As System.Drawing.Design.UITypeEditorEditStyle
        ' Indicates that this editor can display a Form-based ↵
interface.
        Return UITypeEditorEditStyle.Modal
    End Function

    Public Overloads Overrides Function EditValue(ByVal ↵
context As System.ComponentModel.ITypeDescriptorContext, ↵
ByVal provider As System.IServiceProvider, ByVal value As ↵
 Object) As Object
        ' Attempts to obtain an IWindowsFormsEditorService.
        Dim edSvc As IWindowsFormsEditorService = ↵
CType(provider.GetService(GetType ↵
 (IWindowsFormsEditorService)), IWindowsFormsEditorService)
        If edSvc Is Nothing Then
            Return Nothing
        End If

        ' Displays a StringInputDialog Form to get a user-adjustable
        ' string value.
        Dim form As New StringInputDialog(CStr(value))
        If edSvc.ShowDialog(form) = DialogResult.OK Then
            Return form.inputTextBox.Text
        End If

        ' If OK was not pressed, return the original value
        Return value

    End Function
End Class

' Example Form for entering a string.
Friend Class StringInputDialog
    Inherits System.Windows.Forms.Form

    Private ok_button As System.Windows.Forms.Button
    Private cancel_button As System.Windows.Forms.Button
    Public inputTextBox As System.Windows.Forms.TextBox

    Public Sub New(ByVal [text] As String)
        InitializeComponent()
        inputTextBox.Text = [text]
    End Sub

    Private Sub InitializeComponent()
        Me.ok_button = New System.Windows.Forms.Button()
        Me.cancel_button = New System.Windows.Forms.Button()
        Me.inputTextBox = New System.Windows.Forms.TextBox()
        Me.SuspendLayout()
        Me.ok_button.Anchor = ↵
System.Windows.Forms.AnchorStyles.Bottom Or ↵
System.Windows.Forms.AnchorStyles.Right
        Me.ok_button.Location = New System.Drawing.Point(180, 43)
        Me.ok_button.Name = "ok_button"
        Me.ok_button.TabIndex = 1
        Me.ok_button.Text = "OK"
        Me.ok_button.DialogResult = ↵
System.Windows.Forms.DialogResult.OK
        Me.cancel_button.Anchor = ↵
System.Windows.Forms.AnchorStyles.Bottom Or ↵
System.Windows.Forms.AnchorStyles.Right
        Me.cancel_button.Location = New System.Drawing.Point(260, 43)
        Me.cancel_button.Name = "cancel_button"
        Me.cancel_button.TabIndex = 2
        Me.cancel_button.Text = "Cancel"
        Me.cancel_button.DialogResult = ↵
System.Windows.Forms.DialogResult.Cancel
        Me.inputTextBox.Location = New System.Drawing.Point(6, 9)
        Me.inputTextBox.Name = "inputTextBox"
        Me.inputTextBox.Size = New System.Drawing.Size(327, 20)
        Me.inputTextBox.TabIndex = 0
        Me.inputTextBox.Text = ""
        Me.inputTextBox.Anchor = ↵
System.Windows.Forms.AnchorStyles.Top Or ↵
System.Windows.Forms.AnchorStyles.Left Or ↵
System.Windows.Forms.AnchorStyles.Right
        Me.AutoScaleBaseSize = New System.Drawing.Size(5, 13)
        Me.ClientSize = New System.Drawing.Size(342, 73)
        Me.Controls.AddRange(New ↵
System.Windows.Forms.Control() ↵
{Me.inputTextBox, Me.cancel_button, Me.ok_button})
        Me.MinimumSize = New System.Drawing.Size(350, 100)
        Me.Name = "StringInputDialog"
        Me.Text = "String Input Dialog"
        Me.ResumeLayout(False)
    End Sub

End Class
```

```
' Provides an example control that displays instructions in design mode,
' with which the example UITypeEditor is associated.
Public Class WinFormsEdServiceDialogExampleControl
    Inherits UserControl

    <EditorAttribute(GetType(TestDialogEditor), GetType(UITypeEditor))> _
    Public Property TestDialogString() As String
        Get
            Return localDialogTestString
        End Get
        Set(ByVal Value As String)
            localDialogTestString = Value
        End Set
    End Property
    Private localDialogTestString As String

    Public Sub New()
        localDialogTestString = "Test String"
        Me.Size = New Size(210, 74)
        Me.BackColor = Color.Beige
    End Sub

    Protected Overrides Sub OnPaint(ByVal e As System.Windows.Forms.PaintEventArgs)
        If Me.DesignMode Then
            e.Graphics.DrawString("Use the Properties window to show", New Font("Arial", 8), New SolidBrush(Color.Black), 5, 5)
            e.Graphics.DrawString("a Form dialog box, using the", New Font("Arial", 8), New SolidBrush(Color.Black), 5, 17)
            e.Graphics.DrawString("IWindowsFormsEditorService, for", New Font("Arial", 8), New SolidBrush(Color.Black), 5, 29)
            e.Graphics.DrawString("configuring this control's", New Font("Arial", 8), New SolidBrush(Color.Black), 5, 41)
            e.Graphics.DrawString("TestDialogString property.", New Font("Arial", 8), New SolidBrush(Color.Black), 5, 53)
        Else
            e.Graphics.DrawString("This example requires design mode.", New Font("Arial", 8), New SolidBrush(Color.Black), 5, 5)
        End If
    End Sub

End Class
```

[C#]

```
using System;
using System.ComponentModel;
using System.ComponentModel.Design;
using System.Drawing;
using System.Drawing.Design;
using System.Windows.Forms;
using System.Windows.Forms.Design;

namespace IWindowsFormsEditorServiceExample
{
    // Example UITypeEditor that uses the IWindowsFormsEditorService
    // to display a Form.
    [System.Security.Permissions.PermissionSet(System.Security.Permissions.SecurityAction.Demand, Name="FullTrust")]
    public class TestDialogEditor : System.Drawing.Design.UITypeEditor
    {
        public TestDialogEditor()
        {
        }

        public override System.Drawing.Design.UITypeEditorEditStyle GetEditStyle(System.ComponentModel.ITypeDescriptorContext context)
        {
            // Indicates that this editor can display a Form-based interface.
            return UITypeEditorEditStyle.Modal;
        }

        public override object EditValue(System.ComponentModel.ITypeDescriptorContext context, System.IServiceProvider provider, object value)
        {
            // Attempts to obtain an IWindowsFormsEditorService.
            IWindowsFormsEditorService edSvc = (IWindowsFormsEditorService)provider.GetService(typeof(IWindowsFormsEditorService));
            if( edSvc == null )
                return null;

            // Displays a StringInputDialog Form to get a user-adjustable
            // string value.
            StringInputDialog form = new StringInputDialog((string)value);
            if( edSvc.ShowDialog(form) == DialogResult.OK )
                return form.inputTextBox.Text;

            // If OK was not pressed, return the original value
            return value;
        }
    }

    // Example Form for entering a string.
    internal class StringInputDialog : System.Windows.Forms.Form
    {
        private System.Windows.Forms.Button ok_button;
        private System.Windows.Forms.Button cancel_button;
        public System.Windows.Forms.TextBox inputTextBox;

        public StringInputDialog(string text)
        {
            InitializeComponent();
            inputTextBox.Text = text;
        }

        private void InitializeComponent()
        {
            this.ok_button = new System.Windows.Forms.Button();
            this.cancel_button = new System.Windows.Forms.Button();
            this.inputTextBox = new System.Windows.Forms.TextBox();
            this.SuspendLayout();
            this.ok_button.Anchor = (System.Windows.Forms.AnchorStyles.Bottom | System.Windows.Forms.AnchorStyles.Right);
            this.ok_button.Location = new System.Drawing.Point(180, 43);
            this.ok_button.Name = "ok_button";
            this.ok_button.TabIndex = 1;
            this.ok_button.Text = "OK";
            this.ok_button.DialogResult = System.Windows.Forms.DialogResult.OK;
            this.cancel_button.Anchor = (System.Windows.Forms.AnchorStyles.Bottom | System.Windows.Forms.AnchorStyles.Right);
            this.cancel_button.Location = new System.Drawing.Point(260, 43);
            this.cancel_button.Name = "cancel_button";
            this.cancel_button.TabIndex = 2;
            this.cancel_button.Text = "Cancel";
            this.cancel_button.DialogResult = System.Windows.Forms.DialogResult.Cancel;
            this.inputTextBox.Location = new System.Drawing.Point(6, 9);
            this.inputTextBox.Name = "inputTextBox";
            this.inputTextBox.Size = new System.Drawing.Size(327, 20);
            this.inputTextBox.TabIndex = 0;
            this.inputTextBox.Text = "";
            this.inputTextBox.Anchor = ((System.Windows.Forms.AnchorStyles.Top | System.Windows.Forms.AnchorStyles.Left)
                    | System.Windows.Forms.AnchorStyles.Right);
            this.AutoScaleBaseSize = new System.Drawing.Size(5, 13);
            this.ClientSize = new System.Drawing.Size(342, 73);
```

```
            this.Controls.AddRange(new System.Windows.Forms.Control[] {
                                            this.inputTextBox,
                                      this.cancel_button,
                                            this.ok_button});
            this.MinimumSize = new System.Drawing.Size(350, 100);
            this.Name = "StringInputDialog";
            this.Text = "String Input Dialog";
            this.ResumeLayout(false);
        }
    }

    // Provides an example control that displays instructions ↵
in design mode,
    // with which the example UITypeEditor is associated.
    public class WinFormsEdServiceDialogExampleControl : UserControl
    {
        [EditorAttribute(typeof(TestDialogEditor), ↵
typeof(UITypeEditor))]
        public string TestDialogString
        {
            get
            {
                return localDialogTestString;
            }
            set
            {
                localDialogTestString = value;
            }
        }
        private string localDialogTestString;

        public WinFormsEdServiceDialogExampleControl()
        {
            localDialogTestString = "Test String";
            this.Size = new Size(210, 74);
            this.BackColor = Color.Beige;
        }

        protected override void ↵
OnPaint(System.Windows.Forms.PaintEventArgs e)
        {
            if( this.DesignMode )
            {
                e.Graphics.DrawString("Use the Properties ↵
window to show", new Font("Arial", 8), new SolidBrush ↵
 (Color.Black), 5, 5);
                e.Graphics.DrawString("a Form dialog box, ↵
 using the", new Font("Arial", 8), new SolidBrush(Color.Black), 5, 17);
                e.Graphics.DrawString ↵
 ("IWindowsFormsEditorService, for", new Font("Arial", 8), ↵
 new SolidBrush(Color.Black), 5, 29);
                e.Graphics.DrawString("configuring this ↵
control's", new Font("Arial", 8), new SolidBrush(Color.Black), 5, 41);
                e.Graphics.DrawString ↵
 ("TestDialogString property.", new Font("Arial", 8), new ↵
SolidBrush(Color.Black), 5, 53);
            }
            else
            {
                e.Graphics.DrawString("This example requires ↵
design mode.", new Font("Arial", 8), new SolidBrush ↵
 (Color.Black), 5, 5);
            }
        }
    }
}
```

[C++]

```
#using <mscorlib.dll>
#using <System.Windows.Forms.dll>
#using <System.Drawing.dll>
#using <System.dll>

using namespace System;
using namespace System::ComponentModel;
using namespace System::ComponentModel::Design;
using namespace System::Drawing;
using namespace System::Drawing::Design;
using namespace System::Windows::Forms;
using namespace System::Windows::Forms::Design;

namespace IWindowsFormsEditorServiceExample {

   // Example Form for entering a String*.
private __gc class StringInputDialog : public ↵
System::Windows::Forms::Form {
private:
   System::Windows::Forms::Button*  ok_button;
   System::Windows::Forms::Button*  cancel_button;

public:
   System::Windows::Forms::TextBox*  inputTextBox;

   StringInputDialog(String* text) {
      InitializeComponent();
      inputTextBox->Text = text;
   }

private:
   void InitializeComponent() {
      this->ok_button = new System::Windows::Forms::Button();
      this->cancel_button = new System::Windows::Forms::Button();
      this->inputTextBox = new System::Windows::Forms::TextBox();
      this->SuspendLayout();
      this->ok_button->Anchor = ↵
static_cast<AnchorStyles> ↵
 (System::Windows::Forms::AnchorStyles::Bottom | ↵
System::Windows::Forms::AnchorStyles::Right);
      this->ok_button->Location =  System::Drawing::Point(180, 43);
      this->ok_button->Name = S"ok_button";
      this->ok_button->TabIndex = 1;
      this->ok_button->Text = S"OK";
      this->ok_button->DialogResult = ↵
System::Windows::Forms::DialogResult::OK;
      this->cancel_button->Anchor = static_cast<AnchorStyles> ↵
 (System::Windows::Forms::AnchorStyles::Bottom | ↵
System::Windows::Forms::AnchorStyles::Right);
      this->cancel_button->Location =  System::Drawing::Point(260, 43);
      this->cancel_button->Name = S"cancel_button";
      this->cancel_button->TabIndex = 2;
      this->cancel_button->Text = S"Cancel";
      this->cancel_button->DialogResult = ↵
System::Windows::Forms::DialogResult::Cancel;
      this->inputTextBox->Location =  System::Drawing::Point(6, 9);
      this->inputTextBox->Name = S"inputTextBox";
      this->inputTextBox->Size =  System::Drawing::Size(327, 20);
      this->inputTextBox->TabIndex = 0;
      this->inputTextBox->Text = S"";
      this->inputTextBox->Anchor = ↵
static_cast<AnchorStyles> ↵
 (System::Windows::Forms::AnchorStyles::Top | ↵
System::Windows::Forms::AnchorStyles::Left
         | System::Windows::Forms::AnchorStyles::Right);
      this->AutoScaleBaseSize =  System::Drawing::Size(5, 13);
      this->ClientSize =  System::Drawing::Size(342, 73);

      System::Windows::Forms::Control* temp0 [] = {this-> ↵
inputTextBox, this->cancel_button, this->ok_button};
      this->Controls->AddRange(temp0);
      this->MinimumSize =  System::Drawing::Size(350, 100);
      this->Name = S"StringInputDialog";
      this->Text = S"String Input Dialog";
      this->ResumeLayout(false);
   }
};

// Example UITypeEditor that uses the IWindowsFormsEditorService*
// to display a Form.
public __gc class TestDialogEditor : public ↵
System::Drawing::Design::UITypeEditor {
```

```
public:
   TestDialogEditor() {
   }
   [System::Security::Permissions::PermissionSet
 (System::Security::Permissions::SecurityAction::Demand,
Name="FullTrust")]
   System::Drawing::Design::UITypeEditorEditStyle
GetEditStyle(System::ComponentModel::ITypeDescriptorContext* context) {
      // Indicates that this editor can display a Form-based interface.
      return UITypeEditorEditStyle::Modal;
   }

   [System::Security::Permissions::PermissionSet
 (System::Security::Permissions::SecurityAction::Demand,
Name="FullTrust")]
   Object* EditValue
 (System::ComponentModel::ITypeDescriptorContext* context,
System::IServiceProvider* provider, Object* value) {
      // Attempts to obtain an IWindowsFormsEditorService*.
      IWindowsFormsEditorService* edSvc =
dynamic_cast<IWindowsFormsEditorService*>(provider-
>GetService(__typeof(IWindowsFormsEditorService)));
      if (edSvc == 0)
         return 0;

      // Displays a StringInputDialog Form to get a user-adjustable
      // String* value.
      StringInputDialog* form = new
StringInputDialog(dynamic_cast<String*>(value));
      if (edSvc->ShowDialog(form) == DialogResult::OK)
         return form->inputTextBox->Text;

      // If OK was not pressed, return the original value
      return value;
   }
};

// Provides an example control that displays instructions
 in design mode,
// with which the example UITypeEditor is associated.
public __gc class WinFormsEdServiceDialogExampleControl
 : public UserControl {
public:
   [EditorAttribute(__typeof(TestDialogEditor),
__typeof(UITypeEditor))]
   __property String* get_TestDialogString() {
      return localDialogTestString;
   }
   __property void set_TestDialogString(String* value) {
      localDialogTestString = value;
   }

private:
   String*  localDialogTestString;

public:
   WinFormsEdServiceDialogExampleControl() {
      localDialogTestString = S"Test String";
      this->Size =  System::Drawing::Size(210, 74);
      this->BackColor = Color::Beige;
   }

protected:
   void OnPaint(System::Windows::Forms::PaintEventArgs* e) {
      if (this->DesignMode) {
         e->Graphics->DrawString(S"Use the Properties
window to show", new System::Drawing::Font(S"Arial", 8),
new SolidBrush(Color::Black), 5, 5);
         e->Graphics->DrawString(S"a Form dialog box,
 using the", new System::Drawing::Font(S"Arial", 8), new
SolidBrush(Color::Black), 5, 17);
         e->Graphics->DrawString(S"IWindowsFormsEditorService*,
 for", new System::Drawing::Font(S"Arial", 8), new
SolidBrush(Color::Black), 5, 29);
         e->Graphics->DrawString(S"configuring this control's",
 new System::Drawing::Font(S"Arial", 8), new SolidBrush
 (Color::Black), 5, 41);
         e->Graphics->DrawString(S"TestDialogString property.",
 new System::Drawing::Font(S"Arial", 8), new SolidBrush
 (Color::Black), 5, 53);
      } else {
         e->Graphics->DrawString(S"This example requires
design mode.", new System::Drawing::Font(S"Arial", 8), new
SolidBrush(Color::Black), 5, 5);
      }
   }
};
}
```

[Visual Basic, C#, C++] The following example provides an example **UITypeEditor** that uses an **IWindowsFormsEditorService** to display a drop-down **UserControl** for user input.

[Visual Basic]

```
Imports System
Imports System.ComponentModel
Imports System.ComponentModel.Design
Imports System.Drawing
Imports System.Drawing.Design
Imports System.Windows.Forms
Imports System.Windows.Forms.Design

' Example UITypeEditor that uses the IWindowsFormsEditorService to
' display a drop-down control.
Public Class TestDropDownEditor
   Inherits System.Drawing.Design.UITypeEditor

   Public Sub New()
    End Sub

   <System.Security.Permissions.PermissionSetAttribute
 (System.Security.Permissions.SecurityAction.Demand,
Name:="FullTrust")> _
    Public Overloads Overrides Function GetEditStyle(ByVal
context As System.ComponentModel.ITypeDescriptorContext) As
System.Drawing.Design.UITypeEditorEditStyle
        ' Indicates that this editor can display a control-based
        ' drop-down interface.
        Return UITypeEditorEditStyle.DropDown
    End Function

   <System.Security.Permissions.PermissionSetAttribute
 (System.Security.Permissions.SecurityAction.Demand,
Name:="FullTrust")> _
    Public Overloads Overrides Function EditValue
 (ByVal context As System.ComponentModel.ITypeDescriptorContext,
 ByVal provider As System.IServiceProvider, ByVal
 value As Object) As Object

        ' Attempts to obtain an IWindowsFormsEditorService.
        Dim edSvc As IWindowsFormsEditorService =
CType(provider.GetService(GetType
 (IWindowsFormsEditorService)), IWindowsFormsEditorService)
        If edSvc Is Nothing Then
            Return value
        End If

        ' Displays a drop-down control.
        Dim inputControl As New StringInputControl(CStr(value), edSvc)
        edSvc.DropDownControl(inputControl)
        Return inputControl.inputTextBox.Text
    End Function

End Class

' Example control for entering a string.
Friend Class StringInputControl
    Inherits System.Windows.Forms.UserControl

    Public inputTextBox As System.Windows.Forms.TextBox
    Private WithEvents ok_button As System.Windows.Forms.Button
    Private WithEvents cancel_button As System.Windows.Forms.Button
    Private edSvc As IWindowsFormsEditorService
```

```
    Public Sub New(ByVal [text] As String, ByVal edSvc As ↵
IWindowsFormsEditorService)
        InitializeComponent()
        inputTextBox.Text = [text]
        ' Stores IWindowsFormsEditorService reference to use to
        ' close the control.
        Me.edSvc = edSvc
    End Sub

    Private Sub InitializeComponent()
        Me.inputTextBox = New System.Windows.Forms.TextBox()
        Me.ok_button = New System.Windows.Forms.Button()
        Me.cancel_button = New System.Windows.Forms.Button()
        Me.SuspendLayout()
        Me.inputTextBox.Anchor = ↵
System.Windows.Forms.AnchorStyles.Top Or ↵
System.Windows.Forms.AnchorStyles.Left Or ↵
System.Windows.Forms.AnchorStyles.Right
        Me.inputTextBox.Location = New System.Drawing.Point(6, 7)
        Me.inputTextBox.Name = "inputTextBox"
        Me.inputTextBox.Size = New System.Drawing.Size(336, 20)
        Me.inputTextBox.TabIndex = 0
        Me.inputTextBox.Text = ""
        Me.ok_button.Anchor = ↵
System.Windows.Forms.AnchorStyles.Bottom Or ↵
System.Windows.Forms.AnchorStyles.Right
        Me.ok_button.DialogResult = ↵
System.Windows.Forms.DialogResult.OK
        Me.ok_button.Location = New System.Drawing.Point(186, 38)
        Me.ok_button.Name = "ok_button"
        Me.ok_button.TabIndex = 1
        Me.ok_button.Text = "OK"
        Me.cancel_button.Anchor = ↵
System.Windows.Forms.AnchorStyles.Bottom Or ↵
System.Windows.Forms.AnchorStyles.Right
        Me.cancel_button.DialogResult = ↵
System.Windows.Forms.DialogResult.Cancel
        Me.cancel_button.Location = New System.Drawing.Point(267, 38)
        Me.cancel_button.Name = "cancel_button"
        Me.cancel_button.TabIndex = 2
        Me.cancel_button.Text = "Cancel"
        Me.Controls.AddRange(New System.Windows.Forms.Control() ↵
{Me.cancel_button, Me.ok_button, Me.inputTextBox})
        Me.Name = "StringInputControl"
        Me.Size = New System.Drawing.Size(350, 70)
        Me.ResumeLayout(False)
    End Sub

    Private Sub CloseControl(ByVal sender As Object, ByVal e As ↵
EventArgs) Handles ok_button.Click, cancel_button.Click
        edSvc.CloseDropDown()
    End Sub

End Class

' Provides an example control that displays instructions in ↵
 design mode,
' with which the example UITypeEditor is associated.
Public Class WinFormsEdServiceDropDownExampleControl
    Inherits UserControl

    <EditorAttribute(GetType(TestDropDownEditor), ↵
GetType(UITypeEditor))> _
    Public Property TestDropDownString() As String
        Get
            Return localDropDownTestString
        End Get
        Set(ByVal Value As String)
            localDropDownTestString = Value
        End Set
    End Property
    Private localDropDownTestString As String

    Public Sub New()
        localDropDownTestString = "Test String"
        Me.Size = New Size(210, 74)
        Me.BackColor = Color.Beige
    End Sub

    Protected Overrides Sub OnPaint(ByVal e As ↵
System.Windows.Forms.PaintEventArgs)
        If Me.DesignMode Then
            e.Graphics.DrawString("Use the Properties ↵
window to show", New Font("Arial", 8), New SolidBrush ↵
 (Color.Black), 5, 5)
            e.Graphics.DrawString("a drop-down control, ↵
using the", New Font("Arial", 8), New SolidBrush(Color.Black), 5, 17)
            e.Graphics.DrawString("IWindowsFormsEditorService, ↵
 for", New Font("Arial", 8), New SolidBrush(Color.Black), 5, 29)
            e.Graphics.DrawString("configuring this control's", ↵
 New Font("Arial", 8), New SolidBrush(Color.Black), 5, 41)
            e.Graphics.DrawString("TestDropDownString property. ↵
", New Font("Arial", 8), New SolidBrush(Color.Black), 5, 53)
        Else
            e.Graphics.DrawString("This example requires design ↵
 mode.", New Font("Arial", 8), New SolidBrush(Color.Black), 5, 5)
        End If
    End Sub

End Class
```

[C#]

```
using System;
using System.ComponentModel;
using System.ComponentModel.Design;
using System.Drawing;
using System.Drawing.Design;
using System.Windows.Forms;
using System.Windows.Forms.Design;

namespace IWindowsFormsEditorServiceExample
{
    // Example UITypeEditor that uses the IWindowsFormsEditorService to
    // display a drop-down control.
    public class TestDropDownEditor : ↵
System.Drawing.Design.UITypeEditor
    {
        public TestDropDownEditor()
        {
        }

    [System.Security.Permissions.PermissionSet ↵
 (System.Security.Permissions.SecurityAction.Demand, Name="FullTrust")]
        public override System.Drawing.Design.UITypeEditorEditStyle ↵
 ↵
GetEditStyle(System.ComponentModel.ITypeDescriptorContext context)
        {
            // Indicates that this editor can display a control-based
            // drop-down interface.
            return UITypeEditorEditStyle.DropDown;
        }

    [System.Security.Permissions.PermissionSet ↵
 (System.Security.Permissions.SecurityAction.Demand, Name="FullTrust")]
        public override object ↵
EditValue(System.ComponentModel.ITypeDescriptorContext context, ↵
System.IServiceProvider provider, object value)
        {
            // Attempts to obtain an IWindowsFormsEditorService.
            IWindowsFormsEditorService edSvc = ↵
 (IWindowsFormsEditorService)provider.GetService ↵
 (typeof(IWindowsFormsEditorService));
            if( edSvc == null )
                return value;

            // Displays a drop-down control.
            StringInputControl inputControl = new ↵
StringInputControl((string)value, edSvc);
            edSvc.DropDownControl(inputControl);
            return inputControl.inputTextBox.Text;
        }
    }
```

```
    // Example control for entering a string.
    internal class StringInputControl :                              ↵
System.Windows.Forms.UserControl
    {
        public System.Windows.Forms.TextBox inputTextBox;
        private System.Windows.Forms.Button ok_button;
        private System.Windows.Forms.Button cancel_button;
        private IWindowsFormsEditorService edSvc;

        public StringInputControl(string text,                       ↵
IWindowsFormsEditorService edSvc)
        {
            InitializeComponent();
            inputTextBox.Text = text;
            // Stores IWindowsFormsEditorService reference to use to
            // close the control.
            this.edSvc = edSvc;
        }

        private void InitializeComponent()
        {
            this.inputTextBox = new System.Windows.Forms.TextBox();
            this.ok_button = new System.Windows.Forms.Button();
            this.cancel_button = new System.Windows.Forms.Button();
            this.SuspendLayout();
            this.inputTextBox.Anchor =                               ↵
 ((System.Windows.Forms.AnchorStyles.Top |                           ↵
System.Windows.Forms.AnchorStyles.Left)
                | System.Windows.Forms.AnchorStyles.Right);
            this.inputTextBox.Location =                             ↵
new System.Drawing.Point(6, 7);
            this.inputTextBox.Name = "inputTextBox";
            this.inputTextBox.Size = new System.Drawing.Size(336, 20);
            this.inputTextBox.TabIndex = 0;
            this.inputTextBox.Text = "";
            this.ok_button.Anchor =                                  ↵
 (System.Windows.Forms.AnchorStyles.Bottom |                         ↵
System.Windows.Forms.AnchorStyles.Right);
            this.ok_button.DialogResult =                            ↵
System.Windows.Forms.DialogResult.OK;
            this.ok_button.Location = new                            ↵
System.Drawing.Point(186, 38);
            this.ok_button.Name = "ok_button";
            this.ok_button.TabIndex = 1;
            this.ok_button.Text = "OK";
            this.ok_button.Click += new EventHandler(this.CloseControl);
            this.cancel_button.Anchor =                              ↵
 (System.Windows.Forms.AnchorStyles.Bottom |                         ↵
System.Windows.Forms.AnchorStyles.Right);
            this.cancel_button.DialogResult =                        ↵
System.Windows.Forms.DialogResult.Cancel;
            this.cancel_button.Location = new                        ↵
System.Drawing.Point(267, 38);
            this.cancel_button.Name = "cancel_button";
            this.cancel_button.TabIndex = 2;
            this.cancel_button.Text = "Cancel";
            this.cancel_button.Click += new
EventHandler(this.CloseControl);
            this.Controls.AddRange(new System.Windows.Forms.Control[] {
                                                   this.cancel_button,
                                                  this.ok_button,
                                              this.inputTextBox});
            this.Name = "StringInputControl";
            this.Size = new System.Drawing.Size(350, 70);
            this.ResumeLayout(false);
        }

        private void CloseControl(object sender, EventArgs e)
        {
            edSvc.CloseDropDown();
        }
    }

    // Provides an example control that displays instructions       ↵
in design mode,
    // with which the example UITypeEditor is associated.
    public class WinFormsEdServiceDropDownExampleControl : UserControl
    {
        [EditorAttribute(typeof(TestDropDownEditor),                 ↵
typeof(UITypeEditor))]
        public string TestDropDownString
        {
            get
            {
                return localDropDownTestString;
            }
            set
            {
                localDropDownTestString = value;
            }
        }

        private string localDropDownTestString;

        public WinFormsEdServiceDropDownExampleControl()
        {
            localDropDownTestString = "Test String";
            this.Size = new Size(210, 74);
            this.BackColor = Color.Beige;
        }

        protected override void                                      ↵
OnPaint(System.Windows.Forms.PaintEventArgs e)
        {
            if( this.DesignMode )
            {
                e.Graphics.DrawString                                ↵
 ("Use the Properties window to show", new Font("Arial", 8),         ↵
 new SolidBrush(Color.Black), 5, 5);
                e.Graphics.DrawString("a drop-down control,          ↵
using the", new Font("Arial", 8), new SolidBrush(Color.Black), 5, 17);
                e.Graphics.DrawString                                ↵
 ("IWindowsFormsEditorService, for", new Font("Arial", 8),           ↵
 new SolidBrush(Color.Black), 5, 29);
                e.Graphics.DrawString("configuring this              ↵
control's", new Font("Arial", 8), new SolidBrush(Color.Black), 5, 41);
                e.Graphics.DrawString("TestDropDownString            ↵
property.", new Font("Arial", 8), new SolidBrush(Color.Black), 5, 53);
            }
            else
            {
                e.Graphics.DrawString("This example requires         ↵
 design mode.", new Font("Arial", 8), new SolidBrush(Color.Black), 5, 5);
            }
        }
    }
}
```

[C++]

```
#using <mscorlib.dll>
#using <System.Windows.Forms.dll>
#using <System.Drawing.dll>
#using <System.dll>

using namespace System;
using namespace System::ComponentModel;
using namespace System::ComponentModel::Design;
using namespace System::Drawing;
using namespace System::Drawing::Design;
using namespace System::Windows::Forms;
using namespace System::Windows::Forms::Design;

namespace IWindowsFormsEditorServiceExample {
   // Example control for entering a String*.
private __gc class StringInputControl : public
System::Windows::Forms::UserControl {
public:
   System::Windows::Forms::TextBox*  inputTextBox;
private:
   System::Windows::Forms::Button*  ok_button;
   System::Windows::Forms::Button*  cancel_button;
   IWindowsFormsEditorService*  edSvc;
```

```
public:
   StringInputControl(String* text, IWindowsFormsEditorService*        ↵
 edSvc) {
      InitializeComponent();
      inputTextBox->Text = text;
      // Stores IWindowsFormsEditorService* reference to use to
      // close the control.
      this->edSvc = edSvc;
   }

private:
   void InitializeComponent() {
      this->inputTextBox = new System::Windows::Forms::TextBox();
      this->ok_button = new System::Windows::Forms::Button();
      this->cancel_button = new System::Windows::Forms::Button();
      this->SuspendLayout();
      this->inputTextBox->Anchor = static_cast<AnchorStyles>(
         System::Windows::Forms::AnchorStyles::Top
         | System::Windows::Forms::AnchorStyles::Left
         | System::Windows::Forms::AnchorStyles::Right);
      this->inputTextBox->Location =  System::Drawing::Point(6, 7);
      this->inputTextBox->Name = S"inputTextBox";
      this->inputTextBox->Size =  System::Drawing::Size(336, 20);
      this->inputTextBox->TabIndex = 0;
      this->inputTextBox->Text = S"";
      this->ok_button->Anchor = static_cast<AnchorStyles>(
         System::Windows::Forms::AnchorStyles::Bottom
         | System::Windows::Forms::AnchorStyles::Right);
      this->ok_button->DialogResult =                                    ↵
System::Windows::Forms::DialogResult::OK;
      this->ok_button->Location =  System::Drawing::Point(186, 38);
      this->ok_button->Name = S"ok_button";
      this->ok_button->TabIndex = 1;
      this->ok_button->Text = S"OK";
      this->ok_button->Click += new EventHandler(this, CloseControl);
      this->cancel_button->Anchor = static_cast<AnchorStyles>(
         System::Windows::Forms::AnchorStyles::Bottom
         | System::Windows::Forms::AnchorStyles::Right);
      this->cancel_button->DialogResult =                                ↵
System::Windows::Forms::DialogResult::Cancel;
      this->cancel_button->Location =  System::Drawing::Point(267, 38);
      this->cancel_button->Name = S"cancel_button";
      this->cancel_button->TabIndex = 2;
      this->cancel_button->Text = S"Cancel";
      this->cancel_button->Click += new EventHandler(this,               ↵
CloseControl);

      System::Windows::Forms::Control* temp0 [] = {this->cancel_button,
         this->ok_button,
         this->inputTextBox};

      this->Controls->AddRange(temp0);
      this->Name = S"StringInputControl";
      this->Size =  System::Drawing::Size(350, 70);
      this->ResumeLayout(false);
   }

   void CloseControl(Object* sender, EventArgs* e) {
      edSvc->CloseDropDown();
   }
};

// Example UITypeEditor that uses the IWindowsFormsEditorService* to
// display a drop-down control.
public __gc class TestDropDownEditor : public                            ↵
System::Drawing::Design::UITypeEditor {
public:
   TestDropDownEditor() {
   }
[System::Security::Permissions::PermissionSet                            ↵
 (System::Security::Permissions::SecurityAction::Demand,                 ↵
Name="FullTrust")]
   System::Drawing::Design::UITypeEditorEditStyle GetEditStyle(
      System::ComponentModel::ITypeDescriptorContext* context) {
      // Indicates that this editor can display a control-based
      // drop-down interface.
      return UITypeEditorEditStyle::DropDown;
   }
[System::Security::Permissions::PermissionSet                            ↵
 (System::Security::Permissions::SecurityAction::Demand,                 ↵
Name="FullTrust")]
   Object* EditValue(
      System::ComponentModel::ITypeDescriptorContext* context,
      System::IServiceProvider* provider,
      Object* value) {
      // Attempts to obtain an IWindowsFormsEditorService*.
      IWindowsFormsEditorService* edSvc =                                ↵
dynamic_cast<IWindowsFormsEditorService*>(
         provider->GetService(__typeof(IWindowsFormsEditorService)));
      if (edSvc == 0)
         return value;

      // Displays a drop-down control.
      StringInputControl* inputControl = new StringInputControl(
         dynamic_cast<String*>(value), edSvc);
      edSvc->DropDownControl(inputControl);
      return inputControl->inputTextBox->Text;
   }
};

// Provides an example control that displays instructions in             ↵
 design mode,
// with which the example UITypeEditor is associated.
public __gc class WinFormsEdServiceDropDownExampleControl :              ↵
public UserControl {
public:
   [EditorAttribute(__typeof(TestDropDownEditor),                        ↵
__typeof(UITypeEditor))]
   __property String* get_TestDropDownString() {
      return localDropDownTestString;
   }
   __property void set_TestDropDownString(String* value) {
      localDropDownTestString = value;
   }

private:
   String*  localDropDownTestString;

public:
   WinFormsEdServiceDropDownExampleControl() {
      localDropDownTestString = S"Test String";
      this->Size =  System::Drawing::Size(210, 74);
      this->BackColor = Color::Beige;
   }

protected:
   void OnPaint(System::Windows::Forms::PaintEventArgs* e) {
      if (this->DesignMode) {
         e->Graphics->DrawString(S"Use the Properties window to show",
            new System::Drawing::Font(S"Arial", 8), new                  ↵
SolidBrush(Color::Black), 5, 5);
         e->Graphics->DrawString(S"a drop-down control, using the",
            new System::Drawing::Font(S"Arial", 8), new                  ↵
SolidBrush(Color::Black), 5, 17);
         e->Graphics->DrawString(S"IWindowsFormsEditorService*, for",
            new System::Drawing::Font(S"Arial", 8), new                  ↵
SolidBrush(Color::Black), 5, 29);
         e->Graphics->DrawString(S"configuring this control's",
            new System::Drawing::Font(S"Arial", 8), new                  ↵
SolidBrush(Color::Black), 5, 41);
         e->Graphics->DrawString(S"TestDropDownString property.",
            new System::Drawing::Font(S"Arial", 8), new                  ↵
SolidBrush(Color::Black), 5, 53);
      } else {
         e->Graphics->DrawString(S"This example requires design mode.",
            new System::Drawing::Font(S"Arial", 8), new                  ↵
SolidBrush(Color::Black), 5, 5);
      }
   }
};
}
```

Requirements

Namespace: System.Windows.Forms.Design

Platforms: Windows 98, Windows NT 4.0, Windows Millennium Edition, Windows 2000, Windows XP Home Edition, Windows XP Professional, Windows Server 2003 family

Assembly: System.Windows.Forms (in System.Windows.Forms.dll)

IWindowsFormsEditorService.CloseDropDown Method

Closes any previously opened drop down control area.

```
[Visual Basic]
Sub CloseDropDown()
[C#]
void CloseDropDown();
[C++]
void CloseDropDown();
[JScript]
function CloseDropDown();
```

Remarks

This method closes the drop down container area for a control that has been shown using the **DropDownControl** method, and releases the drop down container's reference to the control.

Requirements

Platforms: Windows 98, Windows NT 4.0, Windows Millennium Edition, Windows 2000, Windows XP Home Edition, Windows XP Professional, Windows Server 2003 family

IWindowsFormsEditorService.DropDownControl Method

Displays the specified control in a drop down area below a value field of the property grid that provides this service.

```
[Visual Basic]
Sub DropDownControl( _
   ByVal control As Control _
)
[C#]
void DropDownControl(
   Control control
);
[C++]
void DropDownControl(
   Control* control
);
[JScript]
function DropDownControl(
   control : Control
);
```

Parameters

control

The drop down list **Control** to open.

Remarks

The **EditValue** method of a **UITypeEditor** can call this method to display a specified control in a drop down area over the property grid hosting the editor which uses this service.

When possible, the dimensions of the control will be maintained. If this is not possible due to the screen layout, the control may be resized. To ensure that the control resizes neatly, you should implement docking and anchoring, and possibly any resize event handling update code. If the user performs an action that causes the drop down to close, the control will be hidden and disposed by garbage collection if there is no other stored reference to the control.

Requirements

Platforms: Windows 98, Windows NT 4.0, Windows Millennium Edition, Windows 2000, Windows XP Home Edition, Windows XP Professional, Windows Server 2003 family

IWindowsFormsEditorService.ShowDialog Method

Shows the specified **Form**.

```
[Visual Basic]
Function ShowDialog( _
   ByVal dialog As Form _
) As DialogResult
[C#]
DialogResult ShowDialog(
   Form dialog
);
[C++]
DialogResult ShowDialog(
   Form* dialog
);
[JScript]
function ShowDialog(
   dialog : Form
) : DialogResult;
```

Parameters

dialog

The **Form** to display.

Return Value

A **DialogResult** indicating the result code returned by the **Form**.

Remarks

This method displays the specified form.

Requirements

Platforms: Windows 98, Windows NT 4.0, Windows Millennium Edition, Windows 2000, Windows XP Home Edition, Windows XP Professional, Windows Server 2003 family

MenuCommands Class

Defines a set of **CommandID** fields that each correspond to a command function provided by the host environment.

System.Object
  System.ComponentModel.Design.StandardCommands
    System.Windows.Forms.Design.MenuCommands

[Visual Basic]
```
NotInheritable Public Class MenuCommands
   Inherits StandardCommands
```
[C#]
```
public sealed class MenuCommands : StandardCommands
```
[C++]
```
public __gc __sealed class MenuCommands : public StandardCommands
```
[JScript]
```
public class MenuCommands extends StandardCommands
```

Thread Safety

Any public static (**Shared** in Visual Basic) members of this type are safe for multithreaded operations. Any instance members are not guaranteed to be thread safe.

Remarks

MenuCommands contains a set of **CommandID** fields that can be used to specify a command to link when adding a command using the **AddCommand** method of the **IMenuCommandService**.

Requirements

Namespace: System.Windows.Forms.Design

Platforms: Windows 98, Windows NT 4.0, Windows Millennium Edition, Windows 2000, Windows XP Home Edition, Windows XP Professional, Windows Server 2003 family

Assembly: System.Design (in System.Design.dll)

MenuCommands Constructor

Initializes a new instance of the **MenuCommands** class.

[Visual Basic]
```
Public Sub New()
```
[C#]
```
public MenuCommands();
```
[C++]
```
public: MenuCommands();
```
[JScript]
```
public function MenuCommands();
```

Remarks

The default constructor initializes any fields to their default values.

Requirements

Platforms: Windows 98, Windows NT 4.0, Windows Millennium Edition, Windows 2000, Windows XP Home Edition, Windows XP Professional, Windows Server 2003 family

.NET Framework Security:

- Full trust for the immediate caller. This member cannot be used by partially trusted code.

MenuCommands.ComponentTrayMenu Field

A **CommandID** that can be used to access the component tray menu.

[Visual Basic]
```
Public Shared ReadOnly ComponentTrayMenu As CommandID
```
[C#]
```
public static readonly CommandID ComponentTrayMenu;
```
[C++]
```
public: static CommandID* ComponentTrayMenu;
```
[JScript]
```
public static var ComponentTrayMenu : CommandID;
```

Requirements

Platforms: Windows 98, Windows NT 4.0, Windows Millennium Edition, Windows 2000, Windows XP Home Edition, Windows XP Professional, Windows Server 2003 family

MenuCommands.ContainerMenu Field

A **CommandID** that can be used to access the container menu.

[Visual Basic]
```
Public Shared ReadOnly ContainerMenu As CommandID
```
[C#]
```
public static readonly CommandID ContainerMenu;
```
[C++]
```
public: static CommandID* ContainerMenu;
```
[JScript]
```
public static var ContainerMenu : CommandID;
```

Requirements

Platforms: Windows 98, Windows NT 4.0, Windows Millennium Edition, Windows 2000, Windows XP Home Edition, Windows XP Professional, Windows Server 2003 family

MenuCommands.DesignerProperties Field

A **CommandID** that can be used to access the properties page for the designer.

[Visual Basic]
```
Public Shared ReadOnly DesignerProperties As CommandID
```
[C#]
```
public static readonly CommandID DesignerProperties;
```
[C++]
```
public: static CommandID* DesignerProperties;
```
[JScript]
```
public static var DesignerProperties : CommandID;
```

Requirements

Platforms: Windows 98, Windows NT 4.0, Windows Millennium Edition, Windows 2000, Windows XP Home Edition, Windows XP Professional, Windows Server 2003 family

MenuCommands.KeyCancel Field

A **CommandID** that can be used to access the cancel key handler.

[Visual Basic]
```
Public Shared ReadOnly KeyCancel As CommandID
```
[C#]
```
public static readonly CommandID KeyCancel;
```
[C++]
```
public: static CommandID* KeyCancel;
```
[JScript]
```
public static var KeyCancel : CommandID;
```

Requirements

Platforms: Windows 98, Windows NT 4.0, Windows Millennium Edition, Windows 2000, Windows XP Home Edition, Windows XP Professional, Windows Server 2003 family

MenuCommands.KeyDefaultAction Field

A **CommandID** that can be used to access the default key handler.

[Visual Basic]
```
Public Shared ReadOnly KeyDefaultAction As CommandID
```
[C#]
```
public static readonly CommandID KeyDefaultAction;
```
[C++]
```
public: static CommandID* KeyDefaultAction;
```
[JScript]
```
public static var KeyDefaultAction : CommandID;
```

Requirements

Platforms: Windows 98, Windows NT 4.0, Windows Millennium Edition, Windows 2000, Windows XP Home Edition, Windows XP Professional, Windows Server 2003 family

MenuCommands.KeyMoveDown Field

A **CommandID** that can be used to access the key move down handler.

[Visual Basic]
```
Public Shared ReadOnly KeyMoveDown As CommandID
```
[C#]
```
public static readonly CommandID KeyMoveDown;
```
[C++]
```
public: static CommandID* KeyMoveDown;
```
[JScript]
```
public static var KeyMoveDown : CommandID;
```

Requirements

Platforms: Windows 98, Windows NT 4.0, Windows Millennium Edition, Windows 2000, Windows XP Home Edition, Windows XP Professional, Windows Server 2003 family

MenuCommands.KeyMoveLeft Field

A **CommandID** that can be used to access the key move left handler.

[Visual Basic]
```
Public Shared ReadOnly KeyMoveLeft As CommandID
```
[C#]
```
public static readonly CommandID KeyMoveLeft;
```
[C++]
```
public: static CommandID* KeyMoveLeft;
```
[JScript]
```
public static var KeyMoveLeft : CommandID;
```

Requirements

Platforms: Windows 98, Windows NT 4.0, Windows Millennium Edition, Windows 2000, Windows XP Home Edition, Windows XP Professional, Windows Server 2003 family

MenuCommands.KeyMoveRight Field

A **CommandID** that can be used to access the key move right handler.

[Visual Basic]
```
Public Shared ReadOnly KeyMoveRight As CommandID
```
[C#]
```
public static readonly CommandID KeyMoveRight;
```
[C++]
```
public: static CommandID* KeyMoveRight;
```
[JScript]
```
public static var KeyMoveRight : CommandID;
```

Requirements

Platforms: Windows 98, Windows NT 4.0, Windows Millennium Edition, Windows 2000, Windows XP Home Edition, Windows XP Professional, Windows Server 2003 family

MenuCommands.KeyMoveUp Field

A **CommandID** that can be used to access the key move up handler.

[Visual Basic]
```
Public Shared ReadOnly KeyMoveUp As CommandID
```
[C#]
```
public static readonly CommandID KeyMoveUp;
```
[C++]
```
public: static CommandID* KeyMoveUp;
```
[JScript]
```
public static var KeyMoveUp : CommandID;
```

Requirements

Platforms: Windows 98, Windows NT 4.0, Windows Millennium Edition, Windows 2000, Windows XP Home Edition, Windows XP Professional, Windows Server 2003 family

MenuCommands.KeyNudgeDown Field

A **CommandID** that can be used to access the key nudge down handler.

[Visual Basic]
```
Public Shared ReadOnly KeyNudgeDown As CommandID
```
[C#]
```
public static readonly CommandID KeyNudgeDown;
```
[C++]
```
public: static CommandID* KeyNudgeDown;
```
[JScript]
```
public static var KeyNudgeDown : CommandID;
```

Requirements

Platforms: Windows 98, Windows NT 4.0, Windows Millennium Edition, Windows 2000, Windows XP Home Edition, Windows XP Professional, Windows Server 2003 family

MenuCommands.KeyNudgeHeightDecrease Field

A **CommandID** that can be used to access the key nudge height decrease handler.

[Visual Basic]
```
Public Shared ReadOnly KeyNudgeHeightDecrease As CommandID
```
[C#]
```
public static readonly CommandID KeyNudgeHeightDecrease;
```
[C++]
```
public: static CommandID* KeyNudgeHeightDecrease;
```
[JScript]
```
public static var KeyNudgeHeightDecrease : CommandID;
```

Requirements

Platforms: Windows 98, Windows NT 4.0, Windows Millennium Edition, Windows 2000, Windows XP Home Edition, Windows XP Professional, Windows Server 2003 family

MenuCommands.KeyNudgeHeightIncrease Field

A **CommandID** that can be used to access the key nudge height increase handler.

[Visual Basic]
```
Public Shared ReadOnly KeyNudgeHeightIncrease As CommandID
```
[C#]
```
public static readonly CommandID KeyNudgeHeightIncrease;
```
[C++]
```
public: static CommandID* KeyNudgeHeightIncrease;
```
[JScript]
```
public static var KeyNudgeHeightIncrease : CommandID;
```

Requirements

Platforms: Windows 98, Windows NT 4.0, Windows Millennium Edition, Windows 2000, Windows XP Home Edition, Windows XP Professional, Windows Server 2003 family

MenuCommands.KeyNudgeLeft Field

A **CommandID** that can be used to access the key nudge left handler.

[Visual Basic]
```
Public Shared ReadOnly KeyNudgeLeft As CommandID
```
[C#]
```
public static readonly CommandID KeyNudgeLeft;
```
[C++]
```
public: static CommandID* KeyNudgeLeft;
```
[JScript]
```
public static var KeyNudgeLeft : CommandID;
```

Requirements

Platforms: Windows 98, Windows NT 4.0, Windows Millennium Edition, Windows 2000, Windows XP Home Edition, Windows XP Professional, Windows Server 2003 family

MenuCommands.KeyNudgeRight Field

A **CommandID** that can be used to access the key nudge right handler.

[Visual Basic]
```
Public Shared ReadOnly KeyNudgeRight As CommandID
```
[C#]
```
public static readonly CommandID KeyNudgeRight;
```
[C++]
```
public: static CommandID* KeyNudgeRight;
```
[JScript]
```
public static var KeyNudgeRight : CommandID;
```

Requirements

Platforms: Windows 98, Windows NT 4.0, Windows Millennium Edition, Windows 2000, Windows XP Home Edition, Windows XP Professional, Windows Server 2003 family

MenuCommands.KeyNudgeUp Field

A **CommandID** that can be used to access the key nudge up handler.

[Visual Basic]
```
Public Shared ReadOnly KeyNudgeUp As CommandID
```
[C#]
```
public static readonly CommandID KeyNudgeUp;
```
[C++]
```
public: static CommandID* KeyNudgeUp;
```
[JScript]
```
public static var KeyNudgeUp : CommandID;
```

Requirements

Platforms: Windows 98, Windows NT 4.0, Windows Millennium Edition, Windows 2000, Windows XP Home Edition, Windows XP Professional, Windows Server 2003 family

MenuCommands.KeyNudgeWidthDecrease Field

A **CommandID** that can be used to access the key nudge width decrease handler.

```
[Visual Basic]
Public Shared ReadOnly KeyNudgeWidthDecrease As CommandID
[C#]
public static readonly CommandID KeyNudgeWidthDecrease;
[C++]
public: static CommandID* KeyNudgeWidthDecrease;
[JScript]
public static var KeyNudgeWidthDecrease : CommandID;
```

Requirements

Platforms: Windows 98, Windows NT 4.0, Windows Millennium Edition, Windows 2000, Windows XP Home Edition, Windows XP Professional, Windows Server 2003 family

MenuCommands.KeyNudgeWidthIncrease Field

A **CommandID** that can be used to access the key nudge width increase handler.

```
[Visual Basic]
Public Shared ReadOnly KeyNudgeWidthIncrease As CommandID
[C#]
public static readonly CommandID KeyNudgeWidthIncrease;
[C++]
public: static CommandID* KeyNudgeWidthIncrease;
[JScript]
public static var KeyNudgeWidthIncrease : CommandID;
```

Requirements

Platforms: Windows 98, Windows NT 4.0, Windows Millennium Edition, Windows 2000, Windows XP Home Edition, Windows XP Professional, Windows Server 2003 family

MenuCommands.KeyReverseCancel Field

A **CommandID** that can be used to access the key reverse cancel handler.

```
[Visual Basic]
Public Shared ReadOnly KeyReverseCancel As CommandID
[C#]
public static readonly CommandID KeyReverseCancel;
[C++]
public: static CommandID* KeyReverseCancel;
[JScript]
public static var KeyReverseCancel : CommandID;
```

Requirements

Platforms: Windows 98, Windows NT 4.0, Windows Millennium Edition, Windows 2000, Windows XP Home Edition, Windows XP Professional, Windows Server 2003 family

MenuCommands.KeySelectNext Field

A **CommandID** that can be used to access the key select next handler.

```
[Visual Basic]
Public Shared ReadOnly KeySelectNext As CommandID
[C#]
public static readonly CommandID KeySelectNext;
[C++]
public: static CommandID* KeySelectNext;
[JScript]
public static var KeySelectNext : CommandID;
```

Requirements

Platforms: Windows 98, Windows NT 4.0, Windows Millennium Edition, Windows 2000, Windows XP Home Edition, Windows XP Professional, Windows Server 2003 family

MenuCommands.KeySelectPrevious Field

A **CommandID** that can be used to access the key select previous handler.

```
[Visual Basic]
Public Shared ReadOnly KeySelectPrevious As CommandID
[C#]
public static readonly CommandID KeySelectPrevious;
[C++]
public: static CommandID* KeySelectPrevious;
[JScript]
public static var KeySelectPrevious : CommandID;
```

Requirements

Platforms: Windows 98, Windows NT 4.0, Windows Millennium Edition, Windows 2000, Windows XP Home Edition, Windows XP Professional, Windows Server 2003 family

MenuCommands.KeySizeHeightDecrease Field

A **CommandID** that can be used to access the key size height decrease handler.

```
[Visual Basic]
Public Shared ReadOnly KeySizeHeightDecrease As CommandID
[C#]
public static readonly CommandID KeySizeHeightDecrease;
[C++]
public: static CommandID* KeySizeHeightDecrease;
[JScript]
public static var KeySizeHeightDecrease : CommandID;
```

Requirements

Platforms: Windows 98, Windows NT 4.0, Windows Millennium Edition, Windows 2000, Windows XP Home Edition, Windows XP Professional, Windows Server 2003 family

MenuCommands.KeySizeHeightIncrease Field

A **CommandID** that can be used to access the key size height increase handler.

[Visual Basic]
```
Public Shared ReadOnly KeySizeHeightIncrease As CommandID
```
[C#]
```
public static readonly CommandID KeySizeHeightIncrease;
```
[C++]
```
public: static CommandID* KeySizeHeightIncrease;
```
[JScript]
```
public static var KeySizeHeightIncrease : CommandID;
```

Requirements

Platforms: Windows 98, Windows NT 4.0, Windows Millennium Edition, Windows 2000, Windows XP Home Edition, Windows XP Professional, Windows Server 2003 family

MenuCommands.KeySizeWidthDecrease Field

A **CommandID** that can be used to access the key size width decrease handler.

[Visual Basic]
```
Public Shared ReadOnly KeySizeWidthDecrease As CommandID
```
[C#]
```
public static readonly CommandID KeySizeWidthDecrease;
```
[C++]
```
public: static CommandID* KeySizeWidthDecrease;
```
[JScript]
```
public static var KeySizeWidthDecrease : CommandID;
```

Requirements

Platforms: Windows 98, Windows NT 4.0, Windows Millennium Edition, Windows 2000, Windows XP Home Edition, Windows XP Professional, Windows Server 2003 family

MenuCommands.KeySizeWidthIncrease Field

A **CommandID** that can be used to access the key size width increase handler.

[Visual Basic]
```
Public Shared ReadOnly KeySizeWidthIncrease As CommandID
```
[C#]
```
public static readonly CommandID KeySizeWidthIncrease;
```
[C++]
```
public: static CommandID* KeySizeWidthIncrease;
```
[JScript]
```
public static var KeySizeWidthIncrease : CommandID;
```

Requirements

Platforms: Windows 98, Windows NT 4.0, Windows Millennium Edition, Windows 2000, Windows XP Home Edition, Windows XP Professional, Windows Server 2003 family

MenuCommands.KeyTabOrderSelect Field

A **CommandID** that can be used to access the key tab order select handler.

[Visual Basic]
```
Public Shared ReadOnly KeyTabOrderSelect As CommandID
```
[C#]
```
public static readonly CommandID KeyTabOrderSelect;
```
[C++]
```
public: static CommandID* KeyTabOrderSelect;
```
[JScript]
```
public static var KeyTabOrderSelect : CommandID;
```

Requirements

Platforms: Windows 98, Windows NT 4.0, Windows Millennium Edition, Windows 2000, Windows XP Home Edition, Windows XP Professional, Windows Server 2003 family

MenuCommands.SelectionMenu Field

A **CommandID** that can be used to access the selection menu.

[Visual Basic]
```
Public Shared ReadOnly SelectionMenu As CommandID
```
[C#]
```
public static readonly CommandID SelectionMenu;
```
[C++]
```
public: static CommandID* SelectionMenu;
```
[JScript]
```
public static var SelectionMenu : CommandID;
```

Requirements

Platforms: Windows 98, Windows NT 4.0, Windows Millennium Edition, Windows 2000, Windows XP Home Edition, Windows XP Professional, Windows Server 2003 family

MenuCommands.TraySelectionMenu Field

A **CommandID** that can be used to access the tray selection menu.

[Visual Basic]
```
Public Shared ReadOnly TraySelectionMenu As CommandID
```
[C#]
```
public static readonly CommandID TraySelectionMenu;
```
[C++]
```
public: static CommandID* TraySelectionMenu;
```
[JScript]
```
public static var TraySelectionMenu : CommandID;
```

Requirements

Platforms: Windows 98, Windows NT 4.0, Windows Millennium Edition, Windows 2000, Windows XP Home Edition, Windows XP Professional, Windows Server 2003 family

ParentControlDesigner Class

Base designer class for extending the design mode behavior of a **Control** that supports nested controls.

System.Object
  System.ComponentModel.Design.ComponentDesigner
    System.Windows.Forms.Design.ControlDesigner
      System.Windows.Forms.Design.ParentControlDesigner
        System.Windows.Forms.Design.ScrollableControl-Designer

```
[Visual Basic]
Public Class ParentControlDesigner
   Inherits ControlDesigner
[C#]
public class ParentControlDesigner : ControlDesigner
[C++]
public __gc class ParentControlDesigner : public ControlDesigner
[JScript]
public class ParentControlDesigner extends ControlDesigner
```

Thread Safety

Any public static (**Shared** in Visual Basic) members of this type are safe for multithreaded operations. Any instance members are not guaranteed to be thread safe.

Remarks

ParentControlDesigner provides a base class for designers of controls that can contain child controls. In addition to the methods and functionality inherited from the **ControlDesigner** and **ComponentDesigner** classes, **ParentControlDesigner** enables child controls to be added to, removed from, selected within, and arranged within the control whose behavior it extends at design time.

You can associate a designer with a type using a **DesignerAttribute**. For an overview of customizing design time behavior, see **Enhancing Design-Time Support**.

Requirements

Namespace: System.Windows.Forms.Design

Platforms: Windows 98, Windows NT 4.0, Windows Millennium Edition, Windows 2000, Windows XP Home Edition, Windows XP Professional, Windows Server 2003 family

Assembly: System.Design (in System.Design.dll)

ParentControlDesigner Constructor

Initializes a new instance of the **ParentControlDesigner** class.

```
[Visual Basic]
Public Sub New()
[C#]
public ParentControlDesigner();
[C++]
public: ParentControlDesigner();
[JScript]
public function ParentControlDesigner();
```

Remarks

The default constructor initializes any fields to their default values.

Requirements

Platforms: Windows 98, Windows NT 4.0, Windows Millennium Edition, Windows 2000, Windows XP Home Edition, Windows XP Professional, Windows Server 2003 family

.NET Framework Security:

- Full trust for the immediate caller. This member cannot be used by partially trusted code.

ParentControlDesigner.DefaultControlLocation Property

Gets the default location for a control added to the designer.

```
[Visual Basic]
Protected Overridable ReadOnly Property DefaultControlLocation As _
   Point
[C#]
protected virtual Point DefaultControlLocation {get;}
[C++]
protected: __property virtual Point get_DefaultControlLocation();
[JScript]
protected function get DefaultControlLocation() : Point;
```

Property Value

A **Point** that indicates the default location for a control added to the designer.

Remarks

The default location is usually (0,0). The default location is typically changed if the container has special borders, or for other reasons.

Requirements

Platforms: Windows 98, Windows NT 4.0, Windows Millennium Edition, Windows 2000, Windows XP Home Edition, Windows XP Professional, Windows Server 2003 family

.NET Framework Security:

- Full trust for the immediate caller. This member cannot be used by partially trusted code.

ParentControlDesigner.DrawGrid Property

Gets or sets a value indicating whether a grid should be drawn on the control for this designer.

```
[Visual Basic]
Protected Overridable Property DrawGrid As Boolean
[C#]
protected virtual bool DrawGrid {get; set;}
[C++]
protected: __property virtual bool get_DrawGrid();
protected: __property virtual void set_DrawGrid(bool);
[JScript]
protected function get DrawGrid() : Boolean;
protected function set DrawGrid(Boolean);
```

Property Value

true if a grid should be drawn on the control in the designer; otherwise, **false**.

Requirements

Platforms: Windows 98, Windows NT 4.0, Windows Millennium Edition, Windows 2000, Windows XP Home Edition, Windows XP Professional, Windows Server 2003 family

.NET Framework Security:

- Full trust for the immediate caller. This member cannot be used by partially trusted code.

ParentControlDesigner.EnableDragRect Property

Gets a value indicating whether drag rectangles are drawn by the designer.

```
[Visual Basic]
Overrides Protected ReadOnly Property EnableDragRect As Boolean
[C#]
protected override bool EnableDragRect {get;}
[C++]
protected: __property bool get_EnableDragRect();
[JScript]
protected override function get EnableDragRect() : Boolean;
```

Property Value

true if drag rectangles are drawn; otherwise, **false**.

Remarks

The default value of this property is **true**.

Requirements

Platforms: Windows 98, Windows NT 4.0, Windows Millennium Edition, Windows 2000, Windows XP Home Edition, Windows XP Professional, Windows Server 2003 family

.NET Framework Security:

- Full trust for the immediate caller. This member cannot be used by partially trusted code.

ParentControlDesigner.GridSize Property

Gets or sets the size of each square of the grid that is drawn when the designer is in grid draw mode.

```
[Visual Basic]
Protected Property GridSize As Size
[C#]
protected Size GridSize {get; set;}
[C++]
protected: __property Size get_GridSize();
protected: __property void set_GridSize(Size);
[JScript]
protected function get GridSize() : Size;
protected function set GridSize(Size);
```

Property Value

A **Size** that represents the size of each square of the grid drawn on a form or user control.

Requirements

Platforms: Windows 98, Windows NT 4.0, Windows Millennium Edition, Windows 2000, Windows XP Home Edition, Windows XP Professional, Windows Server 2003 family

.NET Framework Security:

- Full trust for the immediate caller. This member cannot be used by partially trusted code.

ParentControlDesigner.CanParent Method

Indicates whether the specified control can be a child of the control managed by this designer.

Overload List

Indicates whether the specified control can be a child of the control managed by this designer.

[Visual Basic] **Overloads Public Overridable Function CanParent(Control) As Boolean**

[C#] **public virtual bool CanParent(Control);**

[C++] **public: virtual bool CanParent(Control*);**

[JScript] **public function CanParent(Control) : Boolean;**

Indicates whether the control managed by the specified designer can be a child of the control managed by this designer.

[Visual Basic] **Overloads Public Overridable Function CanParent(ControlDesigner) As Boolean**

[C#] **public virtual bool CanParent(ControlDesigner);**

[C++] **public: virtual bool CanParent(ControlDesigner*);**

[JScript] **public function CanParent(ControlDesigner) : Boolean;**

ParentControlDesigner.CanParent Method (Control)

Indicates whether the specified control can be a child of the control managed by this designer.

```
[Visual Basic]
Overloads Public Overridable Function CanParent( _
   ByVal control As Control _
) As Boolean
[C#]
public virtual bool CanParent(
   Control control
);
[C++]
public: virtual bool CanParent(
   Control* control
);
[JScript]
public function CanParent(
   control : Control
) : Boolean;
```

Parameters

control

The **Control** to test.

Return Value

true if the specified control can be a child of the control managed by this designer; otherwise, **false**.

Remarks

This method indicates whether the control managed by the designer can parent the specified **ControlDesigner**.

Requirements

Platforms: Windows 98, Windows NT 4.0, Windows Millennium Edition, Windows 2000, Windows XP Home Edition, Windows XP Professional, Windows Server 2003 family

.NET Framework Security:

- Full trust for the immediate caller. This member cannot be used by partially trusted code.

ParentControlDesigner.CanParent Method (ControlDesigner)

Indicates whether the control managed by the specified designer can be a child of the control managed by this designer.

```
[Visual Basic]
Overloads Public Overridable Function CanParent( _
   ByVal controlDesigner As ControlDesigner _
) As Boolean
[C#]
public virtual bool CanParent(
   ControlDesigner controlDesigner
);
[C++]
public: virtual bool CanParent(
   ControlDesigner* controlDesigner
);
[JScript]
public function CanParent(
   controlDesigner : ControlDesigner
) : Boolean;
```

Parameters

controlDesigner

The designer for the control to test.

Return Value

true if the control managed by the specified designer can be a child of the control managed by this designer; otherwise, **false**.

Remarks

This method indicates whether the control managed by this designer can parent the control of the specified **ControlDesigner**.

Requirements

Platforms: Windows 98, Windows NT 4.0, Windows Millennium Edition, Windows 2000, Windows XP Home Edition, Windows XP Professional, Windows Server 2003 family

.NET Framework Security:

- Full trust for the immediate caller. This member cannot be used by partially trusted code.

ParentControlDesigner.CreateTool Method

Creates a component or control from a tool and adds it to the current design document.

Overload List

Creates a component or control from the specified tool and adds it to the current design document.

[Visual Basic] **Overloads Protected Sub CreateTool(ToolboxItem)**

[C#] **protected void CreateTool(ToolboxItem);**

[C++] **protected: void CreateTool(ToolboxItem*);**

[JScript] **protected function CreateTool(ToolboxItem);**

Creates a component or control from the specified tool and adds it to the current design document at the specified location.

[Visual Basic] **Overloads Protected Sub CreateTool(ToolboxItem, Point)**

[C#] **protected void CreateTool(ToolboxItem, Point);**

[C++] **protected: void CreateTool(ToolboxItem*, Point);**

[JScript] **protected function CreateTool(ToolboxItem, Point);**

Creates a component or control from the specified tool and adds it to the current design document within the bounds of the specified rectangle.

[Visual Basic] **Overloads Protected Sub CreateTool(ToolboxItem, Rectangle)**

[C#] **protected void CreateTool(ToolboxItem, Rectangle);**

[C++] **protected: void CreateTool(ToolboxItem*, Rectangle);**

[JScript] **protected function CreateTool(ToolboxItem, Rectangle);**

ParentControlDesigner.CreateTool Method (ToolboxItem)

Creates a component or control from the specified tool and adds it to the current design document.

```
[Visual Basic]
Overloads Protected Sub CreateTool( _
   ByVal tool As ToolboxItem _
)
[C#]
protected void CreateTool(
   ToolboxItem tool
);
[C++]
protected: void CreateTool(
   ToolboxItem* tool
);
[JScript]
protected function CreateTool(
   tool : ToolboxItem
);
```

Parameters

tool

The **ToolboxItem** to create a component from.

Remarks

The new component or control is positioned at the center of the currently selected control. This method uses the default size for the tool, if the tool has a default size specified.

To specify a location or location and size for the component or control, use one of the other overloaded **CreateTool** methods.

Requirements

Platforms: Windows 98, Windows NT 4.0, Windows Millennium Edition, Windows 2000, Windows XP Home Edition, Windows XP Professional, Windows Server 2003 family

.NET Framework Security:

- Full trust for the immediate caller. This member cannot be used by partially trusted code.

ParentControlDesigner.CreateTool Method (ToolboxItem, Point)

Creates a component or control from the specified tool and adds it to the current design document at the specified location.

```
[Visual Basic]
Overloads Protected Sub CreateTool( _
   ByVal tool As ToolboxItem, _
   ByVal location As Point _
)
[C#]
protected void CreateTool(
   ToolboxItem tool,
   Point location
);
[C++]
protected: void CreateTool(
   ToolboxItem* tool,
   Point location
);
[JScript]
protected function CreateTool(
   tool : ToolboxItem,
   location : Point
);
```

Parameters

tool
The **ToolboxItem** to create a component from.

location
The **Point**, in design-time view screen coordinates, at which to center the component.

Remarks

The new component or control is positioned around the location specified by the *location* parameter. This method uses the default size for the tool's component, if the component has a default size.

To specify a location and size for the component or control, use the appropriate overloaded **CreateTool** method.

Requirements

Platforms: Windows 98, Windows NT 4.0, Windows Millennium Edition, Windows 2000, Windows XP Home Edition, Windows XP Professional, Windows Server 2003 family

.NET Framework Security:

- Full trust for the immediate caller. This member cannot be used by partially trusted code.

ParentControlDesigner.CreateTool Method (ToolboxItem, Rectangle)

Creates a component or control from the specified tool and adds it to the current design document within the bounds of the specified rectangle.

```
[Visual Basic]
Overloads Protected Sub CreateTool( _
   ByVal tool As ToolboxItem, _
   ByVal bounds As Rectangle _
)
[C#]
protected void CreateTool(
   ToolboxItem tool,
   Rectangle bounds
);
[C++]
protected: void CreateTool(
   ToolboxItem* tool,
   Rectangle bounds
);
[JScript]
protected function CreateTool(
   tool : ToolboxItem,
   bounds : Rectangle
);
```

Parameters

tool
The **ToolboxItem** to create a component from.

bounds
A **Rectangle** indicating the location and size for the component created from the tool. The **X** and **Y** values of the **Rectangle** indicate the design-time view screen coordinates of the upper-left corner of the component.

Remarks

The new component or control is positioned with its upper left corner at the location specified by the **X** and **Y** values of the *bounds* parameter. The size of the new component or control will be set to the values specified by the **Height** and **Width** properties of the *bounds* parameter.

Requirements

Platforms: Windows 98, Windows NT 4.0, Windows Millennium Edition, Windows 2000, Windows XP Home Edition, Windows XP Professional, Windows Server 2003 family

.NET Framework Security:

- Full trust for the immediate caller. This member cannot be used by partially trusted code.

ParentControlDesigner.CreateToolCore Method

Provides core functionality for all the **CreateTool** methods.

[Visual Basic]
```
Protected Overridable Function CreateToolCore( _
   ByVal tool As ToolboxItem, _
   ByVal x As Integer, _
   ByVal y As Integer, _
   ByVal width As Integer, _
   ByVal height As Integer, _
   ByVal hasLocation As Boolean, _
   ByVal hasSize As Boolean _
) As IComponent()
```
[C#]
```
protected virtual IComponent[] CreateToolCore(
   ToolboxItem tool,
   int x,
   int y,
   int width,
   int height,
   bool hasLocation,
   bool hasSize
);
```
[C++]
```
protected: virtual IComponent* CreateToolCore(
   ToolboxItem* tool,
   int x,
   int y,
   int width,
   int height,
   bool hasLocation,
   bool hasSize
) [];
```
[JScript]
```
protected function CreateToolCore(
   tool : ToolboxItem,
   x : int,
   y : int,
   width : int,
   height : int,
   hasLocation : Boolean,
   hasSize : Boolean
) : IComponent[];
```

Parameters

tool

The **ToolboxItem** to create a component from.

x

The horizontal position, in design-time view coordinates, of the location of the left edge of the tool, if a size is specified, or of the center of the tool, if no size is specified.

y

The vertical position, in design-time view coordinates, of the location of the top edge of the tool, if a size is specified, or of the center of the tool, if no size is specified.

width

The width of the tool. This parameter is ignored if the *hasSize* parameter is set to **false**.

height

The height of the tool. This parameter is ignored if the *hasSize* parameter is set to **false**.

hasLocation

true if a location for the component is specified; **false** if the component is to be positioned in the center of the currently selected control.

hasSize

true if a size for the component is specified; **false** if the default height and width values for the component are to be used.

Return Value

An array of components created from the tool.

Remarks

This is the only **CreateTool** method that can be overridden.

Requirements

Platforms: Windows 98, Windows NT 4.0, Windows Millennium Edition, Windows 2000, Windows XP Home Edition, Windows XP Professional, Windows Server 2003 family

.NET Framework Security:

- Full trust for the immediate caller. This member cannot be used by partially trusted code.

ParentControlDesigner.Dispose Method

Releases the unmanaged resources used by the **ParentControlDesigner** and optionally releases the managed resources.

Overload List

Releases the unmanaged resources used by the **ParentControlDesigner** and optionally releases the managed resources.

[Visual Basic] **Overloads Overrides Protected Sub Dispose(Boolean)**

[C#] **protected override void Dispose(bool);**

[C++] **protected: void Dispose(bool);**

[JScript] **protected override function Dispose(Boolean);**

Inherited from **ComponentDesigner**.

[Visual Basic] **Overloads Public Overridable Sub Dispose() Implements IDisposable.Dispose**

[C#] **public virtual void Dispose();**

[C++] **public: virtual void Dispose();**

[JScript] **public function Dispose();**

ParentControlDesigner.Dispose Method (Boolean)

Releases the unmanaged resources used by the **ParentControlDesigner** and optionally releases the managed resources.

[Visual Basic]
```
Overrides Overloads Protected Sub Dispose( _
   ByVal disposing As Boolean _
)
```
[C#]
```
protected override void Dispose(
   bool disposing
);
```
[C++]
```
protected: void Dispose(
   bool disposing
);
```

```
[JScript]
protected override function Dispose(
   disposing : Boolean
);
```

Parameters

disposing
: **true** to release both managed and unmanaged resources; **false** to release only unmanaged resources.

Remarks

This method is called by the public **Dispose()** method and the **Finalize** method. **Dispose()** invokes the protected **Dispose(Boolean)** method with the *disposing* parameter set to **true**. **Finalize** invokes **Dispose** with *disposing* set to **false**.

When the *disposing* parameter is **true**, this method releases all resources held by any managed objects that this **ParentControlDesigner** references. This method invokes the **Dispose()** method of each referenced object.

Notes to Inheritors: **Dispose** can be called multiple times by other objects. When overriding **Dispose(Boolean)**, be careful not to reference objects that have been previously disposed of in an earlier call to **Dispose**.

Requirements

Platforms: Windows 98, Windows NT 4.0,
Windows Millennium Edition, Windows 2000,
Windows XP Home Edition, Windows XP Professional,
Windows Server 2003 family

.NET Framework Security:

- Full trust for the immediate caller. This member cannot be used by partially trusted code.

ParentControlDesigner.GetControl Method

Gets the control from the designer of the specified component.

```
[Visual Basic]
Protected Function GetControl( _
   ByVal component As Object _
) As Control
[C#]
protected Control GetControl(
   object component
);
[C++]
protected: Control* GetControl(
   Object* component
);
[JScript]
protected function GetControl(
   component : Object
) : Control;
```

Parameters

component
: The component to retrieve the control for.

Return Value

The **Control** that the specified component belongs to.

Requirements

Platforms: Windows 98, Windows NT 4.0,
Windows Millennium Edition, Windows 2000,
Windows XP Home Edition, Windows XP Professional,
Windows Server 2003 family

.NET Framework Security:

- Full trust for the immediate caller. This member cannot be used by partially trusted code.

ParentControlDesigner.GetUpdatedRect Method

Updates the position of the specified rectangle, adjusting it for grid alignment if gird alignment mode is enabled.

```
[Visual Basic]
Protected Function GetUpdatedRect( _
   ByVal originalRect As Rectangle, _
   ByVal dragRect As Rectangle, _
   ByVal updateSize As Boolean _
) As Rectangle
[C#]
protected Rectangle GetUpdatedRect(
   Rectangle originalRect,
   Rectangle dragRect,
   bool updateSize
);
[C++]
protected: Rectangle GetUpdatedRect(
   Rectangle originalRect,
   Rectangle dragRect,
   bool updateSize
);
[JScript]
protected function GetUpdatedRect(
   originalRect : Rectangle,
   dragRect : Rectangle,
   updateSize : Boolean
) : Rectangle;
```

Parameters

originalRect
: A **Rectangle** indicating the initial position of the component being updated.

dragRect
: A **Rectangle** indicating the new position of the component.

updateSize
: **true** to update the size of the rectangle, if there has been any change; otherwise, **false**.

Return Value

A rectangle indicating the position of the component in design-time view screen coordinates. If no changes have been made, this method returns the original rectangle.

Remarks

This method aligns the specified rectangle to the grid if grid alignment is enabled.

Requirements

Platforms: Windows 98, Windows NT 4.0,
Windows Millennium Edition, Windows 2000,
Windows XP Home Edition, Windows XP Professional,
Windows Server 2003 family

.NET Framework Security:

- Full trust for the immediate caller. This member cannot be used by partially trusted code.

ParentControlDesigner.Initialize Method

Initializes the designer with the specified component.

```
[Visual Basic]
Overrides Public Sub Initialize( _
   ByVal component As IComponent _
) Implements IDesigner.Initialize
[C#]
public override void Initialize(
   IComponent component
);
[C++]
public: void Initialize(
   IComponent* component
);
[JScript]
public override function Initialize(
   component : IComponent
);
```

Parameters

component

The **IComponent** to associate with the designer.

Implements

IDesigner.Initialize

Remarks

This method is called to initialize the designer with the specified primary component.

Requirements

Platforms: Windows 98, Windows NT 4.0, Windows Millennium Edition, Windows 2000, Windows XP Home Edition, Windows XP Professional, Windows Server 2003 family

.NET Framework Security:

- Full trust for the immediate caller. This member cannot be used by partially trusted code.

ParentControlDesigner.InvokeCreateTool Method

Creates a tool from the specified **ToolboxItem**.

```
[Visual Basic]
Protected Shared Sub InvokeCreateTool( _
   ByVal toInvoke As ParentControlDesigner, _
   ByVal tool As ToolboxItem _
)
[C#]
protected static void InvokeCreateTool(
   ParentControlDesigner toInvoke,
   ToolboxItem tool
);
[C++]
protected: static void InvokeCreateTool(
   ParentControlDesigner* toInvoke,
   ToolboxItem* tool
);
[JScript]
protected static function InvokeCreateTool(
   toInvoke : ParentControlDesigner,
   tool : ToolboxItem
);
```

Parameters

toInvoke

The **ParentControlDesigner** that the tool is to be used with.

tool

The **ToolboxItem** to create a tool from.

Requirements

Platforms: Windows 98, Windows NT 4.0, Windows Millennium Edition, Windows 2000, Windows XP Home Edition, Windows XP Professional, Windows Server 2003 family

.NET Framework Security:

- Full trust for the immediate caller. This member cannot be used by partially trusted code.

ParentControlDesigner.OnDragDrop Method

Called when a drag-and-drop object is dropped onto the control designer view.

```
[Visual Basic]
Overrides Protected Sub OnDragDrop( _
   ByVal de As DragEventArgs _
)
[C#]
protected override void OnDragDrop(
   DragEventArgs de
);
[C++]
protected: void OnDragDrop(
   DragEventArgs* de
);
[JScript]
protected override function OnDragDrop(
   de : DragEventArgs
);
```

Parameters

de

A **DragEventArgs** that provides data for the event.

Remarks

This method checks any parent control for a drag-and-drop handler that can handle the operation instead. If one exists, this method passes the **DragEventArgs** to the method and returns. If no parent drag-and-drop handler exists, this method attempts to create a tool if a toolbox item has been dropped on the designer control.

Requirements

Platforms: Windows 98, Windows NT 4.0, Windows Millennium Edition, Windows 2000, Windows XP Home Edition, Windows XP Professional, Windows Server 2003 family

.NET Framework Security:

- Full trust for the immediate caller. This member cannot be used by partially trusted code.

ParentControlDesigner.OnDragEnter Method

Called when a drag-and-drop operation enters the control designer view.

```
[Visual Basic]
Overrides Protected Sub OnDragEnter( _
   ByVal de As DragEventArgs _
)
[C#]
protected override void OnDragEnter(
   DragEventArgs de
);
[C++]
protected: void OnDragEnter(
   DragEventArgs* de
);
[JScript]
protected override function OnDragEnter(
   de : DragEventArgs
);
```

Parameters

de

A **DragEventArgs** that provides data for the event.

Requirements

Platforms: Windows 98, Windows NT 4.0, Windows Millennium Edition, Windows 2000, Windows XP Home Edition, Windows XP Professional, Windows Server 2003 family

.NET Framework Security:

- Full trust for the immediate caller. This member cannot be used by partially trusted code.

ParentControlDesigner.OnDragLeave Method

Called when a drag-and-drop operation leaves the control designer view.

```
[Visual Basic]
Overrides Protected Sub OnDragLeave( _
   ByVal e As EventArgs _
)
[C#]
protected override void OnDragLeave(
   EventArgs e
);
[C++]
protected: void OnDragLeave(
   EventArgs* e
);
[JScript]
protected override function OnDragLeave(
   e : EventArgs
);
```

Parameters

e

An **EventArgs** that provides data for the event.

Requirements

Platforms: Windows 98, Windows NT 4.0, Windows Millennium Edition, Windows 2000, Windows XP Home Edition, Windows XP Professional, Windows Server 2003 family

.NET Framework Security:

- Full trust for the immediate caller. This member cannot be used by partially trusted code.

ParentControlDesigner.OnDragOver Method

Called when a drag-and-drop object is dragged over the control designer view.

```
[Visual Basic]
Overrides Protected Sub OnDragOver( _
   ByVal de As DragEventArgs _
)
[C#]
protected override void OnDragOver(
   DragEventArgs de
);
[C++]
protected: void OnDragOver(
   DragEventArgs* de
);
[JScript]
protected override function OnDragOver(
   de : DragEventArgs
);
```

Parameters

de

A **DragEventArgs** that provides data for the event.

Requirements

Platforms: Windows 98, Windows NT 4.0, Windows Millennium Edition, Windows 2000, Windows XP Home Edition, Windows XP Professional, Windows Server 2003 family

.NET Framework Security:

- Full trust for the immediate caller. This member cannot be used by partially trusted code.

ParentControlDesigner.OnGiveFeedback Method

Called when a drag-and-drop operation is in progress to provide visual cues based on the location of the mouse while a drag operation is in progress.

```
[Visual Basic]
Overrides Protected Sub OnGiveFeedback( _
   ByVal e As GiveFeedbackEventArgs _
)
[C#]
protected override void OnGiveFeedback(
   GiveFeedbackEventArgs e
);
[C++]
protected: void OnGiveFeedback(
   GiveFeedbackEventArgs* e
);
[JScript]
protected override function OnGiveFeedback(
   e : GiveFeedbackEventArgs
);
```

Parameters

e

A **GiveFeedbackEventArgs** that provides data for the event.

Remarks

The designer host calls this method when an OLE drag event occurs.

Requirements

Platforms: Windows 98, Windows NT 4.0, Windows Millennium Edition, Windows 2000, Windows XP Home Edition, Windows XP Professional, Windows Server 2003 family

.NET Framework Security:

- Full trust for the immediate caller. This member cannot be used by partially trusted code.

ParentControlDesigner.OnMouseDragBegin Method

Called in response to the left mouse button being pressed and held while over the component.

```
[Visual Basic]
Overrides Protected Sub OnMouseDragBegin( _
   ByVal x As Integer, _
   ByVal y As Integer _
)
[C#]
protected override void OnMouseDragBegin(
   int x,
   int y
);
[C++]
protected: void OnMouseDragBegin(
   int x,
   int y
);
[JScript]
protected override function OnMouseDragBegin(
   x : int,
   y : int
);
```

Parameters

x

The x position of the mouse in screen coordinates.

y

The y position of the mouse in screen coordinates.

Remarks

This method is called in response to the left mouse button being pressed on a component. The designer overrides the base form of this method to provide a "lasso" selection mechanism for components within the control.

> **Note** You can pass a point in screen coordinates to the **PointToClient** method of the **Control** class to obtain the coordinates of the point relative to the upper-left corner of the control.

Requirements

Platforms: Windows 98, Windows NT 4.0, Windows Millennium Edition, Windows 2000, Windows XP Home Edition, Windows XP Professional, Windows Server 2003 family

.NET Framework Security:

- Full trust for the immediate caller. This member cannot be used by partially trusted code.

ParentControlDesigner.OnMouseDragEnd Method

Called at the end of a drag-and-drop operation to complete or cancel the operation.

```
[Visual Basic]
Overrides Protected Sub OnMouseDragEnd( _
   ByVal cancel As Boolean _
)
[C#]
protected override void OnMouseDragEnd(
   bool cancel
);
[C++]
protected: void OnMouseDragEnd(
   bool cancel
);
[JScript]
protected override function OnMouseDragEnd(
   cancel : Boolean
);
```

Parameters

cancel

true to cancel the drag operation; **false** to commit it.

Remarks

This method is called at the end of a drag operation. This method either commits to or cancels the drag operation.

Requirements

Platforms: Windows 98, Windows NT 4.0, Windows Millennium Edition, Windows 2000, Windows XP Home Edition, Windows XP Professional, Windows Server 2003 family

.NET Framework Security:

- Full trust for the immediate caller. This member cannot be used by partially trusted code.

ParentControlDesigner.OnMouseDragMove Method

Called for each movement of the mouse during a drag-and-drop operation.

```
[Visual Basic]
Overrides Protected Sub OnMouseDragMove( _
   ByVal x As Integer, _
   ByVal y As Integer _
)
[C#]
protected override void OnMouseDragMove(
   int x,
   int y
);
[C++]
protected: void OnMouseDragMove(
   int x,
   int y
);
```

```
[JScript]
protected override function OnMouseDragMove(
   x : int,
   y : int
);
```

Parameters

x

The x position of the mouse in screen coordinates.

y

The y position of the mouse in screen coordinates.

Remarks

This method is called at the start of a drag-and-drop operation.

> **Note** You can pass a point in screen coordinates to the **PointToClient** method of the **Control** class to obtain the coordinates of the point relative to the upper-left corner of the control.

Requirements

Platforms: Windows 98, Windows NT 4.0, Windows Millennium Edition, Windows 2000, Windows XP Home Edition, Windows XP Professional, Windows Server 2003 family

.NET Framework Security:

- Full trust for the immediate caller. This member cannot be used by partially trusted code.

ParentControlDesigner.OnMouseEnter Method

Called when the mouse first enters the control.

```
[Visual Basic]
Overrides Protected Sub OnMouseEnter()
[C#]
protected override void OnMouseEnter();
[C++]
protected: void OnMouseEnter();
[JScript]
protected override function OnMouseEnter();
```

Requirements

Platforms: Windows 98, Windows NT 4.0, Windows Millennium Edition, Windows 2000, Windows XP Home Edition, Windows XP Professional, Windows Server 2003 family

.NET Framework Security:

- Full trust for the immediate caller. This member cannot be used by partially trusted code.

ParentControlDesigner.OnMouseHover Method

Called after the mouse hovers over the control.

```
[Visual Basic]
Overrides Protected Sub OnMouseHover()
[C#]
protected override void OnMouseHover();
[C++]
protected: void OnMouseHover();
[JScript]
protected override function OnMouseHover();
```

Remarks

This method displays the container selector.

> **Note** Because the child controls pass this notification up, this method will display the container selector even if you hover over a child control.

Requirements

Platforms: Windows 98, Windows NT 4.0, Windows Millennium Edition, Windows 2000, Windows XP Home Edition, Windows XP Professional, Windows Server 2003 family

.NET Framework Security:

- Full trust for the immediate caller. This member cannot be used by partially trusted code.

ParentControlDesigner.OnMouseLeave Method

Called when the mouse first enters the control.

```
[Visual Basic]
Overrides Protected Sub OnMouseLeave()
[C#]
protected override void OnMouseLeave();
[C++]
protected: void OnMouseLeave();
[JScript]
protected override function OnMouseLeave();
```

Requirements

Platforms: Windows 98, Windows NT 4.0, Windows Millennium Edition, Windows 2000, Windows XP Home Edition, Windows XP Professional, Windows Server 2003 family

.NET Framework Security:

- Full trust for the immediate caller. This member cannot be used by partially trusted code.

ParentControlDesigner.OnPaintAdornments Method

Called when the control that the designer is managing has painted its surface so the designer can paint any additional adornments on top of the control.

```
[Visual Basic]
Overrides Protected Sub OnPaintAdornments( _
   ByVal pe As PaintEventArgs _
)
[C#]
protected override void OnPaintAdornments(
   PaintEventArgs pe
);
[C++]
protected: void OnPaintAdornments(
   PaintEventArgs* pe
);
[JScript]
protected override function OnPaintAdornments(
   pe : PaintEventArgs
);
```

Parameters

pe

A **PaintEventArgs** that provides data for the event.

Requirements

Platforms: Windows 98, Windows NT 4.0, Windows Millennium Edition, Windows 2000, Windows XP Home Edition, Windows XP Professional, Windows Server 2003 family

.NET Framework Security:

- Full trust for the immediate caller. This member cannot be used by partially trusted code.

ParentControlDesigner.OnSetCursor Method

Provides an opportunity to change the current mouse cursor.

[Visual Basic]
```
Overrides Protected Sub OnSetCursor()
```
[C#]
```
protected override void OnSetCursor();
```
[C++]
```
protected: void OnSetCursor();
```
[JScript]
```
protected override function OnSetCursor();
```

Remarks

This method sets the mouse cursor according to the following rules: If the toolbox service has a tool selected, it allows the toolbox service to set the cursor. Otherwise, the mouse cursor is set to the default mouse cursor.

Requirements

Platforms: Windows 98, Windows NT 4.0, Windows Millennium Edition, Windows 2000, Windows XP Home Edition, Windows XP Professional, Windows Server 2003 family

.NET Framework Security:

- Full trust for the immediate caller. This member cannot be used by partially trusted code.

ParentControlDesigner.PreFilterProperties Method

Adjusts the set of properties the component will expose through a **TypeDescriptor**.

[Visual Basic]
```
Overrides Protected Sub PreFilterProperties( _
   ByVal properties As IDictionary _
)
```
[C#]
```
protected override void PreFilterProperties(
   IDictionary properties
);
```
[C++]
```
protected: void PreFilterProperties(
   IDictionary* properties
);
```
[JScript]
```
protected override function PreFilterProperties(
   properties : IDictionary
);
```

Parameters

properties

An **IDictionary** that contains the properties for the class of the component.

Remarks

This **IDesignerFilter** interface method override adds a set of properties to this designer's control that allow a user to set options related to the grid display and child control alignment. This method adds the following browsable properties: "DrawGrid", "SnapToGrid", and "GridSize".

Requirements

Platforms: Windows 98, Windows NT 4.0, Windows Millennium Edition, Windows 2000, Windows XP Home Edition, Windows XP Professional, Windows Server 2003 family

.NET Framework Security:

- Full trust for the immediate caller. This member cannot be used by partially trusted code.

ParentControlDesigner.WndProc Method

Processes Windows messages.

[Visual Basic]
```
Overrides Protected Sub WndProc( _
   ByRef m As Message _
)
```
[C#]
```
protected override void WndProc(
   ref Message m
);
```
[C++]
```
protected: void WndProc(
   Message* m
);
```
[JScript]
```
protected override function WndProc(
   m : Message
);
```

Parameters

m

The **Message** to process.

Requirements

Platforms: Windows 98, Windows NT 4.0, Windows Millennium Edition, Windows 2000, Windows XP Home Edition, Windows XP Professional, Windows Server 2003 family

.NET Framework Security:

- Full trust for the immediate caller. This member cannot be used by partially trusted code.

PropertyTab Class

Provides a base class for property tabs.

System.Object
  System.Windows.Forms.Design.PropertyTab
    System.Windows.Forms.Design.EventsTab

```
[Visual Basic]
MustInherit Public Class PropertyTab
   Implements IExtenderProvider
[C#]
public abstract class PropertyTab : IExtenderProvider
[C++]
public __gc __abstract class PropertyTab : public IExtenderProvider
[JScript]
public abstract class PropertyTab implements IExtenderProvider
```

Thread Safety

Any public static (**Shared** in Visual Basic) members of this type are safe for multithreaded operations. Any instance members are not guaranteed to be thread safe.

Remarks

PropertyTab provides the base class behavior for a property tab. Property tabs are displayed on the toolbar of the **PropertyGrid** control of the Properties Window, and allow a component to display different views of its properties or other data.

User code will usually not create an instance of a **PropertyTab** directly. Instead, a **PropertyTabAttribute** that indicates the type of the property tab or property tabs to display for a component can be associated with the properties or types that the **PropertyTab** should be displayed for.

The **PropertyGrid** will instantiate a **PropertyTab** of the type specified by a **PropertyTabAttribute** associated with the type or property field of the component that is being browsed.

Requirements

Namespace: System.Windows.Forms.Design

Platforms: Windows 98, Windows NT 4.0, Windows Millennium Edition, Windows 2000, Windows XP Home Edition, Windows XP Professional, Windows Server 2003 family

Assembly: System.Windows.Forms (in System.Windows.Forms.dll)

PropertyTab Constructor

Initializes a new instance of the **PropertyTab** class.

```
[Visual Basic]
Protected Sub New()
[C#]
protected PropertyTab();
[C++]
protected: PropertyTab();
[JScript]
protected function PropertyTab();
```

Remarks

This constructor is called by derived class constructors to initialize state in this type.

Requirements

Platforms: Windows 98, Windows NT 4.0, Windows Millennium Edition, Windows 2000, Windows XP Home Edition, Windows XP Professional, Windows Server 2003 family

PropertyTab.Bitmap Property

Gets the bitmap that is displayed for the **PropertyTab**.

```
[Visual Basic]
Public Overridable ReadOnly Property Bitmap As Bitmap
[C#]
public virtual Bitmap Bitmap {get;}
[C++]
public: __property virtual Bitmap* get_Bitmap();
[JScript]
public function get Bitmap() : Bitmap;
```

Property Value

The **Bitmap** to display for the **PropertyTab**.

Requirements

Platforms: Windows 98, Windows NT 4.0, Windows Millennium Edition, Windows 2000, Windows XP Home Edition, Windows XP Professional, Windows Server 2003 family

PropertyTab.Components Property

Gets or sets the array of components the property tab is associated with.

```
[Visual Basic]
Public Overridable Property Components As Object ()
[C#]
public virtual object[] Components {get; set;}
[C++]
public: __property virtual Object* get_Components();
public: __property virtual void set_Components(Object* __gc[]);
[JScript]
public function get Components() : Object[];
public function set Components(Object[]);
```

Property Value

The array of components the property tab is associated with.

Requirements

Platforms: Windows 98, Windows NT 4.0, Windows Millennium Edition, Windows 2000, Windows XP Home Edition, Windows XP Professional, Windows Server 2003 family

PropertyTab.HelpKeyword Property

Gets the Help keyword that is to be associated with this tab.

```
[Visual Basic]
Public Overridable ReadOnly Property HelpKeyword As String
[C#]
public virtual string HelpKeyword {get;}
[C++]
public: __property virtual String* get_HelpKeyword();
[JScript]
public function get HelpKeyword() : String;
```

Property Value

The Help keyword to be associated with this tab.

Remarks

By default, this is set to the tab name.

Requirements

Platforms: Windows 98, Windows NT 4.0, Windows Millennium Edition, Windows 2000, Windows XP Home Edition, Windows XP Professional, Windows Server 2003 family

PropertyTab.TabName Property

Gets the name for the property tab.

[Visual Basic]
```
Public MustOverride ReadOnly Property TabName As String
```
[C#]
```
public abstract string TabName {get;}
```
[C++]
```
public: __property virtual String* get_TabName() = 0;
```
[JScript]
```
public abstract function get TabName() : String;
```

Property Value

The name for the property tab.

Requirements

Platforms: Windows 98, Windows NT 4.0, Windows Millennium Edition, Windows 2000, Windows XP Home Edition, Windows XP Professional, Windows Server 2003 family

PropertyTab.CanExtend Method

Gets a value indicating whether this **PropertyTab** can display properties for the specified component.

[Visual Basic]
```
Public Overridable Function CanExtend( _
   ByVal extendee As Object _
) As Boolean Implements IExtenderProvider.CanExtend
```
[C#]
```
public virtual bool CanExtend(
   object extendee
);
```
[C++]
```
public: virtual bool CanExtend(
   Object* extendee
);
```
[JScript]
```
public function CanExtend(
   extendee : Object
) : Boolean;
```

Parameters

extendee

The object to test.

Return Value

true if the object can be extended; otherwise, **false**.

Implements

IExtenderProvider.CanExtend

Requirements

Platforms: Windows 98, Windows NT 4.0, Windows Millennium Edition, Windows 2000, Windows XP Home Edition, Windows XP Professional, Windows Server 2003 family

PropertyTab.Dispose Method

Releases all the resources used by the **PropertyTab**.

Overload List

Releases all the resources used by the **PropertyTab**.

[Visual Basic] **Overloads Public Overridable Sub Dispose()**

[C#] **public virtual void Dispose();**

[C++] **public: virtual void Dispose();**

[JScript] **public function Dispose();**

Releases the unmanaged resources used by the **PropertyTab** and optionally releases the managed resources.

[Visual Basic] **Overloads Protected Overridable Sub Dispose(Boolean)**

[C#] **protected virtual void Dispose(bool);**

[C++] **protected: virtual void Dispose(bool);**

[JScript] **protected function Dispose(Boolean);**

PropertyTab.Dispose Method ()

Releases all the resources used by the **PropertyTab**.

[Visual Basic]
```
Overloads Public Overridable Sub Dispose()
```
[C#]
```
public virtual void Dispose();
```
[C++]
```
public: virtual void Dispose();
```
[JScript]
```
public function Dispose();
```

Remarks

Calling **Dispose** allows the resources used by the **PropertyTab** to be reallocated for other purposes. For more information about **Dispose**, see **Cleaning Up Unmanaged Resources**.

Requirements

Platforms: Windows 98, Windows NT 4.0, Windows Millennium Edition, Windows 2000, Windows XP Home Edition, Windows XP Professional, Windows Server 2003 family

PropertyTab.Dispose Method (Boolean)

Releases the unmanaged resources used by the **PropertyTab** and optionally releases the managed resources.

[Visual Basic]
```
Overloads Protected Overridable Sub Dispose( _
   ByVal disposing As Boolean _
)
```
[C#]
```
protected virtual void Dispose(
   bool disposing
);
```

```
[C++]
protected: virtual void Dispose(
   bool disposing
);
[JScript]
protected function Dispose(
   disposing : Boolean
);
```

Parameters

disposing

true to release both managed and unmanaged resources; **false** to release only unmanaged resources.

Remarks

This method is called by the public **Dispose()** method and the **Finalize** method. **Dispose()** invokes the protected **Dispose(Boolean)** method with the *disposing* parameter set to **true**. **Finalize** invokes **Dispose** with *disposing* set to **false**.

When the *disposing* parameter is **true**, this method releases all resources held by any managed objects that this **PropertyTab** references. This method invokes the **Dispose()** method of each referenced object.

Notes to Inheritors: **Dispose** can be called multiple times by other objects. When overriding **Dispose(Boolean)**, be careful not to reference objects that have been previously disposed of in an earlier call to **Dispose**.

Requirements

Platforms: Windows 98, Windows NT 4.0, Windows Millennium Edition, Windows 2000, Windows XP Home Edition, Windows XP Professional, Windows Server 2003 family

PropertyTab.Finalize Method

This member overrides **Object.Finalize**.

```
[Visual Basic]
Overrides Protected Sub Finalize()
[C#]
~PropertyTab();
[C++]
~PropertyTab();
[JScript]
protected override function Finalize();
```

Requirements

Platforms: Windows 98, Windows NT 4.0, Windows Millennium Edition, Windows 2000, Windows XP Home Edition, Windows XP Professional, Windows Server 2003 family

PropertyTab.GetDefaultProperty Method

Gets the default property of the specified component.

```
[Visual Basic]
Public Overridable Function GetDefaultProperty( _
   ByVal component As Object _
) As PropertyDescriptor
[C#]
public virtual PropertyDescriptor GetDefaultProperty(
   object component
);
[C++]
public: virtual PropertyDescriptor* GetDefaultProperty(
   Object* component
);
[JScript]
public function GetDefaultProperty(
   component : Object
) : PropertyDescriptor;
```

Parameters

component

The component to retrieve the default property of.

Return Value

A **PropertyDescriptor** that represents the default property.

Requirements

Platforms: Windows 98, Windows NT 4.0, Windows Millennium Edition, Windows 2000, Windows XP Home Edition, Windows XP Professional, Windows Server 2003 family

PropertyTab.GetProperties Method

Gets the properties of the specified component.

Overload List

Gets the properties of the specified component.

[Visual Basic] **Overloads Public Overridable Function GetProperties(Object) As PropertyDescriptorCollection**

[C#] **public virtual PropertyDescriptorCollection GetProperties(object);**

[C++] **public: virtual PropertyDescriptorCollection* GetProperties(Object*);**

[JScript] **public function GetProperties(Object) : PropertyDescriptorCollection;**

Gets the properties of the specified component that match the specified attributes.

[Visual Basic] **Overloads Public MustOverride Function GetProperties(Object, Attribute()) As PropertyDescriptor-Collection**

[C#] **public abstract PropertyDescriptorCollection GetProperties(object, Attribute[]);**

[C++] **public: virtual PropertyDescriptorCollection* GetProperties(Object*, Attribute[]) = 0;**

[JScript] **public abstract function GetProperties(Object, Attribute[]) : PropertyDescriptorCollection;**

Gets the properties of the specified component that match the specified attributes and context.

[Visual Basic] **Overloads Public Overridable Function GetProperties(ITypeDescriptorContext, Object, Attribute()) As PropertyDescriptorCollection**

[C#] **public virtual PropertyDescriptorCollection GetProperties(ITypeDescriptorContext, object, Attribute[]);**

[C++] **public: virtual PropertyDescriptorCollection* GetProperties(ITypeDescriptorContext*, Object*, Attribute[]);**

[JScript] **public function GetProperties(ITypeDescriptorContext, Object, Attribute[]) : PropertyDescriptorCollection;**

PropertyTab.GetProperties Method (Object)

Gets the properties of the specified component.

[Visual Basic]
```
Overloads Public Overridable Function GetProperties( _
   ByVal component As Object _
) As PropertyDescriptorCollection
```
[C#]
```
public virtual PropertyDescriptorCollection GetProperties(
   object component
);
```
[C++]
```
public: virtual PropertyDescriptorCollection* GetProperties(
   Object* component
);
```
[JScript]
```
public function GetProperties(
   component : Object
) : PropertyDescriptorCollection;
```

Parameters

component

The component to retrieve the properties of.

Return Value

A **PropertyDescriptorCollection** that contains the properties of the component.

Requirements

Platforms: Windows 98, Windows NT 4.0, Windows Millennium Edition, Windows 2000, Windows XP Home Edition, Windows XP Professional, Windows Server 2003 family

PropertyTab.GetProperties Method (Object, Attribute[])

Gets the properties of the specified component that match the specified attributes.

[Visual Basic]
```
Overloads Public MustOverride Function GetProperties( _
   ByVal component As Object, _
   ByVal attributes() As Attribute _
) As PropertyDescriptorCollection
```
[C#]
```
public abstract PropertyDescriptorCollection GetProperties(
   object component,
   Attribute[] attributes
);
```
[C++]
```
public: virtual PropertyDescriptorCollection* GetProperties(
   Object* component,
   Attribute* attributes[]
) = 0;
```
[JScript]
```
public abstract function GetProperties(
   component : Object,
   attributes : Attribute[]
) : PropertyDescriptorCollection;
```

Parameters

component

The component to retrieve properties from.

attributes

An array of type **Attribute** that indicates the attributes of the properties to retrieve.

Return Value

A **PropertyDescriptorCollection** that contains the properties.

Requirements

Platforms: Windows 98, Windows NT 4.0, Windows Millennium Edition, Windows 2000, Windows XP Home Edition, Windows XP Professional, Windows Server 2003 family

PropertyTab.GetProperties Method (ITypeDescriptorContext, Object, Attribute[])

Gets the properties of the specified component that match the specified attributes and context.

[Visual Basic]
```
Overloads Public Overridable Function GetProperties( _
   ByVal context As ITypeDescriptorContext, _
   ByVal component As Object, _
   ByVal attributes() As Attribute _
) As PropertyDescriptorCollection
```
[C#]
```
public virtual PropertyDescriptorCollection GetProperties(
   ITypeDescriptorContext context,
   object component,
   Attribute[] attributes
);
```
[C++]
```
public: virtual PropertyDescriptorCollection* GetProperties(
   ITypeDescriptorContext* context,
   Object* component,
   Attribute* attributes[]
);
```
[JScript]
```
public function GetProperties(
   context : ITypeDescriptorContext,
   component : Object,
   attributes : Attribute[]
) : PropertyDescriptorCollection;
```

Parameters

context

An **ITypeDescriptorContext** that indicates the context to retrieve properties from.

component

The component to retrieve properties from.

attributes

An array of type **Attribute** that indicates the attributes of the properties to retrieve.

Return Value

A **PropertyDescriptorCollection** that contains the properties matching the specified context and attributes.

Requirements

Platforms: Windows 98, Windows NT 4.0, Windows Millennium Edition, Windows 2000, Windows XP Home Edition, Windows XP Professional, Windows Server 2003 family

ScrollableControlDesigner Class

Base designer class for extending the design mode behavior of a **Control** which should receive scroll messages.

System.Object
  System.ComponentModel.Design.ComponentDesigner
    System.Windows.Forms.Design.ControlDesigner
      System.Windows.Forms.Design.ParentControlDesigner
        System.Windows.Forms.Design.ScrollableControlDesigner
          System.Windows.Forms.Design.DocumentDesigner

```
[Visual Basic]
Public Class ScrollableControlDesigner
   Inherits ParentControlDesigner
[C#]
public class ScrollableControlDesigner : ParentControlDesigner
[C++]
public __gc class ScrollableControlDesigner : public
   ParentControlDesigner
[JScript]
public class ScrollableControlDesigner extends
   ParentControlDesigner
```

Thread Safety

Any public static (**Shared** in Visual Basic) members of this type are safe for multithreaded operations. Any instance members are not guaranteed to be thread safe.

Remarks

ScrollableControlDesigner provides a base class for designers of controls that respond to scroll messages. In addition to the methods and functionality inherited from the **ParentControlDesigner**, **ControlDesigner**, and **ComponentDesigner** classes, **ScrollableControlDesigner** provides a **WndProc** method override that passes WM_HSCROLL and WM_VSCROLL messages to the control at design time.

> **Note** If a form has its **AutoScroll** property set to active, the scroll bars are always active in the design-time environment.

You can associate a designer with a type using a **DesignerAttribute**.

Requirements

Namespace: System.Windows.Forms.Design

Platforms: Windows 98, Windows NT 4.0, Windows Millennium Edition, Windows 2000, Windows XP Home Edition, Windows XP Professional, Windows Server 2003 family

Assembly: System.Design (in System.Design.dll)

ScrollableControlDesigner Constructor

Initializes a new instance of the **ScrollableControlDesigner** class.

```
[Visual Basic]
Public Sub New()
[C#]
public ScrollableControlDesigner();
[C++]
public: ScrollableControlDesigner();
[JScript]
public function ScrollableControlDesigner();
```

Remarks

The default constructor initializes any fields to their default values.

Requirements

Platforms: Windows 98, Windows NT 4.0, Windows Millennium Edition, Windows 2000, Windows XP Home Edition, Windows XP Professional, Windows Server 2003 family

.NET Framework Security:

- Full trust for the immediate caller. This member cannot be used by partially trusted code.

ScrollableControlDesigner.GetHitTest Method

Indicates whether a mouse click at the specified point should be handled by the control.

```
[Visual Basic]
Overrides Protected Function GetHitTest( _
   ByVal pt As Point _
) As Boolean
[C#]
protected override bool GetHitTest(
   Point pt
);
[C++]
protected: bool GetHitTest(
   Point pt
);
[JScript]
protected override function GetHitTest(
   pt : Point
) : Boolean;
```

Parameters

pt

A **Point** indicating the position at which the mouse was clicked, in screen coordinates.

Return Value

true if a click at the specified point is to be handled by the control; otherwise, **false**.

Remarks

The **GetHitTest** method determines whether a click at the specified point should be passed to the control, while the control is in design mode. You can override and implement this method to enable your control to receive clicks in the design-time environment.

> **Note** You can pass a point in screen coordinates to the **PointToClient** method of the **Control** class to obtain the coordinates of the point relative to the upper-left corner of the control.

Requirements

Platforms: Windows 98, Windows NT 4.0, Windows Millennium Edition, Windows 2000, Windows XP Home Edition, Windows XP Professional, Windows Server 2003 family

.NET Framework Security:

- Full trust for the immediate caller. This member cannot be used by partially trusted code.

ScrollableControlDesigner.WndProc Method

Processes Windows messages and passes WM_HSCROLL and WM_VSCROLL messages to the control at design time.

```
[Visual Basic]
Overrides Protected Sub WndProc( _
   ByRef m As Message _
)
[C#]
protected override void WndProc(
   ref Message m
);
[C++]
protected: void WndProc(
   Message* m
);
[JScript]
protected override function WndProc(
   m : Message
);
```

Parameters

m

The **Message** to process.

Remarks

This override of the **WndProc** method passes any WM_HSCROLL and WM_VSCROLL messages to the control at design time. All messages are first passed to the base **WndProc** method.

Requirements

Platforms: Windows 98, Windows NT 4.0, Windows Millennium Edition, Windows 2000, Windows XP Home Edition, Windows XP Professional, Windows Server 2003 family

.NET Framework Security:

- Full trust for the immediate caller. This member cannot be used by partially trusted code.

SelectionRules Enumeration

Defines identifiers that are used to indicate selection rules for a component.

This enumeration has a **FlagsAttribute** attribute that allows a bitwise combination of its member values.

[Visual Basic]
```
<Flags>
<Serializable>
Public Enum SelectionRules
```
[C#]
```
[Flags]
[Serializable]
public enum SelectionRules
```
[C++]
```
[Flags]
[Serializable]
__value public enum SelectionRules
```
[JScript]
```
public
   Flags
   Serializable
enum SelectionRules
```

Remarks

These identifiers indicate whether a component has some form of visible user interface and whether the user can take actions to move or alter the size of the component.

Members

Member name	Description	Value
AllSizeable	Indicates the component supports sizing in all directions.	15
BottomSizeable	Indicates the component supports resize from the bottom.	2
LeftSizeable	Indicates the component supports resize from the left.	4
Locked	Indicates the component is locked to its container. Overrides the **Moveable**, **AllSizeable**, **BottomSizeable**, **LeftSizeable**, **RightSizeable**, and **TopSizeable** bit flags of this enumeration.	-2147483648
Moveable	Indicates the component supports a location property that allows it to be moved on the screen.	268435456
None	Indicates no special selection attributes.	0
RightSizeable	Indicates the component supports resize from the right.	8
TopSizeable	Indicates the component supports resize from the top.	1
Visible	Indicates the component has some form of visible user interface and the selection service is drawing a selection border around this user interface. If a selected component has this rule set, you can assume that the component implements **IComponent** and that it is associated with a corresponding designer instance.	1073741824

Requirements

Namespace: System.Windows.Forms.Design

Platforms: Windows 98, Windows NT 4.0, Windows Millennium Edition, Windows 2000, Windows XP Home Edition, Windows XP Professional, Windows Server 2003 family

Assembly: System.Design (in System.Design.dll)

WindowsFormsComponent-Editor Class

Provides a base class for editors that use a modal dialog to display a properties page similar to an ActiveX control's property page.

System.Object
  System.ComponentModel.ComponentEditor
    System.Windows.Forms.Design.WindowsFormsComponent-Editor
      System.Web.UI.Design.WebControls.BaseDataList-ComponentEditor

[Visual Basic]
```
MustInherit Public Class WindowsFormsComponentEditor
   Inherits ComponentEditor
```
[C#]
```
public abstract class WindowsFormsComponentEditor : ComponentEditor
```
[C++]
```
public __gc __abstract class WindowsFormsComponentEditor : public
   ComponentEditor
```
[JScript]
```
public abstract class WindowsFormsComponentEditor extends
   ComponentEditor
```

Thread Safety

Any public static (**Shared** in Visual Basic) members of this type are safe for multithreaded operations. Any instance members are not guaranteed to be thread safe.

Requirements

Namespace: System.Windows.Forms.Design

Platforms: Windows 98, Windows NT 4.0, Windows Millennium Edition, Windows 2000, Windows XP Home Edition, Windows XP Professional, Windows Server 2003 family

Assembly: System.Windows.Forms (in System.Windows.Forms.dll)

WindowsFormsComponentEditor Constructor

Initializes a new instance of the **WindowsFormsComponentEditor** class.

[Visual Basic]
```
Protected Sub New()
```
[C#]
```
protected WindowsFormsComponentEditor();
```
[C++]
```
protected: WindowsFormsComponentEditor();
```
[JScript]
```
protected function WindowsFormsComponentEditor();
```

Remarks

This constructor is called by derived class constructors to initialize state in this type.

Requirements

Platforms: Windows 98, Windows NT 4.0, Windows Millennium Edition, Windows 2000, Windows XP Home Edition, Windows XP Professional, Windows Server 2003 family

WindowsFormsComponentEditor.Edit-Component Method

Creates an editor window that allows the user to edit the specified component.

Overload List

Creates an editor window that allows the user to edit the specified component, using the specified context information.

[Visual Basic] **Overloads Overrides Public Function Edit-Component(ITypeDescriptorContext, Object) As Boolean**

[C#] **public override bool EditComponent(IType-DescriptorContext, object);**

[C++] **public: bool EditComponent(IType-DescriptorContext*, Object*);**

[JScript] **public override function EditComponent(IType-DescriptorContext, Object) : Boolean;**

Creates an editor window that allows the user to edit the specified component, using the specified window which owns the component.

[Visual Basic] **Overloads Public Function EditComponent(Object, IWin32Window) As Boolean**

[C#] **public bool EditComponent(object, IWin32Window);**

[C++] **public: bool EditComponent(Object*, IWin32Window*);**

[JScript] **public function EditComponent(Object, IWin32Window) : Boolean;**

Creates an editor window that allows the user to edit the specified component.

[Visual Basic] **Overloads Public Overridable Function EditComponent(ITypeDescriptorContext, Object, IWin32Window) As Boolean**

[C#] **public virtual bool EditComponent(IType-DescriptorContext, object, IWin32Window);**

[C++] **public: virtual bool EditComponent(IType-DescriptorContext*, Object*, IWin32Window*);**

[JScript] **public function EditComponent(IType-DescriptorContext, Object, IWin32Window) : Boolean;**

Inherited from **ComponentEditor**.

[Visual Basic] **Overloads Public Function EditComponent(Object) As Boolean**

[C#] **public bool EditComponent(object);**

[C++] **public: bool EditComponent(Object*);**

[JScript] **public function EditComponent(Object) : Boolean;**

WindowsFormsComponentEditor.EditComponent Method (ITypeDescriptorContext, Object)

Creates an editor window that allows the user to edit the specified component, using the specified context information.

```
[Visual Basic]
Overrides Overloads Public Function EditComponent( _
   ByVal context As ITypeDescriptorContext, _
   ByVal component As Object _
) As Boolean
[C#]
public override bool EditComponent(
   ITypeDescriptorContext context,
   object component
);
[C++]
public: bool EditComponent(
   ITypeDescriptorContext* context,
   Object* component
);
[JScript]
public override function EditComponent(
   context : ITypeDescriptorContext,
   component : Object
) : Boolean;
```

Parameters

context

An **ITypeDescriptorContext** that can be used to gain additional context information.

component

The component to edit.

Return Value

true if the component was changed during editing; otherwise, **false**.

Requirements

Platforms: Windows 98, Windows NT 4.0, Windows Millennium Edition, Windows 2000, Windows XP Home Edition, Windows XP Professional, Windows Server 2003 family

WindowsFormsComponentEditor.EditComponent Method (Object, IWin32Window)

Creates an editor window that allows the user to edit the specified component, using the specified window which owns the component.

```
[Visual Basic]
Overloads Public Function EditComponent( _
   ByVal component As Object, _
   ByVal owner As IWin32Window _
) As Boolean
[C#]
public bool EditComponent(
   object component,
   IWin32Window owner
);
[C++]
public: bool EditComponent(
   Object* component,
   IWin32Window* owner
);
[JScript]
public function EditComponent(
   component : Object,
   owner : IWin32Window
) : Boolean;
```

Parameters

component

The component to edit.

owner

An **IWin32Window** that the component belongs to.

Return Value

true if the component was changed during editing; otherwise, **false**.

Requirements

Platforms: Windows 98, Windows NT 4.0, Windows Millennium Edition, Windows 2000, Windows XP Home Edition, Windows XP Professional, Windows Server 2003 family

WindowsFormsComponentEditor.EditComponent Method (ITypeDescriptorContext, Object, IWin32Window)

Creates an editor window that allows the user to edit the specified component.

```
[Visual Basic]
Overloads Public Overridable Function EditComponent( _
   ByVal context As ITypeDescriptorContext, _
   ByVal component As Object, _
   ByVal owner As IWin32Window _
) As Boolean
[C#]
public virtual bool EditComponent(
   ITypeDescriptorContext context,
   object component,
   IWin32Window owner
);
[C++]
public: virtual bool EditComponent(
   ITypeDescriptorContext* context,
   Object* component,
   IWin32Window* owner
);
[JScript]
public function EditComponent(
   context : ITypeDescriptorContext,
   component : Object,
   owner : IWin32Window
) : Boolean;
```

Parameters

context

An **ITypeDescriptorContext** that can be used to gain additional context information.

component

The component to edit.

owner

An **IWin32Window** that the component belongs to.

Return Value

true if the component was changed during editing; otherwise, **false**.

Requirements

Platforms: Windows 98, Windows NT 4.0, Windows Millennium Edition, Windows 2000, Windows XP Home Edition, Windows XP Professional, Windows Server 2003 family

WindowsFormsComponentEditor.GetComponentEditorPages Method

Gets the component editor pages associated with the component editor.

[Visual Basic]
```
Protected Overridable Function GetComponentEditorPages() As Type()
```
[C#]
```
protected virtual Type[] GetComponentEditorPages();
```
[C++]
```
protected: virtual Type* GetComponentEditorPages() [];
```
[JScript]
```
protected function GetComponentEditorPages() : Type[];
```

Return Value

An array of component editor pages.

Remarks

Notes to Inheritors: You must override this method to implement the functionality for this method.

Requirements

Platforms: Windows 98, Windows NT 4.0, Windows Millennium Edition, Windows 2000, Windows XP Home Edition, Windows XP Professional, Windows Server 2003 family

WindowsFormsComponentEditor.GetInitialComponentEditorPageIndex Method

Gets the index of the initial component editor page for the component editor to display.

[Visual Basic]
```
Protected Overridable Function GetInitialComponentEditorPageIndex() _
   _
   As Integer
```
[C#]
```
protected virtual int GetInitialComponentEditorPageIndex();
```
[C++]
```
protected: virtual int GetInitialComponentEditorPageIndex();
```
[JScript]
```
protected function GetInitialComponentEditorPageIndex() : int;
```

Return Value

The index of the component editor page that the component editor will initially display.

Requirements

Platforms: Windows 98, Windows NT 4.0, Windows Millennium Edition, Windows 2000, Windows XP Home Edition, Windows XP Professional, Windows Server 2003 family

At Microsoft Press, we use tools to illustrate our books for software developers and IT professionals. Tools very simply and powerfully symbolize human inventiveness. They're a metaphor for people extending their capabilities, precision, and reach. From simple calipers and pliers to digital micrometers and lasers, these stylized illustrations give each book a visual identity, and a personality to the series. With tools and knowledge, there's no limit to creativity and innovation. Our tagline says it all: *the tools you need to put technology to work*.

Proof of Purchase

Use this page as proof of purchase if participating in a promotion or rebate offer on this title. Proof of purchase must be used in conjunction with other proof(s) of payment such as your dated sales receipt—see offer details.

Microsoft® Windows® .NET Framework 1.1 Class Library Reference Volume 7: System.Windows.Forms and System.Drawing

0-7356-1818-6

CUSTOMER NAME

Microsoft Press, PO Box 97017, Redmond, WA 98073-9830

Microsoft®

MICROSOFT®

.NET FRAMEWORK 1.1

CLASS LIBRARY REFERENCE

VOLUME 7b: SYSTEM.DRAWING AND SYSTEM.COMPONENTMODEL

Microsoft®
.net™

PUBLISHED BY
Microsoft Press
A Division of Microsoft Corporation
One Microsoft Way
Redmond, Washington 98052-6399

Library of Congress Cataloging-in-Publication Data pending.

Printed and bound in the United States of America.

1 2 3 4 5 6 7 8 9 QWT 8 7 6 5 4 3

Distributed in Canada by H.B. Fenn and Company Ltd.

A CIP catalogue record for this book is available from the British Library.

Microsoft Press books are available through booksellers and distributors worldwide. For further information about international editions, contact your local Microsoft Corporation office or contact Microsoft Press International directly at fax (425) 936-7329. Visit our Web site at www.microsoft.com/mspress. Send comments to *mspinput@microsoft.com.*

For Microsoft:
Acquisitions Editor: Juliana Aldous Atkinson
Project Editor: Dick Brown

For mediaService, Siegen, Germany:
Project Manager: Gerhard Alfes

SubAssy Part No. X09-56602
Body Part No. X09-56604

Contents

Document Conventions

The following table shows the typographic conventions used in this book.

Convention	Description	Example
Monospace	Indicates source code, code examples, input to the command line, application output, code lines embedded in text, and variables and code elements.	`Public Class`
Bold	Indicates most predefined programming elements, including namespaces, classes, delegates, objects, interfaces, methods, functions, macros, structures, constructors, properties, events, enumerations, fields, operators, statements, directives, data types, keywords, exceptions, non-HTML attributes, and configuration t ags, as well as registry keys, subkeys, and values. Also indicates the following HTML elements: attributes, directives, keywords, values, and headers. In addition, indicates required user input, including command-line options, that must be entered exactly as shown.	**Path** class **Resolve** method
Italic	Indicates placeholders, most often method or function parameters and HTML placeholders; these placeholders represent information that must be supplied by the implementation or the user. For command-line input, indicates parameter values.	*context* parameter
Capital letters	Indicates the names of keys and key sequences.	ENTER CTRL+R
Plus sign	Indicates a combination of keys. For example, ALT+F1 means to h old down the ALT key while pressing the F1 key.	ALT+F1
↵	The "rundown" is a line-continuation character this book uses in code samples for Visual Basic, C#, C++, and JScript. It indicates that a code statement is too long to fit on one line in the book, and so has been continued on the next line. All code samples are available in the .NET Framework 1.1 online documentation, which is also included in the Visual Studio .NET 2003 Help.	`string strSource ="We will ↵` `search on this string";`

System.Drawing Namespace

The **System.Drawing** namespace provides access to GDI+ basic graphics functionality. More advanced functionality is provided in the **System.Drawing.Drawing2D**, **System.Drawing.Imaging**, and **System.Drawing.Text** namespaces.

The **Graphics** class provides methods for drawing to the display device. Classes such as **Rectangle** and **Point** encapsulate GDI+ primitives. The **Pen** class is used to draw lines and curves, while classes derrived from the abstract class **Brush** are used to fill the interiors of shapes.

Bitmap Class

Encapsulates a GDI+ bitmap, which consists of the pixel data for a graphics image and its attributes. A **Bitmap** object is an object used to work with images defined by pixel data.

System.Object
  System.MarshalByRefObject
    System.Drawing.Image
      System.Drawing.Bitmap

```
[Visual Basic]
<Serializable>
<ComVisible(True)>
NotInheritable Public Class Bitmap
   Inherits Image
[C#]
[Serializable]
[ComVisible(true)]
public sealed class Bitmap : Image
[C++]
[Serializable]
[ComVisible(true)]
public __gc __sealed class Bitmap : public Image
[JScript]
public
   Serializable
   ComVisible(true)
class Bitmap extends Image
```

Thread Safety

Any public static (**Shared** in Visual Basic) members of this type are safe for multithreaded operations. Any instance members are not guaranteed to be thread safe.

Remarks

A bitmap consists of the pixel data for a graphics image and its attributes.

Requirements

Namespace: System.Drawing

Platforms: Windows 98, Windows NT 4.0, Windows Millennium Edition, Windows 2000, Windows XP Home Edition, Windows XP Professional, Windows Server 2003 family, .NET Compact Framework - Windows CE .NET

Assembly: System.Drawing (in System.Drawing.dll)

Bitmap Constructor

Initializes a new instance of the **Bitmap** class.

Overload List

Initializes a new instance of the **Bitmap** class from the specified existing image.

Supported by the .NET Compact Framework.

[Visual Basic] **Public Sub New(Image)**
[C#] **public Bitmap(Image);**
[C++] **public: Bitmap(Image*);**
[JScript] **public function Bitmap(Image);**

Initializes a new instance of the **Bitmap** class from the specified data stream.

Supported by the .NET Compact Framework.

[Visual Basic] **Public Sub New(Stream)**
[C#] **public Bitmap(Stream);**
[C++] **public: Bitmap(Stream*);**
[JScript] **public function Bitmap(Stream);**

Initializes a new instance of the **Bitmap** class from the specified file.

Supported by the .NET Compact Framework.

[Visual Basic] **Public Sub New(String)**
[C#] **public Bitmap(string);**
[C++] **public: Bitmap(String*);**
[JScript] **public function Bitmap(String);**

Initializes a new instance of the **Bitmap** class from the specified existing image and with the specified size.

[Visual Basic] **Public Sub New(Image, Size)**
[C#] **public Bitmap(Image, Size);**
[C++] **public: Bitmap(Image*, Size);**
[JScript] **public function Bitmap(Image, Size);**

Initializes a new instance of the **Bitmap** class with the specified size.

Supported by the .NET Compact Framework.

[Visual Basic] **Public Sub New(Integer, Integer)**
[C#] **public Bitmap(int, int);**
[C++] **public: Bitmap(int, int);**
[JScript] **public function Bitmap(int, int);**

Initializes a new instance of the **Bitmap** class from the specified data stream.

[Visual Basic] **Public Sub New(Stream, Boolean)**
[C#] **public Bitmap(Stream, bool);**
[C++] **public: Bitmap(Stream*, bool);**
[JScript] **public function Bitmap(Stream, Boolean);**

Initializes a new instance of the **Bitmap** class from the specified file.

[Visual Basic] **Public Sub New(String, Boolean)**
[C#] **public Bitmap(string, bool);**
[C++] **public: Bitmap(String*, bool);**
[JScript] **public function Bitmap(String, Boolean);**

Initializes a new instance of the **Bitmap** class from a specified resource.

[Visual Basic] **Public Sub New(Type, String)**
[C#] **public Bitmap(Type, string);**
[C++] **public: Bitmap(Type*, String*);**
[JScript] **public function Bitmap(Type, String);**

Initializes a new instance of the **Bitmap** class from the specified existing image and with the specified size.

[Visual Basic] **Public Sub New(Image, Integer, Integer)**

[C#] **public Bitmap(Image, int, int);**

[C++] **public: Bitmap(Image*, int, int);**

[JScript] **public function Bitmap(Image, int, int);**

Initializes a new instance of the **Bitmap** class with the specified size and with the resolution of the specified **Graphics** object.

[Visual Basic] **Public Sub New(Integer, Integer, Graphics)**

[C#] **public Bitmap(int, int, Graphics);**

[C++] **public: Bitmap(int, int, Graphics*);**

[JScript] **public function Bitmap(int, int, Graphics);**

Initializes a new instance of the **Bitmap** class with the specified size and format.

[Visual Basic] **Public Sub New(Integer, Integer, PixelFormat)**

[C#] **public Bitmap(int, int, PixelFormat);**

[C++] **public: Bitmap(int, int, PixelFormat);**

[JScript] **public function Bitmap(int, int, PixelFormat);**

Initializes a new instance of the **Bitmap** class with the specified size, pixel format, and pixel data.

[Visual Basic] **Public Sub New(Integer, Integer, Integer, PixelFormat, IntPtr)**

[C#] **public Bitmap(int, int, int, PixelFormat, IntPtr);**

[C++] **public: Bitmap(int, int, int, PixelFormat, IntPtr);**

[JScript] **public function Bitmap(int, int, int, PixelFormat, IntPtr);**

Bitmap Constructor (Image)

Initializes a new instance of the **Bitmap** class from the specified existing image.

```
[Visual Basic]
Public Sub New( _
   ByVal original As Image _
)
[C#]
public Bitmap(
   Image original
);
[C++]
public: Bitmap(
   Image* original
);
[JScript]
public function Bitmap(
   original : Image
);
```

Parameters

original

The **Image** object from which to create the new **Bitmap** object.

Requirements

Platforms: Windows 98, Windows NT 4.0, Windows Millennium Edition, Windows 2000, Windows XP Home Edition, Windows XP Professional, Windows Server 2003 family, .NET Compact Framework - Windows CE .NET

Bitmap Constructor (Stream)

Initializes a new instance of the **Bitmap** class from the specified data stream.

```
[Visual Basic]
Public Sub New( _
   ByVal stream As Stream _
)
[C#]
public Bitmap(
   Stream stream
);
[C++]
public: Bitmap(
   Stream* stream
);
[JScript]
public function Bitmap(
   stream : Stream
);
```

Parameters

stream

The data stream used to load the image.

Remarks

You must keep the stream open for the lifetime of the **Bitmap** object.

Requirements

Platforms: Windows 98, Windows NT 4.0, Windows Millennium Edition, Windows 2000, Windows XP Home Edition, Windows XP Professional, Windows Server 2003 family, .NET Compact Framework - Windows CE .NET

Bitmap Constructor (String)

Initializes a new instance of the **Bitmap** class from the specified file.

```
[Visual Basic]
Public Sub New( _
   ByVal filename As String _
)
[C#]
public Bitmap(
   string filename
);
[C++]
public: Bitmap(
   String* filename
);
[JScript]
public function Bitmap(
   filename : String
);
```

Parameters

filename

The name of the bitmap file.

Remarks

The file remains locked until the **Bitmap** object is disposed.

Requirements

Platforms: Windows 98, Windows NT 4.0,
Windows Millennium Edition, Windows 2000,
Windows XP Home Edition, Windows XP Professional,
Windows Server 2003 family,
.NET Compact Framework - Windows CE .NET

Bitmap Constructor (Image, Size)

Initializes a new instance of the **Bitmap** class from the specified existing image and with the specified size.

```
[Visual Basic]
Public Sub New( _
   ByVal original As Image, _
   ByVal newSize As Size _
)
[C#]
public Bitmap(
   Image original,
   Size newSize
);
[C++]
public: Bitmap(
   Image* original,
   Size newSize
);
[JScript]
public function Bitmap(
   original : Image,
   newSize : Size
);
```

Parameters

original
The **Image** object from which to create the new **Bitmap** object.

newSize
The **Size** structure that represent the size of the new **Bitmap**.

Requirements

Platforms: Windows 98, Windows NT 4.0,
Windows Millennium Edition, Windows 2000,
Windows XP Home Edition, Windows XP Professional,
Windows Server 2003 family

Bitmap Constructor (Int32, Int32)

Initializes a new instance of the **Bitmap** class with the specified size.

```
[Visual Basic]
Public Sub New( _
   ByVal width As Integer, _
   ByVal height As Integer _
)
[C#]
public Bitmap(
   int width,
   int height
);
[C++]
public: Bitmap(
   int width,
   int height
);
[JScript]
public function Bitmap(
   width : int,
   height : int
);
```

Parameters

width
The width, in pixels, of the new **Bitmap** object.

height
The height, in pixels, of the new **Bitmap** object.

Remarks

This constructor creates a Bitmap with a **PixelFormat** enumeration of **Format32bppARGB**.

Requirements

Platforms: Windows 98, Windows NT 4.0,
Windows Millennium Edition, Windows 2000,
Windows XP Home Edition, Windows XP Professional,
Windows Server 2003 family,
.NET Compact Framework - Windows CE .NET

Bitmap Constructor (Stream, Boolean)

Initializes a new instance of the **Bitmap** class from the specified data stream.

```
[Visual Basic]
Public Sub New( _
   ByVal stream As Stream, _
   ByVal useIcm As Boolean _
)
[C#]
public Bitmap(
   Stream stream,
   bool useIcm
);
[C++]
public: Bitmap(
   Stream* stream,
   bool useIcm
);
[JScript]
public function Bitmap(
   stream : Stream,
   useIcm : Boolean
);
```

Parameters

stream
The data stream used to load the image.

useIcm
Set to **true** to use color correction for this **Bitmap** object; otherwise, **false**.

Remarks

You must keep the stream open for the lifetime of the **Bitmap** object.

Requirements

Platforms: Windows 98, Windows NT 4.0,
Windows Millennium Edition, Windows 2000,
Windows XP Home Edition, Windows XP Professional,
Windows Server 2003 family

Bitmap Constructor (String, Boolean)

Initializes a new instance of the **Bitmap** class from the specified file.

[Visual Basic]
```
Public Sub New( _
   ByVal filename As String, _
   ByVal useIcm As Boolean _
)
```
[C#]
```
public Bitmap(
   string filename,
   bool useIcm
);
```
[C++]
```
public: Bitmap(
   String* filename,
   bool useIcm
);
```
[JScript]
```
public function Bitmap(
   filename : String,
   useIcm : Boolean
);
```

Parameters

filename

The name of the bitmap file.

useIcm

Set to **true** to use color correction for this **Bitmap** object; otherwise, **false**.

Remarks

The file remains locked until the **Bitmap** object is disposed.

Requirements

Platforms: Windows 98, Windows NT 4.0, Windows Millennium Edition, Windows 2000, Windows XP Home Edition, Windows XP Professional, Windows Server 2003 family

Bitmap Constructor (Type, String)

Initializes a new instance of the **Bitmap** class from a specified resource.

[Visual Basic]
```
Public Sub New( _
   ByVal type As Type, _
   ByVal resource As String _
)
```
[C#]
```
public Bitmap(
   Type type,
   string resource
);
```
[C++]
```
public: Bitmap(
   Type* type,
   String* resource
);
```
[JScript]
```
public function Bitmap(
   type : Type,
   resource : String
);
```

Parameters

type

The class used to extract the resource.

resource

The name of the resource.

Requirements

Platforms: Windows 98, Windows NT 4.0, Windows Millennium Edition, Windows 2000, Windows XP Home Edition, Windows XP Professional, Windows Server 2003 family

Bitmap Constructor (Image, Int32, Int32)

Initializes a new instance of the **Bitmap** class from the specified existing image and with the specified size.

[Visual Basic]
```
Public Sub New( _
   ByVal original As Image, _
   ByVal width As Integer, _
   ByVal height As Integer _
)
```
[C#]
```
public Bitmap(
   Image original,
   int width,
   int height
);
```
[C++]
```
public: Bitmap(
   Image* original,
   int width,
   int height
);
```
[JScript]
```
public function Bitmap(
   original : Image,
   width : int,
   height : int
);
```

Parameters

original

The **Image** object from which to create the new **Bitmap** object.

width

The width, in pixels, of the new **Bitmap** object.

height

The height, in pixels, of the new **Bitmap** object.

Requirements

Platforms: Windows 98, Windows NT 4.0, Windows Millennium Edition, Windows 2000, Windows XP Home Edition, Windows XP Professional, Windows Server 2003 family

Bitmap Constructor (Int32, Int32, Graphics)

Initializes a new instance of the **Bitmap** class with the specified size and with the resolution of the specified **Graphics** object.

```
[Visual Basic]
Public Sub New( _
   ByVal width As Integer, _
   ByVal height As Integer, _
   ByVal g As Graphics _
)
[C#]
public Bitmap(
   int width,
   int height,
   Graphics g
);
[C++]
public: Bitmap(
   int width,
   int height,
   Graphics* g
);
[JScript]
public function Bitmap(
   width : int,
   height : int,
   g : Graphics
);
```

Parameters

width
The width, in pixels, of the new **Bitmap** object.

height
The height, in pixels, of the new **Bitmap** object.

g
The **Graphics** object that specifies the resolution for the new **Bitmap** object.

Remarks

The new **Bitmap** object that this method creates takes its horizontal and vertical resolution from the **DpiX** and **DpiY** properties of *g*, respectively.

Requirements

Platforms: Windows 98, Windows NT 4.0, Windows Millennium Edition, Windows 2000, Windows XP Home Edition, Windows XP Professional, Windows Server 2003 family

Bitmap Constructor (Int32, Int32, PixelFormat)

Initializes a new instance of the **Bitmap** class with the specified size and format.

```
[Visual Basic]
Public Sub New( _
   ByVal width As Integer, _
   ByVal height As Integer, _
   ByVal format As PixelFormat _
)
[C#]
public Bitmap(
   int width,
   int height,
   PixelFormat format
);
[C++]
public: Bitmap(
   int width,
   int height,
   PixelFormat format
);
[JScript]
public function Bitmap(
   width : int,
   height : int,
   format : PixelFormat
);
```

Parameters

width
The width, in pixels, of the new **Bitmap** object.

height
The height, in pixels, of the new **Bitmap** object.

format
The **PixelFormat** enumeration for the new **Bitmap**.

Requirements

Platforms: Windows 98, Windows NT 4.0, Windows Millennium Edition, Windows 2000, Windows XP Home Edition, Windows XP Professional, Windows Server 2003 family

Bitmap Constructor (Int32, Int32, Int32, PixelFormat, IntPtr)

Initializes a new instance of the **Bitmap** class with the specified size, pixel format, and pixel data.

```
[Visual Basic]
Public Sub New( _
   ByVal width As Integer, _
   ByVal height As Integer, _
   ByVal stride As Integer, _
   ByVal format As PixelFormat, _
   ByVal scan0 As IntPtr _
)
[C#]
public Bitmap(
   int width,
   int height,
   int stride,
   PixelFormat format,
   IntPtr scan0
);
[C++]
public: Bitmap(
   int width,
   int height,
   int stride,
   PixelFormat format,
   IntPtr scan0
);
```

[JScript]
```
public function Bitmap(
   width : int,
   height : int,
   stride : int,
   format : PixelFormat,
   scan0 : IntPtr
);
```

Parameters

width
The width, in pixels, of the new **Bitmap** object.

height
The height, in pixels, of the new **Bitmap** object.

stride
The memory size of a row in the stream of pixel data.

format
The **PixelFormat** enumeration for the new **Bitmap** object.

scan0
The address of a stream of pixel data.

Remarks

This method requires UnmanagedCode permission. For more information see **SecurityPermissionFlag**.

Requirements

Platforms: Windows 98, Windows NT 4.0, Windows Millennium Edition, Windows 2000, Windows XP Home Edition, Windows XP Professional, Windows Server 2003 family

Bitmap.Clone Method

Creates a copy of the section of this **Bitmap** defined with a specified **PixelFormat**.

Overload List

Creates a copy of the section of this **Bitmap** object defined by **Rectangle** structure and with a specified **PixelFormat** enumeration.

[Visual Basic] **Overloads Public Function Clone(Rectangle, PixelFormat) As Bitmap**

[C#] **public Bitmap Clone(Rectangle, PixelFormat);**

[C++] **public: Bitmap* Clone(Rectangle, PixelFormat);**

[JScript] **public function Clone(Rectangle, PixelFormat) : Bitmap;**

Creates a copy of the section of this **Bitmap** object defined with a specified **PixelFormat** enumeration.

[Visual Basic] **Overloads Public Function Clone(RectangleF, PixelFormat) As Bitmap**

[C#] **public Bitmap Clone(RectangleF, PixelFormat);**

[C++] **public: Bitmap* Clone(RectangleF, PixelFormat);**

[JScript] **public function Clone(RectangleF, PixelFormat) : Bitmap;**

Inherited from **Image**.

[Visual Basic] **Overloads Public Overridable Function Clone() As Object Implements ICloneable.Clone**

[C#] **public virtual object Clone();**

[C++] **public: virtual Object* Clone();**

[JScript] **public function Clone() : Object;**

Example

[Visual Basic, C#] The following example is designed for use with Windows Forms, and it requires **PaintEventArgs** *e*, which is a parameter of the **Paint** event handler. The code performs the following actions:

- Creates a **Bitmap** object from a file.
- Clones a portion of that **Bitmap** object.
- Draws the cloned portion to the screen.

> [Visual Basic, C#] **Note** This example shows how to use one of the overloaded versions of **Clone**. For other examples that might be available, see the individual overload topics.

[Visual Basic]

```
Public Sub Clone_Example(e As PaintEventArgs)
' Create a Bitmap object from a file.
Dim myBitmap As New Bitmap("Grapes.jpg")
' Clone a portion of the Bitmap object.
Dim cloneRect As New RectangleF(0, 0, 100, 100)
Dim format As PixelFormat = myBitmap.PixelFormat
Dim cloneBitmap As Bitmap = myBitmap.Clone(cloneRect, format)
' Draw the cloned portion of the Bitmap object.
e.Graphics.DrawImage(cloneBitmap, 0, 0)
End Sub
```

[C#]
```
public void Clone_Example(PaintEventArgs e)
{
// Create a Bitmap object from a file.
Bitmap myBitmap = new Bitmap("Grapes.jpg");
// Clone a portion of the Bitmap object.
RectangleF cloneRect = new RectangleF(0, 0, 100, 100);
PixelFormat format = myBitmap.PixelFormat;
Bitmap cloneBitmap = myBitmap.Clone(cloneRect, format);
// Draw the cloned portion of the Bitmap object.
e.Graphics.DrawImage(cloneBitmap, 0, 0);
}
```

Bitmap.Clone Method (Rectangle, PixelFormat)

Creates a copy of the section of this **Bitmap** object defined by **Rectangle** structure and with a specified **PixelFormat** enumeration.

[Visual Basic]
```
Overloads Public Function Clone( _
   ByVal rect As Rectangle, _
   ByVal format As PixelFormat _
) As Bitmap
```
[C#]
```
public Bitmap Clone(
   Rectangle rect,
   PixelFormat format
);
```
[C++]
```
public: Bitmap* Clone(
   Rectangle rect,
   PixelFormat format
);
```
[JScript]
```
public function Clone(
   rect : Rectangle,
   format : PixelFormat
) : Bitmap;
```

Parameters

rect

Defines the portion of this **Bitmap** object to copy. Coordinates are relative to this **Bitmap**.

format

Specifies the **PixelFormat** enumeration for the destination **Bitmap** object.

Return Value

The new **Bitmap** object that this method creates.

Remarks

This method might throw an **OutOfMemoryException** if the rectangle specified by the *rect* parameter is outside the bounds of the source bitmap.

Example

[Visual Basic, C#] The following example is designed for use with Windows Forms, and it requires **PaintEventArgs** *e*, which is a parameter of the **Paint** event handler. The code performs the following actions:

- Creates a **Bitmap** object from a file.
- Clones a portion of that **Bitmap** object.
- Draws the cloned portion to the screen.

[Visual Basic]
```
Public Sub Clone_Example(e As PaintEventArgs)
' Create a Bitmap object from a file.
Dim myBitmap As New Bitmap("Grapes.jpg")
' Clone a portion of the Bitmap object.
Dim cloneRect As New Rectangle(0, 0, 100, 100)
Dim format As PixelFormat = myBitmap.PixelFormat
Dim cloneBitmap As Bitmap = myBitmap.Clone(cloneRect, format)
' Draw the cloned portion of the Bitmap object.
e.Graphics.DrawImage(cloneBitmap, 0, 0)
End Sub
```

[C#]
```
public void Clone_Example(PaintEventArgs e)
{
// Create a Bitmap object from a file.
Bitmap myBitmap = new Bitmap("Grapes.jpg");
// Clone a portion of the Bitmap object.
Rectangle cloneRect = new Rectangle(0, 0, 100, 100);
PixelFormat format = myBitmap.PixelFormat;
Bitmap cloneBitmap = myBitmap.Clone(cloneRect, format);
// Draw the cloned portion of the Bitmap object.
e.Graphics.DrawImage(cloneBitmap, 0, 0);
}
```

Requirements

Platforms: Windows 98, Windows NT 4.0, Windows Millennium Edition, Windows 2000, Windows XP Home Edition, Windows XP Professional, Windows Server 2003 family

Bitmap.Clone Method (RectangleF, PixelFormat)

Creates a copy of the section of this **Bitmap** object defined with a specified **PixelFormat** enumeration.

[Visual Basic]
```
Overloads Public Function Clone( _
   ByVal rect As RectangleF, _
   ByVal format As PixelFormat _
) As Bitmap
```
[C#]
```
public Bitmap Clone(
   RectangleF rect,
   PixelFormat format
);
```
[C++]
```
public: Bitmap* Clone(
   RectangleF rect,
   PixelFormat format
);
```
[JScript]
```
public function Clone(
   rect : RectangleF,
   format : PixelFormat
) : Bitmap;
```

Parameters

rect

Defines the portion of this **Bitmap** object to copy.

format

Specifies the **PixelFormat** enumeration for the destination **Bitmap** object.

Return Value

The **Bitmap** object that this method creates.

Remarks

This method might throw an **OutOfMemoryException** if the rectangle specified by the *rect* parameter is outside the bounds of the source bitmap.

Example

[Visual Basic, C#] The following example is designed for use with Windows Forms, and it requires **PaintEventArgs** *e*, which is a parameter of the **Paint** event handler. The code performs the following actions:

- Creates a **Bitmap** object from a file.
- Clones a portion of that **Bitmap** object.
- Draws the cloned portion to the screen.

[Visual Basic]
```
Public Sub Clone_Example(e As PaintEventArgs)
' Create a Bitmap object from a file.
Dim myBitmap As New Bitmap("Grapes.jpg")
' Clone a portion of the Bitmap object.
Dim cloneRect As New RectangleF(0, 0, 100, 100)
Dim format As PixelFormat = myBitmap.PixelFormat
Dim cloneBitmap As Bitmap = myBitmap.Clone(cloneRect, format)
' Draw the cloned portion of the Bitmap object.
e.Graphics.DrawImage(cloneBitmap, 0, 0)
End Sub
```

[C#]
```
public void Clone_Example(PaintEventArgs e)
{
// Create a Bitmap object from a file.
Bitmap myBitmap = new Bitmap("Grapes.jpg");
// Clone a portion of the Bitmap object.
RectangleF cloneRect = new RectangleF(0, 0, 100, 100);
PixelFormat format = myBitmap.PixelFormat;
Bitmap cloneBitmap = myBitmap.Clone(cloneRect, format);
// Draw the cloned portion of the Bitmap object.
e.Graphics.DrawImage(cloneBitmap, 0, 0);
}
```

Requirements

Platforms: Windows 98, Windows NT 4.0, Windows Millennium Edition, Windows 2000, Windows XP Home Edition, Windows XP Professional, Windows Server 2003 family

Bitmap.FromHicon Method

Creates a **Bitmap** from a Windows handle to an icon.

[Visual Basic]
```
Public Shared Function FromHicon( _
   ByVal hicon As IntPtr _
) As Bitmap
```
[C#]
```
public static Bitmap FromHicon(
   IntPtr hicon
);
```
[C++]
```
public: static Bitmap* FromHicon(
   IntPtr hicon
);
```
[JScript]
```
public static function FromHicon(
   hicon : IntPtr
) : Bitmap;
```

Parameters

hicon

A handle to an icon.

Return Value

The **Bitmap** object that this method creates.

Example

[Visual Basic, C#] The following example is designed for use with Windows Forms, and it requires **PaintEventArgs** *e*, which is a parameter of the **Paint** event handler. The code performs the following actions:

- Gets the handle to an existing icon image.
- Creates a **Bitmap** object from the handle.
- Draws the **Bitmap** object to the screen.

[Visual Basic]
```
Private Shared Function
<System.Runtime.InteropServices.DllImportAttribute
 ("user32.dll")> LoadImage(Hinstance As Integer, name As String,
type As Integer, width As Integer, height As Integer, load
As Integer) As IntPtr
Public Sub HICON_Example(e As PaintEventArgs)
' Get a handle to an icon.
Dim Hicon As IntPtr = LoadImage(0, "smile.ico", 1, 0, 0, 16)
' Create a Bitmap object from the icon handle.
Dim iconBitmap As Bitmap = Bitmap.FromHicon(Hicon)
' Draw the Bitmap object to the screen.
e.Graphics.DrawImage(iconBitmap, 0, 0)
End Sub
```

[C#]
```
[System.Runtime.InteropServices.DllImportAttribute("user32.dll")]
private static extern IntPtr LoadImage(
int Hinstance,
string name,
int type,
int width,
int height,
int load);
public void Hicon_Example(PaintEventArgs e)
{
// Get a handle to an icon.
IntPtr Hicon = LoadImage(
0,
"smile.ico",
1,
0,
0,
16);
// Create a Bitmap object from the icon handle.
Bitmap iconBitmap = Bitmap.FromHicon(Hicon);
// Draw the Bitmap object to the screen.
e.Graphics.DrawImage(iconBitmap, 0, 0);
}
```

Requirements

Platforms: Windows 98, Windows NT 4.0, Windows Millennium Edition, Windows 2000, Windows XP Home Edition, Windows XP Professional, Windows Server 2003 family

Bitmap.FromResource Method

Creates a **Bitmap** object from the specified Windows resource.

[Visual Basic]
```
Public Shared Function FromResource( _
   ByVal hinstance As IntPtr, _
   ByVal bitmapName As String _
) As Bitmap
```
[C#]
```
public static Bitmap FromResource(
   IntPtr hinstance,
   string bitmapName
);
```
[C++]
```
public: static Bitmap* FromResource(
   IntPtr hinstance,
   String* bitmapName
);
```
[JScript]
```
public static function FromResource(
   hinstance : IntPtr,
   bitmapName : String
) : Bitmap;
```

Parameters

hinstance

A handle to an instance of the executable file that contains the resource.

bitmapName

A string containing the name of the resource bitmap.

Return Value

The **Bitmap** object that this method creates.

Remarks

This method works only with bitmaps that are named resources in a DLL.

Requirements

Platforms: Windows 98, Windows NT 4.0, Windows Millennium Edition, Windows 2000, Windows XP Home Edition, Windows XP Professional, Windows Server 2003 family

Bitmap.GetHbitmap Method

Creates a GDI bitmap object from a GDI+ **Bitmap** object.

Overload List

Creates a GDI bitmap object from this **Bitmap** object.

[Visual Basic] **Overloads Public Function GetHbitmap() As IntPtr**

[C#] **public IntPtr GetHbitmap();**

[C++] **public: IntPtr GetHbitmap();**

[JScript] **public function GetHbitmap() : IntPtr;**

Creates a GDI bitmap object from this **Bitmap** object.

[Visual Basic] **Overloads Public Function GetHbitmap(Color) As IntPtr**

[C#] **public IntPtr GetHbitmap(Color);**

[C++] **public: IntPtr GetHbitmap(Color);**

[JScript] **public function GetHbitmap(Color) : IntPtr;**

Example

> [Visual Basic, C#] **Note** This example shows how to use one of the overloaded versions of **GetHbitmap**. For other examples that might be available, see the individual overload topics.

[Visual Basic]
```
Imports System.Runtime.InteropServices
...
Declare Function DeleteObject Lib "gdi32.dll"
 (ByVal hObject As IntPtr) As Boolean
...
Dim bm As New Bitmap("Picture.jpg")
Dim hBitmap As IntPtr
hBitmap = bm.GetHbitmap(Color.Blue)
' Do something with hBitmap.
DeleteObject(hBitmap)
```

[C#]
```
using System.Runtime.InteropServices;
...
[DllImport("gdi32.dll")]
public static extern bool DeleteObject(IntPtr hObject);
...
Bitmap bm = new Bitmap("Picture.jpg");
IntPtr hBitmap = bm.GetHbitmap(Color.Blue);
// Do something with hBitmap.
DeleteObject(hBitmap);
```

Bitmap.GetHbitmap Method ()

Creates a GDI bitmap object from this **Bitmap** object.

[Visual Basic]
```
Overloads Public Function GetHbitmap() As IntPtr
```
[C#]
```
public IntPtr GetHbitmap();
```
[C++]
```
public: IntPtr GetHbitmap();
```
[JScript]
```
public function GetHbitmap() : IntPtr;
```

Return Value

A handle to the GDI bitmap object that this method creates.

Remarks

You are responsible for calling DeleteObject to free the memory used by the GDI bitmap object.

Example

[Visual Basic]
```
Imports System.Runtime.InteropServices
...
Declare Function DeleteObject Lib "gdi32.dll"
 (ByVal hObject As IntPtr) As Boolean
...
Dim bm As New Bitmap("Picture.jpg")
Dim hBitmap As IntPtr
hBitmap = bm.GetHbitmap()
' Do something with hBitmap.
DeleteObject(hBitmap)
```

[C#]
```
using System.Runtime.InteropServices;
...
[DllImport("gdi32.dll")]
public static extern bool DeleteObject(IntPtr hObject);
...
Bitmap bm = new Bitmap("Picture.jpg");
IntPtr hBitmap = bm.GetHbitmap();
// Do something with hBitmap.
DeleteObject(hBitmap);
```

Requirements

Platforms: Windows 98, Windows NT 4.0, Windows Millennium Edition, Windows 2000, Windows XP Home Edition, Windows XP Professional, Windows Server 2003 family

Bitmap.GetHbitmap Method (Color)

Creates a GDI bitmap object from this **Bitmap** object.

[Visual Basic]
```
Overloads Public Function GetHbitmap( _
   ByVal background As Color _
) As IntPtr
```
[C#]
```
public IntPtr GetHbitmap(
   Color background
);
```
[C++]
```
public: IntPtr GetHbitmap(
   Color background
);
```
[JScript]
```
public function GetHbitmap(
   background : Color
) : IntPtr;
```

Parameters

background

A **Color** structure that specifies the background color. This parameter is ignored if the bitmap is totally opaque.

Return Value

A handle to the GDI bitmap object that this method creates.

Remarks

You are responsible for calling DeleteObject to free the memory used by the GDI bitmap object.

Example

[Visual Basic]
```
Imports System.Runtime.InteropServices
...
Declare Function DeleteObject Lib "gdi32.dll"
 (ByVal hObject As IntPtr) As Boolean
...
Dim bm As New Bitmap("Picture.jpg")
Dim hBitmap As IntPtr
hBitmap = bm.GetHbitmap(Color.Blue)
' Do something with hBitmap.
DeleteObject(hBitmap)
```

[C#]
```
using System.Runtime.InteropServices;
...
[DllImport("gdi32.dll")]
public static extern bool DeleteObject(IntPtr hObject);
...
Bitmap bm = new Bitmap("Picture.jpg");
IntPtr hBitmap = bm.GetHbitmap(Color.Blue);
// Do something with hBitmap.
DeleteObject(hBitmap);
```

Requirements

Platforms: Windows 98, Windows NT 4.0, Windows Millennium Edition, Windows 2000, Windows XP Home Edition, Windows XP Professional, Windows Server 2003 family

Bitmap.GetHicon Method

Returns the handle to an icon.

[Visual Basic]
```
Public Function GetHicon() As IntPtr
```
[C#]
```
public IntPtr GetHicon();
```
[C++]
```
public: IntPtr GetHicon();
```
[JScript]
```
public function GetHicon() : IntPtr;
```

Return Value

A Windows handle to an icon.

Example

[Visual Basic, C#] The following example is designed for use with Windows Forms, and it requires **PaintEventArgs** *e*, which is a parameter of the **Paint** event handler. The code performs the following actions:

- Creates a **Bitmap** object.
- Draws that object to the screen.
- Gets an icon handle for the **Bitmap** object.
- Does something with the handle.

[Visual Basic]
```
Public Sub GetHicon_Example(e As PaintEventArgs)
' Create a Bitmap object from an image file.
Dim myBitmap As New Bitmap("Grapes.jpg")
' Draw myBitmap to the screen.
e.Graphics.DrawImage(myBitmap, 0, 0)
' Get an Hicon for myBitmap.
Dim HIcon As IntPtr = myBitmap.GetHicon()
End Sub
```

[C#]
```
public void GetHicon_Example(PaintEventArgs e)
{
// Create a Bitmap object from an image file.
Bitmap myBitmap = new Bitmap("Grapes.jpg");
// Draw myBitmap to the screen.
e.Graphics.DrawImage(myBitmap, 0, 0);
// Get an Hicon for myBitmap.
IntPtr Hicon = myBitmap.GetHicon();
// Do something with Hicon.
// ...
}
```

Requirements

Platforms: Windows 98, Windows NT 4.0, Windows Millennium Edition, Windows 2000, Windows XP Home Edition, Windows XP Professional, Windows Server 2003 family

Bitmap.GetPixel Method

Gets the color of the specified pixel in this **Bitmap**.

[Visual Basic]
```
Public Function GetPixel( _
   ByVal x As Integer, _
   ByVal y As Integer _
) As Color
```
[C#]
```
public Color GetPixel(
   int x,
   int y
);
```
[C++]
```
public: Color GetPixel(
   int x,
   int y
);
```
[JScript]
```
public function GetPixel(
   x : int,
   y : int
) : Color;
```

Parameters

x

The x-coordinate of the pixel to retrieve.

y

The y-coordinate of the pixel to retrieve.

Return Value

A **Color** structure that represents the color of the specified pixel.

Example

[Visual Basic, C#] The following example is designed for use with Windows Forms, and it requires **PaintEventArgs** *e*, which is a parameter of the **Paint** event handler. The code gets the color of a pixel in a bitmap, and then fills a rectangle with that color.

[Visual Basic]
```
Public Sub GetPixel_Example(e As PaintEventArgs)
' Create a Bitmap object from an image file.
Dim myBitmap As New Bitmap("Grapes.jpg")
' Get the color of a pixel within myBitmap.
Dim pixelColor As Color = myBitmap.GetPixel(50, 50)
' Fill a rectangle with pixelColor.
```

```
Dim pixelBrush As New SolidBrush(pixelColor)
e.Graphics.FillRectangle(pixelBrush, 0, 0, 100, 100)
End Sub
```

[C#]

```
public void GetPixel_Example(PaintEventArgs e)
{
// Create a Bitmap object from an image file.
Bimap myBitmap = new Bitmap("Grapes.jpg");
// Get the color of a pixel within myBitmap.
Color pixelColor = myBitmap.GetPixel(50, 50);
// Fill a rectangle with pixelColor.
SolidBrush pixelBrush = new SolidBrush(pixelColor);
e.Graphics.FillRectangle(pixelBrush, 0, 0, 100, 100);
}
```

Requirements

Platforms: Windows 98, Windows NT 4.0,
Windows Millennium Edition, Windows 2000,
Windows XP Home Edition, Windows XP Professional,
Windows Server 2003 family,
.NET Compact Framework - Windows CE .NET

Bitmap.LockBits Method

Locks a **Bitmap** object into system memory.

[Visual Basic]

```
Public Function LockBits( _
   ByVal rect As Rectangle, _
   ByVal flags As ImageLockMode, _
   ByVal format As PixelFormat _
) As BitmapData
```

[C#]

```
public BitmapData LockBits(
   Rectangle rect,
   ImageLockMode flags,
   PixelFormat format
);
```

[C++]

```
public: BitmapData* LockBits(
   Rectangle rect,
   ImageLockMode flags,
   PixelFormat format
);
```

[JScript]

```
public function LockBits(
   rect : Rectangle,
   flags : ImageLockMode,
   format : PixelFormat
) : BitmapData;
```

Parameters

rect
: A **Rectangle** structure specifying the portion of the **Bitmap** to lock.

flags
: An **ImageLockMode** enumeration specifying access level (read and write) for the **Bitmap** object.

format
: A **PixelFormat** enumeration specifying the data format of this **Bitmap** object.

Return Value

A **BitmapData** object containing information about this lock operation.

Remarks

The **BitmapData** object specifies the attributes of the Bitmap object, such as size, pixel format, the starting address of the pixel data in memory and length of each scan line (stride).

Requirements

Platforms: Windows 98, Windows NT 4.0,
Windows Millennium Edition, Windows 2000,
Windows XP Home Edition, Windows XP Professional,
Windows Server 2003 family

Bitmap.MakeTransparent Method

Makes the default transparent color transparent for this **Bitmap**.

Overload List

Makes the default transparent color transparent for this **Bitmap** object.

[Visual Basic] **Overloads Public Sub MakeTransparent()**

[C#] **public void MakeTransparent();**

[C++] **public: void MakeTransparent();**

[JScript] **public function MakeTransparent();**

Makes the specified color transparent for this **Bitmap** object.

[Visual Basic] **Overloads Public Sub MakeTransparent(Color)**

[C#] **public void MakeTransparent(Color);**

[C++] **public: void MakeTransparent(Color);**

[JScript] **public function MakeTransparent(Color);**

Example

[Visual Basic, C#] The following example is designed for use with Windows Forms, and it requires **PaintEventArgs** *e*, which is a parameter of the **Paint** event handler. The code performs the following actions:

- Gets the color of a pixel in a **Bitmap** object.
- Makes that color transparent for the bitmap.
- Draws the **Bitmap** object to the screen.

> [Visual Basic, C#] **Note** This example shows how to use one of the overloaded versions of **MakeTransparent**. For other examples that might be available, see the individual overload topics.

[Visual Basic]

```
Public Sub MakeTransparent_Example(e As PaintEventArgs)
' Create a Bitmap object from an image file.
Dim myBitmap As New Bitmap("Grapes.gif")
' Draw myBitmap to the screen.
e.Graphics.DrawImage(myBitmap, 0, 0, myBitmap.Width, _
myBitmap.Height)
' Get the color of a background pixel.
Dim backColor As Color = myBitmap.GetPixel(1, 1)
' Make backColor transparent for myBitmap.
myBitmap.MakeTransparent(backColor)
' Draw the transparent bitmap to the screen.
e.Graphics.DrawImage(myBitmap, myBitmap.Width, 0, myBitmap.Width, _
myBitmap.Height)
End Sub
```

[C#]
```
public void MakeTransparent_Example(PaintEventArgs e)
{
// Create a Bitmap object from an image file.
Bitmap myBitmap = new Bitmap("Grapes.gif");
// Draw myBitmap to the screen.
e.Graphics.DrawImage(
myBitmap,
0,
0,
myBitmap.Width,
myBitmap.Height);
// Get the color of a background pixel.
Color backColor = myBitmap.GetPixel(1, 1);
// Make backColor transparent for myBitmap.
myBitmap.MakeTransparent(backColor);
// Draw the transparent bitmap to the screen.
e.Graphics.DrawImage(
myBitmap,
myBitmap.Width,
0,
myBitmap.Width,
myBitmap.Height);
}
```

Bitmap.MakeTransparent Method ()

Makes the default transparent color transparent for this **Bitmap** object.

[Visual Basic]
```
Overloads Public Sub MakeTransparent()
```
[C#]
```
public void MakeTransparent();
```
[C++]
```
public: void MakeTransparent();
```
[JScript]
```
public function MakeTransparent();
```

Return Value

This method does not return a value.

Remarks

The system palette defines one color as the default transparent, or alpha, color. This method makes the default transparent color transparent for this **Bitmap** object.

Example

[Visual Basic, C#] The following example is designed for use with Windows Forms, and it requires **PaintEventArgs** *e*, which is a parameter of the **Paint** event handler. The code makes the system default transparent color transparent for *myBitmap*, and then draws the **Bitmap** object to the screen.

[Visual Basic]
```
Public Sub MakeTransparent_Example(e As PaintEventArgs)
' Create a Bitmap object from an image file.
Dim myBitmap As New Bitmap("Grapes.gif")
' Draw myBitmap to the screen.
e.Graphics.DrawImage(myBitmap, 0, 0, myBitmap.Width, _
myBitmap.Height)
' Make the default transparent color transparent for myBitmap.
myBitmap.MakeTransparent()
' Draw the transparent bitmap to the screen.
e.Graphics.DrawImage(myBitmap, myBitmap.Width, 0, myBitmap.Width, _
myBitmap.Height)
End Sub
```

[C#]
```
public void MakeTransparent_Example(PaintEventArgs e)
{
// Create a Bitmap object from an image file.
Bitmap myBitmap = new Bitmap("Grapes.gif");
// Draw myBitmap to the screen.
e.Graphics.DrawImage(
myBitmap,
0,
0,
myBitmap.Width,
myBitmap.Height);
// Make the default transparent color transparent for myBitmap.
myBitmap.MakeTransparent();
// Draw the transparent bitmap to the screen.
e.Graphics.DrawImage(
myBitmap,
myBitmap.Width,
0,
myBitmap.Width,
myBitmap.Height);
}
```

Requirements

Platforms: Windows 98, Windows NT 4.0, Windows Millennium Edition, Windows 2000, Windows XP Home Edition, Windows XP Professional, Windows Server 2003 family

Bitmap.MakeTransparent Method (Color)

Makes the specified color transparent for this **Bitmap** object.

[Visual Basic]
```
Overloads Public Sub MakeTransparent( _
   ByVal transparentColor As Color _
)
```
[C#]
```
public void MakeTransparent(
   Color transparentColor
);
```
[C++]
```
public: void MakeTransparent(
   Color transparentColor
);
```
[JScript]
```
public function MakeTransparent(
   transparentColor : Color
);
```

Parameters

transparentColor

The **Color** structure that represents the color to make transparent.

Return Value

This method does not return a value.

Example

[Visual Basic, C#] The following example is designed for use with Windows Forms, and it requires **PaintEventArgs** *e*, which is a parameter of the **Paint** event handler. The code performs the following actions:

- Gets the color of a pixel in a **Bitmap** object.
- Makes that color transparent for the bitmap.
- Draws the **Bitmap** object to the screen.

[Visual Basic]
```
Public Sub MakeTransparent_Example(e As PaintEventArgs)
' Create a Bitmap object from an image file.
Dim myBitmap As New Bitmap("Grapes.gif")
' Draw myBitmap to the screen.
e.Graphics.DrawImage(myBitmap, 0, 0, myBitmap.Width, _
myBitmap.Height)
' Get the color of a background pixel.
Dim backColor As Color = myBitmap.GetPixel(1, 1)
' Make backColor transparent for myBitmap.
myBitmap.MakeTransparent(backColor)
' Draw the transparent bitmap to the screen.
e.Graphics.DrawImage(myBitmap, myBitmap.Width, 0, myBitmap.Width, _
myBitmap.Height)
End Sub
```

[C#]
```
public void MakeTransparent_Example(PaintEventArgs e)
{
// Create a Bitmap object from an image file.
Bitmap myBitmap = new Bitmap("Grapes.gif");
// Draw myBitmap to the screen.
e.Graphics.DrawImage(
myBitmap,
0,
0,
myBitmap.Width,
myBitmap.Height);
// Get the color of a background pixel.
Color backColor = myBitmap.GetPixel(1, 1);
// Make backColor transparent for myBitmap.
myBitmap.MakeTransparent(backColor);
// Draw the transparent bitmap to the screen.
e.Graphics.DrawImage(
myBitmap,
myBitmap.Width,
0,
myBitmap.Width,
myBitmap.Height);
}
```

Requirements

Platforms: Windows 98, Windows NT 4.0, Windows Millennium Edition, Windows 2000, Windows XP Home Edition, Windows XP Professional, Windows Server 2003 family

Bitmap.SetPixel Method

Sets the color of the specified pixel in this **Bitmap** object.

[Visual Basic]
```
Public Sub SetPixel( _
   ByVal x As Integer, _
   ByVal y As Integer, _
   ByVal color As Color _
)
```
[C#]
```
public void SetPixel(
   int x,
   int y,
   Color color
);
```
[C++]
```
public: void SetPixel(
   int x,
   int y,
   Color color
);
```
[JScript]
```
public function SetPixel(
   x : int,
   y : int,
   color : Color
);
```

Parameters

x
The x-coordinate of the pixel to set.

y
The y-coordinate of the pixel to set.

color
A **Color** structure that represents the color to assign to the specified pixel.

Return Value

This method does not return a value.

Example

[Visual Basic, C#] The following example is designed for use with Windows Forms, and it requires **PaintEventArgs** *e*, which is a parameter of the **Paint** event handler. The code performs the following actions:

- Creates a **Bitmap** object.
- Sets the color of each pixel in the bitmap to black.
- Draws the bitmap.

[Visual Basic]
```
Public Sub SetPixel_Example(e As PaintEventArgs)
' Create a Bitmap object from a file.
Dim myBitmap As New Bitmap("Grapes.jpg")
' Draw myBitmap to the screen.
e.Graphics.DrawImage(myBitmap, 0, 0, myBitmap.Width, _
myBitmap.Height)
' Set each pixel in myBitmap to black.
Dim Xcount As Integer
For Xcount = 0 To myBitmap.Width - 1
Dim Ycount As Integer
For Ycount = 0 To myBitmap.Height - 1
myBitmap.SetPixel(Xcount, Ycount, Color.Black)
Next Ycount
Next Xcount
' Draw myBitmap to the screen again.
e.Graphics.DrawImage(myBitmap, myBitmap.Width, 0, myBitmap.Width, _
myBitmap.Height)
End Sub
```

[C#]
```
public void SetPixel_Example(PaintEventArgs e)
{
// Create a Bitmap object from a file.
Bitmap myBitmap = new Bitmap("Grapes.jpg");
// Draw myBitmap to the screen.
e.Graphics.DrawImage(
myBitmap,
0,
0,
myBitmap.Width,
myBitmap.Height);
// Set each pixel in myBitmap to black.
for (int Xcount = 0; Xcount < myBitmap.Width; Xcount++)
{
for (int Ycount = 0; Ycount < myBitmap.Height; Ycount++)
{
myBitmap.SetPixel(Xcount, Ycount, Color.Black);
}
}
// Draw myBitmap to the screen again.
```

```
e.Graphics.DrawImage(
myBitmap,
myBitmap.Width,
0,
myBitmap.Width,
myBitmap.Height);
}
```

Requirements

Platforms: Windows 98, Windows NT 4.0, Windows Millennium Edition, Windows 2000, Windows XP Home Edition, Windows XP Professional, Windows Server 2003 family, .NET Compact Framework - Windows CE .NET

Bitmap.SetResolution Method

Sets the resolution for this **Bitmap**.

```
[Visual Basic]
Public Sub SetResolution( _
   ByVal xDpi As Single, _
   ByVal yDpi As Single _
)
[C#]
public void SetResolution(
   float xDpi,
   float yDpi
);
[C++]
public: void SetResolution(
   float xDpi,
   float yDpi
);
[JScript]
public function SetResolution(
   xDpi : float,
   yDpi : float
);
```

Parameters

xDpi

The horizontal resolution, in dots per inch, of the **Bitmap**.

yDpi

The vertical resolution, in dots per inch, of the **Bitmap**.

Requirements

Platforms: Windows 98, Windows NT 4.0, Windows Millennium Edition, Windows 2000, Windows XP Home Edition, Windows XP Professional, Windows Server 2003 family

Bitmap.UnlockBits Method

Unlocks this **Bitmap** from system memory.

```
[Visual Basic]
Public Sub UnlockBits( _
   ByVal bitmapdata As BitmapData _
)
[C#]
public void UnlockBits(
   BitmapData bitmapdata
);
[C++]
public: void UnlockBits(
   BitmapData* bitmapdata
);
[JScript]
public function UnlockBits(
   bitmapdata : BitmapData
);
```

Parameters

bitmapdata

A **BitmapData** object specifying information about the lock operation.

Remarks

The **BitmapData** object specifies the attributes of the Bitmap object, such as size, pixel format, the starting address of the pixel data in memory and length of each scan line (stride).

Requirements

Platforms: Windows 98, Windows NT 4.0, Windows Millennium Edition, Windows 2000, Windows XP Home Edition, Windows XP Professional, Windows Server 2003 family

Brush Class

Classes derived from this abstract base class define objects used to fill the interiors of graphical shapes such as rectangles, ellipses, pies, polygons, and paths.

System.Object
  System.MarshalByRefObject
    System.Drawing.Brush
      System.Drawing.Drawing2D.HatchBrush
      System.Drawing.Drawing2D.LinearGradientBrush
      System.Drawing.Drawing2D.PathGradientBrush
      System.Drawing.SolidBrush
      System.Drawing.TextureBrush

```
[Visual Basic]
MustInherit Public Class Brush
   Inherits MarshalByRefObject
   Implements ICloneable, IDisposable
[C#]
public abstract class Brush : MarshalByRefObject, ICloneable,
   IDisposable
[C++]
public __gc __abstract class Brush : public MarshalByRefObject,
   ICloneable, IDisposable
[JScript]
public abstract class Brush extends MarshalByRefObject implements
   ICloneable, IDisposable
```

Thread Safety

Any public static (**Shared** in Visual Basic) members of this type are safe for multithreaded operations. Any instance members are not guaranteed to be thread safe.

Remarks

This is an abstract base class and cannot be instantiated. To create a brush object, use classes derived from **Brush**, such as **SolidBrush**, **TextureBrush**, and **LinearGradientBrush**.

Requirements

Namespace: System.Drawing

Platforms: Windows 98, Windows NT 4.0, Windows Millennium Edition, Windows 2000, Windows XP Home Edition, Windows XP Professional, Windows Server 2003 family, .NET Compact Framework - Windows CE .NET

Assembly: System.Drawing (in System.Drawing.dll)

Brush.Clone Method

When overridden in a derived class, creates an exact copy of this **Brush** object.

```
[Visual Basic]
Public MustOverride Function Clone() As Object Implements _
   ICloneable.Clone
[C#]
public abstract object Clone();
[C++]
public: virtual Object* Clone() = 0;
[JScript]
public abstract function Clone() : Object;
```

Return Value

The new **Brush** object that this method creates.

Implements

ICloneable.Clone

Requirements

Platforms: Windows 98, Windows NT 4.0, Windows Millennium Edition, Windows 2000, Windows XP Home Edition, Windows XP Professional, Windows Server 2003 family

Brush.Dispose Method

Overload List

Releases all resources used by this **Brush** object.

Supported by the .NET Compact Framework.

[Visual Basic] **Overloads Public Overridable Sub Dispose() Implements IDisposable.Dispose**

[C#] **public virtual void Dispose();**

[C++] **public: virtual void Dispose();**

[JScript] **public function Dispose();**

This member supports the .NET Framework infrastructure and is not intended to be used directly from your code.

[Visual Basic] **Overloads Protected Overridable Sub Dispose(Boolean)**

[C#] **protected virtual void Dispose(bool);**

[C++] **protected: virtual void Dispose(bool);**

[JScript] **protected function Dispose(Boolean);**

Brush.Dispose Method ()

Releases all resources used by this **Brush** object.

```
[Visual Basic]
Overloads Public Overridable Sub Dispose() Implements _
   IDisposable.Dispose
[C#]
public virtual void Dispose();
[C++]
public: virtual void Dispose();
[JScript]
public function Dispose();
```

Return Value

This method does not return a value.

Implements

IDisposable.Dispose

Remarks

Calling **Dispose** allows the resources used by this **Brush** object to be reallocated for other purposes.

Requirements

Platforms: Windows 98, Windows NT 4.0, Windows Millennium Edition, Windows 2000, Windows XP Home Edition, Windows XP Professional, Windows Server 2003 family, .NET Compact Framework - Windows CE .NET

Brush.Dispose Method (Boolean)

This member supports the .NET Framework infrastructure and is not intended to be used directly from your code.

[Visual Basic]
```
Overloads Protected Overridable Sub Dispose( _
   ByVal disposing As Boolean _
)
```
[C#]
```
protected virtual void Dispose(
   bool disposing
);
```
[C++]
```
protected: virtual void Dispose(
   bool disposing
);
```
[JScript]
```
protected function Dispose(
   disposing : Boolean
);
```

Brush.Finalize Method

This member overrides **Object.Finalize**.

[Visual Basic]
```
Overrides Protected Sub Finalize()
```
[C#]
```
~Brush();
```
[C++]
```
~Brush();
```
[JScript]
```
protected override function Finalize();
```

Requirements

Platforms: Windows 98, Windows NT 4.0, Windows Millennium Edition, Windows 2000, Windows XP Home Edition, Windows XP Professional, Windows Server 2003 family, .NET Compact Framework - Windows CE .NET

Brushes Class

Brushes for all the standard colors. This class cannot be inherited.

System.Object
  System.Drawing.Brushes

[Visual Basic]
```
NotInheritable Public Class Brushes
```
[C#]
```
public sealed class Brushes
```
[C++]
```
public __gc __sealed class Brushes
```
[JScript]
```
public class Brushes
```

Thread Safety

Any public static (**Shared** in Visual Basic) members of this type are safe for multithreaded operations. Any instance members are not guaranteed to be thread safe.

Requirements

Namespace: System.Drawing

Platforms: Windows 98, Windows NT 4.0, Windows Millennium Edition, Windows 2000, Windows XP Home Edition, Windows XP Professional, Windows Server 2003 family

Assembly: System.Drawing (in System.Drawing.dll)

Brushes.AliceBlue Property

Gets a system-defined **Brush** object.

[Visual Basic]
```
Public Shared ReadOnly Property AliceBlue As Brush
```
[C#]
```
public static Brush AliceBlue {get;}
```
[C++]
```
public: __property static Brush* get_AliceBlue();
```
[JScript]
```
public static function get AliceBlue() : Brush;
```

Property Value

A **Brush** object set to a system-defined color.

Requirements

Platforms: Windows 98, Windows NT 4.0, Windows Millennium Edition, Windows 2000, Windows XP Home Edition, Windows XP Professional, Windows Server 2003 family

Brushes.AntiqueWhite Property

Gets a system-defined **Brush** object.

[Visual Basic]
```
Public Shared ReadOnly Property AntiqueWhite As Brush
```
[C#]
```
public static Brush AntiqueWhite {get;}
```
[C++]
```
public: __property static Brush* get_AntiqueWhite();
```
[JScript]
```
public static function get AntiqueWhite() : Brush;
```

Property Value

A **Brush** object set to a system-defined color.

Requirements

Platforms: Windows 98, Windows NT 4.0, Windows Millennium Edition, Windows 2000, Windows XP Home Edition, Windows XP Professional, Windows Server 2003 family

Brushes.Aqua Property

Gets a system-defined **Brush** object.

[Visual Basic]
```
Public Shared ReadOnly Property Aqua As Brush
```
[C#]
```
public static Brush Aqua {get;}
```
[C++]
```
public: __property static Brush* get_Aqua();
```
[JScript]
```
public static function get Aqua() : Brush;
```

Property Value

A **Brush** object set to a system-defined color.

Requirements

Platforms: Windows 98, Windows NT 4.0, Windows Millennium Edition, Windows 2000, Windows XP Home Edition, Windows XP Professional, Windows Server 2003 family

Brushes.Aquamarine Property

Gets a system-defined **Brush** object.

[Visual Basic]
```
Public Shared ReadOnly Property Aquamarine As Brush
```
[C#]
```
public static Brush Aquamarine {get;}
```
[C++]
```
public: __property static Brush* get_Aquamarine();
```
[JScript]
```
public static function get Aquamarine() : Brush;
```

Property Value

A **Brush** object set to a system-defined color.

Requirements

Platforms: Windows 98, Windows NT 4.0, Windows Millennium Edition, Windows 2000, Windows XP Home Edition, Windows XP Professional, Windows Server 2003 family

Brushes.Azure Property

Gets a system-defined **Brush** object.

[Visual Basic]
```
Public Shared ReadOnly Property Azure As Brush
```
[C#]
```
public static Brush Azure {get;}
```

[C++]
```
public: __property static Brush* get_Azure();
```
[JScript]
```
public static function get Azure() : Brush;
```

Property Value

A **Brush** object set to a system-defined color.

Requirements

Platforms: Windows 98, Windows NT 4.0, Windows Millennium Edition, Windows 2000, Windows XP Home Edition, Windows XP Professional, Windows Server 2003 family

Brushes.Beige Property

Gets a system-defined **Brush** object.

[Visual Basic]
```
Public Shared ReadOnly Property Beige As Brush
```
[C#]
```
public static Brush Beige {get;}
```
[C++]
```
public: __property static Brush* get_Beige();
```
[JScript]
```
public static function get Beige() : Brush;
```

Property Value

A **Brush** object set to a system-defined color.

Requirements

Platforms: Windows 98, Windows NT 4.0, Windows Millennium Edition, Windows 2000, Windows XP Home Edition, Windows XP Professional, Windows Server 2003 family

Brushes.Bisque Property

Gets a system-defined **Brush** object.

[Visual Basic]
```
Public Shared ReadOnly Property Bisque As Brush
```
[C#]
```
public static Brush Bisque {get;}
```
[C++]
```
public: __property static Brush* get_Bisque();
```
[JScript]
```
public static function get Bisque() : Brush;
```

Property Value

A **Brush** object set to a system-defined color.

Requirements

Platforms: Windows 98, Windows NT 4.0, Windows Millennium Edition, Windows 2000, Windows XP Home Edition, Windows XP Professional, Windows Server 2003 family

Brushes.Black Property

Gets a system-defined **Brush** object.

[Visual Basic]
```
Public Shared ReadOnly Property Black As Brush
```
[C#]
```
public static Brush Black {get;}
```
[C++]
```
public: __property static Brush* get_Black();
```
[JScript]
```
public static function get Black() : Brush;
```

Property Value

A **Brush** object set to a system-defined color.

Requirements

Platforms: Windows 98, Windows NT 4.0, Windows Millennium Edition, Windows 2000, Windows XP Home Edition, Windows XP Professional, Windows Server 2003 family

Brushes.BlanchedAlmond Property

Gets a system-defined **Brush** object.

[Visual Basic]
```
Public Shared ReadOnly Property BlanchedAlmond As Brush
```
[C#]
```
public static Brush BlanchedAlmond {get;}
```
[C++]
```
public: __property static Brush* get_BlanchedAlmond();
```
[JScript]
```
public static function get BlanchedAlmond() : Brush;
```

Property Value

A **Brush** object set to a system-defined color.

Requirements

Platforms: Windows 98, Windows NT 4.0, Windows Millennium Edition, Windows 2000, Windows XP Home Edition, Windows XP Professional, Windows Server 2003 family

Brushes.Blue Property

Gets a system-defined **Brush** object.

[Visual Basic]
```
Public Shared ReadOnly Property Blue As Brush
```
[C#]
```
public static Brush Blue {get;}
```
[C++]
```
public: __property static Brush* get_Blue();
```
[JScript]
```
public static function get Blue() : Brush;
```

Property Value

A **Brush** object set to a system-defined color.

Requirements

Platforms: Windows 98, Windows NT 4.0, Windows Millennium Edition, Windows 2000, Windows XP Home Edition, Windows XP Professional, Windows Server 2003 family

Brushes.BlueViolet Property

Gets a system-defined **Brush** object.

[Visual Basic]
```
Public Shared ReadOnly Property BlueViolet As Brush
```
[C#]
```
public static Brush BlueViolet {get;}
```
[C++]
```
public: __property static Brush* get_BlueViolet();
```
[JScript]
```
public static function get BlueViolet() : Brush;
```

Property Value

A **Brush** object set to a system-defined color.

Requirements

Platforms: Windows 98, Windows NT 4.0, Windows Millennium Edition, Windows 2000, Windows XP Home Edition, Windows XP Professional, Windows Server 2003 family

Brushes.Brown Property

Gets a system-defined **Brush** object.

[Visual Basic]
```
Public Shared ReadOnly Property Brown As Brush
```
[C#]
```
public static Brush Brown {get;}
```
[C++]
```
public: __property static Brush* get_Brown();
```
[JScript]
```
public static function get Brown() : Brush;
```

Property Value

A **Brush** object set to a system-defined color.

Requirements

Platforms: Windows 98, Windows NT 4.0, Windows Millennium Edition, Windows 2000, Windows XP Home Edition, Windows XP Professional, Windows Server 2003 family

Brushes.BurlyWood Property

Gets a system-defined **Brush** object.

[Visual Basic]
```
Public Shared ReadOnly Property BurlyWood As Brush
```
[C#]
```
public static Brush BurlyWood {get;}
```
[C++]
```
public: __property static Brush* get_BurlyWood();
```
[JScript]
```
public static function get BurlyWood() : Brush;
```

Property Value

A **Brush** object set to a system-defined color.

Requirements

Platforms: Windows 98, Windows NT 4.0, Windows Millennium Edition, Windows 2000, Windows XP Home Edition, Windows XP Professional, Windows Server 2003 family

Brushes.CadetBlue Property

Gets a system-defined **Brush** object.

[Visual Basic]
```
Public Shared ReadOnly Property CadetBlue As Brush
```
[C#]
```
public static Brush CadetBlue {get;}
```
[C++]
```
public: __property static Brush* get_CadetBlue();
```
[JScript]
```
public static function get CadetBlue() : Brush;
```

Property Value

A **Brush** object set to a system-defined color.

Requirements

Platforms: Windows 98, Windows NT 4.0, Windows Millennium Edition, Windows 2000, Windows XP Home Edition, Windows XP Professional, Windows Server 2003 family

Brushes.Chartreuse Property

Gets a system-defined **Brush** object.

[Visual Basic]
```
Public Shared ReadOnly Property Chartreuse As Brush
```
[C#]
```
public static Brush Chartreuse {get;}
```
[C++]
```
public: __property static Brush* get_Chartreuse();
```
[JScript]
```
public static function get Chartreuse() : Brush;
```

Property Value

A **Brush** object set to a system-defined color.

Requirements

Platforms: Windows 98, Windows NT 4.0, Windows Millennium Edition, Windows 2000, Windows XP Home Edition, Windows XP Professional, Windows Server 2003 family

Brushes.Chocolate Property

Gets a system-defined **Brush** object.

[Visual Basic]
```
Public Shared ReadOnly Property Chocolate As Brush
```
[C#]
```
public static Brush Chocolate {get;}
```
[C++]
```
public: __property static Brush* get_Chocolate();
```
[JScript]
```
public static function get Chocolate() : Brush;
```

Property Value

A **Brush** object set to a system-defined color.

Requirements

Platforms: Windows 98, Windows NT 4.0, Windows Millennium Edition, Windows 2000, Windows XP Home Edition, Windows XP Professional, Windows Server 2003 family

Brushes.Coral Property

Gets a system-defined **Brush** object.

[Visual Basic]
```
Public Shared ReadOnly Property Coral As Brush
```
[C#]
```
public static Brush Coral {get;}
```
[C++]
```
public: __property static Brush* get_Coral();
```
[JScript]
```
public static function get Coral() : Brush;
```

Property Value

A **Brush** object set to a system-defined color.

Requirements

Platforms: Windows 98, Windows NT 4.0, Windows Millennium Edition, Windows 2000, Windows XP Home Edition, Windows XP Professional, Windows Server 2003 family

Brushes.CornflowerBlue Property

Gets a system-defined **Brush** object.

[Visual Basic]
```
Public Shared ReadOnly Property CornflowerBlue As Brush
```
[C#]
```
public static Brush CornflowerBlue {get;}
```
[C++]
```
public: __property static Brush* get_CornflowerBlue();
```
[JScript]
```
public static function get CornflowerBlue() : Brush;
```

Property Value

A **Brush** object set to a system-defined color.

Requirements

Platforms: Windows 98, Windows NT 4.0, Windows Millennium Edition, Windows 2000, Windows XP Home Edition, Windows XP Professional, Windows Server 2003 family

Brushes.Cornsilk Property

Gets a system-defined **Brush** object.

[Visual Basic]
```
Public Shared ReadOnly Property Cornsilk As Brush
```
[C#]
```
public static Brush Cornsilk {get;}
```
[C++]
```
public: __property static Brush* get_Cornsilk();
```
[JScript]
```
public static function get Cornsilk() : Brush;
```

Property Value

A **Brush** object set to a system-defined color.

Requirements

Platforms: Windows 98, Windows NT 4.0, Windows Millennium Edition, Windows 2000, Windows XP Home Edition, Windows XP Professional, Windows Server 2003 family

Brushes.Crimson Property

Gets a system-defined **Brush** object.

[Visual Basic]
```
Public Shared ReadOnly Property Crimson As Brush
```
[C#]
```
public static Brush Crimson {get;}
```
[C++]
```
public: __property static Brush* get_Crimson();
```
[JScript]
```
public static function get Crimson() : Brush;
```

Property Value

A **Brush** object set to a system-defined color.

Requirements

Platforms: Windows 98, Windows NT 4.0, Windows Millennium Edition, Windows 2000, Windows XP Home Edition, Windows XP Professional, Windows Server 2003 family

Brushes.Cyan Property

Gets a system-defined **Brush** object.

[Visual Basic]
```
Public Shared ReadOnly Property Cyan As Brush
```
[C#]
```
public static Brush Cyan {get;}
```
[C++]
```
public: __property static Brush* get_Cyan();
```
[JScript]
```
public static function get Cyan() : Brush;
```

Property Value

A **Brush** object set to a system-defined color.

Requirements

Platforms: Windows 98, Windows NT 4.0, Windows Millennium Edition, Windows 2000, Windows XP Home Edition, Windows XP Professional, Windows Server 2003 family

Brushes.DarkBlue Property

Gets a system-defined **Brush** object.

[Visual Basic]
```
Public Shared ReadOnly Property DarkBlue As Brush
```
[C#]
```
public static Brush DarkBlue {get;}
```
[C++]
```
public: __property static Brush* get_DarkBlue();
```
[JScript]
```
public static function get DarkBlue() : Brush;
```

Property Value

A **Brush** object set to a system-defined color.

Requirements

Platforms: Windows 98, Windows NT 4.0, Windows Millennium Edition, Windows 2000, Windows XP Home Edition, Windows XP Professional, Windows Server 2003 family

Brushes.DarkCyan Property

Gets a system-defined **Brush** object.

[Visual Basic]
```
Public Shared ReadOnly Property DarkCyan As Brush
```
[C#]
```
public static Brush DarkCyan {get;}
```
[C++]
```
public: __property static Brush* get_DarkCyan();
```
[JScript]
```
public static function get DarkCyan() : Brush;
```

Property Value

A **Brush** object set to a system-defined color.

Requirements

Platforms: Windows 98, Windows NT 4.0, Windows Millennium Edition, Windows 2000, Windows XP Home Edition, Windows XP Professional, Windows Server 2003 family

Brushes.DarkGoldenrod Property

Gets a system-defined **Brush** object.

[Visual Basic]
```
Public Shared ReadOnly Property DarkGoldenrod As Brush
```
[C#]
```
public static Brush DarkGoldenrod {get;}
```
[C++]
```
public: __property static Brush* get_DarkGoldenrod();
```
[JScript]
```
public static function get DarkGoldenrod() : Brush;
```

Property Value

A **Brush** object set to a system-defined color.

Requirements

Platforms: Windows 98, Windows NT 4.0, Windows Millennium Edition, Windows 2000, Windows XP Home Edition, Windows XP Professional, Windows Server 2003 family

Brushes.DarkGray Property

Gets a system-defined **Brush** object.

[Visual Basic]
```
Public Shared ReadOnly Property DarkGray As Brush
```
[C#]
```
public static Brush DarkGray {get;}
```
[C++]
```
public: __property static Brush* get_DarkGray();
```
[JScript]
```
public static function get DarkGray() : Brush;
```

Property Value

A **Brush** object set to a system-defined color.

Requirements

Platforms: Windows 98, Windows NT 4.0, Windows Millennium Edition, Windows 2000, Windows XP Home Edition, Windows XP Professional, Windows Server 2003 family

Brushes.DarkGreen Property

Gets a system-defined **Brush** object.

[Visual Basic]
```
Public Shared ReadOnly Property DarkGreen As Brush
```
[C#]
```
public static Brush DarkGreen {get;}
```
[C++]
```
public: __property static Brush* get_DarkGreen();
```
[JScript]
```
public static function get DarkGreen() : Brush;
```

Property Value

A **Brush** object set to a system-defined color.

Requirements

Platforms: Windows 98, Windows NT 4.0, Windows Millennium Edition, Windows 2000, Windows XP Home Edition, Windows XP Professional, Windows Server 2003 family

Brushes.DarkKhaki Property

Gets a system-defined **Brush** object.

[Visual Basic]
```
Public Shared ReadOnly Property DarkKhaki As Brush
```
[C#]
```
public static Brush DarkKhaki {get;}
```
[C++]
```
public: __property static Brush* get_DarkKhaki();
```
[JScript]
```
public static function get DarkKhaki() : Brush;
```

Property Value

A **Brush** object set to a system-defined color.

Requirements

Platforms: Windows 98, Windows NT 4.0, Windows Millennium Edition, Windows 2000, Windows XP Home Edition, Windows XP Professional, Windows Server 2003 family

Brushes.DarkMagenta Property

Gets a system-defined **Brush** object.

[Visual Basic]
```
Public Shared ReadOnly Property DarkMagenta As Brush
```
[C#]
```
public static Brush DarkMagenta {get;}
```
[C++]
```
public: __property static Brush* get_DarkMagenta();
```
[JScript]
```
public static function get DarkMagenta() : Brush;
```

Property Value

A **Brush** object set to a system-defined color.

Requirements

Platforms: Windows 98, Windows NT 4.0, Windows Millennium Edition, Windows 2000, Windows XP Home Edition, Windows XP Professional, Windows Server 2003 family

Brushes.DarkOliveGreen Property

Gets a system-defined **Brush** object.

```
[Visual Basic]
Public Shared ReadOnly Property DarkOliveGreen As Brush
[C#]
public static Brush DarkOliveGreen {get;}
[C++]
public: __property static Brush* get_DarkOliveGreen();
[JScript]
public static function get DarkOliveGreen() : Brush;
```

Property Value

A **Brush** object set to a system-defined color.

Requirements

Platforms: Windows 98, Windows NT 4.0, Windows Millennium Edition, Windows 2000, Windows XP Home Edition, Windows XP Professional, Windows Server 2003 family

Brushes.DarkOrange Property

Gets a system-defined **Brush** object.

```
[Visual Basic]
Public Shared ReadOnly Property DarkOrange As Brush
[C#]
public static Brush DarkOrange {get;}
[C++]
public: __property static Brush* get_DarkOrange();
[JScript]
public static function get DarkOrange() : Brush;
```

Property Value

A **Brush** object set to a system-defined color.

Requirements

Platforms: Windows 98, Windows NT 4.0, Windows Millennium Edition, Windows 2000, Windows XP Home Edition, Windows XP Professional, Windows Server 2003 family

Brushes.DarkOrchid Property

Gets a system-defined **Brush** object.

```
[Visual Basic]
Public Shared ReadOnly Property DarkOrchid As Brush
[C#]
public static Brush DarkOrchid {get;}
[C++]
public: __property static Brush* get_DarkOrchid();
[JScript]
public static function get DarkOrchid() : Brush;
```

Property Value

A **Brush** object set to a system-defined color.

Requirements

Platforms: Windows 98, Windows NT 4.0, Windows Millennium Edition, Windows 2000, Windows XP Home Edition, Windows XP Professional, Windows Server 2003 family

Brushes.DarkRed Property

Gets a system-defined **Brush** object.

```
[Visual Basic]
Public Shared ReadOnly Property DarkRed As Brush
[C#]
public static Brush DarkRed {get;}
[C++]
public: __property static Brush* get_DarkRed();
[JScript]
public static function get DarkRed() : Brush;
```

Property Value

A **Brush** object set to a system-defined color.

Requirements

Platforms: Windows 98, Windows NT 4.0, Windows Millennium Edition, Windows 2000, Windows XP Home Edition, Windows XP Professional, Windows Server 2003 family

Brushes.DarkSalmon Property

Gets a system-defined **Brush** object.

```
[Visual Basic]
Public Shared ReadOnly Property DarkSalmon As Brush
[C#]
public static Brush DarkSalmon {get;}
[C++]
public: __property static Brush* get_DarkSalmon();
[JScript]
public static function get DarkSalmon() : Brush;
```

Property Value

A **Brush** object set to a system-defined color.

Requirements

Platforms: Windows 98, Windows NT 4.0, Windows Millennium Edition, Windows 2000, Windows XP Home Edition, Windows XP Professional, Windows Server 2003 family

Brushes.DarkSeaGreen Property

Gets a system-defined **Brush** object.

```
[Visual Basic]
Public Shared ReadOnly Property DarkSeaGreen As Brush
[C#]
public static Brush DarkSeaGreen {get;}
[C++]
public: __property static Brush* get_DarkSeaGreen();
[JScript]
public static function get DarkSeaGreen() : Brush;
```

Property Value

A **Brush** object set to a system-defined color.

Requirements

Platforms: Windows 98, Windows NT 4.0, Windows Millennium Edition, Windows 2000, Windows XP Home Edition, Windows XP Professional, Windows Server 2003 family

Brushes.DarkSlateBlue Property

Gets a system-defined **Brush** object.

[Visual Basic]
```
Public Shared ReadOnly Property DarkSlateBlue As Brush
```
[C#]
```
public static Brush DarkSlateBlue {get;}
```
[C++]
```
public: __property static Brush* get_DarkSlateBlue();
```
[JScript]
```
public static function get DarkSlateBlue() : Brush;
```

Property Value

A **Brush** object set to a system-defined color.

Requirements

Platforms: Windows 98, Windows NT 4.0, Windows Millennium Edition, Windows 2000, Windows XP Home Edition, Windows XP Professional, Windows Server 2003 family

Brushes.DarkSlateGray Property

Gets a system-defined **Brush** object.

[Visual Basic]
```
Public Shared ReadOnly Property DarkSlateGray As Brush
```
[C#]
```
public static Brush DarkSlateGray {get;}
```
[C++]
```
public: __property static Brush* get_DarkSlateGray();
```
[JScript]
```
public static function get DarkSlateGray() : Brush;
```

Property Value

A **Brush** object set to a system-defined color.

Requirements

Platforms: Windows 98, Windows NT 4.0, Windows Millennium Edition, Windows 2000, Windows XP Home Edition, Windows XP Professional, Windows Server 2003 family

Brushes.DarkTurquoise Property

Gets a system-defined **Brush** object.

[Visual Basic]
```
Public Shared ReadOnly Property DarkTurquoise As Brush
```
[C#]
```
public static Brush DarkTurquoise {get;}
```
[C++]
```
public: __property static Brush* get_DarkTurquoise();
```
[JScript]
```
public static function get DarkTurquoise() : Brush;
```

Property Value

A **Brush** object set to a system-defined color.

Requirements

Platforms: Windows 98, Windows NT 4.0, Windows Millennium Edition, Windows 2000, Windows XP Home Edition, Windows XP Professional, Windows Server 2003 family

Brushes.DarkViolet Property

Gets a system-defined **Brush** object.

[Visual Basic]
```
Public Shared ReadOnly Property DarkViolet As Brush
```
[C#]
```
public static Brush DarkViolet {get;}
```
[C++]
```
public: __property static Brush* get_DarkViolet();
```
[JScript]
```
public static function get DarkViolet() : Brush;
```

Property Value

A **Brush** object set to a system-defined color.

Requirements

Platforms: Windows 98, Windows NT 4.0, Windows Millennium Edition, Windows 2000, Windows XP Home Edition, Windows XP Professional, Windows Server 2003 family

Brushes.DeepPink Property

Gets a system-defined **Brush** object.

[Visual Basic]
```
Public Shared ReadOnly Property DeepPink As Brush
```
[C#]
```
public static Brush DeepPink {get;}
```
[C++]
```
public: __property static Brush* get_DeepPink();
```
[JScript]
```
public static function get DeepPink() : Brush;
```

Property Value

A **Brush** object set to a system-defined color.

Requirements

Platforms: Windows 98, Windows NT 4.0, Windows Millennium Edition, Windows 2000, Windows XP Home Edition, Windows XP Professional, Windows Server 2003 family

Brushes.DeepSkyBlue Property

Gets a system-defined **Brush** object.

[Visual Basic]
```
Public Shared ReadOnly Property DeepSkyBlue As Brush
```
[C#]
```
public static Brush DeepSkyBlue {get;}
```
[C++]
```
public: __property static Brush* get_DeepSkyBlue();
```
[JScript]
```
public static function get DeepSkyBlue() : Brush;
```

Property Value

A **Brush** object set to a system-defined color.

Requirements

Platforms: Windows 98, Windows NT 4.0, Windows Millennium Edition, Windows 2000, Windows XP Home Edition, Windows XP Professional, Windows Server 2003 family

Brushes.DimGray Property

Gets a system-defined **Brush** object.

```
[Visual Basic]
Public Shared ReadOnly Property DimGray As Brush
[C#]
public static Brush DimGray {get;}
[C++]
public: __property static Brush* get_DimGray();
[JScript]
public static function get DimGray() : Brush;
```

Property Value

A **Brush** object set to a system-defined color.

Requirements

Platforms: Windows 98, Windows NT 4.0, Windows Millennium Edition, Windows 2000, Windows XP Home Edition, Windows XP Professional, Windows Server 2003 family

Brushes.DodgerBlue Property

Gets a system-defined **Brush** object.

```
[Visual Basic]
Public Shared ReadOnly Property DodgerBlue As Brush
[C#]
public static Brush DodgerBlue {get;}
[C++]
public: __property static Brush* get_DodgerBlue();
[JScript]
public static function get DodgerBlue() : Brush;
```

Property Value

A **Brush** object set to a system-defined color.

Requirements

Platforms: Windows 98, Windows NT 4.0, Windows Millennium Edition, Windows 2000, Windows XP Home Edition, Windows XP Professional, Windows Server 2003 family

Brushes.Firebrick Property

Gets a system-defined **Brush** object.

```
[Visual Basic]
Public Shared ReadOnly Property Firebrick As Brush
[C#]
public static Brush Firebrick {get;}
[C++]
public: __property static Brush* get_Firebrick();
[JScript]
public static function get Firebrick() : Brush;
```

Property Value

A **Brush** object set to a system-defined color.

Requirements

Platforms: Windows 98, Windows NT 4.0, Windows Millennium Edition, Windows 2000, Windows XP Home Edition, Windows XP Professional, Windows Server 2003 family

Brushes.FloralWhite Property

Gets a system-defined **Brush** object.

```
[Visual Basic]
Public Shared ReadOnly Property FloralWhite As Brush
[C#]
public static Brush FloralWhite {get;}
[C++]
public: __property static Brush* get_FloralWhite();
[JScript]
public static function get FloralWhite() : Brush;
```

Property Value

A **Brush** object set to a system-defined color.

Requirements

Platforms: Windows 98, Windows NT 4.0, Windows Millennium Edition, Windows 2000, Windows XP Home Edition, Windows XP Professional, Windows Server 2003 family

Brushes.ForestGreen Property

Gets a system-defined **Brush** object.

```
[Visual Basic]
Public Shared ReadOnly Property ForestGreen As Brush
[C#]
public static Brush ForestGreen {get;}
[C++]
public: __property static Brush* get_ForestGreen();
[JScript]
public static function get ForestGreen() : Brush;
```

Property Value

A **Brush** object set to a system-defined color.

Requirements

Platforms: Windows 98, Windows NT 4.0, Windows Millennium Edition, Windows 2000, Windows XP Home Edition, Windows XP Professional, Windows Server 2003 family

Brushes.Fuchsia Property

Gets a system-defined **Brush** object.

```
[Visual Basic]
Public Shared ReadOnly Property Fuchsia As Brush
[C#]
public static Brush Fuchsia {get;}
[C++]
public: __property static Brush* get_Fuchsia();
[JScript]
public static function get Fuchsia() : Brush;
```

Property Value

A **Brush** object set to a system-defined color.

Requirements

Platforms: Windows 98, Windows NT 4.0, Windows Millennium Edition, Windows 2000, Windows XP Home Edition, Windows XP Professional, Windows Server 2003 family

Brushes.Gainsboro Property

Gets a system-defined **Brush** object.

[Visual Basic]
```
Public Shared ReadOnly Property Gainsboro As Brush
```
[C#]
```
public static Brush Gainsboro {get;}
```
[C++]
```
public: __property static Brush* get_Gainsboro();
```
[JScript]
```
public static function get Gainsboro() : Brush;
```

Property Value

A **Brush** object set to a system-defined color.

Requirements

Platforms: Windows 98, Windows NT 4.0, Windows Millennium Edition, Windows 2000, Windows XP Home Edition, Windows XP Professional, Windows Server 2003 family

Brushes.GhostWhite Property

Gets a system-defined **Brush** object.

[Visual Basic]
```
Public Shared ReadOnly Property GhostWhite As Brush
```
[C#]
```
public static Brush GhostWhite {get;}
```
[C++]
```
public: __property static Brush* get_GhostWhite();
```
[JScript]
```
public static function get GhostWhite() : Brush;
```

Property Value

A **Brush** object set to a system-defined color.

Requirements

Platforms: Windows 98, Windows NT 4.0, Windows Millennium Edition, Windows 2000, Windows XP Home Edition, Windows XP Professional, Windows Server 2003 family

Brushes.Gold Property

Gets a system-defined **Brush** object.

[Visual Basic]
```
Public Shared ReadOnly Property Gold As Brush
```
[C#]
```
public static Brush Gold {get;}
```
[C++]
```
public: __property static Brush* get_Gold();
```
[JScript]
```
public static function get Gold() : Brush;
```

Property Value

A **Brush** object set to a system-defined color.

Requirements

Platforms: Windows 98, Windows NT 4.0, Windows Millennium Edition, Windows 2000, Windows XP Home Edition, Windows XP Professional, Windows Server 2003 family

Brushes.Goldenrod Property

Gets a system-defined **Brush** object.

[Visual Basic]
```
Public Shared ReadOnly Property Goldenrod As Brush
```
[C#]
```
public static Brush Goldenrod {get;}
```
[C++]
```
public: __property static Brush* get_Goldenrod();
```
[JScript]
```
public static function get Goldenrod() : Brush;
```

Property Value

A **Brush** object set to a system-defined color.

Requirements

Platforms: Windows 98, Windows NT 4.0, Windows Millennium Edition, Windows 2000, Windows XP Home Edition, Windows XP Professional, Windows Server 2003 family

Brushes.Gray Property

Gets a system-defined **Brush** object.

[Visual Basic]
```
Public Shared ReadOnly Property Gray As Brush
```
[C#]
```
public static Brush Gray {get;}
```
[C++]
```
public: __property static Brush* get_Gray();
```
[JScript]
```
public static function get Gray() : Brush;
```

Property Value

A **Brush** object set to a system-defined color.

Requirements

Platforms: Windows 98, Windows NT 4.0, Windows Millennium Edition, Windows 2000, Windows XP Home Edition, Windows XP Professional, Windows Server 2003 family

Brushes.Green Property

Gets a system-defined **Brush** object.

[Visual Basic]
```
Public Shared ReadOnly Property Green As Brush
```
[C#]
```
public static Brush Green {get;}
```
[C++]
```
public: __property static Brush* get_Green();
```
[JScript]
```
public static function get Green() : Brush;
```

Property Value

A **Brush** object set to a system-defined color.

Requirements

Platforms: Windows 98, Windows NT 4.0, Windows Millennium Edition, Windows 2000, Windows XP Home Edition, Windows XP Professional, Windows Server 2003 family

Brushes.GreenYellow Property

Gets a system-defined **Brush** object.

[Visual Basic]
```
Public Shared ReadOnly Property GreenYellow As Brush
```
[C#]
```
public static Brush GreenYellow {get;}
```
[C++]
```
public: __property static Brush* get_GreenYellow();
```
[JScript]
```
public static function get GreenYellow() : Brush;
```

Property Value

A **Brush** object set to a system-defined color.

Requirements

Platforms: Windows 98, Windows NT 4.0, Windows Millennium Edition, Windows 2000, Windows XP Home Edition, Windows XP Professional, Windows Server 2003 family

Brushes.Honeydew Property

Gets a system-defined **Brush** object.

[Visual Basic]
```
Public Shared ReadOnly Property Honeydew As Brush
```
[C#]
```
public static Brush Honeydew {get;}
```
[C++]
```
public: __property static Brush* get_Honeydew();
```
[JScript]
```
public static function get Honeydew() : Brush;
```

Property Value

A **Brush** object set to a system-defined color.

Requirements

Platforms: Windows 98, Windows NT 4.0, Windows Millennium Edition, Windows 2000, Windows XP Home Edition, Windows XP Professional, Windows Server 2003 family

Brushes.HotPink Property

Gets a system-defined **Brush** object.

[Visual Basic]
```
Public Shared ReadOnly Property HotPink As Brush
```
[C#]
```
public static Brush HotPink {get;}
```
[C++]
```
public: __property static Brush* get_HotPink();
```
[JScript]
```
public static function get HotPink() : Brush;
```

Property Value

A **Brush** object set to a system-defined color.

Requirements

Platforms: Windows 98, Windows NT 4.0, Windows Millennium Edition, Windows 2000, Windows XP Home Edition, Windows XP Professional, Windows Server 2003 family

Brushes.IndianRed Property

Gets a system-defined **Brush** object.

[Visual Basic]
```
Public Shared ReadOnly Property IndianRed As Brush
```
[C#]
```
public static Brush IndianRed {get;}
```
[C++]
```
public: __property static Brush* get_IndianRed();
```
[JScript]
```
public static function get IndianRed() : Brush;
```

Property Value

A **Brush** object set to a system-defined color.

Requirements

Platforms: Windows 98, Windows NT 4.0, Windows Millennium Edition, Windows 2000, Windows XP Home Edition, Windows XP Professional, Windows Server 2003 family

Brushes.Indigo Property

Gets a system-defined **Brush** object.

[Visual Basic]
```
Public Shared ReadOnly Property Indigo As Brush
```
[C#]
```
public static Brush Indigo {get;}
```
[C++]
```
public: __property static Brush* get_Indigo();
```
[JScript]
```
public static function get Indigo() : Brush;
```

Property Value

A **Brush** object set to a system-defined color.

Requirements

Platforms: Windows 98, Windows NT 4.0, Windows Millennium Edition, Windows 2000, Windows XP Home Edition, Windows XP Professional, Windows Server 2003 family

Brushes.Ivory Property

Gets a system-defined **Brush** object.

[Visual Basic]
```
Public Shared ReadOnly Property Ivory As Brush
```
[C#]
```
public static Brush Ivory {get;}
```
[C++]
```
public: __property static Brush* get_Ivory();
```
[JScript]
```
public static function get Ivory() : Brush;
```

Property Value

A **Brush** object set to a system-defined color.

Requirements

Platforms: Windows 98, Windows NT 4.0, Windows Millennium Edition, Windows 2000, Windows XP Home Edition, Windows XP Professional, Windows Server 2003 family

Brushes.Khaki Property

Gets a system-defined **Brush** object.

[Visual Basic]
```
Public Shared ReadOnly Property Khaki As Brush
```
[C#]
```
public static Brush Khaki {get;}
```
[C++]
```
public: __property static Brush* get_Khaki();
```
[JScript]
```
public static function get Khaki() : Brush;
```

Property Value

A **Brush** object set to a system-defined color.

Requirements

Platforms: Windows 98, Windows NT 4.0, Windows Millennium Edition, Windows 2000, Windows XP Home Edition, Windows XP Professional, Windows Server 2003 family

Brushes.Lavender Property

Gets a system-defined **Brush** object.

[Visual Basic]
```
Public Shared ReadOnly Property Lavender As Brush
```
[C#]
```
public static Brush Lavender {get;}
```
[C++]
```
public: __property static Brush* get_Lavender();
```
[JScript]
```
public static function get Lavender() : Brush;
```

Property Value

A **Brush** object set to a system-defined color.

Requirements

Platforms: Windows 98, Windows NT 4.0, Windows Millennium Edition, Windows 2000, Windows XP Home Edition, Windows XP Professional, Windows Server 2003 family

Brushes.LavenderBlush Property

Gets a system-defined **Brush** object.

[Visual Basic]
```
Public Shared ReadOnly Property LavenderBlush As Brush
```
[C#]
```
public static Brush LavenderBlush {get;}
```
[C++]
```
public: __property static Brush* get_LavenderBlush();
```
[JScript]
```
public static function get LavenderBlush() : Brush;
```

Property Value

A **Brush** object set to a system-defined color.

Requirements

Platforms: Windows 98, Windows NT 4.0, Windows Millennium Edition, Windows 2000, Windows XP Home Edition, Windows XP Professional, Windows Server 2003 family

Brushes.LawnGreen Property

Gets a system-defined **Brush** object.

[Visual Basic]
```
Public Shared ReadOnly Property LawnGreen As Brush
```
[C#]
```
public static Brush LawnGreen {get;}
```
[C++]
```
public: __property static Brush* get_LawnGreen();
```
[JScript]
```
public static function get LawnGreen() : Brush;
```

Property Value

A **Brush** object set to a system-defined color.

Requirements

Platforms: Windows 98, Windows NT 4.0, Windows Millennium Edition, Windows 2000, Windows XP Home Edition, Windows XP Professional, Windows Server 2003 family

Brushes.LemonChiffon Property

Gets a system-defined **Brush** object.

[Visual Basic]
```
Public Shared ReadOnly Property LemonChiffon As Brush
```
[C#]
```
public static Brush LemonChiffon {get;}
```
[C++]
```
public: __property static Brush* get_LemonChiffon();
```
[JScript]
```
public static function get LemonChiffon() : Brush;
```

Property Value

A **Brush** object set to a system-defined color.

Requirements

Platforms: Windows 98, Windows NT 4.0, Windows Millennium Edition, Windows 2000, Windows XP Home Edition, Windows XP Professional, Windows Server 2003 family

Brushes.LightBlue Property

Gets a system-defined **Brush** object.

[Visual Basic]
```
Public Shared ReadOnly Property LightBlue As Brush
```
[C#]
```
public static Brush LightBlue {get;}
```
[C++]
```
public: __property static Brush* get_LightBlue();
```
[JScript]
```
public static function get LightBlue() : Brush;
```

Property Value

A **Brush** object set to a system-defined color.

Requirements

Platforms: Windows 98, Windows NT 4.0, Windows Millennium Edition, Windows 2000, Windows XP Home Edition, Windows XP Professional, Windows Server 2003 family

Brushes.LightCoral Property

Gets a system-defined **Brush** object.

[Visual Basic]
```
Public Shared ReadOnly Property LightCoral As Brush
```
[C#]
```
public static Brush LightCoral {get;}
```
[C++]
```
public: __property static Brush* get_LightCoral();
```
[JScript]
```
public static function get LightCoral() : Brush;
```

Property Value

A **Brush** object set to a system-defined color.

Requirements

Platforms: Windows 98, Windows NT 4.0, Windows Millennium Edition, Windows 2000, Windows XP Home Edition, Windows XP Professional, Windows Server 2003 family

Brushes.LightCyan Property

Gets a system-defined **Brush** object.

[Visual Basic]
```
Public Shared ReadOnly Property LightCyan As Brush
```
[C#]
```
public static Brush LightCyan {get;}
```
[C++]
```
public: __property static Brush* get_LightCyan();
```
[JScript]
```
public static function get LightCyan() : Brush;
```

Property Value

A **Brush** object set to a system-defined color.

Requirements

Platforms: Windows 98, Windows NT 4.0, Windows Millennium Edition, Windows 2000, Windows XP Home Edition, Windows XP Professional, Windows Server 2003 family

Brushes.LightGoldenrodYellow Property

Gets a system-defined **Brush** object.

[Visual Basic]
```
Public Shared ReadOnly Property LightGoldenrodYellow As Brush
```
[C#]
```
public static Brush LightGoldenrodYellow {get;}
```
[C++]
```
public: __property static Brush* get_LightGoldenrodYellow();
```
[JScript]
```
public static function get LightGoldenrodYellow() : Brush;
```

Property Value

A **Brush** object set to a system-defined color.

Requirements

Platforms: Windows 98, Windows NT 4.0, Windows Millennium Edition, Windows 2000, Windows XP Home Edition, Windows XP Professional, Windows Server 2003 family

Brushes.LightGray Property

Gets a system-defined **Brush** object.

[Visual Basic]
```
Public Shared ReadOnly Property LightGray As Brush
```
[C#]
```
public static Brush LightGray {get;}
```
[C++]
```
public: __property static Brush* get_LightGray();
```
[JScript]
```
public static function get LightGray() : Brush;
```

Property Value

A **Brush** object set to a system-defined color.

Requirements

Platforms: Windows 98, Windows NT 4.0, Windows Millennium Edition, Windows 2000, Windows XP Home Edition, Windows XP Professional, Windows Server 2003 family

Brushes.LightGreen Property

Gets a system-defined **Brush** object.

[Visual Basic]
```
Public Shared ReadOnly Property LightGreen As Brush
```
[C#]
```
public static Brush LightGreen {get;}
```
[C++]
```
public: __property static Brush* get_LightGreen();
```
[JScript]
```
public static function get LightGreen() : Brush;
```

Property Value

A **Brush** object set to a system-defined color.

Requirements

Platforms: Windows 98, Windows NT 4.0, Windows Millennium Edition, Windows 2000, Windows XP Home Edition, Windows XP Professional, Windows Server 2003 family

Brushes.LightPink Property

Gets a system-defined **Brush** object.

[Visual Basic]
```
Public Shared ReadOnly Property LightPink As Brush
```
[C#]
```
public static Brush LightPink {get;}
```
[C++]
```
public: __property static Brush* get_LightPink();
```
[JScript]
```
public static function get LightPink() : Brush;
```

Property Value

A **Brush** object set to a system-defined color.

Requirements

Platforms: Windows 98, Windows NT 4.0, Windows Millennium Edition, Windows 2000, Windows XP Home Edition, Windows XP Professional, Windows Server 2003 family

Brushes.LightSalmon Property

Gets a system-defined **Brush** object.

[Visual Basic]
```
Public Shared ReadOnly Property LightSalmon As Brush
```
[C#]
```
public static Brush LightSalmon {get;}
```
[C++]
```
public: __property static Brush* get_LightSalmon();
```
[JScript]
```
public static function get LightSalmon() : Brush;
```

Property Value

A **Brush** object set to a system-defined color.

Requirements

Platforms: Windows 98, Windows NT 4.0, Windows Millennium Edition, Windows 2000, Windows XP Home Edition, Windows XP Professional, Windows Server 2003 family

Brushes.LightSeaGreen Property

Gets a system-defined **Brush** object.

[Visual Basic]
```
Public Shared ReadOnly Property LightSeaGreen As Brush
```
[C#]
```
public static Brush LightSeaGreen {get;}
```
[C++]
```
public: __property static Brush* get_LightSeaGreen();
```
[JScript]
```
public static function get LightSeaGreen() : Brush;
```

Property Value

A **Brush** object set to a system-defined color.

Requirements

Platforms: Windows 98, Windows NT 4.0, Windows Millennium Edition, Windows 2000, Windows XP Home Edition, Windows XP Professional, Windows Server 2003 family

Brushes.LightSkyBlue Property

Gets a system-defined **Brush** object.

[Visual Basic]
```
Public Shared ReadOnly Property LightSkyBlue As Brush
```
[C#]
```
public static Brush LightSkyBlue {get;}
```
[C++]
```
public: __property static Brush* get_LightSkyBlue();
```
[JScript]
```
public static function get LightSkyBlue() : Brush;
```

Property Value

A **Brush** object set to a system-defined color.

Requirements

Platforms: Windows 98, Windows NT 4.0, Windows Millennium Edition, Windows 2000, Windows XP Home Edition, Windows XP Professional, Windows Server 2003 family

Brushes.LightSlateGray Property

Gets a system-defined **Brush** object.

[Visual Basic]
```
Public Shared ReadOnly Property LightSlateGray As Brush
```
[C#]
```
public static Brush LightSlateGray {get;}
```
[C++]
```
public: __property static Brush* get_LightSlateGray();
```
[JScript]
```
public static function get LightSlateGray() : Brush;
```

Property Value

A **Brush** object set to a system-defined color.

Requirements

Platforms: Windows 98, Windows NT 4.0, Windows Millennium Edition, Windows 2000, Windows XP Home Edition, Windows XP Professional, Windows Server 2003 family

Brushes.LightSteelBlue Property

Gets a system-defined **Brush** object.

[Visual Basic]
```
Public Shared ReadOnly Property LightSteelBlue As Brush
```
[C#]
```
public static Brush LightSteelBlue {get;}
```
[C++]
```
public: __property static Brush* get_LightSteelBlue();
```
[JScript]
```
public static function get LightSteelBlue() : Brush;
```

Property Value

A **Brush** object set to a system-defined color.

Requirements

Platforms: Windows 98, Windows NT 4.0, Windows Millennium Edition, Windows 2000, Windows XP Home Edition, Windows XP Professional, Windows Server 2003 family

Brushes.LightYellow Property

Gets a system-defined **Brush** object.

[Visual Basic]
```
Public Shared ReadOnly Property LightYellow As Brush
```
[C#]
```
public static Brush LightYellow {get;}
```
[C++]
```
public: __property static Brush* get_LightYellow();
```
[JScript]
```
public static function get LightYellow() : Brush;
```

Property Value

A **Brush** object set to a system-defined color.

Requirements

Platforms: Windows 98, Windows NT 4.0, Windows Millennium Edition, Windows 2000, Windows XP Home Edition, Windows XP Professional, Windows Server 2003 family

Brushes.Lime Property

Gets a system-defined **Brush** object.

```
[Visual Basic]
Public Shared ReadOnly Property Lime As Brush
[C#]
public static Brush Lime {get;}
[C++]
public: __property static Brush* get_Lime();
[JScript]
public static function get Lime() : Brush;
```

Property Value

A **Brush** object set to a system-defined color.

Requirements

Platforms: Windows 98, Windows NT 4.0, Windows Millennium Edition, Windows 2000, Windows XP Home Edition, Windows XP Professional, Windows Server 2003 family

Brushes.LimeGreen Property

Gets a system-defined **Brush** object.

```
[Visual Basic]
Public Shared ReadOnly Property LimeGreen As Brush
[C#]
public static Brush LimeGreen {get;}
[C++]
public: __property static Brush* get_LimeGreen();
[JScript]
public static function get LimeGreen() : Brush;
```

Property Value

A **Brush** object set to a system-defined color.

Requirements

Platforms: Windows 98, Windows NT 4.0, Windows Millennium Edition, Windows 2000, Windows XP Home Edition, Windows XP Professional, Windows Server 2003 family

Brushes.Linen Property

Gets a system-defined **Brush** object.

```
[Visual Basic]
Public Shared ReadOnly Property Linen As Brush
[C#]
public static Brush Linen {get;}
[C++]
public: __property static Brush* get_Linen();
[JScript]
public static function get Linen() : Brush;
```

Property Value

A **Brush** object set to a system-defined color.

Requirements

Platforms: Windows 98, Windows NT 4.0, Windows Millennium Edition, Windows 2000, Windows XP Home Edition, Windows XP Professional, Windows Server 2003 family

Brushes.Magenta Property

Gets a system-defined **Brush** object.

```
[Visual Basic]
Public Shared ReadOnly Property Magenta As Brush
[C#]
public static Brush Magenta {get;}
[C++]
public: __property static Brush* get_Magenta();
[JScript]
public static function get Magenta() : Brush;
```

Property Value

A **Brush** object set to a system-defined color.

Requirements

Platforms: Windows 98, Windows NT 4.0, Windows Millennium Edition, Windows 2000, Windows XP Home Edition, Windows XP Professional, Windows Server 2003 family

Brushes.Maroon Property

Gets a system-defined **Brush** object.

```
[Visual Basic]
Public Shared ReadOnly Property Maroon As Brush
[C#]
public static Brush Maroon {get;}
[C++]
public: __property static Brush* get_Maroon();
[JScript]
public static function get Maroon() : Brush;
```

Property Value

A **Brush** object set to a system-defined color.

Requirements

Platforms: Windows 98, Windows NT 4.0, Windows Millennium Edition, Windows 2000, Windows XP Home Edition, Windows XP Professional, Windows Server 2003 family

Brushes.MediumAquamarine Property

Gets a system-defined **Brush** object.

```
[Visual Basic]
Public Shared ReadOnly Property MediumAquamarine As Brush
[C#]
public static Brush MediumAquamarine {get;}
[C++]
public: __property static Brush* get_MediumAquamarine();
[JScript]
public static function get MediumAquamarine() : Brush;
```

Property Value

A **Brush** object set to a system-defined color.

Requirements

Platforms: Windows 98, Windows NT 4.0, Windows Millennium Edition, Windows 2000, Windows XP Home Edition, Windows XP Professional, Windows Server 2003 family

Brushes.MediumBlue Property

Gets a system-defined **Brush** object.

[Visual Basic]
```
Public Shared ReadOnly Property MediumBlue As Brush
```
[C#]
```
public static Brush MediumBlue {get;}
```
[C++]
```
public: __property static Brush* get_MediumBlue();
```
[JScript]
```
public static function get MediumBlue() : Brush;
```

Property Value

A **Brush** object set to a system-defined color.

Requirements

Platforms: Windows 98, Windows NT 4.0, Windows Millennium Edition, Windows 2000, Windows XP Home Edition, Windows XP Professional, Windows Server 2003 family

Brushes.MediumOrchid Property

Gets a system-defined **Brush** object.

[Visual Basic]
```
Public Shared ReadOnly Property MediumOrchid As Brush
```
[C#]
```
public static Brush MediumOrchid {get;}
```
[C++]
```
public: __property static Brush* get_MediumOrchid();
```
[JScript]
```
public static function get MediumOrchid() : Brush;
```

Property Value

A **Brush** object set to a system-defined color.

Requirements

Platforms: Windows 98, Windows NT 4.0, Windows Millennium Edition, Windows 2000, Windows XP Home Edition, Windows XP Professional, Windows Server 2003 family

Brushes.MediumPurple Property

Gets a system-defined **Brush** object.

[Visual Basic]
```
Public Shared ReadOnly Property MediumPurple As Brush
```
[C#]
```
public static Brush MediumPurple {get;}
```
[C++]
```
public: __property static Brush* get_MediumPurple();
```
[JScript]
```
public static function get MediumPurple() : Brush;
```

Property Value

A **Brush** object set to a system-defined color.

Requirements

Platforms: Windows 98, Windows NT 4.0, Windows Millennium Edition, Windows 2000, Windows XP Home Edition, Windows XP Professional, Windows Server 2003 family

Brushes.MediumSeaGreen Property

Gets a system-defined **Brush** object.

[Visual Basic]
```
Public Shared ReadOnly Property MediumSeaGreen As Brush
```
[C#]
```
public static Brush MediumSeaGreen {get;}
```
[C++]
```
public: __property static Brush* get_MediumSeaGreen();
```
[JScript]
```
public static function get MediumSeaGreen() : Brush;
```

Property Value

A **Brush** object set to a system-defined color.

Requirements

Platforms: Windows 98, Windows NT 4.0, Windows Millennium Edition, Windows 2000, Windows XP Home Edition, Windows XP Professional, Windows Server 2003 family

Brushes.MediumSlateBlue Property

Gets a system-defined **Brush** object.

[Visual Basic]
```
Public Shared ReadOnly Property MediumSlateBlue As Brush
```
[C#]
```
public static Brush MediumSlateBlue {get;}
```
[C++]
```
public: __property static Brush* get_MediumSlateBlue();
```
[JScript]
```
public static function get MediumSlateBlue() : Brush;
```

Property Value

A **Brush** object set to a system-defined color.

Requirements

Platforms: Windows 98, Windows NT 4.0, Windows Millennium Edition, Windows 2000, Windows XP Home Edition, Windows XP Professional, Windows Server 2003 family

Brushes.MediumSpringGreen Property

Gets a system-defined **Brush** object.

[Visual Basic]
```
Public Shared ReadOnly Property MediumSpringGreen As Brush
```
[C#]
```
public static Brush MediumSpringGreen {get;}
```
[C++]
```
public: __property static Brush* get_MediumSpringGreen();
```
[JScript]
```
public static function get MediumSpringGreen() : Brush;
```

Property Value

A **Brush** object set to a system-defined color.

Requirements

Platforms: Windows 98, Windows NT 4.0, Windows Millennium Edition, Windows 2000, Windows XP Home Edition, Windows XP Professional, Windows Server 2003 family

Brushes.MediumTurquoise Property

Gets a system-defined **Brush** object.

[Visual Basic]
```
Public Shared ReadOnly Property MediumTurquoise As Brush
```
[C#]
```
public static Brush MediumTurquoise {get;}
```
[C++]
```
public: __property static Brush* get_MediumTurquoise();
```
[JScript]
```
public static function get MediumTurquoise() : Brush;
```

Property Value

A **Brush** object set to a system-defined color.

Requirements

Platforms: Windows 98, Windows NT 4.0, Windows Millennium Edition, Windows 2000, Windows XP Home Edition, Windows XP Professional, Windows Server 2003 family

Brushes.MediumVioletRed Property

Gets a system-defined **Brush** object.

[Visual Basic]
```
Public Shared ReadOnly Property MediumVioletRed As Brush
```
[C#]
```
public static Brush MediumVioletRed {get;}
```
[C++]
```
public: __property static Brush* get_MediumVioletRed();
```
[JScript]
```
public static function get MediumVioletRed() : Brush;
```

Property Value

A **Brush** object set to a system-defined color.

Requirements

Platforms: Windows 98, Windows NT 4.0, Windows Millennium Edition, Windows 2000, Windows XP Home Edition, Windows XP Professional, Windows Server 2003 family

Brushes.MidnightBlue Property

Gets a system-defined **Brush** object.

[Visual Basic]
```
Public Shared ReadOnly Property MidnightBlue As Brush
```
[C#]
```
public static Brush MidnightBlue {get;}
```
[C++]
```
public: __property static Brush* get_MidnightBlue();
```
[JScript]
```
public static function get MidnightBlue() : Brush;
```

Property Value

A **Brush** object set to a system-defined color.

Requirements

Platforms: Windows 98, Windows NT 4.0, Windows Millennium Edition, Windows 2000, Windows XP Home Edition, Windows XP Professional, Windows Server 2003 family

Brushes.MintCream Property

Gets a system-defined **Brush** object.

[Visual Basic]
```
Public Shared ReadOnly Property MintCream As Brush
```
[C#]
```
public static Brush MintCream {get;}
```
[C++]
```
public: __property static Brush* get_MintCream();
```
[JScript]
```
public static function get MintCream() : Brush;
```

Property Value

A **Brush** object set to a system-defined color.

Requirements

Platforms: Windows 98, Windows NT 4.0, Windows Millennium Edition, Windows 2000, Windows XP Home Edition, Windows XP Professional, Windows Server 2003 family

Brushes.MistyRose Property

Gets a system-defined **Brush** object.

[Visual Basic]
```
Public Shared ReadOnly Property MistyRose As Brush
```
[C#]
```
public static Brush MistyRose {get;}
```
[C++]
```
public: __property static Brush* get_MistyRose();
```
[JScript]
```
public static function get MistyRose() : Brush;
```

Property Value

A **Brush** object set to a system-defined color.

Requirements

Platforms: Windows 98, Windows NT 4.0, Windows Millennium Edition, Windows 2000, Windows XP Home Edition, Windows XP Professional, Windows Server 2003 family

Brushes.Moccasin Property

Gets a system-defined **Brush** object.

[Visual Basic]
```
Public Shared ReadOnly Property Moccasin As Brush
```
[C#]
```
public static Brush Moccasin {get;}
```
[C++]
```
public: __property static Brush* get_Moccasin();
```
[JScript]
```
public static function get Moccasin() : Brush;
```

Property Value

A **Brush** object set to a system-defined color.

Requirements

Platforms: Windows 98, Windows NT 4.0, Windows Millennium Edition, Windows 2000, Windows XP Home Edition, Windows XP Professional, Windows Server 2003 family

Brushes.NavajoWhite Property

Gets a system-defined **Brush** object.

```
[Visual Basic]
Public Shared ReadOnly Property NavajoWhite As Brush
[C#]
public static Brush NavajoWhite {get;}
[C++]
public: __property static Brush* get_NavajoWhite();
[JScript]
public static function get NavajoWhite() : Brush;
```

Property Value

A **Brush** object set to a system-defined color.

Requirements

Platforms: Windows 98, Windows NT 4.0, Windows Millennium Edition, Windows 2000, Windows XP Home Edition, Windows XP Professional, Windows Server 2003 family

Brushes.Navy Property

Gets a system-defined **Brush** object.

```
[Visual Basic]
Public Shared ReadOnly Property Navy As Brush
[C#]
public static Brush Navy {get;}
[C++]
public: __property static Brush* get_Navy();
[JScript]
public static function get Navy() : Brush;
```

Property Value

A **Brush** object set to a system-defined color.

Requirements

Platforms: Windows 98, Windows NT 4.0, Windows Millennium Edition, Windows 2000, Windows XP Home Edition, Windows XP Professional, Windows Server 2003 family

Brushes.OldLace Property

Gets a system-defined **Brush** object.

```
[Visual Basic]
Public Shared ReadOnly Property OldLace As Brush
[C#]
public static Brush OldLace {get;}
[C++]
public: __property static Brush* get_OldLace();
[JScript]
public static function get OldLace() : Brush;
```

Property Value

A **Brush** object set to a system-defined color.

Requirements

Platforms: Windows 98, Windows NT 4.0, Windows Millennium Edition, Windows 2000, Windows XP Home Edition, Windows XP Professional, Windows Server 2003 family

Brushes.Olive Property

Gets a system-defined **Brush** object.

```
[Visual Basic]
Public Shared ReadOnly Property Olive As Brush
[C#]
public static Brush Olive {get;}
[C++]
public: __property static Brush* get_Olive();
[JScript]
public static function get Olive() : Brush;
```

Property Value

A **Brush** object set to a system-defined color.

Requirements

Platforms: Windows 98, Windows NT 4.0, Windows Millennium Edition, Windows 2000, Windows XP Home Edition, Windows XP Professional, Windows Server 2003 family

Brushes.OliveDrab Property

Gets a system-defined **Brush** object.

```
[Visual Basic]
Public Shared ReadOnly Property OliveDrab As Brush
[C#]
public static Brush OliveDrab {get;}
[C++]
public: __property static Brush* get_OliveDrab();
[JScript]
public static function get OliveDrab() : Brush;
```

Property Value

A **Brush** object set to a system-defined color.

Requirements

Platforms: Windows 98, Windows NT 4.0, Windows Millennium Edition, Windows 2000, Windows XP Home Edition, Windows XP Professional, Windows Server 2003 family

Brushes.Orange Property

Gets a system-defined **Brush** object.

```
[Visual Basic]
Public Shared ReadOnly Property Orange As Brush
[C#]
public static Brush Orange {get;}
[C++]
public: __property static Brush* get_Orange();
[JScript]
public static function get Orange() : Brush;
```

Property Value

A **Brush** object set to a system-defined color.

Requirements

Platforms: Windows 98, Windows NT 4.0, Windows Millennium Edition, Windows 2000, Windows XP Home Edition, Windows XP Professional, Windows Server 2003 family

Brushes.OrangeRed Property

Gets a system-defined **Brush** object.

```
[Visual Basic]
Public Shared ReadOnly Property OrangeRed As Brush
[C#]
public static Brush OrangeRed {get;}
[C++]
public: __property static Brush* get_OrangeRed();
[JScript]
public static function get OrangeRed() : Brush;
```

Property Value

A **Brush** object set to a system-defined color.

Requirements

Platforms: Windows 98, Windows NT 4.0, Windows Millennium Edition, Windows 2000, Windows XP Home Edition, Windows XP Professional, Windows Server 2003 family

Brushes.Orchid Property

Gets a system-defined **Brush** object.

```
[Visual Basic]
Public Shared ReadOnly Property Orchid As Brush
[C#]
public static Brush Orchid {get;}
[C++]
public: __property static Brush* get_Orchid();
[JScript]
public static function get Orchid() : Brush;
```

Property Value

A **Brush** object set to a system-defined color.

Requirements

Platforms: Windows 98, Windows NT 4.0, Windows Millennium Edition, Windows 2000, Windows XP Home Edition, Windows XP Professional, Windows Server 2003 family

Brushes.PaleGoldenrod Property

Gets a system-defined **Brush** object.

```
[Visual Basic]
Public Shared ReadOnly Property PaleGoldenrod As Brush
[C#]
public static Brush PaleGoldenrod {get;}
[C++]
public: __property static Brush* get_PaleGoldenrod();
[JScript]
public static function get PaleGoldenrod() : Brush;
```

Property Value

A **Brush** object set to a system-defined color.

Requirements

Platforms: Windows 98, Windows NT 4.0, Windows Millennium Edition, Windows 2000, Windows XP Home Edition, Windows XP Professional, Windows Server 2003 family

Brushes.PaleGreen Property

Gets a system-defined **Brush** object.

```
[Visual Basic]
Public Shared ReadOnly Property PaleGreen As Brush
[C#]
public static Brush PaleGreen {get;}
[C++]
public: __property static Brush* get_PaleGreen();
[JScript]
public static function get PaleGreen() : Brush;
```

Property Value

A **Brush** object set to a system-defined color.

Requirements

Platforms: Windows 98, Windows NT 4.0, Windows Millennium Edition, Windows 2000, Windows XP Home Edition, Windows XP Professional, Windows Server 2003 family

Brushes.PaleTurquoise Property

Gets a system-defined **Brush** object.

```
[Visual Basic]
Public Shared ReadOnly Property PaleTurquoise As Brush
[C#]
public static Brush PaleTurquoise {get;}
[C++]
public: __property static Brush* get_PaleTurquoise();
[JScript]
public static function get PaleTurquoise() : Brush;
```

Property Value

A **Brush** object set to a system-defined color.

Requirements

Platforms: Windows 98, Windows NT 4.0, Windows Millennium Edition, Windows 2000, Windows XP Home Edition, Windows XP Professional, Windows Server 2003 family

Brushes.PaleVioletRed Property

Gets a system-defined **Brush** object.

```
[Visual Basic]
Public Shared ReadOnly Property PaleVioletRed As Brush
[C#]
public static Brush PaleVioletRed {get;}
[C++]
public: __property static Brush* get_PaleVioletRed();
[JScript]
public static function get PaleVioletRed() : Brush;
```

Property Value

A **Brush** object set to a system-defined color.

Requirements

Platforms: Windows 98, Windows NT 4.0, Windows Millennium Edition, Windows 2000, Windows XP Home Edition, Windows XP Professional, Windows Server 2003 family

Brushes.PapayaWhip Property

Gets a system-defined **Brush** object.

[Visual Basic]
```
Public Shared ReadOnly Property PapayaWhip As Brush
```
[C#]
```
public static Brush PapayaWhip {get;}
```
[C++]
```
public: __property static Brush* get_PapayaWhip();
```
[JScript]
```
public static function get PapayaWhip() : Brush;
```

Property Value

A **Brush** object set to a system-defined color.

Requirements

Platforms: Windows 98, Windows NT 4.0, Windows Millennium Edition, Windows 2000, Windows XP Home Edition, Windows XP Professional, Windows Server 2003 family

Brushes.PeachPuff Property

Gets a system-defined **Brush** object.

[Visual Basic]
```
Public Shared ReadOnly Property PeachPuff As Brush
```
[C#]
```
public static Brush PeachPuff {get;}
```
[C++]
```
public: __property static Brush* get_PeachPuff();
```
[JScript]
```
public static function get PeachPuff() : Brush;
```

Property Value

A **Brush** object set to a system-defined color.

Requirements

Platforms: Windows 98, Windows NT 4.0, Windows Millennium Edition, Windows 2000, Windows XP Home Edition, Windows XP Professional, Windows Server 2003 family

Brushes.Peru Property

Gets a system-defined **Brush** object.

[Visual Basic]
```
Public Shared ReadOnly Property Peru As Brush
```
[C#]
```
public static Brush Peru {get;}
```
[C++]
```
public: __property static Brush* get_Peru();
```
[JScript]
```
public static function get Peru() : Brush;
```

Property Value

A **Brush** object set to a system-defined color.

Requirements

Platforms: Windows 98, Windows NT 4.0, Windows Millennium Edition, Windows 2000, Windows XP Home Edition, Windows XP Professional, Windows Server 2003 family

Brushes.Pink Property

Gets a system-defined **Brush** object.

[Visual Basic]
```
Public Shared ReadOnly Property Pink As Brush
```
[C#]
```
public static Brush Pink {get;}
```
[C++]
```
public: __property static Brush* get_Pink();
```
[JScript]
```
public static function get Pink() : Brush;
```

Property Value

A **Brush** object set to a system-defined color.

Requirements

Platforms: Windows 98, Windows NT 4.0, Windows Millennium Edition, Windows 2000, Windows XP Home Edition, Windows XP Professional, Windows Server 2003 family

Brushes.Plum Property

Gets a system-defined **Brush** object.

[Visual Basic]
```
Public Shared ReadOnly Property Plum As Brush
```
[C#]
```
public static Brush Plum {get;}
```
[C++]
```
public: __property static Brush* get_Plum();
```
[JScript]
```
public static function get Plum() : Brush;
```

Property Value

A **Brush** object set to a system-defined color.

Requirements

Platforms: Windows 98, Windows NT 4.0, Windows Millennium Edition, Windows 2000, Windows XP Home Edition, Windows XP Professional, Windows Server 2003 family

Brushes.PowderBlue Property

Gets a system-defined **Brush** object.

[Visual Basic]
```
Public Shared ReadOnly Property PowderBlue As Brush
```
[C#]
```
public static Brush PowderBlue {get;}
```
[C++]
```
public: __property static Brush* get_PowderBlue();
```
[JScript]
```
public static function get PowderBlue() : Brush;
```

Property Value

A **Brush** object set to a system-defined color.

Requirements

Platforms: Windows 98, Windows NT 4.0, Windows Millennium Edition, Windows 2000, Windows XP Home Edition, Windows XP Professional, Windows Server 2003 family

Brushes.Purple Property

Gets a system-defined **Brush** object.

[Visual Basic]
```
Public Shared ReadOnly Property Purple As Brush
```
[C#]
```
public static Brush Purple {get;}
```
[C++]
```
public: __property static Brush* get_Purple();
```
[JScript]
```
public static function get Purple() : Brush;
```

Property Value

A **Brush** object set to a system-defined color.

Requirements

Platforms: Windows 98, Windows NT 4.0, Windows Millennium Edition, Windows 2000, Windows XP Home Edition, Windows XP Professional, Windows Server 2003 family

Brushes.Red Property

Gets a system-defined **Brush** object.

[Visual Basic]
```
Public Shared ReadOnly Property Red As Brush
```
[C#]
```
public static Brush Red {get;}
```
[C++]
```
public: __property static Brush* get_Red();
```
[JScript]
```
public static function get Red() : Brush;
```

Property Value

A **Brush** object set to a system-defined color.

Requirements

Platforms: Windows 98, Windows NT 4.0, Windows Millennium Edition, Windows 2000, Windows XP Home Edition, Windows XP Professional, Windows Server 2003 family

Brushes.RosyBrown Property

Gets a system-defined **Brush** object.

[Visual Basic]
```
Public Shared ReadOnly Property RosyBrown As Brush
```
[C#]
```
public static Brush RosyBrown {get;}
```
[C++]
```
public: __property static Brush* get_RosyBrown();
```
[JScript]
```
public static function get RosyBrown() : Brush;
```

Property Value

A **Brush** object set to a system-defined color.

Requirements

Platforms: Windows 98, Windows NT 4.0, Windows Millennium Edition, Windows 2000, Windows XP Home Edition, Windows XP Professional, Windows Server 2003 family

Brushes.RoyalBlue Property

Gets a system-defined **Brush** object.

[Visual Basic]
```
Public Shared ReadOnly Property RoyalBlue As Brush
```
[C#]
```
public static Brush RoyalBlue {get;}
```
[C++]
```
public: __property static Brush* get_RoyalBlue();
```
[JScript]
```
public static function get RoyalBlue() : Brush;
```

Property Value

A **Brush** object set to a system-defined color.

Requirements

Platforms: Windows 98, Windows NT 4.0, Windows Millennium Edition, Windows 2000, Windows XP Home Edition, Windows XP Professional, Windows Server 2003 family

Brushes.SaddleBrown Property

Gets a system-defined **Brush** object.

[Visual Basic]
```
Public Shared ReadOnly Property SaddleBrown As Brush
```
[C#]
```
public static Brush SaddleBrown {get;}
```
[C++]
```
public: __property static Brush* get_SaddleBrown();
```
[JScript]
```
public static function get SaddleBrown() : Brush;
```

Property Value

A **Brush** object set to a system-defined color.

Requirements

Platforms: Windows 98, Windows NT 4.0, Windows Millennium Edition, Windows 2000, Windows XP Home Edition, Windows XP Professional, Windows Server 2003 family

Brushes.Salmon Property

Gets a system-defined **Brush** object.

[Visual Basic]
```
Public Shared ReadOnly Property Salmon As Brush
```
[C#]
```
public static Brush Salmon {get;}
```
[C++]
```
public: __property static Brush* get_Salmon();
```
[JScript]
```
public static function get Salmon() : Brush;
```

Property Value

A **Brush** object set to a system-defined color.

Requirements

Platforms: Windows 98, Windows NT 4.0, Windows Millennium Edition, Windows 2000, Windows XP Home Edition, Windows XP Professional, Windows Server 2003 family

Brushes.SandyBrown Property

Gets a system-defined **Brush** object.

[Visual Basic]
```
Public Shared ReadOnly Property SandyBrown As Brush
```
[C#]
```
public static Brush SandyBrown {get;}
```
[C++]
```
public: __property static Brush* get_SandyBrown();
```
[JScript]
```
public static function get SandyBrown() : Brush;
```

Property Value

A **Brush** object set to a system-defined color.

Requirements

Platforms: Windows 98, Windows NT 4.0, Windows Millennium Edition, Windows 2000, Windows XP Home Edition, Windows XP Professional, Windows Server 2003 family

Brushes.SeaGreen Property

Gets a system-defined **Brush** object.

[Visual Basic]
```
Public Shared ReadOnly Property SeaGreen As Brush
```
[C#]
```
public static Brush SeaGreen {get;}
```
[C++]
```
public: __property static Brush* get_SeaGreen();
```
[JScript]
```
public static function get SeaGreen() : Brush;
```

Property Value

A **Brush** object set to a system-defined color.

Requirements

Platforms: Windows 98, Windows NT 4.0, Windows Millennium Edition, Windows 2000, Windows XP Home Edition, Windows XP Professional, Windows Server 2003 family

Brushes.SeaShell Property

Gets a system-defined **Brush** object.

[Visual Basic]
```
Public Shared ReadOnly Property SeaShell As Brush
```
[C#]
```
public static Brush SeaShell {get;}
```
[C++]
```
public: __property static Brush* get_SeaShell();
```
[JScript]
```
public static function get SeaShell() : Brush;
```

Property Value

A **Brush** object set to a system-defined color.

Requirements

Platforms: Windows 98, Windows NT 4.0, Windows Millennium Edition, Windows 2000, Windows XP Home Edition, Windows XP Professional, Windows Server 2003 family

Brushes.Sienna Property

Gets a system-defined **Brush** object.

[Visual Basic]
```
Public Shared ReadOnly Property Sienna As Brush
```
[C#]
```
public static Brush Sienna {get;}
```
[C++]
```
public: __property static Brush* get_Sienna();
```
[JScript]
```
public static function get Sienna() : Brush;
```

Property Value

A **Brush** object set to a system-defined color.

Requirements

Platforms: Windows 98, Windows NT 4.0, Windows Millennium Edition, Windows 2000, Windows XP Home Edition, Windows XP Professional, Windows Server 2003 family

Brushes.Silver Property

Gets a system-defined **Brush** object.

[Visual Basic]
```
Public Shared ReadOnly Property Silver As Brush
```
[C#]
```
public static Brush Silver {get;}
```
[C++]
```
public: __property static Brush* get_Silver();
```
[JScript]
```
public static function get Silver() : Brush;
```

Property Value

A **Brush** object set to a system-defined color.

Requirements

Platforms: Windows 98, Windows NT 4.0, Windows Millennium Edition, Windows 2000, Windows XP Home Edition, Windows XP Professional, Windows Server 2003 family

Brushes.SkyBlue Property

Gets a system-defined **Brush** object.

[Visual Basic]
```
Public Shared ReadOnly Property SkyBlue As Brush
```
[C#]
```
public static Brush SkyBlue {get;}
```
[C++]
```
public: __property static Brush* get_SkyBlue();
```
[JScript]
```
public static function get SkyBlue() : Brush;
```

Property Value

A **Brush** object set to a system-defined color.

Requirements

Platforms: Windows 98, Windows NT 4.0, Windows Millennium Edition, Windows 2000, Windows XP Home Edition, Windows XP Professional, Windows Server 2003 family

Brushes.SlateBlue Property

Gets a system-defined **Brush** object.

[Visual Basic]
```
Public Shared ReadOnly Property SlateBlue As Brush
```
[C#]
```
public static Brush SlateBlue {get;}
```
[C++]
```
public: __property static Brush* get_SlateBlue();
```
[JScript]
```
public static function get SlateBlue() : Brush;
```

Property Value

A **Brush** object set to a system-defined color.

Requirements

Platforms: Windows 98, Windows NT 4.0, Windows Millennium Edition, Windows 2000, Windows XP Home Edition, Windows XP Professional, Windows Server 2003 family

Brushes.SlateGray Property

Gets a system-defined **Brush** object.

[Visual Basic]
```
Public Shared ReadOnly Property SlateGray As Brush
```
[C#]
```
public static Brush SlateGray {get;}
```
[C++]
```
public: __property static Brush* get_SlateGray();
```
[JScript]
```
public static function get SlateGray() : Brush;
```

Property Value

A **Brush** object set to a system-defined color.

Requirements

Platforms: Windows 98, Windows NT 4.0, Windows Millennium Edition, Windows 2000, Windows XP Home Edition, Windows XP Professional, Windows Server 2003 family

Brushes.Snow Property

Gets a system-defined **Brush** object.

[Visual Basic]
```
Public Shared ReadOnly Property Snow As Brush
```
[C#]
```
public static Brush Snow {get;}
```
[C++]
```
public: __property static Brush* get_Snow();
```
[JScript]
```
public static function get Snow() : Brush;
```

Property Value

A **Brush** object set to a system-defined color.

Requirements

Platforms: Windows 98, Windows NT 4.0, Windows Millennium Edition, Windows 2000, Windows XP Home Edition, Windows XP Professional, Windows Server 2003 family

Brushes.SpringGreen Property

Gets a system-defined **Brush** object.

[Visual Basic]
```
Public Shared ReadOnly Property SpringGreen As Brush
```
[C#]
```
public static Brush SpringGreen {get;}
```
[C++]
```
public: __property static Brush* get_SpringGreen();
```
[JScript]
```
public static function get SpringGreen() : Brush;
```

Property Value

A **Brush** object set to a system-defined color.

Requirements

Platforms: Windows 98, Windows NT 4.0, Windows Millennium Edition, Windows 2000, Windows XP Home Edition, Windows XP Professional, Windows Server 2003 family

Brushes.SteelBlue Property

Gets a system-defined **Brush** object.

[Visual Basic]
```
Public Shared ReadOnly Property SteelBlue As Brush
```
[C#]
```
public static Brush SteelBlue {get;}
```
[C++]
```
public: __property static Brush* get_SteelBlue();
```
[JScript]
```
public static function get SteelBlue() : Brush;
```

Property Value

A **Brush** object set to a system-defined color.

Requirements

Platforms: Windows 98, Windows NT 4.0, Windows Millennium Edition, Windows 2000, Windows XP Home Edition, Windows XP Professional, Windows Server 2003 family

Brushes.Tan Property

Gets a system-defined **Brush** object.

[Visual Basic]
```
Public Shared ReadOnly Property Tan As Brush
```
[C#]
```
public static Brush Tan {get;}
```
[C++]
```
public: __property static Brush* get_Tan();
```
[JScript]
```
public static function get Tan() : Brush;
```

Property Value

A **Brush** object set to a system-defined color.

Requirements

Platforms: Windows 98, Windows NT 4.0, Windows Millennium Edition, Windows 2000, Windows XP Home Edition, Windows XP Professional, Windows Server 2003 family

Brushes.Teal Property

Gets a system-defined **Brush** object.

[Visual Basic]
```
Public Shared ReadOnly Property Teal As Brush
```
[C#]
```
public static Brush Teal {get;}
```
[C++]
```
public: __property static Brush* get_Teal();
```
[JScript]
```
public static function get Teal() : Brush;
```

Property Value

A **Brush** object set to a system-defined color.

Requirements

Platforms: Windows 98, Windows NT 4.0, Windows Millennium Edition, Windows 2000, Windows XP Home Edition, Windows XP Professional, Windows Server 2003 family

Brushes.Thistle Property

Gets a system-defined **Brush** object.

[Visual Basic]
```
Public Shared ReadOnly Property Thistle As Brush
```
[C#]
```
public static Brush Thistle {get;}
```
[C++]
```
public: __property static Brush* get_Thistle();
```
[JScript]
```
public static function get Thistle() : Brush;
```

Property Value

A **Brush** object set to a system-defined color.

Requirements

Platforms: Windows 98, Windows NT 4.0, Windows Millennium Edition, Windows 2000, Windows XP Home Edition, Windows XP Professional, Windows Server 2003 family

Brushes.Tomato Property

Gets a system-defined **Brush** object.

[Visual Basic]
```
Public Shared ReadOnly Property Tomato As Brush
```
[C#]
```
public static Brush Tomato {get;}
```
[C++]
```
public: __property static Brush* get_Tomato();
```
[JScript]
```
public static function get Tomato() : Brush;
```

Property Value

A **Brush** object set to a system-defined color.

Requirements

Platforms: Windows 98, Windows NT 4.0, Windows Millennium Edition, Windows 2000, Windows XP Home Edition, Windows XP Professional, Windows Server 2003 family

Brushes.Transparent Property

Gets a system-defined **Brush** object.

[Visual Basic]
```
Public Shared ReadOnly Property Transparent As Brush
```
[C#]
```
public static Brush Transparent {get;}
```
[C++]
```
public: __property static Brush* get_Transparent();
```
[JScript]
```
public static function get Transparent() : Brush;
```

Property Value

A **Brush** object set to a system-defined color.

Requirements

Platforms: Windows 98, Windows NT 4.0, Windows Millennium Edition, Windows 2000, Windows XP Home Edition, Windows XP Professional, Windows Server 2003 family

Brushes.Turquoise Property

Gets a system-defined **Brush** object.

[Visual Basic]
```
Public Shared ReadOnly Property Turquoise As Brush
```
[C#]
```
public static Brush Turquoise {get;}
```
[C++]
```
public: __property static Brush* get_Turquoise();
```
[JScript]
```
public static function get Turquoise() : Brush;
```

Property Value

A **Brush** object set to a system-defined color.

Requirements

Platforms: Windows 98, Windows NT 4.0, Windows Millennium Edition, Windows 2000, Windows XP Home Edition, Windows XP Professional, Windows Server 2003 family

Brushes.Violet Property

Gets a system-defined **Brush** object.

[Visual Basic]
```
Public Shared ReadOnly Property Violet As Brush
```
[C#]
```
public static Brush Violet {get;}
```
[C++]
```
public: __property static Brush* get_Violet();
```
[JScript]
```
public static function get Violet() : Brush;
```

Property Value

A **Brush** object set to a system-defined color.

Requirements

Platforms: Windows 98, Windows NT 4.0, Windows Millennium Edition, Windows 2000, Windows XP Home Edition, Windows XP Professional, Windows Server 2003 family

Brushes.Wheat Property

Gets a system-defined **Brush** object.

[Visual Basic]
```
Public Shared ReadOnly Property Wheat As Brush
```
[C#]
```
public static Brush Wheat {get;}
```
[C++]
```
public: __property static Brush* get_Wheat();
```
[JScript]
```
public static function get Wheat() : Brush;
```

Property Value

A **Brush** object set to a system-defined color.

Requirements

Platforms: Windows 98, Windows NT 4.0, Windows Millennium Edition, Windows 2000, Windows XP Home Edition, Windows XP Professional, Windows Server 2003 family

Brushes.White Property

Gets a system-defined **Brush** object.

[Visual Basic]
```
Public Shared ReadOnly Property White As Brush
```
[C#]
```
public static Brush White {get;}
```
[C++]
```
public: __property static Brush* get_White();
```
[JScript]
```
public static function get White() : Brush;
```

Property Value

A **Brush** object set to a system-defined color.

Requirements

Platforms: Windows 98, Windows NT 4.0, Windows Millennium Edition, Windows 2000, Windows XP Home Edition, Windows XP Professional, Windows Server 2003 family

Brushes.WhiteSmoke Property

Gets a system-defined **Brush** object.

[Visual Basic]
```
Public Shared ReadOnly Property WhiteSmoke As Brush
```
[C#]
```
public static Brush WhiteSmoke {get;}
```
[C++]
```
public: __property static Brush* get_WhiteSmoke();
```
[JScript]
```
public static function get WhiteSmoke() : Brush;
```

Property Value

A **Brush** object set to a system-defined color.

Requirements

Platforms: Windows 98, Windows NT 4.0, Windows Millennium Edition, Windows 2000, Windows XP Home Edition, Windows XP Professional, Windows Server 2003 family

Brushes.Yellow Property

Gets a system-defined **Brush** object.

[Visual Basic]
```
Public Shared ReadOnly Property Yellow As Brush
```
[C#]
```
public static Brush Yellow {get;}
```
[C++]
```
public: __property static Brush* get_Yellow();
```
[JScript]
```
public static function get Yellow() : Brush;
```

Property Value

A **Brush** object set to a system-defined color.

Requirements

Platforms: Windows 98, Windows NT 4.0, Windows Millennium Edition, Windows 2000, Windows XP Home Edition, Windows XP Professional, Windows Server 2003 family

Brushes.YellowGreen Property

Gets a system-defined **Brush** object.

[Visual Basic]
```
Public Shared ReadOnly Property YellowGreen As Brush
```
[C#]
```
public static Brush YellowGreen {get;}
```
[C++]
```
public: __property static Brush* get_YellowGreen();
```
[JScript]
```
public static function get YellowGreen() : Brush;
```

Property Value

A **Brush** object set to a system-defined color.

Requirements

Platforms: Windows 98, Windows NT 4.0, Windows Millennium Edition, Windows 2000, Windows XP Home Edition, Windows XP Professional, Windows Server 2003 family

CharacterRange Structure

Specifies a range of character positions within a string.

System.Object
  System.ValueType
    System.Drawing.CharacterRange

```
[Visual Basic]
Public Structure CharacterRange
[C#]
public struct CharacterRange
[C++]
public __value struct CharacterRange
```

[JScript] In JScript, you can use the structures in the .NET Framework, but you cannot define your own.

Thread Safety

Any public static (**Shared** in Visual Basic) members of this type are safe for multithreaded operations. Any instance members are not guaranteed to be thread safe.

Requirements

Namespace: System.Drawing

Platforms: Windows 98, Windows NT 4.0, Windows Millennium Edition, Windows 2000, Windows XP Home Edition, Windows XP Professional, Windows Server 2003 family

Assembly: System.Drawing (in System.Drawing.dll)

CharacterRange Constructor

Initializes a new instance of the **CharacterRange** structure, specifying a range of character positions within a string.

```
[Visual Basic]
Public Sub New( _
   ByVal First As Integer, _
   ByVal Length As Integer _
)
[C#]
public CharacterRange(
   int First,
   int Length
);
[C++]
public: CharacterRange(
   int First,
   int Length
);
[JScript]
public function CharacterRange(
   First : int,
   Length : int
);
```

Parameters

First
The position of the first character in the range. For example, if *First* is set to 0, then the first position of the range is position 0 in the string.

Length
The number of positions in the range.

Requirements

Platforms: Windows 98, Windows NT 4.0, Windows Millennium Edition, Windows 2000, Windows XP Home Edition, Windows XP Professional, Windows Server 2003 family

CharacterRange.First Property

Gets or sets the position in the string of the first character of this **CharacterRange**.

```
[Visual Basic]
Public Property First As Integer
[C#]
public int First {get; set;}
[C++]
public: __property int get_First();
public: __property void set_First(int);
[JScript]
public function get First() : int;
public function set First(int);
```

Property Value

The first position of this **CharacterRange**. For example, if *First* is set to 0, then the first position of this **CharacterRange** is position 0 in the string.

Requirements

Platforms: Windows 98, Windows NT 4.0, Windows Millennium Edition, Windows 2000, Windows XP Home Edition, Windows XP Professional, Windows Server 2003 family

CharacterRange.Length Property

Gets or sets the number of positions in this **CharacterRange**.

```
[Visual Basic]
Public Property Length As Integer
[C#]
public int Length {get; set;}
[C++]
public: __property int get_Length();
public: __property void set_Length(int);
[JScript]
public function get Length() : int;
public function set Length(int);
```

Property Value

The number of positions in this **CharacterRange**.

Requirements

Platforms: Windows 98, Windows NT 4.0, Windows Millennium Edition, Windows 2000, Windows XP Home Edition, Windows XP Professional, Windows Server 2003 family

Color Structure

Represents an ARGB color.

System.Object
  System.ValueType
    System.Drawing.Color

```
[Visual Basic]
<Serializable>
<ComVisible(True)>
Public Structure Color
[C#]
[Serializable]
[ComVisible(true)]
public struct Color
[C++]
[Serializable]
[ComVisible(true)]
public __value struct Color
```

[JScript] In JScript, you can use the structures in the .NET Framework, but you cannot define your own.

Thread Safety

Any public static (**Shared** in Visual Basic) members of this type are safe for multithreaded operations. Any instance members are not guaranteed to be thread safe.

Requirements

Namespace: System.Drawing

Platforms: Windows 98, Windows NT 4.0,
Windows Millennium Edition, Windows 2000,
Windows XP Home Edition, Windows XP Professional,
Windows Server 2003 family,
.NET Compact Framework - Windows CE .NET

Assembly: System.Drawing (in System.Drawing.dll)

Color.Empty Field

Represents a null color.

```
[Visual Basic]
Public Shared ReadOnly Empty As Color
[C#]
public static readonly Color Empty;
[C++]
public: static Color Empty;
[JScript]
public static var Empty : Color;
```

Requirements

Platforms: Windows 98, Windows NT 4.0,
Windows Millennium Edition, Windows 2000,
Windows XP Home Edition, Windows XP Professional,
Windows Server 2003 family,
.NET Compact Framework - Windows CE .NET

Color.A Property

Gets the alpha component value of this **Color** structure.

```
[Visual Basic]
Public ReadOnly Property A As Byte
[C#]
public byte A {get;}
[C++]
public: __property unsigned char get_A();
[JScript]
public function get A() : Byte;
```

Property Value

The alpha component value of this **Color** structure.

Requirements

Platforms: Windows 98, Windows NT 4.0,
Windows Millennium Edition, Windows 2000,
Windows XP Home Edition, Windows XP Professional,
Windows Server 2003 family,
.NET Compact Framework - Windows CE .NET

Color.AliceBlue Property

Gets a system-defined color.

```
[Visual Basic]
Public Shared ReadOnly Property AliceBlue As Color
[C#]
public static Color AliceBlue {get;}
[C++]
public: __property static Color get_AliceBlue();
[JScript]
public static function get AliceBlue() : Color;
```

Property Value

A **Color** object representing a system-defined color.

Requirements

Platforms: Windows 98, Windows NT 4.0,
Windows Millennium Edition, Windows 2000,
Windows XP Home Edition, Windows XP Professional,
Windows Server 2003 family,
.NET Compact Framework - Windows CE .NET

Color.AntiqueWhite Property

Gets a system-defined color .

```
[Visual Basic]
Public Shared ReadOnly Property AntiqueWhite As Color
[C#]
public static Color AntiqueWhite {get;}
[C++]
public: __property static Color get_AntiqueWhite();
[JScript]
public static function get AntiqueWhite() : Color;
```

Property Value

A **Color** object representing a system-defined color.

Requirements

Platforms: Windows 98, Windows NT 4.0,
Windows Millennium Edition, Windows 2000,
Windows XP Home Edition, Windows XP Professional,
Windows Server 2003 family,
.NET Compact Framework - Windows CE .NET

Color.Aqua Property

Gets a system-defined color.

[Visual Basic]
```
Public Shared ReadOnly Property Aqua As Color
```
[C#]
```
public static Color Aqua {get;}
```
[C++]
```
public: __property static Color get_Aqua();
```
[JScript]
```
public static function get Aqua() : Color;
```

Property Value

A **Color** object representing a system-defined color.

Requirements

Platforms: Windows 98, Windows NT 4.0, Windows Millennium Edition, Windows 2000, Windows XP Home Edition, Windows XP Professional, Windows Server 2003 family, .NET Compact Framework - Windows CE .NET

Color.Aquamarine Property

Gets a system-defined color.

[Visual Basic]
```
Public Shared ReadOnly Property Aquamarine As Color
```
[C#]
```
public static Color Aquamarine {get;}
```
[C++]
```
public: __property static Color get_Aquamarine();
```
[JScript]
```
public static function get Aquamarine() : Color;
```

Property Value

A **Color** structure representing a system-defined color.

Requirements

Platforms: Windows 98, Windows NT 4.0, Windows Millennium Edition, Windows 2000, Windows XP Home Edition, Windows XP Professional, Windows Server 2003 family, .NET Compact Framework - Windows CE .NET

Color.Azure Property

Gets a system-defined color.

[Visual Basic]
```
Public Shared ReadOnly Property Azure As Color
```
[C#]
```
public static Color Azure {get;}
```
[C++]
```
public: __property static Color get_Azure();
```
[JScript]
```
public static function get Azure() : Color;
```

Property Value

A **Color** structure representing a system-defined color.

Requirements

Platforms: Windows 98, Windows NT 4.0, Windows Millennium Edition, Windows 2000, Windows XP Home Edition, Windows XP Professional, Windows Server 2003 family, .NET Compact Framework - Windows CE .NET

Color.B Property

Gets the blue component value of this **Color** structure.

[Visual Basic]
```
Public ReadOnly Property B As Byte
```
[C#]
```
public byte B {get;}
```
[C++]
```
public: __property unsigned char get_B();
```
[JScript]
```
public function get B() : Byte;
```

Property Value

The blue component value of this **Color** structure.

Requirements

Platforms: Windows 98, Windows NT 4.0, Windows Millennium Edition, Windows 2000, Windows XP Home Edition, Windows XP Professional, Windows Server 2003 family, .NET Compact Framework - Windows CE .NET

Color.Beige Property

Gets a system-defined color.

[Visual Basic]
```
Public Shared ReadOnly Property Beige As Color
```
[C#]
```
public static Color Beige {get;}
```
[C++]
```
public: __property static Color get_Beige();
```
[JScript]
```
public static function get Beige() : Color;
```

Property Value

A **Color** structure representing a system-defined color.

Requirements

Platforms: Windows 98, Windows NT 4.0, Windows Millennium Edition, Windows 2000, Windows XP Home Edition, Windows XP Professional, Windows Server 2003 family, .NET Compact Framework - Windows CE .NET

Color.Bisque Property

Gets a system-defined color.

[Visual Basic]
```
Public Shared ReadOnly Property Bisque As Color
```
[C#]
```
public static Color Bisque {get;}
```

```
[C++]
public: __property static Color get_Bisque();
[JScript]
public static function get Bisque() : Color;
```

Property Value

A **Color** structure representing a system-defined color.

Requirements

Platforms: Windows 98, Windows NT 4.0,
Windows Millennium Edition, Windows 2000,
Windows XP Home Edition, Windows XP Professional,
Windows Server 2003 family,
.NET Compact Framework - Windows CE .NET

Color.Black Property

Gets a system-defined color.

```
[Visual Basic]
Public Shared ReadOnly Property Black As Color
[C#]
public static Color Black {get;}
[C++]
public: __property static Color get_Black();
[JScript]
public static function get Black() : Color;
```

Property Value

A **Color** structure representing a system-defined color.

Requirements

Platforms: Windows 98, Windows NT 4.0,
Windows Millennium Edition, Windows 2000,
Windows XP Home Edition, Windows XP Professional,
Windows Server 2003 family,
.NET Compact Framework - Windows CE .NET

Color.BlanchedAlmond Property

Gets a system-defined color.

```
[Visual Basic]
Public Shared ReadOnly Property BlanchedAlmond As Color
[C#]
public static Color BlanchedAlmond {get;}
[C++]
public: __property static Color get_BlanchedAlmond();
[JScript]
public static function get BlanchedAlmond() : Color;
```

Property Value

A **Color** structure representing a system-defined color.

Requirements

Platforms: Windows 98, Windows NT 4.0,
Windows Millennium Edition, Windows 2000,
Windows XP Home Edition, Windows XP Professional,
Windows Server 2003 family,
.NET Compact Framework - Windows CE .NET

Color.Blue Property

Gets a system-defined color.

```
[Visual Basic]
Public Shared ReadOnly Property Blue As Color
[C#]
public static Color Blue {get;}
[C++]
public: __property static Color get_Blue();
[JScript]
public static function get Blue() : Color;
```

Property Value

A **Color** structure representing a system-defined color.

Requirements

Platforms: Windows 98, Windows NT 4.0,
Windows Millennium Edition, Windows 2000,
Windows XP Home Edition, Windows XP Professional,
Windows Server 2003 family,
.NET Compact Framework - Windows CE .NET

Color.BlueViolet Property

Gets a system-defined color.

```
[Visual Basic]
Public Shared ReadOnly Property BlueViolet As Color
[C#]
public static Color BlueViolet {get;}
[C++]
public: __property static Color get_BlueViolet();
[JScript]
public static function get BlueViolet() : Color;
```

Property Value

A **Color** structure representing a system-defined color.

Requirements

Platforms: Windows 98, Windows NT 4.0,
Windows Millennium Edition, Windows 2000,
Windows XP Home Edition, Windows XP Professional,
Windows Server 2003 family,
.NET Compact Framework - Windows CE .NET

Color.Brown Property

Gets a system-defined color.

```
[Visual Basic]
Public Shared ReadOnly Property Brown As Color
[C#]
public static Color Brown {get;}
[C++]
public: __property static Color get_Brown();
[JScript]
public static function get Brown() : Color;
```

Property Value

A **Color** structure representing a system-defined color.

Requirements

Platforms: Windows 98, Windows NT 4.0, Windows Millennium Edition, Windows 2000, Windows XP Home Edition, Windows XP Professional, Windows Server 2003 family, .NET Compact Framework - Windows CE .NET

Color.BurlyWood Property

Gets a system-defined color.

```
[Visual Basic]
Public Shared ReadOnly Property BurlyWood As Color
[C#]
public static Color BurlyWood {get;}
[C++]
public: __property static Color get_BurlyWood();
[JScript]
public static function get BurlyWood() : Color;
```

Property Value

A **Color** structure representing a system-defined color.

Requirements

Platforms: Windows 98, Windows NT 4.0, Windows Millennium Edition, Windows 2000, Windows XP Home Edition, Windows XP Professional, Windows Server 2003 family, .NET Compact Framework - Windows CE .NET

Color.CadetBlue Property

Gets a system-defined color.

```
[Visual Basic]
Public Shared ReadOnly Property CadetBlue As Color
[C#]
public static Color CadetBlue {get;}
[C++]
public: __property static Color get_CadetBlue();
[JScript]
public static function get CadetBlue() : Color;
```

Property Value

A **Color** structure representing a system-defined color.

Requirements

Platforms: Windows 98, Windows NT 4.0, Windows Millennium Edition, Windows 2000, Windows XP Home Edition, Windows XP Professional, Windows Server 2003 family, .NET Compact Framework - Windows CE .NET

Color.Chartreuse Property

Gets a system-defined color.

```
[Visual Basic]
Public Shared ReadOnly Property Chartreuse As Color
[C#]
public static Color Chartreuse {get;}
[C++]
public: __property static Color get_Chartreuse();
[JScript]
public static function get Chartreuse() : Color;
```

Property Value

A **Color** structure representing a system-defined color.

Requirements

Platforms: Windows 98, Windows NT 4.0, Windows Millennium Edition, Windows 2000, Windows XP Home Edition, Windows XP Professional, Windows Server 2003 family, .NET Compact Framework - Windows CE .NET

Color.Chocolate Property

Gets a system-defined color.

```
[Visual Basic]
Public Shared ReadOnly Property Chocolate As Color
[C#]
public static Color Chocolate {get;}
[C++]
public: __property static Color get_Chocolate();
[JScript]
public static function get Chocolate() : Color;
```

Property Value

A **Color** structure representing a system-defined color.

Requirements

Platforms: Windows 98, Windows NT 4.0, Windows Millennium Edition, Windows 2000, Windows XP Home Edition, Windows XP Professional, Windows Server 2003 family, .NET Compact Framework - Windows CE .NET

Color.Coral Property

Gets a system-defined color.

```
[Visual Basic]
Public Shared ReadOnly Property Coral As Color
[C#]
public static Color Coral {get;}
[C++]
public: __property static Color get_Coral();
[JScript]
public static function get Coral() : Color;
```

Property Value

A **Color** structure representing a system-defined color.

Requirements

Platforms: Windows 98, Windows NT 4.0, Windows Millennium Edition, Windows 2000, Windows XP Home Edition, Windows XP Professional, Windows Server 2003 family, .NET Compact Framework - Windows CE .NET

Color.CornflowerBlue Property

Gets a system-defined color.

```
[Visual Basic]
Public Shared ReadOnly Property CornflowerBlue As Color
[C#]
public static Color CornflowerBlue {get;}
[C++]
public: __property static Color get_CornflowerBlue();
[JScript]
public static function get CornflowerBlue() : Color;
```

Property Value

A **Color** structure representing a system-defined color.

Requirements

Platforms: Windows 98, Windows NT 4.0, Windows Millennium Edition, Windows 2000, Windows XP Home Edition, Windows XP Professional, Windows Server 2003 family, .NET Compact Framework - Windows CE .NET

Color.Cornsilk Property

Gets a system-defined color.

```
[Visual Basic]
Public Shared ReadOnly Property Cornsilk As Color
[C#]
public static Color Cornsilk {get;}
[C++]
public: __property static Color get_Cornsilk();
[JScript]
public static function get Cornsilk() : Color;
```

Property Value

A **Color** structure representing a system-defined color.

Requirements

Platforms: Windows 98, Windows NT 4.0, Windows Millennium Edition, Windows 2000, Windows XP Home Edition, Windows XP Professional, Windows Server 2003 family, .NET Compact Framework - Windows CE .NET

Color.Crimson Property

Gets a system-defined color.

```
[Visual Basic]
Public Shared ReadOnly Property Crimson As Color
[C#]
public static Color Crimson {get;}
[C++]
public: __property static Color get_Crimson();
[JScript]
public static function get Crimson() : Color;
```

Property Value

A **Color** structure representing a system-defined color.

Requirements

Platforms: Windows 98, Windows NT 4.0, Windows Millennium Edition, Windows 2000, Windows XP Home Edition, Windows XP Professional, Windows Server 2003 family, .NET Compact Framework - Windows CE .NET

Color.Cyan Property

Gets a system-defined color.

```
[Visual Basic]
Public Shared ReadOnly Property Cyan As Color
[C#]
public static Color Cyan {get;}
[C++]
public: __property static Color get_Cyan();
[JScript]
public static function get Cyan() : Color;
```

Property Value

A **Color** structure representing a system-defined color.

Requirements

Platforms: Windows 98, Windows NT 4.0, Windows Millennium Edition, Windows 2000, Windows XP Home Edition, Windows XP Professional, Windows Server 2003 family, .NET Compact Framework - Windows CE .NET

Color.DarkBlue Property

Gets a system-defined color.

```
[Visual Basic]
Public Shared ReadOnly Property DarkBlue As Color
[C#]
public static Color DarkBlue {get;}
[C++]
public: __property static Color get_DarkBlue();
[JScript]
public static function get DarkBlue() : Color;
```

Property Value

A **Color** structure representing a system-defined color.

Requirements

Platforms: Windows 98, Windows NT 4.0, Windows Millennium Edition, Windows 2000, Windows XP Home Edition, Windows XP Professional, Windows Server 2003 family, .NET Compact Framework - Windows CE .NET

Color.DarkCyan Property

Gets a system-defined color.

```
[Visual Basic]
Public Shared ReadOnly Property DarkCyan As Color
[C#]
public static Color DarkCyan {get;}
```

```
[C++]
public: __property static Color get_DarkCyan();
[JScript]
public static function get DarkCyan() : Color;
```

Property Value

A **Color** structure representing a system-defined color.

Requirements

Platforms: Windows 98, Windows NT 4.0, Windows Millennium Edition, Windows 2000, Windows XP Home Edition, Windows XP Professional, Windows Server 2003 family, .NET Compact Framework - Windows CE .NET

Color.DarkGoldenrod Property

Gets a system-defined color.

```
[Visual Basic]
Public Shared ReadOnly Property DarkGoldenrod As Color
[C#]
public static Color DarkGoldenrod {get;}
[C++]
public: __property static Color get_DarkGoldenrod();
[JScript]
public static function get DarkGoldenrod() : Color;
```

Property Value

A **Color** structure representing a system-defined color.

Requirements

Platforms: Windows 98, Windows NT 4.0, Windows Millennium Edition, Windows 2000, Windows XP Home Edition, Windows XP Professional, Windows Server 2003 family, .NET Compact Framework - Windows CE .NET

Color.DarkGray Property

Gets a system-defined color.

```
[Visual Basic]
Public Shared ReadOnly Property DarkGray As Color
[C#]
public static Color DarkGray {get;}
[C++]
public: __property static Color get_DarkGray();
[JScript]
public static function get DarkGray() : Color;
```

Property Value

A **Color** structure representing a system-defined color.

Requirements

Platforms: Windows 98, Windows NT 4.0, Windows Millennium Edition, Windows 2000, Windows XP Home Edition, Windows XP Professional, Windows Server 2003 family, .NET Compact Framework - Windows CE .NET

Color.DarkGreen Property

Gets a system-defined color.

```
[Visual Basic]
Public Shared ReadOnly Property DarkGreen As Color
[C#]
public static Color DarkGreen {get;}
[C++]
public: __property static Color get_DarkGreen();
[JScript]
public static function get DarkGreen() : Color;
```

Property Value

A **Color** structure representing a system-defined color.

Requirements

Platforms: Windows 98, Windows NT 4.0, Windows Millennium Edition, Windows 2000, Windows XP Home Edition, Windows XP Professional, Windows Server 2003 family, .NET Compact Framework - Windows CE .NET

Color.DarkKhaki Property

Gets a system-defined color.

```
[Visual Basic]
Public Shared ReadOnly Property DarkKhaki As Color
[C#]
public static Color DarkKhaki {get;}
[C++]
public: __property static Color get_DarkKhaki();
[JScript]
public static function get DarkKhaki() : Color;
```

Property Value

A **Color** structure representing a system-defined color.

Requirements

Platforms: Windows 98, Windows NT 4.0, Windows Millennium Edition, Windows 2000, Windows XP Home Edition, Windows XP Professional, Windows Server 2003 family, .NET Compact Framework - Windows CE .NET

Color.DarkMagenta Property

Gets a system-defined color.

```
[Visual Basic]
Public Shared ReadOnly Property DarkMagenta As Color
[C#]
public static Color DarkMagenta {get;}
[C++]
public: __property static Color get_DarkMagenta();
[JScript]
public static function get DarkMagenta() : Color;
```

Property Value

A **Color** structure representing a system-defined color.

Requirements

Platforms: Windows 98, Windows NT 4.0, Windows Millennium Edition, Windows 2000, Windows XP Home Edition, Windows XP Professional, Windows Server 2003 family, .NET Compact Framework - Windows CE .NET

Color.DarkOliveGreen Property

Gets a system-defined color.

```
[Visual Basic]
Public Shared ReadOnly Property DarkOliveGreen As Color
[C#]
public static Color DarkOliveGreen {get;}
[C++]
public: __property static Color get_DarkOliveGreen();
[JScript]
public static function get DarkOliveGreen() : Color;
```

Property Value

A **Color** structure representing a system-defined color.

Requirements

Platforms: Windows 98, Windows NT 4.0, Windows Millennium Edition, Windows 2000, Windows XP Home Edition, Windows XP Professional, Windows Server 2003 family, .NET Compact Framework - Windows CE .NET

Color.DarkOrange Property

Gets a system-defined color.

```
[Visual Basic]
Public Shared ReadOnly Property DarkOrange As Color
[C#]
public static Color DarkOrange {get;}
[C++]
public: __property static Color get_DarkOrange();
[JScript]
public static function get DarkOrange() : Color;
```

Property Value

A **Color** structure representing a system-defined color.

Requirements

Platforms: Windows 98, Windows NT 4.0, Windows Millennium Edition, Windows 2000, Windows XP Home Edition, Windows XP Professional, Windows Server 2003 family, .NET Compact Framework - Windows CE .NET

Color.DarkOrchid Property

Gets a system-defined color.

```
[Visual Basic]
Public Shared ReadOnly Property DarkOrchid As Color
[C#]
public static Color DarkOrchid {get;}
[C++]
public: __property static Color get_DarkOrchid();
[JScript]
public static function get DarkOrchid() : Color;
```

Property Value

A **Color** structure representing a system-defined color.

Requirements

Platforms: Windows 98, Windows NT 4.0, Windows Millennium Edition, Windows 2000, Windows XP Home Edition, Windows XP Professional, Windows Server 2003 family, .NET Compact Framework - Windows CE .NET

Color.DarkRed Property

Gets a system-defined color.

```
[Visual Basic]
Public Shared ReadOnly Property DarkRed As Color
[C#]
public static Color DarkRed {get;}
[C++]
public: __property static Color get_DarkRed();
[JScript]
public static function get DarkRed() : Color;
```

Property Value

A **Color** structure representing a system-defined color.

Requirements

Platforms: Windows 98, Windows NT 4.0, Windows Millennium Edition, Windows 2000, Windows XP Home Edition, Windows XP Professional, Windows Server 2003 family, .NET Compact Framework - Windows CE .NET

Color.DarkSalmon Property

Gets a system-defined color.

```
[Visual Basic]
Public Shared ReadOnly Property DarkSalmon As Color
[C#]
public static Color DarkSalmon {get;}
[C++]
public: __property static Color get_DarkSalmon();
[JScript]
public static function get DarkSalmon() : Color;
```

Property Value

A **Color** structure representing a system-defined color.

Requirements

Platforms: Windows 98, Windows NT 4.0, Windows Millennium Edition, Windows 2000, Windows XP Home Edition, Windows XP Professional, Windows Server 2003 family, .NET Compact Framework - Windows CE .NET

Color.DarkSeaGreen Property

Gets a system-defined color.

```
[Visual Basic]
Public Shared ReadOnly Property DarkSeaGreen As Color
[C#]
public static Color DarkSeaGreen {get;}
[C++]
public: __property static Color get_DarkSeaGreen();
[JScript]
public static function get DarkSeaGreen() : Color;
```

Property Value

A **Color** structure representing a system-defined color.

Requirements

Platforms: Windows 98, Windows NT 4.0, Windows Millennium Edition, Windows 2000, Windows XP Home Edition, Windows XP Professional, Windows Server 2003 family, .NET Compact Framework - Windows CE .NET

Color.DarkSlateBlue Property

Gets a system-defined color.

```
[Visual Basic]
Public Shared ReadOnly Property DarkSlateBlue As Color
[C#]
public static Color DarkSlateBlue {get;}
[C++]
public: __property static Color get_DarkSlateBlue();
[JScript]
public static function get DarkSlateBlue() : Color;
```

Property Value

A **Color** structure representing a system-defined color.

Requirements

Platforms: Windows 98, Windows NT 4.0, Windows Millennium Edition, Windows 2000, Windows XP Home Edition, Windows XP Professional, Windows Server 2003 family, .NET Compact Framework - Windows CE .NET

Color.DarkSlateGray Property

Gets a system-defined color.

```
[Visual Basic]
Public Shared ReadOnly Property DarkSlateGray As Color
[C#]
public static Color DarkSlateGray {get;}
[C++]
public: __property static Color get_DarkSlateGray();
[JScript]
public static function get DarkSlateGray() : Color;
```

Property Value

A **Color** structure representing a system-defined color.

Requirements

Platforms: Windows 98, Windows NT 4.0, Windows Millennium Edition, Windows 2000, Windows XP Home Edition, Windows XP Professional, Windows Server 2003 family, .NET Compact Framework - Windows CE .NET

Color.DarkTurquoise Property

Gets a system-defined color.

```
[Visual Basic]
Public Shared ReadOnly Property DarkTurquoise As Color
[C#]
public static Color DarkTurquoise {get;}
[C++]
public: __property static Color get_DarkTurquoise();
[JScript]
public static function get DarkTurquoise() : Color;
```

Property Value

A **Color** structure representing a system-defined color.

Requirements

Platforms: Windows 98, Windows NT 4.0, Windows Millennium Edition, Windows 2000, Windows XP Home Edition, Windows XP Professional, Windows Server 2003 family, .NET Compact Framework - Windows CE .NET

Color.DarkViolet Property

Gets a system-defined color.

```
[Visual Basic]
Public Shared ReadOnly Property DarkViolet As Color
[C#]
public static Color DarkViolet {get;}
[C++]
public: __property static Color get_DarkViolet();
[JScript]
public static function get DarkViolet() : Color;
```

Property Value

A **Color** structure representing a system-defined color.

Requirements

Platforms: Windows 98, Windows NT 4.0, Windows Millennium Edition, Windows 2000, Windows XP Home Edition, Windows XP Professional, Windows Server 2003 family, .NET Compact Framework - Windows CE .NET

Color.DeepPink Property

Gets a system-defined color.

```
[Visual Basic]
Public Shared ReadOnly Property DeepPink As Color
[C#]
public static Color DeepPink {get;}
```

```
[C++]
public: __property static Color get_DeepPink();
[JScript]
public static function get DeepPink() : Color;
```

Property Value

A **Color** structure representing a system-defined color.

Requirements

Platforms: Windows 98, Windows NT 4.0, Windows Millennium Edition, Windows 2000, Windows XP Home Edition, Windows XP Professional, Windows Server 2003 family, .NET Compact Framework - Windows CE .NET

Color.DeepSkyBlue Property

Gets a system-defined color.

```
[Visual Basic]
Public Shared ReadOnly Property DeepSkyBlue As Color
[C#]
public static Color DeepSkyBlue {get;}
[C++]
public: __property static Color get_DeepSkyBlue();
[JScript]
public static function get DeepSkyBlue() : Color;
```

Property Value

A **Color** structure representing a system-defined color.

Requirements

Platforms: Windows 98, Windows NT 4.0, Windows Millennium Edition, Windows 2000, Windows XP Home Edition, Windows XP Professional, Windows Server 2003 family, .NET Compact Framework - Windows CE .NET

Color.DimGray Property

Gets a system-defined color.

```
[Visual Basic]
Public Shared ReadOnly Property DimGray As Color
[C#]
public static Color DimGray {get;}
[C++]
public: __property static Color get_DimGray();
[JScript]
public static function get DimGray() : Color;
```

Property Value

A **Color** structure representing a system-defined color.

Requirements

Platforms: Windows 98, Windows NT 4.0, Windows Millennium Edition, Windows 2000, Windows XP Home Edition, Windows XP Professional, Windows Server 2003 family, .NET Compact Framework - Windows CE .NET

Color.DodgerBlue Property

Gets a system-defined color.

```
[Visual Basic]
Public Shared ReadOnly Property DodgerBlue As Color
[C#]
public static Color DodgerBlue {get;}
[C++]
public: __property static Color get_DodgerBlue();
[JScript]
public static function get DodgerBlue() : Color;
```

Property Value

A **Color** structure representing a system-defined color.

Requirements

Platforms: Windows 98, Windows NT 4.0, Windows Millennium Edition, Windows 2000, Windows XP Home Edition, Windows XP Professional, Windows Server 2003 family, .NET Compact Framework - Windows CE .NET

Color.Firebrick Property

Gets a system-defined color.

```
[Visual Basic]
Public Shared ReadOnly Property Firebrick As Color
[C#]
public static Color Firebrick {get;}
[C++]
public: __property static Color get_Firebrick();
[JScript]
public static function get Firebrick() : Color;
```

Property Value

A **Color** structure representing a system-defined color.

Requirements

Platforms: Windows 98, Windows NT 4.0, Windows Millennium Edition, Windows 2000, Windows XP Home Edition, Windows XP Professional, Windows Server 2003 family, .NET Compact Framework - Windows CE .NET

Color.FloralWhite Property

Gets a system-defined color.

```
[Visual Basic]
Public Shared ReadOnly Property FloralWhite As Color
[C#]
public static Color FloralWhite {get;}
[C++]
public: __property static Color get_FloralWhite();
[JScript]
public static function get FloralWhite() : Color;
```

Property Value

A **Color** structure representing a system-defined color.

Requirements

Platforms: Windows 98, Windows NT 4.0, Windows Millennium Edition, Windows 2000, Windows XP Home Edition, Windows XP Professional, Windows Server 2003 family, .NET Compact Framework - Windows CE .NET

Color.ForestGreen Property

Gets a system-defined color.

[Visual Basic]
```
Public Shared ReadOnly Property ForestGreen As Color
```
[C#]
```
public static Color ForestGreen {get;}
```
[C++]
```
public: __property static Color get_ForestGreen();
```
[JScript]
```
public static function get ForestGreen() : Color;
```

Property Value

A **Color** structure representing a system-defined color.

Requirements

Platforms: Windows 98, Windows NT 4.0, Windows Millennium Edition, Windows 2000, Windows XP Home Edition, Windows XP Professional, Windows Server 2003 family, .NET Compact Framework - Windows CE .NET

Color.Fuchsia Property

Gets a system-defined color.

[Visual Basic]
```
Public Shared ReadOnly Property Fuchsia As Color
```
[C#]
```
public static Color Fuchsia {get;}
```
[C++]
```
public: __property static Color get_Fuchsia();
```
[JScript]
```
public static function get Fuchsia() : Color;
```

Property Value

A **Color** structure representing a system-defined color.

Requirements

Platforms: Windows 98, Windows NT 4.0, Windows Millennium Edition, Windows 2000, Windows XP Home Edition, Windows XP Professional, Windows Server 2003 family, .NET Compact Framework - Windows CE .NET

Color.G Property

Gets the green component value of this **Color** structure.

[Visual Basic]
```
Public ReadOnly Property G As Byte
```
[C#]
```
public byte G {get;}
```
[C++]
```
public: __property unsigned char get_G();
```
[JScript]
```
public function get G() : Byte;
```

Property Value

The green component value of this **Color** structure.

Requirements

Platforms: Windows 98, Windows NT 4.0, Windows Millennium Edition, Windows 2000, Windows XP Home Edition, Windows XP Professional, Windows Server 2003 family, .NET Compact Framework - Windows CE .NET

Color.Gainsboro Property

Gets a system-defined color.

[Visual Basic]
```
Public Shared ReadOnly Property Gainsboro As Color
```
[C#]
```
public static Color Gainsboro {get;}
```
[C++]
```
public: __property static Color get_Gainsboro();
```
[JScript]
```
public static function get Gainsboro() : Color;
```

Property Value

A **Color** structure representing a system-defined color.

Requirements

Platforms: Windows 98, Windows NT 4.0, Windows Millennium Edition, Windows 2000, Windows XP Home Edition, Windows XP Professional, Windows Server 2003 family, .NET Compact Framework - Windows CE .NET

Color.GhostWhite Property

Gets a system-defined color.

[Visual Basic]
```
Public Shared ReadOnly Property GhostWhite As Color
```
[C#]
```
public static Color GhostWhite {get;}
```
[C++]
```
public: __property static Color get_GhostWhite();
```
[JScript]
```
public static function get GhostWhite() : Color;
```

Property Value

A **Color** structure representing a system-defined color.

Requirements

Platforms: Windows 98, Windows NT 4.0, Windows Millennium Edition, Windows 2000, Windows XP Home Edition, Windows XP Professional, Windows Server 2003 family, .NET Compact Framework - Windows CE .NET

Color.Gold Property

Gets a system-defined color.

```
[Visual Basic]
Public Shared ReadOnly Property Gold As Color
[C#]
public static Color Gold {get;}
[C++]
public: __property static Color get_Gold();
[JScript]
public static function get Gold() : Color;
```

Property Value

A **Color** structure representing a system-defined color.

Requirements

Platforms: Windows 98, Windows NT 4.0, Windows Millennium Edition, Windows 2000, Windows XP Home Edition, Windows XP Professional, Windows Server 2003 family, .NET Compact Framework - Windows CE .NET

Color.Goldenrod Property

Gets a system-defined color.

```
[Visual Basic]
Public Shared ReadOnly Property Goldenrod As Color
[C#]
public static Color Goldenrod {get;}
[C++]
public: __property static Color get_Goldenrod();
[JScript]
public static function get Goldenrod() : Color;
```

Property Value

A **Color** structure representing a system-defined color.

Requirements

Platforms: Windows 98, Windows NT 4.0, Windows Millennium Edition, Windows 2000, Windows XP Home Edition, Windows XP Professional, Windows Server 2003 family, .NET Compact Framework - Windows CE .NET

Color.Gray Property

Gets a system-defined color.

```
[Visual Basic]
Public Shared ReadOnly Property Gray As Color
[C#]
public static Color Gray {get;}
[C++]
public: __property static Color get_Gray();
[JScript]
public static function get Gray() : Color;
```

Property Value

A **Color** structure representing a system-defined color.

Requirements

Platforms: Windows 98, Windows NT 4.0, Windows Millennium Edition, Windows 2000, Windows XP Home Edition, Windows XP Professional, Windows Server 2003 family, .NET Compact Framework - Windows CE .NET

Color.Green Property

Gets a system-defined color.

```
[Visual Basic]
Public Shared ReadOnly Property Green As Color
[C#]
public static Color Green {get;}
[C++]
public: __property static Color get_Green();
[JScript]
public static function get Green() : Color;
```

Property Value

A **Color** structure representing a system-defined color.

Requirements

Platforms: Windows 98, Windows NT 4.0, Windows Millennium Edition, Windows 2000, Windows XP Home Edition, Windows XP Professional, Windows Server 2003 family, .NET Compact Framework - Windows CE .NET

Color.GreenYellow Property

Gets a system-defined color.

```
[Visual Basic]
Public Shared ReadOnly Property GreenYellow As Color
[C#]
public static Color GreenYellow {get;}
[C++]
public: __property static Color get_GreenYellow();
[JScript]
public static function get GreenYellow() : Color;
```

Property Value

A **Color** structure representing a system-defined color.

Requirements

Platforms: Windows 98, Windows NT 4.0, Windows Millennium Edition, Windows 2000, Windows XP Home Edition, Windows XP Professional, Windows Server 2003 family, .NET Compact Framework - Windows CE .NET

Color.Honeydew Property

Gets a system-defined color.

```
[Visual Basic]
Public Shared ReadOnly Property Honeydew As Color
[C#]
public static Color Honeydew {get;}
```

[C++]
```
public: __property static Color get_Honeydew();
```
[JScript]
```
public static function get Honeydew() : Color;
```

Property Value

A **Color** structure representing a system-defined color.

Requirements

Platforms: Windows 98, Windows NT 4.0, Windows Millennium Edition, Windows 2000, Windows XP Home Edition, Windows XP Professional, Windows Server 2003 family, .NET Compact Framework - Windows CE .NET

Color.HotPink Property

Gets a system-defined color.

[Visual Basic]
```
Public Shared ReadOnly Property HotPink As Color
```
[C#]
```
public static Color HotPink {get;}
```
[C++]
```
public: __property static Color get_HotPink();
```
[JScript]
```
public static function get HotPink() : Color;
```

Property Value

A **Color** structure representing a system-defined color.

Requirements

Platforms: Windows 98, Windows NT 4.0, Windows Millennium Edition, Windows 2000, Windows XP Home Edition, Windows XP Professional, Windows Server 2003 family, .NET Compact Framework - Windows CE .NET

Color.IndianRed Property

Gets a system-defined color.

[Visual Basic]
```
Public Shared ReadOnly Property IndianRed As Color
```
[C#]
```
public static Color IndianRed {get;}
```
[C++]
```
public: __property static Color get_IndianRed();
```
[JScript]
```
public static function get IndianRed() : Color;
```

Property Value

A **Color** structure representing a system-defined color.

Requirements

Platforms: Windows 98, Windows NT 4.0, Windows Millennium Edition, Windows 2000, Windows XP Home Edition, Windows XP Professional, Windows Server 2003 family, .NET Compact Framework - Windows CE .NET

Color.Indigo Property

Gets a system-defined color.

[Visual Basic]
```
Public Shared ReadOnly Property Indigo As Color
```
[C#]
```
public static Color Indigo {get;}
```
[C++]
```
public: __property static Color get_Indigo();
```
[JScript]
```
public static function get Indigo() : Color;
```

Property Value

A **Color** structure representing a system-defined color.

Requirements

Platforms: Windows 98, Windows NT 4.0, Windows Millennium Edition, Windows 2000, Windows XP Home Edition, Windows XP Professional, Windows Server 2003 family, .NET Compact Framework - Windows CE .NET

Color.IsEmpty Property

Specifies whether this **Color** structure is uninitialized.

[Visual Basic]
```
Public ReadOnly Property IsEmpty As Boolean
```
[C#]
```
public bool IsEmpty {get;}
```
[C++]
```
public: __property bool get_IsEmpty();
```
[JScript]
```
public function get IsEmpty() : Boolean;
```

Property Value

This property returns **true** if this color is uninitialized; otherwise, **false**.

Requirements

Platforms: Windows 98, Windows NT 4.0, Windows Millennium Edition, Windows 2000, Windows XP Home Edition, Windows XP Professional, Windows Server 2003 family, .NET Compact Framework - Windows CE .NET

Color.IsKnownColor Property

Specifies whether this **Color** structure is a pre-defined color. Pre-defined colors are represented by the elements of the **KnownColor** enumeration.

[Visual Basic]
```
Public ReadOnly Property IsKnownColor As Boolean
```
[C#]
```
public bool IsKnownColor {get;}
```
[C++]
```
public: __property bool get_IsKnownColor();
```
[JScript]
```
public function get IsKnownColor() : Boolean;
```

Property Value

This property returns **true** if this **Color** structure was created from a pre-defined color by using either the **FromName** method or the **FromKnownColor** method; otherwise, **false**.

Remarks

This method does not do a comparison of the ARGB values. Therefore, when the **IsKnownColor** method is applied to a **Color** structure that is created by using the **FromArgb** method, the **IsKnownColor** method returns false, even if the ARGB value matches the ARGB value of a pre-defined color.

Requirements

Platforms: Windows 98, Windows NT 4.0,
Windows Millennium Edition, Windows 2000,
Windows XP Home Edition, Windows XP Professional,
Windows Server 2003 family

Color.IsNamedColor Property

Specifies whether this **Color** structure is a pre-defined color. Pre-defined colors are represented by the elements of the **KnownColor** enumeration.

```
[Visual Basic]
Public ReadOnly Property IsNamedColor As Boolean
[C#]
public bool IsNamedColor {get;}
[C++]
public: __property bool get_IsNamedColor();
[JScript]
public function get IsNamedColor() : Boolean;
```

Property Value

This property returns **true** if this **Color** structure instance was created from a pre-defined color by using either the **FromName** method or the **FromKnownColor** method; otherwise, **false**.

Remarks

This property does not do a comparison of the ARGB values. Therefore, when the **IsNamedColor** property is applied to a **Color** structure that is created by using the **FromArgb** method, the **IsNamedColor** property returns false, even if the ARGB value matches the ARGB value of a pre-defined color.

Requirements

Platforms: Windows 98, Windows NT 4.0,
Windows Millennium Edition, Windows 2000,
Windows XP Home Edition, Windows XP Professional,
Windows Server 2003 family

Color.IsSystemColor Property

Specifies whether this **Color** structure is a system color. A system color is a color that is used in a windows display element. System colors are represented by elements of the **KnownColor** enumeration.

```
[Visual Basic]
Public ReadOnly Property IsSystemColor As Boolean
[C#]
public bool IsSystemColor {get;}
[C++]
public: __property bool get_IsSystemColor();
[JScript]
public function get IsSystemColor() : Boolean;
```

Property Value

This property returns **true** if this **Color** structure was created from a system color by using either the **FromName** method or the **FromKnownColor** method; otherwise, **false**.

Remarks

This method does not do a comparison of the ARGB values. Therefore, when the **IsSystemColor** method is applied to a **Color** structure that is created by using the **FromArgb** method, the **IsSystemColor** method returns false, even if the ARGB value matches the ARGB value of a system color.

Requirements

Platforms: Windows 98, Windows NT 4.0,
Windows Millennium Edition, Windows 2000,
Windows XP Home Edition, Windows XP Professional,
Windows Server 2003 family,
.NET Compact Framework - Windows CE .NET

Color.Ivory Property

Gets a system-defined color.

```
[Visual Basic]
Public Shared ReadOnly Property Ivory As Color
[C#]
public static Color Ivory {get;}
[C++]
public: __property static Color get_Ivory();
[JScript]
public static function get Ivory() : Color;
```

Property Value

A **Color** structure representing a system-defined color.

Requirements

Platforms: Windows 98, Windows NT 4.0,
Windows Millennium Edition, Windows 2000,
Windows XP Home Edition, Windows XP Professional,
Windows Server 2003 family,
.NET Compact Framework - Windows CE .NET

Color.Khaki Property

Gets a system-defined color.

```
[Visual Basic]
Public Shared ReadOnly Property Khaki As Color
[C#]
public static Color Khaki {get;}
[C++]
public: __property static Color get_Khaki();
[JScript]
public static function get Khaki() : Color;
```

Property Value

A **Color** structure representing a system-defined color.

Requirements

Platforms: Windows 98, Windows NT 4.0,
Windows Millennium Edition, Windows 2000,
Windows XP Home Edition, Windows XP Professional,
Windows Server 2003 family,
.NET Compact Framework - Windows CE .NET

Color.Lavender Property

Gets a system-defined color.

[Visual Basic]
```
Public Shared ReadOnly Property Lavender As Color
```
[C#]
```
public static Color Lavender {get;}
```
[C++]
```
public: __property static Color get_Lavender();
```
[JScript]
```
public static function get Lavender() : Color;
```

Property Value

A **Color** structure representing a system-defined color.

Requirements

Platforms: Windows 98, Windows NT 4.0, Windows Millennium Edition, Windows 2000, Windows XP Home Edition, Windows XP Professional, Windows Server 2003 family, .NET Compact Framework - Windows CE .NET

Color.LavenderBlush Property

Gets a system-defined color.

[Visual Basic]
```
Public Shared ReadOnly Property LavenderBlush As Color
```
[C#]
```
public static Color LavenderBlush {get;}
```
[C++]
```
public: __property static Color get_LavenderBlush();
```
[JScript]
```
public static function get LavenderBlush() : Color;
```

Property Value

A **Color** structure representing a system-defined color.

Requirements

Platforms: Windows 98, Windows NT 4.0, Windows Millennium Edition, Windows 2000, Windows XP Home Edition, Windows XP Professional, Windows Server 2003 family, .NET Compact Framework - Windows CE .NET

Color.LawnGreen Property

Gets a system-defined color.

[Visual Basic]
```
Public Shared ReadOnly Property LawnGreen As Color
```
[C#]
```
public static Color LawnGreen {get;}
```
[C++]
```
public: __property static Color get_LawnGreen();
```
[JScript]
```
public static function get LawnGreen() : Color;
```

Property Value

A **Color** structure representing a system-defined color.

Requirements

Platforms: Windows 98, Windows NT 4.0, Windows Millennium Edition, Windows 2000, Windows XP Home Edition, Windows XP Professional, Windows Server 2003 family, .NET Compact Framework - Windows CE .NET

Color.LemonChiffon Property

Gets a system-defined color.

[Visual Basic]
```
Public Shared ReadOnly Property LemonChiffon As Color
```
[C#]
```
public static Color LemonChiffon {get;}
```
[C++]
```
public: __property static Color get_LemonChiffon();
```
[JScript]
```
public static function get LemonChiffon() : Color;
```

Property Value

A **Color** structure representing a system-defined color.

Requirements

Platforms: Windows 98, Windows NT 4.0, Windows Millennium Edition, Windows 2000, Windows XP Home Edition, Windows XP Professional, Windows Server 2003 family, .NET Compact Framework - Windows CE .NET

Color.LightBlue Property

Gets a system-defined color.

[Visual Basic]
```
Public Shared ReadOnly Property LightBlue As Color
```
[C#]
```
public static Color LightBlue {get;}
```
[C++]
```
public: __property static Color get_LightBlue();
```
[JScript]
```
public static function get LightBlue() : Color;
```

Property Value

A **Color** structure representing a system-defined color.

Requirements

Platforms: Windows 98, Windows NT 4.0, Windows Millennium Edition, Windows 2000, Windows XP Home Edition, Windows XP Professional, Windows Server 2003 family, .NET Compact Framework - Windows CE .NET

Color.LightCoral Property

Gets a system-defined color.

[Visual Basic]
```
Public Shared ReadOnly Property LightCoral As Color
```
[C#]
```
public static Color LightCoral {get;}
```

```
[C++]
public: __property static Color get_LightCoral();
[JScript]
public static function get LightCoral() : Color;
```

Property Value

A **Color** structure representing a system-defined color.

Requirements

Platforms: Windows 98, Windows NT 4.0, Windows Millennium Edition, Windows 2000, Windows XP Home Edition, Windows XP Professional, Windows Server 2003 family, .NET Compact Framework - Windows CE .NET

Color.LightCyan Property

Gets a system-defined color.

```
[Visual Basic]
Public Shared ReadOnly Property LightCyan As Color
[C#]
public static Color LightCyan {get;}
[C++]
public: __property static Color get_LightCyan();
[JScript]
public static function get LightCyan() : Color;
```

Property Value

A **Color** structure representing a system-defined color.

Requirements

Platforms: Windows 98, Windows NT 4.0, Windows Millennium Edition, Windows 2000, Windows XP Home Edition, Windows XP Professional, Windows Server 2003 family, .NET Compact Framework - Windows CE .NET

Color.LightGoldenrodYellow Property

Gets a system-defined color.

```
[Visual Basic]
Public Shared ReadOnly Property LightGoldenrodYellow As Color
[C#]
public static Color LightGoldenrodYellow {get;}
[C++]
public: __property static Color get_LightGoldenrodYellow();
[JScript]
public static function get LightGoldenrodYellow() : Color;
```

Property Value

A **Color** structure representing a system-defined color.

Requirements

Platforms: Windows 98, Windows NT 4.0, Windows Millennium Edition, Windows 2000, Windows XP Home Edition, Windows XP Professional, Windows Server 2003 family, .NET Compact Framework - Windows CE .NET

Color.LightGray Property

Gets a system-defined color.

```
[Visual Basic]
Public Shared ReadOnly Property LightGray As Color
[C#]
public static Color LightGray {get;}
[C++]
public: __property static Color get_LightGray();
[JScript]
public static function get LightGray() : Color;
```

Property Value

A **Color** structure representing a system-defined color.

Requirements

Platforms: Windows 98, Windows NT 4.0, Windows Millennium Edition, Windows 2000, Windows XP Home Edition, Windows XP Professional, Windows Server 2003 family, .NET Compact Framework - Windows CE .NET

Color.LightGreen Property

Gets a system-defined color.

```
[Visual Basic]
Public Shared ReadOnly Property LightGreen As Color
[C#]
public static Color LightGreen {get;}
[C++]
public: __property static Color get_LightGreen();
[JScript]
public static function get LightGreen() : Color;
```

Property Value

A **Color** structure representing a system-defined color.

Requirements

Platforms: Windows 98, Windows NT 4.0, Windows Millennium Edition, Windows 2000, Windows XP Home Edition, Windows XP Professional, Windows Server 2003 family, .NET Compact Framework - Windows CE .NET

Color.LightPink Property

Gets a system-defined color.

```
[Visual Basic]
Public Shared ReadOnly Property LightPink As Color
[C#]
public static Color LightPink {get;}
[C++]
public: __property static Color get_LightPink();
[JScript]
public static function get LightPink() : Color;
```

Property Value

A **Color** structure representing a system-defined color.

Requirements

Platforms: Windows 98, Windows NT 4.0, Windows Millennium Edition, Windows 2000, Windows XP Home Edition, Windows XP Professional, Windows Server 2003 family, .NET Compact Framework - Windows CE .NET

Color.LightSalmon Property

Gets a system-defined color.

```
[Visual Basic]
Public Shared ReadOnly Property LightSalmon As Color
[C#]
public static Color LightSalmon {get;}
[C++]
public: __property static Color get_LightSalmon();
[JScript]
public static function get LightSalmon() : Color;
```

Property Value

A **Color** structure representing a system-defined color.

Requirements

Platforms: Windows 98, Windows NT 4.0, Windows Millennium Edition, Windows 2000, Windows XP Home Edition, Windows XP Professional, Windows Server 2003 family, .NET Compact Framework - Windows CE .NET

Color.LightSeaGreen Property

Gets a system-defined color.

```
[Visual Basic]
Public Shared ReadOnly Property LightSeaGreen As Color
[C#]
public static Color LightSeaGreen {get;}
[C++]
public: __property static Color get_LightSeaGreen();
[JScript]
public static function get LightSeaGreen() : Color;
```

Property Value

A **Color** structure representing a system-defined color.

Requirements

Platforms: Windows 98, Windows NT 4.0, Windows Millennium Edition, Windows 2000, Windows XP Home Edition, Windows XP Professional, Windows Server 2003 family, .NET Compact Framework - Windows CE .NET

Color.LightSkyBlue Property

Gets a system-defined color.

```
[Visual Basic]
Public Shared ReadOnly Property LightSkyBlue As Color
[C#]
public static Color LightSkyBlue {get;}
[C++]
public: __property static Color get_LightSkyBlue();
[JScript]
public static function get LightSkyBlue() : Color;
```

Property Value

A **Color** structure representing a system-defined color.

Requirements

Platforms: Windows 98, Windows NT 4.0, Windows Millennium Edition, Windows 2000, Windows XP Home Edition, Windows XP Professional, Windows Server 2003 family, .NET Compact Framework - Windows CE .NET

Color.LightSlateGray Property

Gets a system-defined color.

```
[Visual Basic]
Public Shared ReadOnly Property LightSlateGray As Color
[C#]
public static Color LightSlateGray {get;}
[C++]
public: __property static Color get_LightSlateGray();
[JScript]
public static function get LightSlateGray() : Color;
```

Property Value

A **Color** structure representing a system-defined color.

Requirements

Platforms: Windows 98, Windows NT 4.0, Windows Millennium Edition, Windows 2000, Windows XP Home Edition, Windows XP Professional, Windows Server 2003 family, .NET Compact Framework - Windows CE .NET

Color.LightSteelBlue Property

Gets a system-defined color.

```
[Visual Basic]
Public Shared ReadOnly Property LightSteelBlue As Color
[C#]
public static Color LightSteelBlue {get;}
[C++]
public: __property static Color get_LightSteelBlue();
[JScript]
public static function get LightSteelBlue() : Color;
```

Property Value

A **Color** structure representing a system-defined color.

Requirements

Platforms: Windows 98, Windows NT 4.0, Windows Millennium Edition, Windows 2000, Windows XP Home Edition, Windows XP Professional, Windows Server 2003 family, .NET Compact Framework - Windows CE .NET

Color.LightYellow Property

Gets a system-defined color.

[Visual Basic]
```
Public Shared ReadOnly Property LightYellow As Color
```
[C#]
```
public static Color LightYellow {get;}
```
[C++]
```
public: __property static Color get_LightYellow();
```
[JScript]
```
public static function get LightYellow() : Color;
```

Property Value

A **Color** structure representing a system-defined color.

Requirements

Platforms: Windows 98, Windows NT 4.0, Windows Millennium Edition, Windows 2000, Windows XP Home Edition, Windows XP Professional, Windows Server 2003 family, .NET Compact Framework - Windows CE .NET

Color.Lime Property

Gets a system-defined color.

[Visual Basic]
```
Public Shared ReadOnly Property Lime As Color
```
[C#]
```
public static Color Lime {get;}
```
[C++]
```
public: __property static Color get_Lime();
```
[JScript]
```
public static function get Lime() : Color;
```

Property Value

A **Color** structure representing a system-defined color.

Requirements

Platforms: Windows 98, Windows NT 4.0, Windows Millennium Edition, Windows 2000, Windows XP Home Edition, Windows XP Professional, Windows Server 2003 family, .NET Compact Framework - Windows CE .NET

Color.LimeGreen Property

Gets a system-defined color.

[Visual Basic]
```
Public Shared ReadOnly Property LimeGreen As Color
```
[C#]
```
public static Color LimeGreen {get;}
```
[C++]
```
public: __property static Color get_LimeGreen();
```
[JScript]
```
public static function get LimeGreen() : Color;
```

Property Value

A **Color** structure representing a system-defined color.

Requirements

Platforms: Windows 98, Windows NT 4.0, Windows Millennium Edition, Windows 2000, Windows XP Home Edition, Windows XP Professional, Windows Server 2003 family, .NET Compact Framework - Windows CE .NET

Color.Linen Property

Gets a system-defined color.

[Visual Basic]
```
Public Shared ReadOnly Property Linen As Color
```
[C#]
```
public static Color Linen {get;}
```
[C++]
```
public: __property static Color get_Linen();
```
[JScript]
```
public static function get Linen() : Color;
```

Property Value

A **Color** structure representing a system-defined color.

Requirements

Platforms: Windows 98, Windows NT 4.0, Windows Millennium Edition, Windows 2000, Windows XP Home Edition, Windows XP Professional, Windows Server 2003 family, .NET Compact Framework - Windows CE .NET

Color.Magenta Property

Gets a system-defined color.

[Visual Basic]
```
Public Shared ReadOnly Property Magenta As Color
```
[C#]
```
public static Color Magenta {get;}
```
[C++]
```
public: __property static Color get_Magenta();
```
[JScript]
```
public static function get Magenta() : Color;
```

Property Value

A **Color** structure representing a system-defined color.

Requirements

Platforms: Windows 98, Windows NT 4.0, Windows Millennium Edition, Windows 2000, Windows XP Home Edition, Windows XP Professional, Windows Server 2003 family, .NET Compact Framework - Windows CE .NET

Color.Maroon Property

Gets a system-defined color.

[Visual Basic]
```
Public Shared ReadOnly Property Maroon As Color
```
[C#]
```
public static Color Maroon {get;}
```

```
[C++]
public: __property static Color get_Maroon();
[JScript]
public static function get Maroon() : Color;
```

Property Value

A **Color** structure representing a system-defined color.

Requirements

Platforms: Windows 98, Windows NT 4.0, Windows Millennium Edition, Windows 2000, Windows XP Home Edition, Windows XP Professional, Windows Server 2003 family, .NET Compact Framework - Windows CE .NET

Color.MediumAquamarine Property

Gets a system-defined color.

```
[Visual Basic]
Public Shared ReadOnly Property MediumAquamarine As Color
[C#]
public static Color MediumAquamarine {get;}
[C++]
public: __property static Color get_MediumAquamarine();
[JScript]
public static function get MediumAquamarine() : Color;
```

Property Value

A **Color** structure representing a system-defined color.

Requirements

Platforms: Windows 98, Windows NT 4.0, Windows Millennium Edition, Windows 2000, Windows XP Home Edition, Windows XP Professional, Windows Server 2003 family, .NET Compact Framework - Windows CE .NET

Color.MediumBlue Property

Gets a system-defined color.

```
[Visual Basic]
Public Shared ReadOnly Property MediumBlue As Color
[C#]
public static Color MediumBlue {get;}
[C++]
public: __property static Color get_MediumBlue();
[JScript]
public static function get MediumBlue() : Color;
```

Property Value

A **Color** structure representing a system-defined color.

Requirements

Platforms: Windows 98, Windows NT 4.0, Windows Millennium Edition, Windows 2000, Windows XP Home Edition, Windows XP Professional, Windows Server 2003 family, .NET Compact Framework - Windows CE .NET

Color.MediumOrchid Property

Gets a system-defined color.

```
[Visual Basic]
Public Shared ReadOnly Property MediumOrchid As Color
[C#]
public static Color MediumOrchid {get;}
[C++]
public: __property static Color get_MediumOrchid();
[JScript]
public static function get MediumOrchid() : Color;
```

Property Value

A **Color** structure representing a system-defined color.

Requirements

Platforms: Windows 98, Windows NT 4.0, Windows Millennium Edition, Windows 2000, Windows XP Home Edition, Windows XP Professional, Windows Server 2003 family, .NET Compact Framework - Windows CE .NET

Color.MediumPurple Property

Gets a system-defined color.

```
[Visual Basic]
Public Shared ReadOnly Property MediumPurple As Color
[C#]
public static Color MediumPurple {get;}
[C++]
public: __property static Color get_MediumPurple();
[JScript]
public static function get MediumPurple() : Color;
```

Property Value

A **Color** structure representing a system-defined color.

Requirements

Platforms: Windows 98, Windows NT 4.0, Windows Millennium Edition, Windows 2000, Windows XP Home Edition, Windows XP Professional, Windows Server 2003 family, .NET Compact Framework - Windows CE .NET

Color.MediumSeaGreen Property

Gets a system-defined color.

```
[Visual Basic]
Public Shared ReadOnly Property MediumSeaGreen As Color
[C#]
public static Color MediumSeaGreen {get;}
[C++]
public: __property static Color get_MediumSeaGreen();
[JScript]
public static function get MediumSeaGreen() : Color;
```

Property Value

A **Color** structure representing a system-defined color.

Requirements

Platforms: Windows 98, Windows NT 4.0, Windows Millennium Edition, Windows 2000, Windows XP Home Edition, Windows XP Professional, Windows Server 2003 family, .NET Compact Framework - Windows CE .NET

Color.MediumSlateBlue Property

Gets a system-defined color.

```
[Visual Basic]
Public Shared ReadOnly Property MediumSlateBlue As Color
[C#]
public static Color MediumSlateBlue {get;}
[C++]
public: __property static Color get_MediumSlateBlue();
[JScript]
public static function get MediumSlateBlue() : Color;
```

Property Value

A **Color** structure representing a system-defined color.

Requirements

Platforms: Windows 98, Windows NT 4.0, Windows Millennium Edition, Windows 2000, Windows XP Home Edition, Windows XP Professional, Windows Server 2003 family, .NET Compact Framework - Windows CE .NET

Color.MediumSpringGreen Property

Gets a system-defined color.

```
[Visual Basic]
Public Shared ReadOnly Property MediumSpringGreen As Color
[C#]
public static Color MediumSpringGreen {get;}
[C++]
public: __property static Color get_MediumSpringGreen();
[JScript]
public static function get MediumSpringGreen() : Color;
```

Property Value

A **Color** structure representing a system-defined color.

Requirements

Platforms: Windows 98, Windows NT 4.0, Windows Millennium Edition, Windows 2000, Windows XP Home Edition, Windows XP Professional, Windows Server 2003 family, .NET Compact Framework - Windows CE .NET

Color.MediumTurquoise Property

Gets a system-defined color.

```
[Visual Basic]
Public Shared ReadOnly Property MediumTurquoise As Color
[C#]
public static Color MediumTurquoise {get;}
[C++]
public: __property static Color get_MediumTurquoise();
[JScript]
public static function get MediumTurquoise() : Color;
```

Property Value

A **Color** structure representing a system-defined color.

Requirements

Platforms: Windows 98, Windows NT 4.0, Windows Millennium Edition, Windows 2000, Windows XP Home Edition, Windows XP Professional, Windows Server 2003 family, .NET Compact Framework - Windows CE .NET

Color.MediumVioletRed Property

Gets a system-defined color.

```
[Visual Basic]
Public Shared ReadOnly Property MediumVioletRed As Color
[C#]
public static Color MediumVioletRed {get;}
[C++]
public: __property static Color get_MediumVioletRed();
[JScript]
public static function get MediumVioletRed() : Color;
```

Property Value

A **Color** structure representing a system-defined color.

Requirements

Platforms: Windows 98, Windows NT 4.0, Windows Millennium Edition, Windows 2000, Windows XP Home Edition, Windows XP Professional, Windows Server 2003 family, .NET Compact Framework - Windows CE .NET

Color.MidnightBlue Property

Gets a system-defined color.

```
[Visual Basic]
Public Shared ReadOnly Property MidnightBlue As Color
[C#]
public static Color MidnightBlue {get;}
[C++]
public: __property static Color get_MidnightBlue();
[JScript]
public static function get MidnightBlue() : Color;
```

Property Value

A **Color** structure representing a system-defined color.

Requirements

Platforms: Windows 98, Windows NT 4.0, Windows Millennium Edition, Windows 2000, Windows XP Home Edition, Windows XP Professional, Windows Server 2003 family, .NET Compact Framework - Windows CE .NET

Color.MintCream Property

Gets a system-defined color.

```
[Visual Basic]
Public Shared ReadOnly Property MintCream As Color
[C#]
public static Color MintCream {get;}
[C++]
public: __property static Color get_MintCream();
[JScript]
public static function get MintCream() : Color;
```

Property Value

A **Color** structure representing a system-defined color.

Requirements

Platforms: Windows 98, Windows NT 4.0, Windows Millennium Edition, Windows 2000, Windows XP Home Edition, Windows XP Professional, Windows Server 2003 family, .NET Compact Framework - Windows CE .NET

Color.MistyRose Property

Gets a system-defined color.

```
[Visual Basic]
Public Shared ReadOnly Property MistyRose As Color
[C#]
public static Color MistyRose {get;}
[C++]
public: __property static Color get_MistyRose();
[JScript]
public static function get MistyRose() : Color;
```

Property Value

A **Color** structure representing a system-defined color.

Requirements

Platforms: Windows 98, Windows NT 4.0, Windows Millennium Edition, Windows 2000, Windows XP Home Edition, Windows XP Professional, Windows Server 2003 family, .NET Compact Framework - Windows CE .NET

Color.Moccasin Property

Gets a system-defined color.

```
[Visual Basic]
Public Shared ReadOnly Property Moccasin As Color
[C#]
public static Color Moccasin {get;}
[C++]
public: __property static Color get_Moccasin();
[JScript]
public static function get Moccasin() : Color;
```

Property Value

A **Color** structure representing a system-defined color.

Requirements

Platforms: Windows 98, Windows NT 4.0, Windows Millennium Edition, Windows 2000, Windows XP Home Edition, Windows XP Professional, Windows Server 2003 family, .NET Compact Framework - Windows CE .NET

Color.Name Property

Gets the name of this **Color** Name. This will either return the user-defined name of the color, if the color was created from a name, or the name of the known color. For custom colors, the RGB value will be returned.

```
[Visual Basic]
Public ReadOnly Property Name As String
[C#]
public string Name {get;}
[C++]
public: __property String* get_Name();
[JScript]
public function get Name() : String;
```

Property Value

The name of this **Color**.

Remarks

This method returns either the user defined name of the color, if the color was created from a name, or the name of the known color. For custom colors, the RGB value is returned.

Requirements

Platforms: Windows 98, Windows NT 4.0, Windows Millennium Edition, Windows 2000, Windows XP Home Edition, Windows XP Professional, Windows Server 2003 family

Color.NavajoWhite Property

Gets a system-defined color.

```
[Visual Basic]
Public Shared ReadOnly Property NavajoWhite As Color
[C#]
public static Color NavajoWhite {get;}
[C++]
public: __property static Color get_NavajoWhite();
[JScript]
public static function get NavajoWhite() : Color;
```

Property Value

A **Color** structure representing a system-defined color.

Requirements

Platforms: Windows 98, Windows NT 4.0, Windows Millennium Edition, Windows 2000, Windows XP Home Edition, Windows XP Professional, Windows Server 2003 family, .NET Compact Framework - Windows CE .NET

Color.Navy Property

Gets a system-defined color.

[Visual Basic]
```
Public Shared ReadOnly Property Navy As Color
```
[C#]
```
public static Color Navy {get;}
```
[C++]
```
public: __property static Color get_Navy();
```
[JScript]
```
public static function get Navy() : Color;
```

Property Value

A **Color** structure representing a system-defined color.

Requirements

Platforms: Windows 98, Windows NT 4.0, Windows Millennium Edition, Windows 2000, Windows XP Home Edition, Windows XP Professional, Windows Server 2003 family, .NET Compact Framework - Windows CE .NET

Color.OldLace Property

Gets a system-defined color.

[Visual Basic]
```
Public Shared ReadOnly Property OldLace As Color
```
[C#]
```
public static Color OldLace {get;}
```
[C++]
```
public: __property static Color get_OldLace();
```
[JScript]
```
public static function get OldLace() : Color;
```

Property Value

A **Color** structure representing a system-defined color.

Requirements

Platforms: Windows 98, Windows NT 4.0, Windows Millennium Edition, Windows 2000, Windows XP Home Edition, Windows XP Professional, Windows Server 2003 family, .NET Compact Framework - Windows CE .NET

Color.Olive Property

Gets a system-defined color.

[Visual Basic]
```
Public Shared ReadOnly Property Olive As Color
```
[C#]
```
public static Color Olive {get;}
```
[C++]
```
public: __property static Color get_Olive();
```
[JScript]
```
public static function get Olive() : Color;
```

Property Value

A **Color** structure representing a system-defined color.

Requirements

Platforms: Windows 98, Windows NT 4.0, Windows Millennium Edition, Windows 2000, Windows XP Home Edition, Windows XP Professional, Windows Server 2003 family, .NET Compact Framework - Windows CE .NET

Color.OliveDrab Property

Gets a system-defined color.

[Visual Basic]
```
Public Shared ReadOnly Property OliveDrab As Color
```
[C#]
```
public static Color OliveDrab {get;}
```
[C++]
```
public: __property static Color get_OliveDrab();
```
[JScript]
```
public static function get OliveDrab() : Color;
```

Property Value

A **Color** structure representing a system-defined color.

Requirements

Platforms: Windows 98, Windows NT 4.0, Windows Millennium Edition, Windows 2000, Windows XP Home Edition, Windows XP Professional, Windows Server 2003 family, .NET Compact Framework - Windows CE .NET

Color.Orange Property

Gets a system-defined color.

[Visual Basic]
```
Public Shared ReadOnly Property Orange As Color
```
[C#]
```
public static Color Orange {get;}
```
[C++]
```
public: __property static Color get_Orange();
```
[JScript]
```
public static function get Orange() : Color;
```

Property Value

A **Color** structure representing a system-defined color.

Requirements

Platforms: Windows 98, Windows NT 4.0, Windows Millennium Edition, Windows 2000, Windows XP Home Edition, Windows XP Professional, Windows Server 2003 family, .NET Compact Framework - Windows CE .NET

Color.OrangeRed Property

Gets a system-defined color.

[Visual Basic]
```
Public Shared ReadOnly Property OrangeRed As Color
```
[C#]
```
public static Color OrangeRed {get;}
```

```
[C++]
public: __property static Color get_OrangeRed();
[JScript]
public static function get OrangeRed() : Color;
```

Property Value

A **Color** structure representing a system-defined color.

Requirements

Platforms: Windows 98, Windows NT 4.0, Windows Millennium Edition, Windows 2000, Windows XP Home Edition, Windows XP Professional, Windows Server 2003 family, .NET Compact Framework - Windows CE .NET

Color.Orchid Property

Gets a system-defined color.

```
[Visual Basic]
Public Shared ReadOnly Property Orchid As Color
[C#]
public static Color Orchid {get;}
[C++]
public: __property static Color get_Orchid();
[JScript]
public static function get Orchid() : Color;
```

Property Value

A **Color** structure representing a system-defined color.

Requirements

Platforms: Windows 98, Windows NT 4.0, Windows Millennium Edition, Windows 2000, Windows XP Home Edition, Windows XP Professional, Windows Server 2003 family, .NET Compact Framework - Windows CE .NET

Color.PaleGoldenrod Property

Gets a system-defined color.

```
[Visual Basic]
Public Shared ReadOnly Property PaleGoldenrod As Color
[C#]
public static Color PaleGoldenrod {get;}
[C++]
public: __property static Color get_PaleGoldenrod();
[JScript]
public static function get PaleGoldenrod() : Color;
```

Property Value

A **Color** structure representing a system-defined color.

Requirements

Platforms: Windows 98, Windows NT 4.0, Windows Millennium Edition, Windows 2000, Windows XP Home Edition, Windows XP Professional, Windows Server 2003 family, .NET Compact Framework - Windows CE .NET

Color.PaleGreen Property

Gets a system-defined color.

```
[Visual Basic]
Public Shared ReadOnly Property PaleGreen As Color
[C#]
public static Color PaleGreen {get;}
[C++]
public: __property static Color get_PaleGreen();
[JScript]
public static function get PaleGreen() : Color;
```

Property Value

A **Color** structure representing a system-defined color.

Requirements

Platforms: Windows 98, Windows NT 4.0, Windows Millennium Edition, Windows 2000, Windows XP Home Edition, Windows XP Professional, Windows Server 2003 family, .NET Compact Framework - Windows CE .NET

Color.PaleTurquoise Property

Gets a system-defined color.

```
[Visual Basic]
Public Shared ReadOnly Property PaleTurquoise As Color
[C#]
public static Color PaleTurquoise {get;}
[C++]
public: __property static Color get_PaleTurquoise();
[JScript]
public static function get PaleTurquoise() : Color;
```

Property Value

A **Color** structure representing a system-defined color.

Requirements

Platforms: Windows 98, Windows NT 4.0, Windows Millennium Edition, Windows 2000, Windows XP Home Edition, Windows XP Professional, Windows Server 2003 family, .NET Compact Framework - Windows CE .NET

Color.PaleVioletRed Property

Gets a system-defined color.

```
[Visual Basic]
Public Shared ReadOnly Property PaleVioletRed As Color
[C#]
public static Color PaleVioletRed {get;}
[C++]
public: __property static Color get_PaleVioletRed();
[JScript]
public static function get PaleVioletRed() : Color;
```

Property Value

A **Color** structure representing a system-defined color.

Requirements

Platforms: Windows 98, Windows NT 4.0, Windows Millennium Edition, Windows 2000, Windows XP Home Edition, Windows XP Professional, Windows Server 2003 family, .NET Compact Framework - Windows CE .NET

Color.PapayaWhip Property

Gets a system-defined color.

```
[Visual Basic]
Public Shared ReadOnly Property PapayaWhip As Color
[C#]
public static Color PapayaWhip {get;}
[C++]
public: __property static Color get_PapayaWhip();
[JScript]
public static function get PapayaWhip() : Color;
```

Property Value

A **Color** structure representing a system-defined color.

Requirements

Platforms: Windows 98, Windows NT 4.0, Windows Millennium Edition, Windows 2000, Windows XP Home Edition, Windows XP Professional, Windows Server 2003 family, .NET Compact Framework - Windows CE .NET

Color.PeachPuff Property

Gets a system-defined color.

```
[Visual Basic]
Public Shared ReadOnly Property PeachPuff As Color
[C#]
public static Color PeachPuff {get;}
[C++]
public: __property static Color get_PeachPuff();
[JScript]
public static function get PeachPuff() : Color;
```

Property Value

A **Color** structure representing a system-defined color.

Requirements

Platforms: Windows 98, Windows NT 4.0, Windows Millennium Edition, Windows 2000, Windows XP Home Edition, Windows XP Professional, Windows Server 2003 family, .NET Compact Framework - Windows CE .NET

Color.Peru Property

Gets a system-defined color.

```
[Visual Basic]
Public Shared ReadOnly Property Peru As Color
[C#]
public static Color Peru {get;}
[C++]
public: __property static Color get_Peru();
[JScript]
public static function get Peru() : Color;
```

Property Value

A **Color** structure representing a system-defined color.

Requirements

Platforms: Windows 98, Windows NT 4.0, Windows Millennium Edition, Windows 2000, Windows XP Home Edition, Windows XP Professional, Windows Server 2003 family, .NET Compact Framework - Windows CE .NET

Color.Pink Property

Gets a system-defined color.

```
[Visual Basic]
Public Shared ReadOnly Property Pink As Color
[C#]
public static Color Pink {get;}
[C++]
public: __property static Color get_Pink();
[JScript]
public static function get Pink() : Color;
```

Property Value

A **Color** structure representing a system-defined color.

Requirements

Platforms: Windows 98, Windows NT 4.0, Windows Millennium Edition, Windows 2000, Windows XP Home Edition, Windows XP Professional, Windows Server 2003 family, .NET Compact Framework - Windows CE .NET

Color.Plum Property

Gets a system-defined color.

```
[Visual Basic]
Public Shared ReadOnly Property Plum As Color
[C#]
public static Color Plum {get;}
[C++]
public: __property static Color get_Plum();
[JScript]
public static function get Plum() : Color;
```

Property Value

A **Color** structure representing a system-defined color.

Requirements

Platforms: Windows 98, Windows NT 4.0, Windows Millennium Edition, Windows 2000, Windows XP Home Edition, Windows XP Professional, Windows Server 2003 family, .NET Compact Framework - Windows CE .NET

Color.PowderBlue Property

Gets a system-defined color.

[Visual Basic]
```
Public Shared ReadOnly Property PowderBlue As Color
```
[C#]
```
public static Color PowderBlue {get;}
```
[C++]
```
public: __property static Color get_PowderBlue();
```
[JScript]
```
public static function get PowderBlue() : Color;
```

Property Value

A **Color** structure representing a system-defined color.

Requirements

Platforms: Windows 98, Windows NT 4.0, Windows Millennium Edition, Windows 2000, Windows XP Home Edition, Windows XP Professional, Windows Server 2003 family, .NET Compact Framework - Windows CE .NET

Color.Purple Property

Gets a system-defined color.

[Visual Basic]
```
Public Shared ReadOnly Property Purple As Color
```
[C#]
```
public static Color Purple {get;}
```
[C++]
```
public: __property static Color get_Purple();
```
[JScript]
```
public static function get Purple() : Color;
```

Property Value

A **Color** structure representing a system-defined color.

Requirements

Platforms: Windows 98, Windows NT 4.0, Windows Millennium Edition, Windows 2000, Windows XP Home Edition, Windows XP Professional, Windows Server 2003 family, .NET Compact Framework - Windows CE .NET

Color.R Property

Gets the red component value of this **Color** structure.

[Visual Basic]
```
Public ReadOnly Property R As Byte
```
[C#]
```
public byte R {get;}
```
[C++]
```
public: __property unsigned char get_R();
```
[JScript]
```
public function get R() : Byte;
```

Property Value

The red component value of this **Color** structure.

Requirements

Platforms: Windows 98, Windows NT 4.0, Windows Millennium Edition, Windows 2000, Windows XP Home Edition, Windows XP Professional, Windows Server 2003 family, .NET Compact Framework - Windows CE .NET

Color.Red Property

Gets a system-defined color.

[Visual Basic]
```
Public Shared ReadOnly Property Red As Color
```
[C#]
```
public static Color Red {get;}
```
[C++]
```
public: __property static Color get_Red();
```
[JScript]
```
public static function get Red() : Color;
```

Property Value

A **Color** structure representing a system-defined color.

Requirements

Platforms: Windows 98, Windows NT 4.0, Windows Millennium Edition, Windows 2000, Windows XP Home Edition, Windows XP Professional, Windows Server 2003 family, .NET Compact Framework - Windows CE .NET

Color.RosyBrown Property

Gets a system-defined color.

[Visual Basic]
```
Public Shared ReadOnly Property RosyBrown As Color
```
[C#]
```
public static Color RosyBrown {get;}
```
[C++]
```
public: __property static Color get_RosyBrown();
```
[JScript]
```
public static function get RosyBrown() : Color;
```

Property Value

A **Color** structure representing a system-defined color.

Requirements

Platforms: Windows 98, Windows NT 4.0, Windows Millennium Edition, Windows 2000, Windows XP Home Edition, Windows XP Professional, Windows Server 2003 family, .NET Compact Framework - Windows CE .NET

Color.RoyalBlue Property

Gets a system-defined color.

[Visual Basic]
```
Public Shared ReadOnly Property RoyalBlue As Color
```
[C#]
```
public static Color RoyalBlue {get;}
```

[C++]
```
public: __property static Color get_RoyalBlue();
```
[JScript]
```
public static function get RoyalBlue() : Color;
```

Property Value

A **Color** structure representing a system-defined color.

Requirements

Platforms: Windows 98, Windows NT 4.0, Windows Millennium Edition, Windows 2000, Windows XP Home Edition, Windows XP Professional, Windows Server 2003 family, .NET Compact Framework - Windows CE .NET

Color.SaddleBrown Property

Gets a system-defined color.

[Visual Basic]
```
Public Shared ReadOnly Property SaddleBrown As Color
```
[C#]
```
public static Color SaddleBrown {get;}
```
[C++]
```
public: __property static Color get_SaddleBrown();
```
[JScript]
```
public static function get SaddleBrown() : Color;
```

Property Value

A **Color** structure representing a system-defined color.

Requirements

Platforms: Windows 98, Windows NT 4.0, Windows Millennium Edition, Windows 2000, Windows XP Home Edition, Windows XP Professional, Windows Server 2003 family, .NET Compact Framework - Windows CE .NET

Color.Salmon Property

Gets a system-defined color.

[Visual Basic]
```
Public Shared ReadOnly Property Salmon As Color
```
[C#]
```
public static Color Salmon {get;}
```
[C++]
```
public: __property static Color get_Salmon();
```
[JScript]
```
public static function get Salmon() : Color;
```

Property Value

A **Color** structure representing a system-defined color.

Requirements

Platforms: Windows 98, Windows NT 4.0, Windows Millennium Edition, Windows 2000, Windows XP Home Edition, Windows XP Professional, Windows Server 2003 family, .NET Compact Framework - Windows CE .NET

Color.SandyBrown Property

Gets a system-defined color.

[Visual Basic]
```
Public Shared ReadOnly Property SandyBrown As Color
```
[C#]
```
public static Color SandyBrown {get;}
```
[C++]
```
public: __property static Color get_SandyBrown();
```
[JScript]
```
public static function get SandyBrown() : Color;
```

Property Value

A **Color** structure representing a system-defined color.

Requirements

Platforms: Windows 98, Windows NT 4.0, Windows Millennium Edition, Windows 2000, Windows XP Home Edition, Windows XP Professional, Windows Server 2003 family, .NET Compact Framework - Windows CE .NET

Color.SeaGreen Property

Gets a system-defined color.

[Visual Basic]
```
Public Shared ReadOnly Property SeaGreen As Color
```
[C#]
```
public static Color SeaGreen {get;}
```
[C++]
```
public: __property static Color get_SeaGreen();
```
[JScript]
```
public static function get SeaGreen() : Color;
```

Property Value

A **Color** structure representing a system-defined color.

Requirements

Platforms: Windows 98, Windows NT 4.0, Windows Millennium Edition, Windows 2000, Windows XP Home Edition, Windows XP Professional, Windows Server 2003 family, .NET Compact Framework - Windows CE .NET

Color.SeaShell Property

Gets a system-defined color.

[Visual Basic]
```
Public Shared ReadOnly Property SeaShell As Color
```
[C#]
```
public static Color SeaShell {get;}
```
[C++]
```
public: __property static Color get_SeaShell();
```
[JScript]
```
public static function get SeaShell() : Color;
```

Property Value

A **Color** structure representing a system-defined color.

Requirements

Platforms: Windows 98, Windows NT 4.0, Windows Millennium Edition, Windows 2000, Windows XP Home Edition, Windows XP Professional, Windows Server 2003 family, .NET Compact Framework - Windows CE .NET

Color.Sienna Property

Gets a system-defined color.

```
[Visual Basic]
Public Shared ReadOnly Property Sienna As Color
[C#]
public static Color Sienna {get;}
[C++]
public: __property static Color get_Sienna();
[JScript]
public static function get Sienna() : Color;
```

Property Value

A **Color** structure representing a system-defined color.

Requirements

Platforms: Windows 98, Windows NT 4.0, Windows Millennium Edition, Windows 2000, Windows XP Home Edition, Windows XP Professional, Windows Server 2003 family, .NET Compact Framework - Windows CE .NET

Color.Silver Property

Gets a system-defined color.

```
[Visual Basic]
Public Shared ReadOnly Property Silver As Color
[C#]
public static Color Silver {get;}
[C++]
public: __property static Color get_Silver();
[JScript]
public static function get Silver() : Color;
```

Property Value

A **Color** structure representing a system-defined color.

Requirements

Platforms: Windows 98, Windows NT 4.0, Windows Millennium Edition, Windows 2000, Windows XP Home Edition, Windows XP Professional, Windows Server 2003 family, .NET Compact Framework - Windows CE .NET

Color.SkyBlue Property

Gets a system-defined color.

```
[Visual Basic]
Public Shared ReadOnly Property SkyBlue As Color
[C#]
public static Color SkyBlue {get;}
[C++]
public: __property static Color get_SkyBlue();
[JScript]
public static function get SkyBlue() : Color;
```

Property Value

A **Color** structure representing a system-defined color.

Requirements

Platforms: Windows 98, Windows NT 4.0, Windows Millennium Edition, Windows 2000, Windows XP Home Edition, Windows XP Professional, Windows Server 2003 family, .NET Compact Framework - Windows CE .NET

Color.SlateBlue Property

Gets a system-defined color.

```
[Visual Basic]
Public Shared ReadOnly Property SlateBlue As Color
[C#]
public static Color SlateBlue {get;}
[C++]
public: __property static Color get_SlateBlue();
[JScript]
public static function get SlateBlue() : Color;
```

Property Value

A **Color** structure representing a system-defined color.

Requirements

Platforms: Windows 98, Windows NT 4.0, Windows Millennium Edition, Windows 2000, Windows XP Home Edition, Windows XP Professional, Windows Server 2003 family, .NET Compact Framework - Windows CE .NET

Color.SlateGray Property

Gets a system-defined color.

```
[Visual Basic]
Public Shared ReadOnly Property SlateGray As Color
[C#]
public static Color SlateGray {get;}
[C++]
public: __property static Color get_SlateGray();
[JScript]
public static function get SlateGray() : Color;
```

Property Value

A **Color** structure representing a system-defined color.

Requirements

Platforms: Windows 98, Windows NT 4.0, Windows Millennium Edition, Windows 2000, Windows XP Home Edition, Windows XP Professional, Windows Server 2003 family, .NET Compact Framework - Windows CE .NET

Color.Snow Property

Gets a system-defined color.

[Visual Basic]
```
Public Shared ReadOnly Property Snow As Color
```
[C#]
```
public static Color Snow {get;}
```
[C++]
```
public: __property static Color get_Snow();
```
[JScript]
```
public static function get Snow() : Color;
```

Property Value

A **Color** structure representing a system-defined color.

Requirements

Platforms: Windows 98, Windows NT 4.0, Windows Millennium Edition, Windows 2000, Windows XP Home Edition, Windows XP Professional, Windows Server 2003 family, .NET Compact Framework - Windows CE .NET

Color.SpringGreen Property

Gets a system-defined color.

[Visual Basic]
```
Public Shared ReadOnly Property SpringGreen As Color
```
[C#]
```
public static Color SpringGreen {get;}
```
[C++]
```
public: __property static Color get_SpringGreen();
```
[JScript]
```
public static function get SpringGreen() : Color;
```

Property Value

A **Color** structure representing a system-defined color.

Requirements

Platforms: Windows 98, Windows NT 4.0, Windows Millennium Edition, Windows 2000, Windows XP Home Edition, Windows XP Professional, Windows Server 2003 family, .NET Compact Framework - Windows CE .NET

Color.SteelBlue Property

Gets a system-defined color.

[Visual Basic]
```
Public Shared ReadOnly Property SteelBlue As Color
```
[C#]
```
public static Color SteelBlue {get;}
```
[C++]
```
public: __property static Color get_SteelBlue();
```
[JScript]
```
public static function get SteelBlue() : Color;
```

Property Value

A **Color** structure representing a system-defined color.

Requirements

Platforms: Windows 98, Windows NT 4.0, Windows Millennium Edition, Windows 2000, Windows XP Home Edition, Windows XP Professional, Windows Server 2003 family, .NET Compact Framework - Windows CE .NET

Color.Tan Property

Gets a system-defined color.

[Visual Basic]
```
Public Shared ReadOnly Property Tan As Color
```
[C#]
```
public static Color Tan {get;}
```
[C++]
```
public: __property static Color get_Tan();
```
[JScript]
```
public static function get Tan() : Color;
```

Property Value

A **Color** structure representing a system-defined color.

Requirements

Platforms: Windows 98, Windows NT 4.0, Windows Millennium Edition, Windows 2000, Windows XP Home Edition, Windows XP Professional, Windows Server 2003 family, .NET Compact Framework - Windows CE .NET

Color.Teal Property

Gets a system-defined color.

[Visual Basic]
```
Public Shared ReadOnly Property Teal As Color
```
[C#]
```
public static Color Teal {get;}
```
[C++]
```
public: __property static Color get_Teal();
```
[JScript]
```
public static function get Teal() : Color;
```

Property Value

A **Color** structure representing a system-defined color.

Requirements

Platforms: Windows 98, Windows NT 4.0, Windows Millennium Edition, Windows 2000, Windows XP Home Edition, Windows XP Professional, Windows Server 2003 family, .NET Compact Framework - Windows CE .NET

Color.Thistle Property

Gets a system-defined color.

[Visual Basic]
```
Public Shared ReadOnly Property Thistle As Color
```
[C#]
```
public static Color Thistle {get;}
```

```
[C++]
public: __property static Color get_Thistle();
[JScript]
public static function get Thistle() : Color;
```

Property Value

A **Color** structure representing a system-defined color.

Requirements

Platforms: Windows 98, Windows NT 4.0, Windows Millennium Edition, Windows 2000, Windows XP Home Edition, Windows XP Professional, Windows Server 2003 family, .NET Compact Framework - Windows CE .NET

Color.Tomato Property

Gets a system-defined color.

```
[Visual Basic]
Public Shared ReadOnly Property Tomato As Color
[C#]
public static Color Tomato {get;}
[C++]
public: __property static Color get_Tomato();
[JScript]
public static function get Tomato() : Color;
```

Property Value

A **Color** structure representing a system-defined color.

Requirements

Platforms: Windows 98, Windows NT 4.0, Windows Millennium Edition, Windows 2000, Windows XP Home Edition, Windows XP Professional, Windows Server 2003 family, .NET Compact Framework - Windows CE .NET

Color.Transparent Property

Gets a system-defined color.

```
[Visual Basic]
Public Shared ReadOnly Property Transparent As Color
[C#]
public static Color Transparent {get;}
[C++]
public: __property static Color get_Transparent();
[JScript]
public static function get Transparent() : Color;
```

Property Value

A **Color** structure representing a system-defined color.

Requirements

Platforms: Windows 98, Windows NT 4.0, Windows Millennium Edition, Windows 2000, Windows XP Home Edition, Windows XP Professional, Windows Server 2003 family, .NET Compact Framework - Windows CE .NET

Color.Turquoise Property

Gets a system-defined color.

```
[Visual Basic]
Public Shared ReadOnly Property Turquoise As Color
[C#]
public static Color Turquoise {get;}
[C++]
public: __property static Color get_Turquoise();
[JScript]
public static function get Turquoise() : Color;
```

Property Value

A **Color** structure representing a system-defined color.

Requirements

Platforms: Windows 98, Windows NT 4.0, Windows Millennium Edition, Windows 2000, Windows XP Home Edition, Windows XP Professional, Windows Server 2003 family, .NET Compact Framework - Windows CE .NET

Color.Violet Property

Gets a system-defined color.

```
[Visual Basic]
Public Shared ReadOnly Property Violet As Color
[C#]
public static Color Violet {get;}
[C++]
public: __property static Color get_Violet();
[JScript]
public static function get Violet() : Color;
```

Property Value

A **Color** structure representing a system-defined color.

Requirements

Platforms: Windows 98, Windows NT 4.0, Windows Millennium Edition, Windows 2000, Windows XP Home Edition, Windows XP Professional, Windows Server 2003 family, .NET Compact Framework - Windows CE .NET

Color.Wheat Property

Gets a system-defined color.

```
[Visual Basic]
Public Shared ReadOnly Property Wheat As Color
[C#]
public static Color Wheat {get;}
[C++]
public: __property static Color get_Wheat();
[JScript]
public static function get Wheat() : Color;
```

Property Value

A **Color** structure representing a system-defined color.

Requirements

Platforms: Windows 98, Windows NT 4.0, Windows Millennium Edition, Windows 2000, Windows XP Home Edition, Windows XP Professional, Windows Server 2003 family, .NET Compact Framework - Windows CE .NET

Color.White Property

Gets a system-defined color.

```
[Visual Basic]
Public Shared ReadOnly Property White As Color
[C#]
public static Color White {get;}
[C++]
public: __property static Color get_White();
[JScript]
public static function get White() : Color;
```

Property Value

A **Color** structure representing a system-defined color.

Requirements

Platforms: Windows 98, Windows NT 4.0, Windows Millennium Edition, Windows 2000, Windows XP Home Edition, Windows XP Professional, Windows Server 2003 family, .NET Compact Framework - Windows CE .NET

Color.WhiteSmoke Property

Gets a system-defined color.

```
[Visual Basic]
Public Shared ReadOnly Property WhiteSmoke As Color
[C#]
public static Color WhiteSmoke {get;}
[C++]
public: __property static Color get_WhiteSmoke();
[JScript]
public static function get WhiteSmoke() : Color;
```

Property Value

A **Color** structure representing a system-defined color.

Requirements

Platforms: Windows 98, Windows NT 4.0, Windows Millennium Edition, Windows 2000, Windows XP Home Edition, Windows XP Professional, Windows Server 2003 family, .NET Compact Framework - Windows CE .NET

Color.Yellow Property

Gets a system-defined color.

```
[Visual Basic]
Public Shared ReadOnly Property Yellow As Color
[C#]
public static Color Yellow {get;}
[C++]
public: __property static Color get_Yellow();
[JScript]
public static function get Yellow() : Color;
```

Property Value

A **Color** structure representing a system-defined color.

Requirements

Platforms: Windows 98, Windows NT 4.0, Windows Millennium Edition, Windows 2000, Windows XP Home Edition, Windows XP Professional, Windows Server 2003 family, .NET Compact Framework - Windows CE .NET

Color.YellowGreen Property

Gets a system-defined color.

```
[Visual Basic]
Public Shared ReadOnly Property YellowGreen As Color
[C#]
public static Color YellowGreen {get;}
[C++]
public: __property static Color get_YellowGreen();
[JScript]
public static function get YellowGreen() : Color;
```

Property Value

A **Color** structure representing a system-defined color.

Requirements

Platforms: Windows 98, Windows NT 4.0, Windows Millennium Edition, Windows 2000, Windows XP Home Edition, Windows XP Professional, Windows Server 2003 family, .NET Compact Framework - Windows CE .NET

Color.Equals Method

Tests whether the specified object is a **Color** structure and is equivalent to this **Color** structure.

```
[Visual Basic]
Overrides Public Function Equals( _
   ByVal obj As Object _
) As Boolean
[C#]
public override bool Equals(
   object obj
);
[C++]
public: bool Equals(
   Object* obj
);
[JScript]
public override function Equals(
   obj : Object
) : Boolean;
```

Parameters

obj

The object to test.

Return Value

This method returns **true** if *obj* is a **Color** structure equivalent to this **Color** structure; otherwise, **false**.

Remarks

This structure only does comparisons with other **Color** structures. To compare colors based solely on their ARGB values, you should do the following:

if (color1.ToArgb() == color2.ToArgb()) ...

This is because the .Equals and == operators determine equivalency using more than just the ARGB value of the colors. For example, Color.Black and Color.FromArgb(0,0,0) are not considered equal since Color.Black is a named color and Color.FromArgb(0,0,0) is not.

Requirements

Platforms: Windows 98, Windows NT 4.0, Windows Millennium Edition, Windows 2000, Windows XP Home Edition, Windows XP Professional, Windows Server 2003 family, .NET Compact Framework - Windows CE .NET

Color.FromArgb Method

Creates a **Color** structure from the four 8-bit ARGB component (alpha, red, green, and blue) values.

Overload List

Creates a **Color** structure from a 32-bit ARGB value.

Supported by the .NET Compact Framework.

[Visual Basic] **Overloads Public Shared Function FromArgb(Integer) As Color**

[C#] **public static Color FromArgb(int);**

[C++] **public: static Color FromArgb(int);**

[JScript] **public static function FromArgb(int) : Color;**

Creates a **Color** structure from the specified **Color** structure, but with the new specified alpha value. Although this method allows a 32-bit value to be passed for the alpha value, the value is limited to 8 bits.

[Visual Basic] **Overloads Public Shared Function FromArgb(Integer, Color) As Color**

[C#] **public static Color FromArgb(int, Color);**

[C++] **public: static Color FromArgb(int, Color);**

[JScript] **public static function FromArgb(int, Color) : Color;**

Creates a **Color** structure from the specified 8-bit color values (red, green, and blue). The alpha value is implicitly 255 (fully opaque). Although this method allows a 32-bit value to be passed for each color component, the value of each component is limited to 8 bits.

Supported by the .NET Compact Framework.

[Visual Basic] **Overloads Public Shared Function FromArgb(Integer, Integer, Integer) As Color**

[C#] **public static Color FromArgb(int, int, int);**

[C++] **public: static Color FromArgb(int, int, int);**

[JScript] **public static function FromArgb(int, int, int) : Color;**

Creates a **Color** structure from the four ARGB component (alpha, red, green, and blue) values. Although this method allows a 32-bit value to be passed for each component, the value of each component is limited to 8 bits.

[Visual Basic] **Overloads Public Shared Function FromArgb(Integer, Integer, Integer, Integer) As Color**

[C#] **public static Color FromArgb(int, int, int, int);**

[C++] **public: static Color FromArgb(int, int, int, int);**

[JScript] **public static function FromArgb(int, int, int, int) : Color;**

Example

[Visual Basic, C#] The following example is designed for use with Windows Forms, and it requires **PaintEventArgs** *e*, which is a parameter of the **Paint** event handler. The code performs the following actions:

- Creates three brushes, each a different color. Each **Color** structure that is used to create a brush is created from four component values (alpha, red, green, blue).
- Uses an imaginary triangle to position three circles.
- Paints three overlapping circles, each centered on one vertex of the triangle, using a different brush for each circle.

> [Visual Basic, C#] **Note** This example shows how to use one of the overloaded versions of **FromArgb**. For other examples that might be available, see the individual overload topics.

[Visual Basic]

```
Public Sub FromArgb_1(e As PaintEventArgs)
Dim g As Graphics = e.Graphics
' Transparent red, green, and blue brushes.
Dim trnsRedBrush As New SolidBrush(Color.FromArgb(120, 255, 0, 0))
Dim trnsGreenBrush As New SolidBrush(Color.FromArgb(120, 0, _
255, 0))
Dim trnsBlueBrush As New SolidBrush(Color.FromArgb(120, 0, 0, 255))
' Base and height of the triangle that is used to position the
' circles. Each vertex of the triangle is at the center of one of
' the 3 circles. The base is equal to the diameter of the circle.
Dim triBase As Single = 100
Dim triHeight As Single = CSng(Math.Sqrt((3 *(triBase * _
triBase) / 4)))
' Coordinates of first circle's bounding rectangle.
Dim x1 As Single = 40
Dim y1 As Single = 40
' Fill 3 over-lapping circles. Each circle is a different color.
g.FillEllipse(trnsRedBrush, x1, y1, 2 * triHeight, 2 * triHeight)
g.FillEllipse(trnsGreenBrush, x1 + triBase / 2, y1 + triHeight, _
2 * triHeight, 2 * triHeight)
g.FillEllipse(trnsBlueBrush, x1 + triBase, y1, 2 * triHeight, _
2 * triHeight)
End Sub
```

[C#]

```
public void FromArgb_1(PaintEventArgs e)
{
Graphics     g = e.Graphics;
// Transparent red, green, and blue brushes.
SolidBrush trnsRedBrush = new SolidBrush(Color.FromArgb
(120, 255, 0, 0));
SolidBrush trnsGreenBrush = new SolidBrush(Color.FromArgb
 (120, 0, 255, 0));
SolidBrush trnsBlueBrush = new SolidBrush(Color.FromArgb
 (120, 0, 0, 255));
// Base and height of the triangle that is used to position the
// circles. Each vertex of the triangle is at the center of one of the
// 3 circles. The base is equal to the diameter of the circles.
float   triBase = 100;
float   triHeight = (float)Math.Sqrt(3*(triBase*triBase)/4);
// Coordinates of first circle's bounding rectangle.
float   x1 = 40;
float   y1 = 40;
// Fill 3 over-lapping circles. Each circle is a different color.
g.FillEllipse(trnsRedBrush, x1, y1, 2*triHeight, 2*triHeight);
g.FillEllipse(trnsGreenBrush, x1 + triBase/2, y1 + triHeight,
2*triHeight, 2*triHeight);
g.FillEllipse(trnsBlueBrush, x1 + triBase, y1, 2*triHeight,
2*triHeight);
}
```

Color.FromArgb Method (Int32)

Creates a **Color** structure from a 32-bit ARGB value.

[Visual Basic]
```
Overloads Public Shared Function FromArgb( _
   ByVal argb As Integer _
) As Color
```
[C#]
```
public static Color FromArgb(
   int argb
);
```
[C++]
```
public: static Color FromArgb(
   int argb
);
```
[JScript]
```
public static function FromArgb(
   argb : int
) : Color;
```

Parameters

argb
A value specifying the 32-bit ARGB value.

Return Value

The **Color** structure that this method creates.

Remarks

The byte-ordering of the 32-bit ARGB value is AARRGGBB. The most significant byte (MSB), represented by AA, is the alpha component value. The second, third, and fourth bytes, represented by RR, GG, and BB, respectively, are the color components red, green, and blue, respectively.

Example

[Visual Basic, C#] The following example is designed for use with Windows Forms, and it requires **PaintEventArgs** *e*, which is a parameter of the **Paint** event handler. The code performs the following actions:

- Creates three brushes, each a different color. Each **Color** structure that is used to create a brush is created from a 32-bit ARGB value.
- Uses an imaginary triangle to position three circles.
- Paints three overlapping circles, each centered on one vertex of the triangle, using a different brush for each circle.

[Visual Basic]
```
Public Sub FromArgb_3(e As PaintEventArgs)
Dim g As Graphics = e.Graphics
' Transparent red, green, and blue brushes.
Dim trnsRedBrush As New SolidBrush(Color.FromArgb(&H78FF0000))
Dim trnsGreenBrush As New SolidBrush(Color.FromArgb(&H7800FF00))
Dim trnsBlueBrush As New SolidBrush(Color.FromArgb(&H780000FF))
' Base and height of the triangle that is used to position the
' circles. Each vertex of the triangle is at the center of one of
' the 3 circles. The base is equal to the diameter of the circle.
Dim triBase As Single = 100
Dim triHeight As Single = CSng(Math.Sqrt((3 *(triBase * _
triBase) / 4)))
' Coordinates of first circle's bounding rectangle.
Dim x1 As Single = 40
Dim y1 As Single = 40
' Fill 3 over-lapping circles. Each circle is a different color.
g.FillEllipse(trnsRedBrush, x1, y1, 2 * triHeight, 2 * triHeight)
g.FillEllipse(trnsGreenBrush, x1 + triBase / 2, y1 + triHeight, _
2 * triHeight, 2 * triHeight)
g.FillEllipse(trnsBlueBrush, x1 + triBase, y1, 2 * triHeight, _
2 * triHeight)
End Sub
```

[C#]
```
public void FromArgb_3(PaintEventArgs e)
{
Graphics     g = e.Graphics;
// Transparent red, green, and blue brushes.
SolidBrush trnsRedBrush = new SolidBrush(Color.FromArgb(0x78FF0000));
SolidBrush trnsGreenBrush = new SolidBrush(Color.FromArgb(0x7800FF00));
SolidBrush trnsBlueBrush = new SolidBrush(Color.FromArgb(0x780000FF));
// Base and height of the triangle that is used to position the
// circles. Each vertex of the triangle is at the center of one of the
// 3 circles. The base is equal to the diameter of the circles.
float   triBase = 100;
float   triHeight = (float)Math.Sqrt(3*(triBase*triBase)/4);
// coordinates of first circle's bounding rectangle.
float   x1 = 40;
float   y1 = 40;
// Fill 3 over-lapping circles. Each circle is a different color.
g.FillEllipse(trnsRedBrush, x1, y1, 2*triHeight, 2*triHeight);
g.FillEllipse(trnsGreenBrush, x1 + triBase/2, y1 + triHeight,
2*triHeight, 2*triHeight);
g.FillEllipse(trnsBlueBrush, x1 + triBase, y1, 2*triHeight,          ↵
2*triHeight);
}
```

Requirements

Platforms: Windows 98, Windows NT 4.0, Windows Millennium Edition, Windows 2000, Windows XP Home Edition, Windows XP Professional, Windows Server 2003 family, .NET Compact Framework - Windows CE .NET

Color.FromArgb Method (Int32, Color)

Creates a **Color** structure from the specified **Color** structure, but with the new specified alpha value. Although this method allows a 32-bit value to be passed for the alpha value, the value is limited to 8 bits.

[Visual Basic]
```
Overloads Public Shared Function FromArgb( _
   ByVal alpha As Integer, _
   ByVal baseColor As Color _
) As Color
```
[C#]
```
public static Color FromArgb(
   int alpha,
   Color baseColor
);
```
[C++]
```
public: static Color FromArgb(
   int alpha,
   Color baseColor
);
```
[JScript]
```
public static function FromArgb(
   alpha : int,
   baseColor : Color
) : Color;
```

Parameters

alpha
The alpha value for the new **Color** structure. Valid values are 0 through 255.

baseColor
The **Color** structure from which to create the new **Color** structure.

Return Value

The **Color** structure that this method creates.

Example

[Visual Basic, C#] The following example is designed for use with Windows Forms, and it requires **PaintEventArgs** *e*, which is a parameter of the **Paint** event handler. The code performs the following actions:

- Creates **Color** structures from the three color component values (red, green, blue). Three **Color** structures are created, one for each primary color.
- Iterates through a range of alpha values, changing the alpha value of a color.
- During each iteration: sets the color of a brush to the modified color and paints a rectangle to show the color.
- Repeats steps 2 and 3 for each primary color.

[Visual Basic, C#] The alpha value is never fully opaque and the rectangles overlap so you get color-combination effects.

[Visual Basic]

```
Public Sub FromArgb_2_4(e As PaintEventArgs)
Dim g As Graphics = e.Graphics
' Opaque colors (alpha value defaults to 255 -- max value).
Dim red As Color = Color.FromArgb(255, 0, 0)
Dim green As Color = Color.FromArgb(0, 255, 0)
Dim blue As Color = Color.FromArgb(0, 0, 255)
' Solid brush initialized to red.
Dim myBrush As New SolidBrush(red)
Dim alpha As Integer
Dim x As Integer = 50 ' x coordinate of first red rectangle
Dim y As Integer = 50 ' y coordinate of first red rectangle
' Fill rectangles with red, varying the alpha value from 25 to 250.
For alpha = 25 To 250 Step 25
myBrush.Color = Color.FromArgb(alpha, red)
g.FillRectangle(myBrush, x, y, 50, 100)
g.FillRectangle(myBrush, x, y + 250, 50, 50)
x += 50
Next alpha
x = 50 ' x coordinate of first green rectangle
y += 50 ' y coordinate of first green rectangle
' Fill rectangles with green, varying alpha value from 25 to 250.
For alpha = 25 To 250 Step 25
myBrush.Color = Color.FromArgb(alpha, green)
g.FillRectangle(myBrush, x, y, 50, 150)
x += 50
Next alpha
x = 50 ' x coordinate of first blue rectangle
y += 100 ' y coordinate of first blue rectangle
' Fill rectangles with blue, varying alpha value from 25 to 250.
For alpha = 25 To 250 Step 25
myBrush.Color = Color.FromArgb(alpha, blue)
g.FillRectangle(myBrush, x, y, 50, 150)
x += 50
Next alpha
End Sub
```

[C#]

```
public void FromArgb_2_4(PaintEventArgs e)
{
Graphics     g = e.Graphics;
// Opaque colors (alpha value defaults to 255 -- max value).
Color red = Color.FromArgb(255, 0, 0);
Color green = Color.FromArgb(0, 255, 0);
Color blue = Color.FromArgb(0, 0, 255);
// Solid brush initialized to red.
SolidBrush  myBrush = new SolidBrush(red);
int alpha;
int x = 50;          // x coordinate of first red rectangle
int y = 50;          // y coordinate of first red rectangle
// Fill rectangles with red, varying the alpha value from 25 to 250.
for (alpha = 25; alpha <= 250; alpha += 25)
{
myBrush.Color = Color.FromArgb(alpha, red);
g.FillRectangle(myBrush, x, y, 50, 100);
g.FillRectangle(myBrush, x, y + 250, 50, 50);
x += 50;
}
x = 50;              // x coordinate of first green rectangle
y += 50;             // y coordinate of first green rectangle
// Fill rectangles with green, varying the alpha value from 25 to 250.
for (alpha = 25; alpha <= 250; alpha += 25)
{
myBrush.Color = Color.FromArgb(alpha, green);
g.FillRectangle(myBrush, x, y, 50, 150);
x += 50;
}
x = 50;              // x coordinate of first blue rectangle
y += 100;            // y coordinate of first blue rectangle
// Fill rectangles with blue, varying the alpha value from 25 to 250.
for (alpha = 25; alpha <= 250; alpha += 25)
{
myBrush.Color = Color.FromArgb(alpha, blue);
g.FillRectangle(myBrush, x, y, 50, 150);
x += 50;
}
}
```

Requirements

Platforms: Windows 98, Windows NT 4.0, Windows Millennium Edition, Windows 2000, Windows XP Home Edition, Windows XP Professional, Windows Server 2003 family

Color.FromArgb Method (Int32, Int32, Int32)

Creates a **Color** structure from the specified 8-bit color values (red, green, and blue). The alpha value is implicitly 255 (fully opaque). Although this method allows a 32-bit value to be passed for each color component, the value of each component is limited to 8 bits.

[Visual Basic]

```
Overloads Public Shared Function FromArgb( _
   ByVal red As Integer, _
   ByVal green As Integer, _
   ByVal blue As Integer _
) As Color
```

[C#]

```
public static Color FromArgb(
   int red,
   int green,
   int blue
);
```

[C++]

```
public: static Color FromArgb(
   int red,
   int green,
   int blue
);
```

[JScript]

```
public static function FromArgb(
   red : int,
   green : int,
   blue : int
) : Color;
```

Parameters

red

The red component value for the new **Color** structure. Valid values are 0 through 255.

green

The green component value for the new **Color** structure. Valid values are 0 through 255.

blue

The blue component value for the new **Color** structure. Valid values are 0 through 255.

Return Value

The **Color** structure that this method creates.

Example

[Visual Basic, C#] The following example is designed for use with Windows Forms, and it requires **PaintEventArgs** *e*, which is a parameter of the **Paint** event handler. The code performs the following actions:

- Creates **Color** structures from the three color component values (red, green, blue). Three **Color** structures are created, one for each primary color.
- Iterates through a range of alpha values, changing the alpha value of a color.
- During each iteration: sets the color of a brush to the modified color and paints a rectangle to show the color.
- Repeats steps 2 and 3 for each primary color.

[Visual Basic, C#] The alpha value is never fully opaque and the rectangles overlap so you get color-combination effects.

[Visual Basic]

```
Public Sub FromArgb_2_4(e As PaintEventArgs)
Dim g As Graphics = e.Graphics
' Opaque colors (alpha value defaults to 255 -- max value).
Dim red As Color = Color.FromArgb(255, 0, 0)
Dim green As Color = Color.FromArgb(0, 255, 0)
Dim blue As Color = Color.FromArgb(0, 0, 255)
' Solid brush initialized to red.
Dim myBrush As New SolidBrush(red)
Dim alpha As Integer
Dim x As Integer = 50 ' x coordinate of first red rectangle
Dim y As Integer = 50 ' y coordinate of first red rectangle
' Fill rectangles with red, varying the alpha value from 25 to 250.
For alpha = 25 To 250 Step 25
myBrush.Color = Color.FromArgb(alpha, red)
g.FillRectangle(myBrush, x, y, 50, 100)
g.FillRectangle(myBrush, x, y + 250, 50, 50)
x += 50
Next alpha
x = 50 ' x coordinate of first green rectangle
y += 50 ' y coordinate of first green rectangle
' Fill rectangles with green, varying alpha value from 25 to 250.
For alpha = 25 To 250 Step 25
myBrush.Color = Color.FromArgb(alpha, green)
g.FillRectangle(myBrush, x, y, 50, 150)
x += 50
Next alpha
x = 50 ' x coordinate of first blue rectangle
y += 100 ' y coordinate of first blue rectangle
' Fill rectangles with blue, varying alpha value from 25 to 250.
For alpha = 25 To 250 Step 25
myBrush.Color = Color.FromArgb(alpha, blue)
g.FillRectangle(myBrush, x, y, 50, 150)
x += 50
Next alpha
End Sub
```

[C#]

```
public void FromArgb_2_4(PaintEventArgs e)
{
Graphics     g = e.Graphics;
// Opaque colors (alpha value defaults to 255 -- max value).
Color red = Color.FromArgb(255, 0, 0);
Color green = Color.FromArgb(0, 255, 0);
Color blue = Color.FromArgb(0, 0, 255);
// Solid brush initialized to red.
SolidBrush  myBrush = new SolidBrush(red);
int alpha;
int x = 50;          // x coordinate of first red rectangle
int y = 50;          // y coordinate of first red rectangle
// Fill rectangles with red, varying the alpha value from 25 to 250.
for (alpha = 25; alpha <= 250; alpha += 25)
{
myBrush.Color = Color.FromArgb(alpha, red);
g.FillRectangle(myBrush, x, y, 50, 100);
g.FillRectangle(myBrush, x, y + 250, 50, 50);
x += 50;
}
x = 50;              // x coordinate of first green rectangle
y += 50;             // y coordinate of first green rectangle
// Fill rectangles with green, varying the alpha value from 25 to 250.
for (alpha = 25; alpha <= 250; alpha += 25)
{
myBrush.Color = Color.FromArgb(alpha, green);
g.FillRectangle(myBrush, x, y, 50, 150);
x += 50;
}
x = 50;              // x coordinate of first blue rectangle
y += 100;            // y coordinate of first blue rectangle
// Fill rectangles with blue, varying the alpha value from 25 to 250.
for (alpha = 25; alpha <= 250; alpha += 25)
{
myBrush.Color = Color.FromArgb(alpha, blue);
g.FillRectangle(myBrush, x, y, 50, 150);
x += 50;
}
}
```

Requirements

Platforms: Windows 98, Windows NT 4.0, Windows Millennium Edition, Windows 2000, Windows XP Home Edition, Windows XP Professional, Windows Server 2003 family, .NET Compact Framework - Windows CE .NET

Color.FromArgb Method (Int32, Int32, Int32, Int32)

Creates a **Color** structure from the four ARGB component (alpha, red, green, and blue) values. Although this method allows a 32-bit value to be passed for each component, the value of each component is limited to 8 bits.

[Visual Basic]

```
Overloads Public Shared Function FromArgb( _
   ByVal alpha As Integer, _
   ByVal red As Integer, _
   ByVal green As Integer, _
   ByVal blue As Integer _
) As Color
```

[C#]

```
public static Color FromArgb(
   int alpha,
   int red,
   int green,
   int blue
);
```

```
[C++]
public: static Color FromArgb(
   int alpha,
   int red,
   int green,
   int blue
);
[JScript]
public static function FromArgb(
   alpha : int,
   red : int,
   green : int,
   blue : int
) : Color;
```

Parameters

alpha
: The alpha component. Valid values are 0 through 255.

red
: The red component. Valid values are 0 through 255.

green
: The green component. Valid values are 0 through 255.

blue
: The blue component. Valid values are 0 through 255.

Return Value

The **Color** structure that this method creates.

Example

[Visual Basic, C#] The following example is designed for use with Windows Forms, and it requires **PaintEventArgs** *e*, which is a parameter of the **Paint** event handler. The code performs the following actions:

- Creates three brushes, each a different color. Each **Color** structure that is used to create a brush is created from four component values (alpha, red, green, blue).
- Uses an imaginary triangle to position three circles.
- Paints three overlapping circles, each centered on one vertex of the triangle, using a different brush for each circle.

```
[Visual Basic]
Public Sub FromArgb_1(e As PaintEventArgs)
Dim g As Graphics = e.Graphics
' Transparent red, green, and blue brushes.
Dim trnsRedBrush As New SolidBrush(Color.FromArgb(120, 255, 0, 0))
Dim trnsGreenBrush As New SolidBrush(Color.FromArgb(120, 0, _
255, 0))
Dim trnsBlueBrush As New SolidBrush(Color.FromArgb(120, 0, 0, 255))
' Base and height of the triangle that is used to position the
' circles. Each vertex of the triangle is at the center of one of
' the 3 circles. The base is equal to the diameter of the circle.
Dim triBase As Single = 100
Dim triHeight As Single = CSng(Math.Sqrt((3 *(triBase * _
triBase) / 4)))
' Coordinates of first circle's bounding rectangle.
Dim x1 As Single = 40
Dim y1 As Single = 40
' Fill 3 over-lapping circles. Each circle is a different color.
g.FillEllipse(trnsRedBrush, x1, y1, 2 * triHeight, 2 * triHeight)
g.FillEllipse(trnsGreenBrush, x1 + triBase / 2, y1 + triHeight, _
2 * triHeight, 2 * triHeight)
g.FillEllipse(trnsBlueBrush, x1 + triBase, y1, 2 * triHeight, _
2 * triHeight)
End Sub
```

```
[C#]
public void FromArgb_1(PaintEventArgs e)
{
Graphics    g = e.Graphics;
// Transparent red, green, and blue brushes.
SolidBrush trnsRedBrush = new SolidBrush(Color.FromArgb           ↵
 (120, 255, 0, 0));
SolidBrush trnsGreenBrush = new SolidBrush(Color.FromArgb         ↵
 (120, 0, 255, 0));
SolidBrush trnsBlueBrush = new SolidBrush(Color.FromArgb          ↵
 (120, 0, 0, 255));
// Base and height of the triangle that is used to position the
// circles. Each vertex of the triangle is at the center of one of the
// 3 circles. The base is equal to the diameter of the circles.
float   triBase = 100;
float   triHeight = (float)Math.Sqrt(3*(triBase*triBase)/4);
// Coordinates of first circle's bounding rectangle.
float   x1 = 40;
float   y1 = 40;
// Fill 3 over-lapping circles. Each circle is a different color.
g.FillEllipse(trnsRedBrush, x1, y1, 2*triHeight, 2*triHeight);
g.FillEllipse(trnsGreenBrush, x1 + triBase/2, y1 + triHeight,
2*triHeight, 2*triHeight);
g.FillEllipse(trnsBlueBrush, x1 + triBase, y1, 2*triHeight,       ↵
2*triHeight);
}
```

[C++, JScript] No example is available for C++ or JScript. To view a Visual Basic or C# example, click the Language Filter button <IMG SRC="filter1a.gif" ALT="Language Filter" BORDER=0> in the upper-left corner of the page.

Requirements

Platforms: Windows 98, Windows NT 4.0, Windows Millennium Edition, Windows 2000, Windows XP Home Edition, Windows XP Professional, Windows Server 2003 family

Color.FromKnownColor Method

Creates a **Color** structure from the specified pre-defined color.

```
[Visual Basic]
Public Shared Function FromKnownColor( _
   ByVal color As KnownColor _
) As Color
[C#]
public static Color FromKnownColor(
   KnownColor color
);
[C++]
public: static Color FromKnownColor(
   KnownColor color
);
[JScript]
public static function FromKnownColor(
   color : KnownColor
) : Color;
```

Parameters

color
: An element of the **KnownColor** enumeration.

Return Value

The **Color** structure that this method creates.

Remarks

A pre-defined color is also called a known color and is represented by an element of the **KnownColor** enumeration.

Example

[Visual Basic, C#] The following example is designed for use with Windows Forms, and it requires **PaintEventArgs** *e*, which is a parameter of the **Paint** event handler. The code performs the following actions:

- Creates an instance of a **Color** structure, *redShade*, to be used for comparisons.
- Iterates through the **KnownColor** enumeration elements to find all **KnownColors** that have the same brightness as *redShade*. The iterations are terminated when 15 matches are found or the value of the loop counter is greater than the last **KnownColor** element.
- During each iteration: saves the **KnownColor** element, if it matches the criteria, in an array.
- Uses a brush to paint rectangles.

[Visual Basic, C#] The first rectangle is painted the color represented by *redShade*. Each of the other rectangles is painted a **KnownColor** that matches the brightness of the *redShade*.

[Visual Basic]

```
Public Sub KnownColorBrightnessExample(e As PaintEventArgs)
Dim g As Graphics = e.Graphics
' Color structures. One is used for temporary storage. The other
' is a constant used for comparisons.
Dim someColor As Color = Color.FromArgb(0)
Dim redShade As Color = Color.FromArgb(255, 200, 0, 100)
' Array to store KnownColor values that match the brightness of the
' redShade color.
Dim colorMatches(15) As KnownColor
Dim count As Integer = 0 ' number of matches found
' iterate through the KnownColor enums until 15 matches are found.
Dim enumValue As KnownColor
For enumValue = 0 To KnownColor.YellowGreen
someColor = Color.FromKnownColor(enumValue)
If (someColor.GetBrightness()) = (redShade.GetBrightness()) Then
colorMatches(count) = enumValue
count += 1
If count > 15 Then
Exit For
End If
End If
Next enumValue
' Display the redShade color and its argb value.
Dim myBrush1 As New SolidBrush(redShade)
Dim myFont As New Font("Arial", 12)
Dim x As Integer = 20
Dim y As Integer = 20
someColor = redShade
g.FillRectangle(myBrush1, x, y, 100, 30)
g.DrawString(someColor.ToString(), myFont, Brushes.Black, _
x + 120, y)
' Iterate through the matches that were found and display each
' color that corresponds with the enum value in the array.
' Display the name of the KnownColor.
Dim i As Integer
For i = 0 To count - 1
y += 40
someColor = Color.FromKnownColor(colorMatches(i))
myBrush1.Color = someColor
g.FillRectangle(myBrush1, x, y, 100, 30)
g.DrawString(someColor.ToString(), myFont, Brushes.Black, _
x + 120, y)
Next i
End Sub
```

[C#]

```
public void KnownColorBrightnessExample(PaintEventArgs e)
{
Graphics     g = e.Graphics;
// Color structures. One is a variable used for temporary          ↵
 storage. The other
// is a constant used for comparisons.
Color   someColor = Color.FromArgb(0);
Color   redShade = Color.FromArgb(255, 200, 0, 100);
// Array to store KnownColor values that match the brightness of the
// redShade color.
KnownColor[]  colorMatches = new KnownColor[15];
int  count = 0;  // number of matches found
// Iterate through the KnownColor enums until 15 matches are found.
for (KnownColor enumValue = 0;
enumValue <= KnownColor.YellowGreen && count < 15; enumValue++)
{
someColor = Color.FromKnownColor(enumValue);
if ( someColor.GetBrightness() == redShade.GetBrightness() )
colorMatches[count++] = enumValue;
}
// Display the redShade color and its argb value.
SolidBrush  myBrush1 = new SolidBrush(redShade);
Font        myFont = new Font("Arial", 12);
int         x = 20;
int         y = 20;
someColor = redShade;
g.FillRectangle(myBrush1, x, y, 100, 30);
g.DrawString(someColor.ToString(), myFont, Brushes.Black, x + 120, y);
// Iterate through the matches that were found and display          ↵
each color that
// Corresponds with the enum value in the array. also display       ↵
 the name of
// The KnownColor.
for ( int i = 0; i < count; i++)
{
y += 40;
someColor = Color.FromKnownColor(colorMatches[i]);
myBrush1.Color = someColor;
g.FillRectangle(myBrush1, x, y, 100, 30);
g.DrawString(someColor.ToString(), myFont, Brushes.Black, x + 120, y);
}
}
```

Requirements

Platforms: Windows 98, Windows NT 4.0, Windows Millennium Edition, Windows 2000, Windows XP Home Edition, Windows XP Professional, Windows Server 2003 family

Color.FromName Method

Creates a **Color** structure from the specified name of a pre-defined color.

[Visual Basic]

```
Public Shared Function FromName( _
   ByVal name As String _
) As Color
```

[C#]

```
public static Color FromName(
   string name
);
```

[C++]

```
public: static Color FromName(
   String* name
);
```

[JScript]

```
public static function FromName(
   name : String
) : Color;
```

Parameters

name

A string that is the name of a pre-defined color. Valid names are the same as the names of the elements of the **KnownColor** enumeration.

Return Value

The **Color** structure that this method creates.

Remarks

A pre-defined color is also called a known color and is represented by an element of the **KnownColor** enumeration. If *name* is not the valid name of a pre-defined color, the **FromName** method creates a **Color** structure that has an ARGB value of zero (that is, all ARGB components are 0).

Requirements

Platforms: Windows 98, Windows NT 4.0,
Windows Millennium Edition, Windows 2000,
Windows XP Home Edition, Windows XP Professional,
Windows Server 2003 family

Color.FromSysIcv Method

Note: This namespace, class, or member is supported only in version 1.1 of the .NET Framework.

This member supports the .NET Framework infrastructure and is not intended to be used directly from your code.

[Visual Basic]
```
Public Shared Function FromSysIcv( _
   ByVal icv As Integer _
) As Color
```
[C#]
```
public static Color FromSysIcv(
   int icv
);
```
[C++]
```
public: static Color FromSysIcv(
   int icv
);
```
[JScript]
```
public static function FromSysIcv(
   icv : int
) : Color;
```

Color.GetBrightness Method

Gets the hue-saturation-brightness (HSB) brightness value for this **Color** structure.

[Visual Basic]
```
Public Function GetBrightness() As Single
```
[C#]
```
public float GetBrightness();
```
[C++]
```
public: float GetBrightness();
```
[JScript]
```
public function GetBrightness() : float;
```

Return Value

The brightness of this **Color** structure. The brightness ranges from 0.0 through 1.0, where 0.0 represents black and 1.0 represents white.

Example

[Visual Basic, C#] The following example is designed for use with Windows Forms, and it requires **PaintEventArgs** *e*, which is a parameter of the **Paint** event handler. The code performs the following actions:

- Creates an instance of a **Color** structure, *redShade*, to be used for comparisons.
- Iterates through the **KnownColor** enumeration elements to find all **KnownColors** that have the same brightness as *redShade*. The iterations are terminated when 15 matches are found or the value of the loop counter is greater than the last **KnownColor** element.
- During each iteration: saves the **KnownColor** element, if it matches the criteria, in an array.
- Uses a brush to paint rectangles.

[Visual Basic, C#] The first rectangle is painted the color represented by *redShade*. Each of the other rectangles is painted a **KnownColor** that matches the brightness of the *redShade*.

[Visual Basic]
```
Public Sub KnownColorBrightnessExample(e As PaintEventArgs)
Dim g As Graphics = e.Graphics
' Color structures. One is used for temporary storage. The other
' is a constant used for comparisons.
Dim someColor As Color = Color.FromArgb(0)
Dim redShade As Color = Color.FromArgb(255, 200, 0, 100)
' Array to store KnownColor values that match the brightness of the
' redShade color.
Dim colorMatches(15) As KnownColor
Dim count As Integer = 0 ' number of matches found
' iterate through the KnownColor enums until 15 matches are found.
Dim enumValue As KnownColor
For enumValue = 0 To KnownColor.YellowGreen
someColor = Color.FromKnownColor(enumValue)
If (someColor.GetBrightness()) = (redShade.GetBrightness()) Then
colorMatches(count) = enumValue
count += 1
If count > 15 Then
Exit For
End If
End If
Next enumValue
' Display the redShade color and its argb value.
Dim myBrush1 As New SolidBrush(redShade)
Dim myFont As New Font("Arial", 12)
Dim x As Integer = 20
Dim y As Integer = 20
someColor = redShade
g.FillRectangle(myBrush1, x, y, 100, 30)
g.DrawString(someColor.ToString(), myFont, Brushes.Black, _
x + 120, y)
' Iterate through the matches that were found and display each
' color that corresponds with the enum value in the array.
' Display the name of the KnownColor.
Dim i As Integer
For i = 0 To count - 1
y += 40
someColor = Color.FromKnownColor(colorMatches(i))
myBrush1.Color = someColor
g.FillRectangle(myBrush1, x, y, 100, 30)
g.DrawString(someColor.ToString(), myFont, Brushes.Black, _
x + 120, y)
Next i
End Sub
```

[C#]
```
public void KnownColorBrightnessExample(PaintEventArgs e)
{
Graphics    g = e.Graphics;
// Color structures. One is a variable used for temporary
```

```
storage. The other
// is a constant used for comparisons.
Color   someColor = Color.FromArgb(0);
Color   redShade = Color.FromArgb(255, 200, 0, 100);
// Array to store KnownColor values that match the brightness of the
// redShade color.
KnownColor[]  colorMatches = new KnownColor[15];
int  count = 0;   // number of matches found
// Iterate through the KnownColor enums until 15 matches are found.
for (KnownColor enumValue = 0;
enumValue <= KnownColor.YellowGreen && count < 15; enumValue++)
{
someColor = Color.FromKnownColor(enumValue);
if ( someColor.GetBrightness() == redShade.GetBrightness() )
colorMatches[count++] = enumValue;
}
// display the redShade color and its argb value.
SolidBrush  myBrush1 = new SolidBrush(redShade);
Font        myFont = new Font("Arial", 12);
int         x = 20;
int         y = 20;
someColor = redShade;
g.FillRectangle(myBrush1, x, y, 100, 30);
g.DrawString(someColor.ToString(), myFont, Brushes.Black, x + 120, y);
// Iterate through the matches that were found and display          ↵
 each color that
// corresponds with the enum value in the array. also display        ↵
 the name of
// The KnownColor.
for ( int i = 0; i < count; i++)
{
y += 40;
someColor = Color.FromKnownColor(colorMatches[i]);
myBrush1.Color = someColor;
g.FillRectangle(myBrush1, x, y, 100, 30);
g.DrawString(someColor.ToString(), myFont, Brushes.Black, x + 120, y);
}
}
```

Requirements

Platforms: Windows 98, Windows NT 4.0, Windows Millennium Edition, Windows 2000, Windows XP Home Edition, Windows XP Professional, Windows Server 2003 family

Color.GetHashCode Method

Returns a hash code for this **Color** structure.

[Visual Basic]
```
Overrides Public Function GetHashCode() As Integer
```
[C#]
```
public override int GetHashCode();
```
[C++]
```
public: int GetHashCode();
```
[JScript]
```
public override function GetHashCode() : int;
```

Return Value

An integer value that specifies the hash code for this **Color** structure.

Requirements

Platforms: Windows 98, Windows NT 4.0, Windows Millennium Edition, Windows 2000, Windows XP Home Edition, Windows XP Professional, Windows Server 2003 family, .NET Compact Framework - Windows CE .NET

Color.GetHue Method

Gets the hue-saturation-brightness (HSB) hue value, in degrees, for this **Color** structure.

[Visual Basic]
```
Public Function GetHue() As Single
```
[C#]
```
public float GetHue();
```
[C++]
```
public: float GetHue();
```
[JScript]
```
public function GetHue() : float;
```

Return Value

The hue, in degrees, of this **Color** structure. The hue is measured in degrees, ranging from 0.0 through 360.0, in HSB color space.

Example

[Visual Basic, C#] The following example is designed for use with Windows Forms, and it requires **PaintEventArgs** *e*, which is a parameter of the **Paint** event handler. The code performs the following actions:

- Creates an instance of a **Color** structure, *redShade*, to be used for comparisons.
- Iterates through the **KnownColor** enumeration elements to find all **KnownColors** that have the same hue as *redShade*. The iterations are terminated when 15 matches are found or the value of the loop counter is greater than the last **KnownColor** element.
- During each iteration: saves the **KnownColor** element, if it matches the criteria, in an array.
- Uses a brush to paint rectangles.

[Visual Basic, C#] The first rectangle is painted the color represented by *redShade*. Each of the other rectangles is painted a **KnownColor** that matches the hue of the *redShade*.

[Visual Basic]
```
Public Sub GetHueExample(e As PaintEventArgs)
Dim g As Graphics = e.Graphics
' Color structures. One is used for temporary storage. The other
' is a constant used for comparisons.
Dim someColor As Color = Color.FromArgb(0)
Dim redShade As Color = Color.FromArgb(255, 200, 0, 100)
' Array for KnownColor values that match the hue of redShade
' color.
Dim colorMatches(15) As KnownColor
Dim count As Integer = 0 ' number of matches found
' Iterate through the KnownColor enums until 15 matches are found.
Dim enumValue As KnownColor
For enumValue = 0 To KnownColor.YellowGreen
someColor = Color.FromKnownColor(enumValue)
If (someColor.GetHue()) = (redShade.GetHue()) Then
colorMatches(count) = enumValue
count += 1
If count > 15 Then
Exit For
End If
End If
Next enumValue
' Display the redShade color and its argb value.
Dim myBrush1 As New SolidBrush(redShade)
Dim myFont As New Font("Arial", 12)
Dim x As Integer = 20
Dim y As Integer = 20
someColor = redShade
g.FillRectangle(myBrush1, x, y, 100, 30)
g.DrawString(someColor.ToString(), myFont, Brushes.Black, _
x + 120, y)
```

```
' Iterate through the matches that were found and display each
' color that corresponds with the enum value in the array. Also
' display the name of the KnownColor.
Dim i As Integer
For i = 0 To count - 1
y += 40
someColor = Color.FromKnownColor(colorMatches(i))
myBrush1.Color = someColor
g.FillRectangle(myBrush1, x, y, 100, 30)
g.DrawString(someColor.ToString(), myFont, Brushes.Black, _
x + 120, y)
Next i
End Sub
```

[C#]

```
public void GetHueExample(PaintEventArgs e)
{
Graphics     g = e.Graphics;
// Color structures. One is a variable used for temporary ↵
 storage. The other
// is a constant used for comparisons.
Color   someColor = Color.FromArgb(0);
Color   redShade = Color.FromArgb(255, 200, 0, 100);
// Array to store KnownColor values that match the hue of the redShade
// color.
KnownColor[]  colorMatches = new KnownColor[15];
int  count = 0;   // number of matches found
// Iterate through the KnownColor enums until 15 matches are found.
for (KnownColor enumValue = 0;
enumValue <= KnownColor.YellowGreen && count < 15; enumValue++)
{
someColor = Color.FromKnownColor(enumValue);
if ( someColor.GetHue() == redShade.GetHue() )
colorMatches[count++] = enumValue;
}
// Display the redShade color and its argb value.
SolidBrush  myBrush1 = new SolidBrush(redShade);
Font        myFont = new Font("Arial", 12);
int         x = 20;
int         y = 20;
someColor = redShade;
g.FillRectangle(myBrush1, x, y, 100, 30);
g.DrawString(someColor.ToString(), myFont, Brushes.Black, x + 120, y);
// Iterate through the matches that were found and display ↵
 each color that
// corresponds with the enum value in the array. also display ↵
 the name of
// the KnownColor.
for ( int i = 0; i < count; i++)
{
y += 40;
someColor = Color.FromKnownColor(colorMatches[i]);
myBrush1.Color = someColor;
g.FillRectangle(myBrush1, x, y, 100, 30);
g.DrawString(someColor.ToString(), myFont, Brushes.Black, x + 120, y);
}
}
```

Requirements

Platforms: Windows 98, Windows NT 4.0, Windows Millennium Edition, Windows 2000, Windows XP Home Edition, Windows XP Professional, Windows Server 2003 family

Color.GetSaturation Method

Gets the hue-saturation-brightness (HSB) saturation value for this **Color** structure.

[Visual Basic]
```
Public Function GetSaturation() As Single
```
[C#]
```
public float GetSaturation();
```
[C++]
```
public: float GetSaturation();
```
[JScript]
```
public function GetSaturation() : float;
```

Return Value

The saturation of this **Color** structure. The saturation ranges from 0.0 through 1.0, where 0.0 is grayscale and 1.0 is the most saturated.

Example

[Visual Basic, C#] The following example is designed for use with Windows Forms, and it requires **PaintEventArgs** *e*, which is a parameter of the **Paint** event handler. The code performs the following actions:

- Creates an instance of a **Color** structure, *redShade*, to be used for comparisons.
- Iterates through the **KnownColor** enumeration elements to find all known colors that have the same saturation as *redShade*. The iterations are terminated when 15 matches are found or the value of the loop counter is greater than the last **KnownColor** element.
- During each iteration, saves the **KnownColor** element, if it matches the criteria, in an array.
- Uses a brush to paint rectangles.

[Visual Basic, C#] The first rectangle is painted the color represented by *redShade*. Each of the other rectangles is painted a **KnownColor** that matches the saturation of the *redShade*.

[Visual Basic]

```
Public Sub GetSatExample(e As PaintEventArgs)
Dim g As Graphics = e.Graphics
' Color structures. One is used for temporary storage. The other
' is a constant used for comparisons.
Dim someColor As Color = Color.FromArgb(0)
Dim redShade As Color = Color.FromArgb(255, 200, 0, 100)
' Array to store KnownColor values that match the saturation of the
' redShade color.
Dim colorMatches(15) As KnownColor
Dim count As Integer = 0 ' number of matches found
' Iterate through the KnownColor enums until 15 matches are found
Dim enumValue As KnownColor
For enumValue = 0 To KnownColor.YellowGreen
someColor = Color.FromKnownColor(enumValue)
If (someColor.GetSaturation()) = (redShade.GetSaturation()) Then
colorMatches(count) = enumValue
count += 1
If count > 15 Then
Exit For
End If
End If
Next enumValue
' Display the redShade color and its argb value.
Dim myBrush1 As New SolidBrush(redShade)
Dim myFont As New Font("Arial", 12)
Dim x As Integer = 20
Dim y As Integer = 20
someColor = redShade
g.FillRectangle(myBrush1, x, y, 100, 30)
g.DrawString(someColor.ToString(), myFont, Brushes.Black, _
x + 120, y)
' Iterate through the matches that were found and display each
' color that corresponds with the enum value in the array. also
' display the name of the KnownColor.
Dim i As Integer
For i = 0 To count - 1
y += 40
someColor = Color.FromKnownColor(colorMatches(i))
myBrush1.Color = someColor
g.FillRectangle(myBrush1, x, y, 100, 30)
```

```
g.DrawString(someColor.ToString(), myFont, Brushes.Black, _
x + 120, y)
Next i
End Sub
```

[C#]

```
public void GetSatExample(PaintEventArgs e)
{
Graphics     g = e.Graphics;
// Color structures. One is a variable used for temporary
storage. The other
// is a constant used for comparisons.
Color   someColor = Color.FromArgb(0);
Color   redShade = Color.FromArgb(255, 200, 0, 100);
// Array to store KnownColor values that match the saturation of the
// redShade color.
KnownColor[]  colorMatches = new KnownColor[15];
int  count = 0;   // number of matches found
// Iterate through the KnownColor enums until 15 matches are found.
for (KnownColor enumValue = 0;
enumValue <= KnownColor.YellowGreen && count < 15; enumValue++)
{
someColor = Color.FromKnownColor(enumValue);
if ( someColor.GetSaturation() == redShade.GetSaturation() )
colorMatches[count++] = enumValue;
}
// Display the redShade color and its argb value.
SolidBrush  myBrush1 = new SolidBrush(redShade);
Font        myFont = new Font("Arial", 12);
int         x = 20;
int         y = 20;
someColor = redShade;
g.FillRectangle(myBrush1, x, y, 100, 30);
g.DrawString(someColor.ToString(), myFont, Brushes.Black, x + 120, y);
// Iterate through the matches that were found and display
 each color that
// corresponds with the enum value in the array. also display
 the name of
// the KnownColor.
for ( int i = 0; i < count; i++)
{
y += 40;
someColor = Color.FromKnownColor(colorMatches[i]);
myBrush1.Color = someColor;
g.FillRectangle(myBrush1, x, y, 100, 30);
g.DrawString(someColor.ToString(), myFont, Brushes.Black, x + 120, y);
}
}
```

Requirements

Platforms: Windows 98, Windows NT 4.0, Windows Millennium Edition, Windows 2000, Windows XP Home Edition, Windows XP Professional, Windows Server 2003 family

Color.ToArgb Method

Gets the 32-bit ARGB value of this **Color** structure.

[Visual Basic]
```
Public Function ToArgb() As Integer
```
[C#]
```
public int ToArgb();
```
[C++]
```
public: int ToArgb();
```
[JScript]
```
public function ToArgb() : int;
```

Return Value

The 32-bit ARGB value of this **Color** structure.

Remarks

The byte-ordering of the 32-bit ARGB value is AARRGGBB. The most significant byte (MSB), represented by AA, is the alpha component value. The second, third, and fourth bytes, represented by RR, GG, and BB, respectively, are the color components red, green, and blue, respectively. For example, suppose that a color is created from the four component values. The **ToArgb** method can be used to obtain the 32-bit ARGB value as follows:

Example

[Visual Basic, C#] The following example is designed for use with Windows Forms, and it requires **PaintEventArgs** *e*, which is a parameter of the **Paint** event handler. The code performs the following actions:

- Iterates through the **KnownColor** enumeration elements to find all known colors that have a nonzero green component and a zero-value red component, and that are not system colors.
- During each iteration: saves the **KnownColor** element, if it matches the criteria, in an array.
- Uses a brush to paint rectangles.

[Visual Basic, C#] Each of the rectangles is painted a **KnownColor** that matches the criteria stated in the first step. The name of the KnownColor and its component values are also displayed.

[Visual Basic, C#] This example displays certain known colors, the names of the colors, and their four component values. Use of the **ToArgb** method is a preliminary step to displaying the component values.

[Visual Basic]

```
Public Sub ToArgbToStringExample(e As PaintEventArgs)
Dim g As Graphics = e.Graphics
' Color structure used for temporary storage.
Dim someColor As Color = Color.FromArgb(0)
' Array to store KnownColor values that match the criteria.
Dim colorMatches(167) As KnownColor
Dim count As Integer = 0 ' number of matches found
' Iterate through KnownColor enums to find all corresponding colors
' that have a non-zero green component and zero-valued red
' component and that are not system colors.
Dim enumValue As KnownColor
For enumValue = 0 To KnownColor.YellowGreen
someColor = Color.FromKnownColor(enumValue)
If someColor.G <> 0 And someColor.R = 0 And _
Not someColor.IsSystemColor Then
colorMatches(count) = enumValue
count += 1
End If
Next enumValue
Dim myBrush1 As New SolidBrush(someColor)
Dim myFont As New Font("Arial", 9)
Dim x As Integer = 40
Dim y As Integer = 40
' Iterate through the matches found and display each color that
' corresponds with the enum value in the array. Also display the
' name of the KnownColor and the ARGB components.
Dim i As Integer
For i = 0 To count - 1
' Display the color.
someColor = Color.FromKnownColor(colorMatches(i))
myBrush1.Color = someColor
g.FillRectangle(myBrush1, x, y, 50, 30)
' Display KnownColor name and four component values. To display
' component values:  Use the ToArgb method to get the 32-bit
' ARGB value of someColor (created from a KnownColor). Create
' a Color structure from the 32-bit ARGB value and set someColor
' equal to this new Color structure. Then use the ToString method
' to convert it to a string.
```

```
g.DrawString(someColor.ToString(), myFont, Brushes.Black, _
x + 55, y)
someColor = Color.FromArgb(someColor.ToArgb())
g.DrawString(someColor.ToString(), myFont, Brushes.Black, _
x + 55, y + 15)
y += 40
Next i
End Sub
```

[C#]

```
public void ToArgbToStringExample(PaintEventArgs e)
{
Graphics     g = e.Graphics;
// Color structure used for temporary storage.
Color   someColor = Color.FromArgb(0);
// Array to store KnownColor values that match the criteria.
KnownColor[]  colorMatches = new KnownColor[167];
int  count = 0;   // number of matches found
// Iterate through the KnownColor enums to find all          ↵
corresponding colors
// that have a nonzero green component and zero-value red component and
// that are not system colors.
for (KnownColor enumValue = 0;
enumValue <= KnownColor.YellowGreen; enumValue++)
{
someColor = Color.FromKnownColor(enumValue);
if ( someColor.G != 0 && someColor.R == 0 && !someColor.IsSystemColor )
colorMatches[count++] = enumValue;
}
SolidBrush  myBrush1 = new SolidBrush(someColor);
Font        myFont = new Font("Arial", 9);
int         x = 40;
int         y = 40;
// Iterate through the matches that were found and display       ↵
 each color that
// corresponds with the enum value in the array. also display   ↵
the name of
// the KnownColor and the ARGB components.
for ( int i = 0; i < count; i++)
{
// Display the color.
someColor = Color.FromKnownColor(colorMatches[i]);
myBrush1.Color = someColor;
g.FillRectangle(myBrush1, x, y, 50, 30);
// Display KnownColor name and the four component values.      ↵
To display the
// component values:  Use the ToArgb method to get the 32-bit   ↵
 ARGB value
// of someColor, which was created from a KnownColor. Then create a
// Color structure from the 32-bit ARGB value and set someColor  ↵
 equal to
// this new Color structure. Then use the ToString method to     ↵
convert it to
// a string.
g.DrawString(someColor.ToString(), myFont, Brushes.Black, x + 55, y);
someColor = Color.FromArgb(someColor.ToArgb());
g.DrawString(someColor.ToString(), myFont, Brushes.Black,        ↵
x + 55, y + 15);
y += 40;
}
}
```

Requirements

Platforms: Windows 98, Windows NT 4.0, Windows Millennium Edition, Windows 2000, Windows XP Home Edition, Windows XP Professional, Windows Server 2003 family, .NET Compact Framework - Windows CE .NET

Color.ToKnownColor Method

Gets the **KnownColor** value of this **Color** structure.

[Visual Basic]

```
Public Function ToKnownColor() As KnownColor
```

[C#]

```
public KnownColor ToKnownColor();
```

[C++]

```
public: KnownColor ToKnownColor();
```

[JScript]

```
public function ToKnownColor() : KnownColor;
```

Return Value

An element of the **KnownColor** enumeration, if the **Color** structure is created from a pre-defined color by using either the **FromName** method or the **FromKnownColor** method; otherwise, zero.

Remarks

A pre-defined color is also called a known color and is represented by an element of the **KnownColor** enumeration. When the **ToKnownColor** method is applied to a **Color** structure that is created by using the **FromArgb** method, the **ToKnownColor** method returns zero, even if the ARGB value matches the ARGB value of a pre-defined color. The **ToKnownColor** method also returns zero when it is applied to a **Color** structure that is created by using the **FromName** method with an invalid string name.

Requirements

Platforms: Windows 98, Windows NT 4.0, Windows Millennium Edition, Windows 2000, Windows XP Home Edition, Windows XP Professional, Windows Server 2003 family

Color.ToString Method

Converts this **Color** structure to a human-readable string.

[Visual Basic]

```
Overrides Public Function ToString() As String
```

[C#]

```
public override string ToString();
```

[C++]

```
public: String* ToString();
```

[JScript]

```
public override function ToString() : String;
```

Return Value

A string that is the name of the color of this **Color** structure, if the **Color** structure is created from a pre-defined color by using either the **FromName** method or the **FromKnownColor** method; otherwise, a string that consists of the ARGB component names and their values.

Remarks

A pre-defined color is also called a known color and is represented by an element of the **KnownColor** enumeration. When the **ToString** method is applied to a **Color** structure that is created by using the **FromArgb** method, the **ToString** method returns a string that consists of the ARGB component names and their values, even if the ARGB value matches the ARGB value of a pre-defined color.

Example

[Visual Basic, C#] The following example is designed for use with Windows Forms, and it requires **PaintEventArgs** *e*, which is a parameter of the **Paint** event handler. The code performs the following actions:

- Iterates through the **KnownColor** enumeration elements to find all known colors that have a nonzero green component and a zero-value red component and that are not system colors.
- During each iteration: saves the **KnownColor** element, if it matches the criteria, in an array.
- Uses a brush to paint rectangles. Each of the rectangles is painted a **KnownColor** that matches the criteria stated in the first step. The name of the **KnownColor** and its component values are also displayed.

[Visual Basic, C#] This example displays certain known colors and uses the **ToString** method to display the names of the colors and their four component values.

[Visual Basic]

```
Public Sub ToArgbToStringExample(e As PaintEventArgs)
Dim g As Graphics = e.Graphics
' Color structure used for temporary storage.
Dim someColor As Color = Color.FromArgb(0)
' Array to store KnownColor values that match the criteria.
Dim colorMatches(167) As KnownColor
Dim count As Integer = 0 ' number of matches found
' Iterate through KnownColor enums to find all corresponding colors
' that have a non-zero green component and zero-valued red
' component and that are not system colors.
Dim enumValue As KnownColor
For enumValue = 0 To KnownColor.YellowGreen
someColor = Color.FromKnownColor(enumValue)
If someColor.G <> 0 And someColor.R = 0 And _
Not someColor.IsSystemColor Then
colorMatches(count) = enumValue
count += 1
End If
Next enumValue
Dim myBrush1 As New SolidBrush(someColor)
Dim myFont As New Font("Arial", 9)
Dim x As Integer = 40
Dim y As Integer = 40
' Iterate through the matches found and display each color that
' corresponds with the enum value in the array. Also display the
' name of the KnownColor and the ARGB components.
Dim i As Integer
For i = 0 To count - 1
' Display the color
someColor = Color.FromKnownColor(colorMatches(i))
myBrush1.Color = someColor
g.FillRectangle(myBrush1, x, y, 50, 30)
' Display KnownColor name and four component values. To display
' component values:  Use the ToArgb method to get the 32-bit
' ARGB value of someColor (created from a KnownColor). Create
' a Color structure from the 32-bit ARGB value and set someColor
' equal to this new Color structure. Then use the ToString method
' to convert it to a string.
g.DrawString(someColor.ToString(), myFont, Brushes.Black, _
x + 55, y)
someColor = Color.FromArgb(someColor.ToArgb())
g.DrawString(someColor.ToString(), myFont, Brushes.Black, _
x + 55, y + 15)
y += 40
Next i
End Sub
```

[C#]

```
public void ToArgbToStringExample(PaintEventArgs e)
{
Graphics     g = e.Graphics;
// Color structure used for temporary storage.
Color   someColor = Color.FromArgb(0);
// Array to store KnownColor values that match the criteria.
KnownColor[]  colorMatches = new KnownColor[167];
int  count = 0;  // number of matches found
// Iterate through the KnownColor enums to find all                    ↵
corresponding colors
// that have a nonzero green component and zero-value red component and
// that are not system colors.
for (KnownColor enumValue = 0;
enumValue <= KnownColor.YellowGreen; enumValue++)
{
someColor = Color.FromKnownColor(enumValue);
if ( someColor.G != 0 && someColor.R == 0 && !someColor.IsSystemColor )
colorMatches[count++] = enumValue;
}
SolidBrush  myBrush1 = new SolidBrush(someColor);
Font        myFont = new Font("Arial", 9);
int         x = 40;
int         y = 40;
// Iterate through the matches that were found and display             ↵
 each color that
// corresponds with the enum value in the array. also                  ↵
display the name of
// the KnownColor and the ARGB components.
for ( int i = 0; i < count; i++)
{
// Display the color.
someColor = Color.FromKnownColor(colorMatches[i]);
myBrush1.Color = someColor;
g.FillRectangle(myBrush1, x, y, 50, 30);
// Display KnownColor name and the four component values.              ↵
 To display the
// component values:  Use the ToArgb method to get the 32-bit          ↵
ARGB value
// of someColor, which was created from a KnownColor. Then create a
// Color structure from the 32-bit ARGB value and set                  ↵
someColor equal to
// this new Color structure . Then use the ToString method              ↵
to convert it to
// a string.
g.DrawString(someColor.ToString(), myFont, Brushes.Black, x + 55, y);
someColor = Color.FromArgb(someColor.ToArgb());
g.DrawString(someColor.ToString(), myFont, Brushes.Black,              ↵
x + 55, y + 15);
y += 40;
}
}
```

Requirements

Platforms: Windows 98, Windows NT 4.0, Windows Millennium Edition, Windows 2000, Windows XP Home Edition, Windows XP Professional, Windows Server 2003 family, .NET Compact Framework - Windows CE .NET

Color Equality Operator

Tests whether two specified **Color** structures are equivalent.

[Visual Basic]

```
returnValue = Color.op_Equality(left, right)
```

[C#]

```
public static bool operator ==(
   Color left,
   Color right
);
```

```
[C++]
public: static bool op_Equality(
   Color left,
   Color right
);
[JScript]
returnValue = left == right;
```

[Visual Basic] In Visual Basic, you can use the operators defined by a type, but you cannot define your own.

[JScript] In JScript, you can use the operators defined by a type, but you cannot define your own.

Arguments [Visual Basic, JScript]

left
The **Color** structure that is to the left of the equality operator.

right
The **Color** structure that is to the right of the equality operator.

Parameters [C#, C++]

left
The **Color** structure that is to the left of the equality operator.

right
The **Color** structure that is to the right of the equality operator.

Return Value

This operator returns **true** if the two **Color** structures are equal; otherwise, **false**.

Remarks

This method compares more than the ARGB values of the **Color** structures. It also does a comparison of some state flags. If you want to compare just the ARGB values of two **Color** structures, use Color1.ToArgb() == Color2.ToArgb().

Requirements

Platforms: Windows 98, Windows NT 4.0, Windows Millennium Edition, Windows 2000, Windows XP Home Edition, Windows XP Professional, Windows Server 2003 family, .NET Compact Framework - Windows CE .NET

Color Inequality Operator

Tests whether two specified **Color** structures are different.

```
[Visual Basic]
returnValue = Color.op_Inequality(left, right)
[C#]
public static bool operator !=(
   Color left,
   Color right
);
[C++]
public: static bool op_Inequality(
   Color left,
   Color right
);
[JScript]
returnValue = left != right;
```

[Visual Basic] In Visual Basic, you can use the operators defined by a type, but you cannot define your own.

[JScript] In JScript, you can use the operators defined by a type, but you cannot define your own.

Arguments [Visual Basic, JScript]

left
The **Color** structure that is to the left of the inequality operator.

right
The **Color** structure that is to the right of the inequality operator.

Parameters [C#, C++]

left
The **Color** structure that is to the left of the inequality operator.

right
The **Color** structure that is to the right of the inequality operator.

Return Value

This operator returns **true** if the two **Color** structures are different; otherwise, **false**.

Remarks

This method compares more than the ARGB values of the **Color** structures. It also does a comparison of some state flags. If you want to compare just the ARGB values of two **Color** structures, use Color1.ToArgb() != Color2.ToArgb().

Requirements

Platforms: Windows 98, Windows NT 4.0, Windows Millennium Edition, Windows 2000, Windows XP Home Edition, Windows XP Professional, Windows Server 2003 family, .NET Compact Framework - Windows CE .NET

ColorConverter Class

Converts colors from one data type to another. Access this class through the TypeDescriptor.

System.Object
  System.ComponentModel.TypeConverter
    System.Drawing.ColorConverter
      System.Web.UI.WebControls.WebColorConverter

[Visual Basic]
```
Public Class ColorConverter
   Inherits TypeConverter
```
[C#]
```
public class ColorConverter : TypeConverter
```
[C++]
```
public __gc class ColorConverter : public TypeConverter
```
[JScript]
```
public class ColorConverter extends TypeConverter
```

Thread Safety

Any public static (**Shared** in Visual Basic) members of this type are safe for multithreaded operations. Any instance members are not guaranteed to be thread safe.

Requirements

Namespace: System.Drawing

Platforms: Windows 98, Windows NT 4.0, Windows Millennium Edition, Windows 2000, Windows XP Home Edition, Windows XP Professional, Windows Server 2003 family

Assembly: System.Drawing (in System.Drawing.dll)

ColorConverter Constructor

Initializes a new instance of the **ColorConverter** class.

[Visual Basic]
```
Public Sub New()
```
[C#]
```
public ColorConverter();
```
[C++]
```
public: ColorConverter();
```
[JScript]
```
public function ColorConverter();
```

Requirements

Platforms: Windows 98, Windows NT 4.0, Windows Millennium Edition, Windows 2000, Windows XP Home Edition, Windows XP Professional, Windows Server 2003 family

ColorConverter.CanConvertFrom Method

Overload List

Determines if this converter can convert an object in the given source type to the native type of the converter.

[Visual Basic] **Overloads Overrides Public Function CanConvertFrom(ITypeDescriptorContext, Type) As Boolean**

[C#] **public override bool CanConvertFrom(ITypeDescriptorContext, Type);**

[C++] **public: bool CanConvertFrom(ITypeDescriptorContext*, Type*);**

[JScript] **public override function CanConvertFrom(ITypeDescriptorContext, Type) : Boolean;**

Inherited from **TypeConverter**.

[Visual Basic] **Overloads Public Function CanConvertFrom(Type) As Boolean**

[C#] **public bool CanConvertFrom(Type);**

[C++] **public: bool CanConvertFrom(Type*);**

[JScript] **public function CanConvertFrom(Type) : Boolean;**

ColorConverter.CanConvertFrom Method (ITypeDescriptorContext, Type)

Determines if this converter can convert an object in the given source type to the native type of the converter.

[Visual Basic]
```
Overrides Overloads Public Function CanConvertFrom( _
   ByVal context As ITypeDescriptorContext, _
   ByVal sourceType As Type _
) As Boolean
```
[C#]
```
public override bool CanConvertFrom(
   ITypeDescriptorContext context,
   Type sourceType
);
```
[C++]
```
public: bool CanConvertFrom(
   ITypeDescriptorContext* context,
   Type* sourceType
);
```
[JScript]
```
public override function CanConvertFrom(
   context : ITypeDescriptorContext,
   sourceType : Type
) : Boolean;
```

Parameters

context
An **ITypeDescriptorContext** object that provides a format context. You can use this object to get additional information about the environment from which this converter is being invoked.

sourceType
The type from which you want to convert.

Return Value

This method returns **true** if this object can perform the conversion; otherwise, **false**.

Requirements

Platforms: Windows 98, Windows NT 4.0, Windows Millennium Edition, Windows 2000, Windows XP Home Edition, Windows XP Professional, Windows Server 2003 family

ColorConverter.CanConvertTo Method

Overload List

Returns a value indicating whether this converter can convert an object to the given destination type using the context.

[Visual Basic] **Overloads Overrides Public Function CanConvertTo(ITypeDescriptorContext, Type) As Boolean**

[C#] **public override bool CanConvertTo(ITypeDescriptor-Context, Type);**

[C++] **public: bool CanConvertTo(ITypeDescriptorContext*, Type*);**

[JScript] **public override function CanConvertTo(IType-DescriptorContext, Type) : Boolean;**

Inherited from **TypeConverter**.

[Visual Basic] **Overloads Public Function CanConvertTo(Type) As Boolean**

[C#] **public bool CanConvertTo(Type);**

[C++] **public: bool CanConvertTo(Type*);**

[JScript] **public function CanConvertTo(Type) : Boolean;**

ColorConverter.CanConvertTo Method (ITypeDescriptorContext, Type)

Returns a value indicating whether this converter can convert an object to the given destination type using the context.

```
[Visual Basic]
Overrides Overloads Public Function CanConvertTo( _
   ByVal context As ITypeDescriptorContext, _
   ByVal destinationType As Type _
) As Boolean
[C#]
public override bool CanConvertTo(
   ITypeDescriptorContext context,
   Type destinationType
);
[C++]
public: bool CanConvertTo(
   ITypeDescriptorContext* context,
   Type* destinationType
);
[JScript]
public override function CanConvertTo(
   context : ITypeDescriptorContext,
   destinationType : Type
) : Boolean;
```

Parameters

context

An **ITypeDescriptorContext** object that provides a format context.

destinationType

A **Type** object that represents the type to which you want to convert.

Return Value

This method returns **true** if this converter can perform the operation; otherwise, **false**.

Requirements

Platforms: Windows 98, Windows NT 4.0, Windows Millennium Edition, Windows 2000, Windows XP Home Edition, Windows XP Professional, Windows Server 2003 family

ColorConverter.ConvertFrom Method

Overload List

Converts the given object to the converter's native type.

[Visual Basic] **Overloads Overrides Public Function Convert-From(ITypeDescriptorContext, CultureInfo, Object) As Object**

[C#] **public override object ConvertFrom(ITypeDescriptor-Context, CultureInfo, object);**

[C++] **public: Object* ConvertFrom(ITypeDescriptor-Context*, CultureInfo*, Object*);**

[JScript] **public override function ConvertFrom(IType-DescriptorContext, CultureInfo, Object) : Object;**

Inherited from **TypeConverter**.

[Visual Basic] **Overloads Public Function Convert-From(Object) As Object**

[C#] **public object ConvertFrom(object);**

[C++] **public: Object* ConvertFrom(Object*);**

[JScript] **public function ConvertFrom(Object) : Object;**

ColorConverter.ConvertFrom Method (ITypeDescriptorContext, CultureInfo, Object)

Converts the given object to the converter's native type.

```
[Visual Basic]
Overrides Overloads Public Function ConvertFrom( _
   ByVal context As ITypeDescriptorContext, _
   ByVal culture As CultureInfo, _
   ByVal value As Object _
) As Object
[C#]
public override object ConvertFrom(
   ITypeDescriptorContext context,
   CultureInfo culture,
   object value
);
[C++]
public: Object* ConvertFrom(
   ITypeDescriptorContext* context,
   CultureInfo* culture,
   Object* value
);
[JScript]
public override function ConvertFrom(
   context : ITypeDescriptorContext,
   culture : CultureInfo,
   value : Object
) : Object;
```

Parameters

context

An **TypeDescriptor** object that provides a format context. You can use this object to get additional information about the environment from which this converter is being invoked.

culture

A **CultureInfo** object that specifies the culture to represent the Color.

value

The object to convert.

Return Value

The converted object. This method will throw an exception if the conversion could not be performed.

Requirements

Platforms: Windows 98, Windows NT 4.0, Windows Millennium Edition, Windows 2000, Windows XP Home Edition, Windows XP Professional, Windows Server 2003 family

ColorConverter.ConvertTo Method

Overload List

Converts the specified object to another type. The most common types to convert are to and from a string object.

[Visual Basic] **Overloads Overrides Public Function ConvertTo (ITypeDescriptorContext, CultureInfo, Object, Type) As Object**

[C#] **public override object ConvertTo(ITypeDescriptorContext, CultureInfo, object, Type);**

[C++] **public: Object* ConvertTo(ITypeDescriptorContext*, CultureInfo*, Object*, Type*);**

[JScript] **public override function ConvertTo(ITypeDescriptorContext, CultureInfo, Object, Type) : Object;**

Inherited from **TypeConverter**.

[Visual Basic] **Overloads Public Function ConvertTo(Object, Type) As Object**

[C#] **public object ConvertTo(object, Type);**

[C++] **public: Object* ConvertTo(Object*, Type*);**

[JScript] **public function ConvertTo(Object, Type) : Object;**

ColorConverter.ConvertTo Method (ITypeDescriptorContext, CultureInfo, Object, Type)

Converts the specified object to another type. The most common types to convert are to and from a string object.

```
[Visual Basic]
Overrides Overloads Public Function ConvertTo( _
   ByVal context As ITypeDescriptorContext, _
   ByVal culture As CultureInfo, _
   ByVal value As Object, _
   ByVal destinationType As Type _
) As Object
[C#]
public override object ConvertTo(
   ITypeDescriptorContext context,
   CultureInfo culture,
   object value,
   Type destinationType
);
[C++]
public: Object* ConvertTo(
   ITypeDescriptorContext* context,
   CultureInfo* culture,
   Object* value,
   Type* destinationType
);
[JScript]
public override function ConvertTo(
   context : ITypeDescriptorContext,
   culture : CultureInfo,
   value : Object,
   destinationType : Type
) : Object;
```

Parameters

context

A formatter context. Use this object to extract additional information about the environment from which this converter is being invoked. Always check whether this value is null. Also, properties on the context object may also return null.

culture

A **CultureInfo** object that specifies the culture to represent the Color.

value

The object to convert.

destinationType

The type to convert the object to.

Return Value

The converted object. If this method cannot convert to the destination type, it throws a **NotSupportedException**.

Requirements

Platforms: Windows 98, Windows NT 4.0, Windows Millennium Edition, Windows 2000, Windows XP Home Edition, Windows XP Professional, Windows Server 2003 family

ColorConverter.GetStandardValues Method

Overload List

Retrieves a collection containing a set of standard values for the data type for which this validator is designed. This will return null if the data type does not support a standard set of values.

[Visual Basic] **Overloads Overrides Public Function GetStandardValues(ITypeDescriptorContext) As StandardValuesCollection**

[C#] **public override StandardValuesCollection GetStandardValues(ITypeDescriptorContext);**

[C++] **public: StandardValuesCollection* GetStandardValues(ITypeDescriptorContext*);**

[JScript] **public override function GetStandardValues(ITypeDescriptorContext) : StandardValuesCollection;**

Inherited from **TypeConverter**.

[Visual Basic] **Overloads Public Function GetStandardValues() As ICollection**

[C#] **public ICollection GetStandardValues();**

[C++] **public: ICollection* GetStandardValues();**

[JScript] **public function GetStandardValues() : ICollection;**

ColorConverter.GetStandardValues Method (ITypeDescriptorContext)

Retrieves a collection containing a set of standard values for the data type for which this validator is designed. This will return null if the data type does not support a standard set of values.

```
[Visual Basic]
Overrides Overloads Public Function GetStandardValues( _
   ByVal context As ITypeDescriptorContext _
) As StandardValuesCollection
[C#]
public override StandardValuesCollection GetStandardValues(
   ITypeDescriptorContext context
);
[C++]
public: StandardValuesCollection* GetStandardValues(
   ITypeDescriptorContext* context
);
[JScript]
public override function GetStandardValues(
   context : ITypeDescriptorContext
) : StandardValuesCollection;
```

Parameters

context
A formatter context. Use this object to extract additional information about the environment from which this converter is being invoked. Always check whether this value is null. Also, properties on the context object may also return null.

Return Value

A collection containing null or a standard set of valid values. The default implementation always returns null.

Requirements

Platforms: Windows 98, Windows NT 4.0, Windows Millennium Edition, Windows 2000, Windows XP Home Edition, Windows XP Professional, Windows Server 2003 family

ColorConverter.GetStandardValuesSupported Method

Overload List

Determines if this object supports a standard set of values that can be chosen from a list.

[Visual Basic] **Overloads Overrides Public Function GetStandardValuesSupported(ITypeDescriptorContext) As Boolean**

[C#] **public override bool GetStandardValuesSupported (ITypeDescriptorContext);**

[C++] **public: bool GetStandardValuesSupported (ITypeDescriptorContext*);**

[JScript] **public override function GetStandardValues-Supported(ITypeDescriptorContext) : Boolean;**

Inherited from **TypeConverter**.

[Visual Basic] **Overloads Public Function GetStandardValuesSupported() As Boolean**

[C#] **public bool GetStandardValuesSupported();**

[C++] **public: bool GetStandardValuesSupported();**

[JScript] **public function GetStandardValuesSupported() : Boolean;**

ColorConverter.GetStandardValuesSupported Method (ITypeDescriptorContext)

Determines if this object supports a standard set of values that can be chosen from a list.

```
[Visual Basic]
Overrides Overloads Public Function GetStandardValuesSupported( _
   ByVal context As ITypeDescriptorContext _
) As Boolean
[C#]
public override bool GetStandardValuesSupported(
   ITypeDescriptorContext context
);
[C++]
public: bool GetStandardValuesSupported(
   ITypeDescriptorContext* context
);
[JScript]
public override function GetStandardValuesSupported(
   context : ITypeDescriptorContext
) : Boolean;
```

Parameters

context
A type descriptor through which additional context can be provided.

Return Value

This method returns **true** if **GetStandardValues** must be called to find a common set of values the object supports; otherwise, **false**.

Requirements

Platforms: Windows 98, Windows NT 4.0, Windows Millennium Edition, Windows 2000, Windows XP Home Edition, Windows XP Professional, Windows Server 2003 family

ColorTranslator Class

Translates colors to and from GDI+ **Color** structures. This class cannot be inherited.

System.Object
System.Drawing.ColorTranslator

[Visual Basic]
```
NotInheritable Public Class ColorTranslator
```
[C#]
```
public sealed class ColorTranslator
```
[C++]
```
public __gc __sealed class ColorTranslator
```
[JScript]
```
public class ColorTranslator
```

Thread Safety

Any public static (**Shared** in Visual Basic) members of this type are safe for multithreaded operations. Any instance members are not guaranteed to be thread safe.

Requirements

Namespace: System.Drawing

Platforms: Windows 98, Windows NT 4.0, Windows Millennium Edition, Windows 2000, Windows XP Home Edition, Windows XP Professional, Windows Server 2003 family

Assembly: System.Drawing (in System.Drawing.dll)

ColorTranslator.FromHtml Method

Translates an HTML color representation to a GDI+ **Color** structure.

[Visual Basic]
```
Public Shared Function FromHtml( _
   ByVal htmlColor As String _
) As Color
```
[C#]
```
public static Color FromHtml(
   string htmlColor
);
```
[C++]
```
public: static Color FromHtml(
   String* htmlColor
);
```
[JScript]
```
public static function FromHtml(
   htmlColor : String
) : Color;
```

Parameters

htmlColor
The string representation of the Html color to translate.

Return Value

The **Color** structure that represents the translated HTML color.

Remarks

This method translates a string representation of an HTML color name, such as Blue or Red, to a GDI+ **Color** structure.

Example

[Visual Basic, C#] The following example is designed for use with Windows Forms, and it requires **PaintEventArgs** *e*, which is a parameter of the **Paint** event handler. The code translates an HTML color name to a **Color** structure, and then uses that color to fill a rectangle.

[Visual Basic]
```
Public Sub FromHtml_Example(e As PaintEventArgs)
' Create a string representation of an HTML color.
Dim htmlColor As String = "Blue"
' Translate htmlColor to a GDI+ Color structure.
Dim myColor As Color = ColorTranslator.FromHtml(htmlColor)
' Fill a rectangle with myColor.
e.Graphics.FillRectangle(New SolidBrush(myColor), 0, 0, 100, 100)
End Sub
```

[C#]
```
public void FromHtml_Example(PaintEventArgs e)
{
// Create a string representation of an HTML color.
string htmlColor = "Blue";
// Translate htmlColor to a GDI+ Color structure.
Color myColor = ColorTranslator.FromHtml(htmlColor);
// Fill a rectangle with myColor.
e.Graphics.FillRectangle(
new SolidBrush(myColor),
0,
0,
100,
100);
}
```

Requirements

Platforms: Windows 98, Windows NT 4.0, Windows Millennium Edition, Windows 2000, Windows XP Home Edition, Windows XP Professional, Windows Server 2003 family

ColorTranslator.FromOle Method

Translates an OLE color value to a GDI+ **Color** structure.

[Visual Basic]
```
Public Shared Function FromOle( _
   ByVal oleColor As Integer _
) As Color
```
[C#]
```
public static Color FromOle(
   int oleColor
);
```
[C++]
```
public: static Color FromOle(
   int oleColor
);
```
[JScript]
```
public static function FromOle(
   oleColor : int
) : Color;
```

Parameters

oleColor
The OLE color to translate.

Return Value

The **Color** structure that represents the translated OLE color.

Example

[Visual Basic, C#] The following example is designed for use with Windows Forms, and it requires **PaintEventArgs** *e*, which is a parameter of the **Paint** event handler. The code translates an OLE color value to a **Color** structure, and then uses that color to fill a rectangle.

[Visual Basic]
```
Public Sub FromOle_Example(e As PaintEventArgs)
' Create an integer representation of an HTML color.
Dim oleColor As Integer = &HFF00
' Translate oleColor to a GDI+ Color structure.
Dim myColor As Color = ColorTranslator.FromOle(oleColor)
' Fill a rectangle with myColor.
e.Graphics.FillRectangle(New SolidBrush(myColor), 0, 0, 100, 100)
End Sub
```

[C#]
```
public void FromOle_Example(PaintEventArgs e)
{
// Create an integer representation of an OLE color.
int oleColor = 0xFF00;
// Translate oleColor to a GDI+ Color structure.
Color myColor = ColorTranslator.FromOle(oleColor);
// Fill a rectangle with myColor.
e.Graphics.FillRectangle(
new SolidBrush(myColor),
0,
0,
100,
100);
}
```

Requirements

Platforms: Windows 98, Windows NT 4.0, Windows Millennium Edition, Windows 2000, Windows XP Home Edition, Windows XP Professional, Windows Server 2003 family

ColorTranslator.FromWin32 Method

Translates a Windows color value to a GDI+ **Color** structure.

[Visual Basic]
```
Public Shared Function FromWin32( _
   ByVal win32Color As Integer _
) As Color
```
[C#]
```
public static Color FromWin32(
   int win32Color
);
```
[C++]
```
public: static Color FromWin32(
   int win32Color
);
```
[JScript]
```
public static function FromWin32(
   win32Color : int
) : Color;
```

Parameters

win32Color
: The Windows color to translate.

Return Value

The **Color** structure that represents the translated Windows color.

Example

[Visual Basic, C#] The following example is designed for use with Windows Forms, and it requires **PaintEventArgs** *e*, which is a parameter of the **Paint** event handler. The code translates a Windows color value to a **Color** structure, and then uses that color to fill a rectangle.

[Visual Basic]
```
Public Sub FromWin32_Example(e As PaintEventArgs)
' Create an integer representation of a Win32 color.
Dim winColor As Integer = &HA000
' Translate winColor to a GDI+ Color structure.
Dim myColor As Color = ColorTranslator.FromWin32(winColor)
' Fill a rectangle with myColor.
e.Graphics.FillRectangle(New SolidBrush(myColor), 0, 0, 100, 100)
End Sub
```

[C#]
```
public void FromWin32_Example(PaintEventArgs e)
{
// Create an integer representation of a Windows color.
int winColor = 0xA000;
// Translate winColor to a GDI+ Color structure.
Color myColor = ColorTranslator.FromWin32(winColor);
// Fill a rectangle with myColor.
e.Graphics.FillRectangle(
new SolidBrush(myColor),
0,
0,
100,
100);
}
```

Requirements

Platforms: Windows 98, Windows NT 4.0, Windows Millennium Edition, Windows 2000, Windows XP Home Edition, Windows XP Professional, Windows Server 2003 family

ColorTranslator.ToHtml Method

Translates the specified **Color** structure to an HTML string color representation.

[Visual Basic]
```
Public Shared Function ToHtml( _
   ByVal c As Color _
) As String
```
[C#]
```
public static string ToHtml(
   Color c
);
```
[C++]
```
public: static String* ToHtml(
   Color c
);
```
[JScript]
```
public static function ToHtml(
   c : Color
) : String;
```

Parameters

c
: The **Color** structure to translate.

Return Value

The string that represents the HTML color.

Remarks

This method translates a **Color** structure to a string representation of an HTML color. This is the commonly used name of a color, such as "Red", "Blue", or "Green", and not string representation of a numeric color value, such as "FF33AA".

Example

[Visual Basic, C#] The following example is designed for use with Windows Forms, and it requires **PaintEventArgs** *e*, which is a parameter of the **Paint** event handler. The code translates a **Color** structure to a string representation of an HTML color, and then shows a message box with the resulting string.

```
[Visual Basic]
Public Sub ToHtml_Example(e As PaintEventArgs)
' Create an instance of a Color structure.
Dim myColor As Color = Color.Red
' Translate myColor to an HTML color.
Dim htmlColor As String = ColorTranslator.ToHtml(myColor)
' Show a message box with the value of htmlColor.
MessageBox.Show(htmlColor)
End Sub
```

```
[C#]
public void ToHtml_Example(PaintEventArgs e)
{
// Create an instance of a Color structure.
Color myColor = Color.Red;
// Translate myColor to an HTML color.
string htmlColor = ColorTranslator.ToHtml(myColor);
// Show a message box with the value of htmlColor.
MessageBox.Show(htmlColor);
}
```

Requirements

Platforms: Windows 98, Windows NT 4.0, Windows Millennium Edition, Windows 2000, Windows XP Home Edition, Windows XP Professional, Windows Server 2003 family

ColorTranslator.ToOle Method

Translates the specified **Color** structure to an OLE color.

```
[Visual Basic]
Public Shared Function ToOle( _
   ByVal c As Color _
) As Integer
[C#]
public static int ToOle(
   Color c
);
[C++]
public: static int ToOle(
   Color c
);
[JScript]
public static function ToOle(
   c : Color
) : int;
```

Parameters

c

The **Color** structure to translate.

Return Value

The OLE color value.

Example

[Visual Basic, C#] The following example is designed for use with Windows Forms, and it requires **PaintEventArgs** *e*, which is a parameter of the **Paint** event handler. The code translates a **Color** structure to an integer that represents an OLE color, and then shows a message box with the resulting string.

```
[Visual Basic]
Public Sub ToOle_Example(e As PaintEventArgs)
' Create an instance of a Color structure.
Dim myColor As Color = Color.Green
' Translate myColor to an OLE color.
Dim oleColor As Integer = ColorTranslator.ToOle(myColor)
' Show a message box with the value of htmlColor.
MessageBox.Show(oleColor.ToString())
End Sub
```

```
[C#]
public void ToOle_Example(PaintEventArgs e)
{
// Create an instance of a Color structure.
Color myColor = Color.Red;
// Translate myColor to an OLE color.
int oleColor = ColorTranslator.ToOle(myColor);
// Show a message box with the value of oleColor.
MessageBox.Show(oleColor);
}
```

Requirements

Platforms: Windows 98, Windows NT 4.0, Windows Millennium Edition, Windows 2000, Windows XP Home Edition, Windows XP Professional, Windows Server 2003 family

ColorTranslator.ToWin32 Method

Translates the specified **Color** structure to a Windows color.

```
[Visual Basic]
Public Shared Function ToWin32( _
   ByVal c As Color _
) As Integer
[C#]
public static int ToWin32(
   Color c
);
[C++]
public: static int ToWin32(
   Color c
);
[JScript]
public static function ToWin32(
   c : Color
) : int;
```

Parameters

c

The **Color** structure to translate.

Return Value

The Windows color value.

Example

[Visual Basic, C#] The following example is designed for use with Windows Forms, and it requires **PaintEventArgs** *e*, which is a parameter of the **Paint** event handler. The code translates a **Color** structure to an integer that represents a Windows color, and then shows a message box with the resulting string.

[Visual Basic]
```
Public Sub ToWin32_Example(e As PaintEventArgs)
' Create an instance of a Color structure.
Dim myColor As Color = Color.Red
' Translate myColor to an OLE color.
Dim winColor As Integer = ColorTranslator.ToWin32(myColor)
' Show a message box with the value of winColor.
MessageBox.Show(winColor)
End Sub
```

[C#]
```
public void ToWin32_Example(PaintEventArgs e)
{
// Create an instance of a Color structure.
Color myColor = Color.Red;
// Translate myColor to an OLE color.
int winColor = ColorTranslator.ToWin32(myColor);
// Show a message box with the value of winColor.
MessageBox.Show(winColor);
}
```

Requirements

Platforms: Windows 98, Windows NT 4.0, Windows Millennium Edition, Windows 2000, Windows XP Home Edition, Windows XP Professional, Windows Server 2003 family

ContentAlignment Enumeration

Specifies alignment of content on the drawing surface.

[Visual Basic]
```
<Serializable>
Public Enum ContentAlignment
```
[C#]
```
[Serializable]
public enum ContentAlignment
```
[C++]
```
[Serializable]
__value public enum ContentAlignment
```
[JScript]
```
public
   Serializable
enum ContentAlignment
```

Members

Member name	Description
BottomCenter	Content is vertically aligned at the bottom, and horizontally aligned at the center.
BottomLeft	Content is vertically aligned at the bottom, and horizontally aligned on the left.
BottomRight	Content is vertically aligned at the bottom, and horizontally aligned on the right.
MiddleCenter	Content is vertically aligned in the middle, and horizontally aligned at the center.
MiddleLeft	Content is vertically aligned in the middle, and horizontally aligned on the left.
MiddleRight	Content is vertically aligned in the middle, and horizontally aligned on the right.
TopCenter Supported by the .NET Compact Framework.	Content is vertically aligned at the top, and horizontally aligned at the center.
TopLeft Supported by the .NET Compact Framework.	Content is vertically aligned at the top, and horizontally aligned on the left.
TopRight Supported by the .NET Compact Framework.	Content is vertically aligned at the top, and horizontally aligned on the right.

Requirements

Namespace: System.Drawing

Platforms: Windows 98, Windows NT 4.0, Windows Millennium Edition, Windows 2000, Windows XP Home Edition, Windows XP Professional, Windows Server 2003 family, .NET Compact Framework - Windows CE .NET

Assembly: System.Drawing (in System.Drawing.dll)

Font Class

Defines a particular format for text, including font face, size, and style attributes. This class cannot be inherited.

System.Object
  System.MarshalByRefObject
    System.Drawing.Font

[Visual Basic]
```
<Serializable>
<ComVisible(True)>
NotInheritable Public Class Font
   Inherits MarshalByRefObject
   Implements ICloneable, ISerializable, IDisposable
```
[C#]
```
[Serializable]
[ComVisible(true)]
public sealed class Font : MarshalByRefObject, ICloneable,
   ISerializable, IDisposable
```
[C++]
```
[Serializable]
[ComVisible(true)]
public __gc __sealed class Font : public MarshalByRefObject,
   ICloneable, ISerializable, IDisposable
```
[JScript]
```
public
   Serializable
   ComVisible(true)
class Font extends MarshalByRefObject implements
   ICloneable, ISerializable, IDisposable
```

Thread Safety

Any public static (**Shared** in Visual Basic) members of this type are safe for multithreaded operations. Any instance members are not guaranteed to be thread safe.

Requirements

Namespace: System.Drawing

Platforms: Windows 98, Windows NT 4.0, Windows Millennium Edition, Windows 2000, Windows XP Home Edition, Windows XP Professional, Windows Server 2003 family, .NET Compact Framework - Windows CE .NET

Assembly: System.Drawing (in System.Drawing.dll)

Font Constructor

Note: This namespace, class, or member is supported only in version 1.1 of the .NET Framework.

This member supports the .NET Framework infrastructure and is not intended to be used directly from your code.

Overload List

This member supports the .NET Framework infrastructure and is not intended to be used directly from your code.

Supported only by the .NET Compact Framework.

[Visual Basic] **Public Sub New(IntPtr)**

[C#] **public Font(IntPtr);**

[C++] **public: Font(IntPtr);**

[JScript] **public function Font(IntPtr);**

Initializes a new **Font** object that uses the specified existing **Font** object and **FontStyle** enumeration.

[Visual Basic] **Public Sub New(Font, FontStyle)**

[C#] **public Font(Font, FontStyle);**

[C++] **public: Font(Font*, FontStyle);**

[JScript] **public function Font(Font, FontStyle);**

Initializes a new **Font** object using a specified size. Sets the style to FontStyle.Regular and sets the unit to GraphicsUnit.Point.

[Visual Basic] **Public Sub New(FontFamily, Single)**

[C#] **public Font(FontFamily, float);**

[C++] **public: Font(FontFamily*, float);**

[JScript] **public function Font(FontFamily, float);**

Initializes a new **Font** object using a specified size. Sets the unit to GraphicsUnit.Point and sets the style to FontStyle.Regular.

[Visual Basic] **Public Sub New(String, Single)**

[C#] **public Font(string, float);**

[C++] **public: Font(String*, float);**

[JScript] **public function Font(String, float);**

Initializes a new **Font** object using a specified size and style. Sets the unit to GraphicUnit.Point.

Supported by the .NET Compact Framework.

[Visual Basic] **Public Sub New(FontFamily, Single, FontStyle)**

[C#] **public Font(FontFamily, float, FontStyle);**

[C++] **public: Font(FontFamily*, float, FontStyle);**

[JScript] **public function Font(FontFamily, float, FontStyle);**

Initializes a new **Font** using a specified size and unit. Sets the style to FontStyle.Regular.

[Visual Basic] **Public Sub New(FontFamily, Single, GraphicsUnit)**

[C#] **public Font(FontFamily, float, GraphicsUnit);**

[C++] **public: Font(FontFamily*, float, GraphicsUnit);**

[JScript] **public function Font(FontFamily, float, GraphicsUnit);**

Initializes a new **Font** object using a specified size and style. Sets the unit to GraphicsUnit.Point.

Supported by the .NET Compact Framework.

[Visual Basic] **Public Sub New(String, Single, FontStyle)**

[C#] **public Font(string, float, FontStyle);**

[C++] **public: Font(String*, float, FontStyle);**

[JScript] **public function Font(String, float, FontStyle);**

Initializes a new **Font** object using a specified size and unit. The style is set to FontStyle.Regular.

[Visual Basic] **Public Sub New(String, Single, GraphicsUnit)**

[C#] **public Font(string, float, GraphicsUnit);**

[C++] **public: Font(String*, float, GraphicsUnit);**

[JScript] **public function Font(String, float, GraphicsUnit);**

Initializes a new **Font** using a specified size, style, and unit.

[Visual Basic] **Public Sub New(FontFamily, Single, FontStyle, GraphicsUnit)**

[C#] **public Font(FontFamily, float, FontStyle, GraphicsUnit);**

[C++] **public: Font(FontFamily*, float, FontStyle, GraphicsUnit);**

[JScript] **public function Font(FontFamily, float, FontStyle, GraphicsUnit);**

Initializes a new **Font** object using a specified size, style, and unit.

[Visual Basic] **Public Sub New(String, Single, FontStyle, GraphicsUnit)**

[C#] **public Font(string, float, FontStyle, GraphicsUnit);**

[C++] **public: Font(String*, float, FontStyle, GraphicsUnit);**

[JScript] **public function Font(String, float, FontStyle, GraphicsUnit);**

Initializes a new **Font** object using a specified size, style, unit, and character set.

[Visual Basic] **Public Sub New(FontFamily, Single, FontStyle, GraphicsUnit, Byte)**

[C#] **public Font(FontFamily, float, FontStyle, GraphicsUnit, byte);**

[C++] **public: Font(FontFamily*, float, FontStyle, GraphicsUnit, unsigned char);**

[JScript] **public function Font(FontFamily, float, FontStyle, GraphicsUnit, Byte);**

Initializes a new **Font** using a specified size, style, unit, and character set.

[Visual Basic] **Public Sub New(String, Single, FontStyle, GraphicsUnit, Byte)**

[C#] **public Font(string, float, FontStyle, GraphicsUnit, byte);**

[C++] **public: Font(String*, float, FontStyle, GraphicsUnit, unsigned char);**

[JScript] **public function Font(String, float, FontStyle, GraphicsUnit, Byte);**

Initializes a new **Font** using a specified size, style, unit, and character set.

[Visual Basic] **Public Sub New(FontFamily, Single, FontStyle, GraphicsUnit, Byte, Boolean)**

[C#] **public Font(FontFamily, float, FontStyle, GraphicsUnit, byte, bool);**

[C++] **public: Font(FontFamily*, float, FontStyle, GraphicsUnit, unsigned char, bool);**

[JScript] **public function Font(FontFamily, float, FontStyle, GraphicsUnit, Byte, Boolean);**

Initializes a new **Font** object using the specified size, style, unit, and character set.

[Visual Basic] **Public Sub New(String, Single, FontStyle, GraphicsUnit, Byte, Boolean)**

[C#] **public Font(string, float, FontStyle, GraphicsUnit, byte, bool);**

[C++] **public: Font(String*, float, FontStyle, GraphicsUnit, unsigned char, bool);**

[JScript] **public function Font(String, float, FontStyle, GraphicsUnit, Byte, Boolean);**

Font Constructor (IntPtr)

Note: This namespace, class, or member is supported only in version 1.1 of the .NET Framework.

This member supports the .NET Framework infrastructure and is not intended to be used directly from your code.

```
[Visual Basic]
Public Sub New( _
   ByVal htx As IntPtr _
)
[C#]
public Font(
   IntPtr htx
);
[C++]
public: Font(
   IntPtr htx
);
[JScript]
public function Font(
   htx : IntPtr
);
```

Font Constructor (Font, FontStyle)

Initializes a new **Font** object that uses the specified existing **Font** object and **FontStyle** enumeration.

```
[Visual Basic]
Public Sub New( _
   ByVal prototype As Font, _
   ByVal newStyle As FontStyle _
)
[C#]
public Font(
   Font prototype,
   FontStyle newStyle
);
[C++]
public: Font(
   Font* prototype,
   FontStyle newStyle
);
[JScript]
public function Font(
   prototype : Font,
   newStyle : FontStyle
);
```

Parameters

prototype

The existing **Font** object from which to create the new **Font** object.

newStyle

The **FontStyle** enumeration to apply to the new **Font** object. Multiple values of the **FontStyle** enumeration can be combined with the **OR** operator.

Requirements

Platforms: Windows 98, Windows NT 4.0, Windows Millennium Edition, Windows 2000, Windows XP Home Edition, Windows XP Professional, Windows Server 2003 family

Font Constructor (FontFamily, Single)

Initializes a new **Font** object using a specified size. Sets the style to FontStyle.Regular and sets the unit to GraphicsUnit.Point.

```
[Visual Basic]
Public Sub New( _
   ByVal family As FontFamily, _
   ByVal emSize As Single _
)
```

```
[C#]
public Font(
   FontFamily family,
   float emSize
);
[C++]
public: Font(
   FontFamily* family,
   float emSize
);
[JScript]
public function Font(
   family : FontFamily,
   emSize : float
);
```

Parameters

family
The **FontFamily** object of the new **Font** object.

emSize
The em-size, in points, of the new font.

Requirements

Platforms: Windows 98, Windows NT 4.0, Windows Millennium Edition, Windows 2000, Windows XP Home Edition, Windows XP Professional, Windows Server 2003 family

Font Constructor (String, Single)

Initializes a new **Font** object using a specified size. Sets the unit to GraphicsUnit.Point and sets the style to FontStyle.Regular.

```
[Visual Basic]
Public Sub New( _
   ByVal familyName As String, _
   ByVal emSize As Single _
)
[C#]
public Font(
   string familyName,
   float emSize
);
[C++]
public: Font(
   String* familyName,
   float emSize
);
[JScript]
public function Font(
   familyName : String,
   emSize : float
);
```

Parameters

familyName
A string representation of the **FontFamily** object for the new **Font** object.

emSize
The em-size, in points, of the new font.

Requirements

Platforms: Windows 98, Windows NT 4.0, Windows Millennium Edition, Windows 2000, Windows XP Home Edition, Windows XP Professional, Windows Server 2003 family

Font Constructor (FontFamily, Single, FontStyle)

Initializes a new **Font** object using a specified size and style. Sets the unit to GraphicUnit.Point.

```
[Visual Basic]
Public Sub New( _
   ByVal family As FontFamily, _
   ByVal emSize As Single, _
   ByVal style As FontStyle _
)
[C#]
public Font(
   FontFamily family,
   float emSize,
   FontStyle style
);
[C++]
public: Font(
   FontFamily* family,
   float emSize,
   FontStyle style
);
[JScript]
public function Font(
   family : FontFamily,
   emSize : float,
   style : FontStyle
);
```

Parameters

family
The **FontFamily** object of the new **Font** object.

emSize
The em-size, in points, of the new font.

style
The **FontStyle** of the new font.

Requirements

Platforms: Windows 98, Windows NT 4.0, Windows Millennium Edition, Windows 2000, Windows XP Home Edition, Windows XP Professional, Windows Server 2003 family, .NET Compact Framework - Windows CE .NET

Font Constructor (FontFamily, Single, GraphicsUnit)

Initializes a new **Font** using a specified size and unit. Sets the style to FontStyle.Regular.

```
[Visual Basic]
Public Sub New( _
   ByVal family As FontFamily, _
   ByVal emSize As Single, _
   ByVal unit As GraphicsUnit _
)
```

[C#]
```
public Font(
   FontFamily family,
   float emSize,
   GraphicsUnit unit
);
```
[C++]
```
public: Font(
   FontFamily* family,
   float emSize,
   GraphicsUnit unit
);
```
[JScript]
```
public function Font(
   family : FontFamily,
   emSize : float,
   unit : GraphicsUnit
);
```

Parameters

family

The **FontFamily** object of the new **Font** object.

emSize

The em-size of the new font in the units specified by the *unit* parameter.

unit

The **GraphicsUnit** of the new font.

Requirements

Platforms: Windows 98, Windows NT 4.0, Windows Millennium Edition, Windows 2000, Windows XP Home Edition, Windows XP Professional, Windows Server 2003 family

Font Constructor (String, Single, FontStyle)

Initializes a new **Font** object using a specified size and style. Sets the unit to GraphicsUnit.Point.

[Visual Basic]
```
Public Sub New( _
   ByVal familyName As String, _
   ByVal emSize As Single, _
   ByVal style As FontStyle _
)
```
[C#]
```
public Font(
   string familyName,
   float emSize,
   FontStyle style
);
```
[C++]
```
public: Font(
   String* familyName,
   float emSize,
   FontStyle style
);
```
[JScript]
```
public function Font(
   familyName : String,
   emSize : float,
   style : FontStyle
);
```

Parameters

familyName

A string representation of the **FontFamily** object for the new **Font** object.

emSize

The em-size, in points, of the new font.

style

The **FontStyle** of the new font.

Requirements

Platforms: Windows 98, Windows NT 4.0, Windows Millennium Edition, Windows 2000, Windows XP Home Edition, Windows XP Professional, Windows Server 2003 family, .NET Compact Framework - Windows CE .NET

Font Constructor (String, Single, GraphicsUnit)

Initializes a new **Font** object using a specified size and unit. The style is set to FontStyle.Regular.

[Visual Basic]
```
Public Sub New( _
   ByVal familyName As String, _
   ByVal emSize As Single, _
   ByVal unit As GraphicsUnit _
)
```
[C#]
```
public Font(
   string familyName,
   float emSize,
   GraphicsUnit unit
);
```
[C++]
```
public: Font(
   String* familyName,
   float emSize,
   GraphicsUnit unit
);
```
[JScript]
```
public function Font(
   familyName : String,
   emSize : float,
   unit : GraphicsUnit
);
```

Parameters

familyName

A string representation of the **FontFamily** object for the new **Font** object.

emSize

The em-size of the new font in the units specified by the *unit* parameter.

unit

The **GraphicsUnit** of the new font.

Requirements

Platforms: Windows 98, Windows NT 4.0, Windows Millennium Edition, Windows 2000, Windows XP Home Edition, Windows XP Professional, Windows Server 2003 family

Font Constructor (FontFamily, Single, FontStyle, GraphicsUnit)

Initializes a new **Font** using a specified size, style, and unit.

```
[Visual Basic]
Public Sub New( _
   ByVal family As FontFamily, _
   ByVal emSize As Single, _
   ByVal style As FontStyle, _
   ByVal unit As GraphicsUnit _
)
[C#]
public Font(
   FontFamily family,
   float emSize,
   FontStyle style,
   GraphicsUnit unit
);
[C++]
public: Font(
   FontFamily* family,
   float emSize,
   FontStyle style,
   GraphicsUnit unit
);
[JScript]
public function Font(
   family : FontFamily,
   emSize : float,
   style : FontStyle,
   unit : GraphicsUnit
);
```

Parameters

family
: The **FontFamily** object of the new **Font** object.

emSize
: The em-size of the new font in the units specified by the *unit* parameter.

style
: The **FontStyle** of the new font.

unit
: The **GraphicsUnit** of the new font.

Requirements

Platforms: Windows 98, Windows NT 4.0, Windows Millennium Edition, Windows 2000, Windows XP Home Edition, Windows XP Professional, Windows Server 2003 family

Font Constructor (String, Single, FontStyle, GraphicsUnit)

Initializes a new **Font** object using a specified size, style, and unit.

```
[Visual Basic]
Public Sub New( _
   ByVal familyName As String, _
   ByVal emSize As Single, _
   ByVal style As FontStyle, _
   ByVal unit As GraphicsUnit _
)
[C#]
public Font(
   string familyName,
   float emSize,
   FontStyle style,
   GraphicsUnit unit
);
[C++]
public: Font(
   String* familyName,
   float emSize,
   FontStyle style,
   GraphicsUnit unit
);
[JScript]
public function Font(
   familyName : String,
   emSize : float,
   style : FontStyle,
   unit : GraphicsUnit
);
```

Parameters

familyName
: A string representation of the **FontFamily** object for the new **Font** object.

emSize
: The em-size of the new font in the units specified by the *unit* parameter.

style
: The **FontStyle** of the new font.

unit
: The **GraphicsUnit** of the new font.

Requirements

Platforms: Windows 98, Windows NT 4.0, Windows Millennium Edition, Windows 2000, Windows XP Home Edition, Windows XP Professional, Windows Server 2003 family

Font Constructor (FontFamily, Single, FontStyle, GraphicsUnit, Byte)

Initializes a new **Font** object using a specified size, style, unit, and character set.

```
[Visual Basic]
Public Sub New( _
   ByVal family As FontFamily, _
   ByVal emSize As Single, _
   ByVal style As FontStyle, _
   ByVal unit As GraphicsUnit, _
   ByVal gdiCharSet As Byte _
)
[C#]
public Font(
   FontFamily family,
   float emSize,
   FontStyle style,
   GraphicsUnit unit,
   byte gdiCharSet
);
```

```
[C++]
public: Font(
   FontFamily* family,
   float emSize,
   FontStyle style,
   GraphicsUnit unit,
   unsigned char gdiCharSet
);
[JScript]
public function Font(
   family : FontFamily,
   emSize : float,
   style : FontStyle,
   unit : GraphicsUnit,
   gdiCharSet : Byte
);
```

Parameters

family
The **FontFamily** object of the new **Font** object.

emSize
The em-size of the new font in the units specified by the *unit* parameter.

style
The **FontStyle** of the new font.

unit
The **GraphicsUnit** of the new font.

gdiCharSet
A **Byte** that specifies a GDI character set to use for the new font.

Remarks

The *gdiCharSet* parameter takes a value from the list defined in the platform SDK header file WinGDI.h.

Requirements

Platforms: Windows 98, Windows NT 4.0, Windows Millennium Edition, Windows 2000, Windows XP Home Edition, Windows XP Professional, Windows Server 2003 family

Font Constructor (String, Single, FontStyle, GraphicsUnit, Byte)

Initializes a new **Font** using a specified size, style, unit, and character set.

```
[Visual Basic]
Public Sub New( _
   ByVal familyName As String, _
   ByVal emSize As Single, _
   ByVal style As FontStyle, _
   ByVal unit As GraphicsUnit, _
   ByVal gdiCharSet As Byte _
)
[C#]
public Font(
   string familyName,
   float emSize,
   FontStyle style,
   GraphicsUnit unit,
   byte gdiCharSet
);
[C++]
public: Font(
   String* familyName,
   float emSize,
   FontStyle style,
   GraphicsUnit unit,
   unsigned char gdiCharSet
);
[JScript]
public function Font(
   familyName : String,
   emSize : float,
   style : FontStyle,
   unit : GraphicsUnit,
   gdiCharSet : Byte
);
```

Parameters

familyName
A string representation of the **FontFamily** object for the new **Font** object.

emSize
The em-size of the new font in the units specified by the *unit* parameter.

style
The **FontStyle** of the new font.

unit
The **GraphicsUnit** of the new font.

gdiCharSet
A **Byte** that specifies a GDI character set to use for this font.

Remarks

The *gdiCharSet* parameter takes a value from the list defined in the platform SDK header file WinGDI.h.

Requirements

Platforms: Windows 98, Windows NT 4.0, Windows Millennium Edition, Windows 2000, Windows XP Home Edition, Windows XP Professional, Windows Server 2003 family

Font Constructor (FontFamily, Single, FontStyle, GraphicsUnit, Byte, Boolean)

Initializes a new **Font** using a specified size, style, unit, and character set.

```
[Visual Basic]
Public Sub New( _
   ByVal family As FontFamily, _
   ByVal emSize As Single, _
   ByVal style As FontStyle, _
   ByVal unit As GraphicsUnit, _
   ByVal gdiCharSet As Byte, _
   ByVal gdiVerticalFont As Boolean _
)
[C#]
public Font(
   FontFamily family,
   float emSize,
   FontStyle style,
   GraphicsUnit unit,
```

```
    byte gdiCharSet,
    bool gdiVerticalFont
);
[C++]
public: Font(
    FontFamily* family,
    float emSize,
    FontStyle style,
    GraphicsUnit unit,
    unsigned char gdiCharSet,
    bool gdiVerticalFont
);
[JScript]
public function Font(
    family : FontFamily,
    emSize : float,
    style : FontStyle,
    unit : GraphicsUnit,
    gdiCharSet : Byte,
    gdiVerticalFont : Boolean
);
```

Parameters

family
: The **FontFamily** object of the new **Font** object.

emSize
: The em-size of the new font in the units specified by the *unit* parameter.

style
: The **FontStyle** of the new font.

unit
: The **GraphicsUnit** of the new font.

gdiCharSet
: A **Byte** that specifies a GDI character set to use for this font.

gdiVerticalFont
: A Boolean value indicating whether the new font is derived from a GDI vertical font.

Remarks

The *gdiCharSet* parameter takes a value from the list defined in the platform SDK header file WinGDI.h.

Requirements

Platforms: Windows 98, Windows NT 4.0,
Windows Millennium Edition, Windows 2000,
Windows XP Home Edition, Windows XP Professional,
Windows Server 2003 family

Font Constructor (String, Single, FontStyle, GraphicsUnit, Byte, Boolean)

Initializes a new **Font** object using the specified size, style, unit, and character set.

```
[Visual Basic]
Public Sub New( _
    ByVal familyName As String, _
    ByVal emSize As Single, _
    ByVal style As FontStyle, _
    ByVal unit As GraphicsUnit, _
    ByVal gdiCharSet As Byte, _
    ByVal gdiVerticalFont As Boolean _
)
[C#]
public Font(
    string familyName,
    float emSize,
    FontStyle style,
    GraphicsUnit unit,
    byte gdiCharSet,
    bool gdiVerticalFont
);
[C++]
public: Font(
    String* familyName,
    float emSize,
    FontStyle style,
    GraphicsUnit unit,
    unsigned char gdiCharSet,
    bool gdiVerticalFont
);
[JScript]
public function Font(
    familyName : String,
    emSize : float,
    style : FontStyle,
    unit : GraphicsUnit,
    gdiCharSet : Byte,
    gdiVerticalFont : Boolean
);
```

Parameters

familyName
: A string representation of the **FontFamily** object for the new **Font** object.

emSize
: The em-size of the new font in the units specified by the *unit* parameter.

style
: The **FontStyle** of the new font.

unit
: The **GraphicsUnit** of the new font.

gdiCharSet
: A **Byte** that specifies a GDI character set to use for this font.

gdiVerticalFont
: A Boolean value indicating whether the new **Font** object is derived from a GDI vertical font.

Remarks

The *gdiCharSet* parameter takes a value from the list defined in the platform SDK header file WinGDI.h.

Requirements

Platforms: Windows 98, Windows NT 4.0,
Windows Millennium Edition, Windows 2000,
Windows XP Home Edition, Windows XP Professional,
Windows Server 2003 family

Font.Bold Property

Gets a value that indicates whether this **Font** object is bold.

[Visual Basic]
```
Public ReadOnly Property Bold As Boolean
```
[C#]
```
public bool Bold {get;}
```
[C++]
```
public: __property bool get_Bold();
```
[JScript]
```
public function get Bold() : Boolean;
```

Property Value

This property returns **true** if this **Font** object is bold; otherwise, **false**.

Requirements

Platforms: Windows 98, Windows NT 4.0, Windows Millennium Edition, Windows 2000, Windows XP Home Edition, Windows XP Professional, Windows Server 2003 family

Font.FontFamily Property

Gets the **FontFamily** object associated with this **Font** object.

[Visual Basic]
```
Public ReadOnly Property FontFamily As FontFamily
```
[C#]
```
public FontFamily FontFamily {get;}
```
[C++]
```
public: __property FontFamily* get_FontFamily();
```
[JScript]
```
public function get FontFamily() : FontFamily;
```

Property Value

The **FontFamily** object associated with this **Font** object.

Remarks

A **FontFamily** object represents a group of fonts that have a similar font face, but may have different sizes and styles. For example, Arial, Times New Roman, and Verdana.

Requirements

Platforms: Windows 98, Windows NT 4.0, Windows Millennium Edition, Windows 2000, Windows XP Home Edition, Windows XP Professional, Windows Server 2003 family

Font.GdiCharSet Property

Gets a byte value that specifies the GDI character set that this **Font** object uses.

[Visual Basic]
```
Public ReadOnly Property GdiCharSet As Byte
```
[C#]
```
public byte GdiCharSet {get;}
```
[C++]
```
public: __property unsigned char get_GdiCharSet();
```
[JScript]
```
public function get GdiCharSet() : Byte;
```

Property Value

A byte value that specifies the GDI character set that this **Font** object uses.

Remarks

This property takes a value from the list defined in the platform SDK header file WinGDI.h.

Requirements

Platforms: Windows 98, Windows NT 4.0, Windows Millennium Edition, Windows 2000, Windows XP Home Edition, Windows XP Professional, Windows Server 2003 family

Font.GdiVerticalFont Property

Gets a Boolean value that indicates whether this **Font** object is derived from a GDI vertical font.

[Visual Basic]
```
Public ReadOnly Property GdiVerticalFont As Boolean
```
[C#]
```
public bool GdiVerticalFont {get;}
```
[C++]
```
public: __property bool get_GdiVerticalFont();
```
[JScript]
```
public function get GdiVerticalFont() : Boolean;
```

Property Value

This property returns **true** if this **Font** object is derived from a GDI vertical font; otherwise, **false**.

Requirements

Platforms: Windows 98, Windows NT 4.0, Windows Millennium Edition, Windows 2000, Windows XP Home Edition, Windows XP Professional, Windows Server 2003 family

Font.Height Property

Gets the line spacing of this font.

[Visual Basic]
```
Public ReadOnly Property Height As Integer
```
[C#]
```
public int Height {get;}
```
[C++]
```
public: __property int get_Height();
```
[JScript]
```
public function get Height() : int;
```

Property Value

Gets the line spacing, in pixels, of this font. The line spacing is the vertical distance between the base lines of two consecutive lines of text. Thus, the line spacing includes the blank space between lines along with the height of the character itself.

Remarks

If the **Unit** property of the font is set to anything other than GraphicsUnit.Pixel, the height (in pixels) is calculated using the vertical resolution of the screen display. For example, suppose the font unit is inches and the font size is 0.3. Also suppose that for the corresponding font family, the em height is 2048 and the line spacing is 2355. For a screen display that has a vertical resolution of 96 dots per inch, you can calculate the height as follows:

2355*(0.3/2048)*96 = 33.11719

The value returned by the **GetHeight** method would be 33.11719, and the value returned by the **Height** property would be 34. The **Height** property is the ceiling of the value returned by **GetHeight**.

Requirements

Platforms: Windows 98, Windows NT 4.0, Windows Millennium Edition, Windows 2000, Windows XP Home Edition, Windows XP Professional, Windows Server 2003 family

Font.Italic Property

Gets a value that indicates whether this **Font** object is italic.

```
[Visual Basic]
Public ReadOnly Property Italic As Boolean
[C#]
public bool Italic {get;}
[C++]
public: __property bool get_Italic();
[JScript]
public function get Italic() : Boolean;
```

Property Value

This property returns **true** if this **Font** object is italic; otherwise, **false**.

Requirements

Platforms: Windows 98, Windows NT 4.0, Windows Millennium Edition, Windows 2000, Windows XP Home Edition, Windows XP Professional, Windows Server 2003 family

Font.Name Property

Gets the face name of this **Font** object.

```
[Visual Basic]
Public ReadOnly Property Name As String
[C#]
public string Name {get;}
[C++]
public: __property String* get_Name();
[JScript]
public function get Name() : String;
```

Property Value

A string representation of the face name of this **Font** object.

Requirements

Platforms: Windows 98, Windows NT 4.0, Windows Millennium Edition, Windows 2000, Windows XP Home Edition, Windows XP Professional, Windows Server 2003 family, .NET Compact Framework - Windows CE .NET

Font.Size Property

Gets the em-size of this **Font** object measured in the unit of this **Font** object.

```
[Visual Basic]
Public ReadOnly Property Size As Single
[C#]
public float Size {get;}
[C++]
public: __property float get_Size();
[JScript]
public function get Size() : float;
```

Property Value

The em-size of this **Font** object.

Requirements

Platforms: Windows 98, Windows NT 4.0, Windows Millennium Edition, Windows 2000, Windows XP Home Edition, Windows XP Professional, Windows Server 2003 family, .NET Compact Framework - Windows CE .NET

Font.SizeInPoints Property

Gets the em-size, in points, of this **Font** object.

```
[Visual Basic]
Public ReadOnly Property SizeInPoints As Single
[C#]
public float SizeInPoints {get;}
[C++]
public: __property float get_SizeInPoints();
[JScript]
public function get SizeInPoints() : float;
```

Property Value

The em-size, in points, of this **Font** object.

Requirements

Platforms: Windows 98, Windows NT 4.0, Windows Millennium Edition, Windows 2000, Windows XP Home Edition, Windows XP Professional, Windows Server 2003 family

Font.Strikeout Property

Gets a value that indicates whether this **Font** object specifies a horizontal line through the font.

```
[Visual Basic]
Public ReadOnly Property Strikeout As Boolean
[C#]
public bool Strikeout {get;}
[C++]
public: __property bool get_Strikeout();
[JScript]
public function get Strikeout() : Boolean;
```

Property Value

This property is **true** if this **Font** object has a horizontal line through it; otherwise, **false**.

Requirements

Platforms: Windows 98, Windows NT 4.0, Windows Millennium Edition, Windows 2000, Windows XP Home Edition, Windows XP Professional, Windows Server 2003 family

Font.Style Property

Gets style information for this **Font** object.

[Visual Basic]
```
Public ReadOnly Property Style As FontStyle
```
[C#]
```
public FontStyle Style {get;}
```
[C++]
```
public: __property FontStyle get_Style();
```
[JScript]
```
public function get Style() : FontStyle;
```

Property Value

A **FontStyle** enumeration that contains style information for this **Font** object.

Requirements

Platforms: Windows 98, Windows NT 4.0, Windows Millennium Edition, Windows 2000, Windows XP Home Edition, Windows XP Professional, Windows Server 2003 family, .NET Compact Framework - Windows CE .NET

Font.Underline Property

Gets a value that indicates whether this **Font** object is underlined.

[Visual Basic]
```
Public ReadOnly Property Underline As Boolean
```
[C#]
```
public bool Underline {get;}
```
[C++]
```
public: __property bool get_Underline();
```
[JScript]
```
public function get Underline() : Boolean;
```

Property Value

This property returns **true** if this **Font** object is underlined; otherwise, **false**.

Requirements

Platforms: Windows 98, Windows NT 4.0, Windows Millennium Edition, Windows 2000, Windows XP Home Edition, Windows XP Professional, Windows Server 2003 family

Font.Unit Property

Gets the unit of measure for this **Font** object.

[Visual Basic]
```
Public ReadOnly Property Unit As GraphicsUnit
```
[C#]
```
public GraphicsUnit Unit {get;}
```
[C++]
```
public: __property GraphicsUnit get_Unit();
```
[JScript]
```
public function get Unit() : GraphicsUnit;
```

Property Value

A **GraphicsUnit** enumeration that represents the unit of measure for this **Font** object.

Requirements

Platforms: Windows 98, Windows NT 4.0, Windows Millennium Edition, Windows 2000, Windows XP Home Edition, Windows XP Professional, Windows Server 2003 family

Font.Clone Method

Creates an exact copy of this **Font** object.

[Visual Basic]
```
Public Overridable Function Clone() As Object Implements _
   ICloneable.Clone
```
[C#]
```
public virtual object Clone();
```
[C++]
```
public: virtual Object* Clone();
```
[JScript]
```
public function Clone() : Object;
```

Return Value

The **Font** object this method creates, cast as an **object**.

Implements

ICloneable.Clone

Example

[Visual Basic, C#] The following example is designed for use with Windows Forms, and it requires **PaintEventArgs** *e*, which is a parameter of the **Paint** event handler. The code clones a **Font** object and draws text with that font.

[Visual Basic]
```
Public Sub Clone_Example(e As PaintEventArgs)
' Create a Font object.
Dim myFont As New Font("Arial", 16)
' Create a copy of myFont.
Dim cloneFont As Font = CType(myFont.Clone(), Font)
' Use cloneFont to draw text to the screen.
e.Graphics.DrawString("This is a cloned font", cloneFont, _
Brushes.Black, 0, 0)
End Sub
```

[C#]
```
public void Clone_Example(PaintEventArgs e)
{
// Create a Font object.
Font myFont = new Font("Arial", 16);
// Create a copy of myFont.
Font cloneFont = (Font)myFont.Clone();
// Use cloneFont to draw text to the screen.
e.Graphics.DrawString(
"This is a cloned font",
cloneFont,
Brushes.Black,
0,
0);
}
```

Requirements

Platforms: Windows 98, Windows NT 4.0, Windows Millennium Edition, Windows 2000, Windows XP Home Edition, Windows XP Professional, Windows Server 2003 family

Font.Dispose Method

Releases all resources used by this **Font** object.

[Visual Basic]
```
Public Overridable Sub Dispose() Implements IDisposable.Dispose
```
[C#]
```
public virtual void Dispose();
```
[C++]
```
public: virtual void Dispose();
```
[JScript]
```
public function Dispose();
```

Return Value

This method does not return a value.

Implements

IDisposable.Dispose

Remarks

Calling **Dispose** allows the resources used by this **Font** object to be reallocated for other purposes.

Requirements

Platforms: Windows 98, Windows NT 4.0, Windows Millennium Edition, Windows 2000, Windows XP Home Edition, Windows XP Professional, Windows Server 2003 family, .NET Compact Framework - Windows CE .NET

Font.Equals Method

Indicates whether the specified object is a **Font** object and is identical to this **Font** object.

[Visual Basic]
```
Overrides Public Function Equals( _
   ByVal obj As Object _
) As Boolean
```
[C#]
```
public override bool Equals(
   object obj
);
```
[C++]
```
public: bool Equals(
   Object* obj
);
```
[JScript]
```
public override function Equals(
   obj : Object
) : Boolean;
```

Parameters

obj

The object to test.

Return Value

This method returns **true** if the *obj* parameter is a **Font** object and is identical to this **Font** object; otherwise, **false**.

Example

[Visual Basic, C#] The following example is designed for use with Windows Forms, and it requires **PaintEventArgs** *e*, which is a parameter of the **Paint** event handler. The code creates two **Font** objects and then tests whether they are equivalent.

[Visual Basic]
```
Public Sub Equals_Example(e As PaintEventArgs)
' Create a Font object.
Dim firstFont As New Font("Arial", 16)
' Create a second Font object.
Dim secondFont As New Font(New FontFamily("Arial"), 16)
' Test to see if firstFont is identical to secondFont.
Dim fontTest As Boolean = firstFont.Equals(secondFont)
' Display a message box with the result of the test.
MessageBox.Show(fontTest.ToString())
End Sub
```

[C#]
```
public void Equals_Example(PaintEventArgs e)
{
// Create a Font object.
Font firstFont = new Font("Arial", 16);
// Create a second Font object.
Font secondFont = new Font(new FontFamily("Arial"), 16);
// Test to see if firstFont is identical to secondFont.
bool fontTest = firstFont.Equals(secondFont);
// Display a message box with the result of the test.
MessageBox.Show(fontTest.ToString());
}
```

Requirements

Platforms: Windows 98, Windows NT 4.0, Windows Millennium Edition, Windows 2000, Windows XP Home Edition, Windows XP Professional, Windows Server 2003 family, .NET Compact Framework - Windows CE .NET

Font.Finalize Method

This member overrides **Object.Finalize**.

[Visual Basic]
```
Overrides Protected Sub Finalize()
```
[C#]
```
~Font();
```
[C++]
```
~Font();
```
[JScript]
```
protected override function Finalize();
```

Requirements

Platforms: Windows 98, Windows NT 4.0, Windows Millennium Edition, Windows 2000, Windows XP Home Edition, Windows XP Professional, Windows Server 2003 family, .NET Compact Framework - Windows CE .NET

Font.FromHdc Method

Creates a **Font** object from the specified Windows handle to a device context.

[Visual Basic]
```
Public Shared Function FromHdc( _
   ByVal hdc As IntPtr _
) As Font
```
[C#]
```
public static Font FromHdc(
   IntPtr hdc
);
```

```
[C++]
public: static Font* FromHdc(
   IntPtr hdc
);
[JScript]
public static function FromHdc(
   hdc : IntPtr
) : Font;
```

Parameters

hdc

A handle to a device context.

Return Value

The **Font** object this method creates.

Remarks

For this method to work, the *hdc* parameter must contain a handle to a device context in which a font is selected. This method will not work with an *hdc* acquired from a GDI+ **Graphics** object because the *hdc* does not have a font selected.

Requirements

Platforms: Windows 98, Windows NT 4.0, Windows Millennium Edition, Windows 2000, Windows XP Home Edition, Windows XP Professional, Windows Server 2003 family

Font.FromHfont Method

Creates a **Font** object from the specified Windows handle.

```
[Visual Basic]
Public Shared Function FromHfont( _
   ByVal hfont As IntPtr _
) As Font
[C#]
public static Font FromHfont(
   IntPtr hfont
);
[C++]
public: static Font* FromHfont(
   IntPtr hfont
);
[JScript]
public static function FromHfont(
   hfont : IntPtr
) : Font;
```

Parameters

hfont

A Windows handle to a GDI font.

Return Value

The **Font** object this method creates.

Example

[Visual Basic, C#] The following example is designed for use with Windows Forms, and it requires **PaintEventArgs** *e*, which is a parameter of the **Paint** event handler. The code performs the following actions:

- Gets a handle to a GDI font.
- Creates a **Font** object from that handle.
- Draws text to the screen, using the new **Font** object.

```
[Visual Basic]
<System.Runtime.InteropServices.DllImportAttribute("GDI32.DLL")> _
Private Shared Function GetStockObject(fnObject As Integer) As IntPtr
End Function
Public Sub FromHfont_Example(e As PaintEventArgs)
' Get a handle for a GDI font.
Dim hFont As IntPtr = GetStockObject(0)
' Create a Font object from hFont.
Dim hfontFont As Font = Font.FromHfont(hFont)
' Use hfontFont to draw text to the screen.
e.Graphics.DrawString("This font is from a GDI HFONT", hfontFont, _
Brushes.Black, 0, 0)
End Sub
```

```
[C#]
[System.Runtime.InteropServices.DllImportAttribute("gdi32.dll")]
private static extern IntPtr GetStockObject(int fnObject);
public void FromHfont_Example(PaintEventArgs e)
{
// Get a handle for a GDI font.
IntPtr hFont = GetStockObject(0);
// Create a Font object from hFont.
Font hfontFont = Font.FromHfont(hFont);
// Use hfontFont to draw text to the screen.
e.Graphics.DrawString(
"This font is from a GDI HFONT",
hfontFont,
Brushes.Black,
0,
0);
}
```

Requirements

Platforms: Windows 98, Windows NT 4.0, Windows Millennium Edition, Windows 2000, Windows XP Home Edition, Windows XP Professional, Windows Server 2003 family

Font.FromLogFont Method

Creates a **Font** object from the specified GDI **LOGFONT** structure.

Overload List

Creates a **Font** object from the specified GDI **LOGFONT** structure.

[Visual Basic] **Overloads Public Shared Function FromLogFont(Object) As Font**

[C#] **public static Font FromLogFont(object);**

[C++] **public: static Font* FromLogFont(Object*);**

[JScript] **public static function FromLogFont(Object) : Font;**

Creates a **Font** object from the specified GDI **LOGFONT** structure.

[Visual Basic] **Overloads Public Shared Function FromLogFont(Object, IntPtr) As Font**

[C#] **public static Font FromLogFont(object, IntPtr);**

[C++] **public: static Font* FromLogFont(Object*, IntPtr);**

[JScript] **public static function FromLogFont(Object, IntPtr) : Font;**

Font.FromLogFont Method (Object)

Creates a **Font** object from the specified GDI **LOGFONT** structure.

```
[Visual Basic]
Overloads Public Shared Function FromLogFont( _
   ByVal lf As Object _
) As Font
[C#]
public static Font FromLogFont(
   object lf
);
[C++]
public: static Font* FromLogFont(
   Object* lf
);
[JScript]
public static function FromLogFont(
   lf : Object
) : Font;
```

Parameters

lf

An **Object** object that represents the GDI **LOGFONT** structure from which to create the **Font** object.

Return Value

The **Font** object that this method creates.

Requirements

Platforms: Windows 98, Windows NT 4.0, Windows Millennium Edition, Windows 2000, Windows XP Home Edition, Windows XP Professional, Windows Server 2003 family

Font.FromLogFont Method (Object, IntPtr)

Creates a **Font** object from the specified GDI **LOGFONT** structure.

```
[Visual Basic]
Overloads Public Shared Function FromLogFont( _
   ByVal lf As Object, _
   ByVal hdc As IntPtr _
) As Font
[C#]
public static Font FromLogFont(
   object lf,
   IntPtr hdc
);
[C++]
public: static Font* FromLogFont(
   Object* lf,
   IntPtr hdc
);
[JScript]
public static function FromLogFont(
   lf : Object,
   hdc : IntPtr
) : Font;
```

Parameters

lf

An **Object** object that represents the GDI **LOGFONT** structure from which to create the **Font** object.

hdc

A handle to a device context that contains additional information about the *lf* structure.

Return Value

The **Font** object that this method creates.

Requirements

Platforms: Windows 98, Windows NT 4.0, Windows Millennium Edition, Windows 2000, Windows XP Home Edition, Windows XP Professional, Windows Server 2003 family

Font.GetHashCode Method

Gets the hash code for this **Font** object.

```
[Visual Basic]
Overrides Public Function GetHashCode() As Integer
[C#]
public override int GetHashCode();
[C++]
public: int GetHashCode();
[JScript]
public override function GetHashCode() : int;
```

Return Value

The hash code for this **Font** object.

Example

[Visual Basic, C#] The following example is designed for use with Windows Forms, and it requires **PaintEventArgs** *e*, which is a parameter of the **Paint** event handler. The code performs the following actions:

- Creates a **Font** object.
- Gets the hash code for that font.
- Displays a message box with the value of the hash code.

```
[Visual Basic]
Public Sub GetHashCode_Example(e As PaintEventArgs)
' Create a Font object.
Dim myFont As New Font("Arial", 16)
' Get the hash code for myFont.
Dim hashCode As Integer = myFont.GetHashCode()
' Display the hash code in a message box.
MessageBox.Show(hashCode.ToString())
End Sub
```

```
[C#]
public void GetHashCode_Example(PaintEventArgs e)
{
// Create a Font object.
Font myFont = new Font("Arial", 16);
// Get the hash code for myFont.
int hashCode = myFont.GetHashCode();
// Display the hash code in a message box.
MessageBox.Show(hashCode.ToString());
}
```

Requirements

Platforms: Windows 98, Windows NT 4.0, Windows Millennium Edition, Windows 2000, Windows XP Home Edition, Windows XP Professional, Windows Server 2003 family, .NET Compact Framework - Windows CE .NET

Font.GetHeight Method

Returns the line spacing of this font.

Overload List

Returns the line spacing, in pixels, of this font. The line spacing is the vertical distance between the base lines of two consecutive lines of text. Thus, the line spacing includes the blank space between lines along with the height of the character itself.

[Visual Basic] **Overloads Public Function GetHeight() As Single**

[C#] **public float GetHeight();**

[C++] **public: float GetHeight();**

[JScript] **public function GetHeight() : float;**

Returns the line spacing, in the current unit of a specified **Graphics** object, of this font. The line spacing is the vertical distance between the base lines of two consecutive lines of text. Thus, the line spacing includes the blank space between lines along with the height of the character itself.

[Visual Basic] **Overloads Public Function GetHeight(Graphics) As Single**

[C#] **public float GetHeight(Graphics);**

[C++] **public: float GetHeight(Graphics*);**

[JScript] **public function GetHeight(Graphics) : float;**

Returns the height, in pixels, of this **Font** object when drawn to a device with the specified vertical resolution.

[Visual Basic] **Overloads Public Function GetHeight(Single) As Single**

[C#] **public float GetHeight(float);**

[C++] **public: float GetHeight(float);**

[JScript] **public function GetHeight(float) : float;**

Example

[Visual Basic, C#] The following example is designed for use with Windows Forms, and it requires **PaintEventArgs** *e*, which is a parameter of the **Paint** event handler. The code performs the following actions:

- Creates a **Font** object.
- Draws a line of text to the screen, using the new **Font** object.
- Gets the height of the font.
- Draws a second line of text directly below the first line.

> [Visual Basic, C#] **Note** This example shows how to use one of the overloaded versions of **GetHeight**. For other examples that might be available, see the individual overload topics.

[Visual Basic]

```
Public Sub GetHeight_Example(e As PaintEventArgs)
' Create a Font object.
Dim myFont As New Font("Arial", 16)
'Draw text to the screen with myFont.
e.Graphics.DrawString("This is the first line", myFont, _
Brushes.Black, New PointF(0, 0))
'Get the height of myFont.
Dim height As Single = myFont.GetHeight(e.Graphics)
'Draw text immediately below the first line of text.
e.Graphics.DrawString("This is the second line", myFont, _
Brushes.Black, New PointF(0, height))
End Sub
```

[C#]

```
public void GetHeight_Example(PaintEventArgs e)
{
// Create a Font object.
Font myFont = new Font("Arial", 16);
//Draw text to the screen with myFont.
e.Graphics.DrawString(
"This is the first line",
myFont,
Brushes.Black,
new PointF(0, 0));
//Get the height of myFont.
float height = myFont.GetHeight(e.Graphics);
//Draw text immediately below the first line of text.
e.Graphics.DrawString(
"This is the second line",
myFont,
Brushes.Black,
new PointF(0, height));
}
```

Font.GetHeight Method ()

Returns the line spacing, in pixels, of this font. The line spacing is the vertical distance between the base lines of two consecutive lines of text. Thus, the line spacing includes the blank space between lines along with the height of the character itself.

[Visual Basic]
```
Overloads Public Function GetHeight() As Single
```
[C#]
```
public float GetHeight();
```
[C++]
```
public: float GetHeight();
```
[JScript]
```
public function GetHeight() : float;
```

Return Value

The line spacing, in pixels, of this font.

Remarks

If the **Unit** property of the font is set to anything other than GraphicsUnit.Pixel, the height (in pixels) is calculated using the vertical resolution of the screen display. For example, suppose the font unit is inches and the font size is 0.3. Also suppose that for the corresponding font family, the em height is 2048 and the line spacing is 2355. For a screen display that has a vertical resolution of 96 dots per inch, you can calculate the height as follows:

2355*(0.3/2048)*96 = 33.11719

Requirements

Platforms: Windows 98, Windows NT 4.0, Windows Millennium Edition, Windows 2000, Windows XP Home Edition, Windows XP Professional, Windows Server 2003 family

Font.GetHeight Method (Graphics)

Returns the line spacing, in the current unit of a specified **Graphics** object, of this font. The line spacing is the vertical distance between the base lines of two consecutive lines of text. Thus, the line spacing includes the blank space between lines along with the height of the character itself.

[Visual Basic]
```
Overloads Public Function GetHeight( _
   ByVal graphics As Graphics _
) As Single
```
[C#]
```
public float GetHeight(
   Graphics graphics
);
```

```
[C++]
public: float GetHeight(
   Graphics* graphics
);
[JScript]
public function GetHeight(
   graphics : Graphics
) : float;
```

Parameters

graphics
: A **Graphics** object that holds the vertical resolution (dots per inch) of the display device as well as settings for page unit and page scale.

Return Value

The line spacing, in pixels, of this font.

Remarks

If the **Unit** property of the font is set to anything other than GraphicsUnit.Pixel, the height, in pixels, is calculated using the vertical resolution of the specified **Graphics** object. For example, suppose the font unit is inches and the font size is 0.3. Also suppose that for the corresponding font family, the em height is 2048 and the line spacing is 2355. If the **Graphics** object has a **Unit** of GraphicsUnit.Pixel and a **DpiY** of 96 dots per inch, the height is calculated as follows:

2355*(0.3/2048)*96 = 33.1171875

Continuing with the same example, suppose the **Unit** property of the **Graphics** object is set to something other than GraphicsUnit.Pixel, say GraphicsUnit.Millimeter. Then (using 1 inch = 25.4 millimeters) the height, in millimeters, is calculated as follows:

2355*(0.3/2048)25.4 = 8.762256

Example

[Visual Basic, C#] The following example is designed for use with Windows Forms, and it requires **PaintEventArgs** *e*, which is a parameter of the **Paint** event handler. The code performs the following actions:

- Creates a **Font** object.
- Draws a line of text to the screen, using the new **Font** object.
- Gets the height of the font.
- Draws a second line of text directly below the first line.

```
[Visual Basic]
Public Sub GetHeight_Example(e As PaintEventArgs)
' Create a Font object.
Dim myFont As New Font("Arial", 16)
'Draw text to the screen with myFont.
e.Graphics.DrawString("This is the first line", myFont, _
Brushes.Black, New PointF(0, 0))
'Get the height of myFont.
Dim height As Single = myFont.GetHeight(e.Graphics)
'Draw text immediately below the first line of text.
e.Graphics.DrawString("This is the second line", myFont, _
Brushes.Black, New PointF(0, height))
End Sub
```

```
[C#]
public void GetHeight_Example(PaintEventArgs e)
{
// Create a Font object.
Font myFont = new Font("Arial", 16);
//Draw text to the screen with myFont.
e.Graphics.DrawString(
"This is the first line",
myFont,
Brushes.Black,
new PointF(0, 0));
//Get the height of myFont.
float height = myFont.GetHeight(e.Graphics);
//Draw text immediately below the first line of text.
e.Graphics.DrawString(
"This is the second line",
myFont,
Brushes.Black,
new PointF(0, height));
}
```

Requirements

Platforms: Windows 98, Windows NT 4.0, Windows Millennium Edition, Windows 2000, Windows XP Home Edition, Windows XP Professional, Windows Server 2003 family

Font.GetHeight Method (Single)

Returns the height, in pixels, of this **Font** object when drawn to a device with the specified vertical resolution.

```
[Visual Basic]
Overloads Public Function GetHeight( _
   ByVal dpi As Single _
) As Single
[C#]
public float GetHeight(
   float dpi
);
[C++]
public: float GetHeight(
   float dpi
);
[JScript]
public function GetHeight(
   dpi : float
) : float;
```

Parameters

dpi
: The vertical resolution, in dots per inch, used to calculate the height of the font.

Return Value

The height, in pixels, of this **Font** object.

Remarks

If the **Unit** property of the font is set to anything other than GraphicsUnit.Pixel, the height, in pixels, is calculated using the specified vertical resolution. For example, suppose the font unit is inches and the font size is 0.3. Also suppose that for the corresponding font family, the em height is 2048 and the line spacing is 2355. If the specified vertical resolution is 96 dots per inch, the height is calculated as follows:

2355*(0.3/2048)*96 = 33.1171875

Requirements

Platforms: Windows 98, Windows NT 4.0, Windows Millennium Edition, Windows 2000, Windows XP Home Edition, Windows XP Professional, Windows Server 2003 family

Font.GetHtx Method

Note: This namespace, class, or member is supported only in version 1.1 of the .NET Framework.

This member supports the .NET Framework infrastructure and is not intended to be used directly from your code.

```
[Visual Basic]
Public Function GetHtx() As IntPtr
[C#]
public IntPtr GetHtx();
[C++]
public: IntPtr GetHtx();
[JScript]
public function GetHtx() : IntPtr;
```

Font.ISerializable.GetObjectData Method

This member supports the .NET Framework infrastructure and is not intended to be used directly from your code.

```
[Visual Basic]
Private Sub GetObjectData( _
   ByVal si As SerializationInfo, _
   ByVal context As StreamingContext _
) Implements ISerializable.GetObjectData
[C#]
void ISerializable.GetObjectData(
   SerializationInfo si,
   StreamingContext context
);
[C++]
private: void ISerializable::GetObjectData(
   SerializationInfo* si,
   StreamingContext context
);
[JScript]
private function ISerializable.GetObjectData(
   si : SerializationInfo,
   context : StreamingContext
);
```

Font.ToHfont Method

Returns a handle to this **Font** object.

```
[Visual Basic]
Public Function ToHfont() As IntPtr
[C#]
public IntPtr ToHfont();
[C++]
public: IntPtr ToHfont();
[JScript]
public function ToHfont() : IntPtr;
```

Return Value

A Windows handle to this **Font** object.

Remarks

If the Unit property of the font is set to anything other than GraphicsUnit.Pixel, the height, in pixels, is calculated using the specified vertical resolution. For example, suppose the font unit is inches and the font size is 0.3. Also suppose that for the corresponding font family, the em height is 2048 and the line spacing is 2355. If the specified vertical resolution is 96 dots per inch, the height is calculated as follows:

2355*(0.3/2048)*96 = 33.1171875

Example

[Visual Basic, C#] The following example is designed for use with Windows Forms, and it requires **PaintEventArgs** *e*, which is a parameter of the **Paint** event handler. The code creates a **Font** object and then gets a handle to that **Font** object.

```
[Visual Basic]
Public Sub ToHfont_Example(e As PaintEventArgs)
' Create a Font object.
Dim myFont As New Font("Arial", 16)
' Get a handle to the Font object.
Dim hFont As IntPtr = myFont.ToHfont()
' Display a message box with the value of hFont.
MessageBox.Show(hFont.ToString())
End Sub
```

```
[C#]
public void ToHfont_Example(PaintEventArgs e)
{
// Create a Font object.
Font myFont = new Font("Arial", 16);
// Get a handle to the Font object.
IntPtr hFont = myFont.ToHfont();
// Display a message box with the value of hFont.
MessageBox.Show(hFont.ToString());
}
```

Requirements

Platforms: Windows 98, Windows NT 4.0, Windows Millennium Edition, Windows 2000, Windows XP Home Edition, Windows XP Professional, Windows Server 2003 family

Font.ToLogFont Method

Creates a GDI **LOGFONT** structure from this **Font** object.

Overload List

Creates a GDI **LOGFONT** structure from this **Font** object.

[Visual Basic] **Overloads Public Sub ToLogFont(Object)**

[C#] **public void ToLogFont(object);**

[C++] **public: void ToLogFont(Object*);**

[JScript] **public function ToLogFont(Object);**

Creates a GDI+ **LOGFONT** structure from this **Font** object.

[Visual Basic] **Overloads Public Sub ToLogFont(Object, Graphics)**

[C#] **public void ToLogFont(object, Graphics);**

[C++] **public: void ToLogFont(Object*, Graphics*);**

[JScript] **public function ToLogFont(Object, Graphics);**

Font.ToLogFont Method (Object)

Creates a GDI **LOGFONT** structure from this **Font** object.

```
[Visual Basic]
Overloads Public Sub ToLogFont( _
   ByVal logFont As Object _
)
```

```
[C#]
public void ToLogFont(
   object logFont
);
[C++]
public: void ToLogFont(
   Object* logFont
);
[JScript]
public function ToLogFont(
   logFont : Object
);
```

Parameters

logFont
: An **object** that represents the **LOGFONT** structure that this method creates.

Return Value

This method does not return a value.

Remarks

This method requires UnmanagedCode permission. For more information see **SecurityPermissionFlag**.

Requirements

Platforms: Windows 98, Windows NT 4.0, Windows Millennium Edition, Windows 2000, Windows XP Home Edition, Windows XP Professional, Windows Server 2003 family

Font.ToLogFont Method (Object, Graphics)

Creates a GDI+ **LOGFONT** structure from this **Font** object.

```
[Visual Basic]
Overloads Public Sub ToLogFont( _
   ByVal logFont As Object, _
   ByVal graphics As Graphics _
)
[C#]
public void ToLogFont(
   object logFont,
   Graphics graphics
);
[C++]
public: void ToLogFont(
   Object* logFont,
   Graphics* graphics
);
[JScript]
public function ToLogFont(
   logFont : Object,
   graphics : Graphics
);
```

Parameters

logFont
: An **Object** object that represents the **LOGFONT** structure that this method creates.

graphics
: A **Graphics** object that provides additional information for the **LOGFONT** structure.

Return Value

This method does not return a value.

Remarks

This method requires UnmanagedCode permission. For more information see **SecurityPermissionFlag**.

Requirements

Platforms: Windows 98, Windows NT 4.0, Windows Millennium Edition, Windows 2000, Windows XP Home Edition, Windows XP Professional, Windows Server 2003 family

Font.ToString Method

Returns a human-readable string representation of this **Font** object.

```
[Visual Basic]
Overrides Public Function ToString() As String
[C#]
public override string ToString();
[C++]
public: String* ToString();
[JScript]
public override function ToString() : String;
```

Return Value

A string that represents this **Font** object.

Example

[Visual Basic, C#] The following example is designed for use with Windows Forms, and it requires **PaintEventArgs** *e*, which is a parameter of the **Paint** event handler. The code performs the following actions:

- Creates a **Font** object.
- Gets a string represents the font.
- Displays the string in a message box.

```
[Visual Basic]
Public Sub ToString_Example(e As PaintEventArgs)
' Create a Font object.
Dim myFont As New Font("Arial", 16)
' Get a string that represents myFont.
Dim fontString As String = myFont.ToString()
' Display a message box with fontString.
MessageBox.Show(fontString)
End Sub

[C#]
public void ToString_Example(PaintEventArgs e)
{
// Create a Font object.
Font myFont = new Font("Arial", 16);
// Get a string that represents myFont.
string fontString = myFont.ToString();
// Display a message box with fontString.
MessageBox.Show(fontString);
}
```

Requirements

Platforms: Windows 98, Windows NT 4.0, Windows Millennium Edition, Windows 2000, Windows XP Home Edition, Windows XP Professional, Windows Server 2003 family, .NET Compact Framework - Windows CE .NET

FontConverter Class

Converts **Font** objects from one data type to another. Access the **FontConverter** class through the **TypeDescriptor** object.

System.Object
  System.ComponentModel.TypeConverter
    System.Drawing.FontConverter

[Visual Basic]
```
Public Class FontConverter
   Inherits TypeConverter
```
[C#]
```
public class FontConverter : TypeConverter
```
[C++]
```
public __gc class FontConverter : public TypeConverter
```
[JScript]
```
public class FontConverter extends TypeConverter
```

Thread Safety

Any public static (**Shared** in Visual Basic) members of this type are safe for multithreaded operations. Any instance members are not guaranteed to be thread safe.

Requirements

Namespace: System.Drawing

Platforms: Windows 98, Windows NT 4.0, Windows Millennium Edition, Windows 2000, Windows XP Home Edition, Windows XP Professional, Windows Server 2003 family

Assembly: System.Drawing (in System.Drawing.dll)

FontConverter Constructor

Initializes a new **FontConverter** object.

[Visual Basic]
```
Public Sub New()
```
[C#]
```
public FontConverter();
```
[C++]
```
public: FontConverter();
```
[JScript]
```
public function FontConverter();
```

Requirements

Platforms: Windows 98, Windows NT 4.0, Windows Millennium Edition, Windows 2000, Windows XP Home Edition, Windows XP Professional, Windows Server 2003 family

FontConverter.CanConvertFrom Method

Overload List

Determines whether this converter can convert an object in the specified source type to the native type of the converter.

[Visual Basic] **Overloads Overrides Public Function CanConvertFrom(ITypeDescriptorContext, Type) As Boolean**

[C#] **public override bool CanConvertFrom(ITypeDescriptorContext, Type);**

[C++] **public: bool CanConvertFrom(ITypeDescriptorContext*, Type*);**

[JScript] **public override function CanConvertFrom(ITypeDescriptorContext, Type) : Boolean;**

Inherited from **TypeConverter**.

[Visual Basic] **Overloads Public Function CanConvertFrom(Type) As Boolean**

[C#] **public bool CanConvertFrom(Type);**

[C++] **public: bool CanConvertFrom(Type*);**

[JScript] **public function CanConvertFrom(Type) : Boolean;**

FontConverter.CanConvertFrom Method (ITypeDescriptorContext, Type)

Determines whether this converter can convert an object in the specified source type to the native type of the converter.

[Visual Basic]
```
Overrides Overloads Public Function CanConvertFrom( _
   ByVal context As ITypeDescriptorContext, _
   ByVal sourceType As Type _
) As Boolean
```
[C#]
```
public override bool CanConvertFrom(
   ITypeDescriptorContext context,
   Type sourceType
);
```
[C++]
```
public: bool CanConvertFrom(
   ITypeDescriptorContext* context,
   Type* sourceType
);
```
[JScript]
```
public override function CanConvertFrom(
   context : ITypeDescriptorContext,
   sourceType : Type
) : Boolean;
```

Parameters

context
   A formatter context. This object can be used to get additional information about the environment this converter is being called from. This may be a null reference (**Nothing** in Visual Basic), so you should always check. Also, properties on the context object may also return a null reference (**Nothing**).

sourceType
   The type you want to convert from.

Return Value

This method returns **true** if this object can perform the conversion.

Requirements

Platforms: Windows 98, Windows NT 4.0, Windows Millennium Edition, Windows 2000, Windows XP Home Edition, Windows XP Professional, Windows Server 2003 family

FontConverter.CanConvertTo Method

Overload List

Gets a value indicating whether this converter can convert an object to the given destination type using the context.

[Visual Basic] **Overloads Overrides Public Function CanConvertTo(ITypeDescriptorContext, Type) As Boolean**

[C#] **public override bool CanConvertTo(ITypeDescriptor-Context, Type);**

[C++] **public: bool CanConvertTo(ITypeDescriptorContext*, Type*);**

[JScript] **public override function CanConvertTo(IType-DescriptorContext, Type) : Boolean;**

Inherited from **TypeConverter**.

[Visual Basic] **Overloads Public Function CanConvertTo(Type) As Boolean**

[C#] **public bool CanConvertTo(Type);**

[C++] **public: bool CanConvertTo(Type*);**

[JScript] **public function CanConvertTo(Type) : Boolean;**

FontConverter.CanConvertTo Method (ITypeDescriptorContext, Type)

Gets a value indicating whether this converter can convert an object to the given destination type using the context.

```
[Visual Basic]
Overrides Overloads Public Function CanConvertTo( _
   ByVal context As ITypeDescriptorContext, _
   ByVal destinationType As Type _
) As Boolean
[C#]
public override bool CanConvertTo(
   ITypeDescriptorContext context,
   Type destinationType
);
[C++]
public: bool CanConvertTo(
   ITypeDescriptorContext* context,
   Type* destinationType
);
[JScript]
public override function CanConvertTo(
   context : ITypeDescriptorContext,
   destinationType : Type
) : Boolean;
```

Parameters

context
An **ITypeDescriptorContext** object that provides a format context.

destinationType
A **Type** object that represents the type you want to convert to.

Return Value

This method returns **true** if this converter can perform the conversion; otherwise, **false**.

Remarks

The *context* parameter can be used to extract additional information about the environment this converter is being invoked from. This can be a a null reference (**Nothing** in Visual Basic) reference (**Nothing** in Visual Basic), so always check. Also, properties on the context object can return a null reference (**Nothing**).

Requirements

Platforms: Windows 98, Windows NT 4.0, Windows Millennium Edition, Windows 2000, Windows XP Home Edition, Windows XP Professional, Windows Server 2003 family

FontConverter.ConvertFrom Method

Overload List

Converts the specified object to the native type of the converter.

[Visual Basic] **Overloads Overrides Public Function Convert-From(ITypeDescriptorContext, CultureInfo, Object) As Object**

[C#] **public override object ConvertFrom(ITypeDescriptor-Context, CultureInfo, object);**

[C++] **public: Object* ConvertFrom(ITypeDescriptor-Context*, CultureInfo*, Object*);**

[JScript] **public override function ConvertFrom(IType-DescriptorContext, CultureInfo, Object) : Object;**

Inherited from **TypeConverter**.

[Visual Basic] **Overloads Public Function ConvertFrom(Object) As Object**

[C#] **public object ConvertFrom(object);**

[C++] **public: Object* ConvertFrom(Object*);**

[JScript] **public function ConvertFrom(Object) : Object;**

FontConverter.ConvertFrom Method (ITypeDescriptorContext, CultureInfo, Object)

Converts the specified object to the native type of the converter.

```
[Visual Basic]
Overrides Overloads Public Function ConvertFrom( _
   ByVal context As ITypeDescriptorContext, _
   ByVal culture As CultureInfo, _
   ByVal value As Object _
) As Object
[C#]
public override object ConvertFrom(
   ITypeDescriptorContext context,
   CultureInfo culture,
   object value
);
[C++]
public: Object* ConvertFrom(
   ITypeDescriptorContext* context,
   CultureInfo* culture,
   Object* value
);
[JScript]
public override function ConvertFrom(
   context : ITypeDescriptorContext,
   culture : CultureInfo,
   value : Object
) : Object;
```

Parameters

context

A formatter context. This object can be used to get additional information about the environment this converter is being called from. This may be a null reference (**Nothing** in Visual Basic), so you should always check. Also, properties on the context object may also return a null reference (**Nothing**).

culture

A **CultureInfo** object that specifies the culture used to represent the font.

value

The object to convert.

Return Value

The converted object. This method will throw an exception if the conversion could not be performed.

Requirements

Platforms: Windows 98, Windows NT 4.0, Windows Millennium Edition, Windows 2000, Windows XP Home Edition, Windows XP Professional, Windows Server 2003 family

FontConverter.ConvertTo Method

Overload List

Converts the specified object to another type. The most common type conversion is to and from a string type. The default implementation calls the **ToString** method of the object if the object is valid and if the destination type is string.

[Visual Basic] **Overloads Overrides Public Function ConvertTo(ITypeDescriptorContext, CultureInfo, Object, Type) As Object**

[C#] **public override object ConvertTo(ITypeDescriptorContext, CultureInfo, object, Type);**

[C++] **public: Object* ConvertTo(ITypeDescriptorContext*, CultureInfo*, Object*, Type*);**

[JScript] **public override function ConvertTo(ITypeDescriptorContext, CultureInfo, Object, Type) : Object;**

Inherited from **TypeConverter**.

[Visual Basic] **Overloads Public Function ConvertTo(Object, Type) As Object**

[C#] **public object ConvertTo(object, Type);**

[C++] **public: Object* ConvertTo(Object*, Type*);**

[JScript] **public function ConvertTo(Object, Type) : Object;**

FontConverter.ConvertTo Method (ITypeDescriptorContext, CultureInfo, Object, Type)

Converts the specified object to another type. The most common type conversion is to and from a string type. The default implementation calls the **ToString** method of the object if the object is valid and if the destination type is string.

```
[Visual Basic]
Overrides Overloads Public Function ConvertTo( _
   ByVal context As ITypeDescriptorContext, _
   ByVal culture As CultureInfo, _
   ByVal value As Object, _
   ByVal destinationType As Type _
) As Object
[C#]
public override object ConvertTo(
   ITypeDescriptorContext context,
   CultureInfo culture,
   object value,
   Type destinationType
);
[C++]
public: Object* ConvertTo(
   ITypeDescriptorContext* context,
   CultureInfo* culture,
   Object* value,
   Type* destinationType
);
[JScript]
public override function ConvertTo(
   context : ITypeDescriptorContext,
   culture : CultureInfo,
   value : Object,
   destinationType : Type
) : Object;
```

Parameters

context

A formatter context. This object can be used to get additional information about the environment this converter is being called from. This may be a null reference (**Nothing** in Visual Basic), so you should always check. Also, properties on the context object may also return a null reference (**Nothing**).

culture

A **CultureInfo** object that specifies the culture used to represent the object.

value

The object to convert.

destinationType

The data type to convert the object to.

Return Value

The converted object. If this method cannot convert the specified object to the destination type, it throws a **NotSupportedException** exception.

Requirements

Platforms: Windows 98, Windows NT 4.0, Windows Millennium Edition, Windows 2000, Windows XP Home Edition, Windows XP Professional, Windows Server 2003 family

FontConverter.CreateInstance Method

Overload List

Creates an object of this type by using a specified set of property values for the object. This is useful for creating nonchangeable objects that have changeable properties.

[Visual Basic] **Overloads Overrides Public Function CreateInstance(ITypeDescriptorContext, IDictionary) As Object**

[C#] **public override object CreateInstance(ITypeDescriptorContext, IDictionary);**

[C++] **public: Object* CreateInstance(ITypeDescriptorContext*, IDictionary*);**

[JScript] **public override function CreateInstance(ITypeDescriptorContext, IDictionary) : Object;**

Inherited from **TypeConverter**.

[Visual Basic] **Overloads Public Function CreateInstance(IDictionary) As Object**

[C#] **public object CreateInstance(IDictionary);**

[C++] **public: Object* CreateInstance(IDictionary*);**

[JScript] **public function CreateInstance(IDictionary) : Object;**

FontConverter.CreateInstance Method (ITypeDescriptorContext, IDictionary)

Creates an object of this type by using a specified set of property values for the object. This is useful for creating nonchangeable objects that have changeable properties.

```
[Visual Basic]
Overrides Overloads Public Function CreateInstance( _
   ByVal context As ITypeDescriptorContext, _
   ByVal propertyValues As IDictionary _
) As Object
[C#]
public override object CreateInstance(
   ITypeDescriptorContext context,
   IDictionary propertyValues
);
[C++]
public: Object* CreateInstance(
   ITypeDescriptorContext* context,
   IDictionary* propertyValues
);
[JScript]
public override function CreateInstance(
   context : ITypeDescriptorContext,
   propertyValues : IDictionary
) : Object;
```

Parameters

context

A type descriptor through which additional context can be provided.

propertyValues

A dictionary of new property values. The dictionary contains a series of name-value pairs, one for each property returned from the **GetProperties** object.

Return Value

The newly created object, or a null reference (**Nothing** in Visual Basic) if the object could not be created. The default implementation returns a null reference (**Nothing**).

Requirements

Platforms: Windows 98, Windows NT 4.0, Windows Millennium Edition, Windows 2000, Windows XP Home Edition, Windows XP Professional, Windows Server 2003 family

FontConverter.GetCreateInstanceSupported Method

Overload List

Determines whether changing a value on this object should require a call to the **CreateInstance** method to create a new value.

[Visual Basic] **Overloads Overrides Public Function GetCreateInstanceSupported(ITypeDescriptorContext) As Boolean**

[C#] **public override bool GetCreateInstanceSupported(ITypeDescriptorContext);**

[C++] **public: bool GetCreateInstanceSupported(ITypeDescriptorContext*);**

[JScript] **public override function GetCreateInstanceSupported(ITypeDescriptorContext) : Boolean;**

Inherited from **TypeConverter**.

[Visual Basic] **Overloads Public Function GetCreateInstanceSupported() As Boolean**

[C#] **public bool GetCreateInstanceSupported();**

[C++] **public: bool GetCreateInstanceSupported();**

[JScript] **public function GetCreateInstanceSupported() : Boolean;**

FontConverter.GetCreateInstanceSupported Method (ITypeDescriptorContext)

Determines whether changing a value on this object should require a call to the **CreateInstance** method to create a new value.

```
[Visual Basic]
Overrides Overloads Public Function GetCreateInstanceSupported( _
   ByVal context As ITypeDescriptorContext _
) As Boolean
[C#]
public override bool GetCreateInstanceSupported(
   ITypeDescriptorContext context
);
[C++]
public: bool GetCreateInstanceSupported(
   ITypeDescriptorContext* context
);
[JScript]
public override function GetCreateInstanceSupported(
   context : ITypeDescriptorContext
) : Boolean;
```

Parameters

context

A type descriptor through which additional context can be provided.

Return Value

This method returns **true** if the **CreateInstance** object should be called when a change is made to one or more properties of this object; otherwise, **false**.

Requirements

Platforms: Windows 98, Windows NT 4.0, Windows Millennium Edition, Windows 2000, Windows XP Home Edition, Windows XP Professional, Windows Server 2003 family

FontConverter.GetProperties Method

Overload List

Retrieves the set of properties for this type. By default, a type does not have any properties to return. An easy implementation of this method can call the **TypeDescriptor.GetProperties** method for the correct data type.

[Visual Basic] **Overloads Overrides Public Function GetProperties(ITypeDescriptorContext, Object, Attribute()) As PropertyDescriptorCollection**

[C#] **public override PropertyDescriptorCollection GetProperties(ITypeDescriptorContext, object, Attribute[]);**

[C++] **public: PropertyDescriptorCollection* GetProperties(ITypeDescriptorContext*, Object*, Attribute[]);**

[JScript] **public override function GetProperties(ITypeDescriptorContext, Object, Attribute[]) : PropertyDescriptorCollection;**

Inherited from **TypeConverter**.

[Visual Basic] **Overloads Public Function GetProperties(Object) As PropertyDescriptorCollection**

[C#] **public PropertyDescriptorCollection GetProperties(object);**

[C++] **public: PropertyDescriptorCollection* GetProperties(Object*);**

[JScript] **public function GetProperties(Object) : PropertyDescriptorCollection;**

Inherited from **TypeConverter**.

[Visual Basic] **Overloads Public Function GetProperties(ITypeDescriptorContext, Object) As PropertyDescriptorCollection**

[C#] **public PropertyDescriptorCollection GetProperties(ITypeDescriptorContext, object);**

[C++] **public: PropertyDescriptorCollection* GetProperties(ITypeDescriptorContext*, Object*);**

[JScript] **public function GetProperties(ITypeDescriptorContext, Object) : PropertyDescriptorCollection;**

FontConverter.GetProperties Method (ITypeDescriptorContext, Object, Attribute[])

Retrieves the set of properties for this type. By default, a type does not have any properties to return. An easy implementation of this method can call the **TypeDescriptor.GetProperties** method for the correct data type.

```
[Visual Basic]
Overrides Overloads Public Function GetProperties( _
   ByVal context As ITypeDescriptorContext, _
   ByVal value As Object, _
   ByVal attributes() As Attribute _
) As PropertyDescriptorCollection
[C#]
public override PropertyDescriptorCollection GetProperties(
   ITypeDescriptorContext context,
   object value,
   Attribute[] attributes
);
[C++]
public: PropertyDescriptorCollection* GetProperties(
   ITypeDescriptorContext* context,
   Object* value,
   Attribute* attributes[]
);
[JScript]
public override function GetProperties(
   context : ITypeDescriptorContext,
   value : Object,
   attributes : Attribute[]
) : PropertyDescriptorCollection;
```

Parameters

context

A type descriptor through which additional context can be provided.

value

The value of the object to get the properties for.

attributes

An array of **MemberAttribute** objects that specify the attributes of the properties.

Return Value

The set of properties that should be exposed for this data type. If no properties should be exposed, this may return a null reference (**Nothing** in Visual Basic). The default implementation always returns a null reference (**Nothing**).

Requirements

Platforms: Windows 98, Windows NT 4.0, Windows Millennium Edition, Windows 2000, Windows XP Home Edition, Windows XP Professional, Windows Server 2003 family

FontConverter.GetPropertiesSupported Method

Overload List

Determines whether this object supports properties. By default, this is **false**.

[Visual Basic] **Overloads Overrides Public Function GetPropertiesSupported(ITypeDescriptorContext) As Boolean**

[C#] **public override bool GetPropertiesSupported(ITypeDescriptorContext);**

[C++] **public: bool GetPropertiesSupported(ITypeDescriptorContext*);**

[JScript] **public override function GetPropertiesSupported(ITypeDescriptorContext) : Boolean;**

Inherited from **TypeConverter**.

[Visual Basic] **Overloads Public Function GetPropertiesSupported() As Boolean**

[C#] **public bool GetPropertiesSupported();**

[C++] **public: bool GetPropertiesSupported();**

[JScript] **public function GetPropertiesSupported() : Boolean;**

FontConverter.GetPropertiesSupported Method (ITypeDescriptorContext)

Determines whether this object supports properties. By default, this is **false**.

[Visual Basic]
```
Overrides Overloads Public Function GetPropertiesSupported( _
   ByVal context As ITypeDescriptorContext _
) As Boolean
```
[C#]
```
public override bool GetPropertiesSupported(
   ITypeDescriptorContext context
);
```
[C++]
```
public: bool GetPropertiesSupported(
   ITypeDescriptorContext* context
);
```
[JScript]
```
public override function GetPropertiesSupported(
   context : ITypeDescriptorContext
) : Boolean;
```

Parameters

context
: A type descriptor through which additional context can be provided.

Return Value

This method returns **true** if the **GetProperties** object should be called to find the properties of this object; otherwise, **false**.

Requirements

Platforms: Windows 98, Windows NT 4.0, Windows Millennium Edition, Windows 2000, Windows XP Home Edition, Windows XP Professional, Windows Server 2003 family

FontConverter.FontName-Converter Class

This type supports the .NET Framework infrastructure and is not intended to be used directly from your code.

```
[Visual Basic]
NotInheritable Public Class FontConverter.FontNameConverter
   Inherits TypeConverter
[C#]
public sealed class FontConverter.FontNameConverter : TypeConverter
[C++]
public __gc __sealed class FontConverter.FontNameConverter : public
   TypeConverter
[JScript]
public class FontConverter.FontNameConverter extends TypeConverter
```

FontConverter.FontNameConverter Constructor

This member supports the .NET Framework infrastructure and is not intended to be used directly from your code.

```
[Visual Basic]
Public Sub New()
[C#]
public FontConverter.FontNameConverter();
[C++]
public: FontNameConverter();
[JScript]
public function FontConverter.FontNameConverter();
```

FontConverter.FontNameConverter.CanConvertFrom Method

This member supports the .NET Framework infrastructure and is not intended to be used directly from your code.

Overload List

This member supports the .NET Framework infrastructure and is not intended to be used directly from your code.

[Visual Basic] **Overloads Overrides Public Function CanConvertFrom(ITypeDescriptorContext, Type) As Boolean**

[C#] **public override bool CanConvertFrom(ITypeDescriptorContext, Type);**

[C++] **public: bool CanConvertFrom(ITypeDescriptorContext*, Type*);**

[JScript] **public override function CanConvertFrom(ITypeDescriptorContext, Type) : Boolean;**

This member supports the .NET Framework infrastructure and is not intended to be used directly from your code.

[Visual Basic] **Overloads Public Function CanConvertFrom(Type) As Boolean**

[C#] **public bool CanConvertFrom(Type);**

[C++] **public: bool CanConvertFrom(Type*);**

[JScript] **public function CanConvertFrom(Type) : Boolean;**

FontConverter.FontNameConverter.CanConvertFrom Method (ITypeDescriptorContext, Type)

This member supports the .NET Framework infrastructure and is not intended to be used directly from your code.

```
[Visual Basic]
Overrides Overloads Public Function CanConvertFrom( _
   ByVal context As ITypeDescriptorContext, _
   ByVal sourceType As Type _
) As Boolean
[C#]
public override bool CanConvertFrom(
   ITypeDescriptorContext context,
   Type sourceType
);
[C++]
public: bool CanConvertFrom(
   ITypeDescriptorContext* context,
   Type* sourceType
);
[JScript]
public override function CanConvertFrom(
   context : ITypeDescriptorContext,
   sourceType : Type
) : Boolean;
```

FontConverter.FontNameConverter.ConvertFrom Method

This member supports the .NET Framework infrastructure and is not intended to be used directly from your code.

Overload List

This member supports the .NET Framework infrastructure and is not intended to be used directly from your code.

[Visual Basic] **Overloads Overrides Public Function ConvertFrom(ITypeDescriptorContext, CultureInfo, Object) As Object**

[C#] **public override object ConvertFrom(ITypeDescriptorContext, CultureInfo, object);**

[C++] **public: Object* ConvertFrom(ITypeDescriptorContext*, CultureInfo*, Object*);**

[JScript] **public override function ConvertFrom(ITypeDescriptorContext, CultureInfo, Object) : Object;**

This member supports the .NET Framework infrastructure and is not intended to be used directly from your code.

[Visual Basic] **Overloads Public Function ConvertFrom(Object) As Object**

[C#] **public object ConvertFrom(object);**

[C++] **public: Object* ConvertFrom(Object*);**

[JScript] **public function ConvertFrom(Object) : Object;**

FontConverter.FontNameConverter.ConvertFrom Method (ITypeDescriptorContext, CultureInfo, Object)

This member supports the .NET Framework infrastructure and is not intended to be used directly from your code.

```
[Visual Basic]
Overrides Overloads Public Function ConvertFrom( _
   ByVal context As ITypeDescriptorContext, _
   ByVal culture As CultureInfo, _
   ByVal value As Object _
) As Object
[C#]
public override object ConvertFrom(
   ITypeDescriptorContext context,
   CultureInfo culture,
   object value
);
[C++]
public: Object* ConvertFrom(
   ITypeDescriptorContext* context,
   CultureInfo* culture,
   Object* value
);
[JScript]
public override function ConvertFrom(
   context : ITypeDescriptorContext,
   culture : CultureInfo,
   value : Object
) : Object;
```

FontConverter.FontNameConverter.Finalize Method

This member supports the .NET Framework infrastructure and is not intended to be used directly from your code.

```
[Visual Basic]
Overrides Protected Sub Finalize()
[C#]
~FontNameConverter();
[C++]
~FontNameConverter();
[JScript]
protected override function Finalize();
```

FontConverter.FontNameConverter.GetStandard-Values Method

This member supports the .NET Framework infrastructure and is not intended to be used directly from your code.

Overload List

This member supports the .NET Framework infrastructure and is not intended to be used directly from your code.

[Visual Basic] **Overloads Overrides Public Function GetStandardValues(ITypeDescriptorContext) As StandardValuesCollection**

[C#] **public override StandardValuesCollection GetStandardValues(ITypeDescriptorContext);**

[C++] **public: StandardValuesCollection* GetStandardValues(ITypeDescriptorContext*);**

[JScript] **public override function GetStandardValues(IType-DescriptorContext) : StandardValuesCollection;**

This member supports the .NET Framework infrastructure and is not intended to be used directly from your code.

[Visual Basic] **Overloads Public Function GetStandardValues() As ICollection**

[C#] **public ICollection GetStandardValues();**

[C++] **public: ICollection* GetStandardValues();**

[JScript] **public function GetStandardValues() : ICollection;**

FontConverter.FontNameConverter.GetStandardValues Method (ITypeDescriptorContext)

This member supports the .NET Framework infrastructure and is not intended to be used directly from your code.

```
[Visual Basic]
Overrides Overloads Public Function GetStandardValues( _
   ByVal context As ITypeDescriptorContext _
) As StandardValuesCollection
[C#]
public override StandardValuesCollection GetStandardValues(
   ITypeDescriptorContext context
);
[C++]
public: StandardValuesCollection* GetStandardValues(
   ITypeDescriptorContext* context
);
[JScript]
public override function GetStandardValues(
   context : ITypeDescriptorContext
) : StandardValuesCollection;
```

FontConverter.FontNameConverter.GetStandard-ValuesExclusive Method

This member supports the .NET Framework infrastructure and is not intended to be used directly from your code.

Overload List

This member supports the .NET Framework infrastructure and is not intended to be used directly from your code.

[Visual Basic] **Overloads Overrides Public Function GetStandardValuesExclusive(ITypeDescriptorContext) As Boolean**

[C#] **public override bool GetStandardValues-Exclusive(ITypeDescriptorContext);**

[C++] **public: bool GetStandardValuesExclusive(IType-DescriptorContext*);**

[JScript] **public override function GetStandardValues-Exclusive(ITypeDescriptorContext) : Boolean;**

This member supports the .NET Framework infrastructure and is not intended to be used directly from your code.

[Visual Basic] **Overloads Public Function GetStandardValuesExclusive() As Boolean**

[C#] **public bool GetStandardValuesExclusive();**

[C++] **public: bool GetStandardValuesExclusive();**

[JScript] **public function GetStandardValuesExclusive() : Boolean;**

FontConverter.FontNameConverter.GetStandardValuesExclusive Method (ITypeDescriptorContext)

This member supports the .NET Framework infrastructure and is not intended to be used directly from your code.

[Visual Basic]
```
Overrides Overloads Public Function GetStandardValuesExclusive( _
   ByVal context As ITypeDescriptorContext _
) As Boolean
```
[C#]
```
public override bool GetStandardValuesExclusive(
   ITypeDescriptorContext context
);
```
[C++]
```
public: bool GetStandardValuesExclusive(
   ITypeDescriptorContext* context
);
```
[JScript]
```
public override function GetStandardValuesExclusive(
   context : ITypeDescriptorContext
) : Boolean;
```

FontConverter.FontNameConverter.GetStandardValuesSupported Method

This member supports the .NET Framework infrastructure and is not intended to be used directly from your code.

Overload List

This member supports the .NET Framework infrastructure and is not intended to be used directly from your code.

[Visual Basic] **Overloads Overrides Public Function GetStandardValuesSupported(ITypeDescriptorContext) As Boolean**

[C#] **public override bool GetStandardValuesSupported(ITypeDescriptorContext);**

[C++] **public: bool GetStandardValuesSupported(ITypeDescriptorContext*);**

[JScript] **public override function GetStandardValuesSupported(ITypeDescriptorContext) : Boolean;**

This member supports the .NET Framework infrastructure and is not intended to be used directly from your code.

[Visual Basic] **Overloads Public Function GetStandardValuesSupported() As Boolean**

[C#] **public bool GetStandardValuesSupported();**

[C++] **public: bool GetStandardValuesSupported();**

[JScript] **public function GetStandardValuesSupported() : Boolean;**

FontConverter.FontNameConverter.GetStandardValuesSupported Method (ITypeDescriptorContext)

This member supports the .NET Framework infrastructure and is not intended to be used directly from your code.

[Visual Basic]
```
Overrides Overloads Public Function GetStandardValuesSupported( _
   ByVal context As ITypeDescriptorContext _
) As Boolean
```
[C#]
```
public override bool GetStandardValuesSupported(
   ITypeDescriptorContext context
);
```
[C++]
```
public: bool GetStandardValuesSupported(
   ITypeDescriptorContext* context
);
```
[JScript]
```
public override function GetStandardValuesSupported(
   context : ITypeDescriptorContext
) : Boolean;
```

FontConverter.FontUnitConverter Class

This type supports the .NET Framework infrastructure and is not intended to be used directly from your code.

```
[Visual Basic]
Public Class FontConverter.FontUnitConverter
   Inherits EnumConverter
[C#]
public class FontConverter.FontUnitConverter : EnumConverter
[C++]
public __gc class FontConverter.FontUnitConverter : public
   EnumConverter
[JScript]
public class FontConverter.FontUnitConverter extends EnumConverter
```

FontConverter.FontUnitConverter Constructor

This member supports the .NET Framework infrastructure and is not intended to be used directly from your code.

```
[Visual Basic]
Public Sub New()
[C#]
public FontConverter.FontUnitConverter();
[C++]
public: FontUnitConverter();
[JScript]
public function FontConverter.FontUnitConverter();
```

FontConverter.FontUnitConverter.GetStandardValues Method

This member supports the .NET Framework infrastructure and is not intended to be used directly from your code.

Overload List

This member overrides **TypeConverter.GetStandardValues**.

[Visual Basic] **Overloads Overrides Public Function GetStandardValues(ITypeDescriptorContext) As StandardValuesCollection**

[C#] **public override StandardValuesCollection GetStandardValues(ITypeDescriptorContext);**

[C++] **public: StandardValuesCollection* GetStandardValues(ITypeDescriptorContext*);**

[JScript] **public override function GetStandardValues(ITypeDescriptorContext) : StandardValuesCollection;**

This member supports the .NET Framework infrastructure and is not intended to be used directly from your code.

[Visual Basic] **Overloads Public Function GetStandardValues() As ICollection**

[C#] **public ICollection GetStandardValues();**

[C++] **public: ICollection* GetStandardValues();**

[JScript] **public function GetStandardValues() : ICollection;**

FontConverter.FontUnitConverter.GetStandardValues Method (ITypeDescriptorContext)

This member overrides **TypeConverter.GetStandardValues**.

```
[Visual Basic]
Overrides Overloads Public Function GetStandardValues( _
   ByVal context As ITypeDescriptorContext _
) As StandardValuesCollection
[C#]
public override StandardValuesCollection GetStandardValues(
   ITypeDescriptorContext context
);
[C++]
public: StandardValuesCollection* GetStandardValues(
   ITypeDescriptorContext* context
);
[JScript]
public override function GetStandardValues(
   context : ITypeDescriptorContext
) : StandardValuesCollection;
```

Requirements

Platforms: Windows 98, Windows NT 4.0, Windows Millennium Edition, Windows 2000, Windows XP Home Edition, Windows XP Professional, Windows Server 2003 family

FontFamily Class

Defines a group of type faces having a similar basic design and certain variations in styles. This class cannot be inherited.

System.Object
  System.MarshalByRefObject
    System.Drawing.FontFamily

```
[Visual Basic]
NotInheritable Public Class FontFamily
   Inherits MarshalByRefObject
   Implements IDisposable
[C#]
public sealed class FontFamily : MarshalByRefObject, IDisposable
[C++]
public __gc __sealed class FontFamily : public MarshalByRefObject,
   IDisposable
[JScript]
public class FontFamily extends MarshalByRefObject implements
   IDisposable
```

Thread Safety

Any public static (**Shared** in Visual Basic) members of this type are safe for multithreaded operations. Any instance members are not guaranteed to be thread safe.

Requirements

Namespace: System.Drawing

Platforms: Windows 98, Windows NT 4.0, Windows Millennium Edition, Windows 2000, Windows XP Home Edition, Windows XP Professional, Windows Server 2003 family, .NET Compact Framework - Windows CE .NET

Assembly: System.Drawing (in System.Drawing.dll)

FontFamily Constructor

Initializes a new **FontFamily** object that uses the specified name.

Overload List

Initializes a new **FontFamily** object from the specified generic font family.

[Visual Basic] **Public Sub New(GenericFontFamilies)**

[C#] **public FontFamily(GenericFontFamilies);**

[C++] **public: FontFamily(GenericFontFamilies);**

[JScript] **public function FontFamily(GenericFontFamilies);**

Initializes a new **FontFamily** object with the specified name.

[Visual Basic] **Public Sub New(String)**

[C#] **public FontFamily(string);**

[C++] **public: FontFamily(String*);**

[JScript] **public function FontFamily(String);**

Initializes a new **FontFamily** object in the specified **FontCollection** object with the specified name.

[Visual Basic] **Public Sub New(String, FontCollection)**

[C#] **public FontFamily(string, FontCollection);**

[C++] **public: FontFamily(String*, FontCollection*);**

[JScript] **public function FontFamily(String, FontCollection);**

FontFamily Constructor (GenericFontFamilies)

Initializes a new **FontFamily** object from the specified generic font family.

```
[Visual Basic]
Public Sub New( _
   ByVal genericFamily As GenericFontFamilies _
)
[C#]
public FontFamily(
   GenericFontFamilies genericFamily
);
[C++]
public: FontFamily(
   GenericFontFamilies genericFamily
);
[JScript]
public function FontFamily(
   genericFamily : GenericFontFamilies
);
```

Parameters

genericFamily
  The **GenericFontFamilies** enumeration from which to create the new **FontFamily** object.

Requirements

Platforms: Windows 98, Windows NT 4.0, Windows Millennium Edition, Windows 2000, Windows XP Home Edition, Windows XP Professional, Windows Server 2003 family

FontFamily Constructor (String)

Initializes a new **FontFamily** object with the specified name.

```
[Visual Basic]
Public Sub New( _
   ByVal name As String _
)
[C#]
public FontFamily(
   string name
);
[C++]
public: FontFamily(
   String* name
);
[JScript]
public function FontFamily(
   name : String
);
```

Parameters

name
  The name of the new **FontFamily** object.

Requirements

Platforms: Windows 98, Windows NT 4.0, Windows Millennium Edition, Windows 2000, Windows XP Home Edition, Windows XP Professional, Windows Server 2003 family

FontFamily Constructor (String, FontCollection)

Initializes a new **FontFamily** object in the specified **FontCollection** object with the specified name.

[Visual Basic]
```
Public Sub New( _
   ByVal name As String, _
   ByVal fontCollection As FontCollection _
)
```
[C#]
```
public FontFamily(
   string name,
   FontCollection fontCollection
);
```
[C++]
```
public: FontFamily(
   String* name,
   FontCollection* fontCollection
);
```
[JScript]
```
public function FontFamily(
   name : String,
   fontCollection : FontCollection
);
```

Parameters

name
  A **String** object that represents the name of the new **FontFamily** object.

fontCollection
  The **FontCollection** object that contains this **FontFamily** object.

Requirements

Platforms: Windows 98, Windows NT 4.0, Windows Millennium Edition, Windows 2000, Windows XP Home Edition, Windows XP Professional, Windows Server 2003 family

FontFamily.Families Property

Returns an array that contains all the **FontFamily** objects associated with the current graphics context.

[Visual Basic]
```
Public Shared ReadOnly Property Families As FontFamily ()
```
[C#]
```
public static FontFamily[] Families {get;}
```
[C++]
```
public: __property static FontFamily* get_Families();
```
[JScript]
```
public static function get Families() : FontFamily[];
```

Property Value

An array of **FontFamily** objects associated with the current graphics context.

Requirements

Platforms: Windows 98, Windows NT 4.0, Windows Millennium Edition, Windows 2000, Windows XP Home Edition, Windows XP Professional, Windows Server 2003 family

FontFamily.GenericMonospace Property

Gets a generic monospace **FontFamily** object.

[Visual Basic]
```
Public Shared ReadOnly Property GenericMonospace As FontFamily
```
[C#]
```
public static FontFamily GenericMonospace {get;}
```
[C++]
```
public: __property static FontFamily* get_GenericMonospace();
```
[JScript]
```
public static function get GenericMonospace() : FontFamily;
```

Property Value

A **FontFamily** object that represents a generic monospace font.

Requirements

Platforms: Windows 98, Windows NT 4.0, Windows Millennium Edition, Windows 2000, Windows XP Home Edition, Windows XP Professional, Windows Server 2003 family, .NET Compact Framework - Windows CE .NET

FontFamily.GenericSansSerif Property

Gets a generic sans serif **FontFamily** object.

[Visual Basic]
```
Public Shared ReadOnly Property GenericSansSerif As FontFamily
```
[C#]
```
public static FontFamily GenericSansSerif {get;}
```
[C++]
```
public: __property static FontFamily* get_GenericSansSerif();
```
[JScript]
```
public static function get GenericSansSerif() : FontFamily;
```

Property Value

A **FontFamily** object that represents a generic sans serif font.

Requirements

Platforms: Windows 98, Windows NT 4.0, Windows Millennium Edition, Windows 2000, Windows XP Home Edition, Windows XP Professional, Windows Server 2003 family, .NET Compact Framework - Windows CE .NET

FontFamily.GenericSerif Property

Gets a generic serif **FontFamily** object.

[Visual Basic]
```
Public Shared ReadOnly Property GenericSerif As FontFamily
```
[C#]
```
public static FontFamily GenericSerif {get;}
```
[C++]
```
public: __property static FontFamily* get_GenericSerif();
```
[JScript]
```
public static function get GenericSerif() : FontFamily;
```

Property Value

A **FontFamily** object that represents a generic serif font.

Requirements

Platforms: Windows 98, Windows NT 4.0,
Windows Millennium Edition, Windows 2000,
Windows XP Home Edition, Windows XP Professional,
Windows Server 2003 family,
.NET Compact Framework - Windows CE .NET

FontFamily.Name Property

Gets the name of this **FontFamily** object.

```
[Visual Basic]
Public ReadOnly Property Name As String
[C#]
public string Name {get;}
[C++]
public: __property String* get_Name();
[JScript]
public function get Name() : String;
```

Property Value

A **String** object that represents the name of this **FontFamily** object.

Requirements

Platforms: Windows 98, Windows NT 4.0,
Windows Millennium Edition, Windows 2000,
Windows XP Home Edition, Windows XP Professional,
Windows Server 2003 family

FontFamily.Dispose Method

Releases all resources used by this **FontFamily** object.

```
[Visual Basic]
Public Overridable Sub Dispose() Implements IDisposable.Dispose
[C#]
public virtual void Dispose();
[C++]
public: virtual void Dispose();
[JScript]
public function Dispose();
```

Return Value

This method does not return a value.

Implements

IDisposable.Dispose

Remarks

Calling **Dispose** allows the resources used by this **FontFamily** object to be reallocated for other purposes.

Requirements

Platforms: Windows 98, Windows NT 4.0,
Windows Millennium Edition, Windows 2000,
Windows XP Home Edition, Windows XP Professional,
Windows Server 2003 family,
.NET Compact Framework - Windows CE .NET

FontFamily.Equals Method

Indicates whether the specified object is a **FontFamily** object and is identical to this **FontFamily** object.

```
[Visual Basic]
Overrides Public Function Equals( _
   ByVal obj As Object _
) As Boolean
[C#]
public override bool Equals(
   object obj
);
[C++]
public: bool Equals(
   Object* obj
);
[JScript]
public override function Equals(
   obj : Object
) : Boolean;
```

Parameters

obj

The object to test.

Return Value

This method returns **true** if *obj* is both a **FontFamily** object and is identical to this **FontFamily** object; otherwise, **false**.

Example

[Visual Basic, C#] The following example is designed for use with Windows Forms, and it requires **PaintEventArgs** *e*, which is a parameter of the **Paint** event handler. The code performs the following actions:

- Creates two **Font** objects.
- Tests whether they are equivalent.
- Displays the result of the test in a message box.

```
[Visual Basic]
Public Sub Equals_Example(e As PaintEventArgs)
' Create two FontFamily objects.
Dim firstFontFamily As New FontFamily("Arial")
Dim secondFontFamily As New FontFamily("Times New Roman")
' Check to see if the two font families are equivalent.
Dim equalFonts As Boolean = _
firstFontFamily.Equals(secondFontFamily)
' Display the result of the test in a message box.
MessageBox.Show(equalFonts.ToString())
End Sub
```

```
[C#]
public void Equals_Example(PaintEventArgs e)
{
// Create two FontFamily objects.
FontFamily firstFontFamily = new FontFamily("Arial");
FontFamily secondFontFamily = new FontFamily("Times New Roman");
// Check to see if the two font families are equivalent.
bool equalFonts = firstFontFamily.Equals(secondFontFamily);
// Display the result of the test in a message box.
MessageBox.Show(equalFonts.ToString());
}
```

Requirements

Platforms: Windows 98, Windows NT 4.0,
Windows Millennium Edition, Windows 2000,
Windows XP Home Edition, Windows XP Professional,
Windows Server 2003 family,
.NET Compact Framework - Windows CE .NET

FontFamily.Finalize Method

This member overrides **Object.Finalize**.

[Visual Basic]
```
Overrides Protected Sub Finalize()
```
[C#]
```
~FontFamily();
```
[C++]
```
~FontFamily();
```
[JScript]
```
protected override function Finalize();
```

Requirements

Platforms: Windows 98, Windows NT 4.0, Windows Millennium Edition, Windows 2000, Windows XP Home Edition, Windows XP Professional, Windows Server 2003 family, .NET Compact Framework - Windows CE .NET

FontFamily.GetCellAscent Method

Returns the cell ascent, in design units, of the **FontFamily** object of the specified style. For information about font metrics, see **Obtaining Font Metrics**.

[Visual Basic]
```
Public Function GetCellAscent( _
   ByVal style As FontStyle _
) As Integer
```
[C#]
```
public int GetCellAscent(
   FontStyle style
);
```
[C++]
```
public: int GetCellAscent(
   FontStyle style
);
```
[JScript]
```
public function GetCellAscent(
   style : FontStyle
) : int;
```

Parameters

style
A **FontStyle** enumeration that contains style information for the font.

Return Value

The cell ascent for this **FontFamily** object that uses the specified **FontStyle** enumeration .

Example

[Visual Basic, C#] The following example is designed for use with Windows Forms, and it requires **PaintEventArgs** *e*, which is a parameter of the **Paint** event handler. The code performs the following actions:

- Creates a **FontFamily** object.
- Gets the cell ascent for that font family.
- Draws the value of the cell ascent to the screen as text.

[Visual Basic]
```
Public Sub GetCellAscent_Example(e As PaintEventArgs)
' Create a FontFamily object.
Dim ascentFontFamily As New FontFamily("arial")
' Get the cell ascent of the font family in design units.
Dim cellAscent As Integer = _
ascentFontFamily.GetCellAscent(FontStyle.Regular)
' Draw the result as a string to the screen.
e.Graphics.DrawString("ascentFontFamily.GetCellAscent() returns " _
& cellAscent.ToString() & ".", New Font(ascentFontFamily, 16), _
Brushes.Black, New PointF(0, 0))
End Sub
```

[C#]
```
public void GetCellAscent_Example(PaintEventArgs e)
{
// Create a FontFamily object.
FontFamily ascentFontFamily = new FontFamily("arial");
// Get the cell ascent of the font family in design units.
int cellAscent = ascentFontFamily.GetCellAscent(FontStyle.Regular);
// Draw the result as a string to the screen.
e.Graphics.DrawString(
"ascentFontFamily.GetCellAscent() returns " +                    ↵
cellAscent.ToString() + ".",
new Font(ascentFontFamily, 16),
Brushes.Black,
new PointF(0, 0));
}
```

Requirements

Platforms: Windows 98, Windows NT 4.0, Windows Millennium Edition, Windows 2000, Windows XP Home Edition, Windows XP Professional, Windows Server 2003 family

FontFamily.GetCellDescent Method

Returns the cell descent, in design units, of the **FontFamily** object of the specified style. For information about font metrics, see **Obtaining Font Metrics**.

[Visual Basic]
```
Public Function GetCellDescent( _
   ByVal style As FontStyle _
) As Integer
```
[C#]
```
public int GetCellDescent(
   FontStyle style
);
```
[C++]
```
public: int GetCellDescent(
   FontStyle style
);
```
[JScript]
```
public function GetCellDescent(
   style : FontStyle
) : int;
```

Parameters

style
A **FontStyle** enumeration that contains style information for the font.

Return Value

The cell descent metric for this **FontFamily** object that uses the specified **FontStyle** enumeration .

Example

[Visual Basic, C#] The following example is designed for use with Windows Forms, and it requires **PaintEventArgs** *e*, which is a parameter of the **Paint** event handler. The code performs the following actions:

- Creates a **FontFamily** object.
- Gets the cell descent for that font family.
- Draws the value of the cell ascent to the screen as text.

[Visual Basic]
```
Public Sub GetCellDescent_Example(e As PaintEventArgs)
' Create a FontFamily object.
Dim descentFontFamily As New FontFamily("arial")
' Get the cell descent of the font family in design units.
Dim cellDescent As Integer = _
descentFontFamily.GetCellDescent(FontStyle.Regular)
' Draw the result as a string to the screen.
e.Graphics.DrawString("descentFontFamily.GetCellDescent() returns " _
& cellDescent.ToString() & ".", New Font(descentFontFamily, 16), _
Brushes.Black, New PointF(0, 0))
End Sub
```

[C#]
```
public void GetCellDescent_Example(PaintEventArgs e)
{
// Create a FontFamily object.
FontFamily descentFontFamily = new FontFamily("arial");
// Get the cell descent of the font family in design units.
int cellDescent = descentFontFamily.GetCellDescent(FontStyle.Regular);
// Draw the result as a string to the screen.
e.Graphics.DrawString(
"descentFontFamily.GetCellDescent() returns " +
cellDescent.ToString() + ".",
new Font(descentFontFamily, 16),
Brushes.Black,
new PointF(0, 0));
}
```

Requirements

Platforms: Windows 98, Windows NT 4.0, Windows Millennium Edition, Windows 2000, Windows XP Home Edition, Windows XP Professional, Windows Server 2003 family

FontFamily.GetEmHeight Method

Gets the height, in font design units, of the em square for the specified style. For information about font metrics, see **Obtaining Font Metrics**.

[Visual Basic]
```
Public Function GetEmHeight( _
   ByVal style As FontStyle _
) As Integer
```
[C#]
```
public int GetEmHeight(
   FontStyle style
);
```
[C++]
```
public: int GetEmHeight(
   FontStyle style
);
```
[JScript]
```
public function GetEmHeight(
   style : FontStyle
) : int;
```

Parameters

style

The **FontStyle** enumeration for which to get the em height.

Return Value

The height of the em square.

Example

[Visual Basic, C#] The following example is designed for use with Windows Forms, and it requires **PaintEventArgs** *e*, which is a parameter of the **Paint** event handler. The code performs the following actions:

- Creates a **FontFamily** object.
- Gets the em square height for that font family.
- Draws the value of the em height to the screen as text.

[Visual Basic]
```
Public Sub GetEmHeight_Example(e As PaintEventArgs)
' Create a FontFamily object.
Dim emFontFamily As New FontFamily("arial")
' Get the em height of the font family in design units.
Dim emHeight As Integer = _
emFontFamily.GetEmHeight(FontStyle.Regular)
' Draw the result as a string to the screen.
e.Graphics.DrawString("emFontFamily.GetEmHeight() returns " & _
emHeight.ToString() + ".", New Font(emFontFamily, 16), _
Brushes.Black, New PointF(0, 0))
End Sub
```

[C#]
```
public void GetEmHeight_Example(PaintEventArgs e)
{
// Create a FontFamily object.
FontFamily emFontFamily = new FontFamily("arial");
// Get the em height of the font family in design units.
int emHeight = emFontFamily.GetEmHeight(FontStyle.Regular);
// Draw the result as a string to the screen.
e.Graphics.DrawString(
"emFontFamily.GetEmHeight() returns " + emHeight.ToString() + ".",
new Font(emFontFamily, 16),
Brushes.Black,
new PointF(0, 0));
```

[Visual Basic, C#] }

Requirements

Platforms: Windows 98, Windows NT 4.0, Windows Millennium Edition, Windows 2000, Windows XP Home Edition, Windows XP Professional, Windows Server 2003 family

FontFamily.GetFamilies Method

Returns an array that contains all the **FontFamily** objects available for the specified graphics context.

[Visual Basic]
```
Public Shared Function GetFamilies( _
   ByVal graphics As Graphics _
) As FontFamily()
```
[C#]
```
public static FontFamily[] GetFamilies(
   Graphics graphics
);
```
[C++]
```
public: static FontFamily* GetFamilies(
   Graphics* graphics
) [];
```

```
[JScript]
public static function GetFamilies(
   graphics : Graphics
) : FontFamily[];
```

Parameters

graphics

The **Graphics** object from which to return **FontFamily** objects.

Return Value

An array of **FontFamily** objects available for the specified **Graphics** object.

Example

[Visual Basic, C#] The following example is designed for use with Windows Forms, and it requires **PaintEventArgs** *e*, which is a parameter of the **Paint** event handler. The code gets an array of the available **FontFamily** objects, and then draws text to the screen using each of the font families.

```
[Visual Basic]
Public Sub GetFamilies_Example(e As PaintEventArgs)
' Get an array of the available font families.
Dim families As FontFamily() = FontFamily.GetFamilies(e.Graphics)
' Draw text using each of the font families.
Dim familiesFont As Font
Dim familyString As String
Dim spacing As Single = 0
Dim family As FontFamily
For Each family In families
familiesFont = New Font(family, 16, FontStyle.Bold)
familyString = "This is the " + family.Name + "family."
e.Graphics.DrawString(familyString, familiesFont, _
Brushes.Black, New PointF(0, spacing))
spacing += familiesFont.Height
Next family
End Sub
```

```
[C#]
public void GetFamilies_Example(PaintEventArgs e)
{
// Get an array of the available font families.
FontFamily[] families = FontFamily.GetFamilies(e.Graphics);
// Draw text using each of the font families.
Font familiesFont;
string familyString;
float spacing = 0;
for each (FontFamily family in families)
{
familiesFont = new Font(family, 16, FontStyle.Bold);
familyString = "This is the " + family.Name + "family.";
e.Graphics.DrawString(
familyString,
familiesFont,
Brushes.Black,
new PointF(0, spacing));
spacing += familiesFont.Height;
}
}
```

Requirements

Platforms: Windows 98, Windows NT 4.0, Windows Millennium Edition, Windows 2000, Windows XP Home Edition, Windows XP Professional, Windows Server 2003 family

FontFamily.GetHashCode Method

Gets a hash code for this **FontFamily** object.

```
[Visual Basic]
Overrides Public Function GetHashCode() As Integer
[C#]
public override int GetHashCode();
[C++]
public: int GetHashCode();
[JScript]
public override function GetHashCode() : int;
```

Return Value

The hash code for this **FontFamily** object.

Example

[Visual Basic, C#] The following example is designed for use with Windows Forms, and it requires **PaintEventArgs** *e*, which is a parameter of the **Paint** event handler. The code performs the following actions:

- Creates a **FontFamily** object.
- Gets the hash code for the font family.
- Draws the value of the hash code to the screen as text.

```
[Visual Basic]
Public Sub GetHashCode_Example(e As PaintEventArgs)
' Create a FontFamily object.
Dim myFontFamily As New FontFamily("Arial")
' Get the hash code for myFontFamily.
Dim hashCode As Integer = myFontFamily.GetHashCode()
' Draw the value of hashCode to the screen as a string.
e.Graphics.DrawString("hashCode = " & hashCode.ToString(), _
New Font(myFontFamily, 16), Brushes.Black, New PointF(0, 0))
End Sub
```

```
[C#]
public void GetHashCode_Example(PaintEventArgs e)
{
// Create a FontFamily object.
FontFamily myFontFamily = new FontFamily("Arial");
// Get the hash code for myFontFamily.
int hashCode = myFontFamily.GetHashCode();
// Draw the value of hashCode to the screen as a string.
e.Graphics.DrawString(
"hashCode = " + hashCode.ToString(),
new Font(myFontFamily, 16),
Brushes.Black,
new PointF(0, 0));
}
```

Requirements

Platforms: Windows 98, Windows NT 4.0, Windows Millennium Edition, Windows 2000, Windows XP Home Edition, Windows XP Professional, Windows Server 2003 family, .NET Compact Framework - Windows CE .NET

FontFamily.GetLineSpacing Method

Returns the line spacing, in design units, of the **FontFamily** object of the specified style. The line spacing is the vertical distance between the base lines of two consecutive lines of text. For information about font metrics, see **Obtaining Font Metrics**.

```
[Visual Basic]
Public Function GetLineSpacing( _
   ByVal style As FontStyle _
) As Integer
```

[C#]
```
public int GetLineSpacing(
   FontStyle style
);
```
[C++]
```
public: int GetLineSpacing(
   FontStyle style
);
```
[JScript]
```
public function GetLineSpacing(
   style : FontStyle
) : int;
```

Parameters

style

The **FontStyle** enumeration to apply.

Return Value

The distance between two consecutive lines of text.

Example

[Visual Basic, C#] The following example is designed for use with Windows Forms, and it requires **PaintEventArgs** *e*, which is a parameter of the **Paint** event handler. The code performs the following actions:

- Creates a **FontFamily** object.
- Gets the line spacing for the font family.
- Draws the value of the line spacing to the screen as text.

[Visual Basic]
```
Public Sub GetLineSpacing_Example(e As PaintEventArgs)
' Create a FontFamily object.
Dim myFontFamily As New FontFamily("Arial")
' Get the line spacing for myFontFamily.
Dim lineSpacing As Integer = _
myFontFamily.GetLineSpacing(FontStyle.Regular)
' Draw the value of lineSpacing to the screen as a string.
e.Graphics.DrawString("lineSpacing = " & lineSpacing.ToString(), _
New Font(myFontFamily, 16), Brushes.Black, New PointF(0, 0))
End Sub
```

[C#]
```
public void GetLineSpacing_Example(PaintEventArgs e)
{
// Create a FontFamily object.
FontFamily myFontFamily = new FontFamily("Arial");
// Get the line spacing for myFontFamily.
int lineSpacing = myFontFamily.GetLineSpacing(FontStyle.Regular);
// Draw the value of lineSpacing to the screen as a string.
e.Graphics.DrawString(
"lineSpacing = " + lineSpacing.ToString(),
new Font(myFontFamily, 16),
Brushes.Black,
new PointF(0, 0));
}
```

Requirements

Platforms: Windows 98, Windows NT 4.0, Windows Millennium Edition, Windows 2000, Windows XP Home Edition, Windows XP Professional, Windows Server 2003 family

FontFamily.GetName Method

Returns the name, in the specified language, of this **FontFamily** object.

[Visual Basic]
```
Public Function GetName( _
   ByVal language As Integer _
) As String
```
[C#]
```
public string GetName(
   int language
);
```
[C++]
```
public: String* GetName(
   int language
);
```
[JScript]
```
public function GetName(
   language : int
) : String;
```

Parameters

language

The language in which the name is returned.

Return Value

A **String** object that represents the name, in the specified language, of this **FontFamily** object. It creates a **FontFamily** object, gets the name of that font family, and then draws the name to the screen as text.

Example

[Visual Basic, C#] The following example is designed for use with Windows Forms, and it requires **PaintEventArgs** *e*, which is a parameter of the **Paint** event handler. The code performs the following actions:

- Creates a **FontFamily** object.
- Gets the name of the font family.
- Draws the name of the font family to the screen as text.

[Visual Basic]
```
Public Sub GetName_Example(e As PaintEventArgs)
' Create a FontFamily object.
Dim myFontFamily As New FontFamily("Arial")
' Get the name of myFontFamily.
Dim familyName As String = myFontFamily.GetName(0)
' Draw the name of the myFontFamily to the screen as a string.
e.Graphics.DrawString("The family name is " & familyName, _
New Font(myFontFamily, 16), Brushes.Black, New PointF(0, 0))
End Sub
```

[C#]
```
public void GetName_Example(PaintEventArgs e)
{
// Create a FontFamily object.
FontFamily myFontFamily = new FontFamily("Arial");
// Get the name of myFontFamily.
string familyName = myFontFamily.GetName(0);
// Draw the name of the myFontFamily to the screen as a string.
e.Graphics.DrawString(
"The family name is " + familyName,
new Font(myFontFamily, 16),
Brushes.Black,
new PointF(0, 0));
}
```

Requirements

Platforms: Windows 98, Windows NT 4.0, Windows Millennium Edition, Windows 2000, Windows XP Home Edition, Windows XP Professional, Windows Server 2003 family

FontFamily.IsStyleAvailable Method

Indicates whether the specified **FontStyle** enumeration is available.

```
[Visual Basic]
Public Function IsStyleAvailable( _
   ByVal style As FontStyle _
) As Boolean
[C#]
public bool IsStyleAvailable(
   FontStyle style
);
[C++]
public: bool IsStyleAvailable(
   FontStyle style
);
[JScript]
public function IsStyleAvailable(
   style : FontStyle
) : Boolean;
```

Parameters

style
The **FontStyle** enumeration to test.

Return Value

This method returns **true** if the specified **FontStyle** is available; otherwise, **false**.

Example

[Visual Basic, C#] The following example is designed for use with Windows Forms, and it requires **PaintEventArgs** *e*, which is a parameter of the **Paint** event handler. The code performs the following actions:

- Creates a **FontFamily** object.
- Tests whether the font family is available in an italic font.
- If it is, draws text to the screen.

```
[Visual Basic]
Public Sub IsStyleAvailable_Example(e As PaintEventArgs)
' Create a FontFamily object.
Dim myFontFamily As New FontFamily("Arial")
' Test whether myFontFamily is available in Italic.
If myFontFamily.IsStyleAvailable(FontStyle.Italic) Then
' Create a Font object using myFontFamily.
Dim familyFont As New Font(myFontFamily, 16, FontStyle.Italic)
' Use familyFont to draw text to the screen.
e.Graphics.DrawString(myFontFamily.Name & _
" is available in Italic", familyFont, Brushes.Black, _
New PointF(0, 0))
End If
End Sub
```

```
[C#]
public void IsStyleAvailable_Example(PaintEventArgs e)
{
// Create a FontFamily object.
FontFamily myFontFamily = new FontFamily("Arial");
// Test whether myFontFamily is available in Italic.
if(myFontFamily.IsStyleAvailable(FontStyle.Italic))
{
// Create a Font object using myFontFamily.
Font familyFont = new Font(myFontFamily, 16, FontStyle.Italic);
// Use familyFont to draw text to the screen.
e.Graphics.DrawString(
myFontFamily.Name + " is available in Italic",
familyFont,
Brushes.Black,
new PointF(0, 0));
}
}
```

Requirements

Platforms: Windows 98, Windows NT 4.0, Windows Millennium Edition, Windows 2000, Windows XP Home Edition, Windows XP Professional, Windows Server 2003 family

FontFamily.ToString Method

Converts this **FontFamily** object to a human-readable string representation.

```
[Visual Basic]
Overrides Public Function ToString() As String
[C#]
public override string ToString();
[C++]
public: String* ToString();
[JScript]
public override function ToString() : String;
```

Return Value

The string that represents this **FontFamily** object.

Example

[Visual Basic, C#] The following example is designed for use with Windows Forms, and it requires **PaintEventArgs** *e*, which is a parameter of the **Paint** event handler. The code creates a **FontFamily** object and draws a string representation of the font family to the screen.

```
[Visual Basic]
Public Sub ToString_Example(e As PaintEventArgs)
' Create a FontFamily object.
Dim myFontFamily As New FontFamily("Arial")
' Draw a string representation of myFontFamily to the screen.
e.Graphics.DrawString(myFontFamily.ToString(), _
New Font(myFontFamily, 16), Brushes.Black, New PointF(0, 0))
End Sub
```

```
[C#]
public void ToString_Example(PaintEventArgs e)
{
// Create a FontFamily object.
FontFamily myFontFamily = new FontFamily("Arial");
// Draw a string representation of myFontFamily to the screen.
e.Graphics.DrawString(
myFontFamily.ToString(),
new Font(myFontFamily, 16),
Brushes.Black,
new PointF(0, 0));
}
```

Requirements

Platforms: Windows 98, Windows NT 4.0, Windows Millennium Edition, Windows 2000, Windows XP Home Edition, Windows XP Professional, Windows Server 2003 family, .NET Compact Framework - Windows CE .NET

FontStyle Enumeration

Specifies style information applied to text.

This enumeration has a **FlagsAttribute** attribute that allows a bitwise combination of its member values.

[Visual Basic]
```
<Flags>
<Serializable>
Public Enum FontStyle
```
[C#]
```
[Flags]
[Serializable]
public enum FontStyle
```
[C++]
```
[Flags]
[Serializable]
__value public enum FontStyle
```
[JScript]
```
public
   Flags
   Serializable
enum FontStyle
```

Members

Member name	Description	Value
Bold Supported by the .NET Compact Framework.	Bold text.	1
Italic Supported by the .NET Compact Framework.	Italic text.	2
Regular Supported by the .NET Compact Framework.	Normal text.	0
Strikeout Supported by the .NET Compact Framework.	Text with a line through the middle.	8
Underline Supported by the .NET Compact Framework.	Underlined text.	4

Requirements

Namespace: System.Drawing

Platforms: Windows 98, Windows NT 4.0, Windows Millennium Edition, Windows 2000, Windows XP Home Edition, Windows XP Professional, Windows Server 2003 family, .NET Compact Framework - Windows CE .NET

Assembly: System.Drawing (in System.Drawing.dll)

Graphics Class

Encapsulates a GDI+ drawing surface. This class cannot be inherited.

System.Object
  System.MarshalByRefObject
    System.Drawing.Graphics

```
[Visual Basic]
<ComVisible(False)>
NotInheritable Public Class Graphics
   Inherits MarshalByRefObject
   Implements IDisposable
[C#]
[ComVisible(false)]
public sealed class Graphics : MarshalByRefObject, IDisposable
[C++]
[ComVisible(false)]
public __gc __sealed class Graphics : public MarshalByRefObject,
   IDisposable
[JScript]
public
   ComVisible(false)
class Graphics extends MarshalByRefObject implements
   IDisposable
```

Thread Safety

Any public static (**Shared** in Visual Basic) members of this type are safe for multithreaded operations. Any instance members are not guaranteed to be thread safe.

Remarks

The **Graphics** class provides methods for drawing objects to the display device. A **Graphics** object is associated with a specific device context.

Requirements

Namespace: System.Drawing

Platforms: Windows 98, Windows NT 4.0,
Windows Millennium Edition, Windows 2000,
Windows XP Home Edition, Windows XP Professional,
Windows Server 2003 family,
.NET Compact Framework - Windows CE .NET

Assembly: System.Drawing (in System.Drawing.dll)

Graphics.Clip Property

Gets or sets a **Region** object that limits the drawing region of this **Graphics** object.

```
[Visual Basic]
Public Property Clip As Region
[C#]
public Region Clip {get; set;}
[C++]
public: __property Region* get_Clip();
public: __property void set_Clip(Region*);
[JScript]
public function get Clip() : Region;
public function set Clip(Region);
```

Property Value

This property specifies a **Region** object that limits the portion of this **Graphics** object that is currently available for drawing.

Requirements

Platforms: Windows 98, Windows NT 4.0,
Windows Millennium Edition, Windows 2000,
Windows XP Home Edition, Windows XP Professional,
Windows Server 2003 family,
.NET Compact Framework - Windows CE .NET

Graphics.ClipBounds Property

Gets a **RectangleF** structure that bounds the clipping region of this **Graphics** object.

```
[Visual Basic]
Public ReadOnly Property ClipBounds As RectangleF
[C#]
public RectangleF ClipBounds {get;}
[C++]
public: __property RectangleF get_ClipBounds();
[JScript]
public function get ClipBounds() : RectangleF;
```

Property Value

This property indicates a **RectangleF** structure that represents a bounding rectangle for the clipping region of this **Graphics** object.

Remarks

If the clipping region is infinite, the **ClipBounds** property returns a meaningless large rectangle. To determine whether the clipping region is infinite, retrieve the **Clip** property and call its **IsInfinite** method.

Requirements

Platforms: Windows 98, Windows NT 4.0,
Windows Millennium Edition, Windows 2000,
Windows XP Home Edition, Windows XP Professional,
Windows Server 2003 family,
.NET Compact Framework - Windows CE .NET

Graphics.CompositingMode Property

Gets a value that specifies how composited images are drawn to this **Graphics** object.

```
[Visual Basic]
Public Property CompositingMode As CompositingMode
[C#]
public CompositingMode CompositingMode {get; set;}
[C++]
public: __property CompositingMode get_CompositingMode();
public: __property void set_CompositingMode(CompositingMode);
[JScript]
public function get CompositingMode() : CompositingMode;
public function set CompositingMode(CompositingMode);
```

Property Value

This property specifies a member of the **CompositingMode** enumeration.

Remarks

The compositing mode determines whether pixels from a source image overwrite or are combined with background pixels.

Requirements

Platforms: Windows 98, Windows NT 4.0, Windows Millennium Edition, Windows 2000, Windows XP Home Edition, Windows XP Professional, Windows Server 2003 family

Graphics.CompositingQuality Property

Gets or sets the rendering quality of composited images drawn to this **Graphics** object.

```
[Visual Basic]
Public Property CompositingQuality As CompositingQuality
[C#]
public CompositingQuality CompositingQuality {get; set;}
[C++]
public: __property CompositingQuality get_CompositingQuality();
public: __property void set_CompositingQuality(CompositingQuality);
[JScript]
public function get CompositingQuality() : CompositingQuality;
public function set CompositingQuality(CompositingQuality);
```

Property Value

This property specifies a member of the **CompositingQuality** enumeration.

Remarks

The compositing quality determines the rendering quality level of composited images.

Requirements

Platforms: Windows 98, Windows NT 4.0, Windows Millennium Edition, Windows 2000, Windows XP Home Edition, Windows XP Professional, Windows Server 2003 family

Graphics.DpiX Property

Gets the horizontal resolution of this **Graphics** object.

```
[Visual Basic]
Public ReadOnly Property DpiX As Single
[C#]
public float DpiX {get;}
[C++]
public: __property float get_DpiX();
[JScript]
public function get DpiX() : float;
```

Property Value

This property indicates a value, in dots per inch, for the horizontal resolution supported by this **Graphics** object.

Requirements

Platforms: Windows 98, Windows NT 4.0, Windows Millennium Edition, Windows 2000, Windows XP Home Edition, Windows XP Professional, Windows Server 2003 family

Graphics.DpiY Property

Gets the vertical resolution of this **Graphics** object.

```
[Visual Basic]
Public ReadOnly Property DpiY As Single
[C#]
public float DpiY {get;}
[C++]
public: __property float get_DpiY();
[JScript]
public function get DpiY() : float;
```

Property Value

This property indicates a value, in dots per inch, for the vertical resolution supported by this **Graphics** object.

Requirements

Platforms: Windows 98, Windows NT 4.0, Windows Millennium Edition, Windows 2000, Windows XP Home Edition, Windows XP Professional, Windows Server 2003 family

Graphics.InterpolationMode Property

Gets or sets the interpolation mode associated with this **Graphics** object.

```
[Visual Basic]
Public Property InterpolationMode As InterpolationMode
[C#]
public InterpolationMode InterpolationMode {get; set;}
[C++]
public: __property InterpolationMode get_InterpolationMode();
public: __property void set_InterpolationMode(InterpolationMode);
[JScript]
public function get InterpolationMode() : InterpolationMode;
public function set InterpolationMode(InterpolationMode);
```

Property Value

This property specifies a member of the **InterpolationMode** enumeration associated with this **Graphics** object.

Remarks

The interpolation mode determines how intermediate values between two endpoints are calculated.

Requirements

Platforms: Windows 98, Windows NT 4.0, Windows Millennium Edition, Windows 2000, Windows XP Home Edition, Windows XP Professional, Windows Server 2003 family

Graphics.IsClipEmpty Property

Gets a value indicating whether the clipping region of this **Graphics** object is empty.

```
[Visual Basic]
Public ReadOnly Property IsClipEmpty As Boolean
[C#]
public bool IsClipEmpty {get;}
[C++]
public: __property bool get_IsClipEmpty();
```

```
[JScript]
public function get IsClipEmpty() : Boolean;
```

Property Value

This property is **true** if the clipping region of this **Graphics** object is empty; otherwise, **false**.

Requirements

Platforms: Windows 98, Windows NT 4.0, Windows Millennium Edition, Windows 2000, Windows XP Home Edition, Windows XP Professional, Windows Server 2003 family

Graphics.IsVisibleClipEmpty Property

Gets a value indicating whether the visible clipping region of this **Graphics** object is empty.

```
[Visual Basic]
Public ReadOnly Property IsVisibleClipEmpty As Boolean
[C#]
public bool IsVisibleClipEmpty {get;}
[C++]
public: __property bool get_IsVisibleClipEmpty();
[JScript]
public function get IsVisibleClipEmpty() : Boolean;
```

Property Value

This property is **true** if the visible portion of the clipping region of this **Graphics** object is empty; otherwise, **false**.

Remarks

The visible clipping region is the intersection of the clipping region of this Graphics object and the clipping region of the window.

Requirements

Platforms: Windows 98, Windows NT 4.0, Windows Millennium Edition, Windows 2000, Windows XP Home Edition, Windows XP Professional, Windows Server 2003 family

Graphics.PageScale Property

Gets or sets the scaling between world units and page units for this **Graphics** object.

```
[Visual Basic]
Public Property PageScale As Single
[C#]
public float PageScale {get; set;}
[C++]
public: __property float get_PageScale();
public: __property void set_PageScale(float);
[JScript]
public function get PageScale() : float;
public function set PageScale(float);
```

Property Value

This property specifies a value for the scaling between world units and page units for this **Graphics** object.

Requirements

Platforms: Windows 98, Windows NT 4.0, Windows Millennium Edition, Windows 2000, Windows XP Home Edition, Windows XP Professional, Windows Server 2003 family

Graphics.PageUnit Property

Gets or sets the unit of measure used for page coordinates in this **Graphics** object.

```
[Visual Basic]
Public Property PageUnit As GraphicsUnit
[C#]
public GraphicsUnit PageUnit {get; set;}
[C++]
public: __property GraphicsUnit get_PageUnit();
public: __property void set_PageUnit(GraphicsUnit);
[JScript]
public function get PageUnit() : GraphicsUnit;
public function set PageUnit(GraphicsUnit);
```

Property Value

This property specifies a member of the **GraphicsUnit** enumeration.

Remarks

The graphics unit is the unit of measure used for page coordinates in this **Graphics** object.

Requirements

Platforms: Windows 98, Windows NT 4.0, Windows Millennium Edition, Windows 2000, Windows XP Home Edition, Windows XP Professional, Windows Server 2003 family

Graphics.PixelOffsetMode Property

Gets or set a value specifying how pixels are offset during rendering of this **Graphics** object.

```
[Visual Basic]
Public Property PixelOffsetMode As PixelOffsetMode
[C#]
public PixelOffsetMode PixelOffsetMode {get; set;}
[C++]
public: __property PixelOffsetMode get_PixelOffsetMode();
public: __property void set_PixelOffsetMode(PixelOffsetMode);
[JScript]
public function get PixelOffsetMode() : PixelOffsetMode;
public function set PixelOffsetMode(PixelOffsetMode);
```

Property Value

This property specifies a member of the **PixelOffsetMode** enumeration

Remarks

The pixel offset mode determines how pixels are offset during rendering.

Requirements

Platforms: Windows 98, Windows NT 4.0, Windows Millennium Edition, Windows 2000, Windows XP Home Edition, Windows XP Professional, Windows Server 2003 family

Graphics.RenderingOrigin Property

Gets or sets the rendering origin of this **Graphics** object for dithering and for hatch brushes.

[Visual Basic]
```
Public Property RenderingOrigin As Point
```
[C#]
```
public Point RenderingOrigin {get; set;}
```
[C++]
```
public: __property Point get_RenderingOrigin();
public: __property void set_RenderingOrigin(Point);
```
[JScript]
```
public function get RenderingOrigin() : Point;
public function set RenderingOrigin(Point);
```

Property Value

This property specifies a **Point** structure that represents the dither origin for 8-bits-per-pixel and 16-bits-per-pixel dithering and is also used to set the origin for hatch brushes.

Requirements

Platforms: Windows 98, Windows NT 4.0, Windows Millennium Edition, Windows 2000, Windows XP Home Edition, Windows XP Professional, Windows Server 2003 family

Graphics.SmoothingMode Property

Gets or sets the rendering quality for this **Graphics** object.

[Visual Basic]
```
Public Property SmoothingMode As SmoothingMode
```
[C#]
```
public SmoothingMode SmoothingMode {get; set;}
```
[C++]
```
public: __property SmoothingMode get_SmoothingMode();
public: __property void set_SmoothingMode(SmoothingMode);
```
[JScript]
```
public function get SmoothingMode() : SmoothingMode;
public function set SmoothingMode(SmoothingMode);
```

Property Value

This property specifies a member of the **SmoothingMode** enumeration.

Remarks

The smoothing mode specifies whether lines, curves, and the edges of filled areas use smoothing (also called antialiasing). One exception is that path gradient brushes do not obey the smoothing mode. Areas filled using a **PathGradientBrush** object are rendered the same way (aliased) regardless of the **SmoothingMode** property.

Requirements

Platforms: Windows 98, Windows NT 4.0, Windows Millennium Edition, Windows 2000, Windows XP Home Edition, Windows XP Professional, Windows Server 2003 family

Graphics.TextContrast Property

Gets or sets the gamma correction value for rendering text.

[Visual Basic]
```
Public Property TextContrast As Integer
```
[C#]
```
public int TextContrast {get; set;}
```
[C++]
```
public: __property int get_TextContrast();
public: __property void set_TextContrast(int);
```
[JScript]
```
public function get TextContrast() : int;
public function set TextContrast(int);
```

Property Value

This property specifies a value of the gamma correction used for rendering antialiased and ClearType text.

Remarks

The gamma correction value must be between 0 and 12. The default value is 4.

Requirements

Platforms: Windows 98, Windows NT 4.0, Windows Millennium Edition, Windows 2000, Windows XP Home Edition, Windows XP Professional, Windows Server 2003 family

Graphics.TextRenderingHint Property

Gets or sets the rendering mode for text associated with this **Graphics** object.

[Visual Basic]
```
Public Property TextRenderingHint As TextRenderingHint
```
[C#]
```
public TextRenderingHint TextRenderingHint {get; set;}
```
[C++]
```
public: __property TextRenderingHint get_TextRenderingHint();
public: __property void set_TextRenderingHint(TextRenderingHint);
```
[JScript]
```
public function get TextRenderingHint() : TextRenderingHint;
public function set TextRenderingHint(TextRenderingHint);
```

Property Value

This property specifies a member of the **TextRenderingHint** enumeration.

Remarks

The text rendering hint specifies whether text renders with antialiasing.

Requirements

Platforms: Windows 98, Windows NT 4.0, Windows Millennium Edition, Windows 2000, Windows XP Home Edition, Windows XP Professional, Windows Server 2003 family

Graphics.Transform Property

Gets or sets the world transformation for this **Graphics** object.

[Visual Basic]
```
Public Property Transform As Matrix
```
[C#]
```
public Matrix Transform {get; set;}
```
[C++]
```
public: __property Matrix* get_Transform();
public: __property void set_Transform(Matrix*);
```

```
[JScript]
public function get Transform() : Matrix;
public function set Transform(Matrix);
```

Property Value

This property specifies a **Matrix** object that represents the world transformation for this **Graphics** object.

Requirements

Platforms: Windows 98, Windows NT 4.0, Windows Millennium Edition, Windows 2000, Windows XP Home Edition, Windows XP Professional, Windows Server 2003 family

Graphics.VisibleClipBounds Property

Gets or sets the bounding rectangle of the visible clipping region of this **Graphics** object.

```
[Visual Basic]
Public ReadOnly Property VisibleClipBounds As RectangleF
[C#]
public RectangleF VisibleClipBounds {get;}
[C++]
public: __property RectangleF get_VisibleClipBounds();
[JScript]
public function get VisibleClipBounds() : RectangleF;
```

Property Value

A **RectangleF** structure that represents a bounding rectangle for the visible clipping region of this **Graphics** object.

Remarks

The visible clipping region is the intersection of the clipping region of this Graphics object and the clipping region of the window.

Requirements

Platforms: Windows 98, Windows NT 4.0, Windows Millennium Edition, Windows 2000, Windows XP Home Edition, Windows XP Professional, Windows Server 2003 family

Graphics.AddMetafileComment Method

Adds a comment to the current **Metafile** object.

```
[Visual Basic]
Public Sub AddMetafileComment( _
   ByVal data() As Byte _
)
[C#]
public void AddMetafileComment(
   byte[] data
);
[C++]
public: void AddMetafileComment(
   unsigned char data __gc[]
);
[JScript]
public function AddMetafileComment(
   data : Byte[]
);
```

Parameters

data

Array of bytes that contains the comment.

Return Value

This method does not return a value.

Remarks

This method is valid only if this **Graphics** object is associated with a **Metafile** object.

Example

[Visual Basic, C#] The following example is designed for use with Windows Forms, and it requires **PaintEventArgs** *e*, which is a parameter of the **Paint** event handler, as well as *thisForm*, the **Form** object for the example. The code performs the following actions:

- Creates a temporary **Graphics** object for creating the metafile and gets an *hdc*, a handle to its device context.
- Creates a new metafile using the *hdc*.
- Creates a **Graphics** object for display of the metafile from the **Metafile** object.
- Draws a rectangle to the metafile.
- Adds a comment to the metafile.
- Disposes the **Graphics** object for the metafile-which closes the metafile.
- Disposes the metafile.
- Releases the temporary *hdc*.
- Disposes the temporary **Graphics** object.
- Creates a second metafile from the previously created file.
- Draws the metafile to the screen.
- Disposes the metafile.

```
[Visual Basic]
Public Sub AddMetafileCommentBytes(e As PaintEventArgs)
' Create temporary graphics object for metafile
' creation and get handle to its device context.
Dim newGraphics As Graphics = thisForm.CreateGraphics()
Dim hdc As IntPtr = newGraphics.GetHdc()
' Create metafile object to record.
Dim metaFile1 As New Metafile("SampMeta.emf", hdc)
' Create graphics object to record metaFile.
Dim metaGraphics As Graphics = Graphics.FromImage(metaFile1)
' Draw rectangle in metaFile.
metaGraphics.DrawRectangle(New Pen(Color.Black, 5), 0, 0, 100, 100)
' Create comment and add to metaFile.
Dim metaComment As Byte() = {CByte("T"), CByte("e"), CByte("s"), _
CByte("t")}
metaGraphics.AddMetafileComment(metaComment)
' Dispose of graphics object.
metaGraphics.Dispose()
' Dispose of metafile.
metaFile1.Dispose()
' Release handle to scratch device context.
newGraphics.ReleaseHdc(hdc)
' Dispose of scratch graphics object.
newGraphics.Dispose()
' Create existing metafile object to draw.
Dim metaFile2 As New Metafile("SampMeta.emf")
' Draw metaFile to screen.
e.Graphics.DrawImage(metaFile2, New Point(0, 0))
' Dispose of metafile.
metaFile2.Dispose()
End Sub
```

[C#]
```
public void AddMetafileCommentBytes(PaintEventArgs e)
{
// Create temporary Graphics object for metafile
//  creation and get handle to its device context.
Graphics newGraphics = thisForm.CreateGraphics();
IntPtr hdc = newGraphics.GetHdc();
// Create metafile object to record.
Metafile metaFile1 = new Metafile("SampMeta.emf", hdc);
// Create graphics object to record metaFile.
Graphics metaGraphics = Graphics.FromImage(metaFile1);
// Draw rectangle in metaFile.
metaGraphics.DrawRectangle(new Pen(Color.Black, 5), 0, 0, 100, 100);
// Create comment and add to metaFile.
byte[] metaComment = {(byte)'T', (byte)'e', (byte)'s', (byte)'t'};
metaGraphics.AddMetafileComment(metaComment);
// Dispose of graphics object.
metaGraphics.Dispose();
// Dispose of metafile.
metaFile1.Dispose();
// Release handle to temporary device context.
newGraphics.ReleaseHdc(hdc);
// Dispose of scratch graphics object.
newGraphics.Dispose();
// Create existing metafile object to draw.
Metafile metaFile2 = new Metafile("SampMeta.emf");
// Draw metaFile to screen.
e.Graphics.DrawImage(metaFile2, new Point(0, 0));
// Dispose of metafile.
metaFile2.Dispose();
}
```

Requirements

Platforms: Windows 98, Windows NT 4.0, Windows Millennium Edition, Windows 2000, Windows XP Home Edition, Windows XP Professional, Windows Server 2003 family

Graphics.BeginContainer Method

Saves a graphics container with the current state of this **Graphics** object and opens and uses a new graphics container.

Overload List

Saves a graphics container with the current state of this **Graphics** object and opens and uses a new graphics container.

[Visual Basic] **Overloads Public Function BeginContainer() As GraphicsContainer**

[C#] **public GraphicsContainer BeginContainer();**

[C++] **public: GraphicsContainer* BeginContainer();**

[JScript] **public function BeginContainer() : GraphicsContainer;**

Saves a graphics container with the current state of this **Graphics** object and opens and uses a new graphics container with the specified scale transformation.

[Visual Basic] **Overloads Public Function BeginContainer(Rectangle, Rectangle, GraphicsUnit) As GraphicsContainer**

[C#] **public GraphicsContainer BeginContainer(Rectangle, Rectangle, GraphicsUnit);**

[C++] **public: GraphicsContainer* BeginContainer(Rectangle, Rectangle, GraphicsUnit);**

[JScript] **public function BeginContainer(Rectangle, Rectangle, GraphicsUnit) : GraphicsContainer;**

Saves a graphics container with the current state of this **Graphics** object and opens and uses a new graphics container with the specified scale transformation.

[Visual Basic] **Overloads Public Function BeginContainer(RectangleF, RectangleF, GraphicsUnit) As GraphicsContainer**

[C#] **public GraphicsContainer BeginContainer(RectangleF, RectangleF, GraphicsUnit);**

[C++] **public: GraphicsContainer* BeginContainer(RectangleF, RectangleF, GraphicsUnit);**

[JScript] **public function BeginContainer(RectangleF, RectangleF, GraphicsUnit) : GraphicsContainer;**

Example

[Visual Basic, C#] The following example is designed for use with Windows Forms, and it requires **PaintEventArgs** *e*, which is a parameter of the **Paint** event handler. The code performs the following actions:

- Creates two rectangles to specify a scale transformation for the new container.
- Opens the new graphics container and saves the old container.
- Fills a red rectangle in the (scaled coordinates of the) new container.
- Closes the new container and restores the saved container.
- Fills a green rectangle (to the unscaled coordinates) of the saved container.

[Visual Basic, C#] The result is a green rectangle that overlies a smaller red rectangle.

> [Visual Basic, C#] **Note** This example shows how to use one of the overloaded versions of **BeginContainer**. For other examples that might be available, see the individual overload topics.

[Visual Basic]
```
Public Sub BeginContainerRectangleF(e As PaintEventArgs)
' Define transformation for container.
Dim srcRect As New RectangleF(0F, 0F, 200F, 200F)
Dim destRect As New RectangleF(100F, 100F, 150F, 150F)
' Begin graphics container.
Dim containerState As GraphicsContainer = _
e.Graphics.BeginContainer(destRect, srcRect, GraphicsUnit.Pixel)
' Fill red rectangle in container.
e.Graphics.FillRectangle(New SolidBrush(Color.Red), 0F, 0F, _
200F, 200F)
' End graphics container.
e.Graphics.EndContainer(containerState)
' Fill untransformed rectangle with green.
e.Graphics.FillRectangle(New SolidBrush(Color.Green), 0F, 0F, _
200F, 200F)
End Sub
```

[C#]
```
public void BeginContainerRectangleF(PaintEventArgs e)
{
// Define transformation for container.
RectangleF srcRect = new RectangleF(0.0F, 0.0F, 200.0F, 200.0F);
RectangleF destRect = new RectangleF(100.0F, 100.0F, 150.0F, 150.0F);
// Begin graphics container.
GraphicsContainer containerState = e.Graphics.BeginContainer(
destRect, srcRect,
GraphicsUnit.Pixel);
// Fill red rectangle in container.
e.Graphics.FillRectangle(new SolidBrush(Color.Red), 0.0F, 0.0F,      ↵
200.0F, 200.0F);
// End graphics container.
e.Graphics.EndContainer(containerState);
// Fill untransformed rectangle with green.
e.Graphics.FillRectangle(new SolidBrush(Color.Green), 0.0F,          ↵
0.0F, 200.0F, 200.0F);
}
```

Graphics.BeginContainer Method ()

Saves a graphics container with the current state of this **Graphics** object and opens and uses a new graphics container.

[Visual Basic]
```
Overloads Public Function BeginContainer() As GraphicsContainer
```
[C#]
```
public GraphicsContainer BeginContainer();
```
[C++]
```
public: GraphicsContainer* BeginContainer();
```
[JScript]
```
public function BeginContainer() : GraphicsContainer;
```

Return Value

This method returns a **GraphicsContainer** object that represents the state of this **Graphics** object at the time of the method call.

Remarks

Use this method with the **EndContainer** method to create nested graphics containers. Graphics containers retain graphics state, such as transformation, clipping region, and rendering properties.

When you call the **BeginContainer** method of a **Graphics** object, an information block that holds the state of the **Graphics** object is put on a stack. The **BeginContainer** method returns a **GraphicsContainer** object that identifies that information block. When you pass the identifying object to the **EndContainer** method, the information block is removed from the stack and is used to restore the **Graphics** object to the state it was in at the time of the **BeginContainer** method call.

Containers can be nested; that is, you can call the **BeginContainer** method several times before you call the **EndContainer** method. Each time you call the **BeginContainer** method, an information block is put on the stack, and you receive a **GraphicsContainer** object for the information block. When you pass one of those objects to the **EndContainer** method, the **Graphics** object is returned to the state it was in at the time of the **BeginContainer** method call that returned that particular **GraphicsContainer** object. The information block placed on the stack by that **BeginContainer** method call is removed from the stack, and all information blocks placed on that stack after that **BeginContainer** method call are also removed.

Calls to the **Graphics.Save** method place information blocks on the same stack as calls to the **BeginContainer** method. Just as an **EndContainer** method call is paired with a **BeginContainer** method call, a **Graphics.Restore** method call is paired with a **Save** method call.

When you call the **EndContainer** method, all information blocks placed on the stack (by the **Save** method or by the **BeginContainer** method) after the corresponding call to the **BeginContainer** method are removed from the stack. Likewise, when you call the **Restore** method, all information blocks placed on the stack (by the **Save** method or by the **BeginContainer** method) after the corresponding call to the **Save** method are removed from the stack.

The graphics state established by the **BeginContainer** method includes the rendering qualities of the default graphics state; any rendering-quality state changes existing when the method is called are reset to the default values.

Example

[Visual Basic, C#] The following example is designed for use with Windows Forms, and it requires **PaintEventArgs** *e*, which is a parameter of the **Paint** event handler. The code performs the following actions:

- Opens a new graphics container and saves the old container.
- Translates the world coordinates in the container.
- Fills a red rectangle in the (translated coordinates of the) new container.
- Closes the new container and restores the saved container.
- Fills a green rectangle (to the untranslated coordinates) of the saved container.

[Visual Basic, C#] The result is a green rectangle that overlies a red rectangle of the same size.

[Visual Basic]
```
Public Sub BeginContainerVoid(e As PaintEventArgs)
' Begin graphics container.
Dim containerState As GraphicsContainer = _
e.Graphics.BeginContainer()
' Translate world transformation.
e.Graphics.TranslateTransform(100F, 100F)
' Fill translated rectangle in container with red.
e.Graphics.FillRectangle(New SolidBrush(Color.Red), 0, 0, 200, 200)
' End graphics container.
e.Graphics.EndContainer(containerState)
' Fill untransformed rectangle with green.
e.Graphics.FillRectangle(New SolidBrush(Color.Green), 0, 0, _
200, 200)
End Sub
```

[C#]
```
public void BeginContainerVoid(PaintEventArgs e)
{
// Begin graphics container.
GraphicsContainer containerState = e.Graphics.BeginContainer();
// Translate world transformation.
e.Graphics.TranslateTransform(100.0F, 100.0F);
// Fill translated rectangle in container with red.
e.Graphics.FillRectangle(new SolidBrush(Color.Red), 0, 0, 200, 200);
// End graphics container.
e.Graphics.EndContainer(containerState);
// Fill untransformed rectangle with green.
e.Graphics.FillRectangle(new SolidBrush(Color.Green), 0, 0, 200, 200);
}
```

Requirements

Platforms: Windows 98, Windows NT 4.0, Windows Millennium Edition, Windows 2000, Windows XP Home Edition, Windows XP Professional, Windows Server 2003 family

Graphics.BeginContainer Method (Rectangle, Rectangle, GraphicsUnit)

Saves a graphics container with the current state of this **Graphics** object and opens and uses a new graphics container with the specified scale transformation.

[Visual Basic]
```
Overloads Public Function BeginContainer( _
   ByVal dstrect As Rectangle, _
   ByVal srcrect As Rectangle, _
   ByVal unit As GraphicsUnit _
) As GraphicsContainer
```
[C#]
```
public GraphicsContainer BeginContainer(
   Rectangle dstrect,
   Rectangle srcrect,
   GraphicsUnit unit
);
```

[C++]
```
public: GraphicsContainer* BeginContainer(
   Rectangle dstrect,
   Rectangle srcrect,
   GraphicsUnit unit
);
```
[JScript]
```
public function BeginContainer(
   dstrect : Rectangle,
   srcrect : Rectangle,
   unit : GraphicsUnit
) : GraphicsContainer;
```

Parameters

dstrect

Rectangle structure that, together with the *srcrect* parameter, specifies a scale transformation for the container.

srcrect

Rectangle structure that, together with the *dstrect* parameter, specifies a scale transformation for the container.

unit

Member of the **GraphicsUnit** enumeration that specifies the unit of measure for the container.

Return Value

This method returns a **GraphicsContainer** object that represents the state of this **Graphics** object at the time of the method call.

Remarks

Use this method with the **EndContainer** method to create nested graphics containers. Graphics containers retain graphics state, such as transformation, clipping region, and rendering properties.

When you call the **BeginContainer** method of a **Graphics** object, an information block that holds the state of the **Graphics** object is put on a stack. The **BeginContainer** method returns a **GraphicsContainer** object that identifies that information block. When you pass the identifying object to the **EndContainer** method, the information block is removed from the stack and is used to restore the **Graphics** object to the state it was in at the time of the **BeginContainer** method call.

Containers can be nested; that is, you can call the **BeginContainer** method several times before you call the **EndContainer** method. Each time you call the **BeginContainer** method, an information block is put on the stack, and you receive a **GraphicsContainer** object for the information block. When you pass one of those objects to the **EndContainer** method, the **Graphics** object is returned to the state it was in at the time of the **BeginContainer** method call that returned that particular **GraphicsContainer** object. The information block placed on the stack by that **BeginContainer** method call is removed from the stack, and all information blocks placed on that stack after that **BeginContainer** method call are also removed.

Calls to the **Graphics.Save** method place information blocks on the same stack as calls to the **BeginContainer** method. Just as an **EndContainer** method call is paired with a **BeginContainer** method call, a **Graphics.Restore** method call is paired with a **Save** method call.

When you call the **EndContainer** method, all information blocks placed on the stack (by the **Save** method or by the **BeginContainer** method) after the corresponding call to the **BeginContainer** method are removed from the stack. Likewise, when you call the **Restore** method, all information blocks placed on the stack (by the **Save** method or by the **BeginContainer** method) after the corresponding call to the **Save** method are removed from the stack.

This method specifies a scale transformation for the new graphics container with the *dstrect* and *srcrect* parameters. The scale is equal to the transformation that, when applied to *srcrect*, results in *dstrect*.

The graphics state established by the **BeginContainer** method includes the rendering qualities of the default graphics state; any rendering-quality state changes existing when the method is called are reset to the default values.

Example

[Visual Basic, C#] The following example is designed for use with Windows Forms, and it requires **PaintEventArgs** *e*, which is a parameter of the **Paint** event handler. The code performs the following actions:

- Creates two rectangles to specify a scale transformation for the new container.
- Opens the new graphics container and saves the old container.
- Fills a red rectangle in the (scaled coordinates of the) new container.
- Closes the new container and restores the saved container.
- Fills a green rectangle (to the unscaled coordinates) of the saved container.

[Visual Basic, C#] The result is a green rectangle that overlies a smaller red rectangle.

[Visual Basic]
```
Public Sub BeginContainerRectangle(e As PaintEventArgs)
' Define transformation for container.
Dim srcRect As New Rectangle(0, 0, 200, 200)
Dim destRect As New Rectangle(100, 100, 150, 150)
' Begin graphics container.
Dim containerState As GraphicsContainer = _
e.Graphics.BeginContainer(destRect, srcRect, GraphicsUnit.Pixel)
' Fill red rectangle in container.
e.Graphics.FillRectangle(New SolidBrush(Color.Red), 0, 0, 200, 200)
' End graphics container.
e.Graphics.EndContainer(containerState)
' Fill untransformed rectangle with green.
e.Graphics.FillRectangle(New SolidBrush(Color.Green), 0, 0, _
200, 200)
End Sub
```

[C#]
```
public void BeginContainerRectangle(PaintEventArgs e)
{
// Define transformation for container.
Rectangle srcRect = new Rectangle(0, 0, 200, 200);
Rectangle destRect = new Rectangle(100, 100, 150, 150);
// Begin graphics container.
GraphicsContainer containerState = e.Graphics.BeginContainer(
destRect, srcRect,
GraphicsUnit.Pixel);
// Fill red rectangle in container.
e.Graphics.FillRectangle(new SolidBrush(Color.Red), 0, 0, 200, 200);
// End graphics container.
e.Graphics.EndContainer(containerState);
// Fill untransformed rectangle with green.
e.Graphics.FillRectangle(new SolidBrush(Color.Green), 0, 0, 200, 200);
}
```

Requirements

Platforms: Windows 98, Windows NT 4.0, Windows Millennium Edition, Windows 2000, Windows XP Home Edition, Windows XP Professional, Windows Server 2003 family

Graphics.BeginContainer Method (RectangleF, RectangleF, GraphicsUnit)

Saves a graphics container with the current state of this **Graphics** object and opens and uses a new graphics container with the specified scale transformation.

```
[Visual Basic]
Overloads Public Function BeginContainer( _
   ByVal dstrect As RectangleF, _
   ByVal srcrect As RectangleF, _
   ByVal unit As GraphicsUnit _
) As GraphicsContainer
[C#]
public GraphicsContainer BeginContainer(
   RectangleF dstrect,
   RectangleF srcrect,
   GraphicsUnit unit
);
[C++]
public: GraphicsContainer* BeginContainer(
   RectangleF dstrect,
   RectangleF srcrect,
   GraphicsUnit unit
);
[JScript]
public function BeginContainer(
   dstrect : RectangleF,
   srcrect : RectangleF,
   unit : GraphicsUnit
) : GraphicsContainer;
```

Parameters

dstrect

RectangleF structure that, together with the *srcrect* parameter, specifies a scale transformation for the new graphics container.

srcrect

RectangleF structure that, together with the *dstrect* parameter, specifies a scale transformation for the new graphics container.

unit

Member of the **GraphicsUnit** enumeration that specifies the unit of measure for the container.

Return Value

This method returns a **GraphicsContainer** object that represents the state of this **Graphics** object at the time of the method call.

Remarks

Use this method with the **EndContainer** method to create nested graphics containers. Graphics containers retain graphics state, such as transformation, clipping region, and rendering properties.

When you call the **BeginContainer** method of a **Graphics** object, an information block that holds the state of the **Graphics** object is put on a stack. The **BeginContainer** method returns a **GraphicsContainer** object that identifies that information block. When you pass the identifying object to the **EndContainer** method, the information block is removed from the stack and is used to restore the **Graphics** object to the state it was in at the time of the **BeginContainer** method call.

Containers can be nested; that is, you can call the **BeginContainer** method several times before you call the **EndContainer** method. Each time you call the **BeginContainer** method, an information block is put on the stack, and you receive a **GraphicsContainer** object for the information block. When you pass one of those objects to the **EndContainer** method, the **Graphics** object is returned to the state it was in at the time of the **BeginContainer** method call that returned that particular **GraphicsContainer** object. The information block placed on the stack by that **BeginContainer** method call is removed from the stack, and all information blocks placed on that stack after that **BeginContainer** method call are also removed.

Calls to the **Graphics.Save** method place information blocks on the same stack as calls to the **BeginContainer** method. Just as an **EndContainer** method call is paired with a **BeginContainer** method call, a **Graphics.Restore** method call is paired with a **Save** method call.

When you call the **EndContainer** method, all information blocks placed on the stack (by the **Save** method or by the **BeginContainer** method) after the corresponding call to the **BeginContainer** method are removed from the stack. Likewise, when you call the **Restore** method, all information blocks placed on the stack (by the **Save** method or by the **BeginContainer** method) after the corresponding call to the **Save** method are removed from the stack.

This method specifies a scale transformation for the new graphics container with the *dstrect* and *srcrect* parameters. The scale is equal to the transformation that, when applied to *srcrect*, results in *dstrect*.

The graphics state established by the **BeginContainer** method includes the rendering qualities of the default graphics state; any rendering-quality state changes existing when the method is called are reset to the default values.

Example

[Visual Basic, C#] The following example is designed for use with Windows Forms, and it requires **PaintEventArgs** *e*, which is a parameter of the **Paint** event handler. The code performs the following actions:

- Creates two rectangles to specify a scale transformation for the new container.
- Opens the new graphics container and saves the old container.
- Fills a red rectangle in the (scaled coordinates of the) new container.
- Closes the new container and restores the saved container.
- Fills a green rectangle (to the unscaled coordinates) of the saved container.

[Visual Basic, C#] The result is a green rectangle that overlies a smaller red rectangle.

```
[Visual Basic]
Public Sub BeginContainerRectangleF(e As PaintEventArgs)
' Define transformation for container.
Dim srcRect As New RectangleF(0F, 0F, 200F, 200F)
Dim destRect As New RectangleF(100F, 100F, 150F, 150F)
' Begin graphics container.
Dim containerState As GraphicsContainer = _
e.Graphics.BeginContainer(destRect, srcRect, GraphicsUnit.Pixel)
' Fill red rectangle in container.
e.Graphics.FillRectangle(New SolidBrush(Color.Red), 0F, 0F, _
200F, 200F)
' End graphics container.
e.Graphics.EndContainer(containerState)
' Fill untransformed rectangle with green.
e.Graphics.FillRectangle(New SolidBrush(Color.Green), 0F, 0F, _
200F, 200F)
End Sub
```

[C#]
```
public void BeginContainerRectangleF(PaintEventArgs e)
{
// Define transformation for container.
RectangleF srcRect = new RectangleF(0.0F, 0.0F, 200.0F, 200.0F);
RectangleF destRect = new RectangleF(100.0F, 100.0F, 150.0F, 150.0F);
// Begin graphics container.
GraphicsContainer containerState = e.Graphics.BeginContainer(
destRect, srcRect,
GraphicsUnit.Pixel);
// Fill red rectangle in container.
e.Graphics.FillRectangle(new SolidBrush(Color.Red), 0.0F, 0.0F,           ↵
 200.0F, 200.0F);
// End graphics container.
e.Graphics.EndContainer(containerState);
// Fill untransformed rectangle with green.
e.Graphics.FillRectangle(new SolidBrush(Color.Green), 0.0F,              ↵
0.0F, 200.0F, 200.0F);
}
```

Requirements

Platforms: Windows 98, Windows NT 4.0,
Windows Millennium Edition, Windows 2000,
Windows XP Home Edition, Windows XP Professional,
Windows Server 2003 family

Graphics.Clear Method

Clears the entire drawing surface and fills it with the specified background color.

[Visual Basic]
```
Public Sub Clear( _
   ByVal color As Color _
)
```
[C#]
```
public void Clear(
   Color color
);
```
[C++]
```
public: void Clear(
   Color color
);
```
[JScript]
```
public function Clear(
   color : Color
);
```

Parameters

color
: **Color** structure that represents the background color of the drawing surface.

Return Value

This method does not return a value.

Example

[Visual Basic, C#] The following example is designed for use with Windows Forms, and it requires **PaintEventArgs** *e*, which is a parameter of the **Paint** event handler. The code clears the drawing surface of the **Graphics** object and sets the background color to the system-defined teal color.

[Visual Basic]
```
Public Sub ClearColor(e As PaintEventArgs)
' Clear screen with teal background.
e.Graphics.Clear(Color.Teal)
End Sub
```

[C#]
```
public void ClearColor(PaintEventArgs e)
{
// Clear screen with teal background.
e.Graphics.Clear(Color.Teal);
}
```

Requirements

Platforms: Windows 98, Windows NT 4.0,
Windows Millennium Edition, Windows 2000,
Windows XP Home Edition, Windows XP Professional,
Windows Server 2003 family,
.NET Compact Framework - Windows CE .NET

Graphics.Dispose Method

Releases all resources used by this **Graphics** object.

[Visual Basic]
```
Public Overridable Sub Dispose() Implements IDisposable.Dispose
```
[C#]
```
public virtual void Dispose();
```
[C++]
```
public: virtual void Dispose();
```
[JScript]
```
public function Dispose();
```

Return Value

This method does not return a value.

Implements

IDisposable.Dispose

Remarks

Calling **Dispose** allows the resources used by this **Graphics** object to be reallocated for other purposes.

Example

[Visual Basic, C#] The following example is designed for use with Windows Forms, and it requires **PaintEventArgs** *e*, which is a parameter of the **Paint** event handler. The code performs the following actions:

- Creates an **Image** object from a graphics file SampImag.jpg in the example directory.
- Creates a **Graphics** object from the **Image** object.
- Alters the image by filling a rectangle within it.
- Draws the **Image** object to the screen.
- Releases the created **Graphics** object.

[Visual Basic]
```
Public Sub FromImageImage(e As PaintEventArgs)
' Create image.
Dim imageFile As Image = Image.FromFile("SampImag.jpg")
' Create graphics object for alteration.
Dim newGraphics As Graphics = Graphics.FromImage(imageFile)
' Alter image.
newGraphics.FillRectangle(New SolidBrush(Color.Black), 100, _
50, 100, 100)
' Draw image to screen.
e.Graphics.DrawImage(imageFile, New PointF(0F, 0F))
' Dispose of graphics object.
newGraphics.Dispose()
End Sub
```

[C#]
```
public void FromImageImage(PaintEventArgs e)
{
// Create image.
Image imageFile = Image.FromFile("SampImag.jpg");
// Create graphics object for alteration.
Graphics newGraphics = Graphics.FromImage(imageFile);
// Alter image.
newGraphics.FillRectangle(new SolidBrush(Color.Black), 100,
50, 100, 100);
// Draw image to screen.
e.Graphics.DrawImage(imageFile, new PointF(0.0F, 0.0F));
// Release graphics object.
newGraphics.Dispose();
}
```

Requirements

Platforms: Windows 98, Windows NT 4.0, Windows Millennium Edition, Windows 2000, Windows XP Home Edition, Windows XP Professional, Windows Server 2003 family, .NET Compact Framework - Windows CE .NET

Graphics.DrawArc Method

Draws an arc representing a portion of an ellipse specified by a pair of coordinates, a width, and a height.

Overload List

Draws an arc representing a portion of an ellipse specified by a **Rectangle** structure.

[Visual Basic] **Overloads Public Sub DrawArc(Pen, Rectangle, Single, Single)**

[C#] **public void DrawArc(Pen, Rectangle, float, float);**

[C++] **public: void DrawArc(Pen*, Rectangle, float, float);**

[JScript] **public function DrawArc(Pen, Rectangle, float, float);**

Draws an arc representing a portion of an ellipse specified by a **RectangleF** structure.

[Visual Basic] **Overloads Public Sub DrawArc(Pen, RectangleF, Single, Single)**

[C#] **public void DrawArc(Pen, RectangleF, float, float);**

[C++] **public: void DrawArc(Pen*, RectangleF, float, float);**

[JScript] **public function DrawArc(Pen, RectangleF, float, float);**

Draws an arc representing a portion of an ellipse specified by a pair of coordinates, a width, and a height.

[Visual Basic] **Overloads Public Sub DrawArc(Pen, Integer, Integer, Integer, Integer, Integer, Integer)**

[C#] **public void DrawArc(Pen, int, int, int, int, int, int);**

[C++] **public: void DrawArc(Pen*, int, int, int, int, int, int);**

[JScript] **public function DrawArc(Pen, int, int, int, int, int, int);**

Draws an arc representing a portion of an ellipse specified by a pair of coordinates, a width, and a height.

[Visual Basic] **Overloads Public Sub DrawArc(Pen, Single, Single, Single, Single, Single, Single)**

[C#] **public void DrawArc(Pen, float, float, float, float, float, float);**

[C++] **public: void DrawArc(Pen*, float, float, float, float, float, float);**

[JScript] **public function DrawArc(Pen, float, float, float, float, float, float);**

Example

[Visual Basic, C#] The following example is designed for use with Windows Forms, and it requires **PaintEventArgs** *e*, which is a parameter of the **Paint** event handler. The code performs the following actions:

- Creates a black pen.
- Creates the position and size of a rectangle to bound an ellipse.
- Defines the start (45 degrees) and sweep (270 degrees) angles.
- Draws the elliptical arc to the screen.

[Visual Basic, C#] The result is a partial ellipse missing a segment between + and - 45 degrees of the x axis.

> [Visual Basic, C#] **Note** This example shows how to use one of the overloaded versions of **DrawArc**. For other examples that might be available, see the individual overload topics.

[Visual Basic]
```
Public Sub DrawArcFloat(e As PaintEventArgs)
' Create pen.
Dim blackPen As New Pen(Color.Black, 3)
' Create coordinates of rectangle to bound ellipse.
Dim x As Single = 0F
Dim y As Single = 0F
Dim width As Single = 100F
Dim height As Single = 200F
' Create start and sweep angles on ellipse.
Dim startAngle As Single = 45F
Dim sweepAngle As Single = 270F
' Draw arc to screen.
e.Graphics.DrawArc(blackPen, x, y, width, height, startAngle, _
sweepAngle)
End Sub
```

[C#]
```
public void DrawArcFloat(PaintEventArgs e)
{
// Create pen.
Pen blackPen= new Pen(Color.Black, 3);
// Create coordinates of rectangle to bound ellipse.
float x = 0.0F;
float y = 0.0F;
float width = 100.0F;
float height = 200.0F;
// Create start and sweep angles on ellipse.
float startAngle =  45.0F;
float sweepAngle = 270.0F;
// Draw arc to screen.
e.Graphics.DrawArc(blackPen, x, y, width, height,
startAngle, sweepAngle);
}
```

Graphics.DrawArc Method (Pen, Rectangle, Single, Single)

Draws an arc representing a portion of an ellipse specified by a **Rectangle** structure.

[Visual Basic]
```
Overloads Public Sub DrawArc( _
   ByVal pen As Pen, _
   ByVal rect As Rectangle, _
   ByVal startAngle As Single, _
   ByVal sweepAngle As Single _
)
```
[C#]
```
public void DrawArc(
   Pen pen,
   Rectangle rect,
```

```
   float startAngle,
   float sweepAngle
);
```
[C++]
```
public: void DrawArc(
   Pen* pen,
   Rectangle rect,
   float startAngle,
   float sweepAngle
);
```
[JScript]
```
public function DrawArc(
   pen : Pen,
   rect : Rectangle,
   startAngle : float,
   sweepAngle : float
);
```

Parameters

pen
: **Pen** object that determines the color, width, and style of the arc.

rect
: **RectangleF** structure that defines the boundaries of the ellipse.

startAngle
: Angle in degrees measured clockwise from the x-axis to the starting point of the arc.

sweepAngle
: Angle in degrees measured clockwise from the *startAngle* parameter to ending point of the arc.

Return Value

This method does not return a value.

Remarks

This method draws an arc that is a portion of the perimeter of an ellipse. The ellipse is defined by the boundaries of a rectangle. The arc is the portion of the perimeter of the ellipse between the *startAngle* parameter and the *startAngle* + *sweepAngle* parameters.

Example

[Visual Basic, C#] The following example is designed for use with Windows Forms, and it requires **PaintEventArgs** *e*, which is a parameter of the **Paint** event handler. The code performs the following actions:

- Creates a black pen.
- Creates a rectangle to bound an ellipse.
- Defines the start (45 degrees) and sweep (270 degrees) angles.
- Draws the elliptical arc to the screen.

[Visual Basic, C#] The result is a partial ellipse missing a segment between + and - 45 degrees of the x axis.

[Visual Basic]
```
Public Sub DrawArcRectangle(e As PaintEventArgs)
' Create pen.
Dim blackPen As New Pen(Color.Black, 3)
' Create rectangle to bound ellipse.
Dim rect As New Rectangle(0, 0, 100, 200)
' Create start and sweep angles on ellipse.
Dim startAngle As Single = 45F
Dim sweepAngle As Single = 270F
' Draw arc to screen.
e.Graphics.DrawArc(blackPen, rect, startAngle, sweepAngle)
End Sub
```

[C#]
```
public void DrawArcRectangle(PaintEventArgs e)
{
// Create pen.
Pen blackPen= new Pen(Color.Black, 3);
// Create rectangle to bound ellipse.
Rectangle rect = new Rectangle( 0, 0, 100, 200);
// Create start and sweep angles on ellipse.
float startAngle =  45.0F;
float sweepAngle = 270.0F;
// Draw arc to screen.
e.Graphics.DrawArc(blackPen, rect, startAngle, sweepAngle);
}
```

Requirements

Platforms: Windows 98, Windows NT 4.0, Windows Millennium Edition, Windows 2000, Windows XP Home Edition, Windows XP Professional, Windows Server 2003 family

Graphics.DrawArc Method (Pen, RectangleF, Single, Single)

Draws an arc representing a portion of an ellipse specified by a **RectangleF** structure.

[Visual Basic]
```
Overloads Public Sub DrawArc( _
   ByVal pen As Pen, _
   ByVal rect As RectangleF, _
   ByVal startAngle As Single, _
   ByVal sweepAngle As Single _
)
```
[C#]
```
public void DrawArc(
   Pen pen,
   RectangleF rect,
   float startAngle,
   float sweepAngle
);
```
[C++]
```
public: void DrawArc(
   Pen* pen,
   RectangleF rect,
   float startAngle,
   float sweepAngle
);
```
[JScript]
```
public function DrawArc(
   pen : Pen,
   rect : RectangleF,
   startAngle : float,
   sweepAngle : float
);
```

Parameters

pen
: **Pen** object that determines the color, width, and style of the arc.

rect
: **RectangleF** structure that defines the boundaries of the ellipse.

startAngle
: Angle in degrees measured clockwise from the x-axis to the starting point of the arc.

sweepAngle
: Angle in degrees measured clockwise from the *startAngle* parameter to ending point of the arc.

Return Value

This method does not return a value.

Remarks

This method draws an arc that is a portion of the perimeter of an ellipse. The ellipse is defined by the boundaries of a rectangle. The arc is the portion of the perimeter of the ellipse between the *startAngle* parameter and the *startAngle* + *sweepAngle* parameters.

Example

[Visual Basic, C#] The following example is designed for use with Windows Forms, and it requires **PaintEventArgs** *e*, which is a parameter of the **Paint** event handler. The code performs the following actions:

- Creates a black pen.
- Creates a rectangle to bound an ellipse.
- Defines the start (45 degrees) and sweep (270 degrees) angles.
- Draws the elliptical arc to the screen.

[Visual Basic, C#] The result is a partial ellipse missing a segment between + and - 45 degrees of the x axis.

[Visual Basic]

```
Public Sub DrawArcRectangleF(e As PaintEventArgs)
' Create pen.
Dim blackPen As New Pen(Color.Black, 3)
' Create rectangle to bound ellipse.
Dim rect As New RectangleF(0F, 0F, 100F, 200F)
' Create start and sweep angles on ellipse.
Dim startAngle As Single = 45F
Dim sweepAngle As Single = 270F
' Draw arc to screen.
e.Graphics.DrawArc(blackPen, rect, startAngle, sweepAngle)
End Sub
```

[C#]

```
public void DrawArcRectangleF(PaintEventArgs e)
{
// Create pen.
Pen blackPen= new Pen(Color.Black, 3);
// Create rectangle to bound ellipse.
RectangleF rect = new RectangleF( 0.0F, 0.0F, 100.0F, 200.0F);
// Create start and sweep angles on ellipse.
float startAngle =  45.0F;
float sweepAngle = 270.0F;
// Draw arc to screen.
e.Graphics.DrawArc(blackPen, rect, startAngle, sweepAngle);
}
```

Requirements

Platforms: Windows 98, Windows NT 4.0, Windows Millennium Edition, Windows 2000, Windows XP Home Edition, Windows XP Professional, Windows Server 2003 family

Graphics.DrawArc Method (Pen, Int32, Int32, Int32, Int32, Int32, Int32)

Draws an arc representing a portion of an ellipse specified by a pair of coordinates, a width, and a height.

[Visual Basic]

```
Overloads Public Sub DrawArc( _
   ByVal pen As Pen, _
   ByVal x As Integer, _
   ByVal y As Integer, _
   ByVal width As Integer, _
   ByVal height As Integer, _
   ByVal startAngle As Integer, _
   ByVal sweepAngle As Integer _
)
```

[C#]

```
public void DrawArc(
   Pen pen,
   int x,
   int y,
   int width,
   int height,
   int startAngle,
   int sweepAngle
);
```

[C++]

```
public: void DrawArc(
   Pen* pen,
   int x,
   int y,
   int width,
   int height,
   int startAngle,
   int sweepAngle
);
```

[JScript]

```
public function DrawArc(
   pen : Pen,
   x : int,
   y : int,
   width : int,
   height : int,
   startAngle : int,
   sweepAngle : int
);
```

Parameters

pen
: **Pen** object that determines the color, width, and style of the arc.

x
: x-coordinate of the upper-left corner of the rectangle that defines the ellipse.

y
: y-coordinate of the upper-left corner of the rectangle that defines the ellipse.

width
: Width of the rectangle that defines the ellipse.

height
: Height of the rectangle that defines the ellipse.

startAngle
: Angle in degrees measured clockwise from the x-axis to the starting point of the arc.

sweepAngle
: Angle in degrees measured clockwise from the *startAngle* parameter to ending point of the arc.

Return Value

This method does not return a value.

Remarks

This method draws an arc that is a portion of the perimeter of an ellipse. The ellipse is defined by the boundaries of a rectangle. The arc is the portion of the perimeter of the ellipse between the *startAngle* parameter and the *startAngle* + *sweepAngle* parameters.

Example

[Visual Basic, C#] The following example is designed for use with Windows Forms, and it requires **PaintEventArgs** *e*, which is a parameter of the **Paint** event handler. The code performs the following actions:

- Creates a black pen.
- Creates the position and size of a rectangle to bound an ellipse.
- Defines the start (45 degrees) and sweep (270 degrees) angles.
- Draws the elliptical arc to the screen.

[Visual Basic, C#] The result is a partial ellipse missing a segment between + and - 45 degrees of the x axis.

[Visual Basic]

```
Public Sub DrawArcInt(e As PaintEventArgs)
' Create pen.
Dim blackPen As New Pen(Color.Black, 3)
' Create coordinates of rectangle to bound ellipse.
Dim x As Integer = 0
Dim y As Integer = 0
Dim width As Integer = 100
Dim height As Integer = 200
' Create start and sweep angles on ellipse.
Dim startAngle As Integer = 45
Dim sweepAngle As Integer = 270
' Draw arc to screen.
e.Graphics.DrawArc(blackPen, x, y, width, height, startAngle, _
sweepAngle)
End Sub
```

[C#]

```
public void DrawArcInt(PaintEventArgs e)
{
// Create pen.
Pen blackPen= new Pen(Color.Black, 3);
// Create coordinates of rectangle to bound ellipse.
int x = 0;
int y = 0;
int width = 100;
int height = 200;
// Create start and sweep angles on ellipse.
int startAngle =  45;
int sweepAngle = 270;
// Draw arc to screen.
e.Graphics.DrawArc(blackPen, x, y, width, height, startAngle,      ↵
 sweepAngle);
}
```

Requirements

Platforms: Windows 98, Windows NT 4.0, Windows Millennium Edition, Windows 2000, Windows XP Home Edition, Windows XP Professional, Windows Server 2003 family

Graphics.DrawArc Method (Pen, Single, Single, Single, Single, Single, Single)

Draws an arc representing a portion of an ellipse specified by a pair of coordinates, a width, and a height.

[Visual Basic]

```
Overloads Public Sub DrawArc( _
   ByVal pen As Pen, _
   ByVal x As Single, _
   ByVal y As Single, _
   ByVal width As Single, _
   ByVal height As Single, _
   ByVal startAngle As Single, _
   ByVal sweepAngle As Single _
)
```

[C#]

```
public void DrawArc(
   Pen pen,
   float x,
   float y,
   float width,
   float height,
   float startAngle,
   float sweepAngle
);
```

[C++]

```
public: void DrawArc(
   Pen* pen,
   float x,
   float y,
   float width,
   float height,
   float startAngle,
   float sweepAngle
);
```

[JScript]

```
public function DrawArc(
   pen : Pen,
   x : float,
   y : float,
   width : float,
   height : float,
   startAngle : float,
   sweepAngle : float
);
```

Parameters

pen

Pen object that determines the color, width, and style of the arc.

x

x-coordinate of the upper-left corner of the rectangle that defines the ellipse.

y

y-coordinate of the upper-left corner of the rectangle that defines the ellipse.

width

Width of the rectangle that defines the ellipse.

height

Height of the rectangle that defines the ellipse.

startAngle

Angle in degrees measured clockwise from the x-axis to the starting point of the arc.

sweepAngle

Angle in degrees measured clockwise from the *startAngle* parameter to ending point of the arc.

Return Value

This method does not return a value.

Remarks

This method draws an arc that is a portion of the perimeter of an ellipse. The ellipse is defined by the boundaries of a rectangle. The arc is the portion of the perimeter of the ellipse between the *startAngle* parameter and the *startAngle* + *sweepAngle* parameters.

Example

[Visual Basic, C#] The following example is designed for use with Windows Forms, and it requires **PaintEventArgs** *e*, which is a parameter of the **Paint** event handler. The code performs the following actions:

- Creates a black pen.
- Creates the position and size of a rectangle to bound an ellipse.
- Defines the start (45 degrees) and sweep (270 degrees) angles.
- Draws the elliptical arc to the screen.

[Visual Basic, C#] The result is a partial ellipse missing a segment between + and - 45 degrees of the x axis.

[Visual Basic]
```
Public Sub DrawArcFloat(e As PaintEventArgs)
' Create pen.
Dim blackPen As New Pen(Color.Black, 3)
' Create coordinates of rectangle to bound ellipse.
Dim x As Single = 0F
Dim y As Single = 0F
Dim width As Single = 100F
Dim height As Single = 200F
' Create start and sweep angles on ellipse.
Dim startAngle As Single = 45F
Dim sweepAngle As Single = 270F
' Draw arc to screen.
e.Graphics.DrawArc(blackPen, x, y, width, height, startAngle, _
sweepAngle)
End Sub
```

[C#]
```
public void DrawArcFloat(PaintEventArgs e)
{
// Create pen.
Pen blackPen= new Pen(Color.Black, 3);
// Create coordinates of rectangle to bound ellipse.
float x = 0.0F;
float y = 0.0F;
float width = 100.0F;
float height = 200.0F;
// Create start and sweep angles on ellipse.
float startAngle =  45.0F;
float sweepAngle = 270.0F;
// Draw arc to screen.
e.Graphics.DrawArc(blackPen, x, y, width, height,                ↵
startAngle, sweepAngle);
}
```

Requirements

Platforms: Windows 98, Windows NT 4.0, Windows Millennium Edition, Windows 2000, Windows XP Home Edition, Windows XP Professional, Windows Server 2003 family

Graphics.DrawBezier Method

Draws a Bézier spline defined by four **Point** structures.

Overload List

Draws a Bézier spline defined by four **Point** structures.

[Visual Basic] **Overloads Public Sub DrawBezier(Pen, Point, Point, Point, Point)**

[C#] **public void DrawBezier(Pen, Point, Point, Point, Point);**

[C++] **public: void DrawBezier(Pen*, Point, Point, Point, Point);**

[JScript] **public function DrawBezier(Pen, Point, Point, Point, Point);**

Draws a Bézier spline defined by four **PointF** structures.

[Visual Basic] **Overloads Public Sub DrawBezier(Pen, PointF, PointF, PointF, PointF)**

[C#] **public void DrawBezier(Pen, PointF, PointF, PointF, PointF);**

[C++] **public: void DrawBezier(Pen*, PointF, PointF, PointF, PointF);**

[JScript] **public function DrawBezier(Pen, PointF, PointF, PointF, PointF);**

Draws a Bézier spline defined by four ordered pairs of coordinates that represent points.

[Visual Basic] **Overloads Public Sub DrawBezier(Pen, Single, Single, Single, Single, Single, Single, Single, Single)**

[C#] **public void DrawBezier(Pen, float, float, float, float, float, float, float, float);**

[C++] **public: void DrawBezier(Pen*, float, float, float, float, float, float, float, float);**

[JScript] **public function DrawBezier(Pen, float, float, float, float, float, float, float, float);**

Example

[Visual Basic, C#] The following example is designed for use with Windows Forms, and it requires **PaintEventArgs** *e*, which is a parameter of the **Paint** event handler. The code performs the following actions:

- Creates a black pen.
- Creates the coordinates of the start, end, and two control points for the curve.
- Draws the Bézier curve to the screen.

> [Visual Basic, C#] **Note** This example shows how to use one of the overloaded versions of **DrawBezier**. For other examples that might be available, see the individual overload topics.

[Visual Basic]
```
' Begin Example03.
Public Sub DrawBezierFloat(e As PaintEventArgs)
' Create pen.
Dim blackPen As New Pen(Color.Black, 3)
' Create coordinates of points for curve.
Dim startX As Single = 100F
Dim startY As Single = 100F
Dim controlX1 As Single = 200F
Dim controlY1 As Single = 10F
Dim controlX2 As Single = 350F
Dim controlY2 As Single = 50F
Dim endX As Single = 500F
Dim endY As Single = 100F
' Draw arc to screen.
e.Graphics.DrawBezier(blackPen, startX, startY, controlX1, _
controlY1, controlX2, controlY2, endX, endY)
End Sub
```

[C#]
```
public void DrawBezierFloat(PaintEventArgs e)
{
// Create pen.
Pen blackPen = new Pen(Color.Black, 3);
// Create coordinates of points for curve.
float startX = 100.0F;
float startY = 100.0F;
float controlX1 = 200.0F;
float controlY1 =  10.0F;
float controlX2 = 350.0F;
float controlY2 =  50.0F;
```

```
float endX = 500.0F;
float endY = 100.0F;
// Draw arc to screen.
e.Graphics.DrawBezier(blackPen, startX, startY,
controlX1, controlY1,
controlX2, controlY2,
endX, endY);
}
```

Graphics.DrawBezier Method (Pen, Point, Point, Point, Point)

Draws a Bézier spline defined by four **Point** structures.

[Visual Basic]
```
Overloads Public Sub DrawBezier( _
   ByVal pen As Pen, _
   ByVal pt1 As Point, _
   ByVal pt2 As Point, _
   ByVal pt3 As Point, _
   ByVal pt4 As Point _
)
```
[C#]
```
public void DrawBezier(
   Pen pen,
   Point pt1,
   Point pt2,
   Point pt3,
   Point pt4
);
```
[C++]
```
public: void DrawBezier(
   Pen* pen,
   Point pt1,
   Point pt2,
   Point pt3,
   Point pt4
);
```
[JScript]
```
public function DrawBezier(
   pen : Pen,
   pt1 : Point,
   pt2 : Point,
   pt3 : Point,
   pt4 : Point
);
```

Parameters

pen
  Pen structure that determines the color, width, and style of the curve.

pt1
  Point structure that represents the starting point of the curve.

pt2
  Point structure that represents the first control point for the curve.

pt3
  Point structure that represents the second control point for the curve.

pt4
  Point structure that represents the ending point of the curve.

Return Value

This method does not return a value.

Remarks

The Bézier curve is drawn from the first point to the fourth point. The second and third points are control points that determine the shape of the curve.

Example

[Visual Basic, C#] The following example is designed for use with Windows Forms, and it requires **PaintEventArgs** *e*, which is a parameter of the **Paint** event handler. The code performs the following actions:

- Creates a black pen.
- Creates the start, end, and two control points for the curve.
- Draws the Béziercurve to the screen.

[Visual Basic]
```
Public Sub DrawBezierPoint(e As PaintEventArgs)
' Create pen.
Dim blackPen As New Pen(Color.Black, 3)
' Create points for curve.
Dim start As New Point(100, 100)
Dim control1 As New Point(200, 10)
Dim control2 As New Point(350, 50)
Dim [end] As New Point(500, 100)
' Draw arc to screen.
e.Graphics.DrawBezier(blackPen, start, control1, control2, [end])
End Sub
```

[C#]
```
public void DrawBezierPoint(PaintEventArgs e)
{
// Create pen.
Pen blackPen = new Pen(Color.Black, 3);
// Create points for curve.
Point start = new Point(100, 100);
Point control1 = new Point(200, 10);
Point control2 = new Point(350, 50);
Point end = new Point(500, 100);
// Draw arc to screen.
e.Graphics.DrawBezier(blackPen, start, control1, control2, end);
}
```

Requirements

Platforms: Windows 98, Windows NT 4.0, Windows Millennium Edition, Windows 2000, Windows XP Home Edition, Windows XP Professional, Windows Server 2003 family

Graphics.DrawBezier Method (Pen, PointF, PointF, PointF, PointF)

Draws a Bézier spline defined by four **PointF** structures.

[Visual Basic]
```
Overloads Public Sub DrawBezier( _
   ByVal pen As Pen, _
   ByVal pt1 As PointF, _
   ByVal pt2 As PointF, _
   ByVal pt3 As PointF, _
   ByVal pt4 As PointF _
)
```
[C#]
```
public void DrawBezier(
   Pen pen,
   PointF pt1,
   PointF pt2,
   PointF pt3,
   PointF pt4
);
```

```
[C++]
public: void DrawBezier(
   Pen* pen,
   PointF pt1,
   PointF pt2,
   PointF pt3,
   PointF pt4
);
[JScript]
public function DrawBezier(
   pen : Pen,
   pt1 : PointF,
   pt2 : PointF,
   pt3 : PointF,
   pt4 : PointF
);
```

Parameters

pen
: **Pen** object that determines the color, width, and style of the curve.

pt1
: **PointF** structure that represents the starting point of the curve.

pt2
: **PointF** structure that represents the first control point for the curve.

pt3
: **PointF** structure that represents the second control point for the curve.

pt4
: **PointF** structure that represents the ending point of the curve.

Return Value

This method does not return a value.

Remarks

The Bézier spline is drawn from the first point to the fourth point. The second and third points are control points that determine the shape of the curve.

Example

[Visual Basic, C#] The following example is designed for use with Windows Forms, and it requires **PaintEventArgs** *e*, which is a parameter of the **Paint** event handler. The code performs the following actions:

- Creates a black pen.
- Creates the start, end, and two control points for the curve.
- Draws the Bézier curve to the screen.

```
[Visual Basic]
Public Sub DrawBezierPointF(e As PaintEventArgs)
' Create pen.
Dim blackPen As New Pen(Color.Black, 3)
' Create points for curve.
Dim start As New PointF(100F, 100F)
Dim control1 As New PointF(200F, 10F)
Dim control2 As New PointF(350F, 50F)
Dim [end] As New PointF(500F, 100F)
' Draw arc to screen.
e.Graphics.DrawBezier(blackPen, start, control1, control2, [end])
End Sub
```

```
[C#]
public void DrawBezierPointF(PaintEventArgs e)
{
// Create pen.
Pen blackPen = new Pen(Color.Black, 3);
// Create points for curve.
PointF start = new PointF(100.0F, 100.0F);
PointF control1 = new PointF(200.0F, 10.0F);
PointF control2 = new PointF(350.0F, 50.0F);
PointF end = new PointF(500.0F, 100.0F);
// Draw arc to screen.
e.Graphics.DrawBezier(blackPen, start, control1, control2, end);
}
```

Requirements

Platforms: Windows 98, Windows NT 4.0, Windows Millennium Edition, Windows 2000, Windows XP Home Edition, Windows XP Professional, Windows Server 2003 family

Graphics.DrawBezier Method (Pen, Single, Single, Single, Single, Single, Single, Single, Single)

Draws a Bézier spline defined by four ordered pairs of coordinates that represent points.

```
[Visual Basic]
Overloads Public Sub DrawBezier( _
   ByVal pen As Pen, _
   ByVal x1 As Single, _
   ByVal y1 As Single, _
   ByVal x2 As Single, _
   ByVal y2 As Single, _
   ByVal x3 As Single, _
   ByVal y3 As Single, _
   ByVal x4 As Single, _
   ByVal y4 As Single _
)
[C#]
public void DrawBezier(
   Pen pen,
   float x1,
   float y1,
   float x2,
   float y2,
   float x3,
   float y3,
   float x4,
   float y4
);
[C++]
public: void DrawBezier(
   Pen* pen,
   float x1,
   float y1,
   float x2,
   float y2,
   float x3,
   float y3,
   float x4,
   float y4
);
```

```
[JScript]
public function DrawBezier(
   pen : Pen,
   x1 : float,
   y1 : float,
   x2 : float,
   y2 : float,
   x3 : float,
   x4 : float,
   y3 : float,
   x4 : float,
   y4 : float
);
```

Parameters

pen

Pen object that determines the color, width, and style of the curve.

x1

x-coordinate of the starting point of the curve.

y1

y-coordinate of the starting point of the curve.

x2

x-coordinate of the first control point of the curve.

y2

y-coordinate of the first control point of the curve.

x3

x-coordinate of the second control point of the curve.

y3

y-coordinate of the second control point of the curve.

x4

x-coordinate of the ending point of the curve.

y4

y-coordinate of the ending point of the curve.

Return Value

This method does not return a value.

Remarks

The Bézier spline is drawn from the first point to the fourth point. The second and third points are control points that determine the shape of the curve.

Example

[Visual Basic, C#] The following example is designed for use with Windows Forms, and it requires **PaintEventArgs** *e*, which is a parameter of the **Paint** event handler. The code performs the following actions:

- Creates a black pen.
- Creates the coordinates of the start, end, and two control points for the curve.
- Draws the Bézier curve to the screen.

```
[Visual Basic]
' Begin Example03.
Public Sub DrawBezierFloat(e As PaintEventArgs)
' Create pen.
Dim blackPen As New Pen(Color.Black, 3)
' Create coordinates of points for curve.
Dim startX As Single = 100F
Dim startY As Single = 100F
Dim controlX1 As Single = 200F
Dim controlY1 As Single = 10F
Dim controlX2 As Single = 350F
Dim controlY2 As Single = 50F
Dim endX As Single = 500F
Dim endY As Single = 100F
' Draw arc to screen.
e.Graphics.DrawBezier(blackPen, startX, startY, controlX1, _
controlY1, controlX2, controlY2, endX, endY)
End Sub
```

```
[C#]
public void DrawBezierFloat(PaintEventArgs e)
{
// Create pen.
Pen blackPen = new Pen(Color.Black, 3);
// Create coordinates of points for curve.
float startX = 100.0F;
float startY = 100.0F;
float controlX1 = 200.0F;
float controlY1 =  10.0F;
float controlX2 = 350.0F;
float controlY2 =  50.0F;
float endX = 500.0F;
float endY = 100.0F;
// Draw arc to screen.
e.Graphics.DrawBezier(blackPen, startX, startY,
controlX1, controlY1,
controlX2, controlY2,
endX, endY);
}
```

Requirements

Platforms: Windows 98, Windows NT 4.0, Windows Millennium Edition, Windows 2000, Windows XP Home Edition, Windows XP Professional, Windows Server 2003 family

Graphics.DrawBeziers Method

Draws a series of Bézier splines from an array of **Point** structures.

Overload List

Draws a series of Bézier splines from an array of **Point** structures.

[Visual Basic] **Overloads Public Sub DrawBeziers(Pen, Point())**

[C#] **public void DrawBeziers(Pen, Point[]);**

[C++] **public: void DrawBeziers(Pen*, Point[]);**

[JScript] **public function DrawBeziers(Pen, Point[]);**

Draws a series of Bézier splines from an array of **PointF** structures.

[Visual Basic] **Overloads Public Sub DrawBeziers(Pen, PointF())**

[C#] **public void DrawBeziers(Pen, PointF[]);**

[C++] **public: void DrawBeziers(Pen*, PointF[]);**

[JScript] **public function DrawBeziers(Pen, PointF[]);**

Example

[Visual Basic, C#] The following example is designed for use with Windows Forms, and it requires **PaintEventArgs** *e*, which is a parameter of the **Paint** event handler. The code performs the following actions:

- Creates a black pen.
- Creates the start, end, and two control points for a first curve and end point and two control points for a second curve.
- Draws the successive Bézier curves to the screen.

[Visual Basic, C#] **Note** This example shows how to use one of the overloaded versions of **DrawBeziers**. For other examples that might be available, see the individual overload topics.

[Visual Basic]
```
Public Sub DrawBeziersPointF(e As PaintEventArgs)
' Create pen.
Dim blackPen As New Pen(Color.Black, 3)
' Create points for curve.
Dim start As New PointF(100F, 100F)
Dim control1 As New PointF(200F, 10F)
Dim control2 As New PointF(350F, 50F)
Dim end1 As New PointF(500F, 100F)
Dim control3 As New PointF(600F, 150F)
Dim control4 As New PointF(650F, 250F)
Dim end2 As New PointF(500F, 300F)
Dim bezierPoints As PointF() = {start, control1, control2, _
end1, control3, control4, end2}
' Draw arc to screen.
e.Graphics.DrawBeziers(blackPen, bezierPoints)
End Sub
```

[C#]
```
public void DrawBeziersPointF(PaintEventArgs e)
{
// Create pen.
Pen blackPen = new Pen(Color.Black, 3);
// Create points for curve.
PointF start = new PointF(100.0F, 100.0F);
PointF control1 = new PointF(200.0F, 10.0F);
PointF control2 = new PointF(350.0F, 50.0F);
PointF end1 = new PointF(500.0F, 100.0F);
PointF control3 = new PointF(600.0F, 150.0F);
PointF control4 = new PointF(650.0F, 250.0F);
PointF end2 = new PointF(500.0F, 300.0F);
PointF[] bezierPoints =
{
start, control1, control2, end1,
control3, control4, end2
};
// Draw arc to screen.
e.Graphics.DrawBeziers(blackPen, bezierPoints);
}
```

Graphics.DrawBeziers Method (Pen, Point[])

Draws a series of Bézier splines from an array of **Point** structures.

[Visual Basic]
```
Overloads Public Sub DrawBeziers( _
   ByVal pen As Pen, _
   ByVal points() As Point _
)
```
[C#]
```
public void DrawBeziers(
   Pen pen,
   Point[] points
);
```
[C++]
```
public: void DrawBeziers(
   Pen* pen,
   Point points[]
);
```
[JScript]
```
public function DrawBeziers(
   pen : Pen,
   points : Point[]
);
```

Parameters

pen
: **Pen** object that determines the color, width, and style of the curve.

points
: Array of **Point** structures that represent the points that determine the curve.

Return Value

This method does not return a value.

Remarks

The first Bézier spline is drawn from the first point to the fourth point in the point array. The second and third points are control points that determine the shape of the curve. Each subsequent curve needs exactly three more points: two more control points and an ending point. The ending point of the previous curve is used as the starting point for each additional curve.

Example

[Visual Basic, C#] The following example is designed for use with Windows Forms, and it requires **PaintEventArgs** *e*, which is a parameter of the **Paint** event handler. The code performs the following actions:

- Creates a black pen.
- Creates the start, end, and two control points for a first curve and end point and two control points for a second curve.
- Draws the successive Bézier curves to the screen.

[Visual Basic]
```
Public Sub DrawBeziersPoint(e As PaintEventArgs)
' Create pen.
Dim blackPen As New Pen(Color.Black, 3)
' Create points for curve.
Dim start As New Point(100, 100)
Dim control1 As New Point(200, 10)
Dim control2 As New Point(350, 50)
Dim end1 As New Point(500, 100)
Dim control3 As New Point(600, 150)
Dim control4 As New Point(650, 250)
Dim end2 As New Point(500, 300)
Dim bezierPoints As Point() = {start, control1, control2, _
end1, control3, control4, end2}
' Draw arc to screen.
e.Graphics.DrawBeziers(blackPen, bezierPoints)
End Sub
```

[C#]
```
public void DrawBeziersPoint(PaintEventArgs e)
{
// Create pen.
Pen blackPen = new Pen(Color.Black, 3);
// Create points for curve.
Point start = new Point(100, 100);
Point control1 = new Point(200, 10);
Point control2 = new Point(350, 50);
Point end1 = new Point(500, 100);
Point control3 = new Point(600, 150);
Point control4 = new Point(650, 250);
Point end2 = new Point(500, 300);
Point[] bezierPoints =
{
start, control1, control2, end1,
control3, control4, end2
};
// Draw arc to screen.
e.Graphics.DrawBeziers(blackPen, bezierPoints);
}
```

Requirements

Platforms: Windows 98, Windows NT 4.0, Windows Millennium Edition, Windows 2000, Windows XP Home Edition, Windows XP Professional, Windows Server 2003 family

Graphics.DrawBeziers Method (Pen, PointF[])

Draws a series of Bézier splines from an array of **PointF** structures.

[Visual Basic]
```
Overloads Public Sub DrawBeziers( _
   ByVal pen As Pen, _
   ByVal points() As PointF _
)
```
[C#]
```
public void DrawBeziers(
   Pen pen,
   PointF[] points
);
```
[C++]
```
public: void DrawBeziers(
   Pen* pen,
   PointF points[]
);
```
[JScript]
```
public function DrawBeziers(
   pen : Pen,
   points : PointF[]
);
```

Parameters

pen

Pen object that determines the color, width, and style of the curve.

points

Array of **PointF** structures that represent the points that determine the curve.

Return Value

This method does not return a value.

Remarks

The first Bézier curve is drawn from the first point to the fourth point in the point array. The second and third points are control points that determine the shape of the curve. Each subsequent curve needs exactly three more points: two more control points and an ending point. The ending point of the previous curve is used as the starting point for each additional curve.

Example

[Visual Basic, C#] The following example is designed for use with Windows Forms, and it requires **PaintEventArgs** *e*, which is a parameter of the **Paint** event handler. The code performs the following actions:

- Creates a black pen.
- Creates the start, end, and two control points for a first curve and end point and two control points for a second curve.
- Draws the successive Bézier curves to the screen.

[Visual Basic]
```
Public Sub DrawBeziersPointF(e As PaintEventArgs)
' Create pen.
Dim blackPen As New Pen(Color.Black, 3)
' Create points for curve.
Dim start As New PointF(100F, 100F)
Dim control1 As New PointF(200F, 10F)
Dim control2 As New PointF(350F, 50F)
Dim end1 As New PointF(500F, 100F)
Dim control3 As New PointF(600F, 150F)
Dim control4 As New PointF(650F, 250F)
Dim end2 As New PointF(500F, 300F)
Dim bezierPoints As PointF() = {start, control1, control2, _
end1, control3, control4, end2}
' Draw arc to screen.
e.Graphics.DrawBeziers(blackPen, bezierPoints)
End Sub
```

[C#]
```
public void DrawBeziersPointF(PaintEventArgs e)
{
// Create pen.
Pen blackPen = new Pen(Color.Black, 3);
// Create points for curve.
PointF start = new PointF(100.0F, 100.0F);
PointF control1 = new PointF(200.0F, 10.0F);
PointF control2 = new PointF(350.0F, 50.0F);
PointF end1 = new PointF(500.0F, 100.0F);
PointF control3 = new PointF(600.0F, 150.0F);
PointF control4 = new PointF(650.0F, 250.0F);
PointF end2 = new PointF(500.0F, 300.0F);
PointF[] bezierPoints =
{
start, control1, control2, end1,
control3, control4, end2
};
// Draw arc to screen.
e.Graphics.DrawBeziers(blackPen, bezierPoints);
}
```

Requirements

Platforms: Windows 98, Windows NT 4.0, Windows Millennium Edition, Windows 2000, Windows XP Home Edition, Windows XP Professional, Windows Server 2003 family

Graphics.DrawClosedCurve Method

Draws a closed cardinal spline defined by an array of **Point** structures.

Overload List

Draws a closed cardinal spline defined by an array of **Point** structures.

[Visual Basic] **Overloads Public Sub DrawClosedCurve(Pen, Point())**

[C#] **public void DrawClosedCurve(Pen, Point[]);**

[C++] **public: void DrawClosedCurve(Pen*, Point[]);**

[JScript] **public function DrawClosedCurve(Pen, Point[]);**

Draws a closed cardinal spline defined by an array of **PointF** structures.

[Visual Basic] **Overloads Public Sub DrawClosedCurve(Pen, PointF())**

[C#] **public void DrawClosedCurve(Pen, PointF[]);**

[C++] **public: void DrawClosedCurve(Pen*, PointF[]);**

[JScript] **public function DrawClosedCurve(Pen, PointF[]);**

Draws a closed cardinal spline defined by an array of **Point** structures using a specified tension.

[Visual Basic] **Overloads Public Sub DrawClosedCurve(Pen, Point(), Single, FillMode)**

[C#] **public void DrawClosedCurve(Pen, Point[], float, FillMode);**

[C++] **public: void DrawClosedCurve(Pen*, Point[], float, FillMode);**

[JScript] **public function DrawClosedCurve(Pen, Point[], float, FillMode);**

Draws a closed cardinal spline defined by an array of **PointF** structures using a specified tension.

[Visual Basic] **Overloads Public Sub DrawClosedCurve(Pen, PointF(), Single, FillMode)**

[C#] **public void DrawClosedCurve(Pen, PointF[], float, FillMode);**

[C++] **public: void DrawClosedCurve(Pen*, PointF[], float, FillMode);**

[JScript] **public function DrawClosedCurve(Pen, PointF[], float, FillMode);**

Example

[Visual Basic, C#] The following example is designed for use with Windows Forms, and it requires **PaintEventArgs** *e*, which is a parameter of the **Paint** event handler. The code performs the following actions:

- creates red and green pens.
- Creates seven points to define the curve.
- Draws seven red straight lines between the seven points to form a polygon.
- Creates tension and fill mode settings.
- Draws a green closed curve through the seven points.

[Visual Basic, C#] The method uses the a tension of 1.0 and sets the fill mode to **FillMode.Alternate**.

> [Visual Basic, C#] **Note** This example shows how to use one of the overloaded versions of **DrawClosedCurve**. For other examples that might be available, see the individual overload topics.

[Visual Basic]

```
Public Sub DrawClosedCurvePointFTension(e As PaintEventArgs)
' Create pens.
Dim redPen As New Pen(Color.Red, 3)
Dim greenPen As New Pen(Color.Green, 3)
' Create points that define curve.
Dim point1 As New PointF(50F, 50F)
Dim point2 As New PointF(100F, 25F)
Dim point3 As New PointF(200F, 5F)
Dim point4 As New PointF(250F, 50F)
Dim point5 As New PointF(300F, 100F)
Dim point6 As New PointF(350F, 200F)
Dim point7 As New PointF(250F, 250F)
Dim curvePoints As PointF() = {point1, point2, point3, point4, _
point5, point6, point7}
' Draw lines between original points to screen.
e.Graphics.DrawLines(redPen, curvePoints)
' Create tension and fill mode.
Dim tension As Single = 1F
Dim aFillMode As FillMode = FillMode.Alternate
' Draw closed curve to screen.
e.Graphics.DrawClosedCurve(greenPen, curvePoints, tension, _
aFillMode)
End Sub
```

[C#]

```
public void DrawClosedCurvePointFTension(PaintEventArgs e)
{
// Create pens.
Pen redPen   = new Pen(Color.Red, 3);
Pen greenPen = new Pen(Color.Green, 3);
// Create points that define curve.
PointF point1 = new PointF( 50.0F,  50.0F);
PointF point2 = new PointF(100.0F,  25.0F);
PointF point3 = new PointF(200.0F,   5.0F);
PointF point4 = new PointF(250.0F,  50.0F);
PointF point5 = new PointF(300.0F, 100.0F);
PointF point6 = new PointF(350.0F, 200.0F);
PointF point7 = new PointF(250.0F, 250.0F);
PointF[] curvePoints =
{
point1,
point2,
point3,
point4,
point5,
point6,
point7
};
// Draw lines between original points to screen.
e.Graphics.DrawLines(redPen, curvePoints);
// Create tension and fill mode.
float tension = 1.0F;
FillMode aFillMode = FillMode.Alternate;
// Draw closed curve to screen.
e.Graphics.DrawClosedCurve(greenPen, curvePoints, tension, aFillMode);
}
```

Graphics.DrawClosedCurve Method (Pen, Point[])

Draws a closed cardinal spline defined by an array of **Point** structures.

[Visual Basic]

```
Overloads Public Sub DrawClosedCurve( _
   ByVal pen As Pen, _
   ByVal points() As Point _
)
```

[C#]

```
public void DrawClosedCurve(
   Pen pen,
   Point[] points
);
```

[C++]

```
public: void DrawClosedCurve(
   Pen* pen,
   Point points[]
);
```

[JScript]

```
public function DrawClosedCurve(
   pen : Pen,
   points : Point[]
);
```

Parameters

pen

Pen object that determines the color, width, and height of the curve.

points

Array of **Point** structures that define the spline.

Return Value

This method does not return a value.

Remarks

This method draws a closed cardinal spline that passes through each point in the array. If the last point does not match the first point, an additional curve segment is added from the last point to the first point to close the figure.

The array of points must contain at least four **Point** structures.

This method uses a default tension of 0.5.

Example

[Visual Basic, C#] The following example is designed for use with Windows Forms, and it requires **PaintEventArgs** *e*, which is a parameter of the **Paint** event handler. The code performs the following actions:

- Creates red and green pens.
- Creates seven points to define a curve.
- Draws seven red straight lines between the seven points to form a closed polygon.
- Draws a green closed curve through the seven points.

[Visual Basic, C#] The method uses a default tension of 0.5.

[Visual Basic]
```
Public Sub DrawClosedCurvePoint(e As PaintEventArgs)
' Create pens.
Dim redPen As New Pen(Color.Red, 3)
Dim greenPen As New Pen(Color.Green, 3)
' Create points that define curve.
Dim point1 As New Point(50, 50)
Dim point2 As New Point(100, 25)
Dim point3 As New Point(200, 5)
Dim point4 As New Point(250, 50)
Dim point5 As New Point(300, 100)
Dim point6 As New Point(350, 200)
Dim point7 As New Point(250, 250)
Dim curvePoints As Point() = {point1, point2, point3, point4, _
point5, point6, point7}
' Draw lines between original points to screen.
e.Graphics.DrawLines(redPen, curvePoints)
' Draw closed curve to screen.
e.Graphics.DrawClosedCurve(greenPen, curvePoints)
End Sub
```

[C#]
```
public void DrawClosedCurvePoint(PaintEventArgs e)
{
// Create pens.
Pen redPen   = new Pen(Color.Red, 3);
Pen greenPen = new Pen(Color.Green, 3);
// Create points that define curve.
Point point1 = new Point( 50,  50);
Point point2 = new Point(100,  25);
Point point3 = new Point(200,   5);
Point point4 = new Point(250,  50);
Point point5 = new Point(300, 100);
Point point6 = new Point(350, 200);
Point point7 = new Point(250, 250);
Point[] curvePoints =
{
point1,
point2,
point3,
point4,
point5,
point6,
point7
};
// Draw lines between original points to screen.
e.Graphics.DrawLines(redPen, curvePoints);
// Draw closed curve to screen.
e.Graphics.DrawClosedCurve(greenPen, curvePoints);
}
```

Requirements

Platforms: Windows 98, Windows NT 4.0, Windows Millennium Edition, Windows 2000, Windows XP Home Edition, Windows XP Professional, Windows Server 2003 family

Graphics.DrawClosedCurve Method (Pen, PointF[])

Draws a closed cardinal spline defined by an array of **PointF** structures.

[Visual Basic]
```
Overloads Public Sub DrawClosedCurve( _
   ByVal pen As Pen, _
   ByVal points() As PointF _
)
```
[C#]
```
public void DrawClosedCurve(
   Pen pen,
   PointF[] points
);
```
[C++]
```
public: void DrawClosedCurve(
   Pen* pen,
   PointF points[]
);
```
[JScript]
```
public function DrawClosedCurve(
   pen : Pen,
   points : PointF[]
);
```

Parameters

pen

Pen object that determines the color, width, and height of the curve.

points

Array of **PointF** structures that define the spline.

Return Value

This method does not return a value.

Remarks

This method draws a closed cardinal spline that passes through each point in the array. If the last point does not match the first point, an additional curve segment is added from the last point to the first point to close it.

The array of points must contain at least four **PointF** structures.

This method uses a default tension of 0.5.

Example

[Visual Basic, C#] The following example is designed for use with Windows Forms, and it requires **PaintEventArgs** *e*, which is a parameter of the **Paint** event handler. The code preforms the following actions:

- Creates red and green pens.
- Creates seven points to define a curve.
- Draws seven red straight lines between the seven points to form a closed polygon.
- Draws a green closed curve through the seven points.

[Visual Basic, C#] The method uses a default tension of 0.5.

[Visual Basic]
```
Public Sub DrawClosedCurvePointF(e As PaintEventArgs)
' Create pens.
Dim redPen As New Pen(Color.Red, 3)
Dim greenPen As New Pen(Color.Green, 3)
' Create points that define curve.
Dim point1 As New PointF(50F, 50F)
Dim point2 As New PointF(100F, 25F)
Dim point3 As New PointF(200F, 5F)
Dim point4 As New PointF(250F, 50F)
```

```
Dim point5 As New PointF(300F, 100F)
Dim point6 As New PointF(350F, 200F)
Dim point7 As New PointF(250F, 250F)
Dim curvePoints As PointF() =  {point1, point2, point3, point4, _
point5, point6, point7}
' Draw lines between original points to screen.
e.Graphics.DrawLines(redPen, curvePoints)
' Draw closed curve to screen.
e.Graphics.DrawClosedCurve(greenPen, curvePoints)
End Sub
```

[C#]

```
public void DrawClosedCurvePointF(PaintEventArgs e)
{
// Create pens.
Pen redPen   = new Pen(Color.Red, 3);
Pen greenPen = new Pen(Color.Green, 3);
// Create points that define curve.
PointF point1 = new PointF( 50.0F,  50.0F);
PointF point2 = new PointF(100.0F,  25.0F);
PointF point3 = new PointF(200.0F,   5.0F);
PointF point4 = new PointF(250.0F,  50.0F);
PointF point5 = new PointF(300.0F, 100.0F);
PointF point6 = new PointF(350.0F, 200.0F);
PointF point7 = new PointF(250.0F, 250.0F);
PointF[] curvePoints =
{
point1,
point2,
point3,
point4,
point5,
point6,
point7
};
// Draw lines between original points to screen.
e.Graphics.DrawLines(redPen, curvePoints);
// Draw closed curve to screen.
e.Graphics.DrawClosedCurve(greenPen, curvePoints);
}
```

Requirements

Platforms: Windows 98, Windows NT 4.0, Windows Millennium Edition, Windows 2000, Windows XP Home Edition, Windows XP Professional, Windows Server 2003 family

Graphics.DrawClosedCurve Method (Pen, Point[], Single, FillMode)

Draws a closed cardinal spline defined by an array of **Point** structures using a specified tension.

[Visual Basic]

```
Overloads Public Sub DrawClosedCurve( _
   ByVal pen As Pen, _
   ByVal points() As Point, _
   ByVal tension As Single, _
   ByVal fillmode As FillMode _
)
```

[C#]

```
public void DrawClosedCurve(
   Pen pen,
   Point[] points,
   float tension,
   FillMode fillmode
);
```

[C++]

```
public: void DrawClosedCurve(
   Pen* pen,
   Point points[],
   float tension,
   FillMode fillmode
);
```

[JScript]

```
public function DrawClosedCurve(
   pen : Pen,
   points : Point[],
   tension : float,
   fillmode : FillMode
);
```

Parameters

pen
: **Pen** object that determines the color, width, and height of the curve.

points
: Array of **Point** structures that define the spline.

tension
: Value greater than or equal to 0.0F that specifies the tension of the curve.

fillmode
: Member of the **FillMode** enumeration that determines how the curve is filled. This parameter is required but ignored.

Return Value

This method does not return a value.

Remarks

This method draws a closed cardinal spline that passes through each point in the array. If the last point does not match the first point, an additional curve segment is added from the last point to the first point to close it.

The array of points must contain at least four **Point** structures.

The *tension* parameter determines the shape of the spline. If the value of the *tension* parameter is 0.0F, this method draws straight line segments to connect the points. Usually, the *tension* parameter is less than or equal to 1.0F. Values over 1.0F produce unusual results.

Example

[Visual Basic, C#] The following example is designed for use with Windows Forms, and it requires **PaintEventArgs** *e*, which is a parameter of the **Paint** event handler. The code performs the following actions:

- Creates red and green pens.
- Creates seven points to define the curve.
- Draws seven red straight lines between the seven points to form a polygon.
- Creates tension and fill mode settings.
- Draws a green closed curve through the seven points.

[Visual Basic, C#] The method uses the a tension of 1.0 and sets the fill mode to **FillMode.Alternate**.

[Visual Basic]

```
Public Sub DrawClosedCurvePointTension(e As PaintEventArgs)
' Create pens.
Dim redPen As New Pen(Color.Red, 3)
Dim greenPen As New Pen(Color.Green, 3)
' Create points that define curve.
Dim point1 As New Point(50, 50)
```

```
Dim point2 As New Point(100, 25)
Dim point3 As New Point(200, 5)
Dim point4 As New Point(250, 50)
Dim point5 As New Point(300, 100)
Dim point6 As New Point(350, 200)
Dim point7 As New Point(250, 250)
Dim curvePoints As Point() = {point1, point2, point3, point4, _
point5, point6, point7}
' Draw lines between original points to screen.
e.Graphics.DrawLines(redPen, curvePoints)
' Create tension and fill mode.
Dim tension As Single = 1F
Dim aFillMode As FillMode = FillMode.Alternate
' Draw closed curve to screen.
e.Graphics.DrawClosedCurve(greenPen, curvePoints, tension, _
aFillMode)
End Sub
```

[C#]

```
public void DrawClosedCurvePointTension(PaintEventArgs e)
{
// Create pens.
Pen redPen   = new Pen(Color.Red, 3);
Pen greenPen = new Pen(Color.Green, 3);
// Create points that define curve.
Point point1 = new Point( 50,  50);
Point point2 = new Point(100,  25);
Point point3 = new Point(200,   5);
Point point4 = new Point(250,  50);
Point point5 = new Point(300, 100);
Point point6 = new Point(350, 200);
Point point7 = new Point(250, 250);
Point[] curvePoints =
{
point1,
point2,
point3,
point4,
point5,
point6,
point7
};
// Draw lines between original points to screen.
e.Graphics.DrawLines(redPen, curvePoints);
// Create tension and fill mode.
float tension = 1.0F;
FillMode aFillMode = FillMode.Alternate;
// Draw closed curve to screen.
e.Graphics.DrawClosedCurve(greenPen, curvePoints, tension, aFillMode);
}
```

Requirements

Platforms: Windows 98, Windows NT 4.0, Windows Millennium Edition, Windows 2000, Windows XP Home Edition, Windows XP Professional, Windows Server 2003 family

Graphics.DrawClosedCurve Method (Pen, PointF[], Single, FillMode)

Draws a closed cardinal spline defined by an array of **PointF** structures using a specified tension.

[Visual Basic]

```
Overloads Public Sub DrawClosedCurve( _
   ByVal pen As Pen, _
   ByVal points() As PointF, _
   ByVal tension As Single, _
   ByVal fillmode As FillMode _
)
```

[C#]

```
public void DrawClosedCurve(
   Pen pen,
   PointF[] points,
   float tension,
   FillMode fillmode
);
```

[C++]

```
public: void DrawClosedCurve(
   Pen* pen,
   PointF points[],
   float tension,
   FillMode fillmode
);
```

[JScript]

```
public function DrawClosedCurve(
   pen : Pen,
   points : PointF[],
   tension : float,
   fillmode : FillMode
);
```

Parameters

pen
: **Pen** object that determines the color, width, and height of the curve.

points
: Array of **PointF** structures that define the spline.

tension
: Value greater than or equal to 0.0F that specifies the tension of the curve.

fillmode
: Member of the **FillMode** enumeration that determines how the curve is filled. This parameter is required but is ignored.

Return Value

This method does not return a value.

Remarks

This method draws a closed cardinal spline that passes through each point in the array. If the last point does not match the first point, an additional curve segment is added from the last point to the first point to close it.

The array of points must contain at least four **PointF** structures.

The *tension* parameter determines the shape of the spline. If the value of the *tension* parameter is 0.0F, this method draws straight line segments to connect the points. Usually, the *tension* parameter is less than or equal to 1.0F. Values over 1.0F produce unusual results.

Example

[Visual Basic, C#] The following example is designed for use with Windows Forms, and it requires **PaintEventArgs** *e*, which is a parameter of the **Paint** event handler. The code performs the following actions:

- creates red and green pens.
- Creates seven points to define the curve.
- Draws seven red straight lines between the seven points to form a polygon.
- Creates tension and fill mode settings.
- Draws a green closed curve through the seven points.

[Visual Basic, C#] The method uses the a tension of 1.0 and sets the fill mode to **FillMode.Alternate**.

[Visual Basic]
```
Public Sub DrawClosedCurvePointFTension(e As PaintEventArgs)
' Create pens.
Dim redPen As New Pen(Color.Red, 3)
Dim greenPen As New Pen(Color.Green, 3)
' Create points that define curve.
Dim point1 As New PointF(50F, 50F)
Dim point2 As New PointF(100F, 25F)
Dim point3 As New PointF(200F, 5F)
Dim point4 As New PointF(250F, 50F)
Dim point5 As New PointF(300F, 100F)
Dim point6 As New PointF(350F, 200F)
Dim point7 As New PointF(250F, 250F)
Dim curvePoints As PointF() = {point1, point2, point3, point4, _
point5, point6, point7}
' Draw lines between original points to screen.
e.Graphics.DrawLines(redPen, curvePoints)
' Create tension and fill mode.
Dim tension As Single = 1F
Dim aFillMode As FillMode = FillMode.Alternate
' Draw closed curve to screen.
e.Graphics.DrawClosedCurve(greenPen, curvePoints, tension, _
aFillMode)
End Sub
```

[C#]
```
public void DrawClosedCurvePointFTension(PaintEventArgs e)
{
// Create pens.
Pen redPen   = new Pen(Color.Red, 3);
Pen greenPen = new Pen(Color.Green, 3);
// Create points that define curve.
PointF point1 = new PointF( 50.0F,  50.0F);
PointF point2 = new PointF(100.0F,  25.0F);
PointF point3 = new PointF(200.0F,   5.0F);
PointF point4 = new PointF(250.0F,  50.0F);
PointF point5 = new PointF(300.0F, 100.0F);
PointF point6 = new PointF(350.0F, 200.0F);
PointF point7 = new PointF(250.0F, 250.0F);
PointF[] curvePoints =
{
point1,
point2,
point3,
point4,
point5,
point6,
point7
};
// Draw lines between original points to screen.
e.Graphics.DrawLines(redPen, curvePoints);
// Create tension and fill mode.
float tension = 1.0F;
FillMode aFillMode = FillMode.Alternate;
// Draw closed curve to screen.
e.Graphics.DrawClosedCurve(greenPen, curvePoints, tension, aFillMode);
}
```

Requirements

Platforms: Windows 98, Windows NT 4.0, Windows Millennium Edition, Windows 2000, Windows XP Home Edition, Windows XP Professional, Windows Server 2003 family

Graphics.DrawCurve Method

Draws a cardinal spline through a specified array of **Point** structures.

Overload List

Draws a cardinal spline through a specified array of **Point** structures.

[Visual Basic] **Overloads Public Sub DrawCurve(Pen, Point())**

[C#] **public void DrawCurve(Pen, Point[]);**

[C++] **public: void DrawCurve(Pen*, Point[]);**

[JScript] **public function DrawCurve(Pen, Point[]);**

Draws a cardinal spline through a specified array of **PointF** structures.

[Visual Basic] **Overloads Public Sub DrawCurve(Pen, PointF())**

[C#] **public void DrawCurve(Pen, PointF[]);**

[C++] **public: void DrawCurve(Pen*, PointF[]);**

[JScript] **public function DrawCurve(Pen, PointF[]);**

Draws a cardinal spline through a specified array of **Point** structures using a specified tension.

[Visual Basic] **Overloads Public Sub DrawCurve(Pen, Point(), Single)**

[C#] **public void DrawCurve(Pen, Point[], float);**

[C++] **public: void DrawCurve(Pen*, Point[], float);**

[JScript] **public function DrawCurve(Pen, Point[], float);**

Draws a cardinal spline through a specified array of **PointF** structures using a specified tension.

[Visual Basic] **Overloads Public Sub DrawCurve(Pen, PointF(), Single)**

[C#] **public void DrawCurve(Pen, PointF[], float);**

[C++] **public: void DrawCurve(Pen*, PointF[], float);**

[JScript] **public function DrawCurve(Pen, PointF[], float);**

Draws a cardinal spline through a specified array of **PointF** structures. The drawing begins offset from the beginning of the array.

[Visual Basic] **Overloads Public Sub DrawCurve(Pen, PointF(), Integer, Integer)**

[C#] **public void DrawCurve(Pen, PointF[], int, int);**

[C++] **public: void DrawCurve(Pen*, PointF[], int, int);**

[JScript] **public function DrawCurve(Pen, PointF[], int, int);**

Draws a cardinal spline through a specified array of **Point** structures using a specified tension.

[Visual Basic] **Overloads Public Sub DrawCurve(Pen, Point(), Integer, Integer, Single)**

[C#] **public void DrawCurve(Pen, Point[], int, int, float);**

[C++] **public: void DrawCurve(Pen*, Point[], int, int, float);**

[JScript] **public function DrawCurve(Pen, Point[], int, int, float);**

Draws a cardinal spline through a specified array of **PointF** structures using a specified tension. The drawing begins offset from the beginning of the array.

[Visual Basic] **Overloads Public Sub DrawCurve(Pen, PointF(), Integer, Integer, Single)**

[C#] **public void DrawCurve(Pen, PointF[], int, int, float);**

[C++] **public: void DrawCurve(Pen*, PointF[], int, int, float);**

[JScript] **public function DrawCurve(Pen, PointF[], int, int, float);**

Example

[Visual Basic, C#] The following example is designed for use with Windows Forms, and it requires **PaintEventArgs** *e*, which is a parameter of the **Paint** event handler. The code performs the following actions:

- Creates red and green pens.
- Creates seven points to define a curve.
- Draws six red straight lines between the seven points to form an incomplete polygon.
- Defines the starting point offset and number of segments.
- Defines the tension.
- Draws an open green curve (starting at the third point) through the last five points.

[Visual Basic, C#] The method sets the tension to 1.0.

> [Visual Basic, C#] **Note** This example shows how to use one of the overloaded versions of **DrawCurve**. For other examples that might be available, see the individual overload topics.

[Visual Basic]

```
Public Sub DrawCurvePointFSegmentTension(e As PaintEventArgs)
' Create pens.
Dim redPen As New Pen(Color.Red, 3)
Dim greenPen As New Pen(Color.Green, 3)
' Create points that define curve.
Dim point1 As New PointF(50F, 50F)
Dim point2 As New PointF(100F, 25F)
Dim point3 As New PointF(200F, 5F)
Dim point4 As New PointF(250F, 50F)
Dim point5 As New PointF(300F, 100F)
Dim point6 As New PointF(350F, 200F)
Dim point7 As New PointF(250F, 250F)
Dim curvePoints As PointF() = {point1, point2, point3, point4, _
point5, point6, point7}
' Draw lines between original points to screen.
e.Graphics.DrawLines(redPen, curvePoints)
' Create offset, number of segments, and tension.
Dim offset As Integer = 2
Dim numSegments As Integer = 4
Dim tension As Single = 1F
' Draw curve to screen.
e.Graphics.DrawCurve(greenPen, curvePoints, offset, numSegments, _
tension)
End Sub
```

[C#]

```
public void DrawCurvePointFSegmentTension(PaintEventArgs e)
{
// Create pens.
Pen redPen   = new Pen(Color.Red, 3);
Pen greenPen = new Pen(Color.Green, 3);
// Create points that define curve.
PointF point1 = new PointF( 50.0F,  50.0F);
PointF point2 = new PointF(100.0F,  25.0F);
PointF point3 = new PointF(200.0F,   5.0F);
PointF point4 = new PointF(250.0F,  50.0F);
PointF point5 = new PointF(300.0F, 100.0F);
PointF point6 = new PointF(350.0F, 200.0F);
PointF point7 = new PointF(250.0F, 250.0F);
PointF[] curvePoints =
{
point1,
point2,
point3,
point4,
point5,
point6,
point7
};
// Draw lines between original points to screen.
e.Graphics.DrawLines(redPen, curvePoints);
// Create offset, number of segments, and tension.
int offset = 2;
int numSegments = 4;
float tension = 1.0F;
// Draw curve to screen.
e.Graphics.DrawCurve(greenPen, curvePoints, offset, numSegments,
tension);
}
```

Graphics.DrawCurve Method (Pen, Point[])

Draws a cardinal spline through a specified array of **Point** structures.

[Visual Basic]

```
Overloads Public Sub DrawCurve( _
   ByVal pen As Pen, _
   ByVal points() As Point _
)
```

[C#]

```
public void DrawCurve(
   Pen pen,
   Point[] points
);
```

[C++]

```
public: void DrawCurve(
   Pen* pen,
   Point points[]
);
```

[JScript]

```
public function DrawCurve(
   pen : Pen,
   points : Point[]
);
```

Parameters

pen

Pen object that determines the color, width, and height of the curve.

points

Array of **Point** structures that define the spline.

Return Value

This method does not return a value.

Remarks

This method draws a cardinal spline that passes through each point in the array.

The array of points must contain at least four **Point** structures.

This method uses a default tension of 0.5.

Example

[Visual Basic, C#] The following example is designed for use with Windows Forms, and it requires **PaintEventArgs** *e*, which is a parameter of the **Paint** event handler. The code performs the following actions:

- Creates red and green pens.
- Creates seven points to define a curve.
- Draws six red straight lines between the seven points to form an incomplete polygon.
- Draws an open green curve through the seven points.

[Visual Basic, C#] The method uses a default tension of 0.5.

[Visual Basic]
```
Public Sub DrawCurvePoint(e As PaintEventArgs)
' Create pens.
Dim redPen As New Pen(Color.Red, 3)
Dim greenPen As New Pen(Color.Green, 3)
' Create points that define curve.
Dim point1 As New Point(50, 50)
Dim point2 As New Point(100, 25)
Dim point3 As New Point(200, 5)
Dim point4 As New Point(250, 50)
Dim point5 As New Point(300, 100)
Dim point6 As New Point(350, 200)
Dim point7 As New Point(250, 250)
Dim curvePoints As Point() =  {point1, point2, point3, point4, _
point5, point6, point7}
' Draw lines between original points to screen.
e.Graphics.DrawLines(redPen, curvePoints)
' Draw curve to screen.
e.Graphics.DrawCurve(greenPen, curvePoints)
End Sub
```

[C#]
```
public void DrawCurvePoint(PaintEventArgs e)
{
// Create pens.
Pen redPen   = new Pen(Color.Red, 3);
Pen greenPen = new Pen(Color.Green, 3);
// Create points that define curve.
Point point1 = new Point( 50,  50);
Point point2 = new Point(100,  25);
Point point3 = new Point(200,   5);
Point point4 = new Point(250,  50);
Point point5 = new Point(300, 100);
Point point6 = new Point(350, 200);
Point point7 = new Point(250, 250);
Point[] curvePoints =
{
point1,
point2,
point3,
point4,
point5,
point6,
point7
};
// Draw lines between original points to screen.
e.Graphics.DrawLines(redPen, curvePoints);
// Draw curve to screen.
e.Graphics.DrawCurve(greenPen, curvePoints);
}
```

Requirements

Platforms: Windows 98, Windows NT 4.0, Windows Millennium Edition, Windows 2000, Windows XP Home Edition, Windows XP Professional, Windows Server 2003 family

Graphics.DrawCurve Method (Pen, PointF[])

Draws a cardinal spline through a specified array of **PointF** structures.

[Visual Basic]
```
Overloads Public Sub DrawCurve( _
   ByVal pen As Pen, _
   ByVal points() As PointF _
)
```
[C#]
```
public void DrawCurve(
   Pen pen,
   PointF[] points
);
```
[C++]
```
public: void DrawCurve(
   Pen* pen,
   PointF points[]
);
```
[JScript]
```
public function DrawCurve(
   pen : Pen,
   points : PointF[]
);
```

Parameters

pen

Pen object that determines the color, width, and height of the curve.

points

Array of **PointF** structures that define the spline.

Return Value

This method does not return a value.

Remarks

This method draws a cardinal spline that passes through each point in the array.

The array of points must contain at least four **PointF** structures.

This method uses a default tension of 0.5.

Example

[Visual Basic, C#] The following example is designed for use with Windows Forms, and it requires **PaintEventArgs** *e*, which is a parameter of the **Paint** event handler. The code performs the following actions:

- Creates red and green pens.
- Creates seven points to define a curve.
- Draws six red straight lines between the seven points to form an incomplete polygon.
- Draws an open green curve through the seven points.

[Visual Basic, C#] The method uses a default tension of 0.5.

[Visual Basic]
```
Public Sub DrawCurvePointF(e As PaintEventArgs)
' Create pens.
Dim redPen As New Pen(Color.Red, 3)
Dim greenPen As New Pen(Color.Green, 3)
' Create points that define curve.
Dim point1 As New PointF(50F, 50F)
Dim point2 As New PointF(100F, 25F)
Dim point3 As New PointF(200F, 5F)
Dim point4 As New PointF(250F, 50F)
Dim point5 As New PointF(300F, 100F)
Dim point6 As New PointF(350F, 200F)
Dim point7 As New PointF(250F, 250F)
Dim curvePoints As PointF() =  {point1, point2, point3, point4, _
point5, point6, point7}
' Draw lines between original points to screen.
e.Graphics.DrawLines(redPen, curvePoints)
' Draw curve to screen.
e.Graphics.DrawCurve(greenPen, curvePoints)
End Sub
```

[C#]
```
public void DrawCurvePointF(PaintEventArgs e)
{
// Create pens.
Pen redPen   = new Pen(Color.Red, 3);
Pen greenPen = new Pen(Color.Green, 3);
// Create points that define curve.
PointF point1 = new PointF( 50.0F,  50.0F);
```

```
PointF point2 = new PointF(100.0F,  25.0F);
PointF point3 = new PointF(200.0F,   5.0F);
PointF point4 = new PointF(250.0F,  50.0F);
PointF point5 = new PointF(300.0F, 100.0F);
PointF point6 = new PointF(350.0F, 200.0F);
PointF point7 = new PointF(250.0F, 250.0F);
PointF[] curvePoints =
{
point1,
point2,
point3,
point4,
point5,
point6,
point7
};
// Draw lines between original points to screen.
e.Graphics.DrawLines(redPen, curvePoints);
// Draw curve to screen.
e.Graphics.DrawCurve(greenPen, curvePoints);
}
```

Requirements

Platforms: Windows 98, Windows NT 4.0, Windows Millennium Edition, Windows 2000, Windows XP Home Edition, Windows XP Professional, Windows Server 2003 family

Graphics.DrawCurve Method (Pen, Point[], Single)

Draws a cardinal spline through a specified array of **Point** structures using a specified tension.

[Visual Basic]
```
Overloads Public Sub DrawCurve( _
   ByVal pen As Pen, _
   ByVal points() As Point, _
   ByVal tension As Single _
)
```
[C#]
```
public void DrawCurve(
   Pen pen,
   Point[] points,
   float tension
);
```
[C++]
```
public: void DrawCurve(
   Pen* pen,
   Point points[],
   float tension
);
```
[JScript]
```
public function DrawCurve(
   pen : Pen,
   points : Point[],
   tension : float
);
```

Parameters

pen
: **Pen** object that determines the color, width, and height of the curve.

points
: Array of **Point** structures that define the spline.

tension
: Value greater than or equal to 0.0F that specifies the tension of the curve.

Return Value

This method does not return a value.

Remarks

This method draws a cardinal spline that passes through each point in the array.

The array of points must contain at least four **Point** structures.

The *tension* parameter determines the shape of the spline. If the value of the *tension* parameter is 0.0F, this method draws straight line segments to connect the points. Usually, the *tension* parameter is less than or equal to 1.0F. Values over 1.0F produce unusual results.

Example

[Visual Basic, C#] The following example is designed for use with Windows Forms, and it requires **PaintEventArgs** *e*, which is a parameter of the **Paint** event handler. The code performs the following actions:

[Visual Basic, C#] creates red and green pens.

- Creates seven points to define the curve.
- Draws six red straight lines between the seven points to form an incomplete polygon.
- Creates a tension setting.
- Draws an open green closed curve through the seven points.

[Visual Basic, C#] The method uses the a tension of 1.0.

[Visual Basic]
```
Public Sub DrawCurvePointTension(e As PaintEventArgs)
' Create pens.
Dim redPen As New Pen(Color.Red, 3)
Dim greenPen As New Pen(Color.Green, 3)
' Create points that define curve.
Dim point1 As New Point(50, 50)
Dim point2 As New Point(100, 25)
Dim point3 As New Point(200, 5)
Dim point4 As New Point(250, 50)
Dim point5 As New Point(300, 100)
Dim point6 As New Point(350, 200)
Dim point7 As New Point(250, 250)
Dim curvePoints As Point() =  {point1, point2, point3, point4, _
point5, point6, point7}
' Draw lines between original points to screen.
e.Graphics.DrawLines(redPen, curvePoints)
' Create tension.
Dim tension As Single = 1F
' Draw curve to screen.
e.Graphics.DrawCurve(greenPen, curvePoints, tension)
End Sub
```

[C#]
```
public void DrawCurvePointTension(PaintEventArgs e)
{
// Create pens.
Pen redPen   = new Pen(Color.Red, 3);
Pen greenPen = new Pen(Color.Green, 3);
// Create points that define curve.
Point point1 = new Point( 50,  50);
Point point2 = new Point(100,  25);
Point point3 = new Point(200,   5);
Point point4 = new Point(250,  50);
Point point5 = new Point(300, 100);
Point point6 = new Point(350, 200);
Point point7 = new Point(250, 250);
Point[] curvePoints =
{
point1,
point2,
point3,
point4,
```

```
point5,
point6,
point7
};
// Draw lines between original points to screen.
e.Graphics.DrawLines(redPen, curvePoints);
// Create tension.
float tension = 1.0F;
// Draw curve to screen.
e.Graphics.DrawCurve(greenPen, curvePoints, tension);
}
```

Requirements

Platforms: Windows 98, Windows NT 4.0, Windows Millennium Edition, Windows 2000, Windows XP Home Edition, Windows XP Professional, Windows Server 2003 family

Graphics.DrawCurve Method (Pen, PointF[], Single)

Draws a cardinal spline through a specified array of **PointF** structures using a specified tension.

```
[Visual Basic]
Overloads Public Sub DrawCurve( _
   ByVal pen As Pen, _
   ByVal points() As PointF, _
   ByVal tension As Single _
)
[C#]
public void DrawCurve(
   Pen pen,
   PointF[] points,
   float tension
);
[C++]
public: void DrawCurve(
   Pen* pen,
   PointF points[],
   float tension
);
[JScript]
public function DrawCurve(
   pen : Pen,
   points : PointF[],
   tension : float
);
```

Parameters

pen
: **Pen** object that determines the color, width, and height of the curve.

points
: Array of **PointF** structures that represent the points that define the curve.

tension
: Value greater than or equal to 0.0F that specifies the tension of the curve.

Return Value

This method does not return a value.

Remarks

This method draws a cardinal spline that passes through each point in the array.

The array of points must contain at least four **PointF** structures.

The *tension* parameter determines the shape of the spline. If the value of the *tension* parameter is 0.0F, this method draws straight line segments to connect the points. Usually, the *tension* parameter is less than or equal to 1.0F. Values over 1.0F produce unusual results.

Example

[Visual Basic, C#] The following example is designed for use with Windows Forms, and it requires **PaintEventArgs** *e*, which is a parameter of the **Paint** event handler. The code performs the following actions:

- Creates red and green pens.
- Creates seven points to define the curve.
- Draws six red straight lines between the seven points to form an incomplete polygon.
- Creates a tension setting.
- Draws an open green closed curve through the seven points.

[Visual Basic, C#] The method uses a tension of 1.0.

```
[Visual Basic]
Public Sub DrawCurvePointFTension(e As PaintEventArgs)
' Create pens.
Dim redPen As New Pen(Color.Red, 3)
Dim greenPen As New Pen(Color.Green, 3)
' Create points that define curve.
Dim point1 As New PointF(50F, 50F)
Dim point2 As New PointF(100F, 25F)
Dim point3 As New PointF(200F, 5F)
Dim point4 As New PointF(250F, 50F)
Dim point5 As New PointF(300F, 100F)
Dim point6 As New PointF(350F, 200F)
Dim point7 As New PointF(250F, 250F)
Dim curvePoints As PointF() = {point1, point2, point3, point4, _
point5, point6, point7}
' Draw lines between original points to screen.
e.Graphics.DrawLines(redPen, curvePoints)
' Create tension.
Dim tension As Single = 1F
' Draw curve to screen.
e.Graphics.DrawCurve(greenPen, curvePoints, tension)
End Sub
```

```
[C#]
public void DrawCurvePointFTension(PaintEventArgs e)
{
// Create pens.
Pen redPen   = new Pen(Color.Red, 3);
Pen greenPen = new Pen(Color.Green, 3);
// Create points that define curve.
PointF point1 = new PointF( 50.0F,  50.0F);
PointF point2 = new PointF(100.0F,  25.0F);
PointF point3 = new PointF(200.0F,   5.0F);
PointF point4 = new PointF(250.0F,  50.0F);
PointF point5 = new PointF(300.0F, 100.0F);
PointF point6 = new PointF(350.0F, 200.0F);
PointF point7 = new PointF(250.0F, 250.0F);
PointF[] curvePoints =
{
point1,
point2,
point3,
point4,
point5,
point6,
point7
};
// Draw lines between original points to screen.
e.Graphics.DrawLines(redPen, curvePoints);
// Create tension.
float tension = 1.0F;
// Draw curve to screen.
e.Graphics.DrawCurve(greenPen, curvePoints, tension);
}
```

Requirements

Platforms: Windows 98, Windows NT 4.0, Windows Millennium Edition, Windows 2000, Windows XP Home Edition, Windows XP Professional, Windows Server 2003 family

Graphics.DrawCurve Method (Pen, PointF[], Int32, Int32)

Draws a cardinal spline through a specified array of **PointF** structures. The drawing begins offset from the beginning of the array.

[Visual Basic]
```
Overloads Public Sub DrawCurve( _
   ByVal pen As Pen, _
   ByVal points() As PointF, _
   ByVal offset As Integer, _
   ByVal numberOfSegments As Integer _
)
```
[C#]
```
public void DrawCurve(
   Pen pen,
   PointF[] points,
   int offset,
   int numberOfSegments
);
```
[C++]
```
public: void DrawCurve(
   Pen* pen,
   PointF points[],
   int offset,
   int numberOfSegments
);
```
[JScript]
```
public function DrawCurve(
   pen : Pen,
   points : PointF[],
   offset : int,
   numberOfSegments : int
);
```

Parameters

pen
: **Pen** object that determines the color, width, and height of the curve.

points
: Array of **PointF** structures that define the spline.

offset
: Offset from the first element in the array of the *points* parameter to the starting point in the curve.

numberOfSegments
: Number of segments after the starting point to include in the curve.

Return Value

This method does not return a value.

Remarks

This method draws a cardinal spline that passes through each point in the array.

The array of points must contain at least four **PointF** structures.

The value of the *offset* parameter specifies the number of elements to skip in the array. The first element after the skipped elements represents the starting point of the curve.

The value of the *numberOfSegments* parameter specifies the number of segments, after the starting point, to draw in the curve. The value of the *numberOfSegments* parameter must be at least 1. The value of the *offset* parameter plus the value of the *numberOfSegments* parameter must be less than the number of elements in the array of the *points* parameter.

This method uses a default tension of 0.5.

Example

[Visual Basic, C#] The following example is designed for use with Windows Forms, and it requires **PaintEventArgs** *e*, which is a parameter of the **Paint** event handler. The code performs the following actions:

- Creates red and green pens.
- Creates seven points to define a curve.
- Draws six red straight lines between the seven points to form an incomplete polygon.
- Defines the starting point offset and number of segments.
- Draws an open green curve (starting at the third point) through the last five points.

[Visual Basic, C#] The method uses a default tension of 0.5.

[Visual Basic]
```
Public Sub DrawCurvePointFSegments(e As PaintEventArgs)
' Create pens.
Dim redPen As New Pen(Color.Red, 3)
Dim greenPen As New Pen(Color.Green, 3)
' Create points that define curve.
Dim point1 As New PointF(50F, 50F)
Dim point2 As New PointF(100F, 25F)
Dim point3 As New PointF(200F, 5F)
Dim point4 As New PointF(250F, 50F)
Dim point5 As New PointF(300F, 100F)
Dim point6 As New PointF(350F, 200F)
Dim point7 As New PointF(250F, 250F)
Dim curvePoints As PointF() =  {point1, point2, point3, point4, _
point5, point6, point7}
' Draw lines between original points to screen.
e.Graphics.DrawLines(redPen, curvePoints)
' Create offset and number of segments.
Dim offset As Integer = 2
Dim numSegments As Integer = 4
' Draw curve to screen.
e.Graphics.DrawCurve(greenPen, curvePoints, offset, numSegments)
End Sub
```
[C#]
```
public void DrawCurvePointFSegments(PaintEventArgs e)
{
// Create pens.
Pen redPen   = new Pen(Color.Red, 3);
Pen greenPen = new Pen(Color.Green, 3);
// Create points that define curve.
PointF point1 = new PointF( 50.0F,  50.0F);
PointF point2 = new PointF(100.0F,  25.0F);
PointF point3 = new PointF(200.0F,   5.0F);
PointF point4 = new PointF(250.0F,  50.0F);
PointF point5 = new PointF(300.0F, 100.0F);
PointF point6 = new PointF(350.0F, 200.0F);
PointF point7 = new PointF(250.0F, 250.0F);
PointF[] curvePoints =
{
point1,
point2,
point3,
point4,
point5,
point6,
point7
};
```

```
// Draw lines between original points to screen.
e.Graphics.DrawLines(redPen, curvePoints);
// Create offset and number of segments.
int offset = 2;
int numSegments = 4;
// Draw curve to screen.
e.Graphics.DrawCurve(greenPen, curvePoints, offset, numSegments);
}
```

Requirements

Platforms: Windows 98, Windows NT 4.0, Windows Millennium Edition, Windows 2000, Windows XP Home Edition, Windows XP Professional, Windows Server 2003 family

Graphics.DrawCurve Method (Pen, Point[], Int32, Int32, Single)

Draws a cardinal spline through a specified array of **Point** structures using a specified tension.

[Visual Basic]
```
Overloads Public Sub DrawCurve( _
   ByVal pen As Pen, _
   ByVal points() As Point, _
   ByVal offset As Integer, _
   ByVal numberOfSegments As Integer, _
   ByVal tension As Single _
)
```
[C#]
```
public void DrawCurve(
   Pen pen,
   Point[] points,
   int offset,
   int numberOfSegments,
   float tension
);
```
[C++]
```
public: void DrawCurve(
   Pen* pen,
   Point points[],
   int offset,
   int numberOfSegments,
   float tension
);
```
[JScript]
```
public function DrawCurve(
   pen : Pen,
   points : Point[],
   offset : int,
   numberOfSegments : int,
   tension : float
);
```

Parameters

pen
: **Pen** object that determines the color, width, and height of the curve.

points
: Array of **Point** structures that define the spline.

offset
: Offset from the first element in the array of the *points* parameter to the starting point in the curve.

numberOfSegments
: Number of segments after the starting point to include in the curve.

tension
: Value greater than or equal to 0.0F that specifies the tension of the curve.

Return Value

This method does not return a value.

Remarks

This method draws a cardinal spline that passes through each point in the array.

The array of points must contain at least four **Point** structures.

The value of the *offset* parameter specifies the number of elements to skip in the array. The first element after the skipped elements represents the starting point of the curve.

The value of the *numberOfSegments* parameter specifies the number of segments, after the starting point, to draw in the curve. The value of the *numberOfSegments* parameter must be at least 1. The value of the *offset* parameter plus the value of the *numberOfSegments* parameter must be less than the number of elements in the array of the *points* parameter.

The *tension* parameter determines the shape of the spline. If the value of the *tension* parameter is 0.0F, this method draws straight line segments to connect the points. Usually, the *tension* parameter is less than or equal to 1.0F. Values over 1.0F produce unusual results.

Example

[Visual Basic, C#] The following example is designed for use with Windows Forms, and it requires **PaintEventArgs** *e*, which is a parameter of the **Paint** event handler. The code performs the following actions:

- Creates red and green pens.
- Creates seven points to define a curve.
- Draws six red straight lines between the seven points to form an incomplete polygon.
- Defines the starting point offset and number of segments.
- Defines the tension.
- Draws an open green curve (starting at the third point) through the last five points.

[Visual Basic, C#] The method sets the tension to 1.0.

[Visual Basic]
```
Public Sub DrawCurvePointSegmentTension(e As PaintEventArgs)
' Create pens.
Dim redPen As New Pen(Color.Red, 3)
Dim greenPen As New Pen(Color.Green, 3)
' Create points that define curve.
Dim point1 As New Point(50, 50)
Dim point2 As New Point(100, 25)
Dim point3 As New Point(200, 5)
Dim point4 As New Point(250, 50)
Dim point5 As New Point(300, 100)
Dim point6 As New Point(350, 200)
Dim point7 As New Point(250, 250)
Dim curvePoints As Point() =  {point1, point2, point3, point4, _
point5, point6, point7}
' Draw lines between original points to screen.
e.Graphics.DrawLines(redPen, curvePoints)
' Create offset, number of segments, and tension.
Dim offset As Integer = 2
Dim numSegments As Integer = 4
Dim tension As Single = 1F
' Draw curve to screen.
e.Graphics.DrawCurve(greenPen, curvePoints, offset, numSegments, _
tension)
End Sub
```

[C#]
```
public void DrawCurvePointSegmentTension(PaintEventArgs e)
{
// Create pens.
Pen redPen   = new Pen(Color.Red, 3);
Pen greenPen = new Pen(Color.Green, 3);
// Create points that define curve.
Point point1 = new Point( 50,  50);
Point point2 = new Point(100,  25);
Point point3 = new Point(200,   5);
Point point4 = new Point(250,  50);
Point point5 = new Point(300, 100);
Point point6 = new Point(350, 200);
Point point7 = new Point(250, 250);
Point[] curvePoints =
{
point1,
point2,
point3,
point4,
point5,
point6,
point7
};
// Draw lines between original points to screen.
e.Graphics.DrawLines(redPen, curvePoints);
// Create offset, number of segments, and tension.
int offset = 2;
int numSegments = 4;
float tension = 1.0F;
// Draw curve to screen.
e.Graphics.DrawCurve(greenPen, curvePoints, offset, numSegments,
tension);
}
```

Requirements

Platforms: Windows 98, Windows NT 4.0, Windows Millennium Edition, Windows 2000, Windows XP Home Edition, Windows XP Professional, Windows Server 2003 family

Graphics.DrawCurve Method (Pen, PointF[], Int32, Int32, Single)

Draws a cardinal spline through a specified array of **PointF** structures using a specified tension. The drawing begins offset from the beginning of the array.

[Visual Basic]
```
Overloads Public Sub DrawCurve( _
   ByVal pen As Pen, _
   ByVal points() As PointF, _
   ByVal offset As Integer, _
   ByVal numberOfSegments As Integer, _
   ByVal tension As Single _
)
```
[C#]
```
public void DrawCurve(
   Pen pen,
   PointF[] points,
   int offset,
   int numberOfSegments,
   float tension
);
```
[C++]
```
public: void DrawCurve(
   Pen* pen,
   PointF points[],
   int offset,
   int numberOfSegments,
   float tension
);
```
[JScript]
```
public function DrawCurve(
   pen : Pen,
   points : PointF[],
   offset : int,
   numberOfSegments : int,
   tension : float
);
```

Parameters

pen

Pen object that determines the color, width, and height of the curve.

points

Array of **PointF** structures that define the spline.

offset

Offset from the first element in the array of the *points* parameter to the starting point in the curve.

numberOfSegments

Number of segments after the starting point to include in the curve.

tension

Value greater than or equal to 0.0F that specifies the tension of the curve.

Return Value

This method does not return a value.

Remarks

This method draws a cardinal spline that passes through each point in the array.

The array of points must contain at least four **PointF** structures.

The value of the *offset* parameter specifies the number of elements to skip in the array. The first element after the skipped elements represents the starting point of the curve.

The value of the *numberOfSegments* parameter specifies the number of segments, after the starting point, to draw in the curve. The value of the *numberOfSegments* parameter must be at least 1. The value of the *offset* parameter plus the value of the *numberOfSegments* parameter must be less than the number of elements in the array of the *points* parameter.

The *tension* parameter determines the shape of the spline. If the value of the *tension* parameter is 0.0F, this method draws straight line segments to connect the points. Usually, the *tension* parameter is less than or equal to 1.0F. Values over 1.0F produce unusual results.

Example

[Visual Basic, C#] The following example is designed for use with Windows Forms, and it requires **PaintEventArgs** *e*, which is a parameter of the **Paint** event handler. The code performs the following actions:

- Creates red and green pens.
- Creates seven points to define a curve.
- Draws six red straight lines between the seven points to form an incomplete polygon.
- Defines the starting point offset and number of segments.
- Defines the tension.
- Draws an open green curve (starting at the third point) through the last five points.

[Visual Basic, C#] The method sets the tension to 1.0.

[Visual Basic]
```
Public Sub DrawCurvePointFSegmentTension(e As PaintEventArgs)
' Create pens.
Dim redPen As New Pen(Color.Red, 3)
Dim greenPen As New Pen(Color.Green, 3)
' Create points that define curve.
Dim point1 As New PointF(50F, 50F)
Dim point2 As New PointF(100F, 25F)
Dim point3 As New PointF(200F, 5F)
Dim point4 As New PointF(250F, 50F)
Dim point5 As New PointF(300F, 100F)
Dim point6 As New PointF(350F, 200F)
Dim point7 As New PointF(250F, 250F)
Dim curvePoints As PointF() = {point1, point2, point3, point4, _
point5, point6, point7}
' Draw lines between original points to screen.
e.Graphics.DrawLines(redPen, curvePoints)
' Create offset, number of segments, and tension.
Dim offset As Integer = 2
Dim numSegments As Integer = 4
Dim tension As Single = 1F
' Draw curve to screen.
e.Graphics.DrawCurve(greenPen, curvePoints, offset, numSegments, _
tension)
End Sub
```

[C#]
```
public void DrawCurvePointFSegmentTension(PaintEventArgs e)
{
// Create pens.
Pen redPen   = new Pen(Color.Red, 3);
Pen greenPen = new Pen(Color.Green, 3);
// Create points that define curve.
PointF point1 = new PointF( 50.0F,  50.0F);
PointF point2 = new PointF(100.0F,  25.0F);
PointF point3 = new PointF(200.0F,   5.0F);
PointF point4 = new PointF(250.0F,  50.0F);
PointF point5 = new PointF(300.0F, 100.0F);
PointF point6 = new PointF(350.0F, 200.0F);
PointF point7 = new PointF(250.0F, 250.0F);
PointF[] curvePoints =
{
point1,
point2,
point3,
point4,
point5,
point6,
point7
};
// Draw lines between original points to screen.
e.Graphics.DrawLines(redPen, curvePoints);
// Create offset, number of segments, and tension.
int offset = 2;
int numSegments = 4;
float tension = 1.0F;
// Draw curve to screen.
e.Graphics.DrawCurve(greenPen, curvePoints, offset,
numSegments, tension);
}
```

Requirements

Platforms: Windows 98, Windows NT 4.0, Windows Millennium Edition, Windows 2000, Windows XP Home Edition, Windows XP Professional, Windows Server 2003 family

Graphics.DrawEllipse Method

Draws an ellipse defined by a bounding rectangle specified by a pair of coordinates, a height, and a width.

Overload List

Draws an ellipse specified by a bounding **Rectangle** structure.

Supported by the .NET Compact Framework.

[Visual Basic] **Overloads Public Sub DrawEllipse(Pen, Rectangle)**

[C#] **public void DrawEllipse(Pen, Rectangle);**

[C++] **public: void DrawEllipse(Pen*, Rectangle);**

[JScript] **public function DrawEllipse(Pen, Rectangle);**

Draws an ellipse defined by a bounding **RectangleF**.

[Visual Basic] **Overloads Public Sub DrawEllipse(Pen, RectangleF)**

[C#] **public void DrawEllipse(Pen, RectangleF);**

[C++] **public: void DrawEllipse(Pen*, RectangleF);**

[JScript] **public function DrawEllipse(Pen, RectangleF);**

Draws an ellipse defined by a bounding rectangle specified by a pair of coordinates, a height, and a width.

Supported by the .NET Compact Framework.

[Visual Basic] **Overloads Public Sub DrawEllipse(Pen, Integer, Integer, Integer, Integer)**

[C#] **public void DrawEllipse(Pen, int, int, int, int);**

[C++] **public: void DrawEllipse(Pen*, int, int, int, int);**

[JScript] **public function DrawEllipse(Pen, int, int, int, int);**

Draws an ellipse defined by a bounding rectangle specified by a pair of coordinates, a height, and a width.

[Visual Basic] **Overloads Public Sub DrawEllipse(Pen, Single, Single, Single, Single)**

[C#] **public void DrawEllipse(Pen, float, float, float, float);**

[C++] **public: void DrawEllipse(Pen*, float, float, float, float);**

[JScript] **public function DrawEllipse(Pen, float, float, float, float);**

Example

[Visual Basic, C#] The following example is designed for use with Windows Forms, and it requires **PaintEventArgs** *e*, which is a parameter of the **Paint** event handler. The code performs the following actions:

- Creates a black pen.
- Creates the position and size of a rectangle to bound an ellipse.
- Draws the ellipse to the screen.

> [Visual Basic, C#] **Note** This example shows how to use one of the overloaded versions of **DrawEllipse**. For other examples that might be available, see the individual overload topics.

[Visual Basic]
```
Public Sub DrawEllipseFloat(e As PaintEventArgs)
' Create pen.
Dim blackPen As New Pen(Color.Black, 3)
' Create location and size of ellipse.
Dim x As Single = 0F
Dim y As Single = 0F
Dim width As Single = 200F
Dim height As Single = 100F
' Draw ellipse to screen.
e.Graphics.DrawEllipse(blackPen, x, y, width, height)
End Sub
```

[C#]
```
public void DrawEllipseFloat(PaintEventArgs e)
{
// Create pen.
Pen blackPen = new Pen(Color.Black, 3);
// Create location and size of ellipse.
float x = 0.0F;
float y = 0.0F;
float width = 200.0F;
float height = 100.0F;
// Draw ellipse to screen.
e.Graphics.DrawEllipse(blackPen, x, y, width, height);
}
```

Graphics.DrawEllipse Method (Pen, Rectangle)

Draws an ellipse specified by a bounding **Rectangle** structure.

[Visual Basic]
```
Overloads Public Sub DrawEllipse( _
   ByVal pen As Pen, _
   ByVal rect As Rectangle _
)
```
[C#]
```
public void DrawEllipse(
   Pen pen,
   Rectangle rect
);
```
[C++]
```
public: void DrawEllipse(
   Pen* pen,
   Rectangle rect
);
```
[JScript]
```
public function DrawEllipse(
   pen : Pen,
   rect : Rectangle
);
```

Parameters

pen

Pen object that determines the color, width, and style of the ellipse.

rect

Rectangle structure that defines the boundaries of the ellipse.

Return Value

This method does not return a value.

Remarks

This method draws an ellipse that is defined by the bounding rectangle specified by the *rect* parameter.

Example

[Visual Basic, C#] The following example is designed for use with Windows Forms, and it requires **PaintEventArgs** *e*, which is a parameter of the **Paint** event handler. The code performs the following actions:

- Creates a black pen.
- Creates a rectangle to bound an ellipse.
- Draws the ellipse to the screen.

[Visual Basic]
```
Public Sub DrawEllipseRectangle(e As PaintEventArgs)
' Create pen.
Dim blackPen As New Pen(Color.Black, 3)
' Create rectangle for ellipse.
Dim rect As New Rectangle(0, 0, 200, 100)
' Draw ellipse to screen.
e.Graphics.DrawEllipse(blackPen, rect)
End Sub
```

[C#]
```
public void DrawEllipseRectangle(PaintEventArgs e)
{
// Create pen.
Pen blackPen = new Pen(Color.Black, 3);
// Create rectangle for ellipse.
Rectangle rect = new Rectangle( 0, 0, 200, 100);
// Draw ellipse to screen.
e.Graphics.DrawEllipse(blackPen, rect);
}
```

Requirements

Platforms: Windows 98, Windows NT 4.0, Windows Millennium Edition, Windows 2000, Windows XP Home Edition, Windows XP Professional, Windows Server 2003 family, .NET Compact Framework - Windows CE .NET

Graphics.DrawEllipse Method (Pen, RectangleF)

Draws an ellipse defined by a bounding **RectangleF**.

[Visual Basic]
```
Overloads Public Sub DrawEllipse( _
   ByVal pen As Pen, _
   ByVal rect As RectangleF _
)
```
[C#]
```
public void DrawEllipse(
   Pen pen,
   RectangleF rect
);
```
[C++]
```
public: void DrawEllipse(
   Pen* pen,
   RectangleF rect
);
```
[JScript]
```
public function DrawEllipse(
   pen : Pen,
   rect : RectangleF
);
```

Parameters

pen

Pen object that determines the color, width, and style of the ellipse.

rect

RectangleF structure that defines the boundaries of the ellipse.

Return Value

This method does not return a value.

Remarks

This method draws an ellipse that is defined by the bounding rectangle specified by the *rect* parameter.

Example

[Visual Basic, C#] The following example is designed for use with Windows Forms, and it requires **PaintEventArgs** *e*, which is a parameter of the **Paint** event handler. The code performs the following actions:

- Creates a black pen.
- Creates a rectangle to bound an ellipse.
- Draws the ellipse to the screen.

[Visual Basic]
```
Public Sub DrawEllipseRectangleF(e As PaintEventArgs)
' Create pen.
Dim blackPen As New Pen(Color.Black, 3)
' Create rectangle for ellipse.
Dim rect As New RectangleF(0F, 0F, 200F, 100F)
' Draw ellipse to screen.
e.Graphics.DrawEllipse(blackPen, rect)
End Sub
```

[C#]
```
public void DrawEllipseRectangleF(PaintEventArgs e)
{
// Create pen.
Pen blackPen = new Pen(Color.Black, 3);
// Create rectangle for ellipse.
RectangleF rect = new RectangleF( 0.0F, 0.0F, 200.0F, 100.0F);
// Draw ellipse to screen.
e.Graphics.DrawEllipse(blackPen, rect);
}
```

Requirements

Platforms: Windows 98, Windows NT 4.0, Windows Millennium Edition, Windows 2000, Windows XP Home Edition, Windows XP Professional, Windows Server 2003 family

Graphics.DrawEllipse Method (Pen, Int32, Int32, Int32, Int32)

Draws an ellipse defined by a bounding rectangle specified by a pair of coordinates, a height, and a width.

[Visual Basic]
```
Overloads Public Sub DrawEllipse( _
   ByVal pen As Pen, _
   ByVal x As Integer, _
   ByVal y As Integer, _
   ByVal width As Integer, _
   ByVal height As Integer _
)
```
[C#]
```
public void DrawEllipse(
   Pen pen,
   int x,
   int y,
   int width,
   int height
);
```
[C++]
```
public: void DrawEllipse(
   Pen* pen,
   int x,
   int y,
   int width,
   int height
);
```
[JScript]
```
public function DrawEllipse(
   pen : Pen,
   x : int,
   y : int,
   width : int,
   height : int
);
```

Parameters

pen
: **Pen** object that determines the color, width, and style of the ellipse.

x
: x-coordinate of the upper-left corner of the bounding rectangle that defines the ellipse.

y
: y-coordinate of the upper-left corner of the bounding rectangle that defines the ellipse.

width
: Width of the bounding rectangle that defines the ellipse.

height
: Height of the bounding rectangle that defines the ellipse.

Return Value

This method does not return a value.

Remarks

This method draws an ellipse that is defined by the bounding rectangle described by the *x*, *y*, *width*, and *height* parameters.

Example

[Visual Basic, C#] The following example is designed for use with Windows Forms, and it requires **PaintEventArgs** *e*, which is a parameter of the **Paint** event handler. The code performs the following actions:

- Creates a black pen.
- Creates the position and size of a rectangle to bound an ellipse.
- Draws the ellipse to the screen.

[Visual Basic]
```
Public Sub DrawEllipseInt(e As PaintEventArgs)
' Create pen.
Dim blackPen As New Pen(Color.Black, 3)
' Create location and size of ellipse.
Dim x As Integer = 0
Dim y As Integer = 0
Dim width As Integer = 200
Dim height As Integer = 100
' Draw ellipse to screen.
e.Graphics.DrawEllipse(blackPen, x, y, width, height)
End Sub
```

[C#]
```
public void DrawEllipseInt(PaintEventArgs e)
{
// Create pen.
Pen blackPen = new Pen(Color.Black, 3);
// Create location and size of ellipse.
int x = 0;
int y = 0;
int width = 200;
int height = 100;
// Draw ellipse to screen.
e.Graphics.DrawEllipse(blackPen, x, y, width, height);
}
```

Requirements

Platforms: Windows 98, Windows NT 4.0,
Windows Millennium Edition, Windows 2000,
Windows XP Home Edition, Windows XP Professional,
Windows Server 2003 family,
.NET Compact Framework - Windows CE .NET

Graphics.DrawEllipse Method (Pen, Single, Single, Single, Single)

Draws an ellipse defined by a bounding rectangle specified by a pair of coordinates, a height, and a width.

[Visual Basic]
```
Overloads Public Sub DrawEllipse( _
   ByVal pen As Pen, _
   ByVal x As Single, _
   ByVal y As Single, _
   ByVal width As Single, _
   ByVal height As Single _
)
```
[C#]
```
public void DrawEllipse(
   Pen pen,
   float x,
   float y,
   float width,
   float height
);
```
[C++]
```
public: void DrawEllipse(
   Pen* pen,
   float x,
   float y,
   float width,
   float height
);
```
[JScript]
```
public function DrawEllipse(
   pen : Pen,
   x : float,
   y : float,
   width : float,
   height : float
);
```

Parameters

pen
: **Pen** object that determines the color, width, and style of the ellipse.

x
: x-coordinate of the upper-left corner of the bounding rectangle that defines the ellipse.

y
: y-coordinate of the upper-left corner of the bounding rectangle that defines the ellipse.

width
: Width of the bounding rectangle that defines the ellipse.

height
: Height of the bounding rectangle that defines the ellipse.

Return Value

This method does not return a value.

Remarks

This method draws an ellipse that is defined by the bounding rectangle described by the *x*, *y*, *width*, and *height* parameters.

Example

[Visual Basic, C#] The following example is designed for use with Windows Forms, and it requires **PaintEventArgs** *e*, which is a parameter of the **Paint** event handler. The code performs the following actions:

- Creates a black pen.
- Creates the position and size of a rectangle to bound an ellipse.
- Draws the ellipse to the screen.

[Visual Basic]
```
Public Sub DrawEllipseFloat(e As PaintEventArgs)
' Create pen.
Dim blackPen As New Pen(Color.Black, 3)
' Create location and size of ellipse.
Dim x As Single = 0F
Dim y As Single = 0F
Dim width As Single = 200F
Dim height As Single = 100F
' Draw ellipse to screen.
e.Graphics.DrawEllipse(blackPen, x, y, width, height)
End Sub
```

[C#]
```
public void DrawEllipseFloat(PaintEventArgs e)
{
// Create pen.
Pen blackPen = new Pen(Color.Black, 3);
// Create location and size of ellipse.
float x = 0.0F;
float y = 0.0F;
float width = 200.0F;
float height = 100.0F;
// Draw ellipse to screen.
e.Graphics.DrawEllipse(blackPen, x, y, width, height);
}
```

Requirements

Platforms: Windows 98, Windows NT 4.0,
Windows Millennium Edition, Windows 2000,
Windows XP Home Edition, Windows XP Professional,
Windows Server 2003 family

Graphics.DrawIcon Method

Draws the image represented by the specified **Icon** object at the specified coordinates.

Overload List

Draws the image represented by the specified **Icon** object within the area specified by a **Rectangle** structure.

[Visual Basic] **Overloads Public Sub DrawIcon(Icon, Rectangle)**

[C#] **public void DrawIcon(Icon, Rectangle);**

[C++] **public: void DrawIcon(Icon*, Rectangle);**

[JScript] **public function DrawIcon(Icon, Rectangle);**

Draws the image represented by the specified **Icon** object at the specified coordinates.

Supported by the .NET Compact Framework.

[Visual Basic] **Overloads Public Sub DrawIcon(Icon, Integer, Integer)**

[C#] **public void DrawIcon(Icon, int, int);**

[C++] **public: void DrawIcon(Icon*, int, int);**

[JScript] **public function DrawIcon(Icon, int, int);**

Example

[Visual Basic, C#] The following example is designed for use with Windows Forms, and it requires **PaintEventArgs** *e*, which is a parameter of the **Paint** event handler. The code performs the following actions:

- Creates an icon from a standard Windows icon file SampIcon.ico in the example folder.
- Creates the coordinates of the upper-left corner at which to draw the icon.
- Draws the icon to the screen.

[Visual Basic, C#] The drawn icon is unscaled.

> [Visual Basic, C#] **Note** This example shows how to use one of the overloaded versions of **DrawIcon**. For other examples that might be available, see the individual overload topics.

[Visual Basic]

```
Public Sub DrawIconInt(e As PaintEventArgs)
' Create icon.
Dim newIcon As New Icon("SampIcon.ico")
' Create coordinates for upper-left corner of icon.
Dim x As Integer = 100
Dim y As Integer = 100
' Draw icon to screen.
e.Graphics.DrawIcon(newIcon, x, y)
End Sub
```

[C#]

```
public void DrawIconInt(PaintEventArgs e)
{
// Create icon.
Icon newIcon = new Icon("SampIcon.ico");
// Create coordinates for upper-left corner of icon.
int x = 100;
int y = 100;
// Draw icon to screen.
e.Graphics.DrawIcon(newIcon, x, y);
}
```

Graphics.DrawIcon Method (Icon, Rectangle)

Draws the image represented by the specified **Icon** object within the area specified by a **Rectangle** structure.

[Visual Basic]

```
Overloads Public Sub DrawIcon( _
   ByVal icon As Icon, _
   ByVal targetRect As Rectangle _
)
```

[C#]

```
public void DrawIcon(
   Icon icon,
   Rectangle targetRect
);
```

[C++]

```
public: void DrawIcon(
   Icon* icon,
   Rectangle targetRect
);
```

[JScript]

```
public function DrawIcon(
   icon : Icon,
   targetRect : Rectangle
);
```

Parameters

icon

Icon object to draw.

targetRect

Rectangle structure that specifies the location and size of the resulting image on the display surface. The image contained in the *icon* parameter is scaled to the dimensions of this rectangular area.

Return Value

This method does not return a value.

Example

[Visual Basic, C#] The following example is designed for use with Windows Forms, and it requires **PaintEventArgs** *e*, which is a parameter of the **Paint** event handler. The code performs the following actions:

- Creates an icon from a standard Windows icon file SampIcon.ico in the example folder.
- Creates a rectangle in which to draw the icon.
- Draws the icon to the screen.

[Visual Basic, C#] The position of the rectangle locates the icon on the screen, and the size of the rectangle determines the scaling of the drawn icon.

[Visual Basic]

```
Public Sub DrawIconRectangle(e As PaintEventArgs)
' Create icon.
Dim newIcon As New Icon("SampIcon.ico")
' Create rectangle for icon.
Dim rect As New Rectangle(100, 100, 200, 200)
' Draw icon to screen.
e.Graphics.DrawIcon(newIcon, rect)
End Sub
```

[C#]

```
public void DrawIconRectangle(PaintEventArgs e)
{
// Create icon.
Icon newIcon = new Icon("SampIcon.ico");
// Create rectangle for icon.
Rectangle rect = new Rectangle( 100, 100, 200, 200);
// Draw icon to screen.
e.Graphics.DrawIcon(newIcon, rect);
}
```

Requirements

Platforms: Windows 98, Windows NT 4.0, Windows Millennium Edition, Windows 2000, Windows XP Home Edition, Windows XP Professional, Windows Server 2003 family

Graphics.DrawIcon Method (Icon, Int32, Int32)

Draws the image represented by the specified **Icon** object at the specified coordinates.

```
[Visual Basic]
Overloads Public Sub DrawIcon( _
   ByVal icon As Icon, _
   ByVal x As Integer, _
   ByVal y As Integer _
)
[C#]
public void DrawIcon(
   Icon icon,
   int x,
   int y
);
[C++]
public: void DrawIcon(
   Icon* icon,
   int x,
   int y
);
[JScript]
public function DrawIcon(
   icon : Icon,
   x : int,
   y : int
);
```

Parameters

icon

Icon object to draw.

x

x-coordinate of the upper-left corner of the drawn image.

y

y-coordinate of the upper-left corner of the drawn image.

Return Value

This method does not return a value.

Example

[Visual Basic, C#] The following example is designed for use with Windows Forms, and it requires **PaintEventArgs** *e*, which is a parameter of the **Paint** event handler. The code performs the following actions:

- Creates an icon from a standard Windows icon file SampIcon.ico in the example folder.
- Creates the coordinates of the upper-left corner at which to draw the icon.
- Draws the icon to the screen.

[Visual Basic, C#] The drawn icon is unscaled.

```
[Visual Basic]
Public Sub DrawIconInt(e As PaintEventArgs)
' Create icon.
Dim newIcon As New Icon("SampIcon.ico")
' Create coordinates for upper-left corner of icon.
Dim x As Integer = 100
Dim y As Integer = 100
' Draw icon to screen.
e.Graphics.DrawIcon(newIcon, x, y)
End Sub
```

```
[C#]
public void DrawIconInt(PaintEventArgs e)
{
// Create icon.
Icon newIcon = new Icon("SampIcon.ico");
// Create coordinates for upper-left corner of icon.
int x = 100;
int y = 100;
// Draw icon to screen.
e.Graphics.DrawIcon(newIcon, x, y);
}
```

Requirements

Platforms: Windows 98, Windows NT 4.0, Windows Millennium Edition, Windows 2000, Windows XP Home Edition, Windows XP Professional, Windows Server 2003 family, .NET Compact Framework - Windows CE .NET

Graphics.DrawIconUnstretched Method

Draws the image represented by the specified **Icon** object without scaling the image.

```
[Visual Basic]
Public Sub DrawIconUnstretched( _
   ByVal icon As Icon, _
   ByVal targetRect As Rectangle _
)
[C#]
public void DrawIconUnstretched(
   Icon icon,
   Rectangle targetRect
);
[C++]
public: void DrawIconUnstretched(
   Icon* icon,
   Rectangle targetRect
);
[JScript]
public function DrawIconUnstretched(
   icon : Icon,
   targetRect : Rectangle
);
```

Parameters

icon

Icon object to draw.

targetRect

Rectangle structure that specifies the location and size of the resulting image. The image is not scaled to fit this rectangle, but retains its original size. If the image is larger than the rectangle, it is clipped to fit inside it.

Return Value

This method does not return a value.

Example

[Visual Basic, C#] The following example is designed for use with Windows Forms, and it requires **PaintEventArgs** *e*, which is a parameter of the **Paint** event handler. The code performs the following actions:

- Creates an icon from a standard Windows icon file SampIcon.ico in the example folder.
- Creates a rectangle in which to draw the icon.
- Draws the icon to the screen.

[Visual Basic, C#] The position of the rectangle locates the icon on the screen, and the drawn icon is unscaled and unclipped.

[Visual Basic]
```
Public Sub DrawIconUnstretchedRectangle(e As PaintEventArgs)
' Create icon.
Dim newIcon As New Icon("SampIcon.ico")
' Create rectangle for icon.
Dim rect As New Rectangle(100, 100, 200, 200)
' Draw icon to screen.
e.Graphics.DrawIconUnstretched(newIcon, rect)
End Sub
```

[C#]
```
public void DrawIconUnstretchedRectangle(PaintEventArgs e)
{
// Create icon.
Icon newIcon = new Icon("SampIcon.ico");
// Create rectangle for icon.
Rectangle rect = new Rectangle( 100, 100, 200, 200);
// Draw icon to screen.
e.Graphics.DrawIconUnstretched(newIcon, rect);
}
```

Requirements

Platforms: Windows 98, Windows NT 4.0, Windows Millennium Edition, Windows 2000, Windows XP Home Edition, Windows XP Professional, Windows Server 2003 family

Graphics.DrawImage Method

Draws the specified **Image** object at the specified location and with the original size.

Overload List

Draws the specified **Image** object, using its original physical size, at the specified location.

[Visual Basic] **Overloads Public Sub DrawImage(Image, Point)**

[C#] **public void DrawImage(Image, Point);**

[C++] **public: void DrawImage(Image*, Point);**

[JScript] **public function DrawImage(Image, Point);**

Draws the specified **Image** object at the specified location and with the specified shape and size.

[Visual Basic] **Overloads Public Sub DrawImage(Image, Point())**

[C#] **public void DrawImage(Image, Point[]);**

[C++] **public: void DrawImage(Image*, Point[]);**

[JScript] **public function DrawImage(Image, Point[]);**

Draws the specified **Image** object, using its original physical size, at the specified location.

[Visual Basic] **Overloads Public Sub DrawImage(Image, PointF)**

[C#] **public void DrawImage(Image, PointF);**

[C++] **public: void DrawImage(Image*, PointF);**

[JScript] **public function DrawImage(Image, PointF);**

Draws the specified **Image** object at the specified location and with the specified shape and size.

[Visual Basic] **Overloads Public Sub DrawImage(Image, PointF())**

[C#] **public void DrawImage(Image, PointF[]);**

[C++] **public: void DrawImage(Image*, PointF[]);**

[JScript] **public function DrawImage(Image, PointF[]);**

Draws the specified **Image** object at the specified location and with the specified size.

[Visual Basic] **Overloads Public Sub DrawImage(Image, Rectangle)**

[C#] **public void DrawImage(Image, Rectangle);**

[C++] **public: void DrawImage(Image*, Rectangle);**

[JScript] **public function DrawImage(Image, Rectangle);**

Draws the specified **Image** object at the specified location and with the specified size.

[Visual Basic] **Overloads Public Sub DrawImage(Image, RectangleF)**

[C#] **public void DrawImage(Image, RectangleF);**

[C++] **public: void DrawImage(Image*, RectangleF);**

[JScript] **public function DrawImage(Image, RectangleF);**

Draws the specified image, using its original physical size, at the location specified by a coordinate pair.

Supported by the .NET Compact Framework.

[Visual Basic] **Overloads Public Sub DrawImage(Image, Integer, Integer)**

[C#] **public void DrawImage(Image, int, int);**

[C++] **public: void DrawImage(Image*, int, int);**

[JScript] **public function DrawImage(Image, int, int);**

Draws the specified **Image** object, using its original physical size, at the specified location.

[Visual Basic] **Overloads Public Sub DrawImage(Image, Single, Single)**

[C#] **public void DrawImage(Image, float, float);**

[C++] **public: void DrawImage(Image*, float, float);**

[JScript] **public function DrawImage(Image, float, float);**

Draws the specified portion of the specified **Image** object at the specified location and with the specified size.

[Visual Basic] **Overloads Public Sub DrawImage(Image, Point(), Rectangle, GraphicsUnit)**

[C#] **public void DrawImage(Image, Point[], Rectangle, GraphicsUnit);**

[C++] **public: void DrawImage(Image*, Point[], Rectangle, GraphicsUnit);**

[JScript] **public function DrawImage(Image, Point[], Rectangle, GraphicsUnit);**

Draws the specified portion of the specified **Image** object at the specified location and with the specified size.

[Visual Basic] **Overloads Public Sub DrawImage(Image, PointF(), RectangleF, GraphicsUnit)**

[C#] **public void DrawImage(Image, PointF[], RectangleF, GraphicsUnit);**

[C++] **public: void DrawImage(Image*, PointF[], RectangleF, GraphicsUnit);**

[JScript] **public function DrawImage(Image, PointF[], RectangleF, GraphicsUnit);**

Draws the specified portion of the specified **Image** object at the specified location and with the specified size.

Supported by the .NET Compact Framework.

[Visual Basic] **Overloads Public Sub DrawImage(Image, Rectangle, Rectangle, GraphicsUnit)**

[C#] **public void DrawImage(Image, Rectangle, Rectangle, GraphicsUnit);**

[C++] **public: void DrawImage(Image*, Rectangle, Rectangle, GraphicsUnit);**

[JScript] **public function DrawImage(Image, Rectangle, Rectangle, GraphicsUnit);**

Draws the specified portion of the specified **Image** object at the specified location and with the specified size.

[Visual Basic] **Overloads Public Sub DrawImage(Image, RectangleF, RectangleF, GraphicsUnit)**

[C#] **public void DrawImage(Image, RectangleF, RectangleF, GraphicsUnit);**

[C++] **public: void DrawImage(Image*, RectangleF, RectangleF, GraphicsUnit);**

[JScript] **public function DrawImage(Image, RectangleF, RectangleF, GraphicsUnit);**

Draws the specified **Image** object at the specified location and with the specified size.

[Visual Basic] **Overloads Public Sub DrawImage(Image, Integer, Integer, Integer, Integer)**

[C#] **public void DrawImage(Image, int, int, int, int);**

[C++] **public: void DrawImage(Image*, int, int, int, int);**

[JScript] **public function DrawImage(Image, int, int, int, int);**

Draws a portion of an image at a specified location.

Supported by the .NET Compact Framework.

[Visual Basic] **Overloads Public Sub DrawImage(Image, Integer, Integer, Rectangle, GraphicsUnit)**

[C#] **public void DrawImage(Image, int, int, Rectangle, GraphicsUnit);**

[C++] **public: void DrawImage(Image*, int, int, Rectangle, GraphicsUnit);**

[JScript] **public function DrawImage(Image, int, int, Rectangle, GraphicsUnit);**

Draws the specified portion of the specified **Image** object at the specified location.

[Visual Basic] **Overloads Public Sub DrawImage(Image, Point(), Rectangle, GraphicsUnit, ImageAttributes)**

[C#] **public void DrawImage(Image, Point[], Rectangle, GraphicsUnit, ImageAttributes);**

[C++] **public: void DrawImage(Image*, Point[], Rectangle, GraphicsUnit, ImageAttributes*);**

[JScript] **public function DrawImage(Image, Point[], Rectangle, GraphicsUnit, ImageAttributes);**

Draws the specified portion of the specified **Image** object at the specified location and with the specified size.

[Visual Basic] **Overloads Public Sub DrawImage(Image, PointF(), RectangleF, GraphicsUnit, ImageAttributes)**

[C#] **public void DrawImage(Image, PointF[], RectangleF, GraphicsUnit, ImageAttributes);**

[C++] **public: void DrawImage(Image*, PointF[], RectangleF, GraphicsUnit, ImageAttributes*);**

[JScript] **public function DrawImage(Image, PointF[], RectangleF, GraphicsUnit, ImageAttributes);**

Draws a portion of an image at a specified location.

[Visual Basic] **Overloads Public Sub DrawImage(Image, Single, Single, RectangleF, GraphicsUnit)**

[C#] **public void DrawImage(Image, float, float, RectangleF, GraphicsUnit);**

[C++] **public: void DrawImage(Image*, float, float, RectangleF, GraphicsUnit);**

[JScript] **public function DrawImage(Image, float, float, RectangleF, GraphicsUnit);**

Draws the specified **Image** object at the specified location and with the specified size.

[Visual Basic] **Overloads Public Sub DrawImage(Image, Single, Single, Single, Single)**

[C#] **public void DrawImage(Image, float, float, float, float);**

[C++] **public: void DrawImage(Image*, float, float, float, float);**

[JScript] **public function DrawImage(Image, float, float, float, float);**

Draws the specified portion of the specified **Image** object at the specified location and with the specified size.

[Visual Basic] **Overloads Public Sub DrawImage(Image, Point(), Rectangle, GraphicsUnit, ImageAttributes, Graphics.DrawImageAbort)**

[C#] **public void DrawImage(Image, Point[], Rectangle, GraphicsUnit, ImageAttributes, Graphics.DrawImageAbort);**

[C++] **public: void DrawImage(Image*, Point[], Rectangle, GraphicsUnit, ImageAttributes*, Graphics.DrawImageAbort*);**

[JScript] **public function DrawImage(Image, Point[], Rectangle, GraphicsUnit, ImageAttributes, Graphics.DrawImageAbort);**

Draws the specified portion of the specified **Image** object at the specified location and with the specified size.

[Visual Basic] **Overloads Public Sub DrawImage(Image, PointF(), RectangleF, GraphicsUnit, ImageAttributes, Graphics.DrawImageAbort)**

[C#] **public void DrawImage(Image, PointF[], RectangleF, GraphicsUnit, ImageAttributes, Graphics.DrawImageAbort);**

[C++] **public: void DrawImage(Image*, PointF[], RectangleF, GraphicsUnit, ImageAttributes*, Graphics.DrawImageAbort*);**

[JScript] **public function DrawImage(Image, PointF[], RectangleF, GraphicsUnit, ImageAttributes, Graphics.DrawImageAbort);**

Draws the specified portion of the specified **Image** object at the specified location and with the specified size.

[Visual Basic] **Overloads Public Sub DrawImage(Image, Point(), Rectangle, GraphicsUnit, ImageAttributes, Graphics.DrawImageAbort, Integer)**

[C#] **public void DrawImage(Image, Point[], Rectangle, GraphicsUnit, ImageAttributes, Graphics.DrawImageAbort, int);**

[C++] **public: void DrawImage(Image*, Point[], Rectangle, GraphicsUnit, ImageAttributes*, Graphics.DrawImageAbort*, int);**

[JScript] **public function DrawImage(Image, Point[], Rectangle, GraphicsUnit, ImageAttributes, Graphics.DrawImageAbort, int);**

Draws the specified portion of the specified **Image** object at the specified location and with the specified size.

[Visual Basic] **Overloads Public Sub DrawImage(Image, PointF(), RectangleF, GraphicsUnit, ImageAttributes, Graphics.DrawImageAbort, Integer)**

[C#] **public void DrawImage(Image, PointF[], RectangleF, GraphicsUnit, ImageAttributes, Graphics.DrawImageAbort, int);**

[C++] **public: void DrawImage(Image*, PointF[], RectangleF, GraphicsUnit, ImageAttributes*, Graphics.DrawImageAbort*, int);**

[JScript] **public function DrawImage(Image, PointF[], RectangleF, GraphicsUnit, ImageAttributes, Graphics.DrawImageAbort, int);**

Draws the specified portion of the specified **Image** object at the specified location and with the specified size.

[Visual Basic] **Overloads Public Sub DrawImage(Image, Rectangle, Integer, Integer, Integer, Integer, GraphicsUnit)**

[C#] **public void DrawImage(Image, Rectangle, int, int, int, int, GraphicsUnit);**

[C++] **public: void DrawImage(Image*, Rectangle, int, int, int, int, GraphicsUnit);**

[JScript] **public function DrawImage(Image, Rectangle, int, int, int, int, GraphicsUnit);**

Draws the specified portion of the specified **Image** object at the specified location and with the specified size.

[Visual Basic] **Overloads Public Sub DrawImage(Image, Rectangle, Single, Single, Single, Single, GraphicsUnit)**

[C#] **public void DrawImage(Image, Rectangle, float, float, float, float, GraphicsUnit);**

[C++] **public: void DrawImage(Image*, Rectangle, float, float, float, float, GraphicsUnit);**

[JScript] **public function DrawImage(Image, Rectangle, float, float, float, float, GraphicsUnit);**

Draws the specified portion of the specified **Image** object at the specified location and with the specified size.

Supported by the .NET Compact Framework.

[Visual Basic] **Overloads Public Sub DrawImage(Image, Rectangle, Integer, Integer, Integer, Integer, GraphicsUnit, ImageAttributes)**

[C#] **public void DrawImage(Image, Rectangle, int, int, int, int, GraphicsUnit, ImageAttributes);**

[C++] **public: void DrawImage(Image*, Rectangle, int, int, int, int, GraphicsUnit, ImageAttributes*);**

[JScript] **public function DrawImage(Image, Rectangle, int, int, int, int, GraphicsUnit, ImageAttributes);**

Draws the specified portion of the specified **Image** object at the specified location and with the specified size.

[Visual Basic] **Overloads Public Sub DrawImage(Image, Rectangle, Single, Single, Single, Single, GraphicsUnit, ImageAttributes)**

[C#] **public void DrawImage(Image, Rectangle, float, float, float, float, GraphicsUnit, ImageAttributes);**

[C++] **public: void DrawImage(Image*, Rectangle, float, float, float, float, GraphicsUnit, ImageAttributes*);**

[JScript] **public function DrawImage(Image, Rectangle, float, float, float, float, GraphicsUnit, ImageAttributes);**

Draws the specified portion of the specified **Image** object at the specified location and with the specified size.

[Visual Basic] **Overloads Public Sub DrawImage(Image, Rectangle, Integer, Integer, Integer, Integer, GraphicsUnit, ImageAttributes, Graphics.DrawImageAbort)**

[C#] **public void DrawImage(Image, Rectangle, int, int, int, int, GraphicsUnit, ImageAttributes, Graphics.DrawImageAbort);**

[C++] **public: void DrawImage(Image*, Rectangle, int, int, int, int, GraphicsUnit, ImageAttributes*, Graphics.DrawImageAbort*);**

[JScript] **public function DrawImage(Image, Rectangle, int, int, int, int, GraphicsUnit, ImageAttributes, Graphics.DrawImageAbort);**

Draws the specified portion of the specified **Image** object at the specified location and with the specified size.

[Visual Basic] **Overloads Public Sub DrawImage(Image, Rectangle, Single, Single, Single, Single, GraphicsUnit, ImageAttributes, Graphics.DrawImageAbort)**

[C#] **public void DrawImage(Image, Rectangle, float, float, float, float, GraphicsUnit, ImageAttributes, Graphics.DrawImageAbort);**

[C++] **public: void DrawImage(Image*, Rectangle, float, float, float, float, GraphicsUnit, ImageAttributes*, Graphics.DrawImageAbort*);**

[JScript] **public function DrawImage(Image, Rectangle, float, float, float, float, GraphicsUnit, ImageAttributes, Graphics.DrawImageAbort);**

Draws the specified portion of the specified **Image** object at the specified location and with the specified size.

[Visual Basic] **Overloads Public Sub DrawImage(Image, Rectangle, Integer, Integer, Integer, Integer, GraphicsUnit, ImageAttributes, Graphics.DrawImageAbort, IntPtr)**

[C#] **public void DrawImage(Image, Rectangle, int, int, int, int, GraphicsUnit, ImageAttributes, Graphics.DrawImageAbort, IntPtr);**

[C++] **public: void DrawImage(Image*, Rectangle, int, int, int, int, GraphicsUnit, ImageAttributes*, Graphics.DrawImageAbort*, IntPtr);**

[JScript] **public function DrawImage(Image, Rectangle, int, int, int, int, GraphicsUnit, ImageAttributes, Graphics.DrawImageAbort, IntPtr);**

Draws the specified portion of the specified **Image** object at the specified location and with the specified size.

[Visual Basic] **Overloads Public Sub DrawImage(Image, Rectangle, Single, Single, Single, Single, GraphicsUnit, ImageAttributes, Graphics.DrawImageAbort, IntPtr)**

[C#] **public void DrawImage(Image, Rectangle, float, float, float, float, GraphicsUnit, ImageAttributes, Graphics.DrawImageAbort, IntPtr);**

[C++] **public: void DrawImage(Image*, Rectangle, float, float, float, float, GraphicsUnit, ImageAttributes*, Graphics.DrawImageAbort*, IntPtr);**

[JScript] **public function DrawImage(Image, Rectangle, float, float, float, float, GraphicsUnit, ImageAttributes, Graphics.DrawImageAbort, IntPtr);**

Example

[Visual Basic, C#] The following example is designed for use with Windows Forms, and it requires **PaintEventArgs** *e*, which is a parameter of the **Paint** event handler. The code first defines a callback method for the **DrawImageAbort** delegate; the definition is simplistic and merely tests to see whether the **DrawImage** method calls it with a null *callBackData* parameter. The main body of the example performs the following actions:

- Creates an instance of the **DrawImageAbort** callback method.
- Creates an image from a JPEG file SampImag.jpg in the folder of the example.
- Creates points that define a destination rectangle in which to draw the image.
- Creates a source rectangle to select the portion of the image to draw.
- Sets the graphics drawing unit to pixel.
- Draws the original image to the screen.
- Creates an additional destination rectangle in which to draw an adjusted image.
- Creates and sets the attributes of the adjusted image to have a larger-than-usual gamma value.
- Draws the adjusted image to the screen.

[Visual Basic, C#] For the original, unadjusted destination rectangle, the position locates the image on the screen, and the size of the source rectangle and the size and shape of the destination rectangle determines the scaling of the drawn image.

[Visual Basic, C#] Because this example uses an overload that passes a *callBackData* parameter, the **DrawImageAbort** callback returns **false**, which causes the **DrawImage** method to continue, and the example draws the adjusted image to the screen.

> [Visual Basic, C#] **Note** This example shows how to use one of the overloaded versions of **DrawImage**. For other examples that might be available, see the individual overload topics.

[Visual Basic]
```
Private Function DrawImageCallback(callBackData As IntPtr) As Boolean
' Test for call that passes callBackData parameter.
If callBackData.Equals(IntPtr.Zero) Then
' If no callBackData passed, abort DrawImage method.
Return True
Else
' If callBackData passed, continue DrawImage method.
Return False
End If
End Function
Public Sub DrawImageRect4FloatAttribAbortData(e As PaintEventArgs)
' Create callback method.
Dim imageCallback As New _
Graphics.DrawImageAbort(AddressOf DrawImageCallback)
Dim imageCallbackData As New IntPtr(1)
' Create image.
Dim newImage As Image = Image.FromFile("SampImag.jpg")
' Create rectangle for displaying original image.
Dim destRect1 As New Rectangle(100, 25, 450, 150)
' Create coordinates of rectangle for source image.
Dim x As Single = 50F
Dim y As Single = 50F
Dim width As Single = 150F
Dim height As Single = 150F
Dim units As GraphicsUnit = GraphicsUnit.Pixel
' Draw original image to screen.
e.Graphics.DrawImage(newImage, destRect1, x, y, width, _
height, units)
' Create rectangle for adjusted image.
Dim destRect2 As New Rectangle(100, 175, 450, 150)
' Create image attributes and set large gamma.
Dim imageAttr As New ImageAttributes()
imageAttr.SetGamma(4F)
' Draw adjusted image to screen.
Try
' Draw adjusted image to screen.
e.Graphics.DrawImage(newImage, destRect2, x, y, width, _
height, units, imageAttr, imageCallback, imageCallbackData)
Catch ex As Exception
e.Graphics.DrawString(ex.ToString(), New Font("Arial", 8), _
Brushes.Black, New PointF(0, 0))
End Try
End Sub
```

[C#]
```
// Define DrawImageAbort callback method.
private bool DrawImageCallback(IntPtr callBackData)
{
// Test for call that passes callBackData parameter.
if(callBackData==IntPtr.Zero)
{
// If no callBackData passed, abort DrawImage method.
return true;
}
else
{
// If callBackData passed, continue DrawImage method.
return false;
}
}
public void DrawImageRect4FloatAttribAbortData(PaintEventArgs e)
{
// Create callback method.
Graphics.DrawImageAbort imageCallback
= new Graphics.DrawImageAbort(DrawImageCallback);
IntPtr imageCallbackData = new IntPtr(1);
// Create image.
Image newImage = Image.FromFile("SampImag.jpg");
// Create rectangle for displaying original image.
Rectangle destRect1 = new Rectangle( 100, 25, 450, 150);
// Create coordinates of rectangle for source image.
float x = 50.0F;
float y = 50.0F;
float width = 150.0F;
float height = 150.0F;
GraphicsUnit units = GraphicsUnit.Pixel;
// Draw original image to screen.
e.Graphics.DrawImage(newImage, destRect1, x, y, width, height, units);
// Create rectangle for adjusted image.
Rectangle destRect2 = new Rectangle(100, 175, 450, 150);
// Create image attributes and set large gamma.
ImageAttributes imageAttr = new ImageAttributes();
imageAttr.SetGamma(4.0F);
// Draw adjusted image to screen.
try
{
checked
{
// Draw adjusted image to screen.
e.Graphics.DrawImage(
newImage,
destRect2,
x, y,
width, height,
units,
imageAttr,
```

```
imageCallback,
imageCallbackData);
}
}
catch (Exception ex)
{
e.Graphics.DrawString(
ex.ToString(),
new Font("Arial", 8),
Brushes.Black,
new PointF(0, 0));
}
}
```

Graphics.DrawImage Method (Image, Point)

Draws the specified **Image** object, using its original physical size, at the specified location.

[Visual Basic]
```
Overloads Public Sub DrawImage( _
   ByVal image As Image, _
   ByVal point As Point _
)
```
[C#]
```
public void DrawImage(
   Image image,
   Point point
);
```
[C++]
```
public: void DrawImage(
   Image* image,
   Point point
);
```
[JScript]
```
public function DrawImage(
   image : Image,
   point : Point
);
```

Parameters

image
: **Image** object to draw.

point
: **Point** structure that represents the location of the upper-left corner of the drawn image.

Return Value

This method does not return a value.

Remarks

An **Image** object stores a value for pixel width and a value for horizontal resolution (dots per inch). The physical width, measured in inches, of an image is the pixel width divided by the horizontal resolution. For example, an image with a pixel width of 216 and a horizontal resolution of 72 dots per inch has a physical width of 3 inches. Similar remarks apply to pixel height and physical height.

This method draws an image using its physical size, so the image will have its correct size in inches regardless of the resolution (dots per inch) of the display device. For example, suppose an image has a pixel width of 216 and a horizontal resolution of 72 dots per inch. If you call this method to draw that image on a device that has a resolution of 96 dots per inch, the pixel width of the rendered image will be (216/72)*96 = 288.

Example

[Visual Basic, C#] The following example is designed for use with Windows Forms, and it requires **PaintEventArgs** *e*, which is a parameter of the **Paint** event handler. The code performs the following actions:

- Creates an image from a JPEG file SampImag.jpg in the folder of the example.
- Creates a point at which to draw the upper-left corner of the image.
- Draws the unscaled image to the screen.

[Visual Basic]
```
Public Sub DrawImagePoint(e As PaintEventArgs)
' Create image.
Dim newImage As Image = Image.FromFile("SampImag.jpg")
' Create Point for upper-left corner of image.
Dim ulCorner As New Point(100, 100)
' Draw image to screen.
e.Graphics.DrawImage(newImage, ulCorner)
End Sub
```

[C#]
```
public void DrawImagePoint(PaintEventArgs e)
{
// Create image.
Image newImage = Image.FromFile("SampImag.jpg");
// Create Point for upper-left corner of image.
Point ulCorner = new Point( 100, 100);
// Draw image to screen.
e.Graphics.DrawImage(newImage, ulCorner);
}
```

Requirements

Platforms: Windows 98, Windows NT 4.0, Windows Millennium Edition, Windows 2000, Windows XP Home Edition, Windows XP Professional, Windows Server 2003 family

Graphics.DrawImage Method (Image, Point[])

Draws the specified **Image** object at the specified location and with the specified shape and size.

[Visual Basic]
```
Overloads Public Sub DrawImage( _
   ByVal image As Image, _
   ByVal destPoints() As Point _
)
```
[C#]
```
public void DrawImage(
   Image image,
   Point[] destPoints
);
```
[C++]
```
public: void DrawImage(
   Image* image,
   Point destPoints[]
);
```
[JScript]
```
public function DrawImage(
   image : Image,
   destPoints : Point[]
);
```

Parameters

image

Image object to draw.

destPoints

Array of three **Point** structures that define a parallelogram.

Return Value

This method does not return a value.

Remarks

The *destPoints* parameter specifies three points of a parallelogram. The three **Point** structures represent the upper-left, upper-right, and lower-left corners of the parallelogram. The fourth point is extrapolated from the first three to form a parallelogram.

The image represented by the *image* parameter is scaled and sheared to fit the shape of the parallelogram specified by the *destPoints* parameters.

Example

[Visual Basic, C#] The following example is designed for use with Windows Forms, and it requires **PaintEventArgs** *e*, which is a parameter of the **Paint** event handler. The code performs the following actions:

- Creates an image from a JPEG file SampImag.jpg in the folder of the example.
- Creates points that define a parallelogram in which to draw the image.
- Draws the image to the screen.

[Visual Basic, C#] The position of the parallelogram locates the image on the screen, and the size of the original image and the size and shape of the parallelogram determines the scaling and shearing of the drawn image.

[Visual Basic]

```
Public Sub DrawImagePara(e As PaintEventArgs)
' Create image.
Dim newImage As Image = Image.FromFile("SampImag.jpg")
' Create parallelogram for drawing image.
Dim ulCorner As New Point(100, 100)
Dim urCorner As New Point(550, 100)
Dim llCorner As New Point(150, 250)
Dim destPara As Point() =  {ulCorner, urCorner, llCorner}
' Draw image to screen.
e.Graphics.DrawImage(newImage, destPara)
End Sub
```

[C#]

```
public void DrawImagePara(PaintEventArgs e)
{
// Create image.
Image newImage = Image.FromFile("SampImag.jpg");
// Create parallelogram for drawing image.
Point ulCorner = new Point(100, 100);
Point urCorner = new Point(550, 100);
Point llCorner = new Point(150, 250);
Point[] destPara = {ulCorner, urCorner, llCorner};
// Draw image to screen.
e.Graphics.DrawImage(newImage, destPara);
}
```

Requirements

Platforms: Windows 98, Windows NT 4.0, Windows Millennium Edition, Windows 2000, Windows XP Home Edition, Windows XP Professional, Windows Server 2003 family

Graphics.DrawImage Method (Image, PointF)

Draws the specified **Image** object, using its original physical size, at the specified location.

[Visual Basic]

```
Overloads Public Sub DrawImage( _
   ByVal image As Image, _
   ByVal point As PointF _
)
```

[C#]

```
public void DrawImage(
   Image image,
   PointF point
);
```

[C++]

```
public: void DrawImage(
   Image* image,
   PointF point
);
```

[JScript]

```
public function DrawImage(
   image : Image,
   point : PointF
);
```

Parameters

image

Image object to draw.

point

PointF structure that represents the upper-left corner of the drawn image.

Return Value

This method does not return a value.

Remarks

An **Image** object stores a value for pixel width and a value for horizontal resolution (dots per inch). The physical width, measured in inches, of an image is the pixel width divided by the horizontal resolution. For example, an image with a pixel width of 216 and a horizontal resolution of 72 dots per inch has a physical width of 3 inches. Similar remarks apply to pixel height and physical height.

This method draws an image using its physical size, so the image will have its correct size in inches regardless of the resolution (dots per inch) of the display device. For example, suppose an image has a pixel width of 216 and a horizontal resolution of 72 dots per inch. If you call this method to draw that image on a device that has a resolution of 96 dots per inch, the pixel width of the rendered image will be (216/72)*96 = 288.

Example

[Visual Basic, C#] The following example is designed for use with Windows Forms, and it requires **PaintEventArgs** *e*, which is a parameter of the **Paint** event handler. The code performs the following actions:

- Creates an image from a JPEG file SampImag.jpg in the folder of the example.
- Creates a point at which to draw the upper-left corner of the image.
- Draws the unscaled image to the screen.

[Visual Basic]
```
Public Sub DrawImagePointF(e As PaintEventArgs)
' Create image.
Dim newImage As Image = Image.FromFile("SampImag.jpg")
' Create point for upper-left corner of image.
Dim ulCorner As New PointF(100F, 100F)
' Draw image to screen.
e.Graphics.DrawImage(newImage, ulCorner)
End Sub
```

[C#]
```
public void DrawImagePointF(PaintEventArgs e)
{
// Create image.
Image newImage = Image.FromFile("SampImag.jpg");
// Create point for upper-left corner of image.
PointF ulCorner = new PointF( 100.0F, 100.0F);
// Draw image to screen.
e.Graphics.DrawImage(newImage, ulCorner);
}
```

Requirements

Platforms: Windows 98, Windows NT 4.0, Windows Millennium Edition, Windows 2000, Windows XP Home Edition, Windows XP Professional, Windows Server 2003 family

Graphics.DrawImage Method (Image, PointF[])

Draws the specified **Image** object at the specified location and with the specified shape and size.

[Visual Basic]
```
Overloads Public Sub DrawImage( _
   ByVal image As Image, _
   ByVal destPoints() As PointF _
)
```
[C#]
```
public void DrawImage(
   Image image,
   PointF[] destPoints
);
```
[C++]
```
public: void DrawImage(
   Image* image,
   PointF destPoints[]
);
```
[JScript]
```
public function DrawImage(
   image : Image,
   destPoints : PointF[]
);
```

Parameters

image
  Image object to draw.

destPoints
  Array of three **PointF** structures that define a parallelogram.

Return Value

This method does not return a value.

Remarks

The *destPoints* parameter specifies three points of a parallelogram. The three **PointF** structures represent the upper-left, upper-right, and lower-left corners of the parallelogram. The fourth point is extrapolated from the first three to form a parallelogram.

The image represented by the *image* object is scaled and sheared to fit the shape of the parallelogram specified by the *destPoints* parameter.

Example

[Visual Basic, C#] The following example is designed for use with Windows Forms, and it requires **PaintEventArgs** *e*, which is a parameter of the **Paint** event handler. The code performs the following actions:

- Creates an image from a JPEG file SampImag.jpg in the folder of the example.
- Creates points that define a parallelogram in which to draw the image.
- Draws the image to the screen.

[Visual Basic, C#] The position of the parallelogram locates the image on the screen, and the size of the original image and the size and shape of the parallelogram determines the scaling and shearing of the drawn image.

[Visual Basic]
```
Public Sub DrawImageParaF(e As PaintEventArgs)
' Create image.
Dim newImage As Image = Image.FromFile("SampImag.jpg")
' Create parallelogram for drawing image.
Dim ulCorner As New PointF(100F, 100F)
Dim urCorner As New PointF(550F, 100F)
Dim llCorner As New PointF(150F, 250F)
Dim destPara As PointF() = {ulCorner, urCorner, llCorner}
' Draw image to screen.
e.Graphics.DrawImage(newImage, destPara)
End Sub
```

[C#]
```
public void DrawImageParaF(PaintEventArgs e)
{
// Create image.
Image newImage = Image.FromFile("SampImag.jpg");
// Create parallelogram for drawing image.
PointF ulCorner = new PointF(100.0F, 100.0F);
PointF urCorner = new PointF(550.0F, 100.0F);
PointF llCorner = new PointF(150.0F, 250.0F);
PointF[] destPara = {ulCorner, urCorner, llCorner};
// Draw image to screen.
e.Graphics.DrawImage(newImage, destPara);
}
```

Requirements

Platforms: Windows 98, Windows NT 4.0, Windows Millennium Edition, Windows 2000, Windows XP Home Edition, Windows XP Professional, Windows Server 2003 family

Graphics.DrawImage Method (Image, Rectangle)

Draws the specified **Image** object at the specified location and with the specified size.

[Visual Basic]
```
Overloads Public Sub DrawImage( _
   ByVal image As Image, _
   ByVal rect As Rectangle _
)
```
[C#]
```
public void DrawImage(
   Image image,
   Rectangle rect
);
```

```
[C++]
public: void DrawImage(
   Image* image,
   Rectangle rect
);
[JScript]
public function DrawImage(
   image : Image,
   rect : Rectangle
);
```

Parameters

image

Image object to draw.

rect

Rectangle structure that specifies the location and size of the drawn image.

Return Value

This method does not return a value.

Remarks

The image represented by the *image* object is scaled to the dimensions of the *rect* rectangle.

Example

[Visual Basic, C#] The following example is designed for use with Windows Forms, and it requires **PaintEventArgs** *e*, which is a parameter of the **Paint** event handler. The code performs the following actions:

- Creates an image from a JPEG file SampImag.jpg in the folder of the example.
- Creates a rectangle in which to draw the image.
- Draws the image to the screen.

[Visual Basic, C#] The position of the rectangle locates the image on the screen, and the size of the original image and the size of the rectangle determines the scaling of the drawn image.

```
[Visual Basic]
Public Sub DrawImageRect(e As PaintEventArgs)
' Create image.
Dim newImage As Image = Image.FromFile("SampImag.jpg")
' Create rectangle for displaying image.
Dim destRect As New Rectangle(100, 100, 450, 150)
' Draw image to screen.
e.Graphics.DrawImage(newImage, destRect)
End Sub
```

```
[C#]
public void DrawImageRect(PaintEventArgs e)
{
// Create image.
Image newImage = Image.FromFile("SampImag.jpg");
// Create rectangle for displaying image.
Rectangle destRect = new Rectangle( 100, 100, 450, 150);
// Draw image to screen.
e.Graphics.DrawImage(newImage, destRect);
}
```

Requirements

Platforms: Windows 98, Windows NT 4.0, Windows Millennium Edition, Windows 2000, Windows XP Home Edition, Windows XP Professional, Windows Server 2003 family

Graphics.DrawImage Method (Image, RectangleF)

Draws the specified **Image** object at the specified location and with the specified size.

```
[Visual Basic]
Overloads Public Sub DrawImage( _
   ByVal image As Image, _
   ByVal rect As RectangleF _
)
[C#]
public void DrawImage(
   Image image,
   RectangleF rect
);
[C++]
public: void DrawImage(
   Image* image,
   RectangleF rect
);
[JScript]
public function DrawImage(
   image : Image,
   rect : RectangleF
);
```

Parameters

image

Image object to draw.

rect

RectangleF structure that specifies the location and size of the drawn image.

Return Value

This method does not return a value.

Remarks

The image represented by the *image* object is scaled to the dimensions of the *rect* rectangle.

Example

[Visual Basic, C#] The following example is designed for use with Windows Forms, and it requires **PaintEventArgs** *e*, which is a parameter of the **Paint** event handler. The code performs the following actions:

- Creates an image from a JPEG file SampImag.jpg in the folder of the example.
- Creates a rectangle in which to draw the image.
- Draws the image to the screen.

[Visual Basic, C#] The position of the rectangle locates the image on the screen, and the original size of the image and the size of the rectangle determines the scaling of the drawn image.

```
[Visual Basic]
Public Sub DrawImageRectF(e As PaintEventArgs)
' Create image.
Dim newImage As Image = Image.FromFile("SampImag.jpg")
' Create rectangle for displaying image.
Dim rect As New RectangleF(100F, 100F, 450F, 150F)
' Draw image to screen.
e.Graphics.DrawImage(newImage, rect)
End Sub
```

[C#]
```
public void DrawImageRectF(PaintEventArgs e)
{
// Create image.
Image newImage = Image.FromFile("SampImag.jpg");
// Create rectangle for displaying image.
RectangleF rect = new RectangleF( 100.0F, 100.0F, 450.0F, 150.0F);
// Draw image to screen.
e.Graphics.DrawImage(newImage, rect);
}
```

Requirements

Platforms: Windows 98, Windows NT 4.0, Windows Millennium Edition, Windows 2000, Windows XP Home Edition, Windows XP Professional, Windows Server 2003 family

Graphics.DrawImage Method (Image, Int32, Int32)

Draws the specified image, using its original physical size, at the location specified by a coordinate pair.

[Visual Basic]
```
Overloads Public Sub DrawImage( _
   ByVal image As Image, _
   ByVal x As Integer, _
   ByVal y As Integer _
)
```
[C#]
```
public void DrawImage(
   Image image,
   int x,
   int y
);
```
[C++]
```
public: void DrawImage(
   Image* image,
   int x,
   int y
);
```
[JScript]
```
public function DrawImage(
   image : Image,
   x : int,
   y : int
);
```

Parameters

image
    Image object to draw.

x
    x-coordinate of the upper-left corner of the drawn image.

y
    y-coordinate of the upper-left corner of the drawn image.

Return Value

This method does not return a value.

Remarks

An **Image** object stores a value for pixel width and a value for horizontal resolution (dots per inch). The physical width, measured in inches, of an image is the pixel width divided by the horizontal resolution. For example, an image with a pixel width of 216 and a horizontal resolution of 72 dots per inch has a physical width of 3 inches. Similar remarks apply to pixel height and physical height.

The **DrawImage** method draws an image using its physical size, so the image will have its correct size in inches regardless of the resolution (dots per inch) of the display device. For example, suppose an image has a pixel width of 216 and a horizontal resolution of 72 dots per inch. If you call **DrawImage** to draw that image on a device that has a resolution of 96 dots per inch, the pixel width of the rendered image will be (216/72)*96 = 288.

Example

[Visual Basic, C#] The following example is designed for use with Windows Forms, and it requires **PaintEventArgs** *e*, which is a parameter of the **Paint** event handler. The code performs the following actions:

- Creates an image from a JPEG file SampImag.jpg in the folder of the example SampImag.jpg in the folder of the example.
- Creates the coordinates of a point at which to draw the upper-left corner of the image.
- Draws the unscaled image.

[Visual Basic]
```
Public Sub DrawImage2Int(e As PaintEventArgs)
' Create image.
Dim newImage As Image = Image.FromFile("SampImag.jpg")
' Create coordinates for upper-left corner of image.
Dim x As Integer = 100
Dim y As Integer = 100
' Draw image to screen.
e.Graphics.DrawImage(newImage, x, y)
End Sub
```

[C#]
```
public void DrawImage2Int(PaintEventArgs e)
{
   // Create image.
   Image newImage = Image.FromFile("SampImag.jpg");

   // Create coordinates for upper-left corner of image.
   int x = 100;
   int y = 100;

   // Draw image to screen.
   e.Graphics.DrawImage(newImage, x, y);
}
```

Requirements

Platforms: Windows 98, Windows NT 4.0, Windows Millennium Edition, Windows 2000, Windows XP Home Edition, Windows XP Professional, Windows Server 2003 family, .NET Compact Framework - Windows CE .NET

Graphics.DrawImage Method (Image, Single, Single)

Draws the specified **Image** object, using its original physical size, at the specified location.

[Visual Basic]
```
Overloads Public Sub DrawImage( _
   ByVal image As Image, _
   ByVal x As Single, _
   ByVal y As Single _
)
```
[C#]
```
public void DrawImage(
   Image image,
   float x,
   float y
);
```

[C++]
```
public: void DrawImage(
   Image* image,
   float x,
   float y
);
```
[JScript]
```
public function DrawImage(
   image : Image,
   x : float,
   y : float
);
```

Parameters

image
: **Image** object to draw.

x
: x-coordinate of the upper-left corner of the drawn image.

y
: y-coordinate of the upper-left corner of the drawn image.

Return Value

This method does not return a value.

Remarks

An **Image** object stores a value for pixel width and a value for horizontal resolution (dots per inch). The physical width, measured in inches, of an image is the pixel width divided by the horizontal resolution. For example, an image with a pixel width of 216 and a horizontal resolution of 72 dots per inch has a physical width of 3 inches. Similar remarks apply to pixel height and physical height.

This method draws an image using its physical size, so the image will have its correct size in inches regardless of the resolution (dots per inch) of the display device. For example, suppose an image has a pixel width of 216 and a horizontal resolution of 72 dots per inch. If you call this method to draw that image on a device that has a resolution of 96 dots per inch, the pixel width of the rendered image will be (216/72)*96 = 288.

Example

[Visual Basic, C#] The following example is designed for use with Windows Forms, and it requires **PaintEventArgs** *e*, which is a parameter of the **Paint** event handler. The code performs the following actions:

- Creates an image from a JPEG file SampImag.jpg in the folder of the example.
- Creates the coordinates of a point at which to draw the upper-left corner of the image.
- Draws the unscaled image to the screen.

[Visual Basic]
```
Public Sub DrawImage2Float(e As PaintEventArgs)
' Create image.
Dim newImage As Image = Image.FromFile("SampImag.jpg")
' Create coordinates for upper-left corner of image.
Dim x As Single = 100F
Dim y As Single = 100F
' Draw image to screen.
e.Graphics.DrawImage(newImage, x, y)
End Sub
```

[C#]
```
public void DrawImage2Float(PaintEventArgs e)
{
// Create image.
Image newImage = Image.FromFile("SampImag.jpg");
// Create coordinates for upper-left corner of image.
float x = 100.0F;
float y = 100.0F;
// Draw image to screen.
e.Graphics.DrawImage(newImage, x, y);
}
```

Requirements

Platforms: Windows 98, Windows NT 4.0, Windows Millennium Edition, Windows 2000, Windows XP Home Edition, Windows XP Professional, Windows Server 2003 family

Graphics.DrawImage Method (Image, Point[], Rectangle, GraphicsUnit)

Draws the specified portion of the specified **Image** object at the specified location and with the specified size.

[Visual Basic]
```
Overloads Public Sub DrawImage( _
   ByVal image As Image, _
   ByVal destPoints() As Point, _
   ByVal srcRect As Rectangle, _
   ByVal srcUnit As GraphicsUnit _
)
```
[C#]
```
public void DrawImage(
   Image image,
   Point[] destPoints,
   Rectangle srcRect,
   GraphicsUnit srcUnit
);
```
[C++]
```
public: void DrawImage(
   Image* image,
   Point destPoints[],
   Rectangle srcRect,
   GraphicsUnit srcUnit
);
```
[JScript]
```
public function DrawImage(
   image : Image,
   destPoints : Point[],
   srcRect : Rectangle,
   srcUnit : GraphicsUnit
);
```

Parameters

image
: **Image** object to draw.

destPoints
: Array of three **Point** structures that define a parallelogram.

srcRect
: **Rectangle** structure that specifies the portion of the *image* object to draw.

srcUnit
: Member of the **GraphicsUnit** enumeration that specifies the units of measure used by the *srcRect* parameter.

Return Value

This method does not return a value.

Remarks

The *destPoints* parameter specifies three points of a parallelogram. The three **Point** structures represent the upper-left, upper-right, and lower-left corners of the parallelogram. The fourth point is extrapolated from the first three to form a parallelogram.

The *srcRect* parameter specifies a rectangular portion of the *image* object to draw. This portion is scaled and sheared to fit inside the parallelogram specified by the *destPoints* parameter.

Example

[Visual Basic, C#] The following example is designed for use with Windows Forms, and it requires **PaintEventArgs** *e*, which is a parameter of the **Paint** event handler. The code performs the following actions:

- Creates an image from a JPEG file SampImag.jpg in the folder of the example.
- Creates points that define a parallelogram in which to draw the image.
- Creates a rectangle to select the portion of the image to draw.
- Sets the graphics drawing unit to pixel.
- Draws the image to the screen.

[Visual Basic, C#] The position of the parallelogram locates the image on the screen, and the size of the rectangle and the size and shape of the parallelogram determines the scaling and shearing of the drawn image.

[Visual Basic]
```
Public Sub DrawImageParaRect(e As PaintEventArgs)
' Create image.
Dim newImage As Image = Image.FromFile("SampImag.jpg")
' Create parallelogram for drawing image.
Dim ulCorner As New Point(100, 100)
Dim urCorner As New Point(325, 100)
Dim llCorner As New Point(150, 250)
Dim destPara As Point() =  {ulCorner, urCorner, llCorner}
' Create rectangle for source image.
Dim srcRect As New Rectangle(50, 50, 150, 150)
Dim units As GraphicsUnit = GraphicsUnit.Pixel
' Draw image to screen.
e.Graphics.DrawImage(newImage, destPara, srcRect, units)
End Sub
```

[C#]
```
public void DrawImageParaRect(PaintEventArgs e)
{
// Create image.
Image newImage = Image.FromFile("SampImag.jpg");
// Create parallelogram for drawing image.
Point ulCorner = new Point(100, 100);
Point urCorner = new Point(325, 100);
Point llCorner = new Point(150, 250);
Point[] destPara = {ulCorner, urCorner, llCorner};
// Create rectangle for source image.
Rectangle srcRect = new Rectangle( 50, 50, 150, 150);
GraphicsUnit units = GraphicsUnit.Pixel;
// Draw image to screen.
e.Graphics.DrawImage(newImage, destPara, srcRect, units);
}
```

Requirements

Platforms: Windows 98, Windows NT 4.0, Windows Millennium Edition, Windows 2000, Windows XP Home Edition, Windows XP Professional, Windows Server 2003 family

Graphics.DrawImage Method (Image, PointF[], RectangleF, GraphicsUnit)

Draws the specified portion of the specified **Image** object at the specified location and with the specified size.

[Visual Basic]
```
Overloads Public Sub DrawImage( _
   ByVal image As Image, _
   ByVal destPoints() As PointF, _
   ByVal srcRect As RectangleF, _
   ByVal srcUnit As GraphicsUnit _
)
```
[C#]
```
public void DrawImage(
   Image image,
   PointF[] destPoints,
   RectangleF srcRect,
   GraphicsUnit srcUnit
);
```
[C++]
```
public: void DrawImage(
   Image* image,
   PointF destPoints[],
   RectangleF srcRect,
   GraphicsUnit srcUnit
);
```
[JScript]
```
public function DrawImage(
   image : Image,
   destPoints : PointF[],
   srcRect : RectangleF,
   srcUnit : GraphicsUnit
);
```

Parameters

image
: **Image** object to draw.

destPoints
: Array of three **PointF** structures that define a parallelogram.

srcRect
: **Rectangle** structure that specifies the portion of the *image* object to draw.

srcUnit
: Member of the **GraphicsUnit** enumeration that specifies the units of measure used by the *srcRect* parameter.

Return Value

This method does not return a value.

Remarks

The *destPoints* parameter specifies three points of a parallelogram. The three **PointF** structures represent the upper-left, upper-right, and lower-left corners of the parallelogram. The fourth point is extrapolated from the first three to form a parallelogram.

The *srcRect* parameter specifies a rectangular portion of the *image* object to draw. This portion is scaled and sheared to fit inside the parallelogram specified by the *destPoints* parameter.

Example

[Visual Basic, C#] The following example is designed for use with Windows Forms, and it requires **PaintEventArgs** *e*, which is a parameter of the **Paint** event handler. The code performs the following actions:

- Creates an image from a JPEG file SampImag.jpg in the folder of the example.
- Creates points that define a destination parallelogram in which to draw the image.
- Creates a source rectangle from which to extract a portion of the image.
- Sets the unit of measure of the source rectangle to pixels.
- Draws the image to the screen.

[Visual Basic, C#] The position of the destination parallelogram locates the image on the screen, the size of the source rectangle and the size and shape of the destination parallelogram determines the scaling and shearing of the drawn image, and the size of the rectangle determines what portion of the original image is drawn to the screen.

[Visual Basic]
```
Public Sub DrawImageParaFRectF(e As PaintEventArgs)
' Create image.
Dim newImage As Image = Image.FromFile("SampImag.jpg")
' Create parallelogram for drawing image.
Dim ulCorner As New PointF(100F, 100F)
Dim urCorner As New PointF(550F, 100F)
Dim llCorner As New PointF(150F, 250F)
Dim destPara As PointF() = {ulCorner, urCorner, llCorner}
' Create rectangle for source image.
Dim srcRect As New RectangleF(50F, 50F, 150F, 150F)
Dim units As GraphicsUnit = GraphicsUnit.Pixel
' Draw image to screen.
e.Graphics.DrawImage(newImage, destPara, srcRect, units)
End Sub
```

[C#]
```
public void DrawImageParaFRectF(PaintEventArgs e)
{
// Create image.
Image newImage = Image.FromFile("SampImag.jpg");
// Create parallelogram for drawing image.
PointF ulCorner = new PointF(100.0F, 100.0F);
PointF urCorner = new PointF(550.0F, 100.0F);
PointF llCorner = new PointF(150.0F, 250.0F);
PointF[] destPara = {ulCorner, urCorner, llCorner};
// Create rectangle for source image.
RectangleF srcRect = new RectangleF( 50.0F, 50.0F, 150.0F, 150.0F);
GraphicsUnit units = GraphicsUnit.Pixel;
// Draw image to screen.
e.Graphics.DrawImage(newImage, destPara, srcRect, units);
}
```

Requirements

Platforms: Windows 98, Windows NT 4.0, Windows Millennium Edition, Windows 2000, Windows XP Home Edition, Windows XP Professional, Windows Server 2003 family

Graphics.DrawImage Method (Image, Rectangle, Rectangle, GraphicsUnit)

Draws the specified portion of the specified **Image** object at the specified location and with the specified size.

[Visual Basic]
```
Overloads Public Sub DrawImage( _
   ByVal image As Image, _
   ByVal destRect As Rectangle, _
   ByVal srcRect As Rectangle, _
   ByVal srcUnit As GraphicsUnit _
)
```
[C#]
```
public void DrawImage(
   Image image,
   Rectangle destRect,
   Rectangle srcRect,
   GraphicsUnit srcUnit
);
```
[C++]
```
public: void DrawImage(
   Image* image,
   Rectangle destRect,
   Rectangle srcRect,
   GraphicsUnit srcUnit
);
```
[JScript]
```
public function DrawImage(
   image : Image,
   destRect : Rectangle,
   srcRect : Rectangle,
   srcUnit : GraphicsUnit
);
```

Parameters

image

Image object to draw.

destRect

Rectangle structure that specifies the location and size of the drawn image. The image is scaled to fit the rectangle.

srcRect

Rectangle structure that specifies the portion of the *image* object to draw.

srcUnit

Member of the **GraphicsUnit** enumeration that specifies the units of measure used by the *srcRect* parameter.

Return Value

This method does not return a value.

Remarks

The *srcRect* parameter specifies a rectangular portion of the *image* object to draw. This portion is scaled to fit inside the rectangle specified by the *destRect* parameter.

Example

[Visual Basic, C#] The following example is designed for use with Windows Forms, and it requires **PaintEventArgs** *e*, which is a parameter of the **Paint** event handler. The code performs the following actions:

- Creates an image from a JPEG file SampImag.jpg in the folder of the example.
- Creates a destination rectangle in which to draw the image.

- Creates a source rectangle from which to extract a portion of the image.
- Sets the unit of measure of the source rectangle to pixels.
- Draws the image to the screen.

[Visual Basic, C#] The position of the destination rectangle locates the image on the screen, the sizes of the source and destination rectangles determine the scaling of the drawn image, and the size of the source rectangle determines what portion of the original image is drawn to the screen.

[Visual Basic]
```
Public Sub DrawImageRectRect(e As PaintEventArgs)
' Create image.
Dim newImage As Image = Image.FromFile("SampImag.jpg")
' Create rectangle for displaying image.
Dim destRect As New Rectangle(100, 100, 450, 150)
' Create rectangle for source image.
Dim srcRect As New Rectangle(50, 50, 150, 150)
Dim units As GraphicsUnit = GraphicsUnit.Pixel
' Draw image to screen.
e.Graphics.DrawImage(newImage, destRect, srcRect, units)
End Sub
```

[C#]
```
public void DrawImageRectRect(PaintEventArgs e)
{
// Create image.
Image newImage = Image.FromFile("SampImag.jpg");
// Create rectangle for displaying image.
Rectangle destRect = new Rectangle( 100, 100, 450, 150);
// Create rectangle for source image.
Rectangle srcRect = new Rectangle( 50, 50, 150, 150);
GraphicsUnit units = GraphicsUnit.Pixel;
// Draw image to screen.
e.Graphics.DrawImage(newImage, destRect, srcRect, units);
}
```

Requirements

Platforms: Windows 98, Windows NT 4.0, Windows Millennium Edition, Windows 2000, Windows XP Home Edition, Windows XP Professional, Windows Server 2003 family, .NET Compact Framework - Windows CE .NET

Graphics.DrawImage Method (Image, RectangleF, RectangleF, GraphicsUnit)

Draws the specified portion of the specified **Image** object at the specified location and with the specified size.

[Visual Basic]
```
Overloads Public Sub DrawImage( _
   ByVal image As Image, _
   ByVal destRect As RectangleF, _
   ByVal srcRect As RectangleF, _
   ByVal srcUnit As GraphicsUnit _
)
```
[C#]
```
public void DrawImage(
   Image image,
   RectangleF destRect,
   RectangleF srcRect,
   GraphicsUnit srcUnit
);
```
[C++]
```
public: void DrawImage(
   Image* image,
   RectangleF destRect,
   RectangleF srcRect,
   GraphicsUnit srcUnit
);
```
[JScript]
```
public function DrawImage(
   image : Image,
   destRect : RectangleF,
   srcRect : RectangleF,
   srcUnit : GraphicsUnit
);
```

Parameters

image
: **Image** object to draw.

destRect
: **Rectangle** structure that specifies the location and size of the drawn image. The image is scaled to fit the rectangle.

srcRect
: **Rectangle** structure that specifies the portion of the *image* object to draw.

srcUnit
: Member of the **GraphicsUnit** enumeration that specifies the units of measure used by the *srcRect* parameter.

Return Value

This method does not return a value.

Remarks

The *srcRect* parameter specifies a rectangular portion of the *image* object to draw. This portion is scaled to fit inside the rectangle specified by the *destRect* parameter.

Example

[Visual Basic, C#] The following example is designed for use with Windows Forms, and it requires **PaintEventArgs** *e*, which is a parameter of the **Paint** event handler. The code performs the following actions:

- Creates an image from a JPEG file SampImag.jpg in the folder of the example.
- Creates a destination rectangle in which to draw the image.
- Creates a source rectangle from which to extract a portion of the image.
- Sets the unit of measure of the source rectangle to pixels.
- Draws the image to the screen.

[Visual Basic, C#] The position of the destination rectangle locates the image on the screen, the sizes of the source and destination rectangles determine the scaling of the drawn image, and the size of the source rectangle determines what portion of the original image is drawn to the screen.

[Visual Basic]
```
Public Sub DrawImageRectFRectF(e As PaintEventArgs)
' Create image.
Dim newImage As Image = Image.FromFile("SampImag.jpg")
' Create rectangle for displaying image.
Dim destRect As New RectangleF(100F, 100F, 450F, 150F)
' Create rectangle for source image.
Dim srcRect As New RectangleF(50F, 50F, 150F, 150F)
Dim units As GraphicsUnit = GraphicsUnit.Pixel
```

```
' Draw image to screen.
e.Graphics.DrawImage(newImage, destRect, srcRect, units)
End Sub
```

[C#]

```
public void DrawImageRectFRectF(PaintEventArgs e)
{
// Create image.
Image newImage = Image.FromFile("SampImag.jpg");
// Create rectangle for displaying image.
RectangleF destRect = new RectangleF( 100.0F, 100.0F, 450.0F, 150.0F);
// Create rectangle for source image.
RectangleF srcRect = new RectangleF( 50.0F, 50.0F, 150.0F, 150.0F);
GraphicsUnit units = GraphicsUnit.Pixel;
// Draw image to screen.
e.Graphics.DrawImage(newImage, destRect, srcRect, units);
}
```

Requirements

Platforms: Windows 98, Windows NT 4.0, Windows Millennium Edition, Windows 2000, Windows XP Home Edition, Windows XP Professional, Windows Server 2003 family

Graphics.DrawImage Method (Image, Int32, Int32, Int32, Int32)

Draws the specified **Image** object at the specified location and with the specified size.

[Visual Basic]

```
Overloads Public Sub DrawImage( _
   ByVal image As Image, _
   ByVal x As Integer, _
   ByVal y As Integer, _
   ByVal width As Integer, _
   ByVal height As Integer _
)
```

[C#]

```
public void DrawImage(
   Image image,
   int x,
   int y,
   int width,
   int height
);
```

[C++]

```
public: void DrawImage(
   Image* image,
   int x,
   int y,
   int width,
   int height
);
```

[JScript]

```
public function DrawImage(
   image : Image,
   x : int,
   y : int,
   width : int,
   height : int
);
```

Parameters

image

Image object to draw.

x

x-coordinate of the upper-left corner of the drawn image.

y

y-coordinate of the upper-left corner of the drawn image.

width

Width of the drawn image.

height

Height of the drawn image.

Return Value

This method does not return a value.

Remarks

The rectangle defined by the *x*, *y*, *width*, and *height* parameters determines the position and size of the drawn image.

Example

[Visual Basic, C#] The following example is designed for use with Windows Forms, and it requires **PaintEventArgs** *e*, which is a parameter of the **Paint** event handler. The code performs the following actions:

- Creates an image from a JPEG file SampImag.jpg in the folder of the example.
- Creates the position and size of a rectangle in which to draw the image.
- Draws the image to the screen.

[Visual Basic, C#] The position of the rectangle locates the image on the screen, and the size of the original image and the size of the rectangle determines the scaling of the drawn image.

[Visual Basic]

```
Public Sub DrawImage4Int(e As PaintEventArgs)
' Create image.
Dim newImage As Image = Image.FromFile("SampImag.jpg")
' Create coordinates for upper-left corner
' of image and for size of image.
Dim x As Integer = 100
Dim y As Integer = 100
Dim width As Integer = 450
Dim height As Integer = 150
' Draw image to screen.
e.Graphics.DrawImage(newImage, x, y, width, height)
End Sub
```

[C#]

```
public void DrawImage4Int(PaintEventArgs e)
{
// Create image.
Image newImage = Image.FromFile("SampImag.jpg");
// Create coordinates for upper-left corner.
// of image and for size of image.
int x = 100;
int y = 100;
int width = 450;
int height = 150;
// Draw image to screen.
e.Graphics.DrawImage(newImage, x, y, width, height);
}
```

Requirements

Platforms: Windows 98, Windows NT 4.0, Windows Millennium Edition, Windows 2000, Windows XP Home Edition, Windows XP Professional, Windows Server 2003 family

Graphics.DrawImage Method (Image, Int32, Int32, Rectangle, GraphicsUnit)

Draws a portion of an image at a specified location.

[Visual Basic]
```
Overloads Public Sub DrawImage( _
   ByVal image As Image, _
   ByVal x As Integer, _
   ByVal y As Integer, _
   ByVal srcRect As Rectangle, _
   ByVal srcUnit As GraphicsUnit _
)
```
[C#]
```
public void DrawImage(
   Image image,
   int x,
   int y,
   Rectangle srcRect,
   GraphicsUnit srcUnit
);
```
[C++]
```
public: void DrawImage(
   Image* image,
   int x,
   int y,
   Rectangle srcRect,
   GraphicsUnit srcUnit
);
```
[JScript]
```
public function DrawImage(
   image : Image,
   x : int,
   y : int,
   srcRect : Rectangle,
   srcUnit : GraphicsUnit
);
```

Parameters

image
: **Image** object to draw.

x
: x-coordinate of the upper-left corner of the drawn image.

y
: y-coordinate of the upper-left corner of the drawn image.

srcRect
: **Rectangle** structure that specifies the portion of the *image* object to draw.

srcUnit
: Member of the **GraphicsUnit** enumeration that specifies the units of measure used by the *srcRect* parameter.

Return Value

This method does not return a value.

Remarks

An **Image** object stores a value for pixel width and a value for horizontal resolution (dots per inch). The physical width, measured in inches, of an image is the pixel width divided by the horizontal resolution. For example, an image with a pixel width of 360 and a horizontal resolution of 72 dots per inch has a physical width of 5 inches. Similar remarks apply to pixel height and physical height.

This method draws a portion of an image using its physical size, so the image portion will have its correct size in inches regardless of the resolution (dots per inch) of the display device. For example, suppose an image portion has a pixel width of 216 and a horizontal resolution of 72 dots per inch. If you call this method to draw that image portion on a device that has a resolution of 96 dots per inch, the pixel width of the rendered image portion will be (216/72)*96 = 288.

Example

[Visual Basic, C#] The following example is designed for use with Windows Forms, and it requires **PaintEventArgs** *e*, which is a parameter of the **Paint** event handler. The code performs the following actions:

[Visual Basic, C#] creates an image from a JPEG file SampImag.jpg in the folder of the example.

- Creates the coordinates at which to draw the upper-left corner of the image.
- Creates a source rectangle from which to extract a portion of the image.
- Sets the unit of measure of the source rectangle to pixels.
- Draws the image to the screen.

[Visual Basic, C#] The size of the source rectangle determines what portion of the unscaled original image is drawn to the screen.

[Visual Basic]
```
Public Sub DrawImage2IntRect(e As PaintEventArgs)
' Create image.
Dim newImage As Image = Image.FromFile("SampImag.jpg")
' Create coordinates for upper-left corner of image.
Dim x As Integer = 100
Dim y As Integer = 100
' Create rectangle for source image.
Dim srcRect As New Rectangle(50, 50, 150, 150)
Dim units As GraphicsUnit = GraphicsUnit.Pixel
' Draw image to screen.
e.Graphics.DrawImage(newImage, x, y, srcRect, units)
End Sub
```

[C#]
```
public void DrawImage2IntRect(PaintEventArgs e)
{
// Create image.
Image newImage = Image.FromFile("SampImag.jpg");
// Create coordinates for upper-left corner of image.
int x = 100;
int y = 100;
// Create rectangle for source image.
Rectangle srcRect = new Rectangle( 50, 50, 150, 150);
GraphicsUnit units = GraphicsUnit.Pixel;
// Draw image to screen.
e.Graphics.DrawImage(newImage, x, y, srcRect, units);
}
```

Requirements

Platforms: Windows 98, Windows NT 4.0, Windows Millennium Edition, Windows 2000, Windows XP Home Edition, Windows XP Professional, Windows Server 2003 family, .NET Compact Framework - Windows CE .NET

Graphics.DrawImage Method (Image, Point[], Rectangle, GraphicsUnit, ImageAttributes)

Draws the specified portion of the specified **Image** object at the specified location.

[Visual Basic]
```
Overloads Public Sub DrawImage( _
   ByVal image As Image, _
   ByVal destPoints() As Point, _
   ByVal srcRect As Rectangle, _
   ByVal srcUnit As GraphicsUnit, _
   ByVal imageAttr As ImageAttributes _
)
```
[C#]
```
public void DrawImage(
   Image image,
   Point[] destPoints,
   Rectangle srcRect,
   GraphicsUnit srcUnit,
   ImageAttributes imageAttr
);
```
[C++]
```
public: void DrawImage(
   Image* image,
   Point destPoints[],
   Rectangle srcRect,
   GraphicsUnit srcUnit,
   ImageAttributes* imageAttr
);
```
[JScript]
```
public function DrawImage(
   image : Image,
   destPoints : Point[],
   srcRect : Rectangle,
   srcUnit : GraphicsUnit,
   imageAttr : ImageAttributes
);
```

Parameters

image
  Image object to draw.

destPoints
  Array of three **Point** structures that define a parallelogram.

srcRect
  Rectangle structure that specifies the portion of the *image* object to draw.

srcUnit
  Member of the **GraphicsUnit** enumeration that specifies the units of measure used by the *srcRect* parameter.

imageAttr
  ImageAttributes object that specifies recoloring and gamma information for the *image* object.

Return Value

This method does not return a value.

Remarks

The *destPoints* parameter specifies three points of a parallelogram. The three **Point** structures represent the upper-left, upper-right, and lower-left corners of the parallelogram. The fourth point is extrapolated from the first three to form a parallelogram.

The *srcRect* parameter specifies a rectangular portion of the *image* object to draw. This portion is scaled and sheared to fit inside the parallelogram specified by the *destPoints* parameter.

Example

[Visual Basic, C#] The following example is designed for use with Windows Forms, and it requires **PaintEventArgs** *e*, which is a parameter of the **Paint** event handler. The code performs the following actions:

- Creates an image from a JPEG file SampImag.jpg in the folder of the example.
- Creates points that define a parallelogram in which to draw the image.
- Creates a rectangle to select the portion of the image to draw.
- Sets the graphics drawing unit to pixel.
- Draws the original image to the screen.
- Creates an additional parallelogram in which to draw an adjusted image.
- Creates and sets the attributes of the adjusted image to have a larger-than-usual gamma value.
- Draws the adjusted image to the screen.

[Visual Basic, C#] For the original, unadjusted parallelogram, the position locates the image on the screen, and the size of the rectangle and the size and shape of the parallelogram determines the scaling and shearing of the drawn image.

[Visual Basic]
```
Public Sub DrawImageParaRectAttrib(e As PaintEventArgs)
' Create image.
Dim newImage As Image = Image.FromFile("SampImag.jpg")
' Create parallelogram for drawing image.
Dim ulCorner1 As New Point(100, 100)
Dim urCorner1 As New Point(325, 100)
Dim llCorner1 As New Point(150, 250)
Dim destPara1 As Point() =  {ulCorner1, urCorner1, llCorner1}
' Create rectangle for source image.
Dim srcRect As New Rectangle(50, 50, 150, 150)
Dim units As GraphicsUnit = GraphicsUnit.Pixel
' Draw original image to screen.
e.Graphics.DrawImage(newImage, destPara1, srcRect, units)
' Create parallelogram for drawing adjusted image.
Dim ulCorner2 As New Point(325, 100)
Dim urCorner2 As New Point(550, 100)
Dim llCorner2 As New Point(375, 250)
Dim destPara2 As Point() =  {ulCorner2, urCorner2, llCorner2}
' Create image attributes and set large gamma.
Dim imageAttr As New ImageAttributes()
imageAttr.SetGamma(4F)
' Draw adjusted image to screen.
e.Graphics.DrawImage(newImage, destPara2, srcRect, units, _
imageAttr)
End Sub
```

[C#]
```
public void DrawImageParaRectAttrib(PaintEventArgs e)
{
// Create image.
Image newImage = Image.FromFile("SampImag.jpg");
// Create parallelogram for drawing image.
Point ulCorner1 = new Point(100, 100);
Point urCorner1 = new Point(325, 100);
Point llCorner1 = new Point(150, 250);
Point[] destPara1 = {ulCorner1, urCorner1, llCorner1};
// Create rectangle for source image.
Rectangle srcRect = new Rectangle( 50, 50, 150, 150);
GraphicsUnit units = GraphicsUnit.Pixel;
// Draw original image to screen.
e.Graphics.DrawImage(newImage, destPara1, srcRect, units);
```

```
// Create parallelogram for drawing adjusted image.
Point ulCorner2 = new Point(325, 100);
Point urCorner2 = new Point(550, 100);
Point llCorner2 = new Point(375, 250);
Point[] destPara2 = {ulCorner2, urCorner2, llCorner2};
// Create image attributes and set large gamma.
ImageAttributes imageAttr = new ImageAttributes();
imageAttr.SetGamma(4.0F);
// Draw adjusted image to screen.
e.Graphics.DrawImage(newImage, destPara2, srcRect, units, imageAttr);
}
```

Requirements

Platforms: Windows 98, Windows NT 4.0, Windows Millennium Edition, Windows 2000, Windows XP Home Edition, Windows XP Professional, Windows Server 2003 family

Graphics.DrawImage Method (Image, PointF[], RectangleF, GraphicsUnit, ImageAttributes)

Draws the specified portion of the specified **Image** object at the specified location and with the specified size.

[Visual Basic]

```
Overloads Public Sub DrawImage( _
   ByVal image As Image, _
   ByVal destPoints() As PointF, _
   ByVal srcRect As RectangleF, _
   ByVal srcUnit As GraphicsUnit, _
   ByVal imageAttr As ImageAttributes _
)
```

[C#]

```
public void DrawImage(
   Image image,
   PointF[] destPoints,
   RectangleF srcRect,
   GraphicsUnit srcUnit,
   ImageAttributes imageAttr
);
```

[C++]

```
public: void DrawImage(
   Image* image,
   PointF destPoints[],
   RectangleF srcRect,
   GraphicsUnit srcUnit,
   ImageAttributes* imageAttr
);
```

[JScript]

```
public function DrawImage(
   image : Image,
   destPoints : PointF[],
   srcRect : RectangleF,
   srcUnit : GraphicsUnit,
   imageAttr : ImageAttributes
);
```

Parameters

image

Image object to draw.

destPoints

Array of three **Point** structures that define a parallelogram.

srcRect

RectangleF structure that specifies the portion of the *image* object to draw.

srcUnit

Member of the **GraphicsUnit** enumeration that specifies the units of measure used by the *srcRect* parameter.

imageAttr

ImageAttributes object that specifies recoloring and gamma information for the *image* object.

Return Value

This method does not return a value.

Remarks

The *destPoints* parameter specifies three points of a parallelogram. The three **Point** structures represent the upper-left, upper-right, and lower-left corners of the parallelogram. The fourth point is extrapolated from the first three to form a parallelogram.

The *srcRect* parameter specifies a rectangular portion of the *image* object to draw. This portion is scaled and sheared to fit inside the parallelogram specified by the *destPoints* parameter.

Example

[Visual Basic, C#] The following example is designed for use with Windows Forms, and it requires **PaintEventArgs** *e*, which is a parameter of the **Paint** event handler. The code performs the following actions:

- Creates an image from a JPEG file SampImag.jpg in the folder of the example.
- Creates points that define a destination parallelogram in which to draw the image.
- Creates a source rectangle from which to extract a portion of the image.
- Sets the unit of measure of the source rectangle to pixels.
- Draws the original image to the screen.
- Creates an additional parallelogram in which to draw an adjusted image.
- Creates and sets the attributes of the adjusted image to have a larger-than-usual gamma value.
- Draws the adjusted image to the screen.

[Visual Basic, C#] For the original, unadjusted destination parallelogram, the position locates the image on the screen, the size of the source rectangle and the size and shape of the destination parallelogram determines the scaling and shearing of the drawn image, and the size of the rectangle determines what portion of the original image is drawn to the screen.

[Visual Basic]

```
Public Sub DrawImageParaFRectFAttrib(e As PaintEventArgs)
' Create image.
Dim newImage As Image = Image.FromFile("SampImag.jpg")
' Create parallelogram for drawing original image.
Dim ulCorner1 As New PointF(100F, 100F)
Dim urCorner1 As New PointF(325F, 100F)
Dim llCorner1 As New PointF(150F, 250F)
Dim destPara1 As PointF() = {ulCorner1, urCorner1, llCorner1}
' Create rectangle for source image.
Dim srcRect As New RectangleF(50F, 50F, 150F, 150F)
Dim units As GraphicsUnit = GraphicsUnit.Pixel
' Create parallelogram for drawing adjusted image.
Dim ulCorner2 As New PointF(325F, 100F)
Dim urCorner2 As New PointF(550F, 100F)
Dim llCorner2 As New PointF(375F, 250F)
Dim destPara2 As PointF() = {ulCorner2, urCorner2, llCorner2}
' Draw original image to screen.
e.Graphics.DrawImage(newImage, destPara1, srcRect, units)
' Create image attributes and set large gamma.
Dim imageAttr As New ImageAttributes()
```

```
imageAttr.SetGamma(4F)
' Draw adjusted image to screen.
e.Graphics.DrawImage(newImage, destPara2, srcRect, units, _
imageAttr)
End Sub
```

[C#]
```
public void DrawImageParaFRectFAttrib(PaintEventArgs e)
{
// Create image.
Image newImage = Image.FromFile("SampImag.jpg");
// Create parallelogram for drawing original image.
PointF ulCorner1 = new PointF(100.0F, 100.0F);
PointF urCorner1 = new PointF(325.0F, 100.0F);
PointF llCorner1 = new PointF(150.0F, 250.0F);
PointF[] destPara1 = {ulCorner1, urCorner1, llCorner1};
// Create rectangle for source image.
RectangleF srcRect = new RectangleF( 50.0F, 50.0F, 150.0F, 150.0F);
GraphicsUnit units = GraphicsUnit.Pixel;
// Create parallelogram for drawing adjusted image.
PointF ulCorner2 = new PointF(325.0F, 100.0F);
PointF urCorner2 = new PointF(550.0F, 100.0F);
PointF llCorner2 = new PointF(375.0F, 250.0F);
PointF[] destPara2 = {ulCorner2, urCorner2, llCorner2};
// Draw original image to screen.
e.Graphics.DrawImage(newImage, destPara1, srcRect, units);
// Create image attributes and set large gamma.
ImageAttributes imageAttr = new ImageAttributes();
imageAttr.SetGamma(4.0F);
// Draw adjusted image to screen.
e.Graphics.DrawImage(newImage, destPara2, srcRect, units, imageAttr);
}
```

Requirements

Platforms: Windows 98, Windows NT 4.0, Windows Millennium Edition, Windows 2000, Windows XP Home Edition, Windows XP Professional, Windows Server 2003 family

Graphics.DrawImage Method (Image, Single, Single, RectangleF, GraphicsUnit)

Draws a portion of an image at a specified location.

[Visual Basic]
```
Overloads Public Sub DrawImage( _
   ByVal image As Image, _
   ByVal x As Single, _
   ByVal y As Single, _
   ByVal srcRect As RectangleF, _
   ByVal srcUnit As GraphicsUnit _
)
```
[C#]
```
public void DrawImage(
   Image image,
   float x,
   float y,
   RectangleF srcRect,
   GraphicsUnit srcUnit
);
```
[C++]
```
public: void DrawImage(
   Image* image,
   float x,
   float y,
   RectangleF srcRect,
   GraphicsUnit srcUnit
);
```
[JScript]
```
public function DrawImage(
   image : Image,
   x : float,
   y : float,
   srcRect : RectangleF,
   srcUnit : GraphicsUnit
);
```

Parameters

image

Image object to draw.

x

x-coordinate of the upper-left corner of the drawn image.

y

y-coordinate of the upper-left corner of the drawn image.

srcRect

RectangleF structure that specifies the portion of the **Image** object to draw.

srcUnit

Member of the **GraphicsUnit** enumeration that specifies the units of measure used by the *srcRect* parameter.

Return Value

This method does not return a value.

Remarks

An **Image** object stores a value for pixel width and a value for horizontal resolution (dots per inch). The physical width, measured in inches, of an image is the pixel width divided by the horizontal resolution. For example, an image with a pixel width of 360 and a horizontal resolution of 72 dots per inch has a physical width of 5 inches. Similar remarks apply to pixel height and physical height.

This method draws a portion of an image using its physical size, so the image portion will have its correct size in inches regardless of the resolution (dots per inch) of the display device. For example, suppose an image portion has a pixel width of 216 and a horizontal resolution of 72 dots per inch. If you call this method to draw that image portion on a device that has a resolution of 96 dots per inch, the pixel width of the rendered image portion will be (216/72)*96 = 288.

Example

[Visual Basic, C#] The following example is designed for use with Windows Forms, and it requires **PaintEventArgs** *e*, which is a parameter of the **Paint** event handler. The code performs the following actions:

- Creates an image from a JPEG file SampImag.jpg in the folder of the example.
- Creates the coordinates at which to draw the upper-left corner of the image.
- Creates a source rectangle from which to extract a portion of the image.
- Sets the unit of measure of the source rectangle to pixels.
- Draws the image to the screen.

[Visual Basic, C#] The size of the source rectangle determines what portion of the unscaled original image is drawn to the screen.

[Visual Basic]
```
Public Sub DrawImage2FloatRectF(e As PaintEventArgs)
' Create image.
Dim newImage As Image = Image.FromFile("SampImag.jpg")
' Create coordinates for upper-left corner of image.
Dim x As Single = 100F
```

```
Dim y As Single = 100F
' Create rectangle for source image.
Dim srcRect As New RectangleF(50F, 50F, 150F, 150F)
Dim units As GraphicsUnit = GraphicsUnit.Pixel
' Draw image to screen.
e.Graphics.DrawImage(newImage, x, y, srcRect, units)
End Sub
```

[C#]

```
public void DrawImage2FloatRectF(PaintEventArgs e)
{
// Create image.
Image newImage = Image.FromFile("SampImag.jpg");
// Create coordinates for upper-left corner of image.
float x = 100.0F;
float y = 100.0F;
// Create rectangle for source image.
RectangleF srcRect = new RectangleF( 50.0F, 50.0F, 150.0F, 150.0F);
GraphicsUnit units = GraphicsUnit.Pixel;
// Draw image to screen.
e.Graphics.DrawImage(newImage, x, y, srcRect, units);
}
```

Requirements

Platforms: Windows 98, Windows NT 4.0, Windows Millennium Edition, Windows 2000, Windows XP Home Edition, Windows XP Professional, Windows Server 2003 family

Graphics.DrawImage Method (Image, Single, Single, Single, Single)

Draws the specified **Image** object at the specified location and with the specified size.

[Visual Basic]

```
Overloads Public Sub DrawImage( _
   ByVal image As Image, _
   ByVal x As Single, _
   ByVal y As Single, _
   ByVal width As Single, _
   ByVal height As Single _
)
```

[C#]

```
public void DrawImage(
   Image image,
   float x,
   float y,
   float width,
   float height
);
```

[C++]

```
public: void DrawImage(
   Image* image,
   float x,
   float y,
   float width,
   float height
);
```

[JScript]

```
public function DrawImage(
   image : Image,
   x : float,
   y : float,
   width : float,
   height : float
);
```

Parameters

image
  Image object to draw.

x
  x-coordinate of the upper-left corner of the drawn image.

y
  y-coordinate of the upper-left corner of the drawn image.

width
  Width of the drawn image.

height
  Height of the drawn image.

Return Value

This method does not return a value.

Remarks

The rectangle defined by the *x*, *y*, *width*, and *height* parameters determines the position and size of the drawn image.

Example

[Visual Basic, C#] The following example is designed for use with Windows Forms, and it requires **PaintEventArgs** *e*, which is a parameter of the **Paint** event handler. The code performs the following actions:

- Creates an image from a JPEG file SampImag.jpg in the folder of the example.
- Creates the position and size of a rectangle in which to draw the image.
- Draws the image to the screen.

[Visual Basic, C#] The position of the rectangle locates the image on the screen, and the size of the original image and the size of the rectangle determines the scaling of the drawn image.

[Visual Basic]

```
Public Sub DrawImage4Float(e As PaintEventArgs)
' Create image.
Dim newImage As Image = Image.FromFile("SampImag.jpg")
' Create coordinates for upper-left corner
' of image and for size of image.
Dim x As Single = 100F
Dim y As Single = 100F
Dim width As Single = 450F
Dim height As Single = 150F
' Draw image to screen.
e.Graphics.DrawImage(newImage, x, y, width, height)
End Sub
```

[C#]

```
public void DrawImage4Float(PaintEventArgs e)
{
// Create image.
Image newImage = Image.FromFile("SampImag.jpg");
// Create coordinates for upper-left corner.
// of image and for size of image.
float x = 100.0F;
float y = 100.0F;
float width = 450.0F;
float height = 150.0F;
// Draw image to screen.
e.Graphics.DrawImage(newImage, x, y, width, height);
}
```

Requirements

Platforms: Windows 98, Windows NT 4.0, Windows Millennium Edition, Windows 2000, Windows XP Home Edition, Windows XP Professional, Windows Server 2003 family

Graphics.DrawImage Method (Image, Point[], Rectangle, GraphicsUnit, ImageAttributes, Graphics.DrawImageAbort)

Draws the specified portion of the specified **Image** object at the specified location and with the specified size.

[Visual Basic]
```
Overloads Public Sub DrawImage( _
   ByVal image As Image, _
   ByVal destPoints() As Point, _
   ByVal srcRect As Rectangle, _
   ByVal srcUnit As GraphicsUnit, _
   ByVal imageAttr As ImageAttributes, _
   ByVal callback As Graphics.DrawImageAbort _
)
```
[C#]
```
public void DrawImage(
   Image image,
   Point[] destPoints,
   Rectangle srcRect,
   GraphicsUnit srcUnit,
   ImageAttributes imageAttr,
   Graphics.DrawImageAbort callback
);
```
[C++]
```
public: void DrawImage(
   Image* image,
   Point destPoints[],
   Rectangle srcRect,
   GraphicsUnit srcUnit,
   ImageAttributes* imageAttr,
   Graphics.DrawImageAbort* callback
);
```
[JScript]
```
public function DrawImage(
   image : Image,
   destPoints : Point[],
   srcRect : Rectangle,
   srcUnit : GraphicsUnit,
   imageAttr : ImageAttributes,
   callback : Graphics.DrawImageAbort
);
```

Parameters

image

Image object to draw.

destPoints

Array of three **Point** structures that define a parallelogram.

srcRect

Rectangle structure that specifies the portion of the *image* object to draw.

srcUnit

Member of the **GraphicsUnit** enumeration that specifies the units of measure used by the *srcRect* parameter.

imageAttr

ImageAttributes object that specifies recoloring and gamma information for the *image* object.

callback

Graphics.DrawImageAbort delegate that specifies a method to call during the drawing of the image. This method is called frequently to check whether to stop execution of the **DrawImage** method according to application-determined criteria.

Return Value

This method does not return a value.

Remarks

The *destPoints* parameter specifies three points of a parallelogram. The three **Point** structures represent the upper-left, upper-right, and lower-left corners of the parallelogram. The fourth point is extrapolated from the first three to form a parallelogram.

The *srcRect* parameter specifies a rectangular portion of the *image* object to draw. This portion is scaled and sheared to fit inside the parallelogram specified by the *destPoints* parameter.

This overload with the *callback* parameter provides the means to stop the drawing of an image once it starts according to criteria determined by the application. For example, an application could start drawing a large image and the user might scroll the image off the screen, in which case the application could stop the drawing.

Example

[Visual Basic, C#] The following example is designed for use with Windows Forms, and it requires **PaintEventArgs** *e*, which is a parameter of the **Paint** event handler. The code first defines a callback method for the **DrawImageAbort** delegate; the definition is simplistic and merely tests to see whether the **DrawImage** method calls it with a null *callBackData* parameter. The main body of the example performs the following actions:

- Creates an instance of the **DrawImageAbort** callback method:
- Creates an image from a JPEG file SampImag.jpg in the folder of the example.
- Creates points that define a parallelogram in which to draw the image.
- Creates a rectangle to select the portion of the image to draw.
- Sets the graphics drawing unit to pixel.
- Draws the original image to the screen.
- Creates an additional parallelogram in which to draw an adjusted image.
- Creates and sets the attributes of the adjusted image to have a larger-than-usual gamma value.
- Draws the adjusted image to the screen.

[Visual Basic, C#] For the original, unadjusted parallelogram, the position locates the image on the screen, and the size of the rectangle and the size and shape of the parallelogram determines the scaling and shearing of the drawn image.

[Visual Basic, C#] Because this example uses an overload that does not pass a *callBackData* parameter, the **DrawImageAbort** callback returns **true**, which causes the **DrawImage** method to abort, and the exception-handling code included in the example prints out the exception text rather than drawing the image.

[Visual Basic]
```
Private Function DrawImageCallback(callBackData As IntPtr) As Boolean
' Test for call that passes callBackData parameter.
If callBackData.Equals(IntPtr.Zero) Then
' If no callBackData passed, abort DrawImage method.
Return True
Else
' If callBackData passed, continue DrawImage method.
Return False
End If
End Function
Public Sub DrawImageParaRectAttribAbort(e As PaintEventArgs)
' Create callback method.
Dim imageCallback As New _
Graphics.DrawImageAbort(AddressOf DrawImageCallback)
```

```
' Create image.
Dim newImage As Image = Image.FromFile("SampImag.jpg")
' Create parallelogram for drawing original image.
Dim ulCorner As New Point(100, 100)
Dim urCorner As New Point(550, 100)
Dim llCorner As New Point(150, 250)
Dim destPara1 As Point() = {ulCorner, urCorner, llCorner}
' Create rectangle for source image.
Dim srcRect As New Rectangle(50, 50, 150, 150)
Dim units As GraphicsUnit = GraphicsUnit.Pixel
' Draw original image to screen.
e.Graphics.DrawImage(newImage, destPara1, srcRect, units)
' Create parallelogram for drawing adjusted image.
Dim ulCorner2 As New Point(325, 100)
Dim urCorner2 As New Point(550, 100)
Dim llCorner2 As New Point(375, 250)
Dim destPara2 As Point() = {ulCorner2, urCorner2, llCorner2}
' Create image attributes and set large gamma.
Dim imageAttr As New ImageAttributes()
imageAttr.SetGamma(4F)
Try
' Draw image to screen.
e.Graphics.DrawImage(newImage, destPara2, srcRect, units, _
imageAttr, imageCallback)
Catch ex As Exception
e.Graphics.DrawString(ex.ToString(), New Font("Arial", 8), _
Brushes.Black, New PointF(0, 0))
End Try
End Sub
```

[C#]

```
// Define DrawImageAbort callback method.
private bool DrawImageCallback(IntPtr callBackData)
{
// Test for call that passes callBackData parameter.
if(callBackData==IntPtr.Zero)
{
// If no callBackData passed, abort DrawImage method.
return true;
}
else
{
// If callBackData passed, continue DrawImage method.
return false;
}
}
public void DrawImageParaRectAttribAbort(PaintEventArgs e)
{
// Create callback method.
Graphics.DrawImageAbort imageCallback
= new Graphics.DrawImageAbort(DrawImageCallback);
// Create image.
Image newImage = Image.FromFile("SampImag.jpg");
// Create parallelogram for drawing original image.
Point ulCorner = new Point(100, 100);
Point urCorner = new Point(550, 100);
Point llCorner = new Point(150, 250);
Point[] destPara1 = {ulCorner, urCorner, llCorner};
// Create rectangle for source image.
Rectangle srcRect = new Rectangle( 50, 50, 150, 150);
GraphicsUnit units = GraphicsUnit.Pixel;
// Draw original image to screen.
e.Graphics.DrawImage(newImage, destPara1, srcRect, units);
// Create parallelogram for drawing adjusted image.
Point ulCorner2 = new Point(325, 100);
Point urCorner2 = new Point(550, 100);
Point llCorner2 = new Point(375, 250);
Point[] destPara2 = {ulCorner2, urCorner2, llCorner2};
// Create image attributes and set large gamma.
ImageAttributes imageAttr = new ImageAttributes();
imageAttr.SetGamma(4.0F);
try
{
checked
{
// Draw image to screen.
e.Graphics.DrawImage(
newImage,
destPara2,
srcRect,
units,
imageAttr,
imageCallback);
}
}
catch (Exception ex)
{
e.Graphics.DrawString(
ex.ToString(),
new Font("Arial", 8),
Brushes.Black,
new PointF(0, 0));
}
}
```

Requirements

Platforms: Windows 98, Windows NT 4.0, Windows Millennium Edition, Windows 2000, Windows XP Home Edition, Windows XP Professional, Windows Server 2003 family

Graphics.DrawImage Method (Image, PointF[], RectangleF, GraphicsUnit, ImageAttributes, Graphics.DrawImageAbort)

Draws the specified portion of the specified **Image** object at the specified location and with the specified size.

[Visual Basic]

```
Overloads Public Sub DrawImage( _
   ByVal image As Image, _
   ByVal destPoints() As PointF, _
   ByVal srcRect As RectangleF, _
   ByVal srcUnit As GraphicsUnit, _
   ByVal imageAttr As ImageAttributes, _
   ByVal callback As Graphics.DrawImageAbort _
)
```

[C#]

```
public void DrawImage(
   Image image,
   PointF[] destPoints,
   RectangleF srcRect,
   GraphicsUnit srcUnit,
   ImageAttributes imageAttr,
   Graphics.DrawImageAbort callback
);
```

[C++]

```
public: void DrawImage(
   Image* image,
   PointF destPoints[],
   RectangleF srcRect,
   GraphicsUnit srcUnit,
   ImageAttributes* imageAttr,
   Graphics.DrawImageAbort* callback
);
```

[JScript]

```
public function DrawImage(
   image : Image,
   destPoints : PointF[],
   srcRect : RectangleF,
   srcUnit : GraphicsUnit,
   imageAttr : ImageAttributes,
   callback : Graphics.DrawImageAbort
);
```

Parameters

image

Image object to draw.

destPoints

Array of three **Point** structures that define a parallelogram.

srcRect

Rectangle structure that specifies the portion of the *image* object to draw.

srcUnit

Member of the **GraphicsUnit** enumeration that specifies the units of measure used by the *srcRect* parameter.

imageAttr

ImageAttributes object that specifies recoloring and gamma information for the *image* object.

callback

Graphics.DrawImageAbort delegate that specifies a method to call during the drawing of the image. This method is called frequently to check whether to stop execution of the **DrawImage** method according to application-determined criteria.

Return Value

This method does not return a value.

Remarks

The *destPoints* parameter specifies three points of a parallelogram. The three **Point** structures represent the upper-left, upper-right, and lower-left corners of the parallelogram. The fourth point is extrapolated from the first three to form a parallelogram.

The *srcRect* parameter specifies a rectangular portion of the *image* object to draw. This portion is scaled and sheared to fit inside the parallelogram specified by the *destPoints* parameter.

This overload with the *callback* parameter provides the means to stop the drawing of an image once it starts according to criteria determined by the application. For example, an application could start drawing a large image and the user might scroll the image off the screen, in which case the application could stop the drawing.

Example

[Visual Basic, C#] The following example is designed for use with Windows Forms, and it requires **PaintEventArgs** *e*, which is a parameter of the **Paint** event handler. The code first defines a callback method for the **DrawImageAbort** delegate; the definition is simplistic and merely tests to see whether the **DrawImage** method calls it with a null *callBackData* parameter. The main body of the example performs the following actions:

- Creates an instance of the **DrawImageAbort** callback method.
- Creates an image from a JPEG file SampImag.jpg in the folder of the example.
- Creates points that define a parallelogram in which to draw the image.
- Creates a rectangle to select the portion of the image to draw.
- Sets the graphics drawing unit to pixel.
- Draws the original image to the screen.
- Creates an additional parallelogram in which to draw an adjusted image.
- Creates and sets the attributes of the adjusted image to have a larger-than-usual gamma value.
- Draws the adjusted image to the screen.

[Visual Basic, C#] For the original, unadjusted parallelogram, the position locates the image on the screen, and the size of the rectangle and the size and shape of the parallelogram determines the scaling and shearing of the drawn image.

[Visual Basic, C#] Because this example uses an overload that does not pass a *callBackData* parameter, the **DrawImageAbort** callback returns **true**, which causes the **DrawImage** method to abort, and the exception-handling code included in the example prints out the exception text rather than drawing the image.

[Visual Basic]

```
Private Function DrawImageCallback(callBackData As IntPtr) As Boolean
' Test for call that passes callBackData parameter.
If callBackData.Equals(IntPtr.Zero) Then
' If no callBackData passed, abort DrawImage method.
Return True
Else
' If callBackData passed, continue DrawImage method.
Return False
End If
End Function
Public Sub DrawImageParaFRectAttribAbort(e As PaintEventArgs)
' Create callback method.
Dim imageCallback As New _
Graphics.DrawImageAbort(AddressOf DrawImageCallback)
' Create image.
Dim newImage As Image = Image.FromFile("SampImag.jpg")
' Create parallelogram for drawing original image.
Dim ulCorner1 As New PointF(100F, 100F)
Dim urCorner1 As New PointF(325F, 100F)
Dim llCorner1 As New PointF(150F, 250F)
Dim destPara1 As PointF() = {ulCorner1, urCorner1, llCorner1}
' Create rectangle for source image.
Dim srcRect As New RectangleF(50F, 50F, 150F, 150F)
Dim units As GraphicsUnit = GraphicsUnit.Pixel
' Create parallelogram for drawing adjusted image.
Dim ulCorner2 As New PointF(325F, 100F)
Dim urCorner2 As New PointF(550F, 100F)
Dim llCorner2 As New PointF(375F, 250F)
Dim destPara2 As PointF() = {ulCorner2, urCorner2, llCorner2}
' Draw original image to screen.
e.Graphics.DrawImage(newImage, destPara1, srcRect, units)
' Create image attributes and set large gamma.
Dim imageAttr As New ImageAttributes()
imageAttr.SetGamma(4F)
Try
' Draw adjusted image to screen.
e.Graphics.DrawImage(newImage, destPara2, srcRect, units, _
imageAttr, imageCallback)
Catch ex As Exception
e.Graphics.DrawString(ex.ToString(), New Font("Arial", 8), _
Brushes.Black, New PointF(0, 0))
End Try
End Sub
```

[C#]

```
// Define DrawImageAbort callback method.
private bool DrawImageCallback(IntPtr callBackData)
{
// Test for call that passes callBackData parameter.
if(callBackData==IntPtr.Zero)
{
// If no callBackData passed, abort DrawImage method.
return true;
}
else
{
// If callBackData passed, continue DrawImage method.
return false;
}
}
public void DrawImageParaFRectAttribAbort(PaintEventArgs e)
{
```

```
// Create callback method.
Graphics.DrawImageAbort imageCallback
= new Graphics.DrawImageAbort(DrawImageCallback);
// Create image.
Image newImage = Image.FromFile("SampImag.jpg");
// Create parallelogram for drawing original image.
PointF ulCorner1 = new PointF(100.0F, 100.0F);
PointF urCorner1 = new PointF(325.0F, 100.0F);
PointF llCorner1 = new PointF(150.0F, 250.0F);
PointF[] destPara1 = {ulCorner1, urCorner1, llCorner1};
// Create rectangle for source image.
RectangleF srcRect = new RectangleF( 50.0F, 50.0F, 150.0F, 150.0F);
GraphicsUnit units = GraphicsUnit.Pixel;
// Create parallelogram for drawing adjusted image.
PointF ulCorner2 = new PointF(325.0F, 100.0F);
PointF urCorner2 = new PointF(550.0F, 100.0F);
PointF llCorner2 = new PointF(375.0F, 250.0F);
PointF[] destPara2 = {ulCorner2, urCorner2, llCorner2};
// Draw original image to screen.
e.Graphics.DrawImage(newImage, destPara1, srcRect, units);
// Create image attributes and set large gamma.
ImageAttributes imageAttr = new ImageAttributes();
imageAttr.SetGamma(4.0F);
try
{
checked
{
// Draw adjusted image to screen.
e.Graphics.DrawImage(
newImage,
destPara2,
srcRect,
units,
imageAttr,
imageCallback);
}
}
catch (Exception ex)
{
e.Graphics.DrawString(
ex.ToString(),
new Font("Arial", 8),
Brushes.Black,
new PointF(0, 0));
}
}
```

Requirements

Platforms: Windows 98, Windows NT 4.0, Windows Millennium Edition, Windows 2000, Windows XP Home Edition, Windows XP Professional, Windows Server 2003 family

Graphics.DrawImage Method (Image, Point[], Rectangle, GraphicsUnit, ImageAttributes, Graphics.DrawImageAbort, Int32)

Draws the specified portion of the specified **Image** object at the specified location and with the specified size.

```
[Visual Basic]
Overloads Public Sub DrawImage( _
   ByVal image As Image, _
   ByVal destPoints() As Point, _
   ByVal srcRect As Rectangle, _
   ByVal srcUnit As GraphicsUnit, _
   ByVal imageAttr As ImageAttributes, _
   ByVal callback As Graphics.DrawImageAbort, _
   ByVal callbackData As Integer _
)
```

```
[C#]
public void DrawImage(
   Image image,
   Point[] destPoints,
   Rectangle srcRect,
   GraphicsUnit srcUnit,
   ImageAttributes imageAttr,
   Graphics.DrawImageAbort callback,
   int callbackData
);
[C++]
public: void DrawImage(
   Image* image,
   Point destPoints[],
   Rectangle srcRect,
   GraphicsUnit srcUnit,
   ImageAttributes* imageAttr,
   Graphics.DrawImageAbort* callback,
   int callbackData
);
[JScript]
public function DrawImage(
   image : Image,
   destPoints : Point[],
   srcRect : Rectangle,
   srcUnit : GraphicsUnit,
   imageAttr : ImageAttributes,
   callback : Graphics.DrawImageAbort,
   callbackData : int
);
```

Parameters

image
: **Image** object to draw.

destPoints
: Array of three **Point** structures that define a parallelogram.

srcRect
: **Rectangle** structure that specifies the portion of the *image* object to draw.

srcUnit
: Member of the **GraphicsUnit** enumeration that specifies the units of measure used by the *srcRect* parameter.

imageAttr
: **ImageAttributes** object that specifies recoloring and gamma information for the *image* object.

callback
: **Graphics.DrawImageAbort** delegate that specifies a method to call during the drawing of the image. This method is called frequently to check whether to stop execution of the **DrawImage** method according to application-determined criteria.

callbackData
: Value specifying additional data for the **DrawImageAbort** delegate to use when checking whether to stop execution of the **DrawImage** method.

Return Value

This method does not return a value.

Remarks

The *destPoints* parameter specifies three points of a parallelogram. The three **Point** structures represent the upper-left, upper-right, and lower-left corners of the parallelogram. The fourth point is extrapolated from the first three to form a parallelogram.

The *srcRect* parameter specifies a rectangular portion of the *image* object to draw. This portion is scaled and sheared to fit inside the parallelogram specified by the *destPoints* parameter.

This overload with the *callback* and *callbackData* parameters provides the means to stop the drawing of an image once it starts according to criteria and data determined by the application. For example, an application could start drawing a large image and the user might scroll the image off the screen, in which case the application could stop the drawing.

Example

[Visual Basic, C#] The following example is designed for use with Windows Forms, and it requires **PaintEventArgs** *e*, which is a parameter of the **Paint** event handler. The code first defines a callback method for the **DrawImageAbort** delegate; the definition is simplistic and merely tests to see whether the **DrawImage** method calls it with a null *callBackData* parameter. The main body of the example performs the following actions:

- Creates an instance of the **DrawImageAbort** callback method.
- Creates an image from a JPEG file SampImag.jpg in the folder of the example.
- Creates points that define a parallelogram in which to draw the image.
- Creates a rectangle to select the portion of the image to draw.
- Sets the graphics drawing unit to pixel.
- Draws the original image to the screen.
- Creates an additional parallelogram in which to draw an adjusted image.
- Creates and sets the attributes of the adjusted image to have a larger-than-usual gamma value.
- Draws the adjusted image to the screen.

[Visual Basic, C#] For the original, unadjusted parallelogram, the position locates the image on the screen, and the size of the rectangle and the size and shape of the parallelogram determines the scaling and shearing of the drawn image.

[Visual Basic, C#] Because this example uses an overload that passes a *callBackData* parameter, the **DrawImageAbort** callback returns **false**, which causes the **DrawImage** method to continue, and the example draws the adjusted image to the screen.

[Visual Basic]

```
Private Function DrawImageCallback(callBackData As IntPtr) As Boolean
' Test for call that passes callBackData parameter.
If callBackData.Equals(IntPtr.Zero) Then
' If no callBackData passed, abort DrawImage method.
Return True
Else
' If callBackData passed, continue DrawImage method.
Return False
End If
End Function
Public Sub DrawImageParaRectAttribAbortData(e As PaintEventArgs)
' Create callback method.
Dim imageCallback As New _
Graphics.DrawImageAbort(AddressOf DrawImageCallback)
Dim imageCallbackData As Integer = 1
' Create image.
Dim newImage As Image = Image.FromFile("SampImag.jpg")
' Create parallelogram for drawing original image.
Dim ulCorner As New Point(100, 100)
Dim urCorner As New Point(550, 100)
Dim llCorner As New Point(150, 250)
Dim destPara1 As Point() = {ulCorner, urCorner, llCorner}
' Create rectangle for source image.
Dim srcRect As New Rectangle(50, 50, 150, 150)
Dim units As GraphicsUnit = GraphicsUnit.Pixel
' Draw original image to screen.
e.Graphics.DrawImage(newImage, destPara1, srcRect, units)
' Create parallelogram for drawing adjusted image.
Dim ulCorner2 As New Point(325, 100)
Dim urCorner2 As New Point(550, 100)
Dim llCorner2 As New Point(375, 250)
Dim destPara2 As Point() = {ulCorner2, urCorner2, llCorner2}
' Create image attributes and set large gamma.
Dim imageAttr As New ImageAttributes()
imageAttr.SetGamma(4F)
Try
' Draw image to screen.
e.Graphics.DrawImage(newImage, destPara2, srcRect, units, _
imageAttr, imageCallback, imageCallbackData)
Catch ex As Exception
e.Graphics.DrawString(ex.ToString(), New Font("Arial", 8), _
Brushes.Black, New PointF(0, 0))
End Try
End Sub
```

[C#]

```
// Define DrawImageAbort callback method.
private bool DrawImageCallback(IntPtr callBackData)
{
// Test for call that passes callBackData parameter.
if(callBackData==IntPtr.Zero)
{
// If no callBackData passed, abort DrawImage method.
return true;
}
else
{
// If callBackData passed, continue DrawImage method.
return false;
}
}
public void DrawImageParaRectAttribAbortData(PaintEventArgs e)
{
// Create callback method.
Graphics.DrawImageAbort imageCallback
= new Graphics.DrawImageAbort(DrawImageCallback);
int imageCallbackData = 1;
// Create image.
Image newImage = Image.FromFile("SampImag.jpg");
// Create parallelogram for drawing original image.
Point ulCorner = new Point(100, 100);
Point urCorner = new Point(550, 100);
Point llCorner = new Point(150, 250);
Point[] destPara1 = {ulCorner, urCorner, llCorner};
// Create rectangle for source image.
Rectangle srcRect = new Rectangle( 50, 50, 150, 150);
GraphicsUnit units = GraphicsUnit.Pixel;
// Draw original image to screen.
e.Graphics.DrawImage(newImage, destPara1, srcRect, units);
// Create parallelogram for drawing adjusted image.
Point ulCorner2 = new Point(325, 100);
Point urCorner2 = new Point(550, 100);
Point llCorner2 = new Point(375, 250);
Point[] destPara2 = {ulCorner2, urCorner2, llCorner2};
// Create image attributes and set large gamma.
ImageAttributes imageAttr = new ImageAttributes();
imageAttr.SetGamma(4.0F);
try
{
checked
{
```

```
// Draw image to screen.
e.Graphics.DrawImage(
newImage,
destPara2,
srcRect,
units,
imageAttr,
imageCallback,
imageCallbackData);
}
}
catch (Exception ex)
{
e.Graphics.DrawString(
ex.ToString(),
new Font("Arial", 8),
Brushes.Black,
new PointF(0, 0));
}
}
```

Requirements

Platforms: Windows 98, Windows NT 4.0, Windows Millennium Edition, Windows 2000, Windows XP Home Edition, Windows XP Professional, Windows Server 2003 family

Graphics.DrawImage Method (Image, PointF[], RectangleF, GraphicsUnit, ImageAttributes, Graphics.DrawImageAbort, Int32)

Draws the specified portion of the specified **Image** object at the specified location and with the specified size.

```
[Visual Basic]
Overloads Public Sub DrawImage( _
   ByVal image As Image, _
   ByVal destPoints() As PointF, _
   ByVal srcRect As RectangleF, _
   ByVal srcUnit As GraphicsUnit, _
   ByVal imageAttr As ImageAttributes, _
   ByVal callback As Graphics.DrawImageAbort, _
   ByVal callbackData As Integer _
)
[C#]
public void DrawImage(
   Image image,
   PointF[] destPoints,
   RectangleF srcRect,
   GraphicsUnit srcUnit,
   ImageAttributes imageAttr,
   Graphics.DrawImageAbort callback,
   int callbackData
);
[C++]
public: void DrawImage(
   Image* image,
   PointF destPoints[],
   RectangleF srcRect,
   GraphicsUnit srcUnit,
   ImageAttributes* imageAttr,
   Graphics.DrawImageAbort* callback,
   int callbackData
);
[JScript]
public function DrawImage(
   image : Image,
   destPoints : PointF[],
   srcRect : RectangleF,
   srcUnit : GraphicsUnit,
   imageAttr : ImageAttributes,
   callback : Graphics.DrawImageAbort,
   callbackData : int
);
```

Parameters

image
: **Image** object to draw.

destPoints
: Array of three **Point** structures that define a parallelogram.

srcRect
: **RectangleF** structure that specifies the portion of the *image* object to draw.

srcUnit
: Member of the **GraphicsUnit** enumeration that specifies the units of measure used by the *srcRect* parameter.

imageAttr
: **ImageAttributes** object that specifies recoloring and gamma information for the *image* object.

callback
: **Graphics.DrawImageAbort** delegate that specifies a method to call during the drawing of the image. This method is called frequently to check whether to stop execution of the **DrawImage** method according to application-determined criteria.

callbackData
: Value specifying additional data for the **DrawImageAbort** delegate to use when checking whether to stop execution of the **DrawImage** method.

Return Value

This method does not return a value.

Remarks

The *destPoints* parameter specifies three points of a parallelogram. The three **Point** structures represent the upper-left, upper-right, and lower-left corners of the parallelogram. The fourth point is extrapolated from the first three to form a parallelogram.

The *srcRect* parameter specifies a rectangular portion of the *image* object to draw. This portion is scaled and sheared to fit inside the parallelogram specified by the *destPoints* parameter.

This overload with the *callback* and *callbackData* parameters provides the means to stop the drawing of an image once it starts according to criteria and data determined by the application. For example, an application could start drawing a large image and the user might scroll the image off the screen, in which case the application could stop the drawing.

Example

[Visual Basic, C#] The following example is designed for use with Windows Forms, and it requires **PaintEventArgs** *e*, which is a parameter of the **Paint** event handler. The code first defines a callback method for the **DrawImageAbort** delegate; the definition is simplistic and merely tests to see whether the **DrawImage** method calls it with a null *callBackData* parameter. The main body of the example performs the following actions:

- Creates an instance of the **DrawImageAbort** callback method.
- Creates an image from a JPEG file SampImag.jpg in the folder of the example.
- Creates points that define a parallelogram in which to draw the image.
- Creates a rectangle to select the portion of the image to draw.
- Sets the graphics drawing unit to pixel.
- Draws the original image to the screen.
- Creates an additional parallelogram in which to draw an adjusted image.
- Creates and sets the attributes of the adjusted image to have a larger-than-usual gamma value.
- Draws the adjusted image to the screen.

[Visual Basic, C#] For the original, unadjusted parallelogram, the position locates the image on the screen, and the size of the rectangle and the size and shape of the parallelogram determines the scaling and shearing of the drawn image.

[Visual Basic, C#] Because this example uses an overload that passes a *callBackData* parameter, the **DrawImageAbort** callback returns **false**, which causes the **DrawImage** method to continue, and the example draws the adjusted image to the screen.

[Visual Basic]

```
Private Function DrawImageCallback(callBackData As IntPtr) As Boolean
' Test for call that passes callBackData parameter.
If callBackData.Equals(IntPtr.Zero) Then
' If no callBackData passed, abort DrawImage method.
Return True
Else
' If callBackData passed, continue DrawImage method.
Return False
End If
End Function
Public Sub DrawImageParaFRectAttribAbortData(e As PaintEventArgs)
' Create callback method.
Dim imageCallback As New _
Graphics.DrawImageAbort(AddressOf DrawImageCallback)
Dim imageCallbackData As Integer = 1
' Create image.
Dim newImage As Image = Image.FromFile("SampImag.jpg")
' Create parallelogram for drawing original image.
Dim ulCorner1 As New PointF(100F, 100F)
Dim urCorner1 As New PointF(325F, 100F)
Dim llCorner1 As New PointF(150F, 250F)
Dim destPara1 As PointF() =  {ulCorner1, urCorner1, llCorner1}
' Create rectangle for source image.
Dim srcRect As New RectangleF(50F, 50F, 150F, 150F)
Dim units As GraphicsUnit = GraphicsUnit.Pixel
' Create parallelogram for drawing adjusted image.
Dim ulCorner2 As New PointF(325F, 100F)
Dim urCorner2 As New PointF(550F, 100F)
Dim llCorner2 As New PointF(375F, 250F)
Dim destPara2 As PointF() =  {ulCorner2, urCorner2, llCorner2}
' Draw original image to screen.
e.Graphics.DrawImage(newImage, destPara1, srcRect, units)
' Create image attributes and set large gamma.
Dim imageAttr As New ImageAttributes()
imageAttr.SetGamma(4F)
Try
' Draw adjusted image to screen.
e.Graphics.DrawImage(newImage, destPara2, srcRect, units, _
imageAttr, imageCallback, imageCallbackData)
Catch ex As Exception
e.Graphics.DrawString(ex.ToString(), New Font("Arial", 8), _
Brushes.Black, New PointF(0, 0))
End Try
End Sub
```

[C#]

```
// Define DrawImageAbort callback method.
private bool DrawImageCallback(IntPtr callBackData)
{
// Test for call that passes callBackData parameter.
if(callBackData==IntPtr.Zero)
{
// If no callBackData passed, abort DrawImage method.
return true;
}
else
{
// If callBackData passed, continue DrawImage method.
return false;
}
}
public void DrawImageParaFRectAttribAbortData(PaintEventArgs e)
{
// Create callback method.
Graphics.DrawImageAbort imageCallback
= new Graphics.DrawImageAbort(DrawImageCallback);
int imageCallbackData = 1;
// Create image.
Image newImage = Image.FromFile("SampImag.jpg");
// Create parallelogram for drawing original image.
PointF ulCorner1 = new PointF(100.0F, 100.0F);
PointF urCorner1 = new PointF(325.0F, 100.0F);
PointF llCorner1 = new PointF(150.0F, 250.0F);
PointF[] destPara1 = {ulCorner1, urCorner1, llCorner1};
// Create rectangle for source image.
RectangleF srcRect = new RectangleF( 50.0F, 50.0F, 150.0F, 150.0F);
GraphicsUnit units = GraphicsUnit.Pixel;
// Create parallelogram for drawing adjusted image.
PointF ulCorner2 = new PointF(325.0F, 100.0F);
PointF urCorner2 = new PointF(550.0F, 100.0F);
PointF llCorner2 = new PointF(375.0F, 250.0F);
PointF[] destPara2 = {ulCorner2, urCorner2, llCorner2};
// Draw original image to screen.
e.Graphics.DrawImage(newImage, destPara1, srcRect, units);
// Create image attributes and set large gamma.
ImageAttributes imageAttr = new ImageAttributes();
imageAttr.SetGamma(4.0F);
try
{
checked
{
// Draw adjusted image to screen.
e.Graphics.DrawImage(
newImage,
destPara2,
srcRect,
units,
imageAttr,
imageCallback,
imageCallbackData);
}
}
catch (Exception ex)
{
e.Graphics.DrawString(
ex.ToString(),
new Font("Arial", 8),
Brushes.Black,
new PointF(0, 0));
}
}
```

Requirements

Platforms: Windows 98, Windows NT 4.0, Windows Millennium Edition, Windows 2000, Windows XP Home Edition, Windows XP Professional, Windows Server 2003 family

Graphics.DrawImage Method (Image, Rectangle, Int32, Int32, Int32, Int32, GraphicsUnit)

Draws the specified portion of the specified **Image** object at the specified location and with the specified size.

[Visual Basic]
```
Overloads Public Sub DrawImage( _
   ByVal image As Image, _
   ByVal destRect As Rectangle, _
   ByVal srcX As Integer, _
   ByVal srcY As Integer, _
   ByVal srcWidth As Integer, _
   ByVal srcHeight As Integer, _
   ByVal srcUnit As GraphicsUnit _
)
```
[C#]
```
public void DrawImage(
   Image image,
   Rectangle destRect,
   int srcX,
   int srcY,
   int srcWidth,
   int srcHeight,
   GraphicsUnit srcUnit
);
```
[C++]
```
public: void DrawImage(
   Image* image,
   Rectangle destRect,
   int srcX,
   int srcY,
   int srcWidth,
   int srcHeight,
   GraphicsUnit srcUnit
);
```
[JScript]
```
public function DrawImage(
   image : Image,
   destRect : Rectangle,
   srcX : int,
   srcY : int,
   srcWidth : int,
   srcHeight : int,
   srcUnit : GraphicsUnit
);
```

Parameters

image
: **Image** object to draw.

destRect
: **Rectangle** structure that specifies the location and size of the drawn image. The image is scaled to fit the rectangle.

srcX
: x-coordinate of the upper-left corner of the portion of the source image to draw.

srcY
: y-coordinate of the upper-left corner of the portion of the source image to draw.

srcWidth
: Width of the portion of the source image to draw.

srcHeight
: Height of the portion of the source image to draw.

srcUnit
: Member of the **GraphicsUnit** enumeration that specifies the units of measure used to determine the source rectangle.

Return Value

This method does not return a value.

Remarks

The *srcX*, *srcY*, *srcWidth*, and *srcHeight* parameters specify a rectangular portion, of the *image* object to draw. The rectangle is relative to the upper-left corner of the source image. This portion is scaled to fit inside the rectangle specified by the *destRect* parameter.

Example

[Visual Basic, C#] The following example is designed for use with Windows Forms, and it requires **PaintEventArgs** *e*, which is a parameter of the **Paint** event handler. The code performs the following actions:

- Creates an image from a JPEG file SampImag.jpg in the folder of the example.
- Creates a destination rectangle in which to draw the image.
- Creates the coordinates of a source rectangle from which to extract a portion of the image.
- Sets the unit of measure of the source rectangle to pixels.
- Draws the image to the screen.

[Visual Basic, C#] The position of the destination rectangle locates the image on the screen, and the sizes of the source and destination rectangles determine the scaling of the drawn image, and the size of the source rectangle determines what portion of the original image is drawn to the screen.

[Visual Basic]
```
Public Sub DrawImageRect4Int(e As PaintEventArgs)
' Create image.
Dim newImage As Image = Image.FromFile("SampImag.jpg")
' Create rectangle for displaying image.
Dim destRect As New Rectangle(100, 100, 450, 150)
' Create coordinates of rectangle for source image.
Dim x As Integer = 50
Dim y As Integer = 50
Dim width As Integer = 150
Dim height As Integer = 150
Dim units As GraphicsUnit = GraphicsUnit.Pixel
' Draw image to screen.
e.Graphics.DrawImage(newImage, destRect, x, y, width, height, _
units)
End Sub
```

[C#]
```
public void DrawImageRect4Int(PaintEventArgs e)
{
// Create image.
Image newImage = Image.FromFile("SampImag.jpg");
// Create rectangle for displaying image.
Rectangle destRect = new Rectangle( 100, 100, 450, 150);
// Create coordinates of rectangle for source image.
int x = 50;
int y = 50;
int width = 150;
int height = 150;
GraphicsUnit units = GraphicsUnit.Pixel;
// Draw image to screen.
e.Graphics.DrawImage(newImage, destRect, x, y, width, height, units);
}
```

Requirements

Platforms: Windows 98, Windows NT 4.0, Windows Millennium Edition, Windows 2000, Windows XP Home Edition, Windows XP Professional, Windows Server 2003 family

Graphics.DrawImage Method (Image, Rectangle, Single, Single, Single, Single, GraphicsUnit)

Draws the specified portion of the specified **Image** object at the specified location and with the specified size.

[Visual Basic]
```
Overloads Public Sub DrawImage( _
   ByVal image As Image, _
   ByVal destRect As Rectangle, _
   ByVal srcX As Single, _
   ByVal srcY As Single, _
   ByVal srcWidth As Single, _
   ByVal srcHeight As Single, _
   ByVal srcUnit As GraphicsUnit _
)
```
[C#]
```
public void DrawImage(
   Image image,
   Rectangle destRect,
   float srcX,
   float srcY,
   float srcWidth,
   float srcHeight,
   GraphicsUnit srcUnit
);
```
[C++]
```
public: void DrawImage(
   Image* image,
   Rectangle destRect,
   float srcX,
   float srcY,
   float srcWidth,
   float srcHeight,
   GraphicsUnit srcUnit
);
```
[JScript]
```
public function DrawImage(
   image : Image,
   destRect : Rectangle,
   srcX : float,
   srcY : float,
   srcWidth : float,
   srcHeight : float,
   srcUnit : GraphicsUnit
);
```

Parameters

image
  Image object to draw.

destRect
  Rectangle structure that specifies the location and size of the drawn image. The image is scaled to fit the rectangle.

srcX
  x-coordinate of the upper-left corner of the portion of the source image to draw.

srcY
  y-coordinate of the upper-left corner of the portion of the source image to draw.

srcWidth
  Width of the portion of the source image to draw.

srcHeight
  Height of the portion of the source image to draw.

srcUnit
  Member of the **GraphicsUnit** enumeration that specifies the units of measure used to determine the source rectangle.

Return Value

This method does not return a value.

Remarks

The *srcX*, *srcY*, *srcWidth*, and *srcHeight* parameters specify a rectangular portion, of the *image* object to draw. The rectangle is relative to the upper-left corner of the source image. This portion is scaled to fit inside the rectangle specified by the *destRect* parameter.

Example

[Visual Basic, C#] The following example is designed for use with Windows Forms, and it requires **PaintEventArgs** *e*, which is a parameter of the **Paint** event handler. The code performs the following actions:

- Creates an image from a JPEG file SampImag.jpg in the folder of the example.
- Creates the coordinates of a destination rectangle in which to draw the image.
- Creates a source rectangle from which to extract a portion of the image.
- Sets the unit of measure of the source rectangle to pixels.
- Draws the image to the screen.

[Visual Basic, C#] The position of the destination rectangle locates the image on the screen, the sizes of the source and destination rectangles determine the scaling of the drawn image, and the size of the source rectangle determines what portion of the original image is drawn to the screen.

[Visual Basic]
```
Public Sub DrawImageRect4Float(e As PaintEventArgs)
' Create image.
Dim newImage As Image = Image.FromFile("SampImag.jpg")
' Create rectangle for displaying image.
Dim destRect As New Rectangle(100, 100, 450, 150)
' Create coordinates of rectangle for source image.
Dim x As Single = 50F
Dim y As Single = 50F
Dim width As Single = 150F
Dim height As Single = 150F
Dim units As GraphicsUnit = GraphicsUnit.Pixel
' Draw image to screen.
e.Graphics.DrawImage(newImage, destRect, x, y, width, height, _
units)
End Sub
```

[C#]
```
public void DrawImageRect4Float(PaintEventArgs e)
{
// Create image.
Image newImage = Image.FromFile("SampImag.jpg");
// Create rectangle for displaying image.
Rectangle destRect = new Rectangle( 100, 100, 450, 150);
// Create coordinates of rectangle for source image.
float x = 50.0F;
float y = 50.0F;
float width = 150.0F;
float height = 150.0F;
GraphicsUnit units = GraphicsUnit.Pixel;
// Draw image to screen.
e.Graphics.DrawImage(newImage, destRect, x, y, width, height, units);
}
```

Requirements

Platforms: Windows 98, Windows NT 4.0, Windows Millennium Edition, Windows 2000, Windows XP Home Edition, Windows XP Professional, Windows Server 2003 family

Graphics.DrawImage Method (Image, Rectangle, Int32, Int32, Int32, Int32, GraphicsUnit, ImageAttributes)

Draws the specified portion of the specified **Image** object at the specified location and with the specified size.

[Visual Basic]
```
Overloads Public Sub DrawImage( _
   ByVal image As Image, _
   ByVal destRect As Rectangle, _
   ByVal srcX As Integer, _
   ByVal srcY As Integer, _
   ByVal srcWidth As Integer, _
   ByVal srcHeight As Integer, _
   ByVal srcUnit As GraphicsUnit, _
   ByVal imageAttr As ImageAttributes _
)
```
[C#]
```
public void DrawImage(
   Image image,
   Rectangle destRect,
   int srcX,
   int srcY,
   int srcWidth,
   int srcHeight,
   GraphicsUnit srcUnit,
   ImageAttributes imageAttr
);
```
[C++]
```
public: void DrawImage(
   Image* image,
   Rectangle destRect,
   int srcX,
   int srcY,
   int srcWidth,
   int srcHeight,
   GraphicsUnit srcUnit,
   ImageAttributes* imageAttr
);
```
[JScript]
```
public function DrawImage(
   image : Image,
   destRect : Rectangle,
   srcX : int,
   srcY : int,
   srcWidth : int,
   srcHeight : int,
   srcUnit : GraphicsUnit,
   imageAttr : ImageAttributes
);
```

Parameters

image
: **Image** object to draw.

destRect
: **Rectangle** structure that specifies the location and size of the drawn image. The image is scaled to fit the rectangle.

srcX
: x-coordinate of the upper-left corner of the portion of the source image to draw.

srcY
: y-coordinate of the upper-left corner of the portion of the source image to draw.

srcWidth
: Width of the portion of the source image to draw.

srcHeight
: Height of the portion of the source image to draw.

srcUnit
: Member of the **GraphicsUnit** enumeration that specifies the units of measure used to determine the source rectangle.

imageAttr
: **ImageAttributes** object that specifies recoloring and gamma information for the *image* object.

Return Value

This method does not return a value.

Remarks

The *srcX*, *srcY*, *srcWidth*, and *srcHeight* parameters specify a rectangular portion, of the *image* object to draw. The rectangle is relative to the upper-left corner of the source image. This portion is scaled to fit inside the rectangle specified by the *destRect* parameter.

Example

[Visual Basic, C#] The following example is designed for use with Windows Forms, and it requires **PaintEventArgs** *e*, which is a parameter of the **Paint** event handler. The code performs the following actions:

- Creates an image from a JPEG file SampImag.jpg in the folder of the example.
- Creates a destination rectangle in which to draw the image.
- Creates the coordinates of a source rectangle from which to extract a portion of the image.
- Sets the unit of measure of the source rectangle to pixels.
- Draws the original image to the screen.
- Creates an additional rectangle in which to draw an adjusted image.
- Creates and sets the attributes of the adjusted image to have a larger-than-usual gamma value.
- Draws the adjusted image to the screen.

[Visual Basic, C#] For the original, unadjusted destination rectangle, the position locates the image on the screen, and the sizes of the source and destination rectangles determine the scaling of the drawn image, and the size of the source rectangle determines what portion of the original image is drawn to the screen.

[Visual Basic]
```
Public Sub DrawImageRect4IntAtrrib(e As PaintEventArgs)
' Create image.
Dim newImage As Image = Image.FromFile("SampImag.jpg")
' Create rectangle for displaying original image.
Dim destRect1 As New Rectangle(100, 25, 450, 150)
' Create coordinates of rectangle for source image.
Dim x As Integer = 50
Dim y As Integer = 50
Dim width As Integer = 150
Dim height As Integer = 150
Dim units As GraphicsUnit = GraphicsUnit.Pixel
' Draw original image to screen.
e.Graphics.DrawImage(newImage, destRect1, x, y, width, height, _
units)
```

```
' Create rectangle for adjusted image.
Dim destRect2 As New Rectangle(100, 175, 450, 150)
' Create image attributes and set large gamma.
Dim imageAttr As New ImageAttributes()
imageAttr.SetGamma(4F)
' Draw adjusted image to screen.
e.Graphics.DrawImage(newImage, destRect2, x, y, width, height, _
units, imageAttr)
End Sub
```

[C#]

```
public void DrawImageRect4IntAtrrib(PaintEventArgs e)
{
// Create image.
Image newImage = Image.FromFile("SampImag.jpg");
// Create rectangle for displaying original image.
Rectangle destRect1 = new Rectangle(100, 25, 450, 150);
// Create coordinates of rectangle for source image.
int x = 50;
int y = 50;
int width = 150;
int height = 150;
GraphicsUnit units = GraphicsUnit.Pixel;
// Draw original image to screen.
e.Graphics.DrawImage(newImage, destRect1, x, y, width, height, units);
// Create rectangle for adjusted image.
Rectangle destRect2 = new Rectangle(100, 175, 450, 150);
// Create image attributes and set large gamma.
ImageAttributes imageAttr = new ImageAttributes();
imageAttr.SetGamma(4.0F);
// Draw adjusted image to screen.
e.Graphics.DrawImage(newImage, destRect2, x, y, width, height, units,
imageAttr);
}
```

Requirements

Platforms: Windows 98, Windows NT 4.0,
Windows Millennium Edition, Windows 2000,
Windows XP Home Edition, Windows XP Professional,
Windows Server 2003 family,
.NET Compact Framework - Windows CE .NET

Graphics.DrawImage Method (Image, Rectangle, Single, Single, Single, Single, GraphicsUnit, ImageAttributes)

Draws the specified portion of the specified **Image** object at the specified location and with the specified size.

[Visual Basic]

```
Overloads Public Sub DrawImage( _
   ByVal image As Image, _
   ByVal destRect As Rectangle, _
   ByVal srcX As Single, _
   ByVal srcY As Single, _
   ByVal srcWidth As Single, _
   ByVal srcHeight As Single, _
   ByVal srcUnit As GraphicsUnit, _
   ByVal imageAttrs As ImageAttributes _
)
```

[C#]

```
public void DrawImage(
   Image image,
   Rectangle destRect,
   float srcX,
   float srcY,
   float srcWidth,
   float srcHeight,
   GraphicsUnit srcUnit,
   ImageAttributes imageAttrs
);
```

[C++]

```
public: void DrawImage(
   Image* image,
   Rectangle destRect,
   float srcX,
   float srcY,
   float srcWidth,
   float srcHeight,
   GraphicsUnit srcUnit,
   ImageAttributes* imageAttrs
);
```

[JScript]

```
public function DrawImage(
   image : Image,
   destRect : Rectangle,
   srcX : float,
   srcY : float,
   srcWidth : float,
   srcHeight : float,
   srcUnit : GraphicsUnit,
   imageAttrs : ImageAttributes
);
```

Parameters

image
: **Image** object to draw.

destRect
: **Rectangle** structure that specifies the location and size of the drawn image. The image is scaled to fit the rectangle.

srcX
: x-coordinate of the upper-left corner of the portion of the source image to draw.

srcY
: y-coordinate of the upper-left corner of the portion of the source image to draw.

srcWidth
: Width of the portion of the source image to draw.

srcHeight
: Height of the portion of the source image to draw.

srcUnit
: Member of the **GraphicsUnit** enumeration that specifies the units of measure used to determine the source rectangle.

imageAttrs
: **ImageAttributes** object that specifies recoloring and gamma information for the *image* object.

Return Value

This method does not return a value.

Remarks

The *srcX*, *srcY*, *srcWidth*, and *srcHeight* parameters specify a rectangular portion, of the *image* object to draw. The rectangle is relative to the upper-left corner of the source image. This portion is scaled to fit inside the rectangle specified by the *destRect* parameter.

Example

[Visual Basic, C#] The following example is designed for use with Windows Forms, and it requires **PaintEventArgs** *e*, which is a parameter of the **Paint** event handler. The code performs the following actions:

- Creates an image from a JPEG file SampImag.jpg in the folder of the example.
- Creates a destination rectangle in which to draw the image.
- Creates the coordinates of a source rectangle from which to extract a portion of the image.
- Sets the unit of measure of the source rectangle to pixels.
- Draws the original image to the screen.
- Creates an additional rectangle in which to draw an adjusted image.
- Creates and sets the attributes of the adjusted image to have a larger-than-usual gamma value.
- Draws the adjusted image to the screen.

[Visual Basic, C#] For the original, unadjusted destination rectangle, the position locates the image on the screen, and the sizes of the source and destination rectangles determine the scaling of the drawn image, and the size of the source rectangle determines what portion of the original image is drawn to the screen.

[Visual Basic]

```
Public Sub DrawImageRect4FloatAttrib(e As PaintEventArgs)
' Create image.
Dim newImage As Image = Image.FromFile("SampImag.jpg")
' Create rectangle for displaying original image.
Dim destRect1 As New Rectangle(100, 25, 450, 150)
' Create coordinates of rectangle for source image.
Dim x As Single = 50F
Dim y As Single = 50F
Dim width As Single = 150F
Dim height As Single = 150F
Dim units As GraphicsUnit = GraphicsUnit.Pixel
' Draw original image to screen.
e.Graphics.DrawImage(newImage, destRect1, x, y, width, _
height, units)
' Create rectangle for adjusted image.
Dim destRect2 As New Rectangle(100, 175, 450, 150)
' Create image attributes and set large gamma.
Dim imageAttr As New ImageAttributes()
imageAttr.SetGamma(4F)
' Draw adjusted image to screen.
e.Graphics.DrawImage(newImage, destRect2, x, y, width, height, _
units, imageAttr)
End Sub
```

[C#]

```
public void DrawImageRect4FloatAttrib(PaintEventArgs e)
{
// Create image.
Image newImage = Image.FromFile("SampImag.jpg");
// Create rectangle for displaying original image.
Rectangle destRect1 = new Rectangle( 100, 25, 450, 150);
// Create coordinates of rectangle for source image.
float x = 50.0F;
float y = 50.0F;
float width = 150.0F;
float height = 150.0F;
GraphicsUnit units = GraphicsUnit.Pixel;
// Draw original image to screen.
e.Graphics.DrawImage(newImage, destRect1, x, y, width, height, units);
// Create rectangle for adjusted image.
Rectangle destRect2 = new Rectangle(100, 175, 450, 150);
// Create image attributes and set large gamma.
ImageAttributes imageAttr = new ImageAttributes();
imageAttr.SetGamma(4.0F);
// Draw adjusted image to screen.
e.Graphics.DrawImage(newImage, destRect2, x, y, width, height,
 units, imageAttr);
}
```

Requirements

Platforms: Windows 98, Windows NT 4.0, Windows Millennium Edition, Windows 2000, Windows XP Home Edition, Windows XP Professional, Windows Server 2003 family

Graphics.DrawImage Method (Image, Rectangle, Int32, Int32, Int32, Int32, GraphicsUnit, ImageAttributes, Graphics.DrawImageAbort)

Draws the specified portion of the specified **Image** object at the specified location and with the specified size.

[Visual Basic]

```
Overloads Public Sub DrawImage( _
   ByVal image As Image, _
   ByVal destRect As Rectangle, _
   ByVal srcX As Integer, _
   ByVal srcY As Integer, _
   ByVal srcWidth As Integer, _
   ByVal srcHeight As Integer, _
   ByVal srcUnit As GraphicsUnit, _
   ByVal imageAttr As ImageAttributes, _
   ByVal callback As Graphics.DrawImageAbort _
)
```

[C#]

```
public void DrawImage(
   Image image,
   Rectangle destRect,
   int srcX,
   int srcY,
   int srcWidth,
   int srcHeight,
   GraphicsUnit srcUnit,
   ImageAttributes imageAttr,
   Graphics.DrawImageAbort callback
);
```

[C++]

```
public: void DrawImage(
   Image* image,
   Rectangle destRect,
   int srcX,
   int srcY,
   int srcWidth,
   int srcHeight,
   GraphicsUnit srcUnit,
   ImageAttributes* imageAttr,
   Graphics.DrawImageAbort* callback
);
```

[JScript]

```
public function DrawImage(
   image : Image,
   destRect : Rectangle,
   srcX : int,
   srcY : int,
   srcWidth : int,
   srcHeight : int,
   srcUnit : GraphicsUnit,
   imageAttr : ImageAttributes,
   callback : Graphics.DrawImageAbort
);
```

Parameters

image

Image object to draw.

destRect

Rectangle structure that specifies the location and size of the drawn image. The image is scaled to fit the rectangle.

srcX

x-coordinate of the upper-left corner of the portion of the source image to draw.

srcY

y-coordinate of the upper-left corner of the portion of the source image to draw.

srcWidth

Width of the portion of the source image to draw.

srcHeight

Height of the portion of the source image to draw.

srcUnit

Member of the **GraphicsUnit** enumeration that specifies the units of measure used to determine the source rectangle.

imageAttr

ImageAttributes object that specifies recoloring and gamma information for *image*.

callback

Graphics.DrawImageAbort delegate that specifies a method to call during the drawing of the image. This method is called frequently to check whether to stop execution of the **DrawImage** method according to application-determined criteria.

Return Value

This method does not return a value.

Remarks

The *srcX*, *srcY*, *srcWidth*, and *srcHeight* parameters specify a rectangular portion, of the *image* object to draw. The rectangle is relative to the upper-left corner of the source image. This portion is scaled to fit inside the rectangle specified by the *destRect* object.

This overload with the *callback* parameter provides the means to stop the drawing of an image once it starts according to criteria determined by the application. For example, an application could start drawing a large image and the user might scroll the image off the screen, in which case the application could stop the drawing.

Example

[Visual Basic, C#] The following example is designed for use with Windows Forms, and it requires **PaintEventArgs** *e*, which is a parameter of the **Paint** event handler. The code first defines a callback method for the **DrawImageAbort** delegate; the definition is simplistic and merely tests to see whether the **DrawImage** method calls it with a null *callBackData* parameter. The main body of the example performs the following actions:

- Creates an instance of the **DrawImageAbort** callback method.
- Creates an image from a JPEG file SampImag.jpg in the folder of the example.
- Creates points that define a destination rectangle in which to draw the image.
- Creates a source rectangle to select the portion of the image to draw.
- Sets the graphics drawing unit to pixel.
- Draws the original image to the screen.
- Creates an additional destination rectangle in which to draw an adjusted image.
- Creates and sets the attributes of the adjusted image to have a larger-than-usual gamma value.
- Draws the adjusted image to the screen.

[Visual Basic, C#] For the original, unadjusted destination rectangle, the position locates the image on the screen, and the size of the source rectangle and the size and shape of the destination rectangle determines the scaling of the drawn image.

[Visual Basic, C#] Because this example uses an overload that does not pass a *callBackData* parameter, the **DrawImageAbort** callback returns **true**, which causes the **DrawImage** method to abort, and the exception-handling code included in the example prints out the exception text rather than drawing the image.

[Visual Basic]

```
Private Function DrawImageCallback(callBackData As IntPtr) As Boolean
' Test for call that passes callBackData parameter.
If callBackData.Equals(IntPtr.Zero) Then
' If no callBackData passed, abort DrawImage method.
Return True
Else
' If callBackData passed, continue DrawImage method.
Return False
End If
End Function
Public Sub DrawImageRect4IntAtrribAbort(e As PaintEventArgs)
' Create callback method.
Dim imageCallback As New _
Graphics.DrawImageAbort(AddressOf DrawImageCallback)
' Create image.
Dim newImage As Image = Image.FromFile("SampImag.jpg")
' Create rectangle for displaying original image.
Dim destRect1 As New Rectangle(100, 25, 450, 150)
' Create coordinates of rectangle for source image.
Dim x As Integer = 50
Dim y As Integer = 50
Dim width As Integer = 150
Dim height As Integer = 150
Dim units As GraphicsUnit = GraphicsUnit.Pixel
' Draw original image to screen.
e.Graphics.DrawImage(newImage, destRect1, x, y, width, height, _
units)
' Create rectangle for adjusted image.
Dim destRect2 As New Rectangle(100, 175, 450, 150)
' Create image attributes and set large gamma.
Dim imageAttr As New ImageAttributes()
imageAttr.SetGamma(4F)
Try
' Draw adjusted image to screen.
e.Graphics.DrawImage(newImage, destRect2, x, y, width, _
height, units, imageAttr, imageCallback)
Catch ex As Exception
e.Graphics.DrawString(ex.ToString(), New Font("Arial", 8), _
Brushes.Black, New PointF(0, 0))
End Try
End Sub
```

[C#]

```
// Define DrawImageAbort callback method.
private bool DrawImageCallback(IntPtr callBackData)
{
// Test for call that passes callBackData parameter.
if(callBackData==IntPtr.Zero)
{
// If no callBackData passed, abort DrawImage method.
return true;
}
else
{
// If callBackData passed, continue DrawImage method.
return false;
}
}
```

```
public void DrawImageRect4IntAtrribAbort(PaintEventArgs e)
{
// Create callback method.
Graphics.DrawImageAbort imageCallback
= new Graphics.DrawImageAbort(DrawImageCallback);
// Create image.
Image newImage = Image.FromFile("SampImag.jpg");
// Create rectangle for displaying original image.
Rectangle destRect1 = new Rectangle(100, 25, 450, 150);
// Create coordinates of rectangle for source image.
int x = 50;
int y = 50;
int width = 150;
int height = 150;
GraphicsUnit units = GraphicsUnit.Pixel;
// Draw original image to screen.
e.Graphics.DrawImage(newImage, destRect1, x, y, width, height, units);
// Create rectangle for adjusted image.
Rectangle destRect2 = new Rectangle(100, 175, 450, 150);
// Create image attributes and set large gamma.
ImageAttributes imageAttr = new ImageAttributes();
imageAttr.SetGamma(4.0F);
try
{
checked
{
// Draw adjusted image to screen.
e.Graphics.DrawImage(
newImage,
destRect2,
x, y,
width, height,
units,
imageAttr,
imageCallback);
}
}
catch (Exception ex)
{
e.Graphics.DrawString(
ex.ToString(),
new Font("Arial", 8),
Brushes.Black,
new PointF(0, 0));
}
}
```

Requirements

Platforms: Windows 98, Windows NT 4.0, Windows Millennium Edition, Windows 2000, Windows XP Home Edition, Windows XP Professional, Windows Server 2003 family

Graphics.DrawImage Method (Image, Rectangle, Single, Single, Single, Single, GraphicsUnit, ImageAttributes, Graphics.DrawImageAbort)

Draws the specified portion of the specified **Image** object at the specified location and with the specified size.

[Visual Basic]
```
Overloads Public Sub DrawImage( _
   ByVal image As Image, _
   ByVal destRect As Rectangle, _
   ByVal srcX As Single, _
   ByVal srcY As Single, _
   ByVal srcWidth As Single, _
   ByVal srcHeight As Single, _
   ByVal srcUnit As GraphicsUnit, _
   ByVal imageAttrs As ImageAttributes, _
   ByVal callback As Graphics.DrawImageAbort _
)
```
[C#]
```
public void DrawImage(
   Image image,
   Rectangle destRect,
   float srcX,
   float srcY,
   float srcWidth,
   float srcHeight,
   GraphicsUnit srcUnit,
   ImageAttributes imageAttrs,
   Graphics.DrawImageAbort callback
);
```
[C++]
```
public: void DrawImage(
   Image* image,
   Rectangle destRect,
   float srcX,
   float srcY,
   float srcWidth,
   float srcHeight,
   GraphicsUnit srcUnit,
   ImageAttributes* imageAttrs,
   Graphics.DrawImageAbort* callback
);
```
[JScript]
```
public function DrawImage(
   image : Image,
   destRect : Rectangle,
   srcX : float,
   srcY : float,
   srcWidth : float,
   srcHeight : float,
   srcUnit : GraphicsUnit,
   imageAttrs : ImageAttributes,
   callback : Graphics.DrawImageAbort
);
```

Parameters

image
: **Image** object to draw.

destRect
: **Rectangle** structure that specifies the location and size of the drawn image. The image is scaled to fit the rectangle.

srcX
: x-coordinate of the upper-left corner of the portion of the source image to draw.

srcY
: y-coordinate of the upper-left corner of the portion of the source image to draw.

srcWidth
: Width of the portion of the source image to draw.

srcHeight
: Height of the portion of the source image to draw.

srcUnit
: Member of the **GraphicsUnit** enumeration that specifies the units of measure used to determine the source rectangle.

imageAttrs
: **ImageAttributes** object that specifies recoloring and gamma information for the *image* object.

callback

Graphics.DrawImageAbort delegate that specifies a method to call during the drawing of the image. This method is called frequently to check whether to stop execution of the **DrawImage** method according to application-determined criteria.

Return Value

This method does not return a value.

Remarks

The *srcX*, *srcY*, *srcWidth*, and *srcHeight* parameters specify a rectangular portion, of the *image* object to draw. The rectangle is relative to the upper-left corner of the source image. This portion is scaled to fit inside the rectangle specified by the *destRect* parameter.

This overload with the *callback* parameter provides the means to stop the drawing of an image once it starts according to criteria determined by the application. For example, an application could start drawing a large image and the user might scroll the image off the screen, in which case the application could stop the drawing.

Example

[Visual Basic, C#] The following example is designed for use with Windows Forms, and it requires **PaintEventArgs** *e*, which is a parameter of the **Paint** event handler. The code first defines a callback method for the **DrawImageAbort** delegate; the definition is simplistic and merely tests to see whether the **DrawImage** method calls it with a null *callBackData* parameter. The main body of the example performs the following actions:

- Creates an instance of the **DrawImageAbort** callback method.
- Creates an image from a JPEG file SampImag.jpg in the folder of the example.
- Creates points that define a destination rectangle in which to draw the image.
- Creates a source rectangle to select the portion of the image to draw.
- Sets the graphics drawing unit to pixel.
- Draws the original image to the screen.
- Creates an additional destination rectangle in which to draw an adjusted image.
- Creates and sets the attributes of the adjusted image to have a larger-than-usual gamma value.
- Draws the adjusted image to the screen.

[Visual Basic, C#] For the original, unadjusted destination rectangle, the position locates the image on the screen, and the size of the source rectangle and the size and shape of the destination rectangle determines the scaling of the drawn image.

[Visual Basic, C#] Because this example uses an overload that does not pass a *callBackData* parameter, the **DrawImageAbort** callback returns **true**, which causes the **DrawImage** method to abort, and the exception-handling code included in the example prints out the exception text rather than drawing the image.

[Visual Basic]

```
Private Function DrawImageCallback(callBackData As IntPtr) As Boolean
' Test for call that passes callBackData parameter.
If callBackData.Equals(IntPtr.Zero) Then
' If no callBackData passed, abort DrawImage method.
Return True
Else
' If callBackData passed, continue DrawImage method.
Return False
End If
End Function
Public Sub DrawImageRect4FloatAttribAbort(e As PaintEventArgs)
' Create callback method.
Dim imageCallback As New _
Graphics.DrawImageAbort(AddressOf DrawImageCallback)
' Create image.
Dim newImage As Image = Image.FromFile("SampImag.jpg")
' Create rectangle for displaying original image.
Dim destRect1 As New Rectangle(100, 25, 450, 150)
' Create coordinates of rectangle for source image.
Dim x As Single = 50F
Dim y As Single = 50F
Dim width As Single = 150F
Dim height As Single = 150F
Dim units As GraphicsUnit = GraphicsUnit.Pixel
' Draw original image to screen.
e.Graphics.DrawImage(newImage, destRect1, x, y, width, _
height, units)
' Create rectangle for adjusted image.
Dim destRect2 As New Rectangle(100, 175, 450, 150)
' Create image attributes and set large gamma.
Dim imageAttr As New ImageAttributes()
imageAttr.SetGamma(4F)
Try
' Draw adjusted image to screen.
e.Graphics.DrawImage(newImage, destRect2, x, y, width, _
height, units, imageAttr, imageCallback)
Catch ex As Exception
e.Graphics.DrawString(ex.ToString(), New Font("Arial", 8), _
Brushes.Black, New PointF(0, 0))
End Try
End Sub
```

[C#]

```
// Define DrawImageAbort callback method.
private bool DrawImageCallback(IntPtr callBackData)
{
// Test for call that passes callBackData parameter.
if(callBackData==IntPtr.Zero)
{
// If no callBackData passed, abort DrawImage method.
return true;
}
else
{
// If callBackData passed, continue DrawImage method.
return false;
}
}
public void DrawImageRect4FloatAttribAbort(PaintEventArgs e)
{
// Create callback method.
Graphics.DrawImageAbort imageCallback
= new Graphics.DrawImageAbort(DrawImageCallback);
// Create image.
Image newImage = Image.FromFile("SampImag.jpg");
// Create rectangle for displaying original image.
Rectangle destRect1 = new Rectangle( 100, 25, 450, 150);
// Create coordinates of rectangle for source image.
float x = 50.0F;
float y = 50.0F;
float width = 150.0F;
float height = 150.0F;
GraphicsUnit units = GraphicsUnit.Pixel;
// Draw original image to screen.
e.Graphics.DrawImage(newImage, destRect1, x, y, width, height, units);
// Create rectangle for adjusted image.
Rectangle destRect2 = new Rectangle(100, 175, 450, 150);
// Create image attributes and set large gamma.
ImageAttributes imageAttr = new ImageAttributes();
imageAttr.SetGamma(4.0F);
try
{
checked
{
// Draw adjusted image to screen.
e.Graphics.DrawImage(
newImage,
destRect2,
x, y,
```

```
width, height,
units,
imageAttr,
imageCallback);
}
}
catch (Exception ex)
{
e.Graphics.DrawString(
ex.ToString(),
new Font("Arial", 8),
Brushes.Black,
new PointF(0, 0));
}
}
```

Requirements

Platforms: Windows 98, Windows NT 4.0, Windows Millennium Edition, Windows 2000, Windows XP Home Edition, Windows XP Professional, Windows Server 2003 family

Graphics.DrawImage Method (Image, Rectangle, Int32, Int32, Int32, Int32, GraphicsUnit, ImageAttributes, Graphics.DrawImageAbort, IntPtr)

Draws the specified portion of the specified **Image** object at the specified location and with the specified size.

[Visual Basic]

```
Overloads Public Sub DrawImage( _
   ByVal image As Image, _
   ByVal destRect As Rectangle, _
   ByVal srcX As Integer, _
   ByVal srcY As Integer, _
   ByVal srcWidth As Integer, _
   ByVal srcHeight As Integer, _
   ByVal srcUnit As GraphicsUnit, _
   ByVal imageAttrs As ImageAttributes, _
   ByVal callback As Graphics.DrawImageAbort, _
   ByVal callbackData As IntPtr _
)
```

[C#]

```
public void DrawImage(
   Image image,
   Rectangle destRect,
   int srcX,
   int srcY,
   int srcWidth,
   int srcHeight,
   GraphicsUnit srcUnit,
   ImageAttributes imageAttrs,
   Graphics.DrawImageAbort callback,
   IntPtr callbackData
);
```

[C++]

```
public: void DrawImage(
   Image* image,
   Rectangle destRect,
   int srcX,
   int srcY,
   int srcWidth,
   int srcHeight,
   GraphicsUnit srcUnit,
   ImageAttributes* imageAttrs,
   Graphics.DrawImageAbort* callback,
   IntPtr callbackData
);
```

[JScript]

```
public function DrawImage(
   image : Image,
   destRect : Rectangle,
   srcX : int,
   srcY : int,
   srcWidth : int,
   srcHeight : int,
   srcUnit : GraphicsUnit,
   imageAttrs : ImageAttributes,
   callback : Graphics.DrawImageAbort,
   callbackData : IntPtr
);
```

Parameters

image
: **Image** object to draw.

destRect
: **Rectangle** structure that specifies the location and size of the drawn image. The image is scaled to fit the rectangle.

srcX
: x-coordinate of the upper-left corner of the portion of the source image to draw.

srcY
: y-coordinate of the upper-left corner of the portion of the source image to draw.

srcWidth
: Width of the portion of the source image to draw.

srcHeight
: Height of the portion of the source image to draw.

srcUnit
: Member of the **GraphicsUnit** enumeration that specifies the units of measure used to determine the source rectangle.

imageAttrs
: **ImageAttributes** object that specifies recoloring and gamma information for the *image* object.

callback
: **Graphics.DrawImageAbort** delegate that specifies a method to call during the drawing of the image. This method is called frequently to check whether to stop execution of the **DrawImage** method according to application-determined criteria.

callbackData
: Value specifying additional data for the **DrawImageAbort** delegate to use when checking whether to stop execution of the **DrawImage** method.

Return Value

This method does not return a value.

Remarks

The *srcX*, *srcY*, *srcWidth*, and *srcHeight* parameters specify a rectangular portion, of the *image* object to draw. The rectangle is relative to the upper-left corner of the source image. This portion is scaled to fit inside the rectangle specified by the *destRect* parameter.

This overload with the *callback* and *callbackData* parameters provides the means to stop the drawing of an image once it starts according to criteria and data determined by the application. For example, an application could start drawing a large image and the user might scroll the image off the screen, in which case the application could stop the drawing.

Example

[Visual Basic, C#] The following example is designed for use with Windows Forms, and it requires **PaintEventArgs** *e*, which is a parameter of the **Paint** event handler. The code first defines a callback method for the **DrawImageAbort** delegate; the definition is simplistic and merely tests to see whether the **DrawImage** method calls it with a null *callBackData* parameter. The main body of the example performs the following actions:

- Creates an instance of the **DrawImageAbort** callback method.
- Creates an image from a JPEG file SampImag.jpg in the folder of the example.
- Creates points that define a destination rectangle in which to draw the image.
- Creates a source rectangle to select the portion of the image to draw.
- Sets the graphics drawing unit to pixel.
- Draws the original image to the screen.
- Creates an additional destination rectangle in which to draw an adjusted image.
- Creates and sets the attributes of the adjusted image to have a larger-than-usual gamma value.
- Draws the adjusted image to the screen.

[Visual Basic, C#] For the original, unadjusted destination rectangle, the position locates the image on the screen, and the size of the source rectangle and the size and shape of the destination rectangle determines the scaling of the drawn image.

[Visual Basic, C#] Because this example uses an overload that passes a *callBackData* parameter, the **DrawImageAbort** callback returns **false**, which causes the **DrawImage** method to continue, and the example draws the adjusted image to the screen.

[Visual Basic]

```
Private Function DrawImageCallback(callBackData As IntPtr) As Boolean
' Test for call that passes callBackData parameter.
If callBackData.Equals(IntPtr.Zero) Then
' If no callBackData passed, abort DrawImage method.
Return True
Else
' If callBackData passed, continue DrawImage method.
Return False
End If
End Function
Public Sub DrawImageRect4IntAtrribAbortData(e As PaintEventArgs)
' Create callback method.
Dim imageCallback As New _
Graphics.DrawImageAbort(AddressOf DrawImageCallback)
Dim imageCallbackData As New IntPtr(1)
' Create image.
Dim newImage As Image = Image.FromFile("SampImag.jpg")
' Create rectangle for displaying original image.
Dim destRect1 As New Rectangle(100, 25, 450, 150)
' Create coordinates of rectangle for source image.
Dim x As Integer = 50
Dim y As Integer = 50
Dim width As Integer = 150
Dim height As Integer = 150
Dim units As GraphicsUnit = GraphicsUnit.Pixel
' Draw original image to screen.
e.Graphics.DrawImage(newImage, destRect1, x, y, width, height, _
units)
' Create rectangle for adjusted image.
Dim destRect2 As New Rectangle(100, 175, 450, 150)
' Create image attributes and set large gamma.
Dim imageAttr As New ImageAttributes()
imageAttr.SetGamma(4F)
Try
' Draw adjusted image to screen.
e.Graphics.DrawImage(newImage, destRect2, x, y, width, _
height, units, imageAttr, imageCallback, imageCallbackData)
Catch ex As Exception
e.Graphics.DrawString(ex.ToString(), New Font("Arial", 8), _
Brushes.Black, New PointF(0, 0))
End Try
End Sub
```

[C#]

```
// Define DrawImageAbort callback method.
private bool DrawImageCallback(IntPtr callBackData)
{
// Test for call that passes callBackData parameter.
if(callBackData==IntPtr.Zero)
{
// If no callBackData passed, abort DrawImage method.
return true;
}
else
{
// If callBackData passed, continue DrawImage method.
return false;
}
}
public void DrawImageRect4IntAtrribAbortData(PaintEventArgs e)
{
// Create callback method.
Graphics.DrawImageAbort imageCallback
= new Graphics.DrawImageAbort(DrawImageCallback);
IntPtr imageCallbackData = new IntPtr(1);
// Create image.
Image newImage = Image.FromFile("SampImag.jpg");
// Create rectangle for displaying original image.
Rectangle destRect1 = new Rectangle(100, 25, 450, 150);
// Create coordinates of rectangle for source image.
int x = 50;
int y = 50;
int width = 150;
int height = 150;
GraphicsUnit units = GraphicsUnit.Pixel;
// Draw original image to screen.
e.Graphics.DrawImage(newImage, destRect1, x, y, width, height, units);
// Create rectangle for adjusted image.
Rectangle destRect2 = new Rectangle(100, 175, 450, 150);
// Create image attributes and set large gamma.
ImageAttributes imageAttr = new ImageAttributes();
imageAttr.SetGamma(4.0F);
try
{
checked
{
// Draw adjusted image to screen.
e.Graphics.DrawImage(
newImage,
destRect2,
x, y,
width, height,
units,
imageAttr,
imageCallback,
imageCallbackData);
}
}
catch (Exception ex)
{
e.Graphics.DrawString(
ex.ToString(),
new Font("Arial", 8),
Brushes.Black,
new PointF(0, 0));
}
}
```

Requirements

Platforms: Windows 98, Windows NT 4.0, Windows Millennium Edition, Windows 2000, Windows XP Home Edition, Windows XP Professional, Windows Server 2003 family

Graphics.DrawImage Method (Image, Rectangle, Single, Single, Single, Single, GraphicsUnit, ImageAttributes, Graphics.DrawImageAbort, IntPtr)

Draws the specified portion of the specified **Image** object at the specified location and with the specified size.

[Visual Basic]
```
Overloads Public Sub DrawImage( _
   ByVal image As Image, _
   ByVal destRect As Rectangle, _
   ByVal srcX As Single, _
   ByVal srcY As Single, _
   ByVal srcWidth As Single, _
   ByVal srcHeight As Single, _
   ByVal srcUnit As GraphicsUnit, _
   ByVal imageAttrs As ImageAttributes, _
   ByVal callback As Graphics.DrawImageAbort, _
   ByVal callbackData As IntPtr _
)
```
[C#]
```
public void DrawImage(
   Image image,
   Rectangle destRect,
   float srcX,
   float srcY,
   float srcWidth,
   float srcHeight,
   GraphicsUnit srcUnit,
   ImageAttributes imageAttrs,
   Graphics.DrawImageAbort callback,
   IntPtr callbackData
);
```
[C++]
```
public: void DrawImage(
   Image* image,
   Rectangle destRect,
   float srcX,
   float srcY,
   float srcWidth,
   float srcHeight,
   GraphicsUnit srcUnit,
   ImageAttributes* imageAttrs,
   Graphics.DrawImageAbort* callback,
   IntPtr callbackData
);
```
[JScript]
```
public function DrawImage(
   image : Image,
   destRect : Rectangle,
   srcX : float,
   srcY : float,
   srcWidth : float,
   srcHeight : float,
   srcUnit : GraphicsUnit,
   imageAttrs : ImageAttributes,
   callback : Graphics.DrawImageAbort,
   callbackData : IntPtr
);
```

Parameters

image
: **Image** object to draw.

destRect
: **Rectangle** structure that specifies the location and size of the drawn image. The image is scaled to fit the rectangle.

srcX
: x-coordinate of the upper-left corner of the portion of the source image to draw.

srcY
: y-coordinate of the upper-left corner of the portion of the source image to draw.

srcWidth
: Width of the portion of the source image to draw.

srcHeight
: Height of the portion of the source image to draw.

srcUnit
: Member of the **GraphicsUnit** enumeration that specifies the units of measure used to determine the source rectangle.

imageAttrs
: **ImageAttributes** object that specifies recoloring and gamma information for the *image* object.

callback
: **Graphics.DrawImageAbort** delegate that specifies a method to call during the drawing of the image. This method is called frequently to check whether to stop execution of the **DrawImage** method according to application-determined criteria.

callbackData
: Value specifying additional data for the **DrawImageAbort** delegate to use when checking whether to stop execution of the **DrawImage** method.

Return Value

This method does not return a value.

Remarks

The *srcX*, *srcY*, *srcWidth*, and *srcHeight* parameters specify a rectangular portion, of the *image* object to draw. The rectangle is relative to the upper-left corner of the source image. This portion is scaled to fit inside the rectangle specified by the *destRect* parameter.

This overload with the *callback* and *callbackData* parameters provides the means to stop the drawing of an image once it starts according to criteria and data determined by the application. For example, an application could start drawing a large image and the user might scroll the image off the screen, in which case the application could stop the drawing.

Example

[Visual Basic, C#] The following example is designed for use with Windows Forms, and it requires **PaintEventArgs** *e*, which is a parameter of the **Paint** event handler. The code first defines a callback method for the **DrawImageAbort** delegate; the definition is simplistic and merely tests to see whether the **DrawImage** method calls it with a null *callBackData* parameter. The main body of the example performs the following actions:

- Creates an instance of the **DrawImageAbort** callback method.
- Creates an image from a JPEG file SampImag.jpg in the folder of the example.
- Creates points that define a destination rectangle in which to draw the image.
- Creates a source rectangle to select the portion of the image to draw.
- Sets the graphics drawing unit to pixel.
- Draws the original image to the screen.
- Creates an additional destination rectangle in which to draw an adjusted image.
- Creates and sets the attributes of the adjusted image to have a larger-than-usual gamma value.
- Draws the adjusted image to the screen.

[Visual Basic, C#] For the original, unadjusted destination rectangle, the position locates the image on the screen, and the size of the source rectangle and the size and shape of the destination rectangle determines the scaling of the drawn image.

[Visual Basic, C#] Because this example uses an overload that passes a *callBackData* parameter, the **DrawImageAbort** callback returns **false**, which causes the **DrawImage** method to continue, and the example draws the adjusted image to the screen.

[Visual Basic]

```
Private Function DrawImageCallback(callBackData As IntPtr) As Boolean
' Test for call that passes callBackData parameter.
If callBackData.Equals(IntPtr.Zero) Then
' If no callBackData passed, abort DrawImage method.
Return True
Else
' If callBackData passed, continue DrawImage method.
Return False
End If
End Function
Public Sub DrawImageRect4FloatAttribAbortData(e As PaintEventArgs)
' Create callback method.
Dim imageCallback As New _
Graphics.DrawImageAbort(AddressOf DrawImageCallback)
Dim imageCallbackData As New IntPtr(1)
' Create image.
Dim newImage As Image = Image.FromFile("SampImag.jpg")
' Create rectangle for displaying original image.
Dim destRect1 As New Rectangle(100, 25, 450, 150)
' Create coordinates of rectangle for source image.
Dim x As Single = 50F
Dim y As Single = 50F
Dim width As Single = 150F
Dim height As Single = 150F
Dim units As GraphicsUnit = GraphicsUnit.Pixel
' Draw original image to screen.
e.Graphics.DrawImage(newImage, destRect1, x, y, width, _
height, units)
' Create rectangle for adjusted image.
Dim destRect2 As New Rectangle(100, 175, 450, 150)
' Create image attributes and set large gamma.
Dim imageAttr As New ImageAttributes()
imageAttr.SetGamma(4F)
' Draw adjusted image to screen.
Try
' Draw adjusted image to screen.
e.Graphics.DrawImage(newImage, destRect2, x, y, width, _
height, units, imageAttr, imageCallback, imageCallbackData)
Catch ex As Exception
e.Graphics.DrawString(ex.ToString(), New Font("Arial", 8), _
Brushes.Black, New PointF(0, 0))
End Try
End Sub
```

[C#]

```
// Define DrawImageAbort callback method.
private bool DrawImageCallback(IntPtr callBackData)
{
// Test for call that passes callBackData parameter.
if(callBackData==IntPtr.Zero)
{
// If no callBackData passed, abort DrawImage method.
return true;
}
else
{
// If callBackData passed, continue DrawImage method.
return false;
}
}
public void DrawImageRect4FloatAttribAbortData(PaintEventArgs e)
{
// Create callback method.
Graphics.DrawImageAbort imageCallback
= new Graphics.DrawImageAbort(DrawImageCallback);
IntPtr imageCallbackData = new IntPtr(1);
// Create image.
Image newImage = Image.FromFile("SampImag.jpg");
// Create rectangle for displaying original image.
Rectangle destRect1 = new Rectangle( 100, 25, 450, 150);
// Create coordinates of rectangle for source image.
float x = 50.0F;
float y = 50.0F;
float width = 150.0F;
float height = 150.0F;
GraphicsUnit units = GraphicsUnit.Pixel;
// Draw original image to screen.
e.Graphics.DrawImage(newImage, destRect1, x, y, width, height, units);
// Create rectangle for adjusted image.
Rectangle destRect2 = new Rectangle(100, 175, 450, 150);
// Create image attributes and set large gamma.
ImageAttributes imageAttr = new ImageAttributes();
imageAttr.SetGamma(4.0F);
// Draw adjusted image to screen.
try
{
checked
{
// Draw adjusted image to screen.
e.Graphics.DrawImage(
newImage,
destRect2,
x, y,
width, height,
units,
imageAttr,
imageCallback,
imageCallbackData);
}
}
catch (Exception ex)
{
e.Graphics.DrawString(
ex.ToString(),
new Font("Arial", 8),
Brushes.Black,
new PointF(0, 0));
}
}
```

Requirements

Platforms: Windows 98, Windows NT 4.0, Windows Millennium Edition, Windows 2000, Windows XP Home Edition, Windows XP Professional, Windows Server 2003 family

Graphics.DrawImageUnscaled Method

Draws the specified image using its original physical size at the location specified by a coordinate pair.

Overload List

Draws a specified image using its original physical size at a specified location.

[Visual Basic] **Overloads Public Sub DrawImage-Unscaled(Image, Point)**

[C#] **public void DrawImageUnscaled(Image, Point);**

[C++] **public: void DrawImageUnscaled(Image*, Point);**

[JScript] **public function DrawImageUnscaled(Image, Point);**

Draws a specified image using its original physical size at a specified location.

[Visual Basic] **Overloads Public Sub DrawImage-Unscaled(Image, Rectangle)**

[C#] **public void DrawImageUnscaled(Image, Rectangle);**

[C++] **public: void DrawImageUnscaled(Image*, Rectangle);**

[JScript] **public function DrawImageUnscaled(Image, Rectangle);**

Draws the specified image using its original physical size at the location specified by a coordinate pair.

[Visual Basic] **Overloads Public Sub DrawImage-Unscaled(Image, Integer, Integer)**

[C#] **public void DrawImageUnscaled(Image, int, int);**

[C++] **public: void DrawImageUnscaled(Image*, int, int);**

[JScript] **public function DrawImageUnscaled(Image, int, int);**

Draws a specified image using its original physical size at a specified location.

[Visual Basic] **Overloads Public Sub DrawImageUnscaled(Image, Integer, Integer, Integer, Integer)**

[C#] **public void DrawImageUnscaled(Image, int, int, int, int);**

[C++] **public: void DrawImageUnscaled(Image*, int, int, int, int);**

[JScript] **public function DrawImageUnscaled(Image, int, int, int, int);**

Example

[Visual Basic, C#] The following example is designed for use with Windows Forms, and it requires **PaintEventArgs** *e*, which is a parameter of the **Paint** event handler. The code performs the following actions:

- Creates an image from a JPEG file, SampImag.jpg, in the folder of the example.
- Creates a point at which to draw the upper-left corner of the image.
- Draws the entire image using its physical size.

> [Visual Basic, C#] **Note** This example shows how to use one of the overloaded versions of **DrawImageUnscaled**. For other examples that might be available, see the individual overload topics.

[Visual Basic]
```
Public Sub DrawImageUnscaledInt(e As PaintEventArgs)
' Create image.
Dim newImage As Image = Image.FromFile("SampImag.jpg")
' Create coordinates for upper-left corner of image.
Dim x As Integer = 100
Dim y As Integer = 100
' Draw image to screen.
e.Graphics.DrawImageUnscaled(newImage, x, y)
End Sub
```

[C#]
```
public void DrawImageUnscaledInt(PaintEventArgs e)
{
// Create image.
Image newImage = Image.FromFile("SampImag.jpg");
// Create coordinates for upper-left corner of image.
int x = 100;
int y = 100;
// Draw image to screen.
e.Graphics.DrawImageUnscaled(newImage, x, y);
}
```

Graphics.DrawImageUnscaled Method (Image, Point)

Draws a specified image using its original physical size at a specified location.

[Visual Basic]
```
Overloads Public Sub DrawImageUnscaled( _
   ByVal image As Image, _
   ByVal point As Point _
)
```
[C#]
```
public void DrawImageUnscaled(
   Image image,
   Point point
);
```
[C++]
```
public: void DrawImageUnscaled(
   Image* image,
   Point point
);
```
[JScript]
```
public function DrawImageUnscaled(
   image : Image,
   point : Point
);
```

Parameters

image

Image object to draw.

point

Point structure that specifies the upper-left corner of the drawn image.

Return Value

This method does not return a value.

Remarks

An **Image** object stores a value for pixel width and a value for horizontal resolution (dots per inch). The physical width, measured in inches, of an image is the pixel width divided by the horizontal resolution. For example, an image with a pixel width of 216 and a horizontal resolution of 72 dots per inch has a physical width of 3 inches. Similar remarks apply to pixel height and physical height.

The **DrawImageUnscaled** method draws an image using its physical size, so the image will have its correct size in inches regardless of the resolution (dots per inch) of the display device. For example, suppose an image has a pixel width of 216 and a horizontal resolution of 72 dots per inch. If you call **DrawImageUnscaled** to draw that image on a device that has a resolution of 96 dots per inch, the pixel width of the rendered image will be (216/72)*96 = 288.

The call DrawImageUnscaled(image, point) has exactly the same effect as the call DrawImage(image, point.X, Point.Y).

Example

[Visual Basic, C#] The following example is designed for use with Windows Forms, and it requires **PaintEventArgs** *e*, which is a parameter of the **Paint** event handler. The code performs the following actions:

- Creates an image from a JPEG file SampImag.jpg in the folder of the example.
- Creates a point at which to draw the upper-left corner of the image.
- Draws the entire image using its physical size.

[Visual Basic]
```
Public Sub DrawImageUnscaledPoint(e As PaintEventArgs)
' Create image.
Dim newImage As Image = Image.FromFile("SampImag.jpg")
' Create point for upper-left corner of image.
Dim ulCorner As New Point(100, 100)
' Draw image to screen.
e.Graphics.DrawImageUnscaled(newImage, ulCorner)
End Sub
```

[C#]
```
public void DrawImageUnscaledPoint(PaintEventArgs e)
{
// Create image.
Image newImage = Image.FromFile("SampImag.jpg");
// Create point for upper-left corner of image.
Point ulCorner = new Point(100, 100);
// Draw image to screen.
e.Graphics.DrawImageUnscaled(newImage, ulCorner);
}
```

Requirements

Platforms: Windows 98, Windows NT 4.0, Windows Millennium Edition, Windows 2000, Windows XP Home Edition, Windows XP Professional, Windows Server 2003 family

Graphics.DrawImageUnscaled Method (Image, Rectangle)

Draws a specified image using its original physical size at a specified location.

[Visual Basic]
```
Overloads Public Sub DrawImageUnscaled( _
   ByVal image As Image, _
   ByVal rect As Rectangle _
)
```
[C#]
```
public void DrawImageUnscaled(
   Image image,
   Rectangle rect
);
```
[C++]
```
public: void DrawImageUnscaled(
   Image* image,
   Rectangle rect
);
```
[JScript]
```
public function DrawImageUnscaled(
   image : Image,
   rect : Rectangle
);
```

Parameters

image
: **Image** object to draw.

rect
: **Rectangle** that specifies the upper-left corner of the drawn image. The X and Y properties of the rectangle specify the upper-left corner. The Width and Height properties are ignored.

Return Value

This method does not return a value.

Remarks

An **Image** object stores a value for pixel width and a value for horizontal resolution (dots per inch). The physical width, measured in inches, of an image is the pixel width divided by the horizontal resolution. For example, an image with a pixel width of 216 and a horizontal resolution of 72 dots per inch has a physical width of 3 inches. Similar remarks apply to pixel height and physical height.

The **DrawImageUnscaled** method draws an image using its physical size, so the image will have its correct size in inches regardless of the resolution (dots per inch) of the display device. For example, suppose an image has a pixel width of 216 and a horizontal resolution of 72 dots per inch. If you call **DrawImageUnscaled** to draw that image on a device that has a resolution of 96 dots per inch, the pixel width of the rendered image will be (216/72)*96 = 288.

The call DrawImageUnscaled(image, rect) has exactly the same effect as the call DrawImage(image, rect.X, rect.Y).

Requirements

Platforms: Windows 98, Windows NT 4.0, Windows Millennium Edition, Windows 2000, Windows XP Home Edition, Windows XP Professional, Windows Server 2003 family

Graphics.DrawImageUnscaled Method (Image, Int32, Int32)

Draws the specified image using its original physical size at the location specified by a coordinate pair.

[Visual Basic]
```
Overloads Public Sub DrawImageUnscaled( _
   ByVal image As Image, _
   ByVal x As Integer, _
   ByVal y As Integer _
)
```
[C#]
```
public void DrawImageUnscaled(
   Image image,
   int x,
   int y
);
```

[C++]
```
public: void DrawImageUnscaled(
   Image* image,
   int x,
   int y
);
```
[JScript]
```
public function DrawImageUnscaled(
   image : Image,
   x : int,
   y : int
);
```

Parameters

image
: **Image** object to draw.

x
: x-coordinate of the upper-left corner of the drawn image.

y
: y-coordinate of the upper-left corner of the drawn image.

Return Value

This method does not return a value.

Remarks

An **Image** object stores a value for pixel width and a value for horizontal resolution (dots per inch). The physical width, measured in inches, of an image is the pixel width divided by the horizontal resolution. For example, an image with a pixel width of 216 and a horizontal resolution of 72 dots per inch has a physical width of 3 inches. Similar remarks apply to pixel height and physical height.

The **DrawImageUnscaled** method draws an image using its physical size, so the image will have its correct size in inches regardless of the resolution (dots per inch) of the display device. For example, suppose an image has a pixel width of 216 and a horizontal resolution of 72 dots per inch. If you call **DrawImageUnscaled** to draw that image on a device that has a resolution of 96 dots per inch, the pixel width of the rendered image will be (216/72)*96 = 288.

The call DrawImageUnscaled(image, x, y) has exactly the same effect as the call DrawImage(image, x, y).

Example

[Visual Basic, C#] The following example is designed for use with Windows Forms, and it requires **PaintEventArgs** *e*, which is a parameter of the **Paint** event handler. The code performs the following actions:

- Creates an image from a JPEG file, SampImag.jpg, in the folder of the example.
- Creates a point at which to draw the upper-left corner of the image.
- Draws the entire image using its physical size.

[Visual Basic]
```
Public Sub DrawImageUnscaledInt(e As PaintEventArgs)
' Create image.
Dim newImage As Image = Image.FromFile("SampImag.jpg")
' Create coordinates for upper-left corner of image.
Dim x As Integer = 100
Dim y As Integer = 100
' Draw image to screen.
e.Graphics.DrawImageUnscaled(newImage, x, y)
End Sub
```
[C#]
```
public void DrawImageUnscaledInt(PaintEventArgs e)
{
// Create image.
Image newImage = Image.FromFile("SampImag.jpg");
// Create coordinates for upper-left corner of image.
int x = 100;
int y = 100;
// Draw image to screen.
e.Graphics.DrawImageUnscaled(newImage, x, y);
}
```

Requirements

Platforms: Windows 98, Windows NT 4.0, Windows Millennium Edition, Windows 2000, Windows XP Home Edition, Windows XP Professional, Windows Server 2003 family

Graphics.DrawImageUnscaled Method (Image, Int32, Int32, Int32, Int32)

Draws a specified image using its original physical size at a specified location.

[Visual Basic]
```
Overloads Public Sub DrawImageUnscaled( _
   ByVal image As Image, _
   ByVal x As Integer, _
   ByVal y As Integer, _
   ByVal width As Integer, _
   ByVal height As Integer _
)
```
[C#]
```
public void DrawImageUnscaled(
   Image image,
   int x,
   int y,
   int width,
   int height
);
```
[C++]
```
public: void DrawImageUnscaled(
   Image* image,
   int x,
   int y,
   int width,
   int height
);
```
[JScript]
```
public function DrawImageUnscaled(
   image : Image,
   x : int,
   y : int,
   width : int,
   height : int
);
```

Parameters

image
: **Image** object to draw.

x
: x-coordinate of the upper-left corner of the drawn image.

y
: x-coordinate of the upper-left corner of the drawn image.

width
 Not used.
height
 Not used.

Return Value

This method does not return a value.

Remarks

An **Image** object stores a value for pixel width and a value for horizontal resolution (dots per inch). The physical width, measured in inches, of an image is the pixel width divided by the horizontal resolution. For example, an image with a pixel width of 216 and a horizontal resolution of 72 dots per inch has a physical width of 3 inches. Similar remarks apply to pixel height and physical height.

The **DrawImageUnscaled** method draws an image using its physical size, so the image will have its correct size in inches regardless of the resolution (dots per inch) of the display device. For example, suppose an image has a pixel width of 216 and a horizontal resolution of 72 dots per inch. If you call **DrawImageUnscaled** to draw that image on a device that has a resolution of 96 dots per inch, the pixel width of the rendered image will be (216/72)*96 = 288.

The call DrawImageUnscaled(image, x, y, width, height) has exactly the same effect as the call DrawImage(image, x, y).

Requirements

Platforms: Windows 98, Windows NT 4.0, Windows Millennium Edition, Windows 2000, Windows XP Home Edition, Windows XP Professional, Windows Server 2003 family

Graphics.DrawLine Method

Draws a line connecting the two points specified by coordinate pairs.

Overload List

Draws a line connecting two **Point** structures.

[Visual Basic] **Overloads Public Sub DrawLine(Pen, Point, Point)**

[C#] **public void DrawLine(Pen, Point, Point);**

[C++] **public: void DrawLine(Pen*, Point, Point);**

[JScript] **public function DrawLine(Pen, Point, Point);**

Draws a line connecting two **PointF** structures.

[Visual Basic] **Overloads Public Sub DrawLine(Pen, PointF, PointF)**

[C#] **public void DrawLine(Pen, PointF, PointF);**

[C++] **public: void DrawLine(Pen*, PointF, PointF);**

[JScript] **public function DrawLine(Pen, PointF, PointF);**

Draws a line connecting the two points specified by coordinate pairs.

Supported by the .NET Compact Framework.

[Visual Basic] **Overloads Public Sub DrawLine(Pen, Integer, Integer, Integer, Integer)**

[C#] **public void DrawLine(Pen, int, int, int, int);**

[C++] **public: void DrawLine(Pen*, int, int, int, int);**

[JScript] **public function DrawLine(Pen, int, int, int, int);**

Draws a line connecting the two points specified by coordinate pairs.

[Visual Basic] **Overloads Public Sub DrawLine(Pen, Single, Single, Single, Single)**

[C#] **public void DrawLine(Pen, float, float, float, float);**

[C++] **public: void DrawLine(Pen*, float, float, float, float);**

[JScript] **public function DrawLine(Pen, float, float, float, float);**

Example

[Visual Basic, C#] The following example is designed for use with Windows Forms, and it requires **PaintEventArgs** *e*, which is a parameter of the **Paint** event handler. The code performs the following actions:

- Creates a black pen.
- Creates the coordinates of the endpoints of the line.
- Draws the line to the screen.

> [Visual Basic, C#] **Note** This example shows how to use one of the overloaded versions of **DrawLine**. For other examples that might be available, see the individual overload topics.

[Visual Basic]
```
Public Sub DrawLineFloat(e As PaintEventArgs)
' Create pen.
Dim blackPen As New Pen(Color.Black, 3)
' Create coordinates of points that define line.
Dim x1 As Single = 100F
Dim y1 As Single = 100F
Dim x2 As Single = 500F
Dim y2 As Single = 100F
' Draw line to screen.
e.Graphics.DrawLine(blackPen, x1, y1, x2, y2)
End Sub
```

[C#]
```
public void DrawLineFloat(PaintEventArgs e)
{
// Create pen.
Pen blackPen = new Pen(Color.Black, 3);
// Create coordinates of points that define line.
float x1 = 100.0F;
float y1 = 100.0F;
float x2 = 500.0F;
float y2 = 100.0F;
// Draw line to screen.
e.Graphics.DrawLine(blackPen, x1, y1, x2, y2);
}
```

Graphics.DrawLine Method (Pen, Point, Point)

Draws a line connecting two **Point** structures.

[Visual Basic]
```
Overloads Public Sub DrawLine( _
   ByVal pen As Pen, _
   ByVal pt1 As Point, _
   ByVal pt2 As Point _
)
```
[C#]
```
public void DrawLine(
   Pen pen,
   Point pt1,
   Point pt2
);
```
[C++]
```
public: void DrawLine(
   Pen* pen,
   Point pt1,
   Point pt2
);
```

```
[JScript]
public function DrawLine(
   pen : Pen,
   pt1 : Point,
   pt2 : Point
);
```

Parameters

pen
: **Pen** object that determines the color, width, and style of the line.

pt1
: **Point** structure that represents the first point to connect.

pt2
: **Point** structure that represents the second point to connect.

Return Value

This method does not return a value.

Example

[Visual Basic, C#] The following example is designed for use with Windows Forms, and it requires **PaintEventArgs** *e*, which is a parameter of the **Paint** event handler. The code performs the following actions:

- Creates a black pen.
- Creates points for the endpoints of the line.
- Draws the line to the screen.

```
[Visual Basic]
Public Sub DrawLinePoint(e As PaintEventArgs)
' Create pen.
Dim blackPen As New Pen(Color.Black, 3)
' Create points that define line.
Dim point1 As New Point(100, 100)
Dim point2 As New Point(500, 100)
' Draw line to screen.
e.Graphics.DrawLine(blackPen, point1, point2)
End Sub
```

```
[C#]
public void DrawLinePoint(PaintEventArgs e)
{
// Create pen.
Pen blackPen = new Pen(Color.Black, 3);
// Create points that define line.
Point point1 = new Point(100, 100);
Point point2 = new Point(500, 100);
// Draw line to screen.
e.Graphics.DrawLine(blackPen, point1, point2);
}
```

Requirements

Platforms: Windows 98, Windows NT 4.0, Windows Millennium Edition, Windows 2000, Windows XP Home Edition, Windows XP Professional, Windows Server 2003 family

Graphics.DrawLine Method (Pen, PointF, PointF)

Draws a line connecting two **PointF** structures.

```
[Visual Basic]
Overloads Public Sub DrawLine( _
   ByVal pen As Pen, _
   ByVal pt1 As PointF, _
   ByVal pt2 As PointF _
)
[C#]
public void DrawLine(
   Pen pen,
   PointF pt1,
   PointF pt2
);
[C++]
public: void DrawLine(
   Pen* pen,
   PointF pt1,
   PointF pt2
);
[JScript]
public function DrawLine(
   pen : Pen,
   pt1 : PointF,
   pt2 : PointF
);
```

Parameters

pen
: **Pen** object that determines the color, width, and style of the line.

pt1
: **PointF** structure that represents the first point to connect.

pt2
: **PointF** structure that represents the second point to connect.

Return Value

This method does not return a value.

Example

[Visual Basic, C#] The following example is designed for use with Windows Forms, and it requires **PaintEventArgs** *e*, which is a parameter of the **Paint** event handler. The code performs the following actions:

- Creates a black pen.
- Creates points for the endpoints of the line.
- Draws the line to the screen.

```
[Visual Basic]
Public Sub DrawLinePointF(e As PaintEventArgs)
' Create pen.
Dim blackPen As New Pen(Color.Black, 3)
' Create points that define line.
Dim point1 As New PointF(100F, 100F)
Dim point2 As New PointF(500F, 100F)
' Draw line to screen.
e.Graphics.DrawLine(blackPen, point1, point2)
End Sub
```

```
[C#]
public void DrawLinePointF(PaintEventArgs e)
{
// Create pen.
Pen blackPen = new Pen(Color.Black, 3);
// Create points that define line.
PointF point1 = new PointF(100.0F, 100.0F);
PointF point2 = new PointF(500.0F, 100.0F);
// Draw line to screen.
e.Graphics.DrawLine(blackPen, point1, point2);
}
```

Requirements

Platforms: Windows 98, Windows NT 4.0, Windows Millennium Edition, Windows 2000, Windows XP Home Edition, Windows XP Professional, Windows Server 2003 family

Graphics.DrawLine Method (Pen, Int32, Int32, Int32, Int32)

Draws a line connecting the two points specified by coordinate pairs.

[Visual Basic]
```
Overloads Public Sub DrawLine( _
   ByVal pen As Pen, _
   ByVal x1 As Integer, _
   ByVal y1 As Integer, _
   ByVal x2 As Integer, _
   ByVal y2 As Integer _
)
```
[C#]
```
public void DrawLine(
   Pen pen,
   int x1,
   int y1,
   int x2,
   int y2
);
```
[C++]
```
public: void DrawLine(
   Pen* pen,
   int x1,
   int y1,
   int x2,
   int y2
);
```
[JScript]
```
public function DrawLine(
   pen : Pen,
   x1 : int,
   y1 : int,
   x2 : int,
   y2 : int
);
```

Parameters

pen
: **Pen** object that determines the color, width, and style of the line.

x1
: x-coordinate of the first point.

y1
: y-coordinate of the first point.

x2
: x-coordinate of the second point.

y2
: y-coordinate of the second point.

Return Value

This method does not return a value.

Remarks

This method draws a line connecting the two points specified by the *x1*, *y1*, *x2*, and *y2* parameters.

Example

[Visual Basic, C#] The following example is designed for use with Windows Forms, and it requires **PaintEventArgs** *e*, which is a parameter of the **Paint** event handler. The code performs the following actions:

- Creates a black pen.
- Creates the coordinates of the endpoints of the line.
- Draws the line to the screen.

[Visual Basic]
```
Public Sub DrawLineInt(e As PaintEventArgs)
' Create pen.
Dim blackPen As New Pen(Color.Black, 3)
' Create coordinates of points that define line.
Dim x1 As Integer = 100
Dim y1 As Integer = 100
Dim x2 As Integer = 500
Dim y2 As Integer = 100
' Draw line to screen.
e.Graphics.DrawLine(blackPen, x1, y1, x2, y2)
End Sub
```

[C#]
```
public void DrawLineInt(PaintEventArgs e)
{
// Create pen.
Pen blackPen = new Pen(Color.Black, 3);
// Create coordinates of points that define line.
int x1 = 100;
int y1 = 100;
int x2 = 500;
int y2 = 100;
// Draw line to screen.
e.Graphics.DrawLine(blackPen, x1, y1, x2, y2);
}
```

Requirements

Platforms: Windows 98, Windows NT 4.0, Windows Millennium Edition, Windows 2000, Windows XP Home Edition, Windows XP Professional, Windows Server 2003 family, .NET Compact Framework - Windows CE .NET

Graphics.DrawLine Method (Pen, Single, Single, Single, Single)

Draws a line connecting the two points specified by coordinate pairs.

[Visual Basic]
```
Overloads Public Sub DrawLine( _
   ByVal pen As Pen, _
   ByVal x1 As Single, _
   ByVal y1 As Single, _
   ByVal x2 As Single, _
   ByVal y2 As Single _
)
```
[C#]
```
public void DrawLine(
   Pen pen,
   float x1,
   float y1,
   float x2,
   float y2
);
```
[C++]
```
public: void DrawLine(
   Pen* pen,
   float x1,
   float y1,
   float x2,
   float y2
);
```

```
[JScript]
public function DrawLine(
   pen : Pen,
   x1 : float,
   y1 : float,
   x2 : float,
   y2 : float
);
```

Parameters

pen
: **Pen** object that determines the color, width, and style of the line.

x1
: x-coordinate of the first point.

y1
: y-coordinate of the first point.

x2
: x-coordinate of the second point.

y2
: y-coordinate of the second point.

Return Value

This method does not return a value.

Remarks

This method draws a line connecting the two points specified by the *x1*, *y1*, *x2*, and *y2* parameters.

Example

[Visual Basic, C#] The following example is designed for use with Windows Forms, and it requires **PaintEventArgs** *e*, which is a parameter of the **Paint** event handler. The code performs the following actions:

- Creates a black pen.
- Creates the coordinates of the endpoints of the line.
- Draws the line to the screen.

[Visual Basic]
```
Public Sub DrawLineFloat(e As PaintEventArgs)
' Create pen.
Dim blackPen As New Pen(Color.Black, 3)
' Create coordinates of points that define line.
Dim x1 As Single = 100F
Dim y1 As Single = 100F
Dim x2 As Single = 500F
Dim y2 As Single = 100F
' Draw line to screen.
e.Graphics.DrawLine(blackPen, x1, y1, x2, y2)
End Sub
```

[C#]
```
public void DrawLineFloat(PaintEventArgs e)
{
// Create pen.
Pen blackPen = new Pen(Color.Black, 3);
// Create coordinates of points that define line.
float x1 = 100.0F;
float y1 = 100.0F;
float x2 = 500.0F;
float y2 = 100.0F;
// Draw line to screen.
e.Graphics.DrawLine(blackPen, x1, y1, x2, y2);
}
```

Requirements

Platforms: Windows 98, Windows NT 4.0, Windows Millennium Edition, Windows 2000, Windows XP Home Edition, Windows XP Professional, Windows Server 2003 family

Graphics.DrawLines Method

Draws a series of line segments that connect an array of **Point** structures.

Overload List

Draws a series of line segments that connect an array of **Point** structures.

[Visual Basic] **Overloads Public Sub DrawLines(Pen, Point())**
[C#] **public void DrawLines(Pen, Point[]);**
[C++] **public: void DrawLines(Pen*, Point[]);**
[JScript] **public function DrawLines(Pen, Point[]);**

Draws a series of line segments that connect an array of **PointF** structures.

[Visual Basic] **Overloads Public Sub DrawLines(Pen, PointF())**
[C#] **public void DrawLines(Pen, PointF[]);**
[C++] **public: void DrawLines(Pen*, PointF[]);**
[JScript] **public function DrawLines(Pen, PointF[]);**

Example

[Visual Basic, C#] The following example is designed for use with Windows Forms, and it requires **PaintEventArgs** *e*, which is a parameter of the **Paint** event handler. The performs the following actions:

- Code creates a black pen.
- Creates an array of points of segments of the line.
- Draws the connected line segments to the screen.

> [Visual Basic, C#] **Note** This example shows how to use one of the overloaded versions of **DrawLines**. For other examples that might be available, see the individual overload topics.

[Visual Basic]
```
Public Sub DrawLinesPointF(e As PaintEventArgs)
' Create pen.
Dim blackPen As New Pen(Color.Black, 3)
' Create array of points that define lines to draw.
Dim points As PointF() = {New PointF(10F, 10F), _
New PointF(10F, 100F), New PointF(200F, 50F), _
New PointF(250F, 300F)}
'Draw lines to screen.
e.Graphics.DrawLines(blackPen, points)
End Sub
```

[C#]
```
public void DrawLinesPointF(PaintEventArgs e)
{
// Create pen.
Pen pen = new Pen(Color.Black, 3);
// Create array of points that define lines to draw.
PointF[] points =
{
new PointF( 10.0F,  10.0F),
new PointF( 10.0F, 100.0F),
new PointF(200.0F,  50.0F),
new PointF(250.0F, 300.0F)
};
//Draw lines to screen.
e.Graphics.DrawLines(pen, points);
}
```

Graphics.DrawLines Method (Pen, Point[])

Draws a series of line segments that connect an array of **Point** structures.

[Visual Basic]
```
Overloads Public Sub DrawLines( _
   ByVal pen As Pen, _
   ByVal points() As Point _
)
```
[C#]
```
public void DrawLines(
   Pen pen,
   Point[] points
);
```
[C++]
```
public: void DrawLines(
   Pen* pen,
   Point points[]
);
```
[JScript]
```
public function DrawLines(
   pen : Pen,
   points : Point[]
);
```

Parameters

pen

Pen object that determines the color, width, and style of the line segments.

points

Array of **Point** structures that represent the points to connect.

Return Value

This method does not return a value.

Remarks

This method draws a series of lines connecting an array of ending points. The first two points in the array specify the first line. Each additional point specifies the end of a line segment whose starting point is the ending point of the previous line segment.

Example

[Visual Basic, C#] The following example is designed for use with Windows Forms, and it requires **PaintEventArgs** *e*, which is a parameter of the **Paint** event handler. The code performs the following actions:

- Creates a black pen.
- Creates an array of points of segments of the line.
- Draws the connected line segments to the screen.

[Visual Basic]
```
Public Sub DrawLinesPoint(e As PaintEventArgs)
' Create pen.
Dim blackPen As New Pen(Color.Black, 3)
' Create array of points that define lines to draw.
Dim points As Point() =  {New Point(10, 10), New Point(10, 100), _
New Point(200, 50), New Point(250, 300)}
'Draw lines to screen.
e.Graphics.DrawLines(blackPen, points)
End Sub
```

[C#]
```
public void DrawLinesPoint(PaintEventArgs e)
{
// Create pen.
Pen pen = new Pen(Color.Black, 3);
// Create array of points that define lines to draw.
Point[] points =
{
new Point( 10,  10),
new Point( 10, 100),
new Point(200,  50),
new Point(250, 300)
};
//Draw lines to screen.
e.Graphics.DrawLines(pen, points);
}
```

Requirements

Platforms: Windows 98, Windows NT 4.0, Windows Millennium Edition, Windows 2000, Windows XP Home Edition, Windows XP Professional, Windows Server 2003 family

Graphics.DrawLines Method (Pen, PointF[])

Draws a series of line segments that connect an array of **PointF** structures.

[Visual Basic]
```
Overloads Public Sub DrawLines( _
   ByVal pen As Pen, _
   ByVal points() As PointF _
)
```
[C#]
```
public void DrawLines(
   Pen pen,
   PointF[] points
);
```
[C++]
```
public: void DrawLines(
   Pen* pen,
   PointF points[]
);
```
[JScript]
```
public function DrawLines(
   pen : Pen,
   points : PointF[]
);
```

Parameters

pen

Pen object that determines the color, width, and style of the line segments.

points

Array of **PointF** structures that represent the points to connect.

Return Value

This method does not return a value.

Remarks

This method draws a series of lines connecting an array of ending points. The first two points in the array specify the first line. Each additional point specifies the end of a line segment whose starting point is the ending point of the previous line segment.

Example

[Visual Basic, C#] The following example is designed for use with Windows Forms, and it requires **PaintEventArgs** *e*, which is a parameter of the **Paint** event handler. The performs the following actions:

- Code creates a black pen.
- Creates an array of points of segments of the line.
- Draws the connected line segments to the screen.

[Visual Basic]
```
Public Sub DrawLinesPointF(e As PaintEventArgs)
' Create pen.
Dim blackPen As New Pen(Color.Black, 3)
' Create array of points that define lines to draw.
Dim points As PointF() = {New PointF(10F, 10F), _
New PointF(10F, 100F), New PointF(200F, 50F), _
New PointF(250F, 300F)}
'Draw lines to screen.
e.Graphics.DrawLines(blackPen, points)
End Sub
```

[C#]
```
public void DrawLinesPointF(PaintEventArgs e)
{
// Create pen.
Pen pen = new Pen(Color.Black, 3);
// Create array of points that define lines to draw.
PointF[] points =
{
new PointF( 10.0F,  10.0F),
new PointF( 10.0F, 100.0F),
new PointF(200.0F,  50.0F),
new PointF(250.0F, 300.0F)
};
//Draw lines to screen.
e.Graphics.DrawLines(pen, points);
}
```

Requirements

Platforms: Windows 98, Windows NT 4.0, Windows Millennium Edition, Windows 2000, Windows XP Home Edition, Windows XP Professional, Windows Server 2003 family

Graphics.DrawPath Method

Draws a **GraphicsPath** object.

[Visual Basic]
```
Public Sub DrawPath( _
   ByVal pen As Pen, _
   ByVal path As GraphicsPath _
)
```
[C#]
```
public void DrawPath(
   Pen pen,
   GraphicsPath path
);
```
[C++]
```
public: void DrawPath(
   Pen* pen,
   GraphicsPath* path
);
```
[JScript]
```
public function DrawPath(
   pen : Pen,
   path : GraphicsPath
);
```

Parameters

pen
: **Pen** object that determines the color, width, and style of the path.

path
: **GraphicsPath** object to draw.

Return Value

This method does not return a value.

Remarks

The current transformation in the graphic context is applied to the **GraphicsPath** object before it is drawn.

Example

[Visual Basic, C#] The following example is designed for use with Windows Forms, and it requires **PaintEventArgs** *e*, which is a parameter of the **Paint** event handler. The code performs the following actions:

- Creates a graphics path object and adds an ellipse to it.
- Creates a black pen.
- Draws the graphics path to the screen.

[Visual Basic]
```
Public Sub DrawPathEllipse(e As PaintEventArgs)
' Create graphics path object and add ellipse.
Dim graphPath As New GraphicsPath()
graphPath.AddEllipse(0, 0, 200, 100)
' Create pen.
Dim blackPen As New Pen(Color.Black, 3)
' Draw graphics path to screen.
e.Graphics.DrawPath(blackPen, graphPath)
End Sub
```

[C#]
```
public void DrawPathEllipse(PaintEventArgs e)
{
// Create graphics path object and add ellipse.
GraphicsPath graphPath = new GraphicsPath();
graphPath.AddEllipse(0, 0, 200, 100);
// Create pen.
Pen blackPen = new Pen(Color.Black, 3);
// Draw graphics path to screen.
e.Graphics.DrawPath(blackPen, graphPath);
}
```

Requirements

Platforms: Windows 98, Windows NT 4.0, Windows Millennium Edition, Windows 2000, Windows XP Home Edition, Windows XP Professional, Windows Server 2003 family

Graphics.DrawPie Method

Draws a pie shape defined by an ellipse specified by a coordinate pair, a width, and a height and two radial lines.

Overload List

Draws a pie shape defined by an ellipse specified by a **Rectangle** structure and two radial lines.

[Visual Basic] **Overloads Public Sub DrawPie(Pen, Rectangle, Single, Single)**

[C#] **public void DrawPie(Pen, Rectangle, float, float);**

[C++] **public: void DrawPie(Pen*, Rectangle, float, float);**

[JScript] **public function DrawPie(Pen, Rectangle, float, float);**

Draws a pie shape defined by an ellipse specified by a **RectangleF** structure and two radial lines.

[Visual Basic] **Overloads Public Sub DrawPie(Pen, RectangleF, Single, Single)**

[C#] **public void DrawPie(Pen, RectangleF, float, float);**

[C++] **public: void DrawPie(Pen*, RectangleF, float, float);**

[JScript] **public function DrawPie(Pen, RectangleF, float, float);**

Draws a pie shape defined by an ellipse specified by a coordinate pair, a width, and a height and two radial lines.

[Visual Basic] **Overloads Public Sub DrawPie(Pen, Integer, Integer, Integer, Integer, Integer, Integer)**

[C#] **public void DrawPie(Pen, int, int, int, int, int, int);**

[C++] **public: void DrawPie(Pen*, int, int, int, int, int, int);**

[JScript] **public function DrawPie(Pen, int, int, int, int, int, int);**

Draws a pie shape defined by an ellipse specified by a coordinate pair, a width, and a height and two radial lines.

[Visual Basic] **Overloads Public Sub DrawPie(Pen, Single, Single, Single, Single, Single, Single)**

[C#] **public void DrawPie(Pen, float, float, float, float, float, float);**

[C++] **public: void DrawPie(Pen*, float, float, float, float, float, float);**

[JScript] **public function DrawPie(Pen, float, float, float, float, float, float);**

Example

[Visual Basic, C#] The following example is designed for use with Windows Forms, and it requires **PaintEventArgs** *e*, which is a parameter of the **Paint** event handler. The code performs the following actions:

- Creates a black pen.
- Creates the position and size of a rectangle that bounds a complete ellipse.
- Defines the angles at which to start drawing (relative to the x axis) and through which to draw (both in a clockwise direction).
- Draws the pie segment to the screen.

> [Visual Basic, C#] **Note** This example shows how to use one of the overloaded versions of **DrawPie**. For other examples that might be available, see the individual overload topics.

[Visual Basic]
```
Public Sub DrawPieFloat(e As PaintEventArgs)
' Create pen.
Dim blackPen As New Pen(Color.Black, 3)
' Create location and size of ellipse.
Dim x As Single = 0F
Dim y As Single = 0F
Dim width As Single = 200F
Dim height As Single = 100F
' Create start and sweep angles.
Dim startAngle As Single = 0F
Dim sweepAngle As Single = 45F
' Draw pie to screen.
e.Graphics.DrawPie(blackPen, x, y, width, height, _
startAngle, sweepAngle)
End Sub
```

[C#]
```
public void DrawPieFloat(PaintEventArgs e)
{
// Create pen.
Pen blackPen = new Pen(Color.Black, 3);
// Create location and size of ellipse.
float x = 0.0F;
float y = 0.0F;
float width = 200.0F;
float height = 100.0F;
// Create start and sweep angles.
float startAngle =  0.0F;
float sweepAngle = 45.0F;
// Draw pie to screen.
e.Graphics.DrawPie(blackPen, x, y, width, height,
startAngle, sweepAngle);
}
```

Graphics.DrawPie Method (Pen, Rectangle, Single, Single)

Draws a pie shape defined by an ellipse specified by a **Rectangle** structure and two radial lines.

[Visual Basic]
```
Overloads Public Sub DrawPie( _
   ByVal pen As Pen, _
   ByVal rect As Rectangle, _
   ByVal startAngle As Single, _
   ByVal sweepAngle As Single _
)
```
[C#]
```
public void DrawPie(
   Pen pen,
   Rectangle rect,
   float startAngle,
   float sweepAngle
);
```
[C++]
```
public: void DrawPie(
   Pen* pen,
   Rectangle rect,
   float startAngle,
   float sweepAngle
);
```
[JScript]
```
public function DrawPie(
   pen : Pen,
   rect : Rectangle,
   startAngle : float,
   sweepAngle : float
);
```

Parameters

pen

Pen object that determines the color, width, and style of the pie shape.

rect

Rectangle structure that represents the bounding rectangle that defines the ellipse from which the pie shape comes.

startAngle

Angle measured in degrees clockwise from the x-axis to the first side of the pie shape.

sweepAngle

Angle measured in degrees clockwise from the *startAngle* parameter to the second side of the pie shape.

Return Value

This method does not return a value.

Remarks

This method draws a pie shape defined by an arc of an ellipse and the two radial lines that intersect with the endpoints of the arc. The ellipse is defined by the bounding rectangle. The pie shape consists of the two radial lines defined by the *startAngle* and *sweepAngle* parameters, and the arc between the intersections of those radial lines with the ellipse.

If the *sweepAngle* parameter is greater than 360 degrees or less than -360 degrees, it is treated as if it were 360 degrees or -360 degrees, respectively.

Example

[Visual Basic, C#] The following example is designed for use with Windows Forms, and it requires **PaintEventArgs** *e*, which is a parameter of the **Paint** event handler. The code performs the following actions:

- Creates a black pen.
- Creates a rectangle that bounds a complete ellipse.
- Defines the angles at which to start drawing (relative to the x axis) and through which to draw (both in a clockwise direction).
- Draws the pie segment to the screen.

[Visual Basic]

```
Public Sub DrawPieRectangle(e As PaintEventArgs)
' Create pen.
Dim blackPen As New Pen(Color.Black, 3)
' Create rectangle for ellipse.
Dim rect As New Rectangle(0, 0, 200, 100)
' Create start and sweep angles.
Dim startAngle As Single = 0F
Dim sweepAngle As Single = 45F
' Draw pie to screen.
e.Graphics.DrawPie(blackPen, rect, startAngle, sweepAngle)
End Sub
```

[C#]

```
public void DrawPieRectangle(PaintEventArgs e)
{
// Create pen.
Pen blackPen = new Pen(Color.Black, 3);
// Create rectangle for ellipse.
Rectangle rect = new Rectangle( 0, 0, 200, 100);
// Create start and sweep angles.
float startAngle =  0.0F;
float sweepAngle = 45.0F;
// Draw pie to screen.
e.Graphics.DrawPie(blackPen, rect, startAngle, sweepAngle);
}
```

Requirements

Platforms: Windows 98, Windows NT 4.0, Windows Millennium Edition, Windows 2000, Windows XP Home Edition, Windows XP Professional, Windows Server 2003 family

Graphics.DrawPie Method (Pen, RectangleF, Single, Single)

Draws a pie shape defined by an ellipse specified by a **RectangleF** structure and two radial lines.

[Visual Basic]

```
Overloads Public Sub DrawPie( _
   ByVal pen As Pen, _
   ByVal rect As RectangleF, _
   ByVal startAngle As Single, _
   ByVal sweepAngle As Single _
)
```

[C#]

```
public void DrawPie(
   Pen pen,
   RectangleF rect,
   float startAngle,
   float sweepAngle
);
```

[C++]

```
public: void DrawPie(
   Pen* pen,
   RectangleF rect,
   float startAngle,
   float sweepAngle
);
```

[JScript]

```
public function DrawPie(
   pen : Pen,
   rect : RectangleF,
   startAngle : float,
   sweepAngle : float
);
```

Parameters

pen
: **Pen** object that determines the color, width, and style of the pie shape.

rect
: **RectangleF** structure that represents the bounding rectangle that defines the ellipse from which the pie shape comes.

startAngle
: Angle measured in degrees clockwise from the x-axis to the first side of the pie shape.

sweepAngle
: Angle measured in degrees clockwise from the *startAngle* parameter to the second side of the pie shape.

Return Value

This method does not return a value.

Remarks

This method draws a pie shape defined by an arc of an ellipse and the two radial lines that intersect with the endpoints of the arc. The ellipse is defined by the bounding rectangle. The pie shape consists of the two radial lines defined by the *startAngle* and *sweepAngle* parameters, and the arc between the intersections of those radial lines with the ellipse.

If the *sweepAngle* parameter is greater than 360 degrees or less than -360 degrees, it is treated as if it were 360 degrees or -360 degrees, respectively.

Example

[Visual Basic, C#] The following example is designed for use with Windows Forms, and it requires **PaintEventArgs** *e*, which is a parameter of the **Paint** event handler. The code performs the following actions:

- Creates a black pen.
- Creates a rectangle that bounds a complete ellipse.
- Defines the angles at which to start drawing (relative to the x axis) and through which to draw (both in a clockwise direction).
- Draws the pie segment to the screen.

[Visual Basic]
```
Public Sub DrawPieRectangleF(e As PaintEventArgs)
' Create pen.
Dim blackPen As New Pen(Color.Black, 3)
' Create rectangle for ellipse.
Dim rect As New RectangleF(0F, 0F, 200F, 100F)
' Create start and sweep angles.
Dim startAngle As Single = 0F
Dim sweepAngle As Single = 45F
' Draw pie to screen.
e.Graphics.DrawPie(blackPen, rect, startAngle, sweepAngle)
End Sub
```

[C#]
```
public void DrawPieRectangleF(PaintEventArgs e)
{
// Create pen.
Pen blackPen = new Pen(Color.Black, 3);
// Create rectangle for ellipse.
RectangleF rect = new RectangleF( 0.0F, 0.0F, 200.0F, 100.0F);
// Create start and sweep angles.
float startAngle =  0.0F;
float sweepAngle = 45.0F;
// Draw pie to screen.
e.Graphics.DrawPie(blackPen, rect, startAngle, sweepAngle);
}
```

Requirements

Platforms: Windows 98, Windows NT 4.0, Windows Millennium Edition, Windows 2000, Windows XP Home Edition, Windows XP Professional, Windows Server 2003 family

Graphics.DrawPie Method (Pen, Int32, Int32, Int32, Int32, Int32, Int32)

Draws a pie shape defined by an ellipse specified by a coordinate pair, a width, and a height and two radial lines.

[Visual Basic]
```
Overloads Public Sub DrawPie( _
   ByVal pen As Pen, _
   ByVal x As Integer, _
   ByVal y As Integer, _
   ByVal width As Integer, _
   ByVal height As Integer, _
   ByVal startAngle As Integer, _
   ByVal sweepAngle As Integer _
)
```
[C#]
```
public void DrawPie(
   Pen pen,
   int x,
   int y,
   int width,
   int height,
   int startAngle,
   int sweepAngle
);
```
[C++]
```
public: void DrawPie(
   Pen* pen,
   int x,
   int y,
   int width,
   int height,
   int startAngle,
   int sweepAngle
);
```
[JScript]
```
public function DrawPie(
   pen : Pen,
   x : int,
   y : int,
   width : int,
   height : int,
   startAngle : int,
   sweepAngle : int
);
```

Parameters

pen
: **Pen** object that determines the color, width, and style of the pie shape.

x
: x-coordinate of the upper-left corner of the bounding rectangle that defines the ellipse from which the pie shape comes.

y
: y-coordinate of the upper-left corner of the bounding rectangle that defines the ellipse from which the pie shape comes.

width
: Width of the bounding rectangle that defines the ellipse from which the pie shape comes.

height
: Height of the bounding rectangle that defines the ellipse from which the pie shape comes.

startAngle
: Angle measured in degrees clockwise from the x-axis to the first side of the pie shape.

sweepAngle
: Angle measured in degrees clockwise from the *startAngle* parameter to the second side of the pie shape.

Return Value

This method does not return a value.

Remarks

This method draws a pie shape defined by an arc of an ellipse and the two radial lines that intersect with the endpoints of the arc. The ellipse is defined by the bounding rectangle described by the *x*, *y*, *width*, and *height* parameters. The pie shape consists of the two radial lines defined by the *startAngle* and *sweepAngle* parameters, and the arc between the intersections of those radial lines with the ellipse.

If the *sweepAngle* parameter is greater than 360 degrees or less than -360 degrees, it is treated as if it were 360 degrees or -360 degrees, respectively.

Example

[Visual Basic, C#] The following example is designed for use with Windows Forms, and it requires **PaintEventArgs** *e*, which is a parameter of the **Paint** event handler. The code performs the following actions:

- Creates a black pen.
- Creates the position and size of a rectangle that bounds a complete ellipse.
- Defines the angles at which to start drawing (relative to the x axis) and through which to draw (both in a clockwise direction).
- Draws the pie shape to the screen.

[Visual Basic]
```
Public Sub DrawPieInt(e As PaintEventArgs)
' Create pen.
Dim blackPen As New Pen(Color.Black, 3)
' Create location and size of ellipse.
Dim x As Integer = 0
Dim y As Integer = 0
Dim width As Integer = 200
Dim height As Integer = 100
' Create start and sweep angles.
Dim startAngle As Integer = 0
Dim sweepAngle As Integer = 45
' Draw pie to screen.
e.Graphics.DrawPie(blackPen, x, y, width, height, _
startAngle, sweepAngle)
End Sub
```

[C#]
```
public void DrawPieInt(PaintEventArgs e)
{
// Create pen.
Pen blackPen = new Pen(Color.Black, 3);
// Create location and size of ellipse.
int x = 0;
int y = 0;
int width = 200;
int height = 100;
// Create start and sweep angles.
int startAngle =  0;
int sweepAngle = 45;
// Draw pie to screen.
e.Graphics.DrawPie(blackPen, x, y, width, height,
 startAngle, sweepAngle);
}
```

Requirements

Platforms: Windows 98, Windows NT 4.0, Windows Millennium Edition, Windows 2000, Windows XP Home Edition, Windows XP Professional, Windows Server 2003 family

Graphics.DrawPie Method (Pen, Single, Single, Single, Single, Single, Single)

Draws a pie shape defined by an ellipse specified by a coordinate pair, a width, and a height and two radial lines.

[Visual Basic]
```
Overloads Public Sub DrawPie( _
   ByVal pen As Pen, _
   ByVal x As Single, _
   ByVal y As Single, _
   ByVal width As Single, _
   ByVal height As Single, _
   ByVal startAngle As Single, _
   ByVal sweepAngle As Single _
)
```
[C#]
```
public void DrawPie(
   Pen pen,
   float x,
   float y,
   float width,
   float height,
   float startAngle,
   float sweepAngle
);
```
[C++]
```
public: void DrawPie(
   Pen* pen,
   float x,
   float y,
   float width,
   float height,
   float startAngle,
   float sweepAngle
);
```
[JScript]
```
public function DrawPie(
   pen : Pen,
   x : float,
   y : float,
   width : float,
   height : float,
   startAngle : float,
   sweepAngle : float
);
```

Parameters

pen
: **Pen** object that determines the color, width, and style of the pie shape.

x
: x-coordinate of the upper-left corner of the bounding rectangle that defines the ellipse from which the pie shape comes.

y
: y-coordinate of the upper-left corner of the bounding rectangle that defines the ellipse from which the pie shape comes.

width
: Width of the bounding rectangle that defines the ellipse from which the pie shape comes.

height
: Height of the bounding rectangle that defines the ellipse from which the pie shape comes.

startAngle
: Angle measured in degrees clockwise from the x-axis to the first side of the pie shape.

sweepAngle
: Angle measured in degrees clockwise from the *startAngle* parameter to the second side of the pie shape.

Return Value

This method does not return a value.

Remarks

This method draws a pie shape defined by an arc of an ellipse and the two radial lines that intersect with the endpoints of the arc. The ellipse is defined by the bounding rectangle described by the *x*, *y*, *width*, and *height* parameters. The pie shape consists of the two radial lines defined by the *startAngle* and *sweepAngle* parameters, and the arc between the intersections of those radial lines with the ellipse.

If the *sweepAngle* parameter is greater than 360 degrees or less than -360 degrees, it is treated as if it were 360 degrees or -360 degrees, respectively.

Example

[Visual Basic, C#] The following example is designed for use with Windows Forms, and it requires **PaintEventArgs** *e*, which is a parameter of the **Paint** event handler. The code performs the following actions:

- Creates a black pen.
- Creates the position and size of a rectangle that bounds a complete ellipse.
- Defines the angles at which to start drawing (relative to the x axis) and through which to draw (both in a clockwise direction).
- Draws the pie segment to the screen.

[Visual Basic]
```
Public Sub DrawPieFloat(e As PaintEventArgs)
' Create pen.
Dim blackPen As New Pen(Color.Black, 3)
' Create location and size of ellipse.
Dim x As Single = 0F
Dim y As Single = 0F
Dim width As Single = 200F
Dim height As Single = 100F
' Create start and sweep angles.
Dim startAngle As Single = 0F
Dim sweepAngle As Single = 45F
' Draw pie to screen.
e.Graphics.DrawPie(blackPen, x, y, width, height, _
startAngle, sweepAngle)
End Sub
```

[C#]
```
public void DrawPieFloat(PaintEventArgs e)
{
// Create pen.
Pen blackPen = new Pen(Color.Black, 3);
// Create location and size of ellipse.
float x = 0.0F;
float y = 0.0F;
float width = 200.0F;
float height = 100.0F;
// Create start and sweep angles.
float startAngle =  0.0F;
float sweepAngle = 45.0F;
// Draw pie to screen.
e.Graphics.DrawPie(blackPen, x, y, width, height,                ↵
startAngle, sweepAngle);
}
```

Requirements

Platforms: Windows 98, Windows NT 4.0, Windows Millennium Edition, Windows 2000, Windows XP Home Edition, Windows XP Professional, Windows Server 2003 family

Graphics.DrawPolygon Method

Draws a polygon defined by an array of **Point** structures.

Overload List

Draws a polygon defined by an array of **Point** structures.

Supported by the .NET Compact Framework.

[Visual Basic] **Overloads Public Sub DrawPolygon(Pen, Point())**

[C#] **public void DrawPolygon(Pen, Point[]);**

[C++] **public: void DrawPolygon(Pen*, Point[]);**

[JScript] **public function DrawPolygon(Pen, Point[]);**

Draws a polygon defined by an array of **PointF** structures.

[Visual Basic] **Overloads Public Sub DrawPolygon(Pen, PointF())**

[C#] **public void DrawPolygon(Pen, PointF[]);**

[C++] **public: void DrawPolygon(Pen*, PointF[]);**

[JScript] **public function DrawPolygon(Pen, PointF[]);**

Example

[Visual Basic, C#] The following example is designed for use with Windows Forms, and it requires **PaintEventArgs** *e*, which is a parameter of the **Paint** event handler. The code performs the following actions:

- Creates a black pen.
- Creates an array of seven points for the vertices of the polygon.
- Draws the polygon to the screen.

> [Visual Basic, C#] **Note** This example shows how to use one of the overloaded versions of **DrawPolygon**. For other examples that might be available, see the individual overload topics.

[Visual Basic]
```
Public Sub DrawPolygonPoint(e As PaintEventArgs)
' Create pen.
Dim blackPen As New Pen(Color.Black, 3)
' Create points that define polygon.
Dim point1 As New Point(50, 50)
Dim point2 As New Point(100, 25)
Dim point3 As New Point(200, 5)
Dim point4 As New Point(250, 50)
Dim point5 As New Point(300, 100)
Dim point6 As New Point(350, 200)
Dim point7 As New Point(250, 250)
Dim curvePoints As Point() =  {point1, point2, point3, point4, _
point5, point6, point7}
' Draw polygon to screen.
e.Graphics.DrawPolygon(blackPen, curvePoints)
End Sub
```

[C#]
```
public void DrawPolygonPoint(PaintEventArgs e)
{
// Create pen.
Pen blackPen = new Pen(Color.Black, 3);
// Create points that define polygon.
Point point1 = new Point( 50,  50);
Point point2 = new Point(100,  25);
Point point3 = new Point(200,   5);
Point point4 = new Point(250,  50);
Point point5 = new Point(300, 100);
Point point6 = new Point(350, 200);
Point point7 = new Point(250, 250);
Point[] curvePoints =
{
point1,
point2,
point3,
point4,
point5,
point6,
point7
};
// Draw polygon to screen.
e.Graphics.DrawPolygon(blackPen, curvePoints);
}
```

Graphics.DrawPolygon Method (Pen, Point[])

Draws a polygon defined by an array of **Point** structures.

```
[Visual Basic]
Overloads Public Sub DrawPolygon( _
   ByVal pen As Pen, _
   ByVal points() As Point _
)
[C#]
public void DrawPolygon(
   Pen pen,
   Point[] points
);
[C++]
public: void DrawPolygon(
   Pen* pen,
   Point points[]
);
[JScript]
public function DrawPolygon(
   pen : Pen,
   points : Point[]
);
```

Parameters

pen
: **Pen** object that determines the color, width, and style of the polygon.

points
: Array of **Point** structures that represent the vertices of the polygon.

Return Value

This method does not return a value.

Remarks

Every pair of two consecutive points in the array specify a side of the polygon. In addition, if the last point and the first point of the array do not coincide, they specify the last side of the polygon.

Example

[Visual Basic, C#] The following example is designed for use with Windows Forms, and it requires **PaintEventArgs** *e*, which is a parameter of the **Paint** event handler. The code performs the following actions:

- Creates a black pen.
- Creates an array of seven points for the vertices of the polygon.
- Draws the polygon to the screen.

```
[Visual Basic]
Public Sub DrawPolygonPointF(e As PaintEventArgs)
' Create pen.
Dim blackPen As New Pen(Color.Black, 3)
' Create points that define polygon.
Dim point1 As New PointF(50F, 50F)
Dim point2 As New PointF(100F, 25F)
Dim point3 As New PointF(200F, 5F)
Dim point4 As New PointF(250F, 50F)
Dim point5 As New PointF(300F, 100F)
Dim point6 As New PointF(350F, 200F)
Dim point7 As New PointF(250F, 250F)
Dim curvePoints As PointF() = {point1, point2, point3, point4, _
point5, point6, point7}
' Draw polygon curve to screen.
e.Graphics.DrawPolygon(blackPen, curvePoints)
End Sub
```

```
[C#]
public void DrawPolygonPointF(PaintEventArgs e)
{
// Create pen.
Pen blackPen = new Pen(Color.Black, 3);
// Create points that define polygon.
PointF point1 = new PointF( 50.0F,  50.0F);
PointF point2 = new PointF(100.0F,  25.0F);
PointF point3 = new PointF(200.0F,   5.0F);
PointF point4 = new PointF(250.0F,  50.0F);
PointF point5 = new PointF(300.0F, 100.0F);
PointF point6 = new PointF(350.0F, 200.0F);
PointF point7 = new PointF(250.0F, 250.0F);
PointF[] curvePoints =
{
point1,
point2,
point3,
point4,
point5,
point6,
point7
};
// Draw polygon curve to screen.
e.Graphics.DrawPolygon(blackPen, curvePoints);
}
```

Requirements

Platforms: Windows 98, Windows NT 4.0, Windows Millennium Edition, Windows 2000, Windows XP Home Edition, Windows XP Professional, Windows Server 2003 family, .NET Compact Framework - Windows CE .NET

Graphics.DrawPolygon Method (Pen, PointF[])

Draws a polygon defined by an array of **PointF** structures.

```
[Visual Basic]
Overloads Public Sub DrawPolygon( _
   ByVal pen As Pen, _
   ByVal points() As PointF _
)
[C#]
public void DrawPolygon(
   Pen pen,
   PointF[] points
);
[C++]
public: void DrawPolygon(
   Pen* pen,
   PointF points[]
);
[JScript]
public function DrawPolygon(
   pen : Pen,
   points : PointF[]
);
```

Parameters

pen
: **Pen** object that determines the color, width, and style of the polygon.

points
: Array of **PointF** structures that represent the vertices of the polygon.

Return Value

This method does not return a value.

Remarks

Every pair of two consecutive points in the array specify a side of the polygon. In addition, if the last point and the first of the array point do not coincide, they specify the last side of the polygon.

Example

[Visual Basic, C#] The following example is designed for use with Windows Forms, and it requires **PaintEventArgs** *e*, which is a parameter of the **Paint** event handler. The code performs the following actions:

- Creates a black pen.
- Creates an array of seven points for the vertices of the polygon.
- Draws the polygon to the screen.

[Visual Basic]
```
Public Sub DrawPolygonPoint(e As PaintEventArgs)
' Create pen.
Dim blackPen As New Pen(Color.Black, 3)
' Create points that define polygon.
Dim point1 As New Point(50, 50)
Dim point2 As New Point(100, 25)
Dim point3 As New Point(200, 5)
Dim point4 As New Point(250, 50)
Dim point5 As New Point(300, 100)
Dim point6 As New Point(350, 200)
Dim point7 As New Point(250, 250)
Dim curvePoints As Point() = {point1, point2, point3, point4, _
point5, point6, point7}
' Draw polygon to screen.
e.Graphics.DrawPolygon(blackPen, curvePoints)
End Sub
```

[C#]
```
public void DrawPolygonPoint(PaintEventArgs e)
{
// Create pen.
Pen blackPen = new Pen(Color.Black, 3);
// Create points that define polygon.
Point point1 = new Point( 50,  50);
Point point2 = new Point(100,  25);
Point point3 = new Point(200,   5);
Point point4 = new Point(250,  50);
Point point5 = new Point(300, 100);
Point point6 = new Point(350, 200);
Point point7 = new Point(250, 250);
Point[] curvePoints =
{
point1,
point2,
point3,
point4,
point5,
point6,
point7
};
// Draw polygon to screen.
e.Graphics.DrawPolygon(blackPen, curvePoints);
}
```

Requirements

Platforms: Windows 98, Windows NT 4.0, Windows Millennium Edition, Windows 2000, Windows XP Home Edition, Windows XP Professional, Windows Server 2003 family

Graphics.DrawRectangle Method

Draws a rectangle specified by a coordinate pair, a width, and a height.

Overload List

Draws a rectangle specified by a **Rectangle** structure.

Supported by the .NET Compact Framework.

[Visual Basic] **Overloads Public Sub DrawRectangle(Pen, Rectangle)**

[C#] **public void DrawRectangle(Pen, Rectangle);**

[C++] **public: void DrawRectangle(Pen*, Rectangle);**

[JScript] **public function DrawRectangle(Pen, Rectangle);**

Draws a rectangle specified by a coordinate pair, a width, and a height.

Supported by the .NET Compact Framework.

[Visual Basic] **Overloads Public Sub DrawRectangle(Pen, Integer, Integer, Integer, Integer)**

[C#] **public void DrawRectangle(Pen, int, int, int, int);**

[C++] **public: void DrawRectangle(Pen*, int, int, int, int);**

[JScript] **public function DrawRectangle(Pen, int, int, int, int);**

Draws a rectangle specified by a coordinate pair, a width, and a height.

[Visual Basic] **Overloads Public Sub DrawRectangle(Pen, Single, Single, Single, Single)**

[C#] **public void DrawRectangle(Pen, float, float, float, float);**

[C++] **public: void DrawRectangle(Pen*, float, float, float, float);**

[JScript] **public function DrawRectangle(Pen, float, float, float, float);**

Example

[Visual Basic, C#] The following example is designed for use with Windows Forms, and it requires **PaintEventArgs** *e*, which is a parameter of the **Paint** event handler. The code performs the following actions:

- Creates a black pen.
- Creates the position and size of a rectangle.
- Draws the rectangle to the screen.

> [Visual Basic, C#] **Note** This example shows how to use one of the overloaded versions of **DrawRectangle**. For other examples that might be available, see the individual overload topics.

[Visual Basic]
```
Public Sub DrawRectangleFloat(e As PaintEventArgs)
' Create pen.
Dim blackPen As New Pen(Color.Black, 3)
' Create location and size of rectangle.
Dim x As Single = 0F
Dim y As Single = 0F
Dim width As Single = 200F
Dim height As Single = 200F
' Draw rectangle to screen.
e.Graphics.DrawRectangle(blackPen, x, y, width, height)
End Sub
```

[C#]
```
public void DrawRectangleFloat(PaintEventArgs e)
{
// Create pen.
Pen blackPen = new Pen(Color.Black, 3);
// Create location and size of rectangle.
float x = 0.0F;
float y = 0.0F;
float width = 200.0F;
float height = 200.0F;
// Draw rectangle to screen.
e.Graphics.DrawRectangle(blackPen, x, y, width, height);
}
```

Graphics.DrawRectangle Method (Pen, Rectangle)

Draws a rectangle specified by a **Rectangle** structure.

[Visual Basic]
```
Overloads Public Sub DrawRectangle( _
   ByVal pen As Pen, _
   ByVal rect As Rectangle _
)
```
[C#]
```
public void DrawRectangle(
   Pen pen,
   Rectangle rect
);
```
[C++]
```
public: void DrawRectangle(
   Pen* pen,
   Rectangle rect
);
```
[JScript]
```
public function DrawRectangle(
   pen : Pen,
   rect : Rectangle
);
```

Parameters

pen
A **Pen** object that determines the color, width, and style of the rectangle.

rect
A **Rectangle** structure that represents the rectangle to draw.

Return Value

This method does not return a value.

Example

[Visual Basic, C#] The following example is designed for use with Windows Forms, and it requires **PaintEventArgs** *e*, which is a parameter of the **Paint** event handler. The code performs the following actions:

- Creates a black pen.
- Creates a rectangle.
- Draws the rectangle to the screen.

[Visual Basic]
```
Public Sub DrawRectangleRectangle(e As PaintEventArgs)
' Create pen.
Dim blackPen As New Pen(Color.Black, 3)
' Create rectangle.
Dim rect As New Rectangle(0, 0, 200, 200)
' Draw rectangle to screen.
e.Graphics.DrawRectangle(blackPen, rect)
End Sub
```

[C#]
```
public void DrawRectangleRectangle(PaintEventArgs e)
{
// Create pen.
Pen blackPen = new Pen(Color.Black, 3);
// Create rectangle.
Rectangle rect = new Rectangle( 0, 0, 200, 200);
// Draw rectangle to screen.
e.Graphics.DrawRectangle(blackPen, rect);
}
```

Requirements

Platforms: Windows 98, Windows NT 4.0, Windows Millennium Edition, Windows 2000, Windows XP Home Edition, Windows XP Professional, Windows Server 2003 family, .NET Compact Framework - Windows CE .NET

Graphics.DrawRectangle Method (Pen, Int32, Int32, Int32, Int32)

Draws a rectangle specified by a coordinate pair, a width, and a height.

[Visual Basic]
```
Overloads Public Sub DrawRectangle( _
   ByVal pen As Pen, _
   ByVal x As Integer, _
   ByVal y As Integer, _
   ByVal width As Integer, _
   ByVal height As Integer _
)
```
[C#]
```
public void DrawRectangle(
   Pen pen,
   int x,
   int y,
   int width,
   int height
);
```
[C++]
```
public: void DrawRectangle(
   Pen* pen,
   int x,
   int y,
   int width,
   int height
);
```
[JScript]
```
public function DrawRectangle(
   pen : Pen,
   x : int,
   y : int,
   width : int,
   height : int
);
```

Parameters

pen
Pen object that determines the color, width, and style of the rectangle.

x
x-coordinate of the upper-left corner of the rectangle to draw.

y
y-coordinate of the upper-left corner of the rectangle to draw.

width
Width of the rectangle to draw.

height
Height of the rectangle to draw.

Return Value

This method does not return a value.

Example

[Visual Basic, C#] The following example is designed for use with Windows Forms, and it requires **PaintEventArgs** *e*, which is a parameter of the **Paint** event handler. The code performs the following actions:

- Creates a black pen.
- Creates the position and size of a rectangle.
- Draws the rectangle to the screen.

[Visual Basic]
```
Public Sub DrawRectangleInt(e As PaintEventArgs)
' Create pen.
Dim blackPen As New Pen(Color.Black, 3)
' Create location and size of rectangle.
Dim x As Integer = 0
Dim y As Integer = 0
Dim width As Integer = 200
Dim height As Integer = 200
' Draw rectangle to screen.
e.Graphics.DrawRectangle(blackPen, x, y, width, height)
End Sub
```

[C#]
```
public void DrawRectangleInt(PaintEventArgs e)
{
// Create pen.
Pen blackPen = new Pen(Color.Black, 3);
// Create location and size of rectangle.
int x = 0;
int y = 0;
int width = 200;
int height = 200;
// Draw rectangle to screen.
e.Graphics.DrawRectangle(blackPen, x, y, width, height);
}
```

Requirements

Platforms: Windows 98, Windows NT 4.0, Windows Millennium Edition, Windows 2000, Windows XP Home Edition, Windows XP Professional, Windows Server 2003 family, .NET Compact Framework - Windows CE .NET

Graphics.DrawRectangle Method (Pen, Single, Single, Single, Single)

Draws a rectangle specified by a coordinate pair, a width, and a height.

[Visual Basic]
```
Overloads Public Sub DrawRectangle( _
   ByVal pen As Pen, _
   ByVal x As Single, _
   ByVal y As Single, _
   ByVal width As Single, _
   ByVal height As Single _
)
```
[C#]
```
public void DrawRectangle(
   Pen pen,
   float x,
   float y,
   float width,
   float height
);
```
[C++]
```
public: void DrawRectangle(
   Pen* pen,
   float x,
   float y,
   float width,
   float height
);
```
[JScript]
```
public function DrawRectangle(
   pen : Pen,
   x : float,
   y : float,
   width : float,
   height : float
);
```

Parameters

pen
: A **Pen** object that determines the color, width, and style of the rectangle.

x
: The x-coordinate of the upper-left corner of the rectangle to draw.

y
: The y-coordinate of the upper-left corner of the rectangle to draw.

width
: The width of the rectangle to draw.

height
: The height of the rectangle to draw.

Return Value

This method does not return a value.

Example

[Visual Basic, C#] The following example is designed for use with Windows Forms, and it requires **PaintEventArgs** *e*, which is a parameter of the **Paint** event handler. The code performs the following actions:

- Creates a black pen.
- Creates the position and size of a rectangle.
- Draws the rectangle to the screen.

[Visual Basic]
```
Public Sub DrawRectangleFloat(e As PaintEventArgs)
' Create pen.
Dim blackPen As New Pen(Color.Black, 3)
' Create location and size of rectangle.
Dim x As Single = 0F
Dim y As Single = 0F
Dim width As Single = 200F
Dim height As Single = 200F
' Draw rectangle to screen.
e.Graphics.DrawRectangle(blackPen, x, y, width, height)
End Sub
```

[C#]
```
public void DrawRectangleFloat(PaintEventArgs e)
{
// Create pen.
Pen blackPen = new Pen(Color.Black, 3);
// Create location and size of rectangle.
float x = 0.0F;
float y = 0.0F;
float width = 200.0F;
float height = 200.0F;
// Draw rectangle to screen.
e.Graphics.DrawRectangle(blackPen, x, y, width, height);
}
```

Requirements

Platforms: Windows 98, Windows NT 4.0, Windows Millennium Edition, Windows 2000, Windows XP Home Edition, Windows XP Professional, Windows Server 2003 family

Graphics.DrawRectangles Method

Draws a series of rectangles specified by **Rectangle** structures.

Overload List

Draws a series of rectangles specified by **Rectangle** structures.

[Visual Basic] **Overloads Public Sub DrawRectangles(Pen, Rectangle())**

[C#] **public void DrawRectangles(Pen, Rectangle[]);**

[C++] **public: void DrawRectangles(Pen*, Rectangle[]);**

[JScript] **public function DrawRectangles(Pen, Rectangle[]);**

Draws a series of rectangles specified by **RectangleF** structures.

[Visual Basic] **Overloads Public Sub DrawRectangles(Pen, RectangleF())**

[C#] **public void DrawRectangles(Pen, RectangleF[]);**

[C++] **public: void DrawRectangles(Pen*, RectangleF[]);**

[JScript] **public function DrawRectangles(Pen, RectangleF[]);**

Example

[Visual Basic, C#] The following example is designed for use with Windows Forms, and it requires **PaintEventArgs** *e*, which is a parameter of the **Paint** event handler. The code performs the following actions:

- Creates a black pen.
- Creates an array of three rectangles.
- Draws the rectangles to the screen.

> [Visual Basic, C#] **Note** This example shows how to use one of the overloaded versions of **DrawRectangles**. For other examples that might be available, see the individual overload topics.

[Visual Basic]
```
Public Sub DrawRectanglesRectangleF(e As PaintEventArgs)
' Create pen.
Dim blackPen As New Pen(Color.Black, 3)
' Create array of rectangles.
Dim rects As RectangleF() = {New RectangleF(0F, 0F, 100F, 200F), _
New RectangleF(100F, 200F, 250F, 50F), _
New RectangleF(300F, 0F, 50F, 100F)}
' Draw rectangles to screen.
e.Graphics.DrawRectangles(blackPen, rects)
End Sub
```

[C#]
```
public void DrawRectanglesRectangleF(PaintEventArgs e)
{
// Create pen.
Pen blackPen = new Pen(Color.Black, 3);
// Create array of rectangles.
RectangleF[] rects =
{
new RectangleF(  0.0F,   0.0F, 100.0F, 200.0F),
new RectangleF(100.0F, 200.0F, 250.0F,  50.0F),
new RectangleF(300.0F,   0.0F,  50.0F, 100.0F)
};
// Draw rectangles to screen.
e.Graphics.DrawRectangles(blackPen, rects);
}
```

Graphics.DrawRectangles Method (Pen, Rectangle[])

Draws a series of rectangles specified by **Rectangle** structures.

[Visual Basic]
```
Overloads Public Sub DrawRectangles( _
   ByVal pen As Pen, _
   ByVal rects() As Rectangle _
)
```
[C#]
```
public void DrawRectangles(
   Pen pen,
   Rectangle[] rects
);
```
[C++]
```
public: void DrawRectangles(
   Pen* pen,
   Rectangle rects[]
);
```
[JScript]
```
public function DrawRectangles(
   pen : Pen,
   rects : Rectangle[]
);
```

Parameters

pen
: **Pen** object that determines the color, width, and style of the outlines of the rectangles.

rects
: Array of **Rectangle** structures that represent the rectangles to draw.

Return Value

This method does not return a value.

Example

[Visual Basic, C#] The following example is designed for use with Windows Forms, and it requires **PaintEventArgs** *e*, which is a parameter of the **Paint** event handler. The code performs the following actions:

- Creates a black pen.
- Creates an array of three rectangles.
- Draws the rectangles to the screen.

[Visual Basic]
```
Public Sub DrawRectanglesRectangle(e As PaintEventArgs)
' Create pen.
Dim blackPen As New Pen(Color.Black, 3)
' Create array of rectangles.
Dim rects As Rectangle() = {New Rectangle(0, 0, 100, 200), _
New Rectangle(100, 200, 250, 50), _
New Rectangle(300, 0, 50, 100)}
' Draw rectangles to screen.
e.Graphics.DrawRectangles(blackPen, rects)
End Sub
```

[C#]
```
public void DrawRectanglesRectangle(PaintEventArgs e)
{
// Create pen.
Pen blackPen = new Pen(Color.Black, 3);
// Create array of rectangles.
Rectangle[] rects =
{
new Rectangle(  0,   0, 100, 200),
new Rectangle(100, 200, 250,  50),
new Rectangle(300,   0,  50, 100)
};
```

```
// Draw rectangles to screen.
e.Graphics.DrawRectangles(blackPen, rects);
}
```

Requirements

Platforms: Windows 98, Windows NT 4.0, Windows Millennium Edition, Windows 2000, Windows XP Home Edition, Windows XP Professional, Windows Server 2003 family

Graphics.DrawRectangles Method (Pen, RectangleF[])

Draws a series of rectangles specified by **RectangleF** structures.

[Visual Basic]
```
Overloads Public Sub DrawRectangles( _
   ByVal pen As Pen, _
   ByVal rects() As RectangleF _
)
```
[C#]
```
public void DrawRectangles(
   Pen pen,
   RectangleF[] rects
);
```
[C++]
```
public: void DrawRectangles(
   Pen* pen,
   RectangleF rects[]
);
```
[JScript]
```
public function DrawRectangles(
   pen : Pen,
   rects : RectangleF[]
);
```

Parameters

pen

Pen object that determines the color, width, and style of the outlines of the rectangles.

rects

Array of **RectangleF** structures that represent the rectangles to draw.

Return Value

This method does not return a value.

Example

[Visual Basic, C#] The following example is designed for use with Windows Forms, and it requires **PaintEventArgs** *e*, which is a parameter of the **Paint** event handler. The code performs the following actions:

- Creates a black pen.
- Creates an array of three rectangles.
- Draws the rectangles to the screen.

[Visual Basic]
```
Public Sub DrawRectanglesRectangleF(e As PaintEventArgs)
' Create pen.
Dim blackPen As New Pen(Color.Black, 3)
' Create array of rectangles.
Dim rects As RectangleF() = {New RectangleF(0F, 0F, 100F, 200F), _
New RectangleF(100F, 200F, 250F, 50F), _
New RectangleF(300F, 0F, 50F, 100F)}
' Draw rectangles to screen.
e.Graphics.DrawRectangles(blackPen, rects)
End Sub
```

[C#]
```
public void DrawRectanglesRectangleF(PaintEventArgs e)
{
// Create pen.
Pen blackPen = new Pen(Color.Black, 3);
// Create array of rectangles.
RectangleF[] rects =
{
new RectangleF(  0.0F,   0.0F, 100.0F, 200.0F),
new RectangleF(100.0F, 200.0F, 250.0F,  50.0F),
new RectangleF(300.0F,   0.0F,  50.0F, 100.0F)
};
// Draw rectangles to screen.
e.Graphics.DrawRectangles(blackPen, rects);
}
```

Requirements

Platforms: Windows 98, Windows NT 4.0, Windows Millennium Edition, Windows 2000, Windows XP Home Edition, Windows XP Professional, Windows Server 2003 family

Graphics.DrawString Method

Draws the specified text string at the specified location with the specified **Brush** and **Font** objects.

Overload List

Draws the specified text string at the specified location with the specified **Brush** and **Font** objects.

[Visual Basic] **Overloads Public Sub DrawString(String, Font, Brush, PointF)**

[C#] **public void DrawString(string, Font, Brush, PointF);**

[C++] **public: void DrawString(String*, Font*, Brush*, PointF);**

[JScript] **public function DrawString(String, Font, Brush, PointF);**

Draws the specified text string in the specified rectangle with the specified **Brush** and **Font** objects.

Supported by the .NET Compact Framework.

[Visual Basic] **Overloads Public Sub DrawString(String, Font, Brush, RectangleF)**

[C#] **public void DrawString(string, Font, Brush, RectangleF);**

[C++] **public: void DrawString(String*, Font*, Brush*, RectangleF);**

[JScript] **public function DrawString(String, Font, Brush, RectangleF);**

Draws the specified text string at the specified location with the specified **Brush** and **Font** objects using the formatting attributes of the specified **StringFormat** object.

[Visual Basic] **Overloads Public Sub DrawString(String, Font, Brush, PointF, StringFormat)**

[C#] **public void DrawString(string, Font, Brush, PointF, StringFormat);**

[C++] **public: void DrawString(String*, Font*, Brush*, PointF, StringFormat*);**

[JScript] **public function DrawString(String, Font, Brush, PointF, StringFormat);**

Draws the specified text string in the specified rectangle with the specified **Brush** and **Font** objects using the formatting attributes of the specified **StringFormat** object.

[Visual Basic] **Overloads Public Sub DrawString(String, Font, Brush, RectangleF, StringFormat)**

[C#] **public void DrawString(string, Font, Brush, RectangleF, StringFormat);**

[C++] **public: void DrawString(String*, Font*, Brush*, RectangleF, StringFormat*);**

[JScript] **public function DrawString(String, Font, Brush, RectangleF, StringFormat);**

Draws the specified text string at the specified location with the specified **Brush** and **Font** objects.

Supported by the .NET Compact Framework.

[Visual Basic] **Overloads Public Sub DrawString(String, Font, Brush, Single, Single)**

[C#] **public void DrawString(string, Font, Brush, float, float);**

[C++] **public: void DrawString(String*, Font*, Brush*, float, float);**

[JScript] **public function DrawString(String, Font, Brush, float, float);**

Draws the specified text string at the specified location with the specified **Brush** and **Font** objects using the formatting attributes of the specified **StringFormat** object.

[Visual Basic] **Overloads Public Sub DrawString(String, Font, Brush, Single, Single, StringFormat)**

[C#] **public void DrawString(string, Font, Brush, float, float, StringFormat);**

[C++] **public: void DrawString(String*, Font*, Brush*, float, float, StringFormat*);**

[JScript] **public function DrawString(String, Font, Brush, float, float, StringFormat);**

Example

[Visual Basic, C#] The following example is designed for use with Windows Forms, and it requires **PaintEventArgs** *e*, which is a parameter of the **Paint** event handler. The code performs the following actions:

- Creates a text string to draw.
- Defines the font as Arial (16pt).
- Creates a solid, black brush to draw with.
- Creates the coordinates of a point for the upper-left corner at which to draw the text.
- Sets the format of the string to draw vertically
- Draws the string to the screen using the font, brush, destination point, and format.

[Visual Basic, C#] **Note** This example shows how to use one of the overloaded versions of **DrawString**. For other examples that might be available, see the individual overload topics.

[Visual Basic]
```
Public Sub DrawStringFloatFormat(e As PaintEventArgs)
' Create string to draw.
Dim drawString As [String] = "Sample Text"
' Create font and brush.
Dim drawFont As New Font("Arial", 16)
Dim drawBrush As New SolidBrush(Color.Black)
' Create point for upper-left corner of drawing.
Dim x As Single = 150F
Dim y As Single = 50F
' Set format of string.
Dim drawFormat As New StringFormat()
drawFormat.FormatFlags = StringFormatFlags.DirectionVertical
' Draw string to screen.
e.Graphics.DrawString(drawString, drawFont, drawBrush, _
x, y, drawFormat)
End Sub
```

[C#]
```
public void DrawStringFloatFormat(PaintEventArgs e)
{
// Create string to draw.
String drawString = "Sample Text";
// Create font and brush.
Font drawFont = new Font("Arial", 16);
SolidBrush drawBrush = new SolidBrush(Color.Black);
// Create point for upper-left corner of drawing.
float x = 150.0F;
float y =  50.0F;
// Set format of string.
StringFormat drawFormat = new StringFormat();
drawFormat.FormatFlags = StringFormatFlags.DirectionVertical;
// Draw string to screen.
e.Graphics.DrawString(drawString, drawFont, drawBrush,          ↵
 x, y, drawFormat);
}
```

Graphics.DrawString Method (String, Font, Brush, PointF)

Draws the specified text string at the specified location with the specified **Brush** and **Font** objects.

[Visual Basic]
```
Overloads Public Sub DrawString( _
   ByVal s As String, _
   ByVal font As Font, _
   ByVal brush As Brush, _
   ByVal point As PointF _
)
```
[C#]
```
public void DrawString(
   string s,
   Font font,
   Brush brush,
   PointF point
);
```
[C++]
```
public: void DrawString(
   String* s,
   Font* font,
   Brush* brush,
   PointF point
);
```
[JScript]
```
public function DrawString(
   s : String,
   font : Font,
   brush : Brush,
   point : PointF
);
```

Parameters

s

String to draw.

font

Font object that defines the text format of the string.

brush

Brush object that determines the color and texture of the drawn text.

point

PointF structure that specifies the upper-left corner of the drawn text.

Return Value

This method does not return a value.

Example

[Visual Basic, C#] The following example is designed for use with Windows Forms, and it requires **PaintEventArgs** *e*, which is a parameter of the **Paint** event handler. The code performs the following actions:

- Creates a text string to draw.
- Defines the font as Arial (16pt).
- Creates a solid, black brush to draw with.
- Creates a point for the upper-left corner at which to draw the text.
- Draws the string to the screen using the font, brush, and destination point.

[Visual Basic]

```
Public Sub DrawStringPointF(e As PaintEventArgs)
' Create string to draw.
Dim drawString As [String] = "Sample Text"
' Create font and brush.
Dim drawFont As New Font("Arial", 16)
Dim drawBrush As New SolidBrush(Color.Black)
' Create point for upper-left corner of drawing.
Dim drawPoint As New PointF(150F, 150F)
' Draw string to screen.
e.Graphics.DrawString(drawString, drawFont, drawBrush, drawPoint)
End Sub
```

[C#]

```
public void DrawStringPointF(PaintEventArgs e)
{
// Create string to draw.
String drawString = "Sample Text";
// Create font and brush.
Font drawFont = new Font("Arial", 16);
SolidBrush drawBrush = new SolidBrush(Color.Black);
// Create point for upper-left corner of drawing.
PointF drawPoint = new PointF(150.0F, 150.0F);
// Draw string to screen.
e.Graphics.DrawString(drawString, drawFont, drawBrush, drawPoint);
}
```

Requirements

Platforms: Windows 98, Windows NT 4.0, Windows Millennium Edition, Windows 2000, Windows XP Home Edition, Windows XP Professional, Windows Server 2003 family

Graphics.DrawString Method (String, Font, Brush, RectangleF)

Draws the specified text string in the specified rectangle with the specified **Brush** and **Font** objects.

[Visual Basic]

```
Overloads Public Sub DrawString( _
   ByVal s As String, _
   ByVal font As Font, _
   ByVal brush As Brush, _
   ByVal layoutRectangle As RectangleF _
)
```

[C#]

```
public void DrawString(
   string s,
   Font font,
   Brush brush,
   RectangleF layoutRectangle
);
```

[C++]

```
public: void DrawString(
   String* s,
   Font* font,
   Brush* brush,
   RectangleF layoutRectangle
);
```

[JScript]

```
public function DrawString(
   s : String,
   font : Font,
   brush : Brush,
   layoutRectangle : RectangleF
);
```

Parameters

s

String to draw.

font

Font object that defines the text format of the string.

brush

Brush object that determines the color and texture of the drawn text.

layoutRectangle

RectangleF structure that specifies the location of the drawn text.

Return Value

This method does not return a value.

Remarks

The text represented by the *s* parameter is drawn inside the rectangle represented by the *layoutRectangle* parameter. If the text does not fit inside the rectangle, it is truncated.

Example

[Visual Basic, C#] The following example is designed for use with Windows Forms, and it requires **PaintEventArgs** *e*, which is a parameter of the **Paint** event handler. The code performs the following actions:

- Creates a text string to draw.
- Defines the font as Arial (16pt).
- Creates a solid, black brush to draw with.
- Creates a rectangle in which to draw the text.
- Draws the rectangle to the screen.
- Draws the string to the screen using the font, brush, and destination rectangle.

[Visual Basic]

```
Public Sub DrawStringRectangleF(e As PaintEventArgs)
' Create string to draw.
Dim drawString As [String] = "Sample Text"
' Create font and brush.
Dim drawFont As New Font("Arial", 16)
Dim drawBrush As New SolidBrush(Color.Black)
' Create rectangle for drawing.
Dim x As Single = 150F
Dim y As Single = 150F
Dim width As Single = 200F
```

```
Dim height As Single = 50F
Dim drawRect As New RectangleF(x, y, width, height)
' Draw rectangle to screen.
Dim blackPen As New Pen(Color.Black)
e.Graphics.DrawRectangle(blackPen, x, y, width, height)
' Draw string to screen.
e.Graphics.DrawString(drawString, drawFont, drawBrush, drawRect)
End Sub
```

[C#]

```
public void DrawStringRectangleF(PaintEventArgs e)
{
// Create string to draw.
String drawString = "Sample Text";
// Create font and brush.
Font drawFont = new Font("Arial", 16);
SolidBrush drawBrush = new SolidBrush(Color.Black);
// Create rectangle for drawing.
float x = 150.0F;
float y = 150.0F;
float width = 200.0F;
float height = 50.0F;
RectangleF drawRect = new RectangleF( x, y, width, height);
// Draw rectangle to screen.
Pen blackPen = new Pen(Color.Black);
e.Graphics.DrawRectangle(blackPen, x, y, width, height);
// Draw string to screen.
e.Graphics.DrawString(drawString, drawFont, drawBrush, drawRect);
}
```

Requirements

Platforms: Windows 98, Windows NT 4.0, Windows Millennium Edition, Windows 2000, Windows XP Home Edition, Windows XP Professional, Windows Server 2003 family, .NET Compact Framework - Windows CE .NET

Graphics.DrawString Method (String, Font, Brush, PointF, StringFormat)

Draws the specified text string at the specified location with the specified **Brush** and **Font** objects using the formatting attributes of the specified **StringFormat** object.

[Visual Basic]

```
Overloads Public Sub DrawString( _
   ByVal s As String, _
   ByVal font As Font, _
   ByVal brush As Brush, _
   ByVal point As PointF, _
   ByVal format As StringFormat _
)
```

[C#]

```
public void DrawString(
   string s,
   Font font,
   Brush brush,
   PointF point,
   StringFormat format
);
```

[C++]

```
public: void DrawString(
   String* s,
   Font* font,
   Brush* brush,
   PointF point,
   StringFormat* format
);
```

[JScript]

```
public function DrawString(
   s : String,
   font : Font,
   brush : Brush,
   point : PointF,
   format : StringFormat
);
```

Parameters

s
String to draw.

font
Font object that defines the text format of the string.

brush
Brush object that determines the color and texture of the drawn text.

point
PointF structure that specifies the upper-left corner of the drawn text.

format
StringFormat object that specifies formatting attributes, such as line spacing and alignment, that are applied to the drawn text.

Return Value

This method does not return a value.

Example

[Visual Basic, C#] The following example is designed for use with Windows Forms, and it requires **PaintEventArgs** *e*, which is a parameter of the **Paint** event handler. The code performs the following actions:

- Creates a text string to draw.
- Defines the font as Arial (16pt).
- Creates a solid, black brush to draw with.
- Creates a point for the upper-left corner at which to draw the text.
- Sets the format of the string to draw vertically.
- Draws the string to the screen using the font, brush, destination point and format.

[Visual Basic]

```
Public Sub DrawStringPointFFormat(e As PaintEventArgs)
' Create string to draw.
Dim drawString As [String] = "Sample Text"
' Create font and brush.
Dim drawFont As New Font("Arial", 16)
Dim drawBrush As New SolidBrush(Color.Black)
' Create point for upper-left corner of drawing.
Dim drawPoint As New PointF(150F, 50F)
' Set format of string.
Dim drawFormat As New StringFormat()
drawFormat.FormatFlags = StringFormatFlags.DirectionVertical
' Draw string to screen.
e.Graphics.DrawString(drawString, drawFont, drawBrush, _
drawPoint, drawFormat)
End Sub
```

[C#]

```
public void DrawStringPointFFormat(PaintEventArgs e)
{
// Create string to draw.
String drawString = "Sample Text";
// Create font and brush.
Font drawFont = new Font("Arial", 16);
SolidBrush drawBrush = new SolidBrush(Color.Black);
// Create point for upper-left corner of drawing.
PointF drawPoint = new PointF(150.0F, 50.0F);
```

```
// Set format of string.
StringFormat drawFormat = new StringFormat();
drawFormat.FormatFlags = StringFormatFlags.DirectionVertical;
// Draw string to screen.
e.Graphics.DrawString(drawString, drawFont, drawBrush, ↵
drawPoint, drawFormat);
}
```

Requirements

Platforms: Windows 98, Windows NT 4.0, Windows Millennium Edition, Windows 2000, Windows XP Home Edition, Windows XP Professional, Windows Server 2003 family

Graphics.DrawString Method (String, Font, Brush, RectangleF, StringFormat)

Draws the specified text string in the specified rectangle with the specified **Brush** and **Font** objects using the formatting attributes of the specified **StringFormat** object.

[Visual Basic]
```
Overloads Public Sub DrawString( _
   ByVal s As String, _
   ByVal font As Font, _
   ByVal brush As Brush, _
   ByVal layoutRectangle As RectangleF, _
   ByVal format As StringFormat _
)
```
[C#]
```
public void DrawString(
   string s,
   Font font,
   Brush brush,
   RectangleF layoutRectangle,
   StringFormat format
);
```
[C++]
```
public: void DrawString(
   String* s,
   Font* font,
   Brush* brush,
   RectangleF layoutRectangle,
   StringFormat* format
);
```
[JScript]
```
public function DrawString(
   s : String,
   font : Font,
   brush : Brush,
   layoutRectangle : RectangleF,
   format : StringFormat
);
```

Parameters

s

String to draw.

font

Font object that defines the text format of the string.

brush

Brush object that determines the color and texture of the drawn text.

layoutRectangle

RectangleF structure that specifies the location of the drawn text.

format

StringFormat object that specifies formatting attributes, such as line spacing and alignment, that are applied to the drawn text.

Return Value

This method does not return a value.

Remarks

The text represented by the *s* parameter is drawn inside the rectangle represented by the *layoutRectangle* parameter. If the text does not fit inside the rectangle, it is truncated.

Example

[Visual Basic, C#] The following example is designed for use with Windows Forms, and it requires **PaintEventArgs** *e*, which is a parameter of the **Paint** event handler. The code performs the following actions:

- Creates a text string to draw.
- Defines the font as Arial (16pt).
- Creates a solid, black brush to draw with.
- Creates a rectangle in which to draw the text.
- Draws the rectangle to the screen.
- Sets the format of the string to center it within the rectangle.
- Draws the string to the screen using the font, brush, and destination rectangle.

[Visual Basic]
```
Public Sub DrawStringRectangleFFormat(e As PaintEventArgs)
' Create string to draw.
Dim drawString As [String] = "Sample Text"
' Create font and brush.
Dim drawFont As New Font("Arial", 16)
Dim drawBrush As New SolidBrush(Color.Black)
' Create rectangle for drawing.
Dim x As Single = 150F
Dim y As Single = 150F
Dim width As Single = 200F
Dim height As Single = 50F
Dim drawRect As New RectangleF(x, y, width, height)
' Draw rectangle to screen.
Dim blackPen As New Pen(Color.Black)
e.Graphics.DrawRectangle(blackPen, x, y, width, height)
' Set format of string.
Dim drawFormat As New StringFormat()
drawFormat.Alignment = StringAlignment.Center
' Draw string to screen.
e.Graphics.DrawString(drawString, drawFont, drawBrush, _
drawRect, drawFormat)
End Sub
```

[C#]
```
public void DrawStringRectangleFFormat(PaintEventArgs e)
{
// Create string to draw.
String drawString = "Sample Text";
// Create font and brush.
Font drawFont = new Font("Arial", 16);
SolidBrush drawBrush = new SolidBrush(Color.Black);
// Create rectangle for drawing.
float x = 150.0F;
float y = 150.0F;
float width = 200.0F;
float height = 50.0F;
RectangleF drawRect = new RectangleF( x, y, width, height);
// Draw rectangle to screen.
Pen blackPen = new Pen(Color.Black);
e.Graphics.DrawRectangle(blackPen, x, y, width, height);
// Set format of string.
StringFormat drawFormat = new StringFormat();
drawFormat.Alignment = StringAlignment.Center;
```

```
// Draw string to screen.
e.Graphics.DrawString(drawString, drawFont, drawBrush, ↵
drawRect, drawFormat);
}
```

Requirements

Platforms: Windows 98, Windows NT 4.0, Windows Millennium Edition, Windows 2000, Windows XP Home Edition, Windows XP Professional, Windows Server 2003 family

Graphics.DrawString Method (String, Font, Brush, Single, Single)

Draws the specified text string at the specified location with the specified **Brush** and **Font** objects.

[Visual Basic]
```
Overloads Public Sub DrawString( _
   ByVal s As String, _
   ByVal font As Font, _
   ByVal brush As Brush, _
   ByVal x As Single, _
   ByVal y As Single _
)
```
[C#]
```
public void DrawString(
   string s,
   Font font,
   Brush brush,
   float x,
   float y
);
```
[C++]
```
public: void DrawString(
   String* s,
   Font* font,
   Brush* brush,
   float x,
   float y
);
```
[JScript]
```
public function DrawString(
   s : String,
   font : Font,
   brush : Brush,
   x : float,
   y : float
);
```

Parameters

s
String to draw.

font
Font object that defines the text format of the string.

brush
Brush object that determines the color and texture of the drawn text.

x
x coordinate of the upper-left corner of the drawn text.

y
y coordinate of the upper-left corner of the drawn text.

Return Value

This method does not return a value.

Example

[Visual Basic, C#] The following example is designed for use with Windows Forms, and it requires **PaintEventArgs** *e*, which is a parameter of the **Paint** event handler. The code performs the following actions:

- Creates a text string to draw.
- Defines the font as Arial (16pt).
- Creates a solid black brush to draw with.
- Creates a point for the upper-left corner at which to draw the text.
- Draws the string to the screen using the font, brush, and destination point.

[Visual Basic]
```
Public Sub DrawStringFloat(e As PaintEventArgs)
' Create string to draw.
Dim drawString As [String] = "Sample Text"
' Create font and brush.
Dim drawFont As New Font("Arial", 16)
Dim drawBrush As New SolidBrush(Color.Black)
' Create point for upper-left corner of drawing.
Dim x As Single = 150F
Dim y As Single = 150F
' Draw string to screen.
e.Graphics.DrawString(drawString, drawFont, drawBrush, x, y)
End Sub
```

[C#]
```
public void DrawStringFloat(PaintEventArgs e)
{
// Create string to draw.
String drawString = "Sample Text";
// Create font and brush.
Font drawFont = new Font("Arial", 16);
SolidBrush drawBrush = new SolidBrush(Color.Black);
// Create point for upper-left corner of drawing.
float x = 150.0F;
float y = 150.0F;
// Draw string to screen.
e.Graphics.DrawString(drawString, drawFont, drawBrush, x, y);
}
```

Requirements

Platforms: Windows 98, Windows NT 4.0, Windows Millennium Edition, Windows 2000, Windows XP Home Edition, Windows XP Professional, Windows Server 2003 family, .NET Compact Framework - Windows CE .NET

Graphics.DrawString Method (String, Font, Brush, Single, Single, StringFormat)

Draws the specified text string at the specified location with the specified **Brush** and **Font** objects using the formatting attributes of the specified **StringFormat** object.

[Visual Basic]
```
Overloads Public Sub DrawString( _
   ByVal s As String, _
   ByVal font As Font, _
   ByVal brush As Brush, _
   ByVal x As Single, _
   ByVal y As Single, _
   ByVal format As StringFormat _
)
```

```
[C#]
public void DrawString(
   string s,
   Font font,
   Brush brush,
   float x,
   float y,
   StringFormat format
);
[C++]
public: void DrawString(
   String* s,
   Font* font,
   Brush* brush,
   float x,
   float y,
   StringFormat* format
);
[JScript]
public function DrawString(
   s : String,
   font : Font,
   brush : Brush,
   x : float,
   y : float,
   format : StringFormat
);
```

Parameters

s
: String to draw.

font
: **Font** object that defines the text format of the string.

brush
: **Brush** object that determines the color and texture of the drawn text.

x
: x-coordinate of the upper-left corner of the drawn text.

y
: y-coordinate of the upper-left corner of the drawn text.

format
: **StringFormat** object that specifies formatting attributes, such as line spacing and alignment, that are applied to the drawn text.

Return Value

This method does not return a value.

Example

[Visual Basic, C#] The following example is designed for use with Windows Forms, and it requires **PaintEventArgs** *e*, which is a parameter of the **Paint** event handler. The code performs the following actions:

- Creates a text string to draw.
- Defines the font as Arial (16pt).
- Creates a solid, black brush to draw with.
- Creates the coordinates of a point for the upper-left corner at which to draw the text.
- Sets the format of the string to draw vertically
- Draws the string to the screen using the font, brush, destination point, and format.

```
[Visual Basic]
Public Sub DrawStringFloatFormat(e As PaintEventArgs)
' Create string to draw.
Dim drawString As [String] = "Sample Text"
' Create font and brush.
Dim drawFont As New Font("Arial", 16)
Dim drawBrush As New SolidBrush(Color.Black)
' Create point for upper-left corner of drawing.
Dim x As Single = 150F
Dim y As Single = 50F
' Set format of string.
Dim drawFormat As New StringFormat()
drawFormat.FormatFlags = StringFormatFlags.DirectionVertical
' Draw string to screen.
e.Graphics.DrawString(drawString, drawFont, drawBrush, _
x, y, drawFormat)
End Sub
```

```
[C#]
public void DrawStringFloatFormat(PaintEventArgs e)
{
// Create string to draw.
String drawString = "Sample Text";
// Create font and brush.
Font drawFont = new Font("Arial", 16);
SolidBrush drawBrush = new SolidBrush(Color.Black);
// Create point for upper-left corner of drawing.
float x = 150.0F;
float y =  50.0F;
// Set format of string.
StringFormat drawFormat = new StringFormat();
drawFormat.FormatFlags = StringFormatFlags.DirectionVertical;
// Draw string to screen.
e.Graphics.DrawString(drawString, drawFont, drawBrush, x, y,        ↵
drawFormat);
}
```

Requirements

Platforms: Windows 98, Windows NT 4.0, Windows Millennium Edition, Windows 2000, Windows XP Home Edition, Windows XP Professional, Windows Server 2003 family

Graphics.EndContainer Method

Closes the current graphics container and restores the state of this **Graphics** object to the state saved by a call to the **BeginContainer** method.

```
[Visual Basic]
Public Sub EndContainer( _
   ByVal container As GraphicsContainer _
)
[C#]
public void EndContainer(
   GraphicsContainer container
);
[C++]
public: void EndContainer(
   GraphicsContainer* container
);
[JScript]
public function EndContainer(
   container : GraphicsContainer
);
```

Parameters

container
: **GraphicsContainer** object that represents the container this method restores.

Return Value

This method does not return a value.

Remarks

Use this method with the **BeginContainer** method to create nested graphics containers. Graphics containers retain graphics state, such as transformation, clipping region, and rendering properties.

When you call the **BeginContainer** method of a **Graphics** object, an information block that holds the state of the **Graphics** object is put on a stack. The **BeginContainer** method returns a **GraphicsContainer** object that identifies that information block. When you pass the identifying object to the **EndContainer** method, the information block is removed from the stack and is used to restore the **Graphics** object to the state it was in at the time of the **BeginContainer** method call.

Containers can be nested; that is, you can call the **BeginContainer** method several times before you call the **EndContainer** method. Each time you call the **BeginContainer** method, an information block is put on the stack, and you receive a **GraphicsContainer** object for the information block. When you pass one of those objects to the **EndContainer** method, the **Graphics** object is returned to the state it was in at the time of the **BeginContainer** method call that returned that particular **GraphicsContainer** object. The information block placed on the stack by that **BeginContainer** method call is removed from the stack, and all information blocks placed on that stack after that **BeginContainer** method call are also removed.

Calls to the **Graphics.Save** method place information blocks on the same stack as calls to the **BeginContainer** method. Just as an **EndContainer** method call is paired with a **BeginContainer** method call, a **Graphics.Restore** method call is paired with a **Save** method call.

When you call the **EndContainer** method, all information blocks placed on the stack (by the **Save** method or by the **BeginContainer** method) after the corresponding call to the **BeginContainer** method are removed from the stack. Likewise, when you call the **Restore** method, all information blocks placed on the stack (by the **Save** method or by the **BeginContainer** method) after the corresponding call to the **Save** method are removed from the stack.

Example

[Visual Basic, C#] The following example is designed for use with Windows Forms, and it requires **PaintEventArgs** *e*, which is a parameter of the **Paint** event handler. The code performs the following actions:

- Opens a new graphics container and saves the old container.
- Translates the world coordinates in the container.
- Fills a red rectangle in the (translated coordinates of the) new container.
- Closes the new container and restores the saved container.
- Fills a green rectangle (to the untranslated coordinates) of the saved container.

[Visual Basic, C#] The result is a green rectangle that overlies a red rectangle of the same size.

[Visual Basic]

```
Public Sub EndContainerState(e As PaintEventArgs)
' Begin graphics container.
Dim containerState As GraphicsContainer = _
e.Graphics.BeginContainer()
' Translate world transformation.
e.Graphics.TranslateTransform(100F, 100F)
' Fill translated rectangle in container with red.
e.Graphics.FillRectangle(New SolidBrush(Color.Red), 0, 0, _
200, 200)
' End graphics container.
e.Graphics.EndContainer(containerState)
' Fill untransformed rectangle with green.
e.Graphics.FillRectangle(New SolidBrush(Color.Green), 0, 0, _
200, 200)
End Sub
```

[C#]

```
public void EndContainerState(PaintEventArgs e)
{
// Begin graphics container.
GraphicsContainer containerState = e.Graphics.BeginContainer();
// Translate world transformation.
e.Graphics.TranslateTransform(100.0F, 100.0F);
// Fill translated rectangle in container with red.
e.Graphics.FillRectangle(new SolidBrush(Color.Red), 0, 0, 200, 200);
// End graphics container.
e.Graphics.EndContainer(containerState);
// Fill untransformed rectangle with green.
e.Graphics.FillRectangle(new SolidBrush(Color.Green), 0, 0, 200, 200);
}
```

Requirements

Platforms: Windows 98, Windows NT 4.0, Windows Millennium Edition, Windows 2000, Windows XP Home Edition, Windows XP Professional, Windows Server 2003 family

Graphics.EnumerateMetafile Method

Sends the records in the specified **Metafile** object, one at a time, to a callback method for display at a specified point.

Overload List

Sends the records in the specified **Metafile** object, one at a time, to a callback method for display at a specified point.

[Visual Basic] **Overloads Public Sub EnumerateMetafile(Metafile, Point, Graphics.EnumerateMetafileProc)**

[C#] **public void EnumerateMetafile(Metafile, Point, Graphics.EnumerateMetafileProc);**

[C++] **public: void EnumerateMetafile(Metafile*, Point, Graphics.EnumerateMetafileProc*);**

[JScript] **public function EnumerateMetafile(Metafile, Point, Graphics.EnumerateMetafileProc);**

Sends the records in the specified **Metafile** object, one at a time, to a callback method for display in a specified parallelogram.

[Visual Basic] **Overloads Public Sub EnumerateMetafile(Metafile, Point(), Graphics.EnumerateMetafileProc)**

[C#] **public void EnumerateMetafile(Metafile, Point[], Graphics.EnumerateMetafileProc);**

[C++] **public: void EnumerateMetafile(Metafile*, Point[], Graphics.EnumerateMetafileProc*);**

[JScript] **public function EnumerateMetafile(Metafile, Point[], Graphics.EnumerateMetafileProc);**

Sends the records in the specified **Metafile** object, one at a time, to a callback method for display at a specified point.

[Visual Basic] **Overloads Public Sub EnumerateMetafile(Metafile, PointF, Graphics.EnumerateMetafileProc)**

[C#] **public void EnumerateMetafile(Metafile, PointF, Graphics.EnumerateMetafileProc);**

[C++] **public: void EnumerateMetafile(Metafile*, PointF, Graphics.EnumerateMetafileProc*);**

[JScript] **public function EnumerateMetafile(Metafile, PointF, Graphics.EnumerateMetafileProc);**

Sends the records in the specified **Metafile** object, one at a time, to a callback method for display in a specified parallelogram.

[Visual Basic] **Overloads Public Sub EnumerateMetafile(Metafile, PointF(), Graphics.EnumerateMetafileProc)**

[C#] **public void EnumerateMetafile(Metafile, PointF[], Graphics.EnumerateMetafileProc);**

[C++] **public: void EnumerateMetafile(Metafile*, PointF[], Graphics.EnumerateMetafileProc*);**

[JScript] **public function EnumerateMetafile(Metafile, PointF[], Graphics.EnumerateMetafileProc);**

Sends the records of the specified **Metafile** object, one at a time, to a callback method for display in a specified rectangle.

[Visual Basic] **Overloads Public Sub EnumerateMetafile(Metafile, Rectangle, Graphics.EnumerateMetafileProc)**

[C#] **public void EnumerateMetafile(Metafile, Rectangle, Graphics.EnumerateMetafileProc);**

[C++] **public: void EnumerateMetafile(Metafile*, Rectangle, Graphics.EnumerateMetafileProc*);**

[JScript] **public function EnumerateMetafile(Metafile, Rectangle, Graphics.EnumerateMetafileProc);**

Sends the records of the specified **Metafile** object, one at a time, to a callback method for display in a specified rectangle.

[Visual Basic] **Overloads Public Sub EnumerateMetafile(Metafile, RectangleF, Graphics.EnumerateMetafileProc)**

[C#] **public void EnumerateMetafile(Metafile, RectangleF, Graphics.EnumerateMetafileProc);**

[C++] **public: void EnumerateMetafile(Metafile*, RectangleF, Graphics.EnumerateMetafileProc*);**

[JScript] **public function EnumerateMetafile(Metafile, RectangleF, Graphics.EnumerateMetafileProc);**

Sends the records in the specified **Metafile** object, one at a time, to a callback method for display at a specified point.

[Visual Basic] **Overloads Public Sub EnumerateMetafile(Metafile, Point, Graphics.EnumerateMetafileProc, IntPtr)**

[C#] **public void EnumerateMetafile(Metafile, Point, Graphics.EnumerateMetafileProc, IntPtr);**

[C++] **public: void EnumerateMetafile(Metafile*, Point, Graphics.EnumerateMetafileProc*, IntPtr);**

[JScript] **public function EnumerateMetafile(Metafile, Point, Graphics.EnumerateMetafileProc, IntPtr);**

Sends the records in the specified **Metafile** object, one at a time, to a callback method for display in a specified parallelogram.

[Visual Basic] **Overloads Public Sub EnumerateMetafile(Metafile, Point(), Graphics.EnumerateMetafileProc, IntPtr)**

[C#] **public void EnumerateMetafile(Metafile, Point[], Graphics.EnumerateMetafileProc, IntPtr);**

[C++] **public: void EnumerateMetafile(Metafile*, Point[], Graphics.EnumerateMetafileProc*, IntPtr);**

[JScript] **public function EnumerateMetafile(Metafile, Point[], Graphics.EnumerateMetafileProc, IntPtr);**

Sends the records in the specified **Metafile** object, one at a time, to a callback method for display at a specified point.

[Visual Basic] **Overloads Public Sub EnumerateMetafile(Metafile, PointF, Graphics.EnumerateMetafileProc, IntPtr)**

[C#] **public void EnumerateMetafile(Metafile, PointF, Graphics.EnumerateMetafileProc, IntPtr);**

[C++] **public: void EnumerateMetafile(Metafile*, PointF, Graphics.EnumerateMetafileProc*, IntPtr);**

[JScript] **public function EnumerateMetafile(Metafile, PointF, Graphics.EnumerateMetafileProc, IntPtr);**

Sends the records in the specified **Metafile** object, one at a time, to a callback method for display in a specified parallelogram.

[Visual Basic] **Overloads Public Sub EnumerateMetafile(Metafile, PointF(), Graphics.EnumerateMetafileProc, IntPtr)**

[C#] **public void EnumerateMetafile(Metafile, PointF[], Graphics.EnumerateMetafileProc, IntPtr);**

[C++] **public: void EnumerateMetafile(Metafile*, PointF[], Graphics.EnumerateMetafileProc*, IntPtr);**

[JScript] **public function EnumerateMetafile(Metafile, PointF[], Graphics.EnumerateMetafileProc, IntPtr);**

Sends the records of the specified **Metafile** object, one at a time, to a callback method for display in a specified rectangle.

[Visual Basic] **Overloads Public Sub EnumerateMetafile(Metafile, Rectangle, Graphics.EnumerateMetafileProc, IntPtr)**

[C#] **public void EnumerateMetafile(Metafile, Rectangle, Graphics.EnumerateMetafileProc, IntPtr);**

[C++] **public: void EnumerateMetafile(Metafile*, Rectangle, Graphics.EnumerateMetafileProc*, IntPtr);**

[JScript] **public function EnumerateMetafile(Metafile, Rectangle, Graphics.EnumerateMetafileProc, IntPtr);**

Sends the records of the specified **Metafile** object, one at a time, to a callback method for display in a specified rectangle.

[Visual Basic] **Overloads Public Sub EnumerateMetafile(Metafile, RectangleF, Graphics.EnumerateMetafileProc, IntPtr)**

[C#] **public void EnumerateMetafile(Metafile, RectangleF, Graphics.EnumerateMetafileProc, IntPtr);**

[C++] **public: void EnumerateMetafile(Metafile*, RectangleF, Graphics.EnumerateMetafileProc*, IntPtr);**

[JScript] **public function EnumerateMetafile(Metafile, RectangleF, Graphics.EnumerateMetafileProc, IntPtr);**

Sends the records in the specified **Metafile** object, one at a time, to a callback method for display at a specified point using specified image attributes.

[Visual Basic] **Overloads Public Sub EnumerateMetafile(Metafile, Point, Graphics.EnumerateMetafileProc, IntPtr, ImageAttributes)**

[C#] **public void EnumerateMetafile(Metafile, Point, Graphics.EnumerateMetafileProc, IntPtr, ImageAttributes);**

[C++] **public: void EnumerateMetafile(Metafile*, Point, Graphics.EnumerateMetafileProc*, IntPtr, ImageAttributes*);**

[JScript] **public function EnumerateMetafile(Metafile, Point, Graphics.EnumerateMetafileProc, IntPtr, ImageAttributes);**

Sends the records in a selected rectangle from a **Metafile** object, one at a time, to a callback method for display at a specified point.

[Visual Basic] **Overloads Public Sub EnumerateMetafile(Metafile, Point, Rectangle, GraphicsUnit, Graphics.EnumerateMetafileProc)**

[C#] **public void EnumerateMetafile(Metafile, Point, Rectangle, GraphicsUnit, Graphics.EnumerateMetafileProc);**

[C++] **public: void EnumerateMetafile(Metafile*, Point, Rectangle, GraphicsUnit, Graphics.EnumerateMetafileProc*);**

[JScript] **public function EnumerateMetafile(Metafile, Point, Rectangle, GraphicsUnit, Graphics.EnumerateMetafileProc);**

Sends the records in the specified **Metafile** object, one at a time, to a callback method for display in a specified parallelogram using specified image attributes.

[Visual Basic] **Overloads Public Sub EnumerateMetafile(Metafile, Point(), Graphics.EnumerateMetafileProc, IntPtr, ImageAttributes)**

[C#] **public void EnumerateMetafile(Metafile, Point[], Graphics.EnumerateMetafileProc, IntPtr, ImageAttributes);**

[C++] **public: void EnumerateMetafile(Metafile*, Point[], Graphics.EnumerateMetafileProc*, IntPtr, ImageAttributes*);**

[JScript] **public function EnumerateMetafile(Metafile, Point[], Graphics.EnumerateMetafileProc, IntPtr, ImageAttributes);**

Sends the records in a selected rectangle from a **Metafile** object, one at a time, to a callback method for display in a specified parallelogram.

[Visual Basic] **Overloads Public Sub EnumerateMetafile(Metafile, Point(), Rectangle, GraphicsUnit, Graphics.EnumerateMetafileProc)**

[C#] **public void EnumerateMetafile(Metafile, Point[], Rectangle, GraphicsUnit, Graphics.EnumerateMetafileProc);**

[C++] **public: void EnumerateMetafile(Metafile*, Point[], Rectangle, GraphicsUnit, Graphics.EnumerateMetafileProc*);**

[JScript] **public function EnumerateMetafile(Metafile, Point[], Rectangle, GraphicsUnit, Graphics.EnumerateMetafileProc);**

Sends the records in the specified **Metafile** object, one at a time, to a callback method for display at a specified point using specified image attributes.

[Visual Basic] **Overloads Public Sub EnumerateMetafile(Metafile, PointF, Graphics.EnumerateMetafileProc, IntPtr, ImageAttributes)**

[C#] **public void EnumerateMetafile(Metafile, PointF, Graphics.EnumerateMetafileProc, IntPtr, ImageAttributes);**

[C++] **public: void EnumerateMetafile(Metafile*, PointF, Graphics.EnumerateMetafileProc*, IntPtr, ImageAttributes*);**

[JScript] **public function EnumerateMetafile(Metafile, PointF, Graphics.EnumerateMetafileProc, IntPtr, ImageAttributes);**

Sends the records in a selected rectangle from a **Metafile** object, one at a time, to a callback method for display at a specified point.

[Visual Basic] **Overloads Public Sub EnumerateMetafile(Metafile, PointF, RectangleF, GraphicsUnit, Graphics.EnumerateMetafileProc)**

[C#] **public void EnumerateMetafile(Metafile, PointF, RectangleF, GraphicsUnit, Graphics.EnumerateMetafileProc);**

[C++] **public: void EnumerateMetafile(Metafile*, PointF, RectangleF, GraphicsUnit, Graphics.EnumerateMetafileProc*);**

[JScript] **public function EnumerateMetafile(Metafile, PointF, RectangleF, GraphicsUnit, Graphics.EnumerateMetafileProc);**

Sends the records in the specified **Metafile** object, one at a time, to a callback method for display in a specified parallelogram using specified image attributes.

[Visual Basic] **Overloads Public Sub EnumerateMetafile(Metafile, PointF(), Graphics.EnumerateMetafileProc, IntPtr, ImageAttributes)**

[C#] **public void EnumerateMetafile(Metafile, PointF[], Graphics.EnumerateMetafileProc, IntPtr, ImageAttributes);**

[C++] **public: void EnumerateMetafile(Metafile*, PointF[], Graphics.EnumerateMetafileProc*, IntPtr, ImageAttributes*);**

[JScript] **public function EnumerateMetafile(Metafile, PointF[], Graphics.EnumerateMetafileProc, IntPtr, ImageAttributes);**

Sends the records in a selected rectangle from a **Metafile** object, one at a time, to a callback method for display in a specified parallelogram.

[Visual Basic] **Overloads Public Sub EnumerateMetafile(Metafile, PointF(), RectangleF, GraphicsUnit, Graphics.EnumerateMetafileProc)**

[C#] **public void EnumerateMetafile(Metafile, PointF[], RectangleF, GraphicsUnit, Graphics.EnumerateMetafileProc);**

[C++] **public: void EnumerateMetafile(Metafile*, PointF[], RectangleF, GraphicsUnit, Graphics.EnumerateMetafileProc*);**

[JScript] **public function EnumerateMetafile(Metafile, PointF[], RectangleF, GraphicsUnit, Graphics.EnumerateMetafileProc);**

Sends the records of the specified **Metafile** object, one at a time, to a callback method for display in a specified rectangle using specified image attributes.

[Visual Basic] **Overloads Public Sub EnumerateMetafile(Metafile, Rectangle, Graphics.EnumerateMetafileProc, IntPtr, ImageAttributes)**

[C#] **public void EnumerateMetafile(Metafile, Rectangle, Graphics.EnumerateMetafileProc, IntPtr, ImageAttributes);**

[C++] **public: void EnumerateMetafile(Metafile*, Rectangle, Graphics.EnumerateMetafileProc*, IntPtr, ImageAttributes*);**

[JScript] **public function EnumerateMetafile(Metafile, Rectangle, Graphics.EnumerateMetafileProc, IntPtr, ImageAttributes);**

Sends the records of a selected rectangle from a **Metafile** object, one at a time, to a callback method for display in a specified rectangle.

[Visual Basic] **Overloads Public Sub EnumerateMetafile(Metafile, Rectangle, Rectangle, GraphicsUnit, Graphics.EnumerateMetafileProc)**

[C#] **public void EnumerateMetafile(Metafile, Rectangle, Rectangle, GraphicsUnit, Graphics.EnumerateMetafileProc);**

[C++] **public: void EnumerateMetafile(Metafile*, Rectangle, Rectangle, GraphicsUnit, Graphics.EnumerateMetafileProc*);**

[JScript] **public function EnumerateMetafile(Metafile, Rectangle, Rectangle, GraphicsUnit, Graphics.EnumerateMetafileProc);**

Sends the records of the specified **Metafile** object, one at a time, to a callback method for display in a specified rectangle using specified image attributes.

[Visual Basic] **Overloads Public Sub EnumerateMetafile(Metafile, RectangleF, Graphics.EnumerateMetafileProc, IntPtr, ImageAttributes)**

[C#] **public void EnumerateMetafile(Metafile, RectangleF, Graphics.EnumerateMetafileProc, IntPtr, ImageAttributes);**

[C++] **public: void EnumerateMetafile(Metafile*, RectangleF, Graphics.EnumerateMetafileProc*, IntPtr, ImageAttributes*);**

[JScript] **public function EnumerateMetafile(Metafile, RectangleF, Graphics.EnumerateMetafileProc, IntPtr, ImageAttributes);**

Sends the records of a selected rectangle from a **Metafile** object, one at a time, to a callback method for display in a specified rectangle.

[Visual Basic] **Overloads Public Sub EnumerateMetafile(Metafile, RectangleF, RectangleF, GraphicsUnit, Graphics.EnumerateMetafileProc)**

[C#] **public void EnumerateMetafile(Metafile, RectangleF, RectangleF, GraphicsUnit, Graphics.EnumerateMetafileProc);**

[C++] **public: void EnumerateMetafile(Metafile*, RectangleF, RectangleF, GraphicsUnit, Graphics.EnumerateMetafileProc*);**

[JScript] **public function EnumerateMetafile(Metafile, RectangleF, RectangleF, GraphicsUnit, Graphics.EnumerateMetafileProc);**

Sends the records in a selected rectangle from a **Metafile** object, one at a time, to a callback method for display at a specified point.

[Visual Basic] **Overloads Public Sub EnumerateMetafile(Metafile, Point, Rectangle, GraphicsUnit, Graphics.EnumerateMetafileProc, IntPtr)**

[C#] **public void EnumerateMetafile(Metafile, Point, Rectangle, GraphicsUnit, Graphics.EnumerateMetafileProc, IntPtr);**

[C++] **public: void EnumerateMetafile(Metafile*, Point, Rectangle, GraphicsUnit, Graphics.EnumerateMetafileProc*, IntPtr);**

[JScript] **public function EnumerateMetafile(Metafile, Point, Rectangle, GraphicsUnit, Graphics.EnumerateMetafileProc, IntPtr);**

Sends the records in a selected rectangle from a **Metafile** object, one at a time, to a callback method for display in a specified parallelogram.

[Visual Basic] **Overloads Public Sub EnumerateMetafile(Metafile, Point(), Rectangle, GraphicsUnit, Graphics.EnumerateMetafileProc, IntPtr)**

[C#] **public void EnumerateMetafile(Metafile, Point[], Rectangle, GraphicsUnit, Graphics.EnumerateMetafileProc, IntPtr);**

[C++] **public: void EnumerateMetafile(Metafile*, Point[], Rectangle, GraphicsUnit, Graphics.EnumerateMetafileProc*, IntPtr);**

[JScript] **public function EnumerateMetafile(Metafile, Point[], Rectangle, GraphicsUnit, Graphics.EnumerateMetafileProc, IntPtr);**

Sends the records in a selected rectangle from a **Metafile** object, one at a time, to a callback method for display at a specified point.

[Visual Basic] **Overloads Public Sub EnumerateMetafile(Metafile, PointF, RectangleF, GraphicsUnit, Graphics.EnumerateMetafileProc, IntPtr)**

[C#] **public void EnumerateMetafile(Metafile, PointF, RectangleF, GraphicsUnit, Graphics.EnumerateMetafileProc, IntPtr);**

[C++] **public: void EnumerateMetafile(Metafile*, PointF, RectangleF, GraphicsUnit, Graphics.EnumerateMetafileProc*, IntPtr);**

[JScript] **public function EnumerateMetafile(Metafile, PointF, RectangleF, GraphicsUnit, Graphics.EnumerateMetafileProc, IntPtr);**

Sends the records in a selected rectangle from a **Metafile** object, one at a time, to a callback method for display in a specified parallelogram.

[Visual Basic] **Overloads Public Sub EnumerateMetafile(Metafile, PointF(), RectangleF, GraphicsUnit, Graphics.EnumerateMetafileProc, IntPtr)**

[C#] **public void EnumerateMetafile(Metafile, PointF[], RectangleF, GraphicsUnit, Graphics.EnumerateMetafileProc, IntPtr);**

[C++] **public: void EnumerateMetafile(Metafile*, PointF[], RectangleF, GraphicsUnit, Graphics.EnumerateMetafileProc*, IntPtr);**

[JScript] **public function EnumerateMetafile(Metafile, PointF[], RectangleF, GraphicsUnit, Graphics.EnumerateMetafileProc, IntPtr);**

Sends the records of a selected rectangle from a **Metafile** object, one at a time, to a callback method for display in a specified rectangle.

[Visual Basic] **Overloads Public Sub EnumerateMetafile(Metafile, Rectangle, Rectangle, GraphicsUnit, Graphics.EnumerateMetafileProc, IntPtr)**

[C#] **public void EnumerateMetafile(Metafile, Rectangle, Rectangle, GraphicsUnit, Graphics.EnumerateMetafileProc, IntPtr);**

[C++] **public: void EnumerateMetafile(Metafile*, Rectangle, Rectangle, GraphicsUnit, Graphics.EnumerateMetafileProc*, IntPtr);**

[JScript] **public function EnumerateMetafile(Metafile, Rectangle, Rectangle, GraphicsUnit, Graphics.EnumerateMetafileProc, IntPtr);**

Sends the records of a selected rectangle from a **Metafile** object, one at a time, to a callback method for display in a specified rectangle.

[Visual Basic] **Overloads Public Sub EnumerateMetafile(Metafile, RectangleF, RectangleF, GraphicsUnit, Graphics.EnumerateMetafileProc, IntPtr)**

[C#] **public void EnumerateMetafile(Metafile, RectangleF, RectangleF, GraphicsUnit, Graphics.EnumerateMetafileProc, IntPtr);**

[C++] **public: void EnumerateMetafile(Metafile*, RectangleF, RectangleF, GraphicsUnit, Graphics.EnumerateMetafileProc*, IntPtr);**

[JScript] **public function EnumerateMetafile(Metafile, RectangleF, RectangleF, GraphicsUnit, Graphics.EnumerateMetafileProc, IntPtr);**

Sends the records in a selected rectangle from a **Metafile** object, one at a time, to a callback method for display at a specified point using specified image attributes.

[Visual Basic] **Overloads Public Sub EnumerateMetafile(Metafile, Point, Rectangle, GraphicsUnit, Graphics.EnumerateMetafileProc, IntPtr, ImageAttributes)**

[C#] **public void EnumerateMetafile(Metafile, Point, Rectangle, GraphicsUnit, Graphics.EnumerateMetafileProc, IntPtr, ImageAttributes);**

[C++] **public: void EnumerateMetafile(Metafile*, Point, Rectangle, GraphicsUnit, Graphics.EnumerateMetafileProc*, IntPtr, ImageAttributes*);**

[JScript] **public function EnumerateMetafile(Metafile, Point, Rectangle, GraphicsUnit, Graphics.EnumerateMetafileProc, IntPtr, ImageAttributes);**

Sends the records in a selected rectangle from a **Metafile** object, one at a time, to a callback method for display in a specified parallelogram using specified image attributes.

[Visual Basic] **Overloads Public Sub EnumerateMetafile(Metafile, Point(), Rectangle, GraphicsUnit, Graphics.EnumerateMetafileProc, IntPtr, ImageAttributes)**

[C#] **public void EnumerateMetafile(Metafile, Point[], Rectangle, GraphicsUnit, Graphics.EnumerateMetafileProc, IntPtr, ImageAttributes);**

[C++] **public: void EnumerateMetafile(Metafile*, Point[], Rectangle, GraphicsUnit, Graphics.EnumerateMetafileProc*, IntPtr, ImageAttributes*);**

[JScript] **public function EnumerateMetafile(Metafile, Point[], Rectangle, GraphicsUnit, Graphics.EnumerateMetafileProc, IntPtr, ImageAttributes);**

Sends the records in a selected rectangle from a **Metafile** object, one at a time, to a callback method for display at a specified point using specified image attributes.

[Visual Basic] **Overloads Public Sub EnumerateMetafile(Metafile, PointF, RectangleF, GraphicsUnit, Graphics.EnumerateMetafileProc, IntPtr, ImageAttributes)**

[C#] **public void EnumerateMetafile(Metafile, PointF, RectangleF, GraphicsUnit, Graphics.EnumerateMetafileProc, IntPtr, ImageAttributes);**

[C++] **public: void EnumerateMetafile(Metafile*, PointF, RectangleF, GraphicsUnit, Graphics.EnumerateMetafileProc*, IntPtr, ImageAttributes*);**

[JScript] **public function EnumerateMetafile(Metafile, PointF, RectangleF, GraphicsUnit, Graphics.EnumerateMetafileProc, IntPtr, ImageAttributes);**

Sends the records in a selected rectangle from a **Metafile** object, one at a time, to a callback method for display in a specified parallelogram using specified image attributes.

[Visual Basic] **Overloads Public Sub EnumerateMetafile(Metafile, PointF(), RectangleF, GraphicsUnit, Graphics.EnumerateMetafileProc, IntPtr, ImageAttributes)**

[C#] **public void EnumerateMetafile(Metafile, PointF[], RectangleF, GraphicsUnit, Graphics.EnumerateMetafileProc, IntPtr, ImageAttributes);**

[C++] **public: void EnumerateMetafile(Metafile*, PointF[], RectangleF, GraphicsUnit, Graphics.EnumerateMetafileProc*, IntPtr, ImageAttributes*);**

[JScript] **public function EnumerateMetafile(Metafile, PointF[], RectangleF, GraphicsUnit, Graphics.EnumerateMetafileProc, IntPtr, ImageAttributes);**

Sends the records of a selected rectangle from a **Metafile** object, one at a time, to a callback method for display in a specified rectangle using specified image attributes.

[Visual Basic] **Overloads Public Sub EnumerateMetafile(Metafile, Rectangle, Rectangle, GraphicsUnit, Graphics.EnumerateMetafileProc, IntPtr, ImageAttributes)**

[C#] **public void EnumerateMetafile(Metafile, Rectangle, Rectangle, GraphicsUnit, Graphics.EnumerateMetafileProc, IntPtr, ImageAttributes);**

[C++] **public: void EnumerateMetafile(Metafile*, Rectangle, Rectangle, GraphicsUnit, Graphics.EnumerateMetafileProc*, IntPtr, ImageAttributes*);**

[JScript] **public function EnumerateMetafile(Metafile, Rectangle, Rectangle, GraphicsUnit, Graphics.EnumerateMetafileProc, IntPtr, ImageAttributes);**

Sends the records of a selected rectangle from a **Metafile** object, one at a time, to a callback method for display in a specified rectangle using specified image attributes.

[Visual Basic] **Overloads Public Sub EnumerateMetafile(Metafile, RectangleF, RectangleF, GraphicsUnit, Graphics.EnumerateMetafileProc, IntPtr, ImageAttributes)**

[C#] **public void EnumerateMetafile(Metafile, RectangleF, RectangleF, GraphicsUnit, Graphics.EnumerateMetafileProc, IntPtr, ImageAttributes);**

[C++] **public: void EnumerateMetafile(Metafile*, RectangleF, RectangleF, GraphicsUnit, Graphics.EnumerateMetafileProc*, IntPtr, ImageAttributes*);**

[JScript] **public function EnumerateMetafile(Metafile, RectangleF, RectangleF, GraphicsUnit, Graphics.EnumerateMetafileProc, IntPtr, ImageAttributes);**

Example

For an example see **EnumerateMetafile**.

Graphics.EnumerateMetafile Method (Metafile, Point, Graphics.EnumerateMetafileProc)

Sends the records in the specified **Metafile** object, one at a time, to a callback method for display at a specified point.

[Visual Basic]
```
Overloads Public Sub EnumerateMetafile( _
   ByVal metafile As Metafile, _
   ByVal destPoint As Point, _
   ByVal callback As Graphics.EnumerateMetafileProc _
)
```
[C#]
```
public void EnumerateMetafile(
   Metafile metafile,
   Point destPoint,
   Graphics.EnumerateMetafileProc callback
);
```
[C++]
```
public: void EnumerateMetafile(
   Metafile* metafile,
   Point destPoint,
   Graphics.EnumerateMetafileProc* callback
);
```
[JScript]
```
public function EnumerateMetafile(
   metafile : Metafile,
   destPoint : Point,
   callback : Graphics.EnumerateMetafileProc
);
```

Parameters

metafile
: **Metafile** object to enumerate.

destPoint
: **Point** structure that specifies the location of the upper-left corner of the drawn metafile.

callback
: **Graphics.EnumerateMetafileProc** delegate that specifies the method to which the metafile records are sent.

Return Value

This method does not return a value.

Remarks

This method enumerates the records contained in the specified metafile. Each record is individually sent to a callback method specified by the *callback* parameter. Typically, the callback method calls the **PlayRecord** method to "play back", or draw, the record.

If the callback method calls **Metafile.PlayRecord**, it must do so by calling the **PlayRecord** method of the specific **Metafile** object that is being enumerated.

Example

[C#] The following example creates a form that has a **Metafile** object as one of its private members. The OnPaint method calls **EnumerateMetafile**, which calls the form's MetafileCallback method for each record in the metafile. The MetafileCallback method calls the **PlayRecord** method. Notice that the MetafileCallback method receives the record data as an IntPtr, but the **PlayRecord** method expects the record data to be a byte array. The call to Marshal.Copy copys the record data to a byte array so that it can be passed to **PlayRecord**.

[C#]

```
using System;
using System.Drawing;
using System.Drawing.Imaging;
using System.Windows.Forms;
using System.Runtime.InteropServices; // for Marshal.Copy
public class Form1 : Form
{
   private Metafile m_metafile;
   private Graphics.EnumerateMetafileProc m_delegate;
   private Point m_destPoint;
   public Form1()
   {
      m_metafile = new Metafile("MyMetafile.emf");
      m_delegate = new
Graphics.EnumerateMetafileProc(MetafileCallback);
      m_destPoint = new Point(20, 10);
   }
   protected override void OnPaint(PaintEventArgs e)
   {
      e.Graphics.EnumerateMetafile(m_metafile, m_destPoint,
m_delegate);
   }
   private bool MetafileCallback(
      EmfPlusRecordType recordType,
      int flags,
      int dataSize,
      IntPtr data,
      PlayRecordCallback callbackData)
   {
      byte[] dataArray = null;
      if (data != IntPtr.Zero)
      {
         // Copy the unmanaged record to a managed byte buffer
         // that can be used by PlayRecord.
         dataArray = new byte[dataSize];
         Marshal.Copy(data, dataArray, 0, dataSize);
      }

      m_metafile.PlayRecord(recordType, flags, dataSize, dataArray);

      return true;
   }
   static void Main()
   {
      Application.Run(new Form1());
   }
}
```

Requirements

Platforms: Windows 98, Windows NT 4.0, Windows Millennium Edition, Windows 2000, Windows XP Home Edition, Windows XP Professional, Windows Server 2003 family

Graphics.EnumerateMetafile Method (Metafile, Point[], Graphics.EnumerateMetafileProc)

Sends the records in the specified **Metafile** object, one at a time, to a callback method for display in a specified parallelogram.

[Visual Basic]

```
Overloads Public Sub EnumerateMetafile( _
   ByVal metafile As Metafile, _
   ByVal destPoints() As Point, _
   ByVal callback As Graphics.EnumerateMetafileProc _
)
```

[C#]

```
public void EnumerateMetafile(
   Metafile metafile,
   Point[] destPoints,
   Graphics.EnumerateMetafileProc callback
);
```

[C++]

```
public: void EnumerateMetafile(
   Metafile* metafile,
   Point destPoints[],
   Graphics.EnumerateMetafileProc* callback
);
```

[JScript]

```
public function EnumerateMetafile(
   metafile : Metafile,
   destPoints : Point[],
   callback : Graphics.EnumerateMetafileProc
);
```

Parameters

metafile
: **Metafile** object to enumerate.

destPoints
: Array of three **Point** structures that define a parallelogram that determines the size and location of the drawn metafile.

callback
: **Graphics.EnumerateMetafileProc** delegate that specifies the method to which the metafile records are sent.

Return Value

This method does not return a value.

Remarks

This method enumerates the records contained in the specified metafile. Each record is individually sent to a callback method specified by the *callback* parameter. Typically, the callback method calls the **PlayRecord** method to "play back", or draw, the record.

If the callback method calls **Metafile.PlayRecord**, it must do so by calling the **PlayRecord** method of the specific **Metafile** object that is being enumerated.

Example

For an example see **EnumerateMetafile**.

Requirements

Platforms: Windows 98, Windows NT 4.0, Windows Millennium Edition, Windows 2000, Windows XP Home Edition, Windows XP Professional, Windows Server 2003 family

Graphics.EnumerateMetafile Method (Metafile, PointF, Graphics.EnumerateMetafileProc)

Sends the records in the specified **Metafile** object, one at a time, to a callback method for display at a specified point.

[Visual Basic]
```
Overloads Public Sub EnumerateMetafile( _
   ByVal metafile As Metafile, _
   ByVal destPoint As PointF, _
   ByVal callback As Graphics.EnumerateMetafileProc _
)
```
[C#]
```
public void EnumerateMetafile(
   Metafile metafile,
   PointF destPoint,
   Graphics.EnumerateMetafileProc callback
);
```
[C++]
```
public: void EnumerateMetafile(
   Metafile* metafile,
   PointF destPoint,
   Graphics.EnumerateMetafileProc* callback
);
```
[JScript]
```
public function EnumerateMetafile(
   metafile : Metafile,
   destPoint : PointF,
   callback : Graphics.EnumerateMetafileProc
);
```

Parameters

metafile
: **Metafile** object to enumerate.

destPoint
: **PointF** structure that specifies the location of the upper-left corner of the drawn metafile.

callback
: **Graphics.EnumerateMetafileProc** delegate that specifies the method to which the metafile records are sent.

Return Value

This method does not return a value.

Remarks

This method enumerates the records contained in the specified metafile. Each record is individually sent to a callback method specified by the *callback* parameter. Typically, the callback method calls the **PlayRecord** method to "play back", or draw, the record.

If the callback method calls **Metafile.PlayRecord**, it must do so by calling the **PlayRecord** method of the specific **Metafile** object that is being enumerated.

Example

For an example see **EnumerateMetafile**.

Requirements

Platforms: Windows 98, Windows NT 4.0, Windows Millennium Edition, Windows 2000, Windows XP Home Edition, Windows XP Professional, Windows Server 2003 family

Graphics.EnumerateMetafile Method (Metafile, PointF[], Graphics.EnumerateMetafileProc)

Sends the records in the specified **Metafile** object, one at a time, to a callback method for display in a specified parallelogram.

[Visual Basic]
```
Overloads Public Sub EnumerateMetafile( _
   ByVal metafile As Metafile, _
   ByVal destPoints() As PointF, _
   ByVal callback As Graphics.EnumerateMetafileProc _
)
```
[C#]
```
public void EnumerateMetafile(
   Metafile metafile,
   PointF[] destPoints,
   Graphics.EnumerateMetafileProc callback
);
```
[C++]
```
public: void EnumerateMetafile(
   Metafile* metafile,
   PointF destPoints[],
   Graphics.EnumerateMetafileProc* callback
);
```
[JScript]
```
public function EnumerateMetafile(
   metafile : Metafile,
   destPoints : PointF[],
   callback : Graphics.EnumerateMetafileProc
);
```

Parameters

metafile
: **Metafile** object to enumerate.

destPoints
: Array of three **PointF** structures that define a parallelogram that determines the size and location of the drawn metafile.

callback
: **Graphics.EnumerateMetafileProc** delegate that specifies the method to which the metafile records are sent.

Return Value

This method does not return a value.

Remarks

This method enumerates the records contained in the specified metafile. Each record is individually sent to a callback method specified by the *callback* parameter. Typically, the callback method calls the **PlayRecord** method to "play back", or draw, the record.

If the callback method calls **Metafile.PlayRecord**, it must do so by calling the **PlayRecord** method of the specific **Metafile** object that is being enumerated.

The *destPoints* parameter specifies three points of a parallelogram. The three **PointF** structures represent the upper-left, upper-right, and lower-left corners of the parallelogram. The fourth point is extrapolated from the first three to form a parallelogram. The drawn metafile is scaled and sheared to fit the parallelogram.

Example

For an example see **EnumerateMetafile**.

Requirements

Platforms: Windows 98, Windows NT 4.0, Windows Millennium Edition, Windows 2000, Windows XP Home Edition, Windows XP Professional, Windows Server 2003 family

Graphics.EnumerateMetafile Method (Metafile, Rectangle, Graphics.EnumerateMetafileProc)

Sends the records of the specified **Metafile** object, one at a time, to a callback method for display in a specified rectangle.

[Visual Basic]
```
Overloads Public Sub EnumerateMetafile( _
   ByVal metafile As Metafile, _
   ByVal destRect As Rectangle, _
   ByVal callback As Graphics.EnumerateMetafileProc _
)
```
[C#]
```
public void EnumerateMetafile(
   Metafile metafile,
   Rectangle destRect,
   Graphics.EnumerateMetafileProc callback
);
```
[C++]
```
public: void EnumerateMetafile(
   Metafile* metafile,
   Rectangle destRect,
   Graphics.EnumerateMetafileProc* callback
);
```
[JScript]
```
public function EnumerateMetafile(
   metafile : Metafile,
   destRect : Rectangle,
   callback : Graphics.EnumerateMetafileProc
);
```

Parameters

metafile
  Metafile object to enumerate.

destRect
  Rectangle structure that specifies the location and size of the drawn metafile.

callback
  Graphics.EnumerateMetafileProc delegate that specifies the method to which the metafile records are sent.

Return Value

This method does not return a value.

Remarks

This method enumerates the records contained in the specified metafile. Each record is individually sent to a callback method specified by the *callback* parameter. Typically, the callback method calls the **PlayRecord** method to "play back", or draw, the record.

If the callback method calls **Metafile.PlayRecord**, it must do so by calling the **PlayRecord** method of the specific **Metafile** object that is being enumerated.

Example

For an example see **EnumerateMetafile**.

Requirements

Platforms: Windows 98, Windows NT 4.0, Windows Millennium Edition, Windows 2000, Windows XP Home Edition, Windows XP Professional, Windows Server 2003 family

Graphics.EnumerateMetafile Method (Metafile, RectangleF, Graphics.EnumerateMetafileProc)

Sends the records of the specified **Metafile** object, one at a time, to a callback method for display in a specified rectangle.

[Visual Basic]
```
Overloads Public Sub EnumerateMetafile( _
   ByVal metafile As Metafile, _
   ByVal destRect As RectangleF, _
   ByVal callback As Graphics.EnumerateMetafileProc _
)
```
[C#]
```
public void EnumerateMetafile(
   Metafile metafile,
   RectangleF destRect,
   Graphics.EnumerateMetafileProc callback
);
```
[C++]
```
public: void EnumerateMetafile(
   Metafile* metafile,
   RectangleF destRect,
   Graphics.EnumerateMetafileProc* callback
);
```
[JScript]
```
public function EnumerateMetafile(
   metafile : Metafile,
   destRect : RectangleF,
   callback : Graphics.EnumerateMetafileProc
);
```

Parameters

metafile
  Metafile object to enumerate.

destRect
  RectangleF structure that specifies the location and size of the drawn metafile.

callback
  Graphics.EnumerateMetafileProc delegate that specifies the method to which the metafile records are sent.

Return Value

This method does not return a value.

Remarks

This method enumerates the records contained in the specified metafile. Each record is individually sent to a callback method specified by the *callback* parameter. Typically, the callback method calls the **PlayRecord** method to "play back", or draw, the record.

If the callback method calls **Metafile.PlayRecord**, it must do so by calling the **PlayRecord** method of the specific **Metafile** object that is being enumerated.

Example

For an example see **EnumerateMetafile**.

Requirements

Platforms: Windows 98, Windows NT 4.0, Windows Millennium Edition, Windows 2000, Windows XP Home Edition, Windows XP Professional, Windows Server 2003 family

Graphics.EnumerateMetafile Method (Metafile, Point, Graphics.EnumerateMetafileProc, IntPtr)

Sends the records in the specified **Metafile** object, one at a time, to a callback method for display at a specified point.

[Visual Basic]
```
Overloads Public Sub EnumerateMetafile( _
   ByVal metafile As Metafile, _
   ByVal destPoint As Point, _
   ByVal callback As Graphics.EnumerateMetafileProc, _
   ByVal callbackData As IntPtr _
)
```
[C#]
```
public void EnumerateMetafile(
   Metafile metafile,
   Point destPoint,
   Graphics.EnumerateMetafileProc callback,
   IntPtr callbackData
);
```
[C++]
```
public: void EnumerateMetafile(
   Metafile* metafile,
   Point destPoint,
   Graphics.EnumerateMetafileProc* callback,
   IntPtr callbackData
);
```
[JScript]
```
public function EnumerateMetafile(
   metafile : Metafile,
   destPoint : Point,
   callback : Graphics.EnumerateMetafileProc,
   callbackData : IntPtr
);
```

Parameters

metafile
: **Metafile** object to enumerate.

destPoint
: **Point** structure that specifies the location of the upper-left corner of the drawn metafile.

callback
: **Graphics.EnumerateMetafileProc** delegate that specifies the method to which the metafile records are sent.

callbackData
: Internal pointer that is required, but ignored. You can pass **IntPtr.Zero** for this parameter.

Return Value

This method does not return a value.

Remarks

This method enumerates the records contained in the specified metafile. Each record is individually sent to a callback method specified by the *callback* parameter. Typically, the callback method calls the **PlayRecord** method to "play back", or draw, the record.

If the callback method calls **Metafile.PlayRecord**, it must do so by calling the **PlayRecord** method of the specific **Metafile** object that is being enumerated.

Example

For an example see **EnumerateMetafile**.

Requirements

Platforms: Windows 98, Windows NT 4.0, Windows Millennium Edition, Windows 2000, Windows XP Home Edition, Windows XP Professional, Windows Server 2003 family

Graphics.EnumerateMetafile Method (Metafile, Point[], Graphics.EnumerateMetafileProc, IntPtr)

Sends the records in the specified **Metafile** object, one at a time, to a callback method for display in a specified parallelogram.

[Visual Basic]
```
Overloads Public Sub EnumerateMetafile( _
   ByVal metafile As Metafile, _
   ByVal destPoints() As Point, _
   ByVal callback As Graphics.EnumerateMetafileProc, _
   ByVal callbackData As IntPtr _
)
```
[C#]
```
public void EnumerateMetafile(
   Metafile metafile,
   Point[] destPoints,
   Graphics.EnumerateMetafileProc callback,
   IntPtr callbackData
);
```
[C++]
```
public: void EnumerateMetafile(
   Metafile* metafile,
   Point destPoints[],
   Graphics.EnumerateMetafileProc* callback,
   IntPtr callbackData
);
```
[JScript]
```
public function EnumerateMetafile(
   metafile : Metafile,
   destPoints : Point[],
   callback : Graphics.EnumerateMetafileProc,
   callbackData : IntPtr
);
```

Parameters

metafile
: **Metafile** object to enumerate.

destPoints
: Array of three **Point** structures that define a parallelogram that determines the size and location of the drawn metafile.

callback
: **Graphics.EnumerateMetafileProc** delegate that specifies the method to which the metafile records are sent.

callbackData
: Internal pointer that is required, but ignored. You can pass **IntPtr.Zero** for this parameter.

Return Value

This method does not return a value.

Remarks

This method enumerates the records contained in the specified metafile. Each record is individually sent to a callback method specified by the *callback* parameter. Typically, the callback method calls the **PlayRecord** method to "play back", or draw, the record.

If the callback method calls **Metafile.PlayRecord**, it must do so by calling the **PlayRecord** method of the specific **Metafile** object that is being enumerated.

Example

For an example see **EnumerateMetafile**.

Requirements

Platforms: Windows 98, Windows NT 4.0, Windows Millennium Edition, Windows 2000, Windows XP Home Edition, Windows XP Professional, Windows Server 2003 family

Graphics.EnumerateMetafile Method (Metafile, PointF, Graphics.EnumerateMetafileProc, IntPtr)

Sends the records in the specified **Metafile** object, one at a time, to a callback method for display at a specified point.

```
[Visual Basic]
Overloads Public Sub EnumerateMetafile( _
   ByVal metafile As Metafile, _
   ByVal destPoint As PointF, _
   ByVal callback As Graphics.EnumerateMetafileProc, _
   ByVal callbackData As IntPtr _
)
[C#]
public void EnumerateMetafile(
   Metafile metafile,
   PointF destPoint,
   Graphics.EnumerateMetafileProc callback,
   IntPtr callbackData
);
[C++]
public: void EnumerateMetafile(
   Metafile* metafile,
   PointF destPoint,
   Graphics.EnumerateMetafileProc* callback,
   IntPtr callbackData
);
[JScript]
public function EnumerateMetafile(
   metafile : Metafile,
   destPoint : PointF,
   callback : Graphics.EnumerateMetafileProc,
   callbackData : IntPtr
);
```

Parameters

metafile

Metafile object to enumerate.

destPoint

PointF structure that specifies the location of the upper-left corner of the drawn metafile.

callback

Graphics.EnumerateMetafileProc delegate that specifies the method to which the metafile records are sent.

callbackData

Internal pointer that is required, but ignored. You can pass **IntPtr.Zero** for this parameter.

Return Value

This method does not return a value.

Remarks

This method enumerates the records contained in the specified metafile. Each record is individually sent to a callback method specified by the *callback* parameter. Typically, the callback method calls the **PlayRecord** method to "play back", or draw, the record.

If the callback method calls **Metafile.PlayRecord**, it must do so by calling the **PlayRecord** method of the specific **Metafile** object that is being enumerated.

Example

For an example see **EnumerateMetafile**.

Requirements

Platforms: Windows 98, Windows NT 4.0, Windows Millennium Edition, Windows 2000, Windows XP Home Edition, Windows XP Professional, Windows Server 2003 family

Graphics.EnumerateMetafile Method (Metafile, PointF[], Graphics.EnumerateMetafileProc, IntPtr)

Sends the records in the specified **Metafile** object, one at a time, to a callback method for display in a specified parallelogram.

```
[Visual Basic]
Overloads Public Sub EnumerateMetafile( _
   ByVal metafile As Metafile, _
   ByVal destPoints() As PointF, _
   ByVal callback As Graphics.EnumerateMetafileProc, _
   ByVal callbackData As IntPtr _
)
[C#]
public void EnumerateMetafile(
   Metafile metafile,
   PointF[] destPoints,
   Graphics.EnumerateMetafileProc callback,
   IntPtr callbackData
);
[C++]
public: void EnumerateMetafile(
   Metafile* metafile,
   PointF destPoints[],
   Graphics.EnumerateMetafileProc* callback,
   IntPtr callbackData
);
[JScript]
public function EnumerateMetafile(
   metafile : Metafile,
   destPoints : PointF[],
   callback : Graphics.EnumerateMetafileProc,
   callbackData : IntPtr
);
```

Parameters

metafile

Metafile object to enumerate.

destPoints

Array of three **PointF** structures that define a parallelogram that determines the size and location of the drawn metafile.

callback

Graphics.EnumerateMetafileProc delegate that specifies the method to which the metafile records are sent.

callbackData
Internal pointer that is required, but ignored. You can pass **IntPtr.Zero** for this parameter.

Return Value

This method does not return a value.

Remarks

This method enumerates the records contained in the specified metafile. Each record is individually sent to a callback method specified by the *callback* parameter. Typically, the callback method calls the **PlayRecord** method to "play back", or draw, the record.

If the callback method calls **Metafile.PlayRecord**, it must do so by calling the **PlayRecord** method of the specific **Metafile** object that is being enumerated.

The *destPoints* parameter specifies three points of a parallelogram. The three **PointF** structures represent the upper-left, upper-right, and lower-left corners of the parallelogram. The fourth point is extrapolated from the first three to form a parallelogram. The drawn metafile is scaled and sheared to fit the parallelogram.

Example

For an example see **EnumerateMetafile**.

Requirements

Platforms: Windows 98, Windows NT 4.0, Windows Millennium Edition, Windows 2000, Windows XP Home Edition, Windows XP Professional, Windows Server 2003 family

Graphics.EnumerateMetafile Method (Metafile, Rectangle, Graphics.EnumerateMetafileProc, IntPtr)

Sends the records of the specified **Metafile** object, one at a time, to a callback method for display in a specified rectangle.

[Visual Basic]
```
Overloads Public Sub EnumerateMetafile( _
   ByVal metafile As Metafile, _
   ByVal destRect As Rectangle, _
   ByVal callback As Graphics.EnumerateMetafileProc, _
   ByVal callbackData As IntPtr _
)
```
[C#]
```
public void EnumerateMetafile(
   Metafile metafile,
   Rectangle destRect,
   Graphics.EnumerateMetafileProc callback,
   IntPtr callbackData
);
```
[C++]
```
public: void EnumerateMetafile(
   Metafile* metafile,
   Rectangle destRect,
   Graphics.EnumerateMetafileProc* callback,
   IntPtr callbackData
);
```
[JScript]
```
public function EnumerateMetafile(
   metafile : Metafile,
   destRect : Rectangle,
   callback : Graphics.EnumerateMetafileProc,
   callbackData : IntPtr
);
```

Parameters

metafile
Metafile object to enumerate.

destRect
Rectangle structure that specifies the location and size of the drawn metafile.

callback
Graphics.EnumerateMetafileProc delegate that specifies the method to which the metafile records are sent.

callbackData
Internal pointer that is required, but ignored. You can pass **IntPtr.Zero** for this parameter.

Return Value

This method does not return a value.

Remarks

This method enumerates the records contained in the specified metafile. Each record is individually sent to a callback method specified by the *callback* parameter. Typically, the callback method calls the **PlayRecord** method to "play back", or draw, the record.

If the callback method calls **Metafile.PlayRecord**, it must do so by calling the **PlayRecord** method of the specific **Metafile** object that is being enumerated.

Example

For an example see **EnumerateMetafile**.

Requirements

Platforms: Windows 98, Windows NT 4.0, Windows Millennium Edition, Windows 2000, Windows XP Home Edition, Windows XP Professional, Windows Server 2003 family

Graphics.EnumerateMetafile Method (Metafile, RectangleF, Graphics.EnumerateMetafileProc, IntPtr)

Sends the records of the specified **Metafile** object, one at a time, to a callback method for display in a specified rectangle.

[Visual Basic]
```
Overloads Public Sub EnumerateMetafile( _
   ByVal metafile As Metafile, _
   ByVal destRect As RectangleF, _
   ByVal callback As Graphics.EnumerateMetafileProc, _
   ByVal callbackData As IntPtr _
)
```
[C#]
```
public void EnumerateMetafile(
   Metafile metafile,
   RectangleF destRect,
   Graphics.EnumerateMetafileProc callback,
   IntPtr callbackData
);
```
[C++]
```
public: void EnumerateMetafile(
   Metafile* metafile,
   RectangleF destRect,
   Graphics.EnumerateMetafileProc* callback,
   IntPtr callbackData
);
```

```
[JScript]
public function EnumerateMetafile(
   metafile : Metafile,
   destRect : RectangleF,
   callback : Graphics.EnumerateMetafileProc,
   callbackData : IntPtr
);
```

Parameters

metafile

Metafile object to enumerate.

destRect

RectangleF structure that specifies the location and size of the drawn metafile.

callback

Graphics.EnumerateMetafileProc delegate that specifies the method to which the metafile records are sent.

callbackData

Internal pointer that is required, but ignored. You can pass **IntPtr.Zero** for this parameter.

Return Value

This method does not return a value.

Remarks

This method enumerates the records contained in the specified metafile. Each record is individually sent to a callback method specified by the *callback* parameter. Typically, the callback method calls the **PlayRecord** method to "play back", or draw, the record.

If the callback method calls **Metafile.PlayRecord**, it must do so by calling the **PlayRecord** method of the specific **Metafile** object that is being enumerated.

Example

For an example see **EnumerateMetafile**.

Requirements

Platforms: Windows 98, Windows NT 4.0, Windows Millennium Edition, Windows 2000, Windows XP Home Edition, Windows XP Professional, Windows Server 2003 family

Graphics.EnumerateMetafile Method (Metafile, Point, Graphics.EnumerateMetafileProc, IntPtr, ImageAttributes)

Sends the records in the specified **Metafile** object, one at a time, to a callback method for display at a specified point using specified image attributes.

```
[Visual Basic]
Overloads Public Sub EnumerateMetafile( _
   ByVal metafile As Metafile, _
   ByVal destPoint As Point, _
   ByVal callback As Graphics.EnumerateMetafileProc, _
   ByVal callbackData As IntPtr, _
   ByVal imageAttr As ImageAttributes _
)
[C#]
public void EnumerateMetafile(
   Metafile metafile,
   Point destPoint,
   Graphics.EnumerateMetafileProc callback,
   IntPtr callbackData,
   ImageAttributes imageAttr
);
[C++]
public: void EnumerateMetafile(
   Metafile* metafile,
   Point destPoint,
   Graphics.EnumerateMetafileProc* callback,
   IntPtr callbackData,
   ImageAttributes* imageAttr
);
[JScript]
public function EnumerateMetafile(
   metafile : Metafile,
   destPoint : Point,
   callback : Graphics.EnumerateMetafileProc,
   callbackData : IntPtr,
   imageAttr : ImageAttributes
);
```

Parameters

metafile

Metafile object to enumerate.

destPoint

Point structure that specifies the location of the upper-left corner of the drawn metafile.

callback

Graphics.EnumerateMetafileProc delegate that specifies the method to which the metafile records are sent.

callbackData

Internal pointer that is required, but ignored. You can pass **IntPtr.Zero** for this parameter.

imageAttr

ImageAttributes object that specifies image attribute information for the drawn image.

Return Value

This method does not return a value.

Remarks

This method enumerates the records contained in the specified metafile. Each record is individually sent to a callback method specified by the *callback* parameter. Typically, the callback method calls the **PlayRecord** method to "play back", or draw, the record.

If the callback method calls **Metafile.PlayRecord**, it must do so by calling the **PlayRecord** method of the specific **Metafile** object that is being enumerated.

Example

For an example see **EnumerateMetafile**.

Requirements

Platforms: Windows 98, Windows NT 4.0, Windows Millennium Edition, Windows 2000, Windows XP Home Edition, Windows XP Professional, Windows Server 2003 family

Graphics.EnumerateMetafile Method (Metafile, Point, Rectangle, GraphicsUnit, Graphics.EnumerateMetafileProc)

Sends the records in a selected rectangle from a **Metafile** object, one at a time, to a callback method for display at a specified point.

[Visual Basic]
```
Overloads Public Sub EnumerateMetafile( _
   ByVal metafile As Metafile, _
   ByVal destPoint As Point, _
   ByVal srcRect As Rectangle, _
   ByVal srcUnit As GraphicsUnit, _
   ByVal callback As Graphics.EnumerateMetafileProc _
)
```
[C#]
```
public void EnumerateMetafile(
   Metafile metafile,
   Point destPoint,
   Rectangle srcRect,
   GraphicsUnit srcUnit,
   Graphics.EnumerateMetafileProc callback
);
```
[C++]
```
public: void EnumerateMetafile(
   Metafile* metafile,
   Point destPoint,
   Rectangle srcRect,
   GraphicsUnit srcUnit,
   Graphics.EnumerateMetafileProc* callback
);
```
[JScript]
```
public function EnumerateMetafile(
   metafile : Metafile,
   destPoint : Point,
   srcRect : Rectangle,
   srcUnit : GraphicsUnit,
   callback : Graphics.EnumerateMetafileProc
);
```

Parameters

metafile
: **Metafile** object to enumerate.

destPoint
: **Point** structure that specifies the location of the upper-left corner of the drawn metafile.

srcRect
: **Rectangle** structure that specifies the portion of the metafile, relative to its upper-left corner, to draw.

srcUnit
: Member of the **GraphicsUnit** enumeration that specifies the unit of measure used to determine the portion of the metafile that the rectangle specified by the *srcRect* parameter contains.

callback
: **Graphics.EnumerateMetafileProc** delegate that specifies the method to which the metafile records are sent.

Return Value

This method does not return a value.

Remarks

This method enumerates the records contained in the specified metafile. Each record is individually sent to a callback method specified by the *callback* parameter. Typically, the callback method calls the **PlayRecord** method to "play back", or draw, the record.

If the callback method calls **Metafile.PlayRecord**, it must do so by calling the **PlayRecord** method of the specific **Metafile** object that is being enumerated.

Example

For an example see **EnumerateMetafile**.

Requirements

Platforms: Windows 98, Windows NT 4.0, Windows Millennium Edition, Windows 2000, Windows XP Home Edition, Windows XP Professional, Windows Server 2003 family

Graphics.EnumerateMetafile Method (Metafile, Point[], Graphics.EnumerateMetafileProc, IntPtr, ImageAttributes)

Sends the records in the specified **Metafile** object, one at a time, to a callback method for display in a specified parallelogram using specified image attributes.

[Visual Basic]
```
Overloads Public Sub EnumerateMetafile( _
   ByVal metafile As Metafile, _
   ByVal destPoints() As Point, _
   ByVal callback As Graphics.EnumerateMetafileProc, _
   ByVal callbackData As IntPtr, _
   ByVal imageAttr As ImageAttributes _
)
```
[C#]
```
public void EnumerateMetafile(
   Metafile metafile,
   Point[] destPoints,
   Graphics.EnumerateMetafileProc callback,
   IntPtr callbackData,
   ImageAttributes imageAttr
);
```
[C++]
```
public: void EnumerateMetafile(
   Metafile* metafile,
   Point destPoints[],
   Graphics.EnumerateMetafileProc* callback,
   IntPtr callbackData,
   ImageAttributes* imageAttr
);
```
[JScript]
```
public function EnumerateMetafile(
   metafile : Metafile,
   destPoints : Point[],
   callback : Graphics.EnumerateMetafileProc,
   callbackData : IntPtr,
   imageAttr : ImageAttributes
);
```

Parameters

metafile
: **Metafile** object to enumerate.

destPoints
: Array of three **Point** structures that define a parallelogram that determines the size and location of the drawn metafile.

callback
: **Graphics.EnumerateMetafileProc** delegate that specifies the method to which the metafile records are sent.

callbackData

Internal pointer that is required, but ignored. You can pass **IntPtr.Zero** for this parameter.

imageAttr

ImageAttributes object that specifies image attribute information for the drawn image.

Return Value

This method does not return a value.

Remarks

This method enumerates the records contained in the specified metafile. Each record is individually sent to a callback method specified by the *callback* parameter. Typically, the callback method calls the **PlayRecord** method to "play back", or draw, the record.

If the callback method calls **Metafile.PlayRecord**, it must do so by calling the **PlayRecord** method of the specific **Metafile** object that is being enumerated.

The *destPoints* parameter specifies three points of a parallelogram. The three **Point** structures represent the upper-left, upper-right, and lower-left corners of the parallelogram. The fourth point is extrapolated from the first three to form a parallelogram. The drawn metafile is scaled and sheared to fit the parallelogram.

The image attributes specified by the *imageAttr* parameter replace those specified when the metafile was written.

Example

For an example see **EnumerateMetafile**.

Requirements

Platforms: Windows 98, Windows NT 4.0,
Windows Millennium Edition, Windows 2000,
Windows XP Home Edition, Windows XP Professional,
Windows Server 2003 family

Graphics.EnumerateMetafile Method (Metafile, Point[], Rectangle, GraphicsUnit, Graphics.EnumerateMetafileProc)

Sends the records in a selected rectangle from a **Metafile** object, one at a time, to a callback method for display in a specified parallelogram.

[Visual Basic]
```
Overloads Public Sub EnumerateMetafile( _
   ByVal metafile As Metafile, _
   ByVal destPoints() As Point, _
   ByVal srcRect As Rectangle, _
   ByVal srcUnit As GraphicsUnit, _
   ByVal callback As Graphics.EnumerateMetafileProc _
)
```
[C#]
```
public void EnumerateMetafile(
   Metafile metafile,
   Point[] destPoints,
   Rectangle srcRect,
   GraphicsUnit srcUnit,
   Graphics.EnumerateMetafileProc callback
);
```
[C++]
```
public: void EnumerateMetafile(
   Metafile* metafile,
   Point destPoints[],
   Rectangle srcRect,
   GraphicsUnit srcUnit,
   Graphics.EnumerateMetafileProc* callback
);
```
[JScript]
```
public function EnumerateMetafile(
   metafile : Metafile,
   destPoints : Point[],
   srcRect : Rectangle,
   srcUnit : GraphicsUnit,
   callback : Graphics.EnumerateMetafileProc
);
```

Parameters

metafile

Metafile object to enumerate.

destPoints

Array of three **Point** structures that define a parallelogram that determines the size and location of the drawn metafile.

srcRect

Rectangle structure that specifies the portion of the metafile, relative to its upper-left corner, to draw.

srcUnit

Member of the **GraphicsUnit** enumeration that specifies the unit of measure used to determine the portion of the metafile that the rectangle specified by the *srcRect* parameter contains.

callback

Graphics.EnumerateMetafileProc delegate that specifies the method to which the metafile records are sent.

Return Value

This method does not return a value.

Remarks

This method enumerates the records contained in the specified metafile. Each record is individually sent to a callback method specified by the *callback* parameter. Typically, the callback method calls the **PlayRecord** method to "play back", or draw, the record.

If the callback method calls **Metafile.PlayRecord**, it must do so by calling the **PlayRecord** method of the specific **Metafile** object that is being enumerated.

The *destPoints* parameter specifies three points of a parallelogram. The three **Point** structures represent the upper-left, upper-right, and lower-left corners of the parallelogram. The fourth point is extrapolated from the first three to form a parallelogram. The drawn metafile is scaled and sheared to fit the parallelogram.

Any drawing that takes place outside of the rectangle specified by the *srcRect* parameter is ignored.

Example

For an example see **EnumerateMetafile**.

Requirements

Platforms: Windows 98, Windows NT 4.0,
Windows Millennium Edition, Windows 2000,
Windows XP Home Edition, Windows XP Professional,
Windows Server 2003 family

Graphics.EnumerateMetafile Method (Metafile, PointF, Graphics.EnumerateMetafileProc, IntPtr, ImageAttributes)

Sends the records in the specified **Metafile** object, one at a time, to a callback method for display at a specified point using specified image attributes.

[Visual Basic]
```
Overloads Public Sub EnumerateMetafile( _
   ByVal metafile As Metafile, _
   ByVal destPoint As PointF, _
   ByVal callback As Graphics.EnumerateMetafileProc, _
   ByVal callbackData As IntPtr, _
   ByVal imageAttr As ImageAttributes _
)
```
[C#]
```
public void EnumerateMetafile(
   Metafile metafile,
   PointF destPoint,
   Graphics.EnumerateMetafileProc callback,
   IntPtr callbackData,
   ImageAttributes imageAttr
);
```
[C++]
```
public: void EnumerateMetafile(
   Metafile* metafile,
   PointF destPoint,
   Graphics.EnumerateMetafileProc* callback,
   IntPtr callbackData,
   ImageAttributes* imageAttr
);
```
[JScript]
```
public function EnumerateMetafile(
   metafile : Metafile,
   destPoint : PointF,
   callback : Graphics.EnumerateMetafileProc,
   callbackData : IntPtr,
   imageAttr : ImageAttributes
);
```

Parameters

metafile
: **Metafile** object to enumerate.

destPoint
: **PointF** structure that specifies the location of the upper-left corner of the drawn metafile.

callback
: **Graphics.EnumerateMetafileProc** delegate that specifies the method to which the metafile records are sent.

callbackData
: Internal pointer that is required, but ignored. You can pass **IntPtr.Zero** for this parameter.

imageAttr
: **ImageAttributes** object that specifies image attribute information for the drawn image.

Return Value

This method does not return a value.

Remarks

This method enumerates the records contained in the specified metafile. Each record is individually sent to a callback method specified by the *callback* parameter. Typically, the callback method calls the **PlayRecord** method to "play back", or draw, the record.

If the callback method calls **Metafile.PlayRecord**, it must do so by calling the **PlayRecord** method of the specific **Metafile** object that is being enumerated.

The image attributes specified by the *imageAttr* parameter replace those specified when the metafile was written.

Example

For an example see **EnumerateMetafile**.

Requirements

Platforms: Windows 98, Windows NT 4.0, Windows Millennium Edition, Windows 2000, Windows XP Home Edition, Windows XP Professional, Windows Server 2003 family

Graphics.EnumerateMetafile Method (Metafile, PointF, RectangleF, GraphicsUnit, Graphics.EnumerateMetafileProc)

Sends the records in a selected rectangle from a **Metafile** object, one at a time, to a callback method for display at a specified point.

[Visual Basic]
```
Overloads Public Sub EnumerateMetafile( _
   ByVal metafile As Metafile, _
   ByVal destPoint As PointF, _
   ByVal srcRect As RectangleF, _
   ByVal srcUnit As GraphicsUnit, _
   ByVal callback As Graphics.EnumerateMetafileProc _
)
```
[C#]
```
public void EnumerateMetafile(
   Metafile metafile,
   PointF destPoint,
   RectangleF srcRect,
   GraphicsUnit srcUnit,
   Graphics.EnumerateMetafileProc callback
);
```
[C++]
```
public: void EnumerateMetafile(
   Metafile* metafile,
   PointF destPoint,
   RectangleF srcRect,
   GraphicsUnit srcUnit,
   Graphics.EnumerateMetafileProc* callback
);
```
[JScript]
```
public function EnumerateMetafile(
   metafile : Metafile,
   destPoint : PointF,
   srcRect : RectangleF,
   srcUnit : GraphicsUnit,
   callback : Graphics.EnumerateMetafileProc
);
```

Parameters

metafile
: **Metafile** object to enumerate.

destPoint
: **PointF** structure that specifies the location of the upper-left corner of the drawn metafile.

srcRect

RectangleF structure that specifies the portion of the metafile, relative to its upper-left corner, to draw.

srcUnit

Member of the **GraphicsUnit** enumeration that specifies the unit of measure used to determine the portion of the metafile that the rectangle specified by the *srcRect* parameter contains.

callback

Graphics.EnumerateMetafileProc delegate that specifies the method to which the metafile records are sent.

Return Value

This method does not return a value.

Remarks

This method enumerates the records contained in the specified metafile. Each record is individually sent to a callback method specified by the *callback* parameter. Typically, the callback method calls the **PlayRecord** method to "play back", or draw, the record.

If the callback method calls **Metafile.PlayRecord**, it must do so by calling the **PlayRecord** method of the specific **Metafile** object that is being enumerated.

Any drawing that takes place outside of the rectangle specified by the *srcRect* parameter is ignored.

Example

For an example see **EnumerateMetafile**.

Requirements

Platforms: Windows 98, Windows NT 4.0, Windows Millennium Edition, Windows 2000, Windows XP Home Edition, Windows XP Professional, Windows Server 2003 family

Graphics.EnumerateMetafile Method (Metafile, PointF[], Graphics.EnumerateMetafileProc, IntPtr, ImageAttributes)

Sends the records in the specified **Metafile** object, one at a time, to a callback method for display in a specified parallelogram using specified image attributes.

[Visual Basic]

```
Overloads Public Sub EnumerateMetafile( _
   ByVal metafile As Metafile, _
   ByVal destPoints() As PointF, _
   ByVal callback As Graphics.EnumerateMetafileProc, _
   ByVal callbackData As IntPtr, _
   ByVal imageAttr As ImageAttributes _
)
```

[C#]

```
public void EnumerateMetafile(
   Metafile metafile,
   PointF[] destPoints,
   Graphics.EnumerateMetafileProc callback,
   IntPtr callbackData,
   ImageAttributes imageAttr
);
```

[C++]

```
public: void EnumerateMetafile(
   Metafile* metafile,
   PointF destPoints[],
   Graphics.EnumerateMetafileProc* callback,
   IntPtr callbackData,
   ImageAttributes* imageAttr
);
```

[JScript]

```
public function EnumerateMetafile(
   metafile : Metafile,
   destPoints : PointF[],
   callback : Graphics.EnumerateMetafileProc,
   callbackData : IntPtr,
   imageAttr : ImageAttributes
);
```

Parameters

metafile

Metafile object to enumerate.

destPoints

Array of three **PointF** structures that define a parallelogram that determines the size and location of the drawn metafile.

callback

Graphics.EnumerateMetafileProc delegate that specifies the method to which the metafile records are sent.

callbackData

Internal pointer that is required, but ignored. You can pass **IntPtr.Zero** for this parameter.

imageAttr

ImageAttributes object that specifies image attribute information for the drawn image.

Return Value

This method does not return a value.

Remarks

This method enumerates the records contained in the specified metafile. Each record is individually sent to a callback method specified by the *callback* parameter. Typically, the callback method calls the **PlayRecord** method to "play back", or draw, the record.

If the callback method calls **Metafile.PlayRecord**, it must do so by calling the **PlayRecord** method of the specific **Metafile** object that is being enumerated.

The *destPoints* parameter specifies three points of a parallelogram. The three **PointF** structures represent the upper-left, upper-right, and lower-left corners of the parallelogram. The fourth point is extrapolated from the first three to form a parallelogram. The drawn metafile is scaled and sheared to fit the parallelogram.

The image attributes specified by the *imageAttr* parameter replace those specified when the metafile was written.

Example

For an example see **EnumerateMetafile**.

Requirements

Platforms: Windows 98, Windows NT 4.0, Windows Millennium Edition, Windows 2000, Windows XP Home Edition, Windows XP Professional, Windows Server 2003 family

Graphics.EnumerateMetafile Method (Metafile, PointF[], RectangleF, GraphicsUnit, Graphics.EnumerateMetafileProc)

Sends the records in a selected rectangle from a **Metafile** object, one at a time, to a callback method for display in a specified parallelogram.

[Visual Basic]
```
Overloads Public Sub EnumerateMetafile( _
   ByVal metafile As Metafile, _
   ByVal destPoints() As PointF, _
   ByVal srcRect As RectangleF, _
   ByVal srcUnit As GraphicsUnit, _
   ByVal callback As Graphics.EnumerateMetafileProc _
)
```
[C#]
```
public void EnumerateMetafile(
   Metafile metafile,
   PointF[] destPoints,
   RectangleF srcRect,
   GraphicsUnit srcUnit,
   Graphics.EnumerateMetafileProc callback
);
```
[C++]
```
public: void EnumerateMetafile(
   Metafile* metafile,
   PointF destPoints[],
   RectangleF srcRect,
   GraphicsUnit srcUnit,
   Graphics.EnumerateMetafileProc* callback
);
```
[JScript]
```
public function EnumerateMetafile(
   metafile : Metafile,
   destPoints : PointF[],
   srcRect : RectangleF,
   srcUnit : GraphicsUnit,
   callback : Graphics.EnumerateMetafileProc
);
```

Parameters

metafile

Metafile object to enumerate.

destPoints

Array of three **PointF** structures that define a parallelogram that determines the size and location of the drawn metafile.

srcRect

RectangleF structures that specifies the portion of the metafile, relative to its upper-left corner, to draw.

srcUnit

Member of the **GraphicsUnit** enumeration that specifies the unit of measure used to determine the portion of the metafile that the rectangle specified by the *srcRect* parameter contains.

callback

Graphics.EnumerateMetafileProc delegate that specifies the method to which the metafile records are sent.

Return Value

This method does not return a value.

Remarks

This method enumerates the records contained in the specified metafile. Each record is individually sent to a callback method specified by the *callback* parameter. Typically, the callback method calls the **PlayRecord** method to "play back", or draw, the record.

If the callback method calls **Metafile.PlayRecord**, it must do so by calling the **PlayRecord** method of the specific **Metafile** object that is being enumerated.

The *destPoints* parameter specifies three points of a parallelogram. The three **Point** structures represent the upper-left, upper-right, and lower-left corners of the parallelogram. The fourth point is extrapolated from the first three to form a parallelogram. The drawn metafile is scaled and sheared to fit the parallelogram.

Any drawing that takes place outside of the rectangle specified by the *srcRect* parameter is ignored.

Example

For an example see **EnumerateMetafile**.

Requirements

Platforms: Windows 98, Windows NT 4.0, Windows Millennium Edition, Windows 2000, Windows XP Home Edition, Windows XP Professional, Windows Server 2003 family

Graphics.EnumerateMetafile Method (Metafile, Rectangle, Graphics.EnumerateMetafileProc, IntPtr, ImageAttributes)

Sends the records of the specified **Metafile** object, one at a time, to a callback method for display in a specified rectangle using specified image attributes.

[Visual Basic]
```
Overloads Public Sub EnumerateMetafile( _
   ByVal metafile As Metafile, _
   ByVal destRect As Rectangle, _
   ByVal callback As Graphics.EnumerateMetafileProc, _
   ByVal callbackData As IntPtr, _
   ByVal imageAttr As ImageAttributes _
)
```
[C#]
```
public void EnumerateMetafile(
   Metafile metafile,
   Rectangle destRect,
   Graphics.EnumerateMetafileProc callback,
   IntPtr callbackData,
   ImageAttributes imageAttr
);
```
[C++]
```
public: void EnumerateMetafile(
   Metafile* metafile,
   Rectangle destRect,
   Graphics.EnumerateMetafileProc* callback,
   IntPtr callbackData,
   ImageAttributes* imageAttr
);
```
[JScript]
```
public function EnumerateMetafile(
   metafile : Metafile,
   destRect : Rectangle,
   callback : Graphics.EnumerateMetafileProc,
   callbackData : IntPtr,
   imageAttr : ImageAttributes
);
```

Parameters

metafile

Metafile object to enumerate.

destRect

Rectangle structure that specifies the location and size of the drawn metafile.

callback

Graphics.EnumerateMetafileProc delegate that specifies the method to which the metafile records are sent.

callbackData

Internal pointer that is required, but ignored. You can pass **IntPtr.Zero** for this parameter.

imageAttr

ImageAttributes object that specifies image attribute information for the drawn image.

Return Value

This method does not return a value.

Remarks

This method enumerates the records contained in the specified metafile. Each record is individually sent to a callback method specified by the *callback* parameter. Typically, the callback method calls the **PlayRecord** method to "play back", or draw, the record.

If the callback method calls **Metafile.PlayRecord**, it must do so by calling the **PlayRecord** method of the specific **Metafile** object that is being enumerated.

The image attributes specified by the *imageAttr* parameter replace those specified when the metafile was written.

Example

For an example see **EnumerateMetafile**.

Requirements

Platforms: Windows 98, Windows NT 4.0, Windows Millennium Edition, Windows 2000, Windows XP Home Edition, Windows XP Professional, Windows Server 2003 family

Graphics.EnumerateMetafile Method (Metafile, Rectangle, Rectangle, GraphicsUnit, Graphics.EnumerateMetafileProc)

Sends the records of a selected rectangle from a **Metafile** object, one at a time, to a callback method for display in a specified rectangle.

```
[Visual Basic]
Overloads Public Sub EnumerateMetafile( _
   ByVal metafile As Metafile, _
   ByVal destRect As Rectangle, _
   ByVal srcRect As Rectangle, _
   ByVal srcUnit As GraphicsUnit, _
   ByVal callback As Graphics.EnumerateMetafileProc _
)
[C#]
public void EnumerateMetafile(
   Metafile metafile,
   Rectangle destRect,
   Rectangle srcRect,
   GraphicsUnit srcUnit,
   Graphics.EnumerateMetafileProc callback
);
[C++]
public: void EnumerateMetafile(
   Metafile* metafile,
   Rectangle destRect,
   Rectangle srcRect,
   GraphicsUnit srcUnit,
   Graphics.EnumerateMetafileProc* callback
);
[JScript]
public function EnumerateMetafile(
   metafile : Metafile,
   destRect : Rectangle,
   srcRect : Rectangle,
   srcUnit : GraphicsUnit,
   callback : Graphics.EnumerateMetafileProc
);
```

Parameters

metafile

Metafile object to enumerate.

destRect

Rectangle structure that specifies the location and size of the drawn metafile.

srcRect

Rectangle structure that specifies the portion of the metafile, relative to its upper-left corner, to draw.

srcUnit

Member of the **GraphicsUnit** enumeration that specifies the unit of measure used to determine the portion of the metafile that the rectangle specified by the *srcRect* parameter contains.

callback

Graphics.EnumerateMetafileProc delegate that specifies the method to which the metafile records are sent.

Return Value

This method does not return a value.

Remarks

This method enumerates the records contained in the specified metafile. Each record is individually sent to a callback method specified by the *callback* parameter. Typically, the callback method calls the **PlayRecord** method to "play back", or draw, the record.

If the callback method calls **Metafile.PlayRecord**, it must do so by calling the **PlayRecord** method of the specific **Metafile** object that is being enumerated.

Any drawing that takes place outside of the rectangle specified by the *srcRect* parameter is ignored.

Example

For an example see **EnumerateMetafile**.

Requirements

Platforms: Windows 98, Windows NT 4.0, Windows Millennium Edition, Windows 2000, Windows XP Home Edition, Windows XP Professional, Windows Server 2003 family

Graphics.EnumerateMetafile Method (Metafile, RectangleF, Graphics.EnumerateMetafileProc, IntPtr, ImageAttributes)

Sends the records of the specified **Metafile** object, one at a time, to a callback method for display in a specified rectangle using specified image attributes.

[Visual Basic]
```
Overloads Public Sub EnumerateMetafile( _
   ByVal metafile As Metafile, _
   ByVal destRect As RectangleF, _
   ByVal callback As Graphics.EnumerateMetafileProc, _
   ByVal callbackData As IntPtr, _
   ByVal imageAttr As ImageAttributes _
)
```
[C#]
```
public void EnumerateMetafile(
   Metafile metafile,
   RectangleF destRect,
   Graphics.EnumerateMetafileProc callback,
   IntPtr callbackData,
   ImageAttributes imageAttr
);
```
[C++]
```
public: void EnumerateMetafile(
   Metafile* metafile,
   RectangleF destRect,
   Graphics.EnumerateMetafileProc* callback,
   IntPtr callbackData,
   ImageAttributes* imageAttr
);
```
[JScript]
```
public function EnumerateMetafile(
   metafile : Metafile,
   destRect : RectangleF,
   callback : Graphics.EnumerateMetafileProc,
   callbackData : IntPtr,
   imageAttr : ImageAttributes
);
```

Parameters

metafile
: **Metafile** object to enumerate.

destRect
: **RectangleF** structure that specifies the location and size of the drawn metafile.

callback
: **Graphics.EnumerateMetafileProc** delegate that specifies the method to which the metafile records are sent.

callbackData
: Internal pointer that is required, but ignored. You can pass **IntPtr.Zero** for this parameter.

imageAttr
: **ImageAttributes** object that specifies image attribute information for the drawn image.

Return Value

This method does not return a value.

Remarks

This method enumerates the records contained in the specified metafile. Each record is individually sent to a callback method specified by the *callback* parameter. Typically, the callback method calls the **PlayRecord** method to "play back", or draw, the record.

If the callback method calls **Metafile.PlayRecord**, it must do so by calling the **PlayRecord** method of the specific **Metafile** object that is being enumerated.

The image attributes specified by the *imageAttr* parameter replace those specified when the metafile was written.

Example

For an example see **EnumerateMetafile**.

Requirements

Platforms: Windows 98, Windows NT 4.0, Windows Millennium Edition, Windows 2000, Windows XP Home Edition, Windows XP Professional, Windows Server 2003 family

Graphics.EnumerateMetafile Method (Metafile, RectangleF, RectangleF, GraphicsUnit, Graphics.EnumerateMetafileProc)

Sends the records of a selected rectangle from a **Metafile** object, one at a time, to a callback method for display in a specified rectangle.

[Visual Basic]
```
Overloads Public Sub EnumerateMetafile( _
   ByVal metafile As Metafile, _
   ByVal destRect As RectangleF, _
   ByVal srcRect As RectangleF, _
   ByVal srcUnit As GraphicsUnit, _
   ByVal callback As Graphics.EnumerateMetafileProc _
)
```
[C#]
```
public void EnumerateMetafile(
   Metafile metafile,
   RectangleF destRect,
   RectangleF srcRect,
   GraphicsUnit srcUnit,
   Graphics.EnumerateMetafileProc callback
);
```
[C++]
```
public: void EnumerateMetafile(
   Metafile* metafile,
   RectangleF destRect,
   RectangleF srcRect,
   GraphicsUnit srcUnit,
   Graphics.EnumerateMetafileProc* callback
);
```
[JScript]
```
public function EnumerateMetafile(
   metafile : Metafile,
   destRect : RectangleF,
   srcRect : RectangleF,
   srcUnit : GraphicsUnit,
   callback : Graphics.EnumerateMetafileProc
);
```

Parameters

metafile
: **Metafile** object to enumerate.

destRect
: **RectangleF** structure that specifies the location and size of the drawn metafile.

srcRect
 RectangleF structure that specifies the portion of the metafile, relative to its upper-left corner, to draw.

srcUnit
 Member of the **GraphicsUnit** enumeration that specifies the unit of measure used to determine the portion of the metafile that the rectangle specified by the *srcRect* parameter contains.

callback
 Graphics.EnumerateMetafileProc delegate that specifies the method to which the metafile records are sent.

Return Value

This method does not return a value.

Remarks

This method enumerates the records contained in the specified metafile. Each record is individually sent to a callback method specified by the *callback* parameter. Typically, the callback method calls the **PlayRecord** method to "play back", or draw, the record.

If the callback method calls **Metafile.PlayRecord**, it must do so by calling the **PlayRecord** method of the specific **Metafile** object that is being enumerated.

Any drawing that takes place outside of the rectangle specified by the *srcRect* parameter is ignored.

Example

For an example see **EnumerateMetafile**.

Requirements

Platforms: Windows 98, Windows NT 4.0, Windows Millennium Edition, Windows 2000, Windows XP Home Edition, Windows XP Professional, Windows Server 2003 family

Graphics.EnumerateMetafile Method (Metafile, Point, Rectangle, GraphicsUnit, Graphics.EnumerateMetafileProc, IntPtr)

Sends the records in a selected rectangle from a **Metafile** object, one at a time, to a callback method for display at a specified point.

[Visual Basic]
```
Overloads Public Sub EnumerateMetafile( _
   ByVal metafile As Metafile, _
   ByVal destPoint As Point, _
   ByVal srcRect As Rectangle, _
   ByVal srcUnit As GraphicsUnit, _
   ByVal callback As Graphics.EnumerateMetafileProc, _
   ByVal callbackData As IntPtr _
)
```
[C#]
```
public void EnumerateMetafile(
   Metafile metafile,
   Point destPoint,
   Rectangle srcRect,
   GraphicsUnit srcUnit,
   Graphics.EnumerateMetafileProc callback,
   IntPtr callbackData
);
```
[C++]
```
public: void EnumerateMetafile(
   Metafile* metafile,
   Point destPoint,
   Rectangle srcRect,
   GraphicsUnit srcUnit,
   Graphics.EnumerateMetafileProc* callback,
   IntPtr callbackData
);
```
[JScript]
```
public function EnumerateMetafile(
   metafile : Metafile,
   destPoint : Point,
   srcRect : Rectangle,
   srcUnit : GraphicsUnit,
   callback : Graphics.EnumerateMetafileProc,
   callbackData : IntPtr
);
```

Parameters

metafile
 Metafile object to enumerate.

destPoint
 Point structure that specifies the location of the upper-left corner of the drawn metafile.

srcRect
 Rectangle structure that specifies the portion of the metafile, relative to its upper-left corner, to draw.

srcUnit
 Member of the **GraphicsUnit** enumeration that specifies the unit of measure used to determine the portion of the metafile that the rectangle specified by the *srcRect* parameter contains.

callback
 Graphics.EnumerateMetafileProc delegate that specifies the method to which the metafile records are sent.

callbackData
 Internal pointer that is required, but ignored. You can pass **IntPtr.Zero** for this parameter.

Return Value

This method does not return a value.

Remarks

This method enumerates the records contained in the specified metafile. Each record is individually sent to a callback method specified by the *callback* parameter. Typically, the callback method calls the **PlayRecord** method to "play back", or draw, the record.

If the callback method calls **Metafile.PlayRecord**, it must do so by calling the **PlayRecord** method of the specific **Metafile** object that is being enumerated.

Example

For an example see **EnumerateMetafile**.

Requirements

Platforms: Windows 98, Windows NT 4.0, Windows Millennium Edition, Windows 2000, Windows XP Home Edition, Windows XP Professional, Windows Server 2003 family

Graphics.EnumerateMetafile Method (Metafile, Point[], Rectangle, GraphicsUnit, Graphics.EnumerateMetafileProc, IntPtr)

Sends the records in a selected rectangle from a **Metafile** object, one at a time, to a callback method for display in a specified parallelogram.

```
[Visual Basic]
Overloads Public Sub EnumerateMetafile( _
   ByVal metafile As Metafile, _
   ByVal destPoints() As Point, _
   ByVal srcRect As Rectangle, _
   ByVal srcUnit As GraphicsUnit, _
   ByVal callback As Graphics.EnumerateMetafileProc, _
   ByVal callbackData As IntPtr _
)
[C#]
public void EnumerateMetafile(
   Metafile metafile,
   Point[] destPoints,
   Rectangle srcRect,
   GraphicsUnit srcUnit,
   Graphics.EnumerateMetafileProc callback,
   IntPtr callbackData
);
[C++]
public: void EnumerateMetafile(
   Metafile* metafile,
   Point destPoints[],
   Rectangle srcRect,
   GraphicsUnit srcUnit,
   Graphics.EnumerateMetafileProc* callback,
   IntPtr callbackData
);
[JScript]
public function EnumerateMetafile(
   metafile : Metafile,
   destPoints : Point[],
   srcRect : Rectangle,
   srcUnit : GraphicsUnit,
   callback : Graphics.EnumerateMetafileProc,
   callbackData : IntPtr
);
```

Parameters

metafile
: **Metafile** object to enumerate.

destPoints
: Array of three **Point** structures that define a parallelogram that determines the size and location of the drawn metafile.

srcRect
: **Rectangle** structure that specifies the portion of the metafile, relative to its upper-left corner, to draw.

srcUnit
: Member of the **GraphicsUnit** enumeration that specifies the unit of measure used to determine the portion of the metafile that the rectangle specified by the *srcRect* parameter contains.

callback
: **Graphics.EnumerateMetafileProc** delegate that specifies the method to which the metafile records are sent.

callbackData
: Internal pointer that is required, but ignored. You can pass **IntPtr.Zero** for this parameter.

Return Value

This method does not return a value.

Remarks

This method enumerates the records contained in the specified metafile. Each record is individually sent to a callback method specified by the *callback* parameter. Typically, the callback method calls the **PlayRecord** method to "play back", or draw, the record.

If the callback method calls **Metafile.PlayRecord**, it must do so by calling the **PlayRecord** method of the specific **Metafile** object that is being enumerated.

The *destPoints* parameter specifies three points of a parallelogram. The three **Point** structures represent the upper-left, upper-right, and lower-left corners of the parallelogram. The fourth point is extrapolated from the first three to form a parallelogram. The drawn metafile is scaled and sheared to fit the parallelogram.

Any drawing that takes place outside of the rectangle specified by the *srcRect* parameter is ignored.

Example

For an example see **EnumerateMetafile**.

Requirements

Platforms: Windows 98, Windows NT 4.0, Windows Millennium Edition, Windows 2000, Windows XP Home Edition, Windows XP Professional, Windows Server 2003 family

Graphics.EnumerateMetafile Method (Metafile, PointF, RectangleF, GraphicsUnit, Graphics.EnumerateMetafileProc, IntPtr)

Sends the records in a selected rectangle from a **Metafile** object, one at a time, to a callback method for display at a specified point.

```
[Visual Basic]
Overloads Public Sub EnumerateMetafile( _
   ByVal metafile As Metafile, _
   ByVal destPoint As PointF, _
   ByVal srcRect As RectangleF, _
   ByVal srcUnit As GraphicsUnit, _
   ByVal callback As Graphics.EnumerateMetafileProc, _
   ByVal callbackData As IntPtr _
)
[C#]
public void EnumerateMetafile(
   Metafile metafile,
   PointF destPoint,
   RectangleF srcRect,
   GraphicsUnit srcUnit,
   Graphics.EnumerateMetafileProc callback,
   IntPtr callbackData
);
[C++]
public: void EnumerateMetafile(
   Metafile* metafile,
   PointF destPoint,
   RectangleF srcRect,
   GraphicsUnit srcUnit,
   Graphics.EnumerateMetafileProc* callback,
   IntPtr callbackData
);
```

[JScript]
```
public function EnumerateMetafile(
   metafile : Metafile,
   destPoint : PointF,
   srcRect : RectangleF,
   srcUnit : GraphicsUnit,
   callback : Graphics.EnumerateMetafileProc,
   callbackData : IntPtr
);
```

Parameters

metafile
: **Metafile** object to enumerate.

destPoint
: **PointF** structure that specifies the location of the upper-left corner of the drawn metafile.

srcRect
: **RectangleF** structure that specifies the portion of the metafile, relative to its upper-left corner, to draw.

srcUnit
: Member of the **GraphicsUnit** enumeration that specifies the unit of measure used to determine the portion of the metafile that the rectangle specified by the *srcRect* parameter contains.

callback
: **Graphics.EnumerateMetafileProc** delegate that specifies the method to which the metafile records are sent.

callbackData
: Internal pointer that is required, but ignored. You can pass **IntPtr.Zero** for this parameter.

Return Value

This method does not return a value.

Remarks

This method enumerates the records contained in the specified metafile. Each record is individually sent to a callback method specified by the *callback* parameter. Typically, the callback method calls the **PlayRecord** method to "play back", or draw, the record.

If the callback method calls **Metafile.PlayRecord**, it must do so by calling the **PlayRecord** method of the specific **Metafile** object that is being enumerated.

Any drawing that takes place outside of the rectangle specified by the *srcRect* parameter is ignored.

Example

For an example see **EnumerateMetafile**.

Requirements

Platforms: Windows 98, Windows NT 4.0, Windows Millennium Edition, Windows 2000, Windows XP Home Edition, Windows XP Professional, Windows Server 2003 family

Graphics.EnumerateMetafile Method (Metafile, PointF[], RectangleF, GraphicsUnit, Graphics.EnumerateMetafileProc, IntPtr)

Sends the records in a selected rectangle from a **Metafile** object, one at a time, to a callback method for display in a specified parallelogram.

[Visual Basic]
```
Overloads Public Sub EnumerateMetafile( _
   ByVal metafile As Metafile, _
   ByVal destPoints() As PointF, _
   ByVal srcRect As RectangleF, _
   ByVal srcUnit As GraphicsUnit, _
   ByVal callback As Graphics.EnumerateMetafileProc, _
   ByVal callbackData As IntPtr _
)
```
[C#]
```
public void EnumerateMetafile(
   Metafile metafile,
   PointF[] destPoints,
   RectangleF srcRect,
   GraphicsUnit srcUnit,
   Graphics.EnumerateMetafileProc callback,
   IntPtr callbackData
);
```
[C++]
```
public: void EnumerateMetafile(
   Metafile* metafile,
   PointF destPoints[],
   RectangleF srcRect,
   GraphicsUnit srcUnit,
   Graphics.EnumerateMetafileProc* callback,
   IntPtr callbackData
);
```
[JScript]
```
public function EnumerateMetafile(
   metafile : Metafile,
   destPoints : PointF[],
   srcRect : RectangleF,
   srcUnit : GraphicsUnit,
   callback : Graphics.EnumerateMetafileProc,
   callbackData : IntPtr
);
```

Parameters

metafile
: **Metafile** object to enumerate.

destPoints
: Array of three **PointF** structures that define a parallelogram that determines the size and location of the drawn metafile.

srcRect
: **RectangleF** structure that specifies the portion of the metafile, relative to its upper-left corner, to draw.

srcUnit
: Member of the **GraphicsUnit** enumeration that specifies the unit of measure used to determine the portion of the metafile that the rectangle specified by the *srcRect* parameter contains.

callback
: **Graphics.EnumerateMetafileProc** delegate that specifies the method to which the metafile records are sent.

callbackData
: Internal pointer that is required, but ignored. You can pass **IntPtr.Zero** for this parameter.

Return Value

This method does not return a value.

Remarks

This method enumerates the records contained in the specified metafile. Each record is individually sent to a callback method specified by the *callback* parameter. Typically, the callback method calls the **PlayRecord** method to "play back", or draw, the record.

If the callback method calls **Metafile.PlayRecord**, it must do so by calling the **PlayRecord** method of the specific **Metafile** object that is being enumerated.

The *destPoints* parameter specifies three points of a parallelogram. The three **PointF** structures represent the upper-left, upper-right, and lower-left corners of the parallelogram. The fourth point is extrapolated from the first three to form a parallelogram. The drawn metafile is scaled and sheared to fit the parallelogram.

Any drawing that takes place outside of the rectangle specified by the *srcRect* parameter is ignored.

Example

For an example see **EnumerateMetafile**.

Requirements

Platforms: Windows 98, Windows NT 4.0,
Windows Millennium Edition, Windows 2000,
Windows XP Home Edition, Windows XP Professional,
Windows Server 2003 family

Graphics.EnumerateMetafile Method (Metafile, Rectangle, Rectangle, GraphicsUnit, Graphics.EnumerateMetafileProc, IntPtr)

Sends the records of a selected rectangle from a **Metafile** object, one at a time, to a callback method for display in a specified rectangle.

```
[Visual Basic]
Overloads Public Sub EnumerateMetafile( _
   ByVal metafile As Metafile, _
   ByVal destRect As Rectangle, _
   ByVal srcRect As Rectangle, _
   ByVal srcUnit As GraphicsUnit, _
   ByVal callback As Graphics.EnumerateMetafileProc, _
   ByVal callbackData As IntPtr _
)
[C#]
public void EnumerateMetafile(
   Metafile metafile,
   Rectangle destRect,
   Rectangle srcRect,
   GraphicsUnit srcUnit,
   Graphics.EnumerateMetafileProc callback,
   IntPtr callbackData
);
[C++]
public: void EnumerateMetafile(
   Metafile* metafile,
   Rectangle destRect,
   Rectangle srcRect,
   GraphicsUnit srcUnit,
   Graphics.EnumerateMetafileProc* callback,
   IntPtr callbackData
);
```

```
[JScript]
public function EnumerateMetafile(
   metafile : Metafile,
   destRect : Rectangle,
   srcRect : Rectangle,
   srcUnit : GraphicsUnit,
   callback : Graphics.EnumerateMetafileProc,
   callbackData : IntPtr
);
```

Parameters

metafile
: **Metafile** object to enumerate.

destRect
: **Rectangle** structure that specifies the location and size of the drawn metafile.

srcRect
: **Rectangle** structure that specifies the portion of the metafile, relative to its upper-left corner, to draw.

srcUnit
: Member of the **GraphicsUnit** enumeration that specifies the unit of measure used to determine the portion of the metafile that the rectangle specified by the *srcRect* parameter contains.

callback
: **Graphics.EnumerateMetafileProc** delegate that specifies the method to which the metafile records are sent.

callbackData
: Internal pointer that is required, but ignored. You can pass **IntPtr.Zero** for this parameter.

Return Value

This method does not return a value.

Remarks

This method enumerates the records contained in the specified metafile. Each record is individually sent to a callback method specified by the *callback* parameter. Typically, the callback method calls the **PlayRecord** method to "play back", or draw, the record.

If the callback method calls **Metafile.PlayRecord**, it must do so by calling the **PlayRecord** method of the specific **Metafile** object that is being enumerated.

Any drawing that takes place outside of the rectangle specified by the *srcRect* parameter is ignored.

Example

For an example see **EnumerateMetafile**.

Requirements

Platforms: Windows 98, Windows NT 4.0,
Windows Millennium Edition, Windows 2000,
Windows XP Home Edition, Windows XP Professional,
Windows Server 2003 family

Graphics.EnumerateMetafile Method (Metafile, RectangleF, RectangleF, GraphicsUnit, Graphics.EnumerateMetafileProc, IntPtr)

Sends the records of a selected rectangle from a **Metafile** object, one at a time, to a callback method for display in a specified rectangle.

[Visual Basic]
```
Overloads Public Sub EnumerateMetafile( _
   ByVal metafile As Metafile, _
   ByVal destRect As RectangleF, _
   ByVal srcRect As RectangleF, _
   ByVal srcUnit As GraphicsUnit, _
   ByVal callback As Graphics.EnumerateMetafileProc, _
   ByVal callbackData As IntPtr _
)
```
[C#]
```
public void EnumerateMetafile(
   Metafile metafile,
   RectangleF destRect,
   RectangleF srcRect,
   GraphicsUnit srcUnit,
   Graphics.EnumerateMetafileProc callback,
   IntPtr callbackData
);
```
[C++]
```
public: void EnumerateMetafile(
   Metafile* metafile,
   RectangleF destRect,
   RectangleF srcRect,
   GraphicsUnit srcUnit,
   Graphics.EnumerateMetafileProc* callback,
   IntPtr callbackData
);
```
[JScript]
```
public function EnumerateMetafile(
   metafile : Metafile,
   destRect : RectangleF,
   srcRect : RectangleF,
   srcUnit : GraphicsUnit,
   callback : Graphics.EnumerateMetafileProc,
   callbackData : IntPtr
);
```

Parameters

metafile

Metafile object to enumerate.

destRect

RectangleF structure that specifies the location and size of the drawn metafile.

srcRect

RectangleF structure that specifies the portion of the metafile, relative to its upper-left corner, to draw.

srcUnit

Member of the **GraphicsUnit** enumeration that specifies the unit of measure used to determine the portion of the metafile that the rectangle specified by the *srcRect* parameter contains.

callback

Graphics.EnumerateMetafileProc delegate that specifies the method to which the metafile records are sent.

callbackData

Internal pointer that is required, but ignored. You can pass **IntPtr.Zero** for this parameter.

Return Value

This method does not return a value.

Remarks

This method enumerates the records contained in the specified metafile. Each record is individually sent to a callback method specified by the *callback* parameter. Typically, the callback method calls the **PlayRecord** method to "play back", or draw, the record.

If the callback method calls **Metafile.PlayRecord**, it must do so by calling the **PlayRecord** method of the specific **Metafile** object that is being enumerated.

Any drawing that takes place outside of the rectangle specified by the *srcRect* parameter is ignored.

Example

For an example see **EnumerateMetafile**.

Requirements

Platforms: Windows 98, Windows NT 4.0, Windows Millennium Edition, Windows 2000, Windows XP Home Edition, Windows XP Professional, Windows Server 2003 family

Graphics.EnumerateMetafile Method (Metafile, Point, Rectangle, GraphicsUnit, Graphics.EnumerateMetafileProc, IntPtr, ImageAttributes)

Sends the records in a selected rectangle from a **Metafile** object, one at a time, to a callback method for display at a specified point using specified image attributes.

[Visual Basic]
```
Overloads Public Sub EnumerateMetafile( _
   ByVal metafile As Metafile, _
   ByVal destPoint As Point, _
   ByVal srcRect As Rectangle, _
   ByVal unit As GraphicsUnit, _
   ByVal callback As Graphics.EnumerateMetafileProc, _
   ByVal callbackData As IntPtr, _
   ByVal imageAttr As ImageAttributes _
)
```
[C#]
```
public void EnumerateMetafile(
   Metafile metafile,
   Point destPoint,
   Rectangle srcRect,
   GraphicsUnit unit,
   Graphics.EnumerateMetafileProc callback,
   IntPtr callbackData,
   ImageAttributes imageAttr
);
```
[C++]
```
public: void EnumerateMetafile(
   Metafile* metafile,
   Point destPoint,
   Rectangle srcRect,
   GraphicsUnit unit,
   Graphics.EnumerateMetafileProc* callback,
   IntPtr callbackData,
   ImageAttributes* imageAttr
);
```

[JScript]
```
public function EnumerateMetafile(
   metafile : Metafile,
   destPoint : Point,
   srcRect : Rectangle,
   unit : GraphicsUnit,
   callback : Graphics.EnumerateMetafileProc,
   callbackData : IntPtr,
   imageAttr : ImageAttributes
);
```

Parameters

metafile
: **Metafile** object to enumerate.

destPoint
: **Point** structure that specifies the location of the upper-left corner of the drawn metafile.

srcRect
: **Rectangle** structure that specifies the portion of the metafile, relative to its upper-left corner, to draw.

unit
: Member of the **GraphicsUnit** enumeration that specifies the unit of measure used to determine the portion of the metafile that the rectangle specified by the *srcRect* parameter contains.

callback
: **Graphics.EnumerateMetafileProc** delegate that specifies the method to which the metafile records are sent.

callbackData
: Internal pointer that is required, but ignored. You can pass **IntPtr.Zero** for this parameter.

imageAttr
: **ImageAttributes** object that specifies image attribute information for the drawn image.

Return Value

This method does not return a value.

Remarks

This method enumerates the records contained in the specified metafile. Each record is individually sent to a callback method specified by the *callback* parameter. Typically, the callback method calls the **PlayRecord** method to "play back", or draw, the record.

If the callback method calls **Metafile.PlayRecord**, it must do so by calling the **PlayRecord** method of the specific **Metafile** object that is being enumerated.

Example

For an example see **EnumerateMetafile**.

Requirements

Platforms: Windows 98, Windows NT 4.0, Windows Millennium Edition, Windows 2000, Windows XP Home Edition, Windows XP Professional, Windows Server 2003 family

Graphics.EnumerateMetafile Method (Metafile, Point[], Rectangle, GraphicsUnit, Graphics.EnumerateMetafileProc, IntPtr, ImageAttributes)

Sends the records in a selected rectangle from a **Metafile** object, one at a time, to a callback method for display in a specified parallelogram using specified image attributes.

[Visual Basic]
```
Overloads Public Sub EnumerateMetafile( _
   ByVal metafile As Metafile, _
   ByVal destPoints() As Point, _
   ByVal srcRect As Rectangle, _
   ByVal unit As GraphicsUnit, _
   ByVal callback As Graphics.EnumerateMetafileProc, _
   ByVal callbackData As IntPtr, _
   ByVal imageAttr As ImageAttributes _
)
```
[C#]
```
public void EnumerateMetafile(
   Metafile metafile,
   Point[] destPoints,
   Rectangle srcRect,
   GraphicsUnit unit,
   Graphics.EnumerateMetafileProc callback,
   IntPtr callbackData,
   ImageAttributes imageAttr
);
```
[C++]
```
public: void EnumerateMetafile(
   Metafile* metafile,
   Point destPoints[],
   Rectangle srcRect,
   GraphicsUnit unit,
   Graphics.EnumerateMetafileProc* callback,
   IntPtr callbackData,
   ImageAttributes* imageAttr
);
```
[JScript]
```
public function EnumerateMetafile(
   metafile : Metafile,
   destPoints : Point[],
   srcRect : Rectangle,
   unit : GraphicsUnit,
   callback : Graphics.EnumerateMetafileProc,
   callbackData : IntPtr,
   imageAttr : ImageAttributes
);
```

Parameters

metafile
: **Metafile** object to enumerate.

destPoints
: Array of three **Point** structures that define a parallelogram that determines the size and location of the drawn metafile.

srcRect
: **Rectangle** structure that specifies the portion of the metafile, relative to its upper-left corner, to draw.

unit
: Member of the **GraphicsUnit** enumeration that specifies the unit of measure used to determine the portion of the metafile that the rectangle specified by the *srcRect* parameter contains.

callback
: **Graphics.EnumerateMetafileProc** delegate that specifies the method to which the metafile records are sent.

callbackData
: Internal pointer that is required, but ignored. You can pass **IntPtr.Zero** for this parameter.

imageAttr

ImageAttributes object that specifies image attribute information for the drawn image.

Return Value

This method does not return a value.

Remarks

This method enumerates the records contained in the specified metafile. Each record is individually sent to a callback method specified by the *callback* parameter. Typically, the callback method calls the **PlayRecord** method to "play back", or draw, the record.

If the callback method calls **Metafile.PlayRecord**, it must do so by calling the **PlayRecord** method of the specific **Metafile** object that is being enumerated.

The *destPoints* parameter specifies three points of a parallelogram. The three **Point** structures represent the upper-left, upper-right, and lower-left corners of the parallelogram. The fourth point is extrapolated from the first three to form a parallelogram. The drawn metafile is scaled and sheared to fit the parallelogram.

Any drawing that takes place outside of the rectangle specified by the *srcRect* parameter is ignored.

The image attributes specified by the *imageAttr* parameter replace those specified when the metafile was written.

Example

For an example see **EnumerateMetafile**.

Requirements

Platforms: Windows 98, Windows NT 4.0, Windows Millennium Edition, Windows 2000, Windows XP Home Edition, Windows XP Professional, Windows Server 2003 family

Graphics.EnumerateMetafile Method (Metafile, PointF, RectangleF, GraphicsUnit, Graphics.EnumerateMetafileProc, IntPtr, ImageAttributes)

Sends the records in a selected rectangle from a **Metafile** object, one at a time, to a callback method for display at a specified point using specified image attributes.

[Visual Basic]
```
Overloads Public Sub EnumerateMetafile( _
   ByVal metafile As Metafile, _
   ByVal destPoint As PointF, _
   ByVal srcRect As RectangleF, _
   ByVal unit As GraphicsUnit, _
   ByVal callback As Graphics.EnumerateMetafileProc, _
   ByVal callbackData As IntPtr, _
   ByVal imageAttr As ImageAttributes _
)
```
[C#]
```
public void EnumerateMetafile(
   Metafile metafile,
   PointF destPoint,
   RectangleF srcRect,
   GraphicsUnit unit,
   Graphics.EnumerateMetafileProc callback,
   IntPtr callbackData,
   ImageAttributes imageAttr
);
```
[C++]
```
public: void EnumerateMetafile(
   Metafile* metafile,
   PointF destPoint,
   RectangleF srcRect,
   GraphicsUnit unit,
   Graphics.EnumerateMetafileProc* callback,
   IntPtr callbackData,
   ImageAttributes* imageAttr
);
```
[JScript]
```
public function EnumerateMetafile(
   metafile : Metafile,
   destPoint : PointF,
   srcRect : RectangleF,
   unit : GraphicsUnit,
   callback : Graphics.EnumerateMetafileProc,
   callbackData : IntPtr,
   imageAttr : ImageAttributes
);
```

Parameters

metafile

Metafile object to enumerate.

destPoint

PointF structure that specifies the location of the upper-left corner of the drawn metafile.

srcRect

RectangleF structure that specifies the portion of the metafile, relative to its upper-left corner, to draw.

unit

Member of the **GraphicsUnit** enumeration that specifies the unit of measure used to determine the portion of the metafile that the rectangle specified by the *srcRect* parameter contains.

callback

Graphics.EnumerateMetafileProc delegate that specifies the method to which the metafile records are sent.

callbackData

Internal pointer that is required, but ignored. You can pass **IntPtr.Zero** for this parameter.

imageAttr

ImageAttributes object that specifies image attribute information for the drawn image.

Return Value

This method does not return a value.

Remarks

This method enumerates the records contained in the specified metafile. Each record is individually sent to a callback method specified by the *callback* parameter. Typically, the callback method calls the **PlayRecord** method to "play back", or draw, the record.

If the callback method calls **Metafile.PlayRecord**, it must do so by calling the **PlayRecord** method of the specific **Metafile** object that is being enumerated.

Any drawing that takes place outside of the rectangle specified by the *srcRect* parameter is ignored.

The image attributes specified by the *imageAttr* parameter replace those specified when the metafile was written.

Example

For an example see **EnumerateMetafile**.

Requirements

Platforms: Windows 98, Windows NT 4.0, Windows Millennium Edition, Windows 2000, Windows XP Home Edition, Windows XP Professional, Windows Server 2003 family

Graphics.EnumerateMetafile Method (Metafile, PointF[], RectangleF, GraphicsUnit, Graphics.EnumerateMetafileProc, IntPtr, ImageAttributes)

Sends the records in a selected rectangle from a **Metafile** object, one at a time, to a callback method for display in a specified parallelogram using specified image attributes.

[Visual Basic]
```
Overloads Public Sub EnumerateMetafile( _
   ByVal metafile As Metafile, _
   ByVal destPoints() As PointF, _
   ByVal srcRect As RectangleF, _
   ByVal unit As GraphicsUnit, _
   ByVal callback As Graphics.EnumerateMetafileProc, _
   ByVal callbackData As IntPtr, _
   ByVal imageAttr As ImageAttributes _
)
```
[C#]
```
public void EnumerateMetafile(
   Metafile metafile,
   PointF[] destPoints,
   RectangleF srcRect,
   GraphicsUnit unit,
   Graphics.EnumerateMetafileProc callback,
   IntPtr callbackData,
   ImageAttributes imageAttr
);
```
[C++]
```
public: void EnumerateMetafile(
   Metafile* metafile,
   PointF destPoints[],
   RectangleF srcRect,
   GraphicsUnit unit,
   Graphics.EnumerateMetafileProc* callback,
   IntPtr callbackData,
   ImageAttributes* imageAttr
);
```
[JScript]
```
public function EnumerateMetafile(
   metafile : Metafile,
   destPoints : PointF[],
   srcRect : RectangleF,
   unit : GraphicsUnit,
   callback : Graphics.EnumerateMetafileProc,
   callbackData : IntPtr,
   imageAttr : ImageAttributes
);
```

Parameters

metafile
: **Metafile** object to enumerate.

destPoints
: Array of three **PointF** structures that define a parallelogram that determines the size and location of the drawn metafile.

srcRect
: **RectangleF** structure that specifies the portion of the metafile, relative to its upper-left corner, to draw.

unit
: Member of the **GraphicsUnit** enumeration that specifies the unit of measure used to determine the portion of the metafile that the rectangle specified by the *srcRect* parameter contains.

callback
: **Graphics.EnumerateMetafileProc** delegate that specifies the method to which the metafile records are sent.

callbackData
: Internal pointer that is required, but ignored. You can pass **IntPtr.Zero** for this parameter.

imageAttr
: **ImageAttributes** object that specifies image attribute information for the drawn image.

Return Value

This method does not return a value.

Remarks

This method enumerates the records contained in the specified metafile. Each record is individually sent to a callback method specified by the *callback* parameter. Typically, the callback method calls the **PlayRecord** method to "play back", or draw, the record.

If the callback method calls **Metafile.PlayRecord**, it must do so by calling the **PlayRecord** method of the specific **Metafile** object that is being enumerated.

The *destPoints* parameter specifies three points of a parallelogram. The three **PointF** structures represent the upper-left, upper-right, and lower-left corners of the parallelogram. The fourth point is extrapolated from the first three to form a parallelogram. The drawn metafile is scaled and sheared to fit the parallelogram.

Any drawing that takes place outside of the rectangle specified by the *srcRect* parameter is ignored.

The image attributes specified by the *imageAttr* parameter replace those specified when the metafile was written.

Example

For an example see **EnumerateMetafile**.

Requirements

Platforms: Windows 98, Windows NT 4.0, Windows Millennium Edition, Windows 2000, Windows XP Home Edition, Windows XP Professional, Windows Server 2003 family

Graphics.EnumerateMetafile Method (Metafile, Rectangle, Rectangle, GraphicsUnit, Graphics.EnumerateMetafileProc, IntPtr, ImageAttributes)

Sends the records of a selected rectangle from a **Metafile** object, one at a time, to a callback method for display in a specified rectangle using specified image attributes.

[Visual Basic]
```
Overloads Public Sub EnumerateMetafile( _
   ByVal metafile As Metafile, _
   ByVal destRect As Rectangle, _
   ByVal srcRect As Rectangle, _
   ByVal unit As GraphicsUnit, _
   ByVal callback As Graphics.EnumerateMetafileProc, _
   ByVal callbackData As IntPtr, _
   ByVal imageAttr As ImageAttributes _
)
```
[C#]
```
public void EnumerateMetafile(
   Metafile metafile,
   Rectangle destRect,
   Rectangle srcRect,
   GraphicsUnit unit,
   Graphics.EnumerateMetafileProc callback,
   IntPtr callbackData,
   ImageAttributes imageAttr
);
```
[C++]
```
public: void EnumerateMetafile(
   Metafile* metafile,
   Rectangle destRect,
   Rectangle srcRect,
   GraphicsUnit unit,
   Graphics.EnumerateMetafileProc* callback,
   IntPtr callbackData,
   ImageAttributes* imageAttr
);
```
[JScript]
```
public function EnumerateMetafile(
   metafile : Metafile,
   destRect : Rectangle,
   srcRect : Rectangle,
   unit : GraphicsUnit,
   callback : Graphics.EnumerateMetafileProc,
   callbackData : IntPtr,
   imageAttr : ImageAttributes
);
```

Parameters

metafile

Metafile object to enumerate.

destRect

Rectangle structure that specifies the location and size of the drawn metafile.

srcRect

Rectangle structure that specifies the portion of the metafile, relative to its upper-left corner, to draw.

unit

Member of the **GraphicsUnit** enumeration that specifies the unit of measure used to determine the portion of the metafile that the rectangle specified by the *srcRect* parameter contains.

callback

Graphics.EnumerateMetafileProc delegate that specifies the method to which the metafile records are sent.

callbackData

Internal pointer that is required, but ignored. You can pass **IntPtr.Zero** for this parameter.

imageAttr

ImageAttributes object that specifies image attribute information for the drawn image.

Return Value

This method does not return a value.

Remarks

This method enumerates the records contained in the specified metafile. Each record is individually sent to a callback method specified by the *callback* parameter. Typically, the callback method calls the **PlayRecord** method to "play back", or draw, the record.

If the callback method calls **Metafile.PlayRecord**, it must do so by calling the **PlayRecord** method of the specific **Metafile** object that is being enumerated.

Any drawing that takes place outside of the rectangle specified by the *srcRect* parameter is ignored.

The image attributes specified by the *imageAttr* parameter replace those specified when the metafile was written.

Example

For an example see **EnumerateMetafile**.

Requirements

Platforms: Windows 98, Windows NT 4.0, Windows Millennium Edition, Windows 2000, Windows XP Home Edition, Windows XP Professional, Windows Server 2003 family

Graphics.EnumerateMetafile Method (Metafile, RectangleF, RectangleF, GraphicsUnit, Graphics.EnumerateMetafileProc, IntPtr, ImageAttributes)

Sends the records of a selected rectangle from a **Metafile** object, one at a time, to a callback method for display in a specified rectangle using specified image attributes.

[Visual Basic]
```
Overloads Public Sub EnumerateMetafile( _
   ByVal metafile As Metafile, _
   ByVal destRect As RectangleF, _
   ByVal srcRect As RectangleF, _
   ByVal unit As GraphicsUnit, _
   ByVal callback As Graphics.EnumerateMetafileProc, _
   ByVal callbackData As IntPtr, _
   ByVal imageAttr As ImageAttributes _
)
```
[C#]
```
public void EnumerateMetafile(
   Metafile metafile,
   RectangleF destRect,
   RectangleF srcRect,
   GraphicsUnit unit,
   Graphics.EnumerateMetafileProc callback,
   IntPtr callbackData,
   ImageAttributes imageAttr
);
```

```
[C++]
public: void EnumerateMetafile(
   Metafile* metafile,
   RectangleF destRect,
   RectangleF srcRect,
   GraphicsUnit unit,
   Graphics.EnumerateMetafileProc* callback,
   IntPtr callbackData,
   ImageAttributes* imageAttr
);
[JScript]
public function EnumerateMetafile(
   metafile : Metafile,
   destRect : RectangleF,
   srcRect : RectangleF,
   unit : GraphicsUnit,
   callback : Graphics.EnumerateMetafileProc,
   callbackData : IntPtr,
   imageAttr : ImageAttributes
);
```

Parameters

metafile
: **Metafile** object to enumerate.

destRect
: **RectangleF** structure that specifies the location and size of the drawn metafile.

srcRect
: **RectangleF** structure that specifies the portion of the metafile, relative to its upper-left corner, to draw.

unit
: Member of the **GraphicsUnit** enumeration that specifies the unit of measure used to determine the portion of the metafile that the rectangle specified by the *srcRect* parameter contains.

callback
: **Graphics.EnumerateMetafileProc** delegate that specifies the method to which the metafile records are sent.

callbackData
: Internal pointer that is required, but ignored. You can pass **IntPtr.Zero** for this parameter.

imageAttr
: **ImageAttributes** object that specifies image attribute information for the drawn image.

Return Value

This method does not return a value.

Remarks

This method enumerates the records contained in the specified metafile. Each record is individually sent to a callback method specified by the *callback* parameter. Typically, the callback method calls the **PlayRecord** method to "play back", or draw, the record.

If the callback method calls **Metafile.PlayRecord**, it must do so by calling the **PlayRecord** method of the specific **Metafile** object that is being enumerated.

Any drawing that takes place outside of the rectangle specified by the *srcRect* parameter is ignored.

The image attributes specified by the *imageAttr* parameter replace those specified when the metafile was written.

Example

For an example see **EnumerateMetafile**.

Requirements

Platforms: Windows 98, Windows NT 4.0, Windows Millennium Edition, Windows 2000, Windows XP Home Edition, Windows XP Professional, Windows Server 2003 family

Graphics.ExcludeClip Method

Updates the clip region of this **Graphics** object to exclude the area specified by a **Rectangle** structure.

Overload List

Updates the clip region of this **Graphics** object to exclude the area specified by a **Rectangle** structure.

[Visual Basic] **Overloads Public Sub ExcludeClip(Rectangle)**

[C#] **public void ExcludeClip(Rectangle);**

[C++] **public: void ExcludeClip(Rectangle);**

[JScript] **public function ExcludeClip(Rectangle);**

Updates the clip region of this **Graphics** object to exclude the area specified by a **Region** object.

[Visual Basic] **Overloads Public Sub ExcludeClip(Region)**

[C#] **public void ExcludeClip(Region);**

[C++] **public: void ExcludeClip(Region*);**

[JScript] **public function ExcludeClip(Region);**

Example

[Visual Basic, C#] The following example is designed for use with Windows Forms, and it requires **PaintEventArgs** *e*, which is a parameter of the **Paint** event handler. The code performs the following actions:

- Creates a 100 pixel by 100 pixel rectangle whose upper-left corner is at the coordinate (100, 100).
- Sets the clipping region to exclude the rectangle.
- Fills a 300 pixel by 300 pixel rectangle whose upper-left corner is at the coordinate (0, 0) with a solid blue brush.

[Visual Basic, C#] The result is a blue rectangle with a square area toward its lower-right corner missing.

> [Visual Basic, C#] **Note** This example shows how to use one of the overloaded versions of **ExcludeClip**. For other examples that might be available, see the individual overload topics.

```
[Visual Basic]
Public Sub ExcludeClipRegion(e As PaintEventArgs)
' Create rectangle for exclusion.
Dim excludeRect As New Rectangle(100, 100, 200, 200)
' Set clipping region to exclude rectangle.
e.Graphics.ExcludeClip(excludeRect)
' Fill large rectangle to show clipping region.
e.Graphics.FillRectangle(New SolidBrush(Color.Blue), 0, 0, _
300, 300)
End Sub
```

```
[C#]
public void ExcludeClipRegion(PaintEventArgs e)
{
// Create rectangle for exclusion.
Rectangle excludeRect = new Rectangle(100, 100, 200, 200);
// Set clipping region to exclude rectangle.
e.Graphics.ExcludeClip(excludeRect);
// Fill large rectangle to show clipping region.
e.Graphics.FillRectangle(new SolidBrush(Color.Blue), 0, 0, 300, 300);
}
```

Graphics.ExcludeClip Method (Rectangle)

Updates the clip region of this **Graphics** object to exclude the area specified by a **Rectangle** structure.

```
[Visual Basic]
Overloads Public Sub ExcludeClip( _
   ByVal rect As Rectangle _
)
[C#]
public void ExcludeClip(
   Rectangle rect
);
[C++]
public: void ExcludeClip(
   Rectangle rect
);
[JScript]
public function ExcludeClip(
   rect : Rectangle
);
```

Parameters

rect

Rectangle structure that specifies the rectangle to exclude from the clip region.

Return Value

This method does not return a value.

Remarks

This method excludes the area specified by the *rect* parameter from the current clip region and assigns the resulting area to the **Clip** property of this **Graphics** object.

Example

[Visual Basic, C#] The following example is designed for use with Windows Forms, and it requires **PaintEventArgs** *e*, which is a parameter of the **Paint** event handler. The code performs the following actions:

- Creates a 100 pixel by 100 pixel rectangle whose upper-left corner is at the coordinate (100, 100).
- Creates a region defined by the rectangle.
- Sets the clipping region to exclude the rectangular region.
- Fills a 300 pixel by 300 pixel rectangle whose upper-left corner is at the coordinate (0, 0) with a solid blue brush.

[Visual Basic, C#] The result is a blue rectangle with a square region toward its lower-right corner missing.

```
[Visual Basic]
Public Sub ExcludeClipRectangle(e As PaintEventArgs)
' Create rectangle for region.
Dim excludeRect As New Rectangle(100, 100, 200, 200)
' Create region for exclusion.
Dim excludeRegion As New [Region](excludeRect)
' Set clipping region to exclude region.
e.Graphics.ExcludeClip(excludeRegion)
' Fill large rectangle to show clipping region.
e.Graphics.FillRectangle(New SolidBrush(Color.Blue), 0, 0, _
300, 300)
End Sub
```

```
[C#]
public void ExcludeClipRectangle(PaintEventArgs e)
{
// Create rectangle for region.
Rectangle excludeRect = new Rectangle(100, 100, 200, 200);
// Create region for exclusion.
Region excludeRegion = new Region(excludeRect);
// Set clipping region to exclude region.
e.Graphics.ExcludeClip(excludeRegion);
// Fill large rectangle to show clipping region.
e.Graphics.FillRectangle(new SolidBrush(Color.Blue), 0, 0, 300, 300);
}
```

Requirements

Platforms: Windows 98, Windows NT 4.0, Windows Millennium Edition, Windows 2000, Windows XP Home Edition, Windows XP Professional, Windows Server 2003 family

Graphics.ExcludeClip Method (Region)

Updates the clip region of this **Graphics** object to exclude the area specified by a **Region** object.

```
[Visual Basic]
Overloads Public Sub ExcludeClip( _
   ByVal region As Region _
)
[C#]
public void ExcludeClip(
   Region region
);
[C++]
public: void ExcludeClip(
   Region* region
);
[JScript]
public function ExcludeClip(
   region : Region
);
```

Parameters

region

Region object that specifies the region to exclude from the clip region.

Return Value

This method does not return a value.

Remarks

This method excludes the area specified by the *region* parameter from the current clip region and assigns the resulting area to the **Clip** property of this **Graphics** object.

Example

[Visual Basic, C#] The following example is designed for use with Windows Forms, and it requires **PaintEventArgs** *e*, which is a parameter of the **Paint** event handler. The code performs the following actions:

- Creates a 100 pixel by 100 pixel rectangle whose upper-left corner is at the coordinate (100, 100).
- Sets the clipping region to exclude the rectangle.
- Fills a 300 pixel by 300 pixel rectangle whose upper-left corner is at the coordinate (0, 0) with a solid blue brush.

[Visual Basic, C#] The result is a blue rectangle with a square area toward its lower-right corner missing.

[Visual Basic]
```
Public Sub ExcludeClipRegion(e As PaintEventArgs)
' Create rectangle for exclusion.
Dim excludeRect As New Rectangle(100, 100, 200, 200)
' Set clipping region to exclude rectangle.
e.Graphics.ExcludeClip(excludeRect)
' Fill large rectangle to show clipping region.
e.Graphics.FillRectangle(New SolidBrush(Color.Blue), 0, 0, _
300, 300)
End Sub
```

[C#]
```
public void ExcludeClipRegion(PaintEventArgs e)
{
// Create rectangle for exclusion.
Rectangle excludeRect = new Rectangle(100, 100, 200, 200);
// Set clipping region to exclude rectangle.
e.Graphics.ExcludeClip(excludeRect);
// Fill large rectangle to show clipping region.
e.Graphics.FillRectangle(new SolidBrush(Color.Blue), 0, 0, 300, 300);
}
```

Requirements

Platforms: Windows 98, Windows NT 4.0, Windows Millennium Edition, Windows 2000, Windows XP Home Edition, Windows XP Professional, Windows Server 2003 family

Graphics.FillClosedCurve Method

Fills the interior a closed cardinal spline curve defined by an array of **Point** structures.

Overload List

Fills the interior a closed cardinal spline curve defined by an array of **Point** structures.

[Visual Basic] **Overloads Public Sub FillClosedCurve(Brush, Point())**

[C#] **public void FillClosedCurve(Brush, Point[]);**

[C++] **public: void FillClosedCurve(Brush*, Point[]);**

[JScript] **public function FillClosedCurve(Brush, Point[]);**

Fills the interior a closed cardinal spline curve defined by an array of **PointF** structures.

[Visual Basic] **Overloads Public Sub FillClosedCurve(Brush, PointF())**

[C#] **public void FillClosedCurve(Brush, PointF[]);**

[C++] **public: void FillClosedCurve(Brush*, PointF[]);**

[JScript] **public function FillClosedCurve(Brush, PointF[]);**

Fills the interior a closed cardinal spline curve defined by an array of **Point** structures using the specified fill mode.

[Visual Basic] **Overloads Public Sub FillClosedCurve(Brush, Point(), FillMode)**

[C#] **public void FillClosedCurve(Brush, Point[], FillMode);**

[C++] **public: void FillClosedCurve(Brush*, Point[], FillMode);**

[JScript] **public function FillClosedCurve(Brush, Point[], FillMode);**

Fills the interior a closed cardinal spline curve defined by an array of **PointF** structures using the specified fill mode.

[Visual Basic] **Overloads Public Sub FillClosedCurve(Brush, PointF(), FillMode)**

[C#] **public void FillClosedCurve(Brush, PointF[], FillMode);**

[C++] **public: void FillClosedCurve(Brush*, PointF[], FillMode);**

[JScript] **public function FillClosedCurve(Brush, PointF[], FillMode);**

Fills the interior a closed cardinal spline curve defined by an array of **Point** structures using the specified fill mode and tension.

[Visual Basic] **Overloads Public Sub FillClosedCurve(Brush, Point(), FillMode, Single)**

[C#] **public void FillClosedCurve(Brush, Point[], FillMode, float);**

[C++] **public: void FillClosedCurve(Brush*, Point[], FillMode, float);**

[JScript] **public function FillClosedCurve(Brush, Point[], FillMode, float);**

Fills the interior a closed cardinal spline curve defined by an array of **PointF** structures using the specified fill mode and tension.

[Visual Basic] **Overloads Public Sub FillClosedCurve(Brush, PointF(), FillMode, Single)**

[C#] **public void FillClosedCurve(Brush, PointF[], FillMode, float);**

[C++] **public: void FillClosedCurve(Brush*, PointF[], FillMode, float);**

[JScript] **public function FillClosedCurve(Brush, PointF[], FillMode, float);**

Example

[Visual Basic, C#] The following example is designed for use with Windows Forms, and it requires **PaintEventArgs** *e*, which is a parameter of the **Paint** event handler. The code performs the following actions:

- Creates a solid red brush.
- Creates an array of four points to define a spline.
- Sets the fill mode to **FillMode.Winding**.
- Sets the tension to 1.0.
- Fills the curve on the screen.

> [Visual Basic, C#] **Note** This example shows how to use one of the overloaded versions of **FillClosedCurve**. For other examples that might be available, see the individual overload topics.

[Visual Basic]
```
Public Sub FillClosedCurvePointFFillModeTension(e As PaintEventArgs)
' Create solid brush.
Dim redBrush As New SolidBrush(Color.Red)
' Create array of points for curve.
Dim point1 As New PointF(100F, 100F)
Dim point2 As New PointF(200F, 50F)
Dim point3 As New PointF(250F, 200F)
Dim point4 As New PointF(50F, 150F)
Dim points As PointF() = {point1, point2, point3, point4}
' Set fill mode.
Dim newFillMode As FillMode = FillMode.Winding
' Set tension.
Dim tension As Single = 1F
' Fill curve on screen.
e.Graphics.FillClosedCurve(redBrush, points, newFillMode, tension)
End Sub
```

[C#]

```
public void FillClosedCurvePointFFillModeTension(PaintEventArgs e)
{
// Create solid brush.
SolidBrush redBrush = new SolidBrush(Color.Red);
// Create array of points for curve.
PointF point1 = new PointF(100.0F, 100.0F);
PointF point2 = new PointF(200.0F,  50.0F);
PointF point3 = new PointF(250.0F, 200.0F);
PointF point4 = new PointF( 50.0F, 150.0F);
PointF[] points = {point1, point2, point3, point4};
// Set fill mode.
FillMode newFillMode = FillMode.Winding;
// Set tension.
float tension = 1.0F;
// Fill curve on screen.
e.Graphics.FillClosedCurve(redBrush, points, newFillMode, tension);
}
```

Graphics.FillClosedCurve Method (Brush, Point[])

Fills the interior a closed cardinal spline curve defined by an array of **Point** structures.

[Visual Basic]

```
Overloads Public Sub FillClosedCurve( _
   ByVal brush As Brush, _
   ByVal points() As Point _
)
```

[C#]

```
public void FillClosedCurve(
   Brush brush,
   Point[] points
);
```

[C++]

```
public: void FillClosedCurve(
   Brush* brush,
   Point points[]
);
```

[JScript]

```
public function FillClosedCurve(
   brush : Brush,
   points : Point[]
);
```

Parameters

brush

Brush object that determines the characteristics of the fill.

points

Array of **Point** structures that define the spline.

Return Value

This method does not return a value.

Remarks

This method fills the interior of a closed cardinal spline that passes through each point in the array. If the last point does not match the first point, an additional curve segment is added from the last point to the first point to close it.

The array of points must contain at least four **Point** structures.

This method uses a default tension of 0.5.

Example

[Visual Basic, C#] The following example is designed for use with Windows Forms, and it requires **PaintEventArgs** *e*, which is a parameter of the **Paint** event handler. The code performs the following actions:

- Creates a solid red brush.
- Creates an array of four points to define a spline.
- Fills the curve on the screen.

[Visual Basic, C#] The curve has a default tension of 0.5.

[Visual Basic]

```
Public Sub FillClosedCurvePoint(e As PaintEventArgs)
' Create solid brush.
Dim redBrush As New SolidBrush(Color.Red)
'Create array of points for curve.
Dim point1 As New Point(100, 100)
Dim point2 As New Point(200, 50)
Dim point3 As New Point(250, 200)
Dim point4 As New Point(50, 150)
Dim points As Point() =  {point1, point2, point3, point4}
' Fill curve on screen.
e.Graphics.FillClosedCurve(redBrush, points)
End Sub
```

[C#]

```
public void FillClosedCurvePoint(PaintEventArgs e)
{
// Create solid brush.
SolidBrush redBrush = new SolidBrush(Color.Red);
//Create array of points for curve.
Point point1 = new Point(100, 100);
Point point2 = new Point(200,  50);
Point point3 = new Point(250, 200);
Point point4 = new Point( 50, 150);
Point[] points = {point1, point2, point3, point4};
// Fill curve on screen.
e.Graphics.FillClosedCurve(redBrush, points);
}
```

Requirements

Platforms: Windows 98, Windows NT 4.0, Windows Millennium Edition, Windows 2000, Windows XP Home Edition, Windows XP Professional, Windows Server 2003 family

Graphics.FillClosedCurve Method (Brush, PointF[])

Fills the interior a closed cardinal spline curve defined by an array of **PointF** structures.

[Visual Basic]

```
Overloads Public Sub FillClosedCurve( _
   ByVal brush As Brush, _
   ByVal points() As PointF _
)
```

[C#]

```
public void FillClosedCurve(
   Brush brush,
   PointF[] points
);
```

[C++]

```
public: void FillClosedCurve(
   Brush* brush,
   PointF points[]
);
```

[JScript]

```
public function FillClosedCurve(
   brush : Brush,
   points : PointF[]
);
```

Parameters

brush

Brush object that determines the characteristics of the fill.

points

Array of **PointF** structures that define the spline.

Return Value

This method does not return a value.

Remarks

This method fills the interior of a closed cardinal spline that passes through each point in the array. If the last point does not match the first point, an additional curve segment is added from the last point to the first point to close it.

The array of points must contain at least four **PointF** structures.

This method uses a default tension of 0.5.

Example

[Visual Basic, C#] The following example is designed for use with Windows Forms, and it requires **PaintEventArgs** *e*, which is a parameter of the **Paint** event handler. The code performs the following actions:

- Creates a solid red brush.
- Creates an array of four points to define a spline.
- Fills the curve on the screen.

[Visual Basic, C#] The curve has a default tension of 0.5.

[Visual Basic]
```
Public Sub FillClosedCurvePointF(e As PaintEventArgs)
' Create solid brush.
Dim redBrush As New SolidBrush(Color.Red)
'Create array of points for curve.
Dim point1 As New PointF(100F, 100F)
Dim point2 As New PointF(200F, 50F)
Dim point3 As New PointF(250F, 200F)
Dim point4 As New PointF(50F, 150F)
Dim points As PointF() =  {point1, point2, point3, point4}
' Fill curve on screen.
e.Graphics.FillClosedCurve(redBrush, points)
End Sub
```

[C#]
```
public void FillClosedCurvePointF(PaintEventArgs e)
{
// Create solid brush.
SolidBrush redBrush = new SolidBrush(Color.Red);
//Create array of points for curve.
PointF point1 = new PointF(100.0F, 100.0F);
PointF point2 = new PointF(200.0F,  50.0F);
PointF point3 = new PointF(250.0F, 200.0F);
PointF point4 = new PointF( 50.0F, 150.0F);
PointF[] points = {point1, point2, point3, point4};
// Fill curve on screen.
e.Graphics.FillClosedCurve(redBrush, points);
}
```

Requirements

Platforms: Windows 98, Windows NT 4.0, Windows Millennium Edition, Windows 2000, Windows XP Home Edition, Windows XP Professional, Windows Server 2003 family

Graphics.FillClosedCurve Method (Brush, Point[], FillMode)

Fills the interior a closed cardinal spline curve defined by an array of **Point** structures using the specified fill mode.

[Visual Basic]
```
Overloads Public Sub FillClosedCurve( _
   ByVal brush As Brush, _
   ByVal points() As Point, _
   ByVal fillmode As FillMode _
)
```
[C#]
```
public void FillClosedCurve(
   Brush brush,
   Point[] points,
   FillMode fillmode
);
```
[C++]
```
public: void FillClosedCurve(
   Brush* brush,
   Point points[],
   FillMode fillmode
);
```
[JScript]
```
public function FillClosedCurve(
   brush : Brush,
   points : Point[],
   fillmode : FillMode
);
```

Parameters

brush

Brush object that determines the characteristics of the fill.

points

Array of **Point** structures that define the spline.

fillmode

Member of the **FillMode** enumeration that determines how the curve is filled.

Return Value

This method does not return a value.

Remarks

This method fills the interior of a closed cardinal spline that passes through each point in the array. If the last point does not match the first point, an additional curve segment is added from the last point to the first point to close it.

The array of points must contain at least four **Point** structures.

This method uses a default tension of 0.5.

Example

[Visual Basic, C#] The following example is designed for use with Windows Forms, and it requires **PaintEventArgs** *e*, which is a parameter of the **Paint** event handler. The code performs the following actions:

- Creates a solid red brush.
- Creates an array of four points to define a spline.
- Sets the fill mode to **FillMode.Winding**.
- Fills the curve on the screen.

[Visual Basic, C#] The curve has a default tension of 0.5.

[Visual Basic]
```
Public Sub FillClosedCurvePointFillMode(e As PaintEventArgs)
' Create solid brush.
Dim redBrush As New SolidBrush(Color.Red)
'Create array of points for curve.
Dim point1 As New Point(100, 100)
Dim point2 As New Point(200, 50)
Dim point3 As New Point(250, 200)
Dim point4 As New Point(50, 150)
Dim points As Point() = {point1, point2, point3, point4}
' Set fill mode.
Dim newFillMode As FillMode = FillMode.Winding
' Fill curve on screen.
e.Graphics.FillClosedCurve(redBrush, points, newFillMode)
End Sub
```

[C#]
```
public void FillClosedCurvePointFillMode(PaintEventArgs e)
{
// Create solid brush.
SolidBrush redBrush = new SolidBrush(Color.Red);
//Create array of points for curve.
Point point1 = new Point(100, 100);
Point point2 = new Point(200,  50);
Point point3 = new Point(250, 200);
Point point4 = new Point( 50, 150);
Point[] points = {point1, point2, point3, point4};
// Set fill mode.
FillMode newFillMode = FillMode.Winding;
// Fill curve on screen.
e.Graphics.FillClosedCurve(redBrush, points, newFillMode);
}
```

Requirements

Platforms: Windows 98, Windows NT 4.0, Windows Millennium Edition, Windows 2000, Windows XP Home Edition, Windows XP Professional, Windows Server 2003 family

Graphics.FillClosedCurve Method (Brush, PointF[], FillMode)

Fills the interior a closed cardinal spline curve defined by an array of **PointF** structures using the specified fill mode.

[Visual Basic]
```
Overloads Public Sub FillClosedCurve( _
   ByVal brush As Brush, _
   ByVal points() As PointF, _
   ByVal fillmode As FillMode _
)
```
[C#]
```
public void FillClosedCurve(
   Brush brush,
   PointF[] points,
   FillMode fillmode
);
```
[C++]
```
public: void FillClosedCurve(
   Brush* brush,
   PointF points[],
   FillMode fillmode
);
```
[JScript]
```
public function FillClosedCurve(
   brush : Brush,
   points : PointF[],
   fillmode : FillMode
);
```

Parameters

brush

Brush object that determines the characteristics of the fill.

points

Array of **PointF** structures that define the spline.

fillmode

Member of the **FillMode** enumeration that determines how the curve is filled.

Return Value

This method does not return a value.

Remarks

This method fills the interior of a closed cardinal spline that passes through each point in the array. If the last point does not match the first point, an additional curve segment is added from the last point to the first point to close it.

The array of points must contain at least four **Point** structures.

This method uses a default tension of 0.5.

Example

[Visual Basic, C#] The following example is designed for use with Windows Forms, and it requires **PaintEventArgs** *e*, which is a parameter of the **Paint** event handler. The code performs the following actions:

- Creates a solid red brush.
- Creates an array of four points to define a spline.
- Sets the fill mode to **FillMode.Winding**.
- Fills the curve on the screen.

[Visual Basic, C#] The curve has a default tension of 0.5.

[Visual Basic]
```
Public Sub FillClosedCurvePointFFillMode(e As PaintEventArgs)
' Create solid brush.
Dim redBrush As New SolidBrush(Color.Red)
' Create array of points for curve.
Dim point1 As New PointF(100F, 100F)
Dim point2 As New PointF(200F, 50F)
Dim point3 As New PointF(250F, 200F)
Dim point4 As New PointF(50F, 150F)
Dim points As PointF() = {point1, point2, point3, point4}
' Set fill mode.
Dim newFillMode As FillMode = FillMode.Winding
' Fill curve on screen.
e.Graphics.FillClosedCurve(redBrush, points, newFillMode)
End Sub
```

[C#]
```
public void FillClosedCurvePointFFillMode(PaintEventArgs e)
{
// Create solid brush.
SolidBrush redBrush = new SolidBrush(Color.Red);
// Create array of points for curve.
PointF point1 = new PointF(100.0F, 100.0F);
PointF point2 = new PointF(200.0F,  50.0F);
PointF point3 = new PointF(250.0F, 200.0F);
PointF point4 = new PointF( 50.0F, 150.0F);
PointF[] points = {point1, point2, point3, point4};
// Set fill mode.
FillMode newFillMode = FillMode.Winding;
// Fill curve on screen.
e.Graphics.FillClosedCurve(redBrush, points, newFillMode);
}
```

Requirements

Platforms: Windows 98, Windows NT 4.0, Windows Millennium Edition, Windows 2000, Windows XP Home Edition, Windows XP Professional, Windows Server 2003 family

Graphics.FillClosedCurve Method (Brush, Point[], FillMode, Single)

Fills the interior a closed cardinal spline curve defined by an array of **Point** structures using the specified fill mode and tension.

[Visual Basic]
```
Overloads Public Sub FillClosedCurve( _
   ByVal brush As Brush, _
   ByVal points() As Point, _
   ByVal fillmode As FillMode, _
   ByVal tension As Single _
)
```
[C#]
```
public void FillClosedCurve(
   Brush brush,
   Point[] points,
   FillMode fillmode,
   float tension
);
```
[C++]
```
public: void FillClosedCurve(
   Brush* brush,
   Point points[],
   FillMode fillmode,
   float tension
);
```
[JScript]
```
public function FillClosedCurve(
   brush : Brush,
   points : Point[],
   fillmode : FillMode,
   tension : float
);
```

Parameters

brush
  Brush object that determines the characteristics of the fill.

points
  Array of **Point** structures that define the spline.

fillmode
  Member of the **FillMode** enumeration that determines how the curve is filled.

tension
  Value greater than or equal to 0.0F that specifies the tension of the curve.

Return Value

This method does not return a value.

Remarks

This method fills the interior of a closed cardinal spline that passes through each point in the array. If the last point does not match the first point, an additional curve segment is added from the last point to the first point to close it.

The array of points must contain at least four **Point** structures.

The *tension* parameter determines the shape of the spline. If the value of the *tension* parameter is 0.0F, this method draws straight line segments to connect the points. Usually, the *tension* parameter is less than or equal to 1.0F. Values over 1.0F produce unusual results.

Example

[Visual Basic, C#] The following example is designed for use with Windows Forms, and it requires **PaintEventArgs** *e*, which is a parameter of the **Paint** event handler. The code performs the following actions:

- Creates a solid red brush.
- Creates an array of four points to define a spline.
- Sets the fill mode to **FillMode.Winding**.
- Sets the tension to 1.0.
- Fills the curve on the screen.

[Visual Basic]
```
Public Sub FillClosedCurvePointFillModeTension(e As PaintEventArgs)
' Create solid brush.
Dim redBrush As New SolidBrush(Color.Red)
' Create array of points for curve.
Dim point1 As New Point(100, 100)
Dim point2 As New Point(200, 50)
Dim point3 As New Point(250, 200)
Dim point4 As New Point(50, 150)
Dim points As Point() =  {point1, point2, point3, point4}
' Set fill mode.
Dim newFillMode As FillMode = FillMode.Winding
' Set tension.
Dim tension As Single = 1F
' Fill curve on screen.
e.Graphics.FillClosedCurve(redBrush, points, newFillMode, tension)
End Sub
```

[C#]
```
public void FillClosedCurvePointFillModeTension(PaintEventArgs e)
{
// Create solid brush.
SolidBrush redBrush = new SolidBrush(Color.Red);
// Create array of points for curve.
Point point1 = new Point(100, 100);
Point point2 = new Point(200,  50);
Point point3 = new Point(250, 200);
Point point4 = new Point( 50, 150);
Point[] points = {point1, point2, point3, point4};
// Set fill mode.
FillMode newFillMode = FillMode.Winding;
// Set tension.
float tension = 1.0F;
// Fill curve on screen.
e.Graphics.FillClosedCurve(redBrush, points, newFillMode, tension);
}
```

Requirements

Platforms: Windows 98, Windows NT 4.0, Windows Millennium Edition, Windows 2000, Windows XP Home Edition, Windows XP Professional, Windows Server 2003 family

Graphics.FillClosedCurve Method (Brush, PointF[], FillMode, Single)

Fills the interior a closed cardinal spline curve defined by an array of **PointF** structures using the specified fill mode and tension.

```
[Visual Basic]
Overloads Public Sub FillClosedCurve( _
   ByVal brush As Brush, _
   ByVal points() As PointF, _
   ByVal fillmode As FillMode, _
   ByVal tension As Single _
)
[C#]
public void FillClosedCurve(
   Brush brush,
   PointF[] points,
   FillMode fillmode,
   float tension
);
[C++]
public: void FillClosedCurve(
   Brush* brush,
   PointF points[],
   FillMode fillmode,
   float tension
);
[JScript]
public function FillClosedCurve(
   brush : Brush,
   points : PointF[],
   fillmode : FillMode,
   tension : float
);
```

Parameters

brush

A **Brush** object that determines the characteristics of the fill.

points

Array of **PointF** structures that define the spline.

fillmode

Member of the **FillMode** enumeration that determines how the curve is filled.

tension

Value greater than or equal to 0.0F that specifies the tension of the curve.

Return Value

This method does not return a value.

Remarks

This method fills the interior of a closed cardinal spline that passes through each point in the array. If the last point does not match the first point, an additional curve segment is added from the last point to the first point to close it.

The array of points must contain at least four **Point** structures.

The *tension* parameter determines the shape of the spline. If the value of the *tension* parameter is 0.0F, this method draws straight line segments to connect the points. Usually, the *tension* parameter is less than or equal to 1.0F. Values over 1.0F produce unusual results.

Example

[Visual Basic, C#] The following example is designed for use with Windows Forms, and it requires **PaintEventArgs** *e*, which is a parameter of the **Paint** event handler. The code performs the following actions:

- Creates a solid red brush.
- Creates an array of four points to define a spline.
- Sets the fill mode to **FillMode.Winding**.
- Sets the tension to 1.0.
- Fills the curve on the screen.

```
[Visual Basic]
Public Sub FillClosedCurvePointFFillModeTension(e As PaintEventArgs)
' Create solid brush.
Dim redBrush As New SolidBrush(Color.Red)
' Create array of points for curve.
Dim point1 As New PointF(100F, 100F)
Dim point2 As New PointF(200F, 50F)
Dim point3 As New PointF(250F, 200F)
Dim point4 As New PointF(50F, 150F)
Dim points As PointF() =  {point1, point2, point3, point4}
' Set fill mode.
Dim newFillMode As FillMode = FillMode.Winding
' Set tension.
Dim tension As Single = 1F
' Fill curve on screen.
e.Graphics.FillClosedCurve(redBrush, points, newFillMode, tension)
End Sub
```

```
[C#]
public void FillClosedCurvePointFFillModeTension(PaintEventArgs e)
{
// Create solid brush.
SolidBrush redBrush = new SolidBrush(Color.Red);
// Create array of points for curve.
PointF point1 = new PointF(100.0F, 100.0F);
PointF point2 = new PointF(200.0F,  50.0F);
PointF point3 = new PointF(250.0F, 200.0F);
PointF point4 = new PointF( 50.0F, 150.0F);
PointF[] points = {point1, point2, point3, point4};
// Set fill mode.
FillMode newFillMode = FillMode.Winding;
// Set tension.
float tension = 1.0F;
// Fill curve on screen.
e.Graphics.FillClosedCurve(redBrush, points, newFillMode, tension);
}
```

Requirements

Platforms: Windows 98, Windows NT 4.0, Windows Millennium Edition, Windows 2000, Windows XP Home Edition, Windows XP Professional, Windows Server 2003 family

Graphics.FillEllipse Method

Fills the interior of an ellipse defined by a bounding rectangle specified by a pair of coordinates, a width, and a height.

Overload List

Fills the interior of an ellipse defined by a bounding rectangle specified by a **Rectangle** structure.

Supported by the .NET Compact Framework.

[Visual Basic] **Overloads Public Sub FillEllipse(Brush, Rectangle)**

[C#] **public void FillEllipse(Brush, Rectangle);**

[C++] **public: void FillEllipse(Brush*, Rectangle);**

[JScript] **public function FillEllipse(Brush, Rectangle);**

Fills the interior of an ellipse defined by a bounding rectangle specified by a **RectangleF** structure.

[Visual Basic] **Overloads Public Sub FillEllipse(Brush, RectangleF)**

[C#] **public void FillEllipse(Brush, RectangleF);**

[C++] **public: void FillEllipse(Brush*, RectangleF);**

[JScript] **public function FillEllipse(Brush, RectangleF);**

Fills the interior of an ellipse defined by a bounding rectangle specified by a pair of coordinates, a width, and a height.

Supported by the .NET Compact Framework.

[Visual Basic] **Overloads Public Sub FillEllipse(Brush, Integer, Integer, Integer, Integer)**

[C#] **public void FillEllipse(Brush, int, int, int, int);**

[C++] **public: void FillEllipse(Brush*, int, int, int, int);**

[JScript] **public function FillEllipse(Brush, int, int, int, int);**

Fills the interior of an ellipse defined by a bounding rectangle specified by a pair of coordinates, a width, and a height.

[Visual Basic] **Overloads Public Sub FillEllipse(Brush, Single, Single, Single, Single)**

[C#] **public void FillEllipse(Brush, float, float, float, float);**

[C++] **public: void FillEllipse(Brush*, float, float, float, float);**

[JScript] **public function FillEllipse(Brush, float, float, float, float);**

Example

[Visual Basic, C#] The following example is designed for use with Windows Forms, and it requires **PaintEventArgs** *e*, which is a parameter of the **Paint** event handler. The code performs the following actions:

- Creates a solid red brush.
- Creates the location and size of a rectangle that bounds an ellipse.
- Fills the ellipse on the screen.

> [Visual Basic, C#] **Note** This example shows how to use one of the overloaded versions of **FillEllipse**. For other examples that might be available, see the individual overload topics.

[Visual Basic]
```
Public Sub FillEllipseFloat(e As PaintEventArgs)
' Create solid brush.
Dim redBrush As New SolidBrush(Color.Red)
' Create location and size of ellipse.
Dim x As Single = 0F
Dim y As Single = 0F
Dim width As Single = 200F
Dim height As Single = 100F
' Fill ellipse on screen.
e.Graphics.FillEllipse(redBrush, x, y, width, height)
End Sub
```

[C#]
```
public void FillEllipseFloat(PaintEventArgs e)
{
// Create solid brush.
SolidBrush redBrush = new SolidBrush(Color.Red);
// Create location and size of ellipse.
float x = 0.0F;
float y = 0.0F;
float width = 200.0F;
float height = 100.0F;
// Fill ellipse on screen.
e.Graphics.FillEllipse(redBrush, x, y, width, height);
}
```

Graphics.FillEllipse Method (Brush, Rectangle)

Fills the interior of an ellipse defined by a bounding rectangle specified by a **Rectangle** structure.

[Visual Basic]
```
Overloads Public Sub FillEllipse( _
   ByVal brush As Brush, _
   ByVal rect As Rectangle _
)
```
[C#]
```
public void FillEllipse(
   Brush brush,
   Rectangle rect
);
```
[C++]
```
public: void FillEllipse(
   Brush* brush,
   Rectangle rect
);
```
[JScript]
```
public function FillEllipse(
   brush : Brush,
   rect : Rectangle
);
```

Parameters

brush

Brush object that determines the characteristics of the fill.

rect

Rectangle structure that represents the bounding rectangle that defines the ellipse.

Return Value

This method does not return a value.

Remarks

This method fills the interior of an ellipse with a **Brush** object. The ellipse is defined by the bounding rectangle represented by the *rect* parameter.

Example

[Visual Basic, C#] The following example is designed for use with Windows Forms, and it requires **PaintEventArgs** *e*, which is a parameter of the **Paint** event handler. The code performs the following actions:

- Creates a solid red brush.
- Creates a rectangle that bounds an ellipse.
- Fills the ellipse on the screen.

[Visual Basic]
```
Public Sub FillEllipseRectangle(e As PaintEventArgs)
' Create solid brush.
Dim redBrush As New SolidBrush(Color.Red)
' Create rectangle for ellipse.
Dim x As Integer = 0
Dim y As Integer = 0
Dim width As Integer = 200
Dim height As Integer = 100
Dim rect As New Rectangle(x, y, width, height)
' Fill ellipse on screen.
e.Graphics.FillEllipse(redBrush, rect)
End Sub
```

[C#]
```
public void FillEllipseRectangle(PaintEventArgs e)
{
// Create solid brush.
SolidBrush redBrush = new SolidBrush(Color.Red);
// Create rectangle for ellipse.
int x = 0;
int y = 0;
int width = 200;
int height = 100;
Rectangle rect = new Rectangle( x, y, width, height);
// Fill ellipse on screen.
e.Graphics.FillEllipse(redBrush, rect);
}
```

Requirements

Platforms: Windows 98, Windows NT 4.0, Windows Millennium Edition, Windows 2000, Windows XP Home Edition, Windows XP Professional, Windows Server 2003 family, .NET Compact Framework - Windows CE .NET

Graphics.FillEllipse Method (Brush, RectangleF)

Fills the interior of an ellipse defined by a bounding rectangle specified by a **RectangleF** structure.

[Visual Basic]
```
Overloads Public Sub FillEllipse( _
   ByVal brush As Brush, _
   ByVal rect As RectangleF _
)
```
[C#]
```
public void FillEllipse(
   Brush brush,
   RectangleF rect
);
```
[C++]
```
public: void FillEllipse(
   Brush* brush,
   RectangleF rect
);
```
[JScript]
```
public function FillEllipse(
   brush : Brush,
   rect : RectangleF
);
```

Parameters

brush

Brush object that determines the characteristics of the fill.

rect

RectangleF structure that represents the bounding rectangle that defines the ellipse.

Return Value

This method does not return a value.

Remarks

This method fills the interior of an ellipse with a **Brush** object. The ellipse is defined by the bounding rectangle represented by the *rect* parameter.

Example

[Visual Basic, C#] The following example is designed for use with Windows Forms, and it requires **PaintEventArgs** *e*, which is a parameter of the **Paint** event handler. The code performs the following actions:

- Creates a solid red brush.
- Creates a rectangle that bounds an ellipse.
- Fills the ellipse on the screen.

[Visual Basic]
```
Public Sub FillEllipseRectangleF(e As PaintEventArgs)
' Create solid brush.
Dim redBrush As New SolidBrush(Color.Red)
' Create rectangle for ellipse.
Dim x As Single = 0F
Dim y As Single = 0F
Dim width As Single = 200F
Dim height As Single = 100F
Dim rect As New RectangleF(x, y, width, height)
' Fill ellipse on screen.
e.Graphics.FillEllipse(redBrush, rect)
End Sub
```

[C#]
```
public void FillEllipseRectangleF(PaintEventArgs e)
{
// Create solid brush.
SolidBrush redBrush = new SolidBrush(Color.Red);
// Create rectangle for ellipse.
float x = 0.0F;
float y = 0.0F;
float width = 200.0F;
float height = 100.0F;
RectangleF rect = new RectangleF( x, y, width, height);
// Fill ellipse on screen.
e.Graphics.FillEllipse(redBrush, rect);
}
```

Requirements

Platforms: Windows 98, Windows NT 4.0, Windows Millennium Edition, Windows 2000, Windows XP Home Edition, Windows XP Professional, Windows Server 2003 family

Graphics.FillEllipse Method (Brush, Int32, Int32, Int32, Int32)

Fills the interior of an ellipse defined by a bounding rectangle specified by a pair of coordinates, a width, and a height.

[Visual Basic]
```
Overloads Public Sub FillEllipse( _
   ByVal brush As Brush, _
   ByVal x As Integer, _
   ByVal y As Integer, _
   ByVal width As Integer, _
   ByVal height As Integer _
)
```
[C#]
```
public void FillEllipse(
   Brush brush,
   int x,
   int y,
   int width,
   int height
);
```

```
[C++]
public: void FillEllipse(
   Brush* brush,
   int x,
   int y,
   int width,
   int height
);
[JScript]
public function FillEllipse(
   brush : Brush,
   x : int,
   y : int,
   width : int,
   height : int
);
```

Parameters

brush
: **Brush** object that determines the characteristics of the fill.

x
: x-coordinate of the upper-left corner of the bounding rectangle that defines the ellipse.

y
: y-coordinate of the upper-left corner of the bounding rectangle that defines the ellipse.

width
: Width of the bounding rectangle that defines the ellipse.

height
: Height of the bounding rectangle that defines the ellipse.

Return Value

This method does not return a value.

Remarks

This method fills the interior of an ellipse with a **Brush** object. The ellipse is defined by the bounding rectangle represented by the *x*, *y*, *width*, and *height* parameters.

Example

[Visual Basic, C#] The following example is designed for use with Windows Forms, and it requires **PaintEventArgs** *e*, which is a parameter of the **Paint** event handler. The code performs the following actions:

- Creates a solid red brush.
- Creates the location and size of a rectangle that bounds an ellipse.
- Fills the ellipse on the screen.

```
[Visual Basic]
Public Sub FillEllipseInt(e As PaintEventArgs)
' Create solid brush.
Dim redBrush As New SolidBrush(Color.Red)
' Create location and size of ellipse.
Dim x As Integer = 0
Dim y As Integer = 0
Dim width As Integer = 200
Dim height As Integer = 100
' Fill ellipse on screen.
e.Graphics.FillEllipse(redBrush, x, y, width, height)
End Sub
```

```
[C#]
public void FillEllipseInt(PaintEventArgs e)
{
// Create solid brush.
SolidBrush redBrush = new SolidBrush(Color.Red);
// Create location and size of ellipse.
int x = 0;
int y = 0;
int width = 200;
int height = 100;
// Fill ellipse on screen.
e.Graphics.FillEllipse(redBrush, x, y, width, height);
}
```

Requirements

Platforms: Windows 98, Windows NT 4.0, Windows Millennium Edition, Windows 2000, Windows XP Home Edition, Windows XP Professional, Windows Server 2003 family, .NET Compact Framework - Windows CE .NET

Graphics.FillEllipse Method (Brush, Single, Single, Single, Single)

Fills the interior of an ellipse defined by a bounding rectangle specified by a pair of coordinates, a width, and a height.

```
[Visual Basic]
Overloads Public Sub FillEllipse( _
   ByVal brush As Brush, _
   ByVal x As Single, _
   ByVal y As Single, _
   ByVal width As Single, _
   ByVal height As Single _
)
[C#]
public void FillEllipse(
   Brush brush,
   float x,
   float y,
   float width,
   float height
);
[C++]
public: void FillEllipse(
   Brush* brush,
   float x,
   float y,
   float width,
   float height
);
[JScript]
public function FillEllipse(
   brush : Brush,
   x : float,
   y : float,
   width : float,
   height : float
);
```

Parameters

brush

Brush object that determines the characteristics of the fill.

x

x-coordinate of the upper-left corner of the bounding rectangle that defines the ellipse.

y

y-coordinate of the upper-left corner of the bounding rectangle that defines the ellipse.

width

Width of the bounding rectangle that defines the ellipse.

height

Height of the bounding rectangle that defines the ellipse.

Return Value

This method does not return a value.

Remarks

This method fills the interior of an ellipse with a **Brush** object. The ellipse is defined by the bounding rectangle represented by the *x*, *y*, *width*, and *height* parameters.

Example

[Visual Basic, C#] The following example is designed for use with Windows Forms, and it requires **PaintEventArgs** *e*, which is a parameter of the **Paint** event handler. The code performs the following actions:

- Creates a solid red brush.
- Creates the location and size of a rectangle that bounds an ellipse.
- Fills the ellipse on the screen.

[Visual Basic]
```
Public Sub FillEllipseFloat(e As PaintEventArgs)
' Create solid brush.
Dim redBrush As New SolidBrush(Color.Red)
' Create location and size of ellipse.
Dim x As Single = 0F
Dim y As Single = 0F
Dim width As Single = 200F
Dim height As Single = 100F
' Fill ellipse on screen.
e.Graphics.FillEllipse(redBrush, x, y, width, height)
End Sub
```

[C#]
```
public void FillEllipseFloat(PaintEventArgs e)
{
// Create solid brush.
SolidBrush redBrush = new SolidBrush(Color.Red);
// Create location and size of ellipse.
float x = 0.0F;
float y = 0.0F;
float width = 200.0F;
float height = 100.0F;
// Fill ellipse on screen.
e.Graphics.FillEllipse(redBrush, x, y, width, height);
}
```

Requirements

Platforms: Windows 98, Windows NT 4.0, Windows Millennium Edition, Windows 2000, Windows XP Home Edition, Windows XP Professional, Windows Server 2003 family

Graphics.FillPath Method

Fills the interior of a **GraphicsPath** object.

[Visual Basic]
```
Public Sub FillPath( _
   ByVal brush As Brush, _
   ByVal path As GraphicsPath _
)
```
[C#]
```
public void FillPath(
   Brush brush,
   GraphicsPath path
);
```
[C++]
```
public: void FillPath(
   Brush* brush,
   GraphicsPath* path
);
```
[JScript]
```
public function FillPath(
   brush : Brush,
   path : GraphicsPath
);
```

Parameters

brush

Brush object that determines the characteristics of the fill.

path

GraphicsPath object that represents the path to fill.

Return Value

This method does not return a value.

Remarks

A **GraphicsPath** object consists of a series of line and curve segments. If the path represented by the *path* parameter is not closed, an additional segment is added from the last point to the first point to close the path.

Example

[Visual Basic, C#] The following example is designed for use with Windows Forms, and it requires **PaintEventArgs** *e*, which is a parameter of the **Paint** event handler. The code performs the following actions:

- Creates a solid red brush.
- Creates a graphics path object.
- Adds an ellipse to the graphics path.
- Fills the path on the screen.

[Visual Basic]
```
Public Sub FillPathEllipse(e As PaintEventArgs)
' Create solid brush.
Dim redBrush As New SolidBrush(Color.Red)
' Create graphics path object and add ellipse.
Dim graphPath As New GraphicsPath()
graphPath.AddEllipse(0, 0, 200, 100)
' Fill graphics path to screen.
e.Graphics.FillPath(redBrush, graphPath)
End Sub
```

[C#]
```
public void FillPathEllipse(PaintEventArgs e)
{
// Create solid brush.
SolidBrush redBrush = new SolidBrush(Color.Red);
// Create graphics path object and add ellipse.
```

```
GraphicsPath graphPath = new GraphicsPath();
graphPath.AddEllipse(0, 0, 200, 100);
// Fill graphics path to screen.
e.Graphics.FillPath(redBrush, graphPath);
}
```

Requirements

Platforms: Windows 98, Windows NT 4.0, Windows Millennium Edition, Windows 2000, Windows XP Home Edition, Windows XP Professional, Windows Server 2003 family

Graphics.FillPie Method

Fills the interior of a pie section defined by an ellipse specified by a pair of coordinates, a width, and a height and two radial lines.

Overload List

Fills the interior of a pie section defined by an ellipse specified by a **RectangleF** structure and two radial lines.

[Visual Basic] **Overloads Public Sub FillPie(Brush, Rectangle, Single, Single)**

[C#] **public void FillPie(Brush, Rectangle, float, float);**

[C++] **public: void FillPie(Brush*, Rectangle, float, float);**

[JScript] **public function FillPie(Brush, Rectangle, float, float);**

Fills the interior of a pie section defined by an ellipse specified by a pair of coordinates, a width, and a height and two radial lines.

[Visual Basic] **Overloads Public Sub FillPie(Brush, Integer, Integer, Integer, Integer, Integer, Integer)**

[C#] **public void FillPie(Brush, int, int, int, int, int, int);**

[C++] **public: void FillPie(Brush*, int, int, int, int, int, int);**

[JScript] **public function FillPie(Brush, int, int, int, int, int, int);**

Fills the interior of a pie section defined by an ellipse specified by a pair of coordinates, a width, and a height and two radial lines.

[Visual Basic] **Overloads Public Sub FillPie(Brush, Single, Single, Single, Single, Single, Single)**

[C#] **public void FillPie(Brush, float, float, float, float, float, float);**

[C++] **public: void FillPie(Brush*, float, float, float, float, float, float);**

[JScript] **public function FillPie(Brush, float, float, float, float, float, float);**

Example

[Visual Basic, C#] The following example is designed for use with Windows Forms, and it requires **PaintEventArgs** *e*, which is a parameter of the **Paint** event handler. The code performs the following actions:

- Creates a solid red brush.
- Creates the location and size of a rectangle that bounds an ellipse.
- Defines the start angle (relative to the x axis) and the sweep angle (both in a clockwise direction).
- Fills the pie-shaped area of the ellipse on the screen.

> [Visual Basic, C#] **Note** This example shows how to use one of the overloaded versions of **FillPie**. For other examples that might be available, see the individual overload topics.

[Visual Basic]

```
Public Sub FillPieFloat(e As PaintEventArgs)
' Create solid brush.
Dim redBrush As New SolidBrush(Color.Red)
' Create location and size of ellipse.
Dim x As Single = 0F
Dim y As Single = 0F
Dim width As Single = 200F
Dim height As Single = 100F
' Create start and sweep angles.
Dim startAngle As Single = 0F
Dim sweepAngle As Single = 45F
' Fill pie to screen.
e.Graphics.FillPie(redBrush, x, y, width, height, startAngle, _
sweepAngle)
End Sub
```

[C#]

```
public void FillPieFloat(PaintEventArgs e)
{
// Create solid brush.
SolidBrush redBrush = new SolidBrush(Color.Red);
// Create location and size of ellipse.
float x = 0.0F;
float y = 0.0F;
float width = 200.0F;
float height = 100.0F;
// Create start and sweep angles.
float startAngle =  0.0F;
float sweepAngle = 45.0F;
// Fill pie to screen.
e.Graphics.FillPie(redBrush, x, y, width, height,
startAngle, sweepAngle);
}
```

Graphics.FillPie Method (Brush, Rectangle, Single, Single)

Fills the interior of a pie section defined by an ellipse specified by a **RectangleF** structure and two radial lines.

[Visual Basic]

```
Overloads Public Sub FillPie( _
   ByVal brush As Brush, _
   ByVal rect As Rectangle, _
   ByVal startAngle As Single, _
   ByVal sweepAngle As Single _
)
```

[C#]

```
public void FillPie(
   Brush brush,
   Rectangle rect,
   float startAngle,
   float sweepAngle
);
```

[C++]

```
public: void FillPie(
   Brush* brush,
   Rectangle rect,
   float startAngle,
   float sweepAngle
);
```

[JScript]

```
public function FillPie(
   brush : Brush,
   rect : Rectangle,
   startAngle : float,
   sweepAngle : float
);
```

Parameters

brush

Brush object that determines the characteristics of the fill.

rect

Rectangle structure that represents the bounding rectangle that defines the ellipse from which the pie section comes.

startAngle

Angle in degrees measured clockwise from the x-axis to the first side of the pie section.

sweepAngle

Angle in degrees measured clockwise from the *startAngle* parameter to the second side of the pie section.

Return Value

This method does not return a value.

Remarks

This method fills the interior of a pie section defined by an arc of an ellipse and the two radial lines that intersect with the endpoints of the arc. The ellipse is defined by the bounding rectangle. The pie section consists of the two radial lines defined by the *startAngle* and *sweepAngle* parameters and the arc between the intersections of those radial lines with the ellipse.

If the *sweepAngle* parameter is greater than 360 degrees or less than -360 degrees, it is treated as if it were 360 degrees or -360 degrees, respectively.

Example

[Visual Basic, C#] The following example is designed for use with Windows Forms, and it requires **PaintEventArgs** *e*, which is a parameter of the **Paint** event handler. The code performs the following actions:

- Creates a solid red brush.
- Creates a rectangle that bounds an ellipse.
- Defines the start angle (relative to the x axis) and the sweep angle (both in a clockwise direction).
- Fills the pie-shaped area of the ellipse on the screen.

[Visual Basic]

```
Public Sub FillPieRectangle(e As PaintEventArgs)
' Create solid brush.
Dim redBrush As New SolidBrush(Color.Red)
' Create rectangle for ellipse.
Dim rect As New Rectangle(0, 0, 200, 100)
' Create start and sweep angles.
Dim startAngle As Single = 0F
Dim sweepAngle As Single = 45F
' Fill pie to screen.
e.Graphics.FillPie(redBrush, rect, startAngle, sweepAngle)
End Sub
```

[C#]

```
public void FillPieRectangle(PaintEventArgs e)
{
// Create solid brush.
SolidBrush redBrush = new SolidBrush(Color.Red);
// Create rectangle for ellipse.
Rectangle rect = new Rectangle( 0, 0, 200, 100);
// Create start and sweep angles.
float startAngle =  0.0F;
float sweepAngle = 45.0F;
// Fill pie to screen.
e.Graphics.FillPie(redBrush, rect, startAngle, sweepAngle);
}
```

Requirements

Platforms: Windows 98, Windows NT 4.0, Windows Millennium Edition, Windows 2000, Windows XP Home Edition, Windows XP Professional, Windows Server 2003 family

Graphics.FillPie Method (Brush, Int32, Int32, Int32, Int32, Int32, Int32)

Fills the interior of a pie section defined by an ellipse specified by a pair of coordinates, a width, and a height and two radial lines.

[Visual Basic]

```
Overloads Public Sub FillPie( _
   ByVal brush As Brush, _
   ByVal x As Integer, _
   ByVal y As Integer, _
   ByVal width As Integer, _
   ByVal height As Integer, _
   ByVal startAngle As Integer, _
   ByVal sweepAngle As Integer _
)
```

[C#]

```
public void FillPie(
   Brush brush,
   int x,
   int y,
   int width,
   int height,
   int startAngle,
   int sweepAngle
);
```

[C++]

```
public: void FillPie(
   Brush* brush,
   int x,
   int y,
   int width,
   int height,
   int startAngle,
   int sweepAngle
);
```

[JScript]

```
public function FillPie(
   brush : Brush,
   x : int,
   y : int,
   width : int,
   height : int,
   startAngle : int,
   sweepAngle : int
);
```

Parameters

brush

Brush object that determines the characteristics of the fill.

x

x-coordinate of the upper-left corner of the bounding rectangle that defines the ellipse from which the pie section comes.

y

y-coordinate of the upper-left corner of the bounding rectangle that defines the ellipse from which the pie section comes.

width
Width of the bounding rectangle that defines the ellipse from which the pie section comes.

height
Height of the bounding rectangle that defines the ellipse from which the pie section comes.

startAngle
Angle in degrees measured clockwise from the x-axis to the first side of the pie section.

sweepAngle
Angle in degrees measured clockwise from the *startAngle* parameter to the second side of the pie section.

Return Value

This method does not return a value.

Remarks

This method fills the interior of a pie section defined by an arc of an ellipse and the two radial lines that intersect with the endpoints of the arc. The ellipse is defined by the bounding rectangle. The pie section consists of the two radial lines defined by the *startAngle* and *sweepAngle* parameters and the arc between the intersections of those radial lines with the ellipse.

If the *sweepAngle* parameter is greater than 360 degrees or less than -360 degrees, it is treated as if it were 360 degrees or -360 degrees, respectively.

Example

[Visual Basic, C#] The following example is designed for use with Windows Forms, and it requires **PaintEventArgs** *e*, which is a parameter of the **Paint** event handler. The code performs the following actions:

- Creates a solid red brush.
- Creates the location and size of a rectangle that bounds an ellipse.
- Defines the start angle (relative to the x axis) and the sweep angle (both in a clockwise direction).
- Fills the pie-shaped area of the ellipse on the screen.

[Visual Basic]
```
Public Sub FillPieInt(e As PaintEventArgs)
' Create solid brush.
Dim redBrush As New SolidBrush(Color.Red)
' Create location and size of ellipse.
Dim x As Integer = 0
Dim y As Integer = 0
Dim width As Integer = 200
Dim height As Integer = 100
' Create start and sweep angles.
Dim startAngle As Integer = 0
Dim sweepAngle As Integer = 45
' Fill pie to screen.
e.Graphics.FillPie(redBrush, x, y, width, height, startAngle, _
sweepAngle)
End Sub
```

[C#]
```
public void FillPieInt(PaintEventArgs e)
{
// Create solid brush.
SolidBrush redBrush = new SolidBrush(Color.Red);
// Create location and size of ellipse.
int x = 0;
int y = 0;
int width = 200;
int height = 100;
// Create start and sweep angles.
int startAngle =  0;
int sweepAngle = 45;
// Fill pie to screen.
e.Graphics.FillPie(redBrush, x, y, width, height,
startAngle, sweepAngle);
}
```

Requirements

Platforms: Windows 98, Windows NT 4.0, Windows Millennium Edition, Windows 2000, Windows XP Home Edition, Windows XP Professional, Windows Server 2003 family

Graphics.FillPie Method (Brush, Single, Single, Single, Single, Single, Single)

Fills the interior of a pie section defined by an ellipse specified by a pair of coordinates, a width, and a height and two radial lines.

[Visual Basic]
```
Overloads Public Sub FillPie( _
   ByVal brush As Brush, _
   ByVal x As Single, _
   ByVal y As Single, _
   ByVal width As Single, _
   ByVal height As Single, _
   ByVal startAngle As Single, _
   ByVal sweepAngle As Single _
)
```
[C#]
```
public void FillPie(
   Brush brush,
   float x,
   float y,
   float width,
   float height,
   float startAngle,
   float sweepAngle
);
```
[C++]
```
public: void FillPie(
   Brush* brush,
   float x,
   float y,
   float width,
   float height,
   float startAngle,
   float sweepAngle
);
```
[JScript]
```
public function FillPie(
   brush : Brush,
   x : float,
   y : float,
   width : float,
   height : float,
   startAngle : float,
   sweepAngle : float
);
```

Parameters

brush

Brush object that determines the characteristics of the fill.

x

x-coordinate of the upper-left corner of the bounding rectangle that defines the ellipse from which the pie section comes.

y

y-coordinate of the upper-left corner of the bounding rectangle that defines the ellipse from which the pie section comes.

width

Width of the bounding rectangle that defines the ellipse from which the pie section comes.

height

Height of the bounding rectangle that defines the ellipse from which the pie section comes.

startAngle

Angle in degrees measured clockwise from the x-axis to the first side of the pie section.

sweepAngle

Angle in degrees measured clockwise from the *startAngle* parameter to the second side of the pie section.

Return Value

This method does not return a value.

Remarks

This method fills the interior of a pie section defined by an arc of an ellipse and the two radial lines that intersect with the endpoints of the arc. The ellipse is defined by the bounding rectangle. The pie section consists of the two radial lines defined by the *startAngle* and *sweepAngle* parameters, and the arc between the intersections of those radial lines with the ellipse.

If the *sweepAngle* parameter is greater than 360 degrees or less than -360 degrees, it is treated as if it were 360 degrees or -360 degrees, respectively.

Example

[Visual Basic, C#] The following example is designed for use with Windows Forms, and it requires **PaintEventArgs** *e*, which is a parameter of the **Paint** event handler. The code performs the following actions:

- Creates a solid red brush.
- Creates the location and size of a rectangle that bounds an ellipse.
- Defines the start angle (relative to the x axis) and the sweep angle (both in a clockwise direction).
- Fills the pie-shaped area of the ellipse on the screen.

[Visual Basic]

```
Public Sub FillPieFloat(e As PaintEventArgs)
' Create solid brush.
Dim redBrush As New SolidBrush(Color.Red)
' Create location and size of ellipse.
Dim x As Single = 0F
Dim y As Single = 0F
Dim width As Single = 200F
Dim height As Single = 100F
' Create start and sweep angles.
Dim startAngle As Single = 0F
Dim sweepAngle As Single = 45F
' Fill pie to screen.
e.Graphics.FillPie(redBrush, x, y, width, height, startAngle, _
sweepAngle)
End Sub
```

[C#]

```
public void FillPieFloat(PaintEventArgs e)
{
// Create solid brush.
SolidBrush redBrush = new SolidBrush(Color.Red);
// Create location and size of ellipse.
float x = 0.0F;
float y = 0.0F;
float width = 200.0F;
float height = 100.0F;
// Create start and sweep angles.
float startAngle =  0.0F;
float sweepAngle = 45.0F;
// Fill pie to screen.
e.Graphics.FillPie(redBrush, x, y, width, height,                    ↵
 startAngle, sweepAngle);
}
```

Requirements

Platforms: Windows 98, Windows NT 4.0, Windows Millennium Edition, Windows 2000, Windows XP Home Edition, Windows XP Professional, Windows Server 2003 family

Graphics.FillPolygon Method

Fills the interior of a polygon defined by an array of points specified by **Point** structures.

Overload List

Fills the interior of a polygon defined by an array of points specified by **Point** structures.

Supported by the .NET Compact Framework.

[Visual Basic] **Overloads Public Sub FillPolygon(Brush, Point())**

[C#] **public void FillPolygon(Brush, Point[]);**

[C++] **public: void FillPolygon(Brush*, Point[]);**

[JScript] **public function FillPolygon(Brush, Point[]);**

Fills the interior of a polygon defined by an array of points specified by **PointF** structures .

[Visual Basic] **Overloads Public Sub FillPolygon(Brush, PointF())**

[C#] **public void FillPolygon(Brush, PointF[]);**

[C++] **public: void FillPolygon(Brush*, PointF[]);**

[JScript] **public function FillPolygon(Brush, PointF[]);**

Fills the interior of a polygon defined by an array of points specified by **Point** structures using the specified fill mode.

[Visual Basic] **Overloads Public Sub FillPolygon(Brush, Point(), FillMode)**

[C#] **public void FillPolygon(Brush, Point[], FillMode);**

[C++] **public: void FillPolygon(Brush*, Point[], FillMode);**

[JScript] **public function FillPolygon(Brush, Point[], FillMode);**

Fills the interior of a polygon defined by an array of points specified by **PointF** structures using the specified fill mode.

[Visual Basic] **Overloads Public Sub FillPolygon(Brush, PointF(), FillMode)**

[C#] **public void FillPolygon(Brush, PointF[], FillMode);**

[C++] **public: void FillPolygon(Brush*, PointF[], FillMode);**

[JScript] **public function FillPolygon(Brush, PointF[], FillMode);**

Example

[Visual Basic, C#] The following example is designed for use with Windows Forms, and it requires **PaintEventArgs** *e*, which is a parameter of the **Paint** event handler. The code performs the following action:

- Creates a solid blue brush.
- Creates an array of seven points to define a polygon.
- Sets the fill mode to **FillMode.Winding**.
- Fills the polygonal area on the screen.

> [Visual Basic, C#] **Note** This example shows how to use one of the overloaded versions of **FillPolygon**. For other examples that might be available, see the individual overload topics.

[Visual Basic]

```
Public Sub FillPolygonPointFFillMode(e As PaintEventArgs)
' Create solid brush.
Dim blueBrush As New SolidBrush(Color.Blue)
' Create points that define polygon.
Dim point1 As New PointF(50F, 50F)
Dim point2 As New PointF(100F, 25F)
Dim point3 As New PointF(200F, 5F)
Dim point4 As New PointF(250F, 50F)
Dim point5 As New PointF(300F, 100F)
Dim point6 As New PointF(350F, 200F)
Dim point7 As New PointF(250F, 250F)
Dim curvePoints As PointF() = {point1, point2, point3, point4, _
point5, point6, point7}
' Define fill mode.
Dim newFillMode As FillMode = FillMode.Winding
' Fill polygon to screen.
e.Graphics.FillPolygon(blueBrush, curvePoints, newFillMode)
End Sub
```

[C#]

```
public void FillPolygonPointFFillMode(PaintEventArgs e)
{
// Create solid brush.
SolidBrush blueBrush = new SolidBrush(Color.Blue);
// Create points that define polygon.
PointF point1 = new PointF( 50.0F,  50.0F);
PointF point2 = new PointF(100.0F,  25.0F);
PointF point3 = new PointF(200.0F,   5.0F);
PointF point4 = new PointF(250.0F,  50.0F);
PointF point5 = new PointF(300.0F, 100.0F);
PointF point6 = new PointF(350.0F, 200.0F);
PointF point7 = new PointF(250.0F, 250.0F);
PointF[] curvePoints =
{
point1,
point2,
point3,
point4,
point5,
point6,
point7
};
// Define fill mode.
FillMode newFillMode = FillMode.Winding;
// Fill polygon to screen.
e.Graphics.FillPolygon(blueBrush, curvePoints, newFillModex3);
}
```

Graphics.FillPolygon Method (Brush, Point[])

Fills the interior of a polygon defined by an array of points specified by **Point** structures.

[Visual Basic]

```
Overloads Public Sub FillPolygon( _
   ByVal brush As Brush, _
   ByVal points() As Point _
)
```

[C#]

```
public void FillPolygon(
   Brush brush,
   Point[] points
);
```

[C++]

```
public: void FillPolygon(
   Brush* brush,
   Point points[]
);
```

[JScript]

```
public function FillPolygon(
   brush : Brush,
   points : Point[]
);
```

Parameters

brush
: **Brush** object that determines the characteristics of the fill.

points
: Array of **Point** structures that represent the vertices of the polygon to fill.

Return Value

This method does not return a value.

Remarks

Every two consecutive points in the array specify a side of the polygon. In addition, if the last point and the first point do not coincide, they specify the closing side of the polygon.

Example

[Visual Basic, C#] The following example is designed for use with Windows Forms, and it requires **PaintEventArgs** *e*, which is a parameter of the **Paint** event handler. The code performs the following actions:

- Creates a solid blue brush.
- Creates an array of seven points to define a polygon.
- Fills the polygonal area on the screen.

[Visual Basic]

```
Public Sub FillPolygonPoint(e As PaintEventArgs)
' Create solid brush.
Dim blueBrush As New SolidBrush(Color.Blue)
' Create points that define polygon.
Dim point1 As New Point(50, 50)
Dim point2 As New Point(100, 25)
Dim point3 As New Point(200, 5)
Dim point4 As New Point(250, 50)
Dim point5 As New Point(300, 100)
Dim point6 As New Point(350, 200)
Dim point7 As New Point(250, 250)
Dim curvePoints As Point() = {point1, point2, point3, point4, _
point5, point6, point7}
' Draw polygon to screen.
e.Graphics.FillPolygon(blueBrush, curvePoints)
End Sub
```

[C#]
```
public void FillPolygonPoint(PaintEventArgs e)
{
// Create solid brush.
SolidBrush blueBrush = new SolidBrush(Color.Blue);
// Create points that define polygon.
Point point1 = new Point( 50,  50);
Point point2 = new Point(100,  25);
Point point3 = new Point(200,   5);
Point point4 = new Point(250,  50);
Point point5 = new Point(300, 100);
Point point6 = new Point(350, 200);
Point point7 = new Point(250, 250);
Point[] curvePoints =
{
point1,
point2,
point3,
point4,
point5,
point6,
point7
};
// Draw polygon to screen.
e.Graphics.FillPolygon(blueBrush, curvePoints);
}
```

Requirements

Platforms: Windows 98, Windows NT 4.0, Windows Millennium Edition, Windows 2000, Windows XP Home Edition, Windows XP Professional, Windows Server 2003 family, .NET Compact Framework - Windows CE .NET

Graphics.FillPolygon Method (Brush, PointF[])

Fills the interior of a polygon defined by an array of points specified by **PointF** structures .

[Visual Basic]
```
Overloads Public Sub FillPolygon( _
   ByVal brush As Brush, _
   ByVal points() As PointF _
)
```
[C#]
```
public void FillPolygon(
   Brush brush,
   PointF[] points
);
```
[C++]
```
public: void FillPolygon(
   Brush* brush,
   PointF points[]
);
```
[JScript]
```
public function FillPolygon(
   brush : Brush,
   points : PointF[]
);
```

Parameters

brush

Brush object that determines the characteristics of the fill.

points

Array of **PointF** structures that represent the vertices of the polygon to fill.

Return Value

This method does not return a value.

Remarks

Every two consecutive points in the array specify a side of the polygon. In addition, if the last point and the first point do not coincide, they specify the closing side of the polygon.

Example

[Visual Basic, C#] The following example is designed for use with Windows Forms, and it requires **PaintEventArgs** *e*, which is a parameter of the **Paint** event handler. The code performs the following actions:

- Creates a solid blue brush.
- Creates an array of seven points to define a polygon.
- Fills the polygonal area on the screen.

[Visual Basic]
```
Public Sub FillPolygonPointF(e As PaintEventArgs)
' Create solid brush.
Dim blueBrush As New SolidBrush(Color.Blue)
' Create points that define polygon.
Dim point1 As New PointF(50F, 50F)
Dim point2 As New PointF(100F, 25F)
Dim point3 As New PointF(200F, 5F)
Dim point4 As New PointF(250F, 50F)
Dim point5 As New PointF(300F, 100F)
Dim point6 As New PointF(350F, 200F)
Dim point7 As New PointF(250F, 250F)
Dim curvePoints As PointF() =  {point1, point2, point3, point4, _
point5, point6, point7}
' Fill polygon to screen.
e.Graphics.FillPolygon(blueBrush, curvePoints)
End Sub
```

[C#]
```
public void FillPolygonPointF(PaintEventArgs e)
{
// Create solid brush.
SolidBrush blueBrush = new SolidBrush(Color.Blue);
// Create points that define polygon.
PointF point1 = new PointF( 50.0F,  50.0F);
PointF point2 = new PointF(100.0F,  25.0F);
PointF point3 = new PointF(200.0F,   5.0F);
PointF point4 = new PointF(250.0F,  50.0F);
PointF point5 = new PointF(300.0F, 100.0F);
PointF point6 = new PointF(350.0F, 200.0F);
PointF point7 = new PointF(250.0F, 250.0F);
PointF[] curvePoints =
{
point1,
point2,
point3,
point4,
point5,
point6,
point7
};
// Fill polygon to screen.
e.Graphics.FillPolygon(blueBrush, curvePoints);
}
```

Requirements

Platforms: Windows 98, Windows NT 4.0, Windows Millennium Edition, Windows 2000, Windows XP Home Edition, Windows XP Professional, Windows Server 2003 family

Graphics.FillPolygon Method (Brush, Point[], FillMode)

Fills the interior of a polygon defined by an array of points specified by **Point** structures using the specified fill mode.

```
[Visual Basic]
Overloads Public Sub FillPolygon( _
   ByVal brush As Brush, _
   ByVal points() As Point, _
   ByVal fillMode As FillMode _
)
[C#]
public void FillPolygon(
   Brush brush,
   Point[] points,
   FillMode fillMode
);
[C++]
public: void FillPolygon(
   Brush* brush,
   Point points[],
   FillMode fillMode
);
[JScript]
public function FillPolygon(
   brush : Brush,
   points : Point[],
   fillMode : FillMode
);
```

Parameters

brush
  Brush object that determines the characteristics of the fill.

points
  Array of **Point** structures that represent the vertices of the polygon to fill.

fillMode
  Member of the **FillMode** enumeration that determines the style of the fill.

Return Value

This method does not return a value.

Remarks

Every two consecutive points in the array specify a side of the polygon. In addition, if the last point and the first point do not coincide, they specify the closing side of the polygon.

Example

[Visual Basic, C#] The following example is designed for use with Windows Forms, and it requires **PaintEventArgs** *e*, which is a parameter of the **Paint** event handler. The code performs the following actions:

- Creates a solid blue brush.
- Creates an array of seven points to define a polygon.
- Sets the fill mode to **FillMode.Winding**.
- Fills the polygonal area on the screen.

```
[Visual Basic]
Public Sub FillPolygonPointFillMode(e As PaintEventArgs)
' Create solid brush.
Dim blueBrush As New SolidBrush(Color.Blue)
' Create points that define polygon.
Dim point1 As New Point(50, 50)
Dim point2 As New Point(100, 25)
Dim point3 As New Point(200, 5)
Dim point4 As New Point(250, 50)
Dim point5 As New Point(300, 100)
Dim point6 As New Point(350, 200)
Dim point7 As New Point(250, 250)
Dim curvePoints As Point() = {point1, point2, point3, point4, _
point5, point6, point7}
' Define fill mode.
Dim newFillMode As FillMode = FillMode.Winding
' Draw polygon to screen.
e.Graphics.FillPolygon(blueBrush, curvePoints, newFillMode)
End Sub
```

```
[C#]
public void FillPolygonPointFillMode(PaintEventArgs e)
{
// Create solid brush.
SolidBrush blueBrush = new SolidBrush(Color.Blue);
// Create points that define polygon.
Point point1 = new Point( 50,  50);
Point point2 = new Point(100,  25);
Point point3 = new Point(200,   5);
Point point4 = new Point(250,  50);
Point point5 = new Point(300, 100);
Point point6 = new Point(350, 200);
Point point7 = new Point(250, 250);
Point[] curvePoints =
{
point1,
point2,
point3,
point4,
point5,
point6,
point7
};
// Define fill mode.
FillMode newFillMode = FillMode.Winding;
// Draw polygon to screen.
e.Graphics.FillPolygon(blueBrush, curvePoints, newFillMode);
}
```

Requirements

Platforms: Windows 98, Windows NT 4.0, Windows Millennium Edition, Windows 2000, Windows XP Home Edition, Windows XP Professional, Windows Server 2003 family

Graphics.FillPolygon Method (Brush, PointF[], FillMode)

Fills the interior of a polygon defined by an array of points specified by **PointF** structures using the specified fill mode.

```
[Visual Basic]
Overloads Public Sub FillPolygon( _
   ByVal brush As Brush, _
   ByVal points() As PointF, _
   ByVal fillMode As FillMode _
)
[C#]
public void FillPolygon(
   Brush brush,
   PointF[] points,
   FillMode fillMode
);
[C++]
public: void FillPolygon(
   Brush* brush,
   PointF points[],
   FillMode fillMode
);
```

[JScript]
```
public function FillPolygon(
   brush : Brush,
   points : PointF[],
   fillMode : FillMode
);
```

Parameters

brush
: **Brush** object that determines the characteristics of the fill.

points
: Array of **PointF** structures that represent the vertices of the polygon to fill.

fillMode
: Member of the **FillMode** enumeration that determines the style of the fill.

Return Value

This method does not return a value.

Remarks

Every two consecutive points in the array specify a side of the polygon. In addition, if the last point and the first point do not coincide, they specify the closing side of the polygon.

Example

[Visual Basic, C#] The following example is designed for use with Windows Forms, and it requires **PaintEventArgs** *e*, which is a parameter of the **Paint** event handler. The code performs the following action:

- Creates a solid blue brush.
- Creates an array of seven points to define a polygon.
- Sets the fill mode to **FillMode.Winding**.
- Fills the polygonal area on the screen.

[Visual Basic]
```
Public Sub FillPolygonPointFFillMode(e As PaintEventArgs)
' Create solid brush.
Dim blueBrush As New SolidBrush(Color.Blue)
' Create points that define polygon.
Dim point1 As New PointF(50F, 50F)
Dim point2 As New PointF(100F, 25F)
Dim point3 As New PointF(200F, 5F)
Dim point4 As New PointF(250F, 50F)
Dim point5 As New PointF(300F, 100F)
Dim point6 As New PointF(350F, 200F)
Dim point7 As New PointF(250F, 250F)
Dim curvePoints As PointF() = {point1, point2, point3, point4, _
point5, point6, point7}
' Define fill mode.
Dim newFillMode As FillMode = FillMode.Winding
' Fill polygon to screen.
e.Graphics.FillPolygon(blueBrush, curvePoints, newFillMode)
End Sub
```

[C#]
```
public void FillPolygonPointFFillMode(PaintEventArgs e)
{
// Create solid brush.
SolidBrush blueBrush = new SolidBrush(Color.Blue);
// Create points that define polygon.
PointF point1 = new PointF( 50.0F,  50.0F);
PointF point2 = new PointF(100.0F,  25.0F);
PointF point3 = new PointF(200.0F,   5.0F);
PointF point4 = new PointF(250.0F,  50.0F);
PointF point5 = new PointF(300.0F, 100.0F);
PointF point6 = new PointF(350.0F, 200.0F);
PointF point7 = new PointF(250.0F, 250.0F);
PointF[] curvePoints =
{
point1,
point2,
point3,
point4,
point5,
point6,
point7
};
// Define fill mode.
FillMode newFillMode = FillMode.Winding;
// Fill polygon to screen.
e.Graphics.FillPolygon(blueBrush, curvePoints, newFillModex3);
}
```

Requirements

Platforms: Windows 98, Windows NT 4.0, Windows Millennium Edition, Windows 2000, Windows XP Home Edition, Windows XP Professional, Windows Server 2003 family

Graphics.FillRectangle Method

Fills the interior of a rectangle specified by a pair of coordinates, a width, and a height.

Overload List

Fills the interior of a rectangle specified by a **Rectangle** structure.

Supported by the .NET Compact Framework.

[Visual Basic] **Overloads Public Sub FillRectangle(Brush, Rectangle)**

[C#] **public void FillRectangle(Brush, Rectangle);**

[C++] **public: void FillRectangle(Brush*, Rectangle);**

[JScript] **public function FillRectangle(Brush, Rectangle);**

Fills the interior of a rectangle specified by a **RectangleF** structure.

[Visual Basic] **Overloads Public Sub FillRectangle(Brush, RectangleF)**

[C#] **public void FillRectangle(Brush, RectangleF);**

[C++] **public: void FillRectangle(Brush*, RectangleF);**

[JScript] **public function FillRectangle(Brush, RectangleF);**

Fills the interior of a rectangle specified by a pair of coordinates, a width, and a height.

Supported by the .NET Compact Framework.

[Visual Basic] **Overloads Public Sub FillRectangle(Brush, Integer, Integer, Integer, Integer)**

[C#] **public void FillRectangle(Brush, int, int, int, int);**

[C++] **public: void FillRectangle(Brush*, int, int, int, int);**

[JScript] **public function FillRectangle(Brush, int, int, int, int);**

Fills the interior of a rectangle specified by a pair of coordinates, a width, and a height.

[Visual Basic] **Overloads Public Sub FillRectangle(Brush, Single, Single, Single, Single)**

[C#] **public void FillRectangle(Brush, float, float, float, float);**

[C++] **public: void FillRectangle(Brush*, float, float, float, float);**

[JScript] **public function FillRectangle(Brush, float, float, float, float);**

Example

[Visual Basic, C#] The following example is designed for use with Windows Forms, and it requires **PaintEventArgs** *e*, which is a parameter of the **Paint** event handler. The code performs the following action:

- Creates a solid blue brush.
- Creates the location and size of a rectangle.
- Fills the rectangular area on the screen.

> [Visual Basic, C#] **Note** This example shows how to use one of the overloaded versions of **FillRectangle**. For other examples that might be available, see the individual overload topics.

[Visual Basic]
```
Public Sub FillRectangleFloat(e As PaintEventArgs)
' Create solid brush.
Dim blueBrush As New SolidBrush(Color.Blue)
' Create location and size of rectangle.
Dim x As Single = 0F
Dim y As Single = 0F
Dim width As Single = 200F
Dim height As Single = 200F
' Fill rectangle to screen.
e.Graphics.FillRectangle(blueBrush, x, y, width, height)
End Sub
```

[C#]
```
public void FillRectangleFloat(PaintEventArgs e)
{
// Create solid brush.
SolidBrush blueBrush = new SolidBrush(Color.Blue);
// Create location and size of rectangle.
float x = 0.0F;
float y = 0.0F;
float width = 200.0F;
float height = 200.0F;
// Fill rectangle to screen.
e.Graphics.FillRectangle(blueBrush, x, y, width, height);
}
```

Graphics.FillRectangle Method (Brush, Rectangle)

Fills the interior of a rectangle specified by a **Rectangle** structure.

[Visual Basic]
```
Overloads Public Sub FillRectangle( _
   ByVal brush As Brush, _
   ByVal rect As Rectangle _
)
```
[C#]
```
public void FillRectangle(
   Brush brush,
   Rectangle rect
);
```
[C++]
```
public: void FillRectangle(
   Brush* brush,
   Rectangle rect
);
```
[JScript]
```
public function FillRectangle(
   brush : Brush,
   rect : Rectangle
);
```

Parameters

brush
: **Brush** object that determines the characteristics of the fill.

rect
: **Rectangle** structure that represents the rectangle to fill.

Return Value

This method does not return a value.

Example

[Visual Basic, C#] The following example is designed for use with Windows Forms, and it requires **PaintEventArgs** *e*, which is a parameter of the **Paint** event handler. The code performs the following action:

- Creates a solid blue brush.
- Creates a rectangle.
- Fills the rectangular area on the screen.

[Visual Basic]
```
Public Sub FillRectangleRectangle(e As PaintEventArgs)
' Create solid brush.
Dim blueBrush As New SolidBrush(Color.Blue)
' Create rectangle.
Dim rect As New Rectangle(0, 0, 200, 200)
' Fill rectangle to screen.
e.Graphics.FillRectangle(blueBrush, rect)
End Sub
```

[C#]
```
public void FillRectangleRectangle(PaintEventArgs e)
{
// Create solid brush.
SolidBrush blueBrush = new SolidBrush(Color.Blue);
// Create rectangle.
Rectangle rect = new Rectangle( 0, 0, 200, 200);
// Fill rectangle to screen.
e.Graphics.FillRectangle(blueBrush, rect);
}
```

Requirements

Platforms: Windows 98, Windows NT 4.0, Windows Millennium Edition, Windows 2000, Windows XP Home Edition, Windows XP Professional, Windows Server 2003 family, .NET Compact Framework - Windows CE .NET

Graphics.FillRectangle Method (Brush, RectangleF)

Fills the interior of a rectangle specified by a **RectangleF** structure.

[Visual Basic]
```
Overloads Public Sub FillRectangle( _
   ByVal brush As Brush, _
   ByVal rect As RectangleF _
)
```
[C#]
```
public void FillRectangle(
   Brush brush,
   RectangleF rect
);
```
[C++]
```
public: void FillRectangle(
   Brush* brush,
   RectangleF rect
);
```

```
[JScript]
public function FillRectangle(
   brush : Brush,
   rect : RectangleF
);
```

Parameters

brush

Brush object that determines the characteristics of the fill.

rect

RectangleF structure that represents the rectangle to fill.

Return Value

This method does not return a value.

Example

[Visual Basic, C#] The following example is designed for use with Windows Forms, and it requires **PaintEventArgs** *e*, which is a parameter of the **Paint** event handler. The code performs the following action:

- Creates a solid blue brush.
- Creates a rectangle.
- Fills the rectangular area on the screen.

```
[Visual Basic]
Public Sub FillRectangleRectangleF(e As PaintEventArgs)
' Create solid brush.
Dim blueBrush As New SolidBrush(Color.Blue)
' Create rectangle.
Dim rect As New RectangleF(0F, 0F, 200F, 200F)
' Fill rectangle to screen.
e.Graphics.FillRectangle(blueBrush, rect)
End Sub
```

```
[C#]
public void FillRectangleRectangleF(PaintEventArgs e)
{
// Create solid brush.
SolidBrush blueBrush = new SolidBrush(Color.Blue);
// Create rectangle.
RectangleF rect = new RectangleF( 0.0F, 0.0F, 200.0F, 200.0F);
// Fill rectangle to screen.
e.Graphics.FillRectangle(blueBrush, rect);
}
```

Requirements

Platforms: Windows 98, Windows NT 4.0, Windows Millennium Edition, Windows 2000, Windows XP Home Edition, Windows XP Professional, Windows Server 2003 family

Graphics.FillRectangle Method (Brush, Int32, Int32, Int32, Int32)

Fills the interior of a rectangle specified by a pair of coordinates, a width, and a height.

```
[Visual Basic]
Overloads Public Sub FillRectangle( _
   ByVal brush As Brush, _
   ByVal x As Integer, _
   ByVal y As Integer, _
   ByVal width As Integer, _
   ByVal height As Integer _
)
```

```
[C#]
public void FillRectangle(
   Brush brush,
   int x,
   int y,
   int width,
   int height
);
[C++]
public: void FillRectangle(
   Brush* brush,
   int x,
   int y,
   int width,
   int height
);
[JScript]
public function FillRectangle(
   brush : Brush,
   x : int,
   y : int,
   width : int,
   height : int
);
```

Parameters

brush

Brush object that determines the characteristics of the fill.

x

x-coordinate of the upper-left corner of the rectangle to fill.

y

y-coordinate of the upper-left corner of the rectangle to fill.

width

Width of the rectangle to fill.

height

Height of the rectangle to fill.

Return Value

This method does not return a value.

Remarks

This method fills the interior of the rectangle defined by the *x*, *y*, *width*, and *height* parameters.

Example

[Visual Basic, C#] The following example is designed for use with Windows Forms, and it requires **PaintEventArgs** *e*, which is a parameter of the **Paint** event handler. The code performs the following action:

- Creates a solid blue brush.
- Creates the location and size of a rectangle.
- Fills the rectangular area on the screen.

```
[Visual Basic]
Public Sub FillRectangleInt(e As PaintEventArgs)
' Create solid brush.
Dim blueBrush As New SolidBrush(Color.Blue)
' Create location and size of rectangle.
Dim x As Integer = 0
Dim y As Integer = 0
Dim width As Integer = 200
Dim height As Integer = 200
' Fill rectangle to screen.
e.Graphics.FillRectangle(blueBrush, x, y, width, height)
End Sub
```

[C#]
```
public void FillRectangleInt(PaintEventArgs e)
{
// Create solid brush.
SolidBrush blueBrush = new SolidBrush(Color.Blue);
// Create location and size of rectangle.
int x = 0;
int y = 0;
int width = 200;
int height = 200;
// Fill rectangle to screen.
e.Graphics.FillRectangle(blueBrush, x, y, width, height);
}
```

Requirements

Platforms: Windows 98, Windows NT 4.0, Windows Millennium Edition, Windows 2000, Windows XP Home Edition, Windows XP Professional, Windows Server 2003 family, .NET Compact Framework - Windows CE .NET

Graphics.FillRectangle Method (Brush, Single, Single, Single, Single)

Fills the interior of a rectangle specified by a pair of coordinates, a width, and a height.

[Visual Basic]
```
Overloads Public Sub FillRectangle( _
   ByVal brush As Brush, _
   ByVal x As Single, _
   ByVal y As Single, _
   ByVal width As Single, _
   ByVal height As Single _
)
```
[C#]
```
public void FillRectangle(
   Brush brush,
   float x,
   float y,
   float width,
   float height
);
```
[C++]
```
public: void FillRectangle(
   Brush* brush,
   float x,
   float y,
   float width,
   float height
);
```
[JScript]
```
public function FillRectangle(
   brush : Brush,
   x : float,
   y : float,
   width : float,
   height : float
);
```

Parameters

brush
    Brush object that determines the characteristics of the fill.

x
    x-coordinate of the upper-left corner of the rectangle to fill.

y
    y-coordinate of the upper-left corner of the rectangle to fill.

width
    Width of the rectangle to fill.

height
    Height of the rectangle to fill.

Return Value

This method does not return a value.

Remarks

This method fills the interior of the rectangle defined by the *x*, *y*, *width*, and *height* parameters.

Example

[Visual Basic, C#] The following example is designed for use with Windows Forms, and it requires **PaintEventArgs** *e*, which is a parameter of the **Paint** event handler. The code performs the following action:

- Creates a solid blue brush.
- Creates the location and size of a rectangle.
- Fills the rectangular area on the screen.

[Visual Basic]
```
Public Sub FillRectangleFloat(e As PaintEventArgs)
' Create solid brush.
Dim blueBrush As New SolidBrush(Color.Blue)
' Create location and size of rectangle.
Dim x As Single = 0F
Dim y As Single = 0F
Dim width As Single = 200F
Dim height As Single = 200F
' Fill rectangle to screen.
e.Graphics.FillRectangle(blueBrush, x, y, width, height)
End Sub
```

[C#]
```
public void FillRectangleFloat(PaintEventArgs e)
{
// Create solid brush.
SolidBrush blueBrush = new SolidBrush(Color.Blue);
// Create location and size of rectangle.
float x = 0.0F;
float y = 0.0F;
float width = 200.0F;
float height = 200.0F;
// Fill rectangle to screen.
e.Graphics.FillRectangle(blueBrush, x, y, width, height);
}
```

Requirements

Platforms: Windows 98, Windows NT 4.0, Windows Millennium Edition, Windows 2000, Windows XP Home Edition, Windows XP Professional, Windows Server 2003 family

Graphics.FillRectangles Method

Fills the interiors of a series of rectangles specified by **Rectangle** structures.

Overload List

Fills the interiors of a series of rectangles specified by **Rectangle** structures.

[Visual Basic] **Overloads Public Sub FillRectangles(Brush, Rectangle())**

[C#] **public void FillRectangles(Brush, Rectangle[]);**

[C++] **public: void FillRectangles(Brush*, Rectangle[]);**

[JScript] **public function FillRectangles(Brush, Rectangle[]);**

Fills the interiors of a series of rectangles specified by **RectangleF** structures.

[Visual Basic] **Overloads Public Sub FillRectangles(Brush, RectangleF())**

[C#] **public void FillRectangles(Brush, RectangleF[]);**

[C++] **public: void FillRectangles(Brush*, RectangleF[]);**

[JScript] **public function FillRectangles(Brush, RectangleF[]);**

Example

[Visual Basic, C#] The following example is designed for use with Windows Forms, and it requires **PaintEventArgs** *e*, which is a parameter of the **Paint** event handler. The code performs the following action:

- Creates a solid blue brush.
- Creates an array of three rectangles.
- Fills the three rectangular areas on the screen.

> [Visual Basic, C#] **Note** This example shows how to use one of the overloaded versions of **FillRectangles**. For other examples that might be available, see the individual overload topics.

[Visual Basic]
```
Public Sub FillRectanglesRectangleF(e As PaintEventArgs)
' Create solid brush.
Dim blueBrush As New SolidBrush(Color.Blue)
' Create array of rectangles.
Dim rects As RectangleF() = {New RectangleF(0F, 0F, 100F, 200F), _
New RectangleF(100F, 200F, 250F, 50F), _
New RectangleF(300F, 0F, 50F, 100F)}
' Fill rectangles to screen.
e.Graphics.FillRectangles(blueBrush, rects)
End Sub
```

[C#]
```
public void FillRectanglesRectangleF(PaintEventArgs e)
{
// Create solid brush.
SolidBrush blueBrush = new SolidBrush(Color.Blue);
// Create array of rectangles.
RectangleF[] rects =
{
new RectangleF( 0.0F,   0.0F, 100.0F, 200.0F),
new RectangleF(100.0F, 200.0F, 250.0F,  50.0F),
new RectangleF(300.0F,   0.0F,  50.0F, 100.0F)
};
// Fill rectangles to screen.
e.Graphics.FillRectangles(blueBrush, rects);
}
```

Graphics.FillRectangles Method (Brush, Rectangle[])

Fills the interiors of a series of rectangles specified by **Rectangle** structures.

[Visual Basic]
```
Overloads Public Sub FillRectangles( _
   ByVal brush As Brush, _
   ByVal rects() As Rectangle _
)
```
[C#]
```
public void FillRectangles(
   Brush brush,
   Rectangle[] rects
);
```
[C++]
```
public: void FillRectangles(
   Brush* brush,
   Rectangle rects[]
);
```
[JScript]
```
public function FillRectangles(
   brush : Brush,
   rects : Rectangle[]
);
```

Parameters

brush

Brush object that determines the characteristics of the fill.

rects

Array of **Rectangle** structures that represent the rectangles to fill.

Return Value

This method does not return a value.

Example

[Visual Basic, C#] The following example is designed for use with Windows Forms, and it requires **PaintEventArgs** *e*, which is a parameter of the **Paint** event handler. The code performs the following action:

- Creates a solid blue brush.
- Creates an array of three rectangles.
- Fills the three rectangular areas on the screen.

[Visual Basic]
```
Public Sub FillRectanglesRectangle(e As PaintEventArgs)
' Create solid brush.
Dim blueBrush As New SolidBrush(Color.Blue)
' Create array of rectangles.
Dim rects As Rectangle() = {New Rectangle(0, 0, 100, 200), _
New Rectangle(100, 200, 250, 50), _
New Rectangle(300, 0, 50, 100)}
' Fill rectangles to screen.
e.Graphics.FillRectangles(blueBrush, rects)
End Sub
```

[C#]
```
public void FillRectanglesRectangle(PaintEventArgs e)
{
// Create solid brush.
SolidBrush blueBrush = new SolidBrush(Color.Blue);
// Create array of rectangles.
Rectangle[] rects =
{
new Rectangle( 0,   0, 100, 200),
new Rectangle(100, 200, 250,  50),
new Rectangle(300,   0,  50, 100)
};
```

```
// Fill rectangles to screen.
e.Graphics.FillRectangles(blueBrush, rects);
}
```

Requirements

Platforms: Windows 98, Windows NT 4.0, Windows Millennium Edition, Windows 2000, Windows XP Home Edition, Windows XP Professional, Windows Server 2003 family

Graphics.FillRectangles Method (Brush, RectangleF[])

Fills the interiors of a series of rectangles specified by **RectangleF** structures.

[Visual Basic]
```
Overloads Public Sub FillRectangles( _
   ByVal brush As Brush, _
   ByVal rects() As RectangleF _
)
```
[C#]
```
public void FillRectangles(
   Brush brush,
   RectangleF[] rects
);
```
[C++]
```
public: void FillRectangles(
   Brush* brush,
   RectangleF rects[]
);
```
[JScript]
```
public function FillRectangles(
   brush : Brush,
   rects : RectangleF[]
);
```

Parameters

brush
: **Brush** object that determines the characteristics of the fill.

rects
: Array of **RectangleF** structures that represent the rectangles to fill.

Return Value

This method does not return a value.

Example

[Visual Basic, C#] The following example is designed for use with Windows Forms, and it requires **PaintEventArgs** *e*, which is a parameter of the **Paint** event handler. The code performs the following action:

- Creates a solid blue brush.
- Creates an array of three rectangles.
- Fills the three rectangular areas on the screen.

[Visual Basic]
```
Public Sub FillRectanglesRectangleF(e As PaintEventArgs)
' Create solid brush.
Dim blueBrush As New SolidBrush(Color.Blue)
' Create array of rectangles.
Dim rects As RectangleF() = {New RectangleF(0F, 0F, 100F, 200F), _
New RectangleF(100F, 200F, 250F, 50F), _
New RectangleF(300F, 0F, 50F, 100F)}
' Fill rectangles to screen.
e.Graphics.FillRectangles(blueBrush, rects)
End Sub
```
[C#]
```
public void FillRectanglesRectangleF(PaintEventArgs e)
{
// Create solid brush.
SolidBrush blueBrush = new SolidBrush(Color.Blue);
// Create array of rectangles.
RectangleF[] rects =
{
new RectangleF(  0.0F,   0.0F, 100.0F, 200.0F),
new RectangleF(100.0F, 200.0F, 250.0F,  50.0F),
new RectangleF(300.0F,   0.0F,  50.0F, 100.0F)
};
// Fill rectangles to screen.
e.Graphics.FillRectangles(blueBrush, rects);
}
```

Requirements

Platforms: Windows 98, Windows NT 4.0, Windows Millennium Edition, Windows 2000, Windows XP Home Edition, Windows XP Professional, Windows Server 2003 family

Graphics.FillRegion Method

Fills the interior of a **Region** object.

[Visual Basic]
```
Public Sub FillRegion( _
   ByVal brush As Brush, _
   ByVal region As Region _
)
```
[C#]
```
public void FillRegion(
   Brush brush,
   Region region
);
```
[C++]
```
public: void FillRegion(
   Brush* brush,
   Region* region
);
```
[JScript]
```
public function FillRegion(
   brush : Brush,
   region : Region
);
```

Parameters

brush
: **Brush** object that determines the characteristics of the fill.

region
: **Region** object that represents the area to fill.

Return Value

This method does not return a value.

Remarks

A **Region** object is composed of rectangles and paths. If the region is not closed, an additional segment is added from the last point to the first point to close it.

Example

[Visual Basic, C#] The following example is designed for use with Windows Forms, and it requires **PaintEventArgs** *e*, which is a parameter of the **Paint** event handler. The code performs the following action:

- Creates a solid blue brush.
- Creates a rectangle.
- Creates a rectangular region.
- Fills the rectangular region on the screen.

[Visual Basic]
```
Public Sub FillRegionRectangle(e As PaintEventArgs)
' Create solid brush.
Dim blueBrush As New SolidBrush(Color.Blue)
' Create rectangle for region.
Dim fillRect As New Rectangle(100, 100, 200, 200)
' Create region for fill.
Dim fillRegion As New [Region](fillRect)
' Fill region to screen.
e.Graphics.FillRegion(blueBrush, fillRegion)
End Sub
```

[C#]
```
public void FillRegionRectangle(PaintEventArgs e)
{
// Create solid brush.
SolidBrush blueBrush = new SolidBrush(Color.Blue);
// Create rectangle for region.
Rectangle fillRect = new Rectangle(100, 100, 200, 200);
// Create region for fill.
Region fillRegion = new Region(fillRect);
// Fill region to screen.
e.Graphics.FillRegion(blueBrush, fillRegion);
}
```

Requirements

Platforms: Windows 98, Windows NT 4.0, Windows Millennium Edition, Windows 2000, Windows XP Home Edition, Windows XP Professional, Windows Server 2003 family, .NET Compact Framework - Windows CE .NET

Graphics.Finalize Method

This member overrides **Object.Finalize**.

[Visual Basic]
```
Overrides Protected Sub Finalize()
```
[C#]
```
~Graphics();
```
[C++]
```
~Graphics();
```
[JScript]
```
protected override function Finalize();
```

Requirements

Platforms: Windows 98, Windows NT 4.0, Windows Millennium Edition, Windows 2000, Windows XP Home Edition, Windows XP Professional, Windows Server 2003 family, .NET Compact Framework - Windows CE .NET

Graphics.Flush Method

Forces execution of all pending graphics operations and returns immediately without waiting for the operations to finish.

Overload List

Forces execution of all pending graphics operations and returns immediately without waiting for the operations to finish.

[Visual Basic] **Overloads Public Sub Flush()**

[C#] **public void Flush();**

[C++] **public: void Flush();**

[JScript] **public function Flush();**

Forces execution of all pending graphics operations with the method waiting or not waiting, as specified, to return before the operations finish.

[Visual Basic] **Overloads Public Sub Flush(FlushIntention)**

[C#] **public void Flush(FlushIntention);**

[C++] **public: void Flush(FlushIntention);**

[JScript] **public function Flush(FlushIntention);**

Graphics.Flush Method ()

Forces execution of all pending graphics operations and returns immediately without waiting for the operations to finish.

[Visual Basic]
```
Overloads Public Sub Flush()
```
[C#]
```
public void Flush();
```
[C++]
```
public: void Flush();
```
[JScript]
```
public function Flush();
```

Return Value

This method does not return a value.

Remarks

This method starts a flush and returns immediately without waiting for any currently executing graphics operation to finish.

In version 1.0 of GDI+, this method flushes only GDI operations.

Requirements

Platforms: Windows 98, Windows NT 4.0, Windows Millennium Edition, Windows 2000, Windows XP Home Edition, Windows XP Professional, Windows Server 2003 family

Graphics.Flush Method (FlushIntention)

Forces execution of all pending graphics operations with the method waiting or not waiting, as specified, to return before the operations finish.

[Visual Basic]
```
Overloads Public Sub Flush( _
   ByVal intention As FlushIntention _
)
```
[C#]
```
public void Flush(
   FlushIntention intention
);
```

```
[C++]
public: void Flush(
   FlushIntention intention
);
[JScript]
public function Flush(
   intention : FlushIntention
);
```

Parameters

intention

Member of the **FlushIntention** enumeration that specifies whether the method returns immediately or waits for any existing operations to finish.

Return Value

This method does not return a value.

Remarks

A value of **FlushIntention.Flush** for the *intention* parameter specifies that the method return immediately after beginning the flush, while a value of **FlushIntention.Sync** specifies that the method wait before returning until any existing operations finish.

In version 1.0 of GDI+, this method flushes only GDI operations.

Requirements

Platforms: Windows 98, Windows NT 4.0, Windows Millennium Edition, Windows 2000, Windows XP Home Edition, Windows XP Professional, Windows Server 2003 family

Graphics.FromHdc Method

Creates a new **Graphics** object from the specified handle to a device context.

Overload List

Creates a new **Graphics** object from the specified handle to a device context.

[Visual Basic] **Overloads Public Shared Function FromHdc(IntPtr) As Graphics**

[C#] **public static Graphics FromHdc(IntPtr);**

[C++] **public: static Graphics* FromHdc(IntPtr);**

[JScript] **public static function FromHdc(IntPtr) : Graphics;**

Creates a new **Graphics** object from the specified handle to a device context and handle to a device.

[Visual Basic] **Overloads Public Shared Function FromHdc(IntPtr, IntPtr) As Graphics**

[C#] **public static Graphics FromHdc(IntPtr, IntPtr);**

[C++] **public: static Graphics* FromHdc(IntPtr, IntPtr);**

[JScript] **public static function FromHdc(IntPtr, IntPtr) : Graphics;**

Example

[Visual Basic, C#] The following example is designed for use with Windows Forms, and it requires **PaintEventArgs** *e*, which is a parameter of the **Paint** event handler. The code performs the following action:

- Creates an internal pointer type variable *hdc* and sets it to the handle to the device context of the graphics object of the form.
- Creates a new graphics object using *hdc*.
- Draws a rectangle with the new graphics object (on the screen).
- Releases the new graphics object using *hdc*.

[Visual Basic, C#] **Note** This example shows how to use one of the overloaded versions of **FromHdc**. For other examples that might be available, see the individual overload topics.

```
[Visual Basic]
Public Sub FromHdcHdc(e As PaintEventArgs)
' Get handle to device context.
Dim hdc As IntPtr = e.Graphics.GetHdc()
' Create new graphics object using handle to device context.
Dim newGraphics As Graphics = Graphics.FromHdc(hdc)
' Draw rectangle to screen.
newGraphics.DrawRectangle(New Pen(Color.Red, 3), 0, 0, 200, 100)
' Release handle to device context.
e.Graphics.ReleaseHdc(hdc)
End Sub
```

```
[C#]
public void FromHdcHdc(PaintEventArgs e)
{
// Get handle to device context.
IntPtr hdc = e.Graphics.GetHdc();
// Create new graphics object using handle to device context.
Graphics newGraphics = Graphics.FromHdc(hdc);
// Draw rectangle to screen.
newGraphics.DrawRectangle(new Pen(Color.Red, 3), 0, 0, 200, 100);
// Release handle to device context.
e.Graphics.ReleaseHdc(hdc);
}
```

Graphics.FromHdc Method (IntPtr)

Creates a new **Graphics** object from the specified handle to a device context.

```
[Visual Basic]
Overloads Public Shared Function FromHdc( _
   ByVal hdc As IntPtr _
) As Graphics
[C#]
public static Graphics FromHdc(
   IntPtr hdc
);
[C++]
public: static Graphics* FromHdc(
   IntPtr hdc
);
[JScript]
public static function FromHdc(
   hdc : IntPtr
) : Graphics;
```

Parameters

hdc

Handle to a device context.

Return Value

This method returns a new **Graphics** object for the specified device context.

Remarks

Even if the display device has an associated ICM color profile, GDI+ will not use that profile by default. To enable ICM for a **Graphics** object, construct the **Graphics** object from an HDC after you pass the HDC (and ICM_ON) to the SetICMMode function. Then any drawing done by the **Graphics** object will be adjusted according to the ICM profile associated with the display device.

Enabling ICM will result in slower performance.

The state of the device context (mapping mode, logical unit, and the like) at the time you call **Graphics.FromHdc** can affect rendering done by the **Graphics** object.

Example

[Visual Basic, C#] The following example is designed for use with Windows Forms, and it requires **PaintEventArgs** *e*, which is a parameter of the **Paint** event handler. The code performs the following action:

- Creates an internal pointer type variable *hdc* and sets it to the handle to the device context of the graphics object of the form.
- Creates a new graphics object using *hdc*.
- Draws a rectangle with the new graphics object (on the screen).
- Releases the new graphics object using *hdc*.

[Visual Basic]
```
Public Sub FromHdcHdc(e As PaintEventArgs)
' Get handle to device context.
Dim hdc As IntPtr = e.Graphics.GetHdc()
' Create new graphics object using handle to device context.
Dim newGraphics As Graphics = Graphics.FromHdc(hdc)
' Draw rectangle to screen.
newGraphics.DrawRectangle(New Pen(Color.Red, 3), 0, 0, 200, 100)
' Release handle to device context.
e.Graphics.ReleaseHdc(hdc)
End Sub
```

[C#]
```
public void FromHdcHdc(PaintEventArgs e)
{
// Get handle to device context.
IntPtr hdc = e.Graphics.GetHdc();
// Create new graphics object using handle to device context.
Graphics newGraphics = Graphics.FromHdc(hdc);
// Draw rectangle to screen.
newGraphics.DrawRectangle(new Pen(Color.Red, 3), 0, 0, 200, 100);
// Release handle to device context.
e.Graphics.ReleaseHdc(hdc);
}
```

Requirements

Platforms: Windows 98, Windows NT 4.0, Windows Millennium Edition, Windows 2000, Windows XP Home Edition, Windows XP Professional, Windows Server 2003 family

Graphics.FromHdc Method (IntPtr, IntPtr)

Creates a new **Graphics** object from the specified handle to a device context and handle to a device.

[Visual Basic]
```
Overloads Public Shared Function FromHdc( _
   ByVal hdc As IntPtr, _
   ByVal hdevice As IntPtr _
) As Graphics
```
[C#]
```
public static Graphics FromHdc(
   IntPtr hdc,
   IntPtr hdevice
);
```
[C++]
```
public: static Graphics* FromHdc(
   IntPtr hdc,
   IntPtr hdevice
);
```
[JScript]
```
public static function FromHdc(
   hdc : IntPtr,
   hdevice : IntPtr
) : Graphics;
```

Parameters

hdc
: Handle to a device context.

hdevice
: Handle to a device.

Return Value

This method returns a new **Graphics** object for the specified device context and device.

Remarks

Even if the display device has an associated ICM color profile, GDI+ will not use that profile by default. To enable ICM for a **Graphics** object, construct the **Graphics** object from an HDC after you pass the HDC (and ICM_ON) to the SetICMMode function. Then any drawing done by the **Graphics** object will be adjusted according to the ICM profile associated with the display device. Enabling ICM will result in slower performance.

The state of the device context (mapping mode, logical unit, and the like) at the time you call **Graphics.FromHdc** can affect rendering done by the **Graphics** object.

The device handle is typically used to query specific printer capabilities.

Requirements

Platforms: Windows 98, Windows NT 4.0, Windows Millennium Edition, Windows 2000, Windows XP Home Edition, Windows XP Professional, Windows Server 2003 family

Graphics.FromHdcInternal Method

Internal method. Do not use.

[Visual Basic]
```
Public Shared Function FromHdcInternal( _
   ByVal hdc As IntPtr _
) As Graphics
```
[C#]
```
public static Graphics FromHdcInternal(
   IntPtr hdc
);
```
[C++]
```
public: static Graphics* FromHdcInternal(
   IntPtr hdc
);
```
[JScript]
```
public static function FromHdcInternal(
   hdc : IntPtr
) : Graphics;
```

Parameters

hdc
: Handle to a device context.

Return Value

This method returns a new **Graphics** object for the specified device context.

Remarks

This method is an internal method and should not be used.

Requirements

Platforms: Windows 98, Windows NT 4.0, Windows Millennium Edition, Windows 2000, Windows XP Home Edition, Windows XP Professional, Windows Server 2003 family

Graphics.FromHow Method

Note: This namespace, class, or member is supported only in version 1.1 of the .NET Framework.

This member supports the .NET Framework infrastructure and is not intended to be used directly from your code.

[Visual Basic]
```
Public Shared Function FromHow( _
   ByVal how As IntPtr, _
   ByVal fFree As Boolean _
) As Graphics
```
[C#]
```
public static Graphics FromHow(
   IntPtr how,
   bool fFree
);
```
[C++]
```
public: static Graphics* FromHow(
   IntPtr how,
   bool fFree
);
```
[JScript]
```
public static function FromHow(
   how : IntPtr,
   fFree : Boolean
) : Graphics;
```

Graphics.FromHwnd Method

Creates a new **Graphics** object from the specified handle to a window.

[Visual Basic]
```
Public Shared Function FromHwnd( _
   ByVal hwnd As IntPtr _
) As Graphics
```
[C#]
```
public static Graphics FromHwnd(
   IntPtr hwnd
);
```
[C++]
```
public: static Graphics* FromHwnd(
   IntPtr hwnd
);
```
[JScript]
```
public static function FromHwnd(
   hwnd : IntPtr
) : Graphics;
```

Parameters

hwnd

Handle to a window.

Return Value

This method returns a new **Graphics** object for the specified window handle.

Example

[Visual Basic, C#] The following example is designed for use with Windows Forms, and it requires **PaintEventArgs** *e*, which is a parameter of the **Paint** event handler, as well as *thisForm*, the **Form** object for the example. The code performs the following actions:

- Creates a new internal pointer variable *hwnd* and sets it to the handle of the example's form.
- Creates a new **Graphics** object from the handle.
- Draws a rectangle to the new **Graphics** object using a red pen.
- Disposes the new **Graphics** object.

[Visual Basic]
```
Public Sub FromHwndHwnd(e As PaintEventArgs)
' Get handle to form.
Dim hwnd As New IntPtr()
hwnd = thisForm.Handle
' Create new graphics object using handle to window.
Dim newGraphics As Graphics = Graphics.FromHwnd(hwnd)
' Draw rectangle to screen.
newGraphics.DrawRectangle(New Pen(Color.Red, 3), 0, 0, 200, 100)
' Dispose of new graphics.
newGraphics.Dispose()
End Sub
```

[C#]
```
public void FromHwndHwnd(PaintEventArgs e)
{
// Get handle to form.
IntPtr hwnd = new IntPtr();
hwnd = thisForm.Handle;
// Create new graphics object using handle to window.
Graphics newGraphics = Graphics.FromHwnd(hwnd);
// Draw rectangle to screen.
newGraphics.DrawRectangle(new Pen(Color.Red, 3), 0, 0, 200, 100);
// Dispose of new graphics.
newGraphics.Dispose();
}
```

Requirements

Platforms: Windows 98, Windows NT 4.0, Windows Millennium Edition, Windows 2000, Windows XP Home Edition, Windows XP Professional, Windows Server 2003 family

Graphics.FromHwndInternal Method

Internal method. Do not use.

[Visual Basic]
```
Public Shared Function FromHwndInternal( _
   ByVal hwnd As IntPtr _
) As Graphics
```
[C#]
```
public static Graphics FromHwndInternal(
   IntPtr hwnd
);
```
[C++]
```
public: static Graphics* FromHwndInternal(
   IntPtr hwnd
);
```

```
[JScript]
public static function FromHwndInternal(
   hwnd : IntPtr
) : Graphics;
```

Parameters

hwnd

Handle to a window.

Return Value

This method returns a new **Graphics** object for the specified window handle.

Remarks

This method is an internal method and should not be used.

Requirements

Platforms: Windows 98, Windows NT 4.0, Windows Millennium Edition, Windows 2000, Windows XP Home Edition, Windows XP Professional, Windows Server 2003 family

Graphics.FromImage Method

Creates a new **Graphics** object from the specified **Image** object.

```
[Visual Basic]
Public Shared Function FromImage( _
   ByVal image As Image _
) As Graphics
[C#]
public static Graphics FromImage(
   Image image
);
[C++]
public: static Graphics* FromImage(
   Image* image
);
[JScript]
public static function FromImage(
   image : Image
) : Graphics;
```

Parameters

image

Image object from which to create the new **Graphics** object.

Return Value

This method returns a new **Graphics** for the specified **Image** object.

Remarks

If the image has an indexed pixel format, this method throws an exception with the message, "A Graphics object cannot be created from an image that has an indexed pixel format." The indexed pixel formats are shown in the following list.

- PixelFormat.Format1bppIndexed
- PixelFormat.Format4bppIndexed
- PixelFormat.Format8bppIndexed

This method also throws an exception if the image has any of the following pixel formats.

- PixelFormat.Undefined
- PixelFormat.DontCare
- PixelFormat.Format16bppArgb1555
- PixelFormat.Format16bppGrayScale

Example

[Visual Basic, C#] The following example is designed for use with Windows Forms, and it requires **PaintEventArgs** *e*, which is a parameter of the **Paint** event handler. The code performs the following action:

- Creates an **Image** object from a graphics file SampImag.jpg in the example folder.
- Creates a **Graphics** object from the **Image** object.
- Alters the image by filling a rectangle within it.
- Draws the **Image** object to the screen.
- Releases the created **Graphics** object.

```
[Visual Basic]
Public Sub FromImageImage(e As PaintEventArgs)
' Create image.
Dim imageFile As Image = Image.FromFile("SampImag.jpg")
' Create graphics object for alteration.
Dim newGraphics As Graphics = Graphics.FromImage(imageFile)
' Alter image.
newGraphics.FillRectangle(New SolidBrush(Color.Black), _
100, 50, 100, 100)
' Draw image to screen.
e.Graphics.DrawImage(imageFile, New PointF(0F, 0F))
' Dispose of graphics object.
newGraphics.Dispose()
End Sub
```

```
[C#]
public void FromImageImage(PaintEventArgs e)
{
// Create image.
Image imageFile = Image.FromFile("SampImag.jpg");
// Create graphics object for alteration.
Graphics newGraphics = Graphics.FromImage(imageFile);
// Alter image.
newGraphics.FillRectangle(new SolidBrush(Color.Black), 100,        ↵
 50, 100, 100);
// Draw image to screen.
e.Graphics.DrawImage(imageFile, new PointF(0.0F, 0.0F));
// Release graphics object.
newGraphics.Dispose();
}
```

Requirements

Platforms: Windows 98, Windows NT 4.0, Windows Millennium Edition, Windows 2000, Windows XP Home Edition, Windows XP Professional, Windows Server 2003 family, .NET Compact Framework - Windows CE .NET

Graphics.GetHalftonePalette Method

Gets a handle to the current Windows halftone palette.

```
[Visual Basic]
Public Shared Function GetHalftonePalette() As IntPtr
[C#]
public static IntPtr GetHalftonePalette();
[C++]
public: static IntPtr GetHalftonePalette();
[JScript]
public static function GetHalftonePalette() : IntPtr;
```

Return Value

Internal pointer that specifies the handle to the palette.

Remarks

The purpose of the **GetHalftonePalette** method is to enable GDI+ to produce a better quality halftone when the display uses 8 bits per pixel. To display an image using the halftone palette, use the following procedure.

Example

[Visual Basic, C#] The following example is designed for use with Windows Forms, and it requires **PaintEventArgs** *e*, which is a parameter of the **Paint** event handler. The code performs the following actions:

- Defines interoperability **DllImportAttribute** attributes for the Windows DLL file gdi32.dll, which contains the necessary GDI functions.
- Defines the **SelectPalette** and **RealizePalette** functions in that DLL as external.
- Creates an image from an existing image file SampImag.jpg (which must be in the same folder as the example code file) and draws the image to the screen.
- Creates internal pointer type variables and sets their values to the handle to the *e . Graphics* object and to the current Windows halftone palette, respectively.
- Selects and realizes the halftone palette.
- Creates a new graphics object using the *hdc* parameter.
- Draws the image again.
- Releases the handle to the device context.

[Visual Basic, C#] The result is two renderings of the sample image: one with the 16-bit palette and one with the 8-bit palette.

[Visual Basic]

```
<System.Runtime.InteropServices.DllImportAttribute("gdi32.dll")> _
Private Shared Function SelectPalette(hdc As IntPtr, _
htPalette As IntPtr, bForceBackground As Boolean) As IntPtr
End Function
<System.Runtime.InteropServices.DllImportAttribute("gdi32.dll")> _
Private Shared Function RealizePalette(hdc As IntPtr) As Integer
End Function
Public Sub GetHalftonePaletteVoid(e As PaintEventArgs)
' Create and draw image.
Dim imageFile As Image = Image.FromFile("SampImag.jpg")
e.Graphics.DrawImage(imageFile, New Point(0, 0))
' Get handle to device context.
Dim hdc As IntPtr = e.Graphics.GetHdc()
' Get handle to halftone palette.
Dim htPalette As IntPtr = Graphics.GetHalftonePalette()
' Select and realize new palette.
SelectPalette(hdc, htPalette, True)
RealizePalette(hdc)
' Create new graphics object.
Dim newGraphics As Graphics = Graphics.FromHdc(hdc)
' Draw image with new palette.
newGraphics.DrawImage(imageFile, 300, 0)
' Release handle to device context.
e.Graphics.ReleaseHdc(hdc)
End Sub
```

[C#]

```
[System.Runtime.InteropServices.DllImportAttribute("gdi32.dll")]
private static extern IntPtr SelectPalette(
IntPtr hdc,
IntPtr htPalette,
bool bForceBackground);
[System.Runtime.InteropServices.DllImportAttribute("gdi32.dll")]
private static extern int RealizePalette(IntPtr hdc);
public void GetHalftonePaletteVoid(PaintEventArgs e)
{
// Create and draw image.
Image imageFile = Image.FromFile("SampImag.jpg");
e.Graphics.DrawImage(imageFile, new Point(0, 0));
// Get handle to device context.
IntPtr hdc = e.Graphics.GetHdc();
// Get handle to halftone palette.
IntPtr htPalette = Graphics.GetHalftonePalette();
// Select and realize new palette.
SelectPalette(hdc, htPalette, true);
RealizePalette(hdc);
// Create new graphics object.
Graphics newGraphics = Graphics.FromHdc(hdc);
// Draw image with new palette.
newGraphics.DrawImage(imageFile, 300, 0);
// Release handle to device context.
e.Graphics.ReleaseHdc(hdc);
}
```

Requirements

Platforms: Windows 98, Windows NT 4.0, Windows Millennium Edition, Windows 2000, Windows XP Home Edition, Windows XP Professional, Windows Server 2003 family

Graphics.GetHdc Method

Gets the handle to the device context associated with this **Graphics** object.

[Visual Basic]

```
Public Function GetHdc() As IntPtr
```

[C#]

```
public IntPtr GetHdc();
```

[C++]

```
public: IntPtr GetHdc();
```

[JScript]

```
public function GetHdc() : IntPtr;
```

Return Value

Handle to the device context associated with this **Graphics** object.

Remarks

The device context is a Windows GDI-based structure that defines a set of graphical objects and their associated attributes, as well as the graphical modes that affect output. This method returns that device context with the exception of a font. Because a font is not selected, calls to the **Font.FromHdc** method using a handle returned from the **GetHdc** method will fail.

Calls to the **GetHdc** and **ReleaseHdc** methods must appear in pairs. During the scope of a **GetHdc- ReleaseHdc** method pair, you usually make only calls to GDI functions. Calls in that scope made to GDI+ methods of the **Graphics** object that produced the *hdc* parameter fail with an ObjectBusy error. Also, GDI+ ignores any state changes made to the **Graphics** object of the *hdc* parameter in subsequent operations.

Example

[Visual Basic, C#] The following example is designed for use with Windows Forms, and it requires **PaintEventArgs** *e*, which is a parameter of the **Paint** event handler. The example illustrates calling a Windows GDI function to perform the same task as a GDI+ **Graphics** object method. The code performs the following actions:

- Defines the interoperability **DllImportAttribute** attribute for the Windows DLL file gdi32.dll. This DLL contains the desired GDI function.
- Defines the **Rectangle** function in that DLL as external.

- Creates a red pen.
- With the pen, draws a rectangle to the screen using the GDI+ **DrawRectangle** method.
- Defines an internal pointer type variable *hdc* and sets its value to the handle to the device context of the form.
- Draws a rectangle to the screen using the GDI **Rectangle** function.
- Releases the device context represented by the *hdc* parameter.

[Visual Basic]
```
<System.Runtime.InteropServices.DllImportAttribute("gdi32.dll")> _
Private Shared Function Rectangle(hdc As IntPtr, _
ulCornerX As Integer, ulCornerY As Integer, lrCornerX As Integer, _
lrCornerY As Integer) As Boolean
End Function
Public Sub GetHdcForGDI(e As PaintEventArgs)
' Create pen.
Dim redPen As New Pen(Color.Red, 1)
' Draw rectangle with GDI+.
e.Graphics.DrawRectangle(redPen, 10, 10, 100, 50)
' Get handle to device context.
Dim hdc As IntPtr = e.Graphics.GetHdc()
' Draw rectangle with GDI using default pen.
Rectangle(hdc, 10, 70, 110, 120)
' Release handle to device context.
e.Graphics.ReleaseHdc(hdc)
End Sub
```

[C#]
```
[System.Runtime.InteropServices.DllImportAttribute("gdi32.dll")]
private static extern bool Rectangle(
IntPtr hdc,
int ulCornerX, int ulCornerY,
int lrCornerX, int lrCornerY);
public void GetHdcForGDI(PaintEventArgs e)
{
// Create pen.
Pen redPen = new Pen(Color.Red, 1);
// Draw rectangle with GDI+.
e.Graphics.DrawRectangle(redPen, 10, 10, 100, 50);
// Get handle to device context.
IntPtr hdc = new IntPtr();
hdc = e.Graphics.GetHdc();
// Draw rectangle with GDI using default pen.
Rectangle(hdc, 10, 70, 110, 120);
// Release handle to device context.
e.Graphics.ReleaseHdc(hdc);
}
```

Requirements

Platforms: Windows 98, Windows NT 4.0,
Windows Millennium Edition, Windows 2000,
Windows XP Home Edition, Windows XP Professional,
Windows Server 2003 family

Graphics.GetNearestColor Method

Gets the nearest color to the specified **Color** structure.

[Visual Basic]
```
Public Function GetNearestColor( _
   ByVal color As Color _
) As Color
```
[C#]
```
public Color GetNearestColor(
   Color color
);
```
[C++]
```
public: Color GetNearestColor(
   Color color
);
```
[JScript]
```
public function GetNearestColor(
   color : Color
) : Color;
```

Parameters

color

Color structure for which to find a match.

Return Value

The method returns a **Color** structure that represents the nearest color to the one specified with the *color* parameter.

Example

[Visual Basic, C#] The following example is designed for use with Windows Forms, and it requires **PaintEventArgs** *e*, which is a parameter of the **Paint** event handler. The code performs the following actions:

- Creates an arbitrary color with ARGB coordinates (255, 165, 63, 136).
- Creates a solid brush and sets its color to the specified color.
- Fills an ellipse using the arbitrary color.
- Creates a second color and sets its value to the nearest system ARGB color.
- Fills a second ellipse with this color.

[Visual Basic, C#] The result is two ellipses: the first drawn with the arbitrary, specified color and the second drawn with the system color nearest the specified color.

[Visual Basic]
```
Public Sub GetNearestColorColor(e As PaintEventArgs)
' Create solid brush with arbitrary color.
Dim arbColor As Color = Color.FromArgb(255, 165, 63, 136)
Dim arbBrush As New SolidBrush(arbColor)
' Fill ellipse on screen.
e.Graphics.FillEllipse(arbBrush, 0, 0, 200, 100)
' Get nearest color.
Dim realColor As Color = e.Graphics.GetNearestColor(arbColor)
Dim realBrush As New SolidBrush(realColor)
' Fill ellipse on screen.
e.Graphics.FillEllipse(realBrush, 0, 100, 200, 100)
End Sub
```

[C#]
```
public void GetNearestColorColor(PaintEventArgs e)
{
// Create solid brush with arbitrary color.
Color arbColor = Color.FromArgb(255, 165, 63 , 136);
SolidBrush arbBrush = new SolidBrush(arbColor);
// Fill ellipse on screen.
e.Graphics.FillEllipse(arbBrush, 0, 0, 200, 100);
// Get nearest color.
Color realColor = e.Graphics.GetNearestColor(arbColor);
SolidBrush realBrush = new SolidBrush(realColor);
// Fill ellipse on screen.
e.Graphics.FillEllipse(realBrush, 0, 100, 200, 100);
}
```

Requirements

Platforms: Windows 98, Windows NT 4.0,
Windows Millennium Edition, Windows 2000,
Windows XP Home Edition, Windows XP Professional,
Windows Server 2003 family

Graphics.IntersectClip Method

Updates the clip region of this **Graphics** object to the intersection of the current clip region and the specified **Rectangle** structure.

Overload List

Updates the clip region of this **Graphics** object to the intersection of the current clip region and the specified **Rectangle** structure.

[Visual Basic] **Overloads Public Sub IntersectClip(Rectangle)**

[C#] **public void IntersectClip(Rectangle);**

[C++] **public: void IntersectClip(Rectangle);**

[JScript] **public function IntersectClip(Rectangle);**

Updates the clip region of this **Graphics** object to the intersection of the current clip region and the specified **RectangleF** structure.

[Visual Basic] **Overloads Public Sub IntersectClip(RectangleF)**

[C#] **public void IntersectClip(RectangleF);**

[C++] **public: void IntersectClip(RectangleF);**

[JScript] **public function IntersectClip(RectangleF);**

Updates the clip region of this **Graphics** object to the intersection of the current clip region and the specified **Region** object.

[Visual Basic] **Overloads Public Sub IntersectClip(Region)**

[C#] **public void IntersectClip(Region);**

[C++] **public: void IntersectClip(Region*);**

[JScript] **public function IntersectClip(Region);**

Example

[Visual Basic, C#] The following example is designed for use with Windows Forms, and it requires **PaintEventArgs** *e*, which is a parameter of the **Paint** event handler. The code performs the following actions:

- Creates a rectangle with upper-left corner at (0, 0).
- Creates a region and sets it to the rectangle, and sets the clipping region to this region.
- Creates a second rectangle with upper-left corner at (100, 100).
- Creates a region and sets it to the second rectangle, and sets the clipping region to the intersection of this region and the current clipping region (the first rectangle) using a combine mode of **CombineMode.Replace**.
- Fills a large rectangle that includes both previous regions with a solid blue brush.
- Resets the clipping region to infinite.
- Draws rectangles around the two clipping regions. It uses a black pen for the first clipping region and a red pen for the second clipping region.

[Visual Basic, C#] The result is that only the intersection of the two regions is filled with blue.

> [Visual Basic, C#] **Note** This example shows how to use one of the overloaded versions of **IntersectClip**. For other examples that might be available, see the individual overload topics.

[Visual Basic]
```
Public Sub IntersectClipRegion(e As PaintEventArgs)
' Set clipping region.
Dim clipRect As New Rectangle(0, 0, 200, 200)
Dim clipRegion As New [Region](clipRect)
e.Graphics.SetClip(clipRegion, CombineMode.Replace)
' Update clipping region to intersection of
' existing region with specified rectangle.
Dim intersectRect As New Rectangle(100, 100, 200, 200)
Dim intersectRegion As New [Region](intersectRect)
e.Graphics.IntersectClip(intersectRegion)
' Fill rectangle to demonstrate effective clipping region.
e.Graphics.FillRectangle(New SolidBrush(Color.Blue), 0, 0, _
500, 500)
' Reset clipping region to infinite.
e.Graphics.ResetClip()
' Draw clipRect and intersectRect to screen.
e.Graphics.DrawRectangle(New Pen(Color.Black), clipRect)
e.Graphics.DrawRectangle(New Pen(Color.Red), intersectRect)
End Sub
```

[C#]
```
public void IntersectClipRegion(PaintEventArgs e)
{
// Set clipping region.
Rectangle clipRect = new Rectangle(0, 0, 200, 200);
Region clipRegion = new Region(clipRect);
e.Graphics.SetClip(clipRegion, CombineMode.Replace);
// Update clipping region to intersection of
//  existing region with specified rectangle.
Rectangle intersectRect = new Rectangle(100, 100, 200, 200);
Region intersectRegion = new Region(intersectRect);
e.Graphics.IntersectClip(intersectRegion);
// Fill rectangle to demonstrate effective clipping region.
e.Graphics.FillRectangle(new SolidBrush(Color.Blue), 0, 0, 500, 500);
// Reset clipping region to infinite.
e.Graphics.ResetClip();
// Draw clipRect and intersectRect to screen.
e.Graphics.DrawRectangle(new Pen(Color.Black), clipRect);
e.Graphics.DrawRectangle(new Pen(Color.Red), intersectRect);
}
```

Graphics.IntersectClip Method (Rectangle)

Updates the clip region of this **Graphics** object to the intersection of the current clip region and the specified **Rectangle** structure.

[Visual Basic]
```
Overloads Public Sub IntersectClip( _
   ByVal rect As Rectangle _
)
```
[C#]
```
public void IntersectClip(
   Rectangle rect
);
```
[C++]
```
public: void IntersectClip(
   Rectangle rect
);
```
[JScript]
```
public function IntersectClip(
   rect : Rectangle
);
```

Parameters

rect

Rectangle structure to intersect with the current clip region.

Return Value

This method does not return a value.

Remarks

This method assigns to the **Clip** property of this **Graphics** object the area represented by the intersection of the current clip region and the rectangle specified by the *rect* parameter.

Example

[Visual Basic, C#] The following example is designed for use with Windows Forms, and it requires **PaintEventArgs** *e*, which is a parameter of the **Paint** event handler. The code performs the following actions:

- Creates a rectangle with upper-left corner at (0, 0) and sets the clipping region to this rectangle.
- Creates a second rectangle with upper-left corner at (100, 100) and sets the clipping region to the intersection of this rectangle and the current clipping region (the first rectangle).
- Fills a large rectangle that includes both previous rectangles with a solid blue brush.
- Resets the clipping region to infinite.
- Draws rectangles around the two clipping regions. It uses a black pen for the first clipping rectangle and a red pen for the second clipping region.

[Visual Basic, C#] The result is that only the intersection of the two rectangles is filled with blue.

[Visual Basic]
```
Public Sub IntersectClipRectangle(e As PaintEventArgs)
' Set clipping region.
Dim clipRect As New Rectangle(0, 0, 200, 200)
e.Graphics.SetClip(clipRect)
' Update clipping region to intersection of
' existing region with specified rectangle.
Dim intersectRect As New Rectangle(100, 100, 200, 200)
e.Graphics.IntersectClip(intersectRect)
' Fill rectangle to demonstrate effective clipping region.
e.Graphics.FillRectangle(New SolidBrush(Color.Blue), 0, 0, _
500, 500)
' Reset clipping region to infinite.
e.Graphics.ResetClip()
' Draw clipRect and intersectRect to screen.
e.Graphics.DrawRectangle(New Pen(Color.Black), clipRect)
e.Graphics.DrawRectangle(New Pen(Color.Red), intersectRect)
End Sub
```

[C#]
```
public void IntersectClipRectangle(PaintEventArgs e)
{
// Set clipping region.
Rectangle clipRect = new Rectangle(0, 0, 200, 200);
e.Graphics.SetClip(clipRect);
// Update clipping region to intersection of
// existing region with specified rectangle.
Rectangle intersectRect = new Rectangle(100, 100, 200, 200);
e.Graphics.IntersectClip(intersectRect);
// Fill rectangle to demonstrate effective clipping region.
e.Graphics.FillRectangle(new SolidBrush(Color.Blue), 0, 0, 500, 500);
// Reset clipping region to infinite.
e.Graphics.ResetClip();
// Draw clipRect and intersectRect to screen.
e.Graphics.DrawRectangle(new Pen(Color.Black), clipRect);
e.Graphics.DrawRectangle(new Pen(Color.Red), intersectRect);
}
```

Requirements

Platforms: Windows 98, Windows NT 4.0, Windows Millennium Edition, Windows 2000, Windows XP Home Edition, Windows XP Professional, Windows Server 2003 family

Graphics.IntersectClip Method (RectangleF)

Updates the clip region of this **Graphics** object to the intersection of the current clip region and the specified **RectangleF** structure.

[Visual Basic]
```
Overloads Public Sub IntersectClip( _
   ByVal rect As RectangleF _
)
```
[C#]
```
public void IntersectClip(
   RectangleF rect
);
```
[C++]
```
public: void IntersectClip(
   RectangleF rect
);
```
[JScript]
```
public function IntersectClip(
   rect : RectangleF
);
```

Parameters

rect

RectangleF structure to intersect with the current clip region.

Return Value

This method does not return a value.

Remarks

This method assigns to the **Clip** property of this **Graphics** object the area represented by the intersection of the current clip region and the rectangle specified by the *rect* parameter.

Example

[Visual Basic, C#] The following example is designed for use with Windows Forms, and it requires **PaintEventArgs** *e*, which is a parameter of the **Paint** event handler. The code performs the following actions:

- Creates a rectangle with upper-left corner at (0, 0) and sets the clipping region to this rectangle.
- Creates a second rectangle with upper-left corner at (100, 100) and sets the clipping region to the intersection of this rectangle and the current clipping region (the first rectangle).
- Fills a large rectangle that includes both previous rectangles with a solid blue brush.
- Resets the clipping region to infinite.
- Draws rectangles around the two clipping regions. It uses a black pen for the first clipping rectangle and a red pen for the second clipping region.

[Visual Basic, C#] The result is that only the intersection of the two rectangles is filled with blue.

[Visual Basic]
```
Public Sub IntersectClipRectangleF(e As PaintEventArgs)
' Set clipping region.
Dim clipRect As New Rectangle(0, 0, 200, 200)
e.Graphics.SetClip(clipRect)
' Update clipping region to intersection of
' existing region with specified rectangle.
Dim intersectRectF As New RectangleF(100F, 100F, 200F, 200F)
e.Graphics.IntersectClip(intersectRectF)
' Fill rectangle to demonstrate effective clipping region.
e.Graphics.FillRectangle(New SolidBrush(Color.Blue), 0, 0, _
500, 500)
' Reset clipping region to infinite.
```

```
e.Graphics.ResetClip()
' Draw clipRect and intersectRect to screen.
e.Graphics.DrawRectangle(New Pen(Color.Black), clipRect)
e.Graphics.DrawRectangle(New Pen(Color.Red), _
Rectangle.Round(intersectRectF))
End Sub
```

[C#]

```
public void IntersectClipRectangleF(PaintEventArgs e)
{
// Set clipping region.
Rectangle clipRect = new Rectangle(0, 0, 200, 200);
e.Graphics.SetClip(clipRect);
// Update clipping region to intersection of
// existing region with specified rectangle.
RectangleF intersectRect = new RectangleF(100.0F, 100.0F,
200.0F, 200.0F);
e.Graphics.IntersectClip(intersectRect);
// Fill rectangle to demonstrate effective clipping region.
e.Graphics.FillRectangle(new SolidBrush(Color.Blue), 0, 0, 500, 500);
// Reset clipping region to infinite.
e.Graphics.ResetClip();
// Draw clipRect and intersectRect to screen.
e.Graphics.DrawRectangle(new Pen(Color.Black), clipRect);
e.Graphics.DrawRectangle(new Pen(Color.Red), (Rectangle)intersectRect);
}
```

Requirements

Platforms: Windows 98, Windows NT 4.0, Windows Millennium Edition, Windows 2000, Windows XP Home Edition, Windows XP Professional, Windows Server 2003 family

Graphics.IntersectClip Method (Region)

Updates the clip region of this **Graphics** object to the intersection of the current clip region and the specified **Region** object.

[Visual Basic]

```
Overloads Public Sub IntersectClip( _
   ByVal region As Region _
)
```

[C#]

```
public void IntersectClip(
   Region region
);
```

[C++]

```
public: void IntersectClip(
   Region* region
);
```

[JScript]

```
public function IntersectClip(
   region : Region
);
```

Parameters

region

Region object to intersect with the current region.

Return Value

This method does not return a value.

Remarks

This method assigns to the **Clip** property of this **Graphics** object the area represented by the intersection of the current clip region and the region specified by the *region* parameter.

Example

[Visual Basic, C#] The following example is designed for use with Windows Forms, and it requires **PaintEventArgs** *e*, which is a parameter of the **Paint** event handler. The code performs the following actions:

- Creates a rectangle with upper-left corner at (0, 0).
- Creates a region and sets it to the rectangle, and sets the clipping region to this region.
- Creates a second rectangle with upper-left corner at (100, 100).
- Creates a region and sets it to the second rectangle, and sets the clipping region to the intersection of this region and the current clipping region (the first rectangle) using a combine mode of **CombineMode.Replace**.
- Fills a large rectangle that includes both previous regions with a solid blue brush.
- Resets the clipping region to infinite.
- Draws rectangles around the two clipping regions. It uses a black pen for the first clipping region and a red pen for the second clipping region.

[Visual Basic, C#] The result is that only the intersection of the two regions is filled with blue.

[Visual Basic]

```
Public Sub IntersectClipRegion(e As PaintEventArgs)
' Set clipping region.
Dim clipRect As New Rectangle(0, 0, 200, 200)
Dim clipRegion As New [Region](clipRect)
e.Graphics.SetClip(clipRegion, CombineMode.Replace)
' Update clipping region to intersection of
' existing region with specified rectangle.
Dim intersectRect As New Rectangle(100, 100, 200, 200)
Dim intersectRegion As New [Region](intersectRect)
e.Graphics.IntersectClip(intersectRegion)
' Fill rectangle to demonstrate effective clipping region.
e.Graphics.FillRectangle(New SolidBrush(Color.Blue), 0, 0, _
500, 500)
' Reset clipping region to infinite.
e.Graphics.ResetClip()
' Draw clipRect and intersectRect to screen.
e.Graphics.DrawRectangle(New Pen(Color.Black), clipRect)
e.Graphics.DrawRectangle(New Pen(Color.Red), intersectRect)
End Sub
```

[C#]

```
public void IntersectClipRegion(PaintEventArgs e)
{
// Set clipping region.
Rectangle clipRect = new Rectangle(0, 0, 200, 200);
Region clipRegion = new Region(clipRect);
e.Graphics.SetClip(clipRegion, CombineMode.Replace);
// Update clipping region to intersection of
//  existing region with specified rectangle.
Rectangle intersectRect = new Rectangle(100, 100, 200, 200);
Region intersectRegion = new Region(intersectRect);
e.Graphics.IntersectClip(intersectRegion);
// Fill rectangle to demonstrate effective clipping region.
e.Graphics.FillRectangle(new SolidBrush(Color.Blue), 0, 0, 500, 500);
// Reset clipping region to infinite.
e.Graphics.ResetClip();
// Draw clipRect and intersectRect to screen.
e.Graphics.DrawRectangle(new Pen(Color.Black), clipRect);
e.Graphics.DrawRectangle(new Pen(Color.Red), intersectRect);
}
```

Requirements

Platforms: Windows 98, Windows NT 4.0, Windows Millennium Edition, Windows 2000, Windows XP Home Edition, Windows XP Professional, Windows Server 2003 family

Graphics.IsVisible Method

Indicates whether the point specified by a pair of coordinates is contained within the visible clip region of this **Graphics** object.

Overload List

Indicates whether the specified **Point** structure is contained within the visible clip region of this **Graphics** object.

[Visual Basic] **Overloads Public Function IsVisible(Point) As Boolean**

[C#] **public bool IsVisible(Point);**

[C++] **public: bool IsVisible(Point);**

[JScript] **public function IsVisible(Point) : Boolean;**

Indicates whether the specified **PointF** structure is contained within the visible clip region of this **Graphics** object.

[Visual Basic] **Overloads Public Function IsVisible(PointF) As Boolean**

[C#] **public bool IsVisible(PointF);**

[C++] **public: bool IsVisible(PointF);**

[JScript] **public function IsVisible(PointF) : Boolean;**

Indicates whether the rectangle specified by a **Rectangle** structure is contained within the visible clip region of this **Graphics** object.

[Visual Basic] **Overloads Public Function IsVisible(Rectangle) As Boolean**

[C#] **public bool IsVisible(Rectangle);**

[C++] **public: bool IsVisible(Rectangle);**

[JScript] **public function IsVisible(Rectangle) : Boolean;**

Indicates whether the rectangle specified by a **RectangleF** structure is contained within the visible clip region of this **Graphics** object.

[Visual Basic] **Overloads Public Function IsVisible(RectangleF) As Boolean**

[C#] **public bool IsVisible(RectangleF);**

[C++] **public: bool IsVisible(RectangleF);**

[JScript] **public function IsVisible(RectangleF) : Boolean;**

Indicates whether the point specified by a pair of coordinates is contained within the visible clip region of this **Graphics** object.

[Visual Basic] **Overloads Public Function IsVisible(Integer, Integer) As Boolean**

[C#] **public bool IsVisible(int, int);**

[C++] **public: bool IsVisible(int, int);**

[JScript] **public function IsVisible(int, int) : Boolean;**

Indicates whether the point specified by a pair of coordinates is contained within the visible clip region of this **Graphics** object.

[Visual Basic] **Overloads Public Function IsVisible(Single, Single) As Boolean**

[C#] **public bool IsVisible(float, float);**

[C++] **public: bool IsVisible(float, float);**

[JScript] **public function IsVisible(float, float) : Boolean;**

Indicates whether the rectangle specified by a pair of coordinates, a width, and a height is contained within the visible clip region of this **Graphics** object.

[Visual Basic] **Overloads Public Function IsVisible(Integer, Integer, Integer, Integer) As Boolean**

[C#] **public bool IsVisible(int, int, int, int);**

[C++] **public: bool IsVisible(int, int, int, int);**

[JScript] **public function IsVisible(int, int, int, int) : Boolean;**

Indicates whether the rectangle specified by a pair of coordinates, a width, and a height is contained within the visible clip region of this **Graphics** object.

[Visual Basic] **Overloads Public Function IsVisible(Single, Single, Single, Single) As Boolean**

[C#] **public bool IsVisible(float, float, float, float);**

[C++] **public: bool IsVisible(float, float, float, float);**

[JScript] **public function IsVisible(float, float, float, float) : Boolean;**

Example

[Visual Basic, C#] The following example is designed for use with Windows Forms, and it requires **PaintEventArgs** *e*, which is a parameter of the **Paint** event handler. The code performs the following actions:

- Creates a rectangular clipping region and sets it as the clipping region for the graphics object of the form using **CombineMode.Replace**.
- Creates the location and size of two rectangles, one inside the clipping region and one outside.
- Tests each of the rectangles for visibility and draws only the visible one.

[Visual Basic, C#] The result is one small red rectangle, which is within the clip region.

> [Visual Basic, C#] **Note** This example shows how to use one of the overloaded versions of **IsVisible**. For other examples that might be available, see the individual overload topics.

[Visual Basic]

```
Public Sub IsVisible4Float(e As PaintEventArgs)
' Set clip region.
Dim clipRegion As New [Region](New Rectangle(50, 50, 100, 100))
e.Graphics.SetClip(clipRegion, CombineMode.Replace)
' Set up coordinates of rectangles.
Dim x1 As Single = 100F
Dim y1 As Single = 100F
Dim width1 As Single = 20F
Dim height1 As Single = 20F
Dim x2 As Single = 200F
Dim y2 As Single = 200F
Dim width2 As Single = 20F
Dim height2 As Single = 20F
' If rectangle is visible, fill it.
If e.Graphics.IsVisible(x1, y1, width1, height1) Then
e.Graphics.FillRectangle(New SolidBrush(Color.Red), x1, y1, _
width1, height1)
End If
If e.Graphics.IsVisible(x2, y2, width2, height2) Then
e.Graphics.FillRectangle(New SolidBrush(Color.Blue), x2, y2, _
width2, height2)
End If
End Sub
```

[C#]

```
public void IsVisible4Float(PaintEventArgs e)
{
// Set clip region.
Region clipRegion = new Region(new Rectangle(50, 50, 100, 100));
e.Graphics.SetClip(clipRegion, CombineMode.Replace);
// Set up coordinates of rectangles.
float x1 =  100.0F;
float y1 =  100.0F;
float width1 = 20.0F;
float height1 = 20.0F;
float x2 = 200.0F;
float y2 = 200.0F;
```

```
float width2 = 20.0F;
float height2 = 20.0F;
// If rectangle is visible, fill it.
if (e.Graphics.IsVisible(x1, y1, width1, height1))
e.Graphics.FillRectangle(new SolidBrush(Color.Red), x1, y1,        ↵
width1, height1);
if (e.Graphics.IsVisible(x2, y2, width2, height2))
e.Graphics.FillRectangle(new SolidBrush(Color.Blue), x2, y2,       ↵
width2, height2);
}
```

Graphics.IsVisible Method (Point)

Indicates whether the specified **Point** structure is contained within the visible clip region of this **Graphics** object.

[Visual Basic]
```
Overloads Public Function IsVisible( _
   ByVal point As Point _
) As Boolean
```
[C#]
```
public bool IsVisible(
   Point point
);
```
[C++]
```
public: bool IsVisible(
   Point point
);
```
[JScript]
```
public function IsVisible(
   point : Point
) : Boolean;
```

Parameters

point

Point structure to test for visibility.

Return Value

This method returns **true** if the point specified by the *point* parameter is contained within the visible clip region of this **Graphics** object; otherwise, **false**.

Example

[Visual Basic, C#] The following example is designed for use with Windows Forms, and it requires **PaintEventArgs** *e*, which is a parameter of the **Paint** event handler. The code performs the following actions:

- Creates a rectangular clipping region and sets it as the clipping region for the graphics object of the form using **CombineMode.Replace**.
- Creates two points, one inside the clipping region and one outside.
- Tests each of the points for visibility and draws only the visible one.

[Visual Basic, C#] The result is one small red circle, which is within the clip region.

[Visual Basic]
```
Public Sub IsVisiblePoint(e As PaintEventArgs)
' Set clip region.
Dim clipRegion As New [Region](New Rectangle(50, 50, 100, 100))
e.Graphics.SetClip(clipRegion, CombineMode.Replace)
' Set up coordinates of points.
Dim x1 As Integer = 100
Dim y1 As Integer = 100
Dim x2 As Integer = 200
Dim y2 As Integer = 200
Dim point1 As New Point(x1, y1)
Dim point2 As New Point(x2, y2)
' If point is visible, fill ellipse that represents it.
If e.Graphics.IsVisible(point1) Then
e.Graphics.FillEllipse(New SolidBrush(Color.Red), x1, y1, _
10, 10)
End If
If e.Graphics.IsVisible(point2) Then
e.Graphics.FillEllipse(New SolidBrush(Color.Blue), x2, y2, _
10, 10)
End If
End Sub
```

[C#]
```
public void IsVisiblePoint(PaintEventArgs e)
{
// Set clip region.
Region clipRegion = new Region(new Rectangle(50, 50, 100, 100));
e.Graphics.SetClip(clipRegion, CombineMode.Replace);
// Set up coordinates of points.
int x1 = 100;
int y1 = 100;
int x2 = 200;
int y2 = 200;
Point point1 = new Point(x1, y1);
Point point2 = new Point(x2, y2);
// If point is visible, fill ellipse that represents it.
if (e.Graphics.IsVisible(point1))
e.Graphics.FillEllipse(new SolidBrush(Color.Red), x1, y1, 10, 10);
if (e.Graphics.IsVisible(point2))
e.Graphics.FillEllipse(new SolidBrush(Color.Blue), x2, y2, 10, 10);
}
```

Requirements

Platforms: Windows 98, Windows NT 4.0, Windows Millennium Edition, Windows 2000, Windows XP Home Edition, Windows XP Professional, Windows Server 2003 family

Graphics.IsVisible Method (PointF)

Indicates whether the specified **PointF** structure is contained within the visible clip region of this **Graphics** object.

[Visual Basic]
```
Overloads Public Function IsVisible( _
   ByVal point As PointF _
) As Boolean
```
[C#]
```
public bool IsVisible(
   PointF point
);
```
[C++]
```
public: bool IsVisible(
   PointF point
);
```
[JScript]
```
public function IsVisible(
   point : PointF
) : Boolean;
```

Parameters

point

PointF structure to test for visibility.

Return Value

This method returns **true** if the point specified by the *point* parameter is contained within the visible clip region of this **Graphics** object; otherwise, **false**.

Example

[Visual Basic, C#] The following example is designed for use with Windows Forms, and it requires **PaintEventArgs** *e*, which is a parameter of the **Paint** event handler. The code performs the following actions:

- Creates a rectangular clipping region and sets it as the clipping region for the graphics object of the form using **CombineMode.Replace**.
- Creates two points, one inside the clipping region and one outside.
- Tests each of the points for visibility and draws only the visible one.

[Visual Basic, C#] The result is one small red circle, which is within the clip region.

[Visual Basic]
```
Public Sub IsVisiblePointF(e As PaintEventArgs)
' Set clip region.
Dim clipRegion As New [Region](New Rectangle(50, 50, 100, 100))
e.Graphics.SetClip(clipRegion, CombineMode.Replace)
' Set up coordinates of points.
Dim x1 As Single = 100F
Dim y1 As Single = 100F
Dim x2 As Single = 200F
Dim y2 As Single = 200F
Dim point1 As New PointF(x1, y1)
Dim point2 As New PointF(x2, y2)
' If point is visible, fill ellipse that represents it.
If e.Graphics.IsVisible(point1) Then
e.Graphics.FillEllipse(New SolidBrush(Color.Red), x1, y1, _
10F, 10F)
End If
If e.Graphics.IsVisible(point2) Then
e.Graphics.FillEllipse(New SolidBrush(Color.Blue), x2, y2, _
10F, 10F)
End If
End Sub
```

[C#]
```
public void IsVisiblePointF(PaintEventArgs e)
{
// Set clip region.
Region clipRegion = new Region(new Rectangle(50, 50, 100, 100));
e.Graphics.SetClip(clipRegion, CombineMode.Replace);
// Set up coordinates of points.
float x1 = 100.0F;
float y1 = 100.0F;
float x2 = 200.0F;
float y2 = 200.0F;
PointF point1 = new PointF(x1, y1);
PointF point2 = new PointF(x2, y2);
// If point is visible, fill ellipse that represents it.
if (e.Graphics.IsVisible(point1))
e.Graphics.FillEllipse(new SolidBrush(Color.Red), x1, y1,        ↵
10.0F, 10.0F);
if (e.Graphics.IsVisible(point2))
e.Graphics.FillEllipse(new SolidBrush(Color.Blue), x2, y2,       ↵
 10.0F, 10.0F);
}
```

Requirements

Platforms: Windows 98, Windows NT 4.0, Windows Millennium Edition, Windows 2000, Windows XP Home Edition, Windows XP Professional, Windows Server 2003 family

Graphics.IsVisible Method (Rectangle)

Indicates whether the rectangle specified by a **Rectangle** structure is contained within the visible clip region of this **Graphics** object.

[Visual Basic]
```
Overloads Public Function IsVisible( _
   ByVal rect As Rectangle _
) As Boolean
```
[C#]
```
public bool IsVisible(
   Rectangle rect
);
```
[C++]
```
public: bool IsVisible(
   Rectangle rect
);
```
[JScript]
```
public function IsVisible(
   rect : Rectangle
) : Boolean;
```

Parameters

rect

Rectangle structure to test for visibility.

Return Value

This method returns **true** if the rectangle specified by the *rect* parameter is contained within the visible clip region of this **Graphics** object; otherwise, **false**.

Example

[Visual Basic, C#] The following example is designed for use with Windows Forms, and it requires **PaintEventArgs** *e*, which is a parameter of the **Paint** event handler. The code performs the following actions:

- Creates a rectangular clipping region and sets it as the clipping region for the graphics object of the form using **CombineMode.Replace**.
- Creates the location and size of two rectangles, one inside the clipping region and one outside.
- Tests each of the rectangles for visibility and draws only the visible one.

[Visual Basic, C#] The result is one small red rectangle, which is within the clip region.

[Visual Basic]
```
Public Sub IsVisibleRectangle(e As PaintEventArgs)
' Set clip region.
Dim clipRegion As New [Region](New Rectangle(50, 50, 100, 100))
e.Graphics.SetClip(clipRegion, CombineMode.Replace)
' Set up coordinates of rectangles.
Dim rect1 As New Rectangle(100, 100, 20, 20)
Dim rect2 As New Rectangle(200, 200, 20, 20)
' If rectangle is visible, fill it.
If e.Graphics.IsVisible(rect1) Then
e.Graphics.FillRectangle(New SolidBrush(Color.Red), rect1)
End If
If e.Graphics.IsVisible(rect2) Then
e.Graphics.FillRectangle(New SolidBrush(Color.Blue), rect2)
End If
End Sub
```

[C#]
```
public void IsVisibleRectangle(PaintEventArgs e)
{
// Set clip region.
```

```
Region clipRegion = new Region(new Rectangle(50, 50, 100, 100));
e.Graphics.SetClip(clipRegion, CombineMode.Replace);
// Set up coordinates of rectangles.
Rectangle rect1 = new Rectangle(100, 100, 20, 20);
Rectangle rect2 = new Rectangle(200, 200, 20, 20);
// If rectangle is visible, fill it.
if (e.Graphics.IsVisible(rect1))
e.Graphics.FillRectangle(new SolidBrush(Color.Red), rect1);
if (e.Graphics.IsVisible(rect2))
e.Graphics.FillRectangle(new SolidBrush(Color.Blue), rect2);
}
```

Requirements

Platforms: Windows 98, Windows NT 4.0, Windows Millennium Edition, Windows 2000, Windows XP Home Edition, Windows XP Professional, Windows Server 2003 family

Graphics.IsVisible Method (RectangleF)

Indicates whether the rectangle specified by a **RectangleF** structure is contained within the visible clip region of this **Graphics** object.

[Visual Basic]
```
Overloads Public Function IsVisible( _
   ByVal rect As RectangleF _
) As Boolean
```
[C#]
```
public bool IsVisible(
   RectangleF rect
);
```
[C++]
```
public: bool IsVisible(
   RectangleF rect
);
```
[JScript]
```
public function IsVisible(
   rect : RectangleF
) : Boolean;
```

Parameters

rect

RectangleF structure to test for visibility.

Return Value

This method returns **true** if the rectangle specified by the *rect* parameter is contained within the visible clip region of this **Graphics** object; otherwise, **false**.

Example

[Visual Basic, C#] The following example is designed for use with Windows Forms, and it requires **PaintEventArgs** *e*, which is a parameter of the **Paint** event handler. The code performs the following actions:

- Creates a rectangular clipping region and sets it as the clipping region for the graphics object of the form using **CombineMode.Replace**.
- Creates two rectangles, one inside the clipping region and one outside.
- Tests each of the rectangles for visibility and draws only the visible one.

[Visual Basic, C#] The result is one small red rectangle, which is within the clip region.

[Visual Basic]
```
Public Sub IsVisibleRectangleF(e As PaintEventArgs)
' Set clip region.
Dim clipRegion As New [Region](New Rectangle(50, 50, 100, 100))
e.Graphics.SetClip(clipRegion, CombineMode.Replace)
' Set up coordinates of rectangles.
Dim rect1 As New RectangleF(100F, 100F, 20F, 20F)
Dim rect2 As New RectangleF(200F, 200F, 20F, 20F)
' If rectangle is visible, fill it.
If e.Graphics.IsVisible(rect1) Then
e.Graphics.FillRectangle(New SolidBrush(Color.Red), rect1)
End If
If e.Graphics.IsVisible(rect2) Then
e.Graphics.FillRectangle(New SolidBrush(Color.Blue), rect2)
End If
End Sub
```

[C#]
```
public void IsVisibleRectangleF(PaintEventArgs e)
{
// Set clip region.
Region clipRegion = new Region(new Rectangle(50, 50, 100, 100));
e.Graphics.SetClip(clipRegion, CombineMode.Replace);
// Set up coordinates of rectangles.
RectangleF rect1 = new RectangleF(100.0F, 100.0F, 20.0F, 20.0F);
RectangleF rect2 = new RectangleF(200.0F, 200.0F, 20.0F, 20.0F);
// If rectangle is visible, fill it.
if (e.Graphics.IsVisible(rect1))
e.Graphics.FillRectangle(new SolidBrush(Color.Red), rect1);
if (e.Graphics.IsVisible(rect2))
e.Graphics.FillRectangle(new SolidBrush(Color.Blue), rect2);
}
```

Requirements

Platforms: Windows 98, Windows NT 4.0, Windows Millennium Edition, Windows 2000, Windows XP Home Edition, Windows XP Professional, Windows Server 2003 family

Graphics.IsVisible Method (Int32, Int32)

Indicates whether the point specified by a pair of coordinates is contained within the visible clip region of this **Graphics** object.

[Visual Basic]
```
Overloads Public Function IsVisible( _
   ByVal x As Integer, _
   ByVal y As Integer _
) As Boolean
```
[C#]
```
public bool IsVisible(
   int x,
   int y
);
```
[C++]
```
public: bool IsVisible(
   int x,
   int y
);
```
[JScript]
```
public function IsVisible(
   x : int,
   y : int
) : Boolean;
```

Parameters

x

x coordinate of the point to test for visibility.

y

y coordinate of the point to test for visibility.

Return Value

This method returns **true** if the point defined by the *x* and *y* parameters is contained within the visible clip region of this **Graphics** object; otherwise, **false**.

Example

[Visual Basic, C#] The following example is designed for use with Windows Forms, and it requires **PaintEventArgs** *e*, which is a parameter of the **Paint** event handler. The code performs the following actions:

- Creates a rectangular clipping region and sets it as the clipping region for the graphics object of the form using **CombineMode.Replace**.
- Creates two points, one inside the clipping region and one outside.
- Tests each of the points for visibility and draws only the visible one.

[Visual Basic, C#] The result is one small red circle, which is within the clip region.

[Visual Basic]
```
Public Sub IsVisibleInt(e As PaintEventArgs)
' Set clip region.
Dim clipRegion As New [Region](New Rectangle(50, 50, 100, 100))
e.Graphics.SetClip(clipRegion, CombineMode.Replace)
' Set up coordinates of points.
Dim x1 As Integer = 100
Dim y1 As Integer = 100
Dim x2 As Integer = 200
Dim y2 As Integer = 200
' If point is visible, fill ellipse that represents it.
If e.Graphics.IsVisible(x1, y1) Then
e.Graphics.FillEllipse(New SolidBrush(Color.Red), x1, y1, _
10, 10)
End If
If e.Graphics.IsVisible(x2, y2) Then
e.Graphics.FillEllipse(New SolidBrush(Color.Blue), x2, y2, _
10, 10)
End If
End Sub
```

[C#]
```
public void IsVisibleInt(PaintEventArgs e)
{
// Set clip region.
Region clipRegion = new Region(new Rectangle(50, 50, 100, 100));
e.Graphics.SetClip(clipRegion, CombineMode.Replace);
// Set up coordinates of points.
int x1 = 100;
int y1 = 100;
int x2 = 200;
int y2 = 200;
// If point is visible, fill ellipse that represents it.
if (e.Graphics.IsVisible(x1, y1))
e.Graphics.FillEllipse(new SolidBrush(Color.Red), x1, y1, 10, 10);
if (e.Graphics.IsVisible(x2, y2))
e.Graphics.FillEllipse(new SolidBrush(Color.Blue), x2, y2, 10, 10);
}
```

Requirements

Platforms: Windows 98, Windows NT 4.0, Windows Millennium Edition, Windows 2000, Windows XP Home Edition, Windows XP Professional, Windows Server 2003 family

Graphics.IsVisible Method (Single, Single)

Indicates whether the point specified by a pair of coordinates is contained within the visible clip region of this **Graphics** object.

[Visual Basic]
```
Overloads Public Function IsVisible( _
   ByVal x As Single, _
   ByVal y As Single _
) As Boolean
```
[C#]
```
public bool IsVisible(
   float x,
   float y
);
```
[C++]
```
public: bool IsVisible(
   float x,
   float y
);
```
[JScript]
```
public function IsVisible(
   x : float,
   y : float
) : Boolean;
```

Parameters

x

x coordinate of the point to test for visibility.

y

y coordinate of the point to test for visibility.

Return Value

This method returns **true** if the point defined by the *x* and *y* parameters is contained within the visible clip region of this **Graphics** object; otherwise, **false**.

Example

[Visual Basic, C#] The following example is designed for use with Windows Forms, and it requires **PaintEventArgs** *e*, which is a parameter of the **Paint** event handler. The code performs the following actions:

- Creates a rectangular clipping region and sets it as the clipping region for the graphics object of the form using **CombineMode.Replace**.
- Creates two points, one inside the clipping region and one outside.
- Tests each of the points for visibility and draws only the visible one.

[Visual Basic, C#] The result is one small red circle, which is within the clip region.

[Visual Basic]
```
Public Sub IsVisibleFloat(e As PaintEventArgs)
' Set clip region.
Dim clipRegion As New [Region](New Rectangle(50, 50, 100, 100))
e.Graphics.SetClip(clipRegion, CombineMode.Replace)
' Set up coordinates of points.
Dim x1 As Single = 100F
Dim y1 As Single = 100F
Dim x2 As Single = 200F
Dim y2 As Single = 200F
' If point is visible, fill ellipse that represents it.
If e.Graphics.IsVisible(x1, y1) Then
e.Graphics.FillEllipse(New SolidBrush(Color.Red), x1, y1, _
10F, 10F)
End If
```

```
If e.Graphics.IsVisible(x2, y2) Then
e.Graphics.FillEllipse(New SolidBrush(Color.Blue), x2, y2, _
10F, 10F)
End If
End Sub
```

[C#]

```
public void IsVisibleFloat(PaintEventArgs e)
{
// Set clip region.
Region clipRegion = new Region(new Rectangle(50, 50, 100, 100));
e.Graphics.SetClip(clipRegion, CombineMode.Replace);
// Set up coordinates of points.
float x1 = 100.0F;
float y1 = 100.0F;
float x2 = 200.0F;
float y2 = 200.0F;
// If point is visible, fill ellipse that represents it.
if (e.Graphics.IsVisible(x1, y1))
e.Graphics.FillEllipse(new SolidBrush(Color.Red), x1, y1,        ↵
10.0F, 10.0F);
if (e.Graphics.IsVisible(x2, y2))
e.Graphics.FillEllipse(new SolidBrush(Color.Blue), x2, y2,       ↵
10.0F, 10.0F);
}
```

Requirements

Platforms: Windows 98, Windows NT 4.0, Windows Millennium Edition, Windows 2000, Windows XP Home Edition, Windows XP Professional, Windows Server 2003 family

Graphics.IsVisible Method (Int32, Int32, Int32, Int32)

Indicates whether the rectangle specified by a pair of coordinates, a width, and a height is contained within the visible clip region of this **Graphics** object.

[Visual Basic]

```
Overloads Public Function IsVisible( _
   ByVal x As Integer, _
   ByVal y As Integer, _
   ByVal width As Integer, _
   ByVal height As Integer _
) As Boolean
```

[C#]

```
public bool IsVisible(
   int x,
   int y,
   int width,
   int height
);
```

[C++]

```
public: bool IsVisible(
   int x,
   int y,
   int width,
   int height
);
```

[JScript]

```
public function IsVisible(
   x : int,
   y : int,
   width : int,
   height : int
) : Boolean;
```

Parameters

x
: x coordinate of the upper-left corner of the rectangle to test for visibility.

y
: y coordinate of the upper-left corner of the rectangle to test for visibility.

width
: Width of the rectangle to test for visibility.

height
: Height of the rectangle to test for visibility.

Return Value

This method returns **true** if the rectangle defined by the *x*, *y*, *width*, and *height* parameters is contained within the visible clip region of this **Graphics** object; otherwise, **false**.

Example

[Visual Basic, C#] The following example is designed for use with Windows Forms, and it requires **PaintEventArgs** *e*, which is a parameter of the **Paint** event handler. The code performs the following actions:

- Creates a rectangular clipping region and sets it as the clipping region for the graphics object of the form using **CombineMode.Replace**.
- Creates the location and size of two rectangles, one inside the clipping region and one outside.
- Tests each of the rectangles for visibility and draws only the visible one.

[Visual Basic, C#] The result is one small red rectangle, which is within the clip region.

[Visual Basic]

```
Public Sub IsVisible4Int(e As PaintEventArgs)
' Set clip region.
Dim clipRegion As New [Region](New Rectangle(50, 50, 100, 100))
e.Graphics.SetClip(clipRegion, CombineMode.Replace)
' Set up coordinates of rectangles.
Dim x1 As Integer = 100
Dim y1 As Integer = 100
Dim width1 As Integer = 20
Dim height1 As Integer = 20
Dim x2 As Integer = 200
Dim y2 As Integer = 200
Dim width2 As Integer = 20
Dim height2 As Integer = 20
' If rectangle is visible, fill it.
If e.Graphics.IsVisible(x1, y1, width1, height1) Then
e.Graphics.FillRectangle(New SolidBrush(Color.Red), x1, y1, _
width1, height1)
End If
If e.Graphics.IsVisible(x2, y2, width2, height2) Then
e.Graphics.FillRectangle(New SolidBrush(Color.Blue), x2, y2, _
width2, height2)
End If
End Sub
```

[C#]

```
public void IsVisible4Int(PaintEventArgs e)
{
// Set clip region.
Region clipRegion = new Region(new Rectangle(50, 50, 100, 100));
e.Graphics.SetClip(clipRegion, CombineMode.Replace);
// Set up coordinates of rectangles.
int x1 =  100;
int y1 =  100;
int width1 = 20;
int height1 = 20;
```

```
int x2 = 200;
int y2 = 200;
int width2 = 20;
int height2 = 20;
// If rectangle is visible, fill it.
if (e.Graphics.IsVisible(x1, y1, width1, height1))
e.Graphics.FillRectangle(new SolidBrush(Color.Red), x1, y1,
 width1, height1);
if (e.Graphics.IsVisible(x2, y2, width2, height2))
e.Graphics.FillRectangle(new SolidBrush(Color.Blue), x2, y2,
 width2, height2);
}
```

Requirements

Platforms: Windows 98, Windows NT 4.0, Windows Millennium Edition, Windows 2000, Windows XP Home Edition, Windows XP Professional, Windows Server 2003 family

Graphics.IsVisible Method (Single, Single, Single, Single)

Indicates whether the rectangle specified by a pair of coordinates, a width, and a height is contained within the visible clip region of this **Graphics** object.

[Visual Basic]
```
Overloads Public Function IsVisible( _
   ByVal x As Single, _
   ByVal y As Single, _
   ByVal width As Single, _
   ByVal height As Single _
) As Boolean
```
[C#]
```
public bool IsVisible(
   float x,
   float y,
   float width,
   float height
);
```
[C++]
```
public: bool IsVisible(
   float x,
   float y,
   float width,
   float height
);
```
[JScript]
```
public function IsVisible(
   x : float,
   y : float,
   width : float,
   height : float
) : Boolean;
```

Parameters

x
: x coordinate of the upper-left corner of the rectangle to test for visibility.

y
: y coordinate of the upper-left corner of the rectangle to test for visibility.

width
: Width of the rectangle to test for visibility.

height
: Height of the rectangle to test for visibility.

Return Value

This method returns **true** if the rectangle defined by the *x*, *y*, *width*, and *height* parameters is contained within the visible clip region of this **Graphics** object; otherwise, **false**.

Example

[Visual Basic, C#] The following example is designed for use with Windows Forms, and it requires **PaintEventArgs** *e*, which is a parameter of the **Paint** event handler. The code performs the following actions:

- Creates a rectangular clipping region and sets it as the clipping region for the graphics object of the form using **CombineMode.Replace**.
- Creates the location and size of two rectangles, one inside the clipping region and one outside.
- Tests each of the rectangles for visibility and draws only the visible one.

[Visual Basic, C#] The result is one small red rectangle, which is within the clip region.

[Visual Basic]
```
Public Sub IsVisible4Float(e As PaintEventArgs)
' Set clip region.
Dim clipRegion As New [Region](New Rectangle(50, 50, 100, 100))
e.Graphics.SetClip(clipRegion, CombineMode.Replace)
' Set up coordinates of rectangles.
Dim x1 As Single = 100F
Dim y1 As Single = 100F
Dim width1 As Single = 20F
Dim height1 As Single = 20F
Dim x2 As Single = 200F
Dim y2 As Single = 200F
Dim width2 As Single = 20F
Dim height2 As Single = 20F
' If rectangle is visible, fill it.
If e.Graphics.IsVisible(x1, y1, width1, height1) Then
e.Graphics.FillRectangle(New SolidBrush(Color.Red), x1, y1, _
width1, height1)
End If
If e.Graphics.IsVisible(x2, y2, width2, height2) Then
e.Graphics.FillRectangle(New SolidBrush(Color.Blue), x2, y2, _
width2, height2)
End If
End Sub
```

[C#]
```
public void IsVisible4Float(PaintEventArgs e)
{
// Set clip region.
Region clipRegion = new Region(new Rectangle(50, 50, 100, 100));
e.Graphics.SetClip(clipRegion, CombineMode.Replace);
// Set up coordinates of rectangles.
float x1 =  100.0F;
float y1 =  100.0F;
float width1 = 20.0F;
float height1 = 20.0F;
float x2 = 200.0F;
float y2 = 200.0F;
float width2 = 20.0F;
float height2 = 20.0F;
// If rectangle is visible, fill it.
if (e.Graphics.IsVisible(x1, y1, width1, height1))
e.Graphics.FillRectangle(new SolidBrush(Color.Red), x1, y1,
width1, height1);
if (e.Graphics.IsVisible(x2, y2, width2, height2))
e.Graphics.FillRectangle(new SolidBrush(Color.Blue), x2, y2,
width2, height2);
}
```

Requirements

Platforms: Windows 98, Windows NT 4.0, Windows Millennium Edition, Windows 2000, Windows XP Home Edition, Windows XP Professional, Windows Server 2003 family

Graphics.MeasureCharacterRanges Method

Gets an array of **Region** objects, each of which bounds a range of character positions within the specified string.

[Visual Basic]
```
Public Function MeasureCharacterRanges( _
   ByVal text As String, _
   ByVal font As Font, _
   ByVal layoutRect As RectangleF, _
   ByVal stringFormat As StringFormat _
) As Region()
```
[C#]
```
public Region[] MeasureCharacterRanges(
   string text,
   Font font,
   RectangleF layoutRect,
   StringFormat stringFormat
);
```
[C++]
```
public: Region* MeasureCharacterRanges(
   String* text,
   Font* font,
   RectangleF layoutRect,
   StringFormat* stringFormat
) [];
```
[JScript]
```
public function MeasureCharacterRanges(
   text : String,
   font : Font,
   layoutRect : RectangleF,
   stringFormat : StringFormat
) : Region[];
```

Parameters

text

String to measure.

font

Font object that defines the text format of the string.

layoutRect

RectangleF structure that specifies the layout rectangle for the string.

stringFormat

StringFormat object that represents formatting information, such as line spacing, for the string.

Return Value

This method returns an array of **Region** objects, each of which bounds a range of character positions within the specified string.

Remarks

The regions returned by this method are resolution-dependent, so there might be a slight loss of accuracy if strings are recorded in a metafile at one resolution and later played back at a different resolution.

Example

[Visual Basic, C#] The following example is designed for use with Windows Forms, and it requires **PaintEventArgs** *e*, which is a parameter of the **Paint** event handler. The code performs the following actions:

- Sets a string "First and Second ranges" and a font for display of the string ("Times New Roman", 16pt.).
- Sets two character ranges within the string (which correspond to the words "First" and "Second").
- Creates a rectangle in which to display the string.
- Sets the formatting of the string ¾ including the two character ranges.
- Draws the string to the screen.
- Measures the character ranges, determines rectangles that bound the two specified ranges.
- Draws the two rectangles to the screen.

[Visual Basic, C#] The result is the displayed string with the first range ("First") bounded by a red rectangle and the second range ("Second") bounded by a blue rectangle.

[Visual Basic]
```
Public Sub MeasureCharacterRangesRegions(e As PaintEventArgs)
' Set up string.
Dim measureString As String = "First and Second ranges"
Dim stringFont As New Font("Times New Roman", 16F)
' Set character ranges to "First" and "Second".
Dim characterRanges As CharacterRange() = _
{New CharacterRange(0, 5), New CharacterRange(10, 6)}
' Create rectangle for layout.
Dim x As Single = 50F
Dim y As Single = 50F
Dim width As Single = 35F
Dim height As Single = 200F
Dim layoutRect As New RectangleF(x, y, width, height)
' Set string format.
Dim stringFormat As New StringFormat()
stringFormat.FormatFlags = StringFormatFlags.DirectionVertical
stringFormat.SetMeasurableCharacterRanges(characterRanges)
' Draw string to screen.
e.Graphics.DrawString(measureString, stringFont, Brushes.Black, _
x, y, stringFormat)
' Measure two ranges in string.
Dim stringRegions(2) As [Region]
stringRegions = e.Graphics.MeasureCharacterRanges(measureString, _
stringFont, layoutRect, stringFormat)
' Draw rectangle for first measured range.
Dim measureRect1 As RectangleF = _
stringRegions(0).GetBounds(e.Graphics)
e.Graphics.DrawRectangle(New Pen(Color.Red, 1), _
Rectangle.Round(measureRect1))
' Draw rectangle for second measured range.
Dim measureRect2 As RectangleF = _
stringRegions(1).GetBounds(e.Graphics)
e.Graphics.DrawRectangle(New Pen(Color.Blue, 1), _
Rectangle.Round(measureRect2))
End Sub
```

[C#]
```
public void MeasureCharacterRangesRegions(PaintEventArgs e)
{
// Set up string.
string measureString = "First and Second ranges";
Font stringFont = new Font("Times New Roman", 16.0F);
// Set character ranges to "First" and "Second".
CharacterRange[] characterRanges =
{
new CharacterRange(0, 5),
new CharacterRange(10, 6)
};
```

```
// Create rectangle for layout.
float x = 50.0F;
float y = 50.0F;
float width = 35.0F;
float height = 200.0F;
RectangleF layoutRect = new RectangleF(x, y, width, height);
// Set string format.
StringFormat stringFormat = new StringFormat();
stringFormat.FormatFlags = StringFormatFlags.DirectionVertical;
stringFormat.SetMeasurableCharacterRanges(characterRanges);
// Draw string to screen.
e.Graphics.DrawString(
measureString,
stringFont,
Brushes.Black,
x, y,
stringFormat);
// Measure two ranges in string.
Region[] stringRegions = new Region[2];
stringRegions = e.Graphics.MeasureCharacterRanges(
measureString,
stringFont,
layoutRect,
stringFormat);
// Draw rectangle for first measured range.
RectangleF measureRect1 = stringRegions[0].GetBounds(e.Graphics);
e.Graphics.DrawRectangle(
new Pen(Color.Red, 1),
Rectangle.Round(measureRect1));
// Draw rectangle for second measured range.
RectangleF measureRect2 = stringRegions[1].GetBounds(e.Graphics);
e.Graphics.DrawRectangle(
new Pen(Color.Blue, 1),
Rectangle.Round(measureRect2));
}
```

Requirements

Platforms: Windows 98, Windows NT 4.0, Windows Millennium Edition, Windows 2000, Windows XP Home Edition, Windows XP Professional, Windows Server 2003 family

Graphics.MeasureString Method

Measures the specified string when drawn with the specified **Font** object.

Overload List

Measures the specified string when drawn with the specified **Font** object.

Supported by the .NET Compact Framework.

[Visual Basic] **Overloads Public Function MeasureString(String, Font) As SizeF**

[C#] **public SizeF MeasureString(string, Font);**

[C++] **public: SizeF MeasureString(String*, Font*);**

[JScript] **public function MeasureString(String, Font) : SizeF;**

Measures the specified string when drawn with the specified **Font** object.

[Visual Basic] **Overloads Public Function MeasureString(String, Font, Integer) As SizeF**

[C#] **public SizeF MeasureString(string, Font, int);**

[C++] **public: SizeF MeasureString(String*, Font*, int);**

[JScript] **public function MeasureString(String, Font, int) : SizeF;**

Measures the specified string when drawn with the specified **Font** object within the specified layout area.

[Visual Basic] **Overloads Public Function MeasureString(String, Font, SizeF) As SizeF**

[C#] **public SizeF MeasureString(string, Font, SizeF);**

[C++] **public: SizeF MeasureString(String*, Font*, SizeF);**

[JScript] **public function MeasureString(String, Font, SizeF) : SizeF;**

Measures the specified string when drawn with the specified **Font** object and formatted with the specified **StringFormat** object.

[Visual Basic] **Overloads Public Function MeasureString(String, Font, Integer, StringFormat) As SizeF**

[C#] **public SizeF MeasureString(string, Font, int, StringFormat);**

[C++] **public: SizeF MeasureString(String*, Font*, int, StringFormat*);**

[JScript] **public function MeasureString(String, Font, int, StringFormat) : SizeF;**

Measures the specified string when drawn with the specified **Font** object and formatted with the specified **StringFormat** object.

[Visual Basic] **Overloads Public Function MeasureString(String, Font, PointF, StringFormat) As SizeF**

[C#] **public SizeF MeasureString(string, Font, PointF, StringFormat);**

[C++] **public: SizeF MeasureString(String*, Font*, PointF, StringFormat*);**

[JScript] **public function MeasureString(String, Font, PointF, StringFormat) : SizeF;**

Measures the specified string when drawn with the specified **Font** object and formatted with the specified **StringFormat** object.

[Visual Basic] **Overloads Public Function MeasureString(String, Font, SizeF, StringFormat) As SizeF**

[C#] **public SizeF MeasureString(string, Font, SizeF, StringFormat);**

[C++] **public: SizeF MeasureString(String*, Font*, SizeF, StringFormat*);**

[JScript] **public function MeasureString(String, Font, SizeF, StringFormat) : SizeF;**

Measures the specified string when drawn with the specified **Font** object and formatted with the specified **StringFormat** object.

[Visual Basic] **Overloads Public Function MeasureString(String, Font, SizeF, StringFormat, ByRef Integer, ByRef Integer) As SizeF**

[C#] **public SizeF MeasureString(string, Font, SizeF, StringFormat, int, int);**

[C++] **public: SizeF MeasureString(String*, Font*, SizeF, StringFormat*, int, int);**

[JScript] **public function MeasureString(String, Font, SizeF, StringFormat, int, int) : SizeF;**

Example

[Visual Basic, C#] The following example is designed for use with Windows Forms, and it requires **PaintEventArgs** *e*, which is a parameter of the **Paint** event handler. The code performs the following actions:

- Creates a string to measure and a font object set to Arial (16pt.)
- Sets the maximum layout size of the string.

- Creates a string format object and sets its format flags to **StringFormatFlags.DirectionVertical**.
- Creates the integer variables *charactersFitted* and *linesFilled* and a size object to measure the string.
- Measures the size of the string and determines the number of characters fitted and lines filled, using the string, the font object, the maximum layout size, and the string format.
- Draws a red rectangle using the measured size of the string.
- Draws the string within the drawn rectangle.
- Draws the values of the number of characters fitted and lines filled.

[Visual Basic, C#] The result is a vertical rectangle enclosing a vertical string.

> [Visual Basic, C#] **Note** This example shows how to use one of the overloaded versions of **MeasureString**. For other examples that might be available, see the individual overload topics.

[Visual Basic]
```
Public Sub MeasureStringSizeFFormatInts(e As PaintEventArgs)
' Set up string.
Dim measureString As String = "Measure String"
Dim stringFont As New Font("Arial", 16)
' Set maximum layout size.
Dim layoutSize As New SizeF(100F, 200F)
' Set string format.
Dim newStringFormat As New StringFormat()
newStringFormat.FormatFlags = StringFormatFlags.DirectionVertical
' Measure string.
Dim charactersFitted As Integer
Dim linesFilled As Integer
Dim stringSize As New SizeF()
stringSize = e.Graphics.MeasureString(measureString, stringFont, _
layoutSize, newStringFormat, charactersFitted, linesFilled)
' Draw rectangle representing size of string.
e.Graphics.DrawRectangle(New Pen(Color.Red, 1), 0F, 0F, _
stringSize.Width, stringSize.Height)
' Draw string to screen.
e.Graphics.DrawString(measureString, stringFont, Brushes.Black, _
New PointF(0, 0), newStringFormat)
' Draw output parameters to screen.
Dim outString As String = "chars " & charactersFitted & _
", lines " & linesFilled
e.Graphics.DrawString(outString, stringFont, Brushes.Black, _
New PointF(100, 0))
End Sub
```

[C#]
```
public void MeasureStringSizeFFormatInts(PaintEventArgs e)
{
// Set up string.
string measureString = "Measure String";
Font stringFont = new Font("Arial", 16);
// Set maximum layout size.
SizeF layoutSize = new SizeF(100.0F, 200.0F);
// Set string format.
StringFormat newStringFormat = new StringFormat();
newStringFormat.FormatFlags = StringFormatFlags.DirectionVertical;
// Measure string.
int charactersFitted;
int linesFilled;
SizeF stringSize = new SizeF();
stringSize = e.Graphics.MeasureString(
measureString,
stringFont,
layoutSize,
newStringFormat,
out charactersFitted,
out linesFilled);
// Draw rectangle representing size of string.
e.Graphics.DrawRectangle(
new Pen(Color.Red, 1),
0.0F, 0.0F, stringSize.Width, stringSize.Height);
// Draw string to screen.
e.Graphics.DrawString(
measureString,
stringFont,
Brushes.Black,
new PointF(0, 0),
newStringFormat);
// Draw output parameters to screen.
string outString = "chars " + charactersFitted + ", ↵
 lines " + linesFilled;
e.Graphics.DrawString(
outString,
stringFont,
Brushes.Black,
new PointF(100, 0));
}
```

Graphics.MeasureString Method (String, Font)

Measures the specified string when drawn with the specified **Font** object.

[Visual Basic]
```
Overloads Public Function MeasureString( _
   ByVal text As String, _
   ByVal font As Font _
) As SizeF
```
[C#]
```
public SizeF MeasureString(
   string text,
   Font font
);
```
[C++]
```
public: SizeF MeasureString(
   String* text,
   Font* font
);
```
[JScript]
```
public function MeasureString(
   text : String,
   font : Font
) : SizeF;
```

Parameters

text
String to measure.

font
Font object that defines the text format of the string.

Return Value

This method returns a **SizeF** structure that represents the size, in pixels, of the string specified by the *text* parameter as drawn with the *font* parameter.

Remarks

The **MeasureString** method is designed for use with individual strings and includes a small amount of extra space before and after the string to allow for overhanging glyphs. Also, the **DrawString** method adjusts glyph points to optimize display quality and might display a string narrower than reported by **MeasureString**. To obtain metrics suitable for adjacent strings in layout (for example, when implementing formatted text), use the **MeasureCharacterRanges** method.

Example

[Visual Basic, C#] The following example is designed for use with Windows Forms, and it requires **PaintEventArgs** *e*, which is a parameter of the **Paint** event handler. The code performs the following actions:

- Creates a string to measure.
- Creates a font object and sets it to Arial (16pt.).
- Creates a size object and uses it and the font object to measure the size of the string.
- Draws a red rectangle using the measured size of the string.
- Draws the string within the drawn rectangle.

[Visual Basic]
```
Public Sub MeasureStringMin(e As PaintEventArgs)
' Set up string.
Dim measureString As String = "Measure String"
Dim stringFont As New Font("Arial", 16)
' Measure string.
Dim stringSize As New SizeF()
stringSize = e.Graphics.MeasureString(measureString, stringFont)
' Draw rectangle representing size of string.
e.Graphics.DrawRectangle(New Pen(Color.Red, 1), 0F, 0F, _
stringSize.Width, stringSize.Height)
' Draw string to screen.
e.Graphics.DrawString(measureString, stringFont, Brushes.Black, _
New PointF(0, 0))
End Sub
```

[C#]
```
public void MeasureStringMin(PaintEventArgs e)
{
// Set up string.
string measureString = "Measure String";
Font stringFont = new Font("Arial", 16);
// Measure string.
SizeF stringSize = new SizeF();
stringSize = e.Graphics.MeasureString(measureString, stringFont);
// Draw rectangle representing size of string.
e.Graphics.DrawRectangle(
new Pen(Color.Red, 1),
0.0F, 0.0F, stringSize.Width, stringSize.Height);
// Draw string to screen.
e.Graphics.DrawString(
measureString,
stringFont,
Brushes.Black,
new PointF(0, 0));
}
```

Requirements

Platforms: Windows 98, Windows NT 4.0, Windows Millennium Edition, Windows 2000, Windows XP Home Edition, Windows XP Professional, Windows Server 2003 family, .NET Compact Framework - Windows CE .NET

Graphics.MeasureString Method (String, Font, Int32)

Measures the specified string when drawn with the specified **Font** object.

[Visual Basic]
```
Overloads Public Function MeasureString( _
   ByVal text As String, _
   ByVal font As Font, _
   ByVal width As Integer _
) As SizeF
```
[C#]
```
public SizeF MeasureString(
   string text,
   Font font,
   int width
);
```
[C++]
```
public: SizeF MeasureString(
   String* text,
   Font* font,
   int width
);
```
[JScript]
```
public function MeasureString(
   text : String,
   font : Font,
   width : int
) : SizeF;
```

Parameters

text
: String to measure.

font
: **Font** object that defines the format of the string.

width
: Maximum width of the string in pixels.

Return Value

This method returns a **SizeF** structure that represents the size, in pixels, of the string specified in the *text* parameter as drawn with the *font* parameter.

Remarks

The *width* parameter specifies the maximum value of the width component of the returned **SizeF** structure (**SizeF.Width**). If the *width* parameter is less than the actual width of the string, the returned **SizeF.Width** component is truncated to a value representing the maximum number of characters that will fit within the specified width. To accommodate the entire string, the returned **SizeF.Height** component is adjusted to a value that allows displaying the string with character wrap.

The **MeasureString** method is designed for use with individual strings and includes a small amount of extra space before and after the string to allow for overhanging glyphs. Also, the **DrawString** method adjusts glyph points to optimize display quality and might display a string narrower than reported by **MeasureString**. To obtain metrics suitable for adjacent strings in layout (for example, when implementing formatted text), use the **MeasureCharacterRanges** method.

Example

[Visual Basic, C#] The following example is designed for use with Windows Forms, and it requires **PaintEventArgs** *e*, which is a parameter of the **Paint** event handler. The code performs the following actions:

- Creates a string to measure and a font object set to Arial (16pt.).
- Sets the maximum width of the string.
- Creates a size object and uses it, the font object, and the maximum string width to measure the size of the string.
- Draws a red rectangle using the measured size of the string.
- Draws the string within the drawn rectangle.

[Visual Basic]
```
Public Sub MeasureStringWidth(e As PaintEventArgs)
' Set up string.
Dim measureString As String = "Measure String"
Dim stringFont As New Font("Arial", 16)
' Set maximum width of string.
Dim stringWidth As Integer = 200
' Measure string.
Dim stringSize As New SizeF()
stringSize = e.Graphics.MeasureString(measureString, _
stringFont, stringWidth)
' Draw rectangle representing size of string.
e.Graphics.DrawRectangle(New Pen(Color.Red, 1), 0F, 0F, _
stringSize.Width, stringSize.Height)
' Draw string to screen.
e.Graphics.DrawString(measureString, stringFont, Brushes.Black, _
New PointF(0, 0))
End Sub
```

[C#]
```
public void MeasureStringWidth(PaintEventArgs e)
{
// Set up string.
string measureString = "Measure String";
Font stringFont = new Font("Arial", 16);
// Set maximum width of string.
int stringWidth = 200;
// Measure string.
SizeF stringSize = new SizeF();
stringSize = e.Graphics.MeasureString(measureString,
stringFont, stringWidth);
// Draw rectangle representing size of string.
e.Graphics.DrawRectangle(
new Pen(Color.Red, 1),
0.0F, 0.0F, stringSize.Width, stringSize.Height);
// Draw string to screen.
e.Graphics.DrawString(
measureString,
stringFont,
Brushes.Black,
new PointF(0, 0));
}
```

Requirements

Platforms: Windows 98, Windows NT 4.0, Windows Millennium Edition, Windows 2000, Windows XP Home Edition, Windows XP Professional, Windows Server 2003 family

Graphics.MeasureString Method (String, Font, SizeF)

Measures the specified string when drawn with the specified **Font** object within the specified layout area.

[Visual Basic]
```
Overloads Public Function MeasureString( _
   ByVal text As String, _
   ByVal font As Font, _
   ByVal layoutArea As SizeF _
) As SizeF
```
[C#]
```
public SizeF MeasureString(
   string text,
   Font font,
   SizeF layoutArea
);
```
[C++]
```
public: SizeF MeasureString(
   String* text,
   Font* font,
   SizeF layoutArea
);
```
[JScript]
```
public function MeasureString(
   text : String,
   font : Font,
   layoutArea : SizeF
) : SizeF;
```

Parameters

text
String to measure.

font
Font object defines the text format of the string.

layoutArea
SizeF structure that specifies the maximum layout area for the text.

Return Value

This method returns a **SizeF** structure that represents the size, in pixels, of the string specified in the *text* parameter as drawn with the *font* parameter.

Remarks

The **MeasureString** method is designed for use with individual strings and includes a small amount of extra space before and after the string to allow for overhanging glyphs. Also, the **DrawString** method adjusts glyph points to optimize display quality and might display a string narrower than reported by **MeasureString**. To obtain metrics suitable for adjacent strings in layout (for example, when implementing formatted text), use the **MeasureCharacterRanges** method.

Example

[Visual Basic, C#] The following example is designed for use with Windows Forms, and it requires **PaintEventArgs** *e*, which is a parameter of the **Paint** event handler. The code performs the following actions:

- Creates a string to measure and a font object set to Arial (16pt.).
- Sets the maximum layout size of the string.
- Creates a size object and uses it, the font object, and the maximum layout size to measure the size of the string.
- Draws a red rectangle using the measured size of the string.
- Draws the string within the drawn rectangle.

[Visual Basic]
```
Public Sub MeasureStringSizeF(e As PaintEventArgs)
' Set up string.
Dim measureString As String = "Measure String"
Dim stringFont As New Font("Arial", 16)
' Set maximum layout size.
Dim layoutSize As New SizeF(200F, 50F)
' Measure string.
Dim stringSize As New SizeF()
stringSize = e.Graphics.MeasureString(measureString, stringFont, _
layoutSize)
' Draw rectangle representing size of string.
e.Graphics.DrawRectangle(New Pen(Color.Red, 1), 0F, 0F, _
stringSize.Width, stringSize.Height)
' Draw string to screen.
e.Graphics.DrawString(measureString, stringFont, Brushes.Black, _
New PointF(0, 0))
End Sub
```

[C#]
```
public void MeasureStringSizeF(PaintEventArgs e)
{
// Set up string.
string measureString = "Measure String";
Font stringFont = new Font("Arial", 16);
// Set maximum layout size.
SizeF layoutSize = new SizeF(200.0F, 50.0F);
// Measure string.
SizeF stringSize = new SizeF();
stringSize = e.Graphics.MeasureString(measureString,
stringFont, layoutSize);
// Draw rectangle representing size of string.
e.Graphics.DrawRectangle(
new Pen(Color.Red, 1),
0.0F, 0.0F, stringSize.Width, stringSize.Height);
// Draw string to screen.
e.Graphics.DrawString(
measureString,
stringFont,
Brushes.Black,
new PointF(0, 0));
}
```

Requirements

Platforms: Windows 98, Windows NT 4.0, Windows Millennium Edition, Windows 2000, Windows XP Home Edition, Windows XP Professional, Windows Server 2003 family

Graphics.MeasureString Method (String, Font, Int32, StringFormat)

Measures the specified string when drawn with the specified **Font** object and formatted with the specified **StringFormat** object.

[Visual Basic]
```
Overloads Public Function MeasureString( _
   ByVal text As String, _
   ByVal font As Font, _
   ByVal width As Integer, _
   ByVal format As StringFormat _
) As SizeF
```
[C#]
```
public SizeF MeasureString(
   string text,
   Font font,
   int width,
   StringFormat format
);
```
[C++]
```
public: SizeF MeasureString(
   String* text,
   Font* font,
   int width,
   StringFormat* format
);
```
[JScript]
```
public function MeasureString(
   text : String,
   font : Font,
   width : int,
   format : StringFormat
) : SizeF;
```

Parameters

text

String to measure.

font

Font object that defines the text format of the string.

width

Maximum width of the string.

format

StringFormat object that represents formatting information, such as line spacing, for the string.

Return Value

This method returns a **SizeF** structure that represents the size, in pixels, of the string specified in the *text* parameter as drawn with the *font* parameter and the *stringFormat* parameter.

Remarks

The **MeasureString** method is designed for use with individual strings and includes a small amount of extra space before and after the string to allow for overhanging glyphs. Also, the **DrawString** method adjusts glyph points to optimize display quality and might display a string narrower than reported by **MeasureString**. To obtain metrics suitable for adjacent strings in layout (for example, when implementing formatted text), use the **MeasureCharacterRanges** method.

Example

[Visual Basic, C#] The following example is designed for use with Windows Forms, and it requires **PaintEventArgs** *e*, which is a parameter of the **Paint** event handler. The code performs the following actions:

- Creates a string to measure and a font object set it to Arial (16pt.).
- Sets the maximum width of the string.
- Creates a string format object and sets its format flags to **StringFormatFlags.DirectionVertical**.
- Creates a size object to measure the string.
- Measures the size of the string, using the string, the font object, the maximum width, and the string format.
- Draws a red rectangle using the measured size of the string.
- Draws the string within the drawn rectangle.

[Visual Basic, C#] The result is a vertical rectangle enclosing a vertical string.

[Visual Basic]
```
Public Sub MeasureStringWidthFormat(e As PaintEventArgs)
' Set up string.
Dim measureString As String = "Measure String"
Dim stringFont As New Font("Arial", 16)
' Set maximum width of string.
Dim stringWidth As Integer = 100
' Set string format.
Dim newStringFormat As New StringFormat()
newStringFormat.FormatFlags = StringFormatFlags.DirectionVertical
' Measure string.
Dim stringSize As New SizeF()
stringSize = e.Graphics.MeasureString(measureString, stringFont, _
stringWidth, newStringFormat)
' Draw rectangle representing size of string.
e.Graphics.DrawRectangle(New Pen(Color.Red, 1), 0F, 0F, _
stringSize.Width, stringSize.Height)
' Draw string to screen.
e.Graphics.DrawString(measureString, stringFont, Brushes.Black, _
New PointF(0, 0), newStringFormat)
End Sub
```

[C#]
```
public void MeasureStringWidthFormat(PaintEventArgs e)
{
// Set up string.
string measureString = "Measure String";
Font stringFont = new Font("Arial", 16);
// Set maximum width of string.
int stringWidth = 100;
// Set string format.
StringFormat newStringFormat = new StringFormat();
newStringFormat.FormatFlags = StringFormatFlags.DirectionVertical;
// Measure string.
SizeF stringSize = new SizeF();
stringSize = e.Graphics.MeasureString(
measureString,
stringFont,
stringWidth,
newStringFormat);
// Draw rectangle representing size of string.
e.Graphics.DrawRectangle(
new Pen(Color.Red, 1),
0.0F, 0.0F, stringSize.Width, stringSize.Height);
// Draw string to screen.
e.Graphics.DrawString(
measureString,
stringFont,
Brushes.Black,
new PointF(0, 0),
newStringFormat);
}
```

Requirements

Platforms: Windows 98, Windows NT 4.0, Windows Millennium Edition, Windows 2000, Windows XP Home Edition, Windows XP Professional, Windows Server 2003 family

Graphics.MeasureString Method (String, Font, PointF, StringFormat)

Measures the specified string when drawn with the specified **Font** object and formatted with the specified **StringFormat** object.

[Visual Basic]
```
Overloads Public Function MeasureString( _
   ByVal text As String, _
   ByVal font As Font, _
   ByVal origin As PointF, _
   ByVal stringFormat As StringFormat _
) As SizeF
```
[C#]
```
public SizeF MeasureString(
   string text,
   Font font,
   PointF origin,
   StringFormat stringFormat
);
```
[C++]
```
public: SizeF MeasureString(
   String* text,
   Font* font,
   PointF origin,
   StringFormat* stringFormat
);
```
[JScript]
```
public function MeasureString(
   text : String,
   font : Font,
   origin : PointF,
   stringFormat : StringFormat
) : SizeF;
```

Parameters

text
String to measure.

font
Font object defines the text format of the string.

origin
PointF structure that represents the upper-left corner of the string.

stringFormat
StringFormat object that represents formatting information, such as line spacing, for the string.

Return Value

This method returns a **SizeF** structure that represents the size of the string, in pixels, of the *text* parameter as drawn with the *font* parameter and the *stringFormat* parameter.

Remarks

The **MeasureString** method is designed for use with individual strings and includes a small amount of extra space before and after the string to allow for overhanging glyphs. Also, the **DrawString** method adjusts glyph points to optimize display quality and might display a string narrower than reported by **MeasureString**. To obtain metrics suitable for adjacent strings in layout (for example, when implementing formatted text), use the **MeasureCharacterRanges** method.

Example

[Visual Basic, C#] The following example is designed for use with Windows Forms, and it requires **PaintEventArgs** *e*, which is a parameter of the **Paint** event handler. The code performs the following actions:

- Creates a string to measure and a font object set to Arial (16pt.)
- Creates a point to locate the upper-left corner of the string.
- Creates a string format object and sets its format flags to **StringFormatFlags.DirectionVertical**.
- Creates a size object to measure the string.
- Measures the size of the string, using the string, the font object, the locating point, and the string format.
- Draws a red rectangle using the locating point and the measured size of the string.
- Draws the string within the drawn rectangle.

[Visual Basic, C#] The result is a vertical rectangle enclosing a vertical string.

[Visual Basic]
```
Public Sub MeasureStringPointFFormat(e As PaintEventArgs)
' Set up string.
Dim measureString As String = "Measure String"
Dim stringFont As New Font("Arial", 16)
' Set point for upper-left corner of string.
Dim x As Single = 50F
Dim y As Single = 50F
Dim ulCorner As New PointF(x, y)
' Set string format.
```

```
Dim newStringFormat As New StringFormat()
newStringFormat.FormatFlags = StringFormatFlags.DirectionVertical
' Measure string.
Dim stringSize As New SizeF()
stringSize = e.Graphics.MeasureString(measureString, stringFont, _
ulCorner, newStringFormat)
' Draw rectangle representing size of string.
e.Graphics.DrawRectangle(New Pen(Color.Red, 1), x, y, _
stringSize.Width, stringSize.Height)
' Draw string to screen.
e.Graphics.DrawString(measureString, stringFont, Brushes.Black, _
ulCorner, newStringFormat)
End Sub
```

[C#]

```
public void MeasureStringPointFFormat(PaintEventArgs e)
{
// Set up string.
string measureString = "Measure String";
Font stringFont = new Font("Arial", 16);
// Set point for upper-left corner of string.
float x = 50.0F;
float y = 50.0F;
PointF ulCorner = new PointF(x, y);
// Set string format.
StringFormat newStringFormat = new StringFormat();
newStringFormat.FormatFlags = StringFormatFlags.DirectionVertical;
// Measure string.
SizeF stringSize = new SizeF();
stringSize = e.Graphics.MeasureString(
measureString,
stringFont,
ulCorner,
newStringFormat);
// Draw rectangle representing size of string.
e.Graphics.DrawRectangle(
new Pen(Color.Red, 1),
x, y, stringSize.Width, stringSize.Height);
// Draw string to screen.
e.Graphics.DrawString(
measureString,
stringFont,
Brushes.Black,
ulCorner,
newStringFormat);
}
```

Requirements

Platforms: Windows 98, Windows NT 4.0, Windows Millennium Edition, Windows 2000, Windows XP Home Edition, Windows XP Professional, Windows Server 2003 family

Graphics.MeasureString Method (String, Font, SizeF, StringFormat)

Measures the specified string when drawn with the specified **Font** object and formatted with the specified **StringFormat** object.

[Visual Basic]

```
Overloads Public Function MeasureString( _
   ByVal text As String, _
   ByVal font As Font, _
   ByVal layoutArea As SizeF, _
   ByVal stringFormat As StringFormat _
) As SizeF
```

[C#]

```
public SizeF MeasureString(
   string text,
   Font font,
   SizeF layoutArea,
   StringFormat stringFormat
);
```

[C++]

```
public: SizeF MeasureString(
   String* text,
   Font* font,
   SizeF layoutArea,
   StringFormat* stringFormat
);
```

[JScript]

```
public function MeasureString(
   text : String,
   font : Font,
   layoutArea : SizeF,
   stringFormat : StringFormat
) : SizeF;
```

Parameters

text

String to measure.

font

Font object defines the text format of the string.

layoutArea

SizeF structure that specifies the maximum layout area for the text.

stringFormat

StringFormat object that represents formatting information, such as line spacing, for the string.

Return Value

This method returns a **SizeF** structure that represents the size, in pixels, of the string specified in the *text* parameter as drawn with the *font* parameter and the *stringFormat* parameter.

Remarks

The **MeasureString** method is designed for use with individual strings and includes a small amount of extra space before and after the string to allow for overhanging glyphs. Also, the **DrawString** method adjusts glyph points to optimize display quality and might display a string narrower than reported by **MeasureString**. To obtain metrics suitable for adjacent strings in layout (for example, when implementing formatted text), use the **MeasureCharacterRanges** method.

Example

[Visual Basic, C#] The following example is designed for use with Windows Forms, and it requires **PaintEventArgs** *e*, which is a parameter of the **Paint** event handler. The code performs the following actions:

- Creates a string to measure and a font object set to Arial (16pt.).
- Sets the maximum layout size of the string, creating a size object to measure the string.
- Creates a string format object and sets its format flags to **StringFormatFlags.DirectionVertical**.
- Measures the size of the string, using the string, the font object, the maximum layout size, and the string format.
- Draws a red rectangle using the measured size of the string.
- Draws the string within the drawn rectangle.

[Visual Basic, C#] The result is a vertical rectangle enclosing a vertical string.

[Visual Basic]
```
Public Sub MeasureStringSizeFFormat(e As PaintEventArgs)
' Set up string.
Dim measureString As String = "Measure String"
Dim stringFont As New Font("Arial", 16)
' Set maximum layout size.
Dim layoutSize As New SizeF(100F, 200F)
' Set string format.
Dim newStringFormat As New StringFormat()
newStringFormat.FormatFlags = StringFormatFlags.DirectionVertical
' Measure string.
Dim stringSize As New SizeF()
stringSize = e.Graphics.MeasureString(measureString, stringFont, _
layoutSize, newStringFormat)
' Draw rectangle representing size of string.
e.Graphics.DrawRectangle(New Pen(Color.Red, 1), 0F, 0F, _
stringSize.Width, stringSize.Height)
' Draw string to screen.
e.Graphics.DrawString(measureString, stringFont, Brushes.Black, _
New PointF(0, 0), newStringFormat)
End Sub
```

[C#]
```
public void MeasureStringSizeFFormat(PaintEventArgs e)
{
// Set up string.
string measureString = "Measure String";
Font stringFont = new Font("Arial", 16);
// Set maximum layout size.
SizeF layoutSize = new SizeF(100.0F, 200.0F);
// Set string format.
StringFormat newStringFormat = new StringFormat();
newStringFormat.FormatFlags = StringFormatFlags.DirectionVertical;
// Measure string.
SizeF stringSize = new SizeF();
stringSize = e.Graphics.MeasureString(
measureString,
stringFont,
layoutSize,
newStringFormat);
// Draw rectangle representing size of string.
e.Graphics.DrawRectangle(
new Pen(Color.Red, 1),
0.0F, 0.0F, stringSize.Width, stringSize.Height);
// Draw string to screen.
e.Graphics.DrawString(
measureString,
stringFont,
Brushes.Black,
new PointF(0, 0),
newStringFormat);
}
```

Requirements

Platforms: Windows 98, Windows NT 4.0, Windows Millennium Edition, Windows 2000, Windows XP Home Edition, Windows XP Professional, Windows Server 2003 family

Graphics.MeasureString Method (String, Font, SizeF, StringFormat, Int32, Int32)

Measures the specified string when drawn with the specified **Font** object and formatted with the specified **StringFormat** object.

[Visual Basic]
```
Overloads Public Function MeasureString( _
   ByVal text As String, _
   ByVal font As Font, _
   ByVal layoutArea As SizeF, _
   ByVal stringFormat As StringFormat, _
   <Out()> ByRef charactersFitted As Integer, _
   <Out()> ByRef linesFilled As Integer _
) As SizeF
```
[C#]
```
public SizeF MeasureString(
   string text,
   Font font,
   SizeF layoutArea,
   StringFormat stringFormat,
   out int charactersFitted,
   out int linesFilled
);
```
[C++]
```
public: SizeF MeasureString(
   String* text,
   Font* font,
   SizeF layoutArea,
   StringFormat* stringFormat,
   [
   Out
] int* charactersFitted,
   [
   Out
] int* linesFilled
);
```
[JScript]
```
public function MeasureString(
   text : String,
   font : Font,
   layoutArea : SizeF,
   stringFormat : StringFormat,
   charactersFitted : int,
   linesFilled : int
) : SizeF;
```

Parameters

text
  String to measure.

font
  Font object that defines the text format of the string.

layoutArea
  SizeF structure that specifies the maximum layout area for the text.

stringFormat
  StringFormat object that represents formatting information, such as line spacing, for the string.

charactersFitted
  Number of characters in the string.

linesFilled
  Number of text lines in the string.

Return Value

This method returns a **SizeF** structure that represents the size of the string, in pixels, of the *text* parameter as drawn with the *font* parameter and the *stringFormat* parameter.

Remarks

The **MeasureString** method is designed for use with individual strings and includes a small amount of extra space before and after the string to allow for overhanging glyphs. Also, the **DrawString** method adjusts glyph points to optimize display quality and might display a string narrower than reported by **MeasureString**. To obtain metrics suitable for adjacent strings in layout (for example, when implementing formatted text), use the **MeasureCharacterRanges** method.

Example

[Visual Basic, C#] The following example is designed for use with Windows Forms, and it requires **PaintEventArgs** *e*, which is a parameter of the **Paint** event handler. The code performs the following actions:

- Creates a string to measure and a font object set to Arial (16pt.)
- Sets the maximum layout size of the string.
- Creates a string format object and sets its format flags to **StringFormatFlags.DirectionVertical**.
- Creates the integer variables *charactersFitted* and *linesFilled* and a size object to measure the string.
- Measures the size of the string and determines the number of characters fitted and lines filled, using the string, the font object, the maximum layout size, and the string format.
- Draws a red rectangle using the measured size of the string.
- Draws the string within the drawn rectangle.
- Draws the values of the number of characters fitted and lines filled.

[Visual Basic, C#] The result is a vertical rectangle enclosing a vertical string.

[Visual Basic]
```
Public Sub MeasureStringSizeFFormatInts(e As PaintEventArgs)
' Set up string.
Dim measureString As String = "Measure String"
Dim stringFont As New Font("Arial", 16)
' Set maximum layout size.
Dim layoutSize As New SizeF(100F, 200F)
' Set string format.
Dim newStringFormat As New StringFormat()
newStringFormat.FormatFlags = StringFormatFlags.DirectionVertical
' Measure string.
Dim charactersFitted As Integer
Dim linesFilled As Integer
Dim stringSize As New SizeF()
stringSize = e.Graphics.MeasureString(measureString, stringFont, _
layoutSize, newStringFormat, charactersFitted, linesFilled)
' Draw rectangle representing size of string.
e.Graphics.DrawRectangle(New Pen(Color.Red, 1), 0F, 0F, _
stringSize.Width, stringSize.Height)
' Draw string to screen.
e.Graphics.DrawString(measureString, stringFont, Brushes.Black, _
New PointF(0, 0), newStringFormat)
' Draw output parameters to screen.
Dim outString As String = "chars " & charactersFitted & _
", lines " & linesFilled
e.Graphics.DrawString(outString, stringFont, Brushes.Black, _
New PointF(100, 0))
End Sub
```

[C#]
```
public void MeasureStringSizeFFormatInts(PaintEventArgs e)
{
// Set up string.
string measureString = "Measure String";
Font stringFont = new Font("Arial", 16);
// Set maximum layout size.
SizeF layoutSize = new SizeF(100.0F, 200.0F);
// Set string format.
StringFormat newStringFormat = new StringFormat();
newStringFormat.FormatFlags = StringFormatFlags.DirectionVertical;
// Measure string.
int charactersFitted;
int linesFilled;
SizeF stringSize = new SizeF();
stringSize = e.Graphics.MeasureString(
measureString,
stringFont,
layoutSize,
newStringFormat,
out charactersFitted,
out linesFilled);
// Draw rectangle representing size of string.
e.Graphics.DrawRectangle(
new Pen(Color.Red, 1),
0.0F, 0.0F, stringSize.Width, stringSize.Height);
// Draw string to screen.
e.Graphics.DrawString(
measureString,
stringFont,
Brushes.Black,
new PointF(0, 0),
newStringFormat);
// Draw output parameters to screen.
string outString = "chars " + charactersFitted + ",                ↵
 lines " + linesFilled;
e.Graphics.DrawString(
outString,
stringFont,
Brushes.Black,
new PointF(100, 0));
}
```

Requirements

Platforms: Windows 98, Windows NT 4.0, Windows Millennium Edition, Windows 2000, Windows XP Home Edition, Windows XP Professional, Windows Server 2003 family

Graphics.MultiplyTransform Method

Multiplies the world transformation of this **Graphics** object and specified the **Matrix** object.

Overload List

Multiplies the world transformation of this **Graphics** object and specified the **Matrix** object.

[Visual Basic] **Overloads Public Sub MultiplyTransform(Matrix)**

[C#] **public void MultiplyTransform(Matrix);**

[C++] **public: void MultiplyTransform(Matrix*);**

[JScript] **public function MultiplyTransform(Matrix);**

Multiplies the world transformation of this **Graphics** object and specified the **Matrix** object in the specified order.

[Visual Basic] **Overloads Public Sub MultiplyTransform(Matrix, MatrixOrder)**

[C#] **public void MultiplyTransform(Matrix, MatrixOrder);**

[C++] **public: void MultiplyTransform(Matrix*, MatrixOrder);**

[JScript] **public function MultiplyTransform(Matrix, MatrixOrder);**

Example

[Visual Basic, C#] The following example is designed for use with Windows Forms, and it requires **PaintEventArgs** *e*, which is a parameter of the **Paint** event handler. The code performs the following actions:

- Creates a *transformMatrix* matrix (a two by two identity matrix plus a zero-translation vector).
- Translates the transform matrix by a vector (200, 100).
- Rotates the world transformation matrix of the Windows form by 30 degrees, prepending the rotation matrix for 30 degrees to the form's transformation matrix.
- Multiplies the rotated world transformation matrix by the translated *transformMatrix*, appending the *transformMatrix* to the world transformation matrix.
- Draws a rotated, translated ellipse.

> [Visual Basic, C#] **Note** This example shows how to use one of the overloaded versions of **MultiplyTransform**. For other examples that might be available, see the individual overload topics.

[Visual Basic]
```
Public Sub MultiplyTransformMatrixOrder(e As PaintEventArgs)
' Create transform matrix.
Dim transformMatrix As New Matrix()
' Translate matrix, prepending translation vector.
transformMatrix.Translate(200F, 100F)
' Rotate transformation matrix of graphics object,
' prepending rotation matrix.
e.Graphics.RotateTransform(30F)
' Multiply (append to) transformation matrix of
' graphics object to translate graphics transformation.
e.Graphics.MultiplyTransform(transformMatrix, MatrixOrder.Append)
' Draw rotated, translated ellipse.
e.Graphics.DrawEllipse(New Pen(Color.Blue, 3), - 80, - 40, 160, 80)
End Sub
```

[C#]
```
public void MultiplyTransformMatrixOrder(PaintEventArgs e)
{
// Create transform matrix.
Matrix transformMatrix = new Matrix();
// Translate matrix, prepending translation vector.
transformMatrix.Translate(200.0F, 100.0F);
// Rotate transformation matrix of graphics object,
//  prepending rotation matrix.
e.Graphics.RotateTransform(30.0F);
// Multiply (append to) transformation matrix of
//  graphics object to translate graphics transformation.
e.Graphics.MultiplyTransform(transformMatrix, MatrixOrder.Append);
// Draw rotated, translated ellipse.
e.Graphics.DrawEllipse(new Pen(Color.Blue, 3), -80, -40, 160, 80);
}
```

Graphics.MultiplyTransform Method (Matrix)

Multiplies the world transformation of this **Graphics** object and specified the **Matrix** object.

[Visual Basic]
```
Overloads Public Sub MultiplyTransform( _
   ByVal matrix As Matrix _
)
```
[C#]
```
public void MultiplyTransform(
   Matrix matrix
);
```
[C++]
```
public: void MultiplyTransform(
   Matrix* matrix
);
```
[JScript]
```
public function MultiplyTransform(
   matrix : Matrix
);
```

Parameters

matrix

4x4 **Matrix** object that multiplies the world transformation.

Return Value

This method does not return a value.

Remarks

This method prepends the matrix specified by the *matrix* parameter, so that the result is *matrix* x world transformation.

The **MeasureString** method is designed for use with individual strings and includes a small amount of extra space before and after the string to allow for overhanging glyphs. Also, the **DrawString** method adjusts glyph points to optimize display quality and might display a string narrower than reported by **MeasureString**. To obtain metrics suitable for adjacent strings in layout (for example, when implementing formatted text), use the **MeasureCharacterRanges** method.

Example

[Visual Basic, C#] The following example is designed for use with Windows Forms, and it requires **PaintEventArgs** *e*, which is a parameter of the **Paint** event handler. The code performs the following actions:

- Creates a *transformMatrix* matrix (a two by two identity matrix plus a zero-translation vector).
- Translates the transform matrix by a vector (200, 100).
- Rotates the world transformation matrix of the Windows form by 30 degrees, prepending the rotation matrix for 30 degrees to the form's transformation matrix.
- Multiplies the rotated world transformation matrix by the translated *transformMatrix*, prepending the *transformMatrix* to the world transformation matrix.
- Draws a rotated, translated ellipse.

[Visual Basic]
```
Public Sub MultiplyTransformMatrix(e As PaintEventArgs)
' Create transform matrix.
Dim transformMatrix As New Matrix()
' Translate matrix, prepending translation vector.
transformMatrix.Translate(200F, 100F)
' Rotate transformation matrix of graphics object,
' prepending rotation matrix.
e.Graphics.RotateTransform(30F)
' Multiply (prepend to) transformation matrix of
' graphics object to translate graphics transformation.
e.Graphics.MultiplyTransform(transformMatrix)
' Draw rotated, translated ellipse.
e.Graphics.DrawEllipse(New Pen(Color.Blue, 3), - 80, - 40, 160, 80)
End Sub
```

[C#]
```
public void MultiplyTransformMatrix(PaintEventArgs e)
{
// Create transform matrix.
Matrix transformMatrix = new Matrix();
// Translate matrix, prepending translation vector.
transformMatrix.Translate(200.0F, 100.0F);
// Rotate transformation matrix of graphics object,
//  prepending rotation matrix.
e.Graphics.RotateTransform(30.0F);
// Multiply (prepend to) transformation matrix of
//  graphics object to translate graphics transformation.
e.Graphics.MultiplyTransform(transformMatrix);
// Draw rotated, translated ellipse.
e.Graphics.DrawEllipse(new Pen(Color.Blue, 3), -80, -40, 160, 80);
}
```

Requirements

Platforms: Windows 98, Windows NT 4.0, Windows Millennium Edition, Windows 2000, Windows XP Home Edition, Windows XP Professional, Windows Server 2003 family

Graphics.MultiplyTransform Method (Matrix, MatrixOrder)

Multiplies the world transformation of this **Graphics** object and specified the **Matrix** object in the specified order.

[Visual Basic]
```
Overloads Public Sub MultiplyTransform( _
   ByVal matrix As Matrix, _
   ByVal order As MatrixOrder _
)
```
[C#]
```
public void MultiplyTransform(
   Matrix matrix,
   MatrixOrder order
);
```
[C++]
```
public: void MultiplyTransform(
   Matrix* matrix,
   MatrixOrder order
);
```
[JScript]
```
public function MultiplyTransform(
   matrix : Matrix,
   order : MatrixOrder
);
```

Parameters

matrix

4x4 **Matrix** object that multiplies the world transformation.

order

Member of the **MatrixOrder** enumeration that determines the order of the multiplication.

Return Value

This method does not return a value.

Remarks

A value of **MatrixOrder.Prepend** for the *order* parameter specifies that the order of the multiplication is *matrix* x world transformation. A value of **MatrixOrder.Append** for *order* specifies that the order of the multiplication is world transformation x *matrix*.

Example

[Visual Basic, C#] The following example is designed for use with Windows Forms, and it requires **PaintEventArgs** *e*, which is a parameter of the **Paint** event handler. The code performs the following actions:

- Creates a *transformMatrix* matrix (a two by two identity matrix plus a zero-translation vector).
- Translates the transform matrix by a vector (200, 100).
- Rotates the world transformation matrix of the Windows form by 30 degrees, prepending the rotation matrix for 30 degrees to the form's transformation matrix.
- Multiplies the rotated world transformation matrix by the translated *transformMatrix*, appending the *transformMatrix* to the world transformation matrix.
- Draws a rotated, translated ellipse.

[Visual Basic]
```
Public Sub MultiplyTransformMatrixOrder(e As PaintEventArgs)
' Create transform matrix.
Dim transformMatrix As New Matrix()
' Translate matrix, prepending translation vector.
transformMatrix.Translate(200F, 100F)
' Rotate transformation matrix of graphics object,
' prepending rotation matrix.
e.Graphics.RotateTransform(30F)
' Multiply (append to) transformation matrix of
' graphics object to translate graphics transformation.
e.Graphics.MultiplyTransform(transformMatrix, MatrixOrder.Append)
' Draw rotated, translated ellipse.
e.Graphics.DrawEllipse(New Pen(Color.Blue, 3), - 80, - 40, 160, 80)
End Sub
```

[C#]
```
public void MultiplyTransformMatrixOrder(PaintEventArgs e)
{
// Create transform matrix.
Matrix transformMatrix = new Matrix();
// Translate matrix, prepending translation vector.
transformMatrix.Translate(200.0F, 100.0F);
// Rotate transformation matrix of graphics object,
//  prepending rotation matrix.
e.Graphics.RotateTransform(30.0F);
// Multiply (append to) transformation matrix of
//  graphics object to translate graphics transformation.
e.Graphics.MultiplyTransform(transformMatrix, MatrixOrder.Append);
// Draw rotated, translated ellipse.
e.Graphics.DrawEllipse(new Pen(Color.Blue, 3), -80, -40, 160, 80);
}
```

Requirements

Platforms: Windows 98, Windows NT 4.0, Windows Millennium Edition, Windows 2000, Windows XP Home Edition, Windows XP Professional, Windows Server 2003 family

Graphics.ReleaseHdc Method

Releases a device context handle obtained by a previous call to the **GetHdc** method of this **Graphics** object.

[Visual Basic]
```
Public Sub ReleaseHdc( _
   ByVal hdc As IntPtr _
)
```

[C#]
```
public void ReleaseHdc(
   IntPtr hdc
);
```
[C++]
```
public: void ReleaseHdc(
   IntPtr hdc
);
```
[JScript]
```
public function ReleaseHdc(
   hdc : IntPtr
);
```

Parameters

hdc

Handle to a device context obtained by a previous call to the **GetHdc** method of this **Graphics** object.

Return Value

This method does not return a value.

Remarks

The device context is a Windows GDI-based structure that defines a set of graphical objects and their associated attributes, as well as the graphical modes that affect output.

Calls to the **GetHdc** and **ReleaseHdc** methods must appear in pairs. During the scope of a **GetHdc- ReleaseHdc** method pair, you usually make only calls to GDI functions. Calls in that scope made to GDI+ methods of the **Graphics** object that produced the *hdc* parameter fail with an ObjectBusy error. Also, GDI+ ignores any state changes made to the **Graphics** object of the *hdc* parameter in subsequent operations.

Example

[Visual Basic, C#] The following example is designed for use with Windows Forms, and it requires **PaintEventArgs** *e*, which is a parameter of the **Paint** event handler. The example illustrates calling a Windows GDI function to perform the same task as a GDI+ **Graphics** object method. The code performs the following actions:

- Defines the interoperability **DllImportAttribute** attribute for the Windows DLL file gdi32.dll. This DLL contains the desired GDI function, and it defines the **Rectangle** function in that DLL as external.
- Creates a red pen.
- With the pen, draws a rectangle to the screen using the GDI+ **DrawRectangle** method.
- Defines an internal pointer type variable *hdc* and sets its value to the handle to the device context of the form.
- Draws a rectangle to the screen using the GDI **Rectangle** function.
- Releases the device context represented by the *hdc* parameter.

[Visual Basic]
```
<System.Runtime.InteropServices.DllImportAttribute("gdi32.dll")> _
Private Shared Function Rectangle(hdc As IntPtr, _
ulCornerX As Integer, ulCornerY As Integer, lrCornerX As Integer, _
lrCornerY As Integer) As Boolean
End Function
Public Sub GetHdcForGDI(e As PaintEventArgs)
' Create pen.
Dim redPen As New Pen(Color.Red, 1)
' Draw rectangle with GDI+.
e.Graphics.DrawRectangle(redPen, 10, 10, 100, 50)
' Get handle to device context.
Dim hdc As IntPtr = e.Graphics.GetHdc()
' Draw rectangle with GDI using default pen.
Rectangle(hdc, 10, 70, 110, 120)
' Release handle to device context.
e.Graphics.ReleaseHdc(hdc)
End Sub
```

[C#]
```
[System.Runtime.InteropServices.DllImportAttribute("gdi32.dll")]
private static extern bool Rectangle(
IntPtr hdc,
int ulCornerX, int ulCornerY,
int lrCornerX, int lrCornerY);
public void GetHdcForGDI(PaintEventArgs e)
{
// Create pen.
Pen redPen = new Pen(Color.Red, 1);
// Draw rectangle with GDI+.
e.Graphics.DrawRectangle(redPen, 10, 10, 100, 50);
// Get handle to device context.
IntPtr hdc = new IntPtr();
hdc = e.Graphics.GetHdc();
// Draw rectangle with GDI using default pen.
Rectangle(hdc, 10, 70, 110, 120);
// Release handle to device context.
e.Graphics.ReleaseHdc(hdc);
}
```

Requirements

Platforms: Windows 98, Windows NT 4.0, Windows Millennium Edition, Windows 2000, Windows XP Home Edition, Windows XP Professional, Windows Server 2003 family

Graphics.ReleaseHdcInternal Method

Internal method. Do not use.

[Visual Basic]
```
Public Sub ReleaseHdcInternal( _
   ByVal hdc As IntPtr _
)
```
[C#]
```
public void ReleaseHdcInternal(
   IntPtr hdc
);
```
[C++]
```
public: void ReleaseHdcInternal(
   IntPtr hdc
);
```
[JScript]
```
public function ReleaseHdcInternal(
   hdc : IntPtr
);
```

Parameters

hdc

Handle to a device context.

Return Value

This method does not return a value.

Requirements

Platforms: Windows 98, Windows NT 4.0, Windows Millennium Edition, Windows 2000, Windows XP Home Edition, Windows XP Professional, Windows Server 2003 family

Graphics.ResetClip Method

Resets the clip region of this **Graphics** object to an infinite region.

[Visual Basic]
```
Public Sub ResetClip()
```
[C#]
```
public void ResetClip();
```
[C++]
```
public: void ResetClip();
```
[JScript]
```
public function ResetClip();
```

Return Value

This method does not return a value.

Remarks

When the clipping region of a **Graphics** object is infinite, items that this **Graphics** object draws are not clipped.

Example

[Visual Basic, C#] The following example is designed for use with Windows Forms, and it requires **PaintEventArgs** *e*, which is a parameter of the **Paint** event handler. The code performs the following actions:

- Creates a rectangle with upper-left corner at (0, 0) and sets the clipping region to this rectangle.
- Creates a second rectangle with upper-left corner at (100, 100) and sets the clipping region to the intersection of this rectangle and the current clipping region (the first rectangle).
- Fills a large rectangle that includes both previous rectangles with a solid blue brush.
- Resets the clipping region to infinite.
- Draws rectangles around the two clipping regions; it uses a black pen for the first clipping rectangle and a red pen for the second clipping region.

[Visual Basic, C#] The result is that only the intersection of the two rectangles is filled with blue.

[Visual Basic]
```
Public Sub IntersectClipRectangleF(e As PaintEventArgs)
' Set clipping region.
Dim clipRect As New Rectangle(0, 0, 200, 200)
e.Graphics.SetClip(clipRect)
' Update clipping region to intersection of
' existing region with specified rectangle.
Dim intersectRectF As New RectangleF(100F, 100F, 200F, 200F)
e.Graphics.IntersectClip(intersectRectF)
' Fill rectangle to demonstrate effective clipping region.
e.Graphics.FillRectangle(New SolidBrush(Color.Blue), 0, 0, _
500, 500)
' Reset clipping region to infinite.
e.Graphics.ResetClip()
' Draw clipRect and intersectRect to screen.
e.Graphics.DrawRectangle(New Pen(Color.Black), clipRect)
e.Graphics.DrawRectangle(New Pen(Color.Red), _
Rectangle.Round(intersectRectF))
End Sub
```

[C#]
```
public void IntersectClipRectangleF(PaintEventArgs e)
{
// Set clipping region.
Rectangle clipRect = new Rectangle(0, 0, 200, 200);
e.Graphics.SetClip(clipRect);
// Update clipping region to intersection of existing region     ↵
 with new rectangle.
RectangleF intersectRectF = new RectangleF(100.0F, 100.0F,       ↵
200.0F, 200.0F);
e.Graphics.IntersectClip(intersectRectF);
// Fill rectangle to demonstrate effective clipping region.
e.Graphics.FillRectangle(new SolidBrush(Color.Blue), 0, 0, 500, 500);
// Reset clipping region to infinite.
e.Graphics.ResetClip();
// Draw clipRect and intersectRect to screen.
e.Graphics.DrawRectangle(new Pen(Color.Black), clipRect);
e.Graphics.DrawRectangle(new Pen(Color.Red),
Rectangle.Round(intersectRectF));
}
```

Requirements

Platforms: Windows 98, Windows NT 4.0, Windows Millennium Edition, Windows 2000, Windows XP Home Edition, Windows XP Professional, Windows Server 2003 family, .NET Compact Framework - Windows CE .NET

Graphics.ResetTransform Method

Resets the world transformation matrix of this **Graphics** object to the identity matrix.

[Visual Basic]
```
Public Sub ResetTransform()
```
[C#]
```
public void ResetTransform();
```
[C++]
```
public: void ResetTransform();
```
[JScript]
```
public function ResetTransform();
```

Return Value

This method does not return a value.

Remarks

The identity matrix represents a transformation with no scaling, rotation, or translation. Resetting the world transformation of this **Graphics** object to the identity matrix means that its world transformation doesn't change the geometry of transformed items.

Example

[Visual Basic, C#] The following example is designed for use with Windows Forms, and it requires **PaintEventArgs** *e*, which is a parameter of the **Paint** event handler. The code performs the following actionts:

- Translates the world transform of the Windows form by a vector (100, 0).
- Saves the graphics state of the form.
- Resets the world transform of the form to an identity and fills a rectangle with a solid red brush.
- Restores the translated graphics state and fills a rectangle with a solid blue brush.

[Visual Basic, C#] The result is an untranslated red-filled rectangle and a translated blue-filled rectangle.

[Visual Basic]
```
Public Sub SaveRestore(e As PaintEventArgs)
' Translate transformation matrix.
e.Graphics.TranslateTransform(100, 0)
' Save translated graphics state.
Dim transState As GraphicsState = e.Graphics.Save()
' Reset transformation matrix to identity and fill rectangle.
e.Graphics.ResetTransform()
e.Graphics.FillRectangle(New SolidBrush(Color.Red), 0, 0, 100, 100)
' Restore graphics state to translated state and fill second
' rectangle.
```

```
e.Graphics.Restore(transState)
e.Graphics.FillRectangle(New SolidBrush(Color.Blue), 0, 0, _
100, 100)
End Sub
```

[C#]

```
public void SaveRestore(PaintEventArgs e)
{
// Translate transformation matrix.
e.Graphics.TranslateTransform(100, 0);
// Save translated graphics state.
GraphicsState transState = e.Graphics.Save();
// Reset transformation matrix to identity and fill rectangle.
e.Graphics.ResetTransform();
e.Graphics.FillRectangle(new SolidBrush(Color.Red), 0, 0, 100, 100);
// Restore graphics state to translated state and fill second ↵
rectangle.
e.Graphics.Restore(transState);
e.Graphics.FillRectangle(new SolidBrush(Color.Blue), 0, 0, 100, 100);
}
```

Requirements

Platforms: Windows 98, Windows NT 4.0, Windows Millennium Edition, Windows 2000, Windows XP Home Edition, Windows XP Professional, Windows Server 2003 family

Graphics.Restore Method

Restores the state of this **Graphics** object to the state represented by a **GraphicsState** object.

[Visual Basic]

```
Public Sub Restore( _
   ByVal gstate As GraphicsState _
)
```

[C#]

```
public void Restore(
   GraphicsState gstate
);
```

[C++]

```
public: void Restore(
   GraphicsState* gstate
);
```

[JScript]

```
public function Restore(
   gstate : GraphicsState
);
```

Parameters

gstate

GraphicsState object that represents the state to which to restore this **Graphics** object.

Return Value

This method does not return a value.

Remarks

When you call the **Save** method of a **Graphics** object, an information block that holds the state of the **Graphics** object is put on a stack. The **Save** method returns a **GraphicsState** object that identifies that information block. When you pass the identifying **GraphicsState** object to the **Graphics.Restore** method, the information block is removed from the stack and is used to restore the **Graphics** object to the state it was in at the time of the **Save** method call. Note that the **GraphicsState** object returned by a given call to the **Save** method can be passed only once to the **Restore** method.

Calls to the **Save** method can be nested; that is, you can call the **Save** method several times before you call the **Restore** method. Each time you call the **Save** method, an information block is put on the stack, and you receive a **GraphicsState** object for the information block. When you pass one of those objects to the **Restore** method, the **Graphics** object is returned to the state it was in at the time of the **Save** method call that returned that particular **GraphicsState** object. The information block placed on the stack by that **Save** method call is removed from the stack, and all information blocks placed on that stack after that **Save** method call are also removed.

Calls to the **BeginContainer** method place information blocks on the same stack as calls to the **Save** method. Just as a **Restore** call is paired with a **Save** call, a **EndContainer** method call is paired with a **BeginContainer** method call.

When you call the **Restore** method, all information blocks placed on the stack (by the **Save** method or by the **BeginContainer** method) after the corresponding call to the **Save** method are removed from the stack. Likewise, When you call the **EndContainer** method, all information blocks placed on the stack (by the **Save** method or by the **BeginContainer** method) after the corresponding call to the **BeginContainer** method are removed from the stack.

Example

[Visual Basic, C#] The following example is designed for use with Windows Forms, and it requires **PaintEventArgs** *e*, which is a parameter of the **Paint** event handler. The code performs the following actions:

- Translates the world transform of the Windows form by a vector (100, 0).
- Saves the graphics state of the form.
- Resets the world transform of the form to an identity and fills a rectangle with a solid red brush.
- Restores the translated graphics state and fills a second rectangle with a solid blue brush.

[Visual Basic, C#] The result is an untranslated red-filled rectangle and a translated blue-filled rectangle.

[Visual Basic]

```
Public Sub SaveRestore(e As PaintEventArgs)
' Translate transformation matrix.
e.Graphics.TranslateTransform(100, 0)
' Save translated graphics state.
Dim transState As GraphicsState = e.Graphics.Save()
' Reset transformation matrix to identity and fill rectangle.
e.Graphics.ResetTransform()
e.Graphics.FillRectangle(New SolidBrush(Color.Red), 0, 0, 100, 100)
' Restore graphics state to translated state and fill second
' rectangle.
e.Graphics.Restore(transState)
e.Graphics.FillRectangle(New SolidBrush(Color.Blue), 0, 0, _
100, 100)
End Sub
```

[C#]

```
public void SaveRestore(PaintEventArgs e)
{
// Translate transformation matrix.
e.Graphics.TranslateTransform(100, 0);
// Save translated graphics state.
GraphicsState transState = e.Graphics.Save();
// Reset transformation matrix to identity and fill rectangle.
e.Graphics.ResetTransform();
e.Graphics.FillRectangle(new SolidBrush(Color.Red), 0, 0, 100, 100);
// Restore graphics state to translated state and fill second ↵
rectangle.
e.Graphics.Restore(transState);
e.Graphics.FillRectangle(new SolidBrush(Color.Blue), 0, 0, 100, 100);
}
```

Requirements

Platforms: Windows 98, Windows NT 4.0, Windows Millennium Edition, Windows 2000, Windows XP Home Edition, Windows XP Professional, Windows Server 2003 family

Graphics.RotateTransform Method

Applies the specified rotation to the transformation matrix of this **Graphics** object.

Overload List

Applies the specified rotation to the transformation matrix of this **Graphics** object.

[Visual Basic] **Overloads Public Sub RotateTransform(Single)**

[C#] **public void RotateTransform(float);**

[C++] **public: void RotateTransform(float);**

[JScript] **public function RotateTransform(float);**

Applies the specified rotation to the transformation matrix of this **Graphics** object in the specified order.

[Visual Basic] **Overloads Public Sub RotateTransform(Single, MatrixOrder)**

[C#] **public void RotateTransform(float, MatrixOrder);**

[C++] **public: void RotateTransform(float, MatrixOrder);**

[JScript] **public function RotateTransform(float, MatrixOrder);**

Example

[Visual Basic, C#] The following example is designed for use with Windows Forms, and it requires **PaintEventArgs** *e*, which is a parameter of the **Paint** event handler. The code performs the following actions:

- Translates the world transformation matrix of the Windows form by the vector (100, 0).
- Rotates the world transform by an angle of 30 degrees, appending the rotation matrix to the world transformation matrix with **MatrixOrder.Append**.
- Draws a translated, rotated ellipse with a blue pen.

> [Visual Basic, C#] **Note** This example shows how to use one of the overloaded versions of **RotateTransform**. For other examples that might be available, see the individual overload topics.

[Visual Basic]
```
Public Sub RotateTransformAngleMatrixOrder(e As PaintEventArgs)
' Set world transform of graphics object to translate.
e.Graphics.TranslateTransform(100F, 0F)
' Then to rotate, appending rotation matrix.
e.Graphics.RotateTransform(30F, MatrixOrder.Append)
' Draw translated, rotated ellipse to screen.
e.Graphics.DrawEllipse(New Pen(Color.Blue, 3), 0, 0, 200, 80)
End Sub
```

[C#]
```
public void RotateTransformAngleMatrixOrder(PaintEventArgs e)
{
// Set world transform of graphics object to translate.
e.Graphics.TranslateTransform(100.0F, 0.0F);
// Then to rotate, appending rotation matrix.
e.Graphics.RotateTransform(30.0F, MatrixOrder.Append);
// Draw translated, rotated ellipse to screen.
e.Graphics.DrawEllipse(new Pen(Color.Blue, 3), 0, 0, 200, 80);
}
```

Graphics.RotateTransform Method (Single)

Applies the specified rotation to the transformation matrix of this **Graphics** object.

[Visual Basic]
```
Overloads Public Sub RotateTransform( _
   ByVal angle As Single _
)
```
[C#]
```
public void RotateTransform(
   float angle
);
```
[C++]
```
public: void RotateTransform(
   float angle
);
```
[JScript]
```
public function RotateTransform(
   angle : float
);
```

Parameters

angle

Angle of rotation in degrees.

Return Value

This method does not return a value.

Remarks

The rotation operation consists of multiplying the transformation matrix by a matrix whose elements are derived from the *angle* parameter. This method applies the rotation by prepending it to the transformation matrix.

Example

[Visual Basic, C#] The following example is designed for use with Windows Forms, and it requires **PaintEventArgs** *e*, which is a parameter of the **Paint** event handler. The code performs the following actions:

- Translates the world transformation matrix of the Windows form by the vector (100, 0).
- Rotates the world transformation by an angle of 30 degrees, prepending the rotation matrix to the world transformation matrix.
- Draws a rotated, translated ellipse with a blue pen.

[Visual Basic]
```
Public Sub RotateTransformAngle(e As PaintEventArgs)
' Set world transform of graphics object to translate.
e.Graphics.TranslateTransform(100F, 0F)
' Then to rotate, prepending rotation matrix.
e.Graphics.RotateTransform(30F)
' Draw rotated, translated ellipse to screen.
e.Graphics.DrawEllipse(New Pen(Color.Blue, 3), 0, 0, 200, 80)
End Sub
```

[C#]
```
public void RotateTransformAngle(PaintEventArgs e)
{
// Set world transform of graphics object to translate.
e.Graphics.TranslateTransform(100.0F, 0.0F);
// Then to rotate, prepending rotation matrix.
e.Graphics.RotateTransform(30.0F);
// Draw rotated, translated ellipse to screen.
e.Graphics.DrawEllipse(new Pen(Color.Blue, 3), 0, 0, 200, 80);
}
```

Requirements

Platforms: Windows 98, Windows NT 4.0, Windows Millennium Edition, Windows 2000, Windows XP Home Edition, Windows XP Professional, Windows Server 2003 family

Graphics.RotateTransform Method (Single, MatrixOrder)

Applies the specified rotation to the transformation matrix of this **Graphics** object in the specified order.

```
[Visual Basic]
Overloads Public Sub RotateTransform( _
   ByVal angle As Single, _
   ByVal order As MatrixOrder _
)
[C#]
public void RotateTransform(
   float angle,
   MatrixOrder order
);
[C++]
public: void RotateTransform(
   float angle,
   MatrixOrder order
);
[JScript]
public function RotateTransform(
   angle : float,
   order : MatrixOrder
);
```

Parameters

angle
Angle of rotation in degrees.

order
Member of the **MatrixOrder** enumeration that specifies whether the rotation is appended or prepended to the matrix transformation.

Return Value

This method does not return a value.

Remarks

The rotation operation consists of multiplying the transformation matrix by a matrix whose elements are derived from the *angle* parameter. This method premultiplies (prepends) or postmultiplies (appends) the transformation matrix of the **Graphics** object by the rotation matrix according to the *order* parameter.

Example

[Visual Basic, C#] The following example is designed for use with Windows Forms, and it requires **PaintEventArgs** *e*, which is a parameter of the **Paint** event handler. The code performs the following actions:

- Translates the world transformation matrix of the Windows form by the vector (100, 0).
- Rotates the world transform by an angle of 30 degrees, appending the rotation matrix to the world transformation matrix with **MatrixOrder.Append**.
- Draws a translated, rotated ellipse with a blue pen.

```
[Visual Basic]
Public Sub RotateTransformAngleMatrixOrder(e As PaintEventArgs)
' Set world transform of graphics object to translate.
e.Graphics.TranslateTransform(100F, 0F)
' Then to rotate, appending rotation matrix.
e.Graphics.RotateTransform(30F, MatrixOrder.Append)
' Draw translated, rotated ellipse to screen.
e.Graphics.DrawEllipse(New Pen(Color.Blue, 3), 0, 0, 200, 80)
End Sub
```

```
[C#]
public void RotateTransformAngleMatrixOrder(PaintEventArgs e)
{
// Set world transform of graphics object to translate.
e.Graphics.TranslateTransform(100.0F, 0.0F);
// Then to rotate, appending rotation matrix.
e.Graphics.RotateTransform(30.0F, MatrixOrder.Append);
// Draw translated, rotated ellipse to screen.
e.Graphics.DrawEllipse(new Pen(Color.Blue, 3), 0, 0, 200, 80);
}
```

Requirements

Platforms: Windows 98, Windows NT 4.0, Windows Millennium Edition, Windows 2000, Windows XP Home Edition, Windows XP Professional, Windows Server 2003 family

Graphics.Save Method

Saves the current state of this **Graphics** object and identifies the saved state with a **GraphicsState** object.

```
[Visual Basic]
Public Function Save() As GraphicsState
[C#]
public GraphicsState Save();
[C++]
public: GraphicsState* Save();
[JScript]
public function Save() : GraphicsState;
```

Return Value

This method returns a **GraphicsState** object that represents the saved state of this **Graphics** object.

Remarks

When you call the **Save** method of a **Graphics** object, an information block that holds the state of the **Graphics** object is put on a stack. The **Save** method returns a **GraphicsState** object that identifies that information block. When you pass the identifying **GraphicsState** object to the **Graphics.Restore** method, the information block is removed from the stack and is used to restore the **Graphics** object to the state it was in at the time of the **Save** method call. Note that the **GraphicsState** object returned by a given call to the **Save** method can be passed only once to the **Restore** method.

Calls to the **Save** method can be nested; that is, you can call the **Save** method several times before you call the **Restore** method. Each time you call the **Save** method, an information block is put on the stack, and you receive a **GraphicsState** object for the information block. When you pass one of those objects to the **Restore** method, the **Graphics** object is returned to the state it was in at the time of the **Save** method call that returned that particular **GraphicsState** object. The information block placed on the stack by that **Save** method call is removed from the stack, and all information blocks placed on that stack after that **Save** method call are also removed.

Calls to the **BeginContainer** method place information blocks on the same stack as calls to the **Save** method. Just as a **Restore** call is paired with a **Save** call, a **EndContainer** method call is paired with a **BeginContainer** method call.

When you call the **Restore** method, all information blocks placed on the stack (by the **Save** method or by the **BeginContainer** method) after the corresponding call to the **Save** method are removed from the stack. Likewise, When you call the **EndContainer** method, all information blocks placed on the stack (by the **Save** method or by the **BeginContainer** method) after the corresponding call to the **BeginContainer** method are removed from the stack.

Example

[Visual Basic, C#] The following example is designed for use with Windows Forms, and it requires **PaintEventArgs** *e*, which is a parameter of the **Paint** event handler. The code performs the following actions:

- Translates the world transform of the Windows form by a vector (100, 0).
- Saves the graphics state of the form.
- Resets the world transform of the form to an identity (two by two identity matrix plus a zero-vector translation) and fills a rectangle with a solid red brush.
- Restores the translated graphics state and fills a rectangle with a solid blue brush.

[Visual Basic, C#] The result is an untranslated red-filled rectangle on the left and a translated blue-filled rectangle on the right of the form.

[Visual Basic]
```
Public Sub SaveRestore(e As PaintEventArgs)
' Translate transformation matrix.
e.Graphics.TranslateTransform(100, 0)
' Save translated graphics state.
Dim transState As GraphicsState = e.Graphics.Save()
' Reset transformation matrix to identity and fill rectangle.
e.Graphics.ResetTransform()
e.Graphics.FillRectangle(New SolidBrush(Color.Red), 0, 0, 100, 100)
' Restore graphics state to translated state and fill second
' rectangle.
e.Graphics.Restore(transState)
e.Graphics.FillRectangle(New SolidBrush(Color.Blue), 0, 0, _
100, 100)
End Sub
```

[C#]
```
public void SaveRestore(PaintEventArgs e)
{
// Translate transformation matrix.
e.Graphics.TranslateTransform(100, 0);
// Save translated graphics state.
GraphicsState transState = e.Graphics.Save();
// Reset transformation matrix to identity and fill rectangle.
e.Graphics.ResetTransform();
e.Graphics.FillRectangle(new SolidBrush(Color.Red), 0, 0, 100, 100);
// Restore graphics state to translated state and fill second          ↵
rectangle.
e.Graphics.Restore(transState);
e.Graphics.FillRectangle(new SolidBrush(Color.Blue), 0, 0, 100, 100);
}
```

Requirements

Platforms: Windows 98, Windows NT 4.0, Windows Millennium Edition, Windows 2000, Windows XP Home Edition, Windows XP Professional, Windows Server 2003 family

Graphics.ScaleTransform Method

Applies the specified scaling operation to the transformation matrix of this **Graphics** object by prepending it to the object's transformation matrix.

Overload List

Applies the specified scaling operation to the transformation matrix of this **Graphics** object by prepending it to the object's transformation matrix.

[Visual Basic] **Overloads Public Sub ScaleTransform(Single, Single)**

[C#] **public void ScaleTransform(float, float);**

[C++] **public: void ScaleTransform(float, float);**

[JScript] **public function ScaleTransform(float, float);**

Applies the specified scaling operation to the transformation matrix of this **Graphics** object in the specified order.

[Visual Basic] **Overloads Public Sub ScaleTransform(Single, Single, MatrixOrder)**

[C#] **public void ScaleTransform(float, float, MatrixOrder);**

[C++] **public: void ScaleTransform(float, float, MatrixOrder);**

[JScript] **public function ScaleTransform(float, float, MatrixOrder);**

Example

[Visual Basic, C#] The following example is designed for use with Windows Forms, and it requires **PaintEventArgs** *e*, which is a parameter of the **Paint** event handler. The code performs the following actions:

- Rotates the world transformation matrix of the Windows form by 30 degrees.
- Scales that matrix by a factor of 3 in the x direction and a factor of 1 in the y direction by appending the scaling transformation with the **MatrixOrder.Append** member.
- Draws a rotated, scaled rectangle with a blue pen.

[Visual Basic, C#] The result is a parallelogram.

> [Visual Basic, C#] **Note** This example shows how to use one of the overloaded versions of **ScaleTransform**. For other examples that might be available, see the individual overload topics.

[Visual Basic]
```
Public Sub ScaleTransformFloatMatrixOrder(e As PaintEventArgs)
' Set world transform of graphics object to rotate.
e.Graphics.RotateTransform(30F)
' Then to scale, appending to world transform.
e.Graphics.ScaleTransform(3F, 1F, MatrixOrder.Append)
' Draw rotated, scaled rectangle to screen.
e.Graphics.DrawRectangle(New Pen(Color.Blue, 3), 50, 0, 100, 40)
End Sub
```

[C#]
```
public void ScaleTransformFloatMatrixOrder(PaintEventArgs e)
{
// Set world transform of graphics object to rotate.
e.Graphics.RotateTransform(30.0F);
// Then to scale, appending to world transform.
e.Graphics.ScaleTransform(3.0F, 1.0F, MatrixOrder.Append);
// Draw rotated, scaled rectangle to screen.
e.Graphics.DrawRectangle(new Pen(Color.Blue, 3), 50, 0, 100, 40);
}
```

Graphics.ScaleTransform Method (Single, Single)

Applies the specified scaling operation to the transformation matrix of this **Graphics** object by prepending it to the object's transformation matrix.

```
[Visual Basic]
Overloads Public Sub ScaleTransform( _
   ByVal sx As Single, _
   ByVal sy As Single _
)
[C#]
public void ScaleTransform(
   float sx,
   float sy
);
[C++]
public: void ScaleTransform(
   float sx,
   float sy
);
[JScript]
public function ScaleTransform(
   sx : float,
   sy : float
);
```

Parameters

sx
Scale factor in the x direction.

sy
Scale factor in the y direction.

Return Value

This method does not return a value.

Remarks

The scaling operation consists of multiplying the transformation matrix by a diagonal matrix whose elements are (*sx*, *sy*, 1). This method premultiplies (prepends) the transformation matrix of the **Graphics** object by the scaling matrix.

Example

[Visual Basic, C#] The following example is designed for use with Windows Forms, and it requires **PaintEventArgs** *e*, which is a parameter of the **Paint** event handler. The code performs the following actions:

- Rotates the world transformation matrix of the Windows form by 30 degrees.
- Scales that matrix by a factor of 3 in the x direction and a factor of 1 in the y direction by prepending the scaling transformation.
- Draws a scaled, rotated rectangle with a blue pen.

[Visual Basic, C#] The result is still a rectangle.

```
[Visual Basic]
Public Sub ScaleTransformFloat(e As PaintEventArgs)
' Set world transform of graphics object to rotate.
e.Graphics.RotateTransform(30F)
' Then to scale, prepending to world transform.
e.Graphics.ScaleTransform(3F, 1F)
' Draw scaled, rotated rectangle to screen.
e.Graphics.DrawRectangle(New Pen(Color.Blue, 3), 50, 0, 100, 40)
End Sub
```

```
[C#]
public void ScaleTransformFloat(PaintEventArgs e)
{
// Set world transform of graphics object to rotate.
e.Graphics.RotateTransform(30.0F);
// Then to scale, prepending to world transform.
e.Graphics.ScaleTransform(3.0F, 1.0F);
// Draw scaled, rotated rectangle to screen.
e.Graphics.DrawRectangle(new Pen(Color.Blue, 3), 50, 0, 100, 40);
}
```

Requirements

Platforms: Windows 98, Windows NT 4.0, Windows Millennium Edition, Windows 2000, Windows XP Home Edition, Windows XP Professional, Windows Server 2003 family

Graphics.ScaleTransform Method (Single, Single, MatrixOrder)

Applies the specified scaling operation to the transformation matrix of this **Graphics** object in the specified order.

```
[Visual Basic]
Overloads Public Sub ScaleTransform( _
   ByVal sx As Single, _
   ByVal sy As Single, _
   ByVal order As MatrixOrder _
)
[C#]
public void ScaleTransform(
   float sx,
   float sy,
   MatrixOrder order
);
[C++]
public: void ScaleTransform(
   float sx,
   float sy,
   MatrixOrder order
);
[JScript]
public function ScaleTransform(
   sx : float,
   sy : float,
   order : MatrixOrder
);
```

Parameters

sx
Scale factor in the x direction.

sy
Scale factor in the y direction.

order
Member of the **MatrixOrder** enumeration that specifies whether the scaling operation is prepended or appended to the transformation matrix.

Return Value

This method does not return a value.

Remarks

The scaling operation consists of multiplying the transformation matrix by a diagonal matrix whose elements are (*sx*, *sy*, 1). This method premultiplies (prepends) or postmultiplies (appends) the transformation matrix of the **Graphics** object by the scaling matrix according to the *order* parameter.

Example

[Visual Basic, C#] The following example is designed for use with Windows Forms, and it requires **PaintEventArgs** *e*, which is a parameter of the **Paint** event handler. The code performs the following actions:

- Rotates the world transformation matrix of the Windows form by 30 degrees.
- Scales that matrix by a factor of 3 in the x direction and a factor of 1 in the y direction by appending the scaling transformation with the **MatrixOrder.Append** member.
- Draws a rotated, scaled rectangle with a blue pen.

[Visual Basic, C#] The result is a parallelogram.

[Visual Basic]

```
Public Sub ScaleTransformFloatMatrixOrder(e As PaintEventArgs)
' Set world transform of graphics object to rotate.
e.Graphics.RotateTransform(30F)
' Then to scale, appending to world transform.
e.Graphics.ScaleTransform(3F, 1F, MatrixOrder.Append)
' Draw rotated, scaled rectangle to screen.
e.Graphics.DrawRectangle(New Pen(Color.Blue, 3), 50, 0, 100, 40)
End Sub
```

[C#]

```
public void ScaleTransformFloatMatrixOrder(PaintEventArgs e)
{
// Set world transform of graphics object to rotate.
e.Graphics.RotateTransform(30.0F);
// Then to scale, appending to world transform.
e.Graphics.ScaleTransform(3.0F, 1.0F, MatrixOrder.Append);
// Draw rotated, scaled rectangle to screen.
e.Graphics.DrawRectangle(new Pen(Color.Blue, 3), 50, 0, 100, 40);
}
```

Requirements

Platforms: Windows 98, Windows NT 4.0, Windows Millennium Edition, Windows 2000, Windows XP Home Edition, Windows XP Professional, Windows Server 2003 family

Graphics.SetClip Method

Sets the clipping region of this **Graphics** object to the **Clip** property of the specified **Graphics** object.

Overload List

Sets the clipping region of this **Graphics** object to the **Clip** property of the specified **Graphics** object.

[Visual Basic] **Overloads Public Sub SetClip(Graphics)**

[C#] **public void SetClip(Graphics);**

[C++] **public: void SetClip(Graphics*);**

[JScript] **public function SetClip(Graphics);**

Sets the clipping region of this **Graphics** object to the specified **GraphicsPath** object.

[Visual Basic] **Overloads Public Sub SetClip(GraphicsPath)**

[C#] **public void SetClip(GraphicsPath);**

[C++] **public: void SetClip(GraphicsPath*);**

[JScript] **public function SetClip(GraphicsPath);**

Sets the clipping region of this **Graphics** object to the rectangle specified by a **Rectangle** structure.

[Visual Basic] **Overloads Public Sub SetClip(Rectangle)**

[C#] **public void SetClip(Rectangle);**

[C++] **public: void SetClip(Rectangle);**

[JScript] **public function SetClip(Rectangle);**

Sets the clipping region of this **Graphics** object to the rectangle specified by a **RectangleF** structure.

[Visual Basic] **Overloads Public Sub SetClip(RectangleF)**

[C#] **public void SetClip(RectangleF);**

[C++] **public: void SetClip(RectangleF);**

[JScript] **public function SetClip(RectangleF);**

Sets the clipping region of this **Graphics** object to the result of the specified combining operation of the current clip region and the **Clip** property of the specified **Graphics** object.

[Visual Basic] **Overloads Public Sub SetClip(Graphics, CombineMode)**

[C#] **public void SetClip(Graphics, CombineMode);**

[C++] **public: void SetClip(Graphics*, CombineMode);**

[JScript] **public function SetClip(Graphics, CombineMode);**

Sets the clipping region of this **Graphics** object to the result of the specified operation combining the current clip region and the specified **GraphicsPath** object.

[Visual Basic] **Overloads Public Sub SetClip(GraphicsPath, CombineMode)**

[C#] **public void SetClip(GraphicsPath, CombineMode);**

[C++] **public: void SetClip(GraphicsPath*, CombineMode);**

[JScript] **public function SetClip(GraphicsPath, CombineMode);**

Sets the clipping region of this **Graphics** object to the result of the specified operation combining the current clip region and the rectangle specified by a **Rectangle** structure.

[Visual Basic] **Overloads Public Sub SetClip(Rectangle, CombineMode)**

[C#] **public void SetClip(Rectangle, CombineMode);**

[C++] **public: void SetClip(Rectangle, CombineMode);**

[JScript] **public function SetClip(Rectangle, CombineMode);**

Sets the clipping region of this **Graphics** object to the result of the specified operation combining the current clip region and the rectangle specified by a **RectangleF** structure.

[Visual Basic] **Overloads Public Sub SetClip(RectangleF, CombineMode)**

[C#] **public void SetClip(RectangleF, CombineMode);**

[C++] **public: void SetClip(RectangleF, CombineMode);**

[JScript] **public function SetClip(RectangleF, CombineMode);**

Sets the clipping region of this **Graphics** object to the result of the specified operation combining the current clip region and the specified **Region** object.

[Visual Basic] **Overloads Public Sub SetClip(Region, CombineMode)**

[C#] **public void SetClip(Region, CombineMode);**

[C++] **public: void SetClip(Region*, CombineMode);**

[JScript] **public function SetClip(Region, CombineMode);**

Example

[Visual Basic, C#] The following example is designed for use with Windows Forms, and it requires **PaintEventArgs** *e*, which is a parameter of the **Paint** event handler. The code performs the following actions:

- Creates a small rectangle for the clipping region.
- Sets the clipping region to the rectangle with the **CombineMode.Replace** member.
- Fills a large rectangle with a solid black brush.

[Visual Basic, C#] The result is a small, filled, black rectangle.

> [Visual Basic, C#] **Note** This example shows how to use one of the overloaded versions of **SetClip**. For other examples that might be available, see the individual overload topics.

[Visual Basic]
```
Public Sub SetClipRegionCombine(e As PaintEventArgs)
' Create region for clipping.
Dim clipRegion As New [Region](New Rectangle(0, 0, 100, 100))
' Set clipping region of graphics to region.
e.Graphics.SetClip(clipRegion, CombineMode.Replace)
' Fill rectangle to demonstrate clip region.
e.Graphics.FillRectangle(New SolidBrush(Color.Black), 0, 0, _
500, 300)
End Sub
```

[C#]
```
public void SetClipRegionCombine(PaintEventArgs e)
{
// Create region for clipping.
Region clipRegion = new Region(new Rectangle(0, 0, 100, 100));
// Set clipping region of graphics to region.
e.Graphics.SetClip(clipRegion, CombineMode.Replace);
// Fill rectangle to demonstrate clip region.
e.Graphics.FillRectangle(new SolidBrush(Color.Black), 0, 0, 500, 300);
}
```

Graphics.SetClip Method (Graphics)

Sets the clipping region of this **Graphics** object to the **Clip** property of the specified **Graphics** object.

[Visual Basic]
```
Overloads Public Sub SetClip( _
   ByVal g As Graphics _
)
```
[C#]
```
public void SetClip(
   Graphics g
);
```
[C++]
```
public: void SetClip(
   Graphics* g
);
```
[JScript]
```
public function SetClip(
   g : Graphics
);
```

Parameters

g
: **Graphics** object from which to take the new clip region.

Return Value

This method does not return a value.

Example

[Visual Basic, C#] The following example is designed for use with Windows Forms, and it requires **PaintEventArgs** *e*, which is a parameter of the **Paint** event handler, as well as *thisForm*, the **Form** object for the example. The code performs the following actions:

- Creates a temporary **Graphics** object from the *thisForm* **Form** object of the example.
- Sets the clipping region of the temporary **Graphics** object to a small square.
- Updates the clipping region of the form's graphic object to that of the temporary **Graphics** object.
- Fills a large rectangle with a solid black brush.

[Visual Basic, C#] The result is a small, filled, black square.

[Visual Basic]
```
Public Sub SetClipGraphics(e As PaintEventArgs)
' Create temporary graphics object and set its clipping region.
Dim newGraphics As Graphics = thisForm.CreateGraphics()
newGraphics.SetClip(New Rectangle(0, 0, 100, 100))
' Update clipping region of graphics to clipping region of new
' graphics.
e.Graphics.SetClip(newGraphics)
' Fill rectangle to demonstrate clip region.
e.Graphics.FillRectangle(New SolidBrush(Color.Black), 0, 0, _
500, 300)
' Release new graphics.
newGraphics.Dispose()
End Sub
```

[C#]
```
public void SetClipGraphics(PaintEventArgs e)
{
// Create temporary Graphics object and set its clipping region.
Graphics newGraphics = thisForm.CreateGraphics();
newGraphics.SetClip(new Rectangle(0, 0, 100, 100));
// Update clipping region of graphics to clipping region of new ↵
graphics.
e.Graphics.SetClip(newGraphics);
// Fill rectangle to demonstrate clip region.
e.Graphics.FillRectangle(new SolidBrush(Color.Black), 0, 0, 500, 300);
// Release new graphics.
newGraphics.Dispose();
}
```

Requirements

Platforms: Windows 98, Windows NT 4.0, Windows Millennium Edition, Windows 2000, Windows XP Home Edition, Windows XP Professional, Windows Server 2003 family

Graphics.SetClip Method (GraphicsPath)

Sets the clipping region of this **Graphics** object to the specified **GraphicsPath** object.

[Visual Basic]
```
Overloads Public Sub SetClip( _
   ByVal path As GraphicsPath _
)
```
[C#]
```
public void SetClip(
   GraphicsPath path
);
```

```
[C++]
public: void SetClip(
   GraphicsPath* path
);
[JScript]
public function SetClip(
   path : GraphicsPath
);
```

Parameters

path

GraphicsPath object that represents the new clip region.

Return Value

This method does not return a value.

Remarks

If the graphics path represented by the *path* parameter is not closed, an additional segment is added from the last point to the first point to close the path.

Example

[Visual Basic, C#] The following example is designed for use with Windows Forms, and it requires **PaintEventArgs** *e*, which is a parameter of the **Paint** event handler. The code performs the following actions:

- Creates a graphics path and adds an ellipse to the path.
- Sets the clipping region to the elliptical path.
- Fills a large rectangle with a solid black brush.

[Visual Basic, C#] The result is a filled, black ellipse.

```
[Visual Basic]
Public Sub SetClipPath(e As PaintEventArgs)
' Create graphics path.
Dim clipPath As New GraphicsPath()
clipPath.AddEllipse(0, 0, 200, 100)
' Set clipping region to path.
e.Graphics.SetClip(clipPath)
' Fill rectangle to demonstrate clipping region.
e.Graphics.FillRectangle(New SolidBrush(Color.Black), 0, 0, _
500, 300)
End Sub
```

```
[C#]
public void SetClipPath(PaintEventArgs e)
{
// Create graphics path.
GraphicsPath clipPath = new GraphicsPath();
clipPath.AddEllipse(0, 0, 200, 100);
// Set clipping region to path.
e.Graphics.SetClip(clipPath);
// Fill rectangle to demonstrate clipping region.
e.Graphics.FillRectangle(new SolidBrush(Color.Black), 0, 0, 500, 300);
}
```

Requirements

Platforms: Windows 98, Windows NT 4.0,
Windows Millennium Edition, Windows 2000,
Windows XP Home Edition, Windows XP Professional,
Windows Server 2003 family

Graphics.SetClip Method (Rectangle)

Sets the clipping region of this **Graphics** object to the rectangle specified by a **Rectangle** structure.

```
[Visual Basic]
Overloads Public Sub SetClip( _
   ByVal rect As Rectangle _
)
[C#]
public void SetClip(
   Rectangle rect
);
[C++]
public: void SetClip(
   Rectangle rect
);
[JScript]
public function SetClip(
   rect : Rectangle
);
```

Parameters

rect

Rectangle structure that represents the new clip region.

Return Value

This method does not return a value.

Example

[Visual Basic, C#] The following example is designed for use with Windows Forms, and it requires **PaintEventArgs** *e*, which is a parameter of the **Paint** event handler. The code performs the following actions:

- Creates a small rectangle for the clipping region.
- Sets the clipping region to the rectangle.
- Fills a large rectangle with a solid black brush.

[Visual Basic, C#] The result is a small, filled, black rectangle.

```
[Visual Basic]
Public Sub SetClipRectangle(e As PaintEventArgs)
' Create rectangle for clipping region.
Dim clipRect As New Rectangle(0, 0, 100, 100)
' Set clipping region of graphics to rectangle.
e.Graphics.SetClip(clipRect)
' Fill rectangle to demonstrate clip region.
e.Graphics.FillRectangle(New SolidBrush(Color.Black), 0, 0, _
500, 300)
End Sub
```

```
[C#]
public void SetClipRectangle(PaintEventArgs e)
{
// Create rectangle for clipping region.
Rectangle clipRect = new Rectangle(0, 0, 100, 100);
// Set clipping region of graphics to rectangle.
e.Graphics.SetClip(clipRect);
// Fill rectangle to demonstrate clip region.
e.Graphics.FillRectangle(new SolidBrush(Color.Black), 0, 0, 500, 300);
}
```

Requirements

Platforms: Windows 98, Windows NT 4.0,
Windows Millennium Edition, Windows 2000,
Windows XP Home Edition, Windows XP Professional,
Windows Server 2003 family

Graphics.SetClip Method (RectangleF)

Sets the clipping region of this **Graphics** object to the rectangle specified by a **RectangleF** structure.

```
[Visual Basic]
Overloads Public Sub SetClip( _
   ByVal rect As RectangleF _
)
[C#]
public void SetClip(
   RectangleF rect
);
[C++]
public: void SetClip(
   RectangleF rect
);
[JScript]
public function SetClip(
   rect : RectangleF
);
```

Parameters

rect
: **RectangleF** structure that represents the new clip region.

Return Value

This method does not return a value.

Example

[Visual Basic, C#] The following example is designed for use with Windows Forms, and it requires **PaintEventArgs** *e*, which is a parameter of the **Paint** event handler. The code performs the following actions:

- Creates a small rectangle for the clipping region.
- Sets the clipping region to the rectangle.
- Fills a large rectangle with a solid black brush.

[Visual Basic, C#] The result is a small, filled, black rectangle.

```
[Visual Basic]
Public Sub SetClipRectangleF(e As PaintEventArgs)
' Create rectangle for clipping region.
Dim clipRect As New RectangleF(0F, 0F, 100F, 100F)
' Set clipping region of graphics to rectangle.
e.Graphics.SetClip(clipRect)
' Fill rectangle to demonstrate clip region.
e.Graphics.FillRectangle(New SolidBrush(Color.Black), 0, 0, _
500, 300)
End Sub
```

```
[C#]
public void SetClipRectangleF(PaintEventArgs e)
{
// Create rectangle for clipping region.
RectangleF clipRect = new RectangleF(0.0F, 0.0F, 100.0F, 100.0F);
// Set clipping region of graphics to rectangle.
e.Graphics.SetClip(clipRect);
// Fill rectangle to demonstrate clip region.
e.Graphics.FillRectangle(new SolidBrush(Color.Black), 0, 0, 500, 300);
}
```

Requirements

Platforms: Windows 98, Windows NT 4.0, Windows Millennium Edition, Windows 2000, Windows XP Home Edition, Windows XP Professional, Windows Server 2003 family

Graphics.SetClip Method (Graphics, CombineMode)

Sets the clipping region of this **Graphics** object to the result of the specified combining operation of the current clip region and the **Clip** property of the specified **Graphics** object.

```
[Visual Basic]
Overloads Public Sub SetClip( _
   ByVal g As Graphics, _
   ByVal combineMode As CombineMode _
)
[C#]
public void SetClip(
   Graphics g,
   CombineMode combineMode
);
[C++]
public: void SetClip(
   Graphics* g,
   CombineMode combineMode
);
[JScript]
public function SetClip(
   g : Graphics,
   combineMode : CombineMode
);
```

Parameters

g
: **Graphics** object that specifies the clip region to combine.

combineMode
: Member of the **CombineMode** enumeration that specifies the combining operation to use.

Return Value

This method does not return a value.

Example

[Visual Basic, C#] The following example is designed for use with Windows Forms, and it requires **PaintEventArgs** *e*, which is a parameter of the **Paint** event handler, as well as *thisForm*, the **Form** object for the example. The code performs the following actions:

- Creates a temporary **Graphics** object from the *thisForm* **Form** object of the example.
- Sets the clipping region of the temporary **Graphics** object to a small square.
- Updates the clipping region of the form's graphic object to that of the new **Graphics** object with the **CombineMode.Replace** member.
- Fills a large rectangle with a solid black brush.

[Visual Basic, C#] The result is a small, filled, black square.

```
[Visual Basic]
Public Sub SetClipGraphicsCombine(e As PaintEventArgs)
' Create temporary graphics object and set its clipping region.
Dim newGraphics As Graphics = thisForm.CreateGraphics()
newGraphics.SetClip(New Rectangle(0, 0, 100, 100))
' Update clipping region of graphics to clipping region of new
' graphics.
e.Graphics.SetClip(newGraphics, CombineMode.Replace)
' Fill rectangle to demonstrate clip region.
e.Graphics.FillRectangle(New SolidBrush(Color.Black), 0, 0, _
500, 300)
' Release new graphics.
newGraphics.Dispose()
End Sub
```

[C#]
```
public void SetClipGraphicsCombine(PaintEventArgs e)
{
// Create temporary Graphics object and set its clipping region.
Graphics newGraphics = thisForm.CreateGraphics();
newGraphics.SetClip(new Rectangle(0, 0, 100, 100));
// Update clipping region of graphics to clipping region of new ↵
graphics.
e.Graphics.SetClip(newGraphics, CombineMode.Replace);
// Fill rectangle to demonstrate clip region.
e.Graphics.FillRectangle(new SolidBrush(Color.Black), 0, 0, 500, 300);
// Release new graphics.
newGraphics.Dispose();
}
```

Requirements

Platforms: Windows 98, Windows NT 4.0, Windows Millennium Edition, Windows 2000, Windows XP Home Edition, Windows XP Professional, Windows Server 2003 family

Graphics.SetClip Method (GraphicsPath, CombineMode)

Sets the clipping region of this **Graphics** object to the result of the specified operation combining the current clip region and the specified **GraphicsPath** object.

[Visual Basic]
```
Overloads Public Sub SetClip( _
   ByVal path As GraphicsPath, _
   ByVal combineMode As CombineMode _
)
```
[C#]
```
public void SetClip(
   GraphicsPath path,
   CombineMode combineMode
);
```
[C++]
```
public: void SetClip(
   GraphicsPath* path,
   CombineMode combineMode
);
```
[JScript]
```
public function SetClip(
   path : GraphicsPath,
   combineMode : CombineMode
);
```

Parameters

path

GraphicsPath object to combine.

combineMode

Member of the **CombineMode** enumeration that specifies the combining operation to use.

Return Value

This method does not return a value.

Remarks

If the graphics path represented by the *path* parameter is not closed, an additional segment is added from the last point to the first point to close the path.

Example

[Visual Basic, C#] The following example is designed for use with Windows Forms, and it requires **PaintEventArgs** *e*, which is a parameter of the **Paint** event handler. The code performs the following actions:

- Creates a graphics path and adds an ellipse to the path.
- Sets the clipping region to the elliptical path with the **CombineMode.Replace** member.
- Fills a large rectangle with a solid black brush.

[Visual Basic, C#] The result is a filled, black ellipse.

[Visual Basic]
```
Public Sub SetClipPathCombine(e As PaintEventArgs)
' Create graphics path.
Dim clipPath As New GraphicsPath()
clipPath.AddEllipse(0, 0, 200, 100)
' Set clipping region to path.
e.Graphics.SetClip(clipPath, CombineMode.Replace)
' Fill rectangle to demonstrate clipping region.
e.Graphics.FillRectangle(New SolidBrush(Color.Black), 0, 0, _
500, 300)
End Sub
```

[C#]
```
public void SetClipPathCombine(PaintEventArgs e)
{
// Create graphics path.
GraphicsPath clipPath = new GraphicsPath();
clipPath.AddEllipse(0, 0, 200, 100);
// Set clipping region to path.
e.Graphics.SetClip(clipPath, CombineMode.Replace);
// Fill rectangle to demonstrate clipping region.
e.Graphics.FillRectangle(new SolidBrush(Color.Black), 0, 0, 500, 300);
}
```

Requirements

Platforms: Windows 98, Windows NT 4.0, Windows Millennium Edition, Windows 2000, Windows XP Home Edition, Windows XP Professional, Windows Server 2003 family

Graphics.SetClip Method (Rectangle, CombineMode)

Sets the clipping region of this **Graphics** object to the result of the specified operation combining the current clip region and the rectangle specified by a **Rectangle** structure.

[Visual Basic]
```
Overloads Public Sub SetClip( _
   ByVal rect As Rectangle, _
   ByVal combineMode As CombineMode _
)
```
[C#]
```
public void SetClip(
   Rectangle rect,
   CombineMode combineMode
);
```
[C++]
```
public: void SetClip(
   Rectangle rect,
   CombineMode combineMode
);
```
[JScript]
```
public function SetClip(
   rect : Rectangle,
   combineMode : CombineMode
);
```

Parameters

rect

Rectangle structure to combine.

combineMode

Member of the **CombineMode** enumeration that specifies the combining operation to use.

Return Value

This method does not return a value.

Example

[Visual Basic, C#] The following example is designed for use with Windows Forms, and it requires **PaintEventArgs** *e*, which is a parameter of the **Paint** event handler. The code performs the following actions:

- Creates a small rectangle for the clipping region.
- Sets the clipping region to the rectangle with the **CombineMode.Replace** member.
- Fills a large rectangle with a solid black brush.

[Visual Basic, C#] The result is a small, filled, black rectangle.

```
[Visual Basic]
Public Sub SetClipRectangleCombine(e As PaintEventArgs)
' Create rectangle for clipping region.
Dim clipRect As New Rectangle(0, 0, 100, 100)
' Set clipping region of graphics to rectangle.
e.Graphics.SetClip(clipRect, CombineMode.Replace)
' Fill rectangle to demonstrate clip region.
e.Graphics.FillRectangle(New SolidBrush(Color.Black), 0, 0, _
500, 300)
End Sub
```

```
[C#]
public void SetClipRectangleCombine(PaintEventArgs e)
{
// Create rectangle for clipping region.
Rectangle clipRect = new Rectangle(0, 0, 100, 100);
// Set clipping region of graphics to rectangle.
e.Graphics.SetClip(clipRect, CombineMode.Replace);
// Fill rectangle to demonstrate clip region.
e.Graphics.FillRectangle(new SolidBrush(Color.Black), 0, 0, 500, 300);
}
```

Requirements

Platforms: Windows 98, Windows NT 4.0, Windows Millennium Edition, Windows 2000, Windows XP Home Edition, Windows XP Professional, Windows Server 2003 family

Graphics.SetClip Method (RectangleF, CombineMode)

Sets the clipping region of this **Graphics** object to the result of the specified operation combining the current clip region and the rectangle specified by a **RectangleF** structure.

```
[Visual Basic]
Overloads Public Sub SetClip( _
   ByVal rect As RectangleF, _
   ByVal combineMode As CombineMode _
)
[C#]
public void SetClip(
   RectangleF rect,
   CombineMode combineMode
);
[C++]
public: void SetClip(
   RectangleF rect,
   CombineMode combineMode
);
[JScript]
public function SetClip(
   rect : RectangleF,
   combineMode : CombineMode
);
```

Parameters

rect

RectangleF structure to combine.

combineMode

Member of the **CombineMode** enumeration that specifies the combining operation to use.

Return Value

This method does not return a value.

Example

[Visual Basic, C#] The following example is designed for use with Windows Forms, and it requires **PaintEventArgs** *e*, which is a parameter of the **Paint** event handler. The code performs the following actions:

- Creates a small rectangle for the clipping region.
- Sets the clipping region to the rectangle with the **CombineMode.Replace** member.
- Fills a large rectangle with a solid black brush.

[Visual Basic, C#] The result is a small, filled, black rectangle.

```
[Visual Basic]
Public Sub SetClipRectangleFCombine(e As PaintEventArgs)
' Create rectangle for clipping region.
Dim clipRect As New RectangleF(0F, 0F, 100F, 100F)
' Set clipping region of graphics to rectangle.
e.Graphics.SetClip(clipRect, CombineMode.Replace)
' Fill rectangle to demonstrate clip region.
e.Graphics.FillRectangle(New SolidBrush(Color.Black), 0, 0, _
500, 300)
End Sub
```

```
[C#]
public void SetClipRectangleFCombine(PaintEventArgs e)
{
// Create rectangle for clipping region.
RectangleF clipRect = new RectangleF(0.0F, 0.0F, 100.0F, 100.0F);
// Set clipping region of graphics to rectangle.
e.Graphics.SetClip(clipRect, CombineMode.Replace);
// Fill rectangle to demonstrate clip region.
e.Graphics.FillRectangle(new SolidBrush(Color.Black), 0, 0, 500, 300);
}
```

Requirements

Platforms: Windows 98, Windows NT 4.0, Windows Millennium Edition, Windows 2000, Windows XP Home Edition, Windows XP Professional, Windows Server 2003 family

Graphics.SetClip Method (Region, CombineMode)

Sets the clipping region of this **Graphics** object to the result of the specified operation combining the current clip region and the specified **Region** object.

[Visual Basic]
```
Overloads Public Sub SetClip( _
   ByVal region As Region, _
   ByVal combineMode As CombineMode _
)
```
[C#]
```
public void SetClip(
   Region region,
   CombineMode combineMode
);
```
[C++]
```
public: void SetClip(
   Region* region,
   CombineMode combineMode
);
```
[JScript]
```
public function SetClip(
   region : Region,
   combineMode : CombineMode
);
```

Parameters

region

Region object to combine.

combineMode

Member from the **CombineMode** enumeration that specifies the combining operation to use.

Return Value

This method does not return a value.

Example

[Visual Basic, C#] The following example is designed for use with Windows Forms, and it requires **PaintEventArgs** *e*, which is a parameter of the **Paint** event handler. The code performs the following actions:

- Creates a small rectangle for the clipping region.
- Sets the clipping region to the rectangle with the **CombineMode.Replace** member.
- Fills a large rectangle with a solid black brush.

[Visual Basic, C#] The result is a small, filled, black rectangle.

[Visual Basic]
```
Public Sub SetClipRegionCombine(e As PaintEventArgs)
' Create region for clipping.
Dim clipRegion As New [Region](New Rectangle(0, 0, 100, 100))
' Set clipping region of graphics to region.
e.Graphics.SetClip(clipRegion, CombineMode.Replace)
' Fill rectangle to demonstrate clip region.
e.Graphics.FillRectangle(New SolidBrush(Color.Black), 0, 0, _
500, 300)
End Sub
```

[C#]
```
public void SetClipRegionCombine(PaintEventArgs e)
{
// Create region for clipping.
Region clipRegion = new Region(new Rectangle(0, 0, 100, 100));
// Set clipping region of graphics to region.
e.Graphics.SetClip(clipRegion, CombineMode.Replace);
// Fill rectangle to demonstrate clip region.
e.Graphics.FillRectangle(new SolidBrush(Color.Black), 0, 0, 500, 300);
}
```

Requirements

Platforms: Windows 98, Windows NT 4.0, Windows Millennium Edition, Windows 2000, Windows XP Home Edition, Windows XP Professional, Windows Server 2003 family

Graphics.TransformPoints Method

Transforms an array of points from one coordinate space to another using the current world and page transformations of this **Graphics** object.

Overload List

Transforms an array of points from one coordinate space to another using the current world and page transformations of this **Graphics** object.

[Visual Basic] **Overloads Public Sub TransformPoints(CoordinateSpace, CoordinateSpace, Point())**

[C#] **public void TransformPoints(CoordinateSpace, CoordinateSpace, Point[]);**

[C++] **public: void TransformPoints(CoordinateSpace, CoordinateSpace, Point[]);**

[JScript] **public function TransformPoints(CoordinateSpace, CoordinateSpace, Point[]);**

Transforms an array of points from one coordinate space to another using the current world and page transformations of this **Graphics** object.

[Visual Basic] **Overloads Public Sub TransformPoints(CoordinateSpace, CoordinateSpace, PointF())**

[C#] **public void TransformPoints(CoordinateSpace, CoordinateSpace, PointF[]);**

[C++] **public: void TransformPoints(CoordinateSpace, CoordinateSpace, PointF[]);**

[JScript] **public function TransformPoints(CoordinateSpace, CoordinateSpace, PointF[]);**

Example

[Visual Basic, C#] The following example is designed for use with Windows Forms, and it requires **PaintEventArgs** *e*, which is a parameter of the **Paint** event handler. The code performs the following actions:

- Creates two points and draws a blue line between them.
- Sets the world transform to translate by amounts 40 in the x direction and 30 in the y direction.
- Transforms the points from world coordinates (**CoordinateSpace.World**) to page coordinates (**CoordinateSpace.Page**).
- Resets the world transformation to the identity and draws a red line between the transformed points.

[Visual Basic, C#] The result is a blue line and a translated red line below it.

> [Visual Basic, C#] **Note** This example shows how to use one of the overloaded versions of **TransformPoints**. For other examples that might be available, see the individual overload topics.

[Visual Basic]
```
Public Sub TransformPointsPointF(e As PaintEventArgs)
' Create array of two points.
Dim points As PointF() = {New PointF(0F, 0F), New PointF(100F, _
```

```
50F)}
' Draw line connecting two untransformed points.
e.Graphics.DrawLine(New Pen(Color.Blue, 3), points(0), points(1))
' Set world transformation of Graphics object to translate.
e.Graphics.TranslateTransform(40F, 30F)
' Transform points in array from world to page coordinates.
e.Graphics.TransformPoints(CoordinateSpace.Page, _
CoordinateSpace.World, points)
' Reset world transformation.
e.Graphics.ResetTransform()
' Draw line that connects transformed points.
e.Graphics.DrawLine(New Pen(Color.Red, 3), points(0), points(1))
End Sub
```

[C#]

```
public void TransformPointsPointF(PaintEventArgs e)
{
// Create array of two points.
PointF[] points = {new PointF(0.0F, 0.0F),
new PointF(100.0F, 50.0F)};
// Draw line connecting two untransformed points.
e.Graphics.DrawLine(new Pen(Color.Blue, 3),
points[0],
points[1]);
// Set world transformation of Graphics object to translate.
e.Graphics.TranslateTransform(40.0F, 30.0F);
// Transform points in array from world to page coordinates.
e.Graphics.TransformPoints(CoordinateSpace.Page,
CoordinateSpace.World,
points);
// Reset world transformation.
e.Graphics.ResetTransform();
// Draw line that connects transformed points.
e.Graphics.DrawLine(new Pen(Color.Red, 3),
points[0],
points[1]);
}
```

Graphics.TransformPoints Method (CoordinateSpace, CoordinateSpace, Point[])

Transforms an array of points from one coordinate space to another using the current world and page transformations of this **Graphics** object.

[Visual Basic]

```
Overloads Public Sub TransformPoints( _
   ByVal destSpace As CoordinateSpace, _
   ByVal srcSpace As CoordinateSpace, _
   ByVal pts() As Point _
)
```

[C#]

```
public void TransformPoints(
   CoordinateSpace destSpace,
   CoordinateSpace srcSpace,
   Point[] pts
);
```

[C++]

```
public: void TransformPoints(
   CoordinateSpace destSpace,
   CoordinateSpace srcSpace,
   Point pts[]
);
```

[JScript]

```
public function TransformPoints(
   destSpace : CoordinateSpace,
   srcSpace : CoordinateSpace,
   pts : Point[]
);
```

Parameters

destSpace
: Member of the **CoordinateSpace** enumeration that specifies the destination coordinate space.

srcSpace
: Member of the **CoordinateSpace** enumeration that specifies the source coordinate space.

pts
: Array of **Point** structures that represents the points to transformation.

Return Value

This method does not return a value.

Example

[Visual Basic, C#] The following example is designed for use with Windows Forms, and it requires **PaintEventArgs** *e*, which is a parameter of the **Paint** event handler. The code performs the following actions:

- Creates two points and draws a blue line between them.
- Sets the world transform to translate by amounts 40 in the x direction and 30 in the y direction.
- Transforms the points from world coordinates (**CoordinateSpace.World**) to page coordinates (**CoordinateSpace.Page**).
- Resets the world transformation to the identity.
- Draws a red line between the transformed points.

[Visual Basic, C#] The result is a blue line and a translated red line below it.

[Visual Basic]

```
Public Sub TransformPointsPoint(e As PaintEventArgs)
' Create array of two points.
Dim points As Point() = {New Point(0, 0), New Point(100, 50)}
' Draw line connecting two untransformed points.
e.Graphics.DrawLine(New Pen(Color.Blue, 3), points(0), points(1))
' Set world transformation of Graphics object to translate.
e.Graphics.TranslateTransform(40, 30)
' Transform points in array from world to page coordinates.
e.Graphics.TransformPoints(CoordinateSpace.Page, _
CoordinateSpace.World, points)
' Reset world transformation.
e.Graphics.ResetTransform()
' Draw line that connects transformed points.
e.Graphics.DrawLine(New Pen(Color.Red, 3), points(0), points(1))
End Sub
```

[C#]

```
public void TransformPointsPoint(PaintEventArgs e)
{
// Create array of two points.
Point[] points = {new Point(0, 0),
new Point(100, 50)};
// Draw line connecting two untransformed points.
e.Graphics.DrawLine(new Pen(Color.Blue, 3),
points[0],
points[1]);
// Set world transformation of Graphics object to translate.
e.Graphics.TranslateTransform(40, 30);
// Transform points in array from world to page coordinates.
e.Graphics.TransformPoints(CoordinateSpace.Page,
CoordinateSpace.World,
points);
// Reset world transformation.
e.Graphics.ResetTransform();
// Draw line that connects transformed points.
e.Graphics.DrawLine(new Pen(Color.Red, 3),
points[0],
points[1]);
}
```

Requirements

Platforms: Windows 98, Windows NT 4.0, Windows Millennium Edition, Windows 2000, Windows XP Home Edition, Windows XP Professional, Windows Server 2003 family

Graphics.TransformPoints Method (CoordinateSpace, CoordinateSpace, PointF[])

Transforms an array of points from one coordinate space to another using the current world and page transformations of this **Graphics** object.

[Visual Basic]
```
Overloads Public Sub TransformPoints( _
   ByVal destSpace As CoordinateSpace, _
   ByVal srcSpace As CoordinateSpace, _
   ByVal pts() As PointF _
)
```
[C#]
```
public void TransformPoints(
   CoordinateSpace destSpace,
   CoordinateSpace srcSpace,
   PointF[] pts
);
```
[C++]
```
public: void TransformPoints(
   CoordinateSpace destSpace,
   CoordinateSpace srcSpace,
   PointF pts[]
);
```
[JScript]
```
public function TransformPoints(
   destSpace : CoordinateSpace,
   srcSpace : CoordinateSpace,
   pts : PointF[]
);
```

Parameters

destSpace
: Member of the **CoordinateSpace** enumeration that specifies the destination coordinate space.

srcSpace
: Member of the **CoordinateSpace** enumeration that specifies the source coordinate space.

pts
: Array of **PointF** structures that represent the points to transform.

Return Value

This method does not return a value.

Example

[Visual Basic, C#] The following example is designed for use with Windows Forms, and it requires **PaintEventArgs** *e*, which is a parameter of the **Paint** event handler. The code performs the following actions:

- Creates two points and draws a blue line between them.
- Sets the world transform to translate by amounts 40 in the x direction and 30 in the y direction.
- Transforms the points from world coordinates (**CoordinateSpace.World**) to page coordinates (**CoordinateSpace.Page**).
- Resets the world transformation to the identity and draws a red line between the transformed points.

[Visual Basic, C#] The result is a blue line and a translated red line below it.

[Visual Basic]
```
Public Sub TransformPointsPointF(e As PaintEventArgs)
' Create array of two points.
Dim points As PointF() = {New PointF(0F, 0F), New PointF(100F, _
50F)}
' Draw line connecting two untransformed points.
e.Graphics.DrawLine(New Pen(Color.Blue, 3), points(0), points(1))
' Set world transformation of Graphics object to translate.
e.Graphics.TranslateTransform(40F, 30F)
' Transform points in array from world to page coordinates.
e.Graphics.TransformPoints(CoordinateSpace.Page, _
CoordinateSpace.World, points)
' Reset world transformation.
e.Graphics.ResetTransform()
' Draw line that connects transformed points.
e.Graphics.DrawLine(New Pen(Color.Red, 3), points(0), points(1))
End Sub
```

[C#]
```
public void TransformPointsPointF(PaintEventArgs e)
{
// Create array of two points.
PointF[] points = {new PointF(0.0F, 0.0F),
new PointF(100.0F, 50.0F)};
// Draw line connecting two untransformed points.
e.Graphics.DrawLine(new Pen(Color.Blue, 3),
points[0],
points[1]);
// Set world transformation of Graphics object to translate.
e.Graphics.TranslateTransform(40.0F, 30.0F);
// Transform points in array from world to page coordinates.
e.Graphics.TransformPoints(CoordinateSpace.Page,
CoordinateSpace.World,
points);
// Reset world transformation.
e.Graphics.ResetTransform();
// Draw line that connects transformed points.
e.Graphics.DrawLine(new Pen(Color.Red, 3),
points[0],
points[1]);
}
```

Requirements

Platforms: Windows 98, Windows NT 4.0, Windows Millennium Edition, Windows 2000, Windows XP Home Edition, Windows XP Professional, Windows Server 2003 family

Graphics.TranslateClip Method

Translates the clipping region of this **Graphics** object by specified amounts in the horizontal and vertical directions.

Overload List

Translates the clipping region of this **Graphics** object by specified amounts in the horizontal and vertical directions.

[Visual Basic] **Overloads Public Sub TranslateClip(Integer, Integer)**

[C#] **public void TranslateClip(int, int);**

[C++] **public: void TranslateClip(int, int);**

[JScript] **public function TranslateClip(int, int);**

Translates the clipping region of this **Graphics** object by specified amounts in the horizontal and vertical directions.

[Visual Basic] **Overloads Public Sub TranslateClip(Single, Single)**

[C#] **public void TranslateClip(float, float);**

[C++] **public: void TranslateClip(float, float);**

[JScript] **public function TranslateClip(float, float);**

Example

[Visual Basic, C#] The following example is designed for use with Windows Forms, and it requires **PaintEventArgs** *e*, which is a parameter of the **Paint** event handler. The code performs the following actions:

- Creates a rectangle for the clipping region.
- Sets the clipping region to the rectangle.
- Translates the clipping region by a vector (50.0F, 50.0F).
- Fills a large rectangle with a solid black brush.

[Visual Basic, C#] The result is a translated, small, black rectangle.

> [Visual Basic, C#] **Note** This example shows how to use one of the overloaded versions of **TranslateClip**. For other examples that might be available, see the individual overload topics.

[Visual Basic]
```
Public Sub TranslateClipFloat(e As PaintEventArgs)
' Create rectangle for clipping region.
Dim clipRect As New RectangleF(0F, 0F, 100F, 100F)
' Set clipping region of graphics to rectangle.
e.Graphics.SetClip(clipRect)
' Translate clipping region.
Dim dx As Single = 50F
Dim dy As Single = 50F
e.Graphics.TranslateClip(dx, dy)
' Fill rectangle to demonstrate translated clip region.
e.Graphics.FillRectangle(New SolidBrush(Color.Black), 0, 0, _
500, 300)
End Sub
```

[C#]
```
public void TranslateClipFloat(PaintEventArgs e)
{
// Create rectangle for clipping region.
RectangleF clipRect = new RectangleF(0.0F, 0.0F, 100.0F, 100.0F);
// Set clipping region of graphics to rectangle.
e.Graphics.SetClip(clipRect);
// Translate clipping region.
float dx = 50.0F;
float dy = 50.0F;
e.Graphics.TranslateClip(dx, dy);
// Fill rectangle to demonstrate translated clip region.
e.Graphics.FillRectangle(new SolidBrush(Color.Black), 0, 0, 500, 300);
}
```

Graphics.TranslateClip Method (Int32, Int32)

Translates the clipping region of this **Graphics** object by specified amounts in the horizontal and vertical directions.

[Visual Basic]
```
Overloads Public Sub TranslateClip( _
   ByVal dx As Integer, _
   ByVal dy As Integer _
)
```
[C#]
```
public void TranslateClip(
   int dx,
   int dy
);
```
[C++]
```
public: void TranslateClip(
   int dx,
   int dy
);
```
[JScript]
```
public function TranslateClip(
   dx : int,
   dy : int
);
```

Parameters

dx

x component of the translation.

dy

y component of the translation.

Return Value

This method does not return a value.

Example

[Visual Basic, C#] The following example is designed for use with Windows Forms, and it requires **PaintEventArgs** *e*, which is a parameter of the **Paint** event handler. The code performs the following actions:

- Creates a rectangle for the clipping region.
- Sets the clipping region to the rectangle.
- Translates the clipping region by a vector (50, 50).
- Fills a large rectangle with a solid black brush.

[Visual Basic, C#] The result is a translated, small, black rectangle.

[Visual Basic]
```
Public Sub TranslateClipInt(e As PaintEventArgs)
' Create rectangle for clipping region.
Dim clipRect As New Rectangle(0, 0, 100, 100)
' Set clipping region of graphics to rectangle.
e.Graphics.SetClip(clipRect)
' Translate clipping region.
Dim dx As Integer = 50
Dim dy As Integer = 50
e.Graphics.TranslateClip(dx, dy)
' Fill rectangle to demonstrate translated clip region.
e.Graphics.FillRectangle(New SolidBrush(Color.Black), 0, 0, _
500, 300)
End Sub
```

[C#]
```
public void TranslateClipInt(PaintEventArgs e)
{
// Create rectangle for clipping region.
Rectangle clipRect = new Rectangle(0, 0, 100, 100);
// Set clipping region of graphics to rectangle.
e.Graphics.SetClip(clipRect);
// Translate clipping region.
int dx = 50;
int dy = 50;
e.Graphics.TranslateClip(dx, dy);
// Fill rectangle to demonstrate translated clip region.
e.Graphics.FillRectangle(new SolidBrush(Color.Black), 0, 0, 500, 300);
}
```

Requirements

Platforms: Windows 98, Windows NT 4.0, Windows Millennium Edition, Windows 2000, Windows XP Home Edition, Windows XP Professional, Windows Server 2003 family

Graphics.TranslateClip Method (Single, Single)

Translates the clipping region of this **Graphics** object by specified amounts in the horizontal and vertical directions.

[Visual Basic]
```
Overloads Public Sub TranslateClip( _
   ByVal dx As Single, _
   ByVal dy As Single _
)
```
[C#]
```
public void TranslateClip(
   float dx,
   float dy
);
```
[C++]
```
public: void TranslateClip(
   float dx,
   float dy
);
```
[JScript]
```
public function TranslateClip(
   dx : float,
   dy : float
);
```

Parameters

dx

x component of the translation.

dy

y component of the translation.

Return Value

This method does not return a value.

Example

[Visual Basic, C#] The following example is designed for use with Windows Forms, and it requires **PaintEventArgs** *e*, which is a parameter of the **Paint** event handler. The code performs the following actions:

- Creates a rectangle for the clipping region.
- Sets the clipping region to the rectangle.
- Translates the clipping region by a vector (50.0F, 50.0F).
- Fills a large rectangle with a solid black brush.

[Visual Basic, C#] The result is a translated, small, black rectangle.

[Visual Basic]
```
Public Sub TranslateClipFloat(e As PaintEventArgs)
' Create rectangle for clipping region.
Dim clipRect As New RectangleF(0F, 0F, 100F, 100F)
' Set clipping region of graphics to rectangle.
e.Graphics.SetClip(clipRect)
' Translate clipping region.
Dim dx As Single = 50F
Dim dy As Single = 50F
e.Graphics.TranslateClip(dx, dy)
' Fill rectangle to demonstrate translated clip region.
e.Graphics.FillRectangle(New SolidBrush(Color.Black), 0, 0, _
500, 300)
End Sub
```

[C#]
```
public void TranslateClipFloat(PaintEventArgs e)
{
// Create rectangle for clipping region.
RectangleF clipRect = new RectangleF(0.0F, 0.0F, 100.0F, 100.0F);
// Set clipping region of graphics to rectangle.
e.Graphics.SetClip(clipRect);
// Translate clipping region.
float dx = 50.0F;
float dy = 50.0F;
e.Graphics.TranslateClip(dx, dy);
// Fill rectangle to demonstrate translated clip region.
e.Graphics.FillRectangle(new SolidBrush(Color.Black), 0, 0, 500, 300);
}
```

Requirements

Platforms: Windows 98, Windows NT 4.0, Windows Millennium Edition, Windows 2000, Windows XP Home Edition, Windows XP Professional, Windows Server 2003 family

Graphics.TranslateTransform Method

Prepends the specified translation to the transformation matrix of this **Graphics** object.

Overload List

Prepends the specified translation to the transformation matrix of this **Graphics** object.

[Visual Basic] **Overloads Public Sub TranslateTransform(Single, Single)**

[C#] **public void TranslateTransform(float, float);**

[C++] **public: void TranslateTransform(float, float);**

[JScript] **public function TranslateTransform(float, float);**

Applies the specified translation to the transformation matrix of this **Graphics** object in the specified order.

[Visual Basic] **Overloads Public Sub TranslateTransform(Single, Single, MatrixOrder)**

[C#] **public void TranslateTransform(float, float, MatrixOrder);**

[C++] **public: void TranslateTransform(float, float, MatrixOrder);**

[JScript] **public function TranslateTransform(float, float, MatrixOrder);**

Example

[Visual Basic, C#] The following example is designed for use with Windows Forms, and it requires **PaintEventArgs** *e*, which is a parameter of the **Paint** event handler. The code performs the following actions:

- Rotates the world transformation matrix of the Windows form by 30.0F degrees.
- Translates the world transformation by a vector (100.0F, 0.0F), appending the translation with **MatrixOrder.Append**.
- Draws a rotated, translated ellipse with a blue pen.

> [Visual Basic, C#] **Note** This example shows how to use one of the overloaded versions of **TranslateTransform**. For other examples that might be available, see the individual overload topics.

[Visual Basic]
```
Public Sub TranslateTransformAngleMatrixOrder(e As PaintEventArgs)
' Set world transform of graphics object to rotate.
e.Graphics.RotateTransform(30F)
' Then to translate, appending to world transform.
e.Graphics.TranslateTransform(100F, 0F, MatrixOrder.Append)
' Draw rotated, translated ellipse to screen.
e.Graphics.DrawEllipse(New Pen(Color.Blue, 3), 0, 0, 200, 80)
End Sub
```

[C#]
```
public void TranslateTransformAngleMatrixOrder(PaintEventArgs e)
{
// Set world transform of graphics object to rotate.
e.Graphics.RotateTransform(30.0F);
// Then to translate, appending to world transform.
e.Graphics.TranslateTransform(100.0F, 0.0F, MatrixOrder.Append);
// Draw rotated, translated ellipse to screen.
e.Graphics.DrawEllipse(new Pen(Color.Blue, 3), 0, 0, 200, 80);
}
```

Graphics.TranslateTransform Method (Single, Single)

Prepends the specified translation to the transformation matrix of this **Graphics** object.

[Visual Basic]
```
Overloads Public Sub TranslateTransform( _
   ByVal dx As Single, _
   ByVal dy As Single _
)
```
[C#]
```
public void TranslateTransform(
   float dx,
   float dy
);
```
[C++]
```
public: void TranslateTransform(
   float dx,
   float dy
);
```
[JScript]
```
public function TranslateTransform(
   dx : float,
   dy : float
);
```

Parameters

dx
: x component of the translation.

dy
: y component of the translation.

Return Value

This method does not return a value.

Remarks

The translation operation consists of multiplying the transformation matrix by a matrix whose translation part is the *dx* and *dy* parameters. This method applies the translation by prepending the translation matrix to the transformation matrix.

Example

[Visual Basic, C#] The following example is designed for use with Windows Forms, and it requires **PaintEventArgs** *e*, which is a parameter of the **Paint** event handler. The code performs the following actions:

- Rotates the world transformation matrix of the Windows form by 30.0F degrees.
- Translates the world transformation by a vector (100.0F, 0.0F), prepending the translation.
- Draws a translated, rotated ellipse with a blue pen.

[Visual Basic]
```
Public Sub TranslateTransformAngle(e As PaintEventArgs)
' Set world transform of graphics object to rotate.
e.Graphics.RotateTransform(30F)
' Then to translate, prepending to world transform.
e.Graphics.TranslateTransform(100F, 0F)
' Draw translated, rotated ellipse to screen.
e.Graphics.DrawEllipse(New Pen(Color.Blue, 3), 0, 0, 200, 80)
End Sub
```
[C#]
```
public void TranslateTransformAngle(PaintEventArgs e)
{
// Set world transform of graphics object to rotate.
e.Graphics.RotateTransform(30.0F);
// Then to translate, prepending to world transform.
e.Graphics.TranslateTransform(100.0F, 0.0F);
// Draw translated, rotated ellipse to screen.
e.Graphics.DrawEllipse(new Pen(Color.Blue, 3), 0, 0, 200, 80);
}
```

Requirements

Platforms: Windows 98, Windows NT 4.0, Windows Millennium Edition, Windows 2000, Windows XP Home Edition, Windows XP Professional, Windows Server 2003 family

Graphics.TranslateTransform Method (Single, Single, MatrixOrder)

Applies the specified translation to the transformation matrix of this **Graphics** object in the specified order.

[Visual Basic]
```
Overloads Public Sub TranslateTransform( _
   ByVal dx As Single, _
   ByVal dy As Single, _
   ByVal order As MatrixOrder _
)
```
[C#]
```
public void TranslateTransform(
   float dx,
   float dy,
   MatrixOrder order
);
```
[C++]
```
public: void TranslateTransform(
   float dx,
   float dy,
   MatrixOrder order
);
```
[JScript]
```
public function TranslateTransform(
   dx : float,
   dy : float,
   order : MatrixOrder
);
```

Parameters

dx
: x component of the translation.

dy
: y component of the translation.

order
: Member of the **MatrixOrder** enumeration that specifies whether the translation is prepended or appended to the transformation matrix.

Return Value

This method does not return a value.

Remarks

The translation operation consists of multiplying the transformation matrix by a matrix whose translation part is the *dx* and *dy* parameters. This method premultiplies (prepends) or postmultiplies (appends) the transformation matrix of the **Graphics** object by the translation matrix according to the *order* parameter.

Example

[Visual Basic, C#] The following example is designed for use with Windows Forms, and it requires **PaintEventArgs** *e*, which is a parameter of the **Paint** event handler. The code performs the following actions:

- Rotates the world transformation matrix of the Windows form by 30.0F degrees.
- Translates the world transformation by a vector (100.0F, 0.0F), appending the translation with **MatrixOrder.Append**.
- Draws a rotated, translated ellipse with a blue pen.

[Visual Basic]

```
Public Sub TranslateTransformAngleMatrixOrder(e As PaintEventArgs)
' Set world transform of graphics object to rotate.
e.Graphics.RotateTransform(30F)
' Then to translate, appending to world transform.
e.Graphics.TranslateTransform(100F, 0F, MatrixOrder.Append)
' Draw rotated, translated ellipse to screen.
e.Graphics.DrawEllipse(New Pen(Color.Blue, 3), 0, 0, 200, 80)
End Sub
```

[C#]

```
public void TranslateTransformAngleMatrixOrder(PaintEventArgs e)
{
// Set world transform of graphics object to rotate.
e.Graphics.RotateTransform(30.0F);
// Then to translate, appending to world transform.
e.Graphics.TranslateTransform(100.0F, 0.0F, MatrixOrder.Append);
// Draw rotated, translated ellipse to screen.
e.Graphics.DrawEllipse(new Pen(Color.Blue, 3), 0, 0, 200, 80);
}
```

Requirements

Platforms: Windows 98, Windows NT 4.0, Windows Millennium Edition, Windows 2000, Windows XP Home Edition, Windows XP Professional, Windows Server 2003 family

Graphics.DrawImageAbort Delegate

Provides a callback method for deciding when the **DrawImage** method should prematurely cancel execution and stop drawing an image.

[Visual Basic]
```
<Serializable>
<ComVisible(False)>
Public Delegate Function Sub Graphics.DrawImageAbort( _
   ByVal callbackdata As IntPtr _
) As Boolean
```
[C#]
```
[Serializable]
[ComVisible(false)]
public delegate bool Graphics.DrawImageAbort(
   IntPtr callbackdata
);
```
[C++]
```
[Serializable]
[ComVisible(false)]
public __gc __delegate bool Graphics.DrawImageAbort(
   IntPtr callbackdata
);
```

[JScript] In JScript, you can use the delegates in the .NET Framework, but you cannot define your own.

Parameters [Visual Basic, C#, C++]

The declaration of your callback method must have the same parameters as the **Graphics.DrawImageAbort** delegate declaration.

callbackdata
: Internal pointer that specifies data for the callback method. This parameter is not passed by all **DrawImage** overloads. You can test for its absence by checking for the value **IntPtr.Zero**.

Return Value

This method returns **true** if it decides that the **DrawImage** method should prematurely stop execution. Otherwise it returns **false** to indicate that the **DrawImage** method should continue execution.

Remarks

This method is used in conjunction with the **DrawImage** method of the **Graphics** class. Certain overloads of the **DrawImage** method call an application-defined callback method of this type to find out if the overloads should stop or continue execution.

During execution, the relevant **DrawImage** overloads frequently call this callback method to find out if they should stop drawing the specified image or if they should continue drawing the image. The **Graphics.DrawImageAbort** callback method can determine whether to continue or not based on a chosen algorithm included in it, optionally using the data passed to it by the callbackdata parameter. For example, an algorithm might determine if the image has scrolled off the screen and signal a cancellation to the **DrawImage** method to stop drawing.

A user declaration of this event-handling method must have the same parameters as the **Graphics.DrawImageAbort** delegate declaration.

Example

[Visual Basic, C#] This example is a simplistic implementation of the **Graphics.DrawImageAbort** delegate. It merely checks to see if the **DrawImage** method has passed it data using the callbackdata parameter. (Some **DrawImage** overloads have only a *DrawImageAbort* parameter and pass no data; some overloads have both *DrawImageAbort* and *callbackdata* parameters and can pass data.) If no data was passed, it returns **true** to signal to the calling **DrawImage** method that it should cancel the drawing. If data was passed, it returns **false** to signal that drawing should continue.

[Visual Basic, C#] A realistic implementation of this callback would involve the actual scrutiny of some criteria to cancel or continue the execution.

[Visual Basic]
```
Private Function DrawImageCallback(callBackData As IntPtr) As Boolean
    ' Test for call that passes callBackData parameter.
    If callBackData.Equals(IntPtr.Zero) Then
        ' If no callBackData passed, abort DrawImage method.
        Return True
    Else
        ' If callBackData passed, continue DrawImage method.
        Return False
    End If
End Function 'DrawImageCallback
```

[C#]
```
// Define DrawImageAbort callback method.
private bool DrawImageCallback(IntPtr callbackdata)
{
   // Test for call that passes callBackData parameter.
   if(callbackdata==IntPtr.Zero)
   {
      // If no callbackdata passed, cancel DrawImage method.
      return true;
   }
   else
   {
      // If callbackdata passed, continue DrawImage method.
      return false;
   }
}
```

Requirements

Namespace: System.Drawing

Platforms: Windows 98, Windows NT 4.0, Windows Millennium Edition, Windows 2000, Windows XP Home Edition, Windows XP Professional, Windows Server 2003 family

Assembly: System.Drawing (in System.Drawing.dll)

Graphics.EnumerateMetafileProc Delegate

Provides a callback method for the **EnumerateMetafile** method.

[Visual Basic]
```
<Serializable>
<ComVisible(False)>
Public Delegate Function Sub Graphics.EnumerateMetafileProc( _
   ByVal recordType As EmfPlusRecordType, _
   ByVal flags As Integer, _
   ByVal dataSize As Integer, _
   ByVal data As IntPtr, _
   ByVal callbackData As PlayRecordCallback _
) As Boolean
```
[C#]
```
[Serializable]
[ComVisible(false)]
public delegate bool Graphics.EnumerateMetafileProc(
   EmfPlusRecordType recordType,
   int flags,
   int dataSize,
   IntPtr data,
   PlayRecordCallback callbackData
);
```
[C++]
```
[Serializable]
[ComVisible(false)]
public __gc __delegate bool Graphics.EnumerateMetafileProc(
   EmfPlusRecordType recordType,
   int flags,
   int dataSize,
   IntPtr data,
   PlayRecordCallback* callbackData
);
```
[JScript] In JScript, you can use the delegates in the .NET Framework, but you cannot define your own.

Parameters [Visual Basic, C#, C++]

The declaration of your callback method must have the same parameters as the **Graphics.EnumerateMetafileProc** delegate declaration.

recordType
: Member of the **EmfPlusRecordType** enumeration that specifies the type of metafile record.

flags
: Set of flags that specify attributes of the record.

dataSize
: Number of bytes in the record data.

data
: Pointer to a buffer that contains the record data.

callbackData
: Not used.

Return Value

Return **true** if you want to continue enumerating records; otherwise, **false**.

Remarks

This method is used in conjunction with the **EnumerateMetafile** method of the **Graphics** class. Certain overloads of the **EnumerateMetafile** method call an application-defined callback method of this type for each record in a specified metafile. The callback function can display each record (or selected records) by calling the **PlayRecord** method of the **Metafile** that is being enumerated.

A user declaration of this callback method must have the same parameters as the **Graphics.EnumerateMetafileProc** delegate declaration.

Example

For an example see **EnumerateMetafile**.

Requirements

Namespace: System.Drawing

Platforms: Windows 98, Windows NT 4.0, Windows Millennium Edition, Windows 2000, Windows XP Home Edition, Windows XP Professional, Windows Server 2003 family

Assembly: System.Drawing (in System.Drawing.dll)

GraphicsUnit Enumeration

Specifies the unit of measure for the given data.

[Visual Basic]
```
<Serializable>
Public Enum GraphicsUnit
```
[C#]
```
[Serializable]
public enum GraphicsUnit
```
[C++]
```
[Serializable]
__value public enum GraphicsUnit
```
[JScript]
```
public
   Serializable
enum GraphicsUnit
```

Members

Member name	Description
Display	Specifies 1/75 inch as the unit of measure.
Document	Specifies the document unit (1/300 inch) as the unit of measure.
Inch	Specifies the inch as the unit of measure.
Millimeter	Specifies the millimeter as the unit of measure.
Pixel Supported by the .NET Compact Framework.	Specifies a device pixel as the unit of measure.
Point	Specifies a printer's point (1/72 inch) as the unit of measure.
World	Specifies the world unit as the unit of measure.

Requirements

Namespace: System.Drawing

Platforms: Windows 98, Windows NT 4.0, Windows Millennium Edition, Windows 2000, Windows XP Home Edition, Windows XP Professional, Windows Server 2003 family, .NET Compact Framework - Windows CE .NET

Assembly: System.Drawing (in System.Drawing.dll)

Icon Class

Represents a Windows icon, which is a small bitmap image used to represent an object. Icons can be thought of as transparent bitmaps, although their size is determined by the system.

System.Object
  System.MarshalByRefObject
    System.Drawing.Icon

```
[Visual Basic]
<Serializable>
<ComVisible(False)>
NotInheritable Public Class Icon
   Inherits MarshalByRefObject
   Implements ISerializable, ICloneable, IDisposable
[C#]
[Serializable]
[ComVisible(false)]
public sealed class Icon : MarshalByRefObject, ISerializable,
   ICloneable, IDisposable
[C++]
[Serializable]
[ComVisible(false)]
public __gc __sealed class Icon : public MarshalByRefObject,
   ISerializable, ICloneable, IDisposable
[JScript]
public
   Serializable
   ComVisible(false)
class Icon extends MarshalByRefObject implements
   ISerializable, ICloneable, IDisposable
```

Thread Safety

Any public static (**Shared** in Visual Basic) members of this type are safe for multithreaded operations. Any instance members are not guaranteed to be thread safe.

Requirements

Namespace: System.Drawing

Platforms: Windows 98, Windows NT 4.0, Windows Millennium Edition, Windows 2000, Windows XP Home Edition, Windows XP Professional, Windows Server 2003 family, .NET Compact Framework - Windows CE .NET

Assembly: System.Drawing (in System.Drawing.dll)

Icon Constructor

Initializes a new instance of the **Icon** class from the specified file name.

Overload List

Initializes a new instance of the **Icon** class from the specified data stream.

Supported by the .NET Compact Framework.

[Visual Basic] **Public Sub New(Stream)**

[C#] **public Icon(Stream);**

[C++] **public: Icon(Stream*);**

[JScript] **public function Icon(Stream);**

Initializes a new instance of the **Icon** class from the specified file name.

[Visual Basic] **Public Sub New(String)**

[C#] **public Icon(string);**

[C++] **public: Icon(String*);**

[JScript] **public function Icon(String);**

Initializes a new instance of the **Icon** class and attempts to find a version of the icon that matches the requested size.

[Visual Basic] **Public Sub New(Icon, Size)**

[C#] **public Icon(Icon, Size);**

[C++] **public: Icon(Icon*, Size);**

[JScript] **public function Icon(Icon, Size);**

Initializes a new instance of the **Icon** class from a resource in the specified assembly.

[Visual Basic] **Public Sub New(Type, String)**

[C#] **public Icon(Type, string);**

[C++] **public: Icon(Type*, String*);**

[JScript] **public function Icon(Type, String);**

Initializes a new instance of the **Icon** class and attempts to find a version of the icon that matches the requested size.

[Visual Basic] **Public Sub New(Icon, Integer, Integer)**

[C#] **public Icon(Icon, int, int);**

[C++] **public: Icon(Icon*, int, int);**

[JScript] **public function Icon(Icon, int, int);**

Initializes a new instance of the **Icon** class from the specified data stream and with the specified width and height.

Supported by the .NET Compact Framework.

[Visual Basic] **Public Sub New(Stream, Integer, Integer)**

[C#] **public Icon(Stream, int, int);**

[C++] **public: Icon(Stream*, int, int);**

[JScript] **public function Icon(Stream, int, int);**

Icon Constructor (Stream)

Initializes a new instance of the **Icon** class from the specified data stream.

```
[Visual Basic]
Public Sub New( _
   ByVal stream As Stream _
)
[C#]
public Icon(
   Stream stream
);
[C++]
public: Icon(
   Stream* stream
);
[JScript]
public function Icon(
   stream : Stream
);
```

Parameters

stream
  The data stream from which to load the **Icon** object.

Requirements

Platforms: Windows 98, Windows NT 4.0, Windows Millennium Edition, Windows 2000, Windows XP Home Edition, Windows XP Professional, Windows Server 2003 family, .NET Compact Framework - Windows CE .NET

Icon Constructor (String)

Initializes a new instance of the **Icon** class from the specified file name.

```
[Visual Basic]
Public Sub New( _
   ByVal fileName As String _
)
[C#]
public Icon(
   string fileName
);
[C++]
public: Icon(
   String* fileName
);
[JScript]
public function Icon(
   fileName : String
);
```

Parameters

fileName
: The file to load the **Icon** object from.

Requirements

Platforms: Windows 98, Windows NT 4.0, Windows Millennium Edition, Windows 2000, Windows XP Home Edition, Windows XP Professional, Windows Server 2003 family

Icon Constructor (Icon, Size)

Initializes a new instance of the **Icon** class and attempts to find a version of the icon that matches the requested size.

```
[Visual Basic]
Public Sub New( _
   ByVal original As Icon, _
   ByVal size As Size _
)
[C#]
public Icon(
   Icon original,
   Size size
);
[C++]
public: Icon(
   Icon* original,
   Size size
);
[JScript]
public function Icon(
   original : Icon,
   size : Size
);
```

Parameters

original
: The **Icon** object from which to load the newly sized icon.

size
: A **Size** structure that specifies the height and width of the new **Icon** object.

Remarks

If a version cannot be found that exactly matches the size, the closest match is used. Note that if the *original* parameter is an **Icon** object with a single size, this method only creates a duplicate icon. Use the stretching capabilities of the **DrawImage** method to resize the icon.

Requirements

Platforms: Windows 98, Windows NT 4.0, Windows Millennium Edition, Windows 2000, Windows XP Home Edition, Windows XP Professional, Windows Server 2003 family

Icon Constructor (Type, String)

Initializes a new instance of the **Icon** class from a resource in the specified assembly.

```
[Visual Basic]
Public Sub New( _
   ByVal type As Type, _
   ByVal resource As String _
)
[C#]
public Icon(
   Type type,
   string resource
);
[C++]
public: Icon(
   Type* type,
   String* resource
);
[JScript]
public function Icon(
   type : Type,
   resource : String
);
```

Parameters

type
: A **Type** object that specifies the assembly in which to look for the resource.

resource
: The resource name to load.

Remarks

This constructor creates an **Icon** object from a resource with the name specified by the *resource* parameter in the assembly that contains the type specified by the *type* parameter.

Requirements

Platforms: Windows 98, Windows NT 4.0, Windows Millennium Edition, Windows 2000, Windows XP Home Edition, Windows XP Professional, Windows Server 2003 family

Icon Constructor (Icon, Int32, Int32)

Initializes a new instance of the **Icon** class and attempts to find a version of the icon that matches the requested size.

[Visual Basic]
```
Public Sub New( _
   ByVal original As Icon, _
   ByVal width As Integer, _
   ByVal height As Integer _
)
```
[C#]
```
public Icon(
   Icon original,
   int width,
   int height
);
```
[C++]
```
public: Icon(
   Icon* original,
   int width,
   int height
);
```
[JScript]
```
public function Icon(
   original : Icon,
   width : int,
   height : int
);
```

Parameters

original
    The icon to load the different size from.

width
    The width of the new icon.

height
    The height of the new icon.

Remarks

If a version cannot be found that exactly matches the size, the closest match is used. Note that if the *original* parameter is an **Icon** object with a single size, this method only creates a duplicate icon. Use the stretching capabilities of the **DrawImage** method to resize the icon.

Requirements

Platforms: Windows 98, Windows NT 4.0, Windows Millennium Edition, Windows 2000, Windows XP Home Edition, Windows XP Professional, Windows Server 2003 family

Icon Constructor (Stream, Int32, Int32)

Initializes a new instance of the **Icon** class from the specified data stream and with the specified width and height.

[Visual Basic]
```
Public Sub New( _
   ByVal stream As Stream, _
   ByVal width As Integer, _
   ByVal height As Integer _
)
```
[C#]
```
public Icon(
   Stream stream,
   int width,
   int height
);
```
[C++]
```
public: Icon(
   Stream* stream,
   int width,
   int height
);
```
[JScript]
```
public function Icon(
   stream : Stream,
   width : int,
   height : int
);
```

Parameters

stream
    The data stream from which to load the icon.

width
    The width of the icon.

height
    The height of the icon.

Requirements

Platforms: Windows 98, Windows NT 4.0, Windows Millennium Edition, Windows 2000, Windows XP Home Edition, Windows XP Professional, Windows Server 2003 family, .NET Compact Framework - Windows CE .NET

Icon.Handle Property

Gets the Windows handle for this **Icon** object. This is not a copy of the handle; do not free it.

[Visual Basic]
```
Public ReadOnly Property Handle As IntPtr
```
[C#]
```
public IntPtr Handle {get;}
```
[C++]
```
public: __property IntPtr get_Handle();
```
[JScript]
```
public function get Handle() : IntPtr;
```

Property Value

The Windows handle for the icon.

Requirements

Platforms: Windows 98, Windows NT 4.0, Windows Millennium Edition, Windows 2000, Windows XP Home Edition, Windows XP Professional, Windows Server 2003 family

Icon.Height Property

Gets the height of this **Icon** object.

[Visual Basic]
```
Public ReadOnly Property Height As Integer
```
[C#]
```
public int Height {get;}
```
[C++]
```
public: __property int get_Height();
```
[JScript]
```
public function get Height() : int;
```

Property Value

The height of this **Icon** object.

Requirements

Platforms: Windows 98, Windows NT 4.0, Windows Millennium Edition, Windows 2000, Windows XP Home Edition, Windows XP Professional, Windows Server 2003 family, .NET Compact Framework - Windows CE .NET

Icon.Size Property

Gets the size of this **Icon** object.

[Visual Basic]
```
Public ReadOnly Property Size As Size
```
[C#]
```
public Size Size {get;}
```
[C++]
```
public: __property Size get_Size();
```
[JScript]
```
public function get Size() : Size;
```

Property Value

A **Size** structure that specifies the width and height of this **Icon** object.

Requirements

Platforms: Windows 98, Windows NT 4.0, Windows Millennium Edition, Windows 2000, Windows XP Home Edition, Windows XP Professional, Windows Server 2003 family

Icon.Width Property

Gets the width of this **Icon** object.

[Visual Basic]
```
Public ReadOnly Property Width As Integer
```
[C#]
```
public int Width {get;}
```
[C++]
```
public: __property int get_Width();
```
[JScript]
```
public function get Width() : int;
```

Property Value

The width of this **Icon** object.

Requirements

Platforms: Windows 98, Windows NT 4.0, Windows Millennium Edition, Windows 2000, Windows XP Home Edition, Windows XP Professional, Windows Server 2003 family, .NET Compact Framework - Windows CE .NET

Icon.Clone Method

Clones the **Icon** object, creating a duplicate image.

[Visual Basic]
```
Public Overridable Function Clone() As Object Implements _
   ICloneable.Clone
```
[C#]
```
public virtual object Clone();
```
[C++]
```
public: virtual Object* Clone();
```
[JScript]
```
public function Clone() : Object;
```

Return Value

An object that can be cast to an **Icon** object.

Implements

ICloneable.Clone

Requirements

Platforms: Windows 98, Windows NT 4.0, Windows Millennium Edition, Windows 2000, Windows XP Home Edition, Windows XP Professional, Windows Server 2003 family

Icon.Dispose Method

Releases all resources used by this **Icon** object.

[Visual Basic]
```
Public Overridable Sub Dispose() Implements IDisposable.Dispose
```
[C#]
```
public virtual void Dispose();
```
[C++]
```
public: virtual void Dispose();
```
[JScript]
```
public function Dispose();
```

Return Value

This method does not return a value.

Implements

IDisposable.Dispose

Remarks

Calling **Dispose** allows the resources used by this **Icon** object to be reallocated for other purposes.

Requirements

Platforms: Windows 98, Windows NT 4.0, Windows Millennium Edition, Windows 2000, Windows XP Home Edition, Windows XP Professional, Windows Server 2003 family, .NET Compact Framework - Windows CE .NET

Icon.Finalize Method

This member overrides **Object.Finalize**.

[Visual Basic]
```
Overrides Protected Sub Finalize()
```
[C#]
```
~Icon();
```
[C++]
```
~Icon();
```
[JScript]
```
protected override function Finalize();
```

Requirements

Platforms: Windows 98, Windows NT 4.0, Windows Millennium Edition, Windows 2000, Windows XP Home Edition, Windows XP Professional, Windows Server 2003 family, .NET Compact Framework - Windows CE .NET

Icon.FromHandle Method

Creates a GDI+ **Icon** object from the specified Windows handle to an icon (HICON).

[Visual Basic]
```
Public Shared Function FromHandle( _
   ByVal handle As IntPtr _
) As Icon
```
[C#]
```
public static Icon FromHandle(
   IntPtr handle
);
```
[C++]
```
public: static Icon* FromHandle(
   IntPtr handle
);
```
[JScript]
```
public static function FromHandle(
   handle : IntPtr
) : Icon;
```

Parameters

handle
A Windows handle to an icon.

Return Value

The **Icon** object this method creates.

Requirements

Platforms: Windows 98, Windows NT 4.0, Windows Millennium Edition, Windows 2000, Windows XP Home Edition, Windows XP Professional, Windows Server 2003 family

Icon.GetHicnFromIcon Method

Note: This namespace, class, or member is supported only in version 1.1 of the .NET Framework.

This member supports the .NET Framework infrastructure and is not intended to be used directly from your code.

[Visual Basic]
```
Public Shared Function GetHicnFromIcon( _
   ByVal icn As Icon _
) As IntPtr
```
[C#]
```
public static IntPtr GetHicnFromIcon(
   Icon icn
);
```
[C++]
```
public: static IntPtr GetHicnFromIcon(
   Icon* icn
);
```
[JScript]
```
public static function GetHicnFromIcon(
   icn : Icon
) : IntPtr;
```

Icon.ISerializable.GetObjectData Method

This member supports the .NET Framework infrastructure and is not intended to be used directly from your code.

[Visual Basic]
```
Private Sub GetObjectData( _
   ByVal si As SerializationInfo, _
   ByVal context As StreamingContext _
) Implements ISerializable.GetObjectData
```
[C#]
```
void ISerializable.GetObjectData(
   SerializationInfo si,
   StreamingContext context
);
```
[C++]
```
private: void ISerializable::GetObjectData(
   SerializationInfo* si,
   StreamingContext context
);
```
[JScript]
```
private function ISerializable.GetObjectData(
   si : SerializationInfo,
   context : StreamingContext
);
```

Icon.Save Method

Saves this **Icon** object to the specified output **Stream** object.

[Visual Basic]
```
Public Sub Save( _
   ByVal outputStream As Stream _
)
```
[C#]
```
public void Save(
   Stream outputStream
);
```
[C++]
```
public: void Save(
   Stream* outputStream
);
```
[JScript]
```
public function Save(
   outputStream : Stream
);
```

Parameters

outputStream

The **Stream** object to save to.

Return Value

This method does not return a value.

Requirements

Platforms: Windows 98, Windows NT 4.0, Windows Millennium Edition, Windows 2000, Windows XP Home Edition, Windows XP Professional, Windows Server 2003 family

Icon.ToBitmap Method

Converts this **Icon** object to a GDI+ **Bitmap** object.

[Visual Basic]
```
Public Function ToBitmap() As Bitmap
```
[C#]
```
public Bitmap ToBitmap();
```
[C++]
```
public: Bitmap* ToBitmap();
```
[JScript]
```
public function ToBitmap() : Bitmap;
```

Return Value

A **Bitmap** object representing the converted **Icon** object.

Requirements

Platforms: Windows 98, Windows NT 4.0, Windows Millennium Edition, Windows 2000, Windows XP Home Edition, Windows XP Professional, Windows Server 2003 family

Icon.ToString Method

Gets a human-readable string that describes the **Icon** object.

[Visual Basic]
```
Overrides Public Function ToString() As String
```
[C#]
```
public override string ToString();
```
[C++]
```
public: String* ToString();
```
[JScript]
```
public override function ToString() : String;
```

Return Value

A string that describes the **Icon** object.

Requirements

Platforms: Windows 98, Windows NT 4.0, Windows Millennium Edition, Windows 2000, Windows XP Home Edition, Windows XP Professional, Windows Server 2003 family, .NET Compact Framework - Windows CE .NET

IconConverter Class

Converts an **Icon** object from one data type to another. Access this class through the **TypeDescriptor** object.

System.Object
  System.ComponentModel.TypeConverter
    System.ComponentModel.ExpandableObjectConverter
      System.Drawing.IconConverter

```
[Visual Basic]
Public Class IconConverter
   Inherits ExpandableObjectConverter
[C#]
public class IconConverter : ExpandableObjectConverter
[C++]
public __gc class IconConverter : public ExpandableObjectConverter
[JScript]
public class IconConverter extends ExpandableObjectConverter
```

Thread Safety

Any public static (**Shared** in Visual Basic) members of this type are safe for multithreaded operations. Any instance members are not guaranteed to be thread safe.

Requirements

Namespace: System.Drawing

Platforms: Windows 98, Windows NT 4.0, Windows Millennium Edition, Windows 2000, Windows XP Home Edition, Windows XP Professional, Windows Server 2003 family

Assembly: System.Drawing (in System.Drawing.dll)

IconConverter Constructor

Initializes a new instance of the **IconConverter** class.

```
[Visual Basic]
Public Sub New()
[C#]
public IconConverter();
[C++]
public: IconConverter();
[JScript]
public function IconConverter();
```

Requirements

Platforms: Windows 98, Windows NT 4.0, Windows Millennium Edition, Windows 2000, Windows XP Home Edition, Windows XP Professional, Windows Server 2003 family

IconConverter.CanConvertFrom Method

Overload List

Determines whether this **IconConverter** can convert an instance of a specified type to an **Icon**, using the specified context.

[Visual Basic] **Overloads Overrides Public Function CanConvertFrom(ITypeDescriptorContext, Type) As Boolean**

[C#] **public override bool CanConvertFrom(ITypeDescriptorContext, Type);**

[C++] **public: bool CanConvertFrom(ITypeDescriptorContext*, Type*);**

[JScript] **public override function CanConvertFrom(ITypeDescriptorContext, Type) : Boolean;**

Inherited from **TypeConverter**.

[Visual Basic] **Overloads Public Function CanConvertFrom(Type) As Boolean**

[C#] **public bool CanConvertFrom(Type);**

[C++] **public: bool CanConvertFrom(Type*);**

[JScript] **public function CanConvertFrom(Type) : Boolean;**

IconConverter.CanConvertFrom Method (ITypeDescriptorContext, Type)

Determines whether this **IconConverter** can convert an instance of a specified type to an **Icon**, using the specified context.

```
[Visual Basic]
Overrides Overloads Public Function CanConvertFrom( _
   ByVal context As ITypeDescriptorContext, _
   ByVal sourceType As Type _
) As Boolean
[C#]
public override bool CanConvertFrom(
   ITypeDescriptorContext context,
   Type sourceType
);
[C++]
public: bool CanConvertFrom(
   ITypeDescriptorContext* context,
   Type* sourceType
);
[JScript]
public override function CanConvertFrom(
   context : ITypeDescriptorContext,
   sourceType : Type
) : Boolean;
```

Parameters

context
  An **ITypeDescriptorContext** that provides a format context.

sourceType
  A **Type** that specifies the type you want to convert from.

Return Value

This method returns **true** if this **IconConverter** can perform the conversion; otherwise, **false**.

Remarks

This method returns **true** only if *sourceType* is equal to typeof(System.Byte[]).

Requirements

Platforms: Windows 98, Windows NT 4.0, Windows Millennium Edition, Windows 2000, Windows XP Home Edition, Windows XP Professional, Windows Server 2003 family

IconConverter.CanConvertTo Method

Overload List

Determines whether this **IconConverter** can convert an **Icon** to an instance of a specified type, using the specified context.

[Visual Basic] **Overloads Overrides Public Function CanConvertTo(ITypeDescriptorContext, Type) As Boolean**

[C#] **public override bool CanConvertTo(ITypeDescriptorContext, Type);**

[C++] **public: bool CanConvertTo(ITypeDescriptorContext*, Type*);**

[JScript] **public override function CanConvertTo(ITypeDescriptorContext, Type) : Boolean;**

Inherited from **TypeConverter**.

[Visual Basic] **Overloads Public Function CanConvertTo(Type) As Boolean**

[C#] **public bool CanConvertTo(Type);**

[C++] **public: bool CanConvertTo(Type*);**

[JScript] **public function CanConvertTo(Type) : Boolean;**

IconConverter.CanConvertTo Method (ITypeDescriptorContext, Type)

Determines whether this **IconConverter** can convert an **Icon** to an instance of a specified type, using the specified context.

```
[Visual Basic]
Overrides Overloads Public Function CanConvertTo( _
   ByVal context As ITypeDescriptorContext, _
   ByVal destinationType As Type _
) As Boolean
[C#]
public override bool CanConvertTo(
   ITypeDescriptorContext context,
   Type destinationType
);
[C++]
public: bool CanConvertTo(
   ITypeDescriptorContext* context,
   Type* destinationType
);
[JScript]
public override function CanConvertTo(
   context : ITypeDescriptorContext,
   destinationType : Type
) : Boolean;
```

Parameters

context

An **ITypeDescriptorContext** that provides a format context.

destinationType

A **Type** that specifies the type you want to convert to.

Return Value

This method returns **true** if this **IconConverter** can perform the conversion; otherwise, **false**.

Remarks

This method returns **true** only if *destinationType* is equal to typeof(System.Byte[]) or typeof(System.String).

Requirements

Platforms: Windows 98, Windows NT 4.0, Windows Millennium Edition, Windows 2000, Windows XP Home Edition, Windows XP Professional, Windows Server 2003 family

IconConverter.ConvertFrom Method

Overload List

Converts a specified object to an **Icon**.

[Visual Basic] **Overloads Overrides Public Function ConvertFrom(ITypeDescriptorContext, CultureInfo, Object) As Object**

[C#] **public override object ConvertFrom(ITypeDescriptorContext, CultureInfo, object);**

[C++] **public: Object* ConvertFrom(ITypeDescriptorContext*, CultureInfo*, Object*);**

[JScript] **public override function ConvertFrom(ITypeDescriptorContext, CultureInfo, Object) : Object;**

Inherited from **TypeConverter**.

[Visual Basic] **Overloads Public Function ConvertFrom(Object) As Object**

[C#] **public object ConvertFrom(object);**

[C++] **public: Object* ConvertFrom(Object*);**

[JScript] **public function ConvertFrom(Object) : Object;**

IconConverter.ConvertFrom Method (ITypeDescriptorContext, CultureInfo, Object)

Converts a specified object to an **Icon**.

```
[Visual Basic]
Overrides Overloads Public Function ConvertFrom( _
   ByVal context As ITypeDescriptorContext, _
   ByVal culture As CultureInfo, _
   ByVal value As Object _
) As Object
[C#]
public override object ConvertFrom(
   ITypeDescriptorContext context,
   CultureInfo culture,
   object value
);
[C++]
public: Object* ConvertFrom(
   ITypeDescriptorContext* context,
   CultureInfo* culture,
   Object* value
);
[JScript]
public override function ConvertFrom(
   context : ITypeDescriptorContext,
   culture : CultureInfo,
   value : Object
) : Object;
```

Parameters

context

An **ITypeDescriptorContext** that provides a format context.

culture

A **CultureInfo** that holds information about a specific culture.

value

The **Object** to be converted.

Return Value

If this method succeeds, it returns the **Icon** that it created by converting the specified object. Otherwise, it throws an exception.

Requirements

Platforms: Windows 98, Windows NT 4.0, Windows Millennium Edition, Windows 2000, Windows XP Home Edition, Windows XP Professional, Windows Server 2003 family

IconConverter.ConvertTo Method

Overload List

Converts an **Icon** (or an object that can be cast to an Icon) to a specified type.

[Visual Basic] **Overloads Overrides Public Function ConvertTo(ITypeDescriptorContext, CultureInfo, Object, Type) As Object**

[C#] **public override object ConvertTo(ITypeDescriptor-Context, CultureInfo, object, Type);**

[C++] **public: Object* ConvertTo(ITypeDescriptorContext*, CultureInfo*, Object*, Type*);**

[JScript] **public override function ConvertTo(IType-DescriptorContext, CultureInfo, Object, Type) : Object;**

Inherited from **TypeConverter**.

[Visual Basic] **Overloads Public Function ConvertTo(Object, Type) As Object**

[C#] **public object ConvertTo(object, Type);**

[C++] **public: Object* ConvertTo(Object*, Type*);**

[JScript] **public function ConvertTo(Object, Type) : Object;**

IconConverter.ConvertTo Method (ITypeDescriptorContext, CultureInfo, Object, Type)

Converts an **Icon** (or an object that can be cast to an Icon) to a specified type.

[Visual Basic]

```
Overrides Overloads Public Function ConvertTo( _
   ByVal context As ITypeDescriptorContext, _
   ByVal culture As CultureInfo, _
   ByVal value As Object, _
   ByVal destinationType As Type _
) As Object
```

[C#]

```
public override object ConvertTo(
   ITypeDescriptorContext context,
   CultureInfo culture,
   object value,
   Type destinationType
);
```

[C++]

```
public: Object* ConvertTo(
   ITypeDescriptorContext* context,
   CultureInfo* culture,
   Object* value,
   Type* destinationType
);
```

[JScript]

```
public override function ConvertTo(
   context : ITypeDescriptorContext,
   culture : CultureInfo,
   value : Object,
   destinationType : Type
) : Object;
```

Parameters

context

An **ITypeDescriptorContext** that provides a format context.

culture

A **CultureInfo** object that specifies formatting conventions used by a particular culture.

value

The object to convert. This object should be of type Icon or some type that can be cast Icon.

destinationType

The type to convert the Icon to.

Return Value

This method returns the converted object.

Remarks

The default implementation calls the **ToString** method on the object if the object is valid and if the destination type is **string**. If this method cannot convert to the destination type, it throws a **NotSupportedException** exception.

Requirements

Platforms: Windows 98, Windows NT 4.0, Windows Millennium Edition, Windows 2000, Windows XP Home Edition, Windows XP Professional, Windows Server 2003 family

Image Class

An abstract base class that provides functionality for the **Bitmap** and **Metafile** descended classes.

System.Object
  System.MarshalByRefObject
    System.Drawing.Image
      System.Drawing.Bitmap
      System.Drawing.Imaging.Metafile

[Visual Basic]
```
<Serializable>
<ComVisible(True)>
MustInherit Public Class Image
   Inherits MarshalByRefObject
   Implements ISerializable, ICloneable, IDisposable
```
[C#]
```
[Serializable]
[ComVisible(true)]
public abstract class Image : MarshalByRefObject, ISerializable,
   ICloneable, IDisposable
```
[C++]
```
[Serializable]
[ComVisible(true)]
public __gc __abstract class Image : public MarshalByRefObject,
   ISerializable, ICloneable, IDisposable
```
[JScript]
```
public
   Serializable
   ComVisible(true)
abstract class Image extends MarshalByRefObject implements
   ISerializable, ICloneable, IDisposable
```

Thread Safety

Any public static (**Shared** in Visual Basic) members of this type are safe for multithreaded operations. Any instance members are not guaranteed to be thread safe.

Requirements

Namespace: System.Drawing

Platforms: Windows 98, Windows NT 4.0, Windows Millennium Edition, Windows 2000, Windows XP Home Edition, Windows XP Professional, Windows Server 2003 family, .NET Compact Framework - Windows CE .NET

Assembly: System.Drawing (in System.Drawing.dll)

Image.Flags Property

Gets attribute flags for this **Image** object.

[Visual Basic]
```
Public ReadOnly Property Flags As Integer
```
[C#]
```
public int Flags {get;}
```
[C++]
```
public: __property int get_Flags();
```
[JScript]
```
public function get Flags() : int;
```

Property Value

The attribute flags for this **Image** object.

Requirements

Platforms: Windows 98, Windows NT 4.0, Windows Millennium Edition, Windows 2000, Windows XP Home Edition, Windows XP Professional, Windows Server 2003 family

Image.FrameDimensionsList Property

Gets an array of GUIDs that represent the dimensions of frames within this **Image** object.

[Visual Basic]
```
Public ReadOnly Property FrameDimensionsList As Guid ()
```
[C#]
```
public Guid[] FrameDimensionsList {get;}
```
[C++]
```
public: __property Guid get_FrameDimensionsList();
```
[JScript]
```
public function get FrameDimensionsList() : Guid[];
```

Property Value

An array of GUIDs that specify the dimensions of frames within this **Image** object from most significant to least significant.

Remarks

This method returns information about multiple-frame images, which come in two styles: multiple page and multiple resolution.

A multiple-page image is an image that contains more than one image. Each page contains a single image(or frame). These pages (or images, or frames) are typically displayed in succession to produce an animated sequence, such as an animated .gif file.

A multiple-resolution image is an image that contains more than one copy of an image at different resolutions. This is commonly used by mip-mapping where the displayed image size determines the resolution of the image used for drawing. GDI+ can support an arbitrary number of pages (or images, or frames), as well as an arbitrary number of resolutions. The defined dimensions are properties of the **FrameDimension** object.

Requirements

Platforms: Windows 98, Windows NT 4.0, Windows Millennium Edition, Windows 2000, Windows XP Home Edition, Windows XP Professional, Windows Server 2003 family

Image.Height Property

Gets the height of this **Image** object.

[Visual Basic]
```
Public ReadOnly Property Height As Integer
```
[C#]
```
public int Height {get;}
```
[C++]
```
public: __property int get_Height();
```
[JScript]
```
public function get Height() : int;
```

Property Value

The height of this **Image** object.

Requirements

Platforms: Windows 98, Windows NT 4.0, Windows Millennium Edition, Windows 2000, Windows XP Home Edition, Windows XP Professional, Windows Server 2003 family, .NET Compact Framework - Windows CE .NET

Image.HorizontalResolution Property

Gets the horizontal resolution, in pixels-per-inch, of this **Image** object.

```
[Visual Basic]
Public ReadOnly Property HorizontalResolution As Single
[C#]
public float HorizontalResolution {get;}
[C++]
public: __property float get_HorizontalResolution();
[JScript]
public function get HorizontalResolution() : float;
```

Property Value

The horizontal resolution, in pixels-per-inch, of this **Image** object.

Requirements

Platforms: Windows 98, Windows NT 4.0, Windows Millennium Edition, Windows 2000, Windows XP Home Edition, Windows XP Professional, Windows Server 2003 family

Image.Palette Property

Gets or sets the color palette used for this **Image** object.

```
[Visual Basic]
Public Property Palette As ColorPalette
[C#]
public ColorPalette Palette {get; set;}
[C++]
public: __property ColorPalette* get_Palette();
public: __property void set_Palette(ColorPalette*);
[JScript]
public function get Palette() : ColorPalette;
public function set Palette(ColorPalette);
```

Property Value

A **ColorPalette** object that represents the color palette used for this **Image** object.

Requirements

Platforms: Windows 98, Windows NT 4.0, Windows Millennium Edition, Windows 2000, Windows XP Home Edition, Windows XP Professional, Windows Server 2003 family

Image.PhysicalDimension Property

Gets the width and height of this image.

```
[Visual Basic]
Public ReadOnly Property PhysicalDimension As SizeF
[C#]
public SizeF PhysicalDimension {get;}
[C++]
public: __property SizeF get_PhysicalDimension();
[JScript]
public function get PhysicalDimension() : SizeF;
```

Property Value

A **SizeF** structure that represents the width and height of this **Image** object.

Remarks

If the image is a bitmap, the width and height are returned in pixels. If the image is a metafile, the width and height are returned in 0.01 millimeter units.

Requirements

Platforms: Windows 98, Windows NT 4.0, Windows Millennium Edition, Windows 2000, Windows XP Home Edition, Windows XP Professional, Windows Server 2003 family

Image.PixelFormat Property

Gets the pixel format for this **Image** object.

```
[Visual Basic]
Public ReadOnly Property PixelFormat As PixelFormat
[C#]
public PixelFormat PixelFormat {get;}
[C++]
public: __property PixelFormat get_PixelFormat();
[JScript]
public function get PixelFormat() : PixelFormat;
```

Property Value

A **PixelFormat** enumeration that represents the pixel format for this **Image** object.

Requirements

Platforms: Windows 98, Windows NT 4.0, Windows Millennium Edition, Windows 2000, Windows XP Home Edition, Windows XP Professional, Windows Server 2003 family

Image.PropertyIdList Property

Gets IDs of the property items stored in this **Image** object.

```
[Visual Basic]
Public ReadOnly Property PropertyIdList As Integer ()
[C#]
public int[] PropertyIdList {get;}
[C++]
public: __property int get_PropertyIdList();
[JScript]
public function get PropertyIdList() : int[];
```

Property Value

An array of the property IDs, one for each property item stored in this image.

Remarks

If the image has no property items or if the image format does not support property items, **PropertyIdList** returns an empty array; that is, an array of length zero.

Requirements

Platforms: Windows 98, Windows NT 4.0, Windows Millennium Edition, Windows 2000, Windows XP Home Edition, Windows XP Professional, Windows Server 2003 family

Image.PropertyItems Property

Gets all the property items (pieces of metadata) stored in this **Image** object.

```
[Visual Basic]
Public ReadOnly Property PropertyItems As PropertyItem ()
[C#]
public PropertyItem[] PropertyItems {get;}
[C++]
public: __property PropertyItem* get_PropertyItems();
[JScript]
public function get PropertyItems() : PropertyItem[];
```

Property Value

An array of **PropertyItem** objects, one for each property item stored in the image.

Remarks

If the image has no property items or if the image format does not support property items, **PropertyItems** returns an empty array; that is, an array of length zero.

Requirements

Platforms: Windows 98, Windows NT 4.0, Windows Millennium Edition, Windows 2000, Windows XP Home Edition, Windows XP Professional, Windows Server 2003 family

Image.RawFormat Property

Gets the format of this **Image** object.

```
[Visual Basic]
Public ReadOnly Property RawFormat As ImageFormat
[C#]
public ImageFormat RawFormat {get;}
[C++]
public: __property ImageFormat* get_RawFormat();
[JScript]
public function get RawFormat() : ImageFormat;
```

Property Value

The **ImageFormat** object that represents the format of this **Image** object.

Requirements

Platforms: Windows 98, Windows NT 4.0, Windows Millennium Edition, Windows 2000, Windows XP Home Edition, Windows XP Professional, Windows Server 2003 family

Image.Size Property

Gets the width and height, in pixels, of this image.

```
[Visual Basic]
Public ReadOnly Property Size As Size
[C#]
public Size Size {get;}
[C++]
public: __property Size get_Size();
[JScript]
public function get Size() : Size;
```

Property Value

A **Size** structure that represents the width and height of this image.

Requirements

Platforms: Windows 98, Windows NT 4.0, Windows Millennium Edition, Windows 2000, Windows XP Home Edition, Windows XP Professional, Windows Server 2003 family, .NET Compact Framework - Windows CE .NET

Image.VerticalResolution Property

Gets the vertical resolution, in pixels-per-inch, of this **Image** object.

```
[Visual Basic]
Public ReadOnly Property VerticalResolution As Single
[C#]
public float VerticalResolution {get;}
[C++]
public: __property float get_VerticalResolution();
[JScript]
public function get VerticalResolution() : float;
```

Property Value

The vertical resolution, in pixels-per-inch, of this **Image** object.

Requirements

Platforms: Windows 98, Windows NT 4.0, Windows Millennium Edition, Windows 2000, Windows XP Home Edition, Windows XP Professional, Windows Server 2003 family

Image.Width Property

Gets the width of this **Image** object.

```
[Visual Basic]
Public ReadOnly Property Width As Integer
[C#]
public int Width {get;}
[C++]
public: __property int get_Width();
[JScript]
public function get Width() : int;
```

Property Value

The width of this **Image** object.

Requirements

Platforms: Windows 98, Windows NT 4.0, Windows Millennium Edition, Windows 2000, Windows XP Home Edition, Windows XP Professional, Windows Server 2003 family, .NET Compact Framework - Windows CE .NET

Image.Clone Method

Creates an exact copy of this **Image** object.

```
[Visual Basic]
Public Overridable Function Clone() As Object Implements _
   ICloneable.Clone
[C#]
public virtual object Clone();
[C++]
public: virtual Object* Clone();
[JScript]
public function Clone() : Object;
```

Return Value

The **Image** this method creates, cast as an object.

Implements

ICloneable.Clone

Requirements

Platforms: Windows 98, Windows NT 4.0,
Windows Millennium Edition, Windows 2000,
Windows XP Home Edition, Windows XP Professional,
Windows Server 2003 family

Image.Dispose Method

Overload List

Releases all resources used by this **Image** object.

Supported by the .NET Compact Framework.

[Visual Basic] **Overloads Public Overridable Sub Dispose() Implements IDisposable.Dispose**

[C#] **public virtual void Dispose();**

[C++] **public: virtual void Dispose();**

[JScript] **public function Dispose();**

This member supports the .NET Framework infrastructure and is not intended to be used directly from your code.

[Visual Basic] **Overloads Protected Overridable Sub Dispose(Boolean)**

[C#] **protected virtual void Dispose(bool);**

[C++] **protected: virtual void Dispose(bool);**

[JScript] **protected function Dispose(Boolean);**

Image.Dispose Method ()

Releases all resources used by this **Image** object.

```
[Visual Basic]
Overloads Public Overridable Sub Dispose() Implements _
   IDisposable.Dispose
[C#]
public virtual void Dispose();
[C++]
public: virtual void Dispose();
[JScript]
public function Dispose();
```

Return Value

This method does not return a value.

Implements

IDisposable.Dispose

Remarks

Calling **Dispose** allows the resources used by this **Image** object to be reallocated for other purposes.

Requirements

Platforms: Windows 98, Windows NT 4.0,
Windows Millennium Edition, Windows 2000,
Windows XP Home Edition, Windows XP Professional,
Windows Server 2003 family,
.NET Compact Framework - Windows CE .NET

Image.Dispose Method (Boolean)

This member supports the .NET Framework infrastructure and is not intended to be used directly from your code.

```
[Visual Basic]
Overloads Protected Overridable Sub Dispose( _
   ByVal disposing As Boolean _
)
[C#]
protected virtual void Dispose(
   bool disposing
);
[C++]
protected: virtual void Dispose(
   bool disposing
);
[JScript]
protected function Dispose(
   disposing : Boolean
);
```

Image.Finalize Method

This member overrides **Object.Finalize**.

```
[Visual Basic]
Overrides Protected Sub Finalize()
[C#]
~Image();
[C++]
~Image();
[JScript]
protected override function Finalize();
```

Requirements

Platforms: Windows 98, Windows NT 4.0,
Windows Millennium Edition, Windows 2000,
Windows XP Home Edition, Windows XP Professional,
Windows Server 2003 family,
.NET Compact Framework - Windows CE .NET

Image.FromFile Method

Creates an **Image** object from the specified file.

Overload List

Creates an **Image** object from the specified file.

[Visual Basic] **Overloads Public Shared Function FromFile(String) As Image**

[C#] **public static Image FromFile(string);**

[C++] **public: static Image* FromFile(String*);**

[JScript] **public static function FromFile(String) : Image;**

Creates an **Image** object from the specified file using embedded color management information in that file.

[Visual Basic] **Overloads Public Shared Function FromFile(String, Boolean) As Image**

[C#] **public static Image FromFile(string, bool);**

[C++] **public: static Image* FromFile(String*, bool);**

[JScript] **public static function FromFile(String, Boolean) : Image;**

Image.FromFile Method (String)

Creates an **Image** object from the specified file.

```
[Visual Basic]
Overloads Public Shared Function FromFile( _
   ByVal filename As String _
) As Image
[C#]
public static Image FromFile(
   string filename
);
[C++]
public: static Image* FromFile(
   String* filename
);
[JScript]
public static function FromFile(
   filename : String
) : Image;
```

Parameters

filename

A string that contains the name of the file from which to create the **Image** object.

Return Value

The **Image** object this method creates.

Remarks

The file remains locked until the **Image** object is disposed.

If the file does not have a valid image format or if GDI+ does not support the pixel format of the file, this method throws an **OutOfMemoryException** exception.

Requirements

Platforms: Windows 98, Windows NT 4.0, Windows Millennium Edition, Windows 2000, Windows XP Home Edition, Windows XP Professional, Windows Server 2003 family

Image.FromFile Method (String, Boolean)

Creates an **Image** object from the specified file using embedded color management information in that file.

```
[Visual Basic]
Overloads Public Shared Function FromFile( _
   ByVal filename As String, _
   ByVal useEmbeddedColorManagement As Boolean _
) As Image
[C#]
public static Image FromFile(
   string filename,
   bool useEmbeddedColorManagement
);
[C++]
public: static Image* FromFile(
   String* filename,
   bool useEmbeddedColorManagement
);
[JScript]
public static function FromFile(
   filename : String,
   useEmbeddedColorManagement : Boolean
) : Image;
```

Parameters

filename

A string that contains the name of the file from which to create the **Image** object.

useEmbeddedColorManagement

Set to **true** to use color management information embedded in the image file; otherwise, **false**.

Return Value

The **Image** object this method creates.

Remarks

The file remains locked until the **Image** object is disposed.

If the file does not have a valid image format or if GDI+ does not support the pixel format of the file, this method throws an **OutOfMemoryException** exception.

The *useEmbeddedColorManagement* parameter specifies whether the new **Image** object applies color correction according to color management information that is embedded in the image file. Embedded information can include International Color Consortium (ICC) profiles, gamma values, and chromaticity information.

Requirements

Platforms: Windows 98, Windows NT 4.0, Windows Millennium Edition, Windows 2000, Windows XP Home Edition, Windows XP Professional, Windows Server 2003 family

Image.FromHbitmap Method

Creates a **Bitmap** object from a Windows handle.

Overload List

Creates a **Bitmap** object from a handle to a GDI bitmap.

[Visual Basic] **Overloads Public Shared Function FromHbitmap(IntPtr) As Bitmap**

[C#] **public static Bitmap FromHbitmap(IntPtr);**

[C++] **public: static Bitmap* FromHbitmap(IntPtr);**

[JScript] **public static function FromHbitmap(IntPtr) : Bitmap;**

Creates a **Bitmap** object from a handle to a GDI bitmap and a handle to a GDI palette.

[Visual Basic] **Overloads Public Shared Function FromHbitmap(IntPtr, IntPtr) As Bitmap**

[C#] **public static Bitmap FromHbitmap(IntPtr, IntPtr);**

[C++] **public: static Bitmap* FromHbitmap(IntPtr, IntPtr);**

[JScript] **public static function FromHbitmap(IntPtr, IntPtr) : Bitmap;**

Image.FromHbitmap Method (IntPtr)

Creates a **Bitmap** object from a handle to a GDI bitmap.

[Visual Basic]
```
Overloads Public Shared Function FromHbitmap( _
   ByVal hbitmap As IntPtr _
) As Bitmap
```
[C#]
```
public static Bitmap FromHbitmap(
   IntPtr hbitmap
);
```
[C++]
```
public: static Bitmap* FromHbitmap(
   IntPtr hbitmap
);
```
[JScript]
```
public static function FromHbitmap(
   hbitmap : IntPtr
) : Bitmap;
```

Parameters

hbitmap

The GDI bitmap handle from which to create the **Bitmap** object.

Return Value

The **Bitmap** object this method creates.

Requirements

Platforms: Windows 98, Windows NT 4.0, Windows Millennium Edition, Windows 2000, Windows XP Home Edition, Windows XP Professional, Windows Server 2003 family

Image.FromHbitmap Method (IntPtr, IntPtr)

Creates a **Bitmap** object from a handle to a GDI bitmap and a handle to a GDI palette.

[Visual Basic]
```
Overloads Public Shared Function FromHbitmap( _
   ByVal hbitmap As IntPtr, _
   ByVal hpalette As IntPtr _
) As Bitmap
```
[C#]
```
public static Bitmap FromHbitmap(
   IntPtr hbitmap,
   IntPtr hpalette
);
```
[C++]
```
public: static Bitmap* FromHbitmap(
   IntPtr hbitmap,
   IntPtr hpalette
);
```
[JScript]
```
public static function FromHbitmap(
   hbitmap : IntPtr,
   hpalette : IntPtr
) : Bitmap;
```

Parameters

hbitmap

The GDI bitmap handle from which to create the **Bitmap** object.

hpalette

A handle to a GDI palette used to define the bitmap colors if the bitmap specified in the *hBitmap* parameter is not a device-independent bitmap (DIB).

Return Value

The **Bitmap** object this method creates.

Requirements

Platforms: Windows 98, Windows NT 4.0, Windows Millennium Edition, Windows 2000, Windows XP Home Edition, Windows XP Professional, Windows Server 2003 family

Image.FromStream Method

Creates an **Image** object from the specified data stream.

Overload List

Creates an **Image** object from the specified data stream.

[Visual Basic] **Overloads Public Shared Function FromStream(Stream) As Image**

[C#] **public static Image FromStream(Stream);**

[C++] **public: static Image* FromStream(Stream*);**

[JScript] **public static function FromStream(Stream) : Image;**

Creates an **Image** object from the specified data stream, using embedded color management information in that stream.

[Visual Basic] **Overloads Public Shared Function FromStream(Stream, Boolean) As Image**

[C#] **public static Image FromStream(Stream, bool);**

[C++] **public: static Image* FromStream(Stream*, bool);**

[JScript] **public static function FromStream(Stream, Boolean) : Image;**

Image.FromStream Method (Stream)

Creates an **Image** object from the specified data stream.

[Visual Basic]
```
Overloads Public Shared Function FromStream( _
   ByVal stream As Stream _
) As Image
```

```
[C#]
public static Image FromStream(
   Stream stream
);
[C++]
public: static Image* FromStream(
   Stream* stream
);
[JScript]
public static function FromStream(
   stream : Stream
) : Image;
```

Parameters

stream
A **Stream** object that contains the data for this **Image** object.

Return Value

The **Image** object this method creates.

Remarks

You must keep the stream open for the lifetime of the **Image** object.

Requirements

Platforms: Windows 98, Windows NT 4.0,
Windows Millennium Edition, Windows 2000,
Windows XP Home Edition, Windows XP Professional,
Windows Server 2003 family

Image.FromStream Method (Stream, Boolean)

Creates an **Image** object from the specified data stream, using embedded color management information in that stream.

```
[Visual Basic]
Overloads Public Shared Function FromStream( _
   ByVal stream As Stream, _
   ByVal useEmbeddedColorManagement As Boolean _
) As Image
[C#]
public static Image FromStream(
   Stream stream,
   bool useEmbeddedColorManagement
);
[C++]
public: static Image* FromStream(
   Stream* stream,
   bool useEmbeddedColorManagement
);
[JScript]
public static function FromStream(
   stream : Stream,
   useEmbeddedColorManagement : Boolean
) : Image;
```

Parameters

stream
A **Stream** object that contains the data for this **Image** object.

useEmbeddedColorManagement
Set to **true** to use color management information embedded in the data stream; otherwise, **false**.

Return Value

The **Image** object this method creates.

Remarks

You must keep the stream open for the lifetime of the **Image** object.

The *useEmbeddedColorManagement* parameter specifies whether the new **Image** object applies color correction according to color management information that is embedded in the data stream. Embedded information can include International Color Consortium (ICC) profiles, gamma values, and chromaticity information.

Requirements

Platforms: Windows 98, Windows NT 4.0,
Windows Millennium Edition, Windows 2000,
Windows XP Home Edition, Windows XP Professional,
Windows Server 2003 family

Image.GetBounds Method

Gets a bounding rectangle in the specified units for this **Image** object.

```
[Visual Basic]
Public Function GetBounds( _
   ByRef pageUnit As GraphicsUnit _
) As RectangleF
[C#]
public RectangleF GetBounds(
   ref GraphicsUnit pageUnit
);
[C++]
public: RectangleF GetBounds(
   GraphicsUnit* pageUnit
);
[JScript]
public function GetBounds(
   pageUnit : GraphicsUnit
) : RectangleF;
```

Parameters

pageUnit
A member of the **GraphicsUnit** enumeration that specifies the units for the rectangle.

Return Value

A **RectangleF** structure that represents a bounding rectangle for this **Image** object.

Requirements

Platforms: Windows 98, Windows NT 4.0,
Windows Millennium Edition, Windows 2000,
Windows XP Home Edition, Windows XP Professional,
Windows Server 2003 family

Image.GetEncoderParameterList Method

Returns information about the parameters supported by the specified image encoder.

```
[Visual Basic]
Public Function GetEncoderParameterList( _
   ByVal encoder As Guid _
) As EncoderParameters
[C#]
public EncoderParameters GetEncoderParameterList(
   Guid encoder
);
```

[C++]
```
public: EncoderParameters* GetEncoderParameterList(
   Guid encoder
);
```
[JScript]
```
public function GetEncoderParameterList(
   encoder : Guid
) : EncoderParameters;
```

Parameters

encoder

A GUID that specifies the image encoder.

Return Value

An **EncoderParameters** object that contains an array of **EncoderParameter** objects. Each **EncoderParameter** object contains information about one of he parameters supported by the specified image encoder.

Requirements

Platforms: Windows 98, Windows NT 4.0, Windows Millennium Edition, Windows 2000, Windows XP Home Edition, Windows XP Professional, Windows Server 2003 family

Image.GetFrameCount Method

Returns the number of frames of the specified dimension.

[Visual Basic]
```
Public Function GetFrameCount( _
   ByVal dimension As FrameDimension _
) As Integer
```
[C#]
```
public int GetFrameCount(
   FrameDimension dimension
);
```
[C++]
```
public: int GetFrameCount(
   FrameDimension* dimension
);
```
[JScript]
```
public function GetFrameCount(
   dimension : FrameDimension
) : int;
```

Parameters

dimension

A **FrameDimension** that specifies the identity of the dimension type.

Return Value

The number of frames in the specified dimension.

Requirements

Platforms: Windows 98, Windows NT 4.0, Windows Millennium Edition, Windows 2000, Windows XP Home Edition, Windows XP Professional, Windows Server 2003 family

Image.GetHowFromImage Method

Note: This namespace, class, or member is supported only in version 1.1 of the .NET Framework.

This member supports the .NET Framework infrastructure and is not intended to be used directly from your code.

[Visual Basic]
```
Public Shared Function GetHowFromImage( _
   ByVal img As Image _
) As IntPtr
```
[C#]
```
public static IntPtr GetHowFromImage(
   Image img
);
```
[C++]
```
public: static IntPtr GetHowFromImage(
   Image* img
);
```
[JScript]
```
public static function GetHowFromImage(
   img : Image
) : IntPtr;
```

Image.GetPixelFormatSize Method

Returns the color depth (number of bits per pixel) of the specified pixel format.

[Visual Basic]
```
Public Shared Function GetPixelFormatSize( _
   ByVal pixfmt As PixelFormat _
) As Integer
```
[C#]
```
public static int GetPixelFormatSize(
   PixelFormat pixfmt
);
```
[C++]
```
public: static int GetPixelFormatSize(
   PixelFormat pixfmt
);
```
[JScript]
```
public static function GetPixelFormatSize(
   pixfmt : PixelFormat
) : int;
```

Parameters

pixfmt

The **PixelFormat** enumeration member specifying the format for which to find the size.

Return Value

The color depth of the specified pixel format.

Requirements

Platforms: Windows 98, Windows NT 4.0, Windows Millennium Edition, Windows 2000, Windows XP Home Edition, Windows XP Professional, Windows Server 2003 family

Image.GetPropertyItem Method

Gets the specified property item from this **Image** object.

```
[Visual Basic]
Public Function GetPropertyItem( _
   ByVal propid As Integer _
) As PropertyItem
[C#]
public PropertyItem GetPropertyItem(
   int propid
);
[C++]
public: PropertyItem* GetPropertyItem(
   int propid
);
[JScript]
public function GetPropertyItem(
   propid : int
) : PropertyItem;
```

Parameters

propid
The ID of the property item to get.

Return Value

The **PropertyItem** object this method gets.

Requirements

Platforms: Windows 98, Windows NT 4.0, Windows Millennium Edition, Windows 2000, Windows XP Home Edition, Windows XP Professional, Windows Server 2003 family

Image.GetThumbnailImage Method

Returns a thumbnail for this **Image** object.

```
[Visual Basic]
Public Function GetThumbnailImage( _
   ByVal thumbWidth As Integer, _
   ByVal thumbHeight As Integer, _
   ByVal callback As Image.GetThumbnailImageAbort, _
   ByVal callbackData As IntPtr _
) As Image
[C#]
public Image GetThumbnailImage(
   int thumbWidth,
   int thumbHeight,
   Image.GetThumbnailImageAbort callback,
   IntPtr callbackData
);
[C++]
public: Image* GetThumbnailImage(
   int thumbWidth,
   int thumbHeight,
   Image.GetThumbnailImageAbort* callback,
   IntPtr callbackData
);
[JScript]
public function GetThumbnailImage(
   thumbWidth : int,
   thumbHeight : int,
   callback : Image.GetThumbnailImageAbort,
   callbackData : IntPtr
) : Image;
```

Parameters

thumbWidth
The width, in pixels, of the requested thumbnail image.

thumbHeight
The height, in pixels, of the requested thumbnail image.

callback
A **Image.GetThumbnailImageAbort** delegate. In GDI+ version 1.0, the delegate is not used. Even so, you must create a delegate and pass a reference to that delegate in this parameter.

callbackData
Must be IntPtr.Zero.

Return Value

An **Image** object that represents the thumbnail.

Remarks

If the **Image** object contains an embedded thumbnail image, then this method retrieves the embedded thumbnail and scales it to the requested size. If the **Image** object does not contain an embedded thumbnail image, this method creates a thumbnail image by scaling the main image.

GetThumbnailImage works well when the requested thumbnail image has a size of about 120 x 120. If you request a large thumbnail image (say 300 x 300) from an **Image** object that has an embedded thumbnail, there could be a noticeable loss of quality in the thumbnail image. It might be better to scale the main image (instead of scaling the embedded thumbnail) by calling **DrawImage**.

Example

[C#] The following example creates and displays a thumbnail image. This delegate is never called.

```
[C#]
public bool ThumbnailCallback()
{
return false;
}
public void Example_GetThumb(PaintEventArgs e)
{
Image.GetThumbnailImageAbort myCallback =
new Image.GetThumbnailImageAbort(ThumbnailCallback);
Bitmap myBitmap = new Bitmap("Climber.jpg");
Image myThumbnail = myBitmap.GetThumbnailImage(
40, 40, myCallback, IntPtr.Zero);
e.Graphics.DrawImage(myThumbnail, 150, 75);
}
```

[Visual Basic, C++, JScript] No example is available for Visual Basic, C++, or JScript. To view a C# example, click the Language Filter button <IMG SRC="filter1a.gif" ALT="Language Filter" BORDER=0> in the upper-left corner of the page.

Requirements

Platforms: Windows 98, Windows NT 4.0, Windows Millennium Edition, Windows 2000, Windows XP Home Edition, Windows XP Professional, Windows Server 2003 family

Image.IsAlphaPixelFormat Method

Returns a value that indicates whether the pixel format for this **Image** object contains alpha information.

[Visual Basic]
```
Public Shared Function IsAlphaPixelFormat( _
   ByVal pixfmt As PixelFormat _
) As Boolean
```
[C#]
```
public static bool IsAlphaPixelFormat(
   PixelFormat pixfmt
);
```
[C++]
```
public: static bool IsAlphaPixelFormat(
   PixelFormat pixfmt
);
```
[JScript]
```
public static function IsAlphaPixelFormat(
   pixfmt : PixelFormat
) : Boolean;
```

Parameters

pixfmt

The **PixelFormat** enumeration to test.

Return Value

This method returns **true** if the *pixfmt* parameter contains alpha information; otherwise, **false**.

Requirements

Platforms: Windows 98, Windows NT 4.0, Windows Millennium Edition, Windows 2000, Windows XP Home Edition, Windows XP Professional, Windows Server 2003 family

Image.IsCanonicalPixelFormat Method

Returns a value that indicates whether the pixel format is canonical.

[Visual Basic]
```
Public Shared Function IsCanonicalPixelFormat( _
   ByVal pixfmt As PixelFormat _
) As Boolean
```
[C#]
```
public static bool IsCanonicalPixelFormat(
   PixelFormat pixfmt
);
```
[C++]
```
public: static bool IsCanonicalPixelFormat(
   PixelFormat pixfmt
);
```
[JScript]
```
public static function IsCanonicalPixelFormat(
   pixfmt : PixelFormat
) : Boolean;
```

Parameters

pixfmt

The **PixelFormat** enumeration to test.

Return Value

This method returns **true** if the *pixfmt* parameter is canonical; otherwise, **false**.

Requirements

Platforms: Windows 98, Windows NT 4.0, Windows Millennium Edition, Windows 2000, Windows XP Home Edition, Windows XP Professional, Windows Server 2003 family

Image.ISerializable.GetObjectData Method

This member supports the .NET Framework infrastructure and is not intended to be used directly from your code.

[Visual Basic]
```
Private Sub GetObjectData( _
   ByVal si As SerializationInfo, _
   ByVal context As StreamingContext _
) Implements ISerializable.GetObjectData
```
[C#]
```
void ISerializable.GetObjectData(
   SerializationInfo si,
   StreamingContext context
);
```
[C++]
```
private: void ISerializable::GetObjectData(
   SerializationInfo* si,
   StreamingContext context
);
```
[JScript]
```
private function ISerializable.GetObjectData(
   si : SerializationInfo,
   context : StreamingContext
);
```

Image.IsExtendedPixelFormat Method

Returns a value that indicates whether the pixel format is extended.

[Visual Basic]
```
Public Shared Function IsExtendedPixelFormat( _
   ByVal pixfmt As PixelFormat _
) As Boolean
```
[C#]
```
public static bool IsExtendedPixelFormat(
   PixelFormat pixfmt
);
```
[C++]
```
public: static bool IsExtendedPixelFormat(
   PixelFormat pixfmt
);
```
[JScript]
```
public static function IsExtendedPixelFormat(
   pixfmt : PixelFormat
) : Boolean;
```

Parameters

pixfmt

The **PixelFormat** enumeration to test.

Return Value

This method returns **true** if the *pixfmt* parameter is extended; otherwise, **false**.

Requirements

Platforms: Windows 98, Windows NT 4.0, Windows Millennium Edition, Windows 2000, Windows XP Home Edition, Windows XP Professional, Windows Server 2003 family

Image.RemovePropertyItem Method

Removes the specified property item from this **Image** object.

```
[Visual Basic]
Public Sub RemovePropertyItem( _
   ByVal propid As Integer _
)
[C#]
public void RemovePropertyItem(
   int propid
);
[C++]
public: void RemovePropertyItem(
   int propid
);
[JScript]
public function RemovePropertyItem(
   propid : int
);
```

Parameters

propid
The ID of the property item to remove.

Return Value

This method does not return a value.

Remarks

If the image does not contain the requested property item or if the image format does not support property items, **RemovePropertyItem** throws System.ArgumentException with the message, "Property not found."

Requirements

Platforms: Windows 98, Windows NT 4.0, Windows Millennium Edition, Windows 2000, Windows XP Home Edition, Windows XP Professional, Windows Server 2003 family

Image.RotateFlip Method

This method either rotates, flips, or rotates and flips the **Image** object.

```
[Visual Basic]
Public Sub RotateFlip( _
   ByVal rotateFlipType As RotateFlipType _
)
[C#]
public void RotateFlip(
   RotateFlipType rotateFlipType
);
[C++]
public: void RotateFlip(
   RotateFlipType rotateFlipType
);
[JScript]
public function RotateFlip(
   rotateFlipType : RotateFlipType
);
```

Parameters

rotateFlipType
A **RotateFlipType** enumeration member that specifies the type of rotation and flip to apply to the image.

Return Value

This method does not return a value.

Requirements

Platforms: Windows 98, Windows NT 4.0, Windows Millennium Edition, Windows 2000, Windows XP Home Edition, Windows XP Professional, Windows Server 2003 family

Image.Save Method

Saves this image to the specified stream in the specified format.

Overload List

Saves this **Image** object to the specified file.

[Visual Basic] **Overloads Public Sub Save(String)**

[C#] **public void Save(string);**

[C++] **public: void Save(String*);**

[JScript] **public function Save(String);**

Saves this image to the specified stream in the specified format.

[Visual Basic] **Overloads Public Sub Save(Stream, ImageFormat)**

[C#] **public void Save(Stream, ImageFormat);**

[C++] **public: void Save(Stream*, ImageFormat*);**

[JScript] **public function Save(Stream, ImageFormat);**

Saves this **Image** object to the specified file in the specified format.

[Visual Basic] **Overloads Public Sub Save(String, ImageFormat)**

[C#] **public void Save(string, ImageFormat);**

[C++] **public: void Save(String*, ImageFormat*);**

[JScript] **public function Save(String, ImageFormat);**

Saves this image to the specified stream in the specified format.

[Visual Basic] **Overloads Public Sub Save(Stream, ImageCodecInfo, EncoderParameters)**

[C#] **public void Save(Stream, ImageCodecInfo, EncoderParameters);**

[C++] **public: void Save(Stream*, ImageCodecInfo*, EncoderParameters*);**

[JScript] **public function Save(Stream, ImageCodecInfo, EncoderParameters);**

Saves this **Image** object to the specified file, in the specified format, and with the specified codec parameters.

[Visual Basic] **Overloads Public Sub Save(String, ImageCodecInfo, EncoderParameters)**

[C#] **public void Save(string, ImageCodecInfo, EncoderParameters);**

[C++] **public: void Save(String*, ImageCodecInfo*, EncoderParameters*);**

[JScript] **public function Save(String, ImageCodecInfo, EncoderParameters);**

Image.Save Method (String)

Saves this **Image** object to the specified file.

[Visual Basic]
```
Overloads Public Sub Save( _
   ByVal filename As String _
)
```
[C#]
```
public void Save(
   string filename
);
```
[C++]
```
public: void Save(
   String* filename
);
```
[JScript]
```
public function Save(
   filename : String
);
```

Parameters

filename

A string that contains the name of the file to which to save this **Image** object.

Return Value

This method does not return a value.

Requirements

Platforms: Windows 98, Windows NT 4.0, Windows Millennium Edition, Windows 2000, Windows XP Home Edition, Windows XP Professional, Windows Server 2003 family

Image.Save Method (Stream, ImageFormat)

Saves this image to the specified stream in the specified format.

[Visual Basic]
```
Overloads Public Sub Save( _
   ByVal stream As Stream, _
   ByVal format As ImageFormat _
)
```
[C#]
```
public void Save(
   Stream stream,
   ImageFormat format
);
```
[C++]
```
public: void Save(
   Stream* stream,
   ImageFormat* format
);
```
[JScript]
```
public function Save(
   stream : Stream,
   format : ImageFormat
);
```

Parameters

stream

The **Stream** where the image will be saved.

format

An **ImageFormat** object that specifies the format of the saved image.

Return Value

This method does not return a value.

Remarks

Do not save an image to the same stream that was used to construct the image. Doing so might damage the stream.

[C#]
```
Image myImage = Image.FromStream(myStream);
...
myImage.Save(myStream, ...); // Do not do this.
```

Requirements

Platforms: Windows 98, Windows NT 4.0, Windows Millennium Edition, Windows 2000, Windows XP Home Edition, Windows XP Professional, Windows Server 2003 family

Image.Save Method (String, ImageFormat)

Saves this **Image** object to the specified file in the specified format.

[Visual Basic]
```
Overloads Public Sub Save( _
   ByVal filename As String, _
   ByVal format As ImageFormat _
)
```
[C#]
```
public void Save(
   string filename,
   ImageFormat format
);
```
[C++]
```
public: void Save(
   String* filename,
   ImageFormat* format
);
```
[JScript]
```
public function Save(
   filename : String,
   format : ImageFormat
);
```

Parameters

filename

A string that contains the name of the file to which to save this **Image** object.

format

The **ImageFormat** object for this **Image** object.

Return Value

This method does not return a value.

Requirements

Platforms: Windows 98, Windows NT 4.0, Windows Millennium Edition, Windows 2000, Windows XP Home Edition, Windows XP Professional, Windows Server 2003 family

Image.Save Method (Stream, ImageCodecInfo, EncoderParameters)

Saves this image to the specified stream in the specified format.

```
[Visual Basic]
Overloads Public Sub Save( _
   ByVal stream As Stream, _
   ByVal encoder As ImageCodecInfo, _
   ByVal encoderParams As EncoderParameters _
)
[C#]
public void Save(
   Stream stream,
   ImageCodecInfo encoder,
   EncoderParameters encoderParams
);
[C++]
public: void Save(
   Stream* stream,
   ImageCodecInfo* encoder,
   EncoderParameters* encoderParams
);
[JScript]
public function Save(
   stream : Stream,
   encoder : ImageCodecInfo,
   encoderParams : EncoderParameters
);
```

Parameters

stream
: The **Stream** where the image will be saved.

encoder
: An **ImageFormat** object that specifies the format of the saved image.

encoderParams
: An **EncoderParameters** that specifies parameters used by the image encoder.

Return Value

This method does not return a value.

Remarks

Do not save an image to the same stream that was used to construct the image. Doing so might damage the stream.

```
[C#]
Image myImage = Image.FromStream(myStream);
...
myImage.Save(myStream, ...); // Do not do this.
```

Requirements

Platforms: Windows 98, Windows NT 4.0, Windows Millennium Edition, Windows 2000, Windows XP Home Edition, Windows XP Professional, Windows Server 2003 family

Image.Save Method (String, ImageCodecInfo, EncoderParameters)

Saves this **Image** object to the specified file, in the specified format, and with the specified codec parameters.

```
[Visual Basic]
Overloads Public Sub Save( _
   ByVal filename As String, _
   ByVal encoder As ImageCodecInfo, _
   ByVal encoderParams As EncoderParameters _
)
[C#]
public void Save(
   string filename,
   ImageCodecInfo encoder,
   EncoderParameters encoderParams
);
[C++]
public: void Save(
   String* filename,
   ImageCodecInfo* encoder,
   EncoderParameters* encoderParams
);
[JScript]
public function Save(
   filename : String,
   encoder : ImageCodecInfo,
   encoderParams : EncoderParameters
);
```

Parameters

filename
: A string that contains the name of the file to which to save this **Image** object.

encoder
: The **ImageFormat** object for this **Image** object.

encoderParams
: An **EncoderParameters** object to use for this **Image** object.

Return Value

This method does not return a value.

Requirements

Platforms: Windows 98, Windows NT 4.0, Windows Millennium Edition, Windows 2000, Windows XP Home Edition, Windows XP Professional, Windows Server 2003 family

Image.SaveAdd Method

Adds the information in the specified **Image** object to this **Image** object. The specified **EncoderParameters** object determines how the new information is incorporated into the existing image.

Overload List

Adds a frame to the file or stream specified in a previous call to the **Save** method. Use this method to save selected frames from a multiple-frame image to another multiple-frame image.

[Visual Basic] **Overloads Public Sub SaveAdd(EncoderParameters)**

[C#] **public void SaveAdd(EncoderParameters);**

[C++] **public: void SaveAdd(EncoderParameters*);**

[JScript] **public function SaveAdd(EncoderParameters);**

Adds a frame to the file or stream specified in a previous call to the **Save** method.

[Visual Basic] **Overloads Public Sub SaveAdd(Image, EncoderParameters)**

[C#] **public void SaveAdd(Image, EncoderParameters);**

[C++] **public: void SaveAdd(Image*, EncoderParameters*);**

[JScript] **public function SaveAdd(Image, EncoderParameters);**

Image.SaveAdd Method (EncoderParameters)

Adds a frame to the file or stream specified in a previous call to the **Save** method. Use this method to save selected frames from a multiple-frame image to another multiple-frame image.

```
[Visual Basic]
Overloads Public Sub SaveAdd( _
   ByVal encoderParams As EncoderParameters _
)
[C#]
public void SaveAdd(
   EncoderParameters encoderParams
);
[C++]
public: void SaveAdd(
   EncoderParameters* encoderParams
);
[JScript]
public function SaveAdd(
   encoderParams : EncoderParameters
);
```

Parameters

encoderParams

An **EncoderParameters** object that holds parameters required by the image encoder that is used by the save-add operation.

Return Value

This method does not return a value.

Requirements

Platforms: Windows 98, Windows NT 4.0, Windows Millennium Edition, Windows 2000, Windows XP Home Edition, Windows XP Professional, Windows Server 2003 family

Image.SaveAdd Method (Image, EncoderParameters)

Adds a frame to the file or stream specified in a previous call to the **Save** method.

```
[Visual Basic]
Overloads Public Sub SaveAdd( _
   ByVal image As Image, _
   ByVal encoderParams As EncoderParameters _
)
[C#]
public void SaveAdd(
   Image image,
   EncoderParameters encoderParams
);
[C++]
public: void SaveAdd(
   Image* image,
   EncoderParameters* encoderParams
);
[JScript]
public function SaveAdd(
   image : Image,
   encoderParams : EncoderParameters
);
```

Parameters

image

An **Image** object that contains the frame to add.

encoderParams

An **EncoderParameters** object that holds parameters required by the image encoder that is used by the save-add operation.

Return Value

This method does not return a value.

Requirements

Platforms: Windows 98, Windows NT 4.0, Windows Millennium Edition, Windows 2000, Windows XP Home Edition, Windows XP Professional, Windows Server 2003 family

Image.SelectActiveFrame Method

Selects the frame specified by the dimension and index.

```
[Visual Basic]
Public Function SelectActiveFrame( _
   ByVal dimension As FrameDimension, _
   ByVal frameIndex As Integer _
) As Integer
[C#]
public int SelectActiveFrame(
   FrameDimension dimension,
   int frameIndex
);
[C++]
public: int SelectActiveFrame(
   FrameDimension* dimension,
   int frameIndex
);
[JScript]
public function SelectActiveFrame(
   dimension : FrameDimension,
   frameIndex : int
) : int;
```

Parameters

dimension

A **FrameDimension** object that specifies the identity of the dimension type.

frameIndex

The index of the active frame.

Return Value

The index of the active frame.

Remarks

The possible values of the *dimensionID* parameter are properties of the **FrameDimension** object. Thesecan be used to identify an image by its time, resolution, or page number.

Calling this method causes all changes made to the previous frame to be discarded. Before selecting another frame, save all changes made to the current frame, including changes to pixel values and properties.

Requirements

Platforms: Windows 98, Windows NT 4.0, Windows Millennium Edition, Windows 2000, Windows XP Home Edition, Windows XP Professional, Windows Server 2003 family

Image.SetPropertyItem Method

Stores a property item (piece of metadata) in this **Image** object.

```
[Visual Basic]
Public Sub SetPropertyItem( _
   ByVal propitem As PropertyItem _
)
[C#]
public void SetPropertyItem(
   PropertyItem propitem
);
[C++]
public: void SetPropertyItem(
   PropertyItem* propitem
);
[JScript]
public function SetPropertyItem(
   propitem : PropertyItem
);
```

Parameters

propitem

The **PropertyItem** to be stored.

Return Value

This method does not return a value.

Remarks

If the image format does not support property items, this method throws System.ArgumentException with the message "Property not supported." If the image format supports property items but does not support the particular property you are attempting to set, this method ignores the attempt but does not throw an exception.

It is difficult to set property items because the **PropertyItem** class has no public constructors. One way to work around this restriction is to obtain a **PropertyItem** object by retrieving the **PropertyItems** property or calling the **GetPropertyItem** method of an **Image** object that already has property items. Then you can set the fields of the **PropertyItem** object and pass it to **SetPropertyItem**.

Requirements

Platforms: Windows 98, Windows NT 4.0, Windows Millennium Edition, Windows 2000, Windows XP Home Edition, Windows XP Professional, Windows Server 2003 family

ImageAnimator Class

Animates an image that has time-based frames.

System.Object
  System.Drawing.ImageAnimator

[Visual Basic]
```
NotInheritable Public Class ImageAnimator
```
[C#]
```
public sealed class ImageAnimator
```
[C++]
```
public __gc __sealed class ImageAnimator
```
[JScript]
```
public class ImageAnimator
```

Thread Safety

Any public static (**Shared** in Visual Basic) members of this type are safe for multithreaded operations. Any instance members are not guaranteed to be thread safe.

Requirements

Namespace: System.Drawing

Platforms: Windows 98, Windows NT 4.0, Windows Millennium Edition, Windows 2000, Windows XP Home Edition, Windows XP Professional, Windows Server 2003 family

Assembly: System.Drawing (in System.Drawing.dll)

ImageAnimator.Animate Method

Displays a multiple-frame image as an animation.

[Visual Basic]
```
Public Shared Sub Animate( _
   ByVal image As Image, _
   ByVal onFrameChangedHandler As EventHandler _
)
```
[C#]
```
public static void Animate(
   Image image,
   EventHandler onFrameChangedHandler
);
```
[C++]
```
public: static void Animate(
   Image* image,
   EventHandler* onFrameChangedHandler
);
```
[JScript]
```
public static function Animate(
   image : Image,
   onFrameChangedHandler : EventHandler
);
```

Parameters

image
  The **Image** object to animate.

onFrameChangedHandler
  An **EventHandler** object that specifies the method that is called when the animation frame changes.

Return Value

This method does not return a value.

Example

[Visual Basic, C#] This Windows Forms application demonstrates how to draw an animated image to the screen. The image is created from the animated GIF file SampleAnimation.gif located in the same folder as the application.

[Visual Basic]
```
Imports System
Imports System.Drawing
Imports System.Windows.Forms
Public Class animateImage
Inherits Form
'Create a Bitmpap Object.
Private animatedImage As New Bitmap("SampleAnimation.gif")
Private currentlyAnimating As Boolean = False
'This method begins the animation.
Public Sub AnimateImage()
If Not currentlyAnimating Then
'Begin the animation only once.
ImageAnimator.Animate(animatedImage, _
New EventHandler(AddressOf Me.OnFrameChanged))
currentlyAnimating = True
End If
End Sub
Private Sub OnFrameChanged(o As Object, e As EventArgs)
'Force a call to the Paint event handler.
Me.Invalidate()
End Sub
Protected Overrides Sub OnPaint(e As PaintEventArgs)
'Begin the animation.
AnimateImage()
'Get the next frame ready for rendering.
ImageAnimator.UpdateFrames()
'Draw the next frame in the animation.
e.Graphics.DrawImage(Me.animatedImage, New Point(0, 0))
End Sub
Public Shared Sub Main()
Application.Run(New animateImage())
End Sub
End Class
```

[C#]
```
using System;
using System.Drawing;
using System.Windows.Forms;
public class animateImage : Form {
//Create a Bitmpap Object.
Bitmap animatedImage = new Bitmap("SampleAnimation.gif");
bool currentlyAnimating = false;
//This method begins the animation.
public void AnimateImage() {
if (!currentlyAnimating) {
//Begin the animation only once.
ImageAnimator.Animate(animatedImage, new                          ↵
EventHandler(this.OnFrameChanged));
currentlyAnimating = true;
}
}
private void OnFrameChanged(object o, EventArgs e) {
//Force a call to the Paint event handler.
this.Invalidate();
}
protected override void OnPaint(PaintEventArgs e) {
//Begin the animation.
AnimateImage();
//Get the next frame ready for rendering.
ImageAnimator.UpdateFrames();
//Draw the next frame in the animation.
e.Graphics.DrawImage(this.animatedImage, new Point(0, 0));
}
public static void Main() {
Application.Run(new animateImage());
}
}
```

Requirements

Platforms: Windows 98, Windows NT 4.0, Windows Millennium Edition, Windows 2000, Windows XP Home Edition, Windows XP Professional, Windows Server 2003 family

ImageAnimator.CanAnimate Method

Returns a Boolean value indicating whether the specified image contains time-based frames.

```
[Visual Basic]
Public Shared Function CanAnimate( _
   ByVal image As Image _
) As Boolean
[C#]
public static bool CanAnimate(
   Image image
);
[C++]
public: static bool CanAnimate(
   Image* image
);
[JScript]
public static function CanAnimate(
   image : Image
) : Boolean;
```

Parameters

image
The **Image** object to test.

Return Value

This method returns **true** if the specified image contains time-based frames; otherwise, **false**.

Requirements

Platforms: Windows 98, Windows NT 4.0, Windows Millennium Edition, Windows 2000, Windows XP Home Edition, Windows XP Professional, Windows Server 2003 family

ImageAnimator.StopAnimate Method

Terminates a running animation.

```
[Visual Basic]
Public Shared Sub StopAnimate( _
   ByVal image As Image, _
   ByVal onFrameChangedHandler As EventHandler _
)
[C#]
public static void StopAnimate(
   Image image,
   EventHandler onFrameChangedHandler
);
[C++]
public: static void StopAnimate(
   Image* image,
   EventHandler* onFrameChangedHandler
);
[JScript]
public static function StopAnimate(
   image : Image,
   onFrameChangedHandler : EventHandler
);
```

Parameters

image
The **Image** object to stop animating.

onFrameChangedHandler
An **EventHandler** object that specifies the method that is called when the animation frame changes.

Return Value

This method does not return a value.

Requirements

Platforms: Windows 98, Windows NT 4.0, Windows Millennium Edition, Windows 2000, Windows XP Home Edition, Windows XP Professional, Windows Server 2003 family

ImageAnimator.UpdateFrames Method

Overload List

Advances the frame in all images currently being animated. The new frame is drawn the next time the image is rendered.

[Visual Basic] **Overloads Public Shared Sub UpdateFrames()**

[C#] **public static void UpdateFrames();**

[C++] **public: static void UpdateFrames();**

[JScript] **public static function UpdateFrames();**

Advances the frame in the specified image. The new frame is drawn the next time the image is rendered. This method applies only to images with time-based frames.

[Visual Basic] **Overloads Public Shared Sub UpdateFrames(Image)**

[C#] **public static void UpdateFrames(Image);**

[C++] **public: static void UpdateFrames(Image*);**

[JScript] **public static function UpdateFrames(Image);**

ImageAnimator.UpdateFrames Method ()

Advances the frame in all images currently being animated. The new frame is drawn the next time the image is rendered.

```
[Visual Basic]
Overloads Public Shared Sub UpdateFrames()
[C#]
public static void UpdateFrames();
[C++]
public: static void UpdateFrames();
[JScript]
public static function UpdateFrames();
```

Return Value

This method does not return a value.

Requirements

Platforms: Windows 98, Windows NT 4.0, Windows Millennium Edition, Windows 2000, Windows XP Home Edition, Windows XP Professional, Windows Server 2003 family

ImageAnimator.UpdateFrames Method (Image)

Advances the frame in the specified image. The new frame is drawn the next time the image is rendered. This method applies only to images with time-based frames.

[Visual Basic]
```
Overloads Public Shared Sub UpdateFrames( _
   ByVal image As Image _
)
```
[C#]
```
public static void UpdateFrames(
   Image image
);
```
[C++]
```
public: static void UpdateFrames(
   Image* image
);
```
[JScript]
```
public static function UpdateFrames(
   image : Image
);
```

Parameters

image

The **Image** object for which to update frames.

Return Value

This method does not return a value.

Requirements

Platforms: Windows 98, Windows NT 4.0, Windows Millennium Edition, Windows 2000, Windows XP Home Edition, Windows XP Professional, Windows Server 2003 family

ImageConverter Class

ImageConverter is a class that can be used to convert **Image** objects from one data type to another. Access this class through the **TypeDescriptor** object.

System.Object
  System.ComponentModel.TypeConverter
    System.Drawing.ImageConverter

[Visual Basic]
```
Public Class ImageConverter
   Inherits TypeConverter
```
[C#]
```
public class ImageConverter : TypeConverter
```
[C++]
```
public __gc class ImageConverter : public TypeConverter
```
[JScript]
```
public class ImageConverter extends TypeConverter
```

Thread Safety

Any public static (**Shared** in Visual Basic) members of this type are safe for multithreaded operations. Any instance members are not guaranteed to be thread safe.

Requirements

Namespace: System.Drawing

Platforms: Windows 98, Windows NT 4.0, Windows Millennium Edition, Windows 2000, Windows XP Home Edition, Windows XP Professional, Windows Server 2003 family

Assembly: System.Drawing (in System.Drawing.dll)

ImageConverter Constructor

Initializes a new instance of the **ImageConverter** class.

[Visual Basic]
```
Public Sub New()
```
[C#]
```
public ImageConverter();
```
[C++]
```
public: ImageConverter();
```
[JScript]
```
public function ImageConverter();
```

Requirements

Platforms: Windows 98, Windows NT 4.0, Windows Millennium Edition, Windows 2000, Windows XP Home Edition, Windows XP Professional, Windows Server 2003 family

ImageConverter.CanConvertFrom Method

Overload List

Determines whether this **ImageConverter** can convert an instance of a specified type to an **Image**, using the specified context.

[Visual Basic] **Overloads Overrides Public Function CanConvertFrom(ITypeDescriptorContext, Type) As Boolean**

[C#] **public override bool CanConvertFrom(ITypeDescriptorContext, Type);**

[C++] **public: bool CanConvertFrom(ITypeDescriptorContext*, Type*);**

[JScript] **public override function CanConvertFrom(ITypeDescriptorContext, Type) : Boolean;**

Inherited from **TypeConverter**.

[Visual Basic] **Overloads Public Function CanConvertFrom(Type) As Boolean**

[C#] **public bool CanConvertFrom(Type);**

[C++] **public: bool CanConvertFrom(Type*);**

[JScript] **public function CanConvertFrom(Type) : Boolean;**

ImageConverter.CanConvertFrom Method (ITypeDescriptorContext, Type)

Determines whether this **ImageConverter** can convert an instance of a specified type to an **Image**, using the specified context.

[Visual Basic]
```
Overrides Overloads Public Function CanConvertFrom( _
   ByVal context As ITypeDescriptorContext, _
   ByVal sourceType As Type _
) As Boolean
```
[C#]
```
public override bool CanConvertFrom(
   ITypeDescriptorContext context,
   Type sourceType
);
```
[C++]
```
public: bool CanConvertFrom(
   ITypeDescriptorContext* context,
   Type* sourceType
);
```
[JScript]
```
public override function CanConvertFrom(
   context : ITypeDescriptorContext,
   sourceType : Type
) : Boolean;
```

Parameters

context
  An **ITypeDescriptorContext** that provides a format context.

sourceType
  A **Type** that specifies the type you want to convert from.

Return Value

This method returns **true** if this **ImageConverter** can perform the conversion; otherwise, **false**.

Remarks

This method returns **true** only if *sourceType* is equal to typeof(System.Byte[]).

Requirements

Platforms: Windows 98, Windows NT 4.0, Windows Millennium Edition, Windows 2000, Windows XP Home Edition, Windows XP Professional, Windows Server 2003 family

ImageConverter.CanConvertTo Method

Overload List

Determines whether this **ImageConverter** can convert an **Image** to an instance of a specified type, using the specified context.

[Visual Basic] **Overloads Overrides Public Function CanConvertTo(ITypeDescriptorContext, Type) As Boolean**

[C#] **public override bool CanConvertTo(ITypeDescriptorContext, Type);**

[C++] **public: bool CanConvertTo(ITypeDescriptorContext*, Type*);**

[JScript] **public override function CanConvertTo(ITypeDescriptorContext, Type) : Boolean;**

Inherited from **TypeConverter**.

[Visual Basic] **Overloads Public Function CanConvertTo(Type) As Boolean**

[C#] **public bool CanConvertTo(Type);**

[C++] **public: bool CanConvertTo(Type*);**

[JScript] **public function CanConvertTo(Type) : Boolean;**

ImageConverter.CanConvertTo Method (ITypeDescriptorContext, Type)

Determines whether this **ImageConverter** can convert an **Image** to an instance of a specified type, using the specified context.

```
[Visual Basic]
Overrides Overloads Public Function CanConvertTo( _
   ByVal context As ITypeDescriptorContext, _
   ByVal destinationType As Type _
) As Boolean
[C#]
public override bool CanConvertTo(
   ITypeDescriptorContext context,
   Type destinationType
);
[C++]
public: bool CanConvertTo(
   ITypeDescriptorContext* context,
   Type* destinationType
);
[JScript]
public override function CanConvertTo(
   context : ITypeDescriptorContext,
   destinationType : Type
) : Boolean;
```

Parameters

context

An **ITypeDescriptorContext** that provides a format context.

destinationType

A **Type** that specifies the type you want to convert to.

Return Value

This method returns **true** if this **ImageConverter** can perform the conversion; otherwise, **false**.

Remarks

This method returns **true** only if *sourceType* is equal to typeof(System.Byte[]) or typeof(System.String).

Requirements

Platforms: Windows 98, Windows NT 4.0, Windows Millennium Edition, Windows 2000, Windows XP Home Edition, Windows XP Professional, Windows Server 2003 family

ImageConverter.ConvertFrom Method

Overload List

Converts a specified object to an **Image**.

[Visual Basic] **Overloads Overrides Public Function ConvertFrom(ITypeDescriptorContext, CultureInfo, Object) As Object**

[C#] **public override object ConvertFrom(ITypeDescriptorContext, CultureInfo, object);**

[C++] **public: Object* ConvertFrom(ITypeDescriptorContext*, CultureInfo*, Object*);**

[JScript] **public override function ConvertFrom(ITypeDescriptorContext, CultureInfo, Object) : Object;**

Inherited from **TypeConverter**.

[Visual Basic] **Overloads Public Function ConvertFrom(Object) As Object**

[C#] **public object ConvertFrom(object);**

[C++] **public: Object* ConvertFrom(Object*);**

[JScript] **public function ConvertFrom(Object) : Object;**

ImageConverter.ConvertFrom Method (ITypeDescriptorContext, CultureInfo, Object)

Converts a specified object to an **Image**.

```
[Visual Basic]
Overrides Overloads Public Function ConvertFrom( _
   ByVal context As ITypeDescriptorContext, _
   ByVal culture As CultureInfo, _
   ByVal value As Object _
) As Object
[C#]
public override object ConvertFrom(
   ITypeDescriptorContext context,
   CultureInfo culture,
   object value
);
[C++]
public: Object* ConvertFrom(
   ITypeDescriptorContext* context,
   CultureInfo* culture,
   Object* value
);
[JScript]
public override function ConvertFrom(
   context : ITypeDescriptorContext,
   culture : CultureInfo,
   value : Object
) : Object;
```

Parameters

context

An **ITypeDescriptorContext** that provides a format context.

culture

A **CultureInfo** that holds information about a specific culture.

value

The **Object** to be converted.

Return Value

If this method succeeds, it returns the **Image** that it created by converting the specified object. Otherwise, it throws an exception.

Requirements

Platforms: Windows 98, Windows NT 4.0, Windows Millennium Edition, Windows 2000, Windows XP Home Edition, Windows XP Professional, Windows Server 2003 family

ImageConverter.ConvertTo Method

Overload List

Converts an Image (or an object that can be cast to an Image) to the specified type.

[Visual Basic] **Overloads Overrides Public Function ConvertTo(ITypeDescriptorContext, CultureInfo, Object, Type) As Object**

[C#] **public override object ConvertTo(ITypeDescriptor-Context, CultureInfo, object, Type);**

[C++] **public: Object* ConvertTo(ITypeDescriptorContext*, CultureInfo*, Object*, Type*);**

[JScript] **public override function ConvertTo(IType-DescriptorContext, CultureInfo, Object, Type) : Object;**

Inherited from **TypeConverter**.

[Visual Basic] **Overloads Public Function ConvertTo(Object, Type) As Object**

[C#] **public object ConvertTo(object, Type);**

[C++] **public: Object* ConvertTo(Object*, Type*);**

[JScript] **public function ConvertTo(Object, Type) : Object;**

ImageConverter.ConvertTo Method (ITypeDescriptorContext, CultureInfo, Object, Type)

Converts an Image (or an object that can be cast to an Image) to the specified type.

[Visual Basic]
```
Overrides Overloads Public Function ConvertTo( _
   ByVal context As ITypeDescriptorContext, _
   ByVal culture As CultureInfo, _
   ByVal value As Object, _
   ByVal destinationType As Type _
) As Object
```
[C#]
```
public override object ConvertTo(
   ITypeDescriptorContext context,
   CultureInfo culture,
   object value,
   Type destinationType
);
```
[C++]
```
public: Object* ConvertTo(
   ITypeDescriptorContext* context,
   CultureInfo* culture,
   Object* value,
   Type* destinationType
);
```
[JScript]
```
public override function ConvertTo(
   context : ITypeDescriptorContext,
   culture : CultureInfo,
   value : Object,
   destinationType : Type
) : Object;
```

Parameters

context

A formatter context. This object can be used to get more information about the environment this converter is being called from. This may be a null reference (**Nothing** in Visual Basic), so you should always check. Also, properties on the context object may also return a null reference (**Nothing**).

culture

A **CultureInfo** object that specifies formatting conventions used by a particular culture.

value

The **Image** to convert.

destinationType

The **Type** to convert the **Image** to.

Return Value

This method returns the converted object.

Remarks

The most common type conversion is to and from a string type. The default implementation calls the **ToString** method of the object if the object is valid and if the destination type is string. If this method cannot convert the specified object to the destination type, it throws a **NotSupportedException** exception.

Requirements

Platforms: Windows 98, Windows NT 4.0, Windows Millennium Edition, Windows 2000, Windows XP Home Edition, Windows XP Professional, Windows Server 2003 family

ImageConverter.GetProperties Method

Overload List

Gets the set of properties for this type.

[Visual Basic] **Overloads Overrides Public Function GetProperties(ITypeDescriptorContext, Object, Attribute()) As PropertyDescriptorCollection**

[C#] **public override PropertyDescriptorCollection GetProperties(ITypeDescriptorContext, object, Attribute[]);**

[C++] **public: PropertyDescriptorCollection* Get-Properties(ITypeDescriptorContext*, Object*, Attribute[]);**

[JScript] **public override function GetProperties(IType-DescriptorContext, Object, Attribute[]) : PropertyDescriptorCollection;**

Inherited from **TypeConverter**.

[Visual Basic] **Overloads Public Function GetProperties(Object) As PropertyDescriptorCollection**

[C#] **public PropertyDescriptorCollection GetProperties(object);**

[C++] **public: PropertyDescriptorCollection* GetProperties(Object*);**

[JScript] **public function GetProperties(Object) : PropertyDescriptorCollection;**

Inherited from **TypeConverter**.

[Visual Basic] **Overloads Public Function GetProperties(ITypeDescriptorContext, Object) As PropertyDescriptorCollection**

[C#] **public PropertyDescriptorCollection GetProperties(ITypeDescriptorContext, object);**

[C++] **public: PropertyDescriptorCollection* GetProperties(ITypeDescriptorContext*, Object*);**

[JScript] **public function GetProperties(ITypeDescriptorContext, Object) : PropertyDescriptorCollection;**

ImageConverter.GetProperties Method (ITypeDescriptorContext, Object, Attribute[])

Gets the set of properties for this type.

[Visual Basic]
```
Overrides Overloads Public Function GetProperties( _
   ByVal context As ITypeDescriptorContext, _
   ByVal value As Object, _
   ByVal attributes() As Attribute _
) As PropertyDescriptorCollection
```
[C#]
```
public override PropertyDescriptorCollection GetProperties(
   ITypeDescriptorContext context,
   object value,
   Attribute[] attributes
);
```
[C++]
```
public: PropertyDescriptorCollection* GetProperties(
   ITypeDescriptorContext* context,
   Object* value,
   Attribute* attributes[]
);
```
[JScript]
```
public override function GetProperties(
   context : ITypeDescriptorContext,
   value : Object,
   attributes : Attribute[]
) : PropertyDescriptorCollection;
```

Parameters

context
A type descriptor through which additional context can be provided.

value
The value of the object to get the properties for.

attributes
The value of the object to get the properties for.

Return Value

The set of properties that should be exposed for this data type. If no properties should be exposed, this can return a null reference (**Nothing** in Visual Basic). The default implementation always returns a null reference (**Nothing**).

Remarks

By default, a type does not return any properties. An easy implementation of this method calls the **TypeDescriptor.GetProperties** method for the correct data type.

Requirements

Platforms: Windows 98, Windows NT 4.0, Windows Millennium Edition, Windows 2000, Windows XP Home Edition, Windows XP Professional, Windows Server 2003 family

ImageConverter.GetPropertiesSupported Method

Overload List

Indicates whether this object supports properties. By default, this is **False**.

[Visual Basic] **Overloads Overrides Public Function GetPropertiesSupported(ITypeDescriptorContext) As Boolean**

[C#] **public override bool GetPropertiesSupported(ITypeDescriptorContext);**

[C++] **public: bool GetPropertiesSupported(ITypeDescriptorContext*);**

[JScript] **public override function GetPropertiesSupported(ITypeDescriptorContext) : Boolean;**

Inherited from **TypeConverter**.

[Visual Basic] **Overloads Public Function GetPropertiesSupported() As Boolean**

[C#] **public bool GetPropertiesSupported();**

[C++] **public: bool GetPropertiesSupported();**

[JScript] **public function GetPropertiesSupported() : Boolean;**

ImageConverter.GetPropertiesSupported Method (ITypeDescriptorContext)

Indicates whether this object supports properties. By default, this is **False**.

[Visual Basic]
```
Overrides Overloads Public Function GetPropertiesSupported( _
   ByVal context As ITypeDescriptorContext _
) As Boolean
```
[C#]
```
public override bool GetPropertiesSupported(
   ITypeDescriptorContext context
);
```
[C++]
```
public: bool GetPropertiesSupported(
   ITypeDescriptorContext* context
);
```
[JScript]
```
public override function GetPropertiesSupported(
   context : ITypeDescriptorContext
) : Boolean;
```

Parameters

context

A type descriptor through which additional context can be provided.

Return Value

This method returns **true** if the **GetProperties** method should be called to find the properties of this object.

Requirements

Platforms: Windows 98, Windows NT 4.0,
Windows Millennium Edition, Windows 2000,
Windows XP Home Edition, Windows XP Professional,
Windows Server 2003 family

ImageFormatConverter Class

ImageFormatConverter is a class that can be used to convert colors from one data type to another. Access this class through the **TypeDescriptor** object.

System.Object
  System.ComponentModel.TypeConverter
    System.Drawing.ImageFormatConverter

[Visual Basic]
```
Public Class ImageFormatConverter
   Inherits TypeConverter
```
[C#]
```
public class ImageFormatConverter : TypeConverter
```
[C++]
```
public __gc class ImageFormatConverter : public TypeConverter
```
[JScript]
```
public class ImageFormatConverter extends TypeConverter
```

Thread Safety

Any public static (**Shared** in Visual Basic) members of this type are safe for multithreaded operations. Any instance members are not guaranteed to be thread safe.

Requirements

Namespace: System.Drawing

Platforms: Windows 98, Windows NT 4.0, Windows Millennium Edition, Windows 2000, Windows XP Home Edition, Windows XP Professional, Windows Server 2003 family

Assembly: System.Drawing (in System.Drawing.dll)

ImageFormatConverter Constructor

Initializes a new instance of the **ImageFormatConverter** class.

[Visual Basic]
```
Public Sub New()
```
[C#]
```
public ImageFormatConverter();
```
[C++]
```
public: ImageFormatConverter();
```
[JScript]
```
public function ImageFormatConverter();
```

Requirements

Platforms: Windows 98, Windows NT 4.0, Windows Millennium Edition, Windows 2000, Windows XP Home Edition, Windows XP Professional, Windows Server 2003 family

ImageFormatConverter.CanConvertFrom Method

Overload List

Indicates whether this converter can convert an object in the specified source type to the native type of the converter.

[Visual Basic] **Overloads Overrides Public Function CanConvertFrom(ITypeDescriptorContext, Type) As Boolean**

[C#] **public override bool CanConvertFrom(ITypeDescriptorContext, Type);**

[C++] **public: bool CanConvertFrom(ITypeDescriptorContext*, Type*);**

[JScript] **public override function CanConvertFrom(ITypeDescriptorContext, Type) : Boolean;**

Inherited from **TypeConverter**.

[Visual Basic] **Overloads Public Function CanConvertFrom(Type) As Boolean**

[C#] **public bool CanConvertFrom(Type);**

[C++] **public: bool CanConvertFrom(Type*);**

[JScript] **public function CanConvertFrom(Type) : Boolean;**

ImageFormatConverter.CanConvertFrom Method (ITypeDescriptorContext, Type)

Indicates whether this converter can convert an object in the specified source type to the native type of the converter.

[Visual Basic]
```
Overrides Overloads Public Function CanConvertFrom( _
   ByVal context As ITypeDescriptorContext, _
   ByVal sourceType As Type _
) As Boolean
```
[C#]
```
public override bool CanConvertFrom(
   ITypeDescriptorContext context,
   Type sourceType
);
```
[C++]
```
public: bool CanConvertFrom(
   ITypeDescriptorContext* context,
   Type* sourceType
);
```
[JScript]
```
public override function CanConvertFrom(
   context : ITypeDescriptorContext,
   sourceType : Type
) : Boolean;
```

Parameters

context

A formatter context. This object can be used to get more information about the environment this converter is being called from. This may be a null reference (**Nothing** in Visual Basic), so you should always check. Also, properties on the context object may also return a null reference (**Nothing**).

sourceType

The type you want to convert from.

Return Value

This method returns **true** if this object can perform the conversion.

Requirements

Platforms: Windows 98, Windows NT 4.0, Windows Millennium Edition, Windows 2000, Windows XP Home Edition, Windows XP Professional, Windows Server 2003 family

ImageFormatConverter.CanConvertTo Method

Overload List

Gets a value indicating whether this converter can convert an object to the specified destination type using the context.

[Visual Basic] **Overloads Overrides Public Function CanConvertTo(ITypeDescriptorContext, Type) As Boolean**

[C#] **public override bool CanConvertTo(ITypeDescriptorContext, Type);**

[C++] **public: bool CanConvertTo(ITypeDescriptorContext*, Type*);**

[JScript] **public override function CanConvertTo(ITypeDescriptorContext, Type) : Boolean;**

Inherited from **TypeConverter**.

[Visual Basic] **Overloads Public Function CanConvertTo(Type) As Boolean**

[C#] **public bool CanConvertTo(Type);**

[C++] **public: bool CanConvertTo(Type*);**

[JScript] **public function CanConvertTo(Type) : Boolean;**

ImageFormatConverter.CanConvertTo Method (ITypeDescriptorContext, Type)

Gets a value indicating whether this converter can convert an object to the specified destination type using the context.

```
[Visual Basic]
Overrides Overloads Public Function CanConvertTo( _
   ByVal context As ITypeDescriptorContext, _
   ByVal destinationType As Type _
) As Boolean
[C#]
public override bool CanConvertTo(
   ITypeDescriptorContext context,
   Type destinationType
);
[C++]
public: bool CanConvertTo(
   ITypeDescriptorContext* context,
   Type* destinationType
);
[JScript]
public override function CanConvertTo(
   context : ITypeDescriptorContext,
   destinationType : Type
) : Boolean;
```

Parameters

context

An **ITypeDescriptorContext** that specifies the context for this type conversion.

destinationType

The **Type** that represents the type to which you want to convert this **ImageFormat** object.

Return Value

This method returns **true** if this object can perform the conversion.

Requirements

Platforms: Windows 98, Windows NT 4.0, Windows Millennium Edition, Windows 2000, Windows XP Home Edition, Windows XP Professional, Windows Server 2003 family

ImageFormatConverter.ConvertFrom Method

Overload List

Converts the specified object to an **ImageFormat** object.

[Visual Basic] **Overloads Overrides Public Function ConvertFrom(ITypeDescriptorContext, CultureInfo, Object) As Object**

[C#] **public override object ConvertFrom(ITypeDescriptorContext, CultureInfo, object);**

[C++] **public: Object* ConvertFrom(ITypeDescriptorContext*, CultureInfo*, Object*);**

[JScript] **public override function ConvertFrom(ITypeDescriptorContext, CultureInfo, Object) : Object;**

Inherited from **TypeConverter**.

[Visual Basic] **Overloads Public Function ConvertFrom(Object) As Object**

[C#] **public object ConvertFrom(object);**

[C++] **public: Object* ConvertFrom(Object*);**

[JScript] **public function ConvertFrom(Object) : Object;**

ImageFormatConverter.ConvertFrom Method (ITypeDescriptorContext, CultureInfo, Object)

Converts the specified object to an **ImageFormat** object.

```
[Visual Basic]
Overrides Overloads Public Function ConvertFrom( _
   ByVal context As ITypeDescriptorContext, _
   ByVal culture As CultureInfo, _
   ByVal value As Object _
) As Object
[C#]
public override object ConvertFrom(
   ITypeDescriptorContext context,
   CultureInfo culture,
   object value
);
[C++]
public: Object* ConvertFrom(
   ITypeDescriptorContext* context,
   CultureInfo* culture,
   Object* value
);
[JScript]
public override function ConvertFrom(
   context : ITypeDescriptorContext,
   culture : CultureInfo,
   value : Object
) : Object;
```

Parameters

context

A formatter context. This object can be used to get more information about the environment this converter is being called from. This may be a null reference (**Nothing** in Visual Basic), so you should always check. Also, properties on the context object may also return a null reference (**Nothing**).

culture

A **CultureInfo** object that specifies formatting conventions for a particular culture.

value

The object to convert.

Return Value

The converted object. This will pass an exception if the conversion could not be performed.

Requirements

Platforms: Windows 98, Windows NT 4.0, Windows Millennium Edition, Windows 2000, Windows XP Home Edition, Windows XP Professional, Windows Server 2003 family

ImageFormatConverter.ConvertTo Method

Overload List

Converts the specified object to the specified type.

[Visual Basic] **Overloads Overrides Public Function ConvertTo(ITypeDescriptorContext, CultureInfo, Object, Type) As Object**

[C#] **public override object ConvertTo(ITypeDescriptorContext, CultureInfo, object, Type);**

[C++] **public: Object* ConvertTo(ITypeDescriptorContext*, CultureInfo*, Object*, Type*);**

[JScript] **public override function ConvertTo(ITypeDescriptorContext, CultureInfo, Object, Type) : Object;**

Inherited from **TypeConverter**.

[Visual Basic] **Overloads Public Function ConvertTo(Object, Type) As Object**

[C#] **public object ConvertTo(object, Type);**

[C++] **public: Object* ConvertTo(Object*, Type*);**

[JScript] **public function ConvertTo(Object, Type) : Object;**

ImageFormatConverter.ConvertTo Method (ITypeDescriptorContext, CultureInfo, Object, Type)

Converts the specified object to the specified type.

```
[Visual Basic]
Overrides Overloads Public Function ConvertTo( _
   ByVal context As ITypeDescriptorContext, _
   ByVal culture As CultureInfo, _
   ByVal value As Object, _
   ByVal destinationType As Type _
) As Object
[C#]
public override object ConvertTo(
   ITypeDescriptorContext context,
   CultureInfo culture,
   object value,
   Type destinationType
);
[C++]
public: Object* ConvertTo(
   ITypeDescriptorContext* context,
   CultureInfo* culture,
   Object* value,
   Type* destinationType
);
[JScript]
public override function ConvertTo(
   context : ITypeDescriptorContext,
   culture : CultureInfo,
   value : Object,
   destinationType : Type
) : Object;
```

Parameters

context

A formatter context. This object can be used to get more information about the environment this converter is being called from. This may be a null reference (**Nothing** in Visual Basic), so you should always check. Also, properties on the context object may also return a null reference (**Nothing**).

culture

A **CultureInfo** object that specifies formatting conventions for a particular culture.

value

The object to convert.

destinationType

The type to convert the object to.

Return Value

The converted object.

Remarks

The most common type conversion is to and from a string type. The default implementation calls the **ToString** method of the object if the object is valid and if the destination type is **string**. If this method cannot convert the specified object to the specified destination type, it throws a **NotSupportedException** exception.

Requirements

Platforms: Windows 98, Windows NT 4.0, Windows Millennium Edition, Windows 2000, Windows XP Home Edition, Windows XP Professional, Windows Server 2003 family

ImageFormatConverter.GetStandardValues Method

Overload List

Gets a collection that contains a set of standard values for the data type this validator is designed for. Returns a null reference (**Nothing** in Visual Basic) if the data type does not support a standard set of values.

[Visual Basic] **Overloads Overrides Public Function GetStandardValues(ITypeDescriptorContext) As StandardValuesCollection**

[C#] **public override StandardValuesCollection GetStandardValues(ITypeDescriptorContext);**

[C++] **public: StandardValuesCollection* GetStandardValues(ITypeDescriptorContext*);**

[JScript] **public override function GetStandardValues(ITypeDescriptorContext) : StandardValuesCollection;**

Inherited from **TypeConverter**.

[Visual Basic] **Overloads Public Function GetStandardValues() As ICollection**

[C#] **public ICollection GetStandardValues();**

[C++] **public: ICollection* GetStandardValues();**

[JScript] **public function GetStandardValues() : ICollection;**

ImageFormatConverter.GetStandardValues Method (ITypeDescriptorContext)

Gets a collection that contains a set of standard values for the data type this validator is designed for. Returns a null reference (**Nothing** in Visual Basic) if the data type does not support a standard set of values.

[Visual Basic]
```
Overrides Overloads Public Function GetStandardValues( _
   ByVal context As ITypeDescriptorContext _
) As StandardValuesCollection
```
[C#]
```
public override StandardValuesCollection GetStandardValues(
   ITypeDescriptorContext context
);
```
[C++]
```
public: StandardValuesCollection* GetStandardValues(
   ITypeDescriptorContext* context
);
```
[JScript]
```
public override function GetStandardValues(
   context : ITypeDescriptorContext
) : StandardValuesCollection;
```

Parameters

context

A formatter context. This object can be used to get more information about the environment this converter is being called from. This may be a null reference (**Nothing** in Visual Basic), so you should always check. Also, properties on the context object may also return a null reference (**Nothing**).

Return Value

A collection that contains a standard set of valid values, or a null reference (**Nothing** in Visual Basic). The default implementation always returns a null reference (**Nothing**).

Requirements

Platforms: Windows 98, Windows NT 4.0, Windows Millennium Edition, Windows 2000, Windows XP Home Edition, Windows XP Professional, Windows Server 2003 family

ImageFormatConverter.GetStandardValuesSupported Method

Overload List

Indicates whether this object supports a standard set of values that can be picked from a list.

[Visual Basic] **Overloads Overrides Public Function GetStandardValuesSupported(ITypeDescriptorContext) As Boolean**

[C#] **public override bool GetStandardValuesSupported(ITypeDescriptorContext);**

[C++] **public: bool GetStandardValuesSupported(ITypeDescriptorContext*);**

[JScript] **public override function GetStandardValuesSupported(ITypeDescriptorContext) : Boolean;**

Inherited from **TypeConverter**.

[Visual Basic] **Overloads Public Function GetStandardValuesSupported() As Boolean**

[C#] **public bool GetStandardValuesSupported();**

[C++] **public: bool GetStandardValuesSupported();**

[JScript] **public function GetStandardValuesSupported() : Boolean;**

ImageFormatConverter.GetStandardValuesSupported Method (ITypeDescriptorContext)

Indicates whether this object supports a standard set of values that can be picked from a list.

[Visual Basic]
```
Overrides Overloads Public Function GetStandardValuesSupported( _
   ByVal context As ITypeDescriptorContext _
) As Boolean
```
[C#]
```
public override bool GetStandardValuesSupported(
   ITypeDescriptorContext context
);
```
[C++]
```
public: bool GetStandardValuesSupported(
   ITypeDescriptorContext* context
);
```
[JScript]
```
public override function GetStandardValuesSupported(
   context : ITypeDescriptorContext
) : Boolean;
```

Parameters

context

A type descriptor through which additional context can be provided.

Return Value

This method returns **true** if the **GetStandardValues** method should be called to find a common set of values the object supports.

Requirements

Platforms: Windows 98, Windows NT 4.0, Windows Millennium Edition, Windows 2000, Windows XP Home Edition, Windows XP Professional, Windows Server 2003 family

Image.GetThumbnailImage-Abort Delegate

Provides a callback method for determining when the **GetThumbnailImage** method should prematurely cancel execution.

[Visual Basic]

```
<Serializable>
Public Delegate Function Sub Image.GetThumbnailImageAbort() As _
   Boolean
```

[C#]

```
[Serializable]
public delegate bool Image.GetThumbnailImageAbort();
```

[C++]

```
[Serializable]
public __gc __delegate bool Image.GetThumbnailImageAbort();
```

[JScript] In JScript, you can use the delegates in the .NET Framework, but you cannot define your own.

Parameters [Visual Basic, C#, C++]

The declaration of your callback method must have the same parameters as the **Image.GetThumbnailImageAbort** delegate declaration.

Return Value

This method returns **true** if it decides that the **GetThumbnailImage** method should prematurely stop execution; otherwise, it returns **false**.

Requirements

Namespace: System.Drawing

Platforms: Windows 98, Windows NT 4.0, Windows Millennium Edition, Windows 2000, Windows XP Home Edition, Windows XP Professional, Windows Server 2003 family

Assembly: System.Drawing (in System.Drawing.dll)

KnownColor Enumeration

Specifies the known system colors.

[Visual Basic]
```
<Serializable>
Public Enum KnownColor
```
[C#]
```
[Serializable]
public enum KnownColor
```
[C++]
```
[Serializable]
__value public enum KnownColor
```
[JScript]
```
public
   Serializable
enum KnownColor
```

Members

Member name	Description
ActiveBorder	A system-defined color.
ActiveCaption	A system-defined color.
ActiveCaptionText	A system-defined color.
AliceBlue	A system-defined color.
AntiqueWhite	A system-defined color.
AppWorkspace	A system-defined color.
Aqua	A system-defined color.
Aquamarine	A system-defined color.
Azure	A system-defined color.
Beige	A system-defined color.
Bisque	A system-defined color.
Black	A system-defined color.
BlanchedAlmond	A system-defined color.
Blue	A system-defined color.
BlueViolet	A system-defined color.
Brown	A system-defined color.
BurlyWood	A system-defined color.
CadetBlue	A system-defined color.
Chartreuse	A system-defined color.
Chocolate	A system-defined color.
Control	A system-defined color.
ControlDark	A system-defined color.
ControlDarkDark	A system-defined color.
ControlLight	A system-defined color.
ControlLightLight	A system-defined color.
ControlText	A system-defined color.
Coral	A system-defined color.
CornflowerBlue	[To be supplied.]
Cornsilk	A system-defined color.
Crimson	A system-defined color.
Cyan	A system-defined color.
DarkBlue	A system-defined color.
DarkCyan	A system-defined color.
DarkGoldenrod	A system-defined color.
DarkGray	A system-defined color.
DarkGreen	A system-defined color.
DarkKhaki	A system-defined color.
DarkMagenta	A system-defined color.
DarkOliveGreen	A system-defined color.
DarkOrange	A system-defined color.
DarkOrchid	A system-defined color.
DarkRed	A system-defined color.
DarkSalmon	A system-defined color.
DarkSeaGreen	A system-defined color.
DarkSlateBlue	A system-defined color.
DarkSlateGray	A system-defined color.
DarkTurquoise	A system-defined color.
DarkViolet	A system-defined color.
DeepPink	A system-defined color.
DeepSkyBlue	A system-defined color.
Desktop	A system-defined color.
DimGray	A system-defined color.
DodgerBlue	A system-defined color.
Firebrick	A system-defined color.
FloralWhite	A system-defined color.
ForestGreen	A system-defined color.
Fuchsia	A system-defined color.
Gainsboro	A system-defined color.
GhostWhite	A system-defined color.
Gold	A system-defined color.
Goldenrod	A system-defined color.
Gray	A system-defined color.
GrayText	A system-defined color.
Green	A system-defined color.
GreenYellow	A system-defined color.
Highlight	A system-defined color.
HighlightText	A system-defined color.
Honeydew	A system-defined color.
HotPink	A system-defined color.
HotTrack	A system-defined color.
InactiveBorder	A system-defined color.
InactiveCaption	A system-defined color.
InactiveCaptionText	A system-defined color.
IndianRed	A system-defined color.
Indigo	A system-defined color.
Info	A system-defined color.
InfoText	A system-defined color.
Ivory	A system-defined color.
Khaki	A system-defined color.
Lavender	A system-defined color.
LavenderBlush	A system-defined color.
LawnGreen	A system-defined color.
LemonChiffon	A system-defined color.
LightBlue	A system-defined color.

Member name	Description
LightCoral	A system-defined color.
LightCyan	A system-defined color.
LightGoldenrodYellow	A system-defined color.
LightGray	A system-defined color.
LightGreen	A system-defined color.
LightPink	A system-defined color.
LightSalmon	A system-defined color.
LightSeaGreen	A system-defined color.
LightSkyBlue	A system-defined color.
LightSlateGray	A system-defined color.
LightSteelBlue	A system-defined color.
LightYellow	A system-defined color.
Lime	A system-defined color.
LimeGreen	A system-defined color.
Linen	A system-defined color.
Magenta	A system-defined color.
Maroon	A system-defined color.
MediumAquamarine	A system-defined color.
MediumBlue	A system-defined color.
MediumOrchid	A system-defined color.
MediumPurple	A system-defined color.
MediumSeaGreen	A system-defined color.
MediumSlateBlue	A system-defined color.
MediumSpringGreen	A system-defined color.
MediumTurquoise	A system-defined color.
MediumVioletRed	A system-defined color.
Menu	A system-defined color.
MenuText	A system-defined color.
MidnightBlue	A system-defined color.
MintCream	A system-defined color.
MistyRose	A system-defined color.
Moccasin	A system-defined color.
NavajoWhite	A system-defined color.
Navy	A system-defined color.
OldLace	A system-defined color.
Olive	A system-defined color.
OliveDrab	A system-defined color.
Orange	A system-defined color.
OrangeRed	A system-defined color.
Orchid	A system-defined color.
PaleGoldenrod	A system-defined color.
PaleGreen	A system-defined color.
PaleTurquoise	A system-defined color.
PaleVioletRed	A system-defined color.
PapayaWhip	A system-defined color.
PeachPuff	A system-defined color.
Peru	A system-defined color.
Pink	A system-defined color.
Plum	A system-defined color.
PowderBlue	A system-defined color.
Purple	A system-defined color.
Red	A system-defined color.
RosyBrown	A system-defined color.
RoyalBlue	A system-defined color.
SaddleBrown	A system-defined color.
Salmon	A system-defined color.
SandyBrown	A system-defined color.
ScrollBar	A system-defined color.
SeaGreen	A system-defined color.
SeaShell	A system-defined color.
Sienna	A system-defined color.
Silver	A system-defined color.
SkyBlue	A system-defined color.
SlateBlue	A system-defined color.
SlateGray	A system-defined color.
Snow	A system-defined color.
SpringGreen	A system-defined color.
SteelBlue	A system-defined color.
Tan	A system-defined color.
Teal	A system-defined color.
Thistle	A system-defined color.
Tomato	A system-defined color.
Transparent	A system-defined color.
Turquoise	A system-defined color.
Violet	A system-defined color.
Wheat	A system-defined color.
White	A system-defined color.
WhiteSmoke	A system-defined color.
Window	A system-defined color.
WindowFrame	A system-defined color.
WindowText	A system-defined color.
Yellow	A system-defined color.
YellowGreen	A system-defined color.

Requirements

Namespace: System.Drawing

Platforms: Windows 98, Windows NT 4.0, Windows Millennium Edition, Windows 2000, Windows XP Home Edition, Windows XP Professional, Windows Server 2003 family

Assembly: System.Drawing (in System.Drawing.dll)

Pen Class

Defines an object used to draw lines and curves. This class cannot be inherited.

For a list of all members of this type, see **Pen Members**.

System.Object
  System.MarshalByRefObject
    System.Drawing.Pen

```
[Visual Basic]
NotInheritable Public Class Pen
   Inherits MarshalByRefObject
   Implements ICloneable, IDisposable
[C#]
public sealed class Pen : MarshalByRefObject, ICloneable,
   IDisposable
[C++]
public __gc __sealed class Pen : public MarshalByRefObject,
   ICloneable, IDisposable
[JScript]
public class Pen extends MarshalByRefObject implements ICloneable,
   IDisposable
```

Thread Safety

Any public static (**Shared** in Visual Basic) members of this type are safe for multithreaded operations. Any instance members are not guaranteed to be thread safe.

Remarks

A **Pen** object draws a line of specified width and style. Use the **DashStyle** property to draw several varieties of dashed lines. The line drawn by a **Pen** object can be filled in a variety of fill styles, including solid colors and textures. The fill style depends on brush or texture that is used as the fill object.

Requirements

Namespace: System.Drawing

Platforms: Windows 98, Windows NT 4.0, Windows Millennium Edition, Windows 2000, Windows XP Home Edition, Windows XP Professional, Windows Server 2003 family, .NET Compact Framework - Windows CE .NET

Assembly: System.Drawing (in System.Drawing.dll)

Pen Constructor

Initializes a new instance of the **Pen** class with the specified color.

Overload List

Initializes a new instance of the **Pen** class with the specified **Brush** object.

[Visual Basic] **Public Sub New(Brush)**

[C#] **public Pen(Brush);**

[C++] **public: Pen(Brush*);**

[JScript] **public function Pen(Brush);**

Initializes a new instance of the **Pen** class with the specified color.

Supported by the .NET Compact Framework.

[Visual Basic] **Public Sub New(Color)**

[C#] **public Pen(Color);**

[C++] **public: Pen(Color);**

[JScript] **public function Pen(Color);**

Initializes a new instance of the **Pen** class with the specified **Brush** object and **Width**.

[Visual Basic] **Public Sub New(Brush, Single)**

[C#] **public Pen(Brush, float);**

[C++] **public: Pen(Brush*, float);**

[JScript] **public function Pen(Brush, float);**

Initializes a new instance of the **Pen** class with the specified **Color** and **Width** properties.

[Visual Basic] **Public Sub New(Color, Single)**

[C#] **public Pen(Color, float);**

[C++] **public: Pen(Color, float);**

[JScript] **public function Pen(Color, float);**

Pen Constructor (Brush)

Initializes a new instance of the **Pen** class with the specified **Brush** object.

```
[Visual Basic]
Public Sub New( _
   ByVal brush As Brush _
)
[C#]
public Pen(
   Brush brush
);
[C++]
public: Pen(
   Brush* brush
);
[JScript]
public function Pen(
   brush : Brush
);
```

Parameters

brush
    A **Brush** object that determines the fill properties of this **Pen** object.

Remarks

The **Brush** property determines how the **Pen** object draws lines. Lines are drawn as if they are filled rectangles, with the characteristics of the specified **Brush** object.

The **Width** property of the new **Pen** object is set to 1 (the default).

Requirements

Platforms: Windows 98, Windows NT 4.0, Windows Millennium Edition, Windows 2000, Windows XP Home Edition, Windows XP Professional, Windows Server 2003 family

Pen Constructor (Color)

Initializes a new instance of the **Pen** class with the specified color.

```
[Visual Basic]
Public Sub New( _
   ByVal color As Color _
)
[C#]
public Pen(
   Color color
);
[C++]
public: Pen(
   Color color
);
[JScript]
public function Pen(
   color : Color
);
```

Parameters

color

A **Color** structure that indicates the color of this **Pen** object.

Remarks

The **Color** property is set to the color specified by the *color* parameter. The **Width** property is set to 1 (the default).

Requirements

Platforms: Windows 98, Windows NT 4.0, Windows Millennium Edition, Windows 2000, Windows XP Home Edition, Windows XP Professional, Windows Server 2003 family, .NET Compact Framework - Windows CE .NET

Pen Constructor (Brush, Single)

Initializes a new instance of the **Pen** class with the specified **Brush** object and **Width**.

```
[Visual Basic]
Public Sub New( _
   ByVal brush As Brush, _
   ByVal width As Single _
)
[C#]
public Pen(
   Brush brush,
   float width
);
[C++]
public: Pen(
   Brush* brush,
   float width
);
[JScript]
public function Pen(
   brush : Brush,
   width : float
);
```

Parameters

brush

A **Brush** object that determines the characteristics of this **Pen** object.

width

The width of the new **Pen** object.

Remarks

The **Brush** object is set to the color specified in the *brush* parameter, the **Width** property is set to the value specified in the *width* parameter, and the units are set to **World**.

Note that the *brush* parameter also specifies the **Color** property of this **Pen** object.

Requirements

Platforms: Windows 98, Windows NT 4.0, Windows Millennium Edition, Windows 2000, Windows XP Home Edition, Windows XP Professional, Windows Server 2003 family

Pen Constructor (Color, Single)

Initializes a new instance of the **Pen** class with the specified **Color** and **Width** properties.

```
[Visual Basic]
Public Sub New( _
   ByVal color As Color, _
   ByVal width As Single _
)
[C#]
public Pen(
   Color color,
   float width
);
[C++]
public: Pen(
   Color color,
   float width
);
[JScript]
public function Pen(
   color : Color,
   width : float
);
```

Parameters

color

A **Color** structure that indicates the color of this **Pen** object.

width

A value indicating the width of this **Pen** object.

Remarks

The **Color** property is set to the color specified by the *color* parameter. The **Width** property is set to the value specified in the *width* parameter.

Requirements

Platforms: Windows 98, Windows NT 4.0, Windows Millennium Edition, Windows 2000, Windows XP Home Edition, Windows XP Professional, Windows Server 2003 family

Pen.Alignment Property

Gets or sets the alignment for this **Pen** object.

```
[Visual Basic]
Public Property Alignment As PenAlignment
[C#]
public PenAlignment Alignment {get; set;}
[C++]
public: __property PenAlignment get_Alignment();
public: __property void set_Alignment(PenAlignment);
[JScript]
public function get Alignment() : PenAlignment;
public function set Alignment(PenAlignment);
```

Property Value

A **PenAlignment** enumeration that represents the alignment for this **Pen** object.

Remarks

This property determines how the **Pen** object draws closed curves and polygons. The **PenAlignment** enumeration specifies two values, **Center** and **Inset**. **Center** is the default value for this property and specifies that the width of the pen is centered on the outline of the curve or polygon. A value of **Inset** for this property specifies that the width of the pen is inside the outline of the curve or polygon.

A **Pen** object with its alignment set to **PenAlignment.Inset** cannot be used to draw compound lines and cannot draw dashed lines with **DashCap.Triangle** dash caps.

Requirements

Platforms: Windows 98, Windows NT 4.0, Windows Millennium Edition, Windows 2000, Windows XP Home Edition, Windows XP Professional, Windows Server 2003 family

Pen.Brush Property

Gets or sets the **Brush** object that determines attributes of this **Pen** object.

```
[Visual Basic]
Public Property Brush As Brush
[C#]
public Brush Brush {get; set;}
[C++]
public: __property Brush* get_Brush();
public: __property void set_Brush(Brush*);
[JScript]
public function get Brush() : Brush;
public function set Brush(Brush);
```

Property Value

A **Brush** object that determines attributes of this **Pen**.

Remarks

Assigning this property causes the pen to draw filled lines and curves. It overrides the **Color** property of the **Pen** object .

Requirements

Platforms: Windows 98, Windows NT 4.0, Windows Millennium Edition, Windows 2000, Windows XP Home Edition, Windows XP Professional, Windows Server 2003 family

Pen.Color Property

Gets or sets the color of this **Pen** object.

```
[Visual Basic]
Public Property Color As Color
[C#]
public Color Color {get; set;}
[C++]
public: __property Color get_Color();
public: __property void set_Color(Color);
[JScript]
public function get Color() : Color;
public function set Color(Color);
```

Property Value

A **Color** structure that represents the color of this **Pen** object.

Requirements

Platforms: Windows 98, Windows NT 4.0, Windows Millennium Edition, Windows 2000, Windows XP Home Edition, Windows XP Professional, Windows Server 2003 family, .NET Compact Framework - Windows CE .NET

Pen.CompoundArray Property

Gets or sets an array values that specify a compound pen. A compound pen draws a compound line made up of parallel lines and spaces.

```
[Visual Basic]
Public Property CompoundArray As Single ()
[C#]
public float[] CompoundArray {get; set;}
[C++]
public: __property float get_CompoundArray();
public: __property void set_CompoundArray(float __gc[]);
[JScript]
public function get CompoundArray() : float[];
public function set CompoundArray(float[]);
```

Property Value

An array of real numbers that specifies the compound array. The elements in the array must be in increasing order, not less than 0, and not greater than 1.

Remarks

A compound line is made up of alternating parallel lines and spaces of varying widths. The values in the array specify the starting points of each component of the compound line relative to the pen's width. The first value in the array specifies where the first component (a line) begins as a fraction of the distance across the width of the pen. The second value in the array specifies the beginning of the next component (a space) as a fraction of the distance across the width of the pen. The final value in the array specifies where the last component ends.

Suppose you want a pen to draw two parallel lines where the width of the first line is 20 percent of the pen's width, the width of the space that separates the two lines is 50 percent of the pen' s width, and the width of the second line is 30 percent of the pen's width. Start by creating a **Pen** object and an array of real numbers. Set the compound array by passing the array with the values 0.0, 0.2, 0.7, and 1.0 to this property.

Do not set this property if the **Pen** object has its **Pen.Alignment** property set to **PenAlignment.Inset**.

Requirements

Platforms: Windows 98, Windows NT 4.0, Windows Millennium Edition, Windows 2000, Windows XP Home Edition, Windows XP Professional, Windows Server 2003 family

Pen.CustomEndCap Property

Gets or sets a custom cap to use at the end of lines drawn with this **Pen** object.

```
[Visual Basic]
Public Property CustomEndCap As CustomLineCap
[C#]
public CustomLineCap CustomEndCap {get; set;}
[C++]
public: __property CustomLineCap* get_CustomEndCap();
public: __property void set_CustomEndCap(CustomLineCap*);
[JScript]
public function get CustomEndCap() : CustomLineCap;
public function set CustomEndCap(CustomLineCap);
```

Property Value

A **CustomLineCap** object that represents the cap used at the end of lines drawn with this **Pen** object.

Requirements

Platforms: Windows 98, Windows NT 4.0, Windows Millennium Edition, Windows 2000, Windows XP Home Edition, Windows XP Professional, Windows Server 2003 family

Pen.CustomStartCap Property

Gets or sets a custom cap to use at the beginning of lines drawn with this **Pen** object.

```
[Visual Basic]
Public Property CustomStartCap As CustomLineCap
[C#]
public CustomLineCap CustomStartCap {get; set;}
[C++]
public: __property CustomLineCap* get_CustomStartCap();
public: __property void set_CustomStartCap(CustomLineCap*);
[JScript]
public function get CustomStartCap() : CustomLineCap;
public function set CustomStartCap(CustomLineCap);
```

Property Value

A **CustomLineCap** object that represents the cap used at the beginning of lines drawn with this **Pen** object.

Requirements

Platforms: Windows 98, Windows NT 4.0, Windows Millennium Edition, Windows 2000, Windows XP Home Edition, Windows XP Professional, Windows Server 2003 family

Pen.DashCap Property

Gets or sets the cap style used at the end of the dashes that make up dashed lines drawn with this **Pen** object.

```
[Visual Basic]
Public Property DashCap As DashCap
[C#]
public DashCap DashCap {get; set;}
[C++]
public: __property DashCap get_DashCap();
public: __property void set_DashCap(DashCap);
[JScript]
public function get DashCap() : DashCap;
public function set DashCap(DashCap);
```

Property Value

A **DashCap** enumeration that represents the cap style used at the beginning and end of the dashes that make up dashed lines drawn with this **Pen** object.

Do not set this property to DashCap.Triangle if the Pen object has its Pen.Alignment property set to PenAlignment.Inset.

Requirements

Platforms: Windows 98, Windows NT 4.0, Windows Millennium Edition, Windows 2000, Windows XP Home Edition, Windows XP Professional, Windows Server 2003 family

Pen.DashOffset Property

Gets or sets the distance from the start of a line to the beginning of a dash pattern.

```
[Visual Basic]
Public Property DashOffset As Single
[C#]
public float DashOffset {get; set;}
[C++]
public: __property float get_DashOffset();
public: __property void set_DashOffset(float);
[JScript]
public function get DashOffset() : float;
public function set DashOffset(float);
```

Property Value

The distance from the start of a line to the beginning of a dash pattern.

Requirements

Platforms: Windows 98, Windows NT 4.0, Windows Millennium Edition, Windows 2000, Windows XP Home Edition, Windows XP Professional, Windows Server 2003 family

Pen.DashPattern Property

Gets or sets an array of custom dashes and spaces.

```
[Visual Basic]
Public Property DashPattern As Single ()
[C#]
public float[] DashPattern {get; set;}
```

```
[C++]
public: __property float get_DashPattern();
public: __property void set_DashPattern(float __gc[]);
[JScript]
public function get DashPattern() : float[];
public function set DashPattern(float[]);
```

Property Value

An array of real numbers that specify the lengths of alternating dashes and spaces in dashed lines.

Remarks

Assigning a value other than a null reference (**Nothing** in Visual Basic) to this property will set the **DashStyle** property for this **Pen** object to **DashStyle.Custom**.

The elements in the *dashArray* array set the length of each dash and space in the dash pattern. The first element sets the length of a dash, the second element sets the length of a space, the third element sets the length of a dash, and so on.

The length of each dash and space in the dash pattern is the product of the element value in the array and the width of the **Pen** object.

Requirements

Platforms: Windows 98, Windows NT 4.0, Windows Millennium Edition, Windows 2000, Windows XP Home Edition, Windows XP Professional, Windows Server 2003 family

Pen.DashStyle Property

Gets or sets the style used for dashed lines drawn with this **Pen** object.

```
[Visual Basic]
Public Property DashStyle As DashStyle
[C#]
public DashStyle DashStyle {get; set;}
[C++]
public: __property DashStyle get_DashStyle();
public: __property void set_DashStyle(DashStyle);
[JScript]
public function get DashStyle() : DashStyle;
public function set DashStyle(DashStyle);
```

Property Value

A **DashStyle** enumeration that represents the style used for dashed lines drawn with this **Pen** object.

Remarks

A value of **DashStyle.Custom** for this property specifies that a custom pattern of dashes and spaces, defined by the **DashPattern** property, make up lines drawn with this **Pen** object. If the value of this property is **DashStyle.Custom** and the value of the **DashPattern** property is a null reference (**Nothing** in Visual Basic), the pen draws solid lines.

Requirements

Platforms: Windows 98, Windows NT 4.0, Windows Millennium Edition, Windows 2000, Windows XP Home Edition, Windows XP Professional, Windows Server 2003 family

Pen.EndCap Property

Gets or sets the cap style used at the end of lines drawn with this **Pen** object.

```
[Visual Basic]
Public Property EndCap As LineCap
[C#]
public LineCap EndCap {get; set;}
[C++]
public: __property LineCap get_EndCap();
public: __property void set_EndCap(LineCap);
[JScript]
public function get EndCap() : LineCap;
public function set EndCap(LineCap);
```

Property Value

A **LineCap** enumeration that represents the cap style used at the end of lines drawn with this **Pen** object.

Requirements

Platforms: Windows 98, Windows NT 4.0, Windows Millennium Edition, Windows 2000, Windows XP Home Edition, Windows XP Professional, Windows Server 2003 family

Pen.LineJoin Property

Gets or sets the join style for the ends of two consecutive lines drawn with this **Pen** object.

```
[Visual Basic]
Public Property LineJoin As LineJoin
[C#]
public LineJoin LineJoin {get; set;}
[C++]
public: __property LineJoin get_LineJoin();
public: __property void set_LineJoin(LineJoin);
[JScript]
public function get LineJoin() : LineJoin;
public function set LineJoin(LineJoin);
```

Property Value

A **LineJoin** enumeration that represents the join style for the ends of two consecutive lines drawn with this **Pen** object.

Requirements

Platforms: Windows 98, Windows NT 4.0, Windows Millennium Edition, Windows 2000, Windows XP Home Edition, Windows XP Professional, Windows Server 2003 family

Pen.MiterLimit Property

Gets or sets the limit of the thickness of the join on a mitered corner.

```
[Visual Basic]
Public Property MiterLimit As Single
[C#]
public float MiterLimit {get; set;}
[C++]
public: __property float get_MiterLimit();
public: __property void set_MiterLimit(float);
[JScript]
public function get MiterLimit() : float;
public function set MiterLimit(float);
```

Property Value

The limit of the thickness of the join on a mitered corner.

Remarks

The miter length is the distance from the intersection of the line walls on the inside of the join to the intersection of the line walls outside of the join. The miter length can be large when the angle between two lines is small. The miter limit is the maximum allowed ratio of miter length to stroke width. The default value is 10.0f.

If the miter length of the join of the intersection exceeds the limit of the join, then the join will be beveled to keep it within the limit of the join of the intersection.

Requirements

Platforms: Windows 98, Windows NT 4.0, Windows Millennium Edition, Windows 2000, Windows XP Home Edition, Windows XP Professional, Windows Server 2003 family

Pen.PenType Property

Gets the style of lines drawn with this **Pen** object.

```
[Visual Basic]
Public ReadOnly Property PenType As PenType
[C#]
public PenType PenType {get;}
[C++]
public: __property PenType get_PenType();
[JScript]
public function get PenType() : PenType;
```

Property Value

A **PenType** enumeration that specifies the style of lines drawn with this **Pen** object.

Remarks

A **Pen** object can draw solid lines, filled lines, or textured lines, depending on the style specified by a member of the **PenType** enumeration.

Requirements

Platforms: Windows 98, Windows NT 4.0, Windows Millennium Edition, Windows 2000, Windows XP Home Edition, Windows XP Professional, Windows Server 2003 family

Pen.StartCap Property

Gets or sets the cap style used at the beginning of lines drawn with this **Pen** object.

```
[Visual Basic]
Public Property StartCap As LineCap
[C#]
public LineCap StartCap {get; set;}
[C++]
public: __property LineCap get_StartCap();
public: __property void set_StartCap(LineCap);
[JScript]
public function get StartCap() : LineCap;
public function set StartCap(LineCap);
```

Property Value

A **LineCap** enumeration that represents the cap style used at the beginning of lines drawn with this **Pen** object.

Requirements

Platforms: Windows 98, Windows NT 4.0, Windows Millennium Edition, Windows 2000, Windows XP Home Edition, Windows XP Professional, Windows Server 2003 family

Pen.Transform Property

Gets or sets the geometric transformation for this **Pen** object.

```
[Visual Basic]
Public Property Transform As Matrix
[C#]
public Matrix Transform {get; set;}
[C++]
public: __property Matrix* get_Transform();
public: __property void set_Transform(Matrix*);
[JScript]
public function get Transform() : Matrix;
public function set Transform(Matrix);
```

Property Value

A **Matrix** object that represents the geometric transformation for this **Pen** object.

Remarks

This property defines an elliptical shape for the pen tip. This ellipse is obtained from the default circular shape by applying the transformation matrix. Note that the translation portion of the matrix is ignored.

Requirements

Platforms: Windows 98, Windows NT 4.0, Windows Millennium Edition, Windows 2000, Windows XP Home Edition, Windows XP Professional, Windows Server 2003 family

Pen.Width Property

Gets or sets the width of this **Pen** object.

```
[Visual Basic]
Public Property Width As Single
[C#]
public float Width {get; set;}
[C++]
public: __property float get_Width();
public: __property void set_Width(float);
[JScript]
public function get Width() : float;
public function set Width(float);
```

Property Value

The width of this **Pen** object.

Requirements

Platforms: Windows 98, Windows NT 4.0, Windows Millennium Edition, Windows 2000, Windows XP Home Edition, Windows XP Professional, Windows Server 2003 family

Pen.Clone Method

Creates an exact copy of this **Pen** object.

```
[Visual Basic]
Public Overridable Function Clone() As Object Implements _
   ICloneable.Clone
[C#]
public virtual object Clone();
[C++]
public: virtual Object* Clone();
[JScript]
public function Clone() : Object;
```

Return Value

An **Object** object that can be cast to a **Pen** object.

Implements

ICloneable.Clone

Example

[Visual Basic, C#] The following example is designed for use with Windows Forms, and it requires **PaintEventArgs** *e*, which is a parameter of the **Paint** event handler. The code performs the following actions:

- Creates a **Pen** object.
- Creates a copy of that pen.
- Draws a line to the screen, using the copy of the pen.

```
[Visual Basic]
Public Sub Clone_Example(e As PaintEventArgs)
' Create a Pen object.
Dim myPen As New Pen(Color.Black, 5)
' Clone myPen.
Dim clonePen As Pen = CType(myPen.Clone(), Pen)
' Draw a line with clonePen.
e.Graphics.DrawLine(clonePen, 0, 0, 100, 100)
End Sub
```

```
[C#]
public void Clone_Example(PaintEventArgs e)
{
// Create a Pen object.
Pen myPen = new Pen(Color.Black, 5);
// Clone myPen.
Pen clonePen = (Pen)myPen.Clone();
// Draw a line with clonePen.
e.Graphics.DrawLine(clonePen, 0, 0, 100, 100);
}
```

Requirements

Platforms: Windows 98, Windows NT 4.0, Windows Millennium Edition, Windows 2000, Windows XP Home Edition, Windows XP Professional, Windows Server 2003 family

Pen.Dispose Method

Releases all resources used by this **Pen** object.

```
[Visual Basic]
Public Overridable Sub Dispose() Implements IDisposable.Dispose
[C#]
public virtual void Dispose();
[C++]
public: virtual void Dispose();
[JScript]
public function Dispose();
```

Return Value

This method does not return a value.

Implements

IDisposable.Dispose

Remarks

Calling **Dispose** allows the resources used by this **Brush** object to be reallocated for other purposes.

Requirements

Platforms: Windows 98, Windows NT 4.0, Windows Millennium Edition, Windows 2000, Windows XP Home Edition, Windows XP Professional, Windows Server 2003 family, .NET Compact Framework - Windows CE .NET

Pen.Finalize Method

This member overrides **Object.Finalize**.

```
[Visual Basic]
Overrides Protected Sub Finalize()
[C#]
~Pen();
[C++]
~Pen();
[JScript]
protected override function Finalize();
```

Requirements

Platforms: Windows 98, Windows NT 4.0, Windows Millennium Edition, Windows 2000, Windows XP Home Edition, Windows XP Professional, Windows Server 2003 family, .NET Compact Framework - Windows CE .NET

Pen.MultiplyTransform Method

Multiplies the transformation matrix for this **Pen** object by the specified **Matrix**.

Overload List

Multiplies the transformation matrix for this **Pen** object by the specified **Matrix** object.

[Visual Basic] **Overloads Public Sub Multiply-Transform(Matrix)**

[C#] **public void MultiplyTransform(Matrix);**

[C++] **public: void MultiplyTransform(Matrix*);**

[JScript] **public function MultiplyTransform(Matrix);**

Multiplies the transformation matrix for this **Pen** object by the specified **Matrix** object in the specified order.

[Visual Basic] **Overloads Public Sub Multiply-Transform(Matrix, MatrixOrder)**

[C#] **public void MultiplyTransform(Matrix, MatrixOrder);**

[C++] **public: void MultiplyTransform(Matrix*, MatrixOrder);**

[JScript] **public function MultiplyTransform(Matrix, MatrixOrder);**

Example

[Visual Basic, C#] The following example is designed for use with Windows Forms, and it requires **PaintEventArgs** *e*, which is a parameter of the **Paint** event handler. The code performs the following actions:

- Creates a **Pen** object.
- Draws a line to the screen.
- Multiplies the transformation matrix of the pen by the specified matrix.
- Draws a line with the transformed pen.

> [Visual Basic, C#] **Note** This example shows how to use one of the overloaded versions of **MultiplyTransform**. For other examples that might be available, see the individual overload topics.

[Visual Basic]
```
Public Sub MultiplyTransform_Example(e As PaintEventArgs)
' Create a Pen object.
Dim myPen As New Pen(Color.Black, 5)
' Create a translation matrix.
Dim penMatrix As New Matrix()
penMatrix.Scale(3, 1)
' Multiply the transformation matrix of myPen by transMatrix.
myPen.MultiplyTransform(penMatrix, MatrixOrder.Prepend)
' Draw a line to the screen.
e.Graphics.DrawLine(myPen, 0, 0, 100, 100)
End Sub
```

[C#]
```
public void MultiplyTransform_Example(PaintEventArgs e)
{
// Create a Pen object.
Pen myPen = new Pen(Color.Black, 5);
// Create a translation matrix.
Matrix penMatrix = new Matrix();
penMatrix.Scale(3, 1);
// Multiply the transformation matrix of myPen by transMatrix.
myPen.MultiplyTransform(penMatrix, MatrixOrder.Prepend);
// Draw a line to the screen.
e.Graphics.DrawLine(myPen, 0, 0, 100, 100);
};
```

Pen.MultiplyTransform Method (Matrix)

Multiplies the transformation matrix for this **Pen** object by the specified **Matrix** object.

[Visual Basic]
```
Overloads Public Sub MultiplyTransform( _
   ByVal matrix As Matrix _
)
```
[C#]
```
public void MultiplyTransform(
   Matrix matrix
);
```
[C++]
```
public: void MultiplyTransform(
   Matrix* matrix
);
```
[JScript]
```
public function MultiplyTransform(
   matrix : Matrix
);
```

Parameters

matrix
: The **Matrix** object by which to multiply the transformation matrix.

Return Value

This method does not return a value.

Remarks

This method prepends multiplication matrix specified in the *matrix* parameter to the transformation matrix for the multiplication operation.

Example

[Visual Basic, C#] The following example is designed for use with Windows Forms, and it requires **PaintEventArgs** *e*, which is a parameter of the **Paint** event handler. The code performs the following actions:

- Creates a **Pen** object.
- Draws a line to the screen.
- Multiplies the transformation matrix of the pen by the specified matrix.
- Draws a line with the transformed pen.

[Visual Basic]
```
Public Sub MultiplyTransform_Example(e As PaintEventArgs)
' Create a Pen object.
Dim myPen As New Pen(Color.Black, 5)
' Create a translation matrix.
Dim penMatrix As New Matrix()
penMatrix.Scale(3, 1)
' Multiply the transformation matrix of myPen by transMatrix.
myPen.MultiplyTransform(penMatrix)
' Draw a line to the screen.
e.Graphics.DrawLine(myPen, 0, 0, 100, 100)
End Sub
```

[C#]
```
public void MultiplyTransform_Example(PaintEventArgs e)
{
// Create a Pen object.
Pen myPen = new Pen(Color.Black, 5);
// Create a translation matrix.
Matrix penMatrix = new Matrix();
penMatrix.Scale(3, 1);
// Multiply the transformation matrix of myPen by transMatrix.
myPen.MultiplyTransform(penMatrix);
// Draw a line to the screen.
e.Graphics.DrawLine(myPen, 0, 0, 100, 100);
}
```

Requirements

Platforms: Windows 98, Windows NT 4.0, Windows Millennium Edition, Windows 2000, Windows XP Home Edition, Windows XP Professional, Windows Server 2003 family

Pen.MultiplyTransform Method (Matrix, MatrixOrder)

Multiplies the transformation matrix for this **Pen** object by the specified **Matrix** object in the specified order.

[Visual Basic]
```
Overloads Public Sub MultiplyTransform( _
   ByVal matrix As Matrix, _
   ByVal order As MatrixOrder _
)
```

```
[C#]
public void MultiplyTransform(
   Matrix matrix,
   MatrixOrder order
);
[C++]
public: void MultiplyTransform(
   Matrix* matrix,
   MatrixOrder order
);
[JScript]
public function MultiplyTransform(
   matrix : Matrix,
   order : MatrixOrder
);
```

Parameters

matrix
: The **Matrix** object by which to multiply the transformation matrix.

order
: The order in which to perform the multiplication operation.

Return Value

This method does not return a value.

Remarks

This method uses the **MatrixOrder** enumeration element (either prepend or append) specified by the *order* parameter to carry out the multiplication operation.

Example

[Visual Basic, C#] The following example is designed for use with Windows Forms, and it requires **PaintEventArgs** *e*, which is a parameter of the **Paint** event handler. The code performs the following actions:

- Creates a **Pen** object.
- Draws a line to the screen.
- Multiplies the transformation matrix of the pen by the specified matrix.
- Draws a line with the transformed pen.

```
[Visual Basic]
Public Sub MultiplyTransform_Example(e As PaintEventArgs)
' Create a Pen object.
Dim myPen As New Pen(Color.Black, 5)
' Create a translation matrix.
Dim penMatrix As New Matrix()
penMatrix.Scale(3, 1)
' Multiply the transformation matrix of myPen by transMatrix.
myPen.MultiplyTransform(penMatrix, MatrixOrder.Prepend)
' Draw a line to the screen.
e.Graphics.DrawLine(myPen, 0, 0, 100, 100)
End Sub
```

```
[C#]
public void MultiplyTransform_Example(PaintEventArgs e)
{
// Create a Pen object.
Pen myPen = new Pen(Color.Black, 5);
// Create a translation matrix.
Matrix penMatrix = new Matrix();
penMatrix.Scale(3, 1);
// Multiply the transformation matrix of myPen by transMatrix.
myPen.MultiplyTransform(penMatrix, MatrixOrder.Prepend);
// Draw a line to the screen.
e.Graphics.DrawLine(myPen, 0, 0, 100, 100);
};
```

Requirements

Platforms: Windows 98, Windows NT 4.0, Windows Millennium Edition, Windows 2000, Windows XP Home Edition, Windows XP Professional, Windows Server 2003 family

Pen.ResetTransform Method

Resets the geometric transformation matrix for this **Pen** object to identity.

```
[Visual Basic]
Public Sub ResetTransform()
[C#]
public void ResetTransform();
[C++]
public: void ResetTransform();
[JScript]
public function ResetTransform();
```

Return Value

This method does not return a value.

Example

[Visual Basic, C#] The following example is designed for use with Windows Forms, and it requires **PaintEventArgs** *e*, which is a parameter of the **Paint** event handler. The code performs the following actions:

- Creates a **Pen** object.
- Sets the transformation matrix of the pen to scale 2 times in the x-direction.
- Draws a line to the screen.
- Resets the transformation matrix to identity.
- Draws a second line to the screen.

```
[Visual Basic]
Public Sub ResetTransform_Example(e As PaintEventArgs)
' Create a Pen object.
Dim myPen As New Pen(Color.Black, 3)
' Scale the transformation matrix of myPen.
myPen.ScaleTransform(2, 1)
' Draw a line with myPen.
e.Graphics.DrawLine(myPen, 10, 0, 10, 200)
' Reset the transformation matrix of myPen to identity.
myPen.ResetTransform()
' Draw a second line with myPen.
e.Graphics.DrawLine(myPen, 100, 0, 100, 200)
End Sub
```

```
[C#]
public void ResetTransform_Example(PaintEventArgs e)
{
// Create a Pen object.
Pen myPen = new Pen(Color.Black, 3);
// Scale the transformation matrix of myPen.
myPen.ScaleTransform(2, 1);
// Draw a line with myPen.
e.Graphics.DrawLine(myPen, 10, 0, 10, 200);
// Reset the transformation matrix of myPen to identity.
myPen.ResetTransform();
// Draw a second line with myPen.
e.Graphics.DrawLine(myPen, 100, 0, 100, 200);
}
```

Requirements

Platforms: Windows 98, Windows NT 4.0, Windows Millennium Edition, Windows 2000, Windows XP Home Edition, Windows XP Professional, Windows Server 2003 family

Pen.RotateTransform Method

Rotates the local geometric transformation by the specified angle. This method prepends the rotation to the transformation.

Overload List

Rotates the local geometric transformation by the specified angle. This method prepends the rotation to the transformation.

[Visual Basic] **Overloads Public Sub RotateTransform(Single)**

[C#] **public void RotateTransform(float);**

[C++] **public: void RotateTransform(float);**

[JScript] **public function RotateTransform(float);**

Rotates the local geometric transformation by the specified angle in the specified order.

[Visual Basic] **Overloads Public Sub RotateTransform(Single, MatrixOrder)**

[C#] **public void RotateTransform(float, MatrixOrder);**

[C++] **public: void RotateTransform(float, MatrixOrder);**

[JScript] **public function RotateTransform(float, MatrixOrder);**

Example

[Visual Basic, C#] The following example is designed for use with Windows Forms, and it requires **PaintEventArgs** *e*, which is a parameter of the **Paint** event handler. The code performs the following actions:

- creates a **Pen** object.
- Scales the pen by 2 times in the x-direction.
- Draws a rectangle using the pen.
- Rotates the pen 90 degrees clockwise.
- Draws a second rectangle to demonstrate the difference.

> [Visual Basic, C#] **Note** This example shows how to use one of the overloaded versions of **RotateTransform**. For other examples that might be available, see the individual overload topics.

[Visual Basic]
```
Public Sub RotateTransform_Example(e As PaintEventArgs)
' Create a Pen object.
Dim rotatePen As New Pen(Color.Black, 5)
' Scale rotatePen by 2X in the x-direction.
rotatePen.ScaleTransform(2, 1)
' Draw a rectangle with rotatePen.
e.Graphics.DrawRectangle(rotatePen, 10, 10, 100, 100)
' Rotate rotatePen 90 degrees clockwise.
rotatePen.RotateTransform(90, MatrixOrder.Append)
' Draw a second rectangle with rotatePen.
e.Graphics.DrawRectangle(rotatePen, 120, 10, 100, 100)
End Sub
```

[C#]
```
public void RotateTransform_Example(PaintEventArgs e)
{
// Create a Pen object.
Pen rotatePen = new Pen(Color.Black, 5);
// Scale rotatePen by 2X in the x-direction.
rotatePen.ScaleTransform(2, 1);
// Draw a rectangle with rotatePen.
e.Graphics.DrawRectangle(rotatePen, 10, 10, 100, 100);
// Rotate rotatePen 90 degrees clockwise.
rotatePen.RotateTransform(90, MatrixOrder.Append);
// Draw a second rectangle with rotatePen.
e.Graphics.DrawRectangle(rotatePen, 120, 10, 100, 100);
}
```

Pen.RotateTransform Method (Single)

Rotates the local geometric transformation by the specified angle. This method prepends the rotation to the transformation.

[Visual Basic]
```
Overloads Public Sub RotateTransform( _
   ByVal angle As Single _
)
```
[C#]
```
public void RotateTransform(
   float angle
);
```
[C++]
```
public: void RotateTransform(
   float angle
);
```
[JScript]
```
public function RotateTransform(
   angle : float
);
```

Parameters

angle

The angle of rotation.

Return Value

This method does not return a value.

Remarks

Because the shape of a pen is circular, a rotation does not have any visible effect unless the pen is scaled in the x- or y-direction.

Example

[Visual Basic, C#] The following example is designed for use with Windows Forms, and it requires **PaintEventArgs** *e*, which is a parameter of the **Paint** event handler. The code performs the following actions:

- Creates a **Pen** object.
- Draws a rectangle using the pen.
- Scales the pen by 2 times in the x-direction.
- Rotates the pen 90 degrees clockwise.
- Draws a second rectangle to demonstrate the difference.

[Visual Basic]
```
Public Sub RotateTransform_Example(e As PaintEventArgs)
' Create a Pen object.
Dim rotatePen As New Pen(Color.Black, 5)
' Draw a rectangle with rotatePen.
e.Graphics.DrawRectangle(rotatePen, 10, 10, 100, 100)
' Scale rotatePen by 2X in the x-direction.
rotatePen.ScaleTransform(2, 1)
' Rotate rotatePen 90 degrees clockwise.
rotatePen.RotateTransform(90)
' Draw a second rectangle with rotatePen.
e.Graphics.DrawRectangle(rotatePen, 140, 10, 100, 100)
End Sub
```

[C#]
```
public void RotateTransform_Example(PaintEventArgs e)
{
// Create a Pen object.
Pen rotatePen = new Pen(Color.Black, 5);
// Draw a rectangle with rotatePen.
e.Graphics.DrawRectangle(rotatePen, 10, 10, 100, 100);
// Scale rotatePen by 2X in the x-direction.
rotatePen.ScaleTransform(2, 1);
// Rotate rotatePen 90 degrees clockwise.
rotatePen.RotateTransform(90);
// Draw a second rectangle with rotatePen.
e.Graphics.DrawRectangle(rotatePen, 140, 10, 100, 100);
}
```

Requirements

Platforms: Windows 98, Windows NT 4.0, Windows Millennium Edition, Windows 2000, Windows XP Home Edition, Windows XP Professional, Windows Server 2003 family

Pen.RotateTransform Method (Single, MatrixOrder)

Rotates the local geometric transformation by the specified angle in the specified order.

[Visual Basic]
```
Overloads Public Sub RotateTransform( _
   ByVal angle As Single, _
   ByVal order As MatrixOrder _
)
```
[C#]
```
public void RotateTransform(
   float angle,
   MatrixOrder order
);
```
[C++]
```
public: void RotateTransform(
   float angle,
   MatrixOrder order
);
```
[JScript]
```
public function RotateTransform(
   angle : float,
   order : MatrixOrder
);
```

Parameters

angle
The angle of rotation.

order
A **MatrixOrder** that specifies whether to append or prepend the rotation matrix.

Return Value

This method does not return a value.

Remarks

Because the shape of a pen is circular, a rotation does not have any visible effect unless the pen is scaled in the x- or y-direction.

Example

[Visual Basic, C#] The following example is designed for use with Windows Forms, and it requires **PaintEventArgs** *e*, which is a parameter of the **Paint** event handler. The code performs the following actions:

- creates a **Pen** object.
- Scales the pen by 2 times in the x-direction.
- Draws a rectangle using the pen.
- Rotates the pen 90 degrees clockwise.
- Draws a second rectangle to demonstrate the difference.

[Visual Basic]
```
Public Sub RotateTransform_Example(e As PaintEventArgs)
' Create a Pen object.
Dim rotatePen As New Pen(Color.Black, 5)
' Scale rotatePen by 2X in the x-direction.
rotatePen.ScaleTransform(2, 1)
' Draw a rectangle with rotatePen.
e.Graphics.DrawRectangle(rotatePen, 10, 10, 100, 100)
' Rotate rotatePen 90 degrees clockwise.
rotatePen.RotateTransform(90, MatrixOrder.Append)
' Draw a second rectangle with rotatePen.
e.Graphics.DrawRectangle(rotatePen, 120, 10, 100, 100)
End Sub
```

[C#]
```
public void RotateTransform_Example(PaintEventArgs e)
{
// Create a Pen object.
Pen rotatePen = new Pen(Color.Black, 5);
// Scale rotatePen by 2X in the x-direction.
rotatePen.ScaleTransform(2, 1);
// Draw a rectangle with rotatePen.
e.Graphics.DrawRectangle(rotatePen, 10, 10, 100, 100);
// Rotate rotatePen 90 degrees clockwise.
rotatePen.RotateTransform(90, MatrixOrder.Append);
// Draw a second rectangle with rotatePen.
e.Graphics.DrawRectangle(rotatePen, 120, 10, 100, 100);
}
```

Requirements

Platforms: Windows 98, Windows NT 4.0, Windows Millennium Edition, Windows 2000, Windows XP Home Edition, Windows XP Professional, Windows Server 2003 family

Pen.ScaleTransform Method

Scales the local geometric transformation by the specified factors. This method prepends the scaling matrix to the transformation.

Overload List

Scales the local geometric transformation by the specified factors. This method prepends the scaling matrix to the transformation.

[Visual Basic] **Overloads Public Sub ScaleTransform(Single, Single)**

[C#] **public void ScaleTransform(float, float);**

[C++] **public: void ScaleTransform(float, float);**

[JScript] **public function ScaleTransform(float, float);**

Scales the local geometric transformation by the specified factors in the specified order.

[Visual Basic] **Overloads Public Sub ScaleTransform(Single, Single, MatrixOrder)**

[C#] **public void ScaleTransform(float, float, MatrixOrder);**

[C++] **public: void ScaleTransform(float, float, MatrixOrder);**

[JScript] **public function ScaleTransform(float, float, MatrixOrder);**

Example

[Visual Basic, C#] The following example is designed for use with Windows Forms, and it requires **PaintEventArgs** *e*, which is a parameter of the **Paint** event handler. The code performs the following actions:

- Creates a **Pen** object.
- Draws a rectangle using the pen.
- Scales the pen by 2 times in the x-direction.
- Draws a second rectangle to demonstrate the difference.

[Visual Basic, C#] **Note** This example shows how to use one of the overloaded versions of **ScaleTransform**. For other examples that might be available, see the individual overload topics.

[Visual Basic]
```
Public Sub ScaleTransform_Example(e As PaintEventArgs)
' Create a Pen object.
Dim scalePen As New Pen(Color.Black, 5)
' Draw a rectangle with scalePen.
e.Graphics.DrawRectangle(scalePen, 10, 10, 100, 100)
' Scale scalePen by 2X in the x-direction.
scalePen.ScaleTransform(2, 1, MatrixOrder.Prepend)
' Draw a second rectangle with rotatePen.
e.Graphics.DrawRectangle(scalePen, 120, 10, 100, 100)
End Sub
```

[C#]
```
public void ScaleTransform_Example(PaintEventArgs e)
{
// Create a Pen object.
Pen scalePen = new Pen(Color.Black, 5);
// Draw a rectangle with scalePen.
e.Graphics.DrawRectangle(scalePen, 10, 10, 100, 100);
// Scale scalePen by 2X in the x-direction.
scalePen.ScaleTransform(2, 1, MatrixOrder.Prepend);
// Draw a second rectangle with rotatePen.
e.Graphics.DrawRectangle(scalePen, 120, 10, 100, 100);
}
```

Pen.ScaleTransform Method (Single, Single)

Scales the local geometric transformation by the specified factors. This method prepends the scaling matrix to the transformation.

[Visual Basic]
```
Overloads Public Sub ScaleTransform( _
   ByVal sx As Single, _
   ByVal sy As Single _
)
```
[C#]
```
public void ScaleTransform(
   float sx,
   float sy
);
```
[C++]
```
public: void ScaleTransform(
   float sx,
   float sy
);
```
[JScript]
```
public function ScaleTransform(
   sx : float,
   sy : float
);
```

Parameters

sx

The factor by which to scale the transformation in the x-axis direction.

sy

The factor by which to scale the transformation in the y-axis direction.

Return Value

This method does not return a value.

Example

[Visual Basic, C#] The following example is designed for use with Windows Forms, and it requires **PaintEventArgs** *e*, which is a parameter of the **Paint** event handler. The code performs the following actions:

[Visual Basic, C#] Creates a **Pen** object.

[Visual Basic, C#] Draws a rectangle using the pen.

[Visual Basic, C#] Scales the pen by 2 times in the x-direction.

[Visual Basic, C#] Draws a second rectangle to demonstrate the difference.

[Visual Basic]
```
Public Sub ScaleTransform_Example(e As PaintEventArgs)
' Create a Pen object.
Dim scalePen As New Pen(Color.Black, 5)
' Draw a rectangle with scalePen.
e.Graphics.DrawRectangle(scalePen, 10, 10, 100, 100)
' Scale scalePen by 2X in the x-direction.
scalePen.ScaleTransform(2, 1)
' Draw a second rectangle with rotatePen.
e.Graphics.DrawRectangle(scalePen, 120, 10, 100, 100)
End Sub
```

[C#]
```
public void ScaleTransform_Example(PaintEventArgs e)
{
// Create a Pen object.
Pen scalePen = new Pen(Color.Black, 5);
// Draw a rectangle with scalePen.
e.Graphics.DrawRectangle(scalePen, 10, 10, 100, 100);
// Scale scalePen by 2X in the x-direction.
scalePen.ScaleTransform(2, 1);
// Draw a second rectangle with rotatePen.
e.Graphics.DrawRectangle(scalePen, 120, 10, 100, 100);
}
```

Requirements

Platforms: Windows 98, Windows NT 4.0, Windows Millennium Edition, Windows 2000, Windows XP Home Edition, Windows XP Professional, Windows Server 2003 family

Pen.ScaleTransform Method (Single, Single, MatrixOrder)

Scales the local geometric transformation by the specified factors in the specified order.

[Visual Basic]
```
Overloads Public Sub ScaleTransform( _
   ByVal sx As Single, _
   ByVal sy As Single, _
   ByVal order As MatrixOrder _
)
```
[C#]
```
public void ScaleTransform(
   float sx,
   float sy,
   MatrixOrder order
);
```
[C++]
```
public: void ScaleTransform(
   float sx,
   float sy,
   MatrixOrder order
);
```

```
[JScript]
public function ScaleTransform(
   sx : float,
   sy : float,
   order : MatrixOrder
);
```

Parameters

sx
: The factor by which to scale the transformation in the x-axis direction.

sy
: The factor by which to scale the transformation in the y-axis direction.

order
: A **MatrixOrder** enumeration that specifies whether to append or prepend the scaling matrix.

Return Value

This method does not return a value.

Example

[Visual Basic, C#] The following example is designed for use with Windows Forms, and it requires **PaintEventArgs** *e*, which is a parameter of the **Paint** event handler. The code performs the following actions:

- Creates a **Pen** object.
- Draws a rectangle using the pen.
- Scales the pen by 2 times in the x-direction.
- Draws a second rectangle to demonstrate the difference.

```
[Visual Basic]
Public Sub ScaleTransform_Example(e As PaintEventArgs)
' Create a Pen object.
Dim scalePen As New Pen(Color.Black, 5)
' Draw a rectangle with scalePen.
e.Graphics.DrawRectangle(scalePen, 10, 10, 100, 100)
' Scale scalePen by 2X in the x-direction.
scalePen.ScaleTransform(2, 1, MatrixOrder.Prepend)
' Draw a second rectangle with rotatePen.
e.Graphics.DrawRectangle(scalePen, 120, 10, 100, 100)
End Sub
```

```
[C#]
public void ScaleTransform_Example(PaintEventArgs e)
{
// Create a Pen object.
Pen scalePen = new Pen(Color.Black, 5);
// Draw a rectangle with scalePen.
e.Graphics.DrawRectangle(scalePen, 10, 10, 100, 100);
// Scale scalePen by 2X in the x-direction.
scalePen.ScaleTransform(2, 1, MatrixOrder.Prepend);
// Draw a second rectangle with rotatePen.
e.Graphics.DrawRectangle(scalePen, 120, 10, 100, 100);
}
```

Requirements

Platforms: Windows 98, Windows NT 4.0, Windows Millennium Edition, Windows 2000, Windows XP Home Edition, Windows XP Professional, Windows Server 2003 family

Pen.SetLineCap Method

Sets the values that determine the style of cap used to end lines drawn by this **Pen** object.

```
[Visual Basic]
Public Sub SetLineCap( _
   ByVal startCap As LineCap, _
   ByVal endCap As LineCap, _
   ByVal dashCap As DashCap _
)
[C#]
public void SetLineCap(
   LineCap startCap,
   LineCap endCap,
   DashCap dashCap
);
[C++]
public: void SetLineCap(
   LineCap startCap,
   LineCap endCap,
   DashCap dashCap
);
[JScript]
public function SetLineCap(
   startCap : LineCap,
   endCap : LineCap,
   dashCap : DashCap
);
```

Parameters

startCap
: A **LineCap** enumeration that represents the cap style to use at the beginning of lines drawn with this **Pen** object.

endCap
: A **LineCap** enumeration that represents the cap style to use at the end of lines drawn with this **Pen** object.

dashCap
: A **LineCap** enumeration that represents the cap style to use at the beginning or end of dashed lines drawn with this **Pen** object.

Return Value

This method does not return a value.

Example

[Visual Basic, C#] The following example is designed for use with Windows Forms, and it requires **PaintEventArgs** *e*, which is a parameter of the **Paint** event handler. The code creates a **Pen** and sets it to draw arrow anchor caps at the beginning of lines:

```
[Visual Basic]
Public Sub SetLineCap_Example(e As PaintEventArgs)
' Create a Pen object with a dash pattern.
Dim capPen As New Pen(Color.Black, 5)
capPen.DashStyle = DashStyle.Dash
' Set the start and end caps for capPen.
capPen.SetLineCap(LineCap.ArrowAnchor, LineCap.Flat, DashCap.Flat)
' Draw a line with capPen.
e.Graphics.DrawLine(capPen, 10, 10, 200, 10)
End Sub
```

```
[C#]
public void SetLineCap_Example(PaintEventArgs e)
{
// Create a Pen object with a dash pattern.
Pen capPen = new Pen(Color.Black, 5);
capPen.DashStyle = DashStyle.Dash;
// Set the start and end caps for capPen.
```

```
capPen.SetLineCap(LineCap.Flat, LineCap.Flat, DashCap.Flat);
// Draw a line with capPen.
e.Graphics.DrawLine(capPen, 10, 10, 200, 10);
}
```

Requirements

Platforms: Windows 98, Windows NT 4.0, Windows Millennium Edition, Windows 2000, Windows XP Home Edition, Windows XP Professional, Windows Server 2003 family

Pen.TranslateTransform Method

Translates the local geometric transformation by the specified dimensions. This method prepends the translation to the transformation.

Overload List

Translates the local geometric transformation by the specified dimensions. This method prepends the translation to the transformation.

[Visual Basic] **Overloads Public Sub TranslateTransform(Single, Single)**

[C#] **public void TranslateTransform(float, float);**

[C++] **public: void TranslateTransform(float, float);**

[JScript] **public function TranslateTransform(float, float);**

Translates the local geometric transformation by the specified dimensions in the specified order.

[Visual Basic] **Overloads Public Sub TranslateTransform(Single, Single, MatrixOrder)**

[C#] **public void TranslateTransform(float, float, MatrixOrder);**

[C++] **public: void TranslateTransform(float, float, MatrixOrder);**

[JScript] **public function TranslateTransform(float, float, MatrixOrder);**

Pen.TranslateTransform Method (Single, Single)

Translates the local geometric transformation by the specified dimensions. This method prepends the translation to the transformation.

[Visual Basic]
```
Overloads Public Sub TranslateTransform( _
   ByVal dx As Single, _
   ByVal dy As Single _
)
```
[C#]
```
public void TranslateTransform(
   float dx,
   float dy
);
```
[C++]
```
public: void TranslateTransform(
   float dx,
   float dy
);
```
[JScript]
```
public function TranslateTransform(
   dx : float,
   dy : float
);
```

Parameters

dx

The value of the translation in x.

dy

The value of the translation in y.

Return Value

This method does not return a value.

Requirements

Platforms: Windows 98, Windows NT 4.0, Windows Millennium Edition, Windows 2000, Windows XP Home Edition, Windows XP Professional, Windows Server 2003 family

Pen.TranslateTransform Method (Single, Single, MatrixOrder)

Translates the local geometric transformation by the specified dimensions in the specified order.

[Visual Basic]
```
Overloads Public Sub TranslateTransform( _
   ByVal dx As Single, _
   ByVal dy As Single, _
   ByVal order As MatrixOrder _
)
```
[C#]
```
public void TranslateTransform(
   float dx,
   float dy,
   MatrixOrder order
);
```
[C++]
```
public: void TranslateTransform(
   float dx,
   float dy,
   MatrixOrder order
);
```
[JScript]
```
public function TranslateTransform(
   dx : float,
   dy : float,
   order : MatrixOrder
);
```

Parameters

dx

The value of the translation in x.

dy

The value of the translation in y.

order

The order (prepend or append) in which to apply the translation.

Return Value

This method does not return a value.

Requirements

Platforms: Windows 98, Windows NT 4.0, Windows Millennium Edition, Windows 2000, Windows XP Home Edition, Windows XP Professional, Windows Server 2003 family

Pens Class

Pens for all the standard colors. This class cannot be inherited.

System.Object
  System.Drawing.Pens

[Visual Basic]
```
NotInheritable Public Class Pens
```
[C#]
```
public sealed class Pens
```
[C++]
```
public __gc __sealed class Pens
```
[JScript]
```
public class Pens
```

Thread Safety

Any public static (**Shared** in Visual Basic) members of this type are safe for multithreaded operations. Any instance members are not guaranteed to be thread safe.

Requirements

Namespace: System.Drawing

Platforms: Windows 98, Windows NT 4.0, Windows Millennium Edition, Windows 2000, Windows XP Home Edition, Windows XP Professional, Windows Server 2003 family

Assembly: System.Drawing (in System.Drawing.dll)

Pens.AliceBlue Property

A system-defined **Pen** object with a width of 1.

[Visual Basic]
```
Public Shared ReadOnly Property AliceBlue As Pen
```
[C#]
```
public static Pen AliceBlue {get;}
```
[C++]
```
public: __property static Pen* get_AliceBlue();
```
[JScript]
```
public static function get AliceBlue() : Pen;
```

Property Value

A **Pen** object set to a system-defined color.

Requirements

Platforms: Windows 98, Windows NT 4.0, Windows Millennium Edition, Windows 2000, Windows XP Home Edition, Windows XP Professional, Windows Server 2003 family

Pens.AntiqueWhite Property

A system-defined **Pen** object with a width of 1.

[Visual Basic]
```
Public Shared ReadOnly Property AntiqueWhite As Pen
```
[C#]
```
public static Pen AntiqueWhite {get;}
```
[C++]
```
public: __property static Pen* get_AntiqueWhite();
```
[JScript]
```
public static function get AntiqueWhite() : Pen;
```

Property Value

A **Pen** object set to a system-defined color.

Requirements

Platforms: Windows 98, Windows NT 4.0, Windows Millennium Edition, Windows 2000, Windows XP Home Edition, Windows XP Professional, Windows Server 2003 family

Pens.Aqua Property

A system-defined **Pen** object with a width of 1.

[Visual Basic]
```
Public Shared ReadOnly Property Aqua As Pen
```
[C#]
```
public static Pen Aqua {get;}
```
[C++]
```
public: __property static Pen* get_Aqua();
```
[JScript]
```
public static function get Aqua() : Pen;
```

Property Value

A **Pen** object set to a system-defined color.

Requirements

Platforms: Windows 98, Windows NT 4.0, Windows Millennium Edition, Windows 2000, Windows XP Home Edition, Windows XP Professional, Windows Server 2003 family

Pens.Aquamarine Property

A system-defined **Pen** object with a width of 1.

[Visual Basic]
```
Public Shared ReadOnly Property Aquamarine As Pen
```
[C#]
```
public static Pen Aquamarine {get;}
```
[C++]
```
public: __property static Pen* get_Aquamarine();
```
[JScript]
```
public static function get Aquamarine() : Pen;
```

Property Value

A **Pen** object set to a system-defined color.

Requirements

Platforms: Windows 98, Windows NT 4.0, Windows Millennium Edition, Windows 2000, Windows XP Home Edition, Windows XP Professional, Windows Server 2003 family

Pens.Azure Property

A system-defined **Pen** object with a width of 1.

[Visual Basic]
```
Public Shared ReadOnly Property Azure As Pen
```
[C#]
```
public static Pen Azure {get;}
```

```
[C++]
public: __property static Pen* get_Azure();
[JScript]
public static function get Azure() : Pen;
```

Property Value

A **Pen** object set to a system-defined color.

Requirements

Platforms: Windows 98, Windows NT 4.0, Windows Millennium Edition, Windows 2000, Windows XP Home Edition, Windows XP Professional, Windows Server 2003 family

Pens.Beige Property

A system-defined **Pen** object with a width of 1.

```
[Visual Basic]
Public Shared ReadOnly Property Beige As Pen
[C#]
public static Pen Beige {get;}
[C++]
public: __property static Pen* get_Beige();
[JScript]
public static function get Beige() : Pen;
```

Property Value

A **Pen** object set to a system-defined color.

Requirements

Platforms: Windows 98, Windows NT 4.0, Windows Millennium Edition, Windows 2000, Windows XP Home Edition, Windows XP Professional, Windows Server 2003 family

Pens.Bisque Property

A system-defined **Pen** object with a width of 1.

```
[Visual Basic]
Public Shared ReadOnly Property Bisque As Pen
[C#]
public static Pen Bisque {get;}
[C++]
public: __property static Pen* get_Bisque();
[JScript]
public static function get Bisque() : Pen;
```

Property Value

A **Pen** object set to a system-defined color.

Requirements

Platforms: Windows 98, Windows NT 4.0, Windows Millennium Edition, Windows 2000, Windows XP Home Edition, Windows XP Professional, Windows Server 2003 family

Pens.Black Property

A system-defined **Pen** object with a width of 1.

```
[Visual Basic]
Public Shared ReadOnly Property Black As Pen
[C#]
public static Pen Black {get;}
[C++]
public: __property static Pen* get_Black();
[JScript]
public static function get Black() : Pen;
```

Property Value

A **Pen** object set to a system-defined color.

Requirements

Platforms: Windows 98, Windows NT 4.0, Windows Millennium Edition, Windows 2000, Windows XP Home Edition, Windows XP Professional, Windows Server 2003 family

Pens.BlanchedAlmond Property

A system-defined **Pen** object with a width of 1.

```
[Visual Basic]
Public Shared ReadOnly Property BlanchedAlmond As Pen
[C#]
public static Pen BlanchedAlmond {get;}
[C++]
public: __property static Pen* get_BlanchedAlmond();
[JScript]
public static function get BlanchedAlmond() : Pen;
```

Property Value

A **Pen** object set to a system-defined color.

Requirements

Platforms: Windows 98, Windows NT 4.0, Windows Millennium Edition, Windows 2000, Windows XP Home Edition, Windows XP Professional, Windows Server 2003 family

Pens.Blue Property

A system-defined **Pen** object with a width of 1.

```
[Visual Basic]
Public Shared ReadOnly Property Blue As Pen
[C#]
public static Pen Blue {get;}
[C++]
public: __property static Pen* get_Blue();
[JScript]
public static function get Blue() : Pen;
```

Property Value

A **Pen** object set to a system-defined color.

Requirements

Platforms: Windows 98, Windows NT 4.0, Windows Millennium Edition, Windows 2000, Windows XP Home Edition, Windows XP Professional, Windows Server 2003 family

Pens.BlueViolet Property

A system-defined **Pen** object with a width of 1.

```
[Visual Basic]
Public Shared ReadOnly Property BlueViolet As Pen
[C#]
public static Pen BlueViolet {get;}
[C++]
public: __property static Pen* get_BlueViolet();
[JScript]
public static function get BlueViolet() : Pen;
```

Property Value

A **Pen** object set to a system-defined color.

Requirements

Platforms: Windows 98, Windows NT 4.0, Windows Millennium Edition, Windows 2000, Windows XP Home Edition, Windows XP Professional, Windows Server 2003 family

Pens.Brown Property

A system-defined **Pen** object with a width of 1.

```
[Visual Basic]
Public Shared ReadOnly Property Brown As Pen
[C#]
public static Pen Brown {get;}
[C++]
public: __property static Pen* get_Brown();
[JScript]
public static function get Brown() : Pen;
```

Property Value

A **Pen** object set to a system-defined color.

Requirements

Platforms: Windows 98, Windows NT 4.0, Windows Millennium Edition, Windows 2000, Windows XP Home Edition, Windows XP Professional, Windows Server 2003 family

Pens.BurlyWood Property

A system-defined **Pen** object with a width of 1.

```
[Visual Basic]
Public Shared ReadOnly Property BurlyWood As Pen
[C#]
public static Pen BurlyWood {get;}
[C++]
public: __property static Pen* get_BurlyWood();
[JScript]
public static function get BurlyWood() : Pen;
```

Property Value

A **Pen** object set to a system-defined color.

Requirements

Platforms: Windows 98, Windows NT 4.0, Windows Millennium Edition, Windows 2000, Windows XP Home Edition, Windows XP Professional, Windows Server 2003 family

Pens.CadetBlue Property

A system-defined **Pen** object with a width of 1.

```
[Visual Basic]
Public Shared ReadOnly Property CadetBlue As Pen
[C#]
public static Pen CadetBlue {get;}
[C++]
public: __property static Pen* get_CadetBlue();
[JScript]
public static function get CadetBlue() : Pen;
```

Property Value

A **Pen** object set to a system-defined color.

Requirements

Platforms: Windows 98, Windows NT 4.0, Windows Millennium Edition, Windows 2000, Windows XP Home Edition, Windows XP Professional, Windows Server 2003 family

Pens.Chartreuse Property

A system-defined **Pen** object with a width of 1.

```
[Visual Basic]
Public Shared ReadOnly Property Chartreuse As Pen
[C#]
public static Pen Chartreuse {get;}
[C++]
public: __property static Pen* get_Chartreuse();
[JScript]
public static function get Chartreuse() : Pen;
```

Property Value

A **Pen** object set to a system-defined color.

Requirements

Platforms: Windows 98, Windows NT 4.0, Windows Millennium Edition, Windows 2000, Windows XP Home Edition, Windows XP Professional, Windows Server 2003 family

Pens.Chocolate Property

A system-defined **Pen** object with a width of 1.

```
[Visual Basic]
Public Shared ReadOnly Property Chocolate As Pen
[C#]
public static Pen Chocolate {get;}
[C++]
public: __property static Pen* get_Chocolate();
[JScript]
public static function get Chocolate() : Pen;
```

Property Value

A **Pen** object set to a system-defined color.

Requirements

Platforms: Windows 98, Windows NT 4.0, Windows Millennium Edition, Windows 2000, Windows XP Home Edition, Windows XP Professional, Windows Server 2003 family

Pens.Coral Property

A system-defined **Pen** object with a width of 1.

```
[Visual Basic]
Public Shared ReadOnly Property Coral As Pen
[C#]
public static Pen Coral {get;}
[C++]
public: __property static Pen* get_Coral();
[JScript]
public static function get Coral() : Pen;
```

Property Value

A **Pen** object set to a system-defined color.

Requirements

Platforms: Windows 98, Windows NT 4.0, Windows Millennium Edition, Windows 2000, Windows XP Home Edition, Windows XP Professional, Windows Server 2003 family

Pens.CornflowerBlue Property

A system-defined **Pen** object with a width of 1.

```
[Visual Basic]
Public Shared ReadOnly Property CornflowerBlue As Pen
[C#]
public static Pen CornflowerBlue {get;}
[C++]
public: __property static Pen* get_CornflowerBlue();
[JScript]
public static function get CornflowerBlue() : Pen;
```

Property Value

A **Pen** object set to a system-defined color.

Requirements

Platforms: Windows 98, Windows NT 4.0, Windows Millennium Edition, Windows 2000, Windows XP Home Edition, Windows XP Professional, Windows Server 2003 family

Pens.Cornsilk Property

A system-defined **Pen** object with a width of 1.

```
[Visual Basic]
Public Shared ReadOnly Property Cornsilk As Pen
[C#]
public static Pen Cornsilk {get;}
[C++]
public: __property static Pen* get_Cornsilk();
[JScript]
public static function get Cornsilk() : Pen;
```

Property Value

A **Pen** object set to a system-defined color.

Requirements

Platforms: Windows 98, Windows NT 4.0, Windows Millennium Edition, Windows 2000, Windows XP Home Edition, Windows XP Professional, Windows Server 2003 family

Pens.Crimson Property

A system-defined **Pen** object with a width of 1.

```
[Visual Basic]
Public Shared ReadOnly Property Crimson As Pen
[C#]
public static Pen Crimson {get;}
[C++]
public: __property static Pen* get_Crimson();
[JScript]
public static function get Crimson() : Pen;
```

Property Value

A **Pen** object set to a system-defined color.

Requirements

Platforms: Windows 98, Windows NT 4.0, Windows Millennium Edition, Windows 2000, Windows XP Home Edition, Windows XP Professional, Windows Server 2003 family

Pens.Cyan Property

A system-defined **Pen** object with a width of 1.

```
[Visual Basic]
Public Shared ReadOnly Property Cyan As Pen
[C#]
public static Pen Cyan {get;}
[C++]
public: __property static Pen* get_Cyan();
[JScript]
public static function get Cyan() : Pen;
```

Property Value

A **Pen** object set to a system-defined color.

Requirements

Platforms: Windows 98, Windows NT 4.0, Windows Millennium Edition, Windows 2000, Windows XP Home Edition, Windows XP Professional, Windows Server 2003 family

Pens.DarkBlue Property

A system-defined **Pen** object with a width of 1.

```
[Visual Basic]
Public Shared ReadOnly Property DarkBlue As Pen
[C#]
public static Pen DarkBlue {get;}
[C++]
public: __property static Pen* get_DarkBlue();
[JScript]
public static function get DarkBlue() : Pen;
```

Property Value

A **Pen** object set to a system-defined color.

Requirements

Platforms: Windows 98, Windows NT 4.0, Windows Millennium Edition, Windows 2000, Windows XP Home Edition, Windows XP Professional, Windows Server 2003 family

Pens.DarkCyan Property

A system-defined **Pen** object with a width of 1.

[Visual Basic]
```
Public Shared ReadOnly Property DarkCyan As Pen
```
[C#]
```
public static Pen DarkCyan {get;}
```
[C++]
```
public: __property static Pen* get_DarkCyan();
```
[JScript]
```
public static function get DarkCyan() : Pen;
```

Property Value

A **Pen** object set to a system-defined color.

Requirements

Platforms: Windows 98, Windows NT 4.0, Windows Millennium Edition, Windows 2000, Windows XP Home Edition, Windows XP Professional, Windows Server 2003 family

Pens.DarkGoldenrod Property

A system-defined **Pen** object with a width of 1.

[Visual Basic]
```
Public Shared ReadOnly Property DarkGoldenrod As Pen
```
[C#]
```
public static Pen DarkGoldenrod {get;}
```
[C++]
```
public: __property static Pen* get_DarkGoldenrod();
```
[JScript]
```
public static function get DarkGoldenrod() : Pen;
```

Property Value

A **Pen** object set to a system-defined color.

Requirements

Platforms: Windows 98, Windows NT 4.0, Windows Millennium Edition, Windows 2000, Windows XP Home Edition, Windows XP Professional, Windows Server 2003 family

Pens.DarkGray Property

A system-defined **Pen** object with a width of 1.

[Visual Basic]
```
Public Shared ReadOnly Property DarkGray As Pen
```
[C#]
```
public static Pen DarkGray {get;}
```
[C++]
```
public: __property static Pen* get_DarkGray();
```
[JScript]
```
public static function get DarkGray() : Pen;
```

Property Value

A **Pen** object set to a system-defined color.

Requirements

Platforms: Windows 98, Windows NT 4.0, Windows Millennium Edition, Windows 2000, Windows XP Home Edition, Windows XP Professional, Windows Server 2003 family

Pens.DarkGreen Property

A system-defined **Pen** object with a width of 1.

[Visual Basic]
```
Public Shared ReadOnly Property DarkGreen As Pen
```
[C#]
```
public static Pen DarkGreen {get;}
```
[C++]
```
public: __property static Pen* get_DarkGreen();
```
[JScript]
```
public static function get DarkGreen() : Pen;
```

Property Value

A **Pen** object set to a system-defined color.

Requirements

Platforms: Windows 98, Windows NT 4.0, Windows Millennium Edition, Windows 2000, Windows XP Home Edition, Windows XP Professional, Windows Server 2003 family

Pens.DarkKhaki Property

A system-defined **Pen** object with a width of 1.

[Visual Basic]
```
Public Shared ReadOnly Property DarkKhaki As Pen
```
[C#]
```
public static Pen DarkKhaki {get;}
```
[C++]
```
public: __property static Pen* get_DarkKhaki();
```
[JScript]
```
public static function get DarkKhaki() : Pen;
```

Property Value

A **Pen** object set to a system-defined color.

Requirements

Platforms: Windows 98, Windows NT 4.0, Windows Millennium Edition, Windows 2000, Windows XP Home Edition, Windows XP Professional, Windows Server 2003 family

Pens.DarkMagenta Property

A system-defined **Pen** object with a width of 1.

[Visual Basic]
```
Public Shared ReadOnly Property DarkMagenta As Pen
```
[C#]
```
public static Pen DarkMagenta {get;}
```
[C++]
```
public: __property static Pen* get_DarkMagenta();
```
[JScript]
```
public static function get DarkMagenta() : Pen;
```

Property Value

A **Pen** object set to a system-defined color.

Requirements

Platforms: Windows 98, Windows NT 4.0, Windows Millennium Edition, Windows 2000, Windows XP Home Edition, Windows XP Professional, Windows Server 2003 family

Pens.DarkOliveGreen Property

A system-defined **Pen** object with a width of 1.

```
[Visual Basic]
Public Shared ReadOnly Property DarkOliveGreen As Pen
[C#]
public static Pen DarkOliveGreen {get;}
[C++]
public: __property static Pen* get_DarkOliveGreen();
[JScript]
public static function get DarkOliveGreen() : Pen;
```

Property Value

A **Pen** object set to a system-defined color.

Requirements

Platforms: Windows 98, Windows NT 4.0, Windows Millennium Edition, Windows 2000, Windows XP Home Edition, Windows XP Professional, Windows Server 2003 family

Pens.DarkOrange Property

A system-defined **Pen** object with a width of 1.

```
[Visual Basic]
Public Shared ReadOnly Property DarkOrange As Pen
[C#]
public static Pen DarkOrange {get;}
[C++]
public: __property static Pen* get_DarkOrange();
[JScript]
public static function get DarkOrange() : Pen;
```

Property Value

A **Pen** object set to a system-defined color.

Requirements

Platforms: Windows 98, Windows NT 4.0, Windows Millennium Edition, Windows 2000, Windows XP Home Edition, Windows XP Professional, Windows Server 2003 family

Pens.DarkOrchid Property

A system-defined **Pen** object with a width of 1.

```
[Visual Basic]
Public Shared ReadOnly Property DarkOrchid As Pen
[C#]
public static Pen DarkOrchid {get;}
[C++]
public: __property static Pen* get_DarkOrchid();
[JScript]
public static function get DarkOrchid() : Pen;
```

Property Value

A **Pen** object set to a system-defined color.

Requirements

Platforms: Windows 98, Windows NT 4.0, Windows Millennium Edition, Windows 2000, Windows XP Home Edition, Windows XP Professional, Windows Server 2003 family

Pens.DarkRed Property

A system-defined **Pen** object with a width of 1.

```
[Visual Basic]
Public Shared ReadOnly Property DarkRed As Pen
[C#]
public static Pen DarkRed {get;}
[C++]
public: __property static Pen* get_DarkRed();
[JScript]
public static function get DarkRed() : Pen;
```

Property Value

A **Pen** object set to a system-defined color.

Requirements

Platforms: Windows 98, Windows NT 4.0, Windows Millennium Edition, Windows 2000, Windows XP Home Edition, Windows XP Professional, Windows Server 2003 family

Pens.DarkSalmon Property

A system-defined **Pen** object with a width of 1.

```
[Visual Basic]
Public Shared ReadOnly Property DarkSalmon As Pen
[C#]
public static Pen DarkSalmon {get;}
[C++]
public: __property static Pen* get_DarkSalmon();
[JScript]
public static function get DarkSalmon() : Pen;
```

Property Value

A **Pen** object set to a system-defined color.

Requirements

Platforms: Windows 98, Windows NT 4.0, Windows Millennium Edition, Windows 2000, Windows XP Home Edition, Windows XP Professional, Windows Server 2003 family

Pens.DarkSeaGreen Property

A system-defined **Pen** object with a width of 1.

```
[Visual Basic]
Public Shared ReadOnly Property DarkSeaGreen As Pen
[C#]
public static Pen DarkSeaGreen {get;}
[C++]
public: __property static Pen* get_DarkSeaGreen();
[JScript]
public static function get DarkSeaGreen() : Pen;
```

Property Value

A **Pen** object set to a system-defined color.

Requirements

Platforms: Windows 98, Windows NT 4.0, Windows Millennium Edition, Windows 2000, Windows XP Home Edition, Windows XP Professional, Windows Server 2003 family

Pens.DarkSlateBlue Property

A system-defined **Pen** object with a width of 1.

[Visual Basic]
```
Public Shared ReadOnly Property DarkSlateBlue As Pen
```
[C#]
```
public static Pen DarkSlateBlue {get;}
```
[C++]
```
public: __property static Pen* get_DarkSlateBlue();
```
[JScript]
```
public static function get DarkSlateBlue() : Pen;
```

Property Value

A **Pen** object set to a system-defined color.

Requirements

Platforms: Windows 98, Windows NT 4.0, Windows Millennium Edition, Windows 2000, Windows XP Home Edition, Windows XP Professional, Windows Server 2003 family

Pens.DarkSlateGray Property

A system-defined **Pen** object with a width of 1.

[Visual Basic]
```
Public Shared ReadOnly Property DarkSlateGray As Pen
```
[C#]
```
public static Pen DarkSlateGray {get;}
```
[C++]
```
public: __property static Pen* get_DarkSlateGray();
```
[JScript]
```
public static function get DarkSlateGray() : Pen;
```

Property Value

A **Pen** object set to a system-defined color.

Requirements

Platforms: Windows 98, Windows NT 4.0, Windows Millennium Edition, Windows 2000, Windows XP Home Edition, Windows XP Professional, Windows Server 2003 family

Pens.DarkTurquoise Property

A system-defined **Pen** object with a width of 1.

[Visual Basic]
```
Public Shared ReadOnly Property DarkTurquoise As Pen
```
[C#]
```
public static Pen DarkTurquoise {get;}
```
[C++]
```
public: __property static Pen* get_DarkTurquoise();
```
[JScript]
```
public static function get DarkTurquoise() : Pen;
```

Property Value

A **Pen** object set to a system-defined color.

Requirements

Platforms: Windows 98, Windows NT 4.0, Windows Millennium Edition, Windows 2000, Windows XP Home Edition, Windows XP Professional, Windows Server 2003 family

Pens.DarkViolet Property

A system-defined **Pen** object with a width of 1.

[Visual Basic]
```
Public Shared ReadOnly Property DarkViolet As Pen
```
[C#]
```
public static Pen DarkViolet {get;}
```
[C++]
```
public: __property static Pen* get_DarkViolet();
```
[JScript]
```
public static function get DarkViolet() : Pen;
```

Property Value

A **Pen** object set to a system-defined color.

Requirements

Platforms: Windows 98, Windows NT 4.0, Windows Millennium Edition, Windows 2000, Windows XP Home Edition, Windows XP Professional, Windows Server 2003 family

Pens.DeepPink Property

A system-defined **Pen** object with a width of 1.

[Visual Basic]
```
Public Shared ReadOnly Property DeepPink As Pen
```
[C#]
```
public static Pen DeepPink {get;}
```
[C++]
```
public: __property static Pen* get_DeepPink();
```
[JScript]
```
public static function get DeepPink() : Pen;
```

Property Value

A **Pen** object set to a system-defined color.

Requirements

Platforms: Windows 98, Windows NT 4.0, Windows Millennium Edition, Windows 2000, Windows XP Home Edition, Windows XP Professional, Windows Server 2003 family

Pens.DeepSkyBlue Property

A system-defined **Pen** object with a width of 1.

[Visual Basic]
```
Public Shared ReadOnly Property DeepSkyBlue As Pen
```
[C#]
```
public static Pen DeepSkyBlue {get;}
```
[C++]
```
public: __property static Pen* get_DeepSkyBlue();
```
[JScript]
```
public static function get DeepSkyBlue() : Pen;
```

Property Value

A **Pen** object set to a system-defined color.

Requirements

Platforms: Windows 98, Windows NT 4.0, Windows Millennium Edition, Windows 2000, Windows XP Home Edition, Windows XP Professional, Windows Server 2003 family

Pens.DimGray Property

A system-defined **Pen** object with a width of 1.

[Visual Basic]
```
Public Shared ReadOnly Property DimGray As Pen
```
[C#]
```
public static Pen DimGray {get;}
```
[C++]
```
public: __property static Pen* get_DimGray();
```
[JScript]
```
public static function get DimGray() : Pen;
```

Property Value

A **Pen** object set to a system-defined color.

Requirements

Platforms: Windows 98, Windows NT 4.0, Windows Millennium Edition, Windows 2000, Windows XP Home Edition, Windows XP Professional, Windows Server 2003 family

Pens.DodgerBlue Property

A system-defined **Pen** object with a width of 1.

[Visual Basic]
```
Public Shared ReadOnly Property DodgerBlue As Pen
```
[C#]
```
public static Pen DodgerBlue {get;}
```
[C++]
```
public: __property static Pen* get_DodgerBlue();
```
[JScript]
```
public static function get DodgerBlue() : Pen;
```

Property Value

A **Pen** object set to a system-defined color.

Requirements

Platforms: Windows 98, Windows NT 4.0, Windows Millennium Edition, Windows 2000, Windows XP Home Edition, Windows XP Professional, Windows Server 2003 family

Pens.Firebrick Property

A system-defined **Pen** object with a width of 1.

[Visual Basic]
```
Public Shared ReadOnly Property Firebrick As Pen
```
[C#]
```
public static Pen Firebrick {get;}
```
[C++]
```
public: __property static Pen* get_Firebrick();
```
[JScript]
```
public static function get Firebrick() : Pen;
```

Property Value

A **Pen** object set to a system-defined color.

Requirements

Platforms: Windows 98, Windows NT 4.0, Windows Millennium Edition, Windows 2000, Windows XP Home Edition, Windows XP Professional, Windows Server 2003 family

Pens.FloralWhite Property

A system-defined **Pen** object with a width of 1.

[Visual Basic]
```
Public Shared ReadOnly Property FloralWhite As Pen
```
[C#]
```
public static Pen FloralWhite {get;}
```
[C++]
```
public: __property static Pen* get_FloralWhite();
```
[JScript]
```
public static function get FloralWhite() : Pen;
```

Property Value

A **Pen** object set to a system-defined color.

Requirements

Platforms: Windows 98, Windows NT 4.0, Windows Millennium Edition, Windows 2000, Windows XP Home Edition, Windows XP Professional, Windows Server 2003 family

Pens.ForestGreen Property

A system-defined **Pen** object with a width of 1.

[Visual Basic]
```
Public Shared ReadOnly Property ForestGreen As Pen
```
[C#]
```
public static Pen ForestGreen {get;}
```
[C++]
```
public: __property static Pen* get_ForestGreen();
```
[JScript]
```
public static function get ForestGreen() : Pen;
```

Property Value

A **Pen** object set to a system-defined color.

Requirements

Platforms: Windows 98, Windows NT 4.0, Windows Millennium Edition, Windows 2000, Windows XP Home Edition, Windows XP Professional, Windows Server 2003 family

Pens.Fuchsia Property

A system-defined **Pen** object with a width of 1.

[Visual Basic]
```
Public Shared ReadOnly Property Fuchsia As Pen
```
[C#]
```
public static Pen Fuchsia {get;}
```
[C++]
```
public: __property static Pen* get_Fuchsia();
```
[JScript]
```
public static function get Fuchsia() : Pen;
```

Property Value

A **Pen** object set to a system-defined color.

Requirements

Platforms: Windows 98, Windows NT 4.0, Windows Millennium Edition, Windows 2000, Windows XP Home Edition, Windows XP Professional, Windows Server 2003 family

Pens.Gainsboro Property

A system-defined **Pen** object with a width of 1.

```
[Visual Basic]
Public Shared ReadOnly Property Gainsboro As Pen
[C#]
public static Pen Gainsboro {get;}
[C++]
public: __property static Pen* get_Gainsboro();
[JScript]
public static function get Gainsboro() : Pen;
```

Property Value

A **Pen** object set to a system-defined color.

Requirements

Platforms: Windows 98, Windows NT 4.0, Windows Millennium Edition, Windows 2000, Windows XP Home Edition, Windows XP Professional, Windows Server 2003 family

Pens.GhostWhite Property

A system-defined **Pen** object with a width of 1.

```
[Visual Basic]
Public Shared ReadOnly Property GhostWhite As Pen
[C#]
public static Pen GhostWhite {get;}
[C++]
public: __property static Pen* get_GhostWhite();
[JScript]
public static function get GhostWhite() : Pen;
```

Property Value

A **Pen** object set to a system-defined color.

Requirements

Platforms: Windows 98, Windows NT 4.0, Windows Millennium Edition, Windows 2000, Windows XP Home Edition, Windows XP Professional, Windows Server 2003 family

Pens.Gold Property

A system-defined **Pen** object with a width of 1.

```
[Visual Basic]
Public Shared ReadOnly Property Gold As Pen
[C#]
public static Pen Gold {get;}
[C++]
public: __property static Pen* get_Gold();
[JScript]
public static function get Gold() : Pen;
```

Property Value

A **Pen** object set to a system-defined color.

Requirements

Platforms: Windows 98, Windows NT 4.0, Windows Millennium Edition, Windows 2000, Windows XP Home Edition, Windows XP Professional, Windows Server 2003 family

Pens.Goldenrod Property

A system-defined **Pen** object with a width of 1.

```
[Visual Basic]
Public Shared ReadOnly Property Goldenrod As Pen
[C#]
public static Pen Goldenrod {get;}
[C++]
public: __property static Pen* get_Goldenrod();
[JScript]
public static function get Goldenrod() : Pen;
```

Property Value

A **Pen** object set to a system-defined color.

Requirements

Platforms: Windows 98, Windows NT 4.0, Windows Millennium Edition, Windows 2000, Windows XP Home Edition, Windows XP Professional, Windows Server 2003 family

Pens.Gray Property

A system-defined **Pen** object with a width of 1.

```
[Visual Basic]
Public Shared ReadOnly Property Gray As Pen
[C#]
public static Pen Gray {get;}
[C++]
public: __property static Pen* get_Gray();
[JScript]
public static function get Gray() : Pen;
```

Property Value

A **Pen** object set to a system-defined color.

Requirements

Platforms: Windows 98, Windows NT 4.0, Windows Millennium Edition, Windows 2000, Windows XP Home Edition, Windows XP Professional, Windows Server 2003 family

Pens.Green Property

A system-defined **Pen** object with a width of 1.

```
[Visual Basic]
Public Shared ReadOnly Property Green As Pen
[C#]
public static Pen Green {get;}
[C++]
public: __property static Pen* get_Green();
[JScript]
public static function get Green() : Pen;
```

Property Value

A **Pen** object set to a system-defined color.

Requirements

Platforms: Windows 98, Windows NT 4.0, Windows Millennium Edition, Windows 2000, Windows XP Home Edition, Windows XP Professional, Windows Server 2003 family

Pens.GreenYellow Property

A system-defined **Pen** object with a width of 1.

[Visual Basic]
```
Public Shared ReadOnly Property GreenYellow As Pen
```
[C#]
```
public static Pen GreenYellow {get;}
```
[C++]
```
public: __property static Pen* get_GreenYellow();
```
[JScript]
```
public static function get GreenYellow() : Pen;
```

Property Value

A **Pen** object set to a system-defined color.

Requirements

Platforms: Windows 98, Windows NT 4.0, Windows Millennium Edition, Windows 2000, Windows XP Home Edition, Windows XP Professional, Windows Server 2003 family

Pens.Honeydew Property

A system-defined **Pen** object with a width of 1.

[Visual Basic]
```
Public Shared ReadOnly Property Honeydew As Pen
```
[C#]
```
public static Pen Honeydew {get;}
```
[C++]
```
public: __property static Pen* get_Honeydew();
```
[JScript]
```
public static function get Honeydew() : Pen;
```

Property Value

A **Pen** object set to a system-defined color.

Requirements

Platforms: Windows 98, Windows NT 4.0, Windows Millennium Edition, Windows 2000, Windows XP Home Edition, Windows XP Professional, Windows Server 2003 family

Pens.HotPink Property

A system-defined **Pen** object with a width of 1.

[Visual Basic]
```
Public Shared ReadOnly Property HotPink As Pen
```
[C#]
```
public static Pen HotPink {get;}
```
[C++]
```
public: __property static Pen* get_HotPink();
```
[JScript]
```
public static function get HotPink() : Pen;
```

Property Value

A **Pen** object set to a system-defined color.

Requirements

Platforms: Windows 98, Windows NT 4.0, Windows Millennium Edition, Windows 2000, Windows XP Home Edition, Windows XP Professional, Windows Server 2003 family

Pens.IndianRed Property

A system-defined **Pen** object with a width of 1.

[Visual Basic]
```
Public Shared ReadOnly Property IndianRed As Pen
```
[C#]
```
public static Pen IndianRed {get;}
```
[C++]
```
public: __property static Pen* get_IndianRed();
```
[JScript]
```
public static function get IndianRed() : Pen;
```

Property Value

A **Pen** object set to a system-defined color.

Requirements

Platforms: Windows 98, Windows NT 4.0, Windows Millennium Edition, Windows 2000, Windows XP Home Edition, Windows XP Professional, Windows Server 2003 family

Pens.Indigo Property

A system-defined **Pen** object with a width of 1.

[Visual Basic]
```
Public Shared ReadOnly Property Indigo As Pen
```
[C#]
```
public static Pen Indigo {get;}
```
[C++]
```
public: __property static Pen* get_Indigo();
```
[JScript]
```
public static function get Indigo() : Pen;
```

Property Value

A **Pen** object set to a system-defined color.

Requirements

Platforms: Windows 98, Windows NT 4.0, Windows Millennium Edition, Windows 2000, Windows XP Home Edition, Windows XP Professional, Windows Server 2003 family

Pens.Ivory Property

A system-defined **Pen** object with a width of 1.

[Visual Basic]
```
Public Shared ReadOnly Property Ivory As Pen
```
[C#]
```
public static Pen Ivory {get;}
```
[C++]
```
public: __property static Pen* get_Ivory();
```
[JScript]
```
public static function get Ivory() : Pen;
```

Property Value

A **Pen** object set to a system-defined color.

Requirements

Platforms: Windows 98, Windows NT 4.0, Windows Millennium Edition, Windows 2000, Windows XP Home Edition, Windows XP Professional, Windows Server 2003 family

Pens.Khaki Property

A system-defined **Pen** object with a width of 1.

[Visual Basic]
```
Public Shared ReadOnly Property Khaki As Pen
```
[C#]
```
public static Pen Khaki {get;}
```
[C++]
```
public: __property static Pen* get_Khaki();
```
[JScript]
```
public static function get Khaki() : Pen;
```

Property Value

A **Pen** object set to a system-defined color.

Requirements

Platforms: Windows 98, Windows NT 4.0, Windows Millennium Edition, Windows 2000, Windows XP Home Edition, Windows XP Professional, Windows Server 2003 family

Pens.Lavender Property

A system-defined **Pen** object with a width of 1.

[Visual Basic]
```
Public Shared ReadOnly Property Lavender As Pen
```
[C#]
```
public static Pen Lavender {get;}
```
[C++]
```
public: __property static Pen* get_Lavender();
```
[JScript]
```
public static function get Lavender() : Pen;
```

Property Value

A **Pen** object set to a system-defined color.

Requirements

Platforms: Windows 98, Windows NT 4.0, Windows Millennium Edition, Windows 2000, Windows XP Home Edition, Windows XP Professional, Windows Server 2003 family

Pens.LavenderBlush Property

A system-defined **Pen** object with a width of 1.

[Visual Basic]
```
Public Shared ReadOnly Property LavenderBlush As Pen
```
[C#]
```
public static Pen LavenderBlush {get;}
```
[C++]
```
public: __property static Pen* get_LavenderBlush();
```
[JScript]
```
public static function get LavenderBlush() : Pen;
```

Property Value

A **Pen** object set to a system-defined color.

Requirements

Platforms: Windows 98, Windows NT 4.0, Windows Millennium Edition, Windows 2000, Windows XP Home Edition, Windows XP Professional, Windows Server 2003 family

Pens.LawnGreen Property

A system-defined **Pen** object with a width of 1.

[Visual Basic]
```
Public Shared ReadOnly Property LawnGreen As Pen
```
[C#]
```
public static Pen LawnGreen {get;}
```
[C++]
```
public: __property static Pen* get_LawnGreen();
```
[JScript]
```
public static function get LawnGreen() : Pen;
```

Property Value

A **Pen** object set to a system-defined color.

Requirements

Platforms: Windows 98, Windows NT 4.0, Windows Millennium Edition, Windows 2000, Windows XP Home Edition, Windows XP Professional, Windows Server 2003 family

Pens.LemonChiffon Property

A system-defined **Pen** object with a width of 1.

[Visual Basic]
```
Public Shared ReadOnly Property LemonChiffon As Pen
```
[C#]
```
public static Pen LemonChiffon {get;}
```
[C++]
```
public: __property static Pen* get_LemonChiffon();
```
[JScript]
```
public static function get LemonChiffon() : Pen;
```

Property Value

A **Pen** object set to a system-defined color.

Requirements

Platforms: Windows 98, Windows NT 4.0, Windows Millennium Edition, Windows 2000, Windows XP Home Edition, Windows XP Professional, Windows Server 2003 family

Pens.LightBlue Property

A system-defined **Pen** object with a width of 1.

[Visual Basic]
```
Public Shared ReadOnly Property LightBlue As Pen
```
[C#]
```
public static Pen LightBlue {get;}
```
[C++]
```
public: __property static Pen* get_LightBlue();
```
[JScript]
```
public static function get LightBlue() : Pen;
```

Property Value

A **Pen** object set to a system-defined color.

Requirements

Platforms: Windows 98, Windows NT 4.0, Windows Millennium Edition, Windows 2000, Windows XP Home Edition, Windows XP Professional, Windows Server 2003 family

Pens.LightCoral Property

A system-defined **Pen** object with a width of 1.

[Visual Basic]
```
Public Shared ReadOnly Property LightCoral As Pen
```
[C#]
```
public static Pen LightCoral {get;}
```
[C++]
```
public: __property static Pen* get_LightCoral();
```
[JScript]
```
public static function get LightCoral() : Pen;
```

Property Value

A **Pen** object set to a system-defined color.

Requirements

Platforms: Windows 98, Windows NT 4.0, Windows Millennium Edition, Windows 2000, Windows XP Home Edition, Windows XP Professional, Windows Server 2003 family

Pens.LightCyan Property

A system-defined **Pen** object with a width of 1.

[Visual Basic]
```
Public Shared ReadOnly Property LightCyan As Pen
```
[C#]
```
public static Pen LightCyan {get;}
```
[C++]
```
public: __property static Pen* get_LightCyan();
```
[JScript]
```
public static function get LightCyan() : Pen;
```

Property Value

A **Pen** object set to a system-defined color.

Requirements

Platforms: Windows 98, Windows NT 4.0, Windows Millennium Edition, Windows 2000, Windows XP Home Edition, Windows XP Professional, Windows Server 2003 family

Pens.LightGoldenrodYellow Property

A system-defined **Pen** object with a width of 1.

[Visual Basic]
```
Public Shared ReadOnly Property LightGoldenrodYellow As Pen
```
[C#]
```
public static Pen LightGoldenrodYellow {get;}
```
[C++]
```
public: __property static Pen* get_LightGoldenrodYellow();
```
[JScript]
```
public static function get LightGoldenrodYellow() : Pen;
```

Property Value

A **Pen** object set to a system-defined color.

Requirements

Platforms: Windows 98, Windows NT 4.0, Windows Millennium Edition, Windows 2000, Windows XP Home Edition, Windows XP Professional, Windows Server 2003 family

Pens.LightGray Property

A system-defined **Pen** object with a width of 1.

[Visual Basic]
```
Public Shared ReadOnly Property LightGray As Pen
```
[C#]
```
public static Pen LightGray {get;}
```
[C++]
```
public: __property static Pen* get_LightGray();
```
[JScript]
```
public static function get LightGray() : Pen;
```

Property Value

A **Pen** object set to a system-defined color.

Requirements

Platforms: Windows 98, Windows NT 4.0, Windows Millennium Edition, Windows 2000, Windows XP Home Edition, Windows XP Professional, Windows Server 2003 family

Pens.LightGreen Property

A system-defined **Pen** object with a width of 1.

[Visual Basic]
```
Public Shared ReadOnly Property LightGreen As Pen
```
[C#]
```
public static Pen LightGreen {get;}
```
[C++]
```
public: __property static Pen* get_LightGreen();
```
[JScript]
```
public static function get LightGreen() : Pen;
```

Property Value

A **Pen** object set to a system-defined color.

Requirements

Platforms: Windows 98, Windows NT 4.0, Windows Millennium Edition, Windows 2000, Windows XP Home Edition, Windows XP Professional, Windows Server 2003 family

Pens.LightPink Property

A system-defined **Pen** object with a width of 1.

[Visual Basic]
```
Public Shared ReadOnly Property LightPink As Pen
```
[C#]
```
public static Pen LightPink {get;}
```
[C++]
```
public: __property static Pen* get_LightPink();
```
[JScript]
```
public static function get LightPink() : Pen;
```

Property Value

A **Pen** object set to a system-defined color.

Requirements

Platforms: Windows 98, Windows NT 4.0, Windows Millennium Edition, Windows 2000, Windows XP Home Edition, Windows XP Professional, Windows Server 2003 family

Pens.LightSalmon Property

A system-defined **Pen** object with a width of 1.

[Visual Basic]
```
Public Shared ReadOnly Property LightSalmon As Pen
```
[C#]
```
public static Pen LightSalmon {get;}
```
[C++]
```
public: __property static Pen* get_LightSalmon();
```
[JScript]
```
public static function get LightSalmon() : Pen;
```

Property Value

A **Pen** object set to a system-defined color.

Requirements

Platforms: Windows 98, Windows NT 4.0, Windows Millennium Edition, Windows 2000, Windows XP Home Edition, Windows XP Professional, Windows Server 2003 family

Pens.LightSeaGreen Property

A system-defined **Pen** object with a width of 1.

[Visual Basic]
```
Public Shared ReadOnly Property LightSeaGreen As Pen
```
[C#]
```
public static Pen LightSeaGreen {get;}
```
[C++]
```
public: __property static Pen* get_LightSeaGreen();
```
[JScript]
```
public static function get LightSeaGreen() : Pen;
```

Property Value

A **Pen** object set to a system-defined color.

Requirements

Platforms: Windows 98, Windows NT 4.0, Windows Millennium Edition, Windows 2000, Windows XP Home Edition, Windows XP Professional, Windows Server 2003 family

Pens.LightSkyBlue Property

A system-defined **Pen** object with a width of 1.

[Visual Basic]
```
Public Shared ReadOnly Property LightSkyBlue As Pen
```
[C#]
```
public static Pen LightSkyBlue {get;}
```
[C++]
```
public: __property static Pen* get_LightSkyBlue();
```
[JScript]
```
public static function get LightSkyBlue() : Pen;
```

Property Value

A **Pen** object set to a system-defined color.

Requirements

Platforms: Windows 98, Windows NT 4.0, Windows Millennium Edition, Windows 2000, Windows XP Home Edition, Windows XP Professional, Windows Server 2003 family

Pens.LightSlateGray Property

A system-defined **Pen** object with a width of 1.

[Visual Basic]
```
Public Shared ReadOnly Property LightSlateGray As Pen
```
[C#]
```
public static Pen LightSlateGray {get;}
```
[C++]
```
public: __property static Pen* get_LightSlateGray();
```
[JScript]
```
public static function get LightSlateGray() : Pen;
```

Property Value

A **Pen** object set to a system-defined color.

Requirements

Platforms: Windows 98, Windows NT 4.0, Windows Millennium Edition, Windows 2000, Windows XP Home Edition, Windows XP Professional, Windows Server 2003 family

Pens.LightSteelBlue Property

A system-defined **Pen** object with a width of 1.

[Visual Basic]
```
Public Shared ReadOnly Property LightSteelBlue As Pen
```
[C#]
```
public static Pen LightSteelBlue {get;}
```
[C++]
```
public: __property static Pen* get_LightSteelBlue();
```
[JScript]
```
public static function get LightSteelBlue() : Pen;
```

Property Value

A **Pen** object set to a system-defined color.

Requirements

Platforms: Windows 98, Windows NT 4.0, Windows Millennium Edition, Windows 2000, Windows XP Home Edition, Windows XP Professional, Windows Server 2003 family

Pens.LightYellow Property

A system-defined **Pen** object with a width of 1.

[Visual Basic]
```
Public Shared ReadOnly Property LightYellow As Pen
```
[C#]
```
public static Pen LightYellow {get;}
```
[C++]
```
public: __property static Pen* get_LightYellow();
```
[JScript]
```
public static function get LightYellow() : Pen;
```

Property Value

A **Pen** object set to a system-defined color.

Requirements

Platforms: Windows 98, Windows NT 4.0, Windows Millennium Edition, Windows 2000, Windows XP Home Edition, Windows XP Professional, Windows Server 2003 family

Pens.Lime Property

A system-defined **Pen** object with a width of 1.

```
[Visual Basic]
Public Shared ReadOnly Property Lime As Pen
[C#]
public static Pen Lime {get;}
[C++]
public: __property static Pen* get_Lime();
[JScript]
public static function get Lime() : Pen;
```

Property Value

A **Pen** object set to a system-defined color.

Requirements

Platforms: Windows 98, Windows NT 4.0, Windows Millennium Edition, Windows 2000, Windows XP Home Edition, Windows XP Professional, Windows Server 2003 family

Pens.LimeGreen Property

A system-defined **Pen** object with a width of 1.

```
[Visual Basic]
Public Shared ReadOnly Property LimeGreen As Pen
[C#]
public static Pen LimeGreen {get;}
[C++]
public: __property static Pen* get_LimeGreen();
[JScript]
public static function get LimeGreen() : Pen;
```

Property Value

A **Pen** object set to a system-defined color.

Requirements

Platforms: Windows 98, Windows NT 4.0, Windows Millennium Edition, Windows 2000, Windows XP Home Edition, Windows XP Professional, Windows Server 2003 family

Pens.Linen Property

A system-defined **Pen** object with a width of 1.

```
[Visual Basic]
Public Shared ReadOnly Property Linen As Pen
[C#]
public static Pen Linen {get;}
[C++]
public: __property static Pen* get_Linen();
[JScript]
public static function get Linen() : Pen;
```

Property Value

A **Pen** object set to a system-defined color.

Requirements

Platforms: Windows 98, Windows NT 4.0, Windows Millennium Edition, Windows 2000, Windows XP Home Edition, Windows XP Professional, Windows Server 2003 family

Pens.Magenta Property

A system-defined **Pen** object with a width of 1.

```
[Visual Basic]
Public Shared ReadOnly Property Magenta As Pen
[C#]
public static Pen Magenta {get;}
[C++]
public: __property static Pen* get_Magenta();
[JScript]
public static function get Magenta() : Pen;
```

Property Value

A **Pen** object set to a system-defined color.

Requirements

Platforms: Windows 98, Windows NT 4.0, Windows Millennium Edition, Windows 2000, Windows XP Home Edition, Windows XP Professional, Windows Server 2003 family

Pens.Maroon Property

A system-defined **Pen** object with a width of 1.

```
[Visual Basic]
Public Shared ReadOnly Property Maroon As Pen
[C#]
public static Pen Maroon {get;}
[C++]
public: __property static Pen* get_Maroon();
[JScript]
public static function get Maroon() : Pen;
```

Property Value

A **Pen** object set to a system-defined color.

Requirements

Platforms: Windows 98, Windows NT 4.0, Windows Millennium Edition, Windows 2000, Windows XP Home Edition, Windows XP Professional, Windows Server 2003 family

Pens.MediumAquamarine Property

A system-defined **Pen** object with a width of 1.

```
[Visual Basic]
Public Shared ReadOnly Property MediumAquamarine As Pen
[C#]
public static Pen MediumAquamarine {get;}
[C++]
public: __property static Pen* get_MediumAquamarine();
[JScript]
public static function get MediumAquamarine() : Pen;
```

Property Value

A **Pen** object set to a system-defined color.

Requirements

Platforms: Windows 98, Windows NT 4.0, Windows Millennium Edition, Windows 2000, Windows XP Home Edition, Windows XP Professional, Windows Server 2003 family

Pens.MediumBlue Property

A system-defined **Pen** object with a width of 1.

[Visual Basic]
```
Public Shared ReadOnly Property MediumBlue As Pen
```
[C#]
```
public static Pen MediumBlue {get;}
```
[C++]
```
public: __property static Pen* get_MediumBlue();
```
[JScript]
```
public static function get MediumBlue() : Pen;
```

Property Value

A **Pen** object set to a system-defined color.

Requirements

Platforms: Windows 98, Windows NT 4.0, Windows Millennium Edition, Windows 2000, Windows XP Home Edition, Windows XP Professional, Windows Server 2003 family

Pens.MediumOrchid Property

A system-defined **Pen** object with a width of 1.

[Visual Basic]
```
Public Shared ReadOnly Property MediumOrchid As Pen
```
[C#]
```
public static Pen MediumOrchid {get;}
```
[C++]
```
public: __property static Pen* get_MediumOrchid();
```
[JScript]
```
public static function get MediumOrchid() : Pen;
```

Property Value

A **Pen** object set to a system-defined color.

Requirements

Platforms: Windows 98, Windows NT 4.0, Windows Millennium Edition, Windows 2000, Windows XP Home Edition, Windows XP Professional, Windows Server 2003 family

Pens.MediumPurple Property

A system-defined **Pen** object with a width of 1.

[Visual Basic]
```
Public Shared ReadOnly Property MediumPurple As Pen
```
[C#]
```
public static Pen MediumPurple {get;}
```
[C++]
```
public: __property static Pen* get_MediumPurple();
```
[JScript]
```
public static function get MediumPurple() : Pen;
```

Property Value

A **Pen** object set to a system-defined color.

Requirements

Platforms: Windows 98, Windows NT 4.0, Windows Millennium Edition, Windows 2000, Windows XP Home Edition, Windows XP Professional, Windows Server 2003 family

Pens.MediumSeaGreen Property

A system-defined **Pen** object with a width of 1.

[Visual Basic]
```
Public Shared ReadOnly Property MediumSeaGreen As Pen
```
[C#]
```
public static Pen MediumSeaGreen {get;}
```
[C++]
```
public: __property static Pen* get_MediumSeaGreen();
```
[JScript]
```
public static function get MediumSeaGreen() : Pen;
```

Property Value

A **Pen** object set to a system-defined color.

Requirements

Platforms: Windows 98, Windows NT 4.0, Windows Millennium Edition, Windows 2000, Windows XP Home Edition, Windows XP Professional, Windows Server 2003 family

Pens.MediumSlateBlue Property

A system-defined **Pen** object with a width of 1.

[Visual Basic]
```
Public Shared ReadOnly Property MediumSlateBlue As Pen
```
[C#]
```
public static Pen MediumSlateBlue {get;}
```
[C++]
```
public: __property static Pen* get_MediumSlateBlue();
```
[JScript]
```
public static function get MediumSlateBlue() : Pen;
```

Property Value

A **Pen** object set to a system-defined color.

Requirements

Platforms: Windows 98, Windows NT 4.0, Windows Millennium Edition, Windows 2000, Windows XP Home Edition, Windows XP Professional, Windows Server 2003 family

Pens.MediumSpringGreen Property

A system-defined **Pen** object with a width of 1.

[Visual Basic]
```
Public Shared ReadOnly Property MediumSpringGreen As Pen
```
[C#]
```
public static Pen MediumSpringGreen {get;}
```
[C++]
```
public: __property static Pen* get_MediumSpringGreen();
```
[JScript]
```
public static function get MediumSpringGreen() : Pen;
```

Property Value

A **Pen** object set to a system-defined color.

Requirements

Platforms: Windows 98, Windows NT 4.0, Windows Millennium Edition, Windows 2000, Windows XP Home Edition, Windows XP Professional, Windows Server 2003 family

Pens.MediumTurquoise Property

A system-defined **Pen** object with a width of 1.

```
[Visual Basic]
Public Shared ReadOnly Property MediumTurquoise As Pen
[C#]
public static Pen MediumTurquoise {get;}
[C++]
public: __property static Pen* get_MediumTurquoise();
[JScript]
public static function get MediumTurquoise() : Pen;
```

Property Value

A **Pen** object set to a system-defined color.

Requirements

Platforms: Windows 98, Windows NT 4.0, Windows Millennium Edition, Windows 2000, Windows XP Home Edition, Windows XP Professional, Windows Server 2003 family

Pens.MediumVioletRed Property

A system-defined **Pen** object with a width of 1.

```
[Visual Basic]
Public Shared ReadOnly Property MediumVioletRed As Pen
[C#]
public static Pen MediumVioletRed {get;}
[C++]
public: __property static Pen* get_MediumVioletRed();
[JScript]
public static function get MediumVioletRed() : Pen;
```

Property Value

A **Pen** object set to a system-defined color.

Requirements

Platforms: Windows 98, Windows NT 4.0, Windows Millennium Edition, Windows 2000, Windows XP Home Edition, Windows XP Professional, Windows Server 2003 family

Pens.MidnightBlue Property

A system-defined **Pen** object with a width of 1.

```
[Visual Basic]
Public Shared ReadOnly Property MidnightBlue As Pen
[C#]
public static Pen MidnightBlue {get;}
[C++]
public: __property static Pen* get_MidnightBlue();
[JScript]
public static function get MidnightBlue() : Pen;
```

Property Value

A **Pen** object set to a system-defined color.

Requirements

Platforms: Windows 98, Windows NT 4.0, Windows Millennium Edition, Windows 2000, Windows XP Home Edition, Windows XP Professional, Windows Server 2003 family

Pens.MintCream Property

A system-defined **Pen** object with a width of 1.

```
[Visual Basic]
Public Shared ReadOnly Property MintCream As Pen
[C#]
public static Pen MintCream {get;}
[C++]
public: __property static Pen* get_MintCream();
[JScript]
public static function get MintCream() : Pen;
```

Property Value

A **Pen** object set to a system-defined color.

Requirements

Platforms: Windows 98, Windows NT 4.0, Windows Millennium Edition, Windows 2000, Windows XP Home Edition, Windows XP Professional, Windows Server 2003 family

Pens.MistyRose Property

A system-defined **Pen** object with a width of 1.

```
[Visual Basic]
Public Shared ReadOnly Property MistyRose As Pen
[C#]
public static Pen MistyRose {get;}
[C++]
public: __property static Pen* get_MistyRose();
[JScript]
public static function get MistyRose() : Pen;
```

Property Value

A **Pen** object set to a system-defined color.

Requirements

Platforms: Windows 98, Windows NT 4.0, Windows Millennium Edition, Windows 2000, Windows XP Home Edition, Windows XP Professional, Windows Server 2003 family

Pens.Moccasin Property

A system-defined **Pen** object with a width of 1.

```
[Visual Basic]
Public Shared ReadOnly Property Moccasin As Pen
[C#]
public static Pen Moccasin {get;}
[C++]
public: __property static Pen* get_Moccasin();
[JScript]
public static function get Moccasin() : Pen;
```

Property Value

A **Pen** object set to a system-defined color.

Requirements

Platforms: Windows 98, Windows NT 4.0, Windows Millennium Edition, Windows 2000, Windows XP Home Edition, Windows XP Professional, Windows Server 2003 family

Pens.NavajoWhite Property

A system-defined **Pen** object with a width of 1.

[Visual Basic]
```
Public Shared ReadOnly Property NavajoWhite As Pen
```
[C#]
```
public static Pen NavajoWhite {get;}
```
[C++]
```
public: __property static Pen* get_NavajoWhite();
```
[JScript]
```
public static function get NavajoWhite() : Pen;
```

Property Value

A **Pen** object set to a system-defined color.

Requirements

Platforms: Windows 98, Windows NT 4.0, Windows Millennium Edition, Windows 2000, Windows XP Home Edition, Windows XP Professional, Windows Server 2003 family

Pens.Navy Property

A system-defined **Pen** object with a width of 1.

[Visual Basic]
```
Public Shared ReadOnly Property Navy As Pen
```
[C#]
```
public static Pen Navy {get;}
```
[C++]
```
public: __property static Pen* get_Navy();
```
[JScript]
```
public static function get Navy() : Pen;
```

Property Value

A **Pen** object set to a system-defined color.

Requirements

Platforms: Windows 98, Windows NT 4.0, Windows Millennium Edition, Windows 2000, Windows XP Home Edition, Windows XP Professional, Windows Server 2003 family

Pens.OldLace Property

A system-defined **Pen** object with a width of 1.

[Visual Basic]
```
Public Shared ReadOnly Property OldLace As Pen
```
[C#]
```
public static Pen OldLace {get;}
```
[C++]
```
public: __property static Pen* get_OldLace();
```
[JScript]
```
public static function get OldLace() : Pen;
```

Property Value

A **Pen** object set to a system-defined color.

Requirements

Platforms: Windows 98, Windows NT 4.0, Windows Millennium Edition, Windows 2000, Windows XP Home Edition, Windows XP Professional, Windows Server 2003 family

Pens.Olive Property

A system-defined **Pen** object with a width of 1.

[Visual Basic]
```
Public Shared ReadOnly Property Olive As Pen
```
[C#]
```
public static Pen Olive {get;}
```
[C++]
```
public: __property static Pen* get_Olive();
```
[JScript]
```
public static function get Olive() : Pen;
```

Property Value

A **Pen** object set to a system-defined color.

Requirements

Platforms: Windows 98, Windows NT 4.0, Windows Millennium Edition, Windows 2000, Windows XP Home Edition, Windows XP Professional, Windows Server 2003 family

Pens.OliveDrab Property

A system-defined **Pen** object with a width of 1.

[Visual Basic]
```
Public Shared ReadOnly Property OliveDrab As Pen
```
[C#]
```
public static Pen OliveDrab {get;}
```
[C++]
```
public: __property static Pen* get_OliveDrab();
```
[JScript]
```
public static function get OliveDrab() : Pen;
```

Property Value

A **Pen** object set to a system-defined color.

Requirements

Platforms: Windows 98, Windows NT 4.0, Windows Millennium Edition, Windows 2000, Windows XP Home Edition, Windows XP Professional, Windows Server 2003 family

Pens.Orange Property

A system-defined **Pen** object with a width of 1.

[Visual Basic]
```
Public Shared ReadOnly Property Orange As Pen
```
[C#]
```
public static Pen Orange {get;}
```
[C++]
```
public: __property static Pen* get_Orange();
```
[JScript]
```
public static function get Orange() : Pen;
```

Property Value

A **Pen** object set to a system-defined color.

Requirements

Platforms: Windows 98, Windows NT 4.0, Windows Millennium Edition, Windows 2000, Windows XP Home Edition, Windows XP Professional, Windows Server 2003 family

Pens.OrangeRed Property

A system-defined **Pen** object with a width of 1.

```
[Visual Basic]
Public Shared ReadOnly Property OrangeRed As Pen
[C#]
public static Pen OrangeRed {get;}
[C++]
public: __property static Pen* get_OrangeRed();
[JScript]
public static function get OrangeRed() : Pen;
```

Property Value

A **Pen** object set to a system-defined color.

Requirements

Platforms: Windows 98, Windows NT 4.0, Windows Millennium Edition, Windows 2000, Windows XP Home Edition, Windows XP Professional, Windows Server 2003 family

Pens.Orchid Property

A system-defined **Pen** object with a width of 1.

```
[Visual Basic]
Public Shared ReadOnly Property Orchid As Pen
[C#]
public static Pen Orchid {get;}
[C++]
public: __property static Pen* get_Orchid();
[JScript]
public static function get Orchid() : Pen;
```

Property Value

A **Pen** object set to a system-defined color.

Requirements

Platforms: Windows 98, Windows NT 4.0, Windows Millennium Edition, Windows 2000, Windows XP Home Edition, Windows XP Professional, Windows Server 2003 family

Pens.PaleGoldenrod Property

A system-defined **Pen** object with a width of 1.

```
[Visual Basic]
Public Shared ReadOnly Property PaleGoldenrod As Pen
[C#]
public static Pen PaleGoldenrod {get;}
[C++]
public: __property static Pen* get_PaleGoldenrod();
[JScript]
public static function get PaleGoldenrod() : Pen;
```

Property Value

A **Pen** object set to a system-defined color.

Requirements

Platforms: Windows 98, Windows NT 4.0, Windows Millennium Edition, Windows 2000, Windows XP Home Edition, Windows XP Professional, Windows Server 2003 family

Pens.PaleGreen Property

A system-defined **Pen** object with a width of 1.

```
[Visual Basic]
Public Shared ReadOnly Property PaleGreen As Pen
[C#]
public static Pen PaleGreen {get;}
[C++]
public: __property static Pen* get_PaleGreen();
[JScript]
public static function get PaleGreen() : Pen;
```

Property Value

A **Pen** object set to a system-defined color.

Requirements

Platforms: Windows 98, Windows NT 4.0, Windows Millennium Edition, Windows 2000, Windows XP Home Edition, Windows XP Professional, Windows Server 2003 family

Pens.PaleTurquoise Property

A system-defined **Pen** object with a width of 1.

```
[Visual Basic]
Public Shared ReadOnly Property PaleTurquoise As Pen
[C#]
public static Pen PaleTurquoise {get;}
[C++]
public: __property static Pen* get_PaleTurquoise();
[JScript]
public static function get PaleTurquoise() : Pen;
```

Property Value

A **Pen** object set to a system-defined color.

Requirements

Platforms: Windows 98, Windows NT 4.0, Windows Millennium Edition, Windows 2000, Windows XP Home Edition, Windows XP Professional, Windows Server 2003 family

Pens.PaleVioletRed Property

A system-defined **Pen** object with a width of 1.

```
[Visual Basic]
Public Shared ReadOnly Property PaleVioletRed As Pen
[C#]
public static Pen PaleVioletRed {get;}
[C++]
public: __property static Pen* get_PaleVioletRed();
[JScript]
public static function get PaleVioletRed() : Pen;
```

Property Value

A **Pen** object set to a system-defined color.

Requirements

Platforms: Windows 98, Windows NT 4.0, Windows Millennium Edition, Windows 2000, Windows XP Home Edition, Windows XP Professional, Windows Server 2003 family

Pens.PapayaWhip Property

A system-defined **Pen** object with a width of 1.

[Visual Basic]
```
Public Shared ReadOnly Property PapayaWhip As Pen
```
[C#]
```
public static Pen PapayaWhip {get;}
```
[C++]
```
public: __property static Pen* get_PapayaWhip();
```
[JScript]
```
public static function get PapayaWhip() : Pen;
```

Property Value

A **Pen** object set to a system-defined color.

Requirements

Platforms: Windows 98, Windows NT 4.0, Windows Millennium Edition, Windows 2000, Windows XP Home Edition, Windows XP Professional, Windows Server 2003 family

Pens.PeachPuff Property

A system-defined **Pen** object with a width of 1.

[Visual Basic]
```
Public Shared ReadOnly Property PeachPuff As Pen
```
[C#]
```
public static Pen PeachPuff {get;}
```
[C++]
```
public: __property static Pen* get_PeachPuff();
```
[JScript]
```
public static function get PeachPuff() : Pen;
```

Property Value

A **Pen** object set to a system-defined color.

Requirements

Platforms: Windows 98, Windows NT 4.0, Windows Millennium Edition, Windows 2000, Windows XP Home Edition, Windows XP Professional, Windows Server 2003 family

Pens.Peru Property

A system-defined **Pen** object with a width of 1.

[Visual Basic]
```
Public Shared ReadOnly Property Peru As Pen
```
[C#]
```
public static Pen Peru {get;}
```
[C++]
```
public: __property static Pen* get_Peru();
```
[JScript]
```
public static function get Peru() : Pen;
```

Property Value

A **Pen** object set to a system-defined color.

Requirements

Platforms: Windows 98, Windows NT 4.0, Windows Millennium Edition, Windows 2000, Windows XP Home Edition, Windows XP Professional, Windows Server 2003 family

Pens.Pink Property

A system-defined **Pen** object with a width of 1.

[Visual Basic]
```
Public Shared ReadOnly Property Pink As Pen
```
[C#]
```
public static Pen Pink {get;}
```
[C++]
```
public: __property static Pen* get_Pink();
```
[JScript]
```
public static function get Pink() : Pen;
```

Property Value

A **Pen** object set to a system-defined color.

Requirements

Platforms: Windows 98, Windows NT 4.0, Windows Millennium Edition, Windows 2000, Windows XP Home Edition, Windows XP Professional, Windows Server 2003 family

Pens.Plum Property

A system-defined **Pen** object with a width of 1.

[Visual Basic]
```
Public Shared ReadOnly Property Plum As Pen
```
[C#]
```
public static Pen Plum {get;}
```
[C++]
```
public: __property static Pen* get_Plum();
```
[JScript]
```
public static function get Plum() : Pen;
```

Property Value

A **Pen** object set to a system-defined color.

Requirements

Platforms: Windows 98, Windows NT 4.0, Windows Millennium Edition, Windows 2000, Windows XP Home Edition, Windows XP Professional, Windows Server 2003 family

Pens.PowderBlue Property

A system-defined **Pen** object with a width of 1.

[Visual Basic]
```
Public Shared ReadOnly Property PowderBlue As Pen
```
[C#]
```
public static Pen PowderBlue {get;}
```
[C++]
```
public: __property static Pen* get_PowderBlue();
```
[JScript]
```
public static function get PowderBlue() : Pen;
```

Property Value

A **Pen** object set to a system-defined color.

Requirements

Platforms: Windows 98, Windows NT 4.0, Windows Millennium Edition, Windows 2000, Windows XP Home Edition, Windows XP Professional, Windows Server 2003 family

Pens.Purple Property

A system-defined **Pen** object with a width of 1.

[Visual Basic]
```
Public Shared ReadOnly Property Purple As Pen
```
[C#]
```
public static Pen Purple {get;}
```
[C++]
```
public: __property static Pen* get_Purple();
```
[JScript]
```
public static function get Purple() : Pen;
```

Property Value

A **Pen** object set to a system-defined color.

Requirements

Platforms: Windows 98, Windows NT 4.0, Windows Millennium Edition, Windows 2000, Windows XP Home Edition, Windows XP Professional, Windows Server 2003 family

Pens.Red Property

A system-defined **Pen** object with a width of 1.

[Visual Basic]
```
Public Shared ReadOnly Property Red As Pen
```
[C#]
```
public static Pen Red {get;}
```
[C++]
```
public: __property static Pen* get_Red();
```
[JScript]
```
public static function get Red() : Pen;
```

Property Value

A **Pen** object set to a system-defined color.

Requirements

Platforms: Windows 98, Windows NT 4.0, Windows Millennium Edition, Windows 2000, Windows XP Home Edition, Windows XP Professional, Windows Server 2003 family

Pens.RosyBrown Property

A system-defined **Pen** object with a width of 1.

[Visual Basic]
```
Public Shared ReadOnly Property RosyBrown As Pen
```
[C#]
```
public static Pen RosyBrown {get;}
```
[C++]
```
public: __property static Pen* get_RosyBrown();
```
[JScript]
```
public static function get RosyBrown() : Pen;
```

Property Value

A **Pen** object set to a system-defined color.

Requirements

Platforms: Windows 98, Windows NT 4.0, Windows Millennium Edition, Windows 2000, Windows XP Home Edition, Windows XP Professional, Windows Server 2003 family

Pens.RoyalBlue Property

A system-defined **Pen** object with a width of 1.

[Visual Basic]
```
Public Shared ReadOnly Property RoyalBlue As Pen
```
[C#]
```
public static Pen RoyalBlue {get;}
```
[C++]
```
public: __property static Pen* get_RoyalBlue();
```
[JScript]
```
public static function get RoyalBlue() : Pen;
```

Property Value

A **Pen** object set to a system-defined color.

Requirements

Platforms: Windows 98, Windows NT 4.0, Windows Millennium Edition, Windows 2000, Windows XP Home Edition, Windows XP Professional, Windows Server 2003 family

Pens.SaddleBrown Property

A system-defined **Pen** object with a width of 1.

[Visual Basic]
```
Public Shared ReadOnly Property SaddleBrown As Pen
```
[C#]
```
public static Pen SaddleBrown {get;}
```
[C++]
```
public: __property static Pen* get_SaddleBrown();
```
[JScript]
```
public static function get SaddleBrown() : Pen;
```

Property Value

A **Pen** object set to a system-defined color.

Requirements

Platforms: Windows 98, Windows NT 4.0, Windows Millennium Edition, Windows 2000, Windows XP Home Edition, Windows XP Professional, Windows Server 2003 family

Pens.Salmon Property

A system-defined **Pen** object with a width of 1.

[Visual Basic]
```
Public Shared ReadOnly Property Salmon As Pen
```
[C#]
```
public static Pen Salmon {get;}
```
[C++]
```
public: __property static Pen* get_Salmon();
```
[JScript]
```
public static function get Salmon() : Pen;
```

Property Value

A **Pen** object set to a system-defined color.

Requirements

Platforms: Windows 98, Windows NT 4.0, Windows Millennium Edition, Windows 2000, Windows XP Home Edition, Windows XP Professional, Windows Server 2003 family

Pens.SandyBrown Property

A system-defined **Pen** object with a width of 1.

```
[Visual Basic]
Public Shared ReadOnly Property SandyBrown As Pen
[C#]
public static Pen SandyBrown {get;}
[C++]
public: __property static Pen* get_SandyBrown();
[JScript]
public static function get SandyBrown() : Pen;
```

Property Value

A **Pen** object set to a system-defined color.

Requirements

Platforms: Windows 98, Windows NT 4.0, Windows Millennium Edition, Windows 2000, Windows XP Home Edition, Windows XP Professional, Windows Server 2003 family

Pens.SeaGreen Property

A system-defined **Pen** object with a width of 1.

```
[Visual Basic]
Public Shared ReadOnly Property SeaGreen As Pen
[C#]
public static Pen SeaGreen {get;}
[C++]
public: __property static Pen* get_SeaGreen();
[JScript]
public static function get SeaGreen() : Pen;
```

Property Value

A **Pen** object set to a system-defined color.

Requirements

Platforms: Windows 98, Windows NT 4.0, Windows Millennium Edition, Windows 2000, Windows XP Home Edition, Windows XP Professional, Windows Server 2003 family

Pens.SeaShell Property

A system-defined **Pen** object with a width of 1.

```
[Visual Basic]
Public Shared ReadOnly Property SeaShell As Pen
[C#]
public static Pen SeaShell {get;}
[C++]
public: __property static Pen* get_SeaShell();
[JScript]
public static function get SeaShell() : Pen;
```

Property Value

A **Pen** object set to a system-defined color.

Requirements

Platforms: Windows 98, Windows NT 4.0, Windows Millennium Edition, Windows 2000, Windows XP Home Edition, Windows XP Professional, Windows Server 2003 family

Pens.Sienna Property

A system-defined **Pen** object with a width of 1.

```
[Visual Basic]
Public Shared ReadOnly Property Sienna As Pen
[C#]
public static Pen Sienna {get;}
[C++]
public: __property static Pen* get_Sienna();
[JScript]
public static function get Sienna() : Pen;
```

Property Value

A **Pen** object set to a system-defined color.

Requirements

Platforms: Windows 98, Windows NT 4.0, Windows Millennium Edition, Windows 2000, Windows XP Home Edition, Windows XP Professional, Windows Server 2003 family

Pens.Silver Property

A system-defined **Pen** object with a width of 1.

```
[Visual Basic]
Public Shared ReadOnly Property Silver As Pen
[C#]
public static Pen Silver {get;}
[C++]
public: __property static Pen* get_Silver();
[JScript]
public static function get Silver() : Pen;
```

Property Value

A **Pen** object set to a system-defined color.

Requirements

Platforms: Windows 98, Windows NT 4.0, Windows Millennium Edition, Windows 2000, Windows XP Home Edition, Windows XP Professional, Windows Server 2003 family

Pens.SkyBlue Property

A system-defined **Pen** object with a width of 1.

```
[Visual Basic]
Public Shared ReadOnly Property SkyBlue As Pen
[C#]
public static Pen SkyBlue {get;}
[C++]
public: __property static Pen* get_SkyBlue();
[JScript]
public static function get SkyBlue() : Pen;
```

Property Value

A **Pen** object set to a system-defined color.

Requirements

Platforms: Windows 98, Windows NT 4.0, Windows Millennium Edition, Windows 2000, Windows XP Home Edition, Windows XP Professional, Windows Server 2003 family

Pens.SlateBlue Property

A system-defined **Pen** object with a width of 1.

[Visual Basic]
```
Public Shared ReadOnly Property SlateBlue As Pen
```
[C#]
```
public static Pen SlateBlue {get;}
```
[C++]
```
public: __property static Pen* get_SlateBlue();
```
[JScript]
```
public static function get SlateBlue() : Pen;
```

Property Value

A **Pen** object set to a system-defined color.

Requirements

Platforms: Windows 98, Windows NT 4.0, Windows Millennium Edition, Windows 2000, Windows XP Home Edition, Windows XP Professional, Windows Server 2003 family

Pens.SlateGray Property

A system-defined **Pen** object with a width of 1.

[Visual Basic]
```
Public Shared ReadOnly Property SlateGray As Pen
```
[C#]
```
public static Pen SlateGray {get;}
```
[C++]
```
public: __property static Pen* get_SlateGray();
```
[JScript]
```
public static function get SlateGray() : Pen;
```

Property Value

A **Pen** object set to a system-defined color.

Requirements

Platforms: Windows 98, Windows NT 4.0, Windows Millennium Edition, Windows 2000, Windows XP Home Edition, Windows XP Professional, Windows Server 2003 family

Pens.Snow Property

A system-defined **Pen** object with a width of 1.

[Visual Basic]
```
Public Shared ReadOnly Property Snow As Pen
```
[C#]
```
public static Pen Snow {get;}
```
[C++]
```
public: __property static Pen* get_Snow();
```
[JScript]
```
public static function get Snow() : Pen;
```

Property Value

A **Pen** object set to a system-defined color.

Requirements

Platforms: Windows 98, Windows NT 4.0, Windows Millennium Edition, Windows 2000, Windows XP Home Edition, Windows XP Professional, Windows Server 2003 family

Pens.SpringGreen Property

A system-defined **Pen** object with a width of 1.

[Visual Basic]
```
Public Shared ReadOnly Property SpringGreen As Pen
```
[C#]
```
public static Pen SpringGreen {get;}
```
[C++]
```
public: __property static Pen* get_SpringGreen();
```
[JScript]
```
public static function get SpringGreen() : Pen;
```

Property Value

A **Pen** object set to a system-defined color.

Requirements

Platforms: Windows 98, Windows NT 4.0, Windows Millennium Edition, Windows 2000, Windows XP Home Edition, Windows XP Professional, Windows Server 2003 family

Pens.SteelBlue Property

A system-defined **Pen** object with a width of 1.

[Visual Basic]
```
Public Shared ReadOnly Property SteelBlue As Pen
```
[C#]
```
public static Pen SteelBlue {get;}
```
[C++]
```
public: __property static Pen* get_SteelBlue();
```
[JScript]
```
public static function get SteelBlue() : Pen;
```

Property Value

A **Pen** object set to a system-defined color.

Requirements

Platforms: Windows 98, Windows NT 4.0, Windows Millennium Edition, Windows 2000, Windows XP Home Edition, Windows XP Professional, Windows Server 2003 family

Pens.Tan Property

A system-defined **Pen** object with a width of 1.

[Visual Basic]
```
Public Shared ReadOnly Property Tan As Pen
```
[C#]
```
public static Pen Tan {get;}
```
[C++]
```
public: __property static Pen* get_Tan();
```
[JScript]
```
public static function get Tan() : Pen;
```

Property Value

A **Pen** object set to a system-defined color.

Requirements

Platforms: Windows 98, Windows NT 4.0, Windows Millennium Edition, Windows 2000, Windows XP Home Edition, Windows XP Professional, Windows Server 2003 family

Pens.Teal Property

A system-defined **Pen** object with a width of 1.

[Visual Basic]
```
Public Shared ReadOnly Property Teal As Pen
```
[C#]
```
public static Pen Teal {get;}
```
[C++]
```
public: __property static Pen* get_Teal();
```
[JScript]
```
public static function get Teal() : Pen;
```

Property Value

A **Pen** object set to a system-defined color.

Requirements

Platforms: Windows 98, Windows NT 4.0, Windows Millennium Edition, Windows 2000, Windows XP Home Edition, Windows XP Professional, Windows Server 2003 family

Pens.Thistle Property

A system-defined **Pen** object with a width of 1.

[Visual Basic]
```
Public Shared ReadOnly Property Thistle As Pen
```
[C#]
```
public static Pen Thistle {get;}
```
[C++]
```
public: __property static Pen* get_Thistle();
```
[JScript]
```
public static function get Thistle() : Pen;
```

Property Value

A **Pen** object set to a system-defined color.

Requirements

Platforms: Windows 98, Windows NT 4.0, Windows Millennium Edition, Windows 2000, Windows XP Home Edition, Windows XP Professional, Windows Server 2003 family

Pens.Tomato Property

A system-defined **Pen** object with a width of 1.

[Visual Basic]
```
Public Shared ReadOnly Property Tomato As Pen
```
[C#]
```
public static Pen Tomato {get;}
```
[C++]
```
public: __property static Pen* get_Tomato();
```
[JScript]
```
public static function get Tomato() : Pen;
```

Property Value

A **Pen** object set to a system-defined color.

Requirements

Platforms: Windows 98, Windows NT 4.0, Windows Millennium Edition, Windows 2000, Windows XP Home Edition, Windows XP Professional, Windows Server 2003 family

Pens.Transparent Property

A system-defined **Pen** object with a width of 1.

[Visual Basic]
```
Public Shared ReadOnly Property Transparent As Pen
```
[C#]
```
public static Pen Transparent {get;}
```
[C++]
```
public: __property static Pen* get_Transparent();
```
[JScript]
```
public static function get Transparent() : Pen;
```

Property Value

A **Pen** object set to a system-defined color.

Requirements

Platforms: Windows 98, Windows NT 4.0, Windows Millennium Edition, Windows 2000, Windows XP Home Edition, Windows XP Professional, Windows Server 2003 family

Pens.Turquoise Property

A system-defined **Pen** object with a width of 1.

[Visual Basic]
```
Public Shared ReadOnly Property Turquoise As Pen
```
[C#]
```
public static Pen Turquoise {get;}
```
[C++]
```
public: __property static Pen* get_Turquoise();
```
[JScript]
```
public static function get Turquoise() : Pen;
```

Property Value

A **Pen** object set to a system-defined color.

Requirements

Platforms: Windows 98, Windows NT 4.0, Windows Millennium Edition, Windows 2000, Windows XP Home Edition, Windows XP Professional, Windows Server 2003 family

Pens.Violet Property

A system-defined **Pen** object with a width of 1.

[Visual Basic]
```
Public Shared ReadOnly Property Violet As Pen
```
[C#]
```
public static Pen Violet {get;}
```
[C++]
```
public: __property static Pen* get_Violet();
```
[JScript]
```
public static function get Violet() : Pen;
```

Property Value

A **Pen** object set to a system-defined color.

Requirements

Platforms: Windows 98, Windows NT 4.0, Windows Millennium Edition, Windows 2000, Windows XP Home Edition, Windows XP Professional, Windows Server 2003 family

Pens.Wheat Property

A system-defined **Pen** object with a width of 1.

[Visual Basic]
```
Public Shared ReadOnly Property Wheat As Pen
```
[C#]
```
public static Pen Wheat {get;}
```
[C++]
```
public: __property static Pen* get_Wheat();
```
[JScript]
```
public static function get Wheat() : Pen;
```

Property Value

A **Pen** object set to a system-defined color.

Requirements

Platforms: Windows 98, Windows NT 4.0, Windows Millennium Edition, Windows 2000, Windows XP Home Edition, Windows XP Professional, Windows Server 2003 family

Pens.White Property

A system-defined **Pen** object with a width of 1.

[Visual Basic]
```
Public Shared ReadOnly Property White As Pen
```
[C#]
```
public static Pen White {get;}
```
[C++]
```
public: __property static Pen* get_White();
```
[JScript]
```
public static function get White() : Pen;
```

Property Value

A **Pen** object set to a system-defined color.

Requirements

Platforms: Windows 98, Windows NT 4.0, Windows Millennium Edition, Windows 2000, Windows XP Home Edition, Windows XP Professional, Windows Server 2003 family

Pens.WhiteSmoke Property

A system-defined **Pen** object with a width of 1.

[Visual Basic]
```
Public Shared ReadOnly Property WhiteSmoke As Pen
```
[C#]
```
public static Pen WhiteSmoke {get;}
```
[C++]
```
public: __property static Pen* get_WhiteSmoke();
```
[JScript]
```
public static function get WhiteSmoke() : Pen;
```

Property Value

A **Pen** object set to a system-defined color.

Requirements

Platforms: Windows 98, Windows NT 4.0, Windows Millennium Edition, Windows 2000, Windows XP Home Edition, Windows XP Professional, Windows Server 2003 family

Pens.Yellow Property

A system-defined **Pen** object with a width of 1.

[Visual Basic]
```
Public Shared ReadOnly Property Yellow As Pen
```
[C#]
```
public static Pen Yellow {get;}
```
[C++]
```
public: __property static Pen* get_Yellow();
```
[JScript]
```
public static function get Yellow() : Pen;
```

Property Value

A **Pen** object set to a system-defined color.

Requirements

Platforms: Windows 98, Windows NT 4.0, Windows Millennium Edition, Windows 2000, Windows XP Home Edition, Windows XP Professional, Windows Server 2003 family

Pens.YellowGreen Property

A system-defined **Pen** object with a width of 1.

[Visual Basic]
```
Public Shared ReadOnly Property YellowGreen As Pen
```
[C#]
```
public static Pen YellowGreen {get;}
```
[C++]
```
public: __property static Pen* get_YellowGreen();
```
[JScript]
```
public static function get YellowGreen() : Pen;
```

Property Value

A **Pen** object set to a system-defined color.

Requirements

Platforms: Windows 98, Windows NT 4.0, Windows Millennium Edition, Windows 2000, Windows XP Home Edition, Windows XP Professional, Windows Server 2003 family

Point Structure

Represents an ordered pair of integer x- and y-coordinates that defines a point in a two-dimensional plane.

System.Object
  System.ValueType
    System.Drawing.Point

```
[Visual Basic]
<Serializable>
<ComVisible(True)>
Public Structure Point
[C#]
[Serializable]
[ComVisible(true)]
public struct Point
[C++]
[Serializable]
[ComVisible(true)]
public __value struct Point
```

[JScript] In JScript, you can use the structures in the .NET Framework, but you cannot define your own.

Thread Safety

Any public static (**Shared** in Visual Basic) members of this type are safe for multithreaded operations. Any instance members are not guaranteed to be thread safe.

Requirements

Namespace: System.Drawing

Platforms: Windows 98, Windows NT 4.0, Windows Millennium Edition, Windows 2000, Windows XP Home Edition, Windows XP Professional, Windows Server 2003 family, .NET Compact Framework - Windows CE .NET

Assembly: System.Drawing (in System.Drawing.dll)

Point Constructor

Initializes a new instance of the **Point** class with the specified coordinates.

Overload List

Initializes a new instance of the Point class using coordinates specified by an integer value.

[Visual Basic] **Public Sub New(Integer)**

[C#] **public Point(int);**

[C++] **public: Point(int);**

[JScript] **public function Point(int);**

Initializes a new instance of the **Point** class from a **Size**.

[Visual Basic] **Public Sub New(Size)**

[C#] **public Point(Size);**

[C++] **public: Point(Size);**

[JScript] **public function Point(Size);**

Initializes a new instance of the **Point** class with the specified coordinates.

Supported by the .NET Compact Framework.

[Visual Basic] **Public Sub New(Integer, Integer)**

[C#] **public Point(int, int);**

[C++] **public: Point(int, int);**

[JScript] **public function Point(int, int);**

Point Constructor (Int32)

Initializes a new instance of the Point class using coordinates specified by an integer value.

```
[Visual Basic]
Public Sub New( _
   ByVal dw As Integer _
)
[C#]
public Point(
   int dw
);
[C++]
public: Point(
   int dw
);
[JScript]
public function Point(
   dw : int
);
```

Parameters

dw
  A 32-bit integer that specifies the coordinates for the new **Point**.

Remarks

The low-order 16 bits of *dw* specify the horizontal x-coordinate and the higher 16 bits specify the vertical y-coordinate for the new **Point**.

Requirements

Platforms: Windows 98, Windows NT 4.0, Windows Millennium Edition, Windows 2000, Windows XP Home Edition, Windows XP Professional, Windows Server 2003 family

Point Constructor (Size)

Initializes a new instance of the **Point** class from a **Size**.

```
[Visual Basic]
Public Sub New( _
   ByVal sz As Size _
)
[C#]
public Point(
   Size sz
);
[C++]
public: Point(
   Size sz
);
[JScript]
public function Point(
   sz : Size
);
```

Parameters

sz

A **Size** that specifies the coordinates for the new **Point**.

Requirements

Platforms: Windows 98, Windows NT 4.0, Windows Millennium Edition, Windows 2000, Windows XP Home Edition, Windows XP Professional, Windows Server 2003 family

Point Constructor (Int32, Int32)

Initializes a new instance of the **Point** class with the specified coordinates.

```
[Visual Basic]
Public Sub New( _
   ByVal x As Integer, _
   ByVal y As Integer _
)
[C#]
public Point(
   int x,
   int y
);
[C++]
public: Point(
   int x,
   int y
);
[JScript]
public function Point(
   x : int,
   y : int
);
```

Parameters

x

The horizontal position of the point.

y

The vertical position of the point.

Requirements

Platforms: Windows 98, Windows NT 4.0, Windows Millennium Edition, Windows 2000, Windows XP Home Edition, Windows XP Professional, Windows Server 2003 family, .NET Compact Framework - Windows CE .NET

Point.Empty Field

Represents a null **Point**.

```
[Visual Basic]
Public Shared ReadOnly Empty As Point
[C#]
public static readonly Point Empty;
[C++]
public: static Point Empty;
[JScript]
public static var Empty : Point;
```

Requirements

Platforms: Windows 98, Windows NT 4.0, Windows Millennium Edition, Windows 2000, Windows XP Home Edition, Windows XP Professional, Windows Server 2003 family, .NET Compact Framework - Windows CE .NET

Point.IsEmpty Property

Gets a value indicating whether this **Point** is empty.

```
[Visual Basic]
Public ReadOnly Property IsEmpty As Boolean
[C#]
public bool IsEmpty {get;}
[C++]
public: __property bool get_IsEmpty();
[JScript]
public function get IsEmpty() : Boolean;
```

Property Value

This property returns **true** if both **X** and **Y** are zero; otherwise, **false**.

Requirements

Platforms: Windows 98, Windows NT 4.0, Windows Millennium Edition, Windows 2000, Windows XP Home Edition, Windows XP Professional, Windows Server 2003 family, .NET Compact Framework - Windows CE .NET

Point.X Property

Gets or sets the x-coordinate of this **Point**.

```
[Visual Basic]
Public Property X As Integer
[C#]
public int X {get; set;}
[C++]
public: __property int get_X();
public: __property void set_X(int);
[JScript]
public function get X() : int;
public function set X(int);
```

Property Value

The x-coordinate of this **Point**.

Requirements

Platforms: Windows 98, Windows NT 4.0, Windows Millennium Edition, Windows 2000, Windows XP Home Edition, Windows XP Professional, Windows Server 2003 family, .NET Compact Framework - Windows CE .NET

Point.Y Property

Gets or sets the y-coordinate of this **Point**.

```
[Visual Basic]
Public Property Y As Integer
[C#]
public int Y {get; set;}
```

```
[C++]
public: __property int get_Y();
public: __property void set_Y(int);
[JScript]
public function get Y() : int;
public function set Y(int);
```

Property Value

The y-coordinate of this **Point**.

Requirements

Platforms: Windows 98, Windows NT 4.0, Windows Millennium Edition, Windows 2000, Windows XP Home Edition, Windows XP Professional, Windows Server 2003 family, .NET Compact Framework - Windows CE .NET

Point.Ceiling Method

Converts the specified **PointF** object to a **Point** object by rounding the values of the **PointF** object to the next higher integer values.

```
[Visual Basic]
Public Shared Function Ceiling( _
   ByVal value As PointF _
) As Point
[C#]
public static Point Ceiling(
   PointF value
);
[C++]
public: static Point Ceiling(
   PointF value
);
[JScript]
public static function Ceiling(
   value : PointF
) : Point;
```

Parameters

value
The **PointF** object to convert.

Return Value

The **Point** object this method converts to.

Requirements

Platforms: Windows 98, Windows NT 4.0, Windows Millennium Edition, Windows 2000, Windows XP Home Edition, Windows XP Professional, Windows Server 2003 family

Point.Equals Method

Specifies whether this **Point** contains the same coordinates as the specified **Object**.

```
[Visual Basic]
Overrides Public Function Equals( _
   ByVal obj As Object _
) As Boolean
[C#]
public override bool Equals(
   object obj
);
[C++]
public: bool Equals(
   Object* obj
);
[JScript]
public override function Equals(
   obj : Object
) : Boolean;
```

Parameters

obj
The **Object** to test.

Return Value

This method returns **true** if *obj* is a **Point** and has the same coordinates as this **Point**.

Requirements

Platforms: Windows 98, Windows NT 4.0, Windows Millennium Edition, Windows 2000, Windows XP Home Edition, Windows XP Professional, Windows Server 2003 family, .NET Compact Framework - Windows CE .NET

Point.GetHashCode Method

Returns a hash code for this **Point** object.

```
[Visual Basic]
Overrides Public Function GetHashCode() As Integer
[C#]
public override int GetHashCode();
[C++]
public: int GetHashCode();
[JScript]
public override function GetHashCode() : int;
```

Return Value

An integer value that specifies a hash value for this **Point** object.

Requirements

Platforms: Windows 98, Windows NT 4.0, Windows Millennium Edition, Windows 2000, Windows XP Home Edition, Windows XP Professional, Windows Server 2003 family, .NET Compact Framework - Windows CE .NET

Point.Offset Method

Translates this **Point** by the specified amount.

```
[Visual Basic]
Public Sub Offset( _
   ByVal dx As Integer, _
   ByVal dy As Integer _
)
[C#]
public void Offset(
   int dx,
   int dy
);
```

```
[C++]
public: void Offset(
   int dx,
   int dy
);
[JScript]
public function Offset(
   dx : int,
   dy : int
);
```

Parameters

dx
: The amount to offset the x-coordinate.

dy
: The amount to offset the y-coordinate.

Return Value

This method does not return a value.

Requirements

Platforms: Windows 98, Windows NT 4.0, Windows Millennium Edition, Windows 2000, Windows XP Home Edition, Windows XP Professional, Windows Server 2003 family, .NET Compact Framework - Windows CE .NET

Point.Round Method

Converts the specified **PointF** object to a **Point** object by rounding the **Point** object values to the nearest integer.

```
[Visual Basic]
Public Shared Function Round( _
   ByVal value As PointF _
) As Point
[C#]
public static Point Round(
   PointF value
);
[C++]
public: static Point Round(
   PointF value
);
[JScript]
public static function Round(
   value : PointF
) : Point;
```

Parameters

value
: The **PointF** object to convert.

Return Value

The **Point** object this method converts to.

Requirements

Platforms: Windows 98, Windows NT 4.0, Windows Millennium Edition, Windows 2000, Windows XP Home Edition, Windows XP Professional, Windows Server 2003 family

Point.ToString Method

Converts this **Point** to a human readable string.

```
[Visual Basic]
Overrides Public Function ToString() As String
[C#]
public override string ToString();
[C++]
public: String* ToString();
[JScript]
public override function ToString() : String;
```

Return Value

A string that represents this **Point**.

Requirements

Platforms: Windows 98, Windows NT 4.0, Windows Millennium Edition, Windows 2000, Windows XP Home Edition, Windows XP Professional, Windows Server 2003 family, .NET Compact Framework - Windows CE .NET

Point.Truncate Method

Converts the specified **PointF** object to a **Point** object by truncating the values of the **Point** object.

```
[Visual Basic]
Public Shared Function Truncate( _
   ByVal value As PointF _
) As Point
[C#]
public static Point Truncate(
   PointF value
);
[C++]
public: static Point Truncate(
   PointF value
);
[JScript]
public static function Truncate(
   value : PointF
) : Point;
```

Parameters

value
: The **PointF** object to convert.

Return Value

The **Point** object this method converts to.

Requirements

Platforms: Windows 98, Windows NT 4.0, Windows Millennium Edition, Windows 2000, Windows XP Home Edition, Windows XP Professional, Windows Server 2003 family

Point Addition Operator

Translates a **Point** by a given **Size**.

```
[Visual Basic]
returnValue = Point.op_Addition(pt, sz)
[C#]
public static Point operator +(
   Point pt,
   Size sz
);
[C++]
public: static Point op_Addition(
   Point pt,
   Size sz
);
[JScript]
returnValue = pt + sz;
```

[Visual Basic] In Visual Basic, you can use the operators defined by a type, but you cannot define your own.

[JScript] In JScript, you can use the operators defined by a type, but you cannot define your own.

Arguments [Visual Basic, JScript]

pt

The **Point** to translate.

sz

A **Size** that specifies the pair of numbers to add to the coordinates of *pt*.

Parameters [C#, C++]

pt

The **Point** to translate.

sz

A **Size** that specifies the pair of numbers to add to the coordinates of *pt*.

Return Value

The translated **Point** structure.

Requirements

Platforms: Windows 98, Windows NT 4.0,
Windows Millennium Edition, Windows 2000,
Windows XP Home Edition, Windows XP Professional,
Windows Server 2003 family

Point Equality Operator

Compares two **Point** objects. The result specifies whether the values of the **X** and **Y** properties of the two **Point** objects are equal.

```
[Visual Basic]
returnValue = Point.op_Equality(left, right)
[C#]
public static bool operator ==(
   Point left,
   Point right
);
[C++]
public: static bool op_Equality(
   Point left,
   Point right
);
[JScript]
returnValue = left == right;
```

[Visual Basic] In Visual Basic, you can use the operators defined by a type, but you cannot define your own.

[JScript] In JScript, you can use the operators defined by a type, but you cannot define your own.

Arguments [Visual Basic, JScript]

left

A **Point** to compare.

right

A **Point** to compare.

Parameters [C#, C++]

left

A **Point** to compare.

right

A **Point** to compare.

Return Value

This operator returns **true** if the **X** and **Y** values of *left* and *right* are equal; otherwise, **false**.

Requirements

Platforms: Windows 98, Windows NT 4.0,
Windows Millennium Edition, Windows 2000,
Windows XP Home Edition, Windows XP Professional,
Windows Server 2003 family,
.NET Compact Framework - Windows CE .NET

Point Inequality Operator

Compares two **Point** objects. The result specifies whether the values of the **X** or **Y** properties of the two **Point** objects are unequal.

```
[Visual Basic]
returnValue = Point.op_Inequality(left, right)
[C#]
public static bool operator !=(
   Point left,
   Point right
);
[C++]
public: static bool op_Inequality(
   Point left,
   Point right
);
[JScript]
returnValue = left != right;
```

[Visual Basic] In Visual Basic, you can use the operators defined by a type, but you cannot define your own.

[JScript] In JScript, you can use the operators defined by a type, but you cannot define your own.

Arguments [Visual Basic, JScript]

left

A **Point** to compare.

right

A **Point** to compare.

Parameters [C#, C++]

left

A **Point** to compare.

right

A **Point** to compare.

Return Value

This operator returns **true** if the values of either the **X** properties or the **Y** properties of *left* and *right* differ; otherwise, **false**.

Requirements

Platforms: Windows 98, Windows NT 4.0,
Windows Millennium Edition, Windows 2000,
Windows XP Home Edition, Windows XP Professional,
Windows Server 2003 family,
.NET Compact Framework - Windows CE .NET

Point Subtraction Operator

Translates a **Point** by the negative of a given **Size**.

```
[Visual Basic]
returnValue = Point.op_Subtraction(pt, sz)
[C#]
public static Point operator -(
   Point pt,
   Size sz
);
[C++]
public: static Point op_Subtraction(
   Point pt,
   Size sz
);
[JScript]
returnValue = pt - sz;
```

[Visual Basic] In Visual Basic, you can use the operators defined by a type, but you cannot define your own.

[JScript] In JScript, you can use the operators defined by a type, but you cannot define your own.

Arguments [Visual Basic, JScript]

pt

The **Point** to translate.

sz

A **Size** that specifies the pair of numbers to subtract from the coordinates of *pt*.

Parameters [C#, C++]

pt

The **Point** to translate.

sz

A **Size** that specifies the pair of numbers to subtract from the coordinates of *pt*.

Return Value

A **Point** structure that is translated by the negative of a given **Size** structure.

Requirements

Platforms: Windows 98, Windows NT 4.0,
Windows Millennium Edition, Windows 2000,
Windows XP Home Edition, Windows XP Professional,
Windows Server 2003 family

Point to Size Conversion

Creates a **Size** with the coordinates of the specified **Point**.

```
[Visual Basic]
returnValue = Point.op_Explicit(p)
[C#]
public static explicit operator Size(
   Point p
);
[C++]
public: static Size op_Explicit();
[JScript]
returnValue = Size(p);
```

[Visual Basic] In Visual Basic, you can use the conversion operators defined by a type, but you cannot define your own.

[JScript] In JScript, you can use the conversion operators defined by a type, but you cannot define your own.

Arguments [Visual Basic, JScript]

p

A **Point** that specifies the coordinates for the new **Size**.

Parameters [C#]

p

A **Point** that specifies the coordinates for the new **Size**.

Requirements

Platforms: Windows 98, Windows NT 4.0,
Windows Millennium Edition, Windows 2000,
Windows XP Home Edition, Windows XP Professional,
Windows Server 2003 family

Point to PointF Conversion

Creates a **PointF** with the coordinates of the specified **Point**.

```
[Visual Basic]
returnValue = Point.op_Implicit(p)
[C#]
public static implicit operator PointF(
   Point p
);
[C++]
public: static PointF op_Implicit();
[JScript]
returnValue = p;
```

[Visual Basic] In Visual Basic, you can use the conversion operators defined by a type, but you cannot define your own.

[JScript] In JScript, you can use the conversion operators defined by a type, but you cannot define your own.

Arguments [Visual Basic, JScript]

p

A **Point** that specifies the coordinates for the new **PointF**.

Parameters [C#]

p

A **Point** that specifies the coordinates for the new **PointF**.

Requirements

Platforms: Windows 98, Windows NT 4.0,
Windows Millennium Edition, Windows 2000,
Windows XP Home Edition, Windows XP Professional,
Windows Server 2003 family

PointConverter Class

Converts a **Point** object from one data type to another. Access this class through the **TypeDescriptor** object.

System.Object
  System.ComponentModel.TypeConverter
    System.Drawing.PointConverter

[Visual Basic]
```
Public Class PointConverter
   Inherits TypeConverter
```
[C#]
```
public class PointConverter : TypeConverter
```
[C++]
```
public __gc class PointConverter : public TypeConverter
```
[JScript]
```
public class PointConverter extends TypeConverter
```

Thread Safety

Any public static (**Shared** in Visual Basic) members of this type are safe for multithreaded operations. Any instance members are not guaranteed to be thread safe.

Requirements

Namespace: System.Drawing

Platforms: Windows 98, Windows NT 4.0, Windows Millennium Edition, Windows 2000, Windows XP Home Edition, Windows XP Professional, Windows Server 2003 family

Assembly: System.Drawing (in System.Drawing.dll)

PointConverter Constructor

Initializes a new instance of the **PointConverter** class.

[Visual Basic]
```
Public Sub New()
```
[C#]
```
public PointConverter();
```
[C++]
```
public: PointConverter();
```
[JScript]
```
public function PointConverter();
```

Requirements

Platforms: Windows 98, Windows NT 4.0, Windows Millennium Edition, Windows 2000, Windows XP Home Edition, Windows XP Professional, Windows Server 2003 family

PointConverter.CanConvertFrom Method

Overload List

Determines if this converter can convert an object in the given source type to the native type of the converter.

[Visual Basic] **Overloads Overrides Public Function CanConvertFrom(ITypeDescriptorContext, Type) As Boolean**

[C#] **public override bool CanConvertFrom(ITypeDescriptorContext, Type);**

[C++] **public: bool CanConvertFrom(ITypeDescriptorContext*, Type*);**

[JScript] **public override function CanConvertFrom(ITypeDescriptorContext, Type) : Boolean;**

Inherited from **TypeConverter**.

[Visual Basic] **Overloads Public Function CanConvertFrom(Type) As Boolean**

[C#] **public bool CanConvertFrom(Type);**

[C++] **public: bool CanConvertFrom(Type*);**

[JScript] **public function CanConvertFrom(Type) : Boolean;**

PointConverter.CanConvertFrom Method (ITypeDescriptorContext, Type)

Determines if this converter can convert an object in the given source type to the native type of the converter.

[Visual Basic]
```
Overrides Overloads Public Function CanConvertFrom( _
   ByVal context As ITypeDescriptorContext, _
   ByVal sourceType As Type _
) As Boolean
```
[C#]
```
public override bool CanConvertFrom(
   ITypeDescriptorContext context,
   Type sourceType
);
```
[C++]
```
public: bool CanConvertFrom(
   ITypeDescriptorContext* context,
   Type* sourceType
);
```
[JScript]
```
public override function CanConvertFrom(
   context : ITypeDescriptorContext,
   sourceType : Type
) : Boolean;
```

Parameters

context

A formatter context. This object can be used to get additional information about the environment this converter is being called from. This may be a null reference (**Nothing** in Visual Basic), so you should always check. Also, properties on the context object may also return a null reference (**Nothing**).

sourceType

The type you want to convert from.

Return Value

This method returns **true** if this object can perform the conversion; otherwise, **false**.

Requirements

Platforms: Windows 98, Windows NT 4.0, Windows Millennium Edition, Windows 2000, Windows XP Home Edition, Windows XP Professional, Windows Server 2003 family

PointConverter.CanConvertTo Method

Overload List

Gets a value indicating whether this converter can convert an object to the given destination type using the context.

[Visual Basic] **Overloads Overrides Public Function CanConvertTo(ITypeDescriptorContext, Type) As Boolean**

[C#] **public override bool CanConvertTo(ITypeDescriptor-Context, Type);**

[C++] **public: bool CanConvertTo(ITypeDescriptorContext*, Type*);**

[JScript] **public override function CanConvertTo(IType-DescriptorContext, Type) : Boolean;**

Inherited from **TypeConverter**.

[Visual Basic] **Overloads Public Function CanConvertTo(Type) As Boolean**

[C#] **public bool CanConvertTo(Type);**

[C++] **public: bool CanConvertTo(Type*);**

[JScript] **public function CanConvertTo(Type) : Boolean;**

PointConverter.CanConvertTo Method (ITypeDescriptorContext, Type)

Gets a value indicating whether this converter can convert an object to the given destination type using the context.

```
[Visual Basic]
Overrides Overloads Public Function CanConvertTo( _
   ByVal context As ITypeDescriptorContext, _
   ByVal destinationType As Type _
) As Boolean
[C#]
public override bool CanConvertTo(
   ITypeDescriptorContext context,
   Type destinationType
);
[C++]
public: bool CanConvertTo(
   ITypeDescriptorContext* context,
   Type* destinationType
);
[JScript]
public override function CanConvertTo(
   context : ITypeDescriptorContext,
   destinationType : Type
) : Boolean;
```

Parameters

context

An **ITypeDescriptorContext** object that provides a format context.

destinationType

A **Type** object that represents the type you want to convert to.

Return Value

This method returns **true** if this converter can perform the conversion; otherwise, **false**.

Remarks

The *context* parameter can be used to get additional information about the environment this converter is being called from. This can be a null reference (**Nothing** in Visual Basic), so you should always check. Also, properties on the context object can also return a null reference (**Nothing**).

Requirements

Platforms: Windows 98, Windows NT 4.0, Windows Millennium Edition, Windows 2000, Windows XP Home Edition, Windows XP Professional, Windows Server 2003 family

PointConverter.ConvertFrom Method

Overload List

Converts the specified object to a **Point** object.

[Visual Basic] **Overloads Overrides Public Function Convert-From(ITypeDescriptorContext, CultureInfo, Object) As Object**

[C#] **public override object ConvertFrom(ITypeDescriptor-Context, CultureInfo, object);**

[C++] **public: Object* ConvertFrom(ITypeDescriptor-Context*, CultureInfo*, Object*);**

[JScript] **public override function ConvertFrom(IType-DescriptorContext, CultureInfo, Object) : Object;**

Inherited from **TypeConverter**.

[Visual Basic] **Overloads Public Function ConvertFrom(Object) As Object**

[C#] **public object ConvertFrom(object);**

[C++] **public: Object* ConvertFrom(Object*);**

[JScript] **public function ConvertFrom(Object) : Object;**

PointConverter.ConvertFrom Method (ITypeDescriptorContext, CultureInfo, Object)

Converts the specified object to a **Point** object.

```
[Visual Basic]
Overrides Overloads Public Function ConvertFrom( _
   ByVal context As ITypeDescriptorContext, _
   ByVal culture As CultureInfo, _
   ByVal value As Object _
) As Object
[C#]
public override object ConvertFrom(
   ITypeDescriptorContext context,
   CultureInfo culture,
   object value
);
[C++]
public: Object* ConvertFrom(
   ITypeDescriptorContext* context,
   CultureInfo* culture,
   Object* value
);
[JScript]
public override function ConvertFrom(
   context : ITypeDescriptorContext,
   culture : CultureInfo,
   value : Object
) : Object;
```

Parameters

context
: A formatter context. This object can be used to get additional information about the environment this converter is being called from. This may be a null reference (**Nothing** in Visual Basic), so you should always check. Also, properties on the context object may also return a null reference (**Nothing**).

culture
: An object that contains culture specific information, such as the language, calendar, and cultural conventions associated with a specific culture. It is based on the RFC 1766 standard.

value
: The object to convert.

Return Value

The converted object. This will throw an exception if the conversion could not be performed.

Requirements

Platforms: Windows 98, Windows NT 4.0, Windows Millennium Edition, Windows 2000, Windows XP Home Edition, Windows XP Professional, Windows Server 2003 family

PointConverter.ConvertTo Method

Overload List

Converts the specified object to the specified type.

[Visual Basic] **Overloads Overrides Public Function ConvertTo (ITypeDescriptorContext, CultureInfo, Object, Type) As Object**

[C#] **public override object ConvertTo(ITypeDescriptorContext, CultureInfo, object, Type);**

[C++] **public: Object* ConvertTo(ITypeDescriptorContext*, CultureInfo*, Object*, Type*);**

[JScript] **public override function ConvertTo(ITypeDescriptorContext, CultureInfo, Object, Type) : Object;**

Inherited from **TypeConverter**.

[Visual Basic] **Overloads Public Function ConvertTo(Object, Type) As Object**

[C#] **public object ConvertTo(object, Type);**

[C++] **public: Object* ConvertTo(Object*, Type*);**

[JScript] **public function ConvertTo(Object, Type) : Object;**

PointConverter.ConvertTo Method (ITypeDescriptorContext, CultureInfo, Object, Type)

Converts the specified object to the specified type.

```
[Visual Basic]
Overrides Overloads Public Function ConvertTo( _
   ByVal context As ITypeDescriptorContext, _
   ByVal culture As CultureInfo, _
   ByVal value As Object, _
   ByVal destinationType As Type _
) As Object
[C#]
public override object ConvertTo(
   ITypeDescriptorContext context,
   CultureInfo culture,
   object value,
   Type destinationType
);
[C++]
public: Object* ConvertTo(
   ITypeDescriptorContext* context,
   CultureInfo* culture,
   Object* value,
   Type* destinationType
);
[JScript]
public override function ConvertTo(
   context : ITypeDescriptorContext,
   culture : CultureInfo,
   value : Object,
   destinationType : Type
) : Object;
```

Parameters

context
: A formatter context. This object can be used to get additional information about the environment this converter is being called from. This may be a null reference (**Nothing** in Visual Basic), so you should always check. Also, properties on the context object may also return a null reference (**Nothing**).

culture
: An object that contains culture specific information, such as the language, calendar, and cultural conventions associated with a specific culture. It is based on the RFC 1766 standard.

value
: The object to convert.

destinationType
: The type to convert the object to.

Return Value

The converted object.

Remarks

The most common types to convert are to and from a string object. The default implementation calls the object's **ToString** method if the object is valid and if the destination type is string. If this method cannot convert to the destination type, this will throw a **NotSupportedException** exception.

Requirements

Platforms: Windows 98, Windows NT 4.0, Windows Millennium Edition, Windows 2000, Windows XP Home Edition, Windows XP Professional, Windows Server 2003 family

PointConverter.CreateInstance Method

Overload List

Creates an instance of this type given a set of property values for the object. This is useful for objects that are immutable but still want to provide changeable properties.

[Visual Basic] **Overloads Overrides Public Function CreateInstance(ITypeDescriptorContext, IDictionary) As Object**

[C#] **public override object CreateInstance(ITypeDescriptorContext, IDictionary);**

[C++] **public: Object* CreateInstance(ITypeDescriptorContext*, IDictionary*);**

[JScript] **public override function CreateInstance(ITypeDescriptorContext, IDictionary) : Object;**

Inherited from **TypeConverter**.

[Visual Basic] **Overloads Public Function CreateInstance(IDictionary) As Object**

[C#] **public object CreateInstance(IDictionary);**

[C++] **public: Object* CreateInstance(IDictionary*);**

[JScript] **public function CreateInstance(IDictionary) : Object;**

PointConverter.CreateInstance Method (ITypeDescriptorContext, IDictionary)

Creates an instance of this type given a set of property values for the object. This is useful for objects that are immutable but still want to provide changeable properties.

```
[Visual Basic]
Overrides Overloads Public Function CreateInstance( _
   ByVal context As ITypeDescriptorContext, _
   ByVal propertyValues As IDictionary _
) As Object
[C#]
public override object CreateInstance(
   ITypeDescriptorContext context,
   IDictionary propertyValues
);
[C++]
public: Object* CreateInstance(
   ITypeDescriptorContext* context,
   IDictionary* propertyValues
);
[JScript]
public override function CreateInstance(
   context : ITypeDescriptorContext,
   propertyValues : IDictionary
) : Object;
```

Parameters

context

A type descriptor through which additional context can be provided.

propertyValues

A dictionary of new property values. The dictionary contains a series of name-value pairs, one for each property returned from GetProperties.

Return Value

The newly created object, or a null reference (**Nothing** in Visual Basic) if the object could not be created. The default implementation returns a null reference (**Nothing**).

Requirements

Platforms: Windows 98, Windows NT 4.0, Windows Millennium Edition, Windows 2000, Windows XP Home Edition, Windows XP Professional, Windows Server 2003 family

PointConverter.GetCreateInstanceSupported Method

Overload List

Determines if changing a value on this object should require a call to **CreateInstance** to create a new value.

[Visual Basic] **Overloads Overrides Public Function GetCreateInstanceSupported(ITypeDescriptorContext) As Boolean**

[C#] **public override bool GetCreateInstanceSupported(ITypeDescriptorContext);**

[C++] **public: bool GetCreateInstanceSupported(ITypeDescriptorContext*);**

[JScript] **public override function GetCreateInstanceSupported(ITypeDescriptorContext) : Boolean;**

Inherited from **TypeConverter**.

[Visual Basic] **Overloads Public Function GetCreateInstanceSupported() As Boolean**

[C#] **public bool GetCreateInstanceSupported();**

[C++] **public: bool GetCreateInstanceSupported();**

[JScript] **public function GetCreateInstanceSupported() : Boolean;**

PointConverter.GetCreateInstanceSupported Method (ITypeDescriptorContext)

Determines if changing a value on this object should require a call to **CreateInstance** to create a new value.

```
[Visual Basic]
Overrides Overloads Public Function GetCreateInstanceSupported( _
   ByVal context As ITypeDescriptorContext _
) As Boolean
[C#]
public override bool GetCreateInstanceSupported(
   ITypeDescriptorContext context
);
[C++]
public: bool GetCreateInstanceSupported(
   ITypeDescriptorContext* context
);
[JScript]
public override function GetCreateInstanceSupported(
   context : ITypeDescriptorContext
) : Boolean;
```

Parameters

context

A type descriptor through which additional context can be provided.

Return Value

This method returns **true** if the **CreateInstance** method should be called when a change is made to one or more properties of this object; otherwise, **false**.

Requirements

Platforms: Windows 98, Windows NT 4.0, Windows Millennium Edition, Windows 2000, Windows XP Home Edition, Windows XP Professional, Windows Server 2003 family

PointConverter.GetProperties Method

Overload List

Retrieves the set of properties for this type. By default, a type does not return any properties. A simple implementation of this method can just call **TypeDescriptor.GetProperties** for the correct data type.

[Visual Basic] **Overloads Overrides Public Function GetProperties(ITypeDescriptorContext, Object, Attribute()) As PropertyDescriptorCollection**

[C#] **public override PropertyDescriptorCollection GetProperties(ITypeDescriptorContext, object, Attribute[]);**

[C++] **public: PropertyDescriptorCollection* GetProperties(ITypeDescriptorContext*, Object*, Attribute[]);**

[JScript] **public override function GetProperties(ITypeDescriptorContext, Object, Attribute[]) : PropertyDescriptorCollection;**

Inherited from **TypeConverter**.

[Visual Basic] **Overloads Public Function GetProperties(Object) As PropertyDescriptorCollection**

[C#] **public PropertyDescriptorCollection GetProperties(object);**

[C++] **public: PropertyDescriptorCollection* GetProperties(Object*);**

[JScript] **public function GetProperties(Object) : PropertyDescriptorCollection;**

Inherited from **TypeConverter**.

[Visual Basic] **Overloads Public Function GetProperties(ITypeDescriptorContext, Object) As PropertyDescriptorCollection**

[C#] **public PropertyDescriptorCollection GetProperties(ITypeDescriptorContext, object);**

[C++] **public: PropertyDescriptorCollection* GetProperties(ITypeDescriptorContext*, Object*);**

[JScript] **public function GetProperties(ITypeDescriptorContext, Object) : PropertyDescriptorCollection;**

PointConverter.GetProperties Method (ITypeDescriptorContext, Object, Attribute[])

Retrieves the set of properties for this type. By default, a type does not return any properties. A simple implementation of this method can just call **TypeDescriptor.GetProperties** for the correct data type.

```
[Visual Basic]
Overrides Overloads Public Function GetProperties( _
   ByVal context As ITypeDescriptorContext, _
   ByVal value As Object, _
   ByVal attributes() As Attribute _
) As PropertyDescriptorCollection
[C#]
public override PropertyDescriptorCollection GetProperties(
   ITypeDescriptorContext context,
   object value,
   Attribute[] attributes
);
[C++]
public: PropertyDescriptorCollection* GetProperties(
   ITypeDescriptorContext* context,
   Object* value,
   Attribute* attributes[]
);
[JScript]
public override function GetProperties(
   context : ITypeDescriptorContext,
   value : Object,
   attributes : Attribute[]
) : PropertyDescriptorCollection;
```

Parameters

context
: A type descriptor through which additional context can be provided.

value
: The value of the object to get the properties for.

attributes
: An array of **MemberAttribute** objects that describe the properties.

Return Value

The set of properties that are exposed for this data type. If no properties are exposed, this method might return a null reference (**Nothing** in Visual Basic). The default implementation always returns a null reference (**Nothing**).

Requirements

Platforms: Windows 98, Windows NT 4.0, Windows Millennium Edition, Windows 2000, Windows XP Home Edition, Windows XP Professional, Windows Server 2003 family

PointConverter.GetPropertiesSupported Method

Overload List

Determines if this object supports properties. By default, this is **false**.

[Visual Basic] **Overloads Overrides Public Function GetPropertiesSupported(ITypeDescriptorContext) As Boolean**

[C#] **public override bool GetPropertiesSupported(ITypeDescriptorContext);**

[C++] **public: bool GetPropertiesSupported(ITypeDescriptorContext*);**

[JScript] **public override function GetPropertiesSupported(ITypeDescriptorContext) : Boolean;**

Inherited from **TypeConverter**.

[Visual Basic] **Overloads Public Function GetPropertiesSupported() As Boolean**

[C#] **public bool GetPropertiesSupported();**

[C++] **public: bool GetPropertiesSupported();**

[JScript] **public function GetPropertiesSupported() : Boolean;**

PointConverter.GetPropertiesSupported Method (ITypeDescriptorContext)

Determines if this object supports properties. By default, this is **false**.

[Visual Basic]
```
Overrides Overloads Public Function GetPropertiesSupported( _
   ByVal context As ITypeDescriptorContext _
) As Boolean
```
[C#]
```
public override bool GetPropertiesSupported(
   ITypeDescriptorContext context
);
```
[C++]
```
public: bool GetPropertiesSupported(
   ITypeDescriptorContext* context
);
```
[JScript]
```
public override function GetPropertiesSupported(
   context : ITypeDescriptorContext
) : Boolean;
```

Parameters

context

A type descriptor through which additional context can be provided.

Return Value

This method returns **true** if **GetProperties** should be called to find the properties of this object; otherwise, **false**.

Requirements

Platforms: Windows 98, Windows NT 4.0, Windows Millennium Edition, Windows 2000, Windows XP Home Edition, Windows XP Professional, Windows Server 2003 family

PointF Structure

Represents an ordered pair of floating point x- and y-coordinates that defines a point in a two-dimensional plane.

System.Object
  System.ValueType
    System.Drawing.PointF

```
[Visual Basic]
<Serializable>
<ComVisible(True)>
Public Structure PointF
[C#]
[Serializable]
[ComVisible(true)]
public struct PointF
[C++]
[Serializable]
[ComVisible(true)]
public __value struct PointF
```

[JScript] In JScript, you can use the structures in the .NET Framework, but you cannot define your own.

Thread Safety

Any public static (**Shared** in Visual Basic) members of this type are safe for multithreaded operations. Any instance members are not guaranteed to be thread safe.

Requirements

Namespace: System.Drawing

Platforms: Windows 98, Windows NT 4.0, Windows Millennium Edition, Windows 2000, Windows XP Home Edition, Windows XP Professional, Windows Server 2003 family

Assembly: System.Drawing (in System.Drawing.dll)

PointF Constructor

Initializes a new instance of the **PointF** class with the specified coordinates.

```
[Visual Basic]
Public Sub New( _
   ByVal x As Single, _
   ByVal y As Single _
)
[C#]
public PointF(
   float x,
   float y
);
[C++]
public: PointF(
   float x,
   float y
);
[JScript]
public function PointF(
   x : float,
   y : float
);
```

Parameters

x

The horizontal position of the point.

y

The vertical position of the point.

Requirements

Platforms: Windows 98, Windows NT 4.0, Windows Millennium Edition, Windows 2000, Windows XP Home Edition, Windows XP Professional, Windows Server 2003 family

PointF.Empty Field

Represents a new instance of the **PointF** class with member data left uninitialized.

```
[Visual Basic]
Public Shared ReadOnly Empty As PointF
[C#]
public static readonly PointF Empty;
[C++]
public: static PointF Empty;
[JScript]
public static var Empty : PointF;
```

Requirements

Platforms: Windows 98, Windows NT 4.0, Windows Millennium Edition, Windows 2000, Windows XP Home Edition, Windows XP Professional, Windows Server 2003 family

PointF.IsEmpty Property

Gets a value indicating whether this **PointF** is empty.

```
[Visual Basic]
Public ReadOnly Property IsEmpty As Boolean
[C#]
public bool IsEmpty {get;}
[C++]
public: __property bool get_IsEmpty();
[JScript]
public function get IsEmpty() : Boolean;
```

Property Value

This property returns **true** if both **X** and **Y** are zero; otherwise, **false**.

Requirements

Platforms: Windows 98, Windows NT 4.0, Windows Millennium Edition, Windows 2000, Windows XP Home Edition, Windows XP Professional, Windows Server 2003 family

PointF.X Property

Gets the x-coordinate of this **PointF**.

```
[Visual Basic]
Public Property X As Single
[C#]
public float X {get; set;}
```

```
[C++]
public: __property float get_X();
public: __property void set_X(float);
[JScript]
public function get X() : float;
public function set X(float);
```

Property Value

The x-coordinate of this **PointF**.

Requirements

Platforms: Windows 98, Windows NT 4.0, Windows Millennium Edition, Windows 2000, Windows XP Home Edition, Windows XP Professional, Windows Server 2003 family

PointF.Y Property

Gets the y-coordinate of this **PointF**.

```
[Visual Basic]
Public Property Y As Single
[C#]
public float Y {get; set;}
[C++]
public: __property float get_Y();
public: __property void set_Y(float);
[JScript]
public function get Y() : float;
public function set Y(float);
```

Property Value

The y-coordinate of this **PointF**.

Requirements

Platforms: Windows 98, Windows NT 4.0, Windows Millennium Edition, Windows 2000, Windows XP Home Edition, Windows XP Professional, Windows Server 2003 family

PointF.Equals Method

Specifies whether this **PointF** contains the same coordinates as the specified **Object**.

```
[Visual Basic]
Overrides Public Function Equals( _
   ByVal obj As Object _
) As Boolean
[C#]
public override bool Equals(
   object obj
);
[C++]
public: bool Equals(
   Object* obj
);
[JScript]
public override function Equals(
   obj : Object
) : Boolean;
```

Parameters

obj

The **Object** to test.

Return Value

This method returns **true** if *obj* is a **PointF** and has the same coordinates as this **Point**.

Requirements

Platforms: Windows 98, Windows NT 4.0, Windows Millennium Edition, Windows 2000, Windows XP Home Edition, Windows XP Professional, Windows Server 2003 family

PointF.GetHashCode Method

Returns a hash code for this **PointF** object.

```
[Visual Basic]
Overrides Public Function GetHashCode() As Integer
[C#]
public override int GetHashCode();
[C++]
public: int GetHashCode();
[JScript]
public override function GetHashCode() : int;
```

Return Value

An integer value that specifies a hash value for this **PointF** object.

Requirements

Platforms: Windows 98, Windows NT 4.0, Windows Millennium Edition, Windows 2000, Windows XP Home Edition, Windows XP Professional, Windows Server 2003 family

PointF.ToString Method

Converts this **PointF** to a human readable string.

```
[Visual Basic]
Overrides Public Function ToString() As String
[C#]
public override string ToString();
[C++]
public: String* ToString();
[JScript]
public override function ToString() : String;
```

Return Value

A string that represents this **PointF**.

Requirements

Platforms: Windows 98, Windows NT 4.0, Windows Millennium Edition, Windows 2000, Windows XP Home Edition, Windows XP Professional, Windows Server 2003 family

PointF Addition Operator

Translates a **PointF** by a given **Size**.

[Visual Basic]
```
returnValue = PointF.op_Addition(pt, sz)
```
[C#]
```
public static PointF operator +(
   PointF pt,
   Size sz
);
```
[C++]
```
public: static PointF op_Addition(
   PointF pt,
   Size sz
);
```
[JScript]
```
returnValue = pt + sz;
```

[Visual Basic] In Visual Basic, you can use the operators defined by a type, but you cannot define your own.

[JScript] In JScript, you can use the operators defined by a type, but you cannot define your own.

Arguments [Visual Basic, JScript]

pt
    The **PointF** to translate.

sz
    A **Size** that specifies the pair of numbers to add to the coordinates of *pt*.

Parameters [C#, C++]

pt
    The **PointF** to translate.

sz
    A **Size** that specifies the pair of numbers to add to the coordinates of *pt*.

Return Value

Returns the translated **PointF**.

Requirements

Platforms: Windows 98, Windows NT 4.0, Windows Millennium Edition, Windows 2000, Windows XP Home Edition, Windows XP Professional, Windows Server 2003 family

PointF Equality Operator

Compares two **PointF** structures. The result specifies whether the values of the **X** and **Y** properties of the two **PointF** objects are equal.

[Visual Basic]
```
returnValue = PointF.op_Equality(left, right)
```
[C#]
```
public static bool operator ==(
   PointF left,
   PointF right
);
```
[C++]
```
public: static bool op_Equality(
   PointF left,
   PointF right
);
```
[JScript]
```
returnValue = left == right;
```

[Visual Basic] In Visual Basic, you can use the operators defined by a type, but you cannot define your own.

[JScript] In JScript, you can use the operators defined by a type, but you cannot define your own.

Arguments [Visual Basic, JScript]

left
    A **PointF** to compare.

right
    A **PointF** to compare.

Parameters [C#, C++]

left
    A **PointF** to compare.

right
    A **PointF** to compare.

Return Value

Returns **true** if the **X** and **Y** values of the left and right **PointF** objects are equal; otherwise, **false**.

Requirements

Platforms: Windows 98, Windows NT 4.0, Windows Millennium Edition, Windows 2000, Windows XP Home Edition, Windows XP Professional, Windows Server 2003 family

PointF Inequality Operator

Compares two **PointF** objects. The result specifies whether the values of the **X** or **Y** properties of the two **PointF** objects are unequal.

[Visual Basic]
```
returnValue = PointF.op_Inequality(left, right)
```
[C#]
```
public static bool operator !=(
   PointF left,
   PointF right
);
```
[C++]
```
public: static bool op_Inequality(
   PointF left,
   PointF right
);
```
[JScript]
```
returnValue = left != right;
```

[Visual Basic] In Visual Basic, you can use the operators defined by a type, but you cannot define your own.

[JScript] In JScript, you can use the operators defined by a type, but you cannot define your own.

Arguments [Visual Basic, JScript]

left
    A **PointF** to compare.

right
    A **PointF** to compare.

Parameters [C#, C++]

left
    A **PointF** to compare.

right
    A **PointF** to compare.

Return Value

true if the values of either the X properties or the Y properties of left and right differ; otherwise, **false**.

Requirements

Platforms: Windows 98, Windows NT 4.0,
Windows Millennium Edition, Windows 2000,
Windows XP Home Edition, Windows XP Professional,
Windows Server 2003 family

PointF Subtraction Operator

Translates a **PointF** by the negative of a given **Size**.

[Visual Basic]
```
returnValue = PointF.op_Subtraction(pt, sz)
```
[C#]
```
public static PointF operator -(
   PointF pt,
   Size sz
);
```
[C++]
```
public: static PointF op_Subtraction(
   PointF pt,
   Size sz
);
```
[JScript]
```
returnValue = pt - sz;
```

[Visual Basic] In Visual Basic, you can use the operators defined by a type, but you cannot define your own.

[JScript] In JScript, you can use the operators defined by a type, but you cannot define your own.

Arguments [Visual Basic, JScript]

pt
 A **PointF** to compare.

sz
 A **PointF** to compare.

Parameters [C#, C++]

pt
 A **PointF** to compare.

sz
 A **PointF** to compare.

Return Value

Returns the translated **PointF**.

Requirements

Platforms: Windows 98, Windows NT 4.0,
Windows Millennium Edition, Windows 2000,
Windows XP Home Edition, Windows XP Professional,
Windows Server 2003 family

Rectangle Structure

Stores a set of four integers that represent the location and size of a rectangle. For more advanced region functions, use a **Region** object.

System.Object
  System.ValueType
    System.Drawing.Rectangle

```
[Visual Basic]
<Serializable>
<ComVisible(True)>
Public Structure Rectangle
[C#]
[Serializable]
[ComVisible(true)]
public struct Rectangle
[C++]
[Serializable]
[ComVisible(true)]
public __value struct Rectangle
```

[JScript] In JScript, you can use the structures in the .NET Framework, but you cannot define your own.

Thread Safety

Any public static (**Shared** in Visual Basic) members of this type are safe for multithreaded operations. Any instance members are not guaranteed to be thread safe.

Remarks

A rectangle is defined by its width, height, and upper-left corner.

Requirements

Namespace: System.Drawing

Platforms: Windows 98, Windows NT 4.0, Windows Millennium Edition, Windows 2000, Windows XP Home Edition, Windows XP Professional, Windows Server 2003 family, .NET Compact Framework - Windows CE .NET

Assembly: System.Drawing (in System.Drawing.dll)

Rectangle Constructor

Initializes a new instance of the **Rectangle** class with the specified location and size.

Overload List

Initializes a new instance of the **Rectangle** class with the specified location and size.

[Visual Basic] **Public Sub New(Point, Size)**

[C#] **public Rectangle(Point, Size);**

[C++] **public: Rectangle(Point, Size);**

[JScript] **public function Rectangle(Point, Size);**

Initializes a new instance of the **Rectangle** class with the specified location and size.

Supported by the .NET Compact Framework.

[Visual Basic] **Public Sub New(Integer, Integer, Integer, Integer)**

[C#] **public Rectangle(int, int, int, int);**

[C++] **public: Rectangle(int, int, int, int);**

[JScript] **public function Rectangle(int, int, int, int);**

Rectangle Constructor (Point, Size)

Initializes a new instance of the **Rectangle** class with the specified location and size.

```
[Visual Basic]
Public Sub New( _
   ByVal location As Point, _
   ByVal size As Size _
)
[C#]
public Rectangle(
   Point location,
   Size size
);
[C++]
public: Rectangle(
   Point location,
   Size size
);
[JScript]
public function Rectangle(
   location : Point,
   size : Size
);
```

Parameters

location
  A **Point** that represents the upper-left corner of the rectangular region.

size
  A **Size** that represents the width and height of the rectangular region.

Requirements

Platforms: Windows 98, Windows NT 4.0, Windows Millennium Edition, Windows 2000, Windows XP Home Edition, Windows XP Professional, Windows Server 2003 family

Rectangle Constructor (Int32, Int32, Int32, Int32)

Initializes a new instance of the **Rectangle** class with the specified location and size.

```
[Visual Basic]
Public Sub New( _
   ByVal x As Integer, _
   ByVal y As Integer, _
   ByVal width As Integer, _
   ByVal height As Integer _
)
[C#]
public Rectangle(
   int x,
   int y,
   int width,
   int height
);
```

```
[C++]
public: Rectangle(
   int x,
   int y,
   int width,
   int height
);
[JScript]
public function Rectangle(
   x : int,
   y : int,
   width : int,
   height : int
);
```

Parameters

x
The x-coordinate of the upper-left corner of the rectangle.

y
The y-coordinate of the upper-left corner of the rectangle.

width
The width of the rectangle.

height
The height of the rectangle.

Requirements

Platforms: Windows 98, Windows NT 4.0,
Windows Millennium Edition, Windows 2000,
Windows XP Home Edition, Windows XP Professional,
Windows Server 2003 family,
.NET Compact Framework - Windows CE .NET

Rectangle.Empty Field

Represents a **Rectangle** structure with its properties left uninitialized.

```
[Visual Basic]
Public Shared ReadOnly Empty As Rectangle
[C#]
public static readonly Rectangle Empty;
[C++]
public: static Rectangle Empty;
[JScript]
public static var Empty : Rectangle;
```

Remarks

A rectangle is defined by its width, height and upper-left corner.

Requirements

Platforms: Windows 98, Windows NT 4.0,
Windows Millennium Edition, Windows 2000,
Windows XP Home Edition, Windows XP Professional,
Windows Server 2003 family,
.NET Compact Framework - Windows CE .NET

Rectangle.Bottom Property

Gets the y-coordinate of the bottom edge of this **Rectangle** structure.

```
[Visual Basic]
Public ReadOnly Property Bottom As Integer
[C#]
public int Bottom {get;}
[C++]
public: __property int get_Bottom();
[JScript]
public function get Bottom() : int;
```

Property Value

The y-coordinate of the bottom edge of this **Rectangle** structure.

Requirements

Platforms: Windows 98, Windows NT 4.0,
Windows Millennium Edition, Windows 2000,
Windows XP Home Edition, Windows XP Professional,
Windows Server 2003 family,
.NET Compact Framework - Windows CE .NET

Rectangle.Height Property

Gets or sets the height of this **Rectangle** structure.

```
[Visual Basic]
Public Property Height As Integer
[C#]
public int Height {get; set;}
[C++]
public: __property int get_Height();
public: __property void set_Height(int);
[JScript]
public function get Height() : int;
public function set Height(int);
```

Property Value

The height of this **Rectangle** structure.

Requirements

Platforms: Windows 98, Windows NT 4.0,
Windows Millennium Edition, Windows 2000,
Windows XP Home Edition, Windows XP Professional,
Windows Server 2003 family,
.NET Compact Framework - Windows CE .NET

Rectangle.IsEmpty Property

Tests whether all numeric properties of this **Rectangle** have values of zero.

```
[Visual Basic]
Public ReadOnly Property IsEmpty As Boolean
[C#]
public bool IsEmpty {get;}
[C++]
public: __property bool get_IsEmpty();
[JScript]
public function get IsEmpty() : Boolean;
```

Property Value

This property returns **true** if the **Width**, **Height**, **X**, and **Y** properties of this **Rectangle** all have values of zero; otherwise, **false**.

Requirements

Platforms: Windows 98, Windows NT 4.0,
Windows Millennium Edition, Windows 2000,
Windows XP Home Edition, Windows XP Professional,
Windows Server 2003 family,
.NET Compact Framework - Windows CE .NET

Rectangle.Left Property

Gets the x-coordinate of the left edge of this **Rectangle** structure.

```
[Visual Basic]
Public ReadOnly Property Left As Integer
[C#]
public int Left {get;}
[C++]
public: __property int get_Left();
[JScript]
public function get Left() : int;
```

Property Value

The x-coordinate of the left edge of this **Rectangle** structure.

Requirements

Platforms: Windows 98, Windows NT 4.0, Windows Millennium Edition, Windows 2000, Windows XP Home Edition, Windows XP Professional, Windows Server 2003 family, .NET Compact Framework - Windows CE .NET

Rectangle.Location Property

Gets or sets the coordinates of the upper-left corner of this **Rectangle** structure.

```
[Visual Basic]
Public Property Location As Point
[C#]
public Point Location {get; set;}
[C++]
public: __property Point get_Location();
public: __property void set_Location(Point);
[JScript]
public function get Location() : Point;
public function set Location(Point);
```

Property Value

A **Point** that represents the upper-left corner of this **Rectangle** structure.

Requirements

Platforms: Windows 98, Windows NT 4.0, Windows Millennium Edition, Windows 2000, Windows XP Home Edition, Windows XP Professional, Windows Server 2003 family, .NET Compact Framework - Windows CE .NET

Rectangle.Right Property

Gets the x-coordinate of the right edge of this **Rectangle** structure.

```
[Visual Basic]
Public ReadOnly Property Right As Integer
[C#]
public int Right {get;}
[C++]
public: __property int get_Right();
[JScript]
public function get Right() : int;
```

Property Value

The x-coordinate of the right edge of this **Rectangle** structure.

Requirements

Platforms: Windows 98, Windows NT 4.0, Windows Millennium Edition, Windows 2000, Windows XP Home Edition, Windows XP Professional, Windows Server 2003 family, .NET Compact Framework - Windows CE .NET

Rectangle.Size Property

Gets or sets the size of this **Rectangle**.

```
[Visual Basic]
Public Property Size As Size
[C#]
public Size Size {get; set;}
[C++]
public: __property Size get_Size();
public: __property void set_Size(Size);
[JScript]
public function get Size() : Size;
public function set Size(Size);
```

Property Value

A **Size** that represents the width and height of this **Rectangle** structure.

Requirements

Platforms: Windows 98, Windows NT 4.0, Windows Millennium Edition, Windows 2000, Windows XP Home Edition, Windows XP Professional, Windows Server 2003 family, .NET Compact Framework - Windows CE .NET

Rectangle.Top Property

Gets the y-coordinate of the top edge of this **Rectangle** structure.

```
[Visual Basic]
Public ReadOnly Property Top As Integer
[C#]
public int Top {get;}
[C++]
public: __property int get_Top();
[JScript]
public function get Top() : int;
```

Property Value

The y-coordinate of the top edge of this **Rectangle** structure.

Requirements

Platforms: Windows 98, Windows NT 4.0, Windows Millennium Edition, Windows 2000, Windows XP Home Edition, Windows XP Professional, Windows Server 2003 family, .NET Compact Framework - Windows CE .NET

Rectangle.Width Property

Gets or sets the width of this **Rectangle** structure.

```
[Visual Basic]
Public Property Width As Integer
[C#]
public int Width {get; set;}
```

```
[C++]
public: __property int get_Width();
public: __property void set_Width(int);
[JScript]
public function get Width() : int;
public function set Width(int);
```

Property Value

The width of this **Rectangle** structure.

Requirements

Platforms: Windows 98, Windows NT 4.0,
Windows Millennium Edition, Windows 2000,
Windows XP Home Edition, Windows XP Professional,
Windows Server 2003 family,
.NET Compact Framework - Windows CE .NET

Rectangle.X Property

Gets or sets the x-coordinate of the upper-left corner of this **Rectangle** structure.

```
[Visual Basic]
Public Property X As Integer
[C#]
public int X {get; set;}
[C++]
public: __property int get_X();
public: __property void set_X(int);
[JScript]
public function get X() : int;
public function set X(int);
```

Property Value

The x-coordinate of the upper-left corner of this **Rectangle** structure.

Requirements

Platforms: Windows 98, Windows NT 4.0,
Windows Millennium Edition, Windows 2000,
Windows XP Home Edition, Windows XP Professional,
Windows Server 2003 family,
.NET Compact Framework - Windows CE .NET

Rectangle.Y Property

Gets or sets the y-coordinate of the upper-left corner of this **Rectangle** structure.

```
[Visual Basic]
Public Property Y As Integer
[C#]
public int Y {get; set;}
[C++]
public: __property int get_Y();
public: __property void set_Y(int);
[JScript]
public function get Y() : int;
public function set Y(int);
```

Property Value

The y-coordinate of the upper-left corner of this **Rectangle** structure.

Requirements

Platforms: Windows 98, Windows NT 4.0,
Windows Millennium Edition, Windows 2000,
Windows XP Home Edition, Windows XP Professional,
Windows Server 2003 family,
.NET Compact Framework - Windows CE .NET

Rectangle.Ceiling Method

Converts the specified **RectangleF** structure to a **Rectangle** structure by rounding the **RectangleF** values to the next higher integer values.

```
[Visual Basic]
Public Shared Function Ceiling( _
   ByVal value As RectangleF _
) As Rectangle
[C#]
public static Rectangle Ceiling(
   RectangleF value
);
[C++]
public: static Rectangle Ceiling(
   RectangleF value
);
[JScript]
public static function Ceiling(
   value : RectangleF
) : Rectangle;
```

Parameters

value

The **RectangleF** structure to be converted.

Return Value

Returns a **Rectangle**.

Requirements

Platforms: Windows 98, Windows NT 4.0,
Windows Millennium Edition, Windows 2000,
Windows XP Home Edition, Windows XP Professional,
Windows Server 2003 family,
.NET Compact Framework - Windows CE .NET

Rectangle.Contains Method

Determines if the specified point is contained within the rectangular region defined by this **Rectangle**.

Overload List

Determines if the specified point is contained within this **Rectangle** structure.

[Visual Basic] **Overloads Public Function Contains(Point) As Boolean**

[C#] **public bool Contains(Point);**

[C++] **public: bool Contains(Point);**

[JScript] **public function Contains(Point) : Boolean;**

Determines if the rectangular region represented by *rect* is entirely contained within this **Rectangle** structure.

Supported by the .NET Compact Framework.

[Visual Basic] **Overloads Public Function Contains(Rectangle) As Boolean**

[C#] **public bool Contains(Rectangle);**

[C++] **public: bool Contains(Rectangle);**

[JScript] **public function Contains(Rectangle) : Boolean;**

Determines if the specified point is contained within this **Rectangle** structure.

Supported by the .NET Compact Framework.

[Visual Basic] **Overloads Public Function Contains(Integer, Integer) As Boolean**

[C#] **public bool Contains(int, int);**

[C++] **public: bool Contains(int, int);**

[JScript] **public function Contains(int, int) : Boolean;**

Rectangle.Contains Method (Point)

Determines if the specified point is contained within this **Rectangle** structure.

```
[Visual Basic]
Overloads Public Function Contains( _
   ByVal pt As Point _
) As Boolean
[C#]
public bool Contains(
   Point pt
);
[C++]
public: bool Contains(
   Point pt
);
[JScript]
public function Contains(
   pt : Point
) : Boolean;
```

Parameters

pt

The **Point** to test.

Return Value

This method returns **true** if the point represented by *pt* is contained within this **Rectangle** structure; otherwise **false**.

Requirements

Platforms: Windows 98, Windows NT 4.0, Windows Millennium Edition, Windows 2000, Windows XP Home Edition, Windows XP Professional, Windows Server 2003 family

Rectangle.Contains Method (Rectangle)

Determines if the rectangular region represented by *rect* is entirely contained within this **Rectangle** structure.

```
[Visual Basic]
Overloads Public Function Contains( _
   ByVal rect As Rectangle _
) As Boolean
[C#]
public bool Contains(
   Rectangle rect
);
[C++]
public: bool Contains(
   Rectangle rect
);
[JScript]
public function Contains(
   rect : Rectangle
) : Boolean;
```

Parameters

rect

The **Rectangle** to test.

Return Value

This method returns **true** if the rectangular region represented by *rect* is entirely contained within this **Rectangle** structure; otherwise **false**.

Requirements

Platforms: Windows 98, Windows NT 4.0, Windows Millennium Edition, Windows 2000, Windows XP Home Edition, Windows XP Professional, Windows Server 2003 family, .NET Compact Framework - Windows CE .NET

Rectangle.Contains Method (Int32, Int32)

Determines if the specified point is contained within this **Rectangle** structure.

```
[Visual Basic]
Overloads Public Function Contains( _
   ByVal x As Integer, _
   ByVal y As Integer _
) As Boolean
[C#]
public bool Contains(
   int x,
   int y
);
[C++]
public: bool Contains(
   int x,
   int y
);
[JScript]
public function Contains(
   x : int,
   y : int
) : Boolean;
```

Parameters

x

The x-coordinate of the point to test.

y

The y-coordinate of the point to test.

Return Value

This method returns **true** if the point defined by *x* and *y* is contained within this **Rectangle** structure; otherwise **false**.

Requirements

Platforms: Windows 98, Windows NT 4.0, Windows Millennium Edition, Windows 2000, Windows XP Home Edition, Windows XP Professional, Windows Server 2003 family, .NET Compact Framework - Windows CE .NET

Rectangle.Equals Method

Tests whether *obj* is a **Rectangle** structure with the same location and size of this **Rectangle** structure.

[Visual Basic]
```
Overrides Public Function Equals( _
   ByVal obj As Object _
) As Boolean
```
[C#]
```
public override bool Equals(
   object obj
);
```
[C++]
```
public: bool Equals(
   Object* obj
);
```
[JScript]
```
public override function Equals(
   obj : Object
) : Boolean;
```

Parameters

obj

The **Object** to test.

Return Value

This method returns **true** if *obj* is a **Rectangle** structure and its **X**, **Y**, **Width**, and **Height** properties are equal to the corresponding properties of this **Rectangle** structure; otherwise, **false**.

Requirements

Platforms: Windows 98, Windows NT 4.0, Windows Millennium Edition, Windows 2000, Windows XP Home Edition, Windows XP Professional, Windows Server 2003 family, .NET Compact Framework - Windows CE .NET

Rectangle.FromLTRB Method

Creates a **Rectangle** structure with the specified edge locations.

[Visual Basic]
```
Public Shared Function FromLTRB( _
   ByVal left As Integer, _
   ByVal top As Integer, _
   ByVal right As Integer, _
   ByVal bottom As Integer _
) As Rectangle
```
[C#]
```
public static Rectangle FromLTRB(
   int left,
   int top,
   int right,
   int bottom
);
```
[C++]
```
public: static Rectangle FromLTRB(
   int left,
   int top,
   int right,
   int bottom
);
```
[JScript]
```
public static function FromLTRB(
   left : int,
   top : int,
   right : int,
   bottom : int
) : Rectangle;
```

Parameters

left

The x-coordinate of the upper-left corner of this **Rectangle** structure.

top

The y-coordinate of the upper-left corner of this **Rectangle** structure.

right

The x-coordinate of the lower-right corner of this **Rectangle** structure.

bottom

The y-coordinate of the lower-right corner of this **Rectangle** structure.

Return Value

The new **Rectangle** that this method creates.

Remarks

This method creates a **Rectangle** with the specified upper-left and lower-right corners.

Requirements

Platforms: Windows 98, Windows NT 4.0, Windows Millennium Edition, Windows 2000, Windows XP Home Edition, Windows XP Professional, Windows Server 2003 family, .NET Compact Framework - Windows CE .NET

Rectangle.GetHashCode Method

Returns the hash code for this **Rectangle** structure. For information about the use of hash codes, see **Object.GetHashCode**.

[Visual Basic]
```
Overrides Public Function GetHashCode() As Integer
```
[C#]
```
public override int GetHashCode();
```
[C++]
```
public: int GetHashCode();
```
[JScript]
```
public override function GetHashCode() : int;
```

Return Value

An integer that represents the hashcode for this rectangle.

Requirements

Platforms: Windows 98, Windows NT 4.0, Windows Millennium Edition, Windows 2000, Windows XP Home Edition, Windows XP Professional, Windows Server 2003 family, .NET Compact Framework - Windows CE .NET

Rectangle.Inflate Method

Creates and returns an inflated copy of the specified **Rectangle** structure. The copy is inflated by the specified amount.

Overload List

Inflates this **Rectangle** by the specified amount.

[Visual Basic] **Overloads Public Sub Inflate(Size)**

[C#] **public void Inflate(Size);**

[C++] **public: void Inflate(Size);**

[JScript] **public function Inflate(Size);**

Inflates this **Rectangle** by the specified amount.

Supported by the .NET Compact Framework.

[Visual Basic] **Overloads Public Sub Inflate(Integer, Integer)**

[C#] **public void Inflate(int, int);**

[C++] **public: void Inflate(int, int);**

[JScript] **public function Inflate(int, int);**

Creates and returns an inflated copy of the specified **Rectangle** structure. The copy is inflated by the specified amount. The original **Rectangle** structure remains unmodified.

[Visual Basic] **Overloads Public Shared Function Inflate(Rectangle, Integer, Integer) As Rectangle**

[C#] **public static Rectangle Inflate(Rectangle, int, int);**

[C++] **public: static Rectangle Inflate(Rectangle, int, int);**

[JScript] **public static function Inflate(Rectangle, int, int) : Rectangle;**

Example

[Visual Basic, C#] The following example is designed for use with Windows Forms, and it requires **PaintEventArgs** *e*, which is a parameter of the **Paint** event handler. The code creates a **Rectangle** and inflates it by 50 units in both axes. Notice that the resulting rectangle (red) is 150 units in both axes.

> [Visual Basic, C#] **Note** This example shows how to use one of the overloaded versions of **Inflate**. For other examples that might be available, see the individual overload topics.

[Visual Basic]

```
Public Sub RectangleInflateTest(e As PaintEventArgs)
' Create a rectangle.
Dim rect As New Rectangle(100, 100, 50, 50)
' Draw the uninflated rect to screen.
e.Graphics.DrawRectangle(Pens.Black, rect)
' Call Inflate.
Dim rect2 As Rectangle = Rectangle.Inflate(rect, 50, 50)
' Draw the inflated rect to screen.
e.Graphics.DrawRectangle(Pens.Red, rect2)
End Sub
```

[C#]

```
public void RectangleInflateTest(PaintEventArgs e)
{
// Create a rectangle.
Rectangle rect = new Rectangle(100, 100, 50, 50);
// Draw the uninflated rect to screen.
e.Graphics.DrawRectangle(Pens.Black, rect);
// Call Inflate.
Rectangle rect2 = Rectangle.Inflate(rect, 50, 50);
// Draw the inflated rect to screen.
e.Graphics.DrawRectangle(Pens.Red, rect2);
}
```

Rectangle.Inflate Method (Size)

Inflates this **Rectangle** by the specified amount.

[Visual Basic]

```
Overloads Public Sub Inflate( _
   ByVal size As Size _
)
```

[C#]

```
public void Inflate(
   Size size
);
```

[C++]

```
public: void Inflate(
   Size size
);
```

[JScript]

```
public function Inflate(
   size : Size
);
```

Parameters

size

The amount to inflate this rectangle.

Return Value

This method does not return a value.

Remarks

This method inflates this rectangle, not a copy of it. The inflation along an axis is in two directions (minus direction and plus direction). For example, if a 50 by 50 rectangle is inflated by 50 in the x-axis, the resultant rectangle will be 150 units long (the original 50, the 50 in the minus direction, and the 50 in the plus direction) maintaining the rectangle's geometric center.

Example

[Visual Basic, C#] The following example is designed for use with Windows Forms, and it requires **PaintEventArgs** *e*, which is a parameter of the **Paint** event handler. The code creates a **Rectangle** and inflates it by 50 units in both axes. The rectangle is drawn to screen before inflation (black) and after inflation (red).

[Visual Basic]

```
Public Sub RectangleInflateTest2(e As PaintEventArgs)
' Create a rectangle.
Dim rect As New Rectangle(100, 100, 50, 50)
' Draw the uninflated rect to screen.
e.Graphics.DrawRectangle(Pens.Black, rect)
' Set up the inflate size.
Dim inflateSize As New Size(50, 50)
' Call Inflate.
rect.Inflate(inflateSize)
' Draw the inflated rect to screen.
e.Graphics.DrawRectangle(Pens.Red, rect)
End Sub
```

[C#]

```
public void RectangleInflateTest2(PaintEventArgs e)
{
// Create a rectangle.
Rectangle rect = new Rectangle(100, 100, 50, 50);
// Draw the uninflated rect to screen.
e.Graphics.DrawRectangle(Pens.Black, rect);
// Set up the inflate size.
Size inflateSize = new Size(50, 50);
// Call Inflate.
rect.Inflate(inflateSize);
// Draw the inflated rect to screen.
e.Graphics.DrawRectangle(Pens.Red, rect);
}
```

Requirements

Platforms: Windows 98, Windows NT 4.0, Windows Millennium Edition, Windows 2000, Windows XP Home Edition, Windows XP Professional, Windows Server 2003 family

Rectangle.Inflate Method (Int32, Int32)

Inflates this **Rectangle** by the specified amount.

```
[Visual Basic]
Overloads Public Sub Inflate( _
   ByVal width As Integer, _
   ByVal height As Integer _
)
[C#]
public void Inflate(
   int width,
   int height
);
[C++]
public: void Inflate(
   int width,
   int height
);
[JScript]
public function Inflate(
   width : int,
   height : int
);
```

Parameters

width
: The amount to inflate this **Rectangle** horizontally.

height
: The amount to inflate this **Rectangle** vertically.

Return Value

This method does not return a value.

Remarks

This method inflates this rectangle, not a copy of it. The inflation along an axis is in two directions (minus direction and plus direction). For example, if a 50 by 50 rectangle is inflated by 50 in the x-axis, the resultant rectangle will be 150 units long (the original 50, the 50 in the minus direction, and the 50 in the plus direction) maintaining the rectangle's geometric center.

If either *x* or *y* is negative, the **Rectangle** structure is deflated in the corresponding direction.

Example

[Visual Basic, C#] The following example creates a **Rectangle** structure and inflates it by 100 units in the x-axis direction:

```
[Visual Basic]
Public Sub RectangleInflateTest3(e As PaintEventArgs)
' Create a rectangle.
Dim rect As New Rectangle(100, 100, 50, 50)
' Draw the uninflated rect to screen.
e.Graphics.DrawRectangle(Pens.Black, rect)
' Call Inflate.
rect.Inflate(50, 50)
' Draw the inflated rect to screen.
e.Graphics.DrawRectangle(Pens.Red, rect)
End Sub
```

```
[C#]
public void RectangleInflateTest3(PaintEventArgs e)
{
// Create a rectangle.
Rectangle rect = new Rectangle(100, 100, 50, 50);
// Draw the uninflated rect to screen.
e.Graphics.DrawRectangle(Pens.Black, rect);
// Call Inflate.
rect.Inflate(50, 50);
// Draw the inflated rect to screen.
e.Graphics.DrawRectangle(Pens.Red, rect);
}
```

Requirements

Platforms: Windows 98, Windows NT 4.0, Windows Millennium Edition, Windows 2000, Windows XP Home Edition, Windows XP Professional, Windows Server 2003 family, .NET Compact Framework - Windows CE .NET

Rectangle.Inflate Method (Rectangle, Int32, Int32)

Creates and returns an inflated copy of the specified **Rectangle** structure. The copy is inflated by the specified amount. The original **Rectangle** structure remains unmodified.

```
[Visual Basic]
Overloads Public Shared Function Inflate( _
   ByVal rect As Rectangle, _
   ByVal x As Integer, _
   ByVal y As Integer _
) As Rectangle
[C#]
public static Rectangle Inflate(
   Rectangle rect,
   int x,
   int y
);
[C++]
public: static Rectangle Inflate(
   Rectangle rect,
   int x,
   int y
);
[JScript]
public static function Inflate(
   rect : Rectangle,
   x : int,
   y : int
) : Rectangle;
```

Parameters

rect
: The **Rectangle** with which to start. This rectangle is not modified.

x
: The amount to inflate this **Rectangle** horizontally.

y
: The amount to inflate this **Rectangle** vertically.

Return Value

The inflated **Rectangle**.

Remarks

This method makes a copy of *rect*, inflates the copy, and then returns the inflated copy. The inflation along an axis is in two directions (minus direction and plus direction). For example, if a 50 by 50 rectangle is inflated by 50 in the x-axis, the resultant rectangle will be 150 units long (the original 50, the 50 in the minus direction, and the 50 in the plus direction) maintaining the rectangle's geometric center.

Example

[Visual Basic, C#] The following example is designed for use with Windows Forms, and it requires **PaintEventArgs** *e*, which is a parameter of the **Paint** event handler. The code creates a **Rectangle** and inflates it by 50 units in both axes. Notice that the resulting rectangle (red) is 150 units in both axes.

[Visual Basic]
```
Public Sub RectangleInflateTest(e As PaintEventArgs)
' Create a rectangle.
Dim rect As New Rectangle(100, 100, 50, 50)
' Draw the uninflated rect to screen.
e.Graphics.DrawRectangle(Pens.Black, rect)
' Call Inflate.
Dim rect2 As Rectangle = Rectangle.Inflate(rect, 50, 50)
' Draw the inflated rect to screen.
e.Graphics.DrawRectangle(Pens.Red, rect2)
End Sub
```

[C#]
```
public void RectangleInflateTest(PaintEventArgs e)
{
// Create a rectangle.
Rectangle rect = new Rectangle(100, 100, 50, 50);
// Draw the uninflated rect to screen.
e.Graphics.DrawRectangle(Pens.Black, rect);
// Call Inflate.
Rectangle rect2 = Rectangle.Inflate(rect, 50, 50);
// Draw the inflated rect to screen.
e.Graphics.DrawRectangle(Pens.Red, rect2);
}
```

Requirements

Platforms: Windows 98, Windows NT 4.0, Windows Millennium Edition, Windows 2000, Windows XP Home Edition, Windows XP Professional, Windows Server 2003 family

Rectangle.Intersect Method

Replaces this **Rectangle** structure with the intersection of itself and the specified **Rectangle** structure.

Overload List

Replaces this **Rectangle** with the intersection of itself and the specified **Rectangle**.

Supported by the .NET Compact Framework.

[Visual Basic] **Overloads Public Sub Intersect(Rectangle)**

[C#] **public void Intersect(Rectangle);**

[C++] **public: void Intersect(Rectangle);**

[JScript] **public function Intersect(Rectangle);**

Returns a third **Rectangle** structure that represents the intersection of two other **Rectangle** structures. If there is no intersection, null is returned.

Supported by the .NET Compact Framework.

[Visual Basic] **Overloads Public Shared Function Intersect(Rectangle, Rectangle) As Rectangle**

[C#] **public static Rectangle Intersect(Rectangle, Rectangle);**

[C++] **public: static Rectangle Intersect(Rectangle, Rectangle);**

[JScript] **public static function Intersect(Rectangle, Rectangle) : Rectangle;**

Rectangle.Intersect Method (Rectangle)

Replaces this **Rectangle** with the intersection of itself and the specified **Rectangle**.

[Visual Basic]
```
Overloads Public Sub Intersect( _
   ByVal rect As Rectangle _
)
```
[C#]
```
public void Intersect(
   Rectangle rect
);
```
[C++]
```
public: void Intersect(
   Rectangle rect
);
```
[JScript]
```
public function Intersect(
   rect : Rectangle
);
```

Parameters

rect
The **Rectangle** with which to intersect.

Return Value

This method does not return a value.

Requirements

Platforms: Windows 98, Windows NT 4.0, Windows Millennium Edition, Windows 2000, Windows XP Home Edition, Windows XP Professional, Windows Server 2003 family, .NET Compact Framework - Windows CE .NET

Rectangle.Intersect Method (Rectangle, Rectangle)

Returns a third **Rectangle** structure that represents the intersection of two other **Rectangle** structures. If there is no intersection, null is returned.

[Visual Basic]
```
Overloads Public Shared Function Intersect( _
   ByVal a As Rectangle, _
   ByVal b As Rectangle _
) As Rectangle
```
[C#]
```
public static Rectangle Intersect(
   Rectangle a,
   Rectangle b
);
```

[C++]
```
public: static Rectangle Intersect(
   Rectangle a,
   Rectangle b
);
```
[JScript]
```
public static function Intersect(
   a : Rectangle,
   b : Rectangle
) : Rectangle;
```

Parameters

a

A rectangle to intersect.

b

A rectangle to intersect.

Return Value

A **Rectangle** that represents the intersection of *a* and *b*.

Requirements

Platforms: Windows 98, Windows NT 4.0, Windows Millennium Edition, Windows 2000, Windows XP Home Edition, Windows XP Professional, Windows Server 2003 family, .NET Compact Framework - Windows CE .NET

Rectangle.IntersectsWith Method

Determines if this rectangle intersects with *rect*.

[Visual Basic]
```
Public Function IntersectsWith( _
   ByVal rect As Rectangle _
) As Boolean
```
[C#]
```
public bool IntersectsWith(
   Rectangle rect
);
```
[C++]
```
public: bool IntersectsWith(
   Rectangle rect
);
```
[JScript]
```
public function IntersectsWith(
   rect : Rectangle
) : Boolean;
```

Parameters

rect

The rectangle to test.

Return Value

This method returns **true** if there is any intersection.

Requirements

Platforms: Windows 98, Windows NT 4.0, Windows Millennium Edition, Windows 2000, Windows XP Home Edition, Windows XP Professional, Windows Server 2003 family, .NET Compact Framework - Windows CE .NET

Rectangle.Offset Method

Adjusts the location of this rectangle by the specified amount.

Overload List

Adjusts the location of this rectangle by the specified amount.

[Visual Basic] **Overloads Public Sub Offset(Point)**

[C#] **public void Offset(Point);**

[C++] **public: void Offset(Point);**

[JScript] **public function Offset(Point);**

Adjusts the location of this rectangle by the specified amount. Supported by the .NET Compact Framework.

[Visual Basic] **Overloads Public Sub Offset(Integer, Integer)**

[C#] **public void Offset(int, int);**

[C++] **public: void Offset(int, int);**

[JScript] **public function Offset(int, int);**

Rectangle.Offset Method (Point)

Adjusts the location of this rectangle by the specified amount.

[Visual Basic]
```
Overloads Public Sub Offset( _
   ByVal pos As Point _
)
```
[C#]
```
public void Offset(
   Point pos
);
```
[C++]
```
public: void Offset(
   Point pos
);
```
[JScript]
```
public function Offset(
   pos : Point
);
```

Parameters

pos

Amount to offset the location.

Return Value

This method does not return a value.

Remarks

This method adjusts the location of the upper-left corner horizontally by the x-coordinate of the specified point, and vertically by the y-coordinate of the specified point.

Requirements

Platforms: Windows 98, Windows NT 4.0, Windows Millennium Edition, Windows 2000, Windows XP Home Edition, Windows XP Professional, Windows Server 2003 family

Rectangle.Offset Method (Int32, Int32)

Adjusts the location of this rectangle by the specified amount.

```
[Visual Basic]
Overloads Public Sub Offset( _
   ByVal x As Integer, _
   ByVal y As Integer _
)
[C#]
public void Offset(
   int x,
   int y
);
[C++]
public: void Offset(
   int x,
   int y
);
[JScript]
public function Offset(
   x : int,
   y : int
);
```

Parameters

x
    The horizontal offset.

y
    The vertical offset.

Return Value

This method does not return a value.

Requirements

Platforms: Windows 98, Windows NT 4.0, Windows Millennium Edition, Windows 2000, Windows XP Home Edition, Windows XP Professional, Windows Server 2003 family, .NET Compact Framework - Windows CE .NET

Rectangle.Round Method

Converts the specified **RectangleF** to a **Rectangle** by rounding the **RectangleF** values to the nearest integer values.

```
[Visual Basic]
Public Shared Function Round( _
   ByVal value As RectangleF _
) As Rectangle
[C#]
public static Rectangle Round(
   RectangleF value
);
[C++]
public: static Rectangle Round(
   RectangleF value
);
[JScript]
public static function Round(
   value : RectangleF
) : Rectangle;
```

Parameters

value
    The **RectangleF** to be converted.

Return Value

Returns a **Rectangle**.

Requirements

Platforms: Windows 98, Windows NT 4.0, Windows Millennium Edition, Windows 2000, Windows XP Home Edition, Windows XP Professional, Windows Server 2003 family, .NET Compact Framework - Windows CE .NET

Rectangle.ToString Method

Converts the attributes of this **Rectangle** to a human-readable string.

```
[Visual Basic]
Overrides Public Function ToString() As String
[C#]
public override string ToString();
[C++]
public: String* ToString();
[JScript]
public override function ToString() : String;
```

Return Value

A string that contains the position, width, and height of this **Rectangle** structure ¾ for example, {X=20, Y=20, Width=100, Height=50}

Requirements

Platforms: Windows 98, Windows NT 4.0, Windows Millennium Edition, Windows 2000, Windows XP Home Edition, Windows XP Professional, Windows Server 2003 family, .NET Compact Framework - Windows CE .NET

Rectangle.Truncate Method

Converts the specified **RectangleF** to a **Rectangle** by truncating the **RectangleF** values.

```
[Visual Basic]
Public Shared Function Truncate( _
   ByVal value As RectangleF _
) As Rectangle
[C#]
public static Rectangle Truncate(
   RectangleF value
);
[C++]
public: static Rectangle Truncate(
   RectangleF value
);
[JScript]
public static function Truncate(
   value : RectangleF
) : Rectangle;
```

Parameters

value
    The **RectangleF** to be converted.

Return Value

Returns a **Rectangle**.

Requirements

Platforms: Windows 98, Windows NT 4.0,
Windows Millennium Edition, Windows 2000,
Windows XP Home Edition, Windows XP Professional,
Windows Server 2003 family,
.NET Compact Framework - Windows CE .NET

Rectangle.Union Method

Gets a **Rectangle** structure that contains the union of two R **ectangle** structures.

```
[Visual Basic]
Public Shared Function Union( _
   ByVal a As Rectangle, _
   ByVal b As Rectangle _
) As Rectangle
[C#]
public static Rectangle Union(
   Rectangle a,
   Rectangle b
);
[C++]
public: static Rectangle Union(
   Rectangle a,
   Rectangle b
);
[JScript]
public static function Union(
   a : Rectangle,
   b : Rectangle
) : Rectangle;
```

Parameters

a

A rectangle to union.

b

A rectangle to union.

Return Value

A **Rectangle** structure that bounds the union of the two **Rectangle** structures.

Requirements

Platforms: Windows 98, Windows NT 4.0,
Windows Millennium Edition, Windows 2000,
Windows XP Home Edition, Windows XP Professional,
Windows Server 2003 family,
.NET Compact Framework - Windows CE .NET

Rectangle Equality Operator

Tests whether two **Rectangle** structures have equal location and size.

```
[Visual Basic]
returnValue = Rectangle.op_Equality(left, right)
[C#]
public static bool operator ==(
   Rectangle left,
   Rectangle right
);
[C++]
public: static bool op_Equality(
   Rectangle left,
   Rectangle right
);
[JScript]
returnValue = left == right;
```

[Visual Basic] In Visual Basic, you can use the operators defined by a type, but you cannot define your own.

[JScript] In JScript, you can use the operators defined by a type, but you cannot define your own.

Arguments [Visual Basic, JScript]

left

The **Rectangle** structure that is to the left of the equality operator.

right

The **Rectangle** structure that is to the right of the equality operator.

Parameters [C#, C++]

left

The **Rectangle** structure that is to the left of the equality operator.

right

The **Rectangle** structure that is to the right of the equality operator.

Return Value

This operator returns **true** if the two **Rectangle** structures have equal **X**, **Y**, **Width**, and **Height** properties.

Requirements

Platforms: Windows 98, Windows NT 4.0,
Windows Millennium Edition, Windows 2000,
Windows XP Home Edition, Windows XP Professional,
Windows Server 2003 family,
.NET Compact Framework - Windows CE .NET

Rectangle Inequality Operator

Tests whether two **Rectangle** structures differ in location or size.

```
[Visual Basic]
returnValue = Rectangle.op_Inequality(left, right)
[C#]
public static bool operator !=(
   Rectangle left,
   Rectangle right
);
[C++]
public: static bool op_Inequality(
   Rectangle left,
   Rectangle right
);
[JScript]
returnValue = left != right;
```

[Visual Basic] In Visual Basic, you can use the operators defined by a type, but you cannot define your own.

[JScript] In JScript, you can use the operators defined by a type, but you cannot define your own.

Arguments [Visual Basic, JScript]

left
: The **Rectangle** structure that is to the left of the inequality operator.

right
: The **Rectangle** structure that is to the right of the inequality operator.

Parameters [C#, C++]

left
: The **Rectangle** structure that is to the left of the inequality operator.

right
: The **Rectangle** structure that is to the right of the inequality operator.

Return Value

This operator returns **true** if any of the **X**, **Y**, **Width**, or **Height** properties of the two **Rectangle** structures are unequal; otherwise **false**.

Requirements

Platforms: Windows 98, Windows NT 4.0,
Windows Millennium Edition, Windows 2000,
Windows XP Home Edition, Windows XP Professional,
Windows Server 2003 family,
.NET Compact Framework - Windows CE .NET

RectangleConverter Class

Converts rectangles from one data type to another. Access this class through the TypeDescriptor.

System.Object
  System.ComponentModel.TypeConverter
    System.Drawing.RectangleConverter

[Visual Basic]
```
Public Class RectangleConverter
   Inherits TypeConverter
```
[C#]
```
public class RectangleConverter : TypeConverter
```
[C++]
```
public __gc class RectangleConverter : public TypeConverter
```
[JScript]
```
public class RectangleConverter extends TypeConverter
```

Thread Safety

Any public static (**Shared** in Visual Basic) members of this type are safe for multithreaded operations. Any instance members are not guaranteed to be thread safe.

Requirements

Namespace: System.Drawing

Platforms: Windows 98, Windows NT 4.0, Windows Millennium Edition, Windows 2000, Windows XP Home Edition, Windows XP Professional, Windows Server 2003 family

Assembly: System.Drawing (in System.Drawing.dll)

RectangleConverter Constructor

Initializes a new instance of the **RectangleConverter** class.

[Visual Basic]
```
Public Sub New()
```
[C#]
```
public RectangleConverter();
```
[C++]
```
public: RectangleConverter();
```
[JScript]
```
public function RectangleConverter();
```

Requirements

Platforms: Windows 98, Windows NT 4.0, Windows Millennium Edition, Windows 2000, Windows XP Home Edition, Windows XP Professional, Windows Server 2003 family

RectangleConverter.CanConvertFrom Method

Overload List

Determines if this converter can convert an object in the given source type to the native type of the converter.

[Visual Basic] **Overloads Overrides Public Function CanConvertFrom(ITypeDescriptorContext, Type) As Boolean**

[C#] **public override bool CanConvertFrom(ITypeDescriptorContext, Type);**

[C++] **public: bool CanConvertFrom(ITypeDescriptorContext*, Type*);**

[JScript] **public override function CanConvertFrom(ITypeDescriptorContext, Type) : Boolean;**

Inherited from **TypeConverter**.

[Visual Basic] **Overloads Public Function CanConvertFrom(Type) As Boolean**

[C#] **public bool CanConvertFrom(Type);**

[C++] **public: bool CanConvertFrom(Type*);**

[JScript] **public function CanConvertFrom(Type) : Boolean;**

RectangleConverter.CanConvertFrom Method (ITypeDescriptorContext, Type)

Determines if this converter can convert an object in the given source type to the native type of the converter.

[Visual Basic]
```
Overrides Overloads Public Function CanConvertFrom( _
   ByVal context As ITypeDescriptorContext, _
   ByVal sourceType As Type _
) As Boolean
```
[C#]
```
public override bool CanConvertFrom(
   ITypeDescriptorContext context,
   Type sourceType
);
```
[C++]
```
public: bool CanConvertFrom(
   ITypeDescriptorContext* context,
   Type* sourceType
);
```
[JScript]
```
public override function CanConvertFrom(
   context : ITypeDescriptorContext,
   sourceType : Type
) : Boolean;
```

Parameters

context
  A formatter context. This object can be used to get additional information about the environment this converter is being called from. This may be a null reference (**Nothing** in Visual Basic), so you should always check. Also, properties on the context object may also return a null reference (**Nothing**).

sourceType
  The type you want to convert from.

Return Value

This method returns **true** if this object can perform the conversion; otherwise, **false**.

Requirements

Platforms: Windows 98, Windows NT 4.0, Windows Millennium Edition, Windows 2000, Windows XP Home Edition, Windows XP Professional, Windows Server 2003 family

RectangleConverter.CanConvertTo Method

Overload List

Gets a value indicating whether this converter can convert an object to the given destination type using the context.

[Visual Basic] **Overloads Overrides Public Function CanConvertTo(ITypeDescriptorContext, Type) As Boolean**

[C#] **public override bool CanConvertTo(ITypeDescriptor-Context, Type);**

[C++] **public: bool CanConvertTo(ITypeDescriptorContext*, Type*);**

[JScript] **public override function CanConvertTo(IType-DescriptorContext, Type) : Boolean;**

Inherited from **TypeConverter**.

[Visual Basic] **Overloads Public Function CanConvertTo(Type) As Boolean**

[C#] **public bool CanConvertTo(Type);**

[C++] **public: bool CanConvertTo(Type*);**

[JScript] **public function CanConvertTo(Type) : Boolean;**

RectangleConverter.CanConvertTo Method (ITypeDescriptorContext, Type)

Gets a value indicating whether this converter can convert an object to the given destination type using the context.

```
[Visual Basic]
Overrides Overloads Public Function CanConvertTo( _
   ByVal context As ITypeDescriptorContext, _
   ByVal destinationType As Type _
) As Boolean
[C#]
public override bool CanConvertTo(
   ITypeDescriptorContext context,
   Type destinationType
);
[C++]
public: bool CanConvertTo(
   ITypeDescriptorContext* context,
   Type* destinationType
);
[JScript]
public override function CanConvertTo(
   context : ITypeDescriptorContext,
   destinationType : Type
) : Boolean;
```

Parameters

context

An **ITypeDescriptorContext** object that provides a format context.

destinationType

A **Type** object that represents the type you want to convert to.

Return Value

This method returns **true** if this converter can perform the conversion; otherwise, **false**.

Remarks

The *context* parameter can be used to get additional information about the environment this converter is being called from. This can be a null reference (**Nothing** in Visual Basic), so you should always check. Also, properties on the context object can also return a null reference (**Nothing**).

Requirements

Platforms: Windows 98, Windows NT 4.0, Windows Millennium Edition, Windows 2000, Windows XP Home Edition, Windows XP Professional, Windows Server 2003 family

RectangleConverter.ConvertFrom Method

Overload List

Converts the given object to a **Rectangle** object.

[Visual Basic] **Overloads Overrides Public Function Convert-From(ITypeDescriptorContext, CultureInfo, Object) As Object**

[C#] **public override object ConvertFrom(IType-DescriptorContext, CultureInfo, object);**

[C++] **public: Object* ConvertFrom(ITypeDescriptor-Context*, CultureInfo*, Object*);**

[JScript] **public override function ConvertFrom(IType-DescriptorContext, CultureInfo, Object) : Object;**

Inherited from **TypeConverter**.

[Visual Basic] **Overloads Public Function ConvertFrom(Object) As Object**

[C#] **public object ConvertFrom(object);**

[C++] **public: Object* ConvertFrom(Object*);**

[JScript] **public function ConvertFrom(Object) : Object;**

RectangleConverter.ConvertFrom Method (ITypeDescriptorContext, CultureInfo, Object)

Converts the given object to a **Rectangle** object.

```
[Visual Basic]
Overrides Overloads Public Function ConvertFrom( _
   ByVal context As ITypeDescriptorContext, _
   ByVal culture As CultureInfo, _
   ByVal value As Object _
) As Object
[C#]
public override object ConvertFrom(
   ITypeDescriptorContext context,
   CultureInfo culture,
   object value
);
[C++]
public: Object* ConvertFrom(
   ITypeDescriptorContext* context,
   CultureInfo* culture,
   Object* value
);
[JScript]
public override function ConvertFrom(
   context : ITypeDescriptorContext,
   culture : CultureInfo,
   value : Object
) : Object;
```

Parameters

context

A formatter context. This object can be used to get additional information about the environment this converter is being called from. This may be a null reference (**Nothing** in Visual Basic), so you should always check. Also, properties on the context object may also return a null reference (**Nothing**).

culture

An object that contains culture specific information, such as the language, calendar, and cultural conventions associated with a specific culture. It is based on the RFC 1766 standard.

value

The object to convert.

Return Value

The converted object. This will throw an exception if the conversion could not be performed.

Requirements

Platforms: Windows 98, Windows NT 4.0, Windows Millennium Edition, Windows 2000, Windows XP Home Edition, Windows XP Professional, Windows Server 2003 family

RectangleConverter.ConvertTo Method

Overload List

Converts the specified object to the specified type.

[Visual Basic] **Overloads Overrides Public Function ConvertTo(ITypeDescriptorContext, CultureInfo, Object, Type) As Object**

[C#] **public override object ConvertTo(ITypeDescriptorContext, CultureInfo, object, Type);**

[C++] **public: Object* ConvertTo(ITypeDescriptorContext*, CultureInfo*, Object*, Type*);**

[JScript] **public override function ConvertTo(ITypeDescriptorContext, CultureInfo, Object, Type) : Object;**

Inherited from **TypeConverter**.

[Visual Basic] **Overloads Public Function ConvertTo(Object, Type) As Object**

[C#] **public object ConvertTo(object, Type);**

[C++] **public: Object* ConvertTo(Object*, Type*);**

[JScript] **public function ConvertTo(Object, Type) : Object;**

RectangleConverter.ConvertTo Method (ITypeDescriptorContext, CultureInfo, Object, Type)

Converts the specified object to the specified type.

```
[Visual Basic]
Overrides Overloads Public Function ConvertTo( _
   ByVal context As ITypeDescriptorContext, _
   ByVal culture As CultureInfo, _
   ByVal value As Object, _
   ByVal destinationType As Type _
) As Object
[C#]
public override object ConvertTo(
   ITypeDescriptorContext context,
   CultureInfo culture,
   object value,
   Type destinationType
);
[C++]
public: Object* ConvertTo(
   ITypeDescriptorContext* context,
   CultureInfo* culture,
   Object* value,
   Type* destinationType
);
[JScript]
public override function ConvertTo(
   context : ITypeDescriptorContext,
   culture : CultureInfo,
   value : Object,
   destinationType : Type
) : Object;
```

Parameters

context

A formatter context. This object can be used to get additional information about the environment this converter is being called from. This may be a null reference (**Nothing** in Visual Basic), so you should always check. Also, properties on the context object may also return a null reference (**Nothing**).

culture

An object that contains culture specific information, such as the language, calendar, and cultural conventions associated with a specific culture. It is based on the RFC 1766 standard.

value

The object to convert.

destinationType

The type to convert the object to.

Return Value

The converted object.

Remarks

The most common types to convert are to and from a string object. The default implementation calls the object's **ToString** method if the object is valid and if the destination type is string. If this method cannot convert to the destination type, it throws a **NotSupportedException** exception.

Requirements

Platforms: Windows 98, Windows NT 4.0, Windows Millennium Edition, Windows 2000, Windows XP Home Edition, Windows XP Professional, Windows Server 2003 family

RectangleConverter.CreateInstance Method

Overload List

Creates an instance of this type given a set of property values for the object. This is useful for objects that are immutable but still want to provide changeable properties.

[Visual Basic] **Overloads Overrides Public Function CreateInstance(ITypeDescriptorContext, IDictionary) As Object**

[C#] **public override object CreateInstance(ITypeDescriptorContext, IDictionary);**

[C++] **public: Object* CreateInstance(ITypeDescriptorContext*, IDictionary*);**

[JScript] **public override function CreateInstance(ITypeDescriptorContext, IDictionary) : Object;**

Inherited from **TypeConverter**.

[Visual Basic] **Overloads Public Function CreateInstance(IDictionary) As Object**

[C#] **public object CreateInstance(IDictionary);**

[C++] **public: Object* CreateInstance(IDictionary*);**

[JScript] **public function CreateInstance(IDictionary) : Object;**

RectangleConverter.CreateInstance Method (ITypeDescriptorContext, IDictionary)

Creates an instance of this type given a set of property values for the object. This is useful for objects that are immutable but still want to provide changeable properties.

```
[Visual Basic]
Overrides Overloads Public Function CreateInstance( _
   ByVal context As ITypeDescriptorContext, _
   ByVal propertyValues As IDictionary _
) As Object
[C#]
public override object CreateInstance(
   ITypeDescriptorContext context,
   IDictionary propertyValues
);
[C++]
public: Object* CreateInstance(
   ITypeDescriptorContext* context,
   IDictionary* propertyValues
);
[JScript]
public override function CreateInstance(
   context : ITypeDescriptorContext,
   propertyValues : IDictionary
) : Object;
```

Parameters

context

A type descriptor through which additional context can be provided.

propertyValues

A dictionary of new property values. The dictionary contains a series of name-value pairs, one for each property returned from a call to the **GetProperties** method.

Return Value

The newly created object, or a null reference (**Nothing** in Visual Basic) if the object could not be created. The default implementation returns a null reference (**Nothing**).

Requirements

Platforms: Windows 98, Windows NT 4.0, Windows Millennium Edition, Windows 2000, Windows XP Home Edition, Windows XP Professional, Windows Server 2003 family

RectangleConverter.GetCreateInstanceSupported Method

Overload List

Determines if changing a value on this object should require a call to **CreateInstance** to create a new value.

[Visual Basic] **Overloads Overrides Public Function GetCreateInstanceSupported(ITypeDescriptorContext) As Boolean**

[C#] **public override bool GetCreateInstanceSupported(ITypeDescriptorContext);**

[C++] **public: bool GetCreateInstanceSupported(ITypeDescriptorContext*);**

[JScript] **public override function GetCreateInstanceSupported(ITypeDescriptorContext) : Boolean;**

Inherited from **TypeConverter**.

[Visual Basic] **Overloads Public Function GetCreateInstanceSupported() As Boolean**

[C#] **public bool GetCreateInstanceSupported();**

[C++] **public: bool GetCreateInstanceSupported();**

[JScript] **public function GetCreateInstanceSupported() : Boolean;**

RectangleConverter.GetCreateInstanceSupported Method (ITypeDescriptorContext)

Determines if changing a value on this object should require a call to **CreateInstance** to create a new value.

```
[Visual Basic]
Overrides Overloads Public Function GetCreateInstanceSupported( _
   ByVal context As ITypeDescriptorContext _
) As Boolean
[C#]
public override bool GetCreateInstanceSupported(
   ITypeDescriptorContext context
);
[C++]
public: bool GetCreateInstanceSupported(
   ITypeDescriptorContext* context
);
[JScript]
public override function GetCreateInstanceSupported(
   context : ITypeDescriptorContext
) : Boolean;
```

Parameters

context

A type descriptor through which additional context can be provided.

Return Value

This method returns **true** if **CreateInstance** should be called when a change is made to one or more properties of this object; otherwise, false.

Requirements

Platforms: Windows 98, Windows NT 4.0, Windows Millennium Edition, Windows 2000, Windows XP Home Edition, Windows XP Professional, Windows Server 2003 family

RectangleConverter.GetProperties Method

Overload List

Retrieves the set of properties for this type. By default, a type does not return any properties. A simple implementation of this method can just call the **TypeDescriptor.GetProperties** method for the correct data type.

[Visual Basic] **Overloads Overrides Public Function GetProperties(ITypeDescriptorContext, Object, Attribute()) As PropertyDescriptorCollection**

[C#] **public override PropertyDescriptorCollection GetProperties(ITypeDescriptorContext, object, Attribute[]);**

[C++] **public: PropertyDescriptorCollection* GetProperties(ITypeDescriptorContext*, Object*, Attribute[]);**

[JScript] **public override function GetProperties(ITypeDescriptorContext, Object, Attribute[]) : PropertyDescriptorCollection;**

Inherited from **TypeConverter**.

[Visual Basic] **Overloads Public Function GetProperties(Object) As PropertyDescriptorCollection**

[C#] **public PropertyDescriptorCollection GetProperties(object);**

[C++] **public: PropertyDescriptorCollection* GetProperties(Object*);**

[JScript] **public function GetProperties(Object) : PropertyDescriptorCollection;**

Inherited from **TypeConverter**.

[Visual Basic] **Overloads Public Function GetProperties(ITypeDescriptorContext, Object) As PropertyDescriptorCollection**

[C#] **public PropertyDescriptorCollection GetProperties(ITypeDescriptorContext, object);**

[C++] **public: PropertyDescriptorCollection* GetProperties(ITypeDescriptorContext*, Object*);**

[JScript] **public function GetProperties(ITypeDescriptorContext, Object) : PropertyDescriptorCollection;**

RectangleConverter.GetProperties Method (ITypeDescriptorContext, Object, Attribute[])

Retrieves the set of properties for this type. By default, a type does not return any properties. A simple implementation of this method can just call the **TypeDescriptor.GetProperties** method for the correct data type.

```
[Visual Basic]
Overrides Overloads Public Function GetProperties( _
   ByVal context As ITypeDescriptorContext, _
   ByVal value As Object, _
   ByVal attributes() As Attribute _
) As PropertyDescriptorCollection
[C#]
public override PropertyDescriptorCollection GetProperties(
   ITypeDescriptorContext context,
   object value,
   Attribute[] attributes
);
[C++]
public: PropertyDescriptorCollection* GetProperties(
   ITypeDescriptorContext* context,
   Object* value,
   Attribute* attributes[]
);
[JScript]
public override function GetProperties(
   context : ITypeDescriptorContext,
   value : Object,
   attributes : Attribute[]
) : PropertyDescriptorCollection;
```

Parameters

context
: A type descriptor through which additional context can be provided.

value
: The value of the object to get the properties for.

attributes
: An array of **MemberAttribute** objects that describe the properties.

Return Value

The set of properties that should be exposed for this data type. If no properties should be exposed, this may return a null reference (**Nothing** in Visual Basic). The default implementation always returns a null reference (**Nothing**).

Requirements

Platforms: Windows 98, Windows NT 4.0, Windows Millennium Edition, Windows 2000, Windows XP Home Edition, Windows XP Professional, Windows Server 2003 family

RectangleConverter.GetPropertiesSupported Method

Overload List

Determines if this object supports properties. By default, this is **false**.

[Visual Basic] **Overloads Overrides Public Function GetPropertiesSupported(ITypeDescriptorContext) As Boolean**

[C#] **public override bool GetPropertiesSupported(ITypeDescriptorContext);**

[C++] **public: bool GetPropertiesSupported(ITypeDescriptorContext*);**

[JScript] **public override function GetPropertiesSupported(ITypeDescriptorContext) : Boolean;**

Inherited from **TypeConverter**.

[Visual Basic] **Overloads Public Function GetPropertiesSupported() As Boolean**

[C#] **public bool GetPropertiesSupported();**

[C++] **public: bool GetPropertiesSupported();**

[JScript] **public function GetPropertiesSupported() : Boolean;**

RectangleConverter.GetPropertiesSupported Method (ITypeDescriptorContext)

Determines if this object supports properties. By default, this is **false**.

[Visual Basic]
```
Overrides Overloads Public Function GetPropertiesSupported( _
   ByVal context As ITypeDescriptorContext _
) As Boolean
```
[C#]
```
public override bool GetPropertiesSupported(
   ITypeDescriptorContext context
);
```
[C++]
```
public: bool GetPropertiesSupported(
   ITypeDescriptorContext* context
);
```
[JScript]
```
public override function GetPropertiesSupported(
   context : ITypeDescriptorContext
) : Boolean;
```

Parameters

context

A type descriptor through which additional context can be provided.

Return Value

This method returns **true** if **GetProperties** should be called to find the properties of this object; otherwise, false.

Requirements

Platforms: Windows 98, Windows NT 4.0, Windows Millennium Edition, Windows 2000, Windows XP Home Edition, Windows XP Professional, Windows Server 2003 family

RectangleF Structure

Stores a set of four floating-point numbers that represent the location and size of a rectangle. For more advanced region functions, use a **Region** object.

System.Object
 System.ValueType
  System.Drawing.RectangleF

```
[Visual Basic]
<Serializable>
Public Structure RectangleF
[C#]
[Serializable]
public struct RectangleF
[C++]
[Serializable]
public __value struct RectangleF
```

[JScript] In JScript, you can use the structures in the .NET Framework, but you cannot define your own.

Thread Safety

Any public static (**Shared** in Visual Basic) members of this type are safe for multithreaded operations. Any instance members are not guaranteed to be thread safe.

Remarks

A rectangle is defined by its width, height, and upper-left corner.

Requirements

Namespace: System.Drawing

Platforms: Windows 98, Windows NT 4.0, Windows Millennium Edition, Windows 2000, Windows XP Home Edition, Windows XP Professional, Windows Server 2003 family, .NET Compact Framework - Windows CE .NET

Assembly: System.Drawing (in System.Drawing.dll)

RectangleF Constructor

Initializes a new instance of the **RectangleF** class with the specified location and size.

Overload List

Initializes a new instance of the **RectangleF** class with the specified location and size.

[Visual Basic] **Public Sub New(PointF, SizeF)**

[C#] **public RectangleF(PointF, SizeF);**

[C++] **public: RectangleF(PointF, SizeF);**

[JScript] **public function RectangleF(PointF, SizeF);**

Initializes a new instance of the **RectangleF** class with the specified location and size.

Supported by the .NET Compact Framework.

[Visual Basic] **Public Sub New(Single, Single, Single, Single)**

[C#] **public RectangleF(float, float, float, float);**

[C++] **public: RectangleF(float, float, float, float);**

[JScript] **public function RectangleF(float, float, float, float);**

RectangleF Constructor (PointF, SizeF)

Initializes a new instance of the **RectangleF** class with the specified location and size.

```
[Visual Basic]
Public Sub New( _
   ByVal location As PointF, _
   ByVal size As SizeF _
)
[C#]
public RectangleF(
   PointF location,
   SizeF size
);
[C++]
public: RectangleF(
   PointF location,
   SizeF size
);
[JScript]
public function RectangleF(
   location : PointF,
   size : SizeF
);
```

Parameters

location
 A **PointF** that represents the upper-left corner of the rectangular region.

size
 A **SizeF** that represents the width and height of the rectangular region.

Requirements

Platforms: Windows 98, Windows NT 4.0, Windows Millennium Edition, Windows 2000, Windows XP Home Edition, Windows XP Professional, Windows Server 2003 family

RectangleF Constructor (Single, Single, Single, Single)

Initializes a new instance of the **RectangleF** class with the specified location and size.

```
[Visual Basic]
Public Sub New( _
   ByVal x As Single, _
   ByVal y As Single, _
   ByVal width As Single, _
   ByVal height As Single _
)
[C#]
public RectangleF(
   float x,
   float y,
   float width,
   float height
);
```

```
[C++]
public: RectangleF(
   float x,
   float y,
   float width,
   float height
);
[JScript]
public function RectangleF(
   x : float,
   y : float,
   width : float,
   height : float
);
```

Parameters

x
: The x-coordinate of the upper-left corner of the rectangle.

y
: The y-coordinate of the upper-left corner of the rectangle.

width
: The width of the rectangle.

height
: The height of the rectangle.

Requirements

Platforms: Windows 98, Windows NT 4.0, Windows Millennium Edition, Windows 2000, Windows XP Home Edition, Windows XP Professional, Windows Server 2003 family, .NET Compact Framework - Windows CE .NET

RectangleF.Empty Field

Represents an instance of the **RectangleF** class with its members uninitialized.

```
[Visual Basic]
Public Shared ReadOnly Empty As RectangleF
[C#]
public static readonly RectangleF Empty;
[C++]
public: static RectangleF Empty;
[JScript]
public static var Empty : RectangleF;
```

Remarks

The members of the new **RectangleF** are left uninitialized.

Requirements

Platforms: Windows 98, Windows NT 4.0, Windows Millennium Edition, Windows 2000, Windows XP Home Edition, Windows XP Professional, Windows Server 2003 family, .NET Compact Framework - Windows CE .NET

RectangleF.Bottom Property

Gets the y-coordinate of the bottom edge of this **RectangleF** structure.

```
[Visual Basic]
Public ReadOnly Property Bottom As Single
[C#]
public float Bottom {get;}
[C++]
public: __property float get_Bottom();
[JScript]
public function get Bottom() : float;
```

Property Value

The y-coordinate of the bottom edge of this **RectangleF** structure.

Requirements

Platforms: Windows 98, Windows NT 4.0, Windows Millennium Edition, Windows 2000, Windows XP Home Edition, Windows XP Professional, Windows Server 2003 family, .NET Compact Framework - Windows CE .NET

RectangleF.Height Property

Gets or sets the height of this **RectangleF** structure.

```
[Visual Basic]
Public Property Height As Single
[C#]
public float Height {get; set;}
[C++]
public: __property float get_Height();
public: __property void set_Height(float);
[JScript]
public function get Height() : float;
public function set Height(float);
```

Property Value

The height of this **RectangleF** structure.

Requirements

Platforms: Windows 98, Windows NT 4.0, Windows Millennium Edition, Windows 2000, Windows XP Home Edition, Windows XP Professional, Windows Server 2003 family, .NET Compact Framework - Windows CE .NET

RectangleF.IsEmpty Property

Tests whether all numeric properties of this **RectangleF** have values of zero.

```
[Visual Basic]
Public ReadOnly Property IsEmpty As Boolean
[C#]
public bool IsEmpty {get;}
[C++]
public: __property bool get_IsEmpty();
[JScript]
public function get IsEmpty() : Boolean;
```

Property Value

This property returns **true** if the **Width**, **Height**, **X**, and **Y** properties of this **RectangleF** all have values of zero; otherwise, **false**.

Requirements

Platforms: Windows 98, Windows NT 4.0, Windows Millennium Edition, Windows 2000, Windows XP Home Edition, Windows XP Professional,

Windows Server 2003 family,
.NET Compact Framework - Windows CE .NET

RectangleF.Left Property

Gets the x-coordinate of the left edge of this **RectangleF** structure.

```
[Visual Basic]
Public ReadOnly Property Left As Single
[C#]
public float Left {get;}
[C++]
public: __property float get_Left();
[JScript]
public function get Left() : float;
```

Property Value

The x-coordinate of the left edge of this **RectangleF** structure.

Requirements

Platforms: Windows 98, Windows NT 4.0,
Windows Millennium Edition, Windows 2000,
Windows XP Home Edition, Windows XP Professional,
Windows Server 2003 family,
.NET Compact Framework - Windows CE .NET

RectangleF.Location Property

Gets or sets the coordinates of the upper-left corner of this **RectangleF** structure.

```
[Visual Basic]
Public Property Location As PointF
[C#]
public PointF Location {get; set;}
[C++]
public: __property PointF get_Location();
public: __property void set_Location(PointF);
[JScript]
public function get Location() : PointF;
public function set Location(PointF);
```

Property Value

A **PointF** that represents the upper-left corner of this **RectangleF** structure.

Requirements

Platforms: Windows 98, Windows NT 4.0,
Windows Millennium Edition, Windows 2000,
Windows XP Home Edition, Windows XP Professional,
Windows Server 2003 family

RectangleF.Right Property

Gets the x-coordinate of the right edge of this **RectangleF** structure.

```
[Visual Basic]
Public ReadOnly Property Right As Single
[C#]
public float Right {get;}
[C++]
public: __property float get_Right();
[JScript]
public function get Right() : float;
```

Property Value

The x-coordinate of the right edge of this **RectangleF** structure.

Requirements

Platforms: Windows 98, Windows NT 4.0,
Windows Millennium Edition, Windows 2000,
Windows XP Home Edition, Windows XP Professional,
Windows Server 2003 family,
.NET Compact Framework - Windows CE .NET

RectangleF.Size Property

Gets or sets the size of this **RectangleF**.

```
[Visual Basic]
Public Property Size As SizeF
[C#]
public SizeF Size {get; set;}
[C++]
public: __property SizeF get_Size();
public: __property void set_Size(SizeF);
[JScript]
public function get Size() : SizeF;
public function set Size(SizeF);
```

Property Value

A **SizeF** that represents the width and height of this **RectangleF** structure.

Requirements

Platforms: Windows 98, Windows NT 4.0,
Windows Millennium Edition, Windows 2000,
Windows XP Home Edition, Windows XP Professional,
Windows Server 2003 family

RectangleF.Top Property

Gets the y-coordinate of the top edge of this **RectangleF** structure.

```
[Visual Basic]
Public ReadOnly Property Top As Single
[C#]
public float Top {get;}
[C++]
public: __property float get_Top();
[JScript]
public function get Top() : float;
```

Property Value

The y-coordinate of the top edge of this **RectangleF** structure.

Requirements

Platforms: Windows 98, Windows NT 4.0,
Windows Millennium Edition, Windows 2000,
Windows XP Home Edition, Windows XP Professional,
Windows Server 2003 family,
.NET Compact Framework - Windows CE .NET

RectangleF.Width Property

Gets or sets the width of this **RectangleF** structure.

```
[Visual Basic]
Public Property Width As Single
```

```
[C#]
public float Width {get; set;}
[C++]
public: __property float get_Width();
public: __property void set_Width(float);
[JScript]
public function get Width() : float;
public function set Width(float);
```

Property Value

The width of this **RectangleF** structure.

Requirements

Platforms: Windows 98, Windows NT 4.0, Windows Millennium Edition, Windows 2000, Windows XP Home Edition, Windows XP Professional, Windows Server 2003 family, .NET Compact Framework - Windows CE .NET

RectangleF.X Property

Gets or sets the x-coordinate of the upper-left corner of this **RectangleF** structure.

```
[Visual Basic]
Public Property X As Single
[C#]
public float X {get; set;}
[C++]
public: __property float get_X();
public: __property void set_X(float);
[JScript]
public function get X() : float;
public function set X(float);
```

Property Value

The x-coordinate of the upper-left corner of this **RectangleF** structure.

Requirements

Platforms: Windows 98, Windows NT 4.0, Windows Millennium Edition, Windows 2000, Windows XP Home Edition, Windows XP Professional, Windows Server 2003 family, .NET Compact Framework - Windows CE .NET

RectangleF.Y Property

Gets or sets the y-coordinate of the upper-left corner of this **RectangleF** structure.

```
[Visual Basic]
Public Property Y As Single
[C#]
public float Y {get; set;}
[C++]
public: __property float get_Y();
public: __property void set_Y(float);
[JScript]
public function get Y() : float;
public function set Y(float);
```

Property Value

The y-coordinate of the upper-left corner of this **RectangleF** structure.

Requirements

Platforms: Windows 98, Windows NT 4.0, Windows Millennium Edition, Windows 2000, Windows XP Home Edition, Windows XP Professional, Windows Server 2003 family, .NET Compact Framework - Windows CE .NET

RectangleF.Contains Method

Determines if the specified point is contained within this **RectangleF** structure.

Overload List

Determines if the specified point is contained within this **RectangleF** structure.

[Visual Basic] **Overloads Public Function Contains(PointF) As Boolean**

[C#] **public bool Contains(PointF);**

[C++] **public: bool Contains(PointF);**

[JScript] **public function Contains(PointF) : Boolean;**

Determines if the rectangular region represented by *rect* is entirely contained within this **RectangleF** structure.

[Visual Basic] **Overloads Public Function Contains(RectangleF) As Boolean**

[C#] **public bool Contains(RectangleF);**

[C++] **public: bool Contains(RectangleF);**

[JScript] **public function Contains(RectangleF) : Boolean;**

Determines if the specified point is contained within this **RectangleF** structure.

[Visual Basic] **Overloads Public Function Contains(Single, Single) As Boolean**

[C#] **public bool Contains(float, float);**

[C++] **public: bool Contains(float, float);**

[JScript] **public function Contains(float, float) : Boolean;**

RectangleF.Contains Method (PointF)

Determines if the specified point is contained within this **RectangleF** structure.

```
[Visual Basic]
Overloads Public Function Contains( _
   ByVal pt As PointF _
) As Boolean
[C#]
public bool Contains(
   PointF pt
);
[C++]
public: bool Contains(
   PointF pt
);
[JScript]
public function Contains(
```

```
   pt : PointF
) : Boolean;
```

Parameters

pt

The **PointF** to test.

Return Value

This method returns **true** if the point represented by the *pt* parameter is contained within this **RectangleF** structure; otherwise **false**.

Requirements

Platforms: Windows 98, Windows NT 4.0, Windows Millennium Edition, Windows 2000, Windows XP Home Edition, Windows XP Professional, Windows Server 2003 family

RectangleF.Contains Method (RectangleF)

Determines if the rectangular region represented by *rect* is entirely contained within this **RectangleF** structure.

```
[Visual Basic]
Overloads Public Function Contains( _
   ByVal rect As RectangleF _
) As Boolean
[C#]
public bool Contains(
   RectangleF rect
);
[C++]
public: bool Contains(
   RectangleF rect
);
[JScript]
public function Contains(
   rect : RectangleF
) : Boolean;
```

Parameters

rect

The **RectangleF** to test.

Return Value

This method returns **true** if the rectangular region represented by *rect* is entirely contained within the rectangular region represented by this **RectangleF**; otherwise **false**.

Requirements

Platforms: Windows 98, Windows NT 4.0, Windows Millennium Edition, Windows 2000, Windows XP Home Edition, Windows XP Professional, Windows Server 2003 family

RectangleF.Contains Method (Single, Single)

Determines if the specified point is contained within this **RectangleF** structure.

```
[Visual Basic]
Overloads Public Function Contains( _
   ByVal x As Single, _
   ByVal y As Single _
) As Boolean
[C#]
public bool Contains(
   float x,
   float y
);
[C++]
public: bool Contains(
   float x,
   float y
);
[JScript]
public function Contains(
   x : float,
   y : float
) : Boolean;
```

Parameters

x

The x-coordinate of the point to test.

y

The y-coordinate of the point to test.

Return Value

This method returns **true** if the point defined by *x* and *y* is contained within this **RectangleF** structure; otherwise **false**.

Requirements

Platforms: Windows 98, Windows NT 4.0, Windows Millennium Edition, Windows 2000, Windows XP Home Edition, Windows XP Professional, Windows Server 2003 family

RectangleF.Equals Method

Tests whether *obj* is a **RectangleF** with the same location and size of this **RectangleF**.

```
[Visual Basic]
Overrides Public Function Equals( _
   ByVal obj As Object _
) As Boolean
[C#]
public override bool Equals(
   object obj
);
[C++]
public: bool Equals(
   Object* obj
);
[JScript]
public override function Equals(
   obj : Object
) : Boolean;
```

Parameters

obj

The **Object** to test.

Return Value

This method returns **true** if *obj* is a **RectangleF** and its **X**, **Y**, **Width**, and **Height** properties are equal to the corresponding properties of this **RectangleF**; otherwise, **false**.

Requirements

Platforms: Windows 98, Windows NT 4.0, Windows Millennium Edition, Windows 2000,

Windows XP Home Edition, Windows XP Professional, Windows Server 2003 family, .NET Compact Framework - Windows CE .NET

RectangleF.FromLTRB Method

Creates a **RectangleF** structure with upper-left corner and lower-right corner at the specified locations.

```
[Visual Basic]
Public Shared Function FromLTRB( _
   ByVal left As Single, _
   ByVal top As Single, _
   ByVal right As Single, _
   ByVal bottom As Single _
) As RectangleF
[C#]
public static RectangleF FromLTRB(
   float left,
   float top,
   float right,
   float bottom
);
[C++]
public: static RectangleF FromLTRB(
   float left,
   float top,
   float right,
   float bottom
);
[JScript]
public static function FromLTRB(
   left : float,
   top : float,
   right : float,
   bottom : float
) : RectangleF;
```

Parameters

left
: The x-coordinate of the upper-left corner of the rectangular region.

top
: The y-coordinate of the upper-left corner of the rectangular region.

right
: The x-coordinate of the lower-right corner of the rectangular region.

bottom
: The y-coordinate of the lower-right corner of the rectangular region.

Return Value

The new **RectangleF** that this method creates.

Remarks

This method creates a **RectangleF** with the specified upper-left and lower-right corners.

Requirements

Platforms: Windows 98, Windows NT 4.0, Windows Millennium Edition, Windows 2000, Windows XP Home Edition, Windows XP Professional, Windows Server 2003 family

RectangleF.GetHashCode Method

Gets the hash code for this **RectangleF** structure. For information about the use of hash codes, see **Object.GetHashCode**.

```
[Visual Basic]
Overrides Public Function GetHashCode() As Integer
[C#]
public override int GetHashCode();
[C++]
public: int GetHashCode();
[JScript]
public override function GetHashCode() : int;
```

Return Value

The hash code for this **RectangleF**.

Requirements

Platforms: Windows 98, Windows NT 4.0, Windows Millennium Edition, Windows 2000, Windows XP Home Edition, Windows XP Professional, Windows Server 2003 family, .NET Compact Framework - Windows CE .NET

RectangleF.Inflate Method

Inflates this **RectangleF** by the specified amount.

Overload List

Inflates this **RectangleF** by the specified amount.

[Visual Basic] **Overloads Public Sub Inflate(SizeF)**

[C#] **public void Inflate(SizeF);**

[C++] **public: void Inflate(SizeF);**

[JScript] **public function Inflate(SizeF);**

Inflates this **RectangleF** structure by the specified amount.

[Visual Basic] **Overloads Public Sub Inflate(Single, Single)**

[C#] **public void Inflate(float, float);**

[C++] **public: void Inflate(float, float);**

[JScript] **public function Inflate(float, float);**

Creates and returns an inflated copy of the specified **RectangleF** structure. The copy is inflated by the specified amount. The original rectangle remains unmodified.

[Visual Basic] **Overloads Public Shared Function Inflate(RectangleF, Single, Single) As RectangleF**

[C#] **public static RectangleF Inflate(RectangleF, float, float);**

[C++] **public: static RectangleF Inflate(RectangleF, float, float);**

[JScript] **public static function Inflate(RectangleF, float, float) : RectangleF;**

Example

[Visual Basic, C#] This example is designed for use with Windows Forms, and it requires **PaintEventArgs** e, an OnPaint event object. The code creates a **RectangleF** and draws it to the screen in black. Notice that it has to be converted to a **Rectangle** for drawing purposes. Then the code inflates the **RectangleF**, again converts it to a **Rectangle**, and draws it to the screen in red. Notice that the original (black) rectangle is expanded in both directions along the x-axis by 100 points.

[Visual Basic, C#] **Note** This example shows how to use one of the overloaded versions of **Inflate**. For other examples that might be available, see the individual overload topics.

[Visual Basic]
```
Public Sub RectangleFInflateExample(e As PaintEventArgs)
' Create a RectangleF structure.
Dim myRectF As New RectangleF(100, 20, 100, 100)
' Draw myRect to the screen.
Dim myRect As Rectangle = Rectangle.Truncate(myRectF)
e.Graphics.DrawRectangle(Pens.Black, myRect)
' Create a Size structure.
Dim inflateSize As New SizeF(100, 0)
' Inflate myRect.
myRectF.Inflate(inflateSize)
' Draw the inflated rectangle to the screen.
myRect = Rectangle.Truncate(myRectF)
e.Graphics.DrawRectangle(Pens.Red, myRect)
End Sub
```

[C#]
```
public void RectangleFInflateExample(PaintEventArgs e)
{
// Create a RectangleF structure.
RectangleF myRectF = new RectangleF(100, 20, 100, 100);
// Draw myRect to the screen.
Rectangle myRect = Rectangle.Truncate(myRectF);
e.Graphics.DrawRectangle(Pens.Black, myRect);
// Create a Size structure.
SizeF inflateSize = new SizeF(100, 0);
// Inflate myRect.
myRectF.Inflate(inflateSize);
// Draw the inflated rectangle to the screen.
myRect = Rectangle.Truncate(myRectF);
e.Graphics.DrawRectangle(Pens.Red, myRect);
}
```

This method inflates this rectangle, not a copy of it. The inflation along an axis is in two directions (minus direction and plus direction). For example, if a 50 by 50 rectangle is inflated by 50 in the x-axis, the resultant rectangle will be 150 units long (the original 50, the 50 in the minus direction, and the 50 in the plus direction) maintaining the rectangle's geometric center.

RectangleF.Inflate Method (SizeF)

Inflates this **RectangleF** by the specified amount.

[Visual Basic]
```
Overloads Public Sub Inflate( _
   ByVal size As SizeF _
)
```
[C#]
```
public void Inflate(
   SizeF size
);
```
[C++]
```
public: void Inflate(
   SizeF size
);
```
[JScript]
```
public function Inflate(
   size : SizeF
);
```

Parameters

size

The amount to inflate this rectangle.

Return Value

This method does not return a value.

Example

[Visual Basic, C#] This example is designed for use with Windows Forms, and it requires **PaintEventArgs** e, an OnPaint event object. The code creates a **RectangleF** and draws it to the screen in black. Notice that it has to be converted to a **Rectangle** for drawing purposes. Then the code inflates the **RectangleF**, again converts it to a **Rectangle**, and draws it to the screen in red. Notice that the original (black) rectangle is expanded in both directions along the x-axis by 100 points.

[Visual Basic]
```
Public Sub RectangleFInflateExample(e As PaintEventArgs)
' Create a RectangleF structure.
Dim myRectF As New RectangleF(100, 20, 100, 100)
' Draw myRect to the screen.
Dim myRect As Rectangle = Rectangle.Truncate(myRectF)
e.Graphics.DrawRectangle(Pens.Black, myRect)
' Create a Size structure.
Dim inflateSize As New SizeF(100, 0)
' Inflate myRect.
myRectF.Inflate(inflateSize)
' Draw the inflated rectangle to the screen.
myRect = Rectangle.Truncate(myRectF)
e.Graphics.DrawRectangle(Pens.Red, myRect)
End Sub
```

[C#]
```
public void RectangleFInflateExample(PaintEventArgs e)
{
// Create a RectangleF structure.
RectangleF myRectF = new RectangleF(100, 20, 100, 100);
// Draw myRect to the screen.
Rectangle myRect = Rectangle.Truncate(myRectF);
e.Graphics.DrawRectangle(Pens.Black, myRect);
// Create a Size structure.
SizeF inflateSize = new SizeF(100, 0);
// Inflate myRect.
myRectF.Inflate(inflateSize);
// Draw the inflated rectangle to the screen.
myRect = Rectangle.Truncate(myRectF);
e.Graphics.DrawRectangle(Pens.Red, myRect);
}
```

This method inflates this rectangle, not a copy of it. The inflation along an axis is in two directions (minus direction and plus direction). For example, if a 50 by 50 rectangle is inflated by 50 in the x-axis, the resultant rectangle will be 150 units long (the original 50, the 50 in the minus direction, and the 50 in the plus direction) maintaining the rectangle's geometric center.

Requirements

Platforms: Windows 98, Windows NT 4.0, Windows Millennium Edition, Windows 2000, Windows XP Home Edition, Windows XP Professional, Windows Server 2003 family

RectangleF.Inflate Method (Single, Single)

Inflates this **RectangleF** structure by the specified amount.

[Visual Basic]
```
Overloads Public Sub Inflate( _
   ByVal x As Single, _
   ByVal y As Single _
)
```
[C#]
```
public void Inflate(
```

```
   float x,
   float y
);
[C++]
public: void Inflate(
   float x,
   float y
);
[JScript]
public function Inflate(
   x : float,
   y : float
);
```

Parameters

x

The amount to inflate this **RectangleF** structure horizontally.

y

The amount to inflate this **RectangleF** structure vertically.

Return Value

This method does not return a value.

Remarks

This method inflates this rectangle, not a copy of it. The inflation along an axis is in two directions (minus direction and plus direction). For example, if a 50 by 50 rectangle is inflated by 50 in the x-axis, the resultant rectangle will be 150 units long (the original 50, the 50 in the minus direction, and the 50 in the plus direction) maintaining the rectangle's geometric center.

If either *x* or *y* is negative, the **RectangleF** is deflated in the corresponding direction.

Requirements

Platforms: Windows 98, Windows NT 4.0, Windows Millennium Edition, Windows 2000, Windows XP Home Edition, Windows XP Professional, Windows Server 2003 family

RectangleF.Inflate Method (RectangleF, Single, Single)

Creates and returns an inflated copy of the specified **RectangleF** structure. The copy is inflated by the specified amount. The original rectangle remains unmodified.

```
[Visual Basic]
Overloads Public Shared Function Inflate( _
   ByVal rect As RectangleF, _
   ByVal x As Single, _
   ByVal y As Single _
) As RectangleF
[C#]
public static RectangleF Inflate(
   RectangleF rect,
   float x,
   float y
);
[C++]
public: static RectangleF Inflate(
   RectangleF rect,
   float x,
   float y
);
[JScript]
public static function Inflate(
   rect : RectangleF,
   x : float,
   y : float
) : RectangleF;
```

Parameters

rect

The **RectangleF** to be copied. This rectangle is not modified.

x

The amount to inflate the copy of the rectangle horizontally.

y

The amount to inflate the copy of the rectangle vertically.

Return Value

The inflated **RectangleF**.

Remarks

This method makes a copy of *rect*, inflates the copy, and then returns the inflated copy. The inflation along an axis is in two directions (minus direction and plus direction). For example, if a 50 by 50 rectangle is inflated by 50 in the x-axis, the resultant rectangle will be 150 units long (the original 50, the 50 in the minus direction, and the 50 in the plus direction) maintaining the rectangle's geometric center.

Requirements

Platforms: Windows 98, Windows NT 4.0, Windows Millennium Edition, Windows 2000, Windows XP Home Edition, Windows XP Professional, Windows Server 2003 family

RectangleF.Intersect Method

Returns a **RectangleF** structure that represents the intersection of two rectangles. If there is no intersection, null is returned.

Overload List

Replaces this **RectangleF** structure with the intersection of itself and the specified **RectangleF** structure.

[Visual Basic] **Overloads Public Sub Intersect(RectangleF)**

[C#] **public void Intersect(RectangleF);**

[C++] **public: void Intersect(RectangleF);**

[JScript] **public function Intersect(RectangleF);**

Returns a **RectangleF** structure that represents the intersection of two rectangles. If there is no intersection, null is returned.

[Visual Basic] **Overloads Public Shared Function Intersect(RectangleF, RectangleF) As RectangleF**

[C#] **public static RectangleF Intersect(RectangleF, RectangleF);**

[C++] **public: static RectangleF Intersect(RectangleF, RectangleF);**

[JScript] **public static function Intersect(RectangleF, RectangleF) : RectangleF;**

Example

[Visual Basic, C#] This example is designed for use with Windows Forms, and it requires **PaintEventArgs** e, an OnPaint event object. The code creates two **RectangleF** s and draws them to the screen in black and red. Notice that they have to be converted to **Rectangle** s for drawing purposes. Then the code creates a third **RectangleF** using the **Intersect** method, converts it to a **Rectangle**, and draws it to the screen in blue. Notice the third (blue) rectangle is the area of overlap of the other two rectangles:

> [Visual Basic, C#] **Note** This example shows how to use one of the overloaded versions of **Intersect**. For other examples that might be available, see the individual overload topics.

[Visual Basic]

```
Public Sub RectangleFIntersectExample(e As PaintEventArgs)
' Create two rectangles.
Dim firstRectangleF As New RectangleF(0, 0, 75, 50)
Dim secondRectangleF As New RectangleF(50, 20, 50, 50)
' Convert the RectangleF structures to Rectangle structures and
' draw them to the screen.
Dim firstRect As Rectangle = Rectangle.Truncate(firstRectangleF)
Dim secondRect As Rectangle = Rectangle.Truncate(secondRectangleF)
e.Graphics.DrawRectangle(Pens.Black, firstRect)
e.Graphics.DrawRectangle(Pens.Red, secondRect)
' Get the intersection.
Dim intersectRectangleF As RectangleF = _
RectangleF.Intersect(firstRectangleF, secondRectangleF)
' Draw the intersectRectangleF to the screen.
Dim intersectRect As Rectangle = _
Rectangle.Truncate(intersectRectangleF)
e.Graphics.DrawRectangle(Pens.Blue, intersectRect)
End Sub
```

[C#]

```
public void RectangleFIntersectExample(PaintEventArgs e)
{
// Create two rectangles.
RectangleF firstRectangleF = new RectangleF(0, 0, 75, 50);
RectangleF secondRectangleF = new RectangleF(50, 20, 50, 50);
// Convert the RectangleF structures to Rectangle structures
 and draw them to the
// screen.
Rectangle firstRect = Rectangle.Truncate(firstRectangleF);
Rectangle secondRect = Rectangle.Truncate(secondRectangleF);
e.Graphics.DrawRectangle(Pens.Black, firstRect);
e.Graphics.DrawRectangle(Pens.Red, secondRect);
// Get the intersection.
RectangleF intersectRectangleF =
RectangleF.Intersect(firstRectangleF,
secondRectangleF);
// Draw the intersectRectangleF to the screen.
Rectangle intersectRect =
Rectangle.Truncate(intersectRectangleF);
e.Graphics.DrawRectangle(Pens.Blue, intersectRect);
}
```

RectangleF.Intersect Method (RectangleF)

Replaces this **RectangleF** structure with the intersection of itself and the specified **RectangleF** structure.

[Visual Basic]

```
Overloads Public Sub Intersect( _
   ByVal rect As RectangleF _
)
```

[C#]

```
public void Intersect(
   RectangleF rect
);
```

[C++]

```
public: void Intersect(
   RectangleF rect
);
```

[JScript]

```
public function Intersect(
   rect : RectangleF
);
```

Parameters

rect

The rectangle to intersect.

Return Value

This method does not return a value.

Requirements

Platforms: Windows 98, Windows NT 4.0, Windows Millennium Edition, Windows 2000, Windows XP Home Edition, Windows XP Professional, Windows Server 2003 family

RectangleF.Intersect Method (RectangleF, RectangleF)

Returns a **RectangleF** structure that represents the intersection of two rectangles. If there is no intersection, null is returned.

[Visual Basic]

```
Overloads Public Shared Function Intersect( _
   ByVal a As RectangleF, _
   ByVal b As RectangleF _
) As RectangleF
```

[C#]

```
public static RectangleF Intersect(
   RectangleF a,
   RectangleF b
);
```

[C++]

```
public: static RectangleF Intersect(
   RectangleF a,
   RectangleF b
);
```

[JScript]

```
public static function Intersect(
   a : RectangleF,
   b : RectangleF
) : RectangleF;
```

Parameters

a

A rectangle to intersect.

b

A rectangle to intersect.

Return Value

A third **RectangleF** structure the size of which represents the overlapped area of the two specified rectangles.

Example

[Visual Basic, C#] This example is designed for use with Windows Forms, and it requires **PaintEventArgs** e, an OnPaint event object. The code creates two **RectangleF** s and draws them to the screen in black and red. Notice that they have to be converted to **Rectangle** s for drawing purposes. Then the code creates a third **RectangleF** using the **Intersect** method, converts it to a **Rectangle**, and draws it to the screen in blue. Notice the third (blue) rectangle is the area of overlap of the other two rectangles:

[Visual Basic]

```
Public Sub RectangleFIntersectExample(e As PaintEventArgs)
' Create two rectangles.
```

```
Dim firstRectangleF As New RectangleF(0, 0, 75, 50)
Dim secondRectangleF As New RectangleF(50, 20, 50, 50)
' Convert the RectangleF structures to Rectangle structures and
' draw them to the screen.
Dim firstRect As Rectangle = Rectangle.Truncate(firstRectangleF)
Dim secondRect As Rectangle = Rectangle.Truncate(secondRectangleF)
e.Graphics.DrawRectangle(Pens.Black, firstRect)
e.Graphics.DrawRectangle(Pens.Red, secondRect)
' Get the intersection.
Dim intersectRectangleF As RectangleF = _
RectangleF.Intersect(firstRectangleF, secondRectangleF)
' Draw the intersectRectangleF to the screen.
Dim intersectRect As Rectangle = _
Rectangle.Truncate(intersectRectangleF)
e.Graphics.DrawRectangle(Pens.Blue, intersectRect)
End Sub
```

[C#]

```
public void RectangleFIntersectExample(PaintEventArgs e)
{
// Create two rectangles.
RectangleF firstRectangleF = new RectangleF(0, 0, 75, 50);
RectangleF secondRectangleF = new RectangleF(50, 20, 50, 50);
// Convert the RectangleF structures to Rectangle structures ↵
and draw them to the
// screen.
Rectangle firstRect = Rectangle.Truncate(firstRectangleF);
Rectangle secondRect = Rectangle.Truncate(secondRectangleF);
e.Graphics.DrawRectangle(Pens.Black, firstRect);
e.Graphics.DrawRectangle(Pens.Red, secondRect);
// Get the intersection.
RectangleF intersectRectangleF =
RectangleF.Intersect(firstRectangleF,
secondRectangleF);
// Draw the intersectRectangleF to the screen.
Rectangle intersectRect =
Rectangle.Truncate(intersectRectangleF);
e.Graphics.DrawRectangle(Pens.Blue, intersectRect);
}
```

Requirements

Platforms: Windows 98, Windows NT 4.0, Windows Millennium Edition, Windows 2000, Windows XP Home Edition, Windows XP Professional, Windows Server 2003 family

RectangleF.IntersectsWith Method

Determines if this rectangle intersects with *rect*.

[Visual Basic]

```
Public Function IntersectsWith( _
   ByVal rect As RectangleF _
) As Boolean
```

[C#]

```
public bool IntersectsWith(
   RectangleF rect
);
```

[C++]

```
public: bool IntersectsWith(
   RectangleF rect
);
```

[JScript]

```
public function IntersectsWith(
   rect : RectangleF
) : Boolean;
```

Parameters

rect
The rectangle to test.

Return Value

This method returns **true** if there is any intersection.

Requirements

Platforms: Windows 98, Windows NT 4.0,
Windows Millennium Edition, Windows 2000,
Windows XP Home Edition, Windows XP Professional,
Windows Server 2003 family

RectangleF.Offset Method

Adjusts the location of this rectangle by the specified amount.

Overload List

Adjusts the location of this rectangle by the specified amount.

[Visual Basic] **Overloads Public Sub Offset(PointF)**

[C#] **public void Offset(PointF);**

[C++] **public: void Offset(PointF);**

[JScript] **public function Offset(PointF);**

Adjusts the location of this rectangle by the specified amount.

[Visual Basic] **Overloads Public Sub Offset(Single, Single)**

[C#] **public void Offset(float, float);**

[C++] **public: void Offset(float, float);**

[JScript] **public function Offset(float, float);**

RectangleF.Offset Method (PointF)

Adjusts the location of this rectangle by the specified amount.

```
[Visual Basic]
Overloads Public Sub Offset( _
   ByVal pos As PointF _
)
[C#]
public void Offset(
   PointF pos
);
[C++]
public: void Offset(
   PointF pos
);
[JScript]
public function Offset(
   pos : PointF
);
```

Parameters

pos

The amount to offset the location.

Return Value

This method does not return a value.

Requirements

Platforms: Windows 98, Windows NT 4.0,
Windows Millennium Edition, Windows 2000,
Windows XP Home Edition, Windows XP Professional,
Windows Server 2003 family

RectangleF.Offset Method (Single, Single)

Adjusts the location of this rectangle by the specified amount.

```
[Visual Basic]
Overloads Public Sub Offset( _
   ByVal x As Single, _
   ByVal y As Single _
)
[C#]
public void Offset(
   float x,
   float y
);
[C++]
public: void Offset(
   float x,
   float y
);
[JScript]
public function Offset(
   x : float,
   y : float
);
```

Parameters

x

The amount to offset the location horizontally.

y

The amount to offset the location vertically.

Return Value

This method does not return a value.

Requirements

Platforms: Windows 98, Windows NT 4.0,
Windows Millennium Edition, Windows 2000,
Windows XP Home Edition, Windows XP Professional,
Windows Server 2003 family

RectangleF.ToString Method

Converts the **Location** and **Size** of this **RectangleF** to a human-readable string.

```
[Visual Basic]
Overrides Public Function ToString() As String
[C#]
public override string ToString();
[C++]
public: String* ToString();
[JScript]
public override function ToString() : String;
```

Return Value

A string that contains the position, width, and height of this **RectangleF** structure¾for example, "{X=20, Y=20, Width=100, Height=50}".

Requirements

Platforms: Windows 98, Windows NT 4.0,
Windows Millennium Edition, Windows 2000,
Windows XP Home Edition, Windows XP Professional,
Windows Server 2003 family,
.NET Compact Framework - Windows CE .NET

RectangleF.Union Method

Creates the smallest possible third rectangle that can contain both of two rectangles that form a union.

[Visual Basic]
```
Public Shared Function Union( _
   ByVal a As RectangleF, _
   ByVal b As RectangleF _
) As RectangleF
```
[C#]
```
public static RectangleF Union(
   RectangleF a,
   RectangleF b
);
```
[C++]
```
public: static RectangleF Union(
   RectangleF a,
   RectangleF b
);
```
[JScript]
```
public static function Union(
   a : RectangleF,
   b : RectangleF
) : RectangleF;
```

Parameters

a
  A rectangle to union.

b
  A rectangle to union.

Return Value

A third **RectangleF** structure that contains both of the two rectangles that form the union.

Example

[Visual Basic, C#] This example is designed for use with Windows Forms, and it requires **PaintEventArgs** e, an OnPaint event object. The code creates two **RectangleF** s and draws them to the screen in black and red. Notice that they have to be converted to **Rectangle** s for drawing purposes. Then the code creates a third **RectangleF** using the **Union** method, converts it to a **Rectangle**, and draws it to the screen in blue. Notice the third (blue) rectangle is the smallest possible rectangle that can contain both of the other two rectangles:

[Visual Basic]
```
Public Sub RectangleFUnionExample(e As PaintEventArgs)
' Create two rectangles and draw them to the screen.
Dim firstRectangleF As New RectangleF(0, 0, 75, 50)
Dim secondRectangleF As New RectangleF(100, 100, 20, 20)
' Convert the RectangleF structures to Rectangle structures and
' draw them to the screen.
Dim firstRect As Rectangle = Rectangle.Truncate(firstRectangleF)
Dim secondRect As Rectangle = Rectangle.Truncate(secondRectangleF)
e.Graphics.DrawRectangle(Pens.Black, firstRect)
e.Graphics.DrawRectangle(Pens.Red, secondRect)
' Get the union rectangle.
Dim unionRectangleF As RectangleF = _
RectangleF.Union(firstRectangleF, secondRectangleF)
' Draw the unionRectangleF to the screen.
Dim unionRect As Rectangle = Rectangle.Truncate(unionRectangleF)
e.Graphics.DrawRectangle(Pens.Blue, unionRect)
End Sub
```

[C#]
```
public void RectangleFUnionExample(PaintEventArgs e)
{
// Create two rectangles and draw them to the screen.
RectangleF firstRectangleF = new RectangleF(0, 0, 75, 50);
RectangleF secondRectangleF = new RectangleF(100, 100, 20, 20);
// Convert the RectangleF structures to Rectangle structures ↵
and draw them to the
// screen.
Rectangle firstRect = Rectangle.Truncate(firstRectangleF);
Rectangle secondRect = Rectangle.Truncate(secondRectangleF);
e.Graphics.DrawRectangle(Pens.Black, firstRect);
e.Graphics.DrawRectangle(Pens.Red, secondRect);
// Get the union rectangle.
RectangleF unionRectangleF = RectangleF.Union(firstRectangleF,
secondRectangleF);
// Draw the unionRectangleF to the screen.
Rectangle unionRect = Rectangle.Truncate(unionRectangleF);
e.Graphics.DrawRectangle(Pens.Blue, unionRect);
}
```

Requirements

Platforms: Windows 98, Windows NT 4.0, Windows Millennium Edition, Windows 2000, Windows XP Home Edition, Windows XP Professional, Windows Server 2003 family

RectangleF Equality Operator

Tests whether two **RectangleF** structures have equal location and size.

[Visual Basic]
```
returnValue = RectangleF.op_Equality(left, right)
```
[C#]
```
public static bool operator ==(
   RectangleF left,
   RectangleF right
);
```
[C++]
```
public: static bool op_Equality(
   RectangleF left,
   RectangleF right
);
```
[JScript]
```
returnValue = left == right;
```

[Visual Basic] In Visual Basic, you can use the operators defined by a type, but you cannot define your own.

[JScript] In JScript, you can use the operators defined by a type, but you cannot define your own.

Arguments [Visual Basic, JScript]

left
  The **RectangleF** structure that is to the left of the equality operator.

right
  The **RectangleF** structure that is to the right of the equality operator.

Parameters [C#, C++]

left
  The **RectangleF** structure that is to the left of the equality operator.

right
  The **RectangleF** structure that is to the right of the equality operator.

Return Value

This operator returns **true** if the two specified **RectangleF** structures have equal **X**, **Y**, **Width**, and **Height** properties.

Requirements

Platforms: Windows 98, Windows NT 4.0, Windows Millennium Edition, Windows 2000, Windows XP Home Edition, Windows XP Professional, Windows Server 2003 family, .NET Compact Framework - Windows CE .NET

RectangleF Inequality Operator

Tests whether two **RectangleF** structures differ in location or size.

[Visual Basic]
```
returnValue = RectangleF.op_Inequality(left, right)
```
[C#]
```
public static bool operator !=(
   RectangleF left,
   RectangleF right
);
```
[C++]
```
public: static bool op_Inequality(
   RectangleF left,
   RectangleF right
);
```
[JScript]
```
returnValue = left != right;
```

[Visual Basic] In Visual Basic, you can use the operators defined by a type, but you cannot define your own.

[JScript] In JScript, you can use the operators defined by a type, but you cannot define your own.

Arguments [Visual Basic, JScript]

left

The **RectangleF** structure that is to the left of the inequality operator.

right

The **RectangleF** structure that is to the right of the inequality operator.

Parameters [C#, C++]

left

The **RectangleF** structure that is to the left of the inequality operator.

right

The **RectangleF** structure that is to the right of the inequality operator.

Return Value

This operator returns **true** if any of the **X**, **Y**, **Width**, or **Height** properties of the two **Rectangle** structures are unequal; otherwise **false**.

Requirements

Platforms: Windows 98, Windows NT 4.0, Windows Millennium Edition, Windows 2000, Windows XP Home Edition, Windows XP Professional, Windows Server 2003 family, .NET Compact Framework - Windows CE .NET

Rectangle to RectangleF Conversion

Converts the specified **Rectangle** to a **RectangleF**.

[Visual Basic]
```
returnValue = RectangleF.op_Implicit(r)
```
[C#]
```
public static implicit operator RectangleF(
   Rectangle r
);
```
[C++]
```
public: static RectangleF op_Implicit(
   Rectangle r
);
```
[JScript]
```
returnValue = r;
```

[Visual Basic] In Visual Basic, you can use the conversion operators defined by a type, but you cannot define your own.

[JScript] In JScript, you can use the conversion operators defined by a type, but you cannot define your own.

Arguments [Visual Basic, JScript]

r

The **Rectangle** to convert.

Parameters [C#, C++]

r

The **Rectangle** to convert.

Requirements

Platforms: Windows 98, Windows NT 4.0, Windows Millennium Edition, Windows 2000, Windows XP Home Edition, Windows XP Professional, Windows Server 2003 family, .NET Compact Framework - Windows CE .NET

Region Class

Describes the interior of a graphics shape composed of rectangles and paths. This class cannot be inherited.

System.Object
  System.MarshalByRefObject
    System.Drawing.Region

[Visual Basic]
```
<ComVisible(False)>
NotInheritable Public Class Region
   Inherits MarshalByRefObject
   Implements IDisposable
```
[C#]
```
[ComVisible(false)]
public sealed class Region : MarshalByRefObject, IDisposable
```
[C++]
```
[ComVisible(false)]
public __gc __sealed class Region : public MarshalByRefObject,
   IDisposable
```
[JScript]
```
public
   ComVisible(false)
class Region extends MarshalByRefObject implements
   IDisposable
```

Thread Safety

Any public static (**Shared** in Visual Basic) members of this type are safe for multithreaded operations. Any instance members are not guaranteed to be thread safe.

Remarks

A region is scalable because its coordinates are specified in world coordinates. On a drawing surface, however, its interior is dependent on the size and shape of the pixels representing it. An application can use regions to clamp the output of drawing operations. The window manager uses regions to define the drawing area of windows. These regions are called clipping regions. An application can also use regions in hit-testing operations, such as checking whether a point or a rectangle intersects a region. An application can fill a region by using a **Brush** object.

Requirements

Namespace: System.Drawing

Platforms: Windows 98, Windows NT 4.0, Windows Millennium Edition, Windows 2000, Windows XP Home Edition, Windows XP Professional, Windows Server 2003 family, .NET Compact Framework - Windows CE .NET

Assembly: System.Drawing (in System.Drawing.dll)

Region Constructor

Initializes a new **Region** object.

Overload List

Initializes a new **Region** object.

Supported by the .NET Compact Framework.

[Visual Basic] **Public Sub New()**

[C#] **public Region();**

[C++] **public: Region();**

[JScript] **public function Region();**

Initializes a new **Region** object with the specified **GraphicsPath** object.

[Visual Basic] **Public Sub New(GraphicsPath)**

[C#] **public Region(GraphicsPath);**

[C++] **public: Region(GraphicsPath*);**

[JScript] **public function Region(GraphicsPath);**

Initializes a new **Region** object from the specified **Rectangle** structure.

Supported by the .NET Compact Framework.

[Visual Basic] **Public Sub New(Rectangle)**

[C#] **public Region(Rectangle);**

[C++] **public: Region(Rectangle);**

[JScript] **public function Region(Rectangle);**

Initializes a new **Region** object from the specified **RectangleF** structure.

[Visual Basic] **Public Sub New(RectangleF)**

[C#] **public Region(RectangleF);**

[C++] **public: Region(RectangleF);**

[JScript] **public function Region(RectangleF);**

Initializes a new **Region** object from the specified data.

[Visual Basic] **Public Sub New(RegionData)**

[C#] **public Region(RegionData);**

[C++] **public: Region(RegionData*);**

[JScript] **public function Region(RegionData);**

Region Constructor ()

Initializes a new **Region** object.

[Visual Basic]
```
Public Sub New()
```
[C#]
```
public Region();
```
[C++]
```
public: Region();
```
[JScript]
```
public function Region();
```

Remarks

This constructor initializes a new **Region** object with infinite interior.

Requirements

Platforms: Windows 98, Windows NT 4.0, Windows Millennium Edition, Windows 2000, Windows XP Home Edition, Windows XP Professional, Windows Server 2003 family, .NET Compact Framework - Windows CE .NET

Region Constructor (GraphicsPath)

Initializes a new **Region** object with the specified **GraphicsPath** object.

[Visual Basic]
```
Public Sub New( _
   ByVal path As GraphicsPath _
)
```

```
[C#]
public Region(
   GraphicsPath path
);
[C++]
public: Region(
   GraphicsPath* path
);
[JScript]
public function Region(
   path : GraphicsPath
);
```

Parameters

path

A **GraphicsPath** object that defines the new **Region** object.

Remarks

This method creates a new **Region** object with a **GraphicsPath** object. The new region is defined as the interior of the **GraphicsPath** object specified by the *path* parameter.

Requirements

Platforms: Windows 98, Windows NT 4.0,
Windows Millennium Edition, Windows 2000,
Windows XP Home Edition, Windows XP Professional,
Windows Server 2003 family

Region Constructor (Rectangle)

Initializes a new **Region** object from the specified **Rectangle** structure.

```
[Visual Basic]
Public Sub New( _
   ByVal rect As Rectangle _
)
[C#]
public Region(
   Rectangle rect
);
[C++]
public: Region(
   Rectangle rect
);
[JScript]
public function Region(
   rect : Rectangle
);
```

Parameters

rect

A **Rectangle** structure that defines the interior of the new **Region** object.

Remarks

This method creates a new **Region** object with a rectangular interior. The interior is defined by the *rect* parameter.

Requirements

Platforms: Windows 98, Windows NT 4.0,
Windows Millennium Edition, Windows 2000,
Windows XP Home Edition, Windows XP Professional,
Windows Server 2003 family,
.NET Compact Framework - Windows CE .NET

Region Constructor (RectangleF)

Initializes a new **Region** object from the specified **RectangleF** structure.

```
[Visual Basic]
Public Sub New( _
   ByVal rect As RectangleF _
)
[C#]
public Region(
   RectangleF rect
);
[C++]
public: Region(
   RectangleF rect
);
[JScript]
public function Region(
   rect : RectangleF
);
```

Parameters

rect

A **RectangleF** structure that defines the interior of the new **Region** object.

Remarks

This method creates a new **Region** object with a rectangular interior. The interior is defined by the *rect* parameter.

Requirements

Platforms: Windows 98, Windows NT 4.0,
Windows Millennium Edition, Windows 2000,
Windows XP Home Edition, Windows XP Professional,
Windows Server 2003 family

Region Constructor (RegionData)

Initializes a new **Region** object from the specified data.

```
[Visual Basic]
Public Sub New( _
   ByVal rgnData As RegionData _
)
[C#]
public Region(
   RegionData rgnData
);
[C++]
public: Region(
   RegionData* rgnData
);
[JScript]
public function Region(
   rgnData : RegionData
);
```

Parameters

rgnData

A **RegionData** object that defines the interior of the new **Region** object.

Remarks

This method creates a new **Region** object with an interior defined by an existing **Region** object. The *rgnData* parameter is an array that contains the definition of an existing **Region** object.

Requirements

Platforms: Windows 98, Windows NT 4.0, Windows Millennium Edition, Windows 2000, Windows XP Home Edition, Windows XP Professional, Windows Server 2003 family

Region.Clone Method

Creates an exact copy if this **Region** object.

[Visual Basic]
```
Public Function Clone() As Region
```
[C#]
```
public Region Clone();
```
[C++]
```
public: Region* Clone();
```
[JScript]
```
public function Clone() : Region;
```

Return Value

The **Region** object that this method creates.

Requirements

Platforms: Windows 98, Windows NT 4.0, Windows Millennium Edition, Windows 2000, Windows XP Home Edition, Windows XP Professional, Windows Server 2003 family, .NET Compact Framework - Windows CE .NET

Region.Complement Method

Updates this **Region** object to the portion of the specified **RectangleF** structure that does not intersect with this **Region** object.

Overload List

Updates this **Region** object to contain the portion of the specified **GraphicsPath** object that does not intersect with this **Region** object.

[Visual Basic] **Overloads Public Sub Complement(GraphicsPath)**

[C#] **public void Complement(GraphicsPath);**

[C++] **public: void Complement(GraphicsPath*);**

[JScript] **public function Complement(GraphicsPath);**

Updates this **Region** object to contain the portion of the specified **Rectangle** structure that does not intersect with this **Region** object.

Supported by the .NET Compact Framework.

[Visual Basic] **Overloads Public Sub Complement(Rectangle)**

[C#] **public void Complement(Rectangle);**

[C++] **public: void Complement(Rectangle);**

[JScript] **public function Complement(Rectangle);**

Updates this **Region** object to contain the portion of the specified **RectangleF** structure that does not intersect with this **Region** object.

[Visual Basic] **Overloads Public Sub Complement(RectangleF)**

[C#] **public void Complement(RectangleF);**

[C++] **public: void Complement(RectangleF);**

[JScript] **public function Complement(RectangleF);**

Updates this **Region** object to contain the portion of the specified **Region** object that does not intersect with this **Region** object.

Supported by the .NET Compact Framework.

[Visual Basic] **Overloads Public Sub Complement(Region)**

[C#] **public void Complement(Region);**

[C++] **public: void Complement(Region*);**

[JScript] **public function Complement(Region);**

Example

[Visual Basic, C#] The following example is designed for use with Windows Forms, and it requires **PaintEventArgs** *e*, which is a parameter of the **Paint** event handler. The code performs the following actions:

- Creates a rectangle and draws it o the screen in black
- Creates a second rectangle that intersects with the first and draws it to the screen in red.
- Creates one region using the first rectangle and creates a second region using the second rectangle.
- Gets the complement of that first region when combined with the second region.
- Fills the complement area with blue and draws it to the screen.

[Visual Basic, C#] Notice that the area of the second region that does not intersect with the first region is colored blue.

> [Visual Basic, C#] **Note** This example shows how to use one of the overloaded versions of **Complement**. For other examples that might be available, see the individual overload topics.

[Visual Basic]
```
Public Sub Complement_Region_Example(e As PaintEventArgs)
' Create the first rectangle and draw it to the screen in black.
Dim regionRect As New Rectangle(20, 20, 100, 100)
e.Graphics.DrawRectangle(Pens.Black, regionRect)
' Create the second rectangle and draw it to the screen in red.
Dim complementRect As New Rectangle(90, 30, 100, 100)
e.Graphics.DrawRectangle(Pens.Red, complementRect)
' create a region from the first rectangle.
Dim myRegion As New [Region](regionRect)
' Create a complement region.
Dim complementRegion As New [Region](complementRect)
' Get the complement of myRegion when combined with
' complementRegion.
myRegion.Complement(complementRegion)
' Fill the complement area with blue.
Dim myBrush As New SolidBrush(Color.Blue)
e.Graphics.FillRegion(myBrush, myRegion)
End Sub
```

[C#]
```
public void Complement_Region_Example(PaintEventArgs e)
{
// Create the first rectangle and draw it to the screen in black.
Rectangle regionRect = new Rectangle(20, 20, 100, 100);
e.Graphics.DrawRectangle(Pens.Black, regionRect);
// Create the second rectangle and draw it to the screen in red.
Rectangle complementRect = new Rectangle(90, 30, 100, 100);
e.Graphics.DrawRectangle(Pens.Red, complementRect);
// Create a region from the first rectangle.
Region myRegion = new Region(regionRect);
// Create a complement region.
Region complementRegion = new Region(complementRect);
// Get the complement of myRegion when combined with
// complementRegion.
myRegion.Complement(complementRegion);
// Fill the complement area with blue.
SolidBrush myBrush = new SolidBrush(Color.Blue);
e.Graphics.FillRegion(myBrush, myRegion);
}
```

Region.Complement Method (GraphicsPath)

Updates this **Region** object to contain the portion of the specified **GraphicsPath** object that does not intersect with this **Region** object.

[Visual Basic]
```
Overloads Public Sub Complement( _
   ByVal path As GraphicsPath _
)
```
[C#]
```
public void Complement(
   GraphicsPath path
);
```
[C++]
```
public: void Complement(
   GraphicsPath* path
);
```
[JScript]
```
public function Complement(
   path : GraphicsPath
);
```

Parameters

path

The **GraphicsPath** object to complement this **Region** object.

Return Value

This method does not return a value.

Example

[Visual Basic, C#] The following example is designed for use with Windows Forms, and it requires **PaintEventArgs** *e*, which is a parameter of the **Paint** event handler. The code performs the following actions:

- Creates a rectangle and draws it o the screen in black
- Creates a second rectangle that intersects with the first and draws it to the screen in red.
- Creates a region using the first rectangle.
- Creates a GraphicsPath, and adds the second rectangle to it.
- Gets the complement of the region when combined with the GraphicsPath.
- Fills the complement area with blue and draws it to the screen.

[Visual Basic, C#] Notice that the area of the GraphicsPath that does not intersect with the region is colored blue.

[Visual Basic]
```
Public Sub Complement_Path_Example(e As PaintEventArgs)
' Create the first rectangle and draw it to the screen in black.
Dim regionRect As New Rectangle(20, 20, 100, 100)
e.Graphics.DrawRectangle(Pens.Black, regionRect)
' Create the second rectangle and draw it to the screen in red.
Dim complementRect As New Rectangle(90, 30, 100, 100)
e.Graphics.DrawRectangle(Pens.Red, complementRect)
' Create a graphics path and add the second rectangle to it.
Dim complementPath As New GraphicsPath()
complementPath.AddRectangle(complementRect)
' Create a region using the first rectangle.
Dim myRegion As New [Region](regionRect)
' Get the complement of myRegion when combined with
' complementPath.
myRegion.Complement(complementPath)
' Fill the complement area with blue.
Dim myBrush As New SolidBrush(Color.Blue)
e.Graphics.FillRegion(myBrush, myRegion)
End Sub
```
[C#]
```
public void Complement_Path_Example(PaintEventArgs e)
{
// Create the first rectangle and draw it to the screen in black.
Rectangle regionRect = new Rectangle(20, 20, 100, 100);
e.Graphics.DrawRectangle(Pens.Black, regionRect);
// Create the second rectangle and draw it to the screen in red.
Rectangle complementRect = new Rectangle(90, 30, 100, 100);
e.Graphics.DrawRectangle(Pens.Red, complementRect);
// Create a graphics path and add the second rectangle to it.
GraphicsPath complementPath = new GraphicsPath();
complementPath.AddRectangle(complementRect);
// Create a region using the first rectangle.
Region myRegion = new Region(regionRect);
// Get the complement of myRegion when combined with
// complementPath.
myRegion.Complement(complementPath);
// Fill the complement area with blue.
SolidBrush myBrush = new SolidBrush(Color.Blue);
e.Graphics.FillRegion(myBrush, myRegion);
}
```

Requirements

Platforms: Windows 98, Windows NT 4.0, Windows Millennium Edition, Windows 2000, Windows XP Home Edition, Windows XP Professional, Windows Server 2003 family

Region.Complement Method (Rectangle)

Updates this **Region** object to contain the portion of the specified **Rectangle** structure that does not intersect with this **Region** object.

[Visual Basic]
```
Overloads Public Sub Complement( _
   ByVal rect As Rectangle _
)
```
[C#]
```
public void Complement(
   Rectangle rect
);
```
[C++]
```
public: void Complement(
   Rectangle rect
);
```
[JScript]
```
public function Complement(
   rect : Rectangle
);
```

Parameters

rect

The **Rectangle** structure to complement this **Region** object.

Return Value

This method does not return a value.

Example

For an example, see **Region.Complement Method (RectangleF)**.

Requirements

Platforms: Windows 98, Windows NT 4.0, Windows Millennium Edition, Windows 2000, Windows XP Home Edition, Windows XP Professional, Windows Server 2003 family, .NET Compact Framework - Windows CE .NET

Region.Complement Method (RectangleF)

Updates this **Region** object to contain the portion of the specified **RectangleF** structure that does not intersect with this **Region** object.

```
[Visual Basic]
Overloads Public Sub Complement( _
   ByVal rect As RectangleF _
)
[C#]
public void Complement(
   RectangleF rect
);
[C++]
public: void Complement(
   RectangleF rect
);
[JScript]
public function Complement(
   rect : RectangleF
);
```

Parameters

rect

The **RectangleF** structure to complement this **Region** object.

Return Value

This method does not return a value.

Example

[Visual Basic, C#] The following example is designed for use with Windows Forms, and it requires **PaintEventArgs** *e*, which is a parameter of the **Paint** event handler. The code performs the following actions:

- Creates a rectangle and draws it o the screen in black
- Creates a second rectangle that intersects with the first and draws it to the screen in red.
- Creates a region using the first rectangle.
- Gets the complement of that region combined with the second rectangle.
- Fills the complement area with blue and draws it to the screen.

[Visual Basic, C#] Notice that the area of the second rectangle that does not intersect with the region is colored blue.

```
[Visual Basic]
Public Sub Complement_RectF_Example(e As PaintEventArgs)
' Create the first rectangle and draw it to the screen in black.
Dim regionRect As New Rectangle(20, 20, 100, 100)
e.Graphics.DrawRectangle(Pens.Black, regionRect)
' Create the second rectangle and draw it to the screen in red.
Dim complementRect As New RectangleF(90, 30, 100, 100)
e.Graphics.DrawRectangle(Pens.Red, _
Rectangle.Round(complementRect))
' Create a region using the first rectangle.
Dim myRegion As New [Region](regionRect)
' Get the complement of the region combined with the second
' rectangle.
myRegion.Complement(complementRect)
' Fill the complement area with blue.
Dim myBrush As New SolidBrush(Color.Blue)
e.Graphics.FillRegion(myBrush, myRegion)
End Sub
```

```
[C#]
public void Complement_RectF_Example(PaintEventArgs e)
{
// Create the first rectangle and draw it to the screen in black.
Rectangle regionRect = new Rectangle(20, 20, 100, 100);
e.Graphics.DrawRectangle(Pens.Black, regionRect);
// Create the second rectangle and draw it to the screen in red.
RectangleF complementRect = new RectangleF(90, 30, 100, 100);
e.Graphics.DrawRectangle(Pens.Red,
Rectangle.Round(complementRect));
// Create a region using the first rectangle.
Region myRegion = new Region(regionRect);
// Get the complement of the region combined with the second
// rectangle.
myRegion.Complement(complementRect);
// Fill the complement area with blue.
SolidBrush myBrush = new SolidBrush(Color.Blue);
e.Graphics.FillRegion(myBrush, myRegion);
}
```

Requirements

Platforms: Windows 98, Windows NT 4.0, Windows Millennium Edition, Windows 2000, Windows XP Home Edition, Windows XP Professional, Windows Server 2003 family

Region.Complement Method (Region)

Updates this **Region** object to contain the portion of the specified **Region** object that does not intersect with this **Region** object.

```
[Visual Basic]
Overloads Public Sub Complement( _
   ByVal region As Region _
)
[C#]
public void Complement(
   Region region
);
[C++]
public: void Complement(
   Region* region
);
[JScript]
public function Complement(
   region : Region
);
```

Parameters

region

The **Region** object to complement this **Region** object.

Return Value

This method does not return a value.

Example

[Visual Basic, C#] The following example is designed for use with Windows Forms, and it requires **PaintEventArgs** *e*, which is a parameter of the **Paint** event handler. The code performs the following actions:

- Creates a rectangle and draws it o the screen in black
- Creates a second rectangle that intersects with the first and draws it to the screen in red.
- Creates one region using the first rectangle and creates a second region using the second rectangle.
- Gets the complement of that first region when combined with the second region.
- Fills the complement area with blue and draws it to the screen.

[Visual Basic, C#] Notice that the area of the second region that does not intersect with the first region is colored blue.

[Visual Basic]
```
Public Sub Complement_Region_Example(e As PaintEventArgs)
' Create the first rectangle and draw it to the screen in black.
Dim regionRect As New Rectangle(20, 20, 100, 100)
e.Graphics.DrawRectangle(Pens.Black, regionRect)
' Create the second rectangle and draw it to the screen in red.
Dim complementRect As New Rectangle(90, 30, 100, 100)
e.Graphics.DrawRectangle(Pens.Red, complementRect)
' create a region from the first rectangle.
Dim myRegion As New [Region](regionRect)
' Create a complement region.
Dim complementRegion As New [Region](complementRect)
' Get the complement of myRegion when combined with
' complementRegion.
myRegion.Complement(complementRegion)
' Fill the complement area with blue.
Dim myBrush As New SolidBrush(Color.Blue)
e.Graphics.FillRegion(myBrush, myRegion)
End Sub
```

[C#]
```
public void Complement_Region_Example(PaintEventArgs e)
{
// Create the first rectangle and draw it to the screen in black.
Rectangle regionRect = new Rectangle(20, 20, 100, 100);
e.Graphics.DrawRectangle(Pens.Black, regionRect);
// Create the second rectangle and draw it to the screen in red.
Rectangle complementRect = new Rectangle(90, 30, 100, 100);
e.Graphics.DrawRectangle(Pens.Red, complementRect);
// Create a region from the first rectangle.
Region myRegion = new Region(regionRect);
// Create a complement region.
Region complementRegion = new Region(complementRect);
// Get the complement of myRegion when combined with
// complementRegion.
myRegion.Complement(complementRegion);
// Fill the complement area with blue.
SolidBrush myBrush = new SolidBrush(Color.Blue);
e.Graphics.FillRegion(myBrush, myRegion);
}
```

Requirements

Platforms: Windows 98, Windows NT 4.0,
Windows Millennium Edition, Windows 2000,
Windows XP Home Edition, Windows XP Professional,
Windows Server 2003 family,
.NET Compact Framework - Windows CE .NET

Region.Dispose Method

Releases all resources used by this **Region** object.

[Visual Basic]
```
Public Overridable Sub Dispose() Implements IDisposable.Dispose
```
[C#]
```
public virtual void Dispose();
```
[C++]
```
public: virtual void Dispose();
```
[JScript]
```
public function Dispose();
```

Return Value

This method does not return a value.

Implements

IDisposable.Dispose

Remarks

Calling **Dispose** allows the resources used by this **Region** object to be reallocated for other purposes.

Requirements

Platforms: Windows 98, Windows NT 4.0,
Windows Millennium Edition, Windows 2000,
Windows XP Home Edition, Windows XP Professional,
Windows Server 2003 family,
.NET Compact Framework - Windows CE .NET

Region.Equals Method

Overload List

Tests whether the specified **Region** object is identical to this **Region** object on the specified drawing surface.

Supported by the .NET Compact Framework.

[Visual Basic] **Overloads Public Function Equals(Region, Graphics) As Boolean**

[C#] **public bool Equals(Region, Graphics);**

[C++] **public: bool Equals(Region*, Graphics*);**

[JScript] **public function Equals(Region, Graphics) : Boolean;**

Inherited from **Object**.

Supported by the .NET Compact Framework.

[Visual Basic] **Overloads Public Overridable Function Equals(Object) As Boolean**

[C#] **public virtual bool Equals(object);**

[C++] **public: virtual bool Equals(Object*);**

[JScript] **public function Equals(Object) : Boolean;**

Region.Equals Method (Region, Graphics)

Tests whether the specified **Region** object is identical to this **Region** object on the specified drawing surface.

[Visual Basic]
```
Overloads Public Function Equals( _
   ByVal region As Region, _
   ByVal g As Graphics _
) As Boolean
```
[C#]
```
public bool Equals(
   Region region,
   Graphics g
);
```
[C++]
```
public: bool Equals(
   Region* region,
   Graphics* g
);
```
[JScript]
```
public function Equals(
   region : Region,
   g : Graphics
) : Boolean;
```

Parameters

region

The **Region** object to test.

g

A **Graphics** object that represents a drawing surface.

Return Value

This method returns **true** if the interior of region is identical to the interior of this region when the transformation associated with the *g* parameter is applied; otherwise, **false**.

Remarks

The current transformation of the graphics context *g* is used to compute the region interiors on the drawing surface.

Requirements

Platforms: Windows 98, Windows NT 4.0,
Windows Millennium Edition, Windows 2000,
Windows XP Home Edition, Windows XP Professional,
Windows Server 2003 family,
.NET Compact Framework - Windows CE .NET

Region.Exclude Method

Updates this **Region** object to the portion of its interior that does not intersect with the specified **Rectangle** structure.

Overload List

Updates this **Region** object to contain only the portion of its interior that does not intersect with the specified **GraphicsPath** object.

[Visual Basic] **Overloads Public Sub Exclude(GraphicsPath)**

[C#] **public void Exclude(GraphicsPath);**

[C++] **public: void Exclude(GraphicsPath*);**

[JScript] **public function Exclude(GraphicsPath);**

Updates this **Region** object to contain only the portion of its interior that does not intersect with the specified **Rectangle** structure.

Supported by the .NET Compact Framework.

[Visual Basic] **Overloads Public Sub Exclude(Rectangle)**

[C#] **public void Exclude(Rectangle);**

[C++] **public: void Exclude(Rectangle);**

[JScript] **public function Exclude(Rectangle);**

Updates this **Region** object to contain only the portion of its interior that does not intersect with the specified **RectangleF** structure.

[Visual Basic] **Overloads Public Sub Exclude(RectangleF)**

[C#] **public void Exclude(RectangleF);**

[C++] **public: void Exclude(RectangleF);**

[JScript] **public function Exclude(RectangleF);**

Updates this **Region** object to contain only the portion of its interior that does not intersect with the specified **Region** object.

Supported by the .NET Compact Framework.

[Visual Basic] **Overloads Public Sub Exclude(Region)**

[C#] **public void Exclude(Region);**

[C++] **public: void Exclude(Region*);**

[JScript] **public function Exclude(Region);**

Example

For an example, see **Region.Exclude Method (RectangleF)** and **Region.Complement Method (Region)**.

Region.Exclude Method (GraphicsPath)

Updates this **Region** object to contain only the portion of its interior that does not intersect with the specified **GraphicsPath** object.

```
[Visual Basic]
Overloads Public Sub Exclude( _
   ByVal path As GraphicsPath _
)
[C#]
public void Exclude(
   GraphicsPath path
);
[C++]
public: void Exclude(
   GraphicsPath* path
);
[JScript]
public function Exclude(
   path : GraphicsPath
);
```

Parameters

path

The **GraphicsPath** object to exclude from this **Region** object.

Return Value

This method does not return a value.

Example

For an example, see **Region.Exclude Method (RectangleF)** and **Region.Complement Method (GraphicsPath)**

Requirements

Platforms: Windows 98, Windows NT 4.0,
Windows Millennium Edition, Windows 2000,
Windows XP Home Edition, Windows XP Professional,
Windows Server 2003 family

Region.Exclude Method (Rectangle)

Updates this **Region** object to contain only the portion of its interior that does not intersect with the specified **Rectangle** structure.

```
[Visual Basic]
Overloads Public Sub Exclude( _
   ByVal rect As Rectangle _
)
[C#]
public void Exclude(
   Rectangle rect
);
[C++]
public: void Exclude(
   Rectangle rect
);
[JScript]
public function Exclude(
   rect : Rectangle
);
```

Parameters

rect

The **Rectangle** structure to exclude from this **Region** object.

Return Value

This method does not return a value.

Example

For an example, see **Region.Exclude Method (RectangleF)**.

Requirements

Platforms: Windows 98, Windows NT 4.0, Windows Millennium Edition, Windows 2000, Windows XP Home Edition, Windows XP Professional, Windows Server 2003 family, .NET Compact Framework - Windows CE .NET

Region.Exclude Method (RectangleF)

Updates this **Region** object to contain only the portion of its interior that does not intersect with the specified **RectangleF** structure.

```
[Visual Basic]
Overloads Public Sub Exclude( _
   ByVal rect As RectangleF _
)
[C#]
public void Exclude(
   RectangleF rect
);
[C++]
public: void Exclude(
   RectangleF rect
);
[JScript]
public function Exclude(
   rect : RectangleF
);
```

Parameters

rect

The **RectangleF** structure to exclude from this **Region** object.

Return Value

This method does not return a value.

Example

[Visual Basic, C#] The following example is designed for use with Windows Forms, and it requires **PaintEventArgs** *e*, which is a parameter of the **Paint** event handler. The code performs the following actions:

- Creates a rectangle and draws it o the screen in black
- Creates a second rectangle that intersects with the first and draws it to the screen in red.
- Creates a region using the first rectangle.
- Gets the nonexcluded area of the region when combined with the second rectangle.
- Fills the nonexcluded area with blue and draws it to the screen.

[Visual Basic, C#] Notice that the area of the area of the region that does not intersect with the rectangle is colored blue.

```
[Visual Basic]
Public Sub Exclude_RectF_Example(e As PaintEventArgs)
' Create the first rectangle and draw it to the screen in black.
Dim regionRect As New Rectangle(20, 20, 100, 100)
e.Graphics.DrawRectangle(Pens.Black, regionRect)
' create the second rectangle and draw it to the screen in red.
Dim complementRect As New RectangleF(90, 30, 100, 100)
e.Graphics.DrawRectangle(Pens.Red, _
Rectangle.Round(complementRect))
' Create a region using the first rectangle.
Dim myRegion As New [Region](regionRect)
' Get the nonexcluded area of myRegion when combined with
' complementRect.
myRegion.Exclude(complementRect)
' Fill the nonexcluded area of myRegion with blue.
Dim myBrush As New SolidBrush(Color.Blue)
e.Graphics.FillRegion(myBrush, myRegion)
End Sub
```

```
[C#]
public void Exclude_RectF_Example(PaintEventArgs e)
{
// Create the first rectangle and draw it to the screen in black.
Rectangle regionRect = new Rectangle(20, 20, 100, 100);
e.Graphics.DrawRectangle(Pens.Black, regionRect);
// Create the second rectangle and draw it to the screen in red.
RectangleF complementRect = new RectangleF(90, 30, 100, 100);
e.Graphics.DrawRectangle(Pens.Red,
Rectangle.Round(complementRect));
// Create a region using the first rectangle.
Region myRegion = new Region(regionRect);
// Get the nonexcluded area of myRegion when combined with
// complementRect.
myRegion.Exclude(complementRect);
// Fill the nonexcluded area of myRegion with blue.
SolidBrush myBrush = new SolidBrush(Color.Blue);
e.Graphics.FillRegion(myBrush, myRegion);
}
```

Requirements

Platforms: Windows 98, Windows NT 4.0, Windows Millennium Edition, Windows 2000, Windows XP Home Edition, Windows XP Professional, Windows Server 2003 family

Region.Exclude Method (Region)

Updates this **Region** object to contain only the portion of its interior that does not intersect with the specified **Region** object.

```
[Visual Basic]
Overloads Public Sub Exclude( _
   ByVal region As Region _
)
[C#]
public void Exclude(
   Region region
);
[C++]
public: void Exclude(
   Region* region
);
[JScript]
public function Exclude(
   region : Region
);
```

Parameters

region

The **Region** object to exclude from this **Region** object.

Return Value

This method does not return a value.

Example

For an example, see **Region.Exclude Method (RectangleF)** and **Region.Complement Method (Region)**.

Requirements

Platforms: Windows 98, Windows NT 4.0,
Windows Millennium Edition, Windows 2000,
Windows XP Home Edition, Windows XP Professional,
Windows Server 2003 family,
.NET Compact Framework - Windows CE .NET

Region.Finalize Method

This member overrides **Object.Finalize**.

```
[Visual Basic]
Overrides Protected Sub Finalize()
[C#]
~Region();
[C++]
~Region();
[JScript]
protected override function Finalize();
```

Requirements

Platforms: Windows 98, Windows NT 4.0,
Windows Millennium Edition, Windows 2000,
Windows XP Home Edition, Windows XP Professional,
Windows Server 2003 family,
.NET Compact Framework - Windows CE .NET

Region.FromHrgn Method

Initializes a new **Region** object from a handle to the specified existing GDI region.

```
[Visual Basic]
Public Shared Function FromHrgn( _
   ByVal hrgn As IntPtr _
) As Region
[C#]
public static Region FromHrgn(
   IntPtr hrgn
);
[C++]
public: static Region* FromHrgn(
   IntPtr hrgn
);
[JScript]
public static function FromHrgn(
   hrgn : IntPtr
) : Region;
```

Parameters

hrgn
A handle to an existing **Region** object.

Return Value

The new **Region** object.

Remarks

This method creates a new **Region** object with an interior defined by the existing **Region** object referred to by the handle in the *hrgn* parameter.

Requirements

Platforms: Windows 98, Windows NT 4.0,
Windows Millennium Edition, Windows 2000,
Windows XP Home Edition, Windows XP Professional,
Windows Server 2003 family

Region.GetBounds Method

Gets a **RectangleF** structure that represents a rectangle that bounds this **Region** object on the drawing surface of a **Graphics** object.

```
[Visual Basic]
Public Function GetBounds( _
   ByVal g As Graphics _
) As RectangleF
[C#]
public RectangleF GetBounds(
   Graphics g
);
[C++]
public: RectangleF GetBounds(
   Graphics* g
);
[JScript]
public function GetBounds(
   g : Graphics
) : RectangleF;
```

Parameters

g
The **Graphics** object on which this **Region** object is drawn.

Return Value

A **RectangleF** structure that represents the bounding rectangle for this **Region** object on the specified drawing surface.

Remarks

The current transformation of the graphics context is used to compute the region interior on the drawing surface. The bounding rectangle is not always the smallest possible bounding rectangle depending on the current transformation.

Example

[Visual Basic, C#] The following example is designed for use with Windows Forms, and it requires **PaintEventArgs** *e*, which is a parameter of the **Paint** event handler. The code performs the following actions:

- Creates a GraphicsPath and adds an ellipse to it.
- Fills the path with blue and draws it to the screen.
- Creates a region that uses the GraphicsPath.
- Gets the nonexcluded area of the region when combined with the second rectangle.
- Gets the bounding rectangle for the region and draws it to the screen in red.

```
[Visual Basic]
Public Sub GetBoundsExample(e As PaintEventArgs)
' Create a GraphicsPath and add an ellipse to it.
Dim myPath As New GraphicsPath()
Dim ellipseRect As New Rectangle(20, 20, 100, 100)
myPath.AddEllipse(ellipseRect)
' Fill the path with blue and draw it to the screen.
Dim myBrush As New SolidBrush(Color.Blue)
e.Graphics.FillPath(myBrush, myPath)
```

```
' Create a region using the GraphicsPath.
Dim myRegion As New [Region](myPath)
' Get the bounding rectangle for myRegion and draw it to the
' screen in Red.
Dim boundsRect As RectangleF = myRegion.GetBounds(e.Graphics)
e.Graphics.DrawRectangle(Pens.Red, Rectangle.Round(boundsRect))
End Sub
```

[C#]

```
public void GetBoundsExample(PaintEventArgs e)
{
// Create a GraphicsPath and add an ellipse to it.
GraphicsPath myPath = new GraphicsPath();
Rectangle ellipseRect = new Rectangle(20, 20, 100, 100);
myPath.AddEllipse(ellipseRect);
// Fill the path with blue and draw it to the screen.
SolidBrush myBrush = new SolidBrush(Color.Blue);
e.Graphics.FillPath(myBrush, myPath);
// Create a region using the GraphicsPath.
Region myRegion = new Region(myPath);
// Get the bounding rectangle for myRegion and draw it to the
// screen in Red.
RectangleF boundsRect = myRegion.GetBounds(e.Graphics);
e.Graphics.DrawRectangle(Pens.Red, Rectangle.Round(boundsRect));
}
```

Requirements

Platforms: Windows 98, Windows NT 4.0, Windows Millennium Edition, Windows 2000, Windows XP Home Edition, Windows XP Professional, Windows Server 2003 family, .NET Compact Framework - Windows CE .NET

Region.GetHrgn Method

Returns a Windows handle to this **Region** object in the specified graphics context.

[Visual Basic]

```
Public Function GetHrgn( _
   ByVal g As Graphics _
) As IntPtr
```

[C#]

```
public IntPtr GetHrgn(
   Graphics g
);
```

[C++]

```
public: IntPtr GetHrgn(
   Graphics* g
);
```

[JScript]

```
public function GetHrgn(
   g : Graphics
) : IntPtr;
```

Parameters

g

The **Graphics** object on which this **Region** object is drawn.

Return Value

A Windows handle to this **Region** object.

Requirements

Platforms: Windows 98, Windows NT 4.0, Windows Millennium Edition, Windows 2000, Windows XP Home Edition, Windows XP Professional, Windows Server 2003 family

Region.GetRegionData Method

Returns a **RegionData** object that represents the information that describes this **Region** object.

[Visual Basic]

```
Public Function GetRegionData() As RegionData
```

[C#]

```
public RegionData GetRegionData();
```

[C++]

```
public: RegionData* GetRegionData();
```

[JScript]

```
public function GetRegionData() : RegionData;
```

Return Value

A **RegionData** object that represents the information that describes this **Region** object.

Example

[Visual Basic, C#] The following example is designed for use with Windows Forms, and it requires **PaintEventArgs** *e*, which is a parameter of the **Paint** event handler. The code performs the following actions:

- Creates a rectangle and draw its to the screen in black.
- Creates a region using the rectangle.
- Gets the RegionData.
- Draws the region data (an array of bytes) to the screen, by using the DisplayRegionData helper function.

[Visual Basic]

```
Public Sub GetRegionDataExample(e As PaintEventArgs)
' Create the first rectangle and draw it to the screen in black.
Dim regionRect As New Rectangle(20, 20, 100, 100)
e.Graphics.DrawRectangle(Pens.Black, regionRect)
' Create a region using the first rectangle.
Dim myRegion As New [Region](regionRect)
' Get the RegionData for this region.
Dim myRegionData As RegionData = myRegion.GetRegionData()
Dim myRegionDataLength As Integer = myRegionData.Data.Length
DisplayRegionData(e, myRegionDataLength, myRegionData)
End Sub
' Helper Function for GetRegionData.
Public Sub DisplayRegionData(e As PaintEventArgs, len As Integer, _
dat As RegionData)
' Display the result.
Dim i As Integer
Dim x As Single = 20
Dim y As Single = 140
Dim myFont As New Font("Arial", 8)
Dim myBrush As New SolidBrush(Color.Black)
e.Graphics.DrawString("myRegionData = ", myFont, myBrush, _
New PointF(x, y))
y = 160
For i = 0 To len - 1
If x > 300 Then
y += 20
x = 20
End If
e.Graphics.DrawString(dat.Data(i).ToString(), myFont, _
myBrush, New PointF(x, y))
x += 30
Next i
End Sub
```

[C#]

```
public void GetRegionDataExample(PaintEventArgs e)
{
// Create a rectangle and draw it to the screen in black.
Rectangle regionRect = new Rectangle(20, 20, 100, 100);
e.Graphics.DrawRectangle(Pens.Black, regionRect);
```

```
// Create a region using the first rectangle.
Region myRegion = new Region(regionRect);
// Get the RegionData for this region.
RegionData myRegionData = myRegion.GetRegionData();
int myRegionDataLength = myRegionData.Data.Length;
DisplayRegionData(e, myRegionDataLength, myRegionData);
}
// THIS IS A HELPER FUNCTION FOR GetRegionData.
public void DisplayRegionData(PaintEventArgs e,
int len,
RegionData dat)
{
// Display the result.
int i;
float x = 20, y = 140;
Font myFont = new Font("Arial", 8);
SolidBrush myBrush = new SolidBrush(Color.Black);
e.Graphics.DrawString("myRegionData = ",
myFont,
myBrush,
new PointF(x, y));
y = 160;
for(i = 0; i < len; i++)
{
if(x > 300)
{
y += 20;
x = 20;
}
e.Graphics.DrawString(dat.Data[i].ToString(),
myFont,
myBrush,
new PointF(x, y));
x += 30;
}
}
```

Requirements

Platforms: Windows 98, Windows NT 4.0, Windows Millennium Edition, Windows 2000, Windows XP Home Edition, Windows XP Professional, Windows Server 2003 family

Region.GetRegionScans Method

Returns an array of **RectangleF** structures that approximate this **Region** object.

[Visual Basic]
```
Public Function GetRegionScans( _
   ByVal matrix As Matrix _
) As RectangleF()
```
[C#]
```
public RectangleF[] GetRegionScans(
   Matrix matrix
);
```
[C++]
```
public: RectangleF GetRegionScans(
   Matrix* matrix
) [];
```
[JScript]
```
public function GetRegionScans(
   matrix : Matrix
) : RectangleF[];
```

Parameters

matrix

A **Matrix** object that represents a geometric transformation to apply to the region.

Return Value

An array of **RectangleF** structures that approximate this **Region** object.

Requirements

Platforms: Windows 98, Windows NT 4.0, Windows Millennium Edition, Windows 2000, Windows XP Home Edition, Windows XP Professional, Windows Server 2003 family

Region.Intersect Method

Updates this **Region** object to the intersection of itself with the specified **Region** object.

Overload List

Updates this **Region** object to the intersection of itself with the specified **GraphicsPath** object.

[Visual Basic] **Overloads Public Sub Intersect(GraphicsPath)**

[C#] **public void Intersect(GraphicsPath);**

[C++] **public: void Intersect(GraphicsPath*);**

[JScript] **public function Intersect(GraphicsPath);**

Updates this **Region** object to the intersection of itself with the specified **Rectangle** structure.

Supported by the .NET Compact Framework.

[Visual Basic] **Overloads Public Sub Intersect(Rectangle)**

[C#] **public void Intersect(Rectangle);**

[C++] **public: void Intersect(Rectangle);**

[JScript] **public function Intersect(Rectangle);**

Updates this **Region** object to the intersection of itself with the specified **RectangleF** structure.

[Visual Basic] **Overloads Public Sub Intersect(RectangleF)**

[C#] **public void Intersect(RectangleF);**

[C++] **public: void Intersect(RectangleF);**

[JScript] **public function Intersect(RectangleF);**

Updates this **Region** object to the intersection of itself with the specified **Region** object.

Supported by the .NET Compact Framework.

[Visual Basic] **Overloads Public Sub Intersect(Region)**

[C#] **public void Intersect(Region);**

[C++] **public: void Intersect(Region*);**

[JScript] **public function Intersect(Region);**

Example

For an example, see **Region.Intersect Method (RectangleF)** and **Region.Complement Method (GraphicsPath)**

Region.Intersect Method (GraphicsPath)

Updates this **Region** object to the intersection of itself with the specified **GraphicsPath** object.

[Visual Basic]
```
Overloads Public Sub Intersect( _
   ByVal path As GraphicsPath _
)
```
[C#]
```
public void Intersect(
   GraphicsPath path
);
```

```
[C++]
public: void Intersect(
   GraphicsPath* path
);
[JScript]
public function Intersect(
   path : GraphicsPath
);
```

Parameters

path

The **GraphicsPath** object to intersect with this **Region** object.

Return Value

This method does not return a value.

Example

For an example, see **Region.Intersect Method (RectangleF)** and **Region.Complement Method (GraphicsPath)**

Requirements

Platforms: Windows 98, Windows NT 4.0, Windows Millennium Edition, Windows 2000, Windows XP Home Edition, Windows XP Professional, Windows Server 2003 family

Region.Intersect Method (Rectangle)

Updates this **Region** object to the intersection of itself with the specified **Rectangle** structure.

```
[Visual Basic]
Overloads Public Sub Intersect( _
   ByVal rect As Rectangle _
)
[C#]
public void Intersect(
   Rectangle rect
);
[C++]
public: void Intersect(
   Rectangle rect
);
[JScript]
public function Intersect(
   rect : Rectangle
);
```

Parameters

rect

The **Rectangle** structure to intersect with this **Region** object.

Return Value

This method does not return a value.

Example

For an example, see **Region.Intersect Method (RectangleF)**.

Requirements

Platforms: Windows 98, Windows NT 4.0, Windows Millennium Edition, Windows 2000, Windows XP Home Edition, Windows XP Professional, Windows Server 2003 family, .NET Compact Framework - Windows CE .NET

Region.Intersect Method (RectangleF)

Updates this **Region** object to the intersection of itself with the specified **RectangleF** structure.

```
[Visual Basic]
Overloads Public Sub Intersect( _
   ByVal rect As RectangleF _
)
[C#]
public void Intersect(
   RectangleF rect
);
[C++]
public: void Intersect(
   RectangleF rect
);
[JScript]
public function Intersect(
   rect : RectangleF
);
```

Parameters

rect

The **RectangleF** structure to intersect with this **Region** object.

Return Value

This method does not return a value.

Example

[Visual Basic, C#] The following example is designed for use with Windows Forms, and it requires **PaintEventArgs** *e*, which is a parameter of the **Paint** event handler. The code performs the following actions:

- Creates the first rectangle and draws it to the screen in black.
- Creates the second rectangle and draws it to the screen in red.
- Creates a region that from the first rectangle.
- Gets the area of intersection for the region when combined with the second rectangle.
- Fills the area of intersection with blue and draws it to the screen.

[Visual Basic, C#] Notice that only the overlapped area for the region and rectangle is blue.

```
[Visual Basic]
Public Sub Intersect_RectF_Example(e As PaintEventArgs)
' Create the first rectangle and draw it to the screen in black.
Dim regionRect As New Rectangle(20, 20, 100, 100)
e.Graphics.DrawRectangle(Pens.Black, regionRect)
' create the second rectangle and draw it to the screen in red.
Dim complementRect As New RectangleF(90, 30, 100, 100)
e.Graphics.DrawRectangle(Pens.Red, _
Rectangle.Round(complementRect))
' Create a region using the first rectangle.
Dim myRegion As New [Region](regionRect)
' Get the area of intersection for myRegion when combined with
' complementRect.
myRegion.Intersect(complementRect)
' Fill the intersection area of myRegion with blue.
Dim myBrush As New SolidBrush(Color.Blue)
e.Graphics.FillRegion(myBrush, myRegion)
End Sub
```

```
[C#]
public void Intersect_RectF_Example(PaintEventArgs e)
{
// Create the first rectangle and draw it to the screen in black.
Rectangle regionRect = new Rectangle(20, 20, 100, 100);
e.Graphics.DrawRectangle(Pens.Black, regionRect);
// create the second rectangle and draw it to the screen in red.
RectangleF complementRect = new RectangleF(90, 30, 100, 100);
e.Graphics.DrawRectangle(Pens.Red,
Rectangle.Round(complementRect));
// Create a region using the first rectangle.
Region myRegion = new Region(regionRect);
// Get the area of intersection for myRegion when combined with
// complementRect.
myRegion.Intersect(complementRect);
// Fill the intersection area of myRegion with blue.
SolidBrush myBrush = new SolidBrush(Color.Blue);
e.Graphics.FillRegion(myBrush, myRegion);
}
```

Requirements

Platforms: Windows 98, Windows NT 4.0, Windows Millennium Edition, Windows 2000, Windows XP Home Edition, Windows XP Professional, Windows Server 2003 family

Region.Intersect Method (Region)

Updates this **Region** object to the intersection of itself with the specified **Region** object.

```
[Visual Basic]
Overloads Public Sub Intersect( _
   ByVal region As Region _
)
[C#]
public void Intersect(
   Region region
);
[C++]
public: void Intersect(
   Region* region
);
[JScript]
public function Intersect(
   region : Region
);
```

Parameters

region

The **Region** object to intersect with this **Region** object.

Return Value

This method does not return a value.

Example

For an example, see **Region.Intersect Method (RectangleF)** and **Region.Complement Method (GraphicsPath)**

Requirements

Platforms: Windows 98, Windows NT 4.0, Windows Millennium Edition, Windows 2000, Windows XP Home Edition, Windows XP Professional, Windows Server 2003 family, .NET Compact Framework - Windows CE .NET

Region.IsEmpty Method

Tests whether this **Region** object has an empty interior on the specified drawing surface.

```
[Visual Basic]
Public Function IsEmpty( _
   ByVal g As Graphics _
) As Boolean
[C#]
public bool IsEmpty(
   Graphics g
);
[C++]
public: bool IsEmpty(
   Graphics* g
);
[JScript]
public function IsEmpty(
   g : Graphics
) : Boolean;
```

Parameters

g

A **Graphics** object that represents a drawing surface.

Return Value

This method returns **true** if the interior of this **Region** object is empty when the transformation associated with *g* is applied; otherwise, **false**.

Remarks

The current transformation of the graphics context *g* is used to compute the region interior on the drawing surface.

Requirements

Platforms: Windows 98, Windows NT 4.0, Windows Millennium Edition, Windows 2000, Windows XP Home Edition, Windows XP Professional, Windows Server 2003 family, .NET Compact Framework - Windows CE .NET

Region.IsInfinite Method

Tests whether this **Region** object has an infinite interior on the specified drawing surface.

```
[Visual Basic]
Public Function IsInfinite( _
   ByVal g As Graphics _
) As Boolean
[C#]
public bool IsInfinite(
   Graphics g
);
[C++]
public: bool IsInfinite(
   Graphics* g
);
[JScript]
public function IsInfinite(
   g : Graphics
) : Boolean;
```

Parameters

g

A **Graphics** object that represents a drawing surface.

Return Value

This method returns **true** if the interior of this **Region** object is infinite when the transformation associated with *g* is applied; otherwise, **false**.

Remarks

The current transformation of the graphics context *g* is used to compute the region interior on the drawing surface.

Requirements

Platforms: Windows 98, Windows NT 4.0, Windows Millennium Edition, Windows 2000, Windows XP Home Edition, Windows XP Professional, Windows Server 2003 family, .NET Compact Framework - Windows CE .NET

Region.IsVisible Method

Tests whether the specified rectangle is contained within this **Region** object.

Overload List

Tests whether the specified **Point** structure is contained within this **Region** object.

Supported by the .NET Compact Framework.

[Visual Basic] **Overloads Public Function IsVisible(Point) As Boolean**

[C#] **public bool IsVisible(Point);**

[C++] **public: bool IsVisible(Point);**

[JScript] **public function IsVisible(Point) : Boolean;**

Tests whether the specified **PointF** structure is contained within this **Region** object.

[Visual Basic] **Overloads Public Function IsVisible(PointF) As Boolean**

[C#] **public bool IsVisible(PointF);**

[C++] **public: bool IsVisible(PointF);**

[JScript] **public function IsVisible(PointF) : Boolean;**

Tests whether any portion of the specified **Rectangle** structure is contained within this **Region** object.

Supported by the .NET Compact Framework.

[Visual Basic] **Overloads Public Function IsVisible(Rectangle) As Boolean**

[C#] **public bool IsVisible(Rectangle);**

[C++] **public: bool IsVisible(Rectangle);**

[JScript] **public function IsVisible(Rectangle) : Boolean;**

Tests whether any portion of the specified **RectangleF** structure is contained within this **Region** object.

[Visual Basic] **Overloads Public Function IsVisible(RectangleF) As Boolean**

[C#] **public bool IsVisible(RectangleF);**

[C++] **public: bool IsVisible(RectangleF);**

[JScript] **public function IsVisible(RectangleF) : Boolean;**

Tests whether the specified **Point** structure is contained within this **Region** object when drawn using the specified **Graphics** object.

[Visual Basic] **Overloads Public Function IsVisible(Point, Graphics) As Boolean**

[C#] **public bool IsVisible(Point, Graphics);**

[C++] **public: bool IsVisible(Point, Graphics*);**

[JScript] **public function IsVisible(Point, Graphics) : Boolean;**

Tests whether the specified **PointF** structure is contained within this **Region** object when drawn using the specified **Graphics** object.

[Visual Basic] **Overloads Public Function IsVisible(PointF, Graphics) As Boolean**

[C#] **public bool IsVisible(PointF, Graphics);**

[C++] **public: bool IsVisible(PointF, Graphics*);**

[JScript] **public function IsVisible(PointF, Graphics) : Boolean;**

Tests whether any portion of the specified **Rectangle** structure is contained within this **Region** object when drawn using the specified **Graphics** object.

[Visual Basic] **Overloads Public Function IsVisible(Rectangle, Graphics) As Boolean**

[C#] **public bool IsVisible(Rectangle, Graphics);**

[C++] **public: bool IsVisible(Rectangle, Graphics*);**

[JScript] **public function IsVisible(Rectangle, Graphics) : Boolean;**

Tests whether any portion of the specified **RectangleF** structure is contained within this **Region** when drawn using the specified **Graphics** object.

[Visual Basic] **Overloads Public Function IsVisible(RectangleF, Graphics) As Boolean**

[C#] **public bool IsVisible(RectangleF, Graphics);**

[C++] **public: bool IsVisible(RectangleF, Graphics*);**

[JScript] **public function IsVisible(RectangleF, Graphics) : Boolean;**

Tests whether the specified point is contained within this **Region** object.

Supported by the .NET Compact Framework.

[Visual Basic] **Overloads Public Function IsVisible(Single, Single) As Boolean**

[C#] **public bool IsVisible(float, float);**

[C++] **public: bool IsVisible(float, float);**

[JScript] **public function IsVisible(float, float) : Boolean;**

Tests whether the specified point is contained within this **Region** object when drawn using the specified **Graphics** object.

[Visual Basic] **Overloads Public Function IsVisible(Integer, Integer, Graphics) As Boolean**

[C#] **public bool IsVisible(int, int, Graphics);**

[C++] **public: bool IsVisible(int, int, Graphics*);**

[JScript] **public function IsVisible(int, int, Graphics) : Boolean;**

Tests whether the specified point is contained within this **Region** object when drawn using the specified **Graphics** object.

[Visual Basic] **Overloads Public Function IsVisible(Single, Single, Graphics) As Boolean**

[C#] **public bool IsVisible(float, float, Graphics);**

[C++] **public: bool IsVisible(float, float, Graphics*);**

[JScript] **public function IsVisible(float, float, Graphics) : Boolean;**

Tests whether any portion of the specified rectangle is contained within this **Region** object.

[Visual Basic] **Overloads Public Function IsVisible(Integer, Integer, Integer, Integer) As Boolean**

[C#] **public bool IsVisible(int, int, int, int);**

[C++] **public: bool IsVisible(int, int, int, int);**

[JScript] **public function IsVisible(int, int, int, int) : Boolean;**

Tests whether any portion of the specified rectangle is contained within this **Region** object.

[Visual Basic] **Overloads Public Function IsVisible(Single, Single, Single, Single) As Boolean**

[C#] **public bool IsVisible(float, float, float, float);**

[C++] **public: bool IsVisible(float, float, float, float);**

[JScript] **public function IsVisible(float, float, float, float) : Boolean;**

Tests whether any portion of the specified rectangle is contained within this **Region** object when drawn using the specified **Graphics** object.

[Visual Basic] **Overloads Public Function IsVisible(Integer, Integer, Integer, Integer, Graphics) As Boolean**

[C#] **public bool IsVisible(int, int, int, int, Graphics);**

[C++] **public: bool IsVisible(int, int, int, int, Graphics*);**

[JScript] **public function IsVisible(int, int, int, int, Graphics) : Boolean;**

Tests whether any portion of the specified rectangle is contained within this **Region** object when drawn using the specified **Graphics** object.

[Visual Basic] **Overloads Public Function IsVisible(Single, Single, Single, Single, Graphics) As Boolean**

[C#] **public bool IsVisible(float, float, float, float, Graphics);**

[C++] **public: bool IsVisible(float, float, float, float, Graphics*);**

[JScript] **public function IsVisible(float, float, float, float, Graphics) : Boolean;**

Example

For an example, see **Region.IsVisible Method (RectangleF)**.

Region.IsVisible Method (Point)

Tests whether the specified **Point** structure is contained within this **Region** object.

```
[Visual Basic]
Overloads Public Function IsVisible( _
   ByVal point As Point _
) As Boolean
[C#]
public bool IsVisible(
   Point point
);
[C++]
public: bool IsVisible(
   Point point
);
[JScript]
public function IsVisible(
   point : Point
) : Boolean;
```

Parameters

point

The **Point** structure to test.

Return Value

This method returns **true** when *point* is contained within this **Region** object; otherwise, **false**.

Example

For an example, see **Region.IsVisible Method (RectangleF)**.

Requirements

Platforms: Windows 98, Windows NT 4.0, Windows Millennium Edition, Windows 2000, Windows XP Home Edition, Windows XP Professional, Windows Server 2003 family, .NET Compact Framework - Windows CE .NET

Region.IsVisible Method (PointF)

Tests whether the specified **PointF** structure is contained within this **Region** object.

```
[Visual Basic]
Overloads Public Function IsVisible( _
   ByVal point As PointF _
) As Boolean
[C#]
public bool IsVisible(
   PointF point
);
[C++]
public: bool IsVisible(
   PointF point
);
[JScript]
public function IsVisible(
   point : PointF
) : Boolean;
```

Parameters

point

The **PointF** structure to test.

Return Value

This method returns **true** when *point* is contained within this **Region** object; otherwise, **false**.

Example

For an example, see **Region.IsVisible Method (RectangleF)**.

Requirements

Platforms: Windows 98, Windows NT 4.0, Windows Millennium Edition, Windows 2000, Windows XP Home Edition, Windows XP Professional, Windows Server 2003 family

Region.IsVisible Method (Rectangle)

Tests whether any portion of the specified **Rectangle** structure is contained within this **Region** object.

[Visual Basic]
```
Overloads Public Function IsVisible( _
   ByVal rect As Rectangle _
) As Boolean
```
[C#]
```
public bool IsVisible(
   Rectangle rect
);
```
[C++]
```
public: bool IsVisible(
   Rectangle rect
);
```
[JScript]
```
public function IsVisible(
   rect : Rectangle
) : Boolean;
```

Parameters

rect

The **Rectangle** structure to test.

Return Value

This method returns **true** when any portion of *rect* is contained within this **Region** object; otherwise, **false**.

Example

For an example, see **Region.IsVisible Method (RectangleF)**.

Requirements

Platforms: Windows 98, Windows NT 4.0, Windows Millennium Edition, Windows 2000, Windows XP Home Edition, Windows XP Professional, Windows Server 2003 family, .NET Compact Framework - Windows CE .NET

Region.IsVisible Method (RectangleF)

Tests whether any portion of the specified **RectangleF** structure is contained within this **Region** object.

[Visual Basic]
```
Overloads Public Function IsVisible( _
   ByVal rect As RectangleF _
) As Boolean
```
[C#]
```
public bool IsVisible(
   RectangleF rect
);
```
[C++]
```
public: bool IsVisible(
   RectangleF rect
);
```
[JScript]
```
public function IsVisible(
   rect : RectangleF
) : Boolean;
```

Parameters

rect

The **RectangleF** structure to test.

Return Value

This method returns **true** when any portion of *rect* is contained within this **Region** object; otherwise, **false**.

Example

[Visual Basic, C#] The following example is designed for use with Windows Forms, and it requires **PaintEventArgs** *e*, which is a parameter of the **Paint** event handler. The code performs the following actions:

- Creates the first rectangle and draws it to the screen in blue.
- Creates the second rectangle and draws it to the screen in red.
- Creates a region that from the first rectangle.
- Determines if any portion of the rectangle intersects with the region.
- Displays the **true** or **false** result on the screen.

[Visual Basic, C#] Notice that there one intersect the other so the result is **true**.

[Visual Basic]
```
Public Sub IsVisible_RectF_Example(e As PaintEventArgs)
' Create the first rectangle and draw it to the screen in blue.
Dim regionRect As New Rectangle(20, 20, 100, 100)
e.Graphics.DrawRectangle(Pens.Blue, regionRect)
' create the second rectangle and draw it to the screen in red.
Dim myRect As New RectangleF(90, 30, 100, 100)
e.Graphics.DrawRectangle(Pens.Red, Rectangle.Round(myRect))
' Create a region using the first rectangle.
Dim myRegion As New [Region](regionRect)
' Determine if myRect is contained in the region.
Dim contained As Boolean = myRegion.IsVisible(myRect)
' Display the result.
Dim myFont As New Font("Arial", 8)
Dim myBrush As New SolidBrush(Color.Black)
e.Graphics.DrawString("contained = " & contained.ToString(), _
myFont, myBrush, New PointF(20, 140))
End Sub
```

[C#]
```
public void IsVisible_RectF_Example(PaintEventArgs e)
{
// Create the first rectangle and draw it to the screen in blue.
Rectangle regionRect = new Rectangle(20, 20, 100, 100);
e.Graphics.DrawRectangle(Pens.Blue, regionRect);
// Create the second rectangle and draw it to the screen in red.
RectangleF myRect = new RectangleF(90, 30, 100, 100);
e.Graphics.DrawRectangle(Pens.Red, Rectangle.Round(myRect));
// Create a region using the first rectangle.
Region myRegion = new Region(regionRect);
// Determine if myRect is contained in the region.
bool contained = myRegion.IsVisible(myRect);
// Display the result.
Font myFont = new Font("Arial", 8);
SolidBrush myBrush = new SolidBrush(Color.Black);
e.Graphics.DrawString("contained = " + contained.ToString(),
myFont,
myBrush,
new PointF(20, 140));
}
```

Requirements

Platforms: Windows 98, Windows NT 4.0, Windows Millennium Edition, Windows 2000, Windows XP Home Edition, Windows XP Professional, Windows Server 2003 family

Region.IsVisible Method (Point, Graphics)

Tests whether the specified **Point** structure is contained within this **Region** object when drawn using the specified **Graphics** object.

[Visual Basic]
```
Overloads Public Function IsVisible( _
   ByVal point As Point, _
   ByVal g As Graphics _
) As Boolean
```
[C#]
```
public bool IsVisible(
   Point point,
   Graphics g
);
```
[C++]
```
public: bool IsVisible(
   Point point,
   Graphics* g
);
```
[JScript]
```
public function IsVisible(
   point : Point,
   g : Graphics
) : Boolean;
```

Parameters

point
The **Point** structure to test.

g
A **Graphics** object that represents a graphics context.

Return Value

This method returns **true** when *point* is contained within this **Region** object; otherwise, **false**.

Remarks

The current transformation of the graphics context is used to compute the region interior and the point coordinates on the drawing surface.

Example

For an example, see **Region.IsVisible Method (RectangleF)**.

Requirements

Platforms: Windows 98, Windows NT 4.0,
Windows Millennium Edition, Windows 2000,
Windows XP Home Edition, Windows XP Professional,
Windows Server 2003 family

Region.IsVisible Method (PointF, Graphics)

Tests whether the specified **PointF** structure is contained within this **Region** object when drawn using the specified **Graphics** object.

[Visual Basic]
```
Overloads Public Function IsVisible( _
   ByVal point As PointF, _
   ByVal g As Graphics _
) As Boolean
```
[C#]
```
public bool IsVisible(
   PointF point,
   Graphics g
);
```
[C++]
```
public: bool IsVisible(
   PointF point,
   Graphics* g
);
```
[JScript]
```
public function IsVisible(
   point : PointF,
   g : Graphics
) : Boolean;
```

Parameters

point
The **PointF** structure to test.

g
A **Graphics** object that represents a graphics context.

Return Value

This method returns **true** when *point* is contained within this **Region** object; otherwise, **false**.

Remarks

The current transformation of the graphics context is used to compute the region interior and the point coordinates on the drawing surface.

Example

For an example, see **Region.IsVisible Method (RectangleF)**.

Requirements

Platforms: Windows 98, Windows NT 4.0,
Windows Millennium Edition, Windows 2000,
Windows XP Home Edition, Windows XP Professional,
Windows Server 2003 family

Region.IsVisible Method (Rectangle, Graphics)

Tests whether any portion of the specified **Rectangle** structure is contained within this **Region** object when drawn using the specified **Graphics** object.

[Visual Basic]
```
Overloads Public Function IsVisible( _
   ByVal rect As Rectangle, _
   ByVal g As Graphics _
) As Boolean
```
[C#]
```
public bool IsVisible(
   Rectangle rect,
   Graphics g
);
```
[C++]
```
public: bool IsVisible(
   Rectangle rect,
   Graphics* g
);
```
[JScript]
```
public function IsVisible(
   rect : Rectangle,
   g : Graphics
) : Boolean;
```

Parameters

rect

The **Rectangle** structure to test.

g

A **Graphics** object that represents a graphics context.

Return Value

This method returns **true** when any portion of the *rect* is contained within this **Region** object; otherwise, **false**.

Remarks

The current transformation of the graphics context is used to compute the region interior and the rectangle coordinates on the drawing surface.

Example

For an example, see **Region.IsVisible Method (RectangleF)**.

Requirements

Platforms: Windows 98, Windows NT 4.0,
Windows Millennium Edition, Windows 2000,
Windows XP Home Edition, Windows XP Professional,
Windows Server 2003 family

Region.IsVisible Method (RectangleF, Graphics)

Tests whether any portion of the specified **RectangleF** structure is contained within this **Region** when drawn using the specified **Graphics** object.

```
[Visual Basic]
Overloads Public Function IsVisible( _
   ByVal rect As RectangleF, _
   ByVal g As Graphics _
) As Boolean
[C#]
public bool IsVisible(
   RectangleF rect,
   Graphics g
);
[C++]
public: bool IsVisible(
   RectangleF rect,
   Graphics* g
);
[JScript]
public function IsVisible(
   rect : RectangleF,
   g : Graphics
) : Boolean;
```

Parameters

rect

The **RectangleF** structure to test.

g

A **Graphics** object that represents a graphics context.

Return Value

This method returns **true** when *rect* is contained within this **Region** object; otherwise, **false**.

Remarks

The current transformation of the graphics context is used to compute the region interior and the rectangle coordinates on the drawing surface.

Example

For an example, see **Region.IsVisible Method (RectangleF)**.

Requirements

Platforms: Windows 98, Windows NT 4.0,
Windows Millennium Edition, Windows 2000,
Windows XP Home Edition, Windows XP Professional,
Windows Server 2003 family

Region.IsVisible Method (Single, Single)

Tests whether the specified point is contained within this **Region** object.

```
[Visual Basic]
Overloads Public Function IsVisible( _
   ByVal x As Single, _
   ByVal y As Single _
) As Boolean
[C#]
public bool IsVisible(
   float x,
   float y
);
[C++]
public: bool IsVisible(
   float x,
   float y
);
[JScript]
public function IsVisible(
   x : float,
   y : float
) : Boolean;
```

Parameters

x

The x-coordinate of the point to test.

y

The y-coordinate of the point to test.

Return Value

This method returns **true** when the specified point is contained within this **Region** object; otherwise, **false**.

Example

For an example, see **Region.IsVisible Method (RectangleF)**.

Requirements

Platforms: Windows 98, Windows NT 4.0,
Windows Millennium Edition, Windows 2000,
Windows XP Home Edition, Windows XP Professional,
Windows Server 2003 family,
.NET Compact Framework - Windows CE .NET

Region.IsVisible Method (Int32, Int32, Graphics)

Tests whether the specified point is contained within this **Region** object when drawn using the specified **Graphics** object.

```
[Visual Basic]
Overloads Public Function IsVisible( _
   ByVal x As Integer, _
   ByVal y As Integer, _
   ByVal g As Graphics _
) As Boolean
```

[C#]
```
public bool IsVisible(
   int x,
   int y,
   Graphics g
);
```
[C++]
```
public: bool IsVisible(
   int x,
   int y,
   Graphics* g
);
```
[JScript]
```
public function IsVisible(
   x : int,
   y : int,
   g : Graphics
) : Boolean;
```

Parameters

x

The x-coordinate of the point to test.

y

The y-coordinate of the point to test.

g

A **Graphics** object that represents a graphics context.

Return Value

This method returns **true** when the specified point is contained within this **Region** object; otherwise, **false**.

Remarks

The current transformation of the graphics context is used to compute the region interior and the point coordinates on the drawing surface.

Example

For an example, see **Region.IsVisible Method (RectangleF)**.

Requirements

Platforms: Windows 98, Windows NT 4.0, Windows Millennium Edition, Windows 2000, Windows XP Home Edition, Windows XP Professional, Windows Server 2003 family

Region.IsVisible Method (Single, Single, Graphics)

Tests whether the specified point is contained within this **Region** object when drawn using the specified **Graphics** object.

[Visual Basic]
```
Overloads Public Function IsVisible( _
   ByVal x As Single, _
   ByVal y As Single, _
   ByVal g As Graphics _
) As Boolean
```
[C#]
```
public bool IsVisible(
   float x,
   float y,
   Graphics g
);
```
[C++]
```
public: bool IsVisible(
   float x,
   float y,
   Graphics* g
);
```
[JScript]
```
public function IsVisible(
   x : float,
   y : float,
   g : Graphics
) : Boolean;
```

Parameters

x

The x-coordinate of the point to test.

y

The y-coordinate of the point to test.

g

A **Graphics** object that represents a graphics context.

Return Value

This method returns **true** when the specified point is contained within this **Region** object; otherwise, **false**.

Remarks

The current transformation of the graphics context is used to compute the region interior and the point coordinates on the drawing surface.

Example

For an example, see **Region.IsVisible Method (RectangleF)**.

Requirements

Platforms: Windows 98, Windows NT 4.0, Windows Millennium Edition, Windows 2000, Windows XP Home Edition, Windows XP Professional, Windows Server 2003 family

Region.IsVisible Method (Int32, Int32, Int32, Int32)

Tests whether any portion of the specified rectangle is contained within this **Region** object.

[Visual Basic]
```
Overloads Public Function IsVisible( _
   ByVal x As Integer, _
   ByVal y As Integer, _
   ByVal width As Integer, _
   ByVal height As Integer _
) As Boolean
```
[C#]
```
public bool IsVisible(
   int x,
   int y,
   int width,
   int height
);
```
[C++]
```
public: bool IsVisible(
   int x,
   int y,
   int width,
   int height
);
```

```
[JScript]
public function IsVisible(
   x : int,
   y : int,
   width : int,
   height : int
) : Boolean;
```

Parameters

x

The x-coordinate of the upper-left corner of the rectangle to test.

y

The y-coordinate of the upper-left corner of the rectangle to test.

width

The width of the rectangle to test.

height

The height of the rectangle to test.

Return Value

This method returns **true** when any portion of the specified rectangle is contained within this **Region** object; otherwise, **false**.

Example

For an example, see **Region.IsVisible Method (RectangleF)**.

Requirements

Platforms: Windows 98, Windows NT 4.0, Windows Millennium Edition, Windows 2000, Windows XP Home Edition, Windows XP Professional, Windows Server 2003 family

Region.IsVisible Method (Single, Single, Single, Single)

Tests whether any portion of the specified rectangle is contained within this **Region** object.

```
[Visual Basic]
Overloads Public Function IsVisible( _
   ByVal x As Single, _
   ByVal y As Single, _
   ByVal width As Single, _
   ByVal height As Single _
) As Boolean
[C#]
public bool IsVisible(
   float x,
   float y,
   float width,
   float height
);
[C++]
public: bool IsVisible(
   float x,
   float y,
   float width,
   float height
);
[JScript]
public function IsVisible(
   x : float,
   y : float,
   width : float,
   height : float
) : Boolean;
```

Parameters

x

The x-coordinate of the upper-left corner of the rectangle to test.

y

The y-coordinate of the upper-left corner of the rectangle to test.

width

The width of the rectangle to test.

height

The height of the rectangle to test.

Return Value

This method returns **true** when any portion of the specified rectangle is contained within this **Region** object; otherwise, **false**.

Example

For an example, see **Region.IsVisible Method (RectangleF)**.

Requirements

Platforms: Windows 98, Windows NT 4.0, Windows Millennium Edition, Windows 2000, Windows XP Home Edition, Windows XP Professional, Windows Server 2003 family

Region.IsVisible Method (Int32, Int32, Int32, Int32, Graphics)

Tests whether any portion of the specified rectangle is contained within this **Region** object when drawn using the specified **Graphics** object.

```
[Visual Basic]
Overloads Public Function IsVisible( _
   ByVal x As Integer, _
   ByVal y As Integer, _
   ByVal width As Integer, _
   ByVal height As Integer, _
   ByVal g As Graphics _
) As Boolean
[C#]
public bool IsVisible(
   int x,
   int y,
   int width,
   int height,
   Graphics g
);
[C++]
public: bool IsVisible(
   int x,
   int y,
   int width,
   int height,
   Graphics* g
);
[JScript]
public function IsVisible(
   x : int,
   y : int,
   width : int,
   height : int,
   g : Graphics
) : Boolean;
```

Parameters

x
The x-coordinate of the upper-left corner of the rectangle to test.

y
The y-coordinate of the upper-left corner of the rectangle to test.

width
The width of the rectangle to test.

height
The height of the rectangle to test.

g
A **Graphics** object that represents a graphics context.

Return Value

This method returns **true** when any portion of the specified rectangle is contained within this **Region** object; otherwise, **false**.

Remarks

The current transformation of the graphics context is used to compute the region interior and the rectangle coordinates on the drawing surface.

Example

For an example, see **Region.IsVisible Method (RectangleF)**.

Requirements

Platforms: Windows 98, Windows NT 4.0, Windows Millennium Edition, Windows 2000, Windows XP Home Edition, Windows XP Professional, Windows Server 2003 family

Region.IsVisible Method (Single, Single, Single, Single, Graphics)

Tests whether any portion of the specified rectangle is contained within this **Region** object when drawn using the specified **Graphics** object.

```
[Visual Basic]
Overloads Public Function IsVisible( _
   ByVal x As Single, _
   ByVal y As Single, _
   ByVal width As Single, _
   ByVal height As Single, _
   ByVal g As Graphics _
) As Boolean
[C#]
public bool IsVisible(
   float x,
   float y,
   float width,
   float height,
   Graphics g
);
[C++]
public: bool IsVisible(
   float x,
   float y,
   float width,
   float height,
   Graphics* g
);
[JScript]
public function IsVisible(
   x : float,
   y : float,
   width : float,
   height : float,
   g : Graphics
) : Boolean;
```

Parameters

x
The x-coordinate of the upper-left corner of the rectangle to test.

y
The y-coordinate of the upper-left corner of the rectangle to test.

width
The width of the rectangle to test.

height
The height of the rectangle to test.

g
A **Graphics** object that represents a graphics context.

Return Value

This method returns **true** when any portion of the specified rectangle is contained within this **Region** object; otherwise, **false**.

Remarks

The current transformation of the graphics context is used to compute the region interior and the rectangle coordinates on the drawing surface.

Example

For an example, see **Region.IsVisible Method (RectangleF)**.

Requirements

Platforms: Windows 98, Windows NT 4.0, Windows Millennium Edition, Windows 2000, Windows XP Home Edition, Windows XP Professional, Windows Server 2003 family

Region.MakeEmpty Method

Initializes this **Region** object to an empty interior.

```
[Visual Basic]
Public Sub MakeEmpty()
[C#]
public void MakeEmpty();
[C++]
public: void MakeEmpty();
[JScript]
public function MakeEmpty();
```

Return Value

This method does not return a value.

Requirements

Platforms: Windows 98, Windows NT 4.0, Windows Millennium Edition, Windows 2000, Windows XP Home Edition, Windows XP Professional, Windows Server 2003 family, .NET Compact Framework - Windows CE .NET

Region.MakeInfinite Method

Initializes this **Region** object to an infinite interior.

[Visual Basic]
```
Public Sub MakeInfinite()
```
[C#]
```
public void MakeInfinite();
```
[C++]
```
public: void MakeInfinite();
```
[JScript]
```
public function MakeInfinite();
```

Return Value

This method does not return a value.

Requirements

Platforms: Windows 98, Windows NT 4.0, Windows Millennium Edition, Windows 2000, Windows XP Home Edition, Windows XP Professional, Windows Server 2003 family, .NET Compact Framework - Windows CE .NET

Region.Transform Method

Transforms this **Region** object by the specified **Matrix** object.

[Visual Basic]
```
Public Sub Transform( _
   ByVal matrix As Matrix _
)
```
[C#]
```
public void Transform(
   Matrix matrix
);
```
[C++]
```
public: void Transform(
   Matrix* matrix
);
```
[JScript]
```
public function Transform(
   matrix : Matrix
);
```

Parameters

matrix

The **Matrix** object by which to transform this **Region** object.

Return Value

This method does not return a value.

Example

[Visual Basic, C#] The following example is designed for use with Windows Forms, and it requires **PaintEventArgs** *e*, which is a parameter of the **Paint** event handler. The code performs the following actions:

- Creates a rectangle and draws it to the screen in blue.
- Creates a region from the rectangle.
- Creates a transform matrix and sets it to 45 degrees.
- Apply the transform to the region.
- Fill the transformed region with red and draw the transformed region to the screen in red.

[Visual Basic, C#] Notice that the red rectangle is rotated 45 degrees from the original rectangle, shown in blue.

[Visual Basic]
```
Public Sub TransformExample(e As PaintEventArgs)
' Create the first rectangle and draw it to the screen in blue.
Dim regionRect As New Rectangle(100, 50, 100, 100)
e.Graphics.DrawRectangle(Pens.Blue, regionRect)
' Create a region using the first rectangle.
Dim myRegion As New [Region](regionRect)
' Create a transform matrix and set it to have a 45 degree
' rotation.
Dim transformMatrix As New Matrix()
transformMatrix.RotateAt(45, New PointF(100, 50))
' Apply the transform to the region.
myRegion.Transform(transformMatrix)
' Fill the transformed region with red and draw it to the
' screen in red.
Dim myBrush As New SolidBrush(Color.Red)
e.Graphics.FillRegion(myBrush, myRegion)
End Sub
```

[C#]
```
public void TransformExample(PaintEventArgs e)
{
// Create the first rectangle and draw it to the screen in blue.
Rectangle regionRect = new Rectangle(100, 50, 100, 100);
e.Graphics.DrawRectangle(Pens.Blue, regionRect);
// Create a region using the first rectangle.
Region myRegion = new Region(regionRect);
// Create a transform matrix and set it to have a 45 degree
// rotation.
Matrix transformMatrix = new Matrix();
transformMatrix.RotateAt(45, new Point(100, 50));
// Apply the transform to the region.
myRegion.Transform(transformMatrix);
// Fill the transformed region with red and draw it to the screen
// in red.
SolidBrush myBrush = new SolidBrush(Color.Red);
e.Graphics.FillRegion(myBrush, myRegion);
}
```

Requirements

Platforms: Windows 98, Windows NT 4.0, Windows Millennium Edition, Windows 2000, Windows XP Home Edition, Windows XP Professional, Windows Server 2003 family

Region.Translate Method

Offsets the coordinates of this **Region** object by the specified amount.

Overload List

Offsets the coordinates of this **Region** object by the specified amount.

Supported by the .NET Compact Framework.

[Visual Basic] **Overloads Public Sub Translate(Integer, Integer)**

[C#] **public void Translate(int, int);**

[C++] **public: void Translate(int, int);**

[JScript] **public function Translate(int, int);**

Offsets the coordinates of this **Region** object by the specified amount.

[Visual Basic] **Overloads Public Sub Translate(Single, Single)**

[C#] **public void Translate(float, float);**

[C++] **public: void Translate(float, float);**

[JScript] **public function Translate(float, float);**

Example

For an example, see **Region.Translate Method (Int32, Int32)**.

Region.Translate Method (Int32, Int32)

Offsets the coordinates of this **Region** object by the specified amount.

[Visual Basic]
```
Overloads Public Sub Translate( _
   ByVal dx As Integer, _
   ByVal dy As Integer _
)
```
[C#]
```
public void Translate(
   int dx,
   int dy
);
```
[C++]
```
public: void Translate(
   int dx,
   int dy
);
```
[JScript]
```
public function Translate(
   dx : int,
   dy : int
);
```

Parameters

dx
: The amount to offset this **Region** object horizontally.

dy
: The amount to offset this **Region** object vertically.

Return Value

This method does not return a value.

Example

[Visual Basic, C#] The following example is designed for use with Windows Forms, and it requires **PaintEventArgs** *e*, which is a parameter of the **Paint** event handler. The code performs the following actions:

- Creates a rectangle and draws it to the screen in blue.
- Creates a region from the rectangle.
- Applies the translation to the region.
- Fills the translated region with red and draws the translated region to the screen in red.

[Visual Basic, C#] Notice that the red rectangle is shifted down and to the right from the original rectangle, shown in blue.

[Visual Basic]
```
Public Sub TranslateExample(e As PaintEventArgs)
' Create the first rectangle and draw it to the screen in blue.
Dim regionRect As New Rectangle(100, 50, 100, 100)
e.Graphics.DrawRectangle(Pens.Blue, regionRect)
' Create a region using the first rectangle.
Dim myRegion As New [Region](regionRect)
' Apply the translation to the region.
myRegion.Translate(150, 100)
' Fill the transformed region with red and draw it to the
' screen in red.
Dim myBrush As New SolidBrush(Color.Red)
e.Graphics.FillRegion(myBrush, myRegion)
End Sub
```

[C#]
```
public void TranslateExample(PaintEventArgs e)
{
// Create the first rectangle and draw it to the screen in blue.
Rectangle regionRect = new Rectangle(100, 50, 100, 100);
e.Graphics.DrawRectangle(Pens.Blue, regionRect);
// Create a region using the first rectangle.
Region myRegion = new Region(regionRect);
// Apply the translation to the region.
myRegion.Translate(150, 100);
// Fill the transformed region with red and draw it to the ↵
screen in red.
SolidBrush myBrush = new SolidBrush(Color.Red);
e.Graphics.FillRegion(myBrush, myRegion);
}
```

Requirements

Platforms: Windows 98, Windows NT 4.0, Windows Millennium Edition, Windows 2000, Windows XP Home Edition, Windows XP Professional, Windows Server 2003 family, .NET Compact Framework - Windows CE .NET

Region.Translate Method (Single, Single)

Offsets the coordinates of this **Region** object by the specified amount.

[Visual Basic]
```
Overloads Public Sub Translate( _
   ByVal dx As Single, _
   ByVal dy As Single _
)
```
[C#]
```
public void Translate(
   float dx,
   float dy
);
```
[C++]
```
public: void Translate(
   float dx,
   float dy
);
```
[JScript]
```
public function Translate(
   dx : float,
   dy : float
);
```

Parameters

dx
: The amount to offset this **Region** object horizontally.

dy
: The amount to offset this **Region** object vertically.

Return Value

This method does not return a value.

Example

For an example, see **Region.Translate Method (Int32, Int32)**.

Requirements

Platforms: Windows 98, Windows NT 4.0, Windows Millennium Edition, Windows 2000, Windows XP Home Edition, Windows XP Professional, Windows Server 2003 family

Region.Union Method

Updates this **Region** object to the union of itself and the specified **GraphicsPath** object.

Overload List

Updates this **Region** object to the union of itself and the specified **GraphicsPath** object.

[Visual Basic] **Overloads Public Sub Union(GraphicsPath)**

[C#] **public void Union(GraphicsPath);**

[C++] **public: void Union(GraphicsPath*);**

[JScript] **public function Union(GraphicsPath);**

Updates this **Region** object to the union of itself and the specified **Rectangle** structure.

Supported by the .NET Compact Framework.

[Visual Basic] **Overloads Public Sub Union(Rectangle)**

[C#] **public void Union(Rectangle);**

[C++] **public: void Union(Rectangle);**

[JScript] **public function Union(Rectangle);**

Updates this **Region** object to the union of itself and the specified **RectangleF** structure.

[Visual Basic] **Overloads Public Sub Union(RectangleF)**

[C#] **public void Union(RectangleF);**

[C++] **public: void Union(RectangleF);**

[JScript] **public function Union(RectangleF);**

Updates this **Region** object to the union of itself and the specified **Region** object.

Supported by the .NET Compact Framework.

[Visual Basic] **Overloads Public Sub Union(Region)**

[C#] **public void Union(Region);**

[C++] **public: void Union(Region*);**

[JScript] **public function Union(Region);**

Example

For an example, see **Region.Union Method (RectangleF)** and **Region.Complement Method (Region)**.

Region.Union Method (GraphicsPath)

Updates this **Region** object to the union of itself and the specified **GraphicsPath** object.

```
[Visual Basic]
Overloads Public Sub Union( _
   ByVal path As GraphicsPath _
)
[C#]
public void Union(
   GraphicsPath path
);
[C++]
public: void Union(
   GraphicsPath* path
);
[JScript]
public function Union(
   path : GraphicsPath
);
```

Parameters

path

The **GraphicsPath** object to unite with this **Region** object.

Return Value

This method does not return a value.

Example

For an example, see **Region.Union Method (RectangleF)** and **Region.Complement Method (GraphicsPath)**

Requirements

Platforms: Windows 98, Windows NT 4.0, Windows Millennium Edition, Windows 2000, Windows XP Home Edition, Windows XP Professional, Windows Server 2003 family

Region.Union Method (Rectangle)

Updates this **Region** object to the union of itself and the specified **Rectangle** structure.

```
[Visual Basic]
Overloads Public Sub Union( _
   ByVal rect As Rectangle _
)
[C#]
public void Union(
   Rectangle rect
);
[C++]
public: void Union(
   Rectangle rect
);
[JScript]
public function Union(
   rect : Rectangle
);
```

Parameters

rect

The **Rectangle** structure to unite with this **Region** object.

Return Value

This method does not return a value.

Example

For an example, see **Region.Union Method (RectangleF)**.

Requirements

Platforms: Windows 98, Windows NT 4.0, Windows Millennium Edition, Windows 2000, Windows XP Home Edition, Windows XP Professional, Windows Server 2003 family, .NET Compact Framework - Windows CE .NET

Region.Union Method (RectangleF)

Updates this **Region** object to the union of itself and the specified **RectangleF** structure.

```
[Visual Basic]
Overloads Public Sub Union( _
   ByVal rect As RectangleF _
)
```

```
[C#]
public void Union(
   RectangleF rect
);
[C++]
public: void Union(
   RectangleF rect
);
[JScript]
public function Union(
   rect : RectangleF
);
```

Parameters

rect

The **RectangleF** structure to unite with this **Region** object.

Return Value

This method does not return a value.

Example

[Visual Basic, C#] The following example is designed for use with Windows Forms, and it requires **PaintEventArgs** *e*. The code performs the following actions:

- Creates the first rectangle and draws it to the screen in black.
- Creates a second rectangle and draws it to the screen in red.
- Creates a region using the first rectangle.
- Gets the area of union for myRegion when combined with complementRect.
- Fills the fills the area of union with blue and draws it to the screen.

[Visual Basic, C#] Notice that both rectangles are filled with blue, including the area of overlap.

```
[Visual Basic]
Public Sub Union_RectF_Example(e As PaintEventArgs)
' Create the first rectangle and draw it to the screen in black.
Dim regionRect As New Rectangle(20, 20, 100, 100)
e.Graphics.DrawRectangle(Pens.Black, regionRect)
' create the second rectangle and draw it to the screen in red.
Dim unionRect As New RectangleF(90, 30, 100, 100)
e.Graphics.DrawRectangle(Pens.Red, Rectangle.Round(unionRect))
' Create a region using the first rectangle.
Dim myRegion As New [Region](regionRect)
' Get the area of union for myRegion when combined with
' complementRect.
myRegion.Union(unionRect)
' Fill the intersection area of myRegion with blue.
Dim myBrush As New SolidBrush(Color.Blue)
e.Graphics.FillRegion(myBrush, myRegion)
End Sub
```

```
[C#]
public void Union_RectF_Example(PaintEventArgs e)
{
// Create the first rectangle and draw it to the screen in black.
Rectangle regionRect = new Rectangle(20, 20, 100, 100);
e.Graphics.DrawRectangle(Pens.Black, regionRect);
// create the second rectangle and draw it to the screen in red.
RectangleF unionRect = new RectangleF(90, 30, 100, 100);
e.Graphics.DrawRectangle(Pens.Red,
Rectangle.Round(unionRect));
// Create a region using the first rectangle.
Region myRegion = new Region(regionRect);
// Get the area of union for myRegion when combined with
// complementRect.
myRegion.Union(unionRect);
// Fill the union area of myRegion with blue.
SolidBrush myBrush = new SolidBrush(Color.Blue);
e.Graphics.FillRegion(myBrush, myRegion);
}
```

Requirements

Platforms: Windows 98, Windows NT 4.0, Windows Millennium Edition, Windows 2000, Windows XP Home Edition, Windows XP Professional, Windows Server 2003 family

Region.Union Method (Region)

Updates this **Region** object to the union of itself and the specified **Region** object.

```
[Visual Basic]
Overloads Public Sub Union( _
   ByVal region As Region _
)
[C#]
public void Union(
   Region region
);
[C++]
public: void Union(
   Region* region
);
[JScript]
public function Union(
   region : Region
);
```

Parameters

region

The **Region** object to unite with this **Region** object.

Return Value

This method does not return a value.

Example

For an example, see **Region.Union Method (RectangleF)** and **Region.Complement Method (Region)**.

Requirements

Platforms: Windows 98, Windows NT 4.0, Windows Millennium Edition, Windows 2000, Windows XP Home Edition, Windows XP Professional, Windows Server 2003 family, .NET Compact Framework - Windows CE .NET

Region.Xor Method

Updates this **Region** object to the union minus the intersection of itself with the specified **GraphicsPath** object.

Overload List

Updates this **Region** object to the union minus the intersection of itself with the specified **GraphicsPath** object.

[Visual Basic] **Overloads Public Sub Xor(GraphicsPath)**

[C#] **public void Xor(GraphicsPath);**

[C++] **public: void Xor(GraphicsPath*);**

[JScript] **public function Xor(GraphicsPath);**

Updates this **Region** object to the union minus the intersection of itself with the specified **Rectangle** structure.

Supported by the .NET Compact Framework.

[Visual Basic] **Overloads Public Sub Xor(Rectangle)**

[C#] **public void Xor(Rectangle);**

[C++] **public: void Xor(Rectangle);**

[JScript] **public function Xor(Rectangle);**

Updates this **Region** object to the union minus the intersection of itself with the specified **RectangleF** structure.

[Visual Basic] **Overloads Public Sub Xor(RectangleF)**

[C#] **public void Xor(RectangleF);**

[C++] **public: void Xor(RectangleF);**

[JScript] **public function Xor(RectangleF);**

Updates this **Region** object to the union minus the intersection of itself with the specified **Region** object.

Supported by the .NET Compact Framework.

[Visual Basic] **Overloads Public Sub Xor(Region)**

[C#] **public void Xor(Region);**

[C++] **public: void Xor(Region*);**

[JScript] **public function Xor(Region);**

Example

For an example, see **Region.Xor Method (RectangleF)** and **Region.Complement Method (Region)**.

Region.Xor Method (GraphicsPath)

Updates this **Region** object to the union minus the intersection of itself with the specified **GraphicsPath** object.

```
[Visual Basic]
Overloads Public Sub Xor( _
   ByVal path As GraphicsPath _
)
[C#]
public void Xor(
   GraphicsPath path
);
[C++]
public: void Xor(
   GraphicsPath* path
);
[JScript]
public function Xor(
   path : GraphicsPath
);
```

Parameters

path

The **GraphicsPath** object to **XOR** with this **Region** object.

Return Value

This method does not return a value.

Example

For an example, see **Region.Xor Method (RectangleF)** and **Region.Complement Method (GraphicsPath)**.

Requirements

Platforms: Windows 98, Windows NT 4.0, Windows Millennium Edition, Windows 2000, Windows XP Home Edition, Windows XP Professional, Windows Server 2003 family

Region.Xor Method (Rectangle)

Updates this **Region** object to the union minus the intersection of itself with the specified **Rectangle** structure.

```
[Visual Basic]
Overloads Public Sub Xor( _
   ByVal rect As Rectangle _
)
[C#]
public void Xor(
   Rectangle rect
);
[C++]
public: void Xor(
   Rectangle rect
);
[JScript]
public function Xor(
   rect : Rectangle
);
```

Parameters

rect

The **Rectangle** structure to **XOR** with this **Region** object.

Return Value

This method does not return a value.

Example

For an example, see **Region.Xor Method (RectangleF)**.

Requirements

Platforms: Windows 98, Windows NT 4.0, Windows Millennium Edition, Windows 2000, Windows XP Home Edition, Windows XP Professional, Windows Server 2003 family, .NET Compact Framework - Windows CE .NET

Region.Xor Method (RectangleF)

Updates this **Region** object to the union minus the intersection of itself with the specified **RectangleF** structure.

```
[Visual Basic]
Overloads Public Sub Xor( _
   ByVal rect As RectangleF _
)
[C#]
public void Xor(
   RectangleF rect
);
[C++]
public: void Xor(
   RectangleF rect
);
[JScript]
public function Xor(
   rect : RectangleF
);
```

Parameters

rect

The **RectangleF** structure to **XOR** with this **Region** object.

Return Value

This method does not return a value.

Example

[Visual Basic, C#] The following example is designed for use with Windows Forms, and it requires **PaintEventArgs** *e*, which is a parameter of the **Paint** event handler. The code performs the following actions:

- Creates the first rectangle and draws it to the screen in black.
- Creates a second rectangle and draws it to the screen in red.
- Creates a region using the first rectangle.
- Gets the Xor area for myRegion when combined with complementRect.
- Fills the fills the Xor area with blue and draws it to the screen.

[Visual Basic, C#] Notice that both rectangles are filled with blue, except for the area of overlap.

[Visual Basic]

```
Public Sub XorExample(e As PaintEventArgs)
' Create the first rectangle and draw it to the screen in black.
Dim regionRect As New Rectangle(20, 20, 100, 100)
e.Graphics.DrawRectangle(Pens.Black, regionRect)
' create the second rectangle and draw it to the screen in red.
Dim xorRect As New RectangleF(90, 30, 100, 100)
e.Graphics.DrawRectangle(Pens.Red, Rectangle.Round(xorRect))
' Create a region using the first rectangle.
Dim myRegion As New [Region](regionRect)
' Get the area of overlap for myRegion when combined with
' complementRect.
myRegion.Xor(xorRect)
' Fill the intersection area of myRegion with blue.
Dim myBrush As New SolidBrush(Color.Blue)
e.Graphics.FillRegion(myBrush, myRegion)
End Sub
```

[C#]

```
public void XorExample(PaintEventArgs e)
{
// Create the first rectangle and draw it to the screen in black.
Rectangle regionRect = new Rectangle(20, 20, 100, 100);
e.Graphics.DrawRectangle(Pens.Black, regionRect);
// create the second rectangle and draw it to the screen in red.
RectangleF xorRect = new RectangleF(90, 30, 100, 100);
e.Graphics.DrawRectangle(Pens.Red,
Rectangle.Round(xorRect));
// Create a region using the first rectangle.
Region myRegion = new Region(regionRect);
// Get the area of overlap for myRegion when combined with
// complementRect.
myRegion.Xor(xorRect);
// Fill the Xor area of myRegion with blue.
SolidBrush myBrush = new SolidBrush(Color.Blue);
e.Graphics.FillRegion(myBrush, myRegion);
}
```

Requirements

Platforms: Windows 98, Windows NT 4.0,
Windows Millennium Edition, Windows 2000,
Windows XP Home Edition, Windows XP Professional,
Windows Server 2003 family

Region.Xor Method (Region)

Updates this **Region** object to the union minus the intersection of itself with the specified **Region** object.

[Visual Basic]

```
Overloads Public Sub Xor( _
   ByVal region As Region _
)
```

[C#]

```
public void Xor(
   Region region
);
```

[C++]

```
public: void Xor(
   Region* region
);
```

[JScript]

```
public function Xor(
   region : Region
);
```

Parameters

region
The **Region** object to **XOR** with this **Region** object.

Return Value

This method does not return a value.

Example

For an example, see **Region.Xor Method (RectangleF)** and **Region.Complement Method (Region)**.

Requirements

Platforms: Windows 98, Windows NT 4.0,
Windows Millennium Edition, Windows 2000,
Windows XP Home Edition, Windows XP Professional,
Windows Server 2003 family,
.NET Compact Framework - Windows CE .NET

RotateFlipType Enumeration

Specifies the direction of an image's rotation and the axis used to flip the image.

[Visual Basic]
```
<Serializable>
Public Enum RotateFlipType
```
[C#]
```
[Serializable]
public enum RotateFlipType
```
[C++]
```
[Serializable]
__value public enum RotateFlipType
```
[JScript]
```
public
   Serializable
enum RotateFlipType
```

Members

Member name	Description
Rotate180FlipNone	Specifies a 180-degree rotation without flipping.
Rotate180FlipX	Specifies a 180-degree rotation followed by a horizontal flip.
Rotate180FlipXY	Specifies a 180-degree rotation followed by a horizontal and vertical flip.
Rotate180FlipY	Specifies a 180-degree rotation followed by a vertical flip.
Rotate270FlipNone	Specifies a 270-degree rotation without flipping.
Rotate270FlipX	Specifies a 270-degree rotation followed by a horizontal flip.
Rotate270FlipXY	Specifies a 270-degree rotation followed by a horizontal and vertical flip.
Rotate270FlipY	Specifies a 270-degree rotation followed by a vertical flip.
Rotate90FlipNone	Specifies a 90-degree rotation without flipping.
Rotate90FlipX	Specifies a 90-degree rotation followed by a horizontal flip.
Rotate90FlipXY	Specifies a 90-degree rotation followed by a horizontal and vertical flip.
Rotate90FlipY	Specifies a 90-degree rotation followed by a vertical flip.
RotateNoneFlipNone	Specifies no rotation and no flipping.
RotateNoneFlipX	Specifies no rotation followed by a horizontal flip.
RotateNoneFlipXY	Specifies no rotation followed by a horizontal and vertical flip.
RotateNoneFlipY	Specifies no rotation followed by a vertical flip.

Requirements

Namespace: System.Drawing

Platforms: Windows 98, Windows NT 4.0, Windows Millennium Edition, Windows 2000, Windows XP Home Edition, Windows XP Professional, Windows Server 2003 family

Assembly: System.Drawing (in System.Drawing.dll)

Size Structure

Stores an ordered pair of integers, typically the width and height of a rectangle.

System.Object
  System.ValueType
    System.Drawing.Size

```
[Visual Basic]
<Serializable>
<ComVisible(True)>
Public Structure Size
[C#]
[Serializable]
[ComVisible(true)]
public struct Size
[C++]
[Serializable]
[ComVisible(true)]
public __value struct Size
```

[JScript] In JScript, you can use the structures in the .NET Framework, but you cannot define your own.

Thread Safety

Any public static (**Shared** in Visual Basic) members of this type are safe for multithreaded operations. Any instance members are not guaranteed to be thread safe.

Requirements

Namespace: System.Drawing

Platforms: Windows 98, Windows NT 4.0, Windows Millennium Edition, Windows 2000, Windows XP Home Edition, Windows XP Professional, Windows Server 2003 family, .NET Compact Framework - Windows CE .NET

Assembly: System.Drawing (in System.Drawing.dll)

Size Constructor

Initializes a new instance of the **Size** class from the specified **Point**.

Overload List

Initializes a new instance of the **Size** class from the specified **Point**.

[Visual Basic] **Public Sub New(Point)**

[C#] **public Size(Point);**

[C++] **public: Size(Point);**

[JScript] **public function Size(Point);**

Initializes a new instance of the **Size** class from the specified dimensions.

Supported by the .NET Compact Framework.

[Visual Basic] **Public Sub New(Integer, Integer)**

[C#] **public Size(int, int);**

[C++] **public: Size(int, int);**

[JScript] **public function Size(int, int);**

Size Constructor (Point)

Initializes a new instance of the **Size** class from the specified **Point**.

```
[Visual Basic]
Public Sub New( _
   ByVal pt As Point _
)
[C#]
public Size(
   Point pt
);
[C++]
public: Size(
   Point pt
);
[JScript]
public function Size(
   pt : Point
);
```

Parameters

pt
  The **Point** from which to initialize this **Size**.

Requirements

Platforms: Windows 98, Windows NT 4.0, Windows Millennium Edition, Windows 2000, Windows XP Home Edition, Windows XP Professional, Windows Server 2003 family

Size Constructor (Int32, Int32)

Initializes a new instance of the **Size** class from the specified dimensions.

```
[Visual Basic]
Public Sub New( _
   ByVal width As Integer, _
   ByVal height As Integer _
)
[C#]
public Size(
   int width,
   int height
);
[C++]
public: Size(
   int width,
   int height
);
[JScript]
public function Size(
   width : int,
   height : int
);
```

Parameters

width
  The width component of the new **Size**.

height
  The height component of the new **Size**.

Requirements

Platforms: Windows 98, Windows NT 4.0, Windows Millennium Edition, Windows 2000, Windows XP Home Edition, Windows XP Professional, Windows Server 2003 family, .NET Compact Framework - Windows CE .NET

Size.Empty Field

Initializes a new instance of the **Size** class.

```
[Visual Basic]
Public Shared ReadOnly Empty As Size
[C#]
public static readonly Size Empty;
[C++]
public: static Size Empty;
[JScript]
public static var Empty : Size;
```

Requirements

Platforms: Windows 98, Windows NT 4.0, Windows Millennium Edition, Windows 2000, Windows XP Home Edition, Windows XP Professional, Windows Server 2003 family, .NET Compact Framework - Windows CE .NET

Size.Height Property

Gets or sets the vertical component of this **Size**.

```
[Visual Basic]
Public Property Height As Integer
[C#]
public int Height {get; set;}
[C++]
public: __property int get_Height();
public: __property void set_Height(int);
[JScript]
public function get Height() : int;
public function set Height(int);
```

Property Value

The vertical component of this **Size**.

Requirements

Platforms: Windows 98, Windows NT 4.0, Windows Millennium Edition, Windows 2000, Windows XP Home Edition, Windows XP Professional, Windows Server 2003 family, .NET Compact Framework - Windows CE .NET

Size.IsEmpty Property

Tests whether this **Size** has zero width and height.

```
[Visual Basic]
Public ReadOnly Property IsEmpty As Boolean
[C#]
public bool IsEmpty {get;}
[C++]
public: __property bool get_IsEmpty();
[JScript]
public function get IsEmpty() : Boolean;
```

Property Value

This property returns **true** when this **Size** has both a width and height of zero; otherwise, **false**.

Requirements

Platforms: Windows 98, Windows NT 4.0, Windows Millennium Edition, Windows 2000, Windows XP Home Edition, Windows XP Professional, Windows Server 2003 family, .NET Compact Framework - Windows CE .NET

Size.Width Property

Gets or sets the horizontal component of this **Size**.

```
[Visual Basic]
Public Property Width As Integer
[C#]
public int Width {get; set;}
[C++]
public: __property int get_Width();
public: __property void set_Width(int);
[JScript]
public function get Width() : int;
public function set Width(int);
```

Property Value

The horizontal component of this **Size**.

Requirements

Platforms: Windows 98, Windows NT 4.0, Windows Millennium Edition, Windows 2000, Windows XP Home Edition, Windows XP Professional, Windows Server 2003 family, .NET Compact Framework - Windows CE .NET

Size.Ceiling Method

Converts the specified **SizeF** structure to a **Size** structure by rounding the values of the **Size** structure to the next higher integer values.

```
[Visual Basic]
Public Shared Function Ceiling( _
   ByVal value As SizeF _
) As Size
[C#]
public static Size Ceiling(
   SizeF value
);
[C++]
public: static Size Ceiling(
   SizeF value
);
[JScript]
public static function Ceiling(
   value : SizeF
) : Size;
```

Parameters

value

The **SizeF** structure to convert.

Return Value

The **Size** structure this method converts to.

Requirements

Platforms: Windows 98, Windows NT 4.0, Windows Millennium Edition, Windows 2000, Windows XP Home Edition, Windows XP Professional, Windows Server 2003 family

Size.Equals Method

Tests to see whether the specified object is a **Size** with the same dimensions as this **Size**.

```
[Visual Basic]
Overrides Public Function Equals( _
   ByVal obj As Object _
) As Boolean
[C#]
public override bool Equals(
   object obj
);
[C++]
public: bool Equals(
   Object* obj
);
[JScript]
public override function Equals(
   obj : Object
) : Boolean;
```

Parameters

obj

The **Object** to test.

Return Value

This method returns **true** if *obj* is a **Size** and has the same width and height as this **Size**; otherwise, **false**.

Requirements

Platforms: Windows 98, Windows NT 4.0, Windows Millennium Edition, Windows 2000, Windows XP Home Edition, Windows XP Professional, Windows Server 2003 family, .NET Compact Framework - Windows CE .NET

Size.GetHashCode Method

Returns a hash code for this **Size** structure.

```
[Visual Basic]
Overrides Public Function GetHashCode() As Integer
[C#]
public override int GetHashCode();
[C++]
public: int GetHashCode();
[JScript]
public override function GetHashCode() : int;
```

Return Value

An integer value that specifies a hash value for this **Size** structure.

Requirements

Platforms: Windows 98, Windows NT 4.0, Windows Millennium Edition, Windows 2000, Windows XP Home Edition, Windows XP Professional, Windows Server 2003 family, .NET Compact Framework - Windows CE .NET

Size.Round Method

Converts the specified **SizeF** structure to a **Size** structure by rounding the values of the **Size** structure to the nearest integer values.

```
[Visual Basic]
Public Shared Function Round( _
   ByVal value As SizeF _
) As Size
[C#]
public static Size Round(
   SizeF value
);
[C++]
public: static Size Round(
   SizeF value
);
[JScript]
public static function Round(
   value : SizeF
) : Size;
```

Parameters

value

The **SizeF** structure to convert.

Return Value

The **Size** structure this method converts to.

Requirements

Platforms: Windows 98, Windows NT 4.0, Windows Millennium Edition, Windows 2000, Windows XP Home Edition, Windows XP Professional, Windows Server 2003 family

Size.ToString Method

Creates a human-readable string that represents this **Size**.

```
[Visual Basic]
Overrides Public Function ToString() As String
[C#]
public override string ToString();
[C++]
public: String* ToString();
[JScript]
public override function ToString() : String;
```

Return Value

A string that represents this **Size**.

Requirements

Platforms: Windows 98, Windows NT 4.0, Windows Millennium Edition, Windows 2000,

Windows XP Home Edition, Windows XP Professional,
Windows Server 2003 family,
.NET Compact Framework - Windows CE .NET

Size.Truncate Method

Converts the specified **SizeF** structure to a **Size** structure by truncating the values of the **Size** structure to the next lower integer values.

```
[Visual Basic]
Public Shared Function Truncate( _
   ByVal value As SizeF _
) As Size
[C#]
public static Size Truncate(
   SizeF value
);
[C++]
public: static Size Truncate(
   SizeF value
);
[JScript]
public static function Truncate(
   value : SizeF
) : Size;
```

Parameters

value

The **SizeF** structure to convert.

Return Value

The **Size** structure this method converts to.

Requirements

Platforms: Windows 98, Windows NT 4.0,
Windows Millennium Edition, Windows 2000,
Windows XP Home Edition, Windows XP Professional,
Windows Server 2003 family

Size Addition Operator

Adds the width and height of one **Size** structure to the width and height of another **Size** structure.

```
[Visual Basic]
returnValue = Size.op_Addition(sz1, sz2)
[C#]
public static Size operator +(
   Size sz1,
   Size sz2
);
[C++]
public: static Size op_Addition(
   Size sz1,
   Size sz2
);
[JScript]
returnValue = sz1 + sz2;
```

[Visual Basic] In Visual Basic, you can use the operators defined by a type, but you cannot define your own.

[JScript] In JScript, you can use the operators defined by a type, but you cannot define your own.

Arguments [Visual Basic, JScript]

sz1

The first **Size** to add.

sz2

The second **Size** to add.

Parameters [C#, C++]

sz1

The first **Size** to add.

sz2

The second **Size** to add.

Return Value

A **Size** structure that is the result of the addition operation.

Requirements

Platforms: Windows 98, Windows NT 4.0,
Windows Millennium Edition, Windows 2000,
Windows XP Home Edition, Windows XP Professional,
Windows Server 2003 family

Size Equality Operator

Tests whether two **Size** structures are equal.

```
[Visual Basic]
returnValue = Size.op_Equality(sz1, sz2)
[C#]
public static bool operator ==(
   Size sz1,
   Size sz2
);
[C++]
public: static bool op_Equality(
   Size sz1,
   Size sz2
);
[JScript]
returnValue = sz1 == sz2;
```

[Visual Basic] In Visual Basic, you can use the operators defined by a type, but you cannot define your own.

[JScript] In JScript, you can use the operators defined by a type, but you cannot define your own.

Arguments [Visual Basic, JScript]

sz1

The **Size** structure on the left side of the equality operator.

sz2

The **Size** structure on the right of the equality operator.

Parameters [C#, C++]

sz1

The **Size** structure on the left side of the equality operator.

sz2

The **Size** structure on the right of the equality operator.

Return Value

This operator returns **true** if *sz1* and *sz2* have equal width and height; otherwise, **false**.

Requirements

Platforms: Windows 98, Windows NT 4.0,
Windows Millennium Edition, Windows 2000,
Windows XP Home Edition, Windows XP Professional,

Windows Server 2003 family,
.NET Compact Framework - Windows CE .NET

Size Inequality Operator

Tests whether two **Size** structures are different.

[Visual Basic]
```
returnValue = Size.op_Inequality(sz1, sz2)
```
[C#]
```
public static bool operator !=(
   Size sz1,
   Size sz2
);
```
[C++]
```
public: static bool op_Inequality(
   Size sz1,
   Size sz2
);
```
[JScript]
```
returnValue = sz1 != sz2;
```

[Visual Basic] In Visual Basic, you can use the operators defined by a type, but you cannot define your own.

[JScript] In JScript, you can use the operators defined by a type, but you cannot define your own.

Arguments [Visual Basic, JScript]

sz1
  The **Size** structure on the left of the inequality operator.

sz2
  The **Size** structure on the right of the inequality operator.

Parameters [C#, C++]

sz1
  The **Size** structure on the left of the inequality operator.

sz2
  The **Size** structure on the right of the inequality operator.

Return Value

This operator returns **true** if *sz1* and *sz2* differ either in width or height; **false** if *sz1* and *sz2* are equal.

Requirements

Platforms: Windows 98, Windows NT 4.0,
Windows Millennium Edition, Windows 2000,
Windows XP Home Edition, Windows XP Professional,
Windows Server 2003 family,
.NET Compact Framework - Windows CE .NET

Size Subtraction Operator

Subtracts the width and height of one **Size** structure from the width and height of another **Size** structure.

[Visual Basic]
```
returnValue = Size.op_Subtraction(sz1, sz2)
```
[C#]
```
public static Size operator -(
   Size sz1,
   Size sz2
);
```
[C++]
```
public: static Size op_Subtraction(
   Size sz1,
   Size sz2
);
```
[JScript]
```
returnValue = sz1 - sz2;
```

[Visual Basic] In Visual Basic, you can use the operators defined by a type, but you cannot define your own.

[JScript] In JScript, you can use the operators defined by a type, but you cannot define your own.

Arguments [Visual Basic, JScript]

sz1
  The **Size** structure on the left side of the subtraction operator.

sz2
  The **Size** structure on the right side of the subtraction operator.

Parameters [C#, C++]

sz1
  The **Size** structure on the left side of the subtraction operator.

sz2
  The **Size** structure on the right side of the subtraction operator.

Return Value

A **Size** structure that is the result of the subtraction operation.

Requirements

Platforms: Windows 98, Windows NT 4.0,
Windows Millennium Edition, Windows 2000,
Windows XP Home Edition, Windows XP Professional,
Windows Server 2003 family

Size to Point Conversion

Converts the specified **Size** to a **Point**.

[Visual Basic]
```
returnValue = Size.op_Explicit(size)
```
[C#]
```
public static explicit operator Point(
   Size size
);
```
[C++]
```
public: static Point op_Explicit();
```
[JScript]
```
returnValue = Point(size);
```

[Visual Basic] In Visual Basic, you can use the conversion operators defined by a type, but you cannot define your own.

[JScript] In JScript, you can use the conversion operators defined by a type, but you cannot define your own.

Arguments [Visual Basic, JScript]

size
  The **Size** to convert.

Parameters [C#]

size
  The **Size** to convert.

Requirements

Platforms: Windows 98, Windows NT 4.0,
Windows Millennium Edition, Windows 2000,
Windows XP Home Edition, Windows XP Professional,
Windows Server 2003 family

Size to SizeF Conversion

Converts the specified **Size** to a **SizeF**.

[Visual Basic]
```
returnValue = Size.op_Implicit(p)
```
[C#]
```
public static implicit operator SizeF(
   Size p
);
```
[C++]
```
public: static SizeF op_Implicit();
```
[JScript]
```
returnValue = p;
```

[Visual Basic] In Visual Basic, you can use the conversion operators defined by a type, but you cannot define your own.

[JScript] In JScript, you can use the conversion operators defined by a type, but you cannot define your own.

Arguments [Visual Basic, JScript]

p
  The Size to convert.

Parameters [C#]

p
  The Size to convert.

Return Value

The **SizeF** conversion of *p*.

Requirements

Platforms: Windows 98, Windows NT 4.0, Windows Millennium Edition, Windows 2000, Windows XP Home Edition, Windows XP Professional, Windows Server 2003 family

SizeConverter Class

The **SizeConverter** class is used to convert from one data type to another. Access this class through the **TypeDescriptor** object.

System.Object
  System.ComponentModel.TypeConverter
    System.Drawing.SizeConverter

[Visual Basic]
```
Public Class SizeConverter
   Inherits TypeConverter
```
[C#]
```
public class SizeConverter : TypeConverter
```
[C++]
```
public __gc class SizeConverter : public TypeConverter
```
[JScript]
```
public class SizeConverter extends TypeConverter
```

Thread Safety

Any public static (**Shared** in Visual Basic) members of this type are safe for multithreaded operations. Any instance members are not guaranteed to be thread safe.

Requirements

Namespace: System.Drawing

Platforms: Windows 98, Windows NT 4.0, Windows Millennium Edition, Windows 2000, Windows XP Home Edition, Windows XP Professional, Windows Server 2003 family

Assembly: System.Drawing (in System.Drawing.dll)

SizeConverter Constructor

Initializes a new **SizeConverter** object.

[Visual Basic]
```
Public Sub New()
```
[C#]
```
public SizeConverter();
```
[C++]
```
public: SizeConverter();
```
[JScript]
```
public function SizeConverter();
```

Requirements

Platforms: Windows 98, Windows NT 4.0, Windows Millennium Edition, Windows 2000, Windows XP Home Edition, Windows XP Professional, Windows Server 2003 family

SizeConverter.CanConvertFrom Method

Overload List

Determines whether this converter can convert an object in the specified source type to the native type of the converter.

[Visual Basic] **Overloads Overrides Public Function CanConvertFrom(ITypeDescriptorContext, Type) As Boolean**

[C#] **public override bool CanConvertFrom(ITypeDescriptorContext, Type);**

[C++] **public: bool CanConvertFrom(ITypeDescriptorContext*, Type*);**

[JScript] **public override function CanConvertFrom(ITypeDescriptorContext, Type) : Boolean;**

Inherited from **TypeConverter**.

[Visual Basic] **Overloads Public Function CanConvertFrom(Type) As Boolean**

[C#] **public bool CanConvertFrom(Type);**

[C++] **public: bool CanConvertFrom(Type*);**

[JScript] **public function CanConvertFrom(Type) : Boolean;**

SizeConverter.CanConvertFrom Method (ITypeDescriptorContext, Type)

Determines whether this converter can convert an object in the specified source type to the native type of the converter.

[Visual Basic]
```
Overrides Overloads Public Function CanConvertFrom( _
   ByVal context As ITypeDescriptorContext, _
   ByVal sourceType As Type _
) As Boolean
```
[C#]
```
public override bool CanConvertFrom(
   ITypeDescriptorContext context,
   Type sourceType
);
```
[C++]
```
public: bool CanConvertFrom(
   ITypeDescriptorContext* context,
   Type* sourceType
);
```
[JScript]
```
public override function CanConvertFrom(
   context : ITypeDescriptorContext,
   sourceType : Type
) : Boolean;
```

Parameters

context

A formatter context. This object can be used to get additional information about the environment this converter is being called from. This may be a null reference (**Nothing** in Visual Basic), so you should always check. Also, properties on the context object may also return a null reference (**Nothing**).

sourceType

The type you want to convert from.

Return Value

This method returns **true** if this object can perform the conversion.

Requirements

Platforms: Windows 98, Windows NT 4.0, Windows Millennium Edition, Windows 2000, Windows XP Home Edition, Windows XP Professional, Windows Server 2003 family

SizeConverter.CanConvertTo Method

Overload List

Gets a value indicating whether this converter can convert an object to the given destination type using the context.

[Visual Basic] **Overloads Overrides Public Function CanConvertTo(ITypeDescriptorContext, Type) As Boolean**

[C#] **public override bool CanConvertTo(ITypeDescriptor-Context, Type);**

[C++] **public: bool CanConvertTo(ITypeDescriptorContext*, Type*);**

[JScript] **public override function CanConvertTo(IType-DescriptorContext, Type) : Boolean;**

Inherited from **TypeConverter**.

[Visual Basic] **Overloads Public Function CanConvertTo(Type) As Boolean**

[C#] **public bool CanConvertTo(Type);**

[C++] **public: bool CanConvertTo(Type*);**

[JScript] **public function CanConvertTo(Type) : Boolean;**

SizeConverter.CanConvertTo Method (ITypeDescriptorContext, Type)

Gets a value indicating whether this converter can convert an object to the given destination type using the context.

```
[Visual Basic]
Overrides Overloads Public Function CanConvertTo( _
   ByVal context As ITypeDescriptorContext, _
   ByVal destinationType As Type _
) As Boolean
[C#]
public override bool CanConvertTo(
   ITypeDescriptorContext context,
   Type destinationType
);
[C++]
public: bool CanConvertTo(
   ITypeDescriptorContext* context,
   Type* destinationType
);
[JScript]
public override function CanConvertTo(
   context : ITypeDescriptorContext,
   destinationType : Type
) : Boolean;
```

Parameters

context

An **ITypeDescriptorContext** that provides a format context.

destinationType

A **Type** that represents the type you want to convert to.

Return Value

This method returns **true** if this converter can perform the conversion; otherwise, **false**.

Remarks

The *context* parameter can be used to extract additional information about the environment this converter is being invoked from. This can be a null reference (**Nothing** in Visual Basic), so always check. Also, properties on the context object can return a null reference (**Nothing**).

Requirements

Platforms: Windows 98, Windows NT 4.0, Windows Millennium Edition, Windows 2000, Windows XP Home Edition, Windows XP Professional, Windows Server 2003 family

SizeConverter.ConvertFrom Method

Overload List

Converts the specified object to the converter's native type.

[Visual Basic] **Overloads Overrides Public Function Convert-From(ITypeDescriptorContext, CultureInfo, Object) As Object**

[C#] **public override object ConvertFrom(ITypeDescriptor-Context, CultureInfo, object);**

[C++] **public: Object* ConvertFrom(ITypeDescriptor-Context*, CultureInfo*, Object*);**

[JScript] **public override function ConvertFrom(IType-DescriptorContext, CultureInfo, Object) : Object;**

Inherited from **TypeConverter**.

[Visual Basic] **Overloads Public Function ConvertFrom(Object) As Object**

[C#] **public object ConvertFrom(object);**

[C++] **public: Object* ConvertFrom(Object*);**

[JScript] **public function ConvertFrom(Object) : Object;**

SizeConverter.ConvertFrom Method (ITypeDescriptorContext, CultureInfo, Object)

Converts the specified object to the converter's native type.

```
[Visual Basic]
Overrides Overloads Public Function ConvertFrom( _
   ByVal context As ITypeDescriptorContext, _
   ByVal culture As CultureInfo, _
   ByVal value As Object _
) As Object
[C#]
public override object ConvertFrom(
   ITypeDescriptorContext context,
   CultureInfo culture,
   object value
);
[C++]
public: Object* ConvertFrom(
   ITypeDescriptorContext* context,
   CultureInfo* culture,
   Object* value
);
[JScript]
public override function ConvertFrom(
   context : ITypeDescriptorContext,
   culture : CultureInfo,
   value : Object
) : Object;
```

Parameters

context

A formatter context. This object can be used to get additional information about the environment this converter is being called from. This may be a null reference (**Nothing** in Visual Basic), so you should always check. Also, properties on the context object may also return a null reference (**Nothing**).

culture

An object that contains culture specific information, such as the language, calendar, and cultural conventions associated with a specific culture. It is based on the RFC 1766 standard.

value

The object to convert.

Return Value

The converted object. This will pass an exception if the conversion cannot be performed.

Requirements

Platforms: Windows 98, Windows NT 4.0, Windows Millennium Edition, Windows 2000, Windows XP Home Edition, Windows XP Professional, Windows Server 2003 family

SizeConverter.ConvertTo Method

Overload List

Converts the specified object to the specified type.

[Visual Basic] **Overloads Overrides Public Function ConvertTo(ITypeDescriptorContext, CultureInfo, Object, Type) As Object**

[C#] **public override object ConvertTo(ITypeDescriptor-Context, CultureInfo, object, Type);**

[C++] **public: Object* ConvertTo(ITypeDescriptorContext*, CultureInfo*, Object*, Type*);**

[JScript] **public override function ConvertTo(IType-DescriptorContext, CultureInfo, Object, Type) : Object;**

Inherited from **TypeConverter**.

[Visual Basic] **Overloads Public Function ConvertTo(Object, Type) As Object**

[C#] **public object ConvertTo(object, Type);**

[C++] **public: Object* ConvertTo(Object*, Type*);**

[JScript] **public function ConvertTo(Object, Type) : Object;**

SizeConverter.ConvertTo Method (ITypeDescriptorContext, CultureInfo, Object, Type)

Converts the specified object to the specified type.

```
[Visual Basic]
Overrides Overloads Public Function ConvertTo( _
   ByVal context As ITypeDescriptorContext, _
   ByVal culture As CultureInfo, _
   ByVal value As Object, _
   ByVal destinationType As Type _
) As Object
[C#]
public override object ConvertTo(
   ITypeDescriptorContext context,
   CultureInfo culture,
   object value,
   Type destinationType
);
[C++]
public: Object* ConvertTo(
   ITypeDescriptorContext* context,
   CultureInfo* culture,
   Object* value,
   Type* destinationType
);
[JScript]
public override function ConvertTo(
   context : ITypeDescriptorContext,
   culture : CultureInfo,
   value : Object,
   destinationType : Type
) : Object;
```

Parameters

context

A formatter context. This object can be used to get additional information about the environment this converter is being called from. This may be a null reference (**Nothing** in Visual Basic), so you should always check. Also, properties on the context object may also return a null reference (**Nothing**).

culture

An object that contains culture specific information, such as the language, calendar, and cultural conventions associated with a specific culture. It is based on the RFC 1766 standard.

value

The object to convert.

destinationType

The type to convert the object to.

Return Value

The converted object.

Remarks

The most common type conversion is to and from a string type. The default implementation calls the **ToString** method of the object if the object is valid and if the destination type is string. If this method cannot convert the specified object to the destination type, it passes a **NotSupportedException** exception.

Requirements

Platforms: Windows 98, Windows NT 4.0, Windows Millennium Edition, Windows 2000, Windows XP Home Edition, Windows XP Professional, Windows Server 2003 family

SizeConverter.CreateInstance Method

Overload List

Creates an object of this type by using a specified set of property values for the object. This is useful for creating nonchangeable objects that have changeable properties.

[Visual Basic] **Overloads Overrides Public Function CreateInstance(ITypeDescriptorContext, IDictionary) As Object**

[C#] **public override object CreateInstance(ITypeDescriptorContext, IDictionary);**

[C++] **public: Object* CreateInstance(ITypeDescriptorContext*, IDictionary*);**

[JScript] **public override function CreateInstance(ITypeDescriptorContext, IDictionary) : Object;**

Inherited from **TypeConverter**.

[Visual Basic] **Overloads Public Function CreateInstance(IDictionary) As Object**

[C#] **public object CreateInstance(IDictionary);**

[C++] **public: Object* CreateInstance(IDictionary*);**

[JScript] **public function CreateInstance(IDictionary) : Object;**

SizeConverter.CreateInstance Method (ITypeDescriptorContext, IDictionary)

Creates an object of this type by using a specified set of property values for the object. This is useful for creating nonchangeable objects that have changeable properties.

[Visual Basic]
```
Overrides Overloads Public Function CreateInstance( _
   ByVal context As ITypeDescriptorContext, _
   ByVal propertyValues As IDictionary _
) As Object
```
[C#]
```
public override object CreateInstance(
   ITypeDescriptorContext context,
   IDictionary propertyValues
);
```
[C++]
```
public: Object* CreateInstance(
   ITypeDescriptorContext* context,
   IDictionary* propertyValues
);
```
[JScript]
```
public override function CreateInstance(
   context : ITypeDescriptorContext,
   propertyValues : IDictionary
) : Object;
```

Parameters

context
A type descriptor through which additional context can be provided.

propertyValues
A dictionary of new property values. The dictionary contains a series of name-value pairs, one for each property returned from the **GetProperties** object.

Return Value

The newly created object, or null if the object could not be created. The default implementation returns null.

Requirements

Platforms: Windows 98, Windows NT 4.0, Windows Millennium Edition, Windows 2000, Windows XP Home Edition, Windows XP Professional, Windows Server 2003 family

SizeConverter.GetCreateInstanceSupported Method

Overload List

Determines whether changing a value on this object should require a call to the **CreateInstance** method to create a new value.

[Visual Basic] **Overloads Overrides Public Function GetCreateInstanceSupported(ITypeDescriptorContext) As Boolean**

[C#] **public override bool GetCreateInstanceSupported(ITypeDescriptorContext);**

[C++] **public: bool GetCreateInstanceSupported(ITypeDescriptorContext*);**

[JScript] **public override function GetCreateInstanceSupported(ITypeDescriptorContext) : Boolean;**

Inherited from **TypeConverter**.

[Visual Basic] **Overloads Public Function GetCreateInstanceSupported() As Boolean**

[C#] **public bool GetCreateInstanceSupported();**

[C++] **public: bool GetCreateInstanceSupported();**

[JScript] **public function GetCreateInstanceSupported() : Boolean;**

SizeConverter.GetCreateInstanceSupported Method (ITypeDescriptorContext)

Determines whether changing a value on this object should require a call to the **CreateInstance** method to create a new value.

[Visual Basic]
```
Overrides Overloads Public Function GetCreateInstanceSupported( _
   ByVal context As ITypeDescriptorContext _
) As Boolean
```
[C#]
```
public override bool GetCreateInstanceSupported(
   ITypeDescriptorContext context
);
```
[C++]
```
public: bool GetCreateInstanceSupported(
   ITypeDescriptorContext* context
);
```
[JScript]
```
public override function GetCreateInstanceSupported(
   context : ITypeDescriptorContext
) : Boolean;
```

Parameters

context
A type descriptor through which additional context can be provided.

Return Value

This method returns **true** if the **CreateInstance** object should be called when a change is made to one or more properties of this object.

Requirements

Platforms: Windows 98, Windows NT 4.0, Windows Millennium Edition, Windows 2000, Windows XP Home Edition, Windows XP Professional, Windows Server 2003 family

SizeConverter.GetProperties Method

Overload List

Retrieves the set of properties for this type. By default, a type does not have any properties to return. An easy implementation of this method can call the **TypeDescriptor.GetProperties** method for the correct data type.

[Visual Basic] **Overloads Overrides Public Function GetProperties(ITypeDescriptorContext, Object, Attribute()) As PropertyDescriptorCollection**

[C#] **public override PropertyDescriptorCollection GetProperties(ITypeDescriptorContext, object, Attribute[]);**

[C++] **public: PropertyDescriptorCollection* GetProperties(ITypeDescriptorContext*, Object*, Attribute[]);**

[JScript] **public override function GetProperties(ITypeDescriptorContext, Object, Attribute[]) : PropertyDescriptorCollection;**

Inherited from **TypeConverter**.

[Visual Basic] **Overloads Public Function GetProperties(Object) As PropertyDescriptorCollection**

[C#] **public PropertyDescriptorCollection GetProperties(object);**

[C++] **public: PropertyDescriptorCollection* GetProperties(Object*);**

[JScript] **public function GetProperties(Object) : PropertyDescriptorCollection;**

Inherited from **TypeConverter**.

[Visual Basic] **Overloads Public Function GetProperties(ITypeDescriptorContext, Object) As PropertyDescriptorCollection**

[C#] **public PropertyDescriptorCollection GetProperties(ITypeDescriptorContext, object);**

[C++] **public: PropertyDescriptorCollection* GetProperties(ITypeDescriptorContext*, Object*);**

[JScript] **public function GetProperties(ITypeDescriptorContext, Object) : PropertyDescriptorCollection;**

SizeConverter.GetProperties Method (ITypeDescriptorContext, Object, Attribute[])

Retrieves the set of properties for this type. By default, a type does not have any properties to return. An easy implementation of this method can call the **TypeDescriptor.GetProperties** method for the correct data type.

```
[Visual Basic]
Overrides Overloads Public Function GetProperties( _
   ByVal context As ITypeDescriptorContext, _
   ByVal value As Object, _
   ByVal attributes() As Attribute _
) As PropertyDescriptorCollection
[C#]
public override PropertyDescriptorCollection GetProperties(
   ITypeDescriptorContext context,
   object value,
   Attribute[] attributes
);
[C++]
public: PropertyDescriptorCollection* GetProperties(
   ITypeDescriptorContext* context,
   Object* value,
   Attribute* attributes[]
);
[JScript]
public override function GetProperties(
   context : ITypeDescriptorContext,
   value : Object,
   attributes : Attribute[]
) : PropertyDescriptorCollection;
```

Parameters

context
: A type descriptor through which additional context can be provided.

value
: The value of the object to get the properties for.

attributes
: An array of **MemberAttribute** objects that describe the properties.

Return Value

The set of properties that should be exposed for this data type. If no properties should be exposed, this may return a null reference (**Nothing** in Visual Basic). The default implementation always returns a null reference (**Nothing**).

Requirements

Platforms: Windows 98, Windows NT 4.0, Windows Millennium Edition, Windows 2000, Windows XP Home Edition, Windows XP Professional, Windows Server 2003 family

SizeConverter.GetPropertiesSupported Method

Overload List

Determines whether this object supports properties. By default, this is **false**.

[Visual Basic] **Overloads Overrides Public Function GetPropertiesSupported(ITypeDescriptorContext) As Boolean**

[C#] **public override bool GetPropertiesSupported(ITypeDescriptorContext);**

[C++] **public: bool GetPropertiesSupported(ITypeDescriptorContext*);**

[JScript] **public override function GetPropertiesSupported(ITypeDescriptorContext) : Boolean;**

Inherited from **TypeConverter**.

[Visual Basic] **Overloads Public Function GetPropertiesSupported() As Boolean**

[C#] **public bool GetPropertiesSupported();**

[C++] **public: bool GetPropertiesSupported();**

[JScript] **public function GetPropertiesSupported() : Boolean;**

SizeConverter.GetPropertiesSupported Method (ITypeDescriptorContext)

Determines whether this object supports properties. By default, this is **false**.

[Visual Basic]

```
Overrides Overloads Public Function GetPropertiesSupported( _
   ByVal context As ITypeDescriptorContext _
) As Boolean
```

[C#]

```
public override bool GetPropertiesSupported(
   ITypeDescriptorContext context
);
```

[C++]

```
public: bool GetPropertiesSupported(
   ITypeDescriptorContext* context
);
```

[JScript]

```
public override function GetPropertiesSupported(
   context : ITypeDescriptorContext
) : Boolean;
```

Parameters

context

A type descriptor through which additional context can be provided.

Return Value

This method returns **true** if the **GetProperties** object should be called to find the properties of this object.

Requirements

Platforms: Windows 98, Windows NT 4.0, Windows Millennium Edition, Windows 2000, Windows XP Home Edition, Windows XP Professional, Windows Server 2003 family

SizeF Structure

Stores an ordered pair of floating-point numbers, typically the width and height of a rectangle.

System.Object
 System.ValueType
  System.Drawing.SizeF

```
[Visual Basic]
<Serializable>
<ComVisible(True)>
Public Structure SizeF
[C#]
[Serializable]
[ComVisible(true)]
public struct SizeF
[C++]
[Serializable]
[ComVisible(true)]
public __value struct SizeF
```

[JScript] In JScript, you can use the structures in the .NET Framework, but you cannot define your own.

Thread Safety

Any public static (**Shared** in Visual Basic) members of this type are safe for multithreaded operations. Any instance members are not guaranteed to be thread safe.

Requirements

Namespace: System.Drawing

Platforms: Windows 98, Windows NT 4.0, Windows Millennium Edition, Windows 2000, Windows XP Home Edition, Windows XP Professional, Windows Server 2003 family, .NET Compact Framework - Windows CE .NET

Assembly: System.Drawing (in System.Drawing.dll)

SizeF Constructor

Initializes a new instance of the **SizeF** class from the specified existing **SizeF**.

Overload List

Initializes a new instance of the **SizeF** class from the specified **PointF**.

[Visual Basic] **Public Sub New(PointF)**

[C#] **public SizeF(PointF);**

[C++] **public: SizeF(PointF);**

[JScript] **public function SizeF(PointF);**

Initializes a new instance of the **SizeF** class from the specified existing **SizeF**.

[Visual Basic] **Public Sub New(SizeF)**

[C#] **public SizeF(SizeF);**

[C++] **public: SizeF(SizeF);**

[JScript] **public function SizeF(SizeF);**

Initializes a new instance of the **SizeF** class from the specified dimensions.

Supported by the .NET Compact Framework.

[Visual Basic] **Public Sub New(Single, Single)**

[C#] **public SizeF(float, float);**

[C++] **public: SizeF(float, float);**

[JScript] **public function SizeF(float, float);**

SizeF Constructor (PointF)

Initializes a new instance of the **SizeF** class from the specified **PointF**.

```
[Visual Basic]
Public Sub New( _
   ByVal pt As PointF _
)
[C#]
public SizeF(
   PointF pt
);
[C++]
public: SizeF(
   PointF pt
);
[JScript]
public function SizeF(
   pt : PointF
);
```

Parameters

pt
 The **PointF** from which to initialize this **SizeF**.

Requirements

Platforms: Windows 98, Windows NT 4.0, Windows Millennium Edition, Windows 2000, Windows XP Home Edition, Windows XP Professional, Windows Server 2003 family

SizeF Constructor (SizeF)

Initializes a new instance of the **SizeF** class from the specified existing **SizeF**.

```
[Visual Basic]
Public Sub New( _
   ByVal size As SizeF _
)
[C#]
public SizeF(
   SizeF size
);
[C++]
public: SizeF(
   SizeF size
);
[JScript]
public function SizeF(
   size : SizeF
);
```

Parameters

size
 The **SizeF** from which to create the new **SizeF**.

Requirements

Platforms: Windows 98, Windows NT 4.0,
Windows Millennium Edition, Windows 2000,
Windows XP Home Edition, Windows XP Professional,
Windows Server 2003 family

SizeF Constructor (Single, Single)

Initializes a new instance of the **SizeF** class from the specified dimensions.

[Visual Basic]
```
Public Sub New( _
   ByVal width As Single, _
   ByVal height As Single _
)
```
[C#]
```
public SizeF(
   float width,
   float height
);
```
[C++]
```
public: SizeF(
   float width,
   float height
);
```
[JScript]
```
public function SizeF(
   width : float,
   height : float
);
```

Parameters

width

The width component of the new **SizeF**.

height

The height component of the new **SizeF**.

Requirements

Platforms: Windows 98, Windows NT 4.0,
Windows Millennium Edition, Windows 2000,
Windows XP Home Edition, Windows XP Professional,
Windows Server 2003 family,
.NET Compact Framework - Windows CE .NET

SizeF.Empty Field

Initializes a new instance of the **SizeF** class.

[Visual Basic]
```
Public Shared ReadOnly Empty As SizeF
```
[C#]
```
public static readonly SizeF Empty;
```
[C++]
```
public: static SizeF Empty;
```
[JScript]
```
public static var Empty : SizeF;
```

Requirements

Platforms: Windows 98, Windows NT 4.0,
Windows Millennium Edition, Windows 2000,
Windows XP Home Edition, Windows XP Professional,
Windows Server 2003 family,
.NET Compact Framework - Windows CE .NET

SizeF.Height Property

Gets or sets the vertical component of this **SizeF**.

[Visual Basic]
```
Public Property Height As Single
```
[C#]
```
public float Height {get; set;}
```
[C++]
```
public: __property float get_Height();
public: __property void set_Height(float);
```
[JScript]
```
public function get Height() : float;
public function set Height(float);
```

Property Value

The vertical component of this **SizeF**.

Requirements

Platforms: Windows 98, Windows NT 4.0,
Windows Millennium Edition, Windows 2000,
Windows XP Home Edition, Windows XP Professional,
Windows Server 2003 family,
.NET Compact Framework - Windows CE .NET

SizeF.IsEmpty Property

Gets a value indicating whether this **SizeF** has zero width and height.

[Visual Basic]
```
Public ReadOnly Property IsEmpty As Boolean
```
[C#]
```
public bool IsEmpty {get;}
```
[C++]
```
public: __property bool get_IsEmpty();
```
[JScript]
```
public function get IsEmpty() : Boolean;
```

Property Value

This property returns **true** when this **SizeF** has both a width and height of zero; otherwise, **false**.

Requirements

Platforms: Windows 98, Windows NT 4.0,
Windows Millennium Edition, Windows 2000,
Windows XP Home Edition, Windows XP Professional,
Windows Server 2003 family,
.NET Compact Framework - Windows CE .NET

SizeF.Width Property

Gets or sets the horizontal component of this **SizeF**.

[Visual Basic]
```
Public Property Width As Single
```
[C#]
```
public float Width {get; set;}
```
[C++]
```
public: __property float get_Width();
public: __property void set_Width(float);
```
[JScript]
```
public function get Width() : float;
public function set Width(float);
```

Property Value

The horizontal component of this **SizeF**.

Requirements

Platforms: Windows 98, Windows NT 4.0, Windows Millennium Edition, Windows 2000, Windows XP Home Edition, Windows XP Professional, Windows Server 2003 family, .NET Compact Framework - Windows CE .NET

SizeF.Equals Method

Tests to see whether the specified object is a **SizeF** with the same dimensions as this **SizeF**.

[Visual Basic]
```
Overrides Public Function Equals( _
   ByVal obj As Object _
) As Boolean
```
[C#]
```
public override bool Equals(
   object obj
);
```
[C++]
```
public: bool Equals(
   Object* obj
);
```
[JScript]
```
public override function Equals(
   obj : Object
) : Boolean;
```

Parameters

obj
The **Object** to test.

Return Value

This method returns **true** if *obj* is a **SizeF** and has the same width and height as this **SizeF**; otherwise, **false**.

Requirements

Platforms: Windows 98, Windows NT 4.0, Windows Millennium Edition, Windows 2000, Windows XP Home Edition, Windows XP Professional, Windows Server 2003 family, .NET Compact Framework - Windows CE .NET

SizeF.GetHashCode Method

Returns a hash code for this **Size** structure.

[Visual Basic]
```
Overrides Public Function GetHashCode() As Integer
```
[C#]
```
public override int GetHashCode();
```
[C++]
```
public: int GetHashCode();
```
[JScript]
```
public override function GetHashCode() : int;
```

Return Value

An integer value that specifies a hash value for this **Size** structure.

Requirements

Platforms: Windows 98, Windows NT 4.0, Windows Millennium Edition, Windows 2000, Windows XP Home Edition, Windows XP Professional, Windows Server 2003 family, .NET Compact Framework - Windows CE .NET

SizeF.ToPointF Method

Converts a **SizeF** to a **PointF**.

[Visual Basic]
```
Public Function ToPointF() As PointF
```
[C#]
```
public PointF ToPointF();
```
[C++]
```
public: PointF ToPointF();
```
[JScript]
```
public function ToPointF() : PointF;
```

Requirements

Platforms: Windows 98, Windows NT 4.0, Windows Millennium Edition, Windows 2000, Windows XP Home Edition, Windows XP Professional, Windows Server 2003 family

SizeF.ToSize Method

Converts a **SizeF** to a **Size**.

[Visual Basic]
```
Public Function ToSize() As Size
```
[C#]
```
public Size ToSize();
```
[C++]
```
public: Size ToSize();
```
[JScript]
```
public function ToSize() : Size;
```

Return Value

Returns a **Size** structure.

Requirements

Platforms: Windows 98, Windows NT 4.0, Windows Millennium Edition, Windows 2000, Windows XP Home Edition, Windows XP Professional, Windows Server 2003 family, .NET Compact Framework - Windows CE .NET

SizeF.ToString Method

Creates a human-readable string that represents this **SizeF**.

[Visual Basic]
```
Overrides Public Function ToString() As String
```
[C#]
```
public override string ToString();
```
[C++]
```
public: String* ToString();
```
[JScript]
```
public override function ToString() : String;
```

Return Value

A string that represents this **SizeF**.

Requirements

Platforms: Windows 98, Windows NT 4.0, Windows Millennium Edition, Windows 2000, Windows XP Home Edition, Windows XP Professional, Windows Server 2003 family, .NET Compact Framework - Windows CE .NET

SizeF Addition Operator

Adds the width and height of one **SizeF** structure to the width and height of another **SizeF** structure.

```
[Visual Basic]
returnValue = SizeF.op_Addition(sz1, sz2)
[C#]
public static SizeF operator +(
   SizeF sz1,
   SizeF sz2
);
[C++]
public: static SizeF op_Addition(
   SizeF sz1,
   SizeF sz2
);
[JScript]
returnValue = sz1 + sz2;
```

[Visual Basic] In Visual Basic, you can use the operators defined by a type, but you cannot define your own.

[JScript] In JScript, you can use the operators defined by a type, but you cannot define your own.

Arguments [Visual Basic, JScript]

sz1

The first **SizeF** to add.

sz2

The second **SizeF** to add.

Parameters [C#, C++]

sz1

The first **SizeF** to add.

sz2

The second **SizeF** to add.

Return Value

A **Size** structure that is the result of the addition operation.

Requirements

Platforms: Windows 98, Windows NT 4.0, Windows Millennium Edition, Windows 2000, Windows XP Home Edition, Windows XP Professional, Windows Server 2003 family

SizeF Equality Operator

Tests whether two **SizeF** structures are equal.

```
[Visual Basic]
returnValue = SizeF.op_Equality(sz1, sz2)
[C#]
public static bool operator ==(
   SizeF sz1,
   SizeF sz2
);
[C++]
public: static bool op_Equality(
   SizeF sz1,
   SizeF sz2
);
[JScript]
returnValue = sz1 == sz2;
```

[Visual Basic] In Visual Basic, you can use the operators defined by a type, but you cannot define your own.

[JScript] In JScript, you can use the operators defined by a type, but you cannot define your own.

Arguments [Visual Basic, JScript]

sz1

The **SizeF** structure on the left side of the equality operator.

sz2

The **SizeF** structure on the right of the equality operator.

Parameters [C#, C++]

sz1

The **SizeF** structure on the left side of the equality operator.

sz2

The **SizeF** structure on the right of the equality operator.

Return Value

This operator returns **true** if *sz1* and *sz2* have equal width and height; otherwise, **false**.

Requirements

Platforms: Windows 98, Windows NT 4.0, Windows Millennium Edition, Windows 2000, Windows XP Home Edition, Windows XP Professional, Windows Server 2003 family, .NET Compact Framework - Windows CE .NET

SizeF Inequality Operator

Tests whether two **SizeF** structures are different.

```
[Visual Basic]
returnValue = SizeF.op_Inequality(sz1, sz2)
[C#]
public static bool operator !=(
   SizeF sz1,
   SizeF sz2
);
[C++]
public: static bool op_Inequality(
   SizeF sz1,
   SizeF sz2
);
[JScript]
returnValue = sz1 != sz2;
```

[Visual Basic] In Visual Basic, you can use the operators defined by a type, but you cannot define your own.

[JScript] In JScript, you can use the operators defined by a type, but you cannot define your own.

Arguments [Visual Basic, JScript]

sz1
The **SizeF** structure on the left of the inequality operator.

sz2
The **SizeF** structure on the right of the inequality operator.

Parameters [C#, C++]

sz1
The **SizeF** structure on the left of the inequality operator.

sz2
The **SizeF** structure on the right of the inequality operator.

Return Value

This operator returns **true** if *sz1* and *sz2* differ either in width or height; **false** if *sz1* and *sz2* are equal.

Requirements

Platforms: Windows 98, Windows NT 4.0,
Windows Millennium Edition, Windows 2000,
Windows XP Home Edition, Windows XP Professional,
Windows Server 2003 family,
.NET Compact Framework - Windows CE .NET

SizeF Subtraction Operator

Subtracts the width and height of one **SizeF** structure from the width and height of another **SizeF** structure.

```
[Visual Basic]
returnValue = SizeF.op_Subtraction(sz1, sz2)
[C#]
public static SizeF operator -(
   SizeF sz1,
   SizeF sz2
);
[C++]
public: static SizeF op_Subtraction(
   SizeF sz1,
   SizeF sz2
);
[JScript]
returnValue = sz1 - sz2;
```

[Visual Basic] In Visual Basic, you can use the operators defined by a type, but you cannot define your own.

[JScript] In JScript, you can use the operators defined by a type, but you cannot define your own.

Arguments [Visual Basic, JScript]

sz1
The **SizeF** on the left side of the subtraction operator.

sz2
The **SizeF** on the right side of the subtraction operator.

Parameters [C#, C++]

sz1
The **SizeF** on the left side of the subtraction operator.

sz2
The **SizeF** on the right side of the subtraction operator.

Return Value

A **SizeF** that is the result of the subtraction operation.

Requirements

Platforms: Windows 98, Windows NT 4.0,
Windows Millennium Edition, Windows 2000,
Windows XP Home Edition, Windows XP Professional,
Windows Server 2003 family

SizeF to PointF Conversion

Converts the specified **SizeF** to a **PointF**.

```
[Visual Basic]
returnValue = SizeF.op_Explicit(size)
[C#]
public static explicit operator PointF(
   SizeF size
);
[C++]
public: static PointF op_Explicit();
[JScript]
returnValue = PointF(size);
```

[Visual Basic] In Visual Basic, you can use the conversion operators defined by a type, but you cannot define your own.

[JScript] In JScript, you can use the conversion operators defined by a type, but you cannot define your own.

Arguments [Visual Basic, JScript]

size
The **SizeF** to convert.

Parameters [C#]

size
The **SizeF** to convert.

Requirements

Platforms: Windows 98, Windows NT 4.0,
Windows Millennium Edition, Windows 2000,
Windows XP Home Edition, Windows XP Professional,
Windows Server 2003 family

SolidBrush Class

Defines a brush of a single color. Brushes are used to fill graphics shapes, such as rectangles, ellipses, pies, polygons, and paths. This class cannot be inherited.

System.Object
  System.MarshalByRefObject
    System.Drawing.Brush
      System.Drawing.SolidBrush

[Visual Basic]
```
NotInheritable Public Class SolidBrush
   Inherits Brush
```
[C#]
```
public sealed class SolidBrush : Brush
```
[C++]
```
public __gc __sealed class SolidBrush : public Brush
```
[JScript]
```
public class SolidBrush extends Brush
```

Thread Safety

Any public static (**Shared** in Visual Basic) members of this type are safe for multithreaded operations. Any instance members are not guaranteed to be thread safe.

Remarks

This class inherits from the **Brush** class.

Requirements

Namespace: System.Drawing

Platforms: Windows 98, Windows NT 4.0, Windows Millennium Edition, Windows 2000, Windows XP Home Edition, Windows XP Professional, Windows Server 2003 family, .NET Compact Framework - Windows CE .NET

Assembly: System.Drawing (in System.Drawing.dll)

SolidBrush Constructor

Initializes a new **SolidBrush** object of the specified color.

[Visual Basic]
```
Public Sub New( _
   ByVal color As Color _
)
```
[C#]
```
public SolidBrush(
   Color color
);
```
[C++]
```
public: SolidBrush(
   Color color
);
```
[JScript]
```
public function SolidBrush(
   color : Color
);
```

Parameters

color
  A **Color** structure that represents the color of this brush.

Requirements

Platforms: Windows 98, Windows NT 4.0, Windows Millennium Edition, Windows 2000, Windows XP Home Edition, Windows XP Professional, Windows Server 2003 family, .NET Compact Framework - Windows CE .NET

SolidBrush.Color Property

Gets or sets the color of this **SolidBrush** object.

[Visual Basic]
```
Public Property Color As Color
```
[C#]
```
public Color Color {get; set;}
```
[C++]
```
public: __property Color get_Color();
public: __property void set_Color(Color);
```
[JScript]
```
public function get Color() : Color;
public function set Color(Color);
```

Property Value

A **Color** structure that represents the color of this brush.

Requirements

Platforms: Windows 98, Windows NT 4.0, Windows Millennium Edition, Windows 2000, Windows XP Home Edition, Windows XP Professional, Windows Server 2003 family, .NET Compact Framework - Windows CE .NET

SolidBrush.Clone Method

Creates an exact copy of this **SolidBrush** object.

[Visual Basic]
```
Overrides Public Function Clone() As Object Implements _
   ICloneable.Clone
```
[C#]
```
public override object Clone();
```
[C++]
```
public: Object* Clone();
```
[JScript]
```
public override function Clone() : Object;
```

Return Value

The **SolidBrush** object that this method creates.

Implements

ICloneable.Clone

Requirements

Platforms: Windows 98, Windows NT 4.0, Windows Millennium Edition, Windows 2000, Windows XP Home Edition, Windows XP Professional, Windows Server 2003 family

SolidBrush.Dispose Method

Overload List

This member supports the .NET Framework infrastructure and is not intended to be used directly from your code.

[Visual Basic] **Overloads Overrides Protected Sub Dispose(Boolean)**

[C#] **protected override void Dispose(bool);**

[C++] **protected: void Dispose(bool);**

[JScript] **protected override function Dispose(Boolean);**

Inherited from **Brush**.

Supported by the .NET Compact Framework.

[Visual Basic] **Overloads Public Overridable Sub Dispose() Implements IDisposable.Dispose**

[C#] **public virtual void Dispose();**

[C++] **public: virtual void Dispose();**

[JScript] **public function Dispose();**

SolidBrush.Dispose Method (Boolean)

This member supports the .NET Framework infrastructure and is not intended to be used directly from your code.

```
[Visual Basic]
Overrides Overloads Protected Sub Dispose( _
   ByVal disposing As Boolean _
)
[C#]
protected override void Dispose(
   bool disposing
);
[C++]
protected: void Dispose(
   bool disposing
);
[JScript]
protected override function Dispose(
   disposing : Boolean
);
```

StringAlignment Enumeration

Specifies the alignment of a text string relative to its layout rectangle.

[Visual Basic]
```
<Serializable>
Public Enum StringAlignment
```
[C#]
```
[Serializable]
public enum StringAlignment
```
[C++]
```
[Serializable]
__value public enum StringAlignment
```
[JScript]
```
public
   Serializable
enum StringAlignment
```

Members

Member name	Description
Center	Specifies that text is aligned in the center of the layout rectangle.
Far	Specifies that text is aligned far from the origin position of the layout rectangle. In a left-to-right layout, the far position is right. In a right-to-left layout, the far position is left.
Near	Specifies the text be aligned near the layout. In a left-to-right layout, the near position is left. In a right-to-left layout, the near position is right.

Requirements

Namespace: System.Drawing

Platforms: Windows 98, Windows NT 4.0, Windows Millennium Edition, Windows 2000, Windows XP Home Edition, Windows XP Professional, Windows Server 2003 family

Assembly: System.Drawing (in System.Drawing.dll)

StringDigitSubstitute Enumeration

The **StringDigitSubstitute** enumeration specifies how to substitute digits in a string according to a user's locale or language.

[Visual Basic]
```
<Serializable>
Public Enum StringDigitSubstitute
```
[C#]
```
[Serializable]
public enum StringDigitSubstitute
```
[C++]
```
[Serializable]
__value public enum StringDigitSubstitute
```
[JScript]
```
public
   Serializable
enum StringDigitSubstitute
```

Members

Member name	Description
National	Specifies substitution digits that correspond with the official national language of the user's locale.
None	Specifies to disable substitutions.
Traditional	Specifies substitution digits that correspond with the user's native script or language, which may be different from the official national language of the user's locale.
User	Specifies a user-defined substitution scheme.

Requirements

Namespace: System.Drawing

Platforms: Windows 98, Windows NT 4.0, Windows Millennium Edition, Windows 2000, Windows XP Home Edition, Windows XP Professional, Windows Server 2003 family

Assembly: System.Drawing (in System.Drawing.dll)

StringFormat Class

Encapsulates text layout information (such as alignment and line spacing), display manipulations (such as ellipsis insertion and national digit substitution) and OpenType features. This class cannot be inherited.

System.Object
  System.MarshalByRefObject
    System.Drawing.StringFormat

[Visual Basic]
```
NotInheritable Public Class StringFormat
   Inherits MarshalByRefObject
   Implements ICloneable, IDisposable
```
[C#]
```
public sealed class StringFormat : MarshalByRefObject, ICloneable,
   IDisposable
```
[C++]
```
public __gc __sealed class StringFormat : public
   MarshalByRefObject, ICloneable, IDisposable
```
[JScript]
```
public class StringFormat extends MarshalByRefObject implements
   ICloneable, IDisposable
```

Thread Safety

Any public static (**Shared** in Visual Basic) members of this type are safe for multithreaded operations. Any instance members are not guaranteed to be thread safe.

Remarks

Many common formats are provided through the **StringFormatFlags** enumeration. **StringFormat** objects can be changed.

Requirements

Namespace: System.Drawing

Platforms: Windows 98, Windows NT 4.0, Windows Millennium Edition, Windows 2000, Windows XP Home Edition, Windows XP Professional, Windows Server 2003 family

Assembly: System.Drawing (in System.Drawing.dll)

StringFormat Constructor

Initializes a new **StringFormat** object.

Overload List

Initializes a new **StringFormat** object.

[Visual Basic] **Public Sub New()**

[C#] **public StringFormat();**

[C++] **public: StringFormat();**

[JScript] **public function StringFormat();**

Initializes a new **StringFormat** object from the specified existing **StringFormat** object.

[Visual Basic] **Public Sub New(StringFormat)**

[C#] **public StringFormat(StringFormat);**

[C++] **public: StringFormat(StringFormat*);**

[JScript] **public function StringFormat(StringFormat);**

Initializes a new **StringFormat** object with the specified **StringFormatFlags** enumeration.

[Visual Basic] **Public Sub New(StringFormatFlags)**

[C#] **public StringFormat(StringFormatFlags);**

[C++] **public: StringFormat(StringFormatFlags);**

[JScript] **public function StringFormat(StringFormatFlags);**

Initializes a new **StringFormat** object with the specified **StringFormatFlags** enumeration and language.

[Visual Basic] **Public Sub New(StringFormatFlags, Integer)**

[C#] **public StringFormat(StringFormatFlags, int);**

[C++] **public: StringFormat(StringFormatFlags, int);**

[JScript] **public function StringFormat(StringFormatFlags, int);**

StringFormat Constructor ()

Initializes a new **StringFormat** object.

[Visual Basic]
```
Public Sub New()
```
[C#]
```
public StringFormat();
```
[C++]
```
public: StringFormat();
```
[JScript]
```
public function StringFormat();
```

Requirements

Platforms: Windows 98, Windows NT 4.0, Windows Millennium Edition, Windows 2000, Windows XP Home Edition, Windows XP Professional, Windows Server 2003 family

StringFormat Constructor (StringFormat)

Initializes a new **StringFormat** object from the specified existing **StringFormat** object.

[Visual Basic]
```
Public Sub New( _
   ByVal format As StringFormat _
)
```
[C#]
```
public StringFormat(
   StringFormat format
);
```
[C++]
```
public: StringFormat(
   StringFormat* format
);
```
[JScript]
```
public function StringFormat(
   format : StringFormat
);
```

Parameters

format
  The **StringFormat** object from which to initialize the new **StringFormat** object.

Requirements

Platforms: Windows 98, Windows NT 4.0, Windows Millennium Edition, Windows 2000, Windows XP Home Edition, Windows XP Professional, Windows Server 2003 family

StringFormat Constructor (StringFormatFlags)

Initializes a new **StringFormat** object with the specified **StringFormatFlags** enumeration.

```
[Visual Basic]
Public Sub New( _
   ByVal options As StringFormatFlags _
)
[C#]
public StringFormat(
   StringFormatFlags options
);
[C++]
public: StringFormat(
   StringFormatFlags options
);
[JScript]
public function StringFormat(
   options : StringFormatFlags
);
```

Parameters

options
The **StringFormatFlags** enumeration for the new **StringFormat** object.

Requirements

Platforms: Windows 98, Windows NT 4.0, Windows Millennium Edition, Windows 2000, Windows XP Home Edition, Windows XP Professional, Windows Server 2003 family

StringFormat Constructor (StringFormatFlags, Int32)

Initializes a new **StringFormat** object with the specified **StringFormatFlags** enumeration and language.

```
[Visual Basic]
Public Sub New( _
   ByVal options As StringFormatFlags, _
   ByVal language As Integer _
)
[C#]
public StringFormat(
   StringFormatFlags options,
   int language
);
[C++]
public: StringFormat(
   StringFormatFlags options,
   int language
);
[JScript]
public function StringFormat(
   options : StringFormatFlags,
   language : int
);
```

Parameters

options
The **StringFormatFlags** enumeration for the new **StringFormat** object.

language
A value that indicates the language of the text.

Requirements

Platforms: Windows 98, Windows NT 4.0, Windows Millennium Edition, Windows 2000, Windows XP Home Edition, Windows XP Professional, Windows Server 2003 family

StringFormat.Alignment Property

Gets or sets text alignment information.

```
[Visual Basic]
Public Property Alignment As StringAlignment
[C#]
public StringAlignment Alignment {get; set;}
[C++]
public: __property StringAlignment get_Alignment();
public: __property void set_Alignment(StringAlignment);
[JScript]
public function get Alignment() : StringAlignment;
public function set Alignment(StringAlignment);
```

Property Value

A **StringAlignment** enumeration that specifies text alignment information.

Requirements

Platforms: Windows 98, Windows NT 4.0, Windows Millennium Edition, Windows 2000, Windows XP Home Edition, Windows XP Professional, Windows Server 2003 family

StringFormat.DigitSubstitutionLanguage Property

Gets or sets the language that is used when local digits are substituted for western digits.

```
[Visual Basic]
Public ReadOnly Property DigitSubstitutionLanguage As Integer
[C#]
public int DigitSubstitutionLanguage {get;}
[C++]
public: __property int get_DigitSubstitutionLanguage();
[JScript]
public function get DigitSubstitutionLanguage() : int;
```

Property Value

A National Language Support (NLS) language identifier that identifies the language that will be used when local digits are substituted for western digits. You can pass the **LCID** property of a **CultureInfo** object as the NLS language identifier. For example, suppose you create a **CultureInfo** object by passing the string "ar-EG" to a **CultureInfo** constructor. If you pass the LCID property of that **CultureInfo** object along with StringDigitSubstitue.Traditional to the **SetDigitSubstitution** method, then Arabic-Indic digits will be substituted for western digits at display time.

Requirements

Platforms: Windows 98, Windows NT 4.0, Windows Millennium Edition, Windows 2000, Windows XP Home Edition, Windows XP Professional, Windows Server 2003 family

StringFormat.DigitSubstitutionMethod Property

Gets or sets the method to be used for digit substitution.

[Visual Basic]
```
Public ReadOnly Property DigitSubstitutionMethod As _
   StringDigitSubstitute
```
[C#]
```
public StringDigitSubstitute DigitSubstitutionMethod {get;}
```
[C++]
```
public: __property StringDigitSubstitute
   get_DigitSubstitutionMethod();
```
[JScript]
```
public function get DigitSubstitutionMethod() :
   StringDigitSubstitute;
```

Property Value

Holds a **StringDigitSubstitute** enumeration value that specifies how to substitute characters in a string that cannot be displayed because they are not supported by the current font.

Requirements

Platforms: Windows 98, Windows NT 4.0, Windows Millennium Edition, Windows 2000, Windows XP Home Edition, Windows XP Professional, Windows Server 2003 family

StringFormat.FormatFlags Property

Gets or sets a **StringFormatFlags** enumeration that contains formatting information.

[Visual Basic]
```
Public Property FormatFlags As StringFormatFlags
```
[C#]
```
public StringFormatFlags FormatFlags {get; set;}
```
[C++]
```
public: __property StringFormatFlags get_FormatFlags();
public: __property void set_FormatFlags(StringFormatFlags);
```
[JScript]
```
public function get FormatFlags() : StringFormatFlags;
public function set FormatFlags(StringFormatFlags);
```

Property Value

A **StringFormatFlags** enumeration that contains formatting information.

Requirements

Platforms: Windows 98, Windows NT 4.0, Windows Millennium Edition, Windows 2000, Windows XP Home Edition, Windows XP Professional, Windows Server 2003 family

StringFormat.GenericDefault Property

Gets a generic default **StringFormat** object.

[Visual Basic]
```
Public Shared ReadOnly Property GenericDefault As StringFormat
```
[C#]
```
public static StringFormat GenericDefault {get;}
```
[C++]
```
public: __property static StringFormat* get_GenericDefault();
```
[JScript]
```
public static function get GenericDefault() : StringFormat;
```

Property Value

The generic default **StringFormat** object.

Requirements

Platforms: Windows 98, Windows NT 4.0, Windows Millennium Edition, Windows 2000, Windows XP Home Edition, Windows XP Professional, Windows Server 2003 family

StringFormat.GenericTypographic Property

Gets a generic typographic **StringFormat** object.

[Visual Basic]
```
Public Shared ReadOnly Property GenericTypographic As StringFormat
```
[C#]
```
public static StringFormat GenericTypographic {get;}
```
[C++]
```
public: __property static StringFormat* get_GenericTypographic();
```
[JScript]
```
public static function get GenericTypographic() : StringFormat;
```

Property Value

A generic typographic **StringFormat** object.

Requirements

Platforms: Windows 98, Windows NT 4.0, Windows Millennium Edition, Windows 2000, Windows XP Home Edition, Windows XP Professional, Windows Server 2003 family

StringFormat.HotkeyPrefix Property

Gets or sets the **HotkeyPrefix** object for this **StringFormat** object.

[Visual Basic]
```
Public Property HotkeyPrefix As HotkeyPrefix
```
[C#]
```
public HotkeyPrefix HotkeyPrefix {get; set;}
```
[C++]
```
public: __property HotkeyPrefix get_HotkeyPrefix();
public: __property void set_HotkeyPrefix(HotkeyPrefix);
```
[JScript]
```
public function get HotkeyPrefix() : HotkeyPrefix;
public function set HotkeyPrefix(HotkeyPrefix);
```

Property Value

The **HotkeyPrefix** object for this **StringFormat** object.

Remarks

In a graphical user interface, a hot key is the underlined letter in a word (usually combined with another key, such as the Alt key) that you can press on the keyboard to activate the functionality that the word represents.

Requirements

Platforms: Windows 98, Windows NT 4.0, Windows Millennium Edition, Windows 2000, Windows XP Home Edition, Windows XP Professional, Windows Server 2003 family

StringFormat.LineAlignment Property

Gets or sets the line alignment.

```
[Visual Basic]
Public Property LineAlignment As StringAlignment
[C#]
public StringAlignment LineAlignment {get; set;}
[C++]
public: __property StringAlignment get_LineAlignment();
public: __property void set_LineAlignment(StringAlignment);
[JScript]
public function get LineAlignment() : StringAlignment;
public function set LineAlignment(StringAlignment);
```

Property Value

A **StringAlignment** enumeration that represents the line alignment.

Requirements

Platforms: Windows 98, Windows NT 4.0, Windows Millennium Edition, Windows 2000, Windows XP Home Edition, Windows XP Professional, Windows Server 2003 family

StringFormat.Trimming Property

Gets or sets the **StringTrimming** enumeration for this **StringFormat** object.

```
[Visual Basic]
Public Property Trimming As StringTrimming
[C#]
public StringTrimming Trimming {get; set;}
[C++]
public: __property StringTrimming get_Trimming();
public: __property void set_Trimming(StringTrimming);
[JScript]
public function get Trimming() : StringTrimming;
public function set Trimming(StringTrimming);
```

Property Value

A **StringTrimming** enumeration that indicates how text drawn with this **StringFormat** object is trimmed when it exceeds the edges of the layout rectangle.

Requirements

Platforms: Windows 98, Windows NT 4.0, Windows Millennium Edition, Windows 2000, Windows XP Home Edition, Windows XP Professional, Windows Server 2003 family

StringFormat.Clone Method

Creates an exact copy of this **StringFormat** object.

```
[Visual Basic]
Public Overridable Function Clone() As Object Implements _
   ICloneable.Clone
[C#]
public virtual object Clone();
[C++]
public: virtual Object* Clone();
[JScript]
public function Clone() : Object;
```

Return Value

The **StringFormat** object this method creates.

Implements

ICloneable.Clone

Requirements

Platforms: Windows 98, Windows NT 4.0, Windows Millennium Edition, Windows 2000, Windows XP Home Edition, Windows XP Professional, Windows Server 2003 family

StringFormat.Dispose Method

Releases all resources used by this **StringFormat** object.

```
[Visual Basic]
Public Overridable Sub Dispose() Implements IDisposable.Dispose
[C#]
public virtual void Dispose();
[C++]
public: virtual void Dispose();
[JScript]
public function Dispose();
```

Return Value

This method does not return a value.

Implements

IDisposable.Dispose

Remarks

Calling **Dispose** allows the resources used by this **StringFormat** object to be reallocated for other purposes.

Requirements

Platforms: Windows 98, Windows NT 4.0, Windows Millennium Edition, Windows 2000, Windows XP Home Edition, Windows XP Professional, Windows Server 2003 family

StringFormat.Finalize Method

Cleans up Windows resources for this **StringFormat**.

[C#] In C#, finalizers are expressed using destructor syntax.

[C++] In C++, finalizers are expressed using destructor syntax.

```
[Visual Basic]
Overrides Protected Sub Finalize()
[C#]
~StringFormat();
[C++]
~StringFormat();
[JScript]
protected override function Finalize();
```

Requirements

Platforms: Windows 98, Windows NT 4.0, Windows Millennium Edition, Windows 2000, Windows XP Home Edition, Windows XP Professional, Windows Server 2003 family

StringFormat.GetTabStops Method

Gets the tab stops for this **StringFormat** object.

[Visual Basic]
```
Public Function GetTabStops( _
   <Out()> ByRef firstTabOffset As Single _
) As Single()
```
[C#]
```
public float[] GetTabStops(
   out float firstTabOffset
);
```
[C++]
```
public: float GetTabStops(
   [
   Out
] float* firstTabOffset
) __gc[];
```
[JScript]
```
public function GetTabStops(
   firstTabOffset : float
) : float[];
```

Parameters

firstTabOffset
: The number of spaces between the beginning of a text line and the first tab stop.

Return Value

An array of distances (in number of spaces) between tab stops.

Example

[Visual Basic, C#] The following example is designed for use with Windows Forms, and it requires **PaintEventArgs** *e*, which is a parameter of the **Paint** event handler. The code performs the following actions:

- Sets the tab stops of the **StringFormat**.
- Draws the string and the layout rectangle. Note that the string contains tabs. The tab settings of the **StringFormat** specify the offsets of the tabbed text.
- Gets the tab stops and uses or inspects the values.

[Visual Basic]
```
Public Sub GetSetTabStopsExample(e As PaintEventArgs)
Dim g As Graphics = e.Graphics
' Tools used for drawing, painting.
Dim redPen As New Pen(Color.FromArgb(255, 255, 0, 0))
Dim blueBrush As New SolidBrush(Color.FromArgb(255, 0, 0, 255))
' Layout and format for text.
Dim myFont As New Font("Times New Roman", 12)
Dim myStringFormat As New StringFormat()
Dim enclosingRectangle As New Rectangle(20, 20, 500, 100)
Dim tabStops As Single() =  {150F, 100F, 100F}
' Text with tabbed columns.
Dim myString As String = "Name" & ControlChars.Tab & "Tab 1" _
& ControlChars.Tab & "Tab 2" & ControlChars.Tab & "Tab 3" _
& ControlChars.Cr & "George Brown" & ControlChars.Tab & "One" _
& ControlChars.Tab & "Two" & ControlChars.Tab & "Three"
' Set the tab stops, paint the text specified by myString,the
'  and draw rectangle that encloses the text.
myStringFormat.SetTabStops(0F, tabStops)
g.DrawString(myString, myFont, blueBrush, _
RectangleF.op_implicit(enclosingRectangle), myStringFormat)
g.DrawRectangle(redPen, enclosingRectangle)
' Get the tab stops.
Dim firstTabOffset As Single
Dim tabStopsObtained As Single() = _
myStringFormat.GetTabStops(firstTabOffset)
Dim j As Integer
For j = 0 To tabStopsObtained.Length - 1
' Inspect or use the value in tabStopsObtained[j].
Console.WriteLine(ControlChars.Cr & "  Tab stop {0} = {1}", _
j, tabStopsObtained(j))
Next j
End Sub
```

[C#]
```
public void GetSetTabStopsExample(PaintEventArgs e)
{
Graphics      g = e.Graphics;
// Tools used for drawing, painting.
Pen           redPen = new Pen(Color.FromArgb(255, 255, 0, 0));
SolidBrush    blueBrush = new SolidBrush(Color.FromArgb(255,     ↵
0, 0, 255));
// Layout and format for text.
Font          myFont = new Font("Times New Roman", 12);
StringFormat myStringFormat = new StringFormat();
Rectangle     enclosingRectangle = new Rectangle(20, 20, 500, 100);
float[]       tabStops = {150.0f, 100.0f, 100.0f};
// Text with tabbed columns.
string        myString =
"Name\tTab 1\tTab 2\tTab 3\nGeorge Brown\tOne\tTwo\tThree";
// Set the tab stops, paint the text specified by myString, and     ↵
 draw the
// rectangle that encloses the text.
myStringFormat.SetTabStops(0.0f, tabStops);
g.DrawString(myString, myFont, blueBrush,
enclosingRectangle, myStringFormat);
g.DrawRectangle(redPen, enclosingRectangle);
// Get the tab stops.
float   firstTabOffset;
float[] tabStopsObtained = myStringFormat.GetTabStops(out     ↵
firstTabOffset);
for(int j = 0; j < tabStopsObtained.Length; j++)
{
// Inspect or use the value in tabStopsObtained[j].
Console.WriteLine("\n  Tab stop {0} = {1}", j, tabStopsObtained[j]);
}
}
```

Requirements

Platforms: Windows 98, Windows NT 4.0, Windows Millennium Edition, Windows 2000, Windows XP Home Edition, Windows XP Professional, Windows Server 2003 family

StringFormat.SetDigitSubstitution Method

Specifies the language and method to be used when local digits are substituted for western digits.

[Visual Basic]
```
Public Sub SetDigitSubstitution( _
   ByVal language As Integer, _
   ByVal substitute As StringDigitSubstitute _
)
```
[C#]
```
public void SetDigitSubstitution(
   int language,
   StringDigitSubstitute substitute
);
```
[C++]
```
public: void SetDigitSubstitution(
   int language,
   StringDigitSubstitute substitute
);
```

```
[JScript]
public function SetDigitSubstitution(
   language : int,
   substitute : StringDigitSubstitute
);
```

Parameters

language

A National Language Support (NLS) language identifier that identifies the language that will be used when local digits are substituted for western digits. You can pass the **LCID** property of a **CultureInfo** object as the NLS language identifier. For example, suppose you create a **CultureInfo** object by passing the string "ar-EG" to a **CultureInfo** constructor. If you pass the LCID property of that **CultureInfo** object along with String-DigitSubstitue.Traditional to the **SetDigitSubstitution** method, then Arabic-Indic digits will be substituted for western digits at display time.

substitute

An element of the **StringDigitSubstitute** enumeration that specifies how digits are displayed.

Return Value

This method does not return a value.

Example

[Visual Basic, C#] The following example is designed for use with Windows Forms, and it requires **PaintEventArgs** *e*, which is a parameter of the **Paint** event handler. The code performs the following actions:

- Sets, for the **StringFormat**, the language to be used and the substitution method to be used.
- Draws the string.
- Repeats the above two steps for two different languages (Arabic and Thai).

[Visual Basic, C#] The National substitution method and Traditional substitution method are demonstrated for each of the two languages. The National method displays digits according to the official national language of the user's locale. The Traditional method displays digits according to the user's native script or language, which may be different from the official national language.

```
[Visual Basic]
Public Sub SetDigitSubExample(e As PaintEventArgs)
Dim g As Graphics = e.Graphics
Dim blueBrush As New SolidBrush(Color.FromArgb(255, 0, 0, 255))
Dim myFont As New Font("Courier New", 12)
Dim myStringFormat As New StringFormat()
Dim myString As String = "0 1 2 3 4 5 6 7 8 9"
' Arabic (0x0C01) digits.
' Use National substitution method.
myStringFormat.SetDigitSubstitution(&HC01, _
StringDigitSubstitute.National)
g.DrawString("Arabic:" & ControlChars.Cr & _
"Method of substitution = National:     " & myString, _
myFont, blueBrush, New PointF(10F, 20F), myStringFormat)
' Use Traditional substitution method.
myStringFormat.SetDigitSubstitution(&HC01, _
StringDigitSubstitute.Traditional)
g.DrawString("Method of substitution = Traditional:  " _
& myString, myFont, blueBrush, New PointF(10F, 55F), _
myStringFormat)
' Thai (0x041E) digits.
' Use National substitution method.
myStringFormat.SetDigitSubstitution(&H41E, _
StringDigitSubstitute.National)
g.DrawString("Thai:" & ControlChars.Cr & _
"Method of substitution = National:     " & myString, _
myFont, blueBrush, New PointF(10F, 85F), myStringFormat)
' Use Traditional substitution method.
myStringFormat.SetDigitSubstitution(&H41E, _
StringDigitSubstitute.Traditional)
g.DrawString("Method of substitution = Traditional:  " _
& myString, myFont, blueBrush, New PointF(10F, 120F), _
myStringFormat)
End Sub
```

```
[C#]
public void SetDigitSubExample(PaintEventArgs e)
{
Graphics      g = e.Graphics;
SolidBrush    blueBrush = new SolidBrush(Color.FromArgb(255,
0, 0, 255));
Font          myFont = new Font("Courier New", 12);
StringFormat myStringFormat = new StringFormat();
string        myString = "0 1 2 3 4 5 6 7 8 9";
//
// Arabic (0x0C01) digits.
//
// Use National substitution method.
myStringFormat.SetDigitSubstitution(0x0C01,
StringDigitSubstitute.National);
g.DrawString(
"Arabic:\nMethod of substitution = National:     " + myString,
myFont, blueBrush, new PointF(10.0f, 20.0f), myStringFormat);
// Use Traditional substitution method.
myStringFormat.SetDigitSubstitution(0x0C01,
StringDigitSubstitute.Traditional);
g.DrawString(
"Method of substitution = Traditional:  " + myString,
myFont, blueBrush, new PointF(10.0f, 55.0f), myStringFormat);
//
// Thai (0x041E) digits.
//
// Use National substitution method.
myStringFormat.SetDigitSubstitution(0x041E,
StringDigitSubstitute.National);
g.DrawString(
"Thai:\nMethod of substitution = National:     " + myString,
myFont, blueBrush, new PointF(10.0f, 85.0f), myStringFormat);
// Use Traditional substitution method.
myStringFormat.SetDigitSubstitution(0x041E,
StringDigitSubstitute.Traditional);
g.DrawString(
"Method of substitution = Traditional:  " + myString,
myFont, blueBrush, new PointF(10.0f, 120.0f), myStringFormat);
}
```

Requirements

Platforms: Windows 98, Windows NT 4.0, Windows Millennium Edition, Windows 2000, Windows XP Home Edition, Windows XP Professional, Windows Server 2003 family

StringFormat.SetMeasurableCharacterRanges Method

Specifies an array of **CharacterRange** structures that represent the ranges of characters measured by a call to the **Graphics.MeasureCharacterRanges** method.

```
[Visual Basic]
Public Sub SetMeasurableCharacterRanges( _
   ByVal ranges() As CharacterRange _
)
[C#]
public void SetMeasurableCharacterRanges(
   CharacterRange[] ranges
);
```

[C++]
```
public: void SetMeasurableCharacterRanges(
   CharacterRange ranges[]
);
```
[JScript]
```
public function SetMeasurableCharacterRanges(
   ranges : CharacterRange[]
);
```

Parameters

ranges

An array of **CharacterRange** structures that specifies the ranges of characters measured by a call to the **Graphics.MeasureCharacterRanges** method.

Return Value

This method does not return a value.

Example

[Visual Basic, C#] The following example is designed for use with Windows Forms, and it requires **PaintEventArgs** *e*, which is a parameter of the **Paint** event handler. The code performs the following actions:

- Sets the character ranges of the **StringFormat**.
- Measures the character ranges for a given string and layout rectangle.
- Draws the string and layout rectangle.
- Paints the regions. Each **Region** specifies an area that is occupied by a range of characters. The values in the regions are set when the character ranges are measured by the **Graphics.MeasureCharacterRanges** method.
- Repeats the first four steps, but includes trailing spaces in the measurement of each character range.
- Clears the format flags of the **StringFormat** so that trailing spaces are not included in the measurement of each character range.
- Repeats the first four steps, but uses a different layout rectangle just to demonstrate that the layout rectangle affects the measurements of the character ranges. The size of the font will also affect the measurement.

[Visual Basic]
```
Public Sub SetMeasCharRangesExample(e As PaintEventArgs)
Dim g As Graphics = e.Graphics
Dim redBrush As New SolidBrush(Color.FromArgb(50, 255, 0, 0))
' Layout rectangles, font, and string format used for
' displaying string.
Dim layoutRectA As New Rectangle(20, 20, 165, 80)
Dim layoutRectB As New Rectangle(20, 110, 165, 80)
Dim layoutRectC As New Rectangle(20, 200, 240, 80)
Dim tnrFont As New Font("Times New Roman", 16)
Dim strFormat As New StringFormat()
' Ranges of character positions within a string.
Dim charRanges As CharacterRange() =  {New CharacterRange(3, 5), _
New CharacterRange(15, 2), New CharacterRange(30, 15)}
' Each region specifies the area occupied by the characters within
' a range of positions. The values are obtained by using a method
' that measures the character ranges.
Dim charRegions(charRanges.Length) As [Region]
' String to be displayed.
Dim str As String = _
"The quick, brown fox easily jumps over the lazy dog."
' Set the char ranges for the string format.
strFormat.SetMeasurableCharacterRanges(charRanges)
Dim i As Byte ' loop counter (unsigned 8-bit integer)
' Measure the char ranges for a given string and layout rectangle.
' Each area occupied by the characters in a range is stored as a
' region. then draw the string and layout rectangle and paint the
' regions.
charRegions = g.MeasureCharacterRanges(str, tnrFont, _
RectangleF.op_implicit(layoutRectA), strFormat)
g.DrawString(str, tnrFont, Brushes.Blue, _
RectangleF.op_implicit(layoutRectA), strFormat)
g.DrawRectangle(Pens.Black, layoutRectA)
For i = 0 To charRegions.Length - 1
g.FillRegion(redBrush, charRegions(i)) ' paint the regions
Next i
' Repeat the above steps, but include trailing spaces in the char
' range measurement by setting the appropriate string format flag.
strFormat.FormatFlags = StringFormatFlags.MeasureTrailingSpaces
charRegions = g.MeasureCharacterRanges(str, tnrFont, _
RectangleF.op_implicit(layoutRectB), strFormat)
g.DrawString(str, tnrFont, Brushes.Blue, _
RectangleF.op_implicit(layoutRectB), strFormat)
g.DrawRectangle(Pens.Black, layoutRectB)
For i = 0 To charRegions.Length - 1
g.FillRegion(redBrush, charRegions(i)) 'Paint the regions
Next i
strFormat.FormatFlags = 0 ' clear all the format flags
' Repeat the steps, but use a different layout rectangle. The
' dimensions of the layout rectangle and the size of the font both
' affect the character range measurement.
charRegions = g.MeasureCharacterRanges(str, tnrFont, _
RectangleF.op_implicit(layoutRectC), strFormat)
g.DrawString(str, tnrFont, Brushes.Blue, _
RectangleF.op_implicit(layoutRectC), strFormat)
g.DrawRectangle(Pens.Black, layoutRectC)
For i = 0 To charRegions.Length - 1
g.FillRegion(redBrush, charRegions(i)) ' Paint the regions
Next i
End Sub
```

[C#]
```
public void SetMeasCharRangesExample(PaintEventArgs e)
{
Graphics     g = e.Graphics;
SolidBrush   redBrush = new SolidBrush(Color.FromArgb(50, 255, 0, 0));
// Layout rectangles, font, and string format used for
displaying string.
Rectangle     layoutRectA = new Rectangle(20, 20, 165, 80);
Rectangle     layoutRectB = new Rectangle(20, 110, 165, 80);
Rectangle     layoutRectC = new Rectangle(20, 200, 240, 80);
Font          tnrFont = new Font("Times New Roman", 16);
StringFormat strFormat = new StringFormat();
// Ranges of character positions within a string.
CharacterRange[] charRanges = { new CharacterRange(3, 5),
new CharacterRange(15, 2),
new CharacterRange(30, 15)
};
// Each region specifies the area occupied by the characters within a
// range of positions. the values are obtained by using a method that
// measures the character ranges.
Region[]     charRegions = new Region[charRanges.Length];
// String to be displayed.
string  str =
"The quick, brown fox easily jumps over the lazy dog.";
// Set the char ranges for the string format.
strFormat.SetMeasurableCharacterRanges(charRanges);
byte  i;    // loop counter (unsigned 8-bit integer)
// Measure the char ranges for a given string and layout
rectangle. Each
// area occupied by the characters in a range is stored as a
 region. Then
// draw the string and layout rectangle, and paint the regions.
charRegions = g.MeasureCharacterRanges(str, tnrFont,
layoutRectA, strFormat);
g.DrawString(str, tnrFont, Brushes.Blue, layoutRectA, strFormat );
g.DrawRectangle(Pens.Black, layoutRectA);
for ( i = 0; i < charRegions.Length; i++ )
g.FillRegion(redBrush, charRegions[i]);   // paint the regions
//
```

```
// Repeat the above steps, but include trailing spaces in the char
// range measurement by setting the appropriate string format flag.
strFormat.FormatFlags = StringFormatFlags.MeasureTrailingSpaces;
charRegions = g.MeasureCharacterRanges(str, tnrFont,
layoutRectB, strFormat);
g.DrawString(str, tnrFont, Brushes.Blue, layoutRectB, strFormat );
g.DrawRectangle(Pens.Black, layoutRectB);
for ( i = 0; i < charRegions.Length; i++ )
g.FillRegion(redBrush, charRegions[i]);   // paint the regions
strFormat.FormatFlags = 0;                // clear all the          ↵
format flags
//
// Repeat the steps, but use a different layout rectangle.          ↵
 the dimensions
// of the layout rectangle and the size of the font both affect the
// character range measurement.
charRegions = g.MeasureCharacterRanges(str, tnrFont,
layoutRectC, strFormat);
g.DrawString(str, tnrFont, Brushes.Blue, layoutRectC, strFormat );
g.DrawRectangle(Pens.Black, layoutRectC);
for ( i = 0; i < charRegions.Length; i++ )
g.FillRegion(redBrush, charRegions[i]);  // paint the regions
}
```

Requirements

Platforms: Windows 98, Windows NT 4.0, Windows Millennium Edition, Windows 2000, Windows XP Home Edition, Windows XP Professional, Windows Server 2003 family

StringFormat.SetTabStops Method

Sets tab stops for this **StringFormat** object.

[Visual Basic]
```
Public Sub SetTabStops( _
   ByVal firstTabOffset As Single, _
   ByVal tabStops() As Single _
)
```
[C#]
```
public void SetTabStops(
   float firstTabOffset,
   float[] tabStops
);
```
[C++]
```
public: void SetTabStops(
   float firstTabOffset,
   float tabStops __gc[]
);
```
[JScript]
```
public function SetTabStops(
   firstTabOffset : float,
   tabStops : float[]
);
```

Parameters

firstTabOffset
: The number of spaces between the beginning of a line of text and the first tab stop.

tabStops
: An array of distances (in number of spaces) between tab stops.

Return Value

This method does not return a value.

Example

[Visual Basic, C#] The following example is designed for use with Windows Forms, and it requires **PaintEventArgs** *e*, which is a parameter of the **Paint** event handler. The code performs the following actions:

- Sets the tab stops of the **StringFormat**.
- Draws the string and the layout rectangle. Note that the string contains tabs. The tab settings of the **StringFormat** specify the offsets of the tabbed text.
- Gets the tab stops and uses or inspects the values.

[Visual Basic]
```
Public Sub GetSetTabStopsExample(e As PaintEventArgs)
Dim g As Graphics = e.Graphics
' Tools used for drawing, painting.
Dim redPen As New Pen(Color.FromArgb(255, 255, 0, 0))
Dim blueBrush As New SolidBrush(Color.FromArgb(255, 0, 0, 255))
' Layout and format for text.
Dim myFont As New Font("Times New Roman", 12)
Dim myStringFormat As New StringFormat()
Dim enclosingRectangle As New Rectangle(20, 20, 500, 100)
Dim tabStops As Single() =  {150F, 100F, 100F}
' Text with tabbed columns.
Dim myString As String = "Name" & ControlChars.Tab & "Tab 1" _
& ControlChars.Tab & "Tab 2" & ControlChars.Tab & "Tab 3" _
& ControlChars.Cr & "George Brown" & ControlChars.Tab & "One" _
& ControlChars.Tab & "Two" & ControlChars.Tab & "Three"
' Set the tab stops, paint the text specified by myString,
'  and draw rectangle that encloses the text.
myStringFormat.SetTabStops(0F, tabStops)
g.DrawString(myString, myFont, blueBrush, _
RectangleF.op_implicit(enclosingRectangle), myStringFormat)
g.DrawRectangle(redPen, enclosingRectangle)
' Get the tab stops.
Dim firstTabOffset As Single
Dim tabStopsObtained As Single() = _
myStringFormat.GetTabStops(firstTabOffset)
Dim j As Integer
For j = 0 To tabStopsObtained.Length - 1
' Inspect or use the value in tabStopsObtained[j].
Console.WriteLine(ControlChars.Cr & "  Tab stop {0} = {1}", _
j, tabStopsObtained(j))
Next j
End Sub
```

[C#]
```
public void GetSetTabStopsExample(PaintEventArgs e)
{
Graphics     g = e.Graphics;
// Tools used for drawing, painting.
Pen          redPen = new Pen(Color.FromArgb(255, 255, 0, 0));
SolidBrush   blueBrush = new SolidBrush(Color.FromArgb(255,        ↵
0, 0, 255));
// Layout and format for text.
Font         myFont = new Font("Times New Roman", 12);
StringFormat myStringFormat = new StringFormat();
Rectangle    enclosingRectangle = new Rectangle(20, 20, 500, 100);
float[]      tabStops = {150.0f, 100.0f, 100.0f};
// Text with tabbed columns.
string       myString =
"Name\tTab 1\tTab 2\tTab 3\nGeorge Brown\tOne\tTwo\tThree";
// Set the tab stops, paint the text specified by myString, draw the
// rectangle that encloses the text.
myStringFormat.SetTabStops(0.0f, tabStops);
g.DrawString(myString, myFont, blueBrush,
enclosingRectangle, myStringFormat);
g.DrawRectangle(redPen, enclosingRectangle);
// Get the tab stops.
float   firstTabOffset;
float[] tabStopsObtained = myStringFormat.GetTabStops(out            ↵
firstTabOffset);
for(int j = 0; j < tabStopsObtained.Length; j++)
```

```
{
// Inspect or use the value in tabStopsObtained[j].
Console.WriteLine("\n  Tab stop {0} = {1}", j, tabStopsObtained[j]);
}
}
```

Requirements

Platforms: Windows 98, Windows NT 4.0, Windows Millennium Edition, Windows 2000, Windows XP Home Edition, Windows XP Professional, Windows Server 2003 family

StringFormat.ToString Method

Converts this **StringFormat** object to a human-readable string.

[Visual Basic]
```
Overrides Public Function ToString() As String
```
[C#]
```
public override string ToString();
```
[C++]
```
public: String* ToString();
```
[JScript]
```
public override function ToString() : String;
```

Return Value

A string representation of this **StringFormat** object.

Remarks

Only the value of the FormatFlags property is converted.

Example

[Visual Basic, C#] The following example is designed for use with Windows Forms, and it requires **PaintEventArgs** *e*, which is a parameter of the **Paint** event handler. The code performs the following actions:

- Converts a **StringFormat** object to a string.
- Draws the string.
- Changes some properties in the **StringFormat** object.
- Draws the string. The string will be different because the properties of the **StringFormat** object have changed.

[Visual Basic]
```
Public Sub ToStringExample(e As PaintEventArgs)
Dim g As Graphics = e.Graphics
Dim blueBrush As New SolidBrush(Color.FromArgb(255, 0, 0, 255))
Dim myFont As New Font("Times New Roman", 14)
Dim myStringFormat As New StringFormat()
' String variable to hold the values of the StringFormat object.
Dim strFmtString As String
' Convert the string format object to a string (only certain
' information in the object is converted) and display the string.
strFmtString = myStringFormat.ToString()
g.DrawString("Before changing properties:   ", myFont, blueBrush, _
20, 40, myStringFormat)
' Change some properties of the string format.
myStringFormat.Trimming = StringTrimming.None
myStringFormat.FormatFlags = StringFormatFlags.NoWrap Or _
StringFormatFlags.NoClip
' Convert the string format object to a string and display the
' string. The string will be different because the properties of
' the string format have changed.
strFmtString = myStringFormat.ToString()
g.DrawString("After changing properties:   ", myFont, blueBrush, _
20, 70, myStringFormat)
End Sub
```

[C#]
```
public void ToStringExample(PaintEventArgs e)
{
Graphics     g = e.Graphics;
SolidBrush   blueBrush = new SolidBrush(Color.FromArgb(255,          ↵
 0, 0, 255));
Font         myFont = new Font("Times New Roman", 14);
StringFormat myStringFormat = new StringFormat();
// String variable to hold the values of the StringFormat object.
string    strFmtString;
// Convert the string format object to a string (only certain          ↵
information
// in the object is converted) and display the string.
strFmtString = myStringFormat.ToString();
g.DrawString("Before changing properties:   " + myStringFormat,
myFont, blueBrush, 20, 40);
// Change some properties of the string format
myStringFormat.Trimming = StringTrimming.None;
myStringFormat.FormatFlags =   StringFormatFlags.NoWrap
| StringFormatFlags.NoClip;
// Convert the string format object to a string and display the string.
// The string will be different because the properties of the string
// format have changed.
strFmtString = myStringFormat.ToString();
g.DrawString("After changing properties:   " + myStringFormat,
myFont, blueBrush, 20, 70);
}
```

Requirements

Platforms: Windows 98, Windows NT 4.0, Windows Millennium Edition, Windows 2000, Windows XP Home Edition, Windows XP Professional, Windows Server 2003 family

StringFormatFlags Enumeration

Specifies the display and layout information for text strings.

This enumeration has a **FlagsAttribute** attribute that allows a bitwise combination of its member values.

[Visual Basic]
```
<Flags>
<Serializable>
Public Enum StringFormatFlags
```
[C#]
```
[Flags]
[Serializable]
public enum StringFormatFlags
```
[C++]
```
[Flags]
[Serializable]
__value public enum StringFormatFlags
```
[JScript]
```
public
   Flags
   Serializable
enum StringFormatFlags
```

Members

Member name	Description	Value
DirectionRightToLeft	Specifies that text is right to left.	1
DirectionVertical	Specifies that text is vertical.	2
DisplayFormatControl	Causes control characters such as the left-to-right mark to be shown in the output with a representative glyph.	32
FitBlackBox	Specifies that no part of any glyph overhangs the bounding rectangle. By default some glyphs overhang the rectangle slightly where necessary to appear at the edge visually. For example when an italic lowercase letter f in a font such as Garamond is aligned at the far left of a rectangle, the lower part of the f will reach slightly further left than the left edge of the rectangle. Setting this flag will ensure no painting outside the rectangle but will cause the aligned edges of adjacent lines of text to appear uneven.	4
LineLimit	Only entire lines are laid out in the formatting rectangle. By default layout continues until the end of the text, or until no more lines are visible as a result of clipping, whichever comes first. Note that the default settings allow the last line to be partially obscured by a formatting rectangle that is not a whole multiple of the line height. To ensure that only whole lines are seen, specify this value and be careful to provide a formatting rectangle at least as tall as the height of one line.	8192
MeasureTrailingSpaces	By default the boundary rectangle returned by the **MeasureString** method excludes the space at the end of each line. Set this flag to include that space in measurement.	2048
NoClip	Overhanging parts of glyphs, and unwrapped text reaching outside the formatting rectangle are allowed to show. By default all text and glyph parts reaching outside the formatting rectangle are clipped.	16384
NoFontFallback	Disables fallback to alternate fonts for characters not supported in the requested font. Any missing characters are displayed with the fonts missing glyph, usually an open square.	1024
NoWrap	Disables wrapping of text between lines when formatting within a rectangle. This flag is implied when a point is passed instead of a rectangle, or when the specified rectangle has a zero line length.	4096

Requirements

Namespace: System.Drawing

Platforms: Windows 98, Windows NT 4.0, Windows Millennium Edition, Windows 2000, Windows XP Home Edition, Windows XP Professional, Windows Server 2003 family

Assembly: System.Drawing (in System.Drawing.dll)

StringTrimming Enumeration

Specifies how to trim characters from a string that does not completely fit into a layout shape.

[Visual Basic]
```
<Serializable>
Public Enum StringTrimming
```
[C#]
```
[Serializable]
public enum StringTrimming
```
[C++]
```
[Serializable]
__value public enum StringTrimming
```
[JScript]
```
public
   Serializable
enum StringTrimming
```

Members

Member name	Description
Character	Specifies that the text is trimmed to the nearest character.
EllipsisCharacter	Specifies that the text is trimmed to the nearest character, and an ellipsis is inserted at the end of a trimmed line.
EllipsisPath	The center is removed from trimmed lines and replaced by an ellipsis. The algorithm keeps as much of the last slash-delimited segment of the line as possible.
EllipsisWord	Specifies that text is trimmed to the nearest word, and an ellipsis is inserted at the end of a trimmed line.
None	Specifies no trimming.
Word	Specifies that text is trimmed to the nearest word.

Requirements

Namespace: System.Drawing

Platforms: Windows 98, Windows NT 4.0, Windows Millennium Edition, Windows 2000, Windows XP Home Edition, Windows XP Professional, Windows Server 2003 family

Assembly: System.Drawing (in System.Drawing.dll)

StringUnit Enumeration

Specifies the units of measure for a text string.

[Visual Basic]

```
<Serializable>
Public Enum StringUnit
```

[C#]

```
[Serializable]
public enum StringUnit
```

[C++]

```
[Serializable]
__value public enum StringUnit
```

[JScript]

```
public
   Serializable
enum StringUnit
```

Members

Member name	Description
Display	Specifies the device unit as the unit of measure.
Document	Specifies 1/300 of an inch as the unit of measure.
Em	Specifies a printer's em size of 32 as the unit of measure.
Inch	Specifies an inch as the unit of measure.
Millimeter	Specifies a millimeter as the unit of measure
Pixel	Specifies a pixel as the unit of measure.
Point	Specifies a printer's point (1/72 inch) as the unit of measure.
World	Specifies world units as the unit of measure.

Requirements

Namespace: System.Drawing

Platforms: Windows 98, Windows NT 4.0, Windows Millennium Edition, Windows 2000, Windows XP Home Edition, Windows XP Professional, Windows Server 2003 family

Assembly: System.Drawing (in System.Drawing.dll)

SystemBrushes Class

Each property of the **SystemBrushes** class is a **SolidBrush** object that is the color of a Windows display element.

For a list of all members of this type, see **SystemBrushes Members**.

System.Object
  System.Drawing.SystemBrushes

```
[Visual Basic]
NotInheritable Public Class SystemBrushes
[C#]
public sealed class SystemBrushes
[C++]
public __gc __sealed class SystemBrushes
[JScript]
public class SystemBrushes
```

Thread Safety

Any public static (**Shared** in Visual Basic) members of this type are safe for multithreaded operations. Any instance members are not guaranteed to be thread safe.

Requirements

Namespace: System.Drawing

Platforms: Windows 98, Windows NT 4.0, Windows Millennium Edition, Windows 2000, Windows XP Home Edition, Windows XP Professional, Windows Server 2003 family

Assembly: System.Drawing (in System.Drawing.dll)

SystemBrushes.ActiveBorder Property

Gets a **SolidBrush** object that is the color of the active window's border.

```
[Visual Basic]
Public Shared ReadOnly Property ActiveBorder As Brush
[C#]
public static Brush ActiveBorder {get;}
[C++]
public: __property static Brush* get_ActiveBorder();
[JScript]
public static function get ActiveBorder() : Brush;
```

Property Value

A **SolidBrush** object that is the color of the active window's border.

Requirements

Platforms: Windows 98, Windows NT 4.0, Windows Millennium Edition, Windows 2000, Windows XP Home Edition, Windows XP Professional, Windows Server 2003 family

SystemBrushes.ActiveCaption Property

Gets a **SolidBrush** object that is the color of the background of the active window's title bar.

```
[Visual Basic]
Public Shared ReadOnly Property ActiveCaption As Brush
[C#]
public static Brush ActiveCaption {get;}
[C++]
public: __property static Brush* get_ActiveCaption();
[JScript]
public static function get ActiveCaption() : Brush;
```

Property Value

A **SolidBrush** object that is the color of the background of the active window's title bar.

Requirements

Platforms: Windows 98, Windows NT 4.0, Windows Millennium Edition, Windows 2000, Windows XP Home Edition, Windows XP Professional, Windows Server 2003 family

SystemBrushes.ActiveCaptionText Property

Gets a **SolidBrush** object that is the color of the text in the active window's title bar.

```
[Visual Basic]
Public Shared ReadOnly Property ActiveCaptionText As Brush
[C#]
public static Brush ActiveCaptionText {get;}
[C++]
public: __property static Brush* get_ActiveCaptionText();
[JScript]
public static function get ActiveCaptionText() : Brush;
```

Property Value

A **SolidBrush** object that is the color of the background of the active window's title bar.

Requirements

Platforms: Windows 98, Windows NT 4.0, Windows Millennium Edition, Windows 2000, Windows XP Home Edition, Windows XP Professional, Windows Server 2003 family

SystemBrushes.AppWorkspace Property

Gets a **SolidBrush** object that is the color of the application workspace. The application workspace is the area in a multiple-document view that is not being occupied by documents.

```
[Visual Basic]
Public Shared ReadOnly Property AppWorkspace As Brush
[C#]
public static Brush AppWorkspace {get;}
[C++]
public: __property static Brush* get_AppWorkspace();
[JScript]
public static function get AppWorkspace() : Brush;
```

Property Value

A **SolidBrush** object that is the color of the application workspace.

Requirements

Platforms: Windows 98, Windows NT 4.0, Windows Millennium Edition, Windows 2000, Windows XP Home Edition, Windows XP Professional, Windows Server 2003 family

SystemBrushes.Control Property

Gets a **SolidBrush** object that is the face color of a 3-D element.

```
[Visual Basic]
Public Shared ReadOnly Property Control As Brush
[C#]
public static Brush Control {get;}
[C++]
public: __property static Brush* get_Control();
[JScript]
public static function get Control() : Brush;
```

Property Value

A **SolidBrush** object that is the face color of a 3-D element.

Requirements

Platforms: Windows 98, Windows NT 4.0, Windows Millennium Edition, Windows 2000, Windows XP Home Edition, Windows XP Professional, Windows Server 2003 family

SystemBrushes.ControlDark Property

Gets a **SolidBrush** object that is the shadow color of a 3-D element. The shadow color is applied to parts of a 3-D element that face away from the light source.

```
[Visual Basic]
Public Shared ReadOnly Property ControlDark As Brush
[C#]
public static Brush ControlDark {get;}
[C++]
public: __property static Brush* get_ControlDark();
[JScript]
public static function get ControlDark() : Brush;
```

Property Value

A **SolidBrush** object that is the shadow color of a 3-D element.

Requirements

Platforms: Windows 98, Windows NT 4.0, Windows Millennium Edition, Windows 2000, Windows XP Home Edition, Windows XP Professional, Windows Server 2003 family

SystemBrushes.ControlDarkDark Property

Gets a **SolidBrush** object that is the dark shadow color of a 3-D element. The dark shadow color is applied to the parts of a 3-D element that are the darkest color.

```
[Visual Basic]
Public Shared ReadOnly Property ControlDarkDark As Brush
[C#]
public static Brush ControlDarkDark {get;}
[C++]
public: __property static Brush* get_ControlDarkDark();
[JScript]
public static function get ControlDarkDark() : Brush;
```

Property Value

A **SolidBrush** object that is the dark shadow color of a 3-D element.

Requirements

Platforms: Windows 98, Windows NT 4.0, Windows Millennium Edition, Windows 2000, Windows XP Home Edition, Windows XP Professional, Windows Server 2003 family

SystemBrushes.ControlLight Property

Gets a **SolidBrush** object that is the light color of a 3-D element. The light color is applied to parts of a 3-D element that face the light source.

```
[Visual Basic]
Public Shared ReadOnly Property ControlLight As Brush
[C#]
public static Brush ControlLight {get;}
[C++]
public: __property static Brush* get_ControlLight();
[JScript]
public static function get ControlLight() : Brush;
```

Property Value

A **SolidBrush** object that is the light color of a 3-D element.

Requirements

Platforms: Windows 98, Windows NT 4.0, Windows Millennium Edition, Windows 2000, Windows XP Home Edition, Windows XP Professional, Windows Server 2003 family

SystemBrushes.ControlLightLight Property

Gets a **SolidBrush** object that is the highlight color of a 3-D element. The highlight color is applied to the parts of a 3-D element that are the lightest color.

```
[Visual Basic]
Public Shared ReadOnly Property ControlLightLight As Brush
[C#]
public static Brush ControlLightLight {get;}
[C++]
public: __property static Brush* get_ControlLightLight();
[JScript]
public static function get ControlLightLight() : Brush;
```

Property Value

A **SolidBrush** object that is the highlight color of a 3-D element.

Requirements

Platforms: Windows 98, Windows NT 4.0, Windows Millennium Edition, Windows 2000, Windows XP Home Edition, Windows XP Professional, Windows Server 2003 family

SystemBrushes.ControlText Property

Gets a **SolidBrush** object that is the color of text in a 3-D element.

```
[Visual Basic]
Public Shared ReadOnly Property ControlText As Brush
[C#]
public static Brush ControlText {get;}
```

```
[C++]
public: __property static Brush* get_ControlText();
[JScript]
public static function get ControlText() : Brush;
```

Property Value

A **SolidBrush** object that is the color of text in a 3-D element.

Requirements

Platforms: Windows 98, Windows NT 4.0, Windows Millennium Edition, Windows 2000, Windows XP Home Edition, Windows XP Professional, Windows Server 2003 family

SystemBrushes.Desktop Property

Gets a **SolidBrush** object that is the color of the desktop.

```
[Visual Basic]
Public Shared ReadOnly Property Desktop As Brush
[C#]
public static Brush Desktop {get;}
[C++]
public: __property static Brush* get_Desktop();
[JScript]
public static function get Desktop() : Brush;
```

Property Value

A **SolidBrush** object that is the color of the desktop.

Requirements

Platforms: Windows 98, Windows NT 4.0, Windows Millennium Edition, Windows 2000, Windows XP Home Edition, Windows XP Professional, Windows Server 2003 family

SystemBrushes.Highlight Property

Gets a **SolidBrush** object that is the color of the background of selected items. This includes selected menu items as well as selected text. For example, the brush may be the color used for the background of selected items in a list box.

```
[Visual Basic]
Public Shared ReadOnly Property Highlight As Brush
[C#]
public static Brush Highlight {get;}
[C++]
public: __property static Brush* get_Highlight();
[JScript]
public static function get Highlight() : Brush;
```

Property Value

A **SolidBrush** object that is the color of the background of selected items.

Requirements

Platforms: Windows 98, Windows NT 4.0, Windows Millennium Edition, Windows 2000, Windows XP Home Edition, Windows XP Professional, Windows Server 2003 family

SystemBrushes.HighlightText Property

Gets a **SolidBrush** object that is the color of the text of selected items. This includes selected menu items as well as selected text. For example, the brush may be the color used for the text of selected items in a list box.

```
[Visual Basic]
Public Shared ReadOnly Property HighlightText As Brush
[C#]
public static Brush HighlightText {get;}
[C++]
public: __property static Brush* get_HighlightText();
[JScript]
public static function get HighlightText() : Brush;
```

Property Value

A **SolidBrush** object that is the color of the text of selected items.

Requirements

Platforms: Windows 98, Windows NT 4.0, Windows Millennium Edition, Windows 2000, Windows XP Home Edition, Windows XP Professional, Windows Server 2003 family

SystemBrushes.HotTrack Property

Gets a **SolidBrush** object that is the color used to designate a hot-tracked item. Single-clicking a hot-tracked item executes the item.

```
[Visual Basic]
Public Shared ReadOnly Property HotTrack As Brush
[C#]
public static Brush HotTrack {get;}
[C++]
public: __property static Brush* get_HotTrack();
[JScript]
public static function get HotTrack() : Brush;
```

Property Value

A **SolidBrush** object that is the color used to designate a hot-tracked item.

Requirements

Platforms: Windows 98, Windows NT 4.0, Windows Millennium Edition, Windows 2000, Windows XP Home Edition, Windows XP Professional, Windows Server 2003 family

SystemBrushes.InactiveBorder Property

Gets a **SolidBrush** object that is the color of an inactive window's border.

```
[Visual Basic]
Public Shared ReadOnly Property InactiveBorder As Brush
[C#]
public static Brush InactiveBorder {get;}
[C++]
public: __property static Brush* get_InactiveBorder();
[JScript]
public static function get InactiveBorder() : Brush;
```

Property Value

A **SolidBrush** object that is the color of an inactive window's border.

Requirements

Platforms: Windows 98, Windows NT 4.0, Windows Millennium Edition, Windows 2000, Windows XP Home Edition, Windows XP Professional, Windows Server 2003 family

SystemBrushes.InactiveCaption Property

Gets a **SolidBrush** object that is the color of the background of an inactive window's title bar.

```
[Visual Basic]
Public Shared ReadOnly Property InactiveCaption As Brush
[C#]
public static Brush InactiveCaption {get;}
[C++]
public: __property static Brush* get_InactiveCaption();
[JScript]
public static function get InactiveCaption() : Brush;
```

Property Value

A **SolidBrush** object that is the color of the background of an inactive window's title bar.

Requirements

Platforms: Windows 98, Windows NT 4.0, Windows Millennium Edition, Windows 2000, Windows XP Home Edition, Windows XP Professional, Windows Server 2003 family

SystemBrushes.Info Property

Gets a **SolidBrush** object that is the color of the background of a ToolTip.

```
[Visual Basic]
Public Shared ReadOnly Property Info As Brush
[C#]
public static Brush Info {get;}
[C++]
public: __property static Brush* get_Info();
[JScript]
public static function get Info() : Brush;
```

Property Value

A **SolidBrush** object that is the color of the background of a ToolTip.

Requirements

Platforms: Windows 98, Windows NT 4.0, Windows Millennium Edition, Windows 2000, Windows XP Home Edition, Windows XP Professional, Windows Server 2003 family

SystemBrushes.Menu Property

Gets a **SolidBrush** object that is the color of a menu's background.

```
[Visual Basic]
Public Shared ReadOnly Property Menu As Brush
[C#]
public static Brush Menu {get;}
[C++]
public: __property static Brush* get_Menu();
[JScript]
public static function get Menu() : Brush;
```

Property Value

A **SolidBrush** object that is the color of a menu's background.

Requirements

Platforms: Windows 98, Windows NT 4.0, Windows Millennium Edition, Windows 2000, Windows XP Home Edition, Windows XP Professional, Windows Server 2003 family

SystemBrushes.ScrollBar Property

Gets a **SolidBrush** object that is the color of the background of a scroll bar.

```
[Visual Basic]
Public Shared ReadOnly Property ScrollBar As Brush
[C#]
public static Brush ScrollBar {get;}
[C++]
public: __property static Brush* get_ScrollBar();
[JScript]
public static function get ScrollBar() : Brush;
```

Property Value

A **SolidBrush** object that is the color of the background of a scroll bar.

Requirements

Platforms: Windows 98, Windows NT 4.0, Windows Millennium Edition, Windows 2000, Windows XP Home Edition, Windows XP Professional, Windows Server 2003 family

SystemBrushes.Window Property

Gets a **SolidBrush** object that is the color of the background in the client area of a window.

```
[Visual Basic]
Public Shared ReadOnly Property Window As Brush
[C#]
public static Brush Window {get;}
[C++]
public: __property static Brush* get_Window();
[JScript]
public static function get Window() : Brush;
```

Property Value

A **SolidBrush** object that is the color of the background in the client area of a window.

Requirements

Platforms: Windows 98, Windows NT 4.0, Windows Millennium Edition, Windows 2000, Windows XP Home Edition, Windows XP Professional, Windows Server 2003 family

SystemBrushes.WindowText Property

Gets a **SolidBrush** object that is the color of the text in the client area of a window.

[Visual Basic]
```
Public Shared ReadOnly Property WindowText As Brush
```
[C#]
```
public static Brush WindowText {get;}
```
[C++]
```
public: __property static Brush* get_WindowText();
```
[JScript]
```
public static function get WindowText() : Brush;
```

Property Value

A **SolidBrush** object that is the color of the text in the client area of a window.

Requirements

Platforms: Windows 98, Windows NT 4.0, Windows Millennium Edition, Windows 2000, Windows XP Home Edition, Windows XP Professional, Windows Server 2003 family

SystemBrushes.FromSystemColor Method

Creates a **Brush** object from the specified **Color** color.

[Visual Basic]
```
Public Shared Function FromSystemColor( _
   ByVal c As Color _
) As Brush
```
[C#]
```
public static Brush FromSystemColor(
   Color c
);
```
[C++]
```
public: static Brush* FromSystemColor(
   Color c
);
```
[JScript]
```
public static function FromSystemColor(
   c : Color
) : Brush;
```

Parameters

c

The **Color** structure from which to create the **Brush** object.

Return Value

The **Brush** object this method creates.

Requirements

Platforms: Windows 98, Windows NT 4.0, Windows Millennium Edition, Windows 2000, Windows XP Home Edition, Windows XP Professional, Windows Server 2003 family

SystemColors Class

Each property of the **SystemColors** class is a **Color** structure that is the color of a Windows display element.

System.Object
  System.Drawing.SystemColors

```
[Visual Basic]
NotInheritable Public Class SystemColors
[C#]
public sealed class SystemColors
[C++]
public __gc __sealed class SystemColors
[JScript]
public class SystemColors
```

Thread Safety

Any public static (**Shared** in Visual Basic) members of this type are safe for multithreaded operations. Any instance members are not guaranteed to be thread safe.

Remarks

Better performance is achieved through the use of the **SystemPens** object or **SystemBrushes** object rather than creating a new pen or brush based on a value from the **SystemColors** object. For example, use SystemBrushes.Control because it is a brush that already exists, whereas new SolidBrush(SystemColors.Control) creates a new brush.

Requirements

Namespace: System.Drawing

Platforms: Windows 98, Windows NT 4.0,
Windows Millennium Edition, Windows 2000,
Windows XP Home Edition, Windows XP Professional,
Windows Server 2003 family,
.NET Compact Framework - Windows CE .NET

Assembly: System.Drawing (in System.Drawing.dll)

SystemColors.ActiveBorder Property

Gets a **Color** structure that is the color of the active window's border.

```
[Visual Basic]
Public Shared ReadOnly Property ActiveBorder As Color
[C#]
public static Color ActiveBorder {get;}
[C++]
public: __property static Color get_ActiveBorder();
[JScript]
public static function get ActiveBorder() : Color;
```

Property Value

A **Color** structure that is the color of the active window's border.

Requirements

Platforms: Windows 98, Windows NT 4.0,
Windows Millennium Edition, Windows 2000,
Windows XP Home Edition, Windows XP Professional,
Windows Server 2003 family,
.NET Compact Framework - Windows CE .NET

SystemColors.ActiveCaption Property

Gets a **Color** structure that is the color of the background of the active window's title bar.

```
[Visual Basic]
Public Shared ReadOnly Property ActiveCaption As Color
[C#]
public static Color ActiveCaption {get;}
[C++]
public: __property static Color get_ActiveCaption();
[JScript]
public static function get ActiveCaption() : Color;
```

Property Value

A **Color** structure that is the color of the active window's title bar.

Requirements

Platforms: Windows 98, Windows NT 4.0,
Windows Millennium Edition, Windows 2000,
Windows XP Home Edition, Windows XP Professional,
Windows Server 2003 family,
.NET Compact Framework - Windows CE .NET

SystemColors.ActiveCaptionText Property

Gets a **Color** structure that is the color of the text in the active window's title bar.

```
[Visual Basic]
Public Shared ReadOnly Property ActiveCaptionText As Color
[C#]
public static Color ActiveCaptionText {get;}
[C++]
public: __property static Color get_ActiveCaptionText();
[JScript]
public static function get ActiveCaptionText() : Color;
```

Property Value

A **Color** structure that is the color of the text in the active window's title bar.

Requirements

Platforms: Windows 98, Windows NT 4.0,
Windows Millennium Edition, Windows 2000,
Windows XP Home Edition, Windows XP Professional,
Windows Server 2003 family,
.NET Compact Framework - Windows CE .NET

SystemColors.AppWorkspace Property

Gets a **Color** structure that is the color of the application workspace. The application workspace is the area in a multiple-document view that is not being occupied by documents.

```
[Visual Basic]
Public Shared ReadOnly Property AppWorkspace As Color
[C#]
public static Color AppWorkspace {get;}
[C++]
public: __property static Color get_AppWorkspace();
[JScript]
public static function get AppWorkspace() : Color;
```

Property Value

A **Color** structure that is the color of the application workspace.

Requirements

Platforms: Windows 98, Windows NT 4.0,
Windows Millennium Edition, Windows 2000,
Windows XP Home Edition, Windows XP Professional,
Windows Server 2003 family,
.NET Compact Framework - Windows CE .NET

SystemColors.Control Property

Gets a **Color** structure that is the face color of a 3-D element.

```
[Visual Basic]
Public Shared ReadOnly Property Control As Color
[C#]
public static Color Control {get;}
[C++]
public: __property static Color get_Control();
[JScript]
public static function get Control() : Color;
```

Property Value

A **Color** structure that is the color of the face color of a 3-D element.

Requirements

Platforms: Windows 98, Windows NT 4.0,
Windows Millennium Edition, Windows 2000,
Windows XP Home Edition, Windows XP Professional,
Windows Server 2003 family,
.NET Compact Framework - Windows CE .NET

SystemColors.ControlDark Property

Gets a **Color** structure that is the shadow color of a 3-D element. The shadow color is applied to parts of a 3-D element that face away from the light source.

```
[Visual Basic]
Public Shared ReadOnly Property ControlDark As Color
[C#]
public static Color ControlDark {get;}
[C++]
public: __property static Color get_ControlDark();
[JScript]
public static function get ControlDark() : Color;
```

Property Value

A **Color** structure that is the color of the shadow color of a 3-D element.

Requirements

Platforms: Windows 98, Windows NT 4.0,
Windows Millennium Edition, Windows 2000,
Windows XP Home Edition, Windows XP Professional,
Windows Server 2003 family,
.NET Compact Framework - Windows CE .NET

SystemColors.ControlDarkDark Property

Gets a **Color** structure that is the dark shadow color of a 3-D element. The dark shadow color is applied to the parts of a 3-D element that are the darkest color.

```
[Visual Basic]
Public Shared ReadOnly Property ControlDarkDark As Color
[C#]
public static Color ControlDarkDark {get;}
[C++]
public: __property static Color get_ControlDarkDark();
[JScript]
public static function get ControlDarkDark() : Color;
```

Property Value

A **Color** structure that is the dark shadow color of a 3-D element.

Requirements

Platforms: Windows 98, Windows NT 4.0,
Windows Millennium Edition, Windows 2000,
Windows XP Home Edition, Windows XP Professional,
Windows Server 2003 family,
.NET Compact Framework - Windows CE .NET

SystemColors.ControlLight Property

Gets a **Color** structure that is the light color of a 3-D element. The light color is applied to parts of a 3-D element that face the light source.

```
[Visual Basic]
Public Shared ReadOnly Property ControlLight As Color
[C#]
public static Color ControlLight {get;}
[C++]
public: __property static Color get_ControlLight();
[JScript]
public static function get ControlLight() : Color;
```

Property Value

A **Color** structure that is the light color of a 3-D element.

Requirements

Platforms: Windows 98, Windows NT 4.0,
Windows Millennium Edition, Windows 2000,
Windows XP Home Edition, Windows XP Professional,
Windows Server 2003 family,
.NET Compact Framework - Windows CE .NET

SystemColors.ControlLightLight Property

Gets a **Color** structure that is the highlight color of a 3-D element. The highlight color is applied to the parts of a 3-D element that are the lightest color.

```
[Visual Basic]
Public Shared ReadOnly Property ControlLightLight As Color
[C#]
public static Color ControlLightLight {get;}
[C++]
public: __property static Color get_ControlLightLight();
[JScript]
public static function get ControlLightLight() : Color;
```

Property Value

A **Color** structure that is the highlight color of a 3-D element.

Requirements

Platforms: Windows 98, Windows NT 4.0, Windows Millennium Edition, Windows 2000, Windows XP Home Edition, Windows XP Professional, Windows Server 2003 family, .NET Compact Framework - Windows CE .NET

SystemColors.ControlText Property

Gets a **Color** structure that is the color of text in a 3-D element.

```
[Visual Basic]
Public Shared ReadOnly Property ControlText As Color
[C#]
public static Color ControlText {get;}
[C++]
public: __property static Color get_ControlText();
[JScript]
public static function get ControlText() : Color;
```

Property Value

A **Color** structure that is the color of text in a 3-D element.

Requirements

Platforms: Windows 98, Windows NT 4.0, Windows Millennium Edition, Windows 2000, Windows XP Home Edition, Windows XP Professional, Windows Server 2003 family, .NET Compact Framework - Windows CE .NET

SystemColors.Desktop Property

Gets a **Color** structure that is the color of the desktop.

```
[Visual Basic]
Public Shared ReadOnly Property Desktop As Color
[C#]
public static Color Desktop {get;}
[C++]
public: __property static Color get_Desktop();
[JScript]
public static function get Desktop() : Color;
```

Property Value

A **Color** structure that is the color of the desktop.

Requirements

Platforms: Windows 98, Windows NT 4.0, Windows Millennium Edition, Windows 2000, Windows XP Home Edition, Windows XP Professional, Windows Server 2003 family, .NET Compact Framework - Windows CE .NET

SystemColors.GrayText Property

Gets a **Color** structure that is the color of dimmed text. Items in a list that are disabled are displayed in dimmed text.

```
[Visual Basic]
Public Shared ReadOnly Property GrayText As Color
[C#]
public static Color GrayText {get;}
[C++]
public: __property static Color get_GrayText();
[JScript]
public static function get GrayText() : Color;
```

Property Value

A **Color** structure that is the color of dimmed text.

Requirements

Platforms: Windows 98, Windows NT 4.0, Windows Millennium Edition, Windows 2000, Windows XP Home Edition, Windows XP Professional, Windows Server 2003 family, .NET Compact Framework - Windows CE .NET

SystemColors.Highlight Property

Gets a **Color** structure that is the color of the background of selected items. This includes selected menu items as well as selected text. For example, the **Color** structure may be the color used for the background of selected items in a list box.

```
[Visual Basic]
Public Shared ReadOnly Property Highlight As Color
[C#]
public static Color Highlight {get;}
[C++]
public: __property static Color get_Highlight();
[JScript]
public static function get Highlight() : Color;
```

Property Value

A **Color** structure that is the color of the background of selected items.

Requirements

Platforms: Windows 98, Windows NT 4.0, Windows Millennium Edition, Windows 2000, Windows XP Home Edition, Windows XP Professional, Windows Server 2003 family, .NET Compact Framework - Windows CE .NET

SystemColors.HighlightText Property

Gets a **Color** structure that is the color of the text of selected items. For example, the **Color** structure may be the color used for the text of selected items in a list box.

```
[Visual Basic]
Public Shared ReadOnly Property HighlightText As Color
[C#]
public static Color HighlightText {get;}
[C++]
public: __property static Color get_HighlightText();
[JScript]
public static function get HighlightText() : Color;
```

Property Value

A **Color** structure that is the color of the text of selected items.

Requirements

Platforms: Windows 98, Windows NT 4.0, Windows Millennium Edition, Windows 2000, Windows XP Home Edition, Windows XP Professional, Windows Server 2003 family, .NET Compact Framework - Windows CE .NET

SystemColors.HotTrack Property

Gets a **Color** structure that is the color used to designate a hot-tracked item. Single-clicking a hot-tracked item executes the item.

```
[Visual Basic]
Public Shared ReadOnly Property HotTrack As Color
[C#]
public static Color HotTrack {get;}
[C++]
public: __property static Color get_HotTrack();
[JScript]
public static function get HotTrack() : Color;
```

Property Value

A **Color** structure that is the color used to designate a hot-tracked item.

Requirements

Platforms: Windows 98, Windows NT 4.0,
Windows Millennium Edition, Windows 2000,
Windows XP Home Edition, Windows XP Professional,
Windows Server 2003 family,
.NET Compact Framework - Windows CE .NET

SystemColors.InactiveBorder Property

Gets a **Color** structure that is the color of an inactive window's border.

```
[Visual Basic]
Public Shared ReadOnly Property InactiveBorder As Color
[C#]
public static Color InactiveBorder {get;}
[C++]
public: __property static Color get_InactiveBorder();
[JScript]
public static function get InactiveBorder() : Color;
```

Property Value

A **Color** structure that is the color of an inactive window's border.

Requirements

Platforms: Windows 98, Windows NT 4.0,
Windows Millennium Edition, Windows 2000,
Windows XP Home Edition, Windows XP Professional,
Windows Server 2003 family,
.NET Compact Framework - Windows CE .NET

SystemColors.InactiveCaption Property

Gets a **Color** structure that is the color of the background of an inactive window's title bar.

```
[Visual Basic]
Public Shared ReadOnly Property InactiveCaption As Color
[C#]
public static Color InactiveCaption {get;}
[C++]
public: __property static Color get_InactiveCaption();
[JScript]
public static function get InactiveCaption() : Color;
```

Property Value

A **Color** structure that is the color of the background of an inactive window's title bar.

Requirements

Platforms: Windows 98, Windows NT 4.0,
Windows Millennium Edition, Windows 2000,
Windows XP Home Edition, Windows XP Professional,
Windows Server 2003 family,
.NET Compact Framework - Windows CE .NET

SystemColors.InactiveCaptionText Property

Gets a **Color** structure that is the color of the text in an inactive window's title bar.

```
[Visual Basic]
Public Shared ReadOnly Property InactiveCaptionText As Color
[C#]
public static Color InactiveCaptionText {get;}
[C++]
public: __property static Color get_InactiveCaptionText();
[JScript]
public static function get InactiveCaptionText() : Color;
```

Property Value

A **Color** structure that is the color of the text in an inactive window's title bar.

Requirements

Platforms: Windows 98, Windows NT 4.0,
Windows Millennium Edition, Windows 2000,
Windows XP Home Edition, Windows XP Professional,
Windows Server 2003 family,
.NET Compact Framework - Windows CE .NET

SystemColors.Info Property

Gets a **Color** structure that is the color of the background of a ToolTip.

```
[Visual Basic]
Public Shared ReadOnly Property Info As Color
[C#]
public static Color Info {get;}
[C++]
public: __property static Color get_Info();
[JScript]
public static function get Info() : Color;
```

Property Value

A **Color** structure that is the color of the background of a ToolTip.

Requirements

Platforms: Windows 98, Windows NT 4.0,
Windows Millennium Edition, Windows 2000,
Windows XP Home Edition, Windows XP Professional,
Windows Server 2003 family,
.NET Compact Framework - Windows CE .NET

SystemColors.InfoText Property

Gets a **Color** structure that is the color of the text of a ToolTip.

[Visual Basic]
```
Public Shared ReadOnly Property InfoText As Color
```
[C#]
```
public static Color InfoText {get;}
```
[C++]
```
public: __property static Color get_InfoText();
```
[JScript]
```
public static function get InfoText() : Color;
```

Property Value

A **Color** structure that is the color of the text of a ToolTip.

Requirements

Platforms: Windows 98, Windows NT 4.0, Windows Millennium Edition, Windows 2000, Windows XP Home Edition, Windows XP Professional, Windows Server 2003 family, .NET Compact Framework - Windows CE .NET

SystemColors.Menu Property

Gets a **Color** structure that is the color of a menu's background.

[Visual Basic]
```
Public Shared ReadOnly Property Menu As Color
```
[C#]
```
public static Color Menu {get;}
```
[C++]
```
public: __property static Color get_Menu();
```
[JScript]
```
public static function get Menu() : Color;
```

Property Value

A **Color** structure that is the color of a menu's background.

Requirements

Platforms: Windows 98, Windows NT 4.0, Windows Millennium Edition, Windows 2000, Windows XP Home Edition, Windows XP Professional, Windows Server 2003 family, .NET Compact Framework - Windows CE .NET

SystemColors.MenuText Property

Gets a **Color** structure that is the color of a menu's text.

[Visual Basic]
```
Public Shared ReadOnly Property MenuText As Color
```
[C#]
```
public static Color MenuText {get;}
```
[C++]
```
public: __property static Color get_MenuText();
```
[JScript]
```
public static function get MenuText() : Color;
```

Property Value

A **Color** structure that is the color of a menu's text.

Requirements

Platforms: Windows 98, Windows NT 4.0, Windows Millennium Edition, Windows 2000, Windows XP Home Edition, Windows XP Professional, Windows Server 2003 family, .NET Compact Framework - Windows CE .NET

SystemColors.ScrollBar Property

Gets a **Color** structure that is the color of the background of a scroll bar.

[Visual Basic]
```
Public Shared ReadOnly Property ScrollBar As Color
```
[C#]
```
public static Color ScrollBar {get;}
```
[C++]
```
public: __property static Color get_ScrollBar();
```
[JScript]
```
public static function get ScrollBar() : Color;
```

Property Value

A **Color** structure that is the color of the background of a scroll bar.

Requirements

Platforms: Windows 98, Windows NT 4.0, Windows Millennium Edition, Windows 2000, Windows XP Home Edition, Windows XP Professional, Windows Server 2003 family, .NET Compact Framework - Windows CE .NET

SystemColors.Window Property

Gets a **Color** structure that is the color of the background in the client area of a window.

[Visual Basic]
```
Public Shared ReadOnly Property Window As Color
```
[C#]
```
public static Color Window {get;}
```
[C++]
```
public: __property static Color get_Window();
```
[JScript]
```
public static function get Window() : Color;
```

Property Value

A **Color** structure that is the color of the background in the client area of a window.

Requirements

Platforms: Windows 98, Windows NT 4.0, Windows Millennium Edition, Windows 2000, Windows XP Home Edition, Windows XP Professional, Windows Server 2003 family, .NET Compact Framework - Windows CE .NET

SystemColors.WindowFrame Property

Gets a **Color** structure that is the color of a window frame.

[Visual Basic]
```
Public Shared ReadOnly Property WindowFrame As Color
```
[C#]
```
public static Color WindowFrame {get;}
```
[C++]
```
public: __property static Color get_WindowFrame();
```
[JScript]
```
public static function get WindowFrame() : Color;
```

Property Value

A **Color** structure that is the color of a window frame.

Requirements

Platforms: Windows 98, Windows NT 4.0, Windows Millennium Edition, Windows 2000, Windows XP Home Edition, Windows XP Professional, Windows Server 2003 family, .NET Compact Framework - Windows CE .NET

SystemColors.WindowText Property

Gets a **Color** structure that is the color of the text in the client area of a window.

[Visual Basic]
```
Public Shared ReadOnly Property WindowText As Color
```
[C#]
```
public static Color WindowText {get;}
```
[C++]
```
public: __property static Color get_WindowText();
```
[JScript]
```
public static function get WindowText() : Color;
```

Property Value

A **Color** structure that is the color of the text in the client area of a window.

Requirements

Platforms: Windows 98, Windows NT 4.0, Windows Millennium Edition, Windows 2000, Windows XP Home Edition, Windows XP Professional, Windows Server 2003 family, .NET Compact Framework - Windows CE .NET

SystemIcons Class

Each property of the **SystemIcons** class is an **Icon** object for Windows system-wide icons. This class cannot be inherited.

System.Object
  System.Drawing.SystemIcons

[Visual Basic]
```
NotInheritable Public Class SystemIcons
```
[C#]
```
public sealed class SystemIcons
```
[C++]
```
public __gc __sealed class SystemIcons
```
[JScript]
```
public class SystemIcons
```

Thread Safety

Any public static (**Shared** in Visual Basic) members of this type are safe for multithreaded operations. Any instance members are not guaranteed to be thread safe.

Requirements

Namespace: System.Drawing

Platforms: Windows 98, Windows NT 4.0, Windows Millennium Edition, Windows 2000, Windows XP Home Edition, Windows XP Professional, Windows Server 2003 family

Assembly: System.Drawing (in System.Drawing.dll)

SystemIcons.Application Property

Gets an **Icon** object that contains the default application icon (WIN32: IDI_APPLICATION).

[Visual Basic]
```
Public Shared ReadOnly Property Application As Icon
```
[C#]
```
public static Icon Application {get;}
```
[C++]
```
public: __property static Icon* get_Application();
```
[JScript]
```
public static function get Application() : Icon;
```

Property Value

An **Icon** object that contains the default application icon.

Requirements

Platforms: Windows 98, Windows NT 4.0, Windows Millennium Edition, Windows 2000, Windows XP Home Edition, Windows XP Professional, Windows Server 2003 family

SystemIcons.Asterisk Property

Gets an **Icon** object that contains the system asterisk icon (WIN32: IDI_ASTERISK).

[Visual Basic]
```
Public Shared ReadOnly Property Asterisk As Icon
```
[C#]
```
public static Icon Asterisk {get;}
```
[C++]
```
public: __property static Icon* get_Asterisk();
```
[JScript]
```
public static function get Asterisk() : Icon;
```

Property Value

An **Icon** object that contains the system asterisk icon.

Requirements

Platforms: Windows 98, Windows NT 4.0, Windows Millennium Edition, Windows 2000, Windows XP Home Edition, Windows XP Professional, Windows Server 2003 family

SystemIcons.Error Property

Gets an **Icon** object that contains the system error icon (WIN32: IDI_ERROR).

[Visual Basic]
```
Public Shared ReadOnly Property Error As Icon
```
[C#]
```
public static Icon Error {get;}
```
[C++]
```
public: __property static Icon* get_Error();
```
[JScript]
```
public static function get Error() : Icon;
```

Property Value

An **Icon** object that contains the system error icon.

Requirements

Platforms: Windows 98, Windows NT 4.0, Windows Millennium Edition, Windows 2000, Windows XP Home Edition, Windows XP Professional, Windows Server 2003 family

SystemIcons.Exclamation Property

Gets an **Icon** object that contains the system exclamation icon (WIN32: IDI_EXCLAMATION).

[Visual Basic]
```
Public Shared ReadOnly Property Exclamation As Icon
```
[C#]
```
public static Icon Exclamation {get;}
```
[C++]
```
public: __property static Icon* get_Exclamation();
```
[JScript]
```
public static function get Exclamation() : Icon;
```

Property Value

An **Icon** object that contains the system exclamation icon.

Requirements

Platforms: Windows 98, Windows NT 4.0, Windows Millennium Edition, Windows 2000, Windows XP Home Edition, Windows XP Professional, Windows Server 2003 family

SystemIcons.Hand Property

Gets an **Icon** object that contains the system hand icon (WIN32: IDI_HAND).

```
[Visual Basic]
Public Shared ReadOnly Property Hand As Icon
[C#]
public static Icon Hand {get;}
[C++]
public: __property static Icon* get_Hand();
[JScript]
public static function get Hand() : Icon;
```

Property Value

An **Icon** object that contains the system hand icon.

Requirements

Platforms: Windows 98, Windows NT 4.0, Windows Millennium Edition, Windows 2000, Windows XP Home Edition, Windows XP Professional, Windows Server 2003 family

SystemIcons.Information Property

Gets an **Icon** object that contains the system information icon (WIN32: IDI_INFORMATION).

```
[Visual Basic]
Public Shared ReadOnly Property Information As Icon
[C#]
public static Icon Information {get;}
[C++]
public: __property static Icon* get_Information();
[JScript]
public static function get Information() : Icon;
```

Property Value

An **Icon** object that contains the system information icon.

Requirements

Platforms: Windows 98, Windows NT 4.0, Windows Millennium Edition, Windows 2000, Windows XP Home Edition, Windows XP Professional, Windows Server 2003 family

SystemIcons.Question Property

Gets an **Icon** object that contains the system question icon (WIN32: IDI_QUESTION).

```
[Visual Basic]
Public Shared ReadOnly Property Question As Icon
[C#]
public static Icon Question {get;}
[C++]
public: __property static Icon* get_Question();
[JScript]
public static function get Question() : Icon;
```

Property Value

An **Icon** object that contains the system question icon.

Requirements

Platforms: Windows 98, Windows NT 4.0, Windows Millennium Edition, Windows 2000, Windows XP Home Edition, Windows XP Professional, Windows Server 2003 family

SystemIcons.Warning Property

Gets an **Icon** object that contains the system warning icon (WIN32: IDI_WARNING).

```
[Visual Basic]
Public Shared ReadOnly Property Warning As Icon
[C#]
public static Icon Warning {get;}
[C++]
public: __property static Icon* get_Warning();
[JScript]
public static function get Warning() : Icon;
```

Property Value

An **Icon** object that contains the system warning icon.

Requirements

Platforms: Windows 98, Windows NT 4.0, Windows Millennium Edition, Windows 2000, Windows XP Home Edition, Windows XP Professional, Windows Server 2003 family

SystemIcons.WinLogo Property

Gets an **Icon** object that contains the Windows logo icon (WIN32: IDI_WINLOGO).

```
[Visual Basic]
Public Shared ReadOnly Property WinLogo As Icon
[C#]
public static Icon WinLogo {get;}
[C++]
public: __property static Icon* get_WinLogo();
[JScript]
public static function get WinLogo() : Icon;
```

Property Value

An **Icon** object that contains the Windows logo icon.

Requirements

Platforms: Windows 98, Windows NT 4.0, Windows Millennium Edition, Windows 2000, Windows XP Home Edition, Windows XP Professional, Windows Server 2003 family

SystemPens Class

Each property of the **SystemPens** class is a **Pen** object that is the color of a Windows display element and that is a width of 1.

System.Object
  System.Drawing.SystemPens

```
[Visual Basic]
NotInheritable Public Class SystemPens
[C#]
public sealed class SystemPens
[C++]
public __gc __sealed class SystemPens
[JScript]
public class SystemPens
```

Thread Safety

Any public static (**Shared** in Visual Basic) members of this type are safe for multithreaded operations. Any instance members are not guaranteed to be thread safe.

Requirements

Namespace: System.Drawing

Platforms: Windows 98, Windows NT 4.0, Windows Millennium Edition, Windows 2000, Windows XP Home Edition, Windows XP Professional, Windows Server 2003 family

Assembly: System.Drawing (in System.Drawing.dll)

SystemPens.ActiveCaptionText Property

Gets a **Pen** object that is the color of the text in the active window's title bar.

```
[Visual Basic]
Public Shared ReadOnly Property ActiveCaptionText As Pen
[C#]
public static Pen ActiveCaptionText {get;}
[C++]
public: __property static Pen* get_ActiveCaptionText();
[JScript]
public static function get ActiveCaptionText() : Pen;
```

Property Value

A **Pen** object that is the color of the text in the active window's title bar.

Requirements

Platforms: Windows 98, Windows NT 4.0, Windows Millennium Edition, Windows 2000, Windows XP Home Edition, Windows XP Professional, Windows Server 2003 family

SystemPens.Control Property

Gets a **Pen** object that is the face color of a 3-D element.

```
[Visual Basic]
Public Shared ReadOnly Property Control As Pen
[C#]
public static Pen Control {get;}
[C++]
public: __property static Pen* get_Control();
[JScript]
public static function get Control() : Pen;
```

Property Value

A **Pen** object that is the face color of a 3-D element.

Requirements

Platforms: Windows 98, Windows NT 4.0, Windows Millennium Edition, Windows 2000, Windows XP Home Edition, Windows XP Professional, Windows Server 2003 family

SystemPens.ControlDark Property

Gets a **Pen** object that is the shadow color of a 3-D element. The shadow color is applied to parts of a 3-D element that face away from the light source.

```
[Visual Basic]
Public Shared ReadOnly Property ControlDark As Pen
[C#]
public static Pen ControlDark {get;}
[C++]
public: __property static Pen* get_ControlDark();
[JScript]
public static function get ControlDark() : Pen;
```

Property Value

A **Pen** object that is the shadow color of a 3-D element.

Requirements

Platforms: Windows 98, Windows NT 4.0, Windows Millennium Edition, Windows 2000, Windows XP Home Edition, Windows XP Professional, Windows Server 2003 family

SystemPens.ControlDarkDark Property

Gets a **Pen** object that is the dark shadow color of a 3-D element. The dark shadow color is applied to the parts of a 3-D element that are the darkest color.

```
[Visual Basic]
Public Shared ReadOnly Property ControlDarkDark As Pen
[C#]
public static Pen ControlDarkDark {get;}
[C++]
public: __property static Pen* get_ControlDarkDark();
[JScript]
public static function get ControlDarkDark() : Pen;
```

Property Value

A **Pen** object that is the dark shadow color of a 3-D element.

Requirements

Platforms: Windows 98, Windows NT 4.0, Windows Millennium Edition, Windows 2000, Windows XP Home Edition, Windows XP Professional, Windows Server 2003 family

SystemPens.ControlLight Property

Gets a **Pen** object that is the light color of a 3-D element. The light color is applied to parts of a 3-D element that face the light source.

```
[Visual Basic]
Public Shared ReadOnly Property ControlLight As Pen
[C#]
public static Pen ControlLight {get;}
[C++]
public: __property static Pen* get_ControlLight();
[JScript]
public static function get ControlLight() : Pen;
```

Property Value

A **Pen** object that is the light color of a 3-D element.

Requirements

Platforms: Windows 98, Windows NT 4.0, Windows Millennium Edition, Windows 2000, Windows XP Home Edition, Windows XP Professional, Windows Server 2003 family

SystemPens.ControlLightLight Property

Gets a **Pen** object that is the highlight color of a 3-D element. The highlight color is applied to the parts of a 3-D element that are the lightest color.

```
[Visual Basic]
Public Shared ReadOnly Property ControlLightLight As Pen
[C#]
public static Pen ControlLightLight {get;}
[C++]
public: __property static Pen* get_ControlLightLight();
[JScript]
public static function get ControlLightLight() : Pen;
```

Property Value

A **Pen** object that is the highlight color of a 3-D element.

Requirements

Platforms: Windows 98, Windows NT 4.0, Windows Millennium Edition, Windows 2000, Windows XP Home Edition, Windows XP Professional, Windows Server 2003 family

SystemPens.ControlText Property

Gets a **Pen** object that is the color of text in a 3-D element.

```
[Visual Basic]
Public Shared ReadOnly Property ControlText As Pen
[C#]
public static Pen ControlText {get;}
[C++]
public: __property static Pen* get_ControlText();
[JScript]
public static function get ControlText() : Pen;
```

Property Value

A **Pen** object that is the color of text in a 3-D element.

Requirements

Platforms: Windows 98, Windows NT 4.0, Windows Millennium Edition, Windows 2000, Windows XP Home Edition, Windows XP Professional, Windows Server 2003 family

SystemPens.GrayText Property

Gets a **Pen** object that is the color of dimmed text. Items in a list that are disabled are displayed in dimmed text.

```
[Visual Basic]
Public Shared ReadOnly Property GrayText As Pen
[C#]
public static Pen GrayText {get;}
[C++]
public: __property static Pen* get_GrayText();
[JScript]
public static function get GrayText() : Pen;
```

Property Value

A **Pen** object that is the color of dimmed text.

Requirements

Platforms: Windows 98, Windows NT 4.0, Windows Millennium Edition, Windows 2000, Windows XP Home Edition, Windows XP Professional, Windows Server 2003 family

SystemPens.Highlight Property

Gets a **Pen** object that is the color of the background of selected items. This includes selected menu items as well as selected text. For example, the pen may be the color used for the background of selected items in a list box.

```
[Visual Basic]
Public Shared ReadOnly Property Highlight As Pen
[C#]
public static Pen Highlight {get;}
[C++]
public: __property static Pen* get_Highlight();
[JScript]
public static function get Highlight() : Pen;
```

Property Value

A **Pen** object that is the color of the background of selected items.

Requirements

Platforms: Windows 98, Windows NT 4.0, Windows Millennium Edition, Windows 2000, Windows XP Home Edition, Windows XP Professional, Windows Server 2003 family

SystemPens.HighlightText Property

Gets a **Pen** object that is the color of the text of selected items. This includes selected menu items as well as selected text. For example, the pen may be the color used for the text of selected items in a list box.

```
[Visual Basic]
Public Shared ReadOnly Property HighlightText As Pen
[C#]
public static Pen HighlightText {get;}
```

```
[C++]
public: __property static Pen* get_HighlightText();
[JScript]
public static function get HighlightText() : Pen;
```

Property Value

A **Pen** object that is the color of the text of selected items.

Requirements

Platforms: Windows 98, Windows NT 4.0, Windows Millennium Edition, Windows 2000, Windows XP Home Edition, Windows XP Professional, Windows Server 2003 family

SystemPens.InactiveCaptionText Property

Gets a **Pen** object that is the color of the text in an inactive window's title bar.

```
[Visual Basic]
Public Shared ReadOnly Property InactiveCaptionText As Pen
[C#]
public static Pen InactiveCaptionText {get;}
[C++]
public: __property static Pen* get_InactiveCaptionText();
[JScript]
public static function get InactiveCaptionText() : Pen;
```

Property Value

A **Pen** object that is the color of the text in an inactive window's title bar.

Requirements

Platforms: Windows 98, Windows NT 4.0, Windows Millennium Edition, Windows 2000, Windows XP Home Edition, Windows XP Professional, Windows Server 2003 family

SystemPens.InfoText Property

Gets a **Pen** object that is the color of the text of a ToolTip.

```
[Visual Basic]
Public Shared ReadOnly Property InfoText As Pen
[C#]
public static Pen InfoText {get;}
[C++]
public: __property static Pen* get_InfoText();
[JScript]
public static function get InfoText() : Pen;
```

Property Value

A **Pen** object that is the color of the text of a ToolTip.

Requirements

Platforms: Windows 98, Windows NT 4.0, Windows Millennium Edition, Windows 2000, Windows XP Home Edition, Windows XP Professional, Windows Server 2003 family

SystemPens.MenuText Property

Gets a **Pen** object that is the color of a menu's text.

```
[Visual Basic]
Public Shared ReadOnly Property MenuText As Pen
[C#]
public static Pen MenuText {get;}
[C++]
public: __property static Pen* get_MenuText();
[JScript]
public static function get MenuText() : Pen;
```

Property Value

A **Pen** object that is the color of a menu's text.

Requirements

Platforms: Windows 98, Windows NT 4.0, Windows Millennium Edition, Windows 2000, Windows XP Home Edition, Windows XP Professional, Windows Server 2003 family

SystemPens.WindowFrame Property

Gets a **Pen** object that is the color of a window frame.

```
[Visual Basic]
Public Shared ReadOnly Property WindowFrame As Pen
[C#]
public static Pen WindowFrame {get;}
[C++]
public: __property static Pen* get_WindowFrame();
[JScript]
public static function get WindowFrame() : Pen;
```

Property Value

A **Pen** object that is the color of a window frame.

Requirements

Platforms: Windows 98, Windows NT 4.0, Windows Millennium Edition, Windows 2000, Windows XP Home Edition, Windows XP Professional, Windows Server 2003 family

SystemPens.WindowText Property

Gets a **Pen** object that is the color of the text in the client area of a window.

```
[Visual Basic]
Public Shared ReadOnly Property WindowText As Pen
[C#]
public static Pen WindowText {get;}
[C++]
public: __property static Pen* get_WindowText();
[JScript]
public static function get WindowText() : Pen;
```

Property Value

A **Pen** object that is the color of the text in the client area of a window.

Requirements

Platforms: Windows 98, Windows NT 4.0, Windows Millennium Edition, Windows 2000, Windows XP Home Edition, Windows XP Professional, Windows Server 2003 family

SystemPens.FromSystemColor Method

Creates a **Pen** object from the specified **Color** structure.

[Visual Basic]
```
Public Shared Function FromSystemColor( _
   ByVal c As Color _
) As Pen
```
[C#]
```
public static Pen FromSystemColor(
   Color c
);
```
[C++]
```
public: static Pen* FromSystemColor(
   Color c
);
```
[JScript]
```
public static function FromSystemColor(
   c : Color
) : Pen;
```

Parameters

c

The **Color** structure for the new **Pen** object.

Return Value

The **Pen** object this method creates.

Requirements

Platforms: Windows 98, Windows NT 4.0, Windows Millennium Edition, Windows 2000, Windows XP Home Edition, Windows XP Professional, Windows Server 2003 family

TextureBrush Class

Each property of the **TextureBrush** class is a **Brush** object that uses an image to fill the interior of a shape. This class cannot be inherited.

System.Object
  System.MarshalByRefObject
    System.Drawing.Brush
      System.Drawing.TextureBrush

```
[Visual Basic]
NotInheritable Public Class TextureBrush
   Inherits Brush
[C#]
public sealed class TextureBrush : Brush
[C++]
public __gc __sealed class TextureBrush : public Brush
[JScript]
public class TextureBrush extends Brush
```

Thread Safety

Any public static (**Shared** in Visual Basic) members of this type are safe for multithreaded operations. Any instance members are not guaranteed to be thread safe.

Requirements

Namespace: System.Drawing

Platforms: Windows 98, Windows NT 4.0, Windows Millennium Edition, Windows 2000, Windows XP Home Edition, Windows XP Professional, Windows Server 2003 family

Assembly: System.Drawing (in System.Drawing.dll)

TextureBrush Constructor

Initializes a new **TextureBrush** object that uses the specified image.

Overload List

Initializes a new **TextureBrush** object that uses the specified image.

[Visual Basic] **Public Sub New(Image)**
[C#] **public TextureBrush(Image);**
[C++] **public: TextureBrush(Image*);**
[JScript] **public function TextureBrush(Image);**

Initializes a new **TextureBrush** object that uses the specified image and bounding rectangle.

[Visual Basic] **Public Sub New(Image, Rectangle)**
[C#] **public TextureBrush(Image, Rectangle);**
[C++] **public: TextureBrush(Image*, Rectangle);**
[JScript] **public function TextureBrush(Image, Rectangle);**

Initializes a new **TextureBrush** object that uses the specified image and bounding rectangle.

[Visual Basic] **Public Sub New(Image, RectangleF)**
[C#] **public TextureBrush(Image, RectangleF);**
[C++] **public: TextureBrush(Image*, RectangleF);**
[JScript] **public function TextureBrush(Image, RectangleF);**

Initializes a new **TextureBrush** object that uses the specified image and wrap mode.

[Visual Basic] **Public Sub New(Image, WrapMode)**
[C#] **public TextureBrush(Image, WrapMode);**
[C++] **public: TextureBrush(Image*, WrapMode);**
[JScript] **public function TextureBrush(Image, WrapMode);**

Initializes a new **TextureBrush** object that uses the specified image, bounding rectangle, and image attributes.

[Visual Basic] **Public Sub New(Image, Rectangle, ImageAttributes)**
[C#] **public TextureBrush(Image, Rectangle, ImageAttributes);**
[C++] **public: TextureBrush(Image*, Rectangle, ImageAttributes*);**
[JScript] **public function TextureBrush(Image, Rectangle, ImageAttributes);**

Initializes a new **TextureBrush** object that uses the specified image, bounding rectangle, and image attributes.

[Visual Basic] **Public Sub New(Image, RectangleF, ImageAttributes)**
[C#] **public TextureBrush(Image, RectangleF, ImageAttributes);**
[C++] **public: TextureBrush(Image*, RectangleF, ImageAttributes*);**
[JScript] **public function TextureBrush(Image, RectangleF, ImageAttributes);**

Initializes a new **TextureBrush** object that uses the specified image, wrap mode, and bounding rectangle.

[Visual Basic] **Public Sub New(Image, WrapMode, Rectangle)**
[C#] **public TextureBrush(Image, WrapMode, Rectangle);**
[C++] **public: TextureBrush(Image*, WrapMode, Rectangle);**
[JScript] **public function TextureBrush(Image, WrapMode, Rectangle);**

Initializes a new **TextureBrush** object that uses the specified image, wrap mode, and bounding rectangle.

[Visual Basic] **Public Sub New(Image, WrapMode, RectangleF)**
[C#] **public TextureBrush(Image, WrapMode, RectangleF);**
[C++] **public: TextureBrush(Image*, WrapMode, RectangleF);**
[JScript] **public function TextureBrush(Image, WrapMode, RectangleF);**

TextureBrush Constructor (Image)

Initializes a new **TextureBrush** object that uses the specified image.

```
[Visual Basic]
Public Sub New( _
   ByVal bitmap As Image _
)
[C#]
public TextureBrush(
   Image bitmap
);
[C++]
public: TextureBrush(
   Image* bitmap
);
[JScript]
public function TextureBrush(
   bitmap : Image
);
```

Parameters

bitmap
  The **Image** object with which this **TextureBrush** object fills interiors.

Requirements

Platforms: Windows 98, Windows NT 4.0, Windows Millennium Edition, Windows 2000, Windows XP Home Edition, Windows XP Professional, Windows Server 2003 family

TextureBrush Constructor (Image, Rectangle)

Initializes a new **TextureBrush** object that uses the specified image and bounding rectangle.

```
[Visual Basic]
Public Sub New( _
   ByVal image As Image, _
   ByVal dstRect As Rectangle _
)
[C#]
public TextureBrush(
   Image image,
   Rectangle dstRect
);
[C++]
public: TextureBrush(
   Image* image,
   Rectangle dstRect
);
[JScript]
public function TextureBrush(
   image : Image,
   dstRect : Rectangle
);
```

Parameters

image

The **Image** object with which this **TextureBrush** object fills interiors.

dstRect

A **Rectangle** structure that represents the bounding rectangle for this **TextureBrush** object.

Requirements

Platforms: Windows 98, Windows NT 4.0, Windows Millennium Edition, Windows 2000, Windows XP Home Edition, Windows XP Professional, Windows Server 2003 family

TextureBrush Constructor (Image, RectangleF)

Initializes a new **TextureBrush** object that uses the specified image and bounding rectangle.

```
[Visual Basic]
Public Sub New( _
   ByVal image As Image, _
   ByVal dstRect As RectangleF _
)
[C#]
public TextureBrush(
   Image image,
   RectangleF dstRect
);
[C++]
public: TextureBrush(
   Image* image,
   RectangleF dstRect
);
[JScript]
public function TextureBrush(
   image : Image,
   dstRect : RectangleF
);
```

Parameters

image

The **Image** object with which this **TextureBrush** object fills interiors.

dstRect

A **RectangleF** structure that represents the bounding rectangle for this **TextureBrush** object.

Requirements

Platforms: Windows 98, Windows NT 4.0, Windows Millennium Edition, Windows 2000, Windows XP Home Edition, Windows XP Professional, Windows Server 2003 family

TextureBrush Constructor (Image, WrapMode)

Initializes a new **TextureBrush** object that uses the specified image and wrap mode.

```
[Visual Basic]
Public Sub New( _
   ByVal image As Image, _
   ByVal wrapMode As WrapMode _
)
[C#]
public TextureBrush(
   Image image,
   WrapMode wrapMode
);
[C++]
public: TextureBrush(
   Image* image,
   WrapMode wrapMode
);
[JScript]
public function TextureBrush(
   image : Image,
   wrapMode : WrapMode
);
```

Parameters

image

The **Image** object with which this **TextureBrush** object fills interiors.

wrapMode

A **WrapMode** enumeration that specifies how this **TextureBrush** object is tiled.

Requirements

Platforms: Windows 98, Windows NT 4.0, Windows Millennium Edition, Windows 2000, Windows XP Home Edition, Windows XP Professional, Windows Server 2003 family

TextureBrush Constructor (Image, Rectangle, ImageAttributes)

Initializes a new **TextureBrush** object that uses the specified image, bounding rectangle, and image attributes.

```
[Visual Basic]
Public Sub New( _
   ByVal image As Image, _
   ByVal dstRect As Rectangle, _
   ByVal imageAttr As ImageAttributes _
)
[C#]
public TextureBrush(
   Image image,
   Rectangle dstRect,
   ImageAttributes imageAttr
);
[C++]
public: TextureBrush(
   Image* image,
   Rectangle dstRect,
   ImageAttributes* imageAttr
);
[JScript]
public function TextureBrush(
   image : Image,
   dstRect : Rectangle,
   imageAttr : ImageAttributes
);
```

Parameters

image
: The **Image** object with which this **TextureBrush** object fills interiors.

dstRect
: A **Rectangle** structure that represents the bounding rectangle for this **TextureBrush** object.

imageAttr
: An **ImageAttributes** object that contains additional information about the image used by this **TextureBrush** object.

Requirements

Platforms: Windows 98, Windows NT 4.0, Windows Millennium Edition, Windows 2000, Windows XP Home Edition, Windows XP Professional, Windows Server 2003 family

TextureBrush Constructor (Image, RectangleF, ImageAttributes)

Initializes a new **TextureBrush** object that uses the specified image, bounding rectangle, and image attributes.

```
[Visual Basic]
Public Sub New( _
   ByVal image As Image, _
   ByVal dstRect As RectangleF, _
   ByVal imageAttr As ImageAttributes _
)
[C#]
public TextureBrush(
   Image image,
   RectangleF dstRect,
   ImageAttributes imageAttr
);
[C++]
public: TextureBrush(
   Image* image,
   RectangleF dstRect,
   ImageAttributes* imageAttr
);
[JScript]
public function TextureBrush(
   image : Image,
   dstRect : RectangleF,
   imageAttr : ImageAttributes
);
```

Parameters

image
: The **Image** object with which this **TextureBrush** object fills interiors.

dstRect
: A **RectangleF** structure that represents the bounding rectangle for this **TextureBrush** object.

imageAttr
: An **ImageAttributes** object that contains additional information about the image used by this **TextureBrush** object.

Requirements

Platforms: Windows 98, Windows NT 4.0, Windows Millennium Edition, Windows 2000, Windows XP Home Edition, Windows XP Professional, Windows Server 2003 family

TextureBrush Constructor (Image, WrapMode, Rectangle)

Initializes a new **TextureBrush** object that uses the specified image, wrap mode, and bounding rectangle.

```
[Visual Basic]
Public Sub New( _
   ByVal image As Image, _
   ByVal wrapMode As WrapMode, _
   ByVal dstRect As Rectangle _
)
[C#]
public TextureBrush(
   Image image,
   WrapMode wrapMode,
   Rectangle dstRect
);
[C++]
public: TextureBrush(
   Image* image,
   WrapMode wrapMode,
   Rectangle dstRect
);
```

```
[JScript]
public function TextureBrush(
   image : Image,
   wrapMode : WrapMode,
   dstRect : Rectangle
);
```

Parameters

image

The **Image** object with which this **TextureBrush** object fills interiors.

wrapMode

A **WrapMode** enumeration that specifies how this **TextureBrush** object is tiled.

dstRect

A **Rectangle** structure that represents the bounding rectangle for this **TextureBrush** object.

Requirements

Platforms: Windows 98, Windows NT 4.0, Windows Millennium Edition, Windows 2000, Windows XP Home Edition, Windows XP Professional, Windows Server 2003 family

TextureBrush Constructor (Image, WrapMode, RectangleF)

Initializes a new **TextureBrush** object that uses the specified image, wrap mode, and bounding rectangle.

```
[Visual Basic]
Public Sub New( _
   ByVal image As Image, _
   ByVal wrapMode As WrapMode, _
   ByVal dstRect As RectangleF _
)
[C#]
public TextureBrush(
   Image image,
   WrapMode wrapMode,
   RectangleF dstRect
);
[C++]
public: TextureBrush(
   Image* image,
   WrapMode wrapMode,
   RectangleF dstRect
);
[JScript]
public function TextureBrush(
   image : Image,
   wrapMode : WrapMode,
   dstRect : RectangleF
);
```

Parameters

image

The **Image** object with which this **TextureBrush** object fills interiors.

wrapMode

A **WrapMode** enumeration that specifies how this **TextureBrush** object is tiled.

dstRect

A **RectangleF** structure that represents the bounding rectangle for this **TextureBrush** object.

Requirements

Platforms: Windows 98, Windows NT 4.0, Windows Millennium Edition, Windows 2000, Windows XP Home Edition, Windows XP Professional, Windows Server 2003 family

TextureBrush.Image Property

Gets the **Image** object associated with this **TextureBrush** object.

```
[Visual Basic]
Public ReadOnly Property Image As Image
[C#]
public Image Image {get;}
[C++]
public: __property Image* get_Image();
[JScript]
public function get Image() : Image;
```

Property Value

An **Image** object that represents the image with which this **TextureBrush** object fills shapes.

Requirements

Platforms: Windows 98, Windows NT 4.0, Windows Millennium Edition, Windows 2000, Windows XP Home Edition, Windows XP Professional, Windows Server 2003 family

TextureBrush.Transform Property

Gets or sets a **Matrix** object that defines a local geometric transformation for the image associated with this **TextureBrush** object.

```
[Visual Basic]
Public Property Transform As Matrix
[C#]
public Matrix Transform {get; set;}
[C++]
public: __property Matrix* get_Transform();
public: __property void set_Transform(Matrix*);
[JScript]
public function get Transform() : Matrix;
public function set Transform(Matrix);
```

Property Value

A **Matrix** object that defines a geometric transformation that applies only to fills drawn by using this **TextureBrush** object.

Remarks

A geometric transformation can be used to translate, scale, rotate, or skew the image that defines the texture of this brush.

Requirements

Platforms: Windows 98, Windows NT 4.0, Windows Millennium Edition, Windows 2000, Windows XP Home Edition, Windows XP Professional, Windows Server 2003 family

TextureBrush.WrapMode Property

Gets or sets a **WrapMode** enumeration that indicates the wrap mode for this **TextureBrush** object.

[Visual Basic]
```
Public Property WrapMode As WrapMode
```
[C#]
```
public WrapMode WrapMode {get; set;}
```
[C++]
```
public: __property WrapMode get_WrapMode();
public: __property void set_WrapMode(WrapMode);
```
[JScript]
```
public function get WrapMode() : WrapMode;
public function set WrapMode(WrapMode);
```

Property Value

A **WrapMode** enumeration that specifies how fills drawn by using this **LinearGradientBrush** object are tiled.

Requirements

Platforms: Windows 98, Windows NT 4.0, Windows Millennium Edition, Windows 2000, Windows XP Home Edition, Windows XP Professional, Windows Server 2003 family

TextureBrush.Clone Method

Creates an exact copy of this **TextureBrush** object.

[Visual Basic]
```
Overrides Public Function Clone() As Object Implements _
   ICloneable.Clone
```
[C#]
```
public override object Clone();
```
[C++]
```
public: Object* Clone();
```
[JScript]
```
public override function Clone() : Object;
```

Return Value

The **TextureBrush** object this method creates, cast as an **Object** object.

Implements

ICloneable.Clone

Example

[Visual Basic, C#] The following example is designed for use with Windows Forms, and it requires **PaintEventArgs** *e*, which is a parameter of the **Paint** event handler. The code creates a **TextureBrush** object and an exact copy of that texture brush, and then uses the copy to fill a rectangle on the screen.

[Visual Basic]
```
Public Sub Clone_Example(e As PaintEventArgs)
' Create a TextureBrush object.
Dim tBrush As New TextureBrush(New Bitmap("texture.jpg"))
' Create an exact copy of tBrush.
Dim cloneBrush As TextureBrush = CType(tBrush.Clone(), _
TextureBrush)
' Fill a rectangle with cloneBrush.
e.Graphics.FillRectangle(cloneBrush, 0, 0, 100, 100)
End Sub
```

[C#]
```
public void Clone_Example(PaintEventArgs e)
{
// Create a TextureBrush object.
TextureBrush tBrush = new TextureBrush(new Bitmap("texture.jpg"));
// Create an exact copy of tBrush.
TextureBrush cloneBrush = (TextureBrush)tBrush.Clone();
// Fill a rectangle with cloneBrush.
e.Graphics.FillRectangle(cloneBrush, 0, 0, 100, 100);
}
```

Requirements

Platforms: Windows 98, Windows NT 4.0, Windows Millennium Edition, Windows 2000, Windows XP Home Edition, Windows XP Professional, Windows Server 2003 family

TextureBrush.MultiplyTransform Method

Multiplies the **Matrix** object that represents the local geometric transformation of this **TextureBrush** object by the specified **Matrix** object in the specified order.

Overload List

Multiplies the **Matrix** object that represents the local geometric transformation of this **TextureBrush** object by the specified **Matrix** object by prepending the specified **Matrix** object.

[Visual Basic] **Overloads Public Sub Multiply-Transform(Matrix)**

[C#] **public void MultiplyTransform(Matrix);**

[C++] **public: void MultiplyTransform(Matrix*);**

[JScript] **public function MultiplyTransform(Matrix);**

Multiplies the **Matrix** object that represents the local geometric transformation of this **TextureBrush** object by the specified **Matrix** object in the specified order.

[Visual Basic] **Overloads Public Sub Multiply-Transform(Matrix, MatrixOrder)**

[C#] **public void MultiplyTransform(Matrix, MatrixOrder);**

[C++] **public: void MultiplyTransform(Matrix*, MatrixOrder);**

[JScript] **public function MultiplyTransform(Matrix, MatrixOrder);**

Example

[Visual Basic, C#] The following example is designed for use with Windows Forms, and it requires **PaintEventArgs** *e*, which is a parameter of the **Paint** event handler. The code performs the following actions:

- Creates a **TextureBrush** object.
- Creates a new matrix that specifies a translation of 50 units in the x-direction.
- Multiplies the matrix with the transformation matrix of the texture brush.
- Fills a rectangle, using the texture brush.

[Visual Basic, C#] **Note** This example shows how to use one of the overloaded versions of **MultiplyTransform**. For other examples that might be available, see the individual overload topics.

[Visual Basic]
```
Public Sub MultiplyTransform_Example(e As PaintEventArgs)
' Create a TextureBrush object.
Dim tBrush As New TextureBrush(New Bitmap("texture.jpg"))
' Create a transformation matrix.
Dim translateMatrix As New Matrix()
translateMatrix.Translate(50, 0)
' Multiply the transformation matrix of tBrush by translateMatrix.
tBrush.MultiplyTransform(translateMatrix)
' Fill a rectangle with tBrush.
e.Graphics.FillRectangle(tBrush, 0, 110, 100, 100)
End Sub
```

[C#]
```
public void MultiplyTransform_Example(PaintEventArgs e)
{
// Create a TextureBrush object.
TextureBrush tBrush = new TextureBrush(new Bitmap("texture.jpg"));
// Create a transformation matrix.
Matrix translateMatrix = new Matrix();
translateMatrix.Translate(50, 0);
// Multiply the transformation matrix of tBrush by translateMatrix.
tBrush.MultiplyTransform(translateMatrix);
// Fill a rectangle with tBrush.
e.Graphics.FillRectangle(tBrush, 0, 110, 100, 100);
}
```

TextureBrush.MultiplyTransform Method (Matrix)

Multiplies the **Matrix** object that represents the local geometric transformation of this **TextureBrush** object by the specified **Matrix** object by prepending the specified **Matrix** object.

[Visual Basic]
```
Overloads Public Sub MultiplyTransform( _
   ByVal matrix As Matrix _
)
```
[C#]
```
public void MultiplyTransform(
   Matrix matrix
);
```
[C++]
```
public: void MultiplyTransform(
   Matrix* matrix
);
```
[JScript]
```
public function MultiplyTransform(
   matrix : Matrix
);
```

Parameters

matrix

The **Matrix** object by which to multiply the geometric transformation.

Return Value

This method does not return a value.

Remarks

The transformation matrix of a **TextureBrush** object specifies how the image that defines the texture is transformed. For example, if the transformation matrix specifies a rotation of 90 degrees clockwise, the texture image is rotated by 90 degrees clockwise.

Example

[Visual Basic, C#] The following example is designed for use with Windows Forms, and it requires **PaintEventArgs** *e*, which is a parameter of the **Paint** event handler. The code performs the following actions:

- Creates a **TextureBrush** object.
- Creates a new matrix that specifies a translation of 50 units in the x-direction.
- Multiplies the matrix with the transformation matrix of the texture brush.
- Fills a rectangle, using the texture brush.

[Visual Basic]
```
Public Sub MultiplyTransform_Example(e As PaintEventArgs)
' Create a TextureBrush object.
Dim tBrush As New TextureBrush(New Bitmap("texture.jpg"))
' Create a transformation matrix.
Dim translateMatrix As New Matrix()
translateMatrix.Translate(50, 0)
' Multiply the transformation matrix of tBrush by translateMatrix.
tBrush.MultiplyTransform(translateMatrix, MatrixOrder.Prepend)
' Fill a rectangle with tBrush.
e.Graphics.FillRectangle(tBrush, 0, 110, 100, 100)
End Sub
```

[C#]
```
public void MultiplyTransform_Example(PaintEventArgs e)
{
// Create a TextureBrush object.
TextureBrush tBrush = new TextureBrush(new Bitmap("texture.jpg"));
// Create a transformation matrix.
Matrix translateMatrix = new Matrix();
translateMatrix.Translate(50, 0);
// Multiply the transformation matrix of tBrush by translateMatrix.
tBrush.MultiplyTransform(translateMatrix, MatrixOrder.Prepend);
// Fill a rectangle with tBrush.
e.Graphics.FillRectangle(tBrush, 0, 110, 100, 100);
}
```

Requirements

Platforms: Windows 98, Windows NT 4.0, Windows Millennium Edition, Windows 2000, Windows XP Home Edition, Windows XP Professional, Windows Server 2003 family

TextureBrush.MultiplyTransform Method (Matrix, MatrixOrder)

Multiplies the **Matrix** object that represents the local geometric transformation of this **TextureBrush** object by the specified **Matrix** object in the specified order.

[Visual Basic]
```
Overloads Public Sub MultiplyTransform( _
   ByVal matrix As Matrix, _
   ByVal order As MatrixOrder _
)
```
[C#]
```
public void MultiplyTransform(
   Matrix matrix,
   MatrixOrder order
);
```
[C++]
```
public: void MultiplyTransform(
   Matrix* matrix,
   MatrixOrder order
);
```
[JScript]
```
public function MultiplyTransform(
   matrix : Matrix,
   order : MatrixOrder
);
```

Parameters

matrix
: The **Matrix** object by which to multiply the geometric transformation.

order
: A **MatrixOrder** enumeration that specifies the order in which to multiply the two matrices.

Return Value

This method does not return a value.

Remarks

The transformation matrix of a **TextureBrush** object specifies how the image that defines the texture is transformed. For example, if the transformation matrix specifies a rotation of 90 degrees clockwise, the texture image is rotated by 90 degrees clockwise.

Example

[Visual Basic, C#] The following example is designed for use with Windows Forms, and it requires **PaintEventArgs** *e*, which is a parameter of the **Paint** event handler. The code performs the following actions:

- Creates a **TextureBrush** object.
- Creates a new matrix that specifies a translation of 50 units in the x-direction.
- Multiplies the matrix with the transformation matrix of the texture brush.
- Fills a rectangle, using the texture brush.

[Visual Basic]

```
Public Sub MultiplyTransform_Example(e As PaintEventArgs)
' Create a TextureBrush object.
Dim tBrush As New TextureBrush(New Bitmap("texture.jpg"))
' Create a transformation matrix.
Dim translateMatrix As New Matrix()
translateMatrix.Translate(50, 0)
' Multiply the transformation matrix of tBrush by translateMatrix.
tBrush.MultiplyTransform(translateMatrix)
' Fill a rectangle with tBrush.
e.Graphics.FillRectangle(tBrush, 0, 110, 100, 100)
End Sub
```

[C#]

```
public void MultiplyTransform_Example(PaintEventArgs e)
{
// Create a TextureBrush object.
TextureBrush tBrush = new TextureBrush(new Bitmap("texture.jpg"));
// Create a transformation matrix.
Matrix translateMatrix = new Matrix();
translateMatrix.Translate(50, 0);
// Multiply the transformation matrix of tBrush by translateMatrix.
tBrush.MultiplyTransform(translateMatrix);
// Fill a rectangle with tBrush.
e.Graphics.FillRectangle(tBrush, 0, 110, 100, 100);
}
```

Requirements

Platforms: Windows 98, Windows NT 4.0, Windows Millennium Edition, Windows 2000, Windows XP Home Edition, Windows XP Professional, Windows Server 2003 family

TextureBrush.ResetTransform Method

Resets the **Transform** property of this **TextureBrush** object to identity.

[Visual Basic]
```
Public Sub ResetTransform()
```
[C#]
```
public void ResetTransform();
```
[C++]
```
public: void ResetTransform();
```
[JScript]
```
public function ResetTransform();
```

Return Value

This method does not return a value.

Example

[Visual Basic, C#] The following example is designed for use with Windows Forms, and it requires **PaintEventArgs** *e*, which is a parameter of the **Paint** event handler. The code performs the following actions:

- Creates a **TextureBrush** object.
- Rotates the texture image by 90 degrees.
- Fills a rectangle.
- Resets the transformation matrix to identity.
- Fills a second rectangle.

[Visual Basic]

```
Public Sub ResetTransform_Example(e As PaintEventArgs)
' Create a TextureBrush object.
Dim tBrush As New TextureBrush(New Bitmap("texture.jpg"))
' Rotate the texture image by 90 degrees.
tBrush.RotateTransform(90)
' Fill a rectangle with tBrush.
e.Graphics.FillRectangle(tBrush, 0, 0, 100, 100)
' Reset transformation matrix to identity.
tBrush.ResetTransform()
' Fill a rectangle with tBrush.
e.Graphics.FillRectangle(tBrush, 0, 110, 100, 100)
End Sub 'ResetTransform_Example.
```

[C#]

```
public void ResetTransform_Example(PaintEventArgs e)
{
// Create a TextureBrush object.
TextureBrush tBrush = new TextureBrush(new Bitmap("texture.jpg"));
// Rotate the texture image by 90 degrees.
tBrush.RotateTransform(90);
// Fill a rectangle with tBrush.
e.Graphics.FillRectangle(tBrush, 0, 0, 100, 100);
// Reset transformation matrix to identity.
tBrush.ResetTransform();
// Fill a rectangle with tBrush.
e.Graphics.FillRectangle(tBrush, 0, 110, 100, 100);
}
```

Requirements

Platforms: Windows 98, Windows NT 4.0, Windows Millennium Edition, Windows 2000, Windows XP Home Edition, Windows XP Professional, Windows Server 2003 family

TextureBrush.RotateTransform Method

Rotates the local geometric transformation of this **TextureBrush** object by the specified amount. This method prepends the rotation to the transformation.

Overload List

Rotates the local geometric transformation of this **TextureBrush** object by the specified amount. This method prepends the rotation to the transformation.

[Visual Basic] **Overloads Public Sub RotateTransform(Single)**

[C#] **public void RotateTransform(float);**

[C++] **public: void RotateTransform(float);**

[JScript] **public function RotateTransform(float);**

Rotates the local geometric transformation of this **TextureBrush** object by the specified amount in the specified order.

[Visual Basic] **Overloads Public Sub RotateTransform(Single, MatrixOrder)**

[C#] **public void RotateTransform(float, MatrixOrder);**

[C++] **public: void RotateTransform(float, MatrixOrder);**

[JScript] **public function RotateTransform(float, MatrixOrder);**

Example

[Visual Basic, C#] The following example is designed for use with Windows Forms, and it requires **PaintEventArgs** *e*, which is a parameter of the **Paint** event handler. The code performs the following actions:

- Creates a **TextureBrush** object.
- Rotates the texture image by 90 degrees.
- Fills a rectangle.

> [Visual Basic, C#] **Note** This example shows how to use one of the overloaded versions of **RotateTransform**. For other examples that might be available, see the individual overload topics.

[Visual Basic]
```
Public Sub RotateTransform_Example2(e As PaintEventArgs)
' Create a TextureBrush object.
Dim tBrush As New TextureBrush(New Bitmap("texture.jpg"))
' Rotate the texture image by 90 degrees.
tBrush.RotateTransform(90, MatrixOrder.Prepend)
' Fill a rectangle with tBrush.
e.Graphics.FillRectangle(tBrush, 0, 0, 100, 100)
End Sub
```

[C#]
```
public void RotateTransform_Example2(PaintEventArgs e)
{
// Create a TextureBrush object.
TextureBrush tBrush = new TextureBrush(new Bitmap("texture.jpg"));
// Rotate the texture image by 90 degrees.
tBrush.RotateTransform(90, MatrixOrder.Prepend);
// Fill a rectangle with tBrush.
e.Graphics.FillRectangle(tBrush, 0, 0, 100, 100);
}
```

TextureBrush.RotateTransform Method (Single)

Rotates the local geometric transformation of this **TextureBrush** object by the specified amount. This method prepends the rotation to the transformation.

[Visual Basic]
```
Overloads Public Sub RotateTransform( _
   ByVal angle As Single _
)
```
[C#]
```
public void RotateTransform(
   float angle
);
```
[C++]
```
public: void RotateTransform(
   float angle
);
```
[JScript]
```
public function RotateTransform(
   angle : float
);
```

Parameters

angle

The angle of rotation.

Return Value

This method does not return a value.

Example

[Visual Basic, C#] The following example is designed for use with Windows Forms, and it requires **PaintEventArgs** *e*, which is a parameter of the **Paint** event handler. The code performs the following actions:

- Creates a **TextureBrush** object.
- Rotates the texture image by 90 degrees.
- Fills a rectangle.

[Visual Basic]
```
Public Sub RotateTransform_Example(e As PaintEventArgs)
' Create a TextureBrush object.
Dim tBrush As New TextureBrush(New Bitmap("texture.jpg"))
' Rotate the texture image by 90 degrees.
tBrush.RotateTransform(90)
' Fill a rectangle with tBrush.
e.Graphics.FillRectangle(tBrush, 0, 0, 100, 100)
End Sub
```

[C#]
```
public void RotateTransform_Example(PaintEventArgs e)
{
// Create a TextureBrush object.
TextureBrush tBrush = new TextureBrush(new Bitmap("texture.jpg"));
// Rotate the texture image by 90 degrees.
tBrush.RotateTransform(90);
// Fill a rectangle with tBrush.
e.Graphics.FillRectangle(tBrush, 0, 0, 100, 100);
}
```

Requirements

Platforms: Windows 98, Windows NT 4.0, Windows Millennium Edition, Windows 2000, Windows XP Home Edition, Windows XP Professional, Windows Server 2003 family

TextureBrush.RotateTransform Method (Single, MatrixOrder)

Rotates the local geometric transformation of this **TextureBrush** object by the specified amount in the specified order.

```
[Visual Basic]
Overloads Public Sub RotateTransform( _
   ByVal angle As Single, _
   ByVal order As MatrixOrder _
)
[C#]
public void RotateTransform(
   float angle,
   MatrixOrder order
);
[C++]
public: void RotateTransform(
   float angle,
   MatrixOrder order
);
[JScript]
public function RotateTransform(
   angle : float,
   order : MatrixOrder
);
```

Parameters

angle
The angle of rotation.

order
A **MatrixOrder** enumeration that specifies whether to append or prepend the rotation matrix.

Return Value

This method does not return a value.

Example

[Visual Basic, C#] The following example is designed for use with Windows Forms, and it requires **PaintEventArgs** *e*, which is a parameter of the **Paint** event handler. The code performs the following actions:

- Creates a **TextureBrush** object.
- Rotates the texture image by 90 degrees.
- Fills a rectangle.

```
[Visual Basic]
Public Sub RotateTransform_Example2(e As PaintEventArgs)
' Create a TextureBrush object.
Dim tBrush As New TextureBrush(New Bitmap("texture.jpg"))
' Rotate the texture image by 90 degrees.
tBrush.RotateTransform(90, MatrixOrder.Prepend)
' Fill a rectangle with tBrush.
e.Graphics.FillRectangle(tBrush, 0, 0, 100, 100)
End Sub
```

```
[C#]
public void RotateTransform_Example2(PaintEventArgs e)
{
// Create a TextureBrush object.
TextureBrush tBrush = new TextureBrush(new Bitmap("texture.jpg"));
// Rotate the texture image by 90 degrees.
tBrush.RotateTransform(90, MatrixOrder.Prepend);
// Fill a rectangle with tBrush.
e.Graphics.FillRectangle(tBrush, 0, 0, 100, 100);
}
```

Requirements

Platforms: Windows 98, Windows NT 4.0, Windows Millennium Edition, Windows 2000, Windows XP Home Edition, Windows XP Professional, Windows Server 2003 family

TextureBrush.ScaleTransform Method

Scales the local geometric transformation of this **TextureBrush** object by the specified amounts. This method prepends the scaling matrix to the transformation.

Overload List

Scales the local geometric transformation of this **TextureBrush** object by the specified amounts. This method prepends the scaling matrix to the transformation.

[Visual Basic] **Overloads Public Sub ScaleTransform(Single, Single)**

[C#] **public void ScaleTransform(float, float);**

[C++] **public: void ScaleTransform(float, float);**

[JScript] **public function ScaleTransform(float, float);**

Scales the local geometric transformation of this **TextureBrush** object by the specified amounts in the specified order.

[Visual Basic] **Overloads Public Sub ScaleTransform(Single, Single, MatrixOrder)**

[C#] **public void ScaleTransform(float, float, MatrixOrder);**

[C++] **public: void ScaleTransform(float, float, MatrixOrder);**

[JScript] **public function ScaleTransform(float, float, MatrixOrder);**

Example

[Visual Basic, C#] The following example is designed for use with Windows Forms, and it requires **PaintEventArgs** *e*, which is a parameter of the **Paint** event handler. The code performs the following actions:

- Creates a **TextureBrush** object.
- Scales the texture image by two times in the x-direction.
- Fills a rectangle on the screen, using the texture brush.

> [Visual Basic, C#] **Note** This example shows how to use one of the overloaded versions of **ScaleTransform**. For other examples that might be available, see the individual overload topics.

```
[Visual Basic]
Public Sub ScaleTransform_Example(e As PaintEventArgs)
' Create a TextureBrush object.
Dim tBrush As New TextureBrush(New Bitmap("texture.jpg"))
' Scale the texture image 2X in the x-direction.
tBrush.ScaleTransform(2, 1, MatrixOrder.Prepend)
' Fill a rectangle with tBrush.
e.Graphics.FillRectangle(tBrush, 0, 0, 100, 100)
End Sub
```

```
[C#]
public void ScaleTransform_Example(PaintEventArgs e)
{
// Create a TextureBrush object.
TextureBrush tBrush = new TextureBrush(new Bitmap("texture.jpg"));
// Scale the texture image 2X in the x-direction.
tBrush.ScaleTransform(2, 1, MatrixOrder.Prepend);
// Fill a rectangle with tBrush.
e.Graphics.FillRectangle(tBrush, 0, 0, 100, 100);
}
```

TextureBrush.ScaleTransform Method (Single, Single)

Scales the local geometric transformation of this **TextureBrush** object by the specified amounts. This method prepends the scaling matrix to the transformation.

```
[Visual Basic]
Overloads Public Sub ScaleTransform( _
   ByVal sx As Single, _
   ByVal sy As Single _
)
[C#]
public void ScaleTransform(
   float sx,
   float sy
);
[C++]
public: void ScaleTransform(
   float sx,
   float sy
);
[JScript]
public function ScaleTransform(
   sx : float,
   sy : float
);
```

Parameters

sx

The amount by which to scale the transformation in the x direction.

sy

The amount by which to scale the transformation in the y direction.

Return Value

This method does not return a value.

Example

[Visual Basic, C#] The following example is designed for use with Windows Forms, and it requires **PaintEventArgs** *e*, which is a parameter of the **Paint** event handler. The code performs the following actions:

- Creates a **TextureBrush** object.
- Scales the texture image by two times in the x-direction.
- Fills a rectangle on the screen, using the texture brush.

```
[Visual Basic]
Public Sub ScaleTransform_Example(e As PaintEventArgs)
' Create a TextureBrush object.
Dim tBrush As New TextureBrush(New Bitmap("texture.jpg"))
' Scale the texture image 2X in the x-direction.
tBrush.ScaleTransform(2, 1)
' Fill a rectangle with tBrush.
e.Graphics.FillRectangle(tBrush, 0, 0, 100, 100)
End Sub
```

```
[C#]
public void ScaleTransform_Example(PaintEventArgs e)
{
// Create a TextureBrush object.
TextureBrush tBrush = new TextureBrush(new Bitmap("texture.jpg"));
// Scale the texture image 2X in the x-direction.
tBrush.ScaleTransform(2, 1);
// Fill a rectangle with tBrush.
e.Graphics.FillRectangle(tBrush, 0, 0, 100, 100);
}
```

Requirements

Platforms: Windows 98, Windows NT 4.0, Windows Millennium Edition, Windows 2000, Windows XP Home Edition, Windows XP Professional, Windows Server 2003 family

TextureBrush.ScaleTransform Method (Single, Single, MatrixOrder)

Scales the local geometric transformation of this **TextureBrush** object by the specified amounts in the specified order.

```
[Visual Basic]
Overloads Public Sub ScaleTransform( _
   ByVal sx As Single, _
   ByVal sy As Single, _
   ByVal order As MatrixOrder _
)
[C#]
public void ScaleTransform(
   float sx,
   float sy,
   MatrixOrder order
);
[C++]
public: void ScaleTransform(
   float sx,
   float sy,
   MatrixOrder order
);
[JScript]
public function ScaleTransform(
   sx : float,
   sy : float,
   order : MatrixOrder
);
```

Parameters

sx

The amount by which to scale the transformation in the x direction.

sy

The amount by which to scale the transformation in the y direction.

order

A **MatrixOrder** enumeration that specifies whether to append or prepend the scaling matrix.

Return Value

This method does not return a value.

Example

[Visual Basic, C#] The following example is designed for use with Windows Forms, and it requires **PaintEventArgs** *e*, which is a parameter of the **Paint** event handler. The code performs the following actions:

- Creates a **TextureBrush** object.
- Scales the texture image by two times in the x-direction.
- Fills a rectangle on the screen, using the texture brush.

[Visual Basic]
```
Public Sub ScaleTransform_Example(e As PaintEventArgs)
' Create a TextureBrush object.
Dim tBrush As New TextureBrush(New Bitmap("texture.jpg"))
' Scale the texture image 2X in the x-direction.
tBrush.ScaleTransform(2, 1, MatrixOrder.Prepend)
' Fill a rectangle with tBrush.
e.Graphics.FillRectangle(tBrush, 0, 0, 100, 100)
End Sub
```

[C#]
```
public void ScaleTransform_Example(PaintEventArgs e)
{
// Create a TextureBrush object.
TextureBrush tBrush = new TextureBrush(new Bitmap("texture.jpg"));
// Scale the texture image 2X in the x-direction.
tBrush.ScaleTransform(2, 1, MatrixOrder.Prepend);
// Fill a rectangle with tBrush.
e.Graphics.FillRectangle(tBrush, 0, 0, 100, 100);
}
```

Requirements

Platforms: Windows 98, Windows NT 4.0, Windows Millennium Edition, Windows 2000, Windows XP Home Edition, Windows XP Professional, Windows Server 2003 family

TextureBrush.TranslateTransform Method

Translates the local geometric transformation of this **TextureBrush** object by the specified dimensions in the specified order.

Overload List

Translates the local geometric transformation of this **TextureBrush** object by the specified dimensions. This method prepends the translation to the transformation.

[Visual Basic] **Overloads Public Sub TranslateTransform(Single, Single)**

[C#] **public void TranslateTransform(float, float);**

[C++] **public: void TranslateTransform(float, float);**

[JScript] **public function TranslateTransform(float, float);**

Translates the local geometric transformation of this **TextureBrush** object by the specified dimensions in the specified order.

[Visual Basic] **Overloads Public Sub TranslateTransform(Single, Single, MatrixOrder)**

[C#] **public void TranslateTransform(float, float, MatrixOrder);**

[C++] **public: void TranslateTransform(float, float, MatrixOrder);**

[JScript] **public function TranslateTransform(float, float, MatrixOrder);**

Example

[Visual Basic, C#] The following example is designed for use with Windows Forms, and it requires **PaintEventArgs** *e*, which is a parameter of the **Paint** event handler. The code performs the following actions:

- Creates a **TextureBrush** object.
- Translates the texture image 50 units in the x-direction.
- Fills a rectangle on the screen, using the texture brush.

[Visual Basic, C#] **Note** This example shows how to use one of the overloaded versions of **TranslateTransform**. For other examples that might be available, see the individual overload topics.

[Visual Basic]
```
Public Sub TranslateTransform_Example(e As PaintEventArgs)
' Create a TextureBrush object.
Dim tBrush As New TextureBrush(New Bitmap("texture.jpg"))
' Scale the texture image 2X in the x-direction.
tBrush.TranslateTransform(50, 0)
' Fill a rectangle with tBrush.
e.Graphics.FillRectangle(tBrush, 0, 0, 100, 100)
End Sub
```

[C#]
```
public void TranslateTransform_Example(PaintEventArgs e)
{
// Create a TextureBrush object.
TextureBrush tBrush = new TextureBrush(new Bitmap("texture.jpg"));
// Scale the texture image 2X in the x-direction.
tBrush.TranslateTransform(50, 0);
// Fill a rectangle with tBrush.
e.Graphics.FillRectangle(tBrush, 0, 0, 100, 100);
}
```

TextureBrush.TranslateTransform Method (Single, Single)

Translates the local geometric transformation of this **TextureBrush** object by the specified dimensions. This method prepends the translation to the transformation.

[Visual Basic]
```
Overloads Public Sub TranslateTransform( _
   ByVal dx As Single, _
   ByVal dy As Single _
)
```
[C#]
```
public void TranslateTransform(
   float dx,
   float dy
);
```
[C++]
```
public: void TranslateTransform(
   float dx,
   float dy
);
```
[JScript]
```
public function TranslateTransform(
   dx : float,
   dy : float
);
```

Parameters

dx
: The dimension by which to translate the transformation in the x direction.

dy
: The dimension by which to translate the transformation in the y direction.

Return Value

This method does not return a value.

Example

[Visual Basic, C#] The following example is designed for use with Windows Forms, and it requires **PaintEventArgs** *e*, which is a parameter of the **Paint** event handler. The code performs the following actions:

- Creates a **TextureBrush** object.
- Translates the texture image 50 units in the x-direction.
- Fills a rectangle on the screen, using the texture brush.

[Visual Basic]
```
Public Sub TranslateTransform_Example(e As PaintEventArgs)
' Create a TextureBrush object.
Dim tBrush As New TextureBrush(New Bitmap("texture.jpg"))
' Scale the texture image 2X in the x-direction.
tBrush.TranslateTransform(50, 0, MatrixOrder.Prepend)
' Fill a rectangle with tBrush.
e.Graphics.FillRectangle(tBrush, 0, 0, 100, 100)
End Sub
```

[C#]
```
public void TranslateTransform_Example(PaintEventArgs e)
{
// Create a TextureBrush object.
TextureBrush tBrush = new TextureBrush(new Bitmap("texture.jpg"));
// Scale the texture image 2X in the x-direction.
tBrush.TranslateTransform(50, 0, MatrixOrder.Prepend);
// Fill a rectangle with tBrush.
e.Graphics.FillRectangle(tBrush, 0, 0, 100, 100);
```

Requirements

Platforms: Windows 98, Windows NT 4.0,
Windows Millennium Edition, Windows 2000,
Windows XP Home Edition, Windows XP Professional,
Windows Server 2003 family

TextureBrush.TranslateTransform Method (Single, Single, MatrixOrder)

Translates the local geometric transformation of this **TextureBrush** object by the specified dimensions in the specified order.

[Visual Basic]
```
Overloads Public Sub TranslateTransform( _
   ByVal dx As Single, _
   ByVal dy As Single, _
   ByVal order As MatrixOrder _
)
```
[C#]
```
public void TranslateTransform(
   float dx,
   float dy,
   MatrixOrder order
);
```
[C++]
```
public: void TranslateTransform(
   float dx,
   float dy,
   MatrixOrder order
);
```
[JScript]
```
public function TranslateTransform(
   dx : float,
   dy : float,
   order : MatrixOrder
);
```

Parameters

dx
: The dimension by which to translate the transformation in the x direction.

dy
: The dimension by which to translate the transformation in the y direction.

order
: The order (prepend or append) in which to apply the translation.

Return Value

This method does not return a value.

Example

[Visual Basic, C#] The following example is designed for use with Windows Forms, and it requires **PaintEventArgs** *e*, which is a parameter of the **Paint** event handler. The code performs the following actions:

- Creates a **TextureBrush** object.
- Translates the texture image 50 units in the x-direction.
- Fills a rectangle on the screen, using the texture brush.

[Visual Basic]
```
Public Sub TranslateTransform_Example(e As PaintEventArgs)
' Create a TextureBrush object.
Dim tBrush As New TextureBrush(New Bitmap("texture.jpg"))
' Scale the texture image 2X in the x-direction.
tBrush.TranslateTransform(50, 0)
' Fill a rectangle with tBrush.
e.Graphics.FillRectangle(tBrush, 0, 0, 100, 100)
End Sub
```

[C#]
```
public void TranslateTransform_Example(PaintEventArgs e)
{
// Create a TextureBrush object.
TextureBrush tBrush = new TextureBrush(new Bitmap("texture.jpg"));
// Scale the texture image 2X in the x-direction.
tBrush.TranslateTransform(50, 0);
// Fill a rectangle with tBrush.
e.Graphics.FillRectangle(tBrush, 0, 0, 100, 100);
}
```

Requirements

Platforms: Windows 98, Windows NT 4.0,
Windows Millennium Edition, Windows 2000,
Windows XP Home Edition, Windows XP Professional,
Windows Server 2003 family

ToolboxBitmapAttribute Class

You can apply a **ToolboxBitmapAttribute** to a control so that containers, such as Microsoft Visual Studio Form Designer, can retrieve an icon that represents the control. The bitmap for the icon can be in a file by itself or embedded in the assembly that contains the control.

The size of the bitmap that you embed in the control's assembly (or store in a separate file) should be 16 by 16. The **GetImage** method of a **ToolboxBitmapAttribute** object can return the small 16 by 16 image or a large 32 by 32 image that it creates by scaling the small image.

System.Object
  System.Attribute
    System.Drawing.ToolboxBitmapAttribute

[Visual Basic]
```
<AttributeUsage(AttributeTargets.Class)>
Public Class ToolboxBitmapAttribute
   Inherits Attribute
```
[C#]
```
[AttributeUsage(AttributeTargets.Class)]
public class ToolboxBitmapAttribute : Attribute
```
[C++]
```
[AttributeUsage(AttributeTargets::Class)]
public __gc class ToolboxBitmapAttribute : public Attribute
```
[JScript]
```
public
   AttributeUsage(AttributeTargets.Class)
class ToolboxBitmapAttribute extends Attribute
```

Thread Safety

Any public static (**Shared** in Visual Basic) members of this type are safe for multithreaded operations. Any instance members are not guaranteed to be thread safe.

Requirements

Namespace: System.Drawing

Platforms: Windows 98, Windows NT 4.0, Windows Millennium Edition, Windows 2000, Windows XP Home Edition, Windows XP Professional, Windows Server 2003 family

Assembly: System.Drawing (in System.Drawing.dll)

ToolboxBitmapAttribute Constructor

Overload List

Initializes a new **ToolboxBitmapAttribute** object with an image from a specified file.

[Visual Basic] **Public Sub New(String)**

[C#] **public ToolboxBitmapAttribute(string);**

[C++] **public: ToolboxBitmapAttribute(String*);**

[JScript] **public function ToolboxBitmapAttribute(String);**

Initializes a new **ToolboxBitmapAttribute** object based on a 16 x 16 bitmap that is embedded as a resource in a specified assembly.

[Visual Basic] **Public Sub New(Type)**

[C#] **public ToolboxBitmapAttribute(Type);**

[C++] **public: ToolboxBitmapAttribute(Type*);**

[JScript] **public function ToolboxBitmapAttribute(Type);**

Initializes a new **ToolboxBitmapAttribute** object based on a 16 by 16 bitmap that is embedded as a resource in a specified assembly.

[Visual Basic] **Public Sub New(Type, String)**

[C#] **public ToolboxBitmapAttribute(Type, string);**

[C++] **public: ToolboxBitmapAttribute(Type*, String*);**

[JScript] **public function ToolboxBitmapAttribute(Type, String);**

Example

[C#] The following code shows how to apply a **ToolboxBitmap-Attribute** to a control. Notice that the control class, ControlA, is in the namespace NamespaceA. Assume that NamespaceA is in AssemblyA. Then, the **ToolboxBitmapAttribute** constructor shown in the code will search AssemblyA for a resource named NamespaceA.MyBitmap.bmp.

> [C#] **Note** This example shows how to use one of the overloaded versions of the **ToolboxBitmapAttribute** constructor. For other examples that might be available, see the individual overload topics.

[C#]
```
namespace NamespaceA
{
   [ToolboxBitmap(typeof(ControlA), "MyBitmap.bmp")]
   public class ControlA : System.Windows.Forms.UserControl
   {
      ...
   }
   ...
}
```

[C#] When Microsoft Visual Studio .NET embeds an image file (say MyBitmap.bmp) in an assembly, it prepends the name of the default namespace to the name of the image file. Unless you specify otherwise, the default namespace is the name of the assembly. So in the previous example, the bitmap would get embedded as a resource named AssemblyA.MyBitmap.bmp. To get the correct resource name (MyNamespace.MyBitmap.bmp), you would have to change the default namespace from MyAssembly to MyNamespace. In Solution Explorer, right-click your project, and choose Properties. In the General section of Common Properties, enter the correct default namespace.

ToolboxBitmapAttribute Constructor (String)

Initializes a new **ToolboxBitmapAttribute** object with an image from a specified file.

[Visual Basic]
```
Public Sub New( _
   ByVal imageFile As String _
)
```
[C#]
```
public ToolboxBitmapAttribute(
   string imageFile
);
```
[C++]
```
public: ToolboxBitmapAttribute(
   String* imageFile
);
```
[JScript]
```
public function ToolboxBitmapAttribute(
   imageFile : String
);
```

Parameters

imageFile

The name of a file that contains a 16 by 16 bitmap.

Example

[C#] The following code shows how to apply a **ToolboxBitmap-Attribute** to a control. Assume that NamespaceA is in AssemblyA and that the file BitmapFile.bmp is in the same directory as AssemblyA.dll.

```
[C#]
namespace NamespaceA
{
   [ToolboxBitmap("BitmapFile.bmp")]
   public class ControlA : System.Windows.Forms.UserControl
   {
      ...
   }
   ...
}
```

Requirements

Platforms: Windows 98, Windows NT 4.0, Windows Millennium Edition, Windows 2000, Windows XP Home Edition, Windows XP Professional, Windows Server 2003 family

ToolboxBitmapAttribute Constructor (Type)

Initializes a new **ToolboxBitmapAttribute** object based on a 16 x 16 bitmap that is embedded as a resource in a specified assembly.

```
[Visual Basic]
Public Sub New( _
   ByVal t As Type _
)
[C#]
public ToolboxBitmapAttribute(
   Type t
);
[C++]
public: ToolboxBitmapAttribute(
   Type* t
);
[JScript]
public function ToolboxBitmapAttribute(
   t : Type
);
```

Parameters

t

A **Type** whose defining assembly is searched for the bitmap resource.

Remarks

This constructor searches for an embedded resource in the assembly that defines the type specified by the *t* parameter. The constructor searches for a resource named namespace.classname.bmp, where namespace is the namespace containing the definition of the class specified by the *t* parameter. For example, if ControlA is in NamespaceA in AssemblyA.dll, then the constructor searches AssemblyA.dll for a resource named NamespaceA.ControlA.bmp.

Example

[C#] The following code shows how to apply a **ToolboxBitmap-Attribute** to a control. Notice that the control class, ControlA, is in the namespace NamespaceA. Assume that NamespaceA is in AssemblyA. Then, the **ToolboxBitmapAttribute** constructor shown in the code will search AssemblyA for a resource named NamespaceA.ControlA.bmp.

```
[C#]
namespace NamespaceA
{
   [ToolboxBitmap(typeof(ControlA))]
   public class ControlA : System.Windows.Forms.UserControl
   {
      ...
   }
   ...
}
```

[C#] When Microsoft Visual Studio .NET embeds an image file (say ControlA.bmp) in an assembly, it prepends the name of the default namespace to the name of the image file. Unless you specify otherwise, the default namespace is the name of the assembly. So in the previous example, the bitmap would get embedded as a resource named AssemblyA.ControlA.bmp. To get the correct resource name (MyNamespace.ControlA.bmp), you would have to change the default namespace from MyAssembly to MyNamespace. In Solution Explorer, right-click your project, and choose Properties. In the General section of Common Properties, enter the correct default namespace.

Requirements

Platforms: Windows 98, Windows NT 4.0, Windows Millennium Edition, Windows 2000, Windows XP Home Edition, Windows XP Professional, Windows Server 2003 family

ToolboxBitmapAttribute Constructor (Type, String)

Initializes a new **ToolboxBitmapAttribute** object based on a 16 by 16 bitmap that is embedded as a resource in a specified assembly.

```
[Visual Basic]
Public Sub New( _
   ByVal t As Type, _
   ByVal name As String _
)
[C#]
public ToolboxBitmapAttribute(
   Type t,
   string name
);
[C++]
public: ToolboxBitmapAttribute(
   Type* t,
   String* name
);
[JScript]
public function ToolboxBitmapAttribute(
   t : Type,
   name : String
);
```

Parameters

t

A **Type** whose defining assembly is searched for the bitmap resource.

name

The name of the embedded bitmap resource.

Remarks

This constructor searches for an embedded resource in the assembly that defines the type specified by the *t* parameter. The constructor searches for a resource named namespace.name, where namespace is the namespace containing the definition of the class specified by the *t* parameter. For example, suppose that ControlA is a class in NamespaceA in AssemblyA.dll and that you passed "MyBitmap.bmp" to the *name* parameter. Then the constructor searches AssemblyA.dll for a resource named NamespaceA.MyBitmap.bmp.

Example

[C#] The following code shows how to apply a **ToolboxBitmapAttribute** to a control. Notice that the control class, ControlA, is in the namespace NamespaceA. Assume that NamespaceA is in AssemblyA. Then, the **ToolboxBitmapAttribute** constructor shown in the code will search AssemblyA for a resource named NamespaceA.MyBitmap.bmp.

```
[C#]
namespace NamespaceA
{
   [ToolboxBitmap(typeof(ControlA), "MyBitmap.bmp")]
   public class ControlA : System.Windows.Forms.UserControl
   {
      ...
   }
   ...
}
```

[C#] When Microsoft Visual Studio .NET embeds an image file (say MyBitmap.bmp) in an assembly, it prepends the name of the default namespace to the name of the image file. Unless you specify otherwise, the default namespace is the name of the assembly. So in the previous example, the bitmap would get embedded as a resource named AssemblyA.MyBitmap.bmp. To get the correct resource name (MyNamespace.MyBitmap.bmp), you would have to change the default namespace from MyAssembly to MyNamespace. In Solution Explorer, right-click your project, and choose Properties. In the General section of Common Properties, enter the correct default namespace.

Requirements

Platforms: Windows 98, Windows NT 4.0, Windows Millennium Edition, Windows 2000, Windows XP Home Edition, Windows XP Professional, Windows Server 2003 family

ToolboxBitmapAttribute.Default Field

A **ToolboxBitmapAttribute** object that has its small image and its large image set to a null reference (**Nothing** in Visual Basic).

```
[Visual Basic]
Public Shared ReadOnly Default As ToolboxBitmapAttribute
[C#]
public static readonly ToolboxBitmapAttribute Default;
[C++]
public: static ToolboxBitmapAttribute* Default;
[JScript]
public static var Default : ToolboxBitmapAttribute;
```

Requirements

Platforms: Windows 98, Windows NT 4.0, Windows Millennium Edition, Windows 2000, Windows XP Home Edition, Windows XP Professional, Windows Server 2003 family

ToolboxBitmapAttribute.Equals Method

Indicates whether the specified object is a **ToolboxBitmapAttribute** object and is identical to this **ToolboxBitmapAttribute** object.

```
[Visual Basic]
Overrides Public Function Equals( _
   ByVal value As Object _
) As Boolean
[C#]
public override bool Equals(
   object value
);
[C++]
public: bool Equals(
   Object* value
);
[JScript]
public override function Equals(
   value : Object
) : Boolean;
```

Parameters

value

The **Object** to test.

Return Value

This method returns **true** if *value* is both a **ToolboxBitmapAttribute** object and is identical to this **ToolboxBitmapAttribute** object.

Requirements

Platforms: Windows 98, Windows NT 4.0, Windows Millennium Edition, Windows 2000, Windows XP Home Edition, Windows XP Professional, Windows Server 2003 family

ToolboxBitmapAttribute.GetHashCode Method

Gets a hash code for this **ToolboxBitmapAttribute** object.

```
[Visual Basic]
Overrides Public Function GetHashCode() As Integer
[C#]
public override int GetHashCode();
[C++]
public: int GetHashCode();
[JScript]
public override function GetHashCode() : int;
```

Return Value

The hash code for this **ToolboxBitmapAttribute** object.

Requirements

Platforms: Windows 98, Windows NT 4.0, Windows Millennium Edition, Windows 2000, Windows XP Home Edition, Windows XP Professional, Windows Server 2003 family

ToolboxBitmapAttribute.GetImage Method

Gets the small or large **Image** associated with this **ToolboxBitmap-Attribute** object.

Overload List

Gets the small **Image** associated with this **ToolboxBitmapAttribute** object.

[Visual Basic] **Overloads Public Function GetImage(Object) As Image**

[C#] **public Image GetImage(object);**

[C++] **public: Image* GetImage(Object*);**

[JScript] **public function GetImage(Object) : Image;**

Gets the small **Image** associated with this **ToolboxBitmapAttribute** object.

[Visual Basic] **Overloads Public Function GetImage(Type) As Image**

[C#] **public Image GetImage(Type);**

[C++] **public: Image* GetImage(Type*);**

[JScript] **public function GetImage(Type) : Image;**

Gets the small or large **Image** associated with this **ToolboxBitmap-Attribute** object.

[Visual Basic] **Overloads Public Function GetImage(Object, Boolean) As Image**

[C#] **public Image GetImage(object, bool);**

[C++] **public: Image* GetImage(Object*, bool);**

[JScript] **public function GetImage(Object, Boolean) : Image;**

Gets the small or large **Image** associated with this **ToolboxBitmap-Attribute** object.

[Visual Basic] **Overloads Public Function GetImage(Type, Boolean) As Image**

[C#] **public Image GetImage(Type, bool);**

[C++] **public: Image* GetImage(Type*, bool);**

[JScript] **public function GetImage(Type, Boolean) : Image;**

Gets the small or large **Image** associated with this **ToolboxBitmap-Attribute** object.

[Visual Basic] **Overloads Public Function GetImage(Type, String, Boolean) As Image**

[C#] **public Image GetImage(Type, string, bool);**

[C++] **public: Image* GetImage(Type*, String*, bool);**

[JScript] **public function GetImage(Type, String, Boolean) : Image;**

ToolboxBitmapAttribute.GetImage Method (Object)

Gets the small **Image** associated with this **ToolboxBitmapAttribute** object.

```
[Visual Basic]
Overloads Public Function GetImage( _
   ByVal component As Object _
) As Image
[C#]
public Image GetImage(
   object component
);
[C++]
public: Image* GetImage(
   Object* component
);
[JScript]
public function GetImage(
   component : Object
) : Image;
```

Parameters

component

If this **ToolboxBitmapAttribute** object does not already have a small image, this method searches for a bitmap resource in the assembly that defines the type of the object specified by the component parameter. For example, if you pass an object of type ControlA to the component parameter, then this method searches the assembly that defines ControlA.

Return Value

The small **Image** associated with this **ToolboxBitmapAttributeb** object.

Remarks

This method searches for a resource named namespace.class-name.bmp, where namespace is the namespace containing the definition of the type of the object specified by the *component* parameter. For example, suppose you pass an object of type ControlA to the *component* parameter. If ControlA is in NamespaceA in AssemblyA.dll, then this method searches AssemblyA.dll for a resource named NamespaceA.ControlA.bmp.

Requirements

Platforms: Windows 98, Windows NT 4.0, Windows Millennium Edition, Windows 2000, Windows XP Home Edition, Windows XP Professional, Windows Server 2003 family

ToolboxBitmapAttribute.GetImage Method (Type)

Gets the small **Image** associated with this **ToolboxBitmapAttribute** object.

```
[Visual Basic]
Overloads Public Function GetImage( _
   ByVal type As Type _
) As Image
[C#]
public Image GetImage(
   Type type
);
[C++]
public: Image* GetImage(
   Type* type
);
[JScript]
public function GetImage(
   type : Type
) : Image;
```

Parameters

type

If this **ToolboxBitmapAttribute** object does not already have a small image, this method searches for a bitmap resource in the assembly that defines the type specified by the type parameter. For example, if you pass typeof(ControlA) to the type parameter, then this method searches the assembly that defines ControlA.

Return Value

The small **Image** associated with this **ToolboxBitmapAttributeb** object.

Remarks

This method searches for a resource named namespace.class-name.bmp, where namespace is the namespace containing the definition of the type specified by the *type* parameter. For example, suppose you pass typeof(ControlA) to the *type* parameter. If ControlA is in NamespaceA in AssemblyA.dll, then this method searches AssemblyA.dll for a resource named NamespaceA.ControlA.bmp.

Requirements

Platforms: Windows 98, Windows NT 4.0, Windows Millennium Edition, Windows 2000, Windows XP Home Edition, Windows XP Professional, Windows Server 2003 family

ToolboxBitmapAttribute.GetImage Method (Object, Boolean)

Gets the small or large **Image** associated with this **ToolboxBitmapAttribute** object.

```
[Visual Basic]
Overloads Public Function GetImage( _
   ByVal component As Object, _
   ByVal large As Boolean _
) As Image
[C#]
public Image GetImage(
   object component,
   bool large
);
[C++]
public: Image* GetImage(
   Object* component,
   bool large
);
[JScript]
public function GetImage(
   component : Object,
   large : Boolean
) : Image;
```

Parameters

component

If this **ToolboxBitmapAttribute** object does not already have a small image, this method searches for a bitmap resource in the assembly that defines the type of the object specified by the component parameter. For example, if you pass an object of type ControlA to the component parameter, then this method searches the assembly that defines ControlA.

large

Specifies whether this method returns a large image (**true**) or a small image (**false**). The small image is 16 by 16, and the large image is 32 by 32.

Return Value

An **Image** object associated with this **ToolboxBitmapAttributeb** object.

Remarks

This method searches for a resource named namespace.classname.bmp, where namespace is the namespace containing the definition of the type of the object specified by the *component* parameter. For example, suppose you pass an object of type ControlA to the *component* parameter. If ControlA is in NamespaceA in AssemblyA.dll, then this method searches AssemblyA.dll for a resource named NamespaceA.ControlA.bmp.

If this **ToolboxBitmapAttributeb** object does not already have a large image, this method creates a large image by scaling the small image.

Requirements

Platforms: Windows 98, Windows NT 4.0, Windows Millennium Edition, Windows 2000, Windows XP Home Edition, Windows XP Professional, Windows Server 2003 family

ToolboxBitmapAttribute.GetImage Method (Type, Boolean)

Gets the small or large **Image** associated with this **ToolboxBitmapAttribute** object.

```
[Visual Basic]
Overloads Public Function GetImage( _
   ByVal type As Type, _
   ByVal large As Boolean _
) As Image
[C#]
public Image GetImage(
   Type type,
   bool large
);
[C++]
public: Image* GetImage(
   Type* type,
   bool large
);
[JScript]
public function GetImage(
   type : Type,
   large : Boolean
) : Image;
```

Parameters

type

If this **ToolboxBitmapAttribute** object does not already have a small image, this method searches for a bitmap resource in the assembly that defines the type specified by the component type. For example, if you pass typeof(ControlA) to the type parameter, then this method searches the assembly that defines ControlA.

large

Specifies whether this method returns a large image (**true**) or a small image (**false**). The small image is 16 by 16, and the large image is 32 by 32.

Return Value

An **Image** associated with this **ToolboxBitmapAttributeb** object.

Remarks

This method searches for a resource named namespace.classname.bmp, where namespace is the namespace containing the definition of the type specified by the *type* parameter. For example, suppose you pass an typeof(ControlA) to the *type* parameter. If ControlA is in NamespaceA in AssemblyA.dll, then this method searches AssemblyA.dll for a resource named NamespaceA.ControlA.bmp.

If this **ToolboxBitmapAttribute** object does not already have a large image, this method creates a large image by scaling the small image.

Requirements

Platforms: Windows 98, Windows NT 4.0, Windows Millennium Edition, Windows 2000, Windows XP Home Edition, Windows XP Professional, Windows Server 2003 family

ToolboxBitmapAttribute.GetImage Method (Type, String, Boolean)

Gets the small or large **Image** associated with this **ToolboxBitmapAttribute** object.

[Visual Basic]
```
Overloads Public Function GetImage( _
   ByVal type As Type, _
   ByVal imgName As String, _
   ByVal large As Boolean _
) As Image
```
[C#]
```
public Image GetImage(
   Type type,
   string imgName,
   bool large
);
```
[C++]
```
public: Image* GetImage(
   Type* type,
   String* imgName,
   bool large
);
```
[JScript]
```
public function GetImage(
   type : Type,
   imgName : String,
   large : Boolean
) : Image;
```

Parameters

type
: If this **ToolboxBitmapAttribute** object does not already have a small image, this method searches for an embedded bitmap resource in the assembly that defines the type specified by the component type. For example, if you pass typeof(ControlA) to the type parameter, then this method searches the assembly that defines ControlA.

imgName
: The name of the embedded bitmap resource.

large
: Specifies whether this method returns a large image (**true**) or a small image (**false**). The small image is 16 by 16, and the large image is 32 by 32.

Return Value

An **Image** associated with this **ToolboxBitmapAttributeb** object.

Remarks

This method searches for a resource named namespace.imgName, where namespace is the namespace containing the definition of the type specified by the *type* parameter. For example, suppose you pass typeof(ControlA) to the *type* parameter and that you passed "MyBitmap.bmp" to the imgName parameter. If ControlA is in NamespaceA in AssemblyA.dll, then this method searches AssemblyA.dll for a resource named NamespaceA.MyBitmap.bmp.

If this **ToolboxBitmapAttribute** object does not already have a large image, this method creates a large image by scaling the small image.

Requirements

Platforms: Windows 98, Windows NT 4.0, Windows Millennium Edition, Windows 2000, Windows XP Home Edition, Windows XP Professional, Windows Server 2003 family

ToolboxBitmapAttribute.GetImageFromResource Method

Returns an **Image** object based on a bitmap resource that is embedded in an assembly.

[Visual Basic]
```
Public Shared Function GetImageFromResource( _
   ByVal t As Type, _
   ByVal imageName As String, _
   ByVal large As Boolean _
) As Image
```
[C#]
```
public static Image GetImageFromResource(
   Type t,
   string imageName,
   bool large
);
```
[C++]
```
public: static Image* GetImageFromResource(
   Type* t,
   String* imageName,
   bool large
);
```
[JScript]
```
public static function GetImageFromResource(
   t : Type,
   imageName : String,
   large : Boolean
) : Image;
```

Parameters

t
: This method searches for an embedded bitmap resource in the assembly that defines the type specified by the t parameter. For example, if you pass typeof(ControlA) to the t parameter, then this method searches the assembly that defines ControlA.

imageName
: The name of the embedded bitmap resource.

large
: Specifies whether this method returns a large image (true)or a small image (false). The small image is 16 by 16, and the large image is 32 x 32.

Return Value

An **Image** object based on the retrieved bitmap.

Remarks

This method searches for a resource named namespace.imgName, where namespace is the namespace containing the definition of the type specified by the *t* parameter. For example, suppose you pass typeof(ControlA) to the *t* parameter and you pass "MyBitmap.bmp" to the imgName parameter. If ControlA is in NamespaceA in AssemblyA.dll, then this method searches AssemblyA.dll for a resource named NamespaceA.MyBitmap.bmp.

This method is intended to retrieve a 16 x 16 bitmap resource that is embedded in an assembly. However, there is no requirement that the embedded bitmap has a size of 16 x 16. The bitmap that is retrieved from the assembly (no matter what size) is considered the small image. The large image is created by scaling the "small" image to a size of 32 x 32. So the large image will always be 32 by 32, regardless of the size of the bitmap retrieved from the assembly.

Requirements

Platforms: Windows 98, Windows NT 4.0,
Windows Millennium Edition, Windows 2000,
Windows XP Home Edition, Windows XP Professional,
Windows Server 2003 family

System.Drawing.Design Namespace

The **System.Drawing.Design** namespace contains classes that extend design-time user interface (UI) logic and drawing. The classes in this namespace can be used to create custom toolbox items, type-specific value editors that can edit and graphically represent values of their supported types, and type converters that can convert values between certain types. This namespace provides the basic frameworks for developing extensions to the design-time UI.

BitmapEditor Class

Provides a user interface for selecting bitmap files in a properties window.

System.Object
  System.Drawing.Design.UITypeEditor
    System.Drawing.Design.ImageEditor
      System.Drawing.Design.BitmapEditor

[Visual Basic]
```
Public Class BitmapEditor
   Inherits ImageEditor
```
[C#]
```
public class BitmapEditor : ImageEditor
```
[C++]
```
public __gc class BitmapEditor : public ImageEditor
```
[JScript]
```
public class BitmapEditor extends ImageEditor
```

Thread Safety

Any public static (**Shared** in Visual Basic) members of this type are safe for multithreaded operations. Any instance members are not guaranteed to be thread safe.

Remarks

BitmapEditor provides a simple way to select a bitmap image for a property. Starting the editor displays an open file dialog box that allows directory navigation and selecting a file. The file list is initially filtered for bitmap (.bmp) files.

Example

[Visual Basic]

```
<EditorAttribute(GetType(System.Drawing.Design.BitmapEditor), _
    GetType(System.Drawing.Design.UITypeEditor))> _
Public Property testBitmap() As Bitmap
    Get
        Return testBmp
    End Get
    Set(ByVal Value As Bitmap)
        testBmp = Value
    End Set
End Property

Private testBmp As Bitmap
```

[C#]
```
[EditorAttribute(typeof(System.Drawing.Design.BitmapEditor),
    typeof(System.Drawing.Design.UITypeEditor))]
public Bitmap testBitmap
{
    get
    {
        return testBmp;
    }
    set
    {
        testBmp = value;
    }
}
private Bitmap testBmp;
```

[C++]
```
public:
   [EditorAttribute(__typeof                                   ↵
(System::Drawing::Design::BitmapEditor),                       ↵
 __typeof(System::Drawing::Design::UITypeEditor))]
   __property Bitmap* get_testBitmap() {
      return testBmp;
   }
   __property void set_testBitmap(Bitmap* value) {
      testBmp = value;
   }

private:
   Bitmap*  testBmp;
```

Requirements

Namespace: System.Drawing.Design

Platforms: Windows 98, Windows NT 4.0, Windows Millennium Edition, Windows 2000, Windows XP Home Edition, Windows XP Professional, Windows Server 2003 family

Assembly: System.Drawing.Design (in System.Drawing.Design.dll)

BitmapEditor Constructor

Initializes a new instance of the **BitmapEditor** class.

[Visual Basic]
```
Public Sub New()
```
[C#]
```
public BitmapEditor();
```
[C++]
```
public: BitmapEditor();
```
[JScript]
```
public function BitmapEditor();
```

Remarks

The default constructor initializes any fields to their default values.

Requirements

Platforms: Windows 98, Windows NT 4.0, Windows Millennium Edition, Windows 2000, Windows XP Home Edition, Windows XP Professional, Windows Server 2003 family

.NET Framework Security:

- Full trust for the immediate caller. This member cannot be used by partially trusted code.

BitmapEditor.GetExtensions Method

Gets the extensions for the file list filter that the bitmap editor will initially use to filter the file list.

```
[Visual Basic]
Overrides Protected Function GetExtensions() As String()
[C#]
protected override string[] GetExtensions();
[C++]
protected: String* GetExtensions()  __gc[];
[JScript]
protected override function GetExtensions() : String[];
```

Return Value

The default set of file extensions used to filter the file list.

Requirements

Platforms: Windows 98, Windows NT 4.0, Windows Millennium Edition, Windows 2000, Windows XP Home Edition, Windows XP Professional, Windows Server 2003 family

.NET Framework Security:

- Full trust for the immediate caller. This member cannot be used by partially trusted code.

BitmapEditor.GetFileDialogDescription Method

Gets the description for the default file list filter provided by this editor.

```
[Visual Basic]
Overrides Protected Function GetFileDialogDescription() As String
[C#]
protected override string GetFileDialogDescription();
[C++]
protected: String* GetFileDialogDescription();
[JScript]
protected override function GetFileDialogDescription() : String;
```

Return Value

The description for the default type of files to filter the file list for.

Remarks

The description for the default type of files to filter for appears in the file list filter drop-down.

Requirements

Platforms: Windows 98, Windows NT 4.0, Windows Millennium Edition, Windows 2000, Windows XP Home Edition, Windows XP Professional, Windows Server 2003 family

.NET Framework Security:

- Full trust for the immediate caller. This member cannot be used by partially trusted code.

BitmapEditor.LoadFromStream Method

Loads an image from the specified stream.

```
[Visual Basic]
Overrides Protected Function LoadFromStream( _
   ByVal stream As Stream _
) As Image
[C#]
protected override Image LoadFromStream(
   Stream stream
);
[C++]
protected: Image* LoadFromStream(
   Stream* stream
);
[JScript]
protected override function LoadFromStream(
   stream : Stream
) : Image;
```

Parameters

stream

The stream from which to load the image.

Return Value

The **Image** loaded from the stream.

Requirements

Platforms: Windows 98, Windows NT 4.0, Windows Millennium Edition, Windows 2000, Windows XP Home Edition, Windows XP Professional, Windows Server 2003 family

.NET Framework Security:

- Full trust for the immediate caller. This member cannot be used by partially trusted code.

CategoryNameCollection Class

Represents a collection of category name strings.

System.Object
  System.Collections.ReadOnlyCollectionBase
    System.Drawing.Design.CategoryNameCollection

[Visual Basic]
```
NotInheritable Public Class CategoryNameCollection
   Inherits ReadOnlyCollectionBase
```
[C#]
```
public sealed class CategoryNameCollection : ReadOnlyCollectionBase
```
[C++]
```
public __gc __sealed class CategoryNameCollection : public
   ReadOnlyCollectionBase
```
[JScript]
```
public class CategoryNameCollection extends ReadOnlyCollectionBase
```

Thread Safety

Any public static (**Shared** in Visual Basic) members of this type are safe for multithreaded operations. Any instance members are not guaranteed to be thread safe.

Remarks

This collection is used to store collections of toolbox category names.

Example

[Visual Basic]
```
' categoryNames is a CategoryNameCollection obtained from
' the IToolboxService. CategoryNameCollection is a read-only
' string collection.
' Output each category name in the CategoryNameCollection.
Dim i As Integer
For i = 0 To categoryNames.Count - 1
    e.Graphics.DrawString(categoryNames(i),                          ↵
New Font("Arial", 8), Brushes.Black, 10, 24 + 10 * i)
Next i
```

[C#]
```
// categoryNames is a CategoryNameCollection obtained from
// the IToolboxService. CategoryNameCollection is a read-only
// string collection.

// Output each category name in the CategoryNameCollection.
for( int i=0; i< categoryNames.Count; i++ )
    e.Graphics.DrawString(categoryNames[i], new Font                  ↵
 ("Arial", 8), Brushes.Black, 10, 24+(10*i));
```

[C++]
```
// categoryNames is a CategoryNameCollection obtained from
// the IToolboxService*. CategoryNameCollection is a read-only
// String* collection.

// Output each category name in the CategoryNameCollection.
for (int i=0; i< categoryNames->Count; i++)
   e->Graphics->DrawString(categoryNames->Item[i],
   new System::Drawing::Font(S"Arial", 8), Brushes::Black,            ↵
 (float)10, (float)24+(10*i));
```

[Visual Basic]
```
Imports System
Imports System.Collections
Imports System.ComponentModel
Imports System.ComponentModel.Design
Imports System.Drawing
Imports System.Drawing.Design
Imports System.Data
Imports System.Windows.Forms

Public Class ToolboxCategoryNamesControl
    Inherits System.Windows.Forms.UserControl
    Private toolboxService As System.Drawing.Design.IToolboxService
    Private categoryNames As
System.Drawing.Design.CategoryNameCollection

    Public Sub New()
        Me.BackColor = System.Drawing.Color.Beige
        Me.Name = "Category Names Display Control"
        Me.Size = New System.Drawing.Size(264, 200)
    End Sub

    ' Obtain or reset IToolboxService reference on each siting         ↵
 of control.
    Public Overrides Property Site() As System.ComponentModel.ISite
        Get
            Return MyBase.Site
        End Get
        Set(ByVal Value As System.ComponentModel.ISite)
            MyBase.Site = Value

            ' If the component was sited, attempt to obtain
            ' an IToolboxService instance.
            If Not (MyBase.Site Is Nothing) Then
                toolboxService =
CType(Me.GetService(GetType(IToolboxService)), IToolboxService)
                ' If an IToolboxService was located, update            ↵
the category list.
                If Not (toolboxService Is Nothing) Then
                    categoryNames = toolboxService.CategoryNames
                End If
            Else
                toolboxService = Nothing
            End If
        End Set
    End Property

    Protected Overrides Sub OnPaint(ByVal e As                         ↵
System.Windows.Forms.PaintEventArgs)
        If Not (categoryNames Is Nothing) Then
            e.Graphics.DrawString("IToolboxService category            ↵
names list:", New Font("Arial", 9), Brushes.Black, 10, 10)

            ' categoryNames is a CategoryNameCollection obtained from
            ' the IToolboxService. CategoryNameCollection is a         ↵
 read-only
            ' string collection.
            ' Output each category name in the CategoryNameCollection.
            Dim i As Integer
            For i = 0 To categoryNames.Count - 1
                e.Graphics.DrawString(categoryNames(i), New            ↵
Font("Arial", 8), Brushes.Black, 10, 24 + 10 * i)
            Next i
        End If
    End Sub

End Class
```

[C#]
```
using System;
using System.Collections;
using System.ComponentModel;
using System.ComponentModel.Design;
using System.Drawing;
using System.Drawing.Design;
using System.Data;
using System.Windows.Forms;

namespace ToolboxCategoryNamesControl
{
    public class ToolboxCategoryNamesControl :                         ↵
System.Windows.Forms.UserControl
```

```
    {
        private System.Drawing.Design.IToolboxService toolboxService;
        private System.Drawing.Design.CategoryNameCollection
categoryNames;

        public ToolboxCategoryNamesControl()
        {
            this.BackColor = System.Drawing.Color.Beige;
            this.Name = "Category Names Display Control";
            this.Size = new System.Drawing.Size(264, 200);
        }

        // Obtain or reset IToolboxService reference on each
siting of control.
        public override System.ComponentModel.ISite Site
        {
            get
            {
                return base.Site;
            }
            set
            {
                base.Site = value;

                // If the component was sited, attempt to obtain
                // an IToolboxService instance.
                if( base.Site != null )
                {
                    toolboxService =
(IToolboxService)this.GetService(typeof(IToolboxService));
                    // If an IToolboxService was located, update
the category list.
                    if( toolboxService != null )
                        categoryNames = toolboxService.CategoryNames;
                }
                else
                    toolboxService = null;
            }
        }

        protected override void
OnPaint(System.Windows.Forms.PaintEventArgs e)
        {
            if( categoryNames != null )
            {
                e.Graphics.DrawString("IToolboxService category
names list:", new Font("Arial", 9), Brushes.Black, 10, 10);
                // categoryNames is a CategoryNameCollection
obtained from
                // the IToolboxService. CategoryNameCollection
is a read-only
                // string collection.

                // Output each category name in the
CategoryNameCollection.
                for( int i=0; i< categoryNames.Count; i++ )
                    e.Graphics.DrawString(categoryNames[i], new
Font("Arial", 8), Brushes.Black, 10, 24+(10*i));
            }
        }
    }
}
```

[C++]

```
#using <mscorlib.dll>
#using <System.Windows.Forms.dll>
#using <System.Data.dll>
#using <System.Drawing.dll>
#using <System.dll>

using namespace System;
using namespace System::Collections;
using namespace System::ComponentModel;
using namespace System::ComponentModel::Design;
using namespace System::Drawing;
using namespace System::Drawing::Design;
using namespace System::Data;
using namespace System::Windows::Forms;

namespace ToolboxCategoryNamesControl {
public __gc class ToolboxCategoryNamesControl : public
System::Windows::Forms::UserControl {
private:
   System::Drawing::Design::IToolboxService*  toolboxService;
private:
   System::Drawing::Design::CategoryNameCollection*  categoryNames;

public:
   ToolboxCategoryNamesControl() {
      this->BackColor = System::Drawing::Color::Beige;
      this->Name = S"Category Names Display Control";
      this->Size =  System::Drawing::Size(264, 200);
   }

   // Obtain or reset IToolboxService* reference on each siting
of control.
   __property System::ComponentModel::ISite* get_Site() {
      return UserControl::get_Site();
   }
   __property void set_Site(System::ComponentModel::ISite* value) {
      UserControl::set_Site( value );

      // If the component was sited, attempt to obtain
      // an IToolboxService* instance.
      if (UserControl::Site != 0) {
         toolboxService = dynamic_cast<IToolboxService*>(this-
>GetService(__typeof(IToolboxService)));
         // If an IToolboxService* was located, update the
category list.
         if (toolboxService != 0)
            categoryNames = toolboxService->CategoryNames;
      } else toolboxService = 0;
   }

protected:
   void OnPaint(System::Windows::Forms::PaintEventArgs* e) {
      if (categoryNames != 0) {
         e->Graphics->DrawString(S"IToolboxService category
names list:",
            new System::Drawing::Font(S"Arial", 9),
 Brushes::Black, 10, 10);
         // categoryNames is a CategoryNameCollection obtained from
         // the IToolboxService*. CategoryNameCollection is a read-only
         // String* collection.

         // Output each category name in the CategoryNameCollection.
         for (int i=0; i< categoryNames->Count; i++)
            e->Graphics->DrawString(categoryNames->Item[i],
            new System::Drawing::Font(S"Arial", 8),
 Brushes::Black, (float)10, (float)24+(10*i));
      }
   }
};
}
```

Requirements

Namespace: System.Drawing.Design

Platforms: Windows 98, Windows NT 4.0, Windows Millennium Edition, Windows 2000, Windows XP Home Edition, Windows XP Professional, Windows Server 2003 family

Assembly: System.Drawing (in System.Drawing.dll)

CategoryNameCollection Constructor

Initializes a new instance of the **CategoryNameCollection** class.

Overload List

Initializes a new instance of the **CategoryNameCollection** class using the specified collection.

[Visual Basic] **Public Sub New(CategoryNameCollection)**

[C#] **public CategoryNameCollection(CategoryNameCollection);**

[C++] **public: CategoryNameCollection(CategoryNameCollection*);**

[JScript] **public function CategoryNameCollection(CategoryNameCollection);**

Initializes a new instance of the **CategoryNameCollection** class using the specified array of names.

[Visual Basic] **Public Sub New(String())**

[C#] **public CategoryNameCollection(string[]);**

[C++] **public: CategoryNameCollection(String*[]);**

[JScript] **public function CategoryNameCollection(String[]);**

CategoryNameCollection Constructor (CategoryNameCollection)

Initializes a new instance of the **CategoryNameCollection** class using the specified collection.

```
[Visual Basic]
Public Sub New( _
   ByVal value As CategoryNameCollection _
)
[C#]
public CategoryNameCollection(
   CategoryNameCollection value
);
[C++]
public: CategoryNameCollection(
   CategoryNameCollection* value
);
[JScript]
public function CategoryNameCollection(
   value : CategoryNameCollection
);
```

Parameters

value

A **CategoryNameCollection** that contains the names to initialize the collection values to.

Requirements

Platforms: Windows 98, Windows NT 4.0, Windows Millennium Edition, Windows 2000, Windows XP Home Edition, Windows XP Professional, Windows Server 2003 family

CategoryNameCollection Constructor (String[])

Initializes a new instance of the **CategoryNameCollection** class using the specified array of names.

```
[Visual Basic]
Public Sub New( _
   ByVal value() As String _
)
[C#]
public CategoryNameCollection(
   string[] value
);
[C++]
public: CategoryNameCollection(
   String* value __gc[]
);
[JScript]
public function CategoryNameCollection(
   value : String[]
);
```

Parameters

value

An array of strings that contains the names of the categories to initialize the collection values to.

Requirements

Platforms: Windows 98, Windows NT 4.0, Windows Millennium Edition, Windows 2000, Windows XP Home Edition, Windows XP Professional, Windows Server 2003 family

CategoryNameCollection.Item Property

Gets the category name at the specified index.

[C#] In C#, this property is the indexer for the **CategoryNameCollection** class.

```
[Visual Basic]
Public Default ReadOnly Property Item( _
   ByVal index As Integer _
) As String
[C#]
public string this[
   int index
] {get;}
[C++]
public: __property String* get_Item(
   int index
);
[JScript]
returnValue = CategoryNameCollectionObject.Item(index);
-or-
returnValue = CategoryNameCollectionObject(index);
```

[JScript] In JScript, you can use the default indexed properties defined by a type, but you cannot explicitly define your own. However, specifying the **expando** attribute on a class automatically provides a default indexed property whose type is **Object** and whose index type is **String**.

Arguments [JScript]

index

The index of the collection element to access.

Parameters [Visual Basic, C#, C++]

index

The index of the collection element to access.

Property Value

The category name at the specified index.

Example

[Visual Basic]
```
' categoryNames is a CategoryNameCollection obtained from
' the IToolboxService. CategoryNameCollection is a read-only
' string collection.
' Output each category name in the CategoryNameCollection.
Dim i As Integer
For i = 0 To categoryNames.Count - 1
    e.Graphics.DrawString(categoryNames(i), New Font ↵
 ("Arial", 8), Brushes.Black, 10, 24 + 10 * i)
Next i
```

[C#]
```
// categoryNames is a CategoryNameCollection obtained from
// the IToolboxService. CategoryNameCollection is a read-only
// string collection.

// Output each category name in the CategoryNameCollection.
for( int i=0; i< categoryNames.Count; i++ )
    e.Graphics.DrawString(categoryNames[i], new Font ↵
 ("Arial", 8), Brushes.Black, 10, 24+(10*i));
```

[C++]
```
// categoryNames is a CategoryNameCollection obtained from
// the IToolboxService*. CategoryNameCollection is a read-only
// String* collection.

// Output each category name in the CategoryNameCollection.
for (int i=0; i< categoryNames->Count; i++)
   e->Graphics->DrawString(categoryNames->Item[i],
   new System::Drawing::Font(S"Arial", 8), Brushes::Black, ↵
 (float)10, (float)24+(10*i));
```

Requirements

Platforms: Windows 98, Windows NT 4.0, Windows Millennium Edition, Windows 2000, Windows XP Home Edition, Windows XP Professional, Windows Server 2003 family

CategoryNameCollection.Contains Method

Indicates whether the specified category is contained in the collection.

[Visual Basic]
```
Public Function Contains( _
   ByVal value As String _
) As Boolean
```
[C#]
```
public bool Contains(
   string value
);
```
[C++]
```
public: bool Contains(
   String* value
);
```
[JScript]
```
public function Contains(
   value : String
) : Boolean;
```

Parameters

value

The string to check for in the collection.

Return Value

true if the specified category is contained in the collection; otherwise, **false**.

Requirements

Platforms: Windows 98, Windows NT 4.0, Windows Millennium Edition, Windows 2000, Windows XP Home Edition, Windows XP Professional, Windows Server 2003 family

CategoryNameCollection.CopyTo Method

Copies the collection elements to the specified array at the specified index.

[Visual Basic]
```
Public Sub CopyTo( _
   ByVal array() As String, _
   ByVal index As Integer _
)
```
[C#]
```
public void CopyTo(
   string[] array,
   int index
);
```
[C++]
```
public: void CopyTo(
   String* array __gc[],
   int index
);
```
[JScript]
```
public function CopyTo(
   array : String[],
   index : int
);
```

Parameters

array

The array to copy to.

index

The index of the destination array at which to begin copying.

Requirements

Platforms: Windows 98, Windows NT 4.0, Windows Millennium Edition, Windows 2000, Windows XP Home Edition, Windows XP Professional, Windows Server 2003 family

CategoryNameCollection.IndexOf Method

Gets the index of the specified value.

[Visual Basic]
```
Public Function IndexOf( _
   ByVal value As String _
) As Integer
```
[C#]
```
public int IndexOf(
   string value
);
```
[C++]
```
public: int IndexOf(
   String* value
);
```
[JScript]
```
public function IndexOf(
   value : String
) : int;
```

Parameters

value
   The category name to retrieve the index of in the collection.

Return Value

The index in the collection, or a null reference (**Nothing** in Visual Basic) if the string does not exist in the collection.

Requirements

Platforms: Windows 98, Windows NT 4.0, Windows Millennium Edition, Windows 2000, Windows XP Home Edition, Windows XP Professional, Windows Server 2003 family

ColorEditor Class

This type supports the .NET Framework infrastructure and is not intended to be used directly from your code.

[Visual Basic]
```
Public Class ColorEditor
   Inherits UITypeEditor
```
[C#]
```
public class ColorEditor : UITypeEditor
```
[C++]
```
public __gc class ColorEditor : public UITypeEditor
```
[JScript]
```
public class ColorEditor extends UITypeEditor
```

ColorEditor Constructor

This member supports the .NET Framework infrastructure and is not intended to be used directly from your code.

[Visual Basic]
```
Public Sub New()
```
[C#]
```
public ColorEditor();
```
[C++]
```
public: ColorEditor();
```
[JScript]
```
public function ColorEditor();
```

ColorEditor.EditValue Method

This member supports the .NET Framework infrastructure and is not intended to be used directly from your code.

Overload List

This member supports the .NET Framework infrastructure and is not intended to be used directly from your code.

[Visual Basic] **Overloads Overrides Public Function EditValue(ITypeDescriptorContext, IServiceProvider, Object) As Object**

[C#] **public override object EditValue(ITypeDescriptor-Context, IServiceProvider, object);**

[C++] **public: Object* EditValue(ITypeDescriptorContext*, IServiceProvider*, Object*);**

[JScript] **public override function EditValue(IType-DescriptorContext, IServiceProvider, Object) : Object;**

This member supports the .NET Framework infrastructure and is not intended to be used directly from your code.

[Visual Basic] **Overloads Public Function EditValue(IServiceProvider, Object) As Object**

[C#] **public object EditValue(IServiceProvider, object);**

[C++] **public: Object* EditValue(IServiceProvider*, Object*);**

[JScript] **public function EditValue(IServiceProvider, Object) : Object;**

ColorEditor.EditValue Method (ITypeDescriptorContext, IServiceProvider, Object)

This member supports the .NET Framework infrastructure and is not intended to be used directly from your code.

[Visual Basic]
```
Overrides Overloads Public Function EditValue( _
   ByVal context As ITypeDescriptorContext, _
   ByVal provider As IServiceProvider, _
   ByVal value As Object _
) As Object
```
[C#]
```
public override object EditValue(
   ITypeDescriptorContext context,
   IServiceProvider provider,
   object value
);
```
[C++]
```
public: Object* EditValue(
   ITypeDescriptorContext* context,
   IServiceProvider* provider,
   Object* value
);
```
[JScript]
```
public override function EditValue(
   context : ITypeDescriptorContext,
   provider : IServiceProvider,
   value : Object
) : Object;
```

ColorEditor.GetEditStyle Method

This member supports the .NET Framework infrastructure and is not intended to be used directly from your code.

Overload List

This member supports the .NET Framework infrastructure and is not intended to be used directly from your code.

[Visual Basic] **Overloads Overrides Public Function GetEdit-Style(ITypeDescriptorContext) As UITypeEditorEditStyle**

[C#] **public override UITypeEditorEditStyle GetEdit-Style(ITypeDescriptorContext);**

[C++] **public: UITypeEditorEditStyle GetEdit-Style(ITypeDescriptorContext*);**

[JScript] **public override function GetEdit-Style(ITypeDescriptorContext) : UITypeEditorEditStyle;**

This member supports the .NET Framework infrastructure and is not intended to be used directly from your code.

[Visual Basic] **Overloads Public Function GetEditStyle() As UITypeEditorEditStyle**

[C#] **public UITypeEditorEditStyle GetEditStyle();**

[C++] **public: UITypeEditorEditStyle GetEditStyle();**

[JScript] **public function GetEditStyle() : UITypeEditorEditStyle;**

ColorEditor.GetEditStyle Method (ITypeDescriptorContext)

This member supports the .NET Framework infrastructure and is not intended to be used directly from your code.

```
[Visual Basic]
Overrides Overloads Public Function GetEditStyle( _
   ByVal context As ITypeDescriptorContext _
) As UITypeEditorEditStyle
[C#]
public override UITypeEditorEditStyle GetEditStyle(
   ITypeDescriptorContext context
);
[C++]
public: UITypeEditorEditStyle GetEditStyle(
   ITypeDescriptorContext* context
);
[JScript]
public override function GetEditStyle(
   context : ITypeDescriptorContext
) : UITypeEditorEditStyle;
```

ColorEditor.GetPaintValueSupported Method

This member supports the .NET Framework infrastructure and is not intended to be used directly from your code.

Overload List

This member supports the .NET Framework infrastructure and is not intended to be used directly from your code.

[Visual Basic] **Overloads Overrides Public Function Get-PaintValueSupported(ITypeDescriptorContext) As Boolean**

[C#] **public override bool GetPaintValueSupported(IType-DescriptorContext);**

[C++] **public: bool GetPaintValueSupported(IType-DescriptorContext*);**

[JScript] **public override function GetPaintValue-Supported(ITypeDescriptorContext) : Boolean;**

This member supports the .NET Framework infrastructure and is not intended to be used directly from your code.

[Visual Basic] **Overloads Public Function GetPaintValue-Supported() As Boolean**

[C#] **public bool GetPaintValueSupported();**

[C++] **public: bool GetPaintValueSupported();**

[JScript] **public function GetPaintValueSupported() : Boolean;**

ColorEditor.GetPaintValueSupported Method (ITypeDescriptorContext)

This member supports the .NET Framework infrastructure and is not intended to be used directly from your code.

```
[Visual Basic]
Overrides Overloads Public Function GetPaintValueSupported( _
   ByVal context As ITypeDescriptorContext _
) As Boolean
[C#]
public override bool GetPaintValueSupported(
   ITypeDescriptorContext context
);
[C++]
public: bool GetPaintValueSupported(
   ITypeDescriptorContext* context
);
[JScript]
public override function GetPaintValueSupported(
   context : ITypeDescriptorContext
) : Boolean;
```

ColorEditor.PaintValue Method

This member supports the .NET Framework infrastructure and is not intended to be used directly from your code.

Overload List

This member supports the .NET Framework infrastructure and is not intended to be used directly from your code.

[Visual Basic] **Overloads Overrides Public Sub PaintValue(PaintValueEventArgs)**

[C#] **public override void PaintValue(PaintValueEventArgs);**

[C++] **public: void PaintValue(PaintValueEventArgs*);**

[JScript] **public override function PaintValue(PaintValueEventArgs);**

This member supports the .NET Framework infrastructure and is not intended to be used directly from your code.

[Visual Basic] **Overloads Public Sub PaintValue(Object, Graphics, Rectangle)**

[C#] **public void PaintValue(object, Graphics, Rectangle);**

[C++] **public: void PaintValue(Object*, Graphics*, Rectangle);**

[JScript] **public function PaintValue(Object, Graphics, Rectangle);**

ColorEditor.PaintValue Method (PaintValueEventArgs)

This member supports the .NET Framework infrastructure and is not intended to be used directly from your code.

```
[Visual Basic]
Overrides Overloads Public Sub PaintValue( _
   ByVal e As PaintValueEventArgs _
)
[C#]
public override void PaintValue(
   PaintValueEventArgs e
);
[C++]
public: void PaintValue(
   PaintValueEventArgs* e
);
[JScript]
public override function PaintValue(
   e : PaintValueEventArgs
);
```

ContentAlignmentEditor Class

This type supports the .NET Framework infrastructure and is not intended to be used directly from your code.

[Visual Basic]
```
Public Class ContentAlignmentEditor
   Inherits UITypeEditor
```
[C#]
```
public class ContentAlignmentEditor : UITypeEditor
```
[C++]
```
public __gc class ContentAlignmentEditor : public UITypeEditor
```
[JScript]
```
public class ContentAlignmentEditor extends UITypeEditor
```

ContentAlignmentEditor Constructor

This member supports the .NET Framework infrastructure and is not intended to be used directly from your code.

[Visual Basic]
```
Public Sub New()
```
[C#]
```
public ContentAlignmentEditor();
```
[C++]
```
public: ContentAlignmentEditor();
```
[JScript]
```
public function ContentAlignmentEditor();
```

ContentAlignmentEditor.EditValue Method

This member supports the .NET Framework infrastructure and is not intended to be used directly from your code.

Overload List

This member supports the .NET Framework infrastructure and is not intended to be used directly from your code.

[Visual Basic] **Overloads Overrides Public Function EditValue(ITypeDescriptorContext, IServiceProvider, Object) As Object**

[C#] **public override object EditValue(ITypeDescriptor-Context, IServiceProvider, object);**

[C++] **public: Object* EditValue(ITypeDescriptorContext*, IServiceProvider*, Object*);**

[JScript] **public override function EditValue(IType-DescriptorContext, IServiceProvider, Object) : Object;**

This member supports the .NET Framework infrastructure and is not intended to be used directly from your code.

[Visual Basic] **Overloads Public Function EditValue(IServiceProvider, Object) As Object**

[C#] **public object EditValue(IServiceProvider, object);**

[C++] **public: Object* EditValue(IServiceProvider*, Object*);**

[JScript] **public function EditValue(IServiceProvider, Object) : Object;**

ContentAlignmentEditor.EditValue Method (ITypeDescriptorContext, IServiceProvider, Object)

This member supports the .NET Framework infrastructure and is not intended to be used directly from your code.

[Visual Basic]
```
Overrides Overloads Public Function EditValue( _
   ByVal context As ITypeDescriptorContext, _
   ByVal provider As IServiceProvider, _
   ByVal value As Object _
) As Object
```
[C#]
```
public override object EditValue(
   ITypeDescriptorContext context,
   IServiceProvider provider,
   object value
);
```
[C++]
```
public: Object* EditValue(
   ITypeDescriptorContext* context,
   IServiceProvider* provider,
   Object* value
);
```
[JScript]
```
public override function EditValue(
   context : ITypeDescriptorContext,
   provider : IServiceProvider,
   value : Object
) : Object;
```

ContentAlignmentEditor.GetEditStyle Method

This member supports the .NET Framework infrastructure and is not intended to be used directly from your code.

Overload List

This member supports the .NET Framework infrastructure and is not intended to be used directly from your code.

[Visual Basic] **Overloads Overrides Public Function GetEdit-Style(ITypeDescriptorContext) As UITypeEditorEditStyle**

[C#] **public override UITypeEditorEditStyle GetEditStyle(ITypeDescriptorContext);**

[C++] **public: UITypeEditorEditStyle GetEditStyle(ITypeDescriptorContext*);**

[JScript] **public override function GetEdit-Style(ITypeDescriptorContext) : UITypeEditorEditStyle;**

This member supports the .NET Framework infrastructure and is not intended to be used directly from your code.

[Visual Basic] **Overloads Public Function GetEditStyle() As UITypeEditorEditStyle**

[C#] **public UITypeEditorEditStyle GetEditStyle();**

[C++] **public: UITypeEditorEditStyle GetEditStyle();**

[JScript] **public function GetEditStyle() : UITypeEditorEditStyle;**

ContentAlignmentEditor.GetEditStyle Method (ITypeDescriptorContext)

This member supports the .NET Framework infrastructure and is not intended to be used directly from your code.

[Visual Basic]
```
Overrides Overloads Public Function GetEditStyle( _
   ByVal context As ITypeDescriptorContext _
) As UITypeEditorEditStyle
```
[C#]
```
public override UITypeEditorEditStyle GetEditStyle(
   ITypeDescriptorContext context
);
```
[C++]
```
public: UITypeEditorEditStyle GetEditStyle(
   ITypeDescriptorContext* context
);
```
[JScript]
```
public override function GetEditStyle(
   context : ITypeDescriptorContext
) : UITypeEditorEditStyle;
```

CursorEditor Class

This type supports the .NET Framework infrastructure and is not intended to be used directly from your code.

```
[Visual Basic]
Public Class CursorEditor
   Inherits UITypeEditor
[C#]
public class CursorEditor : UITypeEditor
[C++]
public __gc class CursorEditor : public UITypeEditor
[JScript]
public class CursorEditor extends UITypeEditor
```

CursorEditor Constructor

This member supports the .NET Framework infrastructure and is not intended to be used directly from your code.

```
[Visual Basic]
Public Sub New()
[C#]
public CursorEditor();
[C++]
public: CursorEditor();
[JScript]
public function CursorEditor();
```

CursorEditor.EditValue Method

This member supports the .NET Framework infrastructure and is not intended to be used directly from your code.

Overload List

This member supports the .NET Framework infrastructure and is not intended to be used directly from your code.

[Visual Basic] **Overloads Overrides Public Function EditValue(ITypeDescriptorContext, IServiceProvider, Object) As Object**

[C#] **public override object EditValue(ITypeDescriptorContext, IServiceProvider, object);**

[C++] **public: Object* EditValue(ITypeDescriptorContext*, IServiceProvider*, Object*);**

[JScript] **public override function EditValue(ITypeDescriptorContext, IServiceProvider, Object) : Object;**

This member supports the .NET Framework infrastructure and is not intended to be used directly from your code.

[Visual Basic] **Overloads Public Function EditValue(IServiceProvider, Object) As Object**

[C#] **public object EditValue(IServiceProvider, object);**

[C++] **public: Object* EditValue(IServiceProvider*, Object*);**

[JScript] **public function EditValue(IServiceProvider, Object) : Object;**

CursorEditor.EditValue Method (ITypeDescriptorContext, IServiceProvider, Object)

This member supports the .NET Framework infrastructure and is not intended to be used directly from your code.

```
[Visual Basic]
Overrides Overloads Public Function EditValue( _
   ByVal context As ITypeDescriptorContext, _
   ByVal provider As IServiceProvider, _
   ByVal value As Object _
) As Object
[C#]
public override object EditValue(
   ITypeDescriptorContext context,
   IServiceProvider provider,
   object value
);
[C++]
public: Object* EditValue(
   ITypeDescriptorContext* context,
   IServiceProvider* provider,
   Object* value
);
[JScript]
public override function EditValue(
   context : ITypeDescriptorContext,
   provider : IServiceProvider,
   value : Object
) : Object;
```

CursorEditor.GetEditStyle Method

This member supports the .NET Framework infrastructure and is not intended to be used directly from your code.

Overload List

This member supports the .NET Framework infrastructure and is not intended to be used directly from your code.

[Visual Basic] **Overloads Overrides Public Function GetEditStyle(ITypeDescriptorContext) As UITypeEditorEditStyle**

[C#] **public override UITypeEditorEditStyle GetEditStyle(ITypeDescriptorContext);**

[C++] **public: UITypeEditorEditStyle GetEditStyle(ITypeDescriptorContext*);**

[JScript] **public override function GetEditStyle(ITypeDescriptorContext) : UITypeEditorEditStyle;**

This member supports the .NET Framework infrastructure and is not intended to be used directly from your code.

[Visual Basic] **Overloads Public Function GetEditStyle() As UITypeEditorEditStyle**

[C#] **public UITypeEditorEditStyle GetEditStyle();**

[C++] **public: UITypeEditorEditStyle GetEditStyle();**

[JScript] **public function GetEditStyle() : UITypeEditorEditStyle;**

CursorEditor.GetEditStyle Method (ITypeDescriptorContext)

This member supports the .NET Framework infrastructure and is not intended to be used directly from your code.

[Visual Basic]
```
Overrides Overloads Public Function GetEditStyle( _
   ByVal context As ITypeDescriptorContext _
) As UITypeEditorEditStyle
```
[C#]
```
public override UITypeEditorEditStyle GetEditStyle(
   ITypeDescriptorContext context
);
```
[C++]
```
public: UITypeEditorEditStyle GetEditStyle(
   ITypeDescriptorContext* context
);
```
[JScript]
```
public override function GetEditStyle(
   context : ITypeDescriptorContext
) : UITypeEditorEditStyle;
```

FontEditor Class

Provides a user interface to select and configure a **Font** object.

System.Object
  System.Drawing.Design.UITypeEditor
    System.Drawing.Design.FontEditor

[Visual Basic]
```
Public Class FontEditor
   Inherits UITypeEditor
```
[C#]
```
public class FontEditor : UITypeEditor
```
[C++]
```
public __gc class FontEditor : public UITypeEditor
```
[JScript]
```
public class FontEditor extends UITypeEditor
```

Thread Safety

Any public static (**Shared** in Visual Basic) members of this type are safe for multithreaded operations. Any instance members are not guaranteed to be thread safe.

Remarks

FontEditor is a **UITypeEditor** that provides a user interface for choosing and configuring a **Font** from a list of available fonts.

Example

[Visual Basic]
```
<EditorAttribute(GetType(System.Drawing.Design.FontEditor),  ↵
GetType(System.Drawing.Design.UITypeEditor))> _
Public Property testFont() As Font
   Get
      Return font
   End Get
   Set
      font = value
   End Set
End Property
Private font As Font
```

[C#]
```
[EditorAttribute(typeof(System.Drawing.Design.FontEditor),  ↵
typeof(System.Drawing.Design.UITypeEditor))]
public Font testFont
{
    get
    {
        return font;
    }
    set
    {
        font = value;
    }
}
private Font font;
```

[C++]
```
public:
    [EditorAttribute(__typeof(System::Drawing::Design::FontEditor),
        __typeof(System::Drawing::Design::UITypeEditor))]
    __property System::Drawing::Font* get_testFont() {
        return font;
    }
    [EditorAttribute(__typeof(System::Drawing::Design::FontEditor),
        __typeof(System::Drawing::Design::UITypeEditor))]
    __property void set_testFont(System::Drawing::Font* value) {
        font = value;
    }
private:
    Font*  font;
```

Requirements

Namespace: System.Drawing.Design

Platforms: Windows 98, Windows NT 4.0, Windows Millennium Edition, Windows 2000, Windows XP Home Edition, Windows XP Professional, Windows Server 2003 family

Assembly: System.Drawing.Design (in System.Drawing.Design.dll)

FontEditor Constructor

Initializes a new instance of the **FontEditor** class.

[Visual Basic]
```
Public Sub New()
```
[C#]
```
public FontEditor();
```
[C++]
```
public: FontEditor();
```
[JScript]
```
public function FontEditor();
```

Remarks

The default constructor initializes any fields to their default values.

Requirements

Platforms: Windows 98, Windows NT 4.0, Windows Millennium Edition, Windows 2000, Windows XP Home Edition, Windows XP Professional, Windows Server 2003 family

.NET Framework Security:

- Full trust for the immediate caller. This member cannot be used by partially trusted code.

FontEditor.EditValue Method

Overload List

Edits the value of the specified object using the editor style indicated by **GetEditStyle**.

[Visual Basic] **Overloads Overrides Public Function EditValue(ITypeDescriptorContext, IServiceProvider, Object) As Object**

[C#] **public override object EditValue(ITypeDescriptor-Context, IServiceProvider, object);**

[C++] **public: Object* EditValue(ITypeDescriptorContext*, IServiceProvider*, Object*);**

[JScript] **public override function EditValue(IType-DescriptorContext, IServiceProvider, Object) : Object;**

Inherited from **UITypeEditor**.

[Visual Basic] **Overloads Public Function EditValue(IServiceProvider, Object) As Object**

[C#] **public object EditValue(IServiceProvider, object);**

[C++] **public: Object* EditValue(IServiceProvider*, Object*);**

[JScript] **public function EditValue(IServiceProvider, Object) : Object;**

FontEditor.EditValue Method (ITypeDescriptorContext, IServiceProvider, Object)

Edits the value of the specified object using the editor style indicated by **GetEditStyle**.

[Visual Basic]
```
Overrides Overloads Public Function EditValue( _
   ByVal context As ITypeDescriptorContext, _
   ByVal provider As IServiceProvider, _
   ByVal value As Object _
) As Object
```
[C#]
```
public override object EditValue(
   ITypeDescriptorContext context,
   IServiceProvider provider,
   object value
);
```
[C++]
```
public: Object* EditValue(
   ITypeDescriptorContext* context,
   IServiceProvider* provider,
   Object* value
);
```
[JScript]
```
public override function EditValue(
   context : ITypeDescriptorContext,
   provider : IServiceProvider,
   value : Object
) : Object;
```

Parameters

context
An **ITypeDescriptorContext** that can be used to gain additional context information.

provider
An **IServiceProvider** that this editor can use to obtain services.

value
The object to edit.

Return Value

The new value of the object. If the value of the object has not changed, this should return the same object that was passed to it.

Remarks

A service provider is provided so that any required editing services can be obtained.

Requirements

Platforms: Windows 98, Windows NT 4.0, Windows Millennium Edition, Windows 2000, Windows XP Home Edition, Windows XP Professional, Windows Server 2003 family

.NET Framework Security:

- Full trust for the immediate caller. This member cannot be used by partially trusted code.

FontEditor.GetEditStyle Method

Gets the editor style used by the **EditValue** method.

Overload List

Gets the editor style used by the **EditValue** method.

[Visual Basic] **Overloads Overrides Public Function GetEditStyle(ITypeDescriptorContext) As UITypeEditorEditStyle**

[C#] **public override UITypeEditorEditStyle GetEditStyle(ITypeDescriptorContext);**

[C++] **public: UITypeEditorEditStyle GetEditStyle(ITypeDescriptorContext*);**

[JScript] **public override function GetEditStyle(ITypeDescriptorContext) : UITypeEditorEditStyle;**

Inherited from **UITypeEditor**.

[Visual Basic] **Overloads Public Function GetEditStyle() As UITypeEditorEditStyle**

[C#] **public UITypeEditorEditStyle GetEditStyle();**

[C++] **public: UITypeEditorEditStyle GetEditStyle();**

[JScript] **public function GetEditStyle() : UITypeEditorEditStyle;**

FontEditor.GetEditStyle Method (ITypeDescriptorContext)

Gets the editor style used by the **EditValue** method.

[Visual Basic]
```
Overrides Overloads Public Function GetEditStyle( _
   ByVal context As ITypeDescriptorContext _
) As UITypeEditorEditStyle
```
[C#]
```
public override UITypeEditorEditStyle GetEditStyle(
   ITypeDescriptorContext context
);
```
[C++]
```
public: UITypeEditorEditStyle GetEditStyle(
   ITypeDescriptorContext* context
);
```
[JScript]
```
public override function GetEditStyle(
   context : ITypeDescriptorContext
) : UITypeEditorEditStyle;
```

Parameters

context
An **ITypeDescriptorContext** that can be used to gain additional context information.

Return Value

A **UITypeEditorEditStyle** value that indicates the style of editor used by **EditValue**.

Requirements

Platforms: Windows 98, Windows NT 4.0, Windows Millennium Edition, Windows 2000, Windows XP Home Edition, Windows XP Professional, Windows Server 2003 family

.NET Framework Security:

- Full trust for the immediate caller. This member cannot be used by partially trusted code.

FontNameEditor Class

This type supports the .NET Framework infrastructure and is not intended to be used directly from your code.

```
[Visual Basic]
Public Class FontNameEditor
   Inherits UITypeEditor
[C#]
public class FontNameEditor : UITypeEditor
[C++]
public __gc class FontNameEditor : public UITypeEditor
[JScript]
public class FontNameEditor extends UITypeEditor
```

FontNameEditor Constructor

This member supports the .NET Framework infrastructure and is not intended to be used directly from your code.

```
[Visual Basic]
Public Sub New()
[C#]
public FontNameEditor();
[C++]
public: FontNameEditor();
[JScript]
public function FontNameEditor();
```

FontNameEditor.GetPaintValueSupported Method

This member supports the .NET Framework infrastructure and is not intended to be used directly from your code.

Overload List

This member supports the .NET Framework infrastructure and is not intended to be used directly from your code.

[Visual Basic] **Overloads Overrides Public Function GetPaintValueSupported(ITypeDescriptorContext) As Boolean**

[C#] **public override bool GetPaintValueSupported(ITypeDescriptorContext);**

[C++] **public: bool GetPaintValueSupported(ITypeDescriptorContext*);**

[JScript] **public override function GetPaintValueSupported(ITypeDescriptorContext) : Boolean;**

This member supports the .NET Framework infrastructure and is not intended to be used directly from your code.

[Visual Basic] **Overloads Public Function GetPaintValueSupported() As Boolean**

[C#] **public bool GetPaintValueSupported();**

[C++] **public: bool GetPaintValueSupported();**

[JScript] **public function GetPaintValueSupported() : Boolean;**

FontNameEditor.GetPaintValueSupported Method (ITypeDescriptorContext)

This member supports the .NET Framework infrastructure and is not intended to be used directly from your code.

```
[Visual Basic]
Overrides Overloads Public Function GetPaintValueSupported( _
   ByVal context As ITypeDescriptorContext _
) As Boolean
[C#]
public override bool GetPaintValueSupported(
   ITypeDescriptorContext context
);
[C++]
public: bool GetPaintValueSupported(
   ITypeDescriptorContext* context
);
[JScript]
public override function GetPaintValueSupported(
   context : ITypeDescriptorContext
) : Boolean;
```

FontNameEditor.PaintValue Method

This member supports the .NET Framework infrastructure and is not intended to be used directly from your code.

Overload List

This member supports the .NET Framework infrastructure and is not intended to be used directly from your code.

[Visual Basic] **Overloads Overrides Public Sub PaintValue(PaintValueEventArgs)**

[C#] **public override void PaintValue(PaintValueEventArgs);**

[C++] **public: void PaintValue(PaintValueEventArgs*);**

[JScript] **public override function PaintValue(PaintValueEventArgs);**

This member supports the .NET Framework infrastructure and is not intended to be used directly from your code.

[Visual Basic] **Overloads Public Sub PaintValue(Object, Graphics, Rectangle)**

[C#] **public void PaintValue(object, Graphics, Rectangle);**

[C++] **public: void PaintValue(Object*, Graphics*, Rectangle);**

[JScript] **public function PaintValue(Object, Graphics, Rectangle);**

FontNameEditor.PaintValue Method (PaintValueEventArgs)

This member supports the .NET Framework infrastructure and is not intended to be used directly from your code.

```
[Visual Basic]
Overrides Overloads Public Sub PaintValue( _
   ByVal e As PaintValueEventArgs _
)
[C#]
public override void PaintValue(
   PaintValueEventArgs e
);
[C++]
public: void PaintValue(
   PaintValueEventArgs* e
);
[JScript]
public override function PaintValue(
   e : PaintValueEventArgs
);
```

IconEditor Class

This type supports the .NET Framework infrastructure and is not intended to be used directly from your code.

[Visual Basic]
```
Public Class IconEditor
   Inherits UITypeEditor
```
[C#]
```
public class IconEditor : UITypeEditor
```
[C++]
```
public __gc class IconEditor : public UITypeEditor
```
[JScript]
```
public class IconEditor extends UITypeEditor
```

IconEditor Constructor

This member supports the .NET Framework infrastructure and is not intended to be used directly from your code.

[Visual Basic]
```
Public Sub New()
```
[C#]
```
public IconEditor();
```
[C++]
```
public: IconEditor();
```
[JScript]
```
public function IconEditor();
```

IconEditor.CreateExtensionsString Method

This member supports the .NET Framework infrastructure and is not intended to be used directly from your code.

[Visual Basic]
```
Protected Shared Function CreateExtensionsString( _
   ByVal extensions() As String, _
   ByVal sep As String _
) As String
```
[C#]
```
protected static string CreateExtensionsString(
   string[] extensions,
   string sep
);
```
[C++]
```
protected: static String* CreateExtensionsString(
   String* extensions __gc[],
   String* sep
);
```
[JScript]
```
protected static function CreateExtensionsString(
   extensions : String[],
   sep : String
) : String;
```

IconEditor.CreateFilterEntry Method

This member supports the .NET Framework infrastructure and is not intended to be used directly from your code.

[Visual Basic]
```
Protected Shared Function CreateFilterEntry( _
   ByVal e As IconEditor _
) As String
```
[C#]
```
protected static string CreateFilterEntry(
   IconEditor e
);
```
[C++]
```
protected: static String* CreateFilterEntry(
   IconEditor* e
);
```
[JScript]
```
protected static function CreateFilterEntry(
   e : IconEditor
) : String;
```

IconEditor.EditValue Method

This member supports the .NET Framework infrastructure and is not intended to be used directly from your code.

Overload List

This member supports the .NET Framework infrastructure and is not intended to be used directly from your code.

[Visual Basic] **Overloads Overrides Public Function EditValue(ITypeDescriptorContext, IServiceProvider, Object) As Object**

[C#] **public override object EditValue(ITypeDescriptorContext, IServiceProvider, object);**

[C++] **public: Object* EditValue(ITypeDescriptorContext*, IServiceProvider*, Object*);**

[JScript] **public override function EditValue(ITypeDescriptorContext, IServiceProvider, Object) : Object;**

This member supports the .NET Framework infrastructure and is not intended to be used directly from your code.

[Visual Basic] **Overloads Public Function EditValue(IServiceProvider, Object) As Object**

[C#] **public object EditValue(IServiceProvider, object);**

[C++] **public: Object* EditValue(IServiceProvider*, Object*);**

[JScript] **public function EditValue(IServiceProvider, Object) : Object;**

IconEditor.EditValue Method (ITypeDescriptorContext, IServiceProvider, Object)

This member supports the .NET Framework infrastructure and is not intended to be used directly from your code.

[Visual Basic]
```
Overrides Overloads Public Function EditValue( _
   ByVal context As ITypeDescriptorContext, _
   ByVal provider As IServiceProvider, _
   ByVal value As Object _
) As Object
```

[C#]
```
public override object EditValue(
   ITypeDescriptorContext context,
   IServiceProvider provider,
   object value
);
```
[C++]
```
public: Object* EditValue(
   ITypeDescriptorContext* context,
   IServiceProvider* provider,
   Object* value
);
```
[JScript]
```
public override function EditValue(
   context : ITypeDescriptorContext,
   provider : IServiceProvider,
   value : Object
) : Object;
```

IconEditor.GetEditStyle Method

This member supports the .NET Framework infrastructure and is not intended to be used directly from your code.

Overload List

This member supports the .NET Framework infrastructure and is not intended to be used directly from your code.

[Visual Basic] **Overloads Overrides Public Function GetEditStyle(ITypeDescriptorContext) As UITypeEditorEditStyle**

[C#] **public override UITypeEditorEditStyle GetEditStyle(ITypeDescriptorContext);**

[C++] **public: UITypeEditorEditStyle GetEditStyle(ITypeDescriptorContext*);**

[JScript] **public override function GetEditStyle(ITypeDescriptorContext) : UITypeEditorEditStyle;**

This member supports the .NET Framework infrastructure and is not intended to be used directly from your code.

[Visual Basic] **Overloads Public Function GetEditStyle() As UITypeEditorEditStyle**

[C#] **public UITypeEditorEditStyle GetEditStyle();**

[C++] **public: UITypeEditorEditStyle GetEditStyle();**

[JScript] **public function GetEditStyle() : UITypeEditorEditStyle;**

IconEditor.GetEditStyle Method (ITypeDescriptorContext)

This member supports the .NET Framework infrastructure and is not intended to be used directly from your code.

[Visual Basic]
```
Overrides Overloads Public Function GetEditStyle( _
   ByVal context As ITypeDescriptorContext _
) As UITypeEditorEditStyle
```
[C#]
```
public override UITypeEditorEditStyle GetEditStyle(
   ITypeDescriptorContext context
);
```
[C++]
```
public: UITypeEditorEditStyle GetEditStyle(
   ITypeDescriptorContext* context
);
```
[JScript]
```
public override function GetEditStyle(
   context : ITypeDescriptorContext
) : UITypeEditorEditStyle;
```

IconEditor.GetExtensions Method

This member supports the .NET Framework infrastructure and is not intended to be used directly from your code.

[Visual Basic]
```
Protected Overridable Function GetExtensions() As String()
```
[C#]
```
protected virtual string[] GetExtensions();
```
[C++]
```
protected: virtual String* GetExtensions()  __gc[];
```
[JScript]
```
protected function GetExtensions() : String[];
```

IconEditor.GetFileDialogDescription Method

This member supports the .NET Framework infrastructure and is not intended to be used directly from your code.

[Visual Basic]
```
Protected Overridable Function GetFileDialogDescription() As String
```
[C#]
```
protected virtual string GetFileDialogDescription();
```
[C++]
```
protected: virtual String* GetFileDialogDescription();
```
[JScript]
```
protected function GetFileDialogDescription() : String;
```

IconEditor.GetPaintValueSupported Method

This member supports the .NET Framework infrastructure and is not intended to be used directly from your code.

Overload List

This member supports the .NET Framework infrastructure and is not intended to be used directly from your code.

[Visual Basic] **Overloads Overrides Public Function GetPaintValueSupported(ITypeDescriptorContext) As Boolean**

[C#] **public override bool GetPaintValueSupported(ITypeDescriptorContext);**

[C++] **public: bool GetPaintValueSupported(ITypeDescriptorContext*);**

[JScript] **public override function GetPaintValueSupported(ITypeDescriptorContext) : Boolean;**

This member supports the .NET Framework infrastructure and is not intended to be used directly from your code.

[Visual Basic] **Overloads Public Function GetPaintValueSupported() As Boolean**

[C#] **public bool GetPaintValueSupported();**

[C++] **public: bool GetPaintValueSupported();**

[JScript] **public function GetPaintValueSupported() : Boolean;**

IconEditor.GetPaintValueSupported Method (ITypeDescriptorContext)

This member supports the .NET Framework infrastructure and is not intended to be used directly from your code.

```
[Visual Basic]
Overrides Overloads Public Function GetPaintValueSupported( _
   ByVal context As ITypeDescriptorContext _
) As Boolean
[C#]
public override bool GetPaintValueSupported(
   ITypeDescriptorContext context
);
[C++]
public: bool GetPaintValueSupported(
   ITypeDescriptorContext* context
);
[JScript]
public override function GetPaintValueSupported(
   context : ITypeDescriptorContext
) : Boolean;
```

IconEditor.LoadFromStream Method

This member supports the .NET Framework infrastructure and is not intended to be used directly from your code.

```
[Visual Basic]
Protected Overridable Function LoadFromStream( _
   ByVal stream As Stream _
) As Icon
[C#]
protected virtual Icon LoadFromStream(
   Stream stream
);
[C++]
protected: virtual Icon* LoadFromStream(
   Stream* stream
);
[JScript]
protected function LoadFromStream(
   stream : Stream
) : Icon;
```

IconEditor.PaintValue Method

This member supports the .NET Framework infrastructure and is not intended to be used directly from your code.

Overload List

This member supports the .NET Framework infrastructure and is not intended to be used directly from your code.

[Visual Basic] **Overloads Overrides Public Sub PaintValue(PaintValueEventArgs)**

[C#] **public override void PaintValue(PaintValueEventArgs);**

[C++] **public: void PaintValue(PaintValueEventArgs*);**

[JScript] **public override function PaintValue(PaintValueEventArgs);**

This member supports the .NET Framework infrastructure and is not intended to be used directly from your code.

[Visual Basic] **Overloads Public Sub PaintValue(Object, Graphics, Rectangle)**

[C#] **public void PaintValue(object, Graphics, Rectangle);**

[C++] **public: void PaintValue(Object*, Graphics*, Rectangle);**

[JScript] **public function PaintValue(Object, Graphics, Rectangle);**

IconEditor.PaintValue Method (PaintValueEventArgs)

This member supports the .NET Framework infrastructure and is not intended to be used directly from your code.

```
[Visual Basic]
Overrides Overloads Public Sub PaintValue( _
   ByVal e As PaintValueEventArgs _
)
[C#]
public override void PaintValue(
   PaintValueEventArgs e
);
[C++]
public: void PaintValue(
   PaintValueEventArgs* e
);
[JScript]
public override function PaintValue(
   e : PaintValueEventArgs
);
```

ImageEditor Class

Provides a user interface for selecting an image for a property in a property grid.

System.Object
  System.Drawing.Design.UITypeEditor
    System.Drawing.Design.ImageEditor
      System.Drawing.Design.BitmapEditor

[Visual Basic]
```
Public Class ImageEditor
   Inherits UITypeEditor
```
[C#]
```
public class ImageEditor : UITypeEditor
```
[C++]
```
public __gc class ImageEditor : public UITypeEditor
```
[JScript]
```
public class ImageEditor extends UITypeEditor
```

Thread Safety

Any public static (**Shared** in Visual Basic) members of this type are safe for multithreaded operations. Any instance members are not guaranteed to be thread safe.

Remarks

ImageEditor is a **UITypeEditor** that provides a user interface for selecting an image for a property. Starting the editor displays an open file dialog box that allows directory navigation and selecting a file. The file list is initially filtered by the default file name extensions for the editor.

Example

[Visual Basic]
```
<EditorAttribute(GetType(System.Drawing.Design.ImageEditor),        ↵
GetType(System.Drawing.Design.UITypeEditor))> _
Public Property testImage() As Image
   Get
      Return testImg
   End Get
   Set
      testImg = value
   End Set
End Property
Private testImg As Image
```

[C#]
```
[EditorAttribute(typeof(System.Drawing.Design.ImageEditor),         ↵
typeof(System.Drawing.Design.UITypeEditor))]
public Image testImage
{
    get
    {
        return testImg;
    }
    set
    {
        testImg = value;
    }
}
private Image testImg;
```

[C++]
```
public:
    [EditorAttribute(__typeof(System::Drawing::Design::ImageEditor),
        __typeof(System::Drawing::Design::UITypeEditor))]
    __property Image* get_testImage() {
        return testImg;
    }
    [EditorAttribute(__typeof(System::Drawing::Design::ImageEditor),
        __typeof(System::Drawing::Design::UITypeEditor))]
    __property void set_testImage(Image* value) {
        testImg = value;
    }
private:
    Image*  testImg;
```

Requirements

Namespace: System.Drawing.Design

Platforms: Windows 98, Windows NT 4.0, Windows Millennium Edition, Windows 2000, Windows XP Home Edition, Windows XP Professional, Windows Server 2003 family

Assembly: System.Drawing.Design (in System.Drawing.Design.dll)

ImageEditor Constructor

Initializes a new instance of the **ImageEditor** class.

[Visual Basic]
```
Public Sub New()
```
[C#]
```
public ImageEditor();
```
[C++]
```
public: ImageEditor();
```
[JScript]
```
public function ImageEditor();
```

Remarks

The default constructor initializes any fields to their default values.

Requirements

Platforms: Windows 98, Windows NT 4.0, Windows Millennium Edition, Windows 2000, Windows XP Home Edition, Windows XP Professional, Windows Server 2003 family

.NET Framework Security:

- Full trust for the immediate caller. This member cannot be used by partially trusted code.

ImageEditor.CreateExtensionsString Method

Creates a string of file name extensions using the specified array of file extensions and the specified separator.

[Visual Basic]
```
Protected Shared Function CreateExtensionsString( _
   ByVal extensions() As String, _
   ByVal sep As String _
) As String
```
[C#]
```
protected static string CreateExtensionsString(
   string[] extensions,
   string sep
);
```
[C++]
```
protected: static String* CreateExtensionsString(
   String* extensions __gc[],
   String* sep
);
```

[JScript]
```
protected static function CreateExtensionsString(
   extensions : String[],
   sep : String
) : String;
```

Parameters

extensions
: The extensions to filter for.

sep
: The separator to use.

Return Value

A string containing the specified file name extensions, each separated by the specified separator.

Remarks

The specified extensions indicate the file types for the open file dialog to filter the file list for by default.

Requirements

Platforms: Windows 98, Windows NT 4.0, Windows Millennium Edition, Windows 2000, Windows XP Home Edition, Windows XP Professional, Windows Server 2003 family

.NET Framework Security:

- Full trust for the immediate caller. This member cannot be used by partially trusted code.

ImageEditor.CreateFilterEntry Method

Creates a filter entry for a file dialog box's file list.

[Visual Basic]
```
Protected Shared Function CreateFilterEntry( _
   ByVal e As ImageEditor _
) As String
```
[C#]
```
protected static string CreateFilterEntry(
   ImageEditor e
);
```
[C++]
```
protected: static String* CreateFilterEntry(
   ImageEditor* e
);
```
[JScript]
```
protected static function CreateFilterEntry(
   e : ImageEditor
) : String;
```

Parameters

e
: The image editor to get the filter entry from.

Return Value

The new filter entry string.

Requirements

Platforms: Windows 98, Windows NT 4.0, Windows Millennium Edition, Windows 2000, Windows XP Home Edition, Windows XP Professional, Windows Server 2003 family

.NET Framework Security:

- Full trust for the immediate caller. This member cannot be used by partially trusted code.

ImageEditor.EditValue Method

Edits the specified object value using the edit style provided by **GetEditStyle**.

Overload List

Edits the specified object value using the edit style provided by **GetEditStyle**.

[Visual Basic] **Overloads Overrides Public Function EditValue(ITypeDescriptorContext, IServiceProvider, Object) As Object**

[C#] **public override object EditValue(ITypeDescriptor-Context, IServiceProvider, object);**

[C++] **public: Object* EditValue(ITypeDescriptorContext*, IServiceProvider*, Object*);**

[JScript] **public override function EditValue(IType-DescriptorContext, IServiceProvider, Object) : Object;**

Inherited from **UITypeEditor**.

[Visual Basic] **Overloads Public Function EditValue(IServiceProvider, Object) As Object**

[C#] **public object EditValue(IServiceProvider, object);**

[C++] **public: Object* EditValue(IServiceProvider*, Object*);**

[JScript] **public function EditValue(IServiceProvider, Object) : Object;**

ImageEditor.EditValue Method (ITypeDescriptorContext, IServiceProvider, Object)

Edits the specified object value using the edit style provided by **GetEditStyle**.

[Visual Basic]
```
Overrides Overloads Public Function EditValue( _
   ByVal context As ITypeDescriptorContext, _
   ByVal provider As IServiceProvider, _
   ByVal value As Object _
) As Object
```
[C#]
```
public override object EditValue(
   ITypeDescriptorContext context,
   IServiceProvider provider,
   object value
);
```
[C++]
```
public: Object* EditValue(
   ITypeDescriptorContext* context,
   IServiceProvider* provider,
   Object* value
);
```
[JScript]
```
public override function EditValue(
   context : ITypeDescriptorContext,
   provider : IServiceProvider,
   value : Object
) : Object;
```

Parameters

context

An **ITypeDescriptorContext** that can be used to gain additional context information.

provider

A service provider object through which editing services can be obtained.

value

An instance of the value being edited.

Return Value

The new value of the object. If the value of the object has not changed, this method should return the same object passed to it.

Remarks

This editor uses a service provider to obtain any necessary editing services.

Requirements

Platforms: Windows 98, Windows NT 4.0, Windows Millennium Edition, Windows 2000, Windows XP Home Edition, Windows XP Professional, Windows Server 2003 family

.NET Framework Security:

- Full trust for the immediate caller. This member cannot be used by partially trusted code.

ImageEditor.GetEditStyle Method

Gets the editing style of the **EditValue** method.

Overload List

Gets the editing style of the **EditValue** method.

[Visual Basic] **Overloads Overrides Public Function GetEditStyle(ITypeDescriptorContext) As UITypeEditorEditStyle**

[C#] **public override UITypeEditorEditStyle GetEditStyle(ITypeDescriptorContext);**

[C++] **public: UITypeEditorEditStyle GetEditStyle(ITypeDescriptorContext*);**

[JScript] **public override function GetEditStyle(ITypeDescriptorContext) : UITypeEditorEditStyle;**

Inherited from **UITypeEditor**.

[Visual Basic] **Overloads Public Function GetEditStyle() As UITypeEditorEditStyle**

[C#] **public UITypeEditorEditStyle GetEditStyle();**

[C++] **public: UITypeEditorEditStyle GetEditStyle();**

[JScript] **public function GetEditStyle() : UITypeEditorEditStyle;**

ImageEditor.GetEditStyle Method (ITypeDescriptorContext)

Gets the editing style of the **EditValue** method.

[Visual Basic]
```
Overrides Overloads Public Function GetEditStyle( _
   ByVal context As ITypeDescriptorContext _
) As UITypeEditorEditStyle
```
[C#]
```
public override UITypeEditorEditStyle GetEditStyle(
   ITypeDescriptorContext context
);
```
[C++]
```
public: UITypeEditorEditStyle GetEditStyle(
   ITypeDescriptorContext* context
);
```
[JScript]
```
public override function GetEditStyle(
   context : ITypeDescriptorContext
) : UITypeEditorEditStyle;
```

Parameters

context

An **ITypeDescriptorContext** that can be used to gain additional context information.

Return Value

A **UITypeEditorEditStyle** enumeration value indicating the supported editing style.

Remarks

If the **EditValue** method is not supported, this method will return **None**.

Requirements

Platforms: Windows 98, Windows NT 4.0, Windows Millennium Edition, Windows 2000, Windows XP Home Edition, Windows XP Professional, Windows Server 2003 family

.NET Framework Security:

- Full trust for the immediate caller. This member cannot be used by partially trusted code.

ImageEditor.GetExtensions Method

Gets the extensions for the file list filter that this editor initially uses to filter the file list.

[Visual Basic]
```
Protected Overridable Function GetExtensions() As String()
```
[C#]
```
protected virtual string[] GetExtensions();
```
[C++]
```
protected: virtual String* GetExtensions()  __gc[];
```
[JScript]
```
protected function GetExtensions() : String[];
```

Return Value

A set of file extensions used to filter the file list.

Requirements

Platforms: Windows 98, Windows NT 4.0, Windows Millennium Edition, Windows 2000, Windows XP Home Edition, Windows XP Professional, Windows Server 2003 family

.NET Framework Security:

- Full trust for the immediate caller. This member cannot be used by partially trusted code.

ImageEditor.GetFileDialogDescription Method

Gets the description for the default file list filter provided by this editor.

[Visual Basic]
```
Protected Overridable Function GetFileDialogDescription() As String
```
[C#]
```
protected virtual string GetFileDialogDescription();
```
[C++]
```
protected: virtual String* GetFileDialogDescription();
```
[JScript]
```
protected function GetFileDialogDescription() : String;
```

Return Value

The description for the default type of files to filter the file list for.

Remarks

The file dialog box description appears in the file list filter drop-down.

Requirements

Platforms: Windows 98, Windows NT 4.0, Windows Millennium Edition, Windows 2000, Windows XP Home Edition, Windows XP Professional, Windows Server 2003 family

.NET Framework Security:

- Full trust for the immediate caller. This member cannot be used by partially trusted code.

ImageEditor.GetPaintValueSupported Method

Gets a value indicating whether this editor supports painting a representation of an object's value.

Overload List

Gets a value indicating whether this editor supports painting a representation of an object's value.

[Visual Basic] **Overloads Overrides Public Function GetPaintValueSupported(ITypeDescriptorContext) As Boolean**

[C#] **public override bool GetPaintValueSupported(ITypeDescriptorContext);**

[C++] **public: bool GetPaintValueSupported(ITypeDescriptorContext*);**

[JScript] **public override function GetPaintValueSupported(ITypeDescriptorContext) : Boolean;**

Inherited from **UITypeEditor**.

[Visual Basic] **Overloads Public Function GetPaintValueSupported() As Boolean**

[C#] **public bool GetPaintValueSupported();**

[C++] **public: bool GetPaintValueSupported();**

[JScript] **public function GetPaintValueSupported() : Boolean;**

ImageEditor.GetPaintValueSupported Method (ITypeDescriptorContext)

Gets a value indicating whether this editor supports painting a representation of an object's value.

[Visual Basic]
```
Overrides Overloads Public Function GetPaintValueSupported( _
   ByVal context As ITypeDescriptorContext _
) As Boolean
```
[C#]
```
public override bool GetPaintValueSupported(
   ITypeDescriptorContext context
);
```
[C++]
```
public: bool GetPaintValueSupported(
   ITypeDescriptorContext* context
);
```
[JScript]
```
public override function GetPaintValueSupported(
   context : ITypeDescriptorContext
) : Boolean;
```

Parameters

context
An **ITypeDescriptorContext** that can be used to gain additional context information.

Return Value

true if **PaintValue** is implemented; otherwise, **false**.

Requirements

Platforms: Windows 98, Windows NT 4.0, Windows Millennium Edition, Windows 2000, Windows XP Home Edition, Windows XP Professional, Windows Server 2003 family

.NET Framework Security:

- Full trust for the immediate caller. This member cannot be used by partially trusted code.

ImageEditor.LoadFromStream Method

Loads an image from the specified stream.

[Visual Basic]
```
Protected Overridable Function LoadFromStream( _
   ByVal stream As Stream _
) As Image
```
[C#]
```
protected virtual Image LoadFromStream(
   Stream stream
);
```
[C++]
```
protected: virtual Image* LoadFromStream(
   Stream* stream
);
```
[JScript]
```
protected function LoadFromStream(
   stream : Stream
) : Image;
```

Parameters

stream
A stream that contains the image to load.

Return Value

The **Image** that has been loaded.

Requirements

Platforms: Windows 98, Windows NT 4.0, Windows Millennium Edition, Windows 2000, Windows XP Home Edition, Windows XP Professional, Windows Server 2003 family

.NET Framework Security:

- Full trust for the immediate caller. This member cannot be used by partially trusted code.

ImageEditor.PaintValue Method

Paints a value indicated by the specified **PaintValueEventArgs**.

Overload List

Paints a value indicated by the specified **PaintValueEventArgs**.

[Visual Basic] **Overloads Overrides Public Sub PaintValue(PaintValueEventArgs)**

[C#] **public override void PaintValue(PaintValueEventArgs);**

[C++] **public: void PaintValue(PaintValueEventArgs*);**

[JScript] **public override function PaintValue(PaintValueEventArgs);**

Inherited from **UITypeEditor**.

[Visual Basic] **Overloads Public Sub PaintValue(Object, Graphics, Rectangle)**

[C#] **public void PaintValue(object, Graphics, Rectangle);**

[C++] **public: void PaintValue(Object*, Graphics*, Rectangle);**

[JScript] **public function PaintValue(Object, Graphics, Rectangle);**

ImageEditor.PaintValue Method (PaintValueEventArgs)

Paints a value indicated by the specified **PaintValueEventArgs**.

```
[Visual Basic]
Overrides Overloads Public Sub PaintValue( _
   ByVal e As PaintValueEventArgs _
)
[C#]
public override void PaintValue(
   PaintValueEventArgs e
);
[C++]
public: void PaintValue(
   PaintValueEventArgs* e
);
[JScript]
public override function PaintValue(
   e : PaintValueEventArgs
);
```

Parameters

e

A **PaintValueEventArgs** indicating what to paint and where to paint it.

Remarks

Paint within the boundaries of the **Rectangle** contained within the specified **PaintValueEventArgs** in order to display the representation of the value in typical Properties window format.

Requirements

Platforms: Windows 98, Windows NT 4.0, Windows Millennium Edition, Windows 2000, Windows XP Home Edition, Windows XP Professional, Windows Server 2003 family

.NET Framework Security:

- Full trust for the immediate caller. This member cannot be used by partially trusted code.

IPropertyValueUIService Interface

Provides an interface to manage the images, ToolTips, and event handlers for the properties of a component displayed in a property browser.

```
[Visual Basic]
Public Interface IPropertyValueUIService
[C#]
public interface IPropertyValueUIService
[C++]
public __gc __interface IPropertyValueUIService
[JScript]
public interface IPropertyValueUIService
```

Remarks

A component can use the **IPropertyValueUIService** interface to provide **PropertyValueUIItem** objects for any properties of the component. A **PropertyValueUIItem** associated with a property can provide an image, a ToolTip and an event handler for the event that occurs when the image associated with the property is clicked.

The **IPropertyValueUIService** interface provides methods to add, remove, and retrieve **PropertyValueUIHandler** delegates to or from an internal list. When the properties of a component are displayed in a property browser, each **PropertyValueUIHandler** in the list is given an opportunity to provide a **PropertyValueUIItem** for each property of the component.

When a property browser is set to display the properties of an object, it calls the **GetPropertyUIValueItems** method of this interface for each property of the component, passing a **PropertyDescriptor** that represents the property. The **GetPropertyUIValueItems** method calls each **PropertyValueUIHandler** that has been added to the service. Each **PropertyValueUIHandler** can add a **PropertyValueUIItem** to the **ArrayList** parameter passed in the *valueUIItemList* parameter to supply UI items for the property represented by the **PropertyDescriptor** passed in the *propDesc* parameter.

A **PropertyValueUIItem** can contain an image to display next to the property name, a ToolTip string, and an event handler to invoke when an image associated with the property is double-clicked.

Requirements

Namespace: System.Drawing.Design

Platforms: Windows 98, Windows NT 4.0, Windows Millennium Edition, Windows 2000, Windows XP Home Edition, Windows XP Professional, Windows Server 2003 family

Assembly: System.Drawing (in System.Drawing.dll)

IPropertyValueUIService.AddPropertyValueUIHandler Method

Adds the specified **PropertyValueUIHandler** to this service.

```
[Visual Basic]
Sub AddPropertyValueUIHandler( _
   ByVal newHandler As PropertyValueUIHandler _
)
[C#]
void AddPropertyValueUIHandler(
   PropertyValueUIHandler newHandler
);
[C++]
void AddPropertyValueUIHandler(
   PropertyValueUIHandler* newHandler
);
[JScript]
function AddPropertyValueUIHandler(
   newHandler : PropertyValueUIHandler
);
```

Parameters

newHandler
: The property value UI handler to add.

Remarks

When **GetPropertyUIValueItems** is called, each handler added to this service is called and given the opportunity to add an icon for the property.

Requirements

Platforms: Windows 98, Windows NT 4.0, Windows Millennium Edition, Windows 2000, Windows XP Home Edition, Windows XP Professional, Windows Server 2003 family

IPropertyValueUIService.GetPropertyUIValueItems Method

Gets the **PropertyValueUIItem** objects that match the specified context and property descriptor characteristics.

```
[Visual Basic]
Function GetPropertyUIValueItems( _
   ByVal context As ITypeDescriptorContext, _
   ByVal propDesc As PropertyDescriptor _
) As PropertyValueUIItem()
[C#]
PropertyValueUIItem[] GetPropertyUIValueItems(
   ITypeDescriptorContext context,
   PropertyDescriptor propDesc
);
[C++]
PropertyValueUIItem* GetPropertyUIValueItems(
   ITypeDescriptorContext* context,
   PropertyDescriptor* propDesc
) [];
[JScript]
function GetPropertyUIValueItems(
   context : ITypeDescriptorContext,
   propDesc : PropertyDescriptor
) : PropertyValueUIItem[];
```

Parameters

context
: An **ITypeDescriptorContext** that can be used to gain additional context information.

propDesc
: A **PropertyDescriptor** that indicates the property to match with the properties to return.

Return Value

An array of **PropertyValueUIItem** objects that match the specified parameters.

Requirements

Platforms: Windows 98, Windows NT 4.0,
Windows Millennium Edition, Windows 2000,
Windows XP Home Edition, Windows XP Professional,
Windows Server 2003 family

IPropertyValueUIService.NotifyPropertyValueUIItemsChanged Method

Notifies the **IPropertyValueUIService** implementation that the global list of **PropertyValueUIItem** objects has been modified.

```
[Visual Basic]
Sub NotifyPropertyValueUIItemsChanged()
[C#]
void NotifyPropertyValueUIItemsChanged();
[C++]
void NotifyPropertyValueUIItemsChanged();
[JScript]
function NotifyPropertyValueUIItemsChanged();
```

Requirements

Platforms: Windows 98, Windows NT 4.0,
Windows Millennium Edition, Windows 2000,
Windows XP Home Edition, Windows XP Professional,
Windows Server 2003 family

IPropertyValueUIService.RemovePropertyValueUIHandler Method

Removes the specified **PropertyValueUIHandler** from the property value UI service.

```
[Visual Basic]
Sub RemovePropertyValueUIHandler( _
   ByVal newHandler As PropertyValueUIHandler _
)
[C#]
void RemovePropertyValueUIHandler(
   PropertyValueUIHandler newHandler
);
[C++]
void RemovePropertyValueUIHandler(
   PropertyValueUIHandler* newHandler
);
[JScript]
function RemovePropertyValueUIHandler(
   newHandler : PropertyValueUIHandler
);
```

Parameters

newHandler
The handler to remove.

Requirements

Platforms: Windows 98, Windows NT 4.0,
Windows Millennium Edition, Windows 2000,
Windows XP Home Edition, Windows XP Professional,
Windows Server 2003 family

IPropertyValueUIService.PropertyUIValueItemsChanged Event

Occurs when the list of **PropertyValueUIItem** objects is modified.

```
[Visual Basic]
Event PropertyUIValueItemsChanged As EventHandler
[C#]
event EventHandler PropertyUIValueItemsChanged;
[C++]
__event EventHandler* PropertyUIValueItemsChanged;
```

[JScript] In JScript, you can handle the events defined by a class, but you cannot define your own.

Event Data

The event handler receives an argument of type **EventArgs**.

Remarks

Components that serve **PropertyValueUIItem** objects can call **NotifyPropertyValueUIItemsChanged** when they change their list of items.

Requirements

Platforms: Windows 98, Windows NT 4.0,
Windows Millennium Edition, Windows 2000,
Windows XP Home Edition, Windows XP Professional,
Windows Server 2003 family

IToolboxService Interface

Provides methods and properties to manage and query the toolbox in the development environment.

[Visual Basic]
```
<Guid("4BACD258-DE64-4048-BC4E-FEDBEF9ACB76")>
<InterfaceType(ComInterfaceType.InterfaceIsIUnknown)>
Public Interface IToolboxService
```
[C#]
```
[Guid("4BACD258-DE64-4048-BC4E-FEDBEF9ACB76")]
[InterfaceType(ComInterfaceType.InterfaceIsIUnknown)]
public interface IToolboxService
```
[C++]
```
[Guid("4BACD258-DE64-4048-BC4E-FEDBEF9ACB76")]
[InterfaceType(ComInterfaceType::InterfaceIsIUnknown)]
public __gc __interface IToolboxService
```
[JScript]
```
public
   Guid("4BACD258-DE64-4048-BC4E-FEDBEF9ACB76")
   InterfaceType(ComInterfaceType.InterfaceIsIUnknown)
interface IToolboxService
```

Remarks

The **IToolboxService** interface provides properties and methods for adding and removing toolbox items and toolbox creator callback delegates, serializing and deserializing toolbox items, and retrieving toolbox state information and managing toolbox state.You can retrieve information about the contents of the toolbox with the following methods:

- The **CategoryNames** property indicates the categories currently available on the toolbox.
- The **SelectedCategory** property indicates the currently selected toolbox category.
- The **GetToolboxItems** method retrieves the items on the toolbox, optionally filtered by a specified toolbox category.
- The **GetSelectedToolboxItem** method retrieves the currently selected **ToolboxItem**.
- The **SetSelectedToolboxItem** method selects the specified **ToolboxItem** as the current toolbox item.
- The **IsSupported** method indicates whether the specified serialized object, if it is a **ToolboxItem**, is supported by the specified designer host, or whether it matches the specified attributes.
- The **IsToolboxItem** method indicates whether the specified serialized object is a **ToolboxItem**.

You can add and remove toolbox items with the following methods:

- The **AddToolboxItem** method adds a **ToolboxItem** to the toolbox, creating the optionally specified category if it does not exist.
- The **AddLinkedToolboxItem** method adds a **ToolboxItem** that is only enabled for the current project to the toolbox.
- The **RemoveToolboxItem** method removes the specified **ToolboxItem**.
- The **AddCreator** method adds a **ToolboxItemCreatorCallback** delegate capable of converting some type of data stored on the toolbox to a **ToolboxItem**.
- The **RemoveCreator** method removes any **ToolboxItem-CreatorCallback** delegates for the specified data type.

You can refresh the toolbox, mark a toolbox item as used, or set the mouse cursor to a cursor that represents the current toolbox item using the following methods:

- The **Refresh** method refreshes the toolbox display to reflect the current state of the toolbox items.
- The **SelectedToolboxItemUsed** method signals the toolbox that the selected toolbox item has been used.
- The **SetCursor** method sets the mouse cursor to a cursor that represents the current toolbox item.

You can use the toolbox to serialize or deserialize a toolbox item using the following methods:

- The **DeserializeToolboxItem** method attemps to return a **ToolboxItem** from the specified serialized toolbox item object.
- The **SerializeToolboxItem** method returns a serialized object representing the specified **ToolboxItem**.

Requirements

Namespace: System.Drawing.Design

Platforms: Windows 98, Windows NT 4.0, Windows Millennium Edition, Windows 2000, Windows XP Home Edition, Windows XP Professional, Windows Server 2003 family

Assembly: System.Drawing (in System.Drawing.dll)

IToolboxService.CategoryNames Property

Gets the names of all the tool categories currently on the toolbox.

[Visual Basic]
```
ReadOnly Property CategoryNames As CategoryNameCollection
```
[C#]
```
CategoryNameCollection CategoryNames {get;}
```
[C++]
```
__property CategoryNameCollection* get_CategoryNames();
```
[JScript]
```
function get CategoryNames() : CategoryNameCollection;
```

Property Value

A **CategoryNameCollection** containing the tool categories.

Requirements

Platforms: Windows 98, Windows NT 4.0, Windows Millennium Edition, Windows 2000, Windows XP Home Edition, Windows XP Professional, Windows Server 2003 family

IToolboxService.SelectedCategory Property

Gets or sets the name of the currently selected tool category from the toolbox.

[Visual Basic]
```
Property SelectedCategory As String
```
[C#]
```
string SelectedCategory {get; set;}
```
[C++]
```
__property String* get_SelectedCategory();
__property void set_SelectedCategory(String*);
```
[JScript]
```
function get SelectedCategory() : String;function set
SelectedCategory(String);
```

Property Value

The name of the currently selected category.

Requirements

Platforms: Windows 98, Windows NT 4.0,
Windows Millennium Edition, Windows 2000,
Windows XP Home Edition, Windows XP Professional,
Windows Server 2003 family

IToolboxService.AddCreator Method

Adds a new toolbox item creator for a specified data format.

Overload List

Adds a new toolbox item creator for a specified data format.

[Visual Basic] **Overloads Sub AddCreator(Toolbox-ItemCreatorCallback, String)**

[C#] **void AddCreator(ToolboxItemCreatorCallback, string);**

[C++] **void AddCreator(ToolboxItemCreatorCallback*, String*);**

[JScript] **function AddCreator(ToolboxItemCreatorCallback, String);**

Adds a new toolbox item creator for a specified data format and designer host.

[Visual Basic] **Overloads Sub AddCreator(ToolboxItem-CreatorCallback, String, IDesignerHost)**

[C#] **void AddCreator(ToolboxItemCreatorCallback, string, IDesignerHost);**

[C++] **void AddCreator(ToolboxItemCreatorCallback*, String*, IDesignerHost*);**

[JScript] **function AddCreator(ToolboxItemCreatorCallback, String, IDesignerHost);**

IToolboxService.AddCreator Method (ToolboxItemCreatorCallback, String)

Adds a new toolbox item creator for a specified data format.

```
[Visual Basic]
Sub AddCreator( _
   ByVal creator As ToolboxItemCreatorCallback, _
   ByVal format As String _
)
[C#]
void AddCreator(
   ToolboxItemCreatorCallback creator,
   string format
);
[C++]
void AddCreator(
   ToolboxItemCreatorCallback* creator,
   String* format
);
[JScript]
function AddCreator(
   creator : ToolboxItemCreatorCallback,
   format : String
);
```

Parameters

creator

A **ToolboxItemCreatorCallback** that can create a component when the toolbox item is invoked.

format

The data format that the creator handles.

Remarks

A toolbox item creator can convert data of a particular data format that has been pasted or dropped on the toolbox into a **ToolboxItem**. If a creator handles more than one format, call **AddCreator** more than once. Unexpected behavior may result if you add more than one creator for the same format.

Requirements

Platforms: Windows 98, Windows NT 4.0,
Windows Millennium Edition, Windows 2000,
Windows XP Home Edition, Windows XP Professional,
Windows Server 2003 family

IToolboxService.AddCreator Method (ToolboxItemCreatorCallback, String, IDesignerHost)

Adds a new toolbox item creator for a specified data format and designer host.

```
[Visual Basic]
Sub AddCreator( _
   ByVal creator As ToolboxItemCreatorCallback, _
   ByVal format As String, _
   ByVal host As IDesignerHost _
)
[C#]
void AddCreator(
   ToolboxItemCreatorCallback creator,
   string format,
   IDesignerHost host
);
[C++]
void AddCreator(
   ToolboxItemCreatorCallback* creator,
   String* format,
   IDesignerHost* host
);
[JScript]
function AddCreator(
   creator : ToolboxItemCreatorCallback,
   format : String,
   host : IDesignerHost
);
```

Parameters

creator

A **ToolboxItemCreatorCallback** that can create a component when the toolbox item is invoked.

format

The data format that the creator handles.

host

The **IDesignerHost** that represents the designer host to associate with the creator.

Remarks

A toolbox item creator can convert data of a particular data format that has been pasted or dropped on the toolbox into a **ToolboxItem**. If a creator handles more than one format, call **AddCreator** more than once. Unexpected behavior may result if you add more than one creator for the same format.

If the *host* parameter is set to a null reference (**Nothing** in Visual Basic), the creator will be available to all designers. If a designer host is supplied, the creator will only be available to designers using the specified host.

Requirements

Platforms: Windows 98, Windows NT 4.0, Windows Millennium Edition, Windows 2000, Windows XP Home Edition, Windows XP Professional, Windows Server 2003 family

IToolboxService.AddLinkedToolboxItem Method

Adds a project-linked toolbox item to the toolbox.

Overload List

Adds the specified project-linked toolbox item to the toolbox.

[Visual Basic] **Overloads Sub AddLinkedToolbox-Item(ToolboxItem, IDesignerHost)**

[C#] **void AddLinkedToolboxItem(ToolboxItem, IDesignerHost);**

[C++] **void AddLinkedToolboxItem(ToolboxItem*, IDesignerHost*);**

[JScript] **function AddLinkedToolboxItem(ToolboxItem, IDesignerHost);**

Adds the specified project-linked toolbox item to the toolbox in the specified category.

[Visual Basic] **Overloads Sub AddLinkedToolbox-Item(ToolboxItem, String, IDesignerHost)**

[C#] **void AddLinkedToolboxItem(ToolboxItem, string, IDesignerHost);**

[C++] **void AddLinkedToolboxItem(ToolboxItem*, String*, IDesignerHost*);**

[JScript] **function AddLinkedToolboxItem(ToolboxItem, String, IDesignerHost);**

IToolboxService.AddLinkedToolboxItem Method (ToolboxItem, IDesignerHost)

Adds the specified project-linked toolbox item to the toolbox.

[Visual Basic]
```
Sub AddLinkedToolboxItem( _
   ByVal toolboxItem As ToolboxItem, _
   ByVal host As IDesignerHost _
)
```
[C#]
```
void AddLinkedToolboxItem(
   ToolboxItem toolboxItem,
   IDesignerHost host
);
```
[C++]
```
void AddLinkedToolboxItem(
   ToolboxItem* toolboxItem,
   IDesignerHost* host
);
```
[JScript]
```
function AddLinkedToolboxItem(
   toolboxItem : ToolboxItem,
   host : IDesignerHost
);
```

Parameters

toolboxItem
: The linked **ToolboxItem** to add to the toolbox.

host
: The **IDesignerHost** for the current design document.

Remarks

A linked toolbox item is a toolbox item that is only available for a specific project.

Requirements

Platforms: Windows 98, Windows NT 4.0, Windows Millennium Edition, Windows 2000, Windows XP Home Edition, Windows XP Professional, Windows Server 2003 family

IToolboxService.AddLinkedToolboxItem Method (ToolboxItem, String, IDesignerHost)

Adds the specified project-linked toolbox item to the toolbox in the specified category.

[Visual Basic]
```
Sub AddLinkedToolboxItem( _
   ByVal toolboxItem As ToolboxItem, _
   ByVal category As String, _
   ByVal host As IDesignerHost _
)
```
[C#]
```
void AddLinkedToolboxItem(
   ToolboxItem toolboxItem,
   string category,
   IDesignerHost host
);
```
[C++]
```
void AddLinkedToolboxItem(
   ToolboxItem* toolboxItem,
   String* category,
   IDesignerHost* host
);
```
[JScript]
```
function AddLinkedToolboxItem(
   toolboxItem : ToolboxItem,
   category : String,
   host : IDesignerHost
);
```

Parameters

toolboxItem
: The linked **ToolboxItem** to add to the toolbox.

category
: The toolbox item category to add the toolbox item to.

host
: The **IDesignerHost** for the current design document.

Remarks

A linked toolbox item is a toolbox item that is only available for a specific project.

Requirements

Platforms: Windows 98, Windows NT 4.0, Windows Millennium Edition, Windows 2000, Windows XP Home Edition, Windows XP Professional, Windows Server 2003 family

IToolboxService.AddToolboxItem Method

Adds the specified toolbox item to the toolbox.

Overload List

Adds the specified toolbox item to the toolbox.

[Visual Basic] **Overloads Sub AddToolboxItem(ToolboxItem)**

[C#] **void AddToolboxItem(ToolboxItem);**

[C++] **void AddToolboxItem(ToolboxItem*);**

[JScript] **function AddToolboxItem(ToolboxItem);**

Adds the specified toolbox item to the toolbox in the specified category.

[Visual Basic] **Overloads Sub AddToolboxItem(ToolboxItem, String)**

[C#] **void AddToolboxItem(ToolboxItem, string);**

[C++] **void AddToolboxItem(ToolboxItem*, String*);**

[JScript] **function AddToolboxItem(ToolboxItem, String);**

IToolboxService.AddToolboxItem Method (ToolboxItem)

Adds the specified toolbox item to the toolbox.

```
[Visual Basic]
Sub AddToolboxItem( _
   ByVal toolboxItem As ToolboxItem _
)
[C#]
void AddToolboxItem(
   ToolboxItem toolboxItem
);
[C++]
void AddToolboxItem(
   ToolboxItem* toolboxItem
);
[JScript]
function AddToolboxItem(
   toolboxItem : ToolboxItem
);
```

Parameters

toolboxItem

The **ToolboxItem** to add to the toolbox.

Requirements

Platforms: Windows 98, Windows NT 4.0, Windows Millennium Edition, Windows 2000, Windows XP Home Edition, Windows XP Professional, Windows Server 2003 family

IToolboxService.AddToolboxItem Method (ToolboxItem, String)

Adds the specified toolbox item to the toolbox in the specified category.

```
[Visual Basic]
Sub AddToolboxItem( _
   ByVal toolboxItem As ToolboxItem, _
   ByVal category As String _
)
[C#]
void AddToolboxItem(
   ToolboxItem toolboxItem,
   string category
);
[C++]
void AddToolboxItem(
   ToolboxItem* toolboxItem,
   String* category
);
[JScript]
function AddToolboxItem(
   toolboxItem : ToolboxItem,
   category : String
);
```

Parameters

toolboxItem

The **ToolboxItem** to add to the toolbox.

category

The toolbox item category to add the **ToolboxItem** to.

Requirements

Platforms: Windows 98, Windows NT 4.0, Windows Millennium Edition, Windows 2000, Windows XP Home Edition, Windows XP Professional, Windows Server 2003 family

IToolboxService.DeserializeToolboxItem Method

Gets a toolbox item from the specified object that represents a toolbox item in serialized form.

Overload List

Gets a toolbox item from the specified object that represents a toolbox item in serialized form.

[Visual Basic] **Overloads Function DeserializeToolboxItem(Object) As ToolboxItem**

[C#] **ToolboxItem DeserializeToolboxItem(object);**

[C++] **ToolboxItem* DeserializeToolboxItem(Object*);**

[JScript] **function DeserializeToolboxItem(Object) : ToolboxItem;**

Gets a toolbox item from the specified object that represents a toolbox item in serialized form, using the specified designer host.

[Visual Basic] **Overloads Function DeserializeToolboxItem(Object, IDesignerHost) As ToolboxItem**

[C#] **ToolboxItem DeserializeToolboxItem(object, IDesignerHost);**

[C++] **ToolboxItem* DeserializeToolboxItem(Object*, IDesignerHost*);**

[JScript] **function DeserializeToolboxItem(Object, IDesignerHost) : ToolboxItem;**

IToolboxService.DeserializeToolboxItem Method (Object)

Gets a toolbox item from the specified object that represents a toolbox item in serialized form.

```
[Visual Basic]
Function DeserializeToolboxItem( _
   ByVal serializedObject As Object _
) As ToolboxItem
[C#]
ToolboxItem DeserializeToolboxItem(
   object serializedObject
);
[C++]
ToolboxItem* DeserializeToolboxItem(
   Object* serializedObject
);
[JScript]
function DeserializeToolboxItem(
   serializedObject : Object
) : ToolboxItem;
```

Parameters

serializedObject
The object that contains the **ToolboxItem** to retrieve.

Return Value

The **ToolboxItem** created from the serialized object.

Requirements

Platforms: Windows 98, Windows NT 4.0, Windows Millennium Edition, Windows 2000, Windows XP Home Edition, Windows XP Professional, Windows Server 2003 family

IToolboxService.DeserializeToolboxItem Method (Object, IDesignerHost)

Gets a toolbox item from the specified object that represents a toolbox item in serialized form, using the specified designer host.

```
[Visual Basic]
Function DeserializeToolboxItem( _
   ByVal serializedObject As Object, _
   ByVal host As IDesignerHost _
) As ToolboxItem
[C#]
ToolboxItem DeserializeToolboxItem(
   object serializedObject,
   IDesignerHost host
);
[C++]
ToolboxItem* DeserializeToolboxItem(
   Object* serializedObject,
   IDesignerHost* host
);
[JScript]
function DeserializeToolboxItem(
   serializedObject : Object,
   host : IDesignerHost
) : ToolboxItem;
```

Parameters

serializedObject
The object that contains the **ToolboxItem** to retrieve.

host
The **IDesignerHost** to associate with this **ToolboxItem**.

Return Value

The **ToolboxItem** created from deserialization.

Requirements

Platforms: Windows 98, Windows NT 4.0, Windows Millennium Edition, Windows 2000, Windows XP Home Edition, Windows XP Professional, Windows Server 2003 family

IToolboxService.GetSelectedToolboxItem Method

Gets the currently selected toolbox item.

Overload List

Gets the currently selected toolbox item.

[Visual Basic] **Overloads Function GetSelectedToolboxItem() As ToolboxItem**

[C#] **ToolboxItem GetSelectedToolboxItem();**

[C++] **ToolboxItem* GetSelectedToolboxItem();**

[JScript] **function GetSelectedToolboxItem() : ToolboxItem;**

Gets the currently selected toolbox item if it is available to all designers, or if it supports the specified designer.

[Visual Basic] **Overloads Function GetSelectedToolboxItem(IDesignerHost) As ToolboxItem**

[C#] **ToolboxItem GetSelectedToolboxItem(IDesignerHost);**

[C++] **ToolboxItem* GetSelectedToolboxItem(IDesignerHost*);**

[JScript] **function GetSelectedToolboxItem(IDesignerHost) : ToolboxItem;**

IToolboxService.GetSelectedToolboxItem Method ()

Gets the currently selected toolbox item.

```
[Visual Basic]
Function GetSelectedToolboxItem() As ToolboxItem
[C#]
ToolboxItem GetSelectedToolboxItem();
[C++]
ToolboxItem* GetSelectedToolboxItem();
[JScript]
function GetSelectedToolboxItem() : ToolboxItem;
```

Return Value

The **ToolboxItem** that is currently selected, or a null reference (**Nothing** in Visual Basic) if no toolbox item has been selected.

Requirements

Platforms: Windows 98, Windows NT 4.0, Windows Millennium Edition, Windows 2000, Windows XP Home Edition, Windows XP Professional, Windows Server 2003 family

IToolboxService.GetSelectedToolboxItem Method (IDesignerHost)

Gets the currently selected toolbox item if it is available to all designers, or if it supports the specified designer.

[Visual Basic]
```
Function GetSelectedToolboxItem( _
   ByVal host As IDesignerHost _
) As ToolboxItem
```
[C#]
```
ToolboxItem GetSelectedToolboxItem(
   IDesignerHost host
);
```
[C++]
```
ToolboxItem* GetSelectedToolboxItem(
   IDesignerHost* host
);
```
[JScript]
```
function GetSelectedToolboxItem(
   host : IDesignerHost
) : ToolboxItem;
```

Parameters

host

The **IDesignerHost** that the selected tool must be associated with for it to be returned.

Return Value

The **ToolboxItem** that is currently selected, or a null reference (**Nothing** in Visual Basic) if no toolbox item is currently selected.

Remarks

This method returns the currently selected **ToolboxItem** if it is not designer specific, and only returns a designer-specific currently selected **ToolboxItem** if the type of the designer host specified in the *host* parameter matches the type of designer that the currently selected **ToolboxItem** supports.

Requirements

Platforms: Windows 98, Windows NT 4.0, Windows Millennium Edition, Windows 2000, Windows XP Home Edition, Windows XP Professional, Windows Server 2003 family

IToolboxService.GetToolboxItems Method

Gets a collection of toolbox items from the toolbox.

Overload List

Gets the entire collection of toolbox items from the toolbox.

[Visual Basic] **Overloads Function GetToolboxItems() As ToolboxItemCollection**

[C#] **ToolboxItemCollection GetToolboxItems();**

[C++] **ToolboxItemCollection* GetToolboxItems();**

[JScript] **function GetToolboxItems() : ToolboxItemCollection;**

Gets the collection of toolbox items that are associated with the specified designer host from the toolbox.

[Visual Basic] **Overloads Function GetToolbox-Items(IDesignerHost) As ToolboxItemCollection**

[C#] **ToolboxItemCollection GetToolboxItems(IDesignerHost);**

[C++] **ToolboxItemCollection* GetToolboxItems(IDesigner-Host*);**

[JScript] **function GetToolboxItems(IDesignerHost) : ToolboxItemCollection;**

Gets a collection of toolbox items from the toolbox that match the specified category.

[Visual Basic] **Overloads Function GetToolboxItems(String) As ToolboxItemCollection**

[C#] **ToolboxItemCollection GetToolboxItems(string);**

[C++] **ToolboxItemCollection* GetToolboxItems(String*);**

[JScript] **function GetToolboxItems(String) : ToolboxItemCollection;**

Gets the collection of toolbox items that are associated with the specified designer host and category from the toolbox.

[Visual Basic] **Overloads Function GetToolboxItems(String, IDesignerHost) As ToolboxItemCollection**

[C#] **ToolboxItemCollection GetToolboxItems(string, IDesignerHost);**

[C++] **ToolboxItemCollection* GetToolboxItems(String*, IDesignerHost*);**

[JScript] **function GetToolboxItems(String, IDesignerHost) : ToolboxItemCollection;**

IToolboxService.GetToolboxItems Method ()

Gets the entire collection of toolbox items from the toolbox.

[Visual Basic]
```
Function GetToolboxItems() As ToolboxItemCollection
```
[C#]
```
ToolboxItemCollection GetToolboxItems();
```
[C++]
```
ToolboxItemCollection* GetToolboxItems();
```
[JScript]
```
function GetToolboxItems() : ToolboxItemCollection;
```

Return Value

A **ToolboxItemCollection** that contains the current toolbox items.

Requirements

Platforms: Windows 98, Windows NT 4.0, Windows Millennium Edition, Windows 2000, Windows XP Home Edition, Windows XP Professional, Windows Server 2003 family

IToolboxService.GetToolboxItems Method (IDesignerHost)

Gets the collection of toolbox items that are associated with the specified designer host from the toolbox.

[Visual Basic]
```
Function GetToolboxItems( _
   ByVal host As IDesignerHost _
) As ToolboxItemCollection
```
[C#]
```
ToolboxItemCollection GetToolboxItems(
   IDesignerHost host
);
```
[C++]
```
ToolboxItemCollection* GetToolboxItems(
   IDesignerHost* host
);
```

```
[JScript]
function GetToolboxItems(
   host : IDesignerHost
) : ToolboxItemCollection;
```

Parameters

host

The **IDesignerHost** that is associated with the toolbox items to retrieve.

Return Value

A **ToolboxItemCollection** that contains the current toolbox items that are associated with the specified designer host.

Requirements

Platforms: Windows 98, Windows NT 4.0, Windows Millennium Edition, Windows 2000, Windows XP Home Edition, Windows XP Professional, Windows Server 2003 family

IToolboxService.GetToolboxItems Method (String)

Gets a collection of toolbox items from the toolbox that match the specified category.

```
[Visual Basic]
Function GetToolboxItems( _
   ByVal category As String _
) As ToolboxItemCollection
[C#]
ToolboxItemCollection GetToolboxItems(
   string category
);
[C++]
ToolboxItemCollection* GetToolboxItems(
   String* category
);
[JScript]
function GetToolboxItems(
   category : String
) : ToolboxItemCollection;
```

Parameters

category

The toolbox item category to retrieve all the toolbox items from.

Return Value

A **ToolboxItemCollection** that contains the current toolbox items that are associated with the specified category.

Requirements

Platforms: Windows 98, Windows NT 4.0, Windows Millennium Edition, Windows 2000, Windows XP Home Edition, Windows XP Professional, Windows Server 2003 family

IToolboxService.GetToolboxItems Method (String, IDesignerHost)

Gets the collection of toolbox items that are associated with the specified designer host and category from the toolbox.

```
[Visual Basic]
Function GetToolboxItems( _
   ByVal category As String, _
   ByVal host As IDesignerHost _
) As ToolboxItemCollection
[C#]
ToolboxItemCollection GetToolboxItems(
   string category,
   IDesignerHost host
);
[C++]
ToolboxItemCollection* GetToolboxItems(
   String* category,
   IDesignerHost* host
);
[JScript]
function GetToolboxItems(
   category : String,
   host : IDesignerHost
) : ToolboxItemCollection;
```

Parameters

category

The toolbox item category to retrieve the toolbox items from.

host

The **IDesignerHost** that is associated with the toolbox items to retrieve.

Return Value

A **ToolboxItemCollection** that contains the current toolbox items that are associated with the specified category and designer host.

Requirements

Platforms: Windows 98, Windows NT 4.0, Windows Millennium Edition, Windows 2000, Windows XP Home Edition, Windows XP Professional, Windows Server 2003 family

IToolboxService.IsSupported Method

Gets a value indicating whether the specified object which represents a serialized toolbox item can be used by the specified designer host.

Overload List

Gets a value indicating whether the specified object which represents a serialized toolbox item matches the specified attributes.

[Visual Basic] **Overloads Function IsSupported(Object, ICollection) As Boolean**

[C#] **bool IsSupported(object, ICollection);**

[C++] **bool IsSupported(Object*, ICollection*);**

[JScript] **function IsSupported(Object, ICollection) : Boolean;**

Gets a value indicating whether the specified object which represents a serialized toolbox item can be used by the specified designer host.

[Visual Basic] **Overloads Function IsSupported(Object, IDesignerHost) As Boolean**

[C#] **bool IsSupported(object, IDesignerHost);**

[C++] **bool IsSupported(Object*, IDesignerHost*);**

[JScript] **function IsSupported(Object, IDesignerHost) : Boolean;**

IToolboxService.IsSupported Method (Object, ICollection)

Gets a value indicating whether the specified object which represents a serialized toolbox item matches the specified attributes.

```
[Visual Basic]
Function IsSupported( _
   ByVal serializedObject As Object, _
   ByVal filterAttributes As ICollection _
) As Boolean
[C#]
bool IsSupported(
   object serializedObject,
   ICollection filterAttributes
);
[C++]
bool IsSupported(
   Object* serializedObject,
   ICollection* filterAttributes
);
[JScript]
function IsSupported(
   serializedObject : Object,
   filterAttributes : ICollection
) : Boolean;
```

Parameters

serializedObject
The object that contains the **ToolboxItem** to retrieve.

filterAttributes
An **ICollection** that contains the attributes to test the serialized object for.

Return Value

true if the object matches the specified attributes; otherwise, **false**.

Requirements

Platforms: Windows 98, Windows NT 4.0,
Windows Millennium Edition, Windows 2000,
Windows XP Home Edition, Windows XP Professional,
Windows Server 2003 family

IToolboxService.IsSupported Method (Object, IDesignerHost)

Gets a value indicating whether the specified object which represents a serialized toolbox item can be used by the specified designer host.

```
[Visual Basic]
Function IsSupported( _
   ByVal serializedObject As Object, _
   ByVal host As IDesignerHost _
) As Boolean
[C#]
bool IsSupported(
   object serializedObject,
   IDesignerHost host
);
[C++]
bool IsSupported(
   Object* serializedObject,
   IDesignerHost* host
);
[JScript]
function IsSupported(
   serializedObject : Object,
   host : IDesignerHost
) : Boolean;
```

Parameters

serializedObject
The object that contains the **ToolboxItem** to retrieve.

host
The **IDesignerHost** to test for support for the **ToolboxItem**.

Return Value

true if the specified object is compatible with the specified designer host; otherwise, **false**.

Requirements

Platforms: Windows 98, Windows NT 4.0,
Windows Millennium Edition, Windows 2000,
Windows XP Home Edition, Windows XP Professional,
Windows Server 2003 family

IToolboxService.IsToolboxItem Method

Gets a value indicating whether the specified object is a serialized toolbox item.

Overload List

Gets a value indicating whether the specified object is a serialized toolbox item.

[Visual Basic] **Overloads Function IsToolboxItem(Object) As Boolean**

[C#] **bool IsToolboxItem(object);**

[C++] **bool IsToolboxItem(Object*);**

[JScript] **function IsToolboxItem(Object) : Boolean;**

Gets a value indicating whether the specified object is a serialized toolbox item, using the specified designer host.

[Visual Basic] **Overloads Function IsToolboxItem(Object, IDesignerHost) As Boolean**

[C#] **bool IsToolboxItem(object, IDesignerHost);**

[C++] **bool IsToolboxItem(Object*, IDesignerHost*);**

[JScript] **function IsToolboxItem(Object, IDesignerHost) : Boolean;**

IToolboxService.IsToolboxItem Method (Object)

Gets a value indicating whether the specified object is a serialized toolbox item.

```
[Visual Basic]
Function IsToolboxItem( _
   ByVal serializedObject As Object _
) As Boolean
[C#]
bool IsToolboxItem(
   object serializedObject
);
[C++]
bool IsToolboxItem(
   Object* serializedObject
);
```

```
[JScript]
function IsToolboxItem(
   serializedObject : Object
) : Boolean;
```

Parameters

serializedObject
The object to inspect.

Return Value

true if the object contains a toolbox item object; otherwise, **false**.

Requirements

Platforms: Windows 98, Windows NT 4.0, Windows Millennium Edition, Windows 2000, Windows XP Home Edition, Windows XP Professional, Windows Server 2003 family

IToolboxService.IsToolboxItem Method (Object, IDesignerHost)

Gets a value indicating whether the specified object is a serialized toolbox item, using the specified designer host.

```
[Visual Basic]
Function IsToolboxItem( _
   ByVal serializedObject As Object, _
   ByVal host As IDesignerHost _
) As Boolean
[C#]
bool IsToolboxItem(
   object serializedObject,
   IDesignerHost host
);
[C++]
bool IsToolboxItem(
   Object* serializedObject,
   IDesignerHost* host
);
[JScript]
function IsToolboxItem(
   serializedObject : Object,
   host : IDesignerHost
) : Boolean;
```

Parameters

serializedObject
The object to inspect.

host
The **IDesignerHost** that is making this request.

Return Value

true if the object contains a toolbox item object; otherwise, **false**.

Requirements

Platforms: Windows 98, Windows NT 4.0, Windows Millennium Edition, Windows 2000, Windows XP Home Edition, Windows XP Professional, Windows Server 2003 family

IToolboxService.Refresh Method

Refreshes the state of the toolbox items.

```
[Visual Basic]
Sub Refresh()
[C#]
void Refresh();
[C++]
void Refresh();
[JScript]
function Refresh();
```

Requirements

Platforms: Windows 98, Windows NT 4.0, Windows Millennium Edition, Windows 2000, Windows XP Home Edition, Windows XP Professional, Windows Server 2003 family

IToolboxService.RemoveCreator Method

Removes a previously added toolbox item creator.

Overload List

Removes a previously added toolbox item creator of the specified data format.

[Visual Basic] **Overloads Sub RemoveCreator(String)**
[C#] **void RemoveCreator(string);**
[C++] **void RemoveCreator(String*);**
[JScript] **function RemoveCreator(String);**

Removes a previously added toolbox creator that is associated with the specified data format and the specified designer host.

[Visual Basic] **Overloads Sub RemoveCreator(String, IDesignerHost)**
[C#] **void RemoveCreator(string, IDesignerHost);**
[C++] **void RemoveCreator(String*, IDesignerHost*);**
[JScript] **function RemoveCreator(String, IDesignerHost);**

IToolboxService.RemoveCreator Method (String)

Removes a previously added toolbox item creator of the specified data format.

```
[Visual Basic]
Sub RemoveCreator( _
   ByVal format As String _
)
[C#]
void RemoveCreator(
   string format
);
[C++]
void RemoveCreator(
   String* format
);
[JScript]
function RemoveCreator(
   format : String
);
```

Parameters

format
The data format of the creator to remove.

Requirements

Platforms: Windows 98, Windows NT 4.0, Windows Millennium Edition, Windows 2000, Windows XP Home Edition, Windows XP Professional, Windows Server 2003 family

IToolboxService.RemoveCreator Method (String, IDesignerHost)

Removes a previously added toolbox creator that is associated with the specified data format and the specified designer host.

```
[Visual Basic]
Sub RemoveCreator( _
   ByVal format As String, _
   ByVal host As IDesignerHost _
)
[C#]
void RemoveCreator(
   string format,
   IDesignerHost host
);
[C++]
void RemoveCreator(
   String* format,
   IDesignerHost* host
);
[JScript]
function RemoveCreator(
   format : String,
   host : IDesignerHost
);
```

Parameters

format

The data format of the creator to remove.

host

The **IDesignerHost** that is associated with the creator to remove.

Requirements

Platforms: Windows 98, Windows NT 4.0, Windows Millennium Edition, Windows 2000, Windows XP Home Edition, Windows XP Professional, Windows Server 2003 family

IToolboxService.RemoveToolboxItem Method

Removes the specified toolbox item from the toolbox.

Overload List

Removes the specified toolbox item from the toolbox.

[Visual Basic] **Overloads Sub RemoveToolboxItem(ToolboxItem)**

[C#] **void RemoveToolboxItem(ToolboxItem);**

[C++] **void RemoveToolboxItem(ToolboxItem*);**

[JScript] **function RemoveToolboxItem(ToolboxItem);**

Removes the specified toolbox item from the toolbox.

[Visual Basic] **Overloads Sub RemoveToolboxItem(ToolboxItem, String)**

[C#] **void RemoveToolboxItem(ToolboxItem, string);**

[C++] **void RemoveToolboxItem(ToolboxItem*, String*);**

[JScript] **function RemoveToolboxItem(ToolboxItem, String);**

IToolboxService.RemoveToolboxItem Method (ToolboxItem)

Removes the specified toolbox item from the toolbox.

```
[Visual Basic]
Sub RemoveToolboxItem( _
   ByVal toolboxItem As ToolboxItem _
)
[C#]
void RemoveToolboxItem(
   ToolboxItem toolboxItem
);
[C++]
void RemoveToolboxItem(
   ToolboxItem* toolboxItem
);
[JScript]
function RemoveToolboxItem(
   toolboxItem : ToolboxItem
);
```

Parameters

toolboxItem

The **ToolboxItem** to remove from the toolbox.

Requirements

Platforms: Windows 98, Windows NT 4.0, Windows Millennium Edition, Windows 2000, Windows XP Home Edition, Windows XP Professional, Windows Server 2003 family

IToolboxService.RemoveToolboxItem Method (ToolboxItem, String)

Removes the specified toolbox item from the toolbox.

```
[Visual Basic]
Sub RemoveToolboxItem( _
   ByVal toolboxItem As ToolboxItem, _
   ByVal category As String _
)
[C#]
void RemoveToolboxItem(
   ToolboxItem toolboxItem,
   string category
);
[C++]
void RemoveToolboxItem(
   ToolboxItem* toolboxItem,
   String* category
);
[JScript]
function RemoveToolboxItem(
   toolboxItem : ToolboxItem,
   category : String
);
```

Parameters

toolboxItem

The **ToolboxItem** to remove from the toolbox.

category

The toolbox item category to remove the **ToolboxItem** from.

Requirements

Platforms: Windows 98, Windows NT 4.0, Windows Millennium Edition, Windows 2000, Windows XP Home Edition, Windows XP Professional, Windows Server 2003 family

IToolboxService.SelectedToolboxItemUsed Method

Notifies the toolbox service that the selected tool has been used.

```
[Visual Basic]
Sub SelectedToolboxItemUsed()
[C#]
void SelectedToolboxItemUsed();
[C++]
void SelectedToolboxItemUsed();
[JScript]
function SelectedToolboxItemUsed();
```

Requirements

Platforms: Windows 98, Windows NT 4.0, Windows Millennium Edition, Windows 2000, Windows XP Home Edition, Windows XP Professional, Windows Server 2003 family

IToolboxService.SerializeToolboxItem Method

Gets a serializable object that represents the specified toolbox item.

```
[Visual Basic]
Function SerializeToolboxItem( _
   ByVal toolboxItem As ToolboxItem _
) As Object
[C#]
object SerializeToolboxItem(
   ToolboxItem toolboxItem
);
[C++]
Object* SerializeToolboxItem(
   ToolboxItem* toolboxItem
);
[JScript]
function SerializeToolboxItem(
   toolboxItem : ToolboxItem
) : Object;
```

Parameters

toolboxItem
The **ToolboxItem** to serialize.

Return Value

An object that represents the specified **ToolboxItem**.

Remarks

This method serializes the specified **ToolboxItem** to an object that can be persisted. The returned object can be stored in a stream or passed around in a drag-and-drop or clipboard operation.

Requirements

Platforms: Windows 98, Windows NT 4.0, Windows Millennium Edition, Windows 2000, Windows XP Home Edition, Windows XP Professional, Windows Server 2003 family

IToolboxService.SetCursor Method

Sets the current application's cursor to a cursor that represents the currently selected tool.

```
[Visual Basic]
Function SetCursor() As Boolean
[C#]
bool SetCursor();
[C++]
bool SetCursor();
[JScript]
function SetCursor() : Boolean;
```

Return Value

true if the cursor is set by the currently selected tool, **false** if there is no tool selected and the cursor is set to the standard windows cursor.

Remarks

If no tool is selected, the cursor will default to the standard Windows cursor.

Requirements

Platforms: Windows 98, Windows NT 4.0, Windows Millennium Edition, Windows 2000, Windows XP Home Edition, Windows XP Professional, Windows Server 2003 family

IToolboxService.SetSelectedToolboxItem Method

Selects the specified toolbox item.

```
[Visual Basic]
Sub SetSelectedToolboxItem( _
   ByVal toolboxItem As ToolboxItem _
)
[C#]
void SetSelectedToolboxItem(
   ToolboxItem toolboxItem
);
[C++]
void SetSelectedToolboxItem(
   ToolboxItem* toolboxItem
);
[JScript]
function SetSelectedToolboxItem(
   toolboxItem : ToolboxItem
);
```

Parameters

toolboxItem
The **ToolboxItem** to select.

Requirements

Platforms: Windows 98, Windows NT 4.0, Windows Millennium Edition, Windows 2000, Windows XP Home Edition, Windows XP Professional, Windows Server 2003 family

IToolboxUser Interface

Defines an interface for setting the currently selected toolbox item and indicating whether a designer supports a particular toolbox item.

```
[Visual Basic]
Public Interface IToolboxUser
[C#]
public interface IToolboxUser
[C++]
public __gc __interface IToolboxUser
[JScript]
public interface IToolboxUser
```

Classes that Implement IToolboxUser

Class	Description
ComponentDocument-Designer	Base designer class for extending the design mode behavior of a root design document that supports nested components.
DocumentDesigner	Base designer class for extending the design mode behavior of, and providing a root-level design mode view for, a **Control** that supports nested controls and should receive scroll messages.

Remarks

This interface provides toolbox support functions to designers. The **GetToolSupported** method indicates whether the specified **ToolboxItem** can be used when the current designer is active. The **ToolPicked** method selects the specified **ToolboxItem**.

Requirements

Namespace: System.Drawing.Design

Platforms: Windows 98, Windows NT 4.0, Windows Millennium Edition, Windows 2000, Windows XP Home Edition, Windows XP Professional, Windows Server 2003 family

Assembly: System.Drawing (in System.Drawing.dll)

IToolboxUser.GetToolSupported Method

Gets a value indicating whether the specified tool is supported by the current designer.

```
[Visual Basic]
Function GetToolSupported( _
   ByVal tool As ToolboxItem _
) As Boolean
[C#]
bool GetToolSupported(
   ToolboxItem tool
);
[C++]
bool GetToolSupported(
   ToolboxItem* tool
);
[JScript]
function GetToolSupported(
   tool : ToolboxItem
) : Boolean;
```

Parameters

tool

The **ToolboxItem** to be tested for toolbox support.

Return Value

true if the tool is supported by the toolbox and can be enabled; **false** if the document designer does not know how to use the tool.

Remarks

If the specified tool is supported by the designer implementing the **IToolboxUser** interface, then the tool will be enabled in the toolbox when this designer has focus. Otherwise, it will be disabled. Once a tool is marked as enabled or disabled, it may not be tested for support with the same designer again.

Requirements

Platforms: Windows 98, Windows NT 4.0, Windows Millennium Edition, Windows 2000, Windows XP Home Edition, Windows XP Professional, Windows Server 2003 family

IToolboxUser.ToolPicked Method

Selects the specified tool.

```
[Visual Basic]
Sub ToolPicked( _
   ByVal tool As ToolboxItem _
)
[C#]
void ToolPicked(
   ToolboxItem tool
);
[C++]
void ToolPicked(
   ToolboxItem* tool
);
[JScript]
function ToolPicked(
   tool : ToolboxItem
);
```

Parameters

tool

The **ToolboxItem** to select.

Remarks

ToolPicked is called when the user double-clicks on a toolbox item. The document designer should create a component for the specified tool. The Visual Studio .NET integrated development environment will only call **ToolPicked** on tools that are enabled in the toolbox.

Requirements

Platforms: Windows 98, Windows NT 4.0, Windows Millennium Edition, Windows 2000, Windows XP Home Edition, Windows XP Professional, Windows Server 2003 family

MetafileEditor Class

This type supports the .NET Framework infrastructure and is not intended to be used directly from your code.

```
[Visual Basic]
Public Class MetafileEditor
   Inherits ImageEditor
[C#]
public class MetafileEditor : ImageEditor
[C++]
public __gc class MetafileEditor : public ImageEditor
[JScript]
public class MetafileEditor extends ImageEditor
```

MetafileEditor Constructor

This member supports the .NET Framework infrastructure and is not intended to be used directly from your code.

```
[Visual Basic]
Public Sub New()
[C#]
public MetafileEditor();
[C++]
public: MetafileEditor();
[JScript]
public function MetafileEditor();
```

MetafileEditor.GetExtensions Method

This member supports the .NET Framework infrastructure and is not intended to be used directly from your code.

```
[Visual Basic]
Overrides Protected Function GetExtensions() As String()
[C#]
protected override string[] GetExtensions();
[C++]
protected: String* GetExtensions()  __gc[];
[JScript]
protected override function GetExtensions() : String[];
```

MetafileEditor.GetFileDialogDescription Method

This member supports the .NET Framework infrastructure and is not intended to be used directly from your code.

```
[Visual Basic]
Overrides Protected Function GetFileDialogDescription() As String
[C#]
protected override string GetFileDialogDescription();
[C++]
protected: String* GetFileDialogDescription();
[JScript]
protected override function GetFileDialogDescription() : String;
```

MetafileEditor.LoadFromStream Method

This member supports the .NET Framework infrastructure and is not intended to be used directly from your code.

```
[Visual Basic]
Overrides Protected Function LoadFromStream( _
   ByVal stream As Stream _
) As Image
[C#]
protected override Image LoadFromStream(
   Stream stream
);
[C++]
protected: Image* LoadFromStream(
   Stream* stream
);
[JScript]
protected override function LoadFromStream(
   stream : Stream
) : Image;
```

PaintValueEventArgs Class

Provides data for the **PaintValue** event.

System.Object
  System.EventArgs
    System.Drawing.Design.PaintValueEventArgs

[Visual Basic]
```
Public Class PaintValueEventArgs
   Inherits EventArgs
```
[C#]
```
public class PaintValueEventArgs : EventArgs
```
[C++]
```
public __gc class PaintValueEventArgs : public EventArgs
```
[JScript]
```
public class PaintValueEventArgs extends EventArgs
```

Thread Safety

Any public static (**Shared** in Visual Basic) members of this type are safe for multithreaded operations. Any instance members are not guaranteed to be thread safe.

Remarks

PaintValueEventArgs provides all the information needed for a **UITypeEditor** to paint within an area based on the value of the specified object, including the **Rectangle** in which the drawing should be done and the **Graphics** object with which the drawing should be done.

Example

[Visual Basic, C#, C++] The following example method returns a **PaintValueEventArgs** that provides the data needed to paint a representation of the value of an object within a given area:

[Visual Basic]
```
Public Function CreatePaintValueEventArgs(ByVal context As ↵
System.ComponentModel.ITypeDescriptorContext, ByVal value As ↵
 Object, ByVal graphics As Graphics, ByVal bounds As Rectangle) ↵
 As PaintValueEventArgs
    Dim e As New PaintValueEventArgs(context, value, graphics, bounds)
    ' The context of the paint value event         e.Context
    ' The object representing the value to paint   e.Value
    ' The graphics to use to paint                 e.Graphics
    ' The rectangle in which to paint              e.Bounds
    Return e
End Function
```

[C#]
```
public PaintValueEventArgs ↵
CreatePaintValueEventArgs ↵
 (System.ComponentModel.ITypeDescriptorContext context, object ↵
 value, Graphics graphics, Rectangle bounds)
{
    PaintValueEventArgs e = new PaintValueEventArgs(context, ↵
value, graphics, bounds);
    // The context of the paint value event         e.Context
    // The object representing the value to paint   e.Value
    // The graphics to use to paint                 e.Graphics
    // The rectangle in which to paint              e.Bounds
    return e;
}
```

[C++]
```
public:
   PaintValueEventArgs* CreatePaintValueEventArgs(
      System::ComponentModel::ITypeDescriptorContext* context,
      Object* value,
      Graphics* graphics,
      Rectangle bounds)
   {
      PaintValueEventArgs* e = new PaintValueEventArgs(context, ↵
value, graphics, bounds);
      // The context of the paint value event         e.Context
      // The Object representing the value to paint   e.Value
      // The graphics to use to paint                 e.Graphics
      // The rectangle in which to paint              e.Bounds
      return e;
   }
```

Requirements

Namespace: System.Drawing.Design

Platforms: Windows 98, Windows NT 4.0, Windows Millennium Edition, Windows 2000, Windows XP Home Edition, Windows XP Professional, Windows Server 2003 family

Assembly: System.Drawing (in System.Drawing.dll)

PaintValueEventArgs Constructor

Initializes a new instance of the **PaintValueEventArgs** class using the specified values.

[Visual Basic]
```
Public Sub New( _
   ByVal context As ITypeDescriptorContext, _
   ByVal value As Object, _
   ByVal graphics As Graphics, _
   ByVal bounds As Rectangle _
)
```
[C#]
```
public PaintValueEventArgs(
   ITypeDescriptorContext context,
   object value,
   Graphics graphics,
   Rectangle bounds
);
```
[C++]
```
public: PaintValueEventArgs(
   ITypeDescriptorContext* context,
   Object* value,
   Graphics* graphics,
   Rectangle bounds
);
```
[JScript]
```
public function PaintValueEventArgs(
   context : ITypeDescriptorContext,
   value : Object,
   graphics : Graphics,
   bounds : Rectangle
);
```

Parameters

context
: The context in which the value appears.

value
: The value to paint.

graphics
: The **Graphics** object with which drawing is to be done.

bounds
: The **Rectangle** in which drawing is to be done.

Requirements

Platforms: Windows 98, Windows NT 4.0, Windows Millennium Edition, Windows 2000, Windows XP Home Edition, Windows XP Professional, Windows Server 2003 family

PaintValueEventArgs.Bounds Property

Gets or sets the rectangle that indicates the area in which the painting should be done.

[Visual Basic]
```
Public ReadOnly Property Bounds As Rectangle
```
[C#]
```
public Rectangle Bounds {get;}
```
[C++]
```
public: __property Rectangle get_Bounds();
```
[JScript]
```
public function get Bounds() : Rectangle;
```

Property Value

A **Rectangle**.

Requirements

Platforms: Windows 98, Windows NT 4.0, Windows Millennium Edition, Windows 2000, Windows XP Home Edition, Windows XP Professional, Windows Server 2003 family

PaintValueEventArgs.Context Property

Gets or sets the **ITypeDescriptorContext** object to be used to gain additional information about the context this value appears in.

[Visual Basic]
```
Public ReadOnly Property Context As ITypeDescriptorContext
```
[C#]
```
public ITypeDescriptorContext Context {get;}
```
[C++]
```
public: __property ITypeDescriptorContext* get_Context();
```
[JScript]
```
public function get Context() : ITypeDescriptorContext;
```

Property Value

An **ITypeDescriptorContext** that indicates the context of the event.

Requirements

Platforms: Windows 98, Windows NT 4.0, Windows Millennium Edition, Windows 2000, Windows XP Home Edition, Windows XP Professional, Windows Server 2003 family

PaintValueEventArgs.Graphics Property

Gets or sets the **Graphics** object with which painting should be done.

[Visual Basic]
```
Public ReadOnly Property Graphics As Graphics
```
[C#]
```
public Graphics Graphics {get;}
```
[C++]
```
public: __property Graphics* get_Graphics();
```
[JScript]
```
public function get Graphics() : Graphics;
```

Property Value

A **Graphics** object to use for painting.

Requirements

Platforms: Windows 98, Windows NT 4.0, Windows Millennium Edition, Windows 2000, Windows XP Home Edition, Windows XP Professional, Windows Server 2003 family

PaintValueEventArgs.Value Property

Gets or sets the value to paint.

[Visual Basic]
```
Public ReadOnly Property Value As Object
```
[C#]
```
public object Value {get;}
```
[C++]
```
public: __property Object* get_Value();
```
[JScript]
```
public function get Value() : Object;
```

Property Value

An object indicating what to paint.

Requirements

Platforms: Windows 98, Windows NT 4.0, Windows Millennium Edition, Windows 2000, Windows XP Home Edition, Windows XP Professional, Windows Server 2003 family

PropertyValueUIHandler Delegate

Represents the method that adds a delegate to an implementation of **IPropertyValueUIService**.

[Visual Basic]
```
<Serializable>
Public Delegate Sub PropertyValueUIHandler( _
   ByVal context As ITypeDescriptorContext, _
   ByVal propDesc As PropertyDescriptor, _
   ByVal valueUIItemList As ArrayList _
)
```
[C#]
```
[Serializable]
public delegate void PropertyValueUIHandler(
   ITypeDescriptorContext context,
   PropertyDescriptor propDesc,
   ArrayList valueUIItemList
);
```
[C++]
```
[Serializable]
public __gc __delegate void PropertyValueUIHandler(
   ITypeDescriptorContext* context,
   PropertyDescriptor* propDesc,
   ArrayList* valueUIItemList
);
```

[JScript] In JScript, you can use the delegates in the .NET Framework, but you cannot define your own.

Parameters [Visual Basic, C#, C++]

The declaration of your callback method must have the same parameters as the **PropertyValueUIHandler** delegate declaration.

context
: An **ITypeDescriptorContext** that can be used to obtain context information.

propDesc
: A **PropertyDescriptor** that represents the property being queried.

valueUIItemList
: An **ArrayList** of **PropertyValueUIItem** objects containing the UI items associated with the property.

Remarks

When this delegate is invoked, it can add a **PropertyValueUIItem** containing UI items for the specified property to the **ArrayList** passed as the *valueUIItemList* parameter.

Example

[Visual Basic]
```
' PropertyValueUIHandler delegate that provides PropertyValueUIItem
' objects to any properties named horizontalMargin or verticalMargin.
Private Sub marginPropertyValueUIHandler(ByVal context As ↵
System.ComponentModel.ITypeDescriptorContext, ByVal propDesc As ↵
System.ComponentModel.PropertyDescriptor, ByVal itemList As ArrayList)
    ' A PropertyValueUIHandler added to the IPropertyValueUIService
    ' is queried once for each property of a component and passed
    ' a PropertyDescriptor that represents the characteristics of
    ' the property when the Properties window is set to a new
    ' component. A PropertyValueUIHandler can determine whether
    ' to add a PropertyValueUIItem for the object to its ValueUIItem
    ' list depending on the values of the PropertyDescriptor.
    If propDesc.DisplayName.Equals("horizontalMargin") Then
        Dim img As Image = DeserializeFromBase64Text(imageBlob1)
        itemList.Add(New PropertyValueUIItem(img, New ↵
PropertyValueUIItemInvokeHandler(AddressOf Me.marginInvoke), ↵
"Test ToolTip"))
    End If
    If propDesc.DisplayName.Equals("verticalMargin") Then
        Dim img As Image = DeserializeFromBase64Text(imageBlob1)
        img.RotateFlip(RotateFlipType.Rotate90FlipNone)
        itemList.Add(New PropertyValueUIItem(img, New ↵
PropertyValueUIItemInvokeHandler(AddressOf Me.marginInvoke), ↵
"Test ToolTip"))
    End If
End Sub
```
[C#]
```
// PropertyValueUIHandler delegate that provides PropertyValueUIItem
// objects to any properties named horizontalMargin or verticalMargin.
private void
marginPropertyValueUIHandler(System.ComponentModel.ITypeDescriptorContex
t context, System.ComponentModel.PropertyDescriptor propDesc, ↵
ArrayList itemList)
{
    // A PropertyValueUIHandler added to the IPropertyValueUIService
    // is queried once for each property of a component and passed
    // a PropertyDescriptor that represents the characteristics of
    // the property when the Properties window is set to a new
    // component. A PropertyValueUIHandler can determine whether
    // to add a PropertyValueUIItem for the object to its ValueUIItem
    // list depending on the values of the PropertyDescriptor.
    if( propDesc.DisplayName.Equals( "horizontalMargin" ) )
    {
        Image img = DeserializeFromBase64Text(imageBlob1);
        itemList.Add( new PropertyValueUIItem( img, new ↵
PropertyValueUIItemInvokeHandler(this.marginInvoke), "Test ToolTip") );
    }
    if( propDesc.DisplayName.Equals( "verticalMargin" ) )
    {
        Image img = DeserializeFromBase64Text(imageBlob1);
        img.RotateFlip(RotateFlipType.Rotate90FlipNone);
        itemList.Add( new PropertyValueUIItem( img, new
PropertyValueUIItemInvokeHandler(this.marginInvoke), "Test ToolTip") );
    }
}
```
[C++]
```
// PropertyValueUIHandler delegate that provides PropertyValueUIItem
// objects to any properties named horizontalMargin or verticalMargin.
private:
void
marginPropertyValueUIHandler(System::ComponentModel::ITypeDescriptorCont
ext* context, System::ComponentModel::PropertyDescriptor* ↵
 propDesc, ArrayList* itemList) {
   // A PropertyValueUIHandler added to the IPropertyValueUIService*
   // is queried once for each property of a component and passed
   // a PropertyDescriptor that represents the characteristics of
   // the property when the Properties window is set to a new
   // component. A PropertyValueUIHandler can determine whether
   // to add a PropertyValueUIItem for the Object* to its ValueUIItem
   // list depending on the values of the PropertyDescriptor.
   if (propDesc->DisplayName->Equals(S"horizontalMargin")) {
      Image* img = DeserializeFromBase64Text(imageBlob1);
      itemList->Add(new PropertyValueUIItem(img, new ↵
PropertyValueUIItemInvokeHandler(this, marginInvoke), S"Test ↵
ToolTip"));
   }
   if (propDesc->DisplayName->Equals(S"verticalMargin")) {
      Image* img = DeserializeFromBase64Text(imageBlob1);
      img->RotateFlip(RotateFlipType::Rotate90FlipNone);
      itemList->Add(new PropertyValueUIItem(img, new ↵
PropertyValueUIItemInvokeHandler(this, marginInvoke), ↵
S"Test ToolTip"));
   }
}
```

Requirements

Namespace: **System.Drawing.Design**

Platforms: Windows 98, Windows NT 4.0, Windows Millennium Edition, Windows 2000, Windows XP Home Edition, Windows XP Professional, Windows Server 2003 family

Assembly: System.Drawing (in System.Drawing.dll)

PropertyValueUIItem Class

Provides information about a property displayed on the Properties window, including the associated event handler, pop-up information string, and the icon to display for the property.

System.Object
  System.Drawing.Design.PropertyValueUIItem

```
[Visual Basic]
Public Class PropertyValueUIItem
[C#]
public class PropertyValueUIItem
[C++]
public __gc class PropertyValueUIItem
[JScript]
public class PropertyValueUIItem
```

Thread Safety

Any public static (**Shared** in Visual Basic) members of this type are safe for multithreaded operations. Any instance members are not guaranteed to be thread safe.

Requirements

Namespace: System.Drawing.Design

Platforms: Windows 98, Windows NT 4.0, Windows Millennium Edition, Windows 2000, Windows XP Home Edition, Windows XP Professional, Windows Server 2003 family

Assembly: System.Drawing (in System.Drawing.dll)

PropertyValueUIItem Constructor

Initializes a new instance of the **PropertyValueUIItem** class.

```
[Visual Basic]
Public Sub New( _
   ByVal uiItemImage As Image, _
   ByVal handler As PropertyValueUIItemInvokeHandler, _
   ByVal tooltip As String _
)
[C#]
public PropertyValueUIItem(
   Image uiItemImage,
   PropertyValueUIItemInvokeHandler handler,
   string tooltip
);
[C++]
public: PropertyValueUIItem(
   Image* uiItemImage,
   PropertyValueUIItemInvokeHandler* handler,
   String* tooltip
);
[JScript]
public function PropertyValueUIItem(
   uiItemImage : Image,
   handler : PropertyValueUIItemInvokeHandler,
   tooltip : String
);
```

Parameters

uiItemImage
  The icon to display. The image must must be 8 x 8 pixels.

handler
  The handler to raise when the image is double-clicked.

tooltip
  The **ToolTip** to display for the property that this **PropertyValueUIItem** is associated with.

Requirements

Platforms: Windows 98, Windows NT 4.0, Windows Millennium Edition, Windows 2000, Windows XP Home Edition, Windows XP Professional, Windows Server 2003 family

PropertyValueUIItem.Image Property

Gets or sets the 8 x 8 pixel image that will be drawn on the Properties window.

```
[Visual Basic]
Public Overridable ReadOnly Property Image As Image
[C#]
public virtual Image Image {get;}
[C++]
public: __property virtual Image* get_Image();
[JScript]
public function get Image() : Image;
```

Property Value

The image to use for the property icon.

Remarks

This image must be 8 x 8 pixels. It is advisable to have the image support transparency.

Requirements

Platforms: Windows 98, Windows NT 4.0, Windows Millennium Edition, Windows 2000, Windows XP Home Edition, Windows XP Professional, Windows Server 2003 family

PropertyValueUIItem.InvokeHandler Property

Gets or sets the handler that is raised when a user double-clicks this item.

```
[Visual Basic]
Public Overridable ReadOnly Property InvokeHandler As _
   PropertyValueUIItemInvokeHandler
[C#]
public virtual PropertyValueUIItemInvokeHandler InvokeHandler
   {get;}
[C++]
public: __property virtual PropertyValueUIItemInvokeHandler*
   get_InvokeHandler();
[JScript]
public function get InvokeHandler() :
   PropertyValueUIItemInvokeHandler;
```

Property Value

A **PropertyValueUIItemInvokeHandler** indicating the event handler for this UI Item.

Requirements

Platforms: Windows 98, Windows NT 4.0, Windows Millennium Edition, Windows 2000, Windows XP Home Edition, Windows XP Professional, Windows Server 2003 family

PropertyValueUIItem.ToolTip Property

Gets or sets the information string to display for this item.

[Visual Basic]
```
Public Overridable ReadOnly Property ToolTip As String
```
[C#]
```
public virtual string ToolTip {get;}
```
[C++]
```
public: __property virtual String* get_ToolTip();
```
[JScript]
```
public function get ToolTip() : String;
```

Property Value

A string containing the information string to display for this item.

Requirements

Platforms: Windows 98, Windows NT 4.0, Windows Millennium Edition, Windows 2000, Windows XP Home Edition, Windows XP Professional, Windows Server 2003 family

PropertyValueUIItem.Reset Method

Resets the UI item.

[Visual Basic]
```
Public Overridable Sub Reset()
```
[C#]
```
public virtual void Reset();
```
[C++]
```
public: virtual void Reset();
```
[JScript]
```
public function Reset();
```

Remarks

Notes to Inheritors: Derived classes can override this member to implement the redrawing of the UI item.

Requirements

Platforms: Windows 98, Windows NT 4.0, Windows Millennium Edition, Windows 2000, Windows XP Home Edition, Windows XP Professional, Windows Server 2003 family

PropertyValueUIItemInvoke-Handler Delegate

Represents the method that will handle the **InvokeHandler** event of a **PropertyValueUIItem**.

[Visual Basic]

```
<Serializable>
Public Delegate Sub PropertyValueUIItemInvokeHandler( _
   ByVal context As ITypeDescriptorContext, _
   ByVal descriptor As PropertyDescriptor, _
   ByVal invokedItem As PropertyValueUIItem _
)
```

[C#]

```
[Serializable]
public delegate void PropertyValueUIItemInvokeHandler(
   ITypeDescriptorContext context,
   PropertyDescriptor descriptor,
   PropertyValueUIItem invokedItem
);
```

[C++]

```
[Serializable]
public __gc __delegate void PropertyValueUIItemInvokeHandler(
   ITypeDescriptorContext* context,
   PropertyDescriptor* descriptor,
   PropertyValueUIItem* invokedItem
);
```

[JScript] In JScript, you can use the delegates in the .NET Framework, but you cannot define your own.

Parameters [Visual Basic, C#, C++]

The declaration of your callback method must have the same parameters as the **PropertyValueUIItemInvokeHandler** delegate declaration.

context
: The **ITypeDescriptorContext** for the property associated with the icon that was double-clicked.

descriptor
: The property associated with the icon that was double-clicked.

invokedItem
: The **PropertyValueUIItem** associated with the icon that was double-clicked.

Remarks

Double-clicking an icon in the Properties window will raise the **InvokeHandler** event of the **PropertyValueUIItem** that the icon is associated with. The **InvokeHandler** event typically launches a user interface (UI) to edit the property's value. Add a **PropertyValueUIItemInvokeHandler** to the **InvokeHandler** property of a **PropertyValueUIItem** to assign an event handler to perform the appropriate behavior when the icon displayed next to the property name is double-clicked.

When you create a **PropertyValueUIItemInvokeHandler** delegate, you identify the method that will handle the event. To associate the event with your event handler, add an instance of the delegate to the event. The event handler is called whenever the event occurs, unless you remove the delegate.

Requirements

Namespace: System.Drawing.Design

Platforms: Windows 98, Windows NT 4.0, Windows Millennium Edition, Windows 2000, Windows XP Home Edition, Windows XP Professional, Windows Server 2003 family

Assembly: System.Drawing (in System.Drawing.dll)

ToolboxComponentsCreated-EventArgs Class

Provides data for the **ComponentsCreated** event that occurs when components are added to the toolbox.

System.Object
  System.EventArgs
    System.Drawing.Design.ToolboxComponentsCreated-EventArgs

[Visual Basic]
```
Public Class ToolboxComponentsCreatedEventArgs
   Inherits EventArgs
```
[C#]
```
public class ToolboxComponentsCreatedEventArgs : EventArgs
```
[C++]
```
public __gc class ToolboxComponentsCreatedEventArgs : public
   EventArgs
```
[JScript]
```
public class ToolboxComponentsCreatedEventArgs extends EventArgs
```

Thread Safety

Any public static (**Shared** in Visual Basic) members of this type are safe for multithreaded operations. Any instance members are not guaranteed to be thread safe.

Remarks

The **ComponentsCreated** event is raised when components are added to the toolbox. **ToolboxComponentsCreatedEventArgs** provides data indicating which component or components are being added.

Example

[Visual Basic, C#, C++] The following example method returns a **System.Drawing.Design.ToolboxComponentCreatedEventAgs** that indicates the components that have been created:

[Visual Basic]
```
Public Function CreateToolboxComponentsCreatedEventArgs(ByVal          ↵
components() As System.ComponentModel.IComponent) As                   ↵
ToolboxComponentsCreatedEventArgs
    Dim e As New ToolboxComponentsCreatedEventArgs(components)
    ' The components that were just created       e.Components
    Return e
End Function
```

[C#]
```
public ToolboxComponentsCreatedEventArgs                               ↵
CreateToolboxComponentsCreatedEventArgs                                ↵
 (System.ComponentModel.IComponent[] components)
{
    ToolboxComponentsCreatedEventArgs e = new                          ↵
ToolboxComponentsCreatedEventArgs(components);
    // The components that were just created       e.Components
    return e;
}
```

[C++]
```
public:
   ToolboxComponentsCreatedEventArgs*                                  ↵
CreateToolboxComponentsCreatedEventArgs                                ↵
 (System::ComponentModel::IComponent* components[]) {
      ToolboxComponentsCreatedEventArgs* e = new                       ↵
ToolboxComponentsCreatedEventArgs(components);
      // The components that were just created     e.Components
      return e;
   }
```

Requirements

Namespace: System.Drawing.Design

Platforms: Windows 98, Windows NT 4.0, Windows Millennium Edition, Windows 2000, Windows XP Home Edition, Windows XP Professional, Windows Server 2003 family

Assembly: System.Drawing (in System.Drawing.dll)

ToolboxComponentsCreatedEventArgs Constructor

Initializes a new instance of the **ToolboxComponentsCreated-EventArgs** class.

[Visual Basic]
```
Public Sub New( _
   ByVal components() As IComponent _
)
```
[C#]
```
public ToolboxComponentsCreatedEventArgs(
   IComponent[] components
);
```
[C++]
```
public: ToolboxComponentsCreatedEventArgs(
   IComponent* components[]
);
```
[JScript]
```
public function ToolboxComponentsCreatedEventArgs(
   components : IComponent[]
);
```

Parameters

components
  The components to include in the toolbox.

Requirements

Platforms: Windows 98, Windows NT 4.0, Windows Millennium Edition, Windows 2000, Windows XP Home Edition, Windows XP Professional, Windows Server 2003 family

ToolboxComponentsCreatedEventArgs.Components Property

Gets or sets an array containing the components to add to the toolbox.

[Visual Basic]
```
Public ReadOnly Property Components As IComponent ()
```
[C#]
```
public IComponent[] Components {get;}
```
[C++]
```
public: __property IComponent* get_Components();
```
[JScript]
```
public function get Components() : IComponent[];
```

Property Value

An array of type **IComponent** indicating the components to add to the toolbox.

Requirements

Platforms: Windows 98, Windows NT 4.0, Windows Millennium Edition, Windows 2000, Windows XP Home Edition, Windows XP Professional, Windows Server 2003 family

ToolboxComponentsCreated-EventHandler Delegate

Represents the method that handles the **ComponentsCreated** event.

[Visual Basic]

```
<Serializable>
Public Delegate Sub ToolboxComponentsCreatedEventHandler( _
   ByVal sender As Object, _
   ByVal e As ToolboxComponentsCreatedEventArgs _
)
```

[C#]

```
[Serializable]
public delegate void ToolboxComponentsCreatedEventHandler(
   object sender,
   ToolboxComponentsCreatedEventArgs e
);
```

[C++]

```
[Serializable]
public __gc __delegate void ToolboxComponentsCreatedEventHandler(
   Object* sender,
   ToolboxComponentsCreatedEventArgs* e
);
```

[JScript] In JScript, you can use the delegates in the .NET Framework, but you cannot define your own.

Parameters [Visual Basic, C#, C++]

The declaration of your event handler must have the same parameters as the **ToolboxComponentsCreatedEventHandler** delegate declaration.

sender

The source of the event.

e

A **ToolboxComponentsCreatedEventArgs** that provides data for the event.

Remarks

When you create a **ToolboxComponentsCreatedEventHandler** delegate, you identify the method that will handle the event. To associate the event with your event handler, add an instance of the delegate to the event. The event handler is called whenever the event occurs, unless you remove the delegate. For more information about event-handler delegates, see **Events and Delegates**.

Example

[Visual Basic]

```
Public Sub LinkToolboxComponentsCreatedEvent(ByVal item As ToolboxItem)
    AddHandler item.ComponentsCreated, AddressOf Me.OnComponentsCreated
End Sub

Private Sub OnComponentsCreated(ByVal sender As Object, ByVal e ↵
 As ToolboxComponentsCreatedEventArgs)
    ' Lists created components on the Console.
    Dim i As Integer
    For i = 0 To e.Components.Length - 1
        Console.WriteLine(("Component #" + i.ToString() + ": " + ↵
e.Components(i).Site.Name.ToString()))
    Next i
End Sub
```

[C#]

```
public void LinkToolboxComponentsCreatedEvent(ToolboxItem item)
{
    item.ComponentsCreated += new ↵
ToolboxComponentsCreatedEventHandler(this.OnComponentsCreated);
}

private void OnComponentsCreated(object sender, ↵
ToolboxComponentsCreatedEventArgs e)
{
    // Lists created components on the Console.
    for( int i=0; i< e.Components.Length; i++ )
        Console.WriteLine("Component #"+i.ToString()+": ↵
"+e.Components[i].Site.Name.ToString());
}
```

[C++]

```
public:
   void LinkToolboxComponentsCreatedEvent(ToolboxItem* item) {
      item->ComponentsCreated += new ↵
ToolboxComponentsCreatedEventHandler(this, OnComponentsCreated);
   }

private:
   void OnComponentsCreated(Object* sender, ↵
ToolboxComponentsCreatedEventArgs* e) {
      // Lists created components on the Console.
      for (int i=0; i< e->Components->Length; i++)
         Console::WriteLine(S"Component #{0}: {1}", __box(i), ↵
 e->Components[i]->Site->Name);
   }
```

Requirements

Namespace: System.Drawing.Design

Platforms: Windows 98, Windows NT 4.0, Windows Millennium Edition, Windows 2000, Windows XP Home Edition, Windows XP Professional, Windows Server 2003 family

Assembly: System.Drawing (in System.Drawing.dll)

ToolboxComponentsCreating-EventArgs Class

Provides data for the **ComponentsCreating** event that occurs when components are added to the toolbox.

System.Object
  System.EventArgs
    System.Drawing.Design.ToolboxComponentsCreating-EventArgs

[Visual Basic]
```
Public Class ToolboxComponentsCreatingEventArgs
   Inherits EventArgs
```
[C#]
```
public class ToolboxComponentsCreatingEventArgs : EventArgs
```
[C++]
```
public __gc class ToolboxComponentsCreatingEventArgs : public
   EventArgs
```
[JScript]
```
public class ToolboxComponentsCreatingEventArgs extends EventArgs
```

Thread Safety

Any public static (**Shared** in Visual Basic) members of this type are safe for multithreaded operations. Any instance members are not guaranteed to be thread safe.

Remarks

The **ComponentsCreating** event is raised when components are about to be added to the toolbox. **ToolboxComponentsCreatingEventArgs** provides data indicating the designer that has requested that the components be added.

Example

[Visual Basic, C#, C++] The following example method returns a **System.Drawing.Design.ToolboxComponentCreatingEventArgs** that indicates the designer host that is about to receive a new component or set of components:

[Visual Basic]
```
Public Function CreateToolboxComponentsCreatingEventArgs(ByVal      ↵
host As System.ComponentModel.Design.IDesignerHost) As             ↵
ToolboxComponentsCreatingEventArgs
    Dim e As New ToolboxComponentsCreatingEventArgs(host)
    ' The designer host of the document receiving the components    ↵
  e.DesignerHost
    Return e
End Function
```

[C#]
```
public ToolboxComponentsCreatingEventArgs                           ↵
CreateToolboxComponentsCreatingEventArgs(System.ComponentModel.Design.ID
esignerHost host)
{
    ToolboxComponentsCreatingEventArgs e = new                      ↵
ToolboxComponentsCreatingEventArgs(host);
    // The designer host of the document receiving the components   ↵
  e.DesignerHost
    return e;
}
```

[C++]
```
public:
   ToolboxComponentsCreatingEventArgs*                              ↵
CreateToolboxComponentsCreatingEventArgs                            ↵
 (System::ComponentModel::Design::IDesignerHost* host) {
      ToolboxComponentsCreatingEventArgs* e = new                   ↵
ToolboxComponentsCreatingEventArgs(host);
      // The designer host of the document receiving the            ↵
components        e.DesignerHost
      return e;
   }
```

Requirements

Namespace: System.Drawing.Design

Platforms: Windows 98, Windows NT 4.0, Windows Millennium Edition, Windows 2000, Windows XP Home Edition, Windows XP Professional, Windows Server 2003 family

Assembly: System.Drawing (in System.Drawing.dll)

ToolboxComponentsCreatingEventArgs Constructor

Initializes a new instance of the **ToolboxComponentsCreatingEventArgs** class.

[Visual Basic]
```
Public Sub New( _
   ByVal host As IDesignerHost _
)
```
[C#]
```
public ToolboxComponentsCreatingEventArgs(
   IDesignerHost host
);
```
[C++]
```
public: ToolboxComponentsCreatingEventArgs(
   IDesignerHost* host
);
```
[JScript]
```
public function ToolboxComponentsCreatingEventArgs(
   host : IDesignerHost
);
```

Parameters

host
  The designer host that is making the request.

Requirements

Platforms: Windows 98, Windows NT 4.0, Windows Millennium Edition, Windows 2000, Windows XP Home Edition, Windows XP Professional, Windows Server 2003 family

ToolboxComponentsCreatingEventArgs.DesignerHost Property

Gets or sets an instance of the **IDesignerHost** that made the request to create toolbox components.

[Visual Basic]
```
Public ReadOnly Property DesignerHost As IDesignerHost
```
[C#]
```
public IDesignerHost DesignerHost {get;}
```
[C++]
```
public: __property IDesignerHost* get_DesignerHost();
```
[JScript]
```
public function get DesignerHost() : IDesignerHost;
```

Property Value

The **IDesignerHost** that made the request to create toolbox components, or a null reference (**Nothing** in Visual Basic) if no designer host was provided to the toolbox item.

Remarks

This property can be a null reference (**Nothing** in Visual Basic) if no designer host was provided to the toolbox item.

Requirements

Platforms: Windows 98, Windows NT 4.0, Windows Millennium Edition, Windows 2000, Windows XP Home Edition, Windows XP Professional, Windows Server 2003 family

ToolboxComponentsCreatingEventHandler Delegate

Represents the method that handles the **ComponentsCreating** event.

[Visual Basic]
```
<Serializable>
Public Delegate Sub ToolboxComponentsCreatingEventHandler( _
   ByVal sender As Object, _
   ByVal e As ToolboxComponentsCreatingEventArgs _
)
```
[C#]
```
[Serializable]
public delegate void ToolboxComponentsCreatingEventHandler(
   object sender,
   ToolboxComponentsCreatingEventArgs e
);
```
[C++]
```
[Serializable]
public __gc __delegate void ToolboxComponentsCreatingEventHandler(
   Object* sender,
   ToolboxComponentsCreatingEventArgs* e
);
```
[JScript] In JScript, you can use the delegates in the .NET Framework, but you cannot define your own.

Parameters [Visual Basic, C#, C++]

The declaration of your event handler must have the same parameters as the **ToolboxComponentsCreatingEventHandler** delegate declaration.

sender
   The source of the event.

e
   A **ToolboxComponentsCreatingEventArgs** that provides data for the event.

Remarks

When you create a **ToolboxComponentsCreatingEventHandler** delegate, you identify the method that will handle the event. To associate the event with your event handler, add an instance of the delegate to the event. The event handler is called whenever the event occurs, unless you remove the delegate.

Example

[Visual Basic]
```
Public Sub LinkToolboxComponentsCreatingEvent(ByVal item As ↵
ToolboxItem)
    AddHandler item.ComponentsCreating, AddressOf ↵
Me.OnComponentsCreating
End Sub

Private Sub OnComponentsCreating(ByVal sender As Object, ↵
ByVal e As ToolboxComponentsCreatingEventArgs)
    ' Displays ComponentsCreating event information on the Console.
    Console.WriteLine(("Name of the class of the root component ↵
of the designer host receiving new components: " + ↵
e.DesignerHost.RootComponentClassName))
End Sub
```

[C#]
```
public void LinkToolboxComponentsCreatingEvent(ToolboxItem item)
{
    item.ComponentsCreating += new ↵
ToolboxComponentsCreatingEventHandler(this.OnComponentsCreating);
}

private void OnComponentsCreating(object sender, ↵
ToolboxComponentsCreatingEventArgs e)
{
    // Displays ComponentsCreating event information on the Console.
    Console.WriteLine("Name of the class of the root component of " +
    "the designer host receiving new components: " +
    e.DesignerHost.RootComponentClassName);
}
```

[C++]
```
public:
   void LinkToolboxComponentsCreatingEvent(ToolboxItem* item) {
      item->ComponentsCreating += new ↵
ToolboxComponentsCreatingEventHandler(this, OnComponentsCreating);
   }

private:
   void OnComponentsCreating(Object* sender, ↵
ToolboxComponentsCreatingEventArgs* e) {
      // Displays ComponentsCreating event information on the Console.
      Console::WriteLine(S"Name of the class of the ↵
root component of the designer host receiving new components: ↵
{0}", e->DesignerHost->RootComponentClassName);
   }
```

Requirements

Namespace: System.Drawing.Design

Platforms: Windows 98, Windows NT 4.0, Windows Millennium Edition, Windows 2000, Windows XP Home Edition, Windows XP Professional, Windows Server 2003 family

Assembly: System.Drawing (in System.Drawing.dll)

ToolboxItem Class

Provides a base implementation of a toolbox item.

System.Object
System.Drawing.Design.ToolboxItem
System.Web.UI.Design.WebControlToolboxItem

[Visual Basic]
```
<Serializable>
Public Class ToolboxItem
   Implements ISerializable
```
[C#]
```
[Serializable]
public class ToolboxItem : ISerializable
```
[C++]
```
[Serializable]
public __gc class ToolboxItem : public ISerializable
```
[JScript]
```
public
   Serializable
class ToolboxItem implements ISerializable
```

Thread Safety

Any public static (**Shared** in Visual Basic) members of this type are safe for multithreaded operations. Any instance members are not guaranteed to be thread safe.

Remarks

ToolboxItem is a base class for toolbox items that can be displayed in the toolbox of a design-time environment. A toolbox item typically represents a component to create when invoked on a design mode document. The **ToolboxItem** class provides the methods and properties needed to provide the toolbox with the display properties for the toolbox item, to create a component or components when used, and to serialize and deserialize itself for persistence within the toolbox database.

An instance of the **ToolboxItem** class can be configured with a name, bitmap and type to create, without creating a class that derives from **ToolboxItem**. The **ToolboxItem** class also provides a base class for custom toolbox item implementations. A custom **ToolboxItem** can create multiple components. To implement a custom toolbox item, you must derive from **ToolboxItem** and override the **CreateComponentsCore**, **Serialize**, and **Deserialize** methods.

The following properties and methods must be configured for a **ToolboxItem** to function correctly:

- The **DisplayName** property specifies the label for the toolbox item when displayed in a toolbox.
- The **TypeName** property specifies the fully qualified name of the type of the component that the item creates. If a derived class creates multiple components, the **TypeName** property may or may not be used, depending on whether a **CreateComponents-Core** method override depends on the value of this property.
- The **AssemblyName** property specifies the assembly that contains the type of a component that the item creates.
- The **Bitmap** property optionally specifies a bitmap image to display next to the display name for the toolbox item in the toolbox.
- The **Filter** property optionally contains any **ToolboxItem-FilterAttribute** objects that determine whether the toolbox item can be used on a particular component.
- The **CreateComponentsCore** method returns the component instance or instances to insert where this tool is used.
- The **Serialize** method saves the toolbox item to a specified **SerializationInfo**.
- The **Deserialize** method configures the toolbox item from the state information contained in the specified **SerializationInfo**.
- The **Initialize** method configures the toolbox item to create the specified type of component, if the **CreateComponentsCore** method has not been overridden to behave differently.
- The **Locked** property indicates whether the properties of the toolbox item can be changed. A toolbox item is typically locked after it is added to a toolbox.
- The **Lock** method locks a toolbox item.
- The **CheckUnlocked** method throws an exception if the **Locked** property is **true**.

Example

[Visual Basic, C#, C++] The following example provides a component that uses the **IToolboxService** to add a "Text" data format handler, or **ToolboxItemCreatorCallback**, to the toolbox. The data creator callback delegate passes any text data pasted to the toolbox and dragged onto a form to a custom **ToolboxItem** that creates a **System.Windows.Forms.TextBox** containing the text.

[Visual Basic]
```
Imports System
Imports System.ComponentModel
Imports System.ComponentModel.Design
Imports System.Drawing
Imports System.Drawing.Design
Imports System.Windows.Forms

' Component that adds a "Text" data format ToolboxItemCreatorCallback
' to the Toolbox that creates a custom ToolboxItem that
' creates a TextBox containing the text data.
Public Class TextDataTextBoxComponent
    Inherits System.ComponentModel.Component

   Private creatorAdded As Boolean = False
   Private ts As IToolboxService

   Public Sub New()
    End Sub

    ' ISite override to register TextBox creator
    Public Overrides Property Site() As System.ComponentModel.ISite
        Get
            Return MyBase.Site
        End Get
        Set(ByVal Value As System.ComponentModel.ISite)
            If Not (Value Is Nothing) Then
                MyBase.Site = Value
                If Not creatorAdded Then
                    AddTextTextBoxCreator()
                End If
            Else
                If creatorAdded Then
                    RemoveTextTextBoxCreator()
                End If
                MyBase.Site = Value
            End If
        End Set
    End Property

    ' Adds a "Text" data format creator to the toolbox that creates
    ' a textbox from a text fragment pasted to the toolbox.
    Private Sub AddTextTextBoxCreator()
        ts = CType(GetService(GetType(IToolboxService)),
IToolboxService)
        If Not (ts Is Nothing) Then
            Dim textCreator As New
ToolboxItemCreatorCallback(AddressOf Me.CreateTextBoxForText)
            Try
                ts.AddCreator(textCreator, "Text",
```

```
CType(GetService(GetType(IDesignerHost)), IDesignerHost))
                creatorAdded = True
            Catch ex As Exception
                MessageBox.Show(ex.ToString(), "Exception Information")
            End Try
        End If
    End Sub

    ' Removes any "Text" data format creator from the toolbox.
    Private Sub RemoveTextTextBoxCreator()
        If Not (ts Is Nothing) Then
            ts.RemoveCreator("Text",                                  ↵
CType(GetService(GetType(IDesignerHost)), IDesignerHost))
            creatorAdded = False
        End If
    End Sub

    ' ToolboxItemCreatorCallback delegate format method to create
    ' the toolbox item.
    Private Function CreateTextBoxForText(ByVal serializedObject      ↵
 As Object, ByVal format As String) As ToolboxItem
        Dim formats As String() = CType(serializedObject,             ↵
System.Windows.Forms.DataObject).GetFormats()
        If CType(serializedObject,                                    ↵
System.Windows.Forms.DataObject).GetDataPresent("System.String",      ↵
 True) Then
            Return New TextToolboxItem(CStr(CType                     ↵
 (serializedObject,                                                   ↵
System.Windows.Forms.DataObject).GetData("System.String", True)))
        End If
        Return Nothing
    End Function

    Protected Overloads Overrides Sub Dispose(ByVal disposing As      ↵
Boolean)
        If creatorAdded Then
            RemoveTextTextBoxCreator()
        End If
    End Sub

End Class

' Custom toolbox item creates a TextBox and sets its Text property
' to the constructor-specified text.
Public Class TextToolboxItem
    Inherits System.Drawing.Design.ToolboxItem

    Private [text] As String

    Delegate Sub SetTextMethodHandler(ByVal c As Control, ByVal       ↵
 [text] As String)

    Public Sub New(ByVal [text] As String)
        Me.text = [text]
    End Sub

    ' ToolboxItem.CreateComponentsCore override to create the TextBox
    ' and link a method to set its Text property.
    <System.Security.Permissions.PermissionSetAttribute               ↵
 (System.Security.Permissions.SecurityAction.Demand,                  ↵
Name:="FullTrust")> _
    Protected Overrides Function CreateComponentsCore(ByVal host      ↵
 As System.ComponentModel.Design.IDesignerHost) As                    ↵
System.ComponentModel.IComponent()
        Dim textbox As System.Windows.Forms.TextBox =                 ↵
CType(host.CreateComponent(GetType(TextBox)), TextBox)

        ' Because the designer resets the text of the textbox, use
        ' a SetTextMethodHandler to set the text to the value of
        ' the text data.
        Dim c As Control = host.RootComponent

        c.BeginInvoke(New SetTextMethodHandler(AddressOf              ↵
OnSetText), New Object() {textbox, [text]})

        Return New System.ComponentModel.IComponent() {textbox}
    End Function

    ' Method to set the text property of a TextBox after              ↵
 it is initialized.
    Private Sub OnSetText(ByVal c As Control, ByVal [text] As String)
        c.Text = [text]
    End Sub

End Class
```

[C#]

```
using System;
using System.ComponentModel;
using System.ComponentModel.Design;
using System.Drawing;
using System.Drawing.Design;
using System.Windows.Forms;

namespace TextDataTextBoxComponent
{
    // Component that adds a "Text" data format                       ↵
ToolboxItemCreatorCallback
    // to the Toolbox that creates a custom ToolboxItem that
    // creates a TextBox containing the text data.
    public class TextDataTextBoxComponent :                           ↵
System.ComponentModel.Component
    {
        private bool creatorAdded = false;
        private IToolboxService ts;

        public TextDataTextBoxComponent()
        {
        }

        // ISite override to register TextBox creator
        public override System.ComponentModel.ISite Site
        {
            get
            {
                return base.Site;
            }
            set
            {
                if( value != null )
                {
                    base.Site = value;
                    if( !creatorAdded )
                        AddTextTextBoxCreator();
                }
                else
                {
                    if( creatorAdded )
                        RemoveTextTextBoxCreator();
                    base.Site = value;
                }
            }
        }

        // Adds a "Text" data format creator to the toolbox           ↵
that creates
        // a textbox from a text fragment pasted to the toolbox.
        private void AddTextTextBoxCreator()
        {
            ts = (IToolboxService)GetService(typeof(IToolboxService));
            if (ts != null)
            {
                ToolboxItemCreatorCallback textCreator = new          ↵
ToolboxItemCreatorCallback(this.CreateTextBoxForText);
                try
                {
                    ts.AddCreator(textCreator, "Text",                ↵
(IDesignerHost)GetService(typeof(IDesignerHost)));
                    creatorAdded = true;
                }
                catch(Exception ex)
                {
                    MessageBox.Show(ex.ToString(),                    ↵
"Exception Information");
                }
```

```
            }
        }

        // Removes any "Text" data format creator from the toolbox.
        private void RemoveTextTextBoxCreator()
        {
            if (ts != null)
            {
                ts.RemoveCreator("Text",                                   ↵
(IDesignerHost)GetService(typeof(IDesignerHost)));
                creatorAdded = false;
            }
        }

        // ToolboxItemCreatorCallback delegate format method to create
        // the toolbox item.
        private ToolboxItem CreateTextBoxForText(object                    ↵
serializedObject, string format)
        {
            string[] formats =                                             ↵
((System.Windows.Forms.DataObject)serializedObject).GetFormats();
            if( ((System.Windows.Forms.DataObject)                         ↵
serializedObject).GetDataPresent("System.String", true) )
                return new TextToolboxItem(                                ↵
(string)((System.Windows.Forms.DataObject)                                 ↵
serializedObject).GetData("System.String", true) );
            return null;
        }

        protected override void Dispose(bool disposing)
        {
            if( creatorAdded )
                RemoveTextTextBoxCreator();
        }
    }

    // Custom toolbox item creates a TextBox and sets its Text property
    // to the constructor-specified text.
    public class TextToolboxItem : System.Drawing.Design.ToolboxItem
    {
        private string text;
        private delegate void SetTextMethodHandler(Control c,              ↵
string text);

        public TextToolboxItem(string text) : base()
        {
            this.text = text;
        }

        // ToolboxItem.CreateComponentsCore override to                    ↵
create the TextBox
        // and link a method to set its Text property.
        [System.Security.Permissions.PermissionSet                          ↵
(System.Security.Permissions.SecurityAction.Demand, Name="FullTrust")]
        protected override System.ComponentModel.IComponent[]              ↵
CreateComponentsCore(System.ComponentModel.Design.IDesignerHost host)
        {
            System.Windows.Forms.TextBox textbox =                         ↵
(TextBox)host.CreateComponent(typeof(TextBox));

            // Because the designer resets the text of the textbox, use
            // a SetTextMethodHandler to set the text to the value of
            // the text data.
            Control c = host.RootComponent as Control;
            c.BeginInvoke(new SetTextMethodHandler(OnSetText),             ↵
new object[] {textbox, text});

            return new System.ComponentModel.IComponent[] { textbox };
        }

        // Method to set the text property of a TextBox after             ↵
it is initialized.
        private void OnSetText(Control c, string text)
        {
            c.Text = text;
        }
    }
}
```

[C++]

```
#using <mscorlib.dll>
#using <System.Windows.Forms.dll>
#using <System.Drawing.dll>
#using <System.dll>

using namespace System;
using namespace System::ComponentModel;
using namespace System::ComponentModel::Design;
using namespace System::Drawing;
using namespace System::Drawing::Design;
using namespace System::Windows::Forms;

namespace TextDataTextBoxComponent {

   // Custom toolbox item creates a TextBox and sets its Text property
   // to the constructor-specified text.
public __gc class TextToolboxItem : public                                 ↵
System::Drawing::Design::ToolboxItem {
private:
   String*  text;
   __delegate void SetTextMethodHandler(Control* c, String*  text);

public:
   TextToolboxItem(String* text) : ToolboxItem() {
      this->text = text;
   }

   // ToolboxItem::CreateComponentsCore  to create the TextBox
   // and link a method to set its Text property.
protected:
   [System::Security::Permissions::PermissionSet                           ↵
(System::Security::Permissions::SecurityAction::Demand,                    ↵
Name="FullTrust")]
   System::ComponentModel::IComponent*                                     ↵
CreateComponentsCore                                                       ↵
(System::ComponentModel::Design::IDesignerHost* host)[] {
      System::Windows::Forms::TextBox* textbox =                           ↵
dynamic_cast<TextBox*>(host->CreateComponent(__typeof(TextBox)));

      // Because the designer resets the text of the textbox, use
      // a SetTextMethodHandler to set the text to the value of
      // the text data.
      Control* c = dynamic_cast<Control*>(host->RootComponent);

      Object* temp0 [] = {textbox, text};
      c->BeginInvoke(new SetTextMethodHandler(this, OnSetText), temp0);

      System::ComponentModel::IComponent* temp1 [] = {textbox};
      return temp1;
   }

   // Method to set the text property of a TextBox after                   ↵
it is initialized.
private:
   void OnSetText(Control* c, String* text) {
      c->Text = text;
   }
};

// Component that adds a S"Text" data format ToolboxItemCreatorCallback
// to the Toolbox that creates a custom ToolboxItem that
// creates a TextBox containing the text data.
public __gc class TextDataTextBoxComponent : public                        ↵
System::ComponentModel::Component {
private:
   bool  creatorAdded;
   IToolboxService*  ts;

public:
   TextDataTextBoxComponent() {
      creatorAdded = false;
   }

   // ISite*  to register TextBox creator
   __property System::ComponentModel::ISite* get_Site() {
      return Component::get_Site();
   }
   __property void set_Site(System::ComponentModel::ISite* value) {
```

```
      if (value != 0) {
         Component::set_Site(value);
         if (!creatorAdded)
            AddTextTextBoxCreator();
      } else {
         if (creatorAdded)
            RemoveTextTextBoxCreator();
         Component::set_Site(value);
      }
   }

   // Adds a "Text" data format creator to the toolbox that creates
   // a textbox from a text fragment pasted to the toolbox.
private:
   void AddTextTextBoxCreator() {
      ts =
dynamic_cast<IToolboxService*>(GetService(__typeof(IToolboxService)));
      if (ts != 0) {
         ToolboxItemCreatorCallback* textCreator = new                    ↵
ToolboxItemCreatorCallback(this, CreateTextBoxForText);
         try {
            ts->AddCreator(textCreator, S"Text",                          ↵
dynamic_cast<IDesignerHost*>(GetService(__typeof(IDesignerHost))));
            creatorAdded = true;
         } catch (Exception* ex) {
            MessageBox::Show(ex->ToString(), S"Exception Information");
         }
      }
   }

   // Removes any "Text" data format creator from the toolbox.
   void RemoveTextTextBoxCreator() {
      if (ts != 0) {
         ts->RemoveCreator(S"Text",                                       ↵
dynamic_cast<IDesignerHost*>(GetService(__typeof(IDesignerHost))));
         creatorAdded = false;
      }
   }

   // ToolboxItemCreatorCallback delegate format method to create
   // the toolbox item.
   ToolboxItem* CreateTextBoxForText(Object* serializedObject,           ↵
 String* format) {
      String* formats[] =                                                 ↵
 (dynamic_cast<System::Windows::Forms::DataObject*>                       ↵
 (serializedObject))->GetFormats();
      if ((dynamic_cast<System::Windows::Forms::DataObject*>              ↵
 (serializedObject))->GetDataPresent(S"System::String", true))
         return new
TextToolboxItem(dynamic_cast<String*>((dynamic_cast<System::Windows::For
ms::DataObject*>(serializedObject))->GetData                              ↵
 (S"System::String", true)));
      return 0;
   }

protected:
   void Dispose(bool disposing) {
      if (creatorAdded)
         RemoveTextTextBoxCreator();
   }
};

}
```

Requirements

Namespace: System.Drawing.Design

Platforms: Windows 98, Windows NT 4.0, Windows Millennium Edition, Windows 2000, Windows XP Home Edition, Windows XP Professional, Windows Server 2003 family

Assembly: System.Drawing (in System.Drawing.dll)

ToolboxItem Constructor

Initializes a new instance of the **ToolboxItem** class.

Overload List

Initializes a new instance of the **ToolboxItem** class.

[Visual Basic] **Public Sub New()**

[C#] **public ToolboxItem();**

[C++] **public: ToolboxItem();**

[JScript] **public function ToolboxItem();**

Initializes a new instance of the **ToolboxItem** class that creates the specified type of component.

[Visual Basic] **Public Sub New(Type)**

[C#] **public ToolboxItem(Type);**

[C++] **public: ToolboxItem(Type*);**

[JScript] **public function ToolboxItem(Type);**

ToolboxItem Constructor ()

Initializes a new instance of the **ToolboxItem** class.

[Visual Basic]
```
Public Sub New()
```
[C#]
```
public ToolboxItem();
```
[C++]
```
public: ToolboxItem();
```
[JScript]
```
public function ToolboxItem();
```

Requirements

Platforms: Windows 98, Windows NT 4.0, Windows Millennium Edition, Windows 2000, Windows XP Home Edition, Windows XP Professional, Windows Server 2003 family

ToolboxItem Constructor (Type)

Initializes a new instance of the **ToolboxItem** class that creates the specified type of component.

[Visual Basic]
```
Public Sub New( _
   ByVal toolType As Type _
)
```
[C#]
```
public ToolboxItem(
   Type toolType
);
```
[C++]
```
public: ToolboxItem(
   Type* toolType
);
```
[JScript]
```
public function ToolboxItem(
   toolType : Type
);
```

Parameters

toolType

The type of **IComponent** that the toolbox item will create.

Requirements

Platforms: Windows 98, Windows NT 4.0, Windows Millennium Edition, Windows 2000, Windows XP Home Edition, Windows XP Professional, Windows Server 2003 family

ToolboxItem.AssemblyName Property

Gets or sets the name of the assembly that contains the type or types that the toolbox item creates.

```
[Visual Basic]
Public Property AssemblyName As AssemblyName
[C#]
public AssemblyName AssemblyName {get; set;}
[C++]
public: __property AssemblyName* get_AssemblyName();
public: __property void set_AssemblyName(AssemblyName*);
[JScript]
public function get AssemblyName() : AssemblyName;
public function set AssemblyName(AssemblyName);
```

Property Value

An **AssemblyName** that indicates the assembly containing the type or types to create.

Remarks

This property specifies the assembly that contains the type(s) of the component(s), to create.

Notes to Inheritors: If your derived toolbox item class creates multiple components that are located in different assemblies, you must ensure that references to these assemblies exist in your project. It is advisable to add these references from an overload of the **CreateComponentsCore** method. Even if your **CreateComponentsCore** method does not depend on the value of the **AssemblyName** property, you should ensure that this property is set to the assembly that one of the components to create belongs to, since it is displayed in the **Customize Toolbox** dialog box in Visual Studio .NET.

Requirements

Platforms: Windows 98, Windows NT 4.0, Windows Millennium Edition, Windows 2000, Windows XP Home Edition, Windows XP Professional, Windows Server 2003 family

ToolboxItem.Bitmap Property

Gets or sets a bitmap to represent the toolbox item in the toolbox.

```
[Visual Basic]
Public Property Bitmap As Bitmap
[C#]
public Bitmap Bitmap {get; set;}
[C++]
public: __property Bitmap* get_Bitmap();
public: __property void set_Bitmap(Bitmap*);
[JScript]
public function get Bitmap() : Bitmap;
public function set Bitmap(Bitmap);
```

Property Value

A **Bitmap** that represents the toolbox item in the toolbox.

Requirements

Platforms: Windows 98, Windows NT 4.0, Windows Millennium Edition, Windows 2000, Windows XP Home Edition, Windows XP Professional, Windows Server 2003 family

ToolboxItem.DisplayName Property

Gets or sets the display name for the toolbox item.

```
[Visual Basic]
Public Property DisplayName As String
[C#]
public string DisplayName {get; set;}
[C++]
public: __property String* get_DisplayName();
public: __property void set_DisplayName(String*);
[JScript]
public function get DisplayName() : String;
public function set DisplayName(String);
```

Property Value

The display name for the toolbox item.

Remarks

This property indicates the string that is displayed for the toolbox item in the toolbox.

By default, the base **ToolboxItem** class sets its **DisplayName** property to a short form of the fully qualified type name specified by the **TypeName** property.

Requirements

Platforms: Windows 98, Windows NT 4.0, Windows Millennium Edition, Windows 2000, Windows XP Home Edition, Windows XP Professional, Windows Server 2003 family

ToolboxItem.Filter Property

Gets or sets the filter that determines whether the toolbox item can be used on a destination component.

```
[Visual Basic]
Public Property Filter As ICollection
[C#]
public ICollection Filter {get; set;}
[C++]
public: __property ICollection* get_Filter();
public: __property void set_Filter(ICollection*);
[JScript]
public function get Filter() : ICollection;
public function set Filter(ICollection);
```

Property Value

An **ICollection** collection of **ToolboxItemFilterAttribute** objects.

Remarks

This property's collection contains **ToolboxItemFilterAttribute** objects that specify the policy that the design-time environment uses to determine whether a toolbox item can be used on the destination component.

For more information on restricting the scope in which a **ToolboxItem** can be used, see the documentation for the **ToolboxItemFilter-Attribute** class.

Requirements

Platforms: Windows 98, Windows NT 4.0, Windows Millennium Edition, Windows 2000, Windows XP Home Edition, Windows XP Professional, Windows Server 2003 family

ToolboxItem.Locked Property

Gets a value indicating whether the **ToolboxItem** is currently locked.

```
[Visual Basic]
Protected ReadOnly Property  As Boolean
[C#]
protected bool Locked {get;}
[C++]
protected: __property bool get_Locked();
[JScript]
protected function get Locked() : Boolean;
```

Property Value

true if the toolbox item is locked; otherwise, **false**.

Remarks

When a **ToolboxItem** is locked, you cannot adjust its properties.

Requirements

Platforms: Windows 98, Windows NT 4.0, Windows Millennium Edition, Windows 2000, Windows XP Home Edition, Windows XP Professional, Windows Server 2003 family

ToolboxItem.TypeName Property

Gets or sets the fully qualified name of the type of **IComponent** that the toolbox item creates when invoked.

```
[Visual Basic]
Public Property TypeName As String
[C#]
public string TypeName {get; set;}
[C++]
public: __property String* get_TypeName();
public: __property void set_TypeName(String*);
[JScript]
public function get TypeName() : String;
public function set TypeName(String);
```

Property Value

The fully qualified type name of the type of component that this toolbox item creates.

Remarks

This property specifies the fully qualified type name of the type of component to create.

Notes to Inheritors: If a derived toolbox item class creates multiple components, this property must be set unless your **Create-ComponentsCore** method override does not depend on the value of this property.

Requirements

Platforms: Windows 98, Windows NT 4.0, Windows Millennium Edition, Windows 2000, Windows XP Home Edition, Windows XP Professional, Windows Server 2003 family

ToolboxItem.CheckUnlocked Method

Throws an exception if the toolbox item is currently locked.

```
[Visual Basic]
Protected Sub CheckUnlocked()
[C#]
protected void CheckUnlocked();
[C++]
protected: void CheckUnlocked();
[JScript]
protected function CheckUnlocked();
```

Exceptions

Exception Type	Condition
InvalidOperation-Exception	The **ToolboxItem** was locked.

Remarks

This method throws an **InvalidOperationException** if the **Locked** property of the **ToolboxItem** is set to **true**.

Requirements

Platforms: Windows 98, Windows NT 4.0, Windows Millennium Edition, Windows 2000, Windows XP Home Edition, Windows XP Professional, Windows Server 2003 family

ToolboxItem.CreateComponents Method

Creates the components that the toolbox item is configured to create.

Overload List

Creates the components that the toolbox item is configured to create.

[Visual Basic] **Overloads Public Function CreateComponents() As IComponent()**

[C#] **public IComponent[] CreateComponents();**

[C++] **public: IComponent* CreateComponents() [];**

[JScript] **public function CreateComponents() : IComponent[];**

Creates the components that the toolbox item is configured to create, using the specified designer host.

[Visual Basic] **Overloads Public Function Create-Components(IDesignerHost) As IComponent()**

[C#] **public IComponent[] CreateComponents(IDesignerHost);**

[C++] **public: IComponent* CreateComponents(IDesigner-Host*) [];**

[JScript] **public function CreateComponents(IDesignerHost) : IComponent[];**

ToolboxItem.CreateComponents Method ()

Creates the components that the toolbox item is configured to create.

[Visual Basic]
```
Overloads Public Function CreateComponents() As IComponent()
```
[C#]
```
public IComponent[] CreateComponents();
```
[C++]
```
public: IComponent* CreateComponents() [];
```
[JScript]
```
public function CreateComponents() : IComponent[];
```

Return Value

An array of created **IComponent** objects.

Remarks

This method calls the **CreateComponentsCore** method to retrieve an array of type **IComponent** containing the components to create.

Requirements

Platforms: Windows 98, Windows NT 4.0, Windows Millennium Edition, Windows 2000, Windows XP Home Edition, Windows XP Professional, Windows Server 2003 family

ToolboxItem.CreateComponents Method (IDesignerHost)

Creates the components that the toolbox item is configured to create, using the specified designer host.

[Visual Basic]
```
Overloads Public Function CreateComponents( _
   ByVal host As IDesignerHost _
) As IComponent()
```
[C#]
```
public IComponent[] CreateComponents(
   IDesignerHost host
);
```
[C++]
```
public: IComponent* CreateComponents(
   IDesignerHost* host
) [];
```
[JScript]
```
public function CreateComponents(
   host : IDesignerHost
) : IComponent[];
```

Parameters

host
The **IDesignerHost** to use when creating the components.

Return Value

An array of created **IComponent** objects.

Remarks

This method calls the **CreateComponentsCore** method to retrieve an array of type **IComponent** containing the components to create.

Requirements

Platforms: Windows 98, Windows NT 4.0, Windows Millennium Edition, Windows 2000, Windows XP Home Edition, Windows XP Professional, Windows Server 2003 family

ToolboxItem.CreateComponentsCore Method

Creates a component or an array of components when the toolbox item is invoked.

[Visual Basic]
```
Protected Overridable Function CreateComponentsCore( _
   ByVal host As IDesignerHost _
) As IComponent()
```
[C#]
```
protected virtual IComponent[] CreateComponentsCore(
   IDesignerHost host
);
```
[C++]
```
protected: virtual IComponent* CreateComponentsCore(
   IDesignerHost* host
) [];
```
[JScript]
```
protected function CreateComponentsCore(
   host : IDesignerHost
) : IComponent[];
```

Parameters

host
The **IDesignerHost** to host the toolbox item.

Return Value

An array of created **IComponent** objects.

Remarks

Notes to Inheritors: You can override this method to return the component or components that a toolbox item creates.

Requirements

Platforms: Windows 98, Windows NT 4.0, Windows Millennium Edition, Windows 2000, Windows XP Home Edition, Windows XP Professional, Windows Server 2003 family

ToolboxItem.Deserialize Method

Loads the state of the toolbox item from the specified serialization information object.

[Visual Basic]
```
Protected Overridable Sub Deserialize( _
   ByVal info As SerializationInfo, _
   ByVal context As StreamingContext _
)
```
[C#]
```
protected virtual void Deserialize(
   SerializationInfo info,
   StreamingContext context
);
```
[C++]
```
protected: virtual void Deserialize(
   SerializationInfo* info,
   StreamingContext context
);
```
[JScript]
```
protected function Deserialize(
   info : SerializationInfo,
   context : StreamingContext
);
```

Parameters

info

The **SerializationInfo** to load from.

context

A **StreamingContext** that indicates the stream characteristics.

Remarks

Notes to Implementers: The **Serialize** and **Deserialize** methods must be implemented in classes that derive from **ToolboxItem** in order to support persistence in the toolbox database provided by some development environments.

Requirements

Platforms: Windows 98, Windows NT 4.0, Windows Millennium Edition, Windows 2000, Windows XP Home Edition, Windows XP Professional, Windows Server 2003 family

ToolboxItem.Equals Method

This member overrides **Object.Equals**.

```
[Visual Basic]
Overrides Public Function Equals( _
   ByVal obj As Object _
) As Boolean
[C#]
public override bool Equals(
   object obj
);
[C++]
public: bool Equals(
   Object* obj
);
[JScript]
public override function Equals(
   obj : Object
) : Boolean;
```

Requirements

Platforms: Windows 98, Windows NT 4.0, Windows Millennium Edition, Windows 2000, Windows XP Home Edition, Windows XP Professional, Windows Server 2003 family

ToolboxItem.GetHashCode Method

This member overrides **Object.GetHashCode**.

```
[Visual Basic]
Overrides Public Function GetHashCode() As Integer
[C#]
public override int GetHashCode();
[C++]
public: int GetHashCode();
[JScript]
public override function GetHashCode() : int;
```

Requirements

Platforms: Windows 98, Windows NT 4.0, Windows Millennium Edition, Windows 2000, Windows XP Home Edition, Windows XP Professional, Windows Server 2003 family

ToolboxItem.GetType Method

Creates an instance of the specified type.

Overload List

Creates an instance of the specified type, optionally using a specified designer host and assembly name.

[Visual Basic] **Overloads Protected Overridable Function GetType(IDesignerHost, AssemblyName, String, Boolean) As Type**

[C#] **protected virtual Type GetType(IDesignerHost, AssemblyName, string, bool);**

[C++] **protected: virtual Type* GetType(IDesignerHost*, AssemblyName*, String*, bool);**

[JScript] **protected function GetType(IDesignerHost, AssemblyName, String, Boolean) : Type;**

Inherited from **Object**.

[Visual Basic] **Overloads Public Function GetType() As Type**

[C#] **public Type GetType();**

[C++] **public: Type* GetType();**

[JScript] **public function GetType() : Type;**

ToolboxItem.GetType Method (IDesignerHost, AssemblyName, String, Boolean)

Creates an instance of the specified type, optionally using a specified designer host and assembly name.

```
[Visual Basic]
Overloads Protected Overridable Function GetType( _
   ByVal host As IDesignerHost, _
   ByVal assemblyName As AssemblyName, _
   ByVal typeName As String, _
   ByVal reference As Boolean _
) As Type
[C#]
protected virtual Type GetType(
   IDesignerHost host,
   AssemblyName assemblyName,
   string typeName,
   bool reference
);
[C++]
protected: virtual Type* GetType(
   IDesignerHost* host,
   AssemblyName* assemblyName,
   String* typeName,
   bool reference
);
[JScript]
protected function GetType(
   host : IDesignerHost,
   assemblyName : AssemblyName,
   typeName : String,
   reference : Boolean
) : Type;
```

Parameters

host

The **IDesignerHost** for the current document. This can be a null reference (**Nothing** in Visual Basic).

assemblyName
An **AssemblyName** that indicates the assembly that contains the type to load. This can be a null reference (**Nothing** in Visual Basic).

typeName
The name of the type to create an instance of.

reference
A value indicating whether or not to add a reference to the assembly that contains the specified type to the designer host's set of references.

Return Value

An instance of the specified type, if it could be located.

Exceptions

Exception Type	Condition
ArgumentNull-Exception	The *typeName* parameter was not specified.

Requirements

Platforms: Windows 98, Windows NT 4.0, Windows Millennium Edition, Windows 2000, Windows XP Home Edition, Windows XP Professional, Windows Server 2003 family

ToolboxItem.Initialize Method

Initializes the current toolbox item with the specified type to create.

[Visual Basic]
```
Public Overridable Sub Initialize( _
   ByVal type As Type _
)
```
[C#]
```
public virtual void Initialize(
   Type type
);
```
[C++]
```
public: virtual void Initialize(
   Type* type
);
```
[JScript]
```
public function Initialize(
   type : Type
);
```

Parameters

type
The **Type** that the toolbox item will create.

Remarks

This method configures the toolbox item to create the specified type, if the **CreateComponentsCore** method has not been overridden to behave differently.

This method performs the following operations:

- Sets the **AssemblyName** property to an **AssemblyName** indicating the assembly of the specified type.
- Sets the **DisplayName** property to a short type name based on the name of the specified type.
- Adds any **ToolboxItemFilterAttribute** attributes found on the specified type to the **Filter** property collection.

Requirements

Platforms: Windows 98, Windows NT 4.0, Windows Millennium Edition, Windows 2000, Windows XP Home Edition, Windows XP Professional, Windows Server 2003 family

ToolboxItem.ISerializable.GetObjectData Method

This member supports the .NET Framework infrastructure and is not intended to be used directly from your code.

[Visual Basic]
```
Private Sub GetObjectData( _
   ByVal info As SerializationInfo, _
   ByVal context As StreamingContext _
) Implements ISerializable.GetObjectData
```
[C#]
```
void ISerializable.GetObjectData(
   SerializationInfo info,
   StreamingContext context
);
```
[C++]
```
private: void ISerializable::GetObjectData(
   SerializationInfo* info,
   StreamingContext context
);
```
[JScript]
```
private function ISerializable.GetObjectData(
   info : SerializationInfo,
   context : StreamingContext
);
```

ToolboxItem.Lock Method

Locks the toolbox item and prevents changes to its properties.

[Visual Basic]
```
Public Sub Lock()
```
[C#]
```
public void Lock();
```
[C++]
```
public: void Lock();
```
[JScript]
```
public function Lock();
```

Remarks

The properties of a toolbox item cannot be changed when it is locked.

Requirements

Platforms: Windows 98, Windows NT 4.0, Windows Millennium Edition, Windows 2000, Windows XP Home Edition, Windows XP Professional, Windows Server 2003 family

ToolboxItem.OnComponentsCreated Method

Raises the **ComponentsCreated** event.

[Visual Basic]
```
Protected Overridable Sub OnComponentsCreated( _
   ByVal args As ToolboxComponentsCreatedEventArgs _
)
```

[C#]
```
protected virtual void OnComponentsCreated(
   ToolboxComponentsCreatedEventArgs args
);
```
[C++]
```
protected: virtual void OnComponentsCreated(
   ToolboxComponentsCreatedEventArgs* args
);
```
[JScript]
```
protected function OnComponentsCreated(
   args : ToolboxComponentsCreatedEventArgs
);
```

Parameters

args

A **ToolboxComponentsCreatedEventArgs** that provides data for the event.

Remarks

This method raises the **ComponentsCreated** event. This method is called after a toolbox item is invoked to create components and the **CreateComponentsCore** method has returned.

Requirements

Platforms: Windows 98, Windows NT 4.0, Windows Millennium Edition, Windows 2000, Windows XP Home Edition, Windows XP Professional, Windows Server 2003 family

ToolboxItem.OnComponentsCreating Method

Raises the **ComponentsCreating** event.

[Visual Basic]
```
Protected Overridable Sub OnComponentsCreating( _
   ByVal args As ToolboxComponentsCreatingEventArgs _
)
```
[C#]
```
protected virtual void OnComponentsCreating(
   ToolboxComponentsCreatingEventArgs args
);
```
[C++]
```
protected: virtual void OnComponentsCreating(
   ToolboxComponentsCreatingEventArgs* args
);
```
[JScript]
```
protected function OnComponentsCreating(
   args : ToolboxComponentsCreatingEventArgs
);
```

Parameters

args

A **ToolboxComponentsCreatingEventArgs** that provides data for the event.

Remarks

This method raises the **ComponentsCreating** event. This method is called after a toolbox item is invoked to create components, just before the **CreateComponentsCore** method is called.

Requirements

Platforms: Windows 98, Windows NT 4.0, Windows Millennium Edition, Windows 2000, Windows XP Home Edition, Windows XP Professional, Windows Server 2003 family

ToolboxItem.Serialize Method

Saves the state of the toolbox item to the specified serialization information object.

[Visual Basic]
```
Protected Overridable Sub Serialize( _
   ByVal info As SerializationInfo, _
   ByVal context As StreamingContext _
)
```
[C#]
```
protected virtual void Serialize(
   SerializationInfo info,
   StreamingContext context
);
```
[C++]
```
protected: virtual void Serialize(
   SerializationInfo* info,
   StreamingContext context
);
```
[JScript]
```
protected function Serialize(
   info : SerializationInfo,
   context : StreamingContext
);
```

Parameters

info

The **SerializationInfo** to save to.

context

A **StreamingContext** that indicates the stream characteristics.

Remarks

Notes to Implementers: The **Serialize** and **Deserialize** methods must be implemented in classes that derive from **ToolboxItem** in order to support persistence in the toolbox database provided by some development environments.

Requirements

Platforms: Windows 98, Windows NT 4.0, Windows Millennium Edition, Windows 2000, Windows XP Home Edition, Windows XP Professional, Windows Server 2003 family

ToolboxItem.ToString Method

Provides support for Object's ToString method.

[Visual Basic]
```
Overrides Public Function ToString() As String
```
[C#]
```
public override string ToString();
```
[C++]
```
public: String* ToString();
```
[JScript]
```
public override function ToString() : String;
```

Return Value

A string representation of the current object's value.

Requirements

Platforms: Windows 98, Windows NT 4.0, Windows Millennium Edition, Windows 2000, Windows XP Home Edition, Windows XP Professional, Windows Server 2003 family

ToolboxItem.ComponentsCreated Event

Occurs immediately after components are created.

[Visual Basic]
```
Public Event ComponentsCreated As _
   ToolboxComponentsCreatedEventHandler
```
[C#]
```
public event ToolboxComponentsCreatedEventHandler
   ComponentsCreated;
```
[C++]
```
public: __event ToolboxComponentsCreatedEventHandler*
   ComponentsCreated;
```

[JScript] In JScript, you can handle the events defined by a class, but you cannot define your own.

Event Data

The event handler receives an argument of type **ToolboxComponentsCreatedEventArgs** containing data related to this event. The following **ToolboxComponentsCreatedEventArgs** property provides information specific to this event.

Property	Description
Components	Gets or sets an array containing the components to add to the toolbox.

Remarks

This event is raised each time that components of this toolbox item are created.

Requirements

Platforms: Windows 98, Windows NT 4.0, Windows Millennium Edition, Windows 2000, Windows XP Home Edition, Windows XP Professional, Windows Server 2003 family

ToolboxItem.ComponentsCreating Event

Occurs when components are about to be created.

[Visual Basic]
```
Public Event ComponentsCreating As _
   ToolboxComponentsCreatingEventHandler
```
[C#]
```
public event ToolboxComponentsCreatingEventHandler
   ComponentsCreating;
```
[C++]
```
public: __event ToolboxComponentsCreatingEventHandler*
   ComponentsCreating;
```

[JScript] In JScript, you can handle the events defined by a class, but you cannot define your own.

Event Data

The event handler receives an argument of type **ToolboxComponentsCreatingEventArgs** containing data related to this event. The following **ToolboxComponentsCreatingEventArgs** property provides information specific to this event.

Property	Description
DesignerHost	Gets or sets an instance of the **IDesignerHost** that made the request to create toolbox components.

Remarks

This event is raised each time that components of the toolbox item are about to be created.

Requirements

Platforms: Windows 98, Windows NT 4.0, Windows Millennium Edition, Windows 2000, Windows XP Home Edition, Windows XP Professional, Windows Server 2003 family

ToolboxItemCollection Class

Represents a collection of toolbox items.

System.Object
  System.Collections.ReadOnlyCollectionBase
    System.Drawing.Design.ToolboxItemCollection

```
[Visual Basic]
NotInheritable Public Class ToolboxItemCollection
   Inherits ReadOnlyCollectionBase
[C#]
public sealed class ToolboxItemCollection : ReadOnlyCollectionBase
[C++]
public __gc __sealed class ToolboxItemCollection : public
   ReadOnlyCollectionBase
[JScript]
public class ToolboxItemCollection extends ReadOnlyCollectionBase
```

Thread Safety

Any public static (**Shared** in Visual Basic) members of this type are safe for multithreaded operations. Any instance members are not guaranteed to be thread safe.

Requirements

Namespace: System.Drawing.Design

Platforms: Windows 98, Windows NT 4.0, Windows Millennium Edition, Windows 2000, Windows XP Home Edition, Windows XP Professional, Windows Server 2003 family

Assembly: System.Drawing (in System.Drawing.dll)

ToolboxItemCollection Constructor

Initializes a new instance of the **ToolboxItemCollection** class.

Overload List

Initializes a new instance of the **ToolboxItemCollection** class using the specified array of toolbox items.

[Visual Basic] **Public Sub New(ToolboxItem())**

[C#] **public ToolboxItemCollection(ToolboxItem[]);**

[C++] **public: ToolboxItemCollection(ToolboxItem*[]);**

[JScript] **public function ToolboxItemCollection(ToolboxItem[]);**

Initializes a new instance of the **ToolboxItemCollection** class using the specified collection.

[Visual Basic] **Public Sub New(ToolboxItemCollection)**

[C#] **public ToolboxItemCollection(ToolboxItemCollection);**

[C++] **public: ToolboxItemCollection(ToolboxItemCollection*);**

[JScript] **public function ToolboxItemCollection(ToolboxItemCollection);**

ToolboxItemCollection Constructor (ToolboxItem[])

Initializes a new instance of the **ToolboxItemCollection** class using the specified array of toolbox items.

```
[Visual Basic]
Public Sub New( _
   ByVal value() As ToolboxItem _
)
[C#]
public ToolboxItemCollection(
   ToolboxItem[] value
);
[C++]
public: ToolboxItemCollection(
   ToolboxItem* value[]
);
[JScript]
public function ToolboxItemCollection(
   value : ToolboxItem[]
);
```

Parameters

value

An array of type **ToolboxItem** containing the toolbox items to fill the collection with.

Requirements

Platforms: Windows 98, Windows NT 4.0, Windows Millennium Edition, Windows 2000, Windows XP Home Edition, Windows XP Professional, Windows Server 2003 family

ToolboxItemCollection Constructor (ToolboxItemCollection)

Initializes a new instance of the **ToolboxItemCollection** class using the specified collection.

```
[Visual Basic]
Public Sub New( _
   ByVal value As ToolboxItemCollection _
)
[C#]
public ToolboxItemCollection(
   ToolboxItemCollection value
);
[C++]
public: ToolboxItemCollection(
   ToolboxItemCollection* value
);
[JScript]
public function ToolboxItemCollection(
   value : ToolboxItemCollection
);
```

Parameters

value

A **ToolboxItemCollection** to fill the new collection with.

Requirements

Platforms: Windows 98, Windows NT 4.0, Windows Millennium Edition, Windows 2000, Windows XP Home Edition, Windows XP Professional, Windows Server 2003 family

ToolboxItemCollection.Item Property

Gets the **ToolboxItem** at the specified index.

[C#] In C#, this property is the indexer for the **ToolboxItemCollection** class.

```
[Visual Basic]
Public Default ReadOnly Property Item( _
   ByVal index As Integer _
) As ToolboxItem
[C#]
public ToolboxItem this[
   int index
] {get;}
[C++]
public: __property ToolboxItem* get_Item(
   int index
);
[JScript]
returnValue = ToolboxItemCollectionObject.Item(index);
-or-
returnValue = ToolboxItemCollectionObject(index);
```

[JScript] In JScript, you can use the default indexed properties defined by a type, but you cannot explicitly define your own. However, specifying the **expando** attribute on a class automatically provides a default indexed property whose type is **Object** and whose index type is **String**.

Arguments [JScript]

index
The index of the object to get or set.

Parameters [Visual Basic, C#, C++]

index
The index of the object to get or set.

Property Value

A **ToolboxItem** at each valid index in the collection.

Requirements

Platforms: Windows 98, Windows NT 4.0, Windows Millennium Edition, Windows 2000, Windows XP Home Edition, Windows XP Professional, Windows Server 2003 family

ToolboxItemCollection.Contains Method

Indicates whether the collection contains the specified **ToolboxItem**.

```
[Visual Basic]
Public Function Contains( _
   ByVal value As ToolboxItem _
) As Boolean
[C#]
public bool Contains(
   ToolboxItem value
);
[C++]
public: bool Contains(
   ToolboxItem* value
);
[JScript]
public function Contains(
   value : ToolboxItem
) : Boolean;
```

Parameters

value
A **ToolboxItem** to search the collection for.

Return Value

true if the collection contains the specified object; otherwise, **false**.

Requirements

Platforms: Windows 98, Windows NT 4.0, Windows Millennium Edition, Windows 2000, Windows XP Home Edition, Windows XP Professional, Windows Server 2003 family

ToolboxItemCollection.CopyTo Method

Copies the collection to the specified array beginning with the specified destination index.

```
[Visual Basic]
Public Sub CopyTo( _
   ByVal array() As ToolboxItem, _
   ByVal index As Integer _
)
[C#]
public void CopyTo(
   ToolboxItem[] array,
   int index
);
[C++]
public: void CopyTo(
   ToolboxItem* array[],
   int index
);
[JScript]
public function CopyTo(
   array : ToolboxItem[],
   index : int
);
```

Parameters

array
The array to copy to.

index
The index to begin copying to.

Requirements

Platforms: Windows 98, Windows NT 4.0, Windows Millennium Edition, Windows 2000, Windows XP Home Edition, Windows XP Professional, Windows Server 2003 family

ToolboxItemCollection.IndexOf Method

Gets the index of the specified **ToolboxItem**, if it exists in the collection.

[Visual Basic]
```
Public Function IndexOf( _
   ByVal value As ToolboxItem _
) As Integer
```
[C#]
```
public int IndexOf(
   ToolboxItem value
);
```
[C++]
```
public: int IndexOf(
   ToolboxItem* value
);
```
[JScript]
```
public function IndexOf(
   value : ToolboxItem
) : int;
```

Parameters

value

A **ToolboxItem** to get the index of in the collection.

Return Value

The index of the specified **ToolboxItem**.

Requirements

Platforms: Windows 98, Windows NT 4.0, Windows Millennium Edition, Windows 2000, Windows XP Home Edition, Windows XP Professional, Windows Server 2003 family

ToolboxItemCreatorCallback Delegate

Represents the method that will handle the ToolboxItemCreatorCallback event.

[Visual Basic]
```
<Serializable>
Public Delegate Function Sub ToolboxItemCreatorCallback( _
   ByVal serializedObject As Object, _
   ByVal format As String _
) As ToolboxItem
```
[C#]
```
[Serializable]
public delegate ToolboxItem ToolboxItemCreatorCallback(
   object serializedObject,
   string format
);
```
[C++]
```
[Serializable]
public __gc __delegate ToolboxItem* ToolboxItemCreatorCallback(
   Object* serializedObject,
   String* format
);
```

[JScript] In JScript, you can use the delegates in the .NET Framework, but you cannot define your own.

Parameters [Visual Basic, C#, C++]

The declaration of your callback method must have the same parameters as the **ToolboxItemCreatorCallback** delegate declaration.

serializedObject
: The object which contains the data to create a **ToolboxItem** for.

format
: The name of the clipboard data format to create a **ToolboxItem** for.

Remarks

You can implement a toolbox item creator method with a method signature matching the method signature of this delegate type that creates a toolbox item from any object of a particular clipboard data format placed on the toolbox. For example, you can design a toolbox item creator that creates a **TextBox** to store text pasted to the toolbox from the clipboard. You can use the **AddCreator** method of the **IToolboxService** to add a **ToolboxItemCreatorCallback** event handler for a particular data type to the toolbox. The *serializedObject* parameter contains the data object.

When you create a **ToolboxItemCreatorCallback** delegate, you identify the method that will handle the event. To associate the event with your event handler, add an instance of the delegate to the event. The event handler is called whenever the event occurs, unless you remove the delegate.

Example

[Visual Basic, C#, C++] The following example provides a component that uses the **IToolboxService** to add a "Text" data format handler, or **ToolboxItemCreatorCallback**, to the toolbox. The data creator callback delegate passes any text data pasted to the toolbox and dragged onto a form to a custom **ToolboxItem** that creates a **System.Windows.Forms.TextBox** containing the text.

[Visual Basic]
```
Imports System
Imports System.ComponentModel
Imports System.ComponentModel.Design
Imports System.Drawing
Imports System.Drawing.Design
Imports System.Windows.Forms

' Component that adds a "Text" data format ToolboxItemCreatorCallback
' to the Toolbox that creates a custom ToolboxItem that
' creates a TextBox containing the text data.
Public Class TextDataTextBoxComponent
    Inherits System.ComponentModel.Component

   Private creatorAdded As Boolean = False
   Private ts As IToolboxService

   Public Sub New()
    End Sub

    ' ISite override to register TextBox creator
    Public Overrides Property Site() As System.ComponentModel.ISite
        Get
            Return MyBase.Site
        End Get
        Set(ByVal Value As System.ComponentModel.ISite)
            If Not (Value Is Nothing) Then
                MyBase.Site = Value
                If Not creatorAdded Then
                    AddTextTextBoxCreator()
                End If
            Else
                If creatorAdded Then
                    RemoveTextTextBoxCreator()
                End If
                MyBase.Site = Value
            End If
        End Set
    End Property

    ' Adds a "Text" data format creator to the toolbox that creates
    ' a textbox from a text fragment pasted to the toolbox.
    Private Sub AddTextTextBoxCreator()
        ts = CType(GetService(GetType(IToolboxService)), ↵
IToolboxService)
        If Not (ts Is Nothing) Then
            Dim textCreator As New ↵
ToolboxItemCreatorCallback(AddressOf Me.CreateTextBoxForText)
            Try
                ts.AddCreator(textCreator, "Text", ↵
CType(GetService(GetType(IDesignerHost)), IDesignerHost))
                creatorAdded = True
            Catch ex As Exception
                MessageBox.Show(ex.ToString(), "Exception Information")
            End Try
        End If
    End Sub

    ' Removes any "Text" data format creator from the toolbox.
    Private Sub RemoveTextTextBoxCreator()
        If Not (ts Is Nothing) Then
            ts.RemoveCreator("Text", ↵
CType(GetService(GetType(IDesignerHost)), IDesignerHost))
            creatorAdded = False
        End If
    End Sub

    ' ToolboxItemCreatorCallback delegate format method to create
    ' the toolbox item.
    Private Function CreateTextBoxForText(ByVal ↵
serializedObject As Object, ByVal format As String) As ToolboxItem
        Dim formats As String() = CType(serializedObject, ↵
System.Windows.Forms.DataObject).GetFormats()
        If CType(serializedObject, ↵
System.Windows.Forms.DataObject).GetDataPresent ↵
```

```
("System.String", True) Then
            Return New TextToolboxItem(CStr(CType ↵
(serializedObject, ↵
System.Windows.Forms.DataObject).GetData("System.String", True)))
        End If
        Return Nothing
    End Function

    Protected Overloads Overrides Sub Dispose(ByVal ↵
disposing As Boolean)
        If creatorAdded Then
            RemoveTextTextBoxCreator()
        End If
    End Sub

End Class

' Custom toolbox item creates a TextBox and sets its Text property
' to the constructor-specified text.
Public Class TextToolboxItem
    Inherits System.Drawing.Design.ToolboxItem

    Private [text] As String

    Delegate Sub SetTextMethodHandler(ByVal c As Control, ↵
 ByVal [text] As String)

    Public Sub New(ByVal [text] As String)
        Me.text = [text]
    End Sub

    ' ToolboxItem.CreateComponentsCore override to create the TextBox
    ' and link a method to set its Text property.
    <System.Security.Permissions.PermissionSetAttribute ↵
(System.Security.Permissions.SecurityAction.Demand, Name:="FullTrust")>
_
    Protected Overrides Function CreateComponentsCore(ByVal ↵
host As System.ComponentModel.Design.IDesignerHost) As ↵
System.ComponentModel.IComponent()
        Dim textbox As System.Windows.Forms.TextBox = ↵
CType(host.CreateComponent(GetType(TextBox)), TextBox)

        ' Because the designer resets the text of the textbox, use
        ' a SetTextMethodHandler to set the text to the value of
        ' the text data.
        Dim c As Control = host.RootComponent

        c.BeginInvoke(New SetTextMethodHandler ↵
(AddressOf OnSetText), New Object() {textbox, [text]})

        Return New System.ComponentModel.IComponent() {textbox}
    End Function

    ' Method to set the text property of a TextBox after ↵
it is initialized.
    Private Sub OnSetText(ByVal c As Control, ByVal [text] As String)
        c.Text = [text]
    End Sub

End Class
```

[C#]

```
using System;
using System.ComponentModel;
using System.ComponentModel.Design;
using System.Drawing;
using System.Drawing.Design;
using System.Windows.Forms;

namespace TextDataTextBoxComponent
{
    // Component that adds a "Text" data format ↵
ToolboxItemCreatorCallback
    // to the Toolbox that creates a custom ToolboxItem that
    // creates a TextBox containing the text data.
    public class TextDataTextBoxComponent : ↵
System.ComponentModel.Component
    {
        private bool creatorAdded = false;
        private IToolboxService ts;

        public TextDataTextBoxComponent()
        {
        }

        // ISite override to register TextBox creator
        public override System.ComponentModel.ISite Site
        {
            get
            {
                return base.Site;
            }
            set
            {
                if( value != null )
                {
                    base.Site = value;
                    if( !creatorAdded )
                        AddTextTextBoxCreator();
                }
                else
                {
                    if( creatorAdded )
                        RemoveTextTextBoxCreator();
                    base.Site = value;
                }
            }
        }

        // Adds a "Text" data format creator to the toolbox ↵
that creates
        // a textbox from a text fragment pasted to the toolbox.
        private void AddTextTextBoxCreator()
        {
            ts = (IToolboxService)GetService(typeof(IToolboxService));
            if (ts != null)
            {
                ToolboxItemCreatorCallback textCreator = new ↵
ToolboxItemCreatorCallback(this.CreateTextBoxForText);
                try
                {
                    ts.AddCreator(textCreator, "Text", ↵
 (IDesignerHost)GetService(typeof(IDesignerHost)));
                    creatorAdded = true;
                }
                catch(Exception ex)
                {
                    MessageBox.Show(ex.ToString(), "Exception ↵
Information");
                }
            }
        }

        // Removes any "Text" data format creator from the toolbox.
        private void RemoveTextTextBoxCreator()
        {
            if (ts != null)
            {
                ts.RemoveCreator("Text", ↵
 (IDesignerHost)GetService(typeof(IDesignerHost)));
                creatorAdded = false;
            }
        }

        // ToolboxItemCreatorCallback delegate format method to create
        // the toolbox item.
        private ToolboxItem CreateTextBoxForText(object ↵
serializedObject, string format)
        {
            string[] formats = ↵
```

```
((System.Windows.Forms.DataObject)serializedObject).GetFormats();
            if( ((System.Windows.Forms.DataObject)                     ↵
serializedObject).GetDataPresent("System.String", true) )
                return new TextToolboxItem(
(string)((System.Windows.Forms.DataObject)                              ↵
serializedObject).GetData("System.String", true) );
            return null;
        }

        protected override void Dispose(bool disposing)
        {
            if( creatorAdded )
                RemoveTextTextBoxCreator();
        }
    }

    // Custom toolbox item creates a TextBox and sets its Text property
    // to the constructor-specified text.
    public class TextToolboxItem : System.Drawing.Design.ToolboxItem
    {
        private string text;
        private delegate void SetTextMethodHandler(Control c,          ↵
string text);

        public TextToolboxItem(string text) : base()
        {
            this.text = text;
        }

        // ToolboxItem.CreateComponentsCore override to                 ↵
create the TextBox
        // and link a method to set its Text property.
        [System.Security.Permissions.PermissionSet                      ↵
 (System.Security.Permissions.SecurityAction.Demand, Name="FullTrust")]
        protected override System.ComponentModel.IComponent[]           ↵
CreateComponentsCore(System.ComponentModel.Design.IDesignerHost host)
        {
            System.Windows.Forms.TextBox textbox =                      ↵
 (TextBox)host.CreateComponent(typeof(TextBox));

            // Because the designer resets the text of the textbox, use
            // a SetTextMethodHandler to set the text to the value of
            // the text data.
            Control c = host.RootComponent as Control;
            c.BeginInvoke(new SetTextMethodHandler(OnSetText),          ↵
new object[] {textbox, text});

            return new System.ComponentModel.IComponent[] { textbox };
        }

        // Method to set the text property of a TextBox after           ↵
it is initialized.
        private void OnSetText(Control c, string text)
        {
            c.Text = text;
        }
    }
}
```

[C++]

```
#using <mscorlib.dll>
#using <System.Windows.Forms.dll>
#using <System.Drawing.dll>
#using <System.dll>

using namespace System;
using namespace System::ComponentModel;
using namespace System::ComponentModel::Design;
using namespace System::Drawing;
using namespace System::Drawing::Design;
using namespace System::Windows::Forms;

namespace TextDataTextBoxComponent {

   // Custom toolbox item creates a TextBox and sets its Text property
   // to the constructor-specified text.
public __gc class TextToolboxItem : public                              ↵
System::Drawing::Design::ToolboxItem {
private:
   String*  text;
   __delegate void SetTextMethodHandler(Control* c, String*  text);

public:
   TextToolboxItem(String* text) : ToolboxItem() {
      this->text = text;
   }

   // ToolboxItem::CreateComponentsCore  to create the TextBox
   // and link a method to set its Text property.
protected:
   [System::Security::Permissions::PermissionSet                        ↵
 (System::Security::Permissions::SecurityAction::Demand,                ↵
Name="FullTrust")]
   System::ComponentModel::IComponent* CreateComponentsCore             ↵
 (System::ComponentModel::Design::IDesignerHost* host)[] {
      System::Windows::Forms::TextBox* textbox =                        ↵
dynamic_cast<TextBox*>(host->CreateComponent(__typeof(TextBox)));

      // Because the designer resets the text of the textbox, use
      // a SetTextMethodHandler to set the text to the value of
      // the text data.
      Control* c = dynamic_cast<Control*>(host->RootComponent);

      Object* temp0 [] = {textbox, text};
      c->BeginInvoke(new SetTextMethodHandler(this, OnSetText), temp0);

      System::ComponentModel::IComponent* temp1 [] = {textbox};
      return temp1;
   }

   // Method to set the text property of a TextBox after it             ↵
is initialized.
private:
   void OnSetText(Control* c, String* text) {
      c->Text = text;
   }
};

// Component that adds a S"Text" data format ToolboxItemCreatorCallback
// to the Toolbox that creates a custom ToolboxItem that
// creates a TextBox containing the text data.
public __gc class TextDataTextBoxComponent : public                     ↵
System::ComponentModel::Component {
private:
   bool  creatorAdded;
   IToolboxService*  ts;

public:
   TextDataTextBoxComponent() {
      creatorAdded = false;
   }

   // ISite*  to register TextBox creator
   __property System::ComponentModel::ISite* get_Site() {
      return Component::get_Site();
   }
   __property void set_Site(System::ComponentModel::ISite* value) {
      if (value != 0) {
         Component::set_Site(value);
         if (!creatorAdded)
            AddTextTextBoxCreator();
      } else {
         if (creatorAdded)
            RemoveTextTextBoxCreator();
         Component::set_Site(value);
      }
   }
```

```
   // Adds a "Text" data format creator to the toolbox that creates
   // a textbox from a text fragment pasted to the toolbox.
private:
   void AddTextTextBoxCreator() {
      ts =
dynamic_cast<IToolboxService*>(GetService(__typeof(IToolboxService)));
      if (ts != 0) {
         ToolboxItemCreatorCallback* textCreator = new                    ↵
ToolboxItemCreatorCallback(this, CreateTextBoxForText);
         try {
            ts->AddCreator(textCreator, S"Text",                           ↵
dynamic_cast<IDesignerHost*>(GetService(__typeof(IDesignerHost))));
            creatorAdded = true;
         } catch (Exception* ex) {
            MessageBox::Show(ex->ToString(), S"Exception Information");
         }
      }
   }

   // Removes any "Text" data format creator from the toolbox.
   void RemoveTextTextBoxCreator() {
      if (ts != 0) {
         ts->RemoveCreator(S"Text",                                        ↵
dynamic_cast<IDesignerHost*>(GetService(__typeof(IDesignerHost))));
         creatorAdded = false;
      }
   }

   // ToolboxItemCreatorCallback delegate format method to create
   // the toolbox item.
   ToolboxItem* CreateTextBoxForText(Object* serializedObject,            ↵
String* format) {
      String* formats[] =                                                  ↵
 (dynamic_cast<System::Windows::Forms::DataObject*>                        ↵
 (serializedObject))->GetFormats();
      if ((dynamic_cast<System::Windows::Forms::DataObject*>               ↵
 (serializedObject))->GetDataPresent(S"System::String", true))
         return new TextToolboxItem(dynamic_cast<String*>                  ↵
 ((dynamic_cast<System::Windows::Forms::DataObject*>                       ↵
 (serializedObject))->GetData(S"System::String", true)));
      return 0;
   }

protected:
   void Dispose(bool disposing) {
      if (creatorAdded)
         RemoveTextTextBoxCreator();
   }
};

}
```

Requirements

Namespace: System.Drawing.Design

Platforms: Windows 98, Windows NT 4.0, Windows Millennium Edition, Windows 2000, Windows XP Home Edition, Windows XP Professional, Windows Server 2003 family

Assembly: System.Drawing (in System.Drawing.dll)

UITypeEditor Class

Provides a base class that can be used to design value editors that can provide a user interface for representing and editing the values of objects of the supported data type(s).

System.Object
  System.Drawing.Design.UITypeEditor
    Derived classes

[Visual Basic]
```
Public Class UITypeEditor
```
[C#]
```
public class UITypeEditor
```
[C++]
```
public __gc class UITypeEditor
```
[JScript]
```
public class UITypeEditor
```

Thread Safety

Any public static (**Shared** in Visual Basic) members of this type are safe for multithreaded operations. Any instance members are not guaranteed to be thread safe.

Remarks

UITypeEditor provides a base class that you can derive from and extend to implement a custom type editor for the design-time environment. Custom type editors are useful in situations where a text-box value editor is insufficient to effectively select the values of certain types.

To implement a custom design-time UI type editor, you must at least:

- Define a class that derives from **System.Drawing.Design.UITypeEditor**.
- Override the **EditValue** method to handle the user interface, user input processing, and value assignment.
- Override the **GetEditStyle** method to inform the Properties window of the type of editor style that the editor will use.

You can add additional support for painting a value's representation in the Properties window by implementing the following:

- Override **GetPaintValueSupported** to indicate that the editor supports displaying the value's representation.
- Override **PaintValue** to implement the display of the value's representation.
- Override the **UITypeEditor** constructor method if the editor should have initialization behavior.

Example

[Visual Basic, C#, C++] The following example **UITypeEditor** can be associated with an integer, double, or float property using an **EditorAttribute** to provide an angle selection interface from the properties window in design mode. This example uses the **System.Windows.Forms.Design.IWindowsFormsEditorService** interface to display a drop-down control in the properties window in design mode. Compile the code and add the assembly to the toolbox using the **Customize Toolbox** command on the **Tools** menu of Visual Studio .NET. Create an instance of the `AngleTestControl` and click the drop-down button next to the Angle property in the properties window to configure the property using the editor.

[Visual Basic]
```
Option Strict Off
Imports System
Imports System.ComponentModel
Imports System.Drawing
Imports System.Drawing.Design
Imports System.Reflection
Imports System.Windows.Forms
Imports System.Windows.Forms.Design

' This UITypeEditor can be associated with Int32, Double and Single
' properties to provide a design-mode angle selection interface.
Public Class AngleEditor
   Inherits System.Drawing.Design.UITypeEditor

   Public Sub New()
    End Sub

    ' Indicates whether the UITypeEditor provides a form-based (modal) dialog,
    ' drop down dialog, or no UI outside of the properties window.
    <System.Security.Permissions.PermissionSetAttribute(System.Security.Permissions.SecurityAction.Demand, Name:="FullTrust")> _
    Public Overloads Overrides Function GetEditStyle(ByVal context As System.ComponentModel.ITypeDescriptorContext) As System.Drawing.Design.UITypeEditorEditStyle
        Return UITypeEditorEditStyle.DropDown
    End Function

    ' Displays the UI for value selection.
    <System.Security.Permissions.PermissionSetAttribute(System.Security.Permissions.SecurityAction.Demand, Name:="FullTrust")> _
    Public Overloads Overrides Function EditValue(ByVal context As System.ComponentModel.ITypeDescriptorContext, ByVal provider As System.IServiceProvider, ByVal value As Object) As Object
        ' Return the value if the value is not of type Int32, Double and Single.
        If Not value.GetType() Is GetType(Double) Or value.GetType() Is GetType(Single) Or value.GetType() Is GetType(Integer) Then
            Return value
        End If
        ' Uses the IWindowsFormsEditorService to display a
        ' drop-down UI in the Properties window.
        Dim edSvc As IWindowsFormsEditorService = CType(provider.GetService(GetType(IWindowsFormsEditorService)), IWindowsFormsEditorService)
        If Not (edSvc Is Nothing) Then
            ' Display an angle selection control and retrieve the value.
            Dim angleControl As New AngleControl(System.Convert.ToDouble(value))
            edSvc.DropDownControl(angleControl)

            ' Return the value in the appropraite data format.
            If value Is GetType(Double) Then
                Return angleControl.angle
            ElseIf value Is GetType(Single) Then
                Return System.Convert.ToSingle(angleControl.angle)
            ElseIf value Is GetType(Integer) Then
                Return System.Convert.ToInt32(angleControl.angle)
            End If
        End If
        Return value
    End Function

    ' Draws a representation of the property's value.
    <System.Security.Permissions.PermissionSetAttribute(System.Security.Permissions.SecurityAction.Demand, Name:="FullTrust")> _
    Public Overloads Overrides Sub PaintValue(ByVal e As System.Drawing.Design.PaintValueEventArgs)
        Dim normalX As Integer = e.Bounds.Width / 2
        Dim normalY As Integer = e.Bounds.Height / 2
```

```
        ' Fill background and ellipse and center point.
        e.Graphics.FillRectangle(New SolidBrush(Color.DarkBlue), ↵
e.Bounds.X, e.Bounds.Y, e.Bounds.Width, e.Bounds.Height)
        e.Graphics.FillEllipse(New SolidBrush(Color.White), ↵
 e.Bounds.X + 1, e.Bounds.Y + 1, e.Bounds.Width - 3, ↵
 e.Bounds.Height - 3)
        e.Graphics.FillEllipse(New SolidBrush(Color.SlateGray), ↵
 normalX + e.Bounds.X - 1, normalY + e.Bounds.Y - 1, 3, 3)

        ' Draw line along the current angle.
        Dim radians As Double = System.Convert.ToDouble(e.Value) ↵
 * Math.PI / System.Convert.ToDouble(180)
        e.Graphics.DrawLine(New Pen(New SolidBrush ↵
 (Color.Red), 1), normalX + e.Bounds.X, normalY + e.Bounds.Y, ↵
e.Bounds.X + (normalX + ↵
System.Convert.ToInt32(System.Convert.ToDouble(normalX) * ↵
Math.Cos(radians))), e.Bounds.Y + (normalY + ↵
System.Convert.ToInt32(System.Convert.ToDouble(normalY) * ↵
Math.Sin(radians))))
    End Sub

    ' Indicates whether the UITypeEditor supports painting a
    ' representation of a property's value.
    <System.Security.Permissions.PermissionSetAttribute ↵
 (System.Security.Permissions.SecurityAction.Demand, ↵
Name:="FullTrust")> _
    Public Overloads Overrides Function ↵
GetPaintValueSupported(ByVal context As ↵
System.ComponentModel.ITypeDescriptorContext) As Boolean
        Return True
    End Function
End Class

' Provides a user interface for adjusting an angle value.
Friend Class AngleControl
    Inherits System.Windows.Forms.UserControl

    ' Stores the angle.
    Public angle As Double
    ' Stores the rotation offset.
    Private rotation As Integer = 0
    ' Control state tracking variables.
    Private dbx As Integer = -10
    Private dby As Integer = -10
    Private overButton As Integer = -1

    Public Sub New(ByVal initial_angle As Double)
        Me.angle = initial_angle
        Me.SetStyle(ControlStyles.DoubleBuffer Or ↵
ControlStyles.AllPaintingInWmPaint, True)
    End Sub

    Protected Overrides Sub OnPaint(ByVal e As ↵
System.Windows.Forms.PaintEventArgs)
        ' Set angle origin point at center of control.
        Dim originX As Integer = Me.Width / 2
        Dim originY As Integer = Me.Height / 2

        ' Fill background and ellipse and center point.
        e.Graphics.FillRectangle(New SolidBrush ↵
 (Color.DarkBlue), 0, 0, Me.Width, Me.Height)
        e.Graphics.FillEllipse(New SolidBrush(Color.White), ↵
 1, 1, Me.Width - 3, Me.Height - 3)
        e.Graphics.FillEllipse(New SolidBrush(Color.SlateGray), ↵
originX - 1, originY - 1, 3, 3)

        ' Draw angle markers.
        Dim startangle As Integer = (270 - rotation) Mod 360
        e.Graphics.DrawString(startangle.ToString(), New Font ↵
 ("Arial", 8), New SolidBrush(Color.DarkGray), Me.Width / 2 - 10, 10)
        startangle = (startangle + 90) Mod 360
        e.Graphics.DrawString(startangle.ToString(), New Font ↵
 ("Arial", 8), New SolidBrush(Color.DarkGray), Me.Width - 18, ↵
 Me.Height / 2 - 6)
        startangle = (startangle + 90) Mod 360
        e.Graphics.DrawString(startangle.ToString(), New Font ↵
 ("Arial", 8), New SolidBrush(Color.DarkGray), Me.Width / 2 - 6, ↵
Me.Height - 18)
        startangle = (startangle + 90) Mod 360
        e.Graphics.DrawString(startangle.ToString(), New Font ↵
 ("Arial", 8), New SolidBrush(Color.DarkGray), 10, Me.Height / 2 - 6)

        ' Draw line along the current angle.
        Dim radians As Double = ((angle + rotation + 360) ↵
Mod 360) * Math.PI / System.Convert.ToDouble(180)
        e.Graphics.DrawLine(New Pen(New SolidBrush(Color.Red), ↵
 1), originX, originY, originX + ↵
System.Convert.ToInt32(System.Convert.ToDouble(originX) * ↵
Math.Cos(radians)), originY + ↵
System.Convert.ToInt32(System.Convert.ToDouble(originY) * ↵
Math.Sin(radians)))

        ' Output angle information.
        e.Graphics.FillRectangle(New SolidBrush(Color.Gray), ↵
 Me.Width - 84, 3, 82, 13)
        e.Graphics.DrawString("Angle: " + angle.ToString ↵
 ("F4"), New Font("Arial", 8), New SolidBrush(Color.Yellow), ↵
 Me.Width - 84, 2)
        ' Draw square at mouse position of last angle adjustment.
        e.Graphics.DrawRectangle(New Pen(New SolidBrush ↵
 (Color.Black), 1), dbx - 2, dby - 2, 4, 4)
        ' Draw rotation adjustment buttons.
        If overButton = 1 Then
            e.Graphics.FillRectangle(New SolidBrush ↵
 (Color.Green), Me.Width - 28, Me.Height - 14, 12, 12)
            e.Graphics.FillRectangle(New SolidBrush ↵
 (Color.Gray), 2, Me.Height - 13, 110, 12)
            e.Graphics.DrawString("Rotate 90 degrees left", ↵
 New Font("Arial", 8), New SolidBrush(Color.White), 2, Me.Height - 14)
        Else
            e.Graphics.FillRectangle(New SolidBrush ↵
 (Color.DarkGreen), Me.Width - 28, Me.Height - 14, 12, 12)
        End If
        If overButton = 2 Then
            e.Graphics.FillRectangle(New SolidBrush ↵
 (Color.Green), Me.Width - 14, Me.Height - 14, 12, 12)
            e.Graphics.FillRectangle(New SolidBrush ↵
 (Color.Gray), 2, Me.Height - 13, 116, 12)
            e.Graphics.DrawString("Rotate 90 degrees right", ↵
 New Font("Arial", 8), New SolidBrush(Color.White), 2, Me.Height - 14)
        Else
            e.Graphics.FillRectangle(New SolidBrush ↵
 (Color.DarkGreen), Me.Width - 14, Me.Height - 14, 12, 12)
        End If
        e.Graphics.DrawEllipse(New Pen(New SolidBrush ↵
 (Color.White), 1), Me.Width - 11, Me.Height - 11, 6, 6)
        e.Graphics.DrawEllipse(New Pen(New SolidBrush ↵
 (Color.White), 1), Me.Width - 25, Me.Height - 11, 6, 6)
        If overButton = 1 Then
            e.Graphics.FillRectangle(New SolidBrush ↵
 (Color.Green), Me.Width - 25, Me.Height - 6, 4, 4)
        Else
            e.Graphics.FillRectangle(New SolidBrush ↵
 (Color.DarkGreen), Me.Width - 25, Me.Height - 6, 4, 4)
        End If
        If overButton = 2 Then
            e.Graphics.FillRectangle(New SolidBrush ↵
 (Color.Green), Me.Width - 8, Me.Height - 6, 4, 4)
        Else
            e.Graphics.FillRectangle(New SolidBrush ↵
 (Color.DarkGreen), Me.Width - 8, Me.Height - 6, 4, 4)
        End If
        e.Graphics.FillPolygon(New SolidBrush(Color.White), ↵
 New Point() {New Point(Me.Width - 7, Me.Height - 8), New ↵
Point(Me.Width - 3, Me.Height - 8), New Point(Me.Width - 5, ↵
 Me.Height - 4)})
        e.Graphics.FillPolygon(New SolidBrush(Color.White), ↵
 New Point() {New Point(Me.Width - 26, Me.Height - 8), New ↵
Point(Me.Width - 21, Me.Height - 8), New Point(Me.Width - 25, ↵
 Me.Height - 4)})
    End Sub

    Protected Overrides Sub OnMouseDown(ByVal e As ↵
System.Windows.Forms.MouseEventArgs)
        ' Handle rotation adjustment button clicks.
        If e.X >= Me.Width - 28 AndAlso e.X <= Me.Width - ↵
2 AndAlso e.Y >= Me.Height - 14 AndAlso e.Y <= Me.Height - 2 Then
```

```
            If e.X <= Me.Width - 16 Then
                rotation -= 90
            ElseIf e.X >= Me.Width - 14 Then
                rotation += 90
            End If
            If rotation < 0 Then
                rotation += 360
            End If
            rotation = rotation Mod 360
            dbx = -10
            dby = -10
        Else
            UpdateAngle(e.X, e.Y)
        End If
        Me.Refresh()
    End Sub

    Protected Overrides Sub OnMouseMove(ByVal e As ↵
System.Windows.Forms.MouseEventArgs)
        If e.Button = MouseButtons.Left Then
            UpdateAngle(e.X, e.Y)
            overButton = -1
        ElseIf e.X >= Me.Width - 28 AndAlso e.X <= Me.Width ↵
- 16 AndAlso e.Y >= Me.Height - 14 AndAlso e.Y <= Me.Height - 2 Then
            overButton = 1
        ElseIf e.X >= Me.Width - 14 AndAlso e.X <= Me.Width - 2 ↵
 AndAlso e.Y >= Me.Height - 14 AndAlso e.Y <= Me.Height - 2 Then
            overButton = 2
        Else
            overButton = -1
        End If
        Me.Refresh()
    End Sub

    Private Sub UpdateAngle(ByVal mx As Integer, ByVal my As Integer)
        ' Store mouse coordinates.
        dbx = mx
        dby = my

        ' Translate y coordinate input to GetAngle function ↵
to correct for ellipsoid distortion.
        Dim widthToHeightRatio As Double = ↵
System.Convert.ToDouble(Me.Width) / System.Convert.ToDouble(Me.Height)
        Dim tmy As Integer
        If my = 0 Then
            tmy = my
        ElseIf my < Me.Height / 2 Then
            tmy = Me.Height / 2 - Fix((Me.Height / 2 - my) * ↵
widthToHeightRatio)
        Else
            tmy = Me.Height / 2 + Fix(System.Convert.ToDouble ↵
 (my - Me.Height / 2) * widthToHeightRatio)
        End If
        ' Retrieve updated angle based on rise over run.
        angle = (GetAngle(Me.Width / 2, Me.Height / 2, mx, tmy) ↵
 - rotation) Mod 360
    End Sub

    Private Function GetAngle(ByVal x1 As Integer, ByVal y1 As ↵
 Integer, ByVal x2 As Integer, ByVal y2 As Integer) As Double
        Dim degrees As Double

        ' Avoid divide by zero run values.
        If x2 - x1 = 0 Then
            If y2 > y1 Then
                degrees = 90
            Else
                degrees = 270
            End If
        Else
            ' Calculate angle from offset.
            Dim riseoverrun As Double = ↵
 System.Convert.ToDouble(y2 - y1) / System.Convert.ToDouble(x2 - x1)
            Dim radians As Double = Math.Atan(riseoverrun)
            degrees = radians * (System.Convert.ToDouble(180) / ↵
 Math.PI)
            ' Handle quadrant specific transformations.
            If x2 - x1 < 0 OrElse y2 - y1 < 0 Then
                degrees += 180
            End If
            If x2 - x1 > 0 AndAlso y2 - y1 < 0 Then
                degrees -= 180
            End If
            If degrees < 0 Then
                degrees += 360
            End If
        End If
        Return degrees
    End Function
End Class

Public Class AngleEditorTestControl
    Inherits System.Windows.Forms.UserControl
    Private int_angle As Double

    <BrowsableAttribute(True), EditorAttribute ↵
 (GetType(AngleEditor), GetType(System.Drawing.Design.UITypeEditor))> _
    Public Property Angle() As Double
        Get
            Return int_angle
        End Get
        Set(ByVal Value As Double)
            int_angle = Value
        End Set
    End Property

    Public Sub New()
        int_angle = 90
        Me.Size = New Size(190, 42)
        Me.BackColor = Color.Beige
    End Sub

    Protected Overrides Sub OnPaint(ByVal e As ↵
System.Windows.Forms.PaintEventArgs)
        If Me.DesignMode Then
            e.Graphics.DrawString("Use the Properties ↵
Window to access", New Font("Arial", 8), New ↵
SolidBrush(Color.Black), 3, 2)
            e.Graphics.DrawString("the AngleEditor ↵
UITypeEditor by", New Font("Arial", 8), New SolidBrush ↵
 (Color.Black), 3, 14)
            e.Graphics.DrawString("configuring the ""Angle"" ↵
property.", New Font("Arial", 8), New SolidBrush(Color.Black), 3, 26)
        Else
            e.Graphics.DrawString("This example requires design ↵
 mode.", New Font("Arial", 8), New SolidBrush(Color.Black), 3, 2)
        End If
    End Sub
End Class
```

[C#]

```
using System;
using System.ComponentModel;
using System.Drawing;
using System.Drawing.Design;
using System.Windows.Forms;
using System.Windows.Forms.Design;

namespace AngleEditor
{
    // This UITypeEditor can be associated with Int32, Double ↵
 and Single
    // properties to provide a design-mode angle selection interface.
    public class AngleEditor : System.Drawing.Design.UITypeEditor
    {
        public AngleEditor()
        {
        }

        // Indicates whether the UITypeEditor provides a ↵
form-based (modal) dialog,
        // drop down dialog, or no UI outside of the properties window.
        [System.Security.Permissions.PermissionSet ↵
 (System.Security.Permissions.SecurityAction.Demand, Name="FullTrust")]
```

```
        public override System.Drawing.Design.UITypeEditorEditStyle
GetEditStyle(System.ComponentModel.ITypeDescriptorContext context)
        {
            return UITypeEditorEditStyle.DropDown;
        }

        // Displays the UI for value selection.
        [System.Security.Permissions.PermissionSet                    ↵
 (System.Security.Permissions.SecurityAction.Demand, Name="FullTrust")]
        public override object
EditValue(System.ComponentModel.ITypeDescriptorContext context,       ↵
System.IServiceProvider provider, object value)
        {
            // Return the value if the value is not of type            ↵
Int32, Double and Single.
            if( value.GetType() != typeof(double) &&                   ↵
value.GetType() != typeof(float) && value.GetType() != typeof(int) )
                return value;

            // Uses the IWindowsFormsEditorService to display a
            // drop-down UI in the Properties window.
            IWindowsFormsEditorService edSvc =                         ↵
 (IWindowsFormsEditorService)provider.GetService                       ↵
 (typeof(IWindowsFormsEditorService));
            if( edSvc != null )
            {
                // Display an angle selection control and              ↵
retrieve the value.
                AngleControl angleControl = new                        ↵
AngleControl((double)value);
                edSvc.DropDownControl( angleControl );

                // Return the value in the appropraite data format.
                if( value.GetType() == typeof(double) )
                    return angleControl.angle;
                else if( value.GetType() == typeof(float) )
                    return (float)angleControl.angle;
                else if( value.GetType() == typeof(int) )
                    return (int)angleControl.angle;
            }
            return value;
        }

        // Draws a representation of the property's value.
        [System.Security.Permissions.PermissionSet                    ↵
 (System.Security.Permissions.SecurityAction.Demand, Name="FullTrust")]
        public override void                                           ↵
PaintValue(System.Drawing.Design.PaintValueEventArgs e)
        {
            int normalX = (e.Bounds.Width/2);
            int normalY = (e.Bounds.Height/2);

            // Fill background and ellipse and center point.
            e.Graphics.FillRectangle(new SolidBrush                    ↵
 (Color.DarkBlue), e.Bounds.X, e.Bounds.Y, e.Bounds.Width,             ↵
e.Bounds.Height);
            e.Graphics.FillEllipse(new SolidBrush(Color.White),        ↵
e.Bounds.X+1, e.Bounds.Y+1, e.Bounds.Width-3, e.Bounds.Height-3);
            e.Graphics.FillEllipse(new SolidBrush                      ↵
 (Color.SlateGray), normalX+e.Bounds.X-1, normalY+e.Bounds.Y-1, 3, 3);

            // Draw line along the current angle.
            double radians = ((double)e.Value*Math.PI) / (double)180;
            e.Graphics.DrawLine( new Pen(new SolidBrush                ↵
 (Color.Red), 1), normalX+e.Bounds.X, normalY+e.Bounds.Y,
                e.Bounds.X+ ( normalX + (int)( (double)                ↵
normalX * Math.Cos( radians ) ) ),
                e.Bounds.Y+ ( normalY + (int)( (double)                ↵
normalY * Math.Sin( radians ) ) ) );
        }

        // Indicates whether the UITypeEditor supports painting a
        // representation of a property's value.
        [System.Security.Permissions.PermissionSet                    ↵
 (System.Security.Permissions.SecurityAction.Demand, Name="FullTrust")]
        public override bool GetPaintValueSupported                    ↵
(System.ComponentModel.ITypeDescriptorContext context)
        {
            return true;
        }
    }

    // Provides a user interface for adjusting an angle value.
    internal class AngleControl : System.Windows.Forms.UserControl
    {
        // Stores the angle.
        public double angle;
        // Stores the rotation offset.
        private int rotation = 0;
        // Control state tracking variables.
        private int dbx = -10;
        private int dby = -10;
        private int overButton = -1;

        public AngleControl(double initial_angle)
        {
            this.angle = initial_angle;
            this.SetStyle( ControlStyles.DoubleBuffer |                ↵
ControlStyles.AllPaintingInWmPaint, true );
        }

        protected override void                                        ↵
OnPaint(System.Windows.Forms.PaintEventArgs e)
        {
            // Set angle origin point at center of control.
            int originX = (this.Width/2);
            int originY = (this.Height/2);

            // Fill background and ellipse and center point.
            e.Graphics.FillRectangle(new SolidBrush                    ↵
 (Color.DarkBlue), 0, 0, this.Width, this.Height);
            e.Graphics.FillEllipse(new SolidBrush                      ↵
 (Color.White), 1, 1, this.Width-3, this.Height-3);
            e.Graphics.FillEllipse(new SolidBrush                      ↵
 (Color.SlateGray), originX-1, originY-1, 3, 3);

            // Draw angle markers.
            int startangle = (270-rotation)%360;
            e.Graphics.DrawString(startangle.ToString(), new           ↵
Font("Arial", 8), new SolidBrush(Color.DarkGray),                      ↵
 (this.Width/2)-10, 10);
            startangle = (startangle+90)%360;
            e.Graphics.DrawString(startangle.ToString(), new           ↵
Font("Arial", 8), new SolidBrush(Color.DarkGray),                      ↵
this.Width-18, (this.Height/2)-6);
            startangle = (startangle+90)%360;
            e.Graphics.DrawString(startangle.ToString(), new           ↵
Font("Arial", 8), new SolidBrush(Color.DarkGray),                      ↵
 (this.Width/2)-6, this.Height-18);
            startangle = (startangle+90)%360;
            e.Graphics.DrawString(startangle.ToString(), new           ↵
Font("Arial", 8), new SolidBrush(Color.DarkGray), 10,                  ↵
 (this.Height/2)-6);

            // Draw line along the current angle.
            double radians = ((((angle+rotation)+360)                  ↵
%360)*Math.PI) / (double)180;
            e.Graphics.DrawLine( new Pen(new SolidBrush                ↵
 (Color.Red), 1), originX, originY,
                originX + (int)( (double)originX *                     ↵
 (double)Math.Cos( radians )   ),
                originY + (int)( (double)originY *                     ↵
 (double)Math.Sin( radians ) ) );

            // Output angle information.
            e.Graphics.FillRectangle(new SolidBrush                    ↵
 (Color.Gray), this.Width-84, 3, 82, 13);
            e.Graphics.DrawString("Angle:                              ↵
"+angle.ToString("F4"), new Font("Arial", 8), new                      ↵
SolidBrush(Color.Yellow), this.Width-84, 2);
            // Draw square at mouse position of last angle adjustment.
            e.Graphics.DrawRectangle(new Pen(new                       ↵
SolidBrush(Color.Black), 1), dbx-2, dby-2, 4, 4);
            // Draw rotation adjustment buttons.
            if( overButton == 1 )
            {
```

```
            e.Graphics.FillRectangle(new ↵
SolidBrush(Color.Green), this.Width-28, this.Height-14, 12, 12);
            e.Graphics.FillRectangle(new SolidBrush ↵
(Color.Gray), 2, this.Height-13, 110, 12);
            e.Graphics.DrawString("Rotate 90 degrees left", ↵
new Font("Arial", 8), new SolidBrush(Color.White), 2, this.Height-14);
        }
        else
            e.Graphics.FillRectangle(new ↵
SolidBrush(Color.DarkGreen), this.Width-28, this.Height-14, 12, 12);
        if( overButton == 2 )
        {
            e.Graphics.FillRectangle(new ↵
SolidBrush(Color.Green), this.Width-14, this.Height-14, 12, 12);
            e.Graphics.FillRectangle(new ↵
SolidBrush(Color.Gray), 2, this.Height-13, 116, 12);
            e.Graphics.DrawString("Rotate 90 ↵
degrees right", new Font("Arial", 8), new SolidBrush ↵
(Color.White), 2, this.Height-14);
        }
        else
            e.Graphics.FillRectangle(new ↵
SolidBrush(Color.DarkGreen), this.Width-14, this.Height-14, 12, 12);
        e.Graphics.DrawEllipse(new Pen(new SolidBrush ↵
(Color.White), 1), this.Width-11, this.Height-11, 6, 6);
        e.Graphics.DrawEllipse(new Pen(new SolidBrush ↵
(Color.White), 1), this.Width-25, this.Height-11, 6, 6);
        if( overButton == 1 )
            e.Graphics.FillRectangle(new SolidBrush ↵
(Color.Green), this.Width-25, this.Height-6, 4, 4);
        else
            e.Graphics.FillRectangle(new ↵
SolidBrush(Color.DarkGreen), this.Width-25, this.Height-6, 4, 4);
        if( overButton == 2 )
            e.Graphics.FillRectangle(new SolidBrush ↵
(Color.Green), this.Width-8, this.Height-6, 4, 4);
        else
            e.Graphics.FillRectangle(new ↵
SolidBrush(Color.DarkGreen), this.Width-8, this.Height-6, 4, 4);
        e.Graphics.FillPolygon(new SolidBrush(Color.White), ↵
new Point[] { new Point(this.Width-7, this.Height-8), new ↵
Point(this.Width-3, this.Height-8), new Point(this.Width-5, ↵
this.Height-4) });
        e.Graphics.FillPolygon(new SolidBrush(Color.White), ↵
new Point[] { new Point(this.Width-26, this.Height-8), new ↵
Point(this.Width-21, this.Height-8), new Point(this.Width-25, ↵
this.Height-4) });
    }

    protected override void
OnMouseDown(System.Windows.Forms.MouseEventArgs e)
    {
        // Handle rotation adjustment button clicks.
        if( e.X >= this.Width-28 && e.X <= this.Width-2 ↵
&& e.Y >= this.Height-14 && e.Y <= this.Height-2 )
        {
            if( e.X <= this.Width-16 )
                rotation -= 90;
            else if( e.X >= this.Width-14 )
                rotation += 90;
            if( rotation < 0 )
                rotation += 360;
            rotation = rotation%360;
            dbx=-10;
            dby=-10;
        }
        else
            UpdateAngle(e.X, e.Y);
        this.Refresh();
    }

    protected override void
OnMouseMove(System.Windows.Forms.MouseEventArgs e)
    {
        if( e.Button == MouseButtons.Left )
        {
            UpdateAngle(e.X, e.Y);
            overButton = -1;
        }
        else if( e.X >= this.Width-28 && e.X <= ↵
this.Width-16 && e.Y >= this.Height-14 && e.Y <= this.Height-2 )
            overButton = 1;
        else if( e.X >= this.Width-14 && e.X <= ↵
this.Width-2 && e.Y >= this.Height-14 && e.Y <= this.Height-2 )
            overButton = 2;
        else
            overButton = -1;
        this.Refresh();
    }

    private void UpdateAngle(int mx, int my)
    {
        // Store mouse coordinates.
        dbx = mx;
        dby = my;

        // Translate y coordinate input to GetAngle ↵
function to correct for ellipsoid distortion.
        double widthToHeightRatio = ↵
(double)this.Width/(double)this.Height;
        int tmy;
        if( my == 0 )
            tmy = my;
        else if( my < this.Height/2 )
            tmy = (this.Height/2)-(int)(((this.Height/2)- ↵
my)*widthToHeightRatio);
        else
            tmy = (this.Height/2)+(int)((double)(my- ↵
(this.Height/2))*widthToHeightRatio);

        // Retrieve updated angle based on rise over run.
        angle = (GetAngle(this.Width/2, this.Height/2, ↵
mx, tmy)-rotation)%360;
    }

    private double GetAngle(int x1, int y1, int x2, int y2)
    {
        double degrees;

        // Avoid divide by zero run values.
        if( x2-x1 == 0 )
        {
            if( y2 > y1 )
                degrees = 90;
            else
                degrees = 270;
        }
        else
        {
            // Calculate angle from offset.
            double riseoverrun = (double)(y2-y1)/(double)(x2-x1);
            double radians = Math.Atan( riseoverrun );
            degrees = radians * ((double)180/Math.PI);

            // Handle quadrant specific transformations.
            if( (x2-x1) < 0 || (y2-y1) < 0 )
                degrees += 180;
            if( (x2-x1) > 0 && (y2-y1) < 0 )
                degrees -= 180;
            if( degrees < 0 )
                degrees += 360;
        }
        return degrees;
    }
}

public class AngleEditorTestControl : ↵
System.Windows.Forms.UserControl
{
    private double int_angle;

    [BrowsableAttribute(true)]
    [EditorAttribute(typeof(AngleEditor), ↵
typeof(System.Drawing.Design.UITypeEditor))]
    public double Angle
    {
        get
```

```
            { return int_angle; }
            set
            { int_angle = value; }
        }

        public AngleEditorTestControl()
        {
            int_angle = 90;
            this.Size = new Size(190, 42);
            this.BackColor = Color.Beige;
        }

        protected override void
OnPaint(System.Windows.Forms.PaintEventArgs e)
        {
            if( this.DesignMode )
            {
                e.Graphics.DrawString("Use the Properties
Window to access", new Font("Arial", 8), new SolidBrush
 (Color.Black), 3,2);
                e.Graphics.DrawString("the AngleEditor
UITypeEditor by", new Font("Arial", 8), new SolidBrush
 (Color.Black), 3,14);
                e.Graphics.DrawString("configuring the \"Angle\"
property.", new Font("Arial", 8), new SolidBrush(Color.Black), 3,26);
            }
            else
                e.Graphics.DrawString("This example requires
 design mode.", new Font("Arial", 8), new SolidBrush
 (Color.Black), 3,2);
        }
    }
}
```

[C++]

```
#using <mscorlib.dll>
#using <System.Windows.Forms.dll>
#using <System.Drawing.dll>
#using <System.dll>

using namespace System;
using namespace System::ComponentModel;
using namespace System::Drawing;
using namespace System::Drawing::Design;
using namespace System::Windows::Forms;
using namespace System::Windows::Forms::Design;

namespace AngleEditor {
   // Provides a user interface for adjusting an angle value.
   __gc class AngleControl :
 public System::Windows::Forms::UserControl {
      // Stores the angle.
   public:
      double  angle;
      // Stores the rotation offset.
   private:
      int  rotation;
      // Control state tracking variables.
      int  dbx;
      int  dby;
      int  overButton;

   public:
      AngleControl(double initial_angle) {
         this->angle = initial_angle;
         this->SetStyle(static_cast<ControlStyles>
 (ControlStyles::DoubleBuffer |
ControlStyles::AllPaintingInWmPaint), true);
         rotation = 0;
         dbx = -10;
         dby = -10;
         overButton = -1;
      }

   protected:
      void OnPaint(System::Windows::Forms::PaintEventArgs* e) {
         // Set angle origin point at center of control.
         int originX = (this->Width/2);
         int originY = (this->Height/2);

         // Fill background and ellipse and center point.
         e->Graphics->FillRectangle
 (new SolidBrush(Color::DarkBlue), 0, 0, this->Width, this->Height);
         e->Graphics->FillEllipse(new SolidBrush
 (Color::White), 1, 1, this->Width-3, this->Height-3);
         e->Graphics->FillEllipse(new SolidBrush
 (Color::SlateGray), originX-1, originY-1, 3, 3);

         // Draw angle markers.
         int startangle = (270-rotation)%360;
         e->Graphics->DrawString(startangle.ToString(), new
System::Drawing::Font(S"Arial", 8.0), new SolidBrush
 (Color::DarkGray), (float)(this->Width/2)-10, (float)10);
         startangle = (startangle+90)%360;
         e->Graphics->DrawString(startangle.ToString(), new
System::Drawing::Font(S"Arial", 8), new SolidBrush
 (Color::DarkGray), (float)this->Width-18, (float)(this->Height/2)-6);
         startangle = (startangle+90)%360;
         e->Graphics->DrawString(startangle.ToString(), new
System::Drawing::Font(S"Arial", 8), new SolidBrush
 (Color::DarkGray), ((float)this->Width/2)-6, (float)this->Height-18);
         startangle = (startangle+90)%360;
         e->Graphics->DrawString(startangle.ToString(), new
System::Drawing::Font(S"Arial", 8), new SolidBrush
 (Color::DarkGray), (float)10, (float)(this->Height/2)-6);

         // Draw line along the current angle.
         double radians = ((((int)(angle+rotation)+360)%360)
*Math::PI) / (double)180;
         e->Graphics->DrawLine(new Pen(new SolidBrush
 (Color::Red), 1), originX, originY,
            originX + (int)((double)originX *
 (double)Math::Cos(radians)),
            originY + (int)((double)originY *
 (double)Math::Sin(radians)));

         // Output angle information.
         e->Graphics->FillRectangle(new SolidBrush(Color::Gray),
 this->Width-84, 3, 82, 13);
         e->Graphics->DrawString(String::Format(S"Angle: {0}",
angle.ToString(S"F4")), new System::Drawing::Font(S"Arial", 8),
 new SolidBrush(Color::Yellow), (float)this->Width-84, (float)2);
         // Draw square at mouse position of last angle adjustment.
        e->Graphics->DrawRectangle(new Pen(new SolidBrush(Color::Black),
1), dbx-2, dby-2, 4, 4);
         // Draw rotation adjustment buttons.
         if (overButton == 1) {
            e->Graphics->FillRectangle(new SolidBrush
 (Color::Green), this->Width-28, this->Height-14, 12, 12);
            e->Graphics->FillRectangle(new SolidBrush
 (Color::Gray), 2, this->Height-13, 110, 12);
            e->Graphics->DrawString(S"Rotate 90 degrees left",
 new System::Drawing::Font(S"Arial", 8), new SolidBrush
 (Color::White), (float)2, (float)this->Height-14);
         } else
            e->Graphics->FillRectangle(new
SolidBrush(Color::DarkGreen), this->Width-28, this->Height-14, 12, 12);
         if (overButton == 2) {
            e->Graphics->FillRectangle(new SolidBrush
 (Color::Green), this->Width-14, this->Height-14, 12, 12);
            e->Graphics->FillRectangle(new SolidBrush
 (Color::Gray), 2, this->Height-13, 116, 12);
            e->Graphics->DrawString(S"Rotate 90 degrees
 right", new System::Drawing::Font(S"Arial", 8), new
SolidBrush(Color::White), (float)2, (float)this->Height-14);
         } else
            e->Graphics->FillRectangle(new
SolidBrush(Color::DarkGreen), this->Width-14, this->Height-14, 12, 12);
         e->Graphics->DrawEllipse(new Pen(new SolidBrush
 (Color::White), 1), this->Width-11, this->Height-11, 6, 6);
         e->Graphics->DrawEllipse(new Pen(new SolidBrush
 (Color::White), 1), this->Width-25, this->Height-11, 6, 6);
         if (overButton == 1)
            e->Graphics->FillRectangle(new SolidBrush
 (Color::Green), this->Width-25, this->Height-6, 4, 4);
```

```
        else
           e->Graphics->FillRectangle(new                                    ↵
SolidBrush(Color::DarkGreen), this->Width-25, this->Height-6, 4, 4);
        if (overButton == 2)
           e->Graphics->FillRectangle(new SolidBrush                        ↵
 (Color::Green), this->Width-8, this->Height-6, 4, 4);
        else
           e->Graphics->FillRectangle(new                                    ↵
SolidBrush(Color::DarkGreen), this->Width-8, this->Height-6, 4, 4);

        Point temp0 [] = { Point(this->Width-7, this->                       ↵
Height-8),  Point(this->Width-3, this->Height-8),  Point                     ↵
 (this->Width-5, this->Height-4)};
        e->Graphics->FillPolygon(new SolidBrush(Color::White), temp0);

        Point temp1 [] = { Point(this->Width-26,                             ↵
this->Height-8),  Point(this->Width-21, this->Height-8),                     ↵
Point(this->Width-25, this->Height-4)};
        e->Graphics->FillPolygon(new SolidBrush(Color::White), temp1);
      }

      void OnMouseDown(System::Windows::Forms::MouseEventArgs* e) {
         // Handle rotation adjustment button clicks.
         if (e->X >= this->Width-28 && e->X <= this->Width-2                 ↵
&& e->Y >= this->Height-14 && e->Y <= this->Height-2) {
            if (e->X <= this->Width-16)
               rotation -= 90;
            else if (e->X >= this->Width-14)
               rotation += 90;
            if (rotation < 0)
               rotation += 360;
            rotation = rotation%360;
            dbx=-10;
            dby=-10;
         } else
            UpdateAngle(e->X, e->Y);
         this->Refresh();
      }

      void OnMouseMove(System::Windows::Forms::MouseEventArgs* e) {
         if (e->Button == MouseButtons::Left) {
            UpdateAngle(e->X, e->Y);
            overButton = -1;
         } else if (e->X >= this->Width-28 && e->X <= this->                 ↵
Width-16 && e->Y >= this->Height-14 && e->Y <= this->Height-2)
            overButton = 1;
         else if (e->X >= this->Width-14 && e->X <= this->                   ↵
Width-2 && e->Y >= this->Height-14 && e->Y <= this->Height-2)
            overButton = 2;
         else
            overButton = -1;
         this->Refresh();
      }

   private:
      void UpdateAngle(int mx, int my) {
         // Store mouse coordinates.
         dbx = mx;
         dby = my;

         // Translate y coordinate input to GetAngle                         ↵
 function to correct for ellipsoid distortion.
         double widthToHeightRatio =  (double)this->Width/                   ↵
  (double)this->Height;
         int tmy;
         if (my == 0)
            tmy = my;
         else if (my < this->Height/2)
            tmy = (this->Height/2)-(int)(((this->Height/2)-                  ↵
 my)*widthToHeightRatio);
         else
            tmy = (this->Height/2)+(int)((double)(my-(this-                  ↵
 >Height/2))*widthToHeightRatio);

         // Retrieve updated angle based on rise over run.
         angle = (int)(GetAngle(this->Width/2, this->Height/2,               ↵
  mx, tmy)-rotation)%360;
      }

      double GetAngle(int x1, int y1, int x2, int y2) {
         double degrees;

         // Avoid divide by zero run values.
         if (x2-x1 == 0) {
            if (y2 > y1)
               degrees = 90;
            else
               degrees = 270;
         } else {
            // Calculate angle from offset.
            double riseoverrun = (double)(y2-y1)/(double)(x2-x1);
            double radians = Math::Atan(riseoverrun);
            degrees = radians * ((double)180/Math::PI);

            // Handle quadrant specific transformations.
            if ((x2-x1) < 0 || (y2-y1) < 0)
               degrees += 180;
            if ((x2-x1) > 0 && (y2-y1) < 0)
               degrees -= 180;
            if (degrees < 0)
               degrees += 360;
         }
         return degrees;
      }
   };

   // This UITypeEditor can be associated with Int32, Double and Single
   // properties to provide a design-mode angle selection interface.
public __gc class AngleEditor : public
System::Drawing::Design::UITypeEditor {
public:
   AngleEditor() {
   }

   // Indicates whether the UITypeEditor provides a                          ↵
 form-based (modal) dialog,
   // drop down dialog, or no UI outside of the properties window.
   System::Drawing::Design::UITypeEditorEditStyle
GetEditStyle(System::ComponentModel::ITypeDescriptorContext* context) {
      return UITypeEditorEditStyle::DropDown;
   }

   // Displays the UI for value selection.
   Object* EditValue                                                          ↵
 (System::ComponentModel::ITypeDescriptorContext* context,                    ↵
System::IServiceProvider* provider, Object* value) {
      // Return the value if the value is not of type Int32,                  ↵
Double and Single.
      if (value->GetType() != __typeof(double) && value-                      ↵
>GetType()                                                                    ↵
 != __typeof(float) && value->GetType() != __typeof(int))
         return value;

      // Uses the IWindowsFormsEditorService* to display a
      // drop-down UI in the Properties window.
      IWindowsFormsEditorService* edSvc =                                     ↵
dynamic_cast<IWindowsFormsEditorService*>(provider-                           ↵
>GetService(__typeof(IWindowsFormsEditorService)));
      if (edSvc != 0) {
         // Display an angle selection control and retrieve the value.
         AngleControl* angleControl = new                                     ↵
AngleControl(*dynamic_cast<double __gc *>(value));
         edSvc->DropDownControl(angleControl);

         // Return the value in the appropraite data format.
         if (value->GetType() == __typeof(double))
            return __box(angleControl->angle);
         else if (value->GetType() == __typeof(float))
            return __box((float)angleControl->angle);
         else if (value->GetType() == __typeof(int))
            return __box((int)angleControl->angle);
      }
      return value;
   }

   // Draws a representation of the property's value.
   void PaintValue(System::Drawing::Design::PaintValueEventArgs* e) {
```

```
      int normalX = (e->Bounds.Width/2);
      int normalY = (e->Bounds.Height/2);

      // Fill background and ellipse and center point.
      e->Graphics->FillRectangle(new SolidBrush
 (Color::DarkBlue), e->Bounds.X, e->Bounds.Y, e->Bounds.Width, e-
>Bounds.Height);
      e->Graphics->FillEllipse(new SolidBrush(Color::White), e-
>Bounds.X+1, e->Bounds.Y+1, e->Bounds.Width-3, e->Bounds.Height-3);
      e->Graphics->FillEllipse(new SolidBrush(Color::SlateGray),
normalX+e->Bounds.X-1, normalY+e->Bounds.Y-1, 3, 3);

      // Draw line along the current angle.
      double radians = (*dynamic_cast<double __gc *>(e-
>Value)*Math::PI) / (double)180;
      e->Graphics->DrawLine(new Pen(new SolidBrush(Color::Red),
 1), normalX+e->Bounds.X, normalY+e->Bounds.Y,
         e->Bounds.X+ (normalX + (int)((double)normalX *
Math::Cos(radians))),
         e->Bounds.Y+ (normalY + (int)((double)normalY *
Math::Sin(radians))));
   }

   // Indicates whether the UITypeEditor supports painting a
   // representation of a property's value.
   bool GetPaintValueSupported
 (System::ComponentModel::ITypeDescriptorContext* context) {
      return true;
   }
};

public __gc class AngleEditorTestControl : public
System::Windows::Forms::UserControl {
private:
   double  int_angle;

public:
   [BrowsableAttribute(true)]
   [EditorAttribute(__typeof(AngleEditor),
__typeof(System::Drawing::Design::UITypeEditor))]
   __property double get_Angle() { return int_angle; }
   __property void set_Angle(double value) { int_angle = value; }

   AngleEditorTestControl() {
      int_angle = 90;
      this->Size =  System::Drawing::Size(190, 42);
      this->BackColor = Color::Beige;
   }

protected:
   void OnPaint(System::Windows::Forms::PaintEventArgs* e) {
      if (this->DesignMode) {
         e->Graphics->DrawString(S"Use the Properties Window
 to access", new System::Drawing::Font(S"Arial", 8), new
SolidBrush(Color::Black), 3, 2);
         e->Graphics->DrawString(S"the AngleEditor
 UITypeEditor by", new System::Drawing::Font(S"Arial", 8), new
SolidBrush(Color::Black), 3, 14);
         e->Graphics->DrawString(S"configuring the \"Angle\"
property.", new System::Drawing::Font(S"Arial", 8), new
SolidBrush(Color::Black), 3, 26);
      } else
         e->Graphics->DrawString(S"This example requires design
 mode.", new System::Drawing::Font(S"Arial", 8), new
SolidBrush(Color::Black), 3, 2);
   }
};
}
```

Requirements

Namespace: System.Drawing.Design

Platforms: Windows 98, Windows NT 4.0, Windows Millennium Edition, Windows 2000, Windows XP Home Edition, Windows XP Professional, Windows Server 2003 family

Assembly: System.Drawing (in System.Drawing.dll)

UITypeEditor Constructor

Initializes a new instance of the **UITypeEditor** class.

[Visual Basic]
```
Public Sub New()
```
[C#]
```
public UITypeEditor();
```
[C++]
```
public: UITypeEditor();
```
[JScript]
```
public function UITypeEditor();
```

Requirements

Platforms: Windows 98, Windows NT 4.0, Windows Millennium Edition, Windows 2000, Windows XP Home Edition, Windows XP Professional, Windows Server 2003 family

UITypeEditor.EditValue Method

Edits the value of the specified object using the editor style indicated by **GetEditStyle**.

Overload List

Edits the value of the specified object using the editor style indicated by **GetEditStyle**.

[Visual Basic] **Overloads Public Function EditValue(IServiceProvider, Object) As Object**

[C#] **public object EditValue(IServiceProvider, object);**

[C++] **public: Object* EditValue(IServiceProvider*, Object*);**

[JScript] **public function EditValue(IServiceProvider, Object) : Object;**

Edits the specified object's value using the editor style indicated by **GetEditStyle**.

[Visual Basic] **Overloads Public Overridable Function EditValue(ITypeDescriptorContext, IServiceProvider, Object) As Object**

[C#] **public virtual object EditValue(ITypeDescriptor-Context, IServiceProvider, object);**

[C++] **public: virtual Object* EditValue(IType-DescriptorContext*, IServiceProvider*, Object*);**

[JScript] **public function EditValue(ITypeDescriptorContext, IServiceProvider, Object) : Object;**

UITypeEditor.EditValue Method (IServiceProvider, Object)

Edits the value of the specified object using the editor style indicated by **GetEditStyle**.

[Visual Basic]
```
Overloads Public Function EditValue( _
   ByVal provider As IServiceProvider, _
   ByVal value As Object _
) As Object
```
[C#]
```
public object EditValue(
   IServiceProvider provider,
   object value
);
```

[C++]
```
public: Object* EditValue(
   IServiceProvider* provider,
   Object* value
);
```
[JScript]
```
public function EditValue(
   provider : IServiceProvider,
   value : Object
) : Object;
```

Parameters

provider
An **IServiceProvider** that this editor can use to obtain services.

value
The object to edit.

Return Value

The new value of the object.

Remarks

This method launches the user-interface for value editing, and is called by the Properties window when a user attempts to edit the value of a type that this editor is configured to edit the value of. A service provider is provided so that the editor can obtain any required services.

Requirements

Platforms: Windows 98, Windows NT 4.0, Windows Millennium Edition, Windows 2000, Windows XP Home Edition, Windows XP Professional, Windows Server 2003 family

UITypeEditor.EditValue Method (ITypeDescriptorContext, IServiceProvider, Object)

Edits the specified object's value using the editor style indicated by **GetEditStyle**.

[Visual Basic]
```
Overloads Public Overridable Function EditValue( _
   ByVal context As ITypeDescriptorContext, _
   ByVal provider As IServiceProvider, _
   ByVal value As Object _
) As Object
```
[C#]
```
public virtual object EditValue(
   ITypeDescriptorContext context,
   IServiceProvider provider,
   object value
);
```
[C++]
```
public: virtual Object* EditValue(
   ITypeDescriptorContext* context,
   IServiceProvider* provider,
   Object* value
);
```
[JScript]
```
public function EditValue(
   context : ITypeDescriptorContext,
   provider : IServiceProvider,
   value : Object
) : Object;
```

Parameters

context
An **ITypeDescriptorContext** that can be used to gain additional context information.

provider
An **IServiceProvider** that this editor can use to obtain services.

value
The object to edit.

Return Value

The new value of the object.

Remarks

A service provider is provided so that the editor can obtain any required services.

Requirements

Platforms: Windows 98, Windows NT 4.0, Windows Millennium Edition, Windows 2000, Windows XP Home Edition, Windows XP Professional, Windows Server 2003 family

UITypeEditor.GetEditStyle Method

Gets the editor style used by the **EditValue** method.

Overload List

Gets the editor style used by the **EditValue** method.

[Visual Basic] **Overloads Public Function GetEditStyle() As UITypeEditorEditStyle**

[C#] **public UITypeEditorEditStyle GetEditStyle();**

[C++] **public: UITypeEditorEditStyle GetEditStyle();**

[JScript] **public function GetEditStyle() : UITypeEditorEditStyle;**

Gets the editor style used by the **EditValue** method.

[Visual Basic] **Overloads Public Overridable Function GetEditStyle(ITypeDescriptorContext) As UITypeEditorEditStyle**

[C#] **public virtual UITypeEditorEditStyle GetEditStyle(ITypeDescriptorContext);**

[C++] **public: virtual UITypeEditorEditStyle GetEditStyle(ITypeDescriptorContext*);**

[JScript] **public function GetEditStyle(ITypeDescriptorContext) : UITypeEditorEditStyle;**

UITypeEditor.GetEditStyle Method ()

Gets the editor style used by the **EditValue** method.

[Visual Basic]
```
Overloads Public Function GetEditStyle() As UITypeEditorEditStyle
```
[C#]
```
public UITypeEditorEditStyle GetEditStyle();
```
[C++]
```
public: UITypeEditorEditStyle GetEditStyle();
```
[JScript]
```
public function GetEditStyle() : UITypeEditorEditStyle;
```

Return Value

A **UITypeEditorEditStyle** enumeration value that indicates the style of editor used by the current **UITypeEditor**. By default, this method will return **None**.

Remarks

If a **UITypeEditor** does not overrride and implement this method, **GetEditStyle** will return **None** by default.

Requirements

Platforms: Windows 98, Windows NT 4.0, Windows Millennium Edition, Windows 2000, Windows XP Home Edition, Windows XP Professional, Windows Server 2003 family

UITypeEditor.GetEditStyle Method (ITypeDescriptorContext)

Gets the editor style used by the **EditValue** method.

```
[Visual Basic]
Overloads Public Overridable Function GetEditStyle( _
   ByVal context As ITypeDescriptorContext _
) As UITypeEditorEditStyle
[C#]
public virtual UITypeEditorEditStyle GetEditStyle(
   ITypeDescriptorContext context
);
[C++]
public: virtual UITypeEditorEditStyle GetEditStyle(
   ITypeDescriptorContext* context
);
[JScript]
public function GetEditStyle(
   context : ITypeDescriptorContext
) : UITypeEditorEditStyle;
```

Parameters

context

An **ITypeDescriptorContext** that can be used to gain additional context information.

Return Value

A **UITypeEditorEditStyle** value that indicates the style of editor used by **EditValue**. If the **UITypeEditor** does not support this method, then **GetEditStyle** will return **None**.

Requirements

Platforms: Windows 98, Windows NT 4.0, Windows Millennium Edition, Windows 2000, Windows XP Home Edition, Windows XP Professional, Windows Server 2003 family

UITypeEditor.GetPaintValueSupported Method

Indicates whether this editor supports painting a representation of an object's value.

Overload List

Indicates whether this editor supports painting a representation of an object's value.

[Visual Basic] **Overloads Public Function GetPaintValueSupported() As Boolean**

[C#] **public bool GetPaintValueSupported();**

[C++] **public: bool GetPaintValueSupported();**

[JScript] **public function GetPaintValueSupported() : Boolean;**

Indicates whether the specified context supports painting a representation of an object's value within the specified context.

[Visual Basic] **Overloads Public Overridable Function GetPaintValueSupported(ITypeDescriptorContext) As Boolean**

[C#] **public virtual bool GetPaintValueSupported(ITypeDescriptorContext);**

[C++] **public: virtual bool GetPaintValueSupported(ITypeDescriptorContext*);**

[JScript] **public function GetPaintValueSupported(ITypeDescriptorContext) : Boolean;**

UITypeEditor.GetPaintValueSupported Method ()

Indicates whether this editor supports painting a representation of an object's value.

```
[Visual Basic]
Overloads Public Function GetPaintValueSupported() As Boolean
[C#]
public bool GetPaintValueSupported();
[C++]
public: bool GetPaintValueSupported();
[JScript]
public function GetPaintValueSupported() : Boolean;
```

Return Value

true if **PaintValue** is implemented; otherwise, **false**.

Requirements

Platforms: Windows 98, Windows NT 4.0, Windows Millennium Edition, Windows 2000, Windows XP Home Edition, Windows XP Professional, Windows Server 2003 family

UITypeEditor.GetPaintValueSupported Method (ITypeDescriptorContext)

Indicates whether the specified context supports painting a representation of an object's value within the specified context.

```
[Visual Basic]
Overloads Public Overridable Function GetPaintValueSupported( _
   ByVal context As ITypeDescriptorContext _
) As Boolean
[C#]
public virtual bool GetPaintValueSupported(
   ITypeDescriptorContext context
);
[C++]
public: virtual bool GetPaintValueSupported(
   ITypeDescriptorContext* context
);
[JScript]
public function GetPaintValueSupported(
   context : ITypeDescriptorContext
) : Boolean;
```

Parameters

context

An **ITypeDescriptorContext** that can be used to gain additional context information.

Return Value

true if **PaintValue** is implemented; otherwise, **false**.

Requirements

Platforms: Windows 98, Windows NT 4.0, Windows Millennium Edition, Windows 2000, Windows XP Home Edition, Windows XP Professional, Windows Server 2003 family

UITypeEditor.PaintValue Method

Paints a representation of the value of an object.

Overload List

Paints a representation of the value of an object using the specified **PaintValueEventArgs**.

[Visual Basic] **Overloads Public Overridable Sub PaintValue(PaintValueEventArgs)**

[C#] **public virtual void PaintValue(PaintValueEventArgs);**

[C++] **public: virtual void PaintValue(PaintValueEventArgs*);**

[JScript] **public function PaintValue(PaintValueEventArgs);**

Paints a representation of the value of the specified object to the specified canvas.

[Visual Basic] **Overloads Public Sub PaintValue(Object, Graphics, Rectangle)**

[C#] **public void PaintValue(object, Graphics, Rectangle);**

[C++] **public: void PaintValue(Object*, Graphics*, Rectangle);**

[JScript] **public function PaintValue(Object, Graphics, Rectangle);**

UITypeEditor.PaintValue Method (PaintValueEventArgs)

Paints a representation of the value of an object using the specified **PaintValueEventArgs**.

```
[Visual Basic]
Overloads Public Overridable Sub PaintValue( _
   ByVal e As PaintValueEventArgs _
)
[C#]
public virtual void PaintValue(
   PaintValueEventArgs e
);
[C++]
public: virtual void PaintValue(
   PaintValueEventArgs* e
);
[JScript]
public function PaintValue(
   e : PaintValueEventArgs
);
```

Parameters

e

A **PaintValueEventArgs** that indicates what to paint and where to paint it.

Remarks

Editors should paint within the boundaries of the specified rectangle. This rectangle indicates the area of the Properties window to draw a representation of the value within.

Requirements

Platforms: Windows 98, Windows NT 4.0, Windows Millennium Edition, Windows 2000, Windows XP Home Edition, Windows XP Professional, Windows Server 2003 family

UITypeEditor.PaintValue Method (Object, Graphics, Rectangle)

Paints a representation of the value of the specified object to the specified canvas.

```
[Visual Basic]
Overloads Public Sub PaintValue( _
   ByVal value As Object, _
   ByVal canvas As Graphics, _
   ByVal rectangle As Rectangle _
)
[C#]
public void PaintValue(
   object value,
   Graphics canvas,
   Rectangle rectangle
);
[C++]
public: void PaintValue(
   Object* value,
   Graphics* canvas,
   Rectangle rectangle
);
[JScript]
public function PaintValue(
   value : Object,
   canvas : Graphics,
   rectangle : Rectangle
);
```

Parameters

value

The object whose value this type editor will display.

canvas

A drawing canvas on which to paint the representation of the object's value.

rectangle

A **Rectangle** within whose boundaries to paint the value.

Remarks

Editors should paint within the boundaries of the specified rectangle. This rectangle indicates the area of the Properties window to draw a representation of the value within.

Requirements

Platforms: Windows 98, Windows NT 4.0, Windows Millennium Edition, Windows 2000, Windows XP Home Edition, Windows XP Professional, Windows Server 2003 family

UITypeEditorEditStyle Enumeration

Specifies identifiers that indicate the value editing style of a **UITypeEditor**.

[Visual Basic]

```
<Serializable>
Public Enum UITypeEditorEditStyle
```

[C#]

```
[Serializable]
public enum UITypeEditorEditStyle
```

[C++]

```
[Serializable]
__value public enum UITypeEditorEditStyle
```

[JScript]

```
public
   Serializable
enum UITypeEditorEditStyle
```

Remarks

These identifiers can indicate the value editing style of a **UITypeEditor**.

Members

Member name	Description
DropDown	Displays a down arrow button and the user interface will be hosted in a drop-down dialog.
Modal	Displays an ellipsis (**...**) button to start a modal, or windowed, dialog box.
None	Provides no interactive user interface (UI) component.

Requirements

Namespace: System.Drawing.Design

Platforms: Windows 98, Windows NT 4.0, Windows Millennium Edition, Windows 2000, Windows XP Home Edition, Windows XP Professional, Windows Server 2003 family

Assembly: System.Drawing (in System.Drawing.dll)

System.Drawing.Drawing2D Namespace

The **System.Drawing.Drawing2D** namespace provide advanced 2-dimmensional and vector graphics functionality. This namespace includes the gradient brushes, the **Matrix** class (used to define geometric transforms), and the **GraphicsPath** class.

AdjustableArrowCap Class

Represents an adjustable arrow-shaped line cap. This class cannot be inherited.

System.Object
  System.MarshalByRefObject
    System.Drawing.Drawing2D.CustomLineCap
      System.Drawing.Drawing2D.AdjustableArrowCap

```
[Visual Basic]
NotInheritable Public Class AdjustableArrowCap
   Inherits CustomLineCap
[C#]
public sealed class AdjustableArrowCap : CustomLineCap
[C++]
public __gc __sealed class AdjustableArrowCap : public
   CustomLineCap
[JScript]
public class AdjustableArrowCap extends CustomLineCap
```

Thread Safety

Any public static (**Shared** in Visual Basic) members of this type are safe for multithreaded operations. Any instance members are not guaranteed to be thread safe.

Requirements

Namespace: System.Drawing.Drawing2D

Platforms: Windows 98, Windows NT 4.0, Windows Millennium Edition, Windows 2000, Windows XP Home Edition, Windows XP Professional, Windows Server 2003 family

Assembly: System.Drawing (in System.Drawing.dll)

AdjustableArrowCap Constructor

Initializes a new instance of the **AdjustableArrowCap** class with the specified width and height.

Overload List

Initializes a new instance of the **AdjustableArrowCap** class with the specified width and height. The arrow end caps created with this constructor are always filled.

[Visual Basic] **Public Sub New(Single, Single)**

[C#] **public AdjustableArrowCap(float, float);**

[C++] **public: AdjustableArrowCap(float, float);**

[JScript] **public function AdjustableArrowCap(float, float);**

Initializes a new instance of the **AdjustableArrowCap** class with the specified width, height, and fill property. Whether an arrow end cap is filled depends on the argument passed to the *isFilled* parameter.

[Visual Basic] **Public Sub New(Single, Single, Boolean)**

[C#] **public AdjustableArrowCap(float, float, bool);**

[C++] **public: AdjustableArrowCap(float, float, bool);**

[JScript] **public function AdjustableArrowCap(float, float, Boolean);**

Example

[Visual Basic, C#] The following example is designed for use with Windows Forms, and it requires **PaintEventArgs** *e*, an **OnPaint** event object. The code performs the following actions:

- Creates an **AdjustableArrowCap** object named *myArrow.*
- Creates a **Pen** object named *capPen,* and sets its **CustomStartCap** and **CustomStopCap** properties equal to *myArrow.*
- Uses the **DrawLine** method to draw to screen a line capped by two arrows.

> [Visual Basic, C#] **Note** This example shows how to use one of the overloaded versions of the **AdjustableArrowCap** constructor. For other examples that might be available, see the individual overload topics.

```
[Visual Basic]
Public Sub AdjArrowCap_Sing_Sing_Bool(ByVal e As PaintEventArgs)
    Dim myArrow As New AdjustableArrowCap(6, 6, False)
    Dim customArrow As CustomLineCap = myArrow
    Dim capPen As New Pen(Color.Black)
    capPen.CustomStartCap = myArrow
    capPen.CustomEndCap = myArrow
    e.Graphics.DrawLine(capPen, 50, 50, 200, 50)
End Sub
```

```
[C#]
public void AdjArrowCap_Sing_Sing_Bool(PaintEventArgs e)
{
    AdjustableArrowCap myArrow = new AdjustableArrowCap(6, 6, false);
    Pen capPen = new Pen(Color.Black);
    capPen.CustomStartCap = myArrow;
    capPen.CustomEndCap = myArrow;
    e.Graphics.DrawLine(capPen, 50, 50, 200, 50);
}
```

AdjustableArrowCap Constructor (Single, Single)

Initializes a new instance of the **AdjustableArrowCap** class with the specified width and height. The arrow end caps created with this constructor are always filled.

```
[Visual Basic]
Public Sub New( _
   ByVal width As Single, _
   ByVal height As Single _
)
[C#]
public AdjustableArrowCap(
   float width,
   float height
);
```

[C++]
```
public: AdjustableArrowCap(
   float width,
   float height
);
```
[JScript]
```
public function AdjustableArrowCap(
   width : float,
   height : float
);
```

Parameters

width

The width of the arrow.

height

The height of the arrow.

Example

[Visual Basic, C#] The following example is designed for use with Windows Forms, and it requires **PaintEventArgs** *e*, an **OnPaint** event object. The code performs the following actions:

- Creates an **AdjustableArrowCap** object named *myArrow.*
- Creates a **Pen** object named *capPen,* and sets its **CustomStartCap** and **CustomStopCap** properties equal to *myArrow.*
- Uses the **DrawLine** method to draw to screen a line capped by two arrows.

[Visual Basic]
```
Public Sub AdjArrowCap_Sing_Sing(ByVal e As PaintEventArgs)
    Dim myArrow As New AdjustableArrowCap(6, 6)
    Dim customArrow As CustomLineCap = myArrow
    Dim capPen As New Pen(Color.Black)
    capPen.CustomStartCap = myArrow
    capPen.CustomEndCap = myArrow
    e.Graphics.DrawLine(capPen, 50, 50, 200, 50)
End Sub
```

[C#]
```
public void AdjArrowCap_Sing_Sing(PaintEventArgs e)
{
   AdjustableArrowCap myArrow = new AdjustableArrowCap(6, 6);
   Pen capPen = new Pen(Color.Black);
   capPen.CustomStartCap = myArrow;
   capPen.CustomEndCap = myArrow;
   e.Graphics.DrawLine(capPen, 50, 50, 200, 50);
}
```

Requirements

Platforms: Windows 98, Windows NT 4.0, Windows Millennium Edition, Windows 2000, Windows XP Home Edition, Windows XP Professional, Windows Server 2003 family

AdjustableArrowCap Constructor (Single, Single, Boolean)

Initializes a new instance of the **AdjustableArrowCap** class with the specified width, height, and fill property. Whether an arrow end cap is filled depends on the argument passed to the *isFilled* parameter.

[Visual Basic]
```
Public Sub New( _
   ByVal width As Single, _
   ByVal height As Single, _
   ByVal isFilled As Boolean _
)
```
[C#]
```
public AdjustableArrowCap(
   float width,
   float height,
   bool isFilled
);
```
[C++]
```
public: AdjustableArrowCap(
   float width,
   float height,
   bool isFilled
);
```
[JScript]
```
public function AdjustableArrowCap(
   width : float,
   height : float,
   isFilled : Boolean
);
```

Parameters

width

The width of the arrow.

height

The height of the arrow.

isFilled

true to fill the arrow cap; otherwise, **false**.

Example

[Visual Basic, C#] The following example is designed for use with Windows Forms, and it requires **PaintEventArgs** *e*, an **OnPaint** event object. The code performs the following actions:

- Creates an **AdjustableArrowCap** object named *myArrow.*
- Creates a **Pen** object named *capPen,* and sets its **CustomStartCap** and **CustomStopCap** properties equal to *myArrow.*
- Uses the **DrawLine** method to draw to screen a line capped by two arrows.

[Visual Basic]
```
Public Sub AdjArrowCap_Sing_Sing_Bool(ByVal e As PaintEventArgs)
    Dim myArrow As New AdjustableArrowCap(6, 6, False)
    Dim customArrow As CustomLineCap = myArrow
    Dim capPen As New Pen(Color.Black)
    capPen.CustomStartCap = myArrow
    capPen.CustomEndCap = myArrow
    e.Graphics.DrawLine(capPen, 50, 50, 200, 50)
End Sub
```

[C#]
```
public void AdjArrowCap_Sing_Sing_Bool(PaintEventArgs e)
{
   AdjustableArrowCap myArrow = new AdjustableArrowCap(6, 6, false);
   Pen capPen = new Pen(Color.Black);
   capPen.CustomStartCap = myArrow;
   capPen.CustomEndCap = myArrow;
   e.Graphics.DrawLine(capPen, 50, 50, 200, 50);
}
```

Requirements

Platforms: Windows 98, Windows NT 4.0,
Windows Millennium Edition, Windows 2000,
Windows XP Home Edition, Windows XP Professional,
Windows Server 2003 family

AdjustableArrowCap.Filled Property

Gets or sets whether the arrow cap is filled.

[Visual Basic]
```
Public Property Filled As Boolean
```
[C#]
```
public bool Filled {get; set;}
```
[C++]
```
public: __property bool get_Filled();
public: __property void set_Filled(bool);
```
[JScript]
```
public function get Filled() : Boolean;
public function set Filled(Boolean);
```

Property Value

This property is **true** if the arrow cap is filled; otherwise, **false**.

Requirements

Platforms: Windows 98, Windows NT 4.0,
Windows Millennium Edition, Windows 2000,
Windows XP Home Edition, Windows XP Professional,
Windows Server 2003 family

AdjustableArrowCap.Height Property

Gets or sets the height of the arrow cap.

[Visual Basic]
```
Public Property Height As Single
```
[C#]
```
public float Height {get; set;}
```
[C++]
```
public: __property float get_Height();
public: __property void set_Height(float);
```
[JScript]
```
public function get Height() : float;
public function set Height(float);
```

Property Value

The height of the arrow cap.

Remarks

The height of the arrow cap is scaled by the width of the **Pen** object used to draw the line being capped. For example, if you are drawing a capped line with a pen that has a width of 5 pixels, and the **AdjustableArrowCap** object has a height of 3, then the actual arrow cap is drawn 15 pixels high.

Requirements

Platforms: Windows 98, Windows NT 4.0,
Windows Millennium Edition, Windows 2000,
Windows XP Home Edition, Windows XP Professional,
Windows Server 2003 family

AdjustableArrowCap.MiddleInset Property

Gets or sets the number of units between the outline of the arrow cap and the fill.

[Visual Basic]
```
Public Property MiddleInset As Single
```
[C#]
```
public float MiddleInset {get; set;}
```
[C++]
```
public: __property float get_MiddleInset();
public: __property void set_MiddleInset(float);
```
[JScript]
```
public function get MiddleInset() : float;
public function set MiddleInset(float);
```

Property Value

The number of units between the outline of the arrow cap and the fill of the arrow cap.

Requirements

Platforms: Windows 98, Windows NT 4.0,
Windows Millennium Edition, Windows 2000,
Windows XP Home Edition, Windows XP Professional,
Windows Server 2003 family

AdjustableArrowCap.Width Property

Gets or sets the width of the arrow cap.

[Visual Basic]
```
Public Property Width As Single
```
[C#]
```
public float Width {get; set;}
```
[C++]
```
public: __property float get_Width();
public: __property void set_Width(float);
```
[JScript]
```
public function get Width() : float;
public function set Width(float);
```

Property Value

The width, in units, of the arrow cap.

Remarks

The width of the arrow cap is scaled by the width of the **Pen** object used to draw the line being capped. For example, if you are drawing a capped line with a pen that has a width of 5 pixels, and the **AdjustableArrowCap** object has a width of 3, then the actual arrow cap is drawn 15 pixels wide.

Requirements

Platforms: Windows 98, Windows NT 4.0,
Windows Millennium Edition, Windows 2000,
Windows XP Home Edition, Windows XP Professional,
Windows Server 2003 family

Blend Class

Defines a blend pattern for a **LinearGradientBrush** object. This class cannot be inherited.

System.Object
  System.Drawing.Drawing2D.Blend

[Visual Basic]
```
NotInheritable Public Class Blend
```
[C#]
```
public sealed class Blend
```
[C++]
```
public __gc __sealed class Blend
```
[JScript]
```
public class Blend
```

Thread Safety

Any public static (**Shared** in Visual Basic) members of this type are safe for multithreaded operations. Any instance members are not guaranteed to be thread safe.

Remarks

Gradients are commonly used to smoothly shade the interiors of shapes. A blend pattern is defined by two arrays (**Factors** and **Positions**) that each contain the same number of elements. Each element of the **Positions** array represents a proportion of the distance along the gradient line. Each element of the **Factors** array represents the proportion of the starting and ending colors in the gradient blend at the position along the gradient line represented by the corresponding element in the **Positions** array.

For example, if corresponding elements of the **Positions** and **Factors** arrays are 0.2 and 0.3, respectively, for a linear gradient from blue to red along a 100-pixel line, the color 20 pixels along that line (20 percent of the distance) consists of 30 percent blue and 70 percent red.

Requirements

Namespace: System.Drawing.Drawing2D

Platforms: Windows 98, Windows NT 4.0, Windows Millennium Edition, Windows 2000, Windows XP Home Edition, Windows XP Professional, Windows Server 2003 family

Assembly: System.Drawing (in System.Drawing.dll)

Blend Constructor

Initializes a new instance of the **Blend** class.

Overload List

Initializes a new instance of the **Blend** class.

[Visual Basic] **Public Sub New()**

[C#] **public Blend();**

[C++] **public: Blend();**

[JScript] **public function Blend();**

Initializes a new instance of the **Blend** class with the specified number of factors and positions.

[Visual Basic] **Public Sub New(Integer)**

[C#] **public Blend(int);**

[C++] **public: Blend(int);**

[JScript] **public function Blend(int);**

Example

For an example, see **ctor**.

Blend Constructor ()

Initializes a new instance of the **Blend** class.

[Visual Basic]
```
Public Sub New()
```
[C#]
```
public Blend();
```
[C++]
```
public: Blend();
```
[JScript]
```
public function Blend();
```

Example

[Visual Basic, C#] The following example is intended to be used in a Windows Forms environment. It demonstrates how to use the **Blend** class in conjunction with the **LinearGradientBrush** class to draw an ellipse to screen that has its colors blended. The ellipse is blue on the left, blends to red in the center, and blends back to blue on the right. This is accomplished through the settings in the *myFactors* and *myPositions* arrays used in the **Blend Factors** and **Positions** properties. Note that the **Blend** property of the **LinearGradient-Brush** object named *lgBrush2* must be made equal to the **Blend** object *myBlend*.

[Visual Basic]
```
Public Sub BlendConstExample(e As PaintEventArgs)
' Draw ellipse using Blend.
Dim startPoint2 As New Point(20, 110)
Dim endPoint2 As New Point(140, 110)
Dim myFactors As Single() =  {0.2F, 0.4F, 0.8F, 0.8F, 0.4F, 0.2F}
Dim myPositions As Single() =  {0F, 0.2F, 0.4F, 0.6F, 0.8F, 1F}
Dim myBlend As New Blend()
myBlend.Factors = myFactors
myBlend.Positions = myPositions
Dim lgBrush2 As New LinearGradientBrush(startPoint2, endPoint2, _
Color.Blue, Color.Red)
lgBrush2.Blend = myBlend
Dim ellipseRect2 As New Rectangle(20, 110, 120, 80)
e.Graphics.FillEllipse(lgBrush2, ellipseRect2)
End Sub
```

[C#]
```
public void BlendConstExample(PaintEventArgs e)
{
//Draw ellipse using Blend.
Point startPoint2 = new Point(20, 110);
Point endPoint2 = new Point(140, 110);
float[] myFactors = {.2f,.4f,.8f,.8f,.4f,.2f};
float[] myPositions = {0.0f,.2f,.4f,.6f,.8f,1.0f};
Blend myBlend = new Blend();
myBlend.Factors = myFactors;
myBlend.Positions = myPositions;
LinearGradientBrush lgBrush2 = new LinearGradientBrush(
startPoint2,
endPoint2,
Color.Blue,
Color.Red);
lgBrush2.Blend = myBlend;
Rectangle ellipseRect2 = new Rectangle(20, 110, 120, 80);
e.Graphics.FillEllipse(lgBrush2, ellipseRect2);
// End example.
}
```

Requirements

Platforms: Windows 98, Windows NT 4.0, Windows Millennium Edition, Windows 2000, Windows XP Home Edition, Windows XP Professional, Windows Server 2003 family

Blend Constructor (Int32)

Initializes a new instance of the **Blend** class with the specified number of factors and positions.

```
[Visual Basic]
Public Sub New( _
   ByVal count As Integer _
)
[C#]
public Blend(
   int count
);
[C++]
public: Blend(
   int count
);
[JScript]
public function Blend(
   count : int
);
```

Parameters

count
The number of elements in the **Factors** and **Positions** arrays.

Example

For an example, see **ctor**.

Requirements

Platforms: Windows 98, Windows NT 4.0, Windows Millennium Edition, Windows 2000, Windows XP Home Edition, Windows XP Professional, Windows Server 2003 family

Blend.Factors Property

Gets or sets an array of blend factors for the gradient.

```
[Visual Basic]
Public Property Factors As Single ()
[C#]
public float[] Factors {get; set;}
[C++]
public: __property float get_Factors();
public: __property void set_Factors(float __gc[]);
[JScript]
public function get Factors() : float[];
public function set Factors(float[]);
```

Property Value

An array of blend factors that specify the percentages of the starting color and the ending color to be used at the corresponding position.

Remarks

Typically, the elements of this array are a value from 0.0f through 1.0f. These elements specify the percentages of the starting color and the ending color to use at the corresponding blend position. For example, a value of 0.2 indicates that at the specified position, the blended color is composed of 20 percent of the starting gradient color and 80 percent of the ending gradient color.

Requirements

Platforms: Windows 98, Windows NT 4.0, Windows Millennium Edition, Windows 2000, Windows XP Home Edition, Windows XP Professional, Windows Server 2003 family

Blend.Positions Property

Gets or sets an array of blend positions for the gradient.

```
[Visual Basic]
Public Property Positions As Single ()
[C#]
public float[] Positions {get; set;}
[C++]
public: __property float get_Positions();
public: __property void set_Positions(float __gc[]);
[JScript]
public function get Positions() : float[];
public function set Positions(float[]);
```

Property Value

An array of blend positions that specify the percentages of distance along the gradient line.

Remarks

The elements of this array specify percentages of distance along the gradient line. For example, an element value of 0.2f specifies that this point is 20 percent of the total distance from the starting point. The elements in this array are represented by float values between 0.0f and 1.0f. The first element of the array must be 0.0f, and the last element must be 1.0f.

Requirements

Platforms: Windows 98, Windows NT 4.0, Windows Millennium Edition, Windows 2000, Windows XP Home Edition, Windows XP Professional, Windows Server 2003 family

ColorBlend Class

Defines arrays of colors and positions used for interpolating color blending in a multicolor gradient. This class cannot be inherited.

System.Object
  System.Drawing.Drawing2D.ColorBlend

[Visual Basic]
```
NotInheritable Public Class ColorBlend
```
[C#]
```
public sealed class ColorBlend
```
[C++]
```
public __gc __sealed class ColorBlend
```
[JScript]
```
public class ColorBlend
```

Thread Safety

Any public static (**Shared** in Visual Basic) members of this type are safe for multithreaded operations. Any instance members are not guaranteed to be thread safe.

Requirements

Namespace: System.Drawing.Drawing2D

Platforms: Windows 98, Windows NT 4.0, Windows Millennium Edition, Windows 2000, Windows XP Home Edition, Windows XP Professional, Windows Server 2003 family

Assembly: System.Drawing (in System.Drawing.dll)

ColorBlend Constructor

Initializes a new instance of the **ColorBlend** class.

Overload List

Initializes a new instance of the **ColorBlend** class.

[Visual Basic] **Public Sub New()**

[C#] **public ColorBlend();**

[C++] **public: ColorBlend();**

[JScript] **public function ColorBlend();**

Initializes a new instance of the **ColorBlend** class with the specified number of colors and positions.

[Visual Basic] **Public Sub New(Integer)**

[C#] **public ColorBlend(int);**

[C++] **public: ColorBlend(int);**

[JScript] **public function ColorBlend(int);**

Example

For an example see **ctor**

ColorBlend Constructor ()

Initializes a new instance of the **ColorBlend** class.

[Visual Basic]
```
Public Sub New()
```
[C#]
```
public ColorBlend();
```
[C++]
```
public: ColorBlend();
```
[JScript]
```
public function ColorBlend();
```

Example

[Visual Basic, C#] The following example is intended to be used in a Windows Forms environment. It demonstrates how to use the **ColorBlend** class in conjunction with the **LinearGradientBrush** class to draw an ellipse to screen that has its colors blended. The ellipse is green on the left, blends to yellow, then to blue, and finally to red on the right. This is accomplished through the settings in the *myColors* and *myPositions* arrays used in the **ColorBlend Colors** and **Positions** properties. Note that the **InterpolationColors** property of the **LinearGradientBrush** object named *lgBrush2* must be made equal to the **ColorBlend** object *myBlend*.

[Visual Basic]
```
Public Sub ColorBlendExample(e As PaintEventArgs)
' Begin example.
' Draw ellipse using ColorBlend.
Dim startPoint2 As New Point(20, 110)
Dim endPoint2 As New Point(140, 110)
Dim myColors As Color() =  {Color.Green, Color.Yellow, _
Color.Yellow, Color.Blue, Color.Red, Color.Red}
Dim myPositions As Single() =  {0F, 0.2F, 0.4F, 0.6F, 0.8F, 1F}
Dim myBlend As New ColorBlend()
myBlend.Colors = myColors
myBlend.Positions = myPositions
Dim lgBrush2 As New LinearGradientBrush(startPoint2, endPoint2, _
Color.Green, Color.Red)
lgBrush2.InterpolationColors = myBlend
Dim ellipseRect2 As New Rectangle(20, 110, 120, 80)
e.Graphics.FillEllipse(lgBrush2, ellipseRect2)
End Sub
```

[C#]
```
protected override void OnPaint(PaintEventArgs e)
{
//Draw ellipse using ColorBlend.
Point startPoint2 = new Point(20, 110);
Point endPoint2 = new Point(140, 110);
Color[] myColors = {Color.Green,
Color.Yellow,
Color.Yellow,
Color.Blue,
Color.Red
Color.Red};
float[] myPositions = {0.0f,.20f,.40f,.60f,.80f,1.0f};
ColorBlend myBlend = new ColorBlend();
myBlend.Colors = myColors;
myBlend.Positions = myPositions;
LinearGradientBrush lgBrush2 = new LinearGradientBrush(startPoint2,
endPoint2,
Color.Green,
Color.Red);
lgBrush2.InterpolationColors = myBlend;
Rectangle ellipseRect2 = new Rectangle(20, 110, 120, 80);
e.Graphics.FillEllipse(lgBrush2, ellipseRect2);
}
```

Requirements

Platforms: Windows 98, Windows NT 4.0, Windows Millennium Edition, Windows 2000, Windows XP Home Edition, Windows XP Professional, Windows Server 2003 family

ColorBlend Constructor (Int32)

Initializes a new instance of the **ColorBlend** class with the specified number of colors and positions.

[Visual Basic]
```
Public Sub New( _
   ByVal count As Integer _
)
```
[C#]
```
public ColorBlend(
   int count
);
```
[C++]
```
public: ColorBlend(
   int count
);
```
[JScript]
```
public function ColorBlend(
   count : int
);
```

Parameters

count
The number of colors and positions in this **ColorBlend**.

Example

For an example see **ctor**

Requirements

Platforms: Windows 98, Windows NT 4.0, Windows Millennium Edition, Windows 2000, Windows XP Home Edition, Windows XP Professional, Windows Server 2003 family

ColorBlend.Colors Property

Gets or sets an array of colors that represents the colors to use at corresponding positions along a gradient.

[Visual Basic]
```
Public Property Colors As Color ()
```
[C#]
```
public Color[] Colors {get; set;}
```
[C++]
```
public: __property Color get_Colors();
public: __property void set_Colors(Color[]);
```
[JScript]
```
public function get Colors() : Color[];
public function set Colors(Color[]);
```

Property Value

An array of **Color** structures that represents the colors to use at corresponding positions along a gradient.

Remarks

This property is an array of **Color** structures that represents the colors to use at corresponding positions along a gradient. Along with the **Positions** property, this property defines a multicolor gradient.

Requirements

Platforms: Windows 98, Windows NT 4.0, Windows Millennium Edition, Windows 2000, Windows XP Home Edition, Windows XP Professional, Windows Server 2003 family

ColorBlend.Positions Property

Gets or sets the positions along a gradient line.

[Visual Basic]
```
Public Property Positions As Single ()
```
[C#]
```
public float[] Positions {get; set;}
```
[C++]
```
public: __property float get_Positions();
public: __property void set_Positions(float __gc[]);
```
[JScript]
```
public function get Positions() : float[];
public function set Positions(float[]);
```

Property Value

An array of values that specify percentages of distance along the gradient line.

Remarks

The elements of this array specify percentages of distance along the gradient line. For example, an element value of 0.2f specifies that this point is 20 percent of the total distance from the starting point. The elements in this array are represented by float values between 0.0f and 1.0f, and the first element of the array must be 0.0f and the last element must be 1.0f.

Along with the **Colors** property, this property defines a multicolor gradient.

Requirements

Platforms: Windows 98, Windows NT 4.0, Windows Millennium Edition, Windows 2000, Windows XP Home Edition, Windows XP Professional, Windows Server 2003 family

CombineMode Enumeration

Specifies how different clipping regions can be combined.

[Visual Basic]
```
<Serializable>
Public Enum CombineMode
```
[C#]
```
[Serializable]
public enum CombineMode
```
[C++]
```
[Serializable]
__value public enum CombineMode
```
[JScript]
```
public
   Serializable
enum CombineMode
```

Members

Member name	Description
Complement Supported by the .NET Compact Framework.	Specifies that the existing region is replaced by the result of the existing region being removed from the new region. Said differently, the existing region is excluded from the new region.
Exclude Supported by the .NET Compact Framework.	Specifies that the existing region is replaced by the result of the new region being removed from the existing region. Said differently, the new region is excluded from the existing region.
Intersect Supported by the .NET Compact Framework.	Two clipping regions are combined by taking their intersection.
Replace Supported by the .NET Compact Framework.	One clipping region is replaced by another.
Union Supported by the .NET Compact Framework.	Two clipping regions are combined by taking the union of both.
Xor Supported by the .NET Compact Framework.	Two clipping regions are combined by taking only the areas enclosed by one or the other region, but not both.

Requirements

Namespace: System.Drawing.Drawing2D

Platforms: Windows 98, Windows NT 4.0, Windows Millennium Edition, Windows 2000, Windows XP Home Edition, Windows XP Professional, Windows .NET Server family, .NET Compact Framework - Windows CE .NET

Assembly: System.Drawing (in System.Drawing.dll)

CompositingMode Enumeration

Specifies how the source colors are combined with the background colors.

[Visual Basic]
```
<Serializable>
Public Enum CompositingMode
```
[C#]
```
[Serializable]
public enum CompositingMode
```
[C++]
```
[Serializable]
__value public enum CompositingMode
```
[JScript]
```
public
   Serializable
enum CompositingMode
```

Members

Member name	Description
SourceCopy	Specifies that when a color is rendered, it overwrites the background color.
SourceOver	Specifies that when a color is rendered, it is blended with the background color. The blend is determined by the alpha component of the color being rendered.

Requirements

Namespace: System.Drawing.Drawing2D

Platforms: Windows 98, Windows NT 4.0, Windows Millennium Edition, Windows 2000, Windows XP Home Edition, Windows XP Professional, Windows Server 2003 family

Assembly: System.Drawing (in System.Drawing.dll)

CompositingQuality Enumeration

Specifies the quality level to use during compositing.

[Visual Basic]
```
<Serializable>
Public Enum CompositingQuality
```
[C#]
```
[Serializable]
public enum CompositingQuality
```
[C++]
```
[Serializable]
__value public enum CompositingQuality
```
[JScript]
```
public
   Serializable
enum CompositingQuality
```

Remarks

Compositing is done during rendering when the source pixels are combined with the destination pixels to produce the resultant pixels. The quality of compositing directly relates to the visual quality of the output and is inversely proportional to the render time. The higher the quality, the slower the render time. This is because the higher the quality level, the more surrounding pixels need to be taken into account during the composite. The linear quality setting (**AssumeLinear**) compromises by providing better quality than the default quality at a slightly lower speed.

Members

Member name	Description
AssumeLinear	Assume linear values.
Default	Default quality.
GammaCorrected	Gamma correction is used.
HighQuality	High quality, low speed compositing.
HighSpeed	High speed, low quality.
Invalid	Invalid quality.

Requirements

Namespace: System.Drawing.Drawing2D

Platforms: Windows 98, Windows NT 4.0, Windows Millennium Edition, Windows 2000, Windows XP Home Edition, Windows XP Professional, Windows Server 2003 family

Assembly: System.Drawing (in System.Drawing.dll)

CoordinateSpace Enumeration

Specifies the system to use when evaluating coordinates.

[Visual Basic]
```
<Serializable>
Public Enum CoordinateSpace
```
[C#]
```
[Serializable]
public enum CoordinateSpace
```
[C++]
```
[Serializable]
__value public enum CoordinateSpace
```
[JScript]
```
public
   Serializable
enum CoordinateSpace
```

Members

Member name	Description
Device	Specifies that coordinates are in the device coordinate context. On a computer screen the device coordinates are usually measured in pixels.
Page	Specifies that coordinates are in the page coordinate context. Their units are defined by the **Graphics.PageUnit** property, and must be one of the elements of the **GraphicsUnit** enumeration.
World	Specifies that coordinates are in the world coordinate context. World coordinates are used in a nonphysical environment, such as a modeling environment.

Requirements

Namespace: System.Drawing.Drawing2D

Platforms: Windows 98, Windows NT 4.0, Windows Millennium Edition, Windows 2000, Windows XP Home Edition, Windows XP Professional, Windows Server 2003 family

Assembly: System.Drawing (in System.Drawing.dll)

CustomLineCap Class

Encapsulates a custom user-defined line cap.

System.Object
  System.MarshalByRefObject
    System.Drawing.Drawing2D.CustomLineCap
      System.Drawing.Drawing2D.AdjustableArrowCap

[Visual Basic]
```
Public Class CustomLineCap
   Inherits MarshalByRefObject
   Implements ICloneable, IDisposable
```
[C#]
```
public class CustomLineCap : MarshalByRefObject, ICloneable,
   IDisposable
```
[C++]
```
public __gc class CustomLineCap : public MarshalByRefObject,
   ICloneable, IDisposable
```
[JScript]
```
public class CustomLineCap extends MarshalByRefObject implements
   ICloneable, IDisposable
```

Thread Safety

Any public static (**Shared** in Visual Basic) members of this type are safe for multithreaded operations. Any instance members are not guaranteed to be thread safe.

Remarks

Line caps are used at the beginnings and ends of lines or curves drawn by GDI+ **Pen** objects. GDI+ supports several predefined cap styles, and also allows users to define their own cap styles. This class is used to create custom cap styles.

Requirements

Namespace: System.Drawing.Drawing2D

Platforms: Windows 98, Windows NT 4.0, Windows Millennium Edition, Windows 2000, Windows XP Home Edition, Windows XP Professional, Windows Server 2003 family

Assembly: System.Drawing (in System.Drawing.dll)

CustomLineCap Constructor

Initializes a new instance of the **CustomLineCap** class with the specified outline and fill.

Overload List

Initializes a new instance of the **CustomLineCap** class with the specified outline and fill.

[Visual Basic] **Public Sub New(GraphicsPath, GraphicsPath)**

[C#] **public CustomLineCap(GraphicsPath, GraphicsPath);**

[C++] **public: CustomLineCap(GraphicsPath*, GraphicsPath*);**

[JScript] **public function CustomLineCap(GraphicsPath, GraphicsPath);**

Initializes a new instance of the **CustomLineCap** class from the specified existing **LineCap** enumeration with the specified outline and fill.

[Visual Basic] **Public Sub New(GraphicsPath, GraphicsPath, LineCap)**

[C#] **public CustomLineCap(GraphicsPath, GraphicsPath, LineCap);**

[C++] **public: CustomLineCap(GraphicsPath*, GraphicsPath*, LineCap);**

[JScript] **public function CustomLineCap(GraphicsPath, GraphicsPath, LineCap);**

Initializes a new instance of the **CustomLineCap** class from the specified existing **LineCap** enumeration with the specified outline, fill, and inset.

[Visual Basic] **Public Sub New(GraphicsPath, GraphicsPath, LineCap, Single)**

[C#] **public CustomLineCap(GraphicsPath, GraphicsPath, LineCap, float);**

[C++] **public: CustomLineCap(GraphicsPath*, GraphicsPath*, LineCap, float);**

[JScript] **public function CustomLineCap(GraphicsPath, GraphicsPath, LineCap, float);**

CustomLineCap Constructor (GraphicsPath, GraphicsPath)

Initializes a new instance of the **CustomLineCap** class with the specified outline and fill.

[Visual Basic]
```
Public Sub New( _
   ByVal fillPath As GraphicsPath, _
   ByVal strokePath As GraphicsPath _
)
```
[C#]
```
public CustomLineCap(
   GraphicsPath fillPath,
   GraphicsPath strokePath
);
```
[C++]
```
public: CustomLineCap(
   GraphicsPath* fillPath,
   GraphicsPath* strokePath
);
```
[JScript]
```
public function CustomLineCap(
   fillPath : GraphicsPath,
   strokePath : GraphicsPath
);
```

Parameters

fillPath

A **GraphicsPath** object that defines the fill for the custom cap.

strokePath

A **GraphicsPath** object that defines the outline of the custom cap.

Remarks

CustomLineCap uses a fill mode of "winding" regardless of the fill mode specified for the operation.

The *fillPath* and *strokePath* parameters cannot be used at the same time. One parameter must be passed a null value. If neither parameter is passed a null value, *fillPath* will be ignored.

Requirements

Platforms: Windows 98, Windows NT 4.0, Windows Millennium Edition, Windows 2000, Windows XP Home Edition, Windows XP Professional, Windows Server 2003 family

CustomLineCap Constructor (GraphicsPath, GraphicsPath, LineCap)

Initializes a new instance of the **CustomLineCap** class from the specified existing **LineCap** enumeration with the specified outline and fill.

[Visual Basic]
```
Public Sub New( _
   ByVal fillPath As GraphicsPath, _
   ByVal strokePath As GraphicsPath, _
   ByVal baseCap As LineCap _
)
```
[C#]
```
public CustomLineCap(
   GraphicsPath fillPath,
   GraphicsPath strokePath,
   LineCap baseCap
);
```
[C++]
```
public: CustomLineCap(
   GraphicsPath* fillPath,
   GraphicsPath* strokePath,
   LineCap baseCap
);
```
[JScript]
```
public function CustomLineCap(
   fillPath : GraphicsPath,
   strokePath : GraphicsPath,
   baseCap : LineCap
);
```

Parameters

fillPath
: A **GraphicsPath** object that defines the fill for the custom cap.

strokePath
: A **GraphicsPath** object that defines the outline of the custom cap.

baseCap
: The LineCap from which to create the custom cap.

Remarks

CustomLineCap uses a fill mode of "winding" regardless of the fill mode specified for the operation.

The *fillPath* and *strokePath* parameters cannot be used at the same time. One parameter must be passed a null value. If neither parameter is passed a null value, *fillPath* will be ignored.

Requirements

Platforms: Windows 98, Windows NT 4.0, Windows Millennium Edition, Windows 2000, Windows XP Home Edition, Windows XP Professional, Windows Server 2003 family

CustomLineCap Constructor (GraphicsPath, GraphicsPath, LineCap, Single)

Initializes a new instance of the **CustomLineCap** class from the specified existing **LineCap** enumeration with the specified outline, fill, and inset.

[Visual Basic]
```
Public Sub New( _
   ByVal fillPath As GraphicsPath, _
   ByVal strokePath As GraphicsPath, _
   ByVal baseCap As LineCap, _
   ByVal baseInset As Single _
)
```
[C#]
```
public CustomLineCap(
   GraphicsPath fillPath,
   GraphicsPath strokePath,
   LineCap baseCap,
   float baseInset
);
```
[C++]
```
public: CustomLineCap(
   GraphicsPath* fillPath,
   GraphicsPath* strokePath,
   LineCap baseCap,
   float baseInset
);
```
[JScript]
```
public function CustomLineCap(
   fillPath : GraphicsPath,
   strokePath : GraphicsPath,
   baseCap : LineCap,
   baseInset : float
);
```

Parameters

fillPath
: A **GraphicsPath** object that defines the fill for the custom cap.

strokePath
: A **GraphicsPath** object that defines the outline of the custom cap.

baseCap
: The LineCap from which to create the custom cap.

baseInset
: The distance between the cap and the line.

Remarks

CustomLineCap uses a fill mode of "winding" regardless of the fill mode specified for the operation.

The *fillPath* and *strokePath* parameters cannot be used at the same time. One parameter must be passed a null value. If neither parameter is passed a null value, *fillPath* will be ignored.

Requirements

Platforms: Windows 98, Windows NT 4.0, Windows Millennium Edition, Windows 2000, Windows XP Home Edition, Windows XP Professional, Windows Server 2003 family

CustomLineCap.BaseCap Property

Gets or sets the **LineCap** enumeration on which this **CustomLineCap** is based.

```
[Visual Basic]
Public Property BaseCap As LineCap
[C#]
public LineCap BaseCap {get; set;}
[C++]
public: __property LineCap get_BaseCap();
public: __property void set_BaseCap(LineCap);
[JScript]
public function get BaseCap() : LineCap;
public function set BaseCap(LineCap);
```

Property Value

The **LineCap** enumeration on which this **CustomLineCap** is based.

Requirements

Platforms: Windows 98, Windows NT 4.0,
Windows Millennium Edition, Windows 2000,
Windows XP Home Edition, Windows XP Professional,
Windows Server 2003 family

CustomLineCap.BaseInset Property

Gets or sets the distance between the cap and the line.

```
[Visual Basic]
Public Property BaseInset As Single
[C#]
public float BaseInset {get; set;}
[C++]
public: __property float get_BaseInset();
public: __property void set_BaseInset(float);
[JScript]
public function get BaseInset() : float;
public function set BaseInset(float);
```

Property Value

The distance between the beginning of the cap and the end of the line.

Requirements

Platforms: Windows 98, Windows NT 4.0,
Windows Millennium Edition, Windows 2000,
Windows XP Home Edition, Windows XP Professional,
Windows Server 2003 family

CustomLineCap.StrokeJoin Property

Gets or sets the **LineJoin** enumeration that determines how lines that compose this **CustomLineCap** object are joined.

```
[Visual Basic]
Public Property StrokeJoin As LineJoin
[C#]
public LineJoin StrokeJoin {get; set;}
[C++]
public: __property LineJoin get_StrokeJoin();
public: __property void set_StrokeJoin(LineJoin);
[JScript]
public function get StrokeJoin() : LineJoin;
public function set StrokeJoin(LineJoin);
```

Property Value

The **LineJoin** enumeration this **CustomLineCap** object uses to join lines.

Remarks

This property specifies a **LineJoin** enumeration that is used to join lines and curves that make up the stroked path of this **CustomLineCap** object.

Requirements

Platforms: Windows 98, Windows NT 4.0,
Windows Millennium Edition, Windows 2000,
Windows XP Home Edition, Windows XP Professional,
Windows Server 2003 family

CustomLineCap.WidthScale Property

Gets or sets the amount by which to scale this **CustomLineCap** Class object with respect to the width of the **Pen** object.

```
[Visual Basic]
Public Property WidthScale As Single
[C#]
public float WidthScale {get; set;}
[C++]
public: __property float get_WidthScale();
public: __property void set_WidthScale(float);
[JScript]
public function get WidthScale() : float;
public function set WidthScale(float);
```

Property Value

The amount by which to scale the cap.

Remarks

This property specifies the multiple of the pen width by which to multiply the size of the custom cap. For example, if this property equals 1, the custom cap width is 10, the custom cap height is 5, and a line is drawn with a pen with a width of 3, then the cap is drawn 30 units wide and 15 units high. Setting this property to 3 causes the cap to be drawn 90 units wide and 45 units high.

Requirements

Platforms: Windows 98, Windows NT 4.0,
Windows Millennium Edition, Windows 2000,
Windows XP Home Edition, Windows XP Professional,
Windows Server 2003 family

CustomLineCap.Clone Method

Creates an exact copy of this **CustomLineCap**.

```
[Visual Basic]
Public Overridable Function Clone() As Object Implements _
   ICloneable.Clone
[C#]
public virtual object Clone();
[C++]
public: virtual Object* Clone();
[JScript]
public function Clone() : Object;
```

Return Value

The **CustomLineCap** this method creates, cast as an object.

Implements

ICloneable.Clone

Example

[Visual Basic, C#] The following example is designed for use with Windows Forms, and it requires **PaintEventArgs** *e*, an **OnPaint** event object. The code performs the following actions:

- Creates a custom line cap by using the **GraphicsPath** object.
- Creates a **CustomLineCap** object, *firstCap*,using the **GraphicsPath** object just created.
- Creates a clone of *firstCap* by using *firstCap's* **Clone** method.
- Sets up the **CustomStartCap** and **CustomEndCap** properties of the **Pen** object, and uses that pen to draw a line and the custom caps to the screen.

[Visual Basic]

```
Public Sub CloneExample(e As PaintEventArgs)
Dim points As Point() = New Point(- 5, - 5) New Point(0, 0) _
New Point(5, - 5)
Dim capPath As New GraphicsPath()
' Create a Path and add two lines to it,
' forming a custom line cap.
capPath.AddLines(points)
' Create a CustomLineCap object.
Dim firstCap As New CustomLineCap(Nothing, capPath)
' Create a copy of firstCap.
Dim secondCap As CustomLineCap = CType(firstCap.Clone(), _
CustomLineCap)
' Create a Pen object.
Dim pen As New Pen(Color.Black, 3F)
'Set up the line.
Dim point1 As New Point(20, 20)
Dim point2 As New Point(100, 100)
' Set up the caps.
pen.CustomStartCap = firstCap
pen.CustomEndCap = secondCap
' Draw the line and caps to the screen.
e.Graphics.DrawLine(pen, point1, point2)
End Sub
```

[C#]

```
private void CloneExample(PaintEventArgs e)
{
// Create a Path and add two lines to it,
// forming a custom line cap.
Point[] points =
{
new Point(-5, -5),
new Point(0, 0),
new Point(5, -5)
};
GraphicsPath capPath = new GraphicsPath();
capPath.AddLines(points);
// Create a CustomLineCap object.
CustomLineCap firstCap = new CustomLineCap(null, capPath);
// Create a copy of firstCap.
CustomLineCap secondCap = (CustomLineCap)firstCap.Clone();
// Create a Pen object.
Pen pen = new Pen(Color.Black, 3.0f);
// Set up the line.
Point point1 = new Point(20, 20);
Point point2 = new Point(100, 100);
// Set up the caps.
pen.CustomStartCap = firstCap;
pen.CustomEndCap = secondCap;
// Draw the line and caps to the screen.
e.Graphics.DrawLine(pen, point1, point2);
}
```

Requirements

Platforms: Windows 98, Windows NT 4.0, Windows Millennium Edition, Windows 2000, Windows XP Home Edition, Windows XP Professional, Windows Server 2003 family

CustomLineCap.Dispose Method

Overload List

Releases all resources used by this **CustomLineCap** object.

[Visual Basic] **Overloads Public Overridable Sub Dispose() Implements IDisposable.Dispose**

[C#] **public virtual void Dispose();**

[C++] **public: virtual void Dispose();**

[JScript] **public function Dispose();**

This member supports the .NET Framework infrastructure and is not intended to be used directly from your code.

[Visual Basic] **Overloads Protected Overridable Sub Dispose(Boolean)**

[C#] **protected virtual void Dispose(bool);**

[C++] **protected: virtual void Dispose(bool);**

[JScript] **protected function Dispose(Boolean);**

CustomLineCap.Dispose Method ()

Releases all resources used by this **CustomLineCap** object.

[Visual Basic]

```
Overloads Public Overridable Sub Dispose() Implements _
   IDisposable.Dispose
```

[C#]

```
public virtual void Dispose();
```

[C++]

```
public: virtual void Dispose();
```

[JScript]

```
public function Dispose();
```

Return Value

This method does not return a value.

Implements

IDisposable.Dispose

Remarks

Calling **Dispose** allows the resources used by this **CustomLineCap** object to be reallocated for other purposes.

Requirements

Platforms: Windows 98, Windows NT 4.0, Windows Millennium Edition, Windows 2000, Windows XP Home Edition, Windows XP Professional, Windows Server 2003 family

CustomLineCap.Dispose Method (Boolean)

This member supports the .NET Framework infrastructure and is not intended to be used directly from your code.

[Visual Basic]

```
Overloads Protected Overridable Sub Dispose( _
   ByVal disposing As Boolean _
)
```

[C#]
```
protected virtual void Dispose(
   bool disposing
);
```
[C++]
```
protected: virtual void Dispose(
   bool disposing
);
```
[JScript]
```
protected function Dispose(
   disposing : Boolean
);
```

CustomLineCap.Finalize Method

This member overrides **Object.Finalize**.

[Visual Basic]
```
Overrides Protected Sub Finalize()
```
[C#]
```
~CustomLineCap();
```
[C++]
```
~CustomLineCap();
```
[JScript]
```
protected override function Finalize();
```

Requirements

Platforms: Windows 98, Windows NT 4.0, Windows Millennium Edition, Windows 2000, Windows XP Home Edition, Windows XP Professional, Windows Server 2003 family

CustomLineCap.GetStrokeCaps Method

Gets the caps used to start and end lines that make up this custom cap.

[Visual Basic]
```
Public Sub GetStrokeCaps( _
   <Out()> ByRef startCap As LineCap, _
   <Out()> ByRef endCap As LineCap _
)
```
[C#]
```
public void GetStrokeCaps(
   out LineCap startCap,
   out LineCap endCap
);
```
[C++]
```
public: void GetStrokeCaps(
   [
   Out
] LineCap* startCap,
   [
   Out
] LineCap* endCap
);
```
[JScript]
```
public function GetStrokeCaps(
   startCap : LineCap,
   endCap : LineCap
);
```

Parameters

startCap
: The **LineCap** enumeration used at the beginning of a line within this cap.

endCap
: The **LineCap** enumeration used at the end of a line within this cap.

Example

[Visual Basic, C#] The following example is designed for use with Windows Forms, and it requires **PaintEventArgs** *e*, an **OnPaint** event object. The code performs the following actions:

- Creates a custom line cap, *capPath* using a **GraphicsPath** object.
- Adds stroke caps (triangle and round) to *capPath*.
- Retrieves the stroke caps using the **GetStrokeCaps** method.
- Sets up a pen using the *startStrokeCap* and the *endStrokeCap* parameters.
- Uses the pen to draw a line that uses the stroke caps.

[Visual Basic, C#] Notice that the line is pointed end at one end and round on the other.

[Visual Basic]
```
Public Sub GetStrokeCapsExample(e As PaintEventArgs)
' Create a Path and add two lines to it,
' forming a custom line cap.
Dim points As Point() =  {New Point(- 2, - 2), New Point(0, 0), _
New Point(2, - 2)}
Dim capPath As New GraphicsPath()
capPath.AddLines(points)
' Create a CustomLineCap object.
Dim custCap As New CustomLineCap(Nothing, capPath)
' Set the start and end stroke caps for custCap.
custCap.SetStrokeCaps(LineCap.Triangle, LineCap.Round)
' Retrieve the start and end stroke caps from custCap.
Dim startStrokeCap As New LineCap()
Dim endStrokeCap As New LineCap()
custCap.GetStrokeCaps(startStrokeCap, endStrokeCap)
' Draw a new line that uses the stroke caps retrieved from custCap.
Dim strokeCapPen As New Pen(Color.Black, 15)
strokeCapPen.StartCap = startStrokeCap
strokeCapPen.EndCap = endStrokeCap
e.Graphics.DrawLine(strokeCapPen, New Point(100, 100), _
New Point(300, 100))
End Sub
```

[C#]
```
private void GetStrokeCapsExample(PaintEventArgs e)
{
// Create a Path and add two lines to it,
// forming a custom line cap.
Point[] points =
{
new Point(-2, -2),
new Point(0, 0),
new Point(2, -2)
};
GraphicsPath capPath = new GraphicsPath();
capPath.AddLines(points);
// Create a CustomLineCap object.
CustomLineCap custCap = new CustomLineCap(null, capPath);
// Set the start and end stroke caps for custCap.
custCap.SetStrokeCaps(LineCap.Triangle, LineCap.Round);
// Retrieve the start and end stroke caps from custCap.
LineCap startStrokeCap = new LineCap();
LineCap endStrokeCap = new LineCap();
custCap.GetStrokeCaps(out startStrokeCap, out endStrokeCap);
// Draw a  new line that uses the stroke caps retrieved from
// custCap.
```

```
Pen strokeCapPen = new Pen(Color.Black, 15);
strokeCapPen.StartCap = startStrokeCap;
strokeCapPen.EndCap = endStrokeCap;
e.Graphics.DrawLine(strokeCapPen,
new Point(100, 100),
new Point(300, 100));
}
```

Requirements

Platforms: Windows 98, Windows NT 4.0, Windows Millennium Edition, Windows 2000, Windows XP Home Edition, Windows XP Professional, Windows Server 2003 family

CustomLineCap.SetStrokeCaps Method

Sets the caps used to start and end lines that make up this custom cap.

[Visual Basic]
```
Public Sub SetStrokeCaps( _
   ByVal startCap As LineCap, _
   ByVal endCap As LineCap _
)
```
[C#]
```
public void SetStrokeCaps(
   LineCap startCap,
   LineCap endCap
);
```
[C++]
```
public: void SetStrokeCaps(
   LineCap startCap,
   LineCap endCap
);
```
[JScript]
```
public function SetStrokeCaps(
   startCap : LineCap,
   endCap : LineCap
);
```

Parameters

startCap
The **LineCap** enumeration used at the beginning of a line within this cap.

endCap
The **LineCap** enumeration used at the end of a line within this cap.

Example

[Visual Basic, C#] The following example is designed for use with Windows Forms, and it requires **PaintEventArgs** *e*, an **OnPaint** event object. The code performs the following actions:

- Creates a custom line cap, *capPath* using a **GraphicsPath** object.
- Adds stroke caps (triangle and round) to *capPath*, creating *custCap*.
- Creates a pen that uses *custCap* as the line caps for a new line.

[Visual Basic, C#] Notice that the line caps are arrows (as created in *custCap*) and that each side of the arrows have stroke caps applied, triangle on one side and round on the other.

[Visual Basic]
```
Public Sub SetStrokeCapsExample(e As PaintEventArgs)
' Create a Path and add two lines to it,
' forming a custom line cap.
Dim points As Point() = {New Point(- 2, - 2), New Point(0, 0), _
New Point(2, - 2)}
Dim capPath As New GraphicsPath()
capPath.AddLines(points)
' Create a CustomLineCap object.
Dim custCap As New CustomLineCap(Nothing, capPath)
' Set the start and end caps for custCap.
custCap.SetStrokeCaps(LineCap.Triangle, LineCap.Round)
' Create a Pen object, assign custCap as the start and end caps,
' and draw a line to the screen.
Dim strokeCapPen As New Pen(Color.Black, 15)
strokeCapPen.CustomStartCap = custCap
strokeCapPen.CustomEndCap = custCap
e.Graphics.DrawLine(strokeCapPen, New Point(100, 100), _
New Point(300, 100))
End Sub
```

[C#]
```
private void SetStrokeCapsExample(PaintEventArgs e)
{
// Create a Path and add two lines to it,
// forming a custom line cap.
Point[] points =
{
new Point(-2, -2),
new Point(0, 0),
new Point(2, -2)
};
GraphicsPath capPath = new GraphicsPath();
capPath.AddLines(points);
// Create a CustomLineCap object.
CustomLineCap custCap = new CustomLineCap(null, capPath);
// Set the start and end caps for custCap.
custCap.SetStrokeCaps(LineCap.Triangle, LineCap.Round);
// Create a Pen object, assign custCap as the start and end caps,
 and draw a line to the screen.
Pen strokeCapPen = new Pen(Color.Black, 15);
strokeCapPen.CustomStartCap = custCap;
strokeCapPen.CustomEndCap = custCap;
e.Graphics.DrawLine(strokeCapPen, new Point(100, 100), new
 Point(300, 100));
} // SetStrokeCapsExample
```

Requirements

Platforms: Windows 98, Windows NT 4.0, Windows Millennium Edition, Windows 2000, Windows XP Home Edition, Windows XP Professional, Windows Server 2003 family

DashCap Enumeration

Specifies the type of graphic shape to use on both ends of each dash in a dashed line.

[Visual Basic]
```
<Serializable>
Public Enum DashCap
```
[C#]
```
[Serializable]
public enum DashCap
```
[C++]
```
[Serializable]
__value public enum DashCap
```
[JScript]
```
public
   Serializable
enum DashCap
```

Members

Member name	Description
Flat	Specifies a square cap that squares off both ends of each dash.
Round	Specifies a circular cap that rounds off both ends of each dash.
Triangle	Specifies a triangular cap that points both ends of each dash.

Requirements

Namespace: System.Drawing.Drawing2D

Platforms: Windows 98, Windows NT 4.0, Windows Millennium Edition, Windows 2000, Windows XP Home Edition, Windows XP Professional, Windows Server 2003 family

Assembly: System.Drawing (in System.Drawing.dll)

DashStyle Enumeration

Specifies the style of dashed lines drawn with a **Pen** object.

[Visual Basic]
```
<Serializable>
Public Enum DashStyle
```
[C#]
```
[Serializable]
public enum DashStyle
```
[C++]
```
[Serializable]
__value public enum DashStyle
```
[JScript]
```
public
   Serializable
enum DashStyle
```

Members

Member name	Description
Custom	Specifies a user-defined custom dash style.
Dash	Specifies a line consisting of dashes.
DashDot	Specifies a line consisting of a repeating pattern of dash-dot.
DashDotDot	Specifies a line consisting of a repeating pattern of dash-dot-dot.
Dot	Specifies a line consisting of dots.
Solid	Specifies a solid line.

Requirements

Namespace: System.Drawing.Drawing2D

Platforms: Windows 98, Windows NT 4.0, Windows Millennium Edition, Windows 2000, Windows XP Home Edition, Windows XP Professional, Windows Server 2003 family

Assembly: System.Drawing (in System.Drawing.dll)

FillMode Enumeration

Specifies how the interior of a closed path is filled.

[Visual Basic]

```
<Serializable>
Public Enum FillMode
```

[C#]

```
[Serializable]
public enum FillMode
```

[C++]

```
[Serializable]
__value public enum FillMode
```

[JScript]

```
public
   Serializable
enum FillMode
```

Remarks

An application fills the interior of a path using one of two fill modes: alternate or winding. The mode determines how to fill and clip the interior of a closed figure.

The default mode is **Alternate**. To determine the interiors of closed figures in the alternate mode, draw a line from any arbitrary start point in the path to some point obviously outside the path. If the line crosses an odd number of path segments, the starting point is inside the closed region and is therefore part of the fill or clipping area. An even number of crossings means that the point is not in an area to be filled or clipped. An open figure is filled or clipped by using a line to connect the last point to the first point of the figure.

The **Winding** mode considers the direction of the path segments at each intersection. It adds one for every clockwise intersection, and subtracts one for every counterclockwise intersection. If the result is nonzero, the point is considered inside the fill or clip area. A zero count means that the point lies outside the fill or clip area.

A figure is considered clockwise or counterclockwise based on the order in which the segments of the figure are drawn.

Members

Member name	Description
Alternate	Specifies the alternate fill mode.
Winding	Specifies the winding fill mode.

Requirements

Namespace: System.Drawing.Drawing2D

Platforms: Windows 98, Windows NT 4.0, Windows Millennium Edition, Windows 2000, Windows XP Home Edition, Windows XP Professional, Windows Server 2003 family

Assembly: System.Drawing (in System.Drawing.dll)

FlushIntention Enumeration

Specifies whether commands in the graphics stack are terminated (flushed) immediately or executed as soon as possible.

[Visual Basic]
```
<Serializable>
Public Enum FlushIntention
```
[C#]
```
[Serializable]
public enum FlushIntention
```
[C++]
```
[Serializable]
__value public enum FlushIntention
```
[JScript]
```
public
   Serializable
enum FlushIntention
```

Members

Member name	Description
Flush	Specifies that the stack of all graphics operations is flushed immediately.
Sync	Specifies that all graphics operations on the stack are executed as soon as possible. This synchronizes the graphics state.

Requirements

Namespace: System.Drawing.Drawing2D

Platforms: Windows 98, Windows NT 4.0, Windows Millennium Edition, Windows 2000, Windows XP Home Edition, Windows XP Professional, Windows Server 2003 family

Assembly: System.Drawing (in System.Drawing.dll)

GraphicsContainer Class

Represents the internal data of a graphics container. This class is used when saving the state of a **Graphics** object using the **BeginContainer** and **EndContainer** methods. This class cannot be inherited.

System.Object
  System.MarshalByRefObject
    System.Drawing.Drawing2D.GraphicsContainer

[Visual Basic]

```
NotInheritable Public Class GraphicsContainer
   Inherits MarshalByRefObject
```

[C#]

```
public sealed class GraphicsContainer : MarshalByRefObject
```

[C++]

```
public __gc __sealed class GraphicsContainer : public
   MarshalByRefObject
```

[JScript]

```
public class GraphicsContainer extends MarshalByRefObject
```

Thread Safety

Any public static (**Shared** in Visual Basic) members of this type are safe for multithreaded operations. Any instance members are not guaranteed to be thread safe.

Requirements

Namespace: System.Drawing.Drawing2D

Platforms: Windows 98, Windows NT 4.0, Windows Millennium Edition, Windows 2000, Windows XP Home Edition, Windows XP Professional, Windows Server 2003 family

Assembly: System.Drawing (in System.Drawing.dll)

GraphicsPath Class

Represents a series of connected lines and curves. This class cannot be inherited.

System.Object
  System.MarshalByRefObject
    System.Drawing.Drawing2D.GraphicsPath

[Visual Basic]
```
NotInheritable Public Class GraphicsPath
   Inherits MarshalByRefObject
   Implements ICloneable, IDisposable
```
[C#]
```
public sealed class GraphicsPath : MarshalByRefObject, ICloneable,
   IDisposable
```
[C++]
```
public __gc __sealed class GraphicsPath : public
   MarshalByRefObject, ICloneable, IDisposable
```
[JScript]
```
public class GraphicsPath extends MarshalByRefObject implements
   ICloneable, IDisposable
```

Thread Safety

Any public static (**Shared** in Visual Basic) members of this type are safe for multithreaded operations. Any instance members are not guaranteed to be thread safe.

Remarks

Applications use paths to draw outlines of shapes, fill the interiors of shapes, and create clipping regions. The graphics engine maintains the coordinates of geometric shapes in a path in world coordinate space.

A path may be composed of any number of figures (subpaths). Each figure is either composed of a sequence of connected lines and curves or a geometric shape primitive. The starting point of a figure is the first point in the sequence of connected lines and curves. The ending point is the last point in the sequence. The starting and ending points of a geometric shape primitive are defined by the primitive specification.

A figure that consists of a sequence of connected lines and curves (whose starting and ending points may be coincident) is an open figure, unless it is closed explicitly. A figure can be closed explicitly, by using the **CloseFigure** method, which closes the current figure by connecting a line from the ending point to the starting point. A figure that consists of a geometric shape primitive is a closed figure.

For purposes of filling and clipping (for example, if a path is rendered using **Graphics.FillPath**), all open figures are closed by adding a line from the figure's first point to its last point.

A new figure is implicitly started when a path is created or when a figure is closed. A new figure is explicitly when the **StartFigure** method is called.

When a geometric shape primitive is added to a path, it adds a figure containing the geometric shape, and also implicitly starts a new figure. Consequently, there is always a current figure in a path. When lines and curves are added to a path, an implicit line is added as needed to connect the ending point of the current figure to the starting point of the new lines and curves to form a sequence of connected lines and curves.

A figure has a direction that describes how line and curve segments are traced between the starting point and the ending point. The direction is defined in the order that lines and curves are added to a figure, or is defined by the geometric shape primitive. The direction is used in determining the path interiors for clipping and fill.

Requirements

Namespace: System.Drawing.Drawing2D

Platforms: Windows 98, Windows NT 4.0, Windows Millennium Edition, Windows 2000, Windows XP Home Edition, Windows XP Professional, Windows Server 2003 family

Assembly: System.Drawing (in System.Drawing.dll)

GraphicsPath Constructor

Initializes a new instance of the **GraphicsPath** class with a **FillMode** enumeration of **Alternate**.

Overload List

Initializes a new instance of the **GraphicsPath** class with a **FillMode** enumeration of **Alternate**.

[Visual Basic] **Public Sub New()**

[C#] **public GraphicsPath();**

[C++] **public: GraphicsPath();**

[JScript] **public function GraphicsPath();**

Initializes a new instance of the **GraphicsPath** class with the specified **FillMode** enumeration.

[Visual Basic] **Public Sub New(FillMode)**

[C#] **public GraphicsPath(FillMode);**

[C++] **public: GraphicsPath(FillMode);**

[JScript] **public function GraphicsPath(FillMode);**

Initializes a new instance of the **GraphicsPath** class with the specified **PathPointType** and **Point** arrays.

[Visual Basic] **Public Sub New(Point(), Byte())**

[C#] **public GraphicsPath(Point[], byte[]);**

[C++] **public: GraphicsPath(Point[], unsigned char __gc[]);**

[JScript] **public function GraphicsPath(Point[], Byte[]);**

Initializes a new instance of the **GraphicsPath** array with the specified **PathPointType** and **PointF** arrays.

[Visual Basic] **Public Sub New(PointF(), Byte())**

[C#] **public GraphicsPath(PointF[], byte[]);**

[C++] **public: GraphicsPath(PointF[], unsigned char __gc[]);**

[JScript] **public function GraphicsPath(PointF[], Byte[]);**

Initializes a new instance of the **GraphicsPath** class with the specified **PathPointType** and **Point** arrays and with the specified **FillMode** enumeration element.

[Visual Basic] **Public Sub New(Point(), Byte(), FillMode)**

[C#] **public GraphicsPath(Point[], byte[], FillMode);**

[C++] **public: GraphicsPath(Point[], unsigned char __gc[], FillMode);**

[JScript] **public function GraphicsPath(Point[], Byte[], FillMode);**

Initializes a new instance of the **GraphicsPath** array with the specified **PathPointType** and **PointF** arrays and with the specified **FillMode** enumeration element.

[Visual Basic] **Public Sub New(PointF(), Byte(), FillMode)**

[C#] **public GraphicsPath(PointF[], byte[], FillMode);**

[C++] **public: GraphicsPath(PointF[], unsigned char __gc[], FillMode);**

[JScript] **public function GraphicsPath(PointF[], Byte[], FillMode);**

GraphicsPath Constructor ()

Initializes a new instance of the **GraphicsPath** class with a **FillMode** enumeration of **Alternate**.

```
[Visual Basic]
Public Sub New()
[C#]
public GraphicsPath();
[C++]
public: GraphicsPath();
[JScript]
public function GraphicsPath();
```

Requirements

Platforms: Windows 98, Windows NT 4.0, Windows Millennium Edition, Windows 2000, Windows XP Home Edition, Windows XP Professional, Windows Server 2003 family

GraphicsPath Constructor (FillMode)

Initializes a new instance of the **GraphicsPath** class with the specified **FillMode** enumeration.

```
[Visual Basic]
Public Sub New( _
   ByVal fillMode As FillMode _
)
[C#]
public GraphicsPath(
   FillMode fillMode
);
[C++]
public: GraphicsPath(
   FillMode fillMode
);
[JScript]
public function GraphicsPath(
   fillMode : FillMode
);
```

Parameters

fillMode

The **FillMode** enumeration that determines how the interior of this **GraphicsPath** is filled.

Requirements

Platforms: Windows 98, Windows NT 4.0, Windows Millennium Edition, Windows 2000, Windows XP Home Edition, Windows XP Professional, Windows Server 2003 family

GraphicsPath Constructor (Point[], Byte[])

Initializes a new instance of the **GraphicsPath** class with the specified **PathPointType** and **Point** arrays.

```
[Visual Basic]
Public Sub New( _
   ByVal pts() As Point, _
   ByVal types() As Byte _
)
[C#]
public GraphicsPath(
   Point[] pts,
   byte[] types
);
[C++]
public: GraphicsPath(
   Point pts[],
   unsigned char types __gc[]
);
[JScript]
public function GraphicsPath(
   pts : Point[],
   types : Byte[]
);
```

Parameters

pts

An array of **Point** structures that defines the coordinates of the points that make up this **GraphicsPath**.

types

An array of **PathPointType** enumeration elements that specifies the type of each corresponding point in the *pts* array.

Requirements

Platforms: Windows 98, Windows NT 4.0, Windows Millennium Edition, Windows 2000, Windows XP Home Edition, Windows XP Professional, Windows Server 2003 family

GraphicsPath Constructor (PointF[], Byte[])

Initializes a new instance of the **GraphicsPath** array with the specified **PathPointType** and **PointF** arrays.

```
[Visual Basic]
Public Sub New( _
   ByVal pts() As PointF, _
   ByVal types() As Byte _
)
[C#]
public GraphicsPath(
   PointF[] pts,
   byte[] types
);
[C++]
public: GraphicsPath(
   PointF pts[],
   unsigned char types __gc[]
);
[JScript]
public function GraphicsPath(
   pts : PointF[],
   types : Byte[]
);
```

Parameters

pts
: An array of **PointF** structures that defines the coordinates of the points that make up this **GraphicsPath**.

types
: An array of **PathPointType** enumeration elements that specifies the type of each corresponding point in the *pts* array.

Requirements

Platforms: Windows 98, Windows NT 4.0, Windows Millennium Edition, Windows 2000, Windows XP Home Edition, Windows XP Professional, Windows Server 2003 family

GraphicsPath Constructor (Point[], Byte[], FillMode)

Initializes a new instance of the **GraphicsPath** class with the specified **PathPointType** and **Point** arrays and with the specified **FillMode** enumeration element.

```
[Visual Basic]
Public Sub New( _
   ByVal pts() As Point, _
   ByVal types() As Byte, _
   ByVal fillMode As FillMode _
)
[C#]
public GraphicsPath(
   Point[] pts,
   byte[] types,
   FillMode fillMode
);
[C++]
public: GraphicsPath(
   Point pts[],
   unsigned char types __gc[],
   FillMode fillMode
);
[JScript]
public function GraphicsPath(
   pts : Point[],
   types : Byte[],
   fillMode : FillMode
);
```

Parameters

pts
: An array of **Point** structures that defines the coordinates of the points that make up this **GraphicsPath**.

types
: An array of **PathPointType** enumeration elements that specifies the type of each corresponding point in the *pts* array.

fillMode
: A **FillMode** enumeration that specifies how the interiors of shapes in this **GraphicsPath** are filled.

Requirements

Platforms: Windows 98, Windows NT 4.0, Windows Millennium Edition, Windows 2000, Windows XP Home Edition, Windows XP Professional, Windows Server 2003 family

GraphicsPath Constructor (PointF[], Byte[], FillMode)

Initializes a new instance of the **GraphicsPath** array with the specified **PathPointType** and **PointF** arrays and with the specified **FillMode** enumeration element.

```
[Visual Basic]
Public Sub New( _
   ByVal pts() As PointF, _
   ByVal types() As Byte, _
   ByVal fillMode As FillMode _
)
[C#]
public GraphicsPath(
   PointF[] pts,
   byte[] types,
   FillMode fillMode
);
[C++]
public: GraphicsPath(
   PointF pts[],
   unsigned char types __gc[],
   FillMode fillMode
);
[JScript]
public function GraphicsPath(
   pts : PointF[],
   types : Byte[],
   fillMode : FillMode
);
```

Parameters

pts
: An array of **PointF** structures that defines the coordinates of the points that make up this **GraphicsPath**.

types
: An array of **PathPointType** enumeration elements that specifies the type of each corresponding point in the *pts* array.

fillMode
: A **FillMode** enumeration that specifies how the interiors of shapes in this **GraphicsPath** are filled.

Requirements

Platforms: Windows 98, Windows NT 4.0, Windows Millennium Edition, Windows 2000, Windows XP Home Edition, Windows XP Professional, Windows Server 2003 family

GraphicsPath.FillMode Property

Gets or sets a **FillMode** enumeration that determines how the interiors of shapes in this **GraphicsPath** object are filled.

```
[Visual Basic]
Public Property FillMode As FillMode
[C#]
public FillMode FillMode {get; set;}
[C++]
public: __property FillMode get_FillMode();
public: __property void set_FillMode(FillMode);
[JScript]
public function get FillMode() : FillMode;
public function set FillMode(FillMode);
```

Property Value

A **FillMode** enumeration that specifies how the interiors of shapes in this **GraphicsPath** object are filled.

Requirements

Platforms: Windows 98, Windows NT 4.0, Windows Millennium Edition, Windows 2000, Windows XP Home Edition, Windows XP Professional, Windows Server 2003 family

GraphicsPath.PathData Property

Gets a **PathData** object that encapsulates arrays of points (*points*) and types (*types*) for this **GraphicsPath** object.

```
[Visual Basic]
Public ReadOnly Property PathData As PathData
[C#]
public PathData PathData {get;}
[C++]
public: __property PathData* get_PathData();
[JScript]
public function get PathData() : PathData;
```

Property Value

A **PathData** object that encapsulates arrays for both the points and types for this **GraphicsPath** object.

Requirements

Platforms: Windows 98, Windows NT 4.0, Windows Millennium Edition, Windows 2000, Windows XP Home Edition, Windows XP Professional, Windows Server 2003 family

GraphicsPath.PathPoints Property

Gets the points in the path.

```
[Visual Basic]
Public ReadOnly Property PathPoints As PointF ()
[C#]
public PointF[] PathPoints {get;}
[C++]
public: __property PointF get_PathPoints();
[JScript]
public function get PathPoints() : PointF[];
```

Property Value

A an array of **PointF** objects that represent the path.

Requirements

Platforms: Windows 98, Windows NT 4.0, Windows Millennium Edition, Windows 2000, Windows XP Home Edition, Windows XP Professional, Windows Server 2003 family

GraphicsPath.PathTypes Property

Gets the types of the corresponding points in the **PathPoints** array.

```
[Visual Basic]
Public ReadOnly Property PathTypes As Byte ()
[C#]
public byte[] PathTypes {get;}
[C++]
public: __property unsigned char get_PathTypes();
[JScript]
public function get PathTypes() : Byte[];
```

Property Value

A an array of bytes that specify the types of the corresponding points in the path.

Requirements

Platforms: Windows 98, Windows NT 4.0, Windows Millennium Edition, Windows 2000, Windows XP Home Edition, Windows XP Professional, Windows Server 2003 family

GraphicsPath.PointCount Property

Gets the number of elements in the **PathPoints** or the **PathTypes** array.

```
[Visual Basic]
Public ReadOnly Property PointCount As Integer
[C#]
public int PointCount {get;}
[C++]
public: __property int get_PointCount();
[JScript]
public function get PointCount() : int;
```

Property Value

An integer that specifies the number of elements in the **PathPoints** or the **PathTypes** array.

Requirements

Platforms: Windows 98, Windows NT 4.0, Windows Millennium Edition, Windows 2000, Windows XP Home Edition, Windows XP Professional, Windows Server 2003 family

GraphicsPath.AddArc Method

Appends an elliptical arc to the current figure.

Overload List

Appends an elliptical arc to the current figure.

[Visual Basic] **Overloads Public Sub AddArc(Rectangle, Single, Single)**

[C#] **public void AddArc(Rectangle, float, float);**

[C++] **public: void AddArc(Rectangle, float, float);**

[JScript] **public function AddArc(Rectangle, float, float);**

Appends an elliptical arc to the current figure.

[Visual Basic] **Overloads Public Sub AddArc(RectangleF, Single, Single)**

[C#] **public void AddArc(RectangleF, float, float);**

[C++] **public: void AddArc(RectangleF, float, float);**

[JScript] **public function AddArc(RectangleF, float, float);**

Appends an elliptical arc to the current figure.

[Visual Basic] **Overloads Public Sub AddArc(Integer, Integer, Integer, Integer, Single, Single)**

[C#] **public void AddArc(int, int, int, int, float, float);**

[C++] **public: void AddArc(int, int, int, int, float, float);**

[JScript] **public function AddArc(int, int, int, int, float, float);**

Appends an elliptical arc to the current figure.

[Visual Basic] **Overloads Public Sub AddArc(Single, Single, Single, Single, Single, Single)**

[C#] **public void AddArc(float, float, float, float, float, float);**

[C++] **public: void AddArc(float, float, float, float, float, float);**

[JScript] **public function AddArc(float, float, float, float, float, float);**

Example

For an example, see **GraphicsPath.AddArc Method (Rectangle, Single, Single)**.

GraphicsPath.AddArc Method (Rectangle, Single, Single)

Appends an elliptical arc to the current figure.

```
[Visual Basic]
Overloads Public Sub AddArc( _
   ByVal rect As Rectangle, _
   ByVal startAngle As Single, _
   ByVal sweepAngle As Single _
)
[C#]
public void AddArc(
   Rectangle rect,
   float startAngle,
   float sweepAngle
);
[C++]
public: void AddArc(
   Rectangle rect,
   float startAngle,
   float sweepAngle
);
[JScript]
public function AddArc(
   rect : Rectangle,
   startAngle : float,
   sweepAngle : float
);
```

Parameters

rect

A **Rectangle** structure that represents the rectangular bounds of the ellipse from which the arc is taken.

startAngle

The starting angle of the arc, measured in degrees clockwise from the x-axis.

sweepAngle

The angle between *startAngle* and the end of the arc.

Remarks

If there are previous lines or curves in the figure, a line is added to connect the endpoint of the previous segment to the beginning of the arc.

The arc is traced along the perimeter of the ellipse bounded by the specified rectangle. The starting point of the arc is determined by measuring clockwise from the x-axis of the ellipse (at the 0-degree angle) by the number of degrees in the start angle. The endpoint is similarly located by measuring clockwise from the starting point by the number of degrees in the sweep angle. If the sweep angle is greater than 360 degrees or less than -360 degrees, the arc is swept by exactly 360 degrees or -360 degrees, respectively.

Example

[Visual Basic, C#] The following example is designed for use with Windows Forms, and it requires **PaintEventArgs** *e*, an **OnPaint** event object. The code performs the following actions:

- Creates a rectangle, from which the arc is defined.
- Creates a path, *myPath*.
- Defines a 180-degree elliptical arc that sweeps from 0 degrees to 180 degrees and appends it to a path.
- Draws the path to screen.

```
[Visual Basic]
Public Sub AddArcExample(e As PaintEventArgs)
' Create a GraphicsPath object.
Dim myPath As New GraphicsPath()
' Set up and call AddArc, and close the figure.
Dim rect As New Rectangle(20, 20, 50, 100)
myPath.StartFigure()
myPath.AddArc(rect, 0, 180)
myPath.CloseFigure()
' Draw the path to screen.
e.Graphics.DrawPath(New Pen(Color.Red, 3), myPath)
End Sub
```

```
[C#]
private void AddArcExample(PaintEventArgs e)
{
// Create a GraphicsPath object.
GraphicsPath myPath = new GraphicsPath();
// Set up and call AddArc, and close the figure.
Rectangle rect = new Rectangle(20, 20, 50, 100);
myPath.StartFigure();
myPath.AddArc(rect, 0, 180);
myPath.CloseFigure();
// Draw the path to screen.
e.Graphics.DrawPath(new Pen(Color.Red, 3), myPath);
}
```

Requirements

Platforms: Windows 98, Windows NT 4.0, Windows Millennium Edition, Windows 2000, Windows XP Home Edition, Windows XP Professional, Windows Server 2003 family

GraphicsPath.AddArc Method (RectangleF, Single, Single)

Appends an elliptical arc to the current figure.

```
[Visual Basic]
Overloads Public Sub AddArc( _
   ByVal rect As RectangleF, _
   ByVal startAngle As Single, _
   ByVal sweepAngle As Single _
)
[C#]
public void AddArc(
   RectangleF rect,
   float startAngle,
   float sweepAngle
);
```

[C++]
```
public: void AddArc(
   RectangleF rect,
   float startAngle,
   float sweepAngle
);
```
[JScript]
```
public function AddArc(
   rect : RectangleF,
   startAngle : float,
   sweepAngle : float
);
```

Parameters

rect
: A **RectangleF** structure that represents the rectangular bounds of the ellipse from which the arc is taken.

startAngle
: The starting angle of the arc, measured in degrees clockwise from the x-axis.

sweepAngle
: The angle between *startAngle* and the end of the arc.

Remarks

If there are previous lines or curves in the figure, a line is added to connect the endpoint of the previous segment to the beginning of the arc.

The arc is traced along the perimeter of the ellipse bounded by the specified rectangle. The starting point of the arc is determined by measuring clockwise from the x-axis of the ellipse (at the 0-degree angle) by the number of degrees in the start angle. The endpoint is similarly located by measuring clockwise from the starting point by the number of degrees in the sweep angle. If the sweep angle is greater than 360 degrees or less than -360 degrees, the arc is swept by exactly 360 degrees or -360 degrees, respectively.

Example

For an example, see **GraphicsPath.AddArc Method (Rectangle, Single, Single)**.

Requirements

Platforms: Windows 98, Windows NT 4.0, Windows Millennium Edition, Windows 2000, Windows XP Home Edition, Windows XP Professional, Windows Server 2003 family

GraphicsPath.AddArc Method (Int32, Int32, Int32, Int32, Single, Single)

Appends an elliptical arc to the current figure.

[Visual Basic]
```
Overloads Public Sub AddArc( _
   ByVal x As Integer, _
   ByVal y As Integer, _
   ByVal width As Integer, _
   ByVal height As Integer, _
   ByVal startAngle As Single, _
   ByVal sweepAngle As Single _
)
```
[C#]
```
public void AddArc(
   int x,
   int y,
   int width,
   int height,
   float startAngle,
   float sweepAngle
);
```
[C++]
```
public: void AddArc(
   int x,
   int y,
   int width,
   int height,
   float startAngle,
   float sweepAngle
);
```
[JScript]
```
public function AddArc(
   x : int,
   y : int,
   width : int,
   height : int,
   startAngle : float,
   sweepAngle : float
);
```

Parameters

x
: The x-coordinate of the upper-left corner of the rectangular region that defines the ellipse from which the arc is drawn.

y
: The y-coordinate of the upper-left corner of the rectangular region that defines the ellipse from which the arc is drawn.

width
: The width of the rectangular region that defines the ellipse from which the arc is drawn.

height
: The height of the rectangular region that defines the ellipse from which the arc is drawn.

startAngle
: The starting angle of the arc, measured in degrees clockwise from the x-axis.

sweepAngle
: The angle between *startAngle* and the end of the arc.

Remarks

If there are previous lines or curves in the figure, a line is added to connect the endpoint of the previous segment to the beginning of the arc.

The arc is traced along the perimeter of the ellipse bounded by the specified rectangle. The starting point of the arc is determined by measuring clockwise from the x-axis of the ellipse (at the 0-degree angle) by the number of degrees in the start angle. The endpoint is similarly located by measuring clockwise from the starting point by the number of degrees in the sweep angle. If the sweep angle is greater than 360 degrees or less than -360 degrees, the arc is swept by exactly 360 degrees or -360 degrees, respectively.

Example

For an example, see **GraphicsPath.AddArc Method (Rectangle, Single, Single)**.

Requirements

Platforms: Windows 98, Windows NT 4.0,
Windows Millennium Edition, Windows 2000,
Windows XP Home Edition, Windows XP Professional,
Windows Server 2003 family

GraphicsPath.AddArc Method (Single, Single, Single, Single, Single, Single)

Appends an elliptical arc to the current figure.

```
[Visual Basic]
Overloads Public Sub AddArc( _
   ByVal x As Single, _
   ByVal y As Single, _
   ByVal width As Single, _
   ByVal height As Single, _
   ByVal startAngle As Single, _
   ByVal sweepAngle As Single _
)
[C#]
public void AddArc(
   float x,
   float y,
   float width,
   float height,
   float startAngle,
   float sweepAngle
);
[C++]
public: void AddArc(
   float x,
   float y,
   float width,
   float height,
   float startAngle,
   float sweepAngle
);
[JScript]
public function AddArc(
   x : float,
   y : float,
   width : float,
   height : float,
   startAngle : float,
   sweepAngle : float
);
```

Parameters

x
: The x-coordinate of the upper-left corner of the rectangular region that defines the ellipse from which the arc is drawn.

y
: The y-coordinate of the upper-left corner of the rectangular region that defines the ellipse from which the arc is drawn.

width
: The width of the rectangular region that defines the ellipse from which the arc is drawn.

height
: The height of the rectangular region that defines the ellipse from which the arc is drawn.

startAngle
: The starting angle of the arc, measured in degrees clockwise from the x-axis.

sweepAngle
: The angle between *startAngle* and the end of the arc.

Remarks

If there are previous lines or curves in the figure, a line is added to connect the endpoint of the previous segment to the beginning of the arc.

The arc is traced along the perimeter of the ellipse bounded by the specified rectangle. The starting point of the arc is determined by measuring clockwise from the x-axis of the ellipse (at the 0-degree angle) by the number of degrees in the start angle. The endpoint is similarly located by measuring clockwise from the starting point by the number of degrees in the sweep angle. If the sweep angle is greater than 360 degrees or less than -360 degrees, the arc is swept by exactly 360 degrees or -360 degrees, respectively.

Example

For an example, see **GraphicsPath.AddArc Method (Rectangle, Single, Single)**.

Requirements

Platforms: Windows 98, Windows NT 4.0,
Windows Millennium Edition, Windows 2000,
Windows XP Home Edition, Windows XP Professional,
Windows Server 2003 family

GraphicsPath.AddBezier Method

Adds a cubic Bézier curve to the current figure.

Overload List

Adds a cubic Bézier curve to the current figure.

[Visual Basic] **Overloads Public Sub AddBezier(Point, Point, Point, Point)**

[C#] **public void AddBezier(Point, Point, Point, Point);**

[C++] **public: void AddBezier(Point, Point, Point, Point);**

[JScript] **public function AddBezier(Point, Point, Point, Point);**

Adds a cubic Bézier curve to the current figure.

[Visual Basic] **Overloads Public Sub AddBezier(PointF, PointF, PointF, PointF)**

[C#] **public void AddBezier(PointF, PointF, PointF, PointF);**

[C++] **public: void AddBezier(PointF, PointF, PointF, PointF);**

[JScript] **public function AddBezier(PointF, PointF, PointF, PointF);**

Adds a cubic Bézier curve to the current figure.

[Visual Basic] **Overloads Public Sub AddBezier(Integer, Integer, Integer, Integer, Integer, Integer, Integer, Integer)**

[C#] **public void AddBezier(int, int, int, int, int, int, int, int);**

[C++] **public: void AddBezier(int, int, int, int, int, int, int, int);**

[JScript] **public function AddBezier(int, int, int, int, int, int, int, int);**

Adds a cubic Bézier curve to the current figure.

[Visual Basic] **Overloads Public Sub AddBezier(Single, Single, Single, Single, Single, Single, Single, Single)**

[C#] **public void AddBezier(float, float, float, float, float, float, float, float);**

[C++] **public: void AddBezier(float, float, float, float, float, float, float, float);**

[JScript] **public function AddBezier(float, float, float, float, float, float, float, float);**

Example

For an example, see **GraphicsPath.AddBezier Method (Int32, Int32, Int32, Int32, Int32, Int32, Int32, Int32)**.

GraphicsPath.AddBezier Method (Point, Point, Point, Point)

Adds a cubic Bézier curve to the current figure.

```
[Visual Basic]
Overloads Public Sub AddBezier( _
   ByVal pt1 As Point, _
   ByVal pt2 As Point, _
   ByVal pt3 As Point, _
   ByVal pt4 As Point _
)
[C#]
public void AddBezier(
   Point pt1,
   Point pt2,
   Point pt3,
   Point pt4
);
[C++]
public: void AddBezier(
   Point pt1,
   Point pt2,
   Point pt3,
   Point pt4
);
[JScript]
public function AddBezier(
   pt1 : Point,
   pt2 : Point,
   pt3 : Point,
   pt4 : Point
);
```

Parameters

pt1

A **Point** structure that represents the starting point of the curve.

pt2

A **Point** structure that represents the first control point for the curve.

pt3

A **Point** structure that represents the second control point for the curve.

pt4

A **Point** structure that represents the endpoint of the curve.

Remarks

The cubic curve is constructed from the first point to the fourth point by using the second and third points as control points.

If there is a previous line or curve segment in the figure, a line is added to connect the endpoint of the previous segment to the starting point of the cubic curve.

Example

For an example, see **GraphicsPath.AddBezier Method (Int32, Int32, Int32, Int32, Int32, Int32, Int32, Int32)**.

Requirements

Platforms: Windows 98, Windows NT 4.0, Windows Millennium Edition, Windows 2000, Windows XP Home Edition, Windows XP Professional, Windows Server 2003 family

GraphicsPath.AddBezier Method (PointF, PointF, PointF, PointF)

Adds a cubic Bézier curve to the current figure.

```
[Visual Basic]
Overloads Public Sub AddBezier( _
   ByVal pt1 As PointF, _
   ByVal pt2 As PointF, _
   ByVal pt3 As PointF, _
   ByVal pt4 As PointF _
)
[C#]
public void AddBezier(
   PointF pt1,
   PointF pt2,
   PointF pt3,
   PointF pt4
);
[C++]
public: void AddBezier(
   PointF pt1,
   PointF pt2,
   PointF pt3,
   PointF pt4
);
[JScript]
public function AddBezier(
   pt1 : PointF,
   pt2 : PointF,
   pt3 : PointF,
   pt4 : PointF
);
```

Parameters

pt1

A **PointF** structure that represents the starting point of the curve.

pt2

A **PointF** structure that represents the first control point for the curve.

pt3

A **PointF** structure that represents the second control point for the curve.

pt4

A **PointF** structure that represents the endpoint of the curve.

Remarks

The cubic curve is constructed from the first point to the fourth point by using the second and third points as control points.

If there is a previous line or curve segment in the figure, a line is added to connect the endpoint of the previous segment to the starting point of the cubic curve.

Example

For an example, see **GraphicsPath.AddBezier Method (Int32, Int32, Int32, Int32, Int32, Int32, Int32, Int32)**.

Requirements

Platforms: Windows 98, Windows NT 4.0, Windows Millennium Edition, Windows 2000, Windows XP Home Edition, Windows XP Professional, Windows Server 2003 family

GraphicsPath.AddBezier Method (Int32, Int32, Int32, Int32, Int32, Int32, Int32, Int32)

Adds a cubic Bézier curve to the current figure.

[Visual Basic]
```
Overloads Public Sub AddBezier( _
   ByVal x1 As Integer, _
   ByVal y1 As Integer, _
   ByVal x2 As Integer, _
   ByVal y2 As Integer, _
   ByVal x3 As Integer, _
   ByVal y3 As Integer, _
   ByVal x4 As Integer, _
   ByVal y4 As Integer _
)
```
[C#]
```
public void AddBezier(
   int x1,
   int y1,
   int x2,
   int y2,
   int x3,
   int y3,
   int x4,
   int y4
);
```
[C++]
```
public: void AddBezier(
   int x1,
   int y1,
   int x2,
   int y2,
   int x3,
   int y3,
   int x4,
   int y4
);
```
[JScript]
```
public function AddBezier(
   x1 : int,
   y1 : int,
   x2 : int,
   y2 : int,
   x3 : int,
   y3 : int,
   x4 : int,
   y4 : int
);
```

Parameters

x1
: The x-coordinate of the starting point of the curve.

y1
: The y-coordinate of the starting point of the curve.

x2
: The x-coordinate of the first control point for the curve.

y2
: The y-coordinate of the first control point for the curve.

x3
: The x-coordinate of the second control point for the curve.

y3
: The y-coordinate of the second control point for the curve.

x4
: The x-coordinate of the endpoint of the curve.

y4
: The y-coordinate of the endpoint of the curve.

Remarks

The cubic curve is constructed from the first point to the fourth point by using the second and third points as control points.

If there is a previous line or curve segment in the figure, a line is added to connect the endpoint of the previous segment to the starting point of the cubic curve.

Example

[Visual Basic, C#] The following example is designed for use with Windows Forms, and it requires **PaintEventArgs** *e*, an **OnPaint** event object. The code performs the following actions:

- Creates a path.
- Adds a cubic Bézier curve defined by the points (50, 50), (70, 0), (100, 120), and (150, 50) to the path.
- Closes the curve.
- Draws the path to screen.

[Visual Basic]
```
Public Sub AddBezierExample(e As PaintEventArgs)
' Create a new Path.
Dim myPath As New GraphicsPath()
' Call AddBezier.
myPath.StartFigure()
myPath.AddBezier(50, 50, 70, 0, 100, 120, 150, 50)
' Close the curve.
myPath.CloseFigure()
' Draw the path to screen.
e.Graphics.DrawPath(New Pen(Color.Red, 2), myPath)
End Sub
```

[C#]
```
private void AddBezierExample(PaintEventArgs e)
{
// Create a new Path.
GraphicsPath myPath = new GraphicsPath();
// Call AddBezier.
myPath.StartFigure();
myPath.AddBezier(50, 50, 70, 0, 100, 120, 150, 50);
// Close the curve.
myPath.CloseFigure();
// Draw the path to screen.
e.Graphics.DrawPath(new Pen(Color.Red, 2), myPath);
}
```

Requirements

Platforms: Windows 98, Windows NT 4.0, Windows Millennium Edition, Windows 2000, Windows XP Home Edition, Windows XP Professional, Windows Server 2003 family

GraphicsPath.AddBezier Method (Single, Single, Single, Single, Single, Single, Single, Single)

Adds a cubic Bézier curve to the current figure.

[Visual Basic]
```
Overloads Public Sub AddBezier( _
   ByVal x1 As Single, _
   ByVal y1 As Single, _
   ByVal x2 As Single, _
   ByVal y2 As Single, _
   ByVal x3 As Single, _
   ByVal y3 As Single, _
   ByVal x4 As Single, _
   ByVal y4 As Single _
)
```
[C#]
```
public void AddBezier(
   float x1,
   float y1,
   float x2,
   float y2,
   float x3,
   float y3,
   float x4,
   float y4
);
```
[C++]
```
public: void AddBezier(
   float x1,
   float y1,
   float x2,
   float y2,
   float x3,
   float y3,
   float x4,
   float y4
);
```
[JScript]
```
public function AddBezier(
   x1 : float,
   y1 : float,
   x2 : float,
   y2 : float,
   x3 : float,
   y3 : float,
   x4 : float,
   y4 : float
);
```

Parameters

x1
The x-coordinate of the starting point of the curve.

y1
The y-coordinate of the starting point of the curve.

x2
The x-coordinate of the first control point for the curve.

y2
The y-coordinate of the first control point for the curve.

x3
The x-coordinate of the second control point for the curve.

y3
The y-coordinate of the second control point for the curve.

x4
The x-coordinate of the endpoint of the curve.

y4
The y-coordinate of the endpoint of the curve.

Remarks

The cubic curve is constructed from the first point to the fourth point by using the second and third points as control points.

If there is a previous line or curve segment in the figure, a line is added to connect the endpoint of the previous segment to the starting point of the cubic curve.

Example

For an example, see **GraphicsPath.AddBezier Method (Int32, Int32, Int32, Int32, Int32, Int32, Int32, Int32)**.

Requirements

Platforms: Windows 98, Windows NT 4.0, Windows Millennium Edition, Windows 2000, Windows XP Home Edition, Windows XP Professional, Windows Server 2003 family

GraphicsPath.AddBeziers Method

Adds a sequence of connected cubic Bézier curves to the current figure.

Overload List

Adds a sequence of connected cubic Bézier curves to the current figure.

[Visual Basic] **Overloads Public Sub AddBeziers(Point())**

[C#] **public void AddBeziers(Point[]);**

[C++] **public: void AddBeziers(Point[]);**

[JScript] **public function AddBeziers(Point[]);**

Adds a sequence of connected cubic Bézier curves to the current figure.

[Visual Basic] **Overloads Public Sub AddBeziers(PointF())**

[C#] **public void AddBeziers(PointF[]);**

[C++] **public: void AddBeziers(PointF[]);**

[JScript] **public function AddBeziers(PointF[]);**

Example

For an example, see **GraphicsPath.AddBeziers Method (Point[])**.

GraphicsPath.AddBeziers Method (Point[])

Adds a sequence of connected cubic Bézier curves to the current figure.

[Visual Basic]
```
Overloads Public Sub AddBeziers( _
   ByVal points() As Point _
)
```

[C#]
```
public void AddBeziers(
   Point[] points
);
```
[C++]
```
public: void AddBeziers(
   Point points[]
);
```
[JScript]
```
public function AddBeziers(
   points : Point[]
);
```

Parameters

points

An array of **Point** structures that represents the points that define the curves.

Remarks

The *points* parameter specifies an array of endpoints and control points of the connected curves. The first curve is constructed from the first point to the fourth point in the *points* array by using the second and third points as control points. In addition to the endpoint of the previous curve, each subsequent curve in the sequence needs exactly three more points: the next two points in the sequence are control points, and the third is the endpoint for the added curve.

If there are previous lines or curves in the figure, a line is added to connect the endpoint of the previous segment to the starting point of the first cubic curve in the sequence.

Example

[Visual Basic, C#] The following example is designed for use with Windows Forms, and it requires **PaintEventArgs** *e*, an **OnPaint** event object. The code performs the following actions:

- Creates an array of seven points (representing two connected Bézier curves).
- Creates a path and adds the series of Bézier curve points to the path.
- Draws the path to screen.

[Visual Basic]
```
Public Sub AddBeziersExample(e As PaintEventArgs)
' Adds two Bezier curves.
Dim myArray As Point() = {New Point(20, 100), New Point(40, 75), _
New Point(60, 125), New Point(80, 100), New Point(100, 50), _
New Point(120, 150), New Point(140, 100)}
Dim myPath As New GraphicsPath()
myPath.AddBeziers(myArray)
Dim myPen As New Pen(Color.Black, 2)
e.Graphics.DrawPath(myPen, myPath)
End Sub
```

[C#]
```
private void AddBeziersExample(PaintEventArgs e)
{
// Adds two Bezier curves.
Point[] myArray =
{
new Point(20, 100),
new Point(40, 75),
new Point(60, 125),
new Point(80, 100),
new Point(100, 50),
new Point(120, 150),
new Point(140, 100)
};
// Create the path and add the curves.
GraphicsPath myPath = new GraphicsPath();
myPath.AddBeziers(myArray);
// Draw the path to the screen.
Pen myPen = new Pen(Color.Black, 2);
e.Graphics.DrawPath(myPen, myPath);
}
```

Requirements

Platforms: Windows 98, Windows NT 4.0, Windows Millennium Edition, Windows 2000, Windows XP Home Edition, Windows XP Professional, Windows Server 2003 family

GraphicsPath.AddBeziers Method (PointF[])

Adds a sequence of connected cubic Bézier curves to the current figure.

[Visual Basic]
```
Overloads Public Sub AddBeziers( _
   ByVal points() As PointF _
)
```
[C#]
```
public void AddBeziers(
   PointF[] points
);
```
[C++]
```
public: void AddBeziers(
   PointF points[]
);
```
[JScript]
```
public function AddBeziers(
   points : PointF[]
);
```

Parameters

points

An array of **PointF** structures that represents the points that define the curves.

Remarks

The *points* parameter specifies an array of endpoints and control points of the connected curves. The first curve is constructed from the first point to the fourth point in the *points* array by using the second and third points as control points. In addition to the endpoint of the previous curve, each subsequent curve in the sequence needs exactly three more points: the next two points in the sequence are control points, and the third is the endpoint for the added curve.

If there are previous lines or curves in the figure, a line is added to connect the endpoint of the previous segment to the starting point of the first cubic curve in the sequence.

Example

For an example, see **GraphicsPath.AddBeziers Method (Point[])**.

Requirements

Platforms: Windows 98, Windows NT 4.0, Windows Millennium Edition, Windows 2000, Windows XP Home Edition, Windows XP Professional, Windows Server 2003 family

GraphicsPath.AddClosedCurve Method

Adds a closed curve to this path. A cardinal spline curve is used because the curve travels through each of the points in the array.

Overload List

Adds a closed curve to this path. A cardinal spline curve is used because the curve travels through each of the points in the array.

[Visual Basic] **Overloads Public Sub AddClosedCurve(Point())**

[C#] **public void AddClosedCurve(Point[]);**

[C++] **public: void AddClosedCurve(Point[]);**

[JScript] **public function AddClosedCurve(Point[]);**

Adds a closed curve to this path. A cardinal spline curve is used because the curve travels through each of the points in the array.

[Visual Basic] **Overloads Public Sub AddClosedCurve(PointF())**

[C#] **public void AddClosedCurve(PointF[]);**

[C++] **public: void AddClosedCurve(PointF[]);**

[JScript] **public function AddClosedCurve(PointF[]);**

Adds a closed curve to this path. A cardinal spline curve is used because the curve travels through each of the points in the array.

[Visual Basic] **Overloads Public Sub AddClosedCurve(Point(), Single)**

[C#] **public void AddClosedCurve(Point[], float);**

[C++] **public: void AddClosedCurve(Point[], float);**

[JScript] **public function AddClosedCurve(Point[], float);**

Adds a closed curve to this path. A cardinal spline curve is used because the curve travels through each of the points in the array.

[Visual Basic] **Overloads Public Sub AddClosedCurve(PointF(), Single)**

[C#] **public void AddClosedCurve(PointF[], float);**

[C++] **public: void AddClosedCurve(PointF[], float);**

[JScript] **public function AddClosedCurve(PointF[], float);**

Example

For an example, see **GraphicsPath.AddClosedCurve Method (Point[], Single)**.

GraphicsPath.AddClosedCurve Method (Point[])

Adds a closed curve to this path. A cardinal spline curve is used because the curve travels through each of the points in the array.

```
[Visual Basic]
Overloads Public Sub AddClosedCurve( _
   ByVal points() As Point _
)
[C#]
public void AddClosedCurve(
   Point[] points
);
[C++]
public: void AddClosedCurve(
   Point points[]
);
[JScript]
public function AddClosedCurve(
   points : Point[]
);
```

Parameters

points

An array of **Point** structures that represents the points that define the curve.

Remarks

The user must keep the original points if they are needed. The original points are converted to cubic Bézier control points internally, therefore there is no mechanism for returning the original points. If the first point and the last point in the *points* array are not the same point, the curve is closed by connecting these two points. The tension value cannot be set for this method, and defaults to a value equivalent to 0.5.

Example

For an example, see **GraphicsPath.AddClosedCurve Method (Point[], Single)**.

Requirements

Platforms: Windows 98, Windows NT 4.0, Windows Millennium Edition, Windows 2000, Windows XP Home Edition, Windows XP Professional, Windows Server 2003 family

GraphicsPath.AddClosedCurve Method (PointF[])

Adds a closed curve to this path. A cardinal spline curve is used because the curve travels through each of the points in the array.

```
[Visual Basic]
Overloads Public Sub AddClosedCurve( _
   ByVal points() As PointF _
)
[C#]
public void AddClosedCurve(
   PointF[] points
);
[C++]
public: void AddClosedCurve(
   PointF points[]
);
[JScript]
public function AddClosedCurve(
   points : PointF[]
);
```

Parameters

points

An array of **PointF** structures that represents the points that define the curve.

Remarks

The user must keep the original points if they are needed. The original points are converted to cubic Bézier control points internally, therefore there is no mechanism for returning the original points. If the first point and the last point in the *points* array are not the same point, the curve is closed by connecting these two points. The tension value cannot be set for this method, and defaults to a value equivalent to 0.5.

Example

For an example, see **GraphicsPath.AddClosedCurve Method (Point[], Single)**.

Requirements

Platforms: Windows 98, Windows NT 4.0, Windows Millennium Edition, Windows 2000, Windows XP Home Edition, Windows XP Professional, Windows Server 2003 family

GraphicsPath.AddClosedCurve Method (Point[], Single)

Adds a closed curve to this path. A cardinal spline curve is used because the curve travels through each of the points in the array.

[Visual Basic]
```
Overloads Public Sub AddClosedCurve( _
   ByVal points() As Point, _
   ByVal tension As Single _
)
```
[C#]
```
public void AddClosedCurve(
   Point[] points,
   float tension
);
```
[C++]
```
public: void AddClosedCurve(
   Point points[],
   float tension
);
```
[JScript]
```
public function AddClosedCurve(
   points : Point[],
   tension : float
);
```

Parameters

points
An array of **Point** structures that represents the points that define the curve.

tension
A value between from 0 through 1 that specifies the amount that the curve bends between points, with 0 being the smallest curve (sharpest corner) and 1 being the smoothest curve.

Remarks

The user must keep the original points if they are needed. The original points are converted to cubic Bézier control points internally, therefore there is no mechanism for returning the original points. If the first point and the last point in the *points* array are not the same point, the curve is closed by connecting these two points.

Example

[Visual Basic, C#] The following example is designed for use with Windows Forms, and it requires **PaintEventArgs** *e*, an **OnPaint** event object. The code performs the following actions:

- Creates an array of six points (representing a cardinal spline).
- Creates a path and adds the closed cardinal spline curves to the path (closed from the endpoint to the starting point).
- Draws the path to screen.

[Visual Basic, C#] Notice that a tension of 0.5 is used.

[Visual Basic]
```
Public Sub AddClosedCurveExample(e As PaintEventArgs)
' Creates a symetrical, closed curve.
Dim myArray As Point() = {New Point(20, 100), New Point(40, 150), _
New Point(60, 125), New Point(40, 100), New Point(60, 75), _
New Point(40, 50)}
Dim myPath As New GraphicsPath()
myPath.AddClosedCurve(myArray, 0.5F)
Dim myPen As New Pen(Color.Black, 2)
e.Graphics.DrawPath(myPen, myPath)
End Sub
```

[C#]
```
private void AddClosedCurveExample(PaintEventArgs e)
{
// Creates a symetrical, closed curve.
Point[] myArray =
{
new Point(20,100),
new Point(40,150),
new Point(60,125),
new Point(40,100),
new Point(60,75),
new Point(40,50)
};
// Create a new path and add curve.
GraphicsPath myPath = new GraphicsPath();
myPath.AddClosedCurve(myArray, .5f);
Pen myPen = new Pen(Color.Black, 2);
// Draw the path to screen.
e.Graphics.DrawPath(myPen, myPath);
}
```

Requirements

Platforms: Windows 98, Windows NT 4.0, Windows Millennium Edition, Windows 2000, Windows XP Home Edition, Windows XP Professional, Windows Server 2003 family

GraphicsPath.AddClosedCurve Method (PointF[], Single)

Adds a closed curve to this path. A cardinal spline curve is used because the curve travels through each of the points in the array.

[Visual Basic]
```
Overloads Public Sub AddClosedCurve( _
   ByVal points() As PointF, _
   ByVal tension As Single _
)
```
[C#]
```
public void AddClosedCurve(
   PointF[] points,
   float tension
);
```
[C++]
```
public: void AddClosedCurve(
   PointF points[],
   float tension
);
```
[JScript]
```
public function AddClosedCurve(
   points : PointF[],
   tension : float
);
```

Parameters

points
An array of **PointF** structures that represents the points that define the curve.

tension
A value between from 0 through 1 that specifies the amount that the curve bends between points, with 0 being the smallest curve (sharpest corner) and 1 being the smoothest curve.

Remarks

The user must keep the original points if they are needed. The original points are converted to cubic Bézier control points internally, therefore there is no mechanism for returning the original points. If the first point and the last point in the *points* array are not the same point, the curve is closed by connecting these two points.

Example

For an example, see **GraphicsPath.AddClosedCurve Method (Point[], Single)**.

Requirements

Platforms: Windows 98, Windows NT 4.0,
Windows Millennium Edition, Windows 2000,
Windows XP Home Edition, Windows XP Professional,
Windows Server 2003 family

GraphicsPath.AddCurve Method

Adds a spline curve to the current figure. A cardinal spline curve is used because the curve travels through each of the points in the array.

Overload List

Adds a spline curve to the current figure. A cardinal spline curve is used because the curve travels through each of the points in the array.

[Visual Basic] **Overloads Public Sub AddCurve(Point())**

[C#] **public void AddCurve(Point[]);**

[C++] **public: void AddCurve(Point[]);**

[JScript] **public function AddCurve(Point[]);**

Adds a spline curve to the current figure. A cardinal spline curve is used because the curve travels through each of the points in the array.

[Visual Basic] **Overloads Public Sub AddCurve(PointF())**

[C#] **public void AddCurve(PointF[]);**

[C++] **public: void AddCurve(PointF[]);**

[JScript] **public function AddCurve(PointF[]);**

Adds a spline curve to the current figure.

[Visual Basic] **Overloads Public Sub AddCurve(Point(), Single)**

[C#] **public void AddCurve(Point[], float);**

[C++] **public: void AddCurve(Point[], float);**

[JScript] **public function AddCurve(Point[], float);**

Adds a spline curve to the current figure.

[Visual Basic] **Overloads Public Sub AddCurve(PointF(), Single)**

[C#] **public void AddCurve(PointF[], float);**

[C++] **public: void AddCurve(PointF[], float);**

[JScript] **public function AddCurve(PointF[], float);**

Adds a spline curve to the current figure.

[Visual Basic] **Overloads Public Sub AddCurve(Point(), Integer, Integer, Single)**

[C#] **public void AddCurve(Point[], int, int, float);**

[C++] **public: void AddCurve(Point[], int, int, float);**

[JScript] **public function AddCurve(Point[], int, int, float);**

Adds a spline curve to the current figure.

[Visual Basic] **Overloads Public Sub AddCurve(PointF(), Integer, Integer, Single)**

[C#] **public void AddCurve(PointF[], int, int, float);**

[C++] **public: void AddCurve(PointF[], int, int, float);**

[JScript] **public function AddCurve(PointF[], int, int, float);**

Example

For an example, see **GraphicsPath.AddCurve Method (Point[], Int32, Int32, Single)**.

GraphicsPath.AddCurve Method (Point[])

Adds a spline curve to the current figure. A cardinal spline curve is used because the curve travels through each of the points in the array.

```
[Visual Basic]
Overloads Public Sub AddCurve( _
   ByVal points() As Point _
)
[C#]
public void AddCurve(
   Point[] points
);
[C++]
public: void AddCurve(
   Point points[]
);
[JScript]
public function AddCurve(
   points : Point[]
);
```

Parameters

points
An array of **Point** structures that represents the points that define the curve.

Remarks

The user must keep the original points if they are needed. The original points are converted to cubic Bézier control points internally, therefore there is no mechanism for returning the original points.

Example

For an example, see **GraphicsPath.AddCurve Method (Point[], Int32, Int32, Single)**.

Requirements

Platforms: Windows 98, Windows NT 4.0,
Windows Millennium Edition, Windows 2000,
Windows XP Home Edition, Windows XP Professional,
Windows Server 2003 family

GraphicsPath.AddCurve Method (PointF[])

Adds a spline curve to the current figure. A cardinal spline curve is used because the curve travels through each of the points in the array.

```
[Visual Basic]
Overloads Public Sub AddCurve( _
   ByVal points() As PointF _
)
[C#]
public void AddCurve(
   PointF[] points
);
[C++]
public: void AddCurve(
   PointF points[]
);
[JScript]
public function AddCurve(
   points : PointF[]
);
```

Parameters

points
: An array of **PointF** structures that represents the points that define the curve.

Remarks

The user must keep the original points if they are needed. The original points are converted to cubic Bézier control points internally, therefore there is no mechanism for returning the original points.

Example

For an example, see **GraphicsPath.AddCurve Method (Point[], Int32, Int32, Single)**.

Requirements

Platforms: Windows 98, Windows NT 4.0, Windows Millennium Edition, Windows 2000, Windows XP Home Edition, Windows XP Professional, Windows Server 2003 family

GraphicsPath.AddCurve Method (Point[], Single)

Adds a spline curve to the current figure.

```
[Visual Basic]
Overloads Public Sub AddCurve( _
   ByVal points() As Point, _
   ByVal tension As Single _
)
[C#]
public void AddCurve(
   Point[] points,
   float tension
);
[C++]
public: void AddCurve(
   Point points[],
   float tension
);
[JScript]
public function AddCurve(
   points : Point[],
   tension : float
);
```

Parameters

points
: An array of **Point** structures that represents the points that define the curve.

tension
: A value that specifies the amount that the curve bends between control points. Values greater than 1 produce unpredictable results.

Remarks

The user must keep the original points if they are needed. The original points are converted to cubic Bézier control points internally, therefore there is no mechanism for returning the original points.

Example

For an example, see **GraphicsPath.AddCurve Method (Point[], Int32, Int32, Single)**.

Requirements

Platforms: Windows 98, Windows NT 4.0, Windows Millennium Edition, Windows 2000, Windows XP Home Edition, Windows XP Professional, Windows Server 2003 family

GraphicsPath.AddCurve Method (PointF[], Single)

Adds a spline curve to the current figure.

```
[Visual Basic]
Overloads Public Sub AddCurve( _
   ByVal points() As PointF, _
   ByVal tension As Single _
)
[C#]
public void AddCurve(
   PointF[] points,
   float tension
);
[C++]
public: void AddCurve(
   PointF points[],
   float tension
);
[JScript]
public function AddCurve(
   points : PointF[],
   tension : float
);
```

Parameters

points
: An array of **PointF** structures that represents the points that define the curve.

tension
: A value that specifies the amount that the curve bends between control points. Values greater than 1 produce unpredictable results.

Remarks

The user must keep the original points if they are needed. The original points are converted to cubic Bézier control points internally, therefore there is no mechanism for returning the original points.

Example

For an example, see **GraphicsPath.AddCurve Method (Point[], Int32, Int32, Single)**.

Requirements

Platforms: Windows 98, Windows NT 4.0, Windows Millennium Edition, Windows 2000, Windows XP Home Edition, Windows XP Professional, Windows Server 2003 family

GraphicsPath.AddCurve Method (Point[], Int32, Int32, Single)

Adds a spline curve to the current figure.

[Visual Basic]
```
Overloads Public Sub AddCurve( _
   ByVal points() As Point, _
   ByVal offset As Integer, _
   ByVal numberOfSegments As Integer, _
   ByVal tension As Single _
)
```
[C#]
```
public void AddCurve(
   Point[] points,
   int offset,
   int numberOfSegments,
   float tension
);
```
[C++]
```
public: void AddCurve(
   Point points[],
   int offset,
   int numberOfSegments,
   float tension
);
```
[JScript]
```
public function AddCurve(
   points : Point[],
   offset : int,
   numberOfSegments : int,
   tension : float
);
```

Parameters

points
: An array of **Point** structures that represents the points that define the curve.

offset
: The index of the element in the *points* array that is used as the first point in the curve.

numberOfSegments
: A value that specifies the amount that the curve bends between control points. Values greater than 1 produce unpredictable results.

tension
: A value that specifies the amount that the curve bends between control points. Values greater than 1 produce unpredictable results.

Remarks

The user must keep the original points if they are needed. The original points are converted to cubic Bézier control points internally, therefore there is no mechanism for returning the original points.

The curve begins at the point in the array specified by the *offset* parameter and includes the number of points (segments) specified by *numberOfSegments*.

Example

[Visual Basic, C#] The following example is designed for use with Windows Forms, and it requires **PaintEventArgs** *e*, an **OnPaint** event object. The code performs the following actions:

- Creates an array of four points (representing a cardinal spline).
- Creates a path and using the array of points, adds the curve to the path.
- Draws the path to the screen.

[Visual Basic, C#] Notice that while the array holds four points, there are only three segments - which is number specified in the third argument of the call to **AddCurve**.

[Visual Basic]
```
Public Sub AddCurveExample(e As PaintEventArgs)
' Create some points.
Dim point1 As New Point(20, 20)
Dim point2 As New Point(40, 0)
Dim point3 As New Point(60, 40)
Dim point4 As New Point(80, 20)
' Create an array of the points.
Dim curvePoints As Point() =  {point1, point2, point3, point4}
' Create a GraphicsPath object and add a curve.
Dim myPath As New GraphicsPath()
myPath.AddCurve(curvePoints, 0, 3, 0.8F)
' Draw the path to the screen.
Dim myPen As New Pen(Color.Black, 2)
e.Graphics.DrawPath(myPen, myPath)
End Sub
```

[C#]
```
private void AddCurveExample(PaintEventArgs e)
{
// Create some points.
Point point1 = new Point(20, 20);
Point point2 = new Point(40, 0);
Point point3 = new Point(60, 40);
Point point4 = new Point(80, 20);
// Create an array of the points.
Point[] curvePoints = {point1, point2, point3, point4};
// Create a GraphicsPath object and add a curve.
GraphicsPath myPath = new GraphicsPath();
myPath.AddCurve(curvePoints, 0, 3, 0.8f);
// Draw the path to the screen.
Pen myPen = new Pen(Color.Black, 2);
e.Graphics.DrawPath(myPen, myPath);
}
```

Requirements

Platforms: Windows 98, Windows NT 4.0, Windows Millennium Edition, Windows 2000, Windows XP Home Edition, Windows XP Professional, Windows Server 2003 family

GraphicsPath.AddCurve Method (PointF[], Int32, Int32, Single)

Adds a spline curve to the current figure.

```
[Visual Basic]
Overloads Public Sub AddCurve( _
   ByVal points() As PointF, _
   ByVal offset As Integer, _
   ByVal numberOfSegments As Integer, _
   ByVal tension As Single _
)
[C#]
public void AddCurve(
   PointF[] points,
   int offset,
   int numberOfSegments,
   float tension
);
[C++]
public: void AddCurve(
   PointF points[],
   int offset,
   int numberOfSegments,
   float tension
);
[JScript]
public function AddCurve(
   points : PointF[],
   offset : int,
   numberOfSegments : int,
   tension : float
);
```

Parameters

points
: An array of **PointF** structures that represents the points that define the curve.

offset
: The index of the element in the *points* array that is used as the first point in the curve.

numberOfSegments
: The number of segments used to draw the curve. A segment can be thought of as a line connecting two points.

tension
: A value that specifies the amount that the curve bends between control points. Values greater than 1 produce unpredictable results.

Remarks

The user must keep the original points if they are needed. The original points are converted to cubic Bézier control points internally, therefore there is no mechanism for returning the original points.

The curve begins at the point in the array specified by *offset*, and includes the number of points (segments) specified by *numberOfSegments*.

Example

For an example, see **GraphicsPath.AddCurve Method (Point[], Int32, Int32, Single)**.

Requirements

Platforms: Windows 98, Windows NT 4.0, Windows Millennium Edition, Windows 2000, Windows XP Home Edition, Windows XP Professional, Windows Server 2003 family

GraphicsPath.AddEllipse Method

Adds an ellipse to the current path.

Overload List

Adds an ellipse to the current path.

[Visual Basic] **Overloads Public Sub AddEllipse(Rectangle)**

[C#] **public void AddEllipse(Rectangle);**

[C++] **public: void AddEllipse(Rectangle);**

[JScript] **public function AddEllipse(Rectangle);**

Adds an ellipse to the current path.

[Visual Basic] **Overloads Public Sub AddEllipse(RectangleF)**

[C#] **public void AddEllipse(RectangleF);**

[C++] **public: void AddEllipse(RectangleF);**

[JScript] **public function AddEllipse(RectangleF);**

Adds an ellipse to the current path.

[Visual Basic] **Overloads Public Sub AddEllipse(Integer, Integer, Integer, Integer)**

[C#] **public void AddEllipse(int, int, int, int);**

[C++] **public: void AddEllipse(int, int, int, int);**

[JScript] **public function AddEllipse(int, int, int, int);**

Adds an ellipse to the current path.

[Visual Basic] **Overloads Public Sub AddEllipse(Single, Single, Single, Single)**

[C#] **public void AddEllipse(float, float, float, float);**

[C++] **public: void AddEllipse(float, float, float, float);**

[JScript] **public function AddEllipse(float, float, float, float);**

Example

For an example, see **GraphicsPath.AddEllipse Method (Rectangle)**.

GraphicsPath.AddEllipse Method (Rectangle)

Adds an ellipse to the current path.

```
[Visual Basic]
Overloads Public Sub AddEllipse( _
   ByVal rect As Rectangle _
)
[C#]
public void AddEllipse(
   Rectangle rect
);
[C++]
public: void AddEllipse(
   Rectangle rect
);
[JScript]
public function AddEllipse(
   rect : Rectangle
);
```

Parameters

rect

A **Rectangle** structure that represents the bounding rectangle that defines the ellipse.

Example

[Visual Basic, C#] The following example is designed for use with Windows Forms, and it requires **PaintEventArgs** *e*, an **OnPaint** event object. The code performs the following actions:

[Visual Basic, C#] Creates a bounding rectangle that defines an ellipse.

[Visual Basic, C#] Creates a path and adds the ellipse to the path.

[Visual Basic, C#] Draws the path to screen.

[Visual Basic]
```
Public Sub AddEllipseExample(e As PaintEventArgs)
' Create a path and add an ellipse.
Dim myEllipse As New Rectangle(20, 20, 100, 50)
Dim myPath As New GraphicsPath()
myPath.AddEllipse(myEllipse)
' Draw the path to the screen.
Dim myPen As New Pen(Color.Black, 2)
e.Graphics.DrawPath(myPen, myPath)
End Sub
```

[C#]
```
private void AddEllipseExample(PaintEventArgs e)
{
// Create a path and add an ellipse.
Rectangle myEllipse = new Rectangle(20, 20, 100, 50);
GraphicsPath myPath = new GraphicsPath();
myPath.AddEllipse(myEllipse);
// Draw the path to the screen.
Pen myPen = new Pen(Color.Black, 2);
e.Graphics.DrawPath(myPen, myPath);
}
```

Requirements

Platforms: Windows 98, Windows NT 4.0, Windows Millennium Edition, Windows 2000, Windows XP Home Edition, Windows XP Professional, Windows Server 2003 family

GraphicsPath.AddEllipse Method (RectangleF)

Adds an ellipse to the current path.

[Visual Basic]
```
Overloads Public Sub AddEllipse( _
   ByVal rect As RectangleF _
)
```
[C#]
```
public void AddEllipse(
   RectangleF rect
);
```
[C++]
```
public: void AddEllipse(
   RectangleF rect
);
```
[JScript]
```
public function AddEllipse(
   rect : RectangleF
);
```

Parameters

rect

A **RectangleF** structure that represents the bounding rectangle that defines the ellipse.

Example

For an example, see **GraphicsPath.AddEllipse Method (Rectangle)**.

Requirements

Platforms: Windows 98, Windows NT 4.0, Windows Millennium Edition, Windows 2000, Windows XP Home Edition, Windows XP Professional, Windows Server 2003 family

GraphicsPath.AddEllipse Method (Int32, Int32, Int32, Int32)

Adds an ellipse to the current path.

[Visual Basic]
```
Overloads Public Sub AddEllipse( _
   ByVal x As Integer, _
   ByVal y As Integer, _
   ByVal width As Integer, _
   ByVal height As Integer _
)
```
[C#]
```
public void AddEllipse(
   int x,
   int y,
   int width,
   int height
);
```
[C++]
```
public: void AddEllipse(
   int x,
   int y,
   int width,
   int height
);
```
[JScript]
```
public function AddEllipse(
   x : int,
   y : int,
   width : int,
   height : int
);
```

Parameters

x

The x-coordinate of the upper-left corner of the bounding rectangle that defines the ellipse.

y

The y-coordinate of the upper-left corner of the bounding rectangle that defines the ellipse.

width

The width of the bounding rectangle that defines the ellipse.

height

The height of the bounding rectangle that defines the ellipse.

Example

For an example, see **GraphicsPath.AddEllipse Method (Rectangle)**.

Requirements

Platforms: Windows 98, Windows NT 4.0, Windows Millennium Edition, Windows 2000, Windows XP Home Edition, Windows XP Professional, Windows Server 2003 family

GraphicsPath.AddEllipse Method (Single, Single, Single, Single)

Adds an ellipse to the current path.

```
[Visual Basic]
Overloads Public Sub AddEllipse( _
   ByVal x As Single, _
   ByVal y As Single, _
   ByVal width As Single, _
   ByVal height As Single _
)
[C#]
public void AddEllipse(
   float x,
   float y,
   float width,
   float height
);
[C++]
public: void AddEllipse(
   float x,
   float y,
   float width,
   float height
);
[JScript]
public function AddEllipse(
   x : float,
   y : float,
   width : float,
   height : float
);
```

Parameters

x
: The x-coordinate of the upper-left corner of the bounding rectangle that defines the ellipse.

y
: The y-coordinate of the upper left corner of the bounding rectangle that defines the ellipse.

width
: The width of the bounding rectangle that defines the ellipse.

height
: The height of the bounding rectangle that defines the ellipse.

Example

For an example, see **GraphicsPath.AddEllipse Method (Rectangle)**.

Requirements

Platforms: Windows 98, Windows NT 4.0, Windows Millennium Edition, Windows 2000, Windows XP Home Edition, Windows XP Professional, Windows Server 2003 family

GraphicsPath.AddLine Method

Appends a line segment to this **GraphicsPath** object.

Overload List

Appends a line segment to this **GraphicsPath** object.

[Visual Basic] **Overloads Public Sub AddLine(Point, Point)**

[C#] **public void AddLine(Point, Point);**

[C++] **public: void AddLine(Point, Point);**

[JScript] **public function AddLine(Point, Point);**

Appends a line segment to this **GraphicsPath** object.

[Visual Basic] **Overloads Public Sub AddLine(PointF, PointF)**

[C#] **public void AddLine(PointF, PointF);**

[C++] **public: void AddLine(PointF, PointF);**

[JScript] **public function AddLine(PointF, PointF);**

Appends a line segment to the current figure.

[Visual Basic] **Overloads Public Sub AddLine(Integer, Integer, Integer, Integer)**

[C#] **public void AddLine(int, int, int, int);**

[C++] **public: void AddLine(int, int, int, int);**

[JScript] **public function AddLine(int, int, int, int);**

Appends a line segment to this **GraphicsPath** object.

[Visual Basic] **Overloads Public Sub AddLine(Single, Single, Single, Single)**

[C#] **public void AddLine(float, float, float, float);**

[C++] **public: void AddLine(float, float, float, float);**

[JScript] **public function AddLine(float, float, float, float);**

Example

For an example, see **GraphicsPath.AddLine Method (Int32, Int32, Int32, Int32)**.

GraphicsPath.AddLine Method (Point, Point)

Appends a line segment to this **GraphicsPath** object.

```
[Visual Basic]
Overloads Public Sub AddLine( _
   ByVal pt1 As Point, _
   ByVal pt2 As Point _
)
[C#]
public void AddLine(
   Point pt1,
   Point pt2
);
[C++]
public: void AddLine(
   Point pt1,
   Point pt2
);
[JScript]
public function AddLine(
   pt1 : Point,
   pt2 : Point
);
```

Parameters

pt1

A **Point** structure that represents the starting point of the line.

pt2

A **Point** structure that represents the endpoint of the line.

Remarks

This method adds the line segment defined by the specified points to the end of this **GraphicsPath** object. If there are previous lines or curves in the **GraphicsPath** object, a line segment is drawn to connect the last point in the path to the first point in the new line segment.

Example

For an example, see **GraphicsPath.AddLine Method (Int32, Int32, Int32, Int32)**.

Requirements

Platforms: Windows 98, Windows NT 4.0, Windows Millennium Edition, Windows 2000, Windows XP Home Edition, Windows XP Professional, Windows Server 2003 family

GraphicsPath.AddLine Method (PointF, PointF)

Appends a line segment to this **GraphicsPath** object.

```
[Visual Basic]
Overloads Public Sub AddLine( _
   ByVal pt1 As PointF, _
   ByVal pt2 As PointF _
)
[C#]
public void AddLine(
   PointF pt1,
   PointF pt2
);
[C++]
public: void AddLine(
   PointF pt1,
   PointF pt2
);
[JScript]
public function AddLine(
   pt1 : PointF,
   pt2 : PointF
);
```

Parameters

pt1

A **PointF** structure that represents the starting point of the line.

pt2

A **PointF** structure that represents the endpoint of the line.

Remarks

This method adds the line segment defined by the specified points to the end of this **GraphicsPath** object. If there are previous lines or curves in the **GraphicsPath** object, a line segment is drawn to connect the last point in the path to the first point in the new line segment.

Example

For an example, see **GraphicsPath.AddLine Method (Int32, Int32, Int32, Int32)**.

Requirements

Platforms: Windows 98, Windows NT 4.0, Windows Millennium Edition, Windows 2000, Windows XP Home Edition, Windows XP Professional, Windows Server 2003 family

GraphicsPath.AddLine Method (Int32, Int32, Int32, Int32)

Appends a line segment to the current figure.

```
[Visual Basic]
Overloads Public Sub AddLine( _
   ByVal x1 As Integer, _
   ByVal y1 As Integer, _
   ByVal x2 As Integer, _
   ByVal y2 As Integer _
)
[C#]
public void AddLine(
   int x1,
   int y1,
   int x2,
   int y2
);
[C++]
public: void AddLine(
   int x1,
   int y1,
   int x2,
   int y2
);
[JScript]
public function AddLine(
   x1 : int,
   y1 : int,
   x2 : int,
   y2 : int
);
```

Parameters

x1

The x-coordinate of the starting point of the line.

y1

The y-coordinate of the starting point of the line.

x2

The x-coordinate of the endpoint of the line.

y2

The y-coordinate of the endpoint of the line.

Remarks

This method adds the line segment defined by the specified points to the end of the current figure. If there are previous lines or curves in the **GraphicsPath** object, a line segment is drawn to connect the last point in the path to the first point in the new line segment.

Example

[Visual Basic, C#] The following example is designed for use with Windows Forms, and it requires **PaintEventArgs** *e*, an **OnPaint** event object. The code creates a path, adds three lines that form a triangle, and then draws the path to the screen.

[Visual Basic]
```
Public Sub AddLineExample(e As PaintEventArgs)
' Create a path and add a symetrical triangle using AddLine.
Dim myPath As New GraphicsPath()
myPath.AddLine(30, 30, 60, 60)
myPath.AddLine(60, 60, 0, 60)
myPath.AddLine(0, 60, 30, 30)
' Draw the path to the screen.
Dim myPen As New Pen(Color.Black, 2)
e.Graphics.DrawPath(myPen, myPath)
End Sub
```

[C#]
```
private void AddLineExample(PaintEventArgs e)
{
//Create a path and add a symetrical triangle using AddLine.
GraphicsPath myPath = new GraphicsPath();
myPath.AddLine(30, 30, 60, 60);
myPath.AddLine(60, 60, 0, 60);
myPath.AddLine(0, 60, 30, 30);
// Draw the path to the screen.
Pen myPen = new Pen(Color.Black, 2);
e.Graphics.DrawPath(myPen, myPath);
}
```

Requirements

Platforms: Windows 98, Windows NT 4.0, Windows Millennium Edition, Windows 2000, Windows XP Home Edition, Windows XP Professional, Windows Server 2003 family

GraphicsPath.AddLine Method (Single, Single, Single, Single)

Appends a line segment to this **GraphicsPath** object.

[Visual Basic]
```
Overloads Public Sub AddLine( _
   ByVal x1 As Single, _
   ByVal y1 As Single, _
   ByVal x2 As Single, _
   ByVal y2 As Single _
)
```
[C#]
```
public void AddLine(
   float x1,
   float y1,
   float x2,
   float y2
);
```
[C++]
```
public: void AddLine(
   float x1,
   float y1,
   float x2,
   float y2
);
```
[JScript]
```
public function AddLine(
   x1 : float,
   y1 : float,
   x2 : float,
   y2 : float
);
```

Parameters

x1
: The x-coordinate of the starting point of the line.

y1
: The y-coordinate of the starting point of the line.

x2
: The x-coordinate of the endpoint of the line.

y2
: The y-coordinate of the endpoint of the line.

Remarks

This method adds the line segment defined by the specified points to the end of this **GraphicsPath** object. If there are previous lines or curves in the **GraphicsPath** object, a line segment is drawn to connect the last point in the path to the first point in the new line segment.

Example

For an example, see **GraphicsPath.AddLine Method (Int32, Int32, Int32, Int32)**.

Requirements

Platforms: Windows 98, Windows NT 4.0, Windows Millennium Edition, Windows 2000, Windows XP Home Edition, Windows XP Professional, Windows Server 2003 family

GraphicsPath.AddLines Method

Appends a series of connected line segments to the end of this **GraphicsPath** object.

Overload List

Appends a series of connected line segments to the end of this **GraphicsPath** object.

[Visual Basic] **Overloads Public Sub AddLines(Point())**

[C#] **public void AddLines(Point[]);**

[C++] **public: void AddLines(Point[]);**

[JScript] **public function AddLines(Point[]);**

Appends a series of connected line segments to the end of this **GraphicsPath** object.

[Visual Basic] **Overloads Public Sub AddLines(PointF())**

[C#] **public void AddLines(PointF[]);**

[C++] **public: void AddLines(PointF[]);**

[JScript] **public function AddLines(PointF[]);**

Example

For an example, see **GraphicsPath.AddLines Method (Point[])**.

GraphicsPath.AddLines Method (Point[])

Appends a series of connected line segments to the end of this **GraphicsPath** object.

[Visual Basic]
```
Overloads Public Sub AddLines( _
   ByVal points() As Point _
)
```
[C#]
```
public void AddLines(
   Point[] points
);
```

```
[C++]
public: void AddLines(
   Point points[]
);
[JScript]
public function AddLines(
   points : Point[]
);
```

Parameters

points

An array of **Point** structures that represents the points that define the line segments to add.

Remarks

If there are previous lines or curves in the figure, a line is added to connect the endpoint of the previous segment the starting point of the line. The *points* parameter specifies an array of endpoints. The first two specify the first line. Each additional point specifies the endpoint of a line segment whose starting point is the endpoint of the previous line.

Example

[Visual Basic, C#] The following example is designed for use with Windows Forms, and it requires **PaintEventArgs** *e*, an **OnPaint** event object. The code performs the following actions:

- Creates an array of four points that describe a triangle.
- Creates a path and adds the array of lines.
- Draws the path to screen.

[Visual Basic, C#] Notice that each line after the first point, uses the previous point as the starting point and the new point as the endpoint.

```
[Visual Basic]
Public Sub AddLinesExample(e As PaintEventArgs)
'Create a symetrical triangle using an array of points.
Dim myArray As Point() = {New Point(30, 30), New Point(60, 60), _
New Point(0, 60), New Point(30, 30)}
Dim myPath As New GraphicsPath()
myPath.AddLines(myArray)
' Draw the path to the screen.
Dim myPen As New Pen(Color.Black, 2)
e.Graphics.DrawPath(myPen, myPath)
End Sub
```

```
[C#]
private void AddLinesExample(PaintEventArgs e)
{
// Create a symetrical triangle using an array of points.
Point[] myArray =
{
new Point(30,30),
new Point(60,60),
new Point(0,60),
new Point(30,30)
};
//Create a path and add lines.
GraphicsPath myPath = new GraphicsPath();
myPath.AddLines(myArray);
// Draw the path to the screen.
Pen myPen = new Pen(Color.Black, 2);
e.Graphics.DrawPath(myPen, myPath);
}
```

Requirements

Platforms: Windows 98, Windows NT 4.0, Windows Millennium Edition, Windows 2000, Windows XP Home Edition, Windows XP Professional, Windows Server 2003 family

GraphicsPath.AddLines Method (PointF[])

Appends a series of connected line segments to the end of this **GraphicsPath** object.

```
[Visual Basic]
Overloads Public Sub AddLines( _
   ByVal points() As PointF _
)
[C#]
public void AddLines(
   PointF[] points
);
[C++]
public: void AddLines(
   PointF points[]
);
[JScript]
public function AddLines(
   points : PointF[]
);
```

Parameters

points

An array of **PointF** structures that represents the points that define the line segments to add.

Remarks

If there are previous lines or curves in the figure, a line is added to connect the endpoint of the previous segment the starting point of the line. The *points* parameter specifies an array of endpoints. The first two specify the first line. Each additional point specifies the endpoint of a line segment whose starting point is the endpoint of the previous line.

Example

For an example, see **GraphicsPath.AddLines Method (Point[])**.

Requirements

Platforms: Windows 98, Windows NT 4.0, Windows Millennium Edition, Windows 2000, Windows XP Home Edition, Windows XP Professional, Windows Server 2003 family

GraphicsPath.AddPath Method

Appends the specified **GraphicsPath** object to this path.

```
[Visual Basic]
Public Sub AddPath( _
   ByVal addingPath As GraphicsPath, _
   ByVal connect As Boolean _
)
[C#]
public void AddPath(
   GraphicsPath addingPath,
   bool connect
);
[C++]
public: void AddPath(
   GraphicsPath* addingPath,
   bool connect
);
```

```
[JScript]
public function AddPath(
   addingPath : GraphicsPath,
   connect : Boolean
);
```

Parameters

addingPath
The **GraphicsPath** to add.

connect
A Boolean value that specifies whether the first figure in the added path is part of the last figure in this path. A value of **true** specifies that (if possible) the first figure in the added path is part of the last figure in this path. A value of **false** specifies that the first figure in the added path is separate from the last figure in this path.

Example

[Visual Basic, C#] The following example is designed for use with Windows Forms, and it requires **PaintEventArgs** *e*, an **OnPaint** event object. The code performs the following actions:

- Creates two paths ¾ one a right-side-up triangle and the other an up-side-down triangle.
- Adds the second path to the first.
- Draws the resultant path to the screen.

```
[Visual Basic]
Public Sub AddPathExample(e As PaintEventArgs)
' Creates a symetrical triangle and adds an inverted triangle.
' Create the first path - right side up triangle.
Dim myArray As Point() = {New Point(30, 30), New Point(60, 60), _
New Point(0, 60), New Point(30, 30)}
Dim myPath As New GraphicsPath()
myPath.AddLines(myArray)
' Create the second path - inverted triangle.
Dim myArray2 As Point() = {New Point(30, 30), New Point(0, 0), _
New Point(60, 0), New Point(30, 30)}
Dim myPath2 As New GraphicsPath()
myPath2.AddLines(myArray2)
' Add the second path to the first path.
myPath.AddPath(myPath2, True)
' Draw the combined path to the screen.
Dim myPen As New Pen(Color.Black, 2)
e.Graphics.DrawPath(myPen, myPath)
End Sub
```

```
[C#]
private void AddPathExample(PaintEventArgs e)
{
// Create the first path¾right side up triangle.
Point[] myArray =
{
new Point(30,30),
new Point(60,60),
new Point(0,60),
new Point(30,30)
};
GraphicsPath myPath = new GraphicsPath();
myPath.AddLines(myArray);
// Create the second path¾inverted triangle.
Point[] myArray2 =
{
new Point(30,30),
new Point(0,0),
new Point(60,0),
new Point(30,30)
};
GraphicsPath myPath2 = new GraphicsPath();
myPath2.AddLines(myArray2);
// Add the second path to the first path.
myPath.AddPath(myPath2,true);
// Draw the combined path to the screen.
Pen myPen = new Pen(Color.Black, 2);
e.Graphics.DrawPath(myPen, myPath);
}
```

Requirements

Platforms: Windows 98, Windows NT 4.0, Windows Millennium Edition, Windows 2000, Windows XP Home Edition, Windows XP Professional, Windows Server 2003 family

GraphicsPath.AddPie Method

Adds the outline of a pie shape to this path.

Overload List

Adds the outline of a pie shape to this path.

[Visual Basic] **Overloads Public Sub AddPie(Rectangle, Single, Single)**

[C#] **public void AddPie(Rectangle, float, float);**

[C++] **public: void AddPie(Rectangle, float, float);**

[JScript] **public function AddPie(Rectangle, float, float);**

Adds the outline of a pie shape to this path.

[Visual Basic] **Overloads Public Sub AddPie(Integer, Integer, Integer, Integer, Single, Single)**

[C#] **public void AddPie(int, int, int, int, float, float);**

[C++] **public: void AddPie(int, int, int, int, float, float);**

[JScript] **public function AddPie(int, int, int, int, float, float);**

Adds the outline of a pie shape to this path.

[Visual Basic] **Overloads Public Sub AddPie(Single, Single, Single, Single, Single, Single)**

[C#] **public void AddPie(float, float, float, float, float, float);**

[C++] **public: void AddPie(float, float, float, float, float, float);**

[JScript] **public function AddPie(float, float, float, float, float, float);**

Example

For an example, see **GraphicsPath.AddPie Method (Int32, Int32, Int32, Int32, Single, Single)**.

GraphicsPath.AddPie Method (Rectangle, Single, Single)

Adds the outline of a pie shape to this path.

```
[Visual Basic]
Overloads Public Sub AddPie( _
   ByVal rect As Rectangle, _
   ByVal startAngle As Single, _
   ByVal sweepAngle As Single _
)
[C#]
public void AddPie(
   Rectangle rect,
   float startAngle,
   float sweepAngle
);
```

```
[C++]
public: void AddPie(
   Rectangle rect,
   float startAngle,
   float sweepAngle
);
[JScript]
public function AddPie(
   rect : Rectangle,
   startAngle : float,
   sweepAngle : float
);
```

Parameters

rect
: A **Rectangle** structure that represents the bounding rectangle that defines the ellipse from which the pie is drawn.

startAngle
: The starting angle for the pie section, measured in degrees clockwise from the x-axis.

sweepAngle
: The angle between *startAngle* and the end of the pie section, measured in degrees clockwise from *startAngle*.

Remarks

The pie shape is defined by a partial outline of an ellipse and the two radial lines that intersect the endpoints of the partial outline. The partial outline begins at *startAngle* (measured clockwise from the x-axis) and ends at *startAngle* + *sweepAngle*.

Example

For an example, see **GraphicsPath.AddPie Method (Int32, Int32, Int32, Int32, Single, Single)**.

Requirements

Platforms: Windows 98, Windows NT 4.0, Windows Millennium Edition, Windows 2000, Windows XP Home Edition, Windows XP Professional, Windows Server 2003 family

GraphicsPath.AddPie Method (Int32, Int32, Int32, Int32, Single, Single)

Adds the outline of a pie shape to this path.

```
[Visual Basic]
Overloads Public Sub AddPie( _
   ByVal x As Integer, _
   ByVal y As Integer, _
   ByVal width As Integer, _
   ByVal height As Integer, _
   ByVal startAngle As Single, _
   ByVal sweepAngle As Single _
)
[C#]
public void AddPie(
   int x,
   int y,
   int width,
   int height,
   float startAngle,
   float sweepAngle
);
[C++]
public: void AddPie(
   int x,
   int y,
   int width,
   int height,
   float startAngle,
   float sweepAngle
);
[JScript]
public function AddPie(
   x : int,
   y : int,
   width : int,
   height : int,
   startAngle : float,
   sweepAngle : float
);
```

Parameters

x
: The x-coordinate of the upper-left corner of the bounding rectangle that defines the ellipse from which the pie is drawn.

y
: The y-coordinate of the upper-left corner of the bounding rectangle that defines the ellipse from which the pie is drawn.

width
: The width of the bounding rectangle that defines the ellipse from which the pie is drawn.

height
: The height of the bounding rectangle that defines the ellipse from which the pie is drawn.

startAngle
: The starting angle for the pie section, measured in degrees clockwise from the x-axis.

sweepAngle
: The angle between *startAngle* and the end of the pie section, measured in degrees clockwise from *startAngle*.

Remarks

The pie shape is defined by a partial outline of an ellipse and the two radial lines that intersect the endpoints of the partial outline. The partial outline begins at *startAngle* (measured clockwise from the x-axis) and ends at *startAngle* + *sweepAngle*.

Example

[Visual Basic, C#] The following example is designed for use with Windows Forms, and it requires **PaintEventArgs** *e*, an **OnPaint** event object. The code creates a graphics path, adds the pie shape, and then draws the path to the screen.

```
[Visual Basic]
Public Sub AddPieExample(e As PaintEventArgs)
' Create a pie slice of a circle using the AddPie method.
Dim myPath As New GraphicsPath()
myPath.AddPie(20, 20, 70, 70, - 45, 90)
' Draw the path to the screen.
Dim myPen As New Pen(Color.Black, 2)
e.Graphics.DrawPath(myPen, myPath)
End Sub
```

[C#]
```
private void AddPieExample(PaintEventArgs e)
{
// Create a pie slice of a circle using the AddPie method.
GraphicsPath myPath = new GraphicsPath();
myPath.AddPie(20, 20, 70, 70, -45, 90);
// Draw the path to the screen.
Pen myPen = new Pen(Color.Black, 2);
e.Graphics.DrawPath(myPen, myPath);
}
```

Requirements

Platforms: Windows 98, Windows NT 4.0, Windows Millennium Edition, Windows 2000, Windows XP Home Edition, Windows XP Professional, Windows Server 2003 family

GraphicsPath.AddPie Method (Single, Single, Single, Single, Single, Single)

Adds the outline of a pie shape to this path.

[Visual Basic]
```
Overloads Public Sub AddPie( _
   ByVal x As Single, _
   ByVal y As Single, _
   ByVal width As Single, _
   ByVal height As Single, _
   ByVal startAngle As Single, _
   ByVal sweepAngle As Single _
)
```
[C#]
```
public void AddPie(
   float x,
   float y,
   float width,
   float height,
   float startAngle,
   float sweepAngle
);
```
[C++]
```
public: void AddPie(
   float x,
   float y,
   float width,
   float height,
   float startAngle,
   float sweepAngle
);
```
[JScript]
```
public function AddPie(
   x : float,
   y : float,
   width : float,
   height : float,
   startAngle : float,
   sweepAngle : float
);
```

Parameters

x
: The x-coordinate of the upper-left corner of the bounding rectangle that defines the ellipse from which the pie is drawn.

y
: The y-coordinate of the upper-left corner of the bounding rectangle that defines the ellipse from which the pie is drawn.

width
: The width of the bounding rectangle that defines the ellipse from which the pie is drawn.

height
: The height of the bounding rectangle that defines the ellipse from which the pie is drawn.

startAngle
: The starting angle for the pie section, measured in degrees clockwise from the x-axis.

sweepAngle
: The angle between *startAngle* and the end of the pie section, measured in degrees clockwise from *startAngle*.

Remarks

The pie shape is defined by a partial outline of an ellipse and the two radial lines that intersect the endpoints of the partial outline. The partial outline begins at *startAngle* (measured clockwise from the x-axis) and ends at *startAngle* + *sweepAngle*.

Example

For an example, see **GraphicsPath.AddPie Method (Int32, Int32, Int32, Int32, Single, Single)**.

Requirements

Platforms: Windows 98, Windows NT 4.0, Windows Millennium Edition, Windows 2000, Windows XP Home Edition, Windows XP Professional, Windows Server 2003 family

GraphicsPath.AddPolygon Method

Adds a polygon to this path.

Overload List

Adds a polygon to this path.

[Visual Basic] **Overloads Public Sub AddPolygon(Point())**
[C#] **public void AddPolygon(Point[]);**
[C++] **public: void AddPolygon(Point[]);**
[JScript] **public function AddPolygon(Point[]);**

Adds a polygon to this path.

[Visual Basic] **Overloads Public Sub AddPolygon(PointF())**
[C#] **public void AddPolygon(PointF[]);**
[C++] **public: void AddPolygon(PointF[]);**
[JScript] **public function AddPolygon(PointF[]);**

Example

For an example, see **GraphicsPath.AddPolygon Method (Point[])**.

GraphicsPath.AddPolygon Method (Point[])

Adds a polygon to this path.

[Visual Basic]
```
Overloads Public Sub AddPolygon( _
   ByVal points() As Point _
)
```
[C#]
```
public void AddPolygon(
   Point[] points
);
```

```
[C++]
public: void AddPolygon(
   Point points[]
);
[JScript]
public function AddPolygon(
   points : Point[]
);
```

Parameters

points

An array of **Point** structures that defines the polygon to add.

Remarks

The points in the *points* array specify the vertices of a polygon. If the first point in the array is not the same as the last point, those two points are connected to close the polygon.

Example

[Visual Basic, C#] The following example is designed for use with Windows Forms, and it requires **PaintEventArgs** *e*, an **OnPaint** event object. The code performs the following actions:

- Creates an array of points that defines a polygon.
- Creates a path and adds the polygon to the path.
- Draws the path to the screen.

```
[Visual Basic]
Public Sub AddPolygonExample(e As PaintEventArgs)
' Create an array of points.
Dim myArray As Point() = {New Point(23, 20), New Point(40, 10), _
New Point(57, 20), New Point(50, 40), New Point(30, 40)}
' Create a GraphicsPath object and add a polygon.
Dim myPath As New GraphicsPath()
myPath.AddPolygon(myArray)
' Draw the path to the screen.
Dim myPen As New Pen(Color.Black, 2)
e.Graphics.DrawPath(myPen, myPath)
End Sub
```

```
[C#]
private void AddPolygonExample(PaintEventArgs e)
{
// Create an array of points.
Point[] myArray =
{
new Point(23, 20),
new Point(40, 10),
new Point(57, 20),
new Point(50, 40),
new Point(30, 40)
};
// Create a GraphicsPath object and add a polygon.
GraphicsPath myPath = new GraphicsPath();
myPath.AddPolygon(myArray);
// Draw the path to the screen.
Pen myPen = new Pen(Color.Black, 2);
e.Graphics.DrawPath(myPen, myPath);
}
```

Requirements

Platforms: Windows 98, Windows NT 4.0, Windows Millennium Edition, Windows 2000, Windows XP Home Edition, Windows XP Professional, Windows Server 2003 family

GraphicsPath.AddPolygon Method (PointF[])

Adds a polygon to this path.

```
[Visual Basic]
Overloads Public Sub AddPolygon( _
   ByVal points() As PointF _
)
[C#]
public void AddPolygon(
   PointF[] points
);
[C++]
public: void AddPolygon(
   PointF points[]
);
[JScript]
public function AddPolygon(
   points : PointF[]
);
```

Parameters

points

An array of **PointF** structures that defines the polygon to add.

Remarks

The points in the *points* array specify the vertices of a polygon. If the first point in the array is not the same as the last point, those two points are connected to close the polygon.

Example

For an example, see **GraphicsPath.AddPolygon Method (Point[])**.

Requirements

Platforms: Windows 98, Windows NT 4.0, Windows Millennium Edition, Windows 2000, Windows XP Home Edition, Windows XP Professional, Windows Server 2003 family

GraphicsPath.AddRectangle Method

Adds a rectangle to this path.

Overload List

Adds a rectangle to this path.

[Visual Basic] **Overloads Public Sub AddRectangle(Rectangle)**

[C#] **public void AddRectangle(Rectangle);**

[C++] **public: void AddRectangle(Rectangle);**

[JScript] **public function AddRectangle(Rectangle);**

Adds a rectangle to this path.

[Visual Basic] **Overloads Public Sub AddRectangle(RectangleF)**

[C#] **public void AddRectangle(RectangleF);**

[C++] **public: void AddRectangle(RectangleF);**

[JScript] **public function AddRectangle(RectangleF);**

Example

For an example, see **GraphicsPath.AddRectangle Method (Rectangle)**.

GraphicsPath.AddRectangle Method (Rectangle)

Adds a rectangle to this path.

[Visual Basic]
```
Overloads Public Sub AddRectangle( _
   ByVal rect As Rectangle _
)
```
[C#]
```
public void AddRectangle(
   Rectangle rect
);
```
[C++]
```
public: void AddRectangle(
   Rectangle rect
);
```
[JScript]
```
public function AddRectangle(
   rect : Rectangle
);
```

Parameters

rect
A **Rectangle** structure that represents the rectangle to add.

Example

[Visual Basic, C#] The following example is designed for use with Windows Forms, and it requires **PaintEventArgs** *e*, an **OnPaint** event object. The code performs the following actions:

- Creates a path.
- Creates a rectangle and adds the rectangle to the path.
- Draws the path to the screen.

[Visual Basic]
```
Public Sub AddRectangleExample(e As PaintEventArgs)
' Create a GraphicsPath object and add a rectangle to it.
Dim myPath As New GraphicsPath()
Dim pathRect As New Rectangle(20, 20, 100, 200)
myPath.AddRectangle(pathRect)
' Draw the path to the screen.
Dim myPen As New Pen(Color.Black, 2)
e.Graphics.DrawPath(myPen, myPath)
End Sub
```

[C#]
```
private void AddRectangleExample(PaintEventArgs e)
{
// Create a GraphicsPath object and add a rectangle to it.
GraphicsPath myPath = new GraphicsPath();
Rectangle pathRect = new Rectangle(20, 20, 100, 200);
myPath.AddRectangle(pathRect);
// Draw the path to the screen.
Pen myPen = new Pen(Color.Black, 2);
e.Graphics.DrawPath(myPen, myPath);
}
```

Requirements

Platforms: Windows 98, Windows NT 4.0, Windows Millennium Edition, Windows 2000, Windows XP Home Edition, Windows XP Professional, Windows Server 2003 family

GraphicsPath.AddRectangle Method (RectangleF)

Adds a rectangle to this path.

[Visual Basic]
```
Overloads Public Sub AddRectangle( _
   ByVal rect As RectangleF _
)
```
[C#]
```
public void AddRectangle(
   RectangleF rect
);
```
[C++]
```
public: void AddRectangle(
   RectangleF rect
);
```
[JScript]
```
public function AddRectangle(
   rect : RectangleF
);
```

Parameters

rect
A **RectangleF** structure that represents the rectangle to add.

Example

For an example, see **GraphicsPath.AddRectangle Method (Rectangle)**.

Requirements

Platforms: Windows 98, Windows NT 4.0, Windows Millennium Edition, Windows 2000, Windows XP Home Edition, Windows XP Professional, Windows Server 2003 family

GraphicsPath.AddRectangles Method

Adds a series of rectangles to this path.

Overload List

Adds a series of rectangles to this path.

[Visual Basic] **Overloads Public Sub AddRectangles(Rectangle())**

[C#] **public void AddRectangles(Rectangle[]);**

[C++] **public: void AddRectangles(Rectangle[]);**

[JScript] **public function AddRectangles(Rectangle[]);**

Adds a series of rectangles to this path.

[Visual Basic] **Overloads Public Sub AddRectangles(RectangleF())**

[C#] **public void AddRectangles(RectangleF[]);**

[C++] **public: void AddRectangles(RectangleF[]);**

[JScript] **public function AddRectangles(RectangleF[]);**

Example

For an example, see **GraphicsPath.AddRectangles Method (Rectangle[])**.

GraphicsPath.AddRectangles Method (Rectangle[])

Adds a series of rectangles to this path.

```
[Visual Basic]
Overloads Public Sub AddRectangles( _
   ByVal rects() As Rectangle _
)
[C#]
public void AddRectangles(
   Rectangle[] rects
);
[C++]
public: void AddRectangles(
   Rectangle rects[]
);
[JScript]
public function AddRectangles(
   rects : Rectangle[]
);
```

Parameters

rects

An array of **Rectangle** structures that represents the rectangles to add.

Example

[Visual Basic, C#] The following example is designed for use with Windows Forms, and it requires **PaintEventArgs** *e*, an **OnPaint** event object. The code performs the following actions:

- Creates a path.
- Creates an array of rectangles and adds the rectangles to the path.
- Draws the path to the screen.

```
[Visual Basic]
Public Sub AddRectanglesExample(e As PaintEventArgs)
' Adds a pattern of rectangles to a GraphicsPath object.
Dim myPath As New GraphicsPath()
Dim pathRects As Rectangle() = {New Rectangle(20, 20, 100, 200), _
New Rectangle(40, 40, 120, 220), New Rectangle(60, 60, 240, 140)}
myPath.AddRectangles(pathRects)
' Draw the path to the screen.
Dim myPen As New Pen(Color.Black, 2)
e.Graphics.DrawPath(myPen, myPath)
End Sub
```

```
[C#]
private void AddRectanglesExample(PaintEventArgs e)
{
// Adds a pattern of rectangles to a GraphicsPath object.
GraphicsPath myPath = new GraphicsPath();
Rectangle[] pathRects =
{
new Rectangle(20,20,100,200),
new Rectangle(40,40,120,220),
new Rectangle(60,60,240,140)
};
myPath.AddRectangles(pathRects);
// Draw the path to the screen.
Pen myPen = new Pen(Color.Black, 2);
e.Graphics.DrawPath(myPen, myPath);
}
```

Requirements

Platforms: Windows 98, Windows NT 4.0, Windows Millennium Edition, Windows 2000, Windows XP Home Edition, Windows XP Professional, Windows Server 2003 family

GraphicsPath.AddRectangles Method (RectangleF[])

Adds a series of rectangles to this path.

```
[Visual Basic]
Overloads Public Sub AddRectangles( _
   ByVal rects() As RectangleF _
)
[C#]
public void AddRectangles(
   RectangleF[] rects
);
[C++]
public: void AddRectangles(
   RectangleF rects[]
);
[JScript]
public function AddRectangles(
   rects : RectangleF[]
);
```

Parameters

rects

An array of **RectangleF** structures that represents the rectangles to add.

Example

For an example, see **GraphicsPath.AddRectangles Method (Rectangle[])**.

Requirements

Platforms: Windows 98, Windows NT 4.0, Windows Millennium Edition, Windows 2000, Windows XP Home Edition, Windows XP Professional, Windows Server 2003 family

GraphicsPath.AddString Method

Adds a text string to this path.

Overload List

Adds a text string to this path.

[Visual Basic] **Overloads Public Sub AddString(String, FontFamily, Integer, Single, Point, StringFormat)**

[C#] **public void AddString(string, FontFamily, int, float, Point, StringFormat);**

[C++] **public: void AddString(String*, FontFamily*, int, float, Point, StringFormat*);**

[JScript] **public function AddString(String, FontFamily, int, float, Point, StringFormat);**

Adds a text string to this path.

[Visual Basic] **Overloads Public Sub AddString(String, FontFamily, Integer, Single, PointF, StringFormat)**

[C#] **public void AddString(string, FontFamily, int, float, PointF, StringFormat);**

[C++] **public: void AddString(String*, FontFamily*, int, float, PointF, StringFormat*);**

[JScript] **public function AddString(String, FontFamily, int, float, PointF, StringFormat);**

Adds a text string to this path.

[Visual Basic] **Overloads Public Sub AddString(String, FontFamily, Integer, Single, Rectangle, StringFormat)**

[C#] **public void AddString(string, FontFamily, int, float, Rectangle, StringFormat);**

[C++] **public: void AddString(String*, FontFamily*, int, float, Rectangle, StringFormat*);**

[JScript] **public function AddString(String, FontFamily, int, float, Rectangle, StringFormat);**

Adds a text string to this path.

[Visual Basic] **Overloads Public Sub AddString(String, FontFamily, Integer, Single, RectangleF, StringFormat)**

[C#] **public void AddString(string, FontFamily, int, float, RectangleF, StringFormat);**

[C++] **public: void AddString(String*, FontFamily*, int, float, RectangleF, StringFormat*);**

[JScript] **public function AddString(String, FontFamily, int, float, RectangleF, StringFormat);**

Example

For an example, see **GraphicsPath.AddString Method (String, FontFamily, Int32, Single, Point, StringFormat)**.

GraphicsPath.AddString Method (String, FontFamily, Int32, Single, Point, StringFormat)

Adds a text string to this path.

[Visual Basic]
```
Overloads Public Sub AddString( _
   ByVal s As String, _
   ByVal family As FontFamily, _
   ByVal style As Integer, _
   ByVal emSize As Single, _
   ByVal origin As Point, _
   ByVal format As StringFormat _
)
```
[C#]
```
public void AddString(
   string s,
   FontFamily family,
   int style,
   float emSize,
   Point origin,
   StringFormat format
);
```
[C++]
```
public: void AddString(
   String* s,
   FontFamily* family,
   int style,
   float emSize,
   Point origin,
   StringFormat* format
);
```
[JScript]
```
public function AddString(
   s : String,
   family : FontFamily,
   style : int,
   emSize : float,
   origin : Point,
   format : StringFormat
);
```

Parameters

s
The **String** to add.

family
A **FontFamily** object that represents the name of the font with which the test is drawn.

style
A **FontStyle** enumeration that represents style information about the text (bold, italic, and so on). This must be cast as an integer (see the example code later in this section).

emSize
The height of the Em square box that bounds the character.

origin
A **Point** structure that represents the point where the text starts.

format
A **StringFormat** object that specifies text formatting information, such as line spacing and alignment.

Example

[Visual Basic, C#] The following example is designed for use with Windows Forms, and it requires **PaintEventArgs** *e*, an **OnPaint** event object. The code performs the following actions:

- Creates a path.
- Sets up string and font arguments.
- Adds the string to the path.
- Draws the string to the screen.

[Visual Basic, C#] There are two important things to be pointed out. First, notice that the *fontStyle* argument is cast as an **int**. The **AddString** method requires this so that two or more **FontStyle** members can be combined to create the desired font style (in this case, **Italic** and **Underline**). Secondly, notice that the **FillPath** method is used rather than the **DrawPath** method. If **FillPath** is used, solid text is rendered, whereas if **DrawPath** is used, the text will be an outline style.

[Visual Basic]
```
Public Sub AddStringExample(e As PaintEventArgs)
' Create a GraphicsPath object.
Dim myPath As New GraphicsPath()
' Set up all the string parameters.
Dim stringText As String = "Sample Text"
Dim family As New FontFamily("Arial")
Dim myfontStyle As Integer = CInt(FontStyle.Italic)
Dim emSize As Integer = 26
Dim origin As New Point(20, 20)
Dim format As StringFormat = StringFormat.GenericDefault
' Add the string to the path.
myPath.AddString(stringText, family, myfontStyle, emSize, _
origin, format)
'Draw the path to the screen.
e.Graphics.FillPath(Brushes.Black, myPath)
End Sub
```
[C#]
```
private void AddStringExample(PaintEventArgs e)
{
// Create a GraphicsPath object.
GraphicsPath myPath = new GraphicsPath();
// Set up all the string parameters.
string stringText = "Sample Text";
FontFamily family = new FontFamily("Arial");
int fontStyle = (int)FontStyle.Italic;
int emSize = 26;
Point origin = new Point(20, 20);
StringFormat format = StringFormat.GenericDefault;
// Add the string to the path.
```

```
myPath.AddString(stringText,
family,
fontStyle,
emSize,
origin,
format);
//Draw the path to the screen.
e.Graphics.FillPath(Brushes.Black, myPath);
}
```

Requirements

Platforms: Windows 98, Windows NT 4.0, Windows Millennium Edition, Windows 2000, Windows XP Home Edition, Windows XP Professional, Windows Server 2003 family

GraphicsPath.AddString Method (String, FontFamily, Int32, Single, PointF, StringFormat)

Adds a text string to this path.

[Visual Basic]
```
Overloads Public Sub AddString( _
   ByVal s As String, _
   ByVal family As FontFamily, _
   ByVal style As Integer, _
   ByVal emSize As Single, _
   ByVal origin As PointF, _
   ByVal format As StringFormat _
)
```
[C#]
```
public void AddString(
   string s,
   FontFamily family,
   int style,
   float emSize,
   PointF origin,
   StringFormat format
);
```
[C++]
```
public: void AddString(
   String* s,
   FontFamily* family,
   int style,
   float emSize,
   PointF origin,
   StringFormat* format
);
```
[JScript]
```
public function AddString(
   s : String,
   family : FontFamily,
   style : int,
   emSize : float,
   origin : PointF,
   format : StringFormat
);
```

Parameters

s

The **String** to add.

family

A **FontFamily** object that represents the name of the font with which the test is drawn.

style

A **FontStyle** enumeration that represents style information about the text (bold, italic, and so on). This must be cast as an integer (see the example code later in this section).

emSize

The height of the Em square box that bounds the character.

origin

A **PointF** that represents the point where the text starts.

format

A **StringFormat** object that specifies text formatting information, such as line spacing and alignment.

Example

For an example, see **GraphicsPath.AddString Method (String, FontFamily, Int32, Single, Point, StringFormat)**.

Requirements

Platforms: Windows 98, Windows NT 4.0, Windows Millennium Edition, Windows 2000, Windows XP Home Edition, Windows XP Professional, Windows Server 2003 family

GraphicsPath.AddString Method (String, FontFamily, Int32, Single, Rectangle, StringFormat)

Adds a text string to this path.

[Visual Basic]
```
Overloads Public Sub AddString( _
   ByVal s As String, _
   ByVal family As FontFamily, _
   ByVal style As Integer, _
   ByVal emSize As Single, _
   ByVal layoutRect As Rectangle, _
   ByVal format As StringFormat _
)
```
[C#]
```
public void AddString(
   string s,
   FontFamily family,
   int style,
   float emSize,
   Rectangle layoutRect,
   StringFormat format
);
```
[C++]
```
public: void AddString(
   String* s,
   FontFamily* family,
   int style,
   float emSize,
   Rectangle layoutRect,
   StringFormat* format
);
```
[JScript]
```
public function AddString(
   s : String,
   family : FontFamily,
   style : int,
   emSize : float,
   layoutRect : Rectangle,
   format : StringFormat
);
```

Parameters

s
The **String** to add.

family
A **FontFamily** object that represents the name of the font with which the test is drawn.

style
A **FontStyle** enumeration that represents style information about the text (bold, italic, and so on). This must be cast as an integer (see the example code later in this section).

emSize
The height of the Em square box that bounds the character.

layoutRect
A **Rectangle** structure that represents the rectangle that bounds the text.

format
A **StringFormat** object that specifies text formatting information, such as line spacing and alignment.

Example

For an example, see **GraphicsPath.AddString Method (String, FontFamily, Int32, Single, Point, StringFormat)**.

Requirements

Platforms: Windows 98, Windows NT 4.0,
Windows Millennium Edition, Windows 2000,
Windows XP Home Edition, Windows XP Professional,
Windows Server 2003 family

GraphicsPath.AddString Method (String, FontFamily, Int32, Single, RectangleF, StringFormat)

Adds a text string to this path.

```
[Visual Basic]
Overloads Public Sub AddString( _
   ByVal s As String, _
   ByVal family As FontFamily, _
   ByVal style As Integer, _
   ByVal emSize As Single, _
   ByVal layoutRect As RectangleF, _
   ByVal format As StringFormat _
)
[C#]
public void AddString(
   string s,
   FontFamily family,
   int style,
   float emSize,
   RectangleF layoutRect,
   StringFormat format
);
[C++]
public: void AddString(
   String* s,
   FontFamily* family,
   int style,
   float emSize,
   RectangleF layoutRect,
   StringFormat* format
);
[JScript]
public function AddString(
   s : String,
   family : FontFamily,
   style : int,
   emSize : float,
   layoutRect : RectangleF,
   format : StringFormat
);
```

Parameters

s
The **String** to add.

family
A **FontFamily** object that represents the name of the font with which the test is drawn.

style
A **FontStyle** enumeration that represents style information about the text (bold, italic, and so on). This must be cast as an integer (see the example code later in this section).

emSize
The height of the Em square box that bounds the character.

layoutRect
A **RectangleF** structure that represents the rectangle that bounds the text.

format
A **StringFormat** object that specifies text formatting information, such as line spacing and alignment.

Example

For an example, see **GraphicsPath.AddString Method (String, FontFamily, Int32, Single, Point, StringFormat)**.

Requirements

Platforms: Windows 98, Windows NT 4.0,
Windows Millennium Edition, Windows 2000,
Windows XP Home Edition, Windows XP Professional,
Windows Server 2003 family

GraphicsPath.ClearMarkers Method

Clears all markers from this path.

```
[Visual Basic]
Public Sub ClearMarkers()
[C#]
public void ClearMarkers();
[C++]
public: void ClearMarkers();
[JScript]
public function ClearMarkers();
```

Remarks

Use the **SetMarkers** method to create a marker at the current location in a **GraphicsPath** object. Use the **NextMarker** method to iterate through the existing markers in a path.

Markers are used to separate groups of subpaths. One or more subpaths can be contained between two markers.

Example

[Visual Basic, C#] The following example is designed for use with Windows Forms, and it requires **PaintEventArgs** *e*, an **OnPaint** event object. The code performs the following actions:

- Creates a path.
- Adds several objects to the path.
- Adds markers to the path.
- Clears all markers from the path.
- Draws the path to the screen.

[Visual Basic]
```
Public Sub ClearMarkersExample(e As PaintEventArgs)
' Set several markers in a path.
Dim myPath As New GraphicsPath()
myPath.AddEllipse(0, 0, 100, 200)
myPath.SetMarkers()
myPath.AddLine(New Point(100, 100), New Point(200, 100))
Dim rect As New Rectangle(200, 0, 100, 200)
myPath.AddRectangle(rect)
myPath.SetMarkers()
myPath.AddLine(New Point(250, 200), New Point(250, 300))
myPath.SetMarkers()
' Clear the markers.
myPath.ClearMarkers()
' Draw the path to the screen.
Dim myPen As New Pen(Color.Black, 2)
e.Graphics.DrawPath(myPen, myPath)
End Sub
```

[C#]
```
private void ClearMarkersExample(PaintEventArgs e)
{
// Set several markers in a path.
GraphicsPath myPath = new GraphicsPath();
myPath.AddEllipse(0, 0, 100, 200);
myPath.SetMarkers();
myPath.AddLine(new Point(100, 100), new Point(200, 100));
Rectangle rect = new Rectangle(200, 0, 100, 200);
myPath.AddRectangle(rect);
myPath.SetMarkers();
myPath.AddLine(new Point(250, 200), new Point(250, 300));
myPath.SetMarkers();
// Clear the markers.
myPath.ClearMarkers();
// Draw the path to the screen.
Pen myPen = new Pen(Color.Black, 2);
e.Graphics.DrawPath(myPen, myPath);
}
```

Requirements

Platforms: Windows 98, Windows NT 4.0, Windows Millennium Edition, Windows 2000, Windows XP Home Edition, Windows XP Professional, Windows Server 2003 family

GraphicsPath.Clone Method

Creates an exact copy of this path.

[Visual Basic]
```
Public Overridable Function Clone() As Object Implements _
   ICloneable.Clone
```
[C#]
```
public virtual object Clone();
```
[C++]
```
public: virtual Object* Clone();
```
[JScript]
```
public function Clone() : Object;
```

Return Value

The **GraphicsPath** this method creates, cast as an object.

Implements

ICloneable.Clone

Example

[Visual Basic, C#] The following example is designed for use with Windows Forms, and it requires **PaintEventArgs** *e*, an **OnPaint** event object. The code performs the following actions:

- Creates a path.
- Adds several figures to the path.
- Draws the path to the screen.
- Clones a copy of that path.
- Draws the new path to the screen.

[Visual Basic, C#] Notice that the call the **Clone** method must be cast as a **GraphicsPath** object.

[Visual Basic]
```
Public Sub CloneExample(e As PaintEventArgs)
' Set several markers in a path.
Dim myPath As New GraphicsPath()
myPath.AddEllipse(0, 0, 100, 200)
myPath.AddLine(New Point(100, 100), New Point(200, 100))
Dim rect As New Rectangle(200, 0, 100, 200)
myPath.AddRectangle(rect)
myPath.AddLine(New Point(250, 200), New Point(250, 300))
' Draw the path to the screen.
Dim myPen As New Pen(Color.Black, 2)
e.Graphics.DrawPath(myPen, myPath)
' Clone a copy of myPath.
Dim myPath2 As GraphicsPath = CType(myPath.Clone(), GraphicsPath)
' Draw the path to the screen.
Dim myPen2 As New Pen(Color.Red, 4)
e.Graphics.DrawPath(myPen2, myPath2)
End Sub
```

[C#]
```
private void CloneExample(PaintEventArgs e)
{
// Set several markers in a path.
GraphicsPath myPath = new GraphicsPath();
myPath.AddEllipse(0, 0, 100, 200);
myPath.AddLine(new Point(100, 100), new Point(200, 100));
Rectangle rect = new Rectangle(200, 0, 100, 200);
myPath.AddRectangle(rect);
myPath.AddLine(new Point(250, 200), new Point(250, 300));
// Draw the path to the screen.
Pen myPen = new Pen(Color.Black, 2);
e.Graphics.DrawPath(myPen, myPath);
// Clone a copy of myPath.
GraphicsPath myPath2 = (GraphicsPath)myPath.Clone();
// Draw the path to the screen.
Pen myPen2 = new Pen(Color.Red, 4);
e.Graphics.DrawPath(myPen2, myPath2);
}
```

Requirements

Platforms: Windows 98, Windows NT 4.0, Windows Millennium Edition, Windows 2000, Windows XP Home Edition, Windows XP Professional, Windows Server 2003 family

GraphicsPath.CloseAllFigures Method

Closes all open figures in this path and starts a new figure. It closes each open figure by connecting a line from its endpoint to its starting point.

```
[Visual Basic]
Public Sub CloseAllFigures()
[C#]
public void CloseAllFigures();
[C++]
public: void CloseAllFigures();
[JScript]
public function CloseAllFigures();
```

Example

[Visual Basic, C#] The following example is designed for use with Windows Forms, and it requires **PaintEventArgs** *e*, an **OnPaint** event object. The code performs the following actions:

- Creates a path.
- Adds several open figures to the path.
- Closes all figures in the path.
- Draws the path to the screen.

```
[Visual Basic]
Public Sub CloseAllFiguresExample(e As PaintEventArgs)
' Create a path containing several open-ended figures.
Dim myPath As New GraphicsPath()
myPath.StartFigure()
myPath.AddLine(New Point(10, 10), New Point(150, 10))
myPath.AddLine(New Point(150, 10), New Point(10, 150))
myPath.StartFigure()
myPath.AddArc(200, 200, 100, 100, 0, 90)
myPath.StartFigure()
Dim point1 As New Point(300, 300)
Dim point2 As New Point(400, 325)
Dim point3 As New Point(400, 375)
Dim point4 As New Point(300, 400)
Dim points As Point() =  {point1, point2, point3, point4}
myPath.AddCurve(points)
' close all the figures.
myPath.CloseAllFigures()
' Draw the path to the screen.
e.Graphics.DrawPath(New Pen(Color.Black, 3), myPath)
End Sub
```

```
[C#]
private void CloseAllFiguresExample(PaintEventArgs e)
{
// Create a path containing several open-ended figures.
GraphicsPath myPath = new GraphicsPath();
myPath.StartFigure();
myPath.AddLine(new Point(10, 10), new Point(150, 10));
myPath.AddLine(new Point(150, 10), new Point(10, 150));
myPath.StartFigure();
myPath.AddArc(200, 200, 100, 100, 0, 90);
myPath.StartFigure();
Point point1 = new Point(300, 300);
Point point2 = new Point(400, 325);
Point point3 = new Point(400, 375);
Point point4 = new Point(300, 400);
Point[] points = {point1, point2, point3, point4};
myPath.AddCurve(points);
// Close all the figures.
myPath.CloseAllFigures();
// Draw the path to the screen.
e.Graphics.DrawPath(new Pen(Color.Black, 3), myPath);
}
```

Requirements

Platforms: Windows 98, Windows NT 4.0, Windows Millennium Edition, Windows 2000, Windows XP Home Edition, Windows XP Professional, Windows Server 2003 family

GraphicsPath.CloseFigure Method

Closes the current figure and starts a new figure. If the current figure contains a sequence of connected lines and curves, the method closes the loop by connecting a line from the endpoint to the starting point.

```
[Visual Basic]
Public Sub CloseFigure()
[C#]
public void CloseFigure();
[C++]
public: void CloseFigure();
[JScript]
public function CloseFigure();
```

Example

[Visual Basic, C#] The following example is designed for use with Windows Forms, and it requires **PaintEventArgs** *e*, an **OnPaint** event object. The code creates a triangle by creating a new path, starting a figure, adding two intersecting lines to the figure, and then closing the figure to form a triangle. The path is then drawn to the screen.

```
[Visual Basic]
Public Sub CloseFigureExample(e As PaintEventArgs)
' Create a path consisting of two, open-ended lines and close
' the lines using CloseFigure.
Dim myPath As New GraphicsPath()
myPath.StartFigure()
myPath.AddLine(New Point(10, 10), New Point(200, 10))
myPath.AddLine(New Point(200, 10), New Point(200, 200))
myPath.CloseFigure()
' Draw the path to the screen.
e.Graphics.DrawPath(Pens.Black, myPath)
End Sub
```

```
[C#]
private void CloseFigureExample(PaintEventArgs e)
{
// Create a path consisting of two, open-ended lines and close
// the lines using CloseFigure.
GraphicsPath myPath = new GraphicsPath();
myPath.StartFigure();
myPath.AddLine(new Point(10, 10), new Point(200, 10));
myPath.AddLine(new Point(200, 10), new Point(200, 200));
myPath.CloseFigure();
// Draw the path to the screen.
e.Graphics.DrawPath(Pens.Black, myPath);
}
```

Requirements

Platforms: Windows 98, Windows NT 4.0, Windows Millennium Edition, Windows 2000, Windows XP Home Edition, Windows XP Professional, Windows Server 2003 family

GraphicsPath.Dispose Method

Releases all resources used by this **GraphicsPath** object.

[Visual Basic]
```
Public Overridable Sub Dispose() Implements IDisposable.Dispose
```
[C#]
```
public virtual void Dispose();
```
[C++]
```
public: virtual void Dispose();
```
[JScript]
```
public function Dispose();
```

Return Value

This method does not return a value.

Implements

IDisposable.Dispose

Remarks

Calling **Dispose** allows the resources used by this **GraphicsPath** object to be reallocated for other purposes.

Requirements

Platforms: Windows 98, Windows NT 4.0, Windows Millennium Edition, Windows 2000, Windows XP Home Edition, Windows XP Professional, Windows Server 2003 family

GraphicsPath.Finalize Method

This member overrides **Object.Finalize**.

[Visual Basic]
```
Overrides Protected Sub Finalize()
```
[C#]
```
~GraphicsPath();
```
[C++]
```
~GraphicsPath();
```
[JScript]
```
protected override function Finalize();
```

Requirements

Platforms: Windows 98, Windows NT 4.0, Windows Millennium Edition, Windows 2000, Windows XP Home Edition, Windows XP Professional, Windows Server 2003 family

GraphicsPath.Flatten Method

Converts each curve in this path into a sequence of connected line segments.

Overload List

Converts each curve in this path into a sequence of connected line segments.

[Visual Basic] **Overloads Public Sub Flatten()**

[C#] **public void Flatten();**

[C++] **public: void Flatten();**

[JScript] **public function Flatten();**

Applies the specified transform and then converts each curve in this **GraphicsPath** object into a sequence of connected line segments.

[Visual Basic] **Overloads Public Sub Flatten(Matrix)**

[C#] **public void Flatten(Matrix);**

[C++] **public: void Flatten(Matrix*);**

[JScript] **public function Flatten(Matrix);**

Converts each curve in this **GraphicsPath** object into a sequence of connected line segments.

[Visual Basic] **Overloads Public Sub Flatten(Matrix, Single)**

[C#] **public void Flatten(Matrix, float);**

[C++] **public: void Flatten(Matrix*, float);**

[JScript] **public function Flatten(Matrix, float);**

Example

[Visual Basic, C#] The following example is designed for use with Windows Forms, and it requires **PaintEventArgs** *e*, an **OnPaint** event object. The code performs the following actions:

- Creates a graphics path and a translation matrix.
- Adds a curve to the path using four points.
- Draws the path (curve) to the screen, using a black pen.
- Shifts the curve down 10 pixels and flattens it.
- Draws the curve to the screen using, a red pen.

[Visual Basic, C#] Notice that the red curve has flattened lines connecting the points.

> [Visual Basic, C#] **Note** This example shows how to use one of the overloaded versions of **Flatten**. For other examples that might be available, see the individual overload topics.

[Visual Basic]
```
Public Sub FlattenExample(e As PaintEventArgs)
Dim myPath As New GraphicsPath()
Dim translateMatrix As New Matrix()
translateMatrix.Translate(0, 10)
Dim point1 As New Point(20, 100)
Dim point2 As New Point(70, 10)
Dim point3 As New Point(130, 200)
Dim point4 As New Point(180, 100)
Dim points As Point() = {point1, point2, point3, point4}
myPath.AddCurve(points)
e.Graphics.DrawPath(New Pen(Color.Black, 2), myPath)
myPath.Flatten(translateMatrix, 10F)
e.Graphics.DrawPath(New Pen(Color.Red, 1), myPath)
End Sub 'FlattenExample
```

[C#]
```
private void FlattenExample(PaintEventArgs e)
{
GraphicsPath myPath = new GraphicsPath();
Matrix translateMatrix = new Matrix();
translateMatrix.Translate(0, 10);
Point point1 = new Point(20, 100);
Point point2 = new Point(70, 10);
Point point3 = new Point(130, 200);
Point point4 = new Point(180, 100);
Point[] points = {point1, point2, point3, point4};
myPath.AddCurve(points);
e.Graphics.DrawPath(new Pen(Color.Black, 2), myPath);
myPath.Flatten(translateMatrix, 10f);
e.Graphics.DrawPath(new Pen(Color.Red, 1), myPath);
}
```

GraphicsPath.Flatten Method ()

Converts each curve in this path into a sequence of connected line segments.

```
[Visual Basic]
Overloads Public Sub Flatten()
[C#]
public void Flatten();
[C++]
public: void Flatten();
[JScript]
public function Flatten();
```

Example

For an example, see **GraphicsPath.Flatten Method (Matrix, Single)**.

Requirements

Platforms: Windows 98, Windows NT 4.0, Windows Millennium Edition, Windows 2000, Windows XP Home Edition, Windows XP Professional, Windows Server 2003 family

GraphicsPath.Flatten Method (Matrix)

Applies the specified transform and then converts each curve in this **GraphicsPath** object into a sequence of connected line segments.

```
[Visual Basic]
Overloads Public Sub Flatten( _
   ByVal matrix As Matrix _
)
[C#]
public void Flatten(
   Matrix matrix
);
[C++]
public: void Flatten(
   Matrix* matrix
);
[JScript]
public function Flatten(
   matrix : Matrix
);
```

Parameters

matrix
: A **Matrix** object by which to transform this **GraphicsPath** before flattening.

Example

For an example, see **GraphicsPath.Flatten Method (Matrix, Single)**.

Requirements

Platforms: Windows 98, Windows NT 4.0, Windows Millennium Edition, Windows 2000, Windows XP Home Edition, Windows XP Professional, Windows Server 2003 family

GraphicsPath.Flatten Method (Matrix, Single)

Converts each curve in this **GraphicsPath** object into a sequence of connected line segments.

```
[Visual Basic]
Overloads Public Sub Flatten( _
   ByVal matrix As Matrix, _
   ByVal flatness As Single _
)
[C#]
public void Flatten(
   Matrix matrix,
   float flatness
);
[C++]
public: void Flatten(
   Matrix* matrix,
   float flatness
);
[JScript]
public function Flatten(
   matrix : Matrix,
   flatness : float
);
```

Parameters

matrix
: A **Matrix** object by which to transform this **GraphicsPath** before flattening.

flatness
: Specifies the maximum permitted error between the curve and its flattened approximation. A value of 0.25 is the default. Reducing the flatness value will increase the number of line segments in the approximation.

Example

[Visual Basic, C#] The following example is designed for use with Windows Forms, and it requires **PaintEventArgs** *e*, an **OnPaint** event object. The code performs the following actions:

- Creates a graphics path and a translation matrix.
- Adds a curve to the path using four points.
- Draws the path (curve) to the screen, using a black pen.
- Shifts the curve down 10 pixels and flattens it.
- Draws the curve to the screen using, a red pen.

[Visual Basic, C#] Notice that the red curve has flattened lines connecting the points.

```
[Visual Basic]
Public Sub FlattenExample(e As PaintEventArgs)
Dim myPath As New GraphicsPath()
Dim translateMatrix As New Matrix()
translateMatrix.Translate(0, 10)
Dim point1 As New Point(20, 100)
Dim point2 As New Point(70, 10)
Dim point3 As New Point(130, 200)
Dim point4 As New Point(180, 100)
Dim points As Point() =  {point1, point2, point3, point4}
myPath.AddCurve(points)
e.Graphics.DrawPath(New Pen(Color.Black, 2), myPath)
myPath.Flatten(translateMatrix, 10F)
e.Graphics.DrawPath(New Pen(Color.Red, 1), myPath)
End Sub 'FlattenExample
```

[C#]
```
private void FlattenExample(PaintEventArgs e)
{
GraphicsPath myPath = new GraphicsPath();
Matrix translateMatrix = new Matrix();
translateMatrix.Translate(0, 10);
Point point1 = new Point(20, 100);
Point point2 = new Point(70, 10);
Point point3 = new Point(130, 200);
Point point4 = new Point(180, 100);
Point[] points = {point1, point2, point3, point4};
myPath.AddCurve(points);
e.Graphics.DrawPath(new Pen(Color.Black, 2), myPath);
myPath.Flatten(translateMatrix, 10f);
e.Graphics.DrawPath(new Pen(Color.Red, 1), myPath);
}
```

Requirements

Platforms: Windows 98, Windows NT 4.0, Windows Millennium Edition, Windows 2000, Windows XP Home Edition, Windows XP Professional, Windows Server 2003 family

GraphicsPath.GetBounds Method

Returns a rectangle that bounds this **GraphicsPath** object.

Overload List

Returns a rectangle that bounds this **GraphicsPath** object.

[Visual Basic] **Overloads Public Function GetBounds() As RectangleF**

[C#] **public RectangleF GetBounds();**

[C++] **public: RectangleF GetBounds();**

[JScript] **public function GetBounds() : RectangleF;**

Returns a rectangle that bounds this **GraphicsPath** object when this path is transformed by the specified **Matrix** object.

[Visual Basic] **Overloads Public Function GetBounds(Matrix) As RectangleF**

[C#] **public RectangleF GetBounds(Matrix);**

[C++] **public: RectangleF GetBounds(Matrix*);**

[JScript] **public function GetBounds(Matrix) : RectangleF;**

Returns a rectangle that bounds this **GraphicsPath** object when the current path is transformed by the specified **Matrix** object and drawn with the specified **Pen** object.

[Visual Basic] **Overloads Public Function GetBounds(Matrix, Pen) As RectangleF**

[C#] **public RectangleF GetBounds(Matrix, Pen);**

[C++] **public: RectangleF GetBounds(Matrix*, Pen*);**

[JScript] **public function GetBounds(Matrix, Pen) : RectangleF;**

Example

For an example, see **GraphicsPath.GetBounds()**

GraphicsPath.GetBounds Method ()

Returns a rectangle that bounds this **GraphicsPath** object.

[Visual Basic]
```
Overloads Public Function GetBounds() As RectangleF
```
[C#]
```
public RectangleF GetBounds();
```
[C++]
```
public: RectangleF GetBounds();
```
[JScript]
```
public function GetBounds() : RectangleF;
```

Return Value

A **RectangleF** structure that represents a rectangle that bounds this **GraphicsPath** object.

Remarks

The size of the returned bounding rectangle is influenced by the type of end caps, pen width, and pen miter limit, and therefore produces a "loose fit" to the bounded path. The approximate formula is: the initial bounding rectangle is inflated by pen width, and this result is multiplied by the miter limit, plus some additional margin to allow for end caps.

Example

[Visual Basic, C#] The following example is designed for use with Windows Forms, and it requires **PaintEventArgs** *e*, an **OnPaint** event object. The code performs the following actions:

- Creates a graphics path.
- Adds an ellipse (circle) to it and draws it to the screen.
- Retrieves the bounding rectangle for the circle with a call to **GetBounds()** and draws the rectangle to the screen.
- Creates a second graphics path.
- Adds a circle and widens the path to a width of 10.
- Draws the path to the screen.
- Retrieves the bounding rectangle for the second circle.
- Draws the bounding rectangle to the screen.
- Displays the rectangle size in a dialog box.

[Visual Basic, C#] Notice that the bounding rectangle on the right is larger (to account for the extra width of the line).

[Visual Basic]
```
Public Sub GetBoundsExample(e As PaintEventArgs)
' Create path number 1 and a Pen for drawing.
Dim myPath As New GraphicsPath()
Dim pathPen As New Pen(Color.Black, 1)
' Add an Ellipse to the path and Draw it (circle in start
' position).
myPath.AddEllipse(20, 20, 100, 100)
e.Graphics.DrawPath(pathPen, myPath)
' Get the path bounds for Path number 1 and draw them.
Dim boundRect As RectangleF = myPath.GetBounds()
e.Graphics.DrawRectangle(New Pen(Color.Red, 1), boundRect.X, _
boundRect.Y, boundRect.Height, boundRect.Width)
' Create a second graphics path and a wider Pen.
Dim myPath2 As New GraphicsPath()
Dim pathPen2 As New Pen(Color.Black, 10)
' Create a new ellipse with a width of 10.
myPath2.AddEllipse(150, 20, 100, 100)
myPath2.Widen(pathPen2)
e.Graphics.FillPath(Brushes.Black, myPath2)
' Get the second path bounds.
Dim boundRect2 As RectangleF = myPath2.GetBounds()
' Show the bounds in a message box.
e.Graphics.DrawString("Rectangle2 Bounds: " + _
boundRect2.ToString(), New Font("Arial", 8), Brushes.Black, _
20, 150)
' Draw the bounding rectangle.
e.Graphics.DrawRectangle(New Pen(Color.Red, 1), boundRect2.X, _
boundRect2.Y, boundRect2.Height, boundRect2.Width)
End Sub
```

[C#]
```
public void GetBoundsExample(PaintEventArgs e)
{
// Create path number 1 and a Pen for drawing.
GraphicsPath myPath = new GraphicsPath();
Pen pathPen = new Pen(Color.Black, 1);
// Add an Ellipse to the path and Draw it (circle in start
// position).
myPath.AddEllipse(20, 20, 100, 100);
e.Graphics.DrawPath(pathPen, myPath);
// Get the path bounds for Path number 1 and draw them.
RectangleF boundRect = myPath.GetBounds();
e.Graphics.DrawRectangle(new Pen(Color.Red, 1),
boundRect.X,
boundRect.Y,
boundRect.Height,
boundRect.Width);
// Create a second graphics path and a wider Pen.
GraphicsPath myPath2 = new GraphicsPath();
Pen pathPen2 = new Pen(Color.Black, 10);
// Create a new ellipse with a width of 10.
myPath2.AddEllipse(150, 20, 100, 100);
myPath2.Widen(pathPen2);
e.Graphics.FillPath(Brushes.Black, myPath2);
// Get the second path bounds.
RectangleF boundRect2 = myPath2.GetBounds();
// Draw the bounding rectangle.
e.Graphics.DrawRectangle(new Pen(Color.Red, 1),
boundRect2.X,
boundRect2.Y,
boundRect2.Height,
boundRect2.Width);
// Display the rectangle size.
MessageBox.Show(boundRect2.ToString());
}
```

Requirements

Platforms: Windows 98, Windows NT 4.0, Windows Millennium Edition, Windows 2000, Windows XP Home Edition, Windows XP Professional, Windows Server 2003 family

GraphicsPath.GetBounds Method (Matrix)

Returns a rectangle that bounds this **GraphicsPath** object when this path is transformed by the specified **Matrix** object.

[Visual Basic]
```
Overloads Public Function GetBounds( _
   ByVal matrix As Matrix _
) As RectangleF
```
[C#]
```
public RectangleF GetBounds(
   Matrix matrix
);
```
[C++]
```
public: RectangleF GetBounds(
   Matrix* matrix
);
```
[JScript]
```
public function GetBounds(
   matrix : Matrix
) : RectangleF;
```

Parameters

matrix
The **Matrix** object that specifies a transformation to be applied to this path before the bounding rectangle is calculated. This path is not permanently transformed; the transformation is used only during the process of calculating the bounding rectangle.

Return Value

A **RectangleF** structure that represents a rectangle that bounds this **GraphicsPath** object.

Remarks

The size of the returned bounding rectangle is influenced by the type of end caps, pen width, and pen miter limit, and therefore produces a "loose fit" to the bounded path. The approximate formula is: the initial bounding rectangle is inflated by pen width, and this result is multiplied by the miter limit, plus some additional margin to allow for end caps.

Example

For an example, see **GraphicsPath.GetBounds()**

Requirements

Platforms: Windows 98, Windows NT 4.0, Windows Millennium Edition, Windows 2000, Windows XP Home Edition, Windows XP Professional, Windows Server 2003 family

GraphicsPath.GetBounds Method (Matrix, Pen)

Returns a rectangle that bounds this **GraphicsPath** object when the current path is transformed by the specified **Matrix** object and drawn with the specified **Pen** object.

[Visual Basic]
```
Overloads Public Function GetBounds( _
   ByVal matrix As Matrix, _
   ByVal pen As Pen _
) As RectangleF
```
[C#]
```
public RectangleF GetBounds(
   Matrix matrix,
   Pen pen
);
```
[C++]
```
public: RectangleF GetBounds(
   Matrix* matrix,
   Pen* pen
);
```
[JScript]
```
public function GetBounds(
   matrix : Matrix,
   pen : Pen
) : RectangleF;
```

Parameters

matrix
The **Matrix** object that specifies a transformation to be applied to this path before the bounding rectangle is calculated. This path is not permanently transformed; the transformation is used only during the process of calculating the bounding rectangle.

pen
The **Pen** object with which to draw the **GraphicsPath**.

Return Value

A **RectangleF** structure that represents a rectangle that bounds this **GraphicsPath** object.

Remarks

The size of the returned bounding rectangle is influenced by the type of end caps, pen width, and pen miter limit, and therefore produces a "loose fit" to the bounded path. The approximate formula is: the initial bounding rectangle is inflated by pen width, and this result is multiplied by the miter limit, plus some additional margin to allow for end caps.

Example

For an example, see **GraphicsPath.GetBounds()**

Requirements

Platforms: Windows 98, Windows NT 4.0, Windows Millennium Edition, Windows 2000, Windows XP Home Edition, Windows XP Professional, Windows Server 2003 family

GraphicsPath.GetLastPoint Method

Gets the last point in the **PathPoints** array of this **GraphicsPath** object.

[Visual Basic]
```
Public Function GetLastPoint() As PointF
```
[C#]
```
public PointF GetLastPoint();
```
[C++]
```
public: PointF GetLastPoint();
```
[JScript]
```
public function GetLastPoint() : PointF;
```

Return Value

A **PointF** structure that represents the last point in this **GraphicsPath** object.

Example

[Visual Basic, C#] The following example is designed for use with Windows Forms, and it requires **PaintEventArgs** *e*, an **OnPaint** event object. The code creates a path, adds a line to the path, and then gets the last point in the path.

[Visual Basic]
```
Public Sub GetLastPointExample(e As PaintEventArgs)
Dim myPath As New GraphicsPath()
myPath.AddLine(20, 20, 100, 20)
Dim lastPoint As PointF = myPath.GetLastPoint()
If lastPoint.IsEmpty = False Then
Dim lastPointXString As String = lastPoint.X.ToString()
Dim lastPointYString As String = lastPoint.Y.ToString()
MessageBox.Show((lastPointXString + ", " + lastPointYString))
Else
MessageBox.Show("lastPoint is empty")
End If
End Sub
```

[C#]
```
private void GetLastPointExample(PaintEventArgs e)
{
GraphicsPath myPath = new GraphicsPath();
myPath.AddLine(20, 20, 100, 20);
PointF lastPoint = myPath.GetLastPoint();
if(lastPoint.IsEmpty == false)
{
string lastPointXString = lastPoint.X.ToString();
string lastPointYString = lastPoint.Y.ToString();
MessageBox.Show(lastPointXString + ", " + lastPointYString);
}
else
MessageBox.Show("lastPoint is empty");
}
```

Requirements

Platforms: Windows 98, Windows NT 4.0, Windows Millennium Edition, Windows 2000, Windows XP Home Edition, Windows XP Professional, Windows Server 2003 family

GraphicsPath.IsOutlineVisible Method

Indicates whether the specified point is contained within (under) the outline of this **GraphicsPath** object when drawn with the specified **Pen** object.

Overload List

Indicates whether the specified point is contained within (under) the outline of this **GraphicsPath** object when drawn with the specified **Pen** object.

[Visual Basic] **Overloads Public Function IsOutlineVisible(Point, Pen) As Boolean**

[C#] **public bool IsOutlineVisible(Point, Pen);**

[C++] **public: bool IsOutlineVisible(Point, Pen*);**

[JScript] **public function IsOutlineVisible(Point, Pen) : Boolean;**

Indicates whether the specified point is contained within (under) the outline of this **GraphicsPath** object when drawn with the specified **Pen** object.

[Visual Basic] **Overloads Public Function IsOutlineVisible(PointF, Pen) As Boolean**

[C#] **public bool IsOutlineVisible(PointF, Pen);**

[C++] **public: bool IsOutlineVisible(PointF, Pen*);**

[JScript] **public function IsOutlineVisible(PointF, Pen) : Boolean;**

Indicates whether the specified point is contained within (under) the outline of this **GraphicsPath** object when drawn with the specified **Pen** object.

[Visual Basic] **Overloads Public Function IsOutlineVisible(Integer, Integer, Pen) As Boolean**

[C#] **public bool IsOutlineVisible(int, int, Pen);**

[C++] **public: bool IsOutlineVisible(int, int, Pen*);**

[JScript] **public function IsOutlineVisible(int, int, Pen) : Boolean;**

Indicates whether the specified point is contained within (under) the outline of this **GraphicsPath** object when drawn with the specified **Pen** object and using the specified **Graphics** object.

[Visual Basic] **Overloads Public Function IsOutlineVisible(Point, Pen, Graphics) As Boolean**

[C#] **public bool IsOutlineVisible(Point, Pen, Graphics);**

[C++] **public: bool IsOutlineVisible(Point, Pen*, Graphics*);**

[JScript] **public function IsOutlineVisible(Point, Pen, Graphics) : Boolean;**

Indicates whether the specified point is contained within (under) the outline of this **GraphicsPath** object when drawn with the specified **Pen** object and using the specified **Graphics** object.

[Visual Basic] **Overloads Public Function IsOutlineVisible(PointF, Pen, Graphics) As Boolean**

[C#] **public bool IsOutlineVisible(PointF, Pen, Graphics);**

[C++] **public: bool IsOutlineVisible(PointF, Pen*, Graphics*);**

[JScript] **public function IsOutlineVisible(PointF, Pen, Graphics) : Boolean;**

Indicates whether the specified point is contained within (under) the outline of this **GraphicsPath** object when drawn with the specified **Pen** object.

[Visual Basic] **Overloads Public Function IsOutlineVisible(Single, Single, Pen) As Boolean**

[C#] **public bool IsOutlineVisible(float, float, Pen);**

[C++] **public: bool IsOutlineVisible(float, float, Pen*);**

[JScript] **public function IsOutlineVisible(float, float, Pen) : Boolean;**

Indicates whether the specified point is contained within (under) the outline of this **GraphicsPath** object when drawn with the specified **Pen** object and using the specified **Graphics** object.

[Visual Basic] **Overloads Public Function IsOutlineVisible(Integer, Integer, Pen, Graphics) As Boolean**

[C#] **public bool IsOutlineVisible(int, int, Pen, Graphics);**

[C++] **public: bool IsOutlineVisible(int, int, Pen*, Graphics*);**

[JScript] **public function IsOutlineVisible(int, int, Pen, Graphics) : Boolean;**

Indicates whether the specified point is contained within (under) the outline of this **GraphicsPath** object when drawn with the specified **Pen** object and using the specified **Graphics** object.

[Visual Basic] **Overloads Public Function IsOutlineVisible(Single, Single, Pen, Graphics) As Boolean**

[C#] **public bool IsOutlineVisible(float, float, Pen, Graphics);**

[C++] **public: bool IsOutlineVisible(float, float, Pen*, Graphics*);**

[JScript] **public function IsOutlineVisible(float, float, Pen, Graphics) : Boolean;**

Example

For an example, see **GraphicsPath.IsOutlineVisible Method (Int32, Int32, Pen, Graphics)**.

GraphicsPath.IsOutlineVisible Method (Point, Pen)

Indicates whether the specified point is contained within (under) the outline of this **GraphicsPath** object when drawn with the specified **Pen** object.

```
[Visual Basic]
Overloads Public Function IsOutlineVisible( _
   ByVal point As Point, _
   ByVal pen As Pen _
) As Boolean
[C#]
public bool IsOutlineVisible(
   Point point,
   Pen pen
);
[C++]
public: bool IsOutlineVisible(
   Point point,
   Pen* pen
);
[JScript]
public function IsOutlineVisible(
   point : Point,
   pen : Pen
) : Boolean;
```

Parameters

point

A **Point** structure that specifies the location to test.

pen

The **Pen** object to test.

Return Value

This method returns **true** if the specified point is contained within the outline of this **GraphicsPath** object when drawn with the specified **Pen** object; otherwise, **false**.

Remarks

This method tests to see if the outline of a given path is rendered visible at the specified point.

Example

For an example, see **GraphicsPath.IsOutlineVisible Method (Int32, Int32, Pen, Graphics)**.

Requirements

Platforms: Windows 98, Windows NT 4.0, Windows Millennium Edition, Windows 2000, Windows XP Home Edition, Windows XP Professional, Windows Server 2003 family

GraphicsPath.IsOutlineVisible Method (PointF, Pen)

Indicates whether the specified point is contained within (under) the outline of this **GraphicsPath** object when drawn with the specified **Pen** object.

```
[Visual Basic]
Overloads Public Function IsOutlineVisible( _
   ByVal point As PointF, _
   ByVal pen As Pen _
) As Boolean
[C#]
public bool IsOutlineVisible(
   PointF point,
   Pen pen
);
[C++]
public: bool IsOutlineVisible(
   PointF point,
   Pen* pen
);
[JScript]
public function IsOutlineVisible(
   point : PointF,
   pen : Pen
) : Boolean;
```

Parameters

point

A **PointF** structure that specifies the location to test.

pen

The **Pen** object to test.

Return Value

This method returns **true** if the specified point is contained within the outline of this **GraphicsPath** object when drawn with the specified **Pen** object; otherwise, **false**.

Remarks

This method tests to see if the outline of a given path is rendered visible at the specified point.

Example

For an example, see **GraphicsPath.IsOutlineVisible Method (Int32, Int32, Pen, Graphics)**.

Requirements

Platforms: Windows 98, Windows NT 4.0, Windows Millennium Edition, Windows 2000, Windows XP Home Edition, Windows XP Professional, Windows Server 2003 family

GraphicsPath.IsOutlineVisible Method (Int32, Int32, Pen)

Indicates whether the specified point is contained within (under) the outline of this **GraphicsPath** object when drawn with the specified **Pen** object.

```
[Visual Basic]
Overloads Public Function IsOutlineVisible( _
   ByVal x As Integer, _
   ByVal y As Integer, _
   ByVal pen As Pen _
) As Boolean
[C#]
public bool IsOutlineVisible(
   int x,
   int y,
   Pen pen
);
[C++]
public: bool IsOutlineVisible(
   int x,
   int y,
   Pen* pen
);
[JScript]
public function IsOutlineVisible(
   x : int,
   y : int,
   pen : Pen
) : Boolean;
```

Parameters

x

The x-coordinate of the point to test.

y

The y-coordinate of the point to test.

pen

The **Pen** object to test.

Return Value

This method returns **true** if the specified point is contained within the outline of this **GraphicsPath** object when drawn with the specified **Pen** object; otherwise, **false**.

Remarks

This method tests to see if the outline of a given path is rendered visible at the specified point.

Example

For an example, see **GraphicsPath.IsOutlineVisible Method (Int32, Int32, Pen, Graphics)**.

Requirements

Platforms: Windows 98, Windows NT 4.0, Windows Millennium Edition, Windows 2000, Windows XP Home Edition, Windows XP Professional, Windows Server 2003 family

GraphicsPath.IsOutlineVisible Method (Point, Pen, Graphics)

Indicates whether the specified point is contained within (under) the outline of this **GraphicsPath** object when drawn with the specified **Pen** object and using the specified **Graphics** object.

```
[Visual Basic]
Overloads Public Function IsOutlineVisible( _
   ByVal pt As Point, _
   ByVal pen As Pen, _
   ByVal graphics As Graphics _
) As Boolean
[C#]
public bool IsOutlineVisible(
   Point pt,
   Pen pen,
   Graphics graphics
);
[C++]
public: bool IsOutlineVisible(
   Point pt,
   Pen* pen,
   Graphics* graphics
);
[JScript]
public function IsOutlineVisible(
   pt : Point,
   pen : Pen,
   graphics : Graphics
) : Boolean;
```

Parameters

pt

A **Point** structure that specifies the location to test.

pen

The **Pen** object to test.

graphics

The **Graphics** object for which to test visibility.

Return Value

This method returns **true** if the specified point is contained within the outline of this **GraphicsPath** object as drawn with the specified **Pen** object; otherwise, **false**.

Remarks

This method tests to see if the outline of a given path is rendered visible at the specified point. The coordinates of the point to be tested are given in world coordinates. The transform matrix of *graphics* is temporarily applied before testing for visibility.

Example

For an example, see **GraphicsPath.IsOutlineVisible Method (Int32, Int32, Pen, Graphics)**.

Requirements

Platforms: Windows 98, Windows NT 4.0, Windows Millennium Edition, Windows 2000, Windows XP Home Edition, Windows XP Professional, Windows Server 2003 family

GraphicsPath.IsOutlineVisible Method (PointF, Pen, Graphics)

Indicates whether the specified point is contained within (under) the outline of this **GraphicsPath** object when drawn with the specified **Pen** object and using the specified **Graphics** object.

```
[Visual Basic]
Overloads Public Function IsOutlineVisible( _
   ByVal pt As PointF, _
   ByVal pen As Pen, _
   ByVal graphics As Graphics _
) As Boolean
[C#]
public bool IsOutlineVisible(
   PointF pt,
   Pen pen,
   Graphics graphics
);
[C++]
public: bool IsOutlineVisible(
   PointF pt,
   Pen* pen,
   Graphics* graphics
);
[JScript]
public function IsOutlineVisible(
   pt : PointF,
   pen : Pen,
   graphics : Graphics
) : Boolean;
```

Parameters

pt
A **PointF** structure that specifies the location to test.

pen
The **Pen** object to test.

graphics
The **Graphics** object for which to test visibility.

Return Value

This method returns **true** if the specified point is contained within (under) the outline of this **GraphicsPath** object as drawn with the specified **Pen** object; otherwise, **false**.

Remarks

This method tests to see if the outline of a given path is rendered visible at the specified point. The coordinates of the point to be tested are given in world coordinates. The transform matrix of *graphics* is temporarily applied before testing for visibility.

Example

For an example, see **GraphicsPath.IsOutlineVisible Method (Int32, Int32, Pen, Graphics)**.

Requirements

Platforms: Windows 98, Windows NT 4.0, Windows Millennium Edition, Windows 2000, Windows XP Home Edition, Windows XP Professional, Windows Server 2003 family

GraphicsPath.IsOutlineVisible Method (Single, Single, Pen)

Indicates whether the specified point is contained within (under) the outline of this **GraphicsPath** object when drawn with the specified **Pen** object.

```
[Visual Basic]
Overloads Public Function IsOutlineVisible( _
   ByVal x As Single, _
   ByVal y As Single, _
   ByVal pen As Pen _
) As Boolean
[C#]
public bool IsOutlineVisible(
   float x,
   float y,
   Pen pen
);
[C++]
public: bool IsOutlineVisible(
   float x,
   float y,
   Pen* pen
);
[JScript]
public function IsOutlineVisible(
   x : float,
   y : float,
   pen : Pen
) : Boolean;
```

Parameters

x
The x-coordinate of the point to test.

y
The y-coordinate of the point to test.

pen
The **Pen** object to test.

Return Value

This method returns **true** if the specified point is contained within the outline of this **GraphicsPath** object when drawn with the specified **Pen** object; otherwise, **false**.

Remarks

This method tests to see if the outline of a given path is rendered visible at the specified point.

Example

For an example, see **GraphicsPath.IsOutlineVisible Method (Int32, Int32, Pen, Graphics)**.

Requirements

Platforms: Windows 98, Windows NT 4.0, Windows Millennium Edition, Windows 2000, Windows XP Home Edition, Windows XP Professional, Windows Server 2003 family

GraphicsPath.IsOutlineVisible Method (Int32, Int32, Pen, Graphics)

Indicates whether the specified point is contained within (under) the outline of this **GraphicsPath** object when drawn with the specified **Pen** object and using the specified **Graphics** object.

[Visual Basic]
```
Overloads Public Function IsOutlineVisible( _
   ByVal x As Integer, _
   ByVal y As Integer, _
   ByVal pen As Pen, _
   ByVal graphics As Graphics _
) As Boolean
```
[C#]
```
public bool IsOutlineVisible(
   int x,
   int y,
   Pen pen,
   Graphics graphics
);
```
[C++]
```
public: bool IsOutlineVisible(
   int x,
   int y,
   Pen* pen,
   Graphics* graphics
);
```
[JScript]
```
public function IsOutlineVisible(
   x : int,
   y : int,
   pen : Pen,
   graphics : Graphics
) : Boolean;
```

Parameters

x
The x-coordinate of the point to test.

y
The y-coordinate of the point to test.

pen
The **Pen** object to test.

graphics
The **Graphics** object for which to test visibility.

Return Value

This method returns **true** if the specified point is contained within the outline of this **GraphicsPath** object as drawn with the specified **Pen** object; otherwise, **false**.

Remarks

This method tests to see if the outline of a given path is rendered visible at the specified point. The coordinates of the point to be tested are given in world coordinates. The transform matrix of *graphics* is temporarily applied before testing for visibility.

Example

[Visual Basic, C#] The following example is designed for use with Windows Forms, and it requires **PaintEventArgs** *e*, an **OnPaint** event object. The code performs the following actions:

- Creates a path.
- Adds a rectangle to the path.
- Creates a wide pen and widens the path with that pen (to make the example clearer),
- Tests a point (100, 50) to see if it lies within (under) one of the edges of the rectangle by calling **IsOutlineVisible**.

[Visual Basic, C#] The result is shown in the message box (in this case, true). In other words the edge is rendered over that point.

[Visual Basic]
```
Public Sub IsOutlineVisibleExample(e As PaintEventArgs)
Dim myPath As New GraphicsPath()
Dim rect As New Rectangle(20, 20, 100, 100)
myPath.AddRectangle(rect)
Dim testPen As New Pen(Color.Black, 20)
myPath.Widen(testPen)
e.Graphics.FillPath(Brushes.Black, myPath)
Dim visible As Boolean = myPath.IsOutlineVisible(100, 50, _
testPen, e.Graphics)
MessageBox.Show(("visible = " + visible.ToString()))
End Sub
```
[C#]
```
public void IsOutlineVisibleExample(PaintEventArgs e)
{
GraphicsPath myPath = new GraphicsPath();
Rectangle rect = new Rectangle(20, 20, 100, 100);
myPath.AddRectangle(rect);
Pen testPen = new Pen(Color.Black, 20);
myPath.Widen(testPen);
e.Graphics.FillPath(Brushes.Black, myPath);
bool visible = myPath.IsOutlineVisible(100, 50, testPen,
e.Graphics);
MessageBox.Show("visible = " + visible.ToString());
}
```

Requirements

Platforms: Windows 98, Windows NT 4.0, Windows Millennium Edition, Windows 2000, Windows XP Home Edition, Windows XP Professional, Windows Server 2003 family

GraphicsPath.IsOutlineVisible Method (Single, Single, Pen, Graphics)

Indicates whether the specified point is contained within (under) the outline of this **GraphicsPath** object when drawn with the specified **Pen** object and using the specified **Graphics** object.

[Visual Basic]
```
Overloads Public Function IsOutlineVisible( _
   ByVal x As Single, _
   ByVal y As Single, _
   ByVal pen As Pen, _
   ByVal graphics As Graphics _
) As Boolean
```
[C#]
```
public bool IsOutlineVisible(
   float x,
   float y,
   Pen pen,
   Graphics graphics
);
```
[C++]
```
public: bool IsOutlineVisible(
   float x,
   float y,
   Pen* pen,
   Graphics* graphics
);
```

```
[JScript]
public function IsOutlineVisible(
   x : float,
   y : float,
   pen : Pen,
   graphics : Graphics
) : Boolean;
```

Parameters

x
The x-coordinate of the point to test.

y
The y-coordinate of the point to test.

pen
The **Pen** object to test.

graphics
The **Graphics** object for which to test visibility.

Return Value

This method returns **true** if the specified point is contained within (under) the outline of this **GraphicsPath** object as drawn with the specified **Pen** object; otherwise, **false**.

Remarks

This method tests to see if the outline of a given path is rendered visible at the specified point. The coordinates of the point to be tested are given in world coordinates. The transform matrix of the *graphics* parameter is temporarily applied before testing for visibility.

Example

For an example, see **GraphicsPath.IsOutlineVisible Method (Int32, Int32, Pen, Graphics)**.

Requirements

Platforms: Windows 98, Windows NT 4.0, Windows Millennium Edition, Windows 2000, Windows XP Home Edition, Windows XP Professional, Windows Server 2003 family

GraphicsPath.IsVisible Method

Indicates whether the specified point is contained within this **GraphicsPath** object.

Overload List

Indicates whether the specified point is contained within this **GraphicsPath** object.

[Visual Basic] **Overloads Public Function IsVisible(Point) As Boolean**

[C#] **public bool IsVisible(Point);**

[C++] **public: bool IsVisible(Point);**

[JScript] **public function IsVisible(Point) : Boolean;**

Indicates whether the specified point is contained within this **GraphicsPath** object.

[Visual Basic] **Overloads Public Function IsVisible(PointF) As Boolean**

[C#] **public bool IsVisible(PointF);**

[C++] **public: bool IsVisible(PointF);**

[JScript] **public function IsVisible(PointF) : Boolean;**

Indicates whether the specified point is contained within this **GraphicsPath** object.

[Visual Basic] **Overloads Public Function IsVisible(Integer, Integer) As Boolean**

[C#] **public bool IsVisible(int, int);**

[C++] **public: bool IsVisible(int, int);**

[JScript] **public function IsVisible(int, int) : Boolean;**

Indicates whether the specified point is contained within this **GraphicsPath** object.

[Visual Basic] **Overloads Public Function IsVisible(Point, Graphics) As Boolean**

[C#] **public bool IsVisible(Point, Graphics);**

[C++] **public: bool IsVisible(Point, Graphics*);**

[JScript] **public function IsVisible(Point, Graphics) : Boolean;**

Indicates whether the specified point is contained within this **GraphicsPath** object.

[Visual Basic] **Overloads Public Function IsVisible(PointF, Graphics) As Boolean**

[C#] **public bool IsVisible(PointF, Graphics);**

[C++] **public: bool IsVisible(PointF, Graphics*);**

[JScript] **public function IsVisible(PointF, Graphics) : Boolean;**

Indicates whether the specified point is contained within this **GraphicsPath** object.

[Visual Basic] **Overloads Public Function IsVisible(Single, Single) As Boolean**

[C#] **public bool IsVisible(float, float);**

[C++] **public: bool IsVisible(float, float);**

[JScript] **public function IsVisible(float, float) : Boolean;**

Indicates whether the specified point is contained within this **GraphicsPath** object, using the specified **Graphics** object.

[Visual Basic] **Overloads Public Function IsVisible(Integer, Integer, Graphics) As Boolean**

[C#] **public bool IsVisible(int, int, Graphics);**

[C++] **public: bool IsVisible(int, int, Graphics*);**

[JScript] **public function IsVisible(int, int, Graphics) : Boolean;**

Indicates whether the specified point is contained within this **GraphicsPath** object in the visible clip region of the specified **Graphics** object.

[Visual Basic] **Overloads Public Function IsVisible(Single, Single, Graphics) As Boolean**

[C#] **public bool IsVisible(float, float, Graphics);**

[C++] **public: bool IsVisible(float, float, Graphics*);**

[JScript] **public function IsVisible(float, float, Graphics) : Boolean;**

Example

For an example, see **GraphicsPath.IsVisible Method (Int32, Int32, Graphics)**.

GraphicsPath.IsVisible Method (Point)

Indicates whether the specified point is contained within this **GraphicsPath** object.

[Visual Basic]
```
Overloads Public Function IsVisible( _
   ByVal point As Point _
) As Boolean
```
[C#]
```
public bool IsVisible(
   Point point
);
```
[C++]
```
public: bool IsVisible(
   Point point
);
```
[JScript]
```
public function IsVisible(
   point : Point
) : Boolean;
```

Parameters

point

A **Point** structure that represents the point to test.

Return Value

This method returns **true** if the specified point is contained within this **GraphicsPath** object; otherwise, **false**.

Example

For an example, see **GraphicsPath.IsVisible Method (Int32, Int32, Graphics)**.

Requirements

Platforms: Windows 98, Windows NT 4.0, Windows Millennium Edition, Windows 2000, Windows XP Home Edition, Windows XP Professional, Windows Server 2003 family

GraphicsPath.IsVisible Method (PointF)

Indicates whether the specified point is contained within this **GraphicsPath** object.

[Visual Basic]
```
Overloads Public Function IsVisible( _
   ByVal point As PointF _
) As Boolean
```
[C#]
```
public bool IsVisible(
   PointF point
);
```
[C++]
```
public: bool IsVisible(
   PointF point
);
```
[JScript]
```
public function IsVisible(
   point : PointF
) : Boolean;
```

Parameters

point

A **PointF** structure that represents the point to test.

Return Value

This method returns **true** if the specified point is contained within this **GraphicsPath** object; otherwise, **false**.

Example

For an example, see **GraphicsPath.IsVisible Method (Int32, Int32, Graphics)**.

Requirements

Platforms: Windows 98, Windows NT 4.0, Windows Millennium Edition, Windows 2000, Windows XP Home Edition, Windows XP Professional, Windows Server 2003 family

GraphicsPath.IsVisible Method (Int32, Int32)

Indicates whether the specified point is contained within this **GraphicsPath** object.

[Visual Basic]
```
Overloads Public Function IsVisible( _
   ByVal x As Integer, _
   ByVal y As Integer _
) As Boolean
```
[C#]
```
public bool IsVisible(
   int x,
   int y
);
```
[C++]
```
public: bool IsVisible(
   int x,
   int y
);
```
[JScript]
```
public function IsVisible(
   x : int,
   y : int
) : Boolean;
```

Parameters

x

The x-coordinate of the point to test.

y

The y-coordinate of the point to test.

Return Value

This method returns **true** if the specified point is contained within this **GraphicsPath** object; otherwise, **false**.

Example

For an example, see **GraphicsPath.IsVisible Method (Int32, Int32, Graphics)**.

Requirements

Platforms: Windows 98, Windows NT 4.0, Windows Millennium Edition, Windows 2000, Windows XP Home Edition, Windows XP Professional, Windows Server 2003 family

GraphicsPath.IsVisible Method (Point, Graphics)

Indicates whether the specified point is contained within this **GraphicsPath** object.

```
[Visual Basic]
Overloads Public Function IsVisible( _
   ByVal pt As Point, _
   ByVal graphics As Graphics _
) As Boolean
[C#]
public bool IsVisible(
   Point pt,
   Graphics graphics
);
[C++]
public: bool IsVisible(
   Point pt,
   Graphics* graphics
);
[JScript]
public function IsVisible(
   pt : Point,
   graphics : Graphics
) : Boolean;
```

Parameters

pt
  A **Point** structure that represents the point to test.

graphics
  The **Graphics** object for which to test visibility.

Return Value

This method returns **true** if the specified point is contained within this **GraphicsPath** object; otherwise, **false**.

Remarks

The coordinates of the point to be tested are given in world coordinates. The transform matrix of the *graphics* parameter is temporarily applied before testing for visibility.

Example

For an example, see **GraphicsPath.IsVisible Method (Int32, Int32, Graphics)**.

Requirements

Platforms: Windows 98, Windows NT 4.0, Windows Millennium Edition, Windows 2000, Windows XP Home Edition, Windows XP Professional, Windows Server 2003 family

GraphicsPath.IsVisible Method (PointF, Graphics)

Indicates whether the specified point is contained within this **GraphicsPath** object.

```
[Visual Basic]
Overloads Public Function IsVisible( _
   ByVal pt As PointF, _
   ByVal graphics As Graphics _
) As Boolean
[C#]
public bool IsVisible(
   PointF pt,
   Graphics graphics
);
[C++]
public: bool IsVisible(
   PointF pt,
   Graphics* graphics
);
[JScript]
public function IsVisible(
   pt : PointF,
   graphics : Graphics
) : Boolean;
```

Parameters

pt
  A **PointF** structure that represents the point to test.

graphics
  The **Graphics** object for which to test visibility.

Return Value

This method returns **true** if the specified point is contained within this; otherwise, **false**.

Remarks

The coordinates of the point to be tested are given in world coordinates. The transform matrix of the *graphics* parameter is temporarily applied before testing for visibility.

Example

For an example, see **GraphicsPath.IsVisible Method (Int32, Int32, Graphics)**.

Requirements

Platforms: Windows 98, Windows NT 4.0, Windows Millennium Edition, Windows 2000, Windows XP Home Edition, Windows XP Professional, Windows Server 2003 family

GraphicsPath.IsVisible Method (Single, Single)

Indicates whether the specified point is contained within this **GraphicsPath** object.

```
[Visual Basic]
Overloads Public Function IsVisible( _
   ByVal x As Single, _
   ByVal y As Single _
) As Boolean
[C#]
public bool IsVisible(
   float x,
   float y
);
[C++]
public: bool IsVisible(
   float x,
   float y
);
[JScript]
public function IsVisible(
   x : float,
   y : float
) : Boolean;
```

Parameters

x
The x-coordinate of the point to test.

y
The y-coordinate of the point to test.

Return Value

This method returns **true** if the specified point is contained within this **GraphicsPath** object; otherwise, **false**.

Example

For an example, see **GraphicsPath.IsVisible Method (Int32, Int32, Graphics)**.

Requirements

Platforms: Windows 98, Windows NT 4.0, Windows Millennium Edition, Windows 2000, Windows XP Home Edition, Windows XP Professional, Windows Server 2003 family

GraphicsPath.IsVisible Method (Int32, Int32, Graphics)

Indicates whether the specified point is contained within this **GraphicsPath** object, using the specified **Graphics** object.

[Visual Basic]
```
Overloads Public Function IsVisible( _
   ByVal x As Integer, _
   ByVal y As Integer, _
   ByVal graphics As Graphics _
) As Boolean
```
[C#]
```
public bool IsVisible(
   int x,
   int y,
   Graphics graphics
);
```
[C++]
```
public: bool IsVisible(
   int x,
   int y,
   Graphics* graphics
);
```
[JScript]
```
public function IsVisible(
   x : int,
   y : int,
   graphics : Graphics
) : Boolean;
```

Parameters

x
The x-coordinate of the point to test.

y
The y-coordinate of the point to test.

graphics
The **Graphics** object for which to test visibility.

Return Value

This method returns **true** if the specified point is contained within this **GraphicsPath** object; otherwise, **false**.

Remarks

The coordinates of the point to be tested are given in world coordinates. The transform matrix of *graphics* is temporarily applied before testing for visibility.

Example

[Visual Basic, C#] The following example is designed for use with Windows Forms, and it requires **PaintEventArgs** *e*, an **OnPaint** event object. The code performs the following actions:

- Creates a path and adds an ellipse to the path.
- Tests whether the specified point is contained within the path.
- Displays the result in a dialog box.

[Visual Basic]
```
Public Sub IsVisibleExample(e As PaintEventArgs)
Dim myPath As New GraphicsPath()
myPath.AddEllipse(0, 0, 100, 100)
Dim visible As Boolean = myPath.IsVisible(50, 50, e.Graphics)
MessageBox.Show(visible.ToString())
End Sub
```

[C#]
```
private void IsVisibleExample(PaintEventArgs e)
{
// Create a path and add an ellipse.
GraphicsPath myPath = new GraphicsPath();
myPath.AddEllipse(0, 0, 100, 100);
// Test the visibility of point (50, 50).
bool visible = myPath.IsVisible(50, 50, e.Graphics);
// Show the result.
MessageBox.Show(visible.ToString());
}
```

Requirements

Platforms: Windows 98, Windows NT 4.0, Windows Millennium Edition, Windows 2000, Windows XP Home Edition, Windows XP Professional, Windows Server 2003 family

GraphicsPath.IsVisible Method (Single, Single, Graphics)

Indicates whether the specified point is contained within this **GraphicsPath** object in the visible clip region of the specified **Graphics** object.

[Visual Basic]
```
Overloads Public Function IsVisible( _
   ByVal x As Single, _
   ByVal y As Single, _
   ByVal graphics As Graphics _
) As Boolean
```
[C#]
```
public bool IsVisible(
   float x,
   float y,
   Graphics graphics
);
```
[C++]
```
public: bool IsVisible(
   float x,
   float y,
   Graphics* graphics
);
```
[JScript]
```
public function IsVisible(
   x : float,
   y : float,
   graphics : Graphics
) : Boolean;
```

Parameters

x
: The x-coordinate of the point to test.

y
: The y-coordinate of the point to test.

graphics
: The **Graphics** object for which to test visibility.

Return Value

This method returns **true** if the specified point is contained within this **GraphicsPath** object; otherwise, **false**.

Remarks

The coordinates of the point to be tested are given in world coordinates. The transform matrix of the *graphics* parameter is temporarily applied before testing for visibility.

Example

For an example, see **GraphicsPath.IsVisible Method (Int32, Int32, Graphics)**.

Requirements

Platforms: Windows 98, Windows NT 4.0, Windows Millennium Edition, Windows 2000, Windows XP Home Edition, Windows XP Professional, Windows Server 2003 family

GraphicsPath.Reset Method

Empties the **PathPoints** and **PathTypes** arrays and sets the **FillMode** to **Alternate**.

[Visual Basic]
```
Public Sub Reset()
```
[C#]
```
public void Reset();
```
[C++]
```
public: void Reset();
```
[JScript]
```
public function Reset();
```

Example

[Visual Basic, C#] The following example is designed for use with Windows Forms, and it requires **PaintEventArgs** *e*, an **OnPaint** event object. The code performs the following actions:

- Creates a path.
- Adds several primitives to it.
- Draws the path's points array to the screen.
- Resets the path to an empty state.
- Re-acquires the points array (if it exists).
- Draws the array to the screen.

[Visual Basic, C#] Notice that it finds no array following the reset call.

[Visual Basic]
```
Public Sub GraphicsPathResetExample(e As PaintEventArgs)
Dim myFont As New Font("Arial", 8)
' Create a path and add a line, an ellipse, and an arc.
Dim myPath As New GraphicsPath()
myPath.AddLine(New Point(0, 0), New Point(100, 100))
myPath.AddEllipse(100, 100, 200, 250)
myPath.AddArc(300, 250, 100, 100, 0, 90)
' Draw the pre-reset points array to the screen.
DrawPointsHelper(e, myPath.PathPoints, 20)
' Reset the path.
myPath.Reset()
' See if any points remain.
If myPath.PointCount > 0 Then
' Draw the post-reset points array to the screen.
DrawPointsHelper(e, myPath.PathPoints, 150)
' If there are no points, say so.
Else
e.Graphics.DrawString("No Points", myFont, Brushes.Black, _
150, 20)
End If
End Sub
' A helper function used by GraphicsPathResetExample to draw points.
Public Sub DrawPointsHelper(e As PaintEventArgs, _
pathPoints() As PointF, xOffset As Integer)
Dim y As Integer = 20
Dim myFont As New Font("Arial", 8)
Dim i As Integer
For i = 0 To pathPoints.Length - 1
e.Graphics.DrawString(pathPoints(i).X.ToString() + _
", " + pathPoints(i).Y.ToString(), myFont, Brushes.Black, _
xOffset, y)
y += 20
Next i
End Sub
```

[C#]
```
public void GraphicsPathResetExample(PaintEventArgs e)
{
Font myFont = new Font("Arial", 8);
// Create a path and add a line, an ellipse, and an arc.
GraphicsPath myPath = new GraphicsPath();
myPath.AddLine(new Point(0, 0), new Point(100, 100));
myPath.AddEllipse(100, 100, 200, 250);
myPath.AddArc(300, 250, 100, 100, 0, 90);
// Draw the pre-reset points array to the screen.
DrawPoints(e, myPath.PathPoints, 20);
// Reset the path.
myPath.Reset();
// See if any points remain.
if(myPath.PointCount > 0)
{
// Draw the post-reset points array to the screen.
DrawPoints(e, myPath.PathPoints, 150);
}
else
// If there are no points, say so.
e.Graphics.DrawString("No Points",
myFont,
Brushes.Black,
150,
20);
} //End GraphicsPathResetExample
// A helper function GraphicsPathResetExample uses to draw the points.
// to the screen.
public void DrawPoints(PaintEventArgs e, PointF[] pathPoints,
 int xOffset)
{
int y = 20;
Font myFont = new Font("Arial", 8);
for(int i=0;i < pathPoints.Length; i++)
{
e.Graphics.DrawString(pathPoints[i].X.ToString() + ", " +
pathPoints[i].Y.ToString(),
myFont,
Brushes.Black,
xOffset,
y);
y += 20;
}
} // End DrawPoints
```

Requirements

Platforms: Windows 98, Windows NT 4.0, Windows Millennium Edition, Windows 2000, Windows XP Home Edition, Windows XP Professional, Windows Server 2003 family

GraphicsPath.Reverse Method

Reverses the order of points in the **PathPoints** array of this **GraphicsPath** object.

[Visual Basic]
```
Public Sub Reverse()
```
[C#]
```
public void Reverse();
```
[C++]
```
public: void Reverse();
```
[JScript]
```
public function Reverse();
```

Example

[Visual Basic, C#] The following example is designed for use with Windows Forms, and it requires **PaintEventArgs** *e*, an **OnPaint** event object. The code performs the following actions:

- Creates a path and adds several primitives to the path.
- Draws the path's points array to the screen.
- Draws the reversed points array to the screen.

[Visual Basic, C#] Notice that the second listing of points is in reverse order from the first.

[Visual Basic]
```
Public Sub GraphicsPathReverseExample(e As PaintEventArgs)
' Create a path and add a line, ellipse, and arc.
Dim myPath As New GraphicsPath()
myPath.AddLine(New Point(0, 0), New Point(100, 100))
myPath.AddEllipse(100, 100, 200, 250)
myPath.AddArc(300, 250, 100, 100, 0, 90)
' Draw the first set of points to the screen.
DrawPointsHelper(e, myPath.PathPoints, 20)
' Call GraphicsPath.Reverse.
myPath.Reverse()
' Draw the reversed set of points to the screen.
DrawPointsHelper(e, myPath.PathPoints, 150)
End Sub
' A helper function used by GraphicsPathReverseExample to draw points.
Public Sub DrawPointsHelper(e As PaintEventArgs, _
pathPoints() As PointF, xOffset As Integer)
Dim y As Integer = 20
Dim myFont As New Font("Arial", 8)
Dim i As Integer
For i = 0 To pathPoints.Length - 1
e.Graphics.DrawString(pathPoints(i).X.ToString() + _
", " + pathPoints(i).Y.ToString(), myFont, Brushes.Black, _
xOffset, y)
y += 20
Next i
End Sub
```

[C#]
```
public void GraphicsPathReverseExample(PaintEventArgs e)
{
// Create a path and add a line, ellipse, and arc.
GraphicsPath myPath = new GraphicsPath();
myPath.AddLine(new Point(0, 0), new Point(100, 100));
myPath.AddEllipse(100, 100, 200, 250);
myPath.AddArc(300, 250, 100, 100, 0, 90);
// Draw the first set of points to the screen.
DrawPoints(e, myPath.PathPoints, 20);
// Call GraphicsPath.Reverse.
myPath.Reverse();
// Draw the reversed set of points to the screen.
DrawPoints(e, myPath.PathPoints, 150);
}//End GraphicsPathReverseExample.
// A helper function GraphicsPathReverseExample is used to draw the
// points to the screen.
public void DrawPoints(PaintEventArgs e, PointF[] pathPoints,
 int xOffset)
{
int y = 20;
Font myFont = new Font("Arial", 8);
for(int i=0;i < pathPoints.Length; i++)
{
e.Graphics.DrawString(pathPoints[i].X.ToString() + ", " +
pathPoints[i].Y.ToString(),
myFont,
Brushes.Black,
xOffset,
y);
y += 20;
}
} // End DrawPoints
```

Requirements

Platforms: Windows 98, Windows NT 4.0, Windows Millennium Edition, Windows 2000, Windows XP Home Edition, Windows XP Professional, Windows Server 2003 family

GraphicsPath.SetMarkers Method

Sets a marker on this **GraphicsPath** object.

[Visual Basic]
```
Public Sub SetMarkers()
```
[C#]
```
public void SetMarkers();
```
[C++]
```
public: void SetMarkers();
```
[JScript]
```
public function SetMarkers();
```

Remarks

This method creates a marker on the path that can be used to separate sections of the path. You can then use the **NextMarker** methods to iterate through the markers in the path.

Markers are used to separate groups of subpaths. One or more subpaths can be contained between two markers in the path.

Example

[Visual Basic, C#] The following example is designed for use with Windows Forms, and it requires **PaintEventArgs** *e*, an **OnPaint** event object. The code creates a path and adds several primitives to the path separated by markers, and draws the path to the screen.

[Visual Basic]
```
Public Sub SetMarkersExample(e As PaintEventArgs)
' Create a path and set two markers.
Dim myPath As New GraphicsPath()
myPath.AddLine(New Point(0, 0), New Point(50, 50))
myPath.SetMarkers()
Dim rect As New Rectangle(50, 50, 50, 50)
myPath.AddRectangle(rect)
myPath.SetMarkers()
myPath.AddEllipse(100, 100, 100, 50)
' Draw the path to screen.
e.Graphics.DrawPath(New Pen(Color.Black, 2), myPath)
End Sub
```

[C#]
```
private void SetMarkersExample(PaintEventArgs e)
{
// Create a path and set two markers.
GraphicsPath myPath = new GraphicsPath();
myPath.AddLine(new Point(0, 0), new Point(50, 50));
myPath.SetMarkers();
```

```
Rectangle rect = new Rectangle(50, 50, 50, 50);
myPath.AddRectangle(rect);
myPath.SetMarkers();
myPath.AddEllipse(100, 100, 100, 50);
// Draw the path to screen.
e.Graphics.DrawPath(new Pen(Color.Black, 2), myPath);
}
```

Requirements

Platforms: Windows 98, Windows NT 4.0, Windows Millennium Edition, Windows 2000, Windows XP Home Edition, Windows XP Professional, Windows Server 2003 family

GraphicsPath.StartFigure Method

Starts a new figure without closing the current figure. All subsequent points added to the path are added to this new figure.

[Visual Basic]
```
Public Sub StartFigure()
```
[C#]
```
public void StartFigure();
```
[C++]
```
public: void StartFigure();
```
[JScript]
```
public function StartFigure();
```

Remarks

The user must keep the original points if they are needed. The original points are converted to cubic Bézier control points internally, therefore there is no mechanism for returning the original points.

This method starts a new subpath in the path. Subpaths allow you to separate a path into sections and use the **GraphicsPathIterator** class to iterate through the subpaths.

Example

[Visual Basic, C#] The following example is designed for use with Windows Forms, and it requires **PaintEventArgs** *e*, an **OnPaint** event object. The code performs the following actions:

- Creates a path.
- Adds two sets of figures. The first set of figures combines four primitives into two figures. The second set of figures combines the same four primitives (except that they are offset in the y-axis) into three figures.
- Draws all the figures to the screen.

[Visual Basic, C#] Notice the difference in the appearance between the two sets of figures.

[Visual Basic]
```
Public Sub StartFigureExample(e As PaintEventArgs)
' Create a GraphicsPath object.
Dim myPath As New GraphicsPath()
' First set of figures.
myPath.StartFigure()
myPath.AddArc(10, 10, 50, 50, 0, 270)
myPath.AddLine(New Point(50, 0), New Point(100, 50))
myPath.AddArc(50, 100, 75, 75, 0, 270)
myPath.CloseFigure()
myPath.StartFigure()
myPath.AddArc(100, 10, 50, 50, 0, 270)
' Second set of figures.
myPath.StartFigure()
myPath.AddArc(10, 200, 50, 50, 0, 270)
myPath.CloseFigure()
myPath.StartFigure()
myPath.AddLine(New Point(60, 200), New Point(110, 250))
myPath.AddArc(50, 300, 75, 75, 0, 270)
myPath.CloseFigure()
myPath.StartFigure()
myPath.AddArc(100, 200, 50, 50, 0, 270)
' Draw the path to the screen.
e.Graphics.DrawPath(New Pen(Color.Black), myPath)
End Sub
```

[C#]
```
public void StartFigureExample(PaintEventArgs e)
{
// Create a GraphicsPath object.
GraphicsPath myPath = new GraphicsPath();
// First set of figures.
myPath.StartFigure();
myPath.AddArc(10, 10, 50, 50, 0, 270);
myPath.AddLine(new Point(50, 0), new Point(100, 50));
myPath.AddArc(50, 100, 75, 75, 0, 270);
myPath.CloseFigure();
myPath.StartFigure();
myPath.AddArc(100, 10, 50, 50, 0, 270);
// Second set of figures.
myPath.StartFigure();
myPath.AddArc(10, 200, 50, 50, 0, 270);
myPath.CloseFigure();
myPath.StartFigure();
myPath.AddLine(new Point(60, 200), new Point(110, 250));
myPath.AddArc(50, 300, 75, 75, 0, 270);
myPath.CloseFigure();
myPath.StartFigure();
myPath.AddArc(100, 200, 50, 50, 0, 270);
// Draw the path to the screen.
e.Graphics.DrawPath(new Pen(Color.Black), myPath);
} // End StartFigureExample
```

Requirements

Platforms: Windows 98, Windows NT 4.0, Windows Millennium Edition, Windows 2000, Windows XP Home Edition, Windows XP Professional, Windows Server 2003 family

GraphicsPath.Transform Method

Applies a transform matrix to this **GraphicsPath** object.

[Visual Basic]
```
Public Sub Transform( _
   ByVal matrix As Matrix _
)
```
[C#]
```
public void Transform(
   Matrix matrix
);
```
[C++]
```
public: void Transform(
   Matrix* matrix
);
```
[JScript]
```
public function Transform(
   matrix : Matrix
);
```

Parameters

matrix

A **Matrix** object that represents the transformation to apply.

Remarks

The transformation can scale, translate, rotate, or skew the **GraphicsPath** object.

Example

[Visual Basic, C#] The following example is designed for use with Windows Forms, and it requires **PaintEventArgs** *e*, an **OnPaint** event object. The code performs the following actions:

- Creates a path and adds an ellipse to the path.
- Draws path to the screen.
- Creates a transform matrix to translate the path 100 units in the x-axis direction.
- Draws the transformed path to the screen.

[Visual Basic, C#] Notice that the original ellipse is drawn in black and the transformed ellipse is drawn in red.

[Visual Basic]
```
Public Sub TransformExample(e As PaintEventArgs)
' Create a path and add and ellipse.
Dim myPath As New GraphicsPath()
myPath.AddEllipse(0, 0, 100, 200)
' Draw the starting position to screen.
e.Graphics.DrawPath(Pens.Black, myPath)
' Move the ellipse 100 points to the right.
Dim translateMatrix As New Matrix()
translateMatrix.Translate(100, 0)
myPath.Transform(translateMatrix)
' Draw the transformed ellipse to the screen.
e.Graphics.DrawPath(New Pen(Color.Red, 2), myPath)
End Sub
```

[C#]
```
private void TransformExample(PaintEventArgs e)
{
// Create a path and add and ellipse.
GraphicsPath myPath = new GraphicsPath();
myPath.AddEllipse(0, 0, 100, 200);
// Draw the starting position to screen.
e.Graphics.DrawPath(Pens.Black, myPath);
// Move the ellipse 100 points to the right.
Matrix translateMatrix = new Matrix();
translateMatrix.Translate(100, 0);
myPath.Transform(translateMatrix);
// Draw the transformed ellipse to the screen.
e.Graphics.DrawPath(new Pen(Color.Red, 2), myPath);
}
```

Requirements

Platforms: Windows 98, Windows NT 4.0, Windows Millennium Edition, Windows 2000, Windows XP Home Edition, Windows XP Professional, Windows Server 2003 family

GraphicsPath.Warp Method

Applies a warp transform, defined by a rectangle and a parallelogram, to this **GraphicsPath** object.

Overload List

Applies a warp transform, defined by a rectangle and a parallelogram, to this **GraphicsPath** object.

[Visual Basic] **Overloads Public Sub Warp(PointF(), RectangleF)**

[C#] **public void Warp(PointF[], RectangleF);**

[C++] **public: void Warp(PointF[], RectangleF);**

[JScript] **public function Warp(PointF[], RectangleF);**

Applies a warp transform, defined by a rectangle and a parallelogram, to this **GraphicsPath** object.

[Visual Basic] **Overloads Public Sub Warp(PointF(), RectangleF, Matrix)**

[C#] **public void Warp(PointF[], RectangleF, Matrix);**

[C++] **public: void Warp(PointF[], RectangleF, Matrix*);**

[JScript] **public function Warp(PointF[], RectangleF, Matrix);**

Applies a warp transform, defined by a rectangle and a parallelogram, to this **GraphicsPath** object.

[Visual Basic] **Overloads Public Sub Warp(PointF(), RectangleF, Matrix, WarpMode)**

[C#] **public void Warp(PointF[], RectangleF, Matrix, WarpMode);**

[C++] **public: void Warp(PointF[], RectangleF, Matrix*, WarpMode);**

[JScript] **public function Warp(PointF[], RectangleF, Matrix, WarpMode);**

Applies a warp transform, defined by a rectangle and a parallelogram, to this **GraphicsPath** object.

[Visual Basic] **Overloads Public Sub Warp(PointF(), RectangleF, Matrix, WarpMode, Single)**

[C#] **public void Warp(PointF[], RectangleF, Matrix, WarpMode, float);**

[C++] **public: void Warp(PointF[], RectangleF, Matrix*, WarpMode, float);**

[JScript] **public function Warp(PointF[], RectangleF, Matrix, WarpMode, float);**

Example

[Visual Basic, C#] The following example is designed for use with Windows Forms, and it requires **PaintEventArgs** *e*, an **OnPaint** event object. The code performs the following actions:

- Creates a path and adds a rectangle to the path.
- Draws that rectangle to the screen in black.
- Warps the path with a perspective warp.
- Draws the warped rectangle (path) to the screen in red.

> [Visual Basic, C#] **Note** This example shows how to use one of the overloaded versions of **Warp**. For other examples that might be available, see the individual overload topics.

[Visual Basic]
```
Public Sub WarpExample(e As PaintEventArgs)
' Create a path and add a rectangle.
Dim myPath As New GraphicsPath()
Dim srcRect As New RectangleF(0, 0, 100, 200)
myPath.AddRectangle(srcRect)
' Draw the source path (rectangle)to the screen.
e.Graphics.DrawPath(Pens.Black, myPath)
' Create a destination for the warped rectangle.
Dim point1 As New PointF(200, 200)
Dim point2 As New PointF(400, 250)
Dim point3 As New PointF(220, 400)
Dim destPoints As PointF() =  {point1, point2, point3}
' Create a translation matrix.
Dim translateMatrix As New Matrix()
translateMatrix.Translate(100, 0)
' Warp the source path (rectangle).
myPath.Warp(destPoints, srcRect, translateMatrix, _
WarpMode.Perspective, 0.5F)
' Draw the warped path (rectangle) to the screen.
e.Graphics.DrawPath(New Pen(Color.Red), myPath)
End Sub
```

[C#]
```
private void WarpExample(PaintEventArgs e)
{
// Create a path and add a rectangle.
GraphicsPath myPath = new GraphicsPath();
RectangleF srcRect = new RectangleF(0, 0, 100, 200);
myPath.AddRectangle(srcRect);
// Draw the source path (rectangle)to the screen.
e.Graphics.DrawPath(Pens.Black, myPath);
// Create a destination for the warped rectangle.
PointF point1 = new PointF(200, 200);
PointF point2 = new PointF(400, 250);
PointF point3 = new PointF(220, 400);
PointF[] destPoints = {point1, point2, point3};
// Create a translation matrix.
Matrix translateMatrix = new Matrix();
translateMatrix.Translate(100, 0);
// Warp the source path (rectangle).
myPath.Warp(destPoints, srcRect, translateMatrix,
WarpMode.Perspective, 0.5f);
// Draw the warped path (rectangle) to the screen.
e.Graphics.DrawPath(new Pen(Color.Red), myPath);
}
```

GraphicsPath.Warp Method (PointF[], RectangleF)

Applies a warp transform, defined by a rectangle and a parallelogram, to this **GraphicsPath** object.

[Visual Basic]
```
Overloads Public Sub Warp( _
   ByVal destPoints() As PointF, _
   ByVal srcRect As RectangleF _
)
```
[C#]
```
public void Warp(
   PointF[] destPoints,
   RectangleF srcRect
);
```
[C++]
```
public: void Warp(
   PointF destPoints[],
   RectangleF srcRect
);
```
[JScript]
```
public function Warp(
   destPoints : PointF[],
   srcRect : RectangleF
);
```

Parameters

destPoints

An array of **PointF** structures that define a parallelogram to which the rectangle defined by *srcRect* is transformed. The array can contain either three or four elements. If the array contains three elements, the lower-right corner of the parallelogram is implied by the first three points.

srcRect

A **RectangleF** structure that represents the rectangle that is transformed to the parallelogram defined by *destPoints*.

Example

For an example, see **GraphicsPath.Warp Method (PointF[], RectangleF, Matrix, WarpMode, Single)**.

Requirements

Platforms: Windows 98, Windows NT 4.0, Windows Millennium Edition, Windows 2000, Windows XP Home Edition, Windows XP Professional, Windows Server 2003 family

GraphicsPath.Warp Method (PointF[], RectangleF, Matrix)

Applies a warp transform, defined by a rectangle and a parallelogram, to this **GraphicsPath** object.

[Visual Basic]
```
Overloads Public Sub Warp( _
   ByVal destPoints() As PointF, _
   ByVal srcRect As RectangleF, _
   ByVal matrix As Matrix _
)
```
[C#]
```
public void Warp(
   PointF[] destPoints,
   RectangleF srcRect,
   Matrix matrix
);
```
[C++]
```
public: void Warp(
   PointF destPoints[],
   RectangleF srcRect,
   Matrix* matrix
);
```
[JScript]
```
public function Warp(
   destPoints : PointF[],
   srcRect : RectangleF,
   matrix : Matrix
);
```

Parameters

destPoints

An array of **PointF** structures that define a parallelogram to which the rectangle defined by *srcRect* is transformed. The array can contain either three or four elements. If the array contains three elements, the lower-right corner of the parallelogram is implied by the first three points.

srcRect

A **RectangleF** structure that represents the rectangle that is transformed to the parallelogram defined by *destPoints*.

matrix

A **Matrix** object that specifies a geometric transform to apply to the path.

Example

For an example, see **GraphicsPath.Warp Method (PointF[], RectangleF, Matrix, WarpMode, Single)**.

Requirements

Platforms: Windows 98, Windows NT 4.0, Windows Millennium Edition, Windows 2000, Windows XP Home Edition, Windows XP Professional, Windows Server 2003 family

GraphicsPath.Warp Method (PointF[], RectangleF, Matrix, WarpMode)

Applies a warp transform, defined by a rectangle and a parallelogram, to this **GraphicsPath** object.

[Visual Basic]
```
Overloads Public Sub Warp( _
   ByVal destPoints() As PointF, _
   ByVal srcRect As RectangleF, _
   ByVal matrix As Matrix, _
   ByVal warpMode As WarpMode _
)
```
[C#]
```
public void Warp(
   PointF[] destPoints,
   RectangleF srcRect,
   Matrix matrix,
   WarpMode warpMode
);
```
[C++]
```
public: void Warp(
   PointF destPoints[],
   RectangleF srcRect,
   Matrix* matrix,
   WarpMode warpMode
);
```
[JScript]
```
public function Warp(
   destPoints : PointF[],
   srcRect : RectangleF,
   matrix : Matrix,
   warpMode : WarpMode
);
```

Parameters

destPoints
: An array of **PointF** structures that defines a parallelogram to which the rectangle defined by *srcRect* is transformed. The array can contain either three or four elements. If the array contains three elements, the lower-right corner of the parallelogram is implied by the first three points.

srcRect
: A **RectangleF** structure that represents the rectangle that is transformed to the parallelogram defined by *destPoints*.

matrix
: A **Matrix** object that specifies a geometric transform to apply to the path.

warpMode
: A **WarpMode** enumeration that specifies whether this warp operation uses perspective or bilinear mode.

Example

For an example, see **GraphicsPath.Warp Method (PointF[], RectangleF, Matrix, WarpMode, Single)**.

Requirements

Platforms: Windows 98, Windows NT 4.0, Windows Millennium Edition, Windows 2000, Windows XP Home Edition, Windows XP Professional, Windows Server 2003 family

GraphicsPath.Warp Method (PointF[], RectangleF, Matrix, WarpMode, Single)

Applies a warp transform, defined by a rectangle and a parallelogram, to this **GraphicsPath** object.

[Visual Basic]
```
Overloads Public Sub Warp( _
   ByVal destPoints() As PointF, _
   ByVal srcRect As RectangleF, _
   ByVal matrix As Matrix, _
   ByVal warpMode As WarpMode, _
   ByVal flatness As Single _
)
```
[C#]
```
public void Warp(
   PointF[] destPoints,
   RectangleF srcRect,
   Matrix matrix,
   WarpMode warpMode,
   float flatness
);
```
[C++]
```
public: void Warp(
   PointF destPoints[],
   RectangleF srcRect,
   Matrix* matrix,
   WarpMode warpMode,
   float flatness
);
```
[JScript]
```
public function Warp(
   destPoints : PointF[],
   srcRect : RectangleF,
   matrix : Matrix,
   warpMode : WarpMode,
   flatness : float
);
```

Parameters

destPoints
: An array of **PointF** structures that define a parallelogram to which the rectangle defined by *srcRect* is transformed. The array can contain either three or four elements. If the array contains three elements, the lower-right corner of the parallelogram is implied by the first three points.

srcRect
: A **RectangleF** structure that represents the rectangle that is transformed to the parallelogram defined by *destPoints*.

matrix
: A **Matrix** object that specifies a geometric transform to apply to the path.

warpMode
: A **WarpMode** enumeration that specifies whether this warp operation uses perspective or bilinear mode.

flatness
: A value from 0 through 1 that specifies how flat the resulting path is. For more information, see the **Flatten** methods.

Example

[Visual Basic, C#] The following example is designed for use with Windows Forms, and it requires **PaintEventArgs** *e*, an **OnPaint** event object. The code performs the following actions:

- Creates a path and adds a rectangle to the path.
- Draws that rectangle to the screen in black.
- Warps the path with a perspective warp.
- Draws the warped rectangle (path) to the screen in red.

[Visual Basic]
```
Public Sub WarpExample(e As PaintEventArgs)
' Create a path and add a rectangle.
Dim myPath As New GraphicsPath()
Dim srcRect As New RectangleF(0, 0, 100, 200)
myPath.AddRectangle(srcRect)
' Draw the source path (rectangle)to the screen.
e.Graphics.DrawPath(Pens.Black, myPath)
' Create a destination for the warped rectangle.
Dim point1 As New PointF(200, 200)
Dim point2 As New PointF(400, 250)
Dim point3 As New PointF(220, 400)
Dim destPoints As PointF() =  {point1, point2, point3}
' Create a translation matrix.
Dim translateMatrix As New Matrix()
translateMatrix.Translate(100, 0)
' Warp the source path (rectangle).
myPath.Warp(destPoints, srcRect, translateMatrix, _
WarpMode.Perspective, 0.5F)
' Draw the warped path (rectangle) to the screen.
e.Graphics.DrawPath(New Pen(Color.Red), myPath)
End Sub
```

[C#]
```
private void WarpExample(PaintEventArgs e)
{
// Create a path and add a rectangle.
GraphicsPath myPath = new GraphicsPath();
RectangleF srcRect = new RectangleF(0, 0, 100, 200);
myPath.AddRectangle(srcRect);
// Draw the source path (rectangle)to the screen.
e.Graphics.DrawPath(Pens.Black, myPath);
// Create a destination for the warped rectangle.
PointF point1 = new PointF(200, 200);
PointF point2 = new PointF(400, 250);
PointF point3 = new PointF(220, 400);
PointF[] destPoints = {point1, point2, point3};
// Create a translation matrix.
Matrix translateMatrix = new Matrix();
translateMatrix.Translate(100, 0);
// Warp the source path (rectangle).
myPath.Warp(destPoints, srcRect, translateMatrix,
WarpMode.Perspective, 0.5f);
// Draw the warped path (rectangle) to the screen.
e.Graphics.DrawPath(new Pen(Color.Red), myPath);
}
```

Requirements

Platforms: Windows 98, Windows NT 4.0, Windows Millennium Edition, Windows 2000, Windows XP Home Edition, Windows XP Professional, Windows Server 2003 family

GraphicsPath.Widen Method

Replaces this path with curves that enclose the area that is filled when this path is drawn by the specified pen.

Overload List

Adds an additional outline to the path.

[Visual Basic] **Overloads Public Sub Widen(Pen)**

[C#] **public void Widen(Pen);**

[C++] **public: void Widen(Pen*);**

[JScript] **public function Widen(Pen);**

Adds an additional outline to the **GraphicsPath** object.

[Visual Basic] **Overloads Public Sub Widen(Pen, Matrix)**

[C#] **public void Widen(Pen, Matrix);**

[C++] **public: void Widen(Pen*, Matrix*);**

[JScript] **public function Widen(Pen, Matrix);**

Replaces this **GraphicsPath** object with curves that enclose the area that is filled when this path is drawn by the specified pen.

[Visual Basic] **Overloads Public Sub Widen(Pen, Matrix, Single)**

[C#] **public void Widen(Pen, Matrix, float);**

[C++] **public: void Widen(Pen*, Matrix*, float);**

[JScript] **public function Widen(Pen, Matrix, float);**

Example

[Visual Basic, C#] The following example is designed for use with Windows Forms, and it requires **PaintEventArgs** *e*, an **OnPaint** event object. The code performs the following actions:

- Creates a path and adds two ellipses to the path.
- Draws the path in black.
- Widens the path.
- Draws the path in red.

[Visual Basic, C#] Notice that the second rendering uses **FillPath** instead of **DrawPath**, and hence the rendered figure has the outline filled..

> [Visual Basic, C#] **Note** This example shows how to use one of the overloaded versions of **Widen**. For other examples that might be available, see the individual overload topics.

[Visual Basic]
```
Public Sub WidenExample(e As PaintEventArgs)
Dim myPath As New GraphicsPath()
myPath.AddEllipse(0, 0, 100, 100)
myPath.AddEllipse(100, 0, 100, 100)
e.Graphics.DrawPath(Pens.Black, myPath)
Dim widenPen As New Pen(Color.Black, 10)
Dim widenMatrix As New Matrix()
widenMatrix.Translate(50, 50)
myPath.Widen(widenPen, widenMatrix, 1F) ' Sets tension for curves.
e.Graphics.FillPath(New SolidBrush(Color.Red), myPath)
End Sub
```

[C#]
```
private void WidenExample(PaintEventArgs e)
{
// Create a path and add two ellipses.
GraphicsPath myPath = new GraphicsPath();
myPath.AddEllipse(0, 0, 100, 100);
myPath.AddEllipse(100, 0, 100, 100);
// Draw the original ellipses to the screen in black.
e.Graphics.DrawPath(Pens.Black, myPath);
// Widen the path.
Pen widenPen = new Pen(Color.Black, 10);
Matrix widenMatrix = new Matrix();
widenMatrix.Translate(50, 50);
```

```
myPath.Widen(widenPen, widenMatrix, 1.0f);
// Draw the widened path to the screen in red.
e.Graphics.FillPath(new SolidBrush(Color.Red), myPath);
}
```

GraphicsPath.Widen Method (Pen)

Adds an additional outline to the path.

```
[Visual Basic]
Overloads Public Sub Widen( _
   ByVal pen As Pen _
)
[C#]
public void Widen(
   Pen pen
);
[C++]
public: void Widen(
   Pen* pen
);
[JScript]
public function Widen(
   pen : Pen
);
```

Parameters

pen

A **Pen** object that specifies the width between the original outline of the path and the new outline this method creates.

Remarks

This method creates an outline around the original lines in this **GraphicsPath** object, with a distance between the existing lines and the new outline equal to that of the width of the **Pen** object used in the call to **Widen**. If you want to fill the space between the lines you must use the **FillPath** object rather then the **DrawPath** object.

Example

For an example, see **GraphicsPath.Widen Method (Pen, Matrix, Single)**.

Requirements

Platforms: Windows 98, Windows NT 4.0, Windows Millennium Edition, Windows 2000, Windows XP Home Edition, Windows XP Professional, Windows Server 2003 family

GraphicsPath.Widen Method (Pen, Matrix)

Adds an additional outline to the **GraphicsPath** object.

```
[Visual Basic]
Overloads Public Sub Widen( _
   ByVal pen As Pen, _
   ByVal matrix As Matrix _
)
[C#]
public void Widen(
   Pen pen,
   Matrix matrix
);
[C++]
public: void Widen(
   Pen* pen,
   Matrix* matrix
);
[JScript]
public function Widen(
   pen : Pen,
   matrix : Matrix
);
```

Parameters

pen

A **Pen** object that specifies the width between the original outline of the path and the new outline this method creates.

matrix

A **Matrix** object that specifies a transform to apply to the path before widening.

Remarks

This method creates an outline around the original lines in this **GraphicsPath** object, with a distance between the existing lines and the new outline equal to that of the width of the **Pen** object used in the call to **Widen**. If you want to fill the space between the lines you must use the **FillPath** object rather then the **DrawPath** object.

Example

For an example, see **GraphicsPath.Widen Method (Pen, Matrix, Single)**.

Requirements

Platforms: Windows 98, Windows NT 4.0, Windows Millennium Edition, Windows 2000, Windows XP Home Edition, Windows XP Professional, Windows Server 2003 family

GraphicsPath.Widen Method (Pen, Matrix, Single)

Replaces this **GraphicsPath** object with curves that enclose the area that is filled when this path is drawn by the specified pen.

```
[Visual Basic]
Overloads Public Sub Widen( _
   ByVal pen As Pen, _
   ByVal matrix As Matrix, _
   ByVal flatness As Single _
)
[C#]
public void Widen(
   Pen pen,
   Matrix matrix,
   float flatness
);
[C++]
public: void Widen(
   Pen* pen,
   Matrix* matrix,
   float flatness
);
[JScript]
public function Widen(
   pen : Pen,
   matrix : Matrix,
   flatness : float
);
```

Parameters

pen
: A **Pen** object that specifies the width between the original outline of the path and the new outline this method creates.

matrix
: A **Matrix** object that specifies a transform to apply to the path before widening.

flatness
: A value that specifies the flatness for curves.

Remarks

This method creates an outline around the original lines in this **GraphicsPath** object, with a distance between the existing lines and the new outline equal to that of the width of the **Pen** object used in the call to **Widen**. If you want to fill the space between the lines you must use the **FillPath** object rather then the **DrawPath** object.

Example

[Visual Basic, C#] The following example is designed for use with Windows Forms, and it requires **PaintEventArgs** *e*, an **OnPaint** event object. The code performs the following actions:

- Creates a path and adds two ellipses to the path.
- Draws the path in black.
- Widens the path.
- Draws the path in red.

[Visual Basic, C#] Notice that the second rendering uses **FillPath** instead of **DrawPath**, and hence the rendered figure has the outline filled..

[Visual Basic]

```
Public Sub WidenExample(e As PaintEventArgs)
Dim myPath As New GraphicsPath()
myPath.AddEllipse(0, 0, 100, 100)
myPath.AddEllipse(100, 0, 100, 100)
e.Graphics.DrawPath(Pens.Black, myPath)
Dim widenPen As New Pen(Color.Black, 10)
Dim widenMatrix As New Matrix()
widenMatrix.Translate(50, 50)
myPath.Widen(widenPen, widenMatrix, 1F) ' Sets tension for curves.
e.Graphics.FillPath(New SolidBrush(Color.Red), myPath)
End Sub
```

[C#]

```
private void WidenExample(PaintEventArgs e)
{
// Create a path and add two ellipses.
GraphicsPath myPath = new GraphicsPath();
myPath.AddEllipse(0, 0, 100, 100);
myPath.AddEllipse(100, 0, 100, 100);
// Draw the original ellipses to the screen in black.
e.Graphics.DrawPath(Pens.Black, myPath);
// Widen the path.
Pen widenPen = new Pen(Color.Black, 10);
Matrix widenMatrix = new Matrix();
widenMatrix.Translate(50, 50);
myPath.Widen(widenPen, widenMatrix, 1.0f);
// Draw the widened path to the screen in red.
e.Graphics.FillPath(new SolidBrush(Color.Red), myPath);
}
```

Requirements

Platforms: Windows 98, Windows NT 4.0, Windows Millennium Edition, Windows 2000, Windows XP Home Edition, Windows XP Professional, Windows Server 2003 family

GraphicsPathIterator Class

Provides the ability to iterate through subpaths in a **GraphicsPath** object and test the types of shapes contained in each subpath. This class cannot be inherited.

System.Object
  System.MarshalByRefObject
    System.Drawing.Drawing2D.GraphicsPathIterator

[Visual Basic]
```
NotInheritable Public Class GraphicsPathIterator
   Inherits MarshalByRefObject
   Implements IDisposable
```
[C#]
```
public sealed class GraphicsPathIterator : MarshalByRefObject,
   IDisposable
```
[C++]
```
public __gc __sealed class GraphicsPathIterator : public
   MarshalByRefObject, IDisposable
```
[JScript]
```
public class GraphicsPathIterator extends MarshalByRefObject
   implements IDisposable
```

Thread Safety

Any public static (**Shared** in Visual Basic) members of this type are safe for multithreaded operations. Any instance members are not guaranteed to be thread safe.

Requirements

Namespace: System.Drawing.Drawing2D

Platforms: Windows 98, Windows NT 4.0, Windows Millennium Edition, Windows 2000, Windows XP Home Edition, Windows XP Professional, Windows Server 2003 family

Assembly: System.Drawing (in System.Drawing.dll)

GraphicsPathIterator Constructor

Initializes a new instance of the **GraphicsPathIterator** class with the specified **GraphicsPath** object.

[Visual Basic]
```
Public Sub New( _
   ByVal path As GraphicsPath _
)
```
[C#]
```
public GraphicsPathIterator(
   GraphicsPath path
);
```
[C++]
```
public: GraphicsPathIterator(
   GraphicsPath* path
);
```
[JScript]
```
public function GraphicsPathIterator(
   path : GraphicsPath
);
```

Parameters

path

The **GraphicsPath** object for which this helper class is to be initialized.

Requirements

Platforms: Windows 98, Windows NT 4.0, Windows Millennium Edition, Windows 2000, Windows XP Home Edition, Windows XP Professional, Windows Server 2003 family

GraphicsPathIterator.Count Property

Gets the number of points in the path.

[Visual Basic]
```
Public ReadOnly Property Count As Integer
```
[C#]
```
public int Count {get;}
```
[C++]
```
public: __property int get_Count();
```
[JScript]
```
public function get Count() : int;
```

Property Value

The number of points in the path.

Requirements

Platforms: Windows 98, Windows NT 4.0, Windows Millennium Edition, Windows 2000, Windows XP Home Edition, Windows XP Professional, Windows Server 2003 family

GraphicsPathIterator.SubpathCount Property

Gets the number of subpaths in the path.

[Visual Basic]
```
Public ReadOnly Property SubpathCount As Integer
```
[C#]
```
public int SubpathCount {get;}
```
[C++]
```
public: __property int get_SubpathCount();
```
[JScript]
```
public function get SubpathCount() : int;
```

Property Value

The number of subpaths in the path.

Requirements

Platforms: Windows 98, Windows NT 4.0, Windows Millennium Edition, Windows 2000, Windows XP Home Edition, Windows XP Professional, Windows Server 2003 family

GraphicsPathIterator.CopyData Method

Copies the **PathPoints** property and **System.Drawing.Drawing2D.GraphicsPath.PathTypes** property arrays of the associated **GraphicsPath** object into the two specified arrays.

[Visual Basic]
```
Public Function CopyData( _
   ByRef points() As PointF, _
   ByRef types() As Byte, _
   ByVal startIndex As Integer, _
   ByVal endIndex As Integer _
) As Integer
```

[C#]
```
public int CopyData(
   ref PointF[] points,
   ref byte[] types,
   int startIndex,
   int endIndex
);
```
[C++]
```
public: int CopyData(
   PointF** points[],
   unsigned char* types __gc[],
   int startIndex,
   int endIndex
);
```
[JScript]
```
public function CopyData(
   points : PointF[],
   types : Byte[],
   startIndex : int,
   endIndex : int
) : int;
```

Parameters

points
: Upon return, contains an array of **PointF** structures that represents the points in the path.

types
: Upon return, contains an array of bytes that represents the types of points in the path.

startIndex
: Specifies the starting index of the arrays.

endIndex
: Specifies the ending index of the arrays.

Return Value

The number of points copied.

Remarks

Use the *startIndex* and *endIndex* parameters to copy a specified range of the path data.

Example

[Visual Basic, C#] The following example is designed for use with Windows Forms, and it requires **PaintEventArgs** *e*, an **OnPaint** event object. The code performs the following actions:

- Creates a graphics path.
- Populates it with several primitives and some markers.
- Lists the path data on the left side of the screen.
- Creates a **GraphicsPathIterator** object and rewinds it.
- Increments the path data index to the second marker.
- Calls the **CopyData** method to copy the path data contained between the start and end indexes to the points and types arrays.
- Lists this copied data on the right side of the screen.

[Visual Basic]
```
Public Sub CopyDataExample(e As PaintEventArgs)
' Create a graphics path.
Dim myPath As New GraphicsPath()
' Set up a points array.
Dim myPoints As Point() = {New Point(20, 20), _
New Point(120, 120), New Point(20, 120), New Point(20, 20)}
' Create a rectangle.
Dim myRect As New Rectangle(120, 120, 100, 100)
' Add the points, rectangle, and an ellipse to the path.
myPath.AddLines(myPoints)
myPath.SetMarkers()
myPath.AddRectangle(myRect)
myPath.SetMarkers()
myPath.AddEllipse(220, 220, 100, 100)
' Get the total number of points for the path, and arrays of the
' points and types.
Dim myPathPointCount As Integer = myPath.PointCount
Dim myPathPoints As PointF() = myPath.PathPoints
Dim myPathTypes As Byte() = myPath.PathTypes
' Set up variables for listing the array of points on the left side
' of the screen.
Dim i As Integer
Dim j As Single = 20
Dim myFont As New Font("Arial", 8)
Dim myBrush As New SolidBrush(Color.Black)
' List the set of points and types and types to the left side of
' the screen.
For i = 0 To myPathPointCount - 1
e.Graphics.DrawString(myPathPoints(i).X.ToString() + ", " + _
myPathPoints(i).Y.ToString() + ", " + _
myPathTypes(i).ToString(), myFont, myBrush, 20, j)
j += 20
Next i
' Create a GraphicsPathIterator for myPath and rewind it.
Dim myPathIterator As New GraphicsPathIterator(myPath)
myPathIterator.Rewind()
' Set up the arrays to receive the copied data.
Dim points(myPathIterator.Count) As PointF
Dim types(myPathIterator.Count) As Byte
Dim myStartIndex As Integer
Dim myEndIndex As Integer
' Increment the starting index to the second marker in the path.
myPathIterator.NextMarker(myStartIndex, myEndIndex)
myPathIterator.NextMarker(myStartIndex, myEndIndex)
' Copy all the points and types from the starting index to the
' ending index to the  points array and the types array
' respectively.
Dim numPointsCopied As Integer = myPathIterator.CopyData(points, _
types, myStartIndex, myEndIndex)
' List the copied points to the right side of the screen.
j = 20
Dim copiedStartIndex As Integer = 0
For i = 0 To numPointsCopied - 1
copiedStartIndex = myStartIndex + i
e.Graphics.DrawString("Point: " + _
copiedStartIndex.ToString() + ", Value: " + _
points(i).ToString() + ", Type: " + types(i).ToString(), _
myFont, myBrush, 200, j)
j += 20
Next i
End Sub
```

[C#]
```
public void CopyDataExample(PaintEventArgs e)
{
// Create a graphics path.
GraphicsPath myPath = new GraphicsPath();
// Set up a points array.
Point[] myPoints =
{
new Point(20, 20),
new Point(120, 120),
new Point(20, 120),
new Point(20, 20)
};
// Create a rectangle.
Rectangle myRect = new Rectangle(120, 120, 100, 100);
// Add the points, rectangle, and an ellipse to the path.
myPath.AddLines(myPoints);
myPath.SetMarkers();
myPath.AddRectangle(myRect);
myPath.SetMarkers();
myPath.AddEllipse(220, 220, 100, 100);
```

```
// Get the total number of points for the path, and arrays of
// the  points and types.
int myPathPointCount = myPath.PointCount;
PointF[] myPathPoints = myPath.PathPoints;
byte[] myPathTypes = myPath.PathTypes;
// Set up variables for listing the array of points on the left
// side of the screen.
int i;
float j = 20;
Font myFont = new Font("Arial", 8);
SolidBrush myBrush = new SolidBrush(Color.Black);
// List the set of points and types and types to the left side
// of the screen.
for(i=0; i<myPathPointCount; i++)
{
e.Graphics.DrawString(myPathPoints[i].X.ToString()+
", " + myPathPoints[i].Y.ToString() + ", " +
myPathTypes[i].ToString(),
myFont,
myBrush,
20,
j);
j+=20;
}
// Create a GraphicsPathIterator for myPath and rewind it.
GraphicsPathIterator myPathIterator =
new GraphicsPathIterator(myPath);
myPathIterator.Rewind();
// Set up the arrays to receive the copied data.
PointF[] points = new PointF[myPathIterator.Count];
byte[] types = new byte[myPathIterator.Count];
int myStartIndex;
int myEndIndex;
// Increment the starting index to the second marker in the
// path.
myPathIterator.NextMarker(out myStartIndex, out myEndIndex);
myPathIterator.NextMarker(out myStartIndex, out myEndIndex);
// copy all the points and types from the starting index to the
// ending index to the points array and the types array
//respectively.
int numPointsCopied = myPathIterator.CopyData(
ref points,
ref types,
myStartIndex,
myEndIndex);
// List the copied points to the right side of the screen.
j = 20;
int copiedStartIndex = 0;
for(i=0; i<numPointsCopied; i++)
{
copiedStartIndex = myStartIndex + i;
e.Graphics.DrawString(
"Point: " + copiedStartIndex.ToString() +
", Value: " + points[i].ToString() +
", Type: " + types[i].ToString(),
myFont,
myBrush,
200,
j);
j+=20;
}
}
```

Requirements

Platforms: Windows 98, Windows NT 4.0,
Windows Millennium Edition, Windows 2000,
Windows XP Home Edition, Windows XP Professional,
Windows Server 2003 family

GraphicsPathIterator.Dispose Method

Releases all resources used by this **GraphicsPathIterator** object.

[Visual Basic]
```
Public Overridable Sub Dispose() Implements IDisposable.Dispose
```
[C#]
```
public virtual void Dispose();
```
[C++]
```
public: virtual void Dispose();
```
[JScript]
```
public function Dispose();
```

Return Value

This method does not return a value.

Implements

IDisposable.Dispose

Remarks

Calling **Dispose** allows the resources used by this **GraphicsPathIterator** object to be reallocated for other purposes.

Requirements

Platforms: Windows 98, Windows NT 4.0,
Windows Millennium Edition, Windows 2000,
Windows XP Home Edition, Windows XP Professional,
Windows Server 2003 family

GraphicsPathIterator.Enumerate Method

Copies the **PathPoints** property and **PathTypes** property arrays of the associated **GraphicsPath** object into the two specified arrays.

[Visual Basic]
```
Public Function Enumerate( _
   ByRef points() As PointF, _
   ByRef types() As Byte _
) As Integer
```
[C#]
```
public int Enumerate(
   ref PointF[] points,
   ref byte[] types
);
```
[C++]
```
public: int Enumerate(
   PointF** points[],
   unsigned char* types __gc[]
);
```
[JScript]
```
public function Enumerate(
   points : PointF[],
   types : Byte[]
) : int;
```

Parameters

points

Upon return, contains an array of **PointF** structures that represents the points in the path.

types

Upon return, contains an array of bytes that represents the types of points in the path.

Return Value

The number of points copied.

Example

[Visual Basic, C#] The following example is designed for use with Windows Forms, and it requires **PaintEventArgs** *e*, an **OnPaint** event object. The code performs the following actions:

- Creates a graphics path.
- Populates it with several primitives and some markers.
- Lists the path data on the left side of the screen.
- Creates a **GraphicsPathIterator** object and rewinds it.
- Increments the path data index to the second marker.
- Calls the **Enumerate** method to copy the path data to the *points* and *types* arrays.
- Lists this copied data on the right side of the screen.

[Visual Basic]

```
Public Sub EnumerateExample(e As PaintEventArgs)
Dim myPath As New GraphicsPath()
Dim myPoints As Point() = {New Point(20, 20), _
New Point(120, 120), New Point(20, 120), New Point(20, 20)}
Dim myRect As New Rectangle(120, 120, 100, 100)
myPath.AddLines(myPoints)
myPath.AddRectangle(myRect)
myPath.AddEllipse(220, 220, 100, 100)
' Get the total number of points for the path, and arrays of the
' points and types.
Dim myPathPointCount As Integer = myPath.PointCount
Dim myPathPoints As PointF() = myPath.PathPoints
Dim myPathTypes As Byte() = myPath.PathTypes
' Set up variables for listing the array of points on the left side
' of the screen.
Dim i As Integer
Dim j As Single = 20
Dim myFont As New Font("Arial", 8)
Dim myBrush As New SolidBrush(Color.Black)
' List the set of points and types and types to the left side of
' the screen.
e.Graphics.DrawString("Original Data", myFont, myBrush, 20, j)
j += 20
For i = 0 To myPathPointCount - 1
e.Graphics.DrawString(myPathPoints(i).X.ToString() & ", " & _
myPathPoints(i).Y.ToString() & ", " & _
myPathTypes(i).ToString(), myFont, myBrush, 20, j)
j += 20
Next i
' Create a GraphicsPathIterator for myPath.
Dim myPathIterator As New GraphicsPathIterator(myPath)
myPathIterator.Rewind()
Dim points(myPathIterator.Count) As PointF
Dim types(myPathIterator.Count) As Byte
Dim numPoints As Integer = myPathIterator.Enumerate(points, types)
' Draw the set of copied points and types to the screen.
j = 20
e.Graphics.DrawString("Copied Data", myFont, myBrush, 200, j)
j += 20
For i = 0 To points.Length - 1
e.Graphics.DrawString("Point: " & i & ", " & "Value: " & _
points(i).ToString() & ", " & "Type: " & _
types(i).ToString(), myFont, myBrush, 200, j)
j += 20
Next i
End Sub
```

[C#]

```
public void EnumerateExample(PaintEventArgs e)
{
GraphicsPath myPath = new GraphicsPath();
Point[] myPoints =
{
new Point(20, 20),
new Point(120, 120),
new Point(20, 120),
new Point(20, 20)
};
Rectangle myRect = new Rectangle(120, 120, 100, 100);
myPath.AddLines(myPoints);
myPath.AddRectangle(myRect);
myPath.AddEllipse(220, 220, 100, 100);
// Get the total number of points for the path, and arrays of
//the  points and types.
int myPathPointCount = myPath.PointCount;
PointF[] myPathPoints = myPath.PathPoints;
byte[] myPathTypes = myPath.PathTypes;
// Set up variables for listing the array of points on the left
// side of the screen.
int i;
float j = 20;
Font myFont = new Font("Arial", 8);
SolidBrush myBrush = new SolidBrush(Color.Black);
// List the set of points and types and types to the left side
// of the screen.
e.Graphics.DrawString("Original Data",
myFont,
myBrush,
20,
j);
j += 20;
for(i=0; i<myPathPointCount; i++)
{
e.Graphics.DrawString(myPathPoints[i].X.ToString()+
", " + myPathPoints[i].Y.ToString() + ", " +
myPathTypes[i].ToString(),
myFont,
myBrush,
20,
j);
j+=20;
}
// Create a GraphicsPathIterator for myPath.
GraphicsPathIterator myPathIterator =
new GraphicsPathIterator(myPath);
myPathIterator.Rewind();
PointF[] points = new PointF[myPathIterator.Count];
byte[] types = new byte[myPathIterator.Count];
int numPoints = myPathIterator.Enumerate(ref points, ref types);
// Draw the set of copied points and types to the screen.
j = 20;
e.Graphics.DrawString("Copied Data",
myFont,
myBrush,
200,
j);
j += 20;
for(i=0; i<points.Length; i++)
{
e.Graphics.DrawString("Point: " + i +
", " + "Value: " + points[i].ToString() + ", " +
"Type: " + types[i].ToString(),
myFont,
myBrush,
200,
j);
j+=20;
}
}
```

Requirements

Platforms: Windows 98, Windows NT 4.0, Windows Millennium Edition, Windows 2000, Windows XP Home Edition, Windows XP Professional, Windows Server 2003 family

GraphicsPathIterator.Finalize Method

This member overrides **Object.Finalize**.

[Visual Basic]
```
Overrides Protected Sub Finalize()
```
[C#]
```
~GraphicsPathIterator();
```
[C++]
```
~GraphicsPathIterator();
```
[JScript]
```
protected override function Finalize();
```

Requirements

Platforms: Windows 98, Windows NT 4.0, Windows Millennium Edition, Windows 2000, Windows XP Home Edition, Windows XP Professional, Windows Server 2003 family

GraphicsPathIterator.HasCurve Method

Indicates whether the path associated with this **GraphicsPathIterator** object contains a curve.

[Visual Basic]
```
Public Function HasCurve() As Boolean
```
[C#]
```
public bool HasCurve();
```
[C++]
```
public: bool HasCurve();
```
[JScript]
```
public function HasCurve() : Boolean;
```

Return Value

This method returns **true** if the current subpath contains a curve; otherwise, **false**.

Remarks

All curves in a path are stored as sequences of Bézier splines. For example, when you add an ellipse to a path, you specify the upper-left corner, the width, and the height of the ellipse's bounding rectangle. Those numbers (upper-left corner, width, and height) are not stored in the path; instead; the ellipse is converted to a sequence of four Bézier splines. The path stores the endpoints and control points of those Bézier splines.

A path stores an array of data points, each of which belongs to a line or a Bézier spline. If some of the points in the array belong to Bézier splines, then **HasCurve** returns **true**. If all points in the array belong to lines, then **HasCurve** returns **false**.

Certain methods flatten a path, which means that all the curves in the path are converted to sequences of lines. After a path has been flattened, **HasCurve** will always return **false**. Calling the **Flatten**, **Widen**, or **Warp** method of the **GraphicsPath** class will flatten a path.

Example

[Visual Basic, C#] The following example is designed for use with Windows Forms, and it requires **PaintEventArgs** *e*, an **OnPaint** event object. The code performs the following actions:

- Creates a **GraphicsPath** object, *myPath*.
- Adds three lines, a rectangle, and an ellipse.
- Creates a GraphicsPathIterator object for *myPath*.
- Tests to see if the current path *myPath* contains a curve.
- Shows the result of the test in a message box.

[Visual Basic]
```
Public Sub HasCurveExample(e As PaintEventArgs)
Dim myPath As New GraphicsPath()
Dim myPoints As Point() = {New Point(20, 20), _
New Point(120, 120), New Point(20, 120), New Point(20, 20)}
Dim myRect As New Rectangle(120, 120, 100, 100)
myPath.AddLines(myPoints)
myPath.AddRectangle(myRect)
myPath.AddEllipse(220, 220, 100, 100)
' Create a GraphicsPathIterator for myPath.
Dim myPathIterator As New GraphicsPathIterator(myPath)
Dim myHasCurve As Boolean = myPathIterator.HasCurve()
MessageBox.Show(myHasCurve.ToString())
End Sub
```

[C#]
```
private void HasCurveExample(PaintEventArgs e)
{
// Create a path and add three lines,
// a rectangle and an ellipse.
GraphicsPath myPath = new GraphicsPath();
Point[] myPoints =
{
new Point(20, 20),
new Point(120, 120),
new Point(20, 120),
new Point(20, 20)
};
Rectangle myRect = new Rectangle(120, 120, 100, 100);
myPath.AddLines(myPoints);
myPath.AddRectangle(myRect);
myPath.AddEllipse(220, 220, 100, 100);
// Create a GraphicsPathIterator for myPath.
GraphicsPathIterator myPathIterator = new
GraphicsPathIterator(myPath);
// Test for a curve.
bool myHasCurve = myPathIterator.HasCurve();
// Show the test result.
MessageBox.Show(myHasCurve.ToString());
}
```

Requirements

Platforms: Windows 98, Windows NT 4.0, Windows Millennium Edition, Windows 2000, Windows XP Home Edition, Windows XP Professional, Windows Server 2003 family

GraphicsPathIterator.NextMarker Method

Moves the iterator to the next marker in the path.

Overload List

This **GraphicsPathIterator** object has a **GraphicsPath** object associated with it. The **NextMarker** method increments the associated **GraphicsPath** object to the next marker in its path and copies all the points contained between the current marker and the next marker (or end of path) to a second **GraphicsPath** object passed in to the parameter.

[Visual Basic] **Overloads Public Function NextMarker(GraphicsPath) As Integer**

[C#] **public int NextMarker(GraphicsPath);**

[C++] **public: int NextMarker(GraphicsPath*);**

[JScript] **public function NextMarker(GraphicsPath) : int;**

Increments the **GraphicsPathIterator** object to the next marker in the path and returns the start and stop indexes by way of the out parameters.

[Visual Basic] **Overloads Public Function NextMarker(ByRef Integer, ByRef Integer) As Integer**

[C#] **public int NextMarker(int, int);**

[C++] **public: int NextMarker(int, int);**

[JScript] **public function NextMarker(int, int) : int;**

Example

[Visual Basic, C#] The following example is designed for use with Windows Forms, and it requires **PaintEventArgs** *e*, an **OnPaint** event object. The code performs the following actions:

- Creates a **GraphicsPath** object.
- Adds three lines, a rectangle, and an ellipse ¾ with markers between each.
- Draws the values for the array of points to the screen.
- Creates a **GraphicsPathIterator** object.
- Calls the **NextMarker** method.
- Uses the values returned from the iterative calls to **NextMarker** to draw the start and stop points for each marker to the screen.
- Draws the value for the total number of points to the screen.

> [Visual Basic, C#] **Note** This example shows how to use one of the overloaded versions of **NextMarker**. For other examples that might be available, see the individual overload topics.

[Visual Basic]

```
Public Sub NextMarkerExample(e As PaintEventArgs)
' Create the GraphicsPath.
Dim myPath As New GraphicsPath()
Dim myPoints As Point() = {New Point(20, 20), _
New Point(120, 120), New Point(20, 120), New Point(20, 20)}
Dim myRect As New Rectangle(120, 120, 100, 100)
' Add 3 lines, a rectangle, an ellipse, and 2 markers.
myPath.AddLines(myPoints)
myPath.SetMarkers()
myPath.AddRectangle(myRect)
myPath.SetMarkers()
myPath.AddEllipse(220, 220, 100, 100)
' Get the total number of points for the path,
' and the arrays of the points and types.
Dim myPathPointCount As Integer = myPath.PointCount
Dim myPathPoints As PointF() = myPath.PathPoints
Dim myPathTypes As Byte() = myPath.PathTypes
' Set up variables for drawing the array of points to the screen.
Dim i As Integer
Dim j As Single = 20
Dim myFont As New Font("Arial", 8)
Dim myBrush As New SolidBrush(Color.Black)
' Draw the set of path points and types to the screen.
For i = 0 To myPathPointCount - 1
e.Graphics.DrawString(myPathPoints(i).X.ToString() + ", " + _
myPathPoints(i).Y.ToString() + ", " + _
myPathTypes(i).ToString(), myFont, myBrush, 20, j)
j += 20
Next i
' Create a GraphicsPathIterator.
Dim myPathIterator As New GraphicsPathIterator(myPath)
Dim myStartIndex As Integer
Dim myEndIndex As Integer
' Rewind the Iterator.
myPathIterator.Rewind()
' Draw the Markers and their start and end points to the screen.
j = 20
For i = 0 To 2
myPathIterator.NextMarker(myStartIndex, myEndIndex)
e.Graphics.DrawString("Marker " + i.ToString() + ": _
Start: " + myStartIndex.ToString() + " End: " + _
myEndIndex.ToString(), myFont, myBrush, 200, j)
j += 20
Next i
' Draw the total number of points to the screen.
j += 20
Dim myPathTotalPoints As Integer = myPathIterator.Count
e.Graphics.DrawString("Total Points = " + _
myPathTotalPoints.ToString(), myFont, myBrush, 200, j)
End Sub
```

[C#]

```
private void NextMarkerExample(PaintEventArgs e)
{
// Create the GraphicsPath.
GraphicsPath myPath = new GraphicsPath();
Point[] myPoints =
{
new Point(20, 20),
new Point(120, 120),
new Point(20, 120),
new Point(20, 20)
};
Rectangle myRect = new Rectangle(120, 120, 100, 100);
// Add 3 lines, a rectangle, an ellipse, and 2 markers.
myPath.AddLines(myPoints);
myPath.SetMarkers();
myPath.AddRectangle(myRect);
myPath.SetMarkers();
myPath.AddEllipse(220, 220, 100, 100);
// Get the total number of points for the path,
// and the arrays of the points and types.
int myPathPointCount = myPath.PointCount;
PointF[] myPathPoints = myPath.PathPoints;
byte[] myPathTypes = myPath.PathTypes;
// Set up variables for drawing the array
// of points to the screen.
int i;
float j = 20;
Font myFont = new Font("Arial", 8);
SolidBrush myBrush = new SolidBrush(Color.Black);
// Draw the set of path points and types to the screen.
for(i=0; i<myPathPointCount; i++)
{
e.Graphics.DrawString(myPathPoints[i].X.ToString()+
", " + myPathPoints[i].Y.ToString() + ", " +
myPathTypes[i].ToString(),
myFont,
myBrush,
20,
j);
j+=20;
}
// Create a GraphicsPathIterator.
GraphicsPathIterator myPathIterator = new
GraphicsPathIterator(myPath);
int myStartIndex;
int myEndIndex;
// Rewind the Iterator.
myPathIterator.Rewind();
// Draw the Markers and their start and end points
// to the screen.
j=20;
for(i=0;i<3;i++)
{
myPathIterator.NextMarker(out myStartIndex, out myEndIndex);
e.Graphics.DrawString("Marker " + i.ToString() +
":  Start: " + myStartIndex.ToString()+
"  End: " + myEndIndex.ToString(),
myFont,
myBrush,
200,
j);
j += 20;
```

```
}
// Draw the total number of points to the screen.
j += 20;
int myPathTotalPoints = myPathIterator.Count;
e.Graphics.DrawString("Total Points = " +
myPathTotalPoints.ToString(),
myFont,
myBrush,
200,
j);
}
```

GraphicsPathIterator.NextMarker Method (GraphicsPath)

This **GraphicsPathIterator** object has a **GraphicsPath** object associated with it. The **NextMarker** method increments the associated **GraphicsPath** object to the next marker in its path and copies all the points contained between the current marker and the next marker (or end of path) to a second **GraphicsPath** object passed in to the parameter.

[Visual Basic]
```
Overloads Public Function NextMarker( _
   ByVal path As GraphicsPath _
) As Integer
```
[C#]
```
public int NextMarker(
   GraphicsPath path
);
```
[C++]
```
public: int NextMarker(
   GraphicsPath* path
);
```
[JScript]
```
public function NextMarker(
   path : GraphicsPath
) : int;
```

Parameters

path

The **GraphicsPath** object to which the points will be copied.

Return Value

The number of points between this marker and the next.

Remarks

Use the **SetMarkers** method to set markers in a path. Markers are used to create groups of subpaths. One or more subpaths can be between two markers.

Example

[Visual Basic, C#] The following example is designed for use with Windows Forms, and it requires **PaintEventArgs** *e*, an **OnPaint** event object. The code performs the following actions:

- Creates a **GraphicsPath** object.
- Adds three lines, a rectangle, and an ellipse ¾ plus a couple of markers.
- Lists the values of all the path's points to the left side of the screen.
- Creates a **GraphicsPathIterator** object.
- Creates a **GraphicsPath** object, *myPathSection*, to receive copied points.
- Calls the **NextMarker(GraphicsPath)** method, which iterates to the first marker and copies all the points contained between that marker and the next to *myPathSection*.
- Returns the number of points copied to *markerPoints*.
- Lists the marker number (the first marker) and number of points it contains to the right side of the screen.

[Visual Basic]
```
Public Sub NextMarkerExample2(e As PaintEventArgs)
' Create a graphics path.
Dim myPath As New GraphicsPath()
' Set up primitives to add to myPath.
Dim myPoints As Point() = {New Point(20, 20), _
New Point(120, 120), New Point(20, 120), New Point(20, 20)}
Dim myRect As New Rectangle(120, 120, 100, 100)
' Add 3 lines, a rectangle, an ellipse, and 2 markers.
myPath.AddLines(myPoints)
myPath.SetMarkers()
myPath.AddRectangle(myRect)
myPath.SetMarkers()
myPath.AddEllipse(220, 220, 100, 100)
' Get the total number of points for the path,
' and the arrays of the points and types.
Dim myPathPointCount As Integer = myPath.PointCount
Dim myPathPoints As PointF() = myPath.PathPoints
Dim myPathTypes As Byte() = myPath.PathTypes
' Set up variables for drawing the array
' of points to the screen.
Dim i As Integer
Dim j As Single = 20
Dim myFont As New Font("Arial", 8)
Dim myBrush As New SolidBrush(Color.Black)
' Draw the set of path points and types to the screen.
For i = 0 To myPathPointCount - 1
e.Graphics.DrawString(myPathPoints(i).X.ToString() + _
", " + myPathPoints(i).Y.ToString() + ", " + _
myPathTypes(i).ToString(), myFont, myBrush, 20, j)
j += 20
Next i
' Create a GraphicsPathIterator.
Dim myPathIterator As New GraphicsPathIterator(myPath)
' Rewind the iterator.
myPathIterator.Rewind()
' Create a GraphicsPath section.
Dim myPathSection As New GraphicsPath()
' List the points contained in the first marker
' to the screen.
Dim markerPoints As Integer
markerPoints = myPathIterator.NextMarker(myPathSection)
e.Graphics.DrawString("Marker: 1" + "  Num Points: " + _
markerPoints.ToString(), myFont, myBrush, 200, 20)
End Sub
```

[C#]
```
public void NextMarkerExample2(PaintEventArgs e)
{
// Create a graphics path.
GraphicsPath myPath = new GraphicsPath();
// Set up primitives to add to myPath.
Point[] myPoints =
{
new Point(20, 20),
new Point(120, 120),
new Point(20, 120),
new Point(20, 20)
};
Rectangle myRect = new Rectangle(120, 120, 100, 100);
// Add 3 lines, a rectangle, an ellipse, and 2 markers.
myPath.AddLines(myPoints);
myPath.SetMarkers();
myPath.AddRectangle(myRect);
myPath.SetMarkers();
myPath.AddEllipse(220, 220, 100, 100);
// Get the total number of points for the path,
// and the arrays of the points and types.
int myPathPointCount = myPath.PointCount;
PointF[] myPathPoints = myPath.PathPoints;
byte[] myPathTypes = myPath.PathTypes;
```

```
// Set up variables for listing all the values of the path's
// points to the screen.
int i;
float j = 20;
Font myFont = new Font("Arial", 8);
SolidBrush myBrush = new SolidBrush(Color.Black);
// List the values for all of path points and types to
// the left side of the screen.
for(i=0; i<myPathPointCount; i++)
{
e.Graphics.DrawString(myPathPoints[i].X.ToString()+
", " + myPathPoints[i].Y.ToString() + ", " +
myPathTypes[i].ToString(),
myFont,
myBrush,
20,
j);
j+=20;
}
// Create a GraphicsPathIterator.
GraphicsPathIterator myPathIterator = new
GraphicsPathIterator(myPath);
// Rewind the iterator.
myPathIterator.Rewind();
// Create a GraphicsPath to receive a section of myPath.
GraphicsPath myPathSection = new GraphicsPath();
// Retrieve and list the number of points contained in
// the first marker to the right side of the screen.
int markerPoints;
markerPoints = myPathIterator.NextMarker(myPathSection);
e.Graphics.DrawString("Marker: 1" +
"  Num Points: " +
markerPoints.ToString(),
myFont,
myBrush,
200,
20);
}
```

Requirements

Platforms: Windows 98, Windows NT 4.0, Windows Millennium Edition, Windows 2000, Windows XP Home Edition, Windows XP Professional, Windows Server 2003 family

GraphicsPathIterator.NextMarker Method (Int32, Int32)

Increments the **GraphicsPathIterator** object to the next marker in the path and returns the start and stop indexes by way of the out parameters.

[Visual Basic]
```
Overloads Public Function NextMarker( _
   <Out()> ByRef startIndex As Integer, _
   <Out()> ByRef endIndex As Integer _
) As Integer
```
[C#]
```
public int NextMarker(
   out int startIndex,
   out int endIndex
);
```
[C++]
```
public: int NextMarker(
   [
   Out
] int* startIndex,
   [
   Out
] int* endIndex
);
```
[JScript]
```
public function NextMarker(
   startIndex : int,
   endIndex : int
) : int;
```

Parameters

startIndex
: [out] The integer reference supplied to this parameter receives the index of the point that starts a subpath.

endIndex
: [out] The integer reference supplied to this parameter receives the index of the point that ends the subpath to which *startIndex* points.

Return Value

The number of points between this marker and the next.

Remarks

Use the **SetMarkers** method to set markers in a path. Markers are used to create groups of subpaths. One or more subpaths can be between two markers.

Example

[Visual Basic, C#] The following example is designed for use with Windows Forms, and it requires **PaintEventArgs** *e*, an **OnPaint** event object. The code performs the following actions:

- Creates a **GraphicsPath** object.
- Adds three lines, a rectangle, and an ellipse ¾ with markers between each.
- Draws the values for the array of points to the screen.
- Creates a **GraphicsPathIterator** object.
- Calls the **NextMarker** method.
- Uses the values returned from the iterative calls to **NextMarker** to draw the start and stop points for each marker to the screen.
- Draws the value for the total number of points to the screen.

[Visual Basic]
```
Public Sub NextMarkerExample(e As PaintEventArgs)
' Create the GraphicsPath.
Dim myPath As New GraphicsPath()
Dim myPoints As Point() =  {New Point(20, 20), _
New Point(120, 120), New Point(20, 120), New Point(20, 20)}
Dim myRect As New Rectangle(120, 120, 100, 100)
' Add 3 lines, a rectangle, an ellipse, and 2 markers.
myPath.AddLines(myPoints)
myPath.SetMarkers()
myPath.AddRectangle(myRect)
myPath.SetMarkers()
myPath.AddEllipse(220, 220, 100, 100)
' Get the total number of points for the path,
' and the arrays of the points and types.
Dim myPathPointCount As Integer = myPath.PointCount
Dim myPathPoints As PointF() = myPath.PathPoints
Dim myPathTypes As Byte() = myPath.PathTypes
' Set up variables for drawing the array of points to the screen.
Dim i As Integer
Dim j As Single = 20
Dim myFont As New Font("Arial", 8)
Dim myBrush As New SolidBrush(Color.Black)
' Draw the set of path points and types to the screen.
For i = 0 To myPathPointCount - 1
e.Graphics.DrawString(myPathPoints(i).X.ToString() + ", " + _
myPathPoints(i).Y.ToString() + ", " + _
myPathTypes(i).ToString(), myFont, myBrush, 20, j)
j += 20
Next i
```

```
' Create a GraphicsPathIterator.
Dim myPathIterator As New GraphicsPathIterator(myPath)
Dim myStartIndex As Integer
Dim myEndIndex As Integer
' Rewind the Iterator.
myPathIterator.Rewind()
' Draw the Markers and their start and end points to the screen.
j = 20
For i = 0 To 2
myPathIterator.NextMarker(myStartIndex, myEndIndex)
e.Graphics.DrawString("Marker " + i.ToString() + ":  _
Start: " + myStartIndex.ToString() + "  End: " + _
myEndIndex.ToString(), myFont, myBrush, 200, j)
j += 20
Next i
' Draw the total number of points to the screen.
j += 20
Dim myPathTotalPoints As Integer = myPathIterator.Count
e.Graphics.DrawString("Total Points = " + _
myPathTotalPoints.ToString(), myFont, myBrush, 200, j)
End Sub
```

[C#]

```
private void NextMarkerExample(PaintEventArgs e)
{
// Create the GraphicsPath.
GraphicsPath myPath = new GraphicsPath();
Point[] myPoints =
{
new Point(20, 20),
new Point(120, 120),
new Point(20, 120),
new Point(20, 20)
};
Rectangle myRect = new Rectangle(120, 120, 100, 100);
// Add 3 lines, a rectangle, an ellipse, and 2 markers.
myPath.AddLines(myPoints);
myPath.SetMarkers();
myPath.AddRectangle(myRect);
myPath.SetMarkers();
myPath.AddEllipse(220, 220, 100, 100);
// Get the total number of points for the path,
// and the arrays of the points and types.
int myPathPointCount = myPath.PointCount;
PointF[] myPathPoints = myPath.PathPoints;
byte[] myPathTypes = myPath.PathTypes;
// Set up variables for drawing the array
// of points to the screen.
int i;
float j = 20;
Font myFont = new Font("Arial", 8);
SolidBrush myBrush = new SolidBrush(Color.Black);
// Draw the set of path points and types to the screen.
for(i=0; i<myPathPointCount; i++)
{
e.Graphics.DrawString(myPathPoints[i].X.ToString()+
", " + myPathPoints[i].Y.ToString() + ", " +
myPathTypes[i].ToString(),
myFont,
myBrush,
20,
j);
j+=20;
}
// Create a GraphicsPathIterator.
GraphicsPathIterator myPathIterator = new
GraphicsPathIterator(myPath);
int myStartIndex;
int myEndIndex;
// Rewind the Iterator.
myPathIterator.Rewind();
// Draw the Markers and their start and end points
// to the screen.
j=20;
for(i=0;i<3;i++)
{
myPathIterator.NextMarker(out myStartIndex, out myEndIndex);
e.Graphics.DrawString("Marker " + i.ToString() +
":  Start: " + myStartIndex.ToString()+
"  End: " + myEndIndex.ToString(),
myFont,
myBrush,
200,
j);
j += 20;
}
// Draw the total number of points to the screen.
j += 20;
int myPathTotalPoints = myPathIterator.Count;
e.Graphics.DrawString("Total Points = " +
myPathTotalPoints.ToString(),
myFont,
myBrush,
200,
j);
}
```

Requirements

Platforms: Windows 98, Windows NT 4.0, Windows Millennium Edition, Windows 2000, Windows XP Home Edition, Windows XP Professional, Windows Server 2003 family

GraphicsPathIterator.NextPathType Method

Gets the starting index and the ending index of the next group of data points that all have the same type.

[Visual Basic]

```
Public Function NextPathType( _
   <Out()> ByRef pathType As Byte, _
   <Out()> ByRef startIndex As Integer, _
   <Out()> ByRef endIndex As Integer _
) As Integer
```

[C#]

```
public int NextPathType(
   out byte pathType,
   out int startIndex,
   out int endIndex
);
```

[C++]

```
public: int NextPathType(
   [
   Out
] unsigned char* pathType,
   [
   Out
] int* startIndex,
   [
   Out
] int* endIndex
);
```

[JScript]

```
public function NextPathType(
   pathType : Byte,
   startIndex : int,
   endIndex : int
) : int;
```

Parameters

pathType

[out] Receives the point type shared by all points in the group. Possible types can be retrieved from the **PathPointType** enumeration.

startIndex

[out] Receives the starting index of the group of points.

endIndex

[out] Receives the ending index of the group of points.

Return Value

This method returns the number of data points in the group. If there are no more groups in the path, this method returns 0.

Example

[Visual Basic, C#] The following example is designed for use with Windows Forms, and it requires **PaintEventArgs** *e*, an **OnPaint** event object. The code performs the following actions:

- Creates a **GraphicsPath** object.
- Adds three lines, a rectangle, and an ellipse.
- Lists the values of all the points to the left side of the screen.
- Creates a **GraphicsPathIterator** object and rewinds it.
- In a **for** loop, iterates through the points using the **NextSubpath** and **NextPathType** methods.
- Uses the values returned from the iterative calls to list the subpath number, the number of points in it, and the type of the path points to the right side of the screen.
- Displays the value for the total number of points to the screen.

[Visual Basic, C#] Note that **ListPathPoints** is a helper function that separates most (not all) of the display code from the graphics path code.

[Visual Basic]

```
Public Sub NextPathTypeExample(e As PaintEventArgs)
' Create the GraphicsPath.
Dim myPath As New GraphicsPath()
Dim myPoints As Point() =  {New Point(20, 20), _
New Point(120, 120), New Point(20, 120), New Point(20, 20)}
Dim myRect As New Rectangle(120, 120, 100, 100)
' Add 3 lines, a rectangle, and an ellipse.
myPath.AddLines(myPoints)
myPath.AddRectangle(myRect)
myPath.AddEllipse(220, 220, 100, 100)
' List all of the path points to the screen.
ListPathPointsHelper(e, myPath, Nothing, 20, 1)
' Create a GraphicsPathIterator.
Dim myPathIterator As New GraphicsPathIterator(myPath)
' Rewind the Iterator.
myPathIterator.Rewind()
' Iterate the subpaths and types, and list the results
' to the screen.
Dim j As Integer = 20
Dim i As Integer
Dim mySubPaths, subPathStartIndex, subPathEndIndex As Integer
Dim IsClosed As [Boolean]
Dim subPathPointType As Byte
Dim pointTypeStartIndex, pointTypeEndIndex, _
numPointsFound As Integer
Dim myFont As New Font("Arial", 8)
Dim myBrush As New SolidBrush(Color.Black)
j = 20
For i = 0 To 2
mySubPaths = myPathIterator.NextSubpath(subPathStartIndex, _
subPathEndIndex, IsClosed)
numPointsFound = myPathIterator.NextPathType(subPathPointType, _
pointTypeStartIndex, pointTypeEndIndex)
e.Graphics.DrawString("SubPath: " & i & "  Points Found: " & _
numPointsFound.ToString() & "  Type of Points: " & _
subPathPointType.ToString(), myFont, myBrush, 200, j)
j += 20
Next i
' List the total number of path points to the screen.
ListPathPointsHelper(e, myPath, myPathIterator, 200, 2)
End Sub
' This is a helper function used by NextPathTypeExample.
Public Sub ListPathPointsHelper(e As PaintEventArgs, _
myPath As GraphicsPath, myPathIterator As GraphicsPathIterator, _
xOffset As Integer, listType As Integer)
' Get the total number of points for the path,
' and the arrays of the points and types.
Dim myPathPointCount As Integer = myPath.PointCount
Dim myPathPoints As PointF() = myPath.PathPoints
Dim myPathTypes As Byte() = myPath.PathTypes
' Set up variables for drawing the points to the screen.
Dim i As Integer
Dim j As Single = 20
Dim myFont As New Font("Arial", 8)
Dim myBrush As New SolidBrush(Color.Black)
If listType = 1 Then ' List all the path points to the screen.
' Draw the set of path points and types to the screen.
For i = 0 To myPathPointCount - 1
e.Graphics.DrawString(myPathPoints(i).X.ToString() + ", " + _
myPathPoints(i).Y.ToString() + ", " + _
myPathTypes(i).ToString(), myFont, myBrush, xOffset, j)
j += 20
Next i
Else
If listType = 2 Then ' Display the total number of path points.
' Draw the total number of points to the screen.
Dim myPathTotalPoints As Integer = myPathIterator.Count
e.Graphics.DrawString("Total Points = " + _
myPathTotalPoints.ToString(), myFont, myBrush, xOffset, _
100)
Else
e.Graphics.DrawString("Wrong or no list type argument.", _
myFont, myBrush, xOffset, 200)
End If
End If
End Sub
```

[C#]

```
public void NextPathTypeExample(PaintEventArgs e)
{
// Create the GraphicsPath.
GraphicsPath myPath = new GraphicsPath();
Point[] myPoints =
{
new Point(20, 20),
new Point(120, 120),
new Point(20, 120),
new Point(20, 20)
};
Rectangle myRect = new Rectangle(120, 120, 100, 100);
// Add 3 lines, a rectangle, and an ellipse.
myPath.AddLines(myPoints);
myPath.AddRectangle(myRect);
myPath.AddEllipse(220, 220, 100, 100);
// List all of the path points to the screen.
ListPathPoints(e, myPath, null, 20, 1);
// Create a GraphicsPathIterator.
GraphicsPathIterator myPathIterator = new
GraphicsPathIterator(myPath);
// Rewind the Iterator.
myPathIterator.Rewind();
// Iterate the subpaths and types, and list the results to
// the screen.
int i, j = 20;
int mySubPaths, subPathStartIndex, subPathEndIndex;
Boolean IsClosed;
byte subPathPointType;
int pointTypeStartIndex,  pointTypeEndIndex, numPointsFound;
Font myFont = new Font("Arial", 8);
```

```
SolidBrush myBrush = new SolidBrush(Color.Black);
j = 20;
for(i = 0;i < 3; i++)
{
mySubPaths = myPathIterator.NextSubpath(
out subPathStartIndex,
out subPathEndIndex,
out IsClosed);
numPointsFound = myPathIterator.NextPathType(
out subPathPointType,
out pointTypeStartIndex,
out pointTypeEndIndex);
e.Graphics.DrawString(
"SubPath: " + i +
"  Points Found: " + numPointsFound.ToString() +
"  Type of Points: " + subPathPointType.ToString(),
myFont,
myBrush,
200,
j);
j+=20;
}
// List the total number of path points to the screen.
ListPathPoints(e, myPath, myPathIterator, 200, 2);
}
//-------------------------------------------------------
//This function is a helper function used by
// NextPathTypeExample.
//-------------------------------------------------------
public void ListPathPoints(
PaintEventArgs e,
GraphicsPath myPath,
GraphicsPathIterator myPathIterator,
int xOffset,
int listType)
{
// Get the total number of points for the path,
// and the arrays of the points and types.
int myPathPointCount = myPath.PointCount;
PointF[] myPathPoints = myPath.PathPoints;
byte[] myPathTypes = myPath.PathTypes;
// Set up variables for drawing the points to the screen.
int i;
float j = 20;
Font myFont = new Font("Arial", 8);
SolidBrush myBrush = new SolidBrush(Color.Black);
if (listType == 1) // List all the path points to the screen.
{
// Draw the set of path points and types to the screen.
for(i=0; i<myPathPointCount; i++)
{
e.Graphics.DrawString(myPathPoints[i].X.ToString()+
", " + myPathPoints[i].Y.ToString() + ", " +
myPathTypes[i].ToString(),
myFont,
myBrush,
xOffset,
j);
j+=20;
}
}
else if (listType == 2) // Display the total number of path points.
{
// Draw the total number of points to the screen.
int myPathTotalPoints = myPathIterator.Count;
e.Graphics.DrawString("Total Points = " +
myPathTotalPoints.ToString(),
myFont,
myBrush,
xOffset,
100);
}
else
{
e.Graphics.DrawString("Wrong or no list type argument.",
myFont,
myBrush,
xOffset,
200);
}
```

Requirements

Platforms: Windows 98, Windows NT 4.0, Windows Millennium Edition, Windows 2000, Windows XP Home Edition, Windows XP Professional, Windows Server 2003 family

GraphicsPathIterator.NextSubpath Method

Moves the subpath to the next subpath in the specified **GraphicsPath** object.

Overload List

Gets the next figure (subpath) from this **GraphicsPathIterator** object's associated path.

[Visual Basic] **Overloads Public Function NextSubpath(GraphicsPath, ByRef Boolean) As Integer**

[C#] **public int NextSubpath(GraphicsPath, bool);**

[C++] **public: int NextSubpath(GraphicsPath*, bool);**

[JScript] **public function NextSubpath(GraphicsPath, Boolean) : int;**

Moves the **GraphicsPathIterator** object to the next subpath in the path. The start index and end index of the next subpath are contained in the [out] parameters.

[Visual Basic] **Overloads Public Function NextSubpath(ByRef Integer, ByRef Integer, ByRef Boolean) As Integer**

[C#] **public int NextSubpath(int, int, bool);**

[C++] **public: int NextSubpath(int, int, bool);**

[JScript] **public function NextSubpath(int, int, Boolean) : int;**

Example

[Visual Basic, C#] The following example is designed for use with Windows Forms, and it requires **PaintEventArgs** *e*, an **OnPaint** event object. The code performs the following actions:

- Creates a **GraphicsPath** object.
- Adds three lines, a rectangle, and an ellipse.
- Draws the values for the array of points to the screen.
- Creates a **GraphicsPathIterator** object.
- Calls the **NextSubpath** method.
- Uses the values returned from the iterative calls to **NextSubPath** to draw the start and stop values for each subpath to the screen.
- Draws the value for the total number of subpaths to the screen.

> [Visual Basic, C#] **Note** This example shows how to use one of the overloaded versions of **NextSubpath**. For other examples that might be available, see the individual overload topics.

[Visual Basic]

```
Public Sub NextSubpathExample(e As PaintEventArgs)
' Create the GraphicsPath.
Dim myPath As New GraphicsPath()
Dim myPoints As Point() =  {New Point(20, 20), _
New Point(120, 120), New Point(20, 120), New Point(20, 20)}
Dim myRect As New Rectangle(120, 120, 100, 100)
' Add 3 lines, a rectangle, an ellipse, and 2 markers.
myPath.AddLines(myPoints)
myPath.AddRectangle(myRect)
```

```
myPath.AddEllipse(220, 220, 100, 100)
' Get the total number of points for the path,
' and the arrays of the points and types.
Dim myPathPointCount As Integer = myPath.PointCount
Dim myPathPoints As PointF() = myPath.PathPoints
Dim myPathTypes As Byte() = myPath.PathTypes
' Set up variables for drawing the array of points to the screen.
Dim i As Integer
Dim j As Single = 20
Dim myFont As New Font("Arial", 8)
Dim myBrush As New SolidBrush(Color.Black)
' Draw the set of path points and types to the screen.
For i = 0 To myPathPointCount - 1
e.Graphics.DrawString(myPathPoints(i).X.ToString() + ", " + _
myPathPoints(i).Y.ToString() + ", " + _
myPathTypes(i).ToString(), myFont, myBrush, 20, j)
j += 20
Next i
' Create a GraphicsPathIterator.
Dim myPathIterator As New GraphicsPathIterator(myPath)
Dim myStartIndex As Integer
Dim myEndIndex As Integer
Dim myIsClosed As Boolean
' get the number of Subpaths.
Dim numSubpaths As Integer = myPathIterator.NextSubpath(myPath, _
myIsClosed)
numSubpaths -= 1
' Rewind the Iterator.
myPathIterator.Rewind()
' List the Subpaths to the screen.
j = 20
For i = 0 To numSubpaths - 1
myPathIterator.NextSubpath(myStartIndex, myEndIndex, _
myIsClosed)
e.Graphics.DrawString("Subpath " + i.ToString() + _
":  Start: " + myStartIndex.ToString() + "  End: " + _
myEndIndex.ToString() + "  IsClosed: " + _
myIsClosed.ToString(), myFont, myBrush, 200, j)
j += 20
Next i
' Draw the total number of Subpaths to the screen.
j += 20
e.Graphics.DrawString("Number Subpaths = " + _
numSubpaths.ToString(), myFont, myBrush, 200, j)
End Sub
```

[C#]

```
private void NextSubpathExample(PaintEventArgs e)
{
// Create the GraphicsPath.
GraphicsPath myPath = new GraphicsPath();
Point[] myPoints =
{
new Point(20, 20),
new Point(120, 120),
new Point(20, 120),
new Point(20, 20)
};
Rectangle myRect = new Rectangle(120, 120, 100, 100);
// Add 3 lines, a rectangle, an ellipse, and 2 markers.
myPath.AddLines(myPoints);
myPath.AddRectangle(myRect);
myPath.AddEllipse(220, 220, 100, 100);
// Get the total number of points for the path,
// and the arrays of the points and types.
int myPathPointCount = myPath.PointCount;
PointF[] myPathPoints = myPath.PathPoints;
byte[] myPathTypes = myPath.PathTypes;
// Set up variables for drawing the array of
// points to the screen.
int i;
float j = 20;
Font myFont = new Font("Arial", 8);
SolidBrush myBrush = new SolidBrush(Color.Black);
// Draw the set of path points and types to the screen.
for(i=0; i<myPathPointCount; i++)
{
e.Graphics.DrawString(myPathPoints[i].X.ToString()+
", " + myPathPoints[i].Y.ToString() + ", " +
myPathTypes[i].ToString(),
myFont,
myBrush,
20,
j);
j+=20;
}
// Create a GraphicsPathIterator.
GraphicsPathIterator myPathIterator = new
GraphicsPathIterator(myPath);
int myStartIndex;
int myEndIndex;
bool myIsClosed;
// get the number of Subpaths.
int numSubpaths = myPathIterator.NextSubpath(myPath,
out myIsClosed);
numSubpaths -= 1;
// Rewind the Iterator.
myPathIterator.Rewind();
// List the Subpaths to the screen.
j=20;
for(i=0;i<numSubpaths;i++)
{
myPathIterator.NextSubpath(out myStartIndex,
out myEndIndex,
out myIsClosed);
e.Graphics.DrawString("Subpath " + i.ToString() +
":  Start: " + myStartIndex.ToString()+
"  End: " + myEndIndex.ToString() +
"  IsClosed: " + myIsClosed.ToString(),
myFont,
myBrush,
200,
j);
j += 20;
}
// Draw the total number of Subpaths to the screen.
j += 20;
e.Graphics.DrawString("Number Subpaths = " +
numSubpaths.ToString(),
myFont,
myBrush,
200,
j);
}
```

GraphicsPathIterator.NextSubpath Method (GraphicsPath, Boolean)

Gets the next figure (subpath) from this **GraphicsPathIterator** object's associated path.

[Visual Basic]

```
Overloads Public Function NextSubpath( _
   ByVal path As GraphicsPath, _
   <Out()> ByRef isClosed As Boolean _
) As Integer
```

[C#]

```
public int NextSubpath(
   GraphicsPath path,
   out bool isClosed
);
```

[C++]

```
public: int NextSubpath(
   GraphicsPath* path,
   [
   Out
] bool* isClosed
);
```

[JScript]
```
public function NextSubpath(
   path : GraphicsPath,
   isClosed : Boolean
) : int;
```

Parameters

path

A **GraphicsPath** object that is to have its data points set to match the data points of the retrieved figure (subpath) for this iterator.

isClosed

[out] Indicates whether the current subpath is closed. It is **true** if the if the figure is closed, otherwise it is **false**.

Return Value

The number of data points in the retrieved figure (subpath). If there are no more figures to retrieve, zero is returned.

Example

[Visual Basic, C#] The following example is designed for use with Windows Forms, and it requires **PaintEventArgs** *e*, an **OnPaint** event object. The code performs the following actions:

- Creates a **GraphicsPath** object.
- Adds three lines, a rectangle, and an ellipse ¾ plus a couple of markers.
- Lists the values of all the path's points to the left side of the screen.
- Creates a **GraphicsPathIterator** object.
- Creates a **GraphicsPath** object, *myPathSection*, to receive copied points.
- Calls the **NextSubpath(GraphicsPath)** method, which iterates to the third subpath (figure) and copies all the points contained in that subpath to the *myPathSection* path, and also returns the number of points copied to *subpathPoints*.
- Lists the subpath number and number of points it contains to the right side of the screen.

[Visual Basic]
```
Public Sub NextSubpathExample2(e As PaintEventArgs)
' Create a graphics path.
Dim myPath As New GraphicsPath()
' Set up primitives to add to myPath.
Dim myPoints As Point() = {New Point(20, 20), +
New Point(120, 120), New Point(20, 120), New Point(20, 20)}
Dim myRect As New Rectangle(120, 120, 100, 100)
' Add 3 lines, a rectangle, an ellipse, and 2 markers.
myPath.AddLines(myPoints)
myPath.SetMarkers()
myPath.AddRectangle(myRect)
myPath.SetMarkers()
myPath.AddEllipse(220, 220, 100, 100)
' Get the total number of points for the path,
' and the arrays of the points and types.
Dim myPathPointCount As Integer = myPath.PointCount
Dim myPathPoints As PointF() = myPath.PathPoints
Dim myPathTypes As Byte() = myPath.PathTypes
' Set up variables for drawing the array
' of points to the screen.
Dim i As Integer
Dim j As Single = 20
Dim myFont As New Font("Arial", 8)
Dim myBrush As New SolidBrush(Color.Black)
' Draw the set of path points and types to the screen.
For i = 0 To myPathPointCount - 1
e.Graphics.DrawString(myPathPoints(i).X.ToString() + _
", " + myPathPoints(i).Y.ToString() + ", " + _
myPathTypes(i).ToString(), myFont, myBrush, 20, j)
j += 20
Next i
' Create a GraphicsPathIterator for myPath.
Dim myPathIterator As New GraphicsPathIterator(myPath)
' Rewind the iterator.
myPathIterator.Rewind()
' Create the GraphicsPath section.
Dim myPathSection As New GraphicsPath()
' Draw the 3rd subpath and the number of points therein
' to the screen.
Dim subpathPoints As Integer
Dim IsClosed2 As Boolean
' Iterate to the third subpath.
subpathPoints = myPathIterator.NextSubpath(myPathSection, _
IsClosed2)
subpathPoints = myPathIterator.NextSubpath(myPathSection, _
IsClosed2)
subpathPoints = myPathIterator.NextSubpath(myPathSection, _
IsClosed2)
' Write the number of subpath points to the screen.
e.Graphics.DrawString("Subpath: 3" + "   Num Points: " + _
subpathPoints.ToString(), myFont, myBrush, 200, 20)
End Sub
```

[C#]
```
public void NextSubpathExample2(PaintEventArgs e)
{
// Create a graphics path.
GraphicsPath myPath = new GraphicsPath();
// Set up primitives to add to myPath.
Point[] myPoints =
{
new Point(20, 20),
new Point(120, 120),
new Point(20, 120),
new Point(20, 20)
};
Rectangle myRect = new Rectangle(120, 120, 100, 100);
// Add 3 lines, a rectangle, an ellipse, and 2 markers.
myPath.AddLines(myPoints);
myPath.SetMarkers();
myPath.AddRectangle(myRect);
myPath.SetMarkers();
myPath.AddEllipse(220, 220, 100, 100);
// Get the total number of points for the path,
// and the arrays of the points and types.
int myPathPointCount = myPath.PointCount;
PointF[] myPathPoints = myPath.PathPoints;
byte[] myPathTypes = myPath.PathTypes;
// Set up variables for listing all of the path's
// points to the screen.
int i;
float j = 20;
Font myFont = new Font("Arial", 8);
SolidBrush myBrush = new SolidBrush(Color.Black);
// List the values of all the path points and types to the screen.
for(i=0; i<myPathPointCount; i++)
{
e.Graphics.DrawString(myPathPoints[i].X.ToString()+
", " + myPathPoints[i].Y.ToString() + ", " +
myPathTypes[i].ToString(),
myFont,
myBrush,
20,
j);
j+=20;
}
// Create a GraphicsPathIterator for myPath.
GraphicsPathIterator myPathIterator = new
GraphicsPathIterator(myPath);
// Rewind the iterator.
myPathIterator.Rewind();
// Create the GraphicsPath section.
GraphicsPath myPathSection = new GraphicsPath();
```

```
// Iterate to the 3rd subpath and list the number of points therein
// to the screen.
int subpathPoints;
bool IsClosed2;
// Iterate to the third subpath.
subpathPoints = myPathIterator.NextSubpath(
myPathSection, out IsClosed2);
subpathPoints = myPathIterator.NextSubpath(
myPathSection, out IsClosed2);
subpathPoints = myPathIterator.NextSubpath(
myPathSection, out IsClosed2);
// Write the number of subpath points to the screen.
e.Graphics.DrawString("Subpath: 3" +
"   Num Points: " +
subpathPoints.ToString(),
myFont,
myBrush,
200,
20);
}
```

Requirements

Platforms: Windows 98, Windows NT 4.0, Windows Millennium Edition, Windows 2000, Windows XP Home Edition, Windows XP Professional, Windows Server 2003 family

GraphicsPathIterator.NextSubpath Method (Int32, Int32, Boolean)

Moves the **GraphicsPathIterator** object to the next subpath in the path. The start index and end index of the next subpath are contained in the [out] parameters.

[Visual Basic]

```
Overloads Public Function NextSubpath( _
   <Out()> ByRef startIndex As Integer, _
   <Out()> ByRef endIndex As Integer, _
   <Out()> ByRef isClosed As Boolean _
) As Integer
```

[C#]

```
public int NextSubpath(
   out int startIndex,
   out int endIndex,
   out bool isClosed
);
```

[C++]

```
public: int NextSubpath(
   [
   Out
] int* startIndex,
   [
   Out
] int* endIndex,
   [
   Out
] bool* isClosed
);
```

[JScript]

```
public function NextSubpath(
   startIndex : int,
   endIndex : int,
   isClosed : Boolean
) : int;
```

Parameters

startIndex
: [out] Receives the starting index of the next subpath.

endIndex
: [out] Receives the ending index of the next subpath.

isClosed
: [out] Indicates whether the subpath is closed.

Return Value

The number of subpaths in the **GraphicsPath** object.

Example

[Visual Basic, C#] The following example is designed for use with Windows Forms, and it requires **PaintEventArgs** *e*, an **OnPaint** event object. The code performs the following actions:

- Creates a **GraphicsPath** object.
- Adds three lines, a rectangle, and an ellipse.
- Draws the values for the array of points to the screen.
- Creates a **GraphicsPathIterator** object.
- Calls the **NextSubpath** method.
- Uses the values returned from the iterative calls to **NextSubPath** to draw the start and stop values for each subpath to the screen.
- Draws the value for the total number of subpaths to the screen.

[Visual Basic]

```
Public Sub NextSubpathExample(e As PaintEventArgs)
' Create the GraphicsPath.
Dim myPath As New GraphicsPath()
Dim myPoints As Point() = {New Point(20, 20), _
New Point(120, 120), New Point(20, 120), New Point(20, 20)}
Dim myRect As New Rectangle(120, 120, 100, 100)
' Add 3 lines, a rectangle, an ellipse, and 2 markers.
myPath.AddLines(myPoints)
myPath.AddRectangle(myRect)
myPath.AddEllipse(220, 220, 100, 100)
' Get the total number of points for the path,
' and the arrays of the points and types.
Dim myPathPointCount As Integer = myPath.PointCount
Dim myPathPoints As PointF() = myPath.PathPoints
Dim myPathTypes As Byte() = myPath.PathTypes
' Set up variables for drawing the array of points to the screen.
Dim i As Integer
Dim j As Single = 20
Dim myFont As New Font("Arial", 8)
Dim myBrush As New SolidBrush(Color.Black)
' Draw the set of path points and types to the screen.
For i = 0 To myPathPointCount - 1
e.Graphics.DrawString(myPathPoints(i).X.ToString() + ", " + _
myPathPoints(i).Y.ToString() + ", " + _
myPathTypes(i).ToString(), myFont, myBrush, 20, j)
j += 20
Next i
' Create a GraphicsPathIterator.
Dim myPathIterator As New GraphicsPathIterator(myPath)
Dim myStartIndex As Integer
Dim myEndIndex As Integer
Dim myIsClosed As Boolean
' get the number of Subpaths.
Dim numSubpaths As Integer = myPathIterator.NextSubpath(myPath, _
myIsClosed)
numSubpaths -= 1
' Rewind the Iterator.
myPathIterator.Rewind()
' List the Subpaths to the screen.
j = 20
For i = 0 To numSubpaths - 1
myPathIterator.NextSubpath(myStartIndex, myEndIndex, _
myIsClosed)
e.Graphics.DrawString("Subpath " + i.ToString() + _
```

```
": Start: " + myStartIndex.ToString() + " End: " + _
myEndIndex.ToString() + " IsClosed: " + _
myIsClosed.ToString(), myFont, myBrush, 200, j)
j += 20
Next i
' Draw the total number of Subpaths to the screen.
j += 20
e.Graphics.DrawString("Number Subpaths = " + _
numSubpaths.ToString(), myFont, myBrush, 200, j)
End Sub
```

[C#]

```
private void NextSubpathExample(PaintEventArgs e)
{
// Create the GraphicsPath.
GraphicsPath myPath = new GraphicsPath();
Point[] myPoints =
{
new Point(20, 20),
new Point(120, 120),
new Point(20, 120),
new Point(20, 20)
};
Rectangle myRect = new Rectangle(120, 120, 100, 100);
// Add 3 lines, a rectangle, an ellipse, and 2 markers.
myPath.AddLines(myPoints);
myPath.AddRectangle(myRect);
myPath.AddEllipse(220, 220, 100, 100);
// Get the total number of points for the path,
// and the arrays of the points and types.
int myPathPointCount = myPath.PointCount;
PointF[] myPathPoints = myPath.PathPoints;
byte[] myPathTypes = myPath.PathTypes;
// Set up variables for drawing the array of
// points to the screen.
int i;
float j = 20;
Font myFont = new Font("Arial", 8);
SolidBrush myBrush = new SolidBrush(Color.Black);
// Draw the set of path points and types to the screen.
for(i=0; i<myPathPointCount; i++)
{
e.Graphics.DrawString(myPathPoints[i].X.ToString()+
", " + myPathPoints[i].Y.ToString() + ", " +
myPathTypes[i].ToString(),
myFont,
myBrush,
20,
j);
j+=20;
}
// Create a GraphicsPathIterator.
GraphicsPathIterator myPathIterator = new
GraphicsPathIterator(myPath);
int myStartIndex;
int myEndIndex;
bool myIsClosed;
// get the number of Subpaths.
int numSubpaths = myPathIterator.NextSubpath(myPath,
out myIsClosed);
numSubpaths -= 1;
// Rewind the Iterator.
myPathIterator.Rewind();
// List the Subpaths to the screen.
j=20;
for(i=0;i<numSubpaths;i++)
{
myPathIterator.NextSubpath(out myStartIndex,
out myEndIndex,
out myIsClosed);
e.Graphics.DrawString("Subpath " + i.ToString() +
": Start: " + myStartIndex.ToString()+
" End: " + myEndIndex.ToString() +
" IsClosed: " + myIsClosed.ToString(),
myFont,
myBrush,
200,
j);
j += 20;
}
// Draw the total number of Subpaths to the screen.
j += 20;
e.Graphics.DrawString("Number Subpaths = " +
numSubpaths.ToString(),
myFont,
myBrush,
200,
j);
}
```

Requirements

Platforms: Windows 98, Windows NT 4.0, Windows Millennium Edition, Windows 2000, Windows XP Home Edition, Windows XP Professional, Windows Server 2003 family

GraphicsPathIterator.Rewind Method

Rewinds this **GraphicsPathIterator** object to the beginning of its associated path.

[Visual Basic]

```
Public Sub Rewind()
```

[C#]

```
public void Rewind();
```

[C++]

```
public: void Rewind();
```

[JScript]

```
public function Rewind();
```

Remarks

The first time you call the **NextSubpath** method of an iterator, it gets the first figure (subpath) of that iterator's associated path. The second time, it gets the second figure, and so on. When you call the **Rewind** method, the sequence starts over; that is, after you call **Rewind**, the next call to **NextSubpath** gets the first figure in the path. The **NextMarker** and **NextPathType** methods behave similarly.

Requirements

Platforms: Windows 98, Windows NT 4.0, Windows Millennium Edition, Windows 2000, Windows XP Home Edition, Windows XP Professional, Windows Server 2003 family

GraphicsState Class

Represents the state of a **Graphics** object. This object is returned by a call to the **BeginContainer** methods. This class cannot be inherited.

System.Object
  System.MarshalByRefObject
    System.Drawing.Drawing2D.GraphicsState

[Visual Basic]
```
NotInheritable Public Class GraphicsState
   Inherits MarshalByRefObject
```
[C#]
```
public sealed class GraphicsState : MarshalByRefObject
```
[C++]
```
public __gc __sealed class GraphicsState : public
   MarshalByRefObject
```
[JScript]
```
public class GraphicsState extends MarshalByRefObject
```

Thread Safety

Any public static (**Shared** in Visual Basic) members of this type are safe for multithreaded operations. Any instance members are not guaranteed to be thread safe.

Requirements

Namespace: System.Drawing.Drawing2D

Platforms: Windows 98, Windows NT 4.0, Windows Millennium Edition, Windows 2000, Windows XP Home Edition, Windows XP Professional, Windows Server 2003 family

Assembly: System.Drawing (in System.Drawing.dll)

HatchBrush Class

Defines a rectangular brush with a hatch style, a foreground color, and a background color. This class cannot be inherited.

System.Object
  System.MarshalByRefObject
    System.Drawing.Brush
      System.Drawing.Drawing2D.HatchBrush

```
[Visual Basic]
NotInheritable Public Class HatchBrush
   Inherits Brush
[C#]
public sealed class HatchBrush : Brush
[C++]
public __gc __sealed class HatchBrush : public Brush
[JScript]
public class HatchBrush extends Brush
```

Thread Safety

Any public static (**Shared** in Visual Basic) members of this type are safe for multithreaded operations. Any instance members are not guaranteed to be thread safe.

Remarks

There are six hatch styles. The foreground color defines the color of lines; the background color defines the color of gaps between the lines.

Requirements

Namespace: System.Drawing.Drawing2D

Platforms: Windows 98, Windows NT 4.0, Windows Millennium Edition, Windows 2000, Windows XP Home Edition, Windows XP Professional, Windows Server 2003 family

Assembly: System.Drawing (in System.Drawing.dll)

HatchBrush Constructor

Initializes a new instance of the **HatchBrush** class with the specified **HatchStyle** enumeration and foreground color.

Overload List

Initializes a new instance of the **HatchBrush** class with the specified **HatchStyle** enumeration and foreground color.

[Visual Basic] **Public Sub New(HatchStyle, Color)**

[C#] **public HatchBrush(HatchStyle, Color);**

[C++] **public: HatchBrush(HatchStyle, Color);**

[JScript] **public function HatchBrush(HatchStyle, Color);**

Initializes a new instance of the **HatchBrush** class with the specified **HatchStyle** enumeration, foreground color, and background color.

[Visual Basic] **Public Sub New(HatchStyle, Color, Color)**

[C#] **public HatchBrush(HatchStyle, Color, Color);**

[C++] **public: HatchBrush(HatchStyle, Color, Color);**

[JScript] **public function HatchBrush(HatchStyle, Color, Color);**

HatchBrush Constructor (HatchStyle, Color)

Initializes a new instance of the **HatchBrush** class with the specified **HatchStyle** enumeration and foreground color.

```
[Visual Basic]
Public Sub New( _
   ByVal hatchstyle As HatchStyle, _
   ByVal foreColor As Color _
)
[C#]
public HatchBrush(
   HatchStyle hatchstyle,
   Color foreColor
);
[C++]
public: HatchBrush(
   HatchStyle hatchstyle,
   Color foreColor
);
[JScript]
public function HatchBrush(
   hatchstyle : HatchStyle,
   foreColor : Color
);
```

Parameters

hatchstyle
  The **HatchStyle** enumeration that represents the pattern drawn by this **HatchBrush**.

foreColor
  The **Color** structure that represents the color of lines drawn by this **HatchBrush**.

Remarks

The background color is initialized to black.

Requirements

Platforms: Windows 98, Windows NT 4.0, Windows Millennium Edition, Windows 2000, Windows XP Home Edition, Windows XP Professional, Windows Server 2003 family

HatchBrush Constructor (HatchStyle, Color, Color)

Initializes a new instance of the **HatchBrush** class with the specified **HatchStyle** enumeration, foreground color, and background color.

```
[Visual Basic]
Public Sub New( _
   ByVal hatchstyle As HatchStyle, _
   ByVal foreColor As Color, _
   ByVal backColor As Color _
)
[C#]
public HatchBrush(
   HatchStyle hatchstyle,
   Color foreColor,
   Color backColor
);
```

```
[C++]
public: HatchBrush(
   HatchStyle hatchstyle,
   Color foreColor,
   Color backColor
);
[JScript]
public function HatchBrush(
   hatchstyle : HatchStyle,
   foreColor : Color,
   backColor : Color
);
```

Parameters

hatchstyle
: The **HatchStyle** enumeration that represents the pattern drawn by this **HatchBrush**.

foreColor
: The **Color** structure that represents the color of lines drawn by this **HatchBrush**.

backColor
: The **Color** structure that represents the color of spaces between the lines drawn by this **HatchBrush**.

Requirements

Platforms: Windows 98, Windows NT 4.0, Windows Millennium Edition, Windows 2000, Windows XP Home Edition, Windows XP Professional, Windows Server 2003 family

HatchBrush.BackgroundColor Property

Gets the color of spaces between the hatch lines drawn by this **HatchBrush** object.

```
[Visual Basic]
Public ReadOnly Property BackgroundColor As Color
[C#]
public Color BackgroundColor {get;}
[C++]
public: __property Color get_BackgroundColor();
[JScript]
public function get BackgroundColor() : Color;
```

Property Value

A **Color** structure that represents the background color for this **HatchBrush**.

Requirements

Platforms: Windows 98, Windows NT 4.0, Windows Millennium Edition, Windows 2000, Windows XP Home Edition, Windows XP Professional, Windows Server 2003 family

HatchBrush.ForegroundColor Property

Gets the color of hatch lines drawn by this **HatchBrush** object.

```
[Visual Basic]
Public ReadOnly Property ForegroundColor As Color
[C#]
public Color ForegroundColor {get;}
[C++]
public: __property Color get_ForegroundColor();
[JScript]
public function get ForegroundColor() : Color;
```

Property Value

A **Color** structure that represents the foreground color for this **HatchBrush**.

Requirements

Platforms: Windows 98, Windows NT 4.0, Windows Millennium Edition, Windows 2000, Windows XP Home Edition, Windows XP Professional, Windows Server 2003 family

HatchBrush.HatchStyle Property

Gets the hatch style of this **HatchBrush** object.

```
[Visual Basic]
Public ReadOnly Property HatchStyle As HatchStyle
[C#]
public HatchStyle HatchStyle {get;}
[C++]
public: __property HatchStyle get_HatchStyle();
[JScript]
public function get HatchStyle() : HatchStyle;
```

Property Value

A **HatchStyle** enumeration that represents the pattern of this **HatchBrush**.

Requirements

Platforms: Windows 98, Windows NT 4.0, Windows Millennium Edition, Windows 2000, Windows XP Home Edition, Windows XP Professional, Windows Server 2003 family

HatchBrush.Clone Method

Creates an exact copy of this **HatchBrush** object.

```
[Visual Basic]
Overrides Public Function Clone() As Object Implements _
   ICloneable.Clone
[C#]
public override object Clone();
[C++]
public: Object* Clone();
[JScript]
public override function Clone() : Object;
```

Return Value

The **HatchBrush** this method creates, cast as an object.

Implements

ICloneable.Clone

Requirements

Platforms: Windows 98, Windows NT 4.0, Windows Millennium Edition, Windows 2000, Windows XP Home Edition, Windows XP Professional, Windows Server 2003 family

HatchStyle Enumeration

Specifies the different patterns available for **HatchBrush** objects.

```
[Visual Basic]
<Serializable>
Public Enum HatchStyle
[C#]
[Serializable]
public enum HatchStyle
[C++]
[Serializable]
__value public enum HatchStyle
[JScript]
public
   Serializable
enum HatchStyle
```

Members

Member name	Description
BackwardDiagonal	A pattern of lines on a diagonal from upper right to lower left.
Cross	Specifies horizontal and vertical lines that cross.
DarkDownwardDiagonal	Specifies diagonal lines that slant to the right from top points to bottom points, are spaced 50 percent closer together than, and are twice the width of **ForwardDiagonal**. This hatch pattern is not antialiased.
DarkHorizontal	Specifies horizontal lines that are spaced 50 percent closer together than Horizontal and are twice the width of **HatchStyleHorizontal**.
DarkUpwardDiagonal	Specifies diagonal lines that slant to the left from top points to bottom points, are spaced 50 percent closer together than **BackwardDiagonal**, and are twice its width, but the lines are not antialiased.
DarkVertical	Specifies vertical lines that are spaced 50 percent closer together than **Vertical** and are twice its width.
DashedDownward-Diagonal	Specifies dashed diagonal lines, that slant to the right from top points to bottom points.
DashedHorizontal	Specifies dashed horizontal lines.
DashedUpwardDiagonal	Specifies dashed diagonal lines, that slant to the left from top points to bottom points.
DashedVertical	Specifies dashed vertical lines.
DiagonalBrick	Specifies a hatch that has the appearance of layered bricks that slant to the left from top points to bottom points.
DiagonalCross	Specifies forward diagonal and backward diagonal lines that cross. The lines are antialiased.
Divot	Specifies a hatch that has the appearance of divots.
DottedDiamond	Specifies forward diagonal and backward diagonal lines, each of which is composed of dots, that cross.
DottedGrid	Specifies horizontal and vertical lines, each of which is composed of dots, that cross.
ForwardDiagonal	A pattern of lines on a diagonal from upper left to lower right.
Horizontal	A pattern of horizontal lines.
HorizontalBrick	Specifies a hatch that has the appearance of horizontally layered bricks.
LargeCheckerBoard	Specifies a hatch that has the appearance of a checkerboard with squares that are twice the size of **SmallCheckerBoard**.
LargeConfetti	Specifies a hatch that has the appearance of confetti, and is composed of larger pieces than **SmallConfetti**.
LargeGrid	Specifies the hatch style **Cross**.
LightDownwardDiagonal	
LightHorizontal	Specifies horizontal lines that are spaced 50 percent closer together than **Horizontal**.
LightUpwardDiagonal	Specifies diagonal lines that slant to the left from top points to bottom points and are spaced 50 percent closer together than **BackwardDiagonal**, but they are not antialiased.
LightVertical	Specifies vertical lines that are spaced 50 percent closer together than **Vertical**.
Max	Specifies hatch style **SolidDiamond**.
Min	Specifies hatch style **Horizonal**.
NarrowHorizontal	Specifies horizontal lines that are spaced 75 percent closer together than hatch style **Horizontal** (or 25 percent closer together than **LightHorizontal**).
NarrowVertical	Specifies vertical lines that are spaced 75 percent closer together than hatch style **Vertical** (or 25 percent closer together than **LightVertical**).
OutlinedDiamond	Specifies forward diagonal and backward diagonal lines that cross but are not antialiased.
Percent05	Specifies a 5-percent hatch. The ratio of foreground color to background color is 5:100.

Member name	Description
Percent10	Specifies a 10-percent hatch. The ratio of foreground color to background color is 10:100.
Percent20	Specifies a 20-percent hatch. The ratio of foreground color to background color is 20:100.
Percent25	Specifies a 25-percent hatch. The ratio of foreground color to background color is 25:100.
Percent30	Specifies a 30-percent hatch. The ratio of foreground color to background color is 30:100.
Percent40	Specifies a 40-percent hatch. The ratio of foreground color to background color is 40:100.
Percent50	Specifies a 50-percent hatch. The ratio of foreground color to background color is 50:100.
Percent60	Specifies a 60-percent hatch. The ratio of foreground color to background color is 60:100.
Percent70	Specifies a 70-percent hatch. The ratio of foreground color to background color is 70:100.
Percent75	Specifies a 75-percent hatch. The ratio of foreground color to background color is 75:100.
Percent80	Specifies a 80-percent hatch. The ratio of foreground color to background color is 80:100.
Percent90	Specifies a 90-percent hatch. The ratio of foreground color to background color is 90:100.
Plaid	Specifies a hatch that has the appearance of a plaid material.
Shingle	Specifies a hatch that has the appearance of diagonally-layered shingles that slant to the right from top points to bottom points.
SmallCheckerBoard	Specifies a hatch that has the appearance of a checkerboard.
SmallConfetti	Specifies a hatch that has the appearance of confetti.
SmallGrid	Specifies horizontal and vertical lines that cross and are spaced 50 percent closer together than hatch style **Cross**.
SolidDiamond	Specifies a hatch that has the appearance of a checkerboard placed diagonally.
Sphere	Specifies a hatch that has the appearance of spheres laid adjacent to one another.
Trellis	Specifies a hatch that has the appearance of a trellis.
Vertical	A pattern of vertical lines.
Wave	Specifies horizontal lines that are composed of tildes.
Weave	Specifies a hatch that has the appearance of a woven material.
WideDownwardDiagonal	Specifies diagonal lines that slant to the right from top points to bottom points, have the same spacing as hatch style **ForwardDiagonal**, and are triple its width, but are not antialiased.
WideUpwardDiagonal	Specifies diagonal lines that slant to the left from top points to bottom points, have the same spacing as hatch style **BackwardDiagonal**, and are triple its width, but are not antialiased.
ZigZag	Specifies horizontal lines that are composed of zigzags.

Requirements

Namespace: System.Drawing.Drawing2D

Platforms: Windows 98, Windows NT 4.0, Windows Millennium Edition, Windows 2000, Windows XP Home Edition, Windows XP Professional, Windows Server 2003 family

Assembly: System.Drawing (in System.Drawing.dll)

InterpolationMode Enumeration

Specifies how data is interpolated between endpoints.

[Visual Basic]
```
<Serializable>
Public Enum InterpolationMode
```
[C#]
```
[Serializable]
public enum InterpolationMode
```
[C++]
```
[Serializable]
__value public enum InterpolationMode
```
[JScript]
```
public
   Serializable
enum InterpolationMode
```

Members

Member name	Description
Bicubic	Specifies bicubic interpolation.
Bilinear	Specifies bilinear interpolation.
Default	Specifies default mode.
High	Specifies high quality interpolation.
HighQualityBicubic	Specifies high quality bicubic interpolation.
HighQualityBilinear	Specifies high quality bilinear interpolation.
Invalid	Equivalent to the Invalid element of the **QualityMode** enumeration.
Low	Specifies low quality interpolation.
NearestNeighbor	Specifies nearest-neighbor interpolation.

Requirements

Namespace: System.Drawing.Drawing2D

Platforms: Windows 98, Windows NT 4.0, Windows Millennium Edition, Windows 2000, Windows XP Home Edition, Windows XP Professional, Windows Server 2003 family

Assembly: System.Drawing (in System.Drawing.dll)

LinearGradientBrush Class

Encapsulates a **Brush** object with a linear gradient. This class cannot be inherited.

System.Object
  System.MarshalByRefObject
    System.Drawing.Brush
      System.Drawing.Drawing2D.LinearGradientBrush

[Visual Basic]
```
NotInheritable Public Class LinearGradientBrush
   Inherits Brush
```
[C#]
```
public sealed class LinearGradientBrush : Brush
```
[C++]
```
public __gc __sealed class LinearGradientBrush : public Brush
```
[JScript]
```
public class LinearGradientBrush extends Brush
```

Thread Safety

Any public static (**Shared** in Visual Basic) members of this type are safe for multithreaded operations. Any instance members are not guaranteed to be thread safe.

Remarks

This class encapsulates both two-color gradients and custom multicolor gradients.

All linear gradients are defined along a line specified either by the width of a rectangle or by two points.

By default, a two-color linear gradient is an even horizontal linear blend from the starting color to the ending color along the specified line. Customize the blend pattern using the **Blend** class, the **SetSigmaBellShape** methods, or the **SetBlendTriangularShape** methods. Customize the direction of the gradient by specifying the **LinearGradientMode** enumeration or the angle in the constructor.

Use the **InterpolationColors** property to create a multicolor gradient.

The **Transform** property specifies a local geometric transform applied to the gradient.

Requirements

Namespace: System.Drawing.Drawing2D

Platforms: Windows 98, Windows NT 4.0, Windows Millennium Edition, Windows 2000, Windows XP Home Edition, Windows XP Professional, Windows Server 2003 family

Assembly: System.Drawing (in System.Drawing.dll)

LinearGradientBrush Constructor

Initializes a new instance of the **LinearGradientBrush** class with the specified points and colors.

Overload List

Initializes a new instance of the **LinearGradientBrush** class with the specified points and colors.

[Visual Basic] **Public Sub New(Point, Point, Color, Color)**

[C#] **public LinearGradientBrush(Point, Point, Color, Color);**

[C++] **public: LinearGradientBrush(Point, Point, Color, Color);**

[JScript] **public function LinearGradientBrush(Point, Point, Color, Color);**

Initializes a new instance of the **LinearGradientBrush** class with the specified points and colors.

[Visual Basic] **Public Sub New(PointF, PointF, Color, Color)**

[C#] **public LinearGradientBrush(PointF, PointF, Color, Color);**

[C++] **public: LinearGradientBrush(PointF, PointF, Color, Color);**

[JScript] **public function LinearGradientBrush(PointF, PointF, Color, Color);**

Creates a new instance of the **LinearGradientBrush** class based on a rectangle, starting and ending colors, and orientation.

[Visual Basic] **Public Sub New(Rectangle, Color, Color, LinearGradientMode)**

[C#] **public LinearGradientBrush(Rectangle, Color, Color, LinearGradientMode);**

[C++] **public: LinearGradientBrush(Rectangle, Color, Color, LinearGradientMode);**

[JScript] **public function LinearGradientBrush(Rectangle, Color, Color, LinearGradientMode);**

Creates a new instance of the **LinearGradientBrush** class based on a rectangle, starting and ending colors, and an orientation angle.

[Visual Basic] **Public Sub New(Rectangle, Color, Color, Single)**

[C#] **public LinearGradientBrush(Rectangle, Color, Color, float);**

[C++] **public: LinearGradientBrush(Rectangle, Color, Color, float);**

[JScript] **public function LinearGradientBrush(Rectangle, Color, Color, float);**

Creates a new instance of the **LinearGradientBrush** based on a rectangle, starting and ending colors, and an orientation mode.

[Visual Basic] **Public Sub New(RectangleF, Color, Color, LinearGradientMode)**

[C#] **public LinearGradientBrush(RectangleF, Color, Color, LinearGradientMode);**

[C++] **public: LinearGradientBrush(RectangleF, Color, Color, LinearGradientMode);**

[JScript] **public function LinearGradientBrush(RectangleF, Color, Color, LinearGradientMode);**

Creates a new instance of the **LinearGradientBrush** class based on a rectangle, starting and ending colors, and an orientation angle.

[Visual Basic] **Public Sub New(RectangleF, Color, Color, Single)**

[C#] **public LinearGradientBrush(RectangleF, Color, Color, float);**

[C++] **public: LinearGradientBrush(RectangleF, Color, Color, float);**

[JScript] **public function LinearGradientBrush(RectangleF, Color, Color, float);**

Creates a new instance of the **LinearGradientBrush** class based on a rectangle, starting and ending colors, and an orientation angle.

[Visual Basic] **Public Sub New(Rectangle, Color, Color, Single, Boolean)**

[C#] **public LinearGradientBrush(Rectangle, Color, Color, float, bool);**

[C++] **public: LinearGradientBrush(Rectangle, Color, Color, float, bool);**

[JScript] **public function LinearGradientBrush(Rectangle, Color, Color, float, Boolean);**

Creates a new instance of the **LinearGradientBrush** class based on a rectangle, starting and ending colors, and an orientation angle.

[Visual Basic] **Public Sub New(RectangleF, Color, Color, Single, Boolean)**

[C#] **public LinearGradientBrush(RectangleF, Color, Color, float, bool);**

[C++] **public: LinearGradientBrush(RectangleF, Color, Color, float, bool);**

[JScript] **public function LinearGradientBrush(RectangleF, Color, Color, float, Boolean);**

LinearGradientBrush Constructor (Point, Point, Color, Color)

Initializes a new instance of the **LinearGradientBrush** class with the specified points and colors.

[Visual Basic]
```
Public Sub New( _
   ByVal point1 As Point, _
   ByVal point2 As Point, _
   ByVal color1 As Color, _
   ByVal color2 As Color _
)
```
[C#]
```
public LinearGradientBrush(
   Point point1,
   Point point2,
   Color color1,
   Color color2
);
```
[C++]
```
public: LinearGradientBrush(
   Point point1,
   Point point2,
   Color color1,
   Color color2
);
```
[JScript]
```
public function LinearGradientBrush(
   point1 : Point,
   point2 : Point,
   color1 : Color,
   color2 : Color
);
```

Parameters

point1

A **Point** structure that represents the starting point of the linear gradient.

point2

A **Point** structure that represents the endpoint of the linear gradient.

color1

A **Color** structure that represents the starting color of the linear gradient.

color2

A **Color** structure that represents the ending color of the linear gradient.

Requirements

Platforms: Windows 98, Windows NT 4.0, Windows Millennium Edition, Windows 2000, Windows XP Home Edition, Windows XP Professional, Windows Server 2003 family

LinearGradientBrush Constructor (PointF, PointF, Color, Color)

Initializes a new instance of the **LinearGradientBrush** class with the specified points and colors.

[Visual Basic]
```
Public Sub New( _
   ByVal point1 As PointF, _
   ByVal point2 As PointF, _
   ByVal color1 As Color, _
   ByVal color2 As Color _
)
```
[C#]
```
public LinearGradientBrush(
   PointF point1,
   PointF point2,
   Color color1,
   Color color2
);
```
[C++]
```
public: LinearGradientBrush(
   PointF point1,
   PointF point2,
   Color color1,
   Color color2
);
```
[JScript]
```
public function LinearGradientBrush(
   point1 : PointF,
   point2 : PointF,
   color1 : Color,
   color2 : Color
);
```

Parameters

point1

A **PointF** structure that represents the starting point of the linear gradient.

point2

A **PointF** structure that represents the endpoint of the linear gradient.

color1

A **Color** structure that represents the starting color of the linear gradient.

color2

A **Color** structure that represents the ending color of the linear gradient.

Requirements

Platforms: Windows 98, Windows NT 4.0, Windows Millennium Edition, Windows 2000, Windows XP Home Edition, Windows XP Professional, Windows Server 2003 family

LinearGradientBrush Constructor (Rectangle, Color, Color, LinearGradientMode)

Creates a new instance of the **LinearGradientBrush** class based on a rectangle, starting and ending colors, and orientation.

[Visual Basic]
```
Public Sub New( _
   ByVal rect As Rectangle, _
   ByVal color1 As Color, _
   ByVal color2 As Color, _
   ByVal linearGradientMode As LinearGradientMode _
)
```
[C#]
```
public LinearGradientBrush(
   Rectangle rect,
   Color color1,
   Color color2,
   LinearGradientMode linearGradientMode
);
```
[C++]
```
public: LinearGradientBrush(
   Rectangle rect,
   Color color1,
   Color color2,
   LinearGradientMode linearGradientMode
);
```
[JScript]
```
public function LinearGradientBrush(
   rect : Rectangle,
   color1 : Color,
   color2 : Color,
   linearGradientMode : LinearGradientMode
);
```

Parameters

rect
A **Rectangle** structure that specifies the bounds of the linear gradient.

color1
A **Color** structure that represents the starting color for the gradient.

color2
A **Color** structure that represents the ending color for the gradient.

linearGradientMode
A **LinearGradientMode** enumeration element that specifies the orientation of the gradient. The orientation determines the starting and ending points of the gradient. For example, LinearGradientMode.ForwardDiagonal specifies that the starting point is the upper-left corner of the rectangle and the ending point is the lower-right corner of the rectangle.

Requirements

Platforms: Windows 98, Windows NT 4.0, Windows Millennium Edition, Windows 2000, Windows XP Home Edition, Windows XP Professional, Windows Server 2003 family

LinearGradientBrush Constructor (Rectangle, Color, Color, Single)

Creates a new instance of the **LinearGradientBrush** class based on a rectangle, starting and ending colors, and an orientation angle.

[Visual Basic]
```
Public Sub New( _
   ByVal rect As Rectangle, _
   ByVal color1 As Color, _
   ByVal color2 As Color, _
   ByVal angle As Single _
)
```
[C#]
```
public LinearGradientBrush(
   Rectangle rect,
   Color color1,
   Color color2,
   float angle
);
```
[C++]
```
public: LinearGradientBrush(
   Rectangle rect,
   Color color1,
   Color color2,
   float angle
);
```
[JScript]
```
public function LinearGradientBrush(
   rect : Rectangle,
   color1 : Color,
   color2 : Color,
   angle : float
);
```

Parameters

rect
A **Rectangle** structure that specifies the bounds of the linear gradient.

color1
A **Color** structure that represents the starting color for the gradient.

color2
A **Color** structure that represents the ending color for the gradient.

angle
The angle, measured in degrees clockwise from the x-axis, of the gradient's orientation line.

Remarks

All points along any line perpendicular to the orientation line are the same color.

The starting line is perpendicular to the orientation line and passes through one of the corners of the rectangle. All points on the starting line are the starting color. Then ending line is perpendicular to the orientation line and passes through one of the corners of the rectangle. All points on the ending line are the ending color.

The angle of the orientation line determines which corners the starting and ending lines pass through. For example, if the angle is between 0 and 90 degrees, the starting line passes through the upper-left corner, and the ending line passes through the lower-right corner.

Requirements

Platforms: Windows 98, Windows NT 4.0, Windows Millennium Edition, Windows 2000, Windows XP Home Edition, Windows XP Professional, Windows Server 2003 family

LinearGradientBrush Constructor (RectangleF, Color, Color, LinearGradientMode)

Creates a new instance of the **LinearGradientBrush** based on a rectangle, starting and ending colors, and an orientation mode.

```
[Visual Basic]
Public Sub New( _
   ByVal rect As RectangleF, _
   ByVal color1 As Color, _
   ByVal color2 As Color, _
   ByVal linearGradientMode As LinearGradientMode _
)
[C#]
public LinearGradientBrush(
   RectangleF rect,
   Color color1,
   Color color2,
   LinearGradientMode linearGradientMode
);
[C++]
public: LinearGradientBrush(
   RectangleF rect,
   Color color1,
   Color color2,
   LinearGradientMode linearGradientMode
);
[JScript]
public function LinearGradientBrush(
   rect : RectangleF,
   color1 : Color,
   color2 : Color,
   linearGradientMode : LinearGradientMode
);
```

Parameters

rect
: A **RectangleF** structure that specifies the bounds of the linear gradient.

color1
: A **Color** structure that represents the starting color for the gradient.

color2
: A **Color** structure that represents the ending color for the gradient.

linearGradientMode
: A **LinearGradientMode** enumeration element that specifies the orientation of the gradient. The orientation determines the starting and ending points of the gradient. For example, LinearGradientMode.ForwardDiagonal specifies that the starting point is the upper-left corner of the rectangle and the ending point is the lower-right corner of the rectangle.

Requirements

Platforms: Windows 98, Windows NT 4.0, Windows Millennium Edition, Windows 2000, Windows XP Home Edition, Windows XP Professional, Windows Server 2003 family

LinearGradientBrush Constructor (RectangleF, Color, Color, Single)

Creates a new instance of the **LinearGradientBrush** class based on a rectangle, starting and ending colors, and an orientation angle.

```
[Visual Basic]
Public Sub New( _
   ByVal rect As RectangleF, _
   ByVal color1 As Color, _
   ByVal color2 As Color, _
   ByVal angle As Single _
)
[C#]
public LinearGradientBrush(
   RectangleF rect,
   Color color1,
   Color color2,
   float angle
);
[C++]
public: LinearGradientBrush(
   RectangleF rect,
   Color color1,
   Color color2,
   float angle
);
[JScript]
public function LinearGradientBrush(
   rect : RectangleF,
   color1 : Color,
   color2 : Color,
   angle : float
);
```

Parameters

rect
: A **RectangleF** structure that specifies the bounds of the linear gradient.

color1
: A **Color** structure that represents the starting color for the gradient.

color2
: A **Color** structure that represents the ending color for the gradient.

angle
: The angle, measured in degrees clockwise from the x-axis, of the gradient's orientation line.

Remarks

All points along any line perpendicular to the orientation line are the same color.

The starting line is perpendicular to the orientation line and passes through one of the corners of the rectangle. All points on the starting line are the starting color. Then ending line is perpendicular to the orientation line and passes through one of the corners of the rectangle. All points on the ending line are the ending color.

The angle of the orientation line determines which corners the starting and ending lines pass through. For example, if the angle is between 0 and 90 degrees, the starting line passes through the upper-left corner, and the ending line passes through the lower-right corner.

Requirements

Platforms: Windows 98, Windows NT 4.0,
Windows Millennium Edition, Windows 2000,
Windows XP Home Edition, Windows XP Professional,
Windows Server 2003 family

LinearGradientBrush Constructor (Rectangle, Color, Color, Single, Boolean)

Creates a new instance of the **LinearGradientBrush** class based on a rectangle, starting and ending colors, and an orientation angle.

[Visual Basic]
```
Public Sub New( _
   ByVal rect As Rectangle, _
   ByVal color1 As Color, _
   ByVal color2 As Color, _
   ByVal angle As Single, _
   ByVal isAngleScaleable As Boolean _
)
```
[C#]
```
public LinearGradientBrush(
   Rectangle rect,
   Color color1,
   Color color2,
   float angle,
   bool isAngleScaleable
);
```
[C++]
```
public: LinearGradientBrush(
   Rectangle rect,
   Color color1,
   Color color2,
   float angle,
   bool isAngleScaleable
);
```
[JScript]
```
public function LinearGradientBrush(
   rect : Rectangle,
   color1 : Color,
   color2 : Color,
   angle : float,
   isAngleScaleable : Boolean
);
```

Parameters

rect
A **Rectangle** structure that specifies the bounds of the linear gradient.

color1
A **Color** structure that represents the starting color for the gradient.

color2
A **Color** structure that represents the ending color for the gradient.

angle
The angle, measured in degrees clockwise from the x-axis, of the gradient's orientation line.

isAngleScaleable
Set to **true** to specify that the angle is affected by the transform associated with this **LinearGradientBrush**; otherwise, **false**.

Remarks

All points along any line perpendicular to the orientation line are the same color.

The starting line is perpendicular to the orientation line and passes through one of the corners of the rectangle. All points on the starting line are the starting color. Then ending line is perpendicular to the orientation line and passes through one of the corners of the rectangle. All points on the ending line are the ending color.

The angle of the orientation line determines which corners the starting and ending lines pass through. For example, if the angle is between 0 and 90 degrees, the starting line passes through the upper-left corner, and the ending line passes through the lower-right corner.

Requirements

Platforms: Windows 98, Windows NT 4.0,
Windows Millennium Edition, Windows 2000,
Windows XP Home Edition, Windows XP Professional,
Windows Server 2003 family

LinearGradientBrush Constructor (RectangleF, Color, Color, Single, Boolean)

Creates a new instance of the **LinearGradientBrush** class based on a rectangle, starting and ending colors, and an orientation angle.

[Visual Basic]
```
Public Sub New( _
   ByVal rect As RectangleF, _
   ByVal color1 As Color, _
   ByVal color2 As Color, _
   ByVal angle As Single, _
   ByVal isAngleScaleable As Boolean _
)
```
[C#]
```
public LinearGradientBrush(
   RectangleF rect,
   Color color1,
   Color color2,
   float angle,
   bool isAngleScaleable
);
```
[C++]
```
public: LinearGradientBrush(
   RectangleF rect,
   Color color1,
   Color color2,
   float angle,
   bool isAngleScaleable
);
```

```
[JScript]
public function LinearGradientBrush(
   rect : RectangleF,
   color1 : Color,
   color2 : Color,
   angle : float,
   isAngleScaleable : Boolean
);
```

Parameters

rect

A **RectangleF** structure that specifies the bounds of the linear gradient.

color1

A **Color** structure that represents the starting color for the gradient.

color2

A **Color** structure that represents the ending color for the gradient.

angle

The angle, measured in degrees clockwise from the x-axis, of the gradient's orientation line.

isAngleScaleable

Set to **true** to specify that the angle is affected by the transform associated with this **LinearGradientBrush**; otherwise, **false**.

Remarks

All points along any line perpendicular to the orientation line are the same color.

The starting line is perpendicular to the orientation line and passes through one of the corners of the rectangle. All points on the starting line are the starting color. Then ending line is perpendicular to the orientation line and passes through one of the corners of the rectangle. All points on the ending line are the ending color.

The angle of the orientation line determines which corners the starting and ending lines pass through. For example, if the angle is between 0 and 90 degrees, the starting line passes through the upper-left corner, and the ending line passes through the lower-right corner.

Requirements

Platforms: Windows 98, Windows NT 4.0, Windows Millennium Edition, Windows 2000, Windows XP Home Edition, Windows XP Professional, Windows Server 2003 family

LinearGradientBrush.Blend Property

Gets or sets a **Blend** object that specifies positions and factors that define a custom falloff for the gradient.

```
[Visual Basic]
Public Property Blend As Blend
[C#]
public Blend Blend {get; set;}
[C++]
public: __property Blend* get_Blend();
public: __property void set_Blend(Blend*);
[JScript]
public function get Blend() : Blend;
public function set Blend(Blend);
```

Property Value

A **Blend** object that represents a custom falloff for the gradient.

Remarks

A **Blend** object contains corresponding arrays of blend factors and positions. The blend factors specify the percentages of the starting color and ending color to use at the corresponding position. The positions are given as a percentage of distance along the gradient line.

Requirements

Platforms: Windows 98, Windows NT 4.0, Windows Millennium Edition, Windows 2000, Windows XP Home Edition, Windows XP Professional, Windows Server 2003 family

LinearGradientBrush.GammaCorrection Property

Gets or sets a value indicating whether gamma correction is enabled for this **LinearGradientBrush** object.

```
[Visual Basic]
Public Property GammaCorrection As Boolean
[C#]
public bool GammaCorrection {get; set;}
[C++]
public: __property bool get_GammaCorrection();
public: __property void set_GammaCorrection(bool);
[JScript]
public function get GammaCorrection() : Boolean;
public function set GammaCorrection(Boolean);
```

Property Value

The value is **true** if gamma correction is enabled for this **LinearGradientBrush**; otherwise, **false**.

Requirements

Platforms: Windows 98, Windows NT 4.0, Windows Millennium Edition, Windows 2000, Windows XP Home Edition, Windows XP Professional, Windows Server 2003 family

LinearGradientBrush.InterpolationColors Property

Gets or sets a **ColorBlend** object that defines a multicolor linear gradient.

```
[Visual Basic]
Public Property InterpolationColors As ColorBlend
[C#]
public ColorBlend InterpolationColors {get; set;}
[C++]
public: __property ColorBlend* get_InterpolationColors();
public: __property void set_InterpolationColors(ColorBlend*);
[JScript]
public function get InterpolationColors() : ColorBlend;
public function set InterpolationColors(ColorBlend);
```

Property Value

A **ColorBlend** object that defines a multicolor linear gradient.

Remarks

A **ColorBlend** object contains corresponding arrays of colors and positions. The positions are values from 0 through 1 that specify the percentage of the distance along the gradient line where the corresponding color is located.

Setting this property creates a multicolor gradient with one color at each position along the gradient line. Setting this property nullifies all previous color, position, and falloff settings for this **LinearGradientBrush** object.

Requirements

Platforms: Windows 98, Windows NT 4.0, Windows Millennium Edition, Windows 2000, Windows XP Home Edition, Windows XP Professional, Windows Server 2003 family

LinearGradientBrush.LinearColors Property

Gets or sets the starting and ending colors of the gradient.

```
[Visual Basic]
Public Property LinearColors As Color ()
[C#]
public Color[] LinearColors {get; set;}
[C++]
public: __property Color get_LinearColors();
public: __property void set_LinearColors(Color[]);
[JScript]
public function get LinearColors() : Color[];
public function set LinearColors(Color[]);
```

Property Value

An array of two **Color** structures that represents the starting and ending colors of the gradient.

Requirements

Platforms: Windows 98, Windows NT 4.0, Windows Millennium Edition, Windows 2000, Windows XP Home Edition, Windows XP Professional, Windows Server 2003 family

LinearGradientBrush.Rectangle Property

Gets a rectangular region that defines the starting and ending points of the gradient.

```
[Visual Basic]
Public ReadOnly Property Rectangle As RectangleF
[C#]
public RectangleF Rectangle {get;}
[C++]
public: __property RectangleF get_Rectangle();
[JScript]
public function get Rectangle() : RectangleF;
```

Property Value

A **RectangleF** structure that specifies the starting and ending points of the gradient.

Remarks

The left side of the rectangle specifies the starting point of the linear gradient, and the right side of the rectangle specifies the endpoint.

Requirements

Platforms: Windows 98, Windows NT 4.0, Windows Millennium Edition, Windows 2000, Windows XP Home Edition, Windows XP Professional, Windows Server 2003 family

LinearGradientBrush.Transform Property

Gets or sets a **Matrix** object that defines a local geometric transform for this **LinearGradientBrush** object.

```
[Visual Basic]
Public Property Transform As Matrix
[C#]
public Matrix Transform {get; set;}
[C++]
public: __property Matrix* get_Transform();
public: __property void set_Transform(Matrix*);
[JScript]
public function get Transform() : Matrix;
public function set Transform(Matrix);
```

Property Value

A **Matrix** object that defines a geometric transform that applies only to fills drawn with this **LinearGradientBrush** object.

Remarks

A geometric transform can be used to translate, scale, rotate, or skew the gradient fill.

Requirements

Platforms: Windows 98, Windows NT 4.0, Windows Millennium Edition, Windows 2000, Windows XP Home Edition, Windows XP Professional, Windows Server 2003 family

LinearGradientBrush.WrapMode Property

Gets or sets a **WrapMode** enumeration that indicates the wrap mode for this **LinearGradientBrush**.

```
[Visual Basic]
Public Property WrapMode As WrapMode
[C#]
public WrapMode WrapMode {get; set;}
[C++]
public: __property WrapMode get_WrapMode();
public: __property void set_WrapMode(WrapMode);
[JScript]
public function get WrapMode() : WrapMode;
public function set WrapMode(WrapMode);
```

Property Value

A **WrapMode** enumeration that specifies how fills drawn with this **LinearGradientBrush** are tiled.

Requirements

Platforms: Windows 98, Windows NT 4.0, Windows Millennium Edition, Windows 2000, Windows XP Home Edition, Windows XP Professional, Windows Server 2003 family

LinearGradientBrush.Clone Method

Creates an exact copy of this **LinearGradientBrush** object.

[Visual Basic]
```
Overrides Public Function Clone() As Object Implements _
   ICloneable.Clone
```
[C#]
```
public override object Clone();
```
[C++]
```
public: Object* Clone();
```
[JScript]
```
public override function Clone() : Object;
```

Return Value

The **LinearGradientBrush** this method creates, cast as an object.

Implements

ICloneable.Clone

Example

[Visual Basic, C#] The following example is designed for use with Windows Forms, and it requires **PaintEventArgs** *e*, an **OnPaint** event object. The code performs the following actions:

- Creates a new **LinearGradientBrush** object.
- Draws an ellipse to the screen using this brush.
- Clones the **LinearGradientBrush** object (*clonedLGBrush*).
- Draws an ellipse to the screen directly below the first ellipse, using the cloned brush.

[Visual Basic]
```
Public Sub CloneExample(e As PaintEventArgs)
' Create a LinearGradientBrush.
Dim x As Integer = 20
Dim y As Integer = 20
Dim h As Integer = 100
Dim w As Integer = 200
Dim myRect As New Rectangle(x, y, w, h)
Dim myLGBrush As New LinearGradientBrush(myRect, Color.Blue, _
Color.Aquamarine, 45F, True)
' Draw an ellipse to the screen using the LinearGradientBrush.
e.Graphics.FillEllipse(myLGBrush, x, y, w, h)
' Clone the LinearGradientBrush.
Dim clonedLGBrush As LinearGradientBrush = _
CType(myLGBrush.Clone(), LinearGradientBrush)
' Justify the left edge of the gradient with the left edge of the
' ellipse.
clonedLGBrush.TranslateTransform(- 100F, 0F)
' Draw a second ellipse to the screen using the cloned HBrush.
y = 150
e.Graphics.FillEllipse(clonedLGBrush, x, y, w, h)
End Sub
```

[C#]
```
private void CloneExample(PaintEventArgs e)
{
// Create a LinearGradientBrush.
int x=20, y=20, h=100, w=200;
Rectangle myRect = new Rectangle(x, y, w, h);
LinearGradientBrush myLGBrush = new LinearGradientBrush(
myRect,
Color.Blue,
Color.Aquamarine,
45.0f,
true);
// Draw an ellipse to the screen using the LinearGradientBrush.
e.Graphics.FillEllipse(myLGBrush, x, y, w, h);
// Clone the LinearGradientBrush.
LinearGradientBrush clonedLGBrush =
(LinearGradientBrush)myLGBrush.Clone();
// Justify the left edge of the gradient with the
// left edge of the ellipse.
clonedLGBrush.TranslateTransform(-100.0f, 0.0f);
// Draw a second ellipse to the screen using the cloned HBrush.
y=150;
e.Graphics.FillEllipse(clonedLGBrush, x, y, w, h);
}
```

Requirements

Platforms: Windows 98, Windows NT 4.0, Windows Millennium Edition, Windows 2000, Windows XP Home Edition, Windows XP Professional, Windows Server 2003 family

LinearGradientBrush.MultiplyTransform Method

Multiplies the **Matrix** object that represents the local geometric transform of this **LinearGradientBrush** by the specified **Matrix** by prepending the specified **Matrix**.

Overload List

Multiplies the **Matrix** object that represents the local geometric transform of this **LinearGradientBrush** object by the specified **Matrix** by prepending the specified **Matrix**.

[Visual Basic] **Overloads Public Sub MultiplyTransform(Matrix)**

[C#] **public void MultiplyTransform(Matrix);**

[C++] **public: void MultiplyTransform(Matrix*);**

[JScript] **public function MultiplyTransform(Matrix);**

Multiplies the **Matrix** object that represents the local geometric transform of this **LinearGradientBrush** object by the specified **Matrix** in the specified order.

[Visual Basic] **Overloads Public Sub Multiply-Transform(Matrix, MatrixOrder)**

[C#] **public void MultiplyTransform(Matrix, MatrixOrder);**

[C++] **public: void MultiplyTransform(Matrix*, MatrixOrder);**

[JScript] **public function MultiplyTransform(Matrix, MatrixOrder);**

Example

[Visual Basic, C#] The following example is designed for use with Windows Forms, and it requires **PaintEventArgs** *e*, an **OnPaint** event object. The code performs the following actions:

- Creates a new **LinearGradientBrush** object.
- Draws an ellipse to the screen using this brush.
- Calls the **MultiplyTransform** method, to transform the **LinearGradientBrush** object.
- Draws an ellipse to the screen directly below the first ellipse, using the transformed brush.

[Visual Basic, C#] Notice that the lower ellipse is stretched in the horizontal direction, and that the gradient is stretched to match the new shape.

> [Visual Basic, C#] **Note** This example shows how to use one of the overloaded versions of **MultiplyTransform**. For other examples that might be available, see the individual overload topics.

[Visual Basic]
```
Public Sub MultiplyTransformExample(e As PaintEventArgs)
' Create a LinearGradientBrush.
Dim myRect As New Rectangle(20, 20, 200, 100)
Dim myLGBrush As New LinearGradientBrush(myRect, Color.Blue, _
Color.Red, 0F, True)
' Draw an ellipse to the screen using the LinearGradientBrush.
e.Graphics.FillEllipse(myLGBrush, myRect)
' Transform the LinearGradientBrush.
Dim transformArray As Point() = {New Point(20, 150), _
New Point(400, 150), New Point(20, 200)}
Dim myMatrix As New Matrix(myRect, transformArray)
myLGBrush.MultiplyTransform(myMatrix, MatrixOrder.Prepend)
' Draw a second ellipse to the screen using the transformed brush.
e.Graphics.FillEllipse(myLGBrush, 20, 150, 380, 50)
End Sub
```

[C#]
```
private void MultiplyTransformExample(PaintEventArgs e)
{
// Create a LinearGradientBrush.
Rectangle myRect = new Rectangle(20, 20, 200, 100);
LinearGradientBrush myLGBrush = new LinearGradientBrush(
myRect,
Color.Blue,
Color.Red,
0.0f,
true);
// Draw an ellipse to the screen using the LinearGradientBrush.
e.Graphics.FillEllipse(myLGBrush, myRect);
// Transform the LinearGradientBrush.
Point[] transformArray =
{
new Point(20, 150),
new Point(400,150),
new Point(20, 200)
};
Matrix myMatrix = new Matrix(myRect, transformArray);
myLGBrush.MultiplyTransform(
myMatrix,
MatrixOrder.Prepend);
// Draw a second ellipse to the screen using
// the transformed brush.
e.Graphics.FillEllipse(myLGBrush, 20, 150, 380, 50);
}
```

LinearGradientBrush.MultiplyTransform Method (Matrix)

Multiplies the **Matrix** object that represents the local geometric transform of this **LinearGradientBrush** object by the specified **Matrix** by prepending the specified **Matrix**.

[Visual Basic]
```
Overloads Public Sub MultiplyTransform( _
   ByVal matrix As Matrix _
)
```
[C#]
```
public void MultiplyTransform(
   Matrix matrix
);
```
[C++]
```
public: void MultiplyTransform(
   Matrix* matrix
);
```
[JScript]
```
public function MultiplyTransform(
   matrix : Matrix
);
```

Parameters

matrix

The **Matrix** object by which to multiply the geometric transform.

Example

For an example, see **LinearGradientBrush.MultiplyTransform Method (Matrix, MatrixOrder)**.

Requirements

Platforms: Windows 98, Windows NT 4.0, Windows Millennium Edition, Windows 2000, Windows XP Home Edition, Windows XP Professional, Windows Server 2003 family

LinearGradientBrush.MultiplyTransform Method (Matrix, MatrixOrder)

Multiplies the **Matrix** object that represents the local geometric transform of this **LinearGradientBrush** object by the specified **Matrix** in the specified order.

[Visual Basic]
```
Overloads Public Sub MultiplyTransform( _
   ByVal matrix As Matrix, _
   ByVal order As MatrixOrder _
)
```
[C#]
```
public void MultiplyTransform(
   Matrix matrix,
   MatrixOrder order
);
```
[C++]
```
public: void MultiplyTransform(
   Matrix* matrix,
   MatrixOrder order
);
```
[JScript]
```
public function MultiplyTransform(
   matrix : Matrix,
   order : MatrixOrder
);
```

Parameters

matrix

The **Matrix** object by which to multiply the geometric transform.

order

A **MatrixOrder** enumeration that specifies in which order to multiply the two matrices.

Example

[Visual Basic, C#] The following example is designed for use with Windows Forms, and it requires **PaintEventArgs** *e*, an **OnPaint** event object. The code performs the following actions:

- Creates a new **LinearGradientBrush** object.
- Draws an ellipse to the screen using this brush.
- Calls the **MultiplyTransform** method, to transform the **LinearGradientBrush** object.
- Draws an ellipse to the screen directly below the first ellipse, using the transformed brush.

[Visual Basic, C#] Notice that the lower ellipse is stretched in the horizontal direction, and that the gradient is stretched to match the new shape.

[Visual Basic]
```
Public Sub MultiplyTransformExample(e As PaintEventArgs)
' Create a LinearGradientBrush.
Dim myRect As New Rectangle(20, 20, 200, 100)
Dim myLGBrush As New LinearGradientBrush(myRect, Color.Blue, _
Color.Red, 0F, True)
' Draw an ellipse to the screen using the LinearGradientBrush.
e.Graphics.FillEllipse(myLGBrush, myRect)
' Transform the LinearGradientBrush.
Dim transformArray As Point() = {New Point(20, 150), _
New Point(400, 150), New Point(20, 200)}
Dim myMatrix As New Matrix(myRect, transformArray)
myLGBrush.MultiplyTransform(myMatrix, MatrixOrder.Prepend)
' Draw a second ellipse to the screen using the transformed brush.
e.Graphics.FillEllipse(myLGBrush, 20, 150, 380, 50)
End Sub
```

[C#]
```
private void MultiplyTransformExample(PaintEventArgs e)
{
// Create a LinearGradientBrush.
Rectangle myRect = new Rectangle(20, 20, 200, 100);
LinearGradientBrush myLGBrush = new LinearGradientBrush(
myRect,
Color.Blue,
Color.Red,
0.0f,
true);
// Draw an ellipse to the screen using the LinearGradientBrush.
e.Graphics.FillEllipse(myLGBrush, myRect);
// Transform the LinearGradientBrush.
Point[] transformArray =
{
new Point(20, 150),
new Point(400,150),
new Point(20, 200)
};
Matrix myMatrix = new Matrix(myRect, transformArray);
myLGBrush.MultiplyTransform(
myMatrix,
MatrixOrder.Prepend);
// Draw a second ellipse to the screen using
// the transformed brush.
e.Graphics.FillEllipse(myLGBrush, 20, 150, 380, 50);
}
```

Requirements

Platforms: Windows 98, Windows NT 4.0, Windows Millennium Edition, Windows 2000, Windows XP Home Edition, Windows XP Professional, Windows Server 2003 family

LinearGradientBrush.ResetTransform Method

Resets the **Transform** property to identity.

[Visual Basic]
```
Public Sub ResetTransform()
```
[C#]
```
public void ResetTransform();
```
[C++]
```
public: void ResetTransform();
```
[JScript]
```
public function ResetTransform();
```

Example

[Visual Basic, C#] The following example is designed for use with Windows Forms, and it requires **PaintEventArgs** *e*, an **OnPaint** event object. The code performs the following actions:

- Creates a new **LinearGradientBrush** object.
- Draws an ellipse to the screen using this brush.
- Calls the **MultiplyTransform** method to transform the **LinearGradientBrush** object.
- Draws an ellipse to the screen directly below the first ellipse, using the transformed brush.
- Resets the transform.
- Draws a third ellipse to the screen below the first two.

[Visual Basic, C#] Notice that the lowest ellipse is drawn the same size as the first, and that, due to the call to the **ResetTransform** method, the gradient has been reduced to match.

[Visual Basic]
```
Public Sub ResetTransformExample(e As PaintEventArgs)
' Create a LinearGradientBrush.
Dim myRect As New Rectangle(20, 20, 200, 100)
Dim myLGBrush As New LinearGradientBrush(myRect, Color.Blue, _
Color.Red, 0F, True)
' Draw an ellipse to the screen using the LinearGradientBrush.
e.Graphics.FillEllipse(myLGBrush, myRect)
' Transform the LinearGradientBrush.
Dim transformArray As Point() = {New Point(20, 150), _
New Point(400, 150), New Point(20, 200)}
Dim myMatrix As New Matrix(myRect, transformArray)
myLGBrush.MultiplyTransform(myMatrix, MatrixOrder.Prepend)
' Draw a second ellipse to the screen using the transformed brush.
e.Graphics.FillEllipse(myLGBrush, 20, 150, 380, 50)
' Reset the brush transform.
myLGBrush.ResetTransform()
' Draw a third ellipse to the screen using the reset brush.
e.Graphics.FillEllipse(myLGBrush, 20, 250, 200, 100)
End Sub
```

[C#]
```
private void ResetTransformExample(PaintEventArgs e)
{
// Create a LinearGradientBrush.
Rectangle myRect = new Rectangle(20, 20, 200, 100);
LinearGradientBrush myLGBrush = new LinearGradientBrush(
myRect,
Color.Blue,
Color.Red,
0.0f,
true);
// Draw an ellipse to the screen using the LinearGradientBrush.
e.Graphics.FillEllipse(myLGBrush, myRect);
// Transform the LinearGradientBrush.
Point[] transformArray =
{
new Point(20, 150),
new Point(400,150),
new Point(20, 200)
};
Matrix myMatrix = new Matrix(myRect, transformArray);
myLGBrush.MultiplyTransform(
myMatrix,
MatrixOrder.Prepend);
// Draw a second ellipse to the screen
// using the transformed brush.
e.Graphics.FillEllipse(myLGBrush, 20, 150, 380, 50);
// Reset the brush transform.
myLGBrush.ResetTransform();
// Draw a third ellipse to the screen using the reset brush.
e.Graphics.FillEllipse(myLGBrush, 20, 250, 200, 100);
}
```

Requirements

Platforms: Windows 98, Windows NT 4.0, Windows Millennium Edition, Windows 2000, Windows XP Home Edition, Windows XP Professional, Windows Server 2003 family

LinearGradientBrush.RotateTransform Method

Rotates the local geometric transform by the specified amount. This method prepends the rotation to the transform.

Overload List

Rotates the local geometric transform by the specified amount. This method prepends the rotation to the transform.

[Visual Basic] **Overloads Public Sub RotateTransform(Single)**

[C#] **public void RotateTransform(float);**

[C++] **public: void RotateTransform(float);**

[JScript] **public function RotateTransform(float);**

Rotates the local geometric transform by the specified amount in the specified order.

[Visual Basic] **Overloads Public Sub RotateTransform(Single, MatrixOrder)**

[C#] **public void RotateTransform(float, MatrixOrder);**

[C++] **public: void RotateTransform(float, MatrixOrder);**

[JScript] **public function RotateTransform(float, MatrixOrder);**

Example

[Visual Basic, C#] The following example is designed for use with Windows Forms, and it requires **PaintEventArgs** *e*, an **OnPaint** event object. The code

- Creates a new **LinearGradientBrush** object.
- Draws an ellipse to the screen using this brush.
- Rotates the **LinearGradientBrush** object 45 degrees by calling the **RotateTransform** method.
- Draws an ellipse to the screen directly below the first ellipse, using the rotated brush.

[Visual Basic, C#] Notice that the gradient of the lower ellipse is at a 45 degree angle to the x-axis of the top ellipse. Also notice that a call to the **TranslateTransform** method is used to justify the left edge of the gradient fill with the left edge of the lower ellipse.

> [Visual Basic, C#] **Note** This example shows how to use one of the overloaded versions of **RotateTransform**. For other examples that might be available, see the individual overload topics.

[Visual Basic]
```
Public Sub RotateTransformExample(e As PaintEventArgs)
' Create a LinearGradientBrush.
Dim myRect As New Rectangle(20, 20, 200, 100)
Dim myLGBrush As New LinearGradientBrush(myRect, Color.Blue, _
Color.Red, 0F, True)
' Draw an ellipse to the screen using the LinearGradientBrush.
e.Graphics.FillEllipse(myLGBrush, myRect)
' Rotate the LinearGradientBrush.
myLGBrush.RotateTransform(45F, MatrixOrder.Prepend)
' Rejustify the brush to start at the left edge of the ellipse.
myLGBrush.TranslateTransform(- 100F, 0F)
' Draw a second ellipse to the screen using the transformed brush.
e.Graphics.FillEllipse(myLGBrush, 20, 150, 200, 100)
End Sub
```

[C#]
```
private void RotateTransformExample(PaintEventArgs e)
{
// Create a LinearGradientBrush.
Rectangle myRect = new Rectangle(20, 20, 200, 100);
LinearGradientBrush myLGBrush = new LinearGradientBrush(
myRect,
Color.Blue,
Color.Red,
0.0f,
true);
// Draw an ellipse to the screen using the LinearGradientBrush.
e.Graphics.FillEllipse(myLGBrush, myRect);
// Rotate the LinearGradientBrush.
myLGBrush.RotateTransform(
45.0f,
MatrixOrder.Prepend);
// Rejustify the brush to start at the left edge of the ellipse.
myLGBrush.TranslateTransform(-100.0f, 0.0f);
// Draw a second ellipse to the screen using
// the transformed brush.
e.Graphics.FillEllipse(myLGBrush, 20, 150, 200, 100);
}
```

LinearGradientBrush.RotateTransform Method (Single)

Rotates the local geometric transform by the specified amount. This method prepends the rotation to the transform.

[Visual Basic]
```
Overloads Public Sub RotateTransform( _
   ByVal angle As Single _
)
```
[C#]
```
public void RotateTransform(
   float angle
);
```
[C++]
```
public: void RotateTransform(
   float angle
);
```
[JScript]
```
public function RotateTransform(
   angle : float
);
```

Parameters

angle
The angle of rotation.

Example

For an example, see **LinearGradientBrush.RotateTransform Method (Single, MatrixOrder)**.

Requirements

Platforms: Windows 98, Windows NT 4.0, Windows Millennium Edition, Windows 2000, Windows XP Home Edition, Windows XP Professional, Windows Server 2003 family

LinearGradientBrush.RotateTransform Method (Single, MatrixOrder)

Rotates the local geometric transform by the specified amount in the specified order.

[Visual Basic]
```
Overloads Public Sub RotateTransform( _
   ByVal angle As Single, _
   ByVal order As MatrixOrder _
)
```
[C#]
```
public void RotateTransform(
   float angle,
   MatrixOrder order
);
```
[C++]
```
public: void RotateTransform(
   float angle,
   MatrixOrder order
);
```
[JScript]
```
public function RotateTransform(
   angle : float,
   order : MatrixOrder
);
```

Parameters

angle
The angle of rotation.

order
A **MatrixOrder** enumeration that specifies whether to append or prepend the rotation matrix.

Example

[Visual Basic, C#] The following example is designed for use with Windows Forms, and it requires **PaintEventArgs** *e*, an **OnPaint** event object. The code

- Creates a new **LinearGradientBrush** object.
- Draws an ellipse to the screen using this brush.
- Rotates the **LinearGradientBrush** object 45 degrees by calling the **RotateTransform** method.
- Draws an ellipse to the screen directly below the first ellipse, using the rotated brush.

[Visual Basic, C#] Notice that the gradient of the lower ellipse is at a 45 degree angle to the x-axis of the top ellipse. Also notice that a call to the **TranslateTransform** method is used to justify the left edge of the gradient fill with the left edge of the lower ellipse.

[Visual Basic]
```
Public Sub RotateTransformExample(e As PaintEventArgs)
' Create a LinearGradientBrush.
Dim myRect As New Rectangle(20, 20, 200, 100)
Dim myLGBrush As New LinearGradientBrush(myRect, Color.Blue, _
Color.Red, 0F, True)
' Draw an ellipse to the screen using the LinearGradientBrush.
e.Graphics.FillEllipse(myLGBrush, myRect)
' Rotate the LinearGradientBrush.
myLGBrush.RotateTransform(45F, MatrixOrder.Prepend)
' Rejustify the brush to start at the left edge of the ellipse.
myLGBrush.TranslateTransform(- 100F, 0F)
' Draw a second ellipse to the screen using the transformed brush.
e.Graphics.FillEllipse(myLGBrush, 20, 150, 200, 100)
End Sub
```

[C#]
```
private void RotateTransformExample(PaintEventArgs e)
{
// Create a LinearGradientBrush.
Rectangle myRect = new Rectangle(20, 20, 200, 100);
LinearGradientBrush myLGBrush = new LinearGradientBrush(
myRect,
Color.Blue,
Color.Red,
0.0f,
true);
// Draw an ellipse to the screen using the LinearGradientBrush.
e.Graphics.FillEllipse(myLGBrush, myRect);
// Rotate the LinearGradientBrush.
myLGBrush.RotateTransform(
45.0f,
MatrixOrder.Prepend);
// Rejustify the brush to start at the left edge of the ellipse.
myLGBrush.TranslateTransform(-100.0f, 0.0f);
// Draw a second ellipse to the screen using
// the transformed brush.
e.Graphics.FillEllipse(myLGBrush, 20, 150, 200, 100);
}
```

Requirements

Platforms: Windows 98, Windows NT 4.0, Windows Millennium Edition, Windows 2000, Windows XP Home Edition, Windows XP Professional, Windows Server 2003 family

LinearGradientBrush.ScaleTransform Method

Scales the local geometric transform by the specified amounts. This method prepends the scaling matrix to the transform.

Overload List

Scales the local geometric transform by the specified amounts. This method prepends the scaling matrix to the transform.

[Visual Basic] **Overloads Public Sub ScaleTransform(Single, Single)**

[C#] **public void ScaleTransform(float, float);**

[C++] **public: void ScaleTransform(float, float);**

[JScript] **public function ScaleTransform(float, float);**

Scales the local geometric transform by the specified amounts in the specified order.

[Visual Basic] **Overloads Public Sub ScaleTransform(Single, Single, MatrixOrder)**

[C#] **public void ScaleTransform(float, float, MatrixOrder);**

[C++] **public: void ScaleTransform(float, float, MatrixOrder);**

[JScript] **public function ScaleTransform(float, float, MatrixOrder);**

Example

[Visual Basic, C#] The following example is designed for use with Windows Forms, and it requires **PaintEventArgs** *e*, an **OnPaint** event object. The code performs the following actions:

- Creates a new **LinearGradientBrush** object.
- Draw an ellipse to the screen using this brush.
- Scales the **LinearGradientBrush** object by a factor of two in the x-axis.
- Draws an ellipse to the screen directly below the first ellipse, using the scaled brush.

[Visual Basic, C#] Notice that the gradient of the lower ellipse is stretched by a factor of two. Also notice that a call to the **TranslateTransform** method is used to justify the left edge of the gradient fill with the left edge of ellipse.

> [Visual Basic, C#] **Note** This example shows how to use one of the overloaded versions of **ScaleTransform**. For other examples that might be available, see the individual overload topics.

[Visual Basic]
```
Public Sub ScaleTransformExample(e As PaintEventArgs)
' Create a LinearGradientBrush.
Dim myRect As New Rectangle(20, 20, 200, 100)
Dim myLGBrush As New LinearGradientBrush(myRect, Color.Blue, _
Color.Red, 0F, True)
' Draw an ellipse to the screen using the LinearGradientBrush.
e.Graphics.FillEllipse(myLGBrush, myRect)
' Scale the LinearGradientBrush.
myLGBrush.ScaleTransform(2F, 1F, MatrixOrder.Prepend)
' Rejustify the brush to start at the left edge of the ellipse.
myLGBrush.TranslateTransform(- 20F, 0F)
' Draw a second ellipse to the screen using the transformed brush.
e.Graphics.FillEllipse(myLGBrush, 20, 150, 200, 100)
End Sub
```

[C#]
```
private void ScaleTransformExample(PaintEventArgs e)
{
// Create a LinearGradientBrush.
Rectangle myRect = new Rectangle(20, 20, 200, 100);
LinearGradientBrush myLGBrush = new LinearGradientBrush(
myRect,
Color.Blue,
Color.Red,
0.0f,
true);
// Draw an ellipse to the screen using the LinearGradientBrush.
e.Graphics.FillEllipse(myLGBrush, myRect);
// Scale the LinearGradientBrush.
myLGBrush.ScaleTransform(
2.0f,
1.0f,
MatrixOrder.Prepend);
// Rejustify the brush to start at the left edge of the ellipse.
myLGBrush.TranslateTransform(-20.0f, 0.0f);
// Draw a second ellipse to the screen using
// the transformed brush.
e.Graphics.FillEllipse(myLGBrush, 20, 150, 200, 100);
}
```

LinearGradientBrush.ScaleTransform Method (Single, Single)

Scales the local geometric transform by the specified amounts. This method prepends the scaling matrix to the transform.

[Visual Basic]
```
Overloads Public Sub ScaleTransform( _
   ByVal sx As Single, _
   ByVal sy As Single _
)
```
[C#]
```
public void ScaleTransform(
   float sx,
   float sy
);
```
[C++]
```
public: void ScaleTransform(
   float sx,
   float sy
);
```
[JScript]
```
public function ScaleTransform(
   sx : float,
   sy : float
);
```

Parameters

sx
: The amount by which to scale the transform in the x-axis direction.

sy
: The amount by which to scale the transform in the y-axis direction.

Example

For an example, see **LinearGradientBrush.ScaleTransform Method (Single, Single, MatrixOrder)**.

Requirements

Platforms: Windows 98, Windows NT 4.0, Windows Millennium Edition, Windows 2000, Windows XP Home Edition, Windows XP Professional, Windows Server 2003 family

LinearGradientBrush.ScaleTransform Method (Single, Single, MatrixOrder)

Scales the local geometric transform by the specified amounts in the specified order.

[Visual Basic]
```
Overloads Public Sub ScaleTransform( _
   ByVal sx As Single, _
   ByVal sy As Single, _
   ByVal order As MatrixOrder _
)
```
[C#]
```
public void ScaleTransform(
   float sx,
   float sy,
   MatrixOrder order
);
```
[C++]
```
public: void ScaleTransform(
   float sx,
   float sy,
   MatrixOrder order
);
```
[JScript]
```
public function ScaleTransform(
   sx : float,
   sy : float,
   order : MatrixOrder
);
```

Parameters

sx
: The amount by which to scale the transform in the x-axis direction.

sy
: The amount by which to scale the transform in the y-axis direction.

order
: A **MatrixOrder** enumeration that specifies whether to append or prepend the scaling matrix.

Example

[Visual Basic, C#] The following example is designed for use with Windows Forms, and it requires **PaintEventArgs** *e*, an **OnPaint** event object. The code performs the following actions:

- Creates a new **LinearGradientBrush** object.
- Draw an ellipse to the screen using this brush.
- Scales the **LinearGradientBrush** object by a factor of two in the x-axis.
- Draws an ellipse to the screen directly below the first ellipse, using the scaled brush.

[Visual Basic, C#] Notice that the gradient of the lower ellipse is stretched by a factor of two. Also notice that a call to the **TranslateTransform** method is used to justify the left edge of the gradient fill with the left edge of ellipse.

[Visual Basic]

```
Public Sub ScaleTransformExample(e As PaintEventArgs)
' Create a LinearGradientBrush.
Dim myRect As New Rectangle(20, 20, 200, 100)
Dim myLGBrush As New LinearGradientBrush(myRect, Color.Blue, _
Color.Red, 0F, True)
' Draw an ellipse to the screen using the LinearGradientBrush.
e.Graphics.FillEllipse(myLGBrush, myRect)
' Scale the LinearGradientBrush.
myLGBrush.ScaleTransform(2F, 1F, MatrixOrder.Prepend)
' Rejustify the brush to start at the left edge of the ellipse.
myLGBrush.TranslateTransform(- 20F, 0F)
' Draw a second ellipse to the screen using the transformed brush.
e.Graphics.FillEllipse(myLGBrush, 20, 150, 200, 100)
End Sub
```

[C#]

```
private void ScaleTransformExample(PaintEventArgs e)
{
// Create a LinearGradientBrush.
Rectangle myRect = new Rectangle(20, 20, 200, 100);
LinearGradientBrush myLGBrush = new LinearGradientBrush(
myRect,
Color.Blue,
Color.Red,
0.0f,
true);
// Draw an ellipse to the screen using the LinearGradientBrush.
e.Graphics.FillEllipse(myLGBrush, myRect);
// Scale the LinearGradientBrush.
myLGBrush.ScaleTransform(
2.0f,
1.0f,
MatrixOrder.Prepend);
// Rejustify the brush to start at the left edge of the ellipse.
myLGBrush.TranslateTransform(-20.0f, 0.0f);
// Draw a second ellipse to the screen using
// the transformed brush.
e.Graphics.FillEllipse(myLGBrush, 20, 150, 200, 100);
}
```

Requirements

Platforms: Windows 98, Windows NT 4.0, Windows Millennium Edition, Windows 2000, Windows XP Home Edition, Windows XP Professional, Windows Server 2003 family

LinearGradientBrush.SetBlendTriangularShape Method

Creates a linear gradient with a center color and a linear falloff to a single color on both ends.

Overload List

Creates a linear gradient with a center color and a linear falloff to a single color on both ends.

[Visual Basic] **Overloads Public Sub SetBlendTriangular-Shape(Single)**

[C#] **public void SetBlendTriangularShape(float);**

[C++] **public: void SetBlendTriangularShape(float);**

[JScript] **public function SetBlendTriangularShape(float);**

Creates a linear gradient with a center color and a linear falloff to a single color on both ends.

[Visual Basic] **Overloads Public Sub SetBlendTriangular-Shape(Single, Single)**

[C#] **public void SetBlendTriangularShape(float, float);**

[C++] **public: void SetBlendTriangularShape(float, float);**

[JScript] **public function SetBlendTriangularShape(float, float);**

Example

[Visual Basic, C#] The following example is designed for use with Windows Forms, and it requires **PaintEventArgs** *e*, an **OnPaint** event object. The code performs the following actions:

- Creates a new **LinearGradientBrush** object.
- Uses this brush to draw an ellipse to the screen that has a linear, left-to-right transition of colors.
- Transforms the **LinearGradientBrush** object into a triangular shape with its peak in the center.
- Draws a second ellipse to the screen using the transformed brush.

[Visual Basic, C#] Notice that the gradient of the lower ellipse transitions from blue to red and then back to blue.

> [Visual Basic, C#] **Note** This example shows how to use one of the overloaded versions of **SetBlendTriangularShape**. For other examples that might be available, see the individual overload topics.

[Visual Basic]

```
Public Sub SetBlendTriangularShapeExample(e As PaintEventArgs)
' Create a LinearGradientBrush.
Dim myRect As New Rectangle(20, 20, 200, 100)
Dim myLGBrush As New LinearGradientBrush(myRect, Color.Blue, _
Color.Red, 0F, True)
' Draw an ellipse to the screen using the LinearGradientBrush.
e.Graphics.FillEllipse(myLGBrush, myRect)
' Create a triangular shaped brush with the peak at the center
' of the drawing area.
myLGBrush.SetBlendTriangularShape(0.5F, 1F)
' Use the triangular brush to draw a second ellipse.
myRect.Y = 150
e.Graphics.FillEllipse(myLGBrush, myRect)
End Sub
```

[C#]

```
private void SetBlendTriangularShapeExample(PaintEventArgs e)
{
// Create a LinearGradientBrush.
Rectangle myRect = new Rectangle(20, 20, 200, 100);
LinearGradientBrush myLGBrush = new LinearGradientBrush(
myRect,
```

```
Color.Blue,
Color.Red,
0.0f,
true);
// Draw an ellipse to the screen using the LinearGradientBrush.
e.Graphics.FillEllipse(myLGBrush, myRect);
// Create a triangular shaped brush with the peak at the center
// of the drawing area.
myLGBrush.SetBlendTriangularShape(.5f, 1.0f);
// Use the triangular brush to draw a second ellipse.
myRect.Y = 150;
e.Graphics.FillEllipse(myLGBrush, myRect);
}
```

LinearGradientBrush.SetBlendTriangularShape Method (Single)

Creates a linear gradient with a center color and a linear falloff to a single color on both ends.

[Visual Basic]
```
Overloads Public Sub SetBlendTriangularShape( _
   ByVal focus As Single _
)
```
[C#]
```
public void SetBlendTriangularShape(
   float focus
);
```
[C++]
```
public: void SetBlendTriangularShape(
   float focus
);
```
[JScript]
```
public function SetBlendTriangularShape(
   focus : float
);
```

Parameters

focus

A value from 0 through 1 that specifies the center of the gradient (the point where the gradient is composed of only the ending color).

Remarks

This method specifies a *focus*, which is the point where the gradient is composed only of the ending color. The *focus* parameter represents a location as a proportion of the distance along the gradient line. The gradient falls off to the starting color linearly to either side.

Example

For an example, see **LinearGradientBrush.SetBlendTriangularShape Method (Single, Single)**.

Requirements

Platforms: Windows 98, Windows NT 4.0, Windows Millennium Edition, Windows 2000, Windows XP Home Edition, Windows XP Professional, Windows Server 2003 family

LinearGradientBrush.SetBlendTriangularShape Method (Single, Single)

Creates a linear gradient with a center color and a linear falloff to a single color on both ends.

[Visual Basic]
```
Overloads Public Sub SetBlendTriangularShape( _
   ByVal focus As Single, _
   ByVal scale As Single _
)
```
[C#]
```
public void SetBlendTriangularShape(
   float focus,
   float scale
);
```
[C++]
```
public: void SetBlendTriangularShape(
   float focus,
   float scale
);
```
[JScript]
```
public function SetBlendTriangularShape(
   focus : float,
   scale : float
);
```

Parameters

focus

A value from 0 through 1 that specifies the center of the gradient (the point where the gradient is composed of only the ending color).

scale

A value from 0 through1 that specifies how fast the colors falloff from the starting color to *focus* (ending color)

Remarks

This method specifies a *focus*, which is the point where the gradient is composed only of the ending color. The *focus* parameter represents a location as a proportion of the distance along the gradient line. The gradient falls off to the starting color linearly to either side.

Example

[Visual Basic, C#] The following example is designed for use with Windows Forms, and it requires **PaintEventArgs** *e*, an **OnPaint** event object. The code performs the following actions:

- Creates a new **LinearGradientBrush** object.
- Uses this brush to draw an ellipse to the screen that has a linear, left-to-right transition of colors.
- Transforms the **LinearGradientBrush** object into a triangular shape with its peak in the center.
- Draws a second ellipse to the screen using the transformed brush.

[Visual Basic, C#] Notice that the gradient of the lower ellipse transitions from blue to red and then back to blue.

[Visual Basic]
```
Public Sub SetBlendTriangularShapeExample(e As PaintEventArgs)
' Create a LinearGradientBrush.
Dim myRect As New Rectangle(20, 20, 200, 100)
Dim myLGBrush As New LinearGradientBrush(myRect, Color.Blue, _
Color.Red, 0F, True)
' Draw an ellipse to the screen using the LinearGradientBrush.
e.Graphics.FillEllipse(myLGBrush, myRect)
' Create a triangular shaped brush with the peak at the center
' of the drawing area.
```

```
myLGBrush.SetBlendTriangularShape(0.5F, 1F)
' Use the triangular brush to draw a second ellipse.
myRect.Y = 150
e.Graphics.FillEllipse(myLGBrush, myRect)
End Sub
```

[C#]

```
private void SetBlendTriangularShapeExample(PaintEventArgs e)
{
// Create a LinearGradientBrush.
Rectangle myRect = new Rectangle(20, 20, 200, 100);
LinearGradientBrush myLGBrush = new LinearGradientBrush(
myRect,
Color.Blue,
Color.Red,
0.0f,
true);
// Draw an ellipse to the screen using the LinearGradientBrush.
e.Graphics.FillEllipse(myLGBrush, myRect);
// Create a triangular shaped brush with the peak at the center
// of the drawing area.
myLGBrush.SetBlendTriangularShape(.5f, 1.0f);
// Use the triangular brush to draw a second ellipse.
myRect.Y = 150;
e.Graphics.FillEllipse(myLGBrush, myRect);
}
```

Requirements

Platforms: Windows 98, Windows NT 4.0, Windows Millennium Edition, Windows 2000, Windows XP Home Edition, Windows XP Professional, Windows Server 2003 family

LinearGradientBrush.SetSigmaBellShape Method

Creates a gradient falloff based on a bell-shaped curve.

Overload List

Creates a gradient falloff based on a bell-shaped curve.

[Visual Basic] **Overloads Public Sub SetSigmaBellShape(Single)**

[C#] **public void SetSigmaBellShape(float);**

[C++] **public: void SetSigmaBellShape(float);**

[JScript] **public function SetSigmaBellShape(float);**

Creates a gradient falloff based on a bell-shaped curve.

[Visual Basic] **Overloads Public Sub SetSigmaBellShape(Single, Single)**

[C#] **public void SetSigmaBellShape(float, float);**

[C++] **public: void SetSigmaBellShape(float, float);**

[JScript] **public function SetSigmaBellShape(float, float);**

Example

[Visual Basic, C#] The following example is designed for use with Windows Forms, and it requires **PaintEventArgs** *e*, an **OnPaint** event object. The code performs the following actions:

- Creates a new **LinearGradientBrush** object.
- Uses this brush to draw an ellipse to the screen that has a linear, left-to-right transition of colors.
- Transforms the **LinearGradientBrush** object to have a bell shaped curve with its peak in the center.
- Draws a second ellipse to the screen using the bell-shaped brush.

[Visual Basic, C#] Notice that the gradient of the lower ellipse transitions from blue to red and then back to blue.

> [Visual Basic, C#] **Note** This example shows how to use one of the overloaded versions of **SetSigmaBellShape**. For other examples that might be available, see the individual overload topics.

[Visual Basic]

```
Public Sub SetSigmaBellShapeExample(e As PaintEventArgs)
' Create a LinearGradientBrush.
Dim myRect As New Rectangle(20, 20, 200, 100)
Dim myLGBrush As New LinearGradientBrush(myRect, Color.Blue, _
Color.Red, 0F, True)
' Draw an ellipse to the screen using the LinearGradientBrush.
e.Graphics.FillEllipse(myLGBrush, myRect)
' Create a triangular shaped brush with the peak at the center
' of the drawing area.
myLGBrush.SetSigmaBellShape(0.5F, 1F)
' Use the triangular brush to draw a second ellipse.
myRect.Y = 150
e.Graphics.FillEllipse(myLGBrush, myRect)
End Sub
```

[C#]

```
private void SetSigmaBellShapeExample(PaintEventArgs e)
{
// Create a LinearGradientBrush.
Rectangle myRect = new Rectangle(20, 20, 200, 100);
LinearGradientBrush myLGBrush = new LinearGradientBrush(
myRect,
Color.Blue,
Color.Red,
0.0f,
true);
// Draw an ellipse to the screen using the LinearGradientBrush.
e.Graphics.FillEllipse(myLGBrush, myRect);
// Create a bell-shaped brush with the peak at the
// center of the drawing area.
myLGBrush.SetSigmaBellShape(.5f, 1.0f);
// Use the bell- shaped brush to draw a second
// ellipse.
myRect.Y = 150;
e.Graphics.FillEllipse(myLGBrush, myRect);
}
```

LinearGradientBrush.SetSigmaBellShape Method (Single)

Creates a gradient falloff based on a bell-shaped curve.

[Visual Basic]

```
Overloads Public Sub SetSigmaBellShape( _
   ByVal focus As Single _
)
```

[C#]

```
public void SetSigmaBellShape(
   float focus
);
```

[C++]

```
public: void SetSigmaBellShape(
   float focus
);
```

[JScript]

```
public function SetSigmaBellShape(
   focus : float
);
```

Parameters

focus

A value from 0 through 1 that specifies the center of the gradient (the point where the starting color and ending color are blended equally).

Remarks

This method specifies a *focus*, which is the point where the gradient is composed only of the ending color. The *focus* parameter represents a location as a proportion of the distance along the gradient line. The gradient falls off to the starting color based on a bell curve shape (normal distribution) to either side.

Example

For an example, see **LinearGradientBrush.SetSigmaBellShape Method (Single, Single)**.

Requirements

Platforms: Windows 98, Windows NT 4.0, Windows Millennium Edition, Windows 2000, Windows XP Home Edition, Windows XP Professional, Windows Server 2003 family

LinearGradientBrush.SetSigmaBellShape Method (Single, Single)

Creates a gradient falloff based on a bell-shaped curve.

[Visual Basic]
```
Overloads Public Sub SetSigmaBellShape( _
   ByVal focus As Single, _
   ByVal scale As Single _
)
```
[C#]
```
public void SetSigmaBellShape(
   float focus,
   float scale
);
```
[C++]
```
public: void SetSigmaBellShape(
   float focus,
   float scale
);
```
[JScript]
```
public function SetSigmaBellShape(
   focus : float,
   scale : float
);
```

Parameters

focus

A value from 0 through 1 that specifies the center of the gradient (the point where the gradient is composed of only the ending color).

scale

A value from 0 through 1 that specifies how fast the colors falloff from the *focus*.

Remarks

This method specifies a *focus*, which is the point where the gradient is composed only of the ending color. The *focus* parameter represents a location as a proportion of the distance along the gradient line. The gradient falls off to the starting color based on a bell curve shape (normal distribution) to either side.

Example

[Visual Basic, C#] The following example is designed for use with Windows Forms, and it requires **PaintEventArgs** *e*, an **OnPaint** event object. The code performs the following actions:

- Creates a new **LinearGradientBrush** object.
- Uses this brush to draw an ellipse to the screen that has a linear, left-to-right transition of colors.
- Transforms the **LinearGradientBrush** object to have a bell shaped curve with its peak in the center.
- Draws a second ellipse to the screen using the bell-shaped brush.

[Visual Basic, C#] Notice that the gradient of the lower ellipse transitions from blue to red and then back to blue.

[Visual Basic]
```
Public Sub SetSigmaBellShapeExample(e As PaintEventArgs)
' Create a LinearGradientBrush.
Dim myRect As New Rectangle(20, 20, 200, 100)
Dim myLGBrush As New LinearGradientBrush(myRect, Color.Blue, _
Color.Red, 0F, True)
' Draw an ellipse to the screen using the LinearGradientBrush.
e.Graphics.FillEllipse(myLGBrush, myRect)
' Create a triangular shaped brush with the peak at the center
' of the drawing area.
myLGBrush.SetSigmaBellShape(0.5F, 1F)
' Use the triangular brush to draw a second ellipse.
myRect.Y = 150
e.Graphics.FillEllipse(myLGBrush, myRect)
End Sub
```
[C#]
```
private void SetSigmaBellShapeExample(PaintEventArgs e)
{
// Create a LinearGradientBrush.
Rectangle myRect = new Rectangle(20, 20, 200, 100);
LinearGradientBrush myLGBrush = new LinearGradientBrush(
myRect,
Color.Blue,
Color.Red,
0.0f,
true);
// Draw an ellipse to the screen using the LinearGradientBrush.
e.Graphics.FillEllipse(myLGBrush, myRect);
// Create a bell-shaped brush with the peak at the
// center of the drawing area.
myLGBrush.SetSigmaBellShape(.5f, 1.0f);
// Use the bell- shaped brush to draw a second
// ellipse.
myRect.Y = 150;
e.Graphics.FillEllipse(myLGBrush, myRect);
}
```

Requirements

Platforms: Windows 98, Windows NT 4.0, Windows Millennium Edition, Windows 2000, Windows XP Home Edition, Windows XP Professional, Windows Server 2003 family

LinearGradientBrush.TranslateTransform Method

Translates the local geometric transform by the specified dimensions. This method prepends the translation to the transform.

Overload List

Translates the local geometric transform by the specified dimensions. This method prepends the translation to the transform.

[Visual Basic] **Overloads Public Sub TranslateTransform(Single, Single)**

[C#] **public void TranslateTransform(float, float);**

[C++] **public: void TranslateTransform(float, float);**

[JScript] **public function TranslateTransform(float, float);**

Translates the local geometric transform by the specified dimensions in the specified order.

[Visual Basic] **Overloads Public Sub TranslateTransform(Single, Single, MatrixOrder)**

[C#] **public void TranslateTransform(float, float, MatrixOrder);**

[C++] **public: void TranslateTransform(float, float, MatrixOrder);**

[JScript] **public function TranslateTransform(float, float, MatrixOrder);**

Example

[Visual Basic, C#] The following example is designed for use with Windows Forms, and it requires **PaintEventArgs** *e*, an **OnPaint** event object. The code performs the following actions:

- Creates a new **LinearGradientBrush** object.
- Uses this brush to draw a rectangle to the screen that has a linear, left-to-right transition of colors.
- Rotates the **LinearGradientBrush** object by 90 degrees and scales the gradient.
- Draws the rectangle, with the rotated and scaled gradient, to the screen.
- Translates the rectangle so that it has a linear gradient running from top to bottom.
- Draws the translated rectangle to the screen.

[Visual Basic, C#] Notice that there are three rectangles displayed ¾ the top one showing the left-to-right gradient, the middle one showing the rotated and scaled gradient, and the bottom one showing the final, translated gradient.

> [Visual Basic, C#] **Note** This example shows how to use one of the overloaded versions of **TranslateTransform**. For other examples that might be available, see the individual overload topics.

[Visual Basic]
```
Public Sub TranslateTransformExample(e As PaintEventArgs)
' Create a LinearGradientBrush.
Dim myRect As New Rectangle(20, 20, 200, 100)
Dim myLGBrush As New LinearGradientBrush(myRect, Color.Blue, _
Color.Red, 0F, True)
' Draw a rectangle to the screen using the LinearGradientBrush.
e.Graphics.FillRectangle(myLGBrush, myRect)
' Rotate the LinearGradientBrush.
myLGBrush.RotateTransform(90F)
' Scale the gradient for the height of the rectangle.
myLGBrush.ScaleTransform(0.5F, 1F)
' Draw to the screen, the rotated and scaled gradient.
e.Graphics.FillRectangle(myLGBrush, 20, 150, 200, 100)
' Rejustify the brush to start at the top edge of the rectangle.
myLGBrush.TranslateTransform(- 20F, 0F)
' Draw a third rectangle to the screen using the translated brush.
e.Graphics.FillRectangle(myLGBrush, 20, 300, 200, 100)
End Sub
```

[C#]
```
private void TranslateTransformExample(PaintEventArgs e)
{
// Create a LinearGradientBrush.
Rectangle myRect = new Rectangle(20, 20, 200, 100);
LinearGradientBrush myLGBrush = new LinearGradientBrush(
myRect,
Color.Blue,
Color.Red,
0.0f,
true);
// Draw a rectangle to the screen using the LinearGradientBrush.
e.Graphics.FillRectangle(myLGBrush, myRect);
// Rotate the LinearGradientBrush.
myLGBrush.RotateTransform(90.0f);
// Scale the gradient for the height of the rectangle.
myLGBrush.ScaleTransform(0.5f, 1.0f);
// Draw to the screen, the rotated and scaled gradient.
e.Graphics.FillRectangle(myLGBrush, 20, 150, 200, 100);
// Rejustify the brush to start at the top edge of the
// rectangle.
myLGBrush.TranslateTransform(-20.0f, 0.0f);
// Draw a third rectangle to the screen using the translated
// brush.
e.Graphics.FillRectangle(myLGBrush, 20, 300, 200, 100);
}
```

LinearGradientBrush.TranslateTransform Method (Single, Single)

Translates the local geometric transform by the specified dimensions. This method prepends the translation to the transform.

[Visual Basic]
```
Overloads Public Sub TranslateTransform( _
   ByVal dx As Single, _
   ByVal dy As Single _
)
```
[C#]
```
public void TranslateTransform(
   float dx,
   float dy
);
```
[C++]
```
public: void TranslateTransform(
   float dx,
   float dy
);
```
[JScript]
```
public function TranslateTransform(
   dx : float,
   dy : float
);
```

Parameters

dx

The value of the translation in x.

dy

The value of the translation in y.

Example

For an example, see **LinearGradientBrush.TranslateTransform Method (Single, Single, MatrixOrder)**.

Requirements

Platforms: Windows 98, Windows NT 4.0, Windows Millennium Edition, Windows 2000, Windows XP Home Edition, Windows XP Professional, Windows Server 2003 family

LinearGradientBrush.TranslateTransform Method (Single, Single, MatrixOrder)

Translates the local geometric transform by the specified dimensions in the specified order.

[Visual Basic]
```
Overloads Public Sub TranslateTransform( _
   ByVal dx As Single, _
   ByVal dy As Single, _
   ByVal order As MatrixOrder _
)
```
[C#]
```
public void TranslateTransform(
   float dx,
   float dy,
   MatrixOrder order
);
```
[C++]
```
public: void TranslateTransform(
   float dx,
   float dy,
   MatrixOrder order
);
```
[JScript]
```
public function TranslateTransform(
   dx : float,
   dy : float,
   order : MatrixOrder
);
```

Parameters

dx
: The value of the translation in x.

dy
: The value of the translation in y.

order
: The order (prepend or append) in which to apply the translation.

Example

[Visual Basic, C#] The following example is designed for use with Windows Forms, and it requires **PaintEventArgs** *e*, an **OnPaint** event object. The code performs the following actions:

- Creates a new **LinearGradientBrush** object.
- Uses this brush to draw a rectangle to the screen that has a linear, left-to-right transition of colors.
- Rotates the **LinearGradientBrush** object by 90 degrees and scales the gradient.
- Draws the rectangle, with the rotated and scaled gradient, to the screen.
- Translates the rectangle so that it has a linear gradient running from top to bottom.
- Draws the translated rectangle to the screen.

[Visual Basic, C#] Notice that there are three rectangles displayed ¾ the top one showing the left-to-right gradient, the middle one showing the rotated and scaled gradient, and the bottom one showing the final, translated gradient.

[Visual Basic]
```
Public Sub TranslateTransformExample(e As PaintEventArgs)
' Create a LinearGradientBrush.
Dim myRect As New Rectangle(20, 20, 200, 100)
Dim myLGBrush As New LinearGradientBrush(myRect, Color.Blue, _
Color.Red, 0F, True)
' Draw a rectangle to the screen using the LinearGradientBrush.
e.Graphics.FillRectangle(myLGBrush, myRect)
' Rotate the LinearGradientBrush.
myLGBrush.RotateTransform(90F)
' Scale the gradient for the height of the rectangle.
myLGBrush.ScaleTransform(0.5F, 1F)
' Draw to the screen, the rotated and scaled gradient.
e.Graphics.FillRectangle(myLGBrush, 20, 150, 200, 100)
' Rejustify the brush to start at the top edge of the rectangle.
myLGBrush.TranslateTransform(- 20F, 0F)
' Draw a third rectangle to the screen using the translated brush.
e.Graphics.FillRectangle(myLGBrush, 20, 300, 200, 100)
End Sub
```

[C#]
```
private void TranslateTransformExample(PaintEventArgs e)
{
// Create a LinearGradientBrush.
Rectangle myRect = new Rectangle(20, 20, 200, 100);
LinearGradientBrush myLGBrush = new LinearGradientBrush(
myRect,
Color.Blue,
Color.Red,
0.0f,
true);
// Draw a rectangle to the screen using the LinearGradientBrush.
e.Graphics.FillRectangle(myLGBrush, myRect);
// Rotate the LinearGradientBrush.
myLGBrush.RotateTransform(90.0f);
// Scale the gradient for the height of the rectangle.
myLGBrush.ScaleTransform(0.5f, 1.0f);
// Draw to the screen, the rotated and scaled gradient.
e.Graphics.FillRectangle(myLGBrush, 20, 150, 200, 100);
// Rejustify the brush to start at the top edge of the
// rectangle.
myLGBrush.TranslateTransform(-20.0f, 0.0f);
// Draw a third rectangle to the screen using the translated
// brush.
e.Graphics.FillRectangle(myLGBrush, 20, 300, 200, 100);
}
```

Requirements

Platforms: Windows 98, Windows NT 4.0, Windows Millennium Edition, Windows 2000, Windows XP Home Edition, Windows XP Professional, Windows Server 2003 family

LinearGradientMode Enumeration

Specifies the direction of a linear gradient.

[Visual Basic]
```
<Serializable>
Public Enum LinearGradientMode
```
[C#]
```
[Serializable]
public enum LinearGradientMode
```
[C++]
```
[Serializable]
__value public enum LinearGradientMode
```
[JScript]
```
public
   Serializable
enum LinearGradientMode
```

Members

Member name	Description
BackwardDiagonal	Specifies a gradient from upper right to lower left.
ForwardDiagonal	Specifies a gradient from upper left to lower right.
Horizontal	Specifies a gradient from left to right.
Vertical	Specifies a gradient from top to bottom.

Requirements

Namespace: System.Drawing.Drawing2D

Platforms: Windows 98, Windows NT 4.0, Windows Millennium Edition, Windows 2000, Windows XP Home Edition, Windows XP Professional, Windows Server 2003 family

Assembly: System.Drawing (in System.Drawing.dll)

LineCap Enumeration

Specifies the available cap styles with which a **Pen** object can end a line.

[Visual Basic]
```
<Serializable>
Public Enum LineCap
```
[C#]
```
[Serializable]
public enum LineCap
```
[C++]
```
[Serializable]
__value public enum LineCap
```
[JScript]
```
public
   Serializable
enum LineCap
```

Members

Member name	Description
AnchorMask	Specifies a mask used to check whether a line cap is an anchor cap.
ArrowAnchor	Specifies an arrow-shaped anchor cap.
Custom	Specifies a custom line cap.
DiamondAnchor	Specifies a diamond anchor cap.
Flat	Specifies a flat line cap.
NoAnchor	Specifies no anchor.
Round	Specifies a round line cap.
RoundAnchor	Specifies a round anchor cap.
Square	Specifies a square line cap.
SquareAnchor	Specifies a square anchor line cap.
Triangle	Specifies a triangular line cap.

Requirements

Namespace: System.Drawing.Drawing2D

Platforms: Windows 98, Windows NT 4.0, Windows Millennium Edition, Windows 2000, Windows XP Home Edition, Windows XP Professional, Windows Server 2003 family

Assembly: System.Drawing (in System.Drawing.dll)

LineJoin Enumeration

Specifies how to join consecutive line or curve segments in a figure (subpath) contained in a **GraphicsPath** object.

[Visual Basic]
```
<Serializable>
Public Enum LineJoin
```
[C#]
```
[Serializable]
public enum LineJoin
```
[C++]
```
[Serializable]
__value public enum LineJoin
```
[JScript]
```
public
   Serializable
enum LineJoin
```

Members

Member name	Description
Bevel	Specifies a beveled join. This produces a diagonal corner.
Miter	Specifies a mitered join. This produces a sharp corner or a clipped corner, depending on whether the length of the miter exceeds the miter limit.
MiterClipped	Specifies a mitered join. This produces a sharp corner or a beveled corner, depending on whether the length of the miter exceeds the miter limit.
Round	Specifies a circular join. This produces a smooth, circular arc between the lines.

Requirements

Namespace: System.Drawing.Drawing2D

Platforms: Windows 98, Windows NT 4.0, Windows Millennium Edition, Windows 2000, Windows XP Home Edition, Windows XP Professional, Windows Server 2003 family

Assembly: System.Drawing (in System.Drawing.dll)

Matrix Class

Encapsulates a 3-by-3 affine matrix that represents a geometric transform. This class cannot be inherited.

System.Object
  System.MarshalByRefObject
    System.Drawing.Drawing2D.Matrix

```
[Visual Basic]
NotInheritable Public Class Matrix
   Inherits MarshalByRefObject
   Implements IDisposable
[C#]
public sealed class Matrix : MarshalByRefObject, IDisposable
[C++]
public __gc __sealed class Matrix : public MarshalByRefObject,
   IDisposable
[JScript]
public class Matrix extends MarshalByRefObject implements
   IDisposable
```

Thread Safety

Any public static (**Shared** in Visual Basic) members of this type are safe for multithreaded operations. Any instance members are not guaranteed to be thread safe.

Remarks

The 3-by-3 matrix contains x values in the first column, y values in the second column, and w values in the third column.

Requirements

Namespace: System.Drawing.Drawing2D

Platforms: Windows 98, Windows NT 4.0, Windows Millennium Edition, Windows 2000, Windows XP Home Edition, Windows XP Professional, Windows Server 2003 family

Assembly: System.Drawing (in System.Drawing.dll)

Matrix Constructor

Initializes a new instance of the **Matrix** class.

Overload List

Initializes a new instance of the **Matrix** class as the identity matrix.

[Visual Basic] **Public Sub New()**

[C#] **public Matrix();**

[C++] **public: Matrix();**

[JScript] **public function Matrix();**

Initializes a new instance of the **Matrix** class to the geometric transform defined by the specified rectangle and array of points.

[Visual Basic] **Public Sub New(Rectangle, Point())**

[C#] **public Matrix(Rectangle, Point[]);**

[C++] **public: Matrix(Rectangle, Point[]);**

[JScript] **public function Matrix(Rectangle, Point[]);**

Initializes a new instance of the **Matrix** class to the geometric transform defined by the specified rectangle and array of points.

[Visual Basic] **Public Sub New(RectangleF, PointF())**

[C#] **public Matrix(RectangleF, PointF[]);**

[C++] **public: Matrix(RectangleF, PointF[]);**

[JScript] **public function Matrix(RectangleF, PointF[]);**

Initializes a new instance of the **Matrix** class with the specified elements.

[Visual Basic] **Public Sub New(Single, Single, Single, Single, Single, Single)**

[C#] **public Matrix(float, float, float, float, float, float);**

[C++] **public: Matrix(float, float, float, float, float, float);**

[JScript] **public function Matrix(float, float, float, float, float, float);**

Matrix Constructor ()

Initializes a new instance of the **Matrix** class as the identity matrix.

```
[Visual Basic]
Public Sub New()
[C#]
public Matrix();
[C++]
public: Matrix();
[JScript]
public function Matrix();
```

Requirements

Platforms: Windows 98, Windows NT 4.0, Windows Millennium Edition, Windows 2000, Windows XP Home Edition, Windows XP Professional, Windows Server 2003 family

Matrix Constructor (Rectangle, Point[])

Initializes a new instance of the **Matrix** class to the geometric transform defined by the specified rectangle and array of points.

```
[Visual Basic]
Public Sub New( _
   ByVal rect As Rectangle, _
   ByVal plgpts() As Point _
)
[C#]
public Matrix(
   Rectangle rect,
   Point[] plgpts
);
[C++]
public: Matrix(
   Rectangle rect,
   Point plgpts[]
);
[JScript]
public function Matrix(
   rect : Rectangle,
   plgpts : Point[]
);
```

Parameters

rect
: A **Rectangle** structure that represents the rectangle to be transformed.

plgpts
: An array of three **Point** structures that represents the points of a parallelogram to which the upper-left, upper-right, and lower-left corners of the rectangle is to be transformed. The lower-right corner of the parallelogram is implied by the first three corners.

Remarks

This method initializes the new Matrix such that it represents the geometric transform that maps the rectangle specified by the *rect* parameter to the parallelogram defined by the three points in the *plgpts* parameter. The upper-left corner of the rectangle is mapped to the first point in the *plgpts* array, the upper-right corner is mapped to the second point, and the lower-left corner is mapped to the third point. The lower-left point of the parallelogram is implied by the first three.

Requirements

Platforms: Windows 98, Windows NT 4.0, Windows Millennium Edition, Windows 2000, Windows XP Home Edition, Windows XP Professional, Windows Server 2003 family

Matrix Constructor (RectangleF, PointF[])

Initializes a new instance of the **Matrix** class to the geometric transform defined by the specified rectangle and array of points.

[Visual Basic]
```
Public Sub New( _
   ByVal rect As RectangleF, _
   ByVal plgpts() As PointF _
)
```
[C#]
```
public Matrix(
   RectangleF rect,
   PointF[] plgpts
);
```
[C++]
```
public: Matrix(
   RectangleF rect,
   PointF plgpts[]
);
```
[JScript]
```
public function Matrix(
   rect : RectangleF,
   plgpts : PointF[]
);
```

Parameters

rect

A **RectangleF** structure that represents the rectangle to be transformed.

plgpts

An array of three **PointF** structures that represents the points of a parallelogram to which the upper-left, upper-right, and lower-left corners of the rectangle is to be transformed. The lower-right corner of the parallelogram is implied by the first three corners.

Remarks

This method initializes the new **Matrix** object such that it represents the geometric transform that maps the rectangle specified by the *rect* parameter to the parallelogram defined by the three points in the *plgpts* parameter. The upper-left corner of the rectangle is mapped to the first point in the *plgpts* array, the upper-right corner is mapped to the second point, and the lower-left corner is mapped to the third point. The lower-left point of the parallelogram is implied by the first three.

Requirements

Platforms: Windows 98, Windows NT 4.0, Windows Millennium Edition, Windows 2000, Windows XP Home Edition, Windows XP Professional, Windows Server 2003 family

Matrix Constructor (Single, Single, Single, Single, Single, Single)

Initializes a new instance of the **Matrix** class with the specified elements.

[Visual Basic]
```
Public Sub New( _
   ByVal m11 As Single, _
   ByVal m12 As Single, _
   ByVal m21 As Single, _
   ByVal m22 As Single, _
   ByVal dx As Single, _
   ByVal dy As Single _
)
```
[C#]
```
public Matrix(
   float m11,
   float m12,
   float m21,
   float m22,
   float dx,
   float dy
);
```
[C++]
```
public: Matrix(
   float m11,
   float m12,
   float m21,
   float m22,
   float dx,
   float dy
);
```
[JScript]
```
public function Matrix(
   m11 : float,
   m12 : float,
   m21 : float,
   m22 : float,
   dx : float,
   dy : float
);
```

Parameters

m11

The value in the first row and first column of the new **Matrix**.

m12

The value in the first row and second column of the new **Matrix**.

m21

The value in the second row and first column of the new **Matrix**.

m22

The value in the second row and second column of the new **Matrix**.

dx

The value in the third row and first column of the new **Matrix**.

dy

The value in the third row and second column of the new **Matrix**.

Requirements

Platforms: Windows 98, Windows NT 4.0, Windows Millennium Edition, Windows 2000, Windows XP Home Edition, Windows XP Professional, Windows Server 2003 family

Matrix.Elements Property

Gets an array of floating-point values that represents the elements of this **Matrix** object.

```
[Visual Basic]
Public ReadOnly Property Elements As Single ()
[C#]
public float[] Elements {get;}
[C++]
public: __property float get_Elements();
[JScript]
public function get Elements() : float[];
```

Property Value

An array of floating-point values that represents the elements of this **Matrix** object.

Remarks

The elements m11, m12, m21, m22, dx, dy of the **Matrix** object are represented by the values in the array in that order.

Requirements

Platforms: Windows 98, Windows NT 4.0, Windows Millennium Edition, Windows 2000, Windows XP Home Edition, Windows XP Professional, Windows Server 2003 family

Matrix.IsIdentity Property

Gets a value indicating whether this **Matrix** object is the identity matrix.

```
[Visual Basic]
Public ReadOnly Property IsIdentity As Boolean
[C#]
public bool IsIdentity {get;}
[C++]
public: __property bool get_IsIdentity();
[JScript]
public function get IsIdentity() : Boolean;
```

Property Value

This property is **true** if this **Matrix** is identity; otherwise, **false**.

Requirements

Platforms: Windows 98, Windows NT 4.0, Windows Millennium Edition, Windows 2000, Windows XP Home Edition, Windows XP Professional, Windows Server 2003 family

Matrix.IsInvertible Property

Gets a value indicating whether this **Matrix** object is invertible.

```
[Visual Basic]
Public ReadOnly Property IsInvertible As Boolean
[C#]
public bool IsInvertible {get;}
[C++]
public: __property bool get_IsInvertible();
[JScript]
public function get IsInvertible() : Boolean;
```

Property Value

This property is **true** if this **Matrix** is invertible; otherwise, **false**.

Requirements

Platforms: Windows 98, Windows NT 4.0, Windows Millennium Edition, Windows 2000, Windows XP Home Edition, Windows XP Professional, Windows Server 2003 family

Matrix.OffsetX Property

Gets the x translation value (the dx value, or the element in the third row and first column) of this **Matrix** object.

```
[Visual Basic]
Public ReadOnly Property OffsetX As Single
[C#]
public float OffsetX {get;}
[C++]
public: __property float get_OffsetX();
[JScript]
public function get OffsetX() : float;
```

Property Value

The x translation value of this **Matrix**.

Requirements

Platforms: Windows 98, Windows NT 4.0, Windows Millennium Edition, Windows 2000, Windows XP Home Edition, Windows XP Professional, Windows Server 2003 family

Matrix.OffsetY Property

Gets the y translation value (the dy value, or the element in the third row and second column) of this **Matrix**.

```
[Visual Basic]
Public ReadOnly Property OffsetY As Single
[C#]
public float OffsetY {get;}
[C++]
public: __property float get_OffsetY();
[JScript]
public function get OffsetY() : float;
```

Property Value

The y translation value of this **Matrix**.

Requirements

Platforms: Windows 98, Windows NT 4.0, Windows Millennium Edition, Windows 2000, Windows XP Home Edition, Windows XP Professional, Windows Server 2003 family

Matrix.Clone Method

Creates an exact copy of this **Matrix** object.

```
[Visual Basic]
Public Function Clone() As Matrix
[C#]
public Matrix Clone();
[C++]
public: Matrix* Clone();
[JScript]
public function Clone() : Matrix;
```

Return Value

The **Matrix** object that this method creates.

Requirements

Platforms: Windows 98, Windows NT 4.0, Windows Millennium Edition, Windows 2000, Windows XP Home Edition, Windows XP Professional, Windows Server 2003 family

Matrix.Dispose Method

Releases all resources used by this **Matrix** object.

```
[Visual Basic]
Public Overridable Sub Dispose() Implements IDisposable.Dispose
[C#]
public virtual void Dispose();
[C++]
public: virtual void Dispose();
[JScript]
public function Dispose();
```

Return Value

This method does not return a value.

Implements

IDisposable.Dispose

Remarks

Calling **Dispose** allows the resources used by this **Matrix** object to be reallocated for other purposes.

Requirements

Platforms: Windows 98, Windows NT 4.0, Windows Millennium Edition, Windows 2000, Windows XP Home Edition, Windows XP Professional, Windows Server 2003 family

Matrix.Equals Method

Tests whether the specified object is a **Matrix** object and is identical to this **Matrix** object.

```
[Visual Basic]
Overrides Public Function Equals( _
   ByVal obj As Object _
) As Boolean
[C#]
public override bool Equals(
   object obj
);
[C++]
public: bool Equals(
   Object* obj
);
[JScript]
public override function Equals(
   obj : Object
) : Boolean;
```

Parameters

obj

The object to test.

Return Value

This method returns **true** if *obj* is the specified **Matrix** object identical to this **Matrix** object; otherwise, **false**.

Requirements

Platforms: Windows 98, Windows NT 4.0, Windows Millennium Edition, Windows 2000, Windows XP Home Edition, Windows XP Professional, Windows Server 2003 family

Matrix.Finalize Method

Cleans up resources allocated for this **Matrix**.

[C#] In C#, finalizers are expressed using destructor syntax.

[C++] In C++, finalizers are expressed using destructor syntax.

```
[Visual Basic]
Overrides Protected Sub Finalize()
[C#]
~Matrix();
[C++]
~Matrix();
[JScript]
protected override function Finalize();
```

Requirements

Platforms: Windows 98, Windows NT 4.0, Windows Millennium Edition, Windows 2000, Windows XP Home Edition, Windows XP Professional, Windows Server 2003 family

Matrix.GetHashCode Method

Returns a hash code.

[Visual Basic]
```
Overrides Public Function GetHashCode() As Integer
```
[C#]
```
public override int GetHashCode();
```
[C++]
```
public: int GetHashCode();
```
[JScript]
```
public override function GetHashCode() : int;
```

Return Value

The hash code for this **Matrix** object.

Requirements

Platforms: Windows 98, Windows NT 4.0, Windows Millennium Edition, Windows 2000, Windows XP Home Edition, Windows XP Professional, Windows Server 2003 family

Matrix.Invert Method

Inverts this **Matrix** object, if it is invertible.

[Visual Basic]
```
Public Sub Invert()
```
[C#]
```
public void Invert();
```
[C++]
```
public: void Invert();
```
[JScript]
```
public function Invert();
```

Example

[C#] The following example creates a matrix and inverts it:

[C#]
```
Matrix myMatrix = new Matrix(3, 5, 1, 2, 2, 4);
myMatrix.Invert();
```

Requirements

Platforms: Windows 98, Windows NT 4.0, Windows Millennium Edition, Windows 2000, Windows XP Home Edition, Windows XP Professional, Windows Server 2003 family

Matrix.Multiply Method

Multiplies this **Matrix** object by the specified **Matrix** object by prepending the specified **Matrix**.

Overload List

Multiplies this **Matrix** object by the matrix specified in the *matrix* parameter, by prepending the specified **Matrix** object.

[Visual Basic] **Overloads Public Sub Multiply(Matrix)**

[C#] **public void Multiply(Matrix);**

[C++] **public: void Multiply(Matrix*);**

[JScript] **public function Multiply(Matrix);**

Multiplies this **Matrix** object by the matrix specified in the *matrix* parameter, and in the order specified in the *order* parameter.

[Visual Basic] **Overloads Public Sub Multiply(Matrix, MatrixOrder)**

[C#] **public void Multiply(Matrix, MatrixOrder);**

[C++] **public: void Multiply(Matrix*, MatrixOrder);**

[JScript] **public function Multiply(Matrix, MatrixOrder);**

Example

[Visual Basic, C#] The following example is designed for use with Windows Forms, and it requires **PaintEventArgs** *e*, an **OnPaint** event object. The code performs the following actions:

- Creates three matrices.
- Lists the contents of matrix 1 to the screen.
- Multiplies matrix 1 by matrix 2 and stores the result in matrix 1.
- Lists the contents of matrix 1 to the screen.
- Multiplies the result stored in matrix 1 by matrix 3, and again stores the result in matrix 1.
- Lists the contents of matrix 1 to the screen.
- Draws a rectangle to the screen prior to applying the matrix 1 transform (the blue rectangle).
- Applies the transform to the rectangle.
- Draws the transformed rectangle to the screen (the red rectangle), using the same coordinates as the previous rectangle.

[Visual Basic, C#] Notice that the red rectangle has been scaled by a factor of two in the horizontal direction, then rotated 90 degrees, and then moved (translated) 250 points in the x direction and 50 points in the y direction.

> [Visual Basic, C#] **Note** This example shows how to use one of the overloaded versions of **Multiply**. For other examples that might be available, see the individual overload topics.

[Visual Basic]
```
Public Sub MultiplyExample(e As PaintEventArgs)
Dim myPen As New Pen(Color.Blue, 1)
Dim myPen2 As New Pen(Color.Red, 1)
' Set up the matrices.
Dim myMatrix1 As New Matrix(2F, 0F, 0F, 1F, 0F, 0F)
' Scale.
Dim myMatrix2 As New Matrix(0F, 1F, - 1F, 0F, 0F, 0F)
' Rotate 90.
Dim myMatrix3 As New Matrix(1F, 0F, 0F, 1F, 250F, 50F)
' Translate.
' Display the elements of the starting matrix.
ListMatrixElementsHelper(e, myMatrix1, "Beginning Matrix", 6, 40)
' Multiply Matrix1 by Matrix 2.
myMatrix1.Multiply(myMatrix2, MatrixOrder.Append)
' Display the result of the multiplication of Matrix1 and
' Matrix2.
ListMatrixElementsHelper(e, myMatrix1, _
"Matrix After 1st Multiplication", 6, 60)
' Multiply the result from the pervious multiplication by
' Matrix3.
myMatrix1.Multiply(myMatrix3, MatrixOrder.Append)
' Display the result of the previous multiplication
' multiplied by Matrix3.
ListMatrixElementsHelper(e, myMatrix1, _
"Matrix After 2nd Multiplication", 6, 80)
' Draw the rectangle prior to transformation.
e.Graphics.DrawRectangle(myPen, 0, 0, 100, 100)
e.Graphics.Transform = myMatrix1
' Draw the rectangle after transformation.
e.Graphics.DrawRectangle(myPen2, 0, 0, 100, 100)
End Sub
' A helper function to list the contents of a matrix.
Public Sub ListMatrixElementsHelper(e As PaintEventArgs, _
matrix As Matrix, matrixName As String, numElements As Integer, _
y As Integer)
```

```
' Set up variables for drawing the array
' of points to the screen.
Dim i As Integer
Dim x As Single = 20
Dim j As Single = 200
Dim myFont As New Font("Arial", 8)
Dim myBrush As New SolidBrush(Color.Black)
' Draw the matrix name to the screen.
e.Graphics.DrawString(matrixName + ":  ", myFont, myBrush, x, y)
' Draw the set of path points and types to the screen.
For i = 0 To numElements - 1
e.Graphics.DrawString(matrix.Elements(i).ToString() + ", ", _
myFont, myBrush, j, y)
j += 30
Next i
End Sub
```

[C#]

```
public void MultiplyExample(PaintEventArgs e)
{
Pen myPen = new Pen(Color.Blue, 1);
Pen myPen2 = new Pen(Color.Red, 1);
// Set up the matrices.
Matrix myMatrix1 = new Matrix(
2.0f, 0.0f, 0.0f, 1.0f, 0.0f, 0.0f);  // Scale
Matrix myMatrix2 = new Matrix(
0.0f, 1.0f, -1.0f, 0.0f, 0.0f, 0.0f); // Rotate 90,
Matrix myMatrix3 = new Matrix(
1.0f, 0.0f, 0.0f, 1.0f, 250.0f, 50.0f);  // Translate
// Display the elements of the starting matrix.
ListMatrixElements(e, myMatrix1, "Beginning Matrix", 6, 40);
// Multiply Matrix1 by Matrix 2.
myMatrix1.Multiply(myMatrix2, MatrixOrder.Append);
// Display the result of the multiplication of Matrix1 and
// Matrix2.
ListMatrixElements(e,
myMatrix1,
"Matrix After 1st Multiplication",
6,
60);
// Multiply the result from the pervious multiplication by
// Matrix3.
myMatrix1.Multiply(myMatrix3, MatrixOrder.Append);
// Display the result of the previous multiplication
// multiplied by Matrix3.
ListMatrixElements(e,
myMatrix1,
"Matrix After 2nd Multiplication",
6,
80);
// Draw the rectangle prior to transformation.
e.Graphics.DrawRectangle(myPen, 0, 0, 100, 100);
// Make the transformation.
e.Graphics.Transform = myMatrix1;
// Draw the rectangle after transformation.
e.Graphics.DrawRectangle(myPen2, 0, 0, 100, 100);
}
//-------------------------------------------------------
// The following function is a helper function to
// list the contents of a matrix.
//-------------------------------------------------------
public void ListMatrixElements(
PaintEventArgs e,
Matrix matrix,
string matrixName,
int numElements,
int y)
{
// Set up variables for drawing the array
// of points to the screen.
int i;
float x = 20, X = 200;
Font myFont = new Font("Arial", 8);
SolidBrush myBrush = new SolidBrush(Color.Black);
// Draw the matrix name to the screen.
e.Graphics.DrawString(
matrixName + ":  ",
myFont,
myBrush,
x,
y);
// Draw the set of path points and types to the screen.
for(i=0; i<numElements; i++)
{
e.Graphics.DrawString(
matrix.Elements[i].ToString() + ", ",
myFont,
myBrush,
X,
y);
X += 30;
}
}
```

Matrix.Multiply Method (Matrix)

Multiplies this **Matrix** object by the matrix specified in the *matrix* parameter, by prepending the specified **Matrix** object.

[Visual Basic]

```
Overloads Public Sub Multiply( _
   ByVal matrix As Matrix _
)
```

[C#]

```
public void Multiply(
   Matrix matrix
);
```

[C++]

```
public: void Multiply(
   Matrix* matrix
);
```

[JScript]

```
public function Multiply(
   matrix : Matrix
);
```

Parameters

matrix

The **Matrix** object by which this **Matrix** object is to be multiplied.

Example

For an example, see **Matrix.Multiply Method (Matrix, MatrixOrder)**.

Requirements

Platforms: Windows 98, Windows NT 4.0, Windows Millennium Edition, Windows 2000, Windows XP Home Edition, Windows XP Professional, Windows Server 2003 family

Matrix.Multiply Method (Matrix, MatrixOrder)

Multiplies this **Matrix** object by the matrix specified in the *matrix* parameter, and in the order specified in the *order* parameter.

[Visual Basic]

```
Overloads Public Sub Multiply( _
   ByVal matrix As Matrix, _
   ByVal order As MatrixOrder _
)
```

[C#]

```
public void Multiply(
   Matrix matrix,
   MatrixOrder order
);
```

```
[C++]
public: void Multiply(
   Matrix* matrix,
   MatrixOrder order
);
[JScript]
public function Multiply(
   matrix : Matrix,
   order : MatrixOrder
);
```

Parameters

matrix
: The **Matrix** object by which this **Matrix** object is to be multiplied.

order
: The **MatrixOrder** enumeration that represents the order of the multiplication.

Remarks

If the specified order is **MatrixOrder.Prepend**, this **Matrix** object is multiplied by the specified matrix in a prepended order. If the specified order is **MatrixOrder.Append**, this **Matrix** object is multiplied by the specified matrix in an appended order.

Example

[Visual Basic, C#] The following example is designed for use with Windows Forms, and it requires **PaintEventArgs** *e*, an **OnPaint** event object. The code performs the following actions:

- Creates three matrices.
- Lists the contents of matrix 1 to the screen.
- Multiplies matrix 1 by matrix 2 and stores the result in matrix 1.
- Lists the contents of matrix 1 to the screen.
- Multiplies the result stored in matrix 1 by matrix 3, and again stores the result in matrix 1.
- Lists the contents of matrix 1 to the screen.
- Draws a rectangle to the screen prior to applying the matrix 1 transform (the blue rectangle).
- Applies the transform to the rectangle.
- Draws the transformed rectangle to the screen (the red rectangle), using the same coordinates as the previous rectangle.

[Visual Basic, C#] Notice that the red rectangle has been scaled by a factor of two in the horizontal direction, then rotated 90 degrees, and then moved (translated) 250 points in the x direction and 50 points in the y direction.

```
[Visual Basic]
Public Sub MultiplyExample(e As PaintEventArgs)
Dim myPen As New Pen(Color.Blue, 1)
Dim myPen2 As New Pen(Color.Red, 1)
' Set up the matrices.
Dim myMatrix1 As New Matrix(2F, 0F, 0F, 1F, 0F, 0F)
' Scale.
Dim myMatrix2 As New Matrix(0F, 1F, - 1F, 0F, 0F, 0F)
' Rotate 90.
Dim myMatrix3 As New Matrix(1F, 0F, 0F, 1F, 250F, 50F)
' Translate.
' Display the elements of the starting matrix.
ListMatrixElementsHelper(e, myMatrix1, "Beginning Matrix", 6, 40)
' Multiply Matrix1 by Matrix 2.
myMatrix1.Multiply(myMatrix2, MatrixOrder.Append)
' Display the result of the multiplication of Matrix1 and
' Matrix2.
ListMatrixElementsHelper(e, myMatrix1, _
"Matrix After 1st Multiplication", 6, 60)
' Multiply the result from the pervious multiplication by
' Matrix3.
myMatrix1.Multiply(myMatrix3, MatrixOrder.Append)
' Display the result of the previous multiplication
' multiplied by Matrix3.
ListMatrixElementsHelper(e, myMatrix1, _
"Matrix After 2nd Multiplication", 6, 80)
' Draw the rectangle prior to transformation.
e.Graphics.DrawRectangle(myPen, 0, 0, 100, 100)
e.Graphics.Transform = myMatrix1
' Draw the rectangle after transformation.
e.Graphics.DrawRectangle(myPen2, 0, 0, 100, 100)
End Sub
' A helper function to list the contents of a matrix.
Public Sub ListMatrixElementsHelper(e As PaintEventArgs, _
matrix As Matrix, matrixName As String, numElements As Integer, _
y As Integer)
' Set up variables for drawing the array
' of points to the screen.
Dim i As Integer
Dim x As Single = 20
Dim j As Single = 200
Dim myFont As New Font("Arial", 8)
Dim myBrush As New SolidBrush(Color.Black)
' Draw the matrix name to the screen.
e.Graphics.DrawString(matrixName + ":  ", myFont, myBrush, x, y)
' Draw the set of path points and types to the screen.
For i = 0 To numElements - 1
e.Graphics.DrawString(matrix.Elements(i).ToString() + ", ", _
myFont, myBrush, j, y)
j += 30
Next i
End Sub
```

```
[C#]
public void MultiplyExample(PaintEventArgs e)
{
Pen myPen = new Pen(Color.Blue, 1);
Pen myPen2 = new Pen(Color.Red, 1);
// Set up the matrices.
Matrix myMatrix1 = new Matrix(
2.0f, 0.0f, 0.0f, 1.0f, 0.0f, 0.0f);  // Scale
Matrix myMatrix2 = new Matrix(
0.0f, 1.0f, -1.0f, 0.0f, 0.0f, 0.0f); // Rotate 90,
Matrix myMatrix3 = new Matrix(
1.0f, 0.0f, 0.0f, 1.0f, 250.0f, 50.0f);  // Translate
// Display the elements of the starting matrix.
ListMatrixElements(e, myMatrix1, "Beginning Matrix", 6, 40);
// Multiply Matrix1 by Matrix 2.
myMatrix1.Multiply(myMatrix2, MatrixOrder.Append);
// Display the result of the multiplication of Matrix1 and
// Matrix2.
ListMatrixElements(e,
myMatrix1,
"Matrix After 1st Multiplication",
6,
60);
// Multiply the result from the pervious multiplication by
// Matrix3.
myMatrix1.Multiply(myMatrix3, MatrixOrder.Append);
// Display the result of the previous multiplication
// multiplied by Matrix3.
ListMatrixElements(e,
myMatrix1,
"Matrix After 2nd Multiplication",
6,
80);
// Draw the rectangle prior to transformation.
e.Graphics.DrawRectangle(myPen, 0, 0, 100, 100);
// Make the transformation.
e.Graphics.Transform = myMatrix1;
// Draw the rectangle after transformation.
e.Graphics.DrawRectangle(myPen2, 0, 0, 100, 100);
}
```

```
//-------------------------------------------------------
// The following function is a helper function to
// list the contents of a matrix.
//-------------------------------------------------------
public void ListMatrixElements(
PaintEventArgs e,
Matrix matrix,
string matrixName,
int numElements,
int y)
{
// Set up variables for drawing the array
// of points to the screen.
int i;
float x = 20, X = 200;
Font myFont = new Font("Arial", 8);
SolidBrush myBrush = new SolidBrush(Color.Black);
// Draw the matrix name to the screen.
e.Graphics.DrawString(
matrixName + ":  ",
myFont,
myBrush,
x,
y);
// Draw the set of path points and types to the screen.
for(i=0; i<numElements; i++)
{
e.Graphics.DrawString(
matrix.Elements[i].ToString() + ", ",
myFont,
myBrush,
X,
y);
X += 30;
}
}
```

Requirements

Platforms: Windows 98, Windows NT 4.0, Windows Millennium Edition, Windows 2000, Windows XP Home Edition, Windows XP Professional, Windows Server 2003 family

Matrix.Reset Method

Resets this **Matrix** object to have the elements of the identity matrix.

[Visual Basic]
```
Public Sub Reset()
```
[C#]
```
public void Reset();
```
[C++]
```
public: void Reset();
```
[JScript]
```
public function Reset();
```

Remarks

The elements on the main diagonal of the identity matrix are 1. All other elements of the identity matrix are 0.

Example

[Visual Basic, C#] The following example is designed for use with Windows Forms, and it requires **PaintEventArgs** *e*, an **OnPaint** event object. The code performs the following actions:

- Creates a scaling matrix.
- Lists the matrix elements to the screen.
- Resets the matrix to identity.
- Lists the elements to the screen.
- Translates the matrix by 50 points in the x-axis and 40 points in the y-axis.
- Lists the elements of the translated matrix to the screen.
- Draws a rectangle is drawn to the screen prior to applying the matrix transform (the blue rectangle).
- Applies the transform to the rectangle.
- Draws the transformed rectangle is drawn to the screen (the red rectangle), using the same coordinates as the previous rectangle.

[Visual Basic, C#] Notice that the red rectangle was not scaled (because of the reset) but was translated in the x-axis and y-axis.

[Visual Basic]
```
Public Sub ResetExample(e As PaintEventArgs)
Dim myPen As New Pen(Color.Blue, 1)
Dim myPen2 As New Pen(Color.Red, 1)
Dim myMatrix As New Matrix(5F, 0F, 0F, 3F, 0F, 0F)
' Scale.
ListMatrixElementsHelper(e, myMatrix, "Beginning Matrix", 6, 20)
myMatrix.Reset()
ListMatrixElementsHelper(e, myMatrix, "Matrix After Reset", 6, 40)
myMatrix.Translate(50F, 40F) ' Translate
ListMatrixElementsHelper(e, myMatrix, "Matrix After Translation", _
6, 60)
e.Graphics.DrawRectangle(myPen, 0, 0, 100, 100)
e.Graphics.Transform = myMatrix
e.Graphics.DrawRectangle(myPen2, 0, 0, 100, 100)
End Sub
' A helper function to list the contents of a matrix.
Public Sub ListMatrixElementsHelper(e As PaintEventArgs, _
matrix As Matrix, matrixName As String, numElements As Integer, _
y As Integer)
' Set up variables for drawing the array
' of points to the screen.
Dim i As Integer
Dim x As Single = 20
Dim j As Single = 200
Dim myFont As New Font("Arial", 8)
Dim myBrush As New SolidBrush(Color.Black)
' Draw the matrix name to the screen.
e.Graphics.DrawString(matrixName + ":  ", myFont, myBrush, x, y)
' Draw the set of path points and types to the screen.
For i = 0 To numElements - 1
e.Graphics.DrawString(matrix.Elements(i).ToString() + ", ", _
myFont, myBrush, j, y)
j += 30
Next i
End Sub
```

[C#]
```
public void ResetExample(PaintEventArgs e)
{
Pen myPen = new Pen(Color.Blue, 1);
Pen myPen2 = new Pen(Color.Red, 1);
// Create a matrix that scales by 5 in the x direction and
// by 3 in the y direction.
Matrix myMatrix = new Matrix(
5.0f, 0.0f, 0.0f, 3.0f, 0.0f, 0.0f); // Scale
// List the matrix elements to the screen.
ListMatrixElements(e, myMatrix, "Beginning Matrix", 6, 20);
// Reset the matrix to identity.
myMatrix.Reset();
// Again list the matrix elements to the screen.
ListMatrixElements(e, myMatrix, "Matrix After Reset", 6, 40);
// Translate the matrix by 50 points in the x-axis and 40 points
// in the y-axis.
myMatrix.Translate(50.0f, 40.0f); // Translate
// List the matrix elements to the screen.
ListMatrixElements(e, myMatrix, "Matrix After Translation", 6, 60);
// Draw a rectangle to the screen.
e.Graphics.DrawRectangle(myPen, 0, 0, 100, 100);
// Apply the matrix transform to the Graphics.
e.Graphics.Transform = myMatrix;
```

```
// Draw another rectangle to the screen that has the transform
// applied.
e.Graphics.DrawRectangle(myPen2, 0, 0, 100, 100);
}
//-------------------------------------------------------
// This function is a helper function to
// list the contents of a matrix.
//-------------------------------------------------------
public void ListMatrixElements(
PaintEventArgs e,
Matrix matrix,
string matrixName,
int numElements,
int y)
{
// Set up variables for drawing the array
// of points to the screen.
int i;
float x = 20, X = 200;
Font myFont = new Font("Arial", 8);
SolidBrush myBrush = new SolidBrush(Color.Black);
// Draw the matrix name to the screen.
e.Graphics.DrawString(
matrixName + ":  ",
myFont,
myBrush,
x,
y);
// Draw the set of path points and types to the screen.
for(i=0; i<numElements; i++)
{
e.Graphics.DrawString(
matrix.Elements[i].ToString() + ", ",
myFont,
myBrush,
X,
y);
X += 30;
}
}
```

Requirements

Platforms: Windows 98, Windows NT 4.0, Windows Millennium Edition, Windows 2000, Windows XP Home Edition, Windows XP Professional, Windows Server 2003 family

Matrix.Rotate Method

Applies a clockwise rotation of the specified angle about the origin to this **Matrix** object.

Overload List

Prepend to this **Matrix** object a clockwise rotation, around the origin and by the specified angle.

[Visual Basic] **Overloads Public Sub Rotate(Single)**

[C#] **public void Rotate(float);**

[C++] **public: void Rotate(float);**

[JScript] **public function Rotate(float);**

Applies a clockwise rotation of an amount specified in the *angle* parameter, around the origin (zero x and y coordinates) for this **Matrix** object.

[Visual Basic] **Overloads Public Sub Rotate(Single, MatrixOrder)**

[C#] **public void Rotate(float, MatrixOrder);**

[C++] **public: void Rotate(float, MatrixOrder);**

[JScript] **public function Rotate(float, MatrixOrder);**

Example

[Visual Basic, C#] The following example is designed for use with Windows Forms, and it requires **PaintEventArgs** *e*, an **OnPaint** event object. The code performs the following actions:

- Draws a rectangle to the screen prior to applying a rotation transform (the blue rectangle).
- Creates a matrix and rotates it 45 degrees.
- Applies this matrix transform to the rectangle.
- Draws the transformed rectangle to the screen (the red rectangle).

[Visual Basic, C#] Notice that the red rectangle has been rotated around the 0, 0 screen coordinates.

> [Visual Basic, C#] **Note** This example shows how to use one of the overloaded versions of **Rotate**. For other examples that might be available, see the individual overload topics.

[Visual Basic]

```
Public Sub RotateExample(e As PaintEventArgs)
Dim myPen As New Pen(Color.Blue, 1)
Dim myPen2 As New Pen(Color.Red, 1)
' Draw the rectangle to the screen before applying the transform.
e.Graphics.DrawRectangle(myPen, 150, 50, 200, 100)
' Create a matrix and rotate it 45 degrees.
Dim myMatrix As New Matrix()
myMatrix.Rotate(45, MatrixOrder.Append)
' Draw the rectangle to the screen again after applying the
' transform.
e.Graphics.Transform = myMatrix
e.Graphics.DrawRectangle(myPen2, 150, 50, 200, 100)
End Sub
```

[C#]

```
public void RotateExample(PaintEventArgs e)
{
Pen myPen = new Pen(Color.Blue, 1);
Pen myPen2 = new Pen(Color.Red, 1);
// Draw the rectangle to the screen before applying the transform.
e.Graphics.DrawRectangle(myPen, 150, 50, 200, 100);
// Create a matrix and rotate it 45 degrees.
Matrix myMatrix = new Matrix();
myMatrix.Rotate(45, MatrixOrder.Append);
// Draw the rectangle to the screen again after applying the
// transform.
e.Graphics.Transform = myMatrix;
e.Graphics.DrawRectangle(myPen2, 150, 50, 200, 100);
}
```

Matrix.Rotate Method (Single)

Prepend to this **Matrix** object a clockwise rotation, around the origin and by the specified angle.

[Visual Basic]

```
Overloads Public Sub Rotate( _
   ByVal angle As Single _
)
```

[C#]

```
public void Rotate(
   float angle
);
```

[C++]

```
public: void Rotate(
   float angle
);
```

```
[JScript]
public function Rotate(
   angle : float
);
```

Parameters

angle
The angle of the rotation.

Example

For an example, see **Matrix.Rotate Method (Single, MatrixOrder)**.

Requirements

Platforms: Windows 98, Windows NT 4.0, Windows Millennium Edition, Windows 2000, Windows XP Home Edition, Windows XP Professional, Windows Server 2003 family

Matrix.Rotate Method (Single, MatrixOrder)

Applies a clockwise rotation of an amount specified in the *angle* parameter, around the origin (zero x and y coordinates) for this **Matrix** object.

```
[Visual Basic]
Overloads Public Sub Rotate( _
   ByVal angle As Single, _
   ByVal order As MatrixOrder _
)
[C#]
public void Rotate(
   float angle,
   MatrixOrder order
);
[C++]
public: void Rotate(
   float angle,
   MatrixOrder order
);
[JScript]
public function Rotate(
   angle : float,
   order : MatrixOrder
);
```

Parameters

angle
The angle (extent) of the rotation.

order
A **MatrixOrder** enumeration that specifies the order (append or prepend) in which the rotation is applied to this **Matrix** object.

Example

[Visual Basic, C#] The following example is designed for use with Windows Forms, and it requires **PaintEventArgs** *e*, an **OnPaint** event object. The code performs the following actions:

- Draws a rectangle to the screen prior to applying a rotation transform (the blue rectangle).
- Creates a matrix and rotates it 45 degrees.
- Applies this matrix transform to the rectangle.
- Draws the transformed rectangle to the screen (the red rectangle).

[Visual Basic, C#] Notice that the red rectangle has been rotated around the 0, 0 screen coordinates.

```
[Visual Basic]
Public Sub RotateExample(e As PaintEventArgs)
Dim myPen As New Pen(Color.Blue, 1)
Dim myPen2 As New Pen(Color.Red, 1)
' Draw the rectangle to the screen before applying the transform.
e.Graphics.DrawRectangle(myPen, 150, 50, 200, 100)
' Create a matrix and rotate it 45 degrees.
Dim myMatrix As New Matrix()
myMatrix.Rotate(45, MatrixOrder.Append)
' Draw the rectangle to the screen again after applying the
' transform.
e.Graphics.Transform = myMatrix
e.Graphics.DrawRectangle(myPen2, 150, 50, 200, 100)
End Sub
```

```
[C#]
public void RotateExample(PaintEventArgs e)
{
Pen myPen = new Pen(Color.Blue, 1);
Pen myPen2 = new Pen(Color.Red, 1);
// Draw the rectangle to the screen before applying the transform.
e.Graphics.DrawRectangle(myPen, 150, 50, 200, 100);
// Create a matrix and rotate it 45 degrees.
Matrix myMatrix = new Matrix();
myMatrix.Rotate(45, MatrixOrder.Append);
// Draw the rectangle to the screen again after applying the
// transform.
e.Graphics.Transform = myMatrix;
e.Graphics.DrawRectangle(myPen2, 150, 50, 200, 100);
}
```

Requirements

Platforms: Windows 98, Windows NT 4.0, Windows Millennium Edition, Windows 2000, Windows XP Home Edition, Windows XP Professional, Windows Server 2003 family

Matrix.RotateAt Method

Applies a clockwise rotation about the specified point to this **Matrix** object by prepending the rotation.

Overload List

Applies a clockwise rotation to this **Matrix** object around the point specified in the *point* parameter, and by prepending the rotation.

[Visual Basic] **Overloads Public Sub RotateAt(Single, PointF)**

[C#] **public void RotateAt(float, PointF);**

[C++] **public: void RotateAt(float, PointF);**

[JScript] **public function RotateAt(float, PointF);**

Applies a clockwise rotation about the specified point to this **Matrix** object in the specified order.

[Visual Basic] **Overloads Public Sub RotateAt(Single, PointF, MatrixOrder)**

[C#] **public void RotateAt(float, PointF, MatrixOrder);**

[C++] **public: void RotateAt(float, PointF, MatrixOrder);**

[JScript] **public function RotateAt(float, PointF, MatrixOrder);**

Example

[Visual Basic, C#] The following example is designed for use with Windows Forms, and it requires **PaintEventArgs** *e*, an **OnPaint** event object. The code performs the following actions:

- Draws a rectangle to the screen prior to applying a rotation transform (the blue rectangle).
- Creates a matrix and rotates it 45 degrees around a specified point.
- Applies this matrix transform is to the rectangle.
- Draws the transformed rectangle to the screen (the red rectangle).

[Visual Basic, C#] Notice that the red rectangle has been rotated around the upper left-hand corner of the rectangle (the rotation point specified the **RotateAt** method).

> [Visual Basic, C#] **Note** This example shows how to use one of the overloaded versions of **RotateAt**. For other examples that might be available, see the individual overload topics.

[Visual Basic]
```
Public Sub RotateAtExample(e As PaintEventArgs)
Dim myPen As New Pen(Color.Blue, 1)
Dim myPen2 As New Pen(Color.Red, 1)
Dim rotatePoint As New PointF(150F, 50F)
' Draw the rectangle to the screen before applying the
' transform.
e.Graphics.DrawRectangle(myPen, 150, 50, 200, 100)
' Create a matrix and rotate it 45 degrees.
Dim myMatrix As New Matrix()
myMatrix.RotateAt(45, rotatePoint, MatrixOrder.Append)
' Draw the rectangle to the screen again after applying the
' transform.
e.Graphics.Transform = myMatrix
e.Graphics.DrawRectangle(myPen2, 150, 50, 200, 100)
End Sub
```

[C#]
```
public void RotateAtExample(PaintEventArgs e)
{
Pen myPen = new Pen(Color.Blue, 1);
Pen myPen2 = new Pen(Color.Red, 1);
PointF rotatePoint = new PointF(150.0f, 50.0f);
// Draw the rectangle to the screen before applying the
// transform.
e.Graphics.DrawRectangle(myPen, 150, 50, 200, 100);
// Create a matrix and rotate it 45 degrees.
Matrix myMatrix = new Matrix();
myMatrix.RotateAt(45, rotatePoint, MatrixOrder.Append);
// Draw the rectangle to the screen again after applying the
// transform.
e.Graphics.Transform = myMatrix;
e.Graphics.DrawRectangle(myPen2, 150, 50, 200, 100);
}
```

Matrix.RotateAt Method (Single, PointF)

Applies a clockwise rotation to this **Matrix** object around the point specified in the *point* parameter, and by prepending the rotation.

[Visual Basic]
```
Overloads Public Sub RotateAt( _
   ByVal angle As Single, _
   ByVal point As PointF _
)
```
[C#]
```
public void RotateAt(
   float angle,
   PointF point
);
```
[C++]
```
public: void RotateAt(
   float angle,
   PointF point
);
```
[JScript]
```
public function RotateAt(
   angle : float,
   point : PointF
);
```

Parameters

angle
  The angle (extent) of the rotation.

point
  A **PointF** structure that represents the center of the rotation.

Example

For an example, see **Matrix.RotateAt Method (Single, PointF, MatrixOrder)**.

Requirements

Platforms: Windows 98, Windows NT 4.0, Windows Millennium Edition, Windows 2000, Windows XP Home Edition, Windows XP Professional, Windows Server 2003 family

Matrix.RotateAt Method (Single, PointF, MatrixOrder)

Applies a clockwise rotation about the specified point to this **Matrix** object in the specified order.

[Visual Basic]
```
Overloads Public Sub RotateAt( _
   ByVal angle As Single, _
   ByVal point As PointF, _
   ByVal order As MatrixOrder _
)
```
[C#]
```
public void RotateAt(
   float angle,
   PointF point,
   MatrixOrder order
);
```
[C++]
```
public: void RotateAt(
   float angle,
   PointF point,
   MatrixOrder order
);
```
[JScript]
```
public function RotateAt(
   angle : float,
   point : PointF,
   order : MatrixOrder
);
```

Parameters

angle
The angle of the rotation.

point
A **PointF** structure that represents the center of the rotation.

order
A **MatrixOrder** enumeration that specifies the order (append or prepend) in which the rotation is applied.

Example

[Visual Basic, C#] The following example is designed for use with Windows Forms, and it requires **PaintEventArgs** *e*, an **OnPaint** event object. The code performs the following actions:

- Draws a rectangle to the screen prior to applying a rotation transform (the blue rectangle).
- Creates a matrix and rotates it 45 degrees around a specified point.
- Applies this matrix transform is to the rectangle.
- Draws the transformed rectangle to the screen (the red rectangle).

[Visual Basic, C#] Notice that the red rectangle has been rotated around the upper left-hand corner of the rectangle (the rotation point specified the **RotateAt** method).

[Visual Basic]
```
Public Sub RotateAtExample(e As PaintEventArgs)
Dim myPen As New Pen(Color.Blue, 1)
Dim myPen2 As New Pen(Color.Red, 1)
Dim rotatePoint As New PointF(150F, 50F)
' Draw the rectangle to the screen before applying the
' transform.
e.Graphics.DrawRectangle(myPen, 150, 50, 200, 100)
' Create a matrix and rotate it 45 degrees.
Dim myMatrix As New Matrix()
myMatrix.RotateAt(45, rotatePoint, MatrixOrder.Append)
' Draw the rectangle to the screen again after applying the
' transform.
e.Graphics.Transform = myMatrix
e.Graphics.DrawRectangle(myPen2, 150, 50, 200, 100)
End Sub
```

[C#]
```
public void RotateAtExample(PaintEventArgs e)
{
Pen myPen = new Pen(Color.Blue, 1);
Pen myPen2 = new Pen(Color.Red, 1);
PointF rotatePoint = new PointF(150.0f, 50.0f);
// Draw the rectangle to the screen before applying the
// transform.
e.Graphics.DrawRectangle(myPen, 150, 50, 200, 100);
// Create a matrix and rotate it 45 degrees.
Matrix myMatrix = new Matrix();
myMatrix.RotateAt(45, rotatePoint, MatrixOrder.Append);
// Draw the rectangle to the screen again after applying the
// transform.
e.Graphics.Transform = myMatrix;
e.Graphics.DrawRectangle(myPen2, 150, 50, 200, 100);
}
```

Requirements

Platforms: Windows 98, Windows NT 4.0, Windows Millennium Edition, Windows 2000, Windows XP Home Edition, Windows XP Professional, Windows Server 2003 family

Matrix.Scale Method

Applies the specified scale vector to this **Matrix** object by prepending the scale vector.

Overload List

Applies the specified scale vector to this **Matrix** object by prepending the scale vector.

[Visual Basic] **Overloads Public Sub Scale(Single, Single)**

[C#] **public void Scale(float, float);**

[C++] **public: void Scale(float, float);**

[JScript] **public function Scale(float, float);**

Applies the specified scale vector (*scaleX* and *scaleY*) to this **Matrix** object using the specified order.

[Visual Basic] **Overloads Public Sub Scale(Single, Single, MatrixOrder)**

[C#] **public void Scale(float, float, MatrixOrder);**

[C++] **public: void Scale(float, float, MatrixOrder);**

[JScript] **public function Scale(float, float, MatrixOrder);**

Example

[Visual Basic, C#] The following example is designed for use with Windows Forms, and it requires **PaintEventArgs** *e*, an **OnPaint** event object. The code performs the following actions:

- Draws a rectangle to the screen prior to applying a scaling transform (the blue rectangle).
- Creates a matrix and scales it by 3 in the x-axis and 2 in the y-axis.
- Applies this matrix transform to the rectangle.
- Draws the transformed rectangle to the screen (the red rectangle).

[Visual Basic, C#] Notice that the red rectangle has been scaled by a factor of 3 in the x-axis and by 2 in the y-axis, including the upper left-hand corner of the rectangle (the beginning point of the rectangle).

> [Visual Basic, C#] **Note** This example shows how to use one of the overloaded versions of **Scale**. For other examples that might be available, see the individual overload topics.

[Visual Basic]
```
Public Sub ScaleExample(e As PaintEventArgs)
Dim myPen As New Pen(Color.Blue, 1)
Dim myPen2 As New Pen(Color.Red, 1)
' Draw the rectangle to the screen before applying the
' transform.
e.Graphics.DrawRectangle(myPen, 50, 50, 100, 100)
' Create a matrix and scale it.
Dim myMatrix As New Matrix()
myMatrix.Scale(3, 2, MatrixOrder.Append)
' Draw the rectangle to the screen again after applying the
' transform.
e.Graphics.Transform = myMatrix
e.Graphics.DrawRectangle(myPen2, 50, 50, 100, 100)
End Sub
```

[C#]
```
public void ScaleExample(PaintEventArgs e)
{
Pen myPen = new Pen(Color.Blue, 1);
Pen myPen2 = new Pen(Color.Red, 1);
// Draw the rectangle to the screen before applying the
// transform.
e.Graphics.DrawRectangle(myPen, 50, 50, 100, 100);
// Create a matrix and scale it.
Matrix myMatrix = new Matrix();
myMatrix.Scale(3, 2, MatrixOrder.Append);
```

```
// Draw the rectangle to the screen again after applying the
// transform.
e.Graphics.Transform = myMatrix;
e.Graphics.DrawRectangle(myPen2, 50, 50, 100, 100);
}
```

Matrix.Scale Method (Single, Single)

Applies the specified scale vector to this **Matrix** object by prepending the scale vector.

```
[Visual Basic]
Overloads Public Sub Scale( _
   ByVal scaleX As Single, _
   ByVal scaleY As Single _
)
[C#]
public void Scale(
   float scaleX,
   float scaleY
);
[C++]
public: void Scale(
   float scaleX,
   float scaleY
);
[JScript]
public function Scale(
   scaleX : float,
   scaleY : float
);
```

Parameters

scaleX
: The value by which to scale this **Matrix** in the x-axis direction.

scaleY
: The value by which to scale this **Matrix** in the y-axis direction.

Example

For an example, see **Matrix.Scale Method (Single, Single, MatrixOrder)**.

Requirements

Platforms: Windows 98, Windows NT 4.0, Windows Millennium Edition, Windows 2000, Windows XP Home Edition, Windows XP Professional, Windows Server 2003 family

Matrix.Scale Method (Single, Single, MatrixOrder)

Applies the specified scale vector (*scaleX* and *scaleY*) to this **Matrix** object using the specified order.

```
[Visual Basic]
Overloads Public Sub Scale( _
   ByVal scaleX As Single, _
   ByVal scaleY As Single, _
   ByVal order As MatrixOrder _
)
[C#]
public void Scale(
   float scaleX,
   float scaleY,
   MatrixOrder order
);
[C++]
public: void Scale(
   float scaleX,
   float scaleY,
   MatrixOrder order
);
[JScript]
public function Scale(
   scaleX : float,
   scaleY : float,
   order : MatrixOrder
);
```

Parameters

scaleX
: The value by which to scale this **Matrix** in the x-axis direction.

scaleY
: The value by which to scale this **Matrix** in the y-axis direction.

order
: A **MatrixOrder** enumeration that specifies the order (append or prepend) in which the scale vector is applied to this **Matrix**.

Example

[Visual Basic, C#] The following example is designed for use with Windows Forms, and it requires **PaintEventArgs** *e*, an **OnPaint** event object. The code performs the following actions:

- Draws a rectangle to the screen prior to applying a scaling transform (the blue rectangle).
- Creates a matrix and scales it by 3 in the x-axis and 2 in the y-axis.
- Applies this matrix transform to the rectangle.
- Draws the transformed rectangle to the screen (the red rectangle).

[Visual Basic, C#] Notice that the red rectangle has been scaled by a factor of 3 in the x-axis and by 2 in the y-axis, including the upper left-hand corner of the rectangle (the beginning point of the rectangle).

```
[Visual Basic]
Public Sub ScaleExample(e As PaintEventArgs)
Dim myPen As New Pen(Color.Blue, 1)
Dim myPen2 As New Pen(Color.Red, 1)
' Draw the rectangle to the screen before applying the
' transform.
e.Graphics.DrawRectangle(myPen, 50, 50, 100, 100)
' Create a matrix and scale it.
Dim myMatrix As New Matrix()
myMatrix.Scale(3, 2, MatrixOrder.Append)
' Draw the rectangle to the screen again after applying the
' transform.
e.Graphics.Transform = myMatrix
e.Graphics.DrawRectangle(myPen2, 50, 50, 100, 100)
End Sub
```

```
[C#]
public void ScaleExample(PaintEventArgs e)
{
Pen myPen = new Pen(Color.Blue, 1);
Pen myPen2 = new Pen(Color.Red, 1);
// Draw the rectangle to the screen before applying the
// transform.
e.Graphics.DrawRectangle(myPen, 50, 50, 100, 100);
// Create a matrix and scale it.
Matrix myMatrix = new Matrix();
myMatrix.Scale(3, 2, MatrixOrder.Append);
```

```
// Draw the rectangle to the screen again after applying the
// transform.
e.Graphics.Transform = myMatrix;
e.Graphics.DrawRectangle(myPen2, 50, 50, 100, 100);
}
```

Requirements

Platforms: Windows 98, Windows NT 4.0, Windows Millennium Edition, Windows 2000, Windows XP Home Edition, Windows XP Professional, Windows Server 2003 family

Matrix.Shear Method

Applies the specified shear vector to this **Matrix** by prepending the shear vector.

Overload List

Applies the specified shear vector to this **Matrix** object by prepending the shear transformation.

[Visual Basic] **Overloads Public Sub Shear(Single, Single)**

[C#] **public void Shear(float, float);**

[C++] **public: void Shear(float, float);**

[JScript] **public function Shear(float, float);**

Applies the specified shear vector to this **Matrix** object in the specified order.

[Visual Basic] **Overloads Public Sub Shear(Single, Single, MatrixOrder)**

[C#] **public void Shear(float, float, MatrixOrder);**

[C++] **public: void Shear(float, float, MatrixOrder);**

[JScript] **public function Shear(float, float, MatrixOrder);**

Example

For an example, see **Matrix.Shear Method (Single, Single)**

Matrix.Shear Method (Single, Single)

Applies the specified shear vector to this **Matrix** object by prepending the shear transformation.

[Visual Basic]
```
Overloads Public Sub Shear( _
   ByVal shearX As Single, _
   ByVal shearY As Single _
)
```
[C#]
```
public void Shear(
   float shearX,
   float shearY
);
```
[C++]
```
public: void Shear(
   float shearX,
   float shearY
);
```
[JScript]
```
public function Shear(
   shearX : float,
   shearY : float
);
```

Parameters

shearX
: The horizontal shear factor.

shearY
: The vertical shear factor.

Remarks

The transformation applied in this method is a pure shear only if one of the parameters is 0. Applied to a rectangle at the origin, when the *shearY* factor is 0, the transformation moves the bottom edge horizontally by *shearX* times the height of the rectangle. When the *shearX* factor is 0, it moves the right edge vertically by *shearY* times the width of the rectangle. Caution is in order when both parameters are nonzero, because the results are hard to predict. For example, if both factors are 1, the transformation is singular (hence noninvertible), squeezing the entire plane to a single line.

Example

[Visual Basic, C#] The following example is designed for use with Windows Forms, and it requires **PaintEventArgs** *e*, an **OnPaint** event object. The code performs the following action:

- Draws a rectangle to the screen, using a green pen, prior to applying a scaling transform.
- Creates a **Matrix** object and uses it to set a world-coordinate transform for the **Graphics** object.
- Draws another rectangle using a red pen.
- Draws an ellipse using a blue pen.

[Visual Basic, C#] The result is a green rectangle, a red parallelogram and a transformed, blue ellipse. Notice that the green rectangle (drawn prior to setting the transform) directly uses the coordinates supplied in the **DrawRectangle** method call. The other two figures are transformed prior to drawing. The rectangle is transformed to a parallelogram (red), and the ellipse (blue) is transformed to fit into the transformed parallelogram. Notice the bottom of the rectangle is moved (sheared) in the x-axis by a factor of two times the height of the rectangle, thus forming the parallelogram.

[Visual Basic]
```
Public Sub MatrixShearExample(e As PaintEventArgs)
Dim myMatrix As New Matrix()
myMatrix.Shear(2, 0)
e.Graphics.DrawRectangle(New Pen(Color.Green), 0, 0, 100, 50)
e.Graphics.MultiplyTransform(myMatrix)
e.Graphics.DrawRectangle(New Pen(Color.Red), 0, 0, 100, 50)
e.Graphics.DrawEllipse(New Pen(Color.Blue), 0, 0, 100, 50)
End Sub
```

[C#]
```
public void MatrixShearExample(PaintEventArgs e)
{
Matrix myMatrix = new Matrix();
myMatrix.Shear(2, 0);
e.Graphics.DrawRectangle(new Pen(Color.Green), 0, 0 , 100 , 50);
e.Graphics.MultiplyTransform(myMatrix);
e.Graphics.DrawRectangle(new Pen(Color.Red), 0, 0, 100, 50);
e.Graphics.DrawEllipse(new Pen(Color.Blue), 0, 0, 100, 50);
}
```

Requirements

Platforms: Windows 98, Windows NT 4.0, Windows Millennium Edition, Windows 2000, Windows XP Home Edition, Windows XP Professional, Windows Server 2003 family

Matrix.Shear Method (Single, Single, MatrixOrder)

Applies the specified shear vector to this **Matrix** object in the specified order.

```
[Visual Basic]
Overloads Public Sub Shear( _
   ByVal shearX As Single, _
   ByVal shearY As Single, _
   ByVal order As MatrixOrder _
)
[C#]
public void Shear(
   float shearX,
   float shearY,
   MatrixOrder order
);
[C++]
public: void Shear(
   float shearX,
   float shearY,
   MatrixOrder order
);
[JScript]
public function Shear(
   shearX : float,
   shearY : float,
   order : MatrixOrder
);
```

Parameters

shearX
: The horizontal shear factor.

shearY
: The vertical shear factor.

order
: A **MatrixOrder** enumeration that specifies the order (append or prepend) in which the shear is applied.

Remarks

The transformation applied in this method is a pure shear only if one of the parameters is 0. Applied to a rectangle at the origin, when the *shearY* factor is 0, the transformation moves the bottom edge horizontally by *shearX* times the height of the rectangle. When the *shearX* factor is 0, it moves the right edge vertically by *shearY* times the width of the rectangle. Caution is in order when both parameters are nonzero, because the results are hard to predict. For example, if both factors are 1, the transformation is singular (hence noninvertible), squeezing the entire plane to a single line.

Example

For an example, see **Matrix.Shear Method (Single, Single)**

Requirements

Platforms: Windows 98, Windows NT 4.0, Windows Millennium Edition, Windows 2000, Windows XP Home Edition, Windows XP Professional, Windows Server 2003 family

Matrix.TransformPoints Method

Applies the geometric transform this **Matrix** object represents to an array of points.

Overload List

Applies the geometric transform represented by this **Matrix** object to a specified array of points.

[Visual Basic] **Overloads Public Sub TransformPoints(Point())**
[C#] **public void TransformPoints(Point[]);**
[C++] **public: void TransformPoints(Point[]);**
[JScript] **public function TransformPoints(Point[]);**

Applies the geometric transform represented by this **Matrix** object to a specified array of points.

[Visual Basic] **Overloads Public Sub TransformPoints(PointF())**
[C#] **public void TransformPoints(PointF[]);**
[C++] **public: void TransformPoints(PointF[]);**
[JScript] **public function TransformPoints(PointF[]);**

Example

For an example, see **Matrix.TransformPoints Method (Point[])**.

Matrix.TransformPoints Method (Point[])

Applies the geometric transform represented by this **Matrix** object to a specified array of points.

```
[Visual Basic]
Overloads Public Sub TransformPoints( _
   ByVal pts() As Point _
)
[C#]
public void TransformPoints(
   Point[] pts
);
[C++]
public: void TransformPoints(
   Point pts[]
);
[JScript]
public function TransformPoints(
   pts : Point[]
);
```

Parameters

pts
: An array of **Point** structures that represents the points to transform.

Example

[Visual Basic, C#] The following example is designed for use with Windows Forms, and it requires **PaintEventArgs** *e*, an **OnPaint** event object. The code performs the following actions:

- Creates an array of points that form a rectangle.
- Draws this array of points (to the screen prior to applying a scaling transform (the blue rectangle).
- Creates a matrix and scales it by 3 in the x-axis and 2 in the y-axis.
- Applies this matrix transform to the array of points.
- Draws the transformed array to the screen (the red rectangle).

[Visual Basic, C#] Notice that the red rectangle has been scaled by a factor of 3 in the x-axis and by 2 in the y-axis, including the upper left-hand corner of the rectangle (the beginning point of the rectangle).

[Visual Basic]
```
Public Sub TransformPointsExample(e As PaintEventArgs)
Dim myPen As New Pen(Color.Blue, 1)
Dim myPen2 As New Pen(Color.Red, 1)
' Create an array of points.
Dim myArray As Point() = {New Point(20, 20), New Point(120, 20), _
New Point(120, 120), New Point(20, 120), New Point(20, 20)}
' Draw the Points to the screen before applying the
' transform.
e.Graphics.DrawLines(myPen, myArray)
' Create a matrix and scale it.
Dim myMatrix As New Matrix()
myMatrix.Scale(3, 2, MatrixOrder.Append)
myMatrix.TransformPoints(myArray)
' Draw the Points to the screen again after applying the
' transform.
e.Graphics.DrawLines(myPen2, myArray)
End Sub
```

[C#]
```
public void TransformPointsExample(PaintEventArgs e)
{
Pen myPen = new Pen(Color.Blue, 1);
Pen myPen2 = new Pen(Color.Red, 1);
// Create an array of points.
Point[] myArray =
{
new Point(20, 20),
new Point(120, 20),
new Point(120, 120),
new Point(20, 120),
new Point(20,20)
};
// Draw the Points to the screen before applying the
// transform.
e.Graphics.DrawLines(myPen, myArray);
// Create a matrix and scale it.
Matrix myMatrix = new Matrix();
myMatrix.Scale(3, 2, MatrixOrder.Append);
myMatrix.TransformPoints(myArray);
// Draw the Points to the screen again after applying the
// transform.
e.Graphics.DrawLines(myPen2, myArray);
}
```

Requirements

Platforms: Windows 98, Windows NT 4.0, Windows Millennium Edition, Windows 2000, Windows XP Home Edition, Windows XP Professional, Windows Server 2003 family

Matrix.TransformPoints Method (PointF[])

Applies the geometric transform represented by this **Matrix** object to a specified array of points.

[Visual Basic]
```
Overloads Public Sub TransformPoints( _
   ByVal pts() As PointF _
)
```
[C#]
```
public void TransformPoints(
   PointF[] pts
);
```
[C++]
```
public: void TransformPoints(
   PointF pts[]
);
```
[JScript]
```
public function TransformPoints(
   pts : PointF[]
);
```

Parameters

pts

An array of **PointF** structures that represents the points to transform.

Example

For an example, see **Matrix.TransformPoints Method (Point[])**.

Requirements

Platforms: Windows 98, Windows NT 4.0, Windows Millennium Edition, Windows 2000, Windows XP Home Edition, Windows XP Professional, Windows Server 2003 family

Matrix.TransformVectors Method

Multiplies each vector in an array by the matrix. The translation elements of this matrix (third row) are ignored.

Overload List

Applies only the scale and rotate components of this **Matrix** object to the specified array of points.

[Visual Basic] **Overloads Public Sub TransformVectors(Point())**

[C#] **public void TransformVectors(Point[]);**

[C++] **public: void TransformVectors(Point[]);**

[JScript] **public function TransformVectors(Point[]);**

Multiplies each vector in an array by the matrix. The translation elements of this matrix (third row) are ignored.

[Visual Basic] **Overloads Public Sub TransformVectors(PointF())**

[C#] **public void TransformVectors(PointF[]);**

[C++] **public: void TransformVectors(PointF[]);**

[JScript] **public function TransformVectors(PointF[]);**

Example

For an example, see **Matrix.TransformVectors Method (Point[])**.

Matrix.TransformVectors Method (Point[])

Applies only the scale and rotate components of this **Matrix** object to the specified array of points.

[Visual Basic]
```
Overloads Public Sub TransformVectors( _
   ByVal pts() As Point _
)
```
[C#]
```
public void TransformVectors(
   Point[] pts
);
```
[C++]
```
public: void TransformVectors(
   Point pts[]
);
```
[JScript]
```
public function TransformVectors(
   pts : Point[]
);
```

Parameters

pts

An array of **Point** structures that represents the points to transform.

Example

[Visual Basic, C#] The following example is designed for use with Windows Forms, and it requires **PaintEventArgs** *e*, an **OnPaint** event object. The code performs the following actions:

- Creates an array of points that form a rectangle.
- Draws this array of points to the screen prior to applying a scaling transform (the blue rectangle).
- Creates a matrix and scales it by 3 in the x-axis and 2 in the y-axis, and translates it by 100 in both axes.
- Lists the matrix elements to the screen.
- Applies this matrix transform to the array of points.
- Draws the transformed array to the screen (the red rectangle).

[Visual Basic, C#] Notice that the red rectangle has been scaled by a factor of 3 in the x-axis and by 2 in the y-axis, including the upper left-hand corner of the rectangle (the beginning point of the rectangle) ¾ but the translation vector (the last two elements of the matrix) is ignored.

[Visual Basic]
```
Public Sub TransformVectorsExample(e As PaintEventArgs)
Dim myPen As New Pen(Color.Blue, 1)
Dim myPen2 As New Pen(Color.Red, 1)
' Create an array of points.
Dim myArray As Point() = {New Point(20, 20), New Point(120, 20), _
New Point(120, 120), New Point(20, 120), New Point(20, 20)}
' Draw the Points to the screen before applying the
' transform.
e.Graphics.DrawLines(myPen, myArray)
' Create a matrix and scale it.
Dim myMatrix As New Matrix()
myMatrix.Scale(3, 2, MatrixOrder.Append)
myMatrix.Translate(100, 100, MatrixOrder.Append)
ListMatrixElementsHelper(e, myMatrix, _
"Scaled and Translated Matrix", 6, 20)
myMatrix.TransformVectors(myArray)
' Draw the Points to the screen again after applying the
' transform.
e.Graphics.DrawLines(myPen2, myArray)
End Sub
' A helper function to list the contents of a matrix.
Public Sub ListMatrixElementsHelper(e As PaintEventArgs, _
matrix As Matrix, matrixName As String, numElements As Integer, _
y As Integer)
' Set up variables for drawing the array
' of points to the screen.
Dim i As Integer
Dim x As Single = 20
Dim j As Single = 200
Dim myFont As New Font("Arial", 8)
Dim myBrush As New SolidBrush(Color.Black)
' Draw the matrix name to the screen.
e.Graphics.DrawString(matrixName + ":  ", myFont, myBrush, x, y)
' Draw the set of path points and types to the screen.
For i = 0 To numElements - 1
e.Graphics.DrawString(matrix.Elements(i).ToString() + ", ", _
myFont, myBrush, j, y)
j += 30
Next i
End Sub
```

[C#]
```
public void TransformVectorsExample(PaintEventArgs e)
{
Pen myPen = new Pen(Color.Blue, 1);
Pen myPen2 = new Pen(Color.Red, 1);
// Create an array of points.
Point[] myArray =
{
new Point(20, 20),
new Point(120, 20),
new Point(120, 120),
new Point(20, 120),
new Point(20,20)
};
// Draw the Points to the screen before applying the
// transform.
e.Graphics.DrawLines(myPen, myArray);
// Create a matrix, scale it, and translate it.
Matrix myMatrix = new Matrix();
myMatrix.Scale(3, 2, MatrixOrder.Append);
myMatrix.Translate(100, 100, MatrixOrder.Append);
// List the matrix elements to the screen.
ListMatrixElements(e,
myMatrix,
"Scaled and Translated Matrix",
6,
20);
// Apply the transform to the array.
myMatrix.TransformVectors(myArray);
// Draw the Points to the screen again after applying the
// transform.
e.Graphics.DrawLines(myPen2, myArray);
}
//-------------------------------------------------------
// This function is a helper function to
// list the contents of a matrix.
//-------------------------------------------------------
public void ListMatrixElements(
PaintEventArgs e,
Matrix matrix,
string matrixName,
int numElements,
int y)
{
// Set up variables for drawing the array
// of points to the screen.
int i;
float x = 20, X = 200;
Font myFont = new Font("Arial", 8);
SolidBrush myBrush = new SolidBrush(Color.Black);
// Draw the matrix name to the screen.
e.Graphics.DrawString(
matrixName + ":  ",
myFont,
myBrush,
x,
y);
// Draw the set of path points and types to the screen.
for(i=0; i<numElements; i++)
{
e.Graphics.DrawString(
matrix.Elements[i].ToString() + ", ",
myFont,
myBrush,
X,
y);
X += 30;
}
}
```

Requirements

Platforms: Windows 98, Windows NT 4.0, Windows Millennium Edition, Windows 2000, Windows XP Home Edition, Windows XP Professional, Windows Server 2003 family

Matrix.TransformVectors Method (PointF[])

Multiplies each vector in an array by the matrix. The translation elements of this matrix (third row) are ignored.

```
[Visual Basic]
Overloads Public Sub TransformVectors( _
   ByVal pts() As PointF _
)
[C#]
public void TransformVectors(
   PointF[] pts
);
[C++]
public: void TransformVectors(
   PointF pts[]
);
[JScript]
public function TransformVectors(
   pts : PointF[]
);
```

Parameters

pts

An array of **Point** structures that represents the points to transform.

Example

For an example, see **Matrix.TransformVectors Method (Point[])**.

Requirements

Platforms: Windows 98, Windows NT 4.0, Windows Millennium Edition, Windows 2000, Windows XP Home Edition, Windows XP Professional, Windows Server 2003 family

Matrix.Translate Method

Applies the specified translation vector to this **Matrix** object by prepending the translation vector.

Overload List

Applies the specified translation vector (*offsetX* and *offsetY*) to this **Matrix** object by prepending the translation vector.

[Visual Basic] **Overloads Public Sub Translate(Single, Single)**

[C#] **public void Translate(float, float);**

[C++] **public: void Translate(float, float);**

[JScript] **public function Translate(float, float);**

Applies the specified translation vector to this **Matrix** object in the specified order.

[Visual Basic] **Overloads Public Sub Translate(Single, Single, MatrixOrder)**

[C#] **public void Translate(float, float, MatrixOrder);**

[C++] **public: void Translate(float, float, MatrixOrder);**

[JScript] **public function Translate(float, float, MatrixOrder);**

Example

[Visual Basic, C#] The following example is designed for use with Windows Forms, and it requires **PaintEventArgs** *e*, an **OnPaint** event object. The code performs the following actions:

- Draws a rectangle to the screen prior to applying a translate transform (the blue rectangle).
- Creates a matrix and translates it by 100 in both axes.
- Applies this matrix transform to the rectangle,
- Draws the transformed rectangle to the screen (the red rectangle).

[Visual Basic, C#] Notice that the beginning of the red rectangle is located 100 points in both axes from the beginning of the blue triangle.

> [Visual Basic, C#] **Note** This example shows how to use one of the overloaded versions of **Translate**. For other examples that might be available, see the individual overload topics.

```
[Visual Basic]
Public Sub TranslateExample(e As PaintEventArgs)
Dim myPen As New Pen(Color.Blue, 1)
Dim myPen2 As New Pen(Color.Red, 1)
' Draw a rectangle to the screen before applying the
' transform.
e.Graphics.DrawRectangle(myPen, 20, 20, 100, 50)
' Create a matrix and translate it.
Dim myMatrix As New Matrix()
myMatrix.Translate(100, 100, MatrixOrder.Append)
' Draw the Points to the screen again after applying the
' transform.
e.Graphics.Transform = myMatrix
e.Graphics.DrawRectangle(myPen2, 20, 20, 100, 50)
End Sub
```

```
[C#]
public void TranslateExample(PaintEventArgs e)
{
Pen myPen = new Pen(Color.Blue, 1);
Pen myPen2 = new Pen(Color.Red, 1);
// Draw a rectangle to the screen before applying the
// transform.
e.Graphics.DrawRectangle(myPen, 20, 20, 100, 50);
// Create a matrix and translate it.
Matrix myMatrix = new Matrix();
myMatrix.Translate(100, 100, MatrixOrder.Append);
// Draw the Points to the screen again after applying the
// transform.
e.Graphics.Transform = myMatrix;
e.Graphics.DrawRectangle(myPen2, 20, 20, 100, 50);
}
```

Matrix.Translate Method (Single, Single)

Applies the specified translation vector (*offsetX* and *offsetY*) to this **Matrix** object by prepending the translation vector.

```
[Visual Basic]
Overloads Public Sub Translate( _
   ByVal offsetX As Single, _
   ByVal offsetY As Single _
)
[C#]
public void Translate(
   float offsetX,
   float offsetY
);
[C++]
public: void Translate(
   float offsetX,
   float offsetY
);
[JScript]
public function Translate(
   offsetX : float,
   offsetY : float
);
```

Parameters

offsetX
The x value by which to translate this **Matrix**.

offsetY
The y value by which to translate this **Matrix**.

Example

For an example, see **Matrix.Translate Method (Single, Single, MatrixOrder)**.

Requirements

Platforms: Windows 98, Windows NT 4.0, Windows Millennium Edition, Windows 2000, Windows XP Home Edition, Windows XP Professional, Windows Server 2003 family

Matrix.Translate Method (Single, Single, MatrixOrder)

Applies the specified translation vector to this **Matrix** object in the specified order.

[Visual Basic]
```
Overloads Public Sub Translate( _
   ByVal offsetX As Single, _
   ByVal offsetY As Single, _
   ByVal order As MatrixOrder _
)
```
[C#]
```
public void Translate(
   float offsetX,
   float offsetY,
   MatrixOrder order
);
```
[C++]
```
public: void Translate(
   float offsetX,
   float offsetY,
   MatrixOrder order
);
```
[JScript]
```
public function Translate(
   offsetX : float,
   offsetY : float,
   order : MatrixOrder
);
```

Parameters

offsetX
The x value by which to translate this **Matrix**.

offsetY
The y value by which to translate this **Matrix**.

order
A **MatrixOrder** enumeration that specifies the order (append or prepend) in which the translation is applied to this **Matrix**.

Example

[Visual Basic, C#] The following example is designed for use with Windows Forms, and it requires **PaintEventArgs** *e*, an **OnPaint** event object. The code performs the following actions:

- Draws a rectangle to the screen prior to applying a translate transform (the blue rectangle).
- Creates a matrix and translates it by 100 in both axes.
- Applies this matrix transform to the rectangle,
- Draws the transformed rectangle to the screen (the red rectangle).

[Visual Basic, C#] Notice that the beginning of the red rectangle is located 100 points in both axes from the beginning of the blue triangle.

[Visual Basic]
```
Public Sub TranslateExample(e As PaintEventArgs)
Dim myPen As New Pen(Color.Blue, 1)
Dim myPen2 As New Pen(Color.Red, 1)
' Draw a rectangle to the screen before applying the
' transform.
e.Graphics.DrawRectangle(myPen, 20, 20, 100, 50)
' Create a matrix and translate it.
Dim myMatrix As New Matrix()
myMatrix.Translate(100, 100, MatrixOrder.Append)
' Draw the Points to the screen again after applying the
' transform.
e.Graphics.Transform = myMatrix
e.Graphics.DrawRectangle(myPen2, 20, 20, 100, 50)
End Sub
```

[C#]
```
public void TranslateExample(PaintEventArgs e)
{
Pen myPen = new Pen(Color.Blue, 1);
Pen myPen2 = new Pen(Color.Red, 1);
// Draw a rectangle to the screen before applying the
// transform.
e.Graphics.DrawRectangle(myPen, 20, 20, 100, 50);
// Create a matrix and translate it.
Matrix myMatrix = new Matrix();
myMatrix.Translate(100, 100, MatrixOrder.Append);
// Draw the Points to the screen again after applying the
// transform.
e.Graphics.Transform = myMatrix;
e.Graphics.DrawRectangle(myPen2, 20, 20, 100, 50);
}
```

Requirements

Platforms: Windows 98, Windows NT 4.0, Windows Millennium Edition, Windows 2000, Windows XP Home Edition, Windows XP Professional, Windows Server 2003 family

Matrix.VectorTransformPoints Method

This member supports the .NET Framework infrastructure and is not intended to be used directly from your code.

[Visual Basic]
```
Public Sub VectorTransformPoints( _
   ByVal pts() As Point _
)
```
[C#]
```
public void VectorTransformPoints(
   Point[] pts
);
```
[C++]
```
public: void VectorTransformPoints(
   Point pts[]
);
```
[JScript]
```
public function VectorTransformPoints(
   pts : Point[]
);
```

MatrixOrder Enumeration

Specifies the order for matrix transform operations.

[Visual Basic]
```
<Serializable>
Public Enum MatrixOrder
```
[C#]
```
[Serializable]
public enum MatrixOrder
```
[C++]
```
[Serializable]
__value public enum MatrixOrder
```
[JScript]
```
public
   Serializable
enum MatrixOrder
```

Remarks

Matrix transform operations are not necessarily commutative. The order in which they are applied is important.

Members

Member name	Description
Append	The new operation is applied after the old operation.
Prepend	The new operation is applied before the old operation.

Requirements

Namespace: System.Drawing.Drawing2D

Platforms: Windows 98, Windows NT 4.0, Windows Millennium Edition, Windows 2000, Windows XP Home Edition, Windows XP Professional, Windows Server 2003 family

Assembly: System.Drawing (in System.Drawing.dll)

PathData Class

Contains the graphical data that makes up a **GraphicsPath** object. This class cannot be inherited.

System.Object
  System.Drawing.Drawing2D.PathData

```
[Visual Basic]
NotInheritable Public Class PathData
[C#]
public sealed class PathData
[C++]
public __gc __sealed class PathData
[JScript]
public class PathData
```

Thread Safety

Any public static (**Shared** in Visual Basic) members of this type are safe for multithreaded operations. Any instance members are not guaranteed to be thread safe.

Requirements

Namespace: System.Drawing.Drawing2D

Platforms: Windows 98, Windows NT 4.0, Windows Millennium Edition, Windows 2000, Windows XP Home Edition, Windows XP Professional, Windows Server 2003 family

Assembly: System.Drawing (in System.Drawing.dll)

PathData Constructor

Initializes a new instance of the **PathData** class.

```
[Visual Basic]
Public Sub New()
[C#]
public PathData();
[C++]
public: PathData();
[JScript]
public function PathData();
```

Requirements

Platforms: Windows 98, Windows NT 4.0, Windows Millennium Edition, Windows 2000, Windows XP Home Edition, Windows XP Professional, Windows Server 2003 family

PathData.Points Property

Gets or sets an array of **PointF** structures that represents the points through which the path is constructed.

```
[Visual Basic]
Public Property Points As PointF ()
[C#]
public PointF[] Points {get; set;}
[C++]
public: __property PointF get_Points();
public: __property void set_Points(PointF[]);
[JScript]
public function get Points() : PointF[];
public function set Points(PointF[]);
```

Property Value

An array of **PointF** objects that represents the points through which the path is constructed.

Requirements

Platforms: Windows 98, Windows NT 4.0, Windows Millennium Edition, Windows 2000, Windows XP Home Edition, Windows XP Professional, Windows Server 2003 family

PathData.Types Property

Gets or sets the types of the corresponding points in the path.

```
[Visual Basic]
Public Property Types As Byte ()
[C#]
public byte[] Types {get; set;}
[C++]
public: __property unsigned char get_Types();
public: __property void set_Types(unsigned char __gc[]);
[JScript]
public function get Types() : Byte[];
public function set Types(Byte[]);
```

Property Value

An array of bytes that specify the types of the corresponding points in the path.

Requirements

Platforms: Windows 98, Windows NT 4.0, Windows Millennium Edition, Windows 2000, Windows XP Home Edition, Windows XP Professional, Windows Server 2003 family

PathGradientBrush Class

Encapsulates a **Brush** object that fills the interior of a **GraphicsPath** object with a gradient. This class cannot be inherited.

System.Object
  System.MarshalByRefObject
    System.Drawing.Brush
      System.Drawing.Drawing2D.PathGradientBrush

```
[Visual Basic]
NotInheritable Public Class PathGradientBrush
   Inherits Brush
[C#]
public sealed class PathGradientBrush : Brush
[C++]
public __gc __sealed class PathGradientBrush : public Brush
[JScript]
public class PathGradientBrush extends Brush
```

Thread Safety

Any public static (**Shared** in Visual Basic) members of this type are safe for multithreaded operations. Any instance members are not guaranteed to be thread safe.

Remarks

The color gradient is a smooth shading of colors from the center point of the path to the outside boundary edge of the path. Blend factors, positions, and style affect where the gradient starts and ends, and how fast it changes shade.

Path gradient brushes do not obey the **SmoothingMode** property of the **Graphics** object used to do the drawing. Areas filled using a **PathGradientBrush** object are rendered the same way (aliased) regardless of the smoothing mode.

Requirements

Namespace: System.Drawing.Drawing2D

Platforms: Windows 98, Windows NT 4.0, Windows Millennium Edition, Windows 2000, Windows XP Home Edition, Windows XP Professional, Windows Server 2003 family

Assembly: System.Drawing (in System.Drawing.dll)

PathGradientBrush Constructor

Initializes a new instance of the **PathGradientBrush** class with the specified path.

Overload List

Initializes a new instance of the **PathGradientBrush** class with the specified path.

[Visual Basic] **Public Sub New(GraphicsPath)**

[C#] **public PathGradientBrush(GraphicsPath);**

[C++] **public: PathGradientBrush(GraphicsPath*);**

[JScript] **public function PathGradientBrush(GraphicsPath);**

Initializes a new instance of the **PathGradientBrush** class with the specified points.

[Visual Basic] **Public Sub New(Point())**

[C#] **public PathGradientBrush(Point[]);**

[C++] **public: PathGradientBrush(Point[]);**

[JScript] **public function PathGradientBrush(Point[]);**

Initializes a new instance of the **PathGradientBrush** class with the specified points.

[Visual Basic] **Public Sub New(PointF())**

[C#] **public PathGradientBrush(PointF[]);**

[C++] **public: PathGradientBrush(PointF[]);**

[JScript] **public function PathGradientBrush(PointF[]);**

Initializes a new instance of the **PathGradientBrush** class with the specified points and wrap mode.

[Visual Basic] **Public Sub New(Point(), WrapMode)**

[C#] **public PathGradientBrush(Point[], WrapMode);**

[C++] **public: PathGradientBrush(Point[], WrapMode);**

[JScript] **public function PathGradientBrush(Point[], WrapMode);**

Initializes a new instance of the **PathGradientBrush** class with the specified points and wrap mode.

[Visual Basic] **Public Sub New(PointF(), WrapMode)**

[C#] **public PathGradientBrush(PointF[], WrapMode);**

[C++] **public: PathGradientBrush(PointF[], WrapMode);**

[JScript] **public function PathGradientBrush(PointF[], WrapMode);**

PathGradientBrush Constructor (GraphicsPath)

Initializes a new instance of the **PathGradientBrush** class with the specified path.

```
[Visual Basic]
Public Sub New( _
   ByVal path As GraphicsPath _
)
[C#]
public PathGradientBrush(
   GraphicsPath path
);
[C++]
public: PathGradientBrush(
   GraphicsPath* path
);
[JScript]
public function PathGradientBrush(
   path : GraphicsPath
);
```

Parameters

path
  The **GraphicsPath** object that defines the area filled by this **PathGradientBrush** object.

Requirements

Platforms: Windows 98, Windows NT 4.0, Windows Millennium Edition, Windows 2000, Windows XP Home Edition, Windows XP Professional, Windows Server 2003 family

PathGradientBrush Constructor (Point[])

Initializes a new instance of the **PathGradientBrush** class with the specified points.

```
[Visual Basic]
Public Sub New( _
   ByVal points() As Point _
)
[C#]
public PathGradientBrush(
   Point[] points
);
[C++]
public: PathGradientBrush(
   Point points[]
);
[JScript]
public function PathGradientBrush(
   points : Point[]
);
```

Parameters

points

An array of **Point** structures that represents the points that make up the vertices of the path.

Requirements

Platforms: Windows 98, Windows NT 4.0, Windows Millennium Edition, Windows 2000, Windows XP Home Edition, Windows XP Professional, Windows Server 2003 family

PathGradientBrush Constructor (PointF[])

Initializes a new instance of the **PathGradientBrush** class with the specified points.

```
[Visual Basic]
Public Sub New( _
   ByVal points() As PointF _
)
[C#]
public PathGradientBrush(
   PointF[] points
);
[C++]
public: PathGradientBrush(
   PointF points[]
);
[JScript]
public function PathGradientBrush(
   points : PointF[]
);
```

Parameters

points

An array of **PointF** structures that represents the points that make up the vertices of the path.

Requirements

Platforms: Windows 98, Windows NT 4.0, Windows Millennium Edition, Windows 2000, Windows XP Home Edition, Windows XP Professional, Windows Server 2003 family

PathGradientBrush Constructor (Point[], WrapMode)

Initializes a new instance of the **PathGradientBrush** class with the specified points and wrap mode.

```
[Visual Basic]
Public Sub New( _
   ByVal points() As Point, _
   ByVal wrapMode As WrapMode _
)
[C#]
public PathGradientBrush(
   Point[] points,
   WrapMode wrapMode
);
[C++]
public: PathGradientBrush(
   Point points[],
   WrapMode wrapMode
);
[JScript]
public function PathGradientBrush(
   points : Point[],
   wrapMode : WrapMode
);
```

Parameters

points

An array of **Point** structures that represents the points that make up the vertices of the path.

wrapMode

A **WrapMode** enumeration that specifies how fills drawn with this **PathGradientBrush** object are tiled.

Requirements

Platforms: Windows 98, Windows NT 4.0, Windows Millennium Edition, Windows 2000, Windows XP Home Edition, Windows XP Professional, Windows Server 2003 family

PathGradientBrush Constructor (PointF[], WrapMode)

Initializes a new instance of the **PathGradientBrush** class with the specified points and wrap mode.

```
[Visual Basic]
Public Sub New( _
   ByVal points() As PointF, _
   ByVal wrapMode As WrapMode _
)
[C#]
public PathGradientBrush(
   PointF[] points,
   WrapMode wrapMode
);
[C++]
public: PathGradientBrush(
   PointF points[],
   WrapMode wrapMode
);
```

```
[JScript]
public function PathGradientBrush(
   points : PointF[],
   wrapMode : WrapMode
);
```

Parameters

points

An array of **PointF** structures that represents the points that make up the vertices of the path.

wrapMode

A **WrapMode** enumeration that specifies how fills drawn with this **PathGradientBrush** object are tiled.

Requirements

Platforms: Windows 98, Windows NT 4.0, Windows Millennium Edition, Windows 2000, Windows XP Home Edition, Windows XP Professional, Windows Server 2003 family

PathGradientBrush.Blend Property

Gets or sets a **Blend** object that specifies positions and factors that define a custom falloff for the gradient.

```
[Visual Basic]
Public Property Blend As Blend
[C#]
public Blend Blend {get; set;}
[C++]
public: __property Blend* get_Blend();
public: __property void set_Blend(Blend*);
[JScript]
public function get Blend() : Blend;
public function set Blend(Blend);
```

Property Value

A **Blend** object that represents a custom falloff for the gradient.

Remarks

A **Blend** object contains corresponding arrays of blend factors and positions. The blend factors specify the percentages of the starting color and ending color to use at the corresponding position. The positions are given as a percentage of distance along the gradient path.

Requirements

Platforms: Windows 98, Windows NT 4.0, Windows Millennium Edition, Windows 2000, Windows XP Home Edition, Windows XP Professional, Windows Server 2003 family

PathGradientBrush.CenterColor Property

Gets or sets the color at the center of the path gradient.

```
[Visual Basic]
Public Property CenterColor As Color
[C#]
public Color CenterColor {get; set;}
[C++]
public: __property Color get_CenterColor();
public: __property void set_CenterColor(Color);
[JScript]
public function get CenterColor() : Color;
public function set CenterColor(Color);
```

Property Value

A **Color** structure that represents the color at the center of the path gradient.

Requirements

Platforms: Windows 98, Windows NT 4.0, Windows Millennium Edition, Windows 2000, Windows XP Home Edition, Windows XP Professional, Windows Server 2003 family

PathGradientBrush.CenterPoint Property

Gets or sets the center point of the path gradient.

```
[Visual Basic]
Public Property CenterPoint As PointF
[C#]
public PointF CenterPoint {get; set;}
[C++]
public: __property PointF get_CenterPoint();
public: __property void set_CenterPoint(PointF);
[JScript]
public function get CenterPoint() : PointF;
public function set CenterPoint(PointF);
```

Property Value

A **PointF** structure that represents the center point of the path gradient.

Requirements

Platforms: Windows 98, Windows NT 4.0, Windows Millennium Edition, Windows 2000, Windows XP Home Edition, Windows XP Professional, Windows Server 2003 family

PathGradientBrush.FocusScales Property

Gets or sets the focus point for the gradient falloff.

```
[Visual Basic]
Public Property FocusScales As PointF
[C#]
public PointF FocusScales {get; set;}
[C++]
public: __property PointF get_FocusScales();
public: __property void set_FocusScales(PointF);
[JScript]
public function get FocusScales() : PointF;
public function set FocusScales(PointF);
```

Property Value

A **PointF** structure that represents the focus point for the gradient falloff.

Requirements

Platforms: Windows 98, Windows NT 4.0, Windows Millennium Edition, Windows 2000, Windows XP Home Edition, Windows XP Professional, Windows Server 2003 family

PathGradientBrush.InterpolationColors Property

Gets or sets a **ColorBlend** object that defines a multicolor linear gradient.

```
[Visual Basic]
Public Property InterpolationColors As ColorBlend
[C#]
public ColorBlend InterpolationColors {get; set;}
[C++]
public: __property ColorBlend* get_InterpolationColors();
public: __property void set_InterpolationColors(ColorBlend*);
[JScript]
public function get InterpolationColors() : ColorBlend;
public function set InterpolationColors(ColorBlend);
```

Property Value

A **ColorBlend** object that defines a multicolor linear gradient.

Remarks

A **ColorBlend** object contains corresponding arrays of colors and positions. The positions are values from 0 through 1 that specify the percentage of the distance along the gradient path where the corresponding color is located.

Requirements

Platforms: Windows 98, Windows NT 4.0,
Windows Millennium Edition, Windows 2000,
Windows XP Home Edition, Windows XP Professional,
Windows Server 2003 family

PathGradientBrush.Rectangle Property

Gets a bounding rectangle for this **PathGradientBrush** object.

```
[Visual Basic]
Public ReadOnly Property Rectangle As RectangleF
[C#]
public RectangleF Rectangle {get;}
[C++]
public: __property RectangleF get_Rectangle();
[JScript]
public function get Rectangle() : RectangleF;
```

Property Value

A **RectangleF** structure that represents a rectangular region that bounds the path this **PathGradientBrush** object fills.

Requirements

Platforms: Windows 98, Windows NT 4.0,
Windows Millennium Edition, Windows 2000,
Windows XP Home Edition, Windows XP Professional,
Windows Server 2003 family

PathGradientBrush.SurroundColors Property

Gets or sets an array of colors that correspond to the points in the path this **PathGradientBrush** object fills.

```
[Visual Basic]
Public Property SurroundColors As Color ()
[C#]
public Color[] SurroundColors {get; set;}
[C++]
public: __property Color get_SurroundColors();
public: __property void set_SurroundColors(Color[]);
[JScript]
public function get SurroundColors() : Color[];
public function set SurroundColors(Color[]);
```

Property Value

An array of **Color** structures that represents the colors associated with each point in the path this **PathGradientBrush** object fills.

Remarks

Each **Color** structure in the **SurroundColors** array corresponds to a point in the path.

Requirements

Platforms: Windows 98, Windows NT 4.0,
Windows Millennium Edition, Windows 2000,
Windows XP Home Edition, Windows XP Professional,
Windows Server 2003 family

PathGradientBrush.Transform Property

Gets or sets a **Matrix** object that defines a local geometric transform for this **PathGradientBrush** object.

```
[Visual Basic]
Public Property Transform As Matrix
[C#]
public Matrix Transform {get; set;}
[C++]
public: __property Matrix* get_Transform();
public: __property void set_Transform(Matrix*);
[JScript]
public function get Transform() : Matrix;
public function set Transform(Matrix);
```

Property Value

A **Matrix** object that defines a geometric transform that applies only to fills drawn with this **PathGradientBrush** object.

Remarks

A geometric transform can be used to translate, scale, rotate, or skew the gradient fill.

Requirements

Platforms: Windows 98, Windows NT 4.0,
Windows Millennium Edition, Windows 2000,
Windows XP Home Edition, Windows XP Professional,
Windows Server 2003 family

PathGradientBrush.WrapMode Property

Gets or sets a **WrapMode** enumeration that indicates the wrap mode for this **PathGradientBrush** object.

```
[Visual Basic]
Public Property WrapMode As WrapMode
[C#]
public WrapMode WrapMode {get; set;}
[C++]
public: __property WrapMode get_WrapMode();
public: __property void set_WrapMode(WrapMode);
```

[JScript]
```
public function get WrapMode() : WrapMode;
public function set WrapMode(WrapMode);
```

Property Value

A **WrapMode** enumeration that specifies how fills drawn with this **PathGradientBrush** object are tiled.

Requirements

Platforms: Windows 98, Windows NT 4.0,
Windows Millennium Edition, Windows 2000,
Windows XP Home Edition, Windows XP Professional,
Windows Server 2003 family

PathGradientBrush.Clone Method

Creates an exact copy of this **PathGradientBrush** object.

[Visual Basic]
```
Overrides Public Function Clone() As Object Implements _
   ICloneable.Clone
```
[C#]
```
public override object Clone();
```
[C++]
```
public: Object* Clone();
```
[JScript]
```
public override function Clone() : Object;
```

Return Value

The **PathGradientBrush** this method creates, cast as an object.

Implements

ICloneable.Clone

Requirements

Platforms: Windows 98, Windows NT 4.0,
Windows Millennium Edition, Windows 2000,
Windows XP Home Edition, Windows XP Professional,
Windows Server 2003 family

PathGradientBrush.MultiplyTransform Method

Multiplies the **Matrix** object that represents the local geometric transform of this **PathGradientBrush** by the specified **Matrix** by prepending the specified **Matrix**.

Overload List

Updates the brush's transformation matrix with the product of brush's transformation matrix multiplied by another matrix.

[Visual Basic] **Overloads Public Sub MultiplyTransform(Matrix)**

[C#] **public void MultiplyTransform(Matrix);**

[C++] **public: void MultiplyTransform(Matrix*);**

[JScript] **public function MultiplyTransform(Matrix);**

Updates the brush's transformation matrix with the product of the brush's transformation matrix multiplied by another matrix.

[Visual Basic] **Overloads Public Sub MultiplyTransform(Matrix, MatrixOrder)**

[C#] **public void MultiplyTransform(Matrix, MatrixOrder);**

[C++] **public: void MultiplyTransform(Matrix*, MatrixOrder);**

[JScript] **public function MultiplyTransform(Matrix, MatrixOrder);**

Example

[Visual Basic, C#] The following example is designed for use with Windows Forms, and it requires **PaintEventArgs** *e*, an **OnPaint** event object. The code performs the following actions:

- Creates a graphics path and adds a rectangle to it.
- Creates a **PathGradientBrush** object from the path points (in this example, the points form a rectangle, but it could be most any shape).
- Sets the center color to red and the surrounding color to blue.
- Draws the **PathGradientBrush** to the screen prior to applying the multiply transform.
- Creates s matrix that rotates the brush 90 degrees and translates it by 100 in both axes.
- Applies this matrix to the brush by using the **MultiplyTransform** method,
- Draws the brush to the screen.

> [Visual Basic, C#] **Note** This example shows how to use one of the overloaded versions of **MultiplyTransform**. For other examples that might be available, see the individual overload topics.

[Visual Basic]
```
Public Sub MultiplyTransformExample(e As PaintEventArgs)
' Create a graphics path and add a rectangle.
Dim myPath As New GraphicsPath()
Dim rect As New Rectangle(20, 20, 100, 50)
myPath.AddRectangle(rect)
' Get the path's array of points.
Dim myPathPointArray As PointF() = myPath.PathPoints
' Create a path gradient brush.
Dim myPGBrush As New PathGradientBrush(myPathPointArray)
' Set the color span.
myPGBrush.CenterColor = Color.Red
Dim mySurroundColor As Color() = {Color.Blue}
myPGBrush.SurroundColors = mySurroundColor
' Draw the brush to the screen prior to transformation.
e.Graphics.FillRectangle(myPGBrush, 10, 10, 200, 200)
' Create a new matrix that rotates by 90 degrees, and
' translates by 100 in each direction.
Dim myMatrix As New Matrix(0, 1, - 1, 0, 100, 100)
' Apply the transform to the brush.
myPGBrush.MultiplyTransform(myMatrix, MatrixOrder.Append)
' Draw the brush to the screen again after applying the
' transform.
e.Graphics.FillRectangle(myPGBrush, 10, 10, 200, 300)
End Sub
```

[C#]
```
public void MultiplyTransformExample(PaintEventArgs e)
{
// Create a graphics path and add an rectangle.
GraphicsPath myPath = new GraphicsPath();
Rectangle rect = new Rectangle(20, 20, 100, 50);
myPath.AddRectangle(rect);
// Get the path's array of points.
PointF[] myPathPointArray = myPath.PathPoints;
// Create a path gradient brush.
PathGradientBrush myPGBrush = new
PathGradientBrush(myPathPointArray);
// Set the color span.
myPGBrush.CenterColor = Color.Red;
Color[] mySurroundColor = {Color.Blue};
myPGBrush.SurroundColors = mySurroundColor;
// Draw the brush to the screen prior to transformation.
e.Graphics.FillRectangle(myPGBrush, 10, 10, 200, 200);
// Create a new matrix that rotates by 90 degrees, and
// translates by 100 in each direction.
```

```
Matrix myMatrix = new Matrix(0, 1, -1, 0, 100, 100);
// Apply the transform to the brush.
myPGBrush.MultiplyTransform(myMatrix, MatrixOrder.Append);
// Draw the brush to the screen again after applying the
// transform.
e.Graphics.FillRectangle(myPGBrush, 10, 10, 200, 300);
}
```

PathGradientBrush.MultiplyTransform Method (Matrix)

Updates the brush's transformation matrix with the product of brush's transformation matrix multiplied by another matrix.

[Visual Basic]
```
Overloads Public Sub MultiplyTransform( _
   ByVal matrix As Matrix _
)
```
[C#]
```
public void MultiplyTransform(
   Matrix matrix
);
```
[C++]
```
public: void MultiplyTransform(
   Matrix* matrix
);
```
[JScript]
```
public function MultiplyTransform(
   matrix : Matrix
);
```

Parameters

matrix
: The **Matrix** object that will be multiplied by the brush's current transformation matrix.

Example

For an example, see **PathGradientBrush.MultiplyTransform Method (Matrix, MatrixOrder)**.

Requirements

Platforms: Windows 98, Windows NT 4.0, Windows Millennium Edition, Windows 2000, Windows XP Home Edition, Windows XP Professional, Windows Server 2003 family

PathGradientBrush.MultiplyTransform Method (Matrix, MatrixOrder)

Updates the brush's transformation matrix with the product of the brush's transformation matrix multiplied by another matrix.

[Visual Basic]
```
Overloads Public Sub MultiplyTransform( _
   ByVal matrix As Matrix, _
   ByVal order As MatrixOrder _
)
```
[C#]
```
public void MultiplyTransform(
   Matrix matrix,
   MatrixOrder order
);
```
[C++]
```
public: void MultiplyTransform(
   Matrix* matrix,
   MatrixOrder order
);
```
[JScript]
```
public function MultiplyTransform(
   matrix : Matrix,
   order : MatrixOrder
);
```

Parameters

matrix
: The **Matrix** object that will be multiplied by the brush's current transformation matrix.

order
: A **MatrixOrder** enumeration that specifies in which order to multiply the two matrices.

Example

[Visual Basic, C#] The following example is designed for use with Windows Forms, and it requires **PaintEventArgs** *e*, an **OnPaint** event object. The code performs the following actions:

- Creates a graphics path and adds a rectangle to it.
- Creates a **PathGradientBrush** object from the path points (in this example, the points form a rectangle, but it could be most any shape).
- Sets the center color to red and the surrounding color to blue.
- Draws the **PathGradientBrush** to the screen prior to applying the multiply transform.
- Creates s matrix that rotates the brush 90 degrees and translates it by 100 in both axes.
- Applies this matrix to the brush by using the **MultiplyTransform** method,
- Draws the brush to the screen.

[Visual Basic]
```
Public Sub MultiplyTransformExample(e As PaintEventArgs)
' Create a graphics path and add a rectangle.
Dim myPath As New GraphicsPath()
Dim rect As New Rectangle(20, 20, 100, 50)
myPath.AddRectangle(rect)
' Get the path's array of points.
Dim myPathPointArray As PointF() = myPath.PathPoints
' Create a path gradient brush.
Dim myPGBrush As New PathGradientBrush(myPathPointArray)
' Set the color span.
myPGBrush.CenterColor = Color.Red
Dim mySurroundColor As Color() = {Color.Blue}
myPGBrush.SurroundColors = mySurroundColor
' Draw the brush to the screen prior to transformation.
e.Graphics.FillRectangle(myPGBrush, 10, 10, 200, 200)
' Create a new matrix that rotates by 90 degrees, and
' translates by 100 in each direction.
Dim myMatrix As New Matrix(0, 1, - 1, 0, 100, 100)
' Apply the transform to the brush.
myPGBrush.MultiplyTransform(myMatrix, MatrixOrder.Append)
' Draw the brush to the screen again after applying the
' transform.
e.Graphics.FillRectangle(myPGBrush, 10, 10, 200, 300)
End Sub
```

[C#]
```
public void MultiplyTransformExample(PaintEventArgs e)
{
// Create a graphics path and add an rectangle.
GraphicsPath myPath = new GraphicsPath();
Rectangle rect = new Rectangle(20, 20, 100, 50);
myPath.AddRectangle(rect);
// Get the path's array of points.
PointF[] myPathPointArray = myPath.PathPoints;
// Create a path gradient brush.
PathGradientBrush myPGBrush = new
```

```
PathGradientBrush(myPathPointArray);
// Set the color span.
myPGBrush.CenterColor = Color.Red;
Color[] mySurroundColor = {Color.Blue};
myPGBrush.SurroundColors = mySurroundColor;
// Draw the brush to the screen prior to transformation.
e.Graphics.FillRectangle(myPGBrush, 10, 10, 200, 200);
// Create a new matrix that rotates by 90 degrees, and
// translates by 100 in each direction.
Matrix myMatrix = new Matrix(0, 1, -1, 0, 100, 100);
// Apply the transform to the brush.
myPGBrush.MultiplyTransform(myMatrix, MatrixOrder.Append);
// Draw the brush to the screen again after applying the
// transform.
e.Graphics.FillRectangle(myPGBrush, 10, 10, 200, 300);
}
```

Requirements

Platforms: Windows 98, Windows NT 4.0, Windows Millennium Edition, Windows 2000, Windows XP Home Edition, Windows XP Professional, Windows Server 2003 family

PathGradientBrush.ResetTransform Method

Resets the **Transform** property to identity.

[Visual Basic]
```
Public Sub ResetTransform()
```
[C#]
```
public void ResetTransform();
```
[C++]
```
public: void ResetTransform();
```
[JScript]
```
public function ResetTransform();
```

Example

[C#] The following example resets the geometric transform of *pgBrush* to identity. It is assumed that *myPath* is an existing **GraphicsPath** object.

[C#]
```
PathGradientBrush pgBrush = new PathGradientBrush(myPath);
pgBrush.ResetTransform();
```

Requirements

Platforms: Windows 98, Windows NT 4.0, Windows Millennium Edition, Windows 2000, Windows XP Home Edition, Windows XP Professional, Windows Server 2003 family

PathGradientBrush.RotateTransform Method

Applies a clockwise rotation of the specified angle to the local geometric transform.

Overload List

Rotates the local geometric transform by the specified amount. This method prepends the rotation to the transform.

[Visual Basic] **Overloads Public Sub RotateTransform(Single)**

[C#] **public void RotateTransform(float);**

[C++] **public: void RotateTransform(float);**

[JScript] **public function RotateTransform(float);**

Rotates the local geometric transform by the specified amount in the specified order.

[Visual Basic] **Overloads Public Sub RotateTransform(Single, MatrixOrder)**

[C#] **public void RotateTransform(float, MatrixOrder);**

[C++] **public: void RotateTransform(float, MatrixOrder);**

[JScript] **public function RotateTransform(float, MatrixOrder);**

Example

[Visual Basic, C#] The following example is designed for use with Windows Forms, and it requires **PaintEventArgs** *e*, an **OnPaint** event object. The code performs the following actions:

- Creates a graphics path and adds a rectangle to it.
- Creates a **PathGradientBrush** object from the path points (in this example, the points form a rectangle, but it could be most any shape).
- Sets the center color to red and the surrounding color to blue.
- Draws the **PathGradientBrush** to the screen prior to applying the rotate transform.
- Applies the rotate transform to the brush by using its **RotateTransform** method.
- Draws the rotated brush (rectangle) to the screen.

[Visual Basic, C#] Notice that the bottom rectangle is rotated 45 degrees as compared to the one drawn prior to the translation.

> [Visual Basic, C#] **Note** This example shows how to use one of the overloaded versions of **RotateTransform**. For other examples that might be available, see the individual overload topics.

[Visual Basic]
```
Public Sub RotateTransformExample(e As PaintEventArgs)
' Create a graphics path and add a rectangle.
Dim myPath As New GraphicsPath()
Dim rect As New Rectangle(100, 20, 100, 50)
myPath.AddRectangle(rect)
' Get the path's array of points.
Dim myPathPointArray As PointF() = myPath.PathPoints
' Create a path gradient brush.
Dim myPGBrush As New PathGradientBrush(myPathPointArray)
' Set the color span.
myPGBrush.CenterColor = Color.Red
Dim mySurroundColor As Color() = {Color.Blue}
myPGBrush.SurroundColors = mySurroundColor
' Draw the brush to the screen prior to transformation.
e.Graphics.FillRectangle(myPGBrush, 10, 10, 200, 200)
' Apply the rotate transform to the brush.
myPGBrush.RotateTransform(45, MatrixOrder.Append)
' Draw the brush to the screen again after applying the
' transform.
e.Graphics.FillRectangle(myPGBrush, 10, 10, 200, 300)
End Sub
```

[C#]
```
public void RotateTransformExample(PaintEventArgs e)
{
// Create a graphics path and add an ellipse.
GraphicsPath myPath = new GraphicsPath();
Rectangle rect = new Rectangle(100, 20, 100, 50);
myPath.AddRectangle(rect);
// Get the path's array of points.
PointF[] myPathPointArray = myPath.PathPoints;
// Create a path gradient brush.
PathGradientBrush myPGBrush = new
PathGradientBrush(myPathPointArray);
```

```
// Set the color span.
myPGBrush.CenterColor = Color.Red;
Color[] mySurroundColor = {Color.Blue};
myPGBrush.SurroundColors = mySurroundColor;
// Draw the brush to the screen prior to transformation.
e.Graphics.FillRectangle(myPGBrush, 10, 10, 200, 200);
// Apply the rotate transform to the brush.
myPGBrush.RotateTransform(45, MatrixOrder.Append);
// Draw the brush to the screen again after applying the
// transform.
e.Graphics.FillRectangle(myPGBrush, 10, 10, 200, 300);
}
```

PathGradientBrush.RotateTransform Method (Single)

Rotates the local geometric transform by the specified amount. This method prepends the rotation to the transform.

```
[Visual Basic]
Overloads Public Sub RotateTransform( _
   ByVal angle As Single _
)
[C#]
public void RotateTransform(
   float angle
);
[C++]
public: void RotateTransform(
   float angle
);
[JScript]
public function RotateTransform(
   angle : float
);
```

Parameters

angle
  The angle (extent) of rotation.

Example

For an example, see **PathGradientBrush.RotateTransform Method (Single, MatrixOrder)**.

Requirements

Platforms: Windows 98, Windows NT 4.0, Windows Millennium Edition, Windows 2000, Windows XP Home Edition, Windows XP Professional, Windows Server 2003 family

PathGradientBrush.RotateTransform Method (Single, MatrixOrder)

Rotates the local geometric transform by the specified amount in the specified order.

```
[Visual Basic]
Overloads Public Sub RotateTransform( _
   ByVal angle As Single, _
   ByVal order As MatrixOrder _
)
[C#]
public void RotateTransform(
   float angle,
   MatrixOrder order
);
[C++]
public: void RotateTransform(
   float angle,
   MatrixOrder order
);
[JScript]
public function RotateTransform(
   angle : float,
   order : MatrixOrder
);
```

Parameters

angle
  The angle (extent)of rotation.

order
  A **MatrixOrder** enumeration that specifies whether to append or prepend the rotation matrix.

Example

[Visual Basic, C#] The following example is designed for use with Windows Forms, and it requires **PaintEventArgs** *e*, an **OnPaint** event object. The code performs the following actions:

- Creates a graphics path and adds a rectangle to it.
- Creates a **PathGradientBrush** object from the path points (in this example, the points form a rectangle, but it could be most any shape).
- Sets the center color to red and the surrounding color to blue.
- Draws the **PathGradientBrush** to the screen prior to applying the rotate transform.
- Applies the rotate transform to the brush by using its **RotateTransform** method.
- Draws the rotated brush (rectangle) to the screen.

[Visual Basic, C#] Notice that the bottom rectangle is rotated 45 degrees as compared to the one drawn prior to the translation.

```
[Visual Basic]
Public Sub RotateTransformExample(e As PaintEventArgs)
' Create a graphics path and add a rectangle.
Dim myPath As New GraphicsPath()
Dim rect As New Rectangle(100, 20, 100, 50)
myPath.AddRectangle(rect)
' Get the path's array of points.
Dim myPathPointArray As PointF() = myPath.PathPoints
' Create a path gradient brush.
Dim myPGBrush As New PathGradientBrush(myPathPointArray)
' Set the color span.
myPGBrush.CenterColor = Color.Red
Dim mySurroundColor As Color() = {Color.Blue}
myPGBrush.SurroundColors = mySurroundColor
' Draw the brush to the screen prior to transformation.
e.Graphics.FillRectangle(myPGBrush, 10, 10, 200, 200)
' Apply the rotate transform to the brush.
myPGBrush.RotateTransform(45, MatrixOrder.Append)
' Draw the brush to the screen again after applying the
' transform.
e.Graphics.FillRectangle(myPGBrush, 10, 10, 200, 300)
End Sub
```

```
[C#]
public void RotateTransformExample(PaintEventArgs e)
{
// Create a graphics path and add an ellipse.
GraphicsPath myPath = new GraphicsPath();
Rectangle rect = new Rectangle(100, 20, 100, 50);
myPath.AddRectangle(rect);
// Get the path's array of points.
```

```
PointF[] myPathPointArray = myPath.PathPoints;
// Create a path gradient brush.
PathGradientBrush myPGBrush = new
PathGradientBrush(myPathPointArray);
// Set the color span.
myPGBrush.CenterColor = Color.Red;
Color[] mySurroundColor = {Color.Blue};
myPGBrush.SurroundColors = mySurroundColor;
// Draw the brush to the screen prior to transformation.
e.Graphics.FillRectangle(myPGBrush, 10, 10, 200, 200);
// Apply the rotate transform to the brush.
myPGBrush.RotateTransform(45, MatrixOrder.Append);
// Draw the brush to the screen again after applying the
// transform.
e.Graphics.FillRectangle(myPGBrush, 10, 10, 200, 300);
}
```

Requirements

Platforms: Windows 98, Windows NT 4.0, Windows Millennium Edition, Windows 2000, Windows XP Home Edition, Windows XP Professional, Windows Server 2003 family

PathGradientBrush.ScaleTransform Method

Scales the local geometric transform by the specified amounts. This method prepends the scaling matrix to the transform.

Overload List

Scales the local geometric transform by the specified amounts. This method prepends the scaling matrix to the transform.

[Visual Basic] **Overloads Public Sub ScaleTransform(Single, Single)**

[C#] **public void ScaleTransform(float, float);**

[C++] **public: void ScaleTransform(float, float);**

[JScript] **public function ScaleTransform(float, float);**

Scales the local geometric transform by the specified amounts in the specified order.

[Visual Basic] **Overloads Public Sub ScaleTransform(Single, Single, MatrixOrder)**

[C#] **public void ScaleTransform(float, float, MatrixOrder);**

[C++] **public: void ScaleTransform(float, float, MatrixOrder);**

[JScript] **public function ScaleTransform(float, float, MatrixOrder);**

Example

[Visual Basic, C#] The following example is designed for use with Windows Forms, and it requires **PaintEventArgs** *e*, an **OnPaint** event object. The code

- Creates a graphics path and adds a rectangle to it.
- Creates a **PathGradientBrush** object from the path points (in this example, the points form a rectangle, but it could be most any shape).
- Sets the center color to red and the surrounding color to blue.
- Draws the **PathGradientBrush** to the screen prior to applying the scale transform.
- Applies the scale transform to the brush by using its **ScaleTransform** method.
- Calls the **TranslateTransform** method to move the brush rectangle such that it does not overlay the one drawn to the screen earlier.
- Draws the translated brush rectangle to the screen.

[Visual Basic, C#] Notice that the bottom rectangle is twice as long in the x-axis as is the one drawn prior to the translation.

> [Visual Basic, C#] **Note** This example shows how to use one of the overloaded versions of **ScaleTransform**. For other examples that might be available, see the individual overload topics.

[Visual Basic]
```
Public Sub ScaleTransformExample(e As PaintEventArgs)
' Create a graphics path and add a rectangle.
Dim myPath As New GraphicsPath()
Dim rect As New Rectangle(100, 20, 100, 50)
myPath.AddRectangle(rect)
' Get the path's array of points.
Dim myPathPointArray As PointF() = myPath.PathPoints
' Create a path gradient brush.
Dim myPGBrush As New PathGradientBrush(myPathPointArray)
' Set the color span.
myPGBrush.CenterColor = Color.Red
Dim mySurroundColor As Color() = {Color.Blue}
myPGBrush.SurroundColors = mySurroundColor
' Draw the brush to the screen prior to transformation.
e.Graphics.FillRectangle(myPGBrush, 10, 10, 200, 200)
' Scale by a factor of 2 in the x-axis by applying the scale
' transform to the brush.
myPGBrush.ScaleTransform(2, 1, MatrixOrder.Append)
' Move the brush down by 100 by Applying the translate
' transform to the brush.
myPGBrush.TranslateTransform(- 100, 100, MatrixOrder.Append)
' Draw the brush to the screen again after applying the
' transforms.
e.Graphics.FillRectangle(myPGBrush, 10, 10, 300, 300)
End Sub
```

[C#]
```
public void ScaleTransformExample(PaintEventArgs e)
{
// Create a graphics path and add a rectangle.
GraphicsPath myPath = new GraphicsPath();
Rectangle rect = new Rectangle(100, 20, 100, 50);
myPath.AddRectangle(rect);
// Get the path's array of points.
PointF[] myPathPointArray = myPath.PathPoints;
// Create a path gradient brush.
PathGradientBrush myPGBrush = new
PathGradientBrush(myPathPointArray);
// Set the color span.
myPGBrush.CenterColor = Color.Red;
Color[] mySurroundColor = {Color.Blue};
myPGBrush.SurroundColors = mySurroundColor;
// Draw the brush to the screen prior to transformation.
e.Graphics.FillRectangle(myPGBrush, 10, 10, 200, 200);
// Scale by a factor of 2 in the x-axis by applying the scale
// transform to the brush.
myPGBrush.ScaleTransform(2, 1, MatrixOrder.Append);
// Move the brush down by 100 by Applying the translate
// transform to the brush.
myPGBrush.TranslateTransform(-100, 100, MatrixOrder.Append);
// Draw the brush to the screen again after applying the
// transforms.
e.Graphics.FillRectangle(myPGBrush, 10, 10, 300, 300);
}
```

PathGradientBrush.ScaleTransform Method (Single, Single)

Scales the local geometric transform by the specified amounts. This method prepends the scaling matrix to the transform.

```
[Visual Basic]
Overloads Public Sub ScaleTransform( _
   ByVal sx As Single, _
   ByVal sy As Single _
)
[C#]
public void ScaleTransform(
   float sx,
   float sy
);
[C++]
public: void ScaleTransform(
   float sx,
   float sy
);
[JScript]
public function ScaleTransform(
   sx : float,
   sy : float
);
```

Parameters

sx
: The transform scale factor in the x-axis direction.

sy
: The transform scale factor in the y-axis direction.

Example

for an example, see **PathGradientBrush.ScaleTransform Method (Single, Single, MatrixOrder)**.

Requirements

Platforms: Windows 98, Windows NT 4.0, Windows Millennium Edition, Windows 2000, Windows XP Home Edition, Windows XP Professional, Windows Server 2003 family

PathGradientBrush.ScaleTransform Method (Single, Single, MatrixOrder)

Scales the local geometric transform by the specified amounts in the specified order.

```
[Visual Basic]
Overloads Public Sub ScaleTransform( _
   ByVal sx As Single, _
   ByVal sy As Single, _
   ByVal order As MatrixOrder _
)
[C#]
public void ScaleTransform(
   float sx,
   float sy,
   MatrixOrder order
);
[C++]
public: void ScaleTransform(
   float sx,
   float sy,
   MatrixOrder order
);
[JScript]
public function ScaleTransform(
   sx : float,
   sy : float,
   order : MatrixOrder
);
```

Parameters

sx
: The transform scale factor in the x-axis direction.

sy
: The transform scale factor in the y-axis direction.

order
: A **MatrixOrder** enumeration that specifies whether to append or prepend the scaling matrix.

Example

[Visual Basic, C#] The following example is designed for use with Windows Forms, and it requires **PaintEventArgs** *e*, an **OnPaint** event object. The code

- Creates a graphics path and adds a rectangle to it.
- Creates a **PathGradientBrush** object from the path points (in this example, the points form a rectangle, but it could be most any shape).
- Sets the center color to red and the surrounding color to blue.
- Draws the **PathGradientBrush** to the screen prior to applying the scale transform.
- Applies the scale transform to the brush by using its **ScaleTransform** method.
- Calls the **TranslateTransform** method to move the brush rectangle such that it does not overlay the one drawn to the screen earlier.
- Draws the translated brush rectangle to the screen.

[Visual Basic, C#] Notice that the bottom rectangle is twice as long in the x-axis as is the one drawn prior to the translation.

```
[Visual Basic]
Public Sub ScaleTransformExample(e As PaintEventArgs)
' Create a graphics path and add a rectangle.
Dim myPath As New GraphicsPath()
Dim rect As New Rectangle(100, 20, 100, 50)
myPath.AddRectangle(rect)
' Get the path's array of points.
Dim myPathPointArray As PointF() = myPath.PathPoints
' Create a path gradient brush.
Dim myPGBrush As New PathGradientBrush(myPathPointArray)
' Set the color span.
myPGBrush.CenterColor = Color.Red
Dim mySurroundColor As Color() = {Color.Blue}
myPGBrush.SurroundColors = mySurroundColor
' Draw the brush to the screen prior to transformation.
e.Graphics.FillRectangle(myPGBrush, 10, 10, 200, 200)
' Scale by a factor of 2 in the x-axis by applying the scale
' transform to the brush.
myPGBrush.ScaleTransform(2, 1, MatrixOrder.Append)
' Move the brush down by 100 by Applying the translate
' transform to the brush.
myPGBrush.TranslateTransform(- 100, 100, MatrixOrder.Append)
' Draw the brush to the screen again after applying the
' transforms.
e.Graphics.FillRectangle(myPGBrush, 10, 10, 300, 300)
End Sub
```

[C#]
```
public void ScaleTransformExample(PaintEventArgs e)
{
// Create a graphics path and add a rectangle.
GraphicsPath myPath = new GraphicsPath();
Rectangle rect = new Rectangle(100, 20, 100, 50);
myPath.AddRectangle(rect);
// Get the path's array of points.
PointF[] myPathPointArray = myPath.PathPoints;
// Create a path gradient brush.
PathGradientBrush myPGBrush = new
PathGradientBrush(myPathPointArray);
// Set the color span.
myPGBrush.CenterColor = Color.Red;
Color[] mySurroundColor = {Color.Blue};
myPGBrush.SurroundColors = mySurroundColor;
// Draw the brush to the screen prior to transformation.
e.Graphics.FillRectangle(myPGBrush, 10, 10, 200, 200);
// Scale by a factor of 2 in the x-axis by applying the scale
// transform to the brush.
myPGBrush.ScaleTransform(2, 1, MatrixOrder.Append);
// Move the brush down by 100 by Applying the translate
// transform to the brush.
myPGBrush.TranslateTransform(-100, 100, MatrixOrder.Append);
// Draw the brush to the screen again after applying the
// transforms.
e.Graphics.FillRectangle(myPGBrush, 10, 10, 300, 300);
}
```

Requirements

Platforms: Windows 98, Windows NT 4.0, Windows Millennium Edition, Windows 2000, Windows XP Home Edition, Windows XP Professional, Windows Server 2003 family

PathGradientBrush.SetBlendTriangularShape Method

Creates a gradient with a center color and a linear falloff to one surrounding color.

Overload List

Creates a gradient with a center color and a linear falloff to one surrounding color.

[Visual Basic] **Overloads Public Sub SetBlendTriangularShape(Single)**

[C#] **public void SetBlendTriangularShape(float);**

[C++] **public: void SetBlendTriangularShape(float);**

[JScript] **public function SetBlendTriangularShape(float);**

Creates a gradient with a center color and a linear falloff to each surrounding color.

[Visual Basic] **Overloads Public Sub SetBlendTriangularShape(Single, Single)**

[C#] **public void SetBlendTriangularShape(float, float);**

[C++] **public: void SetBlendTriangularShape(float, float);**

[JScript] **public function SetBlendTriangularShape(float, float);**

Example

[Visual Basic, C#] The following example is designed for use with Windows Forms, and it requires **PaintEventArgs** *e*, an **OnPaint** event object. The code performs the following actions:

- Creates a graphics path and adds a rectangle to it.
- Creates a **PathGradientBrush** from the path points (in this example, the points form a rectangle, but it could be most any shape).
- Sets the center color to red and the surrounding color to blue.
- Draws the **PathGradientBrush** to the screen prior to applying the blend transform.
- Applies the blend transform to the brush by using its **SetBlendTriangularShape** method.
- Calls the **TranslateTransform** method to move the brush rectangle such that it does not overlay the one drawn to the screen earlier.
- Draws the transformed-brush rectangle is drawn to the screen.

[Visual Basic, C#] Notice that the maximum center color (red) is located half way from the center of the path to the path boundary.

> [Visual Basic, C#] **Note** This example shows how to use one of the overloaded versions of **SetBlendTriangularShape**. For other examples that might be available, see the individual overload topics.

[Visual Basic]
```
Public Sub SetBlendTriangularShapeExample(e As PaintEventArgs)
' Create a graphics path and add a rectangle.
Dim myPath As New GraphicsPath()
Dim rect As New Rectangle(100, 20, 100, 50)
myPath.AddRectangle(rect)
' Get the path's array of points.
Dim myPathPointArray As PointF() = myPath.PathPoints
' Create a path gradient brush.
Dim myPGBrush As New PathGradientBrush(myPathPointArray)
' Set the color span.
myPGBrush.CenterColor = Color.Red
Dim mySurroundColor As Color() = {Color.Blue}
myPGBrush.SurroundColors = mySurroundColor
' Draw the brush to the screen prior to blend.
e.Graphics.FillRectangle(myPGBrush, 10, 10, 200, 200)
' Set the Blend factors.
myPGBrush.SetBlendTriangularShape(0.5F, 1F)
' Move the brush down by 100 by Applying the translate
' transform to the brush.
myPGBrush.TranslateTransform(0, 100, MatrixOrder.Append)
' Draw the brush to the screen again after applying the
' transforms.
e.Graphics.FillRectangle(myPGBrush, 10, 10, 300, 300)
End Sub
```

[C#]
```
public void SetBlendTriangularShapeExample(PaintEventArgs e)
{
// Create a graphics path and add a rectangle.
GraphicsPath myPath = new GraphicsPath();
Rectangle rect = new Rectangle(100, 20, 100, 50);
myPath.AddRectangle(rect);
// Get the path's array of points.
PointF[] myPathPointArray = myPath.PathPoints;
// Create a path gradient brush.
PathGradientBrush myPGBrush = new
PathGradientBrush(myPathPointArray);
// Set the color span.
myPGBrush.CenterColor = Color.Red;
Color[] mySurroundColor = {Color.Blue};
myPGBrush.SurroundColors = mySurroundColor;
// Draw the brush to the screen prior to the blend.
e.Graphics.FillRectangle(myPGBrush, 10, 10, 200, 200);
// Set the Blend factors.
myPGBrush.SetBlendTriangularShape(0.5f, 1.0f);
// Move the brush down by 100 by Applying the translate
// transform to the brush.
myPGBrush.TranslateTransform(0, 100, MatrixOrder.Append);
// Draw the brush to the screen again after applying the
// transforms.
e.Graphics.FillRectangle(myPGBrush, 10, 10, 300, 300);
}
```

PathGradientBrush.SetBlendTriangularShape Method (Single)

Creates a gradient with a center color and a linear falloff to one surrounding color.

[Visual Basic]
```
Overloads Public Sub SetBlendTriangularShape( _
   ByVal focus As Single _
)
```
[C#]
```
public void SetBlendTriangularShape(
   float focus
);
```
[C++]
```
public: void SetBlendTriangularShape(
   float focus
);
```
[JScript]
```
public function SetBlendTriangularShape(
   focus : float
);
```

Parameters

focus
A value from 0 through 1 that specifies where, along any radial from the center of the path to the path's boundary, the center color will be at its highest intensity. A value of 1 (the default) places the highest intensity at the center of the path.

Remarks

If there is more than one color in the **SurroundColors** array, the first color in the array is used for the ending color. The colors specified in this array are used for discrete points on the brush's boundary path.

Example

For an example, see **PathGradientBrush.SetBlendTriangularShape Method (Single, Single)**.

Requirements

Platforms: Windows 98, Windows NT 4.0, Windows Millennium Edition, Windows 2000, Windows XP Home Edition, Windows XP Professional, Windows Server 2003 family

PathGradientBrush.SetBlendTriangularShape Method (Single, Single)

Creates a gradient with a center color and a linear falloff to each surrounding color.

[Visual Basic]
```
Overloads Public Sub SetBlendTriangularShape( _
   ByVal focus As Single, _
   ByVal scale As Single _
)
```
[C#]
```
public void SetBlendTriangularShape(
   float focus,
   float scale
);
```
[C++]
```
public: void SetBlendTriangularShape(
   float focus,
   float scale
);
```
[JScript]
```
public function SetBlendTriangularShape(
   focus : float,
   scale : float
);
```

Parameters

focus
A value from 0 through 1 that specifies where, along any radial from the center of the path to the path's boundary, the center color will be at its highest intensity. A value of 1 (the default) places the highest intensity at the center of the path.

scale
A value from 0 through 1 that specifies the maximum intensity of the center color that gets blended with the boundary color. A value of 1 causes the highest possible intensity of the center color, and it is the default value.

Remarks

If there is more than one color in the **SurroundColors** array, the first color in the array is used for the ending color. The colors specified in this array are colors used for discrete points on the brush's boundary path.

By default, as you move from the boundary of a path gradient to the center point, the color changes gradually from the boundary color to the center color. You can customize the positioning and blending of the boundary and center colors by calling this method.

Example

[Visual Basic, C#] The following example is designed for use with Windows Forms, and it requires **PaintEventArgs** *e*, an **OnPaint** event object. The code performs the following actions:

- Creates a graphics path and adds a rectangle to it.
- Creates a **PathGradientBrush** from the path points (in this example, the points form a rectangle, but it could be most any shape).
- Sets the center color to red and the surrounding color to blue.
- Draws the **PathGradientBrush** to the screen prior to applying the blend transform.
- Applies the blend transform to the brush by using its **SetBlendTriangularShape** method.
- Calls the **TranslateTransform** method to move the brush rectangle such that it does not overlay the one drawn to the screen earlier.
- Draws the transformed-brush rectangle is drawn to the screen.

[Visual Basic, C#] Notice that the maximum center color (red) is located half way from the center of the path to the path boundary.

[Visual Basic]
```
Public Sub SetBlendTriangularShapeExample(e As PaintEventArgs)
' Create a graphics path and add a rectangle.
Dim myPath As New GraphicsPath()
Dim rect As New Rectangle(100, 20, 100, 50)
myPath.AddRectangle(rect)
' Get the path's array of points.
Dim myPathPointArray As PointF() = myPath.PathPoints
' Create a path gradient brush.
Dim myPGBrush As New PathGradientBrush(myPathPointArray)
```

```
' Set the color span.
myPGBrush.CenterColor = Color.Red
Dim mySurroundColor As Color() = {Color.Blue}
myPGBrush.SurroundColors = mySurroundColor
' Draw the brush to the screen prior to blend.
e.Graphics.FillRectangle(myPGBrush, 10, 10, 200, 200)
' Set the Blend factors.
myPGBrush.SetBlendTriangularShape(0.5F, 1F)
' Move the brush down by 100 by Applying the translate
' transform to the brush.
myPGBrush.TranslateTransform(0, 100, MatrixOrder.Append)
' Draw the brush to the screen again after applying the
' transforms.
e.Graphics.FillRectangle(myPGBrush, 10, 10, 300, 300)
End Sub
```

[C#]

```
public void SetBlendTriangularShapeExample(PaintEventArgs e)
{
// Create a graphics path and add a rectangle.
GraphicsPath myPath = new GraphicsPath();
Rectangle rect = new Rectangle(100, 20, 100, 50);
myPath.AddRectangle(rect);
// Get the path's array of points.
PointF[] myPathPointArray = myPath.PathPoints;
// Create a path gradient brush.
PathGradientBrush myPGBrush = new
PathGradientBrush(myPathPointArray);
// Set the color span.
myPGBrush.CenterColor = Color.Red;
Color[] mySurroundColor = {Color.Blue};
myPGBrush.SurroundColors = mySurroundColor;
// Draw the brush to the screen prior to the blend.
e.Graphics.FillRectangle(myPGBrush, 10, 10, 200, 200);
// Set the Blend factors.
myPGBrush.SetBlendTriangularShape(0.5f, 1.0f);
// Move the brush down by 100 by Applying the translate
// transform to the brush.
myPGBrush.TranslateTransform(0, 100, MatrixOrder.Append);
// Draw the brush to the screen again after applying the
// transforms.
e.Graphics.FillRectangle(myPGBrush, 10, 10, 300, 300);
}
```

Requirements

Platforms: Windows 98, Windows NT 4.0, Windows Millennium Edition, Windows 2000, Windows XP Home Edition, Windows XP Professional, Windows Server 2003 family

PathGradientBrush.SetSigmaBellShape Method

Creates a gradient falloff between the center color and the first surrounding color based on a bell-shaped curve.

Overload List

Creates a gradient brush that changes color starting from the center of the path outward to the path's boundary. The transition from one color to another is based on a bell-shaped curve.

[Visual Basic] **Overloads Public Sub SetSigmaBellShape(Single)**

[C#] **public void SetSigmaBellShape(float);**

[C++] **public: void SetSigmaBellShape(float);**

[JScript] **public function SetSigmaBellShape(float);**

Creates a gradient brush that changes color starting from the center of the path outward to the path's boundary. The transition from one color to another is based on a bell-shaped curve.

[Visual Basic] **Overloads Public Sub SetSigmaBellShape(Single, Single)**

[C#] **public void SetSigmaBellShape(float, float);**

[C++] **public: void SetSigmaBellShape(float, float);**

[JScript] **public function SetSigmaBellShape(float, float);**

Example

[Visual Basic, C#] The following example is designed for use with Windows Forms, and it requires **PaintEventArgs** *e*, an **OnPaint** event object. The code performs the following actions:

- Creates a graphics path and adds a rectangle to it.
- Creates a **PathGradientBrush** from the path points (in this example, the points form a rectangle, but it could be most any shape).
- Sets the center color to red and the surrounding color to blue.
- Draws the **PathGradientBrush** to the screen prior to applying the blend transform.
- Applies the blend transform to the brush by using its **SetSigmaBellShape** method.
- Calls the **TranslateTransform** method to move the brush rectangle such that it does not overlay the one drawn to the screen earlier.
- Draws the transformed-brush rectangle to the screen.

[Visual Basic, C#] Notice that the maximum center color (red) is located half way from the center of the path to the path boundary.

> [Visual Basic, C#] **Note** This example shows how to use one of the overloaded versions of **SetSigmaBellShape**. For other examples that might be available, see the individual overload topics.

[Visual Basic]

```
Public Sub SetSigmaBellShapeExample(e As PaintEventArgs)
' Create a graphics path and add a rectangle.
Dim myPath As New GraphicsPath()
Dim rect As New Rectangle(100, 20, 100, 50)
myPath.AddRectangle(rect)
' Get the path's array of points.
Dim myPathPointArray As PointF() = myPath.PathPoints
' Create a path gradient brush.
Dim myPGBrush As New PathGradientBrush(myPathPointArray)
' Set the color span.
myPGBrush.CenterColor = Color.Red
Dim mySurroundColor As Color() = {Color.Blue}
myPGBrush.SurroundColors = mySurroundColor
' Draw the brush to the screen prior to blend.
e.Graphics.FillRectangle(myPGBrush, 10, 10, 200, 200)
' Set the Blend factors.
myPGBrush.SetSigmaBellShape(0.5F, 1F)
' Move the brush down by 100 by applying the translate
' transform to the brush.
myPGBrush.TranslateTransform(0, 100, MatrixOrder.Append)
' Draw the brush to the screen again after setting the
' blend and applying the transform.
e.Graphics.FillRectangle(myPGBrush, 10, 10, 300, 300)
End Sub
```

```
[C#]
public void SetSigmaBellShapeExample(PaintEventArgs e)
{
// Create a graphics path and add a rectangle.
GraphicsPath myPath = new GraphicsPath();
Rectangle rect = new Rectangle(100, 20, 100, 50);
myPath.AddRectangle(rect);
// Get the path's array of points.
PointF[] myPathPointArray = myPath.PathPoints;
// Create a path gradient brush.
PathGradientBrush myPGBrush = new
PathGradientBrush(myPathPointArray);
// Set the color span.
myPGBrush.CenterColor = Color.Red;
Color[] mySurroundColor = {Color.Blue};
myPGBrush.SurroundColors = mySurroundColor;
// Draw the brush to the screen prior to blend.
e.Graphics.FillRectangle(myPGBrush, 10, 10, 200, 200);
// Set the Blend factors and transform the brush.
myPGBrush.SetSigmaBellShape(0.5f, 1.0f);
// Move the brush down by 100 by applying the translate
// transform to the brush.
myPGBrush.TranslateTransform(0, 100, MatrixOrder.Append);
// Draw the brush to the screen again after setting the
// blend and applying the transform.
e.Graphics.FillRectangle(myPGBrush, 10, 10, 300, 300);
}
```

PathGradientBrush.SetSigmaBellShape Method (Single)

Creates a gradient brush that changes color starting from the center of the path outward to the path's boundary. The transition from one color to another is based on a bell-shaped curve.

```
[Visual Basic]
Overloads Public Sub SetSigmaBellShape( _
   ByVal focus As Single _
)
[C#]
public void SetSigmaBellShape(
   float focus
);
[C++]
public: void SetSigmaBellShape(
   float focus
);
[JScript]
public function SetSigmaBellShape(
   focus : float
);
```

Parameters

focus
A value from 0 through 1 that specifies where, along any radial from the center of the path to the path's boundary, the center color will be at its highest intensity. A value of 1 (the default) places the highest intensity at the center of the path.

Remarks

If there is more than one color in the **SurroundColors** array, the first color in the array is used for the ending color. The colors specified in this array are colors used for discrete points on the brush's boundary path.

By default, as you move from the boundary of a path gradient to the center point, the color changes gradually from the boundary color to the center color. You can customize the positioning and blending of the boundary and center colors by calling this method.

Example

For an example, see **PathGradientBrush.SetSigmaBellShape Method (Single, Single)**.

Requirements

Platforms: Windows 98, Windows NT 4.0, Windows Millennium Edition, Windows 2000, Windows XP Home Edition, Windows XP Professional, Windows Server 2003 family

PathGradientBrush.SetSigmaBellShape Method (Single, Single)

Creates a gradient brush that changes color starting from the center of the path outward to the path's boundary. The transition from one color to another is based on a bell-shaped curve.

```
[Visual Basic]
Overloads Public Sub SetSigmaBellShape( _
   ByVal focus As Single, _
   ByVal scale As Single _
)
[C#]
public void SetSigmaBellShape(
   float focus,
   float scale
);
[C++]
public: void SetSigmaBellShape(
   float focus,
   float scale
);
[JScript]
public function SetSigmaBellShape(
   focus : float,
   scale : float
);
```

Parameters

focus
A value from 0 through 1 that specifies where, along any radial from the center of the path to the path's boundary, the center color will be at its highest intensity. A value of 1 (the default) places the highest intensity at the center of the path.

scale
A value from 0 through 1 that specifies the maximum intensity of the center color that gets blended with the boundary color. A value of 1 causes the highest possible intensity of the center color, and it is the default value.

Remarks

If there is more than one color in the **SurroundColors** array, the first color in the array is used for the ending color. The colors specified in this array are colors used for discrete points on the brush's boundary path.

By default, as you move from the boundary of a path gradient to the center point, the color changes gradually from the boundary color to the center color. You can customize the positioning and blending of the boundary and center colors by calling this method.

Example

[Visual Basic, C#] The following example is designed for use with Windows Forms, and it requires **PaintEventArgs** *e*, an **OnPaint** event object. The code performs the following actions:

- Creates a graphics path and adds a rectangle to it.
- Creates a **PathGradientBrush** from the path points (in this example, the points form a rectangle, but it could be most any shape).
- Sets the center color to red and the surrounding color to blue.
- Draws the **PathGradientBrush** to the screen prior to applying the blend transform.
- Applies the blend transform to the brush by using its **SetSigmaBellShape** method.
- Calls the **TranslateTransform** method to move the brush rectangle such that it does not overlay the one drawn to the screen earlier.
- Draws the transformed-brush rectangle to the screen.

[Visual Basic, C#] Notice that the maximum center color (red) is located half way from the center of the path to the path boundary.

[Visual Basic]
```
Public Sub SetSigmaBellShapeExample(e As PaintEventArgs)
' Create a graphics path and add a rectangle.
Dim myPath As New GraphicsPath()
Dim rect As New Rectangle(100, 20, 100, 50)
myPath.AddRectangle(rect)
' Get the path's array of points.
Dim myPathPointArray As PointF() = myPath.PathPoints
' Create a path gradient brush.
Dim myPGBrush As New PathGradientBrush(myPathPointArray)
' Set the color span.
myPGBrush.CenterColor = Color.Red
Dim mySurroundColor As Color() = {Color.Blue}
myPGBrush.SurroundColors = mySurroundColor
' Draw the brush to the screen prior to blend.
e.Graphics.FillRectangle(myPGBrush, 10, 10, 200, 200)
' Set the Blend factors.
myPGBrush.SetSigmaBellShape(0.5F, 1F)
' Move the brush down by 100 by applying the translate
' transform to the brush.
myPGBrush.TranslateTransform(0, 100, MatrixOrder.Append)
' Draw the brush to the screen again after setting the
' blend and applying the transform.
e.Graphics.FillRectangle(myPGBrush, 10, 10, 300, 300)
End Sub
```

[C#]
```
public void SetSigmaBellShapeExample(PaintEventArgs e)
{
// Create a graphics path and add a rectangle.
GraphicsPath myPath = new GraphicsPath();
Rectangle rect = new Rectangle(100, 20, 100, 50);
myPath.AddRectangle(rect);
// Get the path's array of points.
PointF[] myPathPointArray = myPath.PathPoints;
// Create a path gradient brush.
PathGradientBrush myPGBrush = new
PathGradientBrush(myPathPointArray);
// Set the color span.
myPGBrush.CenterColor = Color.Red;
Color[] mySurroundColor = {Color.Blue};
myPGBrush.SurroundColors = mySurroundColor;
// Draw the brush to the screen prior to blend.
e.Graphics.FillRectangle(myPGBrush, 10, 10, 200, 200);
// Set the Blend factors and transform the brush.
myPGBrush.SetSigmaBellShape(0.5f, 1.0f);
// Move the brush down by 100 by applying the translate
// transform to the brush.
myPGBrush.TranslateTransform(0, 100, MatrixOrder.Append);
// Draw the brush to the screen again after setting the
// blend and applying the transform.
e.Graphics.FillRectangle(myPGBrush, 10, 10, 300, 300);
}
```

Requirements

Platforms: Windows 98, Windows NT 4.0, Windows Millennium Edition, Windows 2000, Windows XP Home Edition, Windows XP Professional, Windows Server 2003 family

PathGradientBrush.TranslateTransform Method

Applies the specified translation to the local geometric transform. This method prepends the translation to the transform.

Overload List

Applies the specified translation to the local geometric transform. This method prepends the translation to the transform.

[Visual Basic] **Overloads Public Sub TranslateTransform(Single, Single)**

[C#] **public void TranslateTransform(float, float);**

[C++] **public: void TranslateTransform(float, float);**

[JScript] **public function TranslateTransform(float, float);**

Applies the specified translation to the local geometric transform in the specified order.

[Visual Basic] **Overloads Public Sub TranslateTransform(Single, Single, MatrixOrder)**

[C#] **public void TranslateTransform(float, float, MatrixOrder);**

[C++] **public: void TranslateTransform(float, float, MatrixOrder);**

[JScript] **public function TranslateTransform(float, float, MatrixOrder);**

Example

For an example, see **PathGradientBrush.SetBlendTriangular-Shape Method (Single, Single)**.

PathGradientBrush.TranslateTransform Method (Single, Single)

Applies the specified translation to the local geometric transform. This method prepends the translation to the transform.

[Visual Basic]
```
Overloads Public Sub TranslateTransform( _
   ByVal dx As Single, _
   ByVal dy As Single _
)
```
[C#]
```
public void TranslateTransform(
   float dx,
   float dy
);
```
[C++]
```
public: void TranslateTransform(
   float dx,
   float dy
);
```

```
[JScript]
public function TranslateTransform(
   dx : float,
   dy : float
);
```

Parameters

dx
The value of the translation in x.

dy
The value of the translation in y.

Example

For an example, see **PathGradientBrush.SetBlendTriangular-Shape Method (Single, Single)**.

Requirements

Platforms: Windows 98, Windows NT 4.0, Windows Millennium Edition, Windows 2000, Windows XP Home Edition, Windows XP Professional, Windows Server 2003 family

PathGradientBrush.TranslateTransform Method (Single, Single, MatrixOrder)

Applies the specified translation to the local geometric transform in the specified order.

```
[Visual Basic]
Overloads Public Sub TranslateTransform( _
   ByVal dx As Single, _
   ByVal dy As Single, _
   ByVal order As MatrixOrder _
)
[C#]
public void TranslateTransform(
   float dx,
   float dy,
   MatrixOrder order
);
[C++]
public: void TranslateTransform(
   float dx,
   float dy,
   MatrixOrder order
);
[JScript]
public function TranslateTransform(
   dx : float,
   dy : float,
   order : MatrixOrder
);
```

Parameters

dx
The value of the translation in x.

dy
The value of the translation in y.

order
The order (prepend or append) in which to apply the translation.

Example

For an example, see **PathGradientBrush.SetBlendTriangular-Shape Method (Single, Single)**.

Requirements

Platforms: Windows 98, Windows NT 4.0, Windows Millennium Edition, Windows 2000, Windows XP Home Edition, Windows XP Professional, Windows Server 2003 family

PathPointType Enumeration

Specifies the type of point in a **GraphicsPath** object.

[Visual Basic]
```
<Serializable>
Public Enum PathPointType
```
[C#]
```
[Serializable]
public enum PathPointType
```
[C++]
```
[Serializable]
__value public enum PathPointType
```
[JScript]
```
public
   Serializable
enum PathPointType
```

Remarks

Each point in a **GraphicsPath** object has a type associated with it. The type determines how the point is used to draw the path. Point types that make up shapes include start points, stop points, and Bézier curve points. Types also include markers, which allow easy traversal of a path or a mask to show or hide points. The **Line** type and any of the **Bezier** types can be combined with **CloseSubpath** (by using the bitwise operator **OR**) to indicate that the corresponding point is the last point in a figure and that the figure should be closed.

Members

Member name	Description
Bezier	Specifies a default Bezier curve.
Bezier3	Specifies a cubic Bezier curve.
CloseSubpath	Specifies the ending point of a subpath.
DashMode	Specifies that the corresponding segment is dashed.
Line	Specifies a line segment.
PathMarker	Specifies a path marker.
PathTypeMask	Specifies a mask point.
Start	Specifies the starting point of a **GraphicsPath**.

Requirements

Namespace: System.Drawing.Drawing2D

Platforms: Windows 98, Windows NT 4.0, Windows Millennium Edition, Windows 2000, Windows XP Home Edition, Windows XP Professional, Windows Server 2003 family

Assembly: System.Drawing (in System.Drawing.dll)

PenAlignment Enumeration

Specifies the alignment of a **Pen** object in relation to the theoretical, zero-width line.

[Visual Basic]

```
<Serializable>
Public Enum PenAlignment
```

[C#]

```
[Serializable]
public enum PenAlignment
```

[C++]

```
[Serializable]
__value public enum PenAlignment
```

[JScript]

```
public
   Serializable
enum PenAlignment
```

Remarks

A **Pen** object has width. The center point of this pen width is aligned relative to the line being drawn depending on the alignment value. A **Pen** object can be positioned to draw inside of a line or centered over the line.

Members

Member name	Description
Center	Specifies that the **Pen** object is centered over the theoretical line.
Inset	Specifies that the **Pen** is positioned on the inside of the theoretical line.
Left	Specifies that the **Pen** is positioned to the left of the line being drawn.
Outset	Specifies that the **Pen** is positioned on the outside of the line being drawn.
Right	Specifies that the **Pen** is positioned to the right of the line being drawn.

Requirements

Namespace: System.Drawing.Drawing2D

Platforms: Windows 98, Windows NT 4.0, Windows Millennium Edition, Windows 2000, Windows XP Home Edition, Windows XP Professional, Windows Server 2003 family

Assembly: System.Drawing (in System.Drawing.dll)

PenType Enumeration

Specifies the type of fill a **Pen** object uses to fill lines.

[Visual Basic]
```
<Serializable>
Public Enum PenType
```
[C#]
```
[Serializable]
public enum PenType
```
[C++]
```
[Serializable]
__value public enum PenType
```
[JScript]
```
public
   Serializable
enum PenType
```

Remarks

The pen type is determined by the **Brush** property of the **Pen** object.

Members

Member name	Description
HatchFill	Specifies a hatch fill.
LinearGradient	Specifies a linear gradient fill.
PathGradient	Specifies a path gradient fill.
SolidColor	Specifies a solid fill.
TextureFill	Specifies a bitmap texture fill.

Requirements

Namespace: System.Drawing.Drawing2D

Platforms: Windows 98, Windows NT 4.0, Windows Millennium Edition, Windows 2000, Windows XP Home Edition, Windows XP Professional, Windows Server 2003 family

Assembly: System.Drawing (in System.Drawing.dll)

PixelOffsetMode Enumeration

Specifies how pixels are offset during rendering.

[Visual Basic]
```
<Serializable>
Public Enum PixelOffsetMode
```
[C#]
```
[Serializable]
public enum PixelOffsetMode
```
[C++]
```
[Serializable]
__value public enum PixelOffsetMode
```
[JScript]
```
public
   Serializable
enum PixelOffsetMode
```

Remarks

By offsetting pixels during rendering, you can improve render quality at the cost of render speed.

Members

Member name	Description
Default	Specifies the default mode.
Half	Specifies that pixels are offset by -.5 units, both horizontally and vertically, for high speed antialiasing.
HighQuality	Specifies high quality, low speed rendering.
HighSpeed	Specifies high speed, low quality rendering.
Invalid	Specifies an invalid mode.
None	Specifies no pixel offset.

Requirements

Namespace: System.Drawing.Drawing2D

Platforms: Windows 98, Windows NT 4.0, Windows Millennium Edition, Windows 2000, Windows XP Home Edition, Windows XP Professional, Windows Server 2003 family

Assembly: System.Drawing (in System.Drawing.dll)

QualityMode Enumeration

Specifies the overall quality when rendering GDI+ objects.

[Visual Basic]
```
<Serializable>
Public Enum QualityMode
```
[C#]
```
[Serializable]
public enum QualityMode
```
[C++]
```
[Serializable]
__value public enum QualityMode
```
[JScript]
```
public
   Serializable
enum QualityMode
```

Remarks

The quality level is inversely proportional to the amount of time spent rendering. This mode does not affect text. To set the text rendering quality, use the **TextRenderingHint** enumeration.

Members

Member name	Description
Default	Specifies the default mode.
High	Specifies high quality, low speed rendering.
Invalid	Specifies an invalid mode.
Low	Specifies low quality, high speed rendering.

Requirements

Namespace: System.Drawing.Drawing2D

Platforms: Windows 98, Windows NT 4.0, Windows Millennium Edition, Windows 2000, Windows XP Home Edition, Windows XP Professional, Windows .NET Server family

Assembly: System.Drawing (in System.Drawing.dll)

RegionData Class

Encapsulates the data that makes up a **Region** object. This class cannot be inherited.

System.Object
System.Drawing.Drawing2D.RegionData

```
[Visual Basic]
NotInheritable Public Class RegionData
[C#]
public sealed class RegionData
[C++]
public __gc __sealed class RegionData
[JScript]
public class RegionData
```

Thread Safety

Any public static (**Shared** in Visual Basic) members of this type are safe for multithreaded operations. Any instance members are not guaranteed to be thread safe.

Requirements

Namespace: System.Drawing.Drawing2D

Platforms: Windows 98, Windows NT 4.0, Windows Millennium Edition, Windows 2000, Windows XP Home Edition, Windows XP Professional, Windows Server 2003 family

Assembly: System.Drawing (in System.Drawing.dll)

RegionData.Data Property

Gets or sets an array of bytes that specify the **Region** object.

```
[Visual Basic]
Public Property Data As Byte ()
[C#]
public byte[] Data {get; set;}
[C++]
public: __property unsigned char get_Data();
public: __property void set_Data(unsigned char __gc[]);
[JScript]
public function get Data() : Byte[];
public function set Data(Byte[]);
```

Property Value

An array of bytes that specify the **Region** object.

Requirements

Platforms: Windows 98, Windows NT 4.0, Windows Millennium Edition, Windows 2000, Windows XP Home Edition, Windows XP Professional, Windows Server 2003 family

SmoothingMode Enumeration

Specifies whether smoothing (antialiasing) is applied to lines and curves and the edges of filled areas.

[Visual Basic]
```
<Serializable>
Public Enum SmoothingMode
```
[C#]
```
[Serializable]
public enum SmoothingMode
```
[C++]
```
[Serializable]
__value public enum SmoothingMode
```
[JScript]
```
public
   Serializable
enum SmoothingMode
```

Remarks

The SmoothingMode property does not affect text. To set the text rendering quality, use the **TextRenderingHint** enumeration.

The smoothing mode does not affect areas filled by a path gradient brush. Areas filled using a **PathGradientBrush** object are rendered the same way (aliased) regardless of the **SmoothingMode** property.

Members

Member name	Description
AntiAlias	Specifies antialiased rendering.
Default	Specifies the default mode.
HighQuality	Specifies high quality, low speed rendering.
HighSpeed	Specifies high speed, low quality rendering.
Invalid	Specifies an invalid mode.
None	Specifies no antialiasing.

Requirements

Namespace: System.Drawing.Drawing2D

Platforms: Windows 98, Windows NT 4.0, Windows Millennium Edition, Windows 2000, Windows XP Home Edition, Windows XP Professional, Windows Server 2003 family

Assembly: System.Drawing (in System.Drawing.dll)

WarpMode Enumeration

Specifies the type of warp transformation applied in a **Warp** method.

[Visual Basic]

```
<Serializable>
Public Enum WarpMode
```

[C#]

```
[Serializable]
public enum WarpMode
```

[C++]

```
[Serializable]
__value public enum WarpMode
```

[JScript]

```
public
   Serializable
enum WarpMode
```

Remarks

A warp style is used by the **Warp** method to warp or distort the figures in a graphics path. This can be used to create unusual shapes.

Members

Member name	Description
Bilinear	Specifies a bilinear warp.
Perspective	Specifies a perspective warp.

Requirements

Namespace: System.Drawing.Drawing2D

Platforms: Windows 98, Windows NT 4.0, Windows Millennium Edition, Windows 2000, Windows XP Home Edition, Windows XP Professional, Windows Server 2003 family

Assembly: System.Drawing (in System.Drawing.dll)

WrapMode Enumeration

Specifies how a texture or gradient is tiled when it is larger than the area being filled.

[Visual Basic]
```
<Serializable>
Public Enum WrapMode
```
[C#]
```
[Serializable]
public enum WrapMode
```
[C++]
```
[Serializable]
__value public enum WrapMode
```
[JScript]
```
public
   Serializable
enum WrapMode
```

Remarks

Brushes use this enumeration to determine how shapes are filled.

Members

Member name	Description
Clamp	Clamps the texture or gradient to the object boundary.
Tile	Tiles the gradient or texture.
TileFlipX	Reverses the texture or gradient horizontally and then tiles the texture or gradient.
TileFlipXY	Reverses the texture or gradient horizontally and vertically and then tiles the texture or gradient.
TileFlipY	Reverses the texture or gradient vertically and then tiles the texture or gradient.

Requirements

Namespace: System.Drawing.Drawing2D

Platforms: Windows 98, Windows NT 4.0, Windows Millennium Edition, Windows 2000, Windows XP Home Edition, Windows XP Professional, Windows Server 2003 family

Assembly: System.Drawing (in System.Drawing.dll)

System.Drawing.Imaging Namespace

The **System.Drawing.Imaging** namespace provides advanced GDI+ imaging functionality. Basic graphics functionality is provided by the **System.Drawing** namespace.

The **Metafile** class provides methods for recording and saving metafiles. The **Encoder** and **Decoder** classes enable users to extend GDI+ to support any image format. The **PropertyItem** class provides methods for storing and retrieving metadata in image files.

BitmapData Class

Specifies the attributes of a bitmap image. The **BitmapData** class is used by the **LockBits** and **UnlockBits** methods of the **Bitmap** class. Not inheritable.

System.Object
  System.Drawing.Imaging.BitmapData

```
[Visual Basic]
NotInheritable Public Class BitmapData
[C#]
public sealed class BitmapData
[C++]
public __gc __sealed class BitmapData
[JScript]
public class BitmapData
```

Thread Safety

Any public static (**Shared** in Visual Basic) members of this type are safe for multithreaded operations. Any instance members are not guaranteed to be thread safe.

Requirements

Namespace: System.Drawing.Imaging

Platforms: Windows 98, Windows NT 4.0, Windows Millennium Edition, Windows 2000, Windows XP Home Edition, Windows XP Professional, Windows Server 2003 family

Assembly: System.Drawing (in System.Drawing.dll)

BitmapData Constructor

Initializes a new instance of the **BitmapData** class.

```
[Visual Basic]
Public Sub New()
[C#]
public BitmapData();
[C++]
public: BitmapData();
[JScript]
public function BitmapData();
```

Requirements

Platforms: Windows 98, Windows NT 4.0, Windows Millennium Edition, Windows 2000, Windows XP Home Edition, Windows XP Professional, Windows Server 2003 family

BitmapData.Height Property

Gets or sets the pixel height of the **Bitmap** object. Also sometimes referred to as the number of scan lines.

```
[Visual Basic]
Public Property Height As Integer
[C#]
public int Height {get; set;}
[C++]
public: __property int get_Height();
public: __property void set_Height(int);
[JScript]
public function get Height() : int;
public function set Height(int);
```

Property Value

The pixel height of the **Bitmap** object.

Requirements

Platforms: Windows 98, Windows NT 4.0, Windows Millennium Edition, Windows 2000, Windows XP Home Edition, Windows XP Professional, Windows Server 2003 family

BitmapData.PixelFormat Property

Gets or sets the format of the pixel information in the **Bitmap** object that returned this **BitmapData** object.

```
[Visual Basic]
Public Property PixelFormat As PixelFormat
[C#]
public PixelFormat PixelFormat {get; set;}
[C++]
public: __property PixelFormat get_PixelFormat();
public: __property void set_PixelFormat(PixelFormat);
[JScript]
public function get PixelFormat() : PixelFormat;
public function set PixelFormat(PixelFormat);
```

Property Value

A **PixelFormat** that specifies the format of the pixel information in the associated **Bitmap** object.

Remarks

The format defines how many bits of memory are needed to store the color information for a single pixel.

Requirements

Platforms: Windows 98, Windows NT 4.0, Windows Millennium Edition, Windows 2000, Windows XP Home Edition, Windows XP Professional, Windows Server 2003 family

BitmapData.Reserved Property

Reserved. Do not use.

[Visual Basic]
```
Public Property Reserved As Integer
```
[C#]
```
public int Reserved {get; set;}
```
[C++]
```
public: __property int get_Reserved();
public: __property void set_Reserved(int);
```
[JScript]
```
public function get Reserved() : int;
public function set Reserved(int);
```

Property Value

Reserved. Do not use.

Requirements

Platforms: Windows 98, Windows NT 4.0, Windows Millennium Edition, Windows 2000, Windows XP Home Edition, Windows XP Professional, Windows Server 2003 family

BitmapData.Scan0 Property

Gets or sets the address of the first pixel data in the bitmap. This can also be thought of as the first scan line in the bitmap.

[Visual Basic]
```
Public Property Scan0 As IntPtr
```
[C#]
```
public IntPtr Scan0 {get; set;}
```
[C++]
```
public: __property IntPtr get_Scan0();
public: __property void set_Scan0(IntPtr);
```
[JScript]
```
public function get Scan0() : IntPtr;
public function set Scan0(IntPtr);
```

Property Value

The address of the first pixel data in the bitmap.

Requirements

Platforms: Windows 98, Windows NT 4.0, Windows Millennium Edition, Windows 2000, Windows XP Home Edition, Windows XP Professional, Windows Server 2003 family

BitmapData.Stride Property

Gets or sets the stride width (also called scan width) of the **Bitmap** object.

[Visual Basic]
```
Public Property Stride As Integer
```
[C#]
```
public int Stride {get; set;}
```
[C++]
```
public: __property int get_Stride();
public: __property void set_Stride(int);
```
[JScript]
```
public function get Stride() : int;
public function set Stride(int);
```

Property Value

The stride width of the **Bitmap** object.

Remarks

The stride is the width of a single row of pixels (a scan line), rounded up to a four-byte boundary. The stride is always greater than or equal to the actual pixel width. If the stride is positive, the bitmap is top-down. If the stride is negative, the bitmap is bottom-up.

Requirements

Platforms: Windows 98, Windows NT 4.0, Windows Millennium Edition, Windows 2000, Windows XP Home Edition, Windows XP Professional, Windows Server 2003 family

BitmapData.Width Property

Gets or sets the pixel width of the **Bitmap** object. This can also be thought of as the number of pixels in one scan line.

[Visual Basic]
```
Public Property Width As Integer
```
[C#]
```
public int Width {get; set;}
```
[C++]
```
public: __property int get_Width();
public: __property void set_Width(int);
```
[JScript]
```
public function get Width() : int;
public function set Width(int);
```

Property Value

The pixel width of the **Bitmap** object.

Requirements

Platforms: Windows 98, Windows NT 4.0, Windows Millennium Edition, Windows 2000, Windows XP Home Edition, Windows XP Professional, Windows Server 2003 family

ColorAdjustType Enumeration

Specifies which GDI+ objects use color adjustment information.

[Visual Basic]
```
<Serializable>
Public Enum ColorAdjustType
```
[C#]
```
[Serializable]
public enum ColorAdjustType
```
[C++]
```
[Serializable]
__value public enum ColorAdjustType
```
[JScript]
```
public
   Serializable
enum ColorAdjustType
```

Remarks

Bitmap, **Brush**, and **Pen** objects use any color adjustments that have been set in the default **ImageAttributes** object until their own color adjustments have been set.

Members

Member name	Description
Any	The number of types specified.
Bitmap	Color adjustment information for **Bitmap** objects.
Brush	Color adjustment information for **Brush** objects.
Count	The number of types specified.
Default	Color adjustment information that is used by all GDI+ objects that do not have their own color adjustment information.
Pen	Color adjustment information for **Pen** objects.
Text	Color adjustment information for text.

Requirements

Namespace: System.Drawing.Imaging

Platforms: Windows 98, Windows NT 4.0, Windows Millennium Edition, Windows 2000, Windows XP Home Edition, Windows XP Professional, Windows Server 2003 family

Assembly: System.Drawing (in System.Drawing.dll)

ColorChannelFlag Enumeration

Specifies individual channels in the CMYK (cyan, magenta, yellow, black) color space. This enumeration is used by the **SetOutputChannel Methods**.

[Visual Basic]

```
<Serializable>
Public Enum ColorChannelFlag
```

[C#]

```
[Serializable]
public enum ColorChannelFlag
```

[C++]

```
[Serializable]
__value public enum ColorChannelFlag
```

[JScript]

```
public
   Serializable
enum ColorChannelFlag
```

Remarks

The values are flags, which can be combined by using the **OR** operator.

Members

Member name	Description
ColorChannelC	The cyan color channel.
ColorChannelK	The black color channel.
ColorChannelLast	This element specifies to leave the color channel unchanged from the last selected channel.
ColorChannelM	The magenta color channel.
ColorChannelY	The yellow color channel.

Requirements

Namespace: System.Drawing.Imaging

Platforms: Windows 98, Windows NT 4.0, Windows Millennium Edition, Windows 2000, Windows XP Home Edition, Windows XP Professional, Windows Server 2003 family

Assembly: System.Drawing (in System.Drawing.dll)

ColorMap Class

Defines a map for converting colors. Several methods of the **ImageAttributes** class adjust image colors by using a color-remap table, which is an array of **ColorMap** structures. Not inheritable.

System.Object
  System.Drawing.Imaging.ColorMap

```
[Visual Basic]
NotInheritable Public Class ColorMap
[C#]
public sealed class ColorMap
[C++]
public __gc __sealed class ColorMap
[JScript]
public class ColorMap
```

Thread Safety

Any public static (**Shared** in Visual Basic) members of this type are safe for multithreaded operations. Any instance members are not guaranteed to be thread safe.

Remarks

This class defines a mapping between existing colors and the new colors to which they are to be converted. When the map is applied, any pixel of the old color is converted to the new color.

Requirements

Namespace: System.Drawing.Imaging

Platforms: Windows 98, Windows NT 4.0, Windows Millennium Edition, Windows 2000, Windows XP Home Edition, Windows XP Professional, Windows Server 2003 family

Assembly: System.Drawing (in System.Drawing.dll)

ColorMap Constructor

Initializes a new instance of the **ColorMap** class.

```
[Visual Basic]
Public Sub New()
[C#]
public ColorMap();
[C++]
public: ColorMap();
[JScript]
public function ColorMap();
```

Requirements

Platforms: Windows 98, Windows NT 4.0, Windows Millennium Edition, Windows 2000, Windows XP Home Edition, Windows XP Professional, Windows Server 2003 family

ColorMap.NewColor Property

Gets or sets the new **Color** structure to which to convert.

```
[Visual Basic]
Public Property NewColor As Color
[C#]
public Color NewColor {get; set;}
[C++]
public: __property Color get_NewColor();
public: __property void set_NewColor(Color);
[JScript]
public function get NewColor() : Color;
public function set NewColor(Color);
```

Property Value

The new **Color** structure to which to convert.

Requirements

Platforms: Windows 98, Windows NT 4.0, Windows Millennium Edition, Windows 2000, Windows XP Home Edition, Windows XP Professional, Windows Server 2003 family

ColorMap.OldColor Property

Gets or sets the existing **Color** structure to be converted.

```
[Visual Basic]
Public Property OldColor As Color
[C#]
public Color OldColor {get; set;}
[C++]
public: __property Color get_OldColor();
public: __property void set_OldColor(Color);
[JScript]
public function get OldColor() : Color;
public function set OldColor(Color);
```

Property Value

The existing **Color** structure to be converted.

Requirements

Platforms: Windows 98, Windows NT 4.0, Windows Millennium Edition, Windows 2000, Windows XP Home Edition, Windows XP Professional, Windows Server 2003 family

ColorMapType Enumeration

Specifies the types of color maps.

[Visual Basic]
```
<Serializable>
Public Enum ColorMapType
```
[C#]
```
[Serializable]
public enum ColorMapType
```
[C++]
```
[Serializable]
__value public enum ColorMapType
```
[JScript]
```
public
   Serializable
enum ColorMapType
```

Members

Member name	Description
Brush	Specifies a color map for a **Brush**.
Default	A default color map.

Requirements

Namespace: System.Drawing.Imaging

Platforms: Windows 98, Windows NT 4.0, Windows Millennium Edition, Windows 2000, Windows XP Home Edition, Windows XP Professional, Windows Server 2003 family

Assembly: System.Drawing (in System.Drawing.dll)

ColorMatrix Class

Defines a 5x5 matrix that contains the coordinates for the RGBA space. Several methods of the **ImageAttributes** class adjust image colors by using a color matrix. Not inheritable.

System.Object
  System.Drawing.Imaging.ColorMatrix

```
[Visual Basic]
NotInheritable Public Class ColorMatrix
[C#]
public sealed class ColorMatrix
[C++]
public __gc __sealed class ColorMatrix
[JScript]
public class ColorMatrix
```

Thread Safety

Any public static (**Shared** in Visual Basic) members of this type are safe for multithreaded operations. Any instance members are not guaranteed to be thread safe.

Remarks

The matrix coefficients constitute a 5x5 linear transformation that is used for transforming ARGB homogeneous values. For example, an ARGB vector represented as alpha, red, green, blue, and w, where w is always 1.

Requirements

Namespace: System.Drawing.Imaging

Platforms: Windows 98, Windows NT 4.0, Windows Millennium Edition, Windows 2000, Windows XP Home Edition, Windows XP Professional, Windows Server 2003 family

Assembly: System.Drawing (in System.Drawing.dll)

ColorMatrix Constructor

Initializes a new instance of the **ColorMatrix** class.

Overload List

Initializes a new instance of the **ColorMatrix** class.

[Visual Basic] **Public Sub New()**

[C#] **public ColorMatrix();**

[C++] **public: ColorMatrix();**

[JScript] **public function ColorMatrix();**

Initializes a new instance of the **ColorMatrix** class using the elements in the specified matrix *newColorMatrix*. This constructor is not CLS-compliant.

[Visual Basic] **Public Sub New(Single()())**

[C#] **public ColorMatrix(Single[][]);**

[C++] **public: ColorMatrix(Single __gc[] __gc[]);**

[JScript] **public function ColorMatrix(Single[][]);**

ColorMatrix Constructor ()

Initializes a new instance of the **ColorMatrix** class.

```
[Visual Basic]
Public Sub New()
[C#]
public ColorMatrix();
[C++]
public: ColorMatrix();
[JScript]
public function ColorMatrix();
```

Requirements

Platforms: Windows 98, Windows NT 4.0, Windows Millennium Edition, Windows 2000, Windows XP Home Edition, Windows XP Professional, Windows Server 2003 family

ColorMatrix Constructor (Single[][])

Initializes a new instance of the **ColorMatrix** class using the elements in the specified matrix *newColorMatrix*.

This constructor is not CLS-compliant. For more information about CLS compliance, see **What is the Common Language Specification**.

```
[Visual Basic]
<CLSCompliant(False)>
Public Sub New( _
   ByVal newColorMatrix()() As Single _
)
[C#]
[CLSCompliant(false)]
public ColorMatrix(
   float[][] newColorMatrix
);
[C++]
[CLSCompliant(false)]
public: ColorMatrix(
   float* newColorMatrix[]
);
[JScript]
public
   CLSCompliant(false)
function ColorMatrix(
   newColorMatrix : float[][]
);
```

Parameters

newColorMatrix
  The values of the elements for the new **ColorMatrix** object.

Requirements

Platforms: Windows 98, Windows NT 4.0, Windows Millennium Edition, Windows 2000, Windows XP Home Edition, Windows XP Professional, Windows Server 2003 family

ColorMatrix.Item Property

Gets or sets the value of the specified element of this **ColorMatrix**.

[C#] In C#, this property is the indexer for the **ColorMatrix** class.

```
[Visual Basic]
Public Default Property Item( _
   ByVal row As Integer, _
   ByVal column As Integer _
) As Single
[C#]
public float this[
   int row,
   int column
] {get; set;}
[C++]
public: __property float get_Item(
   int row,
   int column
);
public: __property void set_Item(
   int row,
   int column,
   float
);
[JScript]
returnValue = ColorMatrixObject.Item(row, column);
ColorMatrixObject.Item(row, column) = returnValue;
-or-
returnValue = ColorMatrixObject(row, column);
ColorMatrixObject(row, column) = returnValue;
```

[JScript] In JScript, you can use the default indexed properties defined by a type, but you cannot explicitly define your own. However, specifying the **expando** attribute on a class automatically provides a default indexed property whose type is **Object** and whose index type is **String**.

Arguments [JScript]

row
The row of the element.

column
The column of the element.

Parameters [Visual Basic, C#, C++]

row
The row of the element.

column
The column of the element.

Property Value

The value of the specified element of this **ColorMatrix**.

Requirements

Platforms: Windows 98, Windows NT 4.0,
Windows Millennium Edition, Windows 2000,
Windows XP Home Edition, Windows XP Professional,
Windows Server 2003 family

ColorMatrix.Matrix00 Property

Gets or sets the element at the 0th row and 0th column of this **ColorMatrix** object.

```
[Visual Basic]
Public Property Matrix00 As Single
[C#]
public float Matrix00 {get; set;}
[C++]
public: __property float get_Matrix00();
public: __property void set_Matrix00(float);
[JScript]
public function get Matrix00() : float;
public function set Matrix00(float);
```

Property Value

The element at the 0th row and 0th column of this **ColorMatrix** object.

Requirements

Platforms: Windows 98, Windows NT 4.0,
Windows Millennium Edition, Windows 2000,
Windows XP Home Edition, Windows XP Professional,
Windows Server 2003 family

ColorMatrix.Matrix01 Property

Gets or sets the element at the 0th row and 1st column of this **ColorMatrix** object.

```
[Visual Basic]
Public Property Matrix01 As Single
[C#]
public float Matrix01 {get; set;}
[C++]
public: __property float get_Matrix01();
public: __property void set_Matrix01(float);
[JScript]
public function get Matrix01() : float;
public function set Matrix01(float);
```

Property Value

The element at the 0th row and 1st column of this **ColorMatrix** object.

Requirements

Platforms: Windows 98, Windows NT 4.0,
Windows Millennium Edition, Windows 2000,
Windows XP Home Edition, Windows XP Professional,
Windows Server 2003 family

ColorMatrix.Matrix02 Property

Gets or sets the element at the 0th row and 2nd column of this **ColorMatrix** object.

```
[Visual Basic]
Public Property Matrix02 As Single
[C#]
public float Matrix02 {get; set;}
[C++]
public: __property float get_Matrix02();
public: __property void set_Matrix02(float);
[JScript]
public function get Matrix02() : float;
public function set Matrix02(float);
```

Property Value

The element at the 0th row and 2nd column of this **ColorMatrix** object.

Requirements

Platforms: Windows 98, Windows NT 4.0, Windows Millennium Edition, Windows 2000, Windows XP Home Edition, Windows XP Professional, Windows Server 2003 family

ColorMatrix.Matrix03 Property

Gets or sets the element at the 0th row and 3rd column of this **ColorMatrix** object.

```
[Visual Basic]
Public Property Matrix03 As Single
[C#]
public float Matrix03 {get; set;}
[C++]
public: __property float get_Matrix03();
public: __property void set_Matrix03(float);
[JScript]
public function get Matrix03() : float;
public function set Matrix03(float);
```

Property Value

The element at the 0th row and 3rd column of this **ColorMatrix** object.

Requirements

Platforms: Windows 98, Windows NT 4.0, Windows Millennium Edition, Windows 2000, Windows XP Home Edition, Windows XP Professional, Windows Server 2003 family

ColorMatrix.Matrix04 Property

Gets or sets the element at the 0th row and 4th column of this **ColorMatrix** object.

```
[Visual Basic]
Public Property Matrix04 As Single
[C#]
public float Matrix04 {get; set;}
[C++]
public: __property float get_Matrix04();
public: __property void set_Matrix04(float);
[JScript]
public function get Matrix04() : float;
public function set Matrix04(float);
```

Property Value

The element at the 0th row and 4th column of this **ColorMatrix** object.

Requirements

Platforms: Windows 98, Windows NT 4.0, Windows Millennium Edition, Windows 2000, Windows XP Home Edition, Windows XP Professional, Windows Server 2003 family

ColorMatrix.Matrix10 Property

Gets or sets the element at the 1st row and 0th column of this **ColorMatrix** object.

```
[Visual Basic]
Public Property Matrix10 As Single
[C#]
public float Matrix10 {get; set;}
[C++]
public: __property float get_Matrix10();
public: __property void set_Matrix10(float);
[JScript]
public function get Matrix10() : float;
public function set Matrix10(float);
```

Property Value

The element at the 1st row and 0th column of this **ColorMatrix** object.

Requirements

Platforms: Windows 98, Windows NT 4.0, Windows Millennium Edition, Windows 2000, Windows XP Home Edition, Windows XP Professional, Windows Server 2003 family

ColorMatrix.Matrix11 Property

Gets or sets the element at the 1st row and 1st column of this **ColorMatrix** object.

```
[Visual Basic]
Public Property Matrix11 As Single
[C#]
public float Matrix11 {get; set;}
[C++]
public: __property float get_Matrix11();
public: __property void set_Matrix11(float);
[JScript]
public function get Matrix11() : float;
public function set Matrix11(float);
```

Property Value

The element at the 1st row and 1st column of this **ColorMatrix** object.

Requirements

Platforms: Windows 98, Windows NT 4.0, Windows Millennium Edition, Windows 2000, Windows XP Home Edition, Windows XP Professional, Windows Server 2003 family

ColorMatrix.Matrix12 Property

Gets or sets the element at the 1st row and 2nd column of this **ColorMatrix** object.

```
[Visual Basic]
Public Property Matrix12 As Single
[C#]
public float Matrix12 {get; set;}
[C++]
public: __property float get_Matrix12();
public: __property void set_Matrix12(float);
```

```
[JScript]
public function get Matrix12() : float;
public function set Matrix12(float);
```

Property Value

The element at the 1st row and 2nd column of this **ColorMatrix** object.

Requirements

Platforms: Windows 98, Windows NT 4.0, Windows Millennium Edition, Windows 2000, Windows XP Home Edition, Windows XP Professional, Windows Server 2003 family

ColorMatrix.Matrix13 Property

Gets or sets the element at the 1st row and 3rd column of this **ColorMatrix** object.

```
[Visual Basic]
Public Property Matrix13 As Single
[C#]
public float Matrix13 {get; set;}
[C++]
public: __property float get_Matrix13();
public: __property void set_Matrix13(float);
[JScript]
public function get Matrix13() : float;
public function set Matrix13(float);
```

Property Value

The element at the 1st row and 3rd column of this **ColorMatrix** object.

Requirements

Platforms: Windows 98, Windows NT 4.0, Windows Millennium Edition, Windows 2000, Windows XP Home Edition, Windows XP Professional, Windows Server 2003 family

ColorMatrix.Matrix14 Property

Gets or sets the element at the 1st row and 4th column of this **ColorMatrix** object.

```
[Visual Basic]
Public Property Matrix14 As Single
[C#]
public float Matrix14 {get; set;}
[C++]
public: __property float get_Matrix14();
public: __property void set_Matrix14(float);
[JScript]
public function get Matrix14() : float;
public function set Matrix14(float);
```

Property Value

The element at the 1st row and 4th column of this **ColorMatrix** object.

Requirements

Platforms: Windows 98, Windows NT 4.0, Windows Millennium Edition, Windows 2000, Windows XP Home Edition, Windows XP Professional, Windows Server 2003 family

ColorMatrix.Matrix20 Property

Gets or sets the element at the 2nd row and 0th column of this **ColorMatrix** object.

```
[Visual Basic]
Public Property Matrix20 As Single
[C#]
public float Matrix20 {get; set;}
[C++]
public: __property float get_Matrix20();
public: __property void set_Matrix20(float);
[JScript]
public function get Matrix20() : float;
public function set Matrix20(float);
```

Property Value

The element at the 2nd row and 0th column of this **ColorMatrix** object.

Requirements

Platforms: Windows 98, Windows NT 4.0, Windows Millennium Edition, Windows 2000, Windows XP Home Edition, Windows XP Professional, Windows Server 2003 family

ColorMatrix.Matrix21 Property

Gets or sets the element at the 2nd row and 1st column of this **ColorMatrix** object.

```
[Visual Basic]
Public Property Matrix21 As Single
[C#]
public float Matrix21 {get; set;}
[C++]
public: __property float get_Matrix21();
public: __property void set_Matrix21(float);
[JScript]
public function get Matrix21() : float;
public function set Matrix21(float);
```

Property Value

The element at the 2nd row and 1st column of this **ColorMatrix** object.

Requirements

Platforms: Windows 98, Windows NT 4.0, Windows Millennium Edition, Windows 2000, Windows XP Home Edition, Windows XP Professional, Windows Server 2003 family

ColorMatrix.Matrix22 Property

Gets or sets the element at the 2nd row and 2nd column of this **ColorMatrix** object.

```
[Visual Basic]
Public Property Matrix22 As Single
[C#]
public float Matrix22 {get; set;}
[C++]
public: __property float get_Matrix22();
public: __property void set_Matrix22(float);
```

```
[JScript]
public function get Matrix22() : float;
public function set Matrix22(float);
```

Property Value

The element at the 2nd row and 2nd column of this **ColorMatrix** object.

Requirements

Platforms: Windows 98, Windows NT 4.0, Windows Millennium Edition, Windows 2000, Windows XP Home Edition, Windows XP Professional, Windows Server 2003 family

ColorMatrix.Matrix23 Property

Gets or sets the element at the 2nd row and 3rd column of this **ColorMatrix** object.

```
[Visual Basic]
Public Property Matrix23 As Single
[C#]
public float Matrix23 {get; set;}
[C++]
public: __property float get_Matrix23();
public: __property void set_Matrix23(float);
[JScript]
public function get Matrix23() : float;
public function set Matrix23(float);
```

Property Value

The element at the 2nd row and 3rd column of this **ColorMatrix** object.

Requirements

Platforms: Windows 98, Windows NT 4.0, Windows Millennium Edition, Windows 2000, Windows XP Home Edition, Windows XP Professional, Windows Server 2003 family

ColorMatrix.Matrix24 Property

Gets or sets the element at the 2nd row and 4th column of this **ColorMatrix** object.

```
[Visual Basic]
Public Property Matrix24 As Single
[C#]
public float Matrix24 {get; set;}
[C++]
public: __property float get_Matrix24();
public: __property void set_Matrix24(float);
[JScript]
public function get Matrix24() : float;
public function set Matrix24(float);
```

Property Value

The element at the 2nd row and 4th column of this **ColorMatrix** object.

Requirements

Platforms: Windows 98, Windows NT 4.0, Windows Millennium Edition, Windows 2000, Windows XP Home Edition, Windows XP Professional, Windows Server 2003 family

ColorMatrix.Matrix30 Property

Gets or sets the element at the 3rd row and 0th column of this **ColorMatrix** object.

```
[Visual Basic]
Public Property Matrix30 As Single
[C#]
public float Matrix30 {get; set;}
[C++]
public: __property float get_Matrix30();
public: __property void set_Matrix30(float);
[JScript]
public function get Matrix30() : float;
public function set Matrix30(float);
```

Property Value

The element at the 3rd row and 0th column of this **ColorMatrix** object.

Requirements

Platforms: Windows 98, Windows NT 4.0, Windows Millennium Edition, Windows 2000, Windows XP Home Edition, Windows XP Professional, Windows Server 2003 family

ColorMatrix.Matrix31 Property

Gets or sets the element at the 3rd row and 1st column of this **ColorMatrix** object.

```
[Visual Basic]
Public Property Matrix31 As Single
[C#]
public float Matrix31 {get; set;}
[C++]
public: __property float get_Matrix31();
public: __property void set_Matrix31(float);
[JScript]
public function get Matrix31() : float;
public function set Matrix31(float);
```

Property Value

The element at the 3rd row and 1st column of this **ColorMatrix** object.

Requirements

Platforms: Windows 98, Windows NT 4.0, Windows Millennium Edition, Windows 2000, Windows XP Home Edition, Windows XP Professional, Windows Server 2003 family

ColorMatrix.Matrix32 Property

Gets or sets the element at the 3rd row and 2nd column of this **ColorMatrix** object.

```
[Visual Basic]
Public Property Matrix32 As Single
[C#]
public float Matrix32 {get; set;}
[C++]
public: __property float get_Matrix32();
public: __property void set_Matrix32(float);
```

```
[JScript]
public function get Matrix32() : float;
public function set Matrix32(float);
```

Property Value

The element at the 3rd row and 2nd column of this **ColorMatrix** object.

Requirements

Platforms: Windows 98, Windows NT 4.0, Windows Millennium Edition, Windows 2000, Windows XP Home Edition, Windows XP Professional, Windows Server 2003 family

ColorMatrix.Matrix33 Property

Gets or sets the element at the 3rd row and 3rd column of this **ColorMatrix** object.

```
[Visual Basic]
Public Property Matrix33 As Single
[C#]
public float Matrix33 {get; set;}
[C++]
public: __property float get_Matrix33();
public: __property void set_Matrix33(float);
[JScript]
public function get Matrix33() : float;
public function set Matrix33(float);
```

Property Value

The element at the 3rd row and 3rd column of this **ColorMatrix** object.

Requirements

Platforms: Windows 98, Windows NT 4.0, Windows Millennium Edition, Windows 2000, Windows XP Home Edition, Windows XP Professional, Windows Server 2003 family

ColorMatrix.Matrix34 Property

Gets or sets the element at the 3rd row and 4th column of this **ColorMatrix** object.

```
[Visual Basic]
Public Property Matrix34 As Single
[C#]
public float Matrix34 {get; set;}
[C++]
public: __property float get_Matrix34();
public: __property void set_Matrix34(float);
[JScript]
public function get Matrix34() : float;
public function set Matrix34(float);
```

Property Value

The element at the 3rd row and 4th column of this **ColorMatrix** object.

Requirements

Platforms: Windows 98, Windows NT 4.0, Windows Millennium Edition, Windows 2000, Windows XP Home Edition, Windows XP Professional, Windows Server 2003 family

ColorMatrix.Matrix40 Property

Gets or sets the element at the 4th row and 0th column of this **ColorMatrix** object.

```
[Visual Basic]
Public Property Matrix40 As Single
[C#]
public float Matrix40 {get; set;}
[C++]
public: __property float get_Matrix40();
public: __property void set_Matrix40(float);
[JScript]
public function get Matrix40() : float;
public function set Matrix40(float);
```

Property Value

The element at the 4th row and 0th column of this **ColorMatrix** object.

Requirements

Platforms: Windows 98, Windows NT 4.0, Windows Millennium Edition, Windows 2000, Windows XP Home Edition, Windows XP Professional, Windows Server 2003 family

ColorMatrix.Matrix41 Property

Gets or sets the element at the 4th row and 1st column of this **ColorMatrix** object.

```
[Visual Basic]
Public Property Matrix41 As Single
[C#]
public float Matrix41 {get; set;}
[C++]
public: __property float get_Matrix41();
public: __property void set_Matrix41(float);
[JScript]
public function get Matrix41() : float;
public function set Matrix41(float);
```

Property Value

The element at the 4th row and 1st column of this **ColorMatrix** object.

Requirements

Platforms: Windows 98, Windows NT 4.0, Windows Millennium Edition, Windows 2000, Windows XP Home Edition, Windows XP Professional, Windows Server 2003 family

ColorMatrix.Matrix42 Property

Gets or sets the element at the 4th row and 2nd column of this **ColorMatrix** object.

```
[Visual Basic]
Public Property Matrix42 As Single
[C#]
public float Matrix42 {get; set;}
[C++]
public: __property float get_Matrix42();
public: __property void set_Matrix42(float);
```

```
[JScript]
public function get Matrix42() : float;
public function set Matrix42(float);
```

Property Value

The element at the 4th row and 2nd column of this **ColorMatrix** object.

Requirements

Platforms: Windows 98, Windows NT 4.0, Windows Millennium Edition, Windows 2000, Windows XP Home Edition, Windows XP Professional, Windows Server 2003 family

ColorMatrix.Matrix43 Property

Gets or sets the element at the 4th row and 3rd column of this **ColorMatrix** object.

```
[Visual Basic]
Public Property Matrix43 As Single
[C#]
public float Matrix43 {get; set;}
[C++]
public: __property float get_Matrix43();
public: __property void set_Matrix43(float);
[JScript]
public function get Matrix43() : float;
public function set Matrix43(float);
```

Property Value

The element at the 4th row and 3rd column of this **ColorMatrix** object.

Requirements

Platforms: Windows 98, Windows NT 4.0, Windows Millennium Edition, Windows 2000, Windows XP Home Edition, Windows XP Professional, Windows Server 2003 family

ColorMatrix.Matrix44 Property

Gets or sets the element at the 4th row and 4th column of this **ColorMatrix** object.

```
[Visual Basic]
Public Property Matrix44 As Single
[C#]
public float Matrix44 {get; set;}
[C++]
public: __property float get_Matrix44();
public: __property void set_Matrix44(float);
[JScript]
public function get Matrix44() : float;
public function set Matrix44(float);
```

Property Value

The element at the 4th row and 4th column of this **ColorMatrix** object.

Requirements

Platforms: Windows 98, Windows NT 4.0, Windows Millennium Edition, Windows 2000, Windows XP Home Edition, Windows XP Professional, Windows Server 2003 family

ColorMatrixFlag Enumeration

Specifies the types of images and colors that will be affected by the color and grayscale adjustment settings of an **ImageAttributes** object.

[Visual Basic]
```
<Serializable>
Public Enum ColorMatrixFlag
```
[C#]
```
[Serializable]
public enum ColorMatrixFlag
```
[C++]
```
[Serializable]
__value public enum ColorMatrixFlag
```
[JScript]
```
public
   Serializable
enum ColorMatrixFlag
```

Members

Member name	Description
AltGrays	This member supports the .NET Framework infrastructure and is not intended to be used directly from your code.
Default	Specifies that all color values (including gray shades) are adjusted by the same color-adjustment matrix.
SkipGrays	Specifies that colors are adjusted but gray shades are not adjusted. A gray shade is any color that has the same value for its red, green, and blue components.

Requirements

Namespace: System.Drawing.Imaging

Platforms: Windows 98, Windows NT 4.0, Windows Millennium Edition, Windows 2000, Windows XP Home Edition, Windows XP Professional, Windows Server 2003 family

Assembly: System.Drawing (in System.Drawing.dll)

ColorMode Enumeration

Specifies two modes for color component values.

[Visual Basic]
```
<Serializable>
Public Enum ColorMode
```
[C#]
```
[Serializable]
public enum ColorMode
```
[C++]
```
[Serializable]
__value public enum ColorMode
```
[JScript]
```
public
   Serializable
enum ColorMode
```

Remarks

For computers with 32-bit integers, use ARGB32Mode. For computers with 64-bit integers, use ARGB64Mode.

Members

Member name	Description
Argb32Mode	The integer values supplied are 32-bit values.
Argb64Mode	The integer values supplied are 64-bit values.

Requirements

Namespace: System.Drawing.Imaging

Platforms: Windows 98, Windows NT 4.0, Windows Millennium Edition, Windows 2000, Windows XP Home Edition, Windows XP Professional, Windows Server 2003 family

Assembly: System.Drawing (in System.Drawing.dll)

ColorPalette Class

Defines an array of colors that make up a color palette. The colors are 32-bit ARGB colors. Not inheritable.

For a list of all members of this type, see **ColorPalette Members**.

System.Object
  System.Drawing.Imaging.ColorPalette

```
[Visual Basic]
NotInheritable Public Class ColorPalette
[C#]
public sealed class ColorPalette
[C++]
public __gc __sealed class ColorPalette
[JScript]
public class ColorPalette
```

Thread Safety

Any public static (**Shared** in Visual Basic) members of this type are safe for multithreaded operations. Any instance members are not guaranteed to be thread safe.

Remarks

The colors in the palette are limited to 32-bit ARGB colors. A 32-bit ARGB color has 8 bits each for alpha, red, green, and blue values. The lowest 8 bits make up the blue bit, the next 8 bits are green, the next 8 bits are red, and the most significant 8 bits are alpha. This means each component can vary from 0 to 255. Fully on is 255 and fully off is 0. Alpha is used to make the color value transparent (alpha = 0) or opaque (alpha = 255). The number of intensity levels in the image can be increased without increasing the number of colors used. This process creates what is called a halftone, and it offers increased contrast at a cost of decreased resolution.

Requirements

Namespace: System.Drawing.Imaging

Platforms: Windows 98, Windows NT 4.0, Windows Millennium Edition, Windows 2000, Windows XP Home Edition, Windows XP Professional, Windows Server 2003 family

Assembly: System.Drawing (in System.Drawing.dll)

ColorPalette.Entries Property

Gets an array of **Color** structures.

```
[Visual Basic]
Public ReadOnly Property Entries As Color ()
[C#]
public Color[] Entries {get;}
[C++]
public: __property Color get_Entries();
[JScript]
public function get Entries() : Color[];
```

Property Value

The array of **Color** structure that make up this **ColorPalette**.

Requirements

Platforms: Windows 98, Windows NT 4.0, Windows Millennium Edition, Windows 2000, Windows XP Home Edition, Windows XP Professional, Windows Server 2003 family

ColorPalette.Flags Property

Gets a value that specifies how to interpret the color information in the array of colors.

```
[Visual Basic]
Public ReadOnly Property Flags As Integer
[C#]
public int Flags {get;}
[C++]
public: __property int get_Flags();
[JScript]
public function get Flags() : int;
```

Property Value

The following flag values are valid:

0x00000001
  The color values in the array contain alpha information.

0x00000002
  The colors in the array are grayscale values.

0x00000004
  The colors in the array are halftone values.

Requirements

Platforms: Windows 98, Windows NT 4.0, Windows Millennium Edition, Windows 2000, Windows XP Home Edition, Windows XP Professional, Windows Server 2003 family

EmfPlusRecordType Enumeration

Specifies the methods available for use with a metafile to read and write graphic commands. The members of this enumeration come in three groups:

[Visual Basic]
```
<Serializable>
Public Enum EmfPlusRecordType
```
[C#]
```
[Serializable]
public enum EmfPlusRecordType
```
[C++]
```
[Serializable]
__value public enum EmfPlusRecordType
```
[JScript]
```
public
   Serializable
enum EmfPlusRecordType
```

Remarks

GDI+ uses the enhanced Windows metafile image format (EMF). The EMF format contains a comment mechanism for embedding data within the metafile. This comment mechanism is used to embed GDI+ records within an EMF file. EMF files that contain GDI+ data are called EMF+ files. Applications that do not recognize the comment data skip the comment records and render the records they do understand. If the EMF+ file is played back by GDI+, then the GDI+ records are used to render the metafile; otherwise, the GDI records (if present) are used.

Members

Member name	Description
BeginContainer	See **BeginContainer _Methods**.
BeginContainerNoParams	See **BeginContainer _Methods**.
Clear	See **Graphics.Clear**.
Comment	See **Graphics.AddMetafile-Comment**.
DrawArc	See **DrawArc Methods**.
DrawBeziers	See **DrawBeziers Methods**.
DrawClosedCurve	See **DrawClosedCurve Methods**.
DrawCurve	See **DrawCurve Methods**.
DrawDriverString	Specifies a character string, a location, and formatting information.
DrawEllipse	See **DrawEllipse Methods**.
DrawImage	See **DrawImage Methods**.
DrawImagePoints	See **DrawImage Methods**.
DrawLines	See **DrawLines Methods**.
DrawPath	See **Graphics.DrawPath**.
DrawPie	See **DrawPie Methods**.
DrawRects	See **DrawRectangles Methods**.
DrawString	See **DrawString Methods**.
EmfAbortPath	See "Enhanced-Format Metafiles" in the GDI section of the Platform SDK documentation.
EmfAlphaBlend	See "Enhanced-Format Metafiles" in the GDI section of the Platform SDK documentation.
EmfAngleArc	See "Enhanced-Format Metafiles" in the GDI section of the Platform SDK documentation.
EmfArcTo	See "Enhanced-Format Metafiles" in the GDI section of the Platform SDK documentation.
EmfBeginPath	See "Enhanced-Format Metafiles" in the GDI section of the Platform SDK documentation.
EmfBitBlt	See "Enhanced-Format Metafiles" in the GDI section of the Platform SDK documentation.
EmfChord	See "Enhanced-Format Metafiles" in the GDI section of the Platform SDK documentation.
EmfCloseFigure	See "Enhanced-Format Metafiles" in the GDI section of the Platform SDK documentation.
EmfColorCorrectPalette	See "Enhanced-Format Metafiles" in the GDI section of the Platform SDK documentation.
EmfColorMatchTo-TargetW	See "Enhanced-Format Metafiles" in the GDI section of the Platform SDK documentation.
EmfCreateBrushIndirect	See "Enhanced-Format Metafiles" in the GDI section of the Platform SDK documentation.
EmfCreateColorSpace	See "Enhanced-Format Metafiles" in the GDI section of the Platform SDK documentation.
EmfCreateColorSpaceW	See "Enhanced-Format Metafiles" in the GDI section of the Platform SDK documentation.
EmfCreateDibPattern-BrushPt	See "Enhanced-Format Metafiles" in the GDI section of the Platform SDK documentation.
EmfCreateMonoBrush	See "Enhanced-Format Metafiles" in the GDI section of the Platform SDK documentation.
EmfCreatePalette	See "Enhanced-Format Metafiles" in the GDI section of the Platform SDK documentation.
EmfCreatePen	See "Enhanced-Format Metafiles" in the GDI section of the Platform SDK documentation.
EmfDeleteColorSpace	See "Enhanced-Format Metafiles" in the GDI section of the Platform SDK documentation.
EmfDeleteObject	See "Enhanced-Format Metafiles" in the GDI section of the Platform SDK documentation.
EmfDrawEscape	See "Enhanced-Format Metafiles" in the GDI section of the Platform SDK documentation.

Member name	Description
EmfEllipse	See "Enhanced-Format Metafiles" in the GDI section of the Platform SDK documentation.
EmfEndPath	See "Enhanced-Format Metafiles" in the GDI section of the Platform SDK documentation.
EmfEof	See "Enhanced-Format Metafiles" in the GDI section of the Platform SDK documentation.
EmfExcludeClipRect	See "Enhanced-Format Metafiles" in the GDI section of the Platform SDK documentation.
EmfExtCreateFontIndirect	See "Enhanced-Format Metafiles" in the GDI section of the Platform SDK documentation.
EmfExtCreatePen	See "Enhanced-Format Metafiles" in the GDI section of the Platform SDK documentation.
EmfExtEscape	See "Enhanced-Format Metafiles" in the GDI section of the Platform SDK documentation.
EmfExtFloodFill	See "Enhanced-Format Metafiles" in the GDI section of the Platform SDK documentation.
EmfExtSelectClipRgn	See "Enhanced-Format Metafiles" in the GDI section of the Platform SDK documentation.
EmfExtTextOutA	See "Enhanced-Format Metafiles" in the GDI section of the Platform SDK documentation.
EmfExtTextOutW	See "Enhanced-Format Metafiles" in the GDI section of the Platform SDK documentation.
EmfFillPath	See "Enhanced-Format Metafiles" in the GDI section of the Platform SDK documentation.
EmfFillRgn	See "Enhanced-Format Metafiles" in the GDI section of the Platform SDK documentation.
EmfFlattenPath	See "Enhanced-Format Metafiles" in the GDI section of the Platform SDK documentation.
EmfForceUfiMapping	See "Enhanced-Format Metafiles" in the GDI section of the Platform SDK documentation.
EmfFrameRgn	See "Enhanced-Format Metafiles" in the GDI section of the Platform SDK documentation.
EmfGdiComment	See "Enhanced-Format Metafiles" in the GDI section of the Platform SDK documentation.
EmfGlsBoundedRecord	See "Enhanced-Format Metafiles" in the GDI section of the Platform SDK documentation.
EmfGlsRecord	See "Enhanced-Format Metafiles" in the GDI section of the Platform SDK documentation.

Member name	Description
EmfGradientFill	See "Enhanced-Format Metafiles" in the GDI section of the Platform SDK documentation.
EmfHeader	See "Enhanced-Format Metafiles" in the GDI section of the Platform SDK documentation.
EmfIntersectClipRect	See "Enhanced-Format Metafiles" in the GDI section of the Platform SDK documentation.
EmfInvertRgn	See "Enhanced-Format Metafiles" in the GDI section of the Platform SDK documentation.
EmfLineTo	See "Enhanced-Format Metafiles" in the GDI section of the Platform SDK documentation.
EmfMaskBlt	See "Enhanced-Format Metafiles" in the GDI section of the Platform SDK documentation.
EmfMax	See "Enhanced-Format Metafiles" in the GDI section of the Platform SDK documentation.
EmfMin	See "Enhanced-Format Metafiles" in the GDI section of the Platform SDK documentation.
EmfModifyWorld-Transform	See "Enhanced-Format Metafiles" in the GDI section of the Platform SDK documentation.
EmfMoveToEx	See "Enhanced-Format Metafiles" in the GDI section of the Platform SDK documentation.
EmfNamedEscpae	See "Enhanced-Format Metafiles" in the GDI section of the Platform SDK documentation.
EmfOffsetClipRgn	See "Enhanced-Format Metafiles" in the GDI section of the Platform SDK documentation.
EmfPaintRgn	See "Enhanced-Format Metafiles" in the GDI section of the Platform SDK documentation.
EmfPie	See "Enhanced-Format Metafiles" in the GDI section of the Platform SDK documentation.
EmfPixelFormat	See "Enhanced-Format Metafiles" in the GDI section of the Platform SDK documentation.
EmfPlgBlt	See "Enhanced-Format Metafiles" in the GDI section of the Platform SDK documentation.
EmfPlusRecordBase	See "Enhanced-Format Metafiles" in the GDI section of the Platform SDK documentation.
EmfPolyBezier	See "Enhanced-Format Metafiles" in the GDI section of the Platform SDK documentation.
EmfPolyBezier16	See "Enhanced-Format Metafiles" in the GDI section of the Platform SDK documentation.

Member name	Description
EmfPolyBezierTo	See "Enhanced-Format Metafiles" in the GDI section of the Platform SDK documentation.
EmfPolyBezierTo16	See "Enhanced-Format Metafiles" in the GDI section of the Platform SDK documentation.
EmfPolyDraw	See "Enhanced-Format Metafiles" in the GDI section of the Platform SDK documentation.
EmfPolyDraw16	See "Enhanced-Format Metafiles" in the GDI section of the Platform SDK documentation.
EmfPolygon	See "Enhanced-Format Metafiles" in the GDI section of the Platform SDK documentation.
EmfPolygon16	See "Enhanced-Format Metafiles" in the GDI section of the Platform SDK documentation.
EmfPolyline	See "Enhanced-Format Metafiles" in the GDI section of the Platform SDK documentation.
EmfPolyline16	See "Enhanced-Format Metafiles" in the GDI section of the Platform SDK documentation.
EmfPolyLineTo	See "Enhanced-Format Metafiles" in the GDI section of the Platform SDK documentation.
EmfPolylineTo16	See "Enhanced-Format Metafiles" in the GDI section of the Platform SDK documentation.
EmfPolyPolygon	See "Enhanced-Format Metafiles" in the GDI section of the Platform SDK documentation.
EmfPolyPolygon16	See "Enhanced-Format Metafiles" in the GDI section of the Platform SDK documentation.
EmfPolyPolyline	See "Enhanced-Format Metafiles" in the GDI section of the Platform SDK documentation.
EmfPolyPolyline16	See "Enhanced-Format Metafiles" in the GDI section of the Platform SDK documentation.
EmfPolyTextOutA	See "Enhanced-Format Metafiles" in the GDI section of the Platform SDK documentation.
EmfPolyTextOutW	See "Enhanced-Format Metafiles" in the GDI section of the Platform SDK documentation.
EmfRealizePalette	See "Enhanced-Format Metafiles" in the GDI section of the Platform SDK documentation.
EmfRectangle	See "Enhanced-Format Metafiles" in the GDI section of the Platform SDK documentation.
EmfReserved069	See "Enhanced-Format Metafiles" in the GDI section of the Platform SDK documentation.

Member name	Description
EmfReserved117	See "Enhanced-Format Metafiles" in the GDI section of the Platform SDK documentation.
EmfResizePalette	See "Enhanced-Format Metafiles" in the GDI section of the Platform SDK documentation.
EmfRestoreDC	See "Enhanced-Format Metafiles" in the GDI section of the Platform SDK documentation.
EmfRoundArc	See "Enhanced-Format Metafiles" in the GDI section of the Platform SDK documentation.
EmfRoundRect	See "Enhanced-Format Metafiles" in the GDI section of the Platform SDK documentation.
EmfSaveDC	See "Enhanced-Format Metafiles" in the GDI section of the Platform SDK documentation.
EmfScaleViewportExtEx	See "Enhanced-Format Metafiles" in the GDI section of the Platform SDK documentation.
EmfScaleWindowExtEx	See "Enhanced-Format Metafiles" in the GDI section of the Platform SDK documentation.
EmfSelectClipPath	See "Enhanced-Format Metafiles" in the GDI section of the Platform SDK documentation.
EmfSelectObject	See "Enhanced-Format Metafiles" in the GDI section of the Platform SDK documentation.
EmfSelectPalette	See "Enhanced-Format Metafiles" in the GDI section of the Platform SDK documentation.
EmfSetArcDirection	See "Enhanced-Format Metafiles" in the GDI section of the Platform SDK documentation.
EmfSetBkColor	See "Enhanced-Format Metafiles" in the GDI section of the Platform SDK documentation.
EmfSetBkMode	See "Enhanced-Format Metafiles" in the GDI section of the Platform SDK documentation.
EmfSetBrushOrgEx	See "Enhanced-Format Metafiles" in the GDI section of the Platform SDK documentation.
EmfSetColorAdjustment	See "Enhanced-Format Metafiles" in the GDI section of the Platform SDK documentation.
EmfSetColorSpace	See "Enhanced-Format Metafiles" in the GDI section of the Platform SDK documentation.
EmfSetDIBitsToDevice	See "Enhanced-Format Metafiles" in the GDI section of the Platform SDK documentation.
EmfSetIcmMode	See "Enhanced-Format Metafiles" in the GDI section of the Platform SDK documentation.

Member name	Description
EmfSetIcmProfileA	See "Enhanced-Format Metafiles" in the GDI section of the Platform SDK documentation.
EmfSetIcmProfileW	See "Enhanced-Format Metafiles" in the GDI section of the Platform SDK documentation.
EmfSetLayout	See "Enhanced-Format Metafiles" in the GDI section of the Platform SDK documentation.
EmfSetLinkedUfis	See "Enhanced-Format Metafiles" in the GDI section of the Platform SDK documentation.
EmfSetMapMode	See "Enhanced-Format Metafiles" in the GDI section of the Platform SDK documentation.
EmfSetMapperFlags	See "Enhanced-Format Metafiles" in the GDI section of the Platform SDK documentation.
EmfSetMetaRgn	See "Enhanced-Format Metafiles" in the GDI section of the Platform SDK documentation.
EmfSetMiterLimit	See "Enhanced-Format Metafiles" in the GDI section of the Platform SDK documentation.
EmfSetPaletteEntries	See "Enhanced-Format Metafiles" in the GDI section of the Platform SDK documentation.
EmfSetPixelV	See "Enhanced-Format Metafiles" in the GDI section of the Platform SDK documentation.
EmfSetPolyFillMode	See "Enhanced-Format Metafiles" in the GDI section of the Platform SDK documentation.
EmfSetROP2	See "Enhanced-Format Metafiles" in the GDI section of the Platform SDK documentation.
EmfSetStretchBltMode	See "Enhanced-Format Metafiles" in the GDI section of the Platform SDK documentation.
EmfSetTextAlign	See "Enhanced-Format Metafiles" in the GDI section of the Platform SDK documentation.
EmfSetTextColor	See "Enhanced-Format Metafiles" in the GDI section of the Platform SDK documentation.
EmfSetTextJustification	See "Enhanced-Format Metafiles" in the GDI section of the Platform SDK documentation.
EmfSetViewportExtEx	See "Enhanced-Format Metafiles" in the GDI section of the Platform SDK documentation.
EmfSetViewportOrgEx	See "Enhanced-Format Metafiles" in the GDI section of the Platform SDK documentation.
EmfSetWindowExtEx	See "Enhanced-Format Metafiles" in the GDI section of the Platform SDK documentation.

Member name	Description
EmfSetWindowOrgEx	See "Enhanced-Format Metafiles" in the GDI section of the Platform SDK documentation.
EmfSetWorldTransform	See "Enhanced-Format Metafiles" in the GDI section of the Platform SDK documentation.
EmfSmallTextOut	See "Enhanced-Format Metafiles" in the GDI section of the Platform SDK documentation.
EmfStartDoc	See "Enhanced-Format Metafiles" in the GDI section of the Platform SDK documentation.
EmfStretchBlt	See "Enhanced-Format Metafiles" in the GDI section of the Platform SDK documentation.
EmfStretchDIBits	See "Enhanced-Format Metafiles" in the GDI section of the Platform SDK documentation.
EmfStrokeAndFillPath	See "Enhanced-Format Metafiles" in the GDI section of the Platform SDK documentation.
EmfStrokePath	See "Enhanced-Format Metafiles" in the GDI section of the Platform SDK documentation.
EmfTransparentBlt	See "Enhanced-Format Metafiles" in the GDI section of the Platform SDK documentation.
EmfWidenPath	See "Enhanced-Format Metafiles" in the GDI section of the Platform SDK documentation.
EndContainer	See **EndContainer**.
EndOfFile	Identifies a record that marks the last EMF+ record of a metafile.
FillClosedCurve	See **FillClosedCurve Methods**.
FillEllipse	See **FillEllipse Methods**.
FillPath	See **Graphics.FillPath**.
FillPie	See **FillPie Methods**.
FillPolygon	See **FillPolygon Methods**.
FillRects	See **FillRectangles Methods**.
FillRegion	See **Graphics.FillRegion**.
GetDC	See **Graphics.GetHdc**.
Header	Identifies a record that is the EMF+ header.
Invalid	Indicates invalid data.
Max	The maximum value for this enumeration.
Min	The minimum value for this enumeration.
MultiFormatEnd	Marks the end of a multiple-format section.
MultiFormatSection	Marks a multiple-format section.
MultiFormatStart	Marks the start of a multiple-format section.
MultiplyWorldTransform	See **MultiplyTransform Methods**.
Object	Marks an object.

Member name	Description
OffsetClip	See **TranslateClip Methods**.
ResetClip	See **Graphics.ResetClip**.
ResetWorldTransform	See **Graphics.ResetTransform**.
Restore	See **Graphics.Restore**.
RotateWorldTransform	See **RotateTransform Methods**.
Save	See **Graphics.Save**.
ScaleWorldTransform	See **ScaleTransform Methods**.
SetAntiAliasMode	See **Graphics.SmoothingMode**.
SetClipPath	See **SetClip Methods**.
SetClipRect	See **SetClip Methods**.
SetClipRegion	See **SetClip Methods**.
SetCompositingMode	See **Graphics.CompositingMode**.
SetCompositingQuality	See **Graphics.CompositingQuality**.
SetInterpolationMode	See **Graphics.InterpolationMode**.
SetPageTransform	See Graphics. **TransformPoints Methods**.
SetPixelOffsetMode	See **Graphics.PixelOffsetMode**.
SetRenderingOrigin	See **Graphics.RenderingOrigin**.
SetTextContrast	See **Graphics.TextContrast**.
SetTextRenderingHint	See **Graphics.TextRenderingHint**.
SetWorldTransform	See **Graphics.TransformPoints Methods**.
Total	Used internally.
TranslateWorldTransform	See **Graphics.TransformPoints Methods**.
WmfAnimatePalette	See "Windows-Format Metafiles" in the GDI section of the Platform SDK documentation.
WmfArc	See "Windows-Format Metafiles" in the GDI section of the Platform SDK documentation.
WmfBitBlt	See "Windows-Format Metafiles" in the GDI section of the Platform SDK documentation.
WmfChord	See "Windows-Format Metafiles" in the GDI section of the Platform SDK documentation.
WmfCreateBrushIndirect	See "Windows-Format Metafiles" in the GDI section of the Platform SDK documentation.
WmfCreateFontIndirect	See "Windows-Format Metafiles" in the GDI section of the Platform SDK documentation.
WmfCreatePalette	See "Windows-Format Metafiles" in the GDI section of the Platform SDK documentation.
WmfCreatePatternBrush	See "Windows-Format Metafiles" in the GDI section of the Platform SDK documentation.
WmfCreatePenIndirect	See "Windows-Format Metafiles" in the GDI section of the Platform SDK documentation.

Member name	Description
WmfCreateRegion	See "Windows-Format Metafiles" in the GDI section of the Platform SDK documentation.
WmfDeleteObject	See "Windows-Format Metafiles" in the GDI section of the Platform SDK documentation.
WmfDibBitBlt	See "Windows-Format Metafiles" in the GDI section of the Platform SDK documentation.
WmfDibCreatePattern-Brush	See "Windows-Format Metafiles" in the GDI section of the Platform SDK documentation.
WmfDibStretchBlt	See "Windows-Format Metafiles" in the GDI section of the Platform SDK documentation.
WmfEllipse	See "Windows-Format Metafiles" in the GDI section of the Platform SDK documentation.
WmfEscape	See "Windows-Format Metafiles" in the GDI section of the Platform SDK documentation.
WmfExcludeClipRect	See "Windows-Format Metafiles" in the GDI section of the Platform SDK documentation.
WmfExtFloodFill	See "Windows-Format Metafiles" in the GDI section of the Platform SDK documentation.
WmfExtTextOut	See "Windows-Format Metafiles" in the GDI section of the Platform SDK documentation.
WmfFillRegion	See "Windows-Format Metafiles" in the GDI section of the Platform SDK documentation.
WmfFloodFill	See "Windows-Format Metafiles" in the GDI section of the Platform SDK documentation.
WmfFrameRegion	See "Windows-Format Metafiles" in the GDI section of the Platform SDK documentation.
WmfIntersectClipRect	See "Windows-Format Metafiles" in the GDI section of the Platform SDK documentation.
WmfInvertRegion	See "Windows-Format Metafiles" in the GDI section of the Platform SDK documentation.
WmfLineTo	See "Windows-Format Metafiles" in the GDI section of the Platform SDK documentation.
WmfMoveTo	See "Windows-Format Metafiles" in the GDI section of the Platform SDK documentation.
WmfOffsetCilpRgn	See "Windows-Format Metafiles" in the GDI section of the Platform SDK documentation.
WmfOffsetViewportOrg	See "Windows-Format Metafiles" in the GDI section of the Platform SDK documentation.

Member name	Description
WmfOffsetWindowOrg	See "Windows-Format Metafiles" in the GDI section of the Platform SDK documentation.
WmfPaintRegion	See "Windows-Format Metafiles" in the GDI section of the Platform SDK documentation.
WmfPatBlt	See "Windows-Format Metafiles" in the GDI section of the Platform SDK documentation.
WmfPie	See "Windows-Format Metafiles" in the GDI section of the Platform SDK documentation.
WmfPolygon	See "Windows-Format Metafiles" in the GDI section of the Platform SDK documentation.
WmfPolyline	See "Windows-Format Metafiles" in the GDI section of the Platform SDK documentation.
WmfPolyPolygon	See "Windows-Format Metafiles" in the GDI section of the Platform SDK documentation.
WmfRealizePalette	See "Windows-Format Metafiles" in the GDI section of the Platform SDK documentation.
WmfRecordBase	See "Windows-Format Metafiles" in the GDI section of the Platform SDK documentation.
WmfRectangle	See "Windows-Format Metafiles" in the GDI section of the Platform SDK documentation.
WmfResizePalette	Increases or decreases the size of a logical palette based on the specified value.
WmfRestoreDC	See "Windows-Format Metafiles" in the GDI section of the Platform SDK documentation.
WmfRoundRect	See "Windows-Format Metafiles" in the GDI section of the Platform SDK documentation.
WmfSaveDC	See "Windows-Format Metafiles" in the GDI section of the Platform SDK documentation.
WmfScaleViewportExt	See "Windows-Format Metafiles" in the GDI section of the Platform SDK documentation.
WmfScaleWindowExt	See "Windows-Format Metafiles" in the GDI section of the Platform SDK documentation.
WmfSelectClipRegion	See "Windows-Format Metafiles" in the GDI section of the Platform SDK documentation.
WmfSelectObject	See "Windows-Format Metafiles" in the GDI section of the Platform SDK documentation.
WmfSelectPalette	See "Windows-Format Metafiles" in the GDI section of the Platform SDK documentation.

Member name	Description
WmfSetBkColor	See "Windows-Format Metafiles" in the GDI section of the Platform SDK documentation.
WmfSetBkMode	See "Windows-Format Metafiles" in the GDI section of the Platform SDK documentation.
WmfSetDibToDev	See "Windows-Format Metafiles" in the GDI section of the Platform SDK documentation.
WmfSetLayout	See "Windows-Format Metafiles" in the GDI section of the Platform SDK documentation.
WmfSetMapMode	See "Windows-Format Metafiles" in the GDI section of the Platform SDK documentation.
WmfSetMapperFlags	See "Windows-Format Metafiles" in the GDI section of the Platform SDK documentation.
WmfSetPalEntries	See "Windows-Format Metafiles" in the GDI section of the Platform SDK documentation.
WmfSetPixel	See "Windows-Format Metafiles" in the GDI section of the Platform SDK documentation.
WmfSetPolyFillMode	See "Windows-Format Metafiles" in the GDI section of the Platform SDK documentation.
WmfSetRelAbs	See "Windows-Format Metafiles" in the GDI section of the Platform SDK documentation.
WmfSetROP2	See "Windows-Format Metafiles" in the GDI section of the Platform SDK documentation.
WmfSetStretchBltMode	See "Windows-Format Metafiles" in the GDI section of the Platform SDK documentation.
WmfSetTextAlign	See "Windows-Format Metafiles" in the GDI section of the Platform SDK documentation.
WmfSetTextCharExtra	See "Windows-Format Metafiles" in the GDI section of the Platform SDK documentation.
WmfSetTextColor	See "Windows-Format Metafiles" in the GDI section of the Platform SDK documentation.
WmfSetTextJustification	See "Windows-Format Metafiles" in the GDI section of the Platform SDK documentation.
WmfSetViewportExt	See "Windows-Format Metafiles" in the GDI section of the Platform SDK documentation.
WmfSetViewportOrg	See "Windows-Format Metafiles" in the GDI section of the Platform SDK documentation.
WmfSetWindowExt	See "Windows-Format Metafiles" in the GDI section of the Platform SDK documentation.

Member name	Description
WmfSetWindowOrg	See "Windows-Format Metafiles" in the GDI section of the Platform SDK documentation.
WmfStretchBlt	See "Windows-Format Metafiles" in the GDI section of the Platform SDK documentation.
WmfStretchDib	Copies the color data for a rectangle of pixels in a DIB to the specified destination rectangle.
WmfTextOut	See "Windows-Format Metafiles" in the GDI section of the Platform SDK documentation.

Requirements

Namespace: System.Drawing.Imaging

Platforms: Windows 98, Windows NT 4.0, Windows Millennium Edition, Windows 2000, Windows XP Home Edition, Windows XP Professional, Windows Server 2003 family

Assembly: System.Drawing (in System.Drawing.dll)

EmfType Enumeration

Specifies the nature of the records that are placed in an Enhanced Metafile (EMF) file. This enumeration is used by several constructors in the **Metafile** class.

[Visual Basic]
```
<Serializable>
Public Enum EmfType
```
[C#]
```
[Serializable]
public enum EmfType
```
[C++]
```
[Serializable]
__value public enum EmfType
```
[JScript]
```
public
   Serializable
enum EmfType
```

Remarks

GDI+ uses the enhanced Windows metafile image format (EMF). The EMF format contains a comment mechanism for embedding data within the metafile. This comment mechanism is used to embed GDI+ records within an EMF file. EMF files that contain GDI+ data are called EMF+ files. Applications that do not recognize the comment data skip the comment records and render the records they do understand. If the EMF+ file is played back by GDI+, then the GDI+ records are used to render the metafile; otherwise, the GDI records (if present) are used.

Members

Member name	Description
EmfOnly	Specifies that all the records in the metafile are EMF records, which can be displayed by GDI or GDI+.
EmfPlusDual	Specifies that all EMF+ records in the metafile are associated with an alternate EMF record. Metafiles of type **EmfTypeEmfPlusDual** can be displayed by GDI or by GDI+.
EmfPlusOnly	Specifies that all the records in the metafile are EMF+ records, which can be displayed by GDI+ but not by GDI.

Requirements

Namespace: System.Drawing.Imaging

Platforms: Windows 98, Windows NT 4.0, Windows Millennium Edition, Windows 2000, Windows XP Home Edition, Windows XP Professional, Windows Server 2003 family

Assembly: System.Drawing (in System.Drawing.dll)

Encoder Class

An **Encoder** object encapsulates a globally unique identifier (GUID) that identifies the category of an image encoder parameter.

System.Object
  System.Drawing.Imaging.Encoder

```
[Visual Basic]
NotInheritable Public Class Encoder
[C#]
public sealed class Encoder
[C++]
public __gc __sealed class Encoder
[JScript]
public class Encoder
```

Thread Safety

Any public static (**Shared** in Visual Basic) members of this type are safe for multithreaded operations. Any instance members are not guaranteed to be thread safe.

Remarks

When you pass a parameter to an image encoder, the parameter is encapsulated in an **EncoderParameter** object. One of the private fields of the **EncoderParameter** object is a GUID that specifies the category of the parameter. The image encoders that are built into GDI+ receive parameters that belong to the following categories:

Requirements

Namespace: System.Drawing.Imaging

Platforms: Windows 98, Windows NT 4.0, Windows Millennium Edition, Windows 2000, Windows XP Home Edition, Windows XP Professional, Windows Server 2003 family

Assembly: System.Drawing (in System.Drawing.dll)

Encoder Constructor

Initializes a new instance of the **Encoder** class from the specified globally unique identifier (GUID). The GUID specifies an image encoder parameter category.

```
[Visual Basic]
Public Sub New( _
   ByVal guid As Guid _
)
[C#]
public Encoder(
   Guid guid
);
[C++]
public: Encoder(
   Guid guid
);
[JScript]
public function Encoder(
   guid : Guid
);
```

Parameters

guid

A globally unique identifier that identifies an image encoder parameter category.

Requirements

Platforms: Windows 98, Windows NT 4.0, Windows Millennium Edition, Windows 2000, Windows XP Home Edition, Windows XP Professional, Windows Server 2003 family

Encoder.ChrominanceTable Field

An **Encoder** object that is initialized with the globally unique identifier for the chrominance table parameter category.

```
[Visual Basic]
Public Shared ReadOnly ChrominanceTable As Encoder
[C#]
public static readonly Encoder ChrominanceTable;
[C++]
public: static Encoder* ChrominanceTable;
[JScript]
public static var ChrominanceTable : Encoder;
```

Requirements

Platforms: Windows 98, Windows NT 4.0, Windows Millennium Edition, Windows 2000, Windows XP Home Edition, Windows XP Professional, Windows Server 2003 family

Encoder.ColorDepth Field

An **Encoder** object that is initialized with the globally unique identifier for the color depth parameter category.

```
[Visual Basic]
Public Shared ReadOnly ColorDepth As Encoder
[C#]
public static readonly Encoder ColorDepth;
[C++]
public: static Encoder* ColorDepth;
[JScript]
public static var ColorDepth : Encoder;
```

Example

[C#] The following example creates a **Bitmap** object from a BMP file. The code saves the image as a TIFF file with a color depth of 24 bits per pixel.

```
[C#]
using System;
using System.Drawing;
using System.Drawing.Imaging;
class Example_SetColorDepth
{
public static void Main()
{
Bitmap myBitmap;
ImageCodecInfo myImageCodecInfo;
Encoder myEncoder;
EncoderParameter myEncoderParameter;
EncoderParameters myEncoderParameters;
// Create a Bitmap object based on a BMP file.
myBitmap = new Bitmap("Shapes.bmp");
// Get an ImageCodecInfo object that represents the TIFF codec.
```

```
myImageCodecInfo = GetEncoderInfo("image/tiff");
// Create an Encoder object based on the GUID
// for the ColorDepth parameter category.
myEncoder = Encoder.ColorDepth;
// Create an EncoderParameters object.
// An EncoderParameters object has an array of EncoderParameter
// objects. In this case, there is only one
// EncoderParameter object in the array.
myEncoderParameters = new EncoderParameters(1);
// Save the image with a color depth of 24 bits per pixel.
myEncoderParameter =
new EncoderParameter(myEncoder, 24L);
myEncoderParameters.Param[0] = myEncoderParameter;
myBitmap.Save("Shapes24bpp.tiff", myImageCodecInfo,
myEncoderParameters);
}
private static ImageCodecInfo GetEncoderInfo(String mimeType)
{
int j;
ImageCodecInfo[] encoders;
encoders = ImageCodecInfo.GetImageEncoders();
for(j = 0; j < encoders.Length; ++j)
{
if(encoders[j].MimeType == mimeType)
return encoders[j];
}
return null;
}
}
```

Requirements

Platforms: Windows 98, Windows NT 4.0, Windows Millennium Edition, Windows 2000, Windows XP Home Edition, Windows XP Professional, Windows Server 2003 family

Encoder.Compression Field

An **Encoder** object that is initialized with the globally unique identifier for the compression parameter category.

[Visual Basic]
```
Public Shared ReadOnly Compression As Encoder
```
[C#]
```
public static readonly Encoder Compression;
```
[C++]
```
public: static Encoder* Compression;
```
[JScript]
```
public static var Compression : Encoder;
```

Example

[C#] The following example creates a **Bitmap** object from a BMP file. The code saves the image as a TIFF file with LZW compression.

[C#]
```
using System;
using System.Drawing;
using System.Drawing.Imaging;
class Example_SetTIFFCompression
{
public static void Main()
{
Bitmap myBitmap;
ImageCodecInfo myImageCodecInfo;
Encoder myEncoder;
EncoderParameter myEncoderParameter;
EncoderParameters myEncoderParameters;
// Create a Bitmap object based on a BMP file.
myBitmap = new Bitmap("Shapes.bmp");
// Get an ImageCodecInfo object that represents the TIFF codec.
myImageCodecInfo = GetEncoderInfo("image/tiff");
// Create an Encoder object based on the GUID
// for the Compression parameter category.
myEncoder = Encoder.Compression;
// Create an EncoderParameters object.
// An EncoderParameters object has an array of EncoderParameter
// objects. In this case, there is only one
// EncoderParameter object in the array.
myEncoderParameters = new EncoderParameters(1);
// Save the bitmap as a TIFF file with LZW compression.
myEncoderParameter = new EncoderParameter(
myEncoder,
(long)EncoderValue.CompressionLZW);
myEncoderParameters.Param[0] = myEncoderParameter;
myBitmap.Save("ShapesLZW.tif", myImageCodecInfo, myEncoderParameters);
}
private static ImageCodecInfo GetEncoderInfo(String mimeType)
{
int j;
ImageCodecInfo[] encoders;
encoders = ImageCodecInfo.GetImageEncoders();
for(j = 0; j < encoders.Length; ++j)
{
if(encoders[j].MimeType == mimeType)
return encoders[j];
}
return null;
}
}
```

Requirements

Platforms: Windows 98, Windows NT 4.0, Windows Millennium Edition, Windows 2000, Windows XP Home Edition, Windows XP Professional, Windows Server 2003 family

Encoder.LuminanceTable Field

An **Encoder** object that is initialized with the globally unique identifier for the luminance table parameter category.

[Visual Basic]
```
Public Shared ReadOnly LuminanceTable As Encoder
```
[C#]
```
public static readonly Encoder LuminanceTable;
```
[C++]
```
public: static Encoder* LuminanceTable;
```
[JScript]
```
public static var LuminanceTable : Encoder;
```

Requirements

Platforms: Windows 98, Windows NT 4.0, Windows Millennium Edition, Windows 2000, Windows XP Home Edition, Windows XP Professional, Windows Server 2003 family

Encoder.Quality Field

An **Encoder** object that is initialized with the globally unique identifier for the quality parameter category.

[Visual Basic]
```
Public Shared ReadOnly Quality As Encoder
```
[C#]
```
public static readonly Encoder Quality;
```
[C++]
```
public: static Encoder* Quality;
```

```
[JScript]
public static var Quality : Encoder;
```

Example

[C#] The following example creates a **Bitmap** object from a BMP file. The code saves the bitmap to three JPEG files, each with a different quality level.

```
[C#]
using System;
using System.Drawing;
using System.Drawing.Imaging;
class Example_SetJPEGQuality
{
public static void Main()
{
Bitmap myBitmap;
ImageCodecInfo myImageCodecInfo;
Encoder myEncoder;
EncoderParameter myEncoderParameter;
EncoderParameters myEncoderParameters;
// Create a Bitmap object based on a BMP file.
myBitmap = new Bitmap("Shapes.bmp");
// Get an ImageCodecInfo object that represents the JPEG codec.
myImageCodecInfo = GetEncoderInfo("image/jpeg");
// Create an Encoder object based on the GUID
// for the Quality parameter category.
myEncoder = Encoder.Quality;
// Create an EncoderParameters object.
// An EncoderParameters object has an array of EncoderParameter
// objects. In this case, there is only one
// EncoderParameter object in the array.
myEncoderParameters = new EncoderParameters(1);
// Save the bitmap as a JPEG file with quality level 25.
myEncoderParameter = new EncoderParameter(myEncoder, 25L);
myEncoderParameters.Param[0] = myEncoderParameter;
myBitmap.Save("Shapes025.jpg", myImageCodecInfo, myEncoderParameters);
// Save the bitmap as a JPEG file with quality level 50.
myEncoderParameter = new EncoderParameter(myEncoder, 50L);
myEncoderParameters.Param[0] = myEncoderParameter;
myBitmap.Save("Shapes050.jpg", myImageCodecInfo, myEncoderParameters);
// Save the bitmap as a JPEG file with quality level 75.
myEncoderParameter = new EncoderParameter(myEncoder, 75L);
myEncoderParameters.Param[0] = myEncoderParameter;
myBitmap.Save("Shapes075.jpg", myImageCodecInfo, myEncoderParameters);
}
private static ImageCodecInfo GetEncoderInfo(String mimeType)
{
int j;
ImageCodecInfo[] encoders;
encoders = ImageCodecInfo.GetImageEncoders();
for(j = 0; j < encoders.Length; ++j)
{
if(encoders[j].MimeType == mimeType)
return encoders[j];
}
return null;
}
}
```

Requirements

Platforms: Windows 98, Windows NT 4.0, Windows Millennium Edition, Windows 2000, Windows XP Home Edition, Windows XP Professional, Windows Server 2003 family

Encoder.RenderMethod Field

An **Encoder** object that is initialized with the globally unique identifier for the render method parameter category.

```
[Visual Basic]
Public Shared ReadOnly RenderMethod As Encoder
[C#]
public static readonly Encoder RenderMethod;
[C++]
public: static Encoder* RenderMethod;
[JScript]
public static var RenderMethod : Encoder;
```

Requirements

Platforms: Windows 98, Windows NT 4.0, Windows Millennium Edition, Windows 2000, Windows XP Home Edition, Windows XP Professional, Windows Server 2003 family

Encoder.SaveFlag Field

An **Encoder** object that is initialized with the globally unique identifier for the save flag parameter category.

```
[Visual Basic]
Public Shared ReadOnly SaveFlag As Encoder
[C#]
public static readonly Encoder SaveFlag;
[C++]
public: static Encoder* SaveFlag;
[JScript]
public static var SaveFlag : Encoder;
```

Example

[C#] The following example creates three **Bitmap** objects: one from a BMP file, one from a JPEG file, and one from a PNG file. The code saves all three images in a single, multiple-frame TIFF file.

```
[C#]
using System;
using System.Drawing;
using System.Drawing.Imaging;
class Example_MultiFrame
{
public static void Main()
{
Bitmap multi;
Bitmap page2;
Bitmap page3;
ImageCodecInfo myImageCodecInfo;
Encoder myEncoder;
EncoderParameter myEncoderParameter;
EncoderParameters myEncoderParameters;
// Create three Bitmap objects.
multi = new Bitmap("Shapes.bmp");
page2 = new Bitmap("Iron.jpg");
page3 = new Bitmap("House.png");
// Get an ImageCodecInfo object that represents the TIFF codec.
myImageCodecInfo = GetEncoderInfo("image/tiff");
// Create an Encoder object based on the GUID
// for the SaveFlag parameter category.
myEncoder = Encoder.SaveFlag;
// Create an EncoderParameters object.
// An EncoderParameters object has an array of EncoderParameter
// objects. In this case, there is only one
// EncoderParameter object in the array.
myEncoderParameters = new EncoderParameters(1);
// Save the first page (frame).
```

```
myEncoderParameter = new EncoderParameter(
myEncoder,
(long)EncoderValue.MultiFrame);
myEncoderParameters.Param[0] = myEncoderParameter;
multi.Save("Multiframe.tiff", myImageCodecInfo, myEncoderParameters);
// Save the second page (frame).
myEncoderParameter = new EncoderParameter(
myEncoder,
(long)EncoderValue.FrameDimensionPage);
myEncoderParameters.Param[0] = myEncoderParameter;
multi.SaveAdd(page2, myEncoderParameters);
// Save the third page (frame).
myEncoderParameter = new EncoderParameter(
myEncoder,
(long)EncoderValue.FrameDimensionPage);
myEncoderParameters.Param[0] = myEncoderParameter;
multi.SaveAdd(page3, myEncoderParameters);
// Close the multiple-frame file.
myEncoderParameter = new EncoderParameter(
myEncoder,
(long)EncoderValue.Flush);
myEncoderParameters.Param[0] = myEncoderParameter;
multi.SaveAdd(myEncoderParameters);
}
private static ImageCodecInfo GetEncoderInfo(String mimeType)
{
int j;
ImageCodecInfo[] encoders;
encoders = ImageCodecInfo.GetImageEncoders();
for(j = 0; j < encoders.Length; ++j)
{
if(encoders[j].MimeType == mimeType)
return encoders[j];
}
return null;
}
}
```

Requirements

Platforms: Windows 98, Windows NT 4.0, Windows Millennium Edition, Windows 2000, Windows XP Home Edition, Windows XP Professional, Windows Server 2003 family

Encoder.ScanMethod Field

An **Encoder** object that is initialized with the globally unique identifier for the scan method parameter category.

[Visual Basic]
```
Public Shared ReadOnly ScanMethod As Encoder
```
[C#]
```
public static readonly Encoder ScanMethod;
```
[C++]
```
public: static Encoder* ScanMethod;
```
[JScript]
```
public static var ScanMethod : Encoder;
```

Requirements

Platforms: Windows 98, Windows NT 4.0, Windows Millennium Edition, Windows 2000, Windows XP Home Edition, Windows XP Professional, Windows Server 2003 family

Encoder.Transformation Field

An **Encoder** object that is initialized with the globally unique identifier for the transformation parameter category.

[Visual Basic]
```
Public Shared ReadOnly Transformation As Encoder
```
[C#]
```
public static readonly Encoder Transformation;
```
[C++]
```
public: static Encoder* Transformation;
```
[JScript]
```
public static var Transformation : Encoder;
```

Example

[C#] The following example creates a **Bitmap** object from a JPEG file. The code rotates the image 90 degrees and saves it in a separate JPEG file.

[C#]
```
using System;
using System.Drawing;
using System.Drawing.Imaging;
class Example_RotateJPEG
{
public static void Main()
{
Bitmap myBitmap;
ImageCodecInfo myImageCodecInfo;
Encoder myEncoder;
EncoderParameter myEncoderParameter;
EncoderParameters myEncoderParameters;
// Create a Bitmap object based on a JPEG file.
myBitmap = new Bitmap("Shapes.jpg");
// Get an ImageCodecInfo object that represents the JPEG codec.
myImageCodecInfo = GetEncoderInfo("image/jpeg");
// Create an Encoder object based on the GUID
// for the Transformation parameter category.
myEncoder = Encoder.Transformation;
// Create an EncoderParameters object.
// An EncoderParameters object has an array of EncoderParameter
// objects. In this case, there is only one
// EncoderParameter object in the array.
myEncoderParameters = new EncoderParameters(1);
// Rotate the image 90 degrees, and save it as a separate JPEG file.
myEncoderParameter = new EncoderParameter(
myEncoder,
(long)EncoderValue.TransformRotate90);
myEncoderParameters.Param[0] = myEncoderParameter;
myBitmap.Save("ShapesR90.jpg", myImageCodecInfo, myEncoderParameters);
}
private static ImageCodecInfo GetEncoderInfo(String mimeType)
{
int j;
ImageCodecInfo[] encoders;
encoders = ImageCodecInfo.GetImageEncoders();
for(j = 0; j < encoders.Length; ++j)
{
if(encoders[j].MimeType == mimeType)
return encoders[j];
}
return null;
}
}
```

Requirements

Platforms: Windows 98, Windows NT 4.0, Windows Millennium Edition, Windows 2000, Windows XP Home Edition, Windows XP Professional, Windows Server 2003 family

Encoder.Version Field

An **Encoder** object that is initialized with the globally unique identifier for the version parameter category.

[Visual Basic]
```
Public Shared ReadOnly Version As Encoder
```
[C#]
```
public static readonly Encoder Version;
```
[C++]
```
public: static Encoder* Version;
```
[JScript]
```
public static var Version : Encoder;
```

Requirements

Platforms: Windows 98, Windows NT 4.0, Windows Millennium Edition, Windows 2000, Windows XP Home Edition, Windows XP Professional, Windows Server 2003 family

Encoder.Guid Property

Gets a globally unique identifier (GUID) that identifies an image encoder parameter category.

[Visual Basic]
```
Public ReadOnly Property Guid As Guid
```
[C#]
```
public Guid Guid {get;}
```
[C++]
```
public: __property Guid get_Guid();
```
[JScript]
```
public function get Guid() : Guid;
```

Property Value

The GUID that identifies an image encoder parameter category.

Requirements

Platforms: Windows 98, Windows NT 4.0, Windows Millennium Edition, Windows 2000, Windows XP Home Edition, Windows XP Professional, Windows Server 2003 family

EncoderParameter Class

You can use an **EncoderParameter** object to pass an array of values to an image encoder. You can also use an **EncoderParameter** object to receive a list of possible values supported by a particular parameter of a particular image encoder.

System.Object
System.Drawing.Imaging.EncoderParameter

[Visual Basic]
```
NotInheritable Public Class EncoderParameter
   Implements IDisposable
```
[C#]
```
public sealed class EncoderParameter : IDisposable
```
[C++]
```
public __gc __sealed class EncoderParameter : public IDisposable
```
[JScript]
```
public class EncoderParameter implements IDisposable
```

Thread Safety

Any public static (**Shared** in Visual Basic) members of this type are safe for multithreaded operations. Any instance members are not guaranteed to be thread safe.

Requirements

Namespace: System.Drawing.Imaging

Platforms: Windows 98, Windows NT 4.0, Windows Millennium Edition, Windows 2000, Windows XP Home Edition, Windows XP Professional, Windows Server 2003 family

Assembly: System.Drawing (in System.Drawing.dll)

EncoderParameter Constructor

Initializes a new instance of the **EncoderParameter** class with the specified **Encoder** object and one unsigned 8-bit integer.

Overload List

Initializes a new instance of the **EncoderParameter** class with the specified **Encoder** object and one unsigned 8-bit integer. Sets the **ValueType** property to ValueTypeByte, and sets the **NumberOfValues** property to 1.

[Visual Basic] **Public Sub New(Encoder, Byte)**

[C#] **public EncoderParameter(Encoder, byte);**

[C++] **public: EncoderParameter(Encoder*, unsigned char);**

[JScript] **public function EncoderParameter(Encoder, Byte);**

Initializes a new instance of the **EncoderParameter** class with the specified **Encoder** object and an array of unsigned 8-bit integers. Sets the **ValueType** property to ValueTypeByte, and sets the **NumberOfValues** property to the number of elements in the array.

[Visual Basic] **Public Sub New(Encoder, Byte())**

[C#] **public EncoderParameter(Encoder, byte[]);**

[C++] **public: EncoderParameter(Encoder*, unsigned char __gc[]);**

[JScript] **public function EncoderParameter(Encoder, Byte[]);**

Initializes a new instance of the **EncoderParameter** class with the specified **Encoder** object and one, 16-bit integer. Sets the **ValueType** property to ValueTypeShort, and sets the **NumberOfValues** property to 1.

[Visual Basic] **Public Sub New(Encoder, Short)**

[C#] **public EncoderParameter(Encoder, short);**

[C++] **public: EncoderParameter(Encoder*, short);**

[JScript] **public function EncoderParameter(Encoder, Int16);**

Initializes a new instance of the **EncoderParameter** class with the specified **Encoder** object and an array of 16-bit integers. Sets the **ValueType** property to ValueTypeShort, and sets the **NumberOfValues** property to the number of elements in the array.

[Visual Basic] **Public Sub New(Encoder, Short())**

[C#] **public EncoderParameter(Encoder, short[]);**

[C++] **public: EncoderParameter(Encoder*, short __gc[]);**

[JScript] **public function EncoderParameter(Encoder, Int16[]);**

Initializes a new instance of the **EncoderParameter** class with the specified **Encoder** object and one 64-bit integer. Sets the **ValueType** property to **ValueTypeLong** (32 bits), and sets the **NumberOfValues** property to 1.

[Visual Basic] **Public Sub New(Encoder, Long)**

[C#] **public EncoderParameter(Encoder, long);**

[C++] **public: EncoderParameter(Encoder*, __int64);**

[JScript] **public function EncoderParameter(Encoder, long);**

Initializes a new instance of the **EncoderParameter** class with the specified **Encoder** object and an array of 64-bit integers. Sets the **ValueType** property to ValueTypeLong (32-bit), and sets the **NumberOfValues** property to the number of elements in the array.

[Visual Basic] **Public Sub New(Encoder, Long())**

[C#] **public EncoderParameter(Encoder, long[]);**

[C++] **public: EncoderParameter(Encoder*, __int64 __gc[]);**

[JScript] **public function EncoderParameter(Encoder, long[]);**

Initializes a new instance of the **EncoderParameter** class with the specified **Encoder** object and a character string. The string is converted to a null-terminated ASCII string before it is stored in the **EncoderParameter** object. Sets the **ValueType** property to **ValueTypeAscii**, and sets the **NumberOfValues** property to the length of the ASCII string including the NULL terminator.

[Visual Basic] **Public Sub New(Encoder, String)**

[C#] **public EncoderParameter(Encoder, string);**

[C++] **public: EncoderParameter(Encoder*, String*);**

[JScript] **public function EncoderParameter(Encoder, String);**

Initializes a new instance of the **EncoderParameter** class with the specified **Encoder** object and one 8-bit value. Sets the **ValueType** property to ValueTypeUndefined or ValueTypeByte, and sets the **NumberOfValues** property to 1.

[Visual Basic] **Public Sub New(Encoder, Byte, Boolean)**

[C#] **public EncoderParameter(Encoder, byte, bool);**

[C++] **public: EncoderParameter(Encoder*, unsigned char, bool);**

[JScript] **public function EncoderParameter(Encoder, Byte, Boolean);**

Initializes a new instance of the **EncoderParameter** class with the specified **Encoder** object and an array of bytes. Sets the **ValueType** property to ValueTypeUndefined or ValueTypeByte, and sets the **NumberOfValues** property to the number of elements in the array.

[Visual Basic] **Public Sub New(Encoder, Byte(), Boolean)**

[C#] **public EncoderParameter(Encoder, byte[], bool);**

[C++] **public: EncoderParameter(Encoder*, unsigned char __gc[], bool);**

[JScript] **public function EncoderParameter(Encoder, Byte[], Boolean);**

Initializes a new instance of the **EncoderParameter** class with the specified **Encoder** object and a pair of 32-bit integers. The pair of integers represents a fraction, the first integer being the numerator, and the second integer being the denominator. Sets the **ValueType** property to ValueTypeRational, and sets the **NumberOfValues** property to 1.

[Visual Basic] **Public Sub New(Encoder, Integer, Integer)**

[C#] **public EncoderParameter(Encoder, int, int);**

[C++] **public: EncoderParameter(Encoder*, int, int);**

[JScript] **public function EncoderParameter(Encoder, int, int);**

Initializes a new instance of the **EncoderParameter** class with the specified **Encoder** object and two arrays of 32-bit integers. The two arrays represent an array of fractions. Sets the **ValueType** property to **ValueTypeRational**, and sets the **NumberOfValues** property to the number of elements in the *numerator* array, which must be the same as the number of elements in the *denominator* array.

[Visual Basic] **Public Sub New(Encoder, Integer(), Integer())**

[C#] **public EncoderParameter(Encoder, int[], int[]);**

[C++] **public: EncoderParameter(Encoder*, int __gc[], int __gc[]);**

[JScript] **public function EncoderParameter(Encoder, int[], int[]);**

Initializes a new instance of the **EncoderParameter** class with the specified **Encoder** object and a pair of 64-bit integers. The pair of integers represents a range of integers, the first integer being the smallest number in the range, and the second integer being the largest number in the range. Sets the **ValueType** property to **ValueTypeLongRange**, and sets the **NumberOfValues** property to 1.

[Visual Basic] **Public Sub New(Encoder, Long, Long)**

[C#] **public EncoderParameter(Encoder, long, long);**

[C++] **public: EncoderParameter(Encoder*, __int64, __int64);**

[JScript] **public function EncoderParameter(Encoder, long, long);**

Initializes a new instance of the **EncoderParameter** class with the specified **Encoder** object and two arrays of 64-bit integers. The two arrays represent an array integer ranges. Sets the **ValueType** property to ValueTypeLongRange, and sets the **NumberOfValues** property to the number of elements in the *rangebegin* array, which must be the same as the number of elements in the *rangeend* array.

[Visual Basic] **Public Sub New(Encoder, Long(), Long())**

[C#] **public EncoderParameter(Encoder, long[], long[]);**

[C++] **public: EncoderParameter(Encoder*, __int64 __gc[], __int64 __gc[]);**

[JScript] **public function EncoderParameter(Encoder, long[], long[]);**

Initializes a new instance of the **EncoderParameter** class with the specified **Encoder** object and three integers that specify the number of values, the data type of the values, and a pointer to the values stored in the **EncoderParameter** object.

[Visual Basic] **Public Sub New(Encoder, Integer, Integer, Integer)**

[C#] **public EncoderParameter(Encoder, int, int, int);**

[C++] **public: EncoderParameter(Encoder*, int, int, int);**

[JScript] **public function EncoderParameter(Encoder, int, int, int);**

Initializes a new instance of the **EncoderParameter** class with the specified **Encoder** object and four, 32-bit integers. The four integers represent a range of fractions. The first two integers represent the smallest fraction in the range, and the remaining two integers represent the largest fraction in the range. Sets the **ValueType** property to ValueTypeRationalRange, and sets the **NumberOfValues** property to 1.

[Visual Basic] **Public Sub New(Encoder, Integer, Integer, Integer, Integer)**

[C#] **public EncoderParameter(Encoder, int, int, int, int);**

[C++] **public: EncoderParameter(Encoder*, int, int, int, int);**

[JScript] **public function EncoderParameter(Encoder, int, int, int, int);**

Initializes a new instance of the **EncoderParameter** class with the specified **Encoder** object and four arrays of 32-bit integers. The four arrays represent an array rational ranges. A rational range is the set of all fractions from a minimum fractional value through a maximum fractional value. Sets the **ValueType** property to ValueTypeRationalRange, and sets the **NumberOfValues** property to the number of elements in the *numerator1* array, which must be the same as the number of elements in the other three arrays.

[Visual Basic] **Public Sub New(Encoder, Integer(), Integer(), Integer(), Integer())**

[C#] **public EncoderParameter(Encoder, int[], int[], int[], int[]);**

[C++] **public: EncoderParameter(Encoder*, int __gc[], int __gc[], int __gc[], int __gc[]);**

[JScript] **public function EncoderParameter(Encoder, int[], int[], int[], int[]);**

EncoderParameter Constructor (Encoder, Byte)

Initializes a new instance of the **EncoderParameter** class with the specified **Encoder** object and one unsigned 8-bit integer. Sets the **ValueType** property to ValueTypeByte, and sets the **NumberOfValues** property to 1.

```
[Visual Basic]
Public Sub New( _
   ByVal encoder As Encoder, _
   ByVal value As Byte _
)
[C#]
public EncoderParameter(
   Encoder encoder,
   byte value
);
```

```
[C++]
public: EncoderParameter(
   Encoder* encoder,
   unsigned char value
);
[JScript]
public function EncoderParameter(
   encoder : Encoder,
   value : Byte
);
```

Parameters

encoder

An **Encoder** object that encapsulates the globally unique identifier of the parameter category.

value

An 8-bit unsigned integer that specifies the value stored in the **EncoderParameter** object.

Requirements

Platforms: Windows 98, Windows NT 4.0, Windows Millennium Edition, Windows 2000, Windows XP Home Edition, Windows XP Professional, Windows Server 2003 family

EncoderParameter Constructor (Encoder, Byte[])

Initializes a new instance of the **EncoderParameter** class with the specified **Encoder** object and an array of unsigned 8-bit integers. Sets the **ValueType** property to ValueTypeByte, and sets the **NumberOfValues** property to the number of elements in the array.

```
[Visual Basic]
Public Sub New( _
   ByVal encoder As Encoder, _
   ByVal value() As Byte _
)
[C#]
public EncoderParameter(
   Encoder encoder,
   byte[] value
);
[C++]
public: EncoderParameter(
   Encoder* encoder,
   unsigned char value __gc[]
);
[JScript]
public function EncoderParameter(
   encoder : Encoder,
   value : Byte[]
);
```

Parameters

encoder

An **Encoder** object that encapsulates the globally unique identifier of the parameter category.

value

An array of 8-bit unsigned integers that specifies the values stored in the **EncoderParameter** object.

Requirements

Platforms: Windows 98, Windows NT 4.0, Windows Millennium Edition, Windows 2000, Windows XP Home Edition, Windows XP Professional, Windows Server 2003 family

EncoderParameter Constructor (Encoder, Int16)

Initializes a new instance of the **EncoderParameter** class with the specified **Encoder** object and one, 16-bit integer. Sets the **ValueType** property to ValueTypeShort, and sets the **NumberOfValues** property to 1.

```
[Visual Basic]
Public Sub New( _
   ByVal encoder As Encoder, _
   ByVal value As Short _
)
[C#]
public EncoderParameter(
   Encoder encoder,
   short value
);
[C++]
public: EncoderParameter(
   Encoder* encoder,
   short value
);
[JScript]
public function EncoderParameter(
   encoder : Encoder,
   value : Int16
);
```

Parameters

encoder

An **Encoder** object that encapsulates the globally unique identifier of the parameter category.

value

A 16-bit integer that specifies the value stored in the **EncoderParameter** object. Must be nonnegative.

Requirements

Platforms: Windows 98, Windows NT 4.0, Windows Millennium Edition, Windows 2000, Windows XP Home Edition, Windows XP Professional, Windows Server 2003 family

EncoderParameter Constructor (Encoder, Int16[])

Initializes a new instance of the **EncoderParameter** class with the specified **Encoder** object and an array of 16-bit integers. Sets the **ValueType** property to ValueTypeShort, and sets the **NumberOfValues** property to the number of elements in the array.

```
[Visual Basic]
Public Sub New( _
   ByVal encoder As Encoder, _
   ByVal value() As Short _
)
```

```
[C#]
public EncoderParameter(
   Encoder encoder,
   short[] value
);
[C++]
public: EncoderParameter(
   Encoder* encoder,
   short value __gc[]
);
[JScript]
public function EncoderParameter(
   encoder : Encoder,
   value : Int16[]
);
```

Parameters

encoder
An **Encoder** object that encapsulates the globally unique identifier of the parameter category.

value
An array of 16-bit integers that specifies the values stored in the **EncoderParameter** object. The integers in the array must be nonnegative.

Requirements

Platforms: Windows 98, Windows NT 4.0, Windows Millennium Edition, Windows 2000, Windows XP Home Edition, Windows XP Professional, Windows Server 2003 family

EncoderParameter Constructor (Encoder, Int64)

Initializes a new instance of the **EncoderParameter** class with the specified **Encoder** object and one 64-bit integer. Sets the **ValueType** property to **ValueTypeLong** (32 bits), and sets the **NumberOfValues** property to 1.

```
[Visual Basic]
Public Sub New( _
   ByVal encoder As Encoder, _
   ByVal value As Long _
)
[C#]
public EncoderParameter(
   Encoder encoder,
   long value
);
[C++]
public: EncoderParameter(
   Encoder* encoder,
   __int64 value
);
[JScript]
public function EncoderParameter(
   encoder : Encoder,
   value : long
);
```

Parameters

encoder
An **Encoder** object that encapsulates the globally unique identifier of the parameter category.

value
A 64-bit integer that specifies the value stored in the **EncoderParameter** object. Must be nonnegative. This parameter is converted to a 32-bit integer before it is stored in the **EncoderParameter** object.

Requirements

Platforms: Windows 98, Windows NT 4.0, Windows Millennium Edition, Windows 2000, Windows XP Home Edition, Windows XP Professional, Windows Server 2003 family

EncoderParameter Constructor (Encoder, Int64[])

Initializes a new instance of the **EncoderParameter** class with the specified **Encoder** object and an array of 64-bit integers. Sets the **ValueType** property to ValueTypeLong (32-bit), and sets the **NumberOfValues** property to the number of elements in the array.

```
[Visual Basic]
Public Sub New( _
   ByVal encoder As Encoder, _
   ByVal value() As Long _
)
[C#]
public EncoderParameter(
   Encoder encoder,
   long[] value
);
[C++]
public: EncoderParameter(
   Encoder* encoder,
   __int64 value __gc[]
);
[JScript]
public function EncoderParameter(
   encoder : Encoder,
   value : long[]
);
```

Parameters

encoder
An **Encoder** object that encapsulates the globally unique identifier of the parameter category.

value
An array of 64-bit integers that specifies the values stored in the **EncoderParameter** object. The integers in the array must be nonnegative. The 64-bit integers are converted to 32-bit integers before they are stored in the **EncoderParameter** object.

Requirements

Platforms: Windows 98, Windows NT 4.0, Windows Millennium Edition, Windows 2000, Windows XP Home Edition, Windows XP Professional, Windows Server 2003 family

EncoderParameter Constructor (Encoder, String)

Initializes a new instance of the **EncoderParameter** class with the specified **Encoder** object and a character string. The string is converted to a null-terminated ASCII string before it is stored in the **EncoderParameter** object. Sets the **ValueType** property to **ValueTypeAscii**, and sets the **NumberOfValues** property to the length of the ASCII string including the NULL terminator.

```
[Visual Basic]
Public Sub New( _
   ByVal encoder As Encoder, _
   ByVal value As String _
)
[C#]
public EncoderParameter(
   Encoder encoder,
   string value
);
[C++]
public: EncoderParameter(
   Encoder* encoder,
   String* value
);
[JScript]
public function EncoderParameter(
   encoder : Encoder,
   value : String
);
```

Parameters

encoder

An **Encoder** object that encapsulates the globally unique identifier of the parameter category.

value

A **String** that specifies the value stored in the **EncoderParameter** object.

Requirements

Platforms: Windows 98, Windows NT 4.0, Windows Millennium Edition, Windows 2000, Windows XP Home Edition, Windows XP Professional, Windows Server 2003 family

EncoderParameter Constructor (Encoder, Byte, Boolean)

Initializes a new instance of the **EncoderParameter** class with the specified **Encoder** object and one 8-bit value. Sets the **ValueType** property to ValueTypeUndefined or ValueTypeByte, and sets the **NumberOfValues** property to 1.

```
[Visual Basic]
Public Sub New( _
   ByVal encoder As Encoder, _
   ByVal value As Byte, _
   ByVal undefined As Boolean _
)
[C#]
public EncoderParameter(
   Encoder encoder,
   byte value,
   bool undefined
);
[C++]
public: EncoderParameter(
   Encoder* encoder,
   unsigned char value,
   bool undefined
);
[JScript]
public function EncoderParameter(
   encoder : Encoder,
   value : Byte,
   undefined : Boolean
);
```

Parameters

encoder

An **Encoder** object that encapsulates the globally unique identifier of the parameter category.

value

A byte that specifies the value stored in the **EncoderParameter** object.

undefined

If **true**, the **ValueType** property is set to ValueTypeUndefined; otherwise, the **ValueType** property is set to ValueTypeByte.

Requirements

Platforms: Windows 98, Windows NT 4.0, Windows Millennium Edition, Windows 2000, Windows XP Home Edition, Windows XP Professional, Windows Server 2003 family

EncoderParameter Constructor (Encoder, Byte[], Boolean)

Initializes a new instance of the **EncoderParameter** class with the specified **Encoder** object and an array of bytes. Sets the **ValueType** property to ValueTypeUndefined or ValueTypeByte, and sets the **NumberOfValues** property to the number of elements in the array.

```
[Visual Basic]
Public Sub New( _
   ByVal encoder As Encoder, _
   ByVal value() As Byte, _
   ByVal undefined As Boolean _
)
[C#]
public EncoderParameter(
   Encoder encoder,
   byte[] value,
   bool undefined
);
[C++]
public: EncoderParameter(
   Encoder* encoder,
   unsigned char value __gc[],
   bool undefined
);
[JScript]
public function EncoderParameter(
   encoder : Encoder,
   value : Byte[],
   undefined : Boolean
);
```

Parameters

encoder
An **Encoder** object that encapsulates the globally unique identifier of the parameter category.

value
An array of bytes that specifies the values stored in the **EncoderParameter** object.

undefined
If **true**, the **ValueType** property is set to ValueTypeUndefined; otherwise, the **ValueType** property is set to ValueTypeByte.

Requirements

Platforms: Windows 98, Windows NT 4.0, Windows Millennium Edition, Windows 2000, Windows XP Home Edition, Windows XP Professional, Windows Server 2003 family

EncoderParameter Constructor (Encoder, Int32, Int32)

Initializes a new instance of the **EncoderParameter** class with the specified **Encoder** object and a pair of 32-bit integers. The pair of integers represents a fraction, the first integer being the numerator, and the second integer being the denominator. Sets the **ValueType** property to ValueTypeRational, and sets the **NumberOfValues** property to 1.

```
[Visual Basic]
Public Sub New( _
   ByVal encoder As Encoder, _
   ByVal numerator As Integer, _
   ByVal demoninator As Integer _
)
[C#]
public EncoderParameter(
   Encoder encoder,
   int numerator,
   int demoninator
);
[C++]
public: EncoderParameter(
   Encoder* encoder,
   int numerator,
   int demoninator
);
[JScript]
public function EncoderParameter(
   encoder : Encoder,
   numerator : int,
   demoninator : int
);
```

Parameters

encoder
An **Encoder** object that encapsulates the globally unique identifier of the parameter category.

numerator
A 32-bit integer that represents the numerator of a fraction. Must be nonnegative.

demoninator
A 32-bit integer that represents the denominator of a fraction. Must be nonnegative.

Requirements

Platforms: Windows 98, Windows NT 4.0, Windows Millennium Edition, Windows 2000, Windows XP Home Edition, Windows XP Professional, Windows Server 2003 family

EncoderParameter Constructor (Encoder, Int32[], Int32[])

Initializes a new instance of the **EncoderParameter** class with the specified **Encoder** object and two arrays of 32-bit integers. The two arrays represent an array of fractions. Sets the **ValueType** property to **ValueTypeRational**, and sets the **NumberOfValues** property to the number of elements in the *numerator* array, which must be the same as the number of elements in the *denominator* array.

```
[Visual Basic]
Public Sub New( _
   ByVal encoder As Encoder, _
   ByVal numerator() As Integer, _
   ByVal denominator() As Integer _
)
[C#]
public EncoderParameter(
   Encoder encoder,
   int[] numerator,
   int[] denominator
);
[C++]
public: EncoderParameter(
   Encoder* encoder,
   int numerator __gc[],
   int denominator __gc[]
);
[JScript]
public function EncoderParameter(
   encoder : Encoder,
   numerator : int[],
   denominator : int[]
);
```

Parameters

encoder
An **Encoder** object that encapsulates the globally unique identifier of the parameter category.

numerator
An array of 32-bit integers that specifies the numerators of the fractions. The integers in the array must be nonnegative.

denominator
An array of 32-bit integers that specifies the denominators of the fractions. The integers in the array must be nonnegative. A denominator of a given index is paired with the numerator of the same index.

Requirements

Platforms: Windows 98, Windows NT 4.0, Windows Millennium Edition, Windows 2000, Windows XP Home Edition, Windows XP Professional, Windows Server 2003 family

EncoderParameter Constructor (Encoder, Int64, Int64)

Initializes a new instance of the **EncoderParameter** class with the specified **Encoder** object and a pair of 64-bit integers. The pair of integers represents a range of integers, the first integer being the smallest number in the range, and the second integer being the largest number in the range. Sets the **ValueType** property to **ValueTypeLongRange**, and sets the **NumberOfValues** property to 1.

```
[Visual Basic]
Public Sub New( _
   ByVal encoder As Encoder, _
   ByVal rangebegin As Long, _
   ByVal rangeend As Long _
)
[C#]
public EncoderParameter(
   Encoder encoder,
   long rangebegin,
   long rangeend
);
[C++]
public: EncoderParameter(
   Encoder* encoder,
   __int64 rangebegin,
   __int64 rangeend
);
[JScript]
public function EncoderParameter(
   encoder : Encoder,
   rangebegin : long,
   rangeend : long
);
```

Parameters

encoder

An **Encoder** object that encapsulates the globally unique identifier of the parameter category.

rangebegin

A 64-bit integer that represents the smallest number in a range of integers. Must be nonnegative. This parameter is converted to a 32-bit integer before it is stored in the **EncoderParameter** object.

rangeend

A 64-bit integer that represents the largest number in a range of integers. Must be nonnegative. This parameter is converted to a 32-bit integer before it is stored in the **EncoderParameter** object.

Requirements

Platforms: Windows 98, Windows NT 4.0, Windows Millennium Edition, Windows 2000, Windows XP Home Edition, Windows XP Professional, Windows Server 2003 family

EncoderParameter Constructor (Encoder, Int64[], Int64[])

Initializes a new instance of the **EncoderParameter** class with the specified **Encoder** object and two arrays of 64-bit integers. The two arrays represent an array integer ranges. Sets the **ValueType** property to ValueTypeLongRange, and sets the **NumberOfValues** property to the number of elements in the *rangebegin* array, which must be the same as the number of elements in the *rangeend* array.

```
[Visual Basic]
Public Sub New( _
   ByVal encoder As Encoder, _
   ByVal rangebegin() As Long, _
   ByVal rangeend() As Long _
)
[C#]
public EncoderParameter(
   Encoder encoder,
   long[] rangebegin,
   long[] rangeend
);
[C++]
public: EncoderParameter(
   Encoder* encoder,
   __int64 rangebegin __gc[],
   __int64 rangeend __gc[]
);
[JScript]
public function EncoderParameter(
   encoder : Encoder,
   rangebegin : long[],
   rangeend : long[]
);
```

Parameters

encoder

An **Encoder** object that encapsulates the globally unique identifier of the parameter category.

rangebegin

An array of 64-bit integers that specifies the minimum values for the integer ranges. The integers in the array must be nonnegative. The 64-bit integers are converted to 32-bit integers before they are stored in the **EncoderParameter** object.

rangeend

An array of 64-bit integers that specifies the maximum values for the integer ranges. The integers in the array must be nonnegative. The 64-bit integers are converted to 32-bit integers before they are stored in the **EncoderParameters** object. A maximum value of a given index is paired with the minimum value of the same index.

Requirements

Platforms: Windows 98, Windows NT 4.0, Windows Millennium Edition, Windows 2000, Windows XP Home Edition, Windows XP Professional, Windows Server 2003 family

EncoderParameter Constructor (Encoder, Int32, Int32, Int32)

Initializes a new instance of the **EncoderParameter** class with the specified **Encoder** object and three integers that specify the number of values, the data type of the values, and a pointer to the values stored in the **EncoderParameter** object.

[Visual Basic]
```
Public Sub New( _
   ByVal encoder As Encoder, _
   ByVal NumberOfValues As Integer, _
   ByVal Type As Integer, _
   ByVal Value As Integer _
)
```
[C#]
```
public EncoderParameter(
   Encoder encoder,
   int NumberOfValues,
   int Type,
   int Value
);
```
[C++]
```
public: EncoderParameter(
   Encoder* encoder,
   int NumberOfValues,
   int Type,
   int Value
);
```
[JScript]
```
public function EncoderParameter(
   encoder : Encoder,
   NumberOfValues : int,
   Type : int,
   Value : int
);
```

Parameters

encoder
: An **Encoder** object that encapsulates the globally unique identifier of the parameter category.

NumberOfValues
: An integer that specifies the number of values stored in the **EncoderParameter** object. The **NumberOfValues** property is set to this value.

Type
: A member of the **EncoderParameterValueType** enumeration that specifies the data type of the values stored in the **EncoderParameter** object. The **Type** property and the **ValueType** property are set to this value.

Value
: A pointer to an array of values of the type specified by the *Type* parameter. The **ValuePointer** property is set to this address.

Requirements

Platforms: Windows 98, Windows NT 4.0, Windows Millennium Edition, Windows 2000, Windows XP Home Edition, Windows XP Professional, Windows Server 2003 family

EncoderParameter Constructor (Encoder, Int32, Int32, Int32, Int32)

Initializes a new instance of the **EncoderParameter** class with the specified **Encoder** object and four, 32-bit integers. The four integers represent a range of fractions. The first two integers represent the smallest fraction in the range, and the remaining two integers represent the largest fraction in the range. Sets the **ValueType** property to ValueTypeRationalRange, and sets the **NumberOfValues** property to 1.

[Visual Basic]
```
Public Sub New( _
   ByVal encoder As Encoder, _
   ByVal numerator1 As Integer, _
   ByVal demoninator1 As Integer, _
   ByVal numerator2 As Integer, _
   ByVal demoninator2 As Integer _
)
```
[C#]
```
public EncoderParameter(
   Encoder encoder,
   int numerator1,
   int demoninator1,
   int numerator2,
   int demoninator2
);
```
[C++]
```
public: EncoderParameter(
   Encoder* encoder,
   int numerator1,
   int demoninator1,
   int numerator2,
   int demoninator2
);
```
[JScript]
```
public function EncoderParameter(
   encoder : Encoder,
   numerator1 : int,
   demoninator1 : int,
   numerator2 : int,
   demoninator2 : int
);
```

Parameters

encoder
: An **Encoder** object that encapsulates the globally unique identifier of the parameter category.

numerator1
: A 32-bit integer that represents the numerator of the smallest fraction in the range. Must be nonnegative.

demoninator1
: A 32-bit integer that represents the denominator of the smallest fraction in the range. Must be nonnegative.

numerator2
: A 32-bit integer that represents the numerator of the largest fraction in the range. Must be nonnegative.

demoninator2
: A 32-bit integer that represents the denominator of the largest fraction in the range. Must be nonnegative.

Requirements

Platforms: Windows 98, Windows NT 4.0, Windows Millennium Edition, Windows 2000, Windows XP Home Edition, Windows XP Professional, Windows Server 2003 family

EncoderParameter Constructor (Encoder, Int32[], Int32[], Int32[], Int32[])

Initializes a new instance of the **EncoderParameter** class with the specified **Encoder** object and four arrays of 32-bit integers. The four arrays represent an array rational ranges. A rational range is the set of all fractions from a minimum fractional value through a maximum fractional value. Sets the **ValueType** property to ValueTypeRationalRange, and sets the **NumberOfValues** property to the number of elements in the *numerator1* array, which must be the same as the number of elements in the other three arrays.

```
[Visual Basic]
Public Sub New( _
   ByVal encoder As Encoder, _
   ByVal numerator1() As Integer, _
   ByVal denominator1() As Integer, _
   ByVal numerator2() As Integer, _
   ByVal denominator2() As Integer _
)
[C#]
public EncoderParameter(
   Encoder encoder,
   int[] numerator1,
   int[] denominator1,
   int[] numerator2,
   int[] denominator2
);
[C++]
public: EncoderParameter(
   Encoder* encoder,
   int numerator1 __gc[],
   int denominator1 __gc[],
   int numerator2 __gc[],
   int denominator2 __gc[]
);
[JScript]
public function EncoderParameter(
   encoder : Encoder,
   numerator1 : int[],
   denominator1 : int[],
   numerator2 : int[],
   denominator2 : int[]
);
```

Parameters

encoder

An **Encoder** object that encapsulates the globally unique identifier of the parameter category.

numerator1

An array of 32-bit integers that specifies the numerators of the minimum values for the ranges. The integers in the array must be nonnegative.

denominator1

An array of 32-bit integers that specifies the denominators of the minimum values for the ranges. The integers in the array must be nonnegative.

numerator2

An array of 32-bit integers that specifies the numerators of the maximum values for the ranges. The integers in the array must be nonnegative.

denominator2

An array of 32-bit integers that specifies the denominators of the maximum values for the ranges. The integers in the array must be nonnegative.

Remarks

The ith range consists of all fractional numbers from numerator1[i]/denominator1[i] through numerator2[i]/denominator2[i].

Requirements

Platforms: Windows 98, Windows NT 4.0, Windows Millennium Edition, Windows 2000, Windows XP Home Edition, Windows XP Professional, Windows Server 2003 family

EncoderParameter.Encoder Property

Gets or sets the **Encoder** object associated with this **EncoderParameter** object. The **Encoder** object encapsulates the globally unique identifier (GUID) that specifies the category (for example Quality, ColorDepth, or Compression) of the parameter stored in this **EncoderParameter** object.

```
[Visual Basic]
Public Property Encoder As Encoder
[C#]
public Encoder Encoder {get; set;}
[C++]
public: __property Encoder* get_Encoder();
public: __property void set_Encoder(Encoder*);
[JScript]
public function get Encoder() : Encoder;
public function set Encoder(Encoder);
```

Property Value

An **Encoder** object that encapsulates the GUID that specifies the category of the parameter stored in this **EncoderParameter** object.

Requirements

Platforms: Windows 98, Windows NT 4.0, Windows Millennium Edition, Windows 2000, Windows XP Home Edition, Windows XP Professional, Windows Server 2003 family

EncoderParameter.NumberOfValues Property

Gets the number of elements in the array of values stored in this **EncoderParameter** object.

```
[Visual Basic]
Public ReadOnly Property NumberOfValues As Integer
[C#]
public int NumberOfValues {get;}
[C++]
public: __property int get_NumberOfValues();
[JScript]
public function get NumberOfValues() : int;
```

Property Value

An integer that indicates the number of elements in the array of values stored in this **EncoderParameter** object.

Requirements

Platforms: Windows 98, Windows NT 4.0, Windows Millennium Edition, Windows 2000, Windows XP Home Edition, Windows XP Professional, Windows Server 2003 family

EncoderParameter.Type Property

Gets the data type of the values stored in this **EncoderParameter** object.

[Visual Basic]
```
Public ReadOnly Property Type As EncoderParameterValueType
```
[C#]
```
public EncoderParameterValueType Type {get;}
```
[C++]
```
public: __property EncoderParameterValueType get_Type();
```
[JScript]
```
public function get Type() : EncoderParameterValueType;
```

Property Value

A member of the **EncoderParameterValueType** enumeration that indicates the data type of the values stored in this **EncoderParameter** object.

Requirements

Platforms: Windows 98, Windows NT 4.0, Windows Millennium Edition, Windows 2000, Windows XP Home Edition, Windows XP Professional, Windows Server 2003 family

EncoderParameter.ValueType Property

Gets the data type of the values stored in this **EncoderParameter** object.

[Visual Basic]
```
Public ReadOnly Property ValueType As EncoderParameterValueType
```
[C#]
```
public EncoderParameterValueType ValueType {get;}
```
[C++]
```
public: __property EncoderParameterValueType get_ValueType();
```
[JScript]
```
public function get ValueType() : EncoderParameterValueType;
```

Property Value

A member of the **EncoderParameterValueType** enumeration that indicates the data type of the values stored in this **EncoderParameter** object.

Requirements

Platforms: Windows 98, Windows NT 4.0, Windows Millennium Edition, Windows 2000, Windows XP Home Edition, Windows XP Professional, Windows Server 2003 family

EncoderParameter.Dispose Method

Releases all resources used by this **EncoderParameter** object.

[Visual Basic]
```
Public Overridable Sub Dispose() Implements IDisposable.Dispose
```
[C#]
```
public virtual void Dispose();
```
[C++]
```
public: virtual void Dispose();
```
[JScript]
```
public function Dispose();
```

Return Value

This method does not return a value.

Implements

IDisposable.Dispose

Remarks

Calling **Dispose** allows the resources used by this **EncoderParameter** object to be reallocated for other purposes.

Requirements

Platforms: Windows 98, Windows NT 4.0, Windows Millennium Edition, Windows 2000, Windows XP Home Edition, Windows XP Professional, Windows Server 2003 family

EncoderParameter.Finalize Method

This member overrides **Object.Finalize**.

[Visual Basic]
```
Overrides Protected Sub Finalize()
```
[C#]
```
~EncoderParameter();
```
[C++]
```
~EncoderParameter();
```
[JScript]
```
protected override function Finalize();
```

Requirements

Platforms: Windows 98, Windows NT 4.0, Windows Millennium Edition, Windows 2000, Windows XP Home Edition, Windows XP Professional, Windows Server 2003 family

EncoderParameters Class

Encapsulates an array of **EncoderParameter** objects.

System.Object
  System.Drawing.Imaging.EncoderParameters

```
[Visual Basic]
NotInheritable Public Class EncoderParameters
   Implements IDisposable
[C#]
public sealed class EncoderParameters : IDisposable
[C++]
public __gc __sealed class EncoderParameters : public IDisposable
[JScript]
public class EncoderParameters implements IDisposable
```

Thread Safety

Any public static (**Shared** in Visual Basic) members of this type are safe for multithreaded operations. Any instance members are not guaranteed to be thread safe.

Requirements

Namespace: System.Drawing.Imaging

Platforms: Windows 98, Windows NT 4.0, Windows Millennium Edition, Windows 2000, Windows XP Home Edition, Windows XP Professional, Windows Server 2003 family

Assembly: System.Drawing (in System.Drawing.dll)

EncoderParameters Constructor

Initializes a new instance of the **EncoderParameters** class that can contain the specified number of **EncoderParameter** objects.

Overload List

Initializes a new instance of the **EncoderParameters** class that can contain one **EncoderParameter** object.

[Visual Basic] **Public Sub New()**

[C#] **public EncoderParameters();**

[C++] **public: EncoderParameters();**

[JScript] **public function EncoderParameters();**

Initializes a new instance of the **EncoderParameters** class that can contain the specified number of **EncoderParameter** objects.

[Visual Basic] **Public Sub New(Integer)**

[C#] **public EncoderParameters(int);**

[C++] **public: EncoderParameters(int);**

[JScript] **public function EncoderParameters(int);**

EncoderParameters Constructor ()

Initializes a new instance of the **EncoderParameters** class that can contain one **EncoderParameter** object.

```
[Visual Basic]
Public Sub New()
[C#]
public EncoderParameters();
[C++]
public: EncoderParameters();
[JScript]
public function EncoderParameters();
```

Remarks

Some of the **Save** and **SaveAdd** methods receive an **EncoderParameters** object as an argument. The **Image.GetEncoderParameterList** method returns an **EncoderParameters** object.

Requirements

Platforms: Windows 98, Windows NT 4.0, Windows Millennium Edition, Windows 2000, Windows XP Home Edition, Windows XP Professional, Windows Server 2003 family

EncoderParameters Constructor (Int32)

Initializes a new instance of the **EncoderParameters** class that can contain the specified number of **EncoderParameter** objects.

```
[Visual Basic]
Public Sub New( _
   ByVal count As Integer _
)
[C#]
public EncoderParameters(
   int count
);
[C++]
public: EncoderParameters(
   int count
);
[JScript]
public function EncoderParameters(
   count : int
);
```

Parameters

count

An integer that specifies the number of **EncoderParameter** objects that the **EncoderParameters** object can contain.

Requirements

Platforms: Windows 98, Windows NT 4.0, Windows Millennium Edition, Windows 2000, Windows XP Home Edition, Windows XP Professional, Windows Server 2003 family

EncoderParameters.Param Property

Gets or sets an array of **EncoderParameter** objects.

```
[Visual Basic]
Public Property Param As EncoderParameter ()
[C#]
public EncoderParameter[] Param {get; set;}
[C++]
public: __property EncoderParameter* get_Param();
public: __property void set_Param(EncoderParameter*[]);
[JScript]
public function get Param() : EncoderParameter[];
public function set Param(EncoderParameter[]);
```

Property Value

The array of **EncoderParameter** objects.

Requirements

Platforms: Windows 98, Windows NT 4.0, Windows Millennium Edition, Windows 2000, Windows XP Home Edition, Windows XP Professional, Windows Server 2003 family

EncoderParameters.Dispose Method

Releases all resources used by this **EncoderParameters** object.

```
[Visual Basic]
Public Overridable Sub Dispose() Implements IDisposable.Dispose
[C#]
public virtual void Dispose();
[C++]
public: virtual void Dispose();
[JScript]
public function Dispose();
```

Return Value

This method does not return a value.

Implements

IDisposable.Dispose

Remarks

Calling **Dispose** allows the resources used by this **EncoderParameters** object to be reallocated for other purposes.

Requirements

Platforms: Windows 98, Windows NT 4.0, Windows Millennium Edition, Windows 2000, Windows XP Home Edition, Windows XP Professional, Windows Server 2003 family

EncoderParameterValueType Enumeration

GDI+ uses image encoders to convert the images stored in **Bitmap** objects to various file formats. Image encoders are built into GDI+ for the BMP, JPEG, GIF, TIFF, and PNG formats. And encoder is invoked when you call the **Save** or **SaveAdd** method of a **Bitmap** object.

[Visual Basic]
```
<Serializable>
Public Enum EncoderParameterValueType
```
[C#]
```
[Serializable]
public enum EncoderParameterValueType
```
[C++]
```
[Serializable]
__value public enum EncoderParameterValueType
```
[JScript]
```
public
   Serializable
enum EncoderParameterValueType
```

Members

Member name	Description
ValueTypeAscii	Specifies that the array of values is a null-terminated ASCII character string. Note that the **NumberOfValues** data member of the **EncoderParameter** object indicates the length of the character string including the NULL terminator.
ValueTypeByte	Specifies that each value in the array is an 8-bit unsigned integer.
ValueTypeLong	Specifies that each value in the array is a 32-bit unsigned integer.
ValueTypeLongRange	Specifies that each value in the array is a pair of 32-bit unsigned integers. Each pair represents a range of numbers.
ValueTypeRational	Specifies that each value in the array is a pair of 32-bit unsigned integers. Each pair represents a fraction, the first integer being the numerator and the second integer being the denominator.
ValueTypeRational-Range	Specifies that each value in the array is a set of four, 32-bit unsigned integers. The first two integers represent one fraction, and the second two integers represent a second fraction. The two fractions represent a range of rational numbers. The first fraction is the smallest rational number in the range, and the second fraction is the largest rational number in the range.
ValueTypeShort	Specifies that each value in the array is a 16-bit, unsigned integer.
ValueTypeUndefined	Specifies that the array of values is an array of bytes that has no data type defined.

Requirements

Namespace: System.Drawing.Imaging

Platforms: Windows 98, Windows NT 4.0, Windows Millennium Edition, Windows 2000, Windows XP Home Edition, Windows XP Professional, Windows Server 2003 family

Assembly: System.Drawing (in System.Drawing.dll)

EncoderValue Enumeration

When you call the **Save** or **SaveAdd** method of an **Image** object, you can pass parameters to the image encoder by passing an **EncoderParameters** object to the **Save** or **SaveAdd** method. An **EncoderParameters** object contains an array of **EncoderParameter** objects. Each **EncoderParameter** object has an array of values and an **Encoder** property that specifies the parameter category. The **EncoderValue** enumeration provides names for some of the values that can be passed to the JPEG and TIFF image encoders.

```
[Visual Basic]
<Serializable>
Public Enum EncoderValue
[C#]
[Serializable]
public enum EncoderValue
[C++]
[Serializable]
__value public enum EncoderValue
[JScript]
public
   Serializable
enum EncoderValue
```

Members

Member name	Description
ColorTypeCMYK	Not used in GDI+ version 1.0.
ColorTypeYCCK	Not used in GDI+ version 1.0.
CompressionCCITT3	Specifies the CCITT3 compression scheme. Can be passed to the TIFF encoder as a parameter that belongs to the compression category.
CompressionCCITT4	Specifies the CCITT4 compression scheme. Can be passed to the TIFF encoder as a parameter that belongs to the compression category.
CompressionLZW	Specifies the LZW compression scheme. Can be passed to the TIFF encoder as a parameter that belongs to the Compression category.
CompressionNone	Specifies no compression. Can be passed to the TIFF encoder as a parameter that belongs to the compression category.
CompressionRle	Specifies the RLE compression scheme. Can be passed to the TIFF encoder as a parameter that belongs to the compression category.
Flush	Specifies that a multiple-frame file or stream should be closed. Can be passed to the TIFF encoder as a parameter that belongs to the save flag category.
FrameDimensionPage	Specifies that a frame is to be added to the page dimension of an image. Can be passed to the TIFF encoder as a parameter that belongs to the save flag category.
FrameDimension-Resolution	Not used in GDI+ version 1.0.
FrameDimensionTime	Not used in GDI+ version 1.0.
LastFrame	Specifies the last frame in a multiple-frame image. Can be passed to the TIFF encoder as a parameter that belongs to the save flag category.
MultiFrame	Specifies that the image has more than one frame (page). Can be passed to the TIFF encoder as a parameter that belongs to the save flag category.
RenderNonProgressive	Not used in GDI+ version 1.0.
RenderProgressive	Not used in GDI+ version 1.0.
ScanMethodInterlaced	Not used in GDI+ version 1.0.
ScanMethodNon-Interlaced	Not used in GDI+ version 1.0.
TransformFlip-Horizontal	Specifies that the image is to be flipped horizontally (about the vertical axis). Can be passed to the JPEG encoder as a parameter that belongs to the transformation category.
TransformFlipVertical	Specifies that the image is to be flipped vertically (about the horizontal axis). Can be passed to the JPEG encoder as a parameter that belongs to the transformation category.
TransformRotate180	Specifies that the image is to be rotated 180 degrees about its center. Can be passed to the JPEG encoder as a parameter that belongs to the transformation category.
TransformRotate270	Specifies that the image is to be rotated clockwise 270 degrees about its center. Can be passed to the JPEG encoder as a parameter that belongs to the transformation category.
TransformRotate90	Specifies that the image is to be rotated clockwise 90 degrees about its center. Can be passed to the JPEG encoder as a parameter that belongs to the transformation category.
VersionGif87	Not used in GDI+ version 1.0.
VersionGif89	Not used in GDI+ version 1.0.

Requirements

Namespace: System.Drawing.Imaging

Platforms: Windows 98, Windows NT 4.0, Windows Millennium Edition, Windows 2000, Windows XP Home Edition, Windows XP Professional, Windows Server 2003 family

Assembly: System.Drawing (in System.Drawing.dll)

FrameDimension Class

Provides properties that get the frame dimensions of an image. Not inheritable.

System.Object
  System.Drawing.Imaging.FrameDimension

```
[Visual Basic]
NotInheritable Public Class FrameDimension
[C#]
public sealed class FrameDimension
[C++]
public __gc __sealed class FrameDimension
[JScript]
public class FrameDimension
```

Thread Safety

Any public static (**Shared** in Visual Basic) members of this type are safe for multithreaded operations. Any instance members are not guaranteed to be thread safe.

Requirements

Namespace: System.Drawing.Imaging

Platforms: Windows 98, Windows NT 4.0, Windows Millennium Edition, Windows 2000, Windows XP Home Edition, Windows XP Professional, Windows Server 2003 family

Assembly: System.Drawing (in System.Drawing.dll)

FrameDimension Constructor

Initializes a new instance of the **FrameDimension** class using the specified **Guid** structure.

```
[Visual Basic]
Public Sub New( _
   ByVal guid As Guid _
)
[C#]
public FrameDimension(
   Guid guid
);
[C++]
public: FrameDimension(
   Guid guid
);
[JScript]
public function FrameDimension(
   guid : Guid
);
```

Parameters

guid

A **Guid** structure that contains a GUID for this **FrameDimension** object.

Requirements

Platforms: Windows 98, Windows NT 4.0, Windows Millennium Edition, Windows 2000, Windows XP Home Edition, Windows XP Professional, Windows Server 2003 family

FrameDimension.Guid Property

Gets a globally unique identifier (GUID) that represents this **FrameDimension** object.

```
[Visual Basic]
Public ReadOnly Property Guid As Guid
[C#]
public Guid Guid {get;}
[C++]
public: __property Guid get_Guid();
[JScript]
public function get Guid() : Guid;
```

Property Value

A **Guid** structure that contains a GUID that represents this **FrameDimension** object.

Requirements

Platforms: Windows 98, Windows NT 4.0, Windows Millennium Edition, Windows 2000, Windows XP Home Edition, Windows XP Professional, Windows Server 2003 family

FrameDimension.Page Property

Gets the page dimension.

```
[Visual Basic]
Public Shared ReadOnly Property Page As FrameDimension
[C#]
public static FrameDimension Page {get;}
[C++]
public: __property static FrameDimension* get_Page();
[JScript]
public static function get Page() : FrameDimension;
```

Property Value

The page dimension.

Requirements

Platforms: Windows 98, Windows NT 4.0, Windows Millennium Edition, Windows 2000, Windows XP Home Edition, Windows XP Professional, Windows Server 2003 family

FrameDimension.Resolution Property

Gets the resolution dimension.

```
[Visual Basic]
Public Shared ReadOnly Property Resolution As FrameDimension
[C#]
public static FrameDimension Resolution {get;}
[C++]
public: __property static FrameDimension* get_Resolution();
[JScript]
public static function get Resolution() : FrameDimension;
```

Property Value

The resolution dimension.

Requirements

Platforms: Windows 98, Windows NT 4.0, Windows Millennium Edition, Windows 2000, Windows XP Home Edition, Windows XP Professional, Windows Server 2003 family

FrameDimension.Time Property

Gets the time dimension.

```
[Visual Basic]
Public Shared ReadOnly Property Time As FrameDimension
[C#]
public static FrameDimension Time {get;}
[C++]
public: __property static FrameDimension* get_Time();
[JScript]
public static function get Time() : FrameDimension;
```

Property Value

The time dimension.

Requirements

Platforms: Windows 98, Windows NT 4.0, Windows Millennium Edition, Windows 2000, Windows XP Home Edition, Windows XP Professional, Windows Server 2003 family

FrameDimension.Equals Method

Returns a value that indicates whether the specified object is a **FrameDimension** equivalent to this **FrameDimension** object.

```
[Visual Basic]
Overrides Public Function Equals( _
   ByVal o As Object _
) As Boolean
[C#]
public override bool Equals(
   object o
);
[C++]
public: bool Equals(
   Object* o
);
[JScript]
public override function Equals(
   o : Object
) : Boolean;
```

Parameters

o

The object to test.

Return Value

Returns **true** if *o* is a **FrameDimension** equivalent to this **FrameDimension** object; otherwise, **false**.

Requirements

Platforms: Windows 98, Windows NT 4.0, Windows Millennium Edition, Windows 2000, Windows XP Home Edition, Windows XP Professional, Windows Server 2003 family

FrameDimension.GetHashCode Method

Returns a hash code for this **FrameDimension** object.

```
[Visual Basic]
Overrides Public Function GetHashCode() As Integer
[C#]
public override int GetHashCode();
[C++]
public: int GetHashCode();
[JScript]
public override function GetHashCode() : int;
```

Return Value

Returns an **int** value that is the hash code of this **FrameDimension** object.

Requirements

Platforms: Windows 98, Windows NT 4.0, Windows Millennium Edition, Windows 2000, Windows XP Home Edition, Windows XP Professional, Windows Server 2003 family

FrameDimension.ToString Method

Converts this **FrameDimension** object to a human-readable string.

```
[Visual Basic]
Overrides Public Function ToString() As String
[C#]
public override string ToString();
[C++]
public: String* ToString();
[JScript]
public override function ToString() : String;
```

Return Value

A string that represents this **FrameDimension** object.

Requirements

Platforms: Windows 98, Windows NT 4.0, Windows Millennium Edition, Windows 2000, Windows XP Home Edition, Windows XP Professional, Windows Server 2003 family

ImageAttributes Class

An **ImageAttributes** object contains information about how bitmap and metafile colors are manipulated during rendering. An **ImageAttributes** object maintains several color-adjustment settings, including color-adjustment matrices, grayscale-adjustment matrices, gamma-correction values, color-map tables, and color-threshold values.

During rendering colors can be corrected, darkened, lightened, removed, and so on. To apply such manipulations, initialize an **ImageAttributes** object and pass the address of that **ImageAttributes** object (along with the address of an **Image** object) to the **DrawImage** method.

System.Object
  System.Drawing.Imaging.ImageAttributes

```
[Visual Basic]
NotInheritable Public Class ImageAttributes
   Implements ICloneable, IDisposable
[C#]
public sealed class ImageAttributes : ICloneable, IDisposable
[C++]
public __gc __sealed class ImageAttributes : public ICloneable,
   IDisposable
[JScript]
public class ImageAttributes implements ICloneable, IDisposable
```

Thread Safety

Any public static (**Shared** in Visual Basic) members of this type are safe for multithreaded operations. Any instance members are not guaranteed to be thread safe.

Requirements

Namespace: System.Drawing.Imaging

Platforms: Windows 98, Windows NT 4.0, Windows Millennium Edition, Windows 2000, Windows XP Home Edition, Windows XP Professional, Windows Server 2003 family, .NET Compact Framework - Windows CE .NET

Assembly: System.Drawing (in System.Drawing.dll)

ImageAttributes Constructor

Initializes a new instance of the **ImageAttributes** class.

```
[Visual Basic]
Public Sub New()
[C#]
public ImageAttributes();
[C++]
public: ImageAttributes();
[JScript]
public function ImageAttributes();
```

Requirements

Platforms: Windows 98, Windows NT 4.0, Windows Millennium Edition, Windows 2000, Windows XP Home Edition, Windows XP Professional, Windows Server 2003 family, .NET Compact Framework - Windows CE .NET

ImageAttributes.ClearBrushRemapTable Method

This method clears the brush color-remap table of this **ImageAttributes** object.

```
[Visual Basic]
Public Sub ClearBrushRemapTable()
[C#]
public void ClearBrushRemapTable();
[C++]
public: void ClearBrushRemapTable();
[JScript]
public function ClearBrushRemapTable();
```

Return Value

This method does not return a value.

Remarks

An ImageAttributes object maintains color and grayscale settings for five adjustment categories: default, bitmap, brush, pen, and text. For example, you can specify one color-remap table for the default category, a different color-remap table for the bitmap category, and still a different color-remap table for the brush category.

The default color- and grayscale-adjustment settings apply to all categories that don't have adjustment settings of their own. For example, if you never specify any adjustment settings for the brush category, then the default settings apply to the brush category.

As soon as you specify a color- or grayscale-adjustment setting for a certain category, the default adjustment settings no longer apply to that category. For example, suppose you specify a default remap table that converts red to green and you specify a default gamma value of 1.8. If you call SetBrushRemapTable, then the default remap table (red to green) and the default gamma value (1.8) will not apply to brushes. If you later call ClearBrushRemapTable, the brush category will not revert to the default remap table; rather, the brush category will have no remap table. Similarly, the brush category will not revert to the default gamma value; rather, the brush category will have no gamma value.

Requirements

Platforms: Windows 98, Windows NT 4.0, Windows Millennium Edition, Windows 2000, Windows XP Home Edition, Windows XP Professional, Windows Server 2003 family

ImageAttributes.ClearColorKey Method

Clears the color-key (transparency range).

Overload List

Clears the color key (transparency range) for the default category.

Supported by the .NET Compact Framework.

[Visual Basic] **Overloads Public Sub ClearColorKey()**
[C#] **public void ClearColorKey();**
[C++] **public: void ClearColorKey();**
[JScript] **public function ClearColorKey();**

Clears the color key (transparency range) for a specified category.

[Visual Basic] **Overloads Public Sub ClearColorKey(ColorAdjustType)**
[C#] **public void ClearColorKey(ColorAdjustType);**
[C++] **public: void ClearColorKey(ColorAdjustType);**
[JScript] **public function ClearColorKey(ColorAdjustType);**

ImageAttributes.ClearColorKey Method ()

Clears the color key (transparency range) for the default category.

```
[Visual Basic]
Overloads Public Sub ClearColorKey()
[C#]
public void ClearColorKey();
[C++]
public: void ClearColorKey();
[JScript]
public function ClearColorKey();
```

Remarks

An ImageAttributes object maintains color and grayscale settings for five adjustment categories: default, bitmap, brush, pen, and text. For example, you can specify one color key for the default category, a different color key for the bitmap category, and still a different color key for the pen category.

The default color- and grayscale-adjustment settings apply to all categories that don't have adjustment settings of their own. For example, if you never specify any adjustment settings for the pen category, then the default settings apply to the pen category.

Requirements

Platforms: Windows 98, Windows NT 4.0, Windows Millennium Edition, Windows 2000, Windows XP Home Edition, Windows XP Professional, Windows Server 2003 family, .NET Compact Framework - Windows CE .NET

ImageAttributes.ClearColorKey Method (ColorAdjustType)

Clears the color key (transparency range) for a specified category.

```
[Visual Basic]
Overloads Public Sub ClearColorKey( _
   ByVal type As ColorAdjustType _
)
[C#]
public void ClearColorKey(
   ColorAdjustType type
);
[C++]
public: void ClearColorKey(
   ColorAdjustType type
);
[JScript]
public function ClearColorKey(
   type : ColorAdjustType
);
```

Parameters

type
: Element of the **ColorAdjustType** enumeration that specifies the category for which the color key is cleared.

Return Value

This method does not return a value.

Requirements

Platforms: Windows 98, Windows NT 4.0, Windows Millennium Edition, Windows 2000, Windows XP Home Edition, Windows XP Professional, Windows Server 2003 family

ImageAttributes.ClearColorMatrix Method

Clears the color-adjustment matrix.

Overload List

Clears the color-adjustment matrix for the default category.

[Visual Basic] **Overloads Public Sub ClearColorMatrix()**

[C#] **public void ClearColorMatrix();**

[C++] **public: void ClearColorMatrix();**

[JScript] **public function ClearColorMatrix();**

Clears the color-adjustment matrix for a specified category.

[Visual Basic] **Overloads Public Sub ClearColor-Matrix(ColorAdjustType)**

[C#] **public void ClearColorMatrix(ColorAdjustType);**

[C++] **public: void ClearColorMatrix(ColorAdjustType);**

[JScript] **public function ClearColorMatrix(ColorAdjustType);**

ImageAttributes.ClearColorMatrix Method ()

Clears the color-adjustment matrix for the default category.

```
[Visual Basic]
Overloads Public Sub ClearColorMatrix()
[C#]
public void ClearColorMatrix();
[C++]
public: void ClearColorMatrix();
[JScript]
public function ClearColorMatrix();
```

Return Value

This method does not return a value.

Remarks

An ImageAttributes object maintains color and grayscale settings for five adjustment categories: default, bitmap, brush, pen, and text. For example, you can specify a color-adjustment matrix for the default category, a different color-adjustment matrix for the bitmap category, and still a different color-adjustment matrix for the pen category.

The default color- and grayscale-adjustment settings apply to all categories that don't have adjustment settings of their own. For example, if you never specify any adjustment settings for the pen category, then the default settings apply to the pen category.

Requirements

Platforms: Windows 98, Windows NT 4.0, Windows Millennium Edition, Windows 2000, Windows XP Home Edition, Windows XP Professional, Windows Server 2003 family

ImageAttributes.ClearColorMatrix Method (ColorAdjustType)

Clears the color-adjustment matrix for a specified category.

```
[Visual Basic]
Overloads Public Sub ClearColorMatrix( _
   ByVal type As ColorAdjustType _
)
[C#]
public void ClearColorMatrix(
   ColorAdjustType type
);
```

```
[C++]
public: void ClearColorMatrix(
   ColorAdjustType type
);
[JScript]
public function ClearColorMatrix(
   type : ColorAdjustType
);
```

Parameters

type

Element of the **ColorAdjustType** enumeration that specifies the category for which the color-adjustment matrix is cleared.

Return Value

This method does not return a value.

Remarks

An ImageAttributes object maintains color and grayscale settings for five adjustment categories: default, bitmap, brush, pen, and text. For example, you can specify a color-adjustment matrix for the default category, a different color-adjustment matrix for the bitmap category, and still a different color-adjustment matrix for the pen category.

The default color- and grayscale-adjustment settings apply to all categories that don't have adjustment settings of their own. For example, if you never specify any adjustment settings for the pen category, then the default settings apply to the pen category.

As soon as you specify a color- or grayscale-adjustment setting for a certain category, the default adjustment settings no longer apply to that category. For example, suppose you specify a color-adjustment matrix and a gamma value for the default category. If you set a color-adjustment matrix for the pen category by calling SetColorMatrix, then the default color-adjustment matrix will not apply to pens. If you later clear the pen color-adjustment matrix by calling ClearColorMatrix, the pen category will not revert to the default adjustment matrix; rather, the pen category will have no adjustment matrix. Similarly, the pen category will not revert to the default gamma value; rather, the pen category will have no gamma value.

Requirements

Platforms: Windows 98, Windows NT 4.0, Windows Millennium Edition, Windows 2000, Windows XP Home Edition, Windows XP Professional, Windows Server 2003 family

ImageAttributes.ClearGamma Method

Disables gamma correction.

Overload List

Disables gamma correction for the default category.

[Visual Basic] **Overloads Public Sub ClearGamma()**

[C#] **public void ClearGamma();**

[C++] **public: void ClearGamma();**

[JScript] **public function ClearGamma();**

Disables gamma correction for a specified category.

[Visual Basic] **Overloads Public Sub ClearGamma(ColorAdjustType)**

[C#] **public void ClearGamma(ColorAdjustType);**

[C++] **public: void ClearGamma(ColorAdjustType);**

[JScript] **public function ClearGamma(ColorAdjustType);**

ImageAttributes.ClearGamma Method ()

Disables gamma correction for the default category.

```
[Visual Basic]
Overloads Public Sub ClearGamma()
[C#]
public void ClearGamma();
[C++]
public: void ClearGamma();
[JScript]
public function ClearGamma();
```

Remarks

An ImageAttributes object maintains color and grayscale settings for five adjustment categories: default, bitmap, brush, pen, and text. For example, you can specify a gamma value for the default category, a different gamma value for the bitmap category, and still a different gamma value for the pen category.

The default color- and grayscale-adjustment settings apply to all categories that don't have adjustment settings of their own. For example, if you never specify any adjustment settings for the pen category, then the default settings apply to the pen category.

Requirements

Platforms: Windows 98, Windows NT 4.0, Windows Millennium Edition, Windows 2000, Windows XP Home Edition, Windows XP Professional, Windows Server 2003 family

ImageAttributes.ClearGamma Method (ColorAdjustType)

Disables gamma correction for a specified category.

```
[Visual Basic]
Overloads Public Sub ClearGamma( _
   ByVal type As ColorAdjustType _
)
[C#]
public void ClearGamma(
   ColorAdjustType type
);
[C++]
public: void ClearGamma(
   ColorAdjustType type
);
[JScript]
public function ClearGamma(
   type : ColorAdjustType
);
```

Parameters

type

Element of the **ColorAdjustType** enumeration that specifies the category for which gamma correction is disabled.

Return Value

This method does not return a value.

Remarks

An ImageAttributes object maintains color and grayscale settings for five adjustment categories: default, bitmap, brush, pen, and text. For example, you can specify a gamma value for the default category, a different gamma value for the bitmap category, and still a different gamma value for the pen category.

The default color- and grayscale-adjustment settings apply to all categories that don't have adjustment settings of their own. For example, if you never specify any adjustment settings for the pen category, then the default settings apply to the pen category.

As soon as you specify a color- or grayscale-adjustment setting for a certain category, the default adjustment settings no longer apply to that category. For example, suppose you specify a gamma value and a color-adjustment matrix for the default category. If you set the gamma value for the pen category by calling SetGamma, then the default gamma value will not apply to pens. If you later clear the pen gamma value by calling ClearGamma, the pen category will not revert to the default gamma value; rather, the pen category will have no gamma value. Similarly, the pen category will not revert to the default color-adjustment matrix; rather, the pen category will have no color-adjustment matrix.

Requirements

Platforms: Windows 98, Windows NT 4.0, Windows Millennium Edition, Windows 2000, Windows XP Home Edition, Windows XP Professional, Windows Server 2003 family

ImageAttributes.ClearNoOp Method

Clears the NoOp setting.

Overload List

Clears the NoOp setting for the default category.

[Visual Basic] **Overloads Public Sub ClearNoOp()**

[C#] **public void ClearNoOp();**

[C++] **public: void ClearNoOp();**

[JScript] **public function ClearNoOp();**

Clears the NoOp setting for a specified category.

[Visual Basic] **Overloads Public Sub ClearNoOp(ColorAdjustType)**

[C#] **public void ClearNoOp(ColorAdjustType);**

[C++] **public: void ClearNoOp(ColorAdjustType);**

[JScript] **public function ClearNoOp(ColorAdjustType);**

ImageAttributes.ClearNoOp Method ()

Clears the NoOp setting for the default category.

```
[Visual Basic]
Overloads Public Sub ClearNoOp()
[C#]
public void ClearNoOp();
[C++]
public: void ClearNoOp();
[JScript]
public function ClearNoOp();
```

Remarks

An ImageAttributes object maintains color and grayscale settings for five adjustment categories: default, bitmap, brush, pen, and text. For example, you can specify a gamma value for the default category, a different gamma value for the bitmap category, and still a different gamma value for the pen category.

You can disable color adjustment for the default category by calling the SetNoOp() method. Later, you can reinstate color adjustment for the default category by calling the ClearNoOp() method. The color adjustment then returns to what was in place before the call to SetNoOp.

Requirements

Platforms: Windows 98, Windows NT 4.0, Windows Millennium Edition, Windows 2000, Windows XP Home Edition, Windows XP Professional, Windows Server 2003 family

ImageAttributes.ClearNoOp Method (ColorAdjustType)

Clears the NoOp setting for a specified category.

```
[Visual Basic]
Overloads Public Sub ClearNoOp( _
   ByVal type As ColorAdjustType _
)
[C#]
public void ClearNoOp(
   ColorAdjustType type
);
[C++]
public: void ClearNoOp(
   ColorAdjustType type
);
[JScript]
public function ClearNoOp(
   type : ColorAdjustType
);
```

Parameters

type
: Element of the **ColorAdjustType** enumeration that specifies the category for which the NoOp setting is cleared.

Return Value

This method does not return a value.

Remarks

An ImageAttributes object maintains color and grayscale settings for five adjustment categories: default, bitmap, brush, pen, and text. For example, you can specify a gamma value for the default category, a different gamma value for the bitmap category, and still a different gamma value for the pen category.

You can disable color adjustment for a certain category by calling the SetNoOp method. Later, you can reinstate color adjustment for that category by calling the ClearNoOp method. The color adjustment then returns to what was in place before the call to SetNoOp.

Requirements

Platforms: Windows 98, Windows NT 4.0, Windows Millennium Edition, Windows 2000, Windows XP Home Edition, Windows XP Professional, Windows Server 2003 family

ImageAttributes.ClearOutputChannel Method

Clears the CMYK output channel setting.

Overload List

Clears the CMYK output channel setting for the default category.

[Visual Basic] **Overloads Public Sub ClearOutputChannel()**

[C#] **public void ClearOutputChannel();**

[C++] **public: void ClearOutputChannel();**

[JScript] **public function ClearOutputChannel();**

Clears the CMYK output channel setting for a specified category.

[Visual Basic] **Overloads Public Sub ClearOutputChannel(ColorAdjustType)**

[C#] **public void ClearOutputChannel(ColorAdjustType);**

[C++] **public: void ClearOutputChannel(ColorAdjustType);**

[JScript] **public function ClearOutputChannel(ColorAdjustType);**

ImageAttributes.ClearOutputChannel Method ()

Clears the CMYK output channel setting for the default category.

```
[Visual Basic]
Overloads Public Sub ClearOutputChannel()
[C#]
public void ClearOutputChannel();
[C++]
public: void ClearOutputChannel();
[JScript]
public function ClearOutputChannel();
```

Remarks

An ImageAttributes object maintains color and grayscale settings for five adjustment categories: default, bitmap, brush, pen, and text. For example, you can specify an output channel for the default category and a different output channel for the bitmap category.

The default color- and grayscale-adjustment settings apply to all categories that don't have adjustment settings of their own. For example, if you never specify any adjustment settings for the bitmap category, then the default settings apply to the bitmap category.

Requirements

Platforms: Windows 98, Windows NT 4.0, Windows Millennium Edition, Windows 2000, Windows XP Home Edition, Windows XP Professional, Windows Server 2003 family

ImageAttributes.ClearOutputChannel Method (ColorAdjustType)

Clears the CMYK output channel setting for a specified category.

```
[Visual Basic]
Overloads Public Sub ClearOutputChannel( _
   ByVal type As ColorAdjustType _
)
[C#]
public void ClearOutputChannel(
   ColorAdjustType type
);
[C++]
public: void ClearOutputChannel(
   ColorAdjustType type
);
[JScript]
public function ClearOutputChannel(
   type : ColorAdjustType
);
```

Parameters

type

Element of the **ColorAdjustType** enumeration that specifies the category for which the output channel setting is cleared.

Return Value

This method does not return a value.

Remarks

An ImageAttributes object maintains color and grayscale settings for five adjustment categories: default, bitmap, brush, pen, and text. For example, you can specify an output channel for the default category and a different output channel for the bitmap category.

The default color- and grayscale-adjustment settings apply to all categories that don't have adjustment settings of their own. For example, if you never specify any adjustment settings for the bitmap category, then the default settings apply to the bitmap category.

As soon as you specify a color- or grayscale-adjustment setting for a certain category, the default adjustment settings no longer apply to that category. For example, suppose you specify an output channel and an adjustment matrix for the default category. If you set the output channel for the bitmap category by calling SetOutputChannel, then the default output channel will not apply to bitmaps. If you later clear the bitmap output channel by calling ClearOutputChannel, the bitmap category will not revert to the default output channel; rather, the bitmap category will have no output channel setting. Similarly, the bitmap category will not revert to the default color-adjustment matrix; rather, the bitmap category will have no color-adjustment matrix.

Requirements

Platforms: Windows 98, Windows NT 4.0, Windows Millennium Edition, Windows 2000, Windows XP Home Edition, Windows XP Professional, Windows Server 2003 family

ImageAttributes.ClearOutputChannelColorProfile Method

Clears the output channel color profile setting.

Overload List

Clears the output channel color profile setting for the default category.

[Visual Basic] **Overloads Public Sub ClearOutputChannelColorProfile()**

[C#] **public void ClearOutputChannelColorProfile();**

[C++] **public: void ClearOutputChannelColorProfile();**

[JScript] **public function ClearOutputChannelColorProfile();**

Clears the output channel color profile setting for a specified category.

[Visual Basic] **Overloads Public Sub ClearOutputChannel-ColorProfile(ColorAdjustType)**

[C#] **public void ClearOutputChannelColor-Profile(ColorAdjustType);**

[C++] **public: void ClearOutputChannelColor-Profile(ColorAdjustType);**

[JScript] **public function ClearOutputChannelColor-Profile(ColorAdjustType);**

ImageAttributes.ClearOutputChannelColorProfile Method ()

Clears the output channel color profile setting for the default category.

```
[Visual Basic]
Overloads Public Sub ClearOutputChannelColorProfile()
[C#]
public void ClearOutputChannelColorProfile();
[C++]
public: void ClearOutputChannelColorProfile();
[JScript]
public function ClearOutputChannelColorProfile();
```

Remarks

An ImageAttributes object maintains color and grayscale settings for five adjustment categories: default, bitmap, brush, pen, and text. For example, you can specify an output channel profile for the default category and a different output channel profile for the bitmap category.

The default color- and grayscale-adjustment settings apply to all categories that don't have adjustment settings of their own. For example, if you never specify any adjustment settings for the bitmap category, then the default settings apply to the bitmap category.

Requirements

Platforms: Windows 98, Windows NT 4.0, Windows Millennium Edition, Windows 2000, Windows XP Home Edition, Windows XP Professional, Windows Server 2003 family

ImageAttributes.ClearOutputChannelColorProfile Method (ColorAdjustType)

Clears the output channel color profile setting for a specified category.

```
[Visual Basic]
Overloads Public Sub ClearOutputChannelColorProfile( _
   ByVal type As ColorAdjustType _
)
[C#]
public void ClearOutputChannelColorProfile(
   ColorAdjustType type
);
[C++]
public: void ClearOutputChannelColorProfile(
   ColorAdjustType type
);
[JScript]
public function ClearOutputChannelColorProfile(
   type : ColorAdjustType
);
```

Parameters

type
: Element of the **ColorAdjustType** enumeration that specifies the category for which the output channel profile setting is cleared.

Return Value

This method does not return a value.

Remarks

An ImageAttributes object maintains color and grayscale settings for five adjustment categories: default, bitmap, brush, pen, and text. For example, you can specify an output channel profile for the default category and a different output channel profile for the bitmap category.

The default color- and grayscale-adjustment settings apply to all categories that don't have adjustment settings of their own. For example, if you never specify any adjustment settings for the bitmap category, then the default settings apply to the bitmap category.

As soon as you specify a color- or grayscale-adjustment setting for a certain category, the default adjustment settings no longer apply to that category. For example, suppose you specify an output channel profile and an adjustment matrix for the default category. If you set the output channel profile for the bitmap category by calling SetOutputChannelColorProfile, then the default output channel profile will not apply to bitmaps. If you later clear the bitmap output channel profile by calling ClearOutputChannelColorProfile, the bitmap category will not revert to the default output channel profile; rather, the bitmap category will have no output channel profile setting. Similarly, the bitmap category will not revert to the default color-adjustment matrix; rather, the bitmap category will have no color-adjustment matrix.

Requirements

Platforms: Windows 98, Windows NT 4.0, Windows Millennium Edition, Windows 2000, Windows XP Home Edition, Windows XP Professional, Windows Server 2003 family

ImageAttributes.ClearRemapTable Method

Clears the color-remap table.

Overload List

Clears the color-remap table for the default category.

[Visual Basic] **Overloads Public Sub ClearRemapTable()**

[C#] **public void ClearRemapTable();**

[C++] **public: void ClearRemapTable();**

[JScript] **public function ClearRemapTable();**

Clears the color-remap table for a specified category.

[Visual Basic] **Overloads Public Sub ClearRemap-Table(ColorAdjustType)**

[C#] **public void ClearRemapTable(ColorAdjustType);**

[C++] **public: void ClearRemapTable(ColorAdjustType);**

[JScript] **public function ClearRemapTable(ColorAdjustType);**

ImageAttributes.ClearRemapTable Method ()

Clears the color-remap table for the default category.

[Visual Basic]
```
Overloads Public Sub ClearRemapTable()
```
[C#]
```
public void ClearRemapTable();
```
[C++]
```
public: void ClearRemapTable();
```
[JScript]
```
public function ClearRemapTable();
```

Remarks

An ImageAttributes object maintains color and grayscale settings for five adjustment categories: default, bitmap, brush, pen, and text. For example, you can specify a remap table for the default category, a different remap table for the bitmap category, and still a different remap table for the pen category.

The default color- and grayscale-adjustment settings apply to all categories that don't have adjustment settings of their own. For example, if you never specify any adjustment settings for the pen category, then the default settings apply to the pen category.

Requirements

Platforms: Windows 98, Windows NT 4.0, Windows Millennium Edition, Windows 2000, Windows XP Home Edition, Windows XP Professional, Windows Server 2003 family

ImageAttributes.ClearRemapTable Method (ColorAdjustType)

Clears the color-remap table for a specified category.

[Visual Basic]
```
Overloads Public Sub ClearRemapTable( _
   ByVal type As ColorAdjustType _
)
```
[C#]
```
public void ClearRemapTable(
   ColorAdjustType type
);
```
[C++]
```
public: void ClearRemapTable(
   ColorAdjustType type
);
```
[JScript]
```
public function ClearRemapTable(
   type : ColorAdjustType
);
```

Parameters

type

Element of the **ColorAdjustType** enumeration that specifies the category for which the remap table is cleared.

Return Value

This method does not return a value.

Remarks

An ImageAttributes object maintains color and grayscale settings for five adjustment categories: default, bitmap, brush, pen, and text. For example, you can specify a remap table for the default category, a different remap table for the bitmap category, and still a different remap table for the pen category.

The default color- and grayscale-adjustment settings apply to all categories that don't have adjustment settings of their own. For example, if you never specify any adjustment settings for the pen category, then the default settings apply to the pen category.

As soon as you specify a color- or grayscale-adjustment setting for a certain category, the default adjustment settings no longer apply to that category. For example, suppose you specify a remap table and a gamma value for the default category. If you set the remap table for the pen category by calling SetRemapTable, then the default remap table will not apply to pens. If you later clear the pen remap table by calling ClearRemapTable, the pen category will not revert to the default remap table; rather, the pen category will have no remap table. Similarly, the pen category will not revert to the default gamma value; rather, the pen category will have no gamma value.

Requirements

Platforms: Windows 98, Windows NT 4.0, Windows Millennium Edition, Windows 2000, Windows XP Home Edition, Windows XP Professional, Windows Server 2003 family

ImageAttributes.ClearThreshold Method

Clears the threshold value.

Overload List

Clears the threshold value for the default category.

[Visual Basic] **Overloads Public Sub ClearThreshold()**

[C#] **public void ClearThreshold();**

[C++] **public: void ClearThreshold();**

[JScript] **public function ClearThreshold();**

Clears the threshold value for a specified category.

[Visual Basic] **Overloads Public Sub ClearThreshold(ColorAdjustType)**

[C#] **public void ClearThreshold(ColorAdjustType);**

[C++] **public: void ClearThreshold(ColorAdjustType);**

[JScript] **public function ClearThreshold(ColorAdjustType);**

ImageAttributes.ClearThreshold Method ()

Clears the threshold value for the default category.

[Visual Basic]
```
Overloads Public Sub ClearThreshold()
```
[C#]
```
public void ClearThreshold();
```
[C++]
```
public: void ClearThreshold();
```
[JScript]
```
public function ClearThreshold();
```

Return Value

This method does not return a value.

Remarks

The threshold is a value from 0 through 1 that specifies a cutoff point for each color component. For example, suppose the threshold is set to 0.7, and suppose you are rendering a color whose red, green, and blue components are 230, 50, and 220. The red component, 230, is greater than 0.7x255, so the red component will be changed to 255 (full intensity). The green component, 50, is less than 0.7x255, so the green component will be changed to 0. The blue component, 220, is greater than 0.7x255, so the blue component will be changed to 255.

An ImageAttributes object maintains color and grayscale settings for five adjustment categories: default, bitmap, brush, pen, and text. For example, you can specify a threshold for the default category, a different threshold for the bitmap category, and still a different threshold for the pen category.

The default color- and grayscale-adjustment settings apply to all categories that don't have adjustment settings of their own. For example, if you never specify any adjustment settings for the pen category, then the default settings apply to the pen category.

Requirements

Platforms: Windows 98, Windows NT 4.0, Windows Millennium Edition, Windows 2000, Windows XP Home Edition, Windows XP Professional, Windows Server 2003 family

ImageAttributes.ClearThreshold Method (ColorAdjustType)

Clears the threshold value for a specified category.

[Visual Basic]
```
Overloads Public Sub ClearThreshold( _
   ByVal type As ColorAdjustType _
)
```
[C#]
```
public void ClearThreshold(
   ColorAdjustType type
);
```
[C++]
```
public: void ClearThreshold(
   ColorAdjustType type
);
```
[JScript]
```
public function ClearThreshold(
   type : ColorAdjustType
);
```

Parameters

type
: Element of the **ColorAdjustType** enumeration that specifies the category for which the threshold is cleared.

Return Value

This method does not return a value.

Remarks

The threshold is a value from 0 through 1 that specifies a cutoff point for each color component. For example, suppose the threshold is set to 0.7, and suppose you are rendering a color whose red, green, and blue components are 230, 50, and 220. The red component, 230, is greater than 0.7x55, so the red component will be changed to 255 (full intensity). The green component, 50, is less than 0.7x255, so the green component will be changed to 0. The blue component, 220, is greater than 0.7x255, so the blue component will be changed to 255.

An ImageAttributes object maintains color and grayscale settings for five adjustment categories: default, bitmap, brush, pen, and text. For example, you can specify a threshold for the default category, a different threshold for the bitmap category, and still a different threshold for the pen category.

The default color- and grayscale-adjustment settings apply to all categories that don't have adjustment settings of their own. For example, if you never specify any adjustment settings for the pen category, then the default settings apply to the pen category.

As soon as you specify a color- or grayscale-adjustment setting for a certain category, the default adjustment settings no longer apply to that category. For example, suppose you specify a threshold and a gamma value for the default category. If you set the threshold for the pen category by calling SetThreshold, then the default threshold will not apply to pens. If you later clear the pen threshold by calling ClearThreshold, the pen category will not revert to the default threshold; rather, the pen category will have no threshold. Similarly, the pen category will not revert to the default gamma value; rather, the pen category will have no gamma value.

Requirements

Platforms: Windows 98, Windows NT 4.0, Windows Millennium Edition, Windows 2000, Windows XP Home Edition, Windows XP Professional, Windows Server 2003 family

ImageAttributes.Clone Method

Creates an exact copy of this **ImageAttributes** object.

[Visual Basic]
```
Public Overridable Function Clone() As Object Implements _
   ICloneable.Clone
```
[C#]
```
public virtual object Clone();
```
[C++]
```
public: virtual Object* Clone();
```
[JScript]
```
public function Clone() : Object;
```

Return Value

The **ImageAttributes** object this class creates, cast as an object.

Implements

ICloneable.Clone

Requirements

Platforms: Windows 98, Windows NT 4.0, Windows Millennium Edition, Windows 2000, Windows XP Home Edition, Windows XP Professional, Windows Server 2003 family

ImageAttributes.Dispose Method

Releases all resources used by this **ImageAttributes** object.

[Visual Basic]
```
Public Overridable Sub Dispose() Implements IDisposable.Dispose
```
[C#]
```
public virtual void Dispose();
```
[C++]
```
public: virtual void Dispose();
```
[JScript]
```
public function Dispose();
```

Return Value

This method does not return a value.

Implements

IDisposable.Dispose

Remarks

Calling **Dispose** allows the resources used by this **ImageAttributes** object to be reallocated for other purposes.

Requirements

Platforms: Windows 98, Windows NT 4.0, Windows Millennium Edition, Windows 2000, Windows XP Home Edition, Windows XP Professional, Windows Server 2003 family

ImageAttributes.Finalize Method

This member overrides **Object.Finalize**.

```
[Visual Basic]
Overrides Protected Sub Finalize()
[C#]
~ImageAttributes();
[C++]
~ImageAttributes();
[JScript]
protected override function Finalize();
```

Requirements

Platforms: Windows 98, Windows NT 4.0, Windows Millennium Edition, Windows 2000, Windows XP Home Edition, Windows XP Professional, Windows Server 2003 family, .NET Compact Framework - Windows CE .NET

ImageAttributes.GetAdjustedPalette Method

Adjusts the colors in a palette according to the adjustment settings of a specified category.

```
[Visual Basic]
Public Sub GetAdjustedPalette( _
   ByVal palette As ColorPalette, _
   ByVal type As ColorAdjustType _
)
[C#]
public void GetAdjustedPalette(
   ColorPalette palette,
   ColorAdjustType type
);
[C++]
public: void GetAdjustedPalette(
   ColorPalette* palette,
   ColorAdjustType type
);
[JScript]
public function GetAdjustedPalette(
   palette : ColorPalette,
   type : ColorAdjustType
);
```

Parameters

palette

A **ColorPalette** object that on input, contains the palette to be adjusted, and on output, contains the adjusted palette.

type

Element of the **ColorAdjustType** enumeration that specifies the category whose adjustment settings will be applied to the palette.

Return Value

This method does not return a value.

Remarks

An ImageAttributes object maintains color and grayscale settings for five adjustment categories: default, bitmap, brush, pen, and text. For example, you can specify a color-remap table for the default category, a different color-remap table for the bitmap category, and still a different color-remap table for the pen category.

When you call GetAdjustedPalette, you can specify the adjustment category that is used to adjust the palette colors. For example, if you pass ColorAdjustType.Bitmap to the GetAdjustedPalette method, then the adjustment settings of the bitmap category are used to adjust the palette colors.

Requirements

Platforms: Windows 98, Windows NT 4.0, Windows Millennium Edition, Windows 2000, Windows XP Home Edition, Windows XP Professional, Windows Server 2003 family

ImageAttributes.SetBrushRemapTable Method

Sets the color-remap table for the brush category.

```
[Visual Basic]
Public Sub SetBrushRemapTable( _
   ByVal map() As ColorMap _
)
[C#]
public void SetBrushRemapTable(
   ColorMap[] map
);
[C++]
public: void SetBrushRemapTable(
   ColorMap* map[]
);
[JScript]
public function SetBrushRemapTable(
   map : ColorMap[]
);
```

Parameters

map

An array of **ColorMap** objects.

Return Value

This method does not return a value.

Remarks

A color-remap table is an array of ColorMap structures. Each ColorMap structure has two Color objects: one that specifies an old color and one that specifies a corresponding new color. During rendering, any color that matches one of the old colors in the remap table is changed to the corresponding new color.

Calling the SetBrushRemapTable method has the same effect as passing ColorAdjustType.Brush to the SetRemapTable method. The specified remap table applies to items in metafiles that are filled with a brush.

Example

[Visual Basic, C#] The following example is designed for use with Windows Forms, and it requires **PaintEventArgs** *e*, which is a parameter of the **Paint** event handler. The code performs the following actions:

- Creates a single-element **ColorMap** array that holds red as the old color and green as the new color.
- Passes this array to a newly created **ImageAttributes** object.

[Visual Basic]
```
Public Sub SetBrushRemapTableExample(e As PaintEventArgs)
' Create a color map.
Dim myColorMap(0) As ColorMap
myColorMap(0) = New ColorMap()
myColorMap(0).OldColor = Color.Red
myColorMap(0).NewColor = Color.Green
' Create an ImageAttributes object, passing it to the myColorMap
' array.
Dim imageAttr As New ImageAttributes()
imageAttr.SetBrushRemapTable(myColorMap)
End Sub
```

[C#]
```
public void SetBrushRemapTableExample(PaintEventArgs e)
{
// Create a color map.
ColorMap[] myColorMap = new ColorMap[1];
myColorMap[0] = new ColorMap();
myColorMap[0].OldColor = Color.Red;
myColorMap[0].NewColor = Color.Green;
// Create an ImageAttributes object, passing it to the myColorMap
// array.
ImageAttributes imageAttr = new ImageAttributes();
imageAttr.SetBrushRemapTable(myColorMap);
}
```

Requirements

Platforms: Windows 98, Windows NT 4.0, Windows Millennium Edition, Windows 2000, Windows XP Home Edition, Windows XP Professional, Windows Server 2003 family

ImageAttributes.SetColorKey Method

Sets the color key (transparency range).

Overload List

Sets the color key for the default category.

Supported by the .NET Compact Framework.

[Visual Basic] **Overloads Public Sub SetColorKey(Color, Color)**

[C#] **public void SetColorKey(Color, Color);**

[C++] **public: void SetColorKey(Color, Color);**

[JScript] **public function SetColorKey(Color, Color);**

Sets the color key (transparency range) for a specified category.

[Visual Basic] **Overloads Public Sub SetColorKey(Color, Color, ColorAdjustType)**

[C#] **public void SetColorKey(Color, Color, ColorAdjustType);**

[C++] **public: void SetColorKey(Color, Color, ColorAdjustType);**

[JScript] **public function SetColorKey(Color, Color, ColorAdjustType);**

Example

[Visual Basic, C#] The following example is designed for use with Windows Forms, and it requires **PaintEventArgs** *e*, which is a parameter of the **Paint** event handler. The code performs the following actions:

- Opens an **Image** object that uses the file Circle.bmp and draws it to the screen.
- Creates an **ImageAttributes** object and sets its color key by calling the **SetColorKey** method.
- Draws the image to the screen using the color key of the **ImageAttributes** object.

> [Visual Basic, C#] **Note** This example shows how to use one of the overloaded versions of **SetColorKey**. For other examples that might be available, see the individual overload topics.

[Visual Basic]
```
Public Sub SetColorKeyExample(e As PaintEventArgs)
' Open an Image file, and draw it to the screen.
Dim myImage As Image = Image.FromFile("Circle.bmp")
e.Graphics.DrawImage(myImage, 20, 20)
' Create an ImageAttributes object and set the color key.
Dim lowerColor As Color = Color.FromArgb(245, 0, 0)
Dim upperColor As Color = Color.FromArgb(255, 0, 0)
Dim imageAttr As New ImageAttributes()
imageAttr.SetColorKey(lowerColor, upperColor, _
ColorAdjustType.Default)
' Draw the image with the color key set.
Dim rect As New Rectangle(150, 20, 100, 100)
e.Graphics.DrawImage(myImage, rect, 0, 0, 100, 100, _
GraphicsUnit.Pixel, imageAttr) ' Image
End Sub
```

[C#]
```
private void SetColorKeyExample(PaintEventArgs e)
{
// Open an Image file and draw it to the screen.
Image myImage = Image.FromFile("Circle.bmp");
e.Graphics.DrawImage(myImage, 20, 20);
// Create an ImageAttributes object and set the color key.
Color lowerColor = Color.FromArgb(245,0,0);
Color upperColor = Color.FromArgb(255,0,0);
ImageAttributes imageAttr = new ImageAttributes();
imageAttr.SetColorKey(lowerColor,
upperColor,
ColorAdjustType.Default);
// Draw the image with the color key set.
Rectangle rect = new Rectangle(150, 20, 100, 100);
e.Graphics.DrawImage(myImage,         // Image
rect,             // Dest. rect.
0,                // srcX
0,                // srcY
100,              // srcWidth
100,              // srcHeight
GraphicsUnit.Pixel, // srcUnit
imageAttr);       // ImageAttributes
}
```

ImageAttributes.SetColorKey Method (Color, Color)

Sets the color key for the default category.

[Visual Basic]
```
Overloads Public Sub SetColorKey( _
   ByVal colorLow As Color, _
   ByVal colorHigh As Color _
)
```

```
[C#]
public void SetColorKey(
   Color colorLow,
   Color colorHigh
);
[C++]
public: void SetColorKey(
   Color colorLow,
   Color colorHigh
);
[JScript]
public function SetColorKey(
   colorLow : Color,
   colorHigh : Color
);
```

Parameters

colorLow
  The low color-key value.

colorHigh
  The high color-key value.

Return Value

This method does not return a value.

Remarks

This method sets the high and low color-key values so that a range of colors can be made transparent. Any color that has each of its three components (red, green, blue) between the corresponding components of the high and low color keys is made transparent.

An ImageAttributes object maintains color and grayscale settings for five adjustment categories: default, bitmap, brush, pen, and text. For example, you can specify a color key for the default category, a different color key for the bitmap category, and still a different color key for the pen category.

The default color- and grayscale-adjustment settings apply to all categories that don't have adjustment settings of their own. For example, if you never specify any adjustment settings for the pen category, then the default settings apply to the pen category.

Example

For an example, see **ImageAttributes.SetColorKey Method (Color, Color, ColorAdjustType)**.

Requirements

Platforms: Windows 98, Windows NT 4.0, Windows Millennium Edition, Windows 2000, Windows XP Home Edition, Windows XP Professional, Windows Server 2003 family, .NET Compact Framework - Windows CE .NET

ImageAttributes.SetColorKey Method (Color, Color, ColorAdjustType)

Sets the color key (transparency range) for a specified category.

```
[Visual Basic]
Overloads Public Sub SetColorKey( _
   ByVal colorLow As Color, _
   ByVal colorHigh As Color, _
   ByVal type As ColorAdjustType _
)
[C#]
public void SetColorKey(
   Color colorLow,
   Color colorHigh,
   ColorAdjustType type
);
[C++]
public: void SetColorKey(
   Color colorLow,
   Color colorHigh,
   ColorAdjustType type
);
[JScript]
public function SetColorKey(
   colorLow : Color,
   colorHigh : Color,
   type : ColorAdjustType
);
```

Parameters

colorLow
  The low color-key value.

colorHigh
  The high color-key value.

type
  Element of the **ColorAdjustType** enumeration that specifies the category for which the color key is set.

Return Value

This method does not return a value.

Remarks

This method sets the high and low color-key values so that a range of colors can be made transparent. Any color that has each of its three components (red, green, blue) between the corresponding components of the high and low color keys is made transparent.

An ImageAttributes object maintains color and grayscale settings for five adjustment categories: default, bitmap, brush, pen, and text. For example, you can specify a color key for the default category, a different color key for the bitmap category, and still a different color key for the pen category.

The default color- and grayscale-adjustment settings apply to all categories that don't have adjustment settings of their own. For example, if you never specify any adjustment settings for the pen category, then the default settings apply to the pen category.

As soon as you specify a color- or grayscale-adjustment setting for a certain category, the default adjustment settings no longer apply to that category. For example, suppose you specify a collection of adjustment settings for the default category. If you set the color key for the pen category by passing ColorAdjustType.Pen to the SetColorKey method, then none of the default adjustment settings will apply to pens.

Example

[Visual Basic, C#] The following example is designed for use with Windows Forms, and it requires **PaintEventArgs** *e*, which is a parameter of the **Paint** event handler. The code performs the following actions:

- Opens an **Image** object that uses the file Circle.bmp and draws it to the screen.
- Creates an **ImageAttributes** object and sets its color key by calling the **SetColorKey** method.
- Draws the image to the screen using the color key of the **ImageAttributes** object.

[Visual Basic]

```
Public Sub SetColorKeyExample(e As PaintEventArgs)
' Open an Image file, and draw it to the screen.
Dim myImage As Image = Image.FromFile("Circle.bmp")
e.Graphics.DrawImage(myImage, 20, 20)
' Create an ImageAttributes object and set the color key.
Dim lowerColor As Color = Color.FromArgb(245, 0, 0)
Dim upperColor As Color = Color.FromArgb(255, 0, 0)
Dim imageAttr As New ImageAttributes()
imageAttr.SetColorKey(lowerColor, upperColor, _
ColorAdjustType.Default)
' Draw the image with the color key set.
Dim rect As New Rectangle(150, 20, 100, 100)
e.Graphics.DrawImage(myImage, rect, 0, 0, 100, 100, _
GraphicsUnit.Pixel, imageAttr) ' Image
End Sub
```

[C#]

```
private void SetColorKeyExample(PaintEventArgs e)
{
// Open an Image file and draw it to the screen.
Image myImage = Image.FromFile("Circle.bmp");
e.Graphics.DrawImage(myImage, 20, 20);
// Create an ImageAttributes object and set the color key.
Color lowerColor = Color.FromArgb(245,0,0);
Color upperColor = Color.FromArgb(255,0,0);
ImageAttributes imageAttr = new ImageAttributes();
imageAttr.SetColorKey(lowerColor,
upperColor,
ColorAdjustType.Default);
// Draw the image with the color key set.
Rectangle rect = new Rectangle(150, 20, 100, 100);
e.Graphics.DrawImage(myImage,         // Image
rect,           // Dest. rect.
0,              // srcX
0,              // srcY
100,            // srcWidth
100,            // srcHeight
GraphicsUnit.Pixel, // srcUnit
imageAttr);     // ImageAttributes
}
```

Requirements

Platforms: Windows 98, Windows NT 4.0, Windows Millennium Edition, Windows 2000, Windows XP Home Edition, Windows XP Professional, Windows Server 2003 family

ImageAttributes.SetColorMatrices Method

Sets the color-adjustment matrix and the grayscale-adjustment matrix.

Overload List

Sets the color-adjustment matrix and the grayscale-adjustment matrix for the default category.

[Visual Basic] **Overloads Public Sub SetColorMatrices(ColorMatrix, ColorMatrix)**

[C#] **public void SetColorMatrices(ColorMatrix, ColorMatrix);**

[C++] **public: void SetColorMatrices(ColorMatrix*, ColorMatrix*);**

[JScript] **public function SetColorMatrices(ColorMatrix, ColorMatrix);**

Sets the color-adjustment matrix and the grayscale-adjustment matrix for the default category.

[Visual Basic] **Overloads Public Sub SetColorMatrices(ColorMatrix, ColorMatrix, ColorMatrixFlag)**

[C#] **public void SetColorMatrices(ColorMatrix, ColorMatrix, ColorMatrixFlag);**

[C++] **public: void SetColorMatrices(ColorMatrix*, ColorMatrix*, ColorMatrixFlag);**

[JScript] **public function SetColorMatrices(ColorMatrix, ColorMatrix, ColorMatrixFlag);**

Sets the color-adjustment matrix and the grayscale-adjustment matrix for a specified category.

[Visual Basic] **Overloads Public Sub SetColorMatrices(ColorMatrix, ColorMatrix, ColorMatrixFlag, ColorAdjustType)**

[C#] **public void SetColorMatrices(ColorMatrix, ColorMatrix, ColorMatrixFlag, ColorAdjustType);**

[C++] **public: void SetColorMatrices(ColorMatrix*, ColorMatrix*, ColorMatrixFlag, ColorAdjustType);**

[JScript] **public function SetColorMatrices(ColorMatrix, ColorMatrix, ColorMatrixFlag, ColorAdjustType);**

ImageAttributes.SetColorMatrices Method (ColorMatrix, ColorMatrix)

Sets the color-adjustment matrix and the grayscale-adjustment matrix for the default category.

[Visual Basic]

```
Overloads Public Sub SetColorMatrices( _
   ByVal newColorMatrix As ColorMatrix, _
   ByVal grayMatrix As ColorMatrix _
)
```

[C#]

```
public void SetColorMatrices(
   ColorMatrix newColorMatrix,
   ColorMatrix grayMatrix
);
```

[C++]

```
public: void SetColorMatrices(
   ColorMatrix* newColorMatrix,
   ColorMatrix* grayMatrix
);
```

[JScript]

```
public function SetColorMatrices(
   newColorMatrix : ColorMatrix,
   grayMatrix : ColorMatrix
);
```

Parameters

newColorMatrix
: The color-adjustment matrix.

grayMatrix
: The grayscale-adjustment matrix.

Return Value

This method does not return a value.

Remarks

An ImageAttributes object maintains color and grayscale settings for five adjustment categories: default, bitmap, brush, pen, and text. For example, you can specify adjustment matrices for the default category, different adjustment matrices for the bitmap category, and still different adjustment matrices for the pen category.

The default color- and grayscale-adjustment settings apply to all categories that don't have adjustment settings of their own. For example, if you never specify any adjustment settings for the pen category, then the default settings apply to the pen category.

The call myImageAttributes.SetColorMatrices(cm, gsm) is equivalent to the call myImageAttributes.SetColorMatrices(cm, gsm, ColorMatrixFlag.Default). ColorMatrixFlags.Default specifies that all colors (including grays) are adjusted by the color-adjustment matrix, not the grayscale-adjustment matrix. Therefore, the grayscale-adjustment matrix passed to this method has no effect.

Requirements

Platforms: Windows 98, Windows NT 4.0, Windows Millennium Edition, Windows 2000, Windows XP Home Edition, Windows XP Professional, Windows Server 2003 family

ImageAttributes.SetColorMatrices Method (ColorMatrix, ColorMatrix, ColorMatrixFlag)

Sets the color-adjustment matrix and the grayscale-adjustment matrix for the default category.

[Visual Basic]
```
Overloads Public Sub SetColorMatrices( _
   ByVal newColorMatrix As ColorMatrix, _
   ByVal grayMatrix As ColorMatrix, _
   ByVal flags As ColorMatrixFlag _
)
```
[C#]
```
public void SetColorMatrices(
   ColorMatrix newColorMatrix,
   ColorMatrix grayMatrix,
   ColorMatrixFlag flags
);
```
[C++]
```
public: void SetColorMatrices(
   ColorMatrix* newColorMatrix,
   ColorMatrix* grayMatrix,
   ColorMatrixFlag flags
);
```
[JScript]
```
public function SetColorMatrices(
   newColorMatrix : ColorMatrix,
   grayMatrix : ColorMatrix,
   flags : ColorMatrixFlag
);
```

Parameters

newColorMatrix
: The color-adjustment matrix.

grayMatrix
: The grayscale-adjustment matrix.

flags
: Element of the **ColorMatrixFlag** enumeration that specifies the type of image and color that will be affected by the color-adjustment and grayscale-adjustment matrices.

Return Value

This method does not return a value.

Remarks

An ImageAttributes object maintains color and grayscale settings for five adjustment categories: default, bitmap, brush, pen, and text. For example, you can specify adjustment matrices for the default category, different adjustment matrices for the bitmap category, and still different adjustment matrices for the pen category.

The default color- and grayscale-adjustment settings apply to all categories that don't have adjustment settings of their own. For example, if you never specify any adjustment settings for the pen category, then the default settings apply to the pen category.

Requirements

Platforms: Windows 98, Windows NT 4.0, Windows Millennium Edition, Windows 2000, Windows XP Home Edition, Windows XP Professional, Windows Server 2003 family

ImageAttributes.SetColorMatrices Method (ColorMatrix, ColorMatrix, ColorMatrixFlag, ColorAdjustType)

Sets the color-adjustment matrix and the grayscale-adjustment matrix for a specified category.

[Visual Basic]
```
Overloads Public Sub SetColorMatrices( _
   ByVal newColorMatrix As ColorMatrix, _
   ByVal grayMatrix As ColorMatrix, _
   ByVal mode As ColorMatrixFlag, _
   ByVal type As ColorAdjustType _
)
```
[C#]
```
public void SetColorMatrices(
   ColorMatrix newColorMatrix,
   ColorMatrix grayMatrix,
   ColorMatrixFlag mode,
   ColorAdjustType type
);
```
[C++]
```
public: void SetColorMatrices(
   ColorMatrix* newColorMatrix,
   ColorMatrix* grayMatrix,
   ColorMatrixFlag mode,
   ColorAdjustType type
);
```
[JScript]
```
public function SetColorMatrices(
   newColorMatrix : ColorMatrix,
   grayMatrix : ColorMatrix,
   mode : ColorMatrixFlag,
   type : ColorAdjustType
);
```

Parameters

newColorMatrix
: The color-adjustment matrix.

grayMatrix
: The grayscale-adjustment matrix.

mode
: Element of the **ColorMatrixFlag** enumeration that specifies the type of image and color that will be affected by the color-adjustment and grayscale-adjustment matrices.

type
: Element of the **ColorAdjustType** enumeration that specifies the category for which the color-adjustment and grayscale-adjustment matrices are set.

Return Value

This method does not return a value.

Remarks

An ImageAttributes object maintains color and grayscale settings for five adjustment categories: default, bitmap, brush, pen, and text. For example, you can specify adjustment matrices for the default category, different adjustment matrices for the bitmap category, and still different adjustment matrices for the pen category.

The default color- and grayscale-adjustment settings apply to all categories that don't have adjustment settings of their own. For example, if you never specify any adjustment settings for the pen category, then the default settings apply to the pen category.

As soon as you specify a color- or grayscale-adjustment setting for a certain category, the default adjustment settings no longer apply to that category. For example, suppose you specify a collection of adjustment settings for the default category. If you set the color-adjustment and grayscale-adjustment matrices for the pen category by passing ColorAdjustType.Pen to the SetColorMatrices method, then none of the default adjustment settings will apply to pens.

Requirements

Platforms: Windows 98, Windows NT 4.0, Windows Millennium Edition, Windows 2000, Windows XP Home Edition, Windows XP Professional, Windows Server 2003 family

ImageAttributes.SetColorMatrix Method

Sets the color-adjustment matrix.

Overload List

Sets the color-adjustment matrix for the default category.

[Visual Basic] **Overloads Public Sub SetColorMatrix(ColorMatrix)**

[C#] **public void SetColorMatrix(ColorMatrix);**

[C++] **public: void SetColorMatrix(ColorMatrix*);**

[JScript] **public function SetColorMatrix(ColorMatrix);**

Sets the color-adjustment matrix for the default category.

[Visual Basic] **Overloads Public Sub SetColorMatrix(ColorMatrix, ColorMatrixFlag)**

[C#] **public void SetColorMatrix(ColorMatrix, ColorMatrixFlag);**

[C++] **public: void SetColorMatrix(ColorMatrix*, ColorMatrixFlag);**

[JScript] **public function SetColorMatrix(ColorMatrix, ColorMatrixFlag);**

Sets the color-adjustment matrix for a specified category.

[Visual Basic] **Overloads Public Sub SetColorMatrix(ColorMatrix, ColorMatrixFlag, ColorAdjustType)**

[C#] **public void SetColorMatrix(ColorMatrix, ColorMatrixFlag, ColorAdjustType);**

[C++] **public: void SetColorMatrix(ColorMatrix*, ColorMatrixFlag, ColorAdjustType);**

[JScript] **public function SetColorMatrix(ColorMatrix, ColorMatrixFlag, ColorAdjustType);**

Example

For an example, see **ImageAttributes.SetColorMatrix Method (ColorMatrix)**.

ImageAttributes.SetColorMatrix Method (ColorMatrix)

Sets the color-adjustment matrix for the default category.

```
[Visual Basic]
Overloads Public Sub SetColorMatrix( _
   ByVal newColorMatrix As ColorMatrix _
)
[C#]
public void SetColorMatrix(
   ColorMatrix newColorMatrix
);
[C++]
public: void SetColorMatrix(
   ColorMatrix* newColorMatrix
);
[JScript]
public function SetColorMatrix(
   newColorMatrix : ColorMatrix
);
```

Parameters

newColorMatrix
The color-adjustment matrix.

Return Value

This method does not return a value.

Remarks

An ImageAttributes object maintains color and grayscale settings for five adjustment categories: default, bitmap, brush, pen, and text. For example, you can specify a color-adjustment matrix for the default category, a different color-adjustment matrix for the bitmap category, and still a different color-adjustment matrix for the pen category.

The default color- and grayscale-adjustment settings apply to all categories that don't have adjustment settings of their own. For example, if you never specify any adjustment settings for the pen category, then the default settings apply to the pen category.

The call myImageAttributes.SetColorMatrix(cm) is equivalent to the call myImageAttributes.SetColorMatrix(cm, ColorMatrixFlag.Default). ColorMatrixFlag.Default specifies that all colors (including grays) are adjusted by the color-adjustment matrix.

Example

[Visual Basic, C#] The following example is designed for use with Windows Forms, and it requires **PaintEventArgs** *e*, which is a parameter of the **Paint** event handler. The code performs the following actions:

- Creates a rectangle image that has all the color values set to 128, producing a rectangle that is filled with a solid medium gray color. The code then draws this rectangle image to the screen.
- Creates a **ColorMatrix** object and sets its **Matrix00** location to 1.75, which emphasizes the red component of the image.
- Creates an **ImageAttributes** object and calls the **SetColorMatrix** method.
- Draws the image (a second rectangle) to the screen using the **ColorMatrix** object just set in the **ImageAttributes** object.

[Visual Basic, C#] Note that the second rectangle has the color red emphasized.

[Visual Basic]

```
Public Sub SetColorMatrixExample(e As PaintEventArgs)
' Create a rectangle image with all colors set to 128 (medium
' gray).
Dim myBitmap As New Bitmap(50, 50, PixelFormat.Format32bppArgb)
Dim g As Graphics = Graphics.FromImage(myBitmap)
g.FillRectangle(New SolidBrush(Color.FromArgb(255, 128, 128, _
128)), New Rectangle(0, 0, 50, 50))
myBitmap.Save("Rectangle1.jpg")
' Open an Image file and draw it to the screen.
Dim myImage As Image = Image.FromFile("Rectangle1.jpg")
e.Graphics.DrawImage(myImage, 20, 20)
' Initialize the color matrix.
Dim myColorMatrix As New ColorMatrix()
myColorMatrix.Matrix00 = 1.75F ' Red
myColorMatrix.Matrix11 = 1F ' Green
myColorMatrix.Matrix22 = 1F ' Blue
myColorMatrix.Matrix33 = 1F ' alpha
myColorMatrix.Matrix44 = 1F ' w
' Create an ImageAttributes object and set the color matrix.
Dim imageAttr As New ImageAttributes()
imageAttr.SetColorMatrix(myColorMatrix)
' Draw the image using the color matrix.
Dim rect As New Rectangle(100, 20, 200, 200)
e.Graphics.DrawImage(myImage, rect, 0, 0, 200, 200, _
GraphicsUnit.Pixel, imageAttr) ' Image
End Sub 'SetColorMatrixExample
```

[C#]

```
private void SetColorMatrixExample(PaintEventArgs e)
{
// Create a rectangle image with all colors set to 128 (medium
// gray).
Bitmap myBitmap = new Bitmap(50, 50, PixelFormat.Format32bppArgb);
Graphics g = Graphics.FromImage(myBitmap);
g.FillRectangle(new SolidBrush(Color.FromArgb(255, 128, 128, 128)),
new Rectangle(0, 0, 50, 50));
myBitmap.Save("Rectangle1.jpg");
// Open an Image file and draw it to the screen.
Image myImage = Image.FromFile("Rectangle1.jpg");
e.Graphics.DrawImage(myImage, 20, 20);
// Initialize the color matrix.
ColorMatrix myColorMatrix = new ColorMatrix();
myColorMatrix.Matrix00 = 1.75f; // Red
myColorMatrix.Matrix11 = 1.00f; // Green
myColorMatrix.Matrix22 = 1.00f; // Blue
myColorMatrix.Matrix33 = 1.00f; // alpha
myColorMatrix.Matrix44 = 1.00f; // w
// Create an ImageAttributes object and set the color matrix.
ImageAttributes imageAttr = new ImageAttributes();
imageAttr.SetColorMatrix(myColorMatrix);
// Draw the image using the color matrix.
Rectangle rect = new Rectangle(100, 20, 200, 200);
e.Graphics.DrawImage(myImage,          // Image
rect,               // Dest. rect.
0,                  // srcX
0,                  // srcY
200,                // srcWidth
200,                // srcHeight
GraphicsUnit.Pixel, // srcUnit
imageAttr);         // ImageAttributes
}
```

Requirements

Platforms: Windows 98, Windows NT 4.0, Windows Millennium Edition, Windows 2000, Windows XP Home Edition, Windows XP Professional, Windows Server 2003 family

ImageAttributes.SetColorMatrix Method (ColorMatrix, ColorMatrixFlag)

Sets the color-adjustment matrix for the default category.

[Visual Basic]

```
Overloads Public Sub SetColorMatrix( _
   ByVal newColorMatrix As ColorMatrix, _
   ByVal flags As ColorMatrixFlag _
)
```

[C#]

```
public void SetColorMatrix(
   ColorMatrix newColorMatrix,
   ColorMatrixFlag flags
);
```

[C++]

```
public: void SetColorMatrix(
   ColorMatrix* newColorMatrix,
   ColorMatrixFlag flags
);
```

[JScript]

```
public function SetColorMatrix(
   newColorMatrix : ColorMatrix,
   flags : ColorMatrixFlag
);
```

Parameters

newColorMatrix

The color-adjustment matrix.

flags

Element of the **ColorMatrixFlag** enumeration that specifies the type of image and color that will be affected by the color-adjustment matrix.

Return Value

This method does not return a value.

Remarks

An ImageAttributes object maintains color and grayscale settings for five adjustment categories: default, bitmap, brush, pen, and text. For example, you can specify a color-adjustment matrix for the default category, a different color-adjustment matrix for the bitmap category, and still a different color-adjustment matrix for the pen category.

The default color- and grayscale-adjustment settings apply to all categories that don't have adjustment settings of their own. For example, if you never specify any adjustment settings for the pen category, then the default settings apply to the pen category.

Example

For an example, see **ImageAttributes.SetColorMatrix Method (ColorMatrix)**.

Requirements

Platforms: Windows 98, Windows NT 4.0, Windows Millennium Edition, Windows 2000, Windows XP Home Edition, Windows XP Professional, Windows Server 2003 family

ImageAttributes.SetColorMatrix Method (ColorMatrix, ColorMatrixFlag, ColorAdjustType)

Sets the color-adjustment matrix for a specified category.

```
[Visual Basic]
Overloads Public Sub SetColorMatrix( _
   ByVal newColorMatrix As ColorMatrix, _
   ByVal mode As ColorMatrixFlag, _
   ByVal type As ColorAdjustType _
)
[C#]
public void SetColorMatrix(
   ColorMatrix newColorMatrix,
   ColorMatrixFlag mode,
   ColorAdjustType type
);
[C++]
public: void SetColorMatrix(
   ColorMatrix* newColorMatrix,
   ColorMatrixFlag mode,
   ColorAdjustType type
);
[JScript]
public function SetColorMatrix(
   newColorMatrix : ColorMatrix,
   mode : ColorMatrixFlag,
   type : ColorAdjustType
);
```

Parameters

newColorMatrix
: The color-adjustment matrix.

mode
: Element of the **ColorMatrixFlag** enumeration that specifies the type of image and color that will be affected by the color-adjustment matrix.

type
: Element of the **ColorAdjustType** enumeration that specifies the category for which the color-adjustment matrix is set.

Return Value

This method does not return a value.

Remarks

An ImageAttributes object maintains color and grayscale settings for five adjustment categories: default, bitmap, brush, pen, and text. For example, you can specify a color-adjustment matrix for the default category, a different color-adjustment matrix for the bitmap category, and still a different color-adjustment matrix for the pen category.

The default color- and grayscale-adjustment settings apply to all categories that don't have adjustment settings of their own. For example, if you never specify any adjustment settings for the pen category, then the default settings apply to the pen category.

As soon as you specify a color- or grayscale-adjustment setting for a certain category, the default adjustment settings no longer apply to that category. For example, suppose you specify a collection of adjustment settings for the default category. If you set the color-adjustment matrix for the pen category by passing ColorAdjustTypePen to the SetColorMatrix method, then none of the default adjustment settings will apply to pens.

Example

For an example, see **ImageAttributes.SetColorMatrix Method (ColorMatrix)**.

Requirements

Platforms: Windows 98, Windows NT 4.0, Windows Millennium Edition, Windows 2000, Windows XP Home Edition, Windows XP Professional, Windows Server 2003 family

ImageAttributes.SetGamma Method

Sets the gamma value.

Overload List

Sets the gamma value for the default category.

[Visual Basic] **Overloads Public Sub SetGamma(Single)**

[C#] **public void SetGamma(float);**

[C++] **public: void SetGamma(float);**

[JScript] **public function SetGamma(float);**

Sets the gamma value for a specified category.

[Visual Basic] **Overloads Public Sub SetGamma(Single, ColorAdjustType)**

[C#] **public void SetGamma(float, ColorAdjustType);**

[C++] **public: void SetGamma(float, ColorAdjustType);**

[JScript] **public function SetGamma(float, ColorAdjustType);**

Example

For an example, see **ImageAttributes.SetGamma Method (Single)**.

ImageAttributes.SetGamma Method (Single)

Sets the gamma value for the default category.

```
[Visual Basic]
Overloads Public Sub SetGamma( _
   ByVal gamma As Single _
)
[C#]
public void SetGamma(
   float gamma
);
[C++]
public: void SetGamma(
   float gamma
);
[JScript]
public function SetGamma(
   gamma : float
);
```

Parameters

gamma
: Specifies the gamma correction value. Typical values for gamma run from 1.0 to 2.2; however, values from 0.1 to 5.0 could prove useful under some circumstances.

Return Value

This method does not return a value.

Remarks

An ImageAttributes object maintains color and grayscale settings for five adjustment categories: default, bitmap, brush, pen, and text. For example, you can specify a gamma value for the default category, a different gamma value for the bitmap category, and still a different gamma value for the pen category.

The default color- and grayscale-adjustment settings apply to all categories that don't have adjustment settings of their own. For example, if you never specify any adjustment settings for the pen category, then the default settings apply to the pen category.

Example

[Visual Basic, C#] The following example is designed for use with Windows Forms, and it requires **PaintEventArgs** *e*, which is a parameter of the **Paint** event handler. The code performs the following actions:

- Opens an **Image** object that uses the file Camera.jpg and draws it to the screen using the default value for gamma.
- Creates an **ImageAttributes** object and sets its gamma to 2.2 by calling the **SetGamma** method.
- Draws the image (a second camera) to the screen using the gamma value just set in the **ImageAttributes** object.

[Visual Basic]

```
Public Sub SetGammaExample(e As PaintEventArgs)
' Create an Image object from the file Camera.jpg, and draw
' it to screen.
Dim myImage As Image = Image.FromFile("Camera.jpg")
e.Graphics.DrawImage(myImage, 20, 20)
' Create an ImageAttributes object and set the gamma to 2.2.
Dim imageAttr As New ImageAttributes()
imageAttr.SetGamma(2.2F)
' Draw the image with gamma set to 2.2.
Dim rect As New Rectangle(250, 20, 200, 200)
e.Graphics.DrawImage(myImage, rect, 0, 0, 200, 200, _
GraphicsUnit.Pixel, imageAttr) ' Image
End Sub
```

[C#]

```
private void SetGammaExample(PaintEventArgs e)
{
// Create an Image object from the file Camera.jpg, and draw it to
// the screen.
Image myImage = Image.FromFile("Camera.jpg");
e.Graphics.DrawImage(myImage, 20, 20);
// Create an ImageAttributes object and set the gamma to 2.2.
ImageAttributes imageAttr = new ImageAttributes();
imageAttr.SetGamma(2.2f);
// Draw the image with gamma set to 2.2.
Rectangle rect = new Rectangle(250, 20, 200, 200);
e.Graphics.DrawImage(myImage,          // Image
rect,             // Dest. rect.
0,                // srcX
0,                // srcY
200,              // srcWidth
200,              // srcHeight
GraphicsUnit.Pixel, // srcUnit
imageAttr);       // ImageAttributes
}
```

Requirements

Platforms: Windows 98, Windows NT 4.0, Windows Millennium Edition, Windows 2000, Windows XP Home Edition, Windows XP Professional, Windows Server 2003 family

ImageAttributes.SetGamma Method (Single, ColorAdjustType)

Sets the gamma value for a specified category.

[Visual Basic]

```
Overloads Public Sub SetGamma( _
   ByVal gamma As Single, _
   ByVal type As ColorAdjustType _
)
```

[C#]

```
public void SetGamma(
   float gamma,
   ColorAdjustType type
);
```

[C++]

```
public: void SetGamma(
   float gamma,
   ColorAdjustType type
);
```

[JScript]

```
public function SetGamma(
   gamma : float,
   type : ColorAdjustType
);
```

Parameters

gamma

Specifies the gamma correction value. Typical values for gamma run from 1.0 to 2.2; however, values from 0.1 to 5.0 could prove useful under some circumstances.

type

Element of the **ColorAdjustType** enumeration that specifies the category for which the gamma value is set.

Return Value

This method does not return a value.

Remarks

An ImageAttributes object maintains color and grayscale settings for five adjustment categories: default, bitmap, brush, pen, and text. For example, you can specify a gamma value for the default category, a different gamma value for the bitmap category, and still a different gamma value for the pen category.

The default color- and grayscale-adjustment settings apply to all categories that don't have adjustment settings of their own. For example, if you never specify any adjustment settings for the pen category, then the default settings apply to the pen category.

As soon as you specify a color- or grayscale-adjustment setting for a certain category, the default adjustment settings no longer apply to that category. For example, suppose you specify a collection of adjustment settings for the default category. If you set the gamma value for the pen category by passing ColorAdjustType.Pen to the SetGamma method, then none of the default adjustment settings will apply to pens.

Example

For an example, see **ImageAttributes.SetGamma Method (Single)**.

Requirements

Platforms: Windows 98, Windows NT 4.0, Windows Millennium Edition, Windows 2000, Windows XP Home Edition, Windows XP Professional, Windows Server 2003 family

ImageAttributes.SetNoOp Method

Turns off color adjustment.

Overload List

Turns off color adjustment for the default category. You can call ClearNoOp to reinstate the color-adjustment settings that were in place before the call to SetNoOp.

[Visual Basic] **Overloads Public Sub SetNoOp()**

[C#] **public void SetNoOp();**

[C++] **public: void SetNoOp();**

[JScript] **public function SetNoOp();**

Turns off color adjustment for a specified category. You can call ClearNoOp to reinstate the color-adjustment settings that were in place before the call to SetNoOp.

[Visual Basic] **Overloads Public Sub SetNoOp(ColorAdjustType)**

[C#] **public void SetNoOp(ColorAdjustType);**

[C++] **public: void SetNoOp(ColorAdjustType);**

[JScript] **public function SetNoOp(ColorAdjustType);**

Example

For an example, see **ImageAttributes.SetNoOp Method** ().

ImageAttributes.SetNoOp Method ()

Turns off color adjustment for the default category. You can call ClearNoOp to reinstate the color-adjustment settings that were in place before the call to SetNoOp.

[Visual Basic]
```
Overloads Public Sub SetNoOp()
```
[C#]
```
public void SetNoOp();
```
[C++]
```
public: void SetNoOp();
```
[JScript]
```
public function SetNoOp();
```

Return Value

This method does not return a value.

Remarks

An ImageAttributes object maintains color and grayscale settings for five adjustment categories: default, bitmap, brush, pen, and text. For example, you can specify a gamma value for the default category, a different gamma value for the bitmap category, and still a different gamma value for the pen category.

The default color- and grayscale-adjustment settings apply to all categories that don't have adjustment settings of their own. For example, if you never specify any adjustment settings for the pen category, then the default settings apply to the pen category.

Example

[Visual Basic, C#] The following example is designed for use with Windows Forms, and it requires **PaintEventArgs** *e*, which is a parameter of the **Paint** event handler. The code performs the following actions:

- Opens an **Image** object that uses the file, Camera.jpg.
- Sets the gamma value of the **ImageAttributes** object to 0.25.
- Draws the image to the screen.
- Calls the **ImageAttributes SetNoOp** method.
- Draws the image (a second camera) to the screen, but since the **SetNoOp** method was called, the gamma setting defaults to a value of 1.0 and the image is drawn to the screen with the default gamma setting.

[Visual Basic, C#] Note that the image on the left is very washed out (gamma of 0.25) and the image on the right has more contrast (gamma of 1.0).

[Visual Basic]
```
Public Sub SetNoOpExample(e As PaintEventArgs)
' Create an Image object from the file Camera.jpg.
Dim myImage As Image = Image.FromFile("Camera.jpg")
' Create an ImageAttributes object, and set the gamma to 0.25.
Dim imageAttr As New ImageAttributes()
imageAttr.SetGamma(0.25F)
' Draw the image with gamma set to 0.25.
Dim rect1 As New Rectangle(20, 20, 200, 200)
e.Graphics.DrawImage(myImage, rect1, 0, 0, 200, 200, _
GraphicsUnit.Pixel, imageAttr)
' Call the ImageAttributes NoOp method.
imageAttr.SetNoOp()
' Draw the image with gamma set to 0.25, but now NoOp is set,
' so the uncorrected image will be shown.
Dim rect2 As New Rectangle(250, 20, 200, 200)
e.Graphics.DrawImage(myImage, rect2, 0, 0, 200, 200, _
GraphicsUnit.Pixel, imageAttr) ' Image
End Sub
```

[C#]
```
private void SetNoOpExample(PaintEventArgs e)
{
// Create an Image object from the file Camera.jpg.
Image myImage = Image.FromFile("Camera.jpg");
// Create an ImageAttributes object, and set the gamma to 0.25.
ImageAttributes imageAttr = new ImageAttributes();
imageAttr.SetGamma(0.25f);
// Draw the image with gamma set to 0.25.
Rectangle rect1 = new Rectangle(20, 20, 200, 200);
e.Graphics.DrawImage(myImage,        // Image
rect1,            // Dest. rect.
0,                // srcX
0,                // srcY
200,              // srcWidth
200,              // srcHeight
GraphicsUnit.Pixel, // srcUnit
imageAttr);       // ImageAttributes
// Call the ImageAttributes NoOp method.
imageAttr.SetNoOp();
// Draw the image after NoOp is set, so the default gamma value
// of 1.0 will be used.
Rectangle rect2 = new Rectangle(250, 20, 200, 200);
e.Graphics.DrawImage(myImage,        // Image
rect2,            // Dest. rect.
0,                // srcX
0,                // srcY
200,              // srcWidth
200,              // srcHeight
GraphicsUnit.Pixel, // srcUnit
imageAttr);       // ImageAttributes
}
```

Requirements

Platforms: Windows 98, Windows NT 4.0, Windows Millennium Edition, Windows 2000, Windows XP Home Edition, Windows XP Professional, Windows Server 2003 family

ImageAttributes.SetNoOp Method (ColorAdjustType)

Turns off color adjustment for a specified category. You can call ClearNoOp to reinstate the color-adjustment settings that were in place before the call to SetNoOp.

```
[Visual Basic]
Overloads Public Sub SetNoOp( _
   ByVal type As ColorAdjustType _
)
[C#]
public void SetNoOp(
   ColorAdjustType type
);
[C++]
public: void SetNoOp(
   ColorAdjustType type
);
[JScript]
public function SetNoOp(
   type : ColorAdjustType
);
```

Parameters

type

Element of the **ColorAdjustType** enumeration that specifies the category for which color correction is turned off.

Return Value

This method does not return a value.

Remarks

An ImageAttributes object maintains color and grayscale settings for five adjustment categories: default, bitmap, brush, pen, and text. For example, you can specify a gamma value for the default category, a different gamma value for the bitmap category, and still a different gamma value for the pen category.

Example

For an example, see **ImageAttributes.SetNoOp Method** ().

Requirements

Platforms: Windows 98, Windows NT 4.0, Windows Millennium Edition, Windows 2000, Windows XP Home Edition, Windows XP Professional, Windows Server 2003 family

ImageAttributes.SetOutputChannel Method

Sets the CMYK output channel.

Overload List

Sets the CMYK output channel for the default category.

[Visual Basic] **Overloads Public Sub SetOutputChannel(ColorChannelFlag)**

[C#] **public void SetOutputChannel(ColorChannelFlag);**

[C++] **public: void SetOutputChannel(ColorChannelFlag);**

[JScript] **public function SetOutputChannel(ColorChannelFlag);**

Sets the CMYK output channel for a specified category.

[Visual Basic] **Overloads Public Sub SetOutputChannel(ColorChannelFlag, ColorAdjustType)**

[C#] **public void SetOutputChannel(ColorChannelFlag, ColorAdjustType);**

[C++] **public: void SetOutputChannel(ColorChannelFlag, ColorAdjustType);**

[JScript] **public function SetOutputChannel(ColorChannelFlag, ColorAdjustType);**

ImageAttributes.SetOutputChannel Method (ColorChannelFlag)

Sets the CMYK output channel for the default category.

```
[Visual Basic]
Overloads Public Sub SetOutputChannel( _
   ByVal flags As ColorChannelFlag _
)
[C#]
public void SetOutputChannel(
   ColorChannelFlag flags
);
[C++]
public: void SetOutputChannel(
   ColorChannelFlag flags
);
[JScript]
public function SetOutputChannel(
   flags : ColorChannelFlag
);
```

Parameters

flags

Element of the **ColorChannelFlag** enumeration that specifies the output channel.

Return Value

This method does not return a value.

Remarks

You can use the SetOutputChannel method to convert an image to a CMYK (cyan, magenta, yellow, black) color space and examine the intensities of one of the CMYK color channels. For example, suppose you create an ImageAttributes object and set its bitmap output channel to ColorChannelFlag.ColorChannelC. If you pass the address of that ImageAttributes object to the Graphics.DrawImage method, the cyan component of each pixel is calculated, and each pixel in the rendered image is a shade of gray that indicates the intensity of its cyan channel. Similarly, you can render images that indicate the intensities of the magenta, yellow, and black channels.

An ImageAttributes object maintains color and grayscale settings for five adjustment categories: default, bitmap, brush, pen, and text. For example, you can specify an output channel for the default category and a different output channel for the bitmap category.

The default color- and grayscale-adjustment settings apply to all categories that don't have adjustment settings of their own. For example, if you never specify any adjustment settings for the bitmap category, then the default settings apply to the bitmap category.

Requirements

Platforms: Windows 98, Windows NT 4.0, Windows Millennium Edition, Windows 2000, Windows XP Home Edition, Windows XP Professional, Windows Server 2003 family

ImageAttributes.SetOutputChannel Method (ColorChannelFlag, ColorAdjustType)

ets the CMYK output channel for a specified category.

[Visual Basic]
```
Overloads Public Sub SetOutputChannel( _
   ByVal flags As ColorChannelFlag, _
   ByVal type As ColorAdjustType _
)
```
[C#]
```
public void SetOutputChannel(
   ColorChannelFlag flags,
   ColorAdjustType type
);
```
[C++]
```
public: void SetOutputChannel(
   ColorChannelFlag flags,
   ColorAdjustType type
);
```
[JScript]
```
public function SetOutputChannel(
   flags : ColorChannelFlag,
   type : ColorAdjustType
);
```

Parameters

flags
: Element of the **ColorChannelFlag** enumeration that specifies the output channel.

type
: Element of the **ColorAdjustType** enumeration that specifies the category for which the output channel is set.

Return Value

This method does not return a value.

Remarks

You can use the SetOutputChannel method to convert an image to a CMYK (cyan, magenta, yellow, black) color space and examine the intensities of one of the CMYK color channels. For example, suppose you create an ImageAttributes object and set its bitmap output channel to ColorChannelFlag.ColorChannelC. If you pass the address of that ImageAttributes object to the Graphics.DrawImage method, the cyan component of each pixel is calculated, and each pixel in the rendered image is a shade of gray that indicates the intensity of its cyan channel. Similarly, you can render images that indicate the intensities of the magenta, yellow, and black channels.

An ImageAttributes object maintains color and grayscale settings for five adjustment categories: default, bitmap, brush, pen, and text. For example, you can specify an output channel for the default category and a different output channel for the bitmap category.

The default color- and grayscale-adjustment settings apply to all categories that don't have adjustment settings of their own. For example, if you never specify any adjustment settings for the bitmap category, then the default settings apply to the bitmap category.

As soon as you specify a color- or grayscale-adjustment setting for a certain category, the default adjustment settings no longer apply to that category. For example, suppose you specify a collection of adjustment settings for the default category. If you set the output channel for the bitmap category by passing ColorAdjustType.Bitmap to the SetOutputChannel method, then none of the default adjustment settings will apply to bitmaps.

Requirements

Platforms: Windows 98, Windows NT 4.0, Windows Millennium Edition, Windows 2000, Windows XP Home Edition, Windows XP Professional, Windows Server 2003 family

ImageAttributes.SetOutputChannelColorProfile Method

Sets the output channel color-profile file.

Overload List

Sets the output channel color-profile file for the default category.

[Visual Basic] **Overloads Public Sub SetOutputChannelColorProfile(String)**

[C#] **public void SetOutputChannelColorProfile(string);**

[C++] **public: void SetOutputChannelColorProfile(String*);**

[JScript] **public function SetOutputChannelColor-Profile(String);**

Sets the output channel color-profile file for a specified category.

[Visual Basic] **Overloads Public Sub SetOutputChannelColorProfile(String, ColorAdjustType)**

[C#] **public void SetOutputChannelColorProfile(string, ColorAdjustType);**

[C++] **public: void SetOutputChannelColorProfile(String*, ColorAdjustType);**

[JScript] **public function SetOutputChannelColor-Profile(String, ColorAdjustType);**

ImageAttributes.SetOutputChannelColorProfile Method (String)

Sets the output channel color-profile file for the default category.

[Visual Basic]
```
Overloads Public Sub SetOutputChannelColorProfile( _
   ByVal colorProfileFilename As String _
)
```
[C#]
```
public void SetOutputChannelColorProfile(
   string colorProfileFilename
);
```
[C++]
```
public: void SetOutputChannelColorProfile(
   String* colorProfileFilename
);
```
[JScript]
```
public function SetOutputChannelColorProfile(
   colorProfileFilename : String
);
```

Parameters

colorProfileFilename
: Path name of a color-profile file. If the color-profile file is in the %SystemRoot%\System32\Spool\Drivers\Color directory, then this parameter can be the file name. Otherwise, this parameter must be the fully-qualified path name.

Return Value

This method does not return a value.

Remarks

You can use the SetOutputChannel and SetOutputChannelColorProfile methods to convert an image to a CMYK (cyan, magenta, yellow, black) color space and examine the intensities of one of the CMYK color channels. For example, suppose you write code that performs the following steps: Create an Image object. Create an ImageAttributes object. Pass ColorChannelFlag.ColorChannelC to the SetOutputChannel method of the ImageAttributes object. Pass the path name of a color profile file to the SetOutputChannelColorProfile method of the ImageAttributes object. Pass the addresses of the Image and ImageAttributes objects to the Graphics.DrawImage method.

GDI+ will use the color-profile file to calculate the cyan component of each pixel in the image, and each pixel in the rendered image will be a shade of gray that indicates the intensity of its cyan channel.

An ImageAttributes object maintains color and grayscale settings for five adjustment categories: default, bitmap, brush, pen, and text. For example, you can specify an output channel color-profile file for the default category and a different output channel color-profile file for the bitmap category.

The default color- and grayscale-adjustment settings apply to all categories that don't have adjustment settings of their own. For example, if you never specify any adjustment settings for the bitmap category, then the default settings apply to the bitmap category.

Requirements

Platforms: Windows 98, Windows NT 4.0, Windows Millennium Edition, Windows 2000, Windows XP Home Edition, Windows XP Professional, Windows Server 2003 family

ImageAttributes.SetOutputChannelColorProfile Method (String, ColorAdjustType)

Sets the output channel color-profile file for a specified category.

[Visual Basic]
```
Overloads Public Sub SetOutputChannelColorProfile( _
   ByVal colorProfileFilename As String, _
   ByVal type As ColorAdjustType _
)
```
[C#]
```
public void SetOutputChannelColorProfile(
   string colorProfileFilename,
   ColorAdjustType type
);
```
[C++]
```
public: void SetOutputChannelColorProfile(
   String* colorProfileFilename,
   ColorAdjustType type
);
```
[JScript]
```
public function SetOutputChannelColorProfile(
   colorProfileFilename : String,
   type : ColorAdjustType
);
```

Parameters

colorProfileFilename

Path name of a color-profile file. If the color-profile file is in the %SystemRoot%\System32\Spool\Drivers\Color directory, then this parameter can be the file name. Otherwise, this parameter must be the fully-qualified path name.

type

Element of the **ColorAdjustType** enumeration that specifies the category for which the output channel color-profile file is set.

Return Value

This method does not return a value.

Remarks

You can use the SetOutputChannel and SetOutputChannelColorProfile methods to convert an image to a CMYK (cyan, magenta, yellow, black) color space and examine the intensities of one of the CMYK color channels. For example, suppose you write code that performs the following steps: Create an Image object. Create an ImageAttributes object. Pass ColorChannelFlag.ColorChannelC to the SetOutputChannel method of the ImageAttributes object. Pass the path name of a color profile file to the SetOutputChannelColorProfile method of the ImageAttributes object. Pass the addresses of the Image and ImageAttributes objects to the Graphics.DrawImage method.

GDI+ will use the color-profile file to calculate the cyan component of each pixel in the image, and each pixel in the rendered image will be a shade of gray that indicates the intensity of its cyan channel.

An ImageAttributes object maintains color and grayscale settings for five adjustment categories: default, bitmap, brush, pen, and text. For example, you can specify an output channel color-profile file for the default category and a different output channel color-profile file for the bitmap category.

The default color- and grayscale-adjustment settings apply to all categories that don't have adjustment settings of their own. For example, if you never specify any adjustment settings for the bitmap category, then the default settings apply to the bitmap category.

As soon as you specify a color- or grayscale-adjustment setting for a certain category, the default adjustment settings no longer apply to that category. For example, suppose you specify a collection of adjustment settings for the default category. If you set the output channel color-profile file for the bitmap category by passing ColorAdjustTypeBitmap to the SetOutputChannelColorProfile method, then none of the default adjustment settings will apply to bitmaps.

Requirements

Platforms: Windows 98, Windows NT 4.0, Windows Millennium Edition, Windows 2000, Windows XP Home Edition, Windows XP Professional, Windows Server 2003 family

ImageAttributes.SetRemapTable Method

Sets the color-remap table.

Overload List

Sets the color-remap table for the default category.

[Visual Basic] **Overloads Public Sub SetRemapTable(ColorMap())**

[C#] **public void SetRemapTable(ColorMap[]);**

[C++] **public: void SetRemapTable(ColorMap*[]);**

[JScript] **public function SetRemapTable(ColorMap[]);**

Sets the color-remap table for a specified category.

[Visual Basic] **Overloads Public Sub SetRemapTable(ColorMap(), ColorAdjustType)**

[C#] **public void SetRemapTable(ColorMap[], ColorAdjustType);**

[C++] **public: void SetRemapTable(ColorMap*[], ColorAdjustType);**

[JScript] **public function SetRemapTable(ColorMap[], ColorAdjustType);**

Example

For an example, see **ImageAttributes.SetRemapTable Method (ColorMap[])**.

ImageAttributes.SetRemapTable Method (ColorMap[])

Sets the color-remap table for the default category.

[Visual Basic]
```
Overloads Public Sub SetRemapTable( _
   ByVal map() As ColorMap _
)
```
[C#]
```
public void SetRemapTable(
   ColorMap[] map
);
```
[C++]
```
public: void SetRemapTable(
   ColorMap* map[]
);
```
[JScript]
```
public function SetRemapTable(
   map : ColorMap[]
);
```

Parameters

map
An array of color pairs of type **ColorMap**. Each color pair contains an existing color (the first value) and the color that it will be mapped to (the second value).

Return Value

This method does not return a value.

Remarks

A color-remap table is an array of ColorMap structures. Each ColorMap structure has two Color objects: one that specifies an old color and one that specifies a corresponding new color. During rendering, any color that matches one of the old colors in the remap table is changed to the corresponding new color.

An ImageAttributes object maintains color and grayscale settings for five adjustment categories: default, bitmap, brush, pen, and text. For example, you can specify a color remap for the default category, a color-remap table for the bitmap category, and still a different color-remap table for the pen category.

The default color- and grayscale-adjustment settings apply to all categories that don't have adjustment settings of their own. For example, if you never specify any adjustment settings for the pen category, then the default settings apply to the pen category.

Example

[Visual Basic, C#] The following example is designed for use with Windows Forms, and it requires **PaintEventArgs** *e*, which is a parameter of the **Paint** event handler. The code performs the following actions:

- Creates an image (a red circle), saves it to Circle2.jpg, opens that image, and draws it to the screen.
- Creates a color map that maps the color red to the color green.
- Draws the image created earlier to the screen again, but this time using the color map.

[Visual Basic]
```
Public Sub SetRemapTableExample(e As PaintEventArgs)
' Create a filled, red image and save it to Circle2.jpg.
Dim myBitmap As New Bitmap(50, 50)
Dim g As Graphics = Graphics.FromImage(myBitmap)
g.Clear(Color.White)
g.FillEllipse(New SolidBrush(Color.Red), New Rectangle(0, 0, _
50, 50))
myBitmap.Save("Circle2.jpg")
' Create an Image object from the Circle2.jpg file, and draw
' it to the screen.
Dim myImage As Image = Image.FromFile("Circle2.jpg")
e.Graphics.DrawImage(myImage, 20, 20)
' Create a color map.
Dim myColorMap(0) As ColorMap
myColorMap(0) = New ColorMap()
myColorMap(0).OldColor = Color.Red
myColorMap(0).NewColor = Color.Green
' Create an ImageAttributes object, and then pass the
' myColorMap object to the SetRemapTable method.
Dim imageAttr As New ImageAttributes()
imageAttr.SetRemapTable(myColorMap)
' Draw the image with the remap table set.
Dim rect As New Rectangle(150, 20, 50, 50)
e.Graphics.DrawImage(myImage, rect, 0, 0, 50, 50, _
GraphicsUnit.Pixel, imageAttr) ' Image
End Sub
```

[C#]
```
private void SetRemapTableExample(PaintEventArgs e)
{
// Create a filled, red image, and save it to Circle2.jpg.
Bitmap myBitmap = new Bitmap(50, 50);
Graphics g = Graphics.FromImage(myBitmap);
g.Clear(Color.White);
g.FillEllipse(new SolidBrush(Color.Red),
new Rectangle(0, 0, 50, 50));
myBitmap.Save("Circle2.jpg");
// Create an Image object from the Circle2.jpg file, and draw it to
// the screen.
Image myImage = Image.FromFile("Circle2.jpg");
e.Graphics.DrawImage(myImage, 20, 20);
// Create a color map.
ColorMap[] myColorMap = new ColorMap[1];
myColorMap[0] = new ColorMap();
myColorMap[0].OldColor = Color.Red;
myColorMap[0].NewColor = Color.Green;
// Create an ImageAttributes object, and then pass the
// myColorMap object to the SetRemapTable method.
ImageAttributes imageAttr = new ImageAttributes();
imageAttr.SetRemapTable(myColorMap);
// Draw the image with the remap table set.
Rectangle rect = new Rectangle(150, 20, 50, 50);
e.Graphics.DrawImage(myImage,         // Image
rect,               // Dest. rect.
0,                  // srcX
0,                  // srcY
50,                 // srcWidth
50,                 // srcHeight
GraphicsUnit.Pixel, // srcUnit
imageAttr);         // ImageAttributes
}
```

Requirements

Platforms: Windows 98, Windows NT 4.0, Windows Millennium Edition, Windows 2000, Windows XP Home Edition, Windows XP Professional, Windows Server 2003 family

ImageAttributes.SetRemapTable Method (ColorMap[], ColorAdjustType)

Sets the color-remap table for a specified category.

```
[Visual Basic]
Overloads Public Sub SetRemapTable( _
   ByVal map() As ColorMap, _
   ByVal type As ColorAdjustType _
)
[C#]
public void SetRemapTable(
   ColorMap[] map,
   ColorAdjustType type
);
[C++]
public: void SetRemapTable(
   ColorMap* map[],
   ColorAdjustType type
);
[JScript]
public function SetRemapTable(
   map : ColorMap[],
   type : ColorAdjustType
);
```

Parameters

map

An array of color pairs of type **ColorMap**. Each color pair contains an existing color (the first value) and the color that it will be mapped to (the second value).

type

Element of the **ColorAdjustType** enumeration that specifies the category for which the color-remap table is set.

Return Value

This method does not return a value.

Remarks

A color-remap table is an array of ColorMap structures. Each ColorMap structure has two Color objects: one that specifies an old color and one that specifies a corresponding new color. During rendering, any color that matches one of the old colors in the remap table is changed to the corresponding new color.

An ImageAttributes object maintains color and grayscale settings for five adjustment categories: default, bitmap, brush, pen, and text. For example, you can specify a color remap for the default category, a color-remap table for the bitmap category, and still a different color-remap table for the pen category.

The default color- and grayscale-adjustment settings apply to all categories that don't have adjustment settings of their own. For example, if you never specify any adjustment settings for the pen category, then the default settings apply to the pen category.

As soon as you specify a color- or grayscale-adjustment setting for a certain category, the default adjustment settings no longer apply to that category. For example, suppose you specify a collection of adjustment settings for the default category. If you set the color-remap table for the pen category by passing ColorAdjustType.Pen to the SetRemapTable method, then none of the default adjustment settings will apply to pens.

Example

For an example, see **ImageAttributes.SetRemapTable Method (ColorMap[])**.

Requirements

Platforms: Windows 98, Windows NT 4.0, Windows Millennium Edition, Windows 2000, Windows XP Home Edition, Windows XP Professional, Windows Server 2003 family

ImageAttributes.SetThreshold Method

Sets the threshold (transparency range).

Overload List

Sets the threshold (transparency range) for the default category.

[Visual Basic] **Overloads Public Sub SetThreshold(Single)**

[C#] **public void SetThreshold(float);**

[C++] **public: void SetThreshold(float);**

[JScript] **public function SetThreshold(float);**

Sets the threshold (transparency range) for a specified category.

[Visual Basic] **Overloads Public Sub SetThreshold(Single, ColorAdjustType)**

[C#] **public void SetThreshold(float, ColorAdjustType);**

[C++] **public: void SetThreshold(float, ColorAdjustType);**

[JScript] **public function SetThreshold(float, ColorAdjustType);**

Example

For an example, see **ImageAttributes.SetThreshold Method (Single)**.

ImageAttributes.SetThreshold Method (Single)

Sets the threshold (transparency range) for the default category.

```
[Visual Basic]
Overloads Public Sub SetThreshold( _
   ByVal threshold As Single _
)
[C#]
public void SetThreshold(
   float threshold
);
[C++]
public: void SetThreshold(
   float threshold
);
[JScript]
public function SetThreshold(
   threshold : float
);
```

Parameters

threshold

Real number that specifies the threshold value.

Return Value

This method does not return a value.

Remarks

The threshold is a value from 0 through 1 that specifies a cutoff point for each color component. For example, suppose the threshold is set to 0.7, and suppose you are rendering a color whose red, green, and blue components are 230, 50, and 220. The red component, 230, is greater than 0.7x255, so the red component will be changed to 255 (full intensity). The green component, 50, is less than 0.7x255, so the green component will be changed to 0. The blue component, 220, is greater than 0.7x255, so the blue component will be changed to 255.

An ImageAttributes object maintains color and grayscale settings for five adjustment categories: default, bitmap, brush, pen, and text. For example, you can specify a threshold for the default category, a threshold for the bitmap category, and still a different threshold for the pen category.

The default color- and grayscale-adjustment settings apply to all categories that don't have adjustment settings of their own. For example, if you never specify any adjustment settings for the pen category, then the default settings apply to the pen category.

Example

[Visual Basic, C#] The following example is designed for use with Windows Forms, and it requires **PaintEventArgs** *e*, which is a parameter of the **Paint** event handler. The code performs the following actions:

- Opens an **Image** object and draws it to the screen.
- Creates an **ImageAttributes** object and sets its threshold by using the **SetThreshold** method.
- Draws the image to the screen by using the threshold of the **ImageAttributes** object.

[Visual Basic]
```
Public Sub SetThresholdExample(e As PaintEventArgs)
' Open an Image file, and draw it to the screen.
Dim myImage As Image = Image.FromFile("Camera.jpg")
e.Graphics.DrawImage(myImage, 20, 20)
' Create an ImageAttributes object, and set its color threshold.
Dim imageAttr As New ImageAttributes()
imageAttr.SetThreshold(0.7F)
' Draw the image with the colors bifurcated.
Dim rect As New Rectangle(300, 20, 200, 200)
e.Graphics.DrawImage(myImage, rect, 0, 0, 200, 200, _
GraphicsUnit.Pixel, imageAttr)
End Sub
```

[C#]
```
private void SetThresholdExample(PaintEventArgs e)
{
// Open an Image file, and draw it to the screen.
Image myImage = Image.FromFile("Camera.jpg");
e.Graphics.DrawImage(myImage, 20, 20);
// Create an ImageAttributes object, and set its color threshold.
ImageAttributes imageAttr = new ImageAttributes();
imageAttr.SetThreshold(0.7f);
// Draw the image with the colors bifurcated.
Rectangle rect = new Rectangle(300, 20, 200, 200);
e.Graphics.DrawImage(myImage,
rect,
0,
0,
200,
200,
GraphicsUnit.Pixel,
imageAttr);
}
```

Requirements

Platforms: Windows 98, Windows NT 4.0, Windows Millennium Edition, Windows 2000, Windows XP Home Edition, Windows XP Professional, Windows Server 2003 family

ImageAttributes.SetThreshold Method (Single, ColorAdjustType)

Sets the threshold (transparency range) for a specified category.

[Visual Basic]
```
Overloads Public Sub SetThreshold( _
   ByVal threshold As Single, _
   ByVal type As ColorAdjustType _
)
```
[C#]
```
public void SetThreshold(
   float threshold,
   ColorAdjustType type
);
```
[C++]
```
public: void SetThreshold(
   float threshold,
   ColorAdjustType type
);
```
[JScript]
```
public function SetThreshold(
   threshold : float,
   type : ColorAdjustType
);
```

Parameters

threshold
: A threshold value between 0.0 and 1.0 that is used as a breakpoint to sort colors that will be mapped to either a maximum or a minimum value.

type
: Element of the **ColorAdjustType** enumeration that specifies the category for which the color threshold is set.

Return Value

This method does not return a value.

Remarks

The threshold is a value from 0 through 1 that specifies a cutoff point for each color component. For example, suppose the threshold is set to 0.7, and suppose you are rendering a color whose red, green, and blue components are 230, 50, and 220. The red component, 230, is greater than 0.7x255, so the red component will be changed to 255 (full intensity). The green component, 50, is less than 0.7x255, so the green component will be changed to 0. The blue component, 220, is greater than 0.7x255, so the blue component will be changed to 255.

An ImageAttributes object maintains color and grayscale settings for five adjustment categories: default, bitmap, brush, pen, and text. For example, you can specify a threshold for the default category, a threshold for the bitmap category, and still a different threshold for the pen category.

The default color- and grayscale-adjustment settings apply to all categories that don't have adjustment settings of their own. For example, if you never specify any adjustment settings for the pen category, then the default settings apply to the pen category.

As soon as you specify a color- or grayscale-adjustment setting for a certain category, the default adjustment settings no longer apply to that category. For example, suppose you specify a collection of adjustment settings for the default category. If you set the threshold for the pen category by passing ColorAdjustType.Pen to the SetThreshold method, then none of the default adjustment settings will apply to pens.

Example

For an example, see **ImageAttributes.SetThreshold Method (Single)**.

Requirements

Platforms: Windows 98, Windows NT 4.0, Windows Millennium Edition, Windows 2000, Windows XP Home Edition, Windows XP Professional, Windows Server 2003 family

ImageAttributes.SetWrapMode Method

Sets the wrap mode.

Overload List

Sets the wrap mode that is used to decide how to tile a texture across a shape, or at shape boundaries. A texture is tiled across a shape to fill it in when the texture is smaller than the shape it is filling.

[Visual Basic] **Overloads Public Sub SetWrapMode(WrapMode)**

[C#] **public void SetWrapMode(WrapMode);**

[C++] **public: void SetWrapMode(WrapMode);**

[JScript] **public function SetWrapMode(WrapMode);**

Sets the wrap mode and color used to decide how to tile a texture across a shape, or at shape boundaries. A texture is tiled across a shape to fill it in when the texture is smaller than the shape it is filling.

[Visual Basic] **Overloads Public Sub SetWrapMode(WrapMode, Color)**

[C#] **public void SetWrapMode(WrapMode, Color);**

[C++] **public: void SetWrapMode(WrapMode, Color);**

[JScript] **public function SetWrapMode(WrapMode, Color);**

Sets the wrap mode and color used to decide how to tile a texture across a shape, or at shape boundaries. A texture is tiled across a shape to fill it in when the texture is smaller than the shape it is filling.

[Visual Basic] **Overloads Public Sub SetWrapMode(WrapMode, Color, Boolean)**

[C#] **public void SetWrapMode(WrapMode, Color, bool);**

[C++] **public: void SetWrapMode(WrapMode, Color, bool);**

[JScript] **public function SetWrapMode(WrapMode, Color, Boolean);**

Example

For an example, see **ImageAttributes.SetWrapMode Method (WrapMode)**.

ImageAttributes.SetWrapMode Method (WrapMode)

Sets the wrap mode that is used to decide how to tile a texture across a shape, or at shape boundaries. A texture is tiled across a shape to fill it in when the texture is smaller than the shape it is filling.

[Visual Basic]
```
Overloads Public Sub SetWrapMode( _
   ByVal mode As WrapMode _
)
```
[C#]
```
public void SetWrapMode(
   WrapMode mode
);
```
[C++]
```
public: void SetWrapMode(
   WrapMode mode
);
```
[JScript]
```
public function SetWrapMode(
   mode : WrapMode
);
```

Parameters

mode

Element of the **WrapMode** enumeration that specifies how repeated copies of an image are used to tile an area.

Return Value

This method does not return a value.

Remarks

The call myImageAttributes.SetWrapMode(wm) is equivalent to the call myImageAttributes.SetWrapMode(wm, Color.Black). Color.Black specifies the color of pixels outside of a rendered image. This color is visible if the mode parameter is set to WrapMode.Clamp and the source rectangle passed to Graphics.DrawImage is larger than the image itself.

Example

[Visual Basic, C#] The following example is designed for use with Windows Forms, and it requires **PaintEventArgs** *e*, which is a parameter of the **Paint** event handler. The code performs the following actions:

- Opens an **Image** object from the Circle3.jpg file (a small, red-filled circle) and draws it to the screen.
- Creates an **ImageAttributes** object and sets the **WrapMode** enumeration to **Tile**.
- Creates a **TextureBrush** object using the image from the Circle3.jpg file.
- Draws a rectangle to the screen that is filled with the small, red-filled circles.

[Visual Basic]
```
Public Sub SetWrapModeExample(e As PaintEventArgs)
' Create a filled, red circle, and save it to Circle3.jpg.
Dim myBitmap As New Bitmap(50, 50)
Dim g As Graphics = Graphics.FromImage(myBitmap)
g.Clear(Color.White)
g.FillEllipse(New SolidBrush(Color.Red), New Rectangle(0, 0, _
25, 25))
myBitmap.Save("Circle3.jpg")
' Create an Image object from the Circle3.jpg file, and draw
' it to the screen.
Dim myImage As Image = Image.FromFile("Circle3.jpg")
e.Graphics.DrawImage(myImage, 20, 20)
' Set the wrap mode.
Dim imageAttr As New ImageAttributes()
imageAttr.SetWrapMode(WrapMode.Tile)
' Create a TextureBrush.
Dim brushRect As New Rectangle(0, 0, 25, 25)
Dim myTBrush As New TextureBrush(myImage, brushRect, imageAttr)
' Draw to the screen a rectangle filled with red circles.
e.Graphics.FillRectangle(myTBrush, 100, 20, 200, 200)
End Sub
```

[C#]
```
private void SetWrapModeExample(PaintEventArgs e)
{
// Create a filled, red circle, and save it to Circle3.jpg.
Bitmap myBitmap = new Bitmap(50, 50);
Graphics g = Graphics.FromImage(myBitmap);
g.Clear(Color.White);
g.FillEllipse(new SolidBrush(Color.Red),
new Rectangle(0, 0, 25, 25));
myBitmap.Save("Circle3.jpg");
```

```
// Create an Image object from the Circle3.jpg file, and draw it
// to the screen.
Image myImage = Image.FromFile("Circle3.jpg");
e.Graphics.DrawImage(myImage, 20, 20);
// Set the wrap mode.
ImageAttributes imageAttr = new ImageAttributes();
imageAttr.SetWrapMode(WrapMode.Tile);
// Create a TextureBrush.
Rectangle brushRect = new Rectangle(0,0,25,25);
TextureBrush myTBrush = new TextureBrush(myImage, <$RD>
brushRect, imageAttr);
// Draw to the screen a rectangle filled with red circles.
e.Graphics.FillRectangle(myTBrush, 100, 20, 200, 200);
}
```

Requirements

Platforms: Windows 98, Windows NT 4.0, Windows Millennium Edition, Windows 2000, Windows XP Home Edition, Windows XP Professional, Windows Server 2003 family

ImageAttributes.SetWrapMode Method (WrapMode, Color)

Sets the wrap mode and color used to decide how to tile a texture across a shape, or at shape boundaries. A texture is tiled across a shape to fill it in when the texture is smaller than the shape it is filling.

[Visual Basic]
```
Overloads Public Sub SetWrapMode( _
   ByVal mode As WrapMode, _
   ByVal color As Color _
)
```
[C#]
```
public void SetWrapMode(
   WrapMode mode,
   Color color
);
```
[C++]
```
public: void SetWrapMode(
   WrapMode mode,
   Color color
);
```
[JScript]
```
public function SetWrapMode(
   mode : WrapMode,
   color : Color
);
```

Parameters

mode

Element of the **WrapMode** enumeration that specifies how repeated copies of an image are used to tile an area.

color

A Color object that specifies the color of pixels outside of a rendered image. This color is visible if the mode parameter is set to WrapMode.Clamp and the source rectangle passed to Graphics.DrawImage is larger than the image itself.

Return Value

This method does not return a value.

Example

For an example, see **ImageAttributes.SetWrapMode Method (WrapMode)**.

Requirements

Platforms: Windows 98, Windows NT 4.0, Windows Millennium Edition, Windows 2000, Windows XP Home Edition, Windows XP Professional, Windows Server 2003 family

ImageAttributes.SetWrapMode Method (WrapMode, Color, Boolean)

Sets the wrap mode and color used to decide how to tile a texture across a shape, or at shape boundaries. A texture is tiled across a shape to fill it in when the texture is smaller than the shape it is filling.

[Visual Basic]
```
Overloads Public Sub SetWrapMode( _
   ByVal mode As WrapMode, _
   ByVal color As Color, _
   ByVal clamp As Boolean _
)
```
[C#]
```
public void SetWrapMode(
   WrapMode mode,
   Color color,
   bool clamp
);
```
[C++]
```
public: void SetWrapMode(
   WrapMode mode,
   Color color,
   bool clamp
);
```
[JScript]
```
public function SetWrapMode(
   mode : WrapMode,
   color : Color,
   clamp : Boolean
);
```

Parameters

mode

Element of the **WrapMode** enumeration that specifies how repeated copies of an image are used to tile an area.

color

A Color object that specifies the color of pixels outside of a rendered image. This color is visible if the mode parameter is set to WrapMode.Clamp and the source rectangle passed to Graphics.DrawImage is larger than the image itself.

clamp

This parameter has no effect. Set it to false.

Return Value

This method does not return a value.

Example

For an example, see **ImageAttributes.SetWrapMode Method (WrapMode)**.

Requirements

Platforms: Windows 98, Windows NT 4.0, Windows Millennium Edition, Windows 2000, Windows XP Home Edition, Windows XP Professional, Windows Server 2003 family

ImageCodecFlags Enumeration

Provides flags for use with codecs.

This enumeration has a **FlagsAttribute** attribute that allows a bitwise combination of its member values.

[Visual Basic]
```
<Flags>
<Serializable>
Public Enum ImageCodecFlags
```
[C#]
```
[Flags]
[Serializable]
public enum ImageCodecFlags
```
[C++]
```
[Flags]
[Serializable]
__value public enum ImageCodecFlags
```
[JScript]
```
public
   Flags
   Serializable
enum ImageCodecFlags
```

Members

Member name	Description	Value
BlockingDecode	Indicates that a decoder has blocking behavior during the decoding process.	32
Builtin	Indicates that the codec is built into GDI+.	65536
Decoder	Indicates that the codec supports decoding (reading).	2
Encoder	Indicates that the codec supports encoding (saving).	1
SeekableEncode	Indicates that an encoder requires a seekable output stream.	16
SupportBitmap	Indicates that the codec supports raster images (bitmaps).	4
SupportVector	Indicates that the codec supports vector images (metafiles).	8
System	Not used in GDI+ version 1.0.	131072
User	Not used in GDI+ version 1.0.	262144

Requirements

Namespace: System.Drawing.Imaging

Platforms: Windows 98, Windows NT 4.0, Windows Millennium Edition, Windows 2000, Windows XP Home Edition, Windows XP Professional, Windows Server 2003 family

Assembly: System.Drawing (in System.Drawing.dll)

ImageCodecInfo Class

The **ImageCodecInfo** class provides the necessary storage members and methods to retrieve all pertinent information about the installed image codecs. Not inheritable.

System.Object
System.Drawing.Imaging.ImageCodecInfo

```
[Visual Basic]
<ComVisible(False)>
NotInheritable Public Class ImageCodecInfo
[C#]
[ComVisible(false)]
public sealed class ImageCodecInfo
[C++]
[ComVisible(false)]
public __gc __sealed class ImageCodecInfo
[JScript]
public
   ComVisible(false)
class ImageCodecInfo
```

Thread Safety

Any public static (**Shared** in Visual Basic) members of this type are safe for multithreaded operations. Any instance members are not guaranteed to be thread safe.

Requirements

Namespace: System.Drawing.Imaging

Platforms: Windows 98, Windows NT 4.0, Windows Millennium Edition, Windows 2000, Windows XP Home Edition, Windows XP Professional, Windows Server 2003 family

Assembly: System.Drawing (in System.Drawing.dll)

ImageCodecInfo.Clsid Property

Gets or sets a **Guid** structure that contains a GUID that identifies a specific codec.

```
[Visual Basic]
Public Property Clsid As Guid
[C#]
public Guid Clsid {get; set;}
[C++]
public: __property Guid get_Clsid();
public: __property void set_Clsid(Guid);
[JScript]
public function get Clsid() : Guid;
public function set Clsid(Guid);
```

Property Value

A **Guid** structure that contains a GUID that identifies a specific codec.

Requirements

Platforms: Windows 98, Windows NT 4.0, Windows Millennium Edition, Windows 2000, Windows XP Home Edition, Windows XP Professional, Windows Server 2003 family

ImageCodecInfo.CodecName Property

Gets or sets a string that contains the name of the codec.

```
[Visual Basic]
Public Property CodecName As String
[C#]
public string CodecName {get; set;}
[C++]
public: __property String* get_CodecName();
public: __property void set_CodecName(String*);
[JScript]
public function get CodecName() : String;
public function set CodecName(String);
```

Property Value

A string that contains the name of the codec.

Requirements

Platforms: Windows 98, Windows NT 4.0, Windows Millennium Edition, Windows 2000, Windows XP Home Edition, Windows XP Professional, Windows Server 2003 family

ImageCodecInfo.DllName Property

Gets or sets string that contains the path name of the DLL that holds the codec. If the codec is not in a DLL, this pointer is a null reference (**Nothing** in Visual Basic).

```
[Visual Basic]
Public Property DllName As String
[C#]
public string DllName {get; set;}
[C++]
public: __property String* get_DllName();
public: __property void set_DllName(String*);
[JScript]
public function get DllName() : String;
public function set DllName(String);
```

Property Value

A string that contains the path name of the DLL that holds the codec.

Requirements

Platforms: Windows 98, Windows NT 4.0, Windows Millennium Edition, Windows 2000, Windows XP Home Edition, Windows XP Professional, Windows Server 2003 family

ImageCodecInfo.FilenameExtension Property

Gets or sets string that contains the file name extension(s) used in the codec. The extensions are separated by semicolons.

```
[Visual Basic]
Public Property FilenameExtension As String
[C#]
public string FilenameExtension {get; set;}
[C++]
public: __property String* get_FilenameExtension();
public: __property void set_FilenameExtension(String*);
[JScript]
public function get FilenameExtension() : String;
public function set FilenameExtension(String);
```

Property Value

A string that contains the file name extension(s) used in the codec.

Requirements

Platforms: Windows 98, Windows NT 4.0, Windows Millennium Edition, Windows 2000, Windows XP Home Edition, Windows XP Professional, Windows Server 2003 family

ImageCodecInfo.Flags Property

Gets or sets 32-bit value used to store additional information about the codec. This property returns a combination of flags from the **ImageCodecFlags** enumeration.

```
[Visual Basic]
Public Property Flags As ImageCodecFlags
[C#]
public ImageCodecFlags Flags {get; set;}
[C++]
public: __property ImageCodecFlags get_Flags();
public: __property void set_Flags(ImageCodecFlags);
[JScript]
public function get Flags() : ImageCodecFlags;
public function set Flags(ImageCodecFlags);
```

Property Value

A 32-bit value used to store additional information about the codec.

Requirements

Platforms: Windows 98, Windows NT 4.0, Windows Millennium Edition, Windows 2000, Windows XP Home Edition, Windows XP Professional, Windows Server 2003 family

ImageCodecInfo.FormatDescription Property

Gets or sets a string that describes the codec's file format.

```
[Visual Basic]
Public Property FormatDescription As String
[C#]
public string FormatDescription {get; set;}
[C++]
public: __property String* get_FormatDescription();
public: __property void set_FormatDescription(String*);
[JScript]
public function get FormatDescription() : String;
public function set FormatDescription(String);
```

Property Value

A string that describes the codec's file format.

Requirements

Platforms: Windows 98, Windows NT 4.0, Windows Millennium Edition, Windows 2000, Windows XP Home Edition, Windows XP Professional, Windows Server 2003 family

ImageCodecInfo.FormatID Property

Gets or sets a **Guid** structure that contains a GUID that identifies the codec's format.

```
[Visual Basic]
Public Property FormatID As Guid
[C#]
public Guid FormatID {get; set;}
[C++]
public: __property Guid get_FormatID();
public: __property void set_FormatID(Guid);
[JScript]
public function get FormatID() : Guid;
public function set FormatID(Guid);
```

Property Value

A **Guid** structure that contains a GUID that identifies the codec's format.

Requirements

Platforms: Windows 98, Windows NT 4.0, Windows Millennium Edition, Windows 2000, Windows XP Home Edition, Windows XP Professional, Windows Server 2003 family

ImageCodecInfo.MimeType Property

Gets or sets a string that contains the codec's Multipurpose Internet Mail Extensions (MIME) type.

```
[Visual Basic]
Public Property MimeType As String
[C#]
public string MimeType {get; set;}
[C++]
public: __property String* get_MimeType();
public: __property void set_MimeType(String*);
[JScript]
public function get MimeType() : String;
public function set MimeType(String);
```

Property Value

A string that contains the codec's Multipurpose Internet Mail Extensions (MIME) type.

Requirements

Platforms: Windows 98, Windows NT 4.0, Windows Millennium Edition, Windows 2000, Windows XP Home Edition, Windows XP Professional, Windows Server 2003 family

ImageCodecInfo.SignatureMasks Property

Gets or sets a two dimensional array of bytes that can be used as a filter.

```
[Visual Basic]
<CLSCompliant(False)>
Public Property SignatureMasks As Byte ()()
[C#]
[CLSCompliant(false)]
public byte[][] SignatureMasks {get; set;}
```

```
[C++]
[CLSCompliant(false)]
public: __property unsigned char* get_SignatureMasks();
public: __property void set_SignatureMasks(unsigned char*[]);
[JScript]
public
   CLSCompliant(false)
function get SignatureMasks() : Byte[][];
public function set SignatureMasks(Byte[][]);
```

Property Value

A two dimensional array of bytes that can be used as a filter.

Requirements

Platforms: Windows 98, Windows NT 4.0, Windows Millennium Edition, Windows 2000, Windows XP Home Edition, Windows XP Professional, Windows Server 2003 family

ImageCodecInfo.SignaturePatterns Property

Gets or sets a two dimensional array of bytes that represents the signature of the codec.

```
[Visual Basic]
<CLSCompliant(False)>
Public Property SignaturePatterns As Byte ()()
[C#]
[CLSCompliant(false)]
public byte[][] SignaturePatterns {get; set;}
[C++]
[CLSCompliant(false)]
public: __property unsigned char* get_SignaturePatterns();
public: __property void set_SignaturePatterns(unsigned char*[]);
[JScript]
public
   CLSCompliant(false)
function get SignaturePatterns() : Byte[][];
public function set SignaturePatterns(Byte[][]);
```

Property Value

A two dimensional array of bytes that represents the signature of the codec.

Requirements

Platforms: Windows 98, Windows NT 4.0, Windows Millennium Edition, Windows 2000, Windows XP Home Edition, Windows XP Professional, Windows Server 2003 family

ImageCodecInfo.Version Property

Gets or sets the version number of the codec.

```
[Visual Basic]
Public Property Version As Integer
[C#]
public int Version {get; set;}
[C++]
public: __property int get_Version();
public: __property void set_Version(int);
[JScript]
public function get Version() : int;
public function set Version(int);
```

Property Value

A or sets the version number of the codec.

Requirements

Platforms: Windows 98, Windows NT 4.0, Windows Millennium Edition, Windows 2000, Windows XP Home Edition, Windows XP Professional, Windows Server 2003 family

ImageCodecInfo.GetImageDecoders Method

Returns an array of **ImageCodecInfo** objects that contain information about the image decoders built into GDI+.

```
[Visual Basic]
Public Shared Function GetImageDecoders() As ImageCodecInfo()
[C#]
public static ImageCodecInfo[] GetImageDecoders();
[C++]
public: static ImageCodecInfo* GetImageDecoders() [];
[JScript]
public static function GetImageDecoders() : ImageCodecInfo[];
```

Return Value

An array of **ImageCodecInfo** objects. Each **ImageCodecInfo** object in the array contains information about one of the built-in image decoders.

Example

For an example, see **GetImageEncoders**.

Requirements

Platforms: Windows 98, Windows NT 4.0, Windows Millennium Edition, Windows 2000, Windows XP Home Edition, Windows XP Professional, Windows Server 2003 family

ImageCodecInfo.GetImageEncoders Method

Returns an array of **ImageCodecInfo** objects that contain information about the image encoders built into GDI+.

```
[Visual Basic]
Public Shared Function GetImageEncoders() As ImageCodecInfo()
[C#]
public static ImageCodecInfo[] GetImageEncoders();
[C++]
public: static ImageCodecInfo* GetImageEncoders() [];
[JScript]
public static function GetImageEncoders() : ImageCodecInfo[];
```

Return Value

An array of **ImageCodecInfo** objects. Each **ImageCodecInfo** object in the array contains information about one of the built-in image encoders.

Example

[Visual Basic, C#] The following example is designed for use with Windows Forms, and it requires **PaintEventArgs** *e*, which is a parameter of the **Paint** event handler. The code uses the **GetImageEncoders** method to retrieve all the codec information for all installed image encoders and codecs, and then draws all the information about each codec to the screen.

[Visual Basic]

```
Public Sub GetImageEncodersExample(e As PaintEventArgs)
' Get an array of available codecs.
Dim myEncoders() As ImageCodecInfo
myEncoders = ImageCodecInfo.GetImageEncoders()
Dim numEncoders As Integer = myEncoders.GetLength(0)
Dim strNumEncoders As String = numEncoders.ToString()
Dim foreColor As Color = Color.Black
Dim font As New Font("Arial", 8)
Dim i As Integer = 0
' Get the info. for all encoders in the array.
If numEncoders > 0 Then
Dim myEncoderInfo(numEncoders * 10) As String
For i = 0 To numEncoders - 1
myEncoderInfo((i * 10)) = "Codec Name = " _
+ myEncoders(i).CodecName
myEncoderInfo((i * 10 + 1)) = "Class ID = " _
+ myEncoders(i).Clsid.ToString()
myEncoderInfo((i * 10 + 2)) = "DLL Name = " _
+ myEncoders(i).DllName
myEncoderInfo((i * 10 + 3)) = "Filename Ext. = " _
+ myEncoders(i).FilenameExtension
myEncoderInfo((i * 10 + 4)) = "Flags = " _
+ myEncoders(i).Flags.ToString()
myEncoderInfo((i * 10 + 5)) = "Format Descrip. = " _
+ myEncoders(i).FormatDescription
myEncoderInfo((i * 10 + 6)) = "Format ID = " _
+ myEncoders(i).FormatID.ToString()
myEncoderInfo((i * 10 + 7)) = "MimeType = " _
+ myEncoders(i).MimeType
myEncoderInfo((i * 10 + 8)) = "Version = " _
+ myEncoders(i).Version.ToString()
myEncoderInfo((i * 10 + 9)) = " "
Next i
Dim numMyEncoderInfo As Integer = myEncoderInfo.GetLength(0)
' Render to the screen all the information.
Dim j As Integer = 20
For i = 0 To numMyEncoderInfo - 1
e.Graphics.DrawString(myEncoderInfo(i), font, _
New SolidBrush(foreColor), 20, j)
j += 12
Next i
Else
e.Graphics.DrawString("No Encoders Found", font, _
New SolidBrush(foreColor), 20, 20)
End If
End Sub
```

[C#]

```
private void GetImageEncodersExample(PaintEventArgs e)
{
// Get an array of available codecs.
ImageCodecInfo[] myCodecs;
myCodecs = ImageCodecInfo.GetImageEncoders();
int numCodecs = myCodecs.GetLength(0);
//numCodecs = 1;
// Set up display variables.
Color foreColor = Color.Black;
Font font = new Font("Arial", 8);
int i = 0;
// Check to determine whether any codecs were found.
if(numCodecs > 0)
{
// Set up an array to hold codec information. There are 9
// information elements plus 1 space for each codec, so 10 times
// the number of codecs found is allocated.
string[] myCodecInfo = new string[numCodecs*10];
// Write all the codec information to the array.
for(i=0;i<numCodecs;i++)
{
myCodecInfo[i*10] = "Codec Name = " + myCodecs[i].CodecName;
myCodecInfo[(i*10)+1] = "Class ID = " +
myCodecs[i].Clsid.ToString();
myCodecInfo[(i*10)+2] = "DLL Name = " + myCodecs[i].DllName;
myCodecInfo[(i*10)+3] = "Filename Ext. = " +
myCodecs[i].FilenameExtension;
myCodecInfo[(i*10)+4] = "Flags = " +
myCodecs[i].Flags.ToString();
myCodecInfo[(i*10)+5] = "Format Descrip. = " +
myCodecs[i].FormatDescription;
myCodecInfo[(i*10)+6] = "Format ID = " +
myCodecs[i].FormatID.ToString();
myCodecInfo[(i*10)+7] = "MimeType = " + myCodecs[i].MimeType;
myCodecInfo[(i*10)+8] = "Version = " +
myCodecs[i].Version.ToString();
myCodecInfo[(i*10)+9] = " ";
}
int numMyCodecInfo = myCodecInfo.GetLength(0);
// Render all of the information to the screen.
int j=20;
for(i=0;i<numMyCodecInfo;i++)
{
e.Graphics.DrawString(myCodecInfo[i],
font,
new SolidBrush(foreColor),
20,
j);
j+=12;
}
}else
e.Graphics.DrawString("No Codecs Found",
font,
new SolidBrush(foreColor),
20,
20);
}
```

Requirements

Platforms: Windows 98, Windows NT 4.0, Windows Millennium Edition, Windows 2000, Windows XP Home Edition, Windows XP Professional, Windows Server 2003 family

ImageFlags Enumeration

Specifies the attributes of the pixel data contained in an **Image** object. The **Image.Flags** property returns a member of this enumeration.

This enumeration has a **FlagsAttribute** attribute that allows a bitwise combination of its member values.

[Visual Basic]
```
<Flags>
<Serializable>
Public Enum ImageFlags
```
[C#]
```
[Flags]
[Serializable]
public enum ImageFlags
```
[C++]
```
[Flags]
[Serializable]
__value public enum ImageFlags
```
[JScript]
```
public
   Flags
   Serializable
enum ImageFlags
```

Members

Member name	Description	Value
Caching	The pixel data can be cached for faster access.	131072
ColorSpaceCmyk	The pixel data uses a CMYK color space.	32
ColorSpaceGray	The pixel data is grayscale.	64
ColorSpaceRgb	The pixel data uses an RGB color space.	16
ColorSpaceYcbcr	Specifies that the image is stored using a YCBCR color space.	128
ColorSpaceYcck	Specifies that the image is stored using a YCCK color space.	256
HasAlpha	The pixel data contains alpha information.	2
HasRealDpi	Specifies that dots per inch information is stored in the image.	4096
HasRealPixelSize	Specifies that the pixel size is stored in the image.	8192
HasTranslucent	Specifies that the pixel data has alpha values other than 0 (transparent) and 255 (opaque).	4
None	There is no format information.	0
PartiallyScalable	The pixel data is partially scalable, but there are some limitations.	8
ReadOnly	The pixel data is read-only.	65536
Scalable	The pixel data is scalable.	1

Requirements

Namespace: System.Drawing.Imaging

Platforms: Windows 98, Windows NT 4.0, Windows Millennium Edition, Windows 2000, Windows XP Home Edition, Windows XP Professional, Windows Server 2003 family

Assembly: System.Drawing (in System.Drawing.dll)

ImageFormat Class

Specifies the format of the image. Not inheritable.

System.Object
  System.Drawing.Imaging.ImageFormat

```
[Visual Basic]
NotInheritable Public Class ImageFormat
[C#]
public sealed class ImageFormat
[C++]
public __gc __sealed class ImageFormat
[JScript]
public class ImageFormat
```

Thread Safety

Any public static (**Shared** in Visual Basic) members of this type are safe for multithreaded operations. Any instance members are not guaranteed to be thread safe.

Requirements

Namespace: System.Drawing.Imaging

Platforms: Windows 98, Windows NT 4.0, Windows Millennium Edition, Windows 2000, Windows XP Home Edition, Windows XP Professional, Windows Server 2003 family

Assembly: System.Drawing (in System.Drawing.dll)

ImageFormat Constructor

Initializes a new instance of the **ImageFormat** class using the specified **Guid** structure.

```
[Visual Basic]
Public Sub New( _
   ByVal guid As Guid _
)
[C#]
public ImageFormat(
   Guid guid
);
[C++]
public: ImageFormat(
   Guid guid
);
[JScript]
public function ImageFormat(
   guid : Guid
);
```

Parameters

guid

The **Guid** structure that specifies a particular image format.

Requirements

Platforms: Windows 98, Windows NT 4.0, Windows Millennium Edition, Windows 2000, Windows XP Home Edition, Windows XP Professional, Windows Server 2003 family

ImageFormat.Bmp Property

Gets the bitmap image format (BMP).

```
[Visual Basic]
Public Shared ReadOnly Property Bmp As ImageFormat
[C#]
public static ImageFormat Bmp {get;}
[C++]
public: __property static ImageFormat* get_Bmp();
[JScript]
public static function get Bmp() : ImageFormat;
```

Property Value

An **ImageFormat** object that indicates the bitmap image format.

Requirements

Platforms: Windows 98, Windows NT 4.0, Windows Millennium Edition, Windows 2000, Windows XP Home Edition, Windows XP Professional, Windows Server 2003 family

ImageFormat.Emf Property

Gets the enhanced Windows metafile image format (EMF).

```
[Visual Basic]
Public Shared ReadOnly Property Emf As ImageFormat
[C#]
public static ImageFormat Emf {get;}
[C++]
public: __property static ImageFormat* get_Emf();
[JScript]
public static function get Emf() : ImageFormat;
```

Property Value

An **ImageFormat** object that indicates the enhanced Windows metafile image format.

Requirements

Platforms: Windows 98, Windows NT 4.0, Windows Millennium Edition, Windows 2000, Windows XP Home Edition, Windows XP Professional, Windows Server 2003 family

ImageFormat.Exif Property

Gets the Exchangeable Image File (Exif) format.

```
[Visual Basic]
Public Shared ReadOnly Property Exif As ImageFormat
[C#]
public static ImageFormat Exif {get;}
[C++]
public: __property static ImageFormat* get_Exif();
[JScript]
public static function get Exif() : ImageFormat;
```

Property Value

An **ImageFormat** object that indicates the Exif format.

Requirements

Platforms: Windows 98, Windows NT 4.0, Windows Millennium Edition, Windows 2000, Windows XP Home Edition, Windows XP Professional, Windows Server 2003 family

ImageFormat.Gif Property

Gets the Graphics Interchange Format (GIF) image format.

```
[Visual Basic]
Public Shared ReadOnly Property Gif As ImageFormat
[C#]
public static ImageFormat Gif {get;}
[C++]
public: __property static ImageFormat* get_Gif();
[JScript]
public static function get Gif() : ImageFormat;
```

Property Value

An **ImageFormat** object that indicates the GIF image format.

Requirements

Platforms: Windows 98, Windows NT 4.0,
Windows Millennium Edition, Windows 2000,
Windows XP Home Edition, Windows XP Professional,
Windows Server 2003 family

ImageFormat.Guid Property

Gets a **Guid** structure that represents this **ImageFormat** object.

```
[Visual Basic]
Public ReadOnly Property Guid As Guid
[C#]
public Guid Guid {get;}
[C++]
public: __property Guid get_Guid();
[JScript]
public function get Guid() : Guid;
```

Property Value

A **Guid** structure that represents this **ImageFormat** object.

Requirements

Platforms: Windows 98, Windows NT 4.0,
Windows Millennium Edition, Windows 2000,
Windows XP Home Edition, Windows XP Professional,
Windows Server 2003 family

ImageFormat.Icon Property

Gets the Windows icon image format.

```
[Visual Basic]
Public Shared ReadOnly Property Icon As ImageFormat
[C#]
public static ImageFormat Icon {get;}
[C++]
public: __property static ImageFormat* get_Icon();
[JScript]
public static function get Icon() : ImageFormat;
```

Property Value

An **ImageFormat** object that indicates the Windows icon image format.

Requirements

Platforms: Windows 98, Windows NT 4.0,
Windows Millennium Edition, Windows 2000,
Windows XP Home Edition, Windows XP Professional,
Windows Server 2003 family

ImageFormat.Jpeg Property

Gets the Joint Photographic Experts Group (JPEG) image format.

```
[Visual Basic]
Public Shared ReadOnly Property Jpeg As ImageFormat
[C#]
public static ImageFormat Jpeg {get;}
[C++]
public: __property static ImageFormat* get_Jpeg();
[JScript]
public static function get Jpeg() : ImageFormat;
```

Property Value

An **ImageFormat** object that indicates the JPEG image format.

Requirements

Platforms: Windows 98, Windows NT 4.0,
Windows Millennium Edition, Windows 2000,
Windows XP Home Edition, Windows XP Professional,
Windows Server 2003 family

ImageFormat.MemoryBmp Property

Gets a memory bitmap image format.

```
[Visual Basic]
Public Shared ReadOnly Property MemoryBmp As ImageFormat
[C#]
public static ImageFormat MemoryBmp {get;}
[C++]
public: __property static ImageFormat* get_MemoryBmp();
[JScript]
public static function get MemoryBmp() : ImageFormat;
```

Property Value

An **ImageFormat** object that indicates the memory bitmap image format.

Requirements

Platforms: Windows 98, Windows NT 4.0,
Windows Millennium Edition, Windows 2000,
Windows XP Home Edition, Windows XP Professional,
Windows Server 2003 family

ImageFormat.Png Property

Gets the W3C Portable Network Graphics (PNG) image format.

```
[Visual Basic]
Public Shared ReadOnly Property Png As ImageFormat
[C#]
public static ImageFormat Png {get;}
[C++]
public: __property static ImageFormat* get_Png();
[JScript]
public static function get Png() : ImageFormat;
```

Property Value

An **ImageFormat** object that indicates the PNG image format.

Requirements

Platforms: Windows 98, Windows NT 4.0,
Windows Millennium Edition, Windows 2000,
Windows XP Home Edition, Windows XP Professional,
Windows Server 2003 family

ImageFormat.Tiff Property

Gets the Tag Image File Format (TIFF) image format.

```
[Visual Basic]
Public Shared ReadOnly Property Tiff As ImageFormat
[C#]
public static ImageFormat Tiff {get;}
[C++]
public: __property static ImageFormat* get_Tiff();
[JScript]
public static function get Tiff() : ImageFormat;
```

Property Value

An **ImageFormat** object that indicates the TIFF image format.

Requirements

Platforms: Windows 98, Windows NT 4.0, Windows Millennium Edition, Windows 2000, Windows XP Home Edition, Windows XP Professional, Windows Server 2003 family

ImageFormat.Wmf Property

Gets the Windows metafile (WMF) image format.

```
[Visual Basic]
Public Shared ReadOnly Property Wmf As ImageFormat
[C#]
public static ImageFormat Wmf {get;}
[C++]
public: __property static ImageFormat* get_Wmf();
[JScript]
public static function get Wmf() : ImageFormat;
```

Property Value

An **ImageFormat** object that indicates the Windows metafile image format.

Requirements

Platforms: Windows 98, Windows NT 4.0, Windows Millennium Edition, Windows 2000, Windows XP Home Edition, Windows XP Professional, Windows Server 2003 family

ImageFormat.Equals Method

Returns a value that indicates whether the specified object is an **ImageFormat** object that is equivalent to this **ImageFormat** object.

```
[Visual Basic]
Overrides Public Function Equals( _
   ByVal o As Object _
) As Boolean
[C#]
public override bool Equals(
   object o
);
[C++]
public: bool Equals(
   Object* o
);
[JScript]
public override function Equals(
   o : Object
) : Boolean;
```

Parameters

o

The object to test.

Return Value

Returns **true** if *o* is an **ImageFormat** object that is equivalent to this **ImageFormat** object; otherwise, returns **false**.

Requirements

Platforms: Windows 98, Windows NT 4.0, Windows Millennium Edition, Windows 2000, Windows XP Home Edition, Windows XP Professional, Windows Server 2003 family

ImageFormat.GetHashCode Method

Returns a hash code value that represents this object.

```
[Visual Basic]
Overrides Public Function GetHashCode() As Integer
[C#]
public override int GetHashCode();
[C++]
public: int GetHashCode();
[JScript]
public override function GetHashCode() : int;
```

Return Value

Returns a hash code that represents this object.

Requirements

Platforms: Windows 98, Windows NT 4.0, Windows Millennium Edition, Windows 2000, Windows XP Home Edition, Windows XP Professional, Windows Server 2003 family

ImageFormat.ToString Method

Converts this **ImageFormat** object to a human-readable string.

```
[Visual Basic]
Overrides Public Function ToString() As String
[C#]
public override string ToString();
[C++]
public: String* ToString();
[JScript]
public override function ToString() : String;
```

Return Value

A string representing this **ImageFormat** object.

Requirements

Platforms: Windows 98, Windows NT 4.0, Windows Millennium Edition, Windows 2000, Windows XP Home Edition, Windows XP Professional, Windows Server 2003 family

ImageLockMode Enumeration

Specifies flags that are passed to the flags parameter of the **Bitmap.LockBits** method. The **LockBits** method locks a portion of an image so that you can read or write the pixel data.

[Visual Basic]
```
<Serializable>
Public Enum ImageLockMode
```
[C#]
```
[Serializable]
public enum ImageLockMode
```
[C++]
```
[Serializable]
__value public enum ImageLockMode
```
[JScript]
```
public
   Serializable
enum ImageLockMode
```

Members

Member name	Description
ReadOnly	Specifies that a portion of the image is locked for reading.
ReadWrite	Specifies that a portion of the image is locked for reading or writing.
UserInputBuffer	Specifies that the buffer used for reading or writing pixel data is allocated by the user. If this flag is set, the *flags* parameter of the **Bitmap.LockBits** method serves as an input parameter (and possibly as an output parameter). If this flag is cleared, then the *flags* parameter serves only as an output parameter.
WriteOnly	Specifies that a portion of the image is locked for writing.

Requirements

Namespace: System.Drawing.Imaging

Platforms: Windows 98, Windows NT 4.0, Windows Millennium Edition, Windows 2000, Windows XP Home Edition, Windows XP Professional, Windows Server 2003 family

Assembly: System.Drawing (in System.Drawing.dll)

Metafile Class

Defines a graphic metafile. A metafile contains records that describe a sequence of graphics operations that can be recorded (constructed) and played back (displayed). Not inheritable.

System.Object
  System.MarshalByRefObject
    System.Drawing.Image
      System.Drawing.Imaging.Metafile

```
[Visual Basic]
<Serializable>
<ComVisible(False)>
NotInheritable Public Class Metafile
   Inherits Image
[C#]
[Serializable]
[ComVisible(false)]
public sealed class Metafile : Image
[C++]
[Serializable]
[ComVisible(false)]
public __gc __sealed class Metafile : public Image
[JScript]
public
   Serializable
   ComVisible(false)
class Metafile extends Image
```

Thread Safety

Any public static (**Shared** in Visual Basic) members of this type are safe for multithreaded operations. Any instance members are not guaranteed to be thread safe.

Requirements

Namespace: System.Drawing.Imaging

Platforms: Windows 98, Windows NT 4.0, Windows Millennium Edition, Windows 2000, Windows XP Home Edition, Windows XP Professional, Windows Server 2003 family

Assembly: System.Drawing (in System.Drawing.dll)

Metafile Constructor

Initializes a new instance of the **Metafile** class.

Overload List

Initializes a new instance of the **Metafile** class from the specified data stream.

[Visual Basic] **Public Sub New(Stream)**

[C#] **public Metafile(Stream);**

[C++] **public: Metafile(Stream*);**

[JScript] **public function Metafile(Stream);**

Initializes a new instance of the **Metafile** class from the specified file name.

[Visual Basic] **Public Sub New(String)**

[C#] **public Metafile(string);**

[C++] **public: Metafile(String*);**

[JScript] **public function Metafile(String);**

Initializes a new instance of the **Metafile** class from the specified handle.

[Visual Basic] **Public Sub New(IntPtr, Boolean)**

[C#] **public Metafile(IntPtr, bool);**

[C++] **public: Metafile(IntPtr, bool);**

[JScript] **public function Metafile(IntPtr, Boolean);**

Initializes a new instance of the **Metafile** class from the specified handle to a device context and an **EmfType** enumeration that specifies the format of the **Metafile**.

[Visual Basic] **Public Sub New(IntPtr, EmfType)**

[C#] **public Metafile(IntPtr, EmfType);**

[C++] **public: Metafile(IntPtr, EmfType);**

[JScript] **public function Metafile(IntPtr, EmfType);**

Initializes a new instance of the **Metafile** class from the specified device context, bounded by the specified rectangle.

[Visual Basic] **Public Sub New(IntPtr, Rectangle)**

[C#] **public Metafile(IntPtr, Rectangle);**

[C++] **public: Metafile(IntPtr, Rectangle);**

[JScript] **public function Metafile(IntPtr, Rectangle);**

Initializes a new instance of the **Metafile** class from the specified device context, bounded by the specified rectangle.

[Visual Basic] **Public Sub New(IntPtr, RectangleF)**

[C#] **public Metafile(IntPtr, RectangleF);**

[C++] **public: Metafile(IntPtr, RectangleF);**

[JScript] **public function Metafile(IntPtr, RectangleF);**

Initializes a new instance of the **Metafile** class from the specified handle and a **WmfPlaceableFileHeader** object.

[Visual Basic] **Public Sub New(IntPtr, WmfPlaceableFileHeader)**

[C#] **public Metafile(IntPtr, WmfPlaceableFileHeader);**

[C++] **public: Metafile(IntPtr, WmfPlaceableFileHeader*);**

[JScript] **public function Metafile(IntPtr, WmfPlaceableFileHeader);**

Initializes a new instance of the **Metafile** class from the specified data stream.

[Visual Basic] **Public Sub New(Stream, IntPtr)**

[C#] **public Metafile(Stream, IntPtr);**

[C++] **public: Metafile(Stream*, IntPtr);**

[JScript] **public function Metafile(Stream, IntPtr);**

Initializes a new instance of the **Metafile** class with the specified file name.

[Visual Basic] **Public Sub New(String, IntPtr)**

[C#] **public Metafile(string, IntPtr);**

[C++] **public: Metafile(String*, IntPtr);**

[JScript] **public function Metafile(String, IntPtr);**

Initializes a new instance of the **Metafile** class from the specified handle to a device context and an **EmfType** enumeration that specifies the format of the **Metafile** object. A string can be supplied to name the file.

[Visual Basic] **Public Sub New(IntPtr, EmfType, String)**

[C#] **public Metafile(IntPtr, EmfType, string);**

[C++] **public: Metafile(IntPtr, EmfType, String*);**

[JScript] **public function Metafile(IntPtr, EmfType, String);**

Initializes a new instance of the **Metafile** class from the specified device context, bounded by the specified rectangle that uses the supplied units of measure.

[Visual Basic] **Public Sub New(IntPtr, Rectangle, MetafileFrameUnit)**

[C#] **public Metafile(IntPtr, Rectangle, MetafileFrameUnit);**

[C++] **public: Metafile(IntPtr, Rectangle, MetafileFrameUnit);**

[JScript] **public function Metafile(IntPtr, Rectangle, MetafileFrameUnit);**

Initializes a new instance of the **Metafile** class from the specified device context, bounded by the specified rectangle that uses the supplied units of measure.

[Visual Basic] **Public Sub New(IntPtr, RectangleF, MetafileFrameUnit)**

[C#] **public Metafile(IntPtr, RectangleF, MetafileFrameUnit);**

[C++] **public: Metafile(IntPtr, RectangleF, MetafileFrameUnit);**

[JScript] **public function Metafile(IntPtr, RectangleF, MetafileFrameUnit);**

Initializes a new instance of the **Metafile** class from the specified handle and a **WmfPlaceableFileHeader** object. Also, *deleteWmf* can be used to delete the handle when the metafile is deleted.

[Visual Basic] **Public Sub New(IntPtr, WmfPlaceableFileHeader, Boolean)**

[C#] **public Metafile(IntPtr, WmfPlaceableFileHeader, bool);**

[C++] **public: Metafile(IntPtr, WmfPlaceableFileHeader*, bool);**

[JScript] **public function Metafile(IntPtr, WmfPlaceable-FileHeader, Boolean);**

Initializes a new instance of the **Metafile** class from the specified data stream, a Windows handle to a device context, and an **EmfType** enumeration that specifies the format of the **Metafile** object.

[Visual Basic] **Public Sub New(Stream, IntPtr, EmfType)**

[C#] **public Metafile(Stream, IntPtr, EmfType);**

[C++] **public: Metafile(Stream*, IntPtr, EmfType);**

[JScript] **public function Metafile(Stream, IntPtr, EmfType);**

Initializes a new instance of the **Metafile** class from the specified data stream, a Windows handle to a device context, and a **Rectangle** structure that represents the rectangle that bounds the new **Metafile** object.

[Visual Basic] **Public Sub New(Stream, IntPtr, Rectangle)**

[C#] **public Metafile(Stream, IntPtr, Rectangle);**

[C++] **public: Metafile(Stream*, IntPtr, Rectangle);**

[JScript] **public function Metafile(Stream, IntPtr, Rectangle);**

Initializes a new instance of the **Metafile** class from the specified data stream, a Windows handle to a device context, and a **RectangleF** structure that represents the rectangle that bounds the new **Metafile** object.

[Visual Basic] **Public Sub New(Stream, IntPtr, RectangleF)**

[C#] **public Metafile(Stream, IntPtr, RectangleF);**

[C++] **public: Metafile(Stream*, IntPtr, RectangleF);**

[JScript] **public function Metafile(Stream, IntPtr, RectangleF);**

Initializes a new instance of the **Metafile** class with the specified file name, from a Windows handle to a device context, and an **EmfType** enumeration that specifies the format of the **Metafile** object.

[Visual Basic] **Public Sub New(String, IntPtr, EmfType)**

[C#] **public Metafile(string, IntPtr, EmfType);**

[C++] **public: Metafile(String*, IntPtr, EmfType);**

[JScript] **public function Metafile(String, IntPtr, EmfType);**

Initializes a new instance of the **Metafile** class with the specified file name, using a Windows handle to a device context, and a **Rectangle** structure that represents the rectangle that bounds the new **Metafile** object.

[Visual Basic] **Public Sub New(String, IntPtr, Rectangle)**

[C#] **public Metafile(string, IntPtr, Rectangle);**

[C++] **public: Metafile(String*, IntPtr, Rectangle);**

[JScript] **public function Metafile(String, IntPtr, Rectangle);**

Initializes a new instance of the **Metafile** class with the specified file name, using a Windows handle to a device context, and A **RectangleF** structure that represents the rectangle that bounds the new **Metafile** object.

[Visual Basic] **Public Sub New(String, IntPtr, RectangleF)**

[C#] **public Metafile(string, IntPtr, RectangleF);**

[C++] **public: Metafile(String*, IntPtr, RectangleF);**

[JScript] **public function Metafile(String, IntPtr, RectangleF);**

Initializes a new instance of the **Metafile** class from the specified device context, bounded by the specified rectangle that uses the supplied units of measure, and an **EmfType** enumeration that specifies the format of the **Metafile** object.

[Visual Basic] **Public Sub New(IntPtr, Rectangle, MetafileFrameUnit, EmfType)**

[C#] **public Metafile(IntPtr, Rectangle, MetafileFrameUnit, EmfType);**

[C++] **public: Metafile(IntPtr, Rectangle, MetafileFrameUnit, EmfType);**

[JScript] **public function Metafile(IntPtr, Rectangle, MetafileFrameUnit, EmfType);**

Initializes a new instance of the **Metafile** class from the specified device context, bounded by the specified rectangle that uses the supplied units of measure, and an **EmfType** enumeration that specifies the format of the **Metafile** object.

[Visual Basic] **Public Sub New(IntPtr, RectangleF, MetafileFrameUnit, EmfType)**

[C#] **public Metafile(IntPtr, RectangleF, MetafileFrameUnit, EmfType);**

[C++] **public: Metafile(IntPtr, RectangleF, MetafileFrameUnit, EmfType);**

[JScript] **public function Metafile(IntPtr, RectangleF, MetafileFrameUnit, EmfType);**

Initializes a new instance of the **Metafile** class from the specified data stream, a Windows handle to a device context, and an **EmfType** enumeration that specifies the format of the **Metafile** object. Also, a string that contains a descriptive name for the new **Metafile** object can be added.

[Visual Basic] **Public Sub New(Stream, IntPtr, EmfType, String)**

[C#] **public Metafile(Stream, IntPtr, EmfType, string);**

[C++] **public: Metafile(Stream*, IntPtr, EmfType, String*);**

[JScript] **public function Metafile(Stream, IntPtr, EmfType, String);**

Initializes a new instance of the **Metafile** class from the specified data stream, a Windows handle to a device context, and a **Rectangle** structure that represents the rectangle that bounds the new **Metafile** object, and the supplied units of measure.

[Visual Basic] **Public Sub New(Stream, IntPtr, Rectangle, MetafileFrameUnit)**

[C#] **public Metafile(Stream, IntPtr, Rectangle, MetafileFrameUnit);**

[C++] **public: Metafile(Stream*, IntPtr, Rectangle, MetafileFrameUnit);**

[JScript] **public function Metafile(Stream, IntPtr, Rectangle, MetafileFrameUnit);**

Initializes a new instance of the **Metafile** class from the specified data stream, a Windows handle to a device context, and a **RectangleF** structure that represents the rectangle that bounds the new **Metafile** object, and the supplied units of measure.

[Visual Basic] **Public Sub New(Stream, IntPtr, RectangleF, MetafileFrameUnit)**

[C#] **public Metafile(Stream, IntPtr, RectangleF, MetafileFrameUnit);**

[C++] **public: Metafile(Stream*, IntPtr, RectangleF, MetafileFrameUnit);**

[JScript] **public function Metafile(Stream, IntPtr, RectangleF, MetafileFrameUnit);**

Initializes a new instance of the **Metafile** class with the specified file name, from a Windows handle to a device context, and an **EmfType** enumeration that specifies the format of the **Metafile** object. A descriptive string can be added as well.

[Visual Basic] **Public Sub New(String, IntPtr, EmfType, String)**

[C#] **public Metafile(string, IntPtr, EmfType, string);**

[C++] **public: Metafile(String*, IntPtr, EmfType, String*);**

[JScript] **public function Metafile(String, IntPtr, EmfType, String);**

Initializes a new instance of the **Metafile** class with the specified file name, using a Windows handle to a device context, a **Rectangle** structure that represents the rectangle that bounds the new **Metafile** object, and the supplied units of measure.

[Visual Basic] **Public Sub New(String, IntPtr, Rectangle, MetafileFrameUnit)**

[C#] **public Metafile(string, IntPtr, Rectangle, MetafileFrameUnit);**

[C++] **public: Metafile(String*, IntPtr, Rectangle, MetafileFrameUnit);**

[JScript] **public function Metafile(String, IntPtr, Rectangle, MetafileFrameUnit);**

Initializes a new instance of the **Metafile** class with the specified file name, using a Windows handle to a device context, a **RectangleF** structure that represents the rectangle that bounds the new **Metafile** object, and the supplied units of measure.

[Visual Basic] **Public Sub New(String, IntPtr, RectangleF, MetafileFrameUnit)**

[C#] **public Metafile(string, IntPtr, RectangleF, MetafileFrameUnit);**

[C++] **public: Metafile(String*, IntPtr, RectangleF, MetafileFrameUnit);**

[JScript] **public function Metafile(String, IntPtr, RectangleF, MetafileFrameUnit);**

Initializes a new instance of the **Metafile** class from the specified device context, bounded by the specified rectangle that uses the supplied units of measure, and an **EmfType** enumeration that specifies the format of the **Metafile** object. A string can be provided to name the file.

[Visual Basic] **Public Sub New(IntPtr, Rectangle, MetafileFrameUnit, EmfType, String)**

[C#] **public Metafile(IntPtr, Rectangle, MetafileFrameUnit, EmfType, string);**

[C++] **public: Metafile(IntPtr, Rectangle, MetafileFrameUnit, EmfType, String*);**

[JScript] **public function Metafile(IntPtr, Rectangle, MetafileFrameUnit, EmfType, String);**

Initializes a new instance of the **Metafile** class from the specified device context, bounded by the specified rectangle that uses the supplied units of measure, and an **EmfType** enumeration that specifies the format of the **Metafile** object. A string can be provided to name the file.

[Visual Basic] **Public Sub New(IntPtr, RectangleF, MetafileFrameUnit, EmfType, String)**

[C#] **public Metafile(IntPtr, RectangleF, MetafileFrameUnit, EmfType, string);**

[C++] **public: Metafile(IntPtr, RectangleF, MetafileFrameUnit, EmfType, String*);**

[JScript] **public function Metafile(IntPtr, RectangleF, MetafileFrameUnit, EmfType, String);**

Initializes a new instance of the **Metafile** class from the specified data stream, a Windows handle to a device context, a **Rectangle** structure that represents the rectangle that bounds the new **Metafile** object, the supplied units of measure, and an **EmfType** enumeration that specifies the format of the **Metafile** object.

[Visual Basic] **Public Sub New(Stream, IntPtr, Rectangle, MetafileFrameUnit, EmfType)**

[C#] **public Metafile(Stream, IntPtr, Rectangle, MetafileFrameUnit, EmfType);**

[C++] **public: Metafile(Stream*, IntPtr, Rectangle, MetafileFrameUnit, EmfType);**

[JScript] **public function Metafile(Stream, IntPtr, Rectangle, MetafileFrameUnit, EmfType);**

Initializes a new instance of the **Metafile** class from the specified data stream, a Windows handle to a device context, a **RectangleF** structure that represents the rectangle that bounds the new **Metafile** object, the supplied units of measure, and an **EmfType** enumeration that specifies the format of the **Metafile** object.

[Visual Basic] **Public Sub New(Stream, IntPtr, RectangleF, MetafileFrameUnit, EmfType)**

[C#] **public Metafile(Stream, IntPtr, RectangleF, MetafileFrameUnit, EmfType);**

[C++] **public: Metafile(Stream*, IntPtr, RectangleF, MetafileFrameUnit, EmfType);**

[JScript] **public function Metafile(Stream, IntPtr, RectangleF, MetafileFrameUnit, EmfType);**

Initializes a new instance of the **Metafile** class with the specified file name, using a Windows handle to a device context, a **Rectangle** structure that represents the rectangle that bounds the new **Metafile** object, the supplied units of measure, and an **EmfType** enumeration that specifies the format of the **Metafile** object.

[Visual Basic] **Public Sub New(String, IntPtr, Rectangle, MetafileFrameUnit, EmfType)**

[C#] **public Metafile(string, IntPtr, Rectangle, MetafileFrameUnit, EmfType);**

[C++] **public: Metafile(String*, IntPtr, Rectangle, MetafileFrameUnit, EmfType);**

[JScript] **public function Metafile(String, IntPtr, Rectangle, MetafileFrameUnit, EmfType);**

Initializes a new instance of the **Metafile** class with the specified file name, using a Windows handle to a device context, a **Rectangle** structure that represents the rectangle that bounds the new **Metafile** object, and the supplied units of measure. A descriptive string can also be added.

[Visual Basic] **Public Sub New(String, IntPtr, Rectangle, MetafileFrameUnit, String)**

[C#] **public Metafile(string, IntPtr, Rectangle, MetafileFrameUnit, string);**

[C++] **public: Metafile(String*, IntPtr, Rectangle, MetafileFrameUnit, String*);**

[JScript] **public function Metafile(String, IntPtr, Rectangle, MetafileFrameUnit, String);**

Initializes a new instance of the **Metafile** class with the specified file name, using a Windows handle to a device context, a **RectangleF** structure that represents the rectangle that bounds the new **Metafile** object, the supplied units of measure, and an **EmfType** enumeration that specifies the format of the **Metafile** object.

[Visual Basic] **Public Sub New(String, IntPtr, RectangleF, MetafileFrameUnit, EmfType)**

[C#] **public Metafile(string, IntPtr, RectangleF, MetafileFrameUnit, EmfType);**

[C++] **public: Metafile(String*, IntPtr, RectangleF, MetafileFrameUnit, EmfType);**

[JScript] **public function Metafile(String, IntPtr, RectangleF, MetafileFrameUnit, EmfType);**

Initializes a new instance of the **Metafile** class with the specified file name, using a Windows handle to a device context, a **RectangleF** structure that represents the rectangle that bounds the new **Metafile** object, and the supplied units of measure. A descriptive string can also be added.

[Visual Basic] **Public Sub New(String, IntPtr, RectangleF, MetafileFrameUnit, String)**

[C#] **public Metafile(string, IntPtr, RectangleF, MetafileFrameUnit, string);**

[C++] **public: Metafile(String*, IntPtr, RectangleF, MetafileFrameUnit, String*);**

[JScript] **public function Metafile(String, IntPtr, RectangleF, MetafileFrameUnit, String);**

Initializes a new instance of the **Metafile** class from the specified data stream, a Windows handle to a device context, a **Rectangle** structure that represents the rectangle that bounds the new **Metafile** object, the supplied units of measure, and an **EmfType** enumeration that specifies the format of the **Metafile** object. A string that contains a descriptive name for the new **Metafile** object can be added.

[Visual Basic] **Public Sub New(Stream, IntPtr, Rectangle, MetafileFrameUnit, EmfType, String)**

[C#] **public Metafile(Stream, IntPtr, Rectangle, MetafileFrameUnit, EmfType, string);**

[C++] **public: Metafile(Stream*, IntPtr, Rectangle, MetafileFrameUnit, EmfType, String*);**

[JScript] **public function Metafile(Stream, IntPtr, Rectangle, MetafileFrameUnit, EmfType, String);**

Initializes a new instance of the **Metafile** class from the specified data stream, a Windows handle to a device context, a **RectangleF** structure that represents the rectangle that bounds the new **Metafile** object, the supplied units of measure, and an **EmfType** enumeration that specifies the format of the **Metafile** object. A string that contains a descriptive name for the new **Metafile** object can be added.

[Visual Basic] **Public Sub New(Stream, IntPtr, RectangleF, MetafileFrameUnit, EmfType, String)**

[C#] **public Metafile(Stream, IntPtr, RectangleF, MetafileFrameUnit, EmfType, string);**

[C++] **public: Metafile(Stream*, IntPtr, RectangleF, MetafileFrameUnit, EmfType, String*);**

[JScript] **public function Metafile(Stream, IntPtr, RectangleF, MetafileFrameUnit, EmfType, String);**

Initializes a new instance of the **Metafile** class with the specified file name, using a Windows handle to a device context, a **Rectangle** structure that represents the rectangle that bounds the new **Metafile** object, the supplied units of measure, and an **EmfType** enumeration that specifies the format of the **Metafile** object. A descriptive string can also be added.

[Visual Basic] **Public Sub New(String, IntPtr, Rectangle, MetafileFrameUnit, EmfType, String)**

[C#] **public Metafile(string, IntPtr, Rectangle, MetafileFrameUnit, EmfType, string);**

[C++] **public: Metafile(String*, IntPtr, Rectangle, MetafileFrameUnit, EmfType, String*);**

[JScript] **public function Metafile(String, IntPtr, Rectangle, MetafileFrameUnit, EmfType, String);**

Initializes a new instance of the **Metafile** class with the specified file name, using a Windows handle to a device context, a **RectangleF** structure that represents the rectangle that bounds the new **Metafile** object, the supplied units of measure, and an **EmfType** enumeration that specifies the format of the **Metafile** object. A descriptive string can also be added.

[Visual Basic] **Public Sub New(String, IntPtr, RectangleF, MetafileFrameUnit, EmfType, String)**

[C#] **public Metafile(string, IntPtr, RectangleF, MetafileFrameUnit, EmfType, string);**

[C++] **public: Metafile(String*, IntPtr, RectangleF, MetafileFrameUnit, EmfType, String*);**

[JScript] **public function Metafile(String, IntPtr, RectangleF, MetafileFrameUnit, EmfType, String);**

Metafile Constructor (Stream)

Initializes a new instance of the **Metafile** class from the specified data stream.

```
[Visual Basic]
Public Sub New( _
   ByVal stream As Stream _
)
[C#]
public Metafile(
   Stream stream
);
[C++]
public: Metafile(
   Stream* stream
);
[JScript]
public function Metafile(
   stream : Stream
);
```

Parameters

stream

The **Stream** object from which to create the new **Metafile** object.

Requirements

Platforms: Windows 98, Windows NT 4.0, Windows Millennium Edition, Windows 2000, Windows XP Home Edition, Windows XP Professional, Windows Server 2003 family

Metafile Constructor (String)

Initializes a new instance of the **Metafile** class from the specified file name.

```
[Visual Basic]
Public Sub New( _
   ByVal filename As String _
)
[C#]
public Metafile(
   string filename
);
[C++]
public: Metafile(
   String* filename
);
[JScript]
public function Metafile(
   filename : String
);
```

Parameters

filename

A **String** object that represents the file name from which to create the new **Metafile** object.

Requirements

Platforms: Windows 98, Windows NT 4.0, Windows Millennium Edition, Windows 2000, Windows XP Home Edition, Windows XP Professional, Windows Server 2003 family

Metafile Constructor (IntPtr, Boolean)

Initializes a new instance of the **Metafile** class from the specified handle.

```
[Visual Basic]
Public Sub New( _
   ByVal henhmetafile As IntPtr, _
   ByVal deleteEmf As Boolean _
)
[C#]
public Metafile(
   IntPtr henhmetafile,
   bool deleteEmf
);
[C++]
public: Metafile(
   IntPtr henhmetafile,
   bool deleteEmf
);
[JScript]
public function Metafile(
   henhmetafile : IntPtr,
   deleteEmf : Boolean
);
```

Parameters

henhmetafile

A handle to an enhanced metafile .

deleteEmf

Set to **true** to delete the enhanced metafile handle when the **Metafile** object is deleted; otherwise, **false**.

Requirements

Platforms: Windows 98, Windows NT 4.0, Windows Millennium Edition, Windows 2000, Windows XP Home Edition, Windows XP Professional, Windows Server 2003 family

Metafile Constructor (IntPtr, EmfType)

Initializes a new instance of the **Metafile** class from the specified handle to a device context and an **EmfType** enumeration that specifies the format of the **Metafile**.

```
[Visual Basic]
Public Sub New( _
   ByVal referenceHdc As IntPtr, _
   ByVal emfType As EmfType _
)
[C#]
public Metafile(
   IntPtr referenceHdc,
   EmfType emfType
);
[C++]
public: Metafile(
   IntPtr referenceHdc,
   EmfType emfType
);
[JScript]
public function Metafile(
   referenceHdc : IntPtr,
   emfType : EmfType
);
```

Parameters

referenceHdc
The handle to a device context.

emfType
An **EmfType** enumeration that specifies the format of the **Metafile** object.

Requirements

Platforms: Windows 98, Windows NT 4.0, Windows Millennium Edition, Windows 2000, Windows XP Home Edition, Windows XP Professional, Windows Server 2003 family

Metafile Constructor (IntPtr, Rectangle)

Initializes a new instance of the **Metafile** class from the specified device context, bounded by the specified rectangle.

```
[Visual Basic]
Public Sub New( _
   ByVal referenceHdc As IntPtr, _
   ByVal frameRect As Rectangle _
)
[C#]
public Metafile(
   IntPtr referenceHdc,
   Rectangle frameRect
);
[C++]
public: Metafile(
   IntPtr referenceHdc,
   Rectangle frameRect
);
[JScript]
public function Metafile(
   referenceHdc : IntPtr,
   frameRect : Rectangle
);
```

Parameters

referenceHdc
The handle to a device context.

frameRect
A **Rectangle** structure that represents the rectangle that bounds the new **Metafile** object.

Requirements

Platforms: Windows 98, Windows NT 4.0, Windows Millennium Edition, Windows 2000, Windows XP Home Edition, Windows XP Professional, Windows Server 2003 family

Metafile Constructor (IntPtr, RectangleF)

Initializes a new instance of the **Metafile** class from the specified device context, bounded by the specified rectangle.

```
[Visual Basic]
Public Sub New( _
   ByVal referenceHdc As IntPtr, _
   ByVal frameRect As RectangleF _
)
[C#]
public Metafile(
   IntPtr referenceHdc,
   RectangleF frameRect
);
[C++]
public: Metafile(
   IntPtr referenceHdc,
   RectangleF frameRect
);
[JScript]
public function Metafile(
   referenceHdc : IntPtr,
   frameRect : RectangleF
);
```

Parameters

referenceHdc
The handle to a device context.

frameRect
A **RectangleF** structure that represents the rectangle that bounds the new **Metafile** object.

Requirements

Platforms: Windows 98, Windows NT 4.0, Windows Millennium Edition, Windows 2000, Windows XP Home Edition, Windows XP Professional, Windows Server 2003 family

Metafile Constructor (IntPtr, WmfPlaceableFileHeader)

Initializes a new instance of the **Metafile** class from the specified handle and a **WmfPlaceableFileHeader** object.

```
[Visual Basic]
Public Sub New( _
   ByVal hmetafile As IntPtr, _
   ByVal wmfHeader As WmfPlaceableFileHeader _
)
[C#]
public Metafile(
   IntPtr hmetafile,
   WmfPlaceableFileHeader wmfHeader
);
[C++]
public: Metafile(
   IntPtr hmetafile,
   WmfPlaceableFileHeader* wmfHeader
);
[JScript]
public function Metafile(
   hmetafile : IntPtr,
   wmfHeader : WmfPlaceableFileHeader
);
```

Parameters

hmetafile
A windows handle to a **Metafile** object.

wmfHeader
A **WmfPlaceableFileHeader** object.

Requirements

Platforms: Windows 98, Windows NT 4.0, Windows Millennium Edition, Windows 2000, Windows XP Home Edition, Windows XP Professional, Windows Server 2003 family

Metafile Constructor (Stream, IntPtr)

Initializes a new instance of the **Metafile** class from the specified data stream.

```
[Visual Basic]
Public Sub New( _
   ByVal stream As Stream, _
   ByVal referenceHdc As IntPtr _
)
[C#]
public Metafile(
   Stream stream,
   IntPtr referenceHdc
);
[C++]
public: Metafile(
   Stream* stream,
   IntPtr referenceHdc
);
[JScript]
public function Metafile(
   stream : Stream,
   referenceHdc : IntPtr
);
```

Parameters

stream
: A **Stream** object that contains the data for this **Metafile** object.

referenceHdc
: A Windows handle to a device context.

Requirements

Platforms: Windows 98, Windows NT 4.0, Windows Millennium Edition, Windows 2000, Windows XP Home Edition, Windows XP Professional, Windows Server 2003 family

Metafile Constructor (String, IntPtr)

Initializes a new instance of the **Metafile** class with the specified file name.

```
[Visual Basic]
Public Sub New( _
   ByVal fileName As String, _
   ByVal referenceHdc As IntPtr _
)
[C#]
public Metafile(
   string fileName,
   IntPtr referenceHdc
);
[C++]
public: Metafile(
   String* fileName,
   IntPtr referenceHdc
);
[JScript]
public function Metafile(
   fileName : String,
   referenceHdc : IntPtr
);
```

Parameters

fileName
: A **String** object that represents the file name of the new **Metafile** object.

referenceHdc
: A Windows handle to a device context.

Requirements

Platforms: Windows 98, Windows NT 4.0, Windows Millennium Edition, Windows 2000, Windows XP Home Edition, Windows XP Professional, Windows Server 2003 family

Metafile Constructor (IntPtr, EmfType, String)

Initializes a new instance of the **Metafile** class from the specified handle to a device context and an **EmfType** enumeration that specifies the format of the **Metafile** object. A string can be supplied to name the file.

```
[Visual Basic]
Public Sub New( _
   ByVal referenceHdc As IntPtr, _
   ByVal emfType As EmfType, _
   ByVal description As String _
)
[C#]
public Metafile(
   IntPtr referenceHdc,
   EmfType emfType,
   string description
);
[C++]
public: Metafile(
   IntPtr referenceHdc,
   EmfType emfType,
   String* description
);
[JScript]
public function Metafile(
   referenceHdc : IntPtr,
   emfType : EmfType,
   description : String
);
```

Parameters

referenceHdc
: The handle to a device context.

emfType
: An **EmfType** enumeration that specifies the format of the **Metafile** object.

description
: A descriptive name for the new **Metafile** object.

Requirements

Platforms: Windows 98, Windows NT 4.0, Windows Millennium Edition, Windows 2000, Windows XP Home Edition, Windows XP Professional, Windows Server 2003 family

Metafile Constructor (IntPtr, Rectangle, MetafileFrameUnit)

Initializes a new instance of the **Metafile** class from the specified device context, bounded by the specified rectangle that uses the supplied units of measure.

```
[Visual Basic]
Public Sub New( _
   ByVal referenceHdc As IntPtr, _
   ByVal frameRect As Rectangle, _
   ByVal frameUnit As MetafileFrameUnit _
)
[C#]
public Metafile(
   IntPtr referenceHdc,
   Rectangle frameRect,
   MetafileFrameUnit frameUnit
);
[C++]
public: Metafile(
   IntPtr referenceHdc,
   Rectangle frameRect,
   MetafileFrameUnit frameUnit
);
[JScript]
public function Metafile(
   referenceHdc : IntPtr,
   frameRect : Rectangle,
   frameUnit : MetafileFrameUnit
);
```

Parameters

referenceHdc
The handle to a device context.

frameRect
A **Rectangle** structure that represents the rectangle that bounds the new **Metafile** object.

frameUnit
A **MetafileFrameUnit** enumeration that specifies the units of measure for *frameRect*.

Requirements

Platforms: Windows 98, Windows NT 4.0, Windows Millennium Edition, Windows 2000, Windows XP Home Edition, Windows XP Professional, Windows Server 2003 family

Metafile Constructor (IntPtr, RectangleF, MetafileFrameUnit)

Initializes a new instance of the **Metafile** class from the specified device context, bounded by the specified rectangle that uses the supplied units of measure.

```
[Visual Basic]
Public Sub New( _
   ByVal referenceHdc As IntPtr, _
   ByVal frameRect As RectangleF, _
   ByVal frameUnit As MetafileFrameUnit _
)
[C#]
public Metafile(
   IntPtr referenceHdc,
   RectangleF frameRect,
   MetafileFrameUnit frameUnit
);
[C++]
public: Metafile(
   IntPtr referenceHdc,
   RectangleF frameRect,
   MetafileFrameUnit frameUnit
);
[JScript]
public function Metafile(
   referenceHdc : IntPtr,
   frameRect : RectangleF,
   frameUnit : MetafileFrameUnit
);
```

Parameters

referenceHdc
The handle to a device context.

frameRect
A **RectangleF** structure that represents the rectangle that bounds the new **Metafile** object.

frameUnit
A **MetafileFrameUnit** enumeration that specifies the units of measure for *frameRect*.

Requirements

Platforms: Windows 98, Windows NT 4.0, Windows Millennium Edition, Windows 2000, Windows XP Home Edition, Windows XP Professional, Windows Server 2003 family

Metafile Constructor (IntPtr, WmfPlaceableFileHeader, Boolean)

Initializes a new instance of the **Metafile** class from the specified handle and a **WmfPlaceableFileHeader** object. Also, *deleteWmf* can be used to delete the handle when the metafile is deleted.

```
[Visual Basic]
Public Sub New( _
   ByVal hmetafile As IntPtr, _
   ByVal wmfHeader As WmfPlaceableFileHeader, _
   ByVal deleteWmf As Boolean _
)
```

[C#]
```
public Metafile(
   IntPtr hmetafile,
   WmfPlaceableFileHeader wmfHeader,
   bool deleteWmf
);
```
[C++]
```
public: Metafile(
   IntPtr hmetafile,
   WmfPlaceableFileHeader* wmfHeader,
   bool deleteWmf
);
```
[JScript]
```
public function Metafile(
   hmetafile : IntPtr,
   wmfHeader : WmfPlaceableFileHeader,
   deleteWmf : Boolean
);
```

Parameters

hmetafile

A windows handle to a **Metafile**.

wmfHeader

A **WmfPlaceableFileHeader** object.

deleteWmf

Set to **true** to delete the handle to the new **Metafile** object when the **Metafile** object is deleted; otherwise, **false**.

Requirements

Platforms: Windows 98, Windows NT 4.0, Windows Millennium Edition, Windows 2000, Windows XP Home Edition, Windows XP Professional, Windows Server 2003 family

Metafile Constructor (Stream, IntPtr, EmfType)

Initializes a new instance of the **Metafile** class from the specified data stream, a Windows handle to a device context, and an **EmfType** enumeration that specifies the format of the **Metafile** object.

[Visual Basic]
```
Public Sub New( _
   ByVal stream As Stream, _
   ByVal referenceHdc As IntPtr, _
   ByVal type As EmfType _
)
```
[C#]
```
public Metafile(
   Stream stream,
   IntPtr referenceHdc,
   EmfType type
);
```
[C++]
```
public: Metafile(
   Stream* stream,
   IntPtr referenceHdc,
   EmfType type
);
```
[JScript]
```
public function Metafile(
   stream : Stream,
   referenceHdc : IntPtr,
   type : EmfType
);
```

Parameters

stream

A **Stream** object that contains the data for this **Metafile** object.

referenceHdc

A Windows handle to a device context.

type

An **EmfType** enumeration that specifies the format of the **Metafile** object.

Requirements

Platforms: Windows 98, Windows NT 4.0, Windows Millennium Edition, Windows 2000, Windows XP Home Edition, Windows XP Professional, Windows Server 2003 family

Metafile Constructor (Stream, IntPtr, Rectangle)

Initializes a new instance of the **Metafile** class from the specified data stream, a Windows handle to a device context, and a **Rectangle** structure that represents the rectangle that bounds the new **Metafile** object.

[Visual Basic]
```
Public Sub New( _
   ByVal stream As Stream, _
   ByVal referenceHdc As IntPtr, _
   ByVal frameRect As Rectangle _
)
```
[C#]
```
public Metafile(
   Stream stream,
   IntPtr referenceHdc,
   Rectangle frameRect
);
```
[C++]
```
public: Metafile(
   Stream* stream,
   IntPtr referenceHdc,
   Rectangle frameRect
);
```
[JScript]
```
public function Metafile(
   stream : Stream,
   referenceHdc : IntPtr,
   frameRect : Rectangle
);
```

Parameters

stream

A **Stream** object that contains the data for this **Metafile** object.

referenceHdc

A Windows handle to a device context.

frameRect

A **Rectangle** structure that represents the rectangle that bounds the new **Metafile**.

Requirements

Platforms: Windows 98, Windows NT 4.0, Windows Millennium Edition, Windows 2000, Windows XP Home Edition, Windows XP Professional, Windows Server 2003 family

Metafile Constructor (Stream, IntPtr, RectangleF)

Initializes a new instance of the **Metafile** class from the specified data stream, a Windows handle to a device context, and a **RectangleF** structure that represents the rectangle that bounds the new **Metafile** object.

```
[Visual Basic]
Public Sub New( _
   ByVal stream As Stream, _
   ByVal referenceHdc As IntPtr, _
   ByVal frameRect As RectangleF _
)
[C#]
public Metafile(
   Stream stream,
   IntPtr referenceHdc,
   RectangleF frameRect
);
[C++]
public: Metafile(
   Stream* stream,
   IntPtr referenceHdc,
   RectangleF frameRect
);
[JScript]
public function Metafile(
   stream : Stream,
   referenceHdc : IntPtr,
   frameRect : RectangleF
);
```

Parameters

stream
: A **Stream** object that contains the data for this **Metafile** object.

referenceHdc
: A Windows handle to a device context.

frameRect
: A **RectangleF** structure that represents the rectangle that bounds the new **Metafile** object.

Requirements

Platforms: Windows 98, Windows NT 4.0, Windows Millennium Edition, Windows 2000, Windows XP Home Edition, Windows XP Professional, Windows Server 2003 family

Metafile Constructor (String, IntPtr, EmfType)

Initializes a new instance of the **Metafile** class with the specified file name, from a Windows handle to a device context, and an **EmfType** enumeration that specifies the format of the **Metafile** object.

```
[Visual Basic]
Public Sub New( _
   ByVal fileName As String, _
   ByVal referenceHdc As IntPtr, _
   ByVal type As EmfType _
)
[C#]
public Metafile(
   string fileName,
   IntPtr referenceHdc,
   EmfType type
);
[C++]
public: Metafile(
   String* fileName,
   IntPtr referenceHdc,
   EmfType type
);
[JScript]
public function Metafile(
   fileName : String,
   referenceHdc : IntPtr,
   type : EmfType
);
```

Parameters

fileName
: A **String** object that represents the file name of the new **Metafile** object.

referenceHdc
: A Windows handle to a device context.

type
: An **EmfType** enumeration that specifies the format of the **Metafile** object.

Requirements

Platforms: Windows 98, Windows NT 4.0, Windows Millennium Edition, Windows 2000, Windows XP Home Edition, Windows XP Professional, Windows Server 2003 family

Metafile Constructor (String, IntPtr, Rectangle)

Initializes a new instance of the **Metafile** class with the specified file name, using a Windows handle to a device context, and a **Rectangle** structure that represents the rectangle that bounds the new **Metafile** object.

```
[Visual Basic]
Public Sub New( _
   ByVal fileName As String, _
   ByVal referenceHdc As IntPtr, _
   ByVal frameRect As Rectangle _
)
[C#]
public Metafile(
   string fileName,
   IntPtr referenceHdc,
   Rectangle frameRect
);
[C++]
public: Metafile(
   String* fileName,
   IntPtr referenceHdc,
   Rectangle frameRect
);
[JScript]
public function Metafile(
   fileName : String,
   referenceHdc : IntPtr,
   frameRect : Rectangle
);
```

Parameters

fileName

A **String** object that represents the file name of the new **Metafile** object.

referenceHdc

A Windows handle to a device context.

frameRect

A **Rectangle** structure that represents the rectangle that bounds the new **Metafile** object.

Requirements

Platforms: Windows 98, Windows NT 4.0, Windows Millennium Edition, Windows 2000, Windows XP Home Edition, Windows XP Professional, Windows Server 2003 family

Metafile Constructor (String, IntPtr, RectangleF)

Initializes a new instance of the **Metafile** class with the specified file name, using a Windows handle to a device context, and A **RectangleF** structure that represents the rectangle that bounds the new **Metafile** object.

```
[Visual Basic]
Public Sub New( _
   ByVal fileName As String, _
   ByVal referenceHdc As IntPtr, _
   ByVal frameRect As RectangleF _
)
[C#]
public Metafile(
   string fileName,
   IntPtr referenceHdc,
   RectangleF frameRect
);
[C++]
public: Metafile(
   String* fileName,
   IntPtr referenceHdc,
   RectangleF frameRect
);
[JScript]
public function Metafile(
   fileName : String,
   referenceHdc : IntPtr,
   frameRect : RectangleF
);
```

Parameters

fileName

A **String** object that represents the file name of the new **Metafile** object.

referenceHdc

A Windows handle to a device context.

frameRect

A **RectangleF** structure that represents the rectangle that bounds the new **Metafile** object.

Requirements

Platforms: Windows 98, Windows NT 4.0, Windows Millennium Edition, Windows 2000, Windows XP Home Edition, Windows XP Professional, Windows Server 2003 family

Metafile Constructor (IntPtr, Rectangle, MetafileFrameUnit, EmfType)

Initializes a new instance of the **Metafile** class from the specified device context, bounded by the specified rectangle that uses the supplied units of measure, and an **EmfType** enumeration that specifies the format of the **Metafile** object.

```
[Visual Basic]
Public Sub New( _
   ByVal referenceHdc As IntPtr, _
   ByVal frameRect As Rectangle, _
   ByVal frameUnit As MetafileFrameUnit, _
   ByVal type As EmfType _
)
[C#]
public Metafile(
   IntPtr referenceHdc,
   Rectangle frameRect,
   MetafileFrameUnit frameUnit,
   EmfType type
);
[C++]
public: Metafile(
   IntPtr referenceHdc,
   Rectangle frameRect,
   MetafileFrameUnit frameUnit,
   EmfType type
);
[JScript]
public function Metafile(
   referenceHdc : IntPtr,
   frameRect : Rectangle,
   frameUnit : MetafileFrameUnit,
   type : EmfType
);
```

Parameters

referenceHdc

The handle to a device context.

frameRect

A **Rectangle** structure that represents the rectangle that bounds the new **Metafile** object.

frameUnit

A **MetafileFrameUnit** enumeration that specifies the units of measure for *frameRect*.

type

An **EmfType** enumeration that specifies the format of the **Metafile** object.

Requirements

Platforms: Windows 98, Windows NT 4.0, Windows Millennium Edition, Windows 2000, Windows XP Home Edition, Windows XP Professional, Windows Server 2003 family

Metafile Constructor (IntPtr, RectangleF, MetafileFrameUnit, EmfType)

Initializes a new instance of the **Metafile** class from the specified device context, bounded by the specified rectangle that uses the supplied units of measure, and an **EmfType** enumeration that specifies the format of the **Metafile** object.

[Visual Basic]
```
Public Sub New( _
   ByVal referenceHdc As IntPtr, _
   ByVal frameRect As RectangleF, _
   ByVal frameUnit As MetafileFrameUnit, _
   ByVal type As EmfType _
)
```
[C#]
```
public Metafile(
   IntPtr referenceHdc,
   RectangleF frameRect,
   MetafileFrameUnit frameUnit,
   EmfType type
);
```
[C++]
```
public: Metafile(
   IntPtr referenceHdc,
   RectangleF frameRect,
   MetafileFrameUnit frameUnit,
   EmfType type
);
```
[JScript]
```
public function Metafile(
   referenceHdc : IntPtr,
   frameRect : RectangleF,
   frameUnit : MetafileFrameUnit,
   type : EmfType
);
```

Parameters

referenceHdc
  The handle to a device context.

frameRect
  A **RectangleF** structure that represents the rectangle that bounds the new **Metafile** object.

frameUnit
  A **MetafileFrameUnit** enumeration that specifies the units of measure for *frameRect*.

type
  An **EmfType** enumeration that specifies the format of the **Metafile** object.

Requirements

Platforms: Windows 98, Windows NT 4.0, Windows Millennium Edition, Windows 2000, Windows XP Home Edition, Windows XP Professional, Windows Server 2003 family

Metafile Constructor (Stream, IntPtr, EmfType, String)

Initializes a new instance of the **Metafile** class from the specified data stream, a Windows handle to a device context, and an **EmfType** enumeration that specifies the format of the **Metafile** object. Also, a string that contains a descriptive name for the new **Metafile** object can be added.

[Visual Basic]
```
Public Sub New( _
   ByVal stream As Stream, _
   ByVal referenceHdc As IntPtr, _
   ByVal type As EmfType, _
   ByVal description As String _
)
```
[C#]
```
public Metafile(
   Stream stream,
   IntPtr referenceHdc,
   EmfType type,
   string description
);
```
[C++]
```
public: Metafile(
   Stream* stream,
   IntPtr referenceHdc,
   EmfType type,
   String* description
);
```
[JScript]
```
public function Metafile(
   stream : Stream,
   referenceHdc : IntPtr,
   type : EmfType,
   description : String
);
```

Parameters

stream
  A **Stream** object that contains the data for this **Metafile** object.

referenceHdc
  A Windows handle to a device context.

type
  An **EmfType** enumeration that specifies the format of the **Metafile** object.

description
  A **String** object that contains a descriptive name for the new **Metafile** object.

Requirements

Platforms: Windows 98, Windows NT 4.0, Windows Millennium Edition, Windows 2000, Windows XP Home Edition, Windows XP Professional, Windows Server 2003 family

Metafile Constructor (Stream, IntPtr, Rectangle, MetafileFrameUnit)

Initializes a new instance of the **Metafile** class from the specified data stream, a Windows handle to a device context, and a **Rectangle** structure that represents the rectangle that bounds the new **Metafile** object, and the supplied units of measure.

```
[Visual Basic]
Public Sub New( _
   ByVal stream As Stream, _
   ByVal referenceHdc As IntPtr, _
   ByVal frameRect As Rectangle, _
   ByVal frameUnit As MetafileFrameUnit _
)
[C#]
public Metafile(
   Stream stream,
   IntPtr referenceHdc,
   Rectangle frameRect,
   MetafileFrameUnit frameUnit
);
[C++]
public: Metafile(
   Stream* stream,
   IntPtr referenceHdc,
   Rectangle frameRect,
   MetafileFrameUnit frameUnit
);
[JScript]
public function Metafile(
   stream : Stream,
   referenceHdc : IntPtr,
   frameRect : Rectangle,
   frameUnit : MetafileFrameUnit
);
```

Parameters

stream
A **Stream** object that contains the data for this **Metafile** object.

referenceHdc
A Windows handle to a device context.

frameRect
A **Rectangle** structure that represents the rectangle that bounds the new **Metafile** object.

frameUnit
A **MetafileFrameUnit** enumeration that specifies the units of measure for *frameRect*.

Requirements

Platforms: Windows 98, Windows NT 4.0, Windows Millennium Edition, Windows 2000, Windows XP Home Edition, Windows XP Professional, Windows Server 2003 family

Metafile Constructor (Stream, IntPtr, RectangleF, MetafileFrameUnit)

Initializes a new instance of the **Metafile** class from the specified data stream, a Windows handle to a device context, and a **RectangleF** structure that represents the rectangle that bounds the new **Metafile** object, and the supplied units of measure.

```
[Visual Basic]
Public Sub New( _
   ByVal stream As Stream, _
   ByVal referenceHdc As IntPtr, _
   ByVal frameRect As RectangleF, _
   ByVal frameUnit As MetafileFrameUnit _
)
[C#]
public Metafile(
   Stream stream,
   IntPtr referenceHdc,
   RectangleF frameRect,
   MetafileFrameUnit frameUnit
);
[C++]
public: Metafile(
   Stream* stream,
   IntPtr referenceHdc,
   RectangleF frameRect,
   MetafileFrameUnit frameUnit
);
[JScript]
public function Metafile(
   stream : Stream,
   referenceHdc : IntPtr,
   frameRect : RectangleF,
   frameUnit : MetafileFrameUnit
);
```

Parameters

stream
A **Stream** object that contains the data for this **Metafile** object.

referenceHdc
A Windows handle to a device context.

frameRect
A **RectangleF** structure that represents the rectangle that bounds the new **Metafile** object.

frameUnit
A **MetafileFrameUnit** enumeration that specifies the units of measure for *frameRect*.

Requirements

Platforms: Windows 98, Windows NT 4.0, Windows Millennium Edition, Windows 2000, Windows XP Home Edition, Windows XP Professional, Windows Server 2003 family

Metafile Constructor (String, IntPtr, EmfType, String)

Initializes a new instance of the **Metafile** class with the specified file name, from a Windows handle to a device context, and an **EmfType** enumeration that specifies the format of the **Metafile** object. A descriptive string can be added as well.

[Visual Basic]
```
Public Sub New( _
   ByVal fileName As String, _
   ByVal referenceHdc As IntPtr, _
   ByVal type As EmfType, _
   ByVal description As String _
)
```
[C#]
```
public Metafile(
   string fileName,
   IntPtr referenceHdc,
   EmfType type,
   string description
);
```
[C++]
```
public: Metafile(
   String* fileName,
   IntPtr referenceHdc,
   EmfType type,
   String* description
);
```
[JScript]
```
public function Metafile(
   fileName : String,
   referenceHdc : IntPtr,
   type : EmfType,
   description : String
);
```

Parameters

fileName
: A **String** object that represents the file name of the new **Metafile** object.

referenceHdc
: A Windows handle to a device context.

type
: An **EmfType** enumeration that specifies the format of the **Metafile** object.

description
: A **String** object that contains a descriptive name for the new **Metafile** object.

Requirements

Platforms: Windows 98, Windows NT 4.0, Windows Millennium Edition, Windows 2000, Windows XP Home Edition, Windows XP Professional, Windows Server 2003 family

Metafile Constructor (String, IntPtr, Rectangle, MetafileFrameUnit)

Initializes a new instance of the **Metafile** class with the specified file name, using a Windows handle to a device context, a **Rectangle** structure that represents the rectangle that bounds the new **Metafile** object, and the supplied units of measure.

[Visual Basic]
```
Public Sub New( _
   ByVal fileName As String, _
   ByVal referenceHdc As IntPtr, _
   ByVal frameRect As Rectangle, _
   ByVal frameUnit As MetafileFrameUnit _
)
```
[C#]
```
public Metafile(
   string fileName,
   IntPtr referenceHdc,
   Rectangle frameRect,
   MetafileFrameUnit frameUnit
);
```
[C++]
```
public: Metafile(
   String* fileName,
   IntPtr referenceHdc,
   Rectangle frameRect,
   MetafileFrameUnit frameUnit
);
```
[JScript]
```
public function Metafile(
   fileName : String,
   referenceHdc : IntPtr,
   frameRect : Rectangle,
   frameUnit : MetafileFrameUnit
);
```

Parameters

fileName
: A **String** object that represents the file name of the new **Metafile** object.

referenceHdc
: A Windows handle to a device context.

frameRect
: A **Rectangle** structure that represents the rectangle that bounds the new **Metafile** object.

frameUnit
: A **MetafileFrameUnit** enumeration that specifies the units of measure for *frameRect*.

Requirements

Platforms: Windows 98, Windows NT 4.0, Windows Millennium Edition, Windows 2000, Windows XP Home Edition, Windows XP Professional, Windows Server 2003 family

Metafile Constructor (String, IntPtr, RectangleF, MetafileFrameUnit)

Initializes a new instance of the **Metafile** class with the specified file name, using a Windows handle to a device context, a **RectangleF** structure that represents the rectangle that bounds the new **Metafile** object, and the supplied units of measure.

[Visual Basic]
```
Public Sub New( _
   ByVal fileName As String, _
   ByVal referenceHdc As IntPtr, _
   ByVal frameRect As RectangleF, _
   ByVal frameUnit As MetafileFrameUnit _
)
```
[C#]
```
public Metafile(
   string fileName,
   IntPtr referenceHdc,
   RectangleF frameRect,
   MetafileFrameUnit frameUnit
);
```
[C++]
```
public: Metafile(
   String* fileName,
   IntPtr referenceHdc,
   RectangleF frameRect,
   MetafileFrameUnit frameUnit
);
```
[JScript]
```
public function Metafile(
   fileName : String,
   referenceHdc : IntPtr,
   frameRect : RectangleF,
   frameUnit : MetafileFrameUnit
);
```

Parameters

fileName

A **String** object that represents the file name of the new **Metafile** object.

referenceHdc

A Windows handle to a device context.

frameRect

A **RectangleF** structure that represents the rectangle that bounds the new **Metafile** object.

frameUnit

A **MetafileFrameUnit** enumeration that specifies the units of measure for *frameRect*.

Requirements

Platforms: Windows 98, Windows NT 4.0, Windows Millennium Edition, Windows 2000, Windows XP Home Edition, Windows XP Professional, Windows Server 2003 family

Metafile Constructor (IntPtr, Rectangle, MetafileFrameUnit, EmfType, String)

Initializes a new instance of the **Metafile** class from the specified device context, bounded by the specified rectangle that uses the supplied units of measure, and an **EmfType** enumeration that specifies the format of the **Metafile** object. A string can be provided to name the file.

[Visual Basic]
```
Public Sub New( _
   ByVal referenceHdc As IntPtr, _
   ByVal frameRect As Rectangle, _
   ByVal frameUnit As MetafileFrameUnit, _
   ByVal type As EmfType, _
   ByVal desc As String _
)
```
[C#]
```
public Metafile(
   IntPtr referenceHdc,
   Rectangle frameRect,
   MetafileFrameUnit frameUnit,
   EmfType type,
   string desc
);
```
[C++]
```
public: Metafile(
   IntPtr referenceHdc,
   Rectangle frameRect,
   MetafileFrameUnit frameUnit,
   EmfType type,
   String* desc
);
```
[JScript]
```
public function Metafile(
   referenceHdc : IntPtr,
   frameRect : Rectangle,
   frameUnit : MetafileFrameUnit,
   type : EmfType,
   desc : String
);
```

Parameters

referenceHdc

The handle to a device context.

frameRect

A **Rectangle** structure that represents the rectangle that bounds the new **Metafile** object.

frameUnit

A **MetafileFrameUnit** enumeration that specifies the units of measure for *frameRect*.

type

An **EmfType** enumeration that specifies the format of the **Metafile** object.

desc

A **String** object that contains a descriptive name for the new **Metafile** object.

Requirements

Platforms: Windows 98, Windows NT 4.0, Windows Millennium Edition, Windows 2000, Windows XP Home Edition, Windows XP Professional, Windows Server 2003 family

Metafile Constructor (IntPtr, RectangleF, MetafileFrameUnit, EmfType, String)

Initializes a new instance of the **Metafile** class from the specified device context, bounded by the specified rectangle that uses the supplied units of measure, and an **EmfType** enumeration that specifies the format of the **Metafile** object. A string can be provided to name the file.

[Visual Basic]
```
Public Sub New( _
   ByVal referenceHdc As IntPtr, _
   ByVal frameRect As RectangleF, _
   ByVal frameUnit As MetafileFrameUnit, _
   ByVal type As EmfType, _
   ByVal description As String _
)
```
[C#]
```
public Metafile(
   IntPtr referenceHdc,
   RectangleF frameRect,
   MetafileFrameUnit frameUnit,
   EmfType type,
   string description
);
```
[C++]
```
public: Metafile(
   IntPtr referenceHdc,
   RectangleF frameRect,
   MetafileFrameUnit frameUnit,
   EmfType type,
   String* description
);
```
[JScript]
```
public function Metafile(
   referenceHdc : IntPtr,
   frameRect : RectangleF,
   frameUnit : MetafileFrameUnit,
   type : EmfType,
   description : String
);
```

Parameters

referenceHdc
The handle to a device context.

frameRect
A **RectangleF** structure that represents the rectangle that bounds the new **Metafile** object.

frameUnit
A **MetafileFrameUnit** enumeration that specifies the units of measure for *frameRect*.

type
An **EmfType** enumeration that specifies the format of the **Metafile** object.

description
A **String** object that contains a descriptive name for the new **Metafile** object.

Requirements

Platforms: Windows 98, Windows NT 4.0, Windows Millennium Edition, Windows 2000, Windows XP Home Edition, Windows XP Professional, Windows Server 2003 family

Metafile Constructor (Stream, IntPtr, Rectangle, MetafileFrameUnit, EmfType)

Initializes a new instance of the **Metafile** class from the specified data stream, a Windows handle to a device context, a **Rectangle** structure that represents the rectangle that bounds the new **Metafile** object, the supplied units of measure, and an **EmfType** enumeration that specifies the format of the **Metafile** object.

[Visual Basic]
```
Public Sub New( _
   ByVal stream As Stream, _
   ByVal referenceHdc As IntPtr, _
   ByVal frameRect As Rectangle, _
   ByVal frameUnit As MetafileFrameUnit, _
   ByVal type As EmfType _
)
```
[C#]
```
public Metafile(
   Stream stream,
   IntPtr referenceHdc,
   Rectangle frameRect,
   MetafileFrameUnit frameUnit,
   EmfType type
);
```
[C++]
```
public: Metafile(
   Stream* stream,
   IntPtr referenceHdc,
   Rectangle frameRect,
   MetafileFrameUnit frameUnit,
   EmfType type
);
```
[JScript]
```
public function Metafile(
   stream : Stream,
   referenceHdc : IntPtr,
   frameRect : Rectangle,
   frameUnit : MetafileFrameUnit,
   type : EmfType
);
```

Parameters

stream
A **Stream** object that contains the data for this **Metafile** object.

referenceHdc
A Windows handle to a device context.

frameRect
A **Rectangle** structure that represents the rectangle that bounds the new **Metafile** object.

frameUnit
A **MetafileFrameUnit** enumeration that specifies the units of measure for *frameRect*.

type
An **EmfType** enumeration that specifies the format of the **Metafile** object.

Requirements

Platforms: Windows 98, Windows NT 4.0, Windows Millennium Edition, Windows 2000, Windows XP Home Edition, Windows XP Professional, Windows Server 2003 family

Metafile Constructor (Stream, IntPtr, RectangleF, MetafileFrameUnit, EmfType)

Initializes a new instance of the **Metafile** class from the specified data stream, a Windows handle to a device context, a **RectangleF** structure that represents the rectangle that bounds the new **Metafile** object, the supplied units of measure, and an **EmfType** enumeration that specifies the format of the **Metafile** object.

[Visual Basic]
```
Public Sub New( _
   ByVal stream As Stream, _
   ByVal referenceHdc As IntPtr, _
   ByVal frameRect As RectangleF, _
   ByVal frameUnit As MetafileFrameUnit, _
   ByVal type As EmfType _
)
```
[C#]
```
public Metafile(
   Stream stream,
   IntPtr referenceHdc,
   RectangleF frameRect,
   MetafileFrameUnit frameUnit,
   EmfType type
);
```
[C++]
```
public: Metafile(
   Stream* stream,
   IntPtr referenceHdc,
   RectangleF frameRect,
   MetafileFrameUnit frameUnit,
   EmfType type
);
```
[JScript]
```
public function Metafile(
   stream : Stream,
   referenceHdc : IntPtr,
   frameRect : RectangleF,
   frameUnit : MetafileFrameUnit,
   type : EmfType
);
```

Parameters

stream
  A **Stream** object that contains the data for this **Metafile** object.

referenceHdc
  A Windows handle to a device context.

frameRect
  A **RectangleF** structure that represents the rectangle that bounds the new **Metafile** object.

frameUnit
  A **MetafileFrameUnit** enumeration that specifies the units of measure for *frameRect*.

type
  An **EmfType** enumeration that specifies the format of the **Metafile** object.

Requirements

Platforms: Windows 98, Windows NT 4.0, Windows Millennium Edition, Windows 2000, Windows XP Home Edition, Windows XP Professional, Windows Server 2003 family

Metafile Constructor (String, IntPtr, Rectangle, MetafileFrameUnit, EmfType)

Initializes a new instance of the **Metafile** class with the specified file name, using a Windows handle to a device context, a **Rectangle** structure that represents the rectangle that bounds the new **Metafile** object, the supplied units of measure, and an **EmfType** enumeration that specifies the format of the **Metafile** object.

[Visual Basic]
```
Public Sub New( _
   ByVal fileName As String, _
   ByVal referenceHdc As IntPtr, _
   ByVal frameRect As Rectangle, _
   ByVal frameUnit As MetafileFrameUnit, _
   ByVal type As EmfType _
)
```
[C#]
```
public Metafile(
   string fileName,
   IntPtr referenceHdc,
   Rectangle frameRect,
   MetafileFrameUnit frameUnit,
   EmfType type
);
```
[C++]
```
public: Metafile(
   String* fileName,
   IntPtr referenceHdc,
   Rectangle frameRect,
   MetafileFrameUnit frameUnit,
   EmfType type
);
```
[JScript]
```
public function Metafile(
   fileName : String,
   referenceHdc : IntPtr,
   frameRect : Rectangle,
   frameUnit : MetafileFrameUnit,
   type : EmfType
);
```

Parameters

fileName
  A **String** object that represents the file name of the new **Metafile** object.

referenceHdc
  A Windows handle to a device context.

frameRect
  A **Rectangle** structure that represents the rectangle that bounds the new **Metafile** object.

frameUnit
  A **MetafileFrameUnit** enumeration that specifies the units of measure for *frameRect*.

type
  An **EmfType** enumeration that specifies the format of the **Metafile** object.

Requirements

Platforms: Windows 98, Windows NT 4.0, Windows Millennium Edition, Windows 2000, Windows XP Home Edition, Windows XP Professional, Windows Server 2003 family

Metafile Constructor (String, IntPtr, Rectangle, MetafileFrameUnit, String)

Initializes a new instance of the **Metafile** class with the specified file name, using a Windows handle to a device context, a **Rectangle** structure that represents the rectangle that bounds the new **Metafile** object, and the supplied units of measure. A descriptive string can also be added.

[Visual Basic]
```
Public Sub New( _
   ByVal fileName As String, _
   ByVal referenceHdc As IntPtr, _
   ByVal frameRect As Rectangle, _
   ByVal frameUnit As MetafileFrameUnit, _
   ByVal description As String _
)
```
[C#]
```
public Metafile(
   string fileName,
   IntPtr referenceHdc,
   Rectangle frameRect,
   MetafileFrameUnit frameUnit,
   string description
);
```
[C++]
```
public: Metafile(
   String* fileName,
   IntPtr referenceHdc,
   Rectangle frameRect,
   MetafileFrameUnit frameUnit,
   String* description
);
```
[JScript]
```
public function Metafile(
   fileName : String,
   referenceHdc : IntPtr,
   frameRect : Rectangle,
   frameUnit : MetafileFrameUnit,
   description : String
);
```

Parameters

fileName
: A **String** object that represents the file name of the new **Metafile** object.

referenceHdc
: A Windows handle to a device context.

frameRect
: A **Rectangle** structure that represents the rectangle that bounds the new **Metafile** object.

frameUnit
: A **MetafileFrameUnit** enumeration that specifies the units of measure for *frameRect*.

description
: A **String** object that contains a descriptive name for the new **Metafile** object.

Requirements

Platforms: Windows 98, Windows NT 4.0, Windows Millennium Edition, Windows 2000, Windows XP Home Edition, Windows XP Professional, Windows Server 2003 family

Metafile Constructor (String, IntPtr, RectangleF, MetafileFrameUnit, EmfType)

Initializes a new instance of the **Metafile** class with the specified file name, using a Windows handle to a device context, a **RectangleF** structure that represents the rectangle that bounds the new **Metafile** object, the supplied units of measure, and an **EmfType** enumeration that specifies the format of the **Metafile** object.

[Visual Basic]
```
Public Sub New( _
   ByVal fileName As String, _
   ByVal referenceHdc As IntPtr, _
   ByVal frameRect As RectangleF, _
   ByVal frameUnit As MetafileFrameUnit, _
   ByVal type As EmfType _
)
```
[C#]
```
public Metafile(
   string fileName,
   IntPtr referenceHdc,
   RectangleF frameRect,
   MetafileFrameUnit frameUnit,
   EmfType type
);
```
[C++]
```
public: Metafile(
   String* fileName,
   IntPtr referenceHdc,
   RectangleF frameRect,
   MetafileFrameUnit frameUnit,
   EmfType type
);
```
[JScript]
```
public function Metafile(
   fileName : String,
   referenceHdc : IntPtr,
   frameRect : RectangleF,
   frameUnit : MetafileFrameUnit,
   type : EmfType
);
```

Parameters

fileName
: A **String** object that represents the file name of the new **Metafile** object.

referenceHdc
: A Windows handle to a device context.

frameRect
: A **RectangleF** structure that represents the rectangle that bounds the new **Metafile** object.

frameUnit
: A **MetafileFrameUnit** enumeration that specifies the units of measure for *frameRect*.

type
: An **EmfType** enumeration that specifies the format of the **Metafile** object.

Requirements

Platforms: Windows 98, Windows NT 4.0, Windows Millennium Edition, Windows 2000, Windows XP Home Edition, Windows XP Professional, Windows Server 2003 family

Metafile Constructor (String, IntPtr, RectangleF, MetafileFrameUnit, String)

Initializes a new instance of the **Metafile** class with the specified file name, using a Windows handle to a device context, a **RectangleF** structure that represents the rectangle that bounds the new **Metafile** object, and the supplied units of measure. A descriptive string can also be added.

[Visual Basic]
```
Public Sub New( _
   ByVal fileName As String, _
   ByVal referenceHdc As IntPtr, _
   ByVal frameRect As RectangleF, _
   ByVal frameUnit As MetafileFrameUnit, _
   ByVal desc As String _
)
```
[C#]
```
public Metafile(
   string fileName,
   IntPtr referenceHdc,
   RectangleF frameRect,
   MetafileFrameUnit frameUnit,
   string desc
);
```
[C++]
```
public: Metafile(
   String* fileName,
   IntPtr referenceHdc,
   RectangleF frameRect,
   MetafileFrameUnit frameUnit,
   String* desc
);
```
[JScript]
```
public function Metafile(
   fileName : String,
   referenceHdc : IntPtr,
   frameRect : RectangleF,
   frameUnit : MetafileFrameUnit,
   desc : String
);
```

Parameters

fileName
   A **String** object that represents the file name of the new **Metafile** object.

referenceHdc
   A Windows handle to a device context.

frameRect
   A **RectangleF** structure that represents the rectangle that bounds the new **Metafile** object.

frameUnit
   A **MetafileFrameUnit** enumeration that specifies the units of measure for *frameRect*.

desc
   A **String** object that contains a descriptive name for the new **Metafile** object.

Requirements

Platforms: Windows 98, Windows NT 4.0, Windows Millennium Edition, Windows 2000, Windows XP Home Edition, Windows XP Professional, Windows Server 2003 family

Metafile Constructor (Stream, IntPtr, Rectangle, MetafileFrameUnit, EmfType, String)

Initializes a new instance of the **Metafile** class from the specified data stream, a Windows handle to a device context, a **Rectangle** structure that represents the rectangle that bounds the new **Metafile** object, the supplied units of measure, and an **EmfType** enumeration that specifies the format of the **Metafile** object. A string that contains a descriptive name for the new **Metafile** object can be added.

[Visual Basic]
```
Public Sub New( _
   ByVal stream As Stream, _
   ByVal referenceHdc As IntPtr, _
   ByVal frameRect As Rectangle, _
   ByVal frameUnit As MetafileFrameUnit, _
   ByVal type As EmfType, _
   ByVal description As String _
)
```
[C#]
```
public Metafile(
   Stream stream,
   IntPtr referenceHdc,
   Rectangle frameRect,
   MetafileFrameUnit frameUnit,
   EmfType type,
   string description
);
```
[C++]
```
public: Metafile(
   Stream* stream,
   IntPtr referenceHdc,
   Rectangle frameRect,
   MetafileFrameUnit frameUnit,
   EmfType type,
   String* description
);
```
[JScript]
```
public function Metafile(
   stream : Stream,
   referenceHdc : IntPtr,
   frameRect : Rectangle,
   frameUnit : MetafileFrameUnit,
   type : EmfType,
   description : String
);
```

Parameters

stream
   A **Stream** object that contains the data for this **Metafile** object.

referenceHdc
   A Windows handle to a device context.

frameRect
   A **Rectangle** structure that represents the rectangle that bounds the new **Metafile** object.

frameUnit
   A **MetafileFrameUnit** enumeration that specifies the units of measure for *frameRect*.

type
   An **EmfType** enumeration that specifies the format of the **Metafile** object.

description
   A **String** object that contains a descriptive name for the new **Metafile** object.

Requirements

Platforms: Windows 98, Windows NT 4.0, Windows Millennium Edition, Windows 2000, Windows XP Home Edition, Windows XP Professional, Windows Server 2003 family

Metafile Constructor (Stream, IntPtr, RectangleF, MetafileFrameUnit, EmfType, String)

Initializes a new instance of the **Metafile** class from the specified data stream, a Windows handle to a device context, a **RectangleF** structure that represents the rectangle that bounds the new **Metafile** object, the supplied units of measure, and an **EmfType** enumeration that specifies the format of the **Metafile** object. A string that contains a descriptive name for the new **Metafile** object can be added.

```
[Visual Basic]
Public Sub New( _
   ByVal stream As Stream, _
   ByVal referenceHdc As IntPtr, _
   ByVal frameRect As RectangleF, _
   ByVal frameUnit As MetafileFrameUnit, _
   ByVal type As EmfType, _
   ByVal description As String _
)
[C#]
public Metafile(
   Stream stream,
   IntPtr referenceHdc,
   RectangleF frameRect,
   MetafileFrameUnit frameUnit,
   EmfType type,
   string description
);
[C++]
public: Metafile(
   Stream* stream,
   IntPtr referenceHdc,
   RectangleF frameRect,
   MetafileFrameUnit frameUnit,
   EmfType type,
   String* description
);
[JScript]
public function Metafile(
   stream : Stream,
   referenceHdc : IntPtr,
   frameRect : RectangleF,
   frameUnit : MetafileFrameUnit,
   type : EmfType,
   description : String
);
```

Parameters

stream
: A **Stream** object that contains the data for this **Metafile** object.

referenceHdc
: A Windows handle to a device context.

frameRect
: A **RectangleF** structure that represents the rectangle that bounds the new **Metafile** object.

frameUnit
: A **MetafileFrameUnit** enumeration that specifies the units of measure for *frameRect*.

type
: An **EmfType** enumeration that specifies the format of the **Metafile** object.

description
: A **String** object that contains a descriptive name for the new **Metafile** object.

Requirements

Platforms: Windows 98, Windows NT 4.0, Windows Millennium Edition, Windows 2000, Windows XP Home Edition, Windows XP Professional, Windows Server 2003 family

Metafile Constructor (String, IntPtr, Rectangle, MetafileFrameUnit, EmfType, String)

Initializes a new instance of the **Metafile** class with the specified file name, using a Windows handle to a device context, a **Rectangle** structure that represents the rectangle that bounds the new **Metafile** object, the supplied units of measure, and an **EmfType** enumeration that specifies the format of the **Metafile** object. A descriptive string can also be added.

```
[Visual Basic]
Public Sub New( _
   ByVal fileName As String, _
   ByVal referenceHdc As IntPtr, _
   ByVal frameRect As Rectangle, _
   ByVal frameUnit As MetafileFrameUnit, _
   ByVal type As EmfType, _
   ByVal description As String _
)
[C#]
public Metafile(
   string fileName,
   IntPtr referenceHdc,
   Rectangle frameRect,
   MetafileFrameUnit frameUnit,
   EmfType type,
   string description
);
[C++]
public: Metafile(
   String* fileName,
   IntPtr referenceHdc,
   Rectangle frameRect,
   MetafileFrameUnit frameUnit,
   EmfType type,
   String* description
);
[JScript]
public function Metafile(
   fileName : String,
   referenceHdc : IntPtr,
   frameRect : Rectangle,
   frameUnit : MetafileFrameUnit,
   type : EmfType,
   description : String
);
```

Parameters

fileName
A **String** object that represents the file name of the new **Metafile** object.

referenceHdc
A Windows handle to a device context.

frameRect
A **Rectangle** structure that represents the rectangle that bounds the new **Metafile** object.

frameUnit
A **MetafileFrameUnit** enumeration that specifies the units of measure for *frameRect*.

type
An **EmfType** enumeration that specifies the format of the **Metafile** object.

description
A **String** object that contains a descriptive name for the new **Metafile** object.

Requirements

Platforms: Windows 98, Windows NT 4.0, Windows Millennium Edition, Windows 2000, Windows XP Home Edition, Windows XP Professional, Windows Server 2003 family

Metafile Constructor (String, IntPtr, RectangleF, MetafileFrameUnit, EmfType, String)

Initializes a new instance of the **Metafile** class with the specified file name, using a Windows handle to a device context, a **RectangleF** structure that represents the rectangle that bounds the new **Metafile** object, the supplied units of measure, and an **EmfType** enumeration that specifies the format of the **Metafile** object. A descriptive string can also be added.

```
[Visual Basic]
Public Sub New( _
   ByVal fileName As String, _
   ByVal referenceHdc As IntPtr, _
   ByVal frameRect As RectangleF, _
   ByVal frameUnit As MetafileFrameUnit, _
   ByVal type As EmfType, _
   ByVal description As String _
)
[C#]
public Metafile(
   string fileName,
   IntPtr referenceHdc,
   RectangleF frameRect,
   MetafileFrameUnit frameUnit,
   EmfType type,
   string description
);
[C++]
public: Metafile(
   String* fileName,
   IntPtr referenceHdc,
   RectangleF frameRect,
   MetafileFrameUnit frameUnit,
   EmfType type,
   String* description
);
[JScript]
public function Metafile(
   fileName : String,
   referenceHdc : IntPtr,
   frameRect : RectangleF,
   frameUnit : MetafileFrameUnit,
   type : EmfType,
   description : String
);
```

Parameters

fileName
A **String** that represents the file name of the new **Metafile** object.

referenceHdc
A Windows handle to a device context.

frameRect
A **RectangleF** structure that represents the rectangle that bounds the new **Metafile** object.

frameUnit
A **MetafileFrameUnit** enumeration that specifies the units of measure for *frameRect*.

type
An **EmfType** enumeration that specifies the format of the **Metafile** object.

description
A **String** object that contains a descriptive name for the new **Metafile** object.

Requirements

Platforms: Windows 98, Windows NT 4.0, Windows Millennium Edition, Windows 2000, Windows XP Home Edition, Windows XP Professional, Windows Server 2003 family

Metafile.GetHenhmetafile Method

Returns a Windows handle to an enhanced **Metafile** object.

```
[Visual Basic]
Public Function GetHenhmetafile() As IntPtr
[C#]
public IntPtr GetHenhmetafile();
[C++]
public: IntPtr GetHenhmetafile();
[JScript]
public function GetHenhmetafile() : IntPtr;
```

Return Value

A Windows handle to this enhanced **Metafile** object.

Requirements

Platforms: Windows 98, Windows NT 4.0, Windows Millennium Edition, Windows 2000, Windows XP Home Edition, Windows XP Professional, Windows Server 2003 family

Metafile.GetMetafileHeader Method

Returns the **MetafileHeader** object associated with this **Metafile** object.

Overload List

Returns the **MetafileHeader** object associated with this **Metafile** object.

[Visual Basic] **Overloads Public Function GetMetafileHeader() As MetafileHeader**

[C#] **public MetafileHeader GetMetafileHeader();**

[C++] **public: MetafileHeader* GetMetafileHeader();**

[JScript] **public function GetMetafileHeader() : MetafileHeader;**

Returns the **MetafileHeader** object associated with the specified **Metafile** object.

[Visual Basic] **Overloads Public Shared Function GetMetafileHeader(IntPtr) As MetafileHeader**

[C#] **public static MetafileHeader GetMetafileHeader(IntPtr);**

[C++] **public: static MetafileHeader* GetMetafileHeader(IntPtr);**

[JScript] **public static function GetMetafileHeader(IntPtr) : MetafileHeader;**

Returns the **MetafileHeader** object associated with the specified **Metafile** object.

[Visual Basic] **Overloads Public Shared Function GetMetafileHeader(Stream) As MetafileHeader**

[C#] **public static MetafileHeader GetMetafileHeader(Stream);**

[C++] **public: static MetafileHeader* GetMetafileHeader(Stream*);**

[JScript] **public static function GetMetafileHeader(Stream) : MetafileHeader;**

Returns the **MetafileHeader** object associated with the specified **Metafile** object.

[Visual Basic] **Overloads Public Shared Function GetMetafileHeader(String) As MetafileHeader**

[C#] **public static MetafileHeader GetMetafileHeader(string);**

[C++] **public: static MetafileHeader* GetMetafileHeader(String*);**

[JScript] **public static function GetMetafileHeader(String) : MetafileHeader;**

Returns the **MetafileHeader** object associated with the specified **Metafile** object.

[Visual Basic] **Overloads Public Shared Function GetMetafileHeader(IntPtr, WmfPlaceableFileHeader) As MetafileHeader**

[C#] **public static MetafileHeader GetMetafileHeader(IntPtr, WmfPlaceableFileHeader);**

[C++] **public: static MetafileHeader* GetMetafileHeader(IntPtr, WmfPlaceableFileHeader*);**

[JScript] **public static function GetMetafileHeader(IntPtr, WmfPlaceableFileHeader) : MetafileHeader;**

Metafile.GetMetafileHeader Method ()

Returns the **MetafileHeader** object associated with this **Metafile** object.

```
[Visual Basic]
Overloads Public Function GetMetafileHeader() As MetafileHeader
[C#]
public MetafileHeader GetMetafileHeader();
[C++]
public: MetafileHeader* GetMetafileHeader();
[JScript]
public function GetMetafileHeader() : MetafileHeader;
```

Return Value

The **MetafileHeader** object this method retrieves.

Requirements

Platforms: Windows 98, Windows NT 4.0, Windows Millennium Edition, Windows 2000, Windows XP Home Edition, Windows XP Professional, Windows Server 2003 family

Metafile.GetMetafileHeader Method (IntPtr)

Returns the **MetafileHeader** object associated with the specified **Metafile** object.

```
[Visual Basic]
Overloads Public Shared Function GetMetafileHeader( _
   ByVal henhmetafile As IntPtr _
) As MetafileHeader
[C#]
public static MetafileHeader GetMetafileHeader(
   IntPtr henhmetafile
);
[C++]
public: static MetafileHeader* GetMetafileHeader(
   IntPtr henhmetafile
);
[JScript]
public static function GetMetafileHeader(
   henhmetafile : IntPtr
) : MetafileHeader;
```

Parameters

henhmetafile
: The handle to the enhanced **Metafile** object for which a header is returned.

Return Value

The **MetafileHeader** object this method retrieves.

Requirements

Platforms: Windows 98, Windows NT 4.0, Windows Millennium Edition, Windows 2000, Windows XP Home Edition, Windows XP Professional, Windows Server 2003 family

Metafile.GetMetafileHeader Method (Stream)

Returns the **MetafileHeader** object associated with the specified **Metafile** object.

[Visual Basic]
```
Overloads Public Shared Function GetMetafileHeader( _
   ByVal stream As Stream _
) As MetafileHeader
```
[C#]
```
public static MetafileHeader GetMetafileHeader(
   Stream stream
);
```
[C++]
```
public: static MetafileHeader* GetMetafileHeader(
   Stream* stream
);
```
[JScript]
```
public static function GetMetafileHeader(
   stream : Stream
) : MetafileHeader;
```

Parameters

stream

A **Stream** object containing the **Metafile** object for which a header is retrieved.

Return Value

The **MetafileHeader** object this method retrieves.

Requirements

Platforms: Windows 98, Windows NT 4.0, Windows Millennium Edition, Windows 2000, Windows XP Home Edition, Windows XP Professional, Windows Server 2003 family

Metafile.GetMetafileHeader Method (String)

Returns the **MetafileHeader** object associated with the specified **Metafile** object.

[Visual Basic]
```
Overloads Public Shared Function GetMetafileHeader( _
   ByVal fileName As String _
) As MetafileHeader
```
[C#]
```
public static MetafileHeader GetMetafileHeader(
   string fileName
);
```
[C++]
```
public: static MetafileHeader* GetMetafileHeader(
   String* fileName
);
```
[JScript]
```
public static function GetMetafileHeader(
   fileName : String
) : MetafileHeader;
```

Parameters

fileName

A **String** object containing the name of the **Metafile** object for which a header is retrieved.

Return Value

The **MetafileHeader** object this method retrieves.

Requirements

Platforms: Windows 98, Windows NT 4.0, Windows Millennium Edition, Windows 2000, Windows XP Home Edition, Windows XP Professional, Windows Server 2003 family

Metafile.GetMetafileHeader Method (IntPtr, WmfPlaceableFileHeader)

Returns the **MetafileHeader** object associated with the specified **Metafile** object.

[Visual Basic]
```
Overloads Public Shared Function GetMetafileHeader( _
   ByVal hmetafile As IntPtr, _
   ByVal wmfHeader As WmfPlaceableFileHeader _
) As MetafileHeader
```
[C#]
```
public static MetafileHeader GetMetafileHeader(
   IntPtr hmetafile,
   WmfPlaceableFileHeader wmfHeader
);
```
[C++]
```
public: static MetafileHeader* GetMetafileHeader(
   IntPtr hmetafile,
   WmfPlaceableFileHeader* wmfHeader
);
```
[JScript]
```
public static function GetMetafileHeader(
   hmetafile : IntPtr,
   wmfHeader : WmfPlaceableFileHeader
) : MetafileHeader;
```

Parameters

hmetafile

The handle to the **Metafile** object for which to return a header.

wmfHeader

A **WmfPlaceableFileHeader** object.

Return Value

The **MetafileHeader** object this method retrieves.

Requirements

Platforms: Windows 98, Windows NT 4.0, Windows Millennium Edition, Windows 2000, Windows XP Home Edition, Windows XP Professional, Windows Server 2003 family

Metafile.PlayRecord Method

Plays an individual metafile record.

[Visual Basic]
```
Public Sub PlayRecord( _
   ByVal recordType As EmfPlusRecordType, _
   ByVal flags As Integer, _
   ByVal dataSize As Integer, _
   ByVal data() As Byte _
)
```
[C#]
```
public void PlayRecord(
   EmfPlusRecordType recordType,
   int flags,
   int dataSize,
   byte[] data
);
```
[C++]
```
public: void PlayRecord(
   EmfPlusRecordType recordType,
   int flags,
   int dataSize,
   unsigned char data __gc[]
);
```
[JScript]
```
public function PlayRecord(
   recordType : EmfPlusRecordType,
   flags : int,
   dataSize : int,
   data : Byte[]
);
```

Parameters

recordType
Element of the **EmfPlusRecordType** enumeration that specifies the type of metafile record being played.

flags
A set of flags that specify attributes of the record.

dataSize
The number of bytes in the record data.

data
An array of bytes that contains the record data.

Return Value

This method does not return a value.

Requirements

Platforms: Windows 98, Windows NT 4.0, Windows Millennium Edition, Windows 2000, Windows XP Home Edition, Windows XP Professional, Windows Server 2003 family

MetafileFrameUnit Enumeration

Specifies the unit of measurement for the rectangle used to size and position a metafile. This is specified during the creation of the **Metafile** object.

[Visual Basic]
```
<Serializable>
Public Enum MetafileFrameUnit
```
[C#]
```
[Serializable]
public enum MetafileFrameUnit
```
[C++]
```
[Serializable]
__value public enum MetafileFrameUnit
```
[JScript]
```
public
   Serializable
enum MetafileFrameUnit
```

Members

Member name	Description
Document	The unit of measurement is 1/300 of an inch.
GdiCompatible	The unit of measurement is 0.01 millimeter. Provided for compatibility with GDI.
Inch	The unit of measurement is 1 inch.
Millimeter	The unit of measurement is 1 millimeter.
Pixel	The unit of measurement is 1 pixel.
Point	The unit of measurement is 1 printer's point.

Requirements

Namespace: System.Drawing.Imaging

Platforms: Windows 98, Windows NT 4.0, Windows Millennium Edition, Windows 2000, Windows XP Home Edition, Windows XP Professional, Windows Server 2003 family

Assembly: System.Drawing (in System.Drawing.dll)

MetafileHeader Class

Contains attributes of an associated **Metafile** object. Not inheritable.

System.Object
  System.Drawing.Imaging.MetafileHeader

```
[Visual Basic]
NotInheritable Public Class MetafileHeader
[C#]
public sealed class MetafileHeader
[C++]
public __gc __sealed class MetafileHeader
[JScript]
public class MetafileHeader
```

Thread Safety

Any public static (**Shared** in Visual Basic) members of this type are safe for multithreaded operations. Any instance members are not guaranteed to be thread safe.

Requirements

Namespace: System.Drawing.Imaging

Platforms: Windows 98, Windows NT 4.0, Windows Millennium Edition, Windows 2000, Windows XP Home Edition, Windows XP Professional, Windows Server 2003 family

Assembly: System.Drawing (in System.Drawing.dll)

MetafileHeader.Bounds Property

Gets a **Rectangle** structure that bounds the associated **Metafile** object.

```
[Visual Basic]
Public ReadOnly Property Bounds As Rectangle
[C#]
public Rectangle Bounds {get;}
[C++]
public: __property Rectangle get_Bounds();
[JScript]
public function get Bounds() : Rectangle;
```

Property Value

A **Rectangle** structure that bounds the associated **Metafile** object.

Requirements

Platforms: Windows 98, Windows NT 4.0, Windows Millennium Edition, Windows 2000, Windows XP Home Edition, Windows XP Professional, Windows Server 2003 family

MetafileHeader.DpiX Property

Gets the horizontal resolution, in dots per inch, of the associated **Metafile** object.

```
[Visual Basic]
Public ReadOnly Property DpiX As Single
[C#]
public float DpiX {get;}
[C++]
public: __property float get_DpiX();
[JScript]
public function get DpiX() : float;
```

Property Value

The horizontal resolution, in dots per inch, of the associated **Metafile** object.

Requirements

Platforms: Windows 98, Windows NT 4.0, Windows Millennium Edition, Windows 2000, Windows XP Home Edition, Windows XP Professional, Windows Server 2003 family

MetafileHeader.DpiY Property

Gets the vertical resolution, in dots per inch, of the associated **Metafile** object.

```
[Visual Basic]
Public ReadOnly Property DpiY As Single
[C#]
public float DpiY {get;}
[C++]
public: __property float get_DpiY();
[JScript]
public function get DpiY() : float;
```

Property Value

The vertical resolution, in dots per inch, of the associated **Metafile** object.

Requirements

Platforms: Windows 98, Windows NT 4.0, Windows Millennium Edition, Windows 2000, Windows XP Home Edition, Windows XP Professional, Windows Server 2003 family

MetafileHeader.EmfPlusHeaderSize Property

Gets the size, in bytes, of the enhanced metafile plus header file.

```
[Visual Basic]
Public ReadOnly Property EmfPlusHeaderSize As Integer
[C#]
public int EmfPlusHeaderSize {get;}
[C++]
public: __property int get_EmfPlusHeaderSize();
[JScript]
public function get EmfPlusHeaderSize() : int;
```

Property Value

The size, in bytes, of the enhanced metafile plus header file.

Requirements

Platforms: Windows 98, Windows NT 4.0, Windows Millennium Edition, Windows 2000, Windows XP Home Edition, Windows XP Professional, Windows Server 2003 family

MetafileHeader.LogicalDpiX Property

Gets the logical horizontal resolution, in dots per inch, of the associated **Metafile** object.

[Visual Basic]
```
Public ReadOnly Property LogicalDpiX As Integer
```
[C#]
```
public int LogicalDpiX {get;}
```
[C++]
```
public: __property int get_LogicalDpiX();
```
[JScript]
```
public function get LogicalDpiX() : int;
```

Property Value

The logical horizontal resolution, in dots per inch, of the associated **Metafile** object.

Requirements

Platforms: Windows 98, Windows NT 4.0, Windows Millennium Edition, Windows 2000, Windows XP Home Edition, Windows XP Professional, Windows Server 2003 family

MetafileHeader.LogicalDpiY Property

Gets the logical vertical resolution, in dots per inch, of the associated **Metafile** object.

[Visual Basic]
```
Public ReadOnly Property LogicalDpiY As Integer
```
[C#]
```
public int LogicalDpiY {get;}
```
[C++]
```
public: __property int get_LogicalDpiY();
```
[JScript]
```
public function get LogicalDpiY() : int;
```

Property Value

The logical vertical resolution, in dots per inch, of the associated **Metafile** object.

Requirements

Platforms: Windows 98, Windows NT 4.0, Windows Millennium Edition, Windows 2000, Windows XP Home Edition, Windows XP Professional, Windows Server 2003 family

MetafileHeader.MetafileSize Property

Gets the size, in bytes, of the associated **Metafile** object.

[Visual Basic]
```
Public ReadOnly Property MetafileSize As Integer
```
[C#]
```
public int MetafileSize {get;}
```
[C++]
```
public: __property int get_MetafileSize();
```
[JScript]
```
public function get MetafileSize() : int;
```

Property Value

The size, in bytes, of the associated **Metafile** object.

Requirements

Platforms: Windows 98, Windows NT 4.0, Windows Millennium Edition, Windows 2000, Windows XP Home Edition, Windows XP Professional, Windows Server 2003 family

MetafileHeader.Type Property

Gets the type of the associated **Metafile** object.

[Visual Basic]
```
Public ReadOnly Property Type As MetafileType
```
[C#]
```
public MetafileType Type {get;}
```
[C++]
```
public: __property MetafileType get_Type();
```
[JScript]
```
public function get Type() : MetafileType;
```

Property Value

A **MetafileType** enumeration that represents the type of the associated **Metafile** object.

Requirements

Platforms: Windows 98, Windows NT 4.0, Windows Millennium Edition, Windows 2000, Windows XP Home Edition, Windows XP Professional, Windows Server 2003 family

MetafileHeader.Version Property

Gets the version number of the associated **Metafile** object.

[Visual Basic]
```
Public ReadOnly Property Version As Integer
```
[C#]
```
public int Version {get;}
```
[C++]
```
public: __property int get_Version();
```
[JScript]
```
public function get Version() : int;
```

Property Value

The version number of the associated **Metafile** object.

Requirements

Platforms: Windows 98, Windows NT 4.0, Windows Millennium Edition, Windows 2000, Windows XP Home Edition, Windows XP Professional, Windows Server 2003 family

MetafileHeader.WmfHeader Property

Gets the WMF header file for the associated **Metafile** object.

[Visual Basic]
```
Public ReadOnly Property WmfHeader As MetaHeader
```
[C#]
```
public MetaHeader WmfHeader {get;}
```
[C++]
```
public: __property MetaHeader* get_WmfHeader();
```
[JScript]
```
public function get WmfHeader() : MetaHeader;
```

Property Value

A **MetaHeader** object that contains the WMF header file for the associated **Metafile** object.

Requirements

Platforms: Windows 98, Windows NT 4.0, Windows Millennium Edition, Windows 2000, Windows XP Home Edition, Windows XP Professional, Windows Server 2003 family

MetafileHeader.IsDisplay Method

Returns a value that indicates whether the associated **Metafile** object is device dependent.

```
[Visual Basic]
Public Function IsDisplay() As Boolean
[C#]
public bool IsDisplay();
[C++]
public: bool IsDisplay();
[JScript]
public function IsDisplay() : Boolean;
```

Return Value

Returns **true** if the associated **Metafile** object is device dependent; otherwise, **false**.

Requirements

Platforms: Windows 98, Windows NT 4.0, Windows Millennium Edition, Windows 2000, Windows XP Home Edition, Windows XP Professional, Windows Server 2003 family

MetafileHeader.IsEmf Method

Returns a value that indicates whether the associated **Metafile** object is in the Windows enhanced metafile format.

```
[Visual Basic]
Public Function IsEmf() As Boolean
[C#]
public bool IsEmf();
[C++]
public: bool IsEmf();
[JScript]
public function IsEmf() : Boolean;
```

Return Value

Returns **true** if the associated **Metafile** object is in the Windows enhanced metafile format; otherwise, **false**.

Requirements

Platforms: Windows 98, Windows NT 4.0, Windows Millennium Edition, Windows 2000, Windows XP Home Edition, Windows XP Professional, Windows Server 2003 family

MetafileHeader.IsEmfOrEmfPlus Method

Returns a value that indicates whether the associated **Metafile** object is in the Windows enhanced metafile format or the Windows enhanced metafile plus format.

```
[Visual Basic]
Public Function IsEmfOrEmfPlus() As Boolean
[C#]
public bool IsEmfOrEmfPlus();
[C++]
public: bool IsEmfOrEmfPlus();
[JScript]
public function IsEmfOrEmfPlus() : Boolean;
```

Return Value

Returns **true** if the associated **Metafile** object is in the Windows enhanced metafile format or the Windows enhanced metafile plus format; otherwise, **false**.

Requirements

Platforms: Windows 98, Windows NT 4.0, Windows Millennium Edition, Windows 2000, Windows XP Home Edition, Windows XP Professional, Windows Server 2003 family

MetafileHeader.IsEmfPlus Method

Returns a value that indicates whether the associated **Metafile** object is in the Windows enhanced metafile plus format.

```
[Visual Basic]
Public Function IsEmfPlus() As Boolean
[C#]
public bool IsEmfPlus();
[C++]
public: bool IsEmfPlus();
[JScript]
public function IsEmfPlus() : Boolean;
```

Return Value

Returns **true** if the associated **Metafile** object is in the Windows enhanced metafile plus format; otherwise, **false**.

Requirements

Platforms: Windows 98, Windows NT 4.0, Windows Millennium Edition, Windows 2000, Windows XP Home Edition, Windows XP Professional, Windows Server 2003 family

MetafileHeader.IsEmfPlusDual Method

Returns a value that indicates whether the associated **Metafile** object is in the Dual enhanced metafile format. This format supports both the enhanced and the enhanced plus format.

```
[Visual Basic]
Public Function IsEmfPlusDual() As Boolean
[C#]
public bool IsEmfPlusDual();
[C++]
public: bool IsEmfPlusDual();
[JScript]
public function IsEmfPlusDual() : Boolean;
```

Return Value

Returns **true** if the associated **Metafile** object is in the Dual enhanced metafile format; otherwise, **false**.

Requirements

Platforms: Windows 98, Windows NT 4.0, Windows Millennium Edition, Windows 2000, Windows XP Home Edition, Windows XP Professional, Windows Server 2003 family

MetafileHeader.IsEmfPlusOnly Method

Returns a value that indicates whether the associated **Metafile** object supports only the Windows enhanced metafile plus format.

[Visual Basic]
```
Public Function IsEmfPlusOnly() As Boolean
```
[C#]
```
public bool IsEmfPlusOnly();
```
[C++]
```
public: bool IsEmfPlusOnly();
```
[JScript]
```
public function IsEmfPlusOnly() : Boolean;
```

Return Value

Returns **true** if the associated **Metafile** object supports only the Windows enhanced metafile plus format; otherwise, **false**.

Requirements

Platforms: Windows 98, Windows NT 4.0, Windows Millennium Edition, Windows 2000, Windows XP Home Edition, Windows XP Professional, Windows Server 2003 family

MetafileHeader.IsWmf Method

Returns a value that indicates whether the associated **Metafile** object is in the Windows metafile format.

[Visual Basic]
```
Public Function IsWmf() As Boolean
```
[C#]
```
public bool IsWmf();
```
[C++]
```
public: bool IsWmf();
```
[JScript]
```
public function IsWmf() : Boolean;
```

Return Value

Returns **true** if the associated **Metafile** object is in the Windows metafile format; otherwise, **false**.

Requirements

Platforms: Windows 98, Windows NT 4.0, Windows Millennium Edition, Windows 2000, Windows XP Home Edition, Windows XP Professional, Windows Server 2003 family

MetafileHeader.IsWmfPlaceable Method

Returns a value that indicates whether the associated **Metafile** object is in the Windows placeable metafile format.

[Visual Basic]
```
Public Function IsWmfPlaceable() As Boolean
```
[C#]
```
public bool IsWmfPlaceable();
```
[C++]
```
public: bool IsWmfPlaceable();
```
[JScript]
```
public function IsWmfPlaceable() : Boolean;
```

Return Value

Returns **true** if the associated **Metafile** object is in the Windows placeable metafile format; otherwise, **false**.

Requirements

Platforms: Windows 98, Windows NT 4.0, Windows Millennium Edition, Windows 2000, Windows XP Home Edition, Windows XP Professional, Windows Server 2003 family

MetafileType Enumeration

Specifies types of metafiles. The **MetafileHeader.Type** property returns a member of this enumeration.

[Visual Basic]
```
<Serializable>
Public Enum MetafileType
```
[C#]
```
[Serializable]
public enum MetafileType
```
[C++]
```
[Serializable]
__value public enum MetafileType
```
[JScript]
```
public
   Serializable
enum MetafileType
```

Members

Member name	Description
Emf	Specifies an Enhanced Metafile (EMF) file. Such a file contains only GDI records.
EmfPlusDual	Specifies an EMF+ Dual file. Such a file contains GDI+ records along with alternative GDI records and can be displayed by using either GDI or GDI+. Displaying the records using GDI may cause some quality degradation.
EmfPlusOnly	Specifies an EMF+ file. Such a file contains only GDI+ records and must be displayed by using GDI+. Displaying the records using GDI may cause unpredictable results.
Invalid	Specifies a metafile format that is not recognized in GDI+.
Wmf	Specifies a WMF (Windows Metafile) file. Such a file contains only GDI records.
WmfPlaceable	Specifies a WMF (Windows Metafile) file that has a placeable metafile header in front of it.

Requirements

Namespace: System.Drawing.Imaging

Platforms: Windows 98, Windows NT 4.0, Windows Millennium Edition, Windows 2000, Windows XP Home Edition, Windows XP Professional, Windows Server 2003 family

Assembly: System.Drawing (in System.Drawing.dll)

MetaHeader Class

Contains information about a windows-format (WMF) metafile.

System.Object
 System.Drawing.Imaging.MetaHeader

```
[Visual Basic]
NotInheritable Public Class MetaHeader
[C#]
public sealed class MetaHeader
[C++]
public __gc __sealed class MetaHeader
[JScript]
public class MetaHeader
```

Thread Safety

Any public static (**Shared** in Visual Basic) members of this type are safe for multithreaded operations. Any instance members are not guaranteed to be thread safe.

Requirements

Namespace: System.Drawing.Imaging

Platforms: Windows 98, Windows NT 4.0, Windows Millennium Edition, Windows 2000, Windows XP Home Edition, Windows XP Professional, Windows Server 2003 family

Assembly: System.Drawing (in System.Drawing.dll)

MetaHeader Constructor

Initializes a new instance of the **MetaHeader** class.

```
[Visual Basic]
Public Sub New()
[C#]
public MetaHeader();
[C++]
public: MetaHeader();
[JScript]
public function MetaHeader();
```

Remarks

The default constructor initializes all properties to their default values.

Requirements

Platforms: Windows 98, Windows NT 4.0, Windows Millennium Edition, Windows 2000, Windows XP Home Edition, Windows XP Professional, Windows Server 2003 family

MetaHeader.HeaderSize Property

Gets or sets the size, in bytes, of the header file.

```
[Visual Basic]
Public Property HeaderSize As Short
[C#]
public short HeaderSize {get; set;}
[C++]
public: __property short get_HeaderSize();
public: __property void set_HeaderSize(short);
[JScript]
public function get HeaderSize() : Int16;
public function set HeaderSize(Int16);
```

Property Value

The size, in bytes, of the header file.

Requirements

Platforms: Windows 98, Windows NT 4.0, Windows Millennium Edition, Windows 2000, Windows XP Home Edition, Windows XP Professional, Windows Server 2003 family

MetaHeader.MaxRecord Property

Gets or sets the size, in bytes, of the largest record in the associated **Metafile** object.

```
[Visual Basic]
Public Property MaxRecord As Integer
[C#]
public int MaxRecord {get; set;}
[C++]
public: __property int get_MaxRecord();
public: __property void set_MaxRecord(int);
[JScript]
public function get MaxRecord() : int;
public function set MaxRecord(int);
```

Property Value

The size, in bytes, of the largest record in the associated **Metafile** object.

Requirements

Platforms: Windows 98, Windows NT 4.0, Windows Millennium Edition, Windows 2000, Windows XP Home Edition, Windows XP Professional, Windows Server 2003 family

MetaHeader.NoObjects Property

Gets or sets the maximum number of objects that exist in the **Metafile** object at the same time.

```
[Visual Basic]
Public Property NoObjects As Short
[C#]
public short NoObjects {get; set;}
[C++]
public: __property short get_NoObjects();
public: __property void set_NoObjects(short);
[JScript]
public function get NoObjects() : Int16;
public function set NoObjects(Int16);
```

Property Value

The maximum number of objects that exist in the **Metafile** object at the same time.

Requirements

Platforms: Windows 98, Windows NT 4.0, Windows Millennium Edition, Windows 2000, Windows XP Home Edition, Windows XP Professional, Windows Server 2003 family

MetaHeader.NoParameters Property

Reserved.

```
[Visual Basic]
Public Property NoParameters As Short
[C#]
public short NoParameters {get; set;}
[C++]
public: __property short get_NoParameters();
public: __property void set_NoParameters(short);
[JScript]
public function get NoParameters() : Int16;
public function set NoParameters(Int16);
```

Property Value

Reserved.

Requirements

Platforms: Windows 98, Windows NT 4.0, Windows Millennium Edition, Windows 2000, Windows XP Home Edition, Windows XP Professional, Windows Server 2003 family

MetaHeader.Size Property

Gets or sets the size, in bytes, of the associated **Metafile** object.

```
[Visual Basic]
Public Property Size As Integer
[C#]
public int Size {get; set;}
[C++]
public: __property int get_Size();
public: __property void set_Size(int);
[JScript]
public function get Size() : int;
public function set Size(int);
```

Property Value

The size, in bytes, of the associated **Metafile** object.

Requirements

Platforms: Windows 98, Windows NT 4.0, Windows Millennium Edition, Windows 2000, Windows XP Home Edition, Windows XP Professional, Windows Server 2003 family

MetaHeader.Type Property

Gets or sets the type of the associated **Metafile** object.

```
[Visual Basic]
Public Property Type As Short
[C#]
public short Type {get; set;}
[C++]
public: __property short get_Type();
public: __property void set_Type(short);
[JScript]
public function get Type() : Int16;
public function set Type(Int16);
```

Property Value

The type of the associated **Metafile** object.

Remarks

Specifies whether the metafile is in memory or recorded in a disk file. This property can be one of the following values.

Requirements

Platforms: Windows 98, Windows NT 4.0, Windows Millennium Edition, Windows 2000, Windows XP Home Edition, Windows XP Professional, Windows Server 2003 family

MetaHeader.Version Property

Gets or sets the version number of the header format.

```
[Visual Basic]
Public Property Version As Short
[C#]
public short Version {get; set;}
[C++]
public: __property short get_Version();
public: __property void set_Version(short);
[JScript]
public function get Version() : Int16;
public function set Version(Int16);
```

Property Value

The version number of the header format.

Remarks

Specifies the system version number. The version number for metafiles that support device-independent bitmaps (DIBS) is 0x0300. Otherwise, the version number is 0x0100.

Requirements

Platforms: Windows 98, Windows NT 4.0, Windows Millennium Edition, Windows 2000, Windows XP Home Edition, Windows XP Professional, Windows Server 2003 family

PaletteFlags Enumeration

Specifies the type of color data in the system palette. The data can be color data with alpha, grayscale data only, or halftone data.

[Visual Basic]
```
<Serializable>
Public Enum PaletteFlags
```
[C#]
```
[Serializable]
public enum PaletteFlags
```
[C++]
```
[Serializable]
__value public enum PaletteFlags
```
[JScript]
```
public
   Serializable
enum PaletteFlags
```

Members

Member name	Description
GrayScale	Grayscale data.
Halftone	Halftone data.
HasAlpha	Alpha data.

Requirements

Namespace: System.Drawing.Imaging

Platforms: Windows 98, Windows NT 4.0, Windows Millennium Edition, Windows 2000, Windows XP Home Edition, Windows XP Professional, Windows Server 2003 family

Assembly: System.Drawing (in System.Drawing.dll)

PixelFormat Enumeration

Specifies the format of the color data for each pixel in the image.

[Visual Basic]
```
<Serializable>
Public Enum PixelFormat
```
[C#]
```
[Serializable]
public enum PixelFormat
```
[C++]
```
[Serializable]
__value public enum PixelFormat
```
[JScript]
```
public
   Serializable
enum PixelFormat
```

Remarks

The pixel format defines the number of bits of memory associated with one pixel of data. The format also defines the order of the color components within a single pixel of data.

PixelFormat48bppRGB, PixelFormat64bppARGB, and PixelFormat64bppPARGB use 16 bits per color component (channel). GDI+ version 1.0 and 1.1 can read 16-bits-per-channel images, but such images are converted to an 8-bits-per-channel format for processing, displaying, and saving. Each 16-bit color channel can hold a value in the range 0 through 2^13.

Members

Member name	Description
Alpha	The pixel data contains alpha values that are not premultiplied.
Canonical	Reserved.
DontCare	No pixel format is specified.
Extended	Reserved.
Format16bppArgb1555	The pixel format is 16 bits per pixel. The color information specifies 32,768 shades of color, of which 5 bits are red, 5 bits are green, 5 bits are blue, and 1 bit is alpha.
Format16bppGrayScale	The pixel format is 16 bits per pixel. The color information specifies 65536 shades of gray.
Format16bppRgb555	Specifies that the format is 16 bits per pixel; 5 bits each are used for the red, green, and blue components. The remaining bit is not used.
Format16bppRgb565	Specifies that the format is 16 bits per pixel; 5 bits are used for the red component, 6 bits are used for the green component, and 5 bits are used for the blue component.
Format1bppIndexed	Specifies that the pixel format is 1 bit per pixel and that it uses indexed color. The color table therefore has two colors in it.
Format24bppRgb	Specifies that the format is 24 bits per pixel; 8 bits each are used for the red, green, and blue components.
Format32bppArgb	Specifies that the format is 32 bits per pixel; 8 bits each are used for the alpha, red, green, and blue components.
Format32bppPArgb	Specifies that the format is 32 bits per pixel; 8 bits each are used for the alpha, red, green, and blue components. The red, green, and blue components are premultiplied according to the alpha component.
Format32bppRgb	Specifies that the format is 32 bits per pixel; 8 bits each are used for the red, green, and blue components. The remaining 8 bits are not used.
Format48bppRgb	Specifies that the format is 48 bits per pixel; 16 bits each are used for the red, green, and blue components.
Format4bppIndexed	Specifies that the format is 4 bits per pixel, indexed.
Format64bppArgb	Specifies that the format is 64 bits per pixel; 16 bits each are used for the alpha, red, green, and blue components.
Format64bppPArgb	Specifies that the format is 64 bits per pixel; 16 bits each are used for the alpha, red, green, and blue components. The red, green, and blue components are premultiplied according to the alpha component.
Format8bppIndexed	Specifies that the format is 8 bits per pixel, indexed. The color table therefore has 256 colors in it.
Gdi	The pixel data contains GDI colors.
Indexed	The pixel data contains color-indexed values, which means the values are an index to colors in the system color table, as opposed to individual color values.
Max	The maximum value for this enumeration.
PAlpha	The pixel format contains premultiplied alpha values.
Undefined	The pixel format is undefined.

Requirements

Namespace: System.Drawing.Imaging

Platforms: Windows 98, Windows NT 4.0, Windows Millennium Edition, Windows 2000, Windows XP Home Edition, Windows XP Professional, Windows Server 2003 family

Assembly: System.Drawing (in System.Drawing.dll)

PlayRecordCallback Delegate

This delegate is not used. For an example of enumerating the records of a metafile, see **EnumerateMetafile**.

[Visual Basic]
```
<Serializable>
Public Delegate Sub PlayRecordCallback( _
   ByVal recordType As EmfPlusRecordType, _
   ByVal flags As Integer, _
   ByVal dataSize As Integer, _
   ByVal recordData As IntPtr _
)
```
[C#]
```
[Serializable]
public delegate void PlayRecordCallback(
   EmfPlusRecordType recordType,
   int flags,
   int dataSize,
   IntPtr recordData
);
```
[C++]
```
[Serializable]
public __gc __delegate void PlayRecordCallback(
   EmfPlusRecordType recordType,
   int flags,
   int dataSize,
   IntPtr recordData
);
```

[JScript] In JScript, you can use the delegates in the .NET Framework, but you cannot define your own.

Parameters [Visual Basic, C#, C++]

The declaration of your callback method must have the same parameters as the **PlayRecordCallback** delegate declaration.

recordType
Not used.

flags
Not used.

dataSize
Not used.

recordData
Not used.

Requirements

Namespace: System.Drawing.Imaging

Platforms: Windows 98, Windows NT 4.0, Windows Millennium Edition, Windows 2000, Windows XP Home Edition, Windows XP Professional, Windows Server 2003 family

Assembly: System.Drawing (in System.Drawing.dll)

PropertyItem Class

Encapsulates a metadata property to be included in an image file. Not inheritable.

System.Object
  System.Drawing.Imaging.PropertyItem

```
[Visual Basic]
NotInheritable Public Class PropertyItem
[C#]
public sealed class PropertyItem
[C++]
public __gc __sealed class PropertyItem
[JScript]
public class PropertyItem
```

Thread Safety

Any public static (**Shared** in Visual Basic) members of this type are safe for multithreaded operations. Any instance members are not guaranteed to be thread safe.

Remarks

The data consists of: an identifier, the length (in bytes) of the property, the property type, and a pointer to the property value.

Requirements

Namespace: System.Drawing.Imaging

Platforms: Windows 98, Windows NT 4.0, Windows Millennium Edition, Windows 2000, Windows XP Home Edition, Windows XP Professional, Windows Server 2003 family

Assembly: System.Drawing (in System.Drawing.dll)

PropertyItem.Id Property

Gets or sets the ID of the property.

```
[Visual Basic]
Public Property Id As Integer
[C#]
public int Id {get; set;}
[C++]
public: __property int get_Id();
public: __property void set_Id(int);
[JScript]
public function get Id() : int;
public function set Id(int);
```

Property Value

The ID of the property.

Requirements

Platforms: Windows 98, Windows NT 4.0, Windows Millennium Edition, Windows 2000, Windows XP Home Edition, Windows XP Professional, Windows Server 2003 family

PropertyItem.Len Property

Gets or sets the length of the property.

```
[Visual Basic]
Public Property Len As Integer
[C#]
public int Len {get; set;}
[C++]
public: __property int get_Len();
public: __property void set_Len(int);
[JScript]
public function get Len() : int;
public function set Len(int);
```

Property Value

The length of the property.

Requirements

Platforms: Windows 98, Windows NT 4.0, Windows Millennium Edition, Windows 2000, Windows XP Home Edition, Windows XP Professional, Windows Server 2003 family

PropertyItem.Type Property

Gets or sets the type of the property.

```
[Visual Basic]
Public Property Type As Short
[C#]
public short Type {get; set;}
[C++]
public: __property short get_Type();
public: __property void set_Type(short);
[JScript]
public function get Type() : Int16;
public function set Type(Int16);
```

Property Value

The type of the property.

Requirements

Platforms: Windows 98, Windows NT 4.0, Windows Millennium Edition, Windows 2000, Windows XP Home Edition, Windows XP Professional, Windows Server 2003 family

PropertyItem.Value Property

Gets or sets the property value.

```
[Visual Basic]
Public Property Value As Byte ()
[C#]
public byte[] Value {get; set;}
[C++]
public: __property unsigned char get_Value();
public: __property void set_Value(unsigned char __gc[]);
[JScript]
public function get Value() : Byte[];
public function set Value(Byte[]);
```

Property Value

The property value.

Requirements

Platforms: Windows 98, Windows NT 4.0, Windows Millennium Edition, Windows 2000, Windows XP Home Edition, Windows XP Professional, Windows Server 2003 family

WmfPlaceableFileHeader Class

Defines a placeable metafile. Not inheritable.

System.Object
  System.Drawing.Imaging.WmfPlaceableFileHeader

```
[Visual Basic]
NotInheritable Public Class WmfPlaceableFileHeader
[C#]
public sealed class WmfPlaceableFileHeader
[C++]
public __gc __sealed class WmfPlaceableFileHeader
[JScript]
public class WmfPlaceableFileHeader
```

Thread Safety

Any public static (**Shared** in Visual Basic) members of this type are safe for multithreaded operations. Any instance members are not guaranteed to be thread safe.

Remarks

Placeable metafiles provide a nonstandard way to specify how a metafile is mapped and scaled on an output device.

Requirements

Namespace: System.Drawing.Imaging

Platforms: Windows 98, Windows NT 4.0, Windows Millennium Edition, Windows 2000, Windows XP Home Edition, Windows XP Professional, Windows Server 2003 family

Assembly: System.Drawing (in System.Drawing.dll)

WmfPlaceableFileHeader Constructor

Initializes a new instance of the **WmfPlaceableFileHeader** class.

```
[Visual Basic]
Public Sub New()
[C#]
public WmfPlaceableFileHeader();
[C++]
public: WmfPlaceableFileHeader();
[JScript]
public function WmfPlaceableFileHeader();
```

Requirements

Platforms: Windows 98, Windows NT 4.0, Windows Millennium Edition, Windows 2000, Windows XP Home Edition, Windows XP Professional, Windows Server 2003 family

WmfPlaceableFileHeader.BboxBottom Property

Gets or sets the y-coordinate of the lower-right corner of the bounding rectangle of the metafile image on the output device.

```
[Visual Basic]
Public Property BboxBottom As Short
[C#]
public short BboxBottom {get; set;}
[C++]
public: __property short get_BboxBottom();
public: __property void set_BboxBottom(short);
[JScript]
public function get BboxBottom() : Int16;
public function set BboxBottom(Int16);
```

Property Value

The y-coordinate of the lower-right corner of the bounding rectangle of the metafile image on the output device.

Remarks

The coordinates of the bounding rectangle are measured in twips.

Requirements

Platforms: Windows 98, Windows NT 4.0, Windows Millennium Edition, Windows 2000, Windows XP Home Edition, Windows XP Professional, Windows Server 2003 family

WmfPlaceableFileHeader.BboxLeft Property

Gets or sets the x-coordinate of the upper-left corner of the bounding rectangle of the metafile image on the output device.

```
[Visual Basic]
Public Property BboxLeft As Short
[C#]
public short BboxLeft {get; set;}
[C++]
public: __property short get_BboxLeft();
public: __property void set_BboxLeft(short);
[JScript]
public function get BboxLeft() : Int16;
public function set BboxLeft(Int16);
```

Property Value

The x-coordinate of the upper-left corner of the bounding rectangle of the metafile image on the output device.

Remarks

The coordinates of the bounding rectangle are measured in twips.

Requirements

Platforms: Windows 98, Windows NT 4.0, Windows Millennium Edition, Windows 2000, Windows XP Home Edition, Windows XP Professional, Windows Server 2003 family

WmfPlaceableFileHeader.BboxRight Property

Gets or sets the x-coordinate of the lower-right corner of the bounding rectangle of the metafile image on the output device.

```
[Visual Basic]
Public Property BboxRight As Short
[C#]
public short BboxRight {get; set;}
[C++]
public: __property short get_BboxRight();
public: __property void set_BboxRight(short);
[JScript]
public function get BboxRight() : Int16;
public function set BboxRight(Int16);
```

Property Value

The x-coordinate of the lower-right corner of the bounding rectangle of the metafile image on the output device.

Remarks

The coordinates of the bounding rectangle are measured in twips.

Requirements

Platforms: Windows 98, Windows NT 4.0, Windows Millennium Edition, Windows 2000, Windows XP Home Edition, Windows XP Professional, Windows Server 2003 family

WmfPlaceableFileHeader.BboxTop Property

Gets or sets the y-coordinate of the upper-left corner of the bounding rectangle of the metafile image on the output device.

```
[Visual Basic]
Public Property BboxTop As Short
[C#]
public short BboxTop {get; set;}
[C++]
public: __property short get_BboxTop();
public: __property void set_BboxTop(short);
[JScript]
public function get BboxTop() : Int16;
public function set BboxTop(Int16);
```

Property Value

The y-coordinate of the upper-left corner of the bounding rectangle of the metafile image on the output device.

Remarks

The coordinates of the bounding rectangle are measured in twips.

Requirements

Platforms: Windows 98, Windows NT 4.0, Windows Millennium Edition, Windows 2000, Windows XP Home Edition, Windows XP Professional, Windows Server 2003 family

WmfPlaceableFileHeader.Checksum Property

Gets or sets the checksum value for the previous ten **WORD** s in the header.

```
[Visual Basic]
Public Property Checksum As Short
[C#]
public short Checksum {get; set;}
[C++]
public: __property short get_Checksum();
public: __property void set_Checksum(short);
[JScript]
public function get Checksum() : Int16;
public function set Checksum(Int16);
```

Property Value

The checksum value for the previous ten **WORD** s in the header.

Remarks

This value can be used in an attempt to detect whether the metafile has become corrupted. The checksum is calculated by joining each **WORD** value to an initial value of 0 by using the **XOR** operator.

Requirements

Platforms: Windows 98, Windows NT 4.0, Windows Millennium Edition, Windows 2000, Windows XP Home Edition, Windows XP Professional, Windows Server 2003 family

WmfPlaceableFileHeader.Hmf Property

Gets or sets the handle of the metafile in memory.

```
[Visual Basic]
Public Property Hmf As Short
[C#]
public short Hmf {get; set;}
[C++]
public: __property short get_Hmf();
public: __property void set_Hmf(short);
[JScript]
public function get Hmf() : Int16;
public function set Hmf(Int16);
```

Property Value

The handle of the metafile in memory.

Remarks

When written to disk, this property is not used and always contains the value 0.

Requirements

Platforms: Windows 98, Windows NT 4.0, Windows Millennium Edition, Windows 2000, Windows XP Home Edition, Windows XP Professional, Windows Server 2003 family

WmfPlaceableFileHeader.Inch Property

Gets or sets the number of twips per inch.

```
[Visual Basic]
Public Property Inch As Short
[C#]
public short Inch {get; set;}
[C++]
public: __property short get_Inch();
public: __property void set_Inch(short);
[JScript]
public function get Inch() : Int16;
public function set Inch(Int16);
```

Property Value

The number of twips per inch.

Remarks

Normally, there are 1440 twips per inch; however, this number can be changed to scale the image. A value of 720 indicates that the image is double its normal size, or scaled to a factor of 2:1. A value of 360 indicates a scale of 4:1. Conversely, a value of 2880 indicates that the image is scaled down in size by a factor of two. A value of 1440 indicates a 1:1 scale ratio.

Requirements

Platforms: Windows 98, Windows NT 4.0, Windows Millennium Edition, Windows 2000, Windows XP Home Edition, Windows XP Professional, Windows Server 2003 family

WmfPlaceableFileHeader.Key Property

Gets or sets a value indicating the presence of a placeable metafile header.

[Visual Basic]
```
Public Property Key As Integer
```
[C#]
```
public int Key {get; set;}
```
[C++]
```
public: __property int get_Key();
public: __property void set_Key(int);
```
[JScript]
```
public function get Key() : int;
public function set Key(int);
```

Property Value

A value indicating presence of a placeable metafile header.

Remarks

This field always has a value of 0x9AC6CDD7.

Requirements

Platforms: Windows 98, Windows NT 4.0, Windows Millennium Edition, Windows 2000, Windows XP Home Edition, Windows XP Professional, Windows Server 2003 family

WmfPlaceableFileHeader.Reserved Property

Reserved. Do not use.

[Visual Basic]
```
Public Property Reserved As Integer
```
[C#]
```
public int Reserved {get; set;}
```
[C++]
```
public: __property int get_Reserved();
public: __property void set_Reserved(int);
```
[JScript]
```
public function get Reserved() : int;
public function set Reserved(int);
```

Property Value

Reserved. Do not use.

Remarks

Always set this field to zero.

Requirements

Platforms: Windows 98, Windows NT 4.0, Windows Millennium Edition, Windows 2000, Windows XP Home Edition, Windows XP Professional, Windows Server 2003 family

System.Drawing.Printing Namespace

The **System.Drawing.Printing** namespace provides print-related services.

Typically, you create a new instance of the **PrintDocument** class, set the properties that describe what to print, and call the **Print** method to actually print the document.

Use the **PrintPageEventArgs.Graphics** property to specify the output to print. If you are printing a text file, use **StreamReader** in the following manner: read one line at a time from the stream and call the **DrawString** method to draw the line in the graphics object. For more information on this process, see the **Graphics** and **StreamReader** classes.

When implemented in a derived class, the **PrintController** controls how a **PrintDocument** is printed. The **PrintDocument.Print** method invokes the print controller's **OnStartPrint**, **OnEndPrint**, **OnStartPage**, and **OnEndPage** methods, which in turn tell the printer how to print the document. For more information on printing dialogs, see **PrintDialog** and **PageSetupDialog**.

The print-preview process uses a specialized print controller, dialog, and control.

Requirements

Namespace: System.Drawing.Printing

Platforms: Windows 98, Windows NT 4.0, Windows Millennium Edition, Windows 2000, Windows XP Home Edition, Windows XP Professional, Windows Server 2003 family

Assembly: System.Drawing (in System.Drawing.dll)

Duplex Enumeration

Specifies the printer's duplex setting.

[Visual Basic]
```
<Serializable>
Public Enum Duplex
```
[C#]
```
[Serializable]
public enum Duplex
```
[C++]
```
[Serializable]
__value public enum Duplex
```
[JScript]
```
public
   Serializable
enum Duplex
```

Remarks

This enumeration is used by **PrinterSettings**.

For more information on printing, see the **System.Drawing.Printing** namespace overview.

Members

Member name	Description
Default	The printer's default duplex setting.
Horizontal	Double-sided, horizontal printing.
Simplex	Single-sided printing.
Vertical	Double-sided, vertical printing.

InvalidPrinterException Class

Represents the exception that is thrown when trying to access a printer using invalid printer settings.

System.Object
  System.Exception
    System.SystemException
      System.Drawing.Printing.InvalidPrinterException

```
[Visual Basic]
Public Class InvalidPrinterException
   Inherits SystemException
[C#]
public class InvalidPrinterException : SystemException
[C++]
public __gc class InvalidPrinterException : public SystemException
[JScript]
public class InvalidPrinterException extends SystemException
```

Thread Safety

Any public static (**Shared** in Visual Basic) members of this type are safe for multithreaded operations. Any instance members are not guaranteed to be thread safe.

Remarks

The most common cause of invalid printer settings is referencing a printer that does not exist.

For more information on printing, see the **System.Drawing.Printing** namespace overview.

Requirements

Namespace: System.Drawing.Printing

Platforms: Windows 98, Windows NT 4.0, Windows Millennium Edition, Windows 2000, Windows XP Home Edition, Windows XP Professional, Windows Server 2003 family

Assembly: System.Drawing (in System.Drawing.dll)

InvalidPrinterException Constructor

Initializes a new instance of the **InvalidPrinterException** class.

Overload List

Initializes a new instance of the **InvalidPrinterException** class.

[Visual Basic] **Public Sub New(PrinterSettings)**

[C#] **public InvalidPrinterException(PrinterSettings);**

[C++] **public: InvalidPrinterException(PrinterSettings*);**

[JScript] **public function InvalidPrinter-Exception(PrinterSettings);**

Initializes a new instance of the **InvalidPrinterException** class with serialized data.

[Visual Basic] **Protected Sub New(SerializationInfo, StreamingContext)**

[C#] **protected InvalidPrinterException(SerializationInfo, StreamingContext);**

[C++] **protected: InvalidPrinterException(SerializationInfo*, StreamingContext);**

[JScript] **protected function InvalidPrinter-Exception(SerializationInfo, StreamingContext);**

InvalidPrinterException Constructor (PrinterSettings)

Initializes a new instance of the **InvalidPrinterException** class.

```
[Visual Basic]
Public Sub New( _
   ByVal settings As PrinterSettings _
)
[C#]
public InvalidPrinterException(
   PrinterSettings settings
);
[C++]
public: InvalidPrinterException(
   PrinterSettings* settings
);
[JScript]
public function InvalidPrinterException(
   settings : PrinterSettings
);
```

Parameters

settings

A **PrinterSettings** object that specifies the settings for a printer.

Requirements

Platforms: Windows 98, Windows NT 4.0, Windows Millennium Edition, Windows 2000, Windows XP Home Edition, Windows XP Professional, Windows Server 2003 family

InvalidPrinterException Constructor (SerializationInfo, StreamingContext)

Initializes a new instance of the **InvalidPrinterException** class with serialized data.

```
[Visual Basic]
Protected Sub New( _
   ByVal info As SerializationInfo, _
   ByVal context As StreamingContext _
)
[C#]
protected InvalidPrinterException(
   SerializationInfo info,
   StreamingContext context
);
[C++]
protected: InvalidPrinterException(
   SerializationInfo* info,
   StreamingContext context
);
[JScript]
protected function InvalidPrinterException(
   info : SerializationInfo,
   context : StreamingContext
);
```

Parameters

info

The **SerializationInfo** that holds the serialized object data about the exception being thrown.

context

The **StreamingContext** that contains contextual information about the source or destination.

Exceptions

Exception Type	Condition
ArgumentNull-Exception	The *info* parameter is a null reference (**Nothing** in Visual Basic).
SerializationException	The class name is a null reference (**Nothing** in Visual Basic) or **HResult** is zero (0).

Remarks

This constructor is called during deserialization to reconstitute the exception object transmitted over a stream. For more information, see **XML and SOAP Serialization**.

Requirements

Platforms: Windows 98, Windows NT 4.0, Windows Millennium Edition, Windows 2000, Windows XP Home Edition, Windows XP Professional, Windows Server 2003 family

InvalidPrinterException.GetObjectData Method

This member overrides **Exception.GetObjectData**.

[Visual Basic]
```
Overrides Public Sub GetObjectData( _
   ByVal info As SerializationInfo, _
   ByVal context As StreamingContext _
) Implements ISerializable.GetObjectData
```
[C#]
```
public override void GetObjectData(
   SerializationInfo info,
   StreamingContext context
);
```
[C++]
```
public: void GetObjectData(
   SerializationInfo* info,
   StreamingContext context
);
```
[JScript]
```
public override function GetObjectData(
   info : SerializationInfo,
   context : StreamingContext
);
```

Requirements

Platforms: Windows 98, Windows NT 4.0, Windows Millennium Edition, Windows 2000, Windows XP Home Edition, Windows XP Professional, Windows Server 2003 family

Margins Class

Specifies the margins of a printed page.

System.Object
  System.Drawing.Printing.Margins

[Visual Basic]
```
Public Class Margins
   Implements ICloneable
```
[C#]
```
public class Margins : ICloneable
```
[C++]
```
public __gc class Margins : public ICloneable
```
[JScript]
```
public class Margins implements ICloneable
```

Thread Safety

Any public static (**Shared** in Visual Basic) members of this type are safe for multithreaded operations. Any instance members are not guaranteed to be thread safe.

Remarks

This class is used to manipulate margins in **PageSettings** and **PrintController**. **MarginsConverter** is the type descriptor for this class.

Left, **Right**, **Top**, and **Bottom** are properties that define the margins. **Clone** creates an identical **Margins** object. **Equals** determines if another object is equal to a **Margins** object.

For more information on printing, see the **System.Drawing.Printing** namespace overview.

Example

[Visual Basic, C#] Use the **System.Drawing**, **System.Drawing.Printing**, and **System.IO** namespaces for this example.

[Visual Basic, C#] The following example sets the default page settings for a document to margins of 1 inch on each side.

[Visual Basic]

```
Public Sub Printing()
    Try
        ' This assumes that a variable of type string, named filePath,
        ' has been set to the path of the file to print.
        streamToPrint = New StreamReader(filePath)
        Try
            printFont = New Font("Arial", 10)
            Dim pd As New PrintDocument()
            ' This assumes that a method, named pd_PrintPage, has been
            ' defined. pd_PrintPage handles the PrintPage event.
            AddHandler pd.PrintPage, AddressOf pd_PrintPage
            ' This assumes that a variable of type string, named
            ' printer, has been set to the printer's name.
            pd.PrinterSettings.PrinterName = printer
            ' Create a new instance of Margins with one inch margins.
            Dim margins As New Margins(100, 100, 100, 100)
            pd.DefaultPageSettings.Margins = margins
            pd.Print()
        Finally
            streamToPrint.Close()
        End Try
    Catch ex As Exception
        MessageBox.Show("An error occurred printing the file -          ↵
" & ex.Message)
    End Try
End Sub
```

[C#]
```
public void Printing()
{
  try
  {
    /* This assumes that a variable of type string, named filePath,
       has been set to the path of the file to print. */
    streamToPrint = new StreamReader (filePath);
    try
    {
      printFont = new Font("Arial", 10);
      PrintDocument pd = new PrintDocument();
      /* This assumes that a method, named pd_PrintPage, has been
         defined. pd_PrintPage handles the PrintPage event. */
      pd.PrintPage += new PrintPageEventHandler(pd_PrintPage);
      /* This assumes that a variable of type string, named
         printer, has been set to the printer's name. */
      pd.PrinterSettings.PrinterName = printer;
      // Create a new instance of Margins with one inch margins.
      Margins margins = new Margins(100,100,100,100);
      pd.DefaultPageSettings.Margins = margins;
      pd.Print();
    }
    finally
    {
      streamToPrint.Close() ;
    }
  }
  catch(Exception ex)
  {
    MessageBox.Show("An error occurred printing the file - " +          ↵
ex.Message);
  }
}
```

Requirements

Namespace: System.Drawing.Printing

Platforms: Windows 98, Windows NT 4.0, Windows Millennium Edition, Windows 2000, Windows XP Home Edition, Windows XP Professional, Windows Server 2003 family

Assembly: System.Drawing (in System.Drawing.dll)

Margins Constructor

Initializes a new instance of the **Margins** class.

Overload List

Initializes a new instance of the **Margins** class with 1-inch margins.

[Visual Basic] **Public Sub New()**

[C#] **public Margins();**

[C++] **public: Margins();**

[JScript] **public function Margins();**

Initializes a new instance of the **Margins** class with the specified left, right, top, and bottom margins.

[Visual Basic] **Public Sub New(Integer, Integer, Integer, Integer)**

[C#] **public Margins(int, int, int, int);**

[C++] **public: Margins(int, int, int, int);**

[JScript] **public function Margins(int, int, int, int);**

Example

[Visual Basic, C#] Use the **System.Drawing**, **System.Drawing.Printing**, and **System.IO** namespaces for this example.

[Visual Basic, C#] The following example sets the default page settings for a document to margins of 1 inch on each side.

> [Visual Basic, C#] **Note** This example shows how to use one of the overloaded versions of the **Margins** constructor. For other examples that might be available, see the individual overload topics.

[Visual Basic]
```
Public Sub Printing()
    Try
        ' This assumes that a variable of type string, named filePath,
        ' has been set to the path of the file to print.
        streamToPrint = New StreamReader(filePath)
        Try
            printFont = New Font("Arial", 10)
            Dim pd As New PrintDocument()
            ' This assumes that a method, named pd_PrintPage, has been
            ' defined. pd_PrintPage handles the PrintPage event.
            AddHandler pd.PrintPage, AddressOf pd_PrintPage
            ' This assumes that a variable of type string, named
            ' printer, has been set to the printer's name.
            pd.PrinterSettings.PrinterName = printer
            ' Create a new instance of Margins with one inch margins.
            Dim margins As New Margins(100, 100, 100, 100)
            pd.DefaultPageSettings.Margins = margins
            pd.Print()
        Finally
            streamToPrint.Close()
        End Try
    Catch ex As Exception
        MessageBox.Show("An error occurred printing the file -        ↵
" & ex.Message)
    End Try
End Sub
```

[C#]
```
public void Printing()
{
  try
  {
    /* This assumes that a variable of type string, named filePath,
       has been set to the path of the file to print. */
    streamToPrint = new StreamReader (filePath);
    try
    {
      printFont = new Font("Arial", 10);
      PrintDocument pd = new PrintDocument();
      /* This assumes that a method, named pd_PrintPage, has been
         defined. pd_PrintPage handles the PrintPage event. */
      pd.PrintPage += new PrintPageEventHandler(pd_PrintPage);
      /* This assumes that a variable of type string, named
         printer, has been set to the printer's name. */
      pd.PrinterSettings.PrinterName = printer;
      // Create a new instance of Margins with one inch margins.
      Margins margins = new Margins(100,100,100,100);
      pd.DefaultPageSettings.Margins = margins;
      pd.Print();
    }
    finally
    {
      streamToPrint.Close() ;
    }
  }
  catch(Exception ex)
  {
    MessageBox.Show("An error occurred printing the file -         ↵
  " + ex.Message);
  }
}
```

Margins Constructor ()

Initializes a new instance of the **Margins** class with 1-inch margins.

[Visual Basic]
```
Public Sub New()
```
[C#]
```
public Margins();
```
[C++]
```
public: Margins();
```
[JScript]
```
public function Margins();
```

Requirements

Platforms: Windows 98, Windows NT 4.0, Windows Millennium Edition, Windows 2000, Windows XP Home Edition, Windows XP Professional, Windows Server 2003 family

Margins Constructor (Int32, Int32, Int32, Int32)

Initializes a new instance of the **Margins** class with the specified left, right, top, and bottom margins.

[Visual Basic]
```
Public Sub New( _
   ByVal left As Integer, _
   ByVal right As Integer, _
   ByVal top As Integer, _
   ByVal bottom As Integer _
)
```
[C#]
```
public Margins(
   int left,
   int right,
   int top,
   int bottom
);
```
[C++]
```
public: Margins(
   int left,
   int right,
   int top,
   int bottom
);
```
[JScript]
```
public function Margins(
   left : int,
   right : int,
   top : int,
   bottom : int
);
```

Parameters

left
The left margin, in hundredths of an inch.

right
The right margin, in hundredths of an inch.

top
The top margin, in hundredths of an inch.

bottom
The bottom margin, in hundredths of an inch.

Exceptions

Exception Type	Condition
ArgumentException	The *left* parameter value is less than 0. -or- The *right* parameter value is less than 0. -or- The *top* parameter value is less than 0. -or- The *bottom* parameter value is less than 0.

Example

[Visual Basic, C#] Use the **System.Drawing**, **System.Drawing.Printing**, and **System.IO** namespaces for this example.

[Visual Basic, C#] The following example sets the default page settings for a document to margins of 1 inch on each side.

[Visual Basic]
```
Public Sub Printing()
    Try
        ' This assumes that a variable of type string, named filePath,
        ' has been set to the path of the file to print.
        streamToPrint = New StreamReader(filePath)
        Try
            printFont = New Font("Arial", 10)
            Dim pd As New PrintDocument()
            ' This assumes that a method, named pd_PrintPage, has been
            ' defined. pd_PrintPage handles the PrintPage event.
            AddHandler pd.PrintPage, AddressOf pd_PrintPage
            ' This assumes that a variable of type string, named
            ' printer, has been set to the printer's name.
            pd.PrinterSettings.PrinterName = printer
            ' Create a new instance of Margins with one inch margins.
            Dim margins As New Margins(100, 100, 100, 100)
            pd.DefaultPageSettings.Margins = margins
            pd.Print()
        Finally
            streamToPrint.Close()
        End Try
    Catch ex As Exception
        MessageBox.Show("An error occurred printing the file -      ↵
" & ex.Message)
    End Try
End Sub
```

[C#]
```
public void Printing()
{
  try
  {
    /* This assumes that a variable of type string, named filePath,
       has been set to the path of the file to print. */
    streamToPrint = new StreamReader (filePath);
    try
    {
      printFont = new Font("Arial", 10);
      PrintDocument pd = new PrintDocument();
      /* This assumes that a method, named pd_PrintPage, has been
         defined. pd_PrintPage handles the PrintPage event. */
      pd.PrintPage += new PrintPageEventHandler(pd_PrintPage);
      /* This assumes that a variable of type string, named
         printer, has been set to the printer's name. */
      pd.PrinterSettings.PrinterName = printer;
      // Create a new instance of Margins with one inch margins.
      Margins margins = new Margins(100,100,100,100);
      pd.DefaultPageSettings.Margins = margins;
      pd.Print();
    }
    finally
    {
      streamToPrint.Close() ;
    }
  }
  catch(Exception ex)
  {
    MessageBox.Show("An error occurred printing the file -      ↵
" + ex.Message);
  }
}
```

Requirements

Platforms: Windows 98, Windows NT 4.0, Windows Millennium Edition, Windows 2000, Windows XP Home Edition, Windows XP Professional, Windows Server 2003 family

Margins.Bottom Property

Gets or sets the bottom margin, in hundredths of an inch.

[Visual Basic]
```
Public Property Bottom As Integer
```
[C#]
```
public int Bottom {get; set;}
```
[C++]
```
public: __property int get_Bottom();
public: __property void set_Bottom(int);
```
[JScript]
```
public function get Bottom() : int;
public function set Bottom(int);
```

Property Value

The bottom margin, in hundredths of an inch.

Exceptions

Exception Type	Condition
ArgumentException	The **Bottom** property is set to a value that is less than 0.

Example

[Visual Basic, C#] Use the **System.Drawing**, **System.Drawing.Printing**, and **System.IO** namespaces for this example.

[Visual Basic, C#] The following example sets the default page settings for a document to left and right margins of 1 inch, and top and bottom margins of 1.5 inches.

[Visual Basic]
```
Public Sub Printing()
    Try
        ' This assumes that a variable of type string, named filePath,
        ' has been set to the path of the file to print.
        streamToPrint = New StreamReader(filePath)
        Try
            printFont = New Font("Arial", 10)
            Dim pd As New PrintDocument()
            ' This assumes that a method, named pd_PrintPage, has been
            ' defined. pd_PrintPage handles the PrintPage event.
            AddHandler pd.PrintPage, AddressOf pd_PrintPage
            ' This assumes that a variable of type string, named
            ' printer, has been set to the printer's name.
            pd.PrinterSettings.PrinterName = printer

            ' Set the left and right margins to 1 inch.
            pd.DefaultPageSettings.Margins.Left = 100
            pd.DefaultPageSettings.Margins.Right = 100
            ' Set the top and bottom margins to 1.5 inches.
```

```
            pd.DefaultPageSettings.Margins.Top = 150
            pd.DefaultPageSettings.Margins.Bottom = 150

            pd.Print()
        Finally
            streamToPrint.Close()
        End Try
    Catch ex As Exception
        MessageBox.Show("An error occurred printing the file -        ↵
" & ex.Message)
    End Try
End Sub
```

[C#]

```
public void Printing()
{
  try
  {
    /* This assumes that a variable of type string, named filePath,
       has been set to the path of the file to print. */
    streamToPrint = new StreamReader (filePath);
    try
    {
      printFont = new Font("Arial", 10);
      PrintDocument pd = new PrintDocument();
      /* This assumes that a method, named pd_PrintPage, has been
         defined. pd_PrintPage handles the PrintPage event. */
      pd.PrintPage += new PrintPageEventHandler(pd_PrintPage);
      /* This assumes that a variable of type string, named
         printer, has been set to the printer's name. */
      pd.PrinterSettings.PrinterName = printer;

      // Set the left and right margins to 1 inch.
      pd.DefaultPageSettings.Margins.Left = 100;
      pd.DefaultPageSettings.Margins.Right = 100;
      // Set the top and bottom margins to 1.5 inches.
      pd.DefaultPageSettings.Margins.Top = 150;
      pd.DefaultPageSettings.Margins.Bottom = 150;

      pd.Print();
    }
    finally
    {
      streamToPrint.Close() ;
    }
  }
  catch(Exception ex)
  {
    MessageBox.Show("An error occurred printing the file -        ↵
" + ex.Message);
  }
}
```

Requirements

Platforms: Windows 98, Windows NT 4.0, Windows Millennium Edition, Windows 2000, Windows XP Home Edition, Windows XP Professional, Windows Server 2003 family

Margins.Left Property

Gets or sets the left margin, in hundredths of an inch.

[Visual Basic]

```
Public Property Left As Integer
```

[C#]

```
public int Left {get; set;}
```

[C++]

```
public: __property int get_Left();
public: __property void set_Left(int);
```

[JScript]

```
public function get Left() : int;
public function set Left(int);
```

Property Value

The left margin, in hundredths of an inch.

Exceptions

Exception Type	Condition
ArgumentException	The **Left** property is set to a value that is less than 0.

Example

[Visual Basic, C#] Use the **System.Drawing**, **System.Drawing.Printing**, and **System.IO** namespaces for this example.

[Visual Basic, C#] The following example sets the default page settings for a document to left and right margins of 1 inch, and top and bottom margins of 1.5 inches.

[Visual Basic]

```
Public Sub Printing()
    Try
        ' This assumes that a variable of type string, named filePath,
        ' has been set to the path of the file to print.
        streamToPrint = New StreamReader(filePath)
        Try
            printFont = New Font("Arial", 10)
            Dim pd As New PrintDocument()
            ' This assumes that a method, named pd_PrintPage, has been
            ' defined. pd_PrintPage handles the PrintPage event.
            AddHandler pd.PrintPage, AddressOf pd_PrintPage
            ' This assumes that a variable of type string, named
            ' printer, has been set to the printer's name.
            pd.PrinterSettings.PrinterName = printer

            ' Set the left and right margins to 1 inch.
            pd.DefaultPageSettings.Margins.Left = 100
            pd.DefaultPageSettings.Margins.Right = 100
            ' Set the top and bottom margins to 1.5 inches.
            pd.DefaultPageSettings.Margins.Top = 150
            pd.DefaultPageSettings.Margins.Bottom = 150

            pd.Print()
        Finally
            streamToPrint.Close()
        End Try
    Catch ex As Exception
        MessageBox.Show("An error occurred printing the file -        ↵
" & ex.Message)
    End Try
End Sub
```

[C#]

```
public void Printing()
{
  try
  {
    /* This assumes that a variable of type string, named filePath,
       has been set to the path of the file to print. */
    streamToPrint = new StreamReader (filePath);
    try
    {
      printFont = new Font("Arial", 10);
      PrintDocument pd = new PrintDocument();
      /* This assumes that a method, named pd_PrintPage, has been
         defined. pd_PrintPage handles the PrintPage event. */
      pd.PrintPage += new PrintPageEventHandler(pd_PrintPage);
      /* This assumes that a variable of type string, named
         printer, has been set to the printer's name. */
      pd.PrinterSettings.PrinterName = printer;

      // Set the left and right margins to 1 inch.
      pd.DefaultPageSettings.Margins.Left = 100;
      pd.DefaultPageSettings.Margins.Right = 100;
      // Set the top and bottom margins to 1.5 inches.
      pd.DefaultPageSettings.Margins.Top = 150;
      pd.DefaultPageSettings.Margins.Bottom = 150;
```

```
      pd.Print();
    }
    finally
    {
      streamToPrint.Close() ;
    }
  }
  catch(Exception ex)
  {
    MessageBox.Show("An error occurred printing the file -          ↵
" + ex.Message);
  }
}
```

[C++, JScript] No example is available for C++ or JScript. To view a Visual Basic or C# example, click the Language Filter button <IMG SRC="filter1a.gif" ALT="Language Filter" BORDER=0> in the upper-left corner of the page.

Requirements

Platforms: Windows 98, Windows NT 4.0,
Windows Millennium Edition, Windows 2000,
Windows XP Home Edition, Windows XP Professional,
Windows Server 2003 family

Margins.Right Property

Gets or sets the right margin, in hundredths of an inch.

[Visual Basic]
```
Public Property Right As Integer
```
[C#]
```
public int Right {get; set;}
```
[C++]
```
public: __property int get_Right();
public: __property void set_Right(int);
```
[JScript]
```
public function get Right() : int;
public function set Right(int);
```

Property Value

The right margin, in hundredths of an inch.

Exceptions

Exception Type	Condition
ArgumentException	The **Right** property is set to a value that is less than 0.

Example

[Visual Basic, C#] Use the **System.Drawing**, **System.Drawing.Printing**, and **System.IO** namespaces for this example.

[Visual Basic, C#] The following example sets the default page settings for a document to left and right margins of 1 inch, and top and bottom margins of 1.5 inches.

[Visual Basic]
```
Public Sub Printing()
    Try
        ' This assumes that a variable of type string, named filePath,
        ' has been set to the path of the file to print.
        streamToPrint = New StreamReader(filePath)
        Try
            printFont = New Font("Arial", 10)
            Dim pd As New PrintDocument()
            ' This assumes that a method, named pd_PrintPage, has been
            ' defined. pd_PrintPage handles the PrintPage event.
            AddHandler pd.PrintPage, AddressOf pd_PrintPage
            ' This assumes that a variable of type string, named
            ' printer, has been set to the printer's name.
            pd.PrinterSettings.PrinterName = printer

            ' Set the left and right margins to 1 inch.
            pd.DefaultPageSettings.Margins.Left = 100
            pd.DefaultPageSettings.Margins.Right = 100
            ' Set the top and bottom margins to 1.5 inches.
            pd.DefaultPageSettings.Margins.Top = 150
            pd.DefaultPageSettings.Margins.Bottom = 150

            pd.Print()
        Finally
            streamToPrint.Close()
        End Try
    Catch ex As Exception
        MessageBox.Show("An error occurred printing the file -          ↵
" & ex.Message)
    End Try
End Sub
```

[C#]
```
public void Printing()
{
  try
  {
    /* This assumes that a variable of type string, named filePath,
       has been set to the path of the file to print. */
    streamToPrint = new StreamReader (filePath);
    try
    {
      printFont = new Font("Arial", 10);
      PrintDocument pd = new PrintDocument();
      /* This assumes that a method, named pd_PrintPage, has been
         defined. pd_PrintPage handles the PrintPage event. */
      pd.PrintPage += new PrintPageEventHandler(pd_PrintPage);
      /* This assumes that a variable of type string, named
         printer, has been set to the printer's name. */
      pd.PrinterSettings.PrinterName = printer;

      // Set the left and right margins to 1 inch.
      pd.DefaultPageSettings.Margins.Left = 100;
      pd.DefaultPageSettings.Margins.Right = 100;
      // Set the top and bottom margins to 1.5 inches.
      pd.DefaultPageSettings.Margins.Top = 150;
      pd.DefaultPageSettings.Margins.Bottom = 150;

      pd.Print();
    }
    finally
    {
      streamToPrint.Close() ;
    }
  }
  catch(Exception ex)
  {
    MessageBox.Show("An error occurred printing the file -          ↵
" + ex.Message);
  }
}
```

Requirements

Platforms: Windows 98, Windows NT 4.0,
Windows Millennium Edition, Windows 2000,
Windows XP Home Edition, Windows XP Professional,
Windows Server 2003 family

Margins.Top Property

Gets or sets the top margin, in hundredths of an inch.

[Visual Basic]
```
Public Property Top As Integer
```
[C#]
```
public int Top {get; set;}
```
[C++]
```
public: __property int get_Top();
public: __property void set_Top(int);
```
[JScript]
```
public function get Top() : int;
public function set Top(int);
```

Property Value

The top margin, in hundredths of an inch.

Exceptions

Exception Type	Condition
ArgumentException	The **Top** property is set to a value that is less than 0.

Example

[Visual Basic, C#] Use the **System.Drawing**, **System.Drawing.Printing**, and **System.IO** namespaces for this example.

[Visual Basic, C#] The following example sets the default page settings for a document to left and right margins of 1 inch, and top and bottom margins of 1.5 inches.

[Visual Basic]
```
Public Sub Printing()
    Try
        ' This assumes that a variable of type string, named filePath,
        ' has been set to the path of the file to print.
        streamToPrint = New StreamReader(filePath)
        Try
            printFont = New Font("Arial", 10)
            Dim pd As New PrintDocument()
            ' This assumes that a method, named pd_PrintPage, has been
            ' defined. pd_PrintPage handles the PrintPage event.
            AddHandler pd.PrintPage, AddressOf pd_PrintPage
            ' This assumes that a variable of type string, named
            ' printer, has been set to the printer's name.
            pd.PrinterSettings.PrinterName = printer

            ' Set the left and right margins to 1 inch.
            pd.DefaultPageSettings.Margins.Left = 100
            pd.DefaultPageSettings.Margins.Right = 100
            ' Set the top and bottom margins to 1.5 inches.
            pd.DefaultPageSettings.Margins.Top = 150
            pd.DefaultPageSettings.Margins.Bottom = 150

            pd.Print()
        Finally
            streamToPrint.Close()
        End Try
    Catch ex As Exception
        MessageBox.Show("An error occurred printing the file -        ↵
" & ex.Message)
    End Try
End Sub
```

[C#]
```
public void Printing()
{
  try
  {
    /* This assumes that a variable of type string, named filePath,
       has been set to the path of the file to print. */
    streamToPrint = new StreamReader (filePath);
    try
    {
      printFont = new Font("Arial", 10);
      PrintDocument pd = new PrintDocument();
      /* This assumes that a method, named pd_PrintPage, has been
         defined. pd_PrintPage handles the PrintPage event. */
      pd.PrintPage += new PrintPageEventHandler(pd_PrintPage);
      /* This assumes that a variable of type string, named
         printer, has been set to the printer's name. */
      pd.PrinterSettings.PrinterName = printer;

      // Set the left and right margins to 1 inch.
      pd.DefaultPageSettings.Margins.Left = 100;
      pd.DefaultPageSettings.Margins.Right = 100;
      // Set the top and bottom margins to 1.5 inches.
      pd.DefaultPageSettings.Margins.Top = 150;
      pd.DefaultPageSettings.Margins.Bottom = 150;

      pd.Print();
    }
    finally
    {
      streamToPrint.Close() ;
    }
  }
  catch(Exception ex)
  {
    MessageBox.Show("An error occurred printing the file -        ↵
" + ex.Message);
  }
}
```

Requirements

Platforms: Windows 98, Windows NT 4.0, Windows Millennium Edition, Windows 2000, Windows XP Home Edition, Windows XP Professional, Windows Server 2003 family

Margins.Clone Method

Retrieves a duplicate of this object, member by member.

[Visual Basic]
```
Public Overridable Function Clone() As Object Implements _
   ICloneable.Clone
```
[C#]
```
public virtual object Clone();
```
[C++]
```
public: virtual Object* Clone();
```
[JScript]
```
public function Clone() : Object;
```

Return Value

A duplicate of this object.

Implements

ICloneable.Clone

Requirements

Platforms: Windows 98, Windows NT 4.0, Windows Millennium Edition, Windows 2000, Windows XP Home Edition, Windows XP Professional, Windows Server 2003 family

Margins.Equals Method

This member overrides **Object.Equals**.

[Visual Basic]
```
Overrides Public Function Equals( _
   ByVal obj As Object _
) As Boolean
```
[C#]
```
public override bool Equals(
   object obj
);
```
[C++]
```
public: bool Equals(
   Object* obj
);
```
[JScript]
```
public override function Equals(
   obj : Object
) : Boolean;
```

Requirements

Platforms: Windows 98, Windows NT 4.0, Windows Millennium Edition, Windows 2000, Windows XP Home Edition, Windows XP Professional, Windows Server 2003 family

Margins.GetHashCode Method

This member overrides **Object.GetHashCode**.

[Visual Basic]
```
Overrides Public Function GetHashCode() As Integer
```
[C#]
```
public override int GetHashCode();
```
[C++]
```
public: int GetHashCode();
```
[JScript]
```
public override function GetHashCode() : int;
```

Requirements

Platforms: Windows 98, Windows NT 4.0, Windows Millennium Edition, Windows 2000, Windows XP Home Edition, Windows XP Professional, Windows Server 2003 family

Margins.ToString Method

This member overrides **Object.ToString**.

[Visual Basic]
```
Overrides Public Function ToString() As String
```
[C#]
```
public override string ToString();
```
[C++]
```
public: String* ToString();
```
[JScript]
```
public override function ToString() : String;
```

Requirements

Platforms: Windows 98, Windows NT 4.0, Windows Millennium Edition, Windows 2000, Windows XP Home Edition, Windows XP Professional, Windows Server 2003 family

MarginsConverter Class

Provides a **MarginsConverter** for **Margins**.

System.Object
  System.ComponentModel.TypeConverter
    System.ComponentModel.ExpandableObjectConverter
      System.Drawing.Printing.MarginsConverter

[Visual Basic]
```
Public Class MarginsConverter
   Inherits ExpandableObjectConverter
```
[C#]
```
public class MarginsConverter : ExpandableObjectConverter
```
[C++]
```
public __gc class MarginsConverter : public
   ExpandableObjectConverter
```
[JScript]
```
public class MarginsConverter extends ExpandableObjectConverter
```

Thread Safety

Any public static (**Shared** in Visual Basic) members of this type are safe for multithreaded operations. Any instance members are not guaranteed to be thread safe.

Remarks

MarginsConverter provides methods that can convert a string to a **Margins**.

> **Note** You should never access a type converter directly. Instead, call the appropriate converter by using **TypeDescriptor**. For more information, see the examples in the **TypeConverter** base class.

For more information on printing, see the **System.Drawing.Printing** namespace overview.

Requirements

Namespace: System.Drawing.Printing

Platforms: Windows 98, Windows NT 4.0, Windows Millennium Edition, Windows 2000, Windows XP Home Edition, Windows XP Professional, Windows Server 2003 family

Assembly: System.Drawing (in System.Drawing.dll)

MarginsConverter Constructor

Initializes a new instance of the **MarginsConverter** class.

[Visual Basic]
```
Public Sub New()
```
[C#]
```
public MarginsConverter();
```
[C++]
```
public: MarginsConverter();
```
[JScript]
```
public function MarginsConverter();
```

Remarks

The default constructor initializes any fields to their default values.

Requirements

Platforms: Windows 98, Windows NT 4.0, Windows Millennium Edition, Windows 2000, Windows XP Home Edition, Windows XP Professional, Windows Server 2003 family

MarginsConverter.CanConvertFrom Method

Returns whether this converter can convert an object of the specified source type to the native type of the converter.

Overload List

Returns whether this converter can convert an object of the specified source type to the native type of the converter using the specified context.

[Visual Basic] **Overloads Overrides Public Function CanConvertFrom(ITypeDescriptorContext, Type) As Boolean**

[C#] **public override bool CanConvertFrom(ITypeDescriptorContext, Type);**

[C++] **public: bool CanConvertFrom(ITypeDescriptorContext*, Type*);**

[JScript] **public override function CanConvertFrom(ITypeDescriptorContext, Type) : Boolean;**

Inherited from **TypeConverter**.

[Visual Basic] **Overloads Public Function CanConvertFrom(Type) As Boolean**

[C#] **public bool CanConvertFrom(Type);**

[C++] **public: bool CanConvertFrom(Type*);**

[JScript] **public function CanConvertFrom(Type) : Boolean;**

MarginsConverter.CanConvertFrom Method (ITypeDescriptorContext, Type)

Returns whether this converter can convert an object of the specified source type to the native type of the converter using the specified context.

[Visual Basic]
```
Overrides Overloads Public Function CanConvertFrom( _
   ByVal context As ITypeDescriptorContext, _
   ByVal sourceType As Type _
) As Boolean
```
[C#]
```
public override bool CanConvertFrom(
   ITypeDescriptorContext context,
   Type sourceType
);
```
[C++]
```
public: bool CanConvertFrom(
   ITypeDescriptorContext* context,
   Type* sourceType
);
```
[JScript]
```
public override function CanConvertFrom(
   context : ITypeDescriptorContext,
   sourceType : Type
) : Boolean;
```

Parameters

context

An **ITypeDescriptorContext** that provides a format context.

sourceType

A **Type** that represents the type from which you want to convert.

Return Value

true if an object can perform the conversion; otherwise, **false**.

Remarks

The *context* parameter can be used to extract additional information about the environment from which this converter is being invoked. This can be a null reference (**Nothing** in Visual Basic), so always check. Also, properties on the context object can return a null reference (**Nothing**).

Requirements

Platforms: Windows 98, Windows NT 4.0, Windows Millennium Edition, Windows 2000, Windows XP Home Edition, Windows XP Professional, Windows Server 2003 family

MarginsConverter.CanConvertTo Method

Returns whether this converter can convert an object to the given destination type.

Overload List

Returns whether this converter can convert an object to the given destination type using the context.

[Visual Basic] **Overloads Overrides Public Function CanConvertTo(ITypeDescriptorContext, Type) As Boolean**

[C#] **public override bool CanConvertTo(ITypeDescriptor-Context, Type);**

[C++] **public: bool CanConvertTo(ITypeDescriptorContext*, Type*);**

[JScript] **public override function CanConvertTo(IType-DescriptorContext, Type) : Boolean;**

Inherited from **TypeConverter**.

[Visual Basic] **Overloads Public Function CanConvertTo(Type) As Boolean**

[C#] **public bool CanConvertTo(Type);**

[C++] **public: bool CanConvertTo(Type*);**

[JScript] **public function CanConvertTo(Type) : Boolean;**

MarginsConverter.CanConvertTo Method (ITypeDescriptorContext, Type)

Returns whether this converter can convert an object to the given destination type using the context.

```
[Visual Basic]
Overrides Overloads Public Function CanConvertTo( _
   ByVal context As ITypeDescriptorContext, _
   ByVal destinationType As Type _
) As Boolean
[C#]
public override bool CanConvertTo(
   ITypeDescriptorContext context,
   Type destinationType
);
[C++]
public: bool CanConvertTo(
   ITypeDescriptorContext* context,
   Type* destinationType
);
[JScript]
public override function CanConvertTo(
   context : ITypeDescriptorContext,
   destinationType : Type
) : Boolean;
```

Parameters

context

An **ITypeDescriptorContext** that provides a format context.

destinationType

A **Type** that represents the type to which you want to convert.

Return Value

true if this converter can perform the conversion; otherwise, **false**.

Remarks

The *context* parameter can be used to extract additional information about the environment from which this converter is being invoked. This can be a null reference (**Nothing** in Visual Basic), so always check. Also, properties on the context object can return a null reference (**Nothing**).

Notes to Inheritors: Override this method to provide your own conversion requirements.

Requirements

Platforms: Windows 98, Windows NT 4.0, Windows Millennium Edition, Windows 2000, Windows XP Home Edition, Windows XP Professional, Windows Server 2003 family

MarginsConverter.ConvertFrom Method

Converts the specified object to the converter's native type.

Overload List

Converts the specified object to the converter's native type.

[Visual Basic] **Overloads Overrides Public Function Convert-From(ITypeDescriptorContext, CultureInfo, Object) As Object**

[C#] **public override object ConvertFrom(ITypeDescriptor-Context, CultureInfo, object);**

[C++] **public: Object* ConvertFrom(ITypeDescriptor-Context*, CultureInfo*, Object*);**

[JScript] **public override function ConvertFrom(IType-DescriptorContext, CultureInfo, Object) : Object;**

Inherited from **TypeConverter**.

[Visual Basic] **Overloads Public Function ConvertFrom(Object) As Object**

[C#] **public object ConvertFrom(object);**

[C++] **public: Object* ConvertFrom(Object*);**

[JScript] **public function ConvertFrom(Object) : Object;**

MarginsConverter.ConvertFrom Method (ITypeDescriptorContext, CultureInfo, Object)

Converts the specified object to the converter's native type.

```
[Visual Basic]
Overrides Overloads Public Function ConvertFrom( _
   ByVal context As ITypeDescriptorContext, _
   ByVal culture As CultureInfo, _
   ByVal value As Object _
) As Object
[C#]
public override object ConvertFrom(
   ITypeDescriptorContext context,
   CultureInfo culture,
   object value
);
[C++]
public: Object* ConvertFrom(
   ITypeDescriptorContext* context,
   CultureInfo* culture,
   Object* value
);
[JScript]
public override function ConvertFrom(
   context : ITypeDescriptorContext,
   culture : CultureInfo,
   value : Object
) : Object;
```

Parameters

context
An **ITypeDescriptorContext** that provides a format context.

culture
A **CultureInfo** that provides the language to convert to.

value
The **Object** to convert.

Return Value

An **Object** that represents the converted value.

Exceptions

Exception Type	Condition
ArgumentException	The *value* parameter did not contain values for all four margins. For example, "100,100,100,100" specifies 1 inch for the left, right, top, and bottom margins.
NotSupportedException	The conversion could not be performed.

Remarks

The *context* parameter can be used to extract additional information about the environment from which this converter is being invoked. This can be a null reference (**Nothing** in Visual Basic), so always check. Also, properties on the context object can return a null reference (**Nothing**).

Requirements

Platforms: Windows 98, Windows NT 4.0, Windows Millennium Edition, Windows 2000, Windows XP Home Edition, Windows XP Professional, Windows Server 2003 family

MarginsConverter.ConvertTo Method

Converts the given value object to the specified destination type.

Overload List

Converts the given value object to the specified destination type using the specified context and arguments.

[Visual Basic] **Overloads Overrides Public Function ConvertTo(ITypeDescriptorContext, CultureInfo, Object, Type) As Object**

[C#] **public override object ConvertTo(ITypeDescriptor-Context, CultureInfo, object, Type);**

[C++] **public: Object* ConvertTo(ITypeDescriptorContext*, CultureInfo*, Object*, Type*);**

[JScript] **public override function ConvertTo(IType-DescriptorContext, CultureInfo, Object, Type) : Object;**

Inherited from **TypeConverter**.

[Visual Basic] **Overloads Public Function ConvertTo(Object, Type) As Object**

[C#] **public object ConvertTo(object, Type);**

[C++] **public: Object* ConvertTo(Object*, Type*);**

[JScript] **public function ConvertTo(Object, Type) : Object;**

MarginsConverter.ConvertTo Method (ITypeDescriptorContext, CultureInfo, Object, Type)

Converts the given value object to the specified destination type using the specified context and arguments.

```
[Visual Basic]
Overrides Overloads Public Function ConvertTo( _
   ByVal context As ITypeDescriptorContext, _
   ByVal culture As CultureInfo, _
   ByVal value As Object, _
   ByVal destinationType As Type _
) As Object
[C#]
public override object ConvertTo(
   ITypeDescriptorContext context,
   CultureInfo culture,
   object value,
   Type destinationType
);
[C++]
public: Object* ConvertTo(
   ITypeDescriptorContext* context,
   CultureInfo* culture,
   Object* value,
   Type* destinationType
);
[JScript]
public override function ConvertTo(
   context : ITypeDescriptorContext,
   culture : CultureInfo,
   value : Object,
   destinationType : Type
) : Object;
```

Parameters

context

An **ITypeDescriptorContext** that provides a format context.

culture

A **CultureInfo** that provides the language to convert to.

value

The **Object** to convert.

destinationType

The **Type** to which to convert the value.

Return Value

An **Object** that represents the converted value.

Exceptions

Exception Type	Condition
ArgumentNull-Exception	The *destinationType* is a null reference (**Nothing** in Visual Basic).
NotSupportedException	The conversion could not be performed.

Remarks

The *context* parameter can be used to extract additional information about the environment from which this converter is being invoked. This can be a null reference (**Nothing** in Visual Basic), so always check. Also, properties on the context object can return a null reference (**Nothing**).

Requirements

Platforms: Windows 98, Windows NT 4.0, Windows Millennium Edition, Windows 2000, Windows XP Home Edition, Windows XP Professional, Windows Server 2003 family

MarginsConverter.CreateInstance Method

Creates an **Object**.

Overload List

Creates an **Object** given a set of property values for the object.

[Visual Basic] **Overloads Overrides Public Function CreateInstance(ITypeDescriptorContext, IDictionary) As Object**

[C#] **public override object CreateInstance(ITypeDescriptorContext, IDictionary);**

[C++] **public: Object* CreateInstance(ITypeDescriptorContext*, IDictionary*);**

[JScript] **public override function CreateInstance(ITypeDescriptorContext, IDictionary) : Object;**

Inherited from **TypeConverter**.

[Visual Basic] **Overloads Public Function CreateInstance(IDictionary) As Object**

[C#] **public object CreateInstance(IDictionary);**

[C++] **public: Object* CreateInstance(IDictionary*);**

[JScript] **public function CreateInstance(IDictionary) : Object;**

MarginsConverter.CreateInstance Method (ITypeDescriptorContext, IDictionary)

Creates an **Object** given a set of property values for the object.

```
[Visual Basic]
Overrides Overloads Public Function CreateInstance( _
   ByVal context As ITypeDescriptorContext, _
   ByVal propertyValues As IDictionary _
) As Object
[C#]
public override object CreateInstance(
   ITypeDescriptorContext context,
   IDictionary propertyValues
);
[C++]
public: Object* CreateInstance(
   ITypeDescriptorContext* context,
   IDictionary* propertyValues
);
[JScript]
public override function CreateInstance(
   context : ITypeDescriptorContext,
   propertyValues : IDictionary
) : Object;
```

Parameters

context

An **ITypeDescriptorContext** that provides a format context.

propertyValues

An **IDictionary** of new property values.

Return Value

An **Object** representing the specified **IDictionary**; or a null reference (**Nothing** in Visual Basic) if the object cannot be created.

Remarks

The *context* parameter can be used to extract additional information about the environment from which this converter is being invoked. This can be a null reference (**Nothing** in Visual Basic), so always check. Also, properties on the context object can return a null reference (**Nothing**).

Requirements

Platforms: Windows 98, Windows NT 4.0, Windows Millennium Edition, Windows 2000, Windows XP Home Edition, Windows XP Professional, Windows Server 2003 family

MarginsConverter.GetCreateInstanceSupported Method

Returns whether changing a value on this object requires a call to **CreateInstance** to create a new value.

Overload List

Returns whether changing a value on this object requires a call to **CreateInstance** to create a new value, using the specified context.

[Visual Basic] **Overloads Overrides Public Function GetCreateInstanceSupported(ITypeDescriptorContext) As Boolean**

[C#] **public override bool GetCreateInstanceSupported(ITypeDescriptorContext);**

[C++] **public: bool GetCreateInstanceSupported(ITypeDescriptorContext*);**

[JScript] **public override function GetCreateInstanceSupported(ITypeDescriptorContext) : Boolean;**

Inherited from **TypeConverter**.

[Visual Basic] **Overloads Public Function GetCreateInstanceSupported() As Boolean**

[C#] **public bool GetCreateInstanceSupported();**

[C++] **public: bool GetCreateInstanceSupported();**

[JScript] **public function GetCreateInstanceSupported() : Boolean;**

MarginsConverter.GetCreateInstanceSupported Method (ITypeDescriptorContext)

Returns whether changing a value on this object requires a call to **CreateInstance** to create a new value, using the specified context.

[Visual Basic]
```
Overrides Overloads Public Function GetCreateInstanceSupported( _
   ByVal context As ITypeDescriptorContext _
) As Boolean
```
[C#]
```
public override bool GetCreateInstanceSupported(
   ITypeDescriptorContext context
);
```
[C++]
```
public: bool GetCreateInstanceSupported(
   ITypeDescriptorContext* context
);
```
[JScript]
```
public override function GetCreateInstanceSupported(
   context : ITypeDescriptorContext
) : Boolean;
```

Parameters

context

An **ITypeDescriptorContext** that provides a format context.

Return Value

true if changing a property on this object requires a call to **CreateInstance** to create a new value; otherwise, **false**. This method always returns **true**.

Remarks

The *context* parameter can be used to extract additional information about the environment from which this converter is being invoked. This can be a null reference (**Nothing** in Visual Basic), so always check. Also, properties on the context object can return a null reference (**Nothing**).

Requirements

Platforms: Windows 98, Windows NT 4.0, Windows Millennium Edition, Windows 2000, Windows XP Home Edition, Windows XP Professional, Windows Server 2003 family

PageSettings Class

Specifies settings that apply to a single, printed page.

System.Object
System.Drawing.Printing.PageSettings

```
[Visual Basic]
<ComVisible(False)>
Public Class PageSettings
   Implements ICloneable
[C#]
[ComVisible(false)]
public class PageSettings : ICloneable
[C++]
[ComVisible(false)]
public __gc class PageSettings : public ICloneable
[JScript]
public
   ComVisible(false)
class PageSettings implements ICloneable
```

Thread Safety

Any public static (**Shared** in Visual Basic) members of this type are safe for multithreaded operations. Any instance members are not guaranteed to be thread safe.

Remarks

This class is used to specify settings that modify the way a page will be printed. Typically, you set default settings for all pages to be printed through the **PrintDocument.DefaultPageSettings** property. To specify settings on a page-by-page basis, handle the **PrintDocument.PrintPage** or **PrintDocument.QueryPageSettings** event and modify the **PageSettings** argument included in the **PrintPageEventArgs** or **QueryPageSettingsEventArgs**, respectively.

For more information on handling **PrintDocument** events, see the **PrintDocument** class overview. For more information on printing, see the **System.Drawing.Printing** namespace overview.

Example

[Visual Basic, C#] The following example sets the document's default page orientation to landscape through the **PrintDocument.DefaultPageSettings** property, and prints the document using the **Print** method. The example makes three assumptions: that a variable named `filePath` has been set to the path of the file to print; that a method named `pd_PrintPage`, which handles the **PrintPage** event, has been defined; and that a variable named `printer` has been set to the printer's name.

[Visual Basic, C#] Use the **System.Drawing**, **System.Drawing.Printing**, and **System.IO** namespaces for this example.

```
[Visual Basic]
Public Sub Printing()
    Try
        streamToPrint = New StreamReader(filePath)
        Try
            printFont = New Font("Arial", 10)
            Dim pd As New PrintDocument()
            AddHandler pd.PrintPage, AddressOf pd_PrintPage
            pd.PrinterSettings.PrinterName = printer
            ' Set the page orientation to landscape.
            pd.DefaultPageSettings.Landscape = True
            pd.Print()
        Finally
            streamToPrint.Close()
        End Try
    Catch ex As Exception
        MessageBox.Show(ex.Message)
    End Try
End Sub
```

```
[C#]
public void Printing() {
   try {
     streamToPrint = new StreamReader (filePath);
     try {
       printFont = new Font("Arial", 10);
       PrintDocument pd = new PrintDocument();
       pd.PrintPage += new PrintPageEventHandler(pd_PrintPage);
       pd.PrinterSettings.PrinterName = printer;
       // Set the page orientation to landscape.
       pd.DefaultPageSettings.Landscape = true;
       pd.Print();
     }
     finally {
       streamToPrint.Close() ;
     }
   }
   catch(Exception ex) {
     MessageBox.Show(ex.Message);
   }
 }
```

Requirements

Namespace: System.Drawing.Printing

Platforms: Windows 98, Windows NT 4.0, Windows Millennium Edition, Windows 2000, Windows XP Home Edition, Windows XP Professional, Windows Server 2003 family

Assembly: System.Drawing (in System.Drawing.dll)

PageSettings Constructor

Initializes a new instance of the **PageSettings** class .

Overload List

Initializes a new instance of the **PageSettings** class using the default printer.

[Visual Basic] **Public Sub New()**

[C#] **public PageSettings();**

[C++] **public: PageSettings();**

[JScript] **public function PageSettings();**

Initializes a new instance of the **PageSettings** class using a specified printer.

[Visual Basic] **Public Sub New(PrinterSettings)**

[C#] **public PageSettings(PrinterSettings);**

[C++] **public: PageSettings(PrinterSettings*);**

[JScript] **public function PageSettings(PrinterSettings);**

PageSettings Constructor ()

Initializes a new instance of the **PageSettings** class using the default printer.

```
[Visual Basic]
Public Sub New()
[C#]
public PageSettings();
```

```
[C++]
public: PageSettings();
[JScript]
public function PageSettings();
```

Remarks

The default constructor initializes all fields to their default values.

Typically, you do not create an instance of **PageSettings**, but instead use the **PrintDocument.DefaultPageSettings** to set settings for all pages.

Requirements

Platforms: Windows 98, Windows NT 4.0, Windows Millennium Edition, Windows 2000, Windows XP Home Edition, Windows XP Professional, Windows Server 2003 family

PageSettings Constructor (PrinterSettings)

Initializes a new instance of the **PageSettings** class using a specified printer.

```
[Visual Basic]
Public Sub New( _
   ByVal printerSettings As PrinterSettings _
)
[C#]
public PageSettings(
   PrinterSettings printerSettings
);
[C++]
public: PageSettings(
   PrinterSettings* printerSettings
);
[JScript]
public function PageSettings(
   printerSettings : PrinterSettings
);
```

Parameters

printerSettings

The **PrinterSettings** that describes the printer to use.

Remarks

This constructor is similar to initializing a new instance of **PageSettings** and setting the **PrinterSettings** property.

Requirements

Platforms: Windows 98, Windows NT 4.0, Windows Millennium Edition, Windows 2000, Windows XP Home Edition, Windows XP Professional, Windows Server 2003 family

PageSettings.Bounds Property

Gets the size of the page, taking into account the page orientation specified by the **Landscape** property.

```
[Visual Basic]
Public ReadOnly Property Bounds As Rectangle
[C#]
public Rectangle Bounds {get;}
[C++]
public: __property Rectangle get_Bounds();
[JScript]
public function get Bounds() : Rectangle;
```

Property Value

A **Rectangle** that represents the length and width (in hundredths of an inch) of the page.

Exceptions

Exception Type	Condition
InvalidPrinterException	The printer named in the **PrinterSettings.PrinterName** property does not exist.

Remarks

Use this property along with the **Margins** property to calculate the printing area for the page.

Requirements

Platforms: Windows 98, Windows NT 4.0, Windows Millennium Edition, Windows 2000, Windows XP Home Edition, Windows XP Professional, Windows Server 2003 family

PageSettings.Color Property

Gets or sets a value indicating whether the page should be printed in color.

```
[Visual Basic]
Public Property Color As Boolean
[C#]
public bool Color {get; set;}
[C++]
public: __property bool get_Color();
public: __property void set_Color(bool);
[JScript]
public function get Color() : Boolean;
public function set Color(Boolean);
```

Property Value

true if the page should be printed in color; otherwise, **false**. The default is determined by the printer.

Exceptions

Exception Type	Condition
InvalidPrinterException	The printer named in the **PrinterSettings.PrinterName** property does not exist.

Remarks

You can use the **PrinterSettings.SupportsColor** property to determine if the printer supports color printing. If the printer supports color, but you do not want to print in color, set the **Color** property to **false** (the default will be **true**).

Example

[Visual Basic, C#, C++] The following example prints a document with the first page in color, if the printer supports it. The example assumes that a **PrintDocument** variable named `printDoc` has been created, and the **PrintPage** and **QueryPageSettings** events are handled.

[Visual Basic, C#, C++] Use the **System.Drawing** and **System.Drawing.Printing** namespaces for this example.

[Visual Basic]
```
    Private Sub MyButtonPrint_OnClick(ByVal sender As Object, ↵
ByVal e As System.EventArgs)

        ' Set the printer name and ensure it is valid. If not, ↵
 provide a message to the user.
        printDoc.PrinterSettings.PrinterName = "\\mynetworkprinter"

        If printDoc.PrinterSettings.IsValid Then

            ' If the printer supports printing in color, then ↵
override the printer's default behavior.
            if printDoc.PrinterSettings.SupportsColor then

                ' Set the page default's to not print in color.
                printDoc.DefaultPageSettings.Color = False
            End If

            ' Provide a friendly name, set the page number, ↵
and print the document.
            printDoc.DocumentName = "My Presentation"
            currentPageNumber = 1
            printDoc.Print()
        Else
            MessageBox.Show("Printer is not valid")
        End If
    End Sub

    Private Sub MyPrintQueryPageSettingsEvent(ByVal sender As ↵
 Object, ByVal e As QueryPageSettingsEventArgs)

        ' Determines if the printer supports printing in color.
        If printDoc.PrinterSettings.SupportsColor Then

            ' If the printer supports color printing, use color.
            If currentPageNumber = 1 Then

                e.PageSettings.Color = True
            End If

        End If
    End Sub
```

[C#]
```
    private void MyButtonPrint_OnClick(object sender, ↵
System.EventArgs e)
    {

        // Set the printer name and ensure it is valid. If not, ↵
 provide a message to the user.
        printDoc.PrinterSettings.PrinterName = "\\mynetworkprinter";

        if (printDoc.PrinterSettings.IsValid) {

            // If the printer supports printing in color, then ↵
override the printer's default behavior.
            if (printDoc.PrinterSettings.SupportsColor) {

                // Set the page default's to not print in color.
                printDoc.DefaultPageSettings.Color = false;
            }

            // Provide a friendly name, set the page number, ↵
and print the document.
            printDoc.DocumentName = "My Presentation";
            currentPageNumber = 1;
            printDoc.Print();
        }
        else {
            MessageBox.Show("Printer is not valid");
        }
    }

    private void MyPrintQueryPageSettingsEvent(object sender, ↵
QueryPageSettingsEventArgs e)
    {
        // Determines if the printer supports printing in color.
        if (printDoc.PrinterSettings.SupportsColor) {

            // If the printer supports color printing, use color.
            if (currentPageNumber == 1 ) {

                e.PageSettings.Color = true;
            }

        }
    }
```

[C++]
```
private:
   void MyButtonPrint_OnClick(Object* sender, System::EventArgs* e) {

      // Set the printer name and ensure it is valid. If not, ↵
 provide a message to the user.
      printDoc->PrinterSettings->PrinterName = S"\\mynetworkprinter";

      if (printDoc->PrinterSettings->IsValid) {

         // If the printer supports printing in color, then ↵
 the printer's default behavior.
         if (printDoc->PrinterSettings->SupportsColor) {

            // Set the page default's to not print in color.
            printDoc->DefaultPageSettings->Color = false;
         }

         // Provide a friendly name, set the page number, ↵
and print the document.
         printDoc->DocumentName = S"My Presentation";
         currentPageNumber = 1;
         printDoc->Print();
      } else {
         MessageBox::Show(S"Printer is not valid");
      }
   }

private:
   void MyPrintQueryPageSettingsEvent(Object* sender, ↵
QueryPageSettingsEventArgs* e) {
      // Determines if the printer supports printing in color.
      if (printDoc->PrinterSettings->SupportsColor) {

         // If the printer supports color printing, use color.
         if (currentPageNumber == 1) {

            e->PageSettings->Color = true;
         }

      }
   }
```

Requirements

Platforms: Windows 98, Windows NT 4.0, Windows Millennium Edition, Windows 2000, Windows XP Home Edition, Windows XP Professional, Windows Server 2003 family

PageSettings.Landscape Property

Gets or sets a value indicating whether the page is printed in landscape or portrait orientation.

[Visual Basic]
```
Public Property Landscape As Boolean
```
[C#]
```
public bool Landscape {get; set;}
```
[C++]
```
public: __property bool get_Landscape();
public: __property void set_Landscape(bool);
```
[JScript]
```
public function get Landscape() : Boolean;
public function set Landscape(Boolean);
```

Property Value

true if the page should be printed in landscape orientation; otherwise, **false**. The default is determined by the printer.

Exceptions

Exception Type	Condition
InvalidPrinterException	The printer named in the **PrinterSettings.PrinterName** property does not exist.

Remarks

You can use the **PrinterSettings.LandscapeAngle** property to determine the angle, in degrees, that the portrait orientation is rotated to produce the landscape orientation.

Example

[Visual Basic, C#] The following example sets a document's default page orientation to landscape through the **PrintDocument.DefaultPageSettings** property, and prints the document. The example makes three assumptions: that a variable named `filePath` has been set to the path of the file to print; that a method named `pd_PrintPage`, which handles the **PrintPage** event, has been defined; and that a variable named `printer` has been set to the printer's name.

[Visual Basic, C#] Use the **System.Drawing**, **System.Drawing.Printing**, and **System.IO** namespaces for this example.

[Visual Basic]

```
Public Sub Printing()
    Try
        streamToPrint = New StreamReader(filePath)
        Try
            printFont = New Font("Arial", 10)
            Dim pd As New PrintDocument()
            AddHandler pd.PrintPage, AddressOf pd_PrintPage
            pd.PrinterSettings.PrinterName = printer
            ' Set the page orientation to landscape.
            pd.DefaultPageSettings.Landscape = True
            pd.Print()
        Finally
            streamToPrint.Close()
        End Try
    Catch ex As Exception
        MessageBox.Show(ex.Message)
    End Try
End Sub
```

[C#]

```
public void Printing() {
   try {
     streamToPrint = new StreamReader (filePath);
     try {
       printFont = new Font("Arial", 10);
       PrintDocument pd = new PrintDocument();
       pd.PrintPage += new PrintPageEventHandler(pd_PrintPage);
       pd.PrinterSettings.PrinterName = printer;
       // Set the page orientation to landscape.
       pd.DefaultPageSettings.Landscape = true;
       pd.Print();
     }
     finally {
       streamToPrint.Close() ;
     }
   }
   catch(Exception ex) {
     MessageBox.Show(ex.Message);
   }
 }
```

Requirements

Platforms: Windows 98, Windows NT 4.0, Windows Millennium Edition, Windows 2000, Windows XP Home Edition, Windows XP Professional, Windows Server 2003 family

PageSettings.Margins Property

Gets or sets the margins for this page.

[Visual Basic]
```
Public Property Margins As Margins
```
[C#]
```
public Margins Margins {get; set;}
```
[C++]
```
public: __property Margins* get_Margins();
public: __property void set_Margins(Margins*);
```
[JScript]
```
public function get Margins() : Margins;
public function set Margins(Margins);
```

Property Value

A **Margins** that represents the margins (in hundredths of an inch) for the page. The default is 1-inch margins on all sides.

Exceptions

Exception Type	Condition
InvalidPrinterException	The printer named in the **PrinterSettings.PrinterName** property does not exist.

Remarks

When handling the **PrintDocument.PrintPage** event, you can use this property along with the **Bounds** property to calculate the printing area for the page.

Example

[Visual Basic, C#] The following example sets the default page settings for a document to margins to 1 inch on each side. The example makes three assumptions: that a variable named `filePath` has been set to the path of the file to print; that a method named `pd_PrintPage`, which handles the **PrintPage** event, has been defined; and that a variable named `printer` has been set to the printer's name.

[Visual Basic, C#] Use the **System.Drawing**, **System.Drawing.Printing**, and **System.IO** namespaces for this example.

[Visual Basic]

```
Public Sub Printing()
    Try
        streamToPrint = New StreamReader(filePath)
        Try
            printFont = New Font("Arial", 10)
            Dim pd As New PrintDocument()
            AddHandler pd.PrintPage, AddressOf pd_PrintPage
            pd.PrinterSettings.PrinterName = printer
            ' Create a new instance of Margins with 1-inch margins.
            Dim margins As New Margins(100, 100, 100, 100)
            pd.DefaultPageSettings.Margins = margins
            pd.Print()
        Finally
            streamToPrint.Close()
        End Try
    Catch ex As Exception
        MessageBox.Show(ex.Message)
    End Try
End Sub 'Printing
```

[C#]
```
public void Printing(){
   try{
     streamToPrint = new StreamReader (filePath);
     try{
       printFont = new Font("Arial", 10);
       PrintDocument pd = new PrintDocument();
       pd.PrintPage += new PrintPageEventHandler(pd_PrintPage);
       pd.PrinterSettings.PrinterName = printer;
       // Create a new instance of Margins with 1-inch margins.
       Margins margins = new Margins(100,100,100,100);
       pd.DefaultPageSettings.Margins = margins;
       pd.Print();
     }
     finally{
       streamToPrint.Close() ;
     }
   }
   catch(Exception ex){
     MessageBox.Show(ex.Message);
   }
}
```

Requirements

Platforms: Windows 98, Windows NT 4.0, Windows Millennium Edition, Windows 2000, Windows XP Home Edition, Windows XP Professional, Windows Server 2003 family

PageSettings.PaperSize Property

Gets or sets the paper size for the page.

[Visual Basic]
```
Public Property PaperSize As PaperSize
```
[C#]
```
public PaperSize PaperSize {get; set;}
```
[C++]
```
public: __property PaperSize* get_PaperSize();
public: __property void set_PaperSize(PaperSize*);
```
[JScript]
```
public function get PaperSize() : PaperSize;
public function set PaperSize(PaperSize);
```

Property Value

A **PaperSize** that represents the size of the paper. Defaults to the printer's default paper size.

Exceptions

Exception Type	Condition
InvalidPrinterException	The printer named in the **PrinterSettings.PrinterName** property does not exist or there is no default printer installed.

Remarks

An instance of **PaperSize** represents the size of the paper through the **PaperSize.Kind** property, which contains one of the **PaperKind** values.

Set the **PaperSize** property for the page to a valid **PaperSize**, available through the **PrinterSettings.PaperSizes** collection.

See the **PaperSize** constructor to find out how you can specify a custom paper size.

Example

[Visual Basic, C#, C++] The following example sets three properties for the document's default page, including the paper size based upon the size selected in the `comboPaperSize` combo box, and then prints the document using the **Print** method. The example assumes that a **PrintDocument** variable named `printDoc` exists and that the specific combo boxes exists.

[Visual Basic]
```
Private Sub MyButtonPrint_Click(ByVal sender As System.Object, ↵
ByVal e As System.EventArgs) Handles MyButtonPrint.Click

    ' Set the paper size based upon the selection in the combo box.
    If comboPaperSize.SelectedIndex <> -1 Then
        printDoc.DefaultPageSettings.PaperSize = _
        printDoc.PrinterSettings.PaperSizes.Item(combo ↵
PaperSize.SelectedIndex)
    End If

    ' Set the paper source based upon the selection in the combo box.
    If comboPaperSource.SelectedIndex <> -1 Then
        printDoc.DefaultPageSettings.PaperSource = _
        printDoc.PrinterSettings.PaperSources.Item(combo ↵
PaperSource.SelectedIndex)
    End If

    ' Set the printer resolution based upon the selection in the ↵
combo box.
    If comboPrintResolution.SelectedIndex <> -1 Then
        printDoc.DefaultPageSettings.PrinterResolution = _
        printDoc.PrinterSettings.Printer ↵
Resolutions.Item(comboPrintResolution.SelectedIndex)
    End If

    ' Print the document with the specified paper size and source.
    printDoc.Print()

End Sub
```

[C#]
```
private void MyButtonPrint_Click(object sender, System.EventArgs e)
{
    // Set the paper size based upon the selection in the combo box.
    if (comboPaperSize.SelectedIndex != -1) {
        printDoc.DefaultPageSettings.PaperSize =

printDoc.PrinterSettings.PaperSizes[comboPaperSize.SelectedIndex];
    }

    // Set the paper source based upon the selection in the combo box.
    if (comboPaperSource.SelectedIndex != -1) {
        printDoc.DefaultPageSettings.PaperSource =

printDoc.PrinterSettings.PaperSources[comboPaperSource.SelectedIndex];
    }

    // Set the printer resolution based upon the selection in ↵
the combo box.
    if (comboPrintResolution.SelectedIndex != -1)
    {
        printDoc.DefaultPageSettings.PrinterResolution=
            printDoc.PrinterSettings.PrinterResolutions ↵
 [comboPrintResolution.SelectedIndex];
    }

    // Print the document with the specified paper size, ↵
 source, and print resolution.
    printDoc.Print();
}
```

[C++]
```
private:
   void MyButtonPrint_Click(Object* sender, System::EventArgs* e) {
      // Set the paper size based upon the selection in the combo box.
      if (comboPaperSize->SelectedIndex != -1) {
         printDoc->DefaultPageSettings->PaperSize =
            printDoc->PrinterSettings->PaperSizes->Item
 [comboPaperSize->SelectedIndex];
      }

      // Set the paper source based upon the selection in
the combo box.
      if (comboPaperSource->SelectedIndex != -1) {
         printDoc->DefaultPageSettings->PaperSource =
            printDoc->PrinterSettings->PaperSources-
>Item[comboPaperSource->SelectedIndex];
      }

      // Set the printer resolution based upon the selection
 in the combo box.
      if (comboPrintResolution->SelectedIndex != -1) {
         printDoc->DefaultPageSettings->PrinterResolution=
            printDoc->PrinterSettings->PrinterResolutions-
>Item[comboPrintResolution->SelectedIndex];
      }

      // Print the document with the specified paper size,
source, and print resolution.
      printDoc->Print();
   }
```

Requirements

Platforms: Windows 98, Windows NT 4.0, Windows Millennium Edition, Windows 2000, Windows XP Home Edition, Windows XP Professional, Windows Server 2003 family

PageSettings.PaperSource Property

Gets or sets the page's paper source (for example, the printer's upper tray).

[Visual Basic]
```
Public Property PaperSource As PaperSource
```
[C#]
```
public PaperSource PaperSource {get; set;}
```
[C++]
```
public: __property PaperSource* get_PaperSource();
public: __property void set_PaperSource(PaperSource*);
```
[JScript]
```
public function get PaperSource() : PaperSource;
public function set PaperSource(PaperSource);
```

Property Value

A **PaperSource** that specifies the source of the paper. Defaults to the printer's default paper source.

Exceptions

Exception Type	Condition
InvalidPrinterException	The printer named in the **PrinterSettings.PrinterName** property does not exist or there is no default printer installed.

Remarks

An instance of **PaperSource** represents the source of the paper through the **PaperSource.Kind** property, which contains one of the **PaperSourceKind** values.

Set the **PaperSource** property for the page to a valid **PaperSource**, available through the **PrinterSettings.PaperSources** collection.

Example

[Visual Basic, C#, C++] The following example sets three properties for the document's default page, including the paper source based upon the source selected in the `comboPaperSource` combo box, and then prints the document using the **Print** method. The example assumes that a **PrintDocument** variable named `printDoc` exists and that the specific combo boxes exists.

[Visual Basic]
```
Private Sub MyButtonPrint_Click(ByVal sender As System.Object,
ByVal e As System.EventArgs) Handles MyButtonPrint.Click

    ' Set the paper size based upon the selection in the combo box.
    If comboPaperSize.SelectedIndex <> -1 Then
        printDoc.DefaultPageSettings.PaperSize = _
        printDoc.PrinterSettings.PaperSizes.Item(combo
PaperSize.SelectedIndex)
    End If

    ' Set the paper source based upon the selection in the combo box.
    If comboPaperSource.SelectedIndex <> -1 Then
        printDoc.DefaultPageSettings.PaperSource = _
        printDoc.PrinterSettings.PaperSources.Item
 (comboPaperSource.SelectedIndex)
    End If

    ' Set the printer resolution based upon the selection in
 the combo box.
    If comboPrintResolution.SelectedIndex <> -1 Then
        printDoc.DefaultPageSettings.PrinterResolution = _
        printDoc.PrinterSettings.Printer
Resolutions.Item(comboPrintResolution.SelectedIndex)
    End If

    ' Print the document with the specified paper size and source.
    printDoc.Print()

End Sub
```

[C#]
```
private void MyButtonPrint_Click(object sender, System.EventArgs e)
{
    // Set the paper size based upon the selection in the combo box.
    if (comboPaperSize.SelectedIndex != -1) {
        printDoc.DefaultPageSettings.PaperSize =

printDoc.PrinterSettings.PaperSizes[comboPaperSize.SelectedIndex];
    }

    // Set the paper source based upon the selection in the combo box.
    if (comboPaperSource.SelectedIndex != -1) {
        printDoc.DefaultPageSettings.PaperSource =
            printDoc.PrinterSettings.PaperSources[combo
PaperSource.SelectedIndex];
    }

    // Set the printer resolution based upon the selection in
the combo box.
    if (comboPrintResolution.SelectedIndex != -1)
    {
        printDoc.DefaultPageSettings.PrinterResolution=
            printDoc.PrinterSettings.PrinterResolutions
 [comboPrintResolution.SelectedIndex];
    }

    // Print the document with the specified paper size,
 source, and print resolution.
    printDoc.Print();
}
```

[C++]
```
private:
   void MyButtonPrint_Click(Object* sender, System::EventArgs* e) {
      // Set the paper size based upon the selection in the combo box.
      if (comboPaperSize->SelectedIndex != -1) {
         printDoc->DefaultPageSettings->PaperSize =
            printDoc->PrinterSettings->PaperSizes->Item                    ↵
 [comboPaperSize->SelectedIndex];
      }

      // Set the paper source based upon the selection in the            ↵
combo box.
      if (comboPaperSource->SelectedIndex != -1) {
         printDoc->DefaultPageSettings->PaperSource =
            printDoc->PrinterSettings->PaperSources-
>Item[comboPaperSource->SelectedIndex];
      }

      // Set the printer resolution based upon the selection             ↵
 in the combo box.
      if (comboPrintResolution->SelectedIndex != -1) {
         printDoc->DefaultPageSettings->PrinterResolution=
            printDoc->PrinterSettings->PrinterResolutions-               ↵
>Item[comboPrintResolution->SelectedIndex];
      }

      // Print the document with the specified paper size,               ↵
source, and print resolution.
      printDoc->Print();
   }
```

Requirements

Platforms: Windows 98, Windows NT 4.0, Windows Millennium Edition, Windows 2000, Windows XP Home Edition, Windows XP Professional, Windows Server 2003 family

PageSettings.PrinterResolution Property

Gets or sets the printer resolution for the page.

[Visual Basic]
```
Public Property PrinterResolution As PrinterResolution
```
[C#]
```
public PrinterResolution PrinterResolution {get; set;}
```
[C++]
```
public: __property PrinterResolution* get_PrinterResolution();
public: __property void set_PrinterResolution(PrinterResolution*);
```
[JScript]
```
public function get PrinterResolution() : PrinterResolution;
public function set PrinterResolution(PrinterResolution);
```

Property Value

A **PrinterResolution** that specifies the printer resolution for the page. Defaults to the printer's default resolution.

Exceptions

Exception Type	Condition
InvalidPrinterException	The printer named in the **PrinterSettings.PrinterName** property does not exist or there is no default printer installed.

Remarks

An instance of **PrinterResolution** represents the source of the paper through the **PrinterResolution.Kind** property, which contains one of the **PrinterResolutionKind** values.

Set the **PrinterResolution** property for the page to a valid **PrinterResolution**, available through the **PrinterSettings.PrinterResolutions** collection.

Example

[Visual Basic, C#, C++] The following example sets three properties for the document's default page, including the printer's resolution based upon the resolution selected in the `comboPrintResolution` combo box, and then prints the document using the **Print** method. The example assumes that a **PrintDocument** variable named `printDoc` exists and that the specific combo boxes exists.

[Visual Basic]
```
Private Sub MyButtonPrint_Click(ByVal sender As System.Object,              ↵
ByVal e As System.EventArgs) Handles MyButtonPrint.Click

    ' Set the paper size based upon the selection in the combo box.
    If comboPaperSize.SelectedIndex <> -1 Then
        printDoc.DefaultPageSettings.PaperSize = _
        printDoc.PrinterSettings.PaperSizes.Item(combo                      ↵
PaperSize.SelectedIndex)
    End If

    ' Set the paper source based upon the selection in the combo box.
    If comboPaperSource.SelectedIndex <> -1 Then
        printDoc.DefaultPageSettings.PaperSource = _
        printDoc.PrinterSettings.PaperSources.Item                          ↵
 (comboPaperSource.SelectedIndex)
    End If

    ' Set the printer resolution based upon the selection in                ↵
the combo box.
    If comboPrintResolution.SelectedIndex <> -1 Then
        printDoc.DefaultPageSettings.PrinterResolution = _
        printDoc.PrinterSettings.PrinterResolutions.Item                    ↵
 (comboPrintResolution.SelectedIndex)
    End If

    ' Print the document with the specified paper size and source.
    printDoc.Print()

End Sub
```

[C#]
```
private void MyButtonPrint_Click(object sender, System.EventArgs e)
{
    // Set the paper size based upon the selection in the combo box.
    if (comboPaperSize.SelectedIndex != -1) {
        printDoc.DefaultPageSettings.PaperSize =

printDoc.PrinterSettings.PaperSizes[comboPaperSize.SelectedIndex];
    }

    // Set the paper source based upon the selection in the combo box.
    if (comboPaperSource.SelectedIndex != -1) {
        printDoc.DefaultPageSettings.PaperSource =
            printDoc.PrinterSettings.PaperSources[combo                     ↵
PaperSource.SelectedIndex];
    }

    // Set the printer resolution based upon the selection in               ↵
the combo box.
    if (comboPrintResolution.SelectedIndex != -1)
    {
        printDoc.DefaultPageSettings.PrinterResolution=
            printDoc.PrinterSettings.PrinterResolutions                     ↵
 [comboPrintResolution.SelectedIndex];
    }

    // Print the document with the specified paper size,                    ↵
source, and print resolution.
    printDoc.Print();
}
```

[C++]
```
private:
   void MyButtonPrint_Click(Object* sender, System::EventArgs* e) {
      // Set the paper size based upon the selection in the combo box.
      if (comboPaperSize->SelectedIndex != -1) {
         printDoc->DefaultPageSettings->PaperSize =
            printDoc->PrinterSettings->PaperSizes->Item                  ↵
 [comboPaperSize->SelectedIndex];
      }

      // Set the paper source based upon the selection in                ↵
the combo box.
      if (comboPaperSource->SelectedIndex != -1) {
         printDoc->DefaultPageSettings->PaperSource =
            printDoc->PrinterSettings->PaperSources-
>Item[comboPaperSource->SelectedIndex];
      }

      // Set the printer resolution based upon the selection             ↵
 in the combo box.
      if (comboPrintResolution->SelectedIndex != -1) {
         printDoc->DefaultPageSettings->PrinterResolution=
            printDoc->PrinterSettings->PrinterResolutions-               ↵
>Item[comboPrintResolution->SelectedIndex];
      }

      // Print the document with the specified paper size,              ↵
source, and print resolution.
      printDoc->Print();
   }
```

Requirements

Platforms: Windows 98, Windows NT 4.0, Windows Millennium Edition, Windows 2000, Windows XP Home Edition, Windows XP Professional, Windows Server 2003 family

PageSettings.PrinterSettings Property

Gets or sets the printer settings associated with the page.

[Visual Basic]
```
Public Property PrinterSettings As PrinterSettings
```
[C#]
```
public PrinterSettings PrinterSettings {get; set;}
```
[C++]
```
public: __property PrinterSettings* get_PrinterSettings();
public: __property void set_PrinterSettings(PrinterSettings*);
```
[JScript]
```
public function get PrinterSettings() : PrinterSettings;
public function set PrinterSettings(PrinterSettings);
```

Property Value

A **PrinterSettings** that represents the printer settings associated with the page.

Remarks

You can use the printer settings to find default values for properties of the page that are not set.

Requirements

Platforms: Windows 98, Windows NT 4.0, Windows Millennium Edition, Windows 2000, Windows XP Home Edition, Windows XP Professional, Windows Server 2003 family

PageSettings.Clone Method

Creates a copy of this **PageSettings** object.

[Visual Basic]
```
Public Overridable Function Clone() As Object Implements _
   ICloneable.Clone
```
[C#]
```
public virtual object Clone();
```
[C++]
```
public: virtual Object* Clone();
```
[JScript]
```
public function Clone() : Object;
```

Return Value

A copy of this object.

Implements

ICloneable.Clone

Requirements

Platforms: Windows 98, Windows NT 4.0, Windows Millennium Edition, Windows 2000, Windows XP Home Edition, Windows XP Professional, Windows Server 2003 family

PageSettings.CopyToHdevmode Method

Copies the relevant information from the **PageSettings** to the specified DEVMODE structure.

[Visual Basic]
```
Public Sub CopyToHdevmode( _
   ByVal hdevmode As IntPtr _
)
```
[C#]
```
public void CopyToHdevmode(
   IntPtr hdevmode
);
```
[C++]
```
public: void CopyToHdevmode(
   IntPtr hdevmode
);
```
[JScript]
```
public function CopyToHdevmode(
   hdevmode : IntPtr
);
```

Parameters

hdevmode
: The handle to a Win32 DEVMODE structure.

Exceptions

Exception Type	Condition
InvalidPrinterException	The printer named in the **PrinterSettings.PrinterName** property does not exist or there is no default printer installed.

Remarks

Call this method to copy relevant information to a DEVMODE structure from a **PageSettings**. This method is useful when making unmanaged Win32 calls that require a DEVMODE.

To copy information from a DEVMODE structure to the **PageSettings**, call **SetHdevmode**.

Requirements

Platforms: Windows 98, Windows NT 4.0, Windows Millennium Edition, Windows 2000, Windows XP Home Edition, Windows XP Professional, Windows Server 2003 family

.NET Framework Security:

- **PrintingPermission** for printing and access to all printers on the network. Associated enumeration: **PrintingPermissionLevel.AllPrinting**

PageSettings.SetHdevmode Method

Copies relevant information to the **PageSettings** from the specified DEVMODE structure.

[Visual Basic]
```
Public Sub SetHdevmode( _
   ByVal hdevmode As IntPtr _
)
```
[C#]
```
public void SetHdevmode(
   IntPtr hdevmode
);
```
[C++]
```
public: void SetHdevmode(
   IntPtr hdevmode
);
```
[JScript]
```
public function SetHdevmode(
   hdevmode : IntPtr
);
```

Parameters

hdevmode

The handle to a Win32 DEVMODE structure.

Exceptions

Exception Type	Condition
ArgumentException	The printer handle is invalid.
InvalidPrinterException	The printer named in the **PrinterSettings.PrinterName** property does not exist or there is no default printer installed.

Remarks

Use this method to copy relevant information in a DEVMODE structure to the **PageSettings**.

To copy information from the **PageSettings** to a DEVMODE, call **CopyToHdevmode**.

Requirements

Platforms: Windows 98, Windows NT 4.0, Windows Millennium Edition, Windows 2000, Windows XP Home Edition, Windows XP Professional, Windows Server 2003 family

.NET Framework Security:

- **PrintingPermission** for printing and access to all printers on the network. Associated enumeration: **PrintingPermissionLevel.AllPrinting**

PageSettings.ToString Method

This member overrides **Object.ToString**.

[Visual Basic]
```
Overrides Public Function ToString() As String
```
[C#]
```
public override string ToString();
```
[C++]
```
public: String* ToString();
```
[JScript]
```
public override function ToString() : String;
```

Requirements

Platforms: Windows 98, Windows NT 4.0, Windows Millennium Edition, Windows 2000, Windows XP Home Edition, Windows XP Professional, Windows Server 2003 family

PaperKind Enumeration

Specifies the standard paper sizes.

[Visual Basic]
```
<Serializable>
Public Enum PaperKind
```
[C#]
```
[Serializable]
public enum PaperKind
```
[C++]
```
[Serializable]
__value public enum PaperKind
```
[JScript]
```
public
   Serializable
enum PaperKind
```

Remarks

For more information on printing, see the **System.Drawing.Printing** namespace overview.

Members

Member name	Description
A2	A2 paper (420 mm by 594 mm).
A3	A3 paper (297 mm by 420 mm).
A3Extra	A3 extra paper (322 mm by 445 mm).
A3ExtraTransverse	A3 extra transverse paper (322 mm by 445 mm).
A3Rotated	A3 rotated paper (420 mm by 297 mm).
A3Transverse	A3 transverse paper (297 mm by 420 mm).
A4	A4 paper (210 mm by 297 mm).
A4Extra	A4 extra paper (236 mm by 322 mm). This value is specific to the PostScript driver and is used only by Linotronic printers to help save paper.
A4Plus	A4 plus paper (210 mm by 330 mm).
A4Rotated	A4 rotated paper (297 mm by 210 mm). Requires Windows 98, Windows NT 4.0, or later.
A4Small	A4 small paper (210 mm by 297 mm).
A4Transverse	A4 transverse paper (210 mm by 297 mm).
A5	A5 paper (148 mm by 210 mm).
A5Extra	A5 extra paper (174 mm by 235 mm).
A5Rotated	A5 rotated paper (210 mm by 148 mm). Requires Windows 98, Windows NT 4.0, or later.
A5Transverse	A5 transverse paper (148 mm by 210 mm).
A6	A6 paper (105 mm by 148 mm). Requires Windows 98, Windows NT 4.0, or later.
A6Rotated	A6 rotated paper (148 mm by 105 mm). Requires Windows 98, Windows NT 4.0, or later.
APlus	SuperA/SuperA/A4 paper (227 mm by 356 mm).

Member name	Description
B4	B4 paper (250 mm by 353 mm).
B4Envelope	B4 envelope (250 mm by 353 mm).
B4JisRotated	JIS B4 rotated paper (364 mm by 257 mm). Requires Windows 98, Windows NT 4.0, or later.
B5	B5 paper (176 mm by 250 mm).
B5Envelope	B5 envelope (176 mm by 250 mm).
B5Extra	ISO B5 extra paper (201 mm by 276 mm).
B5JisRotated	JIS B5 rotated paper (257 mm by 182 mm). Requires Windows 98, Windows NT 4.0, or later.
B5Transverse	JIS B5 transverse paper (182 mm by 257 mm).
B6Envelope	B6 envelope (176 mm by 125 mm).
B6Jis	JIS B6 paper (128 mm by 182 mm). Requires Windows 98, Windows NT 4.0, or later.
B6JisRotated	JIS B6 rotated paper (182 mm by 128 mm). Requires Windows 98, Windows NT 4.0, or later.
BPlus	SuperB/SuperB/A3 paper (305 mm by 487 mm).
C3Envelope	C3 envelope (324 mm by 458 mm).
C4Envelope	C4 envelope (229 mm by 324 mm).
C5Envelope	C5 envelope (162 mm by 229 mm).
C65Envelope	C65 envelope (114 mm by 229 mm).
C6Envelope	C6 envelope (114 mm by 162 mm).
CSheet	C paper (17 in. by 22 in.).
Custom	The paper size is defined by the user.
DLEnvelope	DL envelope (110 mm by 220 mm).
DSheet	D paper (22 in. by 34 in.).
ESheet	E paper (34 in. by 44 in.).
Executive	Executive paper (7.25 in. by 10.5 in.).
Folio	Folio paper (8.5 in. by 13 in.).
GermanLegalFanfold	German legal fanfold (8.5 in. by 13 in.).
GermanStandard-Fanfold	German standard fanfold (8.5 in. by 12 in.).
InviteEnvelope	Invite envelope (220 mm by 220 mm).
IsoB4	ISO B4 (250 mm by 353 mm).
ItalyEnvelope	Italy envelope (110 mm by 230 mm).
JapaneseDoublePost-card	Japanese double postcard (200 mm by 148 mm). Requires Windows 98, Windows NT 4.0, or later.
JapaneseDouble-PostcardRotated	Japanese rotated double postcard (148 mm by 200 mm). Requires Windows 98, Windows NT 4.0, or later.
JapaneseEnvelope-ChouNumber3	Japanese Chou #3 envelope. Requires Windows 98, Windows NT 4.0, or later.
JapaneseEnvelope-ChouNumber3-Rotated	Japanese rotated Chou #3 envelope. Requires Windows 98, Windows NT 4.0, or later.
JapaneseEnvelope-ChouNumber4	Japanese Chou #4 envelope. Requires Windows 98, Windows NT 4.0, or later.

Member name	Description
JapaneseEnvelope-ChouNumber4-Rotated	Japanese rotated Chou #4 envelope. Requires Windows 98, Windows NT 4.0, or later.
JapaneseEnvelope-KakuNumber2	Japanese Kaku #2 envelope. Requires Windows 98, Windows NT 4.0, or later.
JapaneseEnvelope-KakuNumber2-Rotated	Japanese rotated Kaku #2 envelope. Requires Windows 98, Windows NT 4.0, or later.
JapaneseEnvelope-KakuNumber3	Japanese Kaku #3 envelope. Requires Windows 98, Windows NT 4.0, or later.
JapaneseEnvelope-KakuNumber3-Rotated	Japanese rotated Kaku #3 envelope. Requires Windows 98, Windows NT 4.0, or later.
JapaneseEnvelope-YouNumber4	Japanese You #4 envelope. Requires Windows 98, Windows NT 4.0, or later.
JapaneseEnvelope-YouNumber4Rotated	Japanese You #4 rotated envelope. Requires Windows 98, Windows NT 4.0, or later.
JapanesePostcard	Japanese postcard (100 mm by 148 mm).
JapanesePostcard-Rotated	Japanese rotated postcard (148 mm by 100 mm). Requires Windows 98, Windows NT 4.0, or later.
Ledger	Ledger paper (17 in. by 11 in.).
Legal	Legal paper (8.5 in. by 14 in.).
LegalExtra	Legal extra paper (9.275 in. by 15 in.). This value is specific to the PostScript driver and is used only by Linotronic printers in order to conserve paper.
Letter	Letter paper (8.5 in. by 11 in.).
LetterExtra	Letter extra paper (9.275 in. by 12 in.). This value is specific to the PostScript driver and is used only by Linotronic printers in order to conserve paper.
LetterExtra-Transverse	Letter extra transverse paper (9.275 in. by 12 in.).
LetterPlus	Letter plus paper (8.5 in. by 12.69 in.).
LetterRotated	Letter rotated paper (11 in. by 8.5 in.).
LetterSmall	Letter small paper (8.5 in. by 11 in.).
LetterTransverse	Letter transverse paper (8.275 in. by 11 in.).
MonarchEnvelope	Monarch envelope (3.875 in. by 7.5 in.).
Note	Note paper (8.5 in. by 11 in.).
Number10Envelope	#10 envelope (4.125 in. by 9.5 in.).
Number11Envelope	#11 envelope (4.5 in. by 10.375 in.).
Number12Envelope	#12 envelope (4.75 in. by 11 in.).
Number14Envelope	#14 envelope (5 in. by 11.5 in.).
Number9Envelope	#9 envelope (3.875 in. by 8.875 in.).
PersonalEnvelope	6 3/4 envelope (3.625 in. by 6.5 in.).
Prc16K	People's Republic of China 16K paper (146 mm by 215 mm). Requires Windows 98, Windows NT 4.0, or later.
Prc16KRotated	People's Republic of China 16K rotated paper (146 mm by 215 mm). Requires Windows 98, Windows NT 4.0, or later.
Prc32K	People's Republic of China 32K paper (97 mm by 151 mm). Requires Windows 98, Windows NT 4.0, or later.
Prc32KBig	People's Republic of China 32K big paper (97 mm by 151 mm). Requires Windows 98, Windows NT 4.0, or later.
Prc32KBigRotated	People's Republic of China 32K big rotated paper (97 mm by 151 mm). Requires Windows 98, Windows NT 4.0, or later.
Prc32KRotated	People's Republic of China 32K rotated paper (97 mm by 151 mm). Requires Windows 98, Windows NT 4.0, or later.
PrcEnvelope-Number1	People's Republic of China #1 envelope (102 mm by 165 mm). Requires Windows 98, Windows NT 4.0, or later.
PrcEnvelope-Number10	People's Republic of China #10 envelope (324 mm by 458 mm). Requires Windows 98, Windows NT 4.0, or later.
PrcEnvelope-Number10Rotated	People's Republic of China #10 rotated envelope (458 mm by 324 mm). Requires Windows 98, Windows NT 4.0, or later.
PrcEnvelope-Number1Rotated	People's Republic of China #1 rotated envelope (165 mm by 102 mm). Requires Windows 98, Windows NT 4.0, or later.
PrcEnvelope-Number2	People's Republic of China #2 envelope (102 mm by 176 mm). Requires Windows 98, Windows NT 4.0, or later.
PrcEnvelope-Number2Rotated	People's Republic of China #2 rotated envelope (176 mm by 102 mm). Requires Windows 98, Windows NT 4.0, or later.
PrcEnvelope-Number3	People's Republic of China #3 envelope (125 mm by 176 mm). Requires Windows 98, Windows NT 4.0, or later.
PrcEnvelope-Number3Rotated	People's Republic of China #3 rotated envelope (176 mm by 125 mm). Requires Windows 98, Windows NT 4.0, or later.
PrcEnvelope-Number4	People's Republic of China #4 envelope (110 mm by 208 mm). Requires Windows 98, Windows NT 4.0, or later.
PrcEnvelope-Number4Rotated	People's Republic of China #4 rotated envelope (208 mm by 110 mm). Requires Windows 98, Windows NT 4.0, or later.
PrcEnvelope-Number5	People's Republic of China #5 envelope (110 mm by 220 mm). Requires Windows 98, Windows NT 4.0, or later.
PrcEnvelope-Number5Rotated	People's Republic of China Envelope #5 rotated envelope (220 mm by 110 mm). Requires Windows 98, Windows NT 4.0, or later.
PrcEnvelope-Number6	People's Republic of China #6 envelope (120 mm by 230 mm). Requires Windows 98, Windows NT 4.0, or later.
PrcEnvelope-Number6Rotated	People's Republic of China #6 rotated envelope (230 mm by 120 mm). Requires Windows 98, Windows NT 4.0, or later.

Member name	Description
PrcEnvelope-Number7	People's Republic of China #7 envelope (160 mm by 230 mm). Requires Windows 98, Windows NT 4.0, or later.
PrcEnvelope-Number7Rotated	People's Republic of China #7 rotated envelope (230 mm by 160 mm). Requires Windows 98, Windows NT 4.0, or later.
PrcEnvelope-Number8	People's Republic of China #8 envelope (120 mm by 309 mm). Requires Windows 98, Windows NT 4.0, or later.
PrcEnvelope-Number8Rotated	People's Republic of China #8 rotated envelope (309 mm by 120 mm). Requires Windows 98, Windows NT 4.0, or later.
PrcEnvelope-Number9	People's Republic of China #9 envelope (229 mm by 324 mm). Requires Windows 98, Windows NT 4.0, or later.
PrcEnvelope-Number9Rotated	People's Republic of China #9 rotated envelope (324 mm by 229 mm). Requires Windows 98, Windows NT 4.0, or later.
Quarto	Quarto paper (215 mm by 275 mm).
Standard10x11	Standard paper (10 in. by 11 in.).
Standard10x14	Standard paper (10 in. by 14 in.).
Standard11x17	Standard paper (11 in. by 17 in.).
Standard12x11	Standard paper (12 in. by 11 in.). Requires Windows 98, Windows NT 4.0, or later.
Standard15x11	Standard paper (15 in. by 11 in.).
Standard9x11	Standard paper (9 in. by 11 in.).
Statement	Statement paper (5.5 in. by 8.5 in.).
Tabloid	Tabloid paper (11 in. by 17 in.).
TabloidExtra	Tabloid extra paper (11.69 in. by 18 in.). This value is specific to the PostScript driver and is used only by Linotronic printers in order to conserve paper.
USStandardFanfold	US standard fanfold (14.875 in. by 11 in.).

Requirements

Namespace: System.Drawing.Printing

Platforms: Windows 98, Windows NT 4.0, Windows Millennium Edition, Windows 2000, Windows XP Home Edition, Windows XP Professional, Windows Server 2003 family

Assembly: System.Drawing (in System.Drawing.dll)

PaperSize Class

Specifies the size of a piece of paper.

System.Object
  System.Drawing.Printing.PaperSize

[Visual Basic]
```
Public Class PaperSize
```
[C#]
```
public class PaperSize
```
[C++]
```
public __gc class PaperSize
```
[JScript]
```
public class PaperSize
```

Thread Safety

Any public static (**Shared** in Visual Basic) members of this type are safe for multithreaded operations. Any instance members are not guaranteed to be thread safe.

Remarks

This class is used by **PrinterSettings.PaperSizes** and **PageSettings.PaperSize** properties to get the paper sizes that are available on the printer and to set the paper size for a page, respectively.

You can use the **PaperSize** constructor to specify a custom paper size. Alternatively, you can set the **Width** and **Height** properties by setting the **Kind** property to **Custom**.

For more information on printing, see the **System.Drawing.Printing** namespace overview.

Example

[Visual Basic, C#, C++] The following example populates the `comboPaperSize` combo box with the printer's supported paper sizes. In addition, a custom paper size is created and added to the combo box. The **PaperName** is identified as the property that will provide the display string for the item being added through the **DisplayMember** property of the combo box. The example assumes that a **PrintDocument** variable named `printDoc` exists and that the specific combo box exists.

[Visual Basic]
```
' Add list of supported paper sizes found on the printer.
' The DisplayMember property is used to identify the property ↵
that will provide the display string.
comboPaperSize.DisplayMember = "PaperName"

Dim pkSize As PaperSize
For i = 0 to printDoc.PrinterSettings.PaperSizes.Count - 1
    pkSize = printDoc.PrinterSettings.PaperSizes.Item(i)
    comboPaperSize.Items.Add(pkSize)
Next

' Create a PaperSize and specify the custom paper size ↵
through the constructor and add to combobox.
Dim pkCustomSize1 As New PaperSize("Custom Paper Size", 100, 200)

comboPaperSize.Items.Add(pkCustomSize1)
```

[C#]
```
// Add list of supported paper sizes found on the printer.
// The DisplayMember property is used to identify the property ↵
 that will provide the display string.
comboPaperSize.DisplayMember = "PaperName";

PaperSize pkSize;
for (int i = 0; i < printDoc.PrinterSettings.PaperSizes.Count; i++){
    pkSize = printDoc.PrinterSettings.PaperSizes[i];
    comboPaperSize.Items.Add(pkSize);
}

// Create a PaperSize and specify the custom paper size ↵
through the constructor and add to combobox.
PaperSize pkCustomSize1 = new PaperSize("First custom size", 100, 200);

comboPaperSize.Items.Add(pkCustomSize1);
```

[C++]
```
// Add list of supported paper sizes found on the printer.
// The DisplayMember property is used to identify the ↵
property that will provide the display String*.
comboPaperSize->DisplayMember = S"PaperName";

PaperSize* pkSize;
for (int i = 0; i < printDoc->PrinterSettings->PaperSizes-> ↵
Count; i++) {
   pkSize = printDoc->PrinterSettings->PaperSizes->Item[i];
   comboPaperSize->Items->Add(pkSize);
}

// Create a PaperSize and specify the custom paper size ↵
through the constructor and add to combobox.
PaperSize* pkCustomSize1 = new PaperSize(S"First custom ↵
size", 100, 200);

comboPaperSize->Items->Add(pkCustomSize1);
```

Requirements

Namespace: System.Drawing.Printing

Platforms: Windows 98, Windows NT 4.0, Windows Millennium Edition, Windows 2000, Windows XP Home Edition, Windows XP Professional, Windows Server 2003 family

Assembly: System.Drawing (in System.Drawing.dll)

PaperSize Constructor

Initializes a new instance of the **PaperSize** class.

[Visual Basic]
```
Public Sub New( _
   ByVal name As String, _
   ByVal width As Integer, _
   ByVal height As Integer _
)
```
[C#]
```
public PaperSize(
   string name,
   int width,
   int height
);
```
[C++]
```
public: PaperSize(
   String* name,
   int width,
   int height
);
```
[JScript]
```
public function PaperSize(
   name : String,
   width : int,
   height : int
);
```

Parameters

name

The name of the paper.

width

The width of the paper, in hundredths of an inch.

height

The height of the paper, in hundredths of an inch.

Remarks

Call this constructor to specify a paper size that is custom, providing the name, width and height. Alternatively, you can set the **Width** and **Height** properties by setting the **Kind** property to **Custom**.

Example

[Visual Basic, C#, C++] The following example populates the `comboPaperSize` combo box with the printer's supported paper sizes. In addition, a custom paper size is created and added to the combo box. The **PaperName** is identified as the property that will provide the display string for the item being added through the **DisplayMember** property of the combo box. The example assumes that a **PrintDocument** variable named `printDoc` exists and that the specific combo box exists.

[Visual Basic]

```
' Add list of supported paper sizes found on the printer.
' The DisplayMember property is used to identify the property ↵
that will provide the display string.
comboPaperSize.DisplayMember = "PaperName"

Dim pkSize As PaperSize
For i = 0 to printDoc.PrinterSettings.PaperSizes.Count - 1
    pkSize = printDoc.PrinterSettings.PaperSizes.Item(i)
    comboPaperSize.Items.Add(pkSize)
Next

' Create a PaperSize and specify the custom paper size through ↵
 the constructor and add to combobox.
Dim pkCustomSize1 As New PaperSize("Custom Paper Size", 100, 200)

comboPaperSize.Items.Add(pkCustomSize1)
```

[C#]

```
// Add list of supported paper sizes found on the printer.
// The DisplayMember property is used to identify the property ↵
 that will provide the display string.
comboPaperSize.DisplayMember = "PaperName";

PaperSize pkSize;
for (int i = 0; i < printDoc.PrinterSettings.PaperSizes.Count; i++){
    pkSize = printDoc.PrinterSettings.PaperSizes[i];
    comboPaperSize.Items.Add(pkSize);
}

// Create a PaperSize and specify the custom paper size through ↵
 the constructor and add to combobox.
PaperSize pkCustomSize1 = new PaperSize("First custom size", 100, 200);

comboPaperSize.Items.Add(pkCustomSize1);
```

[C++]

```
// Add list of supported paper sizes found on the printer.
// The DisplayMember property is used to identify the property ↵
 that will provide the display String*.
comboPaperSize->DisplayMember = S"PaperName";

PaperSize* pkSize;
for (int i = 0; i < printDoc->PrinterSettings->PaperSizes-> ↵
Count; i++) {
   pkSize = printDoc->PrinterSettings->PaperSizes->Item[i];
   comboPaperSize->Items->Add(pkSize);
}

// Create a PaperSize and specify the custom paper size through ↵
 the constructor and add to combobox.
PaperSize* pkCustomSize1 = new PaperSize(S"First custom size", ↵
 100, 200);

comboPaperSize->Items->Add(pkCustomSize1);
```

Requirements

Platforms: Windows 98, Windows NT 4.0, Windows Millennium Edition, Windows 2000, Windows XP Home Edition, Windows XP Professional, Windows Server 2003 family

PaperSize.Height Property

Gets or sets the height of the paper, in hundredths of an inch.

[Visual Basic]

```
Public Property Height As Integer
```

[C#]

```
public int Height {get; set;}
```

[C++]

```
public: __property int get_Height();
public: __property void set_Height(int);
```

[JScript]

```
public function get Height() : int;
public function set Height(int);
```

Property Value

The height of the paper, in hundredths of an inch.

Exceptions

Exception Type	Condition
ArgumentException	The **Kind** property is not set to **Custom**.

Remarks

This height measurement is for the portrait orientation of the paper.

Requirements

Platforms: Windows 98, Windows NT 4.0, Windows Millennium Edition, Windows 2000, Windows XP Home Edition, Windows XP Professional, Windows Server 2003 family

PaperSize.Kind Property

Gets the type of paper.

[Visual Basic]

```
Public ReadOnly Property Kind As PaperKind
```

[C#]

```
public PaperKind Kind {get;}
```

[C++]

```
public: __property PaperKind get_Kind();
```

[JScript]

```
public function get Kind() : PaperKind;
```

Property Value

One of the **PaperKind** values.

Remarks

You can use the **PaperSize** constructor to specify a custom paper size.

Requirements

Platforms: Windows 98, Windows NT 4.0, Windows Millennium Edition, Windows 2000, Windows XP Home Edition, Windows XP Professional, Windows Server 2003 family

PaperSize.PaperName Property

Gets or sets the name of the type of paper.

```
[Visual Basic]
Public Property PaperName As String
[C#]
public string PaperName {get; set;}
[C++]
public: __property String* get_PaperName();
public: __property void set_PaperName(String*);
[JScript]
public function get PaperName() : String;
public function set PaperName(String);
```

Property Value

The name of the type of paper.

Exceptions

Exception Type	Condition
ArgumentException	The **Kind** is not set to **Custom**.

Remarks

You can set the paper name only if the **Kind** property is set to **Custom**.

Example

[Visual Basic, C#, C++] The following example populates the `comboPaperSize` combo box with the printer's supported paper sizes. The **PaperName** is identified as the property that will provide the display string for the item being added through the **DisplayMember** property of the combo box. The example assumes that a **PrintDocument** variable named `printDoc` exists and that the specific combo box exists.

```
[Visual Basic]
' Add list of supported paper sizes found on the printer.
' The DisplayMember property is used to identify the property ↵
that will provide the display string.
comboPaperSize.DisplayMember = "PaperName"

Dim pkSize As PaperSize
For i = 0 to printDoc.PrinterSettings.PaperSizes.Count - 1
    pkSize = printDoc.PrinterSettings.PaperSizes.Item(i)
    comboPaperSize.Items.Add(pkSize)
Next

' Create a PaperSize and specify the custom paper size through ↵
 the constructor and add to combobox.
Dim pkCustomSize1 As New PaperSize("Custom Paper Size", 100, 200)

comboPaperSize.Items.Add(pkCustomSize1)
```

```
[C#]
// Add list of supported paper sizes found on the printer.
// The DisplayMember property is used to identify the property ↵
 that will provide the display string.
comboPaperSize.DisplayMember = "PaperName";

PaperSize pkSize;
for (int i = 0; i < printDoc.PrinterSettings.PaperSizes.Count; i++){
    pkSize = printDoc.PrinterSettings.PaperSizes[i];
    comboPaperSize.Items.Add(pkSize);
}

// Create a PaperSize and specify the custom paper size through ↵
 the constructor and add to combobox.
PaperSize pkCustomSize1 = new PaperSize("First custom size", 100, 200);

comboPaperSize.Items.Add(pkCustomSize1);
```

```
[C++]
// Add list of supported paper sizes found on the printer.
// The DisplayMember property is used to identify the property ↵
 that will provide the display String*.
comboPaperSize->DisplayMember = S"PaperName";

PaperSize* pkSize;
for (int i = 0; i < printDoc->PrinterSettings->PaperSizes-> ↵
Count; i++) {
   pkSize = printDoc->PrinterSettings->PaperSizes->Item[i];
   comboPaperSize->Items->Add(pkSize);
}

// Create a PaperSize and specify the custom paper size through ↵
 the constructor and add to combobox.
PaperSize* pkCustomSize1 = new PaperSize(S"First custom size", ↵
 100, 200);

comboPaperSize->Items->Add(pkCustomSize1);
```

Requirements

Platforms: Windows 98, Windows NT 4.0, Windows Millennium Edition, Windows 2000, Windows XP Home Edition, Windows XP Professional, Windows Server 2003 family

PaperSize.Width Property

Gets or sets the width of the paper, in hundredths of an inch.

```
[Visual Basic]
Public Property Width As Integer
[C#]
public int Width {get; set;}
[C++]
public: __property int get_Width();
public: __property void set_Width(int);
[JScript]
public function get Width() : int;
public function set Width(int);
```

Property Value

The width of the paper, in hundredths of an inch.

Exceptions

Exception Type	Condition
ArgumentException	The **Kind** property is not set to **Custom**.

Remarks

This width measurement is for the portrait orientation of the paper.

Requirements

Platforms: Windows 98, Windows NT 4.0, Windows Millennium Edition, Windows 2000, Windows XP Home Edition, Windows XP Professional, Windows Server 2003 family

PaperSize.ToString Method

This member overrides **Object.ToString**.

[Visual Basic]
```
Overrides Public Function ToString() As String
```
[C#]
```
public override string ToString();
```
[C++]
```
public: String* ToString();
```
[JScript]
```
public override function ToString() : String;
```

Requirements

Platforms: Windows 98, Windows NT 4.0, Windows Millennium Edition, Windows 2000, Windows XP Home Edition, Windows XP Professional, Windows Server 2003 family

PaperSource Class

Specifies the paper tray from which the printer gets paper.

System.Object
  System.Drawing.Printing.PaperSource

```
[Visual Basic]
Public Class PaperSource
[C#]
public class PaperSource
[C++]
public __gc class PaperSource
[JScript]
public class PaperSource
```

Thread Safety

Any public static (**Shared** in Visual Basic) members of this type are safe for multithreaded operations. Any instance members are not guaranteed to be thread safe.

Remarks

This class is used by **PrinterSettings.PaperSources** and **PageSettings.PaperSource** properties to get the paper source trays that are available on the printer and to set the paper source for a page, respectively.

For more information on printing, see the **System.Drawing.Printing** namespace overview.

Example

[Visual Basic, C#, C++] The following example populates the `comboPaperSource` combo box with the printer's supported paper sources. The **SourceName** is identified as the property that provides the display string for the item being added through the **DisplayMember** property of the combo box. The example assumes that a **PrintDocument** variable named `printDoc` exists and that the specific combo box exists.

```
[Visual Basic]
' Add list of paper sources found on the printer to the combo box.
' The DisplayMember property is used to identify the property ↵
that will provide the display string.
comboPaperSource.DisplayMember = "SourceName"

Dim pkSource As PaperSource
For i = 0 to printDoc.PrinterSettings.PaperSources.Count - 1
    pkSource = printDoc.PrinterSettings.PaperSources.Item(i)
    comboPaperSource.Items.Add(pkSource)
Next
```

```
[C#]
// Add list of paper sources found on the printer to the combo box.
// The DisplayMember property is used to identify the property ↵
that will provide the display string.
comboPaperSource.DisplayMember="SourceName";

PaperSource pkSource;
for (int i = 0; i < printDoc.PrinterSettings.PaperSources.Count; i++){
    pkSource = printDoc.PrinterSettings.PaperSources[i];
    comboPaperSource.Items.Add(pkSource);
}
```

```
[C++]
// Add list of paper sources found on the printer to the combo box.
// The DisplayMember property is used to identify the property ↵
 that will provide the display String*.
comboPaperSource->DisplayMember=S"SourceName";

PaperSource* pkSource;
for (int i = 0; i < printDoc->PrinterSettings->PaperSources-> ↵
Count; i++) {
   pkSource = printDoc->PrinterSettings->PaperSources->Item[i];
   comboPaperSource->Items->Add(pkSource);
}
```

Requirements

Namespace: System.Drawing.Printing

Platforms: Windows 98, Windows NT 4.0, Windows Millennium Edition, Windows 2000, Windows XP Home Edition, Windows XP Professional, Windows Server 2003 family

Assembly: System.Drawing (in System.Drawing.dll)

PaperSource.Kind Property

Gets the paper source.

```
[Visual Basic]
Public ReadOnly Property Kind As PaperSourceKind
[C#]
public PaperSourceKind Kind {get;}
[C++]
public: __property PaperSourceKind get_Kind();
[JScript]
public function get Kind() : PaperSourceKind;
```

Property Value

One of the **PaperSourceKind** values.

Requirements

Platforms: Windows 98, Windows NT 4.0, Windows Millennium Edition, Windows 2000, Windows XP Home Edition, Windows XP Professional, Windows Server 2003 family

PaperSource.SourceName Property

Gets the name of the paper source.

```
[Visual Basic]
Public ReadOnly Property SourceName As String
[C#]
public string SourceName {get;}
[C++]
public: __property String* get_SourceName();
[JScript]
public function get SourceName() : String;
```

Property Value

The name of the paper source.

Remarks

Call this property when the paper source needs to be displayed. The name of the paper source is generated based upon the **Kind** property.

Example

[Visual Basic, C#, C++] The following example populates the `comboPaperSource` combo box with the printer's supported paper sources. The **SourceName** is identified as the property that provides the display string for the item being added through the **DisplayMember** property of the combo box. The example assumes that a **PrintDocument** variable named `printDoc` exists and that the specific combo box exists.

[Visual Basic]
```
' Add list of paper sources found on the printer to the combo box.
' The DisplayMember property is used to identify the property        ↵
that will provide the display string.
comboPaperSource.DisplayMember = "SourceName"

Dim pkSource As PaperSource
For i = 0 to printDoc.PrinterSettings.PaperSources.Count - 1
    pkSource = printDoc.PrinterSettings.PaperSources.Item(i)
    comboPaperSource.Items.Add(pkSource)
Next
```

[C#]
```
// Add list of paper sources found on the printer to the combo box.
// The DisplayMember property is used to identify the property       ↵
that will provide the display string.
comboPaperSource.DisplayMember="SourceName";

PaperSource pkSource;
for (int i = 0; i < printDoc.PrinterSettings.PaperSources.Count; i++){
    pkSource = printDoc.PrinterSettings.PaperSources[i];
    comboPaperSource.Items.Add(pkSource);
}
```

[C++]
```
// Add list of paper sources found on the printer to the combo box.
// The DisplayMember property is used to identify the property       ↵
that will provide the display String*.
comboPaperSource->DisplayMember=S"SourceName";

PaperSource* pkSource;
for (int i = 0; i < printDoc->PrinterSettings->PaperSources->        ↵
Count; i++) {
   pkSource = printDoc->PrinterSettings->PaperSources->Item[i];
   comboPaperSource->Items->Add(pkSource);
}
```

Requirements

Platforms: Windows 98, Windows NT 4.0, Windows Millennium Edition, Windows 2000, Windows XP Home Edition, Windows XP Professional, Windows Server 2003 family

PaperSource.ToString Method

This member overrides **Object.ToString**.

[Visual Basic]
```
Overrides Public Function ToString() As String
```
[C#]
```
public override string ToString();
```
[C++]
```
public: String* ToString();
```
[JScript]
```
public override function ToString() : String;
```

Requirements

Platforms: Windows 98, Windows NT 4.0, Windows Millennium Edition, Windows 2000, Windows XP Home Edition, Windows XP Professional, Windows Server 2003 family

PaperSourceKind Enumeration

Standard paper sources.

[Visual Basic]
```
<Serializable>
Public Enum PaperSourceKind
```
[C#]
```
[Serializable]
public enum PaperSourceKind
```
[C++]
```
[Serializable]
__value public enum PaperSourceKind
```
[JScript]
```
public
   Serializable
enum PaperSourceKind
```

Remarks

This enumeration is used by **PaperSource.Kind**.

For more information on printing, see the **System.Drawing.Printing** namespace overview.

Members

Member name	Description
AutomaticFeed	Automatically fed paper.
Cassette	A paper cassette.
Custom	A printer-specific paper source.
Envelope	An envelope.
FormSource	The printer's default input bin.
LargeCapacity	The printer's large-capacity bin.
LargeFormat	Large-format paper.
Lower	The lower bin of a printer.
Manual	Manually fed paper.
ManualFeed	Manually fed envelope.
Middle	The middle bin of a printer.
SmallFormat	Small-format paper.
TractorFeed	A tractor feed.
Upper	The upper bin of a printer (or, if the printer only has one bin, that bin).

Requirements

Namespace: System.Drawing.Printing

Platforms: Windows 98, Windows NT 4.0, Windows Millennium Edition, Windows 2000, Windows XP Home Edition, Windows XP Professional, Windows Server 2003 family

Assembly: System.Drawing (in System.Drawing.dll)

PreviewPageInfo Class

Specifies print preview information for a single page. This class cannot be inherited.

System.Object
  System.Drawing.Printing.PreviewPageInfo

[Visual Basic]
```
NotInheritable Public Class PreviewPageInfo
```
[C#]
```
public sealed class PreviewPageInfo
```
[C++]
```
public __gc __sealed class PreviewPageInfo
```
[JScript]
```
public class PreviewPageInfo
```

Thread Safety

Any public static (**Shared** in Visual Basic) members of this type are safe for multithreaded operations. Any instance members are not guaranteed to be thread safe.

Remarks

This class is used extensively by **PreviewPrintController**.

For more information on printing, see the **System.Drawing.Printing** namespace overview.

Requirements

Namespace: System.Drawing.Printing

Platforms: Windows 98, Windows NT 4.0, Windows Millennium Edition, Windows 2000, Windows XP Home Edition, Windows XP Professional, Windows Server 2003 family

Assembly: System.Drawing (in System.Drawing.dll)

PreviewPageInfo Constructor

Initializes a new instance of the **PreviewPageInfo** class.

[Visual Basic]
```
Public Sub New( _
   ByVal image As Image, _
   ByVal physicalSize As Size _
)
```
[C#]
```
public PreviewPageInfo(
   Image image,
   Size physicalSize
);
```
[C++]
```
public: PreviewPageInfo(
   Image* image,
   Size physicalSize
);
```
[JScript]
```
public function PreviewPageInfo(
   image : Image,
   physicalSize : Size
);
```

Parameters

image
  The image of the printed page.

physicalSize
  The size of the printed page, in hundredths of an inch.

Requirements

Platforms: Windows 98, Windows NT 4.0, Windows Millennium Edition, Windows 2000, Windows XP Home Edition, Windows XP Professional, Windows Server 2003 family

PreviewPageInfo.Image Property

Gets the image of the printed page.

[Visual Basic]
```
Public ReadOnly Property Image As Image
```
[C#]
```
public Image Image {get;}
```
[C++]
```
public: __property Image* get_Image();
```
[JScript]
```
public function get Image() : Image;
```

Property Value

An **Image** representing the printed page.

Remarks

See the **System.Drawing** namespace for details on manipulating graphics.

Requirements

Platforms: Windows 98, Windows NT 4.0, Windows Millennium Edition, Windows 2000, Windows XP Home Edition, Windows XP Professional, Windows Server 2003 family

PreviewPageInfo.PhysicalSize Property

Gets the size of the printed page, in hundredths of an inch.

[Visual Basic]
```
Public ReadOnly Property PhysicalSize As Size
```
[C#]
```
public Size PhysicalSize {get;}
```
[C++]
```
public: __property Size get_PhysicalSize();
```
[JScript]
```
public function get PhysicalSize() : Size;
```

Property Value

A **Size** that specifies the size of the printed page, in hundredths of an inch.

Requirements

Platforms: Windows 98, Windows NT 4.0, Windows Millennium Edition, Windows 2000, Windows XP Home Edition, Windows XP Professional, Windows Server 2003 family

PreviewPrintController Class

Specifies a print controller that displays a document on a screen as a series of images.

System.Object
  System.Drawing.Printing.PrintController
    System.Drawing.Printing.PreviewPrintController

[Visual Basic]
```
Public Class PreviewPrintController
   Inherits PrintController
```
[C#]
```
public class PreviewPrintController : PrintController
```
[C++]
```
public __gc class PreviewPrintController : public PrintController
```
[JScript]
```
public class PreviewPrintController extends PrintController
```

Thread Safety

Any public static (**Shared** in Visual Basic) members of this type are safe for multithreaded operations. Any instance members are not guaranteed to be thread safe.

Remarks

Typically, to use the print preview feature, you create an instance of a **PrintPreviewControl** or **PrintPreviewDialog** class and set its **Document** property. The **PreviewPrintController** is used by the **PrintPreviewControl** and **PrintPreviewDialog** classes, though you can use the **PreviewPrintController** when managing the display of your own print preview window.

OnStartPrint creates the **Graphics** that is displayed during the print preview. After **OnStartPrint** is called, the **OnStartPage** method sets the **Graphics** to a graphic of a single page. The **OnEndPage** method clears the **Graphics**, while the **OnEndPrint** method de-allocates the object.

For more information on printing, see the **System.Drawing.Printing** namespace overview.

Requirements

Namespace: System.Drawing.Printing

Platforms: Windows 98, Windows NT 4.0, Windows Millennium Edition, Windows 2000, Windows XP Home Edition, Windows XP Professional, Windows Server 2003 family

Assembly: System.Drawing (in System.Drawing.dll)

PreviewPrintController Constructor

Initializes a new instance of the **PreviewPrintController** class.

[Visual Basic]
```
Public Sub New()
```
[C#]
```
public PreviewPrintController();
```
[C++]
```
public: PreviewPrintController();
```
[JScript]
```
public function PreviewPrintController();
```

Remarks

The default constructor initializes any fields to their default values.

Requirements

Platforms: Windows 98, Windows NT 4.0, Windows Millennium Edition, Windows 2000, Windows XP Home Edition, Windows XP Professional, Windows Server 2003 family

PreviewPrintController.UseAntiAlias Property

Gets or sets a value indicating whether to use anti-aliasing when displaying the print preview.

[Visual Basic]
```
Public Overridable Property UseAntiAlias As Boolean
```
[C#]
```
public virtual bool UseAntiAlias {get; set;}
```
[C++]
```
public: __property virtual bool get_UseAntiAlias();
public: __property virtual void set_UseAntiAlias(bool);
```
[JScript]
```
public function get UseAntiAlias() : Boolean;
public function set UseAntiAlias(Boolean);
```

Property Value

true if the print preview uses anti-aliasing; otherwise, **false**. The default is **false**.

Remarks

Anti-aliasing, also known as gray scaling, uses several shades of gray around areas of curves and diagonals in text to give the text a smoother appearance.

> **Note** While using anti-aliasing makes the print preview look better, it can slow down the rendering speed.

Requirements

Platforms: Windows 98, Windows NT 4.0, Windows Millennium Edition, Windows 2000, Windows XP Home Edition, Windows XP Professional, Windows Server 2003 family

PreviewPrintController.GetPreviewPageInfo Method

Captures the pages of a document as a series of images.

[Visual Basic]
```
Public Function GetPreviewPageInfo() As PreviewPageInfo()
```
[C#]
```
public PreviewPageInfo[] GetPreviewPageInfo();
```
[C++]
```
public: PreviewPageInfo* GetPreviewPageInfo() [];
```
[JScript]
```
public function GetPreviewPageInfo() : PreviewPageInfo[];
```

Return Value

An array of type **PreviewPageInfo** that contains the pages of a **PrintDocument** as a series of images.

Remarks

You can use the **PrintDocument** image representation contained in a **PreviewPageInfo** to implement your own print preview form.

Requirements

Platforms: Windows 98, Windows NT 4.0, Windows Millennium Edition, Windows 2000, Windows XP Home Edition, Windows XP Professional, Windows Server 2003 family

.NET Framework Security:

- **PrintingPermission** for safe printing from a restricted dialog box. Associated enumeration: **PrintingPermissionLevel.SafePrinting**

PreviewPrintController.OnEndPage Method

Completes the control sequence that determines when and how to preview a page in a print document.

```
[Visual Basic]
Overrides Public Sub OnEndPage( _
   ByVal document As PrintDocument, _
   ByVal e As PrintPageEventArgs _
)
[C#]
public override void OnEndPage(
   PrintDocument document,
   PrintPageEventArgs e
);
[C++]
public: void OnEndPage(
   PrintDocument* document,
   PrintPageEventArgs* e
);
[JScript]
public override function OnEndPage(
   document : PrintDocument,
   e : PrintPageEventArgs
);
```

Parameters

document

A **PrintDocument** that represents the document being previewed.

e

A **PrintPageEventArgs** that contains data about how to preview a page in the print document.

Remarks

OnEndPage is called immediately after the **PrintDocument** raises the **PrintPage** event. If an exception is thrown inside a **PrintPage** event of a **PrintDocument**, this method is not called.

OnStartPrint creates the **Graphics** that is displayed during the print preview. After **OnStartPrint** is called, the **OnStartPage** method sets the **Graphics** to a graphic of a single page. The **OnEndPage** method clears the **Graphics**, while the **OnEndPrint** method de-allocates the object.

Requirements

Platforms: Windows 98, Windows NT 4.0, Windows Millennium Edition, Windows 2000, Windows XP Home Edition, Windows XP Professional, Windows Server 2003 family

.NET Framework Security:

- **PrintingPermission** for safe printing from a restricted dialog box. Associated enumeration: **PrintingPermissionLevel.SafePrinting**

PreviewPrintController.OnEndPrint Method

Completes the control sequence that determines when and how to preview a print document.

```
[Visual Basic]
Overrides Public Sub OnEndPrint( _
   ByVal document As PrintDocument, _
   ByVal e As PrintEventArgs _
)
[C#]
public override void OnEndPrint(
   PrintDocument document,
   PrintEventArgs e
);
[C++]
public: void OnEndPrint(
   PrintDocument* document,
   PrintEventArgs* e
);
[JScript]
public override function OnEndPrint(
   document : PrintDocument,
   e : PrintEventArgs
);
```

Parameters

document

A **PrintDocument** that represents the document being previewed.

e

A **PrintEventArgs** that contains data about how to preview the print document.

Remarks

This method is called immediately after **PrintDocument** raises the **EndPrint** event. Even if an uncaught exception was thrown during the print preview process, **OnEndPrint** is called.

OnStartPrint creates the **Graphics** that is displayed during the print preview. After **OnStartPrint** is called, the **OnStartPage** method sets the **Graphics** to a graphic of a single page. The **OnEndPage** method clears the **Graphics**, while the **OnEndPrint** method de-allocates the object.

Requirements

Platforms: Windows 98, Windows NT 4.0, Windows Millennium Edition, Windows 2000, Windows XP Home Edition, Windows XP Professional, Windows Server 2003 family

.NET Framework Security:

- **PrintingPermission** for safe printing from a restricted dialog box. Associated enumeration: **PrintingPermissionLevel.SafePrinting**

PreviewPrintController.OnStartPage Method

Begins the control sequence that determines when and how to preview a page in a print document.

```
[Visual Basic]
Overrides Public Function OnStartPage( _
   ByVal document As PrintDocument, _
   ByVal e As PrintPageEventArgs _
) As Graphics
[C#]
public override Graphics OnStartPage(
   PrintDocument document,
   PrintPageEventArgs e
);
[C++]
public: Graphics* OnStartPage(
   PrintDocument* document,
   PrintPageEventArgs* e
);
[JScript]
public override function OnStartPage(
   document : PrintDocument,
   e : PrintPageEventArgs
) : Graphics;
```

Parameters

document

A **PrintDocument** that represents the document being previewed.

e

A **PrintPageEventArgs** that contains data about how to preview a page in the print document. Initially, the **PrintPageEventArgs.Graphics** property of this parameter will be a null reference (**Nothing** in Visual Basic). The value returned from this method will be used to set this property.

Return Value

A **Graphics** that represents a page from a **PrintDocument**.

Remarks

OnStartPage is called immediately before **PrintDocument** raises the **PrintPage** event.

OnStartPrint creates the **Graphics** that is displayed during the print preview. After **OnStartPrint** is called, the **OnStartPage** method sets the **Graphics** to a graphic of a single page. The **OnEndPage** method clears the **Graphics**, while the **OnEndPrint** method de-allocates the object.

> **Note** Anti-aliasing, also known as gray scaling, makes the print preview look better. However, the use of anti-aliasing can slow down the rendering speed. For more information on anti-aliasing, see the **UseAntiAlias** property.

Requirements

Platforms: Windows 98, Windows NT 4.0, Windows Millennium Edition, Windows 2000, Windows XP Home Edition, Windows XP Professional, Windows Server 2003 family

.NET Framework Security:

- **PrintingPermission** for safe printing from a restricted dialog box. Associated enumeration: **PrintingPermissionLevel.SafePrinting**

PreviewPrintController.OnStartPrint Method

Begins the control sequence that determines when and how to preview a print document.

```
[Visual Basic]
Overrides Public Sub OnStartPrint( _
   ByVal document As PrintDocument, _
   ByVal e As PrintEventArgs _
)
[C#]
public override void OnStartPrint(
   PrintDocument document,
   PrintEventArgs e
);
[C++]
public: void OnStartPrint(
   PrintDocument* document,
   PrintEventArgs* e
);
[JScript]
public override function OnStartPrint(
   document : PrintDocument,
   e : PrintEventArgs
);
```

Parameters

document

A **PrintDocument** that represents the document being previewed.

e

A **PrintEventArgs** that contains data about how to print the document.

Exceptions

Exception Type	Condition
InvalidPrinterException	The printer named in the **PrinterSettings.PrinterName** property does not exist.

Remarks

OnStartPrint is called immediately after **PrintDocument** raises the **BeginPrint** event.

OnStartPrint creates the **Graphics** that is displayed during the print preview. After **OnStartPrint** is called, the **OnStartPage** method sets the **Graphics** to a graphic of a single page. The **OnEndPage** method clears the **Graphics**, while the **OnEndPrint** method de-allocates the object.

OnStartPrint verifies that the printer settings are valid.

Requirements

Platforms: Windows 98, Windows NT 4.0, Windows Millennium Edition, Windows 2000, Windows XP Home Edition, Windows XP Professional, Windows Server 2003 family

.NET Framework Security:

- **PrintingPermission** for safe printing from a restricted dialog box. Associated enumeration: **PrintingPermissionLevel.SafePrinting**

PrintController Class

Controls how a document is printed.

System.Object
  System.Drawing.Printing.PrintController
    System.Drawing.Printing.PreviewPrintController
    System.Drawing.Printing.StandardPrintController
    System.Windows.Forms.PrintControllerWithStatusDialog

[Visual Basic]
```
MustInherit Public Class PrintController
```
[C#]
```
public abstract class PrintController
```
[C++]
```
public __gc __abstract class PrintController
```
[JScript]
```
public abstract class PrintController
```

Thread Safety

Any public static (**Shared** in Visual Basic) members of this type are safe for multithreaded operations. Any instance members are not guaranteed to be thread safe.

Remarks

When implemented in a derived class, **PrintController** controls how a **PrintDocument** is printed. **PrintDocument.Print** invokes the print controller's **OnStartPrint**, **OnEndPrint**, **OnStartPage**, and **OnEndPage** methods, which in turn tell the printer how to print the document. Print preview uses a specialized **PrintController**. For an example of a print controller that is specialized for print preview, see the **PreviewPrintController**.

PrintController is used by **PrintDocument**, and not typically used directly.

The .NET Framework includes two print controllers that are derived from **PrintController**, that help accomplish common tasks. The **StandardPrintController** prints a document to a printer. The **PreviewPrintController** generates a preview of what the document will look like when printed and is used by the **PrintPreviewControl** and **PrintPreviewDialog** classes.

For more information on printing, see the **System.Drawing.Printing** namespace overview.

Requirements

Namespace: System.Drawing.Printing

Platforms: Windows 98, Windows NT 4.0, Windows Millennium Edition, Windows 2000, Windows XP Home Edition, Windows XP Professional, Windows Server 2003 family

Assembly: System.Drawing (in System.Drawing.dll)

PrintController Constructor

Initializes a new instance of the **PrintController** class.

[Visual Basic]
```
Public Sub New()
```
[C#]
```
public PrintController();
```
[C++]
```
public: PrintController();
```
[JScript]
```
public function PrintController();
```

Requirements

Platforms: Windows 98, Windows NT 4.0, Windows Millennium Edition, Windows 2000, Windows XP Home Edition, Windows XP Professional, Windows Server 2003 family

.NET Framework Security:

- **PrintingPermission** for safe printing from a restricted dialog box. Associated enumeration: **PrintingPermissionLevel.SafePrinting**

PrintController.OnEndPage Method

When overridden in a derived class, completes the control sequence that determines when and how to print a page of a document.

[Visual Basic]
```
Public Overridable Sub OnEndPage( _
   ByVal document As PrintDocument, _
   ByVal e As PrintPageEventArgs _
)
```
[C#]
```
public virtual void OnEndPage(
   PrintDocument document,
   PrintPageEventArgs e
);
```
[C++]
```
public: virtual void OnEndPage(
   PrintDocument* document,
   PrintPageEventArgs* e
);
```
[JScript]
```
public function OnEndPage(
   document : PrintDocument,
   e : PrintPageEventArgs
);
```

Parameters

document

A **PrintDocument** that represents the document currently being printed.

e

A **PrintPageEventArgs** that contains the event data.

Remarks

OnEndPage is called immediately after the **PrintDocument** raises the **PrintPage** event. If an exception is thrown inside a **PrintPage** event of a **PrintDocument**, **OnEndPage** is not called.

OnStartPrint creates the **Graphics** object that is sent to the printer. After **OnStartPrint** is called, the **OnStartPage** method sets the **Graphics** object to a graphic of a single page. (Use the **OnStartPage** method to set how to print a page in a document. For example, you can adjust page settings separately for each page.) The **OnEndPage** method clears the **Graphics** object, while the **OnEndPrint** method deallocates the object.

Requirements

Platforms: Windows 98, Windows NT 4.0, Windows Millennium Edition, Windows 2000, Windows XP Home Edition, Windows XP Professional, Windows Server 2003 family

PrintController.OnEndPrint Method

When overridden in a derived class, completes the control sequence that determines when and how to print a document.

```
[Visual Basic]
Public Overridable Sub OnEndPrint( _
   ByVal document As PrintDocument, _
   ByVal e As PrintEventArgs _
)
[C#]
public virtual void OnEndPrint(
   PrintDocument document,
   PrintEventArgs e
);
[C++]
public: virtual void OnEndPrint(
   PrintDocument* document,
   PrintEventArgs* e
);
[JScript]
public function OnEndPrint(
   document : PrintDocument,
   e : PrintEventArgs
);
```

Parameters

document

A **PrintDocument** that represents the document currently being printed.

e

A **PrintEventArgs** that contains the event data.

Remarks

OnEndPrint is called immediately after the **PrintDocument** raises the **EndPrint** event.

OnStartPrint creates the **Graphics** object that is sent to the printer. After **OnStartPrint** is called, the **OnStartPage** method sets the **Graphics** object to a grahpic of a single page. (Use the **OnStartPrint** method to determine when and how to print a document. For example, you can delay printing for 30 minutes or adjust the printer settings for the document.) The **OnEndPage** method clears the **Graphics** object, while the **OnEndPrint** method deallocates the object.

Requirements

Platforms: Windows 98, Windows NT 4.0, Windows Millennium Edition, Windows 2000, Windows XP Home Edition, Windows XP Professional, Windows Server 2003 family

PrintController.OnStartPage Method

When overridden in a derived class, begins the control sequence that determines when and how to print a page of a document.

```
[Visual Basic]
Public Overridable Function OnStartPage( _
   ByVal document As PrintDocument, _
   ByVal e As PrintPageEventArgs _
) As Graphics
[C#]
public virtual Graphics OnStartPage(
   PrintDocument document,
   PrintPageEventArgs e
);
[C++]
public: virtual Graphics* OnStartPage(
   PrintDocument* document,
   PrintPageEventArgs* e
);
[JScript]
public function OnStartPage(
   document : PrintDocument,
   e : PrintPageEventArgs
) : Graphics;
```

Parameters

document

A **PrintDocument** that represents the document currently being printed.

e

A **PrintPageEventArgs** that contains the event data.

Return Value

A **Graphics** object that represents a page from a **PrintDocument**.

Remarks

OnStartPage is called immediately before the **PrintDocument** raises the **PrintPage** event.

OnStartPrint creates the **Graphics** object that is sent to the printer. After **OnStartPrint** is called, the **OnStartPage** method sets the **Graphics** object to a graphic of a single page. The **OnEndPage** method clears the **Graphics** object, while the **OnEndPrint** method deallocates the object.

Use the **OnStartPage** method to set how to print a page in a document. For example, you can adjust page settings separately for each page.

Requirements

Platforms: Windows 98, Windows NT 4.0, Windows Millennium Edition, Windows 2000, Windows XP Home Edition, Windows XP Professional, Windows Server 2003 family

PrintController.OnStartPrint Method

When overridden in a derived class, begins the control sequence that determines when and how to print a document.

```
[Visual Basic]
Public Overridable Sub OnStartPrint( _
   ByVal document As PrintDocument, _
   ByVal e As PrintEventArgs _
)
[C#]
public virtual void OnStartPrint(
   PrintDocument document,
   PrintEventArgs e
);
[C++]
public: virtual void OnStartPrint(
   PrintDocument* document,
   PrintEventArgs* e
);
[JScript]
public function OnStartPrint(
   document : PrintDocument,
   e : PrintEventArgs
);
```

Parameters

document

A **PrintDocument** that represents the document currently being printed.

e

A **PrintEventArgs** that contains the event data.

Remarks

OnStartPrint is called immediately after the **PrintDocument** raises the **BeginPrint** event.

Use the **OnStartPrint** method to determine when and how to print a document. For example, you can delay printing for 30 minutes or adjust the printer settings for the document. **OnStartPrint** creates the **Graphics** object that is sent to the printer. After **OnStartPrint** is called, the **OnStartPage** method sets the **Graphics** object to one of a single page. The **OnEndPage** method clears the **Graphics** object, while the **OnEndPrint** method deallocates the object.

The **OnStartPrint** method is a good place to verify that **PrinterSettings** are valid.

Requirements

Platforms: Windows 98, Windows NT 4.0,
Windows Millennium Edition, Windows 2000,
Windows XP Home Edition, Windows XP Professional,
Windows Server 2003 family

PrintDocument Class

Defines a reusable object that sends output to a printer.

System.Object
  System.MarshalByRefObject
    System.ComponentModel.Component
      System.Drawing.Printing.PrintDocument

[Visual Basic]
```
Public Class PrintDocument
   Inherits Component
```
[C#]
```
public class PrintDocument : Component
```
[C++]
```
public __gc class PrintDocument : public Component
```
[JScript]
```
public class PrintDocument extends Component
```

Thread Safety

Any public static (**Shared** in Visual Basic) members of this type are safe for multithreaded operations. Any instance members are not guaranteed to be thread safe.

Remarks

Typically, you create an instance of the **PrintDocument** class, set the properties that describe how to print, and call the **Print** method to start the printing process. Handle the **PrintPage** event where you specify the output to print, by using the **Graphics** included in the **PrintPageEventArgs**.

For more information on printing, see the **System.Drawing.Printing** namespace overview.

Example

[Visual Basic, C#] The following example prints the file named C:\My Documents\MyFile.txt on the default printer. To run the example, change the path to the file you want to print. You can also modify the `InitializeComponent` procedure through the Windows Forms Designer.

> [Visual Basic, C#] **Note** The example assumes that each line fits within the page width.

[Visual Basic, C#] Use the **System.ComponentModel**, **System.Windows.Forms**, **System.Drawing**, **System.Drawing.Printing**, and **System.IO** namespaces for this example.

[Visual Basic]
```
Public Class PrintingExample
    Inherits System.Windows.Forms.Form
    Private components As System.ComponentModel.Container
    Private printButton As System.Windows.Forms.Button
    Private printFont As Font
    Private streamToPrint As StreamReader

    Public Sub New()
        ' The Windows Forms Designer requires the following call.
        InitializeComponent()
    End Sub

    ' The Click event is raised when the user clicks the Print button.
    Private Sub printButton_Click(sender As Object, e As EventArgs)
        Try
            streamToPrint = New StreamReader("C:\My ↵
Documents\MyFile.txt")
            Try
                printFont = New Font("Arial", 10)
                Dim pd As New PrintDocument()
                AddHandler pd.PrintPage, AddressOf Me.pd_PrintPage
                pd.Print()
            Finally
                streamToPrint.Close()
            End Try
        Catch ex As Exception
            MessageBox.Show(ex.Message)
        End Try
    End Sub

    ' The PrintPage event is raised for each page to be printed.
    Private Sub pd_PrintPage(sender As Object, ev As ↵
PrintPageEventArgs)
        Dim linesPerPage As Single = 0
        Dim yPos As Single = 0
        Dim count As Integer = 0
        Dim leftMargin As Single = ev.MarginBounds.Left
        Dim topMargin As Single = ev.MarginBounds.Top
        Dim line As String = Nothing

        ' Calculate the number of lines per page.
        linesPerPage = ev.MarginBounds.Height / ↵
printFont.GetHeight(ev.Graphics)

        ' Print each line of the file.
        While count < linesPerPage
            line = streamToPrint.ReadLine()
            If line Is Nothing Then
                Exit While
            End If
            yPos = topMargin + count * printFont.GetHeight(ev.Graphics)
            ev.Graphics.DrawString(line, printFont, ↵
 Brushes.Black, leftMargin, yPos, New StringFormat())
            count += 1
        End While

        ' If more lines exist, print another page.
        If Not (line Is Nothing) Then
            ev.HasMorePages = True
        Else
            ev.HasMorePages = False
        End If
    End Sub


    ' The Windows Forms Designer requires the following procedure.
    Private Sub InitializeComponent()
        Me.components = New System.ComponentModel.Container()
        Me.printButton = New System.Windows.Forms.Button()

        Me.AutoScaleBaseSize = New System.Drawing.Size(5, 13)
        Me.ClientSize = New System.Drawing.Size(504, 381)
        Me.Text = "Print Example"

        printButton.ImageAlign = ↵
System.Drawing.ContentAlignment.MiddleLeft
        printButton.Location = New System.Drawing.Point(32, 110)
        printButton.FlatStyle = System.Windows.Forms.FlatStyle.Flat
        printButton.TabIndex = 0
        printButton.Text = "Print the file."
        printButton.Size = New System.Drawing.Size(136, 40)
        AddHandler printButton.Click, AddressOf printButton_Click

        Me.Controls.Add(printButton)
    End Sub

    ' This is the main entry point for the application.
    Public Shared Sub Main()
        Application.Run(New PrintingExample())
    End Sub

End Class
```

[C#]
```
public class PrintingExample : System.Windows.Forms.Form
{
    private System.ComponentModel.Container components;
    private System.Windows.Forms.Button printButton;
    private Font printFont;
    private StreamReader streamToPrint;

   public PrintingExample() : base()
   {
      // The Windows Forms Designer requires the following call.
      InitializeComponent();
   }

   // The Click event is raised when the user clicks the Print button.
   private void printButton_Click(object sender, EventArgs e)
   {
      try
      {
          streamToPrint = new StreamReader
             ("C:\\My Documents\\MyFile.txt");
          try
          {
             printFont = new Font("Arial", 10);
             PrintDocument pd = new PrintDocument();
             pd.PrintPage += new PrintPageEventHandler
                (this.pd_PrintPage);
             pd.Print();
          }
          finally
          {
             streamToPrint.Close();
          }
      }
      catch(Exception ex)
      {
          MessageBox.Show(ex.Message);
      }
   }

   // The PrintPage event is raised for each page to be printed.
   private void pd_PrintPage(object sender, PrintPageEventArgs ev)
   {
      float linesPerPage = 0;
      float yPos = 0;
      int count = 0;
      float leftMargin = ev.MarginBounds.Left;
      float topMargin = ev.MarginBounds.Top;
      string line = null;

      // Calculate the number of lines per page.
      linesPerPage = ev.MarginBounds.Height /
         printFont.GetHeight(ev.Graphics);

      // Print each line of the file.
      while(count < linesPerPage &&
         ((line=streamToPrint.ReadLine()) != null))
      {
         yPos = topMargin + (count *
            printFont.GetHeight(ev.Graphics));
         ev.Graphics.DrawString(line, printFont, Brushes.Black,
            leftMargin, yPos, new StringFormat());
         count++;
      }

      // If more lines exist, print another page.
      if(line != null)
         ev.HasMorePages = true;
      else
         ev.HasMorePages = false;
   }

   // The Windows Forms Designer requires the following procedure.
   private void InitializeComponent()
   {
      this.components = new System.ComponentModel.Container();
      this.printButton = new System.Windows.Forms.Button();

      this.AutoScaleBaseSize = new System.Drawing.Size(5, 13);
      this.ClientSize = new System.Drawing.Size(504, 381);
      this.Text = "Print Example";

      printButton.ImageAlign =
         System.Drawing.ContentAlignment.MiddleLeft;
      printButton.Location = new System.Drawing.Point(32, 110);
      printButton.FlatStyle = System.Windows.Forms.FlatStyle.Flat;
      printButton.TabIndex = 0;
      printButton.Text = "Print the file.";
      printButton.Size = new System.Drawing.Size(136, 40);
      printButton.Click += new System.EventHandler(printButton_Click);

      this.Controls.Add(printButton);
   }

   // This is the main entry point for the application.
   public static void Main(string[] args)
   {
      Application.Run(new PrintingExample());
   }
}
```

Requirements

Namespace: System.Drawing.Printing

Platforms: Windows 98, Windows NT 4.0, Windows Millennium Edition, Windows 2000, Windows XP Home Edition, Windows XP Professional, Windows Server 2003 family

Assembly: System.Drawing (in System.Drawing.dll)

PrintDocument Constructor

Initializes a new instance of the **PrintDocument** class.

[Visual Basic]
```
Public Sub New()
```
[C#]
```
public PrintDocument();
```
[C++]
```
public: PrintDocument();
```
[JScript]
```
public function PrintDocument();
```

Remarks

The default constructor initializes all fields based upon the default printer. Typically, after creating a new **PrintDocument**, you set printer and page settings that affect the output through the **PrinterSettings** and **DefaultPageSettings** properties, respectively.

Example

See related example in the **System.Drawing.Printing.PrintDocument** class topic.

Requirements

Platforms: Windows 98, Windows NT 4.0, Windows Millennium Edition, Windows 2000, Windows XP Home Edition, Windows XP Professional, Windows Server 2003 family

PrintDocument.DefaultPageSettings Property

Gets or sets page settings that are used as defaults for all pages to be printed.

```
[Visual Basic]
Public Property DefaultPageSettings As PageSettings
[C#]
public PageSettings DefaultPageSettings {get; set;}
[C++]
public: __property PageSettings* get_DefaultPageSettings();
public: __property void set_DefaultPageSettings(PageSettings*);
[JScript]
public function get DefaultPageSettings() : PageSettings;
public function set DefaultPageSettings(PageSettings);
```

Property Value

A **PageSettings** that specifies the default page settings for the document.

Remarks

You can specify several default page settings through the **DefaultPageSettings** property. For example, the **PageSettings.Color** property specifies whether the page prints in color, the **PageSettings.Landscape** property specifies landscape or portrait orientation, and the **PageSettings.Margins** property specifies the margins of the page.

To specify settings on a page-by-page basis, handle the **PrintPage** or **QueryPageSettings** event and modify the **PageSettings** argument included in the **PrintPageEventArgs** or **QueryPageSettingsEventArgs**, respectively.

> **Note** After printing has started, changes to page settings through the **DefaultPageSettings** property will not affect pages being printed.

Example

See related example in the **System.Drawing.Printing.PrintDocument** class topic.

Requirements

Platforms: Windows 98, Windows NT 4.0, Windows Millennium Edition, Windows 2000, Windows XP Home Edition, Windows XP Professional, Windows Server 2003 family

PrintDocument.DocumentName Property

Gets or sets the document name to display (for example, in a print status dialog box or printer queue) while printing the document.

```
[Visual Basic]
Public Property DocumentName As String
[C#]
public string DocumentName {get; set;}
[C++]
public: __property String* get_DocumentName();
public: __property void set_DocumentName(String*);
[JScript]
public function get DocumentName() : String;
public function set DocumentName(String);
```

Property Value

The document name to display while printing the document. The default is "document".

Remarks

The **DocumentName** property does not specify the file to print. Rather, you specify the output to print by handling the **PrintPage** event. For an example of this, see the **PrintDocument** class overview.

Example

See related example in the **System.Drawing.Printing.PrintDocument** class topic.

Requirements

Platforms: Windows 98, Windows NT 4.0, Windows Millennium Edition, Windows 2000, Windows XP Home Edition, Windows XP Professional, Windows Server 2003 family

PrintDocument.OriginAtMargins Property

Note: This namespace, class, or member is supported only in version 1.1 of the .NET Framework.

Gets or sets a value indicating whether the position of a graphics object associated with a page is located just inside the user-specified margins or at the top-left corner of the printable area of the page.

```
[Visual Basic]
Public Property OriginAtMargins As Boolean
[C#]
public bool OriginAtMargins {get; set;}
[C++]
public: __property bool get_OriginAtMargins();
public: __property void set_OriginAtMargins(bool);
[JScript]
public function get OriginAtMargins() : Boolean;
public function set OriginAtMargins(Boolean);
```

Property Value

true if the graphics origin starts at the page margins; **false** if the graphics origin is at the top-left corner of the printable page. The default is **false**.

Remarks

Calculating the area available to print requires knowing the physical size of the paper, the margins for the page, and the location of the **Graphics** object origin. When **OriginAtMargins** is **true**, the **Graphics** object location takes into account the **PageSettings.Margins** property value and the printable area of the page. When **OriginAtMargins** is **false**, only the printable are of the page is used to determine the location of the **Graphics** object origin, the **PageSettings.Margins** value is ignored.

For example, if **OriginAtMargins** is **true**, and **PageSettings.Margins** is set for 1 inch on each side, the **Graphics** object included in the **PrintPageEventArgs** is located 1 inch from the left and top of the page. If the printable area of the page is .25 of an inch on each side and **OriginAtMargins** is **false**, the **Graphics** object is located .25 of an inch from the left and top of the page.

> **Note** The printable area of a page varies from printer to printer and is not guaranteed to be symmetrical.

Requirements

Platforms: Windows 98, Windows NT 4.0, Windows Millennium Edition, Windows 2000, Windows XP Home Edition, Windows XP Professional, Windows Server 2003 family

PrintDocument.PrintController Property

Gets or sets the print controller that guides the printing process.

```
[Visual Basic]
Public Property PrintController As PrintController
[C#]
public PrintController PrintController {get; set;}
[C++]
public: __property PrintController* get_PrintController();
public: __property void set_PrintController(PrintController*);
[JScript]
public function get PrintController() : PrintController;
public function set PrintController(PrintController);
```

Property Value

The **PrintController** that guides the printing process. The default is a new instance of the **PrintControllerWithStatusDialog** class.

Remarks

A print controller guides the printing process in several ways. For example, to print a document, you need to convert it to a **Graphics** object. A **PrintController** specifies where to draw the graphic in an image for a print preview or on a printer to actually print the document. A print controller can also specify whether to print a document immediately, or wait a specified interval.

Example

See related example in the **System.Drawing.Printing.PrintDocument** class topic.

Requirements

Platforms: Windows 98, Windows NT 4.0, Windows Millennium Edition, Windows 2000, Windows XP Home Edition, Windows XP Professional, Windows Server 2003 family

.NET Framework Security:

- **PrintingPermission** for safe printing from a restricted dialog box. Associated enumeration: **PrintingPermissionLevel.SafePrinting**

PrintDocument.PrinterSettings Property

Gets or sets the printer that prints the document.

```
[Visual Basic]
Public Property PrinterSettings As PrinterSettings
[C#]
public PrinterSettings PrinterSettings {get; set;}
[C++]
public: __property PrinterSettings* get_PrinterSettings();
public: __property void set_PrinterSettings(PrinterSettings*);
[JScript]
public function get PrinterSettings() : PrinterSettings;
public function set PrinterSettings(PrinterSettings);
```

Property Value

A **PrinterSettings** that specifies where and how the document is printed. The default is a **PrinterSettings** with its properties set to their default values.

Remarks

You can specify several printer settings through the **PrinterSettings** property. For example, use the **PrinterSettings.Copies** property to specify the number of copies you want to print, the **PrinterSettings.PrinterName** property to specify the printer to use, and the **PrinterSettings.PrintRange** property to specify the range of pages you want to print.

Example

See related example in the **System.Drawing.Printing.PrintDocument** class topic.

Requirements

Platforms: Windows 98, Windows NT 4.0, Windows Millennium Edition, Windows 2000, Windows XP Home Edition, Windows XP Professional, Windows Server 2003 family

PrintDocument.OnBeginPrint Method

Raises the **BeginPrint** event. It is called after the **Print** method is called and before the first page of the document prints.

```
[Visual Basic]
Protected Overridable Sub OnBeginPrint( _
   ByVal e As PrintEventArgs _
)
[C#]
protected virtual void OnBeginPrint(
   PrintEventArgs e
);
[C++]
protected: virtual void OnBeginPrint(
   PrintEventArgs* e
);
[JScript]
protected function OnBeginPrint(
   e : PrintEventArgs
);
```

Parameters

e

A **PrintEventArgs** that contains the event data.

Remarks

The **OnBeginPrint** method allows derived classes to handle the event without attaching a delegate. This is the preferred technique for handling the event in a derived class.

When a derived class calls the **OnBeginPrint** method, it raises the **BeginPrint** event by invoking the event handler through a delegate.

Notes to Inheritors: When overriding **OnBeginPrint** in a derived class, be sure to call the base class's **OnBeginPrint** method so that registered delegates receive the event. This method is a good place for initialization.

Requirements

Platforms: Windows 98, Windows NT 4.0, Windows Millennium Edition, Windows 2000, Windows XP Home Edition, Windows XP Professional, Windows Server 2003 family

PrintDocument.OnEndPrint Method

Raises the **EndPrint** event. It is called when the last page of the document has printed.

```
[Visual Basic]
Protected Overridable Sub OnEndPrint( _
   ByVal e As PrintEventArgs _
)
[C#]
protected virtual void OnEndPrint(
   PrintEventArgs e
);
[C++]
protected: virtual void OnEndPrint(
   PrintEventArgs* e
);
[JScript]
protected function OnEndPrint(
   e : PrintEventArgs
);
```

Parameters

e

A **PrintEventArgs** that contains the event data.

Remarks

The **OnEndPrint** method allows derived classes to handle the event without attaching a delegate. This is the preferred technique for handling the event in a derived class. The **OnEndPrint** method is also called if the printing process is canceled or an exception occurs during the printing process.

When a derived class calls the **OnEndPrint** method, it raises the **EndPrint** event by invoking the event handler through a delegate.

Notes to Inheritors: When overriding **OnEndPrint** in a derived class, be sure to call the base class's **OnEndPrint** method so that registered delegates receive the event. This method is a good place for uninitialization.

Requirements

Platforms: Windows 98, Windows NT 4.0, Windows Millennium Edition, Windows 2000, Windows XP Home Edition, Windows XP Professional, Windows Server 2003 family

PrintDocument.OnPrintPage Method

Raises the **PrintPage** event. It is called before a page prints.

```
[Visual Basic]
Protected Overridable Sub OnPrintPage( _
   ByVal e As PrintPageEventArgs _
)
[C#]
protected virtual void OnPrintPage(
   PrintPageEventArgs e
);
[C++]
protected: virtual void OnPrintPage(
   PrintPageEventArgs* e
);
[JScript]
protected function OnPrintPage(
   e : PrintPageEventArgs
);
```

Parameters

e

A **PrintPageEventArgs** that contains the event data.

Remarks

The **OnPrintPage** method allows derived classes to handle the event without attaching a delegate. This is the preferred technique for handling the event in a derived class.

When a derived class calls the **OnPrintPage** method, it raises the **PrintPage** event by invoking the event handler through a delegate.

Notes to Inheritors: When overriding **OnPrintPage** in a derived class, be sure to call the base class's **OnPrintPage** method so that registered delegates receive the event.

Requirements

Platforms: Windows 98, Windows NT 4.0, Windows Millennium Edition, Windows 2000, Windows XP Home Edition, Windows XP Professional, Windows Server 2003 family

PrintDocument.OnQueryPageSettings Method

Raises the **QueryPageSettings** event. It is called immediately before each **PrintPage** event.

```
[Visual Basic]
Protected Overridable Sub OnQueryPageSettings( _
   ByVal e As QueryPageSettingsEventArgs _
)
[C#]
protected virtual void OnQueryPageSettings(
   QueryPageSettingsEventArgs e
);
[C++]
protected: virtual void OnQueryPageSettings(
   QueryPageSettingsEventArgs* e
);
[JScript]
protected function OnQueryPageSettings(
   e : QueryPageSettingsEventArgs
);
```

Parameters

e

A **QueryPageSettingsEventArgs** that contains the event data.

Remarks

The **OnQueryPageSettings** method also allows derived classes to handle the event without attaching a delegate. This is the preferred technique for handling the event in a derived class.

When a derived class calls the **OnQueryPageSettings** method, it raises the **QueryPageSettings** event by invoking the event handler through a delegate.

Notes to Inheritors: When overriding **OnQueryPageSettings** in a derived class, be sure to call the base class's **OnQueryPageSettings** method so that registered delegates receive the event.

Requirements

Platforms: Windows 98, Windows NT 4.0, Windows Millennium Edition, Windows 2000, Windows XP Home Edition, Windows XP Professional, Windows Server 2003 family

PrintDocument.Print Method

Starts the document's printing process.

```
[Visual Basic]
Public Sub Print()
[C#]
public void Print();
[C++]
public: void Print();
[JScript]
public function Print();
```

Exceptions

Exception Type	Condition
InvalidPrinterException	The printer named in the **PrinterSettings.PrinterName** property does not exist.

Remarks

Specify the output to print by handling the **PrintPage** event and by using the **Graphics** included in the **PrintPageEventArgs**.

Use the **PrinterSettings.PrinterName** property to specify which printer should print the document.

The **Print** method prints the document without using a print dialog. Use a **PrintDialog** when you want to offer the user the ability to choose print settings.

> **Note** If an exception that is not handled by the **Print** method is thrown during printing, the printing of the document is aborted.

Example

See related example in the **System.Drawing.Printing.PrintDocument** class topic.

.NET Framework Security:

- **PrintingPermission** for safe printing from a restricted dialog box. Associated enumeration: **PrintingPermissionLevel.SafePrinting**

PrintDocument.ToString Method

This member overrides **Object.ToString**.

```
[Visual Basic]
Overrides Public Function ToString() As String
[C#]
public override string ToString();
[C++]
public: String* ToString();
[JScript]
public override function ToString() : String;
```

Requirements

Platforms: Windows 98, Windows NT 4.0, Windows Millennium Edition, Windows 2000, Windows XP Home Edition, Windows XP Professional, Windows Server 2003 family

PrintDocument.BeginPrint Event

Occurs when the **Print** method is called and before the first page of the document prints.

```
[Visual Basic]
Public Event BeginPrint As PrintEventHandler
[C#]
public event PrintEventHandler BeginPrint;
[C++]
public: __event PrintEventHandler* BeginPrint;
```

[JScript] In JScript, you can handle the events defined by a class, but you cannot define your own.

Event Data

The event handler receives an argument of type **PrintEventArgs** containing data related to this event. The following **PrintEventArgs** property provides information specific to this event.

Property	Description
Cancel (inherited from **CancelEventArgs**)	Gets or sets a value indicating whether the event should be canceled.

Remarks

Typically, you handle the **BeginPrint** event to initialize fonts, file streams, and other resources used during the printing process.

To associate the event with your event handler, add an instance of the **PrintEventHandler** delegate to the event. The event handler is called whenever the event occurs. For more information about handling events with delegates, see **Events and Delegates**.

Requirements

Platforms: Windows 98, Windows NT 4.0, Windows Millennium Edition, Windows 2000, Windows XP Home Edition, Windows XP Professional, Windows Server 2003 family

PrintDocument.EndPrint Event

Occurs when the last page of the document has printed.

```
[Visual Basic]
Public Event EndPrint As PrintEventHandler
[C#]
public event PrintEventHandler EndPrint;
[C++]
public: __event PrintEventHandler* EndPrint;
```

[JScript] In JScript, you can handle the events defined by a class, but you cannot define your own.

Event Data

The event handler receives an argument of type **PrintEventArgs** containing data related to this event. The following **PrintEventArgs** property provides information specific to this event.

Property	Description
Cancel (inherited from **CancelEventArgs**)	Gets or sets a value indicating whether the event should be canceled.

Remarks

Typically, you handle the **EndPrint** event to release fonts, file streams, and other resources used during the printing process, like fonts.

You indicate that there are no more pages to print by setting the **PrintPageEventArgs.HasMorePages** property to **false** in the **PrintPage** event. The **EndPrint** event also occurs if the printing process is canceled or an exception occurs during the printing process.

To associate the event with your event handler, add an instance of the **PrintEventHandler** delegate to the event. The event handler is called whenever the event occurs.

Requirements

Platforms: Windows 98, Windows NT 4.0, Windows Millennium Edition, Windows 2000, Windows XP Home Edition, Windows XP Professional, Windows Server 2003 family

PrintDocument.PrintPage Event

Occurs when the output to print for the current page is needed.

[Visual Basic]
```
Public Event PrintPage As PrintPageEventHandler
```
[C#]
```
public event PrintPageEventHandler PrintPage;
```
[C++]
```
public: __event PrintPageEventHandler* PrintPage;
```

[JScript] In JScript, you can handle the events defined by a class, but you cannot define your own.

Event Data

The event handler receives an argument of type **PrintPageEventArgs** containing data related to this event. The following **PrintPage-EventArgs** properties provide information specific to this event.

Property	Description
Cancel	Gets or sets a value indicating whether the print job should be canceled.
Graphics	Gets the **Graphics** used to paint the page.
HasMorePages	Gets or sets a value indicating whether an additional page should be printed.
MarginBounds	Gets the rectangular area that represents the portion of the page inside the margins.
PageBounds	Gets the rectangular area that represents the total area of the page.
PageSettings	Gets the page settings for the current page.

Remarks

To specify the output to print, use the **Graphics** included in the **PrintPageEventArgs**. For example, to specify a line of text that should be printed, draw the text using the **Graphics.DrawString** method.

In addition to specifying the ouput, you can indicate if there are additional pages to print by setting the **PrintPageEvent-Args.HasMorePages** property to **true**. Individual page settings can also be modified through the **PageSettings** and the print job can be canceled by setting the **PrintPageEventArgs.Cancel** property to **true**. The default is **false**, which indicates that there are no more pages to print. To print each page of a document using different page settings, handle the **QueryPageSettings** event.

To associate the event with your event handler, add an instance of the **PrintPageEventHandler** delegate to the event. The event handler is called whenever the event occurs.

Example

See related example in the **System.Drawing.Printing.PrintDocument** class topic.

Requirements

Platforms: Windows 98, Windows NT 4.0, Windows Millennium Edition, Windows 2000, Windows XP Home Edition, Windows XP Professional, Windows Server 2003 family

PrintDocument.QueryPageSettings Event

Occurs immediately before each **PrintPage** event.

[Visual Basic]
```
Public Event QueryPageSettings As QueryPageSettingsEventHandler
```
[C#]
```
public event QueryPageSettingsEventHandler QueryPageSettings;
```
[C++]
```
public: __event QueryPageSettingsEventHandler* QueryPageSettings;
```

[JScript] In JScript, you can handle the events defined by a class, but you cannot define your own.

Event Data

The event handler receives an argument of type **QueryPage-SettingsEventArgs** containing data related to this event. The following **QueryPageSettingsEventArgs** properties provide information specific to this event.

Property	Description
Cancel (inherited from **CancelEventArgs**)	Gets or sets a value indicating whether the event should be canceled.
PageSettings	Gets or sets the page settings for the page to be printed.

Remarks

It is possible to print each page of a document using different page settings. You set page settings by modifying individual properties of the **QueryPageSettingsEventArgs.PageSettings** property or by setting the property to a **PageSettings**. Changes made to the **PageSettings** affect only the current page, not the document's default page settings. The print job can also be canceled by setting the **Cancel** property to **true** for the **QueryPageSettingsEventArgs**.

To associate the event with your event handler, add an instance of the **QueryPageSettingsEventHandler** delegate to the event. The event handler is called whenever the event occurs. For more information about handling events with delegates, see **Events and Delegates**.

Example

See related example in the **System.Drawing.Printing.PrintDocument** class topic.

Requirements

Platforms: Windows 98, Windows NT 4.0, Windows Millennium Edition, Windows 2000, Windows XP Home Edition, Windows XP Professional, Windows Server 2003 family

PrinterResolution Class

Represents the resolution supported by a printer.

System.Object
 System.Drawing.Printing.PrinterResolution

```
[Visual Basic]
Public Class PrinterResolution
[C#]
public class PrinterResolution
[C++]
public __gc class PrinterResolution
[JScript]
public class PrinterResolution
```

Thread Safety

Any public static (**Shared** in Visual Basic) members of this type are safe for multithreaded operations. Any instance members are not guaranteed to be thread safe.

Remarks

This class is used by **PrinterSettings.PrinterResolutions** and **PageSettings.PrinterResolution** properties to get the printer resolutions that are available on the printer and to set the printing resolution for a page, respectively.

Use the **Kind** property to determine whether the printer resolution type is the **PrinterResolutionKind** value, **Custom**. If so, use the **X** and **Y** properties to determine the printer resolution in the horizontal and vertical directions, respectively.

For more information on printing, see the **System.Drawing.Printing** namespace overview.

Example

[Visual Basic, C#, C++] The following example populates the `comboPrintResolution` combo box with the supported resolutions. The example assumes that a **PrintDocument** variable named `printDoc` exists and that the specific combo box exists.

```
[Visual Basic]
' Add list of printer resolutions found on the printer to the combobox.
' The PrinterResolution's ToString() method will be used to ↵
provide the display string.
Dim pkResolution As PrinterResolution
For i = 0 to printDoc.PrinterSettings.PrinterResolutions.Count - 1
    pkResolution = printDoc.PrinterSettings.PrinterResolutions.Item(i)
    comboPrintResolution.Items.Add(pkResolution)
Next

[C#]
// Add list of printer resolutions found on the printer to the ↵
combobox.
// The PrinterResolution's ToString() method will be used to ↵
provide the display string.

PrinterResolution pkResolution;
for (int i = 0; i < ↵
printDoc.PrinterSettings.PrinterResolutions.Count; i++){
    pkResolution = printDoc.PrinterSettings.PrinterResolutions[i];
    comboPrintResolution.Items.Add(pkResolution);
}

[C++]
// Add list of printer resolutions found on the printer ↵
to the combobox.
// The PrinterResolution's ToString() method will be used ↵
to provide the display String.
PrinterResolution* pkResolution;
for (int i = 0; i < printDoc->PrinterSettings-> ↵
PrinterResolutions->Count; i++) {
   pkResolution = printDoc->PrinterSettings-> ↵
PrinterResolutions->Item[i];
   comboPrintResolution->Items->Add(pkResolution);
}
```

Requirements

Namespace: System.Drawing.Printing

Platforms: Windows 98, Windows NT 4.0, Windows Millennium Edition, Windows 2000, Windows XP Home Edition, Windows XP Professional, Windows Server 2003 family

Assembly: System.Drawing (in System.Drawing.dll)

PrinterResolution.Kind Property

Gets the printer resolution.

```
[Visual Basic]
Public ReadOnly Property Kind As PrinterResolutionKind
[C#]
public PrinterResolutionKind Kind {get;}
[C++]
public: __property PrinterResolutionKind get_Kind();
[JScript]
public function get Kind() : PrinterResolutionKind;
```

Property Value

One of the **PrinterResolutionKind** values.

Requirements

Platforms: Windows 98, Windows NT 4.0, Windows Millennium Edition, Windows 2000, Windows XP Home Edition, Windows XP Professional, Windows Server 2003 family

PrinterResolution.X Property

Gets the horizontal printer resolution, in dots per inch.

```
[Visual Basic]
Public ReadOnly Property X As Integer
[C#]
public int X {get;}
[C++]
public: __property int get_X();
[JScript]
public function get X() : int;
```

Property Value

The horizontal printer resolution, in dots per inch.

Remarks

If the **Kind** property is not set to **Custom**, **X** defaults to -1.

Requirements

Platforms: Windows 98, Windows NT 4.0, Windows Millennium Edition, Windows 2000, Windows XP Home Edition, Windows XP Professional, Windows Server 2003 family

PrinterResolution.Y Property

Gets the vertical printer resolution, in dots per inch.

[Visual Basic]
```
Public ReadOnly Property Y As Integer
```
[C#]
```
public int Y {get;}
```
[C++]
```
public: __property int get_Y();
```
[JScript]
```
public function get Y() : int;
```

Property Value

The vertical printer resolution, in dots per inch.

Remarks

If the **Kind** property is not set to **Custom**, **Y** defaults to -1.

Requirements

Platforms: Windows 98, Windows NT 4.0,
Windows Millennium Edition, Windows 2000,
Windows XP Home Edition, Windows XP Professional,
Windows Server 2003 family

PrinterResolution.ToString Method

This member overrides **Object.ToString**.

[Visual Basic]
```
Overrides Public Function ToString() As String
```
[C#]
```
public override string ToString();
```
[C++]
```
public: String* ToString();
```
[JScript]
```
public override function ToString() : String;
```

Requirements

Platforms: Windows 98, Windows NT 4.0,
Windows Millennium Edition, Windows 2000,
Windows XP Home Edition, Windows XP Professional,
Windows Server 2003 family

PrinterResolutionKind Enumeration

Specifies a printer resolution.

[Visual Basic]
```
<Serializable>
Public Enum PrinterResolutionKind
```
[C#]
```
[Serializable]
public enum PrinterResolutionKind
```
[C++]
```
[Serializable]
__value public enum PrinterResolutionKind
```
[JScript]
```
public
   Serializable
enum PrinterResolutionKind
```

Remarks

All printers support high, medium, low, and draft resolutions, although they can generate the same output.

This enumeration is used by **PrinterResolution**, **PrinterSettings**, and **PageSettings**.

Members

Member name	Description
Custom	Custom resolution.
Draft	Draft-quality resolution.
High	High resolution.
Low	Low resolution.
Medium	Medium resolution.

Requirements

Namespace: System.Drawing.Printing

Platforms: Windows 98, Windows NT 4.0, Windows Millennium Edition, Windows 2000, Windows XP Home Edition, Windows XP Professional, Windows Server 2003 family

Assembly: System.Drawing (in System.Drawing.dll)

PrinterSettings Class

Specifies information about how a document is printed, including the printer that prints it.

System.Object
  System.Drawing.Printing.PrinterSettings

[Visual Basic]
```
<Serializable>
<ComVisible(False)>
Public Class PrinterSettings
   Implements ICloneable
```
[C#]
```
[Serializable]
[ComVisible(false)]
public class PrinterSettings : ICloneable
```
[C++]
```
[Serializable]
[ComVisible(false)]
public __gc class PrinterSettings : public ICloneable
```
[JScript]
```
public
   Serializable
   ComVisible(false)
class PrinterSettings implements ICloneable
```

Thread Safety

Any public static (**Shared** in Visual Basic) members of this type are safe for multithreaded operations. Any instance members are not guaranteed to be thread safe.

Remarks

Typically, you access a **PrinterSettings** through **PrintDocument.PrinterSettings** or **PageSettings.PrinterSettings** properties to modify printer settings. The most common printer setting is **PrinterName**, which specifies the printer to print to.

For more information on printing, see the **System.Drawing.Printing** namespace overview.

Example

[Visual Basic, C#] The following example prints a document on the specified printer. The example makes three assumptions: that a variable names `filePath` has been set to the path of the file to print; that a method named `pd_PrintPage`, which handles the **PrintPage** event, has been defined; and that a variable named `printer` has been set to the printer's name.

[Visual Basic, C#] Use the **System.Drawing**, **System.Drawing.Printing**, and **System.IO** namespaces for this example.

[Visual Basic]
```
Public Sub Printing(printer As String)
    Try
        streamToPrint = New StreamReader(filePath)
        Try
            printFont = New Font("Arial", 10)
            Dim pd As New PrintDocument()
            AddHandler pd.PrintPage, AddressOf pd_PrintPage
            ' Specify the printer to use.
            pd.PrinterSettings.PrinterName = printer

            If pd.PrinterSettings.IsValid then
               pd.Print()
            Else
               MessageBox.Show("Printer is invalid.")
            End If
        Finally
            streamToPrint.Close()
        End Try
    Catch ex As Exception
        MessageBox.Show(ex.Message)
    End Try
End Sub
```

[C#]
```
public void Printing(string printer) {
  try {
    streamToPrint = new StreamReader (filePath);
    try {
      printFont = new Font("Arial", 10);
      PrintDocument pd = new PrintDocument();
      pd.PrintPage += new PrintPageEventHandler(pd_PrintPage);
      // Specify the printer to use.
      pd.PrinterSettings.PrinterName = printer;

      if (pd.PrinterSettings.IsValid) {
         pd.Print();
      }
      else {
         MessageBox.Show("Printer is invalid.");
      }
    }
    finally {
      streamToPrint.Close();
    }
  }
  catch(Exception ex) {
    MessageBox.Show(ex.Message);
  }
}
```

Requirements

Namespace: System.Drawing.Printing

Platforms: Windows 98, Windows NT 4.0, Windows Millennium Edition, Windows 2000, Windows XP Home Edition, Windows XP Professional, Windows Server 2003 family

Assembly: System.Drawing (in System.Drawing.dll)

PrinterSettings Constructor

Initializes a new instance of the **PrinterSettings** class.

[Visual Basic]
```
Public Sub New()
```
[C#]
```
public PrinterSettings();
```
[C++]
```
public: PrinterSettings();
```
[JScript]
```
public function PrinterSettings();
```

Remarks

The default constructor initializes all fields to their default values.

Typically, you do not create an instance of **PrinterSettings**, but instead use the **PrintDocument.PrinterSettings** to set settings for the printer.

Requirements

Platforms: Windows 98, Windows NT 4.0, Windows Millennium Edition, Windows 2000, Windows XP Home Edition, Windows XP Professional, Windows Server 2003 family

PrinterSettings.CanDuplex Property

Gets a value indicating whether the printer supports double-sided printing.

[Visual Basic]
```
Public ReadOnly Property CanDuplex As Boolean
```
[C#]
```
public bool CanDuplex {get;}
```
[C++]
```
public: __property bool get_CanDuplex();
```
[JScript]
```
public function get CanDuplex() : Boolean;
```

Property Value

true if the printer supports double-sided printing; otherwise, **false**.

Remarks

To print using duplex, and if the printer supports it, set **Duplex** to one of the **Duplex** values.

Requirements

Platforms: Windows 98, Windows NT 4.0, Windows Millennium Edition, Windows 2000, Windows XP Home Edition, Windows XP Professional, Windows Server 2003 family

PrinterSettings.Collate Property

Gets or sets a value indicating whether the printed document is collated.

[Visual Basic]
```
Public Property Collate As Boolean
```
[C#]
```
public bool Collate {get; set;}
```
[C++]
```
public: __property bool get_Collate();
public: __property void set_Collate(bool);
```
[JScript]
```
public function get Collate() : Boolean;
public function set Collate(Boolean);
```

Property Value

true if the printed document is collated; otherwise, **false**. The default is **false**.

Remarks

Collating is performed only when the number of copies is greater than 1. Set the **Copies** property to specify the number of copies to print.

Setting **Collate** to **true** will print a complete copy of the document before the first page of the next copy is printed. **False** will print each page by the number of copies specified before printing the next page.

Requirements

Platforms: Windows 98, Windows NT 4.0, Windows Millennium Edition, Windows 2000, Windows XP Home Edition, Windows XP Professional, Windows Server 2003 family

PrinterSettings.Copies Property

Gets or sets the number of copies of the document to print.

[Visual Basic]
```
Public Property Copies As Short
```
[C#]
```
public short Copies {get; set;}
```
[C++]
```
public: __property short get_Copies();
public: __property void set_Copies(short);
```
[JScript]
```
public function get Copies() : Int16;
public function set Copies(Int16);
```

Property Value

The number of copies to print. The default is 1.

Exceptions

Exception Type	Condition
ArgumentException	The value of the **Copies** property is less than zero.

Remarks

Not all printers support printing multiple copes. You can use the **MaximumCopies** property to determine the maximum number of copies the printer supports. If the number of copies is set higher than the maximum copies supported by the printer, it will be ignored, not causing an exception.

> **Note** Some printers might not support printing more than one copy at a time.

Requirements

Platforms: Windows 98, Windows NT 4.0, Windows Millennium Edition, Windows 2000, Windows XP Home Edition, Windows XP Professional, Windows Server 2003 family

PrinterSettings.DefaultPageSettings Property

Gets the default page settings for this printer.

[Visual Basic]
```
Public ReadOnly Property DefaultPageSettings As PageSettings
```
[C#]
```
public PageSettings DefaultPageSettings {get;}
```
[C++]
```
public: __property PageSettings* get_DefaultPageSettings();
```
[JScript]
```
public function get DefaultPageSettings() : PageSettings;
```

Property Value

A **PageSettings** that represents the default page settings for this printer.

Remarks

Page settings include the size of the margins on the page, the size of paper to use, and whether to print in color. For more information on page settings, see the **PageSettings** class.

Requirements

Platforms: Windows 98, Windows NT 4.0, Windows Millennium Edition, Windows 2000, Windows XP Home Edition, Windows XP Professional, Windows Server 2003 family

PrinterSettings.Duplex Property

Gets or sets the printer setting for double-sided printing.

```
[Visual Basic]
Public Property Duplex As Duplex
[C#]
public Duplex Duplex {get; set;}
[C++]
public: __property Duplex get_Duplex();
public: __property void set_Duplex(Duplex);
[JScript]
public function get Duplex() : Duplex;
public function set Duplex(Duplex);
```

Property Value

One of the **Duplex** values. The default is determined by the printer.

Exceptions

Exception Type	Condition
InvalidEnumArgument-Exception	The value of the **Duplex** property is not one of the **Duplex** values.

Remarks

You can use the **CanDuplex** property to check to see if the printer supports duplex printing.

Requirements

Platforms: Windows 98, Windows NT 4.0, Windows Millennium Edition, Windows 2000, Windows XP Home Edition, Windows XP Professional, Windows Server 2003 family

PrinterSettings.FromPage Property

Gets or sets the page number of the first page to print.

```
[Visual Basic]
Public Property FromPage As Integer
[C#]
public int FromPage {get; set;}
[C++]
public: __property int get_FromPage();
public: __property void set_FromPage(int);
[JScript]
public function get FromPage() : int;
public function set FromPage(int);
```

Property Value

The page number of the first page to print.

Exceptions

Exception Type	Condition
ArgumentException	The **FromPage** property's value is less than zero.

Remarks

The **FromPage** and **ToPage** properties are used by the **PrintDialog** when the user selects a print range. The **PrintDialog.AllowSomePages** property must be set to **true** to allow the user to specify a print range. In addition, the **PrintDialog** also requires the **MinimumPage** and **MaximumPage** to be specified and the **FromPage** value to be within that range.

During the printing process, in the **PrintDocument.PrintPage** event, check the **PrintRange** to see what should be printed. If **PrintRange** is **PrintRange.SomePages**, use the **FromPage** and **ToPage** properties to determine what pages should be printed. If **PrintRange** is **PrintRange.Selection**, then specify output only for the selected pages.

The **FromPage**, **ToPage** and **PrintRange** can also be set programmatically, though the **PrintDocument.PrintPage** implementation is the same.

Requirements

Platforms: Windows 98, Windows NT 4.0, Windows Millennium Edition, Windows 2000, Windows XP Home Edition, Windows XP Professional, Windows Server 2003 family

PrinterSettings.InstalledPrinters Property

Gets the names of all printers installed on the computer.

```
[Visual Basic]
Public Shared ReadOnly Property InstalledPrinters As _
   PrinterSettings.StringCollection
[C#]
public static PrinterSettings.StringCollection InstalledPrinters
   {get;}
[C++]
public: __property static PrinterSettings.StringCollection*
   get_InstalledPrinters();
[JScript]
public static function get InstalledPrinters() :
   PrinterSettings.StringCollection;
```

Property Value

A **PrinterSettings.StringCollection** that represents the names of all printers installed on the computer.

Exceptions

Exception Type	Condition
Win32Exception	The available printers could not be enumerated.

Remarks

You can use the collection of installed printer names to provide the user a choice of printers to print to.

Example

[Visual Basic, C#, C++] The following example populates the `comboInstalledPrinters` combo box with the installed printers and also sets the printer to print, using the **PrinterName** property, when the selection changes. The `PopulateInstalledPrintersCombo` routine is called when the form is being initialized. The example assumes that a **PrintDocument** variable named `printDoc` exists and that the specific combo box exists.

```
[Visual Basic]
Private Sub PopulateInstalledPrintersCombo()
    ' Add list of installed printers found to the combo box.
    ' The pkInstalledPrinters string will be used to
provide the display string.
    Dim i as Integer
    Dim pkInstalledPrinters As String

    For i = 0 to PrinterSettings.InstalledPrinters.Count - 1
        pkInstalledPrinters = PrinterSettings.InstalledPrinters.Item(i)
        comboInstalledPrinters.Items.Add(pkInstalledPrinters)
```

```
    Next
End Sub

Private Sub comboInstalledPrinters_SelectionChanged(ByVal ↵
sender As System.Object, ByVal e As System.EventArgs) Handles ↵
comboInstalledPrinters.SelectedIndexChanged
    ' Set the printer to a printer in the combo box when the ↵
selection changes.

    If comboInstalledPrinters.SelectedIndex <> -1 Then
        ' The combo box's Text property returns the selected ↵
item's text, which is the printer name.
        printDoc.PrinterSettings.PrinterName = ↵
comboInstalledPrinters.Text
    End If

End Sub
```

[C#]

```
private void PopulateInstalledPrintersCombo()
{
    // Add list of installed printers found to the combo box.
    // The pkInstalledPrinters string will be used to provide ↵
 the display string.
    String pkInstalledPrinters;
    for (int i = 0; i < PrinterSettings.InstalledPrinters.Count; i++){
        pkInstalledPrinters = PrinterSettings.InstalledPrinters[i];
        comboInstalledPrinters.Items.Add(pkInstalledPrinters);
    }
}

private void comboInstalledPrinters_SelectionChanged(object ↵
sender, System.EventArgs e)
{

    // Set the printer to a printer in the combo box when the ↵
selection changes.

    if (comboInstalledPrinters.SelectedIndex != -1)
    {
        // The combo box's Text property returns the selected ↵
item's text, which is the printer name.
        printDoc.PrinterSettings.PrinterName= ↵
comboInstalledPrinters.Text;
    }

}
```

[C++]

```
private:
   void PopulateInstalledPrintersCombo() {
      // Add list of installed printers found to the combo box.
      // The pkInstalledPrinters String will be used to ↵
provide the display String.
      String* pkInstalledPrinters;
      for (int i = 0; i < PrinterSettings::InstalledPrinters-> ↵
Count; i++) {
         pkInstalledPrinters = ↵
PrinterSettings::InstalledPrinters->Item[i];
         comboInstalledPrinters->Items->Add(pkInstalledPrinters);
      }
   }

private:
   void comboInstalledPrinters_SelectionChanged(Object* ↵
sender, System::EventArgs* e) {

      // Set the printer to a printer in the combo box when ↵
 the selection changes.

      if (comboInstalledPrinters->SelectedIndex != -1) {
         // The combo box's Text property returns the selected ↵
 item's text, which is the printer name.
         printDoc->PrinterSettings->PrinterName= ↵
comboInstalledPrinters->Text;
      }

   }
```

Requirements

Platforms: Windows 98, Windows NT 4.0, Windows Millennium Edition, Windows 2000, Windows XP Home Edition, Windows XP Professional, Windows Server 2003 family

.NET Framework Security:

- **PrintingPermission** for printing and access to all printers on the network. Associated enumeration: **PrintingPermissionLevel.AllPrinting**

PrinterSettings.IsDefaultPrinter Property

Gets a value indicating whether the **PrinterName** property designates the default printer, except when the user explicitly sets **PrinterName**.

[Visual Basic]

```
Public ReadOnly Property IsDefaultPrinter As Boolean
```

[C#]

```
public bool IsDefaultPrinter {get;}
```

[C++]

```
public: __property bool get_IsDefaultPrinter();
```

[JScript]

```
public function get IsDefaultPrinter() : Boolean;
```

Property Value

true if **PrinterName** designates the default printer; otherwise, **false**.

Remarks

IsDefaultPrinter always returns **false** when you explicitly set the **PrinterName** property to a string value other than a null reference (**Nothing** in Visual Basic) (**Nothing** in Visual Basic).

Requirements

Platforms: Windows 98, Windows NT 4.0, Windows Millennium Edition, Windows 2000, Windows XP Home Edition, Windows XP Professional, Windows Server 2003 family

PrinterSettings.IsPlotter Property

Gets a value indicating whether the printer is a plotter.

[Visual Basic]

```
Public ReadOnly Property IsPlotter As Boolean
```

[C#]

```
public bool IsPlotter {get;}
```

[C++]

```
public: __property bool get_IsPlotter();
```

[JScript]

```
public function get IsPlotter() : Boolean;
```

Property Value

true if the printer is a plotter; **false** if the printer is a raster.

Remarks

A plotter is a printer that is vector-based as opposed to raster-based. Most vector-based printers use individual plotting pens to produce output.

Requirements

Platforms: Windows 98, Windows NT 4.0, Windows Millennium Edition, Windows 2000, Windows XP Home Edition, Windows XP Professional, Windows Server 2003 family

PrinterSettings.IsValid Property

Gets a value indicating whether the **PrinterName** property designates a valid printer.

[Visual Basic]
```
Public ReadOnly Property IsValid As Boolean
```
[C#]
```
public bool IsValid {get;}
```
[C++]
```
public: __property bool get_IsValid();
```
[JScript]
```
public function get IsValid() : Boolean;
```

Property Value

true if the **PrinterName** property designates a valid printer; otherwise, **false**.

Remarks

When getting or setting some properties, a valid printer is required or an exception is raised. To avoid exceptions, use the **IsValid** property after setting the **PrinterName** to safely determine if the printer is valid.

Example

[Visual Basic, C#] The following example specifies the target printer by setting the **PrinterName** property, and if the **IsValid** is **true**, prints the document on the specified printer. The example makes three assumptions: that a variable names `filePath` has been set to the path of the file to print; that a method named `pd_PrintPage`, which handles the **PrintPage** event, has been defined; and that a variable named `printer` has been set to the printer's name.

[Visual Basic, C#] Use the **System.Drawing**, **System.Drawing.Printing**, and **System.IO** namespaces for this example.

[Visual Basic]
```
Public Sub Printing(printer As String)
    Try
        streamToPrint = New StreamReader(filePath)
        Try
            printFont = New Font("Arial", 10)
            Dim pd As New PrintDocument()
            AddHandler pd.PrintPage, AddressOf pd_PrintPage
            ' Specify the printer to use.
            pd.PrinterSettings.PrinterName = printer

            If pd.PrinterSettings.IsValid then
               pd.Print()
            Else
               MessageBox.Show("Printer is invalid.")
            End If
        Finally
            streamToPrint.Close()
        End Try
    Catch ex As Exception
        MessageBox.Show(ex.Message)
    End Try
End Sub
```

[C#]
```
public void Printing(string printer) {
  try {
    streamToPrint = new StreamReader (filePath);
    try {
      printFont = new Font("Arial", 10);
      PrintDocument pd = new PrintDocument();
      pd.PrintPage += new PrintPageEventHandler(pd_PrintPage);
      // Specify the printer to use.
      pd.PrinterSettings.PrinterName = printer;

      if (pd.PrinterSettings.IsValid) {
         pd.Print();
      }
      else {
         MessageBox.Show("Printer is invalid.");
      }
    }
    finally {
      streamToPrint.Close();
    }
  }
  catch(Exception ex) {
    MessageBox.Show(ex.Message);
  }
}
```

Requirements

Platforms: Windows 98, Windows NT 4.0, Windows Millennium Edition, Windows 2000, Windows XP Home Edition, Windows XP Professional, Windows Server 2003 family

PrinterSettings.LandscapeAngle Property

Gets the angle, in degrees, that the portrait orientation is rotated to produce the landscape orientation.

[Visual Basic]
```
Public ReadOnly Property LandscapeAngle As Integer
```
[C#]
```
public int LandscapeAngle {get;}
```
[C++]
```
public: __property int get_LandscapeAngle();
```
[JScript]
```
public function get LandscapeAngle() : int;
```

Property Value

The angle, in degrees, that the portrait orientation is rotated to produce the landscape orientation.

Remarks

Valid rotation values are 90 and 270 degrees. If landscape is not supported, the only valid rotation value is 0 degrees. You set the **PageSettings.Landscape** property to **true** to print a page in landscape format.

Requirements

Platforms: Windows 98, Windows NT 4.0, Windows Millennium Edition, Windows 2000, Windows XP Home Edition, Windows XP Professional, Windows Server 2003 family

PrinterSettings.MaximumCopies Property

Gets the maximum number of copies that the printer allows you to print at a time.

[Visual Basic]
```
Public ReadOnly Property MaximumCopies As Integer
```
[C#]
```
public int MaximumCopies {get;}
```
[C++]
```
public: __property int get_MaximumCopies();
```
[JScript]
```
public function get MaximumCopies() : int;
```

Property Value

The maximum number of copies that the printer allows you to print at a time.

Remarks

Set the **Copies** property to the number of copies to print. Use the **MaximumCopies** property to determine if your printer supports printing multiple copies at a time, since some printers do not.

Requirements

Platforms: Windows 98, Windows NT 4.0, Windows Millennium Edition, Windows 2000, Windows XP Home Edition, Windows XP Professional, Windows Server 2003 family

PrinterSettings.MaximumPage Property

Gets or sets the maximum **FromPage** or **ToPage** that can be selected in a **PrintDialog**.

```
[Visual Basic]
Public Property MaximumPage As Integer
[C#]
public int MaximumPage {get; set;}
[C++]
public: __property int get_MaximumPage();
public: __property void set_MaximumPage(int);
[JScript]
public function get MaximumPage() : int;
public function set MaximumPage(int);
```

Property Value

The maximum **FromPage** or **ToPage** that can be selected in a **PrintDialog**.

Exceptions

Exception Type	Condition
ArgumentException	The value of the **MaximumPage** property is less than zero.

Remarks

The **FromPage** and **ToPage** properties are used by the **PrintDialog** when the user selects a print range. The **PrintDialog.AllowSomePages** property must be set to **true** to allow the user to specify a print range. When setting the **FromPage** or **ToPage** values programmatically, ensure that they are within the range defined by the **MinimumPage** and **MaximumPage** properties, or an exception is thrown when displaying the **PrintDialog**.

Requirements

Platforms: Windows 98, Windows NT 4.0, Windows Millennium Edition, Windows 2000, Windows XP Home Edition, Windows XP Professional, Windows Server 2003 family

PrinterSettings.MinimumPage Property

Gets or sets the minimum **FromPage** or **ToPage** that can be selected in a **PrintDialog**.

```
[Visual Basic]
Public Property MinimumPage As Integer
[C#]
public int MinimumPage {get; set;}
[C++]
public: __property int get_MinimumPage();
public: __property void set_MinimumPage(int);
[JScript]
public function get MinimumPage() : int;
public function set MinimumPage(int);
```

Property Value

The minimum **FromPage** or **ToPage** that can be selected in a **PrintDialog**.

Exceptions

Exception Type	Condition
ArgumentException	The value of the **MinimumPage** property is less than zero.

Remarks

The **FromPage** and **ToPage** properties are used by the **PrintDialog** when the user selects a print range. The **PrintDialog.AllowSomePages** property must be set to **true** to allow the user to specify a print range. When setting the **FromPage** or **ToPage** values programmatically, ensure that they are within the range defined by the **MinimumPage** and **MaximumPage** properties, or an exception is thrown when displaying the **PrintDialog**.

Requirements

Platforms: Windows 98, Windows NT 4.0, Windows Millennium Edition, Windows 2000, Windows XP Home Edition, Windows XP Professional, Windows Server 2003 family

PrinterSettings.PaperSizes Property

Gets the paper sizes that are supported by this printer.

```
[Visual Basic]
Public ReadOnly Property PaperSizes As _
   PrinterSettings.PaperSizeCollection
[C#]
public PrinterSettings.PaperSizeCollection PaperSizes {get;}
[C++]
public: __property PrinterSettings.PaperSizeCollection*
   get_PaperSizes();
[JScript]
public function get PaperSizes() :
   PrinterSettings.PaperSizeCollection;
```

Property Value

A **PrinterSettings.PaperSizeCollection** that represents the paper sizes that are supported by this printer.

Remarks

The **PrinterSettings.PaperSizeCollection** contains **PaperSize** instances that represent the paper sizes through the **PaperSize.Kind** property, which contains one of the **PaperKind** values.

Typically, you set a page's paper size through the **PageSettings.PaperSize** property to a valid **PaperSize** available through the **PaperSizes** collection.

To specify a custom paper size, see the **PaperSize** constructor.

Example

[Visual Basic, C#, C++] The following example populates the comboPaperSize combo box with the printer's supported paper sizes. In addition, a custom paper size is created and added to the combo box. The **PaperName** is identified as the property that provides the display string for the item being added through the **DisplayMember** property of the combo box. The example assumes that a **PrintDocument** variable named printDoc exists and that the specific combo box exists.

[Visual Basic]
```
' Add list of supported paper sizes found on the printer.
' The DisplayMember property is used to identify the property ↵
 that will provide the display string.
comboPaperSize.DisplayMember = "PaperName"

Dim pkSize As PaperSize
For i = 0 to printDoc.PrinterSettings.PaperSizes.Count - 1
    pkSize = printDoc.PrinterSettings.PaperSizes.Item(i)
    comboPaperSize.Items.Add(pkSize)
Next

' Create a PaperSize and specify the custom paper size ↵
 through the constructor and add to combobox.
Dim pkCustomSize1 As New PaperSize("Custom Paper Size", 100, 200)

comboPaperSize.Items.Add(pkCustomSize1)
```

[C#]
```
// Add list of supported paper sizes found on the printer.
// The DisplayMember property is used to identify the ↵
 property that will provide the display string.
comboPaperSize.DisplayMember = "PaperName";

PaperSize pkSize;
for (int i = 0; i < printDoc.PrinterSettings.PaperSizes.Count; i++){
    pkSize = printDoc.PrinterSettings.PaperSizes[i];
    comboPaperSize.Items.Add(pkSize);
}

// Create a PaperSize and specify the custom paper size ↵
 through the constructor and add to combobox.
PaperSize pkCustomSize1 = new PaperSize("First custom size", 100, 200);

comboPaperSize.Items.Add(pkCustomSize1);
```

[C++]
```
// Add list of supported paper sizes found on the printer.
// The DisplayMember property is used to identify the ↵
 property that will provide the display String*.
comboPaperSize->DisplayMember = S"PaperName";

PaperSize* pkSize;
for (int i = 0; i < printDoc->PrinterSettings->PaperSizes-> ↵
Count; i++) {
   pkSize = printDoc->PrinterSettings->PaperSizes->Item[i];
   comboPaperSize->Items->Add(pkSize);
}

// Create a PaperSize and specify the custom paper size ↵
through the constructor and add to combobox.
PaperSize* pkCustomSize1 = new PaperSize(S"First custom size", ↵
 100, 200);

comboPaperSize->Items->Add(pkCustomSize1);
```

Requirements

Platforms: Windows 98, Windows NT 4.0, Windows Millennium Edition, Windows 2000, Windows XP Home Edition, Windows XP Professional, Windows Server 2003 family

PrinterSettings.PaperSources Property

Gets the paper source trays that are available on the printer.

[Visual Basic]
```
Public ReadOnly Property PaperSources As _
   PrinterSettings.PaperSourceCollection
```
[C#]
```
public PrinterSettings.PaperSourceCollection PaperSources {get;}
```
[C++]
```
public: __property PrinterSettings.PaperSourceCollection*
   get_PaperSources();
```
[JScript]
```
public function get PaperSources() :
   PrinterSettings.PaperSourceCollection;
```

Property Value

A **PrinterSettings.PaperSourceCollection** that represents the paper source trays that are available on this printer.

Remarks

The **PrinterSettings.PaperSourceCollection** contains **PaperSource** instances that represent the paper source trays through the **PaperSource.Kind** property, which contains one of the **PaperSourceKind** values.

Typically, you set a page's paper source through the **PageSettings.PaperSource** property to a valid **PaperSource** available through the **PaperSources** collection.

Example

[Visual Basic, C#, C++] The following example populates the comboPaperSource combo box with the printer's supported paper sources. The **SourceName** is identified as the property that provides the display string for the item being added through the **DisplayMember** property of the combo box. The example assumes that a **PrintDocument** variable named printDoc exists and that the specific combo box exists.

[Visual Basic]
```
' Add list of paper sources found on the printer to the combo box.
' The DisplayMember property is used to identify the property ↵
that will provide the display string.
comboPaperSource.DisplayMember = "SourceName"

Dim pkSource As PaperSource
For i = 0 to printDoc.PrinterSettings.PaperSources.Count - 1
    pkSource = printDoc.PrinterSettings.PaperSources.Item(i)
    comboPaperSource.Items.Add(pkSource)
Next
```

[C#]
```
// Add list of paper sources found on the printer to the combo box.
// The DisplayMember property is used to identify the property ↵
 that will provide the display string.
comboPaperSource.DisplayMember="SourceName";

PaperSource pkSource;
for (int i = 0; i < printDoc.PrinterSettings.PaperSources.Count; i++){
    pkSource = printDoc.PrinterSettings.PaperSources[i];
    comboPaperSource.Items.Add(pkSource);
}
```

[C++]
```
// Add list of paper sources found on the printer to the combo box.
// The DisplayMember property is used to identify the property ↵
 that will provide the display String*.
comboPaperSource->DisplayMember=S"SourceName";

PaperSource* pkSource;
for (int i = 0; i < printDoc->PrinterSettings->PaperSources-> ↵
Count; i++) {
   pkSource = printDoc->PrinterSettings->PaperSources->Item[i];
   comboPaperSource->Items->Add(pkSource);
}
```

Requirements

Platforms: Windows 98, Windows NT 4.0, Windows Millennium Edition, Windows 2000, Windows XP Home Edition, Windows XP Professional, Windows Server 2003 family

PrinterSettings.PrinterName Property

Gets or sets the name of the printer to use.

[Visual Basic]
```
Public Property PrinterName As String
```
[C#]
```
public string PrinterName {get; set;}
```
[C++]
```
public: __property String* get_PrinterName();
public: __property void set_PrinterName(String*);
```
[JScript]
```
public function get PrinterName() : String;
public function set PrinterName(String);
```

Property Value

The name of the printer to use.

Remarks

After setting the printer name, call **IsValid** to determine if the printer name is recognized as a valid printer on the system.

You can also use the **InstalledPrinters** property to get a list of printers installed on the system.

Example

[Visual Basic, C#] The following example specifies the target printer by setting the **PrinterName** property, and if the **IsValid** is **true**, prints the document on the specified printer. The example makes three assumptions: that a variable named `filePath` has been set to the path of the file to print; that a method named `pd_PrintPage`, which handles the **PrintPage** event, has been defined; and that a variable named `printer` has been set to the printer's name.

[Visual Basic, C#] Use the **System.Drawing**, **System.Drawing.Printing**, and **System.IO** namespaces for this example.

[Visual Basic]
```
Public Sub Printing(printer As String)
    Try
        streamToPrint = New StreamReader(filePath)
        Try
            printFont = New Font("Arial", 10)
            Dim pd As New PrintDocument()
            AddHandler pd.PrintPage, AddressOf pd_PrintPage
            ' Specify the printer to use.
            pd.PrinterSettings.PrinterName = printer

            If pd.PrinterSettings.IsValid then
               pd.Print()
            Else
               MessageBox.Show("Printer is invalid.")
            End If
        Finally
            streamToPrint.Close()
        End Try
    Catch ex As Exception
        MessageBox.Show(ex.Message)
    End Try
End Sub
```

[C#]
```
public void Printing(string printer) {
  try {
    streamToPrint = new StreamReader (filePath);
    try {
      printFont = new Font("Arial", 10);
      PrintDocument pd = new PrintDocument();
      pd.PrintPage += new PrintPageEventHandler(pd_PrintPage);
      // Specify the printer to use.
      pd.PrinterSettings.PrinterName = printer;

      if (pd.PrinterSettings.IsValid) {
         pd.Print();
      }
      else {
         MessageBox.Show("Printer is invalid.");
      }
    }
    finally {
      streamToPrint.Close();
    }
  }
  catch(Exception ex) {
    MessageBox.Show(ex.Message);
  }
}
```

Requirements

Platforms: Windows 98, Windows NT 4.0, Windows Millennium Edition, Windows 2000, Windows XP Home Edition, Windows XP Professional, Windows Server 2003 family

.NET Framework Security:

- **PrintingPermission** for printing and access to all printers on the network. Associated enumeration: **PrintingPermissionLevel.AllPrinting**

PrinterSettings.PrinterResolutions Property

Gets all the resolutions that are supported by this printer.

[Visual Basic]
```
Public ReadOnly Property PrinterResolutions As _
   PrinterSettings.PrinterResolutionCollection
```
[C#]
```
public PrinterSettings.PrinterResolutionCollection
   PrinterResolutions {get;}
```
[C++]
```
public: __property PrinterSettings.PrinterResolutionCollection*
   get_PrinterResolutions();
```
[JScript]
```
public function get PrinterResolutions() :
   PrinterSettings.PrinterResolutionCollection;
```

Property Value

A **PrinterSettings.PrinterResolutionCollection** that represents the resolutions that are supported by this printer.

Remarks

The **PrinterSettings.PrinterResolutionCollection** contains **PrinterResolution** instances that represent the printer resolutions supported through the **PrinterResolution.Kind** property, which contains one of the **PrinterResolutionKind** values.

Typically, you set a page's paper source through the **PageSettings.PrinterResolution** property to a valid **PrinterResolution** available through the **PrinterResolutions** collection.

If **PrinterResolutionKind** is **Custom**, then use the **X** and **Y** properties to determine the custom printer resolution in the horizontal and vertical directions, respectively.

Example

[Visual Basic, C#, C++] The following example populates the `comboPrintResolution` combo box with the supported resolutions. The example assumes that a **PrintDocument** variable named `printDoc` exists and that the specific combo box exists.

[Visual Basic]

```
' Add list of printer resolutions found on the printer to the combobox.
' The PrinterResolution's ToString() method will be used to          ↵
provide the display string.
Dim pkResolution As PrinterResolution
For i = 0 to printDoc.PrinterSettings.PrinterResolutions.Count - 1
    pkResolution = printDoc.PrinterSettings.PrinterResolutions.Item(i)
    comboPrintResolution.Items.Add(pkResolution)
Next
```

[C#]

```
// Add list of printer resolutions found on the printer to the        ↵
combobox.
// The PrinterResolution's ToString() method will be used to          ↵
provide the display string.

PrinterResolution pkResolution;
for (int i = 0; i <                                                   ↵
printDoc.PrinterSettings.PrinterResolutions.Count; i++){
    pkResolution = printDoc.PrinterSettings.PrinterResolutions[i];
    comboPrintResolution.Items.Add(pkResolution);
}
```

[C++]

```
// Add list of printer resolutions found on the printer              ↵
to the combobox.
// The PrinterResolution's ToString() method will be used            ↵
 to provide the display String.

PrinterResolution* pkResolution;
for (int i = 0; i                                                    ↵
< printDoc->PrinterSettings->PrinterResolutions->Count; i++) {
   pkResolution = printDoc->PrinterSettings->                        ↵
PrinterResolutions->Item[i];
   comboPrintResolution->Items->Add(pkResolution);
}
```

Requirements

Platforms: Windows 98, Windows NT 4.0, Windows Millennium Edition, Windows 2000, Windows XP Home Edition, Windows XP Professional, Windows Server 2003 family

PrinterSettings.PrintRange Property

Gets or sets the page numbers that the user has specified to be printed.

[Visual Basic]
```
Public Property PrintRange As PrintRange
```
[C#]
```
public PrintRange PrintRange {get; set;}
```
[C++]
```
public: __property PrintRange get_PrintRange();
public: __property void set_PrintRange(PrintRange);
```
[JScript]
```
public function get PrintRange() : PrintRange;
public function set PrintRange(PrintRange);
```

Property Value

One of the **PrintRange** values.

Exceptions

Exception Type	Condition
InvalidEnumArgument-Exception	The value of the **PrintRange** property is not one of the **PrintRange** values.

Remarks

The **PrintRange** property is used by the **PrintDialog**.when the user selects a print range. The default **PrintRange** is **AllPages**. To allow the user to specify a range of pages to print, the **PrintDialog.Allow-SomePages** property must be set to **true**. To allow the user to specify the selected pages to print, the **PrintDialog.AllowSelection** property must be set to **true**.

During the printing process, in the **PrintDocument.PrintPage** event, check the **PrintRange** to see what should be printed. If **PrintRange** is **PrintRange.SomePages**, use the **FromPage** and **ToPage** properties to determine what pages should be printed. If **PrintRange** is **PrintRange.Selection**, then specify output only for the selected pages.

The **FromPage**, **ToPage** and **PrintRange** can also be set programmatically, though the **PrintDocument.PrintPage** implementation is the same.

Requirements

Platforms: Windows 98, Windows NT 4.0, Windows Millennium Edition, Windows 2000, Windows XP Home Edition, Windows XP Professional, Windows Server 2003 family

PrinterSettings.PrintToFile Property

Gets or sets a value indicating whether the printing output is sent to a file instead of a port.

[Visual Basic]
```
Public Property PrintToFile As Boolean
```
[C#]
```
public bool PrintToFile {get; set;}
```
[C++]
```
public: __property bool get_PrintToFile();
public: __property void set_PrintToFile(bool);
```
[JScript]
```
public function get PrintToFile() : Boolean;
public function set PrintToFile(Boolean);
```

Property Value

true if the printing output is sent to a file; otherwise, **false**. The default is **false**.

Remarks

This property is used by the **PrintDialog** when the user selects the **Print to file** option. In such a case, the output port is set to "FILE", causing the Windows printing subsystem to prompt the user for a file name when the **PrintDocument.Print** method is called.

> **Note** This property is only used by the **PrintDialog** and cannot be set programmatically. The **Print to file** option only appears on the **PrintDialog** when the **PrintDialog.AllowPrintToFile** property is set to **true**.

Requirements

Platforms: Windows 98, Windows NT 4.0, Windows Millennium Edition, Windows 2000, Windows XP Home Edition, Windows XP Professional, Windows Server 2003 family

PrinterSettings.SupportsColor Property

Gets a value indicating whether this printer supports color printing.

[Visual Basic]
```
Public ReadOnly Property SupportsColor As Boolean
```
[C#]
```
public bool SupportsColor {get;}
```
[C++]
```
public: __property bool get_SupportsColor();
```
[JScript]
```
public function get SupportsColor() : Boolean;
```

Property Value

true if this printer supports color; otherwise, **false**.

Remarks

To print using color, and if the printer supports it, set **PageSettings.Color** to **true**.

Example

[Visual Basic, C#, C++] The following example prints a document with the first page in color, if the printer supports it. The example assumes that a **PrintDocument** variable named printDoc has been created, and the **PrintPage** and **QueryPageSettings** events are handled.

[Visual Basic, C#, C++] Use the **System.Drawing** and **System.Drawing.Printing** namespaces for this example.

[Visual Basic]
```
    Private Sub MyButtonPrint_OnClick(ByVal sender As Object, ↵
ByVal e As System.EventArgs)

        ' Set the printer name and ensure it is valid. If not, ↵
provide a message to the user.
        printDoc.PrinterSettings.PrinterName = "\\mynetworkprinter"

        If printDoc.PrinterSettings.IsValid Then

            ' If the printer supports printing in color, then ↵
override the printer's default behavior.
            if printDoc.PrinterSettings.SupportsColor then

                ' Set the page default's to not print in color.
                printDoc.DefaultPageSettings.Color = False
            End If

            ' Provide a friendly name, set the page number, ↵
and print the document.
            printDoc.DocumentName = "My Presentation"
            currentPageNumber = 1
            printDoc.Print()
        Else
            MessageBox.Show("Printer is not valid")
        End If
    End Sub

    Private Sub MyPrintQueryPageSettingsEvent(ByVal sender As ↵
Object, ByVal e As QueryPageSettingsEventArgs)

        ' Determines if the printer supports printing in color.
        If printDoc.PrinterSettings.SupportsColor Then

            ' If the printer supports color printing, use color.
            If currentPageNumber = 1 Then

                e.PageSettings.Color = True
            End If

        End If
    End Sub
```

[C#]
```
    private void MyButtonPrint_OnClick(object sender, ↵
System.EventArgs e)
    {

        // Set the printer name and ensure it is valid. If not, ↵
provide a message to the user.
        printDoc.PrinterSettings.PrinterName = "\\mynetworkprinter";

        if (printDoc.PrinterSettings.IsValid) {

            // If the printer supports printing in color, then ↵
override the printer's default behavior.
            if (printDoc.PrinterSettings.SupportsColor) {

                // Set the page default's to not print in color.
                printDoc.DefaultPageSettings.Color = false;
            }

            // Provide a friendly name, set the page number, ↵
and print the document.
            printDoc.DocumentName = "My Presentation";
            currentPageNumber = 1;
            printDoc.Print();
        }
        else {
            MessageBox.Show("Printer is not valid");
        }
    }

    private void MyPrintQueryPageSettingsEvent(object ↵
sender, QueryPageSettingsEventArgs e)
    {
        // Determines if the printer supports printing in color.
        if (printDoc.PrinterSettings.SupportsColor) {

            // If the printer supports color printing, use color.
            if (currentPageNumber == 1 ) {

                e.PageSettings.Color = true;
            }

        }
    }
```

[C++]
```
private:
    void MyButtonPrint_OnClick(Object* sender, System::EventArgs* e) {

        // Set the printer name and ensure it is valid. If not, ↵
provide a message to the user.
        printDoc->PrinterSettings->PrinterName = S"\\mynetworkprinter";

        if (printDoc->PrinterSettings->IsValid) {

            // If the printer supports printing in color, then ↵
the printer's default behavior.
            if (printDoc->PrinterSettings->SupportsColor) {

                // Set the page default's to not print in color.
                printDoc->DefaultPageSettings->Color = false;
            }

            // Provide a friendly name, set the page number, and ↵
print the document.
            printDoc->DocumentName = S"My Presentation";
            currentPageNumber = 1;
            printDoc->Print();
        } else {
            MessageBox::Show(S"Printer is not valid");
        }
    }
```

```
private:
   void MyPrintQueryPageSettingsEvent(Object* sender, ↵
QueryPageSettingsEventArgs* e) {
      // Determines if the printer supports printing in color.
      if (printDoc->PrinterSettings->SupportsColor) {

         // If the printer supports color printing, use color.
         if (currentPageNumber == 1) {

            e->PageSettings->Color = true;
         }

      }
   }
```

Requirements

Platforms: Windows 98, Windows NT 4.0,
Windows Millennium Edition, Windows 2000,
Windows XP Home Edition, Windows XP Professional,
Windows Server 2003 family

PrinterSettings.ToPage Property

Gets or sets the number of the last page to print.

[Visual Basic]
```
Public Property ToPage As Integer
```
[C#]
```
public int ToPage {get; set;}
```
[C++]
```
public: __property int get_ToPage();
public: __property void set_ToPage(int);
```
[JScript]
```
public function get ToPage() : int;
public function set ToPage(int);
```

Property Value

The number of the last page to print.

Exceptions

Exception Type	Condition
ArgumentException	The value of the **ToPage** property is less than zero.

Remarks

The **FromPage** and **ToPage** properties are used by the **PrintDialog** when the user selects a print range. The **PrintDialog.AllowSomePages** property must be set to **true** to allow the user to specify a print range. In addition, the **PrintDialog** also requires the **MinimumPage** and **MaximumPage** to be specified and the **ToPage** value to be within that range.

During the printing process, in the **PrintDocument.PrintPage** event, check the **PrintRange** to see what should be printed. If **PrintRange** is **PrintRange.SomePages**, use the **FromPage** and **ToPage** properties to determine what pages should be printed. If **PrintRange** is **PrintRange.Selection**, then specify output only for the selected pages.

The **FromPage**, **ToPage** and **PrintRange** can also be set programmatically, though the **PrintDocument.PrintPage** implementation is the same.

Requirements

Platforms: Windows 98, Windows NT 4.0,
Windows Millennium Edition, Windows 2000,
Windows XP Home Edition, Windows XP Professional,
Windows Server 2003 family

PrinterSettings.Clone Method

Creates a copy of this **PrinterSettings** object.

[Visual Basic]
```
Public Overridable Function Clone() As Object Implements _
   ICloneable.Clone
```
[C#]
```
public virtual object Clone();
```
[C++]
```
public: virtual Object* Clone();
```
[JScript]
```
public function Clone() : Object;
```

Return Value

A copy of this object.

Implements

ICloneable.Clone

Requirements

Platforms: Windows 98, Windows NT 4.0,
Windows Millennium Edition, Windows 2000,
Windows XP Home Edition, Windows XP Professional,
Windows Server 2003 family

PrinterSettings.CreateMeasurementGraphics Method

Returns a **Graphics** object that contains printer information that is useful when creating a **PrintDocument**, for example, the **TextMetric** objects for the printer.

[Visual Basic]
```
Public Function CreateMeasurementGraphics() As Graphics
```
[C#]
```
public Graphics CreateMeasurementGraphics();
```
[C++]
```
public: Graphics* CreateMeasurementGraphics();
```
[JScript]
```
public function CreateMeasurementGraphics() : Graphics;
```

Return Value

A **Graphics** object that contains information from a printer.

Exceptions

Exception Type	Condition
InvalidPrinterException	The printer named in the **PrinterName** property does not exist.

Remarks

The **CreateMeasurementGraphics** method allows you to obtain a **Graphics** for the printer without creating a print job. Use the **Graphics** to make decisions on how to layout **TextMetric** elements like fonts, sizes, and type styles of a complex print job.

Requirements

Platforms: Windows 98, Windows NT 4.0,
Windows Millennium Edition, Windows 2000,
Windows XP Home Edition, Windows XP Professional,
Windows Server 2003 family

PrinterSettings.GetHdevmode Method

Creates a handle to a DEVMODE structure that corresponds to the printer settings.

Overload List

Creates a handle to a DEVMODE structure that corresponds to the printer settings.

[Visual Basic] **Overloads Public Function GetHdevmode() As IntPtr**

[C#] **public IntPtr GetHdevmode();**

[C++] **public: IntPtr GetHdevmode();**

[JScript] **public function GetHdevmode() : IntPtr;**

Creates a handle to a DEVMODE structure that corresponds to the printer and the page settings specified through the *pageSettings* parameter.

[Visual Basic] **Overloads Public Function GetHdevmode(PageSettings) As IntPtr**

[C#] **public IntPtr GetHdevmode(PageSettings);**

[C++] **public: IntPtr GetHdevmode(PageSettings*);**

[JScript] **public function GetHdevmode(PageSettings) : IntPtr;**

PrinterSettings.GetHdevmode Method ()

Creates a handle to a DEVMODE structure that corresponds to the printer settings.

```
[Visual Basic]
Overloads Public Function GetHdevmode() As IntPtr
[C#]
public IntPtr GetHdevmode();
[C++]
public: IntPtr GetHdevmode();
[JScript]
public function GetHdevmode() : IntPtr;
```

Return Value

A handle to a DEVMODE structure.

Exceptions

Exception Type	Condition
InvalidPrinterException	The printer named in the **PrinterName** property does not exist.
Win32Exception	The printer's initialization information could not be retrieved.

Remarks

When you are done with the handle that is created through this method, you must deallocate it yourself by calling the Native Win32 GlobalFree method. When you call this method, you pass as a parameter the return value from the **GetHdevmode** method.

Requirements

Platforms: Windows 98, Windows NT 4.0, Windows Millennium Edition, Windows 2000, Windows XP Home Edition, Windows XP Professional, Windows Server 2003 family

.NET Framework Security:

- **PrintingPermission** for printing and access to all printers on the network. Associated enumeration: **PrintingPermissionLevel.AllPrinting**

PrinterSettings.GetHdevmode Method (PageSettings)

Creates a handle to a DEVMODE structure that corresponds to the printer and the page settings specified through the *pageSettings* parameter.

```
[Visual Basic]
Overloads Public Function GetHdevmode( _
   ByVal pageSettings As PageSettings _
) As IntPtr
[C#]
public IntPtr GetHdevmode(
   PageSettings pageSettings
);
[C++]
public: IntPtr GetHdevmode(
   PageSettings* pageSettings
);
[JScript]
public function GetHdevmode(
   pageSettings : PageSettings
) : IntPtr;
```

Parameters

pageSettings
: The **PageSettings** object that the DEVMODE structure's handle corresponds to.

Return Value

A handle to a DEVMODE structure.

Exceptions

Exception Type	Condition
InvalidPrinterException	The printer named in the **PrinterName** property does not exist.
Win32Exception	The printer's initialization information could not be retrieved.

Remarks

When you are done with the handle that is created through this method, you must deallocate it yourself by calling the Native Win32 GlobalFree method. When you call this method, you pass as a parameter the return value from the **GetHdevmode** method.

Requirements

Platforms: Windows 98, Windows NT 4.0, Windows Millennium Edition, Windows 2000, Windows XP Home Edition, Windows XP Professional, Windows Server 2003 family

.NET Framework Security:

- **PrintingPermission** for printing and access to all printers on the network. Associated enumeration: **PrintingPermissionLevel.AllPrinting**

PrinterSettings.GetHdevnames Method

Creates a handle to a DEVNAMES structure that corresponds to the printer settings.

```
[Visual Basic]
Public Function GetHdevnames() As IntPtr
[C#]
public IntPtr GetHdevnames();
```

```
[C++]
public: IntPtr GetHdevnames();
[JScript]
public function GetHdevnames() : IntPtr;
```

Return Value

A handle to a DEVNAMES structure.

Remarks

When you are done with the handle that is created through this method, you must deallocate it yourself by calling the Native Win32 GlobalFree method. When you call this method, you pass as a parameter the return value from the **GetHdevnames** method.

Requirements

Platforms: Windows 98, Windows NT 4.0, Windows Millennium Edition, Windows 2000, Windows XP Home Edition, Windows XP Professional, Windows Server 2003 family

.NET Framework Security:

- **PrintingPermission** for printing and access to all printers on the network. Associated enumeration: **PrintingPermissionLevel.AllPrinting**

PrinterSettings.SetHdevmode Method

Copies the relevant information out of the given handle and into the **PrinterSettings**.

```
[Visual Basic]
Public Sub SetHdevmode( _
   ByVal hdevmode As IntPtr _
)
[C#]
public void SetHdevmode(
   IntPtr hdevmode
);
[C++]
public: void SetHdevmode(
   IntPtr hdevmode
);
[JScript]
public function SetHdevmode(
   hdevmode : IntPtr
);
```

Parameters

hdevmode

The handle to a Win32 DEVMODE structure.

Exceptions

Exception Type	Condition
ArgumentException	The printer handle is invalid.

Requirements

Platforms: Windows 98, Windows NT 4.0, Windows Millennium Edition, Windows 2000, Windows XP Home Edition, Windows XP Professional, Windows Server 2003 family

.NET Framework Security:

- **PrintingPermission** for printing and access to all printers on the network. Associated enumeration: **PrintingPermissionLevel.AllPrinting**

PrinterSettings.SetHdevnames Method

Copies the relevant information out of the given handle and into the **PrinterSettings**.

```
[Visual Basic]
Public Sub SetHdevnames( _
   ByVal hdevnames As IntPtr _
)
[C#]
public void SetHdevnames(
   IntPtr hdevnames
);
[C++]
public: void SetHdevnames(
   IntPtr hdevnames
);
[JScript]
public function SetHdevnames(
   hdevnames : IntPtr
);
```

Parameters

hdevnames

The handle to a Win32 DEVNAMES structure.

Exceptions

Exception Type	Condition
ArgumentException	The printer handle is invalid.

Requirements

Platforms: Windows 98, Windows NT 4.0, Windows Millennium Edition, Windows 2000, Windows XP Home Edition, Windows XP Professional, Windows Server 2003 family

.NET Framework Security:

- **PrintingPermission** for printing and access to all printers on the network. Associated enumeration: **PrintingPermissionLevel.AllPrinting**

PrinterSettings.ToString Method

This member overrides **Object.ToString**.

```
[Visual Basic]
Overrides Public Function ToString() As String
[C#]
public override string ToString();
[C++]
public: String* ToString();
[JScript]
public override function ToString() : String;
```

Requirements

Platforms: Windows 98, Windows NT 4.0, Windows Millennium Edition, Windows 2000, Windows XP Home Edition, Windows XP Professional, Windows Server 2003 family

PrinterSettings.PaperSize-Collection Class

Contains a collection of **PaperSize** objects.

System.Object
System.Drawing.Printing.PrinterSettings.PaperSizeCollection

[Visual Basic]
```
Public Class PrinterSettings.PaperSizeCollection
   Implements ICollection, IEnumerable
```
[C#]
```
public class PrinterSettings.PaperSizeCollection : ICollection,
   IEnumerable
```
[C++]
```
public __gc class PrinterSettings.PaperSizeCollection : public
   ICollection, IEnumerable
```
[JScript]
```
public class PrinterSettings.PaperSizeCollection implements
   ICollection, IEnumerable
```

Thread Safety

Any public static (**Shared** in Visual Basic) members of this type are safe for multithreaded operations. Any instance members are not guaranteed to be thread safe.

Remarks

The **PrinterSettings.PaperSizeCollection** contains **PaperSize** instances that represents the paper sizes through the **PaperSize.Kind** property, which contains one of the **PaperKind** values.

Typically, you set a page's paper size through the **PageSettings.PaperSize** property to a valid **PaperSize** instance available through the **PaperSizes** collection.

See the **PaperSize** constructor to find out how you can specify a custom paper size.

Example

[Visual Basic, C#, C++] The following example populates the `comboPaperSize` combo box with the printer's supported paper sizes. In addition, a custom paper size is created and added to the combo box. The **PaperName** is identified as the property that provides the display string for the item being added through the **DisplayMember** property of the combo box. The example assumes that a **PrintDocument** variable named `printDoc` exists and that the specific combo box exists.

[Visual Basic]
```
' Add list of supported paper sizes found on the printer.
' The DisplayMember property is used to identify the property ↵
that will provide the display string.
comboPaperSize.DisplayMember = "PaperName"

Dim pkSize As PaperSize
For i = 0 to printDoc.PrinterSettings.PaperSizes.Count - 1
    pkSize = printDoc.PrinterSettings.PaperSizes.Item(i)
    comboPaperSize.Items.Add(pkSize)
Next

' Create a PaperSize and specify the custom paper size through ↵
 the constructor and add to combobox.
Dim pkCustomSize1 As New PaperSize("Custom Paper Size", 100, 200)

comboPaperSize.Items.Add(pkCustomSize1)
```

[C#]
```
// Add list of supported paper sizes found on the printer.
// The DisplayMember property is used to identify the property ↵
 that will provide the display string.
comboPaperSize.DisplayMember = "PaperName";

PaperSize pkSize;
for (int i = 0; i < printDoc.PrinterSettings.PaperSizes.Count; i++){
    pkSize = printDoc.PrinterSettings.PaperSizes[i];
    comboPaperSize.Items.Add(pkSize);
}

// Create a PaperSize and specify the custom paper size through ↵
 the constructor and add to combobox.
PaperSize pkCustomSize1 = new PaperSize("First custom size", 100, 200);

comboPaperSize.Items.Add(pkCustomSize1);
```

[C++]
```
// Add list of supported paper sizes found on the printer.
// The DisplayMember property is used to identify the property ↵
 that will provide the display String*.
comboPaperSize->DisplayMember = S"PaperName";

PaperSize* pkSize;
for (int i = 0; i < printDoc->PrinterSettings->PaperSizes-> ↵
Count; i++) {
   pkSize = printDoc->PrinterSettings->PaperSizes->Item[i];
   comboPaperSize->Items->Add(pkSize);
}

// Create a PaperSize and specify the custom paper size through ↵
 the constructor and add to combobox.
PaperSize* pkCustomSize1 = new PaperSize(S"First custom size", ↵
 100, 200);

comboPaperSize->Items->Add(pkCustomSize1);
```

Requirements

Namespace: System.Drawing.Printing

Platforms: Windows 98, Windows NT 4.0, Windows Millennium Edition, Windows 2000, Windows XP Home Edition, Windows XP Professional, Windows Server 2003 family

Assembly: System.Drawing (in System.Drawing.dll)

PrinterSettings.PaperSizeCollection Constructor

Initializes a new instance of the **PrinterSettings.PaperSizeCollection** class.

[Visual Basic]
```
Public Sub New( _
   ByVal array() As PaperSize _
)
```
[C#]
```
public PrinterSettings.PaperSizeCollection(
   PaperSize[] array
);
```
[C++]
```
public: PaperSizeCollection(
   PaperSize* array[]
);
```
[JScript]
```
public function PrinterSettings.PaperSizeCollection(
   array : PaperSize[]
);
```

Parameters

array

An array of type **PaperSize**.

Requirements

Platforms: Windows 98, Windows NT 4.0, Windows Millennium Edition, Windows 2000, Windows XP Home Edition, Windows XP Professional, Windows Server 2003 family

PrinterSettings.PaperSizeCollection.Count Property

Gets the number of different paper sizes in the collection.

[Visual Basic]
```
Public ReadOnly Property Count As Integer
```
[C#]
```
public int Count {get;}
```
[C++]
```
public: __property int get_Count();
```
[JScript]
```
public function get Count() : int;
```

Property Value

The number of different paper sizes in the collection.

Example

[Visual Basic]
```
' Add list of supported paper sizes found on the printer.
' The DisplayMember property is used to identify the property ↵
that will provide the display string.
comboPaperSize.DisplayMember = "PaperName"

Dim pkSize As PaperSize
For i = 0 to printDoc.PrinterSettings.PaperSizes.Count - 1
    pkSize = printDoc.PrinterSettings.PaperSizes.Item(i)
    comboPaperSize.Items.Add(pkSize)
Next

' Create a PaperSize and specify the custom paper size through ↵
the constructor and add to combobox.
Dim pkCustomSize1 As New PaperSize("Custom Paper Size", 100, 200)

comboPaperSize.Items.Add(pkCustomSize1)
```
[C#]
```
// Add list of supported paper sizes found on the printer.
// The DisplayMember property is used to identify the property ↵
that will provide the display string.
comboPaperSize.DisplayMember = "PaperName";

PaperSize pkSize;
for (int i = 0; i < printDoc.PrinterSettings.PaperSizes.Count; i++){
    pkSize = printDoc.PrinterSettings.PaperSizes[i];
    comboPaperSize.Items.Add(pkSize);
}

// Create a PaperSize and specify the custom paper size through ↵
the constructor and add to combobox.
PaperSize pkCustomSize1 = new PaperSize("First custom size", 100, 200);

comboPaperSize.Items.Add(pkCustomSize1);
```
[C++]
```
// Add list of supported paper sizes found on the printer.
// The DisplayMember property is used to identify the property ↵
that will provide the display String*.
comboPaperSize->DisplayMember = S"PaperName";

PaperSize* pkSize;
for (int i = 0; i < printDoc->PrinterSettings->PaperSizes-> ↵
Count; i++) {
   pkSize = printDoc->PrinterSettings->PaperSizes->Item[i];
   comboPaperSize->Items->Add(pkSize);
}

// Create a PaperSize and specify the custom paper size through ↵
 the constructor and add to combobox.
PaperSize* pkCustomSize1 = new PaperSize(S"First custom size", ↵
100, 200);

comboPaperSize->Items->Add(pkCustomSize1);
```

Requirements

Platforms: Windows 98, Windows NT 4.0, Windows Millennium Edition, Windows 2000, Windows XP Home Edition, Windows XP Professional, Windows Server 2003 family

PrinterSettings.PaperSizeCollection.Item Property

Gets the **PaperSize** at a specified index.

[C#] In C#, this property is the indexer for the **PrinterSettings.PaperSizeCollection** class.

[Visual Basic]
```
Public Overridable Default ReadOnly Property Item( _
   ByVal index As Integer _
) As PaperSize
```
[C#]
```
public virtual PaperSize this[
   int index
] {get;}
```
[C++]
```
public: __property virtual PaperSize* get_Item(
   int index
);
```
[JScript]
```
returnValue = PaperSizeCollectionObject.Item(index);
-or-
returnValue = PaperSizeCollectionObject(index);
```

[JScript] In JScript, you can use the default indexed properties defined by a type, but you cannot explicitly define your own. However, specifying the **expando** attribute on a class automatically provides a default indexed property whose type is **Object** and whose index type is **String**.

Arguments [JScript]

index

The index of the **PaperSize** to get.

Parameters [Visual Basic, C#, C++]

index

The index of the **PaperSize** to get.

Property Value

The **PaperSize** at the specified index.

Example

[Visual Basic]
```
' Add list of supported paper sizes found on the printer.
' The DisplayMember property is used to identify the property ↵
 that will provide the display string.
comboPaperSize.DisplayMember = "PaperName"

Dim pkSize As PaperSize
For i = 0 to printDoc.PrinterSettings.PaperSizes.Count - 1
```

```
    pkSize = printDoc.PrinterSettings.PaperSizes.Item(i)
    comboPaperSize.Items.Add(pkSize)
Next

' Create a PaperSize and specify the custom paper size through ↵
 the constructor and add to combobox.
Dim pkCustomSize1 As New PaperSize("Custom Paper Size", 100, 200)

comboPaperSize.Items.Add(pkCustomSize1)
```

[C#]

```
// Add list of supported paper sizes found on the printer.
// The DisplayMember property is used to identify the property ↵
 that will provide the display string.
comboPaperSize.DisplayMember = "PaperName";

PaperSize pkSize;
for (int i = 0; i < printDoc.PrinterSettings.PaperSizes.Count; i++){
    pkSize = printDoc.PrinterSettings.PaperSizes[i];
    comboPaperSize.Items.Add(pkSize);
}

// Create a PaperSize and specify the custom paper size through ↵
 the constructor and add to combobox.
PaperSize pkCustomSize1 = new PaperSize("First custom size", 100, 200);

comboPaperSize.Items.Add(pkCustomSize1);
```

[C++]

```
// Add list of supported paper sizes found on the printer.
// The DisplayMember property is used to identify the property ↵
 that will provide the display String*.
comboPaperSize->DisplayMember = S"PaperName";

PaperSize* pkSize;
for (int i = 0; i < printDoc->PrinterSettings->PaperSizes-> ↵
Count; i++) {
   pkSize = printDoc->PrinterSettings->PaperSizes->Item[i];
   comboPaperSize->Items->Add(pkSize);
}

// Create a PaperSize and specify the custom paper size through ↵
 the constructor and add to combobox.
PaperSize* pkCustomSize1 = new PaperSize(S"First custom size", ↵
100, 200);

comboPaperSize->Items->Add(pkCustomSize1);
```

Requirements

Platforms: Windows 98, Windows NT 4.0, Windows Millennium Edition, Windows 2000, Windows XP Home Edition, Windows XP Professional, Windows Server 2003 family

PrinterSettings.PaperSizeCollection.GetEnumerator Method

Returns an enumerator that can iterate through the collection.

[Visual Basic]

```
Public Function GetEnumerator() As IEnumerator
```

[C#]

```
public IEnumerator GetEnumerator();
```

[C++]

```
public: IEnumerator* GetEnumerator();
```

[JScript]

```
public function GetEnumerator() : IEnumerator;
```

Return Value

An **IEnumerator** for the **PrinterSettings.PaperSizeCollection**.

Remarks

This method instantiates an enumerator that takes a snapshot of the current state of the collection. The enumerator does not have exclusive access to the collection, so multiple enumerators can have access to the same collection at the same time. Therefore, any changes made to the collection, either directly or through another enumerator, can cause **Current** or **MoveNext** to throw an exception.

Two enumerators instantiated from the same collection at the same time can contain different snapshots of the collection.

Removing objects from the enumerator also removes them from the collection.

Requirements

Platforms: Windows 98, Windows NT 4.0, Windows Millennium Edition, Windows 2000, Windows XP Home Edition, Windows XP Professional, Windows Server 2003 family

PrinterSettings.PaperSizeCollection.ICollection.CopyTo Method

This member supports the .NET Framework infrastructure and is not intended to be used directly from your code.

[Visual Basic]

```
Private Sub CopyTo( _
   ByVal array As Array, _
   ByVal index As Integer _
) Implements ICollection.CopyTo
```

[C#]

```
void ICollection.CopyTo(
   Array array,
   int index
);
```

[C++]

```
private: void ICollection::CopyTo(
   Array* array,
   int index
);
```

[JScript]

```
private function ICollection.CopyTo(
   array : Array,
   index : int
);
```

PrinterSettings.PaperSizeCollection.IEnumerable.GetEnumerator Method

This member supports the .NET Framework infrastructure and is not intended to be used directly from your code.

[Visual Basic]

```
Private Function GetEnumerator() As IEnumerator Implements _
   IEnumerable.GetEnumerator
```

[C#]

```
IEnumerator IEnumerable.GetEnumerator();
```

[C++]

```
private: IEnumerator* IEnumerable::GetEnumerator();
```

[JScript]

```
private function IEnumerable.GetEnumerator() : IEnumerator;
```

PrinterSettings.PaperSource-Collection Class

Contains a collection of **PaperSource** objects.

System.Object
  System.Drawing.Printing.PrinterSettings.PaperSourceCollection

[Visual Basic]
```
Public Class PrinterSettings.PaperSourceCollection
   Implements ICollection, IEnumerable
```
[C#]
```
public class PrinterSettings.PaperSourceCollection : ICollection,
   IEnumerable
```
[C++]
```
public __gc class PrinterSettings.PaperSourceCollection : public
   ICollection, IEnumerable
```
[JScript]
```
public class PrinterSettings.PaperSourceCollection implements
   ICollection, IEnumerable
```

Thread Safety

Any public static (**Shared** in Visual Basic) members of this type are safe for multithreaded operations. Any instance members are not guaranteed to be thread safe.

Remarks

The **PrinterSettings.PaperSourceCollection** contains **PaperSource** instances that represents the paper source trays through the **PaperSource.Kind** property, which contains one of the **PaperSourceKind** values.

Typically, you set a page's paper source through the **PageSettings.PaperSource** property to a valid **PaperSource** instance available through the **PaperSources** collection.

Example

[Visual Basic, C#, C++] The following example populates the `comboPaperSource` combo box with the printer's supported paper sources. The **SourceName** is identified as the property that provides the display string for the item being added through the **DisplayMember** property of the combo box. The example assumes that a **PrintDocument** variable named `printDoc` exists and that the specific combo box exists.

[Visual Basic]
```
' Add list of paper sources found on the printer to the combo box.
' The DisplayMember property is used to identify the property ↵
that will provide the display string.
comboPaperSource.DisplayMember = "SourceName"

Dim pkSource As PaperSource
For i = 0 to printDoc.PrinterSettings.PaperSources.Count - 1
    pkSource = printDoc.PrinterSettings.PaperSources.Item(i)
    comboPaperSource.Items.Add(pkSource)
Next
```

[C#]
```
// Add list of paper sources found on the printer to the combo box.
// The DisplayMember property is used to identify the property ↵
 that will provide the display string.
comboPaperSource.DisplayMember="SourceName";

PaperSource pkSource;
for (int i = 0; i < printDoc.PrinterSettings.PaperSources.Count; i++){
    pkSource = printDoc.PrinterSettings.PaperSources[i];
    comboPaperSource.Items.Add(pkSource);
}
```

[C++]
```
// Add list of paper sources found on the printer to the combo box.
// The DisplayMember property is used to identify the property ↵
 that will provide the display String*.
comboPaperSource->DisplayMember=S"SourceName";

PaperSource* pkSource;
for (int i = 0; i < printDoc->PrinterSettings->PaperSources-> ↵
Count; i++) {
   pkSource = printDoc->PrinterSettings->PaperSources->Item[i];
   comboPaperSource->Items->Add(pkSource);
}
```

Requirements

Namespace: System.Drawing.Printing

Platforms: Windows 98, Windows NT 4.0, Windows Millennium Edition, Windows 2000, Windows XP Home Edition, Windows XP Professional, Windows Server 2003 family

Assembly: System.Drawing (in System.Drawing.dll)

PrinterSettings.PaperSourceCollection Constructor

Initializes a new instance of the **PrinterSettings.PaperSourceCollection** class.

[Visual Basic]
```
Public Sub New( _
   ByVal array() As PaperSource _
)
```
[C#]
```
public PrinterSettings.PaperSourceCollection(
   PaperSource[] array
);
```
[C++]
```
public: PaperSourceCollection(
   PaperSource* array[]
);
```
[JScript]
```
public function PrinterSettings.PaperSourceCollection(
   array : PaperSource[]
);
```

Parameters

array
  An array of type **PaperSource**.

Requirements

Platforms: Windows 98, Windows NT 4.0, Windows Millennium Edition, Windows 2000, Windows XP Home Edition, Windows XP Professional, Windows Server 2003 family

PrinterSettings.PaperSourceCollection.Count Property

Gets the number of different paper sources in the collection.

[Visual Basic]
```
Public ReadOnly Property Count As Integer
```
[C#]
```
public int Count {get;}
```

```
[C++]
public: __property int get_Count();
[JScript]
public function get Count() : int;
```

Property Value

The number of different paper sources in the collection.

Example

See related example in the **System.Drawing.Printing.PrinterSettings.PaperSourceCollection** class topic.

Requirements

Platforms: Windows 98, Windows NT 4.0, Windows Millennium Edition, Windows 2000, Windows XP Home Edition, Windows XP Professional, Windows Server 2003 family

PrinterSettings.PaperSourceCollection.Item Property

Gets the **PaperSource** at a specified index.

[C#] In C#, this property is the indexer for the **PrinterSettings.PaperSourceCollection** class.

```
[Visual Basic]
Public Overridable Default ReadOnly Property Item( _
   ByVal index As Integer _
) As PaperSource
[C#]
public virtual PaperSource this[
   int index
] {get;}
[C++]
public: __property virtual PaperSource* get_Item(
   int index
);
[JScript]
returnValue = PaperSourceCollectionObject.Item(index);
-or-
returnValue = PaperSourceCollectionObject(index);
```

[JScript] In JScript, you can use the default indexed properties defined by a type, but you cannot explicitly define your own. However, specifying the **expando** attribute on a class automatically provides a default indexed property whose type is **Object** and whose index type is **String**.

Arguments [JScript]

index

The index of the **PaperSource** to get.

Parameters [Visual Basic, C#, C++]

index

The index of the **PaperSource** to get.

Property Value

The **PaperSource** at the specified index.

Example

See related example in the **System.Drawing.Printing.PrinterSettings.PaperSourceCollection** class topic.

Requirements

Platforms: Windows 98, Windows NT 4.0, Windows Millennium Edition, Windows 2000, Windows XP Home Edition, Windows XP Professional, Windows Server 2003 family

PrinterSettings.PaperSourceCollection.GetEnumerator Method

Returns an enumerator that can iterate through the collection.

```
[Visual Basic]
Public Function GetEnumerator() As IEnumerator
[C#]
public IEnumerator GetEnumerator();
[C++]
public: IEnumerator* GetEnumerator();
[JScript]
public function GetEnumerator() : IEnumerator;
```

Return Value

An **IEnumerator** for the **PrinterSettings.PaperSourceCollection**.

Remarks

This method instantiates an enumerator that takes a snapshot of the current state of the collection. The enumerator does not have exclusive access to the collection, so multiple enumerators can have access to the same collection at the same time. Therefore, any changes made to the collection, either directly or through another enumerator, can cause **Current** or **MoveNext** to throw an exception.

Two enumerators instantiated from the same collection at the same time can contain different snapshots of the collection.

Removing objects from the enumerator also removes them from the collection.

Requirements

Platforms: Windows 98, Windows NT 4.0, Windows Millennium Edition, Windows 2000, Windows XP Home Edition, Windows XP Professional, Windows Server 2003 family

PrinterSettings.PaperSourceCollection.ICollection.CopyTo Method

This member supports the .NET Framework infrastructure and is not intended to be used directly from your code.

```
[Visual Basic]
Private Sub CopyTo( _
   ByVal array As Array, _
   ByVal index As Integer _
) Implements ICollection.CopyTo
[C#]
void ICollection.CopyTo(
   Array array,
   int index
);
[C++]
private: void ICollection::CopyTo(
   Array* array,
   int index
);
```

[JScript]
```
private function ICollection.CopyTo(
   array : Array,
   index : int
);
```

PrinterSettings.PaperSourceCollection.IEnumerable.GetEnumerator Method

This member supports the .NET Framework infrastructure and is not intended to be used directly from your code.

[Visual Basic]
```
Private Function GetEnumerator() As IEnumerator Implements _
   IEnumerable.GetEnumerator
```
[C#]
```
IEnumerator IEnumerable.GetEnumerator();
```
[C++]
```
private: IEnumerator* IEnumerable::GetEnumerator();
```
[JScript]
```
private function IEnumerable.GetEnumerator() : IEnumerator;
```

PrinterSettings.PrinterResolutionCollection Class

Contains a collection of **PrinterResolution** objects.

System.Object
System.Drawing.Printing.PrinterSettings.PrinterResolutionCollection

[Visual Basic]
```
Public Class PrinterSettings.PrinterResolutionCollection
   Implements ICollection, IEnumerable
```
[C#]
```
public class PrinterSettings.PrinterResolutionCollection :
   ICollection, IEnumerable
```
[C++]
```
public __gc class PrinterSettings.PrinterResolutionCollection :
   public ICollection, IEnumerable
```
[JScript]
```
public class PrinterSettings.PrinterResolutionCollection implements
   ICollection, IEnumerable
```

Thread Safety

Any public static (**Shared** in Visual Basic) members of this type are safe for multithreaded operations. Any instance members are not guaranteed to be thread safe.

Remarks

The **PrinterSettings.PrinterResolutionCollection** contains **PrinterResolution** instances that represents the printer resolutions supported through the **PrinterResolution.Kind** property, which contains one of the **PrinterResolutionKind** values.

Typically, you set the printer's resolution through the **PageSettings.PrinterResolution** property to a valid **PrinterResolution** instance available through the **PrinterResolutions** collection.

If **PrinterResolutionKind** is **Custom**, then use the **X** and **Y** properties to determine the custom printer resolution in the horizontal and vertical directions, respectively.

Example

[Visual Basic, C#, C++] The following example populates the `comboPrintResolution` combo box with the supported resolutions. The example assumes that a **PrintDocument** variable named `printDoc` exists and that the specific combo box exists.

[Visual Basic]
```
' Add list of printer resolutions found on the printer to the combobox.
' The PrinterResolution's ToString() method will be used to ↵
provide the display string.
Dim pkResolution As PrinterResolution
For i = 0 to printDoc.PrinterSettings.PrinterResolutions.Count - 1
    pkResolution = printDoc.PrinterSettings.PrinterResolutions.Item(i)
    comboPrintResolution.Items.Add(pkResolution)
Next
```

[C#]
```
// Add list of printer resolutions found on the printer to the ↵
combobox.
// The PrinterResolution's ToString() method will be used to ↵
 provide the display string.

PrinterResolution pkResolution;
for (int i = 0; i < ↵
printDoc.PrinterSettings.PrinterResolutions.Count; i++){
    pkResolution = printDoc.PrinterSettings.PrinterResolutions[i];
    comboPrintResolution.Items.Add(pkResolution);
}
```

[C++]
```
// Add list of printer resolutions found on the printer to ↵
the combobox.
// The PrinterResolution's ToString() method will be used ↵
 to provide the display String.

PrinterResolution* pkResolution;
for (int i = 0; i < ↵
 printDoc->PrinterSettings->PrinterResolutions->Count; i++) {
   pkResolution = printDoc-> ↵
PrinterSettings->PrinterResolutions->Item[i];
   comboPrintResolution->Items->Add(pkResolution);
}
```

Requirements

Namespace: System.Drawing.Printing

Platforms: Windows 98, Windows NT 4.0, Windows Millennium Edition, Windows 2000, Windows XP Home Edition, Windows XP Professional, Windows Server 2003 family

Assembly: System.Drawing (in System.Drawing.dll)

PrinterSettings.PrinterResolutionCollection Constructor

Initializes a new instance of the **PrinterSettings.PrinterResolutionCollection** class.

[Visual Basic]
```
Public Sub New( _
   ByVal array() As PrinterResolution _
)
```
[C#]
```
public PrinterSettings.PrinterResolutionCollection(
   PrinterResolution[] array
);
```
[C++]
```
public: PrinterResolutionCollection(
   PrinterResolution* array[]
);
```
[JScript]
```
public function PrinterSettings.PrinterResolutionCollection(
   array : PrinterResolution[]
);
```

Parameters

array
An array of type **PrinterResolution**.

Requirements

Platforms: Windows 98, Windows NT 4.0, Windows Millennium Edition, Windows 2000, Windows XP Home Edition, Windows XP Professional, Windows Server 2003 family

PrinterSettings.PrinterResolutionCollection.Count Property

Gets the number of available printer resolutions in the collection.

[Visual Basic]
```
Public ReadOnly Property Count As Integer
```
[C#]
```
public int Count {get;}
```

```
[C++]
public: __property int get_Count();
[JScript]
public function get Count() : int;
```

Property Value

The number of available printer resolutions in the collection.

Example

See related example in the **System.Drawing.Printing.PrinterSettings.PrinterResolutionCollection** class topic.

Requirements

Platforms: Windows 98, Windows NT 4.0, Windows Millennium Edition, Windows 2000, Windows XP Home Edition, Windows XP Professional, Windows Server 2003 family

PrinterSettings.PrinterResolutionCollection.Item Property

Gets the **PrinterResolution** at a specified index.

[C#] In C#, this property is the indexer for the **PrinterSettings.PrinterResolutionCollection** class.

```
[Visual Basic]
Public Overridable Default ReadOnly Property Item( _
   ByVal index As Integer _
) As PrinterResolution
[C#]
public virtual PrinterResolution this[
   int index
] {get;}
[C++]
public: __property virtual PrinterResolution* get_Item(
   int index
);
[JScript]
returnValue = PrinterResolutionCollectionObject.Item(index);
-or-
returnValue = PrinterResolutionCollectionObject(index);
```

[JScript] In JScript, you can use the default indexed properties defined by a type, but you cannot explicitly define your own. However, specifying the **expando** attribute on a class automatically provides a default indexed property whose type is **Object** and whose index type is **String**.

Arguments [JScript]

index

The index of the **PrinterResolution** to get.

Parameters [Visual Basic, C#, C++]

index

The index of the **PrinterResolution** to get.

Property Value

The **PrinterResolution** at the specified index.

Example

See related example in the **System.Drawing.Printing.PrinterSettings.PrinterResolutionCollection** class topic.

Requirements

Platforms: Windows 98, Windows NT 4.0, Windows Millennium Edition, Windows 2000, Windows XP Home Edition, Windows XP Professional, Windows Server 2003 family

PrinterSettings.PrinterResolutionCollection.GetEnumerator Method

Returns an enumerator that can iterate through the collection.

```
[Visual Basic]
Public Function GetEnumerator() As IEnumerator
[C#]
public IEnumerator GetEnumerator();
[C++]
public: IEnumerator* GetEnumerator();
[JScript]
public function GetEnumerator() : IEnumerator;
```

Return Value

An **IEnumerator** for the **PrinterSettings.PrinterResolutionCollection**.

Remarks

This method instantiates an enumerator that takes a snapshot of the current state of the collection. The enumerator does not have exclusive access to the collection, so multiple enumerators can have access to the same collection at the same time. Therefore, any changes made to the collection, either directly or through another enumerator, can cause **Current** or **MoveNext** to throw an exception.

Two enumerators instantiated from the same collection at the same time can contain different snapshots of the collection.

Removing objects from the enumerator also removes them from the collection.

Requirements

Platforms: Windows 98, Windows NT 4.0, Windows Millennium Edition, Windows 2000, Windows XP Home Edition, Windows XP Professional, Windows Server 2003 family

PrinterSettings.PrinterResolutionCollection.ICollection.CopyTo Method

This member supports the .NET Framework infrastructure and is not intended to be used directly from your code.

```
[Visual Basic]
Private Sub CopyTo( _
   ByVal array As Array, _
   ByVal index As Integer _
) Implements ICollection.CopyTo
[C#]
void ICollection.CopyTo(
   Array array,
   int index
);
[C++]
private: void ICollection::CopyTo(
   Array* array,
   int index
);
```

[JScript]
```
private function ICollection.CopyTo(
   array : Array,
   index : int
);
```

PrinterSettings.PrinterResolutionCollection.IEnumerable.GetEnumerator Method

This member supports the .NET Framework infrastructure and is not intended to be used directly from your code.

[Visual Basic]
```
Private Function GetEnumerator() As IEnumerator Implements _
   IEnumerable.GetEnumerator
```
[C#]
```
IEnumerator IEnumerable.GetEnumerator();
```
[C++]
```
private: IEnumerator* IEnumerable::GetEnumerator();
```
[JScript]
```
private function IEnumerable.GetEnumerator() : IEnumerator;
```

PrinterSettings.StringCollection Class

This type supports the .NET Framework infrastructure and is not intended to be used directly from your code.

```
[Visual Basic]
Public Class PrinterSettings.StringCollection
   Implements ICollection, IEnumerable
[C#]
public class PrinterSettings.StringCollection : ICollection,
   IEnumerable
[C++]
public __gc class PrinterSettings.StringCollection : public
   ICollection, IEnumerable
[JScript]
public class PrinterSettings.StringCollection implements
   ICollection, IEnumerable
```

PrinterSettings.StringCollection Constructor

This member supports the .NET Framework infrastructure and is not intended to be used directly from your code.

```
[Visual Basic]
Public Sub New( _
   ByVal array() As String _
)
[C#]
public PrinterSettings.StringCollection(
   string[] array
);
[C++]
public: StringCollection(
   String* array __gc[]
);
[JScript]
public function PrinterSettings.StringCollection(
   array : String[]
);
```

PrinterSettings.StringCollection.Count Property

This member supports the .NET Framework infrastructure and is not intended to be used directly from your code.

```
[Visual Basic]
Public ReadOnly Property Count As Integer
[C#]
public int Count {get;}
[C++]
public: __property int get_Count();
[JScript]
public function get Count() : int;
```

PrinterSettings.StringCollection.Item Property

This member supports the .NET Framework infrastructure and is not intended to be used directly from your code.

```
[Visual Basic]
Public Overridable Default ReadOnly Property Item( _
   ByVal index As Integer _
) As String
[C#]
public virtual string this[
   int index
] {get;}
[C++]
public: __property virtual String* get_Item(
   int index
);
[JScript]
returnValue = StringCollectionObject.Item(index);
-or-
returnValue = StringCollectionObject(index);
```

[JScript] In JScript, you can use the default indexed properties defined by a type, but you cannot explicitly define your own. However, specifying the **expando** attribute on a class automatically provides a default indexed property whose type is **Object** and whose index type is **String**.

PrinterSettings.StringCollection.GetEnumerator Method

This member supports the .NET Framework infrastructure and is not intended to be used directly from your code.

```
[Visual Basic]
Public Function GetEnumerator() As IEnumerator
[C#]
public IEnumerator GetEnumerator();
[C++]
public: IEnumerator* GetEnumerator();
[JScript]
public function GetEnumerator() : IEnumerator;
```

PrinterSettings.StringCollection.ICollection.CopyTo Method

This member supports the .NET Framework infrastructure and is not intended to be used directly from your code.

```
[Visual Basic]
Private Sub CopyTo( _
   ByVal array As Array, _
   ByVal index As Integer _
) Implements ICollection.CopyTo
[C#]
void ICollection.CopyTo(
   Array array,
   int index
);
[C++]
private: void ICollection::CopyTo(
   Array* array,
   int index
);
```

[JScript]
```
private function ICollection.CopyTo(
   array : Array,
   index : int
);
```

PrinterSettings.StringCollection.IEnumerable.GetEnumerator Method

This member supports the .NET Framework infrastructure and is not intended to be used directly from your code.

[Visual Basic]
```
Private Function GetEnumerator() As IEnumerator Implements _
   IEnumerable.GetEnumerator
```
[C#]
```
IEnumerator IEnumerable.GetEnumerator();
```
[C++]
```
private: IEnumerator* IEnumerable::GetEnumerator();
```
[JScript]
```
private function IEnumerable.GetEnumerator() : IEnumerator;
```

PrinterUnit Enumeration

Specifies several of the units of measure that the Win32 Application Programming Interface (API) uses for printing.

[Visual Basic]
```
<Serializable>
Public Enum PrinterUnit
```
[C#]
```
[Serializable]
public enum PrinterUnit
```
[C++]
```
[Serializable]
__value public enum PrinterUnit
```
[JScript]
```
public
   Serializable
enum PrinterUnit
```

Remarks

PreviewPrintController, **PrinterSettings**, and **PageSetupDialog** use this enumeration.

For more information on printing, see the **System.Drawing.Printing** namespace overview.

Members

Member name	Description
Display	The default unit (0.01 in.).
HundredthsOfA-Millimeter	One-hundredth of a millimeter (0.01 mm).
TenthsOfAMillimeter	One-tenth of a millimeter (0.1 mm).
ThousandthsOfAnInch	One-thousandth of an inch (0.001 in.).

Requirements

Namespace: System.Drawing.Printing

Platforms: Windows 98, Windows NT 4.0, Windows Millennium Edition, Windows 2000, Windows XP Home Edition, Windows XP Professional, Windows Server 2003 family

Assembly: System.Drawing (in System.Drawing.dll)

PrinterUnitConvert Class

Specifies a series of conversion methods that are useful when interoperating with the Win32 printing Application Program Interface (API). This class cannot be inherited.

System.Object
  System.Drawing.Printing.PrinterUnitConvert

[Visual Basic]
```
NotInheritable Public Class PrinterUnitConvert
```
[C#]
```
public sealed class PrinterUnitConvert
```
[C++]
```
public __gc __sealed class PrinterUnitConvert
```
[JScript]
```
public class PrinterUnitConvert
```

Thread Safety

Any public static (**Shared** in Visual Basic) members of this type are safe for multithreaded operations. Any instance members are not guaranteed to be thread safe.

Remarks

Typically, this class is not called directly.

For more information on printing, see the **System.Drawing.Printing** namespace overview.

Requirements

Namespace: System.Drawing.Printing

Platforms: Windows 98, Windows NT 4.0, Windows Millennium Edition, Windows 2000, Windows XP Home Edition, Windows XP Professional, Windows Server 2003 family

Assembly: System.Drawing (in System.Drawing.dll)

PrinterUnitConvert.Convert Method

Converts a value from one **PrinterUnit** type to another **PrinterUnit** type.

Overload List

Converts a double-precision floating point number from one **PrinterUnit** type to another **PrinterUnit** type.

[Visual Basic] **Overloads Public Shared Function Convert(Double, PrinterUnit, PrinterUnit) As Double**

[C#] **public static double Convert(double, PrinterUnit, PrinterUnit);**

[C++] **public: static double Convert(double, PrinterUnit, PrinterUnit);**

[JScript] **public static function Convert(double, PrinterUnit, PrinterUnit) : double;**

Converts a 32-bit signed integer from one **PrinterUnit** type to another **PrinterUnit** type.

[Visual Basic] **Overloads Public Shared Function Convert(Integer, PrinterUnit, PrinterUnit) As Integer**

[C#] **public static int Convert(int, PrinterUnit, PrinterUnit);**

[C++] **public: static int Convert(int, PrinterUnit, PrinterUnit);**

[JScript] **public static function Convert(int, PrinterUnit, PrinterUnit) : int;**

Converts a **Margins** from one **PrinterUnit** type to another **PrinterUnit** type.

[Visual Basic] **Overloads Public Shared Function Convert(Margins, PrinterUnit, PrinterUnit) As Margins**

[C#] **public static Margins Convert(Margins, PrinterUnit, PrinterUnit);**

[C++] **public: static Margins* Convert(Margins*, PrinterUnit, PrinterUnit);**

[JScript] **public static function Convert(Margins, PrinterUnit, PrinterUnit) : Margins;**

Converts a **Point** from one **PrinterUnit** type to another **PrinterUnit** type.

[Visual Basic] **Overloads Public Shared Function Convert(Point, PrinterUnit, PrinterUnit) As Point**

[C#] **public static Point Convert(Point, PrinterUnit, PrinterUnit);**

[C++] **public: static Point Convert(Point, PrinterUnit, PrinterUnit);**

[JScript] **public static function Convert(Point, PrinterUnit, PrinterUnit) : Point;**

Converts a **Rectangle** from one **PrinterUnit** type to another **PrinterUnit** type.

[Visual Basic] **Overloads Public Shared Function Convert(Rectangle, PrinterUnit, PrinterUnit) As Rectangle**

[C#] **public static Rectangle Convert(Rectangle, PrinterUnit, PrinterUnit);**

[C++] **public: static Rectangle Convert(Rectangle, PrinterUnit, PrinterUnit);**

[JScript] **public static function Convert(Rectangle, PrinterUnit, PrinterUnit) : Rectangle;**

Converts a **Size** from one **PrinterUnit** type to another **PrinterUnit** type.

[Visual Basic] **Overloads Public Shared Function Convert(Size, PrinterUnit, PrinterUnit) As Size**

[C#] **public static Size Convert(Size, PrinterUnit, PrinterUnit);**

[C++] **public: static Size Convert(Size, PrinterUnit, PrinterUnit);**

[JScript] **public static function Convert(Size, PrinterUnit, PrinterUnit) : Size;**

PrinterUnitConvert.Convert Method (Double, PrinterUnit, PrinterUnit)

Converts a double-precision floating point number from one **PrinterUnit** type to another **PrinterUnit** type.

[Visual Basic]
```
Overloads Public Shared Function Convert( _
   ByVal value As Double, _
   ByVal fromUnit As PrinterUnit, _
   ByVal toUnit As PrinterUnit _
) As Double
```
[C#]
```
public static double Convert(
   double value,
   PrinterUnit fromUnit,
   PrinterUnit toUnit
);
```

```
[C++]
public: static double Convert(
   double value,
   PrinterUnit fromUnit,
   PrinterUnit toUnit
);
[JScript]
public static function Convert(
   value : double,
   fromUnit : PrinterUnit,
   toUnit : PrinterUnit
) : double;
```

Parameters

value
: The **Point** being converted.

fromUnit
: The unit to convert from.

toUnit
: The unit to convert to.

Return Value

A double-precision floating point number that represents the converted **PrinterUnit**.

Remarks

The following table shows the **PrinterUnit** values.

Value	Description
Display	The default unit (0.01 in.).
ThousandthsOfAnInch	One thousandth of an inch (0.001 in.).
HundredthsOfAMillimeter	One hundredth of a millimeter (0.01 mm).
TenthsOfAMillimeter	One tenth of a millimeter (0.1 mm).

Requirements

Platforms: Windows 98, Windows NT 4.0, Windows Millennium Edition, Windows 2000, Windows XP Home Edition, Windows XP Professional, Windows Server 2003 family

PrinterUnitConvert.Convert Method (Int32, PrinterUnit, PrinterUnit)

Converts a 32-bit signed integer from one **PrinterUnit** type to another **PrinterUnit** type.

```
[Visual Basic]
Overloads Public Shared Function Convert( _
   ByVal value As Integer, _
   ByVal fromUnit As PrinterUnit, _
   ByVal toUnit As PrinterUnit _
) As Integer
[C#]
public static int Convert(
   int value,
   PrinterUnit fromUnit,
   PrinterUnit toUnit
);
[C++]
public: static int Convert(
   int value,
   PrinterUnit fromUnit,
   PrinterUnit toUnit
);
[JScript]
public static function Convert(
   value : int,
   fromUnit : PrinterUnit,
   toUnit : PrinterUnit
) : int;
```

Parameters

value
: The **Point** being converted.

fromUnit
: The unit to convert from.

toUnit
: The unit to convert to.

Return Value

A 32-bit signed integer that represents the converted **PrinterUnit**.

Remarks

The following table shows the **PrinterUnit** values.

Value	Description
Display	The default unit (0.01 in.).
ThousandthsOfAnInch	One thousandth of an inch (0.001 in.).
HundredthsOfAMillimeter	One hundredth of a millimeter (0.01 mm).
TenthsOfAMillimeter	One tenth of a millimeter (0.1 mm).

Requirements

Platforms: Windows 98, Windows NT 4.0, Windows Millennium Edition, Windows 2000, Windows XP Home Edition, Windows XP Professional, Windows Server 2003 family

PrinterUnitConvert.Convert Method (Margins, PrinterUnit, PrinterUnit)

Converts a **Margins** from one **PrinterUnit** type to another **PrinterUnit** type.

```
[Visual Basic]
Overloads Public Shared Function Convert( _
   ByVal value As Margins, _
   ByVal fromUnit As PrinterUnit, _
   ByVal toUnit As PrinterUnit _
) As Margins
[C#]
public static Margins Convert(
   Margins value,
   PrinterUnit fromUnit,
   PrinterUnit toUnit
);
[C++]
public: static Margins* Convert(
   Margins* value,
   PrinterUnit fromUnit,
   PrinterUnit toUnit
);
```

```
[JScript]
public static function Convert(
   value : Margins,
   fromUnit : PrinterUnit,
   toUnit : PrinterUnit
) : Margins;
```

Parameters

value
The **Margins** being converted.

fromUnit
The unit to convert from.

toUnit
The unit to convert to.

Return Value

A **Margins** that represents the converted **PrinterUnit**.

Remarks

The following table shows the **PrinterUnit** values.

Value	Description
Display	The default unit (0.01 in.).
ThousandthsOfAnInch	One thousandth of an inch (0.001 in.).
HundredthsOfAMillimeter	One hundredth of a millimeter (0.01 mm).
TenthsOfAMillimeter	One tenth of a millimeter (0.1 mm).

Requirements

Platforms: Windows 98, Windows NT 4.0, Windows Millennium Edition, Windows 2000, Windows XP Home Edition, Windows XP Professional, Windows Server 2003 family

PrinterUnitConvert.Convert Method (Point, PrinterUnit, PrinterUnit)

Converts a **Point** from one **PrinterUnit** type to another **PrinterUnit** type.

```
[Visual Basic]
Overloads Public Shared Function Convert( _
   ByVal value As Point, _
   ByVal fromUnit As PrinterUnit, _
   ByVal toUnit As PrinterUnit _
) As Point
[C#]
public static Point Convert(
   Point value,
   PrinterUnit fromUnit,
   PrinterUnit toUnit
);
[C++]
public: static Point Convert(
   Point value,
   PrinterUnit fromUnit,
   PrinterUnit toUnit
);
[JScript]
public static function Convert(
   value : Point,
   fromUnit : PrinterUnit,
   toUnit : PrinterUnit
) : Point;
```

Parameters

value
The **Point** being converted.

fromUnit
The unit to convert from.

toUnit
The unit to convert to.

Return Value

A **Point** that represents the converted **PrinterUnit**.

Remarks

The following table shows the **PrinterUnit** values.

Value	Description
Display	The default unit (0.01 in.).
ThousandthsOfAnInch	One thousandth of an inch (0.001 in.).
HundredthsOfAMillimeter	One hundredth of a millimeter (0.01 mm).
TenthsOfAMillimeter	One tenth of a millimeter (0.1 mm).

Requirements

Platforms: Windows 98, Windows NT 4.0, Windows Millennium Edition, Windows 2000, Windows XP Home Edition, Windows XP Professional, Windows Server 2003 family

PrinterUnitConvert.Convert Method (Rectangle, PrinterUnit, PrinterUnit)

Converts a **Rectangle** from one **PrinterUnit** type to another **PrinterUnit** type.

```
[Visual Basic]
Overloads Public Shared Function Convert( _
   ByVal value As Rectangle, _
   ByVal fromUnit As PrinterUnit, _
   ByVal toUnit As PrinterUnit _
) As Rectangle
[C#]
public static Rectangle Convert(
   Rectangle value,
   PrinterUnit fromUnit,
   PrinterUnit toUnit
);
[C++]
public: static Rectangle Convert(
   Rectangle value,
   PrinterUnit fromUnit,
   PrinterUnit toUnit
);
[JScript]
public static function Convert(
   value : Rectangle,
   fromUnit : PrinterUnit,
   toUnit : PrinterUnit
) : Rectangle;
```

Parameters

value

The **Rectangle** being converted.

fromUnit

The unit to convert from.

toUnit

The unit to convert to.

Return Value

A **Rectangle** that represents the converted **PrinterUnit**.

Remarks

The following table shows the **PrinterUnit** values.

Value	Description
Display	The default unit (0.01 in.).
ThousandthsOfAnInch	One thousandth of an inch (0.001 in.).
HundredthsOfA-Millimeter	One hundredth of a millimeter (0.01 mm).
TenthsOfAMillimeter	One tenth of a millimeter (0.1 mm).

Requirements

Platforms: Windows 98, Windows NT 4.0, Windows Millennium Edition, Windows 2000, Windows XP Home Edition, Windows XP Professional, Windows Server 2003 family

PrinterUnitConvert.Convert Method (Size, PrinterUnit, PrinterUnit)

Converts a **Size** from one **PrinterUnit** type to another **PrinterUnit** type.

```
[Visual Basic]
Overloads Public Shared Function Convert( _
   ByVal value As Size, _
   ByVal fromUnit As PrinterUnit, _
   ByVal toUnit As PrinterUnit _
) As Size
[C#]
public static Size Convert(
   Size value,
   PrinterUnit fromUnit,
   PrinterUnit toUnit
);
[C++]
public: static Size Convert(
   Size value,
   PrinterUnit fromUnit,
   PrinterUnit toUnit
);
[JScript]
public static function Convert(
   value : Size,
   fromUnit : PrinterUnit,
   toUnit : PrinterUnit
) : Size;
```

Parameters

value

The **Size** being converted.

fromUnit

The unit to convert from.

toUnit

The unit to convert to.

Return Value

A **Size** that represents the converted **PrinterUnit**.

Remarks

The following table shows the **PrinterUnit** values.

Value	Description
Display	The default unit (0.01 in.).
ThousandthsOfAnInch	One thousandth of an inch (0.001 in.).
HundredthsOfA-Millimeter	One hundredth of a millimeter (0.01 mm).
TenthsOfAMillimeter	One tenth of a millimeter (0.1 mm).

Requirements

Platforms: Windows 98, Windows NT 4.0, Windows Millennium Edition, Windows 2000, Windows XP Home Edition, Windows XP Professional, Windows Server 2003 family

PrintEventArgs Class

Provides data for the **BeginPrint** and **EndPrint** events.

System.Object
  System.EventArgs
    System.ComponentModel.CancelEventArgs
      System.Drawing.Printing.PrintEventArgs
        System.Drawing.Printing.QueryPageSettingsEventArgs

[Visual Basic]
```
Public Class PrintEventArgs
   Inherits CancelEventArgs
```
[C#]
```
public class PrintEventArgs : CancelEventArgs
```
[C++]
```
public __gc class PrintEventArgs : public CancelEventArgs
```
[JScript]
```
public class PrintEventArgs extends CancelEventArgs
```

Thread Safety

Any public static (**Shared** in Visual Basic) members of this type are safe for multithreaded operations. Any instance members are not guaranteed to be thread safe.

Remarks

In this release, **PrintEventArgs** provides no additional implementation other than **CancelEventArgs**. **PrintEventArgs** is reserved for future use.

For more information on printing, see the **System.Drawing.Printing** namespace overview.

Requirements

Namespace: System.Drawing.Printing

Platforms: Windows 98, Windows NT 4.0, Windows Millennium Edition, Windows 2000, Windows XP Home Edition, Windows XP Professional, Windows Server 2003 family

Assembly: System.Drawing (in System.Drawing.dll)

PrintEventArgs Constructor

Initializes a new instance of the **PrintEventArgs** class.

[Visual Basic]
```
Public Sub New()
```
[C#]
```
public PrintEventArgs();
```
[C++]
```
public: PrintEventArgs();
```
[JScript]
```
public function PrintEventArgs();
```

Requirements

Platforms: Windows 98, Windows NT 4.0, Windows Millennium Edition, Windows 2000, Windows XP Home Edition, Windows XP Professional, Windows Server 2003 family

PrintEventHandler Delegate

Represents the method that will handle the **BeginPrint** or **EndPrint** event of a **PrintDocument**.

[Visual Basic]
```
<Serializable>
Public Delegate Sub PrintEventHandler( _
   ByVal sender As Object, _
   ByVal e As PrintEventArgs _
)
```
[C#]
```
[Serializable]
public delegate void PrintEventHandler(
   object sender,
   PrintEventArgs e
);
```
[C++]
```
[Serializable]
public __gc __delegate void PrintEventHandler(
   Object* sender,
   PrintEventArgs* e
);
```

[JScript] In JScript, you can use the delegates in the .NET Framework, but you cannot define your own.

Parameters [Visual Basic, C#, C++]

The declaration of your event handler must have the same parameters as the **PrintEventHandler** delegate declaration.

sender
: The source of the event.

e
: A **PrintEventArgs** that contains the event data.

Remarks

When you create a **PrintEventHandler** delegate, you identify the method that will handle the event. To associate the event with your event handler, add an instance of the delegate to the event. The event handler is called whenever the event occurs, unless you remove the delegate.

For more information on printing, see the **System.Drawing.Printing** namespace overview.

Requirements

Namespace: System.Drawing.Printing

Platforms: Windows 98, Windows NT 4.0, Windows Millennium Edition, Windows 2000, Windows XP Home Edition, Windows XP Professional, Windows Server 2003 family

Assembly: System.Drawing (in System.Drawing.dll)

PrintingPermission Class

Controls access to printers. This class cannot be inherited.

System.Object
  System.Security.CodeAccessPermission
    System.Drawing.Printing.PrintingPermission

```
[Visual Basic]
<Serializable>
NotInheritable Public Class PrintingPermission
   Inherits CodeAccessPermission
   Implements IUnrestrictedPermission
[C#]
[Serializable]
public sealed class PrintingPermission : CodeAccessPermission,
   IUnrestrictedPermission
[C++]
[Serializable]
public __gc __sealed class PrintingPermission : public
   CodeAccessPermission, IUnrestrictedPermission
[JScript]
public
   Serializable
class PrintingPermission extends CodeAccessPermission
   implements IUnrestrictedPermission
```

Thread Safety

Any public static (**Shared** in Visual Basic) members of this type are safe for multithreaded operations. Any instance members are not guaranteed to be thread safe.

Requirements

Namespace: System.Drawing.Printing

Platforms: Windows 98, Windows NT 4.0, Windows Millennium Edition, Windows 2000, Windows XP Home Edition, Windows XP Professional, Windows Server 2003 family

Assembly: System.Drawing (in System.Drawing.dll)

PrintingPermission Constructor

Initializes a new instance of the **PrintingPermission** class.

Overload List

Initializes a new instance of the **PrintingPermission** class with either fully restricted or unrestricted access, as specified.

[Visual Basic] **Public Sub New(PermissionState)**

[C#] **public PrintingPermission(PermissionState);**

[C++] **public: PrintingPermission(PermissionState);**

[JScript] **public function PrintingPermission(PermissionState);**

Initializes a new instance of the **PrintingPermission** class with the level of printing access specified.

[Visual Basic] **Public Sub New(PrintingPermissionLevel)**

[C#] **public PrintingPermission(PrintingPermissionLevel);**

[C++] **public: PrintingPermission(PrintingPermissionLevel);**

[JScript] **public function PrintingPermission(Printing-PermissionLevel);**

PrintingPermission Constructor (PermissionState)

Initializes a new instance of the **PrintingPermission** class with either fully restricted or unrestricted access, as specified.

```
[Visual Basic]
Public Sub New( _
   ByVal state As PermissionState _
)
[C#]
public PrintingPermission(
   PermissionState state
);
[C++]
public: PrintingPermission(
   PermissionState state
);
[JScript]
public function PrintingPermission(
   state : PermissionState
);
```

Parameters

state
  One of the **PermissionState** values.

Exceptions

Exception Type	Condition
ArgumentException	*state* is not a valid **PermissionState**.

Remarks

This constructor creates either the fully restricted (**None**) or the **Unrestricted** form of the permission.

Requirements

Platforms: Windows 98, Windows NT 4.0, Windows Millennium Edition, Windows 2000, Windows XP Home Edition, Windows XP Professional, Windows Server 2003 family

PrintingPermission Constructor (PrintingPermissionLevel)

Initializes a new instance of the **PrintingPermission** class with the level of printing access specified.

```
[Visual Basic]
Public Sub New( _
   ByVal printingLevel As PrintingPermissionLevel _
)
[C#]
public PrintingPermission(
   PrintingPermissionLevel printingLevel
);
[C++]
public: PrintingPermission(
   PrintingPermissionLevel printingLevel
);
[JScript]
public function PrintingPermission(
   printingLevel : PrintingPermissionLevel
);
```

Parameters

printingLevel

One of the **PrintingPermissionLevel** values.

Requirements

Platforms: Windows 98, Windows NT 4.0, Windows Millennium Edition, Windows 2000, Windows XP Home Edition, Windows XP Professional, Windows Server 2003 family

PrintingPermission.Level Property

Gets or sets the code's level of printing access.

```
[Visual Basic]
Public Property Level As PrintingPermissionLevel
[C#]
public PrintingPermissionLevel Level {get; set;}
[C++]
public: __property PrintingPermissionLevel get_Level();
public: __property void set_Level(PrintingPermissionLevel);
[JScript]
public function get Level() : PrintingPermissionLevel;
public function set Level(PrintingPermissionLevel);
```

Property Value

One of the **PrintingPermissionLevel** values.

Requirements

Platforms: Windows 98, Windows NT 4.0, Windows Millennium Edition, Windows 2000, Windows XP Home Edition, Windows XP Professional, Windows Server 2003 family

PrintingPermission.Copy Method

Creates and returns an identical copy of the current permission object.

```
[Visual Basic]
Overrides Public Function Copy() As IPermission Implements _
   IPermission.Copy
[C#]
public override IPermission Copy();
[C++]
public: IPermission* Copy();
[JScript]
public override function Copy() : IPermission;
```

Return Value

A copy of the current permission object.

Implements

IPermission.Copy

Remarks

A copy of the permission object represents the same access to resources as the original permission object.

Requirements

Platforms: Windows 98, Windows NT 4.0, Windows Millennium Edition, Windows 2000, Windows XP Home Edition, Windows XP Professional, Windows Server 2003 family

PrintingPermission.FromXml Method

Reconstructs a security object with a specified state from an XML encoding.

```
[Visual Basic]
Overrides Public Sub FromXml( _
   ByVal esd As SecurityElement _
) Implements ISecurityEncodable.FromXml
[C#]
public override void FromXml(
   SecurityElement esd
);
[C++]
public: void FromXml(
   SecurityElement* esd
);
[JScript]
public override function FromXml(
   esd : SecurityElement
);
```

Parameters

esd

The XML encoding to use to reconstruct the security object.

Return Value

None.

Implements

ISecurityEncodable.FromXml

Requirements

Platforms: Windows 98, Windows NT 4.0, Windows Millennium Edition, Windows 2000, Windows XP Home Edition, Windows XP Professional, Windows Server 2003 family

PrintingPermission.Intersect Method

Creates and returns a permission that is the intersection of the current permission object and a target permission object.

```
[Visual Basic]
Overrides Public Function Intersect( _
   ByVal target As IPermission _
) As IPermission Implements IPermission.Intersect
[C#]
public override IPermission Intersect(
   IPermission target
);
[C++]
public: IPermission* Intersect(
   IPermission* target
);
[JScript]
public override function Intersect(
   target : IPermission
) : IPermission;
```

Parameters

target

A permission object of the same type as the current permission object.

Return Value

A new permission object that represents the intersection of the current object and the specified target. This object is a null reference (**Nothing** in Visual Basic) if the intersection is empty.

Implements

IPermission.Intersect

Exceptions

Exception Type	Condition
ArgumentException	*target* is an object that is not of the same type as the current permission object.

Remarks

The intersection of two permissions is a permission that describes the set of operations they both hold in common. Specifically, it represents the minimum permissions required for a demand to pass both permissions.

Requirements

Platforms: Windows 98, Windows NT 4.0, Windows Millennium Edition, Windows 2000, Windows XP Home Edition, Windows XP Professional, Windows Server 2003 family

PrintingPermission.IsSubsetOf Method

Determines whether the current permission object is a subset of the specified permission.

```
[Visual Basic]
Overrides Public Function IsSubsetOf( _
   ByVal target As IPermission _
) As Boolean Implements IPermission.IsSubsetOf
[C#]
public override bool IsSubsetOf(
   IPermission target
);
[C++]
public: bool IsSubsetOf(
   IPermission* target
);
[JScript]
public override function IsSubsetOf(
   target : IPermission
) : Boolean;
```

Parameters

target

A permission object that is to be tested for the subset relationship. This object must be of the same type as the current permission object.

Return Value

true if the current permission object is a subset of *target*; otherwise, **false**.

Implements

IPermission.IsSubsetOf

Exceptions

Exception Type	Condition
ArgumentException	*target* is an object that is not of the same type as the current permission object.

Requirements

Platforms: Windows 98, Windows NT 4.0, Windows Millennium Edition, Windows 2000, Windows XP Home Edition, Windows XP Professional, Windows Server 2003 family

PrintingPermission.IsUnrestricted Method

Gets a value indicating whether the permission is unrestricted.

```
[Visual Basic]
Public Overridable Function IsUnrestricted() As Boolean Implements _
   IUnrestrictedPermission.IsUnrestricted
[C#]
public virtual bool IsUnrestricted();
[C++]
public: virtual bool IsUnrestricted();
[JScript]
public function IsUnrestricted() : Boolean;
```

Return Value

true if permission is unrestricted; otherwise, **false**.

Implements

IUnrestrictedPermission.IsUnrestricted

Remarks

An unrestricted permission object represents access to any and all resources protected by the permission.

Requirements

Platforms: Windows 98, Windows NT 4.0, Windows Millennium Edition, Windows 2000, Windows XP Home Edition, Windows XP Professional, Windows Server 2003 family

PrintingPermission.ToXml Method

Creates an XML encoding of the security object and its current state.

```
[Visual Basic]
Overrides Public Function ToXml() As SecurityElement Implements _
   ISecurityEncodable.ToXml
[C#]
public override SecurityElement ToXml();
[C++]
public: SecurityElement* ToXml();
[JScript]
public override function ToXml() : SecurityElement;
```

Return Value

An XML encoding of the security object, including any state information.

Implements

ISecurityEncodable.ToXml

Requirements

Platforms: Windows 98, Windows NT 4.0, Windows Millennium Edition, Windows 2000, Windows XP Home Edition, Windows XP Professional, Windows Server 2003 family

PrintingPermission.Union Method

Creates a permission that combines the permission object and the target permission object.

[Visual Basic]
```
Overrides Public Function Union( _
   ByVal target As IPermission _
) As IPermission Implements IPermission.Union
```
[C#]
```
public override IPermission Union(
   IPermission target
);
```
[C++]
```
public: IPermission* Union(
   IPermission* target
);
```
[JScript]
```
public override function Union(
   target : IPermission
) : IPermission;
```

Parameters

target

A permission object of the same type as the current permission object.

Return Value

A new permission object that represents the union of the current permission object and the specified permission object.

Implements

IPermission.Union

Exceptions

Exception Type	Condition
ArgumentException	*target* is an object that is not of the same type as the current permission object.

Remarks

The result of a call to **Union** is a permission that represents all the operations represented by the current permission object, and all the operations represented by the specified permission object.

Requirements

Platforms: Windows 98, Windows NT 4.0, Windows Millennium Edition, Windows 2000, Windows XP Home Edition, Windows XP Professional, Windows Server 2003 family

PrintingPermissionAttribute Class

Allows declarative printing permission checks.

System.Object
 System.Attribute
  System.Security.Permissions.SecurityAttribute
   System.Security.Permissions.CodeAccessSecurityAttribute
    System.Drawing.Printing.PrintingPermissionAttribute

[Visual Basic]
```
<AttributeUsage(AttributeTargets.All)>
NotInheritable Public Class PrintingPermissionAttribute
   Inherits CodeAccessSecurityAttribute
```
[C#]
```
[AttributeUsage(AttributeTargets.All)]
public sealed class PrintingPermissionAttribute :
   CodeAccessSecurityAttribute
```
[C++]
```
[AttributeUsage(AttributeTargets::All)]
public __gc __sealed class PrintingPermissionAttribute : public
   CodeAccessSecurityAttribute
```
[JScript]
```
public
   AttributeUsage(AttributeTargets.All)
class PrintingPermissionAttribute extends
   CodeAccessSecurityAttribute
```

Thread Safety

Any public static (**Shared** in Visual Basic) members of this type are safe for multithreaded operations. Any instance members are not guaranteed to be thread safe.

Requirements

Namespace: System.Drawing.Printing

Platforms: Windows 98, Windows NT 4.0, Windows Millennium Edition, Windows 2000, Windows XP Home Edition, Windows XP Professional, Windows Server 2003 family

Assembly: System.Drawing (in System.Drawing.dll)

PrintingPermissionAttribute Constructor

Initializes a new instance of the **PrintingPermissionAttribute** class.

[Visual Basic]
```
Public Sub New( _
   ByVal action As SecurityAction _
)
```
[C#]
```
public PrintingPermissionAttribute(
   SecurityAction action
);
```
[C++]
```
public: PrintingPermissionAttribute(
   SecurityAction action
);
```
[JScript]
```
public function PrintingPermissionAttribute(
   action : SecurityAction
);
```

Parameters

action
 One of the **SecurityAction** values.

Requirements

Platforms: Windows 98, Windows NT 4.0, Windows Millennium Edition, Windows 2000, Windows XP Home Edition, Windows XP Professional, Windows Server 2003 family

PrintingPermissionAttribute.Level Property

Gets or sets the type of printing allowed.

[Visual Basic]
```
Public Property Level As PrintingPermissionLevel
```
[C#]
```
public PrintingPermissionLevel Level {get; set;}
```
[C++]
```
public: __property PrintingPermissionLevel get_Level();
public: __property void set_Level(PrintingPermissionLevel);
```
[JScript]
```
public function get Level() : PrintingPermissionLevel;
public function set Level(PrintingPermissionLevel);
```

Property Value

One of the **PrintingPermissionLevel** values.

Exceptions

Exception Type	Condition
ArgumentException	The value is not one of the **PrintingPermissionLevel** values.

Requirements

Platforms: Windows 98, Windows NT 4.0, Windows Millennium Edition, Windows 2000, Windows XP Home Edition, Windows XP Professional, Windows Server 2003 family

PrintingPermissionAttribute.CreatePermission Method

Creates the permission based on the requested access levels, which are set through the **Level** property on the attribute.

[Visual Basic]
```
Overrides Public Function CreatePermission() As IPermission
```
[C#]
```
public override IPermission CreatePermission();
```
[C++]
```
public: IPermission* CreatePermission();
```
[JScript]
```
public override function CreatePermission() : IPermission;
```

Return Value

An **IPermission** that represents the created permission.

Requirements

Platforms: Windows 98, Windows NT 4.0, Windows Millennium Edition, Windows 2000, Windows XP Home Edition, Windows XP Professional, Windows Server 2003 family

PrintingPermissionLevel Enumeration

Specifies the type of printing that code is allowed to do.

[Visual Basic]
```
<Serializable>
Public Enum PrintingPermissionLevel
```
[C#]
```
[Serializable]
public enum PrintingPermissionLevel
```
[C++]
```
[Serializable]
__value public enum PrintingPermissionLevel
```
[JScript]
```
public
   Serializable
enum PrintingPermissionLevel
```

Remarks

This enumeration is used by the **PrintingPermission** class.

Members

Member name	Description
AllPrinting	Provides full access to all printers.
DefaultPrinting	Provides printing programmatically to the default printer, along with safe printing through a less restricted dialog box. **DefaultPrinting** is a subset of **AllPrinting**.
NoPrinting	Prevents access to printers. **NoPrinting** is a subset of **SafePrinting**.
SafePrinting	Provides printing only from a restricted dialog box. **SafePrinting** is a subset of **DefaultPrinting**.

Requirements

Namespace: System.Drawing.Printing

Platforms: Windows 98, Windows NT 4.0, Windows Millennium Edition, Windows 2000, Windows XP Home Edition, Windows XP Professional, Windows Server 2003 family

Assembly: System.Drawing (in System.Drawing.dll)

PrintPageEventArgs Class

Provides data for the **PrintPage** event.

System.Object
  System.EventArgs
    System.Drawing.Printing.PrintPageEventArgs

[Visual Basic]
```
Public Class PrintPageEventArgs
   Inherits EventArgs
```
[C#]
```
public class PrintPageEventArgs : EventArgs
```
[C++]
```
public __gc class PrintPageEventArgs : public EventArgs
```
[JScript]
```
public class PrintPageEventArgs extends EventArgs
```

Thread Safety

Any public static (**Shared** in Visual Basic) members of this type are safe for multithreaded operations. Any instance members are not guaranteed to be thread safe.

Remarks

MarginBounds retrieves the rectangular area that represents the portion of the page between the margins. **PageBounds** retrieves the rectangular area that represents the total area of the page. **Graphics** defines the graphics object with which to do the painting. **PageSettings** retrieves the printer settings for the current page. The remaining properties indicate whether a print job should be canceled or whether a print job has more pages.

For more information on printing, see the **System.Drawing.Printing** namespace overview.

Example

[Visual Basic, C#] Use the **System.ComponentModel**, **System.Collections**, **System.Drawing**, **System.Drawing.Printing**, **System.Resources**, and **System.Windows.Forms** namespaces for this example.

[Visual Basic, C#] The following example assumes a **Button** has been created on a **Form**. The `printButton_Click` method from the example creates an instance of **PrintDocument**, calls the `pd_PrintPage` method, and prints the .bmp file specified in the `pd_PrintPage` method. To run this example, change the path to the bitmap you want to print.

[Visual Basic]
```
' Specifies what happens when the user clicks the Button.
Private Sub printButton_Click(sender As Object, e As EventArgs)
    Try
        ' Assumes the default printer.
        Dim pd As New PrintDocument()
        AddHandler pd.PrintPage, AddressOf Me.pd_PrintPage
        pd.Print()
    Catch ex As Exception
        MessageBox.Show("An error occurred while printing", _
            ex.ToString())
    End Try
End Sub

' Specifies what happens when the PrintPage event is raised.
Private Sub pd_PrintPage(sender As Object, ev As PrintPageEventArgs)
    ' Draw a picture.
    ev.Graphics.DrawImage(Image.FromFile("C:\My Folder\MyFile.bmp"), _
        ev.Graphics.VisibleClipBounds)

    ' Indicate that this is the last page to print.
    ev.HasMorePages = False
End Sub
```

[C#]
```
// Specifies what happens when the user clicks the Button.
 private void printButton_Click(object sender, EventArgs e)
 {
   try
   {
     // Assumes the default printer.
     PrintDocument pd = new PrintDocument();
     pd.PrintPage += new PrintPageEventHandler(this.pd_PrintPage);
     pd.Print();
   }
   catch(Exception ex)
   {
     MessageBox.Show("An error occurred while printing",
ex.ToString());
   }
 }

 // Specifies what happens when the PrintPage event is raised.
 private void pd_PrintPage(object sender, PrintPageEventArgs ev)
 {
   // Draw a picture.
   ev.Graphics.DrawImage(Image.FromFile
 ("C:\\My Folder\\MyFile.bmp"), ev.Graphics.VisibleClipBounds);

   // Indicate that this is the last page to print.
   ev.HasMorePages = false;
 }
```

Requirements

Namespace: System.Drawing.Printing

Platforms: Windows 98, Windows NT 4.0, Windows Millennium Edition, Windows 2000, Windows XP Home Edition, Windows XP Professional, Windows Server 2003 family

Assembly: System.Drawing (in System.Drawing.dll)

PrintPageEventArgs Constructor

Initializes a new instance of the **PrintPageEventArgs** class.

[Visual Basic]
```
Public Sub New( _
   ByVal graphics As Graphics, _
   ByVal marginBounds As Rectangle, _
   ByVal pageBounds As Rectangle, _
   ByVal pageSettings As PageSettings _
)
```
[C#]
```
public PrintPageEventArgs(
   Graphics graphics,
   Rectangle marginBounds,
   Rectangle pageBounds,
   PageSettings pageSettings
);
```
[C++]
```
public: PrintPageEventArgs(
   Graphics* graphics,
   Rectangle marginBounds,
   Rectangle pageBounds,
   PageSettings* pageSettings
);
```

[JScript]
```
public function PrintPageEventArgs(
   graphics : Graphics,
   marginBounds : Rectangle,
   pageBounds : Rectangle,
   pageSettings : PageSettings
);
```

Parameters

graphics
The **Graphics** used to paint the item.

marginBounds
The area between the margins.

pageBounds
The total area of the paper.

pageSettings
The **PageSettings** for the page.

Requirements

Platforms: Windows 98, Windows NT 4.0, Windows Millennium Edition, Windows 2000, Windows XP Home Edition, Windows XP Professional, Windows Server 2003 family

PrintPageEventArgs.Cancel Property

Gets or sets a value indicating whether the print job should be canceled.

[Visual Basic]
```
Public Property Cancel As Boolean
```
[C#]
```
public bool Cancel {get; set;}
```
[C++]
```
public: __property bool get_Cancel();
public: __property void set_Cancel(bool);
```
[JScript]
```
public function get Cancel() : Boolean;
public function set Cancel(Boolean);
```

Property Value

true if the print job should be canceled; otherwise, **false**.

Requirements

Platforms: Windows 98, Windows NT 4.0, Windows Millennium Edition, Windows 2000, Windows XP Home Edition, Windows XP Professional, Windows Server 2003 family

PrintPageEventArgs.Graphics Property

Gets the **Graphics** used to paint the page.

[Visual Basic]
```
Public ReadOnly Property Graphics As Graphics
```
[C#]
```
public Graphics Graphics {get;}
```
[C++]
```
public: __property Graphics* get_Graphics();
```
[JScript]
```
public function get Graphics() : Graphics;
```

Property Value

The **Graphics** used to paint the page.

Example

[Visual Basic, C#] Use the **System.ComponentModel**, **System.Collections**, **System.Drawing**, **System.Drawing.Printing**, **System.Resources**, and **System.Windows.Forms** namespaces for this example.

[Visual Basic, C#] The following example assumes a **Button** has been created on a **Form**. The `printButton_Click` method from the example creates an instance of **PrintDocument**, calls the `pd_PrintPage` method, and prints the .bmp file specified in the `pd_PrintPage` method. To run this example, change the path to the bitmap you want to print.

[Visual Basic]
```
' Specifies what happens when the user clicks the Button.
Private Sub printButton_Click(sender As Object, e As EventArgs)
    Try
        ' Assumes the default printer.
        Dim pd As New PrintDocument()
        AddHandler pd.PrintPage, AddressOf Me.pd_PrintPage
        pd.Print()
    Catch ex As Exception
        MessageBox.Show("An error occurred while printing", _
            ex.ToString())
    End Try
End Sub

' Specifies what happens when the PrintPage event is raised.
Private Sub pd_PrintPage(sender As Object, ev As PrintPageEventArgs)
    ' Draw a picture.
    ev.Graphics.DrawImage(Image.FromFile("C:\My Folder\MyFile.bmp"), _
        ev.Graphics.VisibleClipBounds)

    ' Indicate that this is the last page to print.
    ev.HasMorePages = False
End Sub
```

[C#]
```
// Specifies what happens when the user clicks the Button.
 private void printButton_Click(object sender, EventArgs e)
 {
   try
   {
     // Assumes the default printer.
     PrintDocument pd = new PrintDocument();
     pd.PrintPage += new PrintPageEventHandler(this.pd_PrintPage);
     pd.Print();
   }
   catch(Exception ex)
   {
     MessageBox.Show("An error occurred while printing",                ↵
ex.ToString());
   }
 }

 // Specifies what happens when the PrintPage event is raised.
 private void pd_PrintPage(object sender, PrintPageEventArgs ev)
 {
   // Draw a picture.
   ev.Graphics.DrawImage                                              ↵
(Image.FromFile("C:\\My Folder\\MyFile.bmp"),                         ↵
ev.Graphics.VisibleClipBounds);

   // Indicate that this is the last page to print.
   ev.HasMorePages = false;
 }
```

Requirements

Platforms: Windows 98, Windows NT 4.0, Windows Millennium Edition, Windows 2000, Windows XP Home Edition, Windows XP Professional, Windows Server 2003 family

PrintPageEventArgs.HasMorePages Property

Gets or sets a value indicating whether an additional page should be printed.

[Visual Basic]
```
Public Property HasMorePages As Boolean
```
[C#]
```
public bool HasMorePages {get; set;}
```
[C++]
```
public: __property bool get_HasMorePages();
public: __property void set_HasMorePages(bool);
```
[JScript]
```
public function get HasMorePages() : Boolean;
public function set HasMorePages(Boolean);
```

Property Value

true if an additional page should be printed; otherwise, **false**. The default is **false**.

Example

[Visual Basic, C#] Use the **System.ComponentModel**, **System.Collections**, **System.Drawing**, **System.Drawing.Printing**, **System.Resources**, and **System.Windows.Forms** namespaces for this example.

[Visual Basic, C#] The following example assumes a **Button** has been created on a **Form**. The `printButton_Click` method from the example creates an instance of **PrintDocument**, calls the `pd_PrintPage` method, and prints the .bmp file specified in the `pd_PrintPage` method. To run this example, change the path to the bitmap you want to print.

[Visual Basic]
```
' Specifies what happens when the user clicks the Button.
Private Sub printButton_Click(sender As Object, e As EventArgs)
    Try
        ' Assumes the default printer.
        Dim pd As New PrintDocument()
        AddHandler pd.PrintPage, AddressOf Me.pd_PrintPage
        pd.Print()
    Catch ex As Exception
        MessageBox.Show("An error occurred while printing", _
            ex.ToString())
    End Try
End Sub

' Specifies what happens when the PrintPage event is raised.
Private Sub pd_PrintPage(sender As Object, ev As PrintPageEventArgs)
    ' Draw a picture.
    ev.Graphics.DrawImage(Image.FromFile("C:\My Folder\MyFile.bmp"), _
        ev.Graphics.VisibleClipBounds)

    ' Indicate that this is the last page to print.
    ev.HasMorePages = False
End Sub
```

[C#]
```
// Specifies what happens when the user clicks the Button.
 private void printButton_Click(object sender, EventArgs e)
 {
   try
   {
     // Assumes the default printer.
     PrintDocument pd = new PrintDocument();
     pd.PrintPage += new PrintPageEventHandler(this.pd_PrintPage);
     pd.Print();
   }
   catch(Exception ex)
   {
     MessageBox.Show("An error occurred while printing",            ↵
ex.ToString());
   }
 }

// Specifies what happens when the PrintPage event is raised.
private void pd_PrintPage(object sender, PrintPageEventArgs ev)
{
  // Draw a picture.
  ev.Graphics.DrawImage(Image.FromFile                              ↵
("C:\\My Folder\\MyFile.bmp"), ev.Graphics.VisibleClipBounds);

  // Indicate that this is the last page to print.
  ev.HasMorePages = false;
}
```

Requirements

Platforms: Windows 98, Windows NT 4.0, Windows Millennium Edition, Windows 2000, Windows XP Home Edition, Windows XP Professional, Windows Server 2003 family

PrintPageEventArgs.MarginBounds Property

Gets the rectangular area that represents the portion of the page inside the margins.

[Visual Basic]
```
Public ReadOnly Property MarginBounds As Rectangle
```
[C#]
```
public Rectangle MarginBounds {get;}
```
[C++]
```
public: __property Rectangle get_MarginBounds();
```
[JScript]
```
public function get MarginBounds() : Rectangle;
```

Property Value

The rectangular area that represents the portion of the page inside the margins. Measurement is in hundredths of an inch.

Requirements

Platforms: Windows 98, Windows NT 4.0, Windows Millennium Edition, Windows 2000, Windows XP Home Edition, Windows XP Professional, Windows Server 2003 family

PrintPageEventArgs.PageBounds Property

Gets the rectangular area that represents the total area of the page.

[Visual Basic]
```
Public ReadOnly Property PageBounds As Rectangle
```
[C#]
```
public Rectangle PageBounds {get;}
```
[C++]
```
public: __property Rectangle get_PageBounds();
```
[JScript]
```
public function get PageBounds() : Rectangle;
```

Property Value

The rectangular area that represents the total area of the page.

Remarks

Note Most printers cannot print at the very edge of the page.

Requirements

Platforms: Windows 98, Windows NT 4.0, Windows Millennium Edition, Windows 2000, Windows XP Home Edition, Windows XP Professional, Windows Server 2003 family

PrintPageEventArgs.PageSettings Property

Gets the page settings for the current page.

[Visual Basic]
```
Public ReadOnly Property PageSettings As PageSettings
```
[C#]
```
public PageSettings PageSettings {get;}
```
[C++]
```
public: __property PageSettings* get_PageSettings();
```
[JScript]
```
public function get PageSettings() : PageSettings;
```

Property Value

The page settings for the current page.

Requirements

Platforms: Windows 98, Windows NT 4.0, Windows Millennium Edition, Windows 2000, Windows XP Home Edition, Windows XP Professional, Windows Server 2003 family

PrintPageEventHandler Delegate

Represents the method that will handle the **PrintPage** event of a **PrintDocument**.

[Visual Basic]

```
<Serializable>
Public Delegate Sub PrintPageEventHandler( _
   ByVal sender As Object, _
   ByVal e As PrintPageEventArgs _
)
```

[C#]

```
[Serializable]
public delegate void PrintPageEventHandler(
   object sender,
   PrintPageEventArgs e
);
```

[C++]

```
[Serializable]
public __gc __delegate void PrintPageEventHandler(
   Object* sender,
   PrintPageEventArgs* e
);
```

[JScript] In JScript, you can use the delegates in the .NET Framework, but you cannot define your own.

Parameters [Visual Basic, C#, C++]

The declaration of your event handler must have the same parameters as the **PrintPageEventHandler** delegate declaration.

sender

The source of the event.

e

A **PrintPageEventArgs** that contains the event data.

Remarks

When you create a **PrintPageEventHandler** delegate, you identify the method that will handle the event. To associate the event with your event handler, add an instance of the delegate to the event. The event handler is called whenever the event occurs, unless you remove the delegate.

For more information on printing, see the **System.Drawing.Printing** namespace overview.

Requirements

Namespace: System.Drawing.Printing

Platforms: Windows 98, Windows NT 4.0, Windows Millennium Edition, Windows 2000, Windows XP Home Edition, Windows XP Professional, Windows Server 2003 family

Assembly: System.Drawing (in System.Drawing.dll)

PrintRange Enumeration

Specifies the part of the document to print.

[Visual Basic]
```
<Serializable>
Public Enum PrintRange
```
[C#]
```
[Serializable]
public enum PrintRange
```
[C++]
```
[Serializable]
__value public enum PrintRange
```
[JScript]
```
public
   Serializable
enum PrintRange
```

Remarks

The **PrinterSettings** and **PrintDialog** classes use this enumeration.

For more information on printing, see the **System.Drawing.Printing** namespace overview.

Members

Member name	Description
AllPages	All pages are printed.
Selection	The selected pages are printed.
SomePages	The pages between **FromPage** and **ToPage** are printed.

Requirements

Namespace: System.Drawing.Printing

Platforms: Windows 98, Windows NT 4.0, Windows Millennium Edition, Windows 2000, Windows XP Home Edition, Windows XP Professional, Windows Server 2003 family

Assembly: System.Drawing (in System.Drawing.dll)

QueryPageSettingsEventArgs Class

Provides data for the **QueryPageSettings** event.

System.Object
System.EventArgs
System.ComponentModel.CancelEventArgs
System.Drawing.Printing.PrintEventArgs
System.Drawing.Printing.QueryPageSettingsEventArgs

[Visual Basic]
```
Public Class QueryPageSettingsEventArgs
   Inherits PrintEventArgs
```
[C#]
```
public class QueryPageSettingsEventArgs : PrintEventArgs
```
[C++]
```
public __gc class QueryPageSettingsEventArgs : public
   PrintEventArgs
```
[JScript]
```
public class QueryPageSettingsEventArgs extends PrintEventArgs
```

Thread Safety

Any public static (**Shared** in Visual Basic) members of this type are safe for multithreaded operations. Any instance members are not guaranteed to be thread safe.

Remarks

It is possible to print each page of a document using different page settings. You set page settings by modifying individual properties of the **PageSettings** property or by setting the property to a **PageSettings**. The print job can also be canceled by setting the **Cancel** property to **true**.

To associate the event with your event handler, add an instance of the **QueryPageSettingsEventHandler** delegate to the **QueryPageSettings** event. The event handler is called whenever the event occurs. For more information about handling events with delegates, see **Events and Delegates**.

Example

[Visual Basic, C#, C++] The following example prints a document with the first page in color, if the printer supports it. The example assumes that a **PrintDocument** variable named `printDoc` has been created, and the **PrintPage** and **QueryPageSettings** events are handled.

[Visual Basic, C#, C++] Use the **System.Drawing** and **System.Drawing.Printing** namespaces for this example.

[Visual Basic]
```
    Private Sub MyButtonPrint_OnClick(ByVal sender As Object, ↵
ByVal e As System.EventArgs)

        ' Set the printer name and ensure it is valid. If not, ↵
provide a message to the user.
        printDoc.PrinterSettings.PrinterName = "\\mynetworkprinter"

        If printDoc.PrinterSettings.IsValid Then

            ' If the printer supports printing in color, then ↵
override the printer's default behavior.
            if printDoc.PrinterSettings.SupportsColor then

                ' Set the page default's to not print in color.
                printDoc.DefaultPageSettings.Color = False
            End If

            ' Provide a friendly name, set the page number, ↵
and print the document.
            printDoc.DocumentName = "My Presentation"
            currentPageNumber = 1
            printDoc.Print()
        Else
            MessageBox.Show("Printer is not valid")
        End If
    End Sub

    Private Sub MyPrintQueryPageSettingsEvent(ByVal sender As ↵
Object, ByVal e As QueryPageSettingsEventArgs)

        ' Determines if the printer supports printing in color.
        If printDoc.PrinterSettings.SupportsColor Then

            ' If the printer supports color printing, use color.
            If currentPageNumber = 1 Then

                e.PageSettings.Color = True
            End If

        End If
    End Sub
```
[C#]
```
    private void MyButtonPrint_OnClick(object sender, ↵
System.EventArgs e)
    {

        // Set the printer name and ensure it is valid. If not, ↵
provide a message to the user.
        printDoc.PrinterSettings.PrinterName = "\\mynetworkprinter";

        if (printDoc.PrinterSettings.IsValid) {

            // If the printer supports printing in color, then ↵
override the printer's default behavior.
            if (printDoc.PrinterSettings.SupportsColor) {

                // Set the page default's to not print in color.
                printDoc.DefaultPageSettings.Color = false;
            }

            // Provide a friendly name, set the page number, and ↵
print the document.
            printDoc.DocumentName = "My Presentation";
            currentPageNumber = 1;
            printDoc.Print();
        }
        else {
            MessageBox.Show("Printer is not valid");
        }
    }

    private void MyPrintQueryPageSettingsEvent(object sender, ↵
QueryPageSettingsEventArgs e)
    {
        // Determines if the printer supports printing in color.
        if (printDoc.PrinterSettings.SupportsColor) {

            // If the printer supports color printing, use color.
            if (currentPageNumber == 1 ) {

                e.PageSettings.Color = true;
            }

        }
    }
```
[C++]
```
private:
    void MyButtonPrint_OnClick(Object* sender, System::EventArgs* e) {

        // Set the printer name and ensure it is valid. If not, ↵
provide a message to the user.
        printDoc->PrinterSettings->PrinterName = S"\\mynetworkprinter";

        if (printDoc->PrinterSettings->IsValid) {
```

```
        // If the printer supports printing in color, then  the ↵
printer's default behavior.
        if (printDoc->PrinterSettings->SupportsColor) {

           // Set the page default's to not print in color.
           printDoc->DefaultPageSettings->Color = false;
        }

        // Provide a friendly name, set the page number, and ↵
 print the document.
        printDoc->DocumentName = S"My Presentation";
        currentPageNumber = 1;
        printDoc->Print();
     } else {
        MessageBox::Show(S"Printer is not valid");
     }
  }

private:
   void MyPrintQueryPageSettingsEvent(Object* sender, ↵
QueryPageSettingsEventArgs* e) {
      // Determines if the printer supports printing in color.
      if (printDoc->PrinterSettings->SupportsColor) {

         // If the printer supports color printing, use color.
         if (currentPageNumber == 1) {

            e->PageSettings->Color = true;
         }

      }
  }
```

Requirements

Namespace: System.Drawing.Printing

Platforms: Windows 98, Windows NT 4.0, Windows Millennium Edition, Windows 2000, Windows XP Home Edition, Windows XP Professional, Windows Server 2003 family

Assembly: System.Drawing (in System.Drawing.dll)

QueryPageSettingsEventArgs Constructor

Initializes a new instance of the **QueryPageSettingsEventArgs** class.

[Visual Basic]
```
Public Sub New( _
   ByVal pageSettings As PageSettings _
)
```
[C#]
```
public QueryPageSettingsEventArgs(
   PageSettings pageSettings
);
```
[C++]
```
public: QueryPageSettingsEventArgs(
   PageSettings* pageSettings
);
```
[JScript]
```
public function QueryPageSettingsEventArgs(
   pageSettings : PageSettings
);
```

Parameters

pageSettings

The page settings for the page to be printed.

Requirements

Platforms: Windows 98, Windows NT 4.0, Windows Millennium Edition, Windows 2000, Windows XP Home Edition, Windows XP Professional, Windows Server 2003 family

QueryPageSettingsEventArgs.PageSettings Property

Gets or sets the page settings for the page to be printed.

[Visual Basic]
```
Public Property PageSettings As PageSettings
```
[C#]
```
public PageSettings PageSettings {get; set;}
```
[C++]
```
public: __property PageSettings* get_PageSettings();
public: __property void set_PageSettings(PageSettings*);
```
[JScript]
```
public function get PageSettings() : PageSettings;
public function set PageSettings(PageSettings);
```

Property Value

The page settings for the page to be printed.

Remarks

It is possible to print each page of a document using different page settings. You set page settings by modifying individual properties of the **PageSettings** property or by setting the property to a **PageSettings**. The print job can also be canceled by setting the **Cancel** property to **true**.

To associate the event with your event handler, add an instance of the **QueryPageSettingsEventHandler** delegate to the **QueryPageSettings** event. The event handler is called whenever the event occurs.

Example

[Visual Basic, C#, C++] The following example prints a document with the first page in color, if the printer supports it. The example assumes that a **PrintDocument** variable named `printDoc` has been created, and the **PrintPage** and **QueryPageSettings** events are handled.

[Visual Basic, C#, C++] Use the **System.Drawing** and **System.Drawing.Printing** namespaces for this example.

[Visual Basic]

```
    Private Sub MyButtonPrint_OnClick(ByVal sender As Object, ↵
ByVal e As System.EventArgs)

        ' Set the printer name and ensure it is valid. If not, ↵
 provide a message to the user.
        printDoc.PrinterSettings.PrinterName = "\\mynetworkprinter"

        If printDoc.PrinterSettings.IsValid Then

            ' If the printer supports printing in color, then ↵
override the printer's default behavior.
            if printDoc.PrinterSettings.SupportsColor then

                ' Set the page default's to not print in color.
                printDoc.DefaultPageSettings.Color = False
            End If

            ' Provide a friendly name, set the page number, ↵
and print the document.
```

```
            printDoc.DocumentName = "My Presentation"
            currentPageNumber = 1
            printDoc.Print()
        Else
            MessageBox.Show("Printer is not valid")
        End If
    End Sub

    Private Sub MyPrintQueryPageSettingsEvent(ByVal sender As ↵
Object, ByVal e As QueryPageSettingsEventArgs)

        ' Determines if the printer supports printing in color.
        If printDoc.PrinterSettings.SupportsColor Then

            ' If the printer supports color printing, use color.
            If currentPageNumber = 1 Then

                e.PageSettings.Color = True
            End If

        End If
    End Sub
```

[C#]

```
    private void MyButtonPrint_OnClick(object sender, ↵
System.EventArgs e)
    {

        // Set the printer name and ensure it is valid. If not, ↵
provide a message to the user.
        printDoc.PrinterSettings.PrinterName = "\\mynetworkprinter";

        if (printDoc.PrinterSettings.IsValid) {

            // If the printer supports printing in color, then ↵
override the printer's default behavior.
            if (printDoc.PrinterSettings.SupportsColor) {

                // Set the page default's to not print in color.
                printDoc.DefaultPageSettings.Color = false;
            }

            // Provide a friendly name, set the page number, ↵
and print the document.
            printDoc.DocumentName = "My Presentation";
            currentPageNumber = 1;
            printDoc.Print();
        }
        else {
            MessageBox.Show("Printer is not valid");
        }
    }

    private void MyPrintQueryPageSettingsEvent(object sender, ↵
QueryPageSettingsEventArgs e)
    {
        // Determines if the printer supports printing in color.
        if (printDoc.PrinterSettings.SupportsColor) {

            // If the printer supports color printing, use color.
            if (currentPageNumber == 1 ) {

                e.PageSettings.Color = true;
            }

        }
    }
```

[C++]

```
private:
   void MyButtonPrint_OnClick(Object* sender, System::EventArgs* e) {

      // Set the printer name and ensure it is valid. If not, ↵
provide a message to the user.
      printDoc->PrinterSettings->PrinterName = S"\\mynetworkprinter";

      if (printDoc->PrinterSettings->IsValid) {

         // If the printer supports printing in color, then ↵
the printer's default behavior.
         if (printDoc->PrinterSettings->SupportsColor) {

            // Set the page default's to not print in color.
            printDoc->DefaultPageSettings->Color = false;
         }

         // Provide a friendly name, set the page number, and ↵
print the document.
         printDoc->DocumentName = S"My Presentation";
         currentPageNumber = 1;
         printDoc->Print();
      } else {
         MessageBox::Show(S"Printer is not valid");
      }
   }

private:
   void MyPrintQueryPageSettingsEvent(Object* sender, ↵
QueryPageSettingsEventArgs* e) {
      // Determines if the printer supports printing in color.
      if (printDoc->PrinterSettings->SupportsColor) {

         // If the printer supports color printing, use color.
         if (currentPageNumber == 1) {

            e->PageSettings->Color = true;
         }

      }
   }
```

Requirements

Platforms: Windows 98, Windows NT 4.0, Windows Millennium Edition, Windows 2000, Windows XP Home Edition, Windows XP Professional, Windows Server 2003 family

QueryPageSettingsEventHandler Delegate

Represents the method that handles the **QueryPageSettings** event of a **PrintDocument**.

[Visual Basic]
```
<Serializable>
Public Delegate Sub QueryPageSettingsEventHandler( _
   ByVal sender As Object, _
   ByVal e As QueryPageSettingsEventArgs _
)
```
[C#]
```
[Serializable]
public delegate void QueryPageSettingsEventHandler(
   object sender,
   QueryPageSettingsEventArgs e
);
```
[C++]
```
[Serializable]
public __gc __delegate void QueryPageSettingsEventHandler(
   Object* sender,
   QueryPageSettingsEventArgs* e
);
```
[JScript] In JScript, you can use the delegates in the .NET Framework, but you cannot define your own.

Parameters [Visual Basic, C#, C++]

The declaration of your event handler must have the same parameters as the **QueryPageSettingsEventHandler** delegate declaration.

sender

The source of the event.

e

A **QueryPageSettingsEventArgs** that contains the event data.

Remarks

When you create a **QueryPageSettingsEventHandler** delegate, you identify the method that will handle the event. To associate the event with your event handler, add an instance of the delegate to the event. The event handler is called whenever the event occurs, unless you remove the delegate.

For more information on printing, see the **System.Drawing.Printing** namespace overview.

Requirements

Namespace: System.Drawing.Printing

Platforms: Windows 98, Windows NT 4.0, Windows Millennium Edition, Windows 2000, Windows XP Home Edition, Windows XP Professional, Windows Server 2003 family

Assembly: System.Drawing (in System.Drawing.dll)

StandardPrintController Class

Specifies a print controller that sends information to a printer.

System.Object
  System.Drawing.Printing.PrintController
    System.Drawing.Printing.StandardPrintController

```
[Visual Basic]
Public Class StandardPrintController
   Inherits PrintController
[C#]
public class StandardPrintController : PrintController
[C++]
public __gc class StandardPrintController : public PrintController
[JScript]
public class StandardPrintController extends PrintController
```

Thread Safety

Any public static (**Shared** in Visual Basic) members of this type are safe for multithreaded operations. Any instance members are not guaranteed to be thread safe.

Remarks

PrintDocument uses this class.

For more information on printing, see the **System.Drawing.Printing** namespace overview.

Requirements

Namespace: System.Drawing.Printing

Platforms: Windows 98, Windows NT 4.0, Windows Millennium Edition, Windows 2000, Windows XP Home Edition, Windows XP Professional, Windows Server 2003 family

Assembly: System.Drawing (in System.Drawing.dll)

StandardPrintController Constructor

Initializes a new instance of the **StandardPrintController** class.

```
[Visual Basic]
Public Sub New()
[C#]
public StandardPrintController();
[C++]
public: StandardPrintController();
[JScript]
public function StandardPrintController();
```

Remarks

The default constructor initializes any fields to their default values.

Requirements

Platforms: Windows 98, Windows NT 4.0, Windows Millennium Edition, Windows 2000, Windows XP Home Edition, Windows XP Professional, Windows Server 2003 family

StandardPrintController.OnEndPage Method

Completes the control sequence that determines when and how to print a page of a document.

```
[Visual Basic]
Overrides Public Sub OnEndPage( _
   ByVal document As PrintDocument, _
   ByVal e As PrintPageEventArgs _
)
[C#]
public override void OnEndPage(
   PrintDocument document,
   PrintPageEventArgs e
);
[C++]
public: void OnEndPage(
   PrintDocument* document,
   PrintPageEventArgs* e
);
[JScript]
public override function OnEndPage(
   document : PrintDocument,
   e : PrintPageEventArgs
);
```

Parameters

document
  A **PrintDocument** that represents the document being printed.

e
  A **PrintPageEventArgs** that contains data about how to print a page in the document.

Exceptions

Exception Type	Condition
Win32Exception	The native Win32 Application Programming Interface (API) could not finish writing to a page.

Remarks

OnEndPage is called immediately after the **PrintDocument** raises the **PrintPage** event. If an exception is thrown inside a **PrintPage** event of a **PrintDocument**, **OnEndPage** is not called.

OnStartPrint creates the **Graphics** object that is sent to the printer. After **OnStartPrint** is called, the **OnStartPage** method sets the **Graphics** object to a graphic of a single page. The **OnEndPage** method clears the **Graphics** object, while the **OnEndPrint** method deallocates the object.

Requirements

Platforms: Windows 98, Windows NT 4.0, Windows Millennium Edition, Windows 2000, Windows XP Home Edition, Windows XP Professional, Windows Server 2003 family

StandardPrintController.OnEndPrint Method

Completes the control sequence that determines when and how to print a document.

[Visual Basic]
```
Overrides Public Sub OnEndPrint( _
   ByVal document As PrintDocument, _
   ByVal e As PrintEventArgs _
)
```
[C#]
```
public override void OnEndPrint(
   PrintDocument document,
   PrintEventArgs e
);
```
[C++]
```
public: void OnEndPrint(
   PrintDocument* document,
   PrintEventArgs* e
);
```
[JScript]
```
public override function OnEndPrint(
   document : PrintDocument,
   e : PrintEventArgs
);
```

Parameters

document

A **PrintDocument** that represents the document being printed.

e

A **PrintEventArgs** that contains data about how to print the document.

Exceptions

Exception Type	Condition
Win32Exception	The native Win32 Application Programming Interface (API) could not complete the print job. -or- The native Win32 API could not delete the specified device context (DC).

Remarks

OnEndPrint is called immediately after **PrintDocument** raises the **EndPrint** event. Even if an uncaught exception was thrown during the printing process, **OnEndPrint** is called.

OnStartPrint creates the **Graphics** object that is sent to the printer. After **OnStartPrint** is called, the **OnStartPage** method sets the **Graphics** object to a graphic of a single page. The **OnEndPage** method clears the **Graphics** object, while the **OnEndPrint** method deallocates the object.

Requirements

Platforms: Windows 98, Windows NT 4.0, Windows Millennium Edition, Windows 2000, Windows XP Home Edition, Windows XP Professional, Windows Server 2003 family

StandardPrintController.OnStartPage Method

Begins the control sequence that determines when and how to print a page in a document.

[Visual Basic]
```
Overrides Public Function OnStartPage( _
   ByVal document As PrintDocument, _
   ByVal e As PrintPageEventArgs _
) As Graphics
```
[C#]
```
public override Graphics OnStartPage(
   PrintDocument document,
   PrintPageEventArgs e
);
```
[C++]
```
public: Graphics* OnStartPage(
   PrintDocument* document,
   PrintPageEventArgs* e
);
```
[JScript]
```
public override function OnStartPage(
   document : PrintDocument,
   e : PrintPageEventArgs
) : Graphics;
```

Parameters

document

A **PrintDocument** that represents the document being printed.

e

A **PrintPageEventArgs** that contains data about how to print a page in the document. Initially, the **PrintPageEventArgs.Graphics** property of this parameter will be a null reference (**Nothing** in Visual Basic). The value returned from the **OnStartPage** method will be used to set this property.

Return Value

A **Graphics** object that represents a page from a **PrintDocument**.

Exceptions

Exception Type	Condition
Win32Exception	The native Win32 Application Programming Interface (API) could not prepare the printer driver to accept data. -or- The native Win32 API could not update the specified printer or plotter device context (DC) using the specified information.

Remarks

OnStartPage is called immediately before **PrintDocument** raises the **PrintPage** event.

OnStartPrint creates the **Graphics** object used in printing. After **OnStartPrint** is called, the **OnStartPage** method sets the **Graphics** object to a graphic of a single page. The **OnEndPage** method clears the **Graphics** object, while the **OnEndPrint** method deallocates the object.

Requirements

Platforms: Windows 98, Windows NT 4.0, Windows Millennium Edition, Windows 2000, Windows XP Home Edition, Windows XP Professional, Windows Server 2003 family

StandardPrintController.OnStartPrint Method

Begins the control sequence that determines when and how to print a document.

[Visual Basic]
```
Overrides Public Sub OnStartPrint( _
   ByVal document As PrintDocument, _
   ByVal e As PrintEventArgs _
)
```
[C#]
```
public override void OnStartPrint(
   PrintDocument document,
   PrintEventArgs e
);
```
[C++]
```
public: void OnStartPrint(
   PrintDocument* document,
   PrintEventArgs* e
);
```
[JScript]
```
public override function OnStartPrint(
   document : PrintDocument,
   e : PrintEventArgs
);
```

Parameters

document

A **PrintDocument** that represents the document being printed.

e

A **PrintEventArgs** that contains data about how to print the document.

Exceptions

Exception Type	Condition
InvalidPrinterException	The printer settings are not valid.
Win32Exception	The native Win32 Application Programming Interface (API) could not start a print job.

Remarks

OnStartPrint is called immediately after **PrintDocument** raises the **BeginPrint** event.

OnStartPrint creates the **Graphics** object used in printing. After **OnStartPrint** is called, the **OnStartPage** method sets the **Graphics** object to a graphic of a single page. The **OnEndPage** method clears the **Graphics** object, while the **OnEndPrint** method deallocates the object.

OnStartPrint verifies that the printer settings are valid.

Requirements

Platforms: Windows 98, Windows NT 4.0, Windows Millennium Edition, Windows 2000, Windows XP Home Edition, Windows XP Professional, Windows Server 2003 family

System.Drawing.Text Namespace

The **System.Drawing.Text** namespace provides advanced GDI+ typography functionality. Basic graphics functionality is provided by the **System.Drawing** namespace. The classes in this namespace allow users to create and use collections of fonts.

FontCollection Class

Base class for installed and private font collections. Provides a method to get a list of the font families contained in the collection.

System.Object
  System.Drawing.Text.FontCollection
    System.Drawing.Text.InstalledFontCollection
    System.Drawing.Text.PrivateFontCollection

```
[Visual Basic]
MustInherit Public Class FontCollection
   Implements IDisposable
[C#]
public abstract class FontCollection : IDisposable
[C++]
public __gc __abstract class FontCollection : public IDisposable
[JScript]
public abstract class FontCollection implements IDisposable
```

Thread Safety

Any public static (**Shared** in Visual Basic) members of this type are safe for multithreaded operations. Any instance members are not guaranteed to be thread safe.

Requirements

Namespace: System.Drawing.Text

Platforms: Windows 98, Windows NT 4.0, Windows Millennium Edition, Windows 2000, Windows XP Home Edition, Windows XP Professional, Windows Server 2003 family

Assembly: System.Drawing (in System.Drawing.dll)

FontCollection.Families Property

Gets the array of **FontFamily** objects associated with this **FontCollection** object. For additional information on fonts and text, including example code, see **Fonts and Text** in the Using GDI+ Managed Classes section of these documents.

```
[Visual Basic]
Public ReadOnly Property Families As FontFamily ()
[C#]
public FontFamily[] Families {get;}
[C++]
public: __property FontFamily* get_Families();
[JScript]
public function get Families() : FontFamily[];
```

Property Value

An array of **FontFamily** objects.

Requirements

Platforms: Windows 98, Windows NT 4.0, Windows Millennium Edition, Windows 2000, Windows XP Home Edition, Windows XP Professional, Windows Server 2003 family

FontCollection.Dispose Method

Overload List

Releases all resources used by this **FontCollection** object.

[Visual Basic] **Overloads Public Overridable Sub Dispose() Implements IDisposable.Dispose**

[C#] **public virtual void Dispose();**

[C++] **public: virtual void Dispose();**

[JScript] **public function Dispose();**

This member supports the .NET Framework infrastructure and is not intended to be used directly from your code.

[Visual Basic] **Overloads Protected Overridable Sub Dispose(Boolean)**

[C#] **protected virtual void Dispose(bool);**

[C++] **protected: virtual void Dispose(bool);**

[JScript] **protected function Dispose(Boolean);**

FontCollection.Dispose Method ()

Releases all resources used by this **FontCollection** object.

```
[Visual Basic]
Overloads Public Overridable Sub Dispose() Implements _
   IDisposable.Dispose
[C#]
public virtual void Dispose();
[C++]
public: virtual void Dispose();
[JScript]
public function Dispose();
```

Return Value

This method does not return a value.

Implements

IDisposable.Dispose

Remarks

Calling **Dispose** allows the resources used by this **FontCollection** object to be reallocated for other purposes.

Requirements

Platforms: Windows 98, Windows NT 4.0, Windows Millennium Edition, Windows 2000, Windows XP Home Edition, Windows XP Professional, Windows Server 2003 family

FontCollection.Dispose Method (Boolean)

This member supports the .NET Framework infrastructure and is not intended to be used directly from your code.

```
[Visual Basic]
Overloads Protected Overridable Sub Dispose( _
   ByVal disposing As Boolean _
)
[C#]
protected virtual void Dispose(
   bool disposing
);
[C++]
protected: virtual void Dispose(
   bool disposing
);
[JScript]
protected function Dispose(
   disposing : Boolean
);
```

FontCollection.Finalize Method

This member overrides **Object.Finalize**.

```
[Visual Basic]
Overrides Protected Sub Finalize()
[C#]
~FontCollection();
[C++]
~FontCollection();
[JScript]
protected override function Finalize();
```

Requirements

Platforms: Windows 98, Windows NT 4.0, Windows Millennium Edition, Windows 2000, Windows XP Home Edition, Windows XP Professional, Windows Server 2003 family

GenericFontFamilies Enumeration

Specifies a generic **FontFamily** object.

[Visual Basic]
```
<Serializable>
Public Enum GenericFontFamilies
```
[C#]
```
[Serializable]
public enum GenericFontFamilies
```
[C++]
```
[Serializable]
__value public enum GenericFontFamilies
```
[JScript]
```
public
   Serializable
enum GenericFontFamilies
```

Members

Member name	Description
Monospace	A generic Monospace **FontFamily** object.
SansSerif	A generic Sans Serif **FontFamily** object.
Serif	A generic Serif **FontFamily** object.

Requirements

Namespace: System.Drawing.Text

Platforms: Windows 98, Windows NT 4.0, Windows Millennium Edition, Windows 2000, Windows XP Home Edition, Windows XP Professional, Windows Server 2003 family

Assembly: System.Drawing (in System.Drawing.dll)

HotkeyPrefix Enumeration

Specifies the type of display for hot-key prefixes that relate to text.

[Visual Basic]
```
<Serializable>
Public Enum HotkeyPrefix
```
[C#]
```
[Serializable]
public enum HotkeyPrefix
```
[C++]
```
[Serializable]
__value public enum HotkeyPrefix
```
[JScript]
```
public
   Serializable
enum HotkeyPrefix
```

Remarks

A hot-key prefix allows you to use a keyboard combination (usually CTRL+< *HotKey*> or ALT+< *HotKey*>) to access functionality represented by text displayed on the screen.

Members

Member name	Description
Hide	Do not display the hot-key prefix.
None	No hot-key prefix.
Show	Display the hot-key prefix.

Requirements

Namespace: System.Drawing.Text

Platforms: Windows 98, Windows NT 4.0, Windows Millennium Edition, Windows 2000, Windows XP Home Edition, Windows XP Professional, Windows Server 2003 family

Assembly: System.Drawing (in System.Drawing.dll)

InstalledFontCollection Class

Represents the fonts installed on the system. This class cannot be inherited.

System.Object
  System.Drawing.Text.FontCollection
    System.Drawing.Text.InstalledFontCollection

[Visual Basic]
```
NotInheritable Public Class InstalledFontCollection
   Inherits FontCollection
```
[C#]
```
public sealed class InstalledFontCollection : FontCollection
```
[C++]
```
public __gc __sealed class InstalledFontCollection : public
   FontCollection
```
[JScript]
```
public class InstalledFontCollection extends FontCollection
```

Thread Safety

Any public static (**Shared** in Visual Basic) members of this type are safe for multithreaded operations. Any instance members are not guaranteed to be thread safe.

Remarks

GDI+ applications should not use the **InstalledFontCollection** class to install a font to Windows. Instead use the GDI **AddFontResource** function. An **InstalledFontCollection** object sees only fonts that are installed in Windows before the object is created.

Requirements

Namespace: System.Drawing.Text

Platforms: Windows 98, Windows NT 4.0, Windows Millennium Edition, Windows 2000, Windows XP Home Edition, Windows XP Professional, Windows Server 2003 family

Assembly: System.Drawing (in System.Drawing.dll)

InstalledFontCollection Constructor

Initializes a new instance of the **InstalledFontCollection** class. For additional information on fonts and text, including example code, see **Fonts and Text** in the Using GDI+ Managed Classes section of these documents.

[Visual Basic]
```
Public Sub New()
```
[C#]
```
public InstalledFontCollection();
```
[C++]
```
public: InstalledFontCollection();
```
[JScript]
```
public function InstalledFontCollection();
```

Requirements

Platforms: Windows 98, Windows NT 4.0, Windows Millennium Edition, Windows 2000, Windows XP Home Edition, Windows XP Professional, Windows Server 2003 family

PrivateFontCollection Class

A collection of font families built from font files that are provided by the client application.

System.Object
  System.Drawing.Text.FontCollection
    System.Drawing.Text.PrivateFontCollection

```
[Visual Basic]
<ComVisible(False)>
NotInheritable Public Class PrivateFontCollection
   Inherits FontCollection
[C#]
[ComVisible(false)]
public sealed class PrivateFontCollection : FontCollection
[C++]
[ComVisible(false)]
public __gc __sealed class PrivateFontCollection : public
   FontCollection
[JScript]
public
   ComVisible(false)
class PrivateFontCollection extends FontCollection
```

Thread Safety

Any public static (**Shared** in Visual Basic) members of this type are safe for multithreaded operations. Any instance members are not guaranteed to be thread safe.

Remarks

The **PrivateFontCollection** class allows applications to install a private version of an existing font without the need to replace the system version of the font. For example, GDI+ can create a private version of the Arial font in addition to the Arial font that the system uses. **PrivateFontCollection** can also be used to install fonts that do not exist in the operating system. This is a temporary font install that does not affect the system-installed collection. To see the installed collection, use the **InstalledFontCollection** class.

Requirements

Namespace: System.Drawing.Text

Platforms: Windows 98, Windows NT 4.0, Windows Millennium Edition, Windows 2000, Windows XP Home Edition, Windows XP Professional, Windows Server 2003 family

Assembly: System.Drawing (in System.Drawing.dll)

PrivateFontCollection Constructor

Initializes a new instance of the **PrivateFontCollection** class. For additional information on fonts and text, including example code, see **Fonts and Text** in the Using GDI+ Managed Classes section of these documents.

```
[Visual Basic]
Public Sub New()
[C#]
public PrivateFontCollection();
[C++]
public: PrivateFontCollection();
[JScript]
public function PrivateFontCollection();
```

Requirements

Platforms: Windows 98, Windows NT 4.0, Windows Millennium Edition, Windows 2000, Windows XP Home Edition, Windows XP Professional, Windows Server 2003 family

PrivateFontCollection.AddFontFile Method

Adds a font from the specified file to this **PrivateFontCollection** object. For additional information on fonts and text, including example code, see **Fonts and Text** in the Using GDI+ Managed Classes section of these documents.

```
[Visual Basic]
Public Sub AddFontFile( _
   ByVal filename As String _
)
[C#]
public void AddFontFile(
   string filename
);
[C++]
public: void AddFontFile(
   String* filename
);
[JScript]
public function AddFontFile(
   filename : String
);
```

Parameters

filename
  A **String** containing the file name of the font to add.

Requirements

Platforms: Windows 98, Windows NT 4.0, Windows Millennium Edition, Windows 2000, Windows XP Home Edition, Windows XP Professional, Windows Server 2003 family

PrivateFontCollection.AddMemoryFont Method

Adds a font contained in system memory to this **PrivateFontCollection** object.

```
[Visual Basic]
Public Sub AddMemoryFont( _
   ByVal memory As IntPtr, _
   ByVal length As Integer _
)
[C#]
public void AddMemoryFont(
   IntPtr memory,
   int length
);
[C++]
public: void AddMemoryFont(
   IntPtr memory,
   int length
);
```

```
[JScript]
public function AddMemoryFont(
   memory : IntPtr,
   length : int
);
```

Parameters

memory
The memory address of the font to add.

length
The memory length of the font to add.

Requirements

Platforms: Windows 98, Windows NT 4.0, Windows Millennium Edition, Windows 2000, Windows XP Home Edition, Windows XP Professional, Windows Server 2003 family

PrivateFontCollection.Dispose Method

Overload List

This member supports the .NET Framework infrastructure and is not intended to be used directly from your code.

[Visual Basic] **Overloads Overrides Protected Sub Dispose(Boolean)**

[C#] **protected override void Dispose(bool);**

[C++] **protected: void Dispose(bool);**

[JScript] **protected override function Dispose(Boolean);**

Inherited from **FontCollection**.

[Visual Basic] **Overloads Public Overridable Sub Dispose() Implements IDisposable.Dispose**

[C#] **public virtual void Dispose();**

[C++] **public: virtual void Dispose();**

[JScript] **public function Dispose();**

PrivateFontCollection.Dispose Method (Boolean)

This member supports the .NET Framework infrastructure and is not intended to be used directly from your code.

```
[Visual Basic]
Overrides Overloads Protected Sub Dispose( _
   ByVal disposing As Boolean _
)
[C#]
protected override void Dispose(
   bool disposing
);
[C++]
protected: void Dispose(
   bool disposing
);
[JScript]
protected override function Dispose(
   disposing : Boolean
);
```

TextRenderingHint Enumeration

Specifies the quality of text rendering.

[Visual Basic]
```
<Serializable>
Public Enum TextRenderingHint
```
[C#]
```
[Serializable]
public enum TextRenderingHint
```
[C++]
```
[Serializable]
__value public enum TextRenderingHint
```
[JScript]
```
public
   Serializable
enum TextRenderingHint
```

Remarks

The quality ranges from text (fastest performance and lowest quality) to antialiased text (better quality but slower performance) to ClearType text (best quality on an LCD display).

Members

Member name	Description
AntiAlias	Specifies that each character is drawn using its antialiased glyph bitmap without hinting. Better quality due to antialiasing. Stem width differences may be noticeable because hinting is turned off.
AntiAliasGridFit	Specifies that each character is drawn using its antialiased glyph bitmap with hinting. Much better quality due to antialiasing, but at a higher performance cost.
ClearTypeGridFit	Specifies that each character is drawn using its glyph CT bitmap with hinting. The highest quality setting. Used to take advantage of ClearType font features.
SingleBitPerPixel	Specifies that each character is drawn using its glyph bitmap. Hinting is not used.
SingleBitPerPixelGridFit	Specifies that each character is drawn using its glyph bitmap. Hinting is used to improve character appearance on stems and curvature.
SystemDefault	Specifies that each character is drawn using its glyph bitmap, with the system default rendering hint. The text will be drawn using whatever font smoothing settings the user has selected for the system.

Requirements

Namespace: System.Drawing.Text

Platforms: Windows 98, Windows NT 4.0, Windows Millennium Edition, Windows 2000, Windows XP Home Edition, Windows XP Professional, Windows Server 2003 family

Assembly: System.Drawing (in System.Drawing.dll)

System.ComponentModel Namespace

The **System.ComponentModel** namespace provides classes that are used to implement the run-time and design-time behavior of components and controls. This namespace includes the base classes and interfaces for implementing attributes and type converters, binding to data sources, and licensing components.

The classes in this namespace divide into the following categories:

- Core component classes. See the **Component**, **IComponent**, **Container**, and **IContainer** classes.
- Component licensing. See the **License**, **LicenseManager**, **LicenseProvider**, and **LicenseProviderAttribute** classes.
- Attributes. See the **Attribute** class.
- Descriptors and persistence. See the **TypeDescriptor**, **EventDescriptor**, and **PropertyDescriptor** classes.
- Type converters. See the **TypeConverter** class.

AmbientValueAttribute Class

Specifies the value to pass to a property to cause the property to get its value from another source. This is known as ambience. This class cannot be inherited.

System.Object
  System.Attribute
    System.ComponentModel.AmbientValueAttribute

[Visual Basic]
```
<AttributeUsage(AttributeTargets.All)>
NotInheritable Public Class AmbientValueAttribute
   Inherits Attribute
```
[C#]
```
[AttributeUsage(AttributeTargets.All)]
public sealed class AmbientValueAttribute : Attribute
```
[C++]
```
[AttributeUsage(AttributeTargets::All)]
public __gc __sealed class AmbientValueAttribute : public
   Attribute
```
[JScript]
```
public
   AttributeUsage(AttributeTargets.All)
class AmbientValueAttribute extends Attribute
```

Thread Safety

Any public static (**Shared** in Visual Basic) members of this type are safe for multithreaded operations. Any instance members are not guaranteed to be thread safe.

Remarks

If a property on a control has ambient behavior, this attribute must be present. Ambient properties query their parent for their value, for example, a **Control.Font** property or a **Control.BackColor** property.

Typically, a visual designer uses the **AmbientValueAttribute** attribute to decide which value to persist for a property. This is usually a value that causes the property to get its value from another source. An example of an ambient value is **Color.Empty** as the ambient value for the **BackColor** property. If you have a control on a form and the **BackColor** property of the control is set to a different color than the **BackColor** property of the form, you can reset the **BackColor** property of the control to that of the form by setting the **BackColor** of the control to **Color.Empty**.

Requirements

Namespace: System.ComponentModel

Platforms: Windows 98, Windows NT 4.0, Windows Millennium Edition, Windows 2000, Windows XP Home Edition, Windows XP Professional, Windows Server 2003 family

Assembly: System (in System.dll)

AmbientValueAttribute Constructor

Initializes a new instance of the **AmbientValueAttribute** class.

Overload List

Initializes a new instance of the **AmbientValueAttribute** class, given a Boolean value for its value.

[Visual Basic] **Public Sub New(Boolean)**

[C#] **public AmbientValueAttribute(bool);**

[C++] **public: AmbientValueAttribute(bool);**

[JScript] **public function AmbientValueAttribute(Boolean);**

Initializes a new instance of the **AmbientValueAttribute** class, given an 8-bit unsigned integer for its value.

[Visual Basic] **Public Sub New(Byte)**

[C#] **public AmbientValueAttribute(byte);**

[C++] **public: AmbientValueAttribute(unsigned char);**

[JScript] **public function AmbientValueAttribute(Byte);**

Initializes a new instance of the **AmbientValueAttribute** class, given a Unicode character for its value.

[Visual Basic] **Public Sub New(Char)**

[C#] **public AmbientValueAttribute(char);**

[C++] **public: AmbientValueAttribute(__wchar_t);**

[JScript] **public function AmbientValueAttribute(Char);**

Initializes a new instance of the **AmbientValueAttribute** class, given a double-precision floating-point number for its value.

[Visual Basic] **Public Sub New(Double)**

[C#] **public AmbientValueAttribute(double);**

[C++] **public: AmbientValueAttribute(double);**

[JScript] **public function AmbientValueAttribute(double);**

Initializes a new instance of the **AmbientValueAttribute** class, given a 16-bit signed integer for its value.

[Visual Basic] **Public Sub New(Short)**

[C#] **public AmbientValueAttribute(short);**

[C++] **public: AmbientValueAttribute(short);**

[JScript] **public function AmbientValueAttribute(Int16);**

Initializes a new instance of the **AmbientValueAttribute** class, given a 32-bit signed integer for its value.

[Visual Basic] **Public Sub New(Integer)**

[C#] **public AmbientValueAttribute(int);**

[C++] **public: AmbientValueAttribute(int);**

[JScript] **public function AmbientValueAttribute(int);**

Initializes a new instance of the **AmbientValueAttribute** class, given a 64-bit signed integer for its value.

[Visual Basic] **Public Sub New(Long)**

[C#] **public AmbientValueAttribute(long);**

[C++] **public: AmbientValueAttribute(__int64);**

[JScript] **public function AmbientValueAttribute(long);**

Initializes a new instance of the **AmbientValueAttribute** class, given an object for its value.

[Visual Basic] **Public Sub New(Object)**

[C#] **public AmbientValueAttribute(object);**

[C++] **public: AmbientValueAttribute(Object*);**

[JScript] **public function AmbientValueAttribute(Object);**

Initializes a new instance of the **AmbientValueAttribute** class, given a single-precision floating point number for its value.

[Visual Basic] **Public Sub New(Single)**

[C#] **public AmbientValueAttribute(float);**

[C++] **public: AmbientValueAttribute(float);**

[JScript] **public function AmbientValueAttribute(float);**

Initializes a new instance of the **AmbientValueAttribute** class, given a string for its value.

[Visual Basic] **Public Sub New(String)**

[C#] **public AmbientValueAttribute(string);**

[C++] **public: AmbientValueAttribute(String*);**

[JScript] **public function AmbientValueAttribute(String);**

Initializes a new instance of the **AmbientValueAttribute** class, given the value and its type.

[Visual Basic] **Public Sub New(Type, String)**

[C#] **public AmbientValueAttribute(Type, string);**

[C++] **public: AmbientValueAttribute(Type*, String*);**

[JScript] **public function AmbientValueAttribute(Type, String);**

AmbientValueAttribute Constructor (Boolean)

Initializes a new instance of the **AmbientValueAttribute** class, given a Boolean value for its value.

```
[Visual Basic]
Public Sub New( _
   ByVal value As Boolean _
)
[C#]
public AmbientValueAttribute(
   bool value
);
[C++]
public: AmbientValueAttribute(
   bool value
);
[JScript]
public function AmbientValueAttribute(
   value : Boolean
);
```

Parameters

value

The value of this attribute.

Requirements

Platforms: Windows 98, Windows NT 4.0, Windows Millennium Edition, Windows 2000, Windows XP Home Edition, Windows XP Professional, Windows Server 2003 family

AmbientValueAttribute Constructor (Byte)

Initializes a new instance of the **AmbientValueAttribute** class, given an 8-bit unsigned integer for its value.

```
[Visual Basic]
Public Sub New( _
   ByVal value As Byte _
)
[C#]
public AmbientValueAttribute(
   byte value
);
[C++]
public: AmbientValueAttribute(
   unsigned char value
);
[JScript]
public function AmbientValueAttribute(
   value : Byte
);
```

Parameters

value

The value of this attribute.

Requirements

Platforms: Windows 98, Windows NT 4.0, Windows Millennium Edition, Windows 2000, Windows XP Home Edition, Windows XP Professional, Windows Server 2003 family

AmbientValueAttribute Constructor (Char)

Initializes a new instance of the **AmbientValueAttribute** class, given a Unicode character for its value.

```
[Visual Basic]
Public Sub New( _
   ByVal value As Char _
)
[C#]
public AmbientValueAttribute(
   char value
);
[C++]
public: AmbientValueAttribute(
   __wchar_t value
);
[JScript]
public function AmbientValueAttribute(
   value : Char
);
```

Parameters

value

The value of this attribute.

Requirements

Platforms: Windows 98, Windows NT 4.0, Windows Millennium Edition, Windows 2000, Windows XP Home Edition, Windows XP Professional, Windows Server 2003 family

AmbientValueAttribute Constructor (Double)

Initializes a new instance of the **AmbientValueAttribute** class, given a double-precision floating-point number for its value.

```
[Visual Basic]
Public Sub New( _
   ByVal value As Double _
)
[C#]
public AmbientValueAttribute(
   double value
);
[C++]
public: AmbientValueAttribute(
   double value
);
[JScript]
public function AmbientValueAttribute(
   value : double
);
```

Parameters

value
The value of this attribute.

Requirements

Platforms: Windows 98, Windows NT 4.0, Windows Millennium Edition, Windows 2000, Windows XP Home Edition, Windows XP Professional, Windows Server 2003 family

AmbientValueAttribute Constructor (Int16)

Initializes a new instance of the **AmbientValueAttribute** class, given a 16-bit signed integer for its value.

```
[Visual Basic]
Public Sub New( _
   ByVal value As Short _
)
[C#]
public AmbientValueAttribute(
   short value
);
[C++]
public: AmbientValueAttribute(
   short value
);
[JScript]
public function AmbientValueAttribute(
   value : Int16
);
```

Parameters

value
The value of this attribute.

Requirements

Platforms: Windows 98, Windows NT 4.0, Windows Millennium Edition, Windows 2000, Windows XP Home Edition, Windows XP Professional, Windows Server 2003 family

AmbientValueAttribute Constructor (Int32)

Initializes a new instance of the **AmbientValueAttribute** class, given a 32-bit signed integer for its value.

```
[Visual Basic]
Public Sub New( _
   ByVal value As Integer _
)
[C#]
public AmbientValueAttribute(
   int value
);
[C++]
public: AmbientValueAttribute(
   int value
);
[JScript]
public function AmbientValueAttribute(
   value : int
);
```

Parameters

value
The value of this attribute.

Requirements

Platforms: Windows 98, Windows NT 4.0, Windows Millennium Edition, Windows 2000, Windows XP Home Edition, Windows XP Professional, Windows Server 2003 family

AmbientValueAttribute Constructor (Int64)

Initializes a new instance of the **AmbientValueAttribute** class, given a 64-bit signed integer for its value.

```
[Visual Basic]
Public Sub New( _
   ByVal value As Long _
)
[C#]
public AmbientValueAttribute(
   long value
);
[C++]
public: AmbientValueAttribute(
   __int64 value
);
[JScript]
public function AmbientValueAttribute(
   value : long
);
```

Parameters

value
The value of this attribute.

Requirements

Platforms: Windows 98, Windows NT 4.0, Windows Millennium Edition, Windows 2000, Windows XP Home Edition, Windows XP Professional, Windows Server 2003 family

AmbientValueAttribute Constructor (Object)

Initializes a new instance of the **AmbientValueAttribute** class, given an object for its value.

```
[Visual Basic]
Public Sub New( _
   ByVal value As Object _
)
[C#]
public AmbientValueAttribute(
   object value
);
[C++]
public: AmbientValueAttribute(
   Object* value
);
[JScript]
public function AmbientValueAttribute(
   value : Object
);
```

Parameters

value
The value of this attribute.

Requirements

Platforms: Windows 98, Windows NT 4.0, Windows Millennium Edition, Windows 2000, Windows XP Home Edition, Windows XP Professional, Windows Server 2003 family

AmbientValueAttribute Constructor (Single)

Initializes a new instance of the **AmbientValueAttribute** class, given a single-precision floating point number for its value.

```
[Visual Basic]
Public Sub New( _
   ByVal value As Single _
)
[C#]
public AmbientValueAttribute(
   float value
);
[C++]
public: AmbientValueAttribute(
   float value
);
[JScript]
public function AmbientValueAttribute(
   value : float
);
```

Parameters

value
The value of this attribute.

Requirements

Platforms: Windows 98, Windows NT 4.0, Windows Millennium Edition, Windows 2000, Windows XP Home Edition, Windows XP Professional, Windows Server 2003 family

AmbientValueAttribute Constructor (String)

Initializes a new instance of the **AmbientValueAttribute** class, given a string for its value.

```
[Visual Basic]
Public Sub New( _
   ByVal value As String _
)
[C#]
public AmbientValueAttribute(
   string value
);
[C++]
public: AmbientValueAttribute(
   String* value
);
[JScript]
public function AmbientValueAttribute(
   value : String
);
```

Parameters

value
The value of this attribute.

Requirements

Platforms: Windows 98, Windows NT 4.0, Windows Millennium Edition, Windows 2000, Windows XP Home Edition, Windows XP Professional, Windows Server 2003 family

AmbientValueAttribute Constructor (Type, String)

Initializes a new instance of the **AmbientValueAttribute** class, given the value and its type.

```
[Visual Basic]
Public Sub New( _
   ByVal type As Type, _
   ByVal value As String _
)
[C#]
public AmbientValueAttribute(
   Type type,
   string value
);
[C++]
public: AmbientValueAttribute(
   Type* type,
   String* value
);
[JScript]
public function AmbientValueAttribute(
   type : Type,
   value : String
);
```

Parameters

type
The **Type** of the *value* parameter.

value
The value for this attribute.

Requirements

Platforms: Windows 98, Windows NT 4.0, Windows Millennium Edition, Windows 2000, Windows XP Home Edition, Windows XP Professional, Windows Server 2003 family

AmbientValueAttribute.Value Property

Gets the object that is the value of this **AmbientValueAttribute**.

```
[Visual Basic]
Public ReadOnly Property Value As Object
[C#]
public object Value {get;}
[C++]
public: __property Object* get_Value();
[JScript]
public function get Value() : Object;
```

Property Value

The object that is the value of this **AmbientValueAttribute**.

Requirements

Platforms: Windows 98, Windows NT 4.0, Windows Millennium Edition, Windows 2000, Windows XP Home Edition, Windows XP Professional, Windows Server 2003 family

AmbientValueAttribute.Equals Method

This member overrides **Object.Equals**.

```
[Visual Basic]
Overrides Public Function Equals( _
   ByVal obj As Object _
) As Boolean
[C#]
public override bool Equals(
   object obj
);
[C++]
public: bool Equals(
   Object* obj
);
[JScript]
public override function Equals(
   obj : Object
) : Boolean;
```

Requirements

Platforms: Windows 98, Windows NT 4.0, Windows Millennium Edition, Windows 2000, Windows XP Home Edition, Windows XP Professional, Windows Server 2003 family

AmbientValueAttribute.GetHashCode Method

This member overrides **Attribute.GetHashCode**.

```
[Visual Basic]
Overrides Public Function GetHashCode() As Integer
[C#]
public override int GetHashCode();
[C++]
public: int GetHashCode();
[JScript]
public override function GetHashCode() : int;
```

Requirements

Platforms: Windows 98, Windows NT 4.0, Windows Millennium Edition, Windows 2000, Windows XP Home Edition, Windows XP Professional, Windows Server 2003 family

ArrayConverter Class

Provides a type converter to convert **Array** objects to and from various other representations.

System.Object
  System.ComponentModel.TypeConverter
    System.ComponentModel.CollectionConverter
      System.ComponentModel.ArrayConverter

[Visual Basic]
```
Public Class ArrayConverter
   Inherits CollectionConverter
```
[C#]
```
public class ArrayConverter : CollectionConverter
```
[C++]
```
public __gc class ArrayConverter : public CollectionConverter
```
[JScript]
```
public class ArrayConverter extends CollectionConverter
```

Thread Safety

Any public static (**Shared** in Visual Basic) members of this type are safe for multithreaded operations. Any instance members are not guaranteed to be thread safe.

Remarks

Note You should never create an instance of **ArrayConverter**. Instead, call the **GetConverter** method of **TypeDescriptor**. For more information, see the examples in the **TypeConverter** base class.

Requirements

Namespace: System.ComponentModel

Platforms: Windows 98, Windows NT 4.0, Windows Millennium Edition, Windows 2000, Windows XP Home Edition, Windows XP Professional, Windows Server 2003 family

Assembly: System (in System.dll)

ArrayConverter Constructor

Initializes a new instance of the **ArrayConverter** class.

[Visual Basic]
```
Public Sub New()
```
[C#]
```
public ArrayConverter();
```
[C++]
```
public: ArrayConverter();
```
[JScript]
```
public function ArrayConverter();
```

Remarks

The default constructor initializes any fields to their default values.

Requirements

Platforms: Windows 98, Windows NT 4.0, Windows Millennium Edition, Windows 2000, Windows XP Home Edition, Windows XP Professional, Windows Server 2003 family

ArrayConverter.ConvertTo Method

Overload List

This member supports the .NET Framework infrastructure and is not intended to be used directly from your code.

[Visual Basic] **Overloads Overrides Public Function ConvertTo(ITypeDescriptorContext, CultureInfo, Object, Type) As Object**

[C#] **public override object ConvertTo(ITypeDescriptorContext, CultureInfo, object, Type);**

[C++] **public: Object* ConvertTo(ITypeDescriptorContext*, CultureInfo*, Object*, Type*);**

[JScript] **public override function ConvertTo(ITypeDescriptorContext, CultureInfo, Object, Type) : Object;**

Inherited from **TypeConverter**.

[Visual Basic] **Overloads Public Function ConvertTo(Object, Type) As Object**

[C#] **public object ConvertTo(object, Type);**

[C++] **public: Object* ConvertTo(Object*, Type*);**

[JScript] **public function ConvertTo(Object, Type) : Object;**

ArrayConverter.ConvertTo Method (ITypeDescriptorContext, CultureInfo, Object, Type)

This member overrides **TypeConverter.ConvertTo**.

[Visual Basic]
```
Overrides Overloads Public Function ConvertTo( _
   ByVal context As ITypeDescriptorContext, _
   ByVal culture As CultureInfo, _
   ByVal value As Object, _
   ByVal destinationType As Type _
) As Object
```
[C#]
```
public override object ConvertTo(
   ITypeDescriptorContext context,
   CultureInfo culture,
   object value,
   Type destinationType
);
```
[C++]
```
public: Object* ConvertTo(
   ITypeDescriptorContext* context,
   CultureInfo* culture,
   Object* value,
   Type* destinationType
);
```
[JScript]
```
public override function ConvertTo(
   context : ITypeDescriptorContext,
   culture : CultureInfo,
   value : Object,
   destinationType : Type
) : Object;
```

Requirements

Platforms: Windows 98, Windows NT 4.0, Windows Millennium Edition, Windows 2000, Windows XP Home Edition, Windows XP Professional, Windows Server 2003 family

ArrayConverter.GetProperties Method

Overload List

This member supports the .NET Framework infrastructure and is not intended to be used directly from your code.

[Visual Basic] **Overloads Overrides Public Function GetProperties(ITypeDescriptorContext, Object, Attribute()) As PropertyDescriptorCollection**

[C#] **public override PropertyDescriptorCollection GetProperties(ITypeDescriptorContext, object, Attribute[]);**

[C++] **public: PropertyDescriptorCollection* GetProperties(ITypeDescriptorContext*, Object*, Attribute[]);**

[JScript] **public override function GetProperties(ITypeDescriptorContext, Object, Attribute[]) : PropertyDescriptorCollection;**

Inherited from **TypeConverter**.

[Visual Basic] **Overloads Public Function GetProperties(Object) As PropertyDescriptorCollection**

[C#] **public PropertyDescriptorCollection GetProperties(object);**

[C++] **public: PropertyDescriptorCollection* GetProperties(Object*);**

[JScript] **public function GetProperties(Object) : PropertyDescriptorCollection;**

Inherited from **TypeConverter**.

[Visual Basic] **Overloads Public Function GetProperties(ITypeDescriptorContext, Object) As PropertyDescriptorCollection**

[C#] **public PropertyDescriptorCollection GetProperties(ITypeDescriptorContext, object);**

[C++] **public: PropertyDescriptorCollection* GetProperties(ITypeDescriptorContext*, Object*);**

[JScript] **public function GetProperties(ITypeDescriptorContext, Object) : PropertyDescriptorCollection;**

ArrayConverter.GetProperties Method (ITypeDescriptorContext, Object, Attribute[])

This member overrides **TypeConverter.GetProperties**.

```
[Visual Basic]
Overrides Overloads Public Function GetProperties( _
   ByVal context As ITypeDescriptorContext, _
   ByVal value As Object, _
   ByVal attributes() As Attribute _
) As PropertyDescriptorCollection
[C#]
public override PropertyDescriptorCollection GetProperties(
   ITypeDescriptorContext context,
   object value,
   Attribute[] attributes
);
[C++]
public: PropertyDescriptorCollection* GetProperties(
   ITypeDescriptorContext* context,
   Object* value,
   Attribute* attributes[]
);
[JScript]
public override function GetProperties(
   context : ITypeDescriptorContext,
   value : Object,
   attributes : Attribute[]
) : PropertyDescriptorCollection;
```

Requirements

Platforms: Windows 98, Windows NT 4.0, Windows Millennium Edition, Windows 2000, Windows XP Home Edition, Windows XP Professional, Windows Server 2003 family

ArrayConverter.GetPropertiesSupported Method

Overload List

This member supports the .NET Framework infrastructure and is not intended to be used directly from your code.

[Visual Basic] **Overloads Overrides Public Function GetPropertiesSupported(ITypeDescriptorContext) As Boolean**

[C#] **public override bool GetPropertiesSupported(ITypeDescriptorContext);**

[C++] **public: bool GetPropertiesSupported(ITypeDescriptorContext*);**

[JScript] **public override function GetPropertiesSupported(ITypeDescriptorContext) : Boolean;**

Inherited from **TypeConverter**.

[Visual Basic] **Overloads Public Function GetPropertiesSupported() As Boolean**

[C#] **public bool GetPropertiesSupported();**

[C++] **public: bool GetPropertiesSupported();**

[JScript] **public function GetPropertiesSupported() : Boolean;**

ArrayConverter.GetPropertiesSupported Method (ITypeDescriptorContext)

This member overrides **TypeConverter.GetPropertiesSupported**.

```
[Visual Basic]
Overrides Overloads Public Function GetPropertiesSupported( _
   ByVal context As ITypeDescriptorContext _
) As Boolean
[C#]
public override bool GetPropertiesSupported(
   ITypeDescriptorContext context
);
[C++]
public: bool GetPropertiesSupported(
   ITypeDescriptorContext* context
);
[JScript]
public override function GetPropertiesSupported(
   context : ITypeDescriptorContext
) : Boolean;
```

Requirements

Platforms: Windows 98, Windows NT 4.0, Windows Millennium Edition, Windows 2000, Windows XP Home Edition, Windows XP Professional, Windows Server 2003 family

AttributeCollection Class

Represents a collection of attributes.

System.Object
  System.ComponentModel.AttributeCollection

[Visual Basic]
```
<ComVisible(True)>
Public Class AttributeCollection
   Implements ICollection, IEnumerable
```
[C#]
```
[ComVisible(true)]
public class AttributeCollection : ICollection, IEnumerable
```
[C++]
```
[ComVisible(true)]
public __gc class AttributeCollection : public ICollection,
   IEnumerable
```
[JScript]
```
public
   ComVisible(true)
class AttributeCollection implements ICollection,
   IEnumerable
```

Thread Safety

Any public static (**Shared** in Visual Basic) members of this type are safe for multithreaded operations. Any instance members are not guaranteed to be thread safe.

Remarks

The **AttributeCollection** class is read-only; it does not implement methods to add or remove attributes. You must inherit from this class to implement these methods.

Use the **Count** property to find the number of attributes that exist in the collection.

You can also use the methods of this class to query the collection about its contents. Call **Contains** to verify that a specified attribute or attribute array exists in the collection. Call **Matches** to verify that a specified attribute or array of attributes exists in the collection, and that the values of the specified attributes are the same as the values in the collection.

While most attributes have default values, it is not required. If an attribute has no default value, a null reference (**Nothing** in Visual Basic) is returned from the indexed property that takes a type. When defining your own attributes, you can declare a default value by either providing a constructor that takes no arguments, or defining a public static field of your attribute type named "Default".

Example

When using attributes, verify that an attribute has been set, or access its value. The first example checks to see whether the **BrowsableAttribute** has been set in this collection. It assumes that `button1` and `textBox1`. The second example gets the actual value of the **DescriptionAttribute** for a button. It assumes that `button1` and `textBox1` have been created on a form.

[Visual Basic]
```
Private Sub ContainsAttribute()
    ' Creates a new collection and assigns it the attributes ↵
 for button1.
    Dim attributes As AttributeCollection
    attributes = TypeDescriptor.GetAttributes(button1)

    ' Sets an Attribute to the specific attribute.
    Dim myAttribute As BrowsableAttribute = BrowsableAttribute.Yes

    If attributes.Contains(myAttribute) Then
        textBox1.Text = "button1 has a browsable attribute."
    Else
        textBox1.Text = "button1 does not have a browsable attribute."
    End If
End Sub 'ContainsAttribute
```

[C#]
```
private void ContainsAttribute() {
    // Creates a new collection and assigns it the attributes ↵
for button1.
    AttributeCollection attributes;
    attributes = TypeDescriptor.GetAttributes(button1);

    // Sets an Attribute to the specific attribute.
    BrowsableAttribute myAttribute = BrowsableAttribute.Yes;

    if (attributes.Contains(myAttribute))
       textBox1.Text = "button1 has a browsable attribute.";
    else
       textBox1.Text = "button1 does not have a browsable attribute.";
 }
```

[C++]
```
void ContainsAttribute()
{
    // Creates a new collection and assigns it the attributes ↵
for button1.
    AttributeCollection*    attributes;
    attributes = TypeDescriptor::GetAttributes( button1 );

    // Sets an Attribute to the specific attribute.
    BrowsableAttribute* myAttribute = BrowsableAttribute::Yes;

    if ( attributes->Contains( myAttribute ))
        textBox1->Text = S"button1 has a browsable attribute.";
    else
        textBox1->Text = S"button1 does not have a browsable attribute.";
}
```

[JScript]
```
public function ContainsAttribute() {
    // Creates a new collection and assigns it the attributes ↵
for button1.
    var attributes : AttributeCollection;
    attributes = TypeDescriptor.GetAttributes(button1);

    // Sets an Attribute to the specific attribute.
    var myAttribute : BrowsableAttribute  = BrowsableAttribute.Yes;

    if (attributes.Contains(myAttribute))
       textBox1.Text = "button1 has a browsable attribute.";
    else
       textBox1.Text = "button1 does not have a browsable attribute.";
 }
```

[Visual Basic]
```
Private Sub GetAttributeValue()
    ' Creates a new collection and assigns it the attributes ↵
 for button1.
    Dim attributes As AttributeCollection
    attributes = TypeDescriptor.GetAttributes(button1)

    ' Gets the designer attribute from the collection.
    Dim myDesigner As DesignerAttribute
    myDesigner = CType(attributes(GetType(DesignerAttribute)), ↵
DesignerAttribute)

    ' Prints the value of the attribute in a text box.
    textBox1.Text = myDesigner.DesignerTypeName
End Sub 'GetAttributeValue
```

[C#]
```
private void GetAttributeValue() {
    // Creates a new collection and assigns it the attributes ↵
 for button1.
    AttributeCollection attributes;
    attributes = TypeDescriptor.GetAttributes(button1);

    // Gets the designer attribute from the collection.
    DesignerAttribute myDesigner;
    myDesigner =
(DesignerAttribute)attributes[typeof(DesignerAttribute)];

    // Prints the value of the attribute in a text box.
    textBox1.Text = myDesigner.DesignerTypeName;
 }
```

[C++]
```
void GetAttributeValue()
{
    // Creates a new collection and assigns it the attributes ↵
 for button1.
    AttributeCollection* attributes;
    attributes = TypeDescriptor::GetAttributes( button1 );

    // Gets the designer attribute from the collection.
    DesignerAttribute* myDesigner;
    myDesigner = dynamic_cast<DesignerAttribute*> ↵
 ( attributes->get_Item( __typeof( DesignerAttribute )));

    // Prints the value of the attribute in a text box.
    textBox1->Text = myDesigner->DesignerTypeName;
}
```

[JScript]
```
public function GetAttributeValue() {
    // Creates a new collection and assigns it the attributes ↵
for button1.
    var attributes : AttributeCollection ;
    attributes = TypeDescriptor.GetAttributes(button1);

    // Gets the designer attribute from the collection.
    var myDesigner : DesignerAttribute ;
    myDesigner =
DesignerAttribute(attributes[DesignerAttribute.GetType()]);

    // Prints the value of the attribute in a text box.
    if(myDesigner)
        textBox1.Text = myDesigner.DesignerTypeName;
 }
```

Requirements

Namespace: System.ComponentModel

Platforms: Windows 98, Windows NT 4.0, Windows Millennium Edition, Windows 2000, Windows XP Home Edition, Windows XP Professional, Windows Server 2003 family, .NET Compact Framework - Windows CE .NET

Assembly: System (in System.dll)

AttributeCollection Constructor

Initializes a new instance of the **AttributeCollection** class.

[Visual Basic]
```
Public Sub New( _
   ByVal attributes() As Attribute _
)
```
[C#]
```
public AttributeCollection(
   Attribute[] attributes
);
```
[C++]
```
public: AttributeCollection(
   Attribute* attributes[]
);
```
[JScript]
```
public function AttributeCollection(
   attributes : Attribute[]
);
```

Parameters

attributes
An array of type **Attribute** that provides the attributes for this collection.

Example

The following example creates a new **AttributeCollection** using the attributes on `button1`. It assumes that `button1` has been created on a form.

[Visual Basic]
```
Dim collection1 As AttributeCollection
collection1 = TypeDescriptor.GetAttributes(button1)
```

[C#]
```
AttributeCollection collection1;
collection1 = TypeDescriptor.GetAttributes(button1);
}
```

[C++]
```
AttributeCollection*    collection1;
collection1 = TypeDescriptor::GetAttributes( button1 );
```

[JScript]
```
var collection1 : AttributeCollection;
collection1 = TypeDescriptor.GetAttributes(button1);
textBox1.Text = "The button1 has " + collection1.Count + " attributes";
}
```

Requirements

Platforms: Windows 98, Windows NT 4.0, Windows Millennium Edition, Windows 2000, Windows XP Home Edition, Windows XP Professional, Windows Server 2003 family, .NET Compact Framework - Windows CE .NET

AttributeCollection.Empty Field

Specifies an empty collection that you can use, rather than creating a new one. This field is read-only.

[Visual Basic]
```
Public Shared ReadOnly Empty As AttributeCollection
```
[C#]
```
public static readonly AttributeCollection Empty;
```
[C++]
```
public: static AttributeCollection* Empty;
```
[JScript]
```
public static var Empty : AttributeCollection;
```

Requirements

Platforms: Windows 98, Windows NT 4.0, Windows Millennium Edition, Windows 2000, Windows XP Home Edition, Windows XP Professional, Windows Server 2003 family, .NET Compact Framework - Windows CE .NET

AttributeCollection.Count Property

Gets the number of attributes.

[Visual Basic]
```
Public ReadOnly Property Count As Integer
```
[C#]
```
public int Count {get;}
```
[C++]
```
public: __property int get_Count();
```
[JScript]
```
public function get Count() : int;
```

Property Value

The number of attributes.

Remarks

You can use the **Count** property to set the limits of a loop that iterates through a collection of objects. If the collection is zero-based, be sure to use `Count - 1` as the upper boundary of the loop.

Example

[Visual Basic, C#, C++] The following example uses the **Count** property to print the number of properties on `button1` in a text box. It assumes that `button1` and `textBox1` have been created on a form.

[Visual Basic]
```
Private Sub GetCount
    ' Creates a new collection and assigns it the attributes for    ↵
button 1.
    Dim attributes As AttributeCollection
    attributes = TypeDescriptor.GetAttributes(button1)
    ' Prints the number of items in the collection.
    textBox1.Text = attributes.Count.ToString
End Sub
```

[C#]
```
private void GetCount() {
    // Creates a new collection and assigns it the attributes    ↵
for button1.
    AttributeCollection attributes;
    attributes = TypeDescriptor.GetAttributes(button1);

    // Prints the number of items in the collection.
    textBox1.Text = attributes.Count.ToString();
 }
```

[C++]
```
private:
    void GetCount()
    {
        // Creates a new collection and assigns it the attributes    ↵
 for button1.
        AttributeCollection* attributes;
        attributes = TypeDescriptor::GetAttributes( button1 );

        // Prints the number of items in the collection.
        textBox1->Text = __box( attributes->Count )->ToString();
    }
```

Requirements

Platforms: Windows 98, Windows NT 4.0, Windows Millennium Edition, Windows 2000, Windows XP Home Edition, Windows XP Professional, Windows Server 2003 family, .NET Compact Framework - Windows CE .NET

AttributeCollection.Item Property

Gets the attribute with the specified index.

[C#] In C#, this property is the indexer for the **AttributeCollection** class.

Overload List

Gets the attribute with the specified type.

[Visual Basic] **Overloads Public Overridable Default ReadOnly Property Item(Type) As Attribute**

[C#] **public virtual Attribute this[Type] {get;}**

[C++] **public: __property virtual Attribute* get_Item(Type*);**

[JScript] **AttributeCollection.Item (Type)**

Gets the attribute with the specified index number.

[Visual Basic] **Overloads Public Overridable Default ReadOnly Property Item(Integer) As Attribute**

[C#] **public virtual Attribute this[int] {get;}**

[C++] **public: __property virtual Attribute* get_Item(int);**

[JScript] **AttributeCollection.Item (int)**

Example

The following example uses the **Item** property to print the name of the **Attribute** specified by the index number in a text box. Because the index number is zero-based, this example prints the name of the second **Attribute** in a text box. It assumes `button1` and `textBox1` have been created on a form.

[Visual Basic]
```
Private Sub PrintIndexItem
    ' Creates a new collection and assigns it the attributes    ↵
for button1.
    Dim attributes As AttributeCollection
    attributes = TypeDescriptor.GetAttributes(button1)

    ' Prints the second attribute's name.
    textBox1.Text = attributes(1).ToString
End Sub
```

[C#]
```
private void PrintIndexItem() {
    // Creates a new collection and assigns it the attributes    ↵
for button1.
    AttributeCollection attributes;
    attributes = TypeDescriptor.GetAttributes(button1);

    // Prints the second attribute's name.
    textBox1.Text = attributes[1].ToString();
 }
```

[C++]
```
private:
    void PrintIndexItem()
    {
        // Creates a new collection and assigns it the attributes    ↵
 for button1.
        AttributeCollection* attributes;
        attributes = TypeDescriptor::GetAttributes( button1 );

        // Prints the second attribute's name.
        textBox1->Text = attributes->get_Item( 1 )->ToString();
    }
```

[JScript]
```
private function PrintIndexItem() {
    // Creates a new collection and assigns it the attributes
 for button1.
    var attributes : AttributeCollection;
    attributes = TypeDescriptor.GetAttributes(button1);

    // Prints the second attribute's name.
    textBox1.Text = attributes[1].ToString();
    Console.WriteLine(textBox1.Text);
 }
```

AttributeCollection.Item Property (Type)

Gets the attribute with the specified type.

[C#] In C#, this property is the indexer for the **AttributeCollection** class.

[Visual Basic]
```
Overloads Public Overridable Default ReadOnly Property Item( _
   ByVal attributeType As Type _
) As Attribute
```
[C#]
```
public virtual Attribute this[
   Type attributeType
] {get;}
```
[C++]
```
public: __property virtual Attribute* get_Item(
   Type* attributeType
);
```
[JScript]
```
returnValue = AttributeCollectionObject.Item(attributeType);
-or-
returnValue = AttributeCollectionObject(attributeType);
```

[JScript] In JScript, you can use the default indexed properties defined by a type, but you cannot explicitly define your own. However, specifying the **expando** attribute on a class automatically provides a default indexed property whose type is **Object** and whose index type is **String**.

Arguments [JScript]

attributeType

The **Type** of the **Attribute** to get from the collection.

Parameters [Visual Basic, C#, C++]

attributeType

The **Type** of the **Attribute** to get from the collection.

Property Value

The **Attribute** with the specified type or, if the attribute does not exist, the default value for the attribute type.

Remarks

If the attribute does not exist in the collection, this property returns the default value for the attribute type.

Example

The following example gets the **DesignerAttribute** from the collection and prints its value. It assumes that `button1` and `textBox1` have been created on a form.

For this code example to run, you must provide the fully qualified assembly name. For information about how to obtain the fully qualified assembly name, see **Assembly Names**.

[Visual Basic]
```
Private Sub PrintIndexItem2
    ' Creates a new collection and assigns it the attributes
for button1.
    Dim attributes As AttributeCollection
    attributes = TypeDescriptor.GetAttributes(button1)

    ' Gets the designer attribute from the collection.
    Dim myDesigner As DesignerAttribute
           ' You must supply a valid fully qualified assembly
 name here.
    myDesigner = CType(attributes(Type.GetType("Assembly text
 name, Version, Culture, PublicKeyToken")), DesignerAttribute)
    textBox1.Text = myDesigner.DesignerTypeName
End Sub
```

[C#]
```
private void PrintIndexItem2() {
    // Creates a new collection and assigns it the attributes
 for button1.
    AttributeCollection attributes;
    attributes = TypeDescriptor.GetAttributes(button1);

    // Gets the designer attribute from the collection.
    DesignerAttribute myDesigner;
    // You must supply a valid fully qualified assembly name here.
    myDesigner = (DesignerAttribute)attributes[Type.GetType
 ("Assembly text name, Version, Culture, PublicKeyToken")];
    textBox1.Text = myDesigner.DesignerTypeName;
 }
```

[C++]
```
private:
    void PrintIndexItem2()
    {
        // Creates a new collection and assigns it the attributes
 for button1.
        AttributeCollection* attributes;
        attributes = TypeDescriptor::GetAttributes(button1);

        // Gets the designer attribute from the collection.
        DesignerAttribute* myDesigner;
               // You must supply a valid fully qualified
 assembly name here.
        myDesigner = dynamic_cast<DesignerAttribute*>
 (attributes->get_Item(Type::GetType("Assembly text name,
Version, Culture, PublicKeyToken")));
        textBox1->Text = myDesigner->DesignerTypeName;
    }
```

[JScript]
```
private function PrintIndexItem2() {
    // Creates a new collection and assigns it the attributes
for button1.
    var attributes : AttributeCollection;
    attributes = TypeDescriptor.GetAttributes(button1);

    // Gets the designer attribute from the collection.
    try{
        var myDesigner : DesignerAttribute;
        myDesigner =
DesignerAttribute(attributes[System.ComponentModel.DesignerAttribute]);
        textBox1.Text = myDesigner.DesignerTypeName;
        Console.WriteLine(textBox1.Text);
    }
    catch(e )
    {
        Console.Write(e);
    }
 }
```

Requirements

Platforms: Windows 98, Windows NT 4.0, Windows Millennium Edition, Windows 2000, Windows XP Home Edition, Windows XP Professional, Windows Server 2003 family

AttributeCollection.Item Property (Int32)

Gets the attribute with the specified index number.

[C#] In C#, this property is the indexer for the **AttributeCollection** class.

```
[Visual Basic]
Overloads Public Overridable Default ReadOnly Property Item( _
   ByVal index As Integer _
) As Attribute
[C#]
public virtual Attribute this[
   int index
] {get;}
[C++]
public: __property virtual Attribute* get_Item(
   int index
);
[JScript]
returnValue = AttributeCollectionObject.Item(index);
-or-
returnValue = AttributeCollectionObject(index);
```

[JScript] In JScript, you can use the default indexed properties defined by a type, but you cannot explicitly define your own. However, specifying the **expando** attribute on a class automatically provides a default indexed property whose type is **Object** and whose index type is **String**.

Arguments [JScript]

index

The zero-based index of **AttributeCollection**.

Parameters [Visual Basic, C#, C++]

index

The zero-based index of **AttributeCollection**.

Property Value

The **Attribute** with the specified index number.

Remarks

The index number is zero-based. Therefore, you must subtract one from the numerical position of a particular **Attribute** to access that **Attribute**. For example, to get the third **Attribute**, you need to specify `myColl[2]`.

Example

The following example uses the **Item** property to print the name of the **Attribute** specified by the index number in a text box. Because the index number is zero-based, this example prints the name of the second **Attribute** in a text box. It assumes `button1` and `textBox1` have been created on a form.

```
[Visual Basic]
Private Sub PrintIndexItem
    ' Creates a new collection and assigns it the attributes ↵
for button1.
    Dim attributes As AttributeCollection
    attributes = TypeDescriptor.GetAttributes(button1)

    ' Prints the second attribute's name.
    textBox1.Text = attributes(1).ToString
End Sub
```

```
[C#]
private void PrintIndexItem() {
    // Creates a new collection and assigns it the attributes ↵
for button1.
    AttributeCollection attributes;
    attributes = TypeDescriptor.GetAttributes(button1);

    // Prints the second attribute's name.
    textBox1.Text = attributes[1].ToString();
 }
```

```
[C++]
private:
    void PrintIndexItem()
    {
        // Creates a new collection and assigns it the ↵
attributes for button1.
        AttributeCollection* attributes;
        attributes = TypeDescriptor::GetAttributes( button1 );

        // Prints the second attribute's name.
        textBox1->Text = attributes->get_Item( 1 )->ToString();
    }
```

```
[JScript]
private function PrintIndexItem() {
    // Creates a new collection and assigns it the attributes ↵
 for button1.
    var attributes : AttributeCollection;
    attributes = TypeDescriptor.GetAttributes(button1);

    // Prints the second attribute's name.
    textBox1.Text = attributes[1].ToString();
    Console.WriteLine(textBox1.Text);
 }
```

Requirements

Platforms: Windows 98, Windows NT 4.0, Windows Millennium Edition, Windows 2000, Windows XP Home Edition, Windows XP Professional, Windows Server 2003 family

AttributeCollection.System.Collections.ICollection.Count Property

Note: This namespace, class, or member is supported only in version 1.1 of the .NET Framework.

This member supports the .NET Framework infrastructure and is not intended to be used directly from your code.

```
[Visual Basic]
Private ReadOnly Property Count As Integer Implements _
   ICollection.Count
[C#]
int ICollection.Count {get;}
[C++]
private: __property int
   System::Collections::ICollection::get_Count();
[JScript]
private function get ICollection.Count() : int;
```

AttributeCollection.System.Collections.ICollection.IsSynchronized Property

Note: This namespace, class, or member is supported only in version 1.1 of the .NET Framework.

This member supports the .NET Framework infrastructure and is not intended to be used directly from your code.

[Visual Basic]
```
Private ReadOnly Property IsSynchronized As Boolean Implements _
   ICollection.IsSynchronized
```
[C#]
```
bool ICollection.IsSynchronized {get;}
```
[C++]
```
private: __property bool
   System::Collections::ICollection::get_IsSynchronized();
```
[JScript]
```
private function get ICollection.IsSynchronized() : Boolean;
```

AttributeCollection.System.Collections.ICollection.SyncRoot Property

Note: This namespace, class, or member is supported only in version 1.1 of the .NET Framework.

This member supports the .NET Framework infrastructure and is not intended to be used directly from your code.

[Visual Basic]
```
Private ReadOnly Property SyncRoot As Object Implements _
   ICollection.SyncRoot
```
[C#]
```
object ICollection.SyncRoot {get;}
```
[C++]
```
private: __property Object*
   System::Collections::ICollection::get_SyncRoot();
```
[JScript]
```
private function get ICollection.SyncRoot() : Object;
```

AttributeCollection.Contains Method

Determines whether this collection of attributes has the specified attribute or array of attributes.

Overload List

Determines whether this collection of attributes has the specified attribute.

Supported by the .NET Compact Framework.

[Visual Basic] **Overloads Public Function Contains(Attribute) As Boolean**

[C#] **public bool Contains(Attribute);**

[C++] **public: bool Contains(Attribute*);**

[JScript] **public function Contains(Attribute) : Boolean;**

Determines whether this attribute collection contains all the specified attributes in the attribute array.

[Visual Basic] **Overloads Public Function Contains(Attribute()) As Boolean**

[C#] **public bool Contains(Attribute[]);**

[C++] **public: bool Contains(Attribute*[]);**

[JScript] **public function Contains(Attribute[]) : Boolean;**

Example

The following example compares the attributes in `button1` and `textBox1` to see whether the attributes for the button are contained in the attributes for the text box. It assumes that both `button1` and `textBox1` have been created on a form.

[Visual Basic]
```
Private Sub ContainsAttributes()
    ' Creates a new collection and assigns it the attributes
 for button1.
    Dim myCollection As AttributeCollection
    myCollection = TypeDescriptor.GetAttributes(button1)

    ' Checks to see whether the attributes in myCollection are
 the attributes for textBox1.
    Dim myAttrArray(100) As Attribute
    TypeDescriptor.GetAttributes(textBox1).CopyTo(myAttrArray, 0)
    If myCollection.Contains(myAttrArray) Then
        textBox1.Text = "Both the button and text box have the
same attributes."
    Else
        textBox1.Text = "The button and the text box do not
have the same attributes."
    End If
End Sub
```

[C#]
```
private void ContainsAttributes() {
   // Creates a new collection and assigns it the attributes
for button1.
   AttributeCollection myCollection;
   myCollection = TypeDescriptor.GetAttributes(button1);

   // Checks to see whether the attributes in myCollection
are the attributes for textBox1.
   Attribute[] myAttrArray = new Attribute[100];
   TypeDescriptor.GetAttributes(textBox1).CopyTo(myAttrArray, 0);
   if (myCollection.Contains(myAttrArray))
      textBox1.Text = "Both the button and text box have the
same attributes.";
   else
      textBox1.Text = "The button and the text box do not have
the same attributes.";
}
```

[C++]
```
private:

    void ContainsAttributes()
    {
        // Creates a new collection and assigns it the
 attributes for button1.
        AttributeCollection* myCollection;
        myCollection = TypeDescriptor::GetAttributes( button1 );


        // Checks to see whether the attributes in myCollection
 are the attributes for textBox1.
        Attribute*    myAttrArray[] = new Attribute*[100];

        TypeDescriptor::GetAttributes( textBox1 )->CopyTo
(myAttrArray, 0);
        if (myCollection->Contains(myAttrArray))
            textBox1->Text = S"Both the button and text box
 have the same attributes.";
        else
            textBox1->Text = S"The button and the text box
do not have the same attributes.";
    }
```

[JScript]
```
private function ContainsAttributes() {
   // Creates a new collection and assigns it the attributes ↵
 for button1.
   var myCollection : AttributeCollection;
   myCollection = TypeDescriptor.GetAttributes(button1);

   // Checks to see whether the attributes in myCollection ↵
are the attributes for textBox1.
   var myAttrArray : Attribute[]  = new Attribute[100];
   TypeDescriptor.GetAttributes(textBox1).CopyTo(myAttrArray, 0);
   if (myCollection.Contains(myAttrArray))
      textBox1.Text = "Both the button and text box have the ↵
same attributes.";
   else
      textBox1.Text = "The button and the text box do not have ↵
 the same attributes.";

}
```

AttributeCollection.Contains Method (Attribute)

Determines whether this collection of attributes has the specified attribute.

[Visual Basic]
```
Overloads Public Function Contains( _
   ByVal attribute As Attribute _
) As Boolean
```
[C#]
```
public bool Contains(
   Attribute attribute
);
```
[C++]
```
public: bool Contains(
   Attribute* attribute
);
```
[JScript]
```
public function Contains(
   attribute : Attribute
) : Boolean;
```

Parameters

attribute

An **Attribute** to find in the collection.

Return Value

true if the collection contains the attribute or is the default attribute for the type of attribute; otherwise, **false**.

Remarks

This collection has the specified attribute if the specified type of attribute exists in the collection, and if the value of the specified attribute is the same as the value of the instance of the attribute in the collection.

The difference between **Matches** and **Contains** is that **Matches** calls the **Match** method on an attribute, and **Contains** calls the **Equals** method.

For most attributes these methods do the same thing. For attributes that may have multiple flags, however, **Match** is typically implemented so that it returns **true** if any of the flags are satisified. For example, consider a data binding attribute with the Boolean flags "SupportsSql", "SupportsOleDb" and "SupportsXml". This attribute may be present on a property that supports all three data binding approaches. It will often be the case that a programmer only needs to know if a particlar approach is available, not all three. So a programmer could use **Match** with an instance of the attribute containing only the flags he/she needs.

Example

The following example checks to see whether the collection has a **BrowsableAttribute** set to **true**. It assumes that `button1` and `textBox1` have been created on a form.

[C#]
```
private void ContainsAttribute() {
    // Creates a new collection and assigns it the attributes ↵
for button1.
    AttributeCollection attributes;
    attributes = TypeDescriptor.GetAttributes(button1);

    // Sets an Attribute to the specific attribute.
    BrowsableAttribute myAttribute = BrowsableAttribute.Yes;

    if (attributes.Contains(myAttribute))
       textBox1.Text = "button1 has a browsable attribute.";
    else
       textBox1.Text = "button1 does not have a browsable attribute.";
 }
```

[C++]
```
void ContainsAttribute()
{
    // Creates a new collection and assigns it the attributes ↵
for button1.
    AttributeCollection* attributes;
    attributes = TypeDescriptor::GetAttributes( button1 );

    // Sets an Attribute to the specific attribute.
    BrowsableAttribute* myAttribute = BrowsableAttribute::Yes;

    if (attributes->Contains(myAttribute))
       textBox1->Text = S"button1 has a browsable attribute.";
    else
       textBox1->Text = S"button1 does not have a browsable ↵
attribute.";
}
```

[JScript]
```
private function ContainsAttribute() {
    // Creates a new collection and assigns it the attributes ↵
for button1.
    var attributes : AttributeCollection;
    attributes = TypeDescriptor.GetAttributes(button1);

    // Sets an Attribute to the specific attribute.
    var myAttribute : BrowsableAttribute  = BrowsableAttribute.Yes;

    if (attributes.Contains(myAttribute))
       textBox1.Text = "button1 has a browsable attribute.";
    else
       textBox1.Text = "button1 does not have a browsable attribute.";
 }
```

Requirements

Platforms: Windows 98, Windows NT 4.0, Windows Millennium Edition, Windows 2000, Windows XP Home Edition, Windows XP Professional, Windows Server 2003 family, .NET Compact Framework - Windows CE .NET

AttributeCollection.Contains Method (Attribute[])

Determines whether this attribute collection contains all the specified attributes in the attribute array.

[Visual Basic]
```
Overloads Public Function Contains( _
   ByVal attributes() As Attribute _
) As Boolean
```
[C#]
```
public bool Contains(
   Attribute[] attributes
);
```
[C++]
```
public: bool Contains(
   Attribute* attributes[]
);
```
[JScript]
```
public function Contains(
   attributes : Attribute[]
) : Boolean;
```

Parameters

attributes

An array of type **Attribute** to find in the collection.

Return Value

true if the collection contains all the attributes; otherwise, **false**.

Remarks

This collection has the specified array of attributes if all the specified attribute types exist in the collection and if each attribute in the specified array is the same as an attribute in the collection.

Example

The following example compares the attributes in `button1` and `textBox1` to see whether the attributes for the button are contained in the attributes for the text box. It assumes that both `button1` and `textBox1` have been created on a form.

[Visual Basic]
```
Private Sub ContainsAttributes()
    ' Creates a new collection and assigns it the attributes     ↵
 for button1.
    Dim myCollection As AttributeCollection
    myCollection = TypeDescriptor.GetAttributes(button1)

    ' Checks to see whether the attributes in myCollection are     ↵
the attributes for textBox1.
    Dim myAttrArray(100) As Attribute
    TypeDescriptor.GetAttributes(textBox1).CopyTo(myAttrArray, 0)
    If myCollection.Contains(myAttrArray) Then
        textBox1.Text = "Both the button and text box have the     ↵
same attributes."
    Else
        textBox1.Text = "The button and the text box do not have     ↵
 the same attributes."
    End If
End Sub
```

[C#]
```
private void ContainsAttributes() {
   // Creates a new collection and assigns it the attributes     ↵
for button1.
   AttributeCollection myCollection;
   myCollection = TypeDescriptor.GetAttributes(button1);

   // Checks to see whether the attributes in myCollection are     ↵
the attributes for textBox1.
   Attribute[] myAttrArray = new Attribute[100];
   TypeDescriptor.GetAttributes(textBox1).CopyTo(myAttrArray, 0);
   if (myCollection.Contains(myAttrArray))
      textBox1.Text = "Both the button and text box have the     ↵
same attributes.";
   else
      textBox1.Text = "The button and the text box do not have     ↵
 the same attributes.";
}
```

[C++]
```
private:

    void ContainsAttributes()
    {
        // Creates a new collection and assigns it the     ↵
attributes for button1.
        AttributeCollection* myCollection;
        myCollection = TypeDescriptor::GetAttributes( button1 );


        // Checks to see whether the attributes in myCollection     ↵
 are the attributes for textBox1.
        Attribute*    myAttrArray[] = new Attribute*[100];

        TypeDescriptor::GetAttributes( textBox1 )->CopyTo     ↵
 (myAttrArray, 0);
        if (myCollection->Contains(myAttrArray))
            textBox1->Text = S"Both the button and text box     ↵
have the same attributes.";
        else
            textBox1->Text = S"The button and the text box do     ↵
not have the same attributes.";
    }
```

[JScript]
```
private function ContainsAttributes() {
   // Creates a new collection and assigns it the attributes     ↵
 for button1.
   var myCollection : AttributeCollection;
   myCollection = TypeDescriptor.GetAttributes(button1);

   // Checks to see whether the attributes in myCollection are     ↵
the attributes for textBox1.
   var myAttrArray : Attribute[]  = new Attribute[100];
   TypeDescriptor.GetAttributes(textBox1).CopyTo(myAttrArray, 0);
   if (myCollection.Contains(myAttrArray))
      textBox1.Text = "Both the button and text box have the     ↵
 same attributes.";
   else
      textBox1.Text = "The button and the text box do not have     ↵
the same attributes.";

}
```

Requirements

Platforms: Windows 98, Windows NT 4.0, Windows Millennium Edition, Windows 2000, Windows XP Home Edition, Windows XP Professional, Windows Server 2003 family

AttributeCollection.CopyTo Method

Copies the collection to an array, starting at the specified index.

[Visual Basic]
```
Public Overridable Sub CopyTo( _
   ByVal array As Array, _
   ByVal index As Integer _
) Implements ICollection.CopyTo
```
[C#]
```
public virtual void CopyTo(
   Array array,
   int index
);
```

```
[C++]
public: virtual void CopyTo(
   Array* array,
   int index
);
[JScript]
public function CopyTo(
   array : Array,
   index : int
);
```

Parameters

array

The **Array** to copy the collection to.

index

The index to start from.

Implements

ICollection.CopyTo

Requirements

Platforms: Windows 98, Windows NT 4.0, Windows Millennium Edition, Windows 2000, Windows XP Home Edition, Windows XP Professional, Windows Server 2003 family, .NET Compact Framework - Windows CE .NET

AttributeCollection.GetDefaultAttribute Method

Returns the default **Attribute** of a given **Type**.

```
[Visual Basic]
Protected Function GetDefaultAttribute( _
   ByVal attributeType As Type _
) As Attribute
[C#]
protected Attribute GetDefaultAttribute(
   Type attributeType
);
[C++]
protected: Attribute* GetDefaultAttribute(
   Type* attributeType
);
[JScript]
protected function GetDefaultAttribute(
   attributeType : Type
) : Attribute;
```

Parameters

attributeType

The **Type** of the attribute to retrieve.

Return Value

An **Attribute**.

Requirements

Platforms: Windows 98, Windows NT 4.0, Windows Millennium Edition, Windows 2000, Windows XP Home Edition, Windows XP Professional, Windows Server 2003 family, .NET Compact Framework - Windows CE .NET

AttributeCollection.GetEnumerator Method

Gets an enumerator for this collection.

```
[Visual Basic]
Public Function GetEnumerator() As IEnumerator
[C#]
public IEnumerator GetEnumerator();
[C++]
public: IEnumerator* GetEnumerator();
[JScript]
public function GetEnumerator() : IEnumerator;
```

Return Value

An enumerator of type **IEnumerator**.

Example

[Visual Basic, C#, C++] The following example gets an enumerator for the attributes on `button1`. It uses the enumerator to print the names of the attributes in the collection. It assumes that `button1` and `textBox1` have been created on a form.

```
[Visual Basic]
Private Sub MyEnumerator
    ' Creates a new collection and assigns it the attributes ↵
for button1.
    Dim attributes As AttributeCollection
    attributes = TypeDescriptor.GetAttributes(button1)

    ' Creates an enumerator for the collection.
    Dim ie As System.Collections.IEnumerator = attributes.GetEnumerator

    ' Prints the type of each attribute in the collection.
    Dim myAttribute As Object
    Do While ie.MoveNext
        myAttribute = ie.Current
        textBox1.Text = textBox1.Text & myAttribute.toString & ↵
ControlChars.crlf
    Loop
End Sub
```

```
[C#]
private void MyEnumerator() {
    // Creates a new collection and assigns it the attributes ↵
 for button1.
    AttributeCollection attributes;
    attributes = TypeDescriptor.GetAttributes(button1);

    // Creates an enumerator for the collection.
    System.Collections.IEnumerator ie = attributes.GetEnumerator();

    // Prints the type of each attribute in the collection.
    Object myAttribute;
    while(ie.MoveNext()==true) {
       myAttribute = ie.Current;
       textBox1.Text += myAttribute.ToString();
       textBox1.Text += '\n';
    }
 }
```

```
[C++]
private:
   void MyEnumerator()
   {
       // Creates a new collection and assigns it the ↵
 attributes for button1.
       AttributeCollection*    attributes;
       attributes = TypeDescriptor::GetAttributes(button1);

       // Creates an enumerator for the collection.
       System::Collections::IEnumerator* ie = attributes- ↵
>GetEnumerator();
```

```
        // Prints the type of each attribute in the collection.
        Object*             myAttribute;
        System::Text::StringBuilder*    text = new                    ↵
System::Text::StringBuilder();
        while ( ie->MoveNext() == true )
        {
            myAttribute = ie->Current;
            text->Append( myAttribute );
            text->Append( '\n' );
        }
        textBox1->Text = text->ToString();
 }
```

Requirements

Platforms: Windows 98, Windows NT 4.0, Windows Millennium Edition, Windows 2000, Windows XP Home Edition, Windows XP Professional, Windows Server 2003 family, .NET Compact Framework - Windows CE .NET

AttributeCollection.IEnumerable.GetEnumerator Method

This member supports the .NET Framework infrastructure and is not intended to be used directly from your code.

[Visual Basic]
```
Private Function GetEnumerator() As IEnumerator Implements _
   IEnumerable.GetEnumerator
```
[C#]
```
IEnumerator IEnumerable.GetEnumerator();
```
[C++]
```
private: IEnumerator* IEnumerable::GetEnumerator();
```
[JScript]
```
private function IEnumerable.GetEnumerator() : IEnumerator;
```

AttributeCollection.Matches Method

Determines whether a specified attribute or array of attributes is the same as an attribute or array of attributes in the collection.

Overload List

Determines whether a specified attribute is the same as an attribute in the collection.

Supported by the .NET Compact Framework.

[Visual Basic] **Overloads Public Function Matches(Attribute) As Boolean**

[C#] **public bool Matches(Attribute);**

[C++] **public: bool Matches(Attribute*);**

[JScript] **public function Matches(Attribute) : Boolean;**

Determines whether the attributes in the specified array are the same as the attributes in the collection.

[Visual Basic] **Overloads Public Function Matches(Attribute()) As Boolean**

[C#] **public bool Matches(Attribute[]);**

[C++] **public: bool Matches(Attribute*[]);**

[JScript] **public function Matches(Attribute[]) : Boolean;**

Example

The following example compares the attributes in a button and a text box to see whether they match. It assumes that `button1` and `textBox1` have been created on a form.

[Visual Basic]
```
Private Sub MatchesAttributes()
    ' Creates a new collection and assigns it the attributes for      ↵
button1.
    Dim myCollection As AttributeCollection
    myCollection = TypeDescriptor.GetAttributes(button1)

    ' Checks to see whether the attributes in myCollection match      ↵
the attributes.
    ' for textBox1.
    Dim myAttrArray(100) As Attribute
    TypeDescriptor.GetAttributes(textBox1).CopyTo(myAttrArray, 0)
    If myCollection.Matches(myAttrArray) Then
        textBox1.Text = "The attributes in the button and text        ↵
box match."
    Else
        textBox1.Text = "The attributes in the button and text        ↵
box do not match."
    End If
End Sub
```

[C#]
```
private void MatchesAttributes() {
   // Creates a new collection and assigns it the attributes for      ↵
button1.
   AttributeCollection myCollection;
   myCollection = TypeDescriptor.GetAttributes(button1);

   // Checks to see whether the attributes in myCollection match      ↵
the attributes for textBox1.
   Attribute[] myAttrArray = new Attribute[100];
   TypeDescriptor.GetAttributes(textBox1).CopyTo(myAttrArray, 0);
   if (myCollection.Matches(myAttrArray))
      textBox1.Text = "The attributes in the button and text box match.";
   else
      textBox1.Text = "The attributes in the button and text box      ↵
do not match.";
}
```

[C++]
```
private:
    void MatchesAttributes()
    {
        // Creates a new collection and assigns it the                ↵
 attributes for button1.
        AttributeCollection*    myCollection;
        myCollection = TypeDescriptor::GetAttributes( button1 );

        // Checks to see whether the attributes in myCollection       ↵
 match the attributes for textBox1.
        Attribute*    myAttrArray[] = new Attribute*[100];
        TypeDescriptor::GetAttributes( textBox1 )->CopyTo             ↵
 (myAttrArray, 0);

        if ( myCollection->Matches( myAttrArray ))
            textBox1->Text = S"The attributes in the button and       ↵
 text box match.";
        else
            textBox1->Text = S"The attributes in the button and       ↵
 text box do not match.";
    }
```

[JScript]
```
private function MatchesAttribute() {
    // Creates a new collection and assigns it the attributes         ↵
for button1.
    var myCollection : AttributeCollection;
    myCollection = TypeDescriptor.GetAttributes(button1);

    // Checks to see whether the attributes in myCollection           ↵
match the attributes for textBox1.
    var myAttrArray : Attribute[] = new Attribute[100];
    TypeDescriptor.GetAttributes(textBox1).CopyTo(myAttrArray, 0);
```

```
   if (myCollection.Matches(myAttrArray))
      textBox1.Text = "The attributes in the button and text       ↵
box match.";
   else
      textBox1.Text = "The attributes in the button and text       ↵
box do not match.";
   Console.WriteLine(textBox1.Text);
}
```

AttributeCollection.Matches Method (Attribute)

Determines whether a specified attribute is the same as an attribute in the collection.

[Visual Basic]
```
Overloads Public Function Matches( _
   ByVal attribute As Attribute _
) As Boolean
```
[C#]
```
public bool Matches(
   Attribute attribute
);
```
[C++]
```
public: bool Matches(
   Attribute* attribute
);
```
[JScript]
```
public function Matches(
   attribute : Attribute
) : Boolean;
```

Parameters

attribute

An instance of **Attribute** to compare with the attributes in this collection.

Return Value

true if the attribute is contained within the collection and has the same value as the attribute in the collection; otherwise, **false**.

Remarks

An attribute can provide support for matching.

The difference between **Matches** and **Contains** is that **Matches** calls the **Match** method on an attribute, and **Contains** calls the **Equals** method.

For most attributes these methods do the same thing. For attributes that may have multiple flags, however, **Match** is typically implemented so that it returns **true** if any of the flags are satisified. For example, consider a data binding attribute with the Boolean flags "SupportsSql", "SupportsOleDb" and "SupportsXml". This attribute may be present on a property that supports all three data binding approaches. It will often be the case that a programmer only needs to know if a particlar approach is available, not all three. So a programmer could use **Match** with an instance of the attribute containing only the flags he/she needs.

Example

The following example verifies that the **BrowsableAttribute** is a member of the collection and that it has been set to **true**. It assumes that `button1` and `textBox1` have been created on a form.

[Visual Basic]
```
Private Sub MatchesAttribute
    ' Creates a new collection and assigns it the attributes for button
    Dim attributes As AttributeCollection
    attributes = TypeDescriptor.GetAttributes(button1)

    ' Checks to see if the browsable attribute is true.
    If attributes.Matches(BrowsableAttribute.Yes) Then
        textBox1.Text = "button1 is browsable."
    Else
        textBox1.Text = "button1 is not browsable."
    End If
End Sub
End Class
```

[C#]
```
private void MatchesAttribute() {
    // Creates a new collection and assigns it the attributes       ↵
for button1.
    AttributeCollection attributes;
    attributes = TypeDescriptor.GetAttributes(button1);

    // Checks to see if the browsable attribute is true.
    if (attributes.Matches(BrowsableAttribute.Yes))
       textBox1.Text = "button1 is browsable.";
    else
       textBox1.Text = "button1 is not browsable.";
 }
```

[C++]
```
private:
    void MatchesAttribute()
    {
        // Creates a new collection and assigns it the attributes       ↵
 for button1.
        AttributeCollection* attributes;
        attributes = TypeDescriptor::GetAttributes( button1 );

        // Checks to see if the browsable attribute is true.
        if (attributes->Matches(BrowsableAttribute::Yes))
            textBox1->Text = S"button1 is browsable.";
        else
            textBox1->Text = S"button1 is not browsable.";
    }
```

[JScript]
```
private function MatchesAttribute() {
    // Creates a new collection and assigns it the attributes       ↵
 for button1.
    var attributes : AttributeCollection;
    attributes = TypeDescriptor.GetAttributes(button1);

    // Checks to see if the browsable attribute is true.
    if (attributes.Matches(BrowsableAttribute.Yes))
       textBox1.Text = "button1 is browsable.";
    else
       textBox1.Text = "button1 is not browsable.";
    Console.WriteLine(textBox1.Text);
 }
```

Requirements

Platforms: Windows 98, Windows NT 4.0, Windows Millennium Edition, Windows 2000, Windows XP Home Edition, Windows XP Professional, Windows Server 2003 family, .NET Compact Framework - Windows CE .NET

AttributeCollection.Matches Method (Attribute[])

Determines whether the attributes in the specified array are the same as the attributes in the collection.

```
[Visual Basic]
Overloads Public Function Matches( _
   ByVal attributes() As Attribute _
) As Boolean
[C#]
public bool Matches(
   Attribute[] attributes
);
[C++]
public: bool Matches(
   Attribute* attributes[]
);
[JScript]
public function Matches(
   attributes : Attribute[]
) : Boolean;
```

Parameters

attributes

An array of **MemberAttributes** to compare with the attributes in this collection.

Return Value

true if all the attributes in the array are contained in the collection and have the same values as the attributes in the collection; otherwise, **false**.

Remarks

An attribute can provide support for matching.

Example

The following example compares the attributes in a button and a text box to see whether they match. It assumes that `button1` and `textBox1` have been created on a form.

```
[Visual Basic]
Private Sub MatchesAttributes()
    ' Creates a new collection and assigns it the attributes
 for button1.
    Dim myCollection As AttributeCollection
    myCollection = TypeDescriptor.GetAttributes(button1)

    ' Checks to see whether the attributes in myCollection match
 the attributes.
    ' for textBox1.
    Dim myAttrArray(100) As Attribute
    TypeDescriptor.GetAttributes(textBox1).CopyTo(myAttrArray, 0)
    If myCollection.Matches(myAttrArray) Then
        textBox1.Text = "The attributes in the button and text
 box match."
    Else
        textBox1.Text = "The attributes in the button and text
 box do not match."
    End If
End Sub

[C#]
private void MatchesAttributes() {
   // Creates a new collection and assigns it the attributes
 for button1.
   AttributeCollection myCollection;
   myCollection = TypeDescriptor.GetAttributes(button1);

   // Checks to see whether the attributes in myCollection
 match the attributes for textBox1.
   Attribute[] myAttrArray = new Attribute[100];
   TypeDescriptor.GetAttributes(textBox1).CopyTo(myAttrArray, 0);
   if (myCollection.Matches(myAttrArray))
      textBox1.Text = "The attributes in the button and text
 box match.";
   else
      textBox1.Text = "The attributes in the button and text
 box do not match.";
}

[C++]
private:
    void MatchesAttributes()
    {
        // Creates a new collection and assigns it the attributes
 for button1.
        AttributeCollection*    myCollection;
        myCollection = TypeDescriptor::GetAttributes( button1 );

        // Checks to see whether the attributes in myCollection
 match the attributes for textBox1.
        Attribute*    myAttrArray[] = new Attribute*[100];
        TypeDescriptor::GetAttributes( textBox1 )->CopyTo
 (myAttrArray, 0);

        if ( myCollection->Matches( myAttrArray ))
            textBox1->Text = S"The attributes in the button
 and text box match.";
        else
            textBox1->Text = S"The attributes in the button
 and text box do not match.";
    }

[JScript]
private function MatchesAttribute() {
    // Creates a new collection and assigns it the attributes
 for button1.
    var myCollection : AttributeCollection;
    myCollection = TypeDescriptor.GetAttributes(button1);

    // Checks to see whether the attributes in myCollection
 match the attributes for textBox1.
    var myAttrArray : Attribute[] = new Attribute[100];
    TypeDescriptor.GetAttributes(textBox1).CopyTo(myAttrArray, 0);
    if (myCollection.Matches(myAttrArray))
       textBox1.Text = "The attributes in the button and text
 box match.";
    else
       textBox1.Text = "The attributes in the button and text
 box do not match.";
    Console.WriteLine(textBox1.Text);
 }
```

Requirements

Platforms: Windows 98, Windows NT 4.0, Windows Millennium Edition, Windows 2000, Windows XP Home Edition, Windows XP Professional, Windows Server 2003 family

BaseNumberConverter Class

Provides a base type converter for nonfloating point numerical types.

System.Object
  System.ComponentModel.TypeConverter
    System.ComponentModel.BaseNumberConverter
      Derived classes

[Visual Basic]
```
MustInherit Public Class BaseNumberConverter
   Inherits TypeConverter
```
[C#]
```
public abstract class BaseNumberConverter : TypeConverter
```
[C++]
```
public __gc __abstract class BaseNumberConverter : public
   TypeConverter
```
[JScript]
```
public abstract class BaseNumberConverter extends TypeConverter
```

Thread Safety

Any public static (**Shared** in Visual Basic) members of this type are safe for multithreaded operations. Any instance members are not guaranteed to be thread safe.

Remarks

> **CAUTION** You should never access a type converter directly. Instead, call the appropriate converter by using **TypeDescriptor**. For more information, see the examples in the **TypeConverter** base class.

For more information about type converters, see the **TypeConverter** base class and **Implementing a Type Converter**.

Example

For an example of a converter for a specific data type that inherits from **BaseNumberConverter**, see the example section of each of the classes listed at **BaseNumberConverter Hierarchy**.

Requirements

Namespace: System.ComponentModel

Platforms: Windows 98, Windows NT 4.0, Windows Millennium Edition, Windows 2000, Windows XP Home Edition, Windows XP Professional, Windows Server 2003 family

Assembly: System (in System.dll)

BaseNumberConverter Constructor

Initializes a new instance of the **BaseNumberConverter** class.

[Visual Basic]
```
Protected Sub New()
```
[C#]
```
protected BaseNumberConverter();
```
[C++]
```
protected: BaseNumberConverter();
```
[JScript]
```
protected function BaseNumberConverter();
```

Remarks

This constructor is called by derived class constructors to initialize state in this type.

Requirements

Platforms: Windows 98, Windows NT 4.0, Windows Millennium Edition, Windows 2000, Windows XP Home Edition, Windows XP Professional, Windows Server 2003 family

BaseNumberConverter.CanConvertFrom Method

Overload List

This member supports the .NET Framework infrastructure and is not intended to be used directly from your code.

[Visual Basic] **Overloads Overrides Public Function CanConvertFrom(ITypeDescriptorContext, Type) As Boolean**

[C#] **public override bool CanConvertFrom(ITypeDescriptorContext, Type);**

[C++] **public: bool CanConvertFrom(ITypeDescriptorContext*, Type*);**

[JScript] **public override function CanConvertFrom(ITypeDescriptorContext, Type) : Boolean;**

Inherited from **TypeConverter**.

[Visual Basic] **Overloads Public Function CanConvertFrom(Type) As Boolean**

[C#] **public bool CanConvertFrom(Type);**

[C++] **public: bool CanConvertFrom(Type*);**

[JScript] **public function CanConvertFrom(Type) : Boolean;**

BaseNumberConverter.CanConvertFrom Method (ITypeDescriptorContext, Type)

This member overrides **TypeConverter.CanConvertFrom**.

[Visual Basic]
```
Overrides Overloads Public Function CanConvertFrom( _
   ByVal context As ITypeDescriptorContext, _
   ByVal sourceType As Type _
) As Boolean
```
[C#]
```
public override bool CanConvertFrom(
   ITypeDescriptorContext context,
   Type sourceType
);
```
[C++]
```
public: bool CanConvertFrom(
   ITypeDescriptorContext* context,
   Type* sourceType
);
```
[JScript]
```
public override function CanConvertFrom(
   context : ITypeDescriptorContext,
   sourceType : Type
) : Boolean;
```

Requirements

Platforms: Windows 98, Windows NT 4.0, Windows Millennium Edition, Windows 2000, Windows XP Home Edition, Windows XP Professional, Windows Server 2003 family

BaseNumberConverter.CanConvertTo Method

Overload List

This member supports the .NET Framework infrastructure and is not intended to be used directly from your code.

[Visual Basic] **Overloads Overrides Public Function CanConvertTo(ITypeDescriptorContext, Type) As Boolean**

[C#] **public override bool CanConvertTo(ITypeDescriptorContext, Type);**

[C++] **public: bool CanConvertTo(ITypeDescriptorContext*, Type*);**

[JScript] **public override function CanConvertTo(ITypeDescriptorContext, Type) : Boolean;**

Inherited from **TypeConverter**.

[Visual Basic] **Overloads Public Function CanConvertTo(Type) As Boolean**

[C#] **public bool CanConvertTo(Type);**

[C++] **public: bool CanConvertTo(Type*);**

[JScript] **public function CanConvertTo(Type) : Boolean;**

BaseNumberConverter.CanConvertTo Method (ITypeDescriptorContext, Type)

This member overrides **TypeConverter.CanConvertTo**.

[Visual Basic]
```
Overrides Overloads Public Function CanConvertTo( _
   ByVal context As ITypeDescriptorContext, _
   ByVal t As Type _
) As Boolean
```
[C#]
```
public override bool CanConvertTo(
   ITypeDescriptorContext context,
   Type t
);
```
[C++]
```
public: bool CanConvertTo(
   ITypeDescriptorContext* context,
   Type* t
);
```
[JScript]
```
public override function CanConvertTo(
   context : ITypeDescriptorContext,
   t : Type
) : Boolean;
```

Requirements

Platforms: Windows 98, Windows NT 4.0, Windows Millennium Edition, Windows 2000, Windows XP Home Edition, Windows XP Professional, Windows Server 2003 family

BaseNumberConverter.ConvertFrom Method

Overload List

This member supports the .NET Framework infrastructure and is not intended to be used directly from your code.

[Visual Basic] **Overloads Overrides Public Function ConvertFrom(ITypeDescriptorContext, CultureInfo, Object) As Object**

[C#] **public override object ConvertFrom(ITypeDescriptorContext, CultureInfo, object);**

[C++] **public: Object* ConvertFrom(ITypeDescriptorContext*, CultureInfo*, Object*);**

[JScript] **public override function ConvertFrom(ITypeDescriptorContext, CultureInfo, Object) : Object;**

Inherited from **TypeConverter**.

[Visual Basic] **Overloads Public Function ConvertFrom(Object) As Object**

[C#] **public object ConvertFrom(object);**

[C++] **public: Object* ConvertFrom(Object*);**

[JScript] **public function ConvertFrom(Object) : Object;**

BaseNumberConverter.ConvertFrom Method (ITypeDescriptorContext, CultureInfo, Object)

This member overrides **TypeConverter.ConvertFrom**.

[Visual Basic]
```
Overrides Overloads Public Function ConvertFrom( _
   ByVal context As ITypeDescriptorContext, _
   ByVal culture As CultureInfo, _
   ByVal value As Object _
) As Object
```
[C#]
```
public override object ConvertFrom(
   ITypeDescriptorContext context,
   CultureInfo culture,
   object value
);
```
[C++]
```
public: Object* ConvertFrom(
   ITypeDescriptorContext* context,
   CultureInfo* culture,
   Object* value
);
```
[JScript]
```
public override function ConvertFrom(
   context : ITypeDescriptorContext,
   culture : CultureInfo,
   value : Object
) : Object;
```

Requirements

Platforms: Windows 98, Windows NT 4.0, Windows Millennium Edition, Windows 2000, Windows XP Home Edition, Windows XP Professional, Windows Server 2003 family

BaseNumberConverter.ConvertTo Method

Overload List

This member supports the .NET Framework infrastructure and is not intended to be used directly from your code.

[Visual Basic] **Overloads Overrides Public Function ConvertTo(ITypeDescriptorContext, CultureInfo, Object, Type) As Object**

[C#] **public override object ConvertTo(ITypeDescriptor-Context, CultureInfo, object, Type);**

[C++] **public: Object* ConvertTo(ITypeDescriptorContext*, CultureInfo*, Object*, Type*);**

[JScript] **public override function ConvertTo(IType-DescriptorContext, CultureInfo, Object, Type) : Object;**

Inherited from **TypeConverter**.

[Visual Basic] **Overloads Public Function ConvertTo(Object, Type) As Object**

[C#] **public object ConvertTo(object, Type);**

[C++] **public: Object* ConvertTo(Object*, Type*);**

[JScript] **public function ConvertTo(Object, Type) : Object;**

BaseNumberConverter.ConvertTo Method (ITypeDescriptorContext, CultureInfo, Object, Type)

This member overrides **TypeConverter.ConvertTo**.

```
[Visual Basic]
Overrides Overloads Public Function ConvertTo( _
   ByVal context As ITypeDescriptorContext, _
   ByVal culture As CultureInfo, _
   ByVal value As Object, _
   ByVal destinationType As Type _
) As Object
[C#]
public override object ConvertTo(
   ITypeDescriptorContext context,
   CultureInfo culture,
   object value,
   Type destinationType
);
[C++]
public: Object* ConvertTo(
   ITypeDescriptorContext* context,
   CultureInfo* culture,
   Object* value,
   Type* destinationType
);
[JScript]
public override function ConvertTo(
   context : ITypeDescriptorContext,
   culture : CultureInfo,
   value : Object,
   destinationType : Type
) : Object;
```

Requirements

Platforms: Windows 98, Windows NT 4.0, Windows Millennium Edition, Windows 2000, Windows XP Home Edition, Windows XP Professional, Windows Server 2003 family

BindableAttribute Class

Specifies whether a property is typically used for binding.

System.Object
  System.Attribute
    System.ComponentModel.BindableAttribute

[Visual Basic]
```
<AttributeUsage(AttributeTargets.All)>
NotInheritable Public Class BindableAttribute
   Inherits Attribute
```
[C#]
```
[AttributeUsage(AttributeTargets.All)]
public sealed class BindableAttribute : Attribute
```
[C++]
```
[AttributeUsage(AttributeTargets::All)]
public __gc __sealed class BindableAttribute : public Attribute
```
[JScript]
```
public
   AttributeUsage(AttributeTargets.All)
class BindableAttribute extends Attribute
```

Thread Safety

Any public static (**Shared** in Visual Basic) members of this type are safe for multithreaded operations. Any instance members are not guaranteed to be thread safe.

Remarks

You can specify this attribute for multiple properties on a control.

Initializes a new instance of the **BindableAttribute** class with a Boolean value.

If a property has been marked with the **BindableAttribute** constructor of the value **true**, then a property change notification should be raised for that property. This means that if **Bindable** is **Yes**, then two-way data binding is supported. If **Bindable** is **No**, you can still bind to the property, but it should not be shown in the default set of properties to bind to, because it might or might not raise a property change notification.

Note When you mark a property the **BindableAttribute** constructor of the value **true** , the value of this attribute is set to the constant member **Yes**. For a property marked with the **BindableAttribute** constructor of the value **false,** the value is **No**. Therefore, to check the value of this attribute in your code, you must specify the attribute as **BindableAttribute.Yes** or **BindableAttribute.No**.

CAUTION You can use this attribute at design time only. Nothing prevents you from binding to any property during run time.

Example

[Visual Basic, C#, C++] The following example marks a property as appropriate to bind data to.

[Visual Basic]
```
<Bindable(True)> _
Public Property MyProperty() As Integer
    Get
        ' Insert code here.
        Return 0
    End Get
    Set
        ' Insert code here.
    End Set
End Property
```

[C#]
```
[Bindable(true)]
 public int MyProperty {
    get {
       // Insert code here.
       return 0;
    }
    set {
       // Insert code here.
    }
 }
```

[C++]
```
public:

    [System::ComponentModel::Bindable(true)]
    __property int get_MyProperty() {
        // Insert code here.
        return 0;
    }

    [System::ComponentModel::Bindable(true)]
    __property void set_MyProperty(int) {
        // Insert code here.
    }
```

[Visual Basic, C#, C++] The next example shows how to check the value of the **BindableAttribute** for `MyProperty`. First, the code gets a **PropertyDescriptorCollection** with all the properties for the object. Next, it indexes into the **PropertyDescriptorCollection** to get `MyProperty`. Finally, it returns the attributes for this property and saves them in the attributes variable. The example presents two different ways to check the value of the **BindableAttribute**. In the second code fragment, the example calls the **Equals** method. In the last code fragment, the example uses the **Bindable** property to check the value.

[Visual Basic]
```
' Gets the attributes for the property.
Dim attributes As AttributeCollection = _
    TypeDescriptor.GetProperties(Me)("MyProperty").Attributes

' Checks to see if the value of the BindableAttribute is Yes.
If attributes                                                          ↵
(GetType(BindableAttribute)).Equals(BindableAttribute.Yes) Then
    ' Insert code here.
End If

' This is another way to see whether the property is bindable.
Dim myAttribute As BindableAttribute = _
    CType(attributes(GetType(BindableAttribute)), BindableAttribute)
If myAttribute.Bindable Then
    ' Insert code here.
End If

         ' Yet another way to see whether the property is bindable.
        If attributes.Contains(BindableAttribute.Yes) Then
        ' Insert code here.
        End If
```

[C#]
```
// Gets the attributes for the property.
 AttributeCollection attributes =
    TypeDescriptor.GetProperties(this)["MyProperty"].Attributes;

 // Checks to see if the value of the BindableAttribute is Yes.
 if(attributes                                                          ↵
 [typeof(BindableAttribute)].Equals(BindableAttribute.Yes)) {
    // Insert code here.
 }

 // This is another way to see whether the property is bindable.
 BindableAttribute myAttribute =
    (BindableAttribute)attributes[typeof(BindableAttribute)];
 if(myAttribute.Bindable) {
    // Insert code here.
 }
```

```
      // Yet another way to see whether the property is bindable.
      if (attributes.Contains(BindableAttribute.Yes)) {
// Insert code here.
      }
```

[C++]
```
using namespace System::ComponentModel;

        // Gets the attributes for the property.
AttributeCollection* attributes =
   TypeDescriptor::GetProperties(this)->Item
 [S"MyProperty"]->Attributes;

// Checks to see if the value of the BindableAttribute is Yes.
if(attributes->Item[__typeof(BindableAttribute)]-
>Equals(BindableAttribute::Yes)) {
   // Insert code here.
}

// This is another way to see whether the property is bindable.
BindableAttribute* myAttribute =
   static_cast<BindableAttribute*>(attributes-
>Item[__typeof(BindableAttribute)]);
if(myAttribute->Bindable) {
   // Insert code here.
}

// Yet another way to see whether the property is bindable.
if (attributes->Contains(BindableAttribute::Yes)) {
   // Insert code here.
}
```

[Visual Basic, C#, C++] If you marked a class with the **BindableAttribute**, use the following code to check the value.

[Visual Basic]
```
Dim attributes As AttributeCollection =
TypeDescriptor.GetAttributes(MyProperty)
If attributes(GetType(BindableAttribute)).Equals
 (BindableAttribute.Yes) Then
    ' Insert code here.
End If
```

[C#]
```
AttributeCollection attributes =
    TypeDescriptor.GetAttributes(MyProperty);
 if(attributes[typeof(BindableAttribute)].Equals
 (BindableAttribute.Yes)) {
    // Insert code here.
 }
```

[C++]
```
using namespace System::ComponentModel;

AttributeCollection* attributes =
TypeDescriptor::GetAttributes(__box(MyProperty));

if(attributes->Item[__typeof(BindableAttribute)]-
>Equals(BindableAttribute::Yes)) {
    // Insert code here.
}
```

Requirements

Namespace: System.ComponentModel

Platforms: Windows 98, Windows NT 4.0, Windows Millennium Edition, Windows 2000, Windows XP Home Edition, Windows XP Professional, Windows Server 2003 family

Assembly: System (in System.dll)

BindableAttribute Constructor

Initializes a new instance of the **BindableAttribute** class.

Overload List

Initializes a new instance of the **BindableAttribute** class with one of the **BindableSupport** values.

[Visual Basic] **Public Sub New(BindableSupport)**

[C#] **public BindableAttribute(BindableSupport);**

[C++] **public: BindableAttribute(BindableSupport);**

[JScript] **public function BindableAttribute(BindableSupport);**

Initializes a new instance of the **BindableAttribute** class with a Boolean value.

[Visual Basic] **Public Sub New(Boolean)**

[C#] **public BindableAttribute(bool);**

[C++] **public: BindableAttribute(bool);**

[JScript] **public function BindableAttribute(Boolean);**

Example

See related example in the **System.ComponentModel.BindableAttribute** class topic.

BindableAttribute Constructor (BindableSupport)

Initializes a new instance of the **BindableAttribute** class with one of the **BindableSupport** values.

[Visual Basic]
```
Public Sub New( _
   ByVal flags As BindableSupport _
)
```
[C#]
```
public BindableAttribute(
   BindableSupport flags
);
```
[C++]
```
public: BindableAttribute(
   BindableSupport flags
);
```
[JScript]
```
public function BindableAttribute(
   flags : BindableSupport
);
```

Parameters

flags
  One of the **BindableSupport** values.

Remarks

When you mark a property with the **ctor** constructor of the value **true**, the value of this attribute is set to the constant member **Yes**. For a property marked with the **ctor** constructor of the value **false**, the value is **No**. Therefore, to check the value of this attribute in your code, you must specify the attribute as **BindableAttribute.Yes** or **BindableAttribute.No**.

Example

See related example in the **System.ComponentModel.BindableAttribute** class topic.

Requirements

Platforms: Windows 98, Windows NT 4.0, Windows Millennium Edition, Windows 2000, Windows XP Home Edition, Windows XP Professional, Windows Server 2003 family

BindableAttribute Constructor (Boolean)

Initializes a new instance of the **BindableAttribute** class with a Boolean value.

```
[Visual Basic]
Public Sub New( _
   ByVal bindable As Boolean _
)
[C#]
public BindableAttribute(
   bool bindable
);
[C++]
public: BindableAttribute(
   bool bindable
);
[JScript]
public function BindableAttribute(
   bindable : Boolean
);
```

Parameters

bindable
: **true** if a property is typically used for binding; otherwise, **false**. The default is **false**.

Remarks

When you mark a property with the **ctor** constructor of the value **true**, the value of this attribute is set to the constant member **Yes**. For a property marked with the **ctor** constructor of the value **false**, the value is **No**. Therefore, to check the value of this attribute in your code, you must specify the attribute as **BindableAttribute.Yes** or **BindableAttribute.No**.

Example

See related example in the **System.ComponentModel.BindableAttribute** class topic.

Requirements

Platforms: Windows 98, Windows NT 4.0, Windows Millennium Edition, Windows 2000, Windows XP Home Edition, Windows XP Professional, Windows Server 2003 family

BindableAttribute.Default Field

This member supports the .NET Framework infrastructure and is not intended to be used directly from your code.

```
[Visual Basic]
Public Shared ReadOnly Default As BindableAttribute
[C#]
public static readonly BindableAttribute Default;
[C++]
public: static BindableAttribute* Default;
[JScript]
public static var Default : BindableAttribute;
```

BindableAttribute.No Field

Specifies that a property is not typically used for binding. This static (**Shared** in Visual Basic) field is read-only.

```
[Visual Basic]
Public Shared ReadOnly No As BindableAttribute
[C#]
public static readonly BindableAttribute No;
[C++]
public: static BindableAttribute* No;
[JScript]
public static var No : BindableAttribute;
```

Remarks

This field is the default setting for this attribute.

When you mark a property with the **BindableAttribute** constructor of the value **false,** the value of this attribute is set to the constant member **No**. Therefore, to check whether the attribute is set to this value in your code, you must specify the attribute as **BindableAttribute.No**.

Requirements

Platforms: Windows 98, Windows NT 4.0, Windows Millennium Edition, Windows 2000, Windows XP Home Edition, Windows XP Professional, Windows Server 2003 family

BindableAttribute.Yes Field

Specifies that a property is typically used for binding. This static (**Shared** in Visual Basic) field is read-only.

```
[Visual Basic]
Public Shared ReadOnly Yes As BindableAttribute
[C#]
public static readonly BindableAttribute Yes;
[C++]
public: static BindableAttribute* Yes;
[JScript]
public static var Yes : BindableAttribute;
```

Remarks

When you mark a property with the **BindableAttribute** constructor of the value **true**, the value of this attribute is set to the constant member **Yes**. Therefore, to check whether the attribute is set to this value in your code, you must specify the attribute as **BindableAttribute.Yes**.

Requirements

Platforms: Windows 98, Windows NT 4.0, Windows Millennium Edition, Windows 2000, Windows XP Home Edition, Windows XP Professional, Windows Server 2003 family

BindableAttribute.Bindable Property

Gets a value indicating that a property is typically used for binding.

```
[Visual Basic]
Public ReadOnly Property Bindable As Boolean
[C#]
public bool Bindable {get;}
[C++]
public: __property bool get_Bindable();
[JScript]
public function get Bindable() : Boolean;
```

Property Value

true if the property is typically used for binding; otherwise, **false**.

Requirements

Platforms: Windows 98, Windows NT 4.0, Windows Millennium Edition, Windows 2000, Windows XP Home Edition, Windows XP Professional, Windows Server 2003 family

BindableAttribute.Equals Method

This member overrides **Object.Equals**.

```
[Visual Basic]
Overrides Public Function Equals( _
   ByVal obj As Object _
) As Boolean
[C#]
public override bool Equals(
   object obj
);
[C++]
public: bool Equals(
   Object* obj
);
[JScript]
public override function Equals(
   obj : Object
) : Boolean;
```

Requirements

Platforms: Windows 98, Windows NT 4.0, Windows Millennium Edition, Windows 2000, Windows XP Home Edition, Windows XP Professional, Windows Server 2003 family

BindableAttribute.GetHashCode Method

This member overrides **Attribute.GetHashCode**.

```
[Visual Basic]
Overrides Public Function GetHashCode() As Integer
[C#]
public override int GetHashCode();
[C++]
public: int GetHashCode();
[JScript]
public override function GetHashCode() : int;
```

Requirements

Platforms: Windows 98, Windows NT 4.0, Windows Millennium Edition, Windows 2000, Windows XP Home Edition, Windows XP Professional, Windows Server 2003 family

BindableAttribute.IsDefaultAttribute Method

This member overrides **Attribute.IsDefaultAttribute**.

```
[Visual Basic]
Overrides Public Function IsDefaultAttribute() As Boolean
[C#]
public override bool IsDefaultAttribute();
[C++]
public: bool IsDefaultAttribute();
[JScript]
public override function IsDefaultAttribute() : Boolean;
```

Requirements

Platforms: Windows 98, Windows NT 4.0, Windows Millennium Edition, Windows 2000, Windows XP Home Edition, Windows XP Professional, Windows Server 2003 family

BindableSupport Enumeration

Specifies values to indicate whether a property can be bound to a data element or another property.

[Visual Basic]
```
<Serializable>
Public Enum BindableSupport
```
[C#]
```
[Serializable]
public enum BindableSupport
```
[C++]
```
[Serializable]
__value public enum BindableSupport
```
[JScript]
```
public
   Serializable
enum BindableSupport
```

Remarks

This class is used at design time to indicate whether a designer should offer a property as available for data binding in a visual designer. This class does not affect whether the property can be data bound at runtime.

Members

Member name	Description
Default	The property is set to the default.
No	The property is not bindable at design time.
Yes	The property is bindable at design time.

Example

For an example on how to use the **BindableSupport** enumeration to indicate whether a property can be bound, see the sample code in **BindableAttribute**.

Requirements

Namespace: System.ComponentModel

Platforms: Windows 98, Windows NT 4.0, Windows Millennium Edition, Windows 2000, Windows XP Home Edition, Windows XP Professional, Windows Server 2003 family

Assembly: System (in System.dll)

BooleanConverter Class

Provides a type converter to convert **Boolean** objects to and from various other representations.

System.Object
System.ComponentModel.TypeConverter
System.ComponentModel.BooleanConverter

```
[Visual Basic]
Public Class BooleanConverter
   Inherits TypeConverter
[C#]
public class BooleanConverter : TypeConverter
[C++]
public __gc class BooleanConverter : public TypeConverter
[JScript]
public class BooleanConverter extends TypeConverter
```

Thread Safety

Any public static (**Shared** in Visual Basic) members of this type are safe for multithreaded operations. Any instance members are not guaranteed to be thread safe.

Remarks

This converter can only convert a **Boolean** object to and from a string.

For more information about type converters, see the **TypeConverter** base class and **Implementing a Type Converter**.

> **Note** You should never create an instance of a **BooleanConverter**. Instead, call the **GetConverter** method of **TypeDescriptor**. For more information, see the examples in the **TypeConverter** base class.

Example

[Visual Basic, C#, C++] The following example converts a variable of type **Boolean** to and from a string.

```
[Visual Basic]
Dim bVal As Boolean = True
Dim strA As String = "false"
Console.WriteLine(TypeDescriptor.GetConverter(bVal).ConvertTo ↵
(bVal, GetType(String)))
Console.WriteLine(TypeDescriptor.GetConverter(bVal).ConvertFrom(strA))
```

```
[C#]
bool bVal=true;
string strA="false";
Console.WriteLine(TypeDescriptor.GetConverter(bVal).ConvertTo ↵
 (bVal, typeof(string)));
Console.WriteLine(TypeDescriptor.GetConverter(bVal).ConvertFrom(strA));
```

```
[C++]
bool bVal( true );
String* strA = S"false";
Console::WriteLine(TypeDescriptor::GetConverter(__box(bVal))- ↵
>ConvertTo(__box(bVal), __typeof(String)));
Console::WriteLine(TypeDescriptor::GetConverter(__box(bVal))- ↵
>ConvertFrom(strA));
```

Requirements

Namespace: System.ComponentModel

Platforms: Windows 98, Windows NT 4.0, Windows Millennium Edition, Windows 2000, Windows XP Home Edition, Windows XP Professional, Windows Server 2003 family

Assembly: System (in System.dll)

BooleanConverter Constructor

Initializes a new instance of the **BooleanConverter** class.

```
[Visual Basic]
Public Sub New()
[C#]
public BooleanConverter();
[C++]
public: BooleanConverter();
[JScript]
public function BooleanConverter();
```

Remarks

The default constructor initializes any fields to their default values.

Requirements

Platforms: Windows 98, Windows NT 4.0, Windows Millennium Edition, Windows 2000, Windows XP Home Edition, Windows XP Professional, Windows Server 2003 family

BooleanConverter.CanConvertFrom Method

Overload List

This member supports the .NET Framework infrastructure and is not intended to be used directly from your code.

[Visual Basic] **Overloads Overrides Public Function CanConvertFrom(ITypeDescriptorContext, Type) As Boolean**

[C#] **public override bool CanConvertFrom(ITypeDescriptorContext, Type);**

[C++] **public: bool CanConvertFrom(ITypeDescriptorContext*, Type*);**

[JScript] **public override function CanConvertFrom(ITypeDescriptorContext, Type) : Boolean;**

Inherited from **TypeConverter**.

[Visual Basic] **Overloads Public Function CanConvertFrom(Type) As Boolean**

[C#] **public bool CanConvertFrom(Type);**

[C++] **public: bool CanConvertFrom(Type*);**

[JScript] **public function CanConvertFrom(Type) : Boolean;**

BooleanConverter.CanConvertFrom Method (ITypeDescriptorContext, Type)

This member overrides **TypeConverter.CanConvertFrom**.

```
[Visual Basic]
Overrides Overloads Public Function CanConvertFrom( _
   ByVal context As ITypeDescriptorContext, _
   ByVal sourceType As Type _
) As Boolean
[C#]
public override bool CanConvertFrom(
   ITypeDescriptorContext context,
   Type sourceType
);
[C++]
public: bool CanConvertFrom(
   ITypeDescriptorContext* context,
   Type* sourceType
);
```

```
[JScript]
public override function CanConvertFrom(
   context : ITypeDescriptorContext,
   sourceType : Type
) : Boolean;
```

Requirements

Platforms: Windows 98, Windows NT 4.0, Windows Millennium Edition, Windows 2000, Windows XP Home Edition, Windows XP Professional, Windows Server 2003 family

BooleanConverter.ConvertFrom Method

Overload List

This member supports the .NET Framework infrastructure and is not intended to be used directly from your code.

[Visual Basic] **Overloads Overrides Public Function ConvertFrom(ITypeDescriptorContext, CultureInfo, Object) As Object**

[C#] **public override object ConvertFrom(ITypeDescriptorContext, CultureInfo, object);**

[C++] **public: Object* ConvertFrom(ITypeDescriptorContext*, CultureInfo*, Object*);**

[JScript] **public override function ConvertFrom(ITypeDescriptorContext, CultureInfo, Object) : Object;**

Inherited from **TypeConverter**.

[Visual Basic] **Overloads Public Function ConvertFrom(Object) As Object**

[C#] **public object ConvertFrom(object);**

[C++] **public: Object* ConvertFrom(Object*);**

[JScript] **public function ConvertFrom(Object) : Object;**

BooleanConverter.ConvertFrom Method (ITypeDescriptorContext, CultureInfo, Object)

This member overrides **TypeConverter.ConvertFrom**.

```
[Visual Basic]
Overrides Overloads Public Function ConvertFrom( _
   ByVal context As ITypeDescriptorContext, _
   ByVal culture As CultureInfo, _
   ByVal value As Object _
) As Object
[C#]
public override object ConvertFrom(
   ITypeDescriptorContext context,
   CultureInfo culture,
   object value
);
[C++]
public: Object* ConvertFrom(
   ITypeDescriptorContext* context,
   CultureInfo* culture,
   Object* value
);
[JScript]
public override function ConvertFrom(
   context : ITypeDescriptorContext,
   culture : CultureInfo,
   value : Object
) : Object;
```

Requirements

Platforms: Windows 98, Windows NT 4.0, Windows Millennium Edition, Windows 2000, Windows XP Home Edition, Windows XP Professional, Windows Server 2003 family

BooleanConverter.GetStandardValues Method

Overload List

This member supports the .NET Framework infrastructure and is not intended to be used directly from your code.

[Visual Basic] **Overloads Overrides Public Function GetStandardValues(ITypeDescriptorContext) As StandardValuesCollection**

[C#] **public override StandardValuesCollection GetStandardValues(ITypeDescriptorContext);**

[C++] **public: StandardValuesCollection* GetStandardValues(ITypeDescriptorContext*);**

[JScript] **public override function GetStandardValues(ITypeDescriptorContext) : StandardValuesCollection;**

Inherited from **TypeConverter**.

[Visual Basic] **Overloads Public Function GetStandardValues() As ICollection**

[C#] **public ICollection GetStandardValues();**

[C++] **public: ICollection* GetStandardValues();**

[JScript] **public function GetStandardValues() : ICollection;**

BooleanConverter.GetStandardValues Method (ITypeDescriptorContext)

This member overrides **TypeConverter.GetStandardValues**.

```
[Visual Basic]
Overrides Overloads Public Function GetStandardValues( _
   ByVal context As ITypeDescriptorContext _
) As StandardValuesCollection
[C#]
public override StandardValuesCollection GetStandardValues(
   ITypeDescriptorContext context
);
[C++]
public: StandardValuesCollection* GetStandardValues(
   ITypeDescriptorContext* context
);
[JScript]
public override function GetStandardValues(
   context : ITypeDescriptorContext
) : StandardValuesCollection;
```

Requirements

Platforms: Windows 98, Windows NT 4.0, Windows Millennium Edition, Windows 2000, Windows XP Home Edition, Windows XP Professional, Windows Server 2003 family

BooleanConverter.GetStandardValuesExclusive Method

Overload List

This member supports the .NET Framework infrastructure and is not intended to be used directly from your code.

[Visual Basic] **Overloads Overrides Public Function GetStandardValuesExclusive(ITypeDescriptorContext) As Boolean**

[C#] **public override bool GetStandardValuesExclusive(ITypeDescriptorContext);**

[C++] **public: bool GetStandardValuesExclusive(ITypeDescriptorContext*);**

[JScript] **public override function GetStandardValuesExclusive(ITypeDescriptorContext) : Boolean;**

Inherited from **TypeConverter**.

[Visual Basic] **Overloads Public Function GetStandardValuesExclusive() As Boolean**

[C#] **public bool GetStandardValuesExclusive();**

[C++] **public: bool GetStandardValuesExclusive();**

[JScript] **public function GetStandardValuesExclusive() : Boolean;**

BooleanConverter.GetStandardValuesExclusive Method (ITypeDescriptorContext)

This member overrides **TypeConverter.GetStandardValuesExclusive**.

[Visual Basic]
```
Overrides Overloads Public Function GetStandardValuesExclusive( _
   ByVal context As ITypeDescriptorContext _
) As Boolean
```
[C#]
```
public override bool GetStandardValuesExclusive(
   ITypeDescriptorContext context
);
```
[C++]
```
public: bool GetStandardValuesExclusive(
   ITypeDescriptorContext* context
);
```
[JScript]
```
public override function GetStandardValuesExclusive(
   context : ITypeDescriptorContext
) : Boolean;
```

Requirements

Platforms: Windows 98, Windows NT 4.0, Windows Millennium Edition, Windows 2000, Windows XP Home Edition, Windows XP Professional, Windows Server 2003 family

BooleanConverter.GetStandardValuesSupported Method

Overload List

This member supports the .NET Framework infrastructure and is not intended to be used directly from your code.

[Visual Basic] **Overloads Overrides Public Function GetStandardValuesSupported(ITypeDescriptorContext) As Boolean**

[C#] **public override bool GetStandardValuesSupported(ITypeDescriptorContext);**

[C++] **public: bool GetStandardValuesSupported(ITypeDescriptorContext*);**

[JScript] **public override function GetStandardValuesSupported(ITypeDescriptorContext) : Boolean;**

Inherited from **TypeConverter**.

[Visual Basic] **Overloads Public Function GetStandardValuesSupported() As Boolean**

[C#] **public bool GetStandardValuesSupported();**

[C++] **public: bool GetStandardValuesSupported();**

[JScript] **public function GetStandardValuesSupported() : Boolean;**

BooleanConverter.GetStandardValuesSupported Method (ITypeDescriptorContext)

This member overrides **TypeConverter.GetStandardValuesSupported**.

[Visual Basic]
```
Overrides Overloads Public Function GetStandardValuesSupported( _
   ByVal context As ITypeDescriptorContext _
) As Boolean
```
[C#]
```
public override bool GetStandardValuesSupported(
   ITypeDescriptorContext context
);
```
[C++]
```
public: bool GetStandardValuesSupported(
   ITypeDescriptorContext* context
);
```
[JScript]
```
public override function GetStandardValuesSupported(
   context : ITypeDescriptorContext
) : Boolean;
```

Requirements

Platforms: Windows 98, Windows NT 4.0, Windows Millennium Edition, Windows 2000, Windows XP Home Edition, Windows XP Professional, Windows Server 2003 family

BrowsableAttribute Class

Specifies whether a property or event should be displayed in a Properties window.

System.Object
  System.Attribute
    System.ComponentModel.BrowsableAttribute

[Visual Basic]
```
<AttributeUsage(AttributeTargets.All)>
NotInheritable Public Class BrowsableAttribute
   Inherits Attribute
```
[C#]
```
[AttributeUsage(AttributeTargets.All)]
public sealed class BrowsableAttribute : Attribute
```
[C++]
```
[AttributeUsage(AttributeTargets::All)]
public __gc __sealed class BrowsableAttribute : public Attribute
```
[JScript]
```
public
   AttributeUsage(AttributeTargets.All)
class BrowsableAttribute extends Attribute
```

Thread Safety

Any public static (**Shared** in Visual Basic) members of this type are safe for multithreaded operations. Any instance members are not guaranteed to be thread safe.

Remarks

A visual designer typically displays in the Properties window those members that either have no browsable attribute or are marked with the **BrowsableAttribute** constructor of the value **true**. These members can be modified at design time. Members marked with the **BrowsableAttribute** constructor of the value **false** are not appropriate for design-time editing and therefore are not displayed in a visual designer. The default is **true**.

> **Note** When you mark a property with the **BrowsableAttribute** constructor of the value **true**, the value of this attribute is set to the constant member **Yes**. For a property marked with the **BrowsableAttribute** constructor of the value **false**, the value is **No**. Therefore, when you check the value of this attribute in your code, you must specify the attribute as **BrowsableAttribute.Yes** or **BrowsableAttribute.No**.

Example

[Visual Basic, C#, JScript] The following example marks a property as browsable.

[Visual Basic]
```
<Browsable(True)> _
Public Property MyProperty() As Integer
    Get
        ' Insert code here.
        Return 0
    End Get
    Set
        ' Insert code here.
    End Set
End Property
```

[C#]
```
[Browsable(true)]
 public int MyProperty {
    get {
       // Insert code here.
       return 0;
    }
    set {
       // Insert code here.
    }
 }
```

[JScript]
```
Browsable(true)
public function get MyProperty() : int {
       // Insert code here.
      return 0;
}

public function set MyProperty(value : int) {
}
```

[Visual Basic, C#, JScript] The next example shows how to check the value of the **BrowsableAttribute** for MyProperty. First, the code gets a **PropertyDescriptorCollection** with all the properties for the object. Next, the code indexes into the **PropertyDescriptorCollection** to get MyProperty. Then it returns the attributes for this property and saves them in the attributes variable.

[Visual Basic, C#, JScript] The example presents two different ways of checking the value of the **BrowsableAttribute**. In the second code fragment, the example calls the **Equals** method. In the last code fragment, the example uses the **Browsable** property to check the value.

[Visual Basic]
```
' Gets the attributes for the property.
Dim attributes As AttributeCollection = _
    TypeDescriptor.GetProperties(Me)("MyProperty").Attributes

' Checks to see if the value of the BrowsableAttribute is Yes.
If attributes(GetType(BrowsableAttribute)).Equals
(BrowsableAttribute.Yes) Then
    ' Insert code here.
End If

' This is another way to see whether the property is browsable.
Dim myAttribute As BrowsableAttribute = _
    CType(attributes(GetType(BrowsableAttribute)), BrowsableAttribute)
If myAttribute.Browsable Then
    ' Insert code here.
End If
```

[C#]
```
// Gets the attributes for the property.
 AttributeCollection attributes =
    TypeDescriptor.GetProperties(this)["MyProperty"].Attributes;

 // Checks to see if the value of the BrowsableAttribute is Yes.
 if(attributes[typeof(BrowsableAttribute)].Equals
 (BrowsableAttribute.Yes)) {
    // Insert code here.
 }

 // This is another way to see whether the property is browsable.
 BrowsableAttribute myAttribute =
    (BrowsableAttribute)attributes[typeof(BrowsableAttribute)];
 if(myAttribute.Browsable) {
    // Insert code here.
 }
```

[JScript]
```
// Gets the attributes for the property.
 var attributes : AttributeCollection  =
    TypeDescriptor.GetProperties(this)["MyProperty"].Attributes;

 // Checks to see if the value of the BrowsableAttribute is Yes.
 if(attributes[BrowsableAttribute].Equals(BrowsableAttribute.Yes)) {
    Console.WriteLine("MyProperty is browsable.");
 }
```

```
// This is another way to see whether the property is browsable.
var myAttribute : BrowsableAttribute =
   BrowsableAttribute(attributes[BrowsableAttribute]);
if(myAttribute.Browsable) {
   Console.WriteLine("MyProperty is browsable.");
}
```

[Visual Basic, C#, JScript] If you marked a class with the **BrowsableAttribute**, use the following code to check the value.

[Visual Basic]
```
Dim attributes As AttributeCollection = ↵
TypeDescriptor.GetAttributes(MyProperty)
If attributes(GetType(BrowsableAttribute)).Equals ↵
 (BrowsableAttribute.Yes) Then
    ' Insert code here.
End If
```

[C#]
```
AttributeCollection attributes =
    TypeDescriptor.GetAttributes(MyProperty);
 if(attributes[typeof(BrowsableAttribute)].Equals ↵
 (BrowsableAttribute.Yes)) {
    // Insert code here.
 }
```

[JScript]
```
var attributes : AttributeCollection =
    TypeDescriptor.GetAttributes(MyProperty);
 if(attributes[BrowsableAttribute].Equals(BrowsableAttribute.Yes)) {
    Console.WriteLine("MyProperty is browsable.");
 }
```

Requirements

Namespace: System.ComponentModel

Platforms: Windows 98, Windows NT 4.0, Windows Millennium Edition, Windows 2000, Windows XP Home Edition, Windows XP Professional, Windows Server 2003 family

Assembly: System (in System.dll)

BrowsableAttribute Constructor

Initializes a new instance of the **BrowsableAttribute** class.

[Visual Basic]
```
Public Sub New( _
   ByVal browsable As Boolean _
)
```
[C#]
```
public BrowsableAttribute(
   bool browsable
);
```
[C++]
```
public: BrowsableAttribute(
   bool browsable
);
```
[JScript]
```
public function BrowsableAttribute(
   browsable : Boolean
);
```

Parameters

browsable

true if a property or event can be modified at design time; otherwise, **false**. The default is **true**.

Remarks

When you mark a property with the **ctor** constructor of the value **true**, the value of this attribute is set to the constant member **Yes**. For a property marked with the **ctor** constructor of the value **false**, the value is **No**. Therefore, when you want to check the value of this attribute in your code, you must specify the attribute as **BrowsableAttribute.Yes** or **BrowsableAttribute.No**.

Example

[Visual Basic, C#, JScript] The following example marks a property as browsable. This code creates a new **BrowsableAttribute**, sets its value to **BrowsableAttribute.Yes**, and binds it to the property.

[Visual Basic]
```
<Browsable(True)> _
Public Property MyProperty() As Integer
    Get
        ' Insert code here.
        Return 0
    End Get
    Set
        ' Insert code here.
    End Set
End Property
```

[C#]
```
[Browsable(true)]
 public int MyProperty {
    get {
       // Insert code here.
       return 0;
    }
    set {
       // Insert code here.
    }
 }
```

[JScript]
```
Browsable(true)
public function get MyProperty() : int {
      // Insert code here.
      return 0;
 }

 public function set MyProperty(value : int) {
 }
```

Requirements

Platforms: Windows 98, Windows NT 4.0, Windows Millennium Edition, Windows 2000, Windows XP Home Edition, Windows XP Professional, Windows Server 2003 family

BrowsableAttribute.Default Field

This member supports the .NET Framework infrastructure and is not intended to be used directly from your code.

[Visual Basic]
```
Public Shared ReadOnly Default As BrowsableAttribute
```
[C#]
```
public static readonly BrowsableAttribute Default;
```
[C++]
```
public: static BrowsableAttribute* Default;
```
[JScript]
```
public static var Default : BrowsableAttribute;
```

BrowsableAttribute.No Field

Specifies that a property or event cannot be modified at design time. This static (**Shared** in Visual Basic) field is read-only.

[Visual Basic]
```
Public Shared ReadOnly No As BrowsableAttribute
```
[C#]
```
public static readonly BrowsableAttribute No;
```
[C++]
```
public: static BrowsableAttribute* No;
```
[JScript]
```
public static var No : BrowsableAttribute;
```

Remarks

When you mark a property with the **BrowsableAttribute** constructor of the value **false**, this attribute is set to the constant member **No**. Therefore, when you check whether the attribute is set to this value in your code, you must specify the attribute as **BrowsableAttribute.No**.

Requirements

Platforms: Windows 98, Windows NT 4.0, Windows Millennium Edition, Windows 2000, Windows XP Home Edition, Windows XP Professional, Windows Server 2003 family

BrowsableAttribute.Yes Field

Specifies that a property or event can be modified at design time. This static (**Shared** in Visual Basic) field is read-only.

[Visual Basic]
```
Public Shared ReadOnly Yes As BrowsableAttribute
```
[C#]
```
public static readonly BrowsableAttribute Yes;
```
[C++]
```
public: static BrowsableAttribute* Yes;
```
[JScript]
```
public static var Yes : BrowsableAttribute;
```

Remarks

This field is the default setting for this attribute.

When you mark a property with the **BrowsableAttribute** constructor of the value **true**, this attribute is set to the constant member **Yes**. Therefore, when you check whether the attribute is set to this value in your code, you must specify the attribute as **BrowsableAttribute.Yes**.

Requirements

Platforms: Windows 98, Windows NT 4.0, Windows Millennium Edition, Windows 2000, Windows XP Home Edition, Windows XP Professional, Windows Server 2003 family

BrowsableAttribute.Browsable Property

Gets a value indicating whether an object is browsable.

[Visual Basic]
```
Public ReadOnly Property Browsable As Boolean
```
[C#]
```
public bool Browsable {get;}
```
[C++]
```
public: __property bool get_Browsable();
```
[JScript]
```
public function get Browsable() : Boolean;
```

Property Value

true if the object is browsable; otherwise, **false**.

Example

[Visual Basic, C#, JScript] The following example checks to see whether `MyProperty` is browsable. First the code gets the attributes for `MyProperty` by:

- Retrieving a **PropertyDescriptorCollection** with all the properties for the object.
- Indexing into the **PropertyDescriptorCollection** to get `MyProperty`.
- Saving the attributes for this property in the attributes variable.

[Visual Basic, C#, JScript] Then the code sets `myAttribute` to the value of the **BrowsableAttribute** in the **AttributeCollection** and checks whether the property is browsable.

[Visual Basic]
```
' Gets the attributes for the property.
Dim attributes As AttributeCollection = ↵
TypeDescriptor.GetProperties(Me)("MyProperty").Attributes

' Checks to see if the property is browsable.
Dim myAttribute As BrowsableAttribute = ↵
CType(attributes(GetType(BrowsableAttribute)), BrowsableAttribute)
If myAttribute.Browsable Then
    ' Insert code here.
End If
```

[C#]
```
// Gets the attributes for the property.
 AttributeCollection attributes =
    TypeDescriptor.GetProperties(this)["MyProperty"].Attributes;

 // Checks to see if the property is browsable.
 BrowsableAttribute myAttribute = ↵
 (BrowsableAttribute)attributes[typeof(BrowsableAttribute)];
 if(myAttribute.Browsable) {
    // Insert code here.
 }
```

[JScript]
```
// Gets the attributes for the property.
 var attributes : AttributeCollection =
    TypeDescriptor.GetProperties(this)["MyProperty"].Attributes;

 // Checks to see if the property is browsable.
 var myAttribute : BrowsableAttribute = ↵
BrowsableAttribute(attributes[BrowsableAttribute]);
 if(myAttribute.Browsable) {
    Console.WriteLine("MyProperty is browsable.");
 }
```

Requirements

Platforms: Windows 98, Windows NT 4.0, Windows Millennium Edition, Windows 2000, Windows XP Home Edition, Windows XP Professional, Windows Server 2003 family

BrowsableAttribute.Equals Method

This member overrides **Object.Equals**.

[Visual Basic]
```
Overrides Public Function Equals( _
   ByVal obj As Object _
) As Boolean
```
[C#]
```
public override bool Equals(
   object obj
);
```
[C++]
```
public: bool Equals(
   Object* obj
);
```
[JScript]
```
public override function Equals(
   obj : Object
) : Boolean;
```

Requirements

Platforms: Windows 98, Windows NT 4.0, Windows Millennium Edition, Windows 2000, Windows XP Home Edition, Windows XP Professional, Windows Server 2003 family

BrowsableAttribute.GetHashCode Method

This member overrides **Attribute.GetHashCode**.

[Visual Basic]
```
Overrides Public Function GetHashCode() As Integer
```
[C#]
```
public override int GetHashCode();
```
[C++]
```
public: int GetHashCode();
```
[JScript]
```
public override function GetHashCode() : int;
```

Requirements

Platforms: Windows 98, Windows NT 4.0, Windows Millennium Edition, Windows 2000, Windows XP Home Edition, Windows XP Professional, Windows Server 2003 family

BrowsableAttribute.IsDefaultAttribute Method

This member overrides **Attribute.IsDefaultAttribute**.

[Visual Basic]
```
Overrides Public Function IsDefaultAttribute() As Boolean
```
[C#]
```
public override bool IsDefaultAttribute();
```
[C++]
```
public: bool IsDefaultAttribute();
```
[JScript]
```
public override function IsDefaultAttribute() : Boolean;
```

Requirements

Platforms: Windows 98, Windows NT 4.0, Windows Millennium Edition, Windows 2000, Windows XP Home Edition, Windows XP Professional, Windows Server 2003 family

ByteConverter Class

Provides a type converter to convert 8-bit unsigned integer objects to and from various other representations.

System.Object
  System.ComponentModel.TypeConverter
    System.ComponentModel.BaseNumberConverter
      System.ComponentModel.ByteConverter

[Visual Basic]
```
Public Class ByteConverter
   Inherits BaseNumberConverter
```
[C#]
```
public class ByteConverter : BaseNumberConverter
```
[C++]
```
public __gc class ByteConverter : public BaseNumberConverter
```
[JScript]
```
public class ByteConverter extends BaseNumberConverter
```

Thread Safety

Any public static (**Shared** in Visual Basic) members of this type are safe for multithreaded operations. Any instance members are not guaranteed to be thread safe.

Remarks

This converter can only convert an 8-bit unsigned integer to and from a string.

For more information about type converters, see the **TypeConverter** base class and **Implementing a Type Converter**.

> **Note** You should never create an instance of a **ByteConverter**. Instead, call the **GetConverter** method of **TypeDescriptor**. For more information, see the examples in the **TypeConverter** base class.

Example

[Visual Basic, C#, C++] The following example declares and initializes an 8-bit unsigned integer and a string. The code then converts each of them to the other's type, respectively.

[Visual Basic]
```
Dim myUint As Byte = 5
Dim myUStr As String = "2"
Console.WriteLine                                              ↵
(TypeDescriptor.GetConverter(myUint).ConvertTo(myUint,         ↵
GetType(String)))
Console.WriteLine(TypeDescriptor.GetConverter(myUint).ConvertFrom(myUStr
))
```

[C#]
```
byte myUint = 5;
string myUStr = "2";
Console.WriteLine(TypeDescriptor.GetConverter(myUint).ConvertTo    ↵
 (myUint, typeof(string)));
Console.WriteLine(TypeDescriptor.GetConverter(myUint).ConvertFrom  ↵
 (myUStr));
```

[C++]
```
Byte myUint( 5 );
String* myUStr = S"2";
Console::WriteLine(TypeDescriptor::GetConverter                ↵
 (__box(myUint))->ConvertTo(__box(myUint), __typeof(String)));
Console::WriteLine(TypeDescriptor::GetConverter                ↵
 (__box(myUint))->ConvertFrom(myUStr));
```

Requirements

Namespace: System.ComponentModel

Platforms: Windows 98, Windows NT 4.0, Windows Millennium Edition, Windows 2000, Windows XP Home Edition, Windows XP Professional, Windows Server 2003 family

Assembly: System (in System.dll)

ByteConverter Constructor

Initializes a new instance of the **ByteConverter** class.

[Visual Basic]
```
Public Sub New()
```
[C#]
```
public ByteConverter();
```
[C++]
```
public: ByteConverter();
```
[JScript]
```
public function ByteConverter();
```

Remarks

The default constructor initializes any fields to their default values.

Requirements

Platforms: Windows 98, Windows NT 4.0, Windows Millennium Edition, Windows 2000, Windows XP Home Edition, Windows XP Professional, Windows Server 2003 family

CancelEventArgs Class

Provides data for a cancelable event.

System.Object
  System.EventArgs
    System.ComponentModel.CancelEventArgs
      System.Drawing.Printing.PrintEventArgs
      System.Windows.Forms.InputLanguageChangingEventArgs
      System.Windows.Forms.TreeViewCancelEventArgs

[Visual Basic]
```
Public Class CancelEventArgs
   Inherits EventArgs
```
[C#]
```
public class CancelEventArgs : EventArgs
```
[C++]
```
public __gc class CancelEventArgs : public EventArgs
```
[JScript]
```
public class CancelEventArgs extends EventArgs
```

Thread Safety

Any public static (**Shared** in Visual Basic) members of this type are safe for multithreaded operations. Any instance members are not guaranteed to be thread safe.

Remarks

A cancelable event is raised by a component when it is about to perform an action that can be canceled, such as the **Closing** event of a **Form**.

A **CancelEventArgs** provides the **Cancel** property to indicate whether the event should be canceled.

Example

[Visual Basic, C#, C++] The following example uses a **CancelEventArgs** and a **CancelEventHandler** to handle the **Closing** event of a **Form**. This code assumes that you have created a **Form** with a class-level **Boolean** variable named `myDataIsSaved`.

[Visual Basic]
```
' Calls this method from the InitializeComponent() method of your form.
Private Sub OtherInitialize()
    AddHandler Me.Closing, AddressOf Me.Form1_Cancel
    Me.myDataIsSaved = New Boolean()
    Me.myDataIsSaved = True
End Sub 'OtherInitialize

Protected Sub Form1_Cancel(sender As Object, e As CancelEventArgs)
    If Not myDataIsSaved Then
        e.Cancel = True
        MessageBox.Show("You must save first.")
    Else
        e.Cancel = False
        MessageBox.Show("Goodbye.")
    End If
End Sub 'Form1_Cancel
```

[C#]
```
// Calls this method from the InitializeComponent() method of your form
    private void OtherInitialize() {
       this.Closing += new CancelEventHandler(this.Form1_Cancel);
       this.myDataIsSaved = new Boolean();
       this.myDataIsSaved = true;
    }
    protected void Form1_Cancel (Object sender, CancelEventArgs e) {
       if (!myDataIsSaved) {
          e.Cancel = true;
          MessageBox.Show("You must save first.");
       }
       else {
          e.Cancel = false;
          MessageBox.Show("Goodbye.");
       }
    }
```

[C++]
```
// Calls this method from the InitializeComponent() method of your form
private:

    void OtherInitialize() {
       this->Closing += new CancelEventHandler(this, Form1_Cancel);
       this->myDataIsSaved = true;
    }

protected:

    void Form1_Cancel (Object* sender, CancelEventArgs* e) {
       if (!myDataIsSaved) {
          e->Cancel = true;
          MessageBox::Show(S"You must save first.");
       }
       else {
          e->Cancel = false;
          MessageBox::Show(S"Goodbye.");
       }
    }
```

Requirements

Namespace: System.ComponentModel

Platforms: Windows 98, Windows NT 4.0, Windows Millennium Edition, Windows 2000, Windows XP Home Edition, Windows XP Professional, Windows Server 2003 family, .NET Compact Framework - Windows CE .NET

Assembly: System (in System.dll)

CancelEventArgs Constructor

Initializes a new instance of the **CancelEventArgs** class.

Overload List

Initializes a new instance of the **CancelEventArgs** class with the **Cancel** property set to **false**.

Supported by the .NET Compact Framework.

[Visual Basic] **Public Sub New()**

[C#] **public CancelEventArgs();**

[C++] **public: CancelEventArgs();**

[JScript] **public function CancelEventArgs();**

Initializes a new instance of the **CancelEventArgs** class with the **Cancel** property set to the given value.

Supported by the .NET Compact Framework.

[Visual Basic] **Public Sub New(Boolean)**

[C#] **public CancelEventArgs(bool);**

[C++] **public: CancelEventArgs(bool);**

[JScript] **public function CancelEventArgs(Boolean);**

CancelEventArgs Constructor ()

Initializes a new instance of the **CancelEventArgs** class with the **Cancel** property set to **false**.

```
[Visual Basic]
Public Sub New()
[C#]
public CancelEventArgs();
[C++]
public: CancelEventArgs();
[JScript]
public function CancelEventArgs();
```

Requirements

Platforms: Windows 98, Windows NT 4.0, Windows Millennium Edition, Windows 2000, Windows XP Home Edition, Windows XP Professional, Windows Server 2003 family, .NET Compact Framework - Windows CE .NET

CancelEventArgs Constructor (Boolean)

Initializes a new instance of the **CancelEventArgs** class with the **Cancel** property set to the given value.

```
[Visual Basic]
Public Sub New( _
   ByVal cancel As Boolean _
)
[C#]
public CancelEventArgs(
   bool cancel
);
[C++]
public: CancelEventArgs(
   bool cancel
);
[JScript]
public function CancelEventArgs(
   cancel : Boolean
);
```

Parameters

cancel
true to cancel the event; otherwise, **false**.

Requirements

Platforms: Windows 98, Windows NT 4.0, Windows Millennium Edition, Windows 2000, Windows XP Home Edition, Windows XP Professional, Windows Server 2003 family, .NET Compact Framework - Windows CE .NET

CancelEventArgs.Cancel Property

Gets or sets a value indicating whether the event should be canceled.

```
[Visual Basic]
Public Property Cancel As Boolean
[C#]
public bool Cancel {get; set;}
[C++]
public: __property bool get_Cancel();
public: __property void set_Cancel(bool);
[JScript]
public function get Cancel() : Boolean;
public function set Cancel(Boolean);
```

Property Value

true if the event should be canceled; otherwise, **false**.

Example

[Visual Basic, C#, C++] The following example uses a **CancelEventArgs** and a **CancelEventHandler** to handle the **Closing** event of a **Form**. This code assumes that you have created a **Form** with a class-level **Boolean** variable named `myDataIsSaved`.

```
[Visual Basic]
' Calls this method from the InitializeComponent() method of your form.
Private Sub OtherInitialize()
    AddHandler Me.Closing, AddressOf Me.Form1_Cancel
    Me.myDataIsSaved = New Boolean()
    Me.myDataIsSaved = True
End Sub 'OtherInitialize

Protected Sub Form1_Cancel(sender As Object, e As CancelEventArgs)
    If Not myDataIsSaved Then
        e.Cancel = True
        MessageBox.Show("You must save first.")
    Else
        e.Cancel = False
        MessageBox.Show("Goodbye.")
    End If
End Sub 'Form1_Cancel

[C#]
// Calls this method from the InitializeComponent() method of your form
    private void OtherInitialize() {
       this.Closing += new CancelEventHandler(this.Form1_Cancel);
       this.myDataIsSaved = new Boolean();
       this.myDataIsSaved = true;
    }
    protected void Form1_Cancel (Object sender, CancelEventArgs e) {
       if (!myDataIsSaved) {
          e.Cancel = true;
          MessageBox.Show("You must save first.");
       }
       else {
          e.Cancel = false;
          MessageBox.Show("Goodbye.");
       }
    }

[C++]
// Calls this method from the InitializeComponent() method of your form
private:

    void OtherInitialize() {
       this->Closing += new CancelEventHandler(this, Form1_Cancel);
       this->myDataIsSaved = true;
    }

protected:

    void Form1_Cancel (Object* sender, CancelEventArgs* e) {
       if (!myDataIsSaved) {
          e->Cancel = true;
          MessageBox::Show(S"You must save first.");
       }
       else {
          e->Cancel = false;
          MessageBox::Show(S"Goodbye.");
       }
    }
```

Requirements

Platforms: Windows 98, Windows NT 4.0, Windows Millennium Edition, Windows 2000, Windows XP Home Edition, Windows XP Professional, Windows Server 2003 family, .NET Compact Framework - Windows CE .NET

CancelEventHandler Delegate

Represents the method that handles a cancellable event.

[Visual Basic]
```
<Serializable>
Public Delegate Sub CancelEventHandler( _
   ByVal sender As Object, _
   ByVal e As CancelEventArgs _
)
```
[C#]
```
[Serializable]
public delegate void CancelEventHandler(
   object sender,
   CancelEventArgs e
);
```
[C++]
```
[Serializable]
public __gc __delegate void CancelEventHandler(
   Object* sender,
   CancelEventArgs* e
);
```

[JScript] In JScript, you can use the delegates in the .NET Framework, but you cannot define your own.

Parameters [Visual Basic, C#, C++]

The declaration of your event handler must have the same parameters as the **CancelEventHandler** delegate declaration.

sender

The source of the event.

e

A **CancelEventArgs** that contains the event data.

Remarks

When you create a **CancelEventHandler** delegate, you identify the method that will handle the event. To associate the event with your event handler, add an instance of the delegate to the event. The event-handler method is called whenever the event occurs, unless you remove the delegate.

Example

For an example of how to use the CancelEventHandler delegate, please see the sample code in the **CancelEventArgs** class.

Requirements

Namespace: System.ComponentModel

Platforms: Windows 98, Windows NT 4.0,
Windows Millennium Edition, Windows 2000,
Windows XP Home Edition, Windows XP Professional,
Windows Server 2003 family,
.NET Compact Framework - Windows CE .NET

Assembly: System (in System.dll)

CategoryAttribute Class

Specifies the category in which the property or event will be displayed in a visual designer.

System.Object
  System.Attribute
    System.ComponentModel.CategoryAttribute

[Visual Basic]
```
<AttributeUsage(AttributeTargets.All)>
Public Class CategoryAttribute
   Inherits Attribute
```
[C#]
```
[AttributeUsage(AttributeTargets.All)]
public class CategoryAttribute : Attribute
```
[C++]
```
[AttributeUsage(AttributeTargets::All)]
public __gc class CategoryAttribute : public Attribute
```
[JScript]
```
public
   AttributeUsage(AttributeTargets.All)
class CategoryAttribute extends Attribute
```

Thread Safety

Any public static (**Shared** in Visual Basic) members of this type are safe for multithreaded operations. Any instance members are not guaranteed to be thread safe.

Remarks

A visual designer can use categories to organize members into groups of similar behavior. A category can be created for any name.

This **CategoryAttribute** class provides the **Category** property to get the name of the category. **Category** also provides transparent localization of category names.

Notes to Inheritors: If you use category names other than the predefined names, and you want to localize your category names, you must override the **GetLocalizedString** method. Additionally, you can override the **Category** property to provide your own logic for localization.

The **CategoryAttribute** class defines the following common categories:

Category	Description
Action	Properties regarding available actions.
Appearance	Properties affecting how an entity appears.
Behavior	Properties affecting how an entity acts.
Data	Properties concerning data.
Default	Properties that do not have a category are classified as belonging to the default category.
Design	Properties that are available only at design time.
DragDrop	Properties about drag-and-drop operations.
Focus	Properties pertaining to focus.
Format	Properties that affect format.
Key	Properties affecting the keyboard.
Layout	Properties concerning layout.
Mouse	Properties pertaining to the mouse.
WindowStyle	Properties affecting the window style of top-level forms.

For more information, see **Attributes Overview** and **Extending Metadata Using Attributes**.

Example

[Visual Basic, C#, C++] The following example creates the `MyImage` property. The property has two attributes: a **DescriptionAttribute** and a **CategoryAttribute**.

[Visual Basic]
```
<Description("The image associated with the control"), _
   Category("Appearance")> _
Public Property MyImage() As Image

   Get
      ' Insert code here.
      Return image1
   End Get
   Set
      ' Insert code here.
   End Set
End Property
```

[C#]
```
[Description("The image associated with the
control"),Category("Appearance")]
 public Image MyImage {
    get {
       // Insert code here.
       return image1;
    }
    set {
       // Insert code here.
    }
 }
```

[C++]
```
[Description(S"The image associated with the
control"),Category(S"Appearance")]
__property System::Drawing::Image* get_MyImage() {
    // Insert code here.
    return m_Image1;
}

__property void set_MyImage( System::Drawing::Image* ) {
    // Insert code here.
}
```

[Visual Basic, C#, C++] The next example gets the category for `MyImage`. First, the code gets a **PropertyDescriptorCollection** with all the properties for the object. Next, the code indexes into the **PropertyDescriptorCollection** to get `MyImage`. Then it returns the attributes for this property and saves them in the variable `attributes`.

[Visual Basic, C#, C++] The example then prints the category by retrieving **CategoryAttribute** from the **AttributeCollection**, and writing it to the console screen.

[Visual Basic]
```
' Gets the attributes for the property.
Dim attributes As AttributeCollection = _
    TypeDescriptor.GetProperties(Me)("MyImage").Attributes

' Prints the description by retrieving the CategoryAttribute.
' from the AttributeCollection.
Dim myAttribute As CategoryAttribute = _
    CType(attributes(GetType(CategoryAttribute)), CategoryAttribute)
    Console.WriteLine(myAttribute.Category)
```

[C#]
```
// Gets the attributes for the property.
 AttributeCollection attributes =
    TypeDescriptor.GetProperties(this)["MyImage"].Attributes;

 // Prints the description by retrieving the CategoryAttribute.
 // from the AttributeCollection.
 CategoryAttribute myAttribute =
    (CategoryAttribute)attributes[typeof(CategoryAttribute)];
 Console.WriteLine(myAttribute.Category);
```

[C++]
```
// Gets the attributes for the property.
 AttributeCollection* attributes =
    TypeDescriptor::GetProperties(this)->Item[S"MyImage"]->Attributes;

 // Prints the description by retrieving the CategoryAttribute.
 // from the AttributeCollection.
 CategoryAttribute* myAttribute =
    static_cast<CategoryAttribute*>(attributes-
>Item[__typeof(CategoryAttribute)]);
 Console::WriteLine(myAttribute->Category);
```

Requirements

Namespace: System.ComponentModel

Platforms: Windows 98, Windows NT 4.0, Windows Millennium Edition, Windows 2000, Windows XP Home Edition, Windows XP Professional, Windows .NET Server family

Assembly: System (in System.dll)

CategoryAttribute Constructor

Initializes a new instance of the **CategoryAttribute** class.

Overload List

Initializes a new instance of the **CategoryAttribute** class with the default category.

[Visual Basic] **Public Sub New()**

[C#] **public CategoryAttribute();**

[C++] **public: CategoryAttribute();**

[JScript] **public function CategoryAttribute();**

Initializes a new instance of the **CategoryAttribute** class with the specified category name.

[Visual Basic] **Public Sub New(String)**

[C#] **public CategoryAttribute(string);**

[C++] **public: CategoryAttribute(String*);**

[JScript] **public function CategoryAttribute(String);**

CategoryAttribute Constructor ()

Initializes a new instance of the **CategoryAttribute** class with the default category.

[Visual Basic]
```
Public Sub New()
```
[C#]
```
public CategoryAttribute();
```
[C++]
```
public: CategoryAttribute();
```
[JScript]
```
public function CategoryAttribute();
```

Requirements

Platforms: Windows 98, Windows NT 4.0, Windows Millennium Edition, Windows 2000, Windows XP Home Edition, Windows XP Professional, Windows .NET Server family

CategoryAttribute Constructor (String)

Initializes a new instance of the **CategoryAttribute** class with the specified category name.

[Visual Basic]
```
Public Sub New( _
   ByVal category As String _
)
```
[C#]
```
public CategoryAttribute(
   string category
);
```
[C++]
```
public: CategoryAttribute(
   String* category
);
```
[JScript]
```
public function CategoryAttribute(
   category : String
);
```

Parameters

category

The name of the category.

Remarks

If the name you provide for the *category* parameter is one of the predefined category names, then the name will be automatically localized by the **Category** property. The **Category** property calls **GetLocalizedString** to look up the localized name.

If the name you provide is not a predefined category name, and you do not override **GetLocalizedString** to provide a localized name, then the name will not be localized. In other words, the name you provide to this constructor will be used unmodified.

Requirements

Platforms: Windows 98, Windows NT 4.0, Windows Millennium Edition, Windows 2000, Windows XP Home Edition, Windows XP Professional, Windows .NET Server family

CategoryAttribute.Action Property

Gets the action category attribute.

[Visual Basic]
```
Public Shared ReadOnly Property Action As CategoryAttribute
```
[C#]
```
public static CategoryAttribute Action {get;}
```
[C++]
```
public: __property static CategoryAttribute* get_Action();
```
[JScript]
```
public static function get Action() : CategoryAttribute;
```

Property Value

A **CategoryAttribute** for the action category.

Remarks

This category marks properties having to do with actions.

Requirements

Platforms: Windows 98, Windows NT 4.0, Windows Millennium Edition, Windows 2000, Windows XP Home Edition, Windows XP Professional, Windows .NET Server family

CategoryAttribute.Appearance Property

Gets the appearance category attribute.

[Visual Basic]
```
Public Shared ReadOnly Property Appearance As CategoryAttribute
```
[C#]
```
public static CategoryAttribute Appearance {get;}
```
[C++]
```
public: __property static CategoryAttribute* get_Appearance();
```
[JScript]
```
public static function get Appearance() : CategoryAttribute;
```

Property Value

A **CategoryAttribute** for the appearance category.

Remarks

This category marks properties having to do with appearance.

Requirements

Platforms: Windows 98, Windows NT 4.0, Windows Millennium Edition, Windows 2000, Windows XP Home Edition, Windows XP Professional, Windows .NET Server family

CategoryAttribute.Behavior Property

Gets the behavior category attribute.

[Visual Basic]
```
Public Shared ReadOnly Property Behavior As CategoryAttribute
```
[C#]
```
public static CategoryAttribute Behavior {get;}
```
[C++]
```
public: __property static CategoryAttribute* get_Behavior();
```
[JScript]
```
public static function get Behavior() : CategoryAttribute;
```

Property Value

A **CategoryAttribute** for the behavior category.

Remarks

This category marks properties having to do with behavior.

Requirements

Platforms: Windows 98, Windows NT 4.0, Windows Millennium Edition, Windows 2000, Windows XP Home Edition, Windows XP Professional, Windows .NET Server family

CategoryAttribute.Category Property

Gets the name of the category for the property or event that this attribute is bound to.

[Visual Basic]
```
Public ReadOnly Property Category As String
```
[C#]
```
public string Category {get;}
```
[C++]
```
public: __property String* get_Category();
```
[JScript]
```
public function get Category() : String;
```

Property Value

The name of the category for the property or event that this attribute is bound to.

Remarks

This property calls **GetLocalizedString** to get the localized name of the category the first time it is accessed.

Requirements

Platforms: Windows 98, Windows NT 4.0, Windows Millennium Edition, Windows 2000, Windows XP Home Edition, Windows XP Professional, Windows .NET Server family

CategoryAttribute.Data Property

Gets the data category attribute.

[Visual Basic]
```
Public Shared ReadOnly Property Data As CategoryAttribute
```
[C#]
```
public static CategoryAttribute Data {get;}
```
[C++]
```
public: __property static CategoryAttribute* get_Data();
```
[JScript]
```
public static function get Data() : CategoryAttribute;
```

Property Value

A **CategoryAttribute** for the data category.

Remarks

This category marks properties having to do with data.

Requirements

Platforms: Windows 98, Windows NT 4.0, Windows Millennium Edition, Windows 2000, Windows XP Home Edition, Windows XP Professional, Windows .NET Server family

CategoryAttribute.Default Property

Gets the default category attribute.

[Visual Basic]
```
Public Shared ReadOnly Property Default As CategoryAttribute
```
[C#]
```
public static CategoryAttribute Default {get;}
```
[C++]
```
public: __property static CategoryAttribute* get_Default();
```
[JScript]
```
public static function get Default() : CategoryAttribute;
```

Property Value

A **CategoryAttribute** for the default category.

Remarks

This is the default category. It is used for properties that do not have a category.

Requirements

Platforms: Windows 98, Windows NT 4.0, Windows Millennium Edition, Windows 2000, Windows XP Home Edition, Windows XP Professional, Windows .NET Server family

CategoryAttribute.Design Property

Gets the design category attribute.

[Visual Basic]
```
Public Shared ReadOnly Property Design As CategoryAttribute
```
[C#]
```
public static CategoryAttribute Design {get;}
```
[C++]
```
public: __property static CategoryAttribute* get_Design();
```
[JScript]
```
public static function get Design() : CategoryAttribute;
```

Property Value

A **CategoryAttribute** for the design category.

Remarks

This category marks properties that are only available at design time.

Requirements

Platforms: Windows 98, Windows NT 4.0, Windows Millennium Edition, Windows 2000, Windows XP Home Edition, Windows XP Professional, Windows .NET Server family

CategoryAttribute.DragDrop Property

Gets the drag-and-drop category attribute.

[Visual Basic]
```
Public Shared ReadOnly Property DragDrop As CategoryAttribute
```
[C#]
```
public static CategoryAttribute DragDrop {get;}
```
[C++]
```
public: __property static CategoryAttribute* get_DragDrop();
```
[JScript]
```
public static function get DragDrop() : CategoryAttribute;
```

Property Value

A **CategoryAttribute** for the drag-and-drop category.

Remarks

This category marks properties having to do with drag-and-drop functionality.

Requirements

Platforms: Windows 98, Windows NT 4.0, Windows Millennium Edition, Windows 2000, Windows XP Home Edition, Windows XP Professional, Windows .NET Server family

CategoryAttribute.Focus Property

Gets the focus category attribute.

[Visual Basic]
```
Public Shared ReadOnly Property Focus As CategoryAttribute
```
[C#]
```
public static CategoryAttribute Focus {get;}
```
[C++]
```
public: __property static CategoryAttribute* get_Focus();
```
[JScript]
```
public static function get Focus() : CategoryAttribute;
```

Property Value

A **CategoryAttribute** for the focus category.

Remarks

This category marks properties having to do with focus.

Requirements

Platforms: Windows 98, Windows NT 4.0, Windows Millennium Edition, Windows 2000, Windows XP Home Edition, Windows XP Professional, Windows .NET Server family

CategoryAttribute.Format Property

Gets the format category attribute.

[Visual Basic]
```
Public Shared ReadOnly Property Format As CategoryAttribute
```
[C#]
```
public static CategoryAttribute Format {get;}
```
[C++]
```
public: __property static CategoryAttribute* get_Format();
```
[JScript]
```
public static function get Format() : CategoryAttribute;
```

Property Value

A **CategoryAttribute** for the format category.

Remarks

This category marks properties having to do with formats.

Requirements

Platforms: Windows 98, Windows NT 4.0, Windows Millennium Edition, Windows 2000, Windows XP Home Edition, Windows XP Professional, Windows .NET Server family

CategoryAttribute.Key Property

Gets the keyboard category attribute.

[Visual Basic]
```
Public Shared ReadOnly Property Key As CategoryAttribute
```
[C#]
```
public static CategoryAttribute Key {get;}
```
[C++]
```
public: __property static CategoryAttribute* get_Key();
```
[JScript]
```
public static function get Key() : CategoryAttribute;
```

Property Value

A **CategoryAttribute** for the key category.

Remarks

This category marks properties having to do with the keyboard.

Requirements

Platforms: Windows 98, Windows NT 4.0, Windows Millennium Edition, Windows 2000, Windows XP Home Edition, Windows XP Professional, Windows .NET Server family

CategoryAttribute.Layout Property

Gets the layout category attribute.

```
[Visual Basic]
Public Shared ReadOnly Property Layout As CategoryAttribute
[C#]
public static CategoryAttribute Layout {get;}
[C++]
public: __property static CategoryAttribute* get_Layout();
[JScript]
public static function get Layout() : CategoryAttribute;
```

Property Value

A **CategoryAttribute** for the layout category.

Remarks

This category marks properties having to do with layout.

Requirements

Platforms: Windows 98, Windows NT 4.0, Windows Millennium Edition, Windows 2000, Windows XP Home Edition, Windows XP Professional, Windows .NET Server family

CategoryAttribute.Mouse Property

Gets the mouse category attribute.

```
[Visual Basic]
Public Shared ReadOnly Property Mouse As CategoryAttribute
[C#]
public static CategoryAttribute Mouse {get;}
[C++]
public: __property static CategoryAttribute* get_Mouse();
[JScript]
public static function get Mouse() : CategoryAttribute;
```

Property Value

A **CategoryAttribute** for the mouse category.

Remarks

This category marks properties having to do with the mouse.

Requirements

Platforms: Windows 98, Windows NT 4.0, Windows Millennium Edition, Windows 2000, Windows XP Home Edition, Windows XP Professional, Windows .NET Server family

CategoryAttribute.WindowStyle Property

Gets the window style category attribute.

```
[Visual Basic]
Public Shared ReadOnly Property WindowStyle As CategoryAttribute
[C#]
public static CategoryAttribute WindowStyle {get;}
[C++]
public: __property static CategoryAttribute* get_WindowStyle();
[JScript]
public static function get WindowStyle() : CategoryAttribute;
```

Property Value

A **CategoryAttribute** for the window style category.

Remarks

This category marks properties having to do with window style of top-level forms.

Requirements

Platforms: Windows 98, Windows NT 4.0, Windows Millennium Edition, Windows 2000, Windows XP Home Edition, Windows XP Professional, Windows .NET Server family

CategoryAttribute.Equals Method

This member overrides **Object.Equals**.

```
[Visual Basic]
Overrides Public Function Equals( _
   ByVal obj As Object _
) As Boolean
[C#]
public override bool Equals(
   object obj
);
[C++]
public: bool Equals(
   Object* obj
);
[JScript]
public override function Equals(
   obj : Object
) : Boolean;
```

Requirements

Platforms: Windows 98, Windows NT 4.0, Windows Millennium Edition, Windows 2000, Windows XP Home Edition, Windows XP Professional, Windows .NET Server family

CategoryAttribute.GetHashCode Method

This member overrides **Attribute.GetHashCode**.

[Visual Basic]
```
Overrides Public Function GetHashCode() As Integer
```
[C#]
```
public override int GetHashCode();
```
[C++]
```
public: int GetHashCode();
```
[JScript]
```
public override function GetHashCode() : int;
```

Requirements

Platforms: Windows 98, Windows NT 4.0, Windows Millennium Edition, Windows 2000, Windows XP Home Edition, Windows XP Professional, Windows .NET Server family

CategoryAttribute.GetLocalizedString Method

Looks up the localized name of a given category.

[Visual Basic]
```
Protected Overridable Function GetLocalizedString( _
   ByVal value As String _
) As String
```
[C#]
```
protected virtual string GetLocalizedString(
   string value
);
```
[C++]
```
protected: virtual String* GetLocalizedString(
   String* value
);
```
[JScript]
```
protected function GetLocalizedString(
   value : String
) : String;
```

Parameters

value
   The name of the category to look up.

Return Value

The localized name of the category, or a null reference (**Nothing** in Visual Basic) if a localized name does not exist.

Remarks

The **Category** property calls this method the first time it is accessed to look up the localized name for the given category.

Notes to Inheritors: Override this method to add your own localized names to categories. If a localized string is available for the given value, the method should return it. Otherwise, call the base class's **GetLocalizedString** method to let the base class localize the string.

Requirements

Platforms: Windows 98, Windows NT 4.0, Windows Millennium Edition, Windows 2000, Windows XP Home Edition, Windows XP Professional, Windows .NET Server family

CategoryAttribute.IsDefaultAttribute Method

This member overrides **Attribute.IsDefaultAttribute**.

[Visual Basic]
```
Overrides Public Function IsDefaultAttribute() As Boolean
```
[C#]
```
public override bool IsDefaultAttribute();
```
[C++]
```
public: bool IsDefaultAttribute();
```
[JScript]
```
public override function IsDefaultAttribute() : Boolean;
```

Requirements

Platforms: Windows 98, Windows NT 4.0, Windows Millennium Edition, Windows 2000, Windows XP Home Edition, Windows XP Professional, Windows .NET Server family

CharConverter Class

Provides a type converter to convert Unicode character objects to and from various other representations.

System.Object
  System.ComponentModel.TypeConverter
    System.ComponentModel.CharConverter

```
[Visual Basic]
Public Class CharConverter
   Inherits TypeConverter
[C#]
public class CharConverter : TypeConverter
[C++]
public __gc class CharConverter : public TypeConverter
[JScript]
public class CharConverter extends TypeConverter
```

Thread Safety

Any public static (**Shared** in Visual Basic) members of this type are safe for multithreaded operations. Any instance members are not guaranteed to be thread safe.

Remarks

This converter can only convert a string, with a length of one, to and from a character.

For more information about type converters, see the **TypeConverter** base class and **Implementing a Type Converter**.

> **Note** You should never create an instance of a **CharConverter**. Instead, call the **GetConverter** method of **TypeDescriptor**. For more information, see the examples in the **TypeConverter** base class.

Example

[Visual Basic, C#, C++] The following example converts a variable of type **Char** to a string variable, and vice versa.

```
[Visual Basic]
Dim chrA As [Char] = "a"c
Dim strB As String = "b"
Console.WriteLine(TypeDescriptor.GetConverter(chrA).ConvertTo ↵
(chrA, GetType(String)))
Console.WriteLine(TypeDescriptor.GetConverter(chrA).ConvertFrom(strB))
```

```
[C#]
Char chrA='a';
string strB="b";
Console.WriteLine(TypeDescriptor.GetConverter(chrA).ConvertTo ↵
 (chrA, typeof(string)));
Console.WriteLine(TypeDescriptor.GetConverter(chrA).ConvertFrom(strB));
```

```
[C++]
char chrA( 'a' );
String* strB = S"b";
Console::WriteLine(TypeDescriptor::GetConverter(__box(chrA))- ↵
>ConvertTo(__box(chrA), __typeof(String)));
Console::WriteLine(TypeDescriptor::GetConverter(__box(chrA))- ↵
>ConvertFrom(strB));
```

Requirements

Namespace: System.ComponentModel

Platforms: Windows 98, Windows NT 4.0, Windows Millennium Edition, Windows 2000, Windows XP Home Edition, Windows XP Professional, Windows Server 2003 family

Assembly: System (in System.dll)

CharConverter Constructor

Initializes a new instance of the **CharConverter** class.

```
[Visual Basic]
Public Sub New()
[C#]
public CharConverter();
[C++]
public: CharConverter();
[JScript]
public function CharConverter();
```

Remarks

The default constructor initializes any fields to their default values.

Requirements

Platforms: Windows 98, Windows NT 4.0, Windows Millennium Edition, Windows 2000, Windows XP Home Edition, Windows XP Professional, Windows Server 2003 family

CharConverter.CanConvertFrom Method

Overload List

This member supports the .NET Framework infrastructure and is not intended to be used directly from your code.

[Visual Basic] **Overloads Overrides Public Function CanConvertFrom(ITypeDescriptorContext, Type) As Boolean**

[C#] **public override bool CanConvertFrom(ITypeDescriptorContext, Type);**

[C++] **public: bool CanConvertFrom(ITypeDescriptorContext*, Type*);**

[JScript] **public override function CanConvertFrom(ITypeDescriptorContext, Type) : Boolean;**

Inherited from **TypeConverter**.

[Visual Basic] **Overloads Public Function CanConvertFrom(Type) As Boolean**

[C#] **public bool CanConvertFrom(Type);**

[C++] **public: bool CanConvertFrom(Type*);**

[JScript] **public function CanConvertFrom(Type) : Boolean;**

CharConverter.CanConvertFrom Method (ITypeDescriptorContext, Type)

This member overrides **TypeConverter.CanConvertFrom**.

```
[Visual Basic]
Overrides Overloads Public Function CanConvertFrom( _
   ByVal context As ITypeDescriptorContext, _
   ByVal sourceType As Type _
) As Boolean
[C#]
public override bool CanConvertFrom(
   ITypeDescriptorContext context,
   Type sourceType
);
[C++]
public: bool CanConvertFrom(
   ITypeDescriptorContext* context,
   Type* sourceType
);
```

```
[JScript]
public override function CanConvertFrom(
   context : ITypeDescriptorContext,
   sourceType : Type
) : Boolean;
```

Requirements

Platforms: Windows 98, Windows NT 4.0, Windows Millennium Edition, Windows 2000, Windows XP Home Edition, Windows XP Professional, Windows Server 2003 family

CharConverter.ConvertFrom Method

Overload List

This member supports the .NET Framework infrastructure and is not intended to be used directly from your code.

[Visual Basic] **Overloads Overrides Public Function ConvertFrom(ITypeDescriptorContext, CultureInfo, Object) As Object**

[C#] **public override object ConvertFrom(ITypeDescriptorContext, CultureInfo, object);**

[C++] **public: Object* ConvertFrom(ITypeDescriptorContext*, CultureInfo*, Object*);**

[JScript] **public override function ConvertFrom(ITypeDescriptorContext, CultureInfo, Object) : Object;**

Inherited from **TypeConverter**.

[Visual Basic] **Overloads Public Function ConvertFrom(Object) As Object**

[C#] **public object ConvertFrom(object);**

[C++] **public: Object* ConvertFrom(Object*);**

[JScript] **public function ConvertFrom(Object) : Object;**

CharConverter.ConvertFrom Method (ITypeDescriptorContext, CultureInfo, Object)

This member overrides **TypeConverter.ConvertFrom**.

```
[Visual Basic]
Overrides Overloads Public Function ConvertFrom( _
   ByVal context As ITypeDescriptorContext, _
   ByVal culture As CultureInfo, _
   ByVal value As Object _
) As Object
[C#]
public override object ConvertFrom(
   ITypeDescriptorContext context,
   CultureInfo culture,
   object value
);
[C++]
public: Object* ConvertFrom(
   ITypeDescriptorContext* context,
   CultureInfo* culture,
   Object* value
);
[JScript]
public override function ConvertFrom(
   context : ITypeDescriptorContext,
   culture : CultureInfo,
   value : Object
) : Object;
```

Requirements

Platforms: Windows 98, Windows NT 4.0, Windows Millennium Edition, Windows 2000, Windows XP Home Edition, Windows XP Professional, Windows Server 2003 family

CharConverter.ConvertTo Method

Overload List

This member supports the .NET Framework infrastructure and is not intended to be used directly from your code.

[Visual Basic] **Overloads Overrides Public Function ConvertTo(ITypeDescriptorContext, CultureInfo, Object, Type) As Object**

[C#] **public override object ConvertTo(ITypeDescriptorContext, CultureInfo, object, Type);**

[C++] **public: Object* ConvertTo(ITypeDescriptorContext*, CultureInfo*, Object*, Type*);**

[JScript] **public override function ConvertTo(ITypeDescriptorContext, CultureInfo, Object, Type) : Object;**

Inherited from **TypeConverter**.

[Visual Basic] **Overloads Public Function ConvertTo(Object, Type) As Object**

[C#] **public object ConvertTo(object, Type);**

[C++] **public: Object* ConvertTo(Object*, Type*);**

[JScript] **public function ConvertTo(Object, Type) : Object;**

CharConverter.ConvertTo Method (ITypeDescriptorContext, CultureInfo, Object, Type)

This member overrides **TypeConverter.ConvertTo**.

```
[Visual Basic]
Overrides Overloads Public Function ConvertTo( _
   ByVal context As ITypeDescriptorContext, _
   ByVal culture As CultureInfo, _
   ByVal value As Object, _
   ByVal destinationType As Type _
) As Object
[C#]
public override object ConvertTo(
   ITypeDescriptorContext context,
   CultureInfo culture,
   object value,
   Type destinationType
);
[C++]
public: Object* ConvertTo(
   ITypeDescriptorContext* context,
   CultureInfo* culture,
   Object* value,
   Type* destinationType
);
```

[JScript]
```
public override function ConvertTo(
   context : ITypeDescriptorContext,
   culture : CultureInfo,
   value : Object,
   destinationType : Type
) : Object;
```

Requirements

Platforms: Windows 98, Windows NT 4.0, Windows Millennium Edition, Windows 2000, Windows XP Home Edition, Windows XP Professional, Windows Server 2003 family

CollectionChangeAction Enumeration

Specifies how the collection is changed.

[Visual Basic]
```
<Serializable>
Public Enum CollectionChangeAction
```
[C#]
```
[Serializable]
public enum CollectionChangeAction
```
[C++]
```
[Serializable]
__value public enum CollectionChangeAction
```
[JScript]
```
public
   Serializable
enum CollectionChangeAction
```

Remarks

The **CollectionChangeEventArgs** class uses this enumeration.

Members

Member name	Description
Add Supported by the .NET Compact Framework.	Specifies that an element was added to the collection.
Refresh Supported by the .NET Compact Framework.	Specifies that the entire collection has changed. This is caused by using methods that manipulate the entire collection, such as **Clear**.
Remove Supported by the .NET Compact Framework.	Specifies that an element was removed from the collection.

Requirements

Namespace: System.ComponentModel

Platforms: Windows 98, Windows NT 4.0, Windows Millennium Edition, Windows 2000, Windows XP Home Edition, Windows XP Professional, Windows Server 2003 family, .NET Compact Framework - Windows CE .NET

Assembly: System (in System.dll)

CollectionChangeEventArgs Class

Provides data for the **CollectionChanged** event.

System.Object
  System.EventArgs
    System.ComponentModel.CollectionChangeEventArgs

```
[Visual Basic]
Public Class CollectionChangeEventArgs
   Inherits EventArgs
[C#]
public class CollectionChangeEventArgs : EventArgs
[C++]
public __gc class CollectionChangeEventArgs : public EventArgs
[JScript]
public class CollectionChangeEventArgs extends EventArgs
```

Thread Safety

Any public static (**Shared** in Visual Basic) members of this type are safe for multithreaded operations. Any instance members are not guaranteed to be thread safe.

Remarks

A **CollectionChanged** event is raised when you change which items are in a collection, for example, by adding an element to a collection or removing an element from the collection. This event is not raised when an individual element changes its value.

Example

For an example on using the **CollectionChangeEventArgs** class, see the sample code in the **CollectionChanged** event of the **DataColumnCollection** class.

Requirements

Namespace: System.ComponentModel

Platforms: Windows 98, Windows NT 4.0, Windows Millennium Edition, Windows 2000, Windows XP Home Edition, Windows XP Professional, Windows Server 2003 family, .NET Compact Framework - Windows CE .NET

Assembly: System (in System.dll)

CollectionChangeEventArgs Constructor

Initializes a new instance of the **CollectionChangeEventArgs** class.

```
[Visual Basic]
Public Sub New( _
   ByVal action As CollectionChangeAction, _
   ByVal element As Object _
)
[C#]
public CollectionChangeEventArgs(
   CollectionChangeAction action,
   object element
);
[C++]
public: CollectionChangeEventArgs(
   CollectionChangeAction action,
   Object* element
);
[JScript]
public function CollectionChangeEventArgs(
   action : CollectionChangeAction,
   element : Object
);
```

Parameters

action
  One of the **CollectionChangeAction** values that specifies how the collection changed.

element
  An **Object** that specifies the instance of the collection where the change occurred.

Requirements

Platforms: Windows 98, Windows NT 4.0, Windows Millennium Edition, Windows 2000, Windows XP Home Edition, Windows XP Professional, Windows Server 2003 family, .NET Compact Framework - Windows CE .NET

CollectionChangeEventArgs.Action Property

Gets an action that specifies how the collection changed.

```
[Visual Basic]
Public Overridable ReadOnly Property Action As _
   CollectionChangeAction
[C#]
public virtual CollectionChangeAction Action {get;}
[C++]
public: __property virtual CollectionChangeAction get_Action();
[JScript]
public function get Action() : CollectionChangeAction;
```

Property Value

One of the **CollectionChangeAction** values.

Remarks

This property can have one of the following values:

Action	Property Value
An element was added to the collection	**CollectionChangeAction.Add**
An element was removed from the collection	**CollectionChangeAction.Remove**
The collection was completely changed	**CollectionChangeAction.Refresh**

Requirements

Platforms: Windows 98, Windows NT 4.0, Windows Millennium Edition, Windows 2000, Windows XP Home Edition, Windows XP Professional, Windows Server 2003 family, .NET Compact Framework - Windows CE .NET

CollectionChangeEventArgs.Element Property

Gets the instance of the collection with the change.

[Visual Basic]
```
Public Overridable ReadOnly Property Element As Object
```
[C#]
```
public virtual object Element {get;}
```
[C++]
```
public: __property virtual Object* get_Element();
```
[JScript]
```
public function get Element() : Object;
```

Property Value

An **Object** that represents the instance of the collection with the change; or a null reference (**Nothing** in Visual Basic) if you refresh the collection.

Requirements

Platforms: Windows 98, Windows NT 4.0, Windows Millennium Edition, Windows 2000, Windows XP Home Edition, Windows XP Professional, Windows Server 2003 family, .NET Compact Framework - Windows CE .NET

CollectionChangeEventHandler Delegate

Represents the method that handles the **CollectionChanged** event raised when adding elements to or removing elements from a collection.

[Visual Basic]
```
<Serializable>
Public Delegate Sub CollectionChangeEventHandler( _
   ByVal sender As Object, _
   ByVal e As CollectionChangeEventArgs _
)
```
[C#]
```
[Serializable]
public delegate void CollectionChangeEventHandler(
   object sender,
   CollectionChangeEventArgs e
);
```
[C++]
```
[Serializable]
public __gc __delegate void CollectionChangeEventHandler(
   Object* sender,
   CollectionChangeEventArgs* e
);
```

[JScript] In JScript, you can use the delegates in the .NET Framework, but you cannot define your own.

Parameters [Visual Basic, C#, C++]

The declaration of your event handler must have the same parameters as the **CollectionChangeEventHandler** delegate declaration.

sender
: The source of the event.

e
: A **CollectionChangeEventArgs** that contains the event data.

Remarks

When you create a **CollectionChangeEventHandler** delegate, you identify the method that will handle the event. To associate the event with your event handler, add an instance of the delegate to the event. The event handler is called whenever the event occurs, unless you remove the delegate. For more information about event handler delegates, see **Events and Delegates**.

Example

For an example of using the **CollectionChangeEventHandler** delegate, see the sample code in the **CollectionChanged** event of the **DataColumnCollection** class.

Requirements

Namespace: System.ComponentModel

Platforms: Windows 98, Windows NT 4.0,
Windows Millennium Edition, Windows 2000,
Windows XP Home Edition, Windows XP Professional,
Windows Server 2003 family,
.NET Compact Framework - Windows CE .NET

Assembly: System (in System.dll)

CollectionConverter Class

Provides a type converter to convert collection objects to and from various other representations.

System.Object
  System.ComponentModel.TypeConverter
    System.ComponentModel.CollectionConverter
      System.ComponentModel.ArrayConverter

[Visual Basic]
```
Public Class CollectionConverter
   Inherits TypeConverter
```
[C#]
```
public class CollectionConverter : TypeConverter
```
[C++]
```
public __gc class CollectionConverter : public TypeConverter
```
[JScript]
```
public class CollectionConverter extends TypeConverter
```

Thread Safety

Any public static (**Shared** in Visual Basic) members of this type are safe for multithreaded operations. Any instance members are not guaranteed to be thread safe.

Remarks

The **GetProperties** method for this type converter always returns a null reference (**Nothing** in Visual Basic), and the **GetPropertiesSupported** method always returns **false**.

> **Note** You should never create an instance of **CollectionConverter**. Instead, call the **GetConverter** method of **TypeDescriptor**. For more information, see the examples in the **TypeConverter** base class.

Requirements

Namespace: System.ComponentModel

Platforms: Windows 98, Windows NT 4.0, Windows Millennium Edition, Windows 2000, Windows XP Home Edition, Windows XP Professional, Windows Server 2003 family

Assembly: System (in System.dll)

CollectionConverter Constructor

Initializes a new instance of the **CollectionConverter** class.

[Visual Basic]
```
Public Sub New()
```
[C#]
```
public CollectionConverter();
```
[C++]
```
public: CollectionConverter();
```
[JScript]
```
public function CollectionConverter();
```

Remarks

The default constructor initializes any fields to their default values.

Requirements

Platforms: Windows 98, Windows NT 4.0, Windows Millennium Edition, Windows 2000, Windows XP Home Edition, Windows XP Professional, Windows Server 2003 family

CollectionConverter.ConvertTo Method

Overload List

This member supports the .NET Framework infrastructure and is not intended to be used directly from your code.

[Visual Basic] **Overloads Overrides Public Function ConvertTo(ITypeDescriptorContext, CultureInfo, Object, Type) As Object**

[C#] **public override object ConvertTo(ITypeDescriptorContext, CultureInfo, object, Type);**

[C++] **public: Object* ConvertTo(ITypeDescriptorContext*, CultureInfo*, Object*, Type*);**

[JScript] **public override function ConvertTo(ITypeDescriptorContext, CultureInfo, Object, Type) : Object;**

Inherited from **TypeConverter**.

[Visual Basic] **Overloads Public Function ConvertTo(Object, Type) As Object**

[C#] **public object ConvertTo(object, Type);**

[C++] **public: Object* ConvertTo(Object*, Type*);**

[JScript] **public function ConvertTo(Object, Type) : Object;**

CollectionConverter.ConvertTo Method (ITypeDescriptorContext, CultureInfo, Object, Type)

This member overrides **TypeConverter.ConvertTo**.

[Visual Basic]
```
Overrides Overloads Public Function ConvertTo( _
   ByVal context As ITypeDescriptorContext, _
   ByVal culture As CultureInfo, _
   ByVal value As Object, _
   ByVal destinationType As Type _
) As Object
```
[C#]
```
public override object ConvertTo(
   ITypeDescriptorContext context,
   CultureInfo culture,
   object value,
   Type destinationType
);
```
[C++]
```
public: Object* ConvertTo(
   ITypeDescriptorContext* context,
   CultureInfo* culture,
   Object* value,
   Type* destinationType
);
```
[JScript]
```
public override function ConvertTo(
   context : ITypeDescriptorContext,
   culture : CultureInfo,
   value : Object,
   destinationType : Type
) : Object;
```

Requirements

Platforms: Windows 98, Windows NT 4.0, Windows Millennium Edition, Windows 2000, Windows XP Home Edition, Windows XP Professional, Windows Server 2003 family

CollectionConverter.GetProperties Method

Overload List

This member supports the .NET Framework infrastructure and is not intended to be used directly from your code.

[Visual Basic] **Overloads Overrides Public Function GetProperties(ITypeDescriptorContext, Object, Attribute()) As PropertyDescriptorCollection**

[C#] **public override PropertyDescriptorCollection GetProperties(ITypeDescriptorContext, object, Attribute[]);**

[C++] **public: PropertyDescriptorCollection* GetProperties(ITypeDescriptorContext*, Object*, Attribute[]);**

[JScript] **public override function GetProperties(ITypeDescriptorContext, Object, Attribute[]) : PropertyDescriptorCollection;**

Inherited from **TypeConverter**.

[Visual Basic] **Overloads Public Function GetProperties(Object) As PropertyDescriptorCollection**

[C#] **public PropertyDescriptorCollection GetProperties(object);**

[C++] **public: PropertyDescriptorCollection* GetProperties(Object*);**

[JScript] **public function GetProperties(Object) : PropertyDescriptorCollection;**

Inherited from **TypeConverter**.

[Visual Basic] **Overloads Public Function GetProperties(ITypeDescriptorContext, Object) As PropertyDescriptorCollection**

[C#] **public PropertyDescriptorCollection GetProperties(ITypeDescriptorContext, object);**

[C++] **public: PropertyDescriptorCollection* GetProperties(ITypeDescriptorContext*, Object*);**

[JScript] **public function GetProperties(ITypeDescriptorContext, Object) : PropertyDescriptorCollection;**

CollectionConverter.GetProperties Method (ITypeDescriptorContext, Object, Attribute[])

This member overrides **TypeConverter.GetProperties**.

[Visual Basic]
```
Overrides Overloads Public Function GetProperties( _
   ByVal context As ITypeDescriptorContext, _
   ByVal value As Object, _
   ByVal attributes() As Attribute _
) As PropertyDescriptorCollection
```
[C#]
```
public override PropertyDescriptorCollection GetProperties(
   ITypeDescriptorContext context,
   object value,
   Attribute[] attributes
);
```
[C++]
```
public: PropertyDescriptorCollection* GetProperties(
   ITypeDescriptorContext* context,
   Object* value,
   Attribute* attributes[]
);
```
[JScript]
```
public override function GetProperties(
   context : ITypeDescriptorContext,
   value : Object,
   attributes : Attribute[]
) : PropertyDescriptorCollection;
```

Requirements

Platforms: Windows 98, Windows NT 4.0, Windows Millennium Edition, Windows 2000, Windows XP Home Edition, Windows XP Professional, Windows Server 2003 family

CollectionConverter.GetPropertiesSupported Method

Overload List

This member supports the .NET Framework infrastructure and is not intended to be used directly from your code.

[Visual Basic] **Overloads Overrides Public Function GetPropertiesSupported(ITypeDescriptorContext) As Boolean**

[C#] **public override bool GetPropertiesSupported(ITypeDescriptorContext);**

[C++] **public: bool GetPropertiesSupported(ITypeDescriptorContext*);**

[JScript] **public override function GetPropertiesSupported(ITypeDescriptorContext) : Boolean;**

Inherited from **TypeConverter**.

[Visual Basic] **Overloads Public Function GetPropertiesSupported() As Boolean**

[C#] **public bool GetPropertiesSupported();**

[C++] **public: bool GetPropertiesSupported();**

[JScript] **public function GetPropertiesSupported() : Boolean;**

CollectionConverter.GetPropertiesSupported Method (ITypeDescriptorContext)

This member overrides **TypeConverter.GetPropertiesSupported**.

[Visual Basic]
```
Overrides Overloads Public Function GetPropertiesSupported( _
   ByVal context As ITypeDescriptorContext _
) As Boolean
```
[C#]
```
public override bool GetPropertiesSupported(
   ITypeDescriptorContext context
);
```
[C++]
```
public: bool GetPropertiesSupported(
   ITypeDescriptorContext* context
);
```
[JScript]
```
public override function GetPropertiesSupported(
   context : ITypeDescriptorContext
) : Boolean;
```

Requirements

Platforms: Windows 98, Windows NT 4.0, Windows Millennium Edition, Windows 2000, Windows XP Home Edition, Windows XP Professional, Windows Server 2003 family

Component Class

Provides the base implementation for the **IComponent** interface and enables object-sharing between applications.

System.Object
  System.MarshalByRefObject
    System.ComponentModel.Component
      Derived classes

```
[Visual Basic]
Public Class Component
   Inherits MarshalByRefObject
   Implements IComponent, IDisposable
[C#]
public class Component : MarshalByRefObject, IComponent,
   IDisposable
[C++]
public __gc class Component : public MarshalByRefObject,
   IComponent, IDisposable
[JScript]
public class Component extends MarshalByRefObject implements
   IComponent, IDisposable
```

Thread Safety

Any public static (**Shared** in Visual Basic) members of this type are safe for multithreaded operations. Any instance members are not guaranteed to be thread safe.

Remarks

Component is the base class for all components in the common language runtime which marshal by reference. **Component** is remotable and derives from **MarshalByRefObject**. **Component** provides an implementation of **IComponent**. The **MarshalByValueComponent** provides an implementation of **IComponent** which marshals by value.

You can host a **Component** in any object that implements the **IContainer** interface, and can query and get services from its container. The container creates an **ISite** for each **Component** it contains. The container uses the site to manage the **Component** and is used by the **Component** to communicate with its container.

It is recommended that a **Component** release resources explicitly by calls to its **Dispose** method, without waiting for automatic memory management through an implicit call to **Finalize**. When a **Container** is disposed, all components within the **Container** are also disposed.

Requirements

Namespace: System.ComponentModel

Platforms: Windows 98, Windows NT 4.0, Windows Millennium Edition, Windows 2000, Windows XP Home Edition, Windows XP Professional, Windows Server 2003 family, .NET Compact Framework - Windows CE .NET

Assembly: System (in System.dll)

Component Constructor

Initializes a new instance of the **Component** class.

```
[Visual Basic]
Public Sub New()
[C#]
public Component();
[C++]
public: Component();
[JScript]
public function Component();
```

Remarks

The default constructor initializes any fields to their default values.

Requirements

Platforms: Windows 98, Windows NT 4.0, Windows Millennium Edition, Windows 2000, Windows XP Home Edition, Windows XP Professional, Windows Server 2003 family, .NET Compact Framework - Windows CE .NET

Component.Container Property

Gets the **IContainer** that contains the **Component**.

```
[Visual Basic]
Public ReadOnly Property Container As IContainer
[C#]
public IContainer Container {get;}
[C++]
public: __property IContainer* get_Container();
[JScript]
public function get Container() : IContainer;
```

Property Value

The **IContainer** that contains the **Component**, if any.

This value is a null reference (**Nothing** in Visual Basic) if the **Component** is not encapsulated in an **IContainer**.

Remarks

The components in a container are tracked in a first-in, first-out list, which also defines the order of the components within the container. The last component added is the last component in the list.

Requirements

Platforms: Windows 98, Windows NT 4.0, Windows Millennium Edition, Windows 2000, Windows XP Home Edition, Windows XP Professional, Windows Server 2003 family

Component.DesignMode Property

Gets a value that indicates whether the **Component** is currently in design mode.

```
[Visual Basic]
Protected ReadOnly Property DesignMode As Boolean
[C#]
protected bool DesignMode {get;}
[C++]
protected: __property bool get_DesignMode();
[JScript]
protected function get DesignMode() : Boolean;
```

Property Value

true, if the **Component** is in design mode; otherwise, **false**.

Remarks

The design mode indicator is stored in the **ISite**; therefore, if the **Component** does not have an **ISite** associated with it, this property is always **false**.

Requirements

Platforms: Windows 98, Windows NT 4.0,
Windows Millennium Edition, Windows 2000,
Windows XP Home Edition, Windows XP Professional,
Windows Server 2003 family

Component.Events Property

Gets the list of event handlers that are attached to this **Component**.

[Visual Basic]
```
Protected ReadOnly Property Events As EventHandlerList
```
[C#]
```
protected EventHandlerList Events {get;}
```
[C++]
```
protected: __property EventHandlerList* get_Events();
```
[JScript]
```
protected function get Events() : EventHandlerList;
```

Property Value

An **EventHandlerList** that provides the delegates for this component.

Remarks

For more information about handling events, see **Consuming Events**.

Requirements

Platforms: Windows 98, Windows NT 4.0,
Windows Millennium Edition, Windows 2000,
Windows XP Home Edition, Windows XP Professional,
Windows Server 2003 family

Component.Site Property

Gets or sets the **ISite** of the **Component**.

[Visual Basic]
```
Public Overridable Property Site As ISite  Implements _
   IComponent.Site
```
[C#]
```
public virtual ISite Site {get; set;}
```
[C++]
```
public: __property virtual ISite* get_Site();
public: __property virtual void set_Site(ISite*);
```
[JScript]
```
public function get Site() : ISite;
public function set Site(ISite);
```

Property Value

The **ISite** associated with the **Component**, if any.

This value is a null reference (**Nothing** in Visual Basic) if the **Component** is not encapsulated in an **IContainer**, the **Component** does not have an **ISite** associated with it, or the **Component** is removed from its **IContainer**.

Implements

IComponent.Site

Remarks

A **Component** will have an **ISite** if it has been added to an **IContainer** and the **IContainer** assigns an **ISite** to it. The **IContainer** is responsible to assign the **ISite** to the **Component**. Changing the value of the component's **ISite** does not necessarily change the name of the site the **Component** is assigned to. It is strongly suggested that the setting of the **Site** property only be done by an **IContainer**.

The property value is a null reference (**Nothing** in Visual Basic) if the **Component** is removed from its **IContainer**. Assigning a null reference (**Nothing**) to this property does not necessarily remove the **Component** from the **IContainer**.

A **Component** might or might not have a name. If a **Component** is given a name, the name must be unique among other **Component** objects within its **IContainer**. The **ISite** stores the name of the **Component**; therefore, you can only name a **Component** if it has an **ISite** associated with it.

Requirements

Platforms: Windows 98, Windows NT 4.0,
Windows Millennium Edition, Windows 2000,
Windows XP Home Edition, Windows XP Professional,
Windows Server 2003 family

Component.Dispose Method

Releases the resources used by the **Component**.

Overload List

Releases all resources used by the **Component**.

[Visual Basic] **Overloads Public Overridable Sub Dispose() Implements IDisposable.Dispose**

[C#] **public virtual void Dispose();**

[C++] **public: virtual void Dispose();**

[JScript] **public function Dispose();**

Releases the unmanaged resources used by the **Component** and optionally releases the managed resources.

Supported by the .NET Compact Framework.

[Visual Basic] **Overloads Protected Overridable Sub Dispose(Boolean)**

[C#] **protected virtual void Dispose(bool);**

[C++] **protected: virtual void Dispose(bool);**

[JScript] **protected function Dispose(Boolean);**

Component.Dispose Method ()

Releases all resources used by the **Component**.

[Visual Basic]
```
Overloads Public Overridable Sub Dispose() Implements _
   IDisposable.Dispose
```
[C#]
```
public virtual void Dispose();
```
[C++]
```
public: virtual void Dispose();
```
[JScript]
```
public function Dispose();
```

Implements

IDisposable.Dispose

Remarks

Calling **Dispose** allows the resources used by the **Component** to be reallocated for other purposes. For more information about **Dispose**, see **Cleaning Up Unmanaged Resources**.

Requirements

Platforms: Windows 98, Windows NT 4.0, Windows Millennium Edition, Windows 2000, Windows XP Home Edition, Windows XP Professional, Windows Server 2003 family

Component.Dispose Method (Boolean)

Releases the unmanaged resources used by the **Component** and optionally releases the managed resources.

```
[Visual Basic]
Overloads Protected Overridable Sub Dispose( _
   ByVal disposing As Boolean _
)
[C#]
protected virtual void Dispose(
   bool disposing
);
[C++]
protected: virtual void Dispose(
   bool disposing
);
[JScript]
protected function Dispose(
   disposing : Boolean
);
```

Parameters

disposing

true to release both managed and unmanaged resources; **false** to release only unmanaged resources.

Remarks

This method is called by the public **Dispose()** method and the **Finalize** method. **Dispose()** invokes the protected **Dispose(Boolean)** method with the *disposing* parameter set to **true**. **Finalize** invokes **Dispose** with *disposing* set to **false**.

When the *disposing* parameter is **true**, this method releases all resources held by any managed objects that this **Component** references. This method invokes the **Dispose()** method of each referenced object.

Notes to Inheritors: **Dispose** can be called multiple times by other objects. When overriding **Dispose(Boolean)**, be careful not to reference objects that have been previously disposed of in an earlier call to **Dispose**.

Requirements

Platforms: Windows 98, Windows NT 4.0, Windows Millennium Edition, Windows 2000, Windows XP Home Edition, Windows XP Professional, Windows Server 2003 family, .NET Compact Framework - Windows CE .NET

Component.Finalize Method

Releases unmanaged resources and performs other cleanup operations before the **Component** is reclaimed by garbage collection.

[C#] In C#, finalizers are expressed using destructor syntax.

[C++] In C++, finalizers are expressed using destructor syntax.

```
[Visual Basic]
Overrides Protected Sub Finalize()
[C#]
~Component();
[C++]
~Component();
[JScript]
protected override function Finalize();
```

Remarks

Calls **Dispose** with the *disposing* parameter set to **false** to free unmanaged resources.

This method overrides **Object.Finalize**. Application code should not call this method; an object's **Finalize** method is automatically invoked during garbage collection, unless finalization by the garbage collector has been disabled by a call to the **GC.SuppressFinalize** method.

Requirements

Platforms: Windows 98, Windows NT 4.0, Windows Millennium Edition, Windows 2000, Windows XP Home Edition, Windows XP Professional, Windows Server 2003 family, .NET Compact Framework - Windows CE .NET

Component.GetService Method

Returns an object that represents a service provided by the **Component** or by its **Container**.

```
[Visual Basic]
Protected Overridable Function GetService( _
   ByVal service As Type _
) As Object
[C#]
protected virtual object GetService(
   Type service
);
[C++]
protected: virtual Object* GetService(
   Type* service
);
[JScript]
protected function GetService(
   service : Type
) : Object;
```

Parameters

service

A service provided by the **Component**.

Return Value

An **Object** that represents a service provided by the **Component**.

This value is a null reference (**Nothing** in Visual Basic) if the **Component** does not provide the specified service.

Remarks

This method can be overridden by a derived class.

Requirements

Platforms: Windows 98, Windows NT 4.0, Windows Millennium Edition, Windows 2000, Windows XP Home Edition, Windows XP Professional, Windows Server 2003 family

Component.ToString Method

This member overrides **Object.ToString**.

```
[Visual Basic]
Overrides Public Function ToString() As String
[C#]
public override string ToString();
[C++]
public: String* ToString();
[JScript]
public override function ToString() : String;
```

Requirements

Platforms: Windows 98, Windows NT 4.0, Windows Millennium Edition, Windows 2000, Windows XP Home Edition, Windows XP Professional, Windows Server 2003 family, .NET Compact Framework - Windows CE .NET

Component.Disposed Event

Adds an event handler to listen to the **Disposed** event on the component.

```
[Visual Basic]
Public Overridable Event Disposed As EventHandler
[C#]
public virtual event EventHandler Disposed;
[C++]
public: virtual __event EventHandler* Disposed;
```

[JScript] In JScript, you can handle the events defined by a class, but you cannot define your own.

Event Data

The event handler receives an argument of type **EventArgs**.

Remarks

When you create a **Disposed** delegate, you identify the method that handles the event. To associate the event with your event handler, add an instance of the delegate to the event. The event handler is called whenever the event occurs, unless you remove the delegate.

Requirements

Platforms: Windows 98, Windows NT 4.0, Windows Millennium Edition, Windows 2000, Windows XP Home Edition, Windows XP Professional, Windows Server 2003 family

ComponentCollection Class

Specifies a collection of **Component** objects in the **Container**.

System.Object
System.Collections.ReadOnlyCollectionBase
System.ComponentModel.ComponentCollection

[Visual Basic]
```
<ComVisible(True)>
Public Class ComponentCollection
   Inherits ReadOnlyCollectionBase
```
[C#]
```
[ComVisible(true)]
public class ComponentCollection : ReadOnlyCollectionBase
```
[C++]
```
[ComVisible(true)]
public __gc class ComponentCollection : public
   ReadOnlyCollectionBase
```
[JScript]
```
public
   ComVisible(true)
class ComponentCollection extends ReadOnlyCollectionBase
```

Thread Safety

Any public static (**Shared** in Visual Basic) members of this type are safe for multithreaded operations. Any instance members are not guaranteed to be thread safe.

Requirements

Namespace: System.ComponentModel

Platforms: Windows 98, Windows NT 4.0, Windows Millennium Edition, Windows 2000, Windows XP Home Edition, Windows XP Professional, Windows Server 2003 family

Assembly: System (in System.dll)

ComponentCollection Constructor

Initializes a new instance of the **ComponentCollection** class with an array of components.

[Visual Basic]
```
Public Sub New( _
   ByVal components() As IComponent _
)
```
[C#]
```
public ComponentCollection(
   IComponent[] components
);
```
[C++]
```
public: ComponentCollection(
   IComponent* components[]
);
```
[JScript]
```
public function ComponentCollection(
   components : IComponent[]
);
```

Parameters

components

An array of **IComponent** objects to initialize the collection with.

Requirements

Platforms: Windows 98, Windows NT 4.0, Windows Millennium Edition, Windows 2000, Windows XP Home Edition, Windows XP Professional, Windows Server 2003 family

ComponentCollection.Item Property

Gets the requested component.

[C#] In C#, this property is the indexer for the **ComponentCollection** class.

Overload List

Gets a specific **Component** in the **Container**.

[Visual Basic] **Overloads Public Overridable Default ReadOnly Property Item(String) As IComponent**

[C#] **public virtual IComponent this[string] {get;}**

[C++] **public: __property virtual IComponent* get_Item(String*);**

[JScript] **ComponentCollection.Item (String)**

Gets a specific **Component** in the **Container**.

[Visual Basic] **Overloads Public Overridable Default ReadOnly Property Item(Integer) As IComponent**

[C#] **public virtual IComponent this[int] {get;}**

[C++] **public: __property virtual IComponent* get_Item(int);**

[JScript] **ComponentCollection.Item (int)**

ComponentCollection.Item Property (String)

Gets a specific **Component** in the **Container**.

[C#] In C#, this property is the indexer for the **ComponentCollection** class.

[Visual Basic]
```
Overloads Public Overridable Default ReadOnly Property Item( _
   ByVal name As String _
) As IComponent
```
[C#]
```
public virtual IComponent this[
   string name
] {get;}
```
[C++]
```
public: __property virtual IComponent* get_Item(
   String* name
);
```
[JScript]
```
returnValue = ComponentCollectionObject.Item(name);
-or-
returnValue = ComponentCollectionObject(name);
```

[JScript] In JScript, you can use the default indexed properties defined by a type, but you cannot explicitly define your own. However, specifying the **expando** attribute on a class automatically provides a default indexed property whose type is **Object** and whose index type is **String**.

Arguments [JScript]

name

The name of the **Component** to get.

Parameters [Visual Basic, C#, C++]

name

The name of the **Component** to get.

Property Value

The component specified by the *name* parameter or a null reference (**Nothing** in Visual Basic), if the named component cannot be found.

Remarks

This method can be overridden by a derived class.

> **Note** **Item** works only when the component is sited, which typically occurs only at design time. To site a **Component** at run time, set the **Site** property of the **Component**. Then, **Item** can get the **Component** whose **Site** property **Name** is the *name* parameter.

Requirements

Platforms: Windows 98, Windows NT 4.0, Windows Millennium Edition, Windows 2000, Windows XP Home Edition, Windows XP Professional, Windows Server 2003 family

ComponentCollection.Item Property (Int32)

Gets a specific **Component** in the **Container**.

[C#] In C#, this property is the indexer for the **ComponentCollection** class.

```
[Visual Basic]
Overloads Public Overridable Default ReadOnly Property Item( _
   ByVal index As Integer _
) As IComponent
[C#]
public virtual IComponent this[
   int index
] {get;}
[C++]
public: __property virtual IComponent* get_Item(
   int index
);
[JScript]
returnValue = ComponentCollectionObject.Item(index);
-or-
returnValue = ComponentCollectionObject(index);
```

[JScript] In JScript, you can use the default indexed properties defined by a type, but you cannot explicitly define your own. However, specifying the **expando** attribute on a class automatically provides a default indexed property whose type is **Object** and whose index type is **String**.

Arguments [JScript]

index

The index of the **Component** to get.

Parameters [Visual Basic, C#, C++]

index

The index of the **Component** to get.

Property Value

The **IComponent** object at the given index.

Remarks

This method can be overridden by a derived class.

Requirements

Platforms: Windows 98, Windows NT 4.0, Windows Millennium Edition, Windows 2000, Windows XP Home Edition, Windows XP Professional, Windows Server 2003 family

ComponentCollection.CopyTo Method

Copies the entire collection to an array, starting at the specified index.

```
[Visual Basic]
Public Sub CopyTo( _
   ByVal array() As IComponent, _
   ByVal index As Integer _
)
[C#]
public void CopyTo(
   IComponent[] array,
   int index
);
[C++]
public: void CopyTo(
   IComponent* array[],
   int index
);
[JScript]
public function CopyTo(
   array : IComponent[],
   index : int
);
```

Parameters

array

An array of **IComponent** objects to copy elements of the collection to.

index

The index of the *array* parameter at which copying begins.

Requirements

Platforms: Windows 98, Windows NT 4.0, Windows Millennium Edition, Windows 2000, Windows XP Home Edition, Windows XP Professional, Windows Server 2003 family

ComponentConverter Class

Provides a type converter to convert components to and from various other representations.

System.Object
  System.ComponentModel.TypeConverter
    System.ComponentModel.ReferenceConverter
      System.ComponentModel.ComponentConverter

```
[Visual Basic]
Public Class ComponentConverter
   Inherits ReferenceConverter
[C#]
public class ComponentConverter : ReferenceConverter
[C++]
public __gc class ComponentConverter : public ReferenceConverter
[JScript]
public class ComponentConverter extends ReferenceConverter
```

Thread Safety

Any public static (**Shared** in Visual Basic) members of this type are safe for multithreaded operations. Any instance members are not guaranteed to be thread safe.

Remarks

This class implements **GetPropertiesSupported** and **GetProperties** by returning the properties through the **GetProperties** method of **TypeDescriptor**.

> **Note** You should never create an instance of **ComponentConverter**. Instead, call the **GetConverter** method of **TypeDescriptor**. For more information, see the examples in the **TypeConverter** base class.

This converter converts an object that implements **IComponent** and displays its properties in the Properties window.

Requirements

Namespace: System.ComponentModel

Platforms: Windows 98, Windows NT 4.0, Windows Millennium Edition, Windows 2000, Windows XP Home Edition, Windows XP Professional, Windows .NET Server family

Assembly: System (in System.dll)

ComponentConverter Constructor

This member supports the .NET Framework infrastructure and is not intended to be used directly from your code.

```
[Visual Basic]
Public Sub New( _
   ByVal type As Type _
)
[C#]
public ComponentConverter(
   Type type
);
[C++]
public: ComponentConverter(
   Type* type
);
[JScript]
public function ComponentConverter(
   type : Type
);
```

ComponentConverter.GetProperties Method

Overload List

This member supports the .NET Framework infrastructure and is not intended to be used directly from your code.

[Visual Basic] **Overloads Overrides Public Function GetProperties(ITypeDescriptorContext, Object, Attribute()) As PropertyDescriptorCollection**

[C#] **public override PropertyDescriptorCollection GetProperties(ITypeDescriptorContext, object, Attribute[]);**

[C++] **public: PropertyDescriptorCollection* GetProperties(ITypeDescriptorContext*, Object*, Attribute[]);**

[JScript] **public override function GetProperties(ITypeDescriptorContext, Object, Attribute[]) : PropertyDescriptorCollection;**

Inherited from **TypeConverter**.

[Visual Basic] **Overloads Public Function GetProperties(Object) As PropertyDescriptorCollection**

[C#] **public PropertyDescriptorCollection GetProperties(object);**

[C++] **public: PropertyDescriptorCollection* GetProperties(Object*);**

[JScript] **public function GetProperties(Object) : PropertyDescriptorCollection;**

Inherited from **TypeConverter**.

[Visual Basic] **Overloads Public Function GetProperties(ITypeDescriptorContext, Object) As PropertyDescriptorCollection**

[C#] **public PropertyDescriptorCollection GetProperties(ITypeDescriptorContext, object);**

[C++] **public: PropertyDescriptorCollection* GetProperties(ITypeDescriptorContext*, Object*);**

[JScript] **public function GetProperties(ITypeDescriptorContext, Object) : PropertyDescriptorCollection;**

ComponentConverter.GetProperties Method (ITypeDescriptorContext, Object, Attribute[])

This member overrides **TypeConverter.GetProperties**.

```
[Visual Basic]
Overrides Overloads Public Function GetProperties( _
   ByVal context As ITypeDescriptorContext, _
   ByVal value As Object, _
   ByVal attributes() As Attribute _
) As PropertyDescriptorCollection
[C#]
public override PropertyDescriptorCollection GetProperties(
   ITypeDescriptorContext context,
   object value,
   Attribute[] attributes
);
```

[C++]
```
public: PropertyDescriptorCollection* GetProperties(
   ITypeDescriptorContext* context,
   Object* value,
   Attribute* attributes[]
);
```
[JScript]
```
public override function GetProperties(
   context : ITypeDescriptorContext,
   value : Object,
   attributes : Attribute[]
) : PropertyDescriptorCollection;
```

Requirements

Platforms: Windows 98, Windows NT 4.0, Windows Millennium Edition, Windows 2000, Windows XP Home Edition, Windows XP Professional, Windows .NET Server family

ComponentConverter.GetPropertiesSupported Method

Overload List

This member supports the .NET Framework infrastructure and is not intended to be used directly from your code.

[Visual Basic] **Overloads Overrides Public Function GetPropertiesSupported(ITypeDescriptorContext) As Boolean**

[C#] **public override bool GetPropertiesSupported(ITypeDescriptorContext);**

[C++] **public: bool GetPropertiesSupported(ITypeDescriptorContext*);**

[JScript] **public override function GetPropertiesSupported(ITypeDescriptorContext) : Boolean;**

Inherited from **TypeConverter**.

[Visual Basic] **Overloads Public Function GetPropertiesSupported() As Boolean**

[C#] **public bool GetPropertiesSupported();**

[C++] **public: bool GetPropertiesSupported();**

[JScript] **public function GetPropertiesSupported() : Boolean;**

ComponentConverter.GetPropertiesSupported Method (ITypeDescriptorContext)

This member overrides **TypeConverter.GetPropertiesSupported**.

[Visual Basic]
```
Overrides Overloads Public Function GetPropertiesSupported( _
   ByVal context As ITypeDescriptorContext _
) As Boolean
```
[C#]
```
public override bool GetPropertiesSupported(
   ITypeDescriptorContext context
);
```
[C++]
```
public: bool GetPropertiesSupported(
   ITypeDescriptorContext* context
);
```
[JScript]
```
public override function GetPropertiesSupported(
   context : ITypeDescriptorContext
) : Boolean;
```

Requirements

Platforms: Windows 98, Windows NT 4.0, Windows Millennium Edition, Windows 2000, Windows XP Home Edition, Windows XP Professional, Windows .NET Server family

ComponentEditor Class

Provides the base class for a custom component editor.

System.Object
  System.ComponentModel.ComponentEditor
    System.Windows.Forms.Design.WindowsFormsComponent-Editor

[Visual Basic]
```
MustInherit Public Class ComponentEditor
```
[C#]
```
public abstract class ComponentEditor
```
[C++]
```
public __gc __abstract class ComponentEditor
```
[JScript]
```
public abstract class ComponentEditor
```

Thread Safety

Any public static (**Shared** in Visual Basic) members of this type are safe for multithreaded operations. Any instance members are not guaranteed to be thread safe.

Remarks

A component editor is used to edit a component as a whole and can be used to implement a user interface similar to that of the property pages. You associate a component editor with a component by using the **EditorAttribute** attribute.

Notes to Inheritors: When you inherit from this class, you must override the **EditComponent** method.

Requirements

Namespace: System.ComponentModel

Platforms: Windows 98, Windows NT 4.0,
Windows Millennium Edition, Windows 2000,
Windows XP Home Edition, Windows XP Professional,
Windows Server 2003 family

Assembly: System (in System.dll)

ComponentEditor Constructor

Initializes a new instance of the **ComponentEditor** class.

[Visual Basic]
```
Protected Sub New()
```
[C#]
```
protected ComponentEditor();
```
[C++]
```
protected: ComponentEditor();
```
[JScript]
```
protected function ComponentEditor();
```

Remarks

This constructor is called by derived class constructors to initialize state in this type.

Requirements

Platforms: Windows 98, Windows NT 4.0,
Windows Millennium Edition, Windows 2000,
Windows XP Home Edition, Windows XP Professional,
Windows Server 2003 family

ComponentEditor.EditComponent Method

Edits the component and determines whether the given component was modified.

Overload List

Edits the component and returns a value indicating whether the component was modified.

[Visual Basic] **Overloads Public Function EditComponent(Object) As Boolean**

[C#] **public bool EditComponent(object);**

[C++] **public: bool EditComponent(Object*);**

[JScript] **public function EditComponent(Object) : Boolean;**

Edits the component and returns a value indicating whether the component was modified based upon a given context.

[Visual Basic] **Overloads Public MustOverride Function Edit-Component(ITypeDescriptorContext, Object) As Boolean**

[C#] **public abstract bool EditComponent(IType-DescriptorContext, object);**

[C++] **public: virtual bool EditComponent(IType-DescriptorContext*, Object*) = 0;**

[JScript] **public abstract function EditComponent(IType-DescriptorContext, Object) : Boolean;**

ComponentEditor.EditComponent Method (Object)

Edits the component and returns a value indicating whether the component was modified.

[Visual Basic]
```
Overloads Public Function EditComponent( _
   ByVal component As Object _
) As Boolean
```
[C#]
```
public bool EditComponent(
   object component
);
```
[C++]
```
public: bool EditComponent(
   Object* component
);
```
[JScript]
```
public function EditComponent(
   component : Object
) : Boolean;
```

Parameters

component
  The component to be edited.

Return Value

true if the component was modified; otherwise, **false**.

Remarks

This method opens an advanced user interface that you can use to edit the component. The default implementation opens a dialog box with a collection of component editor control objects and a user interface.

Requirements

Platforms: Windows 98, Windows NT 4.0,
Windows Millennium Edition, Windows 2000,
Windows XP Home Edition, Windows XP Professional,
Windows Server 2003 family

ComponentEditor.EditComponent Method (ITypeDescriptorContext, Object)

Edits the component and returns a value indicating whether the component was modified based upon a given context.

[Visual Basic]
```
Overloads Public MustOverride Function EditComponent( _
   ByVal context As ITypeDescriptorContext, _
   ByVal component As Object _
) As Boolean
```
[C#]
```
public abstract bool EditComponent(
   ITypeDescriptorContext context,
   object component
);
```
[C++]
```
public: virtual bool EditComponent(
   ITypeDescriptorContext* context,
   Object* component
) = 0;
```
[JScript]
```
public abstract function EditComponent(
   context : ITypeDescriptorContext,
   component : Object
) : Boolean;
```

Parameters

context

An optional context object that can be used to obtain further information about the edit.

component

The component to be edited.

Return Value

true if the component was modified; otherwise, **false**.

Remarks

You can override this method to provide a custom editing user interface for a component. From within this method you can display a dialog box or other type of user interface.

Requirements

Platforms: Windows 98, Windows NT 4.0, Windows Millennium Edition, Windows 2000, Windows XP Home Edition, Windows XP Professional, Windows Server 2003 family

ComponentResourceManager Class

Note: This namespace, class, or member is supported only in version 1.1 of the .NET Framework.

The **ComponentResourceManager** class is a **ResourceManager** object that provides simple functionality for enumerating resources for a component or object.

System.Object
  System.Resources.ResourceManager
    System.ComponentModel.ComponentResourceManager

```
[Visual Basic]
Public Class ComponentResourceManager
   Inherits ResourceManager
[C#]
public class ComponentResourceManager : ResourceManager
[C++]
public __gc class ComponentResourceManager : public ResourceManager
[JScript]
public class ComponentResourceManager extends ResourceManager
```

Thread Safety

Any public static (**Shared** in Visual Basic) members of this type are safe for multithreaded operations. Any instance members are not guaranteed to be thread safe.

Requirements

Namespace: System.ComponentModel

Platforms: Windows 98, Windows NT 4.0, Windows Millennium Edition, Windows 2000, Windows XP Home Edition, Windows XP Professional, Windows .NET Server family, .NET Compact Framework - Windows CE .NET

Assembly: System (in System.dll)

ComponentResourceManager Constructor

Note: This namespace, class, or member is supported only in version 1.1 of the .NET Framework.

Overload List

Initializes a new instance of the **ComponentResourceManager** class with default values.

Supported by the .NET Compact Framework.

[Visual Basic] **Public Sub New()**

[C#] **public ComponentResourceManager();**

[C++] **public: ComponentResourceManager();**

[JScript] **public function ComponentResourceManager();**

Creates a **ComponentResourceManager** that looks up resources in satellite assemblies based on information from the specified **Type**.

Supported by the .NET Compact Framework.

[Visual Basic] **Public Sub New(Type)**

[C#] **public ComponentResourceManager(Type);**

[C++] **public: ComponentResourceManager(Type*);**

[JScript] **public function ComponentResourceManager(Type);**

ComponentResourceManager Constructor ()

Note: This namespace, class, or member is supported only in version 1.1 of the .NET Framework.

Initializes a new instance of the **ComponentResourceManager** class with default values.

```
[Visual Basic]
Public Sub New()
[C#]
public ComponentResourceManager();
[C++]
public: ComponentResourceManager();
[JScript]
public function ComponentResourceManager();
```

Requirements

Platforms: Windows 98, Windows NT 4.0, Windows Millennium Edition, Windows 2000, Windows XP Home Edition, Windows XP Professional, Windows .NET Server family, .NET Compact Framework - Windows CE .NET

ComponentResourceManager Constructor (Type)

Note: This namespace, class, or member is supported only in version 1.1 of the .NET Framework.

Creates a **ComponentResourceManager** that looks up resources in satellite assemblies based on information from the specified **Type**.

```
[Visual Basic]
Public Sub New( _
   ByVal t As Type _
)
[C#]
public ComponentResourceManager(
   Type t
);
[C++]
public: ComponentResourceManager(
   Type* t
);
[JScript]
public function ComponentResourceManager(
   t : Type
);
```

Parameters

t

A **Type** from which the **ComponentResourceManager** derives all information for finding .resources files.

Requirements

Platforms: Windows 98, Windows NT 4.0, Windows Millennium Edition, Windows 2000, Windows XP Home Edition, Windows XP Professional, Windows .NET Server family, .NET Compact Framework - Windows CE .NET

ComponentResourceManager.ApplyResources Method

Note: This namespace, class, or member is supported only in version 1.1 of the .NET Framework.

Apply a resource's value to the corresponding property of the object.

Overload List

Apply a resource's value to the corresponding property of the object.

Supported by the .NET Compact Framework.

[Visual Basic] **Overloads Public Sub ApplyResources(Object, String)**

[C#] **public void ApplyResources(object, string);**

[C++] **public: void ApplyResources(Object*, String*);**

[JScript] **public function ApplyResources(Object, String);**

Supported by the .NET Compact Framework.

[Visual Basic] **Overloads Public Overridable Sub ApplyResources(Object, String, CultureInfo)**

[C#] **public virtual void ApplyResources(object, string, CultureInfo);**

[C++] **public: virtual void ApplyResources(Object*, String*, CultureInfo*);**

[JScript] **public function ApplyResources(Object, String, CultureInfo);**

ComponentResourceManager.ApplyResources Method (Object, String)

Note: This namespace, class, or member is supported only in version 1.1 of the .NET Framework.

Apply a resource's value to the corresponding property of the object.

```
[Visual Basic]
Overloads Public Sub ApplyResources( _
   ByVal value As Object, _
   ByVal objectName As String _
)
[C#]
public void ApplyResources(
   object value,
   string objectName
);
[C++]
public: void ApplyResources(
   Object* value,
   String* objectName
);
[JScript]
public function ApplyResources(
   value : Object,
   objectName : String
);
```

Parameters

value

an **Object** that contains the property value to be applied.

objectName

a **String** that contains the name of the object to look up in the resources.

Remarks

This method examines all the resources for the current culture used in the development environment. It attempts to find a resource with a key in the format of `objectName.propertyName`, where `objectName` is passed in as a parameter and `Property` is the name of a property. It will then apply that resource's `Value` to the corresponding property of the object. If there is no matching property, the resource will be ignored.

Requirements

Platforms: Windows 98, Windows NT 4.0, Windows Millennium Edition, Windows 2000, Windows XP Home Edition, Windows XP Professional, Windows .NET Server family, .NET Compact Framework - Windows CE .NET

ComponentResourceManager.ApplyResources Method (Object, String, CultureInfo)

Note: This namespace, class, or member is supported only in version 1.1 of the .NET Framework.

```
[Visual Basic]
Overloads Public Overridable Sub ApplyResources( _
   ByVal value As Object, _
   ByVal objectName As String, _
   ByVal culture As CultureInfo _
)
[C#]
public virtual void ApplyResources(
   object value,
   string objectName,
   CultureInfo culture
);
[C++]
public: virtual void ApplyResources(
   Object* value,
   String* objectName,
   CultureInfo* culture
);
[JScript]
public function ApplyResources(
   value : Object,
   objectName : String,
   culture : CultureInfo
);
```

Parameters

value

objectName

culture

Requirements

Platforms: Windows 98, Windows NT 4.0, Windows Millennium Edition, Windows 2000, Windows XP Home Edition, Windows XP Professional, Windows .NET Server family, .NET Compact Framework - Windows CE .NET

Container Class

Encapsulates zero or more components.

System.Object
  System.ComponentModel.Container

[Visual Basic]
```
Public Class Container
   Implements IContainer, IDisposable
```
[C#]
```
public class Container : IContainer, IDisposable
```
[C++]
```
public __gc class Container : public IContainer, IDisposable
```
[JScript]
```
public class Container implements IContainer, IDisposable
```

Thread Safety

Any public static (**Shared** in Visual Basic) members of this type are safe for multithreaded operations. Any instance members are not guaranteed to be thread safe.

Remarks

The **Container** class is the default implementation for the **IContainer** interface.

Containers are objects that encapsulate and track zero or more components. In this context, containment refers to logical containment, not visual containment. You can use components and containers in a variety of scenarios, including scenarios that are both visual and not visual.

The components in a container are tracked in a first-in, first-out list, which also defines the order of the components within the container. Added components are appended to the end of the list.

Requirements

Namespace: System.ComponentModel

Platforms: Windows 98, Windows NT 4.0,
Windows Millennium Edition, Windows 2000,
Windows XP Home Edition, Windows XP Professional,
Windows Server 2003 family,
.NET Compact Framework - Windows CE .NET

Assembly: System (in System.dll)

Container Constructor

Initializes a new instance of the **Container** class.

[Visual Basic]
```
Public Sub New()
```
[C#]
```
public Container();
```
[C++]
```
public: Container();
```
[JScript]
```
public function Container();
```

Remarks

The default constructor initializes any fields to their default values.

Requirements

Platforms: Windows 98, Windows NT 4.0,
Windows Millennium Edition, Windows 2000,
Windows XP Home Edition, Windows XP Professional,
Windows Server 2003 family,
.NET Compact Framework - Windows CE .NET

Container.Components Property

Gets all the components in the **Container**.

[Visual Basic]
```
Public Overridable ReadOnly Property Components As _
   ComponentCollection  Implements IContainer.Components
```
[C#]
```
public virtual ComponentCollection Components {get;}
```
[C++]
```
public: __property virtual ComponentCollection* get_Components();
```
[JScript]
```
public function get Components() : ComponentCollection;
```

Property Value

A collection that contains the components in the **Container**.

Implements

IContainer.Components

Remarks

This method can be overridden by a derived class.

The components in the collection are stored in the same order as they were added to the **Container**.

Requirements

Platforms: Windows 98, Windows NT 4.0,
Windows Millennium Edition, Windows 2000,
Windows XP Home Edition, Windows XP Professional,
Windows Server 2003 family

Container.Add Method

Adds a **Component** to the **Container**.

Overload List

Adds the specified **Component** to the **Container**. The component is unnamed.

Supported by the .NET Compact Framework.

[Visual Basic] **Overloads Public Overridable Sub Add(IComponent) Implements IContainer.Add**

[C#] **public virtual void Add(IComponent);**

[C++] **public: virtual void Add(IComponent*);**

[JScript] **public function Add(IComponent);**

Adds the specified **Component** to the **Container** and assigns it a name.

Supported by the .NET Compact Framework.

[Visual Basic] **Overloads Public Overridable Sub Add(IComponent, String) Implements IContainer.Add**

[C#] **public virtual void Add(IComponent, string);**

[C++] **public: virtual void Add(IComponent*, String*);**

[JScript] **public function Add(IComponent, String);**

Container.Add Method (IComponent)

Adds the specified **Component** to the **Container**. The component is unnamed.

[Visual Basic]
```
Overloads Public Overridable Sub Add( _
   ByVal component As IComponent _
) Implements IContainer.Add
```

```
[C#]
public virtual void Add(
   IComponent component
);
[C++]
public: virtual void Add(
   IComponent* component
);
[JScript]
public function Add(
   component : IComponent
);
```

Parameters

component

The component to add.

Implements

IContainer.Add

Remarks

This method can be overridden by a derived class.

The new **Component** is added to the end of the list.

Requirements

Platforms: Windows 98, Windows NT 4.0, Windows Millennium Edition, Windows 2000, Windows XP Home Edition, Windows XP Professional, Windows Server 2003 family, .NET Compact Framework - Windows CE .NET

Container.Add Method (IComponent, String)

Adds the specified **Component** to the **Container** and assigns it a name.

```
[Visual Basic]
Overloads Public Overridable Sub Add( _
   ByVal component As IComponent, _
   ByVal name As String _
) Implements IContainer.Add
[C#]
public virtual void Add(
   IComponent component,
   string name
);
[C++]
public: virtual void Add(
   IComponent* component,
   String* name
);
[JScript]
public function Add(
   component : IComponent,
   name : String
);
```

Parameters

component

The component to add.

name

The unique, case insensitive name to assign to the component.

-or-

A null reference (**Nothing** in Visual Basic) that leaves the component unnamed.

Implements

IContainer.Add

Exceptions

Exception Type	Condition
ArgumentException	The *name* parameter is a duplicate.

Remarks

This method can be overridden by a derived class.

The new **Component** is added to the end of the list.

Requirements

Platforms: Windows 98, Windows NT 4.0, Windows Millennium Edition, Windows 2000, Windows XP Home Edition, Windows XP Professional, Windows Server 2003 family, .NET Compact Framework - Windows CE .NET

Container.CreateSite Method

Creates a site **ISite** for the given **IComponent** and assigns the given name to the site.

```
[Visual Basic]
Protected Overridable Function CreateSite( _
   ByVal component As IComponent, _
   ByVal name As String _
) As ISite
[C#]
protected virtual ISite CreateSite(
   IComponent component,
   string name
);
[C++]
protected: virtual ISite* CreateSite(
   IComponent* component,
   String* name
);
[JScript]
protected function CreateSite(
   component : IComponent,
   name : String
) : ISite;
```

Parameters

component

The **IComponent** to create a site for.

name

The name to assign to *component*; or a null reference (**Nothing** in Visual Basic) to skip the name assignment.

Return Value

The newly created site.

Remarks

If *name* is a null reference (**Nothing** in Visual Basic) the **IComponent** is added to the **Container** without an identifying name.

This method can be overridden by a derived class. Implementors wishing to override **CreateSite** can provide a custom implementation through a class implementing **ISite**.

Requirements

Platforms: Windows 98, Windows NT 4.0, Windows Millennium Edition, Windows 2000, Windows XP Home Edition, Windows XP Professional, Windows Server 2003 family, .NET Compact Framework - Windows CE .NET

Container.Dispose Method

Releases the resources used by the **Container**.

Overload List

Releases all resources used by the **Container**.

Supported by the .NET Compact Framework.

[Visual Basic] **Overloads Public Overridable Sub Dispose() Implements IDisposable.Dispose**

[C#] **public virtual void Dispose();**

[C++] **public: virtual void Dispose();**

[JScript] **public function Dispose();**

Releases the unmanaged resources used by the **Container** and optionally releases the managed resources.

[Visual Basic] **Overloads Protected Overridable Sub Dispose(Boolean)**

[C#] **protected virtual void Dispose(bool);**

[C++] **protected: virtual void Dispose(bool);**

[JScript] **protected function Dispose(Boolean);**

Container.Dispose Method ()

Releases all resources used by the **Container**.

```
[Visual Basic]
Overloads Public Overridable Sub Dispose() Implements _
   IDisposable.Dispose
[C#]
public virtual void Dispose();
[C++]
public: virtual void Dispose();
[JScript]
public function Dispose();
```

Implements

IDisposable.Dispose

Remarks

Calling **Dispose** allows the resources used by the **Container** to be reallocated for other purposes. For more information about **Dispose**, see **Cleaning Up Unmanaged Resources**.

Requirements

Platforms: Windows 98, Windows NT 4.0, Windows Millennium Edition, Windows 2000, Windows XP Home Edition, Windows XP Professional, Windows Server 2003 family, .NET Compact Framework - Windows CE .NET

Container.Dispose Method (Boolean)

Releases the unmanaged resources used by the **Container** and optionally releases the managed resources.

```
[Visual Basic]
Overloads Protected Overridable Sub Dispose( _
   ByVal disposing As Boolean _
)
[C#]
protected virtual void Dispose(
   bool disposing
);
[C++]
protected: virtual void Dispose(
   bool disposing
);
[JScript]
protected function Dispose(
   disposing : Boolean
);
```

Parameters

disposing

true to release both managed and unmanaged resources; **false** to release only unmanaged resources.

Remarks

When the *disposing* parameter is **true**, this method releases all resources held by any managed objects that this **Container** references. This method invokes the **Dispose()** method of each referenced object.

Notes to Inheritors: **Dispose** can be called multiple times by other objects. When overriding **Dispose(Boolean)**, be careful not to reference objects that have been previously disposed of in an earlier call to **Dispose**.

This method is called by the public **Dispose()** method and the **Finalize** method. **Dispose()** invokes the protected **Dispose(Boolean)** method with the *disposing* parameter set to **true**. **Finalize** invokes **Dispose** with *disposing* set to **false**.

When the *disposing* parameter is **true**, this method releases all resources held by any managed objects that this **Container** references. This method invokes the **Dispose()** method of each referenced object.

Notes to Inheritors: **Dispose** can be called multiple times by other objects. When overriding **Dispose(Boolean)**, be careful not to reference objects that have been previously disposed of in an earlier call to **Dispose**.

Requirements

Platforms: Windows 98, Windows NT 4.0, Windows Millennium Edition, Windows 2000, Windows XP Home Edition, Windows XP Professional, Windows Server 2003 family

Container.Finalize Method

Releases unmanaged resources and performs other cleanup operations before the **Container** is reclaimed by garbage collection.

[C#] In C#, finalizers are expressed using destructor syntax.

[C++] In C++, finalizers are expressed using destructor syntax.

```
[Visual Basic]
Overrides Protected Sub Finalize()
[C#]
~Container();
[C++]
~Container();
[JScript]
protected override function Finalize();
```

Remarks

Calls **Dispose** with the *disposing* parameter set to **false** to free unmanaged resources.

This method overrides **Object.Finalize**. Application code should not call this method; an object's **Finalize** method is automatically invoked during garbage collection, unless finalization by the garbage collector has been disabled by a call to the **GC.SuppressFinalize** method.

Requirements

Platforms: Windows 98, Windows NT 4.0, Windows Millennium Edition, Windows 2000, Windows XP Home Edition, Windows XP Professional, Windows Server 2003 family, .NET Compact Framework - Windows CE .NET

Container.GetService Method

Gets the service object of the specified type, if it is available.

```
[Visual Basic]
Protected Overridable Function GetService( _
   ByVal service As Type _
) As Object
[C#]
protected virtual object GetService(
   Type service
);
[C++]
protected: virtual Object* GetService(
   Type* service
);
[JScript]
protected function GetService(
   service : Type
) : Object;
```

Parameters

service

The **Type** of the service to retrieve.

Return Value

An **Object** implementing the requested service, or a null reference (**Nothing** in Visual Basic) if the service cannot be resolved.

Remarks

The default implementation of this method returns a null reference (**Nothing** in Visual Basic). Implementors can override this method to provide a custom implementation to return a service object.

Requirements

Platforms: Windows 98, Windows NT 4.0, Windows Millennium Edition, Windows 2000, Windows XP Home Edition, Windows XP Professional, Windows Server 2003 family, .NET Compact Framework - Windows CE .NET

Container.Remove Method

Removes a component from the **Container**.

```
[Visual Basic]
Public Overridable Sub Remove( _
   ByVal component As IComponent _
) Implements IContainer.Remove
[C#]
public virtual void Remove(
   IComponent component
);
[C++]
public: virtual void Remove(
   IComponent* component
);
[JScript]
public function Remove(
   component : IComponent
);
```

Parameters

component

The component to remove.

Implements

IContainer.Remove

Remarks

This method can be overridden by a derived class.

Requirements

Platforms: Windows 98, Windows NT 4.0, Windows Millennium Edition, Windows 2000, Windows XP Home Edition, Windows XP Professional, Windows Server 2003 family, .NET Compact Framework - Windows CE .NET

CultureInfoConverter Class

Provides a type converter to convert **CultureInfo** objects to and from various other representations.

System.Object
  System.ComponentModel.TypeConverter
    System.ComponentModel.CultureInfoConverter

[Visual Basic]
```
Public Class CultureInfoConverter
   Inherits TypeConverter
```
[C#]
```
public class CultureInfoConverter : TypeConverter
```
[C++]
```
public __gc class CultureInfoConverter : public TypeConverter
```
[JScript]
```
public class CultureInfoConverter extends TypeConverter
```

Thread Safety

Any public static (**Shared** in Visual Basic) members of this type are safe for multithreaded operations. Any instance members are not guaranteed to be thread safe.

Remarks

This converter can only convert a **CultureInfo** object to and from a string.

For more information about type converters, see the **TypeConverter** base class and **Implementing a Type Converter**.

> **Note** You should never create an instance of **CultureInfo-Converter**. Instead, call the **GetConverter** method of **Type-Descriptor**. For more information, see the examples in the **TypeConverter** base class.

Example

[Visual Basic, C#, C++] The following sample converts a variable of type **CultureInfo** to a string, and vice versa. First it constructs a **CultureInfo** variable using the Greek culture (represented by "el') and converts it to the string "Greek". Then it converts the string "Russian" to the CultureInfo representation "ru".

[Visual Basic]
```
' The sample first constructs a CultureInfo variable using the
Greek culture - 'el'.
Dim myCulture As New System.Globalization.CultureInfo("el")
Dim myCString As String = "Russian"
Console.WriteLine(TypeDescriptor.GetConverter(myCulture).ConvertTo(myCul
ture, GetType(String)))
' The following line will output 'ru' based on the string being
converted.
Console.WriteLine(TypeDescriptor.GetConverter
 (myCulture).ConvertFrom(myCString))
```

[C#]
```
// The sample first constructs a CultureInfo variable using the
Greek culture - 'el'.
System.Globalization.CultureInfo myCulture= new
System.Globalization.CultureInfo("el");
string myCString="Russian";
Console.WriteLine(TypeDescriptor.GetConverter
 (myCulture).ConvertTo(myCulture, typeof(string)));
// The following line will output 'ru' based on the string
being converted.
Console.WriteLine(TypeDescriptor.GetConverter
 (myCulture).ConvertFrom(myCString));
```

[C++]
```
// The sample first constructs a CultureInfo variable using
the Greek culture - 'el'.
System::Globalization::CultureInfo* myCulture = new
System::Globalization::CultureInfo(S"el");
String* myCString = S"Russian";
Console::WriteLine(TypeDescriptor::GetConverter(myCulture)-
>ConvertTo(myCulture, __typeof(String)));
// The following line will output 'ru' based on the string being
converted.
Console::WriteLine(TypeDescriptor::GetConverter(myCulture)-
>ConvertFrom(myCString));
```

Requirements

Namespace: System.ComponentModel

Platforms: Windows 98, Windows NT 4.0, Windows Millennium Edition, Windows 2000, Windows XP Home Edition, Windows XP Professional, Windows Server 2003 family

Assembly: System (in System.dll)

CultureInfoConverter Constructor

Initializes a new instance of the **CultureInfoConverter** class.

[Visual Basic]
```
Public Sub New()
```
[C#]
```
public CultureInfoConverter();
```
[C++]
```
public: CultureInfoConverter();
```
[JScript]
```
public function CultureInfoConverter();
```

Remarks

The default constructor initializes any fields to their default values.

Requirements

Platforms: Windows 98, Windows NT 4.0, Windows Millennium Edition, Windows 2000, Windows XP Home Edition, Windows XP Professional, Windows Server 2003 family

CultureInfoConverter.CanConvertFrom Method

Overload List

This member supports the .NET Framework infrastructure and is not intended to be used directly from your code.

[Visual Basic] **Overloads Overrides Public Function CanConvertFrom(ITypeDescriptorContext, Type) As Boolean**

[C#] **public override bool CanConvertFrom(ITypeDescriptorContext, Type);**

[C++] **public: bool CanConvertFrom(ITypeDescriptorContext*, Type*);**

[JScript] **public override function CanConvertFrom(ITypeDescriptorContext, Type) : Boolean;**

Inherited from **TypeConverter**.

[Visual Basic] **Overloads Public Function CanConvertFrom(Type) As Boolean**

[C#] **public bool CanConvertFrom(Type);**

[C++] **public: bool CanConvertFrom(Type*);**

[JScript] **public function CanConvertFrom(Type) : Boolean;**

CultureInfoConverter.CanConvertFrom Method (ITypeDescriptorContext, Type)

This member overrides **TypeConverter.CanConvertFrom**.

[Visual Basic]
```
Overrides Overloads Public Function CanConvertFrom( _
   ByVal context As ITypeDescriptorContext, _
   ByVal sourceType As Type _
) As Boolean
```
[C#]
```
public override bool CanConvertFrom(
   ITypeDescriptorContext context,
   Type sourceType
);
```
[C++]
```
public: bool CanConvertFrom(
   ITypeDescriptorContext* context,
   Type* sourceType
);
```
[JScript]
```
public override function CanConvertFrom(
   context : ITypeDescriptorContext,
   sourceType : Type
) : Boolean;
```

Requirements

Platforms: Windows 98, Windows NT 4.0, Windows Millennium Edition, Windows 2000, Windows XP Home Edition, Windows XP Professional, Windows Server 2003 family

CultureInfoConverter.CanConvertTo Method

Overload List

This member supports the .NET Framework infrastructure and is not intended to be used directly from your code.

[Visual Basic] **Overloads Overrides Public Function CanConvertTo(ITypeDescriptorContext, Type) As Boolean**

[C#] **public override bool CanConvertTo(ITypeDescriptorContext, Type);**

[C++] **public: bool CanConvertTo(ITypeDescriptorContext*, Type*);**

[JScript] **public override function CanConvertTo(ITypeDescriptorContext, Type) : Boolean;**

Inherited from **TypeConverter**.

[Visual Basic] **Overloads Public Function CanConvertTo(Type) As Boolean**

[C#] **public bool CanConvertTo(Type);**

[C++] **public: bool CanConvertTo(Type*);**

[JScript] **public function CanConvertTo(Type) : Boolean;**

CultureInfoConverter.CanConvertTo Method (ITypeDescriptorContext, Type)

This member overrides **TypeConverter.CanConvertTo**.

[Visual Basic]
```
Overrides Overloads Public Function CanConvertTo( _
   ByVal context As ITypeDescriptorContext, _
   ByVal destinationType As Type _
) As Boolean
```
[C#]
```
public override bool CanConvertTo(
   ITypeDescriptorContext context,
   Type destinationType
);
```
[C++]
```
public: bool CanConvertTo(
   ITypeDescriptorContext* context,
   Type* destinationType
);
```
[JScript]
```
public override function CanConvertTo(
   context : ITypeDescriptorContext,
   destinationType : Type
) : Boolean;
```

Requirements

Platforms: Windows 98, Windows NT 4.0, Windows Millennium Edition, Windows 2000, Windows XP Home Edition, Windows XP Professional, Windows Server 2003 family

CultureInfoConverter.ConvertFrom Method

Overload List

This member supports the .NET Framework infrastructure and is not intended to be used directly from your code.

[Visual Basic] **Overloads Overrides Public Function ConvertFrom(ITypeDescriptorContext, CultureInfo, Object) As Object**

[C#] **public override object ConvertFrom(ITypeDescriptorContext, CultureInfo, object);**

[C++] **public: Object* ConvertFrom(ITypeDescriptorContext*, CultureInfo*, Object*);**

[JScript] **public override function ConvertFrom(ITypeDescriptorContext, CultureInfo, Object) : Object;**

Inherited from **TypeConverter**.

[Visual Basic] **Overloads Public Function ConvertFrom(Object) As Object**

[C#] **public object ConvertFrom(object);**

[C++] **public: Object* ConvertFrom(Object*);**

[JScript] **public function ConvertFrom(Object) : Object;**

CultureInfoConverter.ConvertFrom Method (ITypeDescriptorContext, CultureInfo, Object)

This member overrides **TypeConverter.ConvertFrom**.

[Visual Basic]
```
Overrides Overloads Public Function ConvertFrom( _
   ByVal context As ITypeDescriptorContext, _
   ByVal culture As CultureInfo, _
   ByVal value As Object _
) As Object
```
[C#]
```
public override object ConvertFrom(
   ITypeDescriptorContext context,
   CultureInfo culture,
   object value
);
```

```
[C++]
public: Object* ConvertFrom(
   ITypeDescriptorContext* context,
   CultureInfo* culture,
   Object* value
);
[JScript]
public override function ConvertFrom(
   context : ITypeDescriptorContext,
   culture : CultureInfo,
   value : Object
) : Object;
```

Requirements

Platforms: Windows 98, Windows NT 4.0, Windows Millennium Edition, Windows 2000, Windows XP Home Edition, Windows XP Professional, Windows Server 2003 family

CultureInfoConverter.ConvertTo Method

Overload List

This member supports the .NET Framework infrastructure and is not intended to be used directly from your code.

[Visual Basic] **Overloads Overrides Public Function ConvertTo(ITypeDescriptorContext, CultureInfo, Object, Type) As Object**

[C#] **public override object ConvertTo(ITypeDescriptor-Context, CultureInfo, object, Type);**

[C++] **public: Object* ConvertTo(ITypeDescriptorContext*, CultureInfo*, Object*, Type*);**

[JScript] **public override function ConvertTo(IType-DescriptorContext, CultureInfo, Object, Type) : Object;**

Inherited from **TypeConverter**.

[Visual Basic] **Overloads Public Function ConvertTo(Object, Type) As Object**

[C#] **public object ConvertTo(object, Type);**

[C++] **public: Object* ConvertTo(Object*, Type*);**

[JScript] **public function ConvertTo(Object, Type) : Object;**

CultureInfoConverter.ConvertTo Method (ITypeDescriptorContext, CultureInfo, Object, Type)

This member overrides **TypeConverter.ConvertTo**.

```
[Visual Basic]
Overrides Overloads Public Function ConvertTo( _
   ByVal context As ITypeDescriptorContext, _
   ByVal culture As CultureInfo, _
   ByVal value As Object, _
   ByVal destinationType As Type _
) As Object
[C#]
public override object ConvertTo(
   ITypeDescriptorContext context,
   CultureInfo culture,
   object value,
   Type destinationType
);
[C++]
public: Object* ConvertTo(
   ITypeDescriptorContext* context,
   CultureInfo* culture,
   Object* value,
   Type* destinationType
);
[JScript]
public override function ConvertTo(
   context : ITypeDescriptorContext,
   culture : CultureInfo,
   value : Object,
   destinationType : Type
) : Object;
```

Requirements

Platforms: Windows 98, Windows NT 4.0, Windows Millennium Edition, Windows 2000, Windows XP Home Edition, Windows XP Professional, Windows Server 2003 family

CultureInfoConverter.GetStandardValues Method

Overload List

This member supports the .NET Framework infrastructure and is not intended to be used directly from your code.

[Visual Basic] **Overloads Overrides Public Function GetStandardValues(ITypeDescriptorContext) As StandardValuesCollection**

[C#] **public override StandardValuesCollection GetStandardValues(ITypeDescriptorContext);**

[C++] **public: StandardValuesCollection* GetStandardValues(ITypeDescriptorContext*);**

[JScript] **public override function GetStandard-Values(ITypeDescriptorContext) : StandardValuesCollection;**

Inherited from **TypeConverter**.

[Visual Basic] **Overloads Public Function GetStandardValues() As ICollection**

[C#] **public ICollection GetStandardValues();**

[C++] **public: ICollection* GetStandardValues();**

[JScript] **public function GetStandardValues() : ICollection;**

CultureInfoConverter.GetStandardValues Method (ITypeDescriptorContext)

This member overrides **TypeConverter.GetStandardValues**.

```
[Visual Basic]
Overrides Overloads Public Function GetStandardValues( _
   ByVal context As ITypeDescriptorContext _
) As StandardValuesCollection
[C#]
public override StandardValuesCollection GetStandardValues(
   ITypeDescriptorContext context
);
[C++]
public: StandardValuesCollection* GetStandardValues(
   ITypeDescriptorContext* context
);
```

```
[JScript]
public override function GetStandardValues(
   context : ITypeDescriptorContext
) : StandardValuesCollection;
```

Requirements

Platforms: Windows 98, Windows NT 4.0, Windows Millennium Edition, Windows 2000, Windows XP Home Edition, Windows XP Professional, Windows Server 2003 family

CultureInfoConverter.GetStandardValues-Exclusive Method

Overload List

This member supports the .NET Framework infrastructure and is not intended to be used directly from your code.

[Visual Basic] **Overloads Overrides Public Function Get-StandardValuesExclusive(ITypeDescriptorContext) As Boolean**

[C#] **public override bool GetStandardValues-Exclusive(ITypeDescriptorContext);**

[C++] **public: bool GetStandardValues-Exclusive(ITypeDescriptorContext*);**

[JScript] **public override function GetStandardValues-Exclusive(ITypeDescriptorContext) : Boolean;**

Inherited from **TypeConverter**.

[Visual Basic] **Overloads Public Function GetStandardValuesExclusive() As Boolean**

[C#] **public bool GetStandardValuesExclusive();**

[C++] **public: bool GetStandardValuesExclusive();**

[JScript] **public function GetStandardValuesExclusive() : Boolean;**

CultureInfoConverter.GetStandardValuesExclusive Method (ITypeDescriptorContext)

This member overrides **TypeConverter.GetStandardValuesExclusive**.

```
[Visual Basic]
Overrides Overloads Public Function GetStandardValuesExclusive( _
   ByVal context As ITypeDescriptorContext _
) As Boolean
[C#]
public override bool GetStandardValuesExclusive(
   ITypeDescriptorContext context
);
[C++]
public: bool GetStandardValuesExclusive(
   ITypeDescriptorContext* context
);
[JScript]
public override function GetStandardValuesExclusive(
   context : ITypeDescriptorContext
) : Boolean;
```

Requirements

Platforms: Windows 98, Windows NT 4.0, Windows Millennium Edition, Windows 2000, Windows XP Home Edition, Windows XP Professional, Windows Server 2003 family

CultureInfoConverter.GetStandardValues-Supported Method

Overload List

This member supports the .NET Framework infrastructure and is not intended to be used directly from your code.

[Visual Basic] **Overloads Overrides Public Function GetStandardValuesSupported(ITypeDescriptorContext) As Boolean**

[C#] **public override bool GetStandardValues-Supported(ITypeDescriptorContext);**

[C++] **public: bool GetStandardValues-Supported(ITypeDescriptorContext*);**

[JScript] **public override function GetStandardValues-Supported(ITypeDescriptorContext) : Boolean;**

Inherited from **TypeConverter**.

[Visual Basic] **Overloads Public Function GetStandardValuesSupported() As Boolean**

[C#] **public bool GetStandardValuesSupported();**

[C++] **public: bool GetStandardValuesSupported();**

[JScript] **public function GetStandardValuesSupported() : Boolean;**

CultureInfoConverter.GetStandardValuesSupported Method (ITypeDescriptorContext)

This member overrides **TypeConverter.GetStandardValuesSupported**.

```
[Visual Basic]
Overrides Overloads Public Function GetStandardValuesSupported( _
   ByVal context As ITypeDescriptorContext _
) As Boolean
[C#]
public override bool GetStandardValuesSupported(
   ITypeDescriptorContext context
);
[C++]
public: bool GetStandardValuesSupported(
   ITypeDescriptorContext* context
);
[JScript]
public override function GetStandardValuesSupported(
   context : ITypeDescriptorContext
) : Boolean;
```

Requirements

Platforms: Windows 98, Windows NT 4.0, Windows Millennium Edition, Windows 2000, Windows XP Home Edition, Windows XP Professional, Windows Server 2003 family

DateTimeConverter Class

Provides a type converter to convert **DateTime** objects to and from various other representations.

System.Object
  System.ComponentModel.TypeConverter
    System.ComponentModel.DateTimeConverter

```
[Visual Basic]
Public Class DateTimeConverter
   Inherits TypeConverter
[C#]
public class DateTimeConverter : TypeConverter
[C++]
public __gc class DateTimeConverter : public TypeConverter
[JScript]
public class DateTimeConverter extends TypeConverter
```

Thread Safety

Any public static (**Shared** in Visual Basic) members of this type are safe for multithreaded operations. Any instance members are not guaranteed to be thread safe.

Remarks

This converter can only convert a **DateTime** object to and from a string.

ConvertFrom uses the **Parse** method of **DateTime** to convert from a string.

ConvertTo uses the current culture, if a **CultureInfo** object is not supplied. Generally, **ConvertTo** uses **ShortDatePattern** to format a date and **ShortDatePattern** with **ShortTimePattern** to format a date and time. If **InvariantCulture** is passed, **ConvertTo** uses yyyy-mm-dd to format a date and **ToString** to format a date and time.

> **Note** You should never create an instance of **DateTimeConverter**. Instead, call the **GetConverter** method of **TypeDescriptor**. For more information, see the examples in the **TypeConverter** base class.

Example

[Visual Basic, C#, C++] The following sample converts a variable of type **DateTime** to a string, and vice versa.

```
[Visual Basic]
Dim dt As New DateTime(1990, 5, 6)
Console.WriteLine(TypeDescriptor.GetConverter(dt).ConvertTo(dt,          ↵
GetType(String)))
Dim myStr As String = "1991-10-10"
Console.WriteLine(TypeDescriptor.GetConverter(dt).ConvertFrom(myStr))
```

```
[C#]
DateTime dt=new DateTime(1990,5,6);
Console.WriteLine(TypeDescriptor.GetConverter(dt).ConvertTo(dt,          ↵
typeof(string)));
string myStr="1991-10-10";
Console.WriteLine(TypeDescriptor.GetConverter(dt).ConvertFrom(myStr));
```

```
[C++]
DateTime dt(1990,5,6);
Console::WriteLine(TypeDescriptor::GetConverter(__box(dt))-          ↵
>ConvertTo(__box(dt), __typeof(String)));
String* myStr = S"1991-10-10";
Console::WriteLine(TypeDescriptor::GetConverter(__box(dt))-          ↵
>ConvertFrom(myStr));
```

Requirements

Namespace: System.ComponentModel

Platforms: Windows 98, Windows NT 4.0, Windows Millennium Edition, Windows 2000, Windows XP Home Edition, Windows XP Professional, Windows .NET Server family

Assembly: System (in System.dll)

DateTimeConverter Constructor

Initializes a new instance of the **DateTimeConverter** class.

```
[Visual Basic]
Public Sub New()
[C#]
public DateTimeConverter();
[C++]
public: DateTimeConverter();
[JScript]
public function DateTimeConverter();
```

Remarks

The default constructor initializes any fields to their default values.

Requirements

Platforms: Windows 98, Windows NT 4.0, Windows Millennium Edition, Windows 2000, Windows XP Home Edition, Windows XP Professional, Windows .NET Server family

DateTimeConverter.CanConvertFrom Method

Overload List

This member supports the .NET Framework infrastructure and is not intended to be used directly from your code.

[Visual Basic] **Overloads Overrides Public Function CanConvertFrom(ITypeDescriptorContext, Type) As Boolean**

[C#] **public override bool CanConvertFrom(ITypeDescriptorContext, Type);**

[C++] **public: bool CanConvertFrom(ITypeDescriptorContext*, Type*);**

[JScript] **public override function CanConvertFrom(ITypeDescriptorContext, Type) : Boolean;**

Inherited from **TypeConverter**.

[Visual Basic] **Overloads Public Function CanConvertFrom(Type) As Boolean**

[C#] **public bool CanConvertFrom(Type);**

[C++] **public: bool CanConvertFrom(Type*);**

[JScript] **public function CanConvertFrom(Type) : Boolean;**

DateTimeConverter.CanConvertFrom Method (ITypeDescriptorContext, Type)

This member overrides **TypeConverter.CanConvertFrom**.

```
[Visual Basic]
Overrides Overloads Public Function CanConvertFrom( _
   ByVal context As ITypeDescriptorContext, _
   ByVal sourceType As Type _
) As Boolean
```

```
[C#]
public override bool CanConvertFrom(
   ITypeDescriptorContext context,
   Type sourceType
);
[C++]
public: bool CanConvertFrom(
   ITypeDescriptorContext* context,
   Type* sourceType
);
[JScript]
public override function CanConvertFrom(
   context : ITypeDescriptorContext,
   sourceType : Type
) : Boolean;
```

Requirements

Platforms: Windows 98, Windows NT 4.0, Windows Millennium Edition, Windows 2000, Windows XP Home Edition, Windows XP Professional, Windows .NET Server family

DateTimeConverter.CanConvertTo Method

Overload List

This member supports the .NET Framework infrastructure and is not intended to be used directly from your code.

[Visual Basic] **Overloads Overrides Public Function CanConvertTo(ITypeDescriptorContext, Type) As Boolean**

[C#] **public override bool CanConvertTo(ITypeDescriptorContext, Type);**

[C++] **public: bool CanConvertTo(ITypeDescriptorContext*, Type*);**

[JScript] **public override function CanConvertTo(ITypeDescriptorContext, Type) : Boolean;**

Inherited from **TypeConverter**.

[Visual Basic] **Overloads Public Function CanConvertTo(Type) As Boolean**

[C#] **public bool CanConvertTo(Type);**

[C++] **public: bool CanConvertTo(Type*);**

[JScript] **public function CanConvertTo(Type) : Boolean;**

DateTimeConverter.CanConvertTo Method (ITypeDescriptorContext, Type)

This member overrides **TypeConverter.CanConvertTo**.

```
[Visual Basic]
Overrides Overloads Public Function CanConvertTo( _
   ByVal context As ITypeDescriptorContext, _
   ByVal destinationType As Type _
) As Boolean
[C#]
public override bool CanConvertTo(
   ITypeDescriptorContext context,
   Type destinationType
);
[C++]
public: bool CanConvertTo(
   ITypeDescriptorContext* context,
   Type* destinationType
);
[JScript]
public override function CanConvertTo(
   context : ITypeDescriptorContext,
   destinationType : Type
) : Boolean;
```

Requirements

Platforms: Windows 98, Windows NT 4.0, Windows Millennium Edition, Windows 2000, Windows XP Home Edition, Windows XP Professional, Windows .NET Server family

DateTimeConverter.ConvertFrom Method

Overload List

This member supports the .NET Framework infrastructure and is not intended to be used directly from your code.

[Visual Basic] **Overloads Overrides Public Function ConvertFrom(ITypeDescriptorContext, CultureInfo, Object) As Object**

[C#] **public override object ConvertFrom(ITypeDescriptorContext, CultureInfo, object);**

[C++] **public: Object* ConvertFrom(ITypeDescriptorContext*, CultureInfo*, Object*);**

[JScript] **public override function ConvertFrom(ITypeDescriptorContext, CultureInfo, Object) : Object;**

Inherited from **TypeConverter**.

[Visual Basic] **Overloads Public Function ConvertFrom(Object) As Object**

[C#] **public object ConvertFrom(object);**

[C++] **public: Object* ConvertFrom(Object*);**

[JScript] **public function ConvertFrom(Object) : Object;**

DateTimeConverter.ConvertFrom Method (ITypeDescriptorContext, CultureInfo, Object)

This member overrides **TypeConverter.ConvertFrom**.

```
[Visual Basic]
Overrides Overloads Public Function ConvertFrom( _
   ByVal context As ITypeDescriptorContext, _
   ByVal culture As CultureInfo, _
   ByVal value As Object _
) As Object
[C#]
public override object ConvertFrom(
   ITypeDescriptorContext context,
   CultureInfo culture,
   object value
);
[C++]
public: Object* ConvertFrom(
   ITypeDescriptorContext* context,
   CultureInfo* culture,
   Object* value
);
```

```
[JScript]
public override function ConvertFrom(
   context : ITypeDescriptorContext,
   culture : CultureInfo,
   value : Object
) : Object;
```

Requirements

Platforms: Windows 98, Windows NT 4.0, Windows Millennium Edition, Windows 2000, Windows XP Home Edition, Windows XP Professional, Windows .NET Server family

DateTimeConverter.ConvertTo Method

Overload List

This member supports the .NET Framework infrastructure and is not intended to be used directly from your code.

[Visual Basic] **Overloads Overrides Public Function ConvertTo(ITypeDescriptorContext, CultureInfo, Object, Type) As Object**

[C#] **public override object ConvertTo(ITypeDescriptorContext, CultureInfo, object, Type);**

[C++] **public: Object* ConvertTo(ITypeDescriptorContext*, CultureInfo*, Object*, Type*);**

[JScript] **public override function ConvertTo(ITypeDescriptorContext, CultureInfo, Object, Type) : Object;**

Inherited from **TypeConverter**.

[Visual Basic] **Overloads Public Function ConvertTo(Object, Type) As Object**

[C#] **public object ConvertTo(object, Type);**

[C++] **public: Object* ConvertTo(Object*, Type*);**

[JScript] **public function ConvertTo(Object, Type) : Object;**

DateTimeConverter.ConvertTo Method (ITypeDescriptorContext, CultureInfo, Object, Type)

This member overrides **TypeConverter.ConvertTo**.

```
[Visual Basic]
Overrides Overloads Public Function ConvertTo( _
   ByVal context As ITypeDescriptorContext, _
   ByVal culture As CultureInfo, _
   ByVal value As Object, _
   ByVal destinationType As Type _
) As Object
[C#]
public override object ConvertTo(
   ITypeDescriptorContext context,
   CultureInfo culture,
   object value,
   Type destinationType
);
[C++]
public: Object* ConvertTo(
   ITypeDescriptorContext* context,
   CultureInfo* culture,
   Object* value,
   Type* destinationType
);
[JScript]
public override function ConvertTo(
   context : ITypeDescriptorContext,
   culture : CultureInfo,
   value : Object,
   destinationType : Type
) : Object;
```

Requirements

Platforms: Windows 98, Windows NT 4.0, Windows Millennium Edition, Windows 2000, Windows XP Home Edition, Windows XP Professional, Windows .NET Server family

DecimalConverter Class

Provides a type converter to convert **Decimal** objects to and from various other representations.

System.Object
  System.ComponentModel.TypeConverter
    System.ComponentModel.BaseNumberConverter
      System.ComponentModel.DecimalConverter

[Visual Basic]
```
Public Class DecimalConverter
   Inherits BaseNumberConverter
```
[C#]
```
public class DecimalConverter : BaseNumberConverter
```
[C++]
```
public __gc class DecimalConverter : public BaseNumberConverter
```
[JScript]
```
public class DecimalConverter extends BaseNumberConverter
```

Thread Safety

Any public static (**Shared** in Visual Basic) members of this type are safe for multithreaded operations. Any instance members are not guaranteed to be thread safe.

Remarks

This converter can only convert a decimal object to and from a string.

> **Note** You should never create an instance of **DecimalConverter**. Instead, call the **GetConverter** method of **TypeDescriptor**. For more information, see the examples in the **TypeConverter** base class.

For more information about type converters, see the **TypeConverter** base class and **Implementing a Type Converter**.

Example

[Visual Basic, C#, C++] The following sample converts a variable of type **Decimal** to a string, and vice versa.

[Visual Basic]
```
Dim myDec As Decimal = 40
Dim myDStr As String = "20"
Console.WriteLine(TypeDescriptor.GetConverter(myDec).ConvertTo ↵
(myDec, GetType(String)))
Console.WriteLine(TypeDescriptor.GetConverter(myDec).ConvertFrom ↵
 (myDStr))
```

[C#]
```
decimal myDec = 40;
string myDStr = "20";
Console.WriteLine(TypeDescriptor.GetConverter(myDec).ConvertTo ↵
 (myDec, typeof(string)));
Console.WriteLine(TypeDescriptor.GetConverter(myDec).ConvertFrom ↵
 (myDStr));
```

[C++]
```
Decimal myDec( 40 );
String* myDStr = S"20";
Console::WriteLine(TypeDescriptor::GetConverter(__box(myDec))- ↵
>ConvertTo(__box(myDec), __typeof(String)));
Console::WriteLine(TypeDescriptor::GetConverter(__box(myDec))- ↵
>ConvertFrom(myDStr));
```

Requirements

Namespace: System.ComponentModel

Platforms: Windows 98, Windows NT 4.0, Windows Millennium Edition, Windows 2000, Windows XP Home Edition, Windows XP Professional, Windows Server 2003 family

Assembly: System (in System.dll)

DecimalConverter Constructor

Initializes a new instance of the **DecimalConverter** class.

[Visual Basic]
```
Public Sub New()
```
[C#]
```
public DecimalConverter();
```
[C++]
```
public: DecimalConverter();
```
[JScript]
```
public function DecimalConverter();
```

Remarks

The default constructor initializes any fields to their default values.

Requirements

Platforms: Windows 98, Windows NT 4.0, Windows Millennium Edition, Windows 2000, Windows XP Home Edition, Windows XP Professional, Windows Server 2003 family

DecimalConverter.CanConvertTo Method

Overload List

This member supports the .NET Framework infrastructure and is not intended to be used directly from your code.

[Visual Basic] **Overloads Overrides Public Function CanConvertTo(ITypeDescriptorContext, Type) As Boolean**

[C#] **public override bool CanConvertTo(ITypeDescriptorContext, Type);**

[C++] **public: bool CanConvertTo(ITypeDescriptorContext*, Type*);**

[JScript] **public override function CanConvertTo(ITypeDescriptorContext, Type) : Boolean;**

Inherited from **TypeConverter**.

[Visual Basic] **Overloads Public Function CanConvertTo(Type) As Boolean**

[C#] **public bool CanConvertTo(Type);**

[C++] **public: bool CanConvertTo(Type*);**

[JScript] **public function CanConvertTo(Type) : Boolean;**

DecimalConverter.CanConvertTo Method (ITypeDescriptorContext, Type)

This member overrides **TypeConverter.CanConvertTo**.

```
[Visual Basic]
Overrides Overloads Public Function CanConvertTo( _
   ByVal context As ITypeDescriptorContext, _
   ByVal destinationType As Type _
) As Boolean
[C#]
public override bool CanConvertTo(
   ITypeDescriptorContext context,
   Type destinationType
);
[C++]
public: bool CanConvertTo(
   ITypeDescriptorContext* context,
   Type* destinationType
);
[JScript]
public override function CanConvertTo(
   context : ITypeDescriptorContext,
   destinationType : Type
) : Boolean;
```

Requirements

Platforms: Windows 98, Windows NT 4.0, Windows Millennium Edition, Windows 2000, Windows XP Home Edition, Windows XP Professional, Windows Server 2003 family

DecimalConverter.ConvertTo Method

Overload List

This member supports the .NET Framework infrastructure and is not intended to be used directly from your code.

[Visual Basic] **Overloads Overrides Public Function ConvertTo(ITypeDescriptorContext, CultureInfo, Object, Type) As Object**

[C#] **public override object ConvertTo(ITypeDescriptorContext, CultureInfo, object, Type);**

[C++] **public: Object* ConvertTo(ITypeDescriptorContext*, CultureInfo*, Object*, Type*);**

[JScript] **public override function ConvertTo(ITypeDescriptorContext, CultureInfo, Object, Type) : Object;**

Inherited from **TypeConverter**.

[Visual Basic] **Overloads Public Function ConvertTo(Object, Type) As Object**

[C#] **public object ConvertTo(object, Type);**

[C++] **public: Object* ConvertTo(Object*, Type*);**

[JScript] **public function ConvertTo(Object, Type) : Object;**

DecimalConverter.ConvertTo Method (ITypeDescriptorContext, CultureInfo, Object, Type)

This member overrides **TypeConverter.ConvertTo**.

```
[Visual Basic]
Overrides Overloads Public Function ConvertTo( _
   ByVal context As ITypeDescriptorContext, _
   ByVal culture As CultureInfo, _
   ByVal value As Object, _
   ByVal destinationType As Type _
) As Object
[C#]
public override object ConvertTo(
   ITypeDescriptorContext context,
   CultureInfo culture,
   object value,
   Type destinationType
);
[C++]
public: Object* ConvertTo(
   ITypeDescriptorContext* context,
   CultureInfo* culture,
   Object* value,
   Type* destinationType
);
[JScript]
public override function ConvertTo(
   context : ITypeDescriptorContext,
   culture : CultureInfo,
   value : Object,
   destinationType : Type
) : Object;
```

Requirements

Platforms: Windows 98, Windows NT 4.0, Windows Millennium Edition, Windows 2000, Windows XP Home Edition, Windows XP Professional, Windows Server 2003 family

DefaultEventAttribute Class

Specifies the default event for a component.

System.Object
  System.Attribute
    System.ComponentModel.DefaultEventAttribute

[Visual Basic]
```
<AttributeUsage(AttributeTargets.Class)>
NotInheritable Public Class DefaultEventAttribute
   Inherits Attribute
```
[C#]
```
[AttributeUsage(AttributeTargets.Class)]
public sealed class DefaultEventAttribute : Attribute
```
[C++]
```
[AttributeUsage(AttributeTargets::Class)]
public __gc __sealed class DefaultEventAttribute : public
   Attribute
```
[JScript]
```
public
   AttributeUsage(AttributeTargets.Class)
class DefaultEventAttribute extends Attribute
```

Thread Safety

Any public static (**Shared** in Visual Basic) members of this type are safe for multithreaded operations. Any instance members are not guaranteed to be thread safe.

Remarks

Use the **Name** property to get the name of the default event.

Example

[Visual Basic, C#] The following example defines a collection class named `MyCollection`. The class is marked with a **DefaultEventAttribute** that specifies `CollectionChanged` as the default event.

[Visual Basic]
```
<DefaultEvent("CollectionChanged")> _
Public Class MyCollection
    Inherits BaseCollection

    Public Event CollectionChanged (ByVal sender As Object, _
        ByVal e As CollectionChangeEventArgs)

    ' Insert additional code.
End Class 'MyCollection
```

[C#]
```
[DefaultEvent("CollectionChanged")]
public class MyCollection : BaseCollection {

    private CollectionChangeEventHandler onCollectionChanged;

    public event CollectionChangeEventHandler CollectionChanged {
       add {
          onCollectionChanged += value;
       }
       remove {
          onCollectionChanged -= value;
       }
    }
    // Insert additional code.
}
```

[Visual Basic, C#] The next example creates an instance of `MyCollection`. Then it gets the attributes for the class, extracts the **DefaultEventAttribute**, and prints the name of the default event.

[Visual Basic]
```
Public Shared Function Main() As Integer
    ' Creates a new collection.
    Dim myNewCollection As New MyCollection()

    ' Gets the attributes for the collection.
    Dim attributes As AttributeCollection =                          ↵
TypeDescriptor.GetAttributes(myNewCollection)

    ' Prints the name of the default event by retrieving the
    ' DefaultEventAttribute from the AttributeCollection.
    Dim myAttribute As DefaultEventAttribute = _
        CType(attributes(GetType(DefaultEventAttribute)),            ↵
DefaultEventAttribute)
    Console.WriteLine(("The default event is: " & myAttribute.Name))
    Return 0
End Function 'Main
```

[C#]
```
public static int Main() {
    // Creates a new collection.
    MyCollection myNewCollection = new MyCollection();

    // Gets the attributes for the collection.
    AttributeCollection attributes =                                 ↵
TypeDescriptor.GetAttributes(myNewCollection);

    /* Prints the name of the default event by retrieving the
     * DefaultEventAttribute from the AttributeCollection. */
    DefaultEventAttribute myAttribute =
       (DefaultEventAttribute)attributes[typeof(DefaultEventAttribute)];
    Console.WriteLine("The default event is: " + myAttribute.Name);
    return 0;
 }
```

Requirements

Namespace: System.ComponentModel

Platforms: Windows 98, Windows NT 4.0, Windows Millennium Edition, Windows 2000, Windows XP Home Edition, Windows XP Professional, Windows Server 2003 family

Assembly: System (in System.dll)

DefaultEventAttribute Constructor

Initializes a new instance of the **DefaultEventAttribute** class.

[Visual Basic]
```
Public Sub New( _
   ByVal name As String _
)
```
[C#]
```
public DefaultEventAttribute(
   string name
);
```
[C++]
```
public: DefaultEventAttribute(
   String* name
);
```
[JScript]
```
public function DefaultEventAttribute(
   name : String
);
```

Parameters

name
  The name of the default event for the component this attribute is bound to.

Requirements

Platforms: Windows 98, Windows NT 4.0, Windows Millennium Edition, Windows 2000, Windows XP Home Edition, Windows XP Professional, Windows Server 2003 family

DefaultEventAttribute.Default Field

This member supports the .NET Framework infrastructure and is not intended to be used directly from your code.

```
[Visual Basic]
Public Shared ReadOnly Default As DefaultEventAttribute
[C#]
public static readonly DefaultEventAttribute Default;
[C++]
public: static DefaultEventAttribute* Default;
[JScript]
public static var Default : DefaultEventAttribute;
```

DefaultEventAttribute.Name Property

Gets the name of the default event for the component this attribute is bound to.

```
[Visual Basic]
Public ReadOnly Property Name As String
[C#]
public string Name {get;}
[C++]
public: __property String* get_Name();
[JScript]
public function get Name() : String;
```

Property Value

The name of the default event for the component this attribute is bound to. The default value is a null reference (**Nothing** in Visual Basic).

Requirements

Platforms: Windows 98, Windows NT 4.0, Windows Millennium Edition, Windows 2000, Windows XP Home Edition, Windows XP Professional, Windows Server 2003 family

DefaultEventAttribute.Equals Method

This member overrides **Object.Equals**.

```
[Visual Basic]
Overrides Public Function Equals( _
   ByVal obj As Object _
) As Boolean
[C#]
public override bool Equals(
   object obj
);
[C++]
public: bool Equals(
   Object* obj
);
[JScript]
public override function Equals(
   obj : Object
) : Boolean;
```

Requirements

Platforms: Windows 98, Windows NT 4.0, Windows Millennium Edition, Windows 2000, Windows XP Home Edition, Windows XP Professional, Windows Server 2003 family

DefaultEventAttribute.GetHashCode Method

This member overrides **Attribute.GetHashCode**.

```
[Visual Basic]
Overrides Public Function GetHashCode() As Integer
[C#]
public override int GetHashCode();
[C++]
public: int GetHashCode();
[JScript]
public override function GetHashCode() : int;
```

Requirements

Platforms: Windows 98, Windows NT 4.0, Windows Millennium Edition, Windows 2000, Windows XP Home Edition, Windows XP Professional, Windows Server 2003 family

DefaultPropertyAttribute Class

Specifies the default property for a component.

System.Object
 System.Attribute
  System.ComponentModel.DefaultPropertyAttribute

[Visual Basic]
```
<AttributeUsage(AttributeTargets.Class)>
NotInheritable Public Class DefaultPropertyAttribute
   Inherits Attribute
```
[C#]
```
[AttributeUsage(AttributeTargets.Class)]
public sealed class DefaultPropertyAttribute : Attribute
```
[C++]
```
[AttributeUsage(AttributeTargets::Class)]
public __gc __sealed class DefaultPropertyAttribute : public
   Attribute
```
[JScript]
```
public
   AttributeUsage(AttributeTargets.Class)
class DefaultPropertyAttribute extends Attribute
```

Thread Safety

Any public static (**Shared** in Visual Basic) members of this type are safe for multithreaded operations. Any instance members are not guaranteed to be thread safe.

Remarks

Use the **Name** property to get the name of the default event.

Example

[Visual Basic, C#] The following example defines a control named `MyControl`. The class is marked with a **DefaultPropertyAttribute** that specifies `MyProperty` as the default property.

[Visual Basic]
```
<DefaultProperty("MyProperty")> _
Public Class MyControl
    Inherits Control

    Public Property MyProperty() As Integer
        Get
            ' Insert code here.
            Return 0
        End Get
        Set
            ' Insert code here.
        End Set
    End Property
    ' Insert any additional code.
End Class 'MyControl
```

[C#]
```
[DefaultProperty("MyProperty")]
 public class MyControl : Control {

    public int MyProperty {
       get {
          // Insert code here.
          return 0;
       }
       set {
          // Insert code here.
       }
    }

    // Insert any additional code.

 }
```

[Visual Basic, C#] The next example creates an instance of `MyControl`. Then it gets the attributes for the class, extracts the **DefaultPropertyAttribute**, and prints the name of the default property.

[Visual Basic]
```
Public Shared Function Main() As Integer
    ' Creates a new control.
    Dim myNewControl As New MyControl()

    ' Gets the attributes for the collection.
    Dim attributes As AttributeCollection =                    ┘
TypeDescriptor.GetAttributes(myNewControl)

    ' Prints the name of the default property by retrieving the
    ' DefaultPropertyAttribute from the AttributeCollection.
    Dim myAttribute As DefaultPropertyAttribute = _
        CType(attributes(GetType(DefaultPropertyAttribute)),   ┘
DefaultPropertyAttribute)
    Console.WriteLine(("The default property is: " + myAttribute.Name))
    Return 0
End Function 'Main
```

[C#]
```
public static int Main() {
    // Creates a new control.
    MyControl myNewControl = new MyControl();

    // Gets the attributes for the collection.
    AttributeCollection attributes =                           ┘
TypeDescriptor.GetAttributes(myNewControl);

    /* Prints the name of the default property by retrieving the
     * DefaultPropertyAttribute from the AttributeCollection. */
    DefaultPropertyAttribute myAttribute =

(DefaultPropertyAttribute)attributes[typeof(DefaultPropertyAttribute)];
    Console.WriteLine("The default property is: " + myAttribute.Name);

    return 0;
 }
```

Requirements

Namespace: System.ComponentModel

Platforms: Windows 98, Windows NT 4.0, Windows Millennium Edition, Windows 2000, Windows XP Home Edition, Windows XP Professional, Windows Server 2003 family

Assembly: System (in System.dll)

DefaultPropertyAttribute Constructor

Initializes a new instance of the **DefaultPropertyAttribute** class.

[Visual Basic]
```
Public Sub New( _
   ByVal name As String _
)
```
[C#]
```
public DefaultPropertyAttribute(
   string name
);
```
[C++]
```
public: DefaultPropertyAttribute(
   String* name
);
```
[JScript]
```
public function DefaultPropertyAttribute(
   name : String
);
```

Parameters

name

The name of the default property for the component this attribute is bound to.

Requirements

Platforms: Windows 98, Windows NT 4.0, Windows Millennium Edition, Windows 2000, Windows XP Home Edition, Windows XP Professional, Windows Server 2003 family

DefaultPropertyAttribute.Default Field

This member supports the .NET Framework infrastructure and is not intended to be used directly from your code.

```
[Visual Basic]
Public Shared ReadOnly Default As DefaultPropertyAttribute
[C#]
public static readonly DefaultPropertyAttribute Default;
[C++]
public: static DefaultPropertyAttribute* Default;
[JScript]
public static var Default : DefaultPropertyAttribute;
```

DefaultPropertyAttribute.Name Property

Gets the name of the default property for the component this attribute is bound to.

```
[Visual Basic]
Public ReadOnly Property Name As String
[C#]
public string Name {get;}
[C++]
public: __property String* get_Name();
[JScript]
public function get Name() : String;
```

Property Value

The name of the default property for the component this attribute is bound to. The default value is a null reference (**Nothing** in Visual Basic).

Requirements

Platforms: Windows 98, Windows NT 4.0, Windows Millennium Edition, Windows 2000, Windows XP Home Edition, Windows XP Professional, Windows Server 2003 family

DefaultPropertyAttribute.Equals Method

This member overrides **Object.Equals**.

```
[Visual Basic]
Overrides Public Function Equals( _
   ByVal obj As Object _
) As Boolean
[C#]
public override bool Equals(
   object obj
);
[C++]
public: bool Equals(
   Object* obj
);
[JScript]
public override function Equals(
   obj : Object
) : Boolean;
```

Requirements

Platforms: Windows 98, Windows NT 4.0, Windows Millennium Edition, Windows 2000, Windows XP Home Edition, Windows XP Professional, Windows Server 2003 family

DefaultPropertyAttribute.GetHashCode Method

This member overrides **Attribute.GetHashCode**.

```
[Visual Basic]
Overrides Public Function GetHashCode() As Integer
[C#]
public override int GetHashCode();
[C++]
public: int GetHashCode();
[JScript]
public override function GetHashCode() : int;
```

Requirements

Platforms: Windows 98, Windows NT 4.0, Windows Millennium Edition, Windows 2000, Windows XP Home Edition, Windows XP Professional, Windows Server 2003 family

DefaultValueAttribute Class

Specifies the default value for a property.

System.Object
System.Attribute
System.ComponentModel.DefaultValueAttribute

[Visual Basic]
```
<AttributeUsage(AttributeTargets.All)>
NotInheritable Public Class DefaultValueAttribute
   Inherits Attribute
```
[C#]
```
[AttributeUsage(AttributeTargets.All)]
public sealed class DefaultValueAttribute : Attribute
```
[C++]
```
[AttributeUsage(AttributeTargets::All)]
public __gc __sealed class DefaultValueAttribute : public
   Attribute
```
[JScript]
```
public
   AttributeUsage(AttributeTargets.All)
class DefaultValueAttribute extends Attribute
```

Thread Safety

Any public static (**Shared** in Visual Basic) members of this type are safe for multithreaded operations. Any instance members are not guaranteed to be thread safe.

Remarks

You can create a **DefaultValueAttribute** with any value. A member's default value is typically its initial value. A visual designer can use the default value to reset the member's value. Code generators can use the default values also to determine whether code should be generated for the member.

Example

[Visual Basic, C#] The following example sets the default value of `MyProperty` to **false**.

[Visual Basic]
```
Private MyVar as Boolean = False
<DefaultValue(False)> _
Public Property MyProperty() As Boolean
    Get
        Return MyVar
    End Get
    Set
        MyVar = Value
    End Set
End Property
```

[C#]
```
private bool myVal=false;

[DefaultValue(false)]
 public bool MyProperty {
    get {
       return myVal;
    }
    set {
       myVal=value;
    }
 }
```

[Visual Basic, C#] The next example checks the default value of `MyProperty`. First the code gets a **PropertyDescriptorCollection** with all the properties for the object. Next it indexes into the **PropertyDescriptorCollection** to get `MyProperty`. Then it returns the attributes for this property and saves them in the attributes variable.

[Visual Basic, C#] The example then prints the default value by retrieving the **DefaultValueAttribute** from the **AttributeCollection**, and writing its name to the console screen.

[Visual Basic]
```
' Gets the attributes for the property.
Dim attributes As AttributeCollection = _
    TypeDescriptor.GetProperties(Me)("MyProperty").Attributes

' Prints the default value by retrieving the DefaultValueAttribute
' from the AttributeCollection.
Dim myAttribute As DefaultValueAttribute = _
    CType(attributes(GetType(DefaultValueAttribute)),                    ↵
DefaultValueAttribute)
Console.WriteLine(("The default value is: " &                            ↵
myAttribute.Value.ToString()))
```

[C#]
```
// Gets the attributes for the property.
 AttributeCollection attributes =
    TypeDescriptor.GetProperties(this)["MyProperty"].Attributes;

 /* Prints the default value by retrieving the DefaultValueAttribute
  * from the AttributeCollection. */
 DefaultValueAttribute myAttribute =
    (DefaultValueAttribute)attributes[typeof(DefaultValueAttribute)];
 Console.WriteLine("The default value is: " +                            ↵
myAttribute.Value.ToString());
```

Requirements

Namespace: System.ComponentModel

Platforms: Windows 98, Windows NT 4.0, Windows Millennium Edition, Windows 2000, Windows XP Home Edition, Windows XP Professional, Windows Server 2003 family, .NET Compact Framework - Windows CE .NET

Assembly: System (in System.dll)

DefaultValueAttribute Constructor

Initializes a new instance of the **DefaultValueAttribute** class.

Overload List

Initializes a new instance of the **DefaultValueAttribute** class using a **Boolean** value.

Supported by the .NET Compact Framework.

[Visual Basic] **Public Sub New(Boolean)**

[C#] **public DefaultValueAttribute(bool);**

[C++] **public: DefaultValueAttribute(bool);**

[JScript] **public function DefaultValueAttribute(Boolean);**

Initializes a new instance of the **DefaultValueAttribute** class using an 8-bit unsigned integer.

Supported by the .NET Compact Framework.

[Visual Basic] **Public Sub New(Byte)**

[C#] **public DefaultValueAttribute(byte);**

[C++] **public: DefaultValueAttribute(unsigned char);**

[JScript] **public function DefaultValueAttribute(Byte);**

Initializes a new instance of the **DefaultValueAttribute** class using a Unicode character.

Supported by the .NET Compact Framework.

[Visual Basic] **Public Sub New(Char)**

[C#] **public DefaultValueAttribute(char);**

[C++] **public: DefaultValueAttribute(__wchar_t);**

[JScript] **public function DefaultValueAttribute(Char);**

Initializes a new instance of the **DefaultValueAttribute** class using a double-precision floating point number.

Supported by the .NET Compact Framework.

[Visual Basic] **Public Sub New(Double)**

[C#] **public DefaultValueAttribute(double);**

[C++] **public: DefaultValueAttribute(double);**

[JScript] **public function DefaultValueAttribute(double);**

Initializes a new instance of the **DefaultValueAttribute** class using a 16-bit signed integer.

Supported by the .NET Compact Framework.

[Visual Basic] **Public Sub New(Short)**

[C#] **public DefaultValueAttribute(short);**

[C++] **public: DefaultValueAttribute(short);**

[JScript] **public function DefaultValueAttribute(Int16);**

Initializes a new instance of the **DefaultValueAttribute** class using a 32-bit signed integer.

Supported by the .NET Compact Framework.

[Visual Basic] **Public Sub New(Integer)**

[C#] **public DefaultValueAttribute(int);**

[C++] **public: DefaultValueAttribute(int);**

[JScript] **public function DefaultValueAttribute(int);**

Initializes a new instance of the **DefaultValueAttribute** class using a 64-bit signed integer.

Supported by the .NET Compact Framework.

[Visual Basic] **Public Sub New(Long)**

[C#] **public DefaultValueAttribute(long);**

[C++] **public: DefaultValueAttribute(__int64);**

[JScript] **public function DefaultValueAttribute(long);**

Initializes a new instance of the **DefaultValueAttribute** class.

Supported by the .NET Compact Framework.

[Visual Basic] **Public Sub New(Object)**

[C#] **public DefaultValueAttribute(object);**

[C++] **public: DefaultValueAttribute(Object*);**

[JScript] **public function DefaultValueAttribute(Object);**

Initializes a new instance of the **DefaultValueAttribute** class using a single-precision floating point number.

Supported by the .NET Compact Framework.

[Visual Basic] **Public Sub New(Single)**

[C#] **public DefaultValueAttribute(float);**

[C++] **public: DefaultValueAttribute(float);**

[JScript] **public function DefaultValueAttribute(float);**

Initializes a new instance of the **DefaultValueAttribute** class using a **String**.

Supported by the .NET Compact Framework.

[Visual Basic] **Public Sub New(String)**

[C#] **public DefaultValueAttribute(string);**

[C++] **public: DefaultValueAttribute(String*);**

[JScript] **public function DefaultValueAttribute(String);**

Initializes a new instance of the **DefaultValueAttribute** class, converting the specified value to the specified type, and using an invariant culture as the translation context.

[Visual Basic] **Public Sub New(Type, String)**

[C#] **public DefaultValueAttribute(Type, string);**

[C++] **public: DefaultValueAttribute(Type*, String*);**

[JScript] **public function DefaultValueAttribute(Type, String);**

DefaultValueAttribute Constructor (Boolean)

Initializes a new instance of the **DefaultValueAttribute** class using a **Boolean** value.

```
[Visual Basic]
Public Sub New( _
   ByVal value As Boolean _
)
[C#]
public DefaultValueAttribute(
   bool value
);
[C++]
public: DefaultValueAttribute(
   bool value
);
[JScript]
public function DefaultValueAttribute(
   value : Boolean
);
```

Parameters

value

A **Boolean** that is the default value.

Requirements

Platforms: Windows 98, Windows NT 4.0, Windows Millennium Edition, Windows 2000, Windows XP Home Edition, Windows XP Professional, Windows Server 2003 family, .NET Compact Framework - Windows CE .NET

DefaultValueAttribute Constructor (Byte)

Initializes a new instance of the **DefaultValueAttribute** class using an 8-bit unsigned integer.

```
[Visual Basic]
Public Sub New( _
   ByVal value As Byte _
)
[C#]
public DefaultValueAttribute(
   byte value
);
```

```
[C++]
public: DefaultValueAttribute(
   unsigned char value
);
[JScript]
public function DefaultValueAttribute(
   value : Byte
);
```

Parameters

value

An 8-bit unsigned integer that is the default value.

Requirements

Platforms: Windows 98, Windows NT 4.0,
Windows Millennium Edition, Windows 2000,
Windows XP Home Edition, Windows XP Professional,
Windows Server 2003 family,
.NET Compact Framework - Windows CE .NET

DefaultValueAttribute Constructor (Char)

Initializes a new instance of the **DefaultValueAttribute** class using a Unicode character.

```
[Visual Basic]
Public Sub New( _
   ByVal value As Char _
)
[C#]
public DefaultValueAttribute(
   char value
);
[C++]
public: DefaultValueAttribute(
   __wchar_t value
);
[JScript]
public function DefaultValueAttribute(
   value : Char
);
```

Parameters

value

A Unicode character that is the default value.

Requirements

Platforms: Windows 98, Windows NT 4.0,
Windows Millennium Edition, Windows 2000,
Windows XP Home Edition, Windows XP Professional,
Windows Server 2003 family,
.NET Compact Framework - Windows CE .NET

DefaultValueAttribute Constructor (Double)

Initializes a new instance of the **DefaultValueAttribute** class using a double-precision floating point number.

```
[Visual Basic]
Public Sub New( _
   ByVal value As Double _
)
[C#]
public DefaultValueAttribute(
   double value
);
[C++]
public: DefaultValueAttribute(
   double value
);
[JScript]
public function DefaultValueAttribute(
   value : double
);
```

Parameters

value

A double-precision floating point number that is the default value.

Requirements

Platforms: Windows 98, Windows NT 4.0,
Windows Millennium Edition, Windows 2000,
Windows XP Home Edition, Windows XP Professional,
Windows Server 2003 family,
.NET Compact Framework - Windows CE .NET

DefaultValueAttribute Constructor (Int16)

Initializes a new instance of the **DefaultValueAttribute** class using a 16-bit signed integer.

```
[Visual Basic]
Public Sub New( _
   ByVal value As Short _
)
[C#]
public DefaultValueAttribute(
   short value
);
[C++]
public: DefaultValueAttribute(
   short value
);
[JScript]
public function DefaultValueAttribute(
   value : Int16
);
```

Parameters

value

A 16-bit signed integer that is the default value.

Requirements

Platforms: Windows 98, Windows NT 4.0,
Windows Millennium Edition, Windows 2000,
Windows XP Home Edition, Windows XP Professional,
Windows Server 2003 family,
.NET Compact Framework - Windows CE .NET

DefaultValueAttribute Constructor (Int32)

Initializes a new instance of the **DefaultValueAttribute** class using a 32-bit signed integer.

```
[Visual Basic]
Public Sub New( _
   ByVal value As Integer _
)
[C#]
public DefaultValueAttribute(
   int value
);
[C++]
public: DefaultValueAttribute(
   int value
);
[JScript]
public function DefaultValueAttribute(
   value : int
);
```

Parameters

value

A 32-bit signed integer that is the default value.

Requirements

Platforms: Windows 98, Windows NT 4.0, Windows Millennium Edition, Windows 2000, Windows XP Home Edition, Windows XP Professional, Windows Server 2003 family, .NET Compact Framework - Windows CE .NET

DefaultValueAttribute Constructor (Int64)

Initializes a new instance of the **DefaultValueAttribute** class using a 64-bit signed integer.

```
[Visual Basic]
Public Sub New( _
   ByVal value As Long _
)
[C#]
public DefaultValueAttribute(
   long value
);
[C++]
public: DefaultValueAttribute(
   __int64 value
);
[JScript]
public function DefaultValueAttribute(
   value : long
);
```

Parameters

value

A 64-bit signed integer that is the default value.

Requirements

Platforms: Windows 98, Windows NT 4.0, Windows Millennium Edition, Windows 2000, Windows XP Home Edition, Windows XP Professional, Windows Server 2003 family, .NET Compact Framework - Windows CE .NET

DefaultValueAttribute Constructor (Object)

Initializes a new instance of the **DefaultValueAttribute** class.

```
[Visual Basic]
Public Sub New( _
   ByVal value As Object _
)
[C#]
public DefaultValueAttribute(
   object value
);
[C++]
public: DefaultValueAttribute(
   Object* value
);
[JScript]
public function DefaultValueAttribute(
   value : Object
);
```

Parameters

value

An **Object** that represents the default value.

Requirements

Platforms: Windows 98, Windows NT 4.0, Windows Millennium Edition, Windows 2000, Windows XP Home Edition, Windows XP Professional, Windows Server 2003 family, .NET Compact Framework - Windows CE .NET

DefaultValueAttribute Constructor (Single)

Initializes a new instance of the **DefaultValueAttribute** class using a single-precision floating point number.

```
[Visual Basic]
Public Sub New( _
   ByVal value As Single _
)
[C#]
public DefaultValueAttribute(
   float value
);
[C++]
public: DefaultValueAttribute(
   float value
);
[JScript]
public function DefaultValueAttribute(
   value : float
);
```

Parameters

value

A single-precision floating point number that is the default value.

Requirements

Platforms: Windows 98, Windows NT 4.0, Windows Millennium Edition, Windows 2000, Windows XP Home Edition, Windows XP Professional, Windows Server 2003 family, .NET Compact Framework - Windows CE .NET

DefaultValueAttribute Constructor (String)

Initializes a new instance of the **DefaultValueAttribute** class using a **String**.

```
[Visual Basic]
Public Sub New( _
   ByVal value As String _
)
[C#]
public DefaultValueAttribute(
   string value
);
[C++]
public: DefaultValueAttribute(
   String* value
);
[JScript]
public function DefaultValueAttribute(
   value : String
);
```

Parameters

value
A **String** that is the default value.

Requirements

Platforms: Windows 98, Windows NT 4.0, Windows Millennium Edition, Windows 2000, Windows XP Home Edition, Windows XP Professional, Windows Server 2003 family, .NET Compact Framework - Windows CE .NET

DefaultValueAttribute Constructor (Type, String)

Initializes a new instance of the **DefaultValueAttribute** class, converting the specified value to the specified type, and using an invariant culture as the translation context.

```
[Visual Basic]
Public Sub New( _
   ByVal type As Type, _
   ByVal value As String _
)
[C#]
public DefaultValueAttribute(
   Type type,
   string value
);
[C++]
public: DefaultValueAttribute(
   Type* type,
   String* value
);
[JScript]
public function DefaultValueAttribute(
   type : Type,
   value : String
);
```

Parameters

type
A **Type** that represents the type to convert the value to.

value
A **String** that can be converted to the type using the **TypeConverter** for the type and the U.S. English culture.

Requirements

Platforms: Windows 98, Windows NT 4.0, Windows Millennium Edition, Windows 2000, Windows XP Home Edition, Windows XP Professional, Windows Server 2003 family

DefaultValueAttribute.Value Property

Gets the default value of the property this attribute is bound to.

```
[Visual Basic]
Public ReadOnly Property Value As Object
[C#]
public object Value {get;}
[C++]
public: __property Object* get_Value();
[JScript]
public function get Value() : Object;
```

Property Value

An **Object** that represents the default value of the property this attribute is bound to.

Requirements

Platforms: Windows 98, Windows NT 4.0, Windows Millennium Edition, Windows 2000, Windows XP Home Edition, Windows XP Professional, Windows Server 2003 family, .NET Compact Framework - Windows CE .NET

DefaultValueAttribute.Equals Method

This member overrides **Object.Equals**.

```
[Visual Basic]
Overrides Public Function Equals( _
   ByVal obj As Object _
) As Boolean
[C#]
public override bool Equals(
   object obj
);
[C++]
public: bool Equals(
   Object* obj
);
[JScript]
public override function Equals(
   obj : Object
) : Boolean;
```

Requirements

Platforms: Windows 98, Windows NT 4.0, Windows Millennium Edition, Windows 2000, Windows XP Home Edition, Windows XP Professional, Windows Server 2003 family, .NET Compact Framework - Windows CE .NET

DefaultValueAttribute.GetHashCode Method

This member overrides **Attribute.GetHashCode**.

[Visual Basic]
```
Overrides Public Function GetHashCode() As Integer
```
[C#]
```
public override int GetHashCode();
```
[C++]
```
public: int GetHashCode();
```
[JScript]
```
public override function GetHashCode() : int;
```

Requirements

Platforms: Windows 98, Windows NT 4.0,
Windows Millennium Edition, Windows 2000,
Windows XP Home Edition, Windows XP Professional,
Windows Server 2003 family,
.NET Compact Framework - Windows CE .NET

DescriptionAttribute Class

Specifies a description for a property or event.

System.Object
  System.Attribute
    System.ComponentModel.DescriptionAttribute
      Derived classes

[Visual Basic]
```
<AttributeUsage(AttributeTargets.All)>
Public Class DescriptionAttribute
   Inherits Attribute
```
[C#]
```
[AttributeUsage(AttributeTargets.All)]
public class DescriptionAttribute : Attribute
```
[C++]
```
[AttributeUsage(AttributeTargets::All)]
public __gc class DescriptionAttribute : public Attribute
```
[JScript]
```
public
   AttributeUsage(AttributeTargets.All)
class DescriptionAttribute extends Attribute
```

Thread Safety

Any public static (**Shared** in Visual Basic) members of this type are safe for multithreaded operations. Any instance members are not guaranteed to be thread safe.

Remarks

A visual designer can display the specified description when referencing the component member, such as in a Properties window. Call **Description** to access the value of this attribute.

Example

[Visual Basic, C#] The following example creates the `MyImage` property. The property has two attributes, a **DescriptionAttribute** and a **CategoryAttribute**.

[Visual Basic]
```
<Description("The image associated with the control"), _
   Category("Appearance")> _
Public Property MyImage() As Image
   Get
      ' Insert code here.
      Return image1
   End Get
   Set
      ' Insert code here.
   End Set
End Property
```

[C#]
```
[Description("The image associated with the                    ┘
control"),Category("Appearance")]
 public Image MyImage {
   get {
      // Insert code here.
      return image1;
   }
   set {
      // Insert code here.
   }
 }
```

[Visual Basic, C#] The next example gets the description of `MyImage`. First the code gets a **PropertyDescriptorCollection** with all the properties for the object. Next it indexes into the **PropertyDescriptorCollection** to get `MyImage`. Then it returns the attributes for this property and saves them in the attributes variable.

[Visual Basic, C#] The example then prints the description by retrieving **DescriptionAttribute** from the **AttributeCollection**, and writing it to the console screen.

[Visual Basic]
```
' Gets the attributes for the property.
Dim attributes As AttributeCollection = _
   TypeDescriptor.GetProperties(Me)("MyImage").Attributes

' Prints the description by retrieving the DescriptionAttribute
' from the AttributeCollection.
Dim myAttribute As DescriptionAttribute = _
   CType(attributes(GetType(DescriptionAttribute)),
DescriptionAttribute)
Console.WriteLine(myAttribute.Description)
```

[C#]
```
// Gets the attributes for the property.
 AttributeCollection attributes =
    TypeDescriptor.GetProperties(this)["MyImage"].Attributes;

 /* Prints the description by retrieving the DescriptionAttribute
  * from the AttributeCollection. */
 DescriptionAttribute myAttribute =
    (DescriptionAttribute)attributes[typeof(DescriptionAttribute)];
 Console.WriteLine(myAttribute.Description);
```

Requirements

Namespace: System.ComponentModel

Platforms: Windows 98, Windows NT 4.0, Windows Millennium Edition, Windows 2000, Windows XP Home Edition, Windows XP Professional, Windows Server 2003 family

Assembly: System (in System.dll)

DescriptionAttribute Constructor

Initializes a new instance of the **DescriptionAttribute** class.

Overload List

Initializes a new instance of the **DescriptionAttribute** class with no parameters.

[Visual Basic] **Public Sub New()**

[C#] **public DescriptionAttribute();**

[C++] **public: DescriptionAttribute();**

[JScript] **public function DescriptionAttribute();**

Initializes a new instance of the **DescriptionAttribute** class with a description.

[Visual Basic] **Public Sub New(String)**

[C#] **public DescriptionAttribute(string);**

[C++] **public: DescriptionAttribute(String*);**

[JScript] **public function DescriptionAttribute(String);**

DescriptionAttribute Constructor ()

Initializes a new instance of the **DescriptionAttribute** class with no parameters.

```
[Visual Basic]
Public Sub New()
[C#]
public DescriptionAttribute();
[C++]
public: DescriptionAttribute();
[JScript]
public function DescriptionAttribute();
```

Requirements

Platforms: Windows 98, Windows NT 4.0, Windows Millennium Edition, Windows 2000, Windows XP Home Edition, Windows XP Professional, Windows Server 2003 family

DescriptionAttribute Constructor (String)

Initializes a new instance of the **DescriptionAttribute** class with a description.

```
[Visual Basic]
Public Sub New( _
   ByVal description As String _
)
[C#]
public DescriptionAttribute(
   string description
);
[C++]
public: DescriptionAttribute(
   String* description
);
[JScript]
public function DescriptionAttribute(
   description : String
);
```

Parameters

description
The description text.

Requirements

Platforms: Windows 98, Windows NT 4.0, Windows Millennium Edition, Windows 2000, Windows XP Home Edition, Windows XP Professional, Windows Server 2003 family

DescriptionAttribute.Default Field

This member supports the .NET Framework infrastructure and is not intended to be used directly from your code.

```
[Visual Basic]
Public Shared ReadOnly Default As DescriptionAttribute
[C#]
public static readonly DescriptionAttribute Default;
[C++]
public: static DescriptionAttribute* Default;
[JScript]
public static var Default : DescriptionAttribute;
```

DescriptionAttribute.Description Property

Gets the description stored in this attribute.

```
[Visual Basic]
Public Overridable ReadOnly Property Description As String
[C#]
public virtual string Description {get;}
[C++]
public: __property virtual String* get_Description();
[JScript]
public function get Description() : String;
```

Property Value

The description stored in this attribute.

Requirements

Platforms: Windows 98, Windows NT 4.0, Windows Millennium Edition, Windows 2000, Windows XP Home Edition, Windows XP Professional, Windows Server 2003 family

DescriptionAttribute.DescriptionValue Property

Gets or sets the string stored as the description.

```
[Visual Basic]
Protected Property DescriptionValue As String
[C#]
protected string DescriptionValue {get; set;}
[C++]
protected: __property String* get_DescriptionValue();
protected: __property void set_DescriptionValue(String*);
[JScript]
protected function get DescriptionValue() : String;
protected function set DescriptionValue(String);
```

Property Value

The string stored as the description. The default value is an empty string ("").

Remarks

The default implementation of the **Description** property simply returns this value.

This extra property exists so that you can derive from **DescriptionAttribute** and provide a localized version. The derived localizable **DescriptionAttribute** will maintain a private Boolean field to indicate if it has been localized. On the first access to the **Description** property, it will look up the localized string and store it back in the **DescriptionValue** property.

Requirements

Platforms: Windows 98, Windows NT 4.0, Windows Millennium Edition, Windows 2000, Windows XP Home Edition, Windows XP Professional, Windows Server 2003 family

DescriptionAttribute.Equals Method

This member overrides **Object.Equals**.

[Visual Basic]
```
Overrides Public Function Equals( _
   ByVal obj As Object _
) As Boolean
```
[C#]
```
public override bool Equals(
   object obj
);
```
[C++]
```
public: bool Equals(
   Object* obj
);
```
[JScript]
```
public override function Equals(
   obj : Object
) : Boolean;
```

Requirements

Platforms: Windows 98, Windows NT 4.0, Windows Millennium Edition, Windows 2000, Windows XP Home Edition, Windows XP Professional, Windows Server 2003 family

DescriptionAttribute.GetHashCode Method

This member overrides **Attribute.GetHashCode**.

[Visual Basic]
```
Overrides Public Function GetHashCode() As Integer
```
[C#]
```
public override int GetHashCode();
```
[C++]
```
public: int GetHashCode();
```
[JScript]
```
public override function GetHashCode() : int;
```

Requirements

Platforms: Windows 98, Windows NT 4.0, Windows Millennium Edition, Windows 2000, Windows XP Home Edition, Windows XP Professional, Windows Server 2003 family

DesignerAttribute Class

Specifies the class used to implement design-time services for a component.

System.Object
  System.Attribute
    System.ComponentModel.DesignerAttribute

[Visual Basic]
```
<AttributeUsage(AttributeTargets.Class Or _
   AttributeTargets.Interface)>
NotInheritable Public Class DesignerAttribute
   Inherits Attribute
```
[C#]
```
[AttributeUsage(AttributeTargets.Class |
   AttributeTargets.Interface)]
public sealed class DesignerAttribute : Attribute
```
[C++]
```
[AttributeUsage(AttributeTargets::Class |
   AttributeTargets::Interface)]
public __gc __sealed class DesignerAttribute : public Attribute
```
[JScript]
```
public
   AttributeUsage(AttributeTargets.Class | AttributeTargets.Interface)
class DesignerAttribute extends Attribute
```

Thread Safety

Any public static (**Shared** in Visual Basic) members of this type are safe for multithreaded operations. Any instance members are not guaranteed to be thread safe.

Remarks

The class you use for the design-time services must implement the **IDesigner** interface.

Use the **DesignerBaseTypeName** property to find the designer's base type. Use the **DesignerTypeName** property to get the name of the type of designer associated with this member.

Example

[Visual Basic, C#] The following example creates a class called `MyForm`. `MyForm` has two attributes, a **DesignerAttribute** that specifies this class uses the **DocumentDesigner**, and a **DesignerCategoryAttribute** that specifies the **Form** category.

[Visual Basic]
```
<Designer("System.Windows.Forms.Design.DocumentDesigner, ↵
System.Windows.Forms.Design.DLL", _
    GetType(IRootDesigner)), DesignerCategory("Form")> _
Public Class MyForm

    Inherits ContainerControl
    ' Insert code here.
End Class 'MyForm
```

[C#]
```
[Designer("System.Windows.Forms.Design.DocumentDesigner, ↵
System.Windows.Forms.Design.DLL",
    typeof(IRootDesigner)),
    DesignerCategory("Form")]
public class MyForm : ContainerControl {
    // Insert code here.
}
```

[Visual Basic, C#] The next example creates an instance of `MyForm`. Then it gets the attributes for the class, extracts the **DesignerAttribute**, and prints the name of the designer.

[Visual Basic]
```
Public Shared Function Main() As Integer
    ' Creates a new form.
    Dim myNewForm As New MyForm()

    ' Gets the attributes for the collection.
    Dim attributes As AttributeCollection = ↵
TypeDescriptor.GetAttributes(myNewForm)

    ' Prints the name of the designer by retrieving the ↵
DesignerAttribute
    ' from the AttributeCollection.
    Dim myAttribute As DesignerAttribute = _
        CType(attributes(GetType(DesignerAttribute)), ↵
DesignerAttribute)
    Console.WriteLine(("The designer for this class is: " & ↵
myAttribute.DesignerTypeName))

    Return 0
End Function 'Main
```

[C#]
```
public static int Main() {
    // Creates a new form.
    MyForm myNewForm = new MyForm();

    // Gets the attributes for the collection.
    AttributeCollection attributes = ↵
TypeDescriptor.GetAttributes(myNewForm);

    /* Prints the name of the designer by retrieving the ↵
DesignerAttribute
     * from the AttributeCollection. */
    DesignerAttribute myAttribute =
       (DesignerAttribute)attributes[typeof(DesignerAttribute)];
    Console.WriteLine("The designer for this class is: " + ↵
myAttribute.DesignerTypeName);

    return 0;
}
```

Requirements

Namespace: System.ComponentModel

Platforms: Windows 98, Windows NT 4.0, Windows Millennium Edition, Windows 2000, Windows XP Home Edition, Windows XP Professional, Windows .NET Server family

Assembly: System (in System.dll)

DesignerAttribute Constructor

Initializes a new instance of the **DesignerAttribute** class.

Overload List

Initializes a new instance of the **DesignerAttribute** class using the name of the type that provides design-time services.

[Visual Basic] **Public Sub New(String)**

[C#] **public DesignerAttribute(string);**

[C++] **public: DesignerAttribute(String*);**

[JScript] **public function DesignerAttribute(String);**

Initializes a new instance of the **DesignerAttribute** class using the type that provides design-time services.

[Visual Basic] **Public Sub New(Type)**

[C#] **public DesignerAttribute(Type);**

[C++] **public: DesignerAttribute(Type*);**

[JScript] **public function DesignerAttribute(Type);**

Initializes a new instance of the **DesignerAttribute** class using the designer type and the base class for the designer.

[Visual Basic] **Public Sub New(String, String)**

[C#] **public DesignerAttribute(string, string);**

[C++] **public: DesignerAttribute(String*, String*);**

[JScript] **public function DesignerAttribute(String, String);**

Initializes a new instance of the **DesignerAttribute** class, using the name of the designer class and the base class for the designer.

[Visual Basic] **Public Sub New(String, Type)**

[C#] **public DesignerAttribute(string, Type);**

[C++] **public: DesignerAttribute(String*, Type*);**

[JScript] **public function DesignerAttribute(String, Type);**

Initializes a new instance of the **DesignerAttribute** class using the types of the designer and designer base class.

[Visual Basic] **Public Sub New(Type, Type)**

[C#] **public DesignerAttribute(Type, Type);**

[C++] **public: DesignerAttribute(Type*, Type*);**

[JScript] **public function DesignerAttribute(Type, Type);**

DesignerAttribute Constructor (String)

Initializes a new instance of the **DesignerAttribute** class using the name of the type that provides design-time services.

```
[Visual Basic]
Public Sub New( _
   ByVal designerTypeName As String _
)
[C#]
public DesignerAttribute(
   string designerTypeName
);
[C++]
public: DesignerAttribute(
   String* designerTypeName
);
[JScript]
public function DesignerAttribute(
   designerTypeName : String
);
```

Parameters

designerTypeName

The concatenation of the fully qualified name of the type that provides design-time services for the component this attribute is bound to, and the name of the assembly this type resides in.

Remarks

The class you use for the design-time services must implement the **IDesigner** interface.

Requirements

Platforms: Windows 98, Windows NT 4.0, Windows Millennium Edition, Windows 2000, Windows XP Home Edition, Windows XP Professional, Windows .NET Server family

DesignerAttribute Constructor (Type)

Initializes a new instance of the **DesignerAttribute** class using the type that provides design-time services.

```
[Visual Basic]
Public Sub New( _
   ByVal designerType As Type _
)
[C#]
public DesignerAttribute(
   Type designerType
);
[C++]
public: DesignerAttribute(
   Type* designerType
);
[JScript]
public function DesignerAttribute(
   designerType : Type
);
```

Parameters

designerType

A **Type** that represents the class that provides design-time services for the component this attribute is bound to.

Remarks

The class you use for the design-time services must implement the **IDesigner** interface.

Requirements

Platforms: Windows 98, Windows NT 4.0, Windows Millennium Edition, Windows 2000, Windows XP Home Edition, Windows XP Professional, Windows .NET Server family

DesignerAttribute Constructor (String, String)

Initializes a new instance of the **DesignerAttribute** class using the designer type and the base class for the designer.

```
[Visual Basic]
Public Sub New( _
   ByVal designerTypeName As String, _
   ByVal designerBaseTypeName As String _
)
[C#]
public DesignerAttribute(
   string designerTypeName,
   string designerBaseTypeName
);
[C++]
public: DesignerAttribute(
   String* designerTypeName,
   String* designerBaseTypeName
);
[JScript]
public function DesignerAttribute(
   designerTypeName : String,
   designerBaseTypeName : String
);
```

Parameters

designerTypeName

The concatenation of the fully qualified name of the type that provides design-time services for the component this attribute is bound to, and the name of the assembly this type resides in.

designerBaseTypeName

The fully qualified name of the base class to associate with the designer class.

Remarks

The class you use for the design-time services must implement the **IDesigner** interface.

The *designerBaseTypeName* parameter allows you to attach more than one type of designer for a given class.

Requirements

Platforms: Windows 98, Windows NT 4.0, Windows Millennium Edition, Windows 2000, Windows XP Home Edition, Windows XP Professional, Windows .NET Server family

DesignerAttribute Constructor (String, Type)

Initializes a new instance of the **DesignerAttribute** class, using the name of the designer class and the base class for the designer.

```
[Visual Basic]
Public Sub New( _
   ByVal designerTypeName As String, _
   ByVal designerBaseType As Type _
)
[C#]
public DesignerAttribute(
   string designerTypeName,
   Type designerBaseType
);
[C++]
public: DesignerAttribute(
   String* designerTypeName,
   Type* designerBaseType
);
[JScript]
public function DesignerAttribute(
   designerTypeName : String,
   designerBaseType : Type
);
```

Parameters

designerTypeName

The concatenation of the fully qualified name of the type that provides design-time services for the component this attribute is bound to, and the name of the assembly this type resides in.

designerBaseType

A **Type** that represents the base class to associate with the *designerTypeName*.

Remarks

The class you use for the design-time services must implement the **IDesigner** interface.

The *designerBaseType* parameter allows you to attach more than one type of designer for a given class.

Requirements

Platforms: Windows 98, Windows NT 4.0, Windows Millennium Edition, Windows 2000, Windows XP Home Edition, Windows XP Professional, Windows .NET Server family

DesignerAttribute Constructor (Type, Type)

Initializes a new instance of the **DesignerAttribute** class using the types of the designer and designer base class.

```
[Visual Basic]
Public Sub New( _
   ByVal designerType As Type, _
   ByVal designerBaseType As Type _
)
[C#]
public DesignerAttribute(
   Type designerType,
   Type designerBaseType
);
[C++]
public: DesignerAttribute(
   Type* designerType,
   Type* designerBaseType
);
[JScript]
public function DesignerAttribute(
   designerType : Type,
   designerBaseType : Type
);
```

Parameters

designerType

A **Type** that represents the class that provides design-time services for the component this attribute is bound to.

designerBaseType

A **Type** that represents the base class to associate with the *designerType*.

Remarks

The class you use for the design-time services must implement the **IDesigner** interface.

The *designerBaseType* parameter allows you to attach more than one type of designer for a given class.

Requirements

Platforms: Windows 98, Windows NT 4.0, Windows Millennium Edition, Windows 2000, Windows XP Home Edition, Windows XP Professional, Windows .NET Server family

DesignerAttribute.DesignerBaseTypeName Property

Gets the name of the base type of this designer.

```
[Visual Basic]
Public ReadOnly Property DesignerBaseTypeName As String
[C#]
public string DesignerBaseTypeName {get;}
[C++]
public: __property String* get_DesignerBaseTypeName();
[JScript]
public function get DesignerBaseTypeName() : String;
```

Property Value

The name of the base type of this designer.

Requirements

Platforms: Windows 98, Windows NT 4.0, Windows Millennium Edition, Windows 2000, Windows XP Home Edition, Windows XP Professional, Windows .NET Server family

DesignerAttribute.DesignerTypeName Property

Gets the name of the designer type associated with this designer attribute.

```
[Visual Basic]
Public ReadOnly Property DesignerTypeName As String
[C#]
public string DesignerTypeName {get;}
[C++]
public: __property String* get_DesignerTypeName();
[JScript]
public function get DesignerTypeName() : String;
```

Property Value

The name of the designer type associated with this designer attribute.

Requirements

Platforms: Windows 98, Windows NT 4.0, Windows Millennium Edition, Windows 2000, Windows XP Home Edition, Windows XP Professional, Windows .NET Server family

DesignerAttribute.TypeId Property

This member overrides **Attribute.TypeId**.

```
[Visual Basic]
Overrides Public ReadOnly Property TypeId As Object
[C#]
public override object TypeId {get;}
[C++]
public: __property Object* get_TypeId();
[JScript]
public override function get TypeId() : Object;
```

Requirements

Platforms: Windows 98, Windows NT 4.0, Windows Millennium Edition, Windows 2000, Windows XP Home Edition, Windows XP Professional, Windows .NET Server family

DesignerAttribute.Equals Method

This member overrides **Object.Equals**.

```
[Visual Basic]
Overrides Public Function Equals( _
   ByVal obj As Object _
) As Boolean
[C#]
public override bool Equals(
   object obj
);
[C++]
public: bool Equals(
   Object* obj
);
[JScript]
public override function Equals(
   obj : Object
) : Boolean;
```

Requirements

Platforms: Windows 98, Windows NT 4.0, Windows Millennium Edition, Windows 2000, Windows XP Home Edition, Windows XP Professional, Windows .NET Server family

DesignerAttribute.GetHashCode Method

This member overrides **Attribute.GetHashCode**.

```
[Visual Basic]
Overrides Public Function GetHashCode() As Integer
[C#]
public override int GetHashCode();
[C++]
public: int GetHashCode();
[JScript]
public override function GetHashCode() : int;
```

Requirements

Platforms: Windows 98, Windows NT 4.0, Windows Millennium Edition, Windows 2000, Windows XP Home Edition, Windows XP Professional, Windows .NET Server family

DesignerCategoryAttribute Class

Specifies that the designer for a class belongs to a certain category.

System.Object
  System.Attribute
    System.ComponentModel.DesignerCategoryAttribute

[Visual Basic]
```
<AttributeUsage(AttributeTargets.Class)>
NotInheritable Public Class DesignerCategoryAttribute
   Inherits Attribute
```
[C#]
```
[AttributeUsage(AttributeTargets.Class)]
public sealed class DesignerCategoryAttribute : Attribute
```
[C++]
```
[AttributeUsage(AttributeTargets::Class)]
public __gc __sealed class DesignerCategoryAttribute : public
   Attribute
```
[JScript]
```
public
   AttributeUsage(AttributeTargets.Class)
class DesignerCategoryAttribute extends Attribute
```

Thread Safety

Any public static (**Shared** in Visual Basic) members of this type are safe for multithreaded operations. Any instance members are not guaranteed to be thread safe.

Remarks

A visual designer can use a designer category to inform a development environment of the type of designer that will be implemented. If no designer category is provided on a class, a development environment may or may not allow the class to be designed. A category can be created for any name.

When you mark a class with this attribute, it is set to a constant member. When you want to check the value of this attribute in your code, you must specify the constant member. The Description column in the table below lists the constant member that each value is set to.

The **DesignerCategoryAttribute** class defines the following common categories:

Category	Description
Component	Designers that are used with components. The attribute is set to the constant member **DesignerCategory-Attribute.Component**.
Form	Designers that are used with forms. The attribute is set to the constant member **DesignerCategory-Attribute.Form**.
Designer	Designers that are used with designers. The attribute is set to the constant member **DesignerCategory-Attribute.Generic**.
Empty String ("")	This is the default category.

For more information, see **Attributes Overview** and **Extending Metadata Using Attributes**.

Example

[Visual Basic, C#] The following example creates a class called `MyForm`. `MyForm` has two attributes, a **DesignerAttribute** that specifies this class uses the **DocumentDesigner**, and a **DesignerCategoryAttribute** that specifies the **Form** category.

[Visual Basic]
```
<Designer("System.Windows.Forms.Design.DocumentDesigner,  ↵
System.Windows.Forms.Design", _
   GetType(IRootDesigner)), DesignerCategory("Form")> _
Public Class MyForm

   Inherits ContainerControl
   ' Insert code here.
End Class 'MyForm
```

[C#]
```
[Designer("System.Windows.Forms.Design.DocumentDesigner,  ↵
System.Windows.Forms.Design",
   typeof(IRootDesigner)),
   DesignerCategory("Form")]

 public class MyForm : ContainerControl {
   // Insert code here.
 }
```

[Visual Basic, C#] The next example creates an instance of `MyForm`. Then it gets the attributes for the class, extracts the **DesignerCategoryAttribute**, and prints the name of the designer.

[Visual Basic]
```
Public Shared Function Main() As Integer
    ' Creates a new form.
    Dim myNewForm As New MyForm()

    ' Gets the attributes for the collection.
    Dim attributes As AttributeCollection =  ↵
TypeDescriptor.GetAttributes(myNewForm)

    ' Prints the name of the designer by retrieving the
    ' DesignerCategoryAttribute from the AttributeCollection.
    Dim myAttribute As DesignerCategoryAttribute = _
        CType(attributes(GetType(DesignerCategoryAttribute)),  ↵
DesignerCategoryAttribute)
    Console.WriteLine(("The category of the designer for this  ↵
class is: " + myAttribute.Category))
    Return 0
End Function 'Main
```

[C#]
```
public static int Main() {
    // Creates a new form.
    MyForm myNewForm = new MyForm();

    // Gets the attributes for the collection.
    AttributeCollection attributes =
TypeDescriptor.GetAttributes(myNewForm);

    /* Prints the name of the designer by retrieving the
     * DesignerCategoryAttribute from the AttributeCollection. */
    DesignerCategoryAttribute myAttribute =

(DesignerCategoryAttribute)attributes[typeof(DesignerCategoryAttribute)]
;
    Console.WriteLine("The category of the designer for this  ↵
 class is: " + myAttribute.Category);

    return 0;
}
```

Requirements

Namespace: System.ComponentModel

Platforms: Windows 98, Windows NT 4.0, Windows Millennium Edition, Windows 2000, Windows XP Home Edition, Windows XP Professional, Windows Server 2003 family, .NET Compact Framework - Windows CE .NET

Assembly: System (in System.dll)

DesignerCategoryAttribute Constructor

Initializes a new instance of the **DesignerCategoryAttribute** class.

Overload List

Initializes a new instance of the **DesignerCategoryAttribute** class with an empty string ("").

Supported by the .NET Compact Framework.

[Visual Basic] **Public Sub New()**

[C#] **public DesignerCategoryAttribute();**

[C++] **public: DesignerCategoryAttribute();**

[JScript] **public function DesignerCategoryAttribute();**

Initializes a new instance of the **DesignerCategoryAttribute** class with the given category name.

Supported by the .NET Compact Framework.

[Visual Basic] **Public Sub New(String)**

[C#] **public DesignerCategoryAttribute(string);**

[C++] **public: DesignerCategoryAttribute(String*);**

[JScript] **public function DesignerCategoryAttribute(String);**

DesignerCategoryAttribute Constructor ()

Initializes a new instance of the **DesignerCategoryAttribute** class with an empty string ("").

```
[Visual Basic]
Public Sub New()
[C#]
public DesignerCategoryAttribute();
[C++]
public: DesignerCategoryAttribute();
[JScript]
public function DesignerCategoryAttribute();
```

Requirements

Platforms: Windows 98, Windows NT 4.0, Windows Millennium Edition, Windows 2000, Windows XP Home Edition, Windows XP Professional, Windows Server 2003 family, .NET Compact Framework - Windows CE .NET

DesignerCategoryAttribute Constructor (String)

Initializes a new instance of the **DesignerCategoryAttribute** class with the given category name.

```
[Visual Basic]
Public Sub New( _
   ByVal category As String _
)
[C#]
public DesignerCategoryAttribute(
   string category
);
[C++]
public: DesignerCategoryAttribute(
   String* category
);
[JScript]
public function DesignerCategoryAttribute(
   category : String
);
```

Parameters

category

The name of the category.

Requirements

Platforms: Windows 98, Windows NT 4.0, Windows Millennium Edition, Windows 2000, Windows XP Home Edition, Windows XP Professional, Windows Server 2003 family, .NET Compact Framework - Windows CE .NET

DesignerCategoryAttribute.Component Field

Specifies that a component marked with this category use a component designer. This field is read-only.

```
[Visual Basic]
Public Shared ReadOnly Component As DesignerCategoryAttribute
[C#]
public static readonly DesignerCategoryAttribute Component;
[C++]
public: static DesignerCategoryAttribute* Component;
[JScript]
public static var Component : DesignerCategoryAttribute;
```

Requirements

Platforms: Windows 98, Windows NT 4.0, Windows Millennium Edition, Windows 2000, Windows XP Home Edition, Windows XP Professional, Windows Server 2003 family, .NET Compact Framework - Windows CE .NET

DesignerCategoryAttribute.Default Field

This member supports the .NET Framework infrastructure and is not intended to be used directly from your code.

```
[Visual Basic]
Public Shared ReadOnly Default As DesignerCategoryAttribute
[C#]
public static readonly DesignerCategoryAttribute Default;
[C++]
public: static DesignerCategoryAttribute* Default;
[JScript]
public static var Default : DesignerCategoryAttribute;
```

DesignerCategoryAttribute.Form Field

Specifies that a component marked with this category use a form designer. This static (**Shared** in Visual Basic) field is read-only.

```
[Visual Basic]
Public Shared ReadOnly Form As DesignerCategoryAttribute
[C#]
public static readonly DesignerCategoryAttribute Form;
[C++]
public: static DesignerCategoryAttribute* Form;
[JScript]
public static var Form : DesignerCategoryAttribute;
```

Requirements

Platforms: Windows 98, Windows NT 4.0, Windows Millennium Edition, Windows 2000, Windows XP Home Edition, Windows XP Professional, Windows Server 2003 family, .NET Compact Framework - Windows CE .NET

DesignerCategoryAttribute.Generic Field

Specifies that a component marked with this category use a generic designer. This static (**Shared** in Visual Basic) field is read-only.

```
[Visual Basic]
Public Shared ReadOnly Generic As DesignerCategoryAttribute
[C#]
public static readonly DesignerCategoryAttribute Generic;
[C++]
public: static DesignerCategoryAttribute* Generic;
[JScript]
public static var Generic : DesignerCategoryAttribute;
```

Requirements

Platforms: Windows 98, Windows NT 4.0, Windows Millennium Edition, Windows 2000, Windows XP Home Edition, Windows XP Professional, Windows Server 2003 family, .NET Compact Framework - Windows CE .NET

DesignerCategoryAttribute.Category Property

Gets the name of the category.

```
[Visual Basic]
Public ReadOnly Property Category As String
[C#]
public string Category {get;}
[C++]
public: __property String* get_Category();
[JScript]
public function get Category() : String;
```

Property Value

The name of the category.

Requirements

Platforms: Windows 98, Windows NT 4.0, Windows Millennium Edition, Windows 2000, Windows XP Home Edition, Windows XP Professional, Windows Server 2003 family, .NET Compact Framework - Windows CE .NET

DesignerCategoryAttribute.TypeId Property

This member overrides **Attribute.TypeId**.

```
[Visual Basic]
Overrides Public ReadOnly Property TypeId As Object
[C#]
public override object TypeId {get;}
[C++]
public: __property Object* get_TypeId();
[JScript]
public override function get TypeId() : Object;
```

Requirements

Platforms: Windows 98, Windows NT 4.0, Windows Millennium Edition, Windows 2000, Windows XP Home Edition, Windows XP Professional, Windows Server 2003 family

DesignerCategoryAttribute.Equals Method

This member overrides **Object.Equals**.

```
[Visual Basic]
Overrides Public Function Equals( _
   ByVal obj As Object _
) As Boolean
[C#]
public override bool Equals(
   object obj
);
[C++]
public: bool Equals(
   Object* obj
);
[JScript]
public override function Equals(
   obj : Object
) : Boolean;
```

Requirements

Platforms: Windows 98, Windows NT 4.0, Windows Millennium Edition, Windows 2000, Windows XP Home Edition, Windows XP Professional, Windows Server 2003 family, .NET Compact Framework - Windows CE .NET

DesignerCategoryAttribute.GetHashCode Method

This member overrides **Attribute.GetHashCode**.

[Visual Basic]
```
Overrides Public Function GetHashCode() As Integer
```
[C#]
```
public override int GetHashCode();
```
[C++]
```
public: int GetHashCode();
```
[JScript]
```
public override function GetHashCode() : int;
```

Requirements

Platforms: Windows 98, Windows NT 4.0, Windows Millennium Edition, Windows 2000, Windows XP Home Edition, Windows XP Professional, Windows Server 2003 family, .NET Compact Framework - Windows CE .NET

DesignerCategoryAttribute.IsDefaultAttribute Method

This member overrides **Attribute.IsDefaultAttribute**.

[Visual Basic]
```
Overrides Public Function IsDefaultAttribute() As Boolean
```
[C#]
```
public override bool IsDefaultAttribute();
```
[C++]
```
public: bool IsDefaultAttribute();
```
[JScript]
```
public override function IsDefaultAttribute() : Boolean;
```

Requirements

Platforms: Windows 98, Windows NT 4.0, Windows Millennium Edition, Windows 2000, Windows XP Home Edition, Windows XP Professional, Windows Server 2003 family

DesignerSerializationVisibility Enumeration

Specifies the visibility a property has to the design-time serializer.

[Visual Basic]
```
<Serializable>
<ComVisible(True)>
Public Enum DesignerSerializationVisibility
```
[C#]
```
[Serializable]
[ComVisible(true)]
public enum DesignerSerializationVisibility
```
[C++]
```
[Serializable]
[ComVisible(true)]
__value public enum DesignerSerializationVisibility
```
[JScript]
```
public
   Serializable
   ComVisible(true)
enum DesignerSerializationVisibility
```

Remarks

A visual designer uses a **DesignerSerializationVisibility** value to indicate which aspects of the property or event should be examined and saved.

Members

Member name	Description
Content	The code generator produces code for the contents of the object, rather than for the object itself.
Hidden	The code generator does not produce code for the object.
Visible	The code generator produces code for the object.

Example

For an example of using the **DesignerSerializationVisibility** enumerator, please see the sample code at **DesignerSerializationVisibilityAttribute**.

Requirements

Namespace: System.ComponentModel

Platforms: Windows 98, Windows NT 4.0, Windows Millennium Edition, Windows 2000, Windows XP Home Edition, Windows XP Professional, Windows Server 2003 family

Assembly: System (in System.dll)

DesignerSerializationVisibility Attribute Class

Specifies the type of persistence to use when serializing a property on a component at design time.

System.Object
  System.Attribute
    System.ComponentModel.DesignerSerializationVisibility-Attribute

[Visual Basic]
```
<AttributeUsage(AttributeTargets.Method Or _
   AttributeTargets.Property)>
NotInheritable Public Class _
   DesignerSerializationVisibilityAttribute
   Inherits Attribute
```
[C#]
```
[AttributeUsage(AttributeTargets.Method |
   AttributeTargets.Property)]
public sealed class DesignerSerializationVisibilityAttribute :
   Attribute
```
[C++]
```
[AttributeUsage(AttributeTargets::Method |
   AttributeTargets::Property)]
public __gc __sealed class
   DesignerSerializationVisibilityAttribute : public Attribute
```
[JScript]
```
public
   AttributeUsage(AttributeTargets.Method | AttributeTargets.Property)
class DesignerSerializationVisibilityAttribute extends
   Attribute
```

Thread Safety

Any public static (**Shared** in Visual Basic) members of this type are safe for multithreaded operations. Any instance members are not guaranteed to be thread safe.

Remarks

When the design time environment saves a project, it often adds code to the initialization method of components in order to persist values of properties that have been set at design time. This happens by default for most basic types, if no attribute has been set to direct other behavior.

The **DesignerSerializationVisibilityAttribute** allows you to indicate whether the value for a property is **Visible**, and should be persisted in initialization code, **Hidden**, and should not be persisted in initialization code, or consists of **Content**, which should have initialization code generated for each public, not hidden property of the object assigned to the property.

Members that do not have a **DesignerSerializationVisibilityAttribute** will be treated as though they have a **DesignerSerializationVisibilityAttribute** with a value of **Visible**. The values of a property marked as **Visible** will be serialized, if possible, by a serializer for the type. To specify custom serialization for a particular type or property, use the **DesignerSerializerAttribute**.

Example

[Visual Basic, C#] The following example demonstrates use of a **DesignerSerializationVisibilityAttribute** set to **Content**, to persist the values of a public property of a user control, which can be configured at design time. To use the example, first compile the following code into a user control library. Next add a reference in a new project to the compiled .DLL file, add the control from the .DLL file to the Toolbox in design mode by right clicking the toolbox, selecting Customize Toolbox..., and selecting the control from the .DLL file containing the user control. Then drag the control from the toolbox to a Form, and set the properties of the DimensionData object listed in the property grid while the control is selected. When you view the code for the form, code will have been added to the InitializeComponent method of the parent form of the control which sets the values of the properties of the control to those which you have set in design mode.

[Visual Basic]
```
Imports System
Imports System.Collections
Imports System.ComponentModel
Imports System.ComponentModel.Design
Imports System.Drawing
Imports System.Windows.Forms

Namespace DesignerSerializationVisibilityTest

    ' The code for this user control declares a public property ↵
 of type DimensionData with a DesignerSerializationVisibility
    ' attribute set to DesignerSerializationVisibility.Content, ↵
indicating that the properties of the object should be serialized.

    ' The public, not hidden properties of the object that are ↵
 set at design time will be persisted in the initialization code
    ' for the class object. Content persistence will not work ↵
for structs without a custom TypeConverter.
    Public Class ContentSerializationExampleControl
        Inherits System.Windows.Forms.UserControl
        Private components As System.ComponentModel.Container = Nothing

        <DesignerSerializationVisibility ↵
 (DesignerSerializationVisibility.Content)> _
        Public ReadOnly Property Dimensions() As DimensionData
            Get
                Return New DimensionData(Me)
            End Get
        End Property

        Public Sub New()
            InitializeComponent()
        End Sub 'New

        Protected Overloads Sub Dispose(ByVal disposing As Boolean)
            If disposing Then
                If Not (components Is Nothing) Then
                    components.Dispose()
                End If
            End If
            MyBase.Dispose(disposing)
        End Sub 'Dispose

        Private Sub InitializeComponent()
        End Sub 'InitializeComponent
    End Class 'ContentSerializationExampleControl

    ' This attribute indicates that the public properties of ↵
 this object should be listed in the property grid.
   <TypeConverterAttribute(GetType ↵
(System.ComponentModel.ExpandableObjectConverter))> _
    Public Class DimensionData
        Private owner As Control

        ' This class reads and writes the Location and Size ↵
 properties from the Control which it is initialized to.
        Friend Sub New(ByVal owner As Control)
            Me.owner = owner
        End Sub 'New
```

```
        Public Property Location() As Point
            Get
                Return owner.Location
            End Get
            Set(ByVal Value As Point)
                owner.Location = Value
            End Set
        End Property

        Public Property FormSize() As Size
            Get
                Return owner.Size
            End Get
            Set(ByVal Value As Size)
                owner.Size = Value
            End Set
        End Property
    End Class 'DimensionData
End Namespace 'DesignerSerializationVisibilityTest
```

[C#]

```
using System;
using System.Collections;
using System.ComponentModel;
using System.ComponentModel.Design;
using System.Drawing;
using System.Windows.Forms;

namespace DesignerSerializationVisibilityTest
{
    // The code for this user control declares a public property ↵
of type DimensionData with a DesignerSerializationVisibility
    // attribute set to DesignerSerializationVisibility.Content, ↵
indicating that the properties of the object should be serialized.

    // The public, not hidden properties of the object that are ↵
set at design time will be persisted in the initialization code
    // for the class object. Content persistence will not work ↵
for structs without a custom TypeConverter.

    public class ContentSerializationExampleControl : ↵
System.Windows.Forms.UserControl
    {
    private System.ComponentModel.Container components = null;

    [DesignerSerializationVisibility ↵
 (DesignerSerializationVisibility.Content)]
    public DimensionData Dimensions
    {
        get
        {
        return new DimensionData(this);
        }
    }

    public ContentSerializationExampleControl()
    {
            InitializeComponent();
    }

    protected override void Dispose( bool disposing )
    {
        if( disposing )
        {
        if( components != null )
            components.Dispose();
        }
        base.Dispose( disposing );
    }

    private void InitializeComponent()
    {
        components = new System.ComponentModel.Container();
    }
    }

    [TypeConverterAttribute(typeof ↵
(System.ComponentModel.ExpandableObjectConverter))]
    // This attribute indicates that the public properties ↵
of this object should be listed in the property grid.
    public class DimensionData
    {
    private Control owner;

    // This class reads and writes the Location and Size ↵
 properties from the Control which it is initialized to.
    internal DimensionData(Control owner)
    {
            this.owner = owner;
    }

    public Point Location
    {
        get
        {
        return owner.Location;
        }
        set
        {
        owner.Location = value;
        }
    }

    public Size FormSize
    {
        get
            {
        return owner.Size;
        }
        set
        {
        owner.Size = value;
        }
    }
    }
}
```

Requirements

Namespace: **System.ComponentModel**

Platforms: Windows 98, Windows NT 4.0, Windows Millennium Edition, Windows 2000, Windows XP Home Edition, Windows XP Professional, Windows Server 2003 family

Assembly: System (in System.dll)

DesignerSerializationVisibilityAttribute Constructor

Initializes a new instance of the **DesignerSerializationVisibilityAttribute** class.

[Visual Basic]

```
Public Sub New( _
   ByVal visibility As DesignerSerializationVisibility _
)
```

[C#]

```
public DesignerSerializationVisibilityAttribute(
   DesignerSerializationVisibility visibility
);
```

[C++]

```
public: DesignerSerializationVisibilityAttribute(
   DesignerSerializationVisibility visibility
);
```

[JScript]
```
public function DesignerSerializationVisibilityAttribute(
   visibility : DesignerSerializationVisibility
);
```

Parameters

visibility
One of the **DesignerSerializationVisibility** values.

Example

[Visual Basic, C#] The following example specifies how a property on a component is saved by a designer. This code creates a new **DesignerSerializationVisibilityAttribute** and sets its value to **DesignerSerializationVisibilityAttribute.Content**.

[Visual Basic]
```
<DesignerSerializationVisibility ↵
 (DesignerSerializationVisibility.Content)> _
Public Property _
    MyProperty() As Integer

    Get
        ' Insert code here.
        Return 0
    End Get
    Set
        ' Insert code here.
    End Set
End Property
```

[C#]
```
[DesignerSerializationVisibility ↵
 (DesignerSerializationVisibility.Content)]
 public int MyProperty {
    get {
       // Insert code here.
       return(0);
    }
    set {
       // Insert code here.
    }
 }
```

Requirements

Platforms: Windows 98, Windows NT 4.0, Windows Millennium Edition, Windows 2000, Windows XP Home Edition, Windows XP Professional, Windows Server 2003 family

DesignerSerializationVisibilityAttribute.Content Field

Specifies that a visual designer serialize the contents of this property, rather than the property itself. This field is read-only.

[Visual Basic]
```
Public Shared ReadOnly Content As _
   DesignerSerializationVisibilityAttribute
```
[C#]
```
public static readonly DesignerSerializationVisibilityAttribute
   Content;
```
[C++]
```
public: static DesignerSerializationVisibilityAttribute* Content;
```
[JScript]
```
public static var Content :
   DesignerSerializationVisibilityAttribute;
```

Remarks

When you mark a property with **DesignerSerializationVisibility-Attribute.Content**, the value of this attribute is set to the constant member **Content**. Therefore, when you want to verify that the attribute is set to this value in your code, you must specify the attribute as **DesignerSerializationVisibilityAttribute.Content**.

Requirements

Platforms: Windows 98, Windows NT 4.0, Windows Millennium Edition, Windows 2000, Windows XP Home Edition, Windows XP Professional, Windows Server 2003 family

DesignerSerializationVisibilityAttribute.Default Field

This member supports the .NET Framework infrastructure and is not intended to be used directly from your code.

[Visual Basic]
```
Public Shared ReadOnly Default As _
   DesignerSerializationVisibilityAttribute
```
[C#]
```
public static readonly DesignerSerializationVisibilityAttribute
   Default;
```
[C++]
```
public: static DesignerSerializationVisibilityAttribute* Default;
```
[JScript]
```
public static var Default :
   DesignerSerializationVisibilityAttribute;
```

DesignerSerializationVisibilityAttribute.Hidden Field

Specifies that a visual designer does not serialize the value of this property. This static (**Shared** in Visual Basic) field is read-only.

[Visual Basic]
```
Public Shared ReadOnly Hidden As _
   DesignerSerializationVisibilityAttribute
```
[C#]
```
public static readonly DesignerSerializationVisibilityAttribute
   Hidden;
```
[C++]
```
public: static DesignerSerializationVisibilityAttribute* Hidden;
```
[JScript]
```
public static var Hidden :
   DesignerSerializationVisibilityAttribute;
```

Remarks

When you mark a property with **DesignerSerializationVisibility-Attribute.Hidden**, the value of this attribute is set to the constant member **Hidden**. Therefore, when you want to verify that the attribute is set to this value in your code, you must specify the attribute as **DesignerSerializationVisibilityAttribute.Hidden**.

Requirements

Platforms: Windows 98, Windows NT 4.0, Windows Millennium Edition, Windows 2000, Windows XP Home Edition, Windows XP Professional, Windows Server 2003 family

DesignerSerializationVisibilityAttribute.Visible Field

Specifies that a visual designer can use default rules when serializing the value of a property. This static (**Shared** in Visual Basic) field is read-only.

[Visual Basic]
```
Public Shared ReadOnly Visible As _
   DesignerSerializationVisibilityAttribute
```
[C#]
```
public static readonly DesignerSerializationVisibilityAttribute
   Visible;
```
[C++]
```
public: static DesignerSerializationVisibilityAttribute* Visible;
```
[JScript]
```
public static var Visible :
   DesignerSerializationVisibilityAttribute;
```

Remarks

This field is the default setting for this attribute.

When you mark a property with **DesignerSerializationVisibilityAttribute.Visible**, the value of this attribute is set to the constant member **Visible**. Therefore, when you want to verify that the attribute is set to this value in your code, you must specify the attribute as **DesignerSerializationVisibilityAttribute.Visible**.

Requirements

Platforms: Windows 98, Windows NT 4.0, Windows Millennium Edition, Windows 2000, Windows XP Home Edition, Windows XP Professional, Windows Server 2003 family

DesignerSerializationVisibilityAttribute.Visibility Property

Gets a value indicating whether a visual designer must generate special code to persist the value of a property.

[Visual Basic]
```
Public ReadOnly Property Visibility As _
   DesignerSerializationVisibility
```
[C#]
```
public DesignerSerializationVisibility Visibility {get;}
```
[C++]
```
public: __property DesignerSerializationVisibility get_Visibility();
```
[JScript]
```
public function get Visibility() : DesignerSerializationVisibility;
```

Property Value

One of the **DesignerSerializationVisibility** values. The default is **Visible**.

Example

[Visual Basic, C#] The following example shows how to check the value of the **DesignerSerializationVisibilityAttribute** for `MyProperty`. First the code gets a **PropertyDescriptorCollection** with all the properties for the object. Next, the code indexes into the **PropertyDescriptorCollection** to get `MyProperty`. Then, the code returns the attributes for this property and saves them in the attributes variable.

[Visual Basic, C#] This example presents two different ways to check the value of the **DesignerSerializationVisibilityAttribute**. In the second code fragment, the example calls the **Equals** method with a static (**Shared** in Visual Basic) value. In the last code fragment, the example uses the **Visibility** property to check the value.

[Visual Basic]
```
' Gets the attributes for the property.
Dim attributes As AttributeCollection = _
    TypeDescriptor.GetProperties(Me)("MyProperty").Attributes

' Checks to see if the value of the                              ↵
DesignerSerializationVisibilityAttribute
' is set to Content.
If attributes(GetType(DesignerSerializationVisibilityAttribute)).Equals(
_
    DesignerSerializationVisibilityAttribute.Content) Then
    ' Insert code here.
End If

' This is another way to see whether the property is marked        ↵
as serializing content.
Dim myAttribute As DesignerSerializationVisibilityAttribute = _
   CType(attributes(GetType(DesignerSerializationVisibilityAttribute)),
_
    DesignerSerializationVisibilityAttribute)
If myAttribute.Visibility =                                      ↵
DesignerSerializationVisibility.Content Then
    ' Insert code here.
End If
```

[C#]
```
// Gets the attributes for the property.
 AttributeCollection attributes =
    TypeDescriptor.GetProperties(this)["MyProperty"].Attributes;

 // Checks to see if the value of the                             ↵
DesignerSerializationVisibilityAttribute is set to Content.

if(attributes[typeof(DesignerSerializationVisibilityAttribute)].Equals(D
esignerSerializationVisibilityAttribute.Content)) {
    // Insert code here.
 }

 // This is another way to see whether the property is marked as    ↵
serializing content.
 DesignerSerializationVisibilityAttribute myAttribute =
    (DesignerSerializationVisibilityAttribute)attributes[typeof     ↵
(DesignerSerializationVisibilityAttribute)];
 if(myAttribute.Visibility ==                                     ↵
DesignerSerializationVisibility.Content) {
    // Insert code here.
 }
```

Requirements

Platforms: Windows 98, Windows NT 4.0, Windows Millennium Edition, Windows 2000, Windows XP Home Edition, Windows XP Professional, Windows Server 2003 family

DesignerSerializationVisibilityAttribute.Equals Method

This member overrides **Object.Equals**.

[Visual Basic]
```
Overrides Public Function Equals( _
   ByVal obj As Object _
) As Boolean
```
[C#]
```
public override bool Equals(
   object obj
);
```
[C++]
```
public: bool Equals(
   Object* obj
);
```
[JScript]
```
public override function Equals(
   obj : Object
) : Boolean;
```

Requirements

Platforms: Windows 98, Windows NT 4.0, Windows Millennium Edition, Windows 2000, Windows XP Home Edition, Windows XP Professional, Windows Server 2003 family

DesignerSerializationVisibilityAttribute.GetHashCode Method

This member overrides **Attribute.GetHashCode**.

[Visual Basic]
```
Overrides Public Function GetHashCode() As Integer
```
[C#]
```
public override int GetHashCode();
```
[C++]
```
public: int GetHashCode();
```
[JScript]
```
public override function GetHashCode() : int;
```

Requirements

Platforms: Windows 98, Windows NT 4.0, Windows Millennium Edition, Windows 2000, Windows XP Home Edition, Windows XP Professional, Windows Server 2003 family

DesignerSerializationVisibilityAttribute.IsDefaultAttribute Method

This member overrides **Attribute.IsDefaultAttribute**.

[Visual Basic]
```
Overrides Public Function IsDefaultAttribute() As Boolean
```
[C#]
```
public override bool IsDefaultAttribute();
```
[C++]
```
public: bool IsDefaultAttribute();
```
[JScript]
```
public override function IsDefaultAttribute() : Boolean;
```

Requirements

Platforms: Windows 98, Windows NT 4.0, Windows Millennium Edition, Windows 2000, Windows XP Home Edition, Windows XP Professional, Windows Server 2003 family

DesignOnlyAttribute Class

Specifies whether a property can only be set at design time.

System.Object
  System.Attribute
    System.ComponentModel.DesignOnlyAttribute

[Visual Basic]
```
<AttributeUsage(AttributeTargets.All)>
NotInheritable Public Class DesignOnlyAttribute
   Inherits Attribute
```
[C#]
```
[AttributeUsage(AttributeTargets.All)]
public sealed class DesignOnlyAttribute : Attribute
```
[C++]
```
[AttributeUsage(AttributeTargets::All)]
public __gc __sealed class DesignOnlyAttribute : public Attribute
```
[JScript]
```
public
   AttributeUsage(AttributeTargets.All)
class DesignOnlyAttribute extends Attribute
```

Thread Safety

Any public static (**Shared** in Visual Basic) members of this type are safe for multithreaded operations. Any instance members are not guaranteed to be thread safe.

Remarks

Members marked with the **DesignOnlyAttribute** constructor of the value **true** can be set only at design time. Typically, these properties exist only at design time and do not correspond to a real property on the object at run time.

Members that either have no attribute or are marked with the **DesignOnlyAttribute** constructor of the value **false** can be set during run time. The default is **false**.

Example

[Visual Basic, C#] The following example creates a GetLanguage property. The property is marked with a **DesignOnlyAttribute**.

[Visual Basic]
```
<DesignOnly(True)> _
Public Property GetLanguage() As CultureInfo
    Get
        ' Insert code here.
        Return myCultureInfo
    End Get
    Set
        ' Insert code here.
    End Set
End Property
```

[C#]
```
[DesignOnly(true)]
 public CultureInfo GetLanguage {
    get {
       // Insert code here.
       return myCultureInfo;
    }
    set {
       // Insert code here.
    }
 }
```

[Visual Basic, C#] The next example gets the value of the **DesignOnlyAttribute**. First the code gets a **PropertyDescriptorCollection** with all the properties for the object. Next it indexes into the **PropertyDescriptorCollection** to find the GetLanguage property. Then it returns the attributes for this property and saves them in the attributes variable.

[Visual Basic, C#] The example then prints whether the property is design only by retrieving **DesignOnlyAttribute** from the **AttributeCollection**, and writing it to the console screen.

[Visual Basic]
```
' Gets the attributes for the property.
Dim attributes As AttributeCollection = _
    TypeDescriptor.GetProperties(Me)("GetLanguage").Attributes

' Prints the description by retrieving the DescriptionAttribute
' from the AttributeCollection.
Dim myAttribute As DesignOnlyAttribute = _
    CType(attributes(GetType(DesignOnlyAttribute)),            ↵
DesignOnlyAttribute)
Console.WriteLine(("This property is design only :" & _
    myAttribute.IsDesignOnly.ToString()))
```

[C#]
```
// Gets the attributes for the property.
 AttributeCollection attributes =
    TypeDescriptor.GetProperties(this)["GetLanguage"].Attributes;

 /* Prints the description by retrieving the DescriptionAttribute
  * from the AttributeCollection. */
 DesignOnlyAttribute myAttribute =
    (DesignOnlyAttribute)attributes[typeof(DesignOnlyAttribute)];
 Console.WriteLine("This property is design only :" +
    myAttribute.IsDesignOnly.ToString());
```

Requirements

Namespace: System.ComponentModel

Platforms: Windows 98, Windows NT 4.0, Windows Millennium Edition, Windows 2000, Windows XP Home Edition, Windows XP Professional, Windows .NET Server family

Assembly: System (in System.dll)

DesignOnlyAttribute Constructor

Initializes a new instance of the **DesignOnlyAttribute** class.

[Visual Basic]
```
Public Sub New( _
   ByVal isDesignOnly As Boolean _
)
```
[C#]
```
public DesignOnlyAttribute(
   bool isDesignOnly
);
```
[C++]
```
public: DesignOnlyAttribute(
   bool isDesignOnly
);
```
[JScript]
```
public function DesignOnlyAttribute(
   isDesignOnly : Boolean
);
```

Parameters

isDesignOnly
: **true** if a property can be set only at design time; **false** if the property can be set at design time and at run time.

Requirements

Platforms: Windows 98, Windows NT 4.0, Windows Millennium Edition, Windows 2000, Windows XP Home Edition, Windows XP Professional, Windows .NET Server family

DesignOnlyAttribute.Default Field

This member supports the .NET Framework infrastructure and is not intended to be used directly from your code.

```
[Visual Basic]
Public Shared ReadOnly Default As DesignOnlyAttribute
[C#]
public static readonly DesignOnlyAttribute Default;
[C++]
public: static DesignOnlyAttribute* Default;
[JScript]
public static var Default : DesignOnlyAttribute;
```

DesignOnlyAttribute.No Field

Specifies that a property can be set at design time or at run time. This static (**Shared** in Visual Basic) field is read-only.

```
[Visual Basic]
Public Shared ReadOnly No As DesignOnlyAttribute
[C#]
public static readonly DesignOnlyAttribute No;
[C++]
public: static DesignOnlyAttribute* No;
[JScript]
public static var No : DesignOnlyAttribute;
```

Remarks

The **No** field is the default setting for this attribute.

Requirements

Platforms: Windows 98, Windows NT 4.0, Windows Millennium Edition, Windows 2000, Windows XP Home Edition, Windows XP Professional, Windows .NET Server family

DesignOnlyAttribute.Yes Field

Specifies that a property can be set only at design time. This static (**Shared** in Visual Basic) field is read-only.

```
[Visual Basic]
Public Shared ReadOnly Yes As DesignOnlyAttribute
[C#]
public static readonly DesignOnlyAttribute Yes;
[C++]
public: static DesignOnlyAttribute* Yes;
[JScript]
public static var Yes : DesignOnlyAttribute;
```

Requirements

Platforms: Windows 98, Windows NT 4.0, Windows Millennium Edition, Windows 2000, Windows XP Home Edition, Windows XP Professional, Windows .NET Server family

DesignOnlyAttribute.IsDesignOnly Property

Gets a value indicating whether a property can be set only at design time.

```
[Visual Basic]
Public ReadOnly Property IsDesignOnly As Boolean
[C#]
public bool IsDesignOnly {get;}
[C++]
public: __property bool get_IsDesignOnly();
[JScript]
public function get IsDesignOnly() : Boolean;
```

Property Value

true if a property can be set only at design time; otherwise, **false**.

Requirements

Platforms: Windows 98, Windows NT 4.0, Windows Millennium Edition, Windows 2000, Windows XP Home Edition, Windows XP Professional, Windows .NET Server family

DesignOnlyAttribute.Equals Method

This member overrides **Object.Equals**.

```
[Visual Basic]
Overrides Public Function Equals( _
   ByVal obj As Object _
) As Boolean
[C#]
public override bool Equals(
   object obj
);
[C++]
public: bool Equals(
   Object* obj
);
[JScript]
public override function Equals(
   obj : Object
) : Boolean;
```

Requirements

Platforms: Windows 98, Windows NT 4.0, Windows Millennium Edition, Windows 2000, Windows XP Home Edition, Windows XP Professional, Windows .NET Server family

DesignOnlyAttribute.GetHashCode Method

This member overrides **Attribute.GetHashCode**.

```
[Visual Basic]
Overrides Public Function GetHashCode() As Integer
[C#]
public override int GetHashCode();
[C++]
public: int GetHashCode();
[JScript]
public override function GetHashCode() : int;
```

Requirements

Platforms: Windows 98, Windows NT 4.0, Windows Millennium Edition, Windows 2000, Windows XP Home Edition, Windows XP Professional, Windows .NET Server family

DesignOnlyAttribute.IsDefaultAttribute Method

This member overrides **Attribute.IsDefaultAttribute**.

[Visual Basic]
```
Overrides Public Function IsDefaultAttribute() As Boolean
```
[C#]
```
public override bool IsDefaultAttribute();
```
[C++]
```
public: bool IsDefaultAttribute();
```
[JScript]
```
public override function IsDefaultAttribute() : Boolean;
```

Requirements

Platforms: Windows 98, Windows NT 4.0, Windows Millennium Edition, Windows 2000, Windows XP Home Edition, Windows XP Professional, Windows .NET Server family

DesignTimeVisibleAttribute Class

DesignTimeVisibleAttribute marks a component's visibility. If **DesignTimeVisibleAttribute.Yes** is present, a visual designer can show this component on a designer.

System.Object
  System.Attribute
    System.ComponentModel.DesignTimeVisibleAttribute

```
[Visual Basic]
<AttributeUsage(AttributeTargets.Class Or _
   AttributeTargets.Interface)>
NotInheritable Public Class DesignTimeVisibleAttribute
   Inherits Attribute
[C#]
[AttributeUsage(AttributeTargets.Class |
   AttributeTargets.Interface)]
public sealed class DesignTimeVisibleAttribute : Attribute
[C++]
[AttributeUsage(AttributeTargets::Class |
   AttributeTargets::Interface)]
public __gc __sealed class DesignTimeVisibleAttribute : public
   Attribute
[JScript]
public
   AttributeUsage(AttributeTargets.Class | AttributeTargets.Interface)
class DesignTimeVisibleAttribute extends Attribute
```

Thread Safety

Any public static (**Shared** in Visual Basic) members of this type are safe for multithreaded operations. Any instance members are not guaranteed to be thread safe.

Requirements

Namespace: System.ComponentModel

Platforms: Windows 98, Windows NT 4.0, Windows Millennium Edition, Windows 2000, Windows XP Home Edition, Windows XP Professional, Windows Server 2003 family

Assembly: System (in System.dll)

DesignTimeVisibleAttribute Constructor

Overload List

Creates a new **DesignTimeVisibleAttribute** set to the default value of **true**.

[Visual Basic] **Public Sub New()**

[C#] **public DesignTimeVisibleAttribute();**

[C++] **public: DesignTimeVisibleAttribute();**

[JScript] **public function DesignTimeVisibleAttribute();**

Creates a new **DesignTimeVisibleAttribute** with the **Visible** property set to the given value in *visible*.

[Visual Basic] **Public Sub New(Boolean)**

[C#] **public DesignTimeVisibleAttribute(bool);**

[C++] **public: DesignTimeVisibleAttribute(bool);**

[JScript] **public function DesignTimeVisibleAttribute(Boolean);**

DesignTimeVisibleAttribute Constructor ()

Creates a new **DesignTimeVisibleAttribute** set to the default value of **true**.

```
[Visual Basic]
Public Sub New()
[C#]
public DesignTimeVisibleAttribute();
[C++]
public: DesignTimeVisibleAttribute();
[JScript]
public function DesignTimeVisibleAttribute();
```

Requirements

Platforms: Windows 98, Windows NT 4.0, Windows Millennium Edition, Windows 2000, Windows XP Home Edition, Windows XP Professional, Windows Server 2003 family

DesignTimeVisibleAttribute Constructor (Boolean)

Creates a new **DesignTimeVisibleAttribute** with the **Visible** property set to the given value in *visible*.

```
[Visual Basic]
Public Sub New( _
   ByVal visible As Boolean _
)
[C#]
public DesignTimeVisibleAttribute(
   bool visible
);
[C++]
public: DesignTimeVisibleAttribute(
   bool visible
);
[JScript]
public function DesignTimeVisibleAttribute(
   visible : Boolean
);
```

Parameters

visible
  The value that the **Visible** property will be set against.

Requirements

Platforms: Windows 98, Windows NT 4.0, Windows Millennium Edition, Windows 2000, Windows XP Home Edition, Windows XP Professional, Windows Server 2003 family

DesignTimeVisibleAttribute.Default Field

The default visibility which is **Yes**.

```
[Visual Basic]
Public Shared ReadOnly Default As DesignTimeVisibleAttribute
[C#]
public static readonly DesignTimeVisibleAttribute Default;
[C++]
public: static DesignTimeVisibleAttribute* Default;
[JScript]
public static var Default : DesignTimeVisibleAttribute;
```

Requirements

Platforms: Windows 98, Windows NT 4.0, Windows Millennium Edition, Windows 2000, Windows XP Home Edition, Windows XP Professional, Windows Server 2003 family

DesignTimeVisibleAttribute.No Field

Marks a component as not visible in a visual designer.

[Visual Basic]
```
Public Shared ReadOnly No As DesignTimeVisibleAttribute
```
[C#]
```
public static readonly DesignTimeVisibleAttribute No;
```
[C++]
```
public: static DesignTimeVisibleAttribute* No;
```
[JScript]
```
public static var No : DesignTimeVisibleAttribute;
```

Requirements

Platforms: Windows 98, Windows NT 4.0, Windows Millennium Edition, Windows 2000, Windows XP Home Edition, Windows XP Professional, Windows Server 2003 family

DesignTimeVisibleAttribute.Yes Field

Marks a component as visible in a visual designer.

[Visual Basic]
```
Public Shared ReadOnly Yes As DesignTimeVisibleAttribute
```
[C#]
```
public static readonly DesignTimeVisibleAttribute Yes;
```
[C++]
```
public: static DesignTimeVisibleAttribute* Yes;
```
[JScript]
```
public static var Yes : DesignTimeVisibleAttribute;
```

Requirements

Platforms: Windows 98, Windows NT 4.0, Windows Millennium Edition, Windows 2000, Windows XP Home Edition, Windows XP Professional, Windows Server 2003 family

DesignTimeVisibleAttribute.Visible Property

Gets or sets whether the component should be shown at design time.

[Visual Basic]
```
Public ReadOnly Property Visible As Boolean
```
[C#]
```
public bool Visible {get;}
```
[C++]
```
public: __property bool get_Visible();
```
[JScript]
```
public function get Visible() : Boolean;
```

Property Value

True if this component should be shown at design time, or **false** if it shouldn't.

Requirements

Platforms: Windows 98, Windows NT 4.0, Windows Millennium Edition, Windows 2000, Windows XP Home Edition, Windows XP Professional, Windows Server 2003 family

DesignTimeVisibleAttribute.Equals Method

This member overrides **Object.Equals**.

[Visual Basic]
```
Overrides Public Function Equals( _
   ByVal obj As Object _
) As Boolean
```
[C#]
```
public override bool Equals(
   object obj
);
```
[C++]
```
public: bool Equals(
   Object* obj
);
```
[JScript]
```
public override function Equals(
   obj : Object
) : Boolean;
```

Requirements

Platforms: Windows 98, Windows NT 4.0, Windows Millennium Edition, Windows 2000, Windows XP Home Edition, Windows XP Professional, Windows Server 2003 family

DesignTimeVisibleAttribute.GetHashCode Method

This member overrides **Attribute.GetHashCode**.

[Visual Basic]
```
Overrides Public Function GetHashCode() As Integer
```
[C#]
```
public override int GetHashCode();
```
[C++]
```
public: int GetHashCode();
```
[JScript]
```
public override function GetHashCode() : int;
```

Requirements

Platforms: Windows 98, Windows NT 4.0, Windows Millennium Edition, Windows 2000, Windows XP Home Edition, Windows XP Professional, Windows Server 2003 family

DesignTimeVisibleAttribute.IsDefaultAttribute Method

This member overrides **Attribute.IsDefaultAttribute**.

[Visual Basic]
```
Overrides Public Function IsDefaultAttribute() As Boolean
```
[C#]
```
public override bool IsDefaultAttribute();
```
[C++]
```
public: bool IsDefaultAttribute();
```
[JScript]
```
public override function IsDefaultAttribute() : Boolean;
```

Requirements

Platforms: Windows 98, Windows NT 4.0, Windows Millennium Edition, Windows 2000, Windows XP Home Edition, Windows XP Professional, Windows Server 2003 family

DoubleConverter Class

Provides a type converter to convert double-precision, floating point number objects to and from various other representations.

System.Object
  System.ComponentModel.TypeConverter
    System.ComponentModel.BaseNumberConverter
      System.ComponentModel.DoubleConverter

[Visual Basic]
```
Public Class DoubleConverter
   Inherits BaseNumberConverter
```
[C#]
```
public class DoubleConverter : BaseNumberConverter
```
[C++]
```
public __gc class DoubleConverter : public BaseNumberConverter
```
[JScript]
```
public class DoubleConverter extends BaseNumberConverter
```

Thread Safety

Any public static (**Shared** in Visual Basic) members of this type are safe for multithreaded operations. Any instance members are not guaranteed to be thread safe.

Remarks

This converter can only convert a **Double** object to and from a string.

> **Note** You should never create an instance of **DoubleConverter**. Instead, call the **GetConverter** method of **TypeDescriptor**. For more information, see the examples in the **TypeConverter** base class.

Example

[Visual Basic, C#, C++] The following sample converts a variable of type **Double** to a string, and vice versa.

[Visual Basic]
```
Dim myDoub As Double = 100.55
Dim myDoStr As String = "4000.425"
Console.WriteLine(TypeDescriptor.GetConverter(myDoub).ConvertTo ↵
(myDoub, GetType(String)))
Console.WriteLine(TypeDescriptor.GetConverter(myDoub).ConvertFrom ↵
 (myDoStr))
```

[C#]
```
double myDoub = 100.55;
string myDoStr = "4000.425";
Console.WriteLine(TypeDescriptor.GetConverter(myDoub).ConvertTo ↵
 (myDoub, typeof(string)));
Console.WriteLine(TypeDescriptor.GetConverter(myDoub).ConvertFrom ↵
 (myDoStr));
```

[C++]
```
double myDoub( 100.55 );
String* myDoStr = S"4000.425";
Console::WriteLine(TypeDescriptor::GetConverter(__box(myDoub))- ↵
>ConvertTo(__box(myDoub), __typeof(String)));
Console::WriteLine(TypeDescriptor::GetConverter(__box(myDoub))- ↵
>ConvertFrom(myDoStr));
```

Requirements

Namespace: System.ComponentModel

Platforms: Windows 98, Windows NT 4.0, Windows Millennium Edition, Windows 2000, Windows XP Home Edition, Windows XP Professional, Windows Server 2003 family

Assembly: System (in System.dll)

DoubleConverter Constructor

Initializes a new instance of the **DoubleConverter** class.

[Visual Basic]
```
Public Sub New()
```
[C#]
```
public DoubleConverter();
```
[C++]
```
public: DoubleConverter();
```
[JScript]
```
public function DoubleConverter();
```

Remarks

The default constructor initializes any fields to their default values.

Requirements

Platforms: Windows 98, Windows NT 4.0, Windows Millennium Edition, Windows 2000, Windows XP Home Edition, Windows XP Professional, Windows Server 2003 family

EditorAttribute Class

Specifies the editor to use to change a property. This class cannot be inherited.

System.Object
  System.Attribute
    System.ComponentModel.EditorAttribute

[Visual Basic]
```
<AttributeUsage(AttributeTargets.All)>
NotInheritable Public Class EditorAttribute
   Inherits Attribute
```
[C#]
```
[AttributeUsage(AttributeTargets.All)]
public sealed class EditorAttribute : Attribute
```
[C++]
```
[AttributeUsage(AttributeTargets::All)]
public __gc __sealed class EditorAttribute : public Attribute
```
[JScript]
```
public
   AttributeUsage(AttributeTargets.All)
class EditorAttribute extends Attribute
```

Thread Safety

Any public static (**Shared** in Visual Basic) members of this type are safe for multithreaded operations. Any instance members are not guaranteed to be thread safe.

Remarks

When editing the property, a visual designer should create a new instance of the specified editor through a dialog box or drop-down window.

Use the **EditorBaseTypeName** property to find this editor's base type. The only available base type is **UITypeEditor**.

Use the **EditorTypeName** property to get the name of the type of editor associated with this attribute.

For general information on using attributes. see **Attributes Overview** and **Extending Metadata Using Attributes**. For more information on design-time attributes, see **Attributes and Design-Time Support**.

Example

[Visual Basic, C#] The following example creates the `MyImage` class. The class is marked with an **EditorAttribute** that specifies the **ImageEditor** as its editor.

[Visual Basic]
```
<Editor("System.Windows.Forms.ImageEditorIndex, System.Design", _
    GetType(UITypeEditor))> _
Public Class MyImage
    ' Insert code here.
End Class 'MyImage
```

[C#]
```
[Editor("System.Windows.Forms.ImageEditorIndex, System.Design",
    typeof(UITypeEditor))]

public class MyImage
{
    // Insert code here.
 }
```

[Visual Basic, C#] The next example creates an instance of the `MyImage` class. Then it gets the attributes for the class, and prints the name of the editor used by `myNewImage`.

[Visual Basic]
```
Public Shared Sub Main()
    ' Creates a new component.
    Dim myNewImage As New MyImage()

    ' Gets the attributes for the component.
    Dim attributes As AttributeCollection =
TypeDescriptor.GetAttributes(myNewImage)

    ' Prints the name of the editor by retrieving the EditorAttribute
    ' from the AttributeCollection.

    Dim myAttribute As EditorAttribute =                                ↵
CType(attributes(GetType(EditorAttribute)), EditorAttribute)
    Console.WriteLine(("The editor for this class is: " &               ↵
myAttribute.EditorTypeName))

End Sub 'Main
```

[C#]
```
public static int Main() {
    // Creates a new component.
    MyImage myNewImage = new MyImage();

    // Gets the attributes for the component.
    AttributeCollection attributes =
TypeDescriptor.GetAttributes(myNewImage);

    /* Prints the name of the editor by retrieving the EditorAttribute
     * from the AttributeCollection. */

    EditorAttribute myAttribute =                                       ↵
 (EditorAttribute)attributes[typeof(EditorAttribute)];
    Console.WriteLine("The editor for this class is: " +                ↵
myAttribute.EditorTypeName);

    return 0;
 }
```

Requirements

Namespace: System.ComponentModel

Platforms: Windows 98, Windows NT 4.0, Windows Millennium Edition, Windows 2000, Windows XP Home Edition, Windows XP Professional, Windows .NET Server family

Assembly: System (in System.dll)

EditorAttribute Constructor

Initializes a new instance of the **EditorAttribute** class.

Overload List

Initializes a new instance of the **EditorAttribute** class with the default editor, which is no editor.

[Visual Basic] **Public Sub New()**

[C#] **public EditorAttribute();**

[C++] **public: EditorAttribute();**

[JScript] **public function EditorAttribute();**

Initializes a new instance of the **EditorAttribute** class with the type name and base type name of the editor.

[Visual Basic] **Public Sub New(String, String)**

[C#] **public EditorAttribute(string, string);**

[C++] **public: EditorAttribute(String*, String*);**

[JScript] **public function EditorAttribute(String, String);**

Initializes a new instance of the **EditorAttribute** class with the type name and the base type.

[Visual Basic] **Public Sub New(String, Type)**

[C#] **public EditorAttribute(string, Type);**

[C++] **public: EditorAttribute(String*, Type*);**

[JScript] **public function EditorAttribute(String, Type);**

Initializes a new instance of the **EditorAttribute** class with the type and the base type.

[Visual Basic] **Public Sub New(Type, Type)**

[C#] **public EditorAttribute(Type, Type);**

[C++] **public: EditorAttribute(Type*, Type*);**

[JScript] **public function EditorAttribute(Type, Type);**

EditorAttribute Constructor ()

Initializes a new instance of the **EditorAttribute** class with the default editor, which is no editor.

```
[Visual Basic]
Public Sub New()
[C#]
public EditorAttribute();
[C++]
public: EditorAttribute();
[JScript]
public function EditorAttribute();
```

Requirements

Platforms: Windows 98, Windows NT 4.0, Windows Millennium Edition, Windows 2000, Windows XP Home Edition, Windows XP Professional, Windows .NET Server family

EditorAttribute Constructor (String, String)

Initializes a new instance of the **EditorAttribute** class with the type name and base type name of the editor.

```
[Visual Basic]
Public Sub New( _
   ByVal typeName As String, _
   ByVal baseTypeName As String _
)
[C#]
public EditorAttribute(
   string typeName,
   string baseTypeName
);
[C++]
public: EditorAttribute(
   String* typeName,
   String* baseTypeName
);
[JScript]
public function EditorAttribute(
   typeName : String,
   baseTypeName : String
);
```

Parameters

typeName

The fully qualified type name of the editor.

baseTypeName

The fully qualified type name of the base class or interface to use as a lookup key for the editor. This class must be or derive from **UITypeEditor**.

Remarks

The *typeName* parameter must be in the **Type.AssemblyQualifiedName** format.

The **Type** represented by the *typeName* parameter must either derive from or implement the base class.

The **Type** represented by the *baseTypeName* parameter is used as a key to find a particular editor, because a data type can have more than one editor associated with it. This can be any class but is typically **UITypeEditor** or **ComponentEditor**.

Requirements

Platforms: Windows 98, Windows NT 4.0, Windows Millennium Edition, Windows 2000, Windows XP Home Edition, Windows XP Professional, Windows .NET Server family

EditorAttribute Constructor (String, Type)

Initializes a new instance of the **EditorAttribute** class with the type name and the base type.

```
[Visual Basic]
Public Sub New( _
   ByVal typeName As String, _
   ByVal baseType As Type _
)
[C#]
public EditorAttribute(
   string typeName,
   Type baseType
);
[C++]
public: EditorAttribute(
   String* typeName,
   Type* baseType
);
[JScript]
public function EditorAttribute(
   typeName : String,
   baseType : Type
);
```

Parameters

typeName

The fully qualified type name of the editor.

baseType

The **Type** of the base class or interface to use as a lookup key for the editor. This class must be or derive from **UITypeEditor**.

Remarks

The *typeName* parameter must be in the **Type.AssemblyQualifiedName** format.

The **Type** represented by the *typeName* must either derive from or implement the base class.

The *baseType* parameter is used as a key to find a particular editor, because a data type can have more than one editor associated with it.

Requirements

Platforms: Windows 98, Windows NT 4.0, Windows Millennium Edition, Windows 2000, Windows XP Home Edition, Windows XP Professional, Windows .NET Server family

EditorAttribute Constructor (Type, Type)

Initializes a new instance of the **EditorAttribute** class with the type and the base type.

```
[Visual Basic]
Public Sub New( _
   ByVal type As Type, _
   ByVal baseType As Type _
)
[C#]
public EditorAttribute(
   Type type,
   Type baseType
);
[C++]
public: EditorAttribute(
   Type* type,
   Type* baseType
);
[JScript]
public function EditorAttribute(
   type : Type,
   baseType : Type
);
```

Parameters

type
A **Type** that represents the type of the editor.

baseType
The **Type** of the base class or interface to use as a lookup key for the editor. This class must be or derive from **UITypeEditor**.

Remarks

The **Type** represented by the *type* parameter must either derive from or implement the base class.

The *baseType* parameter is used as a key to find a particular editor, because a data type can have more than one editor associated with it.

Requirements

Platforms: Windows 98, Windows NT 4.0, Windows Millennium Edition, Windows 2000, Windows XP Home Edition, Windows XP Professional, Windows .NET Server family

EditorAttribute.EditorBaseTypeName Property

Gets the name of the base class or interface serving as a lookup key for this editor.

```
[Visual Basic]
Public ReadOnly Property EditorBaseTypeName As String
[C#]
public string EditorBaseTypeName {get;}
[C++]
public: __property String* get_EditorBaseTypeName();
[JScript]
public function get EditorBaseTypeName() : String;
```

Property Value

The name of the base class or interface serving as a lookup key for this editor.

Remarks

This is an assembly qualified type name. This version of the .NET Framework provides both **UITypeEditor** and **ComponentEditor** as valid base classes, but any value is valid here.

Requirements

Platforms: Windows 98, Windows NT 4.0, Windows Millennium Edition, Windows 2000, Windows XP Home Edition, Windows XP Professional, Windows .NET Server family

EditorAttribute.EditorTypeName Property

Gets the name of the editor class in the **Type.AssemblyQualifiedName** format.

```
[Visual Basic]
Public ReadOnly Property EditorTypeName As String
[C#]
public string EditorTypeName {get;}
[C++]
public: __property String* get_EditorTypeName();
[JScript]
public function get EditorTypeName() : String;
```

Property Value

The name of the editor class in the **Type.AssemblyQualifiedName** format.

Requirements

Platforms: Windows 98, Windows NT 4.0, Windows Millennium Edition, Windows 2000, Windows XP Home Edition, Windows XP Professional, Windows .NET Server family

EditorAttribute.TypeId Property

This member overrides **Attribute.TypeId**.

```
[Visual Basic]
Overrides Public ReadOnly Property TypeId As Object
[C#]
public override object TypeId {get;}
[C++]
public: __property Object* get_TypeId();
[JScript]
public override function get TypeId() : Object;
```

Requirements

Platforms: Windows 98, Windows NT 4.0, Windows Millennium Edition, Windows 2000, Windows XP Home Edition, Windows XP Professional, Windows .NET Server family

EditorAttribute.Equals Method

This member overrides **Object.Equals**.

[Visual Basic]
```
Overrides Public Function Equals( _
   ByVal obj As Object _
) As Boolean
```
[C#]
```
public override bool Equals(
   object obj
);
```
[C++]
```
public: bool Equals(
   Object* obj
);
```
[JScript]
```
public override function Equals(
   obj : Object
) : Boolean;
```

Requirements

Platforms: Windows 98, Windows NT 4.0, Windows Millennium Edition, Windows 2000, Windows XP Home Edition, Windows XP Professional, Windows .NET Server family

EditorAttribute.GetHashCode Method

This member overrides **Attribute.GetHashCode**.

[Visual Basic]
```
Overrides Public Function GetHashCode() As Integer
```
[C#]
```
public override int GetHashCode();
```
[C++]
```
public: int GetHashCode();
```
[JScript]
```
public override function GetHashCode() : int;
```

Requirements

Platforms: Windows 98, Windows NT 4.0, Windows Millennium Edition, Windows 2000, Windows XP Home Edition, Windows XP Professional, Windows .NET Server family

EditorBrowsableAttribute Class

Specifies that a property or method is viewable in an editor. This class cannot be inherited.

System.Object
  System.Attribute
    System.ComponentModel.EditorBrowsableAttribute

[Visual Basic]
```
<AttributeUsage(AttributeTargets.Class Or AttributeTargets.Struct _
   Or AttributeTargets.Enum Or AttributeTargets.Constructor Or _
   AttributeTargets.Method Or AttributeTargets.Property Or _
   AttributeTargets.Field Or AttributeTargets.Event Or _
   AttributeTargets.Interface Or AttributeTargets.Delegate)>
NotInheritable Public Class EditorBrowsableAttribute
   Inherits Attribute
```
[C#]
```
[AttributeUsage(AttributeTargets.Class | AttributeTargets.Struct |
   AttributeTargets.Enum | AttributeTargets.Constructor |
   AttributeTargets.Method | AttributeTargets.Property |
   AttributeTargets.Field | AttributeTargets.Event |
   AttributeTargets.Interface | AttributeTargets.Delegate)]
public sealed class EditorBrowsableAttribute : Attribute
```
[C++]
```
[AttributeUsage(AttributeTargets::Class | AttributeTargets::Struct
   | AttributeTargets::Enum | AttributeTargets::Constructor |
   AttributeTargets::Method | AttributeTargets::Property |
   AttributeTargets::Field | AttributeTargets::Event |
   AttributeTargets::Interface | AttributeTargets::Delegate)]
public __gc __sealed class EditorBrowsableAttribute : public
   Attribute
```
[JScript]
```
public
   AttributeUsage(AttributeTargets.Class | AttributeTargets.Struct |
   AttributeTargets.Enum | AttributeTargets.Constructor |
   AttributeTargets.Method | AttributeTargets.Property |
   AttributeTargets.Field | AttributeTargets.Event |
   AttributeTargets.Interface | AttributeTargets.Delegate)
class EditorBrowsableAttribute extends Attribute
```

Thread Safety

Any public static (**Shared** in Visual Basic) members of this type are safe for multithreaded operations. Any instance members are not guaranteed to be thread safe.

Remarks

You can use this class in a visual designer or text editor to determine what is visible to the user. For example, the IntelliSense engine in Visual Studio .NET uses this attribute to determine whether to show a method or property.

Example

[Visual Basic, C#, C++] The following sample demonstrates how to hide a property of a control from IntelliSense by setting the appropriate value for the **EditorBrowsableAttribute** attribute. After you open a new application, add a reference to the control and declare an instance of the control, IntelliSense does not display the `Age` property in the drop-down list box.

[Visual Basic]
```
Private ageval As Integer

<EditorBrowsable(System.ComponentModel.EditorBrowsableState.Never)> _
Public Property Age() As Integer
    Get
        Return ageval
    End Get
    Set(ByVal Value As Integer)
        If Not ageval.Equals(Value) Then
            ageval = Value
        End If
    End Set
End Property
```

[C#]
```
int ageval;
[EditorBrowsable(EditorBrowsableState.Never)]
public int Age
{
    get { return ageval; }
    set
    {
        if (!ageval.Equals(value))
        {
            ageval = value;
        }
    }
}
```

[C++]
```
int ageval;

[EditorBrowsable(EditorBrowsableState::Never)]
__property int get_Age()
{
    return ageval;
}

[EditorBrowsable(EditorBrowsableState::Never)]
__property void set_Age(int value)
{
    if (ageval != value)
    {
        ageval = value;
    }

}
```

Requirements

Namespace: System.ComponentModel

Platforms: Windows 98, Windows NT 4.0, Windows Millennium Edition, Windows 2000, Windows XP Home Edition, Windows XP Professional, Windows .NET Server family, .NET Compact Framework - Windows CE .NET

Assembly: System (in System.dll)

EditorBrowsableAttribute Constructor

Initializes a new instance of the **EditorBrowsableAttribute** class.

Overload List

Initializes a new instance of the **EditorBrowsableAttribute** class with **State** set to the default state.

Supported by the .NET Compact Framework.

[Visual Basic] **Public Sub New()**

[C#] **public EditorBrowsableAttribute();**

[C++] **public: EditorBrowsableAttribute();**

[JScript] **public function EditorBrowsableAttribute();**

Initializes a new instance of the **EditorBrowsableAttribute** class with an **EditorBrowsableState**.

Supported by the .NET Compact Framework.

[Visual Basic] **Public Sub New(EditorBrowsableState)**

[C#] **public EditorBrowsableAttribute(EditorBrowsableState);**

[C++] **public: EditorBrowsableAttribute(EditorBrowsableState);**

[JScript] **public function EditorBrowsableAttribute(EditorBrowsableState);**

EditorBrowsableAttribute Constructor ()

Initializes a new instance of the **EditorBrowsableAttribute** class with **State** set to the default state.

```
[Visual Basic]
Public Sub New()
[C#]
public EditorBrowsableAttribute();
[C++]
public: EditorBrowsableAttribute();
[JScript]
public function EditorBrowsableAttribute();
```

Remarks

The default for this property is **EditorBrowsableState.Always**.

Requirements

Platforms: Windows 98, Windows NT 4.0, Windows Millennium Edition, Windows 2000, Windows XP Home Edition, Windows XP Professional, Windows .NET Server family, .NET Compact Framework - Windows CE .NET

EditorBrowsableAttribute Constructor (EditorBrowsableState)

Initializes a new instance of the **EditorBrowsableAttribute** class with an **EditorBrowsableState**.

```
[Visual Basic]
Public Sub New( _
   ByVal state As EditorBrowsableState _
)
[C#]
public EditorBrowsableAttribute(
   EditorBrowsableState state
);
[C++]
public: EditorBrowsableAttribute(
   EditorBrowsableState state
);
[JScript]
public function EditorBrowsableAttribute(
   state : EditorBrowsableState
);
```

Parameters

state

The **EditorBrowsableState** to set **State** to.

Requirements

Platforms: Windows 98, Windows NT 4.0, Windows Millennium Edition, Windows 2000, Windows XP Home Edition, Windows XP Professional, Windows .NET Server family, .NET Compact Framework - Windows CE .NET

EditorBrowsableAttribute.State Property

Gets the browsable state of the property or method.

```
[Visual Basic]
Public ReadOnly Property State As EditorBrowsableState
[C#]
public EditorBrowsableState State {get;}
[C++]
public: __property EditorBrowsableState get_State();
[JScript]
public function get State() : EditorBrowsableState;
```

Property Value

An **EditorBrowsableState** that is the browsable state of the property or method.

Remarks

The default for this property is **EditorBrowsableState.Always**.

Requirements

Platforms: Windows 98, Windows NT 4.0, Windows Millennium Edition, Windows 2000, Windows XP Home Edition, Windows XP Professional, Windows .NET Server family, .NET Compact Framework - Windows CE .NET

EditorBrowsableAttribute.Equals Method

This member overrides **Object.Equals**.

```
[Visual Basic]
Overrides Public Function Equals( _
   ByVal obj As Object _
) As Boolean
[C#]
public override bool Equals(
   object obj
);
[C++]
public: bool Equals(
   Object* obj
);
[JScript]
public override function Equals(
   obj : Object
) : Boolean;
```

Requirements

Platforms: Windows 98, Windows NT 4.0, Windows Millennium Edition, Windows 2000, Windows XP Home Edition, Windows XP Professional, Windows .NET Server family, .NET Compact Framework - Windows CE .NET

EditorBrowsableAttribute.GetHashCode Method

This member overrides **Attribute.GetHashCode**.

[Visual Basic]
```
Overrides Public Function GetHashCode() As Integer
```
[C#]
```
public override int GetHashCode();
```
[C++]
```
public: int GetHashCode();
```
[JScript]
```
public override function GetHashCode() : int;
```

Requirements

Platforms: Windows 98, Windows NT 4.0,
Windows Millennium Edition, Windows 2000,
Windows XP Home Edition, Windows XP Professional,
Windows .NET Server family,
.NET Compact Framework - Windows CE .NET

EditorBrowsableState Enumeration

Specifies the browsable state of a property or method from within an editor.

[Visual Basic]
```
<Serializable>
Public Enum EditorBrowsableState
```
[C#]
```
[Serializable]
public enum EditorBrowsableState
```
[C++]
```
[Serializable]
__value public enum EditorBrowsableState
```
[JScript]
```
public
   Serializable
enum EditorBrowsableState
```

Remarks

This class is used by a visual designer to determine what is visible to the user. For example, the IntelliSense engine in Visual Studio .NET never shows those methods or property that are marked as **Never**.

Members

Member name	Description
Advanced Supported by the .NET Compact Framework.	The property or method is a feature that only advanced users should see. An editor can either show or hide such properties.
Always Supported by the .NET Compact Framework.	The property or method is always browsable from within an editor.
Never Supported by the .NET Compact Framework.	The property or method is never browsable from within an editor.

Example

For an example of using the **EditorBrowsableState** enumerator, see the sample code in **EditorBrowsableAttribute** class.

Requirements

Namespace: System.ComponentModel

Platforms: Windows 98, Windows NT 4.0,
Windows Millennium Edition, Windows 2000,
Windows XP Home Edition, Windows XP Professional,
Windows Server 2003 family,
.NET Compact Framework - Windows CE .NET

Assembly: System (in System.dll)

EnumConverter Class

Provides a type converter to convert **Enum** objects to and from various other representations.

System.Object
  System.ComponentModel.TypeConverter
    System.ComponentModel.EnumConverter

[Visual Basic]
```
Public Class EnumConverter
   Inherits TypeConverter
```
[C#]
```
public class EnumConverter : TypeConverter
```
[C++]
```
public __gc class EnumConverter : public TypeConverter
```
[JScript]
```
public class EnumConverter extends TypeConverter
```

Thread Safety

Any public static (**Shared** in Visual Basic) members of this type are safe for multithreaded operations. Any instance members are not guaranteed to be thread safe.

Remarks

This converter can only convert an enumeration object to and from a string. The **EnumConverter** provides the **Comparer** property to get an **IComparer** interface that can be used to sort the values of the enumeration. By default, the enumeration values are sorted in the order they appear in the file.

For more information about type converters, see the **TypeConverter** base class and **Implementing a Type Converter**.

> **Note** You should never create an instance of an **EnumConverter**. Instead, call the **GetConverter** method of **TypeDescriptor**. For more information, see the examples in the **TypeConverter** base class.

Notes to Inheritors: If you want to sort the values into a different order, override the **Comparer** property.

Example

[Visual Basic, C#, C++] The following sample converts a variable of type **Enum** to a string, and vice versa. The code segment assumes that you have declared an **Enum** called `Servers` and that it has the following members, `Windows=1, Exchange=2, BizTalk=3`

[Visual Basic]
```
Dim myServer As Servers = Servers.Exchange
Dim myServerString As string = "BizTalk"
Console.WriteLine(TypeDescriptor.GetConverter(myServer).ConvertTo ↵
(myServer, GetType(String)))
Console.WriteLine(TypeDescriptor.GetConverter ↵
 (myServer).ConvertFrom(myServerString))
```

[C#]
```
Enum myServer= Servers.Exchange;
string myServerString = "BizTalk";
Console.WriteLine(TypeDescriptor.GetConverter(myServer).ConvertTo ↵
 (myServer, typeof(string)));
Console.WriteLine(TypeDescriptor.GetConverter(myServer).ConvertFrom(mySe
rverString));
```

[C++]
```
// Requires public declaration of the following type.
// __value enum Servers {Windows=1, Exchange=2, BizTalk=3};
Servers myServer = Servers::Exchange;
String* myServerString = S"BizTalk";
Console::WriteLine(TypeDescriptor::GetConverter ↵
 (__box(myServer))->ConvertTo(__box(myServer), __typeof(String)));
Console::WriteLine(TypeDescriptor::GetConverter ↵
 (__box(myServer))->ConvertFrom(myServerString));
```

Requirements

Namespace: System.ComponentModel

Platforms: Windows 98, Windows NT 4.0, Windows Millennium Edition, Windows 2000, Windows XP Home Edition, Windows XP Professional, Windows Server 2003 family

Assembly: System (in System.dll)

EnumConverter Constructor

This member supports the .NET Framework infrastructure and is not intended to be used directly from your code.

[Visual Basic]
```
Public Sub New( _
   ByVal type As Type _
)
```
[C#]
```
public EnumConverter(
   Type type
);
```
[C++]
```
public: EnumConverter(
   Type* type
);
```
[JScript]
```
public function EnumConverter(
   type : Type
);
```

EnumConverter.Comparer Property

Gets an **IComparer** that can be used to sort the values of the enumeration.

[Visual Basic]
```
Protected Overridable ReadOnly Property Comparer As IComparer
```
[C#]
```
protected virtual IComparer Comparer {get;}
```
[C++]
```
protected: __property virtual IComparer* get_Comparer();
```
[JScript]
```
protected function get Comparer() : IComparer;
```

Property Value

An **IComparer** for sorting the enumeration values.

Remarks

By default, the enumeration values are sorted in the order they appear in the file.

Notes to Inheritors: If you want to sort the values into a different order, override this property.

Requirements

Platforms: Windows 98, Windows NT 4.0, Windows Millennium Edition, Windows 2000, Windows XP Home Edition, Windows XP Professional, Windows Server 2003 family

EnumConverter.EnumType Property

This member supports the .NET Framework infrastructure and is not intended to be used directly from your code.

[Visual Basic]
```
Protected ReadOnly Property EnumType As Type
```
[C#]
```
protected Type EnumType {get;}
```
[C++]
```
protected: __property Type* get_EnumType();
```
[JScript]
```
protected function get EnumType() : Type;
```

EnumConverter.Values Property

This member supports the .NET Framework infrastructure and is not intended to be used directly from your code.

[Visual Basic]
```
Protected Property Values As TypeConverter.StandardValuesCollection
```
[C#]
```
protected TypeConverter.StandardValuesCollection Values {get; set;}
```
[C++]
```
protected: __property TypeConverter.StandardValuesCollection*
get_Values();
protected: __property void
set_Values(TypeConverter.StandardValuesCollection*);
```
[JScript]
```
protected function get Values() :
TypeConverter.StandardValuesCollection;
protected function set Values(TypeConverter.StandardValuesCollection);
```

EnumConverter.CanConvertFrom Method

Overload List

This member supports the .NET Framework infrastructure and is not intended to be used directly from your code.

[Visual Basic] **Overloads Overrides Public Function CanConvertFrom(ITypeDescriptorContext, Type) As Boolean**

[C#] **public override bool CanConvertFrom(ITypeDescriptorContext, Type);**

[C++] **public: bool CanConvertFrom(ITypeDescriptorContext*, Type*);**

[JScript] **public override function CanConvertFrom(ITypeDescriptorContext, Type) : Boolean;**

Inherited from **TypeConverter**.

[Visual Basic] **Overloads Public Function CanConvertFrom(Type) As Boolean**

[C#] **public bool CanConvertFrom(Type);**

[C++] **public: bool CanConvertFrom(Type*);**

[JScript] **public function CanConvertFrom(Type) : Boolean;**

EnumConverter.CanConvertFrom Method (ITypeDescriptorContext, Type)

This member overrides **TypeConverter.CanConvertFrom**.

[Visual Basic]
```
Overrides Overloads Public Function CanConvertFrom( _
   ByVal context As ITypeDescriptorContext, _
   ByVal sourceType As Type _
) As Boolean
```
[C#]
```
public override bool CanConvertFrom(
   ITypeDescriptorContext context,
   Type sourceType
);
```
[C++]
```
public: bool CanConvertFrom(
   ITypeDescriptorContext* context,
   Type* sourceType
);
```
[JScript]
```
public override function CanConvertFrom(
   context : ITypeDescriptorContext,
   sourceType : Type
) : Boolean;
```

Requirements

Platforms: Windows 98, Windows NT 4.0, Windows Millennium Edition, Windows 2000, Windows XP Home Edition, Windows XP Professional, Windows Server 2003 family

EnumConverter.CanConvertTo Method

Overload List

This member supports the .NET Framework infrastructure and is not intended to be used directly from your code.

[Visual Basic] **Overloads Overrides Public Function CanConvertTo(ITypeDescriptorContext, Type) As Boolean**

[C#] **public override bool CanConvertTo(ITypeDescriptorContext, Type);**

[C++] **public: bool CanConvertTo(ITypeDescriptorContext*, Type*);**

[JScript] **public override function CanConvertTo(ITypeDescriptorContext, Type) : Boolean;**

Inherited from **TypeConverter**.

[Visual Basic] **Overloads Public Function CanConvertTo(Type) As Boolean**

[C#] **public bool CanConvertTo(Type);**

[C++] **public: bool CanConvertTo(Type*);**

[JScript] **public function CanConvertTo(Type) : Boolean;**

EnumConverter.CanConvertTo Method (ITypeDescriptorContext, Type)

This member overrides **TypeConverter.CanConvertTo**.

```
[Visual Basic]
Overrides Overloads Public Function CanConvertTo( _
   ByVal context As ITypeDescriptorContext, _
   ByVal destinationType As Type _
) As Boolean
[C#]
public override bool CanConvertTo(
   ITypeDescriptorContext context,
   Type destinationType
);
[C++]
public: bool CanConvertTo(
   ITypeDescriptorContext* context,
   Type* destinationType
);
[JScript]
public override function CanConvertTo(
   context : ITypeDescriptorContext,
   destinationType : Type
) : Boolean;
```

Requirements

Platforms: Windows 98, Windows NT 4.0, Windows Millennium Edition, Windows 2000, Windows XP Home Edition, Windows XP Professional, Windows Server 2003 family

EnumConverter.ConvertFrom Method

Overload List

This member supports the .NET Framework infrastructure and is not intended to be used directly from your code.

[Visual Basic] **Overloads Overrides Public Function ConvertFrom(ITypeDescriptorContext, CultureInfo, Object) As Object**

[C#] **public override object ConvertFrom(ITypeDescriptorContext, CultureInfo, object);**

[C++] **public: Object* ConvertFrom(ITypeDescriptorContext*, CultureInfo*, Object*);**

[JScript] **public override function ConvertFrom(ITypeDescriptorContext, CultureInfo, Object) : Object;**

Inherited from **TypeConverter**.

[Visual Basic] **Overloads Public Function ConvertFrom(Object) As Object**

[C#] **public object ConvertFrom(object);**

[C++] **public: Object* ConvertFrom(Object*);**

[JScript] **public function ConvertFrom(Object) : Object;**

EnumConverter.ConvertFrom Method (ITypeDescriptorContext, CultureInfo, Object)

This member overrides **TypeConverter.ConvertFrom**.

```
[Visual Basic]
Overrides Overloads Public Function ConvertFrom( _
   ByVal context As ITypeDescriptorContext, _
   ByVal culture As CultureInfo, _
   ByVal value As Object _
) As Object
[C#]
public override object ConvertFrom(
   ITypeDescriptorContext context,
   CultureInfo culture,
   object value
);
[C++]
public: Object* ConvertFrom(
   ITypeDescriptorContext* context,
   CultureInfo* culture,
   Object* value
);
[JScript]
public override function ConvertFrom(
   context : ITypeDescriptorContext,
   culture : CultureInfo,
   value : Object
) : Object;
```

Requirements

Platforms: Windows 98, Windows NT 4.0, Windows Millennium Edition, Windows 2000, Windows XP Home Edition, Windows XP Professional, Windows Server 2003 family

EnumConverter.ConvertTo Method

Overload List

This member supports the .NET Framework infrastructure and is not intended to be used directly from your code.

[Visual Basic] **Overloads Overrides Public Function ConvertTo(ITypeDescriptorContext, CultureInfo, Object, Type) As Object**

[C#] **public override object ConvertTo(ITypeDescriptorContext, CultureInfo, object, Type);**

[C++] **public: Object* ConvertTo(ITypeDescriptorContext*, CultureInfo*, Object*, Type*);**

[JScript] **public override function ConvertTo(ITypeDescriptorContext, CultureInfo, Object, Type) : Object;**

Inherited from **TypeConverter**.

[Visual Basic] **Overloads Public Function ConvertTo(Object, Type) As Object**

[C#] **public object ConvertTo(object, Type);**

[C++] **public: Object* ConvertTo(Object*, Type*);**

[JScript] **public function ConvertTo(Object, Type) : Object;**

EnumConverter.ConvertTo Method (ITypeDescriptorContext, CultureInfo, Object, Type)

This member overrides **TypeConverter.ConvertTo**.

```
[Visual Basic]
Overrides Overloads Public Function ConvertTo( _
   ByVal context As ITypeDescriptorContext, _
   ByVal culture As CultureInfo, _
   ByVal value As Object, _
   ByVal destinationType As Type _
) As Object
```

```
[C#]
public override object ConvertTo(
   ITypeDescriptorContext context,
   CultureInfo culture,
   object value,
   Type destinationType
);
[C++]
public: Object* ConvertTo(
   ITypeDescriptorContext* context,
   CultureInfo* culture,
   Object* value,
   Type* destinationType
);
[JScript]
public override function ConvertTo(
   context : ITypeDescriptorContext,
   culture : CultureInfo,
   value : Object,
   destinationType : Type
) : Object;
```

Requirements

Platforms: Windows 98, Windows NT 4.0, Windows Millennium Edition, Windows 2000, Windows XP Home Edition, Windows XP Professional, Windows Server 2003 family

EnumConverter.GetStandardValues Method

Overload List

This member supports the .NET Framework infrastructure and is not intended to be used directly from your code.

[Visual Basic] **Overloads Overrides Public Function GetStandardValues(ITypeDescriptorContext) As StandardValuesCollection**

[C#] **public override StandardValuesCollection GetStandardValues(ITypeDescriptorContext);**

[C++] **public: StandardValuesCollection* GetStandardValues(ITypeDescriptorContext*);**

[JScript] **public override function GetStandardValues(ITypeDescriptorContext) : StandardValuesCollection;**

Inherited from **TypeConverter**.

[Visual Basic] **Overloads Public Function GetStandardValues() As ICollection**

[C#] **public ICollection GetStandardValues();**

[C++] **public: ICollection* GetStandardValues();**

[JScript] **public function GetStandardValues() : ICollection;**

EnumConverter.GetStandardValues Method (ITypeDescriptorContext)

This member overrides **TypeConverter.GetStandardValues**.

```
[Visual Basic]
Overrides Overloads Public Function GetStandardValues( _
   ByVal context As ITypeDescriptorContext _
) As StandardValuesCollection
[C#]
public override StandardValuesCollection GetStandardValues(
   ITypeDescriptorContext context
);
[C++]
public: StandardValuesCollection* GetStandardValues(
   ITypeDescriptorContext* context
);
[JScript]
public override function GetStandardValues(
   context : ITypeDescriptorContext
) : StandardValuesCollection;
```

Requirements

Platforms: Windows 98, Windows NT 4.0, Windows Millennium Edition, Windows 2000, Windows XP Home Edition, Windows XP Professional, Windows Server 2003 family

EnumConverter.GetStandardValuesExclusive Method

Overload List

This member supports the .NET Framework infrastructure and is not intended to be used directly from your code.

[Visual Basic] **Overloads Overrides Public Function GetStandardValuesExclusive(ITypeDescriptorContext) As Boolean**

[C#] **public override bool GetStandardValues-Exclusive(ITypeDescriptorContext);**

[C++] **public: bool GetStandardValues-Exclusive(ITypeDescriptorContext*);**

[JScript] **public override function GetStandardValues-Exclusive(ITypeDescriptorContext) : Boolean;**

Inherited from **TypeConverter**.

[Visual Basic] **Overloads Public Function GetStandardValuesExclusive() As Boolean**

[C#] **public bool GetStandardValuesExclusive();**

[C++] **public: bool GetStandardValuesExclusive();**

[JScript] **public function GetStandardValuesExclusive() : Boolean;**

EnumConverter.GetStandardValuesExclusive Method (ITypeDescriptorContext)

This member overrides **TypeConverter.GetStandardValuesExclusive**.

```
[Visual Basic]
Overrides Overloads Public Function GetStandardValuesExclusive( _
   ByVal context As ITypeDescriptorContext _
) As Boolean
[C#]
public override bool GetStandardValuesExclusive(
   ITypeDescriptorContext context
);
```

```
[C++]
public: bool GetStandardValuesExclusive(
   ITypeDescriptorContext* context
);
[JScript]
public override function GetStandardValuesExclusive(
   context : ITypeDescriptorContext
) : Boolean;
```

Requirements

Platforms: Windows 98, Windows NT 4.0, Windows Millennium Edition, Windows 2000, Windows XP Home Edition, Windows XP Professional, Windows Server 2003 family

EnumConverter.GetStandardValuesSupported Method

Overload List

This member supports the .NET Framework infrastructure and is not intended to be used directly from your code.

[Visual Basic] **Overloads Overrides Public Function GetStandardValuesSupported(ITypeDescriptorContext) As Boolean**

[C#] **public override bool GetStandardValues-Supported(ITypeDescriptorContext);**

[C++] **public: bool GetStandardValues-Supported(ITypeDescriptorContext*);**

[JScript] **public override function GetStandardValues-Supported(ITypeDescriptorContext) : Boolean;**

Inherited from **TypeConverter**.

[Visual Basic] **Overloads Public Function GetStandardValuesSupported() As Boolean**

[C#] **public bool GetStandardValuesSupported();**

[C++] **public: bool GetStandardValuesSupported();**

[JScript] **public function GetStandardValuesSupported() : Boolean;**

EnumConverter.GetStandardValuesSupported Method (ITypeDescriptorContext)

This member overrides **TypeConverter.GetStandardValuesSupported**.

```
[Visual Basic]
Overrides Overloads Public Function GetStandardValuesSupported( _
   ByVal context As ITypeDescriptorContext _
) As Boolean
[C#]
public override bool GetStandardValuesSupported(
   ITypeDescriptorContext context
);
[C++]
public: bool GetStandardValuesSupported(
   ITypeDescriptorContext* context
);
[JScript]
public override function GetStandardValuesSupported(
   context : ITypeDescriptorContext
) : Boolean;
```

Requirements

Platforms: Windows 98, Windows NT 4.0, Windows Millennium Edition, Windows 2000, Windows XP Home Edition, Windows XP Professional, Windows Server 2003 family

EnumConverter.IsValid Method

Overload List

This member supports the .NET Framework infrastructure and is not intended to be used directly from your code.

[Visual Basic] **Overloads Overrides Public Function IsValid(ITypeDescriptorContext, Object) As Boolean**

[C#] **public override bool IsValid(ITypeDescriptorContext, object);**

[C++] **public: bool IsValid(ITypeDescriptorContext*, Object*);**

[JScript] **public override function IsValid(IType-DescriptorContext, Object) : Boolean;**

Inherited from **TypeConverter**.

[Visual Basic] **Overloads Public Function IsValid(Object) As Boolean**

[C#] **public bool IsValid(object);**

[C++] **public: bool IsValid(Object*);**

[JScript] **public function IsValid(Object) : Boolean;**

EnumConverter.IsValid Method (ITypeDescriptorContext, Object)

This member overrides **TypeConverter.IsValid**.

```
[Visual Basic]
Overrides Overloads Public Function IsValid( _
   ByVal context As ITypeDescriptorContext, _
   ByVal value As Object _
) As Boolean
[C#]
public override bool IsValid(
   ITypeDescriptorContext context,
   object value
);
[C++]
public: bool IsValid(
   ITypeDescriptorContext* context,
   Object* value
);
[JScript]
public override function IsValid(
   context : ITypeDescriptorContext,
   value : Object
) : Boolean;
```

Requirements

Platforms: Windows 98, Windows NT 4.0, Windows Millennium Edition, Windows 2000, Windows XP Home Edition, Windows XP Professional, Windows Server 2003 family

EventDescriptor Class

Provides information about an event.

System.Object
  System.ComponentModel.MemberDescriptor
    System.ComponentModel.EventDescriptor

[Visual Basic]
```
<ComVisible(True)>
MustInherit Public Class EventDescriptor
   Inherits MemberDescriptor
```
[C#]
```
[ComVisible(true)]
public abstract class EventDescriptor : MemberDescriptor
```
[C++]
```
[ComVisible(true)]
public __gc __abstract class EventDescriptor : public
   MemberDescriptor
```
[JScript]
```
public
   ComVisible(true)
abstract class EventDescriptor extends MemberDescriptor
```

Thread Safety

Any public static (**Shared** in Visual Basic) members of this type are safe for multithreaded operations. Any instance members are not guaranteed to be thread safe.

Remarks

An **EventDescriptor** consists of a name, its attributes, the component that the event is bound to, the event delegate, the type of delegate, and whether the delegate is multicast.

EventDescriptor provides the following abstract (**MustOverride** in Visual Basic) properties and methods:

- **ComponentType** contains the type of the component this event is declared on.
- **EventType** contains the type of delegate for the event.
- **IsMulticast** contains a value indicating whether the event delegate is a multicast delegate.
- **AddEventHandler** binds the event to a component.
- **RemoveEventHandler** unbinds the delegate from the component so that the delegate no longer receives events from the component.

Example

[Visual Basic, C#, C++] The following example is built upon the example in the **EventDescriptorCollection** class. It prints the information (category, description, display name) of each event on a button in a text box. It assumes that button1 and textbox1 have been instantiated on a form.

[Visual Basic]
```
Dim events As EventDescriptorCollection =                          ↵
TypeDescriptor.GetEvents(Button1)
' Displays each event's information in the collection in a text box.
Dim myEvent As EventDescriptor
For Each myEvent In events
    TextBox1.Text &= myEvent.Category & ControlChars.Cr
    TextBox1.Text &= myEvent.Description & ControlChars.Cr
    TextBox1.Text &= myEvent.DisplayName & ControlChars.Cr
Next myEvent
```

[C#]
```
EventDescriptorCollection events = TypeDescriptor.GetEvents(button1);
// Displays each event's information in the collection in a text box.
foreach (System.ComponentModel.EventDescriptor myEvent in events) {
    textBox1.Text += myEvent.Category + '\n';
    textBox1.Text += myEvent.Description + '\n';
    textBox1.Text += myEvent.DisplayName + '\n';
}
```

[C++]
```
EventDescriptorCollection* events = TypeDescriptor::GetEvents(button1);
// Displays each event's information in the collection in a text box.
IEnumerator* myEvents = events->GetEnumerator();
while( myEvents->MoveNext() )
{
    textBox1->Text = String::Format( S"{0}\n{1}\n{2}\n",
        static_cast<EventDescriptor*>(myEvents->Current)->Category,
        static_cast<EventDescriptor*>(myEvents->Current)->Description,
        static_cast<EventDescriptor*>(myEvents->Current)->              ↵
DisplayName );
}
```

Requirements

Namespace: System.ComponentModel

Platforms: Windows 98, Windows NT 4.0, Windows Millennium Edition, Windows 2000, Windows XP Home Edition, Windows XP Professional, Windows Server 2003 family, .NET Compact Framework - Windows CE .NET

Assembly: System (in System.dll)

EventDescriptor Constructor

Initializes a new instance of the **EventDescriptor** class.

Overload List

Initializes a new instance of the **EventDescriptor** class with the name and attributes in the specified **MemberDescriptor**.

Supported by the .NET Compact Framework.

[Visual Basic] **Protected Sub New(MemberDescriptor)**

[C#] **protected EventDescriptor(MemberDescriptor);**

[C++] **protected: EventDescriptor(MemberDescriptor*);**

[JScript] **protected function EventDescriptor(Member-Descriptor);**

Initializes a new instance of the **EventDescriptor** class with the name in the specified **MemberDescriptor** and the attributes in both the **MemberDescriptor** and the **Attribute** array.

Supported by the .NET Compact Framework.

[Visual Basic] **Protected Sub New(MemberDescriptor, Attribute())**

[C#] **protected EventDescriptor(MemberDescriptor, Attribute[]);**

[C++] **protected: EventDescriptor(MemberDescriptor*, Attribute[]);**

[JScript] **protected function EventDescriptor(Member-Descriptor, Attribute[]);**

Initializes a new instance of the **EventDescriptor** class with the specified name and attribute array.

Supported by the .NET Compact Framework.

[Visual Basic] **Protected Sub New(String, Attribute())**

[C#] **protected EventDescriptor(string, Attribute[]);**

[C++] **protected: EventDescriptor(String*, Attribute[]);**

[JScript] **protected function EventDescriptor(String, Attribute[]);**

EventDescriptor Constructor (MemberDescriptor)

Initializes a new instance of the **EventDescriptor** class with the name and attributes in the specified **MemberDescriptor**.

[Visual Basic]
```
Protected Sub New( _
   ByVal descr As MemberDescriptor _
)
```
[C#]
```
protected EventDescriptor(
   MemberDescriptor descr
);
```
[C++]
```
protected: EventDescriptor(
   MemberDescriptor* descr
);
```
[JScript]
```
protected function EventDescriptor(
   descr : MemberDescriptor
);
```

Parameters

descr
A **MemberDescriptor** that contains the name of the event and its attributes.

Requirements

Platforms: Windows 98, Windows NT 4.0,
Windows Millennium Edition, Windows 2000,
Windows XP Home Edition, Windows XP Professional,
Windows Server 2003 family,
.NET Compact Framework - Windows CE .NET

EventDescriptor Constructor (MemberDescriptor, Attribute[])

Initializes a new instance of the **EventDescriptor** class with the name in the specified **MemberDescriptor** and the attributes in both the **MemberDescriptor** and the **Attribute** array.

[Visual Basic]
```
Protected Sub New( _
   ByVal descr As MemberDescriptor, _
   ByVal attrs() As Attribute _
)
```
[C#]
```
protected EventDescriptor(
   MemberDescriptor descr,
   Attribute[] attrs
);
```
[C++]
```
protected: EventDescriptor(
   MemberDescriptor* descr,
   Attribute* attrs[]
);
```
[JScript]
```
protected function EventDescriptor(
   descr : MemberDescriptor,
   attrs : Attribute[]
);
```

Parameters

descr
A **MemberDescriptor** that has the name of the member and its attributes.

attrs
An **Attribute** array with the attributes you want to add to this event description.

Remarks

This constructor appends the attributes in the **Attribute** array to the attributes in the **MemberDescriptor**.

Requirements

Platforms: Windows 98, Windows NT 4.0,
Windows Millennium Edition, Windows 2000,
Windows XP Home Edition, Windows XP Professional,
Windows Server 2003 family,
.NET Compact Framework - Windows CE .NET

EventDescriptor Constructor (String, Attribute[])

Initializes a new instance of the **EventDescriptor** class with the specified name and attribute array.

[Visual Basic]
```
Protected Sub New( _
   ByVal name As String, _
   ByVal attrs() As Attribute _
)
```
[C#]
```
protected EventDescriptor(
   string name,
   Attribute[] attrs
);
```
[C++]
```
protected: EventDescriptor(
   String* name,
   Attribute* attrs[]
);
```
[JScript]
```
protected function EventDescriptor(
   name : String,
   attrs : Attribute[]
);
```

Parameters

name
The name of the event.

attrs
An array of type **Attribute** that contains the event attributes.

Requirements

Platforms: Windows 98, Windows NT 4.0,
Windows Millennium Edition, Windows 2000,
Windows XP Home Edition, Windows XP Professional,
Windows Server 2003 family,
.NET Compact Framework - Windows CE .NET

EventDescriptor.ComponentType Property

When overridden in a derived class, gets the type of component this event is bound to.

```
[Visual Basic]
Public MustOverride ReadOnly Property ComponentType As Type
[C#]
public abstract Type ComponentType {get;}
[C++]
public: __property virtual Type* get_ComponentType() = 0;
[JScript]
public abstract function get ComponentType() : Type;
```

Property Value

A **Type** that represents the type of component the event is bound to.

Remarks

Typically, this property is implemented through reflection.

Requirements

Platforms: Windows 98, Windows NT 4.0, Windows Millennium Edition, Windows 2000, Windows XP Home Edition, Windows XP Professional, Windows Server 2003 family, .NET Compact Framework - Windows CE .NET

EventDescriptor.EventType Property

When overridden in a derived class, gets the type of delegate for the event.

```
[Visual Basic]
Public MustOverride ReadOnly Property EventType As Type
[C#]
public abstract Type EventType {get;}
[C++]
public: __property virtual Type* get_EventType() = 0;
[JScript]
public abstract function get EventType() : Type;
```

Property Value

A **Type** that represents the type of delegate for the event.

Remarks

Typically, this property is implemented through reflection.

Requirements

Platforms: Windows 98, Windows NT 4.0, Windows Millennium Edition, Windows 2000, Windows XP Home Edition, Windows XP Professional, Windows Server 2003 family, .NET Compact Framework - Windows CE .NET

EventDescriptor.IsMulticast Property

When overridden in a derived class, gets a value indicating whether the event delegate is a multicast delegate.

```
[Visual Basic]
Public MustOverride ReadOnly Property IsMulticast As Boolean
[C#]
public abstract bool IsMulticast {get;}
[C++]
public: __property virtual bool get_IsMulticast() = 0;
[JScript]
public abstract function get IsMulticast() : Boolean;
```

Property Value

true if the event delegate is multicast; otherwise, **false**.

Remarks

Typically, this property is implemented through reflection.

A multicast delegate differs from a regular delegate in that it can contain references to more than just one method. Methods in a multicast delegate are executed synchronously when the delegate is invoked, in the order in which they appear. If one of the called methods raises an exception, then the delegate ceases and the exception is propagated to the delegate caller.

Requirements

Platforms: Windows 98, Windows NT 4.0, Windows Millennium Edition, Windows 2000, Windows XP Home Edition, Windows XP Professional, Windows Server 2003 family, .NET Compact Framework - Windows CE .NET

EventDescriptor.AddEventHandler Method

When overridden in a derived class, binds the event to the component.

```
[Visual Basic]
Public MustOverride Sub AddEventHandler( _
   ByVal component As Object, _
   ByVal value As Delegate _
)
[C#]
public abstract void AddEventHandler(
   object component,
   Delegate value
);
[C++]
public: virtual void AddEventHandler(
   Object* component,
   Delegate* value
) = 0;
[JScript]
public abstract function AddEventHandler(
   component : Object,
   value : Delegate
);
```

Parameters

component

A component that provides events to the delegate.

value

A delegate that represents the method that handles the event.

Remarks

Typically, this method is implemented through reflection.

Notes to Inheritors: When you override this method, it should add the delegate to the component's event list by invoking the appropriate `add_myHandler` method.

Requirements

Platforms: Windows 98, Windows NT 4.0, Windows Millennium Edition, Windows 2000, Windows XP Home Edition, Windows XP Professional, Windows Server 2003 family, .NET Compact Framework - Windows CE .NET

EventDescriptor.RemoveEventHandler Method

When overridden in a derived class, unbinds the delegate from the component so that the delegate will no longer receive events from the component.

[Visual Basic]
```
Public MustOverride Sub RemoveEventHandler( _
   ByVal component As Object, _
   ByVal value As Delegate _
)
```
[C#]
```
public abstract void RemoveEventHandler(
   object component,
   Delegate value
);
```
[C++]
```
public: virtual void RemoveEventHandler(
   Object* component,
   Delegate* value
) = 0;
```
[JScript]
```
public abstract function RemoveEventHandler(
   component : Object,
   value : Delegate
);
```

Parameters

component

The component that the delegate is bound to.

value

The delegate to unbind from the component.

Remarks

Typically, this method is implemented through reflection.

Notes to Inheritors: When you override this method, it should remove the delegate from the component's event list by invoking the appropriate `remove_myHandler` method.

Requirements

Platforms: Windows 98, Windows NT 4.0, Windows Millennium Edition, Windows 2000, Windows XP Home Edition, Windows XP Professional, Windows Server 2003 family, .NET Compact Framework - Windows CE .NET

EventDescriptorCollection Class

Represents a collection of **EventDescriptor** objects.

System.Object
  System.ComponentModel.EventDescriptorCollection

```
[Visual Basic]
<ComVisible(True)>
Public Class EventDescriptorCollection
   Implements IList, ICollection, IEnumerable
[C#]
[ComVisible(true)]
public class EventDescriptorCollection : IList, ICollection,
   IEnumerable
[C++]
[ComVisible(true)]
public __gc class EventDescriptorCollection : public IList,
   ICollection, IEnumerable
[JScript]
public
   ComVisible(true)
class EventDescriptorCollection implements IList,
   ICollection, IEnumerable
```

Thread Safety

Any public static (**Shared** in Visual Basic) members of this type are safe for multithreaded operations. Any instance members are not guaranteed to be thread safe.

Remarks

EventDescriptorCollection is read-only; it does not implement methods that add or remove events. You must inherit from this class to implement these methods.

Using the properties available in the **EventDescriptorCollection** class, you can query the collection about its contents. Use the **Count** property to determine the number of elements in the collection. Use the **Item** property to get a specific property by index number or by name.

You can also use the **Find** method to get a description of the event with the specified name from the collection.

Example

[Visual Basic, C#] The following example prints all the events on a button in a text box. It assumes that `button1` and `textBox1` have been instantiated on a form.

```
[Visual Basic]
Private Sub MyEventCollection()
    ' Creates a new collection and assigns it the events for button1.
    Dim events As EventDescriptorCollection =
TypeDescriptor.GetEvents(button1)

    ' Displays each event in the collection in a text box.
    Dim myEvent As EventDescriptor
    For Each myEvent In  events
        textBox1.Text &= myEvent.Name & ControlChars.Cr
    Next myEvent
End Sub 'MyEventCollection
```

```
[C#]
private void MyEventCollection() {
    // Creates a new collection and assigns it the events for button1.
    EventDescriptorCollection events =
TypeDescriptor.GetEvents(button1);

    // Displays each event in the collection in a text box.
    foreach (EventDescriptor myEvent in events)
        textBox1.Text += myEvent.Name + '\n';
}
```

Requirements

Namespace: System.ComponentModel

Platforms: Windows 98, Windows NT 4.0, Windows Millennium Edition, Windows 2000, Windows XP Home Edition, Windows XP Professional, Windows .NET Server family, .NET Compact Framework - Windows CE .NET

Assembly: System (in System.dll)

EventDescriptorCollection Constructor

Initializes a new instance of the **EventDescriptorCollection** class.

```
[Visual Basic]
Public Sub New( _
   ByVal events() As EventDescriptor _
)
[C#]
public EventDescriptorCollection(
   EventDescriptor[] events
);
[C++]
public: EventDescriptorCollection(
   EventDescriptor* events[]
);
[JScript]
public function EventDescriptorCollection(
   events : EventDescriptor[]
);
```

Parameters

events
An array of type **EventDescriptor** that provides the events for this collection.

Remarks

If the *events* parameter is empty, this constructor creates an empty **EventDescriptorCollection** class.

Example

[Visual Basic, C#] The following example creates a new **EventDescriptorCollection** class using the events on `button1`. It assumes that `button1` has been instantiated on a form.

```
[Visual Basic]
Dim events As EventDescriptorCollection =
TypeDescriptor.GetEvents(button1)
```

```
[C#]
EventDescriptorCollection events = TypeDescriptor.GetEvents(button1);
```

Requirements

Platforms: Windows 98, Windows NT 4.0, Windows Millennium Edition, Windows 2000, Windows XP Home Edition, Windows XP Professional, Windows .NET Server family, .NET Compact Framework - Windows CE .NET

EventDescriptorCollection.Empty Field

Specifies an empty collection to use, rather than creating a new one with no items. This static (**Shared** in Visual Basic) field is read-only.

[Visual Basic]
```
Public Shared ReadOnly Empty As EventDescriptorCollection
```
[C#]
```
public static readonly EventDescriptorCollection Empty;
```
[C++]
```
public: static EventDescriptorCollection* Empty;
```
[JScript]
```
public static var Empty : EventDescriptorCollection;
```

Requirements

Platforms: Windows 98, Windows NT 4.0, Windows Millennium Edition, Windows 2000, Windows XP Home Edition, Windows XP Professional, Windows .NET Server family, .NET Compact Framework - Windows CE .NET

EventDescriptorCollection.Count Property

Gets the number of event descriptors in the collection.

[Visual Basic]
```
Public ReadOnly Property Count As Integer
```
[C#]
```
public int Count {get;}
```
[C++]
```
public: __property int get_Count();
```
[JScript]
```
public function get Count() : int;
```

Property Value

The number of event descriptors in the collection.

Remarks

The **Count** property can be used to set the limits of a loop that iterates through a collection of objects. If the collection is zero-based, be sure to use `Count - 1` as the upper boundary of the loop.

Example

[Visual Basic, C#] The following example uses the **Count** property to print the number of events attached to `button1`. It assumes that `button1` and `textBox1` have been instantiated on a form.

[Visual Basic]
```
Private Sub GetCount()
    ' Creates a new collection and assigns it the events for button1.
    Dim events As EventDescriptorCollection =                        ↵
TypeDescriptor.GetEvents(button1)

    ' Prints the number of events on button1 in a text box.
    textBox1.Text = events.Count.ToString()
End Sub 'GetCount
```

[C#]
```
private void GetCount() {
    // Creates a new collection and assigns it the events for button1.
    EventDescriptorCollection events =                               ↵
TypeDescriptor.GetEvents(button1);

    // Prints the number of events on button1 in a text box.
    textBox1.Text = events.Count.ToString();
 }
```

Requirements

Platforms: Windows 98, Windows NT 4.0, Windows Millennium Edition, Windows 2000, Windows XP Home Edition, Windows XP Professional, Windows .NET Server family, .NET Compact Framework - Windows CE .NET

EventDescriptorCollection.Item Property

Gets the specified event.

[C#] In C#, this property is the indexer for the **EventDescriptorCollection** class.

Overload List

Gets the event with the specified name.

[Visual Basic] **Overloads Public Overridable Default ReadOnly Property Item(String) As EventDescriptor**

[C#] **public virtual EventDescriptor this[string] {get;}**

[C++] **public: __property virtual EventDescriptor* get_Item(String*);**

[JScript] **EventDescriptorCollection.Item (String)**

Gets the event with the specified index number.

[Visual Basic] **Overloads Public Overridable Default ReadOnly Property Item(Integer) As EventDescriptor**

[C#] **public virtual EventDescriptor this[int] {get;}**

[C++] **public: __property virtual EventDescriptor* get_Item(int);**

[JScript] **EventDescriptorCollection.Item (int)**

Example

[Visual Basic, C#] The following example uses the **Item** property to print the name of the **EventDescriptor** specified by the index number in a text box. Because the index number is zero-based, this example prints the name of the second **EventDescriptor**. It assumes `button1` and `textBox1` have been instantiated on a form.

> [Visual Basic, C#] **Note** This example shows how to use one of the overloaded versions of the **Item** property (**EventDescriptorCollection** indexer). For other examples that might be available, see the individual overload topics.

[Visual Basic]
```
Private Sub PrintIndexItem()
    ' Creates a new collection and assigns it the events for button1.
    Dim events As EventDescriptorCollection =                        ↵
TypeDescriptor.GetEvents(button1)

    ' Prints the second event's name.
    textBox1.Text = events(1).ToString()
End Sub 'PrintIndexItem
```

[C#]
```
private void PrintIndexItem() {
    // Creates a new collection and assigns it the events for button1.
    EventDescriptorCollection events =                               ↵
TypeDescriptor.GetEvents(button1);

    // Prints the second event's name.
    textBox1.Text = events[1].ToString();
 }
```

EventDescriptorCollection.Item Property (String)

Gets the event with the specified name.

[C#] In C#, this property is the indexer for the **EventDescriptorCollection** class.

[Visual Basic]
```
Overloads Public Overridable Default ReadOnly Property Item( _
   ByVal name As String _
) As EventDescriptor
```
[C#]
```
public virtual EventDescriptor this[
   string name
] {get;}
```
[C++]
```
public: __property virtual EventDescriptor* get_Item(
   String* name
);
```
[JScript]
```
returnValue = EventDescriptorCollectionObject.Item(name);
-or-
returnValue = EventDescriptorCollectionObject(name);
```

[JScript] In JScript, you can use the default indexed properties defined by a type, but you cannot explicitly define your own. However, specifying the **expando** attribute on a class automatically provides a default indexed property whose type is **Object** and whose index type is **String**.

Arguments [JScript]

name

The name of the **EventDescriptor** to get from the collection.

Parameters [Visual Basic, C#, C++]

name

The name of the **EventDescriptor** to get from the collection.

Property Value

The **EventDescriptor** with the specified name, or a null reference (**Nothing** in Visual Basic) if the event does not exist.

Remarks

Item is case-sensitive when searching for names. That is, the names "Ename" and "ename" are considered to be two different events.

Example

[Visual Basic, C#] The following example uses the **Item** property to print the type of the component for the **EventDescriptor** specified by the index. It assumes that `button1` and `textBox1` have been instantiated on a form.

[Visual Basic]
```
Private Sub PrintIndexItem2()
    ' Creates a new collection and assigns it the events for button1.
    Dim events As EventDescriptorCollection = ┘
TypeDescriptor.GetEvents(button1)

    ' Sets an EventDescriptor to the specific event.
    Dim myEvent As EventDescriptor = events("KeyDown")

    ' Prints the name of the event.
    textBox1.Text = myEvent.Name
End Sub 'PrintIndexItem2
```

[C#]
```
private void PrintIndexItem2() {
    // Creates a new collection and assigns it the events for button1.
    EventDescriptorCollection events = ┘
TypeDescriptor.GetEvents(button1);

    // Sets an EventDescriptor to the specific event.
    EventDescriptor myEvent = events["KeyDown"];

    // Prints the name of the event.
    textBox1.Text = myEvent.Name;
}
```

Requirements

Platforms: Windows 98, Windows NT 4.0, Windows Millennium Edition, Windows 2000, Windows XP Home Edition, Windows XP Professional, Windows .NET Server family

EventDescriptorCollection.Item Property (Int32)

Gets the event with the specified index number.

[C#] In C#, this property is the indexer for the **EventDescriptorCollection** class.

[Visual Basic]
```
Overloads Public Overridable Default ReadOnly Property Item( _
   ByVal index As Integer _
) As EventDescriptor
```
[C#]
```
public virtual EventDescriptor this[
   int index
] {get;}
```
[C++]
```
public: __property virtual EventDescriptor* get_Item(
   int index
);
```
[JScript]
```
returnValue = EventDescriptorCollectionObject.Item(index);
-or-
returnValue = EventDescriptorCollectionObject(index);
```

[JScript] In JScript, you can use the default indexed properties defined by a type, but you cannot explicitly define your own. However, specifying the **expando** attribute on a class automatically provides a default indexed property whose type is **Object** and whose index type is **String**.

Arguments [JScript]

index

The zero-based index number of the **EventDescriptor** to get from the collection.

Parameters [Visual Basic, C#, C++]

index

The zero-based index number of the **EventDescriptor** to get from the collection.

Property Value

The **EventDescriptor** with the specified index number.

Exceptions

Exception Type	Condition
IndexOutOfRange-Exception	*index* is not a valid index for **Item**.

Remarks

The index number is zero-based. Therefore, you must subtract one from the numerical position of a particular **EventDescriptor** to access that **EventDescriptor**. For example, to get the third **EventDescriptor**, you need to specify `myColl[2]`.

Example

[Visual Basic, C#] The following example uses the **Item** property to print the name of the **EventDescriptor** specified by the index number in a text box. Because the index number is zero-based, this example prints the name of the second **EventDescriptor**. It assumes `button1` and `textBox1` have been instantiated on a form.

```
[Visual Basic]
Private Sub PrintIndexItem()
    ' Creates a new collection and assigns it the events for button1.
    Dim events As EventDescriptorCollection = ↵
TypeDescriptor.GetEvents(button1)

    ' Prints the second event's name.
    textBox1.Text = events(1).ToString()
End Sub 'PrintIndexItem
```

```
[C#]
private void PrintIndexItem() {
    // Creates a new collection and assigns it the events for button1.
    EventDescriptorCollection events = ↵
TypeDescriptor.GetEvents(button1);

    // Prints the second event's name.
    textBox1.Text = events[1].ToString();
 }
```

Requirements

Platforms: Windows 98, Windows NT 4.0, Windows Millennium Edition, Windows 2000, Windows XP Home Edition, Windows XP Professional, Windows .NET Server family

EventDescriptorCollection.System.Collections.ICollection.Count Property

Note: This namespace, class, or member is supported only in version 1.1 of the .NET Framework.

This member supports the .NET Framework infrastructure and is not intended to be used directly from your code.

```
[Visual Basic]
Private ReadOnly Property Count As Integer Implements _
   ICollection.Count
[C#]
int ICollection.Count {get;}
[C++]
private: __property int
   System::Collections::ICollection::get_Count();
[JScript]
private function get ICollection.Count() : int;
```

EventDescriptorCollection.System.Collections.ICollection.IsSynchronized Property

Note: This namespace, class, or member is supported only in version 1.1 of the .NET Framework.

This member supports the .NET Framework infrastructure and is not intended to be used directly from your code.

```
[Visual Basic]
Private ReadOnly Property IsSynchronized As Boolean Implements _
   ICollection.IsSynchronized
[C#]
bool ICollection.IsSynchronized {get;}
[C++]
private: __property bool
   System::Collections::ICollection::get_IsSynchronized();
[JScript]
private function get ICollection.IsSynchronized() : Boolean;
```

EventDescriptorCollection.System.Collections.ICollection.SyncRoot Property

Note: This namespace, class, or member is supported only in version 1.1 of the .NET Framework.

This member supports the .NET Framework infrastructure and is not intended to be used directly from your code.

```
[Visual Basic]
Private ReadOnly Property SyncRoot As Object Implements _
   ICollection.SyncRoot
[C#]
object ICollection.SyncRoot {get;}
[C++]
private: __property Object*
   System::Collections::ICollection::get_SyncRoot();
[JScript]
private function get ICollection.SyncRoot() : Object;
```

EventDescriptorCollection.System.Collections.IList.IsFixedSize Property

Note: This namespace, class, or member is supported only in version 1.1 of the .NET Framework.

This member supports the .NET Framework infrastructure and is not intended to be used directly from your code.

```
[Visual Basic]
Private ReadOnly Property IsFixedSize As Boolean Implements _
   IList.IsFixedSize
[C#]
bool IList.IsFixedSize {get;}
[C++]
private: __property bool
   System::Collections::IList::get_IsFixedSize();
[JScript]
private function get IList.IsFixedSize() : Boolean;
```

EventDescriptorCollection.System.Collections.IList.IsReadOnly Property

Note: This namespace, class, or member is supported only in version 1.1 of the .NET Framework.

This member supports the .NET Framework infrastructure and is not intended to be used directly from your code.

```
[Visual Basic]
Private ReadOnly Property IsReadOnly As Boolean Implements _
   IList.IsReadOnly
[C#]
bool IList.IsReadOnly {get;}
[C++]
private: __property bool
   System::Collections::IList::get_IsReadOnly();
[JScript]
private function get IList.IsReadOnly() : Boolean;
```

EventDescriptorCollection.System.Collections.IList.Item Property

Note: This namespace, class, or member is supported only in version 1.1 of the .NET Framework.

[C#] In C#, this property is the indexer for the **EventDescriptorCollection** class.

```
[Visual Basic]
Private Default Property Item( _
   ByVal index As Integer _
) As Object Implements IList.Item
[C#]
object IList.this[
   int index
] {get; set;}
[C++]
private: __property Object* System::Collections::IList::get_Item(
   int index
);
private: __property void System::Collections::IList::set_Item(
   int index,
   Object*
);
[JScript]
private function get IList.get_Item(index : int) : Object;
private function set IList.set_Item(index : int, value : Object);
-or-
private function get IList.get_Item(index : int) : Object;
private function set IList.set_Item(index : int, value : Object);
```

[JScript] In JScript, you can use the default indexed properties defined by a type, but you cannot explicitly define your own. However, specifying the **expando** attribute on a class automatically provides a default indexed property whose type is **Object** and whose index type is **String**.

Arguments [JScript]

index

Parameters [Visual Basic, C#, C++]

index

Requirements

Platforms: Windows 98, Windows NT 4.0, Windows Millennium Edition, Windows 2000, Windows XP Home Edition, Windows XP Professional, Windows .NET Server family

EventDescriptorCollection.Add Method

Adds an **EventDescriptor** to the end of the collection.

```
[Visual Basic]
Public Function Add( _
   ByVal value As EventDescriptor _
) As Integer
[C#]
public int Add(
   EventDescriptor value
);
[C++]
public: int Add(
   EventDescriptor* value
);
[JScript]
public function Add(
   value : EventDescriptor
) : int;
```

Parameters

value

An **EventDescriptor** to add to the collection.

Return Value

The position of the **EventDescriptor** within the collection.

Requirements

Platforms: Windows 98, Windows NT 4.0, Windows Millennium Edition, Windows 2000, Windows XP Home Edition, Windows XP Professional, Windows .NET Server family, .NET Compact Framework - Windows CE .NET

EventDescriptorCollection.Clear Method

Removes all objects from the collection.

```
[Visual Basic]
Public Sub Clear()
[C#]
public void Clear();
[C++]
public: void Clear();
[JScript]
public function Clear();
```

Requirements

Platforms: Windows 98, Windows NT 4.0, Windows Millennium Edition, Windows 2000, Windows XP Home Edition, Windows XP Professional, Windows .NET Server family, .NET Compact Framework - Windows CE .NET

EventDescriptorCollection.Contains Method

Returns whether the collection contains the given **EventDescriptor**.

```
[Visual Basic]
Public Function Contains( _
   ByVal value As EventDescriptor _
) As Boolean
[C#]
public bool Contains(
   EventDescriptor value
);
[C++]
public: bool Contains(
   EventDescriptor* value
);
[JScript]
public function Contains(
   value : EventDescriptor
) : Boolean;
```

Parameters

value

The **EventDescriptor** to find within the collection.

Return Value

true if the collection contains the *value* parameter given; otherwise, **false**.

Requirements

Platforms: Windows 98, Windows NT 4.0, Windows Millennium Edition, Windows 2000, Windows XP Home Edition, Windows XP Professional, Windows .NET Server family, .NET Compact Framework - Windows CE .NET

EventDescriptorCollection.Find Method

Gets the description of the event with the specified name in the collection.

[Visual Basic]
```
Public Overridable Function Find( _
   ByVal name As String, _
   ByVal ignoreCase As Boolean _
) As EventDescriptor
```
[C#]
```
public virtual EventDescriptor Find(
   string name,
   bool ignoreCase
);
```
[C++]
```
public: virtual EventDescriptor* Find(
   String* name,
   bool ignoreCase
);
```
[JScript]
```
public function Find(
   name : String,
   ignoreCase : Boolean
) : EventDescriptor;
```

Parameters

name
The name of the event to get from the collection.

ignoreCase
true if you want to ignore the case of the event; otherwise, **false**.

Return Value

The **EventDescriptor** with the specified name, or a null reference (**Nothing** in Visual Basic) if the event does not exist.

Example

[Visual Basic, C#] The following example finds a specific **EventDescriptor**. It prints the type of component for this **EventDescriptor** in a text box. It assumes that `button1` and `textBox1` have been instantiated on a form.

[Visual Basic]
```
Private Sub FindEvent()
    ' Creates a new collection and assigns it the events for button1.
    Dim events As EventDescriptorCollection =                          ↵
TypeDescriptor.GetEvents(button1)

    ' Sets an EventDescriptor to the specific event.
    Dim myEvent As EventDescriptor = events.Find("Resize", False)

    ' Prints the event name and event description.
    textBox1.Text = myEvent.Name & ": " & myEvent.Description
End Sub 'FindEvent
```

[C#]
```
private void FindEvent() {
    // Creates a new collection and assigns it the events for button1.
    EventDescriptorCollection events =                                 ↵
TypeDescriptor.GetEvents(button1);

    // Sets an EventDescriptor to the specific event.
    EventDescriptor myEvent = events.Find("Resize", false);

    // Prints the event name and event description.
    textBox1.Text = myEvent.Name + ": " + myEvent.Description;
}
```

Requirements

Platforms: Windows 98, Windows NT 4.0, Windows Millennium Edition, Windows 2000, Windows XP Home Edition, Windows XP Professional, Windows .NET Server family, .NET Compact Framework - Windows CE .NET

EventDescriptorCollection.GetEnumerator Method

Gets an enumerator for this **EventDescriptorCollection**.

[Visual Basic]
```
Public Function GetEnumerator() As IEnumerator
```
[C#]
```
public IEnumerator GetEnumerator();
```
[C++]
```
public: IEnumerator* GetEnumerator();
```
[JScript]
```
public function GetEnumerator() : IEnumerator;
```

Return Value

An enumerator that implements **IEnumerator**.

Example

[Visual Basic, C#] The following example gets an enumerator for the events on `button1`. It uses the enumerator to print the names of the events in the collection. It assumes that `button1` and `textBox1` have been instantiated on a form.

[Visual Basic]
```
Private Sub MyEnumerator()
    ' Creates a new collection, and assigns to it the events           ↵
 for button1.
    Dim events As EventDescriptorCollection =                          ↵
TypeDescriptor.GetEvents(button1)

    ' Creates an enumerator.
    Dim ie As IEnumerator = events.GetEnumerator()

    ' Prints the name of each event in the collection.
    Dim myEvent As Object
    While ie.MoveNext() = True
        myEvent = ie.Current
        textBox1.Text += myEvent.ToString() & ControlChars.Cr
    End While
End Sub 'MyEnumerator
```

[C#]
```
private void MyEnumerator() {
    // Creates a new collection, and assigns to it the                 ↵
events for button1.
    EventDescriptorCollection events =                                 ↵
TypeDescriptor.GetEvents(button1);
```

```
    // Creates an enumerator.
    IEnumerator ie = events.GetEnumerator();

    // Prints the name of each event in the collection.
    Object myEvent;
    while(ie.MoveNext() == true) {
       myEvent = ie.Current;
       textBox1.Text += myEvent.ToString() + '\n';
    }
}
```

Requirements

Platforms: Windows 98, Windows NT 4.0, Windows Millennium Edition, Windows 2000, Windows XP Home Edition, Windows XP Professional, Windows .NET Server family, .NET Compact Framework - Windows CE .NET

EventDescriptorCollection.ICollection.CopyTo Method

This member supports the .NET Framework infrastructure and is not intended to be used directly from your code.

```
[Visual Basic]
Private Sub CopyTo( _
   ByVal array As Array, _
   ByVal index As Integer _
) Implements ICollection.CopyTo
[C#]
void ICollection.CopyTo(
   Array array,
   int index
);
[C++]
private: void ICollection::CopyTo(
   Array* array,
   int index
);
[JScript]
private function ICollection.CopyTo(
   array : Array,
   index : int
);
```

EventDescriptorCollection.IEnumerable.GetEnumerator Method

This member supports the .NET Framework infrastructure and is not intended to be used directly from your code.

```
[Visual Basic]
Private Function GetEnumerator() As IEnumerator Implements _
   IEnumerable.GetEnumerator
[C#]
IEnumerator IEnumerable.GetEnumerator();
[C++]
private: IEnumerator* IEnumerable::GetEnumerator();
[JScript]
private function IEnumerable.GetEnumerator() : IEnumerator;
```

EventDescriptorCollection.IList.Add Method

This member supports the .NET Framework infrastructure and is not intended to be used directly from your code.

```
[Visual Basic]
Private Function Add( _
   ByVal value As Object _
) As Integer Implements IList.Add
[C#]
int IList.Add(
   object value
);
[C++]
private: int IList::Add(
   Object* value
);
[JScript]
private function IList.Add(
   value : Object
) : int;
```

EventDescriptorCollection.IList.Clear Method

This member supports the .NET Framework infrastructure and is not intended to be used directly from your code.

```
[Visual Basic]
Private Sub Clear() Implements IList.Clear
[C#]
void IList.Clear();
[C++]
private: void IList::Clear();
[JScript]
private function IList.Clear();
```

EventDescriptorCollection.IList.Contains Method

This member supports the .NET Framework infrastructure and is not intended to be used directly from your code.

```
[Visual Basic]
Private Function Contains( _
   ByVal value As Object _
) As Boolean Implements IList.Contains
[C#]
bool IList.Contains(
   object value
);
[C++]
private: bool IList::Contains(
   Object* value
);
[JScript]
private function IList.Contains(
   value : Object
) : Boolean;
```

EventDescriptorCollection.IList.IndexOf Method

This member supports the .NET Framework infrastructure and is not intended to be used directly from your code.

```
[Visual Basic]
Private Function IndexOf( _
   ByVal value As Object _
) As Integer Implements IList.IndexOf
[C#]
int IList.IndexOf(
   object value
);
[C++]
private: int IList::IndexOf(
   Object* value
);
[JScript]
private function IList.IndexOf(
   value : Object
) : int;
```

EventDescriptorCollection.IList.Insert Method

This member supports the .NET Framework infrastructure and is not intended to be used directly from your code.

```
[Visual Basic]
Private Sub Insert( _
   ByVal index As Integer, _
   ByVal value As Object _
) Implements IList.Insert
[C#]
void IList.Insert(
   int index,
   object value
);
[C++]
private: void IList::Insert(
   int index,
   Object* value
);
[JScript]
private function IList.Insert(
   index : int,
   value : Object
);
```

EventDescriptorCollection.IList.Remove Method

This member supports the .NET Framework infrastructure and is not intended to be used directly from your code.

```
[Visual Basic]
Private Sub Remove( _
   ByVal value As Object _
) Implements IList.Remove
[C#]
void IList.Remove(
   object value
);
[C++]
private: void IList::Remove(
   Object* value
);
[JScript]
private function IList.Remove(
   value : Object
);
```

EventDescriptorCollection.IList.RemoveAt Method

This member supports the .NET Framework infrastructure and is not intended to be used directly from your code.

```
[Visual Basic]
Private Sub RemoveAt( _
   ByVal index As Integer _
) Implements IList.RemoveAt
[C#]
void IList.RemoveAt(
   int index
);
[C++]
private: void IList::RemoveAt(
   int index
);
[JScript]
private function IList.RemoveAt(
   index : int
);
```

EventDescriptorCollection.IndexOf Method

Returns the index of the **EventDescriptor** given.

```
[Visual Basic]
Public Function IndexOf( _
   ByVal value As EventDescriptor _
) As Integer
[C#]
public int IndexOf(
   EventDescriptor value
);
[C++]
public: int IndexOf(
   EventDescriptor* value
);
[JScript]
public function IndexOf(
   value : EventDescriptor
) : int;
```

Parameters

value

The **EventDescriptor** to find within the collection.

Return Value

The index of the given **EventDescriptor** within the collection.

Exceptions

Exception Type	Condition
ArgumentNull-Exception	The **EventDescriptor** does not exist in the collection.

Requirements

Platforms: Windows 98, Windows NT 4.0,
Windows Millennium Edition, Windows 2000,
Windows XP Home Edition, Windows XP Professional,
Windows .NET Server family,
.NET Compact Framework - Windows CE .NET

EventDescriptorCollection.Insert Method

Inserts an **EventDescriptor** to the collection at a specified index.

```
[Visual Basic]
Public Sub Insert( _
   ByVal index As Integer, _
   ByVal value As EventDescriptor _
)
[C#]
public void Insert(
   int index,
   EventDescriptor value
);
[C++]
public: void Insert(
   int index,
   EventDescriptor* value
);
[JScript]
public function Insert(
   index : int,
   value : EventDescriptor
);
```

Parameters

index
: The index within the collection in which to insert the *value* parameter.

value
: An **EventDescriptor** to insert into the collection.

Requirements

Platforms: Windows 98, Windows NT 4.0,
Windows Millennium Edition, Windows 2000,
Windows XP Home Edition, Windows XP Professional,
Windows .NET Server family,
.NET Compact Framework - Windows CE .NET

EventDescriptorCollection.InternalSort Method

Sorts the members of this **EventDescriptorCollection**.

Overload List

Sorts the members of this **EventDescriptorCollection**, using the specified **IComparer**.

[Visual Basic] **Overloads Protected Sub InternalSort(IComparer)**

[C#] **protected void InternalSort(IComparer);**

[C++] **protected: void InternalSort(IComparer*);**

[JScript] **protected function InternalSort(IComparer);**

Sorts the members of this **EventDescriptorCollection**. The specified order is applied first, followed by the default sort for this collection, which is usually alphabetical.

[Visual Basic] **Overloads Protected Sub InternalSort(String())**

[C#] **protected void InternalSort(string[]);**

[C++] **protected: void InternalSort(String*[]);**

[JScript] **protected function InternalSort(String[]);**

Example

[Visual Basic, C#] If the **EventDescriptorCollection** contains four **EventDescriptor** objects with the names `A`, `B`, `C`, and `D`, the properties of this **EventDescriptorCollection** would be sorted in the order `D`, `B`, `A`, and `C`.

> [Visual Basic, C#] **Note** This example shows how to use one of the overloaded versions of **InternalSort**. For other examples that might be available, see the individual overload topics.

```
[Visual Basic]
Me.InternalSort(New String() {"D", "B"})
```

```
[C#]
this.InternalSort(new string[]{"D", "B"});
```

EventDescriptorCollection.InternalSort Method (IComparer)

Sorts the members of this **EventDescriptorCollection**, using the specified **IComparer**.

```
[Visual Basic]
Overloads Protected Sub InternalSort( _
   ByVal sorter As IComparer _
)
[C#]
protected void InternalSort(
   IComparer sorter
);
[C++]
protected: void InternalSort(
   IComparer* sorter
);
[JScript]
protected function InternalSort(
   sorter : IComparer
);
```

Parameters

sorter
: A comparer to use to sort the **EventDescriptor** objects in this collection.

Remarks

If the *sorter* parameter is a null reference (**Nothing** in Visual Basic), the default sort order is used.

Requirements

Platforms: Windows 98, Windows NT 4.0,
Windows Millennium Edition, Windows 2000,
Windows XP Home Edition, Windows XP Professional,
Windows .NET Server family

EventDescriptorCollection.InternalSort Method (String[])

Sorts the members of this **EventDescriptorCollection**. The specified order is applied first, followed by the default sort for this collection, which is usually alphabetical.

```
[Visual Basic]
Overloads Protected Sub InternalSort( _
   ByVal names() As String _
)
[C#]
protected void InternalSort(
   string[] names
);
[C++]
protected: void InternalSort(
   String* names __gc[]
);
[JScript]
protected function InternalSort(
   names : String[]
);
```

Parameters

names
An array of strings describing the order in which to sort the **EventDescriptor** objects in this collection.

Example

[Visual Basic, C#] If the **EventDescriptorCollection** contains four **EventDescriptor** objects with the names A, B, C, and D, the properties of this **EventDescriptorCollection** would be sorted in the order D, B, A, and C.

```
[Visual Basic]
Me.InternalSort(New String() {"D", "B"})
```

```
[C#]
this.InternalSort(new string[]{"D", "B"});
```

Requirements

Platforms: Windows 98, Windows NT 4.0, Windows Millennium Edition, Windows 2000, Windows XP Home Edition, Windows XP Professional, Windows .NET Server family

EventDescriptorCollection.Remove Method

Removes the specified **EventDescriptor** from the collection.

```
[Visual Basic]
Public Sub Remove( _
   ByVal value As EventDescriptor _
)
[C#]
public void Remove(
   EventDescriptor value
);
[C++]
public: void Remove(
   EventDescriptor* value
);
[JScript]
public function Remove(
   value : EventDescriptor
);
```

Parameters

value
The **EventDescriptor** to remove from the collection.

Requirements

Platforms: Windows 98, Windows NT 4.0, Windows Millennium Edition, Windows 2000, Windows XP Home Edition, Windows XP Professional, Windows .NET Server family, .NET Compact Framework - Windows CE .NET

EventDescriptorCollection.RemoveAt Method

Removes the **EventDescriptor** at the specified index from the collection.

```
[Visual Basic]
Public Sub RemoveAt( _
   ByVal index As Integer _
)
[C#]
public void RemoveAt(
   int index
);
[C++]
public: void RemoveAt(
   int index
);
[JScript]
public function RemoveAt(
   index : int
);
```

Parameters

index
The index of the **EventDescriptor** to remove.

Requirements

Platforms: Windows 98, Windows NT 4.0, Windows Millennium Edition, Windows 2000, Windows XP Home Edition, Windows XP Professional, Windows .NET Server family, .NET Compact Framework - Windows CE .NET

EventDescriptorCollection.Sort Method

Sorts the members of this **EventDescriptorCollection**.

Overload List

Sorts the members of this **EventDescriptorCollection**, using the default sort for this collection, which is usually alphabetical.

[Visual Basic] **Overloads Public Overridable Function Sort() As EventDescriptorCollection**

[C#] **public virtual EventDescriptorCollection Sort();**

[C++] **public: virtual EventDescriptorCollection* Sort();**

[JScript] **public function Sort() : EventDescriptorCollection;**

Sorts the members of this **EventDescriptorCollection**, using the specified **IComparer**.

[Visual Basic] **Overloads Public Overridable Function Sort(IComparer) As EventDescriptorCollection**

[C#] **public virtual EventDescriptorCollection Sort(IComparer);**

[C++] **public: virtual EventDescriptorCollection* Sort(IComparer*);**

[JScript] **public function Sort(IComparer) : EventDescriptorCollection;**

Sorts the members of this **EventDescriptorCollection**, given a specified sort order.

[Visual Basic] **Overloads Public Overridable Function Sort(String()) As EventDescriptorCollection**

[C#] **public virtual EventDescriptorCollection Sort(string[]);**

[C++] **public: virtual EventDescriptorCollection* Sort(String*[]);**

[JScript] **public function Sort(String[]) : EventDescriptorCollection;**

Sorts the members of this **EventDescriptorCollection**, given a specified sort order and an **IComparer**.

[Visual Basic] **Overloads Public Overridable Function Sort(String(), IComparer) As EventDescriptorCollection**

[C#] **public virtual EventDescriptorCollection Sort(string[], IComparer);**

[C++] **public: virtual EventDescriptorCollection* Sort(String*[], IComparer*);**

[JScript] **public function Sort(String[], IComparer) : EventDescriptorCollection;**

Example

[Visual Basic, C#] If the **EventDescriptorCollection** contains four **EventDescriptor** objects with the names `A`, `B`, `C`, and `D`, the properties of `myNewColl` would be sorted in the order `D`, `B`, `A`, and `C`.

> [Visual Basic, C#] **Note** This example shows how to use one of the overloaded versions of **Sort**. For other examples that might be available, see the individual overload topics.

[Visual Basic]
```
myNewColl = Me.Sort(New String() {"D", "B"})
```

[C#]
```
myNewColl = this.Sort(new string[]{"D", "B"});
```

EventDescriptorCollection.Sort Method ()

Sorts the members of this **EventDescriptorCollection**, using the default sort for this collection, which is usually alphabetical.

[Visual Basic]
```
Overloads Public Overridable Function Sort() As
EventDescriptorCollection
```
[C#]
```
public virtual EventDescriptorCollection Sort();
```
[C++]
```
public: virtual EventDescriptorCollection* Sort();
```
[JScript]
```
public function Sort() : EventDescriptorCollection;
```

Return Value

The new **EventDescriptorCollection**.

Example

[Visual Basic, C#] If the **EventDescriptorCollection** contains four **EventDescriptor** objects with the names `A`, `B`, `C`, and `D`, the properties of `myNewColl` would be sorted in the order `D`, `B`, `A`, and `C`.

[Visual Basic]
```
myNewColl = Me.Sort(New String() {"D", "B"})
```

[C#]
```
myNewColl = this.Sort(new string[]{"D", "B"});
```

Requirements

Platforms: Windows 98, Windows NT 4.0, Windows Millennium Edition, Windows 2000, Windows XP Home Edition, Windows XP Professional, Windows .NET Server family

EventDescriptorCollection.Sort Method (IComparer)

Sorts the members of this **EventDescriptorCollection**, using the specified **IComparer**.

[Visual Basic]
```
Overloads Public Overridable Function Sort( _
   ByVal comparer As IComparer _
) As EventDescriptorCollection
```
[C#]
```
public virtual EventDescriptorCollection Sort(
   IComparer comparer
);
```
[C++]
```
public: virtual EventDescriptorCollection* Sort(
   IComparer* comparer
);
```
[JScript]
```
public function Sort(
   comparer : IComparer
) : EventDescriptorCollection;
```

Parameters

comparer

An **IComparer** to use to sort the **EventDescriptor** objects in this collection.

Return Value

The new **EventDescriptorCollection**.

Remarks

The specified **IComparer** is applied first, followed by the default sort for this collection, which is usually alphabetical.

Example

[Visual Basic, C#] If the **EventDescriptorCollection** contains four **EventDescriptor** objects with the names `A`, `B`, `C`, and `D`, the properties of `myNewColl` would be sorted in the order `D`, `B`, `A`, and `C`.

[Visual Basic]
```
myNewColl = Me.Sort(New String() {"D", "B"})
```

[C#]
```
myNewColl = this.Sort(new string[]{"D", "B"});
```

Requirements

Platforms: Windows 98, Windows NT 4.0, Windows Millennium Edition, Windows 2000, Windows XP Home Edition, Windows XP Professional, Windows .NET Server family

EventDescriptorCollection.Sort Method (String[])

Sorts the members of this **EventDescriptorCollection**, given a specified sort order.

[Visual Basic]
```
Overloads Public Overridable Function Sort( _
   ByVal names() As String _
) As EventDescriptorCollection
```
[C#]
```
public virtual EventDescriptorCollection Sort(
   string[] names
);
```
[C++]
```
public: virtual EventDescriptorCollection* Sort(
   String* names __gc[]
);
```
[JScript]
```
public function Sort(
   names : String[]
) : EventDescriptorCollection;
```

Parameters

names
An array of strings describing the order in which to sort the **EventDescriptor** objects in the collection.

Return Value

The new **EventDescriptorCollection**.

Remarks

The specified order is applied first, followed by the default sort for this collection, which is usually alphabetical.

Example

[Visual Basic, C#] If the **EventDescriptorCollection** contains four **EventDescriptor** objects with the names `A`, `B`, `C`, and `D`, the properties of `myNewColl` would be sorted in the order `D`, `B`, `A`, and `C`.

[Visual Basic]
```
myNewColl = Me.Sort(New String() {"D", "B"})
```

[C#]
```
myNewColl = this.Sort(new string[]{"D", "B"});
```

Requirements

Platforms: Windows 98, Windows NT 4.0, Windows Millennium Edition, Windows 2000, Windows XP Home Edition, Windows XP Professional, Windows .NET Server family

EventDescriptorCollection.Sort Method (String[], IComparer)

Sorts the members of this **EventDescriptorCollection**, given a specified sort order and an **IComparer**.

[Visual Basic]
```
Overloads Public Overridable Function Sort( _
   ByVal names() As String, _
   ByVal comparer As IComparer _
) As EventDescriptorCollection
```
[C#]
```
public virtual EventDescriptorCollection Sort(
   string[] names,
   IComparer comparer
);
```
[C++]
```
public: virtual EventDescriptorCollection* Sort(
   String* names __gc[],
   IComparer* comparer
);
```
[JScript]
```
public function Sort(
   names : String[],
   comparer : IComparer
) : EventDescriptorCollection;
```

Parameters

names
An array of strings describing the order in which to sort the **EventDescriptor** objects in the collection.

comparer
An **IComparer** to use to sort the **EventDescriptor** objects in this collection.

Return Value

The new **EventDescriptorCollection**.

Remarks

The specified sort order is applied first, followed by the sort using the specified **IComparer**.

Example

[Visual Basic, C#] If the **EventDescriptorCollection** contains four **EventDescriptor** objects with the names `A`, `B`, `C`, and `D`, the properties of `myNewColl` would be sorted in the order `D`, `B`, `A`, and `C`.

[Visual Basic]
```
myNewColl = Me.Sort(New String() {"D", "B"})
```

[C#]
```
myNewColl = this.Sort(new string[]{"D", "B"});
```

Requirements

Platforms: Windows 98, Windows NT 4.0, Windows Millennium Edition, Windows 2000, Windows XP Home Edition, Windows XP Professional, Windows .NET Server family

EventHandlerList Class

Provides a simple list of delegates. This class cannot be inherited.

System.Object
  System.ComponentModel.EventHandlerList

```
[Visual Basic]
NotInheritable Public Class EventHandlerList
   Implements IDisposable
[C#]
public sealed class EventHandlerList : IDisposable
[C++]
public __gc __sealed class EventHandlerList : public IDisposable
[JScript]
public class EventHandlerList implements IDisposable
```

Thread Safety

Any public static (**Shared** in Visual Basic) members of this type are safe for multithreaded operations. Any instance members are not guaranteed to be thread safe.

Remarks

This class uses a linear search algorithm to find entries in the list of delegates. A linear search algorithm is inefficient when working with a large number of entries. Therefore, when you have a large list, finding entries is slow.

Example

For an example on using an **EventHandlerList**, see the sample in the "Optimizing Event Implementation" section in **Defining an Event**.

Requirements

Namespace: System.ComponentModel

Platforms: Windows 98, Windows NT 4.0, Windows Millennium Edition, Windows 2000, Windows XP Home Edition, Windows XP Professional, Windows Server 2003 family, .NET Compact Framework - Windows CE .NET

Assembly: System (in System.dll)

EventHandlerList Constructor

Initializes a new instance of the **EventHandlerList** class.

```
[Visual Basic]
Public Sub New()
[C#]
public EventHandlerList();
[C++]
public: EventHandlerList();
[JScript]
public function EventHandlerList();
```

Remarks

The default constructor initializes any fields to their default values.

Requirements

Platforms: Windows 98, Windows NT 4.0, Windows Millennium Edition, Windows 2000, Windows XP Home Edition, Windows XP Professional, Windows Server 2003 family, .NET Compact Framework - Windows CE .NET

EventHandlerList.Item Property

Gets or sets the delegate for the specified object.

[C#] In C#, this property is the indexer for the **EventHandlerList** class.

```
[Visual Basic]
Public Default Property Item( _
   ByVal key As Object _
) As Delegate
[C#]
public Delegate this[
   object key
] {get; set;}
[C++]
public: __property Delegate* get_Item(
   Object* key
);
public: __property void set_Item(
   Object* key,
   Delegate*
);
[JScript]
returnValue = EventHandlerListObject.Item(key);
EventHandlerListObject.Item(key) = returnValue;
-or-
returnValue = EventHandlerListObject(key);
EventHandlerListObject(key) = returnValue;
```

[JScript] In JScript, you can use the default indexed properties defined by a type, but you cannot explicitly define your own. However, specifying the **expando** attribute on a class automatically provides a default indexed property whose type is **Object** and whose index type is **String**.

Arguments [JScript]

key
    An object to find in the list.

Parameters [Visual Basic, C#, C++]

key
    An object to find in the list.

Property Value

The delegate for the specified key, or a null reference (**Nothing** in Visual Basic), if a delegate does not exist.

Remarks

When the key is not found in the list and you provide a delegate to set the value of the key, then the key is added to the top of the list and assigned to the delegate as its value.

Requirements

Platforms: Windows 98, Windows NT 4.0, Windows Millennium Edition, Windows 2000, Windows XP Home Edition, Windows XP Professional, Windows Server 2003 family

EventHandlerList.AddHandler Method

Adds a delegate to the list.

```
[Visual Basic]
Public Sub AddHandler( _
   ByVal key As Object, _
   ByVal value As Delegate _
)
```

```
[C#]
public void AddHandler(
   object key,
   Delegate value
);
[C++]
public: void AddHandler(
   Object* key,
   Delegate* value
);
[JScript]
public function AddHandler(
   key : Object,
   value : Delegate
);
```

Parameters

key
: The object that owns the event.

value
: The delegate to add to the list.

Requirements

Platforms: Windows 98, Windows NT 4.0, Windows Millennium Edition, Windows 2000, Windows XP Home Edition, Windows XP Professional, Windows Server 2003 family, .NET Compact Framework - Windows CE .NET

EventHandlerList.Dispose Method

This member supports the .NET Framework infrastructure and is not intended to be used directly from your code.

```
[Visual Basic]
Public Overridable Sub Dispose() Implements IDisposable.Dispose
[C#]
public virtual void Dispose();
[C++]
public: virtual void Dispose();
[JScript]
public function Dispose();
```

EventHandlerList.RemoveHandler Method

Removes a delegate from the list.

```
[Visual Basic]
Public Sub RemoveHandler( _
   ByVal key As Object, _
   ByVal value As Delegate _
)
[C#]
public void RemoveHandler(
   object key,
   Delegate value
);
[C++]
public: void RemoveHandler(
   Object* key,
   Delegate* value
);
[JScript]
public function RemoveHandler(
   key : Object,
   value : Delegate
);
```

Parameters

key
: The object that owns the event.

value
: The delegate to remove from the list.

Requirements

Platforms: Windows 98, Windows NT 4.0, Windows Millennium Edition, Windows 2000, Windows XP Home Edition, Windows XP Professional, Windows Server 2003 family, .NET Compact Framework - Windows CE .NET

ExpandableObjectConverter Class

Provides a type converter to convert expandable objects to and from various other representations.

System.Object
  System.ComponentModel.TypeConverter
    System.ComponentModel.ExpandableObjectConverter
      System.Drawing.IconConverter
      System.Drawing.Printing.MarginsConverter
      System.Windows.Forms.ListViewItemConverter

[Visual Basic]
```
Public Class ExpandableObjectConverter
   Inherits TypeConverter
```
[C#]
```
public class ExpandableObjectConverter : TypeConverter
```
[C++]
```
public __gc class ExpandableObjectConverter : public TypeConverter
```
[JScript]
```
public class ExpandableObjectConverter extends TypeConverter
```

Thread Safety

Any public static (**Shared** in Visual Basic) members of this type are safe for multithreaded operations. Any instance members are not guaranteed to be thread safe.

Remarks

This class adds support for properties on an object to the methods and properties provided by **TypeConverter**. To make a type of property expandable in the **PropertyGrid**, specify this **TypeConverter** for standard implementations of **GetPropertiesSupported** and **GetProperties**.

> **Note** You should never access a type converter directly. Instead, call the appropriate converter by using **TypeDescriptor**. For more information, see the examples in the **TypeConverter** base class.

For more information about type converters, see the **TypeConverter** base class and **Implementing a Type Converter**.

Example

[Visual Basic, C#, C++] The following example converts a variable of type **Margins** to a string variable.

[Visual Basic]
```
Dim strM As String
strM = "1,2,3,4"
Dim m = New System.Drawing.Printing.Margins(1, 2, 3, 4)
Console.WriteLine(TypeDescriptor.GetConverter(strM).CanConvertTo ↵
(GetType(System.Drawing.Printing.Margins)))
Console.WriteLine(TypeDescriptor.GetConverter(m).ConvertToString(m))
```

[C#]
```
string strM="1,2,3,4";
System.Drawing.Printing.Margins  m= new ↵
System.Drawing.Printing.Margins(1,2,3,4);
Console.WriteLine(TypeDescriptor.GetConverter ↵
 (strM).CanConvertTo(typeof(System.Drawing.Printing.Margins)));
Console.WriteLine(TypeDescriptor.GetConverter(m).ConvertToString(m));
```

[C++]
```
String* strM = S"1,2,3,4";
System::Drawing::Printing::Margins* m = new ↵
System::Drawing::Printing::Margins(1,2,3,4);
Console::WriteLine(TypeDescriptor::GetConverter(strM)- ↵
>CanConvertTo(__typeof(System::Drawing::Printing::Margins)));
Console::WriteLine(TypeDescriptor::GetConverter(m)- ↵
>ConvertToString(m));
```

Requirements

Namespace: System.ComponentModel

Platforms: Windows 98, Windows NT 4.0, Windows Millennium Edition, Windows 2000, Windows XP Home Edition, Windows XP Professional, Windows .NET Server family

Assembly: System (in System.dll)

ExpandableObjectConverter Constructor

Initializes a new instance of the **ExpandableObjectConverter** class.

[Visual Basic]
```
Public Sub New()
```
[C#]
```
public ExpandableObjectConverter();
```
[C++]
```
public: ExpandableObjectConverter();
```
[JScript]
```
public function ExpandableObjectConverter();
```

Requirements

Platforms: Windows 98, Windows NT 4.0, Windows Millennium Edition, Windows 2000, Windows XP Home Edition, Windows XP Professional, Windows .NET Server family

ExpandableObjectConverter.GetProperties Method

Overload List

This member supports the .NET Framework infrastructure and is not intended to be used directly from your code.

[Visual Basic] **Overloads Overrides Public Function GetProperties(ITypeDescriptorContext, Object, Attribute()) As PropertyDescriptorCollection**

[C#] **public override PropertyDescriptorCollection GetProperties(ITypeDescriptorContext, object, Attribute[]);**

[C++] **public: PropertyDescriptorCollection* GetProperties(ITypeDescriptorContext*, Object*, Attribute[]);**

[JScript] **public override function GetProperties(ITypeDescriptorContext, Object, Attribute[]) : PropertyDescriptorCollection;**

Inherited from **TypeConverter**.

[Visual Basic] **Overloads Public Function GetProperties(Object) As PropertyDescriptorCollection**

[C#] **public PropertyDescriptorCollection GetProperties(object);**

[C++] **public: PropertyDescriptorCollection* GetProperties(Object*);**

[JScript] **public function GetProperties(Object) : PropertyDescriptorCollection;**

Inherited from **TypeConverter**.

[Visual Basic] **Overloads Public Function GetProperties(ITypeDescriptorContext, Object) As PropertyDescriptorCollection**

[C#] **public PropertyDescriptorCollection GetProperties(ITypeDescriptorContext, object);**

[C++] **public: PropertyDescriptorCollection* GetProperties(ITypeDescriptorContext*, Object*);**

[JScript] **public function GetProperties(ITypeDescriptorContext, Object) : PropertyDescriptorCollection;**

ExpandableObjectConverter.GetProperties Method (ITypeDescriptorContext, Object, Attribute[])

This member overrides **TypeConverter.GetProperties**.

[Visual Basic]
```
Overrides Overloads Public Function GetProperties( _
   ByVal context As ITypeDescriptorContext, _
   ByVal value As Object, _
   ByVal attributes() As Attribute _
) As PropertyDescriptorCollection
```
[C#]
```
public override PropertyDescriptorCollection GetProperties(
   ITypeDescriptorContext context,
   object value,
   Attribute[] attributes
);
```
[C++]
```
public: PropertyDescriptorCollection* GetProperties(
   ITypeDescriptorContext* context,
   Object* value,
   Attribute* attributes[]
);
```
[JScript]
```
public override function GetProperties(
   context : ITypeDescriptorContext,
   value : Object,
   attributes : Attribute[]
) : PropertyDescriptorCollection;
```

Requirements

Platforms: Windows 98, Windows NT 4.0, Windows Millennium Edition, Windows 2000, Windows XP Home Edition, Windows XP Professional, Windows .NET Server family

ExpandableObjectConverter.GetPropertiesSupported Method

Overload List

This member supports the .NET Framework infrastructure and is not intended to be used directly from your code.

[Visual Basic] **Overloads Overrides Public Function GetPropertiesSupported(ITypeDescriptorContext) As Boolean**

[C#] **public override bool GetPropertiesSupported(ITypeDescriptorContext);**

[C++] **public: bool GetPropertiesSupported(ITypeDescriptorContext*);**

[JScript] **public override function GetPropertiesSupported(ITypeDescriptorContext) : Boolean;**

Inherited from **TypeConverter**.

[Visual Basic] **Overloads Public Function GetPropertiesSupported() As Boolean**

[C#] **public bool GetPropertiesSupported();**

[C++] **public: bool GetPropertiesSupported();**

[JScript] **public function GetPropertiesSupported() : Boolean;**

ExpandableObjectConverter.GetPropertiesSupported Method (ITypeDescriptorContext)

This member overrides **TypeConverter.GetPropertiesSupported**.

[Visual Basic]
```
Overrides Overloads Public Function GetPropertiesSupported( _
   ByVal context As ITypeDescriptorContext _
) As Boolean
```
[C#]
```
public override bool GetPropertiesSupported(
   ITypeDescriptorContext context
);
```
[C++]
```
public: bool GetPropertiesSupported(
   ITypeDescriptorContext* context
);
```
[JScript]
```
public override function GetPropertiesSupported(
   context : ITypeDescriptorContext
) : Boolean;
```

Requirements

Platforms: Windows 98, Windows NT 4.0, Windows Millennium Edition, Windows 2000, Windows XP Home Edition, Windows XP Professional, Windows .NET Server family

ExtenderProvidedProperty-Attribute Class

This type supports the .NET Framework infrastructure and is not intended to be used directly from your code.

```
[Visual Basic]
<AttributeUsage(AttributeTargets.All)>
NotInheritable Public Class ExtenderProvidedPropertyAttribute
   Inherits Attribute
[C#]
[AttributeUsage(AttributeTargets.All)]
public sealed class ExtenderProvidedPropertyAttribute : Attribute
[C++]
[AttributeUsage(AttributeTargets::All)]
public __gc __sealed class ExtenderProvidedPropertyAttribute :
   public Attribute
[JScript]
public
   AttributeUsage(AttributeTargets.All)
class ExtenderProvidedPropertyAttribute extends Attribute
```

ExtenderProvidedPropertyAttribute Constructor

This member supports the .NET Framework infrastructure and is not intended to be used directly from your code.

```
[Visual Basic]
Public Sub New()
[C#]
public ExtenderProvidedPropertyAttribute();
[C++]
public: ExtenderProvidedPropertyAttribute();
[JScript]
public function ExtenderProvidedPropertyAttribute();
```

ExtenderProvidedPropertyAttribute.Extender-Property Property

This member supports the .NET Framework infrastructure and is not intended to be used directly from your code.

```
[Visual Basic]
Public ReadOnly Property ExtenderProperty As PropertyDescriptor
[C#]
public PropertyDescriptor ExtenderProperty {get;}
[C++]
public: __property PropertyDescriptor* get_ExtenderProperty();
[JScript]
public function get ExtenderProperty() : PropertyDescriptor;
```

ExtenderProvidedPropertyAttribute.Provider Property

This member supports the .NET Framework infrastructure and is not intended to be used directly from your code.

```
[Visual Basic]
Public ReadOnly Property Provider As IExtenderProvider
[C#]
public IExtenderProvider Provider {get;}
[C++]
public: __property IExtenderProvider* get_Provider();
[JScript]
public function get Provider() : IExtenderProvider;
```

ExtenderProvidedPropertyAttribute.Receiver-Type Property

This member supports the .NET Framework infrastructure and is not intended to be used directly from your code.

```
[Visual Basic]
Public ReadOnly Property ReceiverType As Type
[C#]
public Type ReceiverType {get;}
[C++]
public: __property Type* get_ReceiverType();
[JScript]
public function get ReceiverType() : Type;
```

ExtenderProvidedPropertyAttribute.Equals Method

This member supports the .NET Framework infrastructure and is not intended to be used directly from your code.

```
[Visual Basic]
Overrides Public Function Equals( _
   ByVal obj As Object _
) As Boolean
[C#]
public override bool Equals(
   object obj
);
[C++]
public: bool Equals(
   Object* obj
);
[JScript]
public override function Equals(
   obj : Object
) : Boolean;
```

ExtenderProvidedPropertyAttribute.GetHashCode Method

This member supports the .NET Framework infrastructure and is not intended to be used directly from your code.

[Visual Basic]
```
Overrides Public Function GetHashCode() As Integer
```
[C#]
```
public override int GetHashCode();
```
[C++]
```
public: int GetHashCode();
```
[JScript]
```
public override function GetHashCode() : int;
```

ExtenderProvidedPropertyAttribute.IsDefaultAttribute Method

This member overrides **Attribute.IsDefaultAttribute**.

[Visual Basic]
```
Overrides Public Function IsDefaultAttribute() As Boolean
```
[C#]
```
public override bool IsDefaultAttribute();
```
[C++]
```
public: bool IsDefaultAttribute();
```
[JScript]
```
public override function IsDefaultAttribute() : Boolean;
```

Requirements

Platforms: Windows 98, Windows NT 4.0, Windows Millennium Edition, Windows 2000, Windows XP Home Edition, Windows XP Professional, Windows Server 2003 family

GuidConverter Class

Provides a type converter to convert **Guid** objects to and from various other representations.

System.Object
  System.ComponentModel.TypeConverter
    System.ComponentModel.GuidConverter

```
[Visual Basic]
Public Class GuidConverter
   Inherits TypeConverter
[C#]
public class GuidConverter : TypeConverter
[C++]
public __gc class GuidConverter : public TypeConverter
[JScript]
public class GuidConverter extends TypeConverter
```

Thread Safety

Any public static (**Shared** in Visual Basic) members of this type are safe for multithreaded operations. Any instance members are not guaranteed to be thread safe.

Remarks

This converter can only convert a globally unique identifier (GUID) object to and from a string.

> **CAUTION** You should never create an instance of a **GuidConverter**. Instead, call the **GetConverter** method of **TypeDescriptor**. For more information, see the examples in the **TypeConverter** base class.

Example

[Visual Basic, C#, C++] The following sample converts a variable of type **Guid** to a string, and vice versa.

```
[Visual Basic]
Dim myGuid As New Guid("B80D56EC-5899-459d-83B4-1AE0BB8418E4")
Dim myGuidString As String = "1AA7F83F-C7F5-11D0-A376-00C04FC9DA04"
Console.WriteLine(TypeDescriptor.GetConverter(myGuid).ConvertTo
(myGuid, GetType(String)))
Console.WriteLine(TypeDescriptor.GetConverter(myGuid).ConvertFrom
 (myGuidString))

[C#]
Guid myGuid = new Guid("B80D56EC-5899-459d-83B4-1AE0BB8418E4");
string myGuidString = "1AA7F83F-C7F5-11D0-A376-00C04FC9DA04";
Console.WriteLine(TypeDescriptor.GetConverter(myGuid).ConvertTo
 (myGuid, typeof(string)));
Console.WriteLine(TypeDescriptor.GetConverter(myGuid).ConvertFrom
 (myGuidString));

[C++]
Guid myGuid(S"B80D56EC-5899-459d-83B4-1AE0BB8418E4");
String* myGuidString = S"1AA7F83F-C7F5-11D0-A376-00C04FC9DA04";
Console::WriteLine(TypeDescriptor::GetConverter(__box(myGuid))-
>ConvertTo(__box(myGuid), __typeof(String)));
Console::WriteLine(TypeDescriptor::GetConverter(__box(myGuid))-
>ConvertFrom(myGuidString));
```

Requirements

Namespace: System.ComponentModel

Platforms: Windows 98, Windows NT 4.0, Windows Millennium Edition, Windows 2000, Windows XP Home Edition, Windows XP Professional, Windows Server 2003 family

Assembly: System (in System.dll)

GuidConverter Constructor

Initializes a new instance of the **GuidConverter** class.

```
[Visual Basic]
Public Sub New()
[C#]
public GuidConverter();
[C++]
public: GuidConverter();
[JScript]
public function GuidConverter();
```

Remarks

The default constructor initializes any fields to their default values.

Requirements

Platforms: Windows 98, Windows NT 4.0, Windows Millennium Edition, Windows 2000, Windows XP Home Edition, Windows XP Professional, Windows Server 2003 family

GuidConverter.CanConvertFrom Method

Overload List

This member supports the .NET Framework infrastructure and is not intended to be used directly from your code.

[Visual Basic] **Overloads Overrides Public Function CanConvertFrom(ITypeDescriptorContext, Type) As Boolean**

[C#] **public override bool CanConvertFrom(ITypeDescriptorContext, Type);**

[C++] **public: bool CanConvertFrom(ITypeDescriptorContext*, Type*);**

[JScript] **public override function CanConvertFrom(ITypeDescriptorContext, Type) : Boolean;**

Inherited from **TypeConverter**.

[Visual Basic] **Overloads Public Function CanConvertFrom(Type) As Boolean**

[C#] **public bool CanConvertFrom(Type);**

[C++] **public: bool CanConvertFrom(Type*);**

[JScript] **public function CanConvertFrom(Type) : Boolean;**

GuidConverter.CanConvertFrom Method (ITypeDescriptorContext, Type)

This member overrides **TypeConverter.CanConvertFrom**.

```
[Visual Basic]
Overrides Overloads Public Function CanConvertFrom( _
   ByVal context As ITypeDescriptorContext, _
   ByVal sourceType As Type _
) As Boolean
[C#]
public override bool CanConvertFrom(
   ITypeDescriptorContext context,
   Type sourceType
);
[C++]
public: bool CanConvertFrom(
   ITypeDescriptorContext* context,
   Type* sourceType
);
```

```
[JScript]
public override function CanConvertFrom(
   context : ITypeDescriptorContext,
   sourceType : Type
) : Boolean;
```

Requirements

Platforms: Windows 98, Windows NT 4.0, Windows Millennium Edition, Windows 2000, Windows XP Home Edition, Windows XP Professional, Windows Server 2003 family

GuidConverter.CanConvertTo Method

Overload List

This member supports the .NET Framework infrastructure and is not intended to be used directly from your code.

[Visual Basic] **Overloads Overrides Public Function CanConvertTo(ITypeDescriptorContext, Type) As Boolean**

[C#] **public override bool CanConvertTo(ITypeDescriptor-Context, Type);**

[C++] **public: bool CanConvertTo(ITypeDescriptorContext*, Type*);**

[JScript] **public override function CanConvertTo(IType-DescriptorContext, Type) : Boolean;**

Inherited from **TypeConverter**.

[Visual Basic] **Overloads Public Function CanConvertTo(Type) As Boolean**

[C#] **public bool CanConvertTo(Type);**

[C++] **public: bool CanConvertTo(Type*);**

[JScript] **public function CanConvertTo(Type) : Boolean;**

GuidConverter.CanConvertTo Method (ITypeDescriptorContext, Type)

This member overrides **TypeConverter.CanConvertTo**.

```
[Visual Basic]
Overrides Overloads Public Function CanConvertTo( _
   ByVal context As ITypeDescriptorContext, _
   ByVal destinationType As Type _
) As Boolean
[C#]
public override bool CanConvertTo(
   ITypeDescriptorContext context,
   Type destinationType
);
[C++]
public: bool CanConvertTo(
   ITypeDescriptorContext* context,
   Type* destinationType
);
[JScript]
public override function CanConvertTo(
   context : ITypeDescriptorContext,
   destinationType : Type
) : Boolean;
```

Requirements

Platforms: Windows 98, Windows NT 4.0, Windows Millennium Edition, Windows 2000, Windows XP Home Edition, Windows XP Professional, Windows Server 2003 family

GuidConverter.ConvertFrom Method

Overload List

This member supports the .NET Framework infrastructure and is not intended to be used directly from your code.

[Visual Basic] **Overloads Overrides Public Function ConvertFrom(ITypeDescriptorContext, CultureInfo, Object) As Object**

[C#] **public override object ConvertFrom(IType-DescriptorContext, CultureInfo, object);**

[C++] **public: Object* ConvertFrom(IType-DescriptorContext*, CultureInfo*, Object*);**

[JScript] **public override function ConvertFrom(IType-DescriptorContext, CultureInfo, Object) : Object;**

Inherited from **TypeConverter**.

[Visual Basic] **Overloads Public Function ConvertFrom(Object) As Object**

[C#] **public object ConvertFrom(object);**

[C++] **public: Object* ConvertFrom(Object*);**

[JScript] **public function ConvertFrom(Object) : Object;**

GuidConverter.ConvertFrom Method (ITypeDescriptorContext, CultureInfo, Object)

This member overrides **TypeConverter.ConvertFrom**.

```
[Visual Basic]
Overrides Overloads Public Function ConvertFrom( _
   ByVal context As ITypeDescriptorContext, _
   ByVal culture As CultureInfo, _
   ByVal value As Object _
) As Object
[C#]
public override object ConvertFrom(
   ITypeDescriptorContext context,
   CultureInfo culture,
   object value
);
[C++]
public: Object* ConvertFrom(
   ITypeDescriptorContext* context,
   CultureInfo* culture,
   Object* value
);
[JScript]
public override function ConvertFrom(
   context : ITypeDescriptorContext,
   culture : CultureInfo,
   value : Object
) : Object;
```

Requirements

Platforms: Windows 98, Windows NT 4.0, Windows Millennium Edition, Windows 2000, Windows XP Home Edition, Windows XP Professional, Windows Server 2003 family

GuidConverter.ConvertTo Method

Overload List

This member supports the .NET Framework infrastructure and is not intended to be used directly from your code.

[Visual Basic] **Overloads Overrides Public Function ConvertTo(ITypeDescriptorContext, CultureInfo, Object, Type) As Object**

[C#] **public override object ConvertTo(ITypeDescriptorContext, CultureInfo, object, Type);**

[C++] **public: Object* ConvertTo(ITypeDescriptorContext*, CultureInfo*, Object*, Type*);**

[JScript] **public override function ConvertTo(ITypeDescriptorContext, CultureInfo, Object, Type) : Object;**

Inherited from **TypeConverter**.

[Visual Basic] **Overloads Public Function ConvertTo(Object, Type) As Object**

[C#] **public object ConvertTo(object, Type);**

[C++] **public: Object* ConvertTo(Object*, Type*);**

[JScript] **public function ConvertTo(Object, Type) : Object;**

GuidConverter.ConvertTo Method (ITypeDescriptorContext, CultureInfo, Object, Type)

This member overrides **TypeConverter.ConvertTo**.

```
[Visual Basic]
Overrides Overloads Public Function ConvertTo( _
   ByVal context As ITypeDescriptorContext, _
   ByVal culture As CultureInfo, _
   ByVal value As Object, _
   ByVal destinationType As Type _
) As Object
[C#]
public override object ConvertTo(
   ITypeDescriptorContext context,
   CultureInfo culture,
   object value,
   Type destinationType
);
[C++]
public: Object* ConvertTo(
   ITypeDescriptorContext* context,
   CultureInfo* culture,
   Object* value,
   Type* destinationType
);
[JScript]
public override function ConvertTo(
   context : ITypeDescriptorContext,
   culture : CultureInfo,
   value : Object,
   destinationType : Type
) : Object;
```

Requirements

Platforms: Windows 98, Windows NT 4.0, Windows Millennium Edition, Windows 2000, Windows XP Home Edition, Windows XP Professional, Windows Server 2003 family

IBindingList Interface

Provides the features required to support both complex and simple scenarios when binding to a data source.

```
[Visual Basic]
Public Interface IBindingList
   Inherits IList, ICollection, IEnumerable
[C#]
public interface IBindingList : IList, ICollection, IEnumerable
[C++]
public __gc __interface IBindingList : public IList, ICollection,
   IEnumerable
[JScript]
public interface IBindingList implements IList, ICollection,
   IEnumerable
```

Classes that Implement IBindingList

Class	Description
DataView	Represents a databindable, customized view of a **DataTable** for sorting, filtering, searching, editing, and navigation.
DataViewManager	Contains a default **DataViewSettingCollection** for each **DataTable** in a **DataSet**.

Remarks

This interface is implemented by the **DataView** class. Implementation of a method should exhibit the same behavior as the implementation of that method in the **DataView** class.

When you call the **ApplySort** or **RemoveSort** methods, you should raise a **ListChanged** event with the **Reset** enumeration.

When you call the **AddNew** method, you should raise a **ListChanged** event with the **ItemAdded** enumeration carrying the appropriate index. The added row is in a state where pressing the ESC on a DataGrid control can remove the new row. Raising the **ListChanged** event with the **ItemAdded** enumeration a second time on this row indicates that the item is now a row not in the "new" state.

When you remove an item or call the **CancelEdit** method on a new row (if that row implements **IEditableObject**), you should raise a **ListChanged** event with the **ItemDeleted** enumeration carrying the appropriate index.

Requirements

Namespace: System.ComponentModel

Platforms: Windows 98, Windows NT 4.0, Windows Millennium Edition, Windows 2000, Windows XP Home Edition, Windows XP Professional, Windows Server 2003 family, .NET Compact Framework - Windows CE .NET

Assembly: System (in System.dll)

IBindingList.AllowEdit Property

Gets whether you can update items in the list.

```
[Visual Basic]
ReadOnly Property AllowEdit As Boolean
[C#]
bool AllowEdit {get;}
[C++]
__property bool get_AllowEdit();
[JScript]
function get AllowEdit() : Boolean;
```

Property Value

true if you can update the items in the list; otherwise, **false**.

Requirements

Platforms: Windows 98, Windows NT 4.0, Windows Millennium Edition, Windows 2000, Windows XP Home Edition, Windows XP Professional, Windows Server 2003 family, .NET Compact Framework - Windows CE .NET

IBindingList.AllowNew Property

Gets whether you can add items to the list using **AddNew**.

```
[Visual Basic]
ReadOnly Property AllowNew As Boolean
[C#]
bool AllowNew {get;}
[C++]
__property bool get_AllowNew();
[JScript]
function get AllowNew() : Boolean;
```

Property Value

true if you can add items to the list using **AddNew**; otherwise, **false**.

Remarks

If **IList.IsFixedSize** or **IList.IsReadOnly** is **true**, this property returns **false**.

Requirements

Platforms: Windows 98, Windows NT 4.0, Windows Millennium Edition, Windows 2000, Windows XP Home Edition, Windows XP Professional, Windows Server 2003 family, .NET Compact Framework - Windows CE .NET

IBindingList.AllowRemove Property

Gets whether you can remove items from the list, using **Remove** or **RemoveAt**.

```
[Visual Basic]
ReadOnly Property AllowRemove As Boolean
[C#]
bool AllowRemove {get;}
[C++]
__property bool get_AllowRemove();
[JScript]
function get AllowRemove() : Boolean;
```

Property Value

true if you can remove items from the list; otherwise, **false**.

Remarks

If **IList.IsFixedSize** or **IList.IsReadOnly** is **true**, this property returns **false**.

> **Note** If **AllowRemove** returns **false**, **IList.Remove** and **IList.RemoveAt** throw a **NotSupportedException**.

Requirements

Platforms: Windows 98, Windows NT 4.0, Windows Millennium Edition, Windows 2000, Windows XP Home Edition, Windows XP Professional, Windows Server 2003 family, .NET Compact Framework - Windows CE .NET

IBindingList.IsSorted Property

Gets whether the items in the list are sorted.

[Visual Basic]
```
ReadOnly Property IsSorted As Boolean
```
[C#]
```
bool IsSorted {get;}
```
[C++]
```
__property bool get_IsSorted();
```
[JScript]
```
function get IsSorted() : Boolean;
```

Property Value

true if **ApplySort** has been called and **RemoveSort** has not been called; otherwise, **false**.

Exceptions

Exception Type	Condition
NotSupportedException	This property is not supported.

Remarks

This property is supported if **SupportsSorting** is **true**; otherwise, this property throws a **NotSupportedException**.

If **IsSorted** returns **true**, items are added or removed in the order of the sort.

Requirements

Platforms: Windows 98, Windows NT 4.0, Windows Millennium Edition, Windows 2000, Windows XP Home Edition, Windows XP Professional, Windows Server 2003 family, .NET Compact Framework - Windows CE .NET

IBindingList.SortDirection Property

Gets the direction of the sort.

[Visual Basic]
```
ReadOnly Property SortDirection As ListSortDirection
```
[C#]
```
ListSortDirection SortDirection {get;}
```
[C++]
```
__property ListSortDirection get_SortDirection();
```
[JScript]
```
function get SortDirection() : ListSortDirection;
```

Property Value

One of the **ListSortDirection** values.

Exceptions

Exception Type	Condition
NotSupportedException	This property is not supported.

Remarks

This property is supported if **SupportsSorting** is **true**; otherwise, this property throws a **NotSupportedException**.

Requirements

Platforms: Windows 98, Windows NT 4.0, Windows Millennium Edition, Windows 2000, Windows XP Home Edition, Windows XP Professional, Windows Server 2003 family, .NET Compact Framework - Windows CE .NET

IBindingList.SortProperty Property

Gets the **PropertyDescriptor** that is being used for sorting.

[Visual Basic]
```
ReadOnly Property SortProperty As PropertyDescriptor
```
[C#]
```
PropertyDescriptor SortProperty {get;}
```
[C++]
```
__property PropertyDescriptor* get_SortProperty();
```
[JScript]
```
function get SortProperty() : PropertyDescriptor;
```

Property Value

The **PropertyDescriptor** that is being used for sorting.

Exceptions

Exception Type	Condition
NotSupportedException	This property is not supported.

Remarks

This property is supported if **SupportsSorting** is **true**; otherwise, this property throws a **NotSupportedException**.

Requirements

Platforms: Windows 98, Windows NT 4.0, Windows Millennium Edition, Windows 2000, Windows XP Home Edition, Windows XP Professional, Windows Server 2003 family, .NET Compact Framework - Windows CE .NET

IBindingList.SupportsChangeNotification Property

Gets whether a **ListChanged** event is raised when the list changes or an item in the list changes.

[Visual Basic]
```
ReadOnly Property SupportsChangeNotification As Boolean
```
[C#]
```
bool SupportsChangeNotification {get;}
```
[C++]
```
__property bool get_SupportsChangeNotification();
```
[JScript]
```
function get SupportsChangeNotification() : Boolean;
```

Property Value

true if a **ListChanged** event is raised when the list changes or when an item changes; otherwise, **false**.

Remarks

Objects in the list must notify the list when they change, so the list can raise a **ListChanged** event.

Requirements

Platforms: Windows 98, Windows NT 4.0, Windows Millennium Edition, Windows 2000, Windows XP Home Edition, Windows XP Professional, Windows Server 2003 family, .NET Compact Framework - Windows CE .NET

IBindingList.SupportsSearching Property

Gets whether the list supports searching using the **Find** method.

```
[Visual Basic]
ReadOnly Property SupportsSearching As Boolean
[C#]
bool SupportsSearching {get;}
[C++]
__property bool get_SupportsSearching();
[JScript]
function get SupportsSearching() : Boolean;
```

Property Value

true if the list supports searching using the **Find** method; otherwise, **false**.

Requirements

Platforms: Windows 98, Windows NT 4.0, Windows Millennium Edition, Windows 2000, Windows XP Home Edition, Windows XP Professional, Windows Server 2003 family, .NET Compact Framework - Windows CE .NET

IBindingList.SupportsSorting Property

Gets whether the list supports sorting.

```
[Visual Basic]
ReadOnly Property SupportsSorting As Boolean
[C#]
bool SupportsSorting {get;}
[C++]
__property bool get_SupportsSorting();
[JScript]
function get SupportsSorting() : Boolean;
```

Property Value

true if the list supports sorting; otherwise, **false**.

Remarks

If this property is **true**, then **IsSorted**, **SortProperty**, **SortDirection**, **ApplySort**, and **RemoveSort** are supported.

Requirements

Platforms: Windows 98, Windows NT 4.0, Windows Millennium Edition, Windows 2000, Windows XP Home Edition, Windows XP Professional, Windows Server 2003 family, .NET Compact Framework - Windows CE .NET

IBindingList.AddIndex Method

Adds the **PropertyDescriptor** to the indexes used for searching.

```
[Visual Basic]
Sub AddIndex( _
   ByVal property As PropertyDescriptor _
)
[C#]
void AddIndex(
   PropertyDescriptor property
);
[C++]
void AddIndex(
   PropertyDescriptor* property
);
[JScript]
function AddIndex(
   property : PropertyDescriptor
);
```

Parameters

property
The **PropertyDescriptor** to add to the indexes used for searching.

Remarks

The list must support this method. However, support for this method can be a nonoperation.

Requirements

Platforms: Windows 98, Windows NT 4.0, Windows Millennium Edition, Windows 2000, Windows XP Home Edition, Windows XP Professional, Windows Server 2003 family, .NET Compact Framework - Windows CE .NET

IBindingList.AddNew Method

Adds a new item to the list.

```
[Visual Basic]
Function AddNew() As Object
[C#]
object AddNew();
[C++]
Object* AddNew();
[JScript]
function AddNew() : Object;
```

Return Value

The item added to the list.

Exceptions

Exception Type	Condition
NotSupportedException	This method is not supported.

Remarks

This method is supported only if **AllowNew** is **true**; otherwise, a **NotSupportedException** is thrown.

Implementing this method means that the **IBindingList** list must understand the type of objects to add to the list and must understand how to create a new instance of that type. For example, if you have a collection of `myCustomer` objects, the **AddNew** method should add a new `myCustomer` object to the list.

> **Note** If the objects in this list implement the **IEditableObject** interface, calling the **CancelEdit** method should discard an object, not add it to the list, when the object was created using the **AddNew** method. The object should only be added to the list when the **IEditableObject.EndEdit** method is called. Therefore, you must sychronize the object and the list carefully.

When this method is called, you should raise a **ListChanged** event with the **ItemAdded** enumeration carrying the appropriate index. The added row is in a state where hitting Esc on a DataGrid control can remove the new row. Raising the **ListChanged** event with the **ItemAdded** enumeration a second time on this row indicates that the item is now a normal row (not in new state).

Requirements

Platforms: Windows 98, Windows NT 4.0,
Windows Millennium Edition, Windows 2000,
Windows XP Home Edition, Windows XP Professional,
Windows Server 2003 family,
.NET Compact Framework - Windows CE .NET

IBindingList.ApplySort Method

Sorts the list based on a **PropertyDescriptor** and a **ListSortDirection**.

```
[Visual Basic]
Sub ApplySort( _
   ByVal property As PropertyDescriptor, _
   ByVal direction As ListSortDirection _
)
[C#]
void ApplySort(
   PropertyDescriptor property,
   ListSortDirection direction
);
[C++]
void ApplySort(
   PropertyDescriptor* property,
   ListSortDirection direction
);
[JScript]
function ApplySort(
   property : PropertyDescriptor,
   direction : ListSortDirection
);
```

Parameters

property
The **PropertyDescriptor** to sort by.

direction
One of the **ListSortDirection** values.

Exceptions

Exception Type	Condition
NotSupportedException	This method is not supported.

Remarks

If items are added or removed, these items are placed in the order of the sort.

This method is supported if **SupportsSorting** is **true**; otherwise, this method throws a **NotSupportedException**.

When you call this method, you should raise a **ListChanged** event with the **Reset** enumeration.

Requirements

Platforms: Windows 98, Windows NT 4.0,
Windows Millennium Edition, Windows 2000,
Windows XP Home Edition, Windows XP Professional,
Windows Server 2003 family,
.NET Compact Framework - Windows CE .NET

IBindingList.Find Method

Returns the index of the row that has the given **PropertyDescriptor**.

```
[Visual Basic]
Function Find( _
   ByVal property As PropertyDescriptor, _
   ByVal key As Object _
) As Integer
[C#]
int Find(
   PropertyDescriptor property,
   object key
);
[C++]
int Find(
   PropertyDescriptor* property,
   Object* key
);
[JScript]
function Find(
   property : PropertyDescriptor,
   key : Object
) : int;
```

Parameters

property
The **PropertyDescriptor** to search on.

key
The value of the *property* parameter to search for.

Return Value

The index of the row that has the given **PropertyDescriptor**.

Exceptions

Exception Type	Condition
NotSupportedException	This method is not supported.

Remarks

This method will select the first row where the value of the *property* parameter equals the value of the *key* parameter.

This method is supported if **SupportsSearching** is **true**, otherwise this method throws a **NotSupportedException**.

Requirements

Platforms: Windows 98, Windows NT 4.0,
Windows Millennium Edition, Windows 2000,
Windows XP Home Edition, Windows XP Professional,
Windows Server 2003 family,
.NET Compact Framework - Windows CE .NET

IBindingList.RemoveIndex Method

Removes the **PropertyDescriptor** from the indexes used for searching.

[Visual Basic]
```
Sub RemoveIndex( _
   ByVal property As PropertyDescriptor _
)
```
[C#]
```
void RemoveIndex(
   PropertyDescriptor property
);
```
[C++]
```
void RemoveIndex(
   PropertyDescriptor* property
);
```
[JScript]
```
function RemoveIndex(
   property : PropertyDescriptor
);
```

Parameters

property

The **PropertyDescriptor** to remove from the indexes used for searching.

Remarks

The list must support this method. However, support for this method can be a nonoperation.

Requirements

Platforms: Windows 98, Windows NT 4.0, Windows Millennium Edition, Windows 2000, Windows XP Home Edition, Windows XP Professional, Windows Server 2003 family, .NET Compact Framework - Windows CE .NET

IBindingList.RemoveSort Method

Removes any sort applied using **ApplySort**.

[Visual Basic]
```
Sub RemoveSort()
```
[C#]
```
void RemoveSort();
```
[C++]
```
void RemoveSort();
```
[JScript]
```
function RemoveSort();
```

Exceptions

Exception Type	Condition
NotSupportedException	This method is not supported.

Remarks

This property is supported if **SupportsSorting** is **true**; otherwise, this property throws a **NotSupportedException**.

When you call this method, you should raise a **ListChanged** event with the **Reset** enumeration.

Requirements

Platforms: Windows 98, Windows NT 4.0, Windows Millennium Edition, Windows 2000, Windows XP Home Edition, Windows XP Professional, Windows Server 2003 family, .NET Compact Framework - Windows CE .NET

IBindingList.ListChanged Event

Occurs when the list changes or an item in the list changes.

[Visual Basic]
```
Event ListChanged As ListChangedEventHandler
```
[C#]
```
event ListChangedEventHandler ListChanged;
```
[C++]
```
__event ListChangedEventHandler* ListChanged;
```

[JScript] In JScript, you can handle the events defined by a class, but you cannot define your own.

Event Data

The event handler receives an argument of type **ListChangedEventArgs** containing data related to this event. The following **ListChangedEventArgs** properties provide information specific to this event.

Property	Description
ListChangedType	Gets the way that the list changed.
NewIndex	Gets the new index of the item in the list.
OldIndex	Gets the old index of the item in the list.

Remarks

This event is raised only if the **SupportsChangeNotification** property is **true**.

Requirements

Platforms: Windows 98, Windows NT 4.0, Windows Millennium Edition, Windows 2000, Windows XP Home Edition, Windows XP Professional, Windows Server 2003 family

IComNativeDescriptorHandler Interface

This type supports the .NET Framework infrastructure and is not intended to be used directly from your code.

```
[Visual Basic]
Public Interface IComNativeDescriptorHandler
[C#]
public interface IComNativeDescriptorHandler
[C++]
public __gc __interface IComNativeDescriptorHandler
[JScript]
public interface IComNativeDescriptorHandler
```

IComNativeDescriptorHandler.GetAttributes Method

This member supports the .NET Framework infrastructure and is not intended to be used directly from your code.

```
[Visual Basic]
Function GetAttributes( _
   ByVal component As Object _
) As AttributeCollection
[C#]
AttributeCollection GetAttributes(
   object component
);
[C++]
AttributeCollection* GetAttributes(
   Object* component
);
[JScript]
function GetAttributes(
   component : Object
) : AttributeCollection;
```

IComNativeDescriptorHandler.GetClassName Method

This member supports the .NET Framework infrastructure and is not intended to be used directly from your code.

```
[Visual Basic]
Function GetClassName( _
   ByVal component As Object _
) As String
[C#]
string GetClassName(
   object component
);
[C++]
String* GetClassName(
   Object* component
);
[JScript]
function GetClassName(
   component : Object
) : String;
```

IComNativeDescriptorHandler.GetConverter Method

This member supports the .NET Framework infrastructure and is not intended to be used directly from your code.

```
[Visual Basic]
Function GetConverter( _
   ByVal component As Object _
) As TypeConverter
[C#]
TypeConverter GetConverter(
   object component
);
[C++]
TypeConverter* GetConverter(
   Object* component
);
[JScript]
function GetConverter(
   component : Object
) : TypeConverter;
```

IComNativeDescriptorHandler.GetDefaultEvent Method

This member supports the .NET Framework infrastructure and is not intended to be used directly from your code.

```
[Visual Basic]
Function GetDefaultEvent( _
   ByVal component As Object _
) As EventDescriptor
[C#]
EventDescriptor GetDefaultEvent(
   object component
);
[C++]
EventDescriptor* GetDefaultEvent(
   Object* component
);
[JScript]
function GetDefaultEvent(
   component : Object
) : EventDescriptor;
```

IComNativeDescriptorHandler.GetDefault-Property Method

This member supports the .NET Framework infrastructure and is not intended to be used directly from your code.

```
[Visual Basic]
Function GetDefaultProperty( _
   ByVal component As Object _
) As PropertyDescriptor
[C#]
PropertyDescriptor GetDefaultProperty(
   object component
);
[C++]
PropertyDescriptor* GetDefaultProperty(
   Object* component
);
```

```
[JScript]
function GetDefaultProperty(
   component : Object
) : PropertyDescriptor;
```

IComNativeDescriptorHandler.GetEditor Method

This member supports the .NET Framework infrastructure and is not intended to be used directly from your code.

```
[Visual Basic]
Function GetEditor( _
   ByVal component As Object, _
   ByVal baseEditorType As Type _
) As Object
[C#]
object GetEditor(
   object component,
   Type baseEditorType
);
[C++]
Object* GetEditor(
   Object* component,
   Type* baseEditorType
);
[JScript]
function GetEditor(
   component : Object,
   baseEditorType : Type
) : Object;
```

IComNativeDescriptorHandler.GetEvents Method

This member supports the .NET Framework infrastructure and is not intended to be used directly from your code.

Overload List

This member supports the .NET Framework infrastructure and is not intended to be used directly from your code.

[Visual Basic] **Overloads Function GetEvents(Object) As EventDescriptorCollection**

[C#] **EventDescriptorCollection GetEvents(object);**

[C++] **EventDescriptorCollection* GetEvents(Object*);**

[JScript] **function GetEvents(Object) : EventDescriptorCollection;**

This member supports the .NET Framework infrastructure and is not intended to be used directly from your code.

[Visual Basic] **Overloads Function GetEvents(Object, Attribute()) As EventDescriptorCollection**

[C#] **EventDescriptorCollection GetEvents(object, Attribute[]);**

[C++] **EventDescriptorCollection* GetEvents(Object*, Attribute[]);**

[JScript] **function GetEvents(Object, Attribute[]) : EventDescriptorCollection;**

IComNativeDescriptorHandler.GetEvents Method (Object)

This member supports the .NET Framework infrastructure and is not intended to be used directly from your code.

```
[Visual Basic]
Function GetEvents( _
   ByVal component As Object _
) As EventDescriptorCollection
[C#]
EventDescriptorCollection GetEvents(
   object component
);
[C++]
EventDescriptorCollection* GetEvents(
   Object* component
);
[JScript]
function GetEvents(
   component : Object
) : EventDescriptorCollection;
```

IComNativeDescriptorHandler.GetEvents Method (Object, Attribute[])

This member supports the .NET Framework infrastructure and is not intended to be used directly from your code.

```
[Visual Basic]
Function GetEvents( _
   ByVal component As Object, _
   ByVal attributes() As Attribute _
) As EventDescriptorCollection
[C#]
EventDescriptorCollection GetEvents(
   object component,
   Attribute[] attributes
);
[C++]
EventDescriptorCollection* GetEvents(
   Object* component,
   Attribute* attributes[]
);
[JScript]
function GetEvents(
   component : Object,
   attributes : Attribute[]
) : EventDescriptorCollection;
```

IComNativeDescriptorHandler.GetName Method

This member supports the .NET Framework infrastructure and is not intended to be used directly from your code.

```
[Visual Basic]
Function GetName( _
   ByVal component As Object _
) As String
[C#]
string GetName(
   object component
);
```

```
[C++]
String* GetName(
   Object* component
);
[JScript]
function GetName(
   component : Object
) : String;
```

IComNativeDescriptorHandler.GetProperties Method

This member supports the .NET Framework infrastructure and is not intended to be used directly from your code.

```
[Visual Basic]
Function GetProperties( _
   ByVal component As Object, _
   ByVal attributes() As Attribute _
) As PropertyDescriptorCollection
[C#]
PropertyDescriptorCollection GetProperties(
   object component,
   Attribute[] attributes
);
[C++]
PropertyDescriptorCollection* GetProperties(
   Object* component,
   Attribute* attributes[]
);
[JScript]
function GetProperties(
   component : Object,
   attributes : Attribute[]
) : PropertyDescriptorCollection;
```

IComNativeDescriptorHandler.GetPropertyValue Method

This member supports the .NET Framework infrastructure and is not intended to be used directly from your code.

Overload List

This member supports the .NET Framework infrastructure and is not intended to be used directly from your code.

[Visual Basic] **Overloads Function GetPropertyValue(Object, Integer, ByRef Boolean) As Object**

[C#] **object GetPropertyValue(object, int, ref bool);**

[C++] **Object* GetPropertyValue(Object*, int, bool*);**

[JScript] **function GetPropertyValue(Object, int, Boolean) : Object;**

This member supports the .NET Framework infrastructure and is not intended to be used directly from your code.

[Visual Basic] **Overloads Function GetPropertyValue(Object, String, ByRef Boolean) As Object**

[C#] **object GetPropertyValue(object, string, ref bool);**

[C++] **Object* GetPropertyValue(Object*, String*, bool*);**

[JScript] **function GetPropertyValue(Object, String, Boolean) : Object;**

IComNativeDescriptorHandler.GetPropertyValue Method (Object, Int32, Boolean)

This member supports the .NET Framework infrastructure and is not intended to be used directly from your code.

```
[Visual Basic]
Function GetPropertyValue( _
   ByVal component As Object, _
   ByVal dispid As Integer, _
   ByRef success As Boolean _
) As Object
[C#]
object GetPropertyValue(
   object component,
   int dispid,
   ref bool success
);
[C++]
Object* GetPropertyValue(
   Object* component,
   int dispid,
   bool* success
);
[JScript]
function GetPropertyValue(
   component : Object,
   dispid : int,
   success : Boolean
) : Object;
```

IComNativeDescriptorHandler.GetPropertyValue Method (Object, String, Boolean)

This member supports the .NET Framework infrastructure and is not intended to be used directly from your code.

```
[Visual Basic]
Function GetPropertyValue( _
   ByVal component As Object, _
   ByVal propertyName As String, _
   ByRef success As Boolean _
) As Object
[C#]
object GetPropertyValue(
   object component,
   string propertyName,
   ref bool success
);
[C++]
Object* GetPropertyValue(
   Object* component,
   String* propertyName,
   bool* success
);
[JScript]
function GetPropertyValue(
   component : Object,
   propertyName : String,
   success : Boolean
) : Object;
```

IComponent Interface

Provides functionality required by all components. **Component** is the default implementation of **IComponent** and serves as the base class for all components in the common language runtime.

System.IDisposable
  System.ComponentModel.IComponent

[Visual Basic]
```
<ComVisible(True)>
Public Interface IComponent
   Inherits IDisposable
```
[C#]
```
[ComVisible(true)]
public interface IComponent : IDisposable
```
[C++]
```
[ComVisible(true)]
public __gc __interface IComponent : public IDisposable
```
[JScript]
```
public
   ComVisible(true)
interface IComponent implements IDisposable
```

Classes that Implement IComponent

Class	Description
Component	Provides the base implementation for the **IComponent** interface and enables object-sharing between applications.
Control	Defines the properties, methods, and events that are shared by all ASP.NET server controls.
HttpApplication	Defines the methods, properties, and events common to all application objects within an ASP.NET application. This class is the base class for applications defined by the user in the global.asax file.
MarshalByValue-Component	Implements **IComponent** and provides the base implementation for remotable components that are marshaled by value (a copy of the serialized object is passed).

Remarks

You can contain components in a container. In this context, containment refers to logical containment, not visual containment. You can use components and containers in a variety of scenarios, both visual and non visual.

System.Windows.Forms.Control inherits from **Component**, the default implementation of **IComponent**.

A component interacts with its container primarily through a container-provided **ISite**, which is a repository of container-specific per-component information.

Notes to Implementers: To be a component, a class must implement the **IComponent** interface and provide a basic constructor that requires no parameters or a single parameter of type IContainer. For more information about implementing **IComponent**, see **Developing Components**.

Example

[Visual Basic]
```
'The following example demonstrates the implementation of
'ISite, IComponent, and IContainer for use in a simple library container.
'
'This example imports the System, System.ComponentModel, and System.Collections
'namespaces.

'This code segment implements the ISite and IComponent interfaces.
'The implementation of the IContainer interface can be seen in the documentation
'of IContainer.

'Implement the ISite interface.

'The ISBNSite class represents the ISBN name of the book component

Class ISBNSite
Implements ISite
Private m_curComponent As IComponent
Private m_curContainer As IContainer
Private m_bDesignMode As Boolean
Private m_ISBNCmpName As String

Public Sub New(ByVal actvCntr As IContainer, ByVal prntCmpnt As IComponent)
    m_curComponent = prntCmpnt
    m_curContainer = actvCntr
    m_bDesignMode = False
    m_ISBNCmpName = Nothing
End Sub

'Support the ISite interface.
Public ReadOnly Property Component() As IComponent Implements ISite.Component
    Get
        Return m_curComponent
    End Get
End Property

Public ReadOnly Property Container() As IContainer Implements ISite.Container
    Get
        Return m_curContainer
    End Get
End Property

Public ReadOnly Property DesignMode() As Boolean Implements ISite.DesignMode
    Get
        Return m_bDesignMode
    End Get
End Property

Public Property Name() As String Implements ISite.Name
    Get
        Return m_ISBNCmpName
    End Get
    Set(ByVal Value As String)
        m_ISBNCmpName = Value
    End Set
End Property

'Support the IServiceProvider interface.
Public Function GetService(ByVal serviceType As Type) As Object Implements ISite.GetService
    'This example does not use any service object.
    GetService = Nothing
End Function
End Class
```

```
'The BookComponent class represents the book component ↵
of the library container.
Class BookComponent
Implements IComponent
Public Event Disposed As EventHandler Implements IComponent.Disposed
Private m_curISBNSite As ISite
Private m_bookTitle As String
Private m_bookAuthor As String

Public Sub New(ByVal Title As String, ByVal Author As String)
    m_curISBNSite = Nothing
    m_bookTitle = Title
    m_bookAuthor = Author
End Sub

Public ReadOnly Property Title() As String
    Get
        Return m_bookTitle
    End Get
End Property

Public ReadOnly Property Author() As String
    Get
        Return m_bookAuthor
    End Get
End Property

Public Sub Dispose() Implements IComponent.Dispose
    'There is nothing to clean.
    RaiseEvent Disposed(Me, EventArgs.Empty)
End Sub

Public Property Site() As ISite Implements IComponent.Site
    Get
        Return m_curISBNSite
    End Get
    Set(ByVal Value As ISite)
        m_curISBNSite = Value
    End Set
End Property

Public Overloads Function Equals(ByVal cmp As Object) As Boolean
    Dim cmpObj As BookComponent = CType(cmp, BookComponent)
    If (Me.Title.Equals(cmpObj.Title) And ↵
Me.Author.Equals(cmpObj.Author)) Then
        Equals = True
    Else
        Equals = False
    End If
End Function

Public Overrides Function GetHashCode() As Integer
    GetHashCode = MyBase.GetHashCode()
End Function

End Class
```

[C#]

```
/// <summary>
/// The following example demonstrates the implementation of
/// ISite, IComponent, and IContainer for use in a simple ↵
 library container.
///
/// This example uses the System, System.ComponentModel, ↵
 and System.Collections
/// namespaces.
/// </summary>

//This code segment implements the ISite and IComponent interfaces.
//The implementation of the IContainer interface can be seen in the
documentation
//of IContainer.

//Implement the ISite interface.

// The ISBNSite class represents the ISBN name of the book component
class ISBNSite : ISite
{
    private IComponent m_curComponent;
    private IContainer m_curContainer;
    private bool m_bDesignMode;
    private string m_ISBNCmpName;

    public ISBNSite(IContainer actvCntr, IComponent prntCmpnt)
    {
        m_curComponent = prntCmpnt;
        m_curContainer = actvCntr;
        m_bDesignMode = false;
        m_ISBNCmpName = null;
    }

    //Support the ISite interface.
    public virtual IComponent Component
    {
        get
        {
            return m_curComponent;
        }
    }

    public virtual IContainer Container
    {
        get
        {
            return m_curContainer;
        }
    }

    public virtual bool DesignMode
    {
        get
        {
            return m_bDesignMode;
        }
    }

    public virtual string Name
    {
        get
        {
            return m_ISBNCmpName;
        }

        set
        {
            m_ISBNCmpName = value;
        }
    }

    //Support the IServiceProvider interface.
    public virtual object GetService(Type serviceType)
    {
        //This example does not use any service object.
        return null;
    }

}

// The BookComponent class represents the book component of the ↵
library container.

// This class implements the IComponent interface.

class BookComponent : IComponent
{
    public event EventHandler Disposed;
    private ISite m_curISBNSite;
    private string m_bookTitle;
    private string m_bookAuthor;
```

```
    public BookComponent(string Title, string Author)
    {
        m_curISBNSite = null;
        Disposed = null;
        m_bookTitle = Title;
        m_bookAuthor = Author;
    }

    public string Title
    {
        get
        {
            return m_bookTitle;
        }
    }

    public string Author
    {
        get
        {
            return m_bookAuthor;
        }
    }

    public virtual void Dispose()
    {
        //There is nothing to clean.
        if(Disposed != null)
            Disposed(this,EventArgs.Empty);
    }

    public virtual ISite Site
    {
        get
        {
            return m_curISBNSite;
        }
        set
        {
            m_curISBNSite = value;
        }
    }

    public override bool Equals(object cmp)
    {
        BookComponent cmpObj = (BookComponent)cmp;
        if(this.Title.Equals(cmpObj.Title) &&
this.Author.Equals(cmpObj.Author))
            return true;

        return false;
    }

    public override int GetHashCode()
    {
        return base.GetHashCode();
    }
}
```

[C++]

```
/// <summary>
/// The following example demonstrates the implementation of
/// ISite, IComponent, and IContainer for use in a simple ↵
 library container.
///
/// This example uses the System, System.ComponentModel, ↵
 and System.Collections
/// namespaces.
/// </summary>

//This code segment implements the ISite and IComponent interfaces.
//The implementation of the IContainer interface can be seen ↵
 in the documentation
//of IContainer.

//Implement the ISite interface.

// The ISBNSite class represents the ISBN name of the book component
__gc class ISBNSite : public ISite
{
private:

    IComponent* m_curComponent;
    IContainer* m_curContainer;
    bool m_bDesignMode;
    String* m_ISBNCmpName;

public:
    ISBNSite(IContainer* actvCntr, IComponent* prntCmpnt)
    {
        m_curComponent = prntCmpnt;
        m_curContainer = actvCntr;
        m_bDesignMode = false;
        m_ISBNCmpName = 0;
    }

    //Support the ISite interface.
    __property virtual IComponent* get_Component()
    {
            return m_curComponent;
    }

    __property virtual IContainer* get_Container()
    {
            return m_curContainer;
    }

    __property virtual bool get_DesignMode()
    {
            return m_bDesignMode;
    }

    __property virtual String* get_Name()
    {
            return m_ISBNCmpName;
    }

    __property virtual void set_Name( String* value )
    {
            m_ISBNCmpName = value;
    }

    //Support the IServiceProvider interface.
    virtual Object* GetService(Type* serviceType)
    {
        //This example does not use any service object.
        return 0;
    }

};

// The BookComponent class represents the book component of ↵
 the library container.

// This class implements the IComponent interface.

__gc class BookComponent : public IComponent
{
private:

    ISite* m_curISBNSite;
    String* m_bookTitle;
    String* m_bookAuthor;

public:

    __event virtual EventHandler* Disposed;

    BookComponent(String* Title, String* Author)
    {
```

```
        m_curISBNSite = 0;
        Disposed = 0;
        m_bookTitle = Title;
        m_bookAuthor = Author;
    }

    __property String* get_Title()
    {
            return m_bookTitle;
    }

    __property String* get_Author()
    {
            return m_bookAuthor;
    }

    virtual void Dispose()
    {
        //There is nothing to clean.
        if(Disposed != 0)
            Disposed(this,EventArgs::Empty);
    }

    __property virtual ISite* get_Site()
    {
            return m_curISBNSite;
    }

    __property virtual void set_Site( ISite* value )
    {
            m_curISBNSite = value;
    }

    bool Equals(Object* cmp)
    {
        BookComponent* cmpObj = __try_cast<BookComponent*>(cmp);
        return (this->Title->Equals(cmpObj->Title) && this->
Author->Equals(cmpObj->Author));
    }

    int GetHashCode()
    {
        return IComponent::GetHashCode();
    }
};
```

Requirements

Namespace: System.ComponentModel

Platforms: Windows 98, Windows NT 4.0, Windows Millennium Edition, Windows 2000, Windows XP Home Edition, Windows XP Professional, Windows Server 2003 family, .NET Compact Framework - Windows CE .NET

Assembly: System (in System.dll)

IComponent.Site Property

Gets or sets the **ISite** associated with the **IComponent**.

[Visual Basic]
```
Property Site As ISite
```
[C#]
```
ISite Site {get; set;}
```
[C++]
```
__property ISite* get_Site();
__property void set_Site(ISite*);
```
[JScript]
```
function get Site() : ISite;function set Site(ISite);
```

Property Value

The **ISite** object associated with the component; or a null reference (**Nothing** in Visual Basic), if the component does not have a site.

Remarks

Sites can also serve as a repository for container-specific, per-component information, such as the component name.

Requirements

Platforms: Windows 98, Windows NT 4.0, Windows Millennium Edition, Windows 2000, Windows XP Home Edition, Windows XP Professional, Windows Server 2003 family, .NET Compact Framework - Windows CE .NET

IComponent.Disposed Event

Represents the method that handles the **Disposed** event of a component.

[Visual Basic]
```
Event Disposed As EventHandler
```
[C#]
```
event EventHandler Disposed;
```
[C++]
```
__event EventHandler* Disposed;
```

[JScript] In JScript, you can handle the events defined by a class, but you cannot define your own.

Event Data

The event handler receives an argument of type **EventArgs**.

Remarks

When you create a **IComponent** delegate, you identify the method that handles the event. To associate the event with your event handler, add an instance of the delegate to the event. The event handler is called whenever the event occurs, unless you remove the delegate.

Requirements

Platforms: Windows 98, Windows NT 4.0, Windows Millennium Edition, Windows 2000, Windows XP Home Edition, Windows XP Professional, Windows Server 2003 family

IContainer Interface

Provides functionality for containers. Containers are objects that logically contain zero or more components.

System.IDisposable
  System.ComponentModel.IContainer

[Visual Basic]
```
<ComVisible(True)>
Public Interface IContainer
   Inherits IDisposable
```
[C#]
```
[ComVisible(true)]
public interface IContainer : IDisposable
```
[C++]
```
[ComVisible(true)]
public __gc __interface IContainer : public IDisposable
```
[JScript]
```
public
   ComVisible(true)
interface IContainer implements IDisposable
```

Classes that Implement IContainer

Class	Description
Container	Encapsulates zero or more components.

Remarks

Containers are objects that encapsulate and track zero or more components. In this context, containment refers to logical containment, not visual containment. You can use components and containers in a variety of scenarios, including scenarios that are both visual and not visual.

Notes to Implementers: To be a container, the class must implement the **IContainer** interface, which supports methods for adding, removing, and retrieving components.

Example

[Visual Basic]
```
'This code segment implements the IContainer interface.        ↵
The code segment
'containing the implementation of ISite and IComponent can      ↵
be found in the documentation
'for those interfaces.

'Implement the LibraryContainer using the IContainer interface.

Class LibraryContainer
Implements IContainer
Private m_bookList As ArrayList

Public Sub New()
    m_bookList = New ArrayList()
End Sub

Public Sub Add(ByVal book As IComponent) Implements IContainer.Add
    'The book will be added without creation of the ISite object.
    m_bookList.Add(book)
End Sub

Public Sub Add(ByVal book As IComponent, ByVal ISNDNNum As      ↵
 String) Implements IContainer.Add

    Dim i As Integer
    Dim curObj As IComponent

    For i = 0 To m_bookList.Count - 1
        curObj = CType(m_bookList(i), IComponent)
        If Not curObj.Site Is Nothing Then
            If (curObj.Site.Name.Equals(ISNDNNum)) Then
                Throw New SystemException("The ISBN number          ↵
already exists in the container")
            End If
        End If
    Next i

    Dim data As ISBNSite = New ISBNSite(Me, book)
    data.Name = ISNDNNum
    book.Site = data
    m_bookList.Add(book)

End Sub

Public Sub Remove(ByVal book As IComponent) Implements          ↵
IContainer.Remove
    Dim i As Integer
    Dim curComp As BookComponent = CType(book, BookComponent)

    For i = 0 To m_bookList.Count - 1
        If (curComp.Equals(m_bookList(i)) = True) Then
            m_bookList.RemoveAt(i)
            Exit For
        End If
    Next i
End Sub

Public ReadOnly Property Components() As ComponentCollection    ↵
 Implements IContainer.Components
    Get
        Dim datalist(m_bookList.Count - 1) As IComponent
        Dim i As Integer

        m_bookList.CopyTo(datalist)
        Return New ComponentCollection(datalist)
    End Get
End Property

Public Sub Dispose() Implements IContainer.Dispose
    Dim i As Integer
    For i = 0 To m_bookList.Count - 1
        Dim curObj As IComponent = CType(m_bookList(i), IComponent)
        curObj.Dispose()
    Next i

    m_bookList.Clear()
End Sub

Public Shared Sub Main()
    Dim cntrExmpl As LibraryContainer = New LibraryContainer()

    Try
        Dim book1 As BookComponent = New BookComponent("Wizard's  ↵
 First Rule", "Terry Gooodkind")
        cntrExmpl.Add(book1, "0812548051")
        Dim book2 As BookComponent = New BookComponent("Stone of  ↵
Tears", "Terry Gooodkind")
        cntrExmpl.Add(book2, "0812548094")
        Dim book3 As BookComponent = New BookComponent("Blood of  ↵
 the Fold", "Terry Gooodkind")
        cntrExmpl.Add(book3, "0812551478")
        Dim book4 As BookComponent = New BookComponent("The Soul  ↵
 of the Fire", "Terry Gooodkind")
        'This will generate exception because the ISBN already   ↵
 exists in the container.
        cntrExmpl.Add(book4, "0812551478")
    Catch e As SystemException
        Console.WriteLine("Error description: " + e.Message)
    End Try

    Dim datalist As ComponentCollection = cntrExmpl.Components
    Dim denum As IEnumerator = datalist.GetEnumerator()
```

```
    While (denum.MoveNext())
        Dim cmp As BookComponent = CType(denum.Current, BookComponent)
        Console.WriteLine("Book Title: " + cmp.Title)
        Console.WriteLine("Book Author: " + cmp.Author)
        Console.WriteLine("Book ISBN: " + cmp.Site.Name)
    End While
End Sub
End Class
```

[C#]

```
//This code segment implements the IContainer interface.  The          ↵
code segment
//containing the implementation of ISite and IComponent can be         ↵
found in the documentation
//for those interfaces.

//Implement the LibraryContainer using the IContainer interface.

class LibraryContainer : IContainer
{
    private ArrayList m_bookList;

    public LibraryContainer()
    {
        m_bookList = new ArrayList();
    }

    public virtual void Add(IComponent book)
    {
        //The book will be added without creation of the ISite object.
        m_bookList.Add(book);
    }

    public virtual void Add(IComponent book, string ISNDNNum)
    {
        for(int i =0; i < m_bookList.Count; ++i)
        {
            IComponent curObj = (IComponent)m_bookList[i];
            if(curObj.Site != null)
            {
                if(curObj.Site.Name.Equals(ISNDNNum))
                    throw new SystemException("The ISBN number             ↵
 already exists in the container");
            }
        }

        ISBNSite data = new ISBNSite(this, book);
        data.Name = ISNDNNum;
        book.Site = data;
        m_bookList.Add(book);
    }

    public virtual void Remove(IComponent book)
    {
        for(int i =0; i < m_bookList.Count; ++i)
        {
            if(book.Equals(m_bookList[i]))
            {
                m_bookList.RemoveAt(i);
                    break;
            }
        }
    }

    public ComponentCollection Components
    {
        get
        {
            IComponent[] datalist = new                                ↵
BookComponent[m_bookList.Count];
            m_bookList.CopyTo(datalist);
            return new ComponentCollection(datalist);
        }
    }

    public virtual void Dispose()
    {
        for(int i =0; i < m_bookList.Count; ++i)
        {
            IComponent curObj = (IComponent)m_bookList[i];
            curObj.Dispose();
        }

        m_bookList.Clear();
    }

    static void Main(string[] args)
    {
        LibraryContainer cntrExmpl = new LibraryContainer();

        try
        {
            BookComponent book1 = new BookComponent("Wizard's          ↵
 First Rule", "Terry Gooodkind");
            cntrExmpl.Add(book1, "0812548051");
            BookComponent book2 = new BookComponent("Stone of          ↵
 Tears", "Terry Gooodkind");
            cntrExmpl.Add(book2, "0812548094");
            BookComponent book3 = new BookComponent("Blood of          ↵
 the Fold", "Terry Gooodkind");
            cntrExmpl.Add(book3, "0812551478");
            BookComponent book4 = new BookComponent("The Soul          ↵
 of the Fire", "Terry Gooodkind");
            //This will generate exception because the ISBN        ↵
already exists in the container.
            cntrExmpl.Add(book4, "0812551478");
        }
        catch(SystemException e)
        {
            Console.WriteLine("Error description: " + e.Message);
        }

        ComponentCollection datalist =cntrExmpl.Components;
        IEnumerator denum = datalist.GetEnumerator();

        while(denum.MoveNext())
        {
            BookComponent cmp = (BookComponent)denum.Current;
            Console.WriteLine("Book Title: " + cmp.Title);
            Console.WriteLine("Book Author: " + cmp.Author);
            Console.WriteLine("Book ISBN: " + cmp.Site.Name);
        }
    }
}
```

[C++]

```
//This code segment implements the IContainer interface.  The          ↵
code segment
//containing the implementation of ISite and IComponent can be         ↵
found in the documentation
//for those interfaces.

//Implement the LibraryContainer using the IContainer interface.

__gc class LibraryContainer : public IContainer
{
private:

    ArrayList* m_bookList;

public:

    LibraryContainer()
    {
        m_bookList = new ArrayList();
    }

    virtual void Add(IComponent* book)
    {
        //The book will be added without creation of the ISite object.
```

```
        m_bookList->Add(book);
    }

    virtual void Add(IComponent* book, String* ISNDNNum)
    {
        for(int i =0; i < m_bookList->Count; ++i)
        {
            IComponent* curObj = static_cast<IComponent*>                ↵
(m_bookList->Item[i]);
            if(curObj->Site != 0)
            {
                if(curObj->Site->Name->Equals(ISNDNNum))
                    throw new SystemException(S"The ISBN number          ↵
already exists in the container");
            }
        }

        ISBNSite* data = new ISBNSite(this, book);
        data->Name = ISNDNNum;
        book->Site = data;
        m_bookList->Add(book);
    }

    virtual void Remove(IComponent* book)
    {
        for(int i =0; i < m_bookList->Count; ++i)
        {
            if(book->Equals(m_bookList->Item[i]))
            {
                m_bookList->RemoveAt(i);
                break;
            }
        }
    }

    __property ComponentCollection* get_Components()
    {
        IComponent* datalist[] = new BookComponent*[m_bookList->Count];
        m_bookList->CopyTo(datalist);
        return new ComponentCollection(datalist);
    }

    virtual void Dispose()
    {
        for(int i =0; i < m_bookList->Count; ++i)
        {
            IComponent* curObj = static_cast<IComponent*>                ↵
(m_bookList->Item[i]);
            curObj->Dispose();
        }

        m_bookList->Clear();
    }

    static void Main()
    {
        LibraryContainer* cntrExmpl = new LibraryContainer();

        try
        {
            BookComponent* book1 = new BookComponent(S"Wizard's          ↵
First Rule", S"Terry Gooodkind");
            cntrExmpl->Add(book1, S"0812548051");
            BookComponent* book2 = new BookComponent(S"Stone of          ↵
Tears", S"Terry Gooodkind");
            cntrExmpl->Add(book2, S"0812548094");
            BookComponent* book3 = new BookComponent(S"Blood of          ↵
 the Fold", S"Terry Gooodkind");
            cntrExmpl->Add(book3, S"0812551478");
            BookComponent* book4 = new BookComponent(S"The Soul          ↵
of the Fire", S"Terry Gooodkind");
            //This will generate exception because the ISBN              ↵
already exists in the container.
            cntrExmpl->Add(book4, S"0812551478");
        }
        catch(SystemException* e)
        {
            Console::WriteLine("Error description: {0}", e->Message);
        }

        ComponentCollection* datalist =cntrExmpl->Components;
        IEnumerator* denum = datalist->GetEnumerator();

        while(denum->MoveNext())
        {
            BookComponent* cmp = static_cast<BookComponent*>             ↵
(denum->Current);
            Console::WriteLine(S"Book Title: {0}", cmp->Title);
            Console::WriteLine("Book Author: {0}", cmp->Author);
            Console::WriteLine("Book ISBN: {0}", cmp->Site->Name);
        }
    }
};
```

Requirements

Namespace: System.ComponentModel

Platforms: Windows 98, Windows NT 4.0, Windows Millennium Edition, Windows 2000, Windows XP Home Edition, Windows XP Professional, Windows Server 2003 family, .NET Compact Framework - Windows CE .NET

Assembly: System (in System.dll)

IContainer.Components Property

Gets all the components in the **IContainer**.

[Visual Basic]
`ReadOnly Property Components As ComponentCollection`
[C#]
`ComponentCollection Components {get;}`
[C++]
`__property ComponentCollection* get_Components();`
[JScript]
`function get Components() : ComponentCollection;`

Property Value

A collection of **IComponent** objects that represents all the components in the **IContainer**.

Remarks

For a list of all members of this type, see **ComponentCollection Members**.

Requirements

Platforms: Windows 98, Windows NT 4.0, Windows Millennium Edition, Windows 2000, Windows XP Home Edition, Windows XP Professional, Windows Server 2003 family

IContainer.Add Method

Adds the specified component to the **IContainer**.

Overload List

Adds the specified **IComponent** to the **IContainer** at the end of the list.

Supported by the .NET Compact Framework.

[Visual Basic] **Overloads Sub Add(IComponent)**

[C#] **void Add(IComponent);**

[C++] **void Add(IComponent*);**

[JScript] **function Add(IComponent);**

Adds the specified **IComponent** to the **IContainer** at the end of the list, and assigns a name to the component.

Supported by the .NET Compact Framework.

[Visual Basic] **Overloads Sub Add(IComponent, String)**

[C#] **void Add(IComponent, string);**

[C++] **void Add(IComponent*, String*);**

[JScript] **function Add(IComponent, String);**

IContainer.Add Method (IComponent)

Adds the specified **IComponent** to the **IContainer** at the end of the list.

```
[Visual Basic]
Sub Add( _
   ByVal component As IComponent _
)
[C#]
void Add(
   IComponent component
);
[C++]
void Add(
   IComponent* component
);
[JScript]
function Add(
   component : IComponent
);
```

Parameters

component

The **IComponent** to add.

Remarks

The new **IComponent** is added at the end of the list.

Requirements

Platforms: Windows 98, Windows NT 4.0,
Windows Millennium Edition, Windows 2000,
Windows XP Home Edition, Windows XP Professional,
Windows Server 2003 family,
.NET Compact Framework - Windows CE .NET

IContainer.Add Method (IComponent, String)

Adds the specified **IComponent** to the **IContainer** at the end of the list, and assigns a name to the component.

```
[Visual Basic]
Sub Add( _
   ByVal component As IComponent, _
   ByVal name As String _
)
[C#]
void Add(
   IComponent component,
   string name
);
[C++]
void Add(
   IComponent* component,
   String* name
);
[JScript]
function Add(
   component : IComponent,
   name : String
);
```

Parameters

component

The **IComponent** to add.

name

The unique, case-insensitive name to assign to the component.

-or-

A null reference (**Nothing** in Visual Basic) that leaves the component unnamed.

Remarks

The new **IComponent** is added at the end of the list.

Notes to Inheritors: When you inherit from **Add**, you must assure that *name*, if not a null reference (**Nothing** in Visual Basic), is unique for this **IContainer**.

Requirements

Platforms: Windows 98, Windows NT 4.0,
Windows Millennium Edition, Windows 2000,
Windows XP Home Edition, Windows XP Professional,
Windows Server 2003 family,
.NET Compact Framework - Windows CE .NET

IContainer.Remove Method

Removes a component from the **IContainer**.

```
[Visual Basic]
Sub Remove( _
   ByVal component As IComponent _
)
[C#]
void Remove(
   IComponent component
);
[C++]
void Remove(
   IComponent* component
);
[JScript]
function Remove(
   component : IComponent
);
```

Parameters

component

The **IComponent** to remove.

Remarks

Notes to Inheritors: When you inherit from the **Remove** method, you must also remove the **ISite**, if any, associated with this **IComponent**.

Requirements

Platforms: Windows 98, Windows NT 4.0,
Windows Millennium Edition, Windows 2000,
Windows XP Home Edition, Windows XP Professional,
Windows Server 2003 family,
.NET Compact Framework - Windows CE .NET

ICustomTypeDescriptor Interface

Provides an interface that supplies custom type information for an object.

```
[Visual Basic]
Public Interface ICustomTypeDescriptor
[C#]
public interface ICustomTypeDescriptor
[C++]
public __gc __interface ICustomTypeDescriptor
[JScript]
public interface ICustomTypeDescriptor
```

Classes that Implement ICustomTypeDescriptor

Class	Description
AxHost	Wraps ActiveX controls and exposes them as fully featured Windows Forms controls.
DataRowView	Represents a customized view of a **DataRow** exposed as a fully featured Windows Forms control.
DbDataRecord	Implements **IDataRecord** and **ICustomTypeDescriptor**, and provides data binding support for **DbEnumerator**.

Remarks

ICustomTypeDescriptor allows an object to provide type information about itself. Typically, this interface is used when an object needs dynamic type information. In contrast, **TypeDescriptor** provides static type information that is obtained from metadata.

For example, **ICustomTypeDescriptor** is used in the .NET Framework to provide type information for COM objects. COM objects do not support properties or attributes. The .NET Framework uses **ICustomTypeDescriptor** to implement properties and attributes for COM objects.

Requirements

Namespace: System.ComponentModel

Platforms: Windows 98, Windows NT 4.0, Windows Millennium Edition, Windows 2000, Windows XP Home Edition, Windows XP Professional, Windows Server 2003 family, .NET Compact Framework - Windows CE .NET

Assembly: System (in System.dll)

ICustomTypeDescriptor.GetAttributes Method

Returns a collection of type **Attribute** for this object.

```
[Visual Basic]
Function GetAttributes() As AttributeCollection
[C#]
AttributeCollection GetAttributes();
[C++]
AttributeCollection* GetAttributes();
[JScript]
function GetAttributes() : AttributeCollection;
```

Return Value

An **AttributeCollection** with the attributes for this object.

Remarks

The return value is never a null reference (**Nothing** in Visual Basic).

Implementers can return an empty **AttributeCollection** if no attributes are specified.

Requirements

Platforms: Windows 98, Windows NT 4.0, Windows Millennium Edition, Windows 2000, Windows XP Home Edition, Windows XP Professional, Windows Server 2003 family, .NET Compact Framework - Windows CE .NET

ICustomTypeDescriptor.GetClassName Method

Returns the class name of this object.

```
[Visual Basic]
Function GetClassName() As String
[C#]
string GetClassName();
[C++]
String* GetClassName();
[JScript]
function GetClassName() : String;
```

Return Value

The class name of the object, or a null reference (**Nothing** in Visual Basic) if the class does not have a name.

Remarks

If a null reference (**Nothing** in Visual Basic) is returned, use the type name.

Requirements

Platforms: Windows 98, Windows NT 4.0, Windows Millennium Edition, Windows 2000, Windows XP Home Edition, Windows XP Professional, Windows Server 2003 family, .NET Compact Framework - Windows CE .NET

ICustomTypeDescriptor.GetComponentName Method

Returns the name of this object.

```
[Visual Basic]
Function GetComponentName() As String
[C#]
string GetComponentName();
[C++]
String* GetComponentName();
[JScript]
function GetComponentName() : String;
```

Return Value

The name of the object, or a null reference (**Nothing** in Visual Basic) if object does not have a name.

Remarks

If a null reference (**Nothing** in Visual Basic) is returned, use the default name.

Requirements

Platforms: Windows 98, Windows NT 4.0,
Windows Millennium Edition, Windows 2000,
Windows XP Home Edition, Windows XP Professional,
Windows Server 2003 family,
.NET Compact Framework - Windows CE .NET

ICustomTypeDescriptor.GetConverter Method

Returns a type converter for this object.

```
[Visual Basic]
Function GetConverter() As TypeConverter
[C#]
TypeConverter GetConverter();
[C++]
TypeConverter* GetConverter();
[JScript]
function GetConverter() : TypeConverter;
```

Return Value

A **TypeConverter** that is the converter for this object, or a null reference (**Nothing** in Visual Basic) if there is no **TypeConverter** for this object.

Remarks

If a null reference (**Nothing** in Visual Basic) is returned, use the default **TypeConverter**.

Requirements

Platforms: Windows 98, Windows NT 4.0,
Windows Millennium Edition, Windows 2000,
Windows XP Home Edition, Windows XP Professional,
Windows Server 2003 family,
.NET Compact Framework - Windows CE .NET

ICustomTypeDescriptor.GetDefaultEvent Method

Returns the default event for this object.

```
[Visual Basic]
Function GetDefaultEvent() As EventDescriptor
[C#]
EventDescriptor GetDefaultEvent();
[C++]
EventDescriptor* GetDefaultEvent();
[JScript]
function GetDefaultEvent() : EventDescriptor;
```

Return Value

An **EventDescriptor** that represents the default event for this object, or a null reference (**Nothing** in Visual Basic) if this object does not have events.

Requirements

Platforms: Windows 98, Windows NT 4.0,
Windows Millennium Edition, Windows 2000,
Windows XP Home Edition, Windows XP Professional,
Windows Server 2003 family,
.NET Compact Framework - Windows CE .NET

ICustomTypeDescriptor.GetDefaultProperty Method

Returns the default property for this object.

```
[Visual Basic]
Function GetDefaultProperty() As PropertyDescriptor
[C#]
PropertyDescriptor GetDefaultProperty();
[C++]
PropertyDescriptor* GetDefaultProperty();
[JScript]
function GetDefaultProperty() : PropertyDescriptor;
```

Return Value

A **PropertyDescriptor** that represents the default property for this object, or a null reference (**Nothing** in Visual Basic) if this object does not have properties.

Requirements

Platforms: Windows 98, Windows NT 4.0,
Windows Millennium Edition, Windows 2000,
Windows XP Home Edition, Windows XP Professional,
Windows Server 2003 family,
.NET Compact Framework - Windows CE .NET

ICustomTypeDescriptor.GetEditor Method

Returns an editor of the specified type for this object.

```
[Visual Basic]
Function GetEditor( _
   ByVal editorBaseType As Type _
) As Object
[C#]
object GetEditor(
   Type editorBaseType
);
[C++]
Object* GetEditor(
   Type* editorBaseType
);
[JScript]
function GetEditor(
   editorBaseType : Type
) : Object;
```

Parameters

editorBaseType
A **Type** that represents the editor for this object.

Return Value

An **Object** of the specified type that is the editor for this object, or a null reference (**Nothing** in Visual Basic) if the editor cannot be found.

Requirements

Platforms: Windows 98, Windows NT 4.0,
Windows Millennium Edition, Windows 2000,
Windows XP Home Edition, Windows XP Professional,
Windows Server 2003 family,
.NET Compact Framework - Windows CE .NET

ICustomTypeDescriptor.GetEvents Method

Returns the events for this instance of a component.

Overload List

Returns the events for this instance of a component.

Supported by the .NET Compact Framework.

[Visual Basic] **Overloads Function GetEvents() As EventDescriptorCollection**

[C#] **EventDescriptorCollection GetEvents();**

[C++] **EventDescriptorCollection* GetEvents();**

[JScript] **function GetEvents() : EventDescriptorCollection;**

Returns the events for this instance of a component using the attribute array as a filter.

Supported by the .NET Compact Framework.

[Visual Basic] **Overloads Function GetEvents(Attribute()) As EventDescriptorCollection**

[C#] **EventDescriptorCollection GetEvents(Attribute[]);**

[C++] **EventDescriptorCollection* GetEvents(Attribute*[]);**

[JScript] **function GetEvents(Attribute[]) : EventDescriptorCollection;**

ICustomTypeDescriptor.GetEvents Method ()

Returns the events for this instance of a component.

[Visual Basic]
```
Function GetEvents() As EventDescriptorCollection
```
[C#]
```
EventDescriptorCollection GetEvents();
```
[C++]
```
EventDescriptorCollection* GetEvents();
```
[JScript]
```
function GetEvents() : EventDescriptorCollection;
```

Return Value

An **EventDescriptorCollection** that represents the events for this component instance.

Remarks

The events for this instance can differ from the set of events that the class provides. For example, if the component is site-based, the site can add or remove additional events.

Implementors can return an **EventDescriptorCollection.Empty** if no properties are specified. This method should never return a null reference (**Nothing** in Visual Basic).

Requirements

Platforms: Windows 98, Windows NT 4.0, Windows Millennium Edition, Windows 2000, Windows XP Home Edition, Windows XP Professional, Windows Server 2003 family, .NET Compact Framework - Windows CE .NET

ICustomTypeDescriptor.GetEvents Method (Attribute[])

Returns the events for this instance of a component using the attribute array as a filter.

[Visual Basic]
```
Function GetEvents( _
   ByVal attributes() As Attribute _
) As EventDescriptorCollection
```
[C#]
```
EventDescriptorCollection GetEvents(
   Attribute[] attributes
);
```
[C++]
```
EventDescriptorCollection* GetEvents(
   Attribute* attributes[]
);
```
[JScript]
```
function GetEvents(
   attributes : Attribute[]
) : EventDescriptorCollection;
```

Parameters

attributes

An array of type **Attribute** that is used as a filter.

Return Value

An **EventDescriptorCollection** that represents the events for this component instance that match the given set of attributes.

Remarks

The events for this instance can differ from the set of events that the class provides. For example, if the component is site-based, the site can add or remove additional events.

If an **Attribute** instance is specified in the attributes array and the event does not have an instance of the class for that attribute, the returned array includes the event if the **Attribute** is the default event.

Requirements

Platforms: Windows 98, Windows NT 4.0, Windows Millennium Edition, Windows 2000, Windows XP Home Edition, Windows XP Professional, Windows Server 2003 family, .NET Compact Framework - Windows CE .NET

ICustomTypeDescriptor.GetProperties Method

Returns the properties for this instance of a component.

Overload List

Returns the properties for this instance of a component.

Supported by the .NET Compact Framework.

[Visual Basic] **Overloads Function GetProperties() As PropertyDescriptorCollection**

[C#] **PropertyDescriptorCollection GetProperties();**

[C++] **PropertyDescriptorCollection* GetProperties();**

[JScript] **function GetProperties() : PropertyDescriptorCollection;**

Returns the properties for this instance of a component using the attribute array as a filter.

Supported by the .NET Compact Framework.

[Visual Basic] **Overloads Function GetProperties(Attribute()) As PropertyDescriptorCollection**

[C#] **PropertyDescriptorCollection GetProperties(Attribute[]);**

[C++] **PropertyDescriptorCollection* GetProperties(Attribute*[]);**

[JScript] **function GetProperties(Attribute[]) : PropertyDescriptorCollection;**

ICustomTypeDescriptor.GetProperties Method ()

Returns the properties for this instance of a component.

```
[Visual Basic]
Function GetProperties() As PropertyDescriptorCollection
[C#]
PropertyDescriptorCollection GetProperties();
[C++]
PropertyDescriptorCollection* GetProperties();
[JScript]
function GetProperties() : PropertyDescriptorCollection;
```

Return Value

A **PropertyDescriptorCollection** that represents the properties for this component instance.

Remarks

The properties for this instance can differ from the set of properties that the class provides. For example, if the component is sited, the site can add or remove additional properties.

Implementors can return a **PropertyDescriptorCollection.Empty** if no properties are specified. This method should never return a null reference (**Nothing** in Visual Basic).

Requirements

Platforms: Windows 98, Windows NT 4.0,
Windows Millennium Edition, Windows 2000,
Windows XP Home Edition, Windows XP Professional,
Windows Server 2003 family,
.NET Compact Framework - Windows CE .NET

ICustomTypeDescriptor.GetProperties Method (Attribute[])

Returns the properties for this instance of a component using the attribute array as a filter.

```
[Visual Basic]
Function GetProperties( _
   ByVal attributes() As Attribute _
) As PropertyDescriptorCollection
[C#]
PropertyDescriptorCollection GetProperties(
   Attribute[] attributes
);
[C++]
PropertyDescriptorCollection* GetProperties(
   Attribute* attributes[]
);
[JScript]
function GetProperties(
   attributes : Attribute[]
) : PropertyDescriptorCollection;
```

Parameters

attributes

An array of type **Attribute** that is used as a filter.

Return Value

An array of type **Attribute** that represents the properties for this component instance that match the given set of attributes.

Remarks

The properties for this instance can differ from the set of properties that the class provides. For example, if the component is sited, the site can add or remove additional properties.

If an **Attribute** instance is specified in the attributes array and the property does not have an instance of the class for that attribute, the returned array will include the property if the **Attribute** is the default property.

Requirements

Platforms: Windows 98, Windows NT 4.0,
Windows Millennium Edition, Windows 2000,
Windows XP Home Edition, Windows XP Professional,
Windows Server 2003 family,
.NET Compact Framework - Windows CE .NET

ICustomTypeDescriptor.GetPropertyOwner Method

Returns the object that this value is a member of.

```
[Visual Basic]
Function GetPropertyOwner( _
   ByVal pd As PropertyDescriptor _
) As Object
[C#]
object GetPropertyOwner(
   PropertyDescriptor pd
);
[C++]
Object* GetPropertyOwner(
   PropertyDescriptor* pd
);
[JScript]
function GetPropertyOwner(
   pd : PropertyDescriptor
) : Object;
```

Parameters

pd

A **PropertyDescriptor** that represents the property whose owner is to be found.

Return Value

An **Object** that represents the owner of the specified property.

Remarks

This method retrieves the object that directly depends on this value being edited. Typically, this object is required for the **PropertyDescriptor.GetValue** and **PropertyDescriptor.SetValue** methods.

This method should return an object that you can use as follows:

```
pd.GetValue(GetPropertyOwner(myPd));
```

If the `myPd` is a null reference (**Nothing** in Visual Basic), your implementation of **ICustomTypeDescriptor** should return the default object, typically, the base object that exposes the properties and attributes.

Requirements

Platforms: Windows 98, Windows NT 4.0,
Windows Millennium Edition, Windows 2000,
Windows XP Home Edition, Windows XP Professional,
Windows Server 2003 family,
.NET Compact Framework - Windows CE .NET

IDataErrorInfo Interface

Provides the functionality to offer custom error information that a user interface can bind to.

[Visual Basic]
```
Public Interface IDataErrorInfo
```
[C#]
```
public interface IDataErrorInfo
```
[C++]
```
public __gc __interface IDataErrorInfo
```
[JScript]
```
public interface IDataErrorInfo
```

Classes that Implement IDataErrorInfo

Class	Description
DataRowView	Represents a customized view of a **DataRow** exposed as a fully featured Windows Forms control.

Requirements

Namespace: System.ComponentModel

Platforms: Windows 98, Windows NT 4.0, Windows Millennium Edition, Windows 2000, Windows XP Home Edition, Windows XP Professional, Windows Server 2003 family, .NET Compact Framework - Windows CE .NET

Assembly: System (in System.dll)

IDataErrorInfo.Error Property

Gets an error message indicating what is wrong with this object.

[Visual Basic]
```
ReadOnly Property Error As String
```
[C#]
```
string Error {get;}
```
[C++]
```
__property String* get_Error();
```
[JScript]
```
function get Error() : String;
```

Property Value

An error message indicating what is wrong with this object. The default is an empty string ("").

Requirements

Platforms: Windows 98, Windows NT 4.0, Windows Millennium Edition, Windows 2000, Windows XP Home Edition, Windows XP Professional, Windows Server 2003 family, .NET Compact Framework - Windows CE .NET

IDataErrorInfo.Item Property

Gets the error message for the property with the given name.

[C#] In C#, this property is the indexer for the **IDataErrorInfo** class.

[Visual Basic]
```
Default ReadOnly Property Item( _
   ByVal columnName As String _
) As String
```
[C#]
```
string this[
   string columnName
] {get;}
```
[C++]
```
__property String* get_Item(
   String* columnName
);
```
[JScript]
```
returnValue = IDataErrorInfoObject.Item(columnName);
-or-
returnValue = IDataErrorInfoObject(columnName);
```

[JScript] In JScript, you can use the default indexed properties defined by a type, but you cannot explicitly define your own. However, specifying the **expando** attribute on a class automatically provides a default indexed property whose type is **Object** and whose index type is **String**.

Arguments [JScript]

columnName
: The name of the property whose error message to get.

Parameters [Visual Basic, C#, C++]

columnName
: The name of the property whose error message to get.

Property Value

The error message for the property. The default is an empty string ("").

Requirements

Platforms: Windows 98, Windows NT 4.0, Windows Millennium Edition, Windows 2000, Windows XP Home Edition, Windows XP Professional, Windows Server 2003 family

IEditableObject Interface

Provides functionality to commit or rollback changes to an object that is used as a data source.

[Visual Basic]
```
Public Interface IEditableObject
```
[C#]
```
public interface IEditableObject
```
[C++]
```
public __gc __interface IEditableObject
```
[JScript]
```
public interface IEditableObject
```

Classes that Implement IEditableObject

Class	Description
DataRowView	Represents a customized view of a **DataRow** exposed as a fully featured Windows Forms control.

Remarks

This interface is typically used to capture the **BeginEdit**, **EndEdit**, and **CancelEdit** semantics of a **DataRowView**.

Requirements

Namespace: System.ComponentModel

Platforms: Windows 98, Windows NT 4.0, Windows Millennium Edition, Windows 2000, Windows XP Home Edition, Windows XP Professional, Windows Server 2003 family, .NET Compact Framework - Windows CE .NET

Assembly: System (in System.dll)

IEditableObject.BeginEdit Method

Begins an edit on an object.

[Visual Basic]
```
Sub BeginEdit()
```
[C#]
```
void BeginEdit();
```
[C++]
```
void BeginEdit();
```
[JScript]
```
function BeginEdit();
```

Remarks

This method is typically used to capture the **BeginEdit** semantics of a **DataRowView**.

If **BeginEdit** is called on an object that is already being edited, the second and subsequent calls are ignored.

Notes to Implementers: An object implementing this interface needs to store updates after **BeginEdit** in such a way that they can be discarded if **CancelEdit** is called.

Requirements

Platforms: Windows 98, Windows NT 4.0, Windows Millennium Edition, Windows 2000, Windows XP Home Edition, Windows XP Professional, Windows Server 2003 family, .NET Compact Framework - Windows CE .NET

IEditableObject.CancelEdit Method

Discards changes since the last **BeginEdit** call.

[Visual Basic]
```
Sub CancelEdit()
```
[C#]
```
void CancelEdit();
```
[C++]
```
void CancelEdit();
```
[JScript]
```
function CancelEdit();
```

Remarks

This method is typically used to capture the **CancelEdit** semantics of a **DataRowView**.

This method will be ignored if called on an object that is not being edited.

> **Note** If the owning list implements **IBindingList**, calling **CancelEdit** on an object created using **IBindingList.AddNew** discards the object.

Requirements

Platforms: Windows 98, Windows NT 4.0, Windows Millennium Edition, Windows 2000, Windows XP Home Edition, Windows XP Professional, Windows Server 2003 family, .NET Compact Framework - Windows CE .NET

IEditableObject.EndEdit Method

Pushes changes since the last **BeginEdit** or **IBindingList.AddNew** call into the underlying object.

[Visual Basic]
```
Sub EndEdit()
```
[C#]
```
void EndEdit();
```
[C++]
```
void EndEdit();
```
[JScript]
```
function EndEdit();
```

Remarks

This method is typically used to capture the **EndEdit** semantics of a **DataRowView**.

This method will be ignored if called on an object that is not being edited.

Requirements

Platforms: Windows 98, Windows NT 4.0, Windows Millennium Edition, Windows 2000, Windows XP Home Edition, Windows XP Professional, Windows Server 2003 family, .NET Compact Framework - Windows CE .NET

IExtenderProvider Interface

Defines the interface for extending properties to other components in a container.

[Visual Basic]
```
Public Interface IExtenderProvider
```
[C#]
```
public interface IExtenderProvider
```
[C++]
```
public __gc __interface IExtenderProvider
```
[JScript]
```
public interface IExtenderProvider
```

Classes that Implement IExtenderProvider

Class	Description
ComponentTray	Provides behavior for the component tray of the form designer. The component tray represents components that do not otherwise provide a visible surface at design time and provides a way for users to access and set the properties of those components.
ErrorProvider	Provides a user interface for indicating that a control on a form has an error associated with it.
HelpProvider	Provides pop-up or online Help for controls.
LocalizationExtender-Provider	Provides design-time support for localization features to a root designer.
PropertyTab	Provides a base class for property tabs.
ToolTip	Represents a small rectangular pop-up window that displays a brief description of a control's purpose when the mouse hovers over the control.

Remarks

An extender provider is a component that provides properties to other components. For example, the **ToolTip** control is an extender provider. When you add a **ToolTip** control to a **Form**, all other controls on the form have a **ToolTip** property added to their list of properties.

Any component that provides extender properties must implement **IExtenderProvider**. A visual designer can then call **CanExtend** to determine which objects in a container should receive the extender properties.

Requirements

Namespace: System.ComponentModel

Platforms: Windows 98, Windows NT 4.0, Windows Millennium Edition, Windows 2000, Windows XP Home Edition, Windows XP Professional, Windows Server 2003 family

Assembly: System (in System.dll)

IExtenderProvider.CanExtend Method

Specifies whether this object can provide its extender properties to the specified object.

[Visual Basic]
```
Function CanExtend( _
   ByVal extendee As Object _
) As Boolean
```
[C#]
```
bool CanExtend(
   object extendee
);
```
[C++]
```
bool CanExtend(
   Object* extendee
);
```
[JScript]
```
function CanExtend(
   extendee : Object
) : Boolean;
```

Parameters

extendee

The **Object** to receive the extender properties.

Return Value

true if this object can provide extender properties to the specified object; otherwise, **false**.

Requirements

Platforms: Windows 98, Windows NT 4.0, Windows Millennium Edition, Windows 2000, Windows XP Home Edition, Windows XP Professional, Windows Server 2003 family

IListSource Interface

Provides functionality to an object to return a list that can be bound to a data source.

[Visual Basic]
```
Public Interface IListSource
```
[C#]
```
public interface IListSource
```
[C++]
```
public __gc __interface IListSource
```
[JScript]
```
public interface IListSource
```

Classes that Implement IListSource

Class	Description
DataSet	Represents an in-memory cache of data.
DataTable	Represents one table of in-memory data.

Remarks

You typically use this interface to return a list that can be bound to a data source, from an object that does not implement **IList** itself.

Binding to data can occur at either run time or in a designer, but there are rules for each. At run time, you can bind to data in any of the following:

- **Array**
- Implementer of **IList**, provided the implementer has a strongly typed **Item** property (that is, the **Type** is anything but **Object**). You can accomplish this by making the default implementation of **Item** private. If you want to create an **IList** that follows the rules of a strongly-typed collection, you should derive from **CollectionBase**.
- Implementer of **ITypedList**.

In a designer, you can initialize binding to **Component** objects by following the same rules.

> **Note** Implementers of **IListSource** can return an **IList** that contains a collection of **IList** objects.

Requirements

Namespace: System.ComponentModel

Platforms: Windows 98, Windows NT 4.0,
Windows Millennium Edition, Windows 2000,
Windows XP Home Edition, Windows XP Professional,
Windows Server 2003 family,
.NET Compact Framework - Windows CE .NET

Assembly: System (in System.dll)

IListSource.ContainsListCollection Property

Gets a value indicating whether the collection is a collection of **IList** objects.

[Visual Basic]
```
ReadOnly Property ContainsListCollection As Boolean
```
[C#]
```
bool ContainsListCollection {get;}
```
[C++]
```
__property bool get_ContainsListCollection();
```
[JScript]
```
function get ContainsListCollection() : Boolean;
```

Property Value

true if the collection is a collection of **IList** objects; otherwise, **false**.

Remarks

Using this property in **DataSet** returns **true** because the **DataSet** class contains a collection of collections. Using this property in **DataTable** returns **false** because the **DataTable** class contains a collection of objects.

Requirements

Platforms: Windows 98, Windows NT 4.0,
Windows Millennium Edition, Windows 2000,
Windows XP Home Edition, Windows XP Professional,
Windows Server 2003 family,
.NET Compact Framework - Windows CE .NET

IListSource.GetList Method

Returns an **IList** that can be bound to a data source from an object that does not implement an **IList** itself.

[Visual Basic]
```
Function GetList() As IList
```
[C#]
```
IList GetList();
```
[C++]
```
IList* GetList();
```
[JScript]
```
function GetList() : IList;
```

Return Value

An **IList** that can be bound to a data source from the object.

Requirements

Platforms: Windows 98, Windows NT 4.0,
Windows Millennium Edition, Windows 2000,
Windows XP Home Edition, Windows XP Professional,
Windows Server 2003 family,
.NET Compact Framework - Windows CE .NET

ImmutableObjectAttribute Class

Specifies that an object has no subproperties capable of being edited.

System.Object
System.Attribute
System.ComponentModel.ImmutableObjectAttribute

```
[Visual Basic]
<AttributeUsage(AttributeTargets.All)>
NotInheritable Public Class ImmutableObjectAttribute
   Inherits Attribute
[C#]
[AttributeUsage(AttributeTargets.All)]
public sealed class ImmutableObjectAttribute : Attribute
[C++]
[AttributeUsage(AttributeTargets::All)]
public __gc __sealed class ImmutableObjectAttribute : public
   Attribute
[JScript]
public
   AttributeUsage(AttributeTargets.All)
class ImmutableObjectAttribute extends Attribute
```

Thread Safety

Any public static (**Shared** in Visual Basic) members of this type are safe for multithreaded operations. Any instance members are not guaranteed to be thread safe.

Remarks

This attribute is typically used in the Properties window to determine whether to render an expandable object as read-only. As such, this property is used only at design time.

Requirements

Namespace: System.ComponentModel

Platforms: Windows 98, Windows NT 4.0, Windows Millennium Edition, Windows 2000, Windows XP Home Edition, Windows XP Professional, Windows Server 2003 family

Assembly: System (in System.dll)

ImmutableObjectAttribute Constructor

Initializes a new instance of the **ImmutableObjectAttribute** class.

```
[Visual Basic]
Public Sub New( _
   ByVal immutable As Boolean _
)
[C#]
public ImmutableObjectAttribute(
   bool immutable
);
[C++]
public: ImmutableObjectAttribute(
   bool immutable
);
[JScript]
public function ImmutableObjectAttribute(
   immutable : Boolean
);
```

Parameters

immutable
true if the object is immutable; otherwise, **false**.

Remarks

This attribute is typically used in the Properties window to determine whether to render an expandable object as read-only.

Requirements

Platforms: Windows 98, Windows NT 4.0, Windows Millennium Edition, Windows 2000, Windows XP Home Edition, Windows XP Professional, Windows Server 2003 family

ImmutableObjectAttribute.Default Field

This member supports the .NET Framework infrastructure and is not intended to be used directly from your code.

```
[Visual Basic]
Public Shared ReadOnly Default As ImmutableObjectAttribute
[C#]
public static readonly ImmutableObjectAttribute Default;
[C++]
public: static ImmutableObjectAttribute* Default;
[JScript]
public static var Default : ImmutableObjectAttribute;
```

ImmutableObjectAttribute.No Field

Specifies that an object has at least one editable subproperty. This static (**Shared** in Visual Basic) field is read-only.

```
[Visual Basic]
Public Shared ReadOnly No As ImmutableObjectAttribute
[C#]
public static readonly ImmutableObjectAttribute No;
[C++]
public: static ImmutableObjectAttribute* No;
[JScript]
public static var No : ImmutableObjectAttribute;
```

Remarks

This field is the default setting for this attribute.

This attribute is typically used in the Properties window to determine whether to render an expandable object as read-only.

Requirements

Platforms: Windows 98, Windows NT 4.0, Windows Millennium Edition, Windows 2000, Windows XP Home Edition, Windows XP Professional, Windows Server 2003 family

ImmutableObjectAttribute.Yes Field

Specifies that an object has no subproperties that can be edited. This static (**Shared** in Visual Basic) field is read-only.

```
[Visual Basic]
Public Shared ReadOnly Yes As ImmutableObjectAttribute
[C#]
public static readonly ImmutableObjectAttribute Yes;
[C++]
public: static ImmutableObjectAttribute* Yes;
```

[JScript]
```
public static var Yes : ImmutableObjectAttribute;
```

Remarks

This attribute is typically used in the Properties window to determine whether to render an expandable object as read-only.

Requirements

Platforms: Windows 98, Windows NT 4.0, Windows Millennium Edition, Windows 2000, Windows XP Home Edition, Windows XP Professional, Windows Server 2003 family

ImmutableObjectAttribute.Immutable Property

Gets whether the object is immutable.

[Visual Basic]
```
Public ReadOnly Property Immutable As Boolean
```
[C#]
```
public bool Immutable {get;}
```
[C++]
```
public: __property bool get_Immutable();
```
[JScript]
```
public function get Immutable() : Boolean;
```

Property Value

true if the object is immutable; otherwise, **false**.

Remarks

This attribute is typically used in the Properties window to determine whether to render an expandable object as read-only.

Requirements

Platforms: Windows 98, Windows NT 4.0, Windows Millennium Edition, Windows 2000, Windows XP Home Edition, Windows XP Professional, Windows Server 2003 family

ImmutableObjectAttribute.Equals Method

This member overrides **Object.Equals**.

[Visual Basic]
```
Overrides Public Function Equals( _
   ByVal obj As Object _
) As Boolean
```
[C#]
```
public override bool Equals(
   object obj
);
```
[C++]
```
public: bool Equals(
   Object* obj
);
```
[JScript]
```
public override function Equals(
   obj : Object
) : Boolean;
```

Requirements

Platforms: Windows 98, Windows NT 4.0, Windows Millennium Edition, Windows 2000, Windows XP Home Edition, Windows XP Professional, Windows Server 2003 family

ImmutableObjectAttribute.GetHashCode Method

This member overrides **Attribute.GetHashCode**.

[Visual Basic]
```
Overrides Public Function GetHashCode() As Integer
```
[C#]
```
public override int GetHashCode();
```
[C++]
```
public: int GetHashCode();
```
[JScript]
```
public override function GetHashCode() : int;
```

Requirements

Platforms: Windows 98, Windows NT 4.0, Windows Millennium Edition, Windows 2000, Windows XP Home Edition, Windows XP Professional, Windows Server 2003 family

ImmutableObjectAttribute.IsDefaultAttribute Method

This member overrides **Attribute.IsDefaultAttribute**.

[Visual Basic]
```
Overrides Public Function IsDefaultAttribute() As Boolean
```
[C#]
```
public override bool IsDefaultAttribute();
```
[C++]
```
public: bool IsDefaultAttribute();
```
[JScript]
```
public override function IsDefaultAttribute() : Boolean;
```

Requirements

Platforms: Windows 98, Windows NT 4.0, Windows Millennium Edition, Windows 2000, Windows XP Home Edition, Windows XP Professional, Windows Server 2003 family

InheritanceAttribute Class

Indicates whether the component associated with this attribute has been inherited from a base class. This class cannot be inherited.

System.Object
  System.Attribute
    System.ComponentModel.InheritanceAttribute

```
[Visual Basic]
<AttributeUsage(AttributeTargets.Property Or AttributeTargets.Field _
   Or AttributeTargets.Event)>
NotInheritable Public Class InheritanceAttribute
   Inherits Attribute
[C#]
[AttributeUsage(AttributeTargets.Property | AttributeTargets.Field
   | AttributeTargets.Event)]
public sealed class InheritanceAttribute : Attribute
[C++]
[AttributeUsage(AttributeTargets::Property |
   AttributeTargets::Field | AttributeTargets::Event)]
public __gc __sealed class InheritanceAttribute : public Attribute
[JScript]
public
   AttributeUsage(AttributeTargets.Property | AttributeTargets.Field |
   AttributeTargets.Event)
class InheritanceAttribute extends Attribute
```

Thread Safety

Any public static (**Shared** in Visual Basic) members of this type are safe for multithreaded operations. Any instance members are not guaranteed to be thread safe.

Remarks

InheritanceAttribute represents the type and level of inheritance of a member.

When the **AddInheritedComponents** method of the **IInheritanceService** searches the component fields of a component to identify fields that are inherited from a base class, the method represents the inheritance level of each component using an **InheritanceAttribute**.

Requirements

Namespace: System.ComponentModel

Platforms: Windows 98, Windows NT 4.0, Windows Millennium Edition, Windows 2000, Windows XP Home Edition, Windows XP Professional, Windows Server 2003 family

Assembly: System (in System.dll)

InheritanceAttribute Constructor

Initializes a new instance of the **InheritanceAttribute** class.

Overload List

Initializes a new instance of the **InheritanceAttribute** class.

[Visual Basic] **Public Sub New()**

[C#] **public InheritanceAttribute();**

[C++] **public: InheritanceAttribute();**

[JScript] **public function InheritanceAttribute();**

Initializes a new instance of the **InheritanceAttribute** class with the specified inheritance level.

[Visual Basic] **Public Sub New(InheritanceLevel)**

[C#] **public InheritanceAttribute(InheritanceLevel);**

[C++] **public: InheritanceAttribute(InheritanceLevel);**

[JScript] **public function InheritanceAttribute(InheritanceLevel);**

InheritanceAttribute Constructor ()

Initializes a new instance of the **InheritanceAttribute** class.

```
[Visual Basic]
Public Sub New()
[C#]
public InheritanceAttribute();
[C++]
public: InheritanceAttribute();
[JScript]
public function InheritanceAttribute();
```

Requirements

Platforms: Windows 98, Windows NT 4.0, Windows Millennium Edition, Windows 2000, Windows XP Home Edition, Windows XP Professional, Windows Server 2003 family

InheritanceAttribute Constructor (InheritanceLevel)

Initializes a new instance of the **InheritanceAttribute** class with the specified inheritance level.

```
[Visual Basic]
Public Sub New( _
   ByVal inheritanceLevel As InheritanceLevel _
)
[C#]
public InheritanceAttribute(
   InheritanceLevel inheritanceLevel
);
[C++]
public: InheritanceAttribute(
   InheritanceLevel inheritanceLevel
);
[JScript]
public function InheritanceAttribute(
   inheritanceLevel : InheritanceLevel
);
```

Parameters

inheritanceLevel

An **InheritanceLevel** that indicates the level of inheritance to set this attribute to.

Requirements

Platforms: Windows 98, Windows NT 4.0, Windows Millennium Edition, Windows 2000, Windows XP Home Edition, Windows XP Professional, Windows Server 2003 family

InheritanceAttribute.Default Field

Specifies that the default value for **InheritanceAttribute** is **NotInherited**. This field is read-only.

[Visual Basic]
```
Public Shared ReadOnly Default As InheritanceAttribute
```
[C#]
```
public static readonly InheritanceAttribute Default;
```
[C++]
```
public: static InheritanceAttribute* Default;
```
[JScript]
```
public static var Default : InheritanceAttribute;
```

Remarks

This field creates a new **InheritanceAttribute** that indicates that the associated component is not inherited.

Requirements

Platforms: Windows 98, Windows NT 4.0, Windows Millennium Edition, Windows 2000, Windows XP Home Edition, Windows XP Professional, Windows Server 2003 family

InheritanceAttribute.Inherited Field

Specifies that the component is inherited. This field is read-only.

[Visual Basic]
```
Public Shared ReadOnly Inherited As InheritanceAttribute
```
[C#]
```
public static readonly InheritanceAttribute Inherited;
```
[C++]
```
public: static InheritanceAttribute* Inherited;
```
[JScript]
```
public static var Inherited : InheritanceAttribute;
```

Remarks

This field creates a new **InheritanceAttribute** that indicates that the associated component is inherited.

Requirements

Platforms: Windows 98, Windows NT 4.0, Windows Millennium Edition, Windows 2000, Windows XP Home Edition, Windows XP Professional, Windows Server 2003 family

InheritanceAttribute.InheritedReadOnly Field

Specifies that the component is inherited and is read-only. This field is read-only.

[Visual Basic]
```
Public Shared ReadOnly InheritedReadOnly As InheritanceAttribute
```
[C#]
```
public static readonly InheritanceAttribute InheritedReadOnly;
```
[C++]
```
public: static InheritanceAttribute* InheritedReadOnly;
```
[JScript]
```
public static var InheritedReadOnly : InheritanceAttribute;
```

Remarks

This field creates a new **InheritanceAttribute** that indicates that the associated component is inherited and read-only.

Requirements

Platforms: Windows 98, Windows NT 4.0, Windows Millennium Edition, Windows 2000, Windows XP Home Edition, Windows XP Professional, Windows Server 2003 family

InheritanceAttribute.NotInherited Field

Specifies that the component is not inherited. This field is read-only.

[Visual Basic]
```
Public Shared ReadOnly NotInherited As InheritanceAttribute
```
[C#]
```
public static readonly InheritanceAttribute NotInherited;
```
[C++]
```
public: static InheritanceAttribute* NotInherited;
```
[JScript]
```
public static var NotInherited : InheritanceAttribute;
```

Remarks

This field creates a new **InheritanceAttribute** that indicates that the associated component is not inherited.

Requirements

Platforms: Windows 98, Windows NT 4.0, Windows Millennium Edition, Windows 2000, Windows XP Home Edition, Windows XP Professional, Windows Server 2003 family

InheritanceAttribute.InheritanceLevel Property

Gets or sets the current inheritance level stored in this attribute.

[Visual Basic]
```
Public ReadOnly Property InheritanceLevel As InheritanceLevel
```
[C#]
```
public InheritanceLevel InheritanceLevel {get;}
```
[C++]
```
public: __property InheritanceLevel get_InheritanceLevel();
```
[JScript]
```
public function get InheritanceLevel() : InheritanceLevel;
```

Property Value

The **InheritanceLevel** stored in this attribute.

Requirements

Platforms: Windows 98, Windows NT 4.0, Windows Millennium Edition, Windows 2000, Windows XP Home Edition, Windows XP Professional, Windows Server 2003 family

InheritanceAttribute.Equals Method

This member overrides **Object.Equals**.

[Visual Basic]
```
Overrides Public Function Equals( _
   ByVal value As Object _
) As Boolean
```
[C#]
```
public override bool Equals(
   object value
);
```

```
[C++]
public: bool Equals(
   Object* value
);
[JScript]
public override function Equals(
   value : Object
) : Boolean;
```

Requirements

Platforms: Windows 98, Windows NT 4.0, Windows Millennium Edition, Windows 2000, Windows XP Home Edition, Windows XP Professional, Windows Server 2003 family

InheritanceAttribute.GetHashCode Method

This member overrides **Attribute.GetHashCode**.

```
[Visual Basic]
Overrides Public Function GetHashCode() As Integer
[C#]
public override int GetHashCode();
[C++]
public: int GetHashCode();
[JScript]
public override function GetHashCode() : int;
```

Requirements

Platforms: Windows 98, Windows NT 4.0, Windows Millennium Edition, Windows 2000, Windows XP Home Edition, Windows XP Professional, Windows Server 2003 family

InheritanceAttribute.IsDefaultAttribute Method

Gets a value indicating whether the current value of the attribute is the default value for the attribute.

```
[Visual Basic]
Overrides Public Function IsDefaultAttribute() As Boolean
[C#]
public override bool IsDefaultAttribute();
[C++]
public: bool IsDefaultAttribute();
[JScript]
public override function IsDefaultAttribute() : Boolean;
```

Return Value

true if the current value of the attribute is the default; otherwise, **false**.

Requirements

Platforms: Windows 98, Windows NT 4.0, Windows Millennium Edition, Windows 2000, Windows XP Home Edition, Windows XP Professional, Windows Server 2003 family

InheritanceAttribute.ToString Method

This member overrides **Object.ToString**.

```
[Visual Basic]
Overrides Public Function ToString() As String
[C#]
public override string ToString();
[C++]
public: String* ToString();
[JScript]
public override function ToString() : String;
```

Requirements

Platforms: Windows 98, Windows NT 4.0, Windows Millennium Edition, Windows 2000, Windows XP Home Edition, Windows XP Professional, Windows Server 2003 family

InheritanceLevel Enumeration

Defines identifiers for types of inheritance levels.

[Visual Basic]
```
<Serializable>
Public Enum InheritanceLevel
```
[C#]
```
[Serializable]
public enum InheritanceLevel
```
[C++]
```
[Serializable]
__value public enum InheritanceLevel
```
[JScript]
```
public
   Serializable
enum InheritanceLevel
```

Remarks

InheritanceLevel defines identifiers for numeric IDs that are used with the **InheritanceAttribute** attribute to indicate various levels of inheritance.

Members

Member name	Description
Inherited	The object is inherited.
InheritedReadOnly	The object is inherited, but has read-only access.
NotInherited	The object is not inherited.

Requirements

Namespace: System.ComponentModel

Platforms: Windows 98, Windows NT 4.0, Windows Millennium Edition, Windows 2000, Windows XP Home Edition, Windows XP Professional, Windows Server 2003 family

Assembly: System (in System.dll)

InstallerTypeAttribute Class

Specifies the installer for a type that installs components.

System.Object
  System.Attribute
    System.ComponentModel.InstallerTypeAttribute

```
[Visual Basic]
<AttributeUsage(AttributeTargets.Class)>
Public Class InstallerTypeAttribute
   Inherits Attribute
[C#]
[AttributeUsage(AttributeTargets.Class)]
public class InstallerTypeAttribute : Attribute
[C++]
[AttributeUsage(AttributeTargets::Class)]
public __gc class InstallerTypeAttribute : public Attribute
[JScript]
public
   AttributeUsage(AttributeTargets.Class)
class InstallerTypeAttribute extends Attribute
```

Thread Safety

Any public static (**Shared** in Visual Basic) members of this type are safe for multithreaded operations. Any instance members are not guaranteed to be thread safe.

Remarks

The class used for the installer must implement the **IDesigner** interface. Use the **InstallerType** property to get the installer associated with this attribute.

Requirements

Namespace: System.ComponentModel

Platforms: Windows 98, Windows NT 4.0,
Windows Millennium Edition, Windows 2000,
Windows XP Home Edition, Windows XP Professional,
Windows Server 2003 family

Assembly: System (in System.dll)

InstallerTypeAttribute Constructor

Initializes a new instance of the **InstallerTypeAttribute** class.

Overload List

Initializes a new instance of the **InstallerTypeAttribute** class with the name of the component's installer type.

[Visual Basic] **Public Sub New(String)**

[C#] **public InstallerTypeAttribute(string);**

[C++] **public: InstallerTypeAttribute(String*);**

[JScript] **public function InstallerTypeAttribute(String);**

Initializes a new instance of the **InstallerTypeAttribute** class, when given a **Type** that represents the installer for a component.

[Visual Basic] **Public Sub New(Type)**

[C#] **public InstallerTypeAttribute(Type);**

[C++] **public: InstallerTypeAttribute(Type*);**

[JScript] **public function InstallerTypeAttribute(Type);**

InstallerTypeAttribute Constructor (String)

Initializes a new instance of the **InstallerTypeAttribute** class with the name of the component's installer type.

```
[Visual Basic]
Public Sub New( _
   ByVal typeName As String _
)
[C#]
public InstallerTypeAttribute(
   string typeName
);
[C++]
public: InstallerTypeAttribute(
   String* typeName
);
[JScript]
public function InstallerTypeAttribute(
   typeName : String
);
```

Parameters

typeName
  The name of a **Type** that represents the installer for the component this attribute is bound to. This class must implement **IDesigner**.

Requirements

Platforms: Windows 98, Windows NT 4.0,
Windows Millennium Edition, Windows 2000,
Windows XP Home Edition, Windows XP Professional,
Windows Server 2003 family

InstallerTypeAttribute Constructor (Type)

Initializes a new instance of the **InstallerTypeAttribute** class, when given a **Type** that represents the installer for a component.

```
[Visual Basic]
Public Sub New( _
   ByVal installerType As Type _
)
[C#]
public InstallerTypeAttribute(
   Type installerType
);
[C++]
public: InstallerTypeAttribute(
   Type* installerType
);
[JScript]
public function InstallerTypeAttribute(
   installerType : Type
);
```

Parameters

installerType
  A **Type** that represents the installer for the component this attribute is bound to. This class must implement **IDesigner**.

Requirements

Platforms: Windows 98, Windows NT 4.0,
Windows Millennium Edition, Windows 2000,
Windows XP Home Edition, Windows XP Professional,
Windows Server 2003 family

InstallerTypeAttribute.InstallerType Property

Gets the type of installer associated with this attribute.

```
[Visual Basic]
Public Overridable ReadOnly Property InstallerType As Type
[C#]
public virtual Type InstallerType {get;}
[C++]
public: __property virtual Type* get_InstallerType();
[JScript]
public function get InstallerType() : Type;
```

Property Value

A **Type** that represents the type of installer associated with this attribute, or a null reference (**Nothing** in Visual Basic) if an installer does not exist.

Requirements

Platforms: Windows 98, Windows NT 4.0, Windows Millennium Edition, Windows 2000, Windows XP Home Edition, Windows XP Professional, Windows Server 2003 family

InstallerTypeAttribute.Equals Method

This member overrides **Object.Equals**.

```
[Visual Basic]
Overrides Public Function Equals( _
   ByVal obj As Object _
) As Boolean
[C#]
public override bool Equals(
   object obj
);
[C++]
public: bool Equals(
   Object* obj
);
[JScript]
public override function Equals(
   obj : Object
) : Boolean;
```

Requirements

Platforms: Windows 98, Windows NT 4.0, Windows Millennium Edition, Windows 2000, Windows XP Home Edition, Windows XP Professional, Windows Server 2003 family

InstallerTypeAttribute.GetHashCode Method

This member overrides **Attribute.GetHashCode**.

```
[Visual Basic]
Overrides Public Function GetHashCode() As Integer
[C#]
public override int GetHashCode();
[C++]
public: int GetHashCode();
[JScript]
public override function GetHashCode() : int;
```

Requirements

Platforms: Windows 98, Windows NT 4.0, Windows Millennium Edition, Windows 2000, Windows XP Home Edition, Windows XP Professional, Windows Server 2003 family

Int16Converter Class

Provides a type converter to convert 16-bit signed integer objects to and from other representations.

System.Object
  System.ComponentModel.TypeConverter
    System.ComponentModel.BaseNumberConverter
      System.ComponentModel.Int16Converter

[Visual Basic]
```
Public Class Int16Converter
   Inherits BaseNumberConverter
```
[C#]
```
public class Int16Converter : BaseNumberConverter
```
[C++]
```
public __gc class Int16Converter : public BaseNumberConverter
```
[JScript]
```
public class Int16Converter extends BaseNumberConverter
```

Thread Safety

Any public static (**Shared** in Visual Basic) members of this type are safe for multithreaded operations. Any instance members are not guaranteed to be thread safe.

Remarks

This converter can only convert a 16-bit signed integer object to and from a string. The **Int16** value type represents signed integers with values ranging from negative 32768 through positive 32767.

The **ConvertFrom** method uses the **Parse** method of **Int16** with the integer value of **NumberStyles**.

The **ConvertTo** method uses the general ("G") format for the string returned.

> **Note** You should never create an instance of an **Int16Converter**. Instead, call the **GetConverter** method of **TypeDescriptor**. For more information, see the examples in the **TypeConverter** base class.

Example

[Visual Basic, C#, C++] The following sample converts a variable of type **Int16** to a string, and vice versa.

[Visual Basic]
```
Dim myInt16 As Short = -10000
Dim myInt16String As String = "+20000"
Console.WriteLine(TypeDescriptor.GetConverter(myInt16).                ↵
ConvertTo(myInt16, GetType(String)))
Console.WriteLine(TypeDescriptor.GetConverter(myInt16).                ↵
ConvertFrom(myInt16String))
```

[C#]
```
short myInt16 = -10000;
string myInt16String = "+20000";
Console.WriteLine(TypeDescriptor.GetConverter(myInt16).ConvertTo       ↵
 (myInt16, typeof(string)));
Console.WriteLine(TypeDescriptor.GetConverter(myInt16).ConvertFrom     ↵
 (myInt16String));
```

[C++]
```
short myInt16( -10000 );
String* myInt16String = S"+20000";
Console::WriteLine(TypeDescriptor::GetConverter(__box(myInt16))-       ↵
>ConvertTo(__box(myInt16), __typeof(String)));
Console::WriteLine(TypeDescriptor::GetConverter(__box(myInt16))-       ↵
>ConvertFrom(myInt16String));
```

Requirements

Namespace: System.ComponentModel

Platforms: Windows 98, Windows NT 4.0, Windows Millennium Edition, Windows 2000, Windows XP Home Edition, Windows XP Professional, Windows Server 2003 family

Assembly: System (in System.dll)

Int16Converter Constructor

Initializes a new instance of the **Int16Converter** class.

[Visual Basic]
```
Public Sub New()
```
[C#]
```
public Int16Converter();
```
[C++]
```
public: Int16Converter();
```
[JScript]
```
public function Int16Converter();
```

Remarks

The default constructor initializes any fields to their default values.

Requirements

Platforms: Windows 98, Windows NT 4.0, Windows Millennium Edition, Windows 2000, Windows XP Home Edition, Windows XP Professional, Windows Server 2003 family

Int32Converter Class

Provides a type converter to convert 32-bit signed integer objects to and from other representations.

System.Object
  System.ComponentModel.TypeConverter
    System.ComponentModel.BaseNumberConverter
      System.ComponentModel.Int32Converter
        System.Windows.Forms.ImageIndexConverter

[Visual Basic]
```
Public Class Int32Converter
   Inherits BaseNumberConverter
```
[C#]
```
public class Int32Converter : BaseNumberConverter
```
[C++]
```
public __gc class Int32Converter : public BaseNumberConverter
```
[JScript]
```
public class Int32Converter extends BaseNumberConverter
```

Thread Safety

Any public static (**Shared** in Visual Basic) members of this type are safe for multithreaded operations. Any instance members are not guaranteed to be thread safe.

Remarks

This converter can only convert a 32-bit signed integer object to and from a string. The **Int32** value type represents signed integers with values ranging from negative 2,147,483,648 through positive 2,147,483,647.

The **ConvertFrom** method uses the **Parse** method of **Int32** with the integer value of **NumberStyles**.

The **ConvertTo** method uses the general ("G") format for the string returned.

> **Note** You should never create an instance of an **Int32Converter**. Instead, call the **GetConverter** method of **TypeDescriptor**. For more information, see the examples in the **TypeConverter** base class.

Example

[Visual Basic, C#, C++] The following sample converts a variable of type **Int32** to a string and vice versa.

[Visual Basic]
```
Dim myInt32 As Integer = -967299
Dim myInt32String As String = "+1345556"
Console.WriteLine(TypeDescriptor.GetConverter(myInt32).ConvertTo ↵
(myInt32, GetType(String)))
Console.WriteLine(TypeDescriptor.GetConverter ↵
 (myInt32).ConvertFrom(myInt32String))
```

[C#]
```
int myInt32 = -967299;
string myInt32String = "+1345556";
Console.WriteLine(TypeDescriptor.GetConverter(myInt32).ConvertTo ↵
 (myInt32, typeof(string)));
Console.WriteLine(TypeDescriptor.GetConverter(myInt32).ConvertFrom ↵
 (myInt32String));
```

[C++]
```
int myInt32( -967299 );
String* myInt32String = S"+1345556";
Console::WriteLine(TypeDescriptor::GetConverter(__box(myInt32))- ↵
>ConvertTo(__box(myInt32), __typeof(String)));
Console::WriteLine(TypeDescriptor::GetConverter(__box(myInt32))- ↵
>ConvertFrom(myInt32String));
```

Requirements

Namespace: System.ComponentModel

Platforms: Windows 98, Windows NT 4.0, Windows Millennium Edition, Windows 2000, Windows XP Home Edition, Windows XP Professional, Windows Server 2003 family

Assembly: System (in System.dll)

Int32Converter Constructor

Initializes a new instance of the **Int32Converter** class.

[Visual Basic]
```
Public Sub New()
```
[C#]
```
public Int32Converter();
```
[C++]
```
public: Int32Converter();
```
[JScript]
```
public function Int32Converter();
```

Remarks

The default constructor initializes any fields to their default values.

Requirements

Platforms: Windows 98, Windows NT 4.0, Windows Millennium Edition, Windows 2000, Windows XP Home Edition, Windows XP Professional, Windows Server 2003 family

Int64Converter Class

Provides a type converter to convert 64-bit signed integer objects to and from various other representations.

System.Object
  System.ComponentModel.TypeConverter
    System.ComponentModel.BaseNumberConverter
      System.ComponentModel.Int64Converter

[Visual Basic]
```
Public Class Int64Converter
   Inherits BaseNumberConverter
```
[C#]
```
public class Int64Converter : BaseNumberConverter
```
[C++]
```
public __gc class Int64Converter : public BaseNumberConverter
```
[JScript]
```
public class Int64Converter extends BaseNumberConverter
```

Thread Safety

Any public static (**Shared** in Visual Basic) members of this type are safe for multithreaded operations. Any instance members are not guaranteed to be thread safe.

Remarks

This converter can only convert a 64-bit signed integer object to and from a string. The **Int64** value type represents integers with values ranging from negative 9,223,372,036,854,775,808 through positive 9,223,372,036,854,775,807.

The **ConvertFrom** method uses the **Parse** method of **Int64** with the integer value of **NumberStyles**.

The **ConvertTo** method uses the general ("G") format for the string returned.

For more information about type converters, see the **TypeConverter** base class and **Implementing a Type Converter**.

> **Note** You should never create an instance of an **Int64Converter**. Instead, call the **GetConverter** method of **TypeDescriptor**. For more information, see the examples in the **TypeConverter** base class.

Example

[Visual Basic, C#, C++] The following sample converts a variable of type **Int64** to a string, and vice versa.

[Visual Basic]
```
Dim myInt64 As Long = -123456789123
Dim myInt64String As String = "+184467440737095551"
Console.WriteLine(TypeDescriptor.GetConverter(myInt64).ConvertTo ↵
(myInt64, GetType(String)))
Console.WriteLine(TypeDescriptor.GetConverter ↵
 (myInt64).ConvertFrom(myInt64String))
```

[C#]
```
long myInt64 = -123456789123;
string myInt64String = "+184467440737095551";
Console.WriteLine(TypeDescriptor.GetConverter(myInt64).ConvertTo ↵
 (myInt64, typeof(string)));
Console.WriteLine(TypeDescriptor.GetConverter ↵
 (myInt64).ConvertFrom(myInt64String));
```

[C++]
```
long myInt64( -123456789123 );
String* myInt64String = S"+184467440737095551";
Console::WriteLine(TypeDescriptor::GetConverter(__box(myInt64))- ↵
>ConvertTo(__box(myInt64), __typeof(String)));
Console::WriteLine(TypeDescriptor::GetConverter(__box(myInt64))- ↵
>ConvertFrom(myInt64String));
```

Requirements

Namespace: System.ComponentModel

Platforms: Windows 98, Windows NT 4.0, Windows Millennium Edition, Windows 2000, Windows XP Home Edition, Windows XP Professional, Windows Server 2003 family

Assembly: System (in System.dll)

Int64Converter Constructor

Initializes a new instance of the **Int64Converter** class.

[Visual Basic]
```
Public Sub New()
```
[C#]
```
public Int64Converter();
```
[C++]
```
public: Int64Converter();
```
[JScript]
```
public function Int64Converter();
```

Remarks

The default constructor initializes any fields to their default values.

Requirements

Platforms: Windows 98, Windows NT 4.0, Windows Millennium Edition, Windows 2000, Windows XP Home Edition, Windows XP Professional, Windows Server 2003 family

InvalidEnumArgumentException Class

The exception thrown when using invalid arguments that are enumerators.

System.Object
  System.Exception
    System.SystemException
      System.ArgumentException
        System.ComponentModel.InvalidEnumArgumentException

[Visual Basic]
```
Public Class InvalidEnumArgumentException
   Inherits ArgumentException
```
[C#]
```
public class InvalidEnumArgumentException : ArgumentException
```
[C++]
```
public __gc class InvalidEnumArgumentException : public
   ArgumentException
```
[JScript]
```
public class InvalidEnumArgumentException extends ArgumentException
```

Thread Safety

Any public static (**Shared** in Visual Basic) members of this type are safe for multithreaded operations. Any instance members are not guaranteed to be thread safe.

Remarks

This exception is thrown if you pass an invalid enumeration value to a method or when setting a property.

Example

[Visual Basic, C#, C++] The following example shows how to catch an **InvalidEnumArgumentException** exception and interpret its content. The example attempts to pass an invalid enumeration value (`MessageBoxButtons`) through casting, as the **MessageBox.Show** method's third argument. Upon catching the exception, the example fetches the respective error message, the invalid parameter, stack trace, and origin of the exception.

[Visual Basic]
```
Try
    ' Attempts to pass an invalid enum value (MessageBoxButtons)    ↵
to the Show method
    Dim myButton As MessageBoxButtons
    myButton = CType(123, MessageBoxButtons)
    MessageBox.Show("This is a message", "This is the Caption",    ↵
myButton)
Catch invE As System.ComponentModel.InvalidEnumArgumentException
    Console.WriteLine(invE.Message)
    Console.WriteLine(invE.ParamName)
    Console.WriteLine(invE.StackTrace)
    Console.WriteLine(invE.Source)
End Try
```

[C#]
```
try
{
// Attempts to pass an invalid enum value (MessageBoxButtons)    ↵
 to the Show method
    MessageBoxButtons myButton= (MessageBoxButtons) 123;
    MessageBox.Show("This is a message","This is the    ↵
Caption",myButton);
}
catch(InvalidEnumArgumentException invE)
{
    Console.WriteLine(invE.Message);
    Console.WriteLine(invE.ParamName);
    Console.WriteLine(invE.StackTrace);
    Console.WriteLine(invE.Source);
}
```

[C++]
```
try
{
//Attempting to pass an invalid enum value (MessageBoxButtons)    ↵
 to the Show method
MessageBoxButtons myButton = (MessageBoxButtons) 123;    // to    ↵
 fix use System::Windows::Forms::DialogResult::OK;
MessageBox::Show(this, "This is a message","This is the    ↵
Caption", myButton);
}
catch(InvalidEnumArgumentException* invE)
{
    Console::WriteLine(invE->Message);
    Console::WriteLine(invE->ParamName);
    Console::WriteLine(invE->StackTrace);
    Console::WriteLine(invE->Source);
}
```

Requirements

Namespace: System.ComponentModel

Platforms: Windows 98, Windows NT 4.0, Windows Millennium Edition, Windows 2000, Windows XP Home Edition, Windows XP Professional, Windows Server 2003 family

Assembly: System (in System.dll)

InvalidEnumArgumentException Constructor

Initializes a new instance of the **InvalidEnumArgumentException** class.

Overload List

Initializes a new instance of the **InvalidEnumArgumentException** class without a message.

[Visual Basic] **Public Sub New()**

[C#] **public InvalidEnumArgumentException();**

[C++] **public: InvalidEnumArgumentException();**

[JScript] **public function InvalidEnumArgumentException();**

Initializes a new instance of the **InvalidEnumArgumentException** class with the specified message.

[Visual Basic] **Public Sub New(String)**

[C#] **public InvalidEnumArgumentException(string);**

[C++] **public: InvalidEnumArgumentException(String*);**

[JScript] **public function InvalidEnumArgumentException(String);**

Initializes a new instance of the **InvalidEnumArgumentException** class with a message generated from the argument, the invalid value, and an enumeration class.

[Visual Basic] **Public Sub New(String, Integer, Type)**

[C#] **public InvalidEnumArgumentException(string, int, Type);**

[C++] **public: InvalidEnumArgumentException(String*, int, Type*);**

[JScript] **public function InvalidEnumArgumentException(String, int, Type);**

InvalidEnumArgumentException Constructor ()

Initializes a new instance of the **InvalidEnumArgumentException** class without a message.

[Visual Basic]
```
Public Sub New()
```
[C#]
```
public InvalidEnumArgumentException();
```
[C++]
```
public: InvalidEnumArgumentException();
```
[JScript]
```
public function InvalidEnumArgumentException();
```

Requirements

Platforms: Windows 98, Windows NT 4.0, Windows Millennium Edition, Windows 2000, Windows XP Home Edition, Windows XP Professional, Windows Server 2003 family

InvalidEnumArgumentException Constructor (String)

Initializes a new instance of the **InvalidEnumArgumentException** class with the specified message.

[Visual Basic]
```
Public Sub New( _
   ByVal message As String _
)
```
[C#]
```
public InvalidEnumArgumentException(
   string message
);
```
[C++]
```
public: InvalidEnumArgumentException(
   String* message
);
```
[JScript]
```
public function InvalidEnumArgumentException(
   message : String
);
```

Parameters

message

The message to display with this exception.

Requirements

Platforms: Windows 98, Windows NT 4.0, Windows Millennium Edition, Windows 2000, Windows XP Home Edition, Windows XP Professional, Windows Server 2003 family

InvalidEnumArgumentException Constructor (String, Int32, Type)

Initializes a new instance of the **InvalidEnumArgumentException** class with a message generated from the argument, the invalid value, and an enumeration class.

[Visual Basic]
```
Public Sub New( _
   ByVal argumentName As String, _
   ByVal invalidValue As Integer, _
   ByVal enumClass As Type _
)
```
[C#]
```
public InvalidEnumArgumentException(
   string argumentName,
   int invalidValue,
   Type enumClass
);
```
[C++]
```
public: InvalidEnumArgumentException(
   String* argumentName,
   int invalidValue,
   Type* enumClass
);
```
[JScript]
```
public function InvalidEnumArgumentException(
   argumentName : String,
   invalidValue : int,
   enumClass : Type
);
```

Parameters

argumentName

The name of the argument that caused the exception.

invalidValue

The value of the argument that failed.

enumClass

A **Type** that represents the enumeration class with the valid values.

Remarks

This constructor will create a localized message saying that the *argumentName* parameter was invalid because the value passed in was invalid, and that the value should be one of the values in the enumeration class.

Requirements

Platforms: Windows 98, Windows NT 4.0, Windows Millennium Edition, Windows 2000, Windows XP Home Edition, Windows XP Professional, Windows Server 2003 family

ISite Interface

Provides functionality required by sites.

System.IServiceProvider
  System.ComponentModel.ISite

[Visual Basic]
```
<ComVisible(True)>
Public Interface ISite
   Inherits IServiceProvider
```
[C#]
```
[ComVisible(true)]
public interface ISite : IServiceProvider
```
[C++]
```
[ComVisible(true)]
public __gc __interface ISite : public IServiceProvider
```
[JScript]
```
public
   ComVisible(true)
interface ISite implements IServiceProvider
```

Remarks

Sites bind a **Component** to a **Container** and enable communication between them, as well as provide a way for the container to manage its components.

Sites can also serve as a repository for container-specific, per-component information, such as the component name.

Notes to Implementers: To be a site, a class must implement the **ISite** interface.

Example

[Visual Basic, C#, C++] The following example demonstrates the implementation of **ISite**, **IComponent**, and **IContainer** for use in a library container.

[Visual Basic]
```
'The following example demonstrates the implementation of
'ISite, IComponent, and IContainer for use in a simple library ↵
container.
'
'This example imports the System, System.ComponentModel, and ↵
System.Collections
'namespaces.

'This code segment implements the ISite and IComponent interfaces.
'The implementation of the IContainer interface can be seen ↵
in the documentation
'of IContainer.

'Implement the ISite interface.

'The ISBNSite class represents the ISBN name of the book component

Class ISBNSite
Implements ISite
Private m_curComponent As IComponent
Private m_curContainer As IContainer
Private m_bDesignMode As Boolean
Private m_ISBNCmpName As String

Public Sub New(ByVal actvCntr As IContainer, ByVal prntCmpnt ↵
 As IComponent)
    m_curComponent = prntCmpnt
    m_curContainer = actvCntr
    m_bDesignMode = False
    m_ISBNCmpName = Nothing
End Sub

'Support the ISite interface.
Public ReadOnly Property Component() As IComponent ↵
Implements ISite.Component
    Get
        Return m_curComponent
    End Get
End Property

Public ReadOnly Property Container() As IContainer ↵
Implements ISite.Container
    Get
        Return m_curContainer
    End Get
End Property

Public ReadOnly Property DesignMode() As Boolean ↵
Implements ISite.DesignMode
    Get
        Return m_bDesignMode
    End Get
End Property

Public Property Name() As String Implements ISite.Name
    Get
        Return m_ISBNCmpName
    End Get
    Set(ByVal Value As String)
        m_ISBNCmpName = Value
    End Set
End Property

'Support the IServiceProvider interface.
Public Function GetService(ByVal serviceType As Type) ↵
 As Object Implements ISite.GetService
    'This example does not use any service object.
    GetService = Nothing
End Function
End Class

'The BookComponent class represents the book component ↵
of the library container.
Class BookComponent
Implements IComponent
Public Event Disposed As EventHandler Implements IComponent.Disposed
Private m_curISBNSite As ISite
Private m_bookTitle As String
Private m_bookAuthor As String

Public Sub New(ByVal Title As String, ByVal Author As String)
    m_curISBNSite = Nothing
    m_bookTitle = Title
    m_bookAuthor = Author
End Sub

Public ReadOnly Property Title() As String
    Get
        Return m_bookTitle
    End Get
End Property

Public ReadOnly Property Author() As String
    Get
        Return m_bookAuthor
    End Get
End Property

Public Sub Dispose() Implements IComponent.Dispose
    'There is nothing to clean.
    RaiseEvent Disposed(Me, EventArgs.Empty)
End Sub

Public Property Site() As ISite Implements IComponent.Site
    Get
        Return m_curISBNSite
    End Get
    Set(ByVal Value As ISite)
        m_curISBNSite = Value
```

```
    End Set
End Property

Public Overloads Function Equals(ByVal cmp As Object) As Boolean
    Dim cmpObj As BookComponent = CType(cmp, BookComponent)
    If (Me.Title.Equals(cmpObj.Title) And ↵
Me.Author.Equals(cmpObj.Author)) Then
        Equals = True
    Else
        Equals = False
    End If
End Function

Public Overrides Function GetHashCode() As Integer
    GetHashCode = MyBase.GetHashCode()
End Function

End Class
```

[C#]

```
/// <summary>
/// The following example demonstrates the implementation of
/// ISite, IComponent, and IContainer for use in a simple ↵
library container.
///
/// This example uses the System, System.ComponentModel, ↵
 and System.Collections
/// namespaces.
/// </summary>

//This code segment implements the ISite and IComponent interfaces.
//The implementation of the IContainer interface can be ↵
seen in the documentation
//of IContainer.

//Implement the ISite interface.

// The ISBNSite class represents the ISBN name of the book component
class ISBNSite : ISite
{
    private IComponent m_curComponent;
    private IContainer m_curContainer;
    private bool m_bDesignMode;
    private string m_ISBNCmpName;

    public ISBNSite(IContainer actvCntr, IComponent prntCmpnt)
    {
        m_curComponent = prntCmpnt;
        m_curContainer = actvCntr;
        m_bDesignMode = false;
        m_ISBNCmpName = null;
    }

    //Support the ISite interface.
    public virtual IComponent Component
    {
        get
        {
            return m_curComponent;
        }
    }

    public virtual IContainer Container
    {
        get
        {
            return m_curContainer;
        }
    }

    public virtual bool DesignMode
    {
        get
        {
            return m_bDesignMode;
        }
    }

    public virtual string Name
    {
        get
        {
            return m_ISBNCmpName;
        }

        set
        {
            m_ISBNCmpName = value;
        }
    }

    //Support the IServiceProvider interface.
    public virtual object GetService(Type serviceType)
    {
        //This example does not use any service object.
        return null;
    }

}

// The BookComponent class represents the book component of ↵
the library container.

// This class implements the IComponent interface.

class BookComponent : IComponent
{
    public event EventHandler Disposed;
    private ISite m_curISBNSite;
    private string m_bookTitle;
    private string m_bookAuthor;

    public BookComponent(string Title, string Author)
    {
        m_curISBNSite = null;
        Disposed = null;
        m_bookTitle = Title;
        m_bookAuthor = Author;
    }

    public string Title
    {
        get
        {
            return m_bookTitle;
        }
    }

    public string Author
    {
        get
        {
            return m_bookAuthor;
        }
    }

    public virtual void Dispose()
    {
        //There is nothing to clean.
        if(Disposed != null)
            Disposed(this,EventArgs.Empty);
    }

    public virtual ISite Site
    {
        get
        {
            return m_curISBNSite;
        }
        set
        {
            m_curISBNSite = value;
        }
    }
```

```
    public override bool Equals(object cmp)
    {
        BookComponent cmpObj = (BookComponent)cmp;
        if(this.Title.Equals(cmpObj.Title) &&                    ↲
this.Author.Equals(cmpObj.Author))
            return true;

        return false;
    }

    public override int GetHashCode()
    {
        return base.GetHashCode();
    }
}
```

[C++]

```
/// <summary>
/// The following example demonstrates the implementation of
/// ISite, IComponent, and IContainer for use in a simple        ↲
 library container.
///
/// This example uses the System, System.ComponentModel, and     ↲
System.Collections
/// namespaces.
/// </summary>

//This code segment implements the ISite and IComponent interfaces.
//The implementation of the IContainer interface can be seen     ↲
in the documentation
//of IContainer.

//Implement the ISite interface.

// The ISBNSite class represents the ISBN name of the book component
__gc class ISBNSite : public ISite
{
private:

    IComponent* m_curComponent;
    IContainer* m_curContainer;
    bool m_bDesignMode;
    String* m_ISBNCmpName;

public:
    ISBNSite(IContainer* actvCntr, IComponent* prntCmpnt)
    {
        m_curComponent = prntCmpnt;
        m_curContainer = actvCntr;
        m_bDesignMode = false;
        m_ISBNCmpName = 0;
    }

    //Support the ISite interface.
    __property virtual IComponent* get_Component()
    {
            return m_curComponent;
    }

    __property virtual IContainer* get_Container()
    {
            return m_curContainer;
    }

    __property virtual bool get_DesignMode()
    {
            return m_bDesignMode;
    }

    __property virtual String* get_Name()
    {
            return m_ISBNCmpName;
    }

    __property virtual void set_Name( String* value )
    {
            m_ISBNCmpName = value;
    }

    //Support the IServiceProvider interface.
    virtual Object* GetService(Type* serviceType)
    {
        //This example does not use any service object.
        return 0;
    }

};

// The BookComponent class represents the book component of      ↲
the library container.

// This class implements the IComponent interface.

__gc class BookComponent : public IComponent
{
private:

    ISite* m_curISBNSite;
    String* m_bookTitle;
    String* m_bookAuthor;

public:

    __event virtual EventHandler* Disposed;

    BookComponent(String* Title, String* Author)
    {
        m_curISBNSite = 0;
        Disposed = 0;
        m_bookTitle = Title;
        m_bookAuthor = Author;
    }

    __property String* get_Title()
    {
            return m_bookTitle;
    }

    __property String* get_Author()
    {
            return m_bookAuthor;
    }

    virtual void Dispose()
    {
        //There is nothing to clean.
        if(Disposed != 0)
            Disposed(this,EventArgs::Empty);
    }

    __property virtual ISite* get_Site()
    {
            return m_curISBNSite;
    }

    __property virtual void set_Site( ISite* value )
    {
            m_curISBNSite = value;
    }

    bool Equals(Object* cmp)
    {
        BookComponent* cmpObj = __try_cast<BookComponent*>(cmp);
        return (this->Title->Equals(cmpObj->Title) && this->     ↲
Author->Equals(cmpObj->Author));
    }

    int GetHashCode()
    {
        return IComponent::GetHashCode();
    }
};
```

Requirements

Namespace: System.ComponentModel

Platforms: Windows 98, Windows NT 4.0, Windows Millennium Edition, Windows 2000, Windows XP Home Edition, Windows XP Professional, Windows Server 2003 family, .NET Compact Framework - Windows CE .NET

Assembly: System (in System.dll)

ISite.Component Property

Gets the component associated with the **ISite** when implemented by a class.

```
[Visual Basic]
ReadOnly Property Component As IComponent
[C#]
IComponent Component {get;}
[C++]
__property IComponent* get_Component();
[JScript]
function get Component() : IComponent;
```

Property Value

The **IComponent** instance associated with the **ISite**.

Remarks

A valid value for this property (that is, the value is not a null reference (**Nothing** in Visual Basic)) indicates that the component has been added to a container.

Requirements

Platforms: Windows 98, Windows NT 4.0, Windows Millennium Edition, Windows 2000, Windows XP Home Edition, Windows XP Professional, Windows Server 2003 family, .NET Compact Framework - Windows CE .NET

ISite.Container Property

Gets the **IContainer** associated with the **ISite** when implemented by a class.

```
[Visual Basic]
ReadOnly Property Container As IContainer
[C#]
IContainer Container {get;}
[C++]
__property IContainer* get_Container();
[JScript]
function get Container() : IContainer;
```

Property Value

The **IContainer** instance associated with the **ISite**.

Remarks

A null reference (**Nothing** in Visual Basic) for the **Container** property indicates that the **IComponent** instance does not have an **ISite**.

Requirements

Platforms: Windows 98, Windows NT 4.0, Windows Millennium Edition, Windows 2000, Windows XP Home Edition, Windows XP Professional, Windows Server 2003 family, .NET Compact Framework - Windows CE .NET

ISite.DesignMode Property

Determines whether the component is in design mode when implemented by a class.

```
[Visual Basic]
ReadOnly Property DesignMode As Boolean
[C#]
bool DesignMode {get;}
[C++]
__property bool get_DesignMode();
[JScript]
function get DesignMode() : Boolean;
```

Property Value

true if the component is in design mode; otherwise, **false**.

Remarks

The design mode indicator is stored in the **ISite**; therefore, if the **Component** does not have an **ISite** associated with it, this property is always **false**.

Requirements

Platforms: Windows 98, Windows NT 4.0, Windows Millennium Edition, Windows 2000, Windows XP Home Edition, Windows XP Professional, Windows Server 2003 family, .NET Compact Framework - Windows CE .NET

ISite.Name Property

Gets or sets the name of the component associated with the **ISite** when implemented by a class.

```
[Visual Basic]
Property Name As String
[C#]
string Name {get; set;}
[C++]
__property String* get_Name();
__property void set_Name(String*);
[JScript]
function get Name() : String;function set Name(String);
```

Property Value

The name of the component associated with the **ISite**; or a null reference (**Nothing** in Visual Basic), if no name is assigned to the component.

Remarks

The components within a container might or might not be named. If a component is given a name, the name must be unique among all the components within the container.

Requirements

Platforms: Windows 98, Windows NT 4.0, Windows Millennium Edition, Windows 2000, Windows XP Home Edition, Windows XP Professional, Windows Server 2003 family, .NET Compact Framework - Windows CE .NET

ISupportInitialize Interface

Specifies that this object supports a simple, transacted notification for batch initialization.

```
[Visual Basic]
Public Interface ISupportInitialize
[C#]
public interface ISupportInitialize
[C++]
public __gc __interface ISupportInitialize
[JScript]
public interface ISupportInitialize
```

Classes that Implement ISupportInitialize

Class	Description
AxHost	Wraps ActiveX controls and exposes them as fully featured Windows Forms controls.
DataGrid	Displays ADO.NET data in a scrollable grid.
DataSet	Represents an in-memory cache of data.
DataTable	Represents one table of in-memory data.
DataView	Represents a databindable, customized view of a **DataTable** for sorting, filtering, searching, editing, and navigation.
EventLog	Provides interaction with Windows event logs.
FileSystemWatcher	Listens to the file system change notifications and raises events when a directory, or file in a directory, changes.
NumericUpDown	Represents a Windows up-down control that displays numeric values.
PerformanceCounter	Represents a Windows NT performance counter component.
StatusBarPanel	Represents a panel in a **StatusBar** control.
Timer	Generates recurring events in an application.
TrackBar	Represents a standard Windows track bar.

Remarks

ISupportInitialize allows controls to optimize for multiple sets to properties. As a result, you can initialize co-dependent properties or batch set multiple properties at design time.

Call the **BeginInit** method to signal the object that initialization is starting. Call the **EndInit** method to signal that initialization is complete.

Requirements

Namespace: System.ComponentModel

Platforms: Windows 98, Windows NT 4.0, Windows Millennium Edition, Windows 2000, Windows XP Home Edition, Windows XP Professional, Windows Server 2003 family

Assembly: System (in System.dll)

ISupportInitialize.BeginInit Method

Signals the object that initialization is starting.

```
[Visual Basic]
Sub BeginInit()
[C#]
void BeginInit();
[C++]
void BeginInit();
[JScript]
function BeginInit();
```

Requirements

Platforms: Windows 98, Windows NT 4.0, Windows Millennium Edition, Windows 2000, Windows XP Home Edition, Windows XP Professional, Windows Server 2003 family

ISupportInitialize.EndInit Method

Signals the object that initialization is complete.

```
[Visual Basic]
Sub EndInit()
[C#]
void EndInit();
[C++]
void EndInit();
[JScript]
function EndInit();
```

Requirements

Platforms: Windows 98, Windows NT 4.0, Windows Millennium Edition, Windows 2000, Windows XP Home Edition, Windows XP Professional, Windows Server 2003 family

ISynchronizeInvoke Interface

Provides a way to synchronously or asynchronously execute a delegate.

```
[Visual Basic]
Public Interface ISynchronizeInvoke
[C#]
public interface ISynchronizeInvoke
[C++]
public __gc __interface ISynchronizeInvoke
[JScript]
public interface ISynchronizeInvoke
```

Classes that Implement ISynchronizeInvoke

Class	Description
Control	Defines the base class for controls, which are components with visual representation.

Remarks

The **ISynchronizeInvoke** interface provides synchronous and asynchronous communication between objects about the occurrence of an event. Objects that implement this interface can receive notification that an event has occurred, and they can respond to queries about the event. In this way, clients can make sure that one request has been processed before they submit a subsequent request that depends on completion of the first.

The **ISynchronizeInvoke** class provides two ways to invoke a process:

1. Asynchronously, by using the **BeginInvoke** method. **BeginInvoke** starts a process and then returns immediately. Use **EndInvoke** to wait until the process started by **BeginInvoke** completes.
2. Synchronously, by using the **Invoke** method. **Invoke** starts a process, waits until it completes, and then returns. Use **Invoke** when the control's main thread is different from the calling thread to marshal the call to the proper thread.

Requirements

Namespace: System.ComponentModel

Platforms: Windows 98, Windows NT 4.0, Windows Millennium Edition, Windows 2000, Windows XP Home Edition, Windows XP Professional, Windows Server 2003 family

Assembly: System (in System.dll)

ISynchronizeInvoke.InvokeRequired Property

Gets a value indicating whether the caller must call **Invoke** when calling an object that implements this interface.

```
[Visual Basic]
ReadOnly Property InvokeRequired As Boolean
[C#]
bool InvokeRequired {get;}
[C++]
__property bool get_InvokeRequired();
[JScript]
function get InvokeRequired() : Boolean;
```

Property Value

true if the caller must call **Invoke**; otherwise, **false**.

Remarks

This property determines whether the caller must call **Invoke** when making method calls to an object that implements this interface. Such objects are bound to a specific thread and are not thread-safe. If you are calling a method from a different thread, you must use the **Invoke** method to marshal the call to the proper thread.

Requirements

Platforms: Windows 98, Windows NT 4.0, Windows Millennium Edition, Windows 2000, Windows XP Home Edition, Windows XP Professional, Windows Server 2003 family

ISynchronizeInvoke.BeginInvoke Method

Executes the delegate on the main thread that this object executes on.

```
[Visual Basic]
Function BeginInvoke( _
   ByVal method As Delegate, _
   ByVal args() As Object _
) As IAsyncResult
[C#]
IAsyncResult BeginInvoke(
   Delegate method,
   object[] args
);
[C++]
IAsyncResult* BeginInvoke(
   Delegate* method,
   Object* args __gc[]
);
[JScript]
function BeginInvoke(
   method : Delegate,
   args : Object[]
) : IAsyncResult;
```

Parameters

method

A **Delegate** to a method that takes parameters of the same number and type that are contained in *args*.

args

An array of type **Object** to pass as arguments to the given method. This can be a null reference (**Nothing** in Visual Basic) if no arguments are needed.

Return Value

An **IAsyncResult** interface that represents the asynchronous operation started by calling this method.

Remarks

The delegate is called asynchronously, and this method returns immediately. You can call this method from any thread. If you need the return value from a process started with this method, call **EndInvoke** to get the value.

If you need to call the delegate synchronously, use the **Invoke** method instead.

Requirements

Platforms: Windows 98, Windows NT 4.0, Windows Millennium Edition, Windows 2000, Windows XP Home Edition, Windows XP Professional, Windows Server 2003 family

ISynchronizeInvoke.EndInvoke Method

Waits until the process started by calling **BeginInvoke** completes, and then returns the value generated by the process.

```
[Visual Basic]
Function EndInvoke( _
   ByVal result As IAsyncResult _
) As Object
[C#]
object EndInvoke(
   IAsyncResult result
);
[C++]
Object* EndInvoke(
   IAsyncResult* result
);
[JScript]
function EndInvoke(
   result : IAsyncResult
) : Object;
```

Parameters

result
An **IAsyncResult** interface that represents the asynchronous operation started by calling **BeginInvoke**.

Return Value

An **Object** that represents the return value generated by the asynchronous operation.

Remarks

This method gets the return value of the asynchronous operation represented by the **IAsyncResult** passed by this interface. If the asynchronous operation has not completed, this method will wait until the result is available.

Requirements

Platforms: Windows 98, Windows NT 4.0, Windows Millennium Edition, Windows 2000, Windows XP Home Edition, Windows XP Professional, Windows Server 2003 family

ISynchronizeInvoke.Invoke Method

Executes the delegate on the main thread that this object executes on.

```
[Visual Basic]
Function Invoke( _
   ByVal method As Delegate, _
   ByVal args() As Object _
) As Object
[C#]
object Invoke(
   Delegate method,
   object[] args
);
[C++]
Object* Invoke(
   Delegate* method,
   Object* args __gc[]
);
[JScript]
function Invoke(
   method : Delegate,
   args : Object[]
) : Object;
```

Parameters

method
A **Delegate** that contains a method to call, in the context of the thread for the control.

args
An array of type **Object** that represents the arguments to pass to the given method. This can be a null reference (**Nothing** in Visual Basic) if no arguments are needed.

Return Value

An **Object** that represents the return value from the delegate being invoked, or a null reference (**Nothing** in Visual Basic) if the delegate has no return value.

Remarks

Unlike **BeginInvoke**, this method operates synchronously, that is, it waits until the process completes before returning. Exceptions raised during the call are propagated back to the caller.

Use this method when calling a method from a different thread to marshal the call to the proper thread.

Requirements

Platforms: Windows 98, Windows NT 4.0, Windows Millennium Edition, Windows 2000, Windows XP Home Edition, Windows XP Professional, Windows Server 2003 family

ITypeDescriptorContext Interface

Provides information about the context information of a component, for example, the container that it is in and its **PropertyDescriptor**. The primary use of this interface is in type conversion.

System.IServiceProvider
System.ComponentModel.ITypeDescriptorContext

```
[Visual Basic]
<ComVisible(True)>
Public Interface ITypeDescriptorContext
   Inherits IServiceProvider
[C#]
[ComVisible(true)]
public interface ITypeDescriptorContext : IServiceProvider
[C++]
[ComVisible(true)]
public __gc __interface ITypeDescriptorContext : public
   IServiceProvider
[JScript]
public
   ComVisible(true)
interface ITypeDescriptorContext implements IServiceProvider
```

Remarks

This interface is typically used at design time to provide information about a design-time container.

> **Note** Do not rely on the presence of this interface when you design a type converter. If a particular interface, property, or service is necessary but not available, the type converter should return a null reference (**Nothing** in Visual Basic) rather than throw an exception. This interface's properties can return a null reference (**Nothing**) at any time, and you should plan for this.

The **Instance** property returns the instance of the object invoking this interface. For example, if a type converter is given an instance of a **Color** to convert, and you need to know what the color is used for before you perform the operation, **Instance** returns the actual instance of the control using the color. Then you can query the control for further information about its services and its **Container**.

Requirements

Namespace: System.ComponentModel

Platforms: Windows 98, Windows NT 4.0, Windows Millennium Edition, Windows 2000, Windows XP Home Edition, Windows XP Professional, Windows Server 2003 family

Assembly: System (in System.dll)

ITypeDescriptorContext.Container Property

Gets the container representing this **TypeDescriptor** request.

```
[Visual Basic]
ReadOnly Property Container As IContainer
[C#]
IContainer Container {get;}
[C++]
__property IContainer* get_Container();
[JScript]
function get Container() : IContainer;
```

Property Value

An **IContainer** with the set of objects for this **TypeDescriptor**. It returns a null reference (**Nothing** in Visual Basic) if there is no container, or if the **TypeDescriptor** does not use outside objects.

Requirements

Platforms: Windows 98, Windows NT 4.0, Windows Millennium Edition, Windows 2000, Windows XP Home Edition, Windows XP Professional, Windows Server 2003 family

ITypeDescriptorContext.Instance Property

Gets the instance of the object that is connected with this **TypeDescriptor** request.

```
[Visual Basic]
ReadOnly Property Instance As Object
[C#]
object Instance {get;}
[C++]
__property Object* get_Instance();
[JScript]
function get Instance() : Object;
```

Property Value

The instance that invokes the method on the **TypeDescriptor** object. This returns a null reference (**Nothing** in Visual Basic) if there is no instance responsible for the call.

Requirements

Platforms: Windows 98, Windows NT 4.0, Windows Millennium Edition, Windows 2000, Windows XP Home Edition, Windows XP Professional, Windows Server 2003 family

ITypeDescriptorContext.PropertyDescriptor Property

Gets the **PropertyDescriptor** that describes the given context item.

```
[Visual Basic]
ReadOnly Property PropertyDescriptor As PropertyDescriptor
[C#]
PropertyDescriptor PropertyDescriptor {get;}
[C++]
__property PropertyDescriptor* get_PropertyDescriptor();
[JScript]
function get PropertyDescriptor() : PropertyDescriptor;
```

Property Value

The **PropertyDescriptor** that describes the given context item. This returns a null reference (**Nothing** in Visual Basic) if there is no **PropertyDescriptor** responsible for the call.

Requirements

Platforms: Windows 98, Windows NT 4.0, Windows Millennium Edition, Windows 2000, Windows XP Home Edition, Windows XP Professional, Windows Server 2003 family

ITypeDescriptorContext.OnComponentChanged Method

Raises the **ComponentChanged** event.

[Visual Basic]
```
Sub OnComponentChanged()
```
[C#]
```
void OnComponentChanged();
```
[C++]
```
void OnComponentChanged();
```
[JScript]
```
function OnComponentChanged();
```

Remarks

Use this method to send notification that an instance of an object has changed.

Requirements

Platforms: Windows 98, Windows NT 4.0, Windows Millennium Edition, Windows 2000, Windows XP Home Edition, Windows XP Professional, Windows Server 2003 family

ITypeDescriptorContext.OnComponentChanging Method

Returns a value indicating whether this object can be changed.

[Visual Basic]
```
Function OnComponentChanging() As Boolean
```
[C#]
```
bool OnComponentChanging();
```
[C++]
```
bool OnComponentChanging();
```
[JScript]
```
function OnComponentChanging() : Boolean;
```

Return Value

true if this object can be changed; otherwise, **false**.

Remarks

Use this method before changing an instance of an object to see whether it can be changed. When **false** is returned, do not change the object.

Requirements

Platforms: Windows 98, Windows NT 4.0, Windows Millennium Edition, Windows 2000, Windows XP Home Edition, Windows XP Professional, Windows Server 2003 family

ITypedList Interface

Provides functionality to discover the schema for a bindable list, where the properties available for binding differ from the public properties of the object to bind to. For instance, using a **DataView** object that represents a customer table, you want to bind to the properties on the customer object that the **DataView** represents, not the properties of the **DataView**.

```
[Visual Basic]
Public Interface ITypedList
[C#]
public interface ITypedList
[C++]
public __gc __interface ITypedList
[JScript]
public interface ITypedList
```

Classes that Implement ITypedList

Class	Description
DataView	Represents a databindable, customized view of a **DataTable** for sorting, filtering, searching, editing, and navigation.
DataViewManager	Contains a default **DataViewSettingCollection** for each **DataTable** in a **DataSet**.
PagedDataSource	Encapsulates the properties of the **DataGrid** control that allow it to perform paging. This class cannot be inherited.

Remarks

This interface is not required for design-time support of a bindable list.

Binding to data can occur either at run time or in a designer, but there are rules for each. At run time, you can bind to data in any of the following:

- **Array**
- Implementer of **IList**, provided the implementer has a strongly typed **Item** property (that is, the **Type** is anything but **Object**). You can accomplish this by making the default implementation of **Item** private. If you want to create an **IList** that follows the rules of a strongly typed collection, you should derive from **CollectionBase**.
- Implementer of **ITypedList**.

In a designer, you can initialize binding to **Component** objects by following the same rules.

For more information on binding to a data source, see the **System.Windows.Forms.Binding** class.

Requirements

Namespace: System.ComponentModel

Platforms: Windows 98, Windows NT 4.0, Windows Millennium Edition, Windows 2000, Windows XP Home Edition, Windows XP Professional, Windows Server 2003 family, .NET Compact Framework - Windows CE .NET

Assembly: System (in System.dll)

ITypedList.GetItemProperties Method

Returns the **PropertyDescriptorCollection** that represents the properties on each item used to bind data.

```
[Visual Basic]
Function GetItemProperties( _
   ByVal listAccessors() As PropertyDescriptor _
) As PropertyDescriptorCollection
[C#]
PropertyDescriptorCollection GetItemProperties(
   PropertyDescriptor[] listAccessors
);
[C++]
PropertyDescriptorCollection* GetItemProperties(
   PropertyDescriptor* listAccessors[]
);
[JScript]
function GetItemProperties(
   listAccessors : PropertyDescriptor[]
) : PropertyDescriptorCollection;
```

Parameters

listAccessors

An array of **PropertyDescriptor** objects to find in the collection as bindable. This can be a null reference (**Nothing** in Visual Basic).

Return Value

The **PropertyDescriptorCollection** that represents the properties on each item used to bind data.

Remarks

If the *listAccessors* parameter is not a null reference (**Nothing** in Visual Basic), it typically contains a property descriptor that identifies a list of containers to retrieve for the object that implements **ITypedList**. For example, a **DataSet** containing two tables, `myCustomers` and `myOrders`, with a relationship between them called `myCustOrders`. If you create a **DataView** object to view `myCustomers`, then calling the **GetItemProperties** method with a null reference (**Nothing**) returns the property descriptors for the columns in `myCustomers`. As a result, one of the returned property descriptors is a property descriptor for `myCustOrders`, just as calling the **GetItemProperties** method with a list accessor array containing the property descriptors for `myCustOrders` will return the property descriptors for `myOrders`.

Requirements

Platforms: Windows 98, Windows NT 4.0, Windows Millennium Edition, Windows 2000, Windows XP Home Edition, Windows XP Professional, Windows Server 2003 family, .NET Compact Framework - Windows CE .NET

ITypedList.GetListName Method

Returns the name of the list.

[Visual Basic]
```
Function GetListName( _
   ByVal listAccessors() As PropertyDescriptor _
) As String
```
[C#]
```
string GetListName(
   PropertyDescriptor[] listAccessors
);
```
[C++]
```
String* GetListName(
   PropertyDescriptor* listAccessors[]
);
```
[JScript]
```
function GetListName(
   listAccessors : PropertyDescriptor[]
) : String;
```

Parameters

listAccessors

An array of **PropertyDescriptor** objects, the list name for which is returned. This can be a null reference (**Nothing** in Visual Basic).

Return Value

The name of the list.

Requirements

Platforms: Windows 98, Windows NT 4.0, Windows Millennium Edition, Windows 2000, Windows XP Home Edition, Windows XP Professional, Windows Server 2003 family, .NET Compact Framework - Windows CE .NET

License Class

Provides the abstract (**MustInherit** in Visual Basic) base class for all licenses. A license is granted to a specific instance of a component.

System.Object
  System.ComponentModel.License

[Visual Basic]
```
MustInherit Public Class License
   Implements IDisposable
```
[C#]
```
public abstract class License : IDisposable
```
[C++]
```
public __gc __abstract class License : public IDisposable
```
[JScript]
```
public abstract class License implements IDisposable
```

Thread Safety

Any public static (**Shared** in Visual Basic) members of this type are safe for multithreaded operations. Any instance members are not guaranteed to be thread safe.

Remarks

All components must call **Dispose** for the licenses they grant when the component is disposed or finalized.

Notes to Inheritors: When you inherit from **License**, you must override the following members: **LicenseKey** and **Dispose**.

Requirements

Namespace: System.ComponentModel

Platforms: Windows 98, Windows NT 4.0, Windows Millennium Edition, Windows 2000, Windows XP Home Edition, Windows XP Professional, Windows Server 2003 family

Assembly: System (in System.dll)

License Constructor

Initializes a new instance of the **License** class.

[Visual Basic]
```
Protected Sub New()
```
[C#]
```
protected License();
```
[C++]
```
protected: License();
```
[JScript]
```
protected function License();
```

Remarks

This constructor is called by derived class constructors to initialize state in this type.

Requirements

Platforms: Windows 98, Windows NT 4.0, Windows Millennium Edition, Windows 2000, Windows XP Home Edition, Windows XP Professional, Windows Server 2003 family

License.LicenseKey Property

When overridden in a derived class, gets the license key granted to this component.

[Visual Basic]
```
Public MustOverride ReadOnly Property LicenseKey As String
```
[C#]
```
public abstract string LicenseKey {get;}
```
[C++]
```
public: __property virtual String* get_LicenseKey() = 0;
```
[JScript]
```
public abstract function get LicenseKey() : String;
```

Property Value

A license key granted to this component.

Remarks

A **LicenseProvider** can use any Unicode character string as a license key. The **LicenseKey** should be treated as an opaque cookie, that is, a cookie with a deliberately hidden internal structure.

Requirements

Platforms: Windows 98, Windows NT 4.0, Windows Millennium Edition, Windows 2000, Windows XP Home Edition, Windows XP Professional, Windows Server 2003 family

License.Dispose Method

When overridden in a derived class, disposes of the resources used by the license.

[Visual Basic]
```
Public MustOverride Sub Dispose() Implements IDisposable.Dispose
```
[C#]
```
public abstract void Dispose();
```
[C++]
```
public: virtual void Dispose() = 0;
```
[JScript]
```
public abstract function Dispose();
```

Implements

IDisposable.Dispose

Remarks

All components must call **Dispose** for the licenses that they grant when the component is disposed of or finalized.

A **LicenseProvider** can use the licenses it grants to track its usage.

Call **Dispose** when you are finished using the **License**. The **Dispose** method leaves the **License** in an unusable state. After calling **Dispose**, you must release all references to the **License** so the memory it was occupying can be reclaimed by garbage collection.

> **Note** Always call **Dispose** before you release your last reference to the **License**. Otherwise, the resources the **License** is using will not be freed until garbage collection calls the **License** object's destructor.

Requirements

Platforms: Windows 98, Windows NT 4.0, Windows Millennium Edition, Windows 2000, Windows XP Home Edition, Windows XP Professional, Windows Server 2003 family

LicenseContext Class

Specifies when you can use a licensed object and provides a way of obtaining additional services needed to support licenses running within its domain.

System.Object
  System.ComponentModel.LicenseContext
    System.ComponentModel.Design.DesigntimeLicenseContext

```
[Visual Basic]
Public Class LicenseContext
   Implements IServiceProvider
[C#]
public class LicenseContext : IServiceProvider
[C++]
public __gc class LicenseContext : public IServiceProvider
[JScript]
public class LicenseContext implements IServiceProvider
```

Thread Safety

Any public static (**Shared** in Visual Basic) members of this type are safe for multithreaded operations. Any instance members are not guaranteed to be thread safe.

Remarks

This class provides the default **LicenseContext**. It implements only run-time support and does not support saved license keys.

Notes to Inheritors: If you want to implement design-time license support, you must inherit from this class, and override the following members: **UsageMode**, **GetSavedLicenseKey**, **GetService**, and **SetSavedLicenseKey**. If you want to implement saved license keys, override the **GetSavedLicenseKey** and **SetSavedLicenseKey** methods.

Requirements

Namespace: System.ComponentModel

Platforms: Windows 98, Windows NT 4.0, Windows Millennium Edition, Windows 2000, Windows XP Home Edition, Windows XP Professional, Windows Server 2003 family

Assembly: System (in System.dll)

LicenseContext Constructor

Initializes a new instance of the **LicenseContext** class.

```
[Visual Basic]
Public Sub New()
[C#]
public LicenseContext();
[C++]
public: LicenseContext();
[JScript]
public function LicenseContext();
```

Remarks

The default constructor initializes any fields to their default values.

Requirements

Platforms: Windows 98, Windows NT 4.0, Windows Millennium Edition, Windows 2000, Windows XP Home Edition, Windows XP Professional, Windows Server 2003 family

LicenseContext.UsageMode Property

When overridden in a derived class, gets a value that specifies when you can use a license.

```
[Visual Basic]
Public Overridable ReadOnly Property UsageMode As LicenseUsageMode
[C#]
public virtual LicenseUsageMode UsageMode {get;}
[C++]
public: __property virtual LicenseUsageMode get_UsageMode();
[JScript]
public function get UsageMode() : LicenseUsageMode;
```

Property Value

One of the **LicenseUsageMode** values that specifies when you can use a license. The default is **LicenseUsageMode.Runtime**.

Remarks

Notes to Inheritors: To implement design-time support, override this property in a class that inherits.

Requirements

Platforms: Windows 98, Windows NT 4.0, Windows Millennium Edition, Windows 2000, Windows XP Home Edition, Windows XP Professional, Windows Server 2003 family

LicenseContext.GetSavedLicenseKey Method

When overridden in a derived class, returns a saved license key for the specified type, from the specified resource assembly.

```
[Visual Basic]
Public Overridable Function GetSavedLicenseKey( _
   ByVal type As Type, _
   ByVal resourceAssembly As Assembly _
) As String
[C#]
public virtual string GetSavedLicenseKey(
   Type type,
   Assembly resourceAssembly
);
[C++]
public: virtual String* GetSavedLicenseKey(
   Type* type,
   Assembly* resourceAssembly
);
[JScript]
public function GetSavedLicenseKey(
   type : Type,
   resourceAssembly : Assembly
) : String;
```

Parameters

type
  A **Type** that represents the type of component.

resourceAssembly
  An **Assembly** with the license key.

Return Value

The **LicenseKey** for the specified type. This method returns a null reference (**Nothing** in Visual Basic) unless you override it.

Remarks

Notes to Inheritors: Override this method and the **SetSavedLicenseKey** method to implement a saved license key. If the *resourceAssembly* parameter is a null reference (**Nothing** in Visual Basic), then you can retrieve the resource from the primary executing **Assembly**.

Requirements

Platforms: Windows 98, Windows NT 4.0, Windows Millennium Edition, Windows 2000, Windows XP Home Edition, Windows XP Professional, Windows Server 2003 family

LicenseContext.GetService Method

Gets the requested service, if it is available.

```
[Visual Basic]
Public Overridable Function GetService( _
   ByVal type As Type _
) As Object Implements IServiceProvider.GetService
[C#]
public virtual object GetService(
   Type type
);
[C++]
public: virtual Object* GetService(
   Type* type
);
[JScript]
public function GetService(
   type : Type
) : Object;
```

Parameters

type
: The type of service to retrieve.

Return Value

An instance of the service, or a null reference (**Nothing** in Visual Basic) if the service cannot be found.

Implements

IServiceProvider.GetService

Requirements

Platforms: Windows 98, Windows NT 4.0, Windows Millennium Edition, Windows 2000, Windows XP Home Edition, Windows XP Professional, Windows Server 2003 family

LicenseContext.SetSavedLicenseKey Method

When overridden in a derived class, sets a license key for the specified type.

```
[Visual Basic]
Public Overridable Sub SetSavedLicenseKey( _
   ByVal type As Type, _
   ByVal key As String _
)
[C#]
public virtual void SetSavedLicenseKey(
   Type type,
   string key
);
[C++]
public: virtual void SetSavedLicenseKey(
   Type* type,
   String* key
);
[JScript]
public function SetSavedLicenseKey(
   type : Type,
   key : String
);
```

Parameters

type
: A **Type** that represents the component associated with the license key.

key
: The **LicenseKey** to save for the type of component.

Remarks

Typically, call this method when you set **LicenseUsageMode** at design time. You must override the **UsageMode** property to implement design-time license support.

Notes to Inheritors: This method does not provide support for a saved license key. Override this method and the **GetSavedLicenseKey** method to implement a key.

Requirements

Platforms: Windows 98, Windows NT 4.0, Windows Millennium Edition, Windows 2000, Windows XP Home Edition, Windows XP Professional, Windows Server 2003 family

LicenseException Class

Represents the exception thrown when a component cannot be granted a license.

System.Object
  System.Exception
    System.SystemException
      System.ComponentModel.LicenseException

[Visual Basic]
```
Public Class LicenseException
   Inherits SystemException
```
[C#]
```
public class LicenseException : SystemException
```
[C++]
```
public __gc class LicenseException : public SystemException
```
[JScript]
```
public class LicenseException extends SystemException
```

Thread Safety

Any public static (**Shared** in Visual Basic) members of this type are safe for multithreaded operations. Any instance members are not guaranteed to be thread safe.

Remarks

The **LicenseManager.Validate** method throws **LicenseException** when a component cannot obtain a valid license. This occurs when a component is either not licensed, or is licensed, but cannot be granted a valid license.

For more information on licensing, see **Licensing Components and Controls**.

Example

[Visual Basic, C#] The following example shows how to catch a **LicenseException** and interpret its content. In the sample, the application calls the **Validate** method for a **System.Windows.Forms.Form**, which is not licensed. Upon catching the exception, the sample fetches the respective error message, the type of component that was not granted a license, the stack trace, and the origin of the exception.

[Visual Basic, C#] This example assumes that you have specified the **LicenseProvider** by marking the **System.Windows.Forms.Form** with a **LicenseProviderAttribute** attribute. For more information on how to do this, see the **LicenseManager** class.

[Visual Basic]
```
Try
    Dim licTest As License
    licTest = LicenseManager.Validate(GetType(Form1), Me)
Catch licE As LicenseException
    Console.WriteLine(licE.Message)
    Console.WriteLine(licE.LicensedType)
    Console.WriteLine(licE.StackTrace)
    Console.WriteLine(licE.Source)
End Try
```

[C#]
```
try {
    License licTest = null;
    licTest = LicenseManager.Validate(typeof(Form1), this);
}

catch(LicenseException licE) {
    Console.WriteLine(licE.Message);
    Console.WriteLine(licE.LicensedType);
    Console.WriteLine(licE.StackTrace);
    Console.WriteLine(licE.Source);
}
```

Requirements

Namespace: System.ComponentModel

Platforms: Windows 98, Windows NT 4.0, Windows Millennium Edition, Windows 2000, Windows XP Home Edition, Windows XP Professional, Windows Server 2003 family

Assembly: System (in System.dll)

LicenseException Constructor

Initializes a new instance of the **LicenseException** class.

Overload List

Initializes a new instance of the **LicenseException** class for the type of component that was denied a license.

[Visual Basic] **Public Sub New(Type)**

[C#] **public LicenseException(Type);**

[C++] **public: LicenseException(Type*);**

[JScript] **public function LicenseException(Type);**

Initializes a new instance of the **LicenseException** class for the type and the instance of the component that was denied a license.

[Visual Basic] **Public Sub New(Type, Object)**

[C#] **public LicenseException(Type, object);**

[C++] **public: LicenseException(Type*, Object*);**

[JScript] **public function LicenseException(Type, Object);**

Initializes a new instance of the **LicenseException** class for the type and the instance of the component that was denied a license, along with a message to display.

[Visual Basic] **Public Sub New(Type, Object, String)**

[C#] **public LicenseException(Type, object, string);**

[C++] **public: LicenseException(Type*, Object*, String*);**

[JScript] **public function LicenseException(Type, Object, String);**

Initializes a new instance of the **LicenseException** class for the type and the instance of the component that was denied a license, along with a message to display and the original exception thrown.

[Visual Basic] **Public Sub New(Type, Object, String, Exception)**

[C#] **public LicenseException(Type, object, string, Exception);**

[C++] **public: LicenseException(Type*, Object*, String*, Exception*);**

[JScript] **public function LicenseException(Type, Object, String, Exception);**

LicenseException Constructor (Type)

Initializes a new instance of the **LicenseException** class for the type of component that was denied a license.

[Visual Basic]
```
Public Sub New( _
   ByVal type As Type _
)
```
[C#]
```
public LicenseException(
   Type type
);
```

```
[C++]
public: LicenseException(
   Type* type
);
[JScript]
public function LicenseException(
   type : Type
);
```

Parameters

type
A **Type** that represents the type of component that was not granted a license.

Requirements

Platforms: Windows 98, Windows NT 4.0, Windows Millennium Edition, Windows 2000, Windows XP Home Edition, Windows XP Professional, Windows Server 2003 family

LicenseException Constructor (Type, Object)

Initializes a new instance of the **LicenseException** class for the type and the instance of the component that was denied a license.

```
[Visual Basic]
Public Sub New( _
   ByVal type As Type, _
   ByVal instance As Object _
)
[C#]
public LicenseException(
   Type type,
   object instance
);
[C++]
public: LicenseException(
   Type* type,
   Object* instance
);
[JScript]
public function LicenseException(
   type : Type,
   instance : Object
);
```

Parameters

type
A **Type** that represents the type of component that was not granted a license.

instance
The instance of the component that was not granted a license.

Requirements

Platforms: Windows 98, Windows NT 4.0, Windows Millennium Edition, Windows 2000, Windows XP Home Edition, Windows XP Professional, Windows Server 2003 family

LicenseException Constructor (Type, Object, String)

Initializes a new instance of the **LicenseException** class for the type and the instance of the component that was denied a license, along with a message to display.

```
[Visual Basic]
Public Sub New( _
   ByVal type As Type, _
   ByVal instance As Object, _
   ByVal message As String _
)
[C#]
public LicenseException(
   Type type,
   object instance,
   string message
);
[C++]
public: LicenseException(
   Type* type,
   Object* instance,
   String* message
);
[JScript]
public function LicenseException(
   type : Type,
   instance : Object,
   message : String
);
```

Parameters

type
A **Type** that represents the type of component that was not granted a license.

instance
The instance of the component that was not granted a license.

message
The exception message to display.

Requirements

Platforms: Windows 98, Windows NT 4.0, Windows Millennium Edition, Windows 2000, Windows XP Home Edition, Windows XP Professional, Windows Server 2003 family

LicenseException Constructor (Type, Object, String, Exception)

Initializes a new instance of the **LicenseException** class for the type and the instance of the component that was denied a license, along with a message to display and the original exception thrown.

```
[Visual Basic]
Public Sub New( _
   ByVal type As Type, _
   ByVal instance As Object, _
   ByVal message As String, _
   ByVal innerException As Exception _
)
```

[C#]
```
public LicenseException(
   Type type,
   object instance,
   string message,
   Exception innerException
);
```
[C++]
```
public: LicenseException(
   Type* type,
   Object* instance,
   String* message,
   Exception* innerException
);
```
[JScript]
```
public function LicenseException(
   type : Type,
   instance : Object,
   message : String,
   innerException : Exception
);
```

Parameters

type

A **Type** that represents the type of component that was not granted a license.

instance

The instance of the component that was not granted a license.

message

The exception message to display.

innerException

An **Exception** that represents the original exception.

Requirements

Platforms: Windows 98, Windows NT 4.0, Windows Millennium Edition, Windows 2000, Windows XP Home Edition, Windows XP Professional, Windows Server 2003 family

LicenseException.LicensedType Property

Gets the type of the component that was not granted a license.

[Visual Basic]
```
Public ReadOnly Property LicensedType As Type
```
[C#]
```
public Type LicensedType {get;}
```
[C++]
```
public: __property Type* get_LicensedType();
```
[JScript]
```
public function get LicensedType() : Type;
```

Property Value

A **Type** that represents the type of component that was not granted a license.

Requirements

Platforms: Windows 98, Windows NT 4.0, Windows Millennium Edition, Windows 2000, Windows XP Home Edition, Windows XP Professional, Windows Server 2003 family

LicenseManager Class

Provides properties and methods to add a license to a component and to manage a **LicenseProvider**. This class cannot be inherited.

System.Object
  System.ComponentModel.LicenseManager

```
[Visual Basic]
NotInheritable Public Class LicenseManager
[C#]
public sealed class LicenseManager
[C++]
public __gc __sealed class LicenseManager
[JScript]
public class LicenseManager
```

Thread Safety

Any public static (**Shared** in Visual Basic) members of this type are safe for multithreaded operations. Any instance members are not guaranteed to be thread safe.

Remarks

LicenseManager provides the following static (**Shared** in Visual Basic) properties: **CurrentContext** and **UsageMode**. The class also provides the following static (**Shared** in Visual Basic) methods: **CreateWithContext**, **IsValid**, **Validate**.

When you create a component that you want to license, you must:

1. Specify the **LicenseProvider** by marking the component with a **LicenseProviderAttribute**.
2. Call **Validate** or **IsValid** in the constructor of the component. **Validate** throws a **LicenseException** when it tries to create an instance without a valid license. **IsValid** does not throw an exception.
3. **Dispose** any license that is granted when the component is disposed or finalized.

Requirements

Namespace: System.ComponentModel

Platforms: Windows 98, Windows NT 4.0, Windows Millennium Edition, Windows 2000, Windows XP Home Edition, Windows XP Professional, Windows Server 2003 family

Assembly: System (in System.dll)

LicenseManager.CurrentContext Property

Gets or sets the current **LicenseContext**, which specifies when you can use the licensed object.

```
[Visual Basic]
Public Shared Property CurrentContext As LicenseContext
[C#]
public static LicenseContext CurrentContext {get; set;}
[C++]
public: __property static LicenseContext* get_CurrentContext();
public: __property static void set_CurrentContext(LicenseContext*);
[JScript]
public static function get CurrentContext() : LicenseContext;
public static function set CurrentContext(LicenseContext);
```

Property Value

A **LicenseContext** that specifies when you can use the licensed object.

Remarks

When the user requests a valid **License**, the user must give the context in which the **License** is valid to the **LicenseProvider.GetLicense** method. The **LicenseContext** returned by this property should be passed to all **LicenseProvider** classes.

Requirements

Platforms: Windows 98, Windows NT 4.0, Windows Millennium Edition, Windows 2000, Windows XP Home Edition, Windows XP Professional, Windows Server 2003 family

LicenseManager.UsageMode Property

Gets the **LicenseUsageMode** which specifies when you can use the licensed object for the **CurrentContext**.

```
[Visual Basic]
Public Shared ReadOnly Property UsageMode As LicenseUsageMode
[C#]
public static LicenseUsageMode UsageMode {get;}
[C++]
public: __property static LicenseUsageMode get_UsageMode();
[JScript]
public static function get UsageMode() : LicenseUsageMode;
```

Property Value

One of the **LicenseUsageMode** values, as specified in the **CurrentContext**.

Remarks

If this property cannot find a **CurrentContext** value, it returns **LicenseUsageMode.Runtime**.

Requirements

Platforms: Windows 98, Windows NT 4.0, Windows Millennium Edition, Windows 2000, Windows XP Home Edition, Windows XP Professional, Windows Server 2003 family

LicenseManager.CreateWithContext Method

Creates an instance of an object type with a license context.

Overload List

Creates an instance of the specified type, given a context in which you can use the licensed instance.

[Visual Basic] **Overloads Public Shared Function CreateWithContext(Type, LicenseContext) As Object**

[C#] **public static object CreateWithContext(Type, LicenseContext);**

[C++] **public: static Object* CreateWithContext(Type*, LicenseContext*);**

[JScript] **public static function CreateWithContext(Type, LicenseContext) : Object;**

Creates an instance of the specified type with the specified arguments, given a context in which you can use the licensed instance.

[Visual Basic] **Overloads Public Shared Function CreateWithContext(Type, LicenseContext, Object()) As Object**

[C#] **public static object CreateWithContext(Type, LicenseContext, object[]);**

[C++] **public: static Object* CreateWithContext(Type*, LicenseContext*, Object[]);**

[JScript] **public static function CreateWithContext(Type, LicenseContext, Object[]) : Object;**

LicenseManager.CreateWithContext Method (Type, LicenseContext)

Creates an instance of the specified type, given a context in which you can use the licensed instance.

```
[Visual Basic]
Overloads Public Shared Function CreateWithContext( _
   ByVal type As Type, _
   ByVal creationContext As LicenseContext _
) As Object
[C#]
public static object CreateWithContext(
   Type type,
   LicenseContext creationContext
);
[C++]
public: static Object* CreateWithContext(
   Type* type,
   LicenseContext* creationContext
);
[JScript]
public static function CreateWithContext(
   type : Type,
   creationContext : LicenseContext
) : Object;
```

Parameters

type

A **Type** that represents the type to create.

creationContext

A **LicenseContext** that specifies when you can use the licensed instance.

Return Value

An instance of the specified type.

Remarks

The **LicenseContext** you specify as the *creationContext* parameter is used as the **CurrentContext** for the life of this **License**. This method blocks all other threads in the **AppDomain** from modifying the **CurrentContext**, allowing **CreateWithContext** to behave as an atomic operation.

Requirements

Platforms: Windows 98, Windows NT 4.0, Windows Millennium Edition, Windows 2000, Windows XP Home Edition, Windows XP Professional, Windows Server 2003 family

LicenseManager.CreateWithContext Method (Type, LicenseContext, Object[])

Creates an instance of the specified type with the specified arguments, given a context in which you can use the licensed instance.

```
[Visual Basic]
Overloads Public Shared Function CreateWithContext( _
   ByVal type As Type, _
   ByVal creationContext As LicenseContext, _
   ByVal args() As Object _
) As Object
[C#]
public static object CreateWithContext(
   Type type,
   LicenseContext creationContext,
   object[] args
);
[C++]
public: static Object* CreateWithContext(
   Type* type,
   LicenseContext* creationContext,
   Object* args __gc[]
);
[JScript]
public static function CreateWithContext(
   type : Type,
   creationContext : LicenseContext,
   args : Object[]
) : Object;
```

Parameters

type

A **Type** that represents the type to create.

creationContext

A **LicenseContext** that specifies when you can use the licensed instance.

args

An array of type **Object** that represents the arguments for the type.

Return Value

An instance of the specified type with the given array of arguments.

Remarks

The **LicenseContext** you specify as the *creationContext* parameter is used as the **CurrentContext** for the life of this **License**. This method blocks all other threads in the **AppDomain** from modifying the **CurrentContext**, allowing **CreateWithContext** to behave as an atomic operation.

Requirements

Platforms: Windows 98, Windows NT 4.0, Windows Millennium Edition, Windows 2000, Windows XP Home Edition, Windows XP Professional, Windows Server 2003 family

LicenseManager.IsLicensed Method

Returns whether the given type has a valid license.

```
[Visual Basic]
Public Shared Function IsLicensed( _
   ByVal type As Type _
) As Boolean
```

```
[C#]
public static bool IsLicensed(
   Type type
);
[C++]
public: static bool IsLicensed(
   Type* type
);
[JScript]
public static function IsLicensed(
   type : Type
) : Boolean;
```

Parameters

type

The **Type** to find a valid license for.

Return Value

true if the given type is licensed; otherwise, **false**.

Requirements

Platforms: Windows 98, Windows NT 4.0, Windows Millennium Edition, Windows 2000, Windows XP Home Edition, Windows XP Professional, Windows Server 2003 family

LicenseManager.IsValid Method

Determines whether a valid license can be granted.

Overload List

Determines whether a valid license can be granted for the specified type.

[Visual Basic] **Overloads Public Shared Function IsValid(Type) As Boolean**

[C#] **public static bool IsValid(Type);**

[C++] **public: static bool IsValid(Type*);**

[JScript] **public static function IsValid(Type) : Boolean;**

Determines whether a valid license can be granted for the specified instance of the type. This method creates a valid **License**.

[Visual Basic] **Overloads Public Shared Function IsValid(Type, Object, ByRef License) As Boolean**

[C#] **public static bool IsValid(Type, object, License);**

[C++] **public: static bool IsValid(Type*, Object*, License);**

[JScript] **public static function IsValid(Type, Object, License) : Boolean;**

LicenseManager.IsValid Method (Type)

Determines whether a valid license can be granted for the specified type.

```
[Visual Basic]
Overloads Public Shared Function IsValid( _
   ByVal type As Type _
) As Boolean
[C#]
public static bool IsValid(
   Type type
);
[C++]
public: static bool IsValid(
   Type* type
);
[JScript]
public static function IsValid(
   type : Type
) : Boolean;
```

Parameters

type

A **Type** that represents the type of object that requests the **License**.

Return Value

true if a valid license can be granted; otherwise, **false**.

Remarks

IsValid returns **true** when the type is either not licensed, or is licensed and the license is valid.

This method does not throw a **LicenseException** when it cannot grant a valid **License**. The **Validate** method throws exceptions.

Requirements

Platforms: Windows 98, Windows NT 4.0, Windows Millennium Edition, Windows 2000, Windows XP Home Edition, Windows XP Professional, Windows Server 2003 family

LicenseManager.IsValid Method (Type, Object, License)

Determines whether a valid license can be granted for the specified instance of the type. This method creates a valid **License**.

```
[Visual Basic]
Overloads Public Shared Function IsValid( _
   ByVal type As Type, _
   ByVal instance As Object, _
   <Out()> ByRef license As License _
) As Boolean
[C#]
public static bool IsValid(
   Type type,
   object instance,
   out License license
);
[C++]
public: static bool IsValid(
   Type* type,
   Object* instance,
   [
   Out
] License** license
);
[JScript]
public static function IsValid(
   type : Type,
   instance : Object,
   license : License
) : Boolean;
```

Parameters

type

A **Type** that represents the type of object that requests the license.

instance

An object of the specified type or a type derived from the specified type.

license

When this method returns, it contains a **License** that is a valid license or a null reference (**Nothing** in Visual Basic), if a valid license cannot be granted.

Return Value

true if a valid **License** can be granted; otherwise, **false**.

Remarks

IsValid returns **true** when the *type* parameter is not licensed, or when it is licensed and the *license* parameter is valid.

This method does not throw a **LicenseException** when it cannot grant a valid **License**. The **Validate** method throws exceptions.

If the *license* parameter is not a null reference (**Nothing** in Visual Basic) after this call, the object asking for a **License** must dispose of the license by calling the **Dispose** method when the object is disposed of or finalized.

Requirements

Platforms: Windows 98, Windows NT 4.0, Windows Millennium Edition, Windows 2000, Windows XP Home Edition, Windows XP Professional, Windows Server 2003 family

LicenseManager.LockContext Method

Prevents changes being made to the current **LicenseContext** of the given object.

```
[Visual Basic]
Public Shared Sub LockContext( _
   ByVal contextUser As Object _
)
[C#]
public static void LockContext(
   object contextUser
);
[C++]
public: static void LockContext(
   Object* contextUser
);
[JScript]
public static function LockContext(
   contextUser : Object
);
```

Parameters

contextUser

The object whose current context you want to lock.

Remarks

Use the **LicenseContext** to get the **License** of an object. This method locks the **LicenseContext**, preventing the **License** from being retrieved.

Requirements

Platforms: Windows 98, Windows NT 4.0, Windows Millennium Edition, Windows 2000, Windows XP Home Edition, Windows XP Professional, Windows Server 2003 family

LicenseManager.UnlockContext Method

Allows changes to be made to the current **LicenseContext** of the given object.

```
[Visual Basic]
Public Shared Sub UnlockContext( _
   ByVal contextUser As Object _
)
[C#]
public static void UnlockContext(
   object contextUser
);
[C++]
public: static void UnlockContext(
   Object* contextUser
);
[JScript]
public static function UnlockContext(
   contextUser : Object
);
```

Parameters

contextUser

The object whose current context you want to unlock.

Remarks

Use the **LicenseContext** to get the **License** of an object. This method unlocks the **LicenseContext**, allowing the **License** to be retrieved.

Requirements

Platforms: Windows 98, Windows NT 4.0, Windows Millennium Edition, Windows 2000, Windows XP Home Edition, Windows XP Professional, Windows Server 2003 family

LicenseManager.Validate Method

Determines whether a license can be granted.

Overload List

Determines whether a license can be granted for the specified type.

[Visual Basic] **Overloads Public Shared Sub Validate(Type)**

[C#] **public static void Validate(Type);**

[C++] **public: static void Validate(Type*);**

[JScript] **public static function Validate(Type);**

Determines whether a license can be granted for the instance of the specified type.

[Visual Basic] **Overloads Public Shared Function Validate(Type, Object) As License**

[C#] **public static License Validate(Type, object);**

[C++] **public: static License* Validate(Type*, Object*);**

[JScript] **public static function Validate(Type, Object) : License;**

LicenseManager.Validate Method (Type)

Determines whether a license can be granted for the specified type.

[Visual Basic]
```
Overloads Public Shared Sub Validate( _
   ByVal type As Type _
)
```
[C#]
```
public static void Validate(
   Type type
);
```
[C++]
```
public: static void Validate(
   Type* type
);
```
[JScript]
```
public static function Validate(
   type : Type
);
```

Parameters

type
   A **Type** that represents the type of object that requests the license.

Exceptions

Exception Type	Condition
LicenseException	A **License** cannot be granted.

Remarks

This method throws a **LicenseException** when a valid **License** cannot be granted. **IsValid** does not throw an exception.

Requirements

Platforms: Windows 98, Windows NT 4.0, Windows Millennium Edition, Windows 2000, Windows XP Home Edition, Windows XP Professional, Windows Server 2003 family

LicenseManager.Validate Method (Type, Object)

Determines whether a license can be granted for the instance of the specified type.

[Visual Basic]
```
Overloads Public Shared Function Validate( _
   ByVal type As Type, _
   ByVal instance As Object _
) As License
```
[C#]
```
public static License Validate(
   Type type,
   object instance
);
```
[C++]
```
public: static License* Validate(
   Type* type,
   Object* instance
);
```
[JScript]
```
public static function Validate(
   type : Type,
   instance : Object
) : License;
```

Parameters

type
   A **Type** that represents the type of object that wants the license.

instance
   An **Object** of the specified type or a type derived from the specified type.

Return Value

A valid **License**.

Exceptions

Exception Type	Condition
LicenseException	The type is licensed, but a **License** could not be granted.

Remarks

This method throws a **LicenseException** when a valid **License** cannot be granted. **IsValid** does not throw an exception.

All objects asking for a **License** must dispose of the license by calling the **Dispose** method when the object is disposed of or finalized.

Requirements

Platforms: Windows 98, Windows NT 4.0, Windows Millennium Edition, Windows 2000, Windows XP Home Edition, Windows XP Professional, Windows Server 2003 family

LicenseProvider Class

Provides the abstract (**MustInherit** in Visual Basic) base class for implementing a license provider.

System.Object
  System.ComponentModel.LicenseProvider
    System.ComponentModel.LicFileLicenseProvider

[Visual Basic]
```
MustInherit Public Class LicenseProvider
```
[C#]
```
public abstract class LicenseProvider
```
[C++]
```
public __gc __abstract class LicenseProvider
```
[JScript]
```
public abstract class LicenseProvider
```

Thread Safety

Any public static (**Shared** in Visual Basic) members of this type are safe for multithreaded operations. Any instance members are not guaranteed to be thread safe.

Remarks

Notes to Inheritors: When you inherit from **LicenseProvider**, you must override the **GetLicense** method.

Requirements

Namespace: System.ComponentModel

Platforms: Windows 98, Windows NT 4.0, Windows Millennium Edition, Windows 2000, Windows XP Home Edition, Windows XP Professional, Windows Server 2003 family

Assembly: System (in System.dll)

LicenseProvider Constructor

Initializes a new instance of the **LicenseProvider** class.

[Visual Basic]
```
Protected Sub New()
```
[C#]
```
protected LicenseProvider();
```
[C++]
```
protected: LicenseProvider();
```
[JScript]
```
protected function LicenseProvider();
```

Remarks

This constructor is called by derived class constructors to initialize state in this type.

Requirements

Platforms: Windows 98, Windows NT 4.0, Windows Millennium Edition, Windows 2000, Windows XP Home Edition, Windows XP Professional, Windows Server 2003 family

LicenseProvider.GetLicense Method

When overridden in a derived class, gets a license for an instance or type of component, when given a context and whether the denial of a license throws an exception.

[Visual Basic]
```
Public MustOverride Function GetLicense( _
   ByVal context As LicenseContext, _
   ByVal type As Type, _
   ByVal instance As Object, _
   ByVal allowExceptions As Boolean _
) As License
```
[C#]
```
public abstract License GetLicense(
   LicenseContext context,
   Type type,
   object instance,
   bool allowExceptions
);
```
[C++]
```
public: virtual License* GetLicense(
   LicenseContext* context,
   Type* type,
   Object* instance,
   bool allowExceptions
) = 0;
```
[JScript]
```
public abstract function GetLicense(
   context : LicenseContext,
   type : Type,
   instance : Object,
   allowExceptions : Boolean
) : License;
```

Parameters

context
  A **LicenseContext** that specifies where you can use the licensed object.

type
  A **Type** that represents the component requesting the license.

instance
  An object that is requesting the license.

allowExceptions
  true if a **LicenseException** should be thrown when the component cannot be granted a license; otherwise, **false**.

Return Value

A valid **License**.

Remarks

Notes to Inheritors: The object asking for a **License** must **Dispose** the **License** when the object is disposed of or finalized.

Notes to Inheritors: When you inherit from **LicenseProvider**, you must override **GetLicense** to implement a validation method for the license key.

Requirements

Platforms: Windows 98, Windows NT 4.0, Windows Millennium Edition, Windows 2000, Windows XP Home Edition, Windows XP Professional, Windows Server 2003 family

LicenseProviderAttribute Class

Specifies the **LicenseProvider** to use with a class.

System.Object
  System.Attribute
    System.ComponentModel.LicenseProviderAttribute

```
[Visual Basic]
<AttributeUsage(AttributeTargets.Class)>
NotInheritable Public Class LicenseProviderAttribute
   Inherits Attribute
[C#]
[AttributeUsage(AttributeTargets.Class)]
public sealed class LicenseProviderAttribute : Attribute
[C++]
[AttributeUsage(AttributeTargets::Class)]
public __gc __sealed class LicenseProviderAttribute : public
   Attribute
[JScript]
public
   AttributeUsage(AttributeTargets.Class)
class LicenseProviderAttribute extends Attribute
```

Thread Safety

Any public static (**Shared** in Visual Basic) members of this type are safe for multithreaded operations. Any instance members are not guaranteed to be thread safe.

Remarks

When you create a component that you want to license, you must specify the **LicenseProvider** by marking the component with a **LicenseProviderAttribute**.

Use the **LicenseProvider** property to get the **Type** of the **LicenseProvider**.

Requirements

Namespace: System.ComponentModel

Platforms: Windows 98, Windows NT 4.0, Windows Millennium Edition, Windows 2000, Windows XP Home Edition, Windows XP Professional, Windows Server 2003 family

Assembly: System (in System.dll)

LicenseProviderAttribute Constructor

Initializes a new instance of the **LicenseProviderAttribute** class.

Overload List

Initializes a new instance of the **LicenseProviderAttribute** class without a license provider.

[Visual Basic] **Public Sub New()**

[C#] **public LicenseProviderAttribute();**

[C++] **public: LicenseProviderAttribute();**

[JScript] **public function LicenseProviderAttribute();**

Initializes a new instance of the **LicenseProviderAttribute** class with the specified type.

[Visual Basic] **Public Sub New(String)**

[C#] **public LicenseProviderAttribute(string);**

[C++] **public: LicenseProviderAttribute(String*);**

[JScript] **public function LicenseProviderAttribute(String);**

Initializes a new instance of the **LicenseProviderAttribute** class with the specified type of license provider.

[Visual Basic] **Public Sub New(Type)**

[C#] **public LicenseProviderAttribute(Type);**

[C++] **public: LicenseProviderAttribute(Type*);**

[JScript] **public function LicenseProviderAttribute(Type);**

LicenseProviderAttribute Constructor ()

Initializes a new instance of the **LicenseProviderAttribute** class without a license provider.

```
[Visual Basic]
Public Sub New()
[C#]
public LicenseProviderAttribute();
[C++]
public: LicenseProviderAttribute();
[JScript]
public function LicenseProviderAttribute();
```

Requirements

Platforms: Windows 98, Windows NT 4.0, Windows Millennium Edition, Windows 2000, Windows XP Home Edition, Windows XP Professional, Windows Server 2003 family

LicenseProviderAttribute Constructor (String)

Initializes a new instance of the **LicenseProviderAttribute** class with the specified type.

```
[Visual Basic]
Public Sub New( _
   ByVal typeName As String _
)
[C#]
public LicenseProviderAttribute(
   string typeName
);
[C++]
public: LicenseProviderAttribute(
   String* typeName
);
[JScript]
public function LicenseProviderAttribute(
   typeName : String
);
```

Parameters

typeName
The fully qualified name of the license provider class.

Requirements

Platforms: Windows 98, Windows NT 4.0, Windows Millennium Edition, Windows 2000, Windows XP Home Edition, Windows XP Professional, Windows Server 2003 family

LicenseProviderAttribute Constructor (Type)

Initializes a new instance of the **LicenseProviderAttribute** class with the specified type of license provider.

```
[Visual Basic]
Public Sub New( _
   ByVal type As Type _
)
[C#]
public LicenseProviderAttribute(
   Type type
);
[C++]
public: LicenseProviderAttribute(
   Type* type
);
[JScript]
public function LicenseProviderAttribute(
   type : Type
);
```

Parameters

type

A **Type** that represents the type of the license provider class.

Requirements

Platforms: Windows 98, Windows NT 4.0, Windows Millennium Edition, Windows 2000, Windows XP Home Edition, Windows XP Professional, Windows Server 2003 family

LicenseProviderAttribute.Default Field

This member supports the .NET Framework infrastructure and is not intended to be used directly from your code.

```
[Visual Basic]
Public Shared ReadOnly Default As LicenseProviderAttribute
[C#]
public static readonly LicenseProviderAttribute Default;
[C++]
public: static LicenseProviderAttribute* Default;
[JScript]
public static var Default : LicenseProviderAttribute;
```

LicenseProviderAttribute.LicenseProvider Property

Gets the license provider that must be used with the associated class.

```
[Visual Basic]
Public ReadOnly Property LicenseProvider As Type
[C#]
public Type LicenseProvider {get;}
[C++]
public: __property Type* get_LicenseProvider();
[JScript]
public function get LicenseProvider() : Type;
```

Property Value

A **Type** that represents the type of the license provider. The default value is a null reference (**Nothing** in Visual Basic).

Requirements

Platforms: Windows 98, Windows NT 4.0, Windows Millennium Edition, Windows 2000, Windows XP Home Edition, Windows XP Professional, Windows Server 2003 family

LicenseProviderAttribute.TypeId Property

This member overrides **Attribute.TypeId**.

```
[Visual Basic]
Overrides Public ReadOnly Property TypeId As Object
[C#]
public override object TypeId {get;}
[C++]
public: __property Object* get_TypeId();
[JScript]
public override function get TypeId() : Object;
```

Requirements

Platforms: Windows 98, Windows NT 4.0, Windows Millennium Edition, Windows 2000, Windows XP Home Edition, Windows XP Professional, Windows Server 2003 family

LicenseProviderAttribute.Equals Method

This member overrides **Object.Equals**.

```
[Visual Basic]
Overrides Public Function Equals( _
   ByVal value As Object _
) As Boolean
[C#]
public override bool Equals(
   object value
);
[C++]
public: bool Equals(
   Object* value
);
[JScript]
public override function Equals(
   value : Object
) : Boolean;
```

Requirements

Platforms: Windows 98, Windows NT 4.0, Windows Millennium Edition, Windows 2000, Windows XP Home Edition, Windows XP Professional, Windows Server 2003 family

LicenseProviderAttribute.GetHashCode Method

This member overrides **Attribute.GetHashCode**.

[Visual Basic]
```
Overrides Public Function GetHashCode() As Integer
```
[C#]
```
public override int GetHashCode();
```
[C++]
```
public: int GetHashCode();
```
[JScript]
```
public override function GetHashCode() : int;
```

Requirements

Platforms: Windows 98, Windows NT 4.0, Windows Millennium Edition, Windows 2000, Windows XP Home Edition, Windows XP Professional, Windows Server 2003 family

LicenseUsageMode Enumeration

Specifies when the **License** can be used.

[Visual Basic]
```
<Serializable>
Public Enum LicenseUsageMode
```
[C#]
```
[Serializable]
public enum LicenseUsageMode
```
[C++]
```
[Serializable]
__value public enum LicenseUsageMode
```
[JScript]
```
public
   Serializable
enum LicenseUsageMode
```

Remarks

The **LicenseManager** and the **LicenseContext** classes use this enumeration. It is used to set a component's **CurrentContext**. See the **LicenseManager** class for details.

Members

Member name	Description
Designtime	Used during design time by a visual designer or the compiler.
Runtime	Used during runtime.

Requirements

Namespace: System.ComponentModel

Platforms: Windows 98, Windows NT 4.0, Windows Millennium Edition, Windows 2000, Windows XP Home Edition, Windows XP Professional, Windows Server 2003 family

Assembly: System (in System.dll)

LicFileLicenseProvider Class

Provides an implementation of a **LicenseProvider**. The provider works in a similar fashion to the Microsoft .NET Framework standard licensing module.

System.Object
  System.ComponentModel.LicenseProvider
    System.ComponentModel.LicFileLicenseProvider

[Visual Basic]
```
Public Class LicFileLicenseProvider
   Inherits LicenseProvider
```
[C#]
```
public class LicFileLicenseProvider : LicenseProvider
```
[C++]
```
public __gc class LicFileLicenseProvider : public LicenseProvider
```
[JScript]
```
public class LicFileLicenseProvider extends LicenseProvider
```

Thread Safety

Any public static (**Shared** in Visual Basic) members of this type are safe for multithreaded operations. Any instance members are not guaranteed to be thread safe.

Remarks

The **LicFileLicenseProvider** offers **GetLicense** and **IsKeyValid** methods. The **IsKeyValid** method determines whether the **LicenseKey** retrieved by the **GetLicense** method is valid. When you inherit from this class, you can override the **IsKeyValid** method to provide your own validation logic.

This class exists to provide similar licensing functionality to COM licensing and uses text license files.

Requirements

Namespace: System.ComponentModel

Platforms: Windows 98, Windows NT 4.0, Windows Millennium Edition, Windows 2000, Windows XP Home Edition, Windows XP Professional, Windows Server 2003 family

Assembly: System (in System.dll)

LicFileLicenseProvider Constructor

Initializes a new instance of the **LicFileLicenseProvider** class.

[Visual Basic]
```
Public Sub New()
```
[C#]
```
public LicFileLicenseProvider();
```
[C++]
```
public: LicFileLicenseProvider();
```
[JScript]
```
public function LicFileLicenseProvider();
```

Remarks

The default constructor initializes any fields to their default values.

Requirements

Platforms: Windows 98, Windows NT 4.0, Windows Millennium Edition, Windows 2000, Windows XP Home Edition, Windows XP Professional, Windows Server 2003 family

LicFileLicenseProvider.GetKey Method

Returns a key for the specified type.

[Visual Basic]
```
Protected Overridable Function GetKey( _
   ByVal type As Type _
) As String
```
[C#]
```
protected virtual string GetKey(
   Type type
);
```
[C++]
```
protected: virtual String* GetKey(
   Type* type
);
```
[JScript]
```
protected function GetKey(
   type : Type
) : String;
```

Parameters

type
  The object type to return the key.

Return Value

A confirmation that the *type* parameter is licensed.

Requirements

Platforms: Windows 98, Windows NT 4.0, Windows Millennium Edition, Windows 2000, Windows XP Home Edition, Windows XP Professional, Windows Server 2003 family

LicFileLicenseProvider.GetLicense Method

Returns a license for the instance of the component, if one is available .

[Visual Basic]
```
Overrides Public Function GetLicense( _
   ByVal context As LicenseContext, _
   ByVal type As Type, _
   ByVal instance As Object, _
   ByVal allowExceptions As Boolean _
) As License
```
[C#]
```
public override License GetLicense(
   LicenseContext context,
   Type type,
   object instance,
   bool allowExceptions
);
```
[C++]
```
public: License* GetLicense(
   LicenseContext* context,
   Type* type,
   Object* instance,
   bool allowExceptions
);
```

[JScript]
```
public override function GetLicense(
    context : LicenseContext,
    type : Type,
    instance : Object,
    allowExceptions : Boolean
) : License;
```

Parameters

context
A **LicenseContext** that specifies where you can use the licensed object.

type
A **Type** that represents the component requesting the **License**.

instance
An object that requests the **License**.

allowExceptions
true if a **LicenseException** should be thrown when a component cannot be granted a license; otherwise, **false**.

Return Value

A valid **License**. If this method cannot find a valid **License** or a valid *context* parameter, it returns a null reference (**Nothing** in Visual Basic).

Remarks

At design time, the **GetLicense** method looks for a license file named `myClassName.LIC`, where `myClassName` is the **FullName** of the component to create. This file must be in the same directory as the .dll file that contains the component.

Next, this method checks the first line of the license file against a key specified in the **IsKeyValid** method. If the key is valid, this line is used as the **LicenseKey**.

Requirements

Platforms: Windows 98, Windows NT 4.0,
Windows Millennium Edition, Windows 2000,
Windows XP Home Edition, Windows XP Professional,
Windows Server 2003 family

LicFileLicenseProvider.IsKeyValid Method

Determines whether the key that the **GetLicense** method retrieves is valid for the specified type.

[Visual Basic]
```
Protected Overridable Function IsKeyValid( _
    ByVal key As String, _
    ByVal type As Type _
) As Boolean
```
[C#]
```
protected virtual bool IsKeyValid(
    string key,
    Type type
);
```
[C++]
```
protected: virtual bool IsKeyValid(
    String* key,
    Type* type
);
```
[JScript]
```
protected function IsKeyValid(
    key : String,
    type : Type
) : Boolean;
```

Parameters

key
The **LicenseKey** to check.

type
A **Type** that represents the component requesting the **License**.

Return Value

true if the key is a valid **LicenseKey** for the specified type; otherwise, **false**.

Remarks

This method checks the key against the phrase: "`myClassName is a licensed component.`", where `myClassName` is the **FullName** of the component you want to create.

Notes to Inheritors: When you inherit from this class, you can override this method to provide your own validation logic.

Requirements

Platforms: Windows 98, Windows NT 4.0,
Windows Millennium Edition, Windows 2000,
Windows XP Home Edition, Windows XP Professional,
Windows Server 2003 family

ListBindableAttribute Class

Specifies that a list can be used as a data source. A visual designer should use this attribute to determine whether to display a particular list in a data-binding picker. This class cannot be inherited.

System.Object
  System.Attribute
    System.ComponentModel.ListBindableAttribute

[Visual Basic]
```
<AttributeUsage(AttributeTargets.All)>
NotInheritable Public Class ListBindableAttribute
   Inherits Attribute
```
[C#]
```
[AttributeUsage(AttributeTargets.All)]
public sealed class ListBindableAttribute : Attribute
```
[C++]
```
[AttributeUsage(AttributeTargets::All)]
public __gc __sealed class ListBindableAttribute : public
   Attribute
```
[JScript]
```
public
   AttributeUsage(AttributeTargets.All)
class ListBindableAttribute extends Attribute
```

Thread Safety

Any public static (**Shared** in Visual Basic) members of this type are safe for multithreaded operations. Any instance members are not guaranteed to be thread safe.

Remarks

For more information about using attributes, see **Extending Metadata Using Attributes**.

Requirements

Namespace: System.ComponentModel

Platforms: Windows 98, Windows NT 4.0, Windows Millennium Edition, Windows 2000, Windows XP Home Edition, Windows XP Professional, Windows Server 2003 family

Assembly: System (in System.dll)

ListBindableAttribute Constructor

Initializes a new instance of the **ListBindableAttribute** class.

Overload List

Initializes a new instance of the **ListBindableAttribute** class using **BindableSupport** to indicate whether the list is bindable.

[Visual Basic] **Public Sub New(BindableSupport)**

[C#] **public ListBindableAttribute(BindableSupport);**

[C++] **public: ListBindableAttribute(BindableSupport);**

[JScript] **public function ListBindableAttribute(BindableSupport);**

Initializes a new instance of the **ListBindableAttribute** class using a value to indicate whether the list is bindable.

[Visual Basic] **Public Sub New(Boolean)**

[C#] **public ListBindableAttribute(bool);**

[C++] **public: ListBindableAttribute(bool);**

[JScript] **public function ListBindableAttribute(Boolean);**

ListBindableAttribute Constructor (BindableSupport)

Initializes a new instance of the **ListBindableAttribute** class using **BindableSupport** to indicate whether the list is bindable.

[Visual Basic]
```
Public Sub New( _
   ByVal flags As BindableSupport _
)
```
[C#]
```
public ListBindableAttribute(
   BindableSupport flags
);
```
[C++]
```
public: ListBindableAttribute(
   BindableSupport flags
);
```
[JScript]
```
public function ListBindableAttribute(
   flags : BindableSupport
);
```

Parameters

flags
  A **BindableSupport** that indicates whether the list is bindable.

Requirements

Platforms: Windows 98, Windows NT 4.0, Windows Millennium Edition, Windows 2000, Windows XP Home Edition, Windows XP Professional, Windows Server 2003 family

ListBindableAttribute Constructor (Boolean)

Initializes a new instance of the **ListBindableAttribute** class using a value to indicate whether the list is bindable.

[Visual Basic]
```
Public Sub New( _
   ByVal listBindable As Boolean _
)
```
[C#]
```
public ListBindableAttribute(
   bool listBindable
);
```
[C++]
```
public: ListBindableAttribute(
   bool listBindable
);
```
[JScript]
```
public function ListBindableAttribute(
   listBindable : Boolean
);
```

Parameters

listBindable
  true if the list is bindable; otherwise, **false**.

Requirements

Platforms: Windows 98, Windows NT 4.0, Windows Millennium Edition, Windows 2000, Windows XP Home Edition, Windows XP Professional, Windows Server 2003 family

ListBindableAttribute.Default Field

This member supports the .NET Framework infrastructure and is not intended to be used directly from your code.

```
[Visual Basic]
Public Shared ReadOnly Default As ListBindableAttribute
[C#]
public static readonly ListBindableAttribute Default;
[C++]
public: static ListBindableAttribute* Default;
[JScript]
public static var Default : ListBindableAttribute;
```

ListBindableAttribute.No Field

Specifies that the list is not bindable. This static (**Shared** in Visual Basic) field is read-only.

```
[Visual Basic]
Public Shared ReadOnly No As ListBindableAttribute
[C#]
public static readonly ListBindableAttribute No;
[C++]
public: static ListBindableAttribute* No;
[JScript]
public static var No : ListBindableAttribute;
```

Requirements

Platforms: Windows 98, Windows NT 4.0, Windows Millennium Edition, Windows 2000, Windows XP Home Edition, Windows XP Professional, Windows Server 2003 family

ListBindableAttribute.Yes Field

Specifies that the list is bindable. This static (**Shared** in Visual Basic) field is read-only.

```
[Visual Basic]
Public Shared ReadOnly Yes As ListBindableAttribute
[C#]
public static readonly ListBindableAttribute Yes;
[C++]
public: static ListBindableAttribute* Yes;
[JScript]
public static var Yes : ListBindableAttribute;
```

Remarks

This field is the default setting for this attribute.

Requirements

Platforms: Windows 98, Windows NT 4.0, Windows Millennium Edition, Windows 2000, Windows XP Home Edition, Windows XP Professional, Windows Server 2003 family

ListBindableAttribute.ListBindable Property

Gets whether the list is bindable.

```
[Visual Basic]
Public ReadOnly Property ListBindable As Boolean
[C#]
public bool ListBindable {get;}
[C++]
public: __property bool get_ListBindable();
[JScript]
public function get ListBindable() : Boolean;
```

Property Value

true if the list is bindable; otherwise, **false**.

Requirements

Platforms: Windows 98, Windows NT 4.0, Windows Millennium Edition, Windows 2000, Windows XP Home Edition, Windows XP Professional, Windows Server 2003 family

ListBindableAttribute.Equals Method

This member overrides **Object.Equals**.

```
[Visual Basic]
Overrides Public Function Equals( _
   ByVal obj As Object _
) As Boolean
[C#]
public override bool Equals(
   object obj
);
[C++]
public: bool Equals(
   Object* obj
);
[JScript]
public override function Equals(
   obj : Object
) : Boolean;
```

Requirements

Platforms: Windows 98, Windows NT 4.0, Windows Millennium Edition, Windows 2000, Windows XP Home Edition, Windows XP Professional, Windows Server 2003 family

ListBindableAttribute.GetHashCode Method

This member overrides **Attribute.GetHashCode**.

```
[Visual Basic]
Overrides Public Function GetHashCode() As Integer
[C#]
public override int GetHashCode();
[C++]
public: int GetHashCode();
[JScript]
public override function GetHashCode() : int;
```

Requirements

Platforms: Windows 98, Windows NT 4.0, Windows Millennium Edition, Windows 2000, Windows XP Home Edition, Windows XP Professional, Windows Server 2003 family

ListBindableAttribute.IsDefaultAttribute Method

Returns whether **ListBindable** is set to the default value.

[Visual Basic]
```
Overrides Public Function IsDefaultAttribute() As Boolean
```
[C#]
```
public override bool IsDefaultAttribute();
```
[C++]
```
public: bool IsDefaultAttribute();
```
[JScript]
```
public override function IsDefaultAttribute() : Boolean;
```

Return Value

true if **ListBindable** is set to the default value; otherwise, **false**.

Requirements

Platforms: Windows 98, Windows NT 4.0,
Windows Millennium Edition, Windows 2000,
Windows XP Home Edition, Windows XP Professional,
Windows Server 2003 family

ListChangedEventArgs Class

Provides data for the **ListChanged** event.

System.Object
  System.EventArgs
    System.ComponentModel.ListChangedEventArgs

[Visual Basic]
```
Public Class ListChangedEventArgs
   Inherits EventArgs
```
[C#]
```
public class ListChangedEventArgs : EventArgs
```
[C++]
```
public __gc class ListChangedEventArgs : public EventArgs
```
[JScript]
```
public class ListChangedEventArgs extends EventArgs
```

Thread Safety

Any public static (**Shared** in Visual Basic) members of this type are safe for multithreaded operations. Any instance members are not guaranteed to be thread safe.

Remarks

A **ListChanged** event is raised when the data in an **IBindingList** changes.

When a **ListChanged** event is fired, a single index for deletion needs to be specified. You can set the *newIndex* of **ListChangedEventArgs** to the index you are deleting. If there is only one index in the **IBindingList**, *oldIndex* should be set to -1.

Example

For an example on using this class, see **Working with DataView Events**.

Requirements

Namespace: System.ComponentModel

Platforms: Windows 98, Windows NT 4.0, Windows Millennium Edition, Windows 2000, Windows XP Home Edition, Windows XP Professional, Windows Server 2003 family, .NET Compact Framework - Windows CE .NET

Assembly: System (in System.dll)

ListChangedEventArgs Constructor

Initializes a new instance of the **ListChangedEventArgs** class.

Overload List

Initializes a new instance of the **ListChangedEventArgs** class, when given the way the list changed and the new size of the collection.

Supported by the .NET Compact Framework.

[Visual Basic] **Public Sub New(ListChangedType, Integer)**

[C#] **public ListChangedEventArgs(ListChangedType, int);**

[C++] **public: ListChangedEventArgs(ListChangedType, int);**

[JScript] **public function ListChanged-EventArgs(ListChangedType, int);**

Initializes a new instance of the **ListChangedEventArgs** class, with the way the list changed and a **PropertyDescriptor**.

Supported by the .NET Compact Framework.

[Visual Basic] **Public Sub New(ListChangedType, PropertyDescriptor)**

[C#] **public ListChangedEventArgs(ListChangedType, PropertyDescriptor);**

[C++] **public: ListChangedEventArgs(ListChangedType, PropertyDescriptor*);**

[JScript] **public function ListChanged-EventArgs(ListChangedType, PropertyDescriptor);**

Initializes a new instance of the **ListChangedEventArgs** class.

Supported by the .NET Compact Framework.

[Visual Basic] **Public Sub New(ListChangedType, Integer, Integer)**

[C#] **public ListChangedEventArgs(ListChangedType, int, int);**

[C++] **public: ListChangedEventArgs(ListChangedType, int, int);**

[JScript] **public function ListChanged-EventArgs(ListChangedType, int, int);**

ListChangedEventArgs Constructor (ListChangedType, Int32)

Initializes a new instance of the **ListChangedEventArgs** class, when given the way the list changed and the new size of the collection.

[Visual Basic]
```
Public Sub New( _
   ByVal listChangedType As ListChangedType, _
   ByVal newIndex As Integer _
)
```
[C#]
```
public ListChangedEventArgs(
   ListChangedType listChangedType,
   int newIndex
);
```
[C++]
```
public: ListChangedEventArgs(
   ListChangedType listChangedType,
   int newIndex
);
```
[JScript]
```
public function ListChangedEventArgs(
   listChangedType : ListChangedType,
   newIndex : int
);
```

Parameters

listChangedType
  One of the **ListChangedType** values.

newIndex
  The new index of the item in the list.

Requirements

Platforms: Windows 98, Windows NT 4.0, Windows Millennium Edition, Windows 2000, Windows XP Home Edition, Windows XP Professional, Windows Server 2003 family, .NET Compact Framework - Windows CE .NET

ListChangedEventArgs Constructor (ListChangedType, PropertyDescriptor)

Initializes a new instance of the **ListChangedEventArgs** class, with the way the list changed and a **PropertyDescriptor**.

```
[Visual Basic]
Public Sub New( _
   ByVal listChangedType As ListChangedType, _
   ByVal propDesc As PropertyDescriptor _
)
[C#]
public ListChangedEventArgs(
   ListChangedType listChangedType,
   PropertyDescriptor propDesc
);
[C++]
public: ListChangedEventArgs(
   ListChangedType listChangedType,
   PropertyDescriptor* propDesc
);
[JScript]
public function ListChangedEventArgs(
   listChangedType : ListChangedType,
   propDesc : PropertyDescriptor
);
```

Parameters

listChangedType
One of the **ListChangedType** values.

propDesc
A **PropertyDescriptor** that was added, removed, or changed.

Remarks

This constructor can be used only if the schema of the object has changed.

The *listChangedType* parameter should be **ListChangedType.PropertyDescriptorAdded**, **ListChangedType.PropertyDescriptorChanged**, or **ListChangedType.PropertyDescriptorDeleted**.

Requirements

Platforms: Windows 98, Windows NT 4.0, Windows Millennium Edition, Windows 2000, Windows XP Home Edition, Windows XP Professional, Windows Server 2003 family, .NET Compact Framework - Windows CE .NET

ListChangedEventArgs Constructor (ListChangedType, Int32, Int32)

Initializes a new instance of the **ListChangedEventArgs** class.

```
[Visual Basic]
Public Sub New( _
   ByVal listChangedType As ListChangedType, _
   ByVal newIndex As Integer, _
   ByVal oldIndex As Integer _
)
[C#]
public ListChangedEventArgs(
   ListChangedType listChangedType,
   int newIndex,
[Visual Basic]
   int oldIndex
);
[C++]
public: ListChangedEventArgs(
   ListChangedType listChangedType,
   int newIndex,
   int oldIndex
);
[JScript]
public function ListChangedEventArgs(
   listChangedType : ListChangedType,
   newIndex : int,
   oldIndex : int
);
```

Parameters

listChangedType
One of the **ListChangedType** values.

newIndex
The new index of the item in the list.

oldIndex
The old index of the item in the list.

Requirements

Platforms: Windows 98, Windows NT 4.0, Windows Millennium Edition, Windows 2000, Windows XP Home Edition, Windows XP Professional, Windows Server 2003 family, .NET Compact Framework - Windows CE .NET

ListChangedEventArgs.ListChangedType Property

Gets the way that the list changed.

```
[Visual Basic]
Public ReadOnly Property ListChangedType As ListChangedType
[C#]
public ListChangedType ListChangedType {get;}
[C++]
public: __property ListChangedType get_ListChangedType();
[JScript]
public function get ListChangedType() : ListChangedType;
```

Property Value

One of the **ListChangedType** values.

Requirements

Platforms: Windows 98, Windows NT 4.0, Windows Millennium Edition, Windows 2000, Windows XP Home Edition, Windows XP Professional, Windows Server 2003 family, .NET Compact Framework - Windows CE .NET

ListChangedEventArgs.NewIndex Property

Gets the new index of the item in the list.

[Visual Basic]
```
Public ReadOnly Property NewIndex As Integer
```
[C#]
```
public int NewIndex {get;}
```
[C++]
```
public: __property int get_NewIndex();
```
[JScript]
```
public function get NewIndex() : int;
```

Property Value

The new index of the item in the list.

Requirements

Platforms: Windows 98, Windows NT 4.0, Windows Millennium Edition, Windows 2000, Windows XP Home Edition, Windows XP Professional, Windows Server 2003 family, .NET Compact Framework - Windows CE .NET

ListChangedEventArgs.OldIndex Property

Gets the old index of the item in the list.

[Visual Basic]
```
Public ReadOnly Property OldIndex As Integer
```
[C#]
```
public int OldIndex {get;}
```
[C++]
```
public: __property int get_OldIndex();
```
[JScript]
```
public function get OldIndex() : int;
```

Property Value

The old index of the item in the list.

Requirements

Platforms: Windows 98, Windows NT 4.0, Windows Millennium Edition, Windows 2000, Windows XP Home Edition, Windows XP Professional, Windows Server 2003 family, .NET Compact Framework - Windows CE .NET

ListChangedEventHandler Delegate

Represents the method that will handle the **ListChanged** event of the **IBindingList** class.

[Visual Basic]

```
<Serializable>
Public Delegate Sub ListChangedEventHandler( _
   ByVal sender As Object, _
   ByVal e As ListChangedEventArgs _
)
```

[C#]

```
[Serializable]
public delegate void ListChangedEventHandler(
   object sender,
   ListChangedEventArgs e
);
```

[C++]

```
[Serializable]
public __gc __delegate void ListChangedEventHandler(
   Object* sender,
   ListChangedEventArgs* e
);
```

[JScript] In JScript, you can use the delegates in the .NET Framework, but you cannot define your own.

Parameters [Visual Basic, C#, C++]

The declaration of your event handler must have the same parameters as the **ListChangedEventHandler** delegate declaration.

sender

The source of the event.

e

A **ListChangedEventArgs** that contains the event data.

Remarks

When you create a **ListChangedEventHandler** delegate, you identify a method to handle the event. To associate the event with your event handler, add an instance of the delegate to the event. The event handler is called whenever the event occurs, unless you remove the delegate.

Example

For an example of using this delegate, see **Working with DataView Events**.

Requirements

Namespace: System.ComponentModel

Platforms: Windows 98, Windows NT 4.0, Windows Millennium Edition, Windows 2000, Windows XP Home Edition, Windows XP Professional, Windows Server 2003 family, .NET Compact Framework - Windows CE .NET

Assembly: System (in System.dll)

ListChangedType Enumeration

Specifies how the list changed.

[Visual Basic]
```
<Serializable>
Public Enum ListChangedType
```
[C#]
```
[Serializable]
public enum ListChangedType
```
[C++]
```
[Serializable]
__value public enum ListChangedType
```
[JScript]
```
public
   Serializable
enum ListChangedType
```

Remarks

Used by the **ListChangedType** property of the **ListChangedEventArgs** class to indicate the way an **IBindingList** object changes.

Members

Member name	Description
ItemAdded Supported by the .NET Compact Framework.	An item added to the list. **ListChangedEventArgs.NewIndex** contains the index of the item that was added.
ItemChanged Supported by the .NET Compact Framework.	An item changed in the list. **ListChangedEventArgs.NewIndex** contains the index of the item that was changed.
ItemDeleted Supported by the .NET Compact Framework.	An item deleted from the list. **ListChangedEventArgs.NewIndex** contains the index of the item that was deleted.
ItemMoved Supported by the .NET Compact Framework.	An item moved within the list. **ListChangedEventArgs.OldIndex** contains the previous index for the item, whereas **ListChangedEventArgs.NewIndex** contains the new index for the item.
PropertyDescriptorAdded Supported by the .NET Compact Framework.	A **PropertyDescriptor** was added, which changed the schema.
PropertyDescriptorChanged Supported by the .NET Compact Framework.	A **PropertyDescriptor** was changed, which changed the schema.
PropertyDescriptorDeleted Supported by the .NET Compact Framework.	A **PropertyDescriptor** was deleted, which changed the schema.
Reset Supported by the .NET Compact Framework.	Much of the list has changed. Any listening controls should refresh all their data from the list.

Example

For an example of using this class, see **Working with DataView Events**.

Requirements

Namespace: System.ComponentModel

Platforms: Windows 98, Windows NT 4.0, Windows Millennium Edition, Windows 2000, Windows XP Home Edition, Windows XP Professional, Windows Server 2003 family, .NET Compact Framework - Windows CE .NET

Assembly: System (in System.dll)

ListSortDirection Enumeration

Specifies the direction of a sort operation.

[Visual Basic]
```
<Serializable>
Public Enum ListSortDirection
```
[C#]
```
[Serializable]
public enum ListSortDirection
```
[C++]
```
[Serializable]
__value public enum ListSortDirection
```
[JScript]
```
public
   Serializable
enum ListSortDirection
```

Remarks

IBindingList.ApplySort and **IBindingList.SortDirection** use this enumeration.

Members

Member name	Description
Ascending Supported by the .NET Compact Framework.	Sorts in ascending order.
Descending Supported by the .NET Compact Framework.	Sorts in descending order.

Requirements

Namespace: System.ComponentModel

Platforms: Windows 98, Windows NT 4.0, Windows Millennium Edition, Windows 2000, Windows XP Home Edition, Windows XP Professional, Windows Server 2003 family, .NET Compact Framework - Windows CE .NET

Assembly: System (in System.dll)

LocalizableAttribute Class

Specifies whether a property should be localized.

System.Object
  System.Attribute
    System.ComponentModel.LocalizableAttribute

[Visual Basic]
```
<AttributeUsage(AttributeTargets.All)>
NotInheritable Public Class LocalizableAttribute
   Inherits Attribute
```
[C#]
```
[AttributeUsage(AttributeTargets.All)]
public sealed class LocalizableAttribute : Attribute
```
[C++]
```
[AttributeUsage(AttributeTargets::All)]
public __gc __sealed class LocalizableAttribute : public Attribute
```
[JScript]
```
public
   AttributeUsage(AttributeTargets.All)
class LocalizableAttribute extends Attribute
```

Thread Safety

Any public static (**Shared** in Visual Basic) members of this type are safe for multithreaded operations. Any instance members are not guaranteed to be thread safe.

Remarks

When code is generated for a component, members that are marked with the **LocalizableAttribute** constructor of the value **true** have their property values saved in resource files. You can localize these resource files without modifying the code.

By default, members that have no localizable attribute or are marked with the **LocalizableAttribute** constructor of the value **false** will have their property values persisted to code, if the data type allows. Otherwise, if the main component is set to **Localizable**, all properties will be persisted to the resource file. The default is **false**.

> **Note** When you mark a property with the **LocalizableAttribute** constructor of the value **true**, the value of this attribute is set to the constant member **Yes**. For a property marked with the **LocalizableAttribute** constructor of the value **false**, the value is **No**. Therefore, when you want to check the value of this attribute in your code, you must specify the attribute as **LocalizableAttribute.Yes** or **LocalizableAttribute.No**.

Example

[Visual Basic, C#, JScript] The following example marks a property as needing to be localized.

[Visual Basic]
```
<Localizable(True)> _
Public Property MyProperty() As Integer
    Get
        ' Insert code here.
        Return 0
    End Get
    Set
        ' Insert code here.
    End Set
End Property
```
[C#]
```
[Localizable(true)]
 public int MyProperty {
    get {
       // Insert code here.
       return 0;
    }
    set {
       // Insert code here.
    }
 }
```

[Visual Basic, C#, JScript] The next example shows how to check the value of the **LocalizableAttribute** for `MyProperty`. First, the code gets a **PropertyDescriptorCollection** with all the properties for the object. Then, the code gets `MyProperty` from the **PropertyDescriptorCollection**. Next, it returns the attributes for this property and saves them in the attributes variable.

[Visual Basic, C#, JScript] Finally, the code sets `myAttribute` to the value of the **LocalizableAttribute** in the **AttributeCollection** and checks whether the property needs to be localized.

[Visual Basic]
```
' Gets the attributes for the property.
Dim attributes As AttributeCollection =
TypeDescriptor.GetProperties(Me)("MyProperty").Attributes

' Checks to see if the property needs to be localized.
Dim myAttribute As LocalizableAttribute =
CType(attributes(GetType(LocalizableAttribute)), LocalizableAttribute)
If myAttribute.IsLocalizable Then
    ' Insert code here.
End If
```
[C#]
```
// Gets the attributes for the property.
AttributeCollection attributes =
TypeDescriptor.GetProperties(this)["MyProperty"].Attributes;

// Checks to see if the property needs to be localized.
LocalizableAttribute myAttribute =
(LocalizableAttribute)attributes[typeof(LocalizableAttribute)];
if(myAttribute.IsLocalizable) {
// Insert code here.
}
```
[JScript]
```
// Gets the attributes for the property.
var attributes : AttributeCollection =
TypeDescriptor.GetProperties(this)["MyProperty"].Attributes

// Checks to see if the property needs to be localized.
var myAttribute : LocalizableAttribute =
LocalizableAttribute(attributes(LocalizableAttribute))
if(myAttribute.IsLocalizable){
    // Insert code here.
}
```

Requirements

Namespace: System.ComponentModel

Platforms: Windows 98, Windows NT 4.0, Windows Millennium Edition, Windows 2000, Windows XP Home Edition, Windows XP Professional, Windows Server 2003 family

Assembly: System (in System.dll)

LocalizableAttribute Constructor

Initializes a new instance of the **LocalizableAttribute** class.

[Visual Basic]
```
Public Sub New( _
   ByVal isLocalizable As Boolean _
)
```
[C#]
```
public LocalizableAttribute(
   bool isLocalizable
);
```

```
[C++]
public: LocalizableAttribute(
   bool isLocalizable
);
[JScript]
public function LocalizableAttribute(
   isLocalizable : Boolean
);
```

Parameters

isLocalizable
: **true** if a property should be localized; otherwise, **false**.

Example

[Visual Basic, C#, JScript] The following example marks a property as needing to be localized. This code creates a new **LocalizableAttribute**, sets its value to **LocalizableAttribute.Yes**, and binds it to the property.

```
[Visual Basic]
<Localizable(True)> _
Public Property MyProperty() As Integer
    Get
        ' Insert code here.
        Return 0
    End Get
    Set
        ' Insert code here.
    End Set
End Property
```

```
[C#]
 [Localizable(true)]
 public int MyProperty {
    get {
       // Insert code here.
       return 0;
    }
    set {
       // Insert code here.
    }
 }
```

```
[JScript]
public Localizable(true)
function get MyProperty() : int{
  // Insert code here.  Attribute goes on getter only when
 a property has
  // both a getter and a setter.
  return 0
}

function set MyProperty(value : int){
  // Insert code here.
}
```

Requirements

Platforms: Windows 98, Windows NT 4.0, Windows Millennium Edition, Windows 2000, Windows XP Home Edition, Windows XP Professional, Windows Server 2003 family

LocalizableAttribute.Default Field

This member supports the .NET Framework infrastructure and is not intended to be used directly from your code.

```
[Visual Basic]
Public Shared ReadOnly Default As LocalizableAttribute
[C#]
public static readonly LocalizableAttribute Default;
[C++]
public: static LocalizableAttribute* Default;
[JScript]
public static var Default : LocalizableAttribute;
```

LocalizableAttribute.No Field

Specifies that a property should not be localized. This static (**Shared** in Visual Basic) field is read-only.

```
[Visual Basic]
Public Shared ReadOnly No As LocalizableAttribute
[C#]
public static readonly LocalizableAttribute No;
[C++]
public: static LocalizableAttribute* No;
[JScript]
public static var No : LocalizableAttribute;
```

Remarks

This field is the default setting for this attribute.

When you mark a property with the **LocalizableAttribute** constructor of the value **false**, the value of this attribute is set to the constant member **No**. Therefore, when you want to check whether the attribute is set to this value in your code, you must specify the attribute as **LocalizableAttribute.No**.

Requirements

Platforms: Windows 98, Windows NT 4.0, Windows Millennium Edition, Windows 2000, Windows XP Home Edition, Windows XP Professional, Windows Server 2003 family

LocalizableAttribute.Yes Field

Specifies that a property should be localized. This static (**Shared** in Visual Basic) field is read-only.

```
[Visual Basic]
Public Shared ReadOnly Yes As LocalizableAttribute
[C#]
public static readonly LocalizableAttribute Yes;
[C++]
public: static LocalizableAttribute* Yes;
[JScript]
public static var Yes : LocalizableAttribute;
```

Remarks

When you mark a property with the **LocalizableAttribute** constructor of the value **true**, the value of this attribute is set to the constant member **Yes**. Therefore, when you want to check whether the attribute is set to this value in your code, you must specify the attribute as **LocalizableAttribute.Yes**.

Requirements

Platforms: Windows 98, Windows NT 4.0, Windows Millennium Edition, Windows 2000, Windows XP Home Edition, Windows XP Professional, Windows Server 2003 family

LocalizableAttribute.IsLocalizable Property

Gets a value indicating whether a property should be localized.

```
[Visual Basic]
Public ReadOnly Property IsLocalizable As Boolean
[C#]
public bool IsLocalizable {get;}
[C++]
public: __property bool get_IsLocalizable();
[JScript]
public function get IsLocalizable() : Boolean;
```

Property Value

true if a property should be localized; otherwise, **false**.

Example

[Visual Basic, C#, JScript] The following example shows how to check the value of the **LocalizableAttribute** for `MyProperty`. First, the code gets a **PropertyDescriptorCollection** with all the properties for the object. Then, the code gets `MyProperty` from the **PropertyDescriptorCollection**. Next, it returns the attributes for this property and saves them in the attributes variable.

[Visual Basic, C#, JScript] Finally, the code sets `myAttribute` to the value of the **LocalizableAttribute** in the **AttributeCollection** and checks whether the property needs to be localized.

```
[Visual Basic]
' Gets the attributes for the property.
Dim attributes As AttributeCollection = _
   TypeDescriptor.GetProperties(Me)("MyProperty").Attributes

' Checks to see if the property needs to be localized.
Dim myAttribute As LocalizableAttribute = _
   CType(attributes(GetType(LocalizableAttribute)),
LocalizableAttribute)

If myAttribute.IsLocalizable Then
     ' Insert code here.
End If
```

```
[C#]
// Gets the attributes for the property.
 AttributeCollection attributes =
    TypeDescriptor.GetProperties(this)["MyProperty"].Attributes;

 // Checks to see if the property needs to be localized.
 LocalizableAttribute myAttribute =
    (LocalizableAttribute)attributes[typeof(LocalizableAttribute)];
 if(myAttribute.IsLocalizable) {
    // Insert code here.
 }
```

```
[JScript]
// Gets the attributes for the property.
var attributes : AttributeCollection =
TypeDescriptor.GetProperties(this)["MyProperty"].Attributes

// Checks to see if the property needs to be localized.
var myAttribute : LocalizableAttribute =
LocalizableAttribute(attributes(LocalizableAttribute))

if(myAttribute.IsLocalizable){
     // Insert code here.
}
```

Requirements

Platforms: Windows 98, Windows NT 4.0, Windows Millennium Edition, Windows 2000, Windows XP Home Edition, Windows XP Professional, Windows Server 2003 family

LocalizableAttribute.Equals Method

This member overrides **Object.Equals**.

```
[Visual Basic]
Overrides Public Function Equals( _
   ByVal obj As Object _
) As Boolean
[C#]
public override bool Equals(
   object obj
);
[C++]
public: bool Equals(
   Object* obj
);
[JScript]
public override function Equals(
   obj : Object
) : Boolean;
```

Requirements

Platforms: Windows 98, Windows NT 4.0, Windows Millennium Edition, Windows 2000, Windows XP Home Edition, Windows XP Professional, Windows Server 2003 family

LocalizableAttribute.GetHashCode Method

This member overrides **Attribute.GetHashCode**.

```
[Visual Basic]
Overrides Public Function GetHashCode() As Integer
[C#]
public override int GetHashCode();
[C++]
public: int GetHashCode();
[JScript]
public override function GetHashCode() : int;
```

Requirements

Platforms: Windows 98, Windows NT 4.0, Windows Millennium Edition, Windows 2000, Windows XP Home Edition, Windows XP Professional, Windows Server 2003 family

LocalizableAttribute.IsDefaultAttribute Method

This member overrides **Attribute.IsDefaultAttribute**.

```
[Visual Basic]
Overrides Public Function IsDefaultAttribute() As Boolean
[C#]
public override bool IsDefaultAttribute();
[C++]
public: bool IsDefaultAttribute();
[JScript]
public override function IsDefaultAttribute() : Boolean;
```

Requirements

Platforms: Windows 98, Windows NT 4.0, Windows Millennium Edition, Windows 2000, Windows XP Home Edition, Windows XP Professional, Windows Server 2003 family

MarshalByValueComponent Class

Implements **IComponent** and provides the base implementation for remotable components that are marshaled by value (a copy of the serialized object is passed).

System.Object
  System.ComponentModel.MarshalByValueComponent
    Derived classes

```
[Visual Basic]
Public Class MarshalByValueComponent
   Implements IComponent, IDisposable, IServiceProvider
[C#]
public class MarshalByValueComponent : IComponent, IDisposable,
   IServiceProvider
[C++]
public __gc class MarshalByValueComponent : public IComponent,
   IDisposable, IServiceProvider
[JScript]
public class MarshalByValueComponent implements IComponent,
   IDisposable, IServiceProvider
```

Thread Safety

Any public static (**Shared** in Visual Basic) members of this type are safe for multithreaded operations. Any instance members are not guaranteed to be thread safe.

Remarks

A component can be contained in a container. For each component in a container, the container creates a site that it uses to manage the component. The component interacts with its container primarily through a container-provided **ISite**, which is a repository of container-specific, per-component information.

Notes to Inheritors: When you inherit from this class, you can override the **Dispose**, **Site**, and the **GetService** methods.

Requirements

Namespace: System.ComponentModel

Platforms: Windows 98, Windows NT 4.0,
Windows Millennium Edition, Windows 2000,
Windows XP Home Edition, Windows XP Professional,
Windows Server 2003 family,
.NET Compact Framework - Windows CE .NET

Assembly: System (in System.dll)

MarshalByValueComponent Constructor

Initializes a new instance of the **MarshalByValueComponent** class.

```
[Visual Basic]
Public Sub New()
[C#]
public MarshalByValueComponent();
[C++]
public: MarshalByValueComponent();
[JScript]
public function MarshalByValueComponent();
```

Remarks

A component can be contained in a container. For each component in a container, the container creates a site that it uses to manage the component. The component interacts with its container primarily through a container-provided **ISite**, which is a repository of container-specific, per-component information.

Requirements

Platforms: Windows 98, Windows NT 4.0,
Windows Millennium Edition, Windows 2000,
Windows XP Home Edition, Windows XP Professional,
Windows Server 2003 family,
.NET Compact Framework - Windows CE .NET

MarshalByValueComponent.Container Property

Gets the container for the component.

```
[Visual Basic]
Public Overridable ReadOnly Property Container As IContainer
[C#]
public virtual IContainer Container {get;}
[C++]
public: __property virtual IContainer* get_Container();
[JScript]
public function get Container() : IContainer;
```

Property Value

An object implementing the **IContainer** interface that represents the component's container, or a null reference (**Nothing** in Visual Basic) if the component does not have a site.

Requirements

Platforms: Windows 98, Windows NT 4.0,
Windows Millennium Edition, Windows 2000,
Windows XP Home Edition, Windows XP Professional,
Windows Server 2003 family

MarshalByValueComponent.DesignMode Property

Gets a value indicating whether the component is currently in design mode.

```
[Visual Basic]
Public Overridable ReadOnly Property DesignMode As Boolean
[C#]
public virtual bool DesignMode {get;}
[C++]
public: __property virtual bool get_DesignMode();
[JScript]
public function get DesignMode() : Boolean;
```

Property Value

true if the component is in design mode; otherwise, **false**.

Remarks

If the component does not have a site, this method always returns **false**.

Requirements

Platforms: Windows 98, Windows NT 4.0,
Windows Millennium Edition, Windows 2000,
Windows XP Home Edition, Windows XP Professional,
Windows Server 2003 family

MarshalByValueComponent.Events Property

Gets the list of event handlers that are attached to this component.

```
[Visual Basic]
Protected ReadOnly Property Events As EventHandlerList
[C#]
protected EventHandlerList Events {get;}
[C++]
protected: __property EventHandlerList* get_Events();
[JScript]
protected function get Events() : EventHandlerList;
```

Property Value

An **EventHandlerList** that provides the delegates for this component.

Requirements

Platforms: Windows 98, Windows NT 4.0, Windows Millennium Edition, Windows 2000, Windows XP Home Edition, Windows XP Professional, Windows Server 2003 family

MarshalByValueComponent.Site Property

Gets or sets the site of the component.

```
[Visual Basic]
Public Overridable Property Site As ISite Implements _
   IComponent.Site
[C#]
public virtual ISite Site {get; set;}
[C++]
public: __property virtual ISite* get_Site();
public: __property virtual void set_Site(ISite*);
[JScript]
public function get Site() : ISite;
public function set Site(ISite);
```

Property Value

An object implementing the **ISite** interface that represents the site of the component.

Implements

IComponent.Site

Remarks

A valid value for this property - that is, the value is not a null reference (**Nothing** in Visual Basic), indicates that the component has been added to a container.

When the value of this property is a null reference (**Nothing**), the property indicates that the component is being removed from a container. However, this property does not remove the component from the container.

Notes to Inheritors: To change this behavior, inherit from this class and get and set in this property.

Requirements

Platforms: Windows 98, Windows NT 4.0, Windows Millennium Edition, Windows 2000, Windows XP Home Edition, Windows XP Professional, Windows Server 2003 family

MarshalByValueComponent.Dispose Method

Releases the resources used by the **MarshalByValueComponent**.

Overload List

Releases all resources used by the **MarshalByValueComponent**.

[Visual Basic] **Overloads Public Overridable Sub Dispose() Implements IDisposable.Dispose**

[C#] **public virtual void Dispose();**

[C++] **public: virtual void Dispose();**

[JScript] **public function Dispose();**

Releases the unmanaged resources used by the **MarshalByValueComponent** and optionally releases the managed resources.

[Visual Basic] **Overloads Protected Overridable Sub Dispose(Boolean)**

[C#] **protected virtual void Dispose(bool);**

[C++] **protected: virtual void Dispose(bool);**

[JScript] **protected function Dispose(Boolean);**

MarshalByValueComponent.Dispose Method ()

Releases all resources used by the **MarshalByValueComponent**.

```
[Visual Basic]
Overloads Public Overridable Sub Dispose() Implements _
   IDisposable.Dispose
[C#]
public virtual void Dispose();
[C++]
public: virtual void Dispose();
[JScript]
public function Dispose();
```

Implements

IDisposable.Dispose

Remarks

Calling **Dispose** allows the resources used by the **MarshalByValueComponent** to be reallocated for other purposes. For more information about **Dispose**, see **Cleaning Up Unmanaged Resources**.

Requirements

Platforms: Windows 98, Windows NT 4.0, Windows Millennium Edition, Windows 2000, Windows XP Home Edition, Windows XP Professional, Windows Server 2003 family

MarshalByValueComponent.Dispose Method (Boolean)

Releases the unmanaged resources used by the **MarshalByValueComponent** and optionally releases the managed resources.

```
[Visual Basic]
Overloads Protected Overridable Sub Dispose( _
   ByVal disposing As Boolean _
)
[C#]
protected virtual void Dispose(
   bool disposing
);
[C++]
protected: virtual void Dispose(
   bool disposing
);
```

```
[JScript]
protected function Dispose(
   disposing : Boolean
);
```

Parameters

disposing

true to release both managed and unmanaged resources; **false** to release only unmanaged resources.

Remarks

This method is called by the public **Dispose()** method and the **Finalize** method. **Dispose()** invokes the protected **Dispose(Boolean)** method with the *disposing* parameter set to **true**. **Finalize** invokes **Dispose** with *disposing* set to **false**.

When the *disposing* parameter is **true**, this method releases all resources held by any managed objects that this **MarshalByValueComponent** references. This method invokes the **Dispose()** method of each referenced object.

Notes to Inheritors: **Dispose** can be called multiple times by other objects. When overriding **Dispose(Boolean)**, be careful not to reference objects that have been previously disposed of in an earlier call to **Dispose**.

Requirements

Platforms: Windows 98, Windows NT 4.0, Windows Millennium Edition, Windows 2000, Windows XP Home Edition, Windows XP Professional, Windows Server 2003 family

MarshalByValueComponent.Finalize Method

This member overrides **Object.Finalize**.

```
[Visual Basic]
Overrides Protected Sub Finalize()
[C#]
~MarshalByValueComponent();
[C++]
~MarshalByValueComponent();
[JScript]
protected override function Finalize();
```

Requirements

Platforms: Windows 98, Windows NT 4.0, Windows Millennium Edition, Windows 2000, Windows XP Home Edition, Windows XP Professional, Windows Server 2003 family, .NET Compact Framework - Windows CE .NET

MarshalByValueComponent.GetService Method

Gets the implementer of the **IServiceProvider**.

```
[Visual Basic]
Public Overridable Function GetService( _
   ByVal service As Type _
) As Object Implements IServiceProvider.GetService
[C#]
public virtual object GetService(
   Type service
);
[C++]
public: virtual Object* GetService(
   Type* service
);
[JScript]
public function GetService(
   service : Type
) : Object;
```

Parameters

service

A **Type** that represents the type of service you want.

Return Value

An **Object** that represents the implementer of the **IServiceProvider**.

Implements

IServiceProvider.GetService

Requirements

Platforms: Windows 98, Windows NT 4.0, Windows Millennium Edition, Windows 2000, Windows XP Home Edition, Windows XP Professional, Windows Server 2003 family

MarshalByValueComponent.ToString Method

This member overrides **Object.ToString**.

```
[Visual Basic]
Overrides Public Function ToString() As String
[C#]
public override string ToString();
[C++]
public: String* ToString();
[JScript]
public override function ToString() : String;
```

Requirements

Platforms: Windows 98, Windows NT 4.0, Windows Millennium Edition, Windows 2000, Windows XP Home Edition, Windows XP Professional, Windows Server 2003 family, .NET Compact Framework - Windows CE .NET

MarshalByValueComponent.Disposed Event

Adds an event handler to listen to the **Disposed** event on the component.

```
[Visual Basic]
Public Overridable Event Disposed As EventHandler
[C#]
public virtual event EventHandler Disposed;
[C++]
public: virtual __event EventHandler* Disposed;
```

[JScript] In JScript, you can handle the events defined by a class, but you cannot define your own.

Event Data

The event handler receives an argument of type **EventArgs**.

Requirements

Platforms: Windows 98, Windows NT 4.0, Windows Millennium Edition, Windows 2000, Windows XP Home Edition, Windows XP Professional, Windows Server 2003 family

MemberDescriptor Class

An abstract base class that represents a class member, such as a property, or event.

System.Object
  System.ComponentModel.MemberDescriptor
    System.ComponentModel.EventDescriptor
    System.ComponentModel.PropertyDescriptor

[Visual Basic]
```
<ComVisible(True)>
MustInherit Public Class MemberDescriptor
```
[C#]
```
[ComVisible(true)]
public abstract class MemberDescriptor
```
[C++]
```
[ComVisible(true)]
public __gc __abstract class MemberDescriptor
```
[JScript]
```
public
   ComVisible(true)
abstract class MemberDescriptor
```

Thread Safety

Any public static (**Shared** in Visual Basic) members of this type are safe for multithreaded operations. Any instance members are not guaranteed to be thread safe.

Remarks

MemberDescriptor is the base class for the **EventDescriptor** and the **PropertyDescriptor** classes. The **EventDescriptor** class provides a description of an event, and the **PropertyDescriptor** class provides a description of a property.

This class defines properties and methods to access its stored attributes. **Attributes** gets the collection of attributes. **Category**, **IsBrowsable**, **Description**, and **DesignTimeOnly** retrieve the values of those specific attributes. **Name** and **DisplayName** provide the name of the member.

The **MemberDescriptor** also defines an **Equals** method to compare this **MemberDescriptor** to another.

> **Note** Typically, you inherit from the **EventDescriptor** and **PropertyDescriptor** classes, and not from this class.

Example

Since most of the usage of this class will fall on the inherited classes **EventDescriptor** and **PropertyDescriptor**, refer to the samples in these classes, respectively.

Requirements

Namespace: System.ComponentModel

Platforms: Windows 98, Windows NT 4.0, Windows Millennium Edition, Windows 2000, Windows XP Home Edition, Windows XP Professional, Windows Server 2003 family, .NET Compact Framework - Windows CE .NET

Assembly: System (in System.dll)

MemberDescriptor Constructor

Initializes a new instance of the **MemberDescriptor** class.

Overload List

Initializes a new instance of the **MemberDescriptor** class with the specified **MemberDescriptor**.

Supported by the .NET Compact Framework.

[Visual Basic] **Protected Sub New(MemberDescriptor)**

[C#] **protected MemberDescriptor(MemberDescriptor);**

[C++] **protected: MemberDescriptor(MemberDescriptor*);**

[JScript] **protected function MemberDescriptor(Member-Descriptor);**

Initializes a new instance of the **MemberDescriptor** class with the specified name of the member.

[Visual Basic] **Protected Sub New(String)**

[C#] **protected MemberDescriptor(string);**

[C++] **protected: MemberDescriptor(String*);**

[JScript] **protected function MemberDescriptor(String);**

Initializes a new instance of the **MemberDescriptor** class with the name in the specified **MemberDescriptor** and the attributes in both the old **MemberDescriptor** and the **Attribute** array.

Supported by the .NET Compact Framework.

[Visual Basic] **Protected Sub New(MemberDescriptor, Attribute())**

[C#] **protected MemberDescriptor(MemberDescriptor, Attribute[]);**

[C++] **protected: MemberDescriptor(MemberDescriptor*, Attribute[]);**

[JScript] **protected function MemberDescriptor(Member-Descriptor, Attribute[]);**

Initializes a new instance of the **MemberDescriptor** class with the specified name of the member and an array of attributes.

Supported by the .NET Compact Framework.

[Visual Basic] **Protected Sub New(String, Attribute())**

[C#] **protected MemberDescriptor(string, Attribute[]);**

[C++] **protected: MemberDescriptor(String*, Attribute[]);**

[JScript] **protected function MemberDescriptor(String, Attribute[]);**

MemberDescriptor Constructor (MemberDescriptor)

Initializes a new instance of the **MemberDescriptor** class with the specified **MemberDescriptor**.

[Visual Basic]
```
Protected Sub New( _
   ByVal descr As MemberDescriptor _
)
```
[C#]
```
protected MemberDescriptor(
   MemberDescriptor descr
);
```
[C++]
```
protected: MemberDescriptor(
   MemberDescriptor* descr
);
```

```
[JScript]
protected function MemberDescriptor(
   descr : MemberDescriptor
);
```

Parameters

descr
A **MemberDescriptor** that contains the name of the member and its attributes.

Requirements

Platforms: Windows 98, Windows NT 4.0, Windows Millennium Edition, Windows 2000, Windows XP Home Edition, Windows XP Professional, Windows Server 2003 family, .NET Compact Framework - Windows CE .NET

MemberDescriptor Constructor (String)

Initializes a new instance of the **MemberDescriptor** class with the specified name of the member.

```
[Visual Basic]
Protected Sub New( _
   ByVal name As String _
)
[C#]
protected MemberDescriptor(
   string name
);
[C++]
protected: MemberDescriptor(
   String* name
);
[JScript]
protected function MemberDescriptor(
   name : String
);
```

Parameters

name
The name of the member.

Requirements

Platforms: Windows 98, Windows NT 4.0, Windows Millennium Edition, Windows 2000, Windows XP Home Edition, Windows XP Professional, Windows Server 2003 family

MemberDescriptor Constructor (MemberDescriptor, Attribute[])

Initializes a new instance of the **MemberDescriptor** class with the name in the specified **MemberDescriptor** and the attributes in both the old **MemberDescriptor** and the **Attribute** array.

```
[Visual Basic]
Protected Sub New( _
   ByVal oldMemberDescriptor As MemberDescriptor, _
   ByVal newAttributes() As Attribute _
)
[C#]
protected MemberDescriptor(
   MemberDescriptor oldMemberDescriptor,
   Attribute[] newAttributes
);
[C++]
protected: MemberDescriptor(
   MemberDescriptor* oldMemberDescriptor,
   Attribute* newAttributes[]
);
[JScript]
protected function MemberDescriptor(
   oldMemberDescriptor : MemberDescriptor,
   newAttributes : Attribute[]
);
```

Parameters

oldMemberDescriptor
A **MemberDescriptor** that has the name of the member and its attributes.

newAttributes
An array of **Attribute** objects with the attributes you want to add to the member.

Remarks

This constructor appends the attributes in the **Attribute** array to the attributes in the old **MemberDescriptor**.

Requirements

Platforms: Windows 98, Windows NT 4.0, Windows Millennium Edition, Windows 2000, Windows XP Home Edition, Windows XP Professional, Windows Server 2003 family, .NET Compact Framework - Windows CE .NET

MemberDescriptor Constructor (String, Attribute[])

Initializes a new instance of the **MemberDescriptor** class with the specified name of the member and an array of attributes.

```
[Visual Basic]
Protected Sub New( _
   ByVal name As String, _
   ByVal attributes() As Attribute _
)
[C#]
protected MemberDescriptor(
   string name,
   Attribute[] attributes
);
[C++]
protected: MemberDescriptor(
   String* name,
   Attribute* attributes[]
);
[JScript]
protected function MemberDescriptor(
   name : String,
   attributes : Attribute[]
);
```

Parameters

name

The name of the member.

attributes

An array of type **Attribute** that contains the member attributes.

Exceptions

Exception Type	Condition
ArgumentException	The name is an empty string ("") or a null reference (**Nothing** in Visual Basic).

Requirements

Platforms: Windows 98, Windows NT 4.0,
Windows Millennium Edition, Windows 2000,
Windows XP Home Edition, Windows XP Professional,
Windows Server 2003 family,
.NET Compact Framework - Windows CE .NET

MemberDescriptor.AttributeArray Property

Gets or sets an array of attributes.

[Visual Basic]
```
Protected Overridable Property AttributeArray As Attribute ()
```
[C#]
```
protected virtual Attribute[] AttributeArray {get; set;}
```
[C++]
```
protected: __property virtual Attribute* get_AttributeArray();
protected: __property virtual void
   set_AttributeArray(Attribute*[]);
```
[JScript]
```
protected function get AttributeArray() : Attribute[];
protected function set AttributeArray(Attribute[]);
```

Property Value

An array of type **Attribute** that contains the attributes of this member. Accessing this member allows derived classes to modify the default set of Attributes that are used in CreateAttributeCollection.

Requirements

Platforms: .NET Compact Framework - Windows CE .NET

MemberDescriptor.Attributes Property

Gets the collection of attributes for this member.

[Visual Basic]
```
Public Overridable ReadOnly Property Attributes As _
   AttributeCollection
```
[C#]
```
public virtual AttributeCollection Attributes {get;}
```
[C++]
```
public: __property virtual AttributeCollection* get_Attributes();
```
[JScript]
```
public function get Attributes() : AttributeCollection;
```

Property Value

An **AttributeCollection** that provides the attributes for this member. If there are no attributes in the **AttributeArray**, the property value is an empty collection.

Remarks

If there is no **AttributeCollection** for this member, this property calls **CreateAttributeCollection** to create a new **AttributeCollection** using the array of **Attribute** objects passed to the constructor.

Requirements

Platforms: Windows 98, Windows NT 4.0,
Windows Millennium Edition, Windows 2000,
Windows XP Home Edition, Windows XP Professional,
Windows Server 2003 family

MemberDescriptor.Category Property

Gets the name of the category to which the member belongs, as specified in the **CategoryAttribute**.

[Visual Basic]
```
Public Overridable ReadOnly Property Category As String
```
[C#]
```
public virtual string Category {get;}
```
[C++]
```
public: __property virtual String* get_Category();
```
[JScript]
```
public function get Category() : String;
```

Property Value

The name of the category to which the member belongs. If there is no **CategoryAttribute**, the category name is set to the default category, **Misc**.

Remarks

A visual designer can use this property value to display members in categories.

Requirements

Platforms: Windows 98, Windows NT 4.0,
Windows Millennium Edition, Windows 2000,
Windows XP Home Edition, Windows XP Professional,
Windows Server 2003 family

MemberDescriptor.Description Property

Gets the description of the member, as specified in the **DescriptionAttribute**.

[Visual Basic]
```
Public Overridable ReadOnly Property Description As String
```
[C#]
```
public virtual string Description {get;}
```
[C++]
```
public: __property virtual String* get_Description();
```
[JScript]
```
public function get Description() : String;
```

Property Value

The description of the member. If there is no **DescriptionAttribute**, the property value is set to the default, which is an empty string ("").

Remarks

A visual designer can use this description to display information about this member.

Requirements

Platforms: Windows 98, Windows NT 4.0, Windows Millennium Edition, Windows 2000, Windows XP Home Edition, Windows XP Professional, Windows Server 2003 family

MemberDescriptor.DesignTimeOnly Property

Gets whether this member should be set only at design time, as specified in the **DesignOnlyAttribute**.

[Visual Basic]
```
Public Overridable ReadOnly Property DesignTimeOnly As Boolean
```
[C#]
```
public virtual bool DesignTimeOnly {get;}
```
[C++]
```
public: __property virtual bool get_DesignTimeOnly();
```
[JScript]
```
public function get DesignTimeOnly() : Boolean;
```

Property Value

true if this member should be set only at design time; **false** if the member can be set during run time.

Remarks

If there is no **DesignOnlyAttribute**, the return value is the default, which is **false**.

Requirements

Platforms: Windows 98, Windows NT 4.0, Windows Millennium Edition, Windows 2000, Windows XP Home Edition, Windows XP Professional, Windows Server 2003 family

MemberDescriptor.DisplayName Property

Gets the name that can be displayed in a window, such as a Properties window.

[Visual Basic]
```
Public Overridable ReadOnly Property DisplayName As String
```
[C#]
```
public virtual string DisplayName {get;}
```
[C++]
```
public: __property virtual String* get_DisplayName();
```
[JScript]
```
public function get DisplayName() : String;
```

Property Value

The name to display for the member.

Requirements

Platforms: Windows 98, Windows NT 4.0, Windows Millennium Edition, Windows 2000, Windows XP Home Edition, Windows XP Professional, Windows Server 2003 family, .NET Compact Framework - Windows CE .NET

MemberDescriptor.IsBrowsable Property

Gets a value indicating whether the member is browsable, as specified in the **BrowsableAttribute**.

[Visual Basic]
```
Public Overridable ReadOnly Property IsBrowsable As Boolean
```
[C#]
```
public virtual bool IsBrowsable {get;}
```
[C++]
```
public: __property virtual bool get_IsBrowsable();
```
[JScript]
```
public function get IsBrowsable() : Boolean;
```

Property Value

true if the member is browsable; otherwise, **false**. If there is no **BrowsableAttribute**, the property value is set to the default, which is **true**.

Remarks

A visual designer typically displays the members that are browsable in the Properties window.

Requirements

Platforms: Windows 98, Windows NT 4.0, Windows Millennium Edition, Windows 2000, Windows XP Home Edition, Windows XP Professional, Windows Server 2003 family

MemberDescriptor.Name Property

Gets the name of the member.

[Visual Basic]
```
Public Overridable ReadOnly Property Name As String
```
[C#]
```
public virtual string Name {get;}
```
[C++]
```
public: __property virtual String* get_Name();
```
[JScript]
```
public function get Name() : String;
```

Property Value

The name of the member.

Requirements

Platforms: Windows 98, Windows NT 4.0, Windows Millennium Edition, Windows 2000, Windows XP Home Edition, Windows XP Professional, Windows Server 2003 family, .NET Compact Framework - Windows CE .NET

MemberDescriptor.NameHashCode Property

Gets the hash code for the name of the member, as specified in **GetHashCode**.

[Visual Basic]
```
Protected Overridable ReadOnly Property NameHashCode As Integer
```
[C#]
```
protected virtual int NameHashCode {get;}
```
[C++]
```
protected: __property virtual int get_NameHashCode();
```
[JScript]
```
protected function get NameHashCode() : int;
```

Property Value

The hash code for the name of the member.

Requirements

Platforms: Windows 98, Windows NT 4.0, Windows Millennium Edition, Windows 2000, Windows XP Home Edition, Windows XP Professional, Windows Server 2003 family, .NET Compact Framework - Windows CE .NET

MemberDescriptor.CreateAttributeCollection Method

Creates a collection of attributes using the array of attributes passed to the constructor.

```
[Visual Basic]
Protected Overridable Function CreateAttributeCollection() As _
   AttributeCollection
[C#]
protected virtual AttributeCollection CreateAttributeCollection();
[C++]
protected: virtual AttributeCollection* CreateAttributeCollection();
[JScript]
protected function CreateAttributeCollection() :
   AttributeCollection;
```

Return Value

A new **AttributeCollection** that contains the **AttributeArray** attributes.

Remarks

This method is called from the **Attributes** property when there is no **AttributeCollection** for this member. If there are no attributes in the **AttributeArray**, this will return an empty **AttributeCollection**.

Requirements

Platforms: Windows 98, Windows NT 4.0, Windows Millennium Edition, Windows 2000, Windows XP Home Edition, Windows XP Professional, Windows Server 2003 family, .NET Compact Framework - Windows CE .NET

MemberDescriptor.Equals Method

Compares this instance to the given object to see if they are equivalent.

```
[Visual Basic]
Overrides Public Function Equals( _
   ByVal obj As Object _
) As Boolean
[C#]
public override bool Equals(
   object obj
);
[C++]
public: bool Equals(
   Object* obj
);
[JScript]
public override function Equals(
   obj : Object
) : Boolean;
```

Parameters

obj

The object to compare to the current instance.

Return Value

true if equivalent; otherwise, **false**.

Requirements

Platforms: Windows 98, Windows NT 4.0, Windows Millennium Edition, Windows 2000, Windows XP Home Edition, Windows XP Professional, Windows Server 2003 family, .NET Compact Framework - Windows CE .NET

MemberDescriptor.FillAttributes Method

When overridden in a derived class, adds the attributes of the inheriting class to the specified list of attributes in the parent class.

```
[Visual Basic]
Protected Overridable Sub FillAttributes( _
   ByVal attributeList As IList _
)
[C#]
protected virtual void FillAttributes(
   IList attributeList
);
[C++]
protected: virtual void FillAttributes(
   IList* attributeList
);
[JScript]
protected function FillAttributes(
   attributeList : IList
);
```

Parameters

attributeList

An **IList** that lists the attributes in the parent class. Initially, this is empty.

Remarks

For duplicate attributes, the last one added to the list is kept.

The **IList** with the attributes is created once. If there are duplicate attributes in the list, only the first instance is saved; all subsequent duplicate attributes are removed from the list.

Requirements

Platforms: Windows 98, Windows NT 4.0, Windows Millennium Edition, Windows 2000, Windows XP Home Edition, Windows XP Professional, Windows Server 2003 family, .NET Compact Framework - Windows CE .NET

MemberDescriptor.FindMethod Method

Finds the given method through reflection.

Overload List

Finds the given method through reflection, searching only for public methods.

Supported by the .NET Compact Framework.

[Visual Basic] **Overloads Protected Shared Function FindMethod(Type, String, Type(), Type) As MethodInfo**

[C#] **protected static MethodInfo FindMethod(Type, string, Type[], Type);**

[C++] **protected: static MethodInfo* FindMethod(Type*, String*, Type*[], Type*);**

[JScript] **protected static function FindMethod(Type, String, Type[], Type) : MethodInfo;**

Finds the given method through reflection, with an option to search only public methods.

Supported by the .NET Compact Framework.

[Visual Basic] **Overloads Protected Shared Function FindMethod(Type, String, Type(), Type, Boolean) As MethodInfo**

[C#] **protected static MethodInfo FindMethod(Type, string, Type[], Type, bool);**

[C++] **protected: static MethodInfo* FindMethod(Type*, String*, Type*[], Type*, bool);**

[JScript] **protected static function FindMethod(Type, String, Type[], Type, Boolean) : MethodInfo;**

MemberDescriptor.FindMethod Method (Type, String, Type[], Type)

Finds the given method through reflection, searching only for public methods.

```
[Visual Basic]
Overloads Protected Shared Function FindMethod( _
   ByVal componentClass As Type, _
   ByVal name As String, _
   ByVal args() As Type, _
   ByVal returnType As Type _
) As MethodInfo
[C#]
protected static MethodInfo FindMethod(
   Type componentClass,
   string name,
   Type[] args,
   Type returnType
);
[C++]
protected: static MethodInfo* FindMethod(
   Type* componentClass,
   String* name,
   Type* args[],
   Type* returnType
);
[JScript]
protected static function FindMethod(
   componentClass : Type,
   name : String,
   args : Type[],
   returnType : Type
) : MethodInfo;
```

Parameters

componentClass
: The component that contains the method.

name
: The name of the method to find.

args
: An array of parameters for the method, used to choose between overloaded methods.

returnType
: The type to return for the method.

Return Value

A **MethodInfo** that represents the method. If the method is not found, a null reference (**Nothing** in Visual Basic) is returned.

Requirements

Platforms: Windows 98, Windows NT 4.0, Windows Millennium Edition, Windows 2000, Windows XP Home Edition, Windows XP Professional, Windows Server 2003 family, .NET Compact Framework - Windows CE .NET

MemberDescriptor.FindMethod Method (Type, String, Type[], Type, Boolean)

Finds the given method through reflection, with an option to search only public methods.

```
[Visual Basic]
Overloads Protected Shared Function FindMethod( _
   ByVal componentClass As Type, _
   ByVal name As String, _
   ByVal args() As Type, _
   ByVal returnType As Type, _
   ByVal publicOnly As Boolean _
) As MethodInfo
[C#]
protected static MethodInfo FindMethod(
   Type componentClass,
   string name,
   Type[] args,
   Type returnType,
   bool publicOnly
);
[C++]
protected: static MethodInfo* FindMethod(
   Type* componentClass,
   String* name,
   Type* args[],
   Type* returnType,
   bool publicOnly
);
[JScript]
protected static function FindMethod(
   componentClass : Type,
   name : String,
   args : Type[],
   returnType : Type,
   publicOnly : Boolean
) : MethodInfo;
```

Parameters

componentClass
The component that contains the method.

name
The name of the method to find.

args
An array of parameters for the method, used to choose between overloaded methods.

returnType
The type to return for the method.

publicOnly
Whether to restrict search to public methods.

Return Value

A **MethodInfo** that represents the method. If the method is not found, a null reference (**Nothing** in Visual Basic) is returned.

Requirements

Platforms: Windows 98, Windows NT 4.0, Windows Millennium Edition, Windows 2000, Windows XP Home Edition, Windows XP Professional, Windows Server 2003 family, .NET Compact Framework - Windows CE .NET

MemberDescriptor.GetHashCode Method

This member overrides **Object.GetHashCode**.

```
[Visual Basic]
Overrides Public Function GetHashCode() As Integer
[C#]
public override int GetHashCode();
[C++]
public: int GetHashCode();
[JScript]
public override function GetHashCode() : int;
```

Requirements

Platforms: Windows 98, Windows NT 4.0, Windows Millennium Edition, Windows 2000, Windows XP Home Edition, Windows XP Professional, Windows Server 2003 family, .NET Compact Framework - Windows CE .NET

MemberDescriptor.GetInvokee Method

Gets the component on which to invoke a method.

```
[Visual Basic]
Protected Shared Function GetInvokee( _
   ByVal componentClass As Type, _
   ByVal component As Object _
) As Object
[C#]
protected static object GetInvokee(
   Type componentClass,
   object component
);
[C++]
protected: static Object* GetInvokee(
   Type* componentClass,
   Object* component
);
[JScript]
protected static function GetInvokee(
   componentClass : Type,
   component : Object
) : Object;
```

Parameters

componentClass
A **Type** representing the type of component this **MemberDescriptor** is bound to. For example, if this **MemberDescriptor** describes a property, this parameter should be the class that the property is declared on.

component
An instance of the object to call.

Return Value

An instance of the component to invoke. This method returns a visual designer when the property is attached to a visual designer.

Requirements

Platforms: Windows 98, Windows NT 4.0, Windows Millennium Edition, Windows 2000, Windows XP Home Edition, Windows XP Professional, Windows Server 2003 family

MemberDescriptor.GetSite Method

Gets a component site for the given component.

```
[Visual Basic]
Protected Shared Function GetSite( _
   ByVal component As Object _
) As ISite
[C#]
protected static ISite GetSite(
   object component
);
[C++]
protected: static ISite* GetSite(
   Object* component
);
[JScript]
protected static function GetSite(
   component : Object
) : ISite;
```

Parameters

component
The component for which you want to find a site.

Return Value

The site of the component, or a null reference (**Nothing** in Visual Basic) if a site does not exist.

Requirements

Platforms: Windows 98, Windows NT 4.0, Windows Millennium Edition, Windows 2000, Windows XP Home Edition, Windows XP Professional, Windows Server 2003 family

MergablePropertyAttribute Class

Specifies that this property can be combined with properties belonging to other objects in a Properties window.

System.Object
System.Attribute
System.ComponentModel.MergablePropertyAttribute

[Visual Basic]
```
<AttributeUsage(AttributeTargets.All)>
NotInheritable Public Class MergablePropertyAttribute
   Inherits Attribute
```
[C#]
```
[AttributeUsage(AttributeTargets.All)]
public sealed class MergablePropertyAttribute : Attribute
```
[C++]
```
[AttributeUsage(AttributeTargets::All)]
public __gc __sealed class MergablePropertyAttribute : public
   Attribute
```
[JScript]
```
public
   AttributeUsage(AttributeTargets.All)
class MergablePropertyAttribute extends Attribute
```

Thread Safety

Any public static (**Shared** in Visual Basic) members of this type are safe for multithreaded operations. Any instance members are not guaranteed to be thread safe.

Remarks

Properties that are marked with the **MergablePropertyAttribute** constructor of the value **true** can be combined with properties belonging to other objects in a Properties window. Properties that are marked with the **MergablePropertyAttribute** constructor of the value **false** must be displayed separately. The default is **true**.

> **Note** When you mark a property with the **MergablePropertyAttribute** constructor of the value **true**, the value of this attribute is set to the constant member **Yes**. For a property marked with the **MergablePropertyAttribute** constructor of the value **false**, the value is **No**. Therefore, when you want to check the value of this attribute in your code, you must specify the attribute as **MergablePropertyAttribute.Yes** or **MergablePropertyAttribute.No**.

Example

[Visual Basic, C#, JScript] The following example marks a property as appropriate to merge.

[Visual Basic]
```
<MergableProperty(True)> _
Public Property MyProperty() As Integer
    Get
        ' Insert code here.
        Return 0
    End Get
    Set
        ' Insert code here.
    End Set
End Property
```

[C#]
```
[MergableProperty(true)]
 public int MyProperty {
    get {
       // Insert code here.
       return 0;
    }
    set {
       // Insert code here.
    }
 }
```

[JScript]
```
public MergableProperty(true)
function get MyProperty() : int{
  // Insert code here.
  return 0
}

function set MyProperty(value : int){
  // Insert code here.
}
```

[Visual Basic, C#, JScript] The next example shows how to check the value of the **MergablePropertyAttribute** for `MyProperty`. First the code gets a **PropertyDescriptorCollection** with all the properties for the object. Next it indexes into the **PropertyDescriptorCollection** to get `MyProperty`. Then it returns the attributes for this property and saves them in the attributes variable.

[Visual Basic, C#, JScript] The example presents two different ways of checking the value of the **MergablePropertyAttribute**. In the second code fragment, the example calls the **Equals** method with a static (**Shared** in Visual Basic) value. In the last code fragment, the example uses the **AllowMerge** property to check the value.

[Visual Basic]
```
' Gets the attributes for the property.
Dim attributes As AttributeCollection = _
   TypeDescriptor.GetProperties(Me)("MyProperty").Attributes

' Checks to see if the value of the MergablePropertyAttribute is Yes.
If
attributes(GetType(MergablePropertyAttribute)).Equals(MergablePropertyAt
tribute.Yes) Then
    ' Insert code here.
End If

' This is another way to see if the property is bindable.
Dim myAttribute As MergablePropertyAttribute = _
    CType(attributes(GetType(MergablePropertyAttribute)),               ↵
MergablePropertyAttribute)
If myAttribute.AllowMerge Then
    ' Insert code here.
End If
```

[C#]
```
// Gets the attributes for the property.
 AttributeCollection attributes =
    TypeDescriptor.GetProperties(this)["MyProperty"].Attributes;

 // Checks to see if the value of the MergablePropertyAttribute is Yes.
 if(attributes[typeof(MergablePropertyAttribute)].Equals                ↵
(MergablePropertyAttribute.Yes)) {
    // Insert code here.
 }

 // This is another way to see if the property is bindable.
 MergablePropertyAttribute myAttribute =
    (MergablePropertyAttribute)attributes[typeof                        ↵
(MergablePropertyAttribute)];
 if(myAttribute.AllowMerge) {
    // Insert code here.
 }
```

[JScript]
```
// Gets the attributes for the property.
var attributes : AttributeCollection =
TypeDescriptor.GetProperties(this)["MyProperty"].Attributes

// Checks to see if the value of the MergablePropertyAttribute is Yes.
if(attributes(MergablePropertyAttribute).Equals
 (MergablePropertyAttribute.Yes)){
  // Insert code here.
}

// This is another way to see if the property is bindable.
var myAttribute : MergablePropertyAttribute =
MergablePropertyAttribute(attributes(MergablePropertyAttribute))
if(myAttribute.AllowMerge){
  // Insert code here.
}
```

[Visual Basic, C#, JScript] If you marked a class with the **MergablePropertyAttribute**, use the following code to check the value.

[Visual Basic]
```
Dim attributes As AttributeCollection =
TypeDescriptor.GetAttributes(MyProperty)
If attributes(GetType(MergablePropertyAttribute)).Equals
 (MergablePropertyAttribute.Yes) Then
    ' Insert code here.
End If
```

[C#]
```
AttributeCollection attributes =
    TypeDescriptor.GetAttributes(MyProperty);
 if(attributes[typeof(MergablePropertyAttribute)].Equals
 (MergablePropertyAttribute.Yes)) {
    // Insert code here.
 }
```

[JScript]
```
var attributes : AttributeCollection =
TypeDescriptor.GetAttributes(MyProperty)
if(attributes(MergablePropertyAttribute).Equals
 (MergablePropertyAttribute.Yes)){
    // Insert code here.
}
```

Requirements

Namespace: System.ComponentModel

Platforms: Windows 98, Windows NT 4.0, Windows Millennium Edition, Windows 2000, Windows XP Home Edition, Windows XP Professional, Windows Server 2003 family

Assembly: System (in System.dll)

MergablePropertyAttribute Constructor

Initializes a new instance of the **MergablePropertyAttribute** class.

[Visual Basic]
```
Public Sub New( _
   ByVal allowMerge As Boolean _
)
```
[C#]
```
public MergablePropertyAttribute(
   bool allowMerge
);
```
[C++]
```
public: MergablePropertyAttribute(
   bool allowMerge
);
```
[JScript]
```
public function MergablePropertyAttribute(
   allowMerge : Boolean
);
```

Parameters

allowMerge

true if this property can be combined with properties belonging to other objects in a Properties window; otherwise, **false**.

Example

[Visual Basic, C#, JScript] The following example marks a property as appropriate to merge. This code creates a new **MergablePropertyAttribute**, sets its value to **MergablePropertyAttribute.Yes**, and binds it to the property.

[Visual Basic]
```
<MergableProperty(True)> _
Public Property MyProperty() As Integer
    Get
        ' Insert code here.
        Return 0
    End Get
    Set
        ' Insert code here.
    End Set
End Property
```

[C#]
```
 [MergableProperty(true)]
 public int MyProperty {
    get {
       // Insert code here.
      return 0;
    }
    set {
       // Insert code here.
    }
 }
```

[JScript]
```
public MergableProperty(true)
function get MyProperty() : int{
   // Insert code here.
   return 0
}

function set MyProperty(value : int){
   // Insert code here.
}
```

Requirements

Platforms: Windows 98, Windows NT 4.0, Windows Millennium Edition, Windows 2000, Windows XP Home Edition, Windows XP Professional, Windows Server 2003 family

MergablePropertyAttribute.Default Field

This member supports the .NET Framework infrastructure and is not intended to be used directly from your code.

[Visual Basic]
```
Public Shared ReadOnly Default As MergablePropertyAttribute
```
[C#]
```
public static readonly MergablePropertyAttribute Default;
```

```
[C++]
public: static MergablePropertyAttribute* Default;
[JScript]
public static var Default : MergablePropertyAttribute;
```

MergablePropertyAttribute.No Field

Specifies that a property cannot be combined with properties belonging to other objects in a Properties window. This static (**Shared** in Visual Basic) field is read-only.

```
[Visual Basic]
Public Shared ReadOnly No As MergablePropertyAttribute
[C#]
public static readonly MergablePropertyAttribute No;
[C++]
public: static MergablePropertyAttribute* No;
[JScript]
public static var No : MergablePropertyAttribute;
```

Remarks

When you mark a property with the **MergablePropertyAttribute** constructor of the value **false**, the value of this attribute is set to the constant member **No**. Therefore, when you want to check whether the attribute is set to this value in your code, you must specify the attribute as **MergablePropertyAttribute.No**.

Requirements

Platforms: Windows 98, Windows NT 4.0, Windows Millennium Edition, Windows 2000, Windows XP Home Edition, Windows XP Professional, Windows Server 2003 family

MergablePropertyAttribute.Yes Field

Specifies that a property can be combined with properties belonging to other objects in a Properties window. This static (**Shared** in Visual Basic) field is read-only.

```
[Visual Basic]
Public Shared ReadOnly Yes As MergablePropertyAttribute
[C#]
public static readonly MergablePropertyAttribute Yes;
[C++]
public: static MergablePropertyAttribute* Yes;
[JScript]
public static var Yes : MergablePropertyAttribute;
```

Remarks

This field is the default setting for this attribute.

When you mark a property with the **MergablePropertyAttribute** constructor of the value **true**, the value of this attribute is set to the constant member **Yes**. Therefore, when you want to check whether the attribute is set to this value in your code, you must specify the attribute as **MergablePropertyAttribute.Yes**.

Requirements

Platforms: Windows 98, Windows NT 4.0, Windows Millennium Edition, Windows 2000, Windows XP Home Edition, Windows XP Professional, Windows Server 2003 family

MergablePropertyAttribute.AllowMerge Property

Gets a value indicating whether this property can be combined with properties belonging to other objects in a Properties window.

```
[Visual Basic]
Public ReadOnly Property AllowMerge As Boolean
[C#]
public bool AllowMerge {get;}
[C++]
public: __property bool get_AllowMerge();
[JScript]
public function get AllowMerge() : Boolean;
```

Property Value

true if this property can be combined with properties belonging to other objects in a Properties window; otherwise, **false**.

Example

[Visual Basic, C#, JScript] The following example checks to see whether `MyProperty` is appropriate to merge. First the code gets the attributes for `MyProperty` by:

- Retrieving a **PropertyDescriptorCollection** with all the properties for the object.
- Indexing into the **PropertyDescriptorCollection** to get `MyProperty`.
- Saving the attributes for this property in the attributes variable.

[Visual Basic, C#, JScript] Then the code sets `myAttribute` to the value of the **MergablePropertyAttribute** in the **AttributeCollection** and checks whether the property is appropriate to merge.

```
[Visual Basic]
' Gets the attributes for the property.
Dim attributes As AttributeCollection = _
   TypeDescriptor.GetProperties(Me)("MyPropertyProperty").Attributes

' Checks to see if the property is bindable.
Dim myAttribute As MergablePropertyAttribute = _
   CType(attributes(GetType(MergablePropertyAttribute)), _
   MergablePropertyAttribute)
If myAttribute.AllowMerge Then
    ' Insert code here.
End If
```

```
[C#]
// Gets the attributes for the property.
AttributeCollection attributes =
   TypeDescriptor.GetProperties(this)["MyPropertyProperty"].Attributes;

// Checks to see if the property is bindable.
MergablePropertyAttribute myAttribute =                    ↵
 (MergablePropertyAttribute)attributes[typeof              ↵
 (MergablePropertyAttribute)];
if(myAttribute.AllowMerge) {
   // Insert code here.
}
```

```
[JScript]
// Gets the attributes for the property.
var attributes : AttributeCollection =                     ↵
TypeDescriptor.GetProperties(this)["MyPropertyProperty"].Attributes

// Checks to see if the property is bindable.
var myAttribute : MergablePropertyAttribute =              ↵
MergablePropertyAttribute(attributes(MergablePropertyAttribute))
if(myAttribute.AllowMerge){
  // Insert code here.
}
```

Requirements

Platforms: Windows 98, Windows NT 4.0, Windows Millennium Edition, Windows 2000, Windows XP Home Edition, Windows XP Professional, Windows Server 2003 family

MergablePropertyAttribute.Equals Method

This member overrides **Object.Equals**.

```
[Visual Basic]
Overrides Public Function Equals( _
   ByVal obj As Object _
) As Boolean
[C#]
public override bool Equals(
   object obj
);
[C++]
public: bool Equals(
   Object* obj
);
[JScript]
public override function Equals(
   obj : Object
) : Boolean;
```

Requirements

Platforms: Windows 98, Windows NT 4.0, Windows Millennium Edition, Windows 2000, Windows XP Home Edition, Windows XP Professional, Windows Server 2003 family

MergablePropertyAttribute.GetHashCode Method

This member overrides **Attribute.GetHashCode**.

```
[Visual Basic]
Overrides Public Function GetHashCode() As Integer
[C#]
public override int GetHashCode();
[C++]
public: int GetHashCode();
[JScript]
public override function GetHashCode() : int;
```

Requirements

Platforms: Windows 98, Windows NT 4.0, Windows Millennium Edition, Windows 2000, Windows XP Home Edition, Windows XP Professional, Windows Server 2003 family

MergablePropertyAttribute.IsDefaultAttribute Method

This member overrides **Attribute.IsDefaultAttribute**.

```
[Visual Basic]
Overrides Public Function IsDefaultAttribute() As Boolean
[C#]
public override bool IsDefaultAttribute();
[C++]
public: bool IsDefaultAttribute();
[JScript]
public override function IsDefaultAttribute() : Boolean;
```

Requirements

Platforms: Windows 98, Windows NT 4.0, Windows Millennium Edition, Windows 2000, Windows XP Home Edition, Windows XP Professional, Windows Server 2003 family

NotifyParentPropertyAttribute Class

Indicates that the parent property is notified when the value of the property that this attribute is applied to is modified. This class cannot be inherited.

System.Object
  System.Attribute
    System.ComponentModel.NotifyParentPropertyAttribute

```
[Visual Basic]
<AttributeUsage(AttributeTargets.Property)>
NotInheritable Public Class NotifyParentPropertyAttribute
   Inherits Attribute
[C#]
[AttributeUsage(AttributeTargets.Property)]
public sealed class NotifyParentPropertyAttribute : Attribute
[C++]
[AttributeUsage(AttributeTargets::Property)]
public __gc __sealed class NotifyParentPropertyAttribute : public
   Attribute
[JScript]
public
   AttributeUsage(AttributeTargets.Property)
class NotifyParentPropertyAttribute extends Attribute
```

Thread Safety

Any public static (**Shared** in Visual Basic) members of this type are safe for multithreaded operations. Any instance members are not guaranteed to be thread safe.

Remarks

Apply **NotifyParentPropertyAttribute** to a property if its parent property should receive notification of changes to the property's values. For example, the **Size** property has two nested properties: height and width. These nested properties should be marked with **NotifyParentPropertyAttribute(true)** so they notify the parent property to update its value and display when the property values change.

Requirements

Namespace: System.ComponentModel

Platforms: Windows 98, Windows NT 4.0, Windows Millennium Edition, Windows 2000, Windows XP Home Edition, Windows XP Professional, Windows Server 2003 family

Assembly: System (in System.dll)

NotifyParentPropertyAttribute Constructor

Initializes a new instance of the **NotifyParentPropertyAttribute** class, using the specified value to determine whether the parent property is notified of changes to the value of the property.

```
[Visual Basic]
Public Sub New( _
   ByVal notifyParent As Boolean _
)
[C#]
public NotifyParentPropertyAttribute(
   bool notifyParent
);
[C++]
public: NotifyParentPropertyAttribute(
   bool notifyParent
);
[JScript]
public function NotifyParentPropertyAttribute(
   notifyParent : Boolean
);
```

Parameters

notifyParent
  true if the parent should be notified of changes; otherwise, **false**.

Requirements

Platforms: Windows 98, Windows NT 4.0, Windows Millennium Edition, Windows 2000, Windows XP Home Edition, Windows XP Professional, Windows Server 2003 family

NotifyParentPropertyAttribute.Default Field

Indicates the default attribute state, that the property should not notify the parent property of changes to its value. This field is read-only.

```
[Visual Basic]
Public Shared ReadOnly Default As NotifyParentPropertyAttribute
[C#]
public static readonly NotifyParentPropertyAttribute Default;
[C++]
public: static NotifyParentPropertyAttribute* Default;
[JScript]
public static var Default : NotifyParentPropertyAttribute;
```

Requirements

Platforms: Windows 98, Windows NT 4.0, Windows Millennium Edition, Windows 2000, Windows XP Home Edition, Windows XP Professional, Windows Server 2003 family

NotifyParentPropertyAttribute.No Field

Indicates that the parent property is not be notified of changes to the value of the property. This field is read-only.

```
[Visual Basic]
Public Shared ReadOnly No As NotifyParentPropertyAttribute
[C#]
public static readonly NotifyParentPropertyAttribute No;
[C++]
public: static NotifyParentPropertyAttribute* No;
[JScript]
public static var No : NotifyParentPropertyAttribute;
```

Requirements

Platforms: Windows 98, Windows NT 4.0, Windows Millennium Edition, Windows 2000, Windows XP Home Edition, Windows XP Professional, Windows Server 2003 family

NotifyParentPropertyAttribute.Yes Field

Indicates that the parent property is notified of changes to the value of the property. This field is read-only.

```
[Visual Basic]
Public Shared ReadOnly Yes As NotifyParentPropertyAttribute
[C#]
public static readonly NotifyParentPropertyAttribute Yes;
[C++]
public: static NotifyParentPropertyAttribute* Yes;
[JScript]
public static var Yes : NotifyParentPropertyAttribute;
```

Requirements

Platforms: Windows 98, Windows NT 4.0, Windows Millennium Edition, Windows 2000, Windows XP Home Edition, Windows XP Professional, Windows Server 2003 family

NotifyParentPropertyAttribute.NotifyParent Property

Gets or sets a value indicating whether the parent property should be notified of changes to the value of the property.

```
[Visual Basic]
Public ReadOnly Property NotifyParent As Boolean
[C#]
public bool NotifyParent {get;}
[C++]
public: __property bool get_NotifyParent();
[JScript]
public function get NotifyParent() : Boolean;
```

Property Value

true if the parent property should be notified of changes; otherwise, **false**.

Requirements

Platforms: Windows 98, Windows NT 4.0, Windows Millennium Edition, Windows 2000, Windows XP Home Edition, Windows XP Professional, Windows Server 2003 family

NotifyParentPropertyAttribute.Equals Method

Gets a value indicating whether the specified object is the same as the current object.

```
[Visual Basic]
Overrides Public Function Equals( _
   ByVal obj As Object _
) As Boolean
[C#]
public override bool Equals(
   object obj
);
[C++]
public: bool Equals(
   Object* obj
);
[JScript]
public override function Equals(
   obj : Object
) : Boolean;
```

Parameters

obj

The object to test for equality.

Return Value

true if the object is the same as this object; otherwise, **false**.

Requirements

Platforms: Windows 98, Windows NT 4.0, Windows Millennium Edition, Windows 2000, Windows XP Home Edition, Windows XP Professional, Windows Server 2003 family

NotifyParentPropertyAttribute.GetHashCode Method

Gets the hash code for this object.

```
[Visual Basic]
Overrides Public Function GetHashCode() As Integer
[C#]
public override int GetHashCode();
[C++]
public: int GetHashCode();
[JScript]
public override function GetHashCode() : int;
```

Return Value

The hash code for the object the attribute belongs to.

Requirements

Platforms: Windows 98, Windows NT 4.0, Windows Millennium Edition, Windows 2000, Windows XP Home Edition, Windows XP Professional, Windows Server 2003 family

NotifyParentPropertyAttribute.IsDefaultAttribute Method

Gets a value indicating whether the current value of the attribute is the default value for the attribute.

```
[Visual Basic]
Overrides Public Function IsDefaultAttribute() As Boolean
[C#]
public override bool IsDefaultAttribute();
[C++]
public: bool IsDefaultAttribute();
[JScript]
public override function IsDefaultAttribute() : Boolean;
```

Return Value

true if the current value of the attribute is the default value of the attribute; otherwise, **false**.

Requirements

Platforms: Windows 98, Windows NT 4.0, Windows Millennium Edition, Windows 2000, Windows XP Home Edition, Windows XP Professional, Windows Server 2003 family

ParenthesizePropertyName-Attribute Class

Indicates whether the name of the associated property is displayed with parentheses in the Properties window. This class cannot be inherited.

System.Object
  System.Attribute
    System.ComponentModel.ParenthesizePropertyName-Attribute

```
[Visual Basic]
<AttributeUsage(AttributeTargets.All)>
NotInheritable Public Class ParenthesizePropertyNameAttribute
   Inherits Attribute
[C#]
[AttributeUsage(AttributeTargets.All)]
public sealed class ParenthesizePropertyNameAttribute : Attribute
[C++]
[AttributeUsage(AttributeTargets::All)]
public __gc __sealed class ParenthesizePropertyNameAttribute :
   public Attribute
[JScript]
public
   AttributeUsage(AttributeTargets.All)
class ParenthesizePropertyNameAttribute extends Attribute
```

Thread Safety

Any public static (**Shared** in Visual Basic) members of this type are safe for multithreaded operations. Any instance members are not guaranteed to be thread safe.

Remarks

A **ParenthesizePropertyNameAttribute** with a **NeedParenthesis** value of **true** indicates to the Properties window that the associated property should be displayed with parentheses around its name. The Properties window displays a property with parentheses around its name near the top of the list in alphabetical mode, or near the top of its category if the Properties window is in categorize mode.

Requirements

Namespace: System.ComponentModel

Platforms: Windows 98, Windows NT 4.0, Windows Millennium Edition, Windows 2000, Windows XP Home Edition, Windows XP Professional, Windows Server 2003 family

Assembly: System (in System.dll)

ParenthesizePropertyNameAttribute Constructor

Initializes a new instance of the **ParenthesizeProperty-NameAttribute** class that indicates that the associated property should not be shown with parentheses.

Overload List

Initializes a new instance of the **ParenthesizePropertyNameAttribute** class that indicates that the associated property should not be shown with parentheses.

[Visual Basic] **Public Sub New()**

[C#] **public ParenthesizePropertyNameAttribute();**

[C++] **public: ParenthesizePropertyNameAttribute();**

[JScript] **public function ParenthesizePropertyName-Attribute();**

Initializes a new instance of the **ParenthesizePropertyNameAttribute** class, using the specified value to indicate whether the attribute is displayed with parentheses.

[Visual Basic] **Public Sub New(Boolean)**

[C#] **public ParenthesizePropertyNameAttribute(bool);**

[C++] **public: ParenthesizePropertyNameAttribute(bool);**

[JScript] **public function ParenthesizePropertyName-Attribute(Boolean);**

ParenthesizePropertyNameAttribute Constructor ()

Initializes a new instance of the **ParenthesizePropertyName-Attribute** class that indicates that the associated property should not be shown with parentheses.

```
[Visual Basic]
Public Sub New()
[C#]
public ParenthesizePropertyNameAttribute();
[C++]
public: ParenthesizePropertyNameAttribute();
[JScript]
public function ParenthesizePropertyNameAttribute();
```

Requirements

Platforms: Windows 98, Windows NT 4.0, Windows Millennium Edition, Windows 2000, Windows XP Home Edition, Windows XP Professional, Windows Server 2003 family

ParenthesizePropertyNameAttribute Constructor (Boolean)

Initializes a new instance of the **ParenthesizePropertyName-Attribute** class, using the specified value to indicate whether the attribute is displayed with parentheses.

```
[Visual Basic]
Public Sub New( _
   ByVal needParenthesis As Boolean _
)
[C#]
public ParenthesizePropertyNameAttribute(
   bool needParenthesis
);
[C++]
public: ParenthesizePropertyNameAttribute(
   bool needParenthesis
);
[JScript]
public function ParenthesizePropertyNameAttribute(
   needParenthesis : Boolean
);
```

Parameters

needParenthesis

true if the name should be enclosed in parentheses; otherwise, **false**.

Requirements

Platforms: Windows 98, Windows NT 4.0, Windows Millennium Edition, Windows 2000, Windows XP Home Edition, Windows XP Professional, Windows Server 2003 family

ParenthesizePropertyNameAttribute.Default Field

Initializes a new instance of the **ParenthesizePropertyNameAttribute** class with a default value that indicates that the associated property should not be shown with parentheses. This field is read-only.

```
[Visual Basic]
Public Shared ReadOnly Default As ParenthesizePropertyNameAttribute
[C#]
public static readonly ParenthesizePropertyNameAttribute Default;
[C++]
public: static ParenthesizePropertyNameAttribute* Default;
[JScript]
public static var Default : ParenthesizePropertyNameAttribute;
```

Requirements

Platforms: Windows 98, Windows NT 4.0, Windows Millennium Edition, Windows 2000, Windows XP Home Edition, Windows XP Professional, Windows Server 2003 family

ParenthesizePropertyNameAttribute.NeedParenthesis Property

Gets a value indicating whether the Properties window displays the name of the property in parentheses in the Properties window.

```
[Visual Basic]
Public ReadOnly Property NeedParenthesis As Boolean
[C#]
public bool NeedParenthesis {get;}
[C++]
public: __property bool get_NeedParenthesis();
[JScript]
public function get NeedParenthesis() : Boolean;
```

Property Value

true if the property is displayed with parentheses; otherwise, **false**.

Requirements

Platforms: Windows 98, Windows NT 4.0, Windows Millennium Edition, Windows 2000, Windows XP Home Edition, Windows XP Professional, Windows Server 2003 family

ParenthesizePropertyNameAttribute.Equals Method

This member overrides **Object.Equals**.

```
[Visual Basic]
Overrides Public Function Equals( _
   ByVal o As Object _
) As Boolean
[C#]
public override bool Equals(
   object o
);
[C++]
public: bool Equals(
   Object* o
);
[JScript]
public override function Equals(
   o : Object
) : Boolean;
```

Requirements

Platforms: Windows 98, Windows NT 4.0, Windows Millennium Edition, Windows 2000, Windows XP Home Edition, Windows XP Professional, Windows Server 2003 family

ParenthesizePropertyNameAttribute.GetHashCode Method

This member overrides **Attribute.GetHashCode**.

```
[Visual Basic]
Overrides Public Function GetHashCode() As Integer
[C#]
public override int GetHashCode();
[C++]
public: int GetHashCode();
[JScript]
public override function GetHashCode() : int;
```

Requirements

Platforms: Windows 98, Windows NT 4.0, Windows Millennium Edition, Windows 2000, Windows XP Home Edition, Windows XP Professional, Windows Server 2003 family

ParenthesizePropertyNameAttribute.IsDefaultAttribute Method

Gets a value indicating whether the current value of the attribute is the default value for the attribute.

```
[Visual Basic]
Overrides Public Function IsDefaultAttribute() As Boolean
[C#]
public override bool IsDefaultAttribute();
[C++]
public: bool IsDefaultAttribute();
[JScript]
public override function IsDefaultAttribute() : Boolean;
```

Return Value

true if the current value of the attribute is the default value of the attribute; otherwise, **false**.

Requirements

Platforms: Windows 98, Windows NT 4.0, Windows Millennium Edition, Windows 2000, Windows XP Home Edition, Windows XP Professional, Windows Server 2003 family

PropertyChangedEventArgs Class

Provides data for the **PropertyChanged** event.

System.Object
  System.EventArgs
    System.ComponentModel.PropertyChangedEventArgs

[Visual Basic]
```
Public Class PropertyChangedEventArgs
   Inherits EventArgs
```
[C#]
```
public class PropertyChangedEventArgs : EventArgs
```
[C++]
```
public __gc class PropertyChangedEventArgs : public EventArgs
```
[JScript]
```
public class PropertyChangedEventArgs extends EventArgs
```

Thread Safety

Any public static (**Shared** in Visual Basic) members of this type are safe for multithreaded operations. Any instance members are not guaranteed to be thread safe.

Remarks

A **PropertyChanged** event is raised when a property is changed on a component. A **PropertyChangedEventArgs** object specifies the name of the property that changed.

PropertyChangedEventArgs provides the **PropertyName** property to get the name of the property that changed.

Requirements

Namespace: System.ComponentModel

Platforms: Windows 98, Windows NT 4.0, Windows Millennium Edition, Windows 2000, Windows XP Home Edition, Windows XP Professional, Windows Server 2003 family, .NET Compact Framework - Windows CE .NET

Assembly: System (in System.dll)

PropertyChangedEventArgs Constructor

Initializes a new instance of the **PropertyChangedEventArgs** class.

[Visual Basic]
```
Public Sub New( _
   ByVal propertyName As String _
)
```
[C#]
```
public PropertyChangedEventArgs(
   string propertyName
);
```
[C++]
```
public: PropertyChangedEventArgs(
   String* propertyName
);
```
[JScript]
```
public function PropertyChangedEventArgs(
   propertyName : String
);
```

Parameters

propertyName
  The name of the property that changed.

Requirements

Platforms: Windows 98, Windows NT 4.0, Windows Millennium Edition, Windows 2000, Windows XP Home Edition, Windows XP Professional, Windows Server 2003 family, .NET Compact Framework - Windows CE .NET

PropertyChangedEventArgs.PropertyName Property

Gets the name of the property that changed.

[Visual Basic]
```
Public Overridable ReadOnly Property PropertyName As String
```
[C#]
```
public virtual string PropertyName {get;}
```
[C++]
```
public: __property virtual String* get_PropertyName();
```
[JScript]
```
public function get PropertyName() : String;
```

Property Value

The name of the property that changed.

Requirements

Platforms: Windows 98, Windows NT 4.0, Windows Millennium Edition, Windows 2000, Windows XP Home Edition, Windows XP Professional, Windows Server 2003 family, .NET Compact Framework - Windows CE .NET

PropertyChangedEventHandler Delegate

Represents the method that will handle the **PropertyChanged** event raised when a property is changed on a component.

[Visual Basic]
```
<Serializable>
Public Delegate Sub PropertyChangedEventHandler( _
   ByVal sender As Object, _
   ByVal e As PropertyChangedEventArgs _
)
```
[C#]
```
[Serializable]
public delegate void PropertyChangedEventHandler(
   object sender,
   PropertyChangedEventArgs e
);
```
[C++]
```
[Serializable]
public __gc __delegate void PropertyChangedEventHandler(
   Object* sender,
   PropertyChangedEventArgs* e
);
```

[JScript] In JScript, you can use the delegates in the .NET Framework, but you cannot define your own.

Parameters [Visual Basic, C#, C++]

The declaration of your event handler must have the same parameters as the **PropertyChangedEventHandler** delegate declaration.

sender
: The source of the event.

e
: A **PropertyChangedEventArgs** that contains the event data.

Remarks

When you create a **PropertyChangedEventHandler** delegate, you identify the method that will handle the event. To associate the event with your event handler, add an instance of the delegate to the event. The event-handler method is called whenever the event occurs, unless you remove the delegate.

Requirements

Namespace: System.ComponentModel

Platforms: Windows 98, Windows NT 4.0, Windows Millennium Edition, Windows 2000, Windows XP Home Edition, Windows XP Professional, Windows Server 2003 family, .NET Compact Framework - Windows CE .NET

Assembly: System (in System.dll)

PropertyDescriptor Class

Provides an abstraction of a property on a class.

System.Object
  System.ComponentModel.MemberDescriptor
    System.ComponentModel.PropertyDescriptor
      System.ComponentModel.TypeConverter.SimpleProperty-Descriptor

[Visual Basic]
```
<ComVisible(True)>
MustInherit Public Class PropertyDescriptor
   Inherits MemberDescriptor
```
[C#]
```
[ComVisible(true)]
public abstract class PropertyDescriptor : MemberDescriptor
```
[C++]
```
[ComVisible(true)]
public __gc __abstract class PropertyDescriptor : public
   MemberDescriptor
```
[JScript]
```
public
   ComVisible(true)
abstract class PropertyDescriptor extends MemberDescriptor
```

Thread Safety

Any public static (**Shared** in Visual Basic) members of this type are safe for multithreaded operations. Any instance members are not guaranteed to be thread safe.

Remarks

A description of a property consists of a name, its attributes, the component class that the property is associated with, and the type of the property.

PropertyDescriptor provides the following properties and methods:

- **Converter** contains the **TypeConverter** for this property.
- **IsLocalizable** indicates whether this property should be localized.
- **GetEditor** returns an editor of the specified type.

PropertyDescriptor also provides the following abstract (**MustOverride** in Visual Basic) properties and methods:

- **ComponentType** contains the type of component this property is bound to.
- **IsReadOnly** indicates whether this property is read-only.
- **PropertyType** gets the type of the property.
- **CanResetValue** indicates whether resetting the component changes the value of the component.
- **GetValue** returns the current value of the property on a component.
- **ResetValue** resets the value for this property of the component.
- **SetValue** sets the value of the component to a different value.
- **ShouldSerializeValue** indicates whether the value of this property needs to be persisted.

Typically, the abstract (**MustOverride** in Visual Basic) members are implemented through reflection. For more information about reflection, see **Discovering Type Information at Run Time**.

Example

[Visual Basic, C#] The following example is built upon the example in the **PropertyDescriptorCollection** class. It prints the information (category, description, display name) of the Text of a button in a text box. It assumes that `button1` and `textbox1` have been instantiated on a form.

[Visual Basic]
```
' Creates a new collection and assign it the properties for button1.
Dim properties As PropertyDescriptorCollection =                      ↵
TypeDescriptor.GetProperties(Button1)

' Sets an PropertyDescriptor to the specific property.
Dim myProperty As PropertyDescriptor = properties.Find("Text", False)

' Prints the property and the property description.
TextBox1.Text += myProperty.DisplayName &                             ↵
Microsoft.VisualBasic.ControlChars.Cr
TextBox1.Text += myProperty.Description &                             ↵
Microsoft.VisualBasic.ControlChars.Cr
TextBox1.Text += myProperty.Category &
Microsoft.VisualBasic.ControlChars.Cr
```

[C#]
```
// Creates a new collection and assign it the properties for button1.
PropertyDescriptorCollection properties =                             ↵
TypeDescriptor.GetProperties(button1);

// Sets an PropertyDescriptor to the specific property.
System.ComponentModel.PropertyDescriptor myProperty =                 ↵
properties.Find("Text", false);

// Prints the property and the property description.
textBox1.Text = myProperty.DisplayName+ '\n' ;
textBox1.Text += myProperty.Description + '\n';
textBox1.Text += myProperty.Category + '\n';
```

Requirements

Namespace: System.ComponentModel

Platforms: Windows 98, Windows NT 4.0, Windows Millennium Edition, Windows 2000, Windows XP Home Edition, Windows XP Professional, Windows Server 2003 family, .NET Compact Framework - Windows CE .NET

Assembly: System (in System.dll)

PropertyDescriptor Constructor

Initializes a new instance of the **PropertyDescriptor** class.

Overload List

Initializes a new instance of the **PropertyDescriptor** class with the name and attributes in the specified **MemberDescriptor**.

Supported by the .NET Compact Framework.

[Visual Basic] **Protected Sub New(MemberDescriptor)**

[C#] **protected PropertyDescriptor(MemberDescriptor);**

[C++] **protected: PropertyDescriptor(MemberDescriptor*);**

[JScript] **protected function PropertyDescriptor(Member-Descriptor);**

Initializes a new instance of the **PropertyDescriptor** class with the name in the specified **MemberDescriptor** and the attributes in both the **MemberDescriptor** and the **Attribute** array.

Supported by the .NET Compact Framework.

[Visual Basic] **Protected Sub New(MemberDescriptor, Attribute())**

[C#] **protected PropertyDescriptor(MemberDescriptor, Attribute[]);**

[C++] **protected: PropertyDescriptor(MemberDescriptor*, Attribute[]);**

[JScript] **protected function Property-Descriptor(MemberDescriptor, Attribute[]);**

Initializes a new instance of the **PropertyDescriptor** class with the specified name and attributes.

Supported by the .NET Compact Framework.

[Visual Basic] **Protected Sub New(String, Attribute())**

[C#] **protected PropertyDescriptor(string, Attribute[]);**

[C++] **protected: PropertyDescriptor(String*, Attribute[]);**

[JScript] **protected function PropertyDescriptor(String, Attribute[]);**

PropertyDescriptor Constructor (MemberDescriptor)

Initializes a new instance of the **PropertyDescriptor** class with the name and attributes in the specified **MemberDescriptor**.

```
[Visual Basic]
Protected Sub New( _
   ByVal descr As MemberDescriptor _
)
[C#]
protected PropertyDescriptor(
   MemberDescriptor descr
);
[C++]
protected: PropertyDescriptor(
   MemberDescriptor* descr
);
[JScript]
protected function PropertyDescriptor(
   descr : MemberDescriptor
);
```

Parameters

descr

A **MemberDescriptor** that contains the name of the property and its attributes.

Requirements

Platforms: Windows 98, Windows NT 4.0, Windows Millennium Edition, Windows 2000, Windows XP Home Edition, Windows XP Professional, Windows Server 2003 family, .NET Compact Framework - Windows CE .NET

PropertyDescriptor Constructor (MemberDescriptor, Attribute[])

Initializes a new instance of the **PropertyDescriptor** class with the name in the specified **MemberDescriptor** and the attributes in both the **MemberDescriptor** and the **Attribute** array.

```
[Visual Basic]
Protected Sub New( _
   ByVal descr As MemberDescriptor, _
   ByVal attrs() As Attribute _
)
[C#]
protected PropertyDescriptor(
   MemberDescriptor descr,
   Attribute[] attrs
);
[C++]
protected: PropertyDescriptor(
   MemberDescriptor* descr,
   Attribute* attrs[]
);
[JScript]
protected function PropertyDescriptor(
   descr : MemberDescriptor,
   attrs : Attribute[]
);
```

Parameters

descr

A **MemberDescriptor** containing the name of the member and its attributes.

attrs

An **Attribute** array containing the attributes you want to associate with the property.

Remarks

This constructor appends the attributes in the **Attribute** array to the attributes in the **MemberDescriptor**.

Requirements

Platforms: Windows 98, Windows NT 4.0, Windows Millennium Edition, Windows 2000, Windows XP Home Edition, Windows XP Professional, Windows Server 2003 family, .NET Compact Framework - Windows CE .NET

PropertyDescriptor Constructor (String, Attribute[])

Initializes a new instance of the **PropertyDescriptor** class with the specified name and attributes.

```
[Visual Basic]
Protected Sub New( _
   ByVal name As String, _
   ByVal attrs() As Attribute _
)
[C#]
protected PropertyDescriptor(
   string name,
   Attribute[] attrs
);
```

```
[C++]
protected: PropertyDescriptor(
   String* name,
   Attribute* attrs[]
);
[JScript]
protected function PropertyDescriptor(
   name : String,
   attrs : Attribute[]
);
```

Parameters

name

The name of the property.

attrs

An array of type **Attribute** that contains the property attributes.

Requirements

Platforms: Windows 98, Windows NT 4.0, Windows Millennium Edition, Windows 2000, Windows XP Home Edition, Windows XP Professional, Windows Server 2003 family, .NET Compact Framework - Windows CE .NET

PropertyDescriptor.ComponentType Property

When overridden in a derived class, gets the type of the component this property is bound to.

```
[Visual Basic]
Public MustOverride ReadOnly Property ComponentType As Type
[C#]
public abstract Type ComponentType {get;}
[C++]
public: __property virtual Type* get_ComponentType() = 0;
[JScript]
public abstract function get ComponentType() : Type;
```

Property Value

A **Type** that represents the type of component this property is bound to. When **GetValue** or **SetValue** are invoked, the object specified might be an instance of this type.

Remarks

Typically, this property is implemented through reflection.

Requirements

Platforms: Windows 98, Windows NT 4.0, Windows Millennium Edition, Windows 2000, Windows XP Home Edition, Windows XP Professional, Windows Server 2003 family, .NET Compact Framework - Windows CE .NET

PropertyDescriptor.Converter Property

Gets the type converter for this property.

```
[Visual Basic]
Public Overridable ReadOnly Property Converter As TypeConverter
[C#]
public virtual TypeConverter Converter {get;}
[C++]
public: __property virtual TypeConverter* get_Converter();
[JScript]
public function get Converter() : TypeConverter;
```

Property Value

A **TypeConverter** that is used to convert the **Type** of this property.

Requirements

Platforms: Windows 98, Windows NT 4.0, Windows Millennium Edition, Windows 2000, Windows XP Home Edition, Windows XP Professional, Windows Server 2003 family

PropertyDescriptor.IsLocalizable Property

Gets a value indicating whether this property should be localized, as specified in the **LocalizableAttribute**.

```
[Visual Basic]
Public Overridable ReadOnly Property IsLocalizable As Boolean
[C#]
public virtual bool IsLocalizable {get;}
[C++]
public: __property virtual bool get_IsLocalizable();
[JScript]
public function get IsLocalizable() : Boolean;
```

Property Value

true if the member is marked with the **LocalizableAttribute** constructor of the value **true**; otherwise, **false**.

Remarks

When a property is marked with the **LocalizableAttribute** constructor of the value **true** and used in a visual designer, its values are saved in a resource file. If you mark a property with the attribute and then set the property in code, resource files are not used.

Requirements

Platforms: Windows 98, Windows NT 4.0, Windows Millennium Edition, Windows 2000, Windows XP Home Edition, Windows XP Professional, Windows Server 2003 family

PropertyDescriptor.IsReadOnly Property

When overridden in a derived class, gets a value indicating whether this property is read-only.

```
[Visual Basic]
Public MustOverride ReadOnly Property IsReadOnly As Boolean
[C#]
public abstract bool IsReadOnly {get;}
[C++]
public: __property virtual bool get_IsReadOnly() = 0;
[JScript]
public abstract function get IsReadOnly() : Boolean;
```

Property Value

true if the property is read-only; otherwise, **false**.

Requirements

Platforms: Windows 98, Windows NT 4.0, Windows Millennium Edition, Windows 2000, Windows XP Home Edition, Windows XP Professional, Windows Server 2003 family, .NET Compact Framework - Windows CE .NET

PropertyDescriptor.PropertyType Property

When overridden in a derived class, gets the type of the property.

```
[Visual Basic]
Public MustOverride ReadOnly Property PropertyType As Type
[C#]
public abstract Type PropertyType {get;}
[C++]
public: __property virtual Type* get_PropertyType() = 0;
[JScript]
public abstract function get PropertyType() : Type;
```

Property Value

A **Type** that represents the type of the property.

Remarks

Typically, this property is implemented through reflection.

Requirements

Platforms: Windows 98, Windows NT 4.0, Windows Millennium Edition, Windows 2000, Windows XP Home Edition, Windows XP Professional, Windows Server 2003 family, .NET Compact Framework - Windows CE .NET

PropertyDescriptor.SerializationVisibility Property

Gets a value indicating whether this property should be serialized, as specified in the **DesignerSerializationVisibilityAttribute**.

```
[Visual Basic]
Public ReadOnly Property SerializationVisibility As _
   DesignerSerializationVisibility
[C#]
public DesignerSerializationVisibility SerializationVisibility
   {get;}
[C++]
public: __property DesignerSerializationVisibility
   get_SerializationVisibility();
[JScript]
public function get SerializationVisibility() :
   DesignerSerializationVisibility;
```

Property Value

One of the **DesignerSerializationVisibility** enumeration values that specifies whether this property should be serialized.

Requirements

Platforms: Windows 98, Windows NT 4.0, Windows Millennium Edition, Windows 2000, Windows XP Home Edition, Windows XP Professional, Windows Server 2003 family

PropertyDescriptor.AddValueChanged Method

Enables other objects to be notified when this property changes.

```
[Visual Basic]
Public Overridable Sub AddValueChanged( _
   ByVal component As Object, _
   ByVal handler As EventHandler _
)
[C#]
public virtual void AddValueChanged(
   object component,
   EventHandler handler
);
[C++]
public: virtual void AddValueChanged(
   Object* component,
   EventHandler* handler
);
[JScript]
public function AddValueChanged(
   component : Object,
   handler : EventHandler
);
```

Parameters

component
The component to add the handler for.

handler
The delegate to add as a listener.

Requirements

Platforms: Windows 98, Windows NT 4.0, Windows Millennium Edition, Windows 2000, Windows XP Home Edition, Windows XP Professional, Windows Server 2003 family, .NET Compact Framework - Windows CE .NET

PropertyDescriptor.CanResetValue Method

When overridden in a derived class, returns whether resetting an object changes its value.

```
[Visual Basic]
Public MustOverride Function CanResetValue( _
   ByVal component As Object _
) As Boolean
[C#]
public abstract bool CanResetValue(
   object component
);
[C++]
public: virtual bool CanResetValue(
   Object* component
) = 0;
[JScript]
public abstract function CanResetValue(
   component : Object
) : Boolean;
```

Parameters

component
The component to test for reset capability.

Return Value

true if resetting the component changes its value; otherwise, **false**.

Remarks

Typically, this method is implemented through reflection.

Notes to Inheritors: When overridden in a derived class, this method looks for a **DefaultValueAttribute**. If it finds one, it compares the value of the attribute with the property's current value. It returns **true** when the default value does not match the property's current value. If this method cannot find a **DefaultValueAttribute**, it looks for a "ShouldPersistMyProperty" method that you need to implement yourself. If this is found, **CanResetValue** returns what "ShouldPersistMyProperty" returns. Otherwise, it looks for a "ResetMyProperty" method that you need to implement yourself. If this is found, **CanResetValue** returns **true**. If it cannot find a **DefaultValueAttribute**, a "ShouldPersistMyProperty" method, or a "ResetMyProperty" method, then it returns **false**.

Requirements

Platforms: Windows 98, Windows NT 4.0,
Windows Millennium Edition, Windows 2000,
Windows XP Home Edition, Windows XP Professional,
Windows Server 2003 family,
.NET Compact Framework - Windows CE .NET

PropertyDescriptor.CreateInstance Method

Creates an instance of the specified type.

```
[Visual Basic]
Protected Function CreateInstance( _
   ByVal type As Type _
) As Object
[C#]
protected object CreateInstance(
   Type type
);
[C++]
protected: Object* CreateInstance(
   Type* type
);
[JScript]
protected function CreateInstance(
   type : Type
) : Object;
```

Parameters

type
A **Type** that represents the type to create.

Return Value

A new instance of the type.

Remarks

CreateInstance looks for a constructor that takes the specified type. If it finds a constructor, the type of the property is passed in.

Converters and editors use this method to create versions of a component. This method enables a single component to be reused for more than one type.

Requirements

Platforms: Windows 98, Windows NT 4.0,
Windows Millennium Edition, Windows 2000,
Windows XP Home Edition, Windows XP Professional,
Windows Server 2003 family

PropertyDescriptor.Equals Method

Compares this to another object to see if they are equivalent.

```
[Visual Basic]
Overrides Public Function Equals( _
   ByVal obj As Object _
) As Boolean
[C#]
public override bool Equals(
   object obj
);
[C++]
public: bool Equals(
   Object* obj
);
[JScript]
public override function Equals(
   obj : Object
) : Boolean;
```

Parameters

obj
The object to compare to this **PropertyDescriptor**.

Return Value

true if the values are equivalent; otherwise, **false**.

Requirements

Platforms: Windows 98, Windows NT 4.0,
Windows Millennium Edition, Windows 2000,
Windows XP Home Edition, Windows XP Professional,
Windows Server 2003 family,
.NET Compact Framework - Windows CE .NET

PropertyDescriptor.GetChildProperties Method

Returns a **PropertyDescriptorCollection**.

Overload List

Returns the default **PropertyDescriptorCollection**.

[Visual Basic] **Overloads Public Function GetChildProperties() As PropertyDescriptorCollection**

[C#] **public PropertyDescriptorCollection GetChildProperties();**

[C++] **public: PropertyDescriptorCollection* GetChildProperties();**

[JScript] **public function GetChildProperties() : PropertyDescriptorCollection;**

Returns a **PropertyDescriptorCollection** using a specified array of attributes as a filter.

[Visual Basic] **Overloads Public Function GetChildProperties(Attribute()) As PropertyDescriptorCollection**

[C#] **public PropertyDescriptorCollection GetChildProperties(Attribute[]);**

[C++] **public: PropertyDescriptorCollection* GetChildProperties(Attribute*[]);**

[JScript] **public function GetChildProperties(Attribute[]) : PropertyDescriptorCollection;**

Returns a **PropertyDescriptorCollection** for a given object.

[Visual Basic] **Overloads Public Function GetChildProperties(Object) As PropertyDescriptorCollection**

[C#] **public PropertyDescriptorCollection GetChildProperties(object);**

[C++] **public: PropertyDescriptorCollection* GetChildProperties(Object*);**

[JScript] **public function GetChildProperties(Object) : PropertyDescriptorCollection;**

Returns a **PropertyDescriptorCollection** for a given object using a specified array of attributes as a filter.

[Visual Basic] **Overloads Public Overridable Function GetChildProperties(Object, Attribute()) As PropertyDescriptorCollection**

[C#] **public virtual PropertyDescriptorCollection GetChildProperties(object, Attribute[]);**

[C++] **public: virtual PropertyDescriptorCollection* GetChildProperties(Object*, Attribute[]);**

[JScript] **public function GetChildProperties(Object, Attribute[]) : PropertyDescriptorCollection;**

PropertyDescriptor.GetChildProperties Method ()

Returns the default **PropertyDescriptorCollection**.

[Visual Basic]
```
Overloads Public Function GetChildProperties() As
PropertyDescriptorCollection
```
[C#]
```
public PropertyDescriptorCollection GetChildProperties();
```
[C++]
```
public: PropertyDescriptorCollection* GetChildProperties();
```
[JScript]
```
public function GetChildProperties() : PropertyDescriptorCollection;
```

Return Value

A **PropertyDescriptorCollection**.

Remarks

This method passes a null reference (**Nothing** in Visual Basic) for both the *instance* parameter and the *filter* parameter.

The properties for the *instance* parameter can differ from the properties of a class, because the container can add or remove properties if the *instance* parameter is sited.

The *filter* parameter can mix **Type** and **Attribute** objects. Filtering is defined by the following rules:

- A **Type** object is treated as a wildcard; it matches any property that has the **Type** in its set of attributes.
- If a property does not have an **Attribute** of the same class, the property will not be included in the returned array.
- If the attribute is an instance of **Attribute**, the property must be an exact match to be included in the returned array.
- If you specify an **Attribute** and it is the default property, it will be included in the returned array, even if there is no instance of **Attribute** in the property.

Requirements

Platforms: Windows 98, Windows NT 4.0, Windows Millennium Edition, Windows 2000, Windows XP Home Edition, Windows XP Professional, Windows Server 2003 family

PropertyDescriptor.GetChildProperties Method (Attribute[])

Returns a **PropertyDescriptorCollection** using a specified array of attributes as a filter.

[Visual Basic]
```
Overloads Public Function GetChildProperties( _
   ByVal filter() As Attribute _
) As PropertyDescriptorCollection
```
[C#]
```
public PropertyDescriptorCollection GetChildProperties(
   Attribute[] filter
);
```
[C++]
```
public: PropertyDescriptorCollection* GetChildProperties(
   Attribute* filter[]
);
```
[JScript]
```
public function GetChildProperties(
   filter : Attribute[]
) : PropertyDescriptorCollection;
```

Parameters

filter
: An array of type **Attribute** to use as a filter.

Return Value

A **PropertyDescriptorCollection** with the properties that match the specified attributes.

Remarks

This method passes a null reference (**Nothing** in Visual Basic) for the *instance* parameter.

The properties for the *instance* parameter can differ from the properties of a class, because the site can add or remove properties if the *instance* parameter is sited.

The *filter* parameter can mix **Type** and **Attribute** objects. Filtering is defined by the following rules:

- A **Type** object is treated as a wildcard; it matches any property that has the **Type** in its set of attributes.
- If a property does not have an **Attribute** of the same class, the property will not be included in the returned array.
- If the attribute is an instance of **Attribute**, the property must be an exact match to be included in the returned array.
- If you specify an **Attribute** instance and it is the default property, it will be included in the returned array even if there is no instance of the **Attribute** in the property.

Requirements

Platforms: Windows 98, Windows NT 4.0, Windows Millennium Edition, Windows 2000, Windows XP Home Edition, Windows XP Professional, Windows Server 2003 family

PropertyDescriptor.GetChildProperties Method (Object)

Returns a **PropertyDescriptorCollection** for a given object.

[Visual Basic]
```
Overloads Public Function GetChildProperties( _
   ByVal instance As Object _
) As PropertyDescriptorCollection
```
[C#]
```
public PropertyDescriptorCollection GetChildProperties(
   object instance
);
```
[C++]
```
public: PropertyDescriptorCollection* GetChildProperties(
   Object* instance
);
```

```
[JScript]
public function GetChildProperties(
   instance : Object
) : PropertyDescriptorCollection;
```

Parameters

instance
A component to get the properties for.

Return Value

A **PropertyDescriptorCollection** with the properties for the specified component.

Remarks

This method passes a null reference (**Nothing** in Visual Basic) for the *filter* parameter.

The properties for the *instance* parameter can differ from the properties of a class, because the site can add or remove properties if the *instance* parameter is sited.

The *filter* parameter can mix **Type** and **Attribute** objects. Filtering is defined by the following rules:

- A **Type** object is treated as a wildcard; it matches any property that has the **Type** in its set of attributes.
- If a property does not have an **Attribute** of the same class, the property will not be included in the returned array.
- If the attribute is an instance of **Attribute**, the property must be an exact match to be included in the returned array.
- If you specify an **Attribute** instance and it is the default property, it will be included in the returned array even if there is no instance of the **Attribute** in the property.

Requirements

Platforms: Windows 98, Windows NT 4.0, Windows Millennium Edition, Windows 2000, Windows XP Home Edition, Windows XP Professional, Windows Server 2003 family

PropertyDescriptor.GetChildProperties Method (Object, Attribute[])

Returns a **PropertyDescriptorCollection** for a given object using a specified array of attributes as a filter.

```
[Visual Basic]
Overloads Public Overridable Function GetChildProperties( _
   ByVal instance As Object, _
   ByVal filter() As Attribute _
) As PropertyDescriptorCollection
[C#]
public virtual PropertyDescriptorCollection GetChildProperties(
   object instance,
   Attribute[] filter
);
[C++]
public: virtual PropertyDescriptorCollection* GetChildProperties(
   Object* instance,
   Attribute* filter[]
);
[JScript]
public function GetChildProperties(
   instance : Object,
   filter : Attribute[]
) : PropertyDescriptorCollection;
```

Parameters

instance
A component to get the properties for.

filter
An array of type **Attribute** to use as a filter.

Return Value

A **PropertyDescriptorCollection** with the properties that match the specified attributes for the specified component.

Remarks

The properties for the *instance* parameter can differ from the properties of a class, because the site can add or remove properties if the *instance* parameter is sited.

The *filter* parameter can mix **Type** and **Attribute** objects. Filtering is defined by the following rules:

- A **Type** object is treated as a wildcard; it matches any property that has the **Type** in its set of attributes.
- If a property does not have an **Attribute** of the same class, the property will not be included in the returned array.
- If the attribute is an instance of **Attribute**, the property must be an exact match to be included in the returned array.
- If you specify an **Attribute** instance and it is the default property, it will be included in the returned array even if there is no instance of the **Attribute** in the property.

Generally, child properties should be returned by implementing the **GetProperties** member of the **TypeConverter** returned from this property, however.

Requirements

Platforms: Windows 98, Windows NT 4.0, Windows Millennium Edition, Windows 2000, Windows XP Home Edition, Windows XP Professional, Windows Server 2003 family

PropertyDescriptor.GetEditor Method

Gets an editor of the specified type.

```
[Visual Basic]
Public Overridable Function GetEditor( _
   ByVal editorBaseType As Type _
) As Object
[C#]
public virtual object GetEditor(
   Type editorBaseType
);
[C++]
public: virtual Object* GetEditor(
   Type* editorBaseType
);
[JScript]
public function GetEditor(
   editorBaseType : Type
) : Object;
```

Parameters

editorBaseType
The base type of editor, which is used to differentiate between multiple editors that a property supports.

Return Value

An instance of the requested editor type, or a null reference (**Nothing** in Visual Basic) if an editor cannot be found.

Requirements

Platforms: Windows 98, Windows NT 4.0, Windows Millennium Edition, Windows 2000, Windows XP Home Edition, Windows XP Professional, Windows Server 2003 family

PropertyDescriptor.GetHashCode Method

This member overrides **Object.GetHashCode**.

```
[Visual Basic]
Overrides Public Function GetHashCode() As Integer
[C#]
public override int GetHashCode();
[C++]
public: int GetHashCode();
[JScript]
public override function GetHashCode() : int;
```

Requirements

Platforms: Windows 98, Windows NT 4.0, Windows Millennium Edition, Windows 2000, Windows XP Home Edition, Windows XP Professional, Windows Server 2003 family, .NET Compact Framework - Windows CE .NET

PropertyDescriptor.GetTypeFromName Method

Returns a type using its name.

```
[Visual Basic]
Protected Function GetTypeFromName( _
   ByVal typeName As String _
) As Type
[C#]
protected Type GetTypeFromName(
   string typeName
);
[C++]
protected: Type* GetTypeFromName(
   String* typeName
);
[JScript]
protected function GetTypeFromName(
   typeName : String
) : Type;
```

Parameters

typeName
The assembly-qualified name of the type to retrieve.

Return Value

A **Type** that matches the given type name, or a null reference (**Nothing** in Visual Basic) if a match cannot be found.

Remarks

To find the appropriate type, this method first checks the assembly of the type that this **PropertyDescriptor** references. If it does not find the type in the assembly, it calls **Type.GetType**.

Requirements

Platforms: Windows 98, Windows NT 4.0, Windows Millennium Edition, Windows 2000, Windows XP Home Edition, Windows XP Professional, Windows Server 2003 family

PropertyDescriptor.GetValue Method

When overridden in a derived class, gets the current value of the property on a component.

```
[Visual Basic]
Public MustOverride Function GetValue( _
   ByVal component As Object _
) As Object
[C#]
public abstract object GetValue(
   object component
);
[C++]
public: virtual Object* GetValue(
   Object* component
) = 0;
[JScript]
public abstract function GetValue(
   component : Object
) : Object;
```

Parameters

component
The component with the property for which to retrieve the value.

Return Value

The value of a property for a given component.

Remarks

Typically, this method is implemented through reflection.

This method automatically calls the pre-change method, **OnComponentChanging**, and post-change method, **OnComponentChanged**, of the **IComponentChangeService**.

Notes to Inheritors: When you override this method, it gets the current value of the property by invoking a "GetMyProperty" method that you need to implement. An exception in that method should pass through.

Requirements

Platforms: Windows 98, Windows NT 4.0, Windows Millennium Edition, Windows 2000, Windows XP Home Edition, Windows XP Professional, Windows Server 2003 family, .NET Compact Framework - Windows CE .NET

PropertyDescriptor.OnValueChanged Method

Raises the ValueChanged event that you implemented.

```
[Visual Basic]
Protected Overridable Sub OnValueChanged( _
   ByVal component As Object, _
   ByVal e As EventArgs _
)
[C#]
protected virtual void OnValueChanged(
   object component,
   EventArgs e
);
```

```
[C++]
protected: virtual void OnValueChanged(
   Object* component,
   EventArgs* e
);
[JScript]
protected function OnValueChanged(
   component : Object,
   e : EventArgs
);
```

Parameters

component
: The object that raises the event.

e
: An **EventArgs** that contains the event data.

Remarks

This method should be called by your property descriptor implementation when the property value has changed.

Requirements

Platforms: Windows 98, Windows NT 4.0, Windows Millennium Edition, Windows 2000, Windows XP Home Edition, Windows XP Professional, Windows Server 2003 family, .NET Compact Framework - Windows CE .NET

PropertyDescriptor.RemoveValueChanged Method

Enables other objects to be notified when this property changes.

```
[Visual Basic]
Public Overridable Sub RemoveValueChanged( _
   ByVal component As Object, _
   ByVal handler As EventHandler _
)
[C#]
public virtual void RemoveValueChanged(
   object component,
   EventHandler handler
);
[C++]
public: virtual void RemoveValueChanged(
   Object* component,
   EventHandler* handler
);
[JScript]
public function RemoveValueChanged(
   component : Object,
   handler : EventHandler
);
```

Parameters

component
: The component to remove the handler for.

handler
: The delegate to remove as a listener.

Requirements

Platforms: Windows 98, Windows NT 4.0, Windows Millennium Edition, Windows 2000, Windows XP Home Edition, Windows XP Professional, Windows Server 2003 family, .NET Compact Framework - Windows CE .NET

PropertyDescriptor.ResetValue Method

When overridden in a derived class, resets the value for this property of the component to the default value.

```
[Visual Basic]
Public MustOverride Sub ResetValue( _
   ByVal component As Object _
)
[C#]
public abstract void ResetValue(
   object component
);
[C++]
public: virtual void ResetValue(
   Object* component
) = 0;
[JScript]
public abstract function ResetValue(
   component : Object
);
```

Parameters

component
: The component with the property value that is to be reset to the default value.

Remarks

Typically, this method is implemented through reflection.

This method determines the value to reset the property to in the following order of precedence:

1. There is a shadowed property for this property.
2. There is a **DefaultValueAttribute** for this property.
3. There is a "ResetMyProperty" method that you have implemented, where "MyProperty" is the name of the property you pass to it.

This method creates a **DesignerTransaction** automatically in the following order:

1. The method calls **IDesignerHost.CreateTransaction** to create a new **DesignerTransaction** object to represent the changes.
2. The method calls **IComponentChangeService.OnComponentChanging** to indicate that the transaction has begun and the changes are about to occur.
3. The method resets the property to the value determined by this method's checking order.
4. The method calls **IComponentChangeService.OnComponentChanged** to indicate that the changes have occured.
5. The method calls **DesignerTransaction.Commit** to indicate that the transaction is completed.

The purpose of the transaction is to support **Undo** and **Redo** functionality.

Notes to Inheritors: When overridden in a derived class, this method looks for a **DefaultValueAttribute**. If it finds one, it sets the value of the property to the **DefaultValueAttribute** it found. If this method cannot find a **DefaultValueAttribute**, it looks for a "ResetMyProperty" method that you need to implement. If this is found, **ResetValue** invokes it. If **ResetValue** cannot find a **DefaultValueAttribute** or a "ResetMyProperty" method that you implemented, then it does not perform an operation.

Requirements

Platforms: Windows 98, Windows NT 4.0, Windows Millennium Edition, Windows 2000, Windows XP Home Edition, Windows XP Professional, Windows Server 2003 family, .NET Compact Framework - Windows CE .NET

PropertyDescriptor.SetValue Method

When overridden in a derived class, sets the value of the component to a different value.

```
[Visual Basic]
Public MustOverride Sub SetValue( _
   ByVal component As Object, _
   ByVal value As Object _
)
[C#]
public abstract void SetValue(
   object component,
   object value
);
[C++]
public: virtual void SetValue(
   Object* component,
   Object* value
) = 0;
[JScript]
public abstract function SetValue(
   component : Object,
   value : Object
);
```

Parameters

component
  The component with the property value that is to be set.

value
  The new value.

Remarks

Typically, this method is implemented through reflection.

This method creates a **DesignerTransaction** automatically in the following order:

1. The method calls **IDesignerHost.CreateTransaction** to create a new **DesignerTransaction** object to represent the changes.
2. The method calls **IComponentChangeService.OnComponentChanging** to indicate that the transaction has begun and the changes are about to occur.
3. The method resets the property to the value determined by this method's checking order.
4. The method calls **IComponentChangeService.OnComponentChanged** to indicate that the changes have occurred.
5. The method calls **DesignerTransaction.Commit** to indicate that the transaction is complete.

The purpose of the transaction is to support **Undo** and **Redo** functionality.

Notes to Inheritors: When you override this method, it should set the value of the property by invoking the appropriate "SetMyProperty" method that you need to implement. If the value specified is invalid, the component should throw an exception, which is passed up. You should design the property so that a "GetMyProperty" method (that you have implemented) following a "SetMyProperty" method returns the value passed in when the "SetMyProperty" method does not throw an exception.

Requirements

Platforms: Windows 98, Windows NT 4.0, Windows Millennium Edition, Windows 2000, Windows XP Home Edition, Windows XP Professional, Windows Server 2003 family, .NET Compact Framework - Windows CE .NET

PropertyDescriptor.ShouldSerializeValue Method

When overridden in a derived class, determines a value indicating whether the value of this property needs to be persisted.

```
[Visual Basic]
Public MustOverride Function ShouldSerializeValue( _
   ByVal component As Object _
) As Boolean
[C#]
public abstract bool ShouldSerializeValue(
   object component
);
[C++]
public: virtual bool ShouldSerializeValue(
   Object* component
) = 0;
[JScript]
public abstract function ShouldSerializeValue(
   component : Object
) : Boolean;
```

Parameters

component
  The component with the property to be examined for persistence.

Return Value

true if the property should be persisted; otherwise, **false**.

Remarks

Typically, this method is implemented through reflection.

Notes to Inheritors: When overridden in a derived class, this method returns **true** if the current value of the property is different from its default value. It looks for a default value by first looking for a **DefaultValueAttribute**. If the method finds this attribute, it compares the value of the attribute with the property's current value. If this method cannot find a **DefaultValueAttribute**, it looks for a "ShouldSerializeMyProperty" method that you need to implement. If it is found, **ShouldSerializeValue** invokes it. If this method cannot find a **DefaultValueAttribute** or a "ShouldSerializeMyProperty" method, it cannot create optimizations and it returns **true**.

Requirements

Platforms: Windows 98, Windows NT 4.0, Windows Millennium Edition, Windows 2000, Windows XP Home Edition, Windows XP Professional, Windows Server 2003 family, .NET Compact Framework - Windows CE .NET

PropertyDescriptorCollection Class

Represents a collection of **PropertyDescriptor** objects.

System.Object
System.ComponentModel.PropertyDescriptorCollection

[Visual Basic]
```
Public Class PropertyDescriptorCollection
   Implements IList, ICollection, IEnumerable, IDictionary
```
[C#]
```
public class PropertyDescriptorCollection : IList, ICollection,
   IEnumerable, IDictionary
```
[C++]
```
public __gc class PropertyDescriptorCollection : public IList,
   ICollection, IEnumerable, IDictionary
```
[JScript]
```
public class PropertyDescriptorCollection implements IList,
   ICollection, IEnumerable, IDictionary
```

Thread Safety

Any public static (**Shared** in Visual Basic) members of this type are safe for multithreaded operations. Any instance members are not guaranteed to be thread safe.

Remarks

PropertyDescriptorCollection is read-only; it does not implement methods that add or remove properties. You must inherit from this class to implement these methods.

Using the properties available in the **PropertyDescriptorCollection** class, you can query the collection about its contents. Use the **Count** property to determine the number of elements in the collection. Use the **Item** property to get a specific property by index number or by name.

In addition to properties, you can use the **Find** method to get a description of the property with the specified name from the collection.

Example

[Visual Basic, C#] The following example creates a new **PropertyDescriptorCollection** using the properties on `button1`. It assumes that `button1` has been instantiated on a form.

[Visual Basic]
```
Dim properties As PropertyDescriptorCollection = ↵
TypeDescriptor.GetProperties(button1)
```

[C#]
```
PropertyDescriptorCollection properties = ↵
TypeDescriptor.GetProperties(button1);
```

[Visual Basic, C#] The next example prints all the properties on a button in a text box. It assumes that `button1` and `textBox1` have been instantiated on a form.

[Visual Basic]
```
Private Sub MyPropertyCollection()
    ' Creates a new collection and assign it the properties for ↵
button1.
    Dim properties As PropertyDescriptorCollection = ↵
TypeDescriptor.GetProperties(button1)

    ' Displays each property in the collection in a text box.
    Dim myProperty As PropertyDescriptor
    For Each myProperty In  properties
        textBox1.Text &= myProperty.Name & ControlChars.Cr
    Next myProperty
End Sub 'MyPropertyCollection
```

[C#]
```
private void MyPropertyCollection() {
    // Creates a new collection and assign it the properties ↵
for button1.
    PropertyDescriptorCollection properties = ↵
TypeDescriptor.GetProperties(button1);

    // Displays each property in the collection in a text box.
    foreach (PropertyDescriptor myProperty in properties)
       textBox1.Text += myProperty.Name + '\n';
 }
```

Requirements

Namespace: System.ComponentModel

Platforms: Windows 98, Windows NT 4.0, Windows Millennium Edition, Windows 2000, Windows XP Home Edition, Windows XP Professional, Windows Server 2003 family, .NET Compact Framework - Windows CE .NET

Assembly: System (in System.dll)

PropertyDescriptorCollection Constructor

Initializes a new instance of the **PropertyDescriptorCollection** class.

[Visual Basic]
```
Public Sub New( _
   ByVal properties() As PropertyDescriptor _
)
```
[C#]
```
public PropertyDescriptorCollection(
   PropertyDescriptor[] properties
);
```
[C++]
```
public: PropertyDescriptorCollection(
   PropertyDescriptor* properties[]
);
```
[JScript]
```
public function PropertyDescriptorCollection(
   properties : PropertyDescriptor[]
);
```

Parameters

properties

An array of type **PropertyDescriptor** that provides the properties for this collection.

Requirements

Platforms: Windows 98, Windows NT 4.0, Windows Millennium Edition, Windows 2000, Windows XP Home Edition, Windows XP Professional, Windows Server 2003 family, .NET Compact Framework - Windows CE .NET

PropertyDescriptorCollection.Empty Field

Specifies an empty collection that you can use instead of creating a new one with no items. This static (**Shared** in Visual Basic) field is read-only.

[Visual Basic]
```
Public Shared ReadOnly Empty As PropertyDescriptorCollection
```
[C#]
```
public static readonly PropertyDescriptorCollection Empty;
```
[C++]
```
public: static PropertyDescriptorCollection* Empty;
```
[JScript]
```
public static var Empty : PropertyDescriptorCollection;
```

Requirements

Platforms: Windows 98, Windows NT 4.0, Windows Millennium Edition, Windows 2000, Windows XP Home Edition, Windows XP Professional, Windows Server 2003 family, .NET Compact Framework - Windows CE .NET

PropertyDescriptorCollection.Count Property

Gets the number of property descriptors in the collection.

[Visual Basic]
```
Public ReadOnly Property Count As Integer
```
[C#]
```
public int Count {get;}
```
[C++]
```
public: __property int get_Count();
```
[JScript]
```
public function get Count() : int;
```

Property Value

The number of property descriptors in the collection.

Remarks

You can use the **Count** property to set the limits of a loop that iterates through a collection of objects. Because the collection is zero-based, be sure to use `Count - 1` as the upper boundary of the loop.

Example

[Visual Basic, C#] The following example uses the **Count** property to print the number of properties on `button1`. It assumes that `button1` and `textBox1` have been instantianted on a form.

[Visual Basic]
```
Private Sub GetCount()
    ' Creates a new collection and assign it the properties ↵
 for button1.
    Dim properties As PropertyDescriptorCollection = ↵
TypeDescriptor.GetProperties(button1)

    ' Prints the number of properties on button1 in a textbox.
    textBox1.Text = properties.Count.ToString()
End Sub
```

[C#]
```
private void GetCount() {
    // Creates a new collection and assign it the properties ↵
for button1.
    PropertyDescriptorCollection properties = ↵
TypeDescriptor.GetProperties(button1);

    // Prints the number of properties on button1 in a textbox.
    textBox1.Text = properties.Count.ToString();
 }
```

Requirements

Platforms: Windows 98, Windows NT 4.0, Windows Millennium Edition, Windows 2000, Windows XP Home Edition, Windows XP Professional, Windows Server 2003 family, .NET Compact Framework - Windows CE .NET

PropertyDescriptorCollection.Item Property

Gets the specified **PropertyDescriptor**.

[C#] In C#, this property is the indexer for the **PropertyDescriptor-Collection** class.

Overload List

Gets the **PropertyDescriptor** with the specified name.

[Visual Basic] **Overloads Public Overridable Default ReadOnly Property Item(String) As PropertyDescriptor**

[C#] **public virtual PropertyDescriptor this[string] {get;}**

[C++] **public: __property virtual PropertyDescriptor* get_Item(String*);**

[JScript] **PropertyDescriptorCollection.Item (String)**

Gets the **PropertyDescriptor** at the specified index number.

[Visual Basic] **Overloads Public Overridable Default ReadOnly Property Item(Integer) As PropertyDescriptor**

[C#] **public virtual PropertyDescriptor this[int] {get;}**

[C++] **public: __property virtual PropertyDescriptor* get_Item(int);**

[JScript] **PropertyDescriptorCollection.Item (int)**

Example

[Visual Basic, C#] The following example uses the **Item** property to print the name of the **PropertyDescriptor** specified by the index number in a text box. Because the index number is zero-based, this example prints the name of the second **PropertyDescriptor**. It assumes that `button1` has been instantiated on a form.

> [Visual Basic, C#] **Note** This example shows how to use one of the overloaded versions of the **Item** property (**Property-DescriptorCollection** indexer). For other examples that might be available, see the individual overload topics.

[Visual Basic]
```
Private Sub PrintIndexItem()
    ' Creates a new collection and assigns it the properties ↵
for button1.
    Dim properties As PropertyDescriptorCollection = ↵
TypeDescriptor.GetProperties(button1)

    ' Prints the second property's name.
    textBox1.Text = properties(1).ToString()
End Sub
```

[C#]
```
private void PrintIndexItem() {
    // Creates a new collection and assigns it the properties ↵
 for button1.
    PropertyDescriptorCollection properties = ↵
TypeDescriptor.GetProperties(button1);

    // Prints the second property's name.
    textBox1.Text = properties[1].ToString();
 }
```

PropertyDescriptorCollection.Item Property (String)

Gets the **PropertyDescriptor** with the specified name.

[C#] In C#, this property is the indexer for the **PropertyDescriptor-Collection** class.

```
[Visual Basic]
Overloads Public Overridable Default ReadOnly Property Item( _
   ByVal name As String _
) As PropertyDescriptor
[C#]
public virtual PropertyDescriptor this[
   string name
] {get;}
[C++]
public: __property virtual PropertyDescriptor* get_Item(
   String* name
);
[JScript]
returnValue = PropertyDescriptorCollectionObject.Item(name);
-or-
returnValue = PropertyDescriptorCollectionObject(name);
```

[JScript] In JScript, you can use the default indexed properties defined by a type, but you cannot explicitly define your own. However, specifying the **expando** attribute on a class automatically provides a default indexed property whose type is **Object** and whose index type is **String**.

Arguments [JScript]

name

The name of the **PropertyDescriptor** to get from the collection.

Parameters [Visual Basic, C#, C++]

name

The name of the **PropertyDescriptor** to get from the collection.

Property Value

The **PropertyDescriptor** with the specified name, or a null reference (**Nothing** in Visual Basic) if the property does not exist.

Remarks

Item is case-sensitive when searching for names. That is, the names "Pname" and "pname" are considered to be two different properties.

Example

[Visual Basic, C#] The following example uses the **Item** property to print the type of component for the **PropertyDescriptor** specified by the index. It assumes that `button1` and `textBox1` have been instantiated on a form.

```
[Visual Basic]
Private Sub PrintIndexItem2()
    ' Creates a new collection and assigns it the properties
 for button1.
    Dim properties As PropertyDescriptorCollection = _
       TypeDescriptor.GetProperties(button1)

    ' Sets a PropertyDescriptor to the specific property.
    Dim myProperty As PropertyDescriptor = properties("Opacity")

    ' Prints the display name for the property.
    textBox1.Text = myProperty.DisplayName
End Sub
```

```
[C#]
private void PrintIndexItem2() {
    // Creates a new collection and assigns it the properties
 for button1.
    PropertyDescriptorCollection properties =
        TypeDescriptor.GetProperties(button1);

    // Sets a PropertyDescriptor to the specific property.
    PropertyDescriptor myProperty = properties["Opacity"];

    // Prints the display name for the property.
    textBox1.Text = myProperty.DisplayName;
}
```

Requirements

Platforms: Windows 98, Windows NT 4.0, Windows Millennium Edition, Windows 2000, Windows XP Home Edition, Windows XP Professional, Windows Server 2003 family

PropertyDescriptorCollection.Item Property (Int32)

Gets the **PropertyDescriptor** at the specified index number.

[C#] In C#, this property is the indexer for the **PropertyDescriptor-Collection** class.

```
[Visual Basic]
Overloads Public Overridable Default ReadOnly Property Item( _
   ByVal index As Integer _
) As PropertyDescriptor
[C#]
public virtual PropertyDescriptor this[
   int index
] {get;}
[C++]
public: __property virtual PropertyDescriptor* get_Item(
   int index
);
[JScript]
returnValue = PropertyDescriptorCollectionObject.Item(index);
-or-
returnValue = PropertyDescriptorCollectionObject(index);
```

[JScript] In JScript, you can use the default indexed properties defined by a type, but you cannot explicitly define your own. However, specifying the **expando** attribute on a class automatically provides a default indexed property whose type is **Object** and whose index type is **String**.

Arguments [JScript]

index

The zero-based index of the **PropertyDescriptor** to get from the collection.

Parameters [Visual Basic, C#, C++]

index

The zero-based index of the **PropertyDescriptor** to get from the collection.

Property Value

The **PropertyDescriptor** with the specified index number.

Exceptions

Exception Type	Condition
IndexOutOfRange-Exception	The *index* parameter is not a valid index for **Item**.

Remarks

The index number is zero-based. Therefore, you must subtract one from the numerical position of a particular **PropertyDescriptor** to access that **PropertyDescriptor**. For example, to get the third **PropertyDescriptor**, you need to specify `myColl[2]`.

Example

[Visual Basic, C#] The following example uses the **Item** property to print the name of the **PropertyDescriptor** specified by the index number in a text box. Because the index number is zero-based, this example prints the name of the second **PropertyDescriptor**. It assumes that `button1` has been instantiated on a form.

[Visual Basic]
```
Private Sub PrintIndexItem()
    ' Creates a new collection and assigns it the properties      ↵
 for button1.
    Dim properties As PropertyDescriptorCollection =            ↵
TypeDescriptor.GetProperties(button1)

    ' Prints the second property's name.
    textBox1.Text = properties(1).ToString()
End Sub
```

[C#]
```
private void PrintIndexItem() {
    // Creates a new collection and assigns it the properties     ↵
for button1.
    PropertyDescriptorCollection properties =                   ↵
TypeDescriptor.GetProperties(button1);

    // Prints the second property's name.
    textBox1.Text = properties[1].ToString();
 }
```

Requirements

Platforms: Windows 98, Windows NT 4.0, Windows Millennium Edition, Windows 2000, Windows XP Home Edition, Windows XP Professional, Windows Server 2003 family

PropertyDescriptorCollection.System.Collections.ICollection.Count Property

Note: This namespace, class, or member is supported only in version 1.1 of the .NET Framework.

This member supports the .NET Framework infrastructure and is not intended to be used directly from your code.

[Visual Basic]
```
Private ReadOnly Property Count As Integer Implements _
   ICollection.Count
```
[C#]
```
int ICollection.Count {get;}
```
[C++]
```
private: __property int
   System::Collections::ICollection::get_Count();
```
[JScript]
```
private function get ICollection.Count() : int;
```

PropertyDescriptorCollection.System.Collections.ICollection.IsSynchronized Property

Note: This namespace, class, or member is supported only in version 1.1 of the .NET Framework.

This member supports the .NET Framework infrastructure and is not intended to be used directly from your code.

[Visual Basic]
```
Private ReadOnly Property IsSynchronized As Boolean Implements _
   ICollection.IsSynchronized
```
[C#]
```
bool ICollection.IsSynchronized {get;}
```
[C++]
```
private: __property bool
   System::Collections::ICollection::get_IsSynchronized();
```
[JScript]
```
private function get ICollection.IsSynchronized() : Boolean;
```

PropertyDescriptorCollection.System.Collections.ICollection.SyncRoot Property

Note: This namespace, class, or member is supported only in version 1.1 of the .NET Framework.

This member supports the .NET Framework infrastructure and is not intended to be used directly from your code.

[Visual Basic]
```
Private ReadOnly Property SyncRoot As Object Implements _
   ICollection.SyncRoot
```
[C#]
```
object ICollection.SyncRoot {get;}
```
[C++]
```
private: __property Object*
   System::Collections::ICollection::get_SyncRoot();
```
[JScript]
```
private function get ICollection.SyncRoot() : Object;
```

PropertyDescriptorCollection.System.Collections.IDictionary.IsFixedSize Property

Note: This namespace, class, or member is supported only in version 1.1 of the .NET Framework.

This member supports the .NET Framework infrastructure and is not intended to be used directly from your code.

[Visual Basic]
```
Private ReadOnly Property IsFixedSize As Boolean Implements _
   IDictionary.IsFixedSize
```
[C#]
```
bool IDictionary.IsFixedSize {get;}
```
[C++]
```
private: __property bool
   System::Collections::IDictionary::get_IsFixedSize();
```
[JScript]
```
private function get IDictionary.IsFixedSize() : Boolean;
```

PropertyDescriptorCollection.System.Collections.IDictionary.IsReadOnly Property

Note: This namespace, class, or member is supported only in version 1.1 of the .NET Framework.

This member supports the .NET Framework infrastructure and is not intended to be used directly from your code.

[Visual Basic]
```
Private ReadOnly Property IsReadOnly As Boolean Implements _
   IDictionary.IsReadOnly
```
[C#]
```
bool IDictionary.IsReadOnly {get;}
```
[C++]
```
private: __property bool
   System::Collections::IDictionary::get_IsReadOnly();
```
[JScript]
```
private function get IDictionary.IsReadOnly() : Boolean;
```

PropertyDescriptorCollection.System.Collections.IDictionary.Item Property

Note: This namespace, class, or member is supported only in version 1.1 of the .NET Framework.

[C#] In C#, this property is the indexer for the **PropertyDescriptorCollection** class.

[Visual Basic]
```
Private Default Property Item( _
   ByVal key As Object _
) As Object Implements IDictionary.Item
```
[C#]
```
object IDictionary.this[
   object key
] {get; set;}
```
[C++]
```
private: __property Object*
System::Collections::IDictionary::get_Item(
   Object* key
);
private: __property void
   System::Collections::IDictionary::set_Item(
   Object* key,
   Object*
);
```
[JScript]
```
private function get IDictionary.get_Item(key : Object) : Object;
private function set IDictionary.set_Item(key : Object, value :
Object);
-or-
private function get IDictionary.get_Item(key : Object) : Object;
private function set IDictionary.set_Item(key : Object, value :
Object);
```

[JScript] In JScript, you can use the default indexed properties defined by a type, but you cannot explicitly define your own. However, specifying the **expando** attribute on a class automatically provides a default indexed property whose type is **Object** and whose index type is **String**.

Arguments [JScript]

key

Parameters [Visual Basic, C#, C++]

key

Requirements

Platforms: Windows 98, Windows NT 4.0, Windows Millennium Edition, Windows 2000, Windows XP Home Edition, Windows XP Professional, Windows Server 2003 family

PropertyDescriptorCollection.System.Collections.IDictionary.Keys Property

Note: This namespace, class, or member is supported only in version 1.1 of the .NET Framework.

This member supports the .NET Framework infrastructure and is not intended to be used directly from your code.

[Visual Basic]
```
Private ReadOnly Property Keys As ICollection Implements _
   IDictionary.Keys
```
[C#]
```
ICollection IDictionary.Keys {get;}
```
[C++]
```
private: __property ICollection*
   System::Collections::IDictionary::get_Keys();
```
[JScript]
```
private function get IDictionary.Keys() : ICollection;
```

PropertyDescriptorCollection.System.Collections.IDictionary.Values Property

Note: This namespace, class, or member is supported only in version 1.1 of the .NET Framework.

This member supports the .NET Framework infrastructure and is not intended to be used directly from your code.

[Visual Basic]
```
Private ReadOnly Property Values As ICollection Implements _
   IDictionary.Values
```
[C#]
```
ICollection IDictionary.Values {get;}
```
[C++]
```
private: __property ICollection*
   System::Collections::IDictionary::get_Values();
```
[JScript]
```
private function get IDictionary.Values() : ICollection;
```

PropertyDescriptorCollection.System.Collections.IList.IsFixedSize Property

Note: This namespace, class, or member is supported only in version 1.1 of the .NET Framework.

This member supports the .NET Framework infrastructure and is not intended to be used directly from your code.

[Visual Basic]
```
Private ReadOnly Property IsFixedSize As Boolean Implements _
   IList.IsFixedSize
```
[C#]
```
bool IList.IsFixedSize {get;}
```

```
[C++]
private: __property bool
   System::Collections::IList::get_IsFixedSize();
[JScript]
private function get IList.IsFixedSize() : Boolean;
```

PropertyDescriptorCollection.System.Collections.IList.IsReadOnly Property

Note: This namespace, class, or member is supported only in version 1.1 of the .NET Framework.

This member supports the .NET Framework infrastructure and is not intended to be used directly from your code.

```
[Visual Basic]
Private ReadOnly Property IsReadOnly As Boolean Implements _
   IList.IsReadOnly
[C#]
bool IList.IsReadOnly {get;}
[C++]
private: __property bool
   System::Collections::IList::get_IsReadOnly();
[JScript]
private function get IList.IsReadOnly() : Boolean;
```

PropertyDescriptorCollection.System.Collections.IList.Item Property

Note: This namespace, class, or member is supported only in version 1.1 of the .NET Framework.

[C#] In C#, this property is the indexer for the **PropertyDescriptorCollection** class.

```
[Visual Basic]
Private Default Property Item( _
   ByVal index As Integer _
) As Object Implements IList.Item
[C#]
object IList.this[
   int index
] {get; set;}
[C++]
private: __property Object* System::Collections::IList::get_Item(
   int index
);
private: __property void System::Collections::IList::set_Item(
   int index,
   Object*
);
[JScript]
private function get IList.get_Item(index : int) : Object;
private function set IList.set_Item(index : int, value : Object);
-or-
private function get IList.get_Item(index : int) : Object;
private function set IList.set_Item(index : int, value : Object);
```

[JScript] In JScript, you can use the default indexed properties defined by a type, but you cannot explicitly define your own. However, specifying the **expando** attribute on a class automatically provides a default indexed property whose type is **Object** and whose index type is **String**.

Arguments [JScript]

index

Parameters [Visual Basic, C#, C++]

index

Requirements

Platforms: Windows 98, Windows NT 4.0, Windows Millennium Edition, Windows 2000, Windows XP Home Edition, Windows XP Professional, Windows Server 2003 family

PropertyDescriptorCollection.Add Method

Adds the specified **PropertyDescriptor** to the collection.

```
[Visual Basic]
Public Function Add( _
   ByVal value As PropertyDescriptor _
) As Integer
[C#]
public int Add(
   PropertyDescriptor value
);
[C++]
public: int Add(
   PropertyDescriptor* value
);
[JScript]
public function Add(
   value : PropertyDescriptor
) : int;
```

Parameters

value

The **PropertyDescriptor** to add to the collection.

Return Value

The index of the **PropertyDescriptor** that was added to the collection.

Requirements

Platforms: Windows 98, Windows NT 4.0, Windows Millennium Edition, Windows 2000, Windows XP Home Edition, Windows XP Professional, Windows Server 2003 family, .NET Compact Framework - Windows CE .NET

PropertyDescriptorCollection.Clear Method

Removes all **PropertyDescriptor** objects from the collection.

```
[Visual Basic]
Public Sub Clear()
[C#]
public void Clear();
[C++]
public: void Clear();
[JScript]
public function Clear();
```

Requirements

Platforms: Windows 98, Windows NT 4.0, Windows Millennium Edition, Windows 2000, Windows XP Home Edition, Windows XP Professional, Windows Server 2003 family, .NET Compact Framework - Windows CE .NET

PropertyDescriptorCollection.Contains Method

Returns whether the collection contains the given **PropertyDescriptor**.

```
[Visual Basic]
Public Function Contains( _
   ByVal value As PropertyDescriptor _
) As Boolean
[C#]
public bool Contains(
   PropertyDescriptor value
);
[C++]
public: bool Contains(
   PropertyDescriptor* value
);
[JScript]
public function Contains(
   value : PropertyDescriptor
) : Boolean;
```

Parameters

value
The **PropertyDescriptor** to find in the collection.

Return Value

true if the collection contains the given **PropertyDescriptor**; otherwise, **false**.

Requirements

Platforms: Windows 98, Windows NT 4.0,
Windows Millennium Edition, Windows 2000,
Windows XP Home Edition, Windows XP Professional,
Windows Server 2003 family,
.NET Compact Framework - Windows CE .NET

PropertyDescriptorCollection.CopyTo Method

Copies the entire collection to an array, starting at the specified index number.

```
[Visual Basic]
Public Overridable Sub CopyTo( _
   ByVal array As Array, _
   ByVal index As Integer _
) Implements ICollection.CopyTo
[C#]
public virtual void CopyTo(
   Array array,
   int index
);
[C++]
public: virtual void CopyTo(
   Array* array,
   int index
);
[JScript]
public function CopyTo(
   array : Array,
   index : int
);
```

Parameters

array
An array of **PropertyDescriptor** objects to copy elements of the collection to.

index
The index of the *array* parameter at which copying begins.

Implements

ICollection.CopyTo

Requirements

Platforms: Windows 98, Windows NT 4.0,
Windows Millennium Edition, Windows 2000,
Windows XP Home Edition, Windows XP Professional,
Windows Server 2003 family,
.NET Compact Framework - Windows CE .NET

PropertyDescriptorCollection.Find Method

Returns the **PropertyDescriptor** with the specified name, using a Boolean to indicate whether to ignore case.

```
[Visual Basic]
Public Overridable Function Find( _
   ByVal name As String, _
   ByVal ignoreCase As Boolean _
) As PropertyDescriptor
[C#]
public virtual PropertyDescriptor Find(
   string name,
   bool ignoreCase
);
[C++]
public: virtual PropertyDescriptor* Find(
   String* name,
   bool ignoreCase
);
[JScript]
public function Find(
   name : String,
   ignoreCase : Boolean
) : PropertyDescriptor;
```

Parameters

name
The name of the **PropertyDescriptor** to return from the collection.

ignoreCase
true if you want to ignore the case of the property name; otherwise, **false**.

Return Value

A **PropertyDescriptor** with the specified name, or a null reference (**Nothing** in Visual Basic) if the property does not exist.

Example

See related example in the **System.ComponentModel.PropertyDescriptorCollection** class topic.

Requirements

Platforms: Windows 98, Windows NT 4.0,
Windows Millennium Edition, Windows 2000,
Windows XP Home Edition, Windows XP Professional,
Windows Server 2003 family,
.NET Compact Framework - Windows CE .NET

PropertyDescriptorCollection.GetEnumerator Method

Returns an enumerator for this class.

```
[Visual Basic]
Public Overridable Function GetEnumerator() As IEnumerator
[C#]
public virtual IEnumerator GetEnumerator();
[C++]
public: virtual IEnumerator* GetEnumerator();
[JScript]
public function GetEnumerator() : IEnumerator;
```

Return Value

An enumerator of type **IEnumerator**.

Example

See related example in the **System.ComponentModel.PropertyDescriptorCollection** class topic.

Requirements

Platforms: Windows 98, Windows NT 4.0, Windows Millennium Edition, Windows 2000, Windows XP Home Edition, Windows XP Professional, Windows Server 2003 family, .NET Compact Framework - Windows CE .NET

PropertyDescriptorCollection.IDictionary.Add Method

This member supports the .NET Framework infrastructure and is not intended to be used directly from your code.

```
[Visual Basic]
Private Sub Add( _
   ByVal key As Object, _
   ByVal value As Object _
) Implements IDictionary.Add
[C#]
void IDictionary.Add(
   object key,
   object value
);
[C++]
private: void IDictionary::Add(
   Object* key,
   Object* value
);
[JScript]
private function IDictionary.Add(
   key : Object,
   value : Object
);
```

PropertyDescriptorCollection.IDictionary.Clear Method

This member supports the .NET Framework infrastructure and is not intended to be used directly from your code.

```
[Visual Basic]
Private Sub Clear() Implements IDictionary.Clear
[C#]
void IDictionary.Clear();
[C++]
private: void IDictionary::Clear();
[JScript]
private function IDictionary.Clear();
```

PropertyDescriptorCollection.IDictionary.Contains Method

This member supports the .NET Framework infrastructure and is not intended to be used directly from your code.

```
[Visual Basic]
Private Function Contains( _
   ByVal key As Object _
) As Boolean Implements IDictionary.Contains
[C#]
bool IDictionary.Contains(
   object key
);
[C++]
private: bool IDictionary::Contains(
   Object* key
);
[JScript]
private function IDictionary.Contains(
   key : Object
) : Boolean;
```

PropertyDescriptorCollection.IDictionary.GetEnumerator Method

This member supports the .NET Framework infrastructure and is not intended to be used directly from your code.

```
[Visual Basic]
Private Function GetEnumerator() As IDictionaryEnumerator Implements _
   IDictionary.GetEnumerator
[C#]
IDictionaryEnumerator IDictionary.GetEnumerator();
[C++]
private: IDictionaryEnumerator* IDictionary::GetEnumerator();
[JScript]
private function IDictionary.GetEnumerator() :
   IDictionaryEnumerator;
```

PropertyDescriptorCollection.IDictionary.Remove Method

This member supports the .NET Framework infrastructure and is not intended to be used directly from your code.

```
[Visual Basic]
Private Sub Remove( _
   ByVal key As Object _
) Implements IDictionary.Remove
[C#]
void IDictionary.Remove(
   object key
);
```

```
[C++]
private: void IDictionary::Remove(
   Object* key
);
[JScript]
private function IDictionary.Remove(
   key : Object
);
```

PropertyDescriptorCollection.IEnumerable.GetEnumerator Method

This member supports the .NET Framework infrastructure and is not intended to be used directly from your code.

```
[Visual Basic]
Private Function GetEnumerator() As IEnumerator Implements _
   IEnumerable.GetEnumerator
[C#]
IEnumerator IEnumerable.GetEnumerator();
[C++]
private: IEnumerator* IEnumerable::GetEnumerator();
[JScript]
private function IEnumerable.GetEnumerator() : IEnumerator;
```

PropertyDescriptorCollection.IList.Add Method

This member supports the .NET Framework infrastructure and is not intended to be used directly from your code.

```
[Visual Basic]
Private Function Add( _
   ByVal value As Object _
) As Integer Implements IList.Add
[C#]
int IList.Add(
   object value
);
[C++]
private: int IList::Add(
   Object* value
);
[JScript]
private function IList.Add(
   value : Object
) : int;
```

PropertyDescriptorCollection.IList.Clear Method

This member supports the .NET Framework infrastructure and is not intended to be used directly from your code.

```
[Visual Basic]
Private Sub Clear() Implements IList.Clear
[C#]
void IList.Clear();
[C++]
private: void IList::Clear();
[JScript]
private function IList.Clear();
```

PropertyDescriptorCollection.IList.Contains Method

This member supports the .NET Framework infrastructure and is not intended to be used directly from your code.

```
[Visual Basic]
Private Function Contains( _
   ByVal value As Object _
) As Boolean Implements IList.Contains
[C#]
bool IList.Contains(
   object value
);
[C++]
private: bool IList::Contains(
   Object* value
);
[JScript]
private function IList.Contains(
   value : Object
) : Boolean;
```

PropertyDescriptorCollection.IList.IndexOf Method

This member supports the .NET Framework infrastructure and is not intended to be used directly from your code.

```
[Visual Basic]
Private Function IndexOf( _
   ByVal value As Object _
) As Integer Implements IList.IndexOf
[C#]
int IList.IndexOf(
   object value
);
[C++]
private: int IList::IndexOf(
   Object* value
);
[JScript]
private function IList.IndexOf(
   value : Object
) : int;
```

PropertyDescriptorCollection.IList.Insert Method

This member supports the .NET Framework infrastructure and is not intended to be used directly from your code.

```
[Visual Basic]
Private Sub Insert( _
   ByVal index As Integer, _
   ByVal value As Object _
) Implements IList.Insert
[C#]
void IList.Insert(
   int index,
   object value
);
```

```
[C++]
private: void IList::Insert(
   int index,
   Object* value
);
[JScript]
private function IList.Insert(
   index : int,
   value : Object
);
```

PropertyDescriptorCollection.IList.Remove Method

This member supports the .NET Framework infrastructure and is not intended to be used directly from your code.

```
[Visual Basic]
Private Sub Remove( _
   ByVal value As Object _
) Implements IList.Remove
[C#]
void IList.Remove(
   object value
);
[C++]
private: void IList::Remove(
   Object* value
);
[JScript]
private function IList.Remove(
   value : Object
);
```

PropertyDescriptorCollection.IList.RemoveAt Method

This member supports the .NET Framework infrastructure and is not intended to be used directly from your code.

```
[Visual Basic]
Private Sub RemoveAt( _
   ByVal index As Integer _
) Implements IList.RemoveAt
[C#]
void IList.RemoveAt(
   int index
);
[C++]
private: void IList::RemoveAt(
   int index
);
[JScript]
private function IList.RemoveAt(
   index : int
);
```

PropertyDescriptorCollection.IndexOf Method

Returns the index of the given **PropertyDescriptor**.

```
[Visual Basic]
Public Function IndexOf( _
   ByVal value As PropertyDescriptor _
) As Integer
[C#]
public int IndexOf(
   PropertyDescriptor value
);
[C++]
public: int IndexOf(
   PropertyDescriptor* value
);
[JScript]
public function IndexOf(
   value : PropertyDescriptor
) : int;
```

Parameters

value

The **PropertyDescriptor** to return the index of.

Return Value

The index of the given **PropertyDescriptor**.

Requirements

Platforms: Windows 98, Windows NT 4.0, Windows Millennium Edition, Windows 2000, Windows XP Home Edition, Windows XP Professional, Windows Server 2003 family, .NET Compact Framework - Windows CE .NET

PropertyDescriptorCollection.Insert Method

Adds the **PropertyDescriptor** to the collection at the specified index number.

```
[Visual Basic]
Public Sub Insert( _
   ByVal index As Integer, _
   ByVal value As PropertyDescriptor _
)
[C#]
public void Insert(
   int index,
   PropertyDescriptor value
);
[C++]
public: void Insert(
   int index,
   PropertyDescriptor* value
);
[JScript]
public function Insert(
   index : int,
   value : PropertyDescriptor
);
```

Parameters

index

The index at which to add the *value* parameter to the collection.

value

The **PropertyDescriptor** to add to the collection.

Requirements

Platforms: Windows 98, Windows NT 4.0, Windows Millennium Edition, Windows 2000, Windows XP Home Edition, Windows XP Professional, Windows Server 2003 family, .NET Compact Framework - Windows CE .NET

PropertyDescriptorCollection.InternalSort Method

Sorts the members of this collection.

Overload List

Sorts the members of this collection, using the specified **IComparer**.

[Visual Basic] **Overloads Protected Sub InternalSort(IComparer)**

[C#] **protected void InternalSort(IComparer);**

[C++] **protected: void InternalSort(IComparer*);**

[JScript] **protected function InternalSort(IComparer);**

Sorts the members of this collection. The specified order is applied first, followed by the default sort for this collection, which is usually alphabetical.

[Visual Basic] **Overloads Protected Sub InternalSort(String())**

[C#] **protected void InternalSort(string[]);**

[C++] **protected: void InternalSort(String*[]);**

[JScript] **protected function InternalSort(String[]);**

Example

[Visual Basic, C#] If the **PropertyDescriptorCollection** contains four **PropertyDescriptor** objects with the names `A`, `B`, `C`, and `D`, this results in the properties of `myNewColl` sorted in the order `D`, `B`, `A`, and `C`.

> [Visual Basic, C#] **Note** This example shows how to use one of the overloaded versions of **InternalSort**. For other examples that might be available, see the individual overload topics.

[Visual Basic]
```
Me.InternalSort(New String() {"D", "B"})
```

[C#]
```
this.InternalSort(new string[]{"D", "B"});
```

PropertyDescriptorCollection.InternalSort Method (IComparer)

Sorts the members of this collection, using the specified **IComparer**.

[Visual Basic]
```
Overloads Protected Sub InternalSort( _
   ByVal sorter As IComparer _
)
```
[C#]
```
protected void InternalSort(
   IComparer sorter
);
```
[C++]
```
protected: void InternalSort(
   IComparer* sorter
);
```
[JScript]
```
protected function InternalSort(
   sorter : IComparer
);
```

Parameters

sorter

A comparer to use to sort the **PropertyDescriptor** objects in this collection.

Requirements

Platforms: Windows 98, Windows NT 4.0, Windows Millennium Edition, Windows 2000, Windows XP Home Edition, Windows XP Professional, Windows Server 2003 family

PropertyDescriptorCollection.InternalSort Method (String[])

Sorts the members of this collection. The specified order is applied first, followed by the default sort for this collection, which is usually alphabetical.

[Visual Basic]
```
Overloads Protected Sub InternalSort( _
   ByVal names() As String _
)
```
[C#]
```
protected void InternalSort(
   string[] names
);
```
[C++]
```
protected: void InternalSort(
   String* names __gc[]
);
```
[JScript]
```
protected function InternalSort(
   names : String[]
);
```

Parameters

names

An array of strings describing the order in which to sort the **PropertyDescriptor** objects in this collection.

Example

[Visual Basic, C#] If the **PropertyDescriptorCollection** contains four **PropertyDescriptor** objects with the names `A`, `B`, `C`, and `D`, this results in the properties of `myNewColl` sorted in the order `D`, `B`, `A`, and `C`.

[Visual Basic]
```
Me.InternalSort(New String() {"D", "B"})
```

[C#]
```
this.InternalSort(new string[]{"D", "B"});
```

Requirements

Platforms: Windows 98, Windows NT 4.0, Windows Millennium Edition, Windows 2000, Windows XP Home Edition, Windows XP Professional, Windows Server 2003 family

PropertyDescriptorCollection.Remove Method

Removes the specified **PropertyDescriptor** from the collection.

[Visual Basic]
```
Public Sub Remove( _
   ByVal value As PropertyDescriptor _
)
```
[C#]
```
public void Remove(
   PropertyDescriptor value
);
```
[C++]
```
public: void Remove(
   PropertyDescriptor* value
);
```
[JScript]
```
public function Remove(
   value : PropertyDescriptor
);
```

Parameters

value
The **PropertyDescriptor** to remove from the collection.

Requirements

Platforms: Windows 98, Windows NT 4.0, Windows Millennium Edition, Windows 2000, Windows XP Home Edition, Windows XP Professional, Windows Server 2003 family, .NET Compact Framework - Windows CE .NET

PropertyDescriptorCollection.RemoveAt Method

Removes the **PropertyDescriptor** at the specified index from the collection.

[Visual Basic]
```
Public Sub RemoveAt( _
   ByVal index As Integer _
)
```
[C#]
```
public void RemoveAt(
   int index
);
```
[C++]
```
public: void RemoveAt(
   int index
);
```
[JScript]
```
public function RemoveAt(
   index : int
);
```

Parameters

index
The index of the **PropertyDescriptor** to remove from the collection.

Requirements

Platforms: Windows 98, Windows NT 4.0, Windows Millennium Edition, Windows 2000, Windows XP Home Edition, Windows XP Professional, Windows Server 2003 family, .NET Compact Framework - Windows CE .NET

PropertyDescriptorCollection.Sort Method

Sorts the members of this collection.

Overload List

Sorts the members of this collection, using the default sort for this collection, which is usually alphabetical.

[Visual Basic] **Overloads Public Overridable Function Sort() As PropertyDescriptorCollection**

[C#] **public virtual PropertyDescriptorCollection Sort();**

[C++] **public: virtual PropertyDescriptorCollection* Sort();**

[JScript] **public function Sort() : PropertyDescriptorCollection;**

Sorts the members of this collection, using the specified **IComparer**.

[Visual Basic] **Overloads Public Overridable Function Sort(IComparer) As PropertyDescriptorCollection**

[C#] **public virtual PropertyDescriptorCollection Sort(IComparer);**

[C++] **public: virtual PropertyDescriptorCollection* Sort(IComparer*);**

[JScript] **public function Sort(IComparer) : PropertyDescriptorCollection;**

Sorts the members of this collection. The specified order is applied first, followed by the default sort for this collection, which is usually alphabetical.

[Visual Basic] **Overloads Public Overridable Function Sort(String()) As PropertyDescriptorCollection**

[C#] **public virtual PropertyDescriptorCollection Sort(string[]);**

[C++] **public: virtual PropertyDescriptorCollection* Sort(String*[]);**

[JScript] **public function Sort(String[]) : PropertyDescriptorCollection;**

Sorts the members of this collection. The specified order is applied first, followed by the sort using the specified **IComparer**.

[Visual Basic] **Overloads Public Overridable Function Sort(String(), IComparer) As PropertyDescriptorCollection**

[C#] **public virtual PropertyDescriptorCollection Sort(string[], IComparer);**

[C++] **public: virtual PropertyDescriptorCollection* Sort(String*[], IComparer*);**

[JScript] **public function Sort(String[], IComparer) : PropertyDescriptorCollection;**

Example

[Visual Basic, C#] If the **PropertyDescriptorCollection** contains four **PropertyDescriptor** objects with the names `A`, `B`, `C`, and `D`, this results in the properties of `myNewColl` sorted in the order `D`, `B`, `A`, and `C`.

> [Visual Basic, C#] **Note** This example shows how to use one of the overloaded versions of **Sort**. For other examples that might be available, see the individual overload topics.

[Visual Basic]
```
myNewColl = Me.Sort(New String() {"D", "B"})
```

[C#]
```
myNewColl = this.Sort(new string[]{"D", "B"});
```

PropertyDescriptorCollection.Sort Method ()

Sorts the members of this collection, using the default sort for this collection, which is usually alphabetical.

[Visual Basic]
```
Overloads Public Overridable Function Sort() As
PropertyDescriptorCollection
```
[C#]
```
public virtual PropertyDescriptorCollection Sort();
```
[C++]
```
public: virtual PropertyDescriptorCollection* Sort();
```
[JScript]
```
public function Sort() : PropertyDescriptorCollection;
```

Return Value

A new **PropertyDescriptorCollection** that contains the sorted **PropertyDescriptor** objects.

Requirements

Platforms: Windows 98, Windows NT 4.0, Windows Millennium Edition, Windows 2000, Windows XP Home Edition, Windows XP Professional, Windows Server 2003 family

PropertyDescriptorCollection.Sort Method (IComparer)

Sorts the members of this collection, using the specified **IComparer**.

[Visual Basic]
```
Overloads Public Overridable Function Sort( _
   ByVal comparer As IComparer _
) As PropertyDescriptorCollection
```
[C#]
```
public virtual PropertyDescriptorCollection Sort(
   IComparer comparer
);
```
[C++]
```
public: virtual PropertyDescriptorCollection* Sort(
   IComparer* comparer
);
```
[JScript]
```
public function Sort(
   comparer : IComparer
) : PropertyDescriptorCollection;
```

Parameters

comparer
  A comparer to use to sort the **PropertyDescriptor** objects in this collection.

Return Value

A new **PropertyDescriptorCollection** that contains the sorted **PropertyDescriptor** objects.

Requirements

Platforms: Windows 98, Windows NT 4.0, Windows Millennium Edition, Windows 2000, Windows XP Home Edition, Windows XP Professional, Windows Server 2003 family

PropertyDescriptorCollection.Sort Method (String[])

Sorts the members of this collection. The specified order is applied first, followed by the default sort for this collection, which is usually alphabetical.

[Visual Basic]
```
Overloads Public Overridable Function Sort( _
   ByVal names() As String _
) As PropertyDescriptorCollection
```
[C#]
```
public virtual PropertyDescriptorCollection Sort(
   string[] names
);
```
[C++]
```
public: virtual PropertyDescriptorCollection* Sort(
   String* names __gc[]
);
```
[JScript]
```
public function Sort(
   names : String[]
) : PropertyDescriptorCollection;
```

Parameters

names
  An array of strings describing the order in which to sort the **PropertyDescriptor** objects in this collection.

Return Value

A new **PropertyDescriptorCollection** that contains the sorted **PropertyDescriptor** objects.

Example

[Visual Basic, C#] If the **PropertyDescriptorCollection** contains four **PropertyDescriptor** objects with the names `A`, `B`, `C`, and `D`, this results in the properties of `myNewColl` sorted in the order `D`, `B`, `A`, and `C`.

[Visual Basic]
```
myNewColl = Me.Sort(New String() {"D", "B"})
```

[C#]
```
myNewColl = this.Sort(new string[]{"D", "B"});
```

[C++, JScript] No example is available for C++ or JScript. To view a Visual Basic or C# example, click the Language Filter button <IMG SRC="filter1a.gif" ALT="Language Filter" BORDER=0> in the upper-left corner of the page.

Requirements

Platforms: Windows 98, Windows NT 4.0, Windows Millennium Edition, Windows 2000, Windows XP Home Edition, Windows XP Professional, Windows Server 2003 family

PropertyDescriptorCollection.Sort Method (String[], IComparer)

Sorts the members of this collection. The specified order is applied first, followed by the sort using the specified **IComparer**.

[Visual Basic]
```
Overloads Public Overridable Function Sort( _
   ByVal names() As String, _
   ByVal comparer As IComparer _
) As PropertyDescriptorCollection
```
[C#]
```
public virtual PropertyDescriptorCollection Sort(
   string[] names,
   IComparer comparer
);
```
[C++]
```
public: virtual PropertyDescriptorCollection* Sort(
   String* names __gc[],
   IComparer* comparer
);
```
[JScript]
```
public function Sort(
   names : String[],
   comparer : IComparer
) : PropertyDescriptorCollection;
```

Parameters

names

An array of strings describing the order in which to sort the **PropertyDescriptor** objects in this collection.

comparer

A comparer to use to sort the **PropertyDescriptor** objects in this collection.

Return Value

A new **PropertyDescriptorCollection** that contains the sorted **PropertyDescriptor** objects.

Example

[Visual Basic, C#] If the **PropertyDescriptorCollection** contains four **PropertyDescriptor** objects with the names `A`, `B`, `C`, and `D`, this results in the properties of `myNewColl` sorted in the order `D`, `B`, `A`, and `C`.

[Visual Basic]
```
myNewColl = Me.Sort(New String() {"D", "B"})
```

[C#]
```
myNewColl = this.Sort(new string[]{"D", "B"});
```

Requirements

Platforms: Windows 98, Windows NT 4.0, Windows Millennium Edition, Windows 2000, Windows XP Home Edition, Windows XP Professional, Windows Server 2003 family

PropertyTabAttribute Class

Identifies the property tab or tabs to display for the specified class or classes.

System.Object
System.Attribute
System.ComponentModel.PropertyTabAttribute

```
[Visual Basic]
<AttributeUsage(AttributeTargets.All)>
Public Class PropertyTabAttribute
   Inherits Attribute
[C#]
[AttributeUsage(AttributeTargets.All)]
public class PropertyTabAttribute : Attribute
[C++]
[AttributeUsage(AttributeTargets::All)]
public __gc class PropertyTabAttribute : public Attribute
[JScript]
public
   AttributeUsage(AttributeTargets.All)
class PropertyTabAttribute extends Attribute
```

Thread Safety

Any public static (**Shared** in Visual Basic) members of this type are safe for multithreaded operations. Any instance members are not guaranteed to be thread safe.

Remarks

A property tab can add additional property tabs to expose property information other than its default set of properties.

Requirements

Namespace: System.ComponentModel

Platforms: Windows 98, Windows NT 4.0, Windows Millennium Edition, Windows 2000, Windows XP Home Edition, Windows XP Professional, Windows Server 2003 family

Assembly: System (in System.dll)

PropertyTabAttribute Constructor

Initializes a new instance of the **PropertyTabAttribute** class.

Overload List

Initializes a new instance of the **PropertyTabAttribute** class.

[Visual Basic] **Public Sub New()**

[C#] **public PropertyTabAttribute();**

[C++] **public: PropertyTabAttribute();**

[JScript] **public function PropertyTabAttribute();**

Initializes a new instance of the **PropertyTabAttribute** class using the specified tab class name.

[Visual Basic] **Public Sub New(String)**

[C#] **public PropertyTabAttribute(string);**

[C++] **public: PropertyTabAttribute(String*);**

[JScript] **public function PropertyTabAttribute(String);**

Initializes a new instance of the **PropertyTabAttribute** class using the specified type of tab.

[Visual Basic] **Public Sub New(Type)**

[C#] **public PropertyTabAttribute(Type);**

[C++] **public: PropertyTabAttribute(Type*);**

[JScript] **public function PropertyTabAttribute(Type);**

Initializes a new instance of the **PropertyTabAttribute** class using the specified tab class name and tab scope.

[Visual Basic] **Public Sub New(String, PropertyTabScope)**

[C#] **public PropertyTabAttribute(string, PropertyTabScope);**

[C++] **public: PropertyTabAttribute(String*, PropertyTabScope);**

[JScript] **public function PropertyTabAttribute(String, PropertyTabScope);**

Initializes a new instance of the **PropertyTabAttribute** class using the specified type of tab and tab scope.

[Visual Basic] **Public Sub New(Type, PropertyTabScope)**

[C#] **public PropertyTabAttribute(Type, PropertyTabScope);**

[C++] **public: PropertyTabAttribute(Type*, PropertyTabScope);**

[JScript] **public function PropertyTabAttribute(Type, PropertyTabScope);**

PropertyTabAttribute Constructor ()

Initializes a new instance of the **PropertyTabAttribute** class.

```
[Visual Basic]
Public Sub New()
[C#]
public PropertyTabAttribute();
[C++]
public: PropertyTabAttribute();
[JScript]
public function PropertyTabAttribute();
```

Remarks

This is a default constructor that creates an uninitialized **PropertyTabAttribute**. This constructor can be used to derive from this attribute and specify multiple tab types by calling **InitializeArrays**.

Requirements

Platforms: Windows 98, Windows NT 4.0, Windows Millennium Edition, Windows 2000, Windows XP Home Edition, Windows XP Professional, Windows Server 2003 family

PropertyTabAttribute Constructor (String)

Initializes a new instance of the **PropertyTabAttribute** class using the specified tab class name.

```
[Visual Basic]
Public Sub New( _
   ByVal tabClassName As String _
)
[C#]
public PropertyTabAttribute(
   string tabClassName
);
[C++]
public: PropertyTabAttribute(
   String* tabClassName
);
```

```
[JScript]
public function PropertyTabAttribute(
   tabClassName : String
);
```

Parameters

tabClassName

The assembly qualified name of the type of tab to create. For an example of this format convention, see **AssemblyQualifiedName**.

Requirements

Platforms: Windows 98, Windows NT 4.0, Windows Millennium Edition, Windows 2000, Windows XP Home Edition, Windows XP Professional, Windows Server 2003 family

PropertyTabAttribute Constructor (Type)

Initializes a new instance of the **PropertyTabAttribute** class using the specified type of tab.

```
[Visual Basic]
Public Sub New( _
   ByVal tabClass As Type _
)
[C#]
public PropertyTabAttribute(
   Type tabClass
);
[C++]
public: PropertyTabAttribute(
   Type* tabClass
);
[JScript]
public function PropertyTabAttribute(
   tabClass : Type
);
```

Parameters

tabClass

The type of tab to create.

Requirements

Platforms: Windows 98, Windows NT 4.0, Windows Millennium Edition, Windows 2000, Windows XP Home Edition, Windows XP Professional, Windows Server 2003 family

PropertyTabAttribute Constructor (String, PropertyTabScope)

Initializes a new instance of the **PropertyTabAttribute** class using the specified tab class name and tab scope.

```
[Visual Basic]
Public Sub New( _
   ByVal tabClassName As String, _
   ByVal tabScope As PropertyTabScope _
)
[C#]
public PropertyTabAttribute(
   string tabClassName,
   PropertyTabScope tabScope
);
[C++]
public: PropertyTabAttribute(
   String* tabClassName,
   PropertyTabScope tabScope
);
[JScript]
public function PropertyTabAttribute(
   tabClassName : String,
   tabScope : PropertyTabScope
);
```

Parameters

tabClassName

The assembly qualified name of the type of tab to create.

tabScope

A **PropertyTabScope** that indicates the scope of this tab. If the scope is **Component**, it is shown only for components with the corresponding **PropertyTabAttribute**. If it is **Document**, it is shown for all components on the document.

Requirements

Platforms: Windows 98, Windows NT 4.0, Windows Millennium Edition, Windows 2000, Windows XP Home Edition, Windows XP Professional, Windows Server 2003 family

PropertyTabAttribute Constructor (Type, PropertyTabScope)

Initializes a new instance of the **PropertyTabAttribute** class using the specified type of tab and tab scope.

```
[Visual Basic]
Public Sub New( _
   ByVal tabClass As Type, _
   ByVal tabScope As PropertyTabScope _
)
[C#]
public PropertyTabAttribute(
   Type tabClass,
   PropertyTabScope tabScope
);
[C++]
public: PropertyTabAttribute(
   Type* tabClass,
   PropertyTabScope tabScope
);
[JScript]
public function PropertyTabAttribute(
   tabClass : Type,
   tabScope : PropertyTabScope
);
```

Parameters

tabClass

The type of tab to create.

tabScope

A **PropertyTabScope** that indicates the scope of this tab. If the scope is **Component**, it is shown only for components with the corresponding **PropertyTabAttribute**. If it is **Document**, it is shown for all components on the document.

Requirements

Platforms: Windows 98, Windows NT 4.0, Windows Millennium Edition, Windows 2000, Windows XP Home Edition, Windows XP Professional, Windows Server 2003 family

PropertyTabAttribute.TabClasses Property

Gets the types of tab that this attribute uses.

```
[Visual Basic]
Public ReadOnly Property TabClasses As Type ()
[C#]
public Type[] TabClasses {get;}
[C++]
public: __property Type* get_TabClasses();
[JScript]
public function get TabClasses() : Type[];
```

Property Value

An array of types indicating the types of tab that this attribute uses.

Remarks

All specified types must be able to be assigned to a **PropertyTab**.

Requirements

Platforms: Windows 98, Windows NT 4.0, Windows Millennium Edition, Windows 2000, Windows XP Home Edition, Windows XP Professional, Windows Server 2003 family

PropertyTabAttribute.TabClassNames Property

Gets the names of the tab classes that this attribute uses.

```
[Visual Basic]
Protected ReadOnly Property TabClassNames As String ()
[C#]
protected string[] TabClassNames {get;}
[C++]
protected: __property String* get_TabClassNames();
[JScript]
protected function get TabClassNames() : String[];
```

Property Value

The names of the tab classes that this attribute uses.

Requirements

Platforms: Windows 98, Windows NT 4.0, Windows Millennium Edition, Windows 2000, Windows XP Home Edition, Windows XP Professional, Windows Server 2003 family

PropertyTabAttribute.TabScopes Property

Gets an array of tab scopes of each tab of this **PropertyTabAttribute**.

```
[Visual Basic]
Public ReadOnly Property TabScopes As PropertyTabScope ()
[C#]
public PropertyTabScope[] TabScopes {get;}
[C++]
public: __property PropertyTabScope get_TabScopes();
[JScript]
public function get TabScopes() : PropertyTabScope[];
```

Property Value

An array of **PropertyTabScope** objects that indicate the scopes of the tabs.

Requirements

Platforms: Windows 98, Windows NT 4.0, Windows Millennium Edition, Windows 2000, Windows XP Home Edition, Windows XP Professional, Windows Server 2003 family

PropertyTabAttribute.Equals Method

This member supports the .NET Framework infrastructure and is not intended to be used directly from your code.

Overload List

This member overrides **Object.Equals**.

[Visual Basic] **Overloads Overrides Public Function Equals(Object) As Boolean**

[C#] **public override bool Equals(object);**

[C++] **public: bool Equals(Object*);**

[JScript] **public override function Equals(Object) : Boolean;**

This member supports the .NET Framework infrastructure and is not intended to be used directly from your code.

[Visual Basic] **Overloads Public Function Equals(PropertyTabAttribute) As Boolean**

[C#] **public bool Equals(PropertyTabAttribute);**

[C++] **public: bool Equals(PropertyTabAttribute*);**

[JScript] **public function Equals(PropertyTabAttribute) : Boolean;**

PropertyTabAttribute.Equals Method (Object)

This member overrides **Object.Equals**.

```
[Visual Basic]
Overrides Overloads Public Function Equals( _
   ByVal other As Object _
) As Boolean
[C#]
public override bool Equals(
   object other
);
[C++]
public: bool Equals(
   Object* other
);
[JScript]
public override function Equals(
   other : Object
) : Boolean;
```

Requirements

Platforms: Windows 98, Windows NT 4.0, Windows Millennium Edition, Windows 2000, Windows XP Home Edition, Windows XP Professional, Windows Server 2003 family

PropertyTabAttribute.Equals Method (PropertyTabAttribute)

This member supports the .NET Framework infrastructure and is not intended to be used directly from your code.

```
[Visual Basic]
Overloads Public Function Equals( _
   ByVal other As PropertyTabAttribute _
) As Boolean
[C#]
public bool Equals(
   PropertyTabAttribute other
);
[C++]
public: bool Equals(
   PropertyTabAttribute* other
);
[JScript]
public function Equals(
   other : PropertyTabAttribute
) : Boolean;
```

PropertyTabAttribute.GetHashCode Method

This member overrides **Attribute.GetHashCode**.

```
[Visual Basic]
Overrides Public Function GetHashCode() As Integer
[C#]
public override int GetHashCode();
[C++]
public: int GetHashCode();
[JScript]
public override function GetHashCode() : int;
```

Requirements

Platforms: Windows 98, Windows NT 4.0, Windows Millennium Edition, Windows 2000, Windows XP Home Edition, Windows XP Professional, Windows Server 2003 family

PropertyTabAttribute.InitializeArrays Method

Initializes the attribute.

Overload List

Initializes the attribute using the specified names of tab classes and array of tab scopes.

[Visual Basic] **Overloads Protected Sub InitializeArrays(String(), PropertyTabScope())**

[C#] **protected void InitializeArrays(string[], PropertyTabScope[]);**

[C++] **protected: void InitializeArrays(String*[], PropertyTabScope[]);**

[JScript] **protected function InitializeArrays(String[], PropertyTabScope[]);**

Initializes the attribute using the specified names of tab classes and array of tab scopes.

[Visual Basic] **Overloads Protected Sub InitializeArrays(Type(), PropertyTabScope())**

[C#] **protected void InitializeArrays(Type[], PropertyTabScope[]);**

[C++] **protected: void InitializeArrays(Type*[], PropertyTabScope[]);**

[JScript] **protected function InitializeArrays(Type[], PropertyTabScope[]);**

PropertyTabAttribute.InitializeArrays Method (String[], PropertyTabScope[])

Initializes the attribute using the specified names of tab classes and array of tab scopes.

```
[Visual Basic]
Overloads Protected Sub InitializeArrays( _
   ByVal tabClassNames() As String, _
   ByVal tabScopes() As PropertyTabScope _
)
[C#]
protected void InitializeArrays(
   string[] tabClassNames,
   PropertyTabScope[] tabScopes
);
[C++]
protected: void InitializeArrays(
   String* tabClassNames __gc[],
   PropertyTabScope tabScopes[]
);
[JScript]
protected function InitializeArrays(
   tabClassNames : String[],
   tabScopes : PropertyTabScope[]
);
```

Parameters

tabClassNames

An array of fully qualified type names of the types to create for tabs on the Properties window.

tabScopes

The scope of each tab. If the scope is **Component**, it is shown only for components with the corresponding **PropertyTabAttribute**. If it is **Document**, it is shown for all components on the document.

Remarks

InitializeArrays provides a utility function that can be used to set the types of tab classes that this **PropertyTabAttribute** specifies.

Requirements

Platforms: Windows 98, Windows NT 4.0, Windows Millennium Edition, Windows 2000, Windows XP Home Edition, Windows XP Professional, Windows Server 2003 family

PropertyTabAttribute.InitializeArrays Method (Type[], PropertyTabScope[])

Initializes the attribute using the specified names of tab classes and array of tab scopes.

[Visual Basic]
```
Overloads Protected Sub InitializeArrays( _
   ByVal tabClasses() As Type, _
   ByVal tabScopes() As PropertyTabScope _
)
```
[C#]
```
protected void InitializeArrays(
   Type[] tabClasses,
   PropertyTabScope[] tabScopes
);
```
[C++]
```
protected: void InitializeArrays(
   Type* tabClasses[],
   PropertyTabScope tabScopes[]
);
```
[JScript]
```
protected function InitializeArrays(
   tabClasses : Type[],
   tabScopes : PropertyTabScope[]
);
```

Parameters

tabClasses

The types of tabs to create.

tabScopes

The scope of each tab. If the scope is **Component**, it is shown only for components with the corresponding **PropertyTabAttribute**. If it is **Document**, it is shown for all components on the document.

Remarks

InitializeArrays provides a utility function that can be used to set the types of tab classes that this **PropertyTabAttribute** specifies.

Requirements

Platforms: Windows 98, Windows NT 4.0, Windows Millennium Edition, Windows 2000, Windows XP Home Edition, Windows XP Professional, Windows Server 2003 family

PropertyTabScope Enumeration

Defines identifiers that indicate the persistence scope of a tab in the Properties window.

[Visual Basic]
```
<Serializable>
Public Enum PropertyTabScope
```
[C#]
```
[Serializable]
public enum PropertyTabScope
```
[C++]
```
[Serializable]
__value public enum PropertyTabScope
```
[JScript]
```
public
   Serializable
enum PropertyTabScope
```

Remarks

PropertyTabScope indicates the persistence scope of a tab that is displayed in the Properties window when a component of a design document has an associated **PropertyTabAttribute**.

Members

Member name	Description
Component	This tab is specific to the current component. This tab is added to the Properties window for the current component only and is removed when the component is no longer selected.
Document	This tab is specific to the current document. This tab is added to the Properties window and is removed when the currently selected document changes.
Global	This tab is added to the Properties window and can only be removed explicitly by a parent component.
Static	This tab is added to the Properties window and cannot be removed.

Requirements

Namespace: System.ComponentModel

Platforms: Windows 98, Windows NT 4.0, Windows Millennium Edition, Windows 2000, Windows XP Home Edition, Windows XP Professional, Windows Server 2003 family

Assembly: System (in System.dll)

ProvidePropertyAttribute Class

Specifies the name of the property that an implementor of **IExtenderProvider** offers to other components.

System.Object
  System.Attribute
    System.ComponentModel.ProvidePropertyAttribute

[Visual Basic]
```
<AttributeUsage(AttributeTargets.Class)>
NotInheritable Public Class ProvidePropertyAttribute
   Inherits Attribute
```
[C#]
```
[AttributeUsage(AttributeTargets.Class)]
public sealed class ProvidePropertyAttribute : Attribute
```
[C++]
```
[AttributeUsage(AttributeTargets::Class)]
public __gc __sealed class ProvidePropertyAttribute : public
   Attribute
```
[JScript]
```
public
   AttributeUsage(AttributeTargets.Class)
class ProvidePropertyAttribute extends Attribute
```

Thread Safety

Any public static (**Shared** in Visual Basic) members of this type are safe for multithreaded operations. Any instance members are not guaranteed to be thread safe.

Remarks

When you mark a class with this attribute, you tell the code generator to create an extender property with the name you provide. The marked class must implement **IExtenderProvider**. As a result, the new property can be used by other components in a container.

Within the marked class, you must implement **Get** <name> and **Set** <name> methods. For example, if you mark a class with [ProvideProperty("PropertyName")], you must implement **GetPropertyName** and **SetPropertyName** methods. To specify that the new property will be an extender property, you must implement from **IExtenderProvider**, you must also implement a **CanExtend** method.

Example

[Visual Basic, C#] The following example marks `MyClass` with a **ProvidePropertyAttribute** that tells the compiler to create a property called `MyProperty` from the `GetMyProperty` and `SetMyProperty` methods.

[Visual Basic]
```
<ProvideProperty("MyProperty", GetType(Control))> _
Public Class SampleClass
    Implements IExtenderProvider
    Protected ciMine As CultureInfo = Nothing

    ' Provides the Get portion of MyProperty.
    Public Function GetMyProperty(myControl As Control) As CultureInfo
        ' Insert code here.
        Return ciMine
    End Function 'GetMyProperty

    ' Provides the Set portion of MyProperty.
    Public Sub SetMyProperty(myControl As Control, value As String)
        ' Insert code here.
    End Sub 'SetMyProperty

    ' When you inherit from IExtenderProvider, you must implement the
    ' CanExtend method.
    Public Function CanExtend(target As [Object]) As Boolean
 Implements IExtenderProvider.CanExtend
        Return TypeOf target Is Control
    End Function 'CanExtend

    ' Insert additional code here.

End Class
```

[C#]
```
[ProvideProperty("MyProperty", typeof(Control))]
public class MyClass : IExtenderProvider {
    protected CultureInfo ciMine = null;
    // Provides the Get portion of MyProperty.
    public CultureInfo GetMyProperty(Control myControl) {
        // Insert code here.
        return ciMine;
    }

    // Provides the Set portion of MyProperty.
    public void SetMyProperty(Control myControl, string value) {
        // Insert code here.
    }

    /* When you inherit from IExtenderProvider, you must implement the
     * CanExtend method. */
    public bool CanExtend(Object target) {
        return(target is Control);
    }

    // Insert additional code here.
 }
```

Requirements

Namespace: System.ComponentModel

Platforms: Windows 98, Windows NT 4.0, Windows Millennium Edition, Windows 2000, Windows XP Home Edition, Windows XP Professional, Windows Server 2003 family

Assembly: System (in System.dll)

ProvidePropertyAttribute Constructor

Initializes a new instance of the **ProvidePropertyAttribute** class.

Overload List

Initializes a new instance of the **ProvidePropertyAttribute** class with the name of the property and the type of its receiver.

[Visual Basic] **Public Sub New(String, String)**

[C#] **public ProvidePropertyAttribute(string, string);**

[C++] **public: ProvidePropertyAttribute(String*, String*);**

[JScript] **public function ProvidePropertyAttribute(String, String);**

Initializes a new instance of the **ProvidePropertyAttribute** class with the name of the property and its **Type**.

[Visual Basic] **Public Sub New(String, Type)**

[C#] **public ProvidePropertyAttribute(string, Type);**

[C++] **public: ProvidePropertyAttribute(String*, Type*);**

[JScript] **public function ProvidePropertyAttribute(String, Type);**

ProvidePropertyAttribute Constructor (String, String)

Initializes a new instance of the **ProvidePropertyAttribute** class with the name of the property and the type of its receiver.

```
[Visual Basic]
Public Sub New( _
   ByVal propertyName As String, _
   ByVal receiverTypeName As String _
)
[C#]
public ProvidePropertyAttribute(
   string propertyName,
   string receiverTypeName
);
[C++]
public: ProvidePropertyAttribute(
   String* propertyName,
   String* receiverTypeName
);
[JScript]
public function ProvidePropertyAttribute(
   propertyName : String,
   receiverTypeName : String
);
```

Parameters

propertyName
The name of the property extending to an object of the specified type.

receiverTypeName
The name of the data type this property can extend.

Requirements

Platforms: Windows 98, Windows NT 4.0, Windows Millennium Edition, Windows 2000, Windows XP Home Edition, Windows XP Professional, Windows Server 2003 family

ProvidePropertyAttribute Constructor (String, Type)

Initializes a new instance of the **ProvidePropertyAttribute** class with the name of the property and its **Type**.

```
[Visual Basic]
Public Sub New( _
   ByVal propertyName As String, _
   ByVal receiverType As Type _
)
[C#]
public ProvidePropertyAttribute(
   string propertyName,
   Type receiverType
);
[C++]
public: ProvidePropertyAttribute(
   String* propertyName,
   Type* receiverType
);
[JScript]
public function ProvidePropertyAttribute(
   propertyName : String,
   receiverType : Type
);
```

Parameters

propertyName
The name of the property extending to an object of the specified type.

receiverType
The **Type** of the data type of the object that can receive the property.

Requirements

Platforms: Windows 98, Windows NT 4.0, Windows Millennium Edition, Windows 2000, Windows XP Home Edition, Windows XP Professional, Windows Server 2003 family

ProvidePropertyAttribute.PropertyName Property

Gets the name of a property that this class provides.

```
[Visual Basic]
Public ReadOnly Property PropertyName As String
[C#]
public string PropertyName {get;}
[C++]
public: __property String* get_PropertyName();
[JScript]
public function get PropertyName() : String;
```

Property Value

The name of a property that this class provides.

Requirements

Platforms: Windows 98, Windows NT 4.0, Windows Millennium Edition, Windows 2000, Windows XP Home Edition, Windows XP Professional, Windows Server 2003 family

ProvidePropertyAttribute.ReceiverTypeName Property

Gets the name of the data type this property can extend.

```
[Visual Basic]
Public ReadOnly Property ReceiverTypeName As String
[C#]
public string ReceiverTypeName {get;}
[C++]
public: __property String* get_ReceiverTypeName();
[JScript]
public function get ReceiverTypeName() : String;
```

Property Value

The name of the data type this property can extend.

Requirements

Platforms: Windows 98, Windows NT 4.0, Windows Millennium Edition, Windows 2000, Windows XP Home Edition, Windows XP Professional, Windows Server 2003 family

ProvidePropertyAttribute.TypeId Property

This member overrides **Attribute.TypeId**.

```
[Visual Basic]
Overrides Public ReadOnly Property TypeId As Object
[C#]
public override object TypeId {get;}
[C++]
public: __property Object* get_TypeId();
[JScript]
public override function get TypeId() : Object;
```

Requirements

Platforms: Windows 98, Windows NT 4.0, Windows Millennium Edition, Windows 2000, Windows XP Home Edition, Windows XP Professional, Windows Server 2003 family

ProvidePropertyAttribute.Equals Method

This member overrides **Object.Equals**.

```
[Visual Basic]
Overrides Public Function Equals( _
   ByVal obj As Object _
) As Boolean
[C#]
public override bool Equals(
   object obj
);
[C++]
public: bool Equals(
   Object* obj
);
[JScript]
public override function Equals(
   obj : Object
) : Boolean;
```

Requirements

Platforms: Windows 98, Windows NT 4.0, Windows Millennium Edition, Windows 2000, Windows XP Home Edition, Windows XP Professional, Windows Server 2003 family

ProvidePropertyAttribute.GetHashCode Method

This member overrides **Attribute.GetHashCode**.

```
[Visual Basic]
Overrides Public Function GetHashCode() As Integer
[C#]
public override int GetHashCode();
[C++]
public: int GetHashCode();
[JScript]
public override function GetHashCode() : int;
```

Requirements

Platforms: Windows 98, Windows NT 4.0, Windows Millennium Edition, Windows 2000, Windows XP Home Edition, Windows XP Professional, Windows Server 2003 family

ReadOnlyAttribute Class

Specifies whether the property this attribute is bound to is read-only or read/write at design time.

System.Object
  System.Attribute
    System.ComponentModel.ReadOnlyAttribute

[Visual Basic]
```
<AttributeUsage(AttributeTargets.All)>
NotInheritable Public Class ReadOnlyAttribute
   Inherits Attribute
```
[C#]
```
[AttributeUsage(AttributeTargets.All)]
public sealed class ReadOnlyAttribute : Attribute
```
[C++]
```
[AttributeUsage(AttributeTargets::All)]
public __gc __sealed class ReadOnlyAttribute : public Attribute
```
[JScript]
```
public
   AttributeUsage(AttributeTargets.All)
class ReadOnlyAttribute extends Attribute
```

Thread Safety

Any public static (**Shared** in Visual Basic) members of this type are safe for multithreaded operations. Any instance members are not guaranteed to be thread safe.

Remarks

Members that are marked with the **ReadOnlyAttribute** constructor of the value **true** or that do not have a **Set** method cannot be changed. Members that do not have this attribute or that are marked with the **ReadOnlyAttribute** constructor of the value **false** are read/write, and they can be changed. The default is **No**.

> **Note** When you mark a property with the **ReadOnlyAttribute** constructor of the value **true**, the value of this attribute is set to the constant member **Yes**. For a property marked with the **ReadOnlyAttribute** constructor of the value **false**, the value is **No**. Therefore, when you want to check the value of this attribute in your code, you must specify the attribute as **ReadOnlyAttribute.Yes** or **ReadOnlyAttribute.No**.

For more information, see **Attributes Overview** and **Extending Metadata Using Attributes**.

Example

[Visual Basic, C#] The following example marks a property as read-only.

[Visual Basic]
```
Public ReadOnly Property MyProperty() As Integer
    Get
        ' Insert code here.
        Return 0
    End Get
End Property
```

[C#]
```
[ReadOnly(true)]
 public int MyProperty {
    get {
       // Insert code here.
       return 0;
    }
}
```

[Visual Basic, C#] The next example shows how to check the value of the **ReadOnlyAttribute** for `MyProperty`. First the code gets a **PropertyDescriptorCollection** with all the properties for the object. Next it indexes into the **PropertyDescriptorCollection** to get `MyProperty`. Then it returns the attributes for this property and saves them in the attributes variable.

[Visual Basic, C#] The example presents two different ways of checking the value of the **ReadOnlyAttribute**. In the second code fragment, the example calls the **Equals** method. In the last code fragment, the example uses the **IsReadOnly** property to check the value.

[Visual Basic]
```
' Gets the attributes for the property.
Dim attributes As AttributeCollection = _
    TypeDescriptor.GetProperties(Me)("MyProperty").Attributes

' Checks to see whether the value of the ReadOnlyAttribute is Yes.
If attributes(GetType(ReadOnlyAttribute)).Equals
(ReadOnlyAttribute.Yes) Then
    ' Insert code here.
End If

' This is another way to see whether the property is read-only.
Dim myAttribute As ReadOnlyAttribute = _
    CType(attributes(GetType(ReadOnlyAttribute)), ReadOnlyAttribute)

If myAttribute.IsReadOnly Then
    ' Insert code here.
End If
```

[C#]
```
// Gets the attributes for the property.
AttributeCollection attributes =
   TypeDescriptor.GetProperties(this)["MyProperty"].Attributes;

// Checks to see whether the value of the ReadOnlyAttribute is Yes.
if(attributes[typeof(ReadOnlyAttribute)].Equals
 (ReadOnlyAttribute.Yes)) {
   // Insert code here.
}

// This is another way to see whether the property is read-only.
ReadOnlyAttribute myAttribute =
   (ReadOnlyAttribute)attributes[typeof(ReadOnlyAttribute)];
if(myAttribute.IsReadOnly) {
   // Insert code here.
}
```

[Visual Basic, C#] If you marked a class with the **ReadOnly-Attribute**, use the following code example to check the value.

[Visual Basic]
```
Dim attributes As AttributeCollection =
TypeDescriptor.GetAttributes(MyProperty)
If attributes(GetType(ReadOnlyAttribute)).Equals
 (ReadOnlyAttribute.Yes) Then
    ' Insert code here.
End If
```

[C#]
```
AttributeCollection attributes =
   TypeDescriptor.GetAttributes(MyProperty);
if(attributes[typeof(ReadOnlyAttribute)].Equals
 (ReadOnlyAttribute.Yes)) {
   // Insert code here.
}
```

Requirements

Namespace: System.ComponentModel

Platforms: Windows 98, Windows NT 4.0, Windows Millennium Edition, Windows 2000, Windows XP Home Edition, Windows XP Professional, Windows Server 2003 family

Assembly: System (in System.dll)

ReadOnlyAttribute Constructor

Initializes a new instance of the **ReadOnlyAttribute** class.

[Visual Basic]
```
Public Sub New( _
   ByVal isReadOnly As Boolean _
)
```
[C#]
```
public ReadOnlyAttribute(
   bool isReadOnly
);
```
[C++]
```
public: ReadOnlyAttribute(
   bool isReadOnly
);
```
[JScript]
```
public function ReadOnlyAttribute(
   isReadOnly : Boolean
);
```

Parameters

isReadOnly

true if the property this attribute is bound to is read-only; **false** if the property is read/write.

Remarks

Members that are marked with the **ctor** constructor of the value **true** or that do not have a **Set** method cannot be changed. Members that do not have this attribute or that are marked with the **ctor** constructor of the value **false** are read/write, and they can be changed. The default is **No**.

> **Note** When you mark a property with the **ctor** constructor of the value **true**, the value of this attribute is set to the constant member **Yes**. For a property marked with the **ctor** constructor of the value **false**, the value is **No**. Therefore, when you want to check the value of this attribute in your code, you must specify the attribute as **ReadOnlyAttribute.Yes** or **ReadOnlyAttribute.No**.

Example

[Visual Basic, C#] The following example marks a property as read-only. This code creates a new **ReadOnlyAttribute**, sets its value to **ReadOnlyAttribute.Yes**, and binds it to the property.

[Visual Basic]
```
<ReadOnlyAttribute(True)> _
Public Property MyProperty() As Integer
   Get
       ' Insert code here.
       Return 0
   End Get
   Set
       ' Insert code here.
   End Set
End Property
```
[C#]
```
[ReadOnly(true)]
public int MyProperty {
   get {
      // Insert code here.
      return 0;
   }
   set {
      // Insert code here.
   }
}
```

Requirements

Platforms: Windows 98, Windows NT 4.0, Windows Millennium Edition, Windows 2000, Windows XP Home Edition, Windows XP Professional, Windows Server 2003 family

ReadOnlyAttribute.Default Field

This member supports the .NET Framework infrastructure and is not intended to be used directly from your code.

[Visual Basic]
```
Public Shared ReadOnly Default As ReadOnlyAttribute
```
[C#]
```
public static readonly ReadOnlyAttribute Default;
```
[C++]
```
public: static ReadOnlyAttribute* Default;
```
[JScript]
```
public static var Default : ReadOnlyAttribute;
```

ReadOnlyAttribute.No Field

Specifies that the property this attribute is bound to is read/write and can be modified at design time. This static (**Shared** in Visual Basic) field is read-only.

[Visual Basic]
```
Public Shared ReadOnly No As ReadOnlyAttribute
```
[C#]
```
public static readonly ReadOnlyAttribute No;
```
[C++]
```
public: static ReadOnlyAttribute* No;
```
[JScript]
```
public static var No : ReadOnlyAttribute;
```

Remarks

This field is the default setting for this attribute.

When you mark a property with the **ReadOnlyAttribute** constructor of the value **false**, the value of this attribute is set to the constant member **No**. Therefore, when you want to check whether the attribute is set to this value in your code, you must specify the attribute as **ReadOnlyAttribute.No**.

Requirements

Platforms: Windows 98, Windows NT 4.0, Windows Millennium Edition, Windows 2000, Windows XP Home Edition, Windows XP Professional, Windows Server 2003 family

ReadOnlyAttribute.Yes Field

Specifies that the property this attribute is bound to is read-only and cannot be modified in the server explorer. This static (**Shared** in Visual Basic) field is read-only.

[Visual Basic]
```
Public Shared ReadOnly Yes As ReadOnlyAttribute
```
[C#]
```
public static readonly ReadOnlyAttribute Yes;
```
[C++]
```
public: static ReadOnlyAttribute* Yes;
```
[JScript]
```
public static var Yes : ReadOnlyAttribute;
```

Remarks

When you mark a property with the **ReadOnlyAttribute** constructor of the value **true**, the value of this attribute is set to the constant member **Yes**. Therefore, when you want to check whether the attribute is set to this value in your code, you must specify the attribute as **ReadOnlyAttribute.Yes**.

Requirements

Platforms: Windows 98, Windows NT 4.0, Windows Millennium Edition, Windows 2000, Windows XP Home Edition, Windows XP Professional, Windows Server 2003 family

ReadOnlyAttribute.IsReadOnly Property

Gets a value indicating whether the property this attribute is bound to is read-only.

[Visual Basic]
```
Public ReadOnly Property IsReadOnly As Boolean
```
[C#]
```
public bool IsReadOnly {get;}
```
[C++]
```
public: __property bool get_IsReadOnly();
```
[JScript]
```
public function get IsReadOnly() : Boolean;
```

Property Value

true if the property this attribute is bound to is read-only; **false** if the property is read/write.

Example

[Visual Basic, C#] The following example checks to see whether `MyProperty` is read-only. First the code gets the attributes for `MyProperty` by:

- Retrieving a **PropertyDescriptorCollection** with all the properties for the object.
- Indexing into the **PropertyDescriptorCollection** to get `MyProperty`.
- Saving the attributes for this property in the attributes variable.

[Visual Basic, C#] Then the code sets `myAttribute` to the value of the **ReadOnlyAttribute** in the **AttributeCollection** and checks a whether the property is read-only.

[Visual Basic]
```
' Gets the attributes for the property.
Dim attributes As AttributeCollection = _
   TypeDescriptor.GetProperties(Me)("MyProperty").Attributes

' Checks to see whether the property is read-only.
Dim myAttribute As ReadOnlyAttribute = _
   CType(attributes(GetType(ReadOnlyAttribute)), ReadOnlyAttribute)

If myAttribute.IsReadOnly Then
    ' Insert code here.
End If
```

[C#]
```
// Gets the attributes for the property.
AttributeCollection attributes =
   TypeDescriptor.GetProperties(this)["MyProperty"].Attributes;

// Checks to see whether the property is read-only.
ReadOnlyAttribute myAttribute =
   (ReadOnlyAttribute)attributes[typeof(ReadOnlyAttribute)];

if(myAttribute.IsReadOnly) {
   // Insert code here.
}
```

Requirements

Platforms: Windows 98, Windows NT 4.0, Windows Millennium Edition, Windows 2000, Windows XP Home Edition, Windows XP Professional, Windows Server 2003 family

ReadOnlyAttribute.Equals Method

This member overrides **Object.Equals**.

[Visual Basic]
```
Overrides Public Function Equals( _
   ByVal value As Object _
) As Boolean
```
[C#]
```
public override bool Equals(
   object value
);
```
[C++]
```
public: bool Equals(
   Object* value
);
```
[JScript]
```
public override function Equals(
   value : Object
) : Boolean;
```

Requirements

Platforms: Windows 98, Windows NT 4.0, Windows Millennium Edition, Windows 2000, Windows XP Home Edition, Windows XP Professional, Windows Server 2003 family

ReadOnlyAttribute.GetHashCode Method

This member overrides **Attribute.GetHashCode**.

[Visual Basic]
```
Overrides Public Function GetHashCode() As Integer
```
[C#]
```
public override int GetHashCode();
```
[C++]
```
public: int GetHashCode();
```
[JScript]
```
public override function GetHashCode() : int;
```

Requirements

Platforms: Windows 98, Windows NT 4.0, Windows Millennium Edition, Windows 2000, Windows XP Home Edition, Windows XP Professional, Windows Server 2003 family

ReadOnlyAttribute.IsDefaultAttribute Method

This member overrides **Attribute.IsDefaultAttribute**.

[Visual Basic]
```
Overrides Public Function IsDefaultAttribute() As Boolean
```
[C#]
```
public override bool IsDefaultAttribute();
```
[C++]
```
public: bool IsDefaultAttribute();
```
[JScript]
```
public override function IsDefaultAttribute() : Boolean;
```

Requirements

Platforms: Windows 98, Windows NT 4.0, Windows Millennium Edition, Windows 2000, Windows XP Home Edition, Windows XP Professional, Windows Server 2003 family

RecommendedAsConfigurable-Attribute Class

Specifies that the property can be used as an application setting.

System.Object
  System.Attribute
    System.ComponentModel.RecommendedAsConfigurable-Attribute

[Visual Basic]
```
<AttributeUsage(AttributeTargets.Property)>
Public Class RecommendedAsConfigurableAttribute
   Inherits Attribute
```
[C#]
```
[AttributeUsage(AttributeTargets.Property)]
public class RecommendedAsConfigurableAttribute : Attribute
```
[C++]
```
[AttributeUsage(AttributeTargets::Property)]
public __gc class RecommendedAsConfigurableAttribute : public
   Attribute
```
[JScript]
```
public
   AttributeUsage(AttributeTargets.Property)
class RecommendedAsConfigurableAttribute extends Attribute
```

Thread Safety

Any public static (**Shared** in Visual Basic) members of this type are safe for multithreaded operations. Any instance members are not guaranteed to be thread safe.

Remarks

Properties that are marked with the **RecommendedAsConfigurableAttribute** constructor of the value **true** display when you expand the ConfigurableProperties line in the Properties window in Visual Studio .NET. A property that has no recommended setting or that is marked with **RecommendedAs-ConfigurableAttribute** constructor of the value **false** is not shown and is an unlikely candidate for being an application setting. The default is **false**.

You can bind a property that does not have a **RecommendedAsCon-figurableAttribute** to a setting in Visual Studio .NET by clicking the ellipsis button (...) under Settingsin the Propertieswindow and selecting the appropriate property from the list.

> **Note** When you mark a property with **RecommendedAsCon-figurableAttribute** constructor of the value **true**, the value of this attribute is set to the constant member **Yes**. For a property marked with **RecommendedAsConfigurableAttribute** constructor of the value **false**, the value is **No**. Therefore, when you want to check the value of this attribute in your code, you must specify the attribute as **RecommendedAsConfigurable-Attribute.Yes** or **RecommendedAsConfigurableAttribute.No**.

For more information, see **Attributes Overview** and **Extending Metadata Using Attributes**.

Example

[Visual Basic, C#] The following example marks a property as usable as an application setting.

[Visual Basic]
```
<RecommendedAsConfigurable(True)> _
Public Property MyProperty() As Integer
    Get
        ' Insert code here.
        Return 0
    End Get
    Set
        ' Insert code here.
    End Set
End Property
```

[C#]
```
[RecommendedAsConfigurable(true)]
 public int MyProperty {
    get {
       // Insert code here.
       return 0;
    }
    set {
       // Insert code here.
    }
 }
```

[Visual Basic, C#] The next example shows how to check the value of the **RecommendedAsConfigurableAttribute** for `MyProperty`. First the code gets a **PropertyDescriptorCollection** with all the properties for the object. Next it indexes into the **Property-DescriptorCollection** to get `MyProperty`. Then it returns the attributes for this property and saves them in the attributes variable.

[Visual Basic, C#] This example presents two different ways of checking the value of the **RecommendedAsConfigurable-Attribute**. In the second code fragment, the example calls the **Equals** method. In the last code fragment, the example uses the **RecommendedAsConfigurable** property to check the value.

[Visual Basic]
```
' Gets the attributes for the property.
Dim attributes As AttributeCollection =
TypeDescriptor.GetProperties(Me)("MyProperty").Attributes

' Checks to see if the value of the                                   ↵
RecommendedAsConfigurableAttribute is Yes.
If attributes(GetType(RecommendedAsConfigurableAttribute)).Equals     ↵
 (RecommendedAsConfigurableAttribute.Yes) Then
    ' Insert code here.
End If

' This is another way to see if the property is recommended as       ↵
configurable.
Dim myAttribute As RecommendedAsConfigurableAttribute = _
    CType(attributes(GetType                                          ↵
 (RecommendedAsConfigurableAttribute)),                               ↵
RecommendedAsConfigurableAttribute)
If myAttribute.RecommendedAsConfigurable Then
    ' Insert code here.
End If
```

[C#]
```
// Gets the attributes for the property.
AttributeCollection attributes =
   TypeDescriptor.GetProperties(this)["MyProperty"].Attributes;

// Checks to see if the value of the                                  ↵
RecommendedAsConfigurableAttribute is Yes.
if(attributes[typeof(RecommendedAsConfigurableAttribute)].Equals      ↵
 (RecommendedAsConfigurableAttribute.Yes)) {
   // Insert code here.
}
```

```
// This is another way to see if the property is recommended as ↵
configurable.
RecommendedAsConfigurableAttribute myAttribute =
   (RecommendedAsConfigurableAttribute)attributes[typeof ↵
 (RecommendedAsConfigurableAttribute)];
if(myAttribute.RecommendedAsConfigurable) {
   // Insert code here.
}
```

[Visual Basic, C#] If you marked a class with the **RecommendedAs-ConfigurableAttribute**, use the following code to check the value.

[Visual Basic]
```
Dim attributes As AttributeCollection = ↵
TypeDescriptor.GetAttributes(MyProperty)
If attributes(GetType(RecommendedAsConfigurableAttribute)).Equals ↵
 (RecommendedAsConfigurableAttribute.Yes) Then
    ' Insert code here.
End If
```

[C#]
```
AttributeCollection attributes =
   TypeDescriptor.GetAttributes(MyProperty);
if(attributes[typeof(RecommendedAsConfigurableAttribute)].Equals ↵
 (RecommendedAsConfigurableAttribute.Yes)) {
   // Insert code here.
}
```

Requirements

Namespace: System.ComponentModel

Platforms: Windows 98, Windows NT 4.0, Windows Millennium Edition, Windows 2000, Windows XP Home Edition, Windows XP Professional, Windows Server 2003 family

Assembly: System (in System.dll)

RecommendedAsConfigurableAttribute Constructor

Initializes a new instance of the **RecommendedAsConfigurable-Attribute** class.

[Visual Basic]
```
Public Sub New( _
   ByVal recommendedAsConfigurable As Boolean _
)
```
[C#]
```
public RecommendedAsConfigurableAttribute(
   bool recommendedAsConfigurable
);
```
[C++]
```
public: RecommendedAsConfigurableAttribute(
   bool recommendedAsConfigurable
);
```
[JScript]
```
public function RecommendedAsConfigurableAttribute(
   recommendedAsConfigurable : Boolean
);
```

Parameters

recommendedAsConfigurable

true if the property this attribute is bound to can be used as an application setting; otherwise, **false**.

Example

[Visual Basic, C#] The following example marks a property as usable as an application setting. This code creates a new **RecommendedAsConfigurableAttribute**, sets its value to **RecommendedAsConfigurableAttribute.Yes**, and binds it to the property.

[Visual Basic]
```
<RecommendedAsConfigurable(True)> _
Public Property MyProperty() As Integer
    Get
        ' Insert code here.
        Return 0
    End Get
    Set
        ' Insert code here.
    End Set
End Property
```

[C#]
```
[RecommendedAsConfigurable(true)]
public int MyProperty {
   get {
      // Insert code here.
      return 0;
   }
   set {
      // Insert code here.
   }
}
```

Requirements

Platforms: Windows 98, Windows NT 4.0, Windows Millennium Edition, Windows 2000, Windows XP Home Edition, Windows XP Professional, Windows Server 2003 family

RecommendedAsConfigurableAttribute.Default Field

This member supports the .NET Framework infrastructure and is not intended to be used directly from your code.

[Visual Basic]
```
Public Shared ReadOnly Default As _
   RecommendedAsConfigurableAttribute
```
[C#]
```
public static readonly RecommendedAsConfigurableAttribute Default;
```
[C++]
```
public: static RecommendedAsConfigurableAttribute* Default;
```
[JScript]
```
public static var Default : RecommendedAsConfigurableAttribute;
```

RecommendedAsConfigurableAttribute.No Field

Specifies that a property cannot be used as an application setting. This static (**Shared** in Visual Basic) field is read-only.

[Visual Basic]
```
Public Shared ReadOnly No As RecommendedAsConfigurableAttribute
```
[C#]
```
public static readonly RecommendedAsConfigurableAttribute No;
```
[C++]
```
public: static RecommendedAsConfigurableAttribute* No;
```
[JScript]
```
public static var No : RecommendedAsConfigurableAttribute;
```

Remarks

This field is the default setting for this attribute.

When you mark a property with **RecommendedAsConfigurableAttribute** constructor of the value **false**, the value of this attribute is set to the constant member **No**. Therefore, when you want to check whether the attribute is set to this value in your code, you must specify the attribute **RecommendedAsConfigurableAttribute.No**.

Requirements

Platforms: Windows 98, Windows NT 4.0, Windows Millennium Edition, Windows 2000, Windows XP Home Edition, Windows XP Professional, Windows Server 2003 family

RecommendedAsConfigurableAttribute.Yes Field

Specifies that a property can be used as an application setting. This static (**Shared** in Visual Basic) field is read-only.

[Visual Basic]
```
Public Shared ReadOnly Yes As RecommendedAsConfigurableAttribute
```
[C#]
```
public static readonly RecommendedAsConfigurableAttribute Yes;
```
[C++]
```
public: static RecommendedAsConfigurableAttribute* Yes;
```
[JScript]
```
public static var Yes : RecommendedAsConfigurableAttribute;
```

Remarks

When you mark a property with **RecommendedAsConfigurableAttribute** constructor of the value **true**, the value of this attribute is set to the constant member **Yes**.

Therefore, when you want to check whether the attribute is set to this value in your code, you must specify the attribute as **RecommendedAsConfigurableAttribute.Yes**.

Requirements

Platforms: Windows 98, Windows NT 4.0, Windows Millennium Edition, Windows 2000, Windows XP Home Edition, Windows XP Professional, Windows Server 2003 family

RecommendedAsConfigurableAttribute.RecommendedAsConfigurable Property

Gets a value indicating whether the property this attribute is bound to can be used as an application setting.

[Visual Basic]
```
Public ReadOnly Property RecommendedAsConfigurable As Boolean
```
[C#]
```
public bool RecommendedAsConfigurable {get;}
```
[C++]
```
public: __property bool get_RecommendedAsConfigurable();
```
[JScript]
```
public function get RecommendedAsConfigurable() : Boolean;
```

Property Value

true if the property this attribute is bound to can be used as an application setting; otherwise, **false**.

Example

[Visual Basic, C#] The following example checks to see whether `MyProperty` is bindable. First the code gets the attributes for `MyProperty` by:

- Retrieving a **PropertyDescriptorCollection** with all the properties for the object.
- Indexing into the **PropertyDescriptorCollection** to get `MyProperty`.
- Saving the attributes for this property in the attributes variable.

[Visual Basic, C#] Then the code sets `myAttribute` to the value of the **RecommendedAsConfigurableAttribute** in the **AttributeCollection** and checks whether the property is bindable.

[Visual Basic]
```
' Gets the attributes for the property.
Dim attributes As AttributeCollection = _
   TypeDescriptor.GetProperties(Me)("MyProperty").Attributes

' Checks to see if the property is recommended as configurable.
Dim myAttribute As RecommendedAsConfigurableAttribute = _
   CType(attributes(GetType(RecommendedAsConfigurableAttribute)), _
   RecommendedAsConfigurableAttribute)

If myAttribute.RecommendedAsConfigurable Then
    ' Insert code here.
End If
```

[C#]
```
// Gets the attributes for the property.
AttributeCollection attributes =
   TypeDescriptor.GetProperties(this)["MyProperty"].Attributes;

// Checks to see if the property is recommended as configurable.
RecommendedAsConfigurableAttribute myAttribute =
   (RecommendedAsConfigurableAttribute)attributes[typeof
 (RecommendedAsConfigurableAttribute)];
if(myAttribute.RecommendedAsConfigurable) {
   // Insert code here.
}
```

Requirements

Platforms: Windows 98, Windows NT 4.0, Windows Millennium Edition, Windows 2000, Windows XP Home Edition, Windows XP Professional, Windows Server 2003 family

RecommendedAsConfigurableAttribute.Equals Method

This member overrides **Object.Equals**.

[Visual Basic]
```
Overrides Public Function Equals( _
   ByVal obj As Object _
) As Boolean
```
[C#]
```
public override bool Equals(
   object obj
);
```
[C++]
```
public: bool Equals(
   Object* obj
);
```

[JScript]
```
public override function Equals(
   obj : Object
) : Boolean;
```

Requirements

Platforms: Windows 98, Windows NT 4.0, Windows Millennium Edition, Windows 2000, Windows XP Home Edition, Windows XP Professional, Windows Server 2003 family

RecommendedAsConfigurableAttribute.GetHashCode Method

This member overrides **Attribute.GetHashCode**.

[Visual Basic]
```
Overrides Public Function GetHashCode() As Integer
```
[C#]
```
public override int GetHashCode();
```
[C++]
```
public: int GetHashCode();
```
[JScript]
```
public override function GetHashCode() : int;
```

Requirements

Platforms: Windows 98, Windows NT 4.0, Windows Millennium Edition, Windows 2000, Windows XP Home Edition, Windows XP Professional, Windows Server 2003 family

RecommendedAsConfigurableAttribute.IsDefaultAttribute Method

This member overrides **Attribute.IsDefaultAttribute**.

[Visual Basic]
```
Overrides Public Function IsDefaultAttribute() As Boolean
```
[C#]
```
public override bool IsDefaultAttribute();
```
[C++]
```
public: bool IsDefaultAttribute();
```
[JScript]
```
public override function IsDefaultAttribute() : Boolean;
```

Requirements

Platforms: Windows 98, Windows NT 4.0, Windows Millennium Edition, Windows 2000, Windows XP Home Edition, Windows XP Professional, Windows Server 2003 family

ReferenceConverter Class

Provides a type converter to convert object references to and from other representations.

System.Object
  System.ComponentModel.TypeConverter
    System.ComponentModel.ReferenceConverter
      System.ComponentModel.ComponentConverter

```
[Visual Basic]
Public Class ReferenceConverter
   Inherits TypeConverter
[C#]
public class ReferenceConverter : TypeConverter
[C++]
public __gc class ReferenceConverter : public TypeConverter
[JScript]
public class ReferenceConverter extends TypeConverter
```

Thread Safety

Any public static (**Shared** in Visual Basic) members of this type are safe for multithreaded operations. Any instance members are not guaranteed to be thread safe.

Remarks

The **ReferenceConverter** is typically used within the context of sited components or a design environment. Without a component site or a usable **ITypeDescriptorContext**, this converter is of little use.

This converter converts a reference of an object that implements **IComponent** and displays its properties in the Properties window.

For more information about type converters, see the **TypeConverter** base class and **Implementing a Type Converter**.

> **Note** You should never create an instance of **Reference-Converter**. Instead, call the **GetConverter** method of **TypeDescriptor**. For more information, see the examples in the **TypeConverter** base class.

This class provides the **IsValueAllowed** method to check whether a particular value can be added to the standard values collection. If you do not want to add the value to the collection, override this method.

Notes to Inheritors: Override **IsValueAllowed** when you do not want to add a value to the standard values collection.

Requirements

Namespace: System.ComponentModel

Platforms: Windows 98, Windows NT 4.0, Windows Millennium Edition, Windows 2000, Windows XP Home Edition, Windows XP Professional, Windows Server 2003 family

Assembly: System (in System.dll)

ReferenceConverter Constructor

This member supports the .NET Framework infrastructure and is not intended to be used directly from your code.

```
[Visual Basic]
Public Sub New( _
   ByVal type As Type _
)
[C#]
public ReferenceConverter(
   Type type
);
[C++]
public: ReferenceConverter(
   Type* type
);
[JScript]
public function ReferenceConverter(
   type : Type
);
```

ReferenceConverter.CanConvertFrom Method

Overload List

This member supports the .NET Framework infrastructure and is not intended to be used directly from your code.

[Visual Basic] **Overloads Overrides Public Function Can-ConvertFrom(ITypeDescriptorContext, Type) As Boolean**

[C#] **public override bool CanConvertFrom(IType-DescriptorContext, Type);**

[C++] **public: bool CanConvertFrom(ITypeDescriptor-Context*, Type*);**

[JScript] **public override function CanConvertFrom(IType-DescriptorContext, Type) : Boolean;**

Inherited from **TypeConverter**.

[Visual Basic] **Overloads Public Function CanConvert-From(Type) As Boolean**

[C#] **public bool CanConvertFrom(Type);**

[C++] **public: bool CanConvertFrom(Type*);**

[JScript] **public function CanConvertFrom(Type) : Boolean;**

ReferenceConverter.CanConvertFrom Method (ITypeDescriptorContext, Type)

This member overrides **TypeConverter.CanConvertFrom**.

```
[Visual Basic]
Overrides Overloads Public Function CanConvertFrom( _
   ByVal context As ITypeDescriptorContext, _
   ByVal sourceType As Type _
) As Boolean
[C#]
public override bool CanConvertFrom(
   ITypeDescriptorContext context,
   Type sourceType
);
[C++]
public: bool CanConvertFrom(
   ITypeDescriptorContext* context,
   Type* sourceType
);
[JScript]
public override function CanConvertFrom(
   context : ITypeDescriptorContext,
   sourceType : Type
) : Boolean;
```

Requirements

Platforms: Windows 98, Windows NT 4.0, Windows Millennium Edition, Windows 2000, Windows XP Home Edition, Windows XP Professional, Windows Server 2003 family

ReferenceConverter.ConvertFrom Method

Overload List

This member supports the .NET Framework infrastructure and is not intended to be used directly from your code.

[Visual Basic] **Overloads Overrides Public Function ConvertFrom(ITypeDescriptorContext, CultureInfo, Object) As Object**

[C#] **public override object ConvertFrom(ITypeDescriptorContext, CultureInfo, object);**

[C++] **public: Object* ConvertFrom(ITypeDescriptorContext*, CultureInfo*, Object*);**

[JScript] **public override function ConvertFrom(ITypeDescriptorContext, CultureInfo, Object) : Object;**

Inherited from **TypeConverter**.

[Visual Basic] **Overloads Public Function ConvertFrom(Object) As Object**

[C#] **public object ConvertFrom(object);**

[C++] **public: Object* ConvertFrom(Object*);**

[JScript] **public function ConvertFrom(Object) : Object;**

ReferenceConverter.ConvertFrom Method (ITypeDescriptorContext, CultureInfo, Object)

This member overrides **TypeConverter.ConvertFrom**.

```
[Visual Basic]
Overrides Overloads Public Function ConvertFrom( _
   ByVal context As ITypeDescriptorContext, _
   ByVal culture As CultureInfo, _
   ByVal value As Object _
) As Object
[C#]
public override object ConvertFrom(
   ITypeDescriptorContext context,
   CultureInfo culture,
   object value
);
[C++]
public: Object* ConvertFrom(
   ITypeDescriptorContext* context,
   CultureInfo* culture,
   Object* value
);
[JScript]
public override function ConvertFrom(
   context : ITypeDescriptorContext,
   culture : CultureInfo,
   value : Object
) : Object;
```

Requirements

Platforms: Windows 98, Windows NT 4.0, Windows Millennium Edition, Windows 2000, Windows XP Home Edition, Windows XP Professional, Windows Server 2003 family

ReferenceConverter.ConvertTo Method

Overload List

This member supports the .NET Framework infrastructure and is not intended to be used directly from your code.

[Visual Basic] **Overloads Overrides Public Function ConvertTo(ITypeDescriptorContext, CultureInfo, Object, Type) As Object**

[C#] **public override object ConvertTo(ITypeDescriptorContext, CultureInfo, object, Type);**

[C++] **public: Object* ConvertTo(ITypeDescriptorContext*, CultureInfo*, Object*, Type*);**

[JScript] **public override function ConvertTo(ITypeDescriptorContext, CultureInfo, Object, Type) : Object;**

Inherited from **TypeConverter**.

[Visual Basic] **Overloads Public Function ConvertTo(Object, Type) As Object**

[C#] **public object ConvertTo(object, Type);**

[C++] **public: Object* ConvertTo(Object*, Type*);**

[JScript] **public function ConvertTo(Object, Type) : Object;**

ReferenceConverter.ConvertTo Method (ITypeDescriptorContext, CultureInfo, Object, Type)

This member overrides **TypeConverter.ConvertTo**.

```
[Visual Basic]
Overrides Overloads Public Function ConvertTo( _
   ByVal context As ITypeDescriptorContext, _
   ByVal culture As CultureInfo, _
   ByVal value As Object, _
   ByVal destinationType As Type _
) As Object
[C#]
public override object ConvertTo(
   ITypeDescriptorContext context,
   CultureInfo culture,
   object value,
   Type destinationType
);
[C++]
public: Object* ConvertTo(
   ITypeDescriptorContext* context,
   CultureInfo* culture,
   Object* value,
   Type* destinationType
);
[JScript]
public override function ConvertTo(
   context : ITypeDescriptorContext,
   culture : CultureInfo,
   value : Object,
   destinationType : Type
) : Object;
```

Requirements

Platforms: Windows 98, Windows NT 4.0, Windows Millennium Edition, Windows 2000, Windows XP Home Edition, Windows XP Professional, Windows Server 2003 family

ReferenceConverter.GetStandardValues Method

Overload List

This member supports the .NET Framework infrastructure and is not intended to be used directly from your code.

[Visual Basic] **Overloads Overrides Public Function GetStandardValues(ITypeDescriptorContext) As StandardValuesCollection**

[C#] **public override StandardValuesCollection GetStandardValues(ITypeDescriptorContext);**

[C++] **public: StandardValuesCollection* GetStandardValues(ITypeDescriptorContext*);**

[JScript] **public override function GetStandardValues(ITypeDescriptorContext) : StandardValuesCollection;**

Inherited from **TypeConverter**.

[Visual Basic] **Overloads Public Function GetStandardValues() As ICollection**

[C#] **public ICollection GetStandardValues();**

[C++] **public: ICollection* GetStandardValues();**

[JScript] **public function GetStandardValues() : ICollection;**

ReferenceConverter.GetStandardValues Method (ITypeDescriptorContext)

This member overrides **TypeConverter.GetStandardValues**.

```
[Visual Basic]
Overrides Overloads Public Function GetStandardValues( _
   ByVal context As ITypeDescriptorContext _
) As StandardValuesCollection
[C#]
public override StandardValuesCollection GetStandardValues(
   ITypeDescriptorContext context
);
[C++]
public: StandardValuesCollection* GetStandardValues(
   ITypeDescriptorContext* context
);
[JScript]
public override function GetStandardValues(
   context : ITypeDescriptorContext
) : StandardValuesCollection;
```

Requirements

Platforms: Windows 98, Windows NT 4.0, Windows Millennium Edition, Windows 2000, Windows XP Home Edition, Windows XP Professional, Windows Server 2003 family

ReferenceConverter.GetStandardValuesExclusive Method

Overload List

This member supports the .NET Framework infrastructure and is not intended to be used directly from your code.

[Visual Basic] **Overloads Overrides Public Function GetStandardValuesExclusive(ITypeDescriptorContext) As Boolean**

[C#] **public override bool GetStandardValues-Exclusive(ITypeDescriptorContext);**

[C++] **public: bool GetStandardValues-Exclusive(ITypeDescriptorContext*);**

[JScript] **public override function GetStandardValues-Exclusive(ITypeDescriptorContext) : Boolean;**

Inherited from **TypeConverter**.

[Visual Basic] **Overloads Public Function GetStandardValuesExclusive() As Boolean**

[C#] **public bool GetStandardValuesExclusive();**

[C++] **public: bool GetStandardValuesExclusive();**

[JScript] **public function GetStandardValuesExclusive() : Boolean;**

ReferenceConverter.GetStandardValuesExclusive Method (ITypeDescriptorContext)

This member overrides **TypeConverter.GetStandardValuesExclusive**.

```
[Visual Basic]
Overrides Overloads Public Function GetStandardValuesExclusive( _
   ByVal context As ITypeDescriptorContext _
) As Boolean
[C#]
public override bool GetStandardValuesExclusive(
   ITypeDescriptorContext context
);
[C++]
public: bool GetStandardValuesExclusive(
   ITypeDescriptorContext* context
);
[JScript]
public override function GetStandardValuesExclusive(
   context : ITypeDescriptorContext
) : Boolean;
```

Requirements

Platforms: Windows 98, Windows NT 4.0, Windows Millennium Edition, Windows 2000, Windows XP Home Edition, Windows XP Professional, Windows Server 2003 family

ReferenceConverter.GetStandardValues-Supported Method

Overload List

This member supports the .NET Framework infrastructure and is not intended to be used directly from your code.

[Visual Basic] **Overloads Overrides Public Function GetStandardValuesSupported(ITypeDescriptorContext) As Boolean**

[C#] **public override bool GetStandardValues-Supported(ITypeDescriptorContext);**

[C++] **public: bool GetStandardValues-Supported(ITypeDescriptorContext*);**

[JScript] **public override function GetStandardValues-Supported(ITypeDescriptorContext) : Boolean;**

Inherited from **TypeConverter**.

[Visual Basic] **Overloads Public Function GetStandardValuesSupported() As Boolean**

[C#] **public bool GetStandardValuesSupported();**

[C++] **public: bool GetStandardValuesSupported();**

[JScript] **public function GetStandardValuesSupported() : Boolean;**

ReferenceConverter.GetStandardValuesSupported Method (ITypeDescriptorContext)

This member overrides **TypeConverter.GetStandardValuesSupported**.

```
[Visual Basic]
Overrides Overloads Public Function GetStandardValuesSupported( _
   ByVal context As ITypeDescriptorContext _
) As Boolean
[C#]
public override bool GetStandardValuesSupported(
   ITypeDescriptorContext context
);
[C++]
public: bool GetStandardValuesSupported(
   ITypeDescriptorContext* context
);
[JScript]
public override function GetStandardValuesSupported(
   context : ITypeDescriptorContext
) : Boolean;
```

Requirements

Platforms: Windows 98, Windows NT 4.0, Windows Millennium Edition, Windows 2000, Windows XP Home Edition, Windows XP Professional, Windows Server 2003 family

ReferenceConverter.IsValueAllowed Method

Returns a value indicating whether a particular value can be added to the standard values collection.

```
[Visual Basic]
Protected Overridable Function IsValueAllowed( _
   ByVal context As ITypeDescriptorContext, _
   ByVal value As Object _
) As Boolean
[C#]
protected virtual bool IsValueAllowed(
   ITypeDescriptorContext context,
   object value
);
[C++]
protected: virtual bool IsValueAllowed(
   ITypeDescriptorContext* context,
   Object* value
);
[JScript]
protected function IsValueAllowed(
   context : ITypeDescriptorContext,
   value : Object
) : Boolean;
```

Parameters

context

An **ITypeDescriptorContext** that provides an additional context.

value

The value to check.

Return Value

true if the value is allowed and can be added to the standard values collection; **false** if the value cannot be added to the standard values collection.

Remarks

This method is called for each value that matches the type associated with this **ReferenceConverter** and for each component found that is of the associated type. By default, this method returns **true**, that is, it allows adding the value into the standard values collection.

Notes to Inheritors: Override this method when you do not want to add a value to the standard values collection.

Requirements

Platforms: Windows 98, Windows NT 4.0, Windows Millennium Edition, Windows 2000, Windows XP Home Edition, Windows XP Professional, Windows Server 2003 family

RefreshEventArgs Class

Provides data for the **Refreshed** event.

System.Object
  System.EventArgs
    System.ComponentModel.RefreshEventArgs

```
[Visual Basic]
Public Class RefreshEventArgs
   Inherits EventArgs
[C#]
public class RefreshEventArgs : EventArgs
[C++]
public __gc class RefreshEventArgs : public EventArgs
[JScript]
public class RefreshEventArgs extends EventArgs
```

Thread Safety

Any public static (**Shared** in Visual Basic) members of this type are safe for multithreaded operations. Any instance members are not guaranteed to be thread safe.

Remarks

Typically, component information does not change for the life of a process. During design time, however, you can change the component's properties or events. As a result, the component's information in **TypeDescriptor** becomes out-of-date, and a **Refreshed** event is raised. A **Refreshed** event is also raised when a **Type** is changed during design time.

A **RefreshEventArgs** object specifies the data associated with the **Refreshed** event; that is, the component and the type of component that changed.

The **RefreshEventArgs** class provides **ComponentChanged** and **TypeChanged** properties to get the component or type that raised the event.

Example

For an example of the **RefreshEventArgs** class, see the sample code in the **RefreshEventHandler** delegate.

Requirements

Namespace: System.ComponentModel

Platforms: Windows 98, Windows NT 4.0, Windows Millennium Edition, Windows 2000, Windows XP Home Edition, Windows XP Professional, Windows Server 2003 family

Assembly: System (in System.dll)

RefreshEventArgs Constructor

Initializes a new instance of the **RefreshEventArgs** class.

Overload List

Initializes a new instance of the **RefreshEventArgs** class with the component that has changed.

[Visual Basic] **Public Sub New(Object)**

[C#] **public RefreshEventArgs(object);**

[C++] **public: RefreshEventArgs(Object*);**

[JScript] **public function RefreshEventArgs(Object);**

Initializes a new instance of the **RefreshEventArgs** class with the type of component that has changed.

[Visual Basic] **Public Sub New(Type)**

[C#] **public RefreshEventArgs(Type);**

[C++] **public: RefreshEventArgs(Type*);**

[JScript] **public function RefreshEventArgs(Type);**

RefreshEventArgs Constructor (Object)

Initializes a new instance of the **RefreshEventArgs** class with the component that has changed.

```
[Visual Basic]
Public Sub New( _
   ByVal componentChanged As Object _
)
[C#]
public RefreshEventArgs(
   object componentChanged
);
[C++]
public: RefreshEventArgs(
   Object* componentChanged
);
[JScript]
public function RefreshEventArgs(
   componentChanged : Object
);
```

Parameters

componentChanged
  The component that changed.

Requirements

Platforms: Windows 98, Windows NT 4.0, Windows Millennium Edition, Windows 2000, Windows XP Home Edition, Windows XP Professional, Windows Server 2003 family

RefreshEventArgs Constructor (Type)

Initializes a new instance of the **RefreshEventArgs** class with the type of component that has changed.

```
[Visual Basic]
Public Sub New( _
   ByVal typeChanged As Type _
)
[C#]
public RefreshEventArgs(
   Type typeChanged
);
[C++]
public: RefreshEventArgs(
   Type* typeChanged
);
[JScript]
public function RefreshEventArgs(
   typeChanged : Type
);
```

Parameters

typeChanged

The **Type** that changed.

Requirements

Platforms: Windows 98, Windows NT 4.0, Windows Millennium Edition, Windows 2000, Windows XP Home Edition, Windows XP Professional, Windows Server 2003 family

RefreshEventArgs.ComponentChanged Property

Gets the component that changed its properties, events, or extenders.

```
[Visual Basic]
Public ReadOnly Property ComponentChanged As Object
[C#]
public object ComponentChanged {get;}
[C++]
public: __property Object* get_ComponentChanged();
[JScript]
public function get ComponentChanged() : Object;
```

Property Value

The component that changed its properties, events, or extenders, or a null reference (**Nothing** in Visual Basic) if all components of the same type have changed.

Requirements

Platforms: Windows 98, Windows NT 4.0, Windows Millennium Edition, Windows 2000, Windows XP Home Edition, Windows XP Professional, Windows Server 2003 family

RefreshEventArgs.TypeChanged Property

Gets the **Type** that changed its properties or events.

```
[Visual Basic]
Public ReadOnly Property TypeChanged As Type
[C#]
public Type TypeChanged {get;}
[C++]
public: __property Type* get_TypeChanged();
[JScript]
public function get TypeChanged() : Type;
```

Property Value

The **Type** that changed its properties or events.

Requirements

Platforms: Windows 98, Windows NT 4.0, Windows Millennium Edition, Windows 2000, Windows XP Home Edition, Windows XP Professional, Windows Server 2003 family

RefreshEventHandler Delegate

Represents the method that handles the **Refreshed** event raised when a **Type** or component is changed during design time.

[Visual Basic]
```
<Serializable>
Public Delegate Sub RefreshEventHandler( _
   ByVal e As RefreshEventArgs _
)
```
[C#]
```
[Serializable]
public delegate void RefreshEventHandler(
   RefreshEventArgs e
);
```
[C++]
```
[Serializable]
public __gc __delegate void RefreshEventHandler(
   RefreshEventArgs* e
);
```

[JScript] In JScript, you can use the delegates in the .NET Framework, but you cannot define your own.

Parameters [Visual Basic, C#, C++]

The declaration of your event handler must have the same parameters as the **RefreshEventHandler** delegate declaration.

e

A **RefreshEventArgs** that contains the component or **Type** that changed.

Remarks

When you create a **RefreshEventHandler** delegate, you identify the method that will handle the event. To associate the event with your event handler, add an instance of the delegate to the event. The event handler is called whenever the event occurs, unless you remove the delegate.

Example

[Visual Basic, C#] The following sample demonstrates how to use a **RefreshEventHandler** delegate to handle the **Refreshed** event when a type or component changes. In the code, the `OnRefreshed` event handles the event and displays the component being changed.

[Visual Basic, C#] The code assumes that a `TextBox` control is already sited on the form.

[Visual Basic]
```
Private Sub Form1_Load(ByVal sender As System.Object, ByVal e
As System.EventArgs) Handles MyBase.Load
    TextBox1.Text = "changed"
    AddHandler System.ComponentModel.TypeDescriptor.Refreshed,
AddressOf OnRefreshed
    System.ComponentModel.TypeDescriptor.GetProperties(TextBox1)
    System.ComponentModel.TypeDescriptor.Refresh(TextBox1)
End Sub

Private Sub OnRefreshed(ByVal e As
System.ComponentModel.RefreshEventArgs)
    Console.WriteLine(e.ComponentChanged.ToString())
End Sub
```

[C#]
```
private void Form1_Load(object sender, System.EventArgs e)
{
    textBox1.Text = "changed";
    System.ComponentModel.TypeDescriptor.Refreshed += new
    System.ComponentModel.RefreshEventHandler(OnRefresh);
    System.ComponentModel.TypeDescriptor.GetProperties(textBox1);
    System.ComponentModel.TypeDescriptor.Refresh(textBox1);
}

protected static void OnRefresh
 (System.ComponentModel.RefreshEventArgs e)
{
    Console.WriteLine(e.ComponentChanged.ToString());
}
```

Requirements

Namespace: System.ComponentModel

Platforms: Windows 98, Windows NT 4.0, Windows Millennium Edition, Windows 2000, Windows XP Home Edition, Windows XP Professional, Windows Server 2003 family

Assembly: System (in System.dll)

RefreshProperties Enumeration

Defines identifiers that indicate the type of a refresh of the Properties window.

[Visual Basic]
```
<Serializable>
Public Enum RefreshProperties
```
[C#]
```
[Serializable]
public enum RefreshProperties
```
[C++]
```
[Serializable]
__value public enum RefreshProperties
```
[JScript]
```
public
   Serializable
enum RefreshProperties
```

Remarks

RefreshProperties defines identifiers for types of refresh methods that can be used when refreshing the view of the Properties window.

Members

Member name	Description
All	The properties should be requeried and the view should be refreshed.
None	No refresh is necessary.
Repaint	The view should be should refreshed.

Requirements

Namespace: System.ComponentModel

Platforms: Windows 98, Windows NT 4.0, Windows Millennium Edition, Windows 2000, Windows XP Home Edition, Windows XP Professional, Windows Server 2003 family

Assembly: System (in System.dll)

RefreshPropertiesAttribute Class

Indicates how a designer refreshes when the associated property value changes. This class cannot be inherited.

System.Object
 System.Attribute
  System.ComponentModel.RefreshPropertiesAttribute

```
[Visual Basic]
<AttributeUsage(AttributeTargets.All)>
NotInheritable Public Class RefreshPropertiesAttribute
   Inherits Attribute
[C#]
[AttributeUsage(AttributeTargets.All)]
public sealed class RefreshPropertiesAttribute : Attribute
[C++]
[AttributeUsage(AttributeTargets::All)]
public __gc __sealed class RefreshPropertiesAttribute : public
   Attribute
[JScript]
public
   AttributeUsage(AttributeTargets.All)
class RefreshPropertiesAttribute extends Attribute
```

Thread Safety

Any public static (**Shared** in Visual Basic) members of this type are safe for multithreaded operations. Any instance members are not guaranteed to be thread safe.

Remarks

RefreshProperties indicates the type of refresh mode to use when refreshing the Properties window.

Requirements

Namespace: System.ComponentModel

Platforms: Windows 98, Windows NT 4.0, Windows Millennium Edition, Windows 2000, Windows XP Home Edition, Windows XP Professional, Windows Server 2003 family

Assembly: System (in System.dll)

RefreshPropertiesAttribute Constructor

This member supports the .NET Framework infrastructure and is not intended to be used directly from your code.

```
[Visual Basic]
Public Sub New( _
   ByVal refresh As RefreshProperties _
)
[C#]
public RefreshPropertiesAttribute(
   RefreshProperties refresh
);
[C++]
public: RefreshPropertiesAttribute(
   RefreshProperties refresh
);
[JScript]
public function RefreshPropertiesAttribute(
   refresh : RefreshProperties
);
```

RefreshPropertiesAttribute.All Field

Indicates that all properties are requeried and refreshed if the property value is changed. This field is read-only.

```
[Visual Basic]
Public Shared ReadOnly All As RefreshPropertiesAttribute
[C#]
public static readonly RefreshPropertiesAttribute All;
[C++]
public: static RefreshPropertiesAttribute* All;
[JScript]
public static var All : RefreshPropertiesAttribute;
```

Remarks

Specify this attribute on a property to requery and refresh all properties in the **PropertyGrid** when the property value changes. The **PropertyGrid** caches data. The **All** mode causes the Properties window to requery each property and refresh its view.

Requirements

Platforms: Windows 98, Windows NT 4.0, Windows Millennium Edition, Windows 2000, Windows XP Home Edition, Windows XP Professional, Windows Server 2003 family

RefreshPropertiesAttribute.Default Field

Indicates that no other properties are refreshed if the property value is changed. This field is read-only.

```
[Visual Basic]
Public Shared ReadOnly Default As RefreshPropertiesAttribute
[C#]
public static readonly RefreshPropertiesAttribute Default;
[C++]
public: static RefreshPropertiesAttribute* Default;
[JScript]
public static var Default : RefreshPropertiesAttribute;
```

Remarks

Specify this attribute on a property to refresh only the associated property when the property value is changed.

Requirements

Platforms: Windows 98, Windows NT 4.0, Windows Millennium Edition, Windows 2000, Windows XP Home Edition, Windows XP Professional, Windows Server 2003 family

RefreshPropertiesAttribute.Repaint Field

Indicates that all properties are repainted if the property value is changed. This field is read-only.

```
[Visual Basic]
Public Shared ReadOnly Repaint As RefreshPropertiesAttribute
[C#]
public static readonly RefreshPropertiesAttribute Repaint;
[C++]
public: static RefreshPropertiesAttribute* Repaint;
[JScript]
public static var Repaint : RefreshPropertiesAttribute;
```

Remarks

Specify this attribute on a property to repaint all properties in the **PropertyGrid** when the property value changes.

Requirements

Platforms: Windows 98, Windows NT 4.0, Windows Millennium Edition, Windows 2000, Windows XP Home Edition, Windows XP Professional, Windows Server 2003 family

RefreshPropertiesAttribute.RefreshProperties Property

Gets or sets the refresh properties for the member.

```
[Visual Basic]
Public ReadOnly Property RefreshProperties As RefreshProperties
[C#]
public RefreshProperties RefreshProperties {get;}
[C++]
public: __property RefreshProperties get_RefreshProperties();
[JScript]
public function get RefreshProperties() : RefreshProperties;
```

Property Value

A **RefreshProperties** that indicates the current refresh properties for the member.

Requirements

Platforms: Windows 98, Windows NT 4.0, Windows Millennium Edition, Windows 2000, Windows XP Home Edition, Windows XP Professional, Windows Server 2003 family

RefreshPropertiesAttribute.Equals Method

This member overrides **Object.Equals**.

```
[Visual Basic]
Overrides Public Function Equals( _
   ByVal value As Object _
) As Boolean
[C#]
public override bool Equals(
   object value
);
[C++]
public: bool Equals(
   Object* value
);
[JScript]
public override function Equals(
   value : Object
) : Boolean;
```

Requirements

Platforms: Windows 98, Windows NT 4.0, Windows Millennium Edition, Windows 2000, Windows XP Home Edition, Windows XP Professional, Windows Server 2003 family

RefreshPropertiesAttribute.GetHashCode Method

Returns the hash code for this object.

```
[Visual Basic]
Overrides Public Function GetHashCode() As Integer
[C#]
public override int GetHashCode();
[C++]
public: int GetHashCode();
[JScript]
public override function GetHashCode() : int;
```

Return Value

The hash code for the object that the attribute belongs to.

Requirements

Platforms: Windows 98, Windows NT 4.0, Windows Millennium Edition, Windows 2000, Windows XP Home Edition, Windows XP Professional, Windows Server 2003 family

RefreshPropertiesAttribute.IsDefaultAttribute Method

Gets a value indicating whether the current value of the attribute is the default value for the attribute.

```
[Visual Basic]
Overrides Public Function IsDefaultAttribute() As Boolean
[C#]
public override bool IsDefaultAttribute();
[C++]
public: bool IsDefaultAttribute();
[JScript]
public override function IsDefaultAttribute() : Boolean;
```

Return Value

true if the current value of the attribute is the default; otherwise, **false**.

Requirements

Platforms: Windows 98, Windows NT 4.0, Windows Millennium Edition, Windows 2000, Windows XP Home Edition, Windows XP Professional, Windows Server 2003 family

RunInstallerAttribute Class

Specifies whether the Visual Studio .NET Custom Action Installer or the **Installer Tool (Installutil.exe)** should be invoked when the assembly is installed.

System.Object
  System.Attribute
    System.ComponentModel.RunInstallerAttribute

[Visual Basic]
```
<AttributeUsage(AttributeTargets.Class)>
Public Class RunInstallerAttribute
   Inherits Attribute
```
[C#]
```
[AttributeUsage(AttributeTargets.Class)]
public class RunInstallerAttribute : Attribute
```
[C++]
```
[AttributeUsage(AttributeTargets::Class)]
public __gc class RunInstallerAttribute : public Attribute
```
[JScript]
```
public
   AttributeUsage(AttributeTargets.Class)
class RunInstallerAttribute extends Attribute
```

Thread Safety

Any public static (**Shared** in Visual Basic) members of this type are safe for multithreaded operations. Any instance members are not guaranteed to be thread safe.

Remarks

If a class that inherits from **Installer** is marked with the **RunInstallerAttribute** constructor of the value **true**, Visual Studio .NET's Custom Action Installer or the InstallUtil.exe will be invoked when the assembly is installed. Members marked with the **RunInstallerAttribute** constructor of the value **false** will not invoke an installer. The default is **false**.

> **Note** When you mark a property with the **RunInstallerAttribute** constructor of the value **true**, the value of this attribute is set to the constant member **Yes**. For a property marked with the **RunInstallerAttribute** constructor of the value **false**, the value is **No**. Therefore, when you want to check the value of this attribute in your code, you must specify the attribute as **RunInstallerAttribute.Yes** or **RunInstallerAttribute.No**.

Example

[Visual Basic, C#] The following example specifies that the installer should be run for `MyProjectInstaller`.

[Visual Basic]
```
<RunInstallerAttribute(True)> _
Public Class MyProjectInstaller
    Inherits Installer

    ' Insert code here.
End Class 'MyProjectInstaller
```

[C#]
```
[RunInstallerAttribute(true)]
 public class MyProjectInstaller : Installer {
    // Insert code here.
 }
```

[Visual Basic, C#] The next example creates an instance of `MyProjectInstaller`. Then it gets the attributes for the class, extracts the **RunInstallerAttribute**, and prints whether to run the installer.

[Visual Basic]
```
Public Shared Function Main() As Integer
    ' Creates a new installer.
    Dim myNewProjectInstaller As New MyProjectInstaller()

    ' Gets the attributes for the collection.
    Dim attributes As AttributeCollection =                        ↵
TypeDescriptor.GetAttributes(myNewProjectInstaller)

    ' Prints whether to run the installer by retrieving the
    ' RunInstallerAttribute from the AttributeCollection.
    Dim myAttribute As RunInstallerAttribute = _
       CType(attributes(GetType(RunInstallerAttribute)),           ↵
RunInstallerAttribute)

    Console.WriteLine(("Run the installer? " &                     ↵
myAttribute.RunInstaller.ToString()))
    Return 0
End Function 'Main
```

[C#]
```
public static int Main() {
    // Creates a new installer.
    MyProjectInstaller myNewProjectInstaller = new                 ↵
MyProjectInstaller();

    // Gets the attributes for the collection.
    AttributeCollection attributes =                               ↵
TypeDescriptor.GetAttributes(myNewProjectInstaller);

    /* Prints whether to run the installer by retrieving the
     * RunInstallerAttribute from the AttributeCollection. */
    RunInstallerAttribute myAttribute =
       (RunInstallerAttribute)attributes[typeof(RunInstallerAttribute)];
    Console.WriteLine("Run the installer? " +                      ↵
myAttribute.RunInstaller.ToString());

    return 0;
 }
```

Requirements

Namespace: System.ComponentModel

Platforms: Windows 98, Windows NT 4.0, Windows Millennium Edition, Windows 2000, Windows XP Home Edition, Windows XP Professional, Windows Server 2003 family

Assembly: System (in System.dll)

RunInstallerAttribute Constructor

Initializes a new instance of the **RunInstallerAttribute** class.

[Visual Basic]
```
Public Sub New( _
   ByVal runInstaller As Boolean _
)
```
[C#]
```
public RunInstallerAttribute(
   bool runInstaller
);
```
[C++]
```
public: RunInstallerAttribute(
   bool runInstaller
);
```

```
[JScript]
public function RunInstallerAttribute(
   runInstaller : Boolean
);
```

Parameters

runInstaller

true if an installer should be invoked during installation of an assembly; otherwise, **false**.

Requirements

Platforms: Windows 98, Windows NT 4.0, Windows Millennium Edition, Windows 2000, Windows XP Home Edition, Windows XP Professional, Windows Server 2003 family

RunInstallerAttribute.Default Field

This member supports the .NET Framework infrastructure and is not intended to be used directly from your code.

```
[Visual Basic]
Public Shared ReadOnly Default As RunInstallerAttribute
[C#]
public static readonly RunInstallerAttribute Default;
[C++]
public: static RunInstallerAttribute* Default;
[JScript]
public static var Default : RunInstallerAttribute;
```

RunInstallerAttribute.No Field

Specifies that the Visual Studio .NET Custom Action Installer or the **Installer Tool (Installutil.exe)** should not be invoked when the assembly is installed. This static (**Shared** in Visual Basic) field is read-only.

```
[Visual Basic]
Public Shared ReadOnly No As RunInstallerAttribute
[C#]
public static readonly RunInstallerAttribute No;
[C++]
public: static RunInstallerAttribute* No;
[JScript]
public static var No : RunInstallerAttribute;
```

Remarks

This field is the default setting for this attribute.

When you mark a property with the **RunInstallerAttribute** constructor of the value **false**, the value of this attribute is set to the constant member **No**. Therefore, when you want to check whether the attribute is set to this value in your code, you must specify the attribute as **RunInstallerAttribute.No**.

Requirements

Platforms: Windows 98, Windows NT 4.0, Windows Millennium Edition, Windows 2000, Windows XP Home Edition, Windows XP Professional, Windows Server 2003 family

RunInstallerAttribute.Yes Field

Specifies that the Visual Studio .NET Custom Action Installer or the **Installer Tool (Installutil.exe)** should be invoked when the assembly is installed. This static (**Shared** in Visual Basic) field is read-only.

```
[Visual Basic]
Public Shared ReadOnly Yes As RunInstallerAttribute
[C#]
public static readonly RunInstallerAttribute Yes;
[C++]
public: static RunInstallerAttribute* Yes;
[JScript]
public static var Yes : RunInstallerAttribute;
```

Remarks

When you mark a property with the **RunInstallerAttribute** constructor of the value **true**, the value of this attribute is set to the constant member **Yes**. Therefore, when you want to check whether the attribute is set to this value in your code, you must specify the attribute as **RunInstallerAttribute.Yes**.

Requirements

Platforms: Windows 98, Windows NT 4.0, Windows Millennium Edition, Windows 2000, Windows XP Home Edition, Windows XP Professional, Windows Server 2003 family

RunInstallerAttribute.RunInstaller Property

Gets a value indicating whether an installer should be invoked during installation of an assembly.

```
[Visual Basic]
Public ReadOnly Property RunInstaller As Boolean
[C#]
public bool RunInstaller {get;}
[C++]
public: __property bool get_RunInstaller();
[JScript]
public function get RunInstaller() : Boolean;
```

Property Value

true if an installer should be invoked during installation of an assembly; otherwise, **false**.

Requirements

Platforms: Windows 98, Windows NT 4.0, Windows Millennium Edition, Windows 2000, Windows XP Home Edition, Windows XP Professional, Windows Server 2003 family

RunInstallerAttribute.Equals Method

This member overrides **Object.Equals**.

```
[Visual Basic]
Overrides Public Function Equals( _
   ByVal obj As Object _
) As Boolean
[C#]
public override bool Equals(
   object obj
);
```

[C++]
```
public: bool Equals(
   Object* obj
);
```
[JScript]
```
public override function Equals(
   obj : Object
) : Boolean;
```

Requirements

Platforms: Windows 98, Windows NT 4.0, Windows Millennium Edition, Windows 2000, Windows XP Home Edition, Windows XP Professional, Windows Server 2003 family

RunInstallerAttribute.GetHashCode Method

This member overrides **Attribute.GetHashCode**.

[Visual Basic]
```
Overrides Public Function GetHashCode() As Integer
```
[C#]
```
public override int GetHashCode();
```
[C++]
```
public: int GetHashCode();
```
[JScript]
```
public override function GetHashCode() : int;
```

Requirements

Platforms: Windows 98, Windows NT 4.0, Windows Millennium Edition, Windows 2000, Windows XP Home Edition, Windows XP Professional, Windows Server 2003 family

RunInstallerAttribute.IsDefaultAttribute Method

This member overrides **Attribute.IsDefaultAttribute**.

[Visual Basic]
```
Overrides Public Function IsDefaultAttribute() As Boolean
```
[C#]
```
public override bool IsDefaultAttribute();
```
[C++]
```
public: bool IsDefaultAttribute();
```
[JScript]
```
public override function IsDefaultAttribute() : Boolean;
```

Requirements

Platforms: Windows 98, Windows NT 4.0, Windows Millennium Edition, Windows 2000, Windows XP Home Edition, Windows XP Professional, Windows Server 2003 family

SByteConverter Class

Provides a type converter to convert 8-bit unsigned integer objects to and from a string.

For a list of all members of this type, see **SByteConverter Members**.

System.Object
  System.ComponentModel.TypeConverter
    System.ComponentModel.BaseNumberConverter
      System.ComponentModel.SByteConverter

[Visual Basic]
```
Public Class SByteConverter
   Inherits BaseNumberConverter
```
[C#]
```
public class SByteConverter : BaseNumberConverter
```
[C++]
```
public __gc class SByteConverter : public BaseNumberConverter
```
[JScript]
```
public class SByteConverter extends BaseNumberConverter
```

Thread Safety

Any public static (**Shared** in Visual Basic) members of this type are safe for multithreaded operations. Any instance members are not guaranteed to be thread safe.

Remarks

This converter can convert only an 8-bit unsigned integer object to and from a string.

The **SByte** value type represents integers with values ranging from negative 128 to positive 127. This data type is not supported in Visual Basic.

> **Note** You should never create an instance of **SByteConverter**. Instead, call the **GetConverter** method of **TypeDescriptor**.

Example

[Visual Basic, C#, C++] The following sample converts a variable of type **SByte** to a string, and vice versa.

[Visual Basic]
```
'This data type is not supported in Visual Basic.
```

[C#]
```
sbyte mySByte=+121;
string mySByteStr="-100";
Console.WriteLine(TypeDescriptor.GetConverter(mySByte).ConvertTo
(mySByte, typeof(string)));
Console.WriteLine(TypeDescriptor.GetConverter(mySByte).ConvertFrom
 (mySByteStr));
```

[C++]
```
SByte mySByte( +121 );
String* mySByteStr = S"-100";
Console::WriteLine(TypeDescriptor::GetConverter(__box(mySByte))-
>ConvertTo(__box(mySByte), __typeof(String)));
Console::WriteLine(TypeDescriptor::GetConverter(__box(mySByte))-
>ConvertFrom(mySByteStr));
```

Requirements

Namespace: System.ComponentModel

Platforms: Windows 98, Windows NT 4.0, Windows Millennium Edition, Windows 2000, Windows XP Home Edition, Windows XP Professional, Windows Server 2003 family

Assembly: System (in System.dll)

SByteConverter Constructor

Initializes a new instance of the **SByteConverter** class.

[Visual Basic]
```
Public Sub New()
```
[C#]
```
public SByteConverter();
```
[C++]
```
public: SByteConverter();
```
[JScript]
```
public function SByteConverter();
```

Remarks

The default constructor initializes any fields to their default values.

Requirements

Platforms: Windows 98, Windows NT 4.0, Windows Millennium Edition, Windows 2000, Windows XP Home Edition, Windows XP Professional, Windows Server 2003 family

SingleConverter Class

Provides a type converter to convert single-precision, floating point number objects to and from various other representations.

System.Object
  System.ComponentModel.TypeConverter
    System.ComponentModel.BaseNumberConverter
      System.ComponentModel.SingleConverter

```
[Visual Basic]
Public Class SingleConverter
   Inherits BaseNumberConverter
[C#]
public class SingleConverter : BaseNumberConverter
[C++]
public __gc class SingleConverter : public BaseNumberConverter
[JScript]
public class SingleConverter extends BaseNumberConverter
```

Thread Safety

Any public static (**Shared** in Visual Basic) members of this type are safe for multithreaded operations. Any instance members are not guaranteed to be thread safe.

Remarks

This converter can only convert a single-precision, floating point number object to and from a string. The **Single** value type represents a single-precision 32-bit number with values ranging from negative 3.402823e38 to positive 3.402823e38.

> **Note** You should never create an instance of **SingleConverter**. Instead, call the **GetConverter** method of **TypeDescriptor**.

Example

[Visual Basic, C#, C++] The following sample converts a variable of type **Single** to a string, and vice versa.

```
[Visual Basic]
Dim s As [Single] = 3.402823E+10F
Dim mySStr As String = "3.402823E+10"
Console.WriteLine(TypeDescriptor.GetConverter(s).ConvertTo(s,        ↵
GetType(String)))
Console.WriteLine(TypeDescriptor.GetConverter(s).ConvertFrom(mySStr))
```

```
[C#]
Single s=3.402823E+10F;
string mySStr="3.402823E+10";
Console.WriteLine(TypeDescriptor.GetConverter(s).ConvertTo(s,        ↵
typeof(string)));
Console.WriteLine(TypeDescriptor.GetConverter(s).ConvertFrom(mySStr));
```

```
[C++]
Single s( 3.402823E+10F );
String* mySStr = S"3.402823E+10";
Console::WriteLine(TypeDescriptor::GetConverter(__box(s))-           ↵
>ConvertTo(__box(s), __typeof(String)));
Console::WriteLine(TypeDescriptor::GetConverter(__box(s))-           ↵
>ConvertFrom(mySStr));
```

Requirements

Namespace: System.ComponentModel

Platforms: Windows 98, Windows NT 4.0, Windows Millennium Edition, Windows 2000, Windows XP Home Edition, Windows XP Professional, Windows Server 2003 family

Assembly: System (in System.dll)

SingleConverter Constructor

Initializes a new instance of the **SingleConverter** class.

```
[Visual Basic]
Public Sub New()
[C#]
public SingleConverter();
[C++]
public: SingleConverter();
[JScript]
public function SingleConverter();
```

Remarks

The default constructor initializes any fields to their default values.

Requirements

Platforms: Windows 98, Windows NT 4.0, Windows Millennium Edition, Windows 2000, Windows XP Home Edition, Windows XP Professional, Windows Server 2003 family

StringConverter Class

Provides a type converter to convert string objects to and from other representations.

System.Object
  System.ComponentModel.TypeConverter
    System.ComponentModel.StringConverter
      System.Web.UI.WebControls.TargetConverter
      System.Web.UI.WebControls.ValidatedControlConverter

```
[Visual Basic]
Public Class StringConverter
   Inherits TypeConverter
[C#]
public class StringConverter : TypeConverter
[C++]
public __gc class StringConverter : public TypeConverter
[JScript]
public class StringConverter extends TypeConverter
```

Thread Safety

Any public static (**Shared** in Visual Basic) members of this type are safe for multithreaded operations. Any instance members are not guaranteed to be thread safe.

Remarks

This converter can only convert to a string. It works as a pass through for other converters that want to convert an object to a string.

For more information about type converters, see the **TypeConverter** base class and **Implementing a Type Converter**.

> **Note** You should never create an instance of **StringConverter**. Instead, call the **GetConverter** method of **TypeDescriptor**. For more information, see the examples in the **TypeConverter** base class.

Requirements

Namespace: System.ComponentModel

Platforms: Windows 98, Windows NT 4.0, Windows Millennium Edition, Windows 2000, Windows XP Home Edition, Windows XP Professional, Windows Server 2003 family

Assembly: System (in System.dll)

StringConverter Constructor

Initializes a new instance of the **StringConverter** class.

```
[Visual Basic]
Public Sub New()
[C#]
public StringConverter();
[C++]
public: StringConverter();
[JScript]
public function StringConverter();
```

Remarks

The default constructor initializes any fields to their default values.

Requirements

Platforms: Windows 98, Windows NT 4.0, Windows Millennium Edition, Windows 2000, Windows XP Home Edition, Windows XP Professional, Windows Server 2003 family

StringConverter.CanConvertFrom Method

Overload List

This member supports the .NET Framework infrastructure and is not intended to be used directly from your code.

[Visual Basic] **Overloads Overrides Public Function CanConvertFrom(ITypeDescriptorContext, Type) As Boolean**

[C#] **public override bool CanConvertFrom(ITypeDescriptorContext, Type);**

[C++] **public: bool CanConvertFrom(ITypeDescriptorContext*, Type*);**

[JScript] **public override function CanConvertFrom(ITypeDescriptorContext, Type) : Boolean;**

Inherited from **TypeConverter**.

[Visual Basic] **Overloads Public Function CanConvertFrom(Type) As Boolean**

[C#] **public bool CanConvertFrom(Type);**

[C++] **public: bool CanConvertFrom(Type*);**

[JScript] **public function CanConvertFrom(Type) : Boolean;**

StringConverter.CanConvertFrom Method (ITypeDescriptorContext, Type)

This member overrides **TypeConverter.CanConvertFrom**.

```
[Visual Basic]
Overrides Overloads Public Function CanConvertFrom( _
   ByVal context As ITypeDescriptorContext, _
   ByVal sourceType As Type _
) As Boolean
[C#]
public override bool CanConvertFrom(
   ITypeDescriptorContext context,
   Type sourceType
);
[C++]
public: bool CanConvertFrom(
   ITypeDescriptorContext* context,
   Type* sourceType
);
[JScript]
public override function CanConvertFrom(
   context : ITypeDescriptorContext,
   sourceType : Type
) : Boolean;
```

Requirements

Platforms: Windows 98, Windows NT 4.0, Windows Millennium Edition, Windows 2000, Windows XP Home Edition, Windows XP Professional, Windows Server 2003 family

StringConverter.ConvertFrom Method

Overload List

Converts the specified value object to a **String** object.

[Visual Basic] **Overloads Overrides Public Function ConvertFrom(ITypeDescriptorContext, CultureInfo, Object) As Object**

[C#] **public override object ConvertFrom(ITypeDescriptorContext, CultureInfo, object);**

[C++] **public: Object* ConvertFrom(ITypeDescriptorContext*, CultureInfo*, Object*);**

[JScript] **public override function ConvertFrom(ITypeDescriptorContext, CultureInfo, Object) : Object;**

Inherited from **TypeConverter**.

[Visual Basic] **Overloads Public Function ConvertFrom(Object) As Object**

[C#] **public object ConvertFrom(object);**

[C++] **public: Object* ConvertFrom(Object*);**

[JScript] **public function ConvertFrom(Object) : Object;**

StringConverter.ConvertFrom Method (ITypeDescriptorContext, CultureInfo, Object)

Converts the specified value object to a **String** object.

```
[Visual Basic]
Overrides Overloads Public Function ConvertFrom( _
   ByVal context As ITypeDescriptorContext, _
   ByVal culture As CultureInfo, _
   ByVal value As Object _
) As Object
[C#]
public override object ConvertFrom(
   ITypeDescriptorContext context,
   CultureInfo culture,
   object value
);
[C++]
public: Object* ConvertFrom(
   ITypeDescriptorContext* context,
   CultureInfo* culture,
   Object* value
);
[JScript]
public override function ConvertFrom(
   context : ITypeDescriptorContext,
   culture : CultureInfo,
   value : Object
) : Object;
```

Parameters

context

An **ITypeDescriptorContext** that provides a format context.

culture

The **CultureInfo** to use.

value

The **Object** to convert.

Return Value

An **Object** that represents the converted value.

Exceptions

Exception Type	Condition
NotSupportedException	The conversion could not be performed.

Remarks

The *context* parameter can be used to extract additional information about the environment this converter is being invoked from. This can be a null reference (**Nothing** in Visual Basic), so you always need to check its value. In addition, properties on the context object can return a null reference (**Nothing**).

Requirements

Platforms: Windows 98, Windows NT 4.0, Windows Millennium Edition, Windows 2000, Windows XP Home Edition, Windows XP Professional, Windows Server 2003 family

SyntaxCheck Class

This type supports the .NET Framework infrastructure and is not intended to be used directly from your code.

[Visual Basic]
```
Public Class SyntaxCheck
```
[C#]
```
public class SyntaxCheck
```
[C++]
```
public __gc class SyntaxCheck
```
[JScript]
```
public class SyntaxCheck
```

SyntaxCheck.CheckMachineName Method

This member supports the .NET Framework infrastructure and is not intended to be used directly from your code.

[Visual Basic]
```
Public Shared Function CheckMachineName( _
   ByVal value As String _
) As Boolean
```
[C#]
```
public static bool CheckMachineName(
   string value
);
```
[C++]
```
public: static bool CheckMachineName(
   String* value
);
```
[JScript]
```
public static function CheckMachineName(
   value : String
) : Boolean;
```

SyntaxCheck.CheckPath Method

This member supports the .NET Framework infrastructure and is not intended to be used directly from your code.

[Visual Basic]
```
Public Shared Function CheckPath( _
   ByVal value As String _
) As Boolean
```
[C#]
```
public static bool CheckPath(
   string value
);
```
[C++]
```
public: static bool CheckPath(
   String* value
);
```
[JScript]
```
public static function CheckPath(
   value : String
) : Boolean;
```

SyntaxCheck.CheckRootedPath Method

This member supports the .NET Framework infrastructure and is not intended to be used directly from your code.

[Visual Basic]
```
Public Shared Function CheckRootedPath( _
   ByVal value As String _
) As Boolean
```
[C#]
```
public static bool CheckRootedPath(
   string value
);
```
[C++]
```
public: static bool CheckRootedPath(
   String* value
);
```
[JScript]
```
public static function CheckRootedPath(
   value : String
) : Boolean;
```

TimeSpanConverter Class

Provides a type converter to convert **TimeSpan** objects to and from other representations.

System.Object
  System.ComponentModel.TypeConverter
    System.ComponentModel.TimeSpanConverter

[Visual Basic]
```
Public Class TimeSpanConverter
   Inherits TypeConverter
```
[C#]
```
public class TimeSpanConverter : TypeConverter
```
[C++]
```
public __gc class TimeSpanConverter : public TypeConverter
```
[JScript]
```
public class TimeSpanConverter extends TypeConverter
```

Thread Safety

Any public static (**Shared** in Visual Basic) members of this type are safe for multithreaded operations. Any instance members are not guaranteed to be thread safe.

Remarks

This converter can only convert a **TimeSpan** object to and from a string.

For more information about type converters, see the **TypeConverter** base class and **Implementing a Type Converter**.

> **Note** You should never create an instance of a **TimeSpanConverter**. Instead, call the **GetConverter** method of **TypeDescriptor**. For more information, see the examples in the **TypeConverter** base class.

Example

[Visual Basic, C#, C++] The following sample converts a variable of type **TimeSpan** to a string, and vice versa. Both variables are represented in **Ticks** format.

[Visual Basic]
```
Dim ts As New TimeSpan(133333330)
Dim myTSStr As String = "5000000"
Console.WriteLine(TypeDescriptor.GetConverter(ts).ConvertTo(ts,     ↵
GetType(String)))
Console.WriteLine(TypeDescriptor.GetConverter(ts).ConvertFrom(myTSStr))
```
[C#]
```
TimeSpan ts=new TimeSpan(133333330);
string myTSStr = "5000000";
Console.WriteLine(TypeDescriptor.GetConverter(ts).ConvertTo(ts,     ↵
typeof(string)));
Console.WriteLine(TypeDescriptor.GetConverter(ts).ConvertFrom(myTSStr));
```
[C++]
```
TimeSpan ts(133333330);
String* myTSStr = S"5000000";
Console::WriteLine(TypeDescriptor::GetConverter(__box(ts))-     ↵
>ConvertTo(__box(ts), __typeof(String)));
Console::WriteLine(TypeDescriptor::GetConverter(__box(ts))-     ↵
>ConvertFrom(myTSStr));
```

Requirements

Namespace: System.ComponentModel

Platforms: Windows 98, Windows NT 4.0, Windows Millennium Edition, Windows 2000, Windows XP Home Edition, Windows XP Professional, Windows Server 2003 family

Assembly: System (in System.dll)

TimeSpanConverter Constructor

Initializes a new instance of the **TimeSpanConverter** class.

[Visual Basic]
```
Public Sub New()
```
[C#]
```
public TimeSpanConverter();
```
[C++]
```
public: TimeSpanConverter();
```
[JScript]
```
public function TimeSpanConverter();
```

Remarks

The default constructor initializes any fields to their default values.

Requirements

Platforms: Windows 98, Windows NT 4.0, Windows Millennium Edition, Windows 2000, Windows XP Home Edition, Windows XP Professional, Windows Server 2003 family

TimeSpanConverter.CanConvertFrom Method

Overload List

This member supports the .NET Framework infrastructure and is not intended to be used directly from your code.

[Visual Basic] **Overloads Overrides Public Function CanConvertFrom(ITypeDescriptorContext, Type) As Boolean**

[C#] **public override bool CanConvertFrom(ITypeDescriptorContext, Type);**

[C++] **public: bool CanConvertFrom(ITypeDescriptorContext*, Type*);**

[JScript] **public override function CanConvertFrom(ITypeDescriptorContext, Type) : Boolean;**

Inherited from **TypeConverter**.

[Visual Basic] **Overloads Public Function CanConvertFrom(Type) As Boolean**

[C#] **public bool CanConvertFrom(Type);**

[C++] **public: bool CanConvertFrom(Type*);**

[JScript] **public function CanConvertFrom(Type) : Boolean;**

TimeSpanConverter.CanConvertFrom Method (ITypeDescriptorContext, Type)

This member overrides **TypeConverter.CanConvertFrom**.

[Visual Basic]
```
Overrides Overloads Public Function CanConvertFrom( _
   ByVal context As ITypeDescriptorContext, _
   ByVal sourceType As Type _
) As Boolean
```

```
[C#]
public override bool CanConvertFrom(
   ITypeDescriptorContext context,
   Type sourceType
);
[C++]
public: bool CanConvertFrom(
   ITypeDescriptorContext* context,
   Type* sourceType
);
[JScript]
public override function CanConvertFrom(
   context : ITypeDescriptorContext,
   sourceType : Type
) : Boolean;
```

Requirements

Platforms: Windows 98, Windows NT 4.0, Windows Millennium Edition, Windows 2000, Windows XP Home Edition, Windows XP Professional, Windows Server 2003 family

TimeSpanConverter.CanConvertTo Method

Overload List

This member supports the .NET Framework infrastructure and is not intended to be used directly from your code.

[Visual Basic] **Overloads Overrides Public Function CanConvertTo(ITypeDescriptorContext, Type) As Boolean**

[C#] **public override bool CanConvertTo(ITypeDescriptorContext, Type);**

[C++] **public: bool CanConvertTo(ITypeDescriptorContext*, Type*);**

[JScript] **public override function CanConvertTo(ITypeDescriptorContext, Type) : Boolean;**

Inherited from **TypeConverter**.

[Visual Basic] **Overloads Public Function CanConvertTo(Type) As Boolean**

[C#] **public bool CanConvertTo(Type);**

[C++] **public: bool CanConvertTo(Type*);**

[JScript] **public function CanConvertTo(Type) : Boolean;**

TimeSpanConverter.CanConvertTo Method (ITypeDescriptorContext, Type)

This member overrides **TypeConverter.CanConvertTo**.

```
[Visual Basic]
Overrides Overloads Public Function CanConvertTo( _
   ByVal context As ITypeDescriptorContext, _
   ByVal destinationType As Type _
) As Boolean
[C#]
public override bool CanConvertTo(
   ITypeDescriptorContext context,
   Type destinationType
);
[C++]
public: bool CanConvertTo(
   ITypeDescriptorContext* context,
   Type* destinationType
);
[JScript]
public override function CanConvertTo(
   context : ITypeDescriptorContext,
   destinationType : Type
) : Boolean;
```

Requirements

Platforms: Windows 98, Windows NT 4.0, Windows Millennium Edition, Windows 2000, Windows XP Home Edition, Windows XP Professional, Windows Server 2003 family

TimeSpanConverter.ConvertFrom Method

Overload List

This member supports the .NET Framework infrastructure and is not intended to be used directly from your code.

[Visual Basic] **Overloads Overrides Public Function ConvertFrom(ITypeDescriptorContext, CultureInfo, Object) As Object**

[C#] **public override object ConvertFrom(ITypeDescriptorContext, CultureInfo, object);**

[C++] **public: Object* ConvertFrom(ITypeDescriptorContext*, CultureInfo*, Object*);**

[JScript] **public override function ConvertFrom(ITypeDescriptorContext, CultureInfo, Object) : Object;**

Inherited from **TypeConverter**.

[Visual Basic] **Overloads Public Function ConvertFrom(Object) As Object**

[C#] **public object ConvertFrom(object);**

[C++] **public: Object* ConvertFrom(Object*);**

[JScript] **public function ConvertFrom(Object) : Object;**

TimeSpanConverter.ConvertFrom Method (ITypeDescriptorContext, CultureInfo, Object)

This member overrides **TypeConverter.ConvertFrom**.

```
[Visual Basic]
Overrides Overloads Public Function ConvertFrom( _
   ByVal context As ITypeDescriptorContext, _
   ByVal culture As CultureInfo, _
   ByVal value As Object _
) As Object
[C#]
public override object ConvertFrom(
   ITypeDescriptorContext context,
   CultureInfo culture,
   object value
);
[C++]
public: Object* ConvertFrom(
   ITypeDescriptorContext* context,
   CultureInfo* culture,
   Object* value
);
[JScript]
public override function ConvertFrom(
   context : ITypeDescriptorContext,
   culture : CultureInfo,
   value : Object
) : Object;
```

Requirements

Platforms: Windows 98, Windows NT 4.0, Windows Millennium Edition, Windows 2000, Windows XP Home Edition, Windows XP Professional, Windows Server 2003 family

TimeSpanConverter.ConvertTo Method

Overload List

This member supports the .NET Framework infrastructure and is not intended to be used directly from your code.

[Visual Basic] **Overloads Overrides Public Function ConvertTo(ITypeDescriptorContext, CultureInfo, Object, Type) As Object**

[C#] **public override object ConvertTo(ITypeDescriptorContext, CultureInfo, object, Type);**

[C++] **public: Object* ConvertTo(ITypeDescriptorContext*, CultureInfo*, Object*, Type*);**

[JScript] **public override function ConvertTo(ITypeDescriptorContext, CultureInfo, Object, Type) : Object;**

Inherited from **TypeConverter**.

[Visual Basic] **Overloads Public Function ConvertTo(Object, Type) As Object**

[C#] **public object ConvertTo(object, Type);**

[C++] **public: Object* ConvertTo(Object*, Type*);**

[JScript] **public function ConvertTo(Object, Type) : Object;**

TimeSpanConverter.ConvertTo Method (ITypeDescriptorContext, CultureInfo, Object, Type)

This member overrides **TypeConverter.ConvertTo**.

```
[Visual Basic]
Overrides Overloads Public Function ConvertTo( _
   ByVal context As ITypeDescriptorContext, _
   ByVal culture As CultureInfo, _
   ByVal value As Object, _
   ByVal destinationType As Type _
) As Object
[C#]
public override object ConvertTo(
   ITypeDescriptorContext context,
   CultureInfo culture,
   object value,
   Type destinationType
);
[C++]
public: Object* ConvertTo(
   ITypeDescriptorContext* context,
   CultureInfo* culture,
   Object* value,
   Type* destinationType
);
[JScript]
public override function ConvertTo(
   context : ITypeDescriptorContext,
   culture : CultureInfo,
   value : Object,
   destinationType : Type
) : Object;
```

Requirements

Platforms: Windows 98, Windows NT 4.0, Windows Millennium Edition, Windows 2000, Windows XP Home Edition, Windows XP Professional, Windows Server 2003 family

ToolboxItemAttribute Class

Represents an attribute of a toolbox item.

System.Object
  System.Attribute
    System.ComponentModel.ToolboxItemAttribute

```
[Visual Basic]
<AttributeUsage(AttributeTargets.All)>
Public Class ToolboxItemAttribute
   Inherits Attribute
[C#]
[AttributeUsage(AttributeTargets.All)]
public class ToolboxItemAttribute : Attribute
[C++]
[AttributeUsage(AttributeTargets::All)]
public __gc class ToolboxItemAttribute : public Attribute
[JScript]
public
   AttributeUsage(AttributeTargets.All)
class ToolboxItemAttribute extends Attribute
```

Thread Safety

Any public static (**Shared** in Visual Basic) members of this type are safe for multithreaded operations. Any instance members are not guaranteed to be thread safe.

Remarks

ToolboxItemAttribute provides a way to specify an attribute for a **ToolboxItem**. In addition to what **Attribute** provides, this class of object stores the type of the toolbox item.

Requirements

Namespace: System.ComponentModel

Platforms: Windows 98, Windows NT 4.0, Windows Millennium Edition, Windows 2000, Windows XP Home Edition, Windows XP Professional, Windows Server 2003 family

Assembly: System (in System.dll)

ToolboxItemAttribute Constructor

Initializes a new instance of **ToolboxItemAttribute** and specifies whether to use default initialization values.

Overload List

Initializes a new instance of **ToolboxItemAttribute** and specifies whether to use default initialization values.

[Visual Basic] **Public Sub New(Boolean)**

[C#] **public ToolboxItemAttribute(bool);**

[C++] **public: ToolboxItemAttribute(bool);**

[JScript] **public function ToolboxItemAttribute(Boolean);**

Initializes a new instance of the **ToolboxItemAttribute** class using the specified name of the type.

[Visual Basic] **Public Sub New(String)**

[C#] **public ToolboxItemAttribute(string);**

[C++] **public: ToolboxItemAttribute(String*);**

[JScript] **public function ToolboxItemAttribute(String);**

Initializes a new instance of the **ToolboxItemAttribute** class using the specified type of the toolbox item.

[Visual Basic] **Public Sub New(Type)**

[C#] **public ToolboxItemAttribute(Type);**

[C++] **public: ToolboxItemAttribute(Type*);**

[JScript] **public function ToolboxItemAttribute(Type);**

ToolboxItemAttribute Constructor (Boolean)

Initializes a new instance of **ToolboxItemAttribute** and specifies whether to use default initialization values.

```
[Visual Basic]
Public Sub New( _
   ByVal defaultType As Boolean _
)
[C#]
public ToolboxItemAttribute(
   bool defaultType
);
[C++]
public: ToolboxItemAttribute(
   bool defaultType
);
[JScript]
public function ToolboxItemAttribute(
   defaultType : Boolean
);
```

Parameters

defaultType
  true to create a toolbox item attribute for a default type; **false** to associate no default toolbox item support for this attribute.

Remarks

By default, the **ToolboxItemType** property is set to **ToolboxItem**.

Requirements

Platforms: Windows 98, Windows NT 4.0, Windows Millennium Edition, Windows 2000, Windows XP Home Edition, Windows XP Professional, Windows Server 2003 family

ToolboxItemAttribute Constructor (String)

Initializes a new instance of the **ToolboxItemAttribute** class using the specified name of the type.

```
[Visual Basic]
Public Sub New( _
   ByVal toolboxItemTypeName As String _
)
[C#]
public ToolboxItemAttribute(
   string toolboxItemTypeName
);
[C++]
public: ToolboxItemAttribute(
   String* toolboxItemTypeName
);
[JScript]
public function ToolboxItemAttribute(
   toolboxItemTypeName : String
);
```

Parameters

toolboxItemTypeName

The names of the type of the toolbox item and of the assembly that contains the type.

Remarks

This constructor expects the *toolboxItemTypeName* parameter to be in the form: <name of the item type>, <name of the assembly>. For example, System.Drawing.Design.ToolboxItem, System.Drawing.Design.

Requirements

Platforms: Windows 98, Windows NT 4.0, Windows Millennium Edition, Windows 2000, Windows XP Home Edition, Windows XP Professional, Windows Server 2003 family

ToolboxItemAttribute Constructor (Type)

Initializes a new instance of the **ToolboxItemAttribute** class using the specified type of the toolbox item.

```
[Visual Basic]
Public Sub New( _
   ByVal toolboxItemType As Type _
)
[C#]
public ToolboxItemAttribute(
   Type toolboxItemType
);
[C++]
public: ToolboxItemAttribute(
   Type* toolboxItemType
);
[JScript]
public function ToolboxItemAttribute(
   toolboxItemType : Type
);
```

Parameters

toolboxItemType

The type of the toolbox item.

Requirements

Platforms: Windows 98, Windows NT 4.0, Windows Millennium Edition, Windows 2000, Windows XP Home Edition, Windows XP Professional, Windows Server 2003 family

ToolboxItemAttribute.Default Field

Initializes a new instance of the **ToolboxItemAttribute** class and sets the type to the default, **ToolboxItem**. This field is read-only.

```
[Visual Basic]
Public Shared ReadOnly Default As ToolboxItemAttribute
[C#]
public static readonly ToolboxItemAttribute Default;
[C++]
public: static ToolboxItemAttribute* Default;
[JScript]
public static var Default : ToolboxItemAttribute;
```

Remarks

By default, the **ToolboxItemType** property is set to **ToolboxItem**.

Requirements

Platforms: Windows 98, Windows NT 4.0, Windows Millennium Edition, Windows 2000, Windows XP Home Edition, Windows XP Professional, Windows Server 2003 family

ToolboxItemAttribute.None Field

Initializes a new instance of the **ToolboxItemAttribute** class and sets the type to a null reference (**Nothing** in Visual Basic). This field is read-only.

```
[Visual Basic]
Public Shared ReadOnly None As ToolboxItemAttribute
[C#]
public static readonly ToolboxItemAttribute None;
[C++]
public: static ToolboxItemAttribute* None;
[JScript]
public static var None : ToolboxItemAttribute;
```

Requirements

Platforms: Windows 98, Windows NT 4.0, Windows Millennium Edition, Windows 2000, Windows XP Home Edition, Windows XP Professional, Windows Server 2003 family

ToolboxItemAttribute.ToolboxItemType Property

Gets or sets the type of the toolbox item.

```
[Visual Basic]
Public ReadOnly Property ToolboxItemType As Type
[C#]
public Type ToolboxItemType {get;}
[C++]
public: __property Type* get_ToolboxItemType();
[JScript]
public function get ToolboxItemType() : Type;
```

Property Value

The type of the toolbox item.

Requirements

Platforms: Windows 98, Windows NT 4.0, Windows Millennium Edition, Windows 2000, Windows XP Home Edition, Windows XP Professional, Windows Server 2003 family

ToolboxItemAttribute.ToolboxItemTypeName Property

Gets or sets the name of the type of the current **ToolboxItem**.

```
[Visual Basic]
Public ReadOnly Property ToolboxItemTypeName As String
[C#]
public string ToolboxItemTypeName {get;}
[C++]
public: __property String* get_ToolboxItemTypeName();
[JScript]
public function get ToolboxItemTypeName() : String;
```

Property Value

The fully qualified type name of the current toolbox item.

Requirements

Platforms: Windows 98, Windows NT 4.0, Windows Millennium Edition, Windows 2000, Windows XP Home Edition, Windows XP Professional, Windows Server 2003 family

ToolboxItemAttribute.Equals Method

This member overrides **Object.Equals**.

[Visual Basic]
```
Overrides Public Function Equals( _
   ByVal obj As Object _
) As Boolean
```
[C#]
```
public override bool Equals(
   object obj
);
```
[C++]
```
public: bool Equals(
   Object* obj
);
```
[JScript]
```
public override function Equals(
   obj : Object
) : Boolean;
```

Requirements

Platforms: Windows 98, Windows NT 4.0, Windows Millennium Edition, Windows 2000, Windows XP Home Edition, Windows XP Professional, Windows Server 2003 family

ToolboxItemAttribute.GetHashCode Method

This member overrides **Attribute.GetHashCode**.

[Visual Basic]
```
Overrides Public Function GetHashCode() As Integer
```
[C#]
```
public override int GetHashCode();
```
[C++]
```
public: int GetHashCode();
```
[JScript]
```
public override function GetHashCode() : int;
```

Requirements

Platforms: Windows 98, Windows NT 4.0, Windows Millennium Edition, Windows 2000, Windows XP Home Edition, Windows XP Professional, Windows Server 2003 family

ToolboxItemAttribute.IsDefaultAttribute Method

Gets a value indicating whether the current value of the attribute is the default value for the attribute.

[Visual Basic]
```
Overrides Public Function IsDefaultAttribute() As Boolean
```
[C#]
```
public override bool IsDefaultAttribute();
```
[C++]
```
public: bool IsDefaultAttribute();
```
[JScript]
```
public override function IsDefaultAttribute() : Boolean;
```

Return Value

true if the current value of the attribute is the default; otherwise, **false**.

Remarks

By default, this value returns **false** from the method defined in the **Attribute** class.

Requirements

Platforms: Windows 98, Windows NT 4.0, Windows Millennium Edition, Windows 2000, Windows XP Home Edition, Windows XP Professional, Windows Server 2003 family

ToolboxItemFilterAttribute Class

Specifies the filter string and filter type to use for a toolbox item.

System.Object
  System.Attribute
    System.ComponentModel.ToolboxItemFilterAttribute

```
[Visual Basic]
<AttributeUsage(AttributeTargets.Class)>
<Serializable>
NotInheritable Public Class ToolboxItemFilterAttribute
   Inherits Attribute
[C#]
[AttributeUsage(AttributeTargets.Class)]
[Serializable]
public sealed class ToolboxItemFilterAttribute : Attribute
[C++]
[AttributeUsage(AttributeTargets::Class)]
[Serializable]
public __gc __sealed class ToolboxItemFilterAttribute : public
   Attribute
[JScript]
public
   AttributeUsage(AttributeTargets.Class)
   Serializable
class ToolboxItemFilterAttribute extends Attribute
```

Thread Safety

Any public static (**Shared** in Visual Basic) members of this type are safe for multithreaded operations. Any instance members are not guaranteed to be thread safe.

Remarks

ToolboxItemFilterAttribute provides a mechanism by which toolbox items can be marked for use only with designers that have a matching attribute or code that determines whether the item should be enabled or disabled in the toolbox.

A **ToolboxItemFilterAttribute** can be applied to a **ToolboxItem** to indicate a filter string and filter type that specify when to enable or disable the item. **ToolboxItemFilterAttribute** can also be applied to a designer to indicate its requirements for enabling items in the toolbox. This type of attribute can be used to indicate that a toolbox item can only be enabled when a designer with a matching filter string is being used. The type of the filter is indicated in the **FilterType** property by a **ToolboxItemFilterType** that indicates whether and how a filter string match is used, or whether to use custom code to determine whether to enable an item.

Requirements

Namespace: System.ComponentModel

Platforms: Windows 98, Windows NT 4.0, Windows Millennium Edition, Windows 2000, Windows XP Home Edition, Windows XP Professional, Windows Server 2003 family

Assembly: System (in System.dll)

ToolboxItemFilterAttribute Constructor

Initializes a new instance of the **ToolboxItemFilterAttribute** class.

Overload List

Initializes a new instance of the **ToolboxItemFilterAttribute** class using the specified filter string.

[Visual Basic] **Public Sub New(String)**

[C#] **public ToolboxItemFilterAttribute(string);**

[C++] **public: ToolboxItemFilterAttribute(String*);**

[JScript] **public function ToolboxItemFilterAttribute(String);**

Initializes a new instance of the **ToolboxItemFilterAttribute** class using the specified filter string and type.

[Visual Basic] **Public Sub New(String, ToolboxItemFilterType)**

[C#] **public ToolboxItemFilterAttribute(string, ToolboxItemFilterType);**

[C++] **public: ToolboxItemFilterAttribute(String*, ToolboxItemFilterType);**

[JScript] **public function ToolboxItemFilterAttribute(String, ToolboxItemFilterType);**

ToolboxItemFilterAttribute Constructor (String)

Initializes a new instance of the **ToolboxItemFilterAttribute** class using the specified filter string.

```
[Visual Basic]
Public Sub New( _
   ByVal filterString As String _
)
[C#]
public ToolboxItemFilterAttribute(
   string filterString
);
[C++]
public: ToolboxItemFilterAttribute(
   String* filterString
);
[JScript]
public function ToolboxItemFilterAttribute(
   filterString : String
);
```

Parameters

filterString
  The filter string for the toolbox item.

Requirements

Platforms: Windows 98, Windows NT 4.0, Windows Millennium Edition, Windows 2000, Windows XP Home Edition, Windows XP Professional, Windows Server 2003 family

ToolboxItemFilterAttribute Constructor (String, ToolboxItemFilterType)

Initializes a new instance of the **ToolboxItemFilterAttribute** class using the specified filter string and type.

```
[Visual Basic]
Public Sub New( _
   ByVal filterString As String, _
   ByVal filterType As ToolboxItemFilterType _
)
[C#]
public ToolboxItemFilterAttribute(
   string filterString,
   ToolboxItemFilterType filterType
);
[C++]
public: ToolboxItemFilterAttribute(
   String* filterString,
   ToolboxItemFilterType filterType
);
[JScript]
public function ToolboxItemFilterAttribute(
   filterString : String,
   filterType : ToolboxItemFilterType
);
```

Parameters

filterString
The filter string for the toolbox item.

filterType
A **ToolboxItemFilterType** indicating the type of the filter.

Requirements

Platforms: Windows 98, Windows NT 4.0, Windows Millennium Edition, Windows 2000, Windows XP Home Edition, Windows XP Professional, Windows Server 2003 family

ToolboxItemFilterAttribute.FilterString Property

Gets the filter string for the toolbox item.

```
[Visual Basic]
Public ReadOnly Property FilterString As String
[C#]
public string FilterString {get;}
[C++]
public: __property String* get_FilterString();
[JScript]
public function get FilterString() : String;
```

Property Value

The filter string for the toolbox item.

Requirements

Platforms: Windows 98, Windows NT 4.0, Windows Millennium Edition, Windows 2000, Windows XP Home Edition, Windows XP Professional, Windows Server 2003 family

ToolboxItemFilterAttribute.FilterType Property

Gets the type of the filter.

```
[Visual Basic]
Public ReadOnly Property FilterType As ToolboxItemFilterType
[C#]
public ToolboxItemFilterType FilterType {get;}
[C++]
public: __property ToolboxItemFilterType get_FilterType();
[JScript]
public function get FilterType() : ToolboxItemFilterType;
```

Property Value

A **ToolboxItemFilterType** that indicates the type of the filter.

Remarks

The type of the filter, along with any existing **ToolboxItemFilterAttribute** on the current designer, indicates the rules to use to determine whether a particular toolbox item should be enabled in the toolbox.

Requirements

Platforms: Windows 98, Windows NT 4.0, Windows Millennium Edition, Windows 2000, Windows XP Home Edition, Windows XP Professional, Windows Server 2003 family

ToolboxItemFilterAttribute.TypeId Property

Gets the type ID for the attribute.

```
[Visual Basic]
Overrides Public ReadOnly Property TypeId As Object
[C#]
public override object TypeId {get;}
[C++]
public: __property Object* get_TypeId();
[JScript]
public override function get TypeId() : Object;
```

Property Value

The type ID for this attribute. All **ToolboxItemFilterAttribute** objects with the same filter string return the same type ID.

Requirements

Platforms: Windows 98, Windows NT 4.0, Windows Millennium Edition, Windows 2000, Windows XP Home Edition, Windows XP Professional, Windows Server 2003 family

ToolboxItemFilterAttribute.Equals Method

This member overrides **Object.Equals**.

```
[Visual Basic]
Overrides Public Function Equals( _
   ByVal obj As Object _
) As Boolean
[C#]
public override bool Equals(
   object obj
);
```

```
[C++]
public: bool Equals(
   Object* obj
);
[JScript]
public override function Equals(
   obj : Object
) : Boolean;
```

Requirements

Platforms: Windows 98, Windows NT 4.0, Windows Millennium Edition, Windows 2000, Windows XP Home Edition, Windows XP Professional, Windows Server 2003 family

ToolboxItemFilterAttribute.GetHashCode Method

This member overrides **Attribute.GetHashCode**.

```
[Visual Basic]
Overrides Public Function GetHashCode() As Integer
[C#]
public override int GetHashCode();
[C++]
public: int GetHashCode();
[JScript]
public override function GetHashCode() : int;
```

Requirements

Platforms: Windows 98, Windows NT 4.0, Windows Millennium Edition, Windows 2000, Windows XP Home Edition, Windows XP Professional, Windows Server 2003 family

ToolboxItemFilterAttribute.Match Method

Indicates whether the specified object has a matching filter string.

```
[Visual Basic]
Overrides Public Function Match( _
   ByVal obj As Object _
) As Boolean
[C#]
public override bool Match(
   object obj
);
[C++]
public: bool Match(
   Object* obj
);
[JScript]
public override function Match(
   obj : Object
) : Boolean;
```

Parameters

obj

The object to test for a matching filter string.

Return Value

true if the specified object has a matching filter string; otherwise, **false**.

Requirements

Platforms: Windows 98, Windows NT 4.0, Windows Millennium Edition, Windows 2000, Windows XP Home Edition, Windows XP Professional, Windows Server 2003 family

ToolboxItemFilterType Enumeration

Defines identifiers used to indicate the type of filter that a **ToolboxItemFilterAttribute** uses.

[Visual Basic]

```
<Serializable>
Public Enum ToolboxItemFilterType
```

[C#]

```
[Serializable]
public enum ToolboxItemFilterType
```

[C++]

```
[Serializable]
__value public enum ToolboxItemFilterType
```

[JScript]

```
public
   Serializable
enum ToolboxItemFilterType
```

Members

Member name	Description
Allow	Indicates that a toolbox item filter string is allowed, but not required.
Custom	Indicates that custom processing is required to determine whether to use a toolbox item filter string. This type of **ToolboxItemFilterType** is typically specified on a root designer class to indicate that the designer wishes to accept or reject a toolbox item through code. The designer must implement the **GetToolSupported** method of the **IToolboxUser** interface.
Prevent	Indicates that a toolbox item filter string is not allowed. If a designer and a component class both have a filter string and one has a **ToolboxItemFilterType** of **Prevent**, the toolbox item will not be available.
Require	Indicates that a toolbox item filter string must be present for a toolbox item to be enabled. For a toolbox item with a filter type of **Require** to be enabled, the designer and the component class must have a matching filter string. Additionally, neither the designer or component class can have a **ToolboxItemFilterType** of **Prevent** for the toolbox item to be enabled.

Requirements

Namespace: System.ComponentModel

Platforms: Windows 98, Windows NT 4.0, Windows Millennium Edition, Windows 2000, Windows XP Home Edition, Windows XP Professional, Windows Server 2003 family

Assembly: System (in System.dll)

TypeConverter Class

Provides a unified way of converting types of values to other types, as well as for accessing standard values and subproperties.

System.Object
  System.ComponentModel.TypeConverter
    Derived classes

[Visual Basic]
```
<ComVisible(True)>
Public Class TypeConverter
```
[C#]
```
[ComVisible(true)]
public class TypeConverter
```
[C++]
```
[ComVisible(true)]
public __gc class TypeConverter
```
[JScript]
```
public
   ComVisible(true)
class TypeConverter
```

Thread Safety

Any public static (**Shared** in Visual Basic) members of this type are safe for multithreaded operations. Any instance members are not guaranteed to be thread safe.

Remarks

The most common type of converter is one that converts to and from a text representation. The type converter for a class is bound to the class with a **TypeConverterAttribute**. Unless this attribute is overridden, all classes that inherit from this class use the same type converter as the base class.

> **Note** Never access a type converter directly. Instead, access the appropriate converter by using **TypeDescriptor**. For more information, see the code examples provided.

Notes to Inheritors: Inherit from **TypeConverter** to implement your own conversion requirements. When you inherit from this class, you can override the following methods:

- To support custom type conversion, override the following methods: **CanConvertFrom**, **CanConvertTo**, **ConvertFrom**, and **ConvertTo**.
- To convert types that must re-create the object to change its value, override **CreateInstance** and **GetCreateInstanceSupported**.
- To convert types that support properties, override **GetProperties** and **GetPropertiesSupported**. If the class you are converting does not have properties, and you need to implement properties, you can use the **TypeConverter.SimplePropertyDescriptor** class as a base for implementing the property descriptors. When you inherit from **TypeConverter.SimplePropertyDescriptor**, you must override the **GetValue** and **SetValue** methods.
- To convert types that support standard values, override the following methods: **GetStandardValues**, **GetStandardValuesExclusive**, **GetStandardValuesSupported** and **IsValid**.

Example

[Visual Basic, C#] The following example shows how to create an instance of a type converter and bind it to a class. The class implementing the converter, `MyClassConverter`, must inherit from the **TypeConverter** class.

[Visual Basic]
```
<TypeConverter(GetType(MyClassConverter))> _
Public Class Class1
    ' Insert code here.
End Class 'MyClass
```

[C#]
```
[TypeConverter(typeof(MyClassConverter))]
 public class MyClass {
    // Insert code here.
}
```

[Visual Basic, C#] When you have a property that has an enumeration, check to see whether an enumeration value is valid before setting the property. The next code example assumes that an enumeration called `MyPropertyEnum` has been declared.

[Visual Basic]
```
Public WriteOnly Property MyProperty() As MyPropertyEnum
    Set
        ' Checks to see if the value passed is valid.
        If Not
TypeDescriptor.GetConverter(GetType(MyPropertyEnum)).IsValid      ↵
(value) Then
            Throw New ArgumentException()
        End If
        ' The value is valid. Insert code to set the property.
    End Set
End Property
```

[C#]
```
public MyPropertyEnum MyProperty {
    set {
        // Checks to see if the value passed is valid.
        if
(!TypeDescriptor.GetConverter(typeof(MyPropertyEnum)).IsValid(value)) {
            throw new ArgumentException();
        }
        // The value is valid. Insert code to set the property.
    }
 }
```

[Visual Basic, C#] Another common type converter usage is to convert an object to a string. The following example prints out the name of the **Color** stored in the variable `c`.

[Visual Basic]
```
Dim c As Color = Color.Red
Console.WriteLine(TypeDescriptor.GetConverter(c).ConvertToString(c))
```

[C#]
```
Color c = Color.Red;

Console.WriteLine(TypeDescriptor.GetConverter(c).ConvertToString(c));
```

[Visual Basic, C#] You can also use a type converter to convert a value from its name, as shown in the next code example.

[Visual Basic]
```
Dim c As Color =                                                  ↵
CType(TypeDescriptor.GetConverter                                 ↵
 (GetType(Color)).ConvertFromString("Red"), Color)
```

[C#]
```
Color c = (Color)TypeDescriptor.GetConverter                      ↵
 (typeof(Color)).ConvertFromString("Red");
```

[Visual Basic, C#] In this example, you can use a type converter to print out the set of standard values that the object supports.

[Visual Basic]
```
Dim c As Color
For Each c In                                                     ↵
TypeDescriptor.GetConverter(GetType(Color)).GetStandardValues()
    Console.WriteLine(TypeDescriptor.GetConverter(c).ConvertToString(c))
Next c
```

[C#]
```
foreach(Color c in
TypeDescriptor.GetConverter(typeof(Color)).GetStandardValues()) {

Console.WriteLine(TypeDescriptor.GetConverter(c).ConvertToString(c));
 }
```

Requirements

Namespace: System.ComponentModel

Platforms: Windows 98, Windows NT 4.0, Windows Millennium Edition, Windows 2000, Windows XP Home Edition, Windows XP Professional, Windows Server 2003 family, .NET Compact Framework - Windows CE .NET

Assembly: System (in System.dll)

TypeConverter Constructor

Initializes a new instance of the **TypeConverter** class.

[Visual Basic]
```
Public Sub New()
```
[C#]
```
public TypeConverter();
```
[C++]
```
public: TypeConverter();
```
[JScript]
```
public function TypeConverter();
```

Remarks

The default constructor initializes any fields to their default values.

Requirements

Platforms: Windows 98, Windows NT 4.0, Windows Millennium Edition, Windows 2000, Windows XP Home Edition, Windows XP Professional, Windows Server 2003 family, .NET Compact Framework - Windows CE .NET

TypeConverter.CanConvertFrom Method

Returns whether this converter can convert an object of one type to the type of this converter.

Overload List

Returns whether this converter can convert an object of the given type to the type of this converter.

[Visual Basic] **Overloads Public Function CanConvertFrom(Type) As Boolean**

[C#] **public bool CanConvertFrom(Type);**

[C++] **public: bool CanConvertFrom(Type*);**

[JScript] **public function CanConvertFrom(Type) : Boolean;**

Returns whether this converter can convert an object of the given type to the type of this converter, using the specified context.

[Visual Basic] **Overloads Public Overridable Function Can-ConvertFrom(ITypeDescriptorContext, Type) As Boolean**

[C#] **public virtual bool CanConvertFrom(IType-DescriptorContext, Type);**

[C++] **public: virtual bool CanConvertFrom(IType-DescriptorContext*, Type*);**

[JScript] **public function CanConvertFrom(IType-DescriptorContext, Type) : Boolean;**

TypeConverter.CanConvertFrom Method (Type)

Returns whether this converter can convert an object of the given type to the type of this converter.

[Visual Basic]
```
Overloads Public Function CanConvertFrom( _
   ByVal sourceType As Type _
) As Boolean
```
[C#]
```
public bool CanConvertFrom(
   Type sourceType
);
```
[C++]
```
public: bool CanConvertFrom(
   Type* sourceType
);
```
[JScript]
```
public function CanConvertFrom(
   sourceType : Type
) : Boolean;
```

Parameters

sourceType

A **Type** that represents the type you want to convert from.

Return Value

true if this converter can perform the conversion; otherwise, **false**.

Remarks

As implemented in this class, this method always returns **false**. It never returns **true**.

Requirements

Platforms: Windows 98, Windows NT 4.0, Windows Millennium Edition, Windows 2000, Windows XP Home Edition, Windows XP Professional, Windows Server 2003 family

TypeConverter.CanConvertFrom Method (ITypeDescriptorContext, Type)

Returns whether this converter can convert an object of the given type to the type of this converter, using the specified context.

[Visual Basic]
```
Overloads Public Overridable Function CanConvertFrom( _
   ByVal context As ITypeDescriptorContext, _
   ByVal sourceType As Type _
) As Boolean
```
[C#]
```
public virtual bool CanConvertFrom(
   ITypeDescriptorContext context,
   Type sourceType
);
```
[C++]
```
public: virtual bool CanConvertFrom(
   ITypeDescriptorContext* context,
   Type* sourceType
);
```
[JScript]
```
public function CanConvertFrom(
   context : ITypeDescriptorContext,
   sourceType : Type
) : Boolean;
```

Parameters

context

An **ITypeDescriptorContext** that provides a format context.

sourceType

A **Type** that represents the type you want to convert from.

Return Value

true if this converter can perform the conversion; otherwise, **false**.

Remarks

As implemented in this class, this method always returns **false**. It never returns **true**.

Notes to Inheritors: Override this method to provide your own conversion requirements.

Use the *context* parameter to extract additional information about the environment from which this converter is invoked. This parameter can be a null reference (**Nothing** in Visual Basic), so always check it. Also, properties on the context object can return a null reference (**Nothing**).

Requirements

Platforms: Windows 98, Windows NT 4.0, Windows Millennium Edition, Windows 2000, Windows XP Home Edition, Windows XP Professional, Windows Server 2003 family

TypeConverter.CanConvertTo Method

Returns whether this converter can convert the object to the specified type.

Overload List

Returns whether this converter can convert the object to the specified type.

[Visual Basic] **Overloads Public Function CanConvertTo(Type) As Boolean**

[C#] **public bool CanConvertTo(Type);**

[C++] **public: bool CanConvertTo(Type*);**

[JScript] **public function CanConvertTo(Type) : Boolean;**

Returns whether this converter can convert the object to the specified type, using the specified context.

[Visual Basic] **Overloads Public Overridable Function CanConvertTo(ITypeDescriptorContext, Type) As Boolean**

[C#] **public virtual bool CanConvertTo(ITypeDescriptorContext, Type);**

[C++] **public: virtual bool CanConvertTo(ITypeDescriptorContext*, Type*);**

[JScript] **public function CanConvertTo(ITypeDescriptorContext, Type) : Boolean;**

TypeConverter.CanConvertTo Method (Type)

Returns whether this converter can convert the object to the specified type.

```
[Visual Basic]
Overloads Public Function CanConvertTo( _
   ByVal destinationType As Type _
) As Boolean
[C#]
public bool CanConvertTo(
   Type destinationType
);
[C++]
public: bool CanConvertTo(
   Type* destinationType
);
[JScript]
public function CanConvertTo(
   destinationType : Type
) : Boolean;
```

Parameters

destinationType

A **Type** that represents the type you want to convert to.

Return Value

true if this converter can perform the conversion; otherwise, **false**.

Requirements

Platforms: Windows 98, Windows NT 4.0, Windows Millennium Edition, Windows 2000, Windows XP Home Edition, Windows XP Professional, Windows Server 2003 family

TypeConverter.CanConvertTo Method (ITypeDescriptorContext, Type)

Returns whether this converter can convert the object to the specified type, using the specified context.

```
[Visual Basic]
Overloads Public Overridable Function CanConvertTo( _
   ByVal context As ITypeDescriptorContext, _
   ByVal destinationType As Type _
) As Boolean
[C#]
public virtual bool CanConvertTo(
   ITypeDescriptorContext context,
   Type destinationType
);
[C++]
public: virtual bool CanConvertTo(
   ITypeDescriptorContext* context,
   Type* destinationType
);
[JScript]
public function CanConvertTo(
   context : ITypeDescriptorContext,
   destinationType : Type
) : Boolean;
```

Parameters

context

An **ITypeDescriptorContext** that provides a format context.

destinationType

A **Type** that represents the type you want to convert to.

Return Value

true if this converter can perform the conversion; otherwise, **false**.

Remarks

Use the *context* parameter to extract additional information about the environment from which this converter is invoked. This parameter can be a null reference (**Nothing** in Visual Basic), so always check it. Also, properties on the context object can return a null reference (**Nothing**).

Notes to Inheritors: Override this method to provide your own conversion requirements.

Requirements

Platforms: Windows 98, Windows NT 4.0, Windows Millennium Edition, Windows 2000, Windows XP Home Edition, Windows XP Professional, Windows Server 2003 family

TypeConverter.ConvertFrom Method

Converts the given value to the type of this converter.

Overload List

Converts the given value to the type of this converter.

[Visual Basic] **Overloads Public Function ConvertFrom(Object) As Object**

[C#] **public object ConvertFrom(object);**

[C++] **public: Object* ConvertFrom(Object*);**

[JScript] **public function ConvertFrom(Object) : Object;**

Converts the given object to the type of this converter, using the specified context and culture information.

[Visual Basic] **Overloads Public Overridable Function ConvertFrom(ITypeDescriptorContext, CultureInfo, Object) As Object**

[C#] **public virtual object ConvertFrom(ITypeDescriptorContext, CultureInfo, object);**

[C++] **public: virtual Object* ConvertFrom(ITypeDescriptorContext*, CultureInfo*, Object*);**

[JScript] **public function ConvertFrom(ITypeDescriptorContext, CultureInfo, Object) : Object;**

TypeConverter.ConvertFrom Method (Object)

Converts the given value to the type of this converter.

```
[Visual Basic]
Overloads Public Function ConvertFrom( _
   ByVal value As Object _
) As Object
[C#]
public object ConvertFrom(
   object value
);
[C++]
public: Object* ConvertFrom(
   Object* value
);
[JScript]
public function ConvertFrom(
   value : Object
) : Object;
```

Parameters

value
The **Object** to convert.

Return Value

An **Object** that represents the converted value.

Exceptions

Exception Type	Condition
NotSupportedException	The conversion could not be performed.

Requirements

Platforms: Windows 98, Windows NT 4.0, Windows Millennium Edition, Windows 2000, Windows XP Home Edition, Windows XP Professional, Windows Server 2003 family

TypeConverter.ConvertFrom Method (ITypeDescriptorContext, CultureInfo, Object)

Converts the given object to the type of this converter, using the specified context and culture information.

```
[Visual Basic]
Overloads Public Overridable Function ConvertFrom( _
   ByVal context As ITypeDescriptorContext, _
   ByVal culture As CultureInfo, _
   ByVal value As Object _
) As Object
[C#]
public virtual object ConvertFrom(
   ITypeDescriptorContext context,
   CultureInfo culture,
   object value
);
[C++]
public: virtual Object* ConvertFrom(
   ITypeDescriptorContext* context,
   CultureInfo* culture,
   Object* value
);
[JScript]
public function ConvertFrom(
   context : ITypeDescriptorContext,
   culture : CultureInfo,
   value : Object
) : Object;
```

Parameters

context
An **ITypeDescriptorContext** that provides a format context.

culture
The **CultureInfo** to use as the current culture.

value
The **Object** to convert.

Return Value

An **Object** that represents the converted value.

Exceptions

Exception Type	Condition
NotSupportedException	The conversion could not be performed.

Remarks

Notes to Inheritors: Override this method to provide your own conversion requirements.

Use the *context* parameter to extract additional information about the environment from which this converter is invoked. This parameter can be a null reference (**Nothing** in Visual Basic), so always check it. Also, properties on the context object can return a null reference (**Nothing**).

Requirements

Platforms: Windows 98, Windows NT 4.0,
Windows Millennium Edition, Windows 2000,
Windows XP Home Edition, Windows XP Professional,
Windows Server 2003 family

TypeConverter.ConvertFromInvariantString Method

Converts the value to a type of this converter, using the invariant culture.

Overload List

Converts the given string to the type of this converter, using the invariant culture.

[Visual Basic] **Overloads Public Function ConvertFromInvariantString(String) As Object**

[C#] **public object ConvertFromInvariantString(string);**

[C++] **public: Object* ConvertFromInvariantString(String*);**

[JScript] **public function ConvertFromInvariantString(String) : Object;**

Converts the given string to the type of this converter, using the invariant culture.

[Visual Basic] **Overloads Public Function ConvertFrom-InvariantString(ITypeDescriptorContext, String) As Object**

[C#] **public object ConvertFromInvariant-String(ITypeDescriptorContext, string);**

[C++] **public: Object* ConvertFromInvariant-String(ITypeDescriptorContext*, String*);**

[JScript] **public function ConvertFromInvariant-String(ITypeDescriptorContext, String) : Object;**

TypeConverter.ConvertFromInvariantString Method (String)

Converts the given string to the type of this converter, using the invariant culture.

```
[Visual Basic]
Overloads Public Function ConvertFromInvariantString( _
   ByVal text As String _
) As Object
[C#]
public object ConvertFromInvariantString(
   string text
);
[C++]
public: Object* ConvertFromInvariantString(
   String* text
);
[JScript]
public function ConvertFromInvariantString(
   text : String
) : Object;
```

Parameters

text

The **String** to convert.

Return Value

An **Object** that represents the converted text.

Exceptions

Exception Type	Condition
NotSupportedException	The conversion could not be performed.

Requirements

Platforms: Windows 98, Windows NT 4.0,
Windows Millennium Edition, Windows 2000,
Windows XP Home Edition, Windows XP Professional,
Windows Server 2003 family

TypeConverter.ConvertFromInvariantString Method (ITypeDescriptorContext, String)

Converts the given string to the type of this converter, using the invariant culture.

```
[Visual Basic]
Overloads Public Function ConvertFromInvariantString( _
   ByVal context As ITypeDescriptorContext, _
   ByVal text As String _
) As Object
[C#]
public object ConvertFromInvariantString(
   ITypeDescriptorContext context,
   string text
);
[C++]
public: Object* ConvertFromInvariantString(
   ITypeDescriptorContext* context,
   String* text
);
[JScript]
public function ConvertFromInvariantString(
   context : ITypeDescriptorContext,
   text : String
) : Object;
```

Parameters

context

An **ITypeDescriptorContext** that provides a format context.

text

The **String** to convert.

Return Value

An **Object** that represents the converted text.

Exceptions

Exception Type	Condition
NotSupportedException	The conversion could not be performed.

Requirements

Platforms: Windows 98, Windows NT 4.0,
Windows Millennium Edition, Windows 2000,
Windows XP Home Edition, Windows XP Professional,
Windows Server 2003 family

TypeConverter.ConvertFromString Method

Converts the specified text to an object.

Overload List

Converts the specified text to an object.

[Visual Basic] **Overloads Public Function ConvertFromString(String) As Object**

[C#] **public object ConvertFromString(string);**

[C++] **public: Object* ConvertFromString(String*);**

[JScript] **public function ConvertFromString(String) : Object;**

Converts the given text to an object, using the specified context.

[Visual Basic] **Overloads Public Function ConvertFromString(ITypeDescriptorContext, String) As Object**

[C#] **public object ConvertFromString(ITypeDescriptorContext, string);**

[C++] **public: Object* ConvertFromString(ITypeDescriptorContext*, String*);**

[JScript] **public function ConvertFromString(ITypeDescriptorContext, String) : Object;**

Converts the given text to an object, using the specified context and culture information.

[Visual Basic] **Overloads Public Function ConvertFromString(ITypeDescriptorContext, CultureInfo, String) As Object**

[C#] **public object ConvertFromString(ITypeDescriptorContext, CultureInfo, string);**

[C++] **public: Object* ConvertFromString(ITypeDescriptorContext*, CultureInfo*, String*);**

[JScript] **public function ConvertFromString(ITypeDescriptorContext, CultureInfo, String) : Object;**

Example

For an example on this function, see the sample in **TypeConverter**.

TypeConverter.ConvertFromString Method (String)

Converts the specified text to an object.

[Visual Basic]
```
Overloads Public Function ConvertFromString( _
   ByVal text As String _
) As Object
```
[C#]
```
public object ConvertFromString(
   string text
);
```
[C++]
```
public: Object* ConvertFromString(
   String* text
);
```
[JScript]
```
public function ConvertFromString(
   text : String
) : Object;
```

Parameters

text
The text representation of the object to convert.

Return Value

An **Object** that represents the converted text.

Exceptions

Exception Type	Condition
NotSupportedException	The string could not be converted into the appropriate object.

Remarks

The default implementation always returns a null reference (**Nothing** in Visual Basic).

Example

For an example on this function, see the sample in **TypeConverter**.

Requirements

Platforms: Windows 98, Windows NT 4.0, Windows Millennium Edition, Windows 2000, Windows XP Home Edition, Windows XP Professional, Windows Server 2003 family

TypeConverter.ConvertFromString Method (ITypeDescriptorContext, String)

Converts the given text to an object, using the specified context.

[Visual Basic]
```
Overloads Public Function ConvertFromString( _
   ByVal context As ITypeDescriptorContext, _
   ByVal text As String _
) As Object
```
[C#]
```
public object ConvertFromString(
   ITypeDescriptorContext context,
   string text
);
```
[C++]
```
public: Object* ConvertFromString(
   ITypeDescriptorContext* context,
   String* text
);
```
[JScript]
```
public function ConvertFromString(
   context : ITypeDescriptorContext,
   text : String
) : Object;
```

Parameters

context
An **ITypeDescriptorContext** that provides a format context.

text
The **String** to convert.

Return Value

An **Object** that represents the converted text.

Exceptions

Exception Type	Condition
NotSupportedException	The conversion could not be performed.

Remarks

An exception is raised if the string cannot be converted into the appropriate object. The default implementation always returns a null reference (**Nothing** in Visual Basic).

Use the *context* parameter to extract additional information about the environment from which this converter is invoked. This parameter can be a null reference (**Nothing**), so always check it. Also, properties on the context object can return a null reference (**Nothing**).

Requirements

Platforms: Windows 98, Windows NT 4.0, Windows Millennium Edition, Windows 2000, Windows XP Home Edition, Windows XP Professional, Windows Server 2003 family

TypeConverter.ConvertFromString Method (ITypeDescriptorContext, CultureInfo, String)

Converts the given text to an object, using the specified context and culture information.

[Visual Basic]
```
Overloads Public Function ConvertFromString( _
   ByVal context As ITypeDescriptorContext, _
   ByVal culture As CultureInfo, _
   ByVal text As String _
) As Object
```
[C#]
```
public object ConvertFromString(
   ITypeDescriptorContext context,
   CultureInfo culture,
   string text
);
```
[C++]
```
public: Object* ConvertFromString(
   ITypeDescriptorContext* context,
   CultureInfo* culture,
   String* text
);
```
[JScript]
```
public function ConvertFromString(
   context : ITypeDescriptorContext,
   culture : CultureInfo,
   text : String
) : Object;
```

Parameters

context
: An **ITypeDescriptorContext** that provides a format context.

culture
: A **CultureInfo** object. If a null reference (**Nothing** in Visual Basic) is passed, the current culture is assumed.

text
: The **String** to convert.

Return Value

An **Object** that represents the converted text.

Exceptions

Exception Type	Condition
NotSupportedException	The conversion could not be performed.

Remarks

An exception is raised if the string cannot be converted into the appropriate object. The default implementation always returns a null reference (**Nothing** in Visual Basic).

Use the *context* parameter to extract additional information about the environment from which this converter is invoked. This parameter can be a null reference (**Nothing**), so always check it. Also, properties on the context object can return a null reference (**Nothing**).

Requirements

Platforms: Windows 98, Windows NT 4.0, Windows Millennium Edition, Windows 2000, Windows XP Home Edition, Windows XP Professional, Windows Server 2003 family

TypeConverter.ConvertTo Method

Converts the given value object to the specified type.

Overload List

Converts the given value object to the specified type, using the arguments.

[Visual Basic] **Overloads Public Function ConvertTo(Object, Type) As Object**

[C#] **public object ConvertTo(object, Type);**

[C++] **public: Object* ConvertTo(Object*, Type*);**

[JScript] **public function ConvertTo(Object, Type) : Object;**

Converts the given value object to the specified type, using the specified context and culture information.

[Visual Basic] **Overloads Public Overridable Function ConvertTo(ITypeDescriptorContext, CultureInfo, Object, Type) As Object**

[C#] **public virtual object ConvertTo(ITypeDescriptorContext, CultureInfo, object, Type);**

[C++] **public: virtual Object* ConvertTo(ITypeDescriptorContext*, CultureInfo*, Object*, Type*);**

[JScript] **public function ConvertTo(ITypeDescriptorContext, CultureInfo, Object, Type) : Object;**

TypeConverter.ConvertTo Method (Object, Type)

Converts the given value object to the specified type, using the arguments.

[Visual Basic]
```
Overloads Public Function ConvertTo( _
   ByVal value As Object, _
   ByVal destinationType As Type _
) As Object
```
[C#]
```
public object ConvertTo(
   object value,
   Type destinationType
);
```
[C++]
```
public: Object* ConvertTo(
   Object* value,
   Type* destinationType
);
```

```
[JScript]
public function ConvertTo(
   value : Object,
   destinationType : Type
) : Object;
```

Parameters

value
The **Object** to convert.

destinationType
The **Type** to convert the *value* parameter to.

Return Value

An **Object** that represents the converted value.

Exceptions

Exception Type	Condition
ArgumentNull-Exception	The *destinationType* parameter is a null reference (**Nothing** in Visual Basic).
NotSupportedException	The conversion could not be performed.

Remarks

The most common type to convert to and from is a string object. This implementation calls **ToString** on the object, if the object is valid and if the destination type is string.

Requirements

Platforms: Windows 98, Windows NT 4.0, Windows Millennium Edition, Windows 2000, Windows XP Home Edition, Windows XP Professional, Windows Server 2003 family

TypeConverter.ConvertTo Method (ITypeDescriptorContext, CultureInfo, Object, Type)

Converts the given value object to the specified type, using the specified context and culture information.

```
[Visual Basic]
Overloads Public Overridable Function ConvertTo( _
   ByVal context As ITypeDescriptorContext, _
   ByVal culture As CultureInfo, _
   ByVal value As Object, _
   ByVal destinationType As Type _
) As Object
[C#]
public virtual object ConvertTo(
   ITypeDescriptorContext context,
   CultureInfo culture,
   object value,
   Type destinationType
);
[C++]
public: virtual Object* ConvertTo(
   ITypeDescriptorContext* context,
   CultureInfo* culture,
   Object* value,
   Type* destinationType
);
[JScript]
public function ConvertTo(
   context : ITypeDescriptorContext,
   culture : CultureInfo,
   value : Object,
   destinationType : Type
) : Object;
```

Parameters

context
An **ITypeDescriptorContext** that provides a format context.

culture
A **CultureInfo** object. If a null reference (**Nothing** in Visual Basic) is passed, the current culture is assumed.

value
The **Object** to convert.

destinationType
The **Type** to convert the *value* parameter to.

Return Value

An **Object** that represents the converted value.

Exceptions

Exception Type	Condition
ArgumentNull-Exception	The *destinationType* parameter is a null reference (**Nothing** in Visual Basic).
NotSupportedException	The conversion could not be performed.

Remarks

The most common types to convert are to and from a string object. This implementation calls **ToString** on the object if the object is valid and if the destination type is string.

Use the *context* parameter to extract additional information about the environment from which this converter is invoked. This parameter can be a null reference (**Nothing** in Visual Basic), so always check it. Also, properties on the context object can return a null reference (**Nothing**).

Notes to Inheritors: Override this method to provide your own conversion requirements.

Requirements

Platforms: Windows 98, Windows NT 4.0, Windows Millennium Edition, Windows 2000, Windows XP Home Edition, Windows XP Professional, Windows Server 2003 family

TypeConverter.ConvertToInvariantString Method

Converts the specified value to a culture-invariant string representation.

Overload List

Converts the specified value to a culture-invariant string representation.

[Visual Basic] **Overloads Public Function ConvertToInvariantString(Object) As String**

[C#] **public string ConvertToInvariantString(object);**

[C++] **public: String* ConvertToInvariantString(Object*);**

[JScript] **public function ConvertToInvariantString(Object) : String;**

Converts the specified value to a culture-invariant string representation, using the specified context.

[Visual Basic] **Overloads Public Function ConvertTo-InvariantString(ITypeDescriptorContext, Object) As String**

[C#] **public string ConvertToInvariant-String(ITypeDescriptorContext, object);**

[C++] **public: String* ConvertToInvariant-String(ITypeDescriptorContext*, Object*);**

[JScript] **public function ConvertToInvariant-String(ITypeDescriptorContext, Object) : String;**

TypeConverter.ConvertToInvariantString Method (Object)

Converts the specified value to a culture-invariant string representation.

[Visual Basic]
```
Overloads Public Function ConvertToInvariantString( _
   ByVal value As Object _
) As String
```
[C#]
```
public string ConvertToInvariantString(
   object value
);
```
[C++]
```
public: String* ConvertToInvariantString(
   Object* value
);
```
[JScript]
```
public function ConvertToInvariantString(
   value : Object
) : String;
```

Parameters

value
The **Object** to convert.

Return Value

A **String** that represents the converted value.

Exceptions

Exception Type	Condition
NotSupportedException	The conversion could not be performed.

Remarks

The *context* parameter can be used to extract additional information about the environment from which this converter is being invoked. This can be a null reference (**Nothing** in Visual Basic), so always check. Also, properties on the context object can return a null reference (**Nothing**).

Depending on the implementation of the value formatter, it might be possible to pass the returned string back into the value formatter to re-create an instance of the object.

Requirements

Platforms: Windows 98, Windows NT 4.0, Windows Millennium Edition, Windows 2000, Windows XP Home Edition, Windows XP Professional, Windows Server 2003 family

TypeConverter.ConvertToInvariantString Method (ITypeDescriptorContext, Object)

Converts the specified value to a culture-invariant string representation, using the specified context.

[Visual Basic]
```
Overloads Public Function ConvertToInvariantString( _
   ByVal context As ITypeDescriptorContext, _
   ByVal value As Object _
) As String
```
[C#]
```
public string ConvertToInvariantString(
   ITypeDescriptorContext context,
   object value
);
```
[C++]
```
public: String* ConvertToInvariantString(
   ITypeDescriptorContext* context,
   Object* value
);
```
[JScript]
```
public function ConvertToInvariantString(
   context : ITypeDescriptorContext,
   value : Object
) : String;
```

Parameters

context
An **ITypeDescriptorContext** that provides a format context.

value
The **Object** to convert.

Return Value

A **String** that represents the converted value.

Exceptions

Exception Type	Condition
NotSupportedException	The conversion could not be performed.

Remarks

Use the *context* parameter to extract additional information about the environment from which this converter is invoked. This parameter can be a null reference (**Nothing** in Visual Basic), so always check it. Also, properties on the context object can return a null reference (**Nothing**).

Depending on the implementation of the value formatter, it might be possible to pass the returned string back into the value formatter to re-create an instance of the object.

Requirements

Platforms: Windows 98, Windows NT 4.0, Windows Millennium Edition, Windows 2000, Windows XP Home Edition, Windows XP Professional, Windows Server 2003 family

TypeConverter.ConvertToString Method

Converts the specified value to a string representation.

Overload List

Converts the specified value to a string representation.

[Visual Basic] **Overloads Public Function ConvertToString(Object) As String**

[C#] **public string ConvertToString(object);**

[C++] **public: String* ConvertToString(Object*);**

[JScript] **public function ConvertToString(Object) : String;**

Converts the given value to a string representation, using the given context.

[Visual Basic] **Overloads Public Function ConvertToString(ITypeDescriptorContext, Object) As String**

[C#] **public string ConvertToString(ITypeDescriptorContext, object);**

[C++] **public: String* ConvertToString(ITypeDescriptor-Context*, Object*);**

[JScript] **public function ConvertToString(ITypeDescriptor-Context, Object) : String;**

Converts the given value to a string representation, using the specified context and culture information.

[Visual Basic] **Overloads Public Function ConvertTo-String(ITypeDescriptorContext, CultureInfo, Object) As String**

[C#] **public string ConvertToString(ITypeDescriptorContext, CultureInfo, object);**

[C++] **public: String* ConvertToString(ITypeDescriptor-Context*, CultureInfo*, Object*);**

[JScript] **public function ConvertToString(ITypeDescriptor-Context, CultureInfo, Object) : String;**

Example

For an example on this function, see the sample in **TypeConverter**.

TypeConverter.ConvertToString Method (Object)

Converts the specified value to a string representation.

```
[Visual Basic]
Overloads Public Function ConvertToString( _
   ByVal value As Object _
) As String
[C#]
public string ConvertToString(
   object value
);
[C++]
public: String* ConvertToString(
   Object* value
);
[JScript]
public function ConvertToString(
   value : Object
) : String;
```

Parameters

value
The **Object** to convert.

Return Value

An **Object** that represents the converted value.

Exceptions

Exception Type	Condition
NotSupportedException	The conversion could not be performed.

Remarks

Depending on the implementation of the value formatter, it might be possible to pass the returned string back into the value formatter to re-create an instance of the object.

Example

For an example on this function, see the sample in **TypeConverter**.

Requirements

Platforms: Windows 98, Windows NT 4.0, Windows Millennium Edition, Windows 2000, Windows XP Home Edition, Windows XP Professional, Windows Server 2003 family

TypeConverter.ConvertToString Method (ITypeDescriptorContext, Object)

Converts the given value to a string representation, using the given context.

```
[Visual Basic]
Overloads Public Function ConvertToString( _
   ByVal context As ITypeDescriptorContext, _
   ByVal value As Object _
) As String
[C#]
public string ConvertToString(
   ITypeDescriptorContext context,
   object value
);
[C++]
public: String* ConvertToString(
   ITypeDescriptorContext* context,
   Object* value
);
[JScript]
public function ConvertToString(
   context : ITypeDescriptorContext,
   value : Object
) : String;
```

Parameters

context
An **ITypeDescriptorContext** that provides a format context.

value
The **Object** to convert.

Return Value

An **Object** that represents the converted value.

Exceptions

Exception Type	Condition
NotSupportedException	The conversion could not be performed.

Remarks

Use the *context* parameter to extract additional information about the environment from which this converter is invoked. This parameter can be a null reference (**Nothing** in Visual Basic), so always check it. Also, properties on the context object can return a null reference (**Nothing**).

Depending on the implementation of the value formatter, it might be possible to pass the returned string back into the value formatter to re-create an instance of the object.

Requirements

Platforms: Windows 98, Windows NT 4.0, Windows Millennium Edition, Windows 2000, Windows XP Home Edition, Windows XP Professional, Windows Server 2003 family

TypeConverter.ConvertToString Method (ITypeDescriptorContext, CultureInfo, Object)

Converts the given value to a string representation, using the specified context and culture information.

```
[Visual Basic]
Overloads Public Function ConvertToString( _
   ByVal context As ITypeDescriptorContext, _
   ByVal culture As CultureInfo, _
   ByVal value As Object _
) As String
[C#]
public string ConvertToString(
   ITypeDescriptorContext context,
   CultureInfo culture,
   object value
);
[C++]
public: String* ConvertToString(
   ITypeDescriptorContext* context,
   CultureInfo* culture,
   Object* value
);
[JScript]
public function ConvertToString(
   context : ITypeDescriptorContext,
   culture : CultureInfo,
   value : Object
) : String;
```

Parameters

context
An **ITypeDescriptorContext** that provides a format context.

culture
A **CultureInfo** object. If a null reference (**Nothing** in Visual Basic) is passed, the current culture is assumed.

value
The **Object** to convert.

Return Value

An **Object** that represents the converted value.

Exceptions

Exception Type	Condition
NotSupportedException	The conversion could not be performed.

Remarks

Use the *context* parameter to extract additional information about the environment from which this converter is invoked. This parameter can be a null reference (**Nothing** in Visual Basic), so always check it. Also, properties on the context object can return a null reference (**Nothing**).

Depending on the implementation of the value formatter, it might be possible to pass the returned string back into the value formatter to re-create an instance of the object.

Requirements

Platforms: Windows 98, Windows NT 4.0, Windows Millennium Edition, Windows 2000, Windows XP Home Edition, Windows XP Professional, Windows Server 2003 family

TypeConverter.CreateInstance Method

Re-creates an **Object** given a set of property values for the object.

Overload List

Re-creates an **Object** given a set of property values for the object.

[Visual Basic] **Overloads Public Function CreateInstance(IDictionary) As Object**

[C#] **public object CreateInstance(IDictionary);**

[C++] **public: Object* CreateInstance(IDictionary*);**

[JScript] **public function CreateInstance(IDictionary) : Object;**

Creates an instance of the Type that this **TypeConverter** is associated with, using the specified context, given a set of property values for the object.

[Visual Basic] **Overloads Public Overridable Function CreateInstance(ITypeDescriptorContext, IDictionary) As Object**

[C#] **public virtual object CreateInstance(ITypeDescriptorContext, IDictionary);**

[C++] **public: virtual Object* CreateInstance(ITypeDescriptorContext*, IDictionary*);**

[JScript] **public function CreateInstance(ITypeDescriptorContext, IDictionary) : Object;**

TypeConverter.CreateInstance Method (IDictionary)

Re-creates an **Object** given a set of property values for the object.

```
[Visual Basic]
Overloads Public Function CreateInstance( _
   ByVal propertyValues As IDictionary _
) As Object
[C#]
public object CreateInstance(
   IDictionary propertyValues
);
[C++]
public: Object* CreateInstance(
   IDictionary* propertyValues
);
[JScript]
public function CreateInstance(
   propertyValues : IDictionary
) : Object;
```

Parameters

propertyValues
An **IDictionary** that represents a dictionary of new property values.

Return Value

An **Object** representing the given **IDictionary**, or a null reference (**Nothing** in Visual Basic) if the object cannot be created. This method always returns a null reference (**Nothing**).

Remarks

Use this method for objects that are immutable, but for which you want to provide changeable properties.

The dictionary provided by the *propertyValues* parameter has a series of name/value pairs, one for each property returned from **GetProperties**.

Requirements

Platforms: Windows 98, Windows NT 4.0, Windows Millennium Edition, Windows 2000, Windows XP Home Edition, Windows XP Professional, Windows Server 2003 family

TypeConverter.CreateInstance Method (ITypeDescriptorContext, IDictionary)

Creates an instance of the Type that this **TypeConverter** is associated with, using the specified context, given a set of property values for the object.

```
[Visual Basic]
Overloads Public Overridable Function CreateInstance( _
   ByVal context As ITypeDescriptorContext, _
   ByVal propertyValues As IDictionary _
) As Object
[C#]
public virtual object CreateInstance(
   ITypeDescriptorContext context,
   IDictionary propertyValues
);
[C++]
public: virtual Object* CreateInstance(
   ITypeDescriptorContext* context,
   IDictionary* propertyValues
);
[JScript]
public function CreateInstance(
   context : ITypeDescriptorContext,
   propertyValues : IDictionary
) : Object;
```

Parameters

context
An **ITypeDescriptorContext** that provides a format context.

propertyValues
An **IDictionary** of new property values.

Return Value

An **Object** representing the given **IDictionary**, or a null reference (**Nothing** in Visual Basic) if the object cannot be created. This method always returns a null reference (**Nothing**).

Remarks

Use this method for objects that are immutable, but for which you want to provide changeable properties.

Notes to Inheritors: Override this method if the type you want to convert must re-create the object to change its value.

Use the *context* parameter to extract additional information about the environment from which this converter is invoked. This parameter can be a null reference (**Nothing** in Visual Basic), so always check it. Also, properties on the context object can return a null reference (**Nothing**).

The dictionary provided by the *propertyValues* parameter has a series of name/value pairs, one for each property returned from **GetProperties**.

Requirements

Platforms: Windows 98, Windows NT 4.0, Windows Millennium Edition, Windows 2000, Windows XP Home Edition, Windows XP Professional, Windows Server 2003 family

TypeConverter.GetConvertFromException Method

Returns an exception to throw when a conversion cannot be performed.

```
[Visual Basic]
Protected Function GetConvertFromException( _
   ByVal value As Object _
) As Exception
[C#]
protected Exception GetConvertFromException(
   object value
);
[C++]
protected: Exception* GetConvertFromException(
   Object* value
);
[JScript]
protected function GetConvertFromException(
   value : Object
) : Exception;
```

Parameters

value
The **Object** to convert, or a null reference (**Nothing** in Visual Basic) if the object is not available.

Return Value

An **Exception** that represents the exception to throw when a conversion cannot be performed.

Exceptions

Exception Type	Condition
NotSupportedException	Automatically thrown by this method.

Requirements

Platforms: Windows 98, Windows NT 4.0, Windows Millennium Edition, Windows 2000, Windows XP Home Edition, Windows XP Professional, Windows Server 2003 family

TypeConverter.GetConvertToException Method

Returns an exception to throw when a conversion cannot be performed.

[Visual Basic]
```
Protected Function GetConvertToException( _
   ByVal value As Object, _
   ByVal destinationType As Type _
) As Exception
```
[C#]
```
protected Exception GetConvertToException(
   object value,
   Type destinationType
);
```
[C++]
```
protected: Exception* GetConvertToException(
   Object* value,
   Type* destinationType
);
```
[JScript]
```
protected function GetConvertToException(
   value : Object,
   destinationType : Type
) : Exception;
```

Parameters

value

The **Object** to convert, or a null reference (**Nothing** in Visual Basic) if the object is not available.

destinationType

A **Type** that represents the type the conversion was trying to convert to.

Return Value

An **Exception** that represents the exception to throw when a conversion cannot be performed.

Exceptions

Exception Type	Condition
NotSupportedException	Automatically thrown by this method.

Requirements

Platforms: Windows 98, Windows NT 4.0, Windows Millennium Edition, Windows 2000, Windows XP Home Edition, Windows XP Professional, Windows Server 2003 family

TypeConverter.GetCreateInstanceSupported Method

Returns whether changing a value on this object requires a call to **CreateInstance** to create a new value.

Overload List

Returns whether changing a value on this object requires a call to **CreateInstance** to create a new value.

[Visual Basic] **Overloads Public Function GetCreateInstanceSupported() As Boolean**

[C#] **public bool GetCreateInstanceSupported();**

[C++] **public: bool GetCreateInstanceSupported();**

[JScript] **public function GetCreateInstanceSupported() : Boolean;**

Returns whether changing a value on this object requires a call to **CreateInstance** to create a new value, using the specified context.

[Visual Basic] **Overloads Public Overridable Function GetCreateInstanceSupported(ITypeDescriptorContext) As Boolean**

[C#] **public virtual bool GetCreateInstance-Supported(ITypeDescriptorContext);**

[C++] **public: virtual bool GetCreateInstance-Supported(ITypeDescriptorContext*);**

[JScript] **public function GetCreateInstance-Supported(ITypeDescriptorContext) : Boolean;**

TypeConverter.GetCreateInstanceSupported Method ()

Returns whether changing a value on this object requires a call to **CreateInstance** to create a new value.

[Visual Basic]
```
Overloads Public Function GetCreateInstanceSupported() As Boolean
```
[C#]
```
public bool GetCreateInstanceSupported();
```
[C++]
```
public: bool GetCreateInstanceSupported();
```
[JScript]
```
public function GetCreateInstanceSupported() : Boolean;
```

Return Value

true if changing a property on this object requires a call to **CreateInstance** to create a new value; otherwise, **false**.

Requirements

Platforms: Windows 98, Windows NT 4.0, Windows Millennium Edition, Windows 2000, Windows XP Home Edition, Windows XP Professional, Windows Server 2003 family

TypeConverter.GetCreateInstanceSupported Method (ITypeDescriptorContext)

Returns whether changing a value on this object requires a call to **CreateInstance** to create a new value, using the specified context.

[Visual Basic]
```
Overloads Public Overridable Function GetCreateInstanceSupported( _
   ByVal context As ITypeDescriptorContext _
) As Boolean
```
[C#]
```
public virtual bool GetCreateInstanceSupported(
   ITypeDescriptorContext context
);
```
[C++]
```
public: virtual bool GetCreateInstanceSupported(
   ITypeDescriptorContext* context
);
```
[JScript]
```
public function GetCreateInstanceSupported(
   context : ITypeDescriptorContext
) : Boolean;
```

Parameters

context

An **ITypeDescriptorContext** that provides a format context.

Return Value

true if changing a property on this object requires a call to **CreateInstance** to create a new value; otherwise, **false**.

Remarks

As implemented in this class, this method always returns **false**.

Notes to Inheritors: Override this method if the type you want to convert must re-create the object to change its value.

Use the *context* parameter to extract additional information about the environment from which this converter is invoked. This parameter can be a null reference (**Nothing** in Visual Basic), so always check it. Also, properties on the context object can return a null reference (**Nothing**).

Requirements

Platforms: Windows 98, Windows NT 4.0, Windows Millennium Edition, Windows 2000, Windows XP Home Edition, Windows XP Professional, Windows Server 2003 family

TypeConverter.GetProperties Method

Returns a collection of properties for the type of array specified by the value parameter.

Overload List

Returns a collection of properties for the type of array specified by the value parameter.

[Visual Basic] **Overloads Public Function GetProperties(Object) As PropertyDescriptorCollection**

[C#] **public PropertyDescriptorCollection GetProperties(object);**

[C++] **public: PropertyDescriptorCollection* GetProperties(Object*);**

[JScript] **public function GetProperties(Object) : PropertyDescriptorCollection;**

Returns a collection of properties for the type of array specified by the value parameter, using the specified context.

[Visual Basic] **Overloads Public Function GetProperties(ITypeDescriptorContext, Object) As PropertyDescriptorCollection**

[C#] **public PropertyDescriptorCollection GetProperties(ITypeDescriptorContext, object);**

[C++] **public: PropertyDescriptorCollection* GetProperties(ITypeDescriptorContext*, Object*);**

[JScript] **public function GetProperties(ITypeDescriptorContext, Object) : PropertyDescriptorCollection;**

Returns a collection of properties for the type of array specified by the value parameter, using the specified context and attributes.

[Visual Basic] **Overloads Public Overridable Function GetProperties(ITypeDescriptorContext, Object, Attribute()) As PropertyDescriptorCollection**

[C#] **public virtual PropertyDescriptorCollection GetProperties(ITypeDescriptorContext, object, Attribute[]);**

[C++] **public: virtual PropertyDescriptorCollection* GetProperties(ITypeDescriptorContext*, Object*, Attribute[]);**

[JScript] **public function GetProperties(ITypeDescriptorContext, Object, Attribute[]) : PropertyDescriptorCollection;**

TypeConverter.GetProperties Method (Object)

Returns a collection of properties for the type of array specified by the value parameter.

```
[Visual Basic]
Overloads Public Function GetProperties( _
   ByVal value As Object _
) As PropertyDescriptorCollection
[C#]
public PropertyDescriptorCollection GetProperties(
   object value
);
[C++]
public: PropertyDescriptorCollection* GetProperties(
   Object* value
);
[JScript]
public function GetProperties(
   value : Object
) : PropertyDescriptorCollection;
```

Parameters

value

An **Object** that specifies the type of array for which to get properties.

Return Value

A **PropertyDescriptorCollection** with the properties that are exposed for this data type, or a null reference (**Nothing** in Visual Basic) if there are no properties.

Remarks

As implemented in this class, this method always returns a null reference (**Nothing** in Visual Basic).

By default, a type does not return properties. An easy implementation of this method can call **GetProperties** for the correct data type.

Requirements

Platforms: Windows 98, Windows NT 4.0, Windows Millennium Edition, Windows 2000, Windows XP Home Edition, Windows XP Professional, Windows Server 2003 family

TypeConverter.GetProperties Method (ITypeDescriptorContext, Object)

Returns a collection of properties for the type of array specified by the value parameter, using the specified context.

```
[Visual Basic]
Overloads Public Function GetProperties( _
   ByVal context As ITypeDescriptorContext, _
   ByVal value As Object _
) As PropertyDescriptorCollection
[C#]
public PropertyDescriptorCollection GetProperties(
   ITypeDescriptorContext context,
   object value
);
[C++]
public: PropertyDescriptorCollection* GetProperties(
   ITypeDescriptorContext* context,
   Object* value
);
```

```
[JScript]
public function GetProperties(
   context : ITypeDescriptorContext,
   value : Object
) : PropertyDescriptorCollection;
```

Parameters

context
: An **ITypeDescriptorContext** that provides a format context.

value
: An **Object** that specifies the type of array for which to get properties.

Return Value

A **PropertyDescriptorCollection** with the properties that are exposed for this data type, or a null reference (**Nothing** in Visual Basic) if there are no properties.

Remarks

Use the *context* parameter to extract additional information about the environment from which this converter is invoked. This parameter can be a null reference (**Nothing** in Visual Basic), so always check it. Also, properties on the context object can return a null reference (**Nothing**).

As implemented in this class, this method always returns a null reference (**Nothing**).

By default, a type does not return properties. An easy implementation of this method can call **GetProperties** for the correct data type.

Requirements

Platforms: Windows 98, Windows NT 4.0, Windows Millennium Edition, Windows 2000, Windows XP Home Edition, Windows XP Professional, Windows Server 2003 family

TypeConverter.GetProperties Method (ITypeDescriptorContext, Object, Attribute[])

Returns a collection of properties for the type of array specified by the value parameter, using the specified context and attributes.

```
[Visual Basic]
Overloads Public Overridable Function GetProperties( _
   ByVal context As ITypeDescriptorContext, _
   ByVal value As Object, _
   ByVal attributes() As Attribute _
) As PropertyDescriptorCollection
[C#]
public virtual PropertyDescriptorCollection GetProperties(
   ITypeDescriptorContext context,
   object value,
   Attribute[] attributes
);
[C++]
public: virtual PropertyDescriptorCollection* GetProperties(
   ITypeDescriptorContext* context,
   Object* value,
   Attribute* attributes[]
);
[JScript]
public function GetProperties(
   context : ITypeDescriptorContext,
   value : Object,
   attributes : Attribute[]
) : PropertyDescriptorCollection;
```

Parameters

context
: An **ITypeDescriptorContext** that provides a format context.

value
: An **Object** that specifies the type of array for which to get properties.

attributes
: An array of type **Attribute** that is used as a filter.

Return Value

A **PropertyDescriptorCollection** with the properties that are exposed for this data type, or a null reference (**Nothing** in Visual Basic) if there are no properties.

Remarks

As implemented in this class, this method always returns a null reference (**Nothing** in Visual Basic).

Notes to Inheritors: Override this method if the type you want to convert supports properties.

Use the *context* parameter to extract additional information about the environment from which this converter is invoked. This parameter can be a null reference (**Nothing**), so always check it. Also, properties on the context object can return a null reference (**Nothing**).

The attributes array is used to filter the array. The attributes can have a mix of **Type** and **Attribute** objects. Filtering is defined by the following rules:

- A **Type** object is treated as a wildcard; it matches a property that has the **Type** in its set of attributes.
- If a property does not have an **Attribute** of the same class, the property is not included in the returned array.
- If the attribute is an instance of **Attribute**, the property must be an exact match or it is not included in the returned array.
- If an **Attribute** instance is specified and it is the default property, it is included in the returned array even if there is no instance of the **Attribute** in the property.

Requirements

Platforms: Windows 98, Windows NT 4.0, Windows Millennium Edition, Windows 2000, Windows XP Home Edition, Windows XP Professional, Windows Server 2003 family

TypeConverter.GetPropertiesSupported Method

Returns whether this object supports properties.

Overload List

Returns whether this object supports properties.

[Visual Basic] **Overloads Public Function GetPropertiesSupported() As Boolean**

[C#] **public bool GetPropertiesSupported();**

[C++] **public: bool GetPropertiesSupported();**

[JScript] **public function GetPropertiesSupported() : Boolean;**

Returns whether this object supports properties, using the specified context.

[Visual Basic] **Overloads Public Overridable Function Get-PropertiesSupported(ITypeDescriptorContext) As Boolean**

[C#] **public virtual bool GetProperties-Supported(ITypeDescriptorContext);**

[C++] **public: virtual bool GetProperties-Supported(ITypeDescriptorContext*);**

[JScript] **public function GetProperties-Supported(ITypeDescriptorContext) : Boolean;**

TypeConverter.GetPropertiesSupported Method ()

Returns whether this object supports properties.

```
[Visual Basic]
Overloads Public Function GetPropertiesSupported() As Boolean
[C#]
public bool GetPropertiesSupported();
[C++]
public: bool GetPropertiesSupported();
[JScript]
public function GetPropertiesSupported() : Boolean;
```

Return Value

true if **GetProperties** should be called to find the properties of this object; otherwise, **false**.

Remarks

As implemented in this class, this method always returns **false**.

Requirements

Platforms: Windows 98, Windows NT 4.0, Windows Millennium Edition, Windows 2000, Windows XP Home Edition, Windows XP Professional, Windows Server 2003 family

TypeConverter.GetPropertiesSupported Method (ITypeDescriptorContext)

Returns whether this object supports properties, using the specified context.

```
[Visual Basic]
Overloads Public Overridable Function GetPropertiesSupported( _
   ByVal context As ITypeDescriptorContext _
) As Boolean
[C#]
public virtual bool GetPropertiesSupported(
   ITypeDescriptorContext context
);
[C++]
public: virtual bool GetPropertiesSupported(
   ITypeDescriptorContext* context
);
[JScript]
public function GetPropertiesSupported(
   context : ITypeDescriptorContext
) : Boolean;
```

Parameters

context
An **ITypeDescriptorContext** that provides a format context.

Return Value

true if **GetProperties** should be called to find the properties of this object; otherwise, **false**.

Remarks

As implemented in this class, this method always returns **false**.

Notes to Inheritors: Override this method if the type you want to convert supports properties.

Use the *context* parameter to extract additional information about the environment from which this converter is invoked. This parameter can be a null reference (**Nothing** in Visual Basic), so always check it. Also, properties on the context object can return a null reference (**Nothing**).

Requirements

Platforms: Windows 98, Windows NT 4.0, Windows Millennium Edition, Windows 2000, Windows XP Home Edition, Windows XP Professional, Windows Server 2003 family

TypeConverter.GetStandardValues Method

Returns a collection of standard values for the data type this type converter is designed for.

Overload List

Returns a collection of standard values from the default context for the data type this type converter is designed for.

[Visual Basic] **Overloads Public Function GetStandardValues() As ICollection**

[C#] **public ICollection GetStandardValues();**

[C++] **public: ICollection* GetStandardValues();**

[JScript] **public function GetStandardValues() : ICollection;**

Returns a collection of standard values for the data type this type converter is designed for when provided with a format context.

[Visual Basic] **Overloads Public Overridable Function GetStandardValues(ITypeDescriptorContext) As StandardValuesCollection**

[C#] **public virtual StandardValuesCollection GetStandardValues(ITypeDescriptorContext);**

[C++] **public: virtual StandardValuesCollection* GetStandardValues(ITypeDescriptorContext*);**

[JScript] **public function GetStandardValues(IType-DescriptorContext) : StandardValuesCollection;**

Example

For an example on this function, see the sample in **TypeConverter**.

TypeConverter.GetStandardValues Method ()

Returns a collection of standard values from the default context for the data type this type converter is designed for.

```
[Visual Basic]
Overloads Public Function GetStandardValues() As ICollection
[C#]
public ICollection GetStandardValues();
[C++]
public: ICollection* GetStandardValues();
[JScript]
public function GetStandardValues() : ICollection;
```

Return Value

A **TypeConverter.StandardValuesCollection** containing a standard set of valid values, or a null reference (**Nothing** in Visual Basic) if the data type does not support a standard set of values.

Remarks

As implemented in this class, this method always returns a null reference (**Nothing** in Visual Basic).

Requirements

Platforms: Windows 98, Windows NT 4.0, Windows Millennium Edition, Windows 2000, Windows XP Home Edition, Windows XP Professional, Windows Server 2003 family

TypeConverter.GetStandardValues Method (ITypeDescriptorContext)

Returns a collection of standard values for the data type this type converter is designed for when provided with a format context.

[Visual Basic]
```
Overloads Public Overridable Function GetStandardValues( _
   ByVal context As ITypeDescriptorContext _
) As StandardValuesCollection
```
[C#]
```
public virtual StandardValuesCollection GetStandardValues(
   ITypeDescriptorContext context
);
```
[C++]
```
public: virtual StandardValuesCollection* GetStandardValues(
   ITypeDescriptorContext* context
);
```
[JScript]
```
public function GetStandardValues(
   context : ITypeDescriptorContext
) : StandardValuesCollection;
```

Parameters

context

An **ITypeDescriptorContext** that provides a format context that can be used to extract additional information about the environment from which this converter is invoked. This parameter or properties of this parameter can be a null reference (**Nothing** in Visual Basic).

Return Value

A **TypeConverter.StandardValuesCollection** that holds a standard set of valid values, or a null reference (**Nothing** in Visual Basic) if the data type does not support a standard set of values.

Remarks

As implemented in **TypeConverter**, this method always returns a null reference (**Nothing** in Visual Basic).

Notes to Inheritors: Override this method if the type you want to convert supports standard values.

Example

For an example on this function, see the sample in **TypeConverter**.

Requirements

Platforms: Windows 98, Windows NT 4.0, Windows Millennium Edition, Windows 2000, Windows XP Home Edition, Windows XP Professional, Windows Server 2003 family

TypeConverter.GetStandardValuesExclusive Method

Returns whether the collection of standard values returned from **GetStandardValues** is an exclusive list.

Overload List

Returns whether the collection of standard values returned from **GetStandardValues** is an exclusive list.

[Visual Basic] **Overloads Public Function GetStandardValuesExclusive() As Boolean**

[C#] **public bool GetStandardValuesExclusive();**

[C++] **public: bool GetStandardValuesExclusive();**

[JScript] **public function GetStandardValuesExclusive() : Boolean;**

Returns whether the collection of standard values returned from **GetStandardValues** is an exclusive list of possible values, using the specified context.

[Visual Basic] **Overloads Public Overridable Function GetStandardValuesExclusive(ITypeDescriptorContext) As Boolean**

[C#] **public virtual bool GetStandardValues-Exclusive(ITypeDescriptorContext);**

[C++] **public: virtual bool GetStandardValues-Exclusive(ITypeDescriptorContext*);**

[JScript] **public function GetStandardValues-Exclusive(ITypeDescriptorContext) : Boolean;**

TypeConverter.GetStandardValuesExclusive Method ()

Returns whether the collection of standard values returned from **GetStandardValues** is an exclusive list.

[Visual Basic]
```
Overloads Public Function GetStandardValuesExclusive() As Boolean
```
[C#]
```
public bool GetStandardValuesExclusive();
```
[C++]
```
public: bool GetStandardValuesExclusive();
```
[JScript]
```
public function GetStandardValuesExclusive() : Boolean;
```

Return Value

true if the **TypeConverter.StandardValuesCollection** returned from **GetStandardValues** is an exhaustive list of possible values; **false** if other values are possible.

Remarks

As implemented in this class, this method always returns **false**.

If the list is exclusive, such as in an enumeration data type, then no other values are valid. If the list is not exclusive, then other valid values might exist in addition to the list of standard values that **GetStandardValues** provides.

Requirements

Platforms: Windows 98, Windows NT 4.0, Windows Millennium Edition, Windows 2000, Windows XP Home Edition, Windows XP Professional, Windows Server 2003 family

TypeConverter.GetStandardValuesExclusive Method (ITypeDescriptorContext)

Returns whether the collection of standard values returned from **GetStandardValues** is an exclusive list of possible values, using the specified context.

```
[Visual Basic]
Overloads Public Overridable Function GetStandardValuesExclusive( _
   ByVal context As ITypeDescriptorContext _
) As Boolean
[C#]
public virtual bool GetStandardValuesExclusive(
   ITypeDescriptorContext context
);
[C++]
public: virtual bool GetStandardValuesExclusive(
   ITypeDescriptorContext* context
);
[JScript]
public function GetStandardValuesExclusive(
   context : ITypeDescriptorContext
) : Boolean;
```

Parameters

context
An **ITypeDescriptorContext** that provides a format context.

Return Value

true if the **TypeConverter.StandardValuesCollection** returned from **GetStandardValues** is an exhaustive list of possible values; **false** if other values are possible.

Remarks

As implemented in this class, this method always returns **false**.

If the list is exclusive, such as in an enumeration data type, then no other values are valid. If the list is not exclusive, then other valid values might exist in addition to the list of standard values that **GetStandardValues** provides.

Notes to Inheritors: Override this method if the type you want to convert supports standard values.

Use the *context* parameter to extract additional information about the environment from which this converter is invoked. This parameter can be a null reference (**Nothing** in Visual Basic), so always check it. Also, properties on the context object can return a null reference (**Nothing**).

Requirements

Platforms: Windows 98, Windows NT 4.0, Windows Millennium Edition, Windows 2000, Windows XP Home Edition, Windows XP Professional, Windows Server 2003 family

TypeConverter.GetStandardValuesSupported Method

Returns whether this object supports a standard set of values that can be picked from a list.

Overload List

Returns whether this object supports a standard set of values that can be picked from a list.

[Visual Basic] **Overloads Public Function GetStandardValuesSupported() As Boolean**

[C#] **public bool GetStandardValuesSupported();**

[C++] **public: bool GetStandardValuesSupported();**

[JScript] **public function GetStandardValuesSupported() : Boolean;**

Returns whether this object supports a standard set of values that can be picked from a list, using the specified context.

[Visual Basic] **Overloads Public Overridable Function GetStandardValuesSupported(ITypeDescriptorContext) As Boolean**

[C#] **public virtual bool GetStandardValuesSupported(ITypeDescriptorContext);**

[C++] **public: virtual bool GetStandardValuesSupported(ITypeDescriptorContext*);**

[JScript] **public function GetStandardValuesSupported(ITypeDescriptorContext) : Boolean;**

TypeConverter.GetStandardValuesSupported Method ()

Returns whether this object supports a standard set of values that can be picked from a list.

```
[Visual Basic]
Overloads Public Function GetStandardValuesSupported() As Boolean
[C#]
public bool GetStandardValuesSupported();
[C++]
public: bool GetStandardValuesSupported();
[JScript]
public function GetStandardValuesSupported() : Boolean;
```

Return Value

true if **GetStandardValues** should be called to find a common set of values the object supports; otherwise, **false**.

Requirements

Platforms: Windows 98, Windows NT 4.0, Windows Millennium Edition, Windows 2000, Windows XP Home Edition, Windows XP Professional, Windows Server 2003 family

TypeConverter.GetStandardValuesSupported Method (ITypeDescriptorContext)

Returns whether this object supports a standard set of values that can be picked from a list, using the specified context.

```
[Visual Basic]
Overloads Public Overridable Function GetStandardValuesSupported( _
   ByVal context As ITypeDescriptorContext _
) As Boolean
```

```
[C#]
public virtual bool GetStandardValuesSupported(
   ITypeDescriptorContext context
);
[C++]
public: virtual bool GetStandardValuesSupported(
   ITypeDescriptorContext* context
);
[JScript]
public function GetStandardValuesSupported(
   context : ITypeDescriptorContext
) : Boolean;
```

Parameters

context

An **ITypeDescriptorContext** that provides a format context.

Return Value

true if **GetStandardValues** should be called to find a common set of values the object supports; otherwise, **false**.

Remarks

As implemented in this class, this method always returns **false**.

Use the *context* parameter to extract additional information about the environment from which this converter is invoked. This parameter can be a null reference (**Nothing** in Visual Basic), so always check it. Also, properties on the context object can return a null reference (**Nothing**).

Notes to Inheritors: Override this method if the type you want to convert supports standard values.

Requirements

Platforms: Windows 98, Windows NT 4.0, Windows Millennium Edition, Windows 2000, Windows XP Home Edition, Windows XP Professional, Windows Server 2003 family

TypeConverter.IsValid Method

Returns whether the given value object is valid for this type.

Overload List

Returns whether the given value object is valid for this type.

[Visual Basic] **Overloads Public Function IsValid(Object) As Boolean**

[C#] **public bool IsValid(object);**

[C++] **public: bool IsValid(Object*);**

[JScript] **public function IsValid(Object) : Boolean;**

Returns whether the given value object is valid for this type and for the specified context.

[Visual Basic] **Overloads Public Overridable Function IsValid(ITypeDescriptorContext, Object) As Boolean**

[C#] **public virtual bool IsValid(ITypeDescriptorContext, object);**

[C++] **public: virtual bool IsValid(ITypeDescriptorContext*, Object*);**

[JScript] **public function IsValid(ITypeDescriptorContext, Object) : Boolean;**

Example

For an example on this function, see the sample in **TypeConverter**.

TypeConverter.IsValid Method (Object)

Returns whether the given value object is valid for this type.

```
[Visual Basic]
Overloads Public Function IsValid( _
   ByVal value As Object _
) As Boolean
[C#]
public bool IsValid(
   object value
);
[C++]
public: bool IsValid(
   Object* value
);
[JScript]
public function IsValid(
   value : Object
) : Boolean;
```

Parameters

value

The object to test for validity.

Return Value

true if the specified value is valid for this object; otherwise, **false**.

Requirements

Platforms: Windows 98, Windows NT 4.0, Windows Millennium Edition, Windows 2000, Windows XP Home Edition, Windows XP Professional, Windows Server 2003 family

TypeConverter.IsValid Method (ITypeDescriptorContext, Object)

Returns whether the given value object is valid for this type and for the specified context.

```
[Visual Basic]
Overloads Public Overridable Function IsValid( _
   ByVal context As ITypeDescriptorContext, _
   ByVal value As Object _
) As Boolean
[C#]
public virtual bool IsValid(
   ITypeDescriptorContext context,
   object value
);
[C++]
public: virtual bool IsValid(
   ITypeDescriptorContext* context,
   Object* value
);
[JScript]
public function IsValid(
   context : ITypeDescriptorContext,
   value : Object
) : Boolean;
```

Parameters

context

An **ITypeDescriptorContext** that provides a format context.

value

The **Object** to test for validity.

Return Value

true if the specified value is valid for this object; otherwise, **false**.

Remarks

As implemented in this class, this method always returns **true**.

Use the *context* parameter to extract additional information about the environment from which this converter is invoked. This parameter can be a null reference (**Nothing** in Visual Basic), so always check it. Also, properties on the context object can return a null reference (**Nothing**).

Notes to Inheritors: Override this method if the type you want to convert supports standard values that can be validated.

Example

For an example on this function, see the sample in **TypeConverter**.

Requirements

Platforms: Windows 98, Windows NT 4.0, Windows Millennium Edition, Windows 2000, Windows XP Home Edition, Windows XP Professional, Windows Server 2003 family

TypeConverter.SortProperties Method

Sorts a collection of properties.

```
[Visual Basic]
Protected Function SortProperties( _
   ByVal props As PropertyDescriptorCollection, _
   ByVal names() As String _
) As PropertyDescriptorCollection
[C#]
protected PropertyDescriptorCollection SortProperties(
   PropertyDescriptorCollection props,
   string[] names
);
[C++]
protected: PropertyDescriptorCollection* SortProperties(
   PropertyDescriptorCollection* props,
   String* names __gc[]
);
[JScript]
protected function SortProperties(
   props : PropertyDescriptorCollection,
   names : String[]
) : PropertyDescriptorCollection;
```

Parameters

props

A **PropertyDescriptorCollection** that has the properties to sort.

names

An array of names in the order you want the properties to appear in the collection.

Return Value

A **PropertyDescriptorCollection** that contains the sorted properties.

Remarks

All properties in the collection that are not already in the array of names are added alphabetically to the end. If the *names* parameter is an empty array or a null reference (**Nothing** in Visual Basic), all the properties in the collection are sorted alphabetically.

Requirements

Platforms: Windows 98, Windows NT 4.0, Windows Millennium Edition, Windows 2000, Windows XP Home Edition, Windows XP Professional, Windows Server 2003 family

TypeConverterAttribute Class

Specifies what type to use as a converter for the object this attribute is bound to. This class cannot be inherited.

System.Object
  System.Attribute
    System.ComponentModel.TypeConverterAttribute

[Visual Basic]
```
<AttributeUsage(AttributeTargets.All)>
NotInheritable Public Class TypeConverterAttribute
   Inherits Attribute
```
[C#]
```
[AttributeUsage(AttributeTargets.All)]
public sealed class TypeConverterAttribute : Attribute
```
[C++]
```
[AttributeUsage(AttributeTargets::All)]
public __gc __sealed class TypeConverterAttribute : public
   Attribute
```
[JScript]
```
public
   AttributeUsage(AttributeTargets.All)
class TypeConverterAttribute extends Attribute
```

Thread Safety

Any public static (**Shared** in Visual Basic) members of this type are safe for multithreaded operations. Any instance members are not guaranteed to be thread safe.

Remarks

The class you use for conversion must inherit from **TypeConverter**. Use the **ConverterTypeName** property to get the name of the class that provides the data conversion for the object this attribute is bound to.

Example

[Visual Basic, C#] The following example tells `MyClass` to use the type converter called `MyClassConverter`. This example assumes that `MyClassConverter` has been implemented elsewhere. The class implementing the converter (`MyClassConverter`) must inherit from the **TypeConverter** class.

[Visual Basic]
```
<TypeConverter(GetType(MyClassConverter))> _
Public Class ClassA
    ' Insert code here.
End Class 'MyClass
```

[C#]
```
[TypeConverter(typeof(MyClassConverter))]
 public class MyClass {
    // Insert code here.
 }
```

[Visual Basic, C#] The next example creates an instance of `MyClass`. Then it gets the attributes for the class, and prints the name of the type converter used by `MyClass`.

[Visual Basic]
```
Public Shared Function Main() As Integer
    ' Creates a new instance of ClassA.
    Dim myNewClass As New ClassA()

    ' Gets the attributes for the instance.
    Dim attributes As AttributeCollection =                          ↵
TypeDescriptor.GetAttributes(myNewClass)

    ' Prints the name of the type converter by retrieving the
    ' TypeConverterAttribute from the AttributeCollection.
    Dim myAttribute As TypeConverterAttribute = _
        CType(attributes(GetType(TypeConverterAttribute)),            ↵
TypeConverterAttribute)

    Console.WriteLine(("The type conveter for this class is: " _
        + myAttribute.ConverterTypeName))
    Return 0
End Function 'Main
```

[C#]
```
public static int Main() {
    // Creates a new instance of MyClass.
    MyClass myNewClass = new MyClass();

    // Gets the attributes for the instance.
    AttributeCollection attributes =                                   ↵
TypeDescriptor.GetAttributes(myNewClass);

    /* Prints the name of the type converter by retrieving the
     * TypeConverterAttribute from the AttributeCollection. */
    TypeConverterAttribute myAttribute =

(TypeConverterAttribute)attributes[typeof(TypeConverterAttribute)];

    Console.WriteLine("The type conveter for this class is: " +
        myAttribute.ConverterTypeName);

    return 0;
 }
```

Requirements

Namespace: System.ComponentModel

Platforms: Windows 98, Windows NT 4.0, Windows Millennium Edition, Windows 2000, Windows XP Home Edition, Windows XP Professional, Windows Server 2003 family

Assembly: System (in System.dll)

TypeConverterAttribute Constructor

Initializes a new instance of the **TypeConverterAttribute** class.

Overload List

Initializes a new instance of the **TypeConverterAttribute** class with the default type converter, which is an empty string ("").

[Visual Basic] **Public Sub New()**

[C#] **public TypeConverterAttribute();**

[C++] **public: TypeConverterAttribute();**

[JScript] **public function TypeConverterAttribute();**

Initializes a new instance of the **TypeConverterAttribute** class, using the specified type name as the data converter for the object this attribute is bound to.

[Visual Basic] **Public Sub New(String)**

[C#] **public TypeConverterAttribute(string);**

[C++] **public: TypeConverterAttribute(String*);**

[JScript] **public function TypeConverterAttribute(String);**

Initializes a new instance of the **TypeConverterAttribute** class, using the specified type as the data converter for the object this attribute is bound to.

[Visual Basic] **Public Sub New(Type)**

[C#] **public TypeConverterAttribute(Type);**

[C++] **public: TypeConverterAttribute(Type*);**

[JScript] **public function TypeConverterAttribute(Type);**

TypeConverterAttribute Constructor ()

Initializes a new instance of the **TypeConverterAttribute** class with the default type converter, which is an empty string ("").

```
[Visual Basic]
Public Sub New()
[C#]
public TypeConverterAttribute();
[C++]
public: TypeConverterAttribute();
[JScript]
public function TypeConverterAttribute();
```

Remarks

The class that provides the data conversion must inherit from **TypeConverter**.

Requirements

Platforms: Windows 98, Windows NT 4.0, Windows Millennium Edition, Windows 2000, Windows XP Home Edition, Windows XP Professional, Windows Server 2003 family

TypeConverterAttribute Constructor (String)

Initializes a new instance of the **TypeConverterAttribute** class, using the specified type name as the data converter for the object this attribute is bound to.

```
[Visual Basic]
Public Sub New( _
   ByVal typeName As String _
)
[C#]
public TypeConverterAttribute(
   string typeName
);
[C++]
public: TypeConverterAttribute(
   String* typeName
);
[JScript]
public function TypeConverterAttribute(
   typeName : String
);
```

Parameters

typeName

The fully qualified name of the class to use for data conversion for the object this attribute is bound to.

Remarks

The class that provides the data conversion must inherit from **TypeConverter**.

Requirements

Platforms: Windows 98, Windows NT 4.0, Windows Millennium Edition, Windows 2000, Windows XP Home Edition, Windows XP Professional, Windows Server 2003 family

TypeConverterAttribute Constructor (Type)

Initializes a new instance of the **TypeConverterAttribute** class, using the specified type as the data converter for the object this attribute is bound to.

```
[Visual Basic]
Public Sub New( _
   ByVal type As Type _
)
[C#]
public TypeConverterAttribute(
   Type type
);
[C++]
public: TypeConverterAttribute(
   Type* type
);
[JScript]
public function TypeConverterAttribute(
   type : Type
);
```

Parameters

type

A **Type** that represents the type of the converter class to use for data conversion for the object this attribute is bound to.

Remarks

The class that provides the data conversion must inherit from **TypeConverter**.

Requirements

Platforms: Windows 98, Windows NT 4.0, Windows Millennium Edition, Windows 2000, Windows XP Home Edition, Windows XP Professional, Windows Server 2003 family

TypeConverterAttribute.Default Field

This member supports the .NET Framework infrastructure and is not intended to be used directly from your code.

```
[Visual Basic]
Public Shared ReadOnly Default As TypeConverterAttribute
[C#]
public static readonly TypeConverterAttribute Default;
[C++]
public: static TypeConverterAttribute* Default;
[JScript]
public static var Default : TypeConverterAttribute;
```

TypeConverterAttribute.ConverterTypeName Property

Gets the fully qualified type name of the **Type** to use as a converter for the object this attribute is bound to.

```
[Visual Basic]
Public ReadOnly Property ConverterTypeName As String
[C#]
public string ConverterTypeName {get;}
[C++]
public: __property String* get_ConverterTypeName();
[JScript]
public function get ConverterTypeName() : String;
```

Property Value

The fully qualified type name of the **Type** to use as a converter for the object this attribute is bound to, or an empty string ("") if none exists. The default value is an empty string ("").

Requirements

Platforms: Windows 98, Windows NT 4.0,
Windows Millennium Edition, Windows 2000,
Windows XP Home Edition, Windows XP Professional,
Windows Server 2003 family

TypeConverterAttribute.Equals Method

Returns whether the value of the given object is equal to the current **TypeConverterAttribute**.

```
[Visual Basic]
Overrides Public Function Equals( _
   ByVal obj As Object _
) As Boolean
[C#]
public override bool Equals(
   object obj
);
[C++]
public: bool Equals(
   Object* obj
);
[JScript]
public override function Equals(
   obj : Object
) : Boolean;
```

Parameters

obj
The object to test the value equality of.

Return Value

true if the value of the given object is equal to that of the current; otherwise, **false**.

Requirements

Platforms: Windows 98, Windows NT 4.0,
Windows Millennium Edition, Windows 2000,
Windows XP Home Edition, Windows XP Professional,
Windows Server 2003 family

TypeConverterAttribute.GetHashCode Method

This member overrides **Attribute.GetHashCode**.

```
[Visual Basic]
Overrides Public Function GetHashCode() As Integer
[C#]
public override int GetHashCode();
[C++]
public: int GetHashCode();
[JScript]
public override function GetHashCode() : int;
```

Requirements

Platforms: Windows 98, Windows NT 4.0,
Windows Millennium Edition, Windows 2000,
Windows XP Home Edition, Windows XP Professional,
Windows Server 2003 family

TypeConverter.SimpleProperty Descriptor Class

Represents an abstract (**MustInherit** in Visual Basic) class that provides properties for objects that do not have properties.

System.Object
  System.ComponentModel.MemberDescriptor
    System.ComponentModel.PropertyDescriptor
      System.ComponentModel.TypeConverter.SimplePropertyDescriptor

[Visual Basic]
```
MustInherit Protected Class TypeConverter.SimplePropertyDescriptor
   Inherits PropertyDescriptor
```
[C#]
```
protected abstract class TypeConverter.SimplePropertyDescriptor :
   PropertyDescriptor
```
[C++]
```
protected __gc __abstract class
   TypeConverter.SimplePropertyDescriptor : public
   PropertyDescriptor
```
[JScript]
```
protected abstract class TypeConverter.SimplePropertyDescriptor
   extends PropertyDescriptor
```

Thread Safety

Any public static (**Shared** in Visual Basic) members of this type are safe for multithreaded operations. Any instance members are not guaranteed to be thread safe.

Remarks

Notes to Inheritors: When you inherit from **TypeConverter.SimplePropertyDescriptor**, you must override the **GetValue** and **SetValue** methods.

Example

For an example on this class, see the example in **PropertyDescriptor**.

Requirements

Namespace: System.ComponentModel

Platforms: Windows 98, Windows NT 4.0, Windows Millennium Edition, Windows 2000, Windows XP Home Edition, Windows XP Professional, Windows Server 2003 family

Assembly: System (in System.dll)

TypeConverter.SimpleProperty-Descriptor Constructor

Initializes a new instance of the **TypeConverter.SimplePropertyDescriptor** class.

Overload List

Initializes a new instance of the **TypeConverter.SimplePropertyDescriptor** class.

[Visual Basic] **Public Sub New(Type, String, Type)**

[C#] **public TypeConverter.SimplePropertyDescriptor(Type, string, Type);**

[C++] **public: SimplePropertyDescriptor(Type*, String*, Type*);**

[JScript] **public function TypeConverter.SimplePropertyDescriptor(Type, String, Type);**

Initializes a new instance of the **TypeConverter.SimplePropertyDescriptor** class.

[Visual Basic] **Public Sub New(Type, String, Type, Attribute())**

[C#] **public TypeConverter.SimplePropertyDescriptor(Type, string, Type, Attribute[]);**

[C++] **public: SimplePropertyDescriptor(Type*, String*, Type*, Attribute[]);**

[JScript] **public function TypeConverter.SimplePropertyDescriptor(Type, String, Type, Attribute[]);**

TypeConverter.SimplePropertyDescriptor Constructor (Type, String, Type)

Initializes a new instance of the **TypeConverter.SimplePropertyDescriptor** class.

[Visual Basic]
```
Public Sub New( _
   ByVal componentType As Type, _
   ByVal name As String, _
   ByVal propertyType As Type _
)
```
[C#]
```
public TypeConverter.SimplePropertyDescriptor(
   Type componentType,
   string name,
   Type propertyType
);
```
[C++]
```
public: SimplePropertyDescriptor(
   Type* componentType,
   String* name,
   Type* propertyType
);
```
[JScript]
```
public function TypeConverter.SimplePropertyDescriptor(
   componentType : Type,
   name : String,
   propertyType : Type
);
```

Parameters

componentType
  A **Type** that represents the type of component to which this property descriptor binds.

name
  The name of the property.

propertyType
  A **Type** that represents the data type for this property.

Requirements

Platforms: Windows 98, Windows NT 4.0, Windows Millennium Edition, Windows 2000, Windows XP Home Edition, Windows XP Professional, Windows Server 2003 family

TypeConverter.SimplePropertyDescriptor Constructor (Type, String, Type, Attribute[])

Initializes a new instance of the **TypeConverter.SimplePropertyDescriptor** class.

```
[Visual Basic]
Public Sub New( _
   ByVal componentType As Type, _
   ByVal name As String, _
   ByVal propertyType As Type, _
   ByVal attributes() As Attribute _
)
[C#]
public TypeConverter.SimplePropertyDescriptor(
   Type componentType,
   string name,
   Type propertyType,
   Attribute[] attributes
);
[C++]
public: SimplePropertyDescriptor(
   Type* componentType,
   String* name,
   Type* propertyType,
   Attribute* attributes[]
);
[JScript]
public function TypeConverter.SimplePropertyDescriptor(
   componentType : Type,
   name : String,
   propertyType : Type,
   attributes : Attribute[]
);
```

Parameters

componentType
A **Type** that represents the type of component to which this property descriptor binds.

name
The name of the property.

propertyType
A **Type** that represents the data type for this property.

attributes
An **Attribute** array with the attributes to associate with the property.

Requirements

Platforms: Windows 98, Windows NT 4.0, Windows Millennium Edition, Windows 2000, Windows XP Home Edition, Windows XP Professional, Windows Server 2003 family

TypeConverter.SimplePropertyDescriptor.ComponentType Property

Gets the type of component to which this property description binds.

```
[Visual Basic]
Overrides Public ReadOnly Property ComponentType As Type
[C#]
public override Type ComponentType {get;}
[C++]
public: __property Type* get_ComponentType();
[JScript]
public override function get ComponentType() : Type;
```

Property Value

A **Type** that represents the type of component to which this property binds.

Requirements

Platforms: Windows 98, Windows NT 4.0, Windows Millennium Edition, Windows 2000, Windows XP Home Edition, Windows XP Professional, Windows Server 2003 family

TypeConverter.SimplePropertyDescriptor.IsReadOnly Property

Gets a value indicating whether this property is read-only.

```
[Visual Basic]
Overrides Public ReadOnly Property IsReadOnly As Boolean
[C#]
public override bool IsReadOnly {get;}
[C++]
public: __property bool get_IsReadOnly();
[JScript]
public override function get IsReadOnly() : Boolean;
```

Property Value

true if the property is read-only; **false** if the property is read/write.

Requirements

Platforms: Windows 98, Windows NT 4.0, Windows Millennium Edition, Windows 2000, Windows XP Home Edition, Windows XP Professional, Windows Server 2003 family

TypeConverter.SimplePropertyDescriptor.PropertyType Property

Gets the type of the property.

```
[Visual Basic]
Overrides Public ReadOnly Property PropertyType As Type
[C#]
public override Type PropertyType {get;}
[C++]
public: __property Type* get_PropertyType();
[JScript]
public override function get PropertyType() : Type;
```

Property Value

A **Type** that represents the type of the property.

Requirements

Platforms: Windows 98, Windows NT 4.0, Windows Millennium Edition, Windows 2000, Windows XP Home Edition, Windows XP Professional, Windows Server 2003 family

TypeConverter.SimplePropertyDescriptor.CanResetValue Method

Returns whether resetting the component changes the value of the component.

[Visual Basic]
```
Overrides Public Function CanResetValue( _
   ByVal component As Object _
) As Boolean
```
[C#]
```
public override bool CanResetValue(
   object component
);
```
[C++]
```
public: bool CanResetValue(
   Object* component
);
```
[JScript]
```
public override function CanResetValue(
   component : Object
) : Boolean;
```

Parameters

component
The component to test for reset capability.

Return Value

true if resetting the component changes the value of the component; otherwise, **false**.

Remarks

This method looks for a **DefaultValueAttribute**. If it finds one, it compares the value of the attribute with the current value of the property. It returns **true** when the default value does not match the current value of the property. If this method cannot find a **DefaultValueAttribute**, it looks for a `ShouldSerializeMyProperty` method. If it finds a `ShouldSerializeMyProperty` method, it returns what `ShouldSerializeMyProperty` returns. If this method cannot find a `ShouldSerializeMyProperty` method, it looks for a `ResetMyProperty` method. If it finds a `ResetMyProperty` method, it returns **true**. If this method cannot find a **DefaultValueAttribute**, a `ShouldSerializeMyProperty` method, or a `ResetMyProperty` method, then it returns **false**.

Requirements

Platforms: Windows 98, Windows NT 4.0, Windows Millennium Edition, Windows 2000, Windows XP Home Edition, Windows XP Professional, Windows Server 2003 family

TypeConverter.SimplePropertyDescriptor.ResetValue Method

Resets the value for this property of the component.

[Visual Basic]
```
Overrides Public Sub ResetValue( _
   ByVal component As Object _
)
```
[C#]
```
public override void ResetValue(
   object component
);
```
[C++]
```
public: void ResetValue(
   Object* component
);
```
[JScript]
```
public override function ResetValue(
   component : Object
);
```

Parameters

component
The component with the property value to be reset.

Remarks

This method looks for a **DefaultValueAttribute**. If it finds one, it sets the value of the property to the value specified in the attribute. If this method cannot find a **DefaultValueAttribute**, it looks for a `ResetMyProperty` method. If it finds a `ResetMyProperty` method, it invokes it. If this method cannot find a **DefaultValueAttribute** or a `ResetMyProperty` method, then it does not perform an operation.

Requirements

Platforms: Windows 98, Windows NT 4.0, Windows Millennium Edition, Windows 2000, Windows XP Home Edition, Windows XP Professional, Windows Server 2003 family

TypeConverter.SimplePropertyDescriptor.ShouldSerializeValue Method

Returns whether the value of this property can persist.

[Visual Basic]
```
Overrides Public Function ShouldSerializeValue( _
   ByVal component As Object _
) As Boolean
```
[C#]
```
public override bool ShouldSerializeValue(
   object component
);
```
[C++]
```
public: bool ShouldSerializeValue(
   Object* component
);
```
[JScript]
```
public override function ShouldSerializeValue(
   component : Object
) : Boolean;
```

Parameters

component
The component with the property that is to be examined for persistence.

Return Value

true if the value of the property can persist; otherwise, **false**.

Remarks

As implemented in this class, this method returns **false**.

Notes to Inheritors: When overridden in a derived class, this method returns **true** if the current value of the property is different from its default value. It looks for a default value by first looking for a **DefaultValueAttribute**. If the method finds this attribute, it compares the value of the attribute with the current value of the property. If this method cannot find a **DefaultValueAttribute**, it looks for a `ShouldSerializeMyProperty` method. If this method finds a `ShouldSerializeMyProperty` method, it invokes it. If this method cannot find a **DefaultValueAttribute** or a `ShouldSerializeMyProperty` method, it cannot create optimizations and it returns **true**.

Requirements

Platforms: Windows 98, Windows NT 4.0,
Windows Millennium Edition, Windows 2000,
Windows XP Home Edition, Windows XP Professional,
Windows Server 2003 family

TypeConverter.Standard-ValuesCollection Class

Represents a collection of values.

System.Object
System.ComponentModel.TypeConverter.StandardValues-Collection

[Visual Basic]
```
Public Class TypeConverter.StandardValuesCollection
   Implements ICollection, IEnumerable
```
[C#]
```
public class TypeConverter.StandardValuesCollection : ICollection,
   IEnumerable
```
[C++]
```
public __gc class TypeConverter.StandardValuesCollection : public
   ICollection, IEnumerable
```
[JScript]
```
public class TypeConverter.StandardValuesCollection implements
   ICollection, IEnumerable
```

Thread Safety

Any public static (**Shared** in Visual Basic) members of this type are safe for multithreaded operations. Any instance members are not guaranteed to be thread safe.

Remarks

This is a simple collection class that takes an array of values and converts it to a collection. It is lightweight and is well suited for use in **GetStandardValues**.

Requirements

Namespace: System.ComponentModel

Platforms: Windows 98, Windows NT 4.0, Windows Millennium Edition, Windows 2000, Windows XP Home Edition, Windows XP Professional, Windows Server 2003 family

Assembly: System (in System.dll)

TypeConverter.StandardValuesCollection Constructor

Initializes a new instance of the **TypeConverter.StandardValuesCollection** class.

[Visual Basic]
```
Public Sub New( _
   ByVal values As ICollection _
)
```
[C#]
```
public TypeConverter.StandardValuesCollection(
   ICollection values
);
```
[C++]
```
public: StandardValuesCollection(
   ICollection* values
);
```
[JScript]
```
public function TypeConverter.StandardValuesCollection(
   values : ICollection
);
```

Parameters

values
An **ICollection** that represents the objects to put into the collection.

Requirements

Platforms: Windows 98, Windows NT 4.0, Windows Millennium Edition, Windows 2000, Windows XP Home Edition, Windows XP Professional, Windows Server 2003 family

TypeConverter.StandardValuesCollection.Count Property

Gets the number of objects in the collection.

[Visual Basic]
```
Public ReadOnly Property Count As Integer
```
[C#]
```
public int Count {get;}
```
[C++]
```
public: __property int get_Count();
```
[JScript]
```
public function get Count() : int;
```

Property Value

The number of objects in the collection.

Remarks

The **Count** property can be used to set the limits of a loop that iterates through a collection of objects. Since collection is zero-based, be sure to use `Count - 1` as the upper bound of the loop.

Requirements

Platforms: Windows 98, Windows NT 4.0, Windows Millennium Edition, Windows 2000, Windows XP Home Edition, Windows XP Professional, Windows Server 2003 family

TypeConverter.StandardValuesCollection.Item Property

Gets the object at the specified index number.

[C#] In C#, this property is the indexer for the **TypeConverter.StandardValuesCollection** class.

[Visual Basic]
```
Public Default ReadOnly Property Item( _
   ByVal index As Integer _
) As Object
```
[C#]
```
public object this[
   int index
] {get;}
```
[C++]
```
public: __property Object* get_Item(
   int index
);
```
[JScript]
```
returnValue = StandardValuesCollectionObject.Item(index);
-or-
returnValue = StandardValuesCollectionObject(index);
```

[JScript] In JScript, you can use the default indexed properties defined by a type, but you cannot explicitly define your own. However, specifying the **expando** attribute on a class automatically provides a default indexed property whose type is **Object** and whose index type is **String**.

Arguments [JScript]

index

The zero-based index of the **Object** to get from the collection.

Parameters [Visual Basic, C#, C++]

index

The zero-based index of the **Object** to get from the collection.

Property Value

The **Object** with the specified index.

Remarks

The index number is zero-based. Therefore, you must subtract one from the numerical position of a particular **Object** to access that **Object**. For example, to get the third **Object**, you need to specify `myColl[2]`.

Requirements

Platforms: Windows 98, Windows NT 4.0, Windows Millennium Edition, Windows 2000, Windows XP Home Edition, Windows XP Professional, Windows Server 2003 family

TypeConverter.StandardValuesCollection.CopyTo Method

Copies the contents of this collection to an array.

```
[Visual Basic]
Public Sub CopyTo( _
   ByVal array As Array, _
   ByVal index As Integer _
)
[C#]
public void CopyTo(
   Array array,
   int index
);
[C++]
public: void CopyTo(
   Array* array,
   int index
);
[JScript]
public function CopyTo(
   array : Array,
   index : int
);
```

Parameters

array

An **Array** that represents the array to copy to.

index

The index to start from.

Remarks

The index number is zero-based. Therefore, you must subtract one from the numerical position of a particular **Object** to access that **Object**. For example, to get the third **Object**, you need to specify `myColl[2]`.

Requirements

Platforms: Windows 98, Windows NT 4.0, Windows Millennium Edition, Windows 2000, Windows XP Home Edition, Windows XP Professional, Windows Server 2003 family

TypeConverter.StandardValuesCollection.GetEnumerator Method

Returns an enumerator for this collection.

```
[Visual Basic]
Public Function GetEnumerator() As IEnumerator
[C#]
public IEnumerator GetEnumerator();
[C++]
public: IEnumerator* GetEnumerator();
[JScript]
public function GetEnumerator() : IEnumerator;
```

Return Value

An enumerator of type **IEnumerator**.

Requirements

Platforms: Windows 98, Windows NT 4.0, Windows Millennium Edition, Windows 2000, Windows XP Home Edition, Windows XP Professional, Windows Server 2003 family

TypeConverter.StandardValuesCollection.ICollection.CopyTo Method

This member supports the .NET Framework infrastructure and is not intended to be used directly from your code.

```
[Visual Basic]
Private Sub CopyTo( _
   ByVal array As Array, _
   ByVal index As Integer _
) Implements ICollection.CopyTo
[C#]
void ICollection.CopyTo(
   Array array,
   int index
);
[C++]
private: void ICollection::CopyTo(
   Array* array,
   int index
);
[JScript]
private function ICollection.CopyTo(
   array : Array,
   index : int
);
```

TypeConverter.StandardValuesCollection.IEnumerable.GetEnumerator Method

This member supports the .NET Framework infrastructure and is not intended to be used directly from your code.

[Visual Basic]
```
Private Function GetEnumerator() As IEnumerator Implements _
   IEnumerable.GetEnumerator
```
[C#]
```
IEnumerator IEnumerable.GetEnumerator();
```
[C++]
```
private: IEnumerator* IEnumerable::GetEnumerator();
```
[JScript]
```
private function IEnumerable.GetEnumerator() : IEnumerator;
```

TypeDescriptor Class

Provides information about the properties and events for a component. This class cannot be inherited.

System.Object
  System.ComponentModel.TypeDescriptor

```
[Visual Basic]
NotInheritable Public Class TypeDescriptor
[C#]
public sealed class TypeDescriptor
[C++]
public __gc __sealed class TypeDescriptor
[JScript]
public class TypeDescriptor
```

Thread Safety

Any public static (**Shared** in Visual Basic) members of this type are safe for multithreaded operations. Any instance members are not guaranteed to be thread safe.

Remarks

All the methods in this class are static (**Shared** in Visual Basic) . You cannot create an instance of this class.

You can set property and event values two different ways: specify them in the component class or change them at design time. Because you can set these values two ways, the overloaded methods in this class take two different types of parameters. A method can take the type of class or an instance of an object. At design time, these two kinds of methods can be different; at run time, they are usually the same.

When you want to access **TypeDescriptor** information and you have an instance of the object, use the method that calls for a component. Use the method that calls for the type of the class method only when you do not have an instance of the object.

Requirements

Namespace: System.ComponentModel

Platforms: Windows 98, Windows NT 4.0, Windows Millennium Edition, Windows 2000, Windows XP Home Edition, Windows XP Professional, Windows Server 2003 family, .NET Compact Framework - Windows CE .NET

Assembly: System (in System.dll)

TypeDescriptor.ComNativeDescriptorHandler Property

This member supports the .NET Framework infrastructure and is not intended to be used directly from your code.

```
[Visual Basic]
Public Shared Property ComNativeDescriptorHandler As _
   IComNativeDescriptorHandler
[C#]
public static IComNativeDescriptorHandler
   ComNativeDescriptorHandler {get; set;}
[C++]
public: __property static IComNativeDescriptorHandler*
get_ComNativeDescriptorHandler();
public: __property static void
set_ComNativeDescriptorHandler(IComNativeDescriptorHandler*);
[JScript]
public static function get ComNativeDescriptorHandler() :
IComNativeDescriptorHandler;
public static function set
ComNativeDescriptorHandler(IComNativeDescriptorHandler);
```

TypeDescriptor.AddEditorTable Method

This member supports the .NET Framework infrastructure and is not intended to be used directly from your code.

```
[Visual Basic]
Public Shared Sub AddEditorTable( _
   ByVal editorBaseType As Type, _
   ByVal table As Hashtable _
)
[C#]
public static void AddEditorTable(
   Type editorBaseType,
   Hashtable table
);
[C++]
public: static void AddEditorTable(
   Type* editorBaseType,
   Hashtable* table
);
[JScript]
public static function AddEditorTable(
   editorBaseType : Type,
   table : Hashtable
);
```

TypeDescriptor.CreateDesigner Method

Creates an instance of the designer associated with the specified component and the type of designer to create.

```
[Visual Basic]
Public Shared Function CreateDesigner( _
   ByVal component As IComponent, _
   ByVal designerBaseType As Type _
) As IDesigner
[C#]
public static IDesigner CreateDesigner(
   IComponent component,
   Type designerBaseType
);
[C++]
public: static IDesigner* CreateDesigner(
   IComponent* component,
   Type* designerBaseType
);
[JScript]
public static function CreateDesigner(
   component : IComponent,
   designerBaseType : Type
) : IDesigner;
```

Parameters

component
An **IComponent** that specifies the component to associate with the designer.

designerBaseType
A **Type** that represents the type of designer to create.

Return Value

An **IDesigner** that is an instance of the designer for the component, or a null reference (**Nothing** in Visual Basic) if no designer can be found.

Remarks

If this method cannot find a valid **DesignerAttribute**, it searches up the class hierarchy for a designer. If it cannot find a designer in the class hierarchy, it returns a null reference (**Nothing** in Visual Basic).

Requirements

Platforms: Windows 98, Windows NT 4.0, Windows Millennium Edition, Windows 2000, Windows XP Home Edition, Windows XP Professional, Windows Server 2003 family

TypeDescriptor.CreateEvent Method

Creates a new event descriptor that is identical to an existing event descriptor.

Overload List

Creates a new event descriptor that is identical to an existing event descriptor, when passed the existing **EventDescriptor**.

[Visual Basic] **Overloads Public Shared Function CreateEvent(Type, EventDescriptor, ParamArray Attribute()) As EventDescriptor**

[C#] **public static EventDescriptor CreateEvent(Type, EventDescriptor, params Attribute[]);**

[C++] **public: static EventDescriptor* CreateEvent(Type*, EventDescriptor*, Attribute[]);**

[JScript] **public static function CreateEvent(Type, EventDescriptor, Attribute[]) : EventDescriptor;**

Creates a new event descriptor that is identical to an existing event descriptor by dynamically generating descriptor information from a specified event on a type.

[Visual Basic] **Overloads Public Shared Function CreateEvent(Type, String, Type, ParamArray Attribute()) As EventDescriptor**

[C#] **public static EventDescriptor CreateEvent(Type, string, Type, params Attribute[]);**

[C++] **public: static EventDescriptor* CreateEvent(Type*, String*, Type*, Attribute[]);**

[JScript] **public static function CreateEvent(Type, String, Type, Attribute[]) : EventDescriptor;**

TypeDescriptor.CreateEvent Method (Type, EventDescriptor, Attribute[])

Creates a new event descriptor that is identical to an existing event descriptor, when passed the existing **EventDescriptor**.

```
[Visual Basic]
Overloads Public Shared Function CreateEvent( _
   ByVal componentType As Type, _
   ByVal oldEventDescriptor As EventDescriptor, _
   ByVal ParamArray attributes() As Attribute _
) As EventDescriptor
[C#]
public static EventDescriptor CreateEvent(
   Type componentType,
   EventDescriptor oldEventDescriptor,
   params Attribute[] attributes
);
[C++]
public: static EventDescriptor* CreateEvent(
   Type* componentType,
   EventDescriptor* oldEventDescriptor,
   Attribute* attributes[]
);
[JScript]
public static function CreateEvent(
   componentType : Type,
   oldEventDescriptor : EventDescriptor,
   attributes : Attribute[]
) : EventDescriptor;
```

Parameters

componentType
: The type of the component the event lives on.

oldEventDescriptor
: The existing event information.

attributes
: The new attributes.

Return Value

A new **EventDescriptor** that has merged the specified metadata attributes with the existing metadata attributes.

Requirements

Platforms: Windows 98, Windows NT 4.0, Windows Millennium Edition, Windows 2000, Windows XP Home Edition, Windows XP Professional, Windows Server 2003 family

TypeDescriptor.CreateEvent Method (Type, String, Type, Attribute[])

Creates a new event descriptor that is identical to an existing event descriptor by dynamically generating descriptor information from a specified event on a type.

```
[Visual Basic]
Overloads Public Shared Function CreateEvent( _
   ByVal componentType As Type, _
   ByVal name As String, _
   ByVal type As Type, _
   ByVal ParamArray attributes() As Attribute _
) As EventDescriptor
[C#]
public static EventDescriptor CreateEvent(
   Type componentType,
   string name,
   Type type,
   params Attribute[] attributes
);
```

```
[C++]
public: static EventDescriptor* CreateEvent(
   Type* componentType,
   String* name,
   Type* type,
   Attribute* attributes[]
);
[JScript]
public static function CreateEvent(
   componentType : Type,
   name : String,
   type : Type,
   attributes : Attribute[]
) : EventDescriptor;
```

Parameters

componentType
: The type of the component the event lives on.

name
: The name of the event.

type
: The type of the delegate that handles the event.

attributes
: The attributes for this event.

Return Value

An **EventDescriptor** that is bound to a type.

Requirements

Platforms: Windows 98, Windows NT 4.0, Windows Millennium Edition, Windows 2000, Windows XP Home Edition, Windows XP Professional, Windows Server 2003 family

TypeDescriptor.CreateProperty Method

Creates a new property descriptor that is identical to an existing property descriptor.

Overload List

Creates a new property descriptor that is identical to an existing property descriptor, when passed the existing **PropertyDescriptor**.

[Visual Basic] **Overloads Public Shared Function CreateProperty(Type, PropertyDescriptor, ParamArray Attribute()) As PropertyDescriptor**

[C#] **public static PropertyDescriptor CreateProperty(Type, PropertyDescriptor, params Attribute[]);**

[C++] **public: static PropertyDescriptor* CreateProperty(Type*, PropertyDescriptor*, Attribute[]);**

[JScript] **public static function CreateProperty(Type, PropertyDescriptor, Attribute[]) : PropertyDescriptor;**

Creates a new property descriptor that is identical to an existing property descriptor by dynamically generating descriptor information from a specified property on a type.

[Visual Basic] **Overloads Public Shared Function CreateProperty(Type, String, Type, ParamArray Attribute()) As PropertyDescriptor**

[C#] **public static PropertyDescriptor CreateProperty(Type, string, Type, params Attribute[]);**

[C++] **public: static PropertyDescriptor* CreateProperty(Type*, String*, Type*, Attribute[]);**

[JScript] **public static function CreateProperty(Type, String, Type, Attribute[]) : PropertyDescriptor;**

Example

For an example on this method, see the sample in **Web Forms Templated Data-Bound Control Designer Sample**.

TypeDescriptor.CreateProperty Method (Type, PropertyDescriptor, Attribute[])

Creates a new property descriptor that is identical to an existing property descriptor, when passed the existing **PropertyDescriptor**.

```
[Visual Basic]
Overloads Public Shared Function CreateProperty( _
   ByVal componentType As Type, _
   ByVal oldPropertyDescriptor As PropertyDescriptor, _
   ByVal ParamArray attributes() As Attribute _
) As PropertyDescriptor
[C#]
public static PropertyDescriptor CreateProperty(
   Type componentType,
   PropertyDescriptor oldPropertyDescriptor,
   params Attribute[] attributes
);
[C++]
public: static PropertyDescriptor* CreateProperty(
   Type* componentType,
   PropertyDescriptor* oldPropertyDescriptor,
   Attribute* attributes[]
);
[JScript]
public static function CreateProperty(
   componentType : Type,
   oldPropertyDescriptor : PropertyDescriptor,
   attributes : Attribute[]
) : PropertyDescriptor;
```

Parameters

componentType
: The type of the component the property lives on.

oldPropertyDescriptor
: The existing property descriptor.

attributes
: The new attributes for this property.

Return Value

A new **PropertyDescriptor** has the specified metadata attributes merged with the existing metadata attributes.

Example

For an example on this method, see the sample in **Web Forms Templated Data-Bound Control Designer Sample**.

Requirements

Platforms: Windows 98, Windows NT 4.0, Windows Millennium Edition, Windows 2000, Windows XP Home Edition, Windows XP Professional, Windows Server 2003 family

TypeDescriptor.CreateProperty Method (Type, String, Type, Attribute[])

Creates a new property descriptor that is identical to an existing property descriptor by dynamically generating descriptor information from a specified property on a type.

[Visual Basic]
```
Overloads Public Shared Function CreateProperty( _
   ByVal componentType As Type, _
   ByVal name As String, _
   ByVal type As Type, _
   ByVal ParamArray attributes() As Attribute _
) As PropertyDescriptor
```
[C#]
```
public static PropertyDescriptor CreateProperty(
   Type componentType,
   string name,
   Type type,
   params Attribute[] attributes
);
```
[C++]
```
public: static PropertyDescriptor* CreateProperty(
   Type* componentType,
   String* name,
   Type* type,
   Attribute* attributes[]
);
```
[JScript]
```
public static function CreateProperty(
   componentType : Type,
   name : String,
   type : Type,
   attributes : Attribute[]
) : PropertyDescriptor;
```

Parameters

componentType
The type of the component the property lives on.

name
The name of the property.

type
The type of the property.

attributes
The attributes for this property.

Return Value

A **PropertyDescriptor** that is bound to a type.

Requirements

Platforms: Windows 98, Windows NT 4.0, Windows Millennium Edition, Windows 2000, Windows XP Home Edition, Windows XP Professional, Windows Server 2003 family

TypeDescriptor.GetAttributes Method

Gets the collection of attributes.

Overload List

Gets the collection of attributes for the specified component.

[Visual Basic] **Overloads Public Shared Function GetAttributes(Object) As AttributeCollection**

[C#] **public static AttributeCollection GetAttributes(object);**

[C++] **public: static AttributeCollection* GetAttributes(Object*);**

[JScript] **public static function GetAttributes(Object) : AttributeCollection;**

Gets the collection of attributes for the specified type of component.

[Visual Basic] **Overloads Public Shared Function GetAttributes(Type) As AttributeCollection**

[C#] **public static AttributeCollection GetAttributes(Type);**

[C++] **public: static AttributeCollection* GetAttributes(Type*);**

[JScript] **public static function GetAttributes(Type) : AttributeCollection;**

Gets a collection of attributes for the specified component and a Boolean indicating that a custom type descriptor has been created.

[Visual Basic] **Overloads Public Shared Function GetAttributes(Object, Boolean) As AttributeCollection**

[C#] **public static AttributeCollection GetAttributes(object, bool);**

[C++] **public: static AttributeCollection* GetAttributes(Object*, bool);**

[JScript] **public static function GetAttributes(Object, Boolean) : AttributeCollection;**

Example

For an example on this method, see the sample in **Matches**

TypeDescriptor.GetAttributes Method (Object)

Gets the collection of attributes for the specified component.

[Visual Basic]
```
Overloads Public Shared Function GetAttributes( _
   ByVal component As Object _
) As AttributeCollection
```
[C#]
```
public static AttributeCollection GetAttributes(
   object component
);
```
[C++]
```
public: static AttributeCollection* GetAttributes(
   Object* component
);
```
[JScript]
```
public static function GetAttributes(
   component : Object
) : AttributeCollection;
```

Parameters

component
The component for which you want to get attributes.

Return Value

An **AttributeCollection** with the attributes for the component. If the component is a null reference (**Nothing** in Visual Basic), this method returns an empty collection.

Example

For an example on this method, see the sample in **Matches**

Requirements

Platforms: Windows 98, Windows NT 4.0, Windows Millennium Edition, Windows 2000, Windows XP Home Edition, Windows XP Professional, Windows Server 2003 family

TypeDescriptor.GetAttributes Method (Type)

Gets the collection of attributes for the specified type of component.

```
[Visual Basic]
Overloads Public Shared Function GetAttributes( _
   ByVal componentType As Type _
) As AttributeCollection
[C#]
public static AttributeCollection GetAttributes(
   Type componentType
);
[C++]
public: static AttributeCollection* GetAttributes(
   Type* componentType
);
[JScript]
public static function GetAttributes(
   componentType : Type
) : AttributeCollection;
```

Parameters

componentType
A **Type** that represents the class of the component for which to get the attribute.

Return Value

An **AttributeCollection** with the attributes for the type of the component. If the component is a null reference (**Nothing** in Visual Basic), this method returns an empty collection.

Remarks

Call this version of this method only when you do not have an instance of the object.

Requirements

Platforms: Windows 98, Windows NT 4.0, Windows Millennium Edition, Windows 2000, Windows XP Home Edition, Windows XP Professional, Windows Server 2003 family

TypeDescriptor.GetAttributes Method (Object, Boolean)

Gets a collection of attributes for the specified component and a Boolean indicating that a custom type descriptor has been created.

```
[Visual Basic]
Overloads Public Shared Function GetAttributes( _
   ByVal component As Object, _
   ByVal noCustomTypeDesc As Boolean _
) As AttributeCollection
[C#]
public static AttributeCollection GetAttributes(
   object component,
   bool noCustomTypeDesc
);
[C++]
public: static AttributeCollection* GetAttributes(
   Object* component,
   bool noCustomTypeDesc
);
[JScript]
public static function GetAttributes(
   component : Object,
   noCustomTypeDesc : Boolean
) : AttributeCollection;
```

Parameters

component
The component for which you want to get attributes.

noCustomTypeDesc
true if an instance of **ICustomTypeDescriptor** calls **TypeDescriptor**; otherwise, **false**.

Return Value

An **AttributeCollection** with the attributes for the component. If the component is a null reference (**Nothing** in Visual Basic), this method returns an empty collection.

Requirements

Platforms: Windows 98, Windows NT 4.0, Windows Millennium Edition, Windows 2000, Windows XP Home Edition, Windows XP Professional, Windows Server 2003 family

TypeDescriptor.GetClassName Method

Gets the name of the class for the specified component.

Overload List

Gets the name of the class for the specified component using the default type descriptor.

[Visual Basic] **Overloads Public Shared Function GetClassName(Object) As String**

[C#] **public static string GetClassName(object);**

[C++] **public: static String* GetClassName(Object*);**

[JScript] **public static function GetClassName(Object) : String;**

Gets the name of the class for the specified component using a custom type descriptor.

[Visual Basic] **Overloads Public Shared Function GetClassName(Object, Boolean) As String**

[C#] **public static string GetClassName(object, bool);**

[C++] **public: static String* GetClassName(Object*, bool);**

[JScript] **public static function GetClassName(Object, Boolean) : String;**

TypeDescriptor.GetClassName Method (Object)

Gets the name of the class for the specified component using the default type descriptor.

```
[Visual Basic]
Overloads Public Shared Function GetClassName( _
   ByVal component As Object _
) As String
[C#]
public static string GetClassName(
   object component
);
[C++]
public: static String* GetClassName(
   Object* component
);
[JScript]
public static function GetClassName(
   component : Object
) : String;
```

Parameters

component

The **Object** for which you want the class name.

Return Value

The name of the class for the specified component.

Exceptions

Exception Type	Condition
ArgumentNull-Exception	The *component* parameter is a null reference (**Nothing** in Visual Basic).

Remarks

Typically, this method returns the full **Type** name for the *component* parameter type. If the *component* parameter implements **ICustomTypeDescriptor**, it can return an alternate name.

For example, the class name for a button is **System.Windows.Forms.Button**.

Requirements

Platforms: Windows 98, Windows NT 4.0, Windows Millennium Edition, Windows 2000, Windows XP Home Edition, Windows XP Professional, Windows Server 2003 family

TypeDescriptor.GetClassName Method (Object, Boolean)

Gets the name of the class for the specified component using a custom type descriptor.

```
[Visual Basic]
Overloads Public Shared Function GetClassName( _
   ByVal component As Object, _
   ByVal noCustomTypeDesc As Boolean _
) As String
[C#]
public static string GetClassName(
   object component,
   bool noCustomTypeDesc
);
[C++]
public: static String* GetClassName(
   Object* component,
   bool noCustomTypeDesc
);
[JScript]
public static function GetClassName(
   component : Object,
   noCustomTypeDesc : Boolean
) : String;
```

Parameters

component

The **Object** for which you want the class name.

noCustomTypeDesc

true if an instance of **ICustomTypeDescriptor** calls **TypeDescriptor**; otherwise, **false**.

Return Value

The name of the class for the specified component.

Exceptions

Exception Type	Condition
ArgumentNull-Exception	The *component* parameter is a null reference (**Nothing** in Visual Basic).

Remarks

Typically, this method returns the full **Type** name for the *component* parameter type. If the *component* parameter implements **ICustomTypeDescriptor**, it can return an alternate name.

For example, the class name for a button is **System.Windows.Forms.Button**.

Requirements

Platforms: Windows 98, Windows NT 4.0, Windows Millennium Edition, Windows 2000, Windows XP Home Edition, Windows XP Professional, Windows Server 2003 family

TypeDescriptor.GetComponentName Method

Gets the name of the specified component.

Overload List

Gets the name of the specified component using the default type descriptor.

[Visual Basic] **Overloads Public Shared Function GetComponentName(Object) As String**

[C#] **public static string GetComponentName(object);**

[C++] **public: static String* GetComponentName(Object*);**

[JScript] **public static function GetComponentName(Object) : String;**

Gets the name of the specified component using a custom type descriptor.

[Visual Basic] **Overloads Public Shared Function GetComponentName(Object, Boolean) As String**

[C#] **public static string GetComponentName(object, bool);**

[C++] **public: static String* GetComponentName(Object*, bool);**

[JScript] **public static function GetComponentName(Object, Boolean) : String;**

TypeDescriptor.GetComponentName Method (Object)

Gets the name of the specified component using the default type descriptor.

```
[Visual Basic]
Overloads Public Shared Function GetComponentName( _
   ByVal component As Object _
) As String
[C#]
public static string GetComponentName(
   object component
);
[C++]
public: static String* GetComponentName(
   Object* component
);
```

```
[JScript]
public static function GetComponentName(
   component : Object
) : String;
```

Parameters

component
The **Object** for which you want the class name.

Return Value

The name of the specified component. If there is no component name, a null reference (**Nothing** in Visual Basic) is returned.

Exceptions

Exception Type	Condition
ArgumentNull-Exception	The *component* parameter is a null reference (**Nothing** in Visual Basic).

Remarks

This method is used at design time to retrieve the name of an instance of a component. Typically, this method returns the name for the site of the component, if one exists.

For example, the class name for a button is **System.Windows.Forms.Button**.

Requirements

Platforms: Windows 98, Windows NT 4.0, Windows Millennium Edition, Windows 2000, Windows XP Home Edition, Windows XP Professional, Windows Server 2003 family

TypeDescriptor.GetComponentName Method (Object, Boolean)

Gets the name of the specified component using a custom type descriptor.

```
[Visual Basic]
Overloads Public Shared Function GetComponentName( _
   ByVal component As Object, _
   ByVal noCustomTypeDesc As Boolean _
) As String
[C#]
public static string GetComponentName(
   object component,
   bool noCustomTypeDesc
);
[C++]
public: static String* GetComponentName(
   Object* component,
   bool noCustomTypeDesc
);
[JScript]
public static function GetComponentName(
   component : Object,
   noCustomTypeDesc : Boolean
) : String;
```

Parameters

component
The **Object** for which you want the class name.

noCustomTypeDesc
true if an instance of **ICustomTypeDescriptor** calls **TypeDescriptor**; otherwise, **false**.

Return Value

The name of the class for the specified component. If there is no component name, a null reference (**Nothing** in Visual Basic) is returned.

Exceptions

Exception Type	Condition
ArgumentNull-Exception	The *component* parameter is a null reference (**Nothing** in Visual Basic).

Remarks

This method is used at design time to retrieve the name of an instance of a component. Typically, this method returns the name for the site of the component, if one exists. If the component implements **ICustomTypeDescriptor**, it can return an alternate name.

For example, the class name for a button is **System.Windows.Forms.Button**.

Requirements

Platforms: Windows 98, Windows NT 4.0, Windows Millennium Edition, Windows 2000, Windows XP Home Edition, Windows XP Professional, Windows Server 2003 family

TypeDescriptor.GetConverter Method

Gets a type converter for a component.

Overload List

Gets a type converter for the type of the specified component.

[Visual Basic] **Overloads Public Shared Function GetConverter(Object) As TypeConverter**

[C#] **public static TypeConverter GetConverter(object);**

[C++] **public: static TypeConverter* GetConverter(Object*);**

[JScript] **public static function GetConverter(Object) : TypeConverter;**

Gets a type converter for the specified type.

[Visual Basic] **Overloads Public Shared Function GetConverter(Type) As TypeConverter**

[C#] **public static TypeConverter GetConverter(Type);**

[C++] **public: static TypeConverter* GetConverter(Type*);**

[JScript] **public static function GetConverter(Type) : TypeConverter;**

Gets a type converter for the type of the specified component with a custom type descriptor.

[Visual Basic] **Overloads Public Shared Function GetConverter(Object, Boolean) As TypeConverter**

[C#] **public static TypeConverter GetConverter(object, bool);**

[C++] **public: static TypeConverter* GetConverter(Object*, bool);**

[JScript] **public static function GetConverter(Object, Boolean) : TypeConverter;**

Example

For an example on using this method, see the sample in **TypeConverter**.

TypeDescriptor.GetConverter Method (Object)

Gets a type converter for the type of the specified component.

```
[Visual Basic]
Overloads Public Shared Function GetConverter( _
   ByVal component As Object _
) As TypeConverter
[C#]
public static TypeConverter GetConverter(
   object component
);
[C++]
public: static TypeConverter* GetConverter(
   Object* component
);
[JScript]
public static function GetConverter(
   component : Object
) : TypeConverter;
```

Parameters

component

A component to get the converter for.

Return Value

A **TypeConverter** for the specified component, or a null reference (**Nothing** in Visual Basic) if a **TypeConverter** cannot be found.

Exceptions

Exception Type	Condition
ArgumentNull-Exception	The specified component is a null reference (**Nothing** in Visual Basic).

Remarks

This method looks for the appropriate type converter by looking for a **TypeConverterAttribute**. If it cannot find a **TypeConverter-Attribute**, it traverses the base class hierarchy of the class until it finds a primitive type.

Example

For an example on using this method, see the sample in **TypeConverter**.

Requirements

Platforms: Windows 98, Windows NT 4.0, Windows Millennium Edition, Windows 2000, Windows XP Home Edition, Windows XP Professional, Windows Server 2003 family

TypeDescriptor.GetConverter Method (Type)

Gets a type converter for the specified type.

```
[Visual Basic]
Overloads Public Shared Function GetConverter( _
   ByVal type As Type _
) As TypeConverter
[C#]
public static TypeConverter GetConverter(
   Type type
);
[C++]
public: static TypeConverter* GetConverter(
   Type* type
);
[JScript]
public static function GetConverter(
   type : Type
) : TypeConverter;
```

Parameters

type

A **Type** that represents the type of component to get the converter for.

Return Value

A **TypeConverter** for the specified type, or a null reference (**Nothing** in Visual Basic) if a **TypeConverter** cannot be found.

Remarks

Call this version of this method only when you do not have an instance of the object.

This method looks for the appropriate type converter by looking for a **TypeConverterAttribute**. If it cannot find a **TypeConverter-Attribute**, it traverses the base class hierarchy of the class until it finds a primitive type.

Requirements

Platforms: Windows 98, Windows NT 4.0, Windows Millennium Edition, Windows 2000, Windows XP Home Edition, Windows XP Professional, Windows Server 2003 family

TypeDescriptor.GetConverter Method (Object, Boolean)

Gets a type converter for the type of the specified component with a custom type descriptor.

```
[Visual Basic]
Overloads Public Shared Function GetConverter( _
   ByVal component As Object, _
   ByVal noCustomTypeDesc As Boolean _
) As TypeConverter
[C#]
public static TypeConverter GetConverter(
   object component,
   bool noCustomTypeDesc
);
[C++]
public: static TypeConverter* GetConverter(
   Object* component,
   bool noCustomTypeDesc
);
[JScript]
public static function GetConverter(
   component : Object,
   noCustomTypeDesc : Boolean
) : TypeConverter;
```

Parameters

component

A component to get the converter for.

noCustomTypeDesc

true if an instance of **ICustomTypeDescriptor** calls **TypeDescriptor**; otherwise, **false**.

Return Value

A **TypeConverter** for the specified component, or a null reference (**Nothing** in Visual Basic) if a **TypeConverter** cannot be found.

Exceptions

Exception Type	Condition
ArgumentNull-Exception	The specified component is a null reference (**Nothing** in Visual Basic).

Remarks

This method looks for the appropriate type converter by trying to find a **TypeConverterAttribute**. If it cannot find a **TypeConverter-Attribute**, it traverses the base class hierarchy of the class until it finds a primitive type.

Requirements

Platforms: Windows 98, Windows NT 4.0, Windows Millennium Edition, Windows 2000, Windows XP Home Edition, Windows XP Professional, Windows Server 2003 family

TypeDescriptor.GetDefaultEvent Method

Gets the default event for a component.

Overload List

Gets the default event for the specified component.

[Visual Basic] **Overloads Public Shared Function GetDefaultEvent(Object) As EventDescriptor**

[C#] **public static EventDescriptor GetDefaultEvent(object);**

[C++] **public: static EventDescriptor* GetDefault-Event(Object*);**

[JScript] **public static function GetDefaultEvent(Object) : EventDescriptor;**

Gets the default event for the specified type of component.

[Visual Basic] **Overloads Public Shared Function GetDefaultEvent(Type) As EventDescriptor**

[C#] **public static EventDescriptor GetDefaultEvent(Type);**

[C++] **public: static EventDescriptor* GetDefaultEvent(Type*);**

[JScript] **public static function GetDefaultEvent(Type) : EventDescriptor;**

Gets the default event for a component with a custom type descriptor.

[Visual Basic] **Overloads Public Shared Function GetDefaultEvent(Object, Boolean) As EventDescriptor**

[C#] **public static EventDescriptor GetDefaultEvent(object, bool);**

[C++] **public: static EventDescriptor* GetDefault-Event(Object*, bool);**

[JScript] **public static function GetDefaultEvent(Object, Boolean) : EventDescriptor;**

TypeDescriptor.GetDefaultEvent Method (Object)

Gets the default event for the specified component.

[Visual Basic]
```
Overloads Public Shared Function GetDefaultEvent( _
   ByVal component As Object _
) As EventDescriptor
```
[C#]
```
public static EventDescriptor GetDefaultEvent(
   object component
);
```
[C++]
```
public: static EventDescriptor* GetDefaultEvent(
   Object* component
);
```
[JScript]
```
public static function GetDefaultEvent(
   component : Object
) : EventDescriptor;
```

Parameters

component

The component to get the event for.

Return Value

An **EventDescriptor** with the default event, or a null reference (**Nothing** in Visual Basic) if there are no events.

Requirements

Platforms: Windows 98, Windows NT 4.0, Windows Millennium Edition, Windows 2000, Windows XP Home Edition, Windows XP Professional, Windows Server 2003 family

TypeDescriptor.GetDefaultEvent Method (Type)

Gets the default event for the specified type of component.

[Visual Basic]
```
Overloads Public Shared Function GetDefaultEvent( _
   ByVal componentType As Type _
) As EventDescriptor
```
[C#]
```
public static EventDescriptor GetDefaultEvent(
   Type componentType
);
```
[C++]
```
public: static EventDescriptor* GetDefaultEvent(
   Type* componentType
);
```
[JScript]
```
public static function GetDefaultEvent(
   componentType : Type
) : EventDescriptor;
```

Parameters

componentType

A **Type** that represents the type of component to get the event for.

Return Value

An **EventDescriptor** with the default event, or a null reference (**Nothing** in Visual Basic) if there are no events.

Remarks

Call this version of this method only when you do not have an instance of the object.

Requirements

Platforms: Windows 98, Windows NT 4.0, Windows Millennium Edition, Windows 2000, Windows XP Home Edition, Windows XP Professional, Windows Server 2003 family

TypeDescriptor.GetDefaultEvent Method (Object, Boolean)

Gets the default event for a component with a custom type descriptor.

```
[Visual Basic]
Overloads Public Shared Function GetDefaultEvent( _
   ByVal component As Object, _
   ByVal noCustomTypeDesc As Boolean _
) As EventDescriptor
[C#]
public static EventDescriptor GetDefaultEvent(
   object component,
   bool noCustomTypeDesc
);
[C++]
public: static EventDescriptor* GetDefaultEvent(
   Object* component,
   bool noCustomTypeDesc
);
[JScript]
public static function GetDefaultEvent(
   component : Object,
   noCustomTypeDesc : Boolean
) : EventDescriptor;
```

Parameters

component
The component to get the event for.

noCustomTypeDesc
true if an instance of **ICustomTypeDescriptor** calls **TypeDescriptor**; otherwise, **false**.

Return Value

An **EventDescriptor** with the default event, or a null reference (**Nothing** in Visual Basic) if there are no events.

Requirements

Platforms: Windows 98, Windows NT 4.0, Windows Millennium Edition, Windows 2000, Windows XP Home Edition, Windows XP Professional, Windows Server 2003 family

TypeDescriptor.GetDefaultProperty Method

Gets the default property for a component.

Overload List

Gets the default property for the specified component.

[Visual Basic] **Overloads Public Shared Function GetDefaultProperty(Object) As PropertyDescriptor**

[C#] **public static PropertyDescriptor GetDefault-Property(object);**

[C++] **public: static PropertyDescriptor* GetDefault-Property(Object*);**

[JScript] **public static function GetDefaultProperty(Object) : PropertyDescriptor;**

Gets the default property for the specified type of component.

[Visual Basic] **Overloads Public Shared Function GetDefaultProperty(Type) As PropertyDescriptor**

[C#] **public static PropertyDescriptor GetDefault-Property(Type);**

[C++] **public: static PropertyDescriptor* GetDefaultProperty(Type*);**

[JScript] **public static function GetDefaultProperty(Type) : PropertyDescriptor;**

Gets the default property for the specified component with a custom type descriptor.

[Visual Basic] **Overloads Public Shared Function GetDefaultProperty(Object, Boolean) As PropertyDescriptor**

[C#] **public static PropertyDescriptor GetDefault-Property(object, bool);**

[C++] **public: static PropertyDescriptor* GetDefault-Property(Object*, bool);**

[JScript] **public static function GetDefaultProperty(Object, Boolean) : PropertyDescriptor;**

TypeDescriptor.GetDefaultProperty Method (Object)

Gets the default property for the specified component.

```
[Visual Basic]
Overloads Public Shared Function GetDefaultProperty( _
   ByVal component As Object _
) As PropertyDescriptor
[C#]
public static PropertyDescriptor GetDefaultProperty(
   object component
);
[C++]
public: static PropertyDescriptor* GetDefaultProperty(
   Object* component
);
[JScript]
public static function GetDefaultProperty(
   component : Object
) : PropertyDescriptor;
```

Parameters

component
The component to get the default property for.

Return Value

A **PropertyDescriptor** with the default property, or a null reference (**Nothing** in Visual Basic) if there are no properties.

Requirements

Platforms: Windows 98, Windows NT 4.0, Windows Millennium Edition, Windows 2000, Windows XP Home Edition, Windows XP Professional, Windows Server 2003 family

TypeDescriptor.GetDefaultProperty Method (Type)

Gets the default property for the specified type of component.

```
[Visual Basic]
Overloads Public Shared Function GetDefaultProperty( _
   ByVal componentType As Type _
) As PropertyDescriptor
[C#]
public static PropertyDescriptor GetDefaultProperty(
   Type componentType
);
```

```
[C++]
public: static PropertyDescriptor* GetDefaultProperty(
   Type* componentType
);
[JScript]
public static function GetDefaultProperty(
   componentType : Type
) : PropertyDescriptor;
```

Parameters

componentType
A **Type** that represents the class to get the property for.

Return Value

A **PropertyDescriptor** with the default property, or a null reference (**Nothing** in Visual Basic) if there are no properties.

Remarks

Call this version of this method only when you do not have an instance of the object.

Requirements

Platforms: Windows 98, Windows NT 4.0, Windows Millennium Edition, Windows 2000, Windows XP Home Edition, Windows XP Professional, Windows Server 2003 family

TypeDescriptor.GetDefaultProperty Method (Object, Boolean)

Gets the default property for the specified component with a custom type descriptor.

```
[Visual Basic]
Overloads Public Shared Function GetDefaultProperty( _
   ByVal component As Object, _
   ByVal noCustomTypeDesc As Boolean _
) As PropertyDescriptor
[C#]
public static PropertyDescriptor GetDefaultProperty(
   object component,
   bool noCustomTypeDesc
);
[C++]
public: static PropertyDescriptor* GetDefaultProperty(
   Object* component,
   bool noCustomTypeDesc
);
[JScript]
public static function GetDefaultProperty(
   component : Object,
   noCustomTypeDesc : Boolean
) : PropertyDescriptor;
```

Parameters

component
The component to get the default property for.

noCustomTypeDesc
true if an instance of **ICustomTypeDescriptor** calls **TypeDescriptor**; otherwise, **false**.

Return Value

A **PropertyDescriptor** with the default property, or a null reference (**Nothing** in Visual Basic) if there are no properties.

Requirements

Platforms: Windows 98, Windows NT 4.0, Windows Millennium Edition, Windows 2000, Windows XP Home Edition, Windows XP Professional, Windows Server 2003 family

TypeDescriptor.GetEditor Method

Gets an editor with the specified base type.

Overload List

Gets an editor with the specified base type for the specified component.

[Visual Basic] **Overloads Public Shared Function GetEditor(Object, Type) As Object**

[C#] **public static object GetEditor(object, Type);**

[C++] **public: static Object* GetEditor(Object*, Type*);**

[JScript] **public static function GetEditor(Object, Type) : Object;**

Gets an editor with the specified base type for the specified type.

[Visual Basic] **Overloads Public Shared Function GetEditor(Type, Type) As Object**

[C#] **public static object GetEditor(Type, Type);**

[C++] **public: static Object* GetEditor(Type*, Type*);**

[JScript] **public static function GetEditor(Type, Type) : Object;**

Gets an editor with the specified base type and with a custom type descriptor for the specified component.

[Visual Basic] **Overloads Public Shared Function GetEditor(Object, Type, Boolean) As Object**

[C#] **public static object GetEditor(object, Type, bool);**

[C++] **public: static Object* GetEditor(Object*, Type*, bool);**

[JScript] **public static function GetEditor(Object, Type, Boolean) : Object;**

TypeDescriptor.GetEditor Method (Object, Type)

Gets an editor with the specified base type for the specified component.

```
[Visual Basic]
Overloads Public Shared Function GetEditor( _
   ByVal component As Object, _
   ByVal editorBaseType As Type _
) As Object
[C#]
public static object GetEditor(
   object component,
   Type editorBaseType
);
[C++]
public: static Object* GetEditor(
   Object* component,
   Type* editorBaseType
);
[JScript]
public static function GetEditor(
   component : Object,
   editorBaseType : Type
) : Object;
```

Parameters

component
The component to get the editor for.

editorBaseType
A **Type** that represents the base type of the editor you want to find.

Return Value

An instance of the editor that can be cast to the specified editor type. This returns a null reference (**Nothing** in Visual Basic) if no editor of the requested type can be found.

Exceptions

Exception Type	Condition
ArgumentNull-Exception	The *component* parameter is a null reference (**Nothing** in Visual Basic).

Remarks

You can define multiple editors for a property. You use this method to select the editor you want to use.

Requirements

Platforms: Windows 98, Windows NT 4.0, Windows Millennium Edition, Windows 2000, Windows XP Home Edition, Windows XP Professional, Windows Server 2003 family

TypeDescriptor.GetEditor Method (Type, Type)

Gets an editor with the specified base type for the specified type.

```
[Visual Basic]
Overloads Public Shared Function GetEditor( _
   ByVal type As Type, _
   ByVal editorBaseType As Type _
) As Object
[C#]
public static object GetEditor(
   Type type,
   Type editorBaseType
);
[C++]
public: static Object* GetEditor(
   Type* type,
   Type* editorBaseType
);
[JScript]
public static function GetEditor(
   type : Type,
   editorBaseType : Type
) : Object;
```

Parameters

type
A **Type** that represents the type to get the editor for.

editorBaseType
A **Type** that represents the base type of the editor you are trying to find.

Return Value

An instance of the editor object that can be cast to the given base type. This returns a null reference (**Nothing** in Visual Basic) if no editor of the requested type can be found.

Remarks

You can define multiple editors for a type. You use this method to select the one you want to use.

Call this version of this method only when you do not have an instance of the object.

Requirements

Platforms: Windows 98, Windows NT 4.0, Windows Millennium Edition, Windows 2000, Windows XP Home Edition, Windows XP Professional, Windows Server 2003 family

TypeDescriptor.GetEditor Method (Object, Type, Boolean)

Gets an editor with the specified base type and with a custom type descriptor for the specified component.

```
[Visual Basic]
Overloads Public Shared Function GetEditor( _
   ByVal component As Object, _
   ByVal editorBaseType As Type, _
   ByVal noCustomTypeDesc As Boolean _
) As Object
[C#]
public static object GetEditor(
   object component,
   Type editorBaseType,
   bool noCustomTypeDesc
);
[C++]
public: static Object* GetEditor(
   Object* component,
   Type* editorBaseType,
   bool noCustomTypeDesc
);
[JScript]
public static function GetEditor(
   component : Object,
   editorBaseType : Type,
   noCustomTypeDesc : Boolean
) : Object;
```

Parameters

component
The component to get the editor for.

editorBaseType
A **Type** that represents the base type of the editor you want to find.

noCustomTypeDesc
true if an instance of **ICustomTypeDescriptor** calls **TypeDescriptor**; otherwise, **false**.

Return Value

An instance of the editor that can be cast to the specified editor type. This returns a null reference (**Nothing** in Visual Basic) if no editor of the requested type can be found.

Exceptions

Exception Type	Condition
ArgumentNull-Exception	The *component* parameter is a null reference (**Nothing** in Visual Basic).

Remarks

You can define multiple editors for a property. You use this method to select the editor you want to use.

Requirements

Platforms: Windows 98, Windows NT 4.0, Windows Millennium Edition, Windows 2000, Windows XP Home Edition, Windows XP Professional, Windows Server 2003 family

TypeDescriptor.GetEvents Method

Gets the collection of events.

Overload List

Gets the collection of events for a specified component.

Supported by the .NET Compact Framework.

[Visual Basic] **Overloads Public Shared Function GetEvents(Object) As EventDescriptorCollection**

[C#] **public static EventDescriptorCollection GetEvents(object);**

[C++] **public: static EventDescriptorCollection* GetEvents(Object*);**

[JScript] **public static function GetEvents(Object) : EventDescriptorCollection;**

Gets the collection of events for a specified type of component.

Supported by the .NET Compact Framework.

[Visual Basic] **Overloads Public Shared Function GetEvents(Type) As EventDescriptorCollection**

[C#] **public static EventDescriptorCollection GetEvents(Type);**

[C++] **public: static EventDescriptorCollection* GetEvents(Type*);**

[JScript] **public static function GetEvents(Type) : EventDescriptorCollection;**

Gets the collection of events for a specified component using a specified array of attributes as a filter.

Supported by the .NET Compact Framework.

[Visual Basic] **Overloads Public Shared Function GetEvents(Object, Attribute()) As EventDescriptorCollection**

[C#] **public static EventDescriptorCollection GetEvents(object, Attribute[]);**

[C++] **public: static EventDescriptorCollection* GetEvents(Object*, Attribute[]);**

[JScript] **public static function GetEvents(Object, Attribute[]) : EventDescriptorCollection;**

Gets the collection of events for a specified component with a custom type descriptor.

Supported by the .NET Compact Framework.

[Visual Basic] **Overloads Public Shared Function GetEvents(Object, Boolean) As EventDescriptorCollection**

[C#] **public static EventDescriptorCollection GetEvents(object, bool);**

[C++] **public: static EventDescriptorCollection* GetEvents(Object*, bool);**

[JScript] **public static function GetEvents(Object, Boolean) : EventDescriptorCollection;**

Gets the collection of events for a specified type of component using a specified array of attributes as a filter.

Supported by the .NET Compact Framework.

[Visual Basic] **Overloads Public Shared Function GetEvents(Type, Attribute()) As EventDescriptorCollection**

[C#] **public static EventDescriptorCollection GetEvents(Type, Attribute[]);**

[C++] **public: static EventDescriptorCollection* GetEvents(Type*, Attribute[]);**

[JScript] **public static function GetEvents(Type, Attribute[]) : EventDescriptorCollection;**

Gets the collection of events for a specified component using a specified array of attributes as a filter and using a custom type descriptor.

Supported by the .NET Compact Framework.

[Visual Basic] **Overloads Public Shared Function GetEvents(Object, Attribute(), Boolean) As EventDescriptorCollection**

[C#] **public static EventDescriptorCollection GetEvents(object, Attribute[], bool);**

[C++] **public: static EventDescriptorCollection* GetEvents(Object*, Attribute[], bool);**

[JScript] **public static function GetEvents(Object, Attribute[], Boolean) : EventDescriptorCollection;**

Example

For an example on this method, see the sample in **Count**

TypeDescriptor.GetEvents Method (Object)

Gets the collection of events for a specified component.

```
[Visual Basic]
Overloads Public Shared Function GetEvents( _
   ByVal component As Object _
) As EventDescriptorCollection
[C#]
public static EventDescriptorCollection GetEvents(
   object component
);
[C++]
public: static EventDescriptorCollection* GetEvents(
   Object* component
);
[JScript]
public static function GetEvents(
   component : Object
) : EventDescriptorCollection;
```

Parameters

component

A component to get the events for.

Return Value

An **EventDescriptorCollection** with the events for this component.

Remarks

Retrieves a collection of events that the given *component* parameter instance provides. This collection can differ from the set of events the class provides. If the *component* parameter is sited, the site can add or remove additional events.

Example

For an example on this method, see the sample in **Count**

Requirements

Platforms: Windows 98, Windows NT 4.0, Windows Millennium Edition, Windows 2000, Windows XP Home Edition, Windows XP Professional, Windows Server 2003 family, .NET Compact Framework - Windows CE .NET

TypeDescriptor.GetEvents Method (Type)

Gets the collection of events for a specified type of component.

[Visual Basic]
```
Overloads Public Shared Function GetEvents( _
   ByVal componentType As Type _
) As EventDescriptorCollection
```
[C#]
```
public static EventDescriptorCollection GetEvents(
   Type componentType
);
```
[C++]
```
public: static EventDescriptorCollection* GetEvents(
   Type* componentType
);
```
[JScript]
```
public static function GetEvents(
   componentType : Type
) : EventDescriptorCollection;
```

Parameters

componentType
A **Type** that represents the component to get events for.

Return Value

An **EventDescriptorCollection** with the events for this component.

Remarks

Call this version of this method only when you do not have an instance of the object.

Requirements

Platforms: Windows 98, Windows NT 4.0, Windows Millennium Edition, Windows 2000, Windows XP Home Edition, Windows XP Professional, Windows Server 2003 family, .NET Compact Framework - Windows CE .NET

TypeDescriptor.GetEvents Method (Object, Attribute[])

Gets the collection of events for a specified component using a specified array of attributes as a filter.

[Visual Basic]
```
Overloads Public Shared Function GetEvents( _
   ByVal component As Object, _
   ByVal attributes() As Attribute _
) As EventDescriptorCollection
```
[C#]
```
public static EventDescriptorCollection GetEvents(
   object component,
   Attribute[] attributes
);
```
[C++]
```
public: static EventDescriptorCollection* GetEvents(
   Object* component,
   Attribute* attributes[]
);
```
[JScript]
```
public static function GetEvents(
   component : Object,
   attributes : Attribute[]
) : EventDescriptorCollection;
```

Parameters

component
A component to get the events for.

attributes
An array of type **Attribute** that you can use as a filter.

Return Value

An **EventDescriptorCollection** with the events that match the specified attributes for this component.

Remarks

The events for the *component* parameter can differ from the events of a class, because the site can add or remove events if the *component* parameter is sited.

The *attributes* array can have a mix of **Type** and **Attribute** objects. Filtering is defined by the following rules:

- A **Type** object is treated as a wildcard; it matches any event that has the **Type** in its set of attributes.
- If an event does not have an **Attribute** of the same class, the event is not included in the returned array.
- If the attribute is an instance of **Attribute**, the event must be an exact match or it is not included in the returned array.
- If an **Attribute** instance is specified and it is the default event, it is included in the returned array even if there is no instance of the **Attribute** in the event.

Requirements

Platforms: Windows 98, Windows NT 4.0, Windows Millennium Edition, Windows 2000, Windows XP Home Edition, Windows XP Professional, Windows Server 2003 family, .NET Compact Framework - Windows CE .NET

TypeDescriptor.GetEvents Method (Object, Boolean)

Gets the collection of events for a specified component with a custom type descriptor.

[Visual Basic]
```
Overloads Public Shared Function GetEvents( _
   ByVal component As Object, _
   ByVal noCustomTypeDesc As Boolean _
) As EventDescriptorCollection
```
[C#]
```
public static EventDescriptorCollection GetEvents(
   object component,
   bool noCustomTypeDesc
);
```
[C++]
```
public: static EventDescriptorCollection* GetEvents(
   Object* component,
   bool noCustomTypeDesc
);
```

```
[JScript]
public static function GetEvents(
   component : Object,
   noCustomTypeDesc : Boolean
) : EventDescriptorCollection;
```

Parameters

component

A component to get the events for.

noCustomTypeDesc

true if an instance of **ICustomTypeDescriptor** calls **TypeDescriptor**; otherwise, **false**.

Return Value

An **EventDescriptorCollection** with the events for this component.

Remarks

Retrieves a collection of events that the given *component* parameter instance provides. This can differ from the set of events the class provides. If the *component* parameter is sited, the site can add or remove additional events.

Requirements

Platforms: Windows 98, Windows NT 4.0, Windows Millennium Edition, Windows 2000, Windows XP Home Edition, Windows XP Professional, Windows Server 2003 family, .NET Compact Framework - Windows CE .NET

TypeDescriptor.GetEvents Method (Type, Attribute[])

Gets the collection of events for a specified type of component using a specified array of attributes as a filter.

```
[Visual Basic]
Overloads Public Shared Function GetEvents( _
   ByVal componentType As Type, _
   ByVal attributes() As Attribute _
) As EventDescriptorCollection
[C#]
public static EventDescriptorCollection GetEvents(
   Type componentType,
   Attribute[] attributes
);
[C++]
public: static EventDescriptorCollection* GetEvents(
   Type* componentType,
   Attribute* attributes[]
);
[JScript]
public static function GetEvents(
   componentType : Type,
   attributes : Attribute[]
) : EventDescriptorCollection;
```

Parameters

componentType

A **Type** that represents the component to get events for.

attributes

An array of type **Attribute** that you can use as a filter.

Return Value

An **EventDescriptorCollection** with the events that match the specified attributes for this component.

Remarks

Call this version of this method only when you do not have an instance of the object.

The *attributes* parameter array can have a mix of **Type** and **Attribute** objects. Filtering is defined by the following rules:

- A **Type** object is treated as a wildcard; it matches any event that has the **Type** in its set of attributes.
- If an event does not have an **Attribute** of the same class, the event is not included in the returned array.
- If the attribute is an instance of **Attribute**, the event must be an exact match or it is not included in the returned array.
- If an **Attribute** instance is specified and it is the default event, it is included in the returned array even if there is no instance of the **Attribute** in the event.

Requirements

Platforms: Windows 98, Windows NT 4.0, Windows Millennium Edition, Windows 2000, Windows XP Home Edition, Windows XP Professional, Windows Server 2003 family, .NET Compact Framework - Windows CE .NET

TypeDescriptor.GetEvents Method (Object, Attribute[], Boolean)

Gets the collection of events for a specified component using a specified array of attributes as a filter and using a custom type descriptor.

```
[Visual Basic]
Overloads Public Shared Function GetEvents( _
   ByVal component As Object, _
   ByVal attributes() As Attribute, _
   ByVal noCustomTypeDesc As Boolean _
) As EventDescriptorCollection
[C#]
public static EventDescriptorCollection GetEvents(
   object component,
   Attribute[] attributes,
   bool noCustomTypeDesc
);
[C++]
public: static EventDescriptorCollection* GetEvents(
   Object* component,
   Attribute* attributes[],
   bool noCustomTypeDesc
);
[JScript]
public static function GetEvents(
   component : Object,
   attributes : Attribute[],
   noCustomTypeDesc : Boolean
) : EventDescriptorCollection;
```

Parameters

component

A component to get the events for.

attributes

An array of type **Attribute** to use as a filter.

noCustomTypeDesc

true if an instance of **ICustomTypeDescriptor** calls **TypeDescriptor**; otherwise, **false**.

Return Value

An **EventDescriptorCollection** with the events that match the specified attributes for this component.

Remarks

The events for the *component* parameter can differ from the events of a class, because the site can add or remove events if the *component* parameter is sited.

The *attributes* parameter array can have a mix of **Type** and **Attribute** objects. Filtering is defined by the following rules:

- A **Type** object is treated as a wildcard; it matches any event that has the **Type** in its set of attributes.
- If an event does not have an **Attribute** of the same class, the event is not included in the returned array.
- If the attribute is an instance of **Attribute**, the event must be an exact match or it is not included in the returned array.
- If an **Attribute** instance is specified and it is the default event, it is included in the returned array even if there is no instance of the **Attribute** in the event.

Requirements

Platforms: Windows 98, Windows NT 4.0, Windows Millennium Edition, Windows 2000, Windows XP Home Edition, Windows XP Professional, Windows Server 2003 family, .NET Compact Framework - Windows CE .NET

TypeDescriptor.GetProperties Method

Gets the collection of properties.

Overload List

Gets the collection of properties for a specified component.

Supported by the .NET Compact Framework.

[Visual Basic] **Overloads Public Shared Function GetProperties(Object) As PropertyDescriptorCollection**

[C#] **public static PropertyDescriptorCollection GetProperties(object);**

[C++] **public: static PropertyDescriptorCollection* GetProperties(Object*);**

[JScript] **public static function GetProperties(Object) : PropertyDescriptorCollection;**

Gets the collection of properties for a specified type of component.

Supported by the .NET Compact Framework.

[Visual Basic] **Overloads Public Shared Function GetProperties(Type) As PropertyDescriptorCollection**

[C#] **public static PropertyDescriptorCollection GetProperties(Type);**

[C++] **public: static PropertyDescriptorCollection* GetProperties(Type*);**

[JScript] **public static function GetProperties(Type) : PropertyDescriptorCollection;**

Gets the collection of properties for a specified component using a specified array of attributes as a filter.

[Visual Basic] **Overloads Public Shared Function GetProperties(Object, Attribute()) As PropertyDescriptorCollection**

[C#] **public static PropertyDescriptorCollection GetProperties(object, Attribute[]);**

[C++] **public: static PropertyDescriptorCollection* GetProperties(Object*, Attribute[]);**

[JScript] **public static function GetProperties(Object, Attribute[]) : PropertyDescriptorCollection;**

Gets the collection of properties for a specified component using the default type descriptor.

Supported by the .NET Compact Framework.

[Visual Basic] **Overloads Public Shared Function GetProperties(Object, Boolean) As PropertyDescriptorCollection**

[C#] **public static PropertyDescriptorCollection GetProperties(object, bool);**

[C++] **public: static PropertyDescriptorCollection* GetProperties(Object*, bool);**

[JScript] **public static function GetProperties(Object, Boolean) : PropertyDescriptorCollection;**

Gets the collection of properties for a specified type of component using a specified array of attributes as a filter.

[Visual Basic] **Overloads Public Shared Function GetProperties(Type, Attribute()) As PropertyDescriptorCollection**

[C#] **public static PropertyDescriptorCollection GetProperties(Type, Attribute[]);**

[C++] **public: static PropertyDescriptorCollection* GetProperties(Type*, Attribute[]);**

[JScript] **public static function GetProperties(Type, Attribute[]) : PropertyDescriptorCollection;**

Gets the collection of properties for a specified component using a specified array of attributes as a filter and using a custom type descriptor.

[Visual Basic] **Overloads Public Shared Function GetProperties(Object, Attribute(), Boolean) As PropertyDescriptorCollection**

[C#] **public static PropertyDescriptorCollection GetProperties(object, Attribute[], bool);**

[C++] **public: static PropertyDescriptorCollection* GetProperties(Object*, Attribute[], bool);**

[JScript] **public static function GetProperties(Object, Attribute[], Boolean) : PropertyDescriptorCollection;**

Example

For an example on this method, see the sample in **Contains**

TypeDescriptor.GetProperties Method (Object)

Gets the collection of properties for a specified component.

```
[Visual Basic]
Overloads Public Shared Function GetProperties( _
   ByVal component As Object _
) As PropertyDescriptorCollection
[C#]
public static PropertyDescriptorCollection GetProperties(
   object component
);
[C++]
public: static PropertyDescriptorCollection* GetProperties(
   Object* component
);
```

```
[JScript]
public static function GetProperties(
   component : Object
) : PropertyDescriptorCollection;
```

Parameters

component

A component to get the properties for.

Return Value

A **PropertyDescriptorCollection** with the properties for the specified component.

Exceptions

Exception Type	Condition
ArgumentNull-Exception	The *component* parameter is a null reference (**Nothing** in Visual Basic).

Remarks

The properties for a component can differ from the properties of a class, because the site can add or remove properties if the component is sited.

Example

For an example on this method, see the sample in **Contains**

Requirements

Platforms: Windows 98, Windows NT 4.0, Windows Millennium Edition, Windows 2000, Windows XP Home Edition, Windows XP Professional, Windows Server 2003 family, .NET Compact Framework - Windows CE .NET

TypeDescriptor.GetProperties Method (Type)

Gets the collection of properties for a specified type of component.

```
[Visual Basic]
Overloads Public Shared Function GetProperties( _
   ByVal componentType As Type _
) As PropertyDescriptorCollection
[C#]
public static PropertyDescriptorCollection GetProperties(
   Type componentType
);
[C++]
public: static PropertyDescriptorCollection* GetProperties(
   Type* componentType
);
[JScript]
public static function GetProperties(
   componentType : Type
) : PropertyDescriptorCollection;
```

Parameters

componentType

A **Type** that represents the component to get properties for.

Return Value

A **PropertyDescriptorCollection** with the properties for a specified type of component.

Remarks

Call this version of this method only when you do not have an instance of the object.

Requirements

Platforms: Windows 98, Windows NT 4.0, Windows Millennium Edition, Windows 2000, Windows XP Home Edition, Windows XP Professional, Windows Server 2003 family, .NET Compact Framework - Windows CE .NET

TypeDescriptor.GetProperties Method (Object, Attribute[])

Gets the collection of properties for a specified component using a specified array of attributes as a filter.

```
[Visual Basic]
Overloads Public Shared Function GetProperties( _
   ByVal component As Object, _
   ByVal attributes() As Attribute _
) As PropertyDescriptorCollection
[C#]
public static PropertyDescriptorCollection GetProperties(
   object component,
   Attribute[] attributes
);
[C++]
public: static PropertyDescriptorCollection* GetProperties(
   Object* component,
   Attribute* attributes[]
);
[JScript]
public static function GetProperties(
   component : Object,
   attributes : Attribute[]
) : PropertyDescriptorCollection;
```

Parameters

component

A component to get the properties for.

attributes

An array of type **Attribute** to use as a filter.

Return Value

A **PropertyDescriptorCollection** with the properties that match the specified attributes for the specified component.

Exceptions

Exception Type	Condition
ArgumentNull-Exception	The *component* parameter is a null reference (**Nothing** in Visual Basic).

Remarks

The properties for the *component* parameter can differ from the properties of a class, because the site can add or remove properties if the *component* parameter is sited.

The *attributes* parameter array is used to filter the array. The *attributes* parameter can have a mix of **Type** and **Attribute** objects. Filtering is defined by the following rules:

- A **Type** object is treated as a wildcard; it matches any property that has the **Type** in its set of attributes.
- If a property does not have an **Attribute** of the same class, the property is not included in the returned array.
- If the attribute is an instance of **Attribute**, the property must be an exact match or it is not included in the returned array.

- If an **Attribute** instance is specified and it is the default property, it is included in the returned array even if there is no instance of the **Attribute** in the property.

Requirements

Platforms: Windows 98, Windows NT 4.0,
Windows Millennium Edition, Windows 2000,
Windows XP Home Edition, Windows XP Professional,
Windows Server 2003 family

TypeDescriptor.GetProperties Method (Object, Boolean)

Gets the collection of properties for a specified component using the default type descriptor.

```
[Visual Basic]
Overloads Public Shared Function GetProperties( _
   ByVal component As Object, _
   ByVal noCustomTypeDesc As Boolean _
) As PropertyDescriptorCollection
[C#]
public static PropertyDescriptorCollection GetProperties(
   object component,
   bool noCustomTypeDesc
);
[C++]
public: static PropertyDescriptorCollection* GetProperties(
   Object* component,
   bool noCustomTypeDesc
);
[JScript]
public static function GetProperties(
   component : Object,
   noCustomTypeDesc : Boolean
) : PropertyDescriptorCollection;
```

Parameters

component
A component to get the properties for.

noCustomTypeDesc
true if an instance of **ICustomTypeDescriptor** calls **TypeDescriptor**; otherwise, **false**.

Return Value

A **PropertyDescriptorCollection** with the properties for a specified component.

Exceptions

Exception Type	Condition
ArgumentNull-Exception	The *component* parameter is a null reference (**Nothing** in Visual Basic).

Remarks

The properties for the *component* parameter can differ from the properties of a class, because the site can add or remove properties if the *component* parameter is sited.

Requirements

Platforms: Windows 98, Windows NT 4.0,
Windows Millennium Edition, Windows 2000,
Windows XP Home Edition, Windows XP Professional,
Windows Server 2003 family,
.NET Compact Framework - Windows CE .NET

TypeDescriptor.GetProperties Method (Type, Attribute[])

Gets the collection of properties for a specified type of component using a specified array of attributes as a filter.

```
[Visual Basic]
Overloads Public Shared Function GetProperties( _
   ByVal componentType As Type, _
   ByVal attributes() As Attribute _
) As PropertyDescriptorCollection
[C#]
public static PropertyDescriptorCollection GetProperties(
   Type componentType,
   Attribute[] attributes
);
[C++]
public: static PropertyDescriptorCollection* GetProperties(
   Type* componentType,
   Attribute* attributes[]
);
[JScript]
public static function GetProperties(
   componentType : Type,
   attributes : Attribute[]
) : PropertyDescriptorCollection;
```

Parameters

componentType
A **Type** that represents the component to get properties for.

attributes
An array of type **Attribute** to use as a filter.

Return Value

A **PropertyDescriptorCollection** with the properties that match the specified attributes for this type of component.

Remarks

Call this version of this method only when you do not have an instance of the object.

The *attributes* parameter array can have a mix of **Type** and **Attribute** objects. Filtering is defined by the following rules:

- A **Type** object is treated as a wildcard; it matches any property that has the **Type** in its set of attributes.
- If a property does not have an **Attribute** of the same class, the property is not included in the returned array.
- If the attribute is an instance of **Attribute**, the property must be an exact match or it is not included in the returned array.
- If an **Attribute** instance is specified and it is the default property, it is included in the returned array even if there is no instance of the **Attribute** in the property.

Requirements

Platforms: Windows 98, Windows NT 4.0,
Windows Millennium Edition, Windows 2000,
Windows XP Home Edition, Windows XP Professional,
Windows Server 2003 family

TypeDescriptor.GetProperties Method (Object, Attribute[], Boolean)

Gets the collection of properties for a specified component using a specified array of attributes as a filter and using a custom type descriptor.

```
[Visual Basic]
Overloads Public Shared Function GetProperties( _
   ByVal component As Object, _
   ByVal attributes() As Attribute, _
   ByVal noCustomTypeDesc As Boolean _
) As PropertyDescriptorCollection
[C#]
public static PropertyDescriptorCollection GetProperties(
   object component,
   Attribute[] attributes,
   bool noCustomTypeDesc
);
[C++]
public: static PropertyDescriptorCollection* GetProperties(
   Object* component,
   Attribute* attributes[],
   bool noCustomTypeDesc
);
[JScript]
public static function GetProperties(
   component : Object,
   attributes : Attribute[],
   noCustomTypeDesc : Boolean
) : PropertyDescriptorCollection;
```

Parameters

component
A component to get the properties for.

attributes
An array of type **Attribute** to use as a filter.

noCustomTypeDesc
true if an instance of **ICustomTypeDescriptor** calls **TypeDescriptor**; otherwise, **false**.

Return Value

A **PropertyDescriptorCollection** with the events that match the specified attributes for the specified component.

Exceptions

Exception Type	Condition
ArgumentNull-Exception	The *component* parameter is a null reference (**Nothing** in Visual Basic).

Remarks

The properties for a component can differ from the properties of a class, because the site can add or remove properties if the component is sited.

The *attributes* array can have a mix of **Type** and **Attribute** objects. Filtering is defined by the following rules:

- A **Type** object is treated as a wildcard; it matches any property that has the **Type** in its set of attributes.
- If a property does not have an **Attribute** of the same class, the property is not included in the returned array.
- If the attribute is an instance of **Attribute**, the property must be an exact match or it is not included in the returned array.
- If a **Attribute** instance is specified and it is the default property, it is included in the returned array even if there is no instance of the **Attribute** in the property.

Requirements

Platforms: Windows 98, Windows NT 4.0, Windows Millennium Edition, Windows 2000, Windows XP Home Edition, Windows XP Professional, Windows Server 2003 family

TypeDescriptor.Refresh Method

Clears the properties and events from the cache.

Overload List

Clears the properties and events for the specified assembly from the cache.

[Visual Basic] **Overloads Public Shared Sub Refresh(Assembly)**

[C#] **public static void Refresh(Assembly);**

[C++] **public: static void Refresh(Assembly*);**

[JScript] **public static function Refresh(Assembly);**

Clears the properties and events for the specified module from the cache.

[Visual Basic] **Overloads Public Shared Sub Refresh(Module)**

[C#] **public static void Refresh(Module);**

[C++] **public: static void Refresh(Module*);**

[JScript] **public static function Refresh(Module);**

Clears the properties and events for the specified component from the cache.

[Visual Basic] **Overloads Public Shared Sub Refresh(Object)**

[C#] **public static void Refresh(object);**

[C++] **public: static void Refresh(Object*);**

[JScript] **public static function Refresh(Object);**

Clears the properties and events for the specified type of component from the cache.

[Visual Basic] **Overloads Public Shared Sub Refresh(Type)**

[C#] **public static void Refresh(Type);**

[C++] **public: static void Refresh(Type*);**

[JScript] **public static function Refresh(Type);**

Example

For an example on using this method, see the sample in **RefreshEventHandler**.

TypeDescriptor.Refresh Method (Assembly)

Clears the properties and events for the specified assembly from the cache.

```
[Visual Basic]
Overloads Public Shared Sub Refresh( _
   ByVal assembly As Assembly _
)
[C#]
public static void Refresh(
   Assembly assembly
);
```

```
[C++]
public: static void Refresh(
   Assembly* assembly
);
[JScript]
public static function Refresh(
   assembly : Assembly
);
```

Parameters

assembly

The **Assembly** that represents the assembly to refresh. Each **Type** in this assembly will be refreshed.

Remarks

Properties and events are cached by **TypeDescriptor** for speed. Typically, they are constant for the lifetime of an object. However, extender providers and designers can change the set of properties on an object. If they do, they can call this method to clear the property and event descriptors of the object. This method is used only at design time. It is not used during run time.

Before you make a call to **Refresh** to clear the cache, you need to call **GetProperties** for the specific assembly to cache the information first.

This method also raises a **Refreshed** event to notify all classes that want to be notified when the property set of a component changes.

Requirements

Platforms: Windows 98, Windows NT 4.0, Windows Millennium Edition, Windows 2000, Windows XP Home Edition, Windows XP Professional, Windows Server 2003 family

TypeDescriptor.Refresh Method (Module)

Clears the properties and events for the specified module from the cache.

```
[Visual Basic]
Overloads Public Shared Sub Refresh( _
   ByVal module As Module _
)
[C#]
public static void Refresh(
   Module module
);
[C++]
public: static void Refresh(
   Module* module
);
[JScript]
public static function Refresh(
   module : Module
);
```

Parameters

module

The **Module** that represents the module to refresh. Each **Type** in this module will be refreshed.

Remarks

Properties and events are cached by **TypeDescriptor** for speed. Typically, they are constant for the lifetime of an object. However, extender providers and designers can change the set of properties on an object. If they do, they can call this method to clear the property and event descriptors of the object. This method is used only at design time. It is not used during run time.

Before you make a call to **Refresh** to clear the cache, you need to call **GetProperties** for the specific module to cache the information first.

This method also raises a **Refreshed** event to notify all classes that want to be notified when the property set of a component changes.

Requirements

Platforms: Windows 98, Windows NT 4.0, Windows Millennium Edition, Windows 2000, Windows XP Home Edition, Windows XP Professional, Windows Server 2003 family

TypeDescriptor.Refresh Method (Object)

Clears the properties and events for the specified component from the cache.

```
[Visual Basic]
Overloads Public Shared Sub Refresh( _
   ByVal component As Object _
)
[C#]
public static void Refresh(
   object component
);
[C++]
public: static void Refresh(
   Object* component
);
[JScript]
public static function Refresh(
   component : Object
);
```

Parameters

component

A component the properties or events of which have changed.

Remarks

Properties and events are cached by **TypeDescriptor** for speed. Typically, they are constant for the lifetime of an object. However, extender providers and designers can change the set of properties on an object. If they do, they should call this method to clear the property and event descriptors of the object. This method is used only at design time. It is not used during run time.

This method also raises a **Refreshed** event when the properties or events of a component change. This event is only raised if there was a prior call to **GetProperties** or **GetEvents** that cached the information.

Example

For an example on using this method, see the sample in **RefreshEventHandler**.

Requirements

Platforms: Windows 98, Windows NT 4.0, Windows Millennium Edition, Windows 2000, Windows XP Home Edition, Windows XP Professional, Windows Server 2003 family

TypeDescriptor.Refresh Method (Type)

Clears the properties and events for the specified type of component from the cache.

```
[Visual Basic]
Overloads Public Shared Sub Refresh( _
   ByVal type As Type _
)
[C#]
public static void Refresh(
   Type type
);
[C++]
public: static void Refresh(
   Type* type
);
[JScript]
public static function Refresh(
   type : Type
);
```

Parameters

type

A **Type** that represents the type with properties or events that have changed.

Remarks

Call this version of this method only when you do not have an instance of the object.

Properties and events are cached by **TypeDescriptor** for speed. Typically, they are constant for the lifetime of an object. However, extender providers and designers can change the set of properties on an object. If they do, they can call this method to clear the property and event descriptorsof the object. This method is used only at design time. It is not used during run time.

This method also raises a **Refreshed** event when the properties or events of a component change. This event is only raised if there was a prior call to **GetProperties** or **GetEvents** that cached the information.

Requirements

Platforms: Windows 98, Windows NT 4.0, Windows Millennium Edition, Windows 2000, Windows XP Home Edition, Windows XP Professional, Windows Server 2003 family

TypeDescriptor.SortDescriptorArray Method

Sorts descriptors by name of the descriptor.

```
[Visual Basic]
Public Shared Sub SortDescriptorArray( _
   ByVal infos As IList _
)
[C#]
public static void SortDescriptorArray(
   IList infos
);
[C++]
public: static void SortDescriptorArray(
   IList* infos
);
[JScript]
public static function SortDescriptorArray(
   infos : IList
);
```

Parameters

infos

An **IList** that contains the descriptors to sort.

Requirements

Platforms: Windows 98, Windows NT 4.0, Windows Millennium Edition, Windows 2000, Windows XP Home Edition, Windows XP Professional, Windows Server 2003 family

TypeDescriptor.Refreshed Event

Occurs when the **Refreshed** event is raised for a component.

```
[Visual Basic]
Public Shared Event Refreshed As RefreshEventHandler
[C#]
public static event RefreshEventHandler Refreshed;
[C++]
public: static __event RefreshEventHandler* Refreshed;
```

[JScript] In JScript, you can handle the events defined by a class, but you cannot define your own.

Event Data

The event handler receives an argument of type **RefreshEventArgs** containing data related to this event. The following **RefreshEventArgs** properties provide information specific to this event.

Property	Description
ComponentChanged	Gets the component that changed its properties, events, or extenders.
TypeChanged	Gets the **Type** that changed its properties or events.

Example

For an example on using this event, see the sample in **RefreshEventHandler**.

Requirements

Platforms: Windows 98, Windows NT 4.0, Windows Millennium Edition, Windows 2000, Windows XP Home Edition, Windows XP Professional, Windows Server 2003 family

TypeListConverter Class

Provides a type converter that can be used to populate a list box with available types.

System.Object
  System.ComponentModel.TypeConverter
    System.ComponentModel.TypeListConverter

```
[Visual Basic]
MustInherit Public Class TypeListConverter
   Inherits TypeConverter
[C#]
public abstract class TypeListConverter : TypeConverter
[C++]
public __gc __abstract class TypeListConverter : public
   TypeConverter
[JScript]
public abstract class TypeListConverter extends TypeConverter
```

Thread Safety

Any public static (**Shared** in Visual Basic) members of this type are safe for multithreaded operations. Any instance members are not guaranteed to be thread safe.

Remarks

You must provide the list of types to the constructor of this abstract (**MustInherit** in Visual Basic) class.

For more information about type converters, see the **TypeConverter** base class and **Implementing a Type Converter**.

> **Note** You should never create an instance of a **TypeListConverter**. Instead, call the **GetConverter** method of **TypeDescriptor**. For more information, see the examples in the **TypeConverter** base class.

Notes to Inheritors: When you inherit from **TypeListConverter**, you can override the following methods:

- To support custom type conversion, override the following methods: **CanConvertFrom**, **CanConvertTo**, **ConvertFrom**, and **ConvertTo**.
- To convert types that must re-create the object to change its value, override **CreateInstance** and **GetCreateInstanceSupported**.
- To convert types that support properties, override **GetProperties** and **GetPropertiesSupported**. If the class you are converting does not have properties, and you need to implement properties, you can use the **TypeConverter.SimplePropertyDescriptor** class as a base for implementing the property descriptors. When you inherit from **TypeConverter.SimplePropertyDescriptor**, you must override the **GetValue** and **SetValue** methods.
- To convert types that support standard values, override **GetStandardValues**, **GetStandardValuesExclusive**, **GetStandardValuesSupported** and **IsValid**.

Requirements

Namespace: System.ComponentModel

Platforms: Windows 98, Windows NT 4.0, Windows Millennium Edition, Windows 2000, Windows XP Home Edition, Windows XP Professional, Windows Server 2003 family

Assembly: System (in System.dll)

TypeListConverter Constructor

This member supports the .NET Framework infrastructure and is not intended to be used directly from your code.

```
[Visual Basic]
Protected Sub New( _
   ByVal types() As Type _
)
[C#]
protected TypeListConverter(
   Type[] types
);
[C++]
protected: TypeListConverter(
   Type* types[]
);
[JScript]
protected function TypeListConverter(
   types : Type[]
);
```

TypeListConverter.CanConvertFrom Method

Overload List

This member supports the .NET Framework infrastructure and is not intended to be used directly from your code.

[Visual Basic] **Overloads Overrides Public Function CanConvertFrom(ITypeDescriptorContext, Type) As Boolean**

[C#] **public override bool CanConvertFrom(ITypeDescriptorContext, Type);**

[C++] **public: bool CanConvertFrom(ITypeDescriptorContext*, Type*);**

[JScript] **public override function CanConvertFrom(ITypeDescriptorContext, Type) : Boolean;**

Inherited from **TypeConverter**.

[Visual Basic] **Overloads Public Function CanConvertFrom(Type) As Boolean**

[C#] **public bool CanConvertFrom(Type);**

[C++] **public: bool CanConvertFrom(Type*);**

[JScript] **public function CanConvertFrom(Type) : Boolean;**

TypeListConverter.CanConvertFrom Method (ITypeDescriptorContext, Type)

This member overrides **TypeConverter.CanConvertFrom**.

```
[Visual Basic]
Overrides Overloads Public Function CanConvertFrom( _
   ByVal context As ITypeDescriptorContext, _
   ByVal sourceType As Type _
) As Boolean
[C#]
public override bool CanConvertFrom(
   ITypeDescriptorContext context,
   Type sourceType
);
[C++]
public: bool CanConvertFrom(
   ITypeDescriptorContext* context,
   Type* sourceType
);
```

```
[JScript]
public override function CanConvertFrom(
   context : ITypeDescriptorContext,
   sourceType : Type
) : Boolean;
```

Requirements

Platforms: Windows 98, Windows NT 4.0, Windows Millennium Edition, Windows 2000, Windows XP Home Edition, Windows XP Professional, Windows Server 2003 family

TypeListConverter.CanConvertTo Method

Overload List

This member supports the .NET Framework infrastructure and is not intended to be used directly from your code.

[Visual Basic] **Overloads Overrides Public Function CanConvertTo(ITypeDescriptorContext, Type) As Boolean**

[C#] **public override bool CanConvertTo(ITypeDescriptorContext, Type);**

[C++] **public: bool CanConvertTo(ITypeDescriptorContext*, Type*);**

[JScript] **public override function CanConvertTo(ITypeDescriptorContext, Type) : Boolean;**

Inherited from **TypeConverter**.

[Visual Basic] **Overloads Public Function CanConvertTo(Type) As Boolean**

[C#] **public bool CanConvertTo(Type);**

[C++] **public: bool CanConvertTo(Type*);**

[JScript] **public function CanConvertTo(Type) : Boolean;**

TypeListConverter.CanConvertTo Method (ITypeDescriptorContext, Type)

This member overrides **TypeConverter.CanConvertTo**.

```
[Visual Basic]
Overrides Overloads Public Function CanConvertTo( _
   ByVal context As ITypeDescriptorContext, _
   ByVal destinationType As Type _
) As Boolean
[C#]
public override bool CanConvertTo(
   ITypeDescriptorContext context,
   Type destinationType
);
[C++]
public: bool CanConvertTo(
   ITypeDescriptorContext* context,
   Type* destinationType
);
[JScript]
public override function CanConvertTo(
   context : ITypeDescriptorContext,
   destinationType : Type
) : Boolean;
```

Requirements

Platforms: Windows 98, Windows NT 4.0, Windows Millennium Edition, Windows 2000, Windows XP Home Edition, Windows XP Professional, Windows Server 2003 family

TypeListConverter.ConvertFrom Method

Overload List

This member supports the .NET Framework infrastructure and is not intended to be used directly from your code.

[Visual Basic] **Overloads Overrides Public Function ConvertFrom(ITypeDescriptorContext, CultureInfo, Object) As Object**

[C#] **public override object ConvertFrom(ITypeDescriptorContext, CultureInfo, object);**

[C++] **public: Object* ConvertFrom(ITypeDescriptorContext*, CultureInfo*, Object*);**

[JScript] **public override function ConvertFrom(ITypeDescriptorContext, CultureInfo, Object) : Object;**

Inherited from **TypeConverter**.

[Visual Basic] **Overloads Public Function ConvertFrom(Object) As Object**

[C#] **public object ConvertFrom(object);**

[C++] **public: Object* ConvertFrom(Object*);**

[JScript] **public function ConvertFrom(Object) : Object;**

TypeListConverter.ConvertFrom Method (ITypeDescriptorContext, CultureInfo, Object)

This member overrides **TypeConverter.ConvertFrom**.

```
[Visual Basic]
Overrides Overloads Public Function ConvertFrom( _
   ByVal context As ITypeDescriptorContext, _
   ByVal culture As CultureInfo, _
   ByVal value As Object _
) As Object
[C#]
public override object ConvertFrom(
   ITypeDescriptorContext context,
   CultureInfo culture,
   object value
);
[C++]
public: Object* ConvertFrom(
   ITypeDescriptorContext* context,
   CultureInfo* culture,
   Object* value
);
[JScript]
public override function ConvertFrom(
   context : ITypeDescriptorContext,
   culture : CultureInfo,
   value : Object
) : Object;
```

Requirements

Platforms: Windows 98, Windows NT 4.0, Windows Millennium Edition, Windows 2000, Windows XP Home Edition, Windows XP Professional, Windows Server 2003 family

TypeListConverter.ConvertTo Method

Overload List

This member supports the .NET Framework infrastructure and is not intended to be used directly from your code.

[Visual Basic] **Overloads Overrides Public Function ConvertTo(ITypeDescriptorContext, CultureInfo, Object, Type) As Object**

[C#] **public override object ConvertTo(ITypeDescriptorContext, CultureInfo, object, Type);**

[C++] **public: Object* ConvertTo(ITypeDescriptorContext*, CultureInfo*, Object*, Type*);**

[JScript] **public override function ConvertTo(ITypeDescriptorContext, CultureInfo, Object, Type) : Object;**

Inherited from **TypeConverter**.

[Visual Basic] **Overloads Public Function ConvertTo(Object, Type) As Object**

[C#] **public object ConvertTo(object, Type);**

[C++] **public: Object* ConvertTo(Object*, Type*);**

[JScript] **public function ConvertTo(Object, Type) : Object;**

TypeListConverter.ConvertTo Method (ITypeDescriptorContext, CultureInfo, Object, Type)

This member overrides **TypeConverter.ConvertTo**.

[Visual Basic]
```
Overrides Overloads Public Function ConvertTo( _
   ByVal context As ITypeDescriptorContext, _
   ByVal culture As CultureInfo, _
   ByVal value As Object, _
   ByVal destinationType As Type _
) As Object
```
[C#]
```
public override object ConvertTo(
   ITypeDescriptorContext context,
   CultureInfo culture,
   object value,
   Type destinationType
);
```
[C++]
```
public: Object* ConvertTo(
   ITypeDescriptorContext* context,
   CultureInfo* culture,
   Object* value,
   Type* destinationType
);
```
[JScript]
```
public override function ConvertTo(
   context : ITypeDescriptorContext,
   culture : CultureInfo,
   value : Object,
   destinationType : Type
) : Object;
```

Requirements

Platforms: Windows 98, Windows NT 4.0, Windows Millennium Edition, Windows 2000, Windows XP Home Edition, Windows XP Professional, Windows Server 2003 family

TypeListConverter.GetStandardValues Method

Overload List

This member supports the .NET Framework infrastructure and is not intended to be used directly from your code.

[Visual Basic] **Overloads Overrides Public Function GetStandardValues(ITypeDescriptorContext) As StandardValuesCollection**

[C#] **public override StandardValuesCollection GetStandardValues(ITypeDescriptorContext);**

[C++] **public: StandardValuesCollection* GetStandardValues(ITypeDescriptorContext*);**

[JScript] **public override function GetStandardValues(ITypeDescriptorContext) : StandardValuesCollection;**

Inherited from **TypeConverter**.

[Visual Basic] **Overloads Public Function GetStandardValues() As ICollection**

[C#] **public ICollection GetStandardValues();**

[C++] **public: ICollection* GetStandardValues();**

[JScript] **public function GetStandardValues() : ICollection;**

TypeListConverter.GetStandardValues Method (ITypeDescriptorContext)

This member overrides **TypeConverter.GetStandardValues**.

[Visual Basic]
```
Overrides Overloads Public Function GetStandardValues( _
   ByVal context As ITypeDescriptorContext _
) As StandardValuesCollection
```
[C#]
```
public override StandardValuesCollection GetStandardValues(
   ITypeDescriptorContext context
);
```
[C++]
```
public: StandardValuesCollection* GetStandardValues(
   ITypeDescriptorContext* context
);
```
[JScript]
```
public override function GetStandardValues(
   context : ITypeDescriptorContext
) : StandardValuesCollection;
```

Requirements

Platforms: Windows 98, Windows NT 4.0, Windows Millennium Edition, Windows 2000, Windows XP Home Edition, Windows XP Professional, Windows Server 2003 family

TypeListConverter.GetStandardValuesExclusive Method

Overload List

This member supports the .NET Framework infrastructure and is not intended to be used directly from your code.

[Visual Basic] **Overloads Overrides Public Function GetStandardValuesExclusive(ITypeDescriptorContext) As Boolean**

[C#] **public override bool GetStandardValues-Exclusive(ITypeDescriptorContext);**

[C++] **public: bool GetStandardValues-Exclusive(ITypeDescriptorContext*);**

[JScript] **public override function GetStandardValues-Exclusive(ITypeDescriptorContext) : Boolean;**

Inherited from **TypeConverter**.

[Visual Basic] **Overloads Public Function GetStandardValuesExclusive() As Boolean**

[C#] **public bool GetStandardValuesExclusive();**

[C++] **public: bool GetStandardValuesExclusive();**

[JScript] **public function GetStandardValuesExclusive() : Boolean;**

TypeListConverter.GetStandardValuesExclusive Method (ITypeDescriptorContext)

This member overrides **TypeConverter.GetStandardValuesExclusive**.

```
[Visual Basic]
Overrides Overloads Public Function GetStandardValuesExclusive( _
   ByVal context As ITypeDescriptorContext _
) As Boolean
[C#]
public override bool GetStandardValuesExclusive(
   ITypeDescriptorContext context
);
[C++]
public: bool GetStandardValuesExclusive(
   ITypeDescriptorContext* context
);
[JScript]
public override function GetStandardValuesExclusive(
   context : ITypeDescriptorContext
) : Boolean;
```

Requirements

Platforms: Windows 98, Windows NT 4.0, Windows Millennium Edition, Windows 2000, Windows XP Home Edition, Windows XP Professional, Windows Server 2003 family

TypeListConverter.GetStandardValuesSupported Method

Overload List

This member supports the .NET Framework infrastructure and is not intended to be used directly from your code.

[Visual Basic] **Overloads Overrides Public Function GetStandardValuesSupported(ITypeDescriptorContext) As Boolean**

[C#] **public override bool GetStandardValues-Supported(ITypeDescriptorContext);**

[C++] **public: bool GetStandardValues-Supported(ITypeDescriptorContext*);**

[JScript] **public override function GetStandardValues-Supported(ITypeDescriptorContext) : Boolean;**

Inherited from **TypeConverter**.

[Visual Basic] **Overloads Public Function GetStandardValuesSupported() As Boolean**

[C#] **public bool GetStandardValuesSupported();**

[C++] **public: bool GetStandardValuesSupported();**

[JScript] **public function GetStandardValuesSupported() : Boolean;**

TypeListConverter.GetStandardValuesSupported Method (ITypeDescriptorContext)

This member overrides **TypeConverter.GetStandardValuesSupported**.

```
[Visual Basic]
Overrides Overloads Public Function GetStandardValuesSupported( _
   ByVal context As ITypeDescriptorContext _
) As Boolean
[C#]
public override bool GetStandardValuesSupported(
   ITypeDescriptorContext context
);
[C++]
public: bool GetStandardValuesSupported(
   ITypeDescriptorContext* context
);
[JScript]
public override function GetStandardValuesSupported(
   context : ITypeDescriptorContext
) : Boolean;
```

Requirements

Platforms: Windows 98, Windows NT 4.0, Windows Millennium Edition, Windows 2000, Windows XP Home Edition, Windows XP Professional, Windows Server 2003 family

UInt16Converter Class

Provides a type converter to convert 16-bit unsigned integer objects to and from other representations.

System.Object
  System.ComponentModel.TypeConverter
    System.ComponentModel.BaseNumberConverter
      System.ComponentModel.UInt16Converter

[Visual Basic]
```
Public Class UInt16Converter
   Inherits BaseNumberConverter
```
[C#]
```
public class UInt16Converter : BaseNumberConverter
```
[C++]
```
public __gc class UInt16Converter : public BaseNumberConverter
```
[JScript]
```
public class UInt16Converter extends BaseNumberConverter
```

Thread Safety

Any public static (**Shared** in Visual Basic) members of this type are safe for multithreaded operations. Any instance members are not guaranteed to be thread safe.

Remarks

This converter can only convert a 16-bit unsigned integer object to and from a string.

The **UInt16** value type represents unsigned integers with values ranging from 0 to 65535. This data type is not supported in Visual Basic.

> **Note** You should never create an instance of a **UInt16Converter**. Instead, call the **GetConverter** method of **TypeDescriptor**.

Example

[Visual Basic, C#, C++] The following example converts a variable of type **UInt16** to a string and vice versa.

[Visual Basic]
```
'This data type is not supported in Visual Basic.
```

[C#]
```
ushort myUInt16 = 10000;
string myUInt16String = "20000";
Console.WriteLine(TypeDescriptor.GetConverter(myUInt16).ConvertTo
 (myUInt16, typeof(string)));
Console.WriteLine(TypeDescriptor.GetConverter
 (myUInt16).ConvertFrom(myUInt16String));
```

[C++]
```
unsigned short myUInt16( 10000 );
String* myUInt16String = S"20000";
Console::WriteLine(TypeDescriptor::GetConverter
 (__box(myUInt16))->ConvertTo(__box(myUInt16), __typeof(String)));
Console::WriteLine(TypeDescriptor::GetConverter
 (__box(myUInt16))->ConvertFrom(myUInt16String));
```

Requirements

Namespace: System.ComponentModel

Platforms: Windows 98, Windows NT 4.0, Windows Millennium Edition, Windows 2000, Windows XP Home Edition, Windows XP Professional, Windows Server 2003 family

Assembly: System (in System.dll)

UInt16Converter Constructor

Initializes a new instance of the **UInt16Converter** class.

[Visual Basic]
```
Public Sub New()
```
[C#]
```
public UInt16Converter();
```
[C++]
```
public: UInt16Converter();
```
[JScript]
```
public function UInt16Converter();
```

Remarks

The default constructor initializes any fields to their default values.

Requirements

Platforms: Windows 98, Windows NT 4.0, Windows Millennium Edition, Windows 2000, Windows XP Home Edition, Windows XP Professional, Windows Server 2003 family

UInt32Converter Class

Provides a type converter to convert 32-bit unsigned integer objects to and from various other representations.

System.Object
  System.ComponentModel.TypeConverter
    System.ComponentModel.BaseNumberConverter
      System.ComponentModel.UInt32Converter

[Visual Basic]
```
Public Class UInt32Converter
   Inherits BaseNumberConverter
```
[C#]
```
public class UInt32Converter : BaseNumberConverter
```
[C++]
```
public __gc class UInt32Converter : public BaseNumberConverter
```
[JScript]
```
public class UInt32Converter extends BaseNumberConverter
```

Thread Safety

Any public static (**Shared** in Visual Basic) members of this type are safe for multithreaded operations. Any instance members are not guaranteed to be thread safe.

Remarks

This converter can only convert a 32-bit unsigned integer object to and from a string.

The **UInt32** value type represents unsigned integers with values ranging from 0 to 4,294,967,295. This data type is not supported in Visual Basic.

> **Note** You should never create an instance of a **UInt32Converter**. Instead, call the **GetConverter** method of **TypeDescriptor**. For more information, see the examples in the **TypeConverter** base class and **Implementing a Type Converter**.

Example

[Visual Basic, C#, C++] The following example converts a variable of type **UInt32** to a string, and vice versa.

[Visual Basic]
```
'This data type is not supported in Visual Basic.
   . . .
'This data type is not supported in Visual Basic.
```

[C#]
```
uint myUInt32 = 967299;
string myUInt32String = "1345556";
Console.WriteLine(TypeDescriptor.GetConverter                    ↵
(myUInt32).ConvertTo(myUInt32, typeof(string)));
Console.WriteLine(TypeDescriptor.GetConverter                    ↵
 (myUInt32).ConvertFrom(myUInt32String));
   . . .
uint myUInt32 = 967299;
string myUInt32String = "1345556";
Console.WriteLine(TypeDescriptor.GetConverter                    ↵
 (myUInt32).ConvertTo(myUInt32, typeof(string)));
Console.WriteLine(TypeDescriptor.GetConverter                    ↵
 (myUInt32).ConvertFrom(myUInt32String));
```

[C++]
```
unsigned int myUInt32( 967299 );
String* myUInt32String = S"1345556";
Console::WriteLine(TypeDescriptor::GetConverter                  ↵
 (__box(myUInt32))->ConvertTo(__box(myUInt32), __typeof(String)));
Console::WriteLine(TypeDescriptor::GetConverter                  ↵
 (__box(myUInt32))->ConvertFrom(myUInt32String));
   . . .
unsigned int myUInt32( 967299 );
String* myUInt32String = S"1345556";
Console::WriteLine(TypeDescriptor::GetConverter                  ↵
 (__box(myUInt32))->ConvertTo(__box(myUInt32), __typeof(String)));
Console::WriteLine(TypeDescriptor::GetConverter                  ↵
 (__box(myUInt32))->ConvertFrom(myUInt32String));
```

Requirements

Namespace: System.ComponentModel

Platforms: Windows 98, Windows NT 4.0, Windows Millennium Edition, Windows 2000, Windows XP Home Edition, Windows XP Professional, Windows Server 2003 family

Assembly: System (in System.dll)

UInt32Converter Constructor

Initializes a new instance of the **UInt32Converter** class.

[Visual Basic]
```
Public Sub New()
```
[C#]
```
public UInt32Converter();
```
[C++]
```
public: UInt32Converter();
```
[JScript]
```
public function UInt32Converter();
```

Remarks

The default constructor initializes any fields to their default values.

Requirements

Platforms: Windows 98, Windows NT 4.0, Windows Millennium Edition, Windows 2000, Windows XP Home Edition, Windows XP Professional, Windows Server 2003 family

UInt64Converter Class

Provides a type converter to convert 64-bit unsigned integer objects to and from other representations.

System.Object
  System.ComponentModel.TypeConverter
    System.ComponentModel.BaseNumberConverter
      System.ComponentModel.UInt64Converter

[Visual Basic]
```
Public Class UInt64Converter
   Inherits BaseNumberConverter
```
[C#]
```
public class UInt64Converter : BaseNumberConverter
```
[C++]
```
public __gc class UInt64Converter : public BaseNumberConverter
```
[JScript]
```
public class UInt64Converter extends BaseNumberConverter
```

Thread Safety

Any public static (**Shared** in Visual Basic) members of this type are safe for multithreaded operations. Any instance members are not guaranteed to be thread safe.

Remarks

This converter can only convert a 64-bit unsigned integer object to and from a string.

The **UInt64** value type represents unsigned integers with values ranging from 0 to 184,467,440,737,095,551,615. This data type is not supported in Visual Basic.

> **Note** You should never create an instance of a **UInt64Converter**. Instead, call the **GetConverter** method of **TypeDescriptor**.

Example

[Visual Basic, C#, C++] The following example converts a variable of type **UInt64** to a string, and vice versa.

[Visual Basic]
```
'This data type is not supported in Visual Basic.
   . . .
'This data type is not supported in Visual Basic.
```

[C#]
```
ulong myUInt64 = 123456789123;
string myUInt64String = "184467440737095551";
Console.WriteLine(TypeDescriptor.GetConverter
(myUInt64).ConvertTo(myUInt64, typeof(string)));
Console.WriteLine(TypeDescriptor.GetConverter
 (myUInt64).ConvertFrom(myUInt64String));
   . . .
ulong myUInt64 = 123456789123;
string myUInt64String = "184467440737095551";
Console.WriteLine(TypeDescriptor.GetConverter
 (myUInt64).ConvertTo(myUInt64, typeof(string)));
Console.WriteLine(TypeDescriptor.GetConverter
 (myUInt64).ConvertFrom(myUInt64String));
```

[C++]
```
UInt64 myUInt64( 123456789123 );
String* myUInt64String = S"184467440737095551";
Console::WriteLine(TypeDescriptor::GetConverter
 (__box(myUInt64))->ConvertTo(__box(myUInt64), __typeof(String)));
Console::WriteLine(TypeDescriptor::GetConverter
 (__box(myUInt64))->ConvertFrom(myUInt64String));
   . . .
UInt64 myUInt64( 123456789123 );
String* myUInt64String = S"184467440737095551";
Console::WriteLine(TypeDescriptor::GetConverter
 (__box(myUInt64))->ConvertTo(__box(myUInt64), __typeof(String)));
Console::WriteLine(TypeDescriptor::GetConverter
 (__box(myUInt64))->ConvertFrom(myUInt64String));
```

Requirements

Namespace: System.ComponentModel

Platforms: Windows 98, Windows NT 4.0, Windows Millennium Edition, Windows 2000, Windows XP Home Edition, Windows XP Professional, Windows Server 2003 family

Assembly: System (in System.dll)

UInt64Converter Constructor

Initializes a new instance of the **UInt64Converter** class.

[Visual Basic]
```
Public Sub New()
```
[C#]
```
public UInt64Converter();
```
[C++]
```
public: UInt64Converter();
```
[JScript]
```
public function UInt64Converter();
```

Remarks

The default constructor initializes any fields to their default values.

Requirements

Platforms: Windows 98, Windows NT 4.0, Windows Millennium Edition, Windows 2000, Windows XP Home Edition, Windows XP Professional, Windows Server 2003 family

WarningException Class

Specifies an exception that is handled as a warning instead of an error.

System.Object
  System.Exception
    System.SystemException
      System.ComponentModel.WarningException

```
[Visual Basic]
Public Class WarningException
   Inherits SystemException
[C#]
public class WarningException : SystemException
[C++]
public __gc class WarningException : public SystemException
[JScript]
public class WarningException extends SystemException
```

Thread Safety

Any public static (**Shared** in Visual Basic) members of this type are safe for multithreaded operations. Any instance members are not guaranteed to be thread safe.

Remarks

If this exception is not caught, it is presented to the user as a warning message. In the **WarningException** constructor, you can specify the Help file and Help topic to display if the user requests more information.

Example

[Visual Basic, C#, C++] The following example shows how to catch a warning and interpret its warning message.

```
[Visual Basic]
Dim myEx As New WarningException("This is a warning")
Console.WriteLine(myEx.Message)
Console.WriteLine(myEx.ToString())

[C#]
WarningException myEx=new WarningException("This is a warning");
Console.WriteLine(myEx.Message);
Console.WriteLine(myEx.ToString());

[C++]
WarningException* myEx = new WarningException(S"This is a warning");
Console::WriteLine(myEx->Message);
Console::WriteLine(myEx->ToString());
```

Requirements

Namespace: System.ComponentModel

Platforms: Windows 98, Windows NT 4.0, Windows Millennium Edition, Windows 2000, Windows XP Home Edition, Windows XP Professional, Windows Server 2003 family

Assembly: System (in System.dll)

WarningException Constructor

Initializes a new instance of the **WarningException** class.

Overload List

Initializes a new instance of the **WarningException** class with the specified message and no Help file.

[Visual Basic] **Public Sub New(String)**

[C#] **public WarningException(string);**

[C++] **public: WarningException(String*);**

[JScript] **public function WarningException(String);**

Initializes a new instance of the **WarningException** class with the specified message, and with access to the specified Help file.

[Visual Basic] **Public Sub New(String, String)**

[C#] **public WarningException(string, string);**

[C++] **public: WarningException(String*, String*);**

[JScript] **public function WarningException(String, String);**

Initializes a new instance of the **WarningException** class with the specified message, and with access to the specified Help file and topic.

[Visual Basic] **Public Sub New(String, String, String)**

[C#] **public WarningException(string, string, string);**

[C++] **public: WarningException(String*, String*, String*);**

[JScript] **public function WarningException(String, String, String);**

WarningException Constructor (String)

Initializes a new instance of the **WarningException** class with the specified message and no Help file.

```
[Visual Basic]
Public Sub New( _
   ByVal message As String _
)
[C#]
public WarningException(
   string message
);
[C++]
public: WarningException(
   String* message
);
[JScript]
public function WarningException(
   message : String
);
```

Parameters

message
  The message to display to the end user.

Requirements

Platforms: Windows 98, Windows NT 4.0, Windows Millennium Edition, Windows 2000, Windows XP Home Edition, Windows XP Professional, Windows Server 2003 family

WarningException Constructor (String, String)

Initializes a new instance of the **WarningException** class with the specified message, and with access to the specified Help file.

```
[Visual Basic]
Public Sub New( _
   ByVal message As String, _
   ByVal helpUrl As String _
)
[C#]
public WarningException(
   string message,
   string helpUrl
);
[C++]
public: WarningException(
   String* message,
   String* helpUrl
);
[JScript]
public function WarningException(
   message : String,
   helpUrl : String
);
```

Parameters

message

The message to display to the end user.

helpUrl

The Help file to display if the user requests help.

Requirements

Platforms: Windows 98, Windows NT 4.0, Windows Millennium Edition, Windows 2000, Windows XP Home Edition, Windows XP Professional, Windows Server 2003 family

WarningException Constructor (String, String, String)

Initializes a new instance of the **WarningException** class with the specified message, and with access to the specified Help file and topic.

```
[Visual Basic]
Public Sub New( _
   ByVal message As String, _
   ByVal helpUrl As String, _
   ByVal helpTopic As String _
)
[C#]
public WarningException(
   string message,
   string helpUrl,
   string helpTopic
);
[C++]
public: WarningException(
   String* message,
   String* helpUrl,
   String* helpTopic
);
[JScript]
public function WarningException(
   message : String,
   helpUrl : String,
   helpTopic : String
);
```

Parameters

message

The message to display to the end user.

helpUrl

The Help file to display if the user requests help.

helpTopic

The Help topic to display if the user requests help.

Requirements

Platforms: Windows 98, Windows NT 4.0, Windows Millennium Edition, Windows 2000, Windows XP Home Edition, Windows XP Professional, Windows Server 2003 family

WarningException.HelpTopic Property

Gets the Help topic associated with the warning.

```
[Visual Basic]
Public ReadOnly Property HelpTopic As String
[C#]
public string HelpTopic {get;}
[C++]
public: __property String* get_HelpTopic();
[JScript]
public function get HelpTopic() : String;
```

Property Value

The Help topic associated with the warning.

Requirements

Platforms: Windows 98, Windows NT 4.0, Windows Millennium Edition, Windows 2000, Windows XP Home Edition, Windows XP Professional, Windows Server 2003 family

WarningException.HelpUrl Property

Gets the Help file associated with the warning.

```
[Visual Basic]
Public ReadOnly Property HelpUrl As String
[C#]
public string HelpUrl {get;}
[C++]
public: __property String* get_HelpUrl();
[JScript]
public function get HelpUrl() : String;
```

Property Value

The Help file associated with the warning.

Requirements

Platforms: Windows 98, Windows NT 4.0, Windows Millennium Edition, Windows 2000, Windows XP Home Edition, Windows XP Professional, Windows Server 2003 family

Win32Exception Class

The exception that is thrown for a Win32 error code.

System.Object
  System.Exception
    System.SystemException
      System.Runtime.InteropServices.ExternalException
        System.ComponentModel.Win32Exception
          System.Net.Sockets.SocketException

[Visual Basic]
```
<Serializable>
Public Class Win32Exception
   Inherits ExternalException
```
[C#]
```
[Serializable]
public class Win32Exception : ExternalException
```
[C++]
```
[Serializable]
public __gc class Win32Exception : public ExternalException
```
[JScript]
```
public
   Serializable
class Win32Exception extends ExternalException
```

Thread Safety

Any public static (**Shared** in Visual Basic) members of this type are safe for multithreaded operations. Any instance members are not guaranteed to be thread safe.

Remarks

Win32 error codes are translated from their numeric representations into a system message when they are displayed. Use **NativeErrorCode** to access the numeric representation of the error code associated with this exception. For information about the error codes, see "Win32 Error Codes" in the Platform SDK or in MSDN.

Example

[Visual Basic, C#, C++] The following example shows how to catch a Win32 exception and interpret its content. The sample attempts to start a nonexisting executable which results in throwing a Win32 exception. Upon catching the exception, the sample fetches the respective error message, code, and origin of the exception.

[Visual Basic]
```
Dim myEx As New Win32Exception(-2147467259)
Console.WriteLine(myEx.Message)
Console.WriteLine(myEx.ErrorCode)
Console.WriteLine(myEx.HelpLink)
Console.WriteLine(myEx.Source)
```

[C#]
```
Win32Exception myEx=new Win32Exception(-2147467259);
Console.WriteLine(myEx.Message);
Console.WriteLine(myEx.ErrorCode);
Console.WriteLine(myEx.HelpLink);
Console.WriteLine(myEx.Source);
```

[C++]
```
Win32Exception* myEx = new Win32Exception(-2147467259);
Console::WriteLine(myEx->Message);
Console::WriteLine(myEx->ErrorCode);
Console::WriteLine(myEx->HelpLink);
Console::WriteLine(myEx->Source);
```

Requirements

Namespace: System.ComponentModel

Platforms: Windows 98, Windows NT 4.0, Windows Millennium Edition, Windows 2000, Windows XP Home Edition, Windows XP Professional, Windows Server 2003 family, .NET Compact Framework - Windows CE .NET

Assembly: System (in System.dll)

Win32Exception Constructor

Initializes a new instance of the **Win32Exception** class.

Overload List

Initializes a new instance of the **Win32Exception** class with the last Win32 error that occurred.

Supported by the .NET Compact Framework.

[Visual Basic] **Public Sub New()**

[C#] **public Win32Exception();**

[C++] **public: Win32Exception();**

[JScript] **public function Win32Exception();**

Initializes a new instance of the **Win32Exception** class with the specified error.

Supported by the .NET Compact Framework.

[Visual Basic] **Public Sub New(Integer)**

[C#] **public Win32Exception(int);**

[C++] **public: Win32Exception(int);**

[JScript] **public function Win32Exception(int);**

Initializes a new instance of the **Win32Exception** class with the specified error and the specified detailed description.

Supported by the .NET Compact Framework.

[Visual Basic] **Public Sub New(Integer, String)**

[C#] **public Win32Exception(int, string);**

[C++] **public: Win32Exception(int, String*);**

[JScript] **public function Win32Exception(int, String);**

Initializes a new instance of the **Win32Exception** class with the specified context and the serialization information.

[Visual Basic] **Protected Sub New(SerializationInfo, StreamingContext)**

[C#] **protected Win32Exception(SerializationInfo, StreamingContext);**

[C++] **protected: Win32Exception(SerializationInfo*, StreamingContext);**

[JScript] **protected function Win32-Exception(SerializationInfo, StreamingContext);**

Win32Exception Constructor ()

Initializes a new instance of the **Win32Exception** class with the last Win32 error that occurred.

[Visual Basic]
```
Public Sub New()
```
[C#]
```
public Win32Exception();
```

```
[C++]
public: Win32Exception();
[JScript]
public function Win32Exception();
```

Remarks

The detail description of the error will be determined by the Win32 error message associated with the error.

This constructor uses the **GetLastWin32Error** method of **Marshal** to get its error code.

Requirements

Platforms: Windows 98, Windows NT 4.0, Windows Millennium Edition, Windows 2000, Windows XP Home Edition, Windows XP Professional, Windows Server 2003 family, .NET Compact Framework - Windows CE .NET

Win32Exception Constructor (Int32)

Initializes a new instance of the **Win32Exception** class with the specified error.

```
[Visual Basic]
Public Sub New( _
   ByVal error As Integer _
)
[C#]
public Win32Exception(
   int error
);
[C++]
public: Win32Exception(
   int error
);
[JScript]
public function Win32Exception(
   error : int
);
```

Parameters

error
The Win32 error code associated with this exception.

Remarks

The detail description of the error is determined by the Win32 error message associated with the error.

Requirements

Platforms: Windows 98, Windows NT 4.0, Windows Millennium Edition, Windows 2000, Windows XP Home Edition, Windows XP Professional, Windows Server 2003 family, .NET Compact Framework - Windows CE .NET

Win32Exception Constructor (Int32, String)

Initializes a new instance of the **Win32Exception** class with the specified error and the specified detailed description.

```
[Visual Basic]
Public Sub New( _
   ByVal error As Integer, _
   ByVal message As String _
)
[C#]
public Win32Exception(
   int error,
   string message
);
[C++]
public: Win32Exception(
   int error,
   String* message
);
[JScript]
public function Win32Exception(
   error : int,
   message : String
);
```

Parameters

error
The Win32 error code associated with this exception.

message
A detailed description of the error.

Requirements

Platforms: Windows 98, Windows NT 4.0, Windows Millennium Edition, Windows 2000, Windows XP Home Edition, Windows XP Professional, Windows Server 2003 family, .NET Compact Framework - Windows CE .NET

Win32Exception Constructor (SerializationInfo, StreamingContext)

Initializes a new instance of the **Win32Exception** class with the specified context and the serialization information.

```
[Visual Basic]
Protected Sub New( _
   ByVal info As SerializationInfo, _
   ByVal context As StreamingContext _
)
[C#]
protected Win32Exception(
   SerializationInfo info,
   StreamingContext context
);
[C++]
protected: Win32Exception(
   SerializationInfo* info,
   StreamingContext context
);
[JScript]
protected function Win32Exception(
   info : SerializationInfo,
   context : StreamingContext
);
```

Parameters

info
The **SerializationInfo** object associated with this exception.

context
A **StreamingContext** object that represents the context of this exception.

Requirements

Platforms: Windows 98, Windows NT 4.0,
Windows Millennium Edition, Windows 2000,
Windows XP Home Edition, Windows XP Professional,
Windows Server 2003 family

Win32Exception.NativeErrorCode Property

Gets the Win32 error code associated with this exception.

[Visual Basic]
```
Public ReadOnly Property NativeErrorCode As Integer
```
[C#]
```
public int NativeErrorCode {get;}
```
[C++]
```
public: __property int get_NativeErrorCode();
```
[JScript]
```
public function get NativeErrorCode() : int;
```

Property Value

The Win32 error code associated with this exception.

Requirements

Platforms: Windows 98, Windows NT 4.0,
Windows Millennium Edition, Windows 2000,
Windows XP Home Edition, Windows XP Professional,
Windows Server 2003 family,
.NET Compact Framework - Windows CE .NET

Win32Exception.GetObjectData Method

This member overrides **Exception.GetObjectData**.

[Visual Basic]
```
Overrides Public Sub GetObjectData( _
   ByVal info As SerializationInfo, _
   ByVal context As StreamingContext _
) Implements ISerializable.GetObjectData
```
[C#]
```
public override void GetObjectData(
   SerializationInfo info,
   StreamingContext context
);
```
[C++]
```
public: void GetObjectData(
   SerializationInfo* info,
   StreamingContext context
);
```
[JScript]
```
public override function GetObjectData(
   info : SerializationInfo,
   context : StreamingContext
);
```

Requirements

Platforms: Windows 98, Windows NT 4.0,
Windows Millennium Edition, Windows 2000,
Windows XP Home Edition, Windows XP Professional,
Windows Server 2003 family

System.Component-Model.Design Namespace

The **System.ComponentModel.Design** namespace contains classes that developers can use to build custom design-time behavior for components and user interfaces for configuring components at design time. The design time environment provides systems that enable developers to arrange components and configure their properties. Some components may require specific design-time only behavior to function properly in a design time environment. It may also be valuable to provide custom user interfaces which assist developers in configuring components or the values of complex data types. The classes and interfaces defined within this namespace can be used to build design-time behavior for components, access design-time services, and implement customized design-time configuration interfaces.

The classes in this namespace include:

- A basic **IDesigner** interface that you can use to customize design-time behavior for specific types of components.
- A **ComponentDesigner** class that provides a more sophisticated designer base class which implements the **IDesigner**, **IDisposable**, and **IDesignerFilter** interfaces.
- Designer interfaces and services that enable a designer to support additional functionality, including: **IComponentChangeService**, **IDesignerEventService**, **IDesignerFilter**, **IDesignerHost**, **IDesignerOptionService**, **IDictionaryService**, **IEventBindingService**, **IExtenderListService**, **IExtenderProviderService**, **IHelpService**, **IInheritanceService**, **IMenuCommandService**, **IReferenceService**, **IResourceService**, **IRootDesigner**, **ISelectionService**, **IServiceContainer**, **ITypeDescriptorFilterService**, and **ITypeResolutionService**.
- Classes that can be used to customize design-time license context management and serialization: **DesigntimeLicenseContext** and **DesigntimeLicenseContextSerializer**.
- Simple collection editors that can be extended: **ArrayEditor** and **CollectionEditor**.

Namespace hierarchy

ActiveDesignerEventArgs Class

Provides data for the **ActiveDesigner** event.

System.Object
  System.EventArgs
    System.ComponentModel.Design.ActiveDesignerEventArgs

[Visual Basic]
```
Public Class ActiveDesignerEventArgs
   Inherits EventArgs
```
[C#]
```
public class ActiveDesignerEventArgs : EventArgs
```
[C++]
```
public __gc class ActiveDesignerEventArgs : public EventArgs
```
[JScript]
```
public class ActiveDesignerEventArgs extends EventArgs
```

Thread Safety

Any public static (**Shared** in Visual Basic) members of this type are safe for multithreaded operations. Any instance members are not guaranteed to be thread safe.

Remarks

The **ActiveDesigner** event occurs when the currently active document changes. The active document changes when a new document is created, an existing document is opened, or a document is closed.

When you create an **ActiveDesignerEventArgs** delegate, you identify the method that will handle the event. To associate the event with your event handler, add an instance of the delegate to the event. The event handler is called whenever the event occurs, unless you remove the delegate.

Example

[Visual Basic, C#, C++] The following example method returns an **ActiveDesignerEventArgs** that contains a specified reference to the **IDesignerHost** for the designer losing focus and a specified reference to the **IDesignerHost** for the designer gaining focus.

[Visual Basic]
```
Public Function CreateActiveDesignerEventArgs(ByVal losingFocus ↵
As IDesignerHost, ByVal gainingFocus As IDesignerHost) As ↵
ActiveDesignerEventArgs
    Dim e As New ActiveDesignerEventArgs(losingFocus, gainingFocus)
    Return e
End Function
```

[C#]
```
public ActiveDesignerEventArgs
CreateActiveDesignerEventArgs(IDesignerHost losingFocus, ↵
 IDesignerHost gainingFocus)
{
    ActiveDesignerEventArgs e = new ↵
ActiveDesignerEventArgs(losingFocus, gainingFocus);
    return e;
}
```

[C++]
```
ActiveDesignerEventArgs* CreateActiveDesignerEventArgs ↵
 (IDesignerHost* losingFocus, IDesignerHost* gainingFocus) {
    ActiveDesignerEventArgs* e = new ↵
ActiveDesignerEventArgs(losingFocus, gainingFocus);
    return e;
}
```

Requirements

Namespace: System.ComponentModel.Design

Platforms: Windows 98, Windows NT 4.0, Windows Millennium Edition, Windows 2000, Windows XP Home Edition, Windows XP Professional, Windows Server 2003 family

Assembly: System (in System.dll)

ActiveDesignerEventArgs Constructor

Initializes a new instance of the **ActiveDesignerEventArgs** class.

[Visual Basic]
```
Public Sub New( _
   ByVal oldDesigner As IDesignerHost, _
   ByVal newDesigner As IDesignerHost _
)
```

```
[C#]
public ActiveDesignerEventArgs(
   IDesignerHost oldDesigner,
   IDesignerHost newDesigner
);
[C++]
public: ActiveDesignerEventArgs(
   IDesignerHost* oldDesigner,
   IDesignerHost* newDesigner
);
[JScript]
public function ActiveDesignerEventArgs(
   oldDesigner : IDesignerHost,
   newDesigner : IDesignerHost
);
```

Parameters

oldDesigner
  The document that is losing activation.

newDesigner
  The document that is gaining activation.

Requirements

Platforms: Windows 98, Windows NT 4.0,
Windows Millennium Edition, Windows 2000,
Windows XP Home Edition, Windows XP Professional,
Windows Server 2003 family

ActiveDesignerEventArgs.NewDesigner Property

Gets the document that is gaining activation.

```
[Visual Basic]
Public ReadOnly Property NewDesigner As IDesignerHost
[C#]
public IDesignerHost NewDesigner {get;}
[C++]
public: __property IDesignerHost* get_NewDesigner();
[JScript]
public function get NewDesigner() : IDesignerHost;
```

Property Value

An **IDesignerHost** that represents the document gaining activation.

Requirements

Platforms: Windows 98, Windows NT 4.0,
Windows Millennium Edition, Windows 2000,
Windows XP Home Edition, Windows XP Professional,
Windows Server 2003 family

ActiveDesignerEventArgs.OldDesigner Property

Gets the document that is losing activation.

```
[Visual Basic]
Public ReadOnly Property OldDesigner As IDesignerHost
[C#]
public IDesignerHost OldDesigner {get;}
[C++]
public: __property IDesignerHost* get_OldDesigner();
[JScript]
public function get OldDesigner() : IDesignerHost;
```

Property Value

An **IDesignerHost** that represents the document losing activation.

Requirements

Platforms: Windows 98, Windows NT 4.0,
Windows Millennium Edition, Windows 2000,
Windows XP Home Edition, Windows XP Professional,
Windows Server 2003 family

ActiveDesignerEventHandler Delegate

Represents the method that will handle the **ActiveDesignerChanged** event.

[Visual Basic]
```
<Serializable>
Public Delegate Sub ActiveDesignerEventHandler( _
   ByVal sender As Object, _
   ByVal e As ActiveDesignerEventArgs _
)
```
[C#]
```
[Serializable]
public delegate void ActiveDesignerEventHandler(
   object sender,
   ActiveDesignerEventArgs e
);
```
[C++]
```
[Serializable]
public __gc __delegate void ActiveDesignerEventHandler(
   Object* sender,
   ActiveDesignerEventArgs* e
);
```

[JScript] In JScript, you can use the delegates in the .NET Framework, but you cannot define your own.

Parameters [Visual Basic, C#, C++]

The declaration of your event handler must have the same parameters as the **ActiveDesignerEventHandler** delegate declaration.

sender
: The source of the event.

e
: An **ActiveDesignerEventArgs** that contains the event data.

Remarks

The **ActiveDesignerChanged** event is raised when the currently active document has been modified.

When you create an **ActiveDesignerEventHandler** delegate, you identify the method that will handle the event. To associate the event with your event handler, add an instance of the delegate to the event. The event handler is called whenever the event occurs, unless you remove the delegate. For more information about event-handler delegates, see **Events and Delegates**.

Example

[Visual Basic, C#, C++] The following example demonstrates registering an **ActiveDesignerEventHandler** and handling an **ActiveDesignerChanged** event.

[Visual Basic]
```
Public Sub LinkActiveDesignerEvent(ByVal eventService As
IDesignerEventService)
    ' Registers an event handler for the ActiveDesignerChanged event.
    AddHandler eventService.ActiveDesignerChanged, AddressOf
Me.OnActiveDesignerEvent
End Sub

Private Sub OnActiveDesignerEvent(ByVal sender As Object, ByVal
 e As ActiveDesignerEventArgs)
    ' Displays changed designer information on the console.
    If Not (e.NewDesigner.RootComponent.Site Is Nothing) Then
        Console.WriteLine(("Name of the component of the new
 active designer: " + e.NewDesigner.RootComponent.Site.Name))
    End If
    Console.WriteLine(("Type of the component of the new
active designer: " + e.NewDesigner.RootComponentClassName))
    If Not (e.OldDesigner.RootComponent.Site Is Nothing) Then
        Console.WriteLine(("Name of the component of the
previously active designer: " + e.OldDesigner.RootComponent.Site.Name))
    End If
    Console.WriteLine(("Type of the component of the previously
 active designer: " + e.OldDesigner.RootComponentClassName))
End Sub
```

[C#]
```
public void LinkActiveDesignerEvent(IDesignerEventService eventService)
{
    // Registers an event handler for the ActiveDesignerChanged event.
    eventService.ActiveDesignerChanged += new
ActiveDesignerEventHandler(this.OnActiveDesignerEvent);
}

private void OnActiveDesignerEvent(object sender,
ActiveDesignerEventArgs e)
{
    // Displays changed designer information on the console.
    if( e.NewDesigner.RootComponent.Site != null )
        Console.WriteLine("Name of the component of the new
 active designer: "+e.NewDesigner.RootComponent.Site.Name);
    Console.WriteLine("Type of the component of the new active
designer: "+e.NewDesigner.RootComponentClassName);
    if( e.OldDesigner.RootComponent.Site != null )
        Console.WriteLine("Name of the component of the
previously active designer: "+e.OldDesigner.RootComponent.Site.Name);
    Console.WriteLine("Type of the component of the previously
 active designer: "+e.OldDesigner.RootComponentClassName);
}
```

[C++]
```
public:

    void LinkActiveDesignerEvent(IDesignerEventService* eventService)
    {
        // Registers an event handler for the
ActiveDesignerChanged event.
        eventService->ActiveDesignerChanged += new
ActiveDesignerEventHandler(this, OnActiveDesignerEvent);
    }

private:

    void OnActiveDesignerEvent(Object* sender,
ActiveDesignerEventArgs* e)
    {
        // Displays changed designer information on the console.
        if( e->NewDesigner->RootComponent->Site != 0 )
            Console::WriteLine(S"Name of the component of
 the new active designer: {0}", e->NewDesigner->RootComponent->
Site->Name);
        Console::WriteLine(S"Type of the component of the new
active designer: {0}", e->NewDesigner->RootComponentClassName);
        if( e->OldDesigner->RootComponent->Site != 0 )
            Console::WriteLine(S"Name of the component of the
previously active designer: {0}", e->OldDesigner->RootComponent->
Site->Name);
        Console::WriteLine(S"Type of the component of the
 previously active designer: {0}", e->OldDesigner-
>RootComponentClassName);
    }
```

Requirements

Namespace: System.ComponentModel.Design

Platforms: Windows 98, Windows NT 4.0, Windows Millennium Edition, Windows 2000, Windows XP Home Edition, Windows XP Professional, Windows Server 2003 family

Assembly: System (in System.dll)

ArrayEditor Class

Provides a user interface for editing arrays at design time.

System.Object
  System.Drawing.Design.UITypeEditor
    System.ComponentModel.Design.CollectionEditor
      System.ComponentModel.Design.ArrayEditor

```
[Visual Basic]
Public Class ArrayEditor
   Inherits CollectionEditor
[C#]
public class ArrayEditor : CollectionEditor
[C++]
public __gc class ArrayEditor : public CollectionEditor
[JScript]
public class ArrayEditor extends CollectionEditor
```

Thread Safety

Any public static (**Shared** in Visual Basic) members of this type are safe for multithreaded operations. Any instance members are not guaranteed to be thread safe.

Remarks

This editor can be used to edit arrays within the design-time environment.

Requirements

Namespace: System.ComponentModel.Design

Platforms: Windows 98, Windows NT 4.0, Windows Millennium Edition, Windows 2000, Windows XP Home Edition, Windows XP Professional, Windows Server 2003 family

Assembly: System.Design (in System.Design.dll)

ArrayEditor Constructor

Initializes a new instance of **ArrayEditor** using the specified data type for the array.

```
[Visual Basic]
Public Sub New( _
   ByVal type As Type _
)
[C#]
public ArrayEditor(
   Type type
);
[C++]
public: ArrayEditor(
   Type* type
);
[JScript]
public function ArrayEditor(
   type : Type
);
```

Parameters

type
    The data type of the items in the array.

Requirements

Platforms: Windows 98, Windows NT 4.0, Windows Millennium Edition, Windows 2000, Windows XP Home Edition, Windows XP Professional, Windows Server 2003 family

.NET Framework Security:

- Full trust for the immediate caller. This member cannot be used by partially trusted code.

ArrayEditor.CreateCollectionItemType Method

Gets the data type that this collection is designed to contain.

```
[Visual Basic]
Overrides Protected Function CreateCollectionItemType() As Type
[C#]
protected override Type CreateCollectionItemType();
[C++]
protected: Type* CreateCollectionItemType();
[JScript]
protected override function CreateCollectionItemType() : Type;
```

Return Value

A **Type** that indicates the data type that the collection is designed to contain.

Remarks

The default implementation returns the item type of the array.

Requirements

Platforms: Windows 98, Windows NT 4.0, Windows Millennium Edition, Windows 2000, Windows XP Home Edition, Windows XP Professional, Windows Server 2003 family

.NET Framework Security:

- Full trust for the immediate caller. This member cannot be used by partially trusted code.

ArrayEditor.GetItems Method

Gets the items in the array.

```
[Visual Basic]
Overrides Protected Function GetItems( _
   ByVal editValue As Object _
) As Object()
[C#]
protected override object[] GetItems(
   object editValue
);
[C++]
protected: Object* GetItems(
   Object* editValue
) __gc[];
[JScript]
protected override function GetItems(
   editValue : Object
) : Object[];
```

Parameters

editValue
    The array from which to retrieve the items.

Return Value

An array consisting of the items within the specified array. If the object specified in the *editValue* parameter is not an array, a new empty object is returned.

Requirements

Platforms: Windows 98, Windows NT 4.0, Windows Millennium Edition, Windows 2000, Windows XP Home Edition, Windows XP Professional, Windows Server 2003 family

.NET Framework Security:

- Full trust for the immediate caller. This member cannot be used by partially trusted code.

ArrayEditor.SetItems Method

Sets the items in the array.

[Visual Basic]

```
Overrides Protected Function SetItems( _
   ByVal editValue As Object, _
   ByVal value() As Object _
) As Object
```

[C#]

```
protected override object SetItems(
   object editValue,
   object[] value
);
```

[C++]

```
protected: Object* SetItems(
   Object* editValue,
   Object* value __gc[]
);
```

[JScript]

```
protected override function SetItems(
   editValue : Object,
   value : Object[]
) : Object;
```

Parameters

editValue
: The array to set the items to.

value
: The array of objects to set as the items of the array.

Return Value

An instance of the new array. If the object specified by the *editValue* parameter is not an array, the object specified by the *editValue* parameter is returned.

Requirements

Platforms: Windows 98, Windows NT 4.0, Windows Millennium Edition, Windows 2000, Windows XP Home Edition, Windows XP Professional, Windows Server 2003 family

.NET Framework Security:

- Full trust for the immediate caller. This member cannot be used by partially trusted code.

BinaryEditor Class

This type supports the .NET Framework infrastructure and is not intended to be used directly from your code.

[Visual Basic]
```
NotInheritable Public Class BinaryEditor
   Inherits UITypeEditor
```
[C#]
```
public sealed class BinaryEditor : UITypeEditor
```
[C++]
```
public __gc __sealed class BinaryEditor : public UITypeEditor
```
[JScript]
```
public class BinaryEditor extends UITypeEditor
```

BinaryEditor Constructor

This member supports the .NET Framework infrastructure and is not intended to be used directly from your code.

[Visual Basic]
```
Public Sub New()
```
[C#]
```
public BinaryEditor();
```
[C++]
```
public: BinaryEditor();
```
[JScript]
```
public function BinaryEditor();
```

BinaryEditor.EditValue Method

This member supports the .NET Framework infrastructure and is not intended to be used directly from your code.

Overload List

This member supports the .NET Framework infrastructure and is not intended to be used directly from your code.

[Visual Basic] **Overloads Overrides Public Function EditValue(ITypeDescriptorContext, IServiceProvider, Object) As Object**

[C#] **public override object EditValue(ITypeDescriptorContext, IServiceProvider, object);**

[C++] **public: Object* EditValue(ITypeDescriptorContext*, IServiceProvider*, Object*);**

[JScript] **public override function EditValue(ITypeDescriptorContext, IServiceProvider, Object) : Object;**

This member supports the .NET Framework infrastructure and is not intended to be used directly from your code.

[Visual Basic] **Overloads Public Function EditValue(IServiceProvider, Object) As Object**

[C#] **public object EditValue(IServiceProvider, object);**

[C++] **public: Object* EditValue(IServiceProvider*, Object*);**

[JScript] **public function EditValue(IServiceProvider, Object) : Object;**

BinaryEditor.EditValue Method (ITypeDescriptorContext, IServiceProvider, Object)

This member supports the .NET Framework infrastructure and is not intended to be used directly from your code.

[Visual Basic]
```
Overrides Overloads Public Function EditValue( _
   ByVal context As ITypeDescriptorContext, _
   ByVal provider As IServiceProvider, _
   ByVal value As Object _
) As Object
```
[C#]
```
public override object EditValue(
   ITypeDescriptorContext context,
   IServiceProvider provider,
   object value
);
```
[C++]
```
public: Object* EditValue(
   ITypeDescriptorContext* context,
   IServiceProvider* provider,
   Object* value
);
```
[JScript]
```
public override function EditValue(
   context : ITypeDescriptorContext,
   provider : IServiceProvider,
   value : Object
) : Object;
```

BinaryEditor.GetEditStyle Method

This member supports the .NET Framework infrastructure and is not intended to be used directly from your code.

Overload List

This member supports the .NET Framework infrastructure and is not intended to be used directly from your code.

[Visual Basic] **Overloads Overrides Public Function GetEditStyle(ITypeDescriptorContext) As UITypeEditorEditStyle**

[C#] **public override UITypeEditorEditStyle GetEditStyle(ITypeDescriptorContext);**

[C++] **public: UITypeEditorEditStyle GetEditStyle(ITypeDescriptorContext*);**

[JScript] **public override function GetEditStyle(ITypeDescriptorContext) : UITypeEditorEditStyle;**

This member supports the .NET Framework infrastructure and is not intended to be used directly from your code.

[Visual Basic] **Overloads Public Function GetEditStyle() As UITypeEditorEditStyle**

[C#] **public UITypeEditorEditStyle GetEditStyle();**

[C++] **public: UITypeEditorEditStyle GetEditStyle();**

[JScript] **public function GetEditStyle() : UITypeEditorEditStyle;**

BinaryEditor.GetEditStyle Method (ITypeDescriptorContext)

This member supports the .NET Framework infrastructure and is not intended to be used directly from your code.

[Visual Basic]
```
Overrides Overloads Public Function GetEditStyle( _
   ByVal context As ITypeDescriptorContext _
) As UITypeEditorEditStyle
```
[C#]
```
public override UITypeEditorEditStyle GetEditStyle(
   ITypeDescriptorContext context
);
```
[C++]
```
public: UITypeEditorEditStyle GetEditStyle(
   ITypeDescriptorContext* context
);
```
[JScript]
```
public override function GetEditStyle(
   context : ITypeDescriptorContext
) : UITypeEditorEditStyle;
```

ByteViewer Class

Displays byte arrays in hexadecimal, ANSI, and Unicode formats.

System.Object
  System.MarshalByRefObject
    System.ComponentModel.Component
      System.Windows.Forms.Control
        System.ComponentModel.Design.ByteViewer

[Visual Basic]
```
Public Class ByteViewer
   Inherits Control
```
[C#]
```
public class ByteViewer : Control
```
[C++]
```
public __gc class ByteViewer : public Control
```
[JScript]
```
public class ByteViewer extends Control
```

Thread Safety

Any public static (**Shared** in Visual Basic) members of this type are safe for multithreaded operations. Any instance members are not guaranteed to be thread safe.

Remarks

ByteViewer provides an interface for viewing hexadecimal, ANSI, and Unicode formatted data.

The **DisplayMode** enumeration specifies the identifiers that are used to indicate the display mode to use. The **Auto** display mode selects a default display mode based on the contents of the byte array. **ByteViewer** uses a simple algorithm to determine what kind of data is stored in the buffer. The hexadecimal **Hexdump** view displays the hexadecimal values and corresponding byte representations (chars) in a read-only edit box. The default number of columns is 16. The **Ansi** and **Unicode** views show the byte array in a read-only edit box. In these views, the a null reference (**Nothing** in Visual Basic) characters are replaced with Unicode block characters.

Requirements

Namespace: System.ComponentModel.Design

Platforms: Windows 98, Windows NT 4.0, Windows Millennium Edition, Windows 2000, Windows XP Home Edition, Windows XP Professional, Windows Server 2003 family

Assembly: System.Design (in System.Design.dll)

ByteViewer Constructor

Initializes a new instance of the **ByteViewer** class.

[Visual Basic]
```
Public Sub New()
```
[C#]
```
public ByteViewer();
```
[C++]
```
public: ByteViewer();
```
[JScript]
```
public function ByteViewer();
```

Requirements

Platforms: Windows 98, Windows NT 4.0, Windows Millennium Edition, Windows 2000, Windows XP Home Edition, Windows XP Professional, Windows Server 2003 family

.NET Framework Security:

- Full trust for the immediate caller. This member cannot be used by partially trusted code.

ByteViewer.GetBytes Method

Gets the bytes in the buffer.

[Visual Basic]
```
Public Overridable Function GetBytes() As Byte()
```
[C#]
```
public virtual byte[] GetBytes();
```
[C++]
```
public: virtual unsigned char GetBytes()  __gc[];
```
[JScript]
```
public function GetBytes() : Byte[];
```

Return Value

The unsigned byte array reference.

Requirements

Platforms: Windows 98, Windows NT 4.0, Windows Millennium Edition, Windows 2000, Windows XP Home Edition, Windows XP Professional, Windows Server 2003 family

.NET Framework Security:

- Full trust for the immediate caller. This member cannot be used by partially trusted code.

ByteViewer.GetDisplayMode Method

Gets the display mode for the control.

[Visual Basic]
```
Public Overridable Function GetDisplayMode() As DisplayMode
```
[C#]
```
public virtual DisplayMode GetDisplayMode();
```
[C++]
```
public: virtual DisplayMode GetDisplayMode();
```
[JScript]
```
public function GetDisplayMode() : DisplayMode;
```

Return Value

The display mode that this control uses. The returned value is defined in **DisplayMode**.

Requirements

Platforms: Windows 98, Windows NT 4.0, Windows Millennium Edition, Windows 2000, Windows XP Home Edition, Windows XP Professional, Windows Server 2003 family

.NET Framework Security:

- Full trust for the immediate caller. This member cannot be used by partially trusted code.

ByteViewer.OnKeyDown Method

This member overrides **Control.OnKeyDown**.

```
[Visual Basic]
Overrides Protected Sub OnKeyDown( _
   ByVal e As KeyEventArgs _
)
[C#]
protected override void OnKeyDown(
   KeyEventArgs e
);
[C++]
protected: void OnKeyDown(
   KeyEventArgs* e
);
[JScript]
protected override function OnKeyDown(
   e : KeyEventArgs
);
```

Requirements

Platforms: Windows 98, Windows NT 4.0, Windows Millennium Edition, Windows 2000, Windows XP Home Edition, Windows XP Professional, Windows Server 2003 family

.NET Framework Security:

- Full trust for the immediate caller. This member cannot be used by partially trusted code.

ByteViewer.OnPaint Method

This member overrides **Control.OnPaint**.

```
[Visual Basic]
Overrides Protected Sub OnPaint( _
   ByVal e As PaintEventArgs _
)
[C#]
protected override void OnPaint(
   PaintEventArgs e
);
[C++]
protected: void OnPaint(
   PaintEventArgs* e
);
[JScript]
protected override function OnPaint(
   e : PaintEventArgs
);
```

Requirements

Platforms: Windows 98, Windows NT 4.0, Windows Millennium Edition, Windows 2000, Windows XP Home Edition, Windows XP Professional, Windows Server 2003 family

.NET Framework Security:

- Full trust for the immediate caller. This member cannot be used by partially trusted code.

ByteViewer.OnResize Method

This member overrides **Control.OnResize**.

```
[Visual Basic]
Overrides Protected Sub OnResize( _
   ByVal e As EventArgs _
)
[C#]
protected override void OnResize(
   EventArgs e
);
[C++]
protected: void OnResize(
   EventArgs* e
);
[JScript]
protected override function OnResize(
   e : EventArgs
);
```

Requirements

Platforms: Windows 98, Windows NT 4.0, Windows Millennium Edition, Windows 2000, Windows XP Home Edition, Windows XP Professional, Windows Server 2003 family

.NET Framework Security:

- Full trust for the immediate caller. This member cannot be used by partially trusted code.

ByteViewer.SaveToFile Method

Writes the raw data from the data buffer to a file.

```
[Visual Basic]
Public Overridable Sub SaveToFile( _
   ByVal path As String _
)
[C#]
public virtual void SaveToFile(
   string path
);
[C++]
public: virtual void SaveToFile(
   String* path
);
[JScript]
public function SaveToFile(
   path : String
);
```

Parameters

path

The file path to save to.

Exceptions

Exception Type	Condition
IOException	The file write failed.

Requirements

Platforms: Windows 98, Windows NT 4.0, Windows Millennium Edition, Windows 2000, Windows XP Home Edition, Windows XP Professional, Windows Server 2003 family

.NET Framework Security:

- Full trust for the immediate caller. This member cannot be used by partially trusted code.

ByteViewer.ScrollChanged Method

This member supports the .NET Framework infrastructure and is not intended to be used directly from your code.

```
[Visual Basic]
Protected Overridable Sub ScrollChanged( _
   ByVal source As Object, _
   ByVal e As EventArgs _
)
[C#]
protected virtual void ScrollChanged(
   object source,
   EventArgs e
);
[C++]
protected: virtual void ScrollChanged(
   Object* source,
   EventArgs* e
);
[JScript]
protected function ScrollChanged(
   source : Object,
   e : EventArgs
);
```

ByteViewer.SetBytes Method

Sets the byte array to display in the viewer.

```
[Visual Basic]
Public Overridable Sub SetBytes( _
   ByVal bytes() As Byte _
)
[C#]
public virtual void SetBytes(
   byte[] bytes
);
[C++]
public: virtual void SetBytes(
   unsigned char bytes __gc[]
);
[JScript]
public function SetBytes(
   bytes : Byte[]
);
```

Parameters

bytes

The byte array to display.

Exceptions

Exception Type	Condition
ArgumentNull-Exception	The specified byte array is a null reference (**Nothing** in Visual Basic).

Requirements

Platforms: Windows 98, Windows NT 4.0, Windows Millennium Edition, Windows 2000, Windows XP Home Edition, Windows XP Professional, Windows Server 2003 family

.NET Framework Security:

- Full trust for the immediate caller. This member cannot be used by partially trusted code.

ByteViewer.SetDisplayMode Method

Sets the current display mode.

```
[Visual Basic]
Public Overridable Sub SetDisplayMode( _
   ByVal mode As DisplayMode _
)
[C#]
public virtual void SetDisplayMode(
   DisplayMode mode
);
[C++]
public: virtual void SetDisplayMode(
   DisplayMode mode
);
[JScript]
public function SetDisplayMode(
   mode : DisplayMode
);
```

Parameters

mode

The display mode to set.

Exceptions

Exception Type	Condition
InvalidEnumArgument-Exception	The specified display mode is not from the **DisplayMode** enumeration.

Requirements

Platforms: Windows 98, Windows NT 4.0, Windows Millennium Edition, Windows 2000, Windows XP Home Edition, Windows XP Professional, Windows Server 2003 family

.NET Framework Security:

- Full trust for the immediate caller. This member cannot be used by partially trusted code.

ByteViewer.SetFile Method

Sets the file to display in the viewer.

```
[Visual Basic]
Public Overridable Sub SetFile( _
   ByVal path As String _
)
```

```
[C#]
public virtual void SetFile(
   string path
);
[C++]
public: virtual void SetFile(
   String* path
);
[JScript]
public function SetFile(
   path : String
);
```

Parameters

path

The file path to load from.

Exceptions

Exception Type	Condition
IOException	The file load failed.

Remarks

The viewer loads the data to view from the specified file. This method throws an exception if the file load fails.

Requirements

Platforms: Windows 98, Windows NT 4.0, Windows Millennium Edition, Windows 2000, Windows XP Home Edition, Windows XP Professional, Windows Server 2003 family

.NET Framework Security:

- Full trust for the immediate caller. This member cannot be used by partially trusted code.

ByteViewer.SetStartLine Method

Sets the current line for the **Hexdump** view.

```
[Visual Basic]
Public Overridable Sub SetStartLine( _
   ByVal line As Integer _
)
[C#]
public virtual void SetStartLine(
   int line
);
[C++]
public: virtual void SetStartLine(
   int line
);
[JScript]
public function SetStartLine(
   line : int
);
```

Parameters

line

The current line to display from.

Remarks

The **Hexdump** display mode displays the buffer starting at the specified line. If the specified line is out of range, the start line is set to zero.

Requirements

Platforms: Windows 98, Windows NT 4.0, Windows Millennium Edition, Windows 2000, Windows XP Home Edition, Windows XP Professional, Windows Server 2003 family

.NET Framework Security:

- Full trust for the immediate caller. This member cannot be used by partially trusted code.

CheckoutException Class

The exception that is thrown when an attempt to check out a file that is checked into a source code management program is canceled or fails.

System.Object
  System.Exception
    System.SystemException
      System.Runtime.InteropServices.ExternalException
        System.ComponentModel.Design.CheckoutException

[Visual Basic]
```
Public Class CheckoutException
   Inherits ExternalException
```
[C#]
```
public class CheckoutException : ExternalException
```
[C++]
```
public __gc class CheckoutException : public ExternalException
```
[JScript]
```
public class CheckoutException extends ExternalException
```

Thread Safety

Any public static (**Shared** in Visual Basic) members of this type are safe for multithreaded operations. Any instance members are not guaranteed to be thread safe.

Example

[Visual Basic, C#, C++] The following example demonstrates throwing a **CheckoutException**.

[Visual Basic]
```
' Throws a checkout exception with a message and error code.
Throw New CheckoutException("This is an example exception", 0)
```

[C#]
```
// Throws a checkout exception with a message and error code.
throw new CheckoutException("This is an example exception", 0);
```

[C++]
```
// Throws a checkout exception with a message and error code.
throw new CheckoutException(S"This is an example exception", 0);
```

Requirements

Namespace: System.ComponentModel.Design

Platforms: Windows 98, Windows NT 4.0, Windows Millennium Edition, Windows 2000, Windows XP Home Edition, Windows XP Professional, Windows Server 2003 family

Assembly: System (in System.dll)

CheckoutException Constructor

Initializes a new instance of the **CheckoutException** class.

Overload List

Initializes a new instance of the **CheckoutException** class with no associated message or error code.

[Visual Basic] **Public Sub New()**

[C#] **public CheckoutException();**

[C++] **public: CheckoutException();**

[JScript] **public function CheckoutException();**

Initializes a new instance of the **CheckoutException** class with the specified message.

[Visual Basic] **Public Sub New(String)**

[C#] **public CheckoutException(string);**

[C++] **public: CheckoutException(String*);**

[JScript] **public function CheckoutException(String);**

Initializes a new instance of the **CheckoutException** class with the specified message and error code.

[Visual Basic] **Public Sub New(String, Integer)**

[C#] **public CheckoutException(string, int);**

[C++] **public: CheckoutException(String*, int);**

[JScript] **public function CheckoutException(String, int);**

CheckoutException Constructor ()

Initializes a new instance of the **CheckoutException** class with no associated message or error code.

[Visual Basic]
```
Public Sub New()
```
[C#]
```
public CheckoutException();
```
[C++]
```
public: CheckoutException();
```
[JScript]
```
public function CheckoutException();
```

Requirements

Platforms: Windows 98, Windows NT 4.0, Windows Millennium Edition, Windows 2000, Windows XP Home Edition, Windows XP Professional, Windows Server 2003 family

CheckoutException Constructor (String)

Initializes a new instance of the **CheckoutException** class with the specified message.

[Visual Basic]
```
Public Sub New( _
   ByVal message As String _
)
```
[C#]
```
public CheckoutException(
   string message
);
```
[C++]
```
public: CheckoutException(
   String* message
);
```
[JScript]
```
public function CheckoutException(
   message : String
);
```

Parameters

message
  A message describing the exception.

Requirements

Platforms: Windows 98, Windows NT 4.0, Windows Millennium Edition, Windows 2000, Windows XP Home Edition, Windows XP Professional, Windows Server 2003 family

CheckoutException Constructor (String, Int32)

Initializes a new instance of the **CheckoutException** class with the specified message and error code.

```
[Visual Basic]
Public Sub New( _
   ByVal message As String, _
   ByVal errorCode As Integer _
)
[C#]
public CheckoutException(
   string message,
   int errorCode
);
[C++]
public: CheckoutException(
   String* message,
   int errorCode
);
[JScript]
public function CheckoutException(
   message : String,
   errorCode : int
);
```

Parameters

message
: A message describing the exception.

errorCode
: The error code to pass.

Requirements

Platforms: Windows 98, Windows NT 4.0, Windows Millennium Edition, Windows 2000, Windows XP Home Edition, Windows XP Professional, Windows Server 2003 family

CheckoutException.Canceled Field

Initializes a new instance of the **CheckoutException** class that specifies that the checkout was canceled. This field is read-only.

```
[Visual Basic]
Public Shared ReadOnly Canceled As CheckoutException
[C#]
public static readonly CheckoutException Canceled;
[C++]
public: static CheckoutException* Canceled;
[JScript]
public static var Canceled : CheckoutException;
```

Remarks

This exception occurs if the user selects **Cancel** on the checkout dialog box.

Requirements

Platforms: Windows 98, Windows NT 4.0, Windows Millennium Edition, Windows 2000, Windows XP Home Edition, Windows XP Professional, Windows Server 2003 family

CollectionEditor Class

Provides a user interface that can edit most types of collections at design time.

System.Object
 System.Drawing.Design.UITypeEditor
  System.ComponentModel.Design.CollectionEditor
   System.ComponentModel.Design.ArrayEditor
   System.Web.UI.Design.WebControls.ListItemsCollectionEditor
   System.Web.UI.Design.WebControls.TableCellsCollectionEditor
   System.Web.UI.Design.WebControls.TableRowsCollectionEditor

[Visual Basic]
```
Public Class CollectionEditor
   Inherits UITypeEditor
```
[C#]
```
public class CollectionEditor : UITypeEditor
```
[C++]
```
public __gc class CollectionEditor : public UITypeEditor
```
[JScript]
```
public class CollectionEditor extends UITypeEditor
```

Thread Safety

Any public static (**Shared** in Visual Basic) members of this type are safe for multithreaded operations. Any instance members are not guaranteed to be thread safe.

Remarks

Notes to Inheritors: This editor can edit collections that have an **Item** property. The editor can determine the type of the collection from the **Item** property, if it exists. If the collection does not have this property, or if you want to provide collections of more than one type, you can override certain protected members of this class to customize the editor to support other types of collections.

Example

[Visual Basic]
```
<EditorAttribute(GetType                                              ↵
(System.ComponentModel.Design.CollectionEditor),                      ↵
GetType(System.Drawing.Design.UITypeEditor))> _
Public Property testCollection() As ICollection
   Get
      Return Icollection
   End Get
   Set
      Icollection = value
   End Set
End Property
Private Icollection As ICollection
```

[C#]
```
[EditorAttribute(typeof                                               ↵
 (System.ComponentModel.Design.CollectionEditor),                     ↵
typeof(System.Drawing.Design.UITypeEditor))]
public ICollection testCollection
{
    get
    {
       return Icollection;
    }
    set
    {
       Icollection = value;
    }
}
private ICollection Icollection;
```

[C++]
```
public:
    [EditorAttribute(__typeof                                         ↵
 (System::ComponentModel::Design::CollectionEditor),
        __typeof(System::Drawing::Design::UITypeEditor))]
    __property ICollection* get_testCollection() {
        return Icollection;
    }
    [EditorAttribute(__typeof                                         ↵
 (System::ComponentModel::Design::CollectionEditor),
        __typeof(System::Drawing::Design::UITypeEditor))]
    __property void set_testCollection(ICollection* value) {
        Icollection = value;
    }
private:
    ICollection*  Icollection;
```

Requirements

Namespace: System.ComponentModel.Design

Platforms: Windows 98, Windows NT 4.0, Windows Millennium Edition, Windows 2000, Windows XP Home Edition, Windows XP Professional, Windows Server 2003 family

Assembly: System.Design (in System.Design.dll)

CollectionEditor Constructor

Initializes a new instance of the **CollectionEditor** class using the specified collection type.

[Visual Basic]
```
Public Sub New( _
   ByVal type As Type _
)
```
[C#]
```
public CollectionEditor(
   Type type
);
```
[C++]
```
public: CollectionEditor(
   Type* type
);
```
[JScript]
```
public function CollectionEditor(
   type : Type
);
```

Parameters

type
  The type of the collection for this editor to edit.

Requirements

Platforms: Windows 98, Windows NT 4.0, Windows Millennium Edition, Windows 2000, Windows XP Home Edition, Windows XP Professional, Windows Server 2003 family

.NET Framework Security:

- Full trust for the immediate caller. This member cannot be used by partially trusted code.

CollectionEditor.CollectionItemType Property

Gets the data type of each item in the collection.

[Visual Basic]
```
Protected ReadOnly Property CollectionItemType As Type
```
[C#]
```
protected Type CollectionItemType {get;}
```
[C++]
```
protected: __property Type* get_CollectionItemType();
```
[JScript]
```
protected function get CollectionItemType() : Type;
```

Property Value

The data type of the collection items.

Remarks

This property represents the data type of the items of the collection.

Requirements

Platforms: Windows 98, Windows NT 4.0, Windows Millennium Edition, Windows 2000, Windows XP Home Edition, Windows XP Professional, Windows Server 2003 family

.NET Framework Security:

- Full trust for the immediate caller. This member cannot be used by partially trusted code.

CollectionEditor.CollectionType Property

Gets the data type of the collection object.

[Visual Basic]
```
Protected ReadOnly Property CollectionType As Type
```
[C#]
```
protected Type CollectionType {get;}
```
[C++]
```
protected: __property Type* get_CollectionType();
```
[JScript]
```
protected function get CollectionType() : Type;
```

Property Value

The data type of the collection object.

Remarks

This property represents the data type of the collection object.

Requirements

Platforms: Windows 98, Windows NT 4.0, Windows Millennium Edition, Windows 2000, Windows XP Home Edition, Windows XP Professional, Windows Server 2003 family

.NET Framework Security:

- Full trust for the immediate caller. This member cannot be used by partially trusted code.

CollectionEditor.Context Property

Gets a type descriptor that indicates the current context.

[Visual Basic]
```
Protected ReadOnly Property Context As ITypeDescriptorContext
```
[C#]
```
protected ITypeDescriptorContext Context {get;}
```
[C++]
```
protected: __property ITypeDescriptorContext* get_Context();
```
[JScript]
```
protected function get Context() : ITypeDescriptorContext;
```

Property Value

An **ITypeDescriptorContext** that indicates the context currently in use, or a null reference (**Nothing** in Visual Basic) if no context is available.

Requirements

Platforms: Windows 98, Windows NT 4.0, Windows Millennium Edition, Windows 2000, Windows XP Home Edition, Windows XP Professional, Windows Server 2003 family

.NET Framework Security:

- Full trust for the immediate caller. This member cannot be used by partially trusted code.

CollectionEditor.HelpTopic Property

Gets the Help keyword to display the Help topic or topic list for when the editor's dialog **Help** button or the F1 key is pressed.

[Visual Basic]
```
Protected Overridable ReadOnly Property HelpTopic As String
```
[C#]
```
protected virtual string HelpTopic {get;}
```
[C++]
```
protected: __property virtual String* get_HelpTopic();
```
[JScript]
```
protected function get HelpTopic() : String;
```

Property Value

The Help keyword to display the Help topic or topic list for when Help is requested from the editor.

Remarks

Override this property to display a different Help topic.

Requirements

Platforms: Windows 98, Windows NT 4.0, Windows Millennium Edition, Windows 2000, Windows XP Home Edition, Windows XP Professional, Windows Server 2003 family

.NET Framework Security:

- Full trust for the immediate caller. This member cannot be used by partially trusted code.

CollectionEditor.NewItemTypes Property

Gets the available types of items that can be created for this collection.

[Visual Basic]
```
Protected ReadOnly Property NewItemTypes As Type ()
```
[C#]
```
protected Type[] NewItemTypes {get;}
```
[C++]
```
protected: __property Type* get_NewItemTypes();
```
[JScript]
```
protected function get NewItemTypes() : Type[];
```

Property Value

The types of items that can be created.

Remarks

This property indicates the data types that can be added to the collection. By default, this returns a single type of **CollectionItemType**. If more than one type is returned, the collection editor UI provides a way to choose which item type to create.

Requirements

Platforms: Windows 98, Windows NT 4.0, Windows Millennium Edition, Windows 2000, Windows XP Home Edition, Windows XP Professional, Windows Server 2003 family

.NET Framework Security:

- Full trust for the immediate caller. This member cannot be used by partially trusted code.

CollectionEditor.CanRemoveInstance Method

Indicates whether original members of the collection can be removed.

```
[Visual Basic]
Protected Overridable Function CanRemoveInstance( _
   ByVal value As Object _
) As Boolean
[C#]
protected virtual bool CanRemoveInstance(
   object value
);
[C++]
protected: virtual bool CanRemoveInstance(
   Object* value
);
[JScript]
protected function CanRemoveInstance(
   value : Object
) : Boolean;
```

Parameters

value

The value to remove.

Return Value

true if it is permissible to remove this value from the collection; otherwise, **false**. The default implementation always returns **true**.

Remarks

When implemented in a derived class, this method indicates whether the specified value can be removed from the collection. By default, this method always returns **true**.

This method is called when the user tries to remove an item that is an original member of the collection. This method is not called when removing items that were added in the current editing session because they are not yet part of the collection.

Requirements

Platforms: Windows 98, Windows NT 4.0, Windows Millennium Edition, Windows 2000, Windows XP Home Edition, Windows XP Professional, Windows Server 2003 family

.NET Framework Security:

- Full trust for the immediate caller. This member cannot be used by partially trusted code.

CollectionEditor.CanSelectMultipleInstances Method

Indicates whether multiple collection items can be selected at once.

```
[Visual Basic]
Protected Overridable Function CanSelectMultipleInstances() As _
   Boolean
[C#]
protected virtual bool CanSelectMultipleInstances();
[C++]
protected: virtual bool CanSelectMultipleInstances();
[JScript]
protected function CanSelectMultipleInstances() : Boolean;
```

Return Value

true if it multiple collection members can be selected at the same time; otherwise, **false**. By default, this returns **true**.

Remarks

This method indicates whether multiple collection members can be selected within the collection editor dialog box.

Requirements

Platforms: Windows 98, Windows NT 4.0, Windows Millennium Edition, Windows 2000, Windows XP Home Edition, Windows XP Professional, Windows Server 2003 family

.NET Framework Security:

- Full trust for the immediate caller. This member cannot be used by partially trusted code.

CollectionEditor.CreateCollectionForm Method

Creates a new form to display and edit the current collection.

```
[Visual Basic]
Protected Overridable Function CreateCollectionForm() As _
   CollectionForm
[C#]
protected virtual CollectionForm CreateCollectionForm();
[C++]
protected: virtual CollectionForm* CreateCollectionForm();
[JScript]
protected function CreateCollectionForm() : CollectionForm;
```

Return Value

An instance of **CollectionEditor.CollectionForm** to provide as the user interface for editing the collection.

Remarks

Notes to Inheritors: You can inherit from **CollectionEditor.CollectionForm** to provide your own form.

Requirements

Platforms: Windows 98, Windows NT 4.0, Windows Millennium Edition, Windows 2000, Windows XP Home Edition, Windows XP Professional, Windows Server 2003 family

.NET Framework Security:

- Full trust for the immediate caller. This member cannot be used by partially trusted code.

CollectionEditor.CreateCollectionItemType Method

Gets the data type that this collection contains.

```
[Visual Basic]
Protected Overridable Function CreateCollectionItemType() As Type
[C#]
protected virtual Type CreateCollectionItemType();
[C++]
protected: virtual Type* CreateCollectionItemType();
[JScript]
protected function CreateCollectionItemType() : Type;
```

Return Value

The data type of the items in the collection, or an instance of **Object** if no **Item** property can be located on the collection.

Remarks

You can retrieve the data type of the items of the collection from the **CollectionItemType** property, which is faster than this method.

This method does not need to be called by users, except in derived classes where this method has been overridden and implemented.

The default implementation of this method returns the data type of the **Item** property of the collection, if it exists.

Notes to Implementers: Developers can choose to override this method to support collections that do not follow the typical and supported collection model, or when performance is critical, and reflection-based type resolution is too slow.

Requirements

Platforms: Windows 98, Windows NT 4.0, Windows Millennium Edition, Windows 2000, Windows XP Home Edition, Windows XP Professional, Windows Server 2003 family

.NET Framework Security:

- Full trust for the immediate caller. This member cannot be used by partially trusted code.

CollectionEditor.CreateInstance Method

Creates a new instance of the specified collection item type.

```
[Visual Basic]
Protected Overridable Function CreateInstance( _
   ByVal itemType As Type _
) As Object
[C#]
protected virtual object CreateInstance(
   Type itemType
);
[C++]
protected: virtual Object* CreateInstance(
   Type* itemType
);
[JScript]
protected function CreateInstance(
   itemType : Type
) : Object;
```

Parameters

itemType

The type of item to create.

Return Value

A new instance of the specified object.

Remarks

Notes to Implementers: This method should throw an exception if it cannot create a new instance of the specified type.

Requirements

Platforms: Windows 98, Windows NT 4.0, Windows Millennium Edition, Windows 2000, Windows XP Home Edition, Windows XP Professional, Windows Server 2003 family

.NET Framework Security:

- Full trust for the immediate caller. This member cannot be used by partially trusted code.

CollectionEditor.CreateNewItemTypes Method

Gets the data types that this collection editor can contain.

```
[Visual Basic]
Protected Overridable Function CreateNewItemTypes() As Type()
[C#]
protected virtual Type[] CreateNewItemTypes();
[C++]
protected: virtual Type* CreateNewItemTypes() [];
[JScript]
protected function CreateNewItemTypes() : Type[];
```

Return Value

An array of data types that this collection can contain.

Remarks

You can retrieve the data type of the items of the collection from the **NewItemTypes** property, which is faster than this method.

This method does not need to be called by users, except in derived classes where this method has been overridden and implemented.

The default implementation of this method returns the type of all the collection items in a Type array.

Notes to Inheritors: This method must be overridden to support collections with multiple types. The default implementation of this method returns the data type of the **Item** property of the collection, if it exists. Use this method to override the default implementation.

Requirements

Platforms: Windows 98, Windows NT 4.0, Windows Millennium Edition, Windows 2000, Windows XP Home Edition, Windows XP Professional, Windows Server 2003 family

.NET Framework Security:

- Full trust for the immediate caller. This member cannot be used by partially trusted code.

CollectionEditor.DestroyInstance Method

Destroys the specified instance of the object.

[Visual Basic]
```
Protected Overridable Sub DestroyInstance( _
   ByVal instance As Object _
)
```
[C#]
```
protected virtual void DestroyInstance(
   object instance
);
```
[C++]
```
protected: virtual void DestroyInstance(
   Object* instance
);
```
[JScript]
```
protected function DestroyInstance(
   instance : Object
);
```

Parameters

instance
The object to destroy.

Requirements

Platforms: Windows 98, Windows NT 4.0, Windows Millennium Edition, Windows 2000, Windows XP Home Edition, Windows XP Professional, Windows Server 2003 family

.NET Framework Security:

- Full trust for the immediate caller. This member cannot be used by partially trusted code.

CollectionEditor.EditValue Method

Edits the value of the specified object.

Overload List

Edits the value of the specified object using the specified service provider and context.

[Visual Basic] **Overloads Overrides Public Function EditValue(ITypeDescriptorContext, IServiceProvider, Object) As Object**

[C#] **public override object EditValue(ITypeDescriptorContext, IServiceProvider, object);**

[C++] **public: Object* EditValue(ITypeDescriptorContext*, IServiceProvider*, Object*);**

[JScript] **public override function EditValue(ITypeDescriptorContext, IServiceProvider, Object) : Object;**

Inherited from **UITypeEditor**.

[Visual Basic] **Overloads Public Function EditValue(IServiceProvider, Object) As Object**

[C#] **public object EditValue(IServiceProvider, object);**

[C++] **public: Object* EditValue(IServiceProvider*, Object*);**

[JScript] **public function EditValue(IServiceProvider, Object) : Object;**

CollectionEditor.EditValue Method (ITypeDescriptorContext, IServiceProvider, Object)

Edits the value of the specified object using the specified service provider and context.

[Visual Basic]
```
Overrides Overloads Public Function EditValue( _
   ByVal context As ITypeDescriptorContext, _
   ByVal provider As IServiceProvider, _
   ByVal value As Object _
) As Object
```
[C#]
```
public override object EditValue(
   ITypeDescriptorContext context,
   IServiceProvider provider,
   object value
);
```
[C++]
```
public: Object* EditValue(
   ITypeDescriptorContext* context,
   IServiceProvider* provider,
   Object* value
);
```
[JScript]
```
public override function EditValue(
   context : ITypeDescriptorContext,
   provider : IServiceProvider,
   value : Object
) : Object;
```

Parameters

context
An **ITypeDescriptorContext** that can be used to gain additional context information.

provider
A service provider object through which editing services can be obtained.

value
The object to edit the value of.

Return Value

The new value of the object. If the value of the object has not changed, this should return the same object it was passed.

Requirements

Platforms: Windows 98, Windows NT 4.0, Windows Millennium Edition, Windows 2000, Windows XP Home Edition, Windows XP Professional, Windows Server 2003 family

.NET Framework Security:

- Full trust for the immediate caller. This member cannot be used by partially trusted code.

CollectionEditor.GetEditStyle Method

Gets the edit style used by the **EditValue** method.

Overload List

Gets the edit style used by the **EditValue** method.

[Visual Basic] **Overloads Overrides Public Function GetEditStyle(ITypeDescriptorContext) As UITypeEditorEditStyle**

[C#] **public override UITypeEditorEditStyle GetEditStyle(ITypeDescriptorContext);**

[C++] **public: UITypeEditorEditStyle GetEditStyle(ITypeDescriptorContext*);**

[JScript] **public override function GetEditStyle(ITypeDescriptorContext) : UITypeEditorEditStyle;**

Inherited from **UITypeEditor**.

[Visual Basic] **Overloads Public Function GetEditStyle() As UITypeEditorEditStyle**

[C#] **public UITypeEditorEditStyle GetEditStyle();**

[C++] **public: UITypeEditorEditStyle GetEditStyle();**

[JScript] **public function GetEditStyle() : UITypeEditorEditStyle;**

CollectionEditor.GetEditStyle Method (ITypeDescriptorContext)

Gets the edit style used by the **EditValue** method.

```
[Visual Basic]
Overrides Overloads Public Function GetEditStyle( _
   ByVal context As ITypeDescriptorContext _
) As UITypeEditorEditStyle
[C#]
public override UITypeEditorEditStyle GetEditStyle(
   ITypeDescriptorContext context
);
[C++]
public: UITypeEditorEditStyle GetEditStyle(
   ITypeDescriptorContext* context
);
[JScript]
public override function GetEditStyle(
   context : ITypeDescriptorContext
) : UITypeEditorEditStyle;
```

Parameters

context

An **ITypeDescriptorContext** that can be used to gain additional context information.

Return Value

A **UITypeEditorEditStyle** enumeration value indicating the provided editing style. If the method is not supported in the specified context, this method will return the **None** identifier.

Requirements

Platforms: Windows 98, Windows NT 4.0, Windows Millennium Edition, Windows 2000, Windows XP Home Edition, Windows XP Professional, Windows Server 2003 family

.NET Framework Security:

- Full trust for the immediate caller. This member cannot be used by partially trusted code.

CollectionEditor.GetItems Method

Gets an array of objects containing the specified collection.

```
[Visual Basic]
Protected Overridable Function GetItems( _
   ByVal editValue As Object _
) As Object()
[C#]
protected virtual object[] GetItems(
   object editValue
);
[C++]
protected: virtual Object* GetItems(
   Object* editValue
) __gc[];
[JScript]
protected function GetItems(
   editValue : Object
) : Object[];
```

Parameters

editValue

The collection to edit.

Return Value

An array containing the collection objects, or an empty object array if the specified collection does not inherit from **ICollection**.

Requirements

Platforms: Windows 98, Windows NT 4.0, Windows Millennium Edition, Windows 2000, Windows XP Home Edition, Windows XP Professional, Windows Server 2003 family

.NET Framework Security:

- Full trust for the immediate caller. This member cannot be used by partially trusted code.

CollectionEditor.GetService Method

Gets the requested service, if it is available.

```
[Visual Basic]
Protected Function GetService( _
   ByVal serviceType As Type _
) As Object
[C#]
protected object GetService(
   Type serviceType
);
[C++]
protected: Object* GetService(
   Type* serviceType
);
[JScript]
protected function GetService(
   serviceType : Type
) : Object;
```

Parameters

serviceType

The type of service to retrieve.

Return Value

An instance of the service, or a null reference (**Nothing** in Visual Basic) if the service cannot be found.

Requirements

Platforms: Windows 98, Windows NT 4.0, Windows Millennium Edition, Windows 2000, Windows XP Home Edition, Windows XP Professional, Windows Server 2003 family

.NET Framework Security:

- Full trust for the immediate caller. This member cannot be used by partially trusted code.

CollectionEditor.SetItems Method

Sets the specified array as the items of the collection.

```
[Visual Basic]
Protected Overridable Function SetItems( _
   ByVal editValue As Object, _
   ByVal value() As Object _
) As Object
[C#]
protected virtual object SetItems(
   object editValue,
   object[] value
);
[C++]
protected: virtual Object* SetItems(
   Object* editValue,
   Object* value __gc[]
);
[JScript]
protected function SetItems(
   editValue : Object,
   value : Object[]
) : Object;
```

Parameters

editValue
    The collection to edit.

value
    An array of objects to set as the collection items.

Return Value

The newly created collection object or, otherwise, the collection indicated by the *editValue* parameter.

Remarks

If setting requires that a new object be created, the new object is returned. Otherwise, the *editValue* parameter is returned.

Requirements

Platforms: Windows 98, Windows NT 4.0, Windows Millennium Edition, Windows 2000, Windows XP Home Edition, Windows XP Professional, Windows Server 2003 family

.NET Framework Security:

- Full trust for the immediate caller. This member cannot be used by partially trusted code.

CollectionEditor.ShowHelp Method

Displays the default Help topic for the collection editor.

```
[Visual Basic]
Protected Overridable Sub ShowHelp()
[C#]
protected virtual void ShowHelp();
[C++]
protected: virtual void ShowHelp();
[JScript]
protected function ShowHelp();
```

Requirements

Platforms: Windows 98, Windows NT 4.0, Windows Millennium Edition, Windows 2000, Windows XP Home Edition, Windows XP Professional, Windows Server 2003 family

.NET Framework Security:

- Full trust for the immediate caller. This member cannot be used by partially trusted code.

CollectionEditor.Collection-Form Class

Provides a modal dialog box for editing the contents of a collection using a **UITypeEditor**.

System.Object
 System.MarshalByRefObject
  System.ComponentModel.Component
   System.Windows.Forms.Control
    System.Windows.Forms.ScrollableControl
     System.Windows.Forms.ContainerControl
      System.Windows.Forms.Form
       System.ComponentModel.Design.Collection-Editor.CollectionForm

[Visual Basic]
```
MustInherit Protected Class CollectionEditor.CollectionForm
   Inherits Form
```
[C#]
```
protected abstract class CollectionEditor.CollectionForm : Form
```
[C++]
```
protected __gc __abstract class CollectionEditor.CollectionForm :
   public Form
```
[JScript]
```
protected abstract class CollectionEditor.CollectionForm extends
   Form
```

Thread Safety

Any public static (**Shared** in Visual Basic) members of this type are safe for multithreaded operations. Any instance members are not guaranteed to be thread safe.

Remarks

Notes to Implementers: You can provide implementations for the abstract methods on this form, together with your own user interface.

Requirements

Namespace: System.ComponentModel.Design

Platforms: Windows 98, Windows NT 4.0, Windows Millennium Edition, Windows 2000, Windows XP Home Edition, Windows XP Professional, Windows Server 2003 family

Assembly: System.Design (in System.Design.dll)

CollectionEditor.CollectionForm Constructor

Initializes a new instance of the **CollectionEditor.CollectionForm** class.

[Visual Basic]
```
Public Sub New( _
   ByVal editor As CollectionEditor _
)
```
[C#]
```
public CollectionEditor.CollectionForm(
   CollectionEditor editor
);
```
[C++]
```
public: CollectionForm(
   CollectionEditor* editor
);
```
[JScript]
```
public function CollectionEditor.CollectionForm(
   editor : CollectionEditor
);
```

Parameters

editor

The **CollectionEditor** to use for editing the collection.

Requirements

Platforms: Windows 98, Windows NT 4.0, Windows Millennium Edition, Windows 2000, Windows XP Home Edition, Windows XP Professional, Windows Server 2003 family

.NET Framework Security:

- Full trust for the immediate caller. This member cannot be used by partially trusted code.

CollectionEditor.CollectionForm.Collection-ItemType Property

Gets the data type of each item in the collection.

[Visual Basic]
```
Protected ReadOnly Property CollectionItemType As Type
```
[C#]
```
protected Type CollectionItemType {get;}
```
[C++]
```
protected: __property Type* get_CollectionItemType();
```
[JScript]
```
protected function get CollectionItemType() : Type;
```

Property Value

The data type of the collection items.

Remarks

This property represents the data type of the items of the collection.

Requirements

Platforms: Windows 98, Windows NT 4.0, Windows Millennium Edition, Windows 2000, Windows XP Home Edition, Windows XP Professional, Windows Server 2003 family

.NET Framework Security:

- Full trust for the immediate caller. This member cannot be used by partially trusted code.

CollectionEditor.CollectionForm.CollectionType Property

Gets the data type of the collection object.

[Visual Basic]
```
Protected ReadOnly Property CollectionType As Type
```
[C#]
```
protected Type CollectionType {get;}
```
[C++]
```
protected: __property Type* get_CollectionType();
```
[JScript]
```
protected function get CollectionType() : Type;
```

Property Value

The data type of the collection object.

Remarks

This property represents the data type of the collection object.

Requirements

Platforms: Windows 98, Windows NT 4.0, Windows Millennium Edition, Windows 2000, Windows XP Home Edition, Windows XP Professional, Windows Server 2003 family

.NET Framework Security:

- Full trust for the immediate caller. This member cannot be used by partially trusted code.

CollectionEditor.CollectionForm.Context Property

Gets a type descriptor that indicates the current context.

[Visual Basic]
```
Protected ReadOnly Property Context As ITypeDescriptorContext
```
[C#]
```
protected ITypeDescriptorContext Context {get;}
```
[C++]
```
protected: __property ITypeDescriptorContext* get_Context();
```
[JScript]
```
protected function get Context() : ITypeDescriptorContext;
```

Property Value

An **ITypeDescriptorContext** that indicates the context currently in use, or a null reference (**Nothing** in Visual Basic) if no context is available.

Requirements

Platforms: Windows 98, Windows NT 4.0, Windows Millennium Edition, Windows 2000, Windows XP Home Edition, Windows XP Professional, Windows Server 2003 family

.NET Framework Security:

- Full trust for the immediate caller. This member cannot be used by partially trusted code.

CollectionEditor.CollectionForm.EditValue Property

Gets or sets the collection object to edit.

[Visual Basic]
```
Public Property EditValue As Object
```
[C#]
```
public object EditValue {get; set;}
```
[C++]
```
public: __property Object* get_EditValue();
public: __property void set_EditValue(Object*);
```
[JScript]
```
public function get EditValue() : Object;
public function set EditValue(Object);
```

Property Value

The collection object to edit.

Requirements

Platforms: Windows 98, Windows NT 4.0, Windows Millennium Edition, Windows 2000, Windows XP Home Edition, Windows XP Professional, Windows Server 2003 family

.NET Framework Security:

- Full trust for the immediate caller. This member cannot be used by partially trusted code.

CollectionEditor.CollectionForm.Items Property

Gets or sets the array of items for this form to display.

[Visual Basic]
```
Protected Property Items As Object ()
```
[C#]
```
protected object[] Items {get; set;}
```
[C++]
```
protected: __property Object* get_Items();
protected: __property void set_Items(Object* __gc[]);
```
[JScript]
```
protected function get Items() : Object[];
protected function set Items(Object[]);
```

Property Value

An array of objects for the form to display.

Remarks

The default implementation retrieves the current set of items from the **Item** property of the collection.

Requirements

Platforms: Windows 98, Windows NT 4.0, Windows Millennium Edition, Windows 2000, Windows XP Home Edition, Windows XP Professional, Windows Server 2003 family

.NET Framework Security:

- Full trust for the immediate caller. This member cannot be used by partially trusted code.

CollectionEditor.CollectionForm.NewItemTypes Property

Gets the available item types that can be created for this collection.

[Visual Basic]
```
Protected ReadOnly Property NewItemTypes As Type ()
```
[C#]
```
protected Type[] NewItemTypes {get;}
```
[C++]
```
protected: __property Type* get_NewItemTypes();
```
[JScript]
```
protected function get NewItemTypes() : Type[];
```

Property Value

The types of items that can be created.

Remarks

This property indicates the data types that can be added to the collection. By default, this returns a single type of **CollectionItemType**. If more than one type is returned, the collection editor UI provides a way to choose which item type to create.

Requirements

Platforms: Windows 98, Windows NT 4.0, Windows Millennium Edition, Windows 2000, Windows XP Home Edition, Windows XP Professional, Windows Server 2003 family

.NET Framework Security:

- Full trust for the immediate caller. This member cannot be used by partially trusted code.

CollectionEditor.CollectionForm.CanRemoveInstance Method

Indicates whether you can remove the original members of the collection.

```
[Visual Basic]
Protected Function CanRemoveInstance( _
   ByVal value As Object _
) As Boolean
[C#]
protected bool CanRemoveInstance(
   object value
);
[C++]
protected: bool CanRemoveInstance(
   Object* value
);
[JScript]
protected function CanRemoveInstance(
   value : Object
) : Boolean;
```

Parameters

value
The value to remove.

Return Value

true if it is permissible to remove this value from the collection; otherwise, **false**. By default, this method returns the value from **CanRemoveInstance** of the **CollectionEditor** for this form.

Remarks

When implemented in a derived class, this method indicates whether the specified value can be removed from the collection. By default, this returns the value from **CanRemoveInstance** of the **CollectionEditor** for this form.

This method is called when the user tries to remove from the collection an item that is an original member of the collection. This method is not called when removing items that were added in this editing session, because they are not yet part of the collection.

Requirements

Platforms: Windows 98, Windows NT 4.0, Windows Millennium Edition, Windows 2000, Windows XP Home Edition, Windows XP Professional, Windows Server 2003 family

.NET Framework Security:

- Full trust for the immediate caller. This member cannot be used by partially trusted code.

CollectionEditor.CollectionForm.CanSelectMultipleInstances Method

Indicates whether multiple collection items can be selected at once.

```
[Visual Basic]
Protected Overridable Function CanSelectMultipleInstances() As _
   Boolean
[C#]
protected virtual bool CanSelectMultipleInstances();
[C++]
protected: virtual bool CanSelectMultipleInstances();
[JScript]
protected function CanSelectMultipleInstances() : Boolean;
```

Return Value

true if it multiple collection members can be selected at the same time; otherwise, **false**. By default, this method returns the value from **CanSelectMultipleInstances** of the **CollectionEditor** for this form.

Remarks

This method indicates whether multiple collection members can be selected within the collection editor dialog box.

Requirements

Platforms: Windows 98, Windows NT 4.0, Windows Millennium Edition, Windows 2000, Windows XP Home Edition, Windows XP Professional, Windows Server 2003 family

.NET Framework Security:

- Full trust for the immediate caller. This member cannot be used by partially trusted code.

CollectionEditor.CollectionForm.CreateInstance Method

Creates a new instance of the specified collection item type.

```
[Visual Basic]
Protected Function CreateInstance( _
   ByVal itemType As Type _
) As Object
[C#]
protected object CreateInstance(
   Type itemType
);
[C++]
protected: Object* CreateInstance(
   Type* itemType
);
[JScript]
protected function CreateInstance(
   itemType : Type
) : Object;
```

Parameters

itemType
The type of item to create.

Return Value

A new instance of the specified object, or a null reference (**Nothing** in Visual Basic) if the user chose to cancel the creation of this instance.

Remarks

This method throws an exception if a new instance cannot be created. If the user chooses to cancel the creation of this instance, this method returns a null reference (**Nothing** in Visual Basic).

Requirements

Platforms: Windows 98, Windows NT 4.0, Windows Millennium Edition, Windows 2000, Windows XP Home Edition, Windows XP Professional, Windows Server 2003 family

.NET Framework Security:

- Full trust for the immediate caller. This member cannot be used by partially trusted code.

CollectionEditor.CollectionForm.DestroyInstance Method

Destroys the specified instance of the object.

```
[Visual Basic]
Protected Sub DestroyInstance( _
   ByVal instance As Object _
)
[C#]
protected void DestroyInstance(
   object instance
);
[C++]
protected: void DestroyInstance(
   Object* instance
);
[JScript]
protected function DestroyInstance(
   instance : Object
);
```

Parameters

instance

The object to destroy.

Requirements

Platforms: Windows 98, Windows NT 4.0, Windows Millennium Edition, Windows 2000, Windows XP Home Edition, Windows XP Professional, Windows Server 2003 family

.NET Framework Security:

- Full trust for the immediate caller. This member cannot be used by partially trusted code.

CollectionEditor.CollectionForm.DisplayError Method

Displays the specified exception to the user.

```
[Visual Basic]
Protected Overridable Sub DisplayError( _
   ByVal e As Exception _
)
[C#]
protected virtual void DisplayError(
   Exception e
);
[C++]
protected: virtual void DisplayError(
   Exception* e
);
[JScript]
protected function DisplayError(
   e : Exception
);
```

Parameters

e

The exception to display.

Requirements

Platforms: Windows 98, Windows NT 4.0, Windows Millennium Edition, Windows 2000, Windows XP Home Edition, Windows XP Professional, Windows Server 2003 family

.NET Framework Security:

- Full trust for the immediate caller. This member cannot be used by partially trusted code.

CollectionEditor.CollectionForm.GetService Method

Gets the requested service, if it is available.

```
[Visual Basic]
Overrides Protected Function GetService( _
   ByVal serviceType As Type _
) As Object
[C#]
protected override object GetService(
   Type serviceType
);
[C++]
protected: Object* GetService(
   Type* serviceType
);
[JScript]
protected override function GetService(
   serviceType : Type
) : Object;
```

Parameters

serviceType

The type of service to retrieve.

Return Value

An instance of the service, or a null reference (**Nothing** in Visual Basic) if the service cannot be found.

Requirements

Platforms: Windows 98, Windows NT 4.0, Windows Millennium Edition, Windows 2000, Windows XP Home Edition, Windows XP Professional, Windows Server 2003 family

.NET Framework Security:

- Full trust for the immediate caller. This member cannot be used by partially trusted code.

CollectionEditor.CollectionForm.OnEditValueChanged Method

Provides an opportunity to perform processing when a collection value has changed.

```
[Visual Basic]
Protected MustOverride Sub OnEditValueChanged()
[C#]
protected abstract void OnEditValueChanged();
[C++]
protected: virtual void OnEditValueChanged() = 0;
[JScript]
protected abstract function OnEditValueChanged();
```

Remarks

This method is raised when the value of a collection item has changed.

Notes to Implementers: In this method, update your user interface to reflect the current value.

Requirements

Platforms: Windows 98, Windows NT 4.0, Windows Millennium Edition, Windows 2000, Windows XP Home Edition, Windows XP Professional, Windows Server 2003 family

.NET Framework Security:

- Full trust for the immediate caller. This member cannot be used by partially trusted code.

CollectionEditor.CollectionForm.ShowEditorDialog Method

Shows the dialog box for the collection editor using the specified **IWindowsFormsEditorService** object.

```
[Visual Basic]
Protected Friend Overridable Function ShowEditorDialog( _
   ByVal edSvc As IWindowsFormsEditorService _
) As DialogResult
[C#]
protected internal virtual DialogResult ShowEditorDialog(
   IWindowsFormsEditorService edSvc
);
[C++]
protected public: virtual DialogResult ShowEditorDialog(
   IWindowsFormsEditorService* edSvc
);
[JScript]
protected internal function ShowEditorDialog(
   edSvc : IWindowsFormsEditorService
) : DialogResult;
```

Parameters

edSvc

An **IWindowsFormsEditorService** that can be used to show the dialog box.

Return Value

A **DialogResult** that indicates the result code returned from the dialog box.

Requirements

Platforms: Windows 98, Windows NT 4.0, Windows Millennium Edition, Windows 2000, Windows XP Home Edition, Windows XP Professional, Windows Server 2003 family

.NET Framework Security:

- Full trust for the immediate caller. This member cannot be used by partially trusted code.

CommandID Class

Represents a unique command identifier that consists of a numeric command ID and a GUID menu group identifier.

System.Object
  System.ComponentModel.Design.CommandID

```
[Visual Basic]
<ComVisible(True)>
Public Class CommandID
[C#]
[ComVisible(true)]
public class CommandID
[C++]
[ComVisible(true)]
public __gc class CommandID
[JScript]
public
   ComVisible(true)
class CommandID
```

Thread Safety

Any public static (**Shared** in Visual Basic) members of this type are safe for multithreaded operations. Any instance members are not guaranteed to be thread safe.

Remarks

A **CommandID** uniquely identifies a command. A unique command identification system prevents conflicts between command identifiers. Command IDs consist of a menu group GUID and a numeric command identifier.

Requirements

Namespace: System.ComponentModel.Design

Platforms: Windows 98, Windows NT 4.0, Windows Millennium Edition, Windows 2000, Windows XP Home Edition, Windows XP Professional, Windows Server 2003 family

Assembly: System (in System.dll)

CommandID Constructor

Initializes a new instance of the **CommandID** class using the specified menu group GUID and command ID number.

```
[Visual Basic]
Public Sub New( _
   ByVal menuGroup As Guid, _
   ByVal commandID As Integer _
)
[C#]
public CommandID(
   Guid menuGroup,
   int commandID
);
[C++]
public: CommandID(
   Guid menuGroup,
   int commandID
);
[JScript]
public function CommandID(
   menuGroup : Guid,
   commandID : int
);
```

Parameters

menuGroup
  The GUID of the group that this menu command belongs to.

commandID
  The numeric identifier of this menu command.

Remarks

This method creates a new command ID.

Requirements

Platforms: Windows 98, Windows NT 4.0, Windows Millennium Edition, Windows 2000, Windows XP Home Edition, Windows XP Professional, Windows Server 2003 family

CommandID.Guid Property

Gets the GUID of the menu group that the menu command identified by this **CommandID** belongs to.

```
[Visual Basic]
Public Overridable ReadOnly Property Guid As Guid
[C#]
public virtual Guid Guid {get;}
[C++]
public: __property virtual Guid get_Guid();
[JScript]
public function get Guid() : Guid;
```

Property Value

The GUID of the command group for this command.

Requirements

Platforms: Windows 98, Windows NT 4.0, Windows Millennium Edition, Windows 2000, Windows XP Home Edition, Windows XP Professional, Windows Server 2003 family

CommandID.ID Property

Gets the numeric command ID.

```
[Visual Basic]
Public Overridable ReadOnly Property ID As Integer
[C#]
public virtual int ID {get;}
[C++]
public: __property virtual int get_ID();
[JScript]
public function get ID() : int;
```

Property Value

The command ID number.

Requirements

Platforms: Windows 98, Windows NT 4.0, Windows Millennium Edition, Windows 2000, Windows XP Home Edition, Windows XP Professional, Windows Server 2003 family

CommandID.Equals Method

This member overrides **Object.Equals**.

[Visual Basic]
```
Overrides Public Function Equals( _
   ByVal obj As Object _
) As Boolean
```
[C#]
```
public override bool Equals(
   object obj
);
```
[C++]
```
public: bool Equals(
   Object* obj
);
```
[JScript]
```
public override function Equals(
   obj : Object
) : Boolean;
```

Requirements

Platforms: Windows 98, Windows NT 4.0, Windows Millennium Edition, Windows 2000, Windows XP Home Edition, Windows XP Professional, Windows Server 2003 family

CommandID.GetHashCode Method

This member overrides **Object.GetHashCode**.

[Visual Basic]
```
Overrides Public Function GetHashCode() As Integer
```
[C#]
```
public override int GetHashCode();
```
[C++]
```
public: int GetHashCode();
```
[JScript]
```
public override function GetHashCode() : int;
```

Requirements

Platforms: Windows 98, Windows NT 4.0, Windows Millennium Edition, Windows 2000, Windows XP Home Edition, Windows XP Professional, Windows Server 2003 family

CommandID.ToString Method

Returns a **String** that represents the current object.

[Visual Basic]
```
Overrides Public Function ToString() As String
```
[C#]
```
public override string ToString();
```
[C++]
```
public: String* ToString();
```
[JScript]
```
public override function ToString() : String;
```

Return Value

A string that contains the command ID information, both the GUID and integer identifier.

Remarks

This method returns a string that contains the significant information of the **CommandID**, a concatenation that consists of the menu group GUID and the numeric ID for the **CommandID**.

Requirements

Platforms: Windows 98, Windows NT 4.0, Windows Millennium Edition, Windows 2000, Windows XP Home Edition, Windows XP Professional, Windows Server 2003 family

ComponentChangedEventArgs Class

Provides data for the **ComponentChanged** event. This class cannot be inherited.

System.Object
 System.EventArgs
  System.ComponentModel.Design.ComponentChanged-EventArgs

[Visual Basic]
```
<ComVisible(True)>
NotInheritable Public Class ComponentChangedEventArgs
   Inherits EventArgs
```
[C#]
```
[ComVisible(true)]
public sealed class ComponentChangedEventArgs : EventArgs
```
[C++]
```
[ComVisible(true)]
public __gc __sealed class ComponentChangedEventArgs : public
   EventArgs
```
[JScript]
```
public
   ComVisible(true)
class ComponentChangedEventArgs extends EventArgs
```

Thread Safety

Any public static (**Shared** in Visual Basic) members of this type are safe for multithreaded operations. Any instance members are not guaranteed to be thread safe.

Remarks

ComponentChangedEventArgs provides data for a **ComponentChanged** event. The **ComponentChanged** event notifies the **IComponentChangeService** and registered event handlers that a particular component in the currently active document has been changed.

A **ComponentChangedEventArgs** provides the following information:

- A **Component** property that indicates the component that was modified.
- A **Member** property that indicates the member that was changed.
- A **NewValue** property that indicates the new value of the member.
- An **OldValue** property that indicates the old value of the member.

Component designers typically raise the **ComponentChanged** event automatically when components are added, removed, or modified. A **ComponentChanged** event is not raised during form load and unload because changes at this time are expected. A component designer might raise the **ComponentChanged** event after it changes a property of the component; this ensures that the Properties window will display the updated property.

Notes to Inheritors: A compiler error occurs if this class is specified as the base class of another class.

Example

[Visual Basic, C#, C++] The following example demonstrates creating a **ComponentChangedEventArgs**.

[Visual Basic]
```
' This example method creates a ComponentChangedEventArgs ↵
using the specified arguments.
' Typically, this type of event args is created by a design ↵
 mode subsystem.
Public Function CreateComponentChangedEventArgs(ByVal ↵
 component As Object, ByVal member As MemberDescriptor, ↵
 ByVal oldValue As Object, ByVal newValue As Object) As ↵
ComponentChangedEventArgs
    ' Creates a component changed event args with the ↵
specified arguments.
    Dim args As New ComponentChangedEventArgs(component, ↵
 member, oldValue, newValue)

    ' The component that has changed:            args.Component
    ' The member of the component that changed:  args.Member
    ' The old value of the member:               args.oldValue
    ' The new value of the member:               args.newValue
    Return args
End Function
```

[C#]
```
// This example method creates a ComponentChangedEventArgs ↵
 using the specified arguments.
// Typically, this type of event args is created by a design ↵
 mode subsystem.
public ComponentChangedEventArgs ↵
CreateComponentChangedEventArgs(object component, ↵
MemberDescriptor member, object oldValue, object newValue)
{
    // Creates a component changed event args with the ↵
 specified arguments.
    ComponentChangedEventArgs args = new ↵
ComponentChangedEventArgs(component, member, oldValue, newValue);

    // The component that has changed:            args.Component
    // The member of the component that changed:  args.Member
    // The old value of the member:               args.oldValue
    // The new value of the member:               args.newValue

    return args;
}
```

[C++]
```
// This example method creates a ComponentChangedEventArgs ↵
 using the specified arguments.
// Typically, this type of event args is created by a ↵
 design mode subsystem.
ComponentChangedEventArgs* CreateComponentChangedEventArgs ↵
 (Object* component, MemberDescriptor* member, Object* ↵
oldValue, Object* newValue)
{
    // Creates a component changed event args with the ↵
specified arguments.
    ComponentChangedEventArgs* args = new ↵
ComponentChangedEventArgs(component, member, oldValue, newValue);

    // The component that has changed:            args.Component
    // The member of the component that changed:  args.Member
    // The old value of the member:               args.oldValue
    // The new value of the member:               args.newValue

    return args;
}
```

Requirements

Namespace: System.ComponentModel.Design

Platforms: Windows 98, Windows NT 4.0, Windows Millennium Edition, Windows 2000, Windows XP Home Edition, Windows XP Professional, Windows Server 2003 family

Assembly: System (in System.dll)

ComponentChangedEventArgs Constructor

Initializes a new instance of the **ComponentChangedEventArgs** class.

[Visual Basic]
```
Public Sub New( _
   ByVal component As Object, _
   ByVal member As MemberDescriptor, _
   ByVal oldValue As Object, _
   ByVal newValue As Object _
)
```
[C#]
```
public ComponentChangedEventArgs(
   object component,
   MemberDescriptor member,
   object oldValue,
   object newValue
);
```
[C++]
```
public: ComponentChangedEventArgs(
   Object* component,
   MemberDescriptor* member,
   Object* oldValue,
   Object* newValue
);
```
[JScript]
```
public function ComponentChangedEventArgs(
   component : Object,
   member : MemberDescriptor,
   oldValue : Object,
   newValue : Object
);
```

Parameters

component
The component that was changed.

member
A **MemberDescriptor** that represents the member that was changed.

oldValue
The old value of the changed member.

newValue
The new value of the changed member.

Remarks

The designer for a component calls this constructor after it has changed a property of the component. This ensures that the Properties window will display the property's updated value.

Requirements

Platforms: Windows 98, Windows NT 4.0, Windows Millennium Edition, Windows 2000, Windows XP Home Edition, Windows XP Professional, Windows Server 2003 family

ComponentChangedEventArgs.Component Property

Gets the component that was modified.

[Visual Basic]
```
Public ReadOnly Property Component As Object
```
[C#]
```
public object Component {get;}
```
[C++]
```
public: __property Object* get_Component();
```
[JScript]
```
public function get Component() : Object;
```

Property Value

An **Object** that represents the component that was modified.

Requirements

Platforms: Windows 98, Windows NT 4.0, Windows Millennium Edition, Windows 2000, Windows XP Home Edition, Windows XP Professional, Windows Server 2003 family

ComponentChangedEventArgs.Member Property

Gets the member that has been changed.

[Visual Basic]
```
Public ReadOnly Property Member As MemberDescriptor
```
[C#]
```
public MemberDescriptor Member {get;}
```
[C++]
```
public: __property MemberDescriptor* get_Member();
```
[JScript]
```
public function get Member() : MemberDescriptor;
```

Property Value

A **MemberDescriptor** that indicates the member that has been changed.

Remarks

This property can be a null reference (**Nothing** in Visual Basic) if the member is unknown.

Requirements

Platforms: Windows 98, Windows NT 4.0, Windows Millennium Edition, Windows 2000, Windows XP Home Edition, Windows XP Professional, Windows Server 2003 family

ComponentChangedEventArgs.NewValue Property

Gets the new value of the changed member.

[Visual Basic]
```
Public ReadOnly Property NewValue As Object
```
[C#]
```
public object NewValue {get;}
```
[C++]
```
public: __property Object* get_NewValue();
```
[JScript]
```
public function get NewValue() : Object;
```

Property Value

The new value of the changed member. This property can be a null reference (**Nothing** in Visual Basic).

Remarks

This property has meaning only if the member is not a null reference (**Nothing** in Visual Basic).

Requirements

Platforms: Windows 98, Windows NT 4.0, Windows Millennium Edition, Windows 2000, Windows XP Home Edition, Windows XP Professional, Windows Server 2003 family

ComponentChangedEventArgs.OldValue Property

Gets the old value of the changed member.

[Visual Basic]
```
Public ReadOnly Property OldValue As Object
```
[C#]
```
public object OldValue {get;}
```
[C++]
```
public: __property Object* get_OldValue();
```
[JScript]
```
public function get OldValue() : Object;
```

Property Value

The old value of the changed member. This property can be a null reference (**Nothing** in Visual Basic).

Remarks

This property has meaning only if the member is not a null reference (**Nothing** in Visual Basic).

Requirements

Platforms: Windows 98, Windows NT 4.0, Windows Millennium Edition, Windows 2000, Windows XP Home Edition, Windows XP Professional, Windows Server 2003 family

ComponentChangedEvent-Handler Delegate

Represents the method that will handle a **ComponentChanged** event.

```
[Visual Basic]
<Serializable>
<ComVisible(True)>
Public Delegate Sub ComponentChangedEventHandler( _
   ByVal sender As Object, _
   ByVal e As ComponentChangedEventArgs _
)
[C#]
[Serializable]
[ComVisible(true)]
public delegate void ComponentChangedEventHandler(
   object sender,
   ComponentChangedEventArgs e
);
[C++]
[Serializable]
[ComVisible(true)]
public __gc __delegate void ComponentChangedEventHandler(
   Object* sender,
   ComponentChangedEventArgs* e
);
```

[JScript] In JScript, you can use the delegates in the .NET Framework, but you cannot define your own.

Parameters [Visual Basic, C#, C++]

The declaration of your event handler must have the same parameters as the **ComponentChangedEventHandler** delegate declaration.

sender
: The source of the event.

e
: A **ComponentChangedEventArgs** that contains the event data.

Remarks

When you create a **ComponentChangedEventHandler** delegate, you identify the method that will handle the event. To associate the event with your event handler, add an instance of the delegate to the event. The event handler is called whenever the event occurs, unless you remove the delegate. For more information about event-handler delegates, see **Events and Delegates**.

A **ComponentChanged** event will not occur during the loading or unloading of a form because changes are expected during these operations.

Example

[Visual Basic, C#, C++] This example demonstrates registering a **ComponentChangedEventHandler** and handling the **ComponentChanged** event.

```
[Visual Basic]
Public Sub LinkComponentChangedEvent(ByVal changeService As ↵
IComponentChangeService)
    ' Registers an event handler for the ComponentChanged event.
    AddHandler changeService.ComponentChanged, AddressOf ↵
Me.OnComponentChanged
End Sub

Private Sub OnComponentChanged(ByVal sender As Object, ByVal ↵
e As ComponentChangedEventArgs)
    ' Displays changed component information on the console.
    Console.WriteLine(("Type of the component that has changed: ↵
" + e.Component.GetType().FullName))
    Console.WriteLine(("Name of the member of the component that ↵
 has changed: " + e.Member.Name))
    Console.WriteLine(("Old value of the member: " + ↵
e.OldValue.ToString()))
    Console.WriteLine(("New value of the member: " + ↵
e.NewValue.ToString()))
End Sub
```

```
[C#]
public void LinkComponentChangedEvent(IComponentChangeService ↵
changeService)
{
    // Registers an event handler for the ComponentChanged event.
    changeService.ComponentChanged += new ↵
ComponentChangedEventHandler(this.OnComponentChanged);
}

private void OnComponentChanged(object sender, ↵
ComponentChangedEventArgs e)
{
    // Displays changed component information on the console.
    Console.WriteLine("Type of the component that has changed: ↵
"+e.Component.GetType().FullName);
    Console.WriteLine("Name of the member of the component ↵
that has changed: "+e.Member.Name);
    Console.WriteLine("Old value of the member: ↵
"+e.OldValue.ToString());
    Console.WriteLine("New value of the member: ↵
"+e.NewValue.ToString());
}
```

```
[C++]
public:
    void LinkComponentChangedEvent(IComponentChangeService* ↵
changeService)
    {
        // Registers an event handler for the ComponentChanged event.
        changeService->ComponentChanged += new ↵
ComponentChangedEventHandler(this, OnComponentChanged);
    }

private:
    void OnComponentChanged(Object* sender, ↵
ComponentChangedEventArgs* e)
    {
        // Displays changed component information on the console.
        Console::WriteLine(S"Type of the component that has ↵
changed: {0}", e->Component->GetType()->FullName);
        Console::WriteLine(S"Name of the member of the ↵
component that has changed: {0}", e->Member->Name);
        Console::WriteLine(S"Old value of the member: {0}", e- ↵
>OldValue);
        Console::WriteLine(S"New value of the member: {0}", e- ↵
>NewValue);
    }
```

Requirements

Namespace: System.ComponentModel.Design

Platforms: Windows 98, Windows NT 4.0, Windows Millennium Edition, Windows 2000, Windows XP Home Edition, Windows XP Professional, Windows Server 2003 family

Assembly: System (in System.dll)

ComponentChangingEvent-Args Class

Provides data for the **ComponentChanging** event. This class cannot be inherited.

System.Object
  System.EventArgs
    System.ComponentModel.Design.ComponentChanging-EventArgs

[Visual Basic]
```
<ComVisible(True)>
NotInheritable Public Class ComponentChangingEventArgs
   Inherits EventArgs
```
[C#]
```
[ComVisible(true)]
public sealed class ComponentChangingEventArgs : EventArgs
```
[C++]
```
[ComVisible(true)]
public __gc __sealed class ComponentChangingEventArgs : public
   EventArgs
```
[JScript]
```
public
   ComVisible(true)
class ComponentChangingEventArgs extends EventArgs
```

Thread Safety

Any public static (**Shared** in Visual Basic) members of this type are safe for multithreaded operations. Any instance members are not guaranteed to be thread safe.

Remarks

ComponentChangingEventArgs provides data about a **ComponentChanging** event. The **ComponentChanging** event notifies the **IComponentChangeService** and registered event handlers that a particular component in the current design document is about to be changed. This event provides a widely accessible method to prevent a component from changing.

A **ComponentChanging** event is raised before a component is changed. This event provides an opportunity for a designer to abort the change. Component designers typically raise the **ComponentChanging** event automatically. If a property cannot be changed, the method that handles the event can throw an exception. For example, if a designer file is checked into source code control, the handler of this event typically throws an exception if the user refuses to check out the file.

A **ComponentChangingEventArgs** provides the following information:

- A **Component** property that indicates the component that is about to be modified.
- A **Member** property that indicates the member that is about to be changed.

Notes to Inheritors: A compiler error occurs if this class is specified as the base class of another class.

Example

[Visual Basic, C#, C++] The following example demonstrates creating a **ComponentChangingEventArgs**.

[Visual Basic]
```
' This example method creates a ComponentChangingEventArgs using ↵
 the specified arguments.
' Typically, this type of event args is created by a design mode ↵
subsystem.
Public Function CreateComponentChangingEventArgs(ByVal component ↵
As Object, ByVal member As MemberDescriptor) As ↵
ComponentChangingEventArgs
    Dim args As New ComponentChangingEventArgs(component, member)

    ' The component that is about to change:      args.Component
    ' The member that is about to change:         args.Member

    Return args
End Function
```

[C#]
```
// This example method creates a ComponentChangingEventArgs ↵
using the specified arguments.
// Typically, this type of event args is created by a design ↵
 mode subsystem.
public ComponentChangingEventArgs
CreateComponentChangingEventArgs(object component, ↵
MemberDescriptor member)
{
    ComponentChangingEventArgs args = new ↵
ComponentChangingEventArgs(component, member);

    // The component that is about to change:      args.Component
    // The member that is about to change:         args.Member

    return args;
}
```

[C++]
```
// This example method creates a ComponentChangingEventArgs ↵
 using the specified arguments.
// Typically, this type of event args is created by a design ↵
 mode subsystem.
ComponentChangingEventArgs* CreateComponentChangingEventArgs ↵
 (Object* component, MemberDescriptor* member)
{
    // The component that is about to change:      args.Component
    // The member that is about to change:         args.Member

    return new ComponentChangingEventArgs(component, member);
}
```

Requirements

Namespace: System.ComponentModel.Design

Platforms: Windows 98, Windows NT 4.0, Windows Millennium Edition, Windows 2000, Windows XP Home Edition, Windows XP Professional, Windows Server 2003 family

Assembly: System (in System.dll)

ComponentChangingEventArgs Constructor

Initializes a new instance of the **ComponentChangingEventArgs** class.

[Visual Basic]
```
Public Sub New( _
   ByVal component As Object, _
   ByVal member As MemberDescriptor _
)
```

```
[C#]
public ComponentChangingEventArgs(
   object component,
   MemberDescriptor member
);
[C++]
public: ComponentChangingEventArgs(
   Object* component,
   MemberDescriptor* member
);
[JScript]
public function ComponentChangingEventArgs(
   component : Object,
   member : MemberDescriptor
);
```

Parameters

component

The component that is about to be changed.

member

A **MemberDescriptor** indicating the member of the component that is about to be changed.

Remarks

A **ComponentChangingEventArgs** indicates the component and member that are about to be changed.

Requirements

Platforms: Windows 98, Windows NT 4.0, Windows Millennium Edition, Windows 2000, Windows XP Home Edition, Windows XP Professional, Windows Server 2003 family

ComponentChangingEventArgs.Component Property

Gets the component that is about to be changed or the component that is the parent container of the member that is about to be changed.

```
[Visual Basic]
Public ReadOnly Property Component As Object
[C#]
public object Component {get;}
[C++]
public: __property Object* get_Component();
[JScript]
public function get Component() : Object;
```

Property Value

The component that is about to have a member changed.

Requirements

Platforms: Windows 98, Windows NT 4.0, Windows Millennium Edition, Windows 2000, Windows XP Home Edition, Windows XP Professional, Windows Server 2003 family

ComponentChangingEventArgs.Member Property

Gets the member that is about to be changed.

```
[Visual Basic]
Public ReadOnly Property Member As MemberDescriptor
[C#]
public MemberDescriptor Member {get;}
[C++]
public: __property MemberDescriptor* get_Member();
[JScript]
public function get Member() : MemberDescriptor;
```

Property Value

A **MemberDescriptor** indicating the member that is about to be changed, if known, or a null reference (**Nothing** in Visual Basic) otherwise.

Remarks

This property is a null reference (**Nothing** in Visual Basic) if the member is unknown.

Requirements

Platforms: Windows 98, Windows NT 4.0, Windows Millennium Edition, Windows 2000, Windows XP Home Edition, Windows XP Professional, Windows Server 2003 family

ComponentChangingEvent-Handler Delegate

Represents the method that will handle a **ComponentChanging** event.

[Visual Basic]
```
<Serializable>
<ComVisible(True)>
Public Delegate Sub ComponentChangingEventHandler( _
   ByVal sender As Object, _
   ByVal e As ComponentChangingEventArgs _
)
```
[C#]
```
[Serializable]
[ComVisible(true)]
public delegate void ComponentChangingEventHandler(
   object sender,
   ComponentChangingEventArgs e
);
```
[C++]
```
[Serializable]
[ComVisible(true)]
public __gc __delegate void ComponentChangingEventHandler(
   Object* sender,
   ComponentChangingEventArgs* e
);
```

[JScript] In JScript, you can use the delegates in the .NET Framework, but you cannot define your own.

Parameters [Visual Basic, C#, C++]

The declaration of your event handler must have the same parameters as the **ComponentChangingEventHandler** delegate declaration.

sender

The source of the event.

e

A **ComponentChangingEventArgs** event that contains the event data.

Remarks

When you create a **ComponentChangingEventHandler** delegate, you identify the method that will handle the event. To associate the event with your event handler, add an instance of the delegate to the event. The event handler is called whenever the event occurs, unless you remove the delegate.

Example

[Visual Basic, C#, C++] This example demonstrates registering a **ComponentChangingEventHandler** and handling the **ComponentChanging** event.

[Visual Basic]
```
Public Sub LinkComponentChangingEvent(ByVal changeService As ↵
IComponentChangeService)
    ' Registers an event handler for the ComponentChanging event.
    AddHandler changeService.ComponentChanging, AddressOf ↵
Me.OnComponentChanging
End Sub

Private Sub OnComponentChanging(ByVal sender As Object, ByVal ↵
e As ComponentChangingEventArgs)
    ' Displays changing component information on the console.
    Console.WriteLine(("Type of the component that is about to ↵
change: " + e.Component.GetType().FullName))
    Console.WriteLine(("Name of the member of the component ↵
that is about to change: " + e.Member.Name))
End Sub
```

[C#]
```
public void LinkComponentChangingEvent(IComponentChangeService ↵
changeService)
{
    // Registers an event handler for the ComponentChanging event.
    changeService.ComponentChanging += new ↵
ComponentChangingEventHandler(this.OnComponentChanging);
}

private void OnComponentChanging(object sender, ↵
ComponentChangingEventArgs e)
{
    // Displays changing component information on the console.
    Console.WriteLine("Type of the component that is about to ↵
 change: "+e.Component.GetType().FullName);
    Console.WriteLine("Name of the member of the component ↵
that is about to change: "+e.Member.Name);
}
```

[C++]
```
public:

    void LinkComponentChangingEvent(IComponentChangeService* ↵
changeService)
    {
        // Registers an event handler for the ComponentChanging event.
        changeService->ComponentChanging += new ↵
ComponentChangingEventHandler(this, OnComponentChanging);
    }

private:

    void OnComponentChanging(Object* sender, ↵
ComponentChangingEventArgs* e)
    {
        // Displays changing component information on the console.
        Console::WriteLine(S"Type of the component that is ↵
 about to change: ", e->Component->GetType()->FullName);
        Console::WriteLine(S"Name of the member of the ↵
component that is about to change: {0}", e->Member->Name);
    }
```

Requirements

Namespace: System.ComponentModel.Design

Platforms: Windows 98, Windows NT 4.0, Windows Millennium Edition, Windows 2000, Windows XP Home Edition, Windows XP Professional, Windows Server 2003 family

Assembly: System (in System.dll)

ComponentDesigner Class

Base designer class for extending the design mode behavior of a component.

System.Object
System.ComponentModel.Design.ComponentDesigner
System.Web.UI.Design.HtmlControlDesigner
System.Windows.Forms.Design.ComponentDocument-Designer
System.Windows.Forms.Design.ControlDesigner

[Visual Basic]
```
Public Class ComponentDesigner
   Implements IDesigner, IDisposable, IDesignerFilter
```
[C#]
```
public class ComponentDesigner : IDesigner, IDisposable,
   IDesignerFilter
```
[C++]
```
public __gc class ComponentDesigner : public IDesigner,
   IDisposable, IDesignerFilter
```
[JScript]
```
public class ComponentDesigner implements IDesigner, IDisposable,
   IDesignerFilter
```

Thread Safety

Any public static (**Shared** in Visual Basic) members of this type are safe for multithreaded operations. Any instance members are not guaranteed to be thread safe.

Remarks

ComponentDesigner provides a simple designer that can extend the behavior of an associated component in design mode.

ComponentDesigner provides an empty **IDesignerFilter** interface implementation, whose methods can be overridden to adjust the attributes, properties and events of the associated component at design time.

You can associate a designer with a type using a **DesignerAttribute**.

Example

[Visual Basic, C#, C++] The following example provides an example **ComponentDesigner** implementation and an example component associated with the designer. The designer implements an override of the **Initialize** method that calls the base **Initialize** method, an override of the **DoDefaultAction** method that displays a **MessageBox** when the component is double-clicked, and an override of the **Verbs** property accessor that supplies a custom **DesignerVerb** menu command to the shortcut menu for the component.

[Visual Basic]
```
Imports System
Imports System.Collections
Imports System.ComponentModel
Imports System.ComponentModel.Design
Imports System.Drawing
Imports System.Windows.Forms

Namespace ExampleComponent

    ' Provides an example component designer.
    Public Class ExampleComponentDesigner
        Inherits System.ComponentModel.Design.ComponentDesigner

        Public Sub New()
        End Sub 'New

        ' This method provides an opportunity to perform ↵
 processing when a designer is initialized.
        ' The component parameter is the component that the ↵
 designer is associated with.
        Public Overrides Sub Initialize(ByVal component As ↵
System.ComponentModel.IComponent)
            ' Always call the base Initialize method in an ↵
override of this method.
            MyBase.Initialize(component)
        End Sub 'Initialize

        ' This method is invoked when the associated component ↵
 is double-clicked.
        Public Overrides Sub DoDefaultAction()
            MessageBox.Show("The event handler for the default ↵
action was invoked.")
        End Sub 'DoDefaultAction

        ' This method provides designer verbs.
        Public Overrides ReadOnly Property Verbs() As ↵
System.ComponentModel.Design.DesignerVerbCollection
            Get
                Return New DesignerVerbCollection(New ↵
 DesignerVerb() {New DesignerVerb("Example Designer Verb ↵
Command", New EventHandler(AddressOf Me.onVerb))})
            End Get
        End Property

        ' Event handling method for the example designer verb
        Private Sub onVerb(ByVal sender As Object, ByVal e ↵
As EventArgs)
            MessageBox.Show("The event handler for the Example ↵
 Designer Verb Command was invoked.")
        End Sub 'onVerb
    End Class 'ExampleComponentDesigner

    ' Provides an example component associated with the ↵
example component designer.
    <DesignerAttribute(GetType(ExampleComponentDesigner), ↵
GetType(IDesigner))> _
     Public Class ExampleComponent
        Inherits System.ComponentModel.Component

        Public Sub New()
        End Sub 'New
    End Class 'ExampleComponent

End Namespace 'ExampleComponent
```

[C#]
```
using System;
using System.Collections;
using System.ComponentModel;
using System.ComponentModel.Design;
using System.Drawing;
using System.Windows.Forms;

namespace ExampleComponent
{
    // Provides an example component designer.
    public class ExampleComponentDesigner : ↵
System.ComponentModel.Design.ComponentDesigner
    {
        public ExampleComponentDesigner()
        {
        }

        // This method provides an opportunity to perform ↵
processing when a designer is initialized.
        // The component parameter is the component that ↵
the designer is associated with.
       public override void Initialize(System.ComponentModel.IComponent
component)
        {
            // Always call the base Initialize method in an ↵
```

```
override of this method.
            base.Initialize(component);
        }

        // This method is invoked when the associated                ↵
component is double-clicked.
        public override void DoDefaultAction()
        {
            MessageBox.Show("The event handler for the               ↵
default action was invoked.");
        }

        // This method provides designer verbs.
        public override
System.ComponentModel.Design.DesignerVerbCollection Verbs
        {
            get
            {
                return new DesignerVerbCollection( new               ↵
DesignerVerb[] { new DesignerVerb("Example Designer Verb             ↵
Command", new EventHandler(this.onVerb)) } );
            }
        }

        // Event handling method for the example designer verb
        private void onVerb(object sender, EventArgs e)
        {
            MessageBox.Show("The event handler for the Example       ↵
Designer Verb Command was invoked.");
        }
    }

    // Provides an example component associated with the             ↵
 example component designer.
    [DesignerAttribute(typeof(ExampleComponentDesigner),             ↵
typeof(IDesigner))]
    public class ExampleComponent : System.ComponentModel.Component
    {
        public ExampleComponent()
        {
        }
    }
}
```

[C++]

```
#using <mscorlib.dll>
#using <System.dll>
#using <System.Design.dll>
#using <System.Drawing.dll>
#using <System.Windows.Forms.dll>

using namespace System;
using namespace System::Collections;
using namespace System::ComponentModel;
using namespace System::ComponentModel::Design;
using namespace System::Drawing;
using namespace System::Windows::Forms;

// Provides an example component designer.
__gc class ExampleComponentDesigner : public ComponentDesigner {
public:
    ExampleComponentDesigner() {}

    // This method provides an opportunity to perform processing    ↵
 when a designer is initialized.
    // The component parameter is the component that the designer   ↵
 is associated with.
    void Initialize(IComponent* component) {
        // Always call the base Initialize method in an of this method.
        ComponentDesigner::Initialize(component);
    }

    // This method is invoked when the associated component is      ↵
 double-clicked.
    void DoDefaultAction() {
        MessageBox::Show(S"The event handler for the default         ↵
 action was invoked.");
    }

    // This method provides designer verbs.
    __property DesignerVerbCollection* get_Verbs() {
        DesignerVerb* newDesignerVerbs[] = {
            new DesignerVerb(S"Example Designer Verb Command",
                new EventHandler(this,
&ExampleComponentDesigner::onVerb))};

            return new DesignerVerbCollection(newDesignerVerbs);
    }

private:
    // Event handling method for the example designer verb
    void onVerb(Object* sender, EventArgs* e) {
        MessageBox::Show(S"The event handler for the Example         ↵
 Designer Verb Command was invoked.");
    }
};

// Provides an example component associated with the example        ↵
 component designer.
[DesignerAttribute(__typeof(ExampleComponentDesigner),               ↵
__typeof(IDesigner))]
__gc class ExampleComponent : public Component {
public:
    ExampleComponent() {}
};
```

Requirements

Namespace: System.ComponentModel.Design

Platforms: Windows 98, Windows NT 4.0, Windows Millennium Edition, Windows 2000, Windows XP Home Edition, Windows XP Professional, Windows Server 2003 family

Assembly: System.Design (in System.Design.dll)

ComponentDesigner Constructor

Initializes a new instance of the **ComponentDesigner** class.

[Visual Basic]

```
Public Sub New()
```

[C#]

```
public ComponentDesigner();
```

[C++]

```
public: ComponentDesigner();
```

[JScript]

```
public function ComponentDesigner();
```

Remarks

The default constructor initializes any fields to their default values.

Requirements

Platforms: Windows 98, Windows NT 4.0, Windows Millennium Edition, Windows 2000, Windows XP Home Edition, Windows XP Professional, Windows Server 2003 family

.NET Framework Security:

- Full trust for the immediate caller. This member cannot be used by partially trusted code.

ComponentDesigner.AssociatedComponents Property

Gets the collection of components associated with the component managed by the designer.

```
[Visual Basic]
Public Overridable ReadOnly Property AssociatedComponents As _
   ICollection
[C#]
public virtual ICollection AssociatedComponents {get;}
[C++]
public: __property virtual ICollection* get_AssociatedComponents();
[JScript]
public function get AssociatedComponents() : ICollection;
```

Property Value

The components that are associated with the component managed by the designer.

Remarks

This property indicates any components to copy or move along with the component managed by the designer during a copy, drag or move operation.

If this collection contains references to other components in the current design mode document, those components will be copied along with the component managed by the designer during a copy operation.

When the component managed by the designer is selected, this collection is filled with any nested controls. This collection can also include other components, such as the buttons of a toolbar.

Requirements

Platforms: Windows 98, Windows NT 4.0, Windows Millennium Edition, Windows 2000, Windows XP Home Edition, Windows XP Professional, Windows Server 2003 family

.NET Framework Security:

- Full trust for the immediate caller. This member cannot be used by partially trusted code.

ComponentDesigner.Component Property

Gets the component this designer is designing.

```
[Visual Basic]
Public Overridable ReadOnly Property Component As IComponent _
   Implements IDesigner.Component
[C#]
public virtual IComponent Component {get;}
[C++]
public: __property virtual IComponent* get_Component();
[JScript]
public function get Component() : IComponent;
```

Property Value

The component managed by the designer.

Implements

IDesigner.Component

Remarks

The **Initialize** method of **ComponentDesigner** sets this property.

> **Note** When overriding the **Initialize** method, be sure to call the base class **Initialize** method before using this property.

Requirements

Platforms: Windows 98, Windows NT 4.0, Windows Millennium Edition, Windows 2000, Windows XP Home Edition, Windows XP Professional, Windows Server 2003 family

.NET Framework Security:

- Full trust for the immediate caller. This member cannot be used by partially trusted code.

ComponentDesigner.InheritanceAttribute Property

Gets an attribute that indicates the type of inheritance of the associated component.

```
[Visual Basic]
Protected ReadOnly Property InheritanceAttribute As _
   InheritanceAttribute
[C#]
protected InheritanceAttribute InheritanceAttribute {get;}
[C++]
protected: __property InheritanceAttribute*
   get_InheritanceAttribute();
[JScript]
protected function get InheritanceAttribute() :
   InheritanceAttribute;
```

Property Value

The **InheritanceAttribute** for the associated component.

Requirements

Platforms: Windows 98, Windows NT 4.0, Windows Millennium Edition, Windows 2000, Windows XP Home Edition, Windows XP Professional, Windows Server 2003 family

.NET Framework Security:

- Full trust for the immediate caller. This member cannot be used by partially trusted code.

ComponentDesigner.Inherited Property

Gets a value indicating whether this component is inherited.

```
[Visual Basic]
Protected ReadOnly Property Inherited As Boolean
[C#]
protected bool Inherited {get;}
[C++]
protected: __property bool get_Inherited();
[JScript]
protected function get Inherited() : Boolean;
```

Property Value

true if the component is inherited; otherwise, **false**.

Requirements

Platforms: Windows 98, Windows NT 4.0, Windows Millennium Edition, Windows 2000, Windows XP Home Edition, Windows XP Professional, Windows Server 2003 family

.NET Framework Security:

- Full trust for the immediate caller. This member cannot be used by partially trusted code.

ComponentDesigner.ShadowProperties Property

Gets a collection of property values that override user settings.

```
[Visual Basic]
Protected ReadOnly Property ShadowProperties As _
   ComponentDesigner.ShadowPropertyCollection
[C#]
protected ComponentDesigner.ShadowPropertyCollection
   ShadowProperties {get;}
[C++]
protected: __property ComponentDesigner.ShadowPropertyCollection*
   get_ShadowProperties();
[JScript]
protected function get ShadowProperties() :
   ComponentDesigner.ShadowPropertyCollection;
```

Property Value

A **ComponentDesigner.ShadowPropertyCollection** that indicates the shadow properties of the design document.

Requirements

Platforms: Windows 98, Windows NT 4.0, Windows Millennium Edition, Windows 2000, Windows XP Home Edition, Windows XP Professional, Windows Server 2003 family

.NET Framework Security:

- Full trust for the immediate caller. This member cannot be used by partially trusted code.

ComponentDesigner.Verbs Property

Gets the design-time verbs supported by the component that is associated with the designer.

```
[Visual Basic]
Public Overridable ReadOnly Property Verbs As _
   DesignerVerbCollection  Implements IDesigner.Verbs
[C#]
public virtual DesignerVerbCollection Verbs {get;}
[C++]
public: __property virtual DesignerVerbCollection* get_Verbs();
[JScript]
public function get Verbs() : DesignerVerbCollection;
```

Property Value

A **DesignerVerbCollection** of **DesignerVerb** objects, or a null reference (**Nothing** in Visual Basic) if no designer verbs are available. This default implementation always returns a null reference (**Nothing**).

Implements

IDesigner.Verbs

Remarks

This method returns a null reference (**Nothing** in Visual Basic) if the component has no design-time verbs.

The design-time environment typically displays verbs returned by this method in a right-click menu. When a user selects one of the verbs, the **Invoke** method of the corresponding **DesignerVerb** is invoked.

> **Note** A design-time environment typically provides a **Properties...** entry on a component's right-click menu. Therefore, do not include such an entry in the collection of designer-specified verbs.

Requirements

Platforms: Windows 98, Windows NT 4.0, Windows Millennium Edition, Windows 2000, Windows XP Home Edition, Windows XP Professional, Windows Server 2003 family

.NET Framework Security:

- Full trust for the immediate caller. This member cannot be used by partially trusted code.

ComponentDesigner.Dispose Method

Releases the resources used by the **ComponentDesigner**.

Overload List

Releases all resources used by the **ComponentDesigner**.

[Visual Basic] **Overloads Public Overridable Sub Dispose() Implements IDisposable.Dispose**

[C#] **public virtual void Dispose();**

[C++] **public: virtual void Dispose();**

[JScript] **public function Dispose();**

Releases the unmanaged resources used by the **ComponentDesigner** and optionally releases the managed resources.

[Visual Basic] **Overloads Protected Overridable Sub Dispose(Boolean)**

[C#] **protected virtual void Dispose(bool);**

[C++] **protected: virtual void Dispose(bool);**

[JScript] **protected function Dispose(Boolean);**

ComponentDesigner.Dispose Method ()

Releases all resources used by the **ComponentDesigner**.

```
[Visual Basic]
Overloads Public Overridable Sub Dispose() Implements _
   IDisposable.Dispose
[C#]
public virtual void Dispose();
[C++]
public: virtual void Dispose();
[JScript]
public function Dispose();
```

Implements

IDisposable.Dispose

Remarks

Calling **Dispose** allows the resources used by the **ComponentDesigner**. to be reallocated for other purposes. For more information about **Dispose**, see **Cleaning Up Unmanaged Resources**.

Requirements

Platforms: Windows 98, Windows NT 4.0, Windows Millennium Edition, Windows 2000, Windows XP Home Edition, Windows XP Professional, Windows Server 2003 family

.NET Framework Security:

- Full trust for the immediate caller. This member cannot be used by partially trusted code.

ComponentDesigner.Dispose Method (Boolean)

Releases the unmanaged resources used by the **ComponentDesigner** and optionally releases the managed resources.

```
[Visual Basic]
Overloads Protected Overridable Sub Dispose( _
   ByVal disposing As Boolean _
)
[C#]
protected virtual void Dispose(
   bool disposing
);
[C++]
protected: virtual void Dispose(
   bool disposing
);
[JScript]
protected function Dispose(
   disposing : Boolean
);
```

Parameters

disposing

true to release both managed and unmanaged resources; **false** to release only unmanaged resources.

Remarks

This method is called by the public **Dispose()** method and the **Finalize** method. **Dispose()** invokes the protected **Dispose(Boolean)** method with the *disposing* parameter set to **true**. **Finalize** invokes **Dispose** with *disposing* set to **false**.

When the *disposing* parameter is **true**, this method releases all resources held by any managed objects that this **ComponentDesigner** references. This method invokes the **Dispose()** method of each referenced object.

Notes to Inheritors: **Dispose** can be called multiple times by other objects. When overriding **Dispose(Boolean)**, be careful not to reference objects that have been previously disposed of in an earlier call to **Dispose**.

Requirements

Platforms: Windows 98, Windows NT 4.0, Windows Millennium Edition, Windows 2000, Windows XP Home Edition, Windows XP Professional, Windows Server 2003 family

.NET Framework Security:

- Full trust for the immediate caller. This member cannot be used by partially trusted code.

ComponentDesigner.DoDefaultAction Method

Creates a method signature in the source code file for the default event on the component and navigates the user's cursor to that location.

```
[Visual Basic]
Public Overridable Sub DoDefaultAction() Implements _
   IDesigner.DoDefaultAction
[C#]
public virtual void DoDefaultAction();
[C++]
public: virtual void DoDefaultAction();
[JScript]
public function DoDefaultAction();
```

Implements

IDesigner.DoDefaultAction

Remarks

In Windows Forms and Web Forms designers, this method is invoked when a user double-clicks a component.

Requirements

Platforms: Windows 98, Windows NT 4.0, Windows Millennium Edition, Windows 2000, Windows XP Home Edition, Windows XP Professional, Windows Server 2003 family

.NET Framework Security:

- Full trust for the immediate caller. This member cannot be used by partially trusted code.

ComponentDesigner.Finalize Method

Attempts to free resources by calling **Dispose(false)** before the object is reclaimed by garbage collection.

[C#] In C#, finalizers are expressed using destructor syntax.

[C++] In C++, finalizers are expressed using destructor syntax.

```
[Visual Basic]
Overrides Protected Sub Finalize()
[C#]
~ComponentDesigner();
[C++]
~ComponentDesigner();
[JScript]
protected override function Finalize();
```

Remarks

This method overrides **Object.Finalize** and cleans up resources by calling **Dispose(false)**. Override **Dispose(Boolean)** to customize the cleanup.

Application code should not call this method; an object's **Finalize** method is automatically invoked during garbage collection, unless finalization by the garbage collector has been disabled by a call to the **GC.SuppressFinalize** method.

Requirements

Platforms: Windows 98, Windows NT 4.0, Windows Millennium Edition, Windows 2000, Windows XP Home Edition, Windows XP Professional, Windows Server 2003 family

.NET Framework Security:

- Full trust for the immediate caller. This member cannot be used by partially trusted code.

ComponentDesigner.GetService Method

Attempts to retrieve the specified type of service from the designer's component's design mode site.

```
[Visual Basic]
Protected Overridable Function GetService( _
   ByVal serviceType As Type _
) As Object
[C#]
protected virtual object GetService(
   Type serviceType
);
[C++]
protected: virtual Object* GetService(
   Type* serviceType
);
[JScript]
protected function GetService(
   serviceType : Type
) : Object;
```

Parameters

serviceType
The type of service to request.

Return Value

An object implementing the requested service, or a null reference (**Nothing** in Visual Basic) if the service cannot be resolved.

Remarks

The default implementation of this method requests the service from the site of the component.

Requirements

Platforms: Windows 98, Windows NT 4.0, Windows Millennium Edition, Windows 2000, Windows XP Home Edition, Windows XP Professional, Windows Server 2003 family

.NET Framework Security:

- Full trust for the immediate caller. This member cannot be used by partially trusted code.

ComponentDesigner.IDesignerFilter.PostFilterAttributes Method

This member supports the .NET Framework infrastructure and is not intended to be used directly from your code.

```
[Visual Basic]
Private Sub PostFilterAttributes( _
   ByVal attributes As IDictionary _
) Implements IDesignerFilter.PostFilterAttributes
[C#]
void IDesignerFilter.PostFilterAttributes(
   IDictionary attributes
);
[C++]
private: void IDesignerFilter::PostFilterAttributes(
   IDictionary* attributes
);
[JScript]
private function IDesignerFilter.PostFilterAttributes(
   attributes : IDictionary
);
```

ComponentDesigner.IDesignerFilter.PostFilterEvents Method

This member supports the .NET Framework infrastructure and is not intended to be used directly from your code.

```
[Visual Basic]
Private Sub PostFilterEvents( _
   ByVal events As IDictionary _
) Implements IDesignerFilter.PostFilterEvents
[C#]
void IDesignerFilter.PostFilterEvents(
   IDictionary events
);
[C++]
private: void IDesignerFilter::PostFilterEvents(
   IDictionary* events
);
[JScript]
private function IDesignerFilter.PostFilterEvents(
   events : IDictionary
);
```

ComponentDesigner.IDesignerFilter.PostFilterProperties Method

This member supports the .NET Framework infrastructure and is not intended to be used directly from your code.

```
[Visual Basic]
Private Sub PostFilterProperties( _
   ByVal properties As IDictionary _
) Implements IDesignerFilter.PostFilterProperties
[C#]
void IDesignerFilter.PostFilterProperties(
   IDictionary properties
);
[C++]
private: void IDesignerFilter::PostFilterProperties(
   IDictionary* properties
);
```

```
[JScript]
private function IDesignerFilter.PostFilterProperties(
   properties : IDictionary
);
```

ComponentDesigner.IDesignerFilter.PreFilterAttributes Method

This member supports the .NET Framework infrastructure and is not intended to be used directly from your code.

```
[Visual Basic]
Private Sub PreFilterAttributes( _
   ByVal attributes As IDictionary _
) Implements IDesignerFilter.PreFilterAttributes
[C#]
void IDesignerFilter.PreFilterAttributes(
   IDictionary attributes
);
[C++]
private: void IDesignerFilter::PreFilterAttributes(
   IDictionary* attributes
);
[JScript]
private function IDesignerFilter.PreFilterAttributes(
   attributes : IDictionary
);
```

ComponentDesigner.IDesignerFilter.PreFilterEvents Method

This member supports the .NET Framework infrastructure and is not intended to be used directly from your code.

```
[Visual Basic]
Private Sub PreFilterEvents( _
   ByVal events As IDictionary _
) Implements IDesignerFilter.PreFilterEvents
[C#]
void IDesignerFilter.PreFilterEvents(
   IDictionary events
);
[C++]
private: void IDesignerFilter::PreFilterEvents(
   IDictionary* events
);
[JScript]
private function IDesignerFilter.PreFilterEvents(
   events : IDictionary
);
```

ComponentDesigner.IDesignerFilter.PreFilterProperties Method

This member supports the .NET Framework infrastructure and is not intended to be used directly from your code.

```
[Visual Basic]
Private Sub PreFilterProperties( _
   ByVal properties As IDictionary _
) Implements IDesignerFilter.PreFilterProperties
[C#]
void IDesignerFilter.PreFilterProperties(
   IDictionary properties
);
[C++]
private: void IDesignerFilter::PreFilterProperties(
   IDictionary* properties
);
[JScript]
private function IDesignerFilter.PreFilterProperties(
   properties : IDictionary
);
```

ComponentDesigner.Initialize Method

Prepares the designer to view, edit, and design the specified component.

```
[Visual Basic]
Public Overridable Sub Initialize( _
   ByVal component As IComponent _
) Implements IDesigner.Initialize
[C#]
public virtual void Initialize(
   IComponent component
);
[C++]
public: virtual void Initialize(
   IComponent* component
);
[JScript]
public function Initialize(
   component : IComponent
);
```

Parameters

component

The component for this designer.

Implements

IDesigner.Initialize

Remarks

The designer host calls this method when it is ready to use the designer.

Requirements

Platforms: Windows 98, Windows NT 4.0, Windows Millennium Edition, Windows 2000, Windows XP Home Edition, Windows XP Professional, Windows Server 2003 family

.NET Framework Security:

- Full trust for the immediate caller. This member cannot be used by partially trusted code.

ComponentDesigner.InitializeNonDefault Method

Initializes the settings for an imported component that is already initialized to settings other than the defaults.

[Visual Basic]
```
Public Overridable Sub InitializeNonDefault()
```
[C#]
```
public virtual void InitializeNonDefault();
```
[C++]
```
public: virtual void InitializeNonDefault();
```
[JScript]
```
public function InitializeNonDefault();
```

Remarks

This method is called when the designer is associated with a control that is not in its default state, such as a control that you paste or move with a drag-and-drop operation onto the designer. This method provides an opportunity for implementers to modify or shadow the properties of the component rather than initialize the properties for the component to their defaults. This method is called after the other initialization functions.

Requirements

Platforms: Windows 98, Windows NT 4.0, Windows Millennium Edition, Windows 2000, Windows XP Home Edition, Windows XP Professional, Windows Server 2003 family

.NET Framework Security:

- Full trust for the immediate caller. This member cannot be used by partially trusted code.

ComponentDesigner.InvokeGetInheritance-Attribute Method

Gets the **InheritanceAttribute** of the specified **ComponentDesigner**.

[Visual Basic]
```
Protected Function InvokeGetInheritanceAttribute( _
   ByVal toInvoke As ComponentDesigner _
) As InheritanceAttribute
```
[C#]
```
protected InheritanceAttribute InvokeGetInheritanceAttribute(
   ComponentDesigner toInvoke
);
```
[C++]
```
protected: InheritanceAttribute* InvokeGetInheritanceAttribute(
   ComponentDesigner* toInvoke
);
```
[JScript]
```
protected function InvokeGetInheritanceAttribute(
   toInvoke : ComponentDesigner
) : InheritanceAttribute;
```

Parameters

toInvoke

The **ComponentDesigner** whose inheritance attribute to retrieve.

Return Value

The **InheritanceAttribute** of the specified designer.

Example

[Visual Basic]
```
Public Class DesignerSample
   Inherits ComponentDesigner

   Public Overrides ReadOnly Property Verbs() As DesignerVerbCollection
      Get
         ' Specifies a new verb that will show up in the context ↵
 menu for the component.
         Dim clickVerb As New DesignerVerb("Click Me!", New ↵
EventHandler(AddressOf OnVerbClicked))
         Return New DesignerVerbCollection(New DesignerVerb() ↵
{clickVerb})
      End Get
   End Property


   Private Sub OnVerbClicked(sender As Object, e As EventArgs)
      MessageBox.Show("This verb was clicked")
   End Sub 'OnVerbClicked
End Class 'DesignerSample
 . . .
<Designer(GetType(DesignerSample))> _
Public Class DesignerComponent
   Inherits Component
End Class 'DesignerComponent
 _
```

[C#]
```
public class DesignerSample : ComponentDesigner
{
    public override DesignerVerbCollection Verbs
    {
        get
        {
            // Specifies a new verb that will show up in the ↵
 shortcut menu for the component.
            DesignerVerb clickVerb = new DesignerVerb("Click ↵
Me!", new EventHandler(OnVerbClicked));
            return new DesignerVerbCollection(new DesignerVerb[] ↵
{clickVerb});
        }
    }

    private void OnVerbClicked(object sender, EventArgs e)
    {
        MessageBox.Show("This verb was clicked");
    }
}
 . . .
[Designer(typeof(DesignerSample))]
public class DesignerComponent : Component
{
}
```

[C++]
```
public __gc class DesignerSample : public ComponentDesigner {
public:

    __property DesignerVerbCollection* get_Verbs()
    {
        // Specifies a new verb that will show up in the shortcut ↵
 menu for the component.
        DesignerVerb* clickVerb = new DesignerVerb(S"Click Me!", ↵
 new EventHandler(this, OnVerbClicked));
        DesignerVerb* myArray[] = {clickVerb};
        return new DesignerVerbCollection(myArray);
    }
```

```
private:

    void OnVerbClicked(Object* sender, EventArgs* e)
    {
        MessageBox::Show(S"This verb was clicked");
    }
};
. . .
[Designer(__typeof(DesignerSample))]
public __gc class DesignerComponent : public Component
{
};
```

Requirements

Platforms: Windows 98, Windows NT 4.0, Windows Millennium Edition, Windows 2000, Windows XP Home Edition, Windows XP Professional, Windows Server 2003 family

.NET Framework Security:

- Full trust for the immediate caller. This member cannot be used by partially trusted code.

ComponentDesigner.OnSetComponentDefaults Method

Sets the default properties for the component.

```
[Visual Basic]
Public Overridable Sub OnSetComponentDefaults()
[C#]
public virtual void OnSetComponentDefaults();
[C++]
public: virtual void OnSetComponentDefaults();
[JScript]
public function OnSetComponentDefaults();
```

Remarks

OnSetComponentDefaults is called when the designer is initialized. This allows the designer to provide default values for the base component.

The default implementation of this method sets the default property of the component to the name of the component if the default property is a string and the property is not already set. This method can be implemented in a derived class to customize the initialization of the component that this designer is designing.

Requirements

Platforms: Windows 98, Windows NT 4.0, Windows Millennium Edition, Windows 2000, Windows XP Home Edition, Windows XP Professional, Windows Server 2003 family

.NET Framework Security:

- Full trust for the immediate caller. This member cannot be used by partially trusted code.

ComponentDesigner.PostFilterAttributes Method

Allows a designer to change or remove items from the set of attributes that it exposes through a **TypeDescriptor**.

```
[Visual Basic]
Protected Overridable Sub PostFilterAttributes( _
   ByVal attributes As IDictionary _
)
[C#]
protected virtual void PostFilterAttributes(
   IDictionary attributes
);
[C++]
protected: virtual void PostFilterAttributes(
   IDictionary* attributes
);
[JScript]
protected function PostFilterAttributes(
   attributes : IDictionary
);
```

Parameters

attributes

The attributes for the class of the component.

Remarks

This method provides a way to change or remove the items within the dictionary of attributes that are exposed through a **TypeDescriptor**.

The keys in the dictionary of attributes are the type identifers of the attributes, as specified by the value of their **TypeId** property. The objects are of type **PropertyDescriptor**. This method is called immediately after **PreFilterAttributes**.

Notes to Implementers: You can directly filter the dictionary that is accessible through the *attributes* parameter, or you can leave it unchanged. If you override this method, call the base implementation after you perform your own filtering.

Requirements

Platforms: Windows 98, Windows NT 4.0, Windows Millennium Edition, Windows 2000, Windows XP Home Edition, Windows XP Professional, Windows Server 2003 family

.NET Framework Security:

- Full trust for the immediate caller. This member cannot be used by partially trusted code.

ComponentDesigner.PostFilterEvents Method

Allows a designer to change or remove items from the set of events that it exposes through a **TypeDescriptor**.

```
[Visual Basic]
Protected Overridable Sub PostFilterEvents( _
   ByVal events As IDictionary _
)
[C#]
protected virtual void PostFilterEvents(
   IDictionary events
);
```

```
[C++]
protected: virtual void PostFilterEvents(
   IDictionary* events
);
[JScript]
protected function PostFilterEvents(
   events : IDictionary
);
```

Parameters

events

The events for the class of the component.

Remarks

This method provides a way to change or remove the items within the dictionary of events that are exposed through a **TypeDescriptor**.

The keys in the dictionary of events are the names of the events. The objects are of type **PropertyDescriptor**. This method is called immediately after **PreFilterEvents**.

Notes to Implementers: You can directly filter the dictionary that is accessible through the *events* parameter, or you can leave it unchanged. If you override this method, call the base implementation after you perform your own filtering.

Requirements

Platforms: Windows 98, Windows NT 4.0, Windows Millennium Edition, Windows 2000, Windows XP Home Edition, Windows XP Professional, Windows Server 2003 family

.NET Framework Security:

- Full trust for the immediate caller. This member cannot be used by partially trusted code.

ComponentDesigner.PostFilterProperties Method

Allows a designer to change or remove items from the set of properties that it exposes through a **TypeDescriptor**.

```
[Visual Basic]
Protected Overridable Sub PostFilterProperties( _
   ByVal properties As IDictionary _
)
[C#]
protected virtual void PostFilterProperties(
   IDictionary properties
);
[C++]
protected: virtual void PostFilterProperties(
   IDictionary* properties
);
[JScript]
protected function PostFilterProperties(
   properties : IDictionary
);
```

Parameters

properties

The properties for the class of the component.

Remarks

This method provides a way to change or remove the items within the dictionary of properties that are exposed through a **TypeDescriptor**.

The keys in the dictionary of properties are the names of the properties. The objects are of type **PropertyDescriptor**. This method is called immediately after **PreFilterProperties**.

Notes to Implementers: You can directly filter the dictionary that is accessible through the *properties* parameter, or you can leave it unchanged. If you override this method, call the base implementation after you perform your own filtering.

Requirements

Platforms: Windows 98, Windows NT 4.0, Windows Millennium Edition, Windows 2000, Windows XP Home Edition, Windows XP Professional, Windows Server 2003 family

.NET Framework Security:

- Full trust for the immediate caller. This member cannot be used by partially trusted code.

ComponentDesigner.PreFilterAttributes Method

Allows a designer to add to the set of attributes that it exposes through a **TypeDescriptor**.

```
[Visual Basic]
Protected Overridable Sub PreFilterAttributes( _
   ByVal attributes As IDictionary _
)
[C#]
protected virtual void PreFilterAttributes(
   IDictionary attributes
);
[C++]
protected: virtual void PreFilterAttributes(
   IDictionary* attributes
);
[JScript]
protected function PreFilterAttributes(
   attributes : IDictionary
);
```

Parameters

attributes

The attributes for the class of the component.

Remarks

This method provides a way to add items to the dictionary of attributes that a designer exposes through a **TypeDescriptor**.

The keys in the dictionary of attributes are the type identifers of the attributes, as specified by the value of their **TypeId** property. The objects are of type **PropertyDescriptor**. This method is called immediately before **PostFilterAttributes**.

Notes to Implementers: You can directly modify the dictionary that is accessible through the *attributes* parameter, or you can leave it unchanged. If you override this method, call the base implementation before you perform your own filtering.

Requirements

Platforms: Windows 98, Windows NT 4.0, Windows Millennium Edition, Windows 2000, Windows XP Home Edition, Windows XP Professional, Windows Server 2003 family

.NET Framework Security:

- Full trust for the immediate caller. This member cannot be used by partially trusted code.

ComponentDesigner.PreFilterEvents Method

Allows a designer to add to the set of events that it exposes through a **TypeDescriptor**.

```
[Visual Basic]
Protected Overridable Sub PreFilterEvents( _
   ByVal events As IDictionary _
)
[C#]
protected virtual void PreFilterEvents(
   IDictionary events
);
[C++]
protected: virtual void PreFilterEvents(
   IDictionary* events
);
[JScript]
protected function PreFilterEvents(
   events : IDictionary
);
```

Parameters

events

The events for the class of the component.

Remarks

This method provides a way to add items to the dictionary of events that a designer exposes through a **TypeDescriptor**.

The keys in the dictionary of events are the names of the events. The objects are of type **PropertyDescriptor**. This method is called immediately before **PostFilterEvents**.

Notes to Implementers: You can directly modify the dictionary that is accessible through the *events* parameter, or you can leave it unchanged. If you override this method, call the base implementation before you perform your own filtering.

Requirements

Platforms: Windows 98, Windows NT 4.0, Windows Millennium Edition, Windows 2000, Windows XP Home Edition, Windows XP Professional, Windows Server 2003 family

.NET Framework Security:

- Full trust for the immediate caller. This member cannot be used by partially trusted code.

ComponentDesigner.PreFilterProperties Method

Allows a designer to add to the set of properties that it exposes through a **TypeDescriptor**.

```
[Visual Basic]
Protected Overridable Sub PreFilterProperties( _
   ByVal properties As IDictionary _
)
[C#]
protected virtual void PreFilterProperties(
   IDictionary properties
);
[C++]
protected: virtual void PreFilterProperties(
   IDictionary* properties
);
[JScript]
protected function PreFilterProperties(
   properties : IDictionary
);
```

Parameters

properties

The properties for the class of the component.

Remarks

This method provides a way to add items to the dictionary of properties that a designer exposes through a **TypeDescriptor**.

The keys in the dictionary of properties are the names of the properties. The objects are of type **PropertyDescriptor**. This method is called immediately before **PostFilterProperties**.

Notes to Implementers: You can directly modify the dictionary that is accessible through the *properties* parameter, or you can leave it unchanged. If you override this method, call the base implementation before you perform your own filtering.

Requirements

Platforms: Windows 98, Windows NT 4.0, Windows Millennium Edition, Windows 2000, Windows XP Home Edition, Windows XP Professional, Windows Server 2003 family

.NET Framework Security:

- Full trust for the immediate caller. This member cannot be used by partially trusted code.

ComponentDesigner.RaiseComponentChanged Method

Notifies the **IComponentChangeService** that this component has been changed.

```
[Visual Basic]
Protected Sub RaiseComponentChanged( _
   ByVal member As MemberDescriptor, _
   ByVal oldValue As Object, _
   ByVal newValue As Object _
)
```

[C#]
```
protected void RaiseComponentChanged(
   MemberDescriptor member,
   object oldValue,
   object newValue
);
```
[C++]
```
protected: void RaiseComponentChanged(
   MemberDescriptor* member,
   Object* oldValue,
   Object* newValue
);
```
[JScript]
```
protected function RaiseComponentChanged(
   member : MemberDescriptor,
   oldValue : Object,
   newValue : Object
);
```

Parameters

member
  A **MemberDescriptor** that indicates the member that has been changed.

oldValue
  The old value of the member.

newValue
  The new value of the member.

Remarks

Call this method only when you affect component properties directly and not through the accessors provided by **MemberDescriptor**.

Requirements

Platforms: Windows 98, Windows NT 4.0,
Windows Millennium Edition, Windows 2000,
Windows XP Home Edition, Windows XP Professional,
Windows Server 2003 family

.NET Framework Security:

- Full trust for the immediate caller. This member cannot be used by partially trusted code.

ComponentDesigner.RaiseComponentChanging Method

Notifies the **IComponentChangeService** that this component is about to be changed.

[Visual Basic]
```
Protected Sub RaiseComponentChanging( _
   ByVal member As MemberDescriptor _
)
```
[C#]
```
protected void RaiseComponentChanging(
   MemberDescriptor member
);
```
[C++]
```
protected: void RaiseComponentChanging(
   MemberDescriptor* member
);
```
[JScript]
```
protected function RaiseComponentChanging(
   member : MemberDescriptor
);
```

Parameters

member
  A **MemberDescriptor** that indicates the member that is about to be changed.

Remarks

Call this method only when you affect component properties directly and not through accessors provided by **MemberDescriptor**.

Requirements

Platforms: Windows 98, Windows NT 4.0,
Windows Millennium Edition, Windows 2000,
Windows XP Home Edition, Windows XP Professional,
Windows Server 2003 family

.NET Framework Security:

- Full trust for the immediate caller. This member cannot be used by partially trusted code.

ComponentDesigner.ShadowPropertyCollection Class

Represents a collection of shadow properties that should override inherited default or assigned values for specific properties. This class cannot be inherited.

System.Object
  System.ComponentModel.Design.ComponentDesigner.ShadowPropertyCollection

```
[Visual Basic]
NotInheritable Protected Class _
   ComponentDesigner.ShadowPropertyCollection
[C#]
protected sealed class ComponentDesigner.ShadowPropertyCollection
[C++]
protected __gc __sealed class
   ComponentDesigner.ShadowPropertyCollection
[JScript]
protected class ComponentDesigner.ShadowPropertyCollection
```

Thread Safety

Any public static (**Shared** in Visual Basic) members of this type are safe for multithreaded operations. Any instance members are not guaranteed to be thread safe.

Remarks

ComponentDesigner.ShadowPropertyCollection stores a collection of values for specific properties that override any other value for these properties at design time. This is useful for ensuring that a specific property is set to a specific value, for example, in situations when the background form should always have its visible property set to **true**.

Requirements

Namespace: System.ComponentModel.Design

Platforms: Windows 98, Windows NT 4.0, Windows Millennium Edition, Windows 2000, Windows XP Home Edition, Windows XP Professional, Windows Server 2003 family

Assembly: System.Design (in System.Design.dll)

ComponentDesigner.ShadowPropertyCollection.Item Property

Gets or sets the object at the specified index.

[C#] In C#, this property is the indexer for the **ComponentDesigner.ShadowPropertyCollection** class.

```
[Visual Basic]
Public Default Property Item( _
   ByVal propertyName As String _
) As Object
[C#]
public object this[
   string propertyName
] {get; set;}
[C++]
public: __property Object* get_Item(
   String* propertyName
);
public: __property void set_Item(
   String* propertyName,
   Object*
);
[JScript]
returnValue = ShadowPropertyCollectionObject.Item(propertyName);
ShadowPropertyCollectionObject.Item(propertyName) = returnValue;
-or-
returnValue = ShadowPropertyCollectionObject(propertyName);
ShadowPropertyCollectionObject(propertyName) = returnValue;
```

[JScript] In JScript, you can use the default indexed properties defined by a type, but you cannot explicitly define your own. However, specifying the **expando** attribute on a class automatically provides a default indexed property whose type is **Object** and whose index type is **String**.

Arguments [JScript]

propertyName
  The name of the property to access in the collection.

Parameters [Visual Basic, C#, C++]

propertyName
  The name of the property to access in the collection.

Property Value

The value of the specified property, if it exists in the collection. Otherwise, the value is retrieved from the current value of the nonshadowed property.

Remarks

This method returns the current value of a property, if the property has not been shadowed. Therefore, it is important to determine whether the property is shadowed by calling **Contains**.

Requirements

Platforms: Windows 98, Windows NT 4.0, Windows Millennium Edition, Windows 2000, Windows XP Home Edition, Windows XP Professional, Windows Server 2003 family

.NET Framework Security:

- Full trust for the immediate caller. This member cannot be used by partially trusted code.

ComponentDesigner.ShadowPropertyCollection.Contains Method

Indicates whether a property matching the specified name exists in the collection.

```
[Visual Basic]
Public Function Contains( _
   ByVal propertyName As String _
) As Boolean
[C#]
public bool Contains(
   string propertyName
);
```

```
[C++]
public: bool Contains(
   String* propertyName
);
[JScript]
public function Contains(
   propertyName : String
) : Boolean;
```

Parameters

propertyName
The name of the property to check for in the collection.

Return Value

true if the property exists in the collection; otherwise, **false**.

Requirements

Platforms: Windows 98, Windows NT 4.0, Windows Millennium Edition, Windows 2000, Windows XP Home Edition, Windows XP Professional, Windows Server 2003 family

.NET Framework Security:

- Full trust for the immediate caller. This member cannot be used by partially trusted code.

ComponentEventArgs Class

Provides data for the **ComponentAdded**, **ComponentAdding**, **ComponentRemoved**, and **ComponentRemoving** events.

System.Object
  System.EventArgs
    System.ComponentModel.Design.ComponentEventArgs

[Visual Basic]
```
<ComVisible(True)>
Public Class ComponentEventArgs
   Inherits EventArgs
```
[C#]
```
[ComVisible(true)]
public class ComponentEventArgs : EventArgs
```
[C++]
```
[ComVisible(true)]
public __gc class ComponentEventArgs : public EventArgs
```
[JScript]
```
public
   ComVisible(true)
class ComponentEventArgs extends EventArgs
```

Thread Safety

Any public static (**Shared** in Visual Basic) members of this type are safe for multithreaded operations. Any instance members are not guaranteed to be thread safe.

Remarks

ComponentEventArgs is the root event arguments class for all component management events. This type of event occurs when you add or remove components using a designer.

Example

[Visual Basic, C#, C++] The following example demonstrates creating a **ComponentEventArgs**.

[Visual Basic]
```
' This example method creates a ComponentEventArgs using the ↵
specified argument.
' Typically, this type of event args is created by a design ↵
mode subsystem.
Public Function CreateComponentEventArgs(ByVal component As ↵
 IComponent) As ComponentEventArgs

    Dim args As New ComponentEventArgs(component)

    ' The component that is related to the event:  args.Component

    Return args
End Function
```

[C#]
```
// This example method creates a ComponentEventArgs using ↵
the specified argument.
// Typically, this type of event args is created by a design ↵
mode subsystem.
public ComponentEventArgs CreateComponentEventArgs(IComponent ↵
component)
{
    ComponentEventArgs args = new ComponentEventArgs(component);

    // The component that is related to the event:  args.Component

    return args;
}
```

[C++]
```
// This example method creates a ComponentEventArgs using the ↵
specified argument.
// Typically, this type of event args is created by a design ↵
 mode subsystem.
ComponentEventArgs* CreateComponentEventArgs(IComponent* component)
{
    // The component that is related to the event:  args.Component

    return new ComponentEventArgs(component);
}
```

Requirements

Namespace: System.ComponentModel.Design

Platforms: Windows 98, Windows NT 4.0, Windows Millennium Edition, Windows 2000, Windows XP Home Edition, Windows XP Professional, Windows Server 2003 family

Assembly: System (in System.dll)

ComponentEventArgs Constructor

Initializes a new instance of the **ComponentEventArgs** class.

[Visual Basic]
```
Public Sub New( _
   ByVal component As IComponent _
)
```
[C#]
```
public ComponentEventArgs(
   IComponent component
);
```
[C++]
```
public: ComponentEventArgs(
   IComponent* component
);
```
[JScript]
```
public function ComponentEventArgs(
   component : IComponent
);
```

Parameters

component
  The component that is the source of the event.

Requirements

Platforms: Windows 98, Windows NT 4.0, Windows Millennium Edition, Windows 2000, Windows XP Home Edition, Windows XP Professional, Windows Server 2003 family

ComponentEventArgs.Component Property

Gets the component associated with the event.

[Visual Basic]
```
Public Overridable ReadOnly Property Component As IComponent
```
[C#]
```
public virtual IComponent Component {get;}
```
[C++]
```
public: __property virtual IComponent* get_Component();
```
[JScript]
```
public function get Component() : IComponent;
```

Property Value

The component associated with the event.

Requirements

Platforms: Windows 98, Windows NT 4.0, Windows Millennium Edition, Windows 2000, Windows XP Home Edition, Windows XP Professional, Windows Server 2003 family

ComponentEventHandler Delegate

Represents the method that will handle the **ComponentAdding**, **ComponentAdded**, **ComponentRemoving**, and **ComponentRemoved** events raised for component-level events.

[Visual Basic]
```
<Serializable>
<ComVisible(True)>
Public Delegate Sub ComponentEventHandler( _
   ByVal sender As Object, _
   ByVal e As ComponentEventArgs _
)
```
[C#]
```
[Serializable]
[ComVisible(true)]
public delegate void ComponentEventHandler(
   object sender,
   ComponentEventArgs e
);
```
[C++]
```
[Serializable]
[ComVisible(true)]
public __gc __delegate void ComponentEventHandler(
   Object* sender,
   ComponentEventArgs* e
);
```

[JScript] In JScript, you can use the delegates in the .NET Framework, but you cannot define your own.

Parameters [Visual Basic, C#, C++]

The declaration of your event handler must have the same parameters as the **ComponentEventHandler** delegate declaration.

sender
The source of the event.

e
A **ComponentEventArgs** that contains the event data.

Remarks

When you create a **ComponentEventHandler** delegate, you identify the method that will handle the event. To associate the event with your event handler, add an instance of the delegate to the event. The event handler is called whenever the event occurs, unless you remove the delegate. For more information about event-handler delegates, see **Events and Delegates**.

Example

[Visual Basic, C#, C++] The following example demonstrates registering a **ComponentEventHandler** and handling the **ComponentAdded**, **ComponentAdding**, **ComponentRemoved** and **ComponentRemoving** events.

[Visual Basic]
```
Public Sub LinkComponentEvent(ByVal changeService As ↵
IComponentChangeService)
    ' Registers an event handler for the ComponentAdded,
    ' ComponentAdding, ComponentRemoved, and ComponentRemoving events.
    AddHandler changeService.ComponentAdded, AddressOf ↵
Me.OnComponentEvent
    AddHandler changeService.ComponentAdding, AddressOf ↵
Me.OnComponentEvent
    AddHandler changeService.ComponentRemoved, AddressOf ↵
Me.OnComponentEvent
    AddHandler changeService.ComponentRemoving, AddressOf ↵
Me.OnComponentEvent
End Sub

Private Sub OnComponentEvent(ByVal sender As Object, ByVal e As ↵
ComponentEventArgs)
    ' Displays changed component information on the console.
    If Not (e.Component.Site Is Nothing) Then
        Console.WriteLine(("Name of the component related to ↵
 the event: " + e.Component.Site.Name))
    End If
End Sub
```
[C#]
```
public void LinkComponentEvent(IComponentChangeService changeService)
{
    // Registers an event handler for the ComponentAdded,
    // ComponentAdding, ComponentRemoved, and ComponentRemoving events.
    changeService.ComponentAdded += new ↵
ComponentEventHandler(this.OnComponentEvent);
    changeService.ComponentAdding += new ↵
ComponentEventHandler(this.OnComponentEvent);
    changeService.ComponentRemoved += new ↵
ComponentEventHandler(this.OnComponentEvent);
    changeService.ComponentRemoving += new ↵
ComponentEventHandler(this.OnComponentEvent);
}

private void OnComponentEvent(object sender, ComponentEventArgs e)
{
    // Displays changed component information on the console.
    if( e.Component.Site != null )
        Console.WriteLine("Name of the component related to the ↵
event: "+e.Component.Site.Name);
    Console.WriteLine("Type of the component related to the ↵
event: "+e.Component.GetType().FullName);
}
```
[C++]
```
public:

    void LinkComponentEvent(IComponentChangeService* changeService)
    {
        // Registers an event handler for the ComponentAdded,
        // ComponentAdding, ComponentRemoved, and ↵
ComponentRemoving events.
        changeService->ComponentAdded += new ↵
ComponentEventHandler(this, OnComponentEvent);
        changeService->ComponentAdding += new ↵
ComponentEventHandler(this, OnComponentEvent);
        changeService->ComponentRemoved += new ↵
ComponentEventHandler(this, OnComponentEvent);
        changeService->ComponentRemoving += new ↵
ComponentEventHandler(this, OnComponentEvent);
    }

private:

    void OnComponentEvent(Object* sender, ComponentEventArgs* e)
    {
        // Displays changed component information on the console.
        if( e->Component->Site != 0 )
            Console::WriteLine(S"Name of the component related ↵
to the event: {0}", e->Component->Site->Name);
        Console::WriteLine(S"Type of the component related to ↵
 the event: {0}", e->Component->GetType()->FullName);
    }
```

Requirements

Namespace: System.ComponentModel.Design

Platforms: Windows 98, Windows NT 4.0, Windows Millennium Edition, Windows 2000, Windows XP Home Edition, Windows XP Professional, Windows Server 2003 family

Assembly: System (in System.dll)

ComponentRenameEventArgs Class

Provides data for the **ComponentRename** event.

System.Object
  System.EventArgs
    System.ComponentModel.Design.ComponentRename-EventArgs

[Visual Basic]
```
<ComVisible(True)>
Public Class ComponentRenameEventArgs
   Inherits EventArgs
```
[C#]
```
[ComVisible(true)]
public class ComponentRenameEventArgs : EventArgs
```
[C++]
```
[ComVisible(true)]
public __gc class ComponentRenameEventArgs : public EventArgs
```
[JScript]
```
public
   ComVisible(true)
class ComponentRenameEventArgs extends EventArgs
```

Thread Safety

Any public static (**Shared** in Visual Basic) members of this type are safe for multithreaded operations. Any instance members are not guaranteed to be thread safe.

Remarks

A **ComponentRenameEventArgs** provides data about a **ComponentRename** event.

A **ComponentRenameEventArgs** object provides the following information:

- A **Component** property that references the component being renamed.
- An **OldName** property that indicates the old name of the component.
- A **NewName** property that indicates the new name of the component.

Example

[Visual Basic, C#, C++] The following example demonstrates creating a **ComponentRenameEventArgs**.

[Visual Basic]
```
' This example method creates a ComponentRenameEventArgs          ↵
 using the specified arguments.
' Typically, this type of event args is created by a design       ↵
mode subsystem.
Public Function CreateComponentRenameEventArgs(ByVal component    ↵
 As Object, ByVal oldName As String, ByVal newName As String)     ↵
As ComponentRenameEventArgs
    Dim args As New ComponentRenameEventArgs(component,           ↵
 oldName, newName)

    ' The component that was renamed:        args.Component
    ' The previous name of the component:    args.OldName
    ' The new name of the component:         args.NewName

    Return args
End Function
```

[C#]
```
// This example method creates a ComponentRenameEventArgs using     ↵
 the specified arguments.
// Typically, this type of event args is created by a design        ↵
 mode subsystem.
public ComponentRenameEventArgs CreateComponentRenameEventArgs      ↵
 (object component, string oldName, string newName)
{
    ComponentRenameEventArgs args = new                             ↵
ComponentRenameEventArgs(component, oldName, newName);

    // The component that was renamed:        args.Component
    // The previous name of the component:    args.OldName
    // The new name of the component:         args.NewName

    return args;
}
```

[C++]
```
// This example method creates a ComponentRenameEventArgs using     ↵
 the specified arguments.
// Typically, this type of event args is created by a design        ↵
mode subsystem.
ComponentRenameEventArgs* CreateComponentRenameEventArgs            ↵
 (Object* component, String* oldName, String* newName)
{
    // The component that was renamed:        args.Component
    // The previous name of the component:    args.OldName
    // The new name of the component:         args.NewName

    return new ComponentRenameEventArgs(component, oldName, newName);
}
```

Requirements

Namespace: System.ComponentModel.Design

Platforms: Windows 98, Windows NT 4.0, Windows Millennium Edition, Windows 2000, Windows XP Home Edition, Windows XP Professional, Windows Server 2003 family

Assembly: System (in System.dll)

ComponentRenameEventArgs Constructor

Initializes a new instance of the **ComponentRenameEventArgs** class.

[Visual Basic]
```
Public Sub New( _
   ByVal component As Object, _
   ByVal oldName As String, _
   ByVal newName As String _
)
```
[C#]
```
public ComponentRenameEventArgs(
   object component,
   string oldName,
   string newName
);
```
[C++]
```
public: ComponentRenameEventArgs(
   Object* component,
   String* oldName,
   String* newName
);
```

[JScript]
```
public function ComponentRenameEventArgs(
   component : Object,
   oldName : String,
   newName : String
);
```

Parameters

component
  The component to be renamed.

oldName
  The old name of the component.

newName
  The new name of the component.

Requirements

Platforms: Windows 98, Windows NT 4.0, Windows Millennium Edition, Windows 2000, Windows XP Home Edition, Windows XP Professional, Windows Server 2003 family

ComponentRenameEventArgs.Component Property

Gets the component that is being renamed.

[Visual Basic]
```
Public ReadOnly Property Component As Object
```
[C#]
```
public object Component {get;}
```
[C++]
```
public: __property Object* get_Component();
```
[JScript]
```
public function get Component() : Object;
```

Property Value

The component that is being renamed.

Requirements

Platforms: Windows 98, Windows NT 4.0, Windows Millennium Edition, Windows 2000, Windows XP Home Edition, Windows XP Professional, Windows Server 2003 family

ComponentRenameEventArgs.NewName Property

Gets the name of the component after the rename event.

[Visual Basic]
```
Public Overridable ReadOnly Property NewName As String
```
[C#]
```
public virtual string NewName {get;}
```
[C++]
```
public: __property virtual String* get_NewName();
```
[JScript]
```
public function get NewName() : String;
```

Property Value

The name of the component after the rename event.

Requirements

Platforms: Windows 98, Windows NT 4.0, Windows Millennium Edition, Windows 2000, Windows XP Home Edition, Windows XP Professional, Windows Server 2003 family

ComponentRenameEventArgs.OldName Property

Gets the name of the component before the rename event.

[Visual Basic]
```
Public Overridable ReadOnly Property OldName As String
```
[C#]
```
public virtual string OldName {get;}
```
[C++]
```
public: __property virtual String* get_OldName();
```
[JScript]
```
public function get OldName() : String;
```

Property Value

The previous name of the component.

Requirements

Platforms: Windows 98, Windows NT 4.0, Windows Millennium Edition, Windows 2000, Windows XP Home Edition, Windows XP Professional, Windows Server 2003 family

ComponentRenameEvent-Handler Delegate

Represents the method that will handle a **ComponentRename** event.

[Visual Basic]
```
<Serializable>
<ComVisible(True)>
Public Delegate Sub ComponentRenameEventHandler( _
   ByVal sender As Object, _
   ByVal e As ComponentRenameEventArgs _
)
```
[C#]
```
[Serializable]
[ComVisible(true)]
public delegate void ComponentRenameEventHandler(
   object sender,
   ComponentRenameEventArgs e
);
```
[C++]
```
[Serializable]
[ComVisible(true)]
public __gc __delegate void ComponentRenameEventHandler(
   Object* sender,
   ComponentRenameEventArgs* e
);
```
[JScript] In JScript, you can use the delegates in the .NET Framework, but you cannot define your own.

Parameters [Visual Basic, C#, C++]

The declaration of your event handler must have the same parameters as the **ComponentRenameEventHandler** delegate declaration.

sender
    The source of the event.

e
    A **ComponentRenameEventArgs** that contains the event data.

Remarks

When you create a **ComponentRenameEventHandler** delegate, you identify the method that will handle the event. To associate the event with your event handler, add an instance of the delegate to the event. The event handler is called whenever the event occurs, unless you remove the delegate.

Example

[Visual Basic, C#, C++] The following example demonstrates registering a **ComponentRenameEventHandler** and handling the **ComponentRename** event.

[Visual Basic]
```
Public Sub LinkComponentRenameEvent(ByVal changeService As
IComponentChangeService)
    ' Registers an event handler for the ComponentRename event.
    AddHandler changeService.ComponentRename, AddressOf
Me.OnComponentRename
End Sub

Private Sub OnComponentRename(ByVal sender As Object, ByVal e
As ComponentRenameEventArgs)
    ' Displays component renamed information on the console.
    Console.WriteLine(("Type of the component that has been
 renamed: " + e.Component.GetType().FullName))
    Console.WriteLine(("New name of the component that has
 been renamed: " + e.NewName))
    Console.WriteLine(("Old name of the component that has
been renamed: " + e.OldName))
End Sub
```

[C#]
```
public void LinkComponentRenameEvent(IComponentChangeService
changeService)
{
    // Registers an event handler for the ComponentRename event.
    changeService.ComponentRename += new
ComponentRenameEventHandler(this.OnComponentRename);
}

private void OnComponentRename(object sender,
ComponentRenameEventArgs e)
{
    // Displayss component renamed information on the console.
    Console.WriteLine("Type of the component that has been
renamed:
"+e.Component.GetType().FullName);
    Console.WriteLine("New name of the component that has been
 renamed: "+e.NewName);
    Console.WriteLine("Old name of the component that has been
renamed: "+e.OldName);
}
```

[C++]
```
public:

    void LinkComponentRenameEvent(IComponentChangeService*
changeService)
    {
        // Registers an event handler for the ComponentRename event.
        changeService->ComponentRename += new
ComponentRenameEventHandler(this, OnComponentRename);
    }

private:

    void OnComponentRename(Object* sender, ComponentRenameEventArgs* e)
    {
        // Displayss component renamed information on the console.
        Console::WriteLine(S"Type of the component that has
 been renamed: {0}", e->Component->GetType()->FullName);
        Console::WriteLine(S"New name of the component that
 has been renamed: {0}", e->NewName);
        Console::WriteLine(S"Old name of the component that
 has been renamed: {0}", e->OldName);
    }
```

Requirements

Namespace: System.ComponentModel.Design

Platforms: Windows 98, Windows NT 4.0, Windows Millennium Edition, Windows 2000, Windows XP Home Edition, Windows XP Professional, Windows Server 2003 family

Assembly: System (in System.dll)

DateTimeEditor Class

This type supports the .NET Framework infrastructure and is not intended to be used directly from your code.

```
[Visual Basic]
Public Class DateTimeEditor
   Inherits UITypeEditor
[C#]
public class DateTimeEditor : UITypeEditor
[C++]
public __gc class DateTimeEditor : public UITypeEditor
[JScript]
public class DateTimeEditor extends UITypeEditor
```

DateTimeEditor Constructor

This member supports the .NET Framework infrastructure and is not intended to be used directly from your code.

```
[Visual Basic]
Public Sub New()
[C#]
public DateTimeEditor();
[C++]
public: DateTimeEditor();
[JScript]
public function DateTimeEditor();
```

DateTimeEditor.EditValue Method

This member supports the .NET Framework infrastructure and is not intended to be used directly from your code.

Overload List

This member supports the .NET Framework infrastructure and is not intended to be used directly from your code.

[Visual Basic] **Overloads Overrides Public Function EditValue(ITypeDescriptorContext, IServiceProvider, Object) As Object**

[C#] **public override object EditValue(ITypeDescriptorContext, IServiceProvider, object);**

[C++] **public: Object* EditValue(ITypeDescriptorContext*, IServiceProvider*, Object*);**

[JScript] **public override function EditValue(ITypeDescriptorContext, IServiceProvider, Object) : Object;**

This member supports the .NET Framework infrastructure and is not intended to be used directly from your code.

[Visual Basic] **Overloads Public Function EditValue(IServiceProvider, Object) As Object**

[C#] **public object EditValue(IServiceProvider, object);**

[C++] **public: Object* EditValue(IServiceProvider*, Object*);**

[JScript] **public function EditValue(IServiceProvider, Object) : Object;**

DateTimeEditor.EditValue Method (ITypeDescriptorContext, IServiceProvider, Object)

This member supports the .NET Framework infrastructure and is not intended to be used directly from your code.

```
[Visual Basic]
Overrides Overloads Public Function EditValue( _
   ByVal context As ITypeDescriptorContext, _
   ByVal provider As IServiceProvider, _
   ByVal value As Object _
) As Object
[C#]
public override object EditValue(
   ITypeDescriptorContext context,
   IServiceProvider provider,
   object value
);
[C++]
public: Object* EditValue(
   ITypeDescriptorContext* context,
   IServiceProvider* provider,
   Object* value
);
[JScript]
public override function EditValue(
   context : ITypeDescriptorContext,
   provider : IServiceProvider,
   value : Object
) : Object;
```

DateTimeEditor.GetEditStyle Method

This member supports the .NET Framework infrastructure and is not intended to be used directly from your code.

Overload List

This member supports the .NET Framework infrastructure and is not intended to be used directly from your code.

[Visual Basic] **Overloads Overrides Public Function GetEditStyle(ITypeDescriptorContext) As UITypeEditorEditStyle**

[C#] **public override UITypeEditorEditStyle GetEditStyle(ITypeDescriptorContext);**

[C++] **public: UITypeEditorEditStyle GetEditStyle(ITypeDescriptorContext*);**

[JScript] **public override function GetEditStyle(ITypeDescriptorContext) : UITypeEditorEditStyle;**

This member supports the .NET Framework infrastructure and is not intended to be used directly from your code.

[Visual Basic] **Overloads Public Function GetEditStyle() As UITypeEditorEditStyle**

[C#] **public UITypeEditorEditStyle GetEditStyle();**

[C++] **public: UITypeEditorEditStyle GetEditStyle();**

[JScript] **public function GetEditStyle() : UITypeEditorEditStyle;**

DateTimeEditor.GetEditStyle Method (ITypeDescriptorContext)

This member supports the .NET Framework infrastructure and is not intended to be used directly from your code.

[Visual Basic]
```
Overrides Overloads Public Function GetEditStyle( _
   ByVal context As ITypeDescriptorContext _
) As UITypeEditorEditStyle
```
[C#]
```
public override UITypeEditorEditStyle GetEditStyle(
   ITypeDescriptorContext context
);
```
[C++]
```
public: UITypeEditorEditStyle GetEditStyle(
   ITypeDescriptorContext* context
);
```
[JScript]
```
public override function GetEditStyle(
   context : ITypeDescriptorContext
) : UITypeEditorEditStyle;
```

DesignerCollection Class

Represents a collection of designers.

System.Object
  System.ComponentModel.Design.DesignerCollection

[Visual Basic]
```
Public Class DesignerCollection
   Implements ICollection, IEnumerable
```
[C#]
```
public class DesignerCollection : ICollection, IEnumerable
```
[C++]
```
public __gc class DesignerCollection : public ICollection,
   IEnumerable
```
[JScript]
```
public class DesignerCollection implements ICollection, IEnumerable
```

Thread Safety

Any public static (**Shared** in Visual Basic) members of this type are safe for multithreaded operations. Any instance members are not guaranteed to be thread safe.

Remarks

This collection object can store references to a set of designers.

Requirements

Namespace: System.ComponentModel.Design

Platforms: Windows 98, Windows NT 4.0, Windows Millennium Edition, Windows 2000, Windows XP Home Edition, Windows XP Professional, Windows Server 2003 family

Assembly: System (in System.dll)

DesignerCollection Constructor

Initializes a new instance of the **DesignerCollection** class.

Overload List

Initializes a new instance of the **DesignerCollection** class that contains the specified designers.

[Visual Basic] **Public Sub New(IDesignerHost())**

[C#] **public DesignerCollection(IDesignerHost[]);**

[C++] **public: DesignerCollection(IDesignerHost*[]);**

[JScript] **public function DesignerCollection(IDesignerHost[]);**

Initializes a new instance of the **DesignerCollection** class that contains the specified set of designers.

[Visual Basic] **Public Sub New(IList)**

[C#] **public DesignerCollection(IList);**

[C++] **public: DesignerCollection(IList*);**

[JScript] **public function DesignerCollection(IList);**

DesignerCollection Constructor (IDesignerHost[])

Initializes a new instance of the **DesignerCollection** class that contains the specified designers.

[Visual Basic]
```
Public Sub New( _
   ByVal designers() As IDesignerHost _
)
```
[C#]
```
public DesignerCollection(
   IDesignerHost[] designers
);
```
[C++]
```
public: DesignerCollection(
   IDesignerHost* designers[]
);
```
[JScript]
```
public function DesignerCollection(
   designers : IDesignerHost[]
);
```

Parameters

designers
   An array of **IDesignerHost** objects to store.

Remarks

Creates a new designer collection from an array of designers. The collection does not clone the array.

Requirements

Platforms: Windows 98, Windows NT 4.0, Windows Millennium Edition, Windows 2000, Windows XP Home Edition, Windows XP Professional, Windows Server 2003 family

DesignerCollection Constructor (IList)

Initializes a new instance of the **DesignerCollection** class that contains the specified set of designers.

[Visual Basic]
```
Public Sub New( _
   ByVal designers As IList _
)
```
[C#]
```
public DesignerCollection(
   IList designers
);
```
[C++]
```
public: DesignerCollection(
   IList* designers
);
```
[JScript]
```
public function DesignerCollection(
   designers : IList
);
```

Parameters

designers
   A list that contains the collection of designers to add.

Requirements

Platforms: Windows 98, Windows NT 4.0, Windows Millennium Edition, Windows 2000, Windows XP Home Edition, Windows XP Professional, Windows Server 2003 family

DesignerCollection.Count Property

Gets the number of designers in the collection.

[Visual Basic]
```
Public ReadOnly Property Count As Integer
```

```
[C#]
public int Count {get;}
[C++]
public: __property int get_Count();
[JScript]
public function get Count() : int;
```

Property Value

The number of designers in the collection.

Requirements

Platforms: Windows 98, Windows NT 4.0, Windows Millennium Edition, Windows 2000, Windows XP Home Edition, Windows XP Professional, Windows Server 2003 family

DesignerCollection.Item Property

Gets the designer at the specified index.

[C#] In C#, this property is the indexer for the **DesignerCollection** class.

```
[Visual Basic]
Public Overridable Default ReadOnly Property Item( _
   ByVal index As Integer _
) As IDesignerHost
[C#]
public virtual IDesignerHost this[
   int index
] {get;}
[C++]
public: __property virtual IDesignerHost* get_Item(
   int index
);
[JScript]
returnValue = DesignerCollectionObject.Item(index);
-or-
returnValue = DesignerCollectionObject(index);
```

[JScript] In JScript, you can use the default indexed properties defined by a type, but you cannot explicitly define your own. However, specifying the **expando** attribute on a class automatically provides a default indexed property whose type is **Object** and whose index type is **String**.

Arguments [JScript]

index
The index of the designer to return.

Parameters [Visual Basic, C#, C++]

index
The index of the designer to return.

Property Value

The designer at the specified index.

Requirements

Platforms: Windows 98, Windows NT 4.0, Windows Millennium Edition, Windows 2000, Windows XP Home Edition, Windows XP Professional, Windows Server 2003 family

DesignerCollection.GetEnumerator Method

Gets a new enumerator for this collection.

```
[Visual Basic]
Public Function GetEnumerator() As IEnumerator
[C#]
public IEnumerator GetEnumerator();
[C++]
public: IEnumerator* GetEnumerator();
[JScript]
public function GetEnumerator() : IEnumerator;
```

Return Value

An **IEnumerator** that enumerates the collection.

Requirements

Platforms: Windows 98, Windows NT 4.0, Windows Millennium Edition, Windows 2000, Windows XP Home Edition, Windows XP Professional, Windows Server 2003 family

DesignerCollection.ICollection.CopyTo Method

This member supports the .NET Framework infrastructure and is not intended to be used directly from your code.

```
[Visual Basic]
Private Sub CopyTo( _
   ByVal array As Array, _
   ByVal index As Integer _
) Implements ICollection.CopyTo
[C#]
void ICollection.CopyTo(
   Array array,
   int index
);
[C++]
private: void ICollection::CopyTo(
   Array* array,
   int index
);
[JScript]
private function ICollection.CopyTo(
   array : Array,
   index : int
);
```

DesignerCollection.IEnumerable.Get-Enumerator Method

This member supports the .NET Framework infrastructure and is not intended to be used directly from your code.

```
[Visual Basic]
Private Function GetEnumerator() As IEnumerator Implements _
   IEnumerable.GetEnumerator
[C#]
IEnumerator IEnumerable.GetEnumerator();
[C++]
private: IEnumerator* IEnumerable::GetEnumerator();
[JScript]
private function IEnumerable.GetEnumerator() : IEnumerator;
```

DesignerEventArgs Class

Provides data for the **DesignerCreated** and **DesignerDisposed** events.

System.Object
  System.EventArgs
    System.ComponentModel.Design.DesignerEventArgs

[Visual Basic]
```
Public Class DesignerEventArgs
   Inherits EventArgs
```
[C#]
```
public class DesignerEventArgs : EventArgs
```
[C++]
```
public __gc class DesignerEventArgs : public EventArgs
```
[JScript]
```
public class DesignerEventArgs extends EventArgs
```

Thread Safety

Any public static (**Shared** in Visual Basic) members of this type are safe for multithreaded operations. Any instance members are not guaranteed to be thread safe.

Remarks

The **DesignerCreated** and **DesignerDisposed** events are raised when a document is created or disposed of.

Example

[Visual Basic, C#, C++] The following example demonstrates creating a **DesignerEventArgs**.

[Visual Basic]
```
' This example method creates a DesignerEventArgs using the ↵
 specified designer host.
' Typically, this type of event args is created by the ↵
IDesignerEventService.
Public Function CreateComponentEventArgs(ByVal host As ↵
 IDesignerHost) As DesignerEventArgs

    Dim args As New DesignerEventArgs(host)

    ' The designer host of the created or disposed document: ↵
 args.Component

    Return args

End Function
```
[C#]
```
// This example method creates a DesignerEventArgs using the ↵
specified designer host.
// Typically, this type of event args is created by the ↵
IDesignerEventService.
public DesignerEventArgs CreateComponentEventArgs(IDesignerHost host)
{
    DesignerEventArgs args = new DesignerEventArgs(host);

    // The designer host of the created or disposed document: ↵
args.Component

    return args;
}
```
[C++]
```
// This example method creates a DesignerEventArgs using the ↵
specified designer host.
// Typically, this type of event args is created by the ↵
IDesignerEventService.
DesignerEventArgs* CreateComponentEventArgs(IDesignerHost* host)
{
    // The designer host of the created or disposed document: ↵
args.Component

    return new DesignerEventArgs(host);
}
```

Requirements

Namespace: System.ComponentModel.Design

Platforms: Windows 98, Windows NT 4.0, Windows Millennium Edition, Windows 2000, Windows XP Home Edition, Windows XP Professional, Windows Server 2003 family

Assembly: System (in System.dll)

DesignerEventArgs Constructor

Initializes a new instance of the **DesignerEventArgs** class.

[Visual Basic]
```
Public Sub New( _
   ByVal host As IDesignerHost _
)
```
[C#]
```
public DesignerEventArgs(
   IDesignerHost host
);
```
[C++]
```
public: DesignerEventArgs(
   IDesignerHost* host
);
```
[JScript]
```
public function DesignerEventArgs(
   host : IDesignerHost
);
```

Parameters

host
  The **IDesignerHost** of the document.

Requirements

Platforms: Windows 98, Windows NT 4.0, Windows Millennium Edition, Windows 2000, Windows XP Home Edition, Windows XP Professional, Windows Server 2003 family

DesignerEventArgs.Designer Property

Gets the host of the document.

[Visual Basic]
```
Public ReadOnly Property Designer As IDesignerHost
```
[C#]
```
public IDesignerHost Designer {get;}
```
[C++]
```
public: __property IDesignerHost* get_Designer();
```
[JScript]
```
public function get Designer() : IDesignerHost;
```

Property Value

The **IDesignerHost** of the document.

Requirements

Platforms: Windows 98, Windows NT 4.0, Windows Millennium Edition, Windows 2000, Windows XP Home Edition, Windows XP Professional, Windows Server 2003 family

DesignerEventHandler Delegate

Represents the method that will handle the **DesignerCreated** and **DesignerDisposed** events that are raised when a document is created or disposed of.

[Visual Basic]
```
<Serializable>
Public Delegate Sub DesignerEventHandler( _
   ByVal sender As Object, _
   ByVal e As DesignerEventArgs _
)
```
[C#]
```
[Serializable]
public delegate void DesignerEventHandler(
   object sender,
   DesignerEventArgs e
);
```
[C++]
```
[Serializable]
public __gc __delegate void DesignerEventHandler(
   Object* sender,
   DesignerEventArgs* e
);
```

[JScript] In JScript, you can use the delegates in the .NET Framework, but you cannot define your own.

Parameters [Visual Basic, C#, C++]

The declaration of your event handler must have the same parameters as the **DesignerEventHandler** delegate declaration.

sender
: The source of the event.

e
: A **DesignerEventArgs** that contains the event data.

Remarks

When you create a **DesignerEventHandler** delegate, you identify the method that will handle the event. To associate the event with your event handler, add an instance of the delegate to the event. The event handler is called whenever the event occurs, unless you remove the delegate.

Example

[Visual Basic, C#, C++] The following example demonstrates registering a **DesignerEventHandler** and handling the **DesignerCreated** and **DesignerDisposed** events.

[Visual Basic]
```
Public Sub LinkDesignerEvent(ByVal eventService As                ↵
IDesignerEventService)
    ' Registers an event handler for the DesignerCreated          ↵
and DesignerDisposed events.
    AddHandler eventService.DesignerCreated, AddressOf            ↵
Me.OnDesignerEvent
    AddHandler eventService.DesignerDisposed, AddressOf           ↵
Me.OnDesignerEvent
End Sub

Private Sub OnDesignerEvent(ByVal sender As Object, ByVal e       ↵
 As DesignerEventArgs)
    ' Displays designer event information on the console.
    Console.WriteLine(("Name of the root component of the         ↵
created or disposed designer: " + e.Designer.RootComponentClassName))
End Sub
```

[C#]
```
public void LinkDesignerEvent(IDesignerEventService eventService)
{
    // Registers an event handler for the DesignerCreated         ↵
 and DesignerDisposed events.
    eventService.DesignerCreated += new                           ↵
DesignerEventHandler(this.OnDesignerEvent);
    eventService.DesignerDisposed += new                          ↵
DesignerEventHandler(this.OnDesignerEvent);
}

private void OnDesignerEvent(object sender, DesignerEventArgs e)
{
    // Displays designer event information on the console.
    Console.WriteLine("Name of the root component of the created  ↵
 or disposed designer: "+e.Designer.RootComponentClassName);
}
```

[C++]
```
public:

    void LinkDesignerEvent(IDesignerEventService* eventService)
    {
        // Registers an event handler for the DesignerCreated     ↵
 and DesignerDisposed events.
        eventService->DesignerCreated += new DesignerEventHandler ↵
 (this, OnDesignerEvent);
        eventService->DesignerDisposed += new                     ↵
DesignerEventHandler(this, OnDesignerEvent);
    }

private:

    void OnDesignerEvent(Object* sender, DesignerEventArgs* e)
    {
        // Displays designer event information on the console.
        Console::WriteLine(S"Name of the root component of the    ↵
 created or disposed designer: {0}", +e->Designer             ↵
RootComponentClassName);
    }
```

Requirements

Namespace: System.ComponentModel.Design

Platforms: Windows 98, Windows NT 4.0, Windows Millennium Edition, Windows 2000, Windows XP Home Edition, Windows XP Professional, Windows Server 2003 family

Assembly: System (in System.dll)

DesignerTransaction Class

Provides a way to group a series of design-time actions to improve performance and enable most types of changes to be undone.

System.Object
  System.ComponentModel.Design.DesignerTransaction

[Visual Basic]
```
MustInherit Public Class DesignerTransaction
   Implements IDisposable
```
[C#]
```
public abstract class DesignerTransaction : IDisposable
```
[C++]
```
public __gc __abstract class DesignerTransaction : public
   IDisposable
```
[JScript]
```
public abstract class DesignerTransaction implements IDisposable
```

Thread Safety

Any public static (**Shared** in Visual Basic) members of this type are safe for multithreaded operations. Any instance members are not guaranteed to be thread safe.

Remarks

Transactions can track actions that can be undone later. Changes made during a transaction can be reversed by cancelling a transaction, which automatically attempts to reverse each change by setting each changed property to its pre-change value. Transactions can also improve performance during a series of operations by deferring updates to the display until the completion of the transaction.

When a transaction is in progress, some components defer their processing until the transaction has completed by listening to the **TransactionOpening** and **TransactionClosed** events. The Properties window, for example, does not update its display after a transaction has opened until the transaction has closed.

To use transactions for undoable or multiple operations, have your designer create a **DesignerTransaction** for each operation or series of operations which should be undoable. Be careful not to perform actions outside the transactions that might prevent a sequence of undo events from completing successfully.

You can obtain a new **DesignerTransaction** by calling the **CreateTransaction** method of an **IDesignerHost**. Be sure to obtain each **DesignerTransaction** from the active **IDesignerHost** in order to correctly integrate with the designer transaction processing mechanism, rather than creating a new **DesignerTransaction** directly.

To perform an action within a transaction, you must first create a transaction. Then you must call the **OnComponentChanging** method before each change or set of changes occurs, and the **OnComponentChanged** method after each change or set of changes occur. Finally, complete and close the transaction by calling the **Commit** method.

> **Note** When making changes to property values, use the **SetValue** method of a **PropertyDescriptor**, which calls the component change methods of the **IComponentChangeService** and creates a **DesignerTransaction** representing the change automatically.

To perform a transaction:

1. Call **CreateTransaction** to obtain a **DesignerTransaction** that can be used to control the transaction.
2. Within a **try** block, for each action that you want to track with a **DesignerTransaction**, call the **OnComponentChanging** event, make the change or changes, then call the **OnComponentChanged** event to signal that the change or changes have been made.
3. To complete the transaction, call **Commit** from within a **finally** block.

In C#, you can use the **using** statement rather than a **try...finally** block, such as in the following example.

```
using (host.CreateTransaction() {
// do work here
}
```

To cancel and attempt to roll back a transaction before it has been committed, call the **Cancel** method. When the **Cancel** method is invoked, the actions tracked by the **DesignerTransaction** are reversed to attempt to roll back the changes. To undo actions which occurred as part of earlier transactions, you must use the undo command provided by the development environment.

Example

[Visual Basic, C#, C++] The following example program demonstrates how to create a **DesignerTransaction** from a designer. The designer can optionally display notifications about designer transaction events. To run this sample, compile the source code into a class library, add a reference to the compiled DLL to a project and add the component in the library to the Toolbox by right-clicking the toolbox, clicking **Customize Toolbox**, and selecting the .dll file that contains the DTComponent sample. Add an instance of the DTComponent to a form while in design mode, and a message box appears asking whether you would like to receive designer transaction event notifications. You may toggle these notifications using the shortcut menu that appears when you right-click an instance of the DTComponent. Transactions are created when you change values using the Properties window. You can also have the designer perform a transaction by clicking **Perform Example Transaction** on the shortcut menu for the component.

[Visual Basic]
```
Imports System
Imports System.ComponentModel
Imports System.ComponentModel.Design
Imports System.Windows.Forms
Imports System.Windows.Forms.Design

'   This sample demonstrates how to perform a series of actions      ↵
in a designer
'   transaction, how to change values of properties of a             ↵
component from a
'   designer, and how to complete transactions without being         ↵
interrupted
'   by other activities.

'   To run this sample, add this code to a class library project     ↵
 and compile.
'   Create a new Windows Forms project or load a form in the         ↵
designer. Add a
'   reference to the class library that was compiled in the first step.
'   Right-click the Toolbox in design mode and click Customize Toolbox.
'   Browse to the class library that was compiled in the first step and
'   select OK until the DTComponent item appears in the Toolbox.     ↵
 Add an
'   instance of this component to the form.

'   When the component is created and added to the component         ↵
 tray for your
'   design project, the Initialize method of the designer is called.
```

```
'   This method displays a message box informing you that ↵
 designer transaction
'   event handlers are being registered unless you click Cancel. ↵
 When you set
'   properties in the properties window, each change will be ↵
encapsulated in
'   a designer transaction, allowing the change to be undone later.

'   When you right-click the component, the shortcut menu for ↵
the component
'   is displayed. The designer constructs this menu according ↵
to whether
'   designer transaction notifications are enabled, and offers ↵
 the option
'   of enabling or disabling the notifications, depending on the ↵
current
'   mode. The shortcut menu also presents a Perform Example Transaction
'   item which will set the values of the component's ↵
StringProperty and
'   CountProperty properties. You can undo the last designer ↵
transaction using
'   the Undo command provided by the Visual Studio .NET ↵
development environment.

Namespace DesignerTransactionSample

    ' Associate the DTDesigner with this component
    <DesignerAttribute(GetType(DTDesigner))> _
    Public Class DTComponent
        Inherits System.ComponentModel.Component
        Private m_String As String
        Private m_Count As Integer

        Public Property StringProperty() As String
            Get
                Return m_String
            End Get
            Set(ByVal Value As String)
                m_String = Value
            End Set
        End Property

        Public Property CountProperty() As Integer
            Get
                Return m_Count
            End Get
            Set(ByVal Value As Integer)
                m_Count = Value
            End Set
        End Property

        Private Sub InitializeComponent()
            m_String = "Initial Value"
            m_Count = 0
        End Sub 'InitializeComponent

    End Class 'DTComponent

    Friend Class DTDesigner
        Inherits ComponentDesigner

        Private notification_mode As Boolean = False
        Private count As Integer = 10

        ' The Verbs property is overridden from ComponentDesigner
        Public Overrides ReadOnly Property Verbs() As ↵
 DesignerVerbCollection
            Get
                Dim dvc As New DesignerVerbCollection()
                dvc.Add(New DesignerVerb("Perform Example ↵
 Transaction", AddressOf Me.DoTransaction))
                If notification_mode Then
                    dvc.Add(New DesignerVerb("End Designer ↵
 Transaction Notifications", AddressOf Me.UnlinkDTNotifications))
                Else
                    dvc.Add(New DesignerVerb("Show Designer ↵
Transaction Notifications", AddressOf Me.LinkDTNotifications))
                End If
                Return dvc
            End Get
        End Property

        Public Overrides Sub Initialize(ByVal component As ↵
System.ComponentModel.IComponent)
            MyBase.Initialize(component)

            Dim host As IDesignerHost = ↵
CType(GetService(GetType(IDesignerHost)), IDesignerHost)
            If host Is Nothing Then
                MessageBox.Show("The IDesignerHost service ↵
interface could not be obtained.")
                Return
            End If

            If MessageBox.Show("Press the Yes button to ↵
display notification message boxes for the designer ↵
transaction opened and closed notifications.", "Link ↵
DesignerTransaction Notifications?", MessageBoxButtons.YesNo, ↵
MessageBoxIcon.Question, MessageBoxDefaultButton.Button1, ↵
MessageBoxOptions.RightAlign) = DialogResult.Yes Then
                AddHandler host.TransactionOpened, AddressOf ↵
OnDesignerTransactionOpened
                AddHandler host.TransactionClosed, AddressOf ↵
OnDesignerTransactionClosed
                notification_mode = True
            End If
        End Sub 'Initialize

        Private Sub LinkDTNotifications(ByVal sender As Object, ↵
 ByVal e As EventArgs)
            If notification_mode = False Then
                Dim host As IDesignerHost = ↵
CType(GetService(GetType(IDesignerHost)), IDesignerHost)
                If Not (host Is Nothing) Then
                    notification_mode = True
                    AddHandler host.TransactionOpened, AddressOf ↵
OnDesignerTransactionOpened
                    AddHandler host.TransactionClosed, AddressOf ↵
OnDesignerTransactionClosed
                End If
            End If
        End Sub 'LinkDTNotifications

        Private Sub UnlinkDTNotifications(ByVal sender As ↵
Object, ByVal e As EventArgs)
            If notification_mode Then
                Dim host As IDesignerHost = ↵
CType(GetService(GetType(IDesignerHost)), IDesignerHost)
                If Not (host Is Nothing) Then
                    notification_mode = False
                    RemoveHandler host.TransactionOpened, ↵
AddressOf Me.OnDesignerTransactionOpened
                    RemoveHandler host.TransactionClosed, ↵
AddressOf Me.OnDesignerTransactionClosed
                End If
            End If
        End Sub 'UnlinkDTNotifications

        Private Sub OnDesignerTransactionOpened(ByVal sender As ↵
Object, ByVal e As EventArgs)
            System.Windows.Forms.MessageBox.Show("A Designer ↵
Transaction was started. (TransactionOpened)")
        End Sub 'OnDesignerTransactionOpened

        Private Sub OnDesignerTransactionClosed(ByVal sender As ↵
Object, ByVal e As DesignerTransactionCloseEventArgs)
            System.Windows.Forms.MessageBox.Show("A Designer ↵
Transaction was completed. (TransactionClosed)")
        End Sub 'OnDesignerTransactionClosed
```

```
        Private Sub DoTransaction(ByVal sender As Object, ByVal ↵
 e As EventArgs)
            Dim host As IDesignerHost = ↵
CType(GetService(GetType(IDesignerHost)), IDesignerHost)
            Dim t As DesignerTransaction = ↵
host.CreateTransaction("Change Text and Size")

            ' The code within the using statement is considered ↵
 to be a single transaction.
            ' When the user selects Undo, the system will undo ↵
everything executed in this code block.
            Try
                If (notification_mode) Then
                    System.Windows.Forms.MessageBox.Show ↵
 ("Entering a Designer-Initiated Designer Transaction")
                End If

                Dim someText As PropertyDescriptor = ↵
TypeDescriptor.GetProperties(Component)("StringProperty")
                someText.SetValue(Component, "This text was set ↵
by the designer for this component.")
                Dim anInteger As PropertyDescriptor = ↵
TypeDescriptor.GetProperties(Component)("CountProperty")
                anInteger.SetValue(Component, count)
                count = count + 1

                Exit Try
            Finally
                t.Commit()
            End Try
            If (notification_mode) Then
                System.Windows.Forms.MessageBox.Show("Designer- ↵
Initiated Designer Transaction Completed")
            End If
        End Sub 'DoTransaction

        Protected Overloads Overrides Sub Dispose(ByVal ↵
disposing As Boolean)
            UnlinkDTNotifications(Me, New EventArgs())
            MyBase.Dispose(disposing)
        End Sub 'Dispose

    End Class 'DTDesigner
End Namespace 'DesignerTransactionSample
```

[C#]

```
using System;
using System.ComponentModel;
using System.ComponentModel.Design;
using System.Windows.Forms;
using System.Windows.Forms.Design;

/*
    This sample demonstrates how to perform a series of actions ↵
 in a designer
    transaction, how to change values of properties of a ↵
component ↵
 from a
    designer, and how to complete transactions without being ↵
interrupted
    by other activities.

    To run this sample, add this code to a class library project ↵
and compile.
    Create a new Windows Forms project or load a form in the ↵
designer. Add a
    reference to the class library that was compiled in the first step.
    Right-click the Toolbox in design mode and click Customize Toolbox.
    Browse to the class library that was compiled in the first step and
    select OK until the DTComponent item appears in the Toolbox. ↵
 Add an
    instance of this component to the form.

    When the component is created and added to the component ↵
 tray for your
    design project, the Initialize method of the designer is called.
    This method displays a message box informing you that ↵
designer transaction
    event handlers will be registered unless you click Cancel. ↵
When you set
    properties in the properties window, each change will be ↵
encapsulated in
    a designer transaction, allowing the change to be undone later.

    When you right-click the component,   the shortcut menu ↵
for the component
    is displayed. The designer constructs this menu according ↵
to whether
    designer transaction notifications are enabled, and offers ↵
the option
    of enabling or disabling the notifications, depending on ↵
the current
    mode. The shortcut menu also presents a Perform Example Transaction
    item, which will set the values of the component's ↵
StringProperty and
    CountProperty properties. You can undo the last designer ↵
transaction using
    the Undo command provided by the Visual Studio .NET ↵
development environment.
*/

namespace DesignerTransactionSample
{
    // Associate the DTDesigner with this component
    [DesignerAttribute(typeof(DTDesigner))]
    public class DTComponent : System.ComponentModel.Component
    {
        private string m_String;
    private int m_Count;

    public string StringProperty
    {
        get
            { return m_String; }
        set
        { m_String = value; }
    }

    public int CountProperty
    {
        get
        { return m_Count; }
        set
        { m_Count = value; }
    }

    private void InitializeComponent()
    {
        m_String = "Initial Value";
        m_Count = 0;
    }
    }

    internal class DTDesigner : ComponentDesigner
    {
    private bool notification_mode = false;
    private int count = 10;

    // The Verbs property is overridden from ComponentDesigner
    public override DesignerVerbCollection Verbs
    {
        get
        {
            DesignerVerbCollection dvc = new DesignerVerbCollection();
        dvc.Add( new DesignerVerb("Perform Example Transaction", ↵
 new EventHandler(this.DoTransaction)) );
        if(notification_mode)
            dvc.Add(new DesignerVerb("End Designer Transaction ↵
Notifications", new EventHandler(this.UnlinkDTNotifications)));
        else
```

```
            dvc.Add(new DesignerVerb("Show Designer Transaction        ↵
Notifications", new EventHandler(this.LinkDTNotifications)));          ↵
\ return dvc;
        }
    }

        public override void Initialize(System.ComponentModel.IComponent
component)
        {
            base.Initialize(component);

            IDesignerHost host =                                        ↵
 (IDesignerHost)GetService(typeof(IDesignerHost));
            if(host == null)
            {
                MessageBox.Show("The IDesignerHost service              ↵
 interface could not be obtained.");
                return;
            }

            if( MessageBox.Show("Press the Yes button to                ↵
 display notification message boxes for the designer                   ↵
 transaction opened and closed notifications.","Link                   ↵
DesignerTransaction Notifications?", MessageBoxButtons.YesNo,          ↵
MessageBoxIcon.Question, MessageBoxDefaultButton.Button1,              ↵
MessageBoxOptions.RightAlign) == DialogResult.Yes )
            {
            host.TransactionOpened += new                               ↵
EventHandler(OnDesignerTransactionOpened);
                host.TransactionClosed += new                           ↵
DesignerTransactionCloseEventHandler(OnDesignerTransactionClosed);
                notification_mode = true;
            }
        }

        private void LinkDTNotifications(object sender, EventArgs e)
        {
            if(notification_mode == false)
            {
            IDesignerHost host =                                        ↵
 (IDesignerHost)GetService(typeof(IDesignerHost));
                if(host != null)
            {
            notification_mode = true;
                    host.TransactionOpened += new                       ↵
EventHandler(OnDesignerTransactionOpened);
                    host.TransactionClosed += new                       ↵
DesignerTransactionCloseEventHandler(OnDesignerTransactionClosed);
            }
        }
        }

        private void UnlinkDTNotifications(object sender, EventArgs e)
        {
        if(notification_mode)
            {
                IDesignerHost host =                                    ↵
 (IDesignerHost)GetService(typeof(IDesignerHost));
            if(host != null)
                {
            notification_mode = false;
                    host.TransactionOpened -= new                       ↵
 EventHandler(OnDesignerTransactionOpened);
                    host.TransactionClosed -= new                       ↵
 DesignerTransactionCloseEventHandler(OnDesignerTransactionClosed);
                }
            }
        }

        private void OnDesignerTransactionOpened(object sender,         ↵
 EventArgs e)
        {
        System.Windows.Forms.MessageBox.Show("A Designer                ↵
 Transaction was started. (TransactionOpened)");
        }

        private void OnDesignerTransactionClosed(object sender,         ↵
DesignerTransactionCloseEventArgs e)
        {
        System.Windows.Forms.MessageBox.Show("A Designer                ↵
Transaction was completed. (TransactionClosed)");
        }

        private void DoTransaction(object sender, EventArgs e)
        {
            IDesignerHost host =                                        ↵
 (IDesignerHost)GetService(typeof(IDesignerHost));
            DesignerTransaction t = host.CreateTransaction              ↵
 ("Change Text and Size");

            /* The code within the using statement is considered        ↵
 to be a single transaction.
           When the user selects Undo, the system will undo             ↵
everything executed in this code block. */
            using (t)
            {
            if(notification_mode)
                System.Windows.Forms.MessageBox.Show                    ↵
 ("Entering a Designer-Initiated Designer Transaction");

                // The .NET Framework automatically associates          ↵
the TypeDescriptor with the correct component
            PropertyDescriptor someText =                               ↵
TypeDescriptor.GetProperties(Component)["StringProperty"];
                someText.SetValue(Component, "This text was set         ↵
 by the designer for this component.");

                PropertyDescriptor anInteger =                          ↵
TypeDescriptor.GetProperties(Component)["CountProperty"];
            anInteger.SetValue(Component, count);
            count++;

                // Complete the designer transaction.
            t.Commit();

            if(notification_mode)
                System.Windows.Forms.MessageBox.Show                    ↵
 ("Designer-Initiated Designer Transaction Completed");
            }
        }

    protected override void Dispose(bool disposing)
    {
        UnlinkDTNotifications(this, new EventArgs());
        base.Dispose(disposing);
    }
    }
}
```

[C++]

```
#using <mscorlib.dll>
#using <system.dll>
#using <system.design.dll>
#using <system.windows.forms.dll>

using namespace System;
using namespace System::ComponentModel;
using namespace System::ComponentModel::Design;
using namespace System::Windows::Forms;
using namespace System::Windows::Forms::Design;

/*
    This sample demonstrates how to perform a series of                 ↵
actions in a designer
    transaction, how to change values of properties of a               ↵
component from a
    designer, and how to complete transactions without being          ↵
interrupted
    by other activities.
```

```
    To run this sample, add this code to a class library project    ↵
 and compile.
    Create a new Windows Forms project or load a form in the        ↵
 designer. Add a
    reference to the class library that was compiled in the first step.
    Right-click the Toolbox in design mode and click Customize Toolbox.
    Browse to the class library that was compiled in the first step and
    select OK until the DTComponent item appears in the Toolbox.    ↵
 Add an
    instance of this component to the form.

    When the component is created and added to the component        ↵
 tray for your
    design project, the Initialize method of the designer is called.
    This method displays a message box informing you that           ↵
designer transaction
    event handlers will be registered unless you click Cancel.      ↵
 When you set
    properties in the properties window, each change will be        ↵
encapsulated in
    a designer transaction, allowing the change to be undone later.

    When you right-click the component,   the shortcut menu         ↵
 for the component
    is displayed. The designer constructs this menu according       ↵
to whether
    designer transaction notifications are enabled, and offers      ↵
 the option
    of enabling or disabling the notifications, depending on        ↵
the current
    mode. The shortcut menu also presents a Perform Example Transaction
    item, which will set the values of the component's              ↵
StringProperty and
    CountProperty properties. You can undo the last designer        ↵
transaction using
    the Undo command provided by the Visual Studio .NET             ↵
development environment.
*/

namespace DesignerTransactionSample
{
    private __gc class DTDesigner : public ComponentDesigner {
    private:

        bool notification_mode;
        int count;

        void LinkDTNotifications(Object* sender, EventArgs* e)
        {
            if(!notification_mode)
            {
                IDesignerHost* host =                               ↵
dynamic_cast<IDesignerHost*>(GetService(__typeof(IDesignerHost)));
                if(host != 0)
                {
                    notification_mode = true;
                       host->TransactionOpened += new               ↵
EventHandler(this, OnDesignerTransactionOpened);
                       host->TransactionClosed += new               ↵
DesignerTransactionCloseEventHandler(this,                          ↵
OnDesignerTransactionClosed);
                }
            }
        }

        void UnlinkDTNotifications(Object* sender, EventArgs* e)
        {
            if(notification_mode)
            {
                IDesignerHost* host =                               ↵
dynamic_cast<IDesignerHost*>(GetService(__typeof(IDesignerHost)));
                if(host != 0)
                {
                    notification_mode = false;
                    host->TransactionOpened -= new                  ↵
 EventHandler(this, OnDesignerTransactionOpened);
                       host->TransactionClosed -= new               ↵
DesignerTransactionCloseEventHandler(this,                          ↵
OnDesignerTransactionClosed);
                }
            }
        }

        void OnDesignerTransactionOpened(Object* sender, EventArgs* e)
        {
            MessageBox::Show(S"A Designer Transaction was               ↵
 started. (TransactionOpened)");
        }

        void OnDesignerTransactionClosed(Object* sender,                ↵
DesignerTransactionCloseEventArgs* e)
        {
            MessageBox::Show(S"A Designer Transaction was               ↵
 completed. (TransactionClosed)");
        }

        void DoTransaction(Object* sender, EventArgs* e)
        {
            IDesignerHost* host =                                       ↵
static_cast<IDesignerHost*>(GetService(__typeof(IDesignerHost)));
            DesignerTransaction* t = host->CreateTransaction            ↵
 (S"Change Text and Size");

            /* The code within the using statement is                   ↵
considered to be a single transaction.
               When the user selects Undo, the system will              ↵
 undo everything executed in this code block.
            */
            if(notification_mode)
                MessageBox::Show(S"Entering a Designer-Initiated        ↵
 Designer Transaction");

            // The .NET Framework automatically associates the          ↵
TypeDescriptor with the correct component
            PropertyDescriptor* someText =                              ↵
TypeDescriptor::GetProperties(Component)->Item[S"StringProperty"];
            someText->SetValue(Component, S"This text was set           ↵
by the designer for this component.");

            PropertyDescriptor* anInteger =                             ↵
TypeDescriptor::GetProperties(Component)->Item[S"CountProperty"];
            anInteger->SetValue(Component, __box(count));
            count++;

            // Complete the designer transaction.
            t->Commit();

            if(notification_mode)
                MessageBox::Show(S"Designer-Initiated                   ↵
Designer Transaction Completed");
        }

    public:

        // The Verbs property is overridden from ComponentDesigner
        __property DesignerVerbCollection* get_Verbs()
        {
            DesignerVerbCollection* dvc = new DesignerVerbCollection();
            dvc->Add( new DesignerVerb(S"Perform Example                ↵
Transaction", new EventHandler(this, DoTransaction)) );
            if(notification_mode)
                dvc->Add(new DesignerVerb(S"End Designer                ↵
Transaction Notifications", new EventHandler(this,                      ↵
UnlinkDTNotifications)));
            else
                dvc->Add(new DesignerVerb(S"Show Designer               ↵
Transaction Notifications", new EventHandler(this,                      ↵
LinkDTNotifications)));
```

```
            return dvc;
        }

        void Initialize(IComponent* component)
        {
            ComponentDesigner::Initialize(component);

            notification_mode = false;
            count = 10;

            IDesignerHost* host =
dynamic_cast<IDesignerHost*>(GetService(__typeof(IDesignerHost)));
            if(host == 0)
            {
                MessageBox::Show(S"The IDesignerHost service
 interface could not be obtained.");
                return;
            }

            if( MessageBox::Show(S"Press the Yes button to
 display notification message boxes for the designer transaction
opened and closed notifications.",
                S"Link DesignerTransaction Notifications?",
MessageBoxButtons::YesNo, MessageBoxIcon::Question,
MessageBoxDefaultButton::Button1,
                MessageBoxOptions::RightAlign) == DialogResult::Yes )
            {
                host->TransactionOpened += new EventHandler
 (this, OnDesignerTransactionOpened);
                host->TransactionClosed += new
DesignerTransactionCloseEventHandler(this,
OnDesignerTransactionClosed);
                notification_mode = true;
            }
        }

    protected:

        void Dispose(bool disposing)
        {
            UnlinkDTNotifications(this, new EventArgs());
            ComponentDesigner::Dispose(disposing);
        }
    };

    // Associate the DTDesigner with this component
    [DesignerAttribute(__typeof(DTDesigner))]
    public __gc class DTComponent : public
System::ComponentModel::Component {
    private:

        String* m_String;
        int m_Count;

        void InitializeComponent()
        {
            m_String = S"Initial Value";
            m_Count = 0;
        }

    public:

        __property String* get_StringProperty()
        {
            return m_String;
        }

        __property void set_StringProperty(String* value)
        {
            m_String = value;
        }

        __property int get_CountProperty()
        {
            return m_Count;
        }

        __property void set_CountProperty(int value)
        {
            m_Count = value;
        }
    };
}
```

Requirements

Namespace: System.ComponentModel.Design

Platforms: Windows 98, Windows NT 4.0, Windows Millennium Edition, Windows 2000, Windows XP Home Edition, Windows XP Professional, Windows Server 2003 family

Assembly: System (in System.dll)

DesignerTransaction Constructor

Initializes a new instance of the **DesignerTransaction** class.

Overload List

Initializes a new instance of the **DesignerTransaction** class with no description.

[Visual Basic] **Public Sub New()**

[C#] **public DesignerTransaction();**

[C++] **public: DesignerTransaction();**

[JScript] **public function DesignerTransaction();**

Initializes a new instance of the **DesignerTransaction** class using the specified transaction description.

[Visual Basic] **Public Sub New(String)**

[C#] **public DesignerTransaction(string);**

[C++] **public: DesignerTransaction(String*);**

[JScript] **public function DesignerTransaction(String);**

DesignerTransaction Constructor ()

Initializes a new instance of the **DesignerTransaction** class with no description.

[Visual Basic]
```
Public Sub New()
```
[C#]
```
public DesignerTransaction();
```
[C++]
```
public: DesignerTransaction();
```
[JScript]
```
public function DesignerTransaction();
```

Requirements

Platforms: Windows 98, Windows NT 4.0, Windows Millennium Edition, Windows 2000, Windows XP Home Edition, Windows XP Professional, Windows Server 2003 family

DesignerTransaction Constructor (String)

Initializes a new instance of the **DesignerTransaction** class using the specified transaction description.

```
[Visual Basic]
Public Sub New( _
   ByVal description As String _
)
[C#]
public DesignerTransaction(
   string description
);
[C++]
public: DesignerTransaction(
   String* description
);
[JScript]
public function DesignerTransaction(
   description : String
);
```

Parameters

description

A description for this transaction.

Remarks

This constructor initializes the transaction with the specified description.

Requirements

Platforms: Windows 98, Windows NT 4.0, Windows Millennium Edition, Windows 2000, Windows XP Home Edition, Windows XP Professional, Windows Server 2003 family

DesignerTransaction.Canceled Property

Gets a value indicating whether the transaction was canceled.

```
[Visual Basic]
Public ReadOnly Property Canceled As Boolean
[C#]
public bool Canceled {get;}
[C++]
public: __property bool get_Canceled();
[JScript]
public function get Canceled() : Boolean;
```

Property Value

true if the transaction was canceled; otherwise, **false**.

Remarks

When a designer transaction is canceled, the transaction processing mechanism attempts to roll back the changes that have been made so far in the transaction. Whether this succeeds is dependent upon such factors as the type of each operation, whether other operations interfered with any of the involved code's state, and whether a sequence of expected operations failed to complete.

Requirements

Platforms: Windows 98, Windows NT 4.0, Windows Millennium Edition, Windows 2000, Windows XP Home Edition, Windows XP Professional, Windows Server 2003 family

DesignerTransaction.Committed Property

Gets a value indicating whether the transaction was committed.

```
[Visual Basic]
Public ReadOnly Property Committed As Boolean
[C#]
public bool Committed {get;}
[C++]
public: __property bool get_Committed();
[JScript]
public function get Committed() : Boolean;
```

Property Value

true if the transaction was committed; otherwise, **false**.

Remarks

When a designer transaction is committed, the transaction is considered complete, and does not track further changes.

Requirements

Platforms: Windows 98, Windows NT 4.0, Windows Millennium Edition, Windows 2000, Windows XP Home Edition, Windows XP Professional, Windows Server 2003 family

DesignerTransaction.Description Property

Gets a description for the transaction.

```
[Visual Basic]
Public ReadOnly Property Description As String
[C#]
public string Description {get;}
[C++]
public: __property String* get_Description();
[JScript]
public function get Description() : String;
```

Property Value

A description for the transaction.

Remarks

A transaction can have a description that is useful in identifying the nature of the operation or operations.

Requirements

Platforms: Windows 98, Windows NT 4.0, Windows Millennium Edition, Windows 2000, Windows XP Home Edition, Windows XP Professional, Windows Server 2003 family

DesignerTransaction.Cancel Method

Cancels the transaction and attempts to roll back the changes made by the events of the transaction.

```
[Visual Basic]
Public Sub Cancel()
[C#]
public void Cancel();
[C++]
public: void Cancel();
[JScript]
public function Cancel();
```

Requirements

Platforms: Windows 98, Windows NT 4.0, Windows Millennium Edition, Windows 2000, Windows XP Home Edition, Windows XP Professional, Windows Server 2003 family

DesignerTransaction.Commit Method

Commits this transaction.

[Visual Basic]
```
Public Sub Commit()
```
[C#]
```
public void Commit();
```
[C++]
```
public: void Commit();
```
[JScript]
```
public function Commit();
```

Remarks

When a designer transaction is committed, the transaction is considered complete, and does not track further changes.

Once a transaction has been committed, further calls to this method do nothing. Always call this method after creating a transaction, to ensure that the transaction closes properly.

Requirements

Platforms: Windows 98, Windows NT 4.0, Windows Millennium Edition, Windows 2000, Windows XP Home Edition, Windows XP Professional, Windows Server 2003 family

DesignerTransaction.Dispose Method

Releases the unmanaged resources used by the **DesignerTransaction** and optionally releases the managed resources.

[Visual Basic]
```
Protected Overridable Sub Dispose( _
   ByVal disposing As Boolean _
)
```
[C#]
```
protected virtual void Dispose(
   bool disposing
);
```
[C++]
```
protected: virtual void Dispose(
   bool disposing
);
```
[JScript]
```
protected function Dispose(
   disposing : Boolean
);
```

Parameters

disposing

true to release both managed and unmanaged resources; **false** to release only unmanaged resources.

Remarks

This method is called by the public **Dispose()** method and the **Finalize** method. **Dispose()** invokes the protected **Dispose(Boolean)** method with the *disposing* parameter set to **true**. **Finalize** invokes **Dispose** with *disposing* set to **false**.

When the *disposing* parameter is **true**, this method releases all resources held by any managed objects that this **DesignerTransaction** references. This method invokes the **Dispose()** method of each referenced object.

Notes to Inheritors: **Dispose** can be called multiple times by other objects. When overriding **Dispose(Boolean)**, be careful not to reference objects that have been previously disposed of in an earlier call to **Dispose**. For more information about how to implement **Dispose(Boolean)**, see **Implementing a Dispose Method**.

For more information about **Dispose** and **Finalize**, see **Cleaning Up Unmanaged Resources** and **Overriding the Finalize Method**.

Requirements

Platforms: Windows 98, Windows NT 4.0, Windows Millennium Edition, Windows 2000, Windows XP Home Edition, Windows XP Professional, Windows Server 2003 family

DesignerTransaction.Finalize Method

Releases the resources associated with this object. This override commits this transaction if it was not already committed.

[C#] In C#, finalizers are expressed using destructor syntax.

[C++] In C++, finalizers are expressed using destructor syntax.

[Visual Basic]
```
Overrides Protected Sub Finalize()
```
[C#]
```
~DesignerTransaction();
```
[C++]
```
~DesignerTransaction();
```
[JScript]
```
protected override function Finalize();
```

Remarks

This method overrides **Object.Finalize** and cleans up resources by calling **Dispose(false)**. Override **Dispose(Boolean)** to customize the cleanup.

Application code should not call this method; an object's **Finalize** method is automatically invoked during garbage collection, unless finalization by the garbage collector has been disabled by a call to the **GC.SuppressFinalize** method.

Requirements

Platforms: Windows 98, Windows NT 4.0, Windows Millennium Edition, Windows 2000, Windows XP Home Edition, Windows XP Professional, Windows Server 2003 family

DesignerTransaction.IDisposable.Dispose Method

This member supports the .NET Framework infrastructure and is not intended to be used directly from your code.

[Visual Basic]
```
Private Sub Dispose() Implements IDisposable.Dispose
```
[C#]
```
void IDisposable.Dispose();
```

[C++]
```
private: void IDisposable::Dispose();
```
[JScript]
```
private function IDisposable.Dispose();
```

DesignerTransaction.OnCancel Method

Raises the **Cancel** event.

[Visual Basic]
```
Protected MustOverride Sub OnCancel()
```
[C#]
```
protected abstract void OnCancel();
```
[C++]
```
protected: virtual void OnCancel() = 0;
```
[JScript]
```
protected abstract function OnCancel();
```

Remarks

When a designer transaction is canceled, the transaction processing mechanism attempts to roll back the changes that have been made so far in the transaction. Whether this succeeds is dependent upon such factors as the type of each operation, whether other operations interfered with any of the involved code's state, and whether a sequence of expected operations failed to complete.

Notes to Inheritors: When implemented in a derived class, this method cancels a transaction.

Requirements

Platforms: Windows 98, Windows NT 4.0,
Windows Millennium Edition, Windows 2000,
Windows XP Home Edition, Windows XP Professional,
Windows Server 2003 family

DesignerTransaction.OnCommit Method

Raises the **Commit** event.

[Visual Basic]
```
Protected MustOverride Sub OnCommit()
```
[C#]
```
protected abstract void OnCommit();
```
[C++]
```
protected: virtual void OnCommit() = 0;
```
[JScript]
```
protected abstract function OnCommit();
```

Remarks

When a designer transaction is committed, the transaction is considered complete, and does not track further changes.

Notes to Inheritors: When implemented in a derived class, this method performs work associated with processing the transaction.

Requirements

Platforms: Windows 98, Windows NT 4.0,
Windows Millennium Edition, Windows 2000,
Windows XP Home Edition, Windows XP Professional,
Windows Server 2003 family

DesignerTransactionClose-EventArgs Class

Provides data for the **TransactionClosed** and **TransactionClosing** events.

System.Object
  System.EventArgs
    System.ComponentModel.Design.DesignerTransaction-CloseEventArgs

[Visual Basic]
```
<ComVisible(True)>
Public Class DesignerTransactionCloseEventArgs
   Inherits EventArgs
```
[C#]
```
[ComVisible(true)]
public class DesignerTransactionCloseEventArgs : EventArgs
```
[C++]
```
[ComVisible(true)]
public __gc class DesignerTransactionCloseEventArgs : public
   EventArgs
```
[JScript]
```
public
   ComVisible(true)
class DesignerTransactionCloseEventArgs extends EventArgs
```

Thread Safety

Any public static (**Shared** in Visual Basic) members of this type are safe for multithreaded operations. Any instance members are not guaranteed to be thread safe.

Remarks

The **TransactionClosed** event occurs when a designer finalizes a transaction.

Example

[Visual Basic, C#, C++] The following example demonstrates creating a **DesignerTransactionCloseEventArgs**.

[Visual Basic]
```
' This example method creates a DesignerTransactionCloseEventArgs    ↲
 using the specified argument.
' Typically, this type of event args is created by a design mode     ↲
subsystem.
Public Function CreateDesignerTransactionCloseEventArgs(ByVal        ↲
 commit As Boolean) As DesignerTransactionCloseEventArgs

    ' Creates a component changed event args with the specified      ↲
arguments.
    Dim args As New DesignerTransactionCloseEventArgs(commit)

    ' Whether the transaction has been committed:                    ↲
args.TransactionCommitted

    Return args
End Function
```

[C#]
```
// This example method creates a                                     ↲
DesignerTransactionCloseEventArgs using the specified argument.
// Typically, this type of event args is created by a design         ↲
 mode subsystem.
public DesignerTransactionCloseEventArgs                             ↲
CreateDesignerTransactionCloseEventArgs(bool commit)
{
    // Creates a component changed event args with the               ↲
specified arguments.
    DesignerTransactionCloseEventArgs args = new                     ↲
DesignerTransactionCloseEventArgs(commit);

    // Whether the transaction has been committed:                   ↲
args.TransactionCommitted

    return args;
}
```

[C++]
```
// This example method creates a                                     ↲
DesignerTransactionCloseEventArgs using the specified argument.
// Typically, this type of event args is created by a                ↲
design mode subsystem.
DesignerTransactionCloseEventArgs*                                   ↲
CreateDesignerTransactionCloseEventArgs(bool commit)
{
    // Creates a component changed event args with the               ↲
specified arguments.
    // Whether the transaction has been committed:                   ↲
args.TransactionCommitted

    return new DesignerTransactionCloseEventArgs(commit);
}
```

Requirements

Namespace: System.ComponentModel.Design

Platforms: Windows 98, Windows NT 4.0, Windows Millennium Edition, Windows 2000, Windows XP Home Edition, Windows XP Professional, Windows Server 2003 family

Assembly: System (in System.dll)

DesignerTransactionCloseEventArgs Constructor

Initializes a new instance of the **DesignerTransactionCloseEventArgs** class, using the specified value that indicates whether the designer called **Commit** on the transaction.

[Visual Basic]
```
Public Sub New( _
   ByVal commit As Boolean _
)
```
[C#]
```
public DesignerTransactionCloseEventArgs(
   bool commit
);
```
[C++]
```
public: DesignerTransactionCloseEventArgs(
   bool commit
);
```
[JScript]
```
public function DesignerTransactionCloseEventArgs(
   commit : Boolean
);
```

Parameters

commit

  A value indicating whether the transaction was committed.

Requirements

Platforms: Windows 98, Windows NT 4.0, Windows Millennium Edition, Windows 2000, Windows XP Home Edition, Windows XP Professional, Windows Server 2003 family

DesignerTransactionCloseEventArgs.TransactionCommitted Property

Indicates whether the designer called **Commit** on the transaction.

[Visual Basic]
```
Public ReadOnly Property TransactionCommitted As Boolean
```
[C#]
```
public bool TransactionCommitted {get;}
```
[C++]
```
public: __property bool get_TransactionCommitted();
```
[JScript]
```
public function get TransactionCommitted() : Boolean;
```

Property Value

true if the designer called **Commit** on the transaction; otherwise, **false**.

Requirements

Platforms: Windows 98, Windows NT 4.0,
Windows Millennium Edition, Windows 2000,
Windows XP Home Edition, Windows XP Professional,
Windows Server 2003 family

DesignerTransactionClose-EventHandler Delegate

Represents the method that handles the **TransactionClosed** and **TransactionClosing** events of a designer.

[Visual Basic]
```
<Serializable>
<ComVisible(True)>
Public Delegate Sub DesignerTransactionCloseEventHandler( _
   ByVal sender As Object, _
   ByVal e As DesignerTransactionCloseEventArgs _
)
```
[C#]
```
[Serializable]
[ComVisible(true)]
public delegate void DesignerTransactionCloseEventHandler(
   object sender,
   DesignerTransactionCloseEventArgs e
);
```
[C++]
```
[Serializable]
[ComVisible(true)]
public __gc __delegate void DesignerTransactionCloseEventHandler(
   Object* sender,
   DesignerTransactionCloseEventArgs* e
);
```

[JScript] In JScript, you can use the delegates in the .NET Framework, but you cannot define your own.

Parameters [Visual Basic, C#, C++]

The declaration of your event handler must have the same parameters as the **DesignerTransactionCloseEventHandler** delegate declaration.

Remarks

When you create a **DesignerTransactionCloseEventHandler** delegate, you identify the method that will handle the event. To associate the event with your event handler, add an instance of the delegate to the event. The event handler is called whenever the event occurs, unless you remove the delegate.

Requirements

Namespace: System.ComponentModel.Design

Platforms: Windows 98, Windows NT 4.0, Windows Millennium Edition, Windows 2000, Windows XP Home Edition, Windows XP Professional, Windows Server 2003 family

Assembly: System (in System.dll)

DesignerVerb Class

Represents a verb that can be invoked from a designer.

System.Object
  System.ComponentModel.Design.MenuCommand
    System.ComponentModel.Design.DesignerVerb
      System.Web.UI.Design.TemplateEditingVerb

[Visual Basic]
```
<ComVisible(True)>
Public Class DesignerVerb
   Inherits MenuCommand
```
[C#]
```
[ComVisible(true)]
public class DesignerVerb : MenuCommand
```
[C++]
```
[ComVisible(true)]
public __gc class DesignerVerb : public MenuCommand
```
[JScript]
```
public
   ComVisible(true)
class DesignerVerb extends MenuCommand
```

Thread Safety

Any public static (**Shared** in Visual Basic) members of this type are safe for multithreaded operations. Any instance members are not guaranteed to be thread safe.

Remarks

A designer verb is a menu command linked to an event handler. Designer verbs are added to a component's context menu and the Properties window at run time.

Example

[Visual Basic, C#, C++] The following example demonstrates how to create **DesignerVerb** objects and add them to the design-time context menu for a component.

[Visual Basic]
```
Imports System
Imports System.ComponentModel
Imports System.Collections
Imports System.ComponentModel.Design

'  This sample demonstrates a designer that adds menu commands
'   to the design-time context menu for a component.
'
'   To test this sample, build the code for the component as        ↵
 a class library,
'   add the resulting component to the toolbox, open a form in      ↵
design mode,
'   and drag the component from the toolbox onto the form.
'
'   The component should appear in the component tray beneath the form.
'   Right-click the component.  The verbs should appear in the      ↵
 context menu.

Namespace VBDesignerVerb
    ' Associate MyDesigner with this component type using a         ↵
DesignerAttribute
    <Designer(GetType(MyDesigner))> _
    Public Class Component1
        Inherits System.ComponentModel.Component
    End Class 'Component1

    '  This is a designer class which provides designer verb         ↵
menu commands for
    '  the associated component. This code is called by the          ↵
design environment at design-time.
    Friend Class MyDesigner
        Inherits ComponentDesigner

        Private m_Verbs As DesignerVerbCollection

        ' DesignerVerbCollection is overridden from ComponentDesigner
        Public Overrides ReadOnly Property Verbs() As               ↵
DesignerVerbCollection
            Get
                If m_Verbs Is Nothing Then
                    ' Create and initialize the collection of verbs
                    m_Verbs = New DesignerVerbCollection()
            m_Verbs.Add( New DesignerVerb("First Designer Verb",    ↵
New EventHandler(AddressOf OnFirstItemSelected)) )
            m_Verbs.Add( New DesignerVerb("Second Designer Verb",   ↵
 New EventHandler(AddressOf OnSecondItemSelected)) )
                End If
                Return m_Verbs
            End Get
        End Property

        Sub New()
        End Sub 'New

        Private Sub OnFirstItemSelected(ByVal sender As Object,     ↵
ByVal args As EventArgs)
            ' Display a message
            System.Windows.Forms.MessageBox.Show("The first         ↵
designer verb was invoked.")
        End Sub 'OnFirstItemSelected

        Private Sub OnSecondItemSelected(ByVal sender As Object,    ↵
 ByVal args As EventArgs)
            ' Display a message
            System.Windows.Forms.MessageBox.Show("The second        ↵
designer verb was invoked.")
        End Sub 'OnSecondItemSelected
    End Class 'MyDesigner
End Namespace
```

[C#]
```
using System;
using System.ComponentModel;
using System.ComponentModel.Design;
using System.Collections;

/* This sample demonstrates a designer that adds menu commands
    to the design-time context menu for a component.

    To test this sample, build the code for the component as        ↵
class library,
    add the resulting component to the toolbox, open a form in      ↵
design mode,
    and drag the component from the toolbox onto the form.

    The component should appear in the component tray beneath the form.
    Right-click the component.  The verbs should appear in the      ↵
context menu.
*/

namespace CSDesignerVerb
{
    // Associate MyDesigner with this component type using a        ↵
DesignerAttribute
    [Designer(typeof(MyDesigner))]
    public class Component1 : System.ComponentModel.Component
    {
    }

    // This is a designer class which provides designer verb         ↵
menu commands for
    // the associated component. This code is called by the          ↵
design environment at design-time.
    internal class MyDesigner : ComponentDesigner
    {
        DesignerVerbCollection m_Verbs;
```

```
        // DesignerVerbCollection is overridden from ComponentDesigner
        public override DesignerVerbCollection Verbs
        {
            get {
                if (m_Verbs == null)
                {
                    // Create and initialize the collection of verbs
                    m_Verbs = new DesignerVerbCollection();

            m_Verbs.Add( new DesignerVerb("First Designer Verb",     ↵
 new EventHandler(OnFirstItemSelected)) );
            m_Verbs.Add( new DesignerVerb("Second Designer Verb",    ↵
 new EventHandler(OnSecondItemSelected)) );
                }
                return m_Verbs;
            }
        }

        MyDesigner()
        {
        }

        private void OnFirstItemSelected(object sender, EventArgs args)
        {
            // Display a message
            System.Windows.Forms.MessageBox.Show("The first          ↵
designer verb was invoked.");
        }

        private void OnSecondItemSelected(object sender,             ↵
EventArgs args)
        {
            // Display a message
            System.Windows.Forms.MessageBox.Show("The second         ↵
designer verb was invoked.");
        }
    }
}
```

[C++]

```
#using <mscorlib.dll>
#using <system.dll>
#using <system.design.dll>
#using <system.windows.forms.dll>

using namespace System;
using namespace System::ComponentModel;
using namespace System::ComponentModel::Design;
using namespace System::Windows::Forms;

/* This sample demonstrates a designer that adds menu commands
    to the design-time context menu for a component.

    To test this sample, build the code for the component as a       ↵
class library,
    add the resulting component to the toolbox, open a form in       ↵
design mode,
    and drag the component from the toolbox onto the form.

    The component should appear in the component tray beneath the form.
    Right-click the component.  The verbs should appear in the       ↵
context menu.
*/

namespace CSDesignerVerb
{
    // This is a designer class which provides designer verb         ↵
menu commands for
    // the associated component. This code is called by the          ↵
 design environment at design-time.
    private __gc class MyDesigner : public ComponentDesigner {
    public:

        // DesignerVerbCollection is overridden from ComponentDesigner
        __property DesignerVerbCollection* get_Verbs()
        {
            if (m_Verbs == 0)
            {
                // Create and initialize the collection of verbs
                m_Verbs = new DesignerVerbCollection();

                m_Verbs->Add( new DesignerVerb(S"First Designer       ↵
Verb", new EventHandler(this, OnFirstItemSelected)) );
                m_Verbs->Add( new DesignerVerb(S"Second Designer      ↵
Verb", new EventHandler(this, OnSecondItemSelected)) );
            }

            return m_Verbs;
        }

        MyDesigner()
        {
        }

    private:

        DesignerVerbCollection* m_Verbs;

        void OnFirstItemSelected(Object* sender, EventArgs* args)
        {
            // Display a message
            MessageBox::Show(S"The first designer verb was invoked.");
        }

        void OnSecondItemSelected(Object* sender, EventArgs* args)
        {
            // Display a message
            MessageBox::Show(S"The second designer verb was invoked.");
        }
    };

    // Associate MyDesigner with this component type using a         ↵
DesignerAttribute
    [Designer(__typeof(MyDesigner))]
    public __gc class Component1 : public                            ↵
System::ComponentModel::Component
    {
    };

}
```

Requirements

Namespace: System.ComponentModel.Design

Platforms: Windows 98, Windows NT 4.0, Windows Millennium Edition, Windows 2000, Windows XP Home Edition, Windows XP Professional, Windows Server 2003 family

Assembly: System (in System.dll)

DesignerVerb Constructor

Initializes a new instance of the **DesignerVerb** class.

Overload List

Initializes a new instance of the **DesignerVerb** class.

[Visual Basic] **Public Sub New(String, EventHandler)**

[C#] **public DesignerVerb(string, EventHandler);**

[C++] **public: DesignerVerb(String*, EventHandler*);**

[JScript] **public function DesignerVerb(String, EventHandler);**

Initializes a new instance of the **DesignerVerb** class.

[Visual Basic] **Public Sub New(String, EventHandler, CommandID)**

[C#] **public DesignerVerb(string, EventHandler, CommandID);**

[C++] **public: DesignerVerb(String*, EventHandler*, CommandID*);**

[JScript] **public function DesignerVerb(String, EventHandler, CommandID);**

DesignerVerb Constructor (String, EventHandler)

Initializes a new instance of the **DesignerVerb** class.

```
[Visual Basic]
Public Sub New( _
   ByVal text As String, _
   ByVal handler As EventHandler _
)
[C#]
public DesignerVerb(
   string text,
   EventHandler handler
);
[C++]
public: DesignerVerb(
   String* text,
   EventHandler* handler
);
[JScript]
public function DesignerVerb(
   text : String,
   handler : EventHandler
);
```

Parameters

text

The text of the menu command that is shown to the user.

handler

The event handler that performs the actions of the verb.

Remarks

Verbs are menu commands that are dynamically inserted into the menu at run time. Verb commands are usually displayed on either an edit menu or on a component's context menu.

Requirements

Platforms: Windows 98, Windows NT 4.0, Windows Millennium Edition, Windows 2000, Windows XP Home Edition, Windows XP Professional, Windows Server 2003 family

DesignerVerb Constructor (String, EventHandler, CommandID)

Initializes a new instance of the **DesignerVerb** class.

```
[Visual Basic]
Public Sub New( _
   ByVal text As String, _
   ByVal handler As EventHandler, _
   ByVal startCommandID As CommandID _
)
[C#]
public DesignerVerb(
   string text,
   EventHandler handler,
   CommandID startCommandID
);
[C++]
public: DesignerVerb(
   String* text,
   EventHandler* handler,
   CommandID* startCommandID
);
[JScript]
public function DesignerVerb(
   text : String,
   handler : EventHandler,
   startCommandID : CommandID
);
```

Parameters

text

The text of the menu command that is shown to the user.

handler

The event handler that performs the actions of the verb.

startCommandID

The starting command ID for this verb. By default, the designer architecture sets aside a range of command IDs for verbs. You can override this by providing a custom command ID.

Remarks

Verbs are menu commands that are dynamically inserted into the menu at run time. Verb commands are usually displayed on either an edit menu or on a component's context menu.

Requirements

Platforms: Windows 98, Windows NT 4.0, Windows Millennium Edition, Windows 2000, Windows XP Home Edition, Windows XP Professional, Windows Server 2003 family

DesignerVerb.Text Property

Gets the text description that describes the verb command on the menu.

```
[Visual Basic]
Public ReadOnly Property Text As String
[C#]
public string Text {get;}
[C++]
public: __property String* get_Text();
[JScript]
public function get Text() : String;
```

Property Value

A description that describes the the verb command.

Requirements

Platforms: Windows 98, Windows NT 4.0, Windows Millennium Edition, Windows 2000, Windows XP Home Edition, Windows XP Professional, Windows Server 2003 family

DesignerVerb.ToString Method

This member overrides **MenuCommand.ToString**.

[Visual Basic]
```
Overrides Public Function ToString() As String
```
[C#]
```
public override string ToString();
```
[C++]
```
public: String* ToString();
```
[JScript]
```
public override function ToString() : String;
```

Requirements

Platforms: Windows 98, Windows NT 4.0, Windows Millennium Edition, Windows 2000, Windows XP Home Edition, Windows XP Professional, Windows Server 2003 family

DesignerVerbCollection Class

Represents a collection of **DesignerVerb** objects.

System.Object
System.Collections.CollectionBase
System.ComponentModel.Design.DesignerVerbCollection

[Visual Basic]
```
<ComVisible(True)>
Public Class DesignerVerbCollection
   Inherits CollectionBase
```
[C#]
```
[ComVisible(true)]
public class DesignerVerbCollection : CollectionBase
```
[C++]
```
[ComVisible(true)]
public __gc class DesignerVerbCollection : public CollectionBase
```
[JScript]
```
public
   ComVisible(true)
class DesignerVerbCollection extends CollectionBase
```

Thread Safety

Any public static (**Shared** in Visual Basic) members of this type are safe for multithreaded operations. Any instance members are not guaranteed to be thread safe.

Remarks

This class provides a collection that can contain **DesignerVerb** objects.

Example

[Visual Basic]
```
' Creates an empty DesignerVerbCollection.
Dim collection As New DesignerVerbCollection()

' Adds a DesignerVerb to the collection.
collection.Add(New DesignerVerb("Example designer verb", New ↵
EventHandler(AddressOf Me.ExampleEvent)))

' Adds an array of DesignerVerb objects to the collection.
Dim verbs As DesignerVerb() = {New DesignerVerb("Example ↵
designer verb", New EventHandler(AddressOf Me.ExampleEvent)), ↵
New DesignerVerb("Example designer verb", New EventHandler ↵
 (AddressOf Me.ExampleEvent))}
collection.AddRange(verbs)

' Adds a collection of DesignerVerb objects to the collection.
Dim verbsCollection As New DesignerVerbCollection()
verbsCollection.Add(New DesignerVerb("Example designer verb", ↵
 New EventHandler(AddressOf Me.ExampleEvent)))
verbsCollection.Add(New DesignerVerb("Example designer verb", ↵
 New EventHandler(AddressOf Me.ExampleEvent)))
collection.AddRange(verbsCollection)

' Tests for the presence of a DesignerVerb in the collection,
' and retrieves its index if it is found.
Dim testVerb As New DesignerVerb("Example designer verb", New ↵
EventHandler(AddressOf Me.ExampleEvent))
Dim itemIndex As Integer = -1
If collection.Contains(testVerb) Then
    itemIndex = collection.IndexOf(testVerb)
End If

' Copies the contents of the collection, beginning at index 0,
' to the specified DesignerVerb array.
' 'verbs' is a DesignerVerb array.
collection.CopyTo(verbs, 0)

' Retrieves the count of the items in the collection.
Dim collectionCount As Integer = collection.Count

' Inserts a DesignerVerb at index 0 of the collection.
collection.Insert(0, New DesignerVerb("Example designer verb", ↵
 New EventHandler(AddressOf Me.ExampleEvent)))

' Removes the specified DesignerVerb from the collection.
Dim verb As New DesignerVerb("Example designer verb", New ↵
EventHandler(AddressOf Me.ExampleEvent))
collection.Remove(verb)

' Removes the DesignerVerb at index 0.
collection.RemoveAt(0)
```

[C#]
```
// Creates an empty DesignerVerbCollection.
DesignerVerbCollection collection = new DesignerVerbCollection();

// Adds a DesignerVerb to the collection.
collection.Add( new DesignerVerb("Example designer verb", new ↵
EventHandler(this.ExampleEvent)) );

// Adds an array of DesignerVerb objects to the collection.
DesignerVerb[] verbs = { new DesignerVerb("Example designer ↵
 verb", new EventHandler(this.ExampleEvent)), new DesignerVerb ↵
 ("Example designer verb", new EventHandler(this.ExampleEvent)) };
collection.AddRange( verbs );

// Adds a collection of DesignerVerb objects to the collection.
DesignerVerbCollection verbsCollection = new DesignerVerbCollection();
verbsCollection.Add( new DesignerVerb("Example designer verb", ↵
 new EventHandler(this.ExampleEvent)) );
verbsCollection.Add( new DesignerVerb("Example designer verb", ↵
 new EventHandler(this.ExampleEvent)) );
collection.AddRange( verbsCollection );

// Tests for the presence of a DesignerVerb in the collection,
// and retrieves its index if it is found.
DesignerVerb testVerb = new DesignerVerb("Example designer verb", ↵
 new EventHandler(this.ExampleEvent));
int itemIndex = -1;
if( collection.Contains( testVerb ) )
    itemIndex = collection.IndexOf( testVerb );

// Copies the contents of the collection, beginning at index 0,
// to the specified DesignerVerb array.
// 'verbs' is a DesignerVerb array.
collection.CopyTo( verbs, 0 );

// Retrieves the count of the items in the collection.
int collectionCount = collection.Count;

// Inserts a DesignerVerb at index 0 of the collection.
collection.Insert( 0, new DesignerVerb("Example designer verb", ↵
 new EventHandler(this.ExampleEvent)) );

// Removes the specified DesignerVerb from the collection.
DesignerVerb verb = new DesignerVerb("Example designer verb", ↵
new EventHandler(this.ExampleEvent));
collection.Remove( verb );

// Removes the DesignerVerb at index 0.
collection.RemoveAt(0);
```

[C++]
```
// Creates an empty DesignerVerbCollection.
DesignerVerbCollection* collection = new DesignerVerbCollection();

// Adds a DesignerVerb to the collection.
collection->Add( new DesignerVerb(S"Example designer verb", ↵
 new EventHandler(this, ExampleEvent)) );

// Adds an array of DesignerVerb objects to the collection.
DesignerVerb* verbs[] = { new DesignerVerb(S"Example designer ↵
```

```
verb", new EventHandler(this, ExampleEvent)), new                   ↵
DesignerVerb(S"Example designer verb", new EventHandler(this,       ↵
ExampleEvent)) };
collection->AddRange( verbs );

// Adds a collection of DesignerVerb objects to the collection.
DesignerVerbCollection* verbsCollection = new DesignerVerbCollection();
verbsCollection->Add( new DesignerVerb(S"Example designer verb",    ↵
new EventHandler(this, ExampleEvent)) );
verbsCollection->Add( new DesignerVerb(S"Example designer verb",    ↵
new EventHandler(this, ExampleEvent)) );
collection->AddRange( verbsCollection );

// Tests for the presence of a DesignerVerb in the collection,
// and retrieves its index if it is found.
DesignerVerb* testVerb = new DesignerVerb(S"Example designer        ↵
 verb", new EventHandler(this, ExampleEvent));
int itemIndex = -1;
if( collection->Contains( testVerb ) )
    itemIndex = collection->IndexOf( testVerb );

// Copies the contents of the collection, beginning at index 0,
// to the specified DesignerVerb array.
// 'verbs' is a DesignerVerb array.
collection->CopyTo( verbs, 0 );

// Retrieves the count of the items in the collection.
int collectionCount = collection->Count;

// Inserts a DesignerVerb at index 0 of the collection.
collection->Insert( 0, new DesignerVerb(S"Example designer verb",   ↵
 new EventHandler(this, ExampleEvent)) );

// Removes the specified DesignerVerb from the collection.
DesignerVerb* verb = new DesignerVerb(S"Example designer verb",     ↵
 new EventHandler(this, ExampleEvent));
collection->Remove( verb );

// Removes the DesignerVerb at index 0.
collection->RemoveAt(0);
```

Requirements

Namespace: System.ComponentModel.Design

Platforms: Windows 98, Windows NT 4.0, Windows Millennium Edition, Windows 2000, Windows XP Home Edition, Windows XP Professional, Windows Server 2003 family

Assembly: System (in System.dll)

DesignerVerbCollection Constructor

Initializes a new instance of the **DesignerVerbCollection** class.

Overload List

Initializes a new instance of the **DesignerVerbCollection** class.

[Visual Basic] **Public Sub New()**

[C#] **public DesignerVerbCollection();**

[C++] **public: DesignerVerbCollection();**

[JScript] **public function DesignerVerbCollection();**

Initializes a new instance of the **DesignerVerbCollection** class using the specified array of **DesignerVerb** objects.

[Visual Basic] **Public Sub New(DesignerVerb())**

[C#] **public DesignerVerbCollection(DesignerVerb[]);**

[C++] **public: DesignerVerbCollection(DesignerVerb*[]);**

[JScript] **public function DesignerVerb-Collection(DesignerVerb[]);**

Example

[Visual Basic, C#, C++] **Note** This example shows how to use one of the overloaded versions of the **DesignerVerbCollection** constructor. For other examples that might be available, see the individual overload topics.

[Visual Basic]
```
' Creates an empty DesignerVerbCollection.
Dim collection As New DesignerVerbCollection()
```

[C#]
```
// Creates an empty DesignerVerbCollection.
DesignerVerbCollection collection = new DesignerVerbCollection();
```

[C++]
```
// Creates an empty DesignerVerbCollection.
DesignerVerbCollection* collection = new DesignerVerbCollection();
```

DesignerVerbCollection Constructor ()

Initializes a new instance of the **DesignerVerbCollection** class.

[Visual Basic]
```
Public Sub New()
```
[C#]
```
public DesignerVerbCollection();
```
[C++]
```
public: DesignerVerbCollection();
```
[JScript]
```
public function DesignerVerbCollection();
```

Remarks

This is a default empty collection constructor.

Example

[Visual Basic]
```
' Creates an empty DesignerVerbCollection.
Dim collection As New DesignerVerbCollection()
```

[C#]
```
// Creates an empty DesignerVerbCollection.
DesignerVerbCollection collection = new DesignerVerbCollection();
```

[C++]
```
// Creates an empty DesignerVerbCollection.
DesignerVerbCollection* collection = new DesignerVerbCollection();
```

Requirements

Platforms: Windows 98, Windows NT 4.0, Windows Millennium Edition, Windows 2000, Windows XP Home Edition, Windows XP Professional, Windows Server 2003 family

DesignerVerbCollection Constructor (DesignerVerb[])

Initializes a new instance of the **DesignerVerbCollection** class using the specified array of **DesignerVerb** objects.

[Visual Basic]
```
Public Sub New( _
   ByVal value() As DesignerVerb _
)
```
[C#]
```
public DesignerVerbCollection(
   DesignerVerb[] value
);
```

```
[C++]
public: DesignerVerbCollection(
   DesignerVerb* value[]
);
[JScript]
public function DesignerVerbCollection(
   value : DesignerVerb[]
);
```

Parameters

value

A **DesignerVerb** array that indicates the verbs to contain within the collection.

Requirements

Platforms: Windows 98, Windows NT 4.0, Windows Millennium Edition, Windows 2000, Windows XP Home Edition, Windows XP Professional, Windows Server 2003 family

DesignerVerbCollection.Item Property

Gets or sets the **DesignerVerb** at the specified index.

[C#] In C#, this property is the indexer for the **DesignerVerbCollection** class.

```
[Visual Basic]
Public Default Property Item( _
   ByVal index As Integer _
) As DesignerVerb
[C#]
public DesignerVerb this[
   int index
] {get; set;}
[C++]
public: __property DesignerVerb* get_Item(
   int index
);
public: __property void set_Item(
   int index,
   DesignerVerb*
);
[JScript]
returnValue = DesignerVerbCollectionObject.Item(index);
DesignerVerbCollectionObject.Item(index) = returnValue;
-or-
returnValue = DesignerVerbCollectionObject(index);
DesignerVerbCollectionObject(index) = returnValue;
```

[JScript] In JScript, you can use the default indexed properties defined by a type, but you cannot explicitly define your own. However, specifying the **expando** attribute on a class automatically provides a default indexed property whose type is **Object** and whose index type is **String**.

Arguments [JScript]

index

The index at which to get or set the **DesignerVerb**.

Parameters [Visual Basic, C#, C++]

index

The index at which to get or set the **DesignerVerb**.

Property Value

A **DesignerVerb** at each valid index in the collection.

Requirements

Platforms: Windows 98, Windows NT 4.0, Windows Millennium Edition, Windows 2000, Windows XP Home Edition, Windows XP Professional, Windows Server 2003 family

DesignerVerbCollection.Add Method

Adds the specified **DesignerVerb** to the collection.

```
[Visual Basic]
Public Function Add( _
   ByVal value As DesignerVerb _
) As Integer
[C#]
public int Add(
   DesignerVerb value
);
[C++]
public: int Add(
   DesignerVerb* value
);
[JScript]
public function Add(
   value : DesignerVerb
) : int;
```

Parameters

value

The **DesignerVerb** to add to the collection.

Return Value

The index in the collection at which the verb was added.

Example

```
[Visual Basic]
' Adds a DesignerVerb to the collection.
collection.Add(New DesignerVerb("Example designer verb", New ↵
EventHandler(AddressOf Me.ExampleEvent)))
```

```
[C#]
// Adds a DesignerVerb to the collection.
collection.Add( new DesignerVerb("Example designer verb", new ↵
EventHandler(this.ExampleEvent)) );
```

```
[C++]
// Adds a DesignerVerb to the collection.
collection->Add( new DesignerVerb(S"Example designer verb", new ↵
EventHandler(this, ExampleEvent)) );
```

Requirements

Platforms: Windows 98, Windows NT 4.0, Windows Millennium Edition, Windows 2000, Windows XP Home Edition, Windows XP Professional, Windows Server 2003 family

DesignerVerbCollection.AddRange Method

Adds the specified set of designer verbs to the collection.

Overload List

Adds the specified set of designer verbs to the collection.

[Visual Basic] **Overloads Public Sub AddRange(DesignerVerb())**

[C#] **public void AddRange(DesignerVerb[]);**

[C++] **public: void AddRange(DesignerVerb*[]);**

[JScript] **public function AddRange(DesignerVerb[]);**

Adds the specified collection of designer verbs to the collection.

[Visual Basic] **Overloads Public Sub AddRange(DesignerVerbCollection)**

[C#] **public void AddRange(DesignerVerbCollection);**

[C++] **public: void AddRange(DesignerVerbCollection*);**

[JScript] **public function AddRange(DesignerVerbCollection);**

Example

[Visual Basic, C#, C++] **Note** This example shows how to use one of the overloaded versions of **AddRange**. For other examples that might be available, see the individual overload topics.

[Visual Basic]

```
' Adds an array of DesignerVerb objects to the collection.
Dim verbs As DesignerVerb() = {New DesignerVerb("Example designer verb",
New EventHandler(AddressOf Me.ExampleEvent)), New
DesignerVerb("Example designer verb", New EventHandler(AddressOf
Me.ExampleEvent))}
collection.AddRange(verbs)

' Adds a collection of DesignerVerb objects to the collection.
Dim verbsCollection As New DesignerVerbCollection()
verbsCollection.Add(New DesignerVerb("Example designer verb",
 New EventHandler(AddressOf Me.ExampleEvent)))
verbsCollection.Add(New DesignerVerb("Example designer verb",
 New EventHandler(AddressOf Me.ExampleEvent)))
collection.AddRange(verbsCollection)
```

[C#]

```
// Adds an array of DesignerVerb objects to the collection.
DesignerVerb[] verbs = { new DesignerVerb("Example designer
verb", new EventHandler(this.ExampleEvent)), new DesignerVerb
 ("Example designer verb", new EventHandler(this.ExampleEvent)) };
collection.AddRange( verbs );

// Adds a collection of DesignerVerb objects to the collection.
DesignerVerbCollection verbsCollection = new DesignerVerbCollection();
verbsCollection.Add( new DesignerVerb("Example designer verb",
 new EventHandler(this.ExampleEvent)) );
verbsCollection.Add( new DesignerVerb("Example designer verb",
 new EventHandler(this.ExampleEvent)) );
collection.AddRange( verbsCollection );
```

[C++]

```
// Adds an array of DesignerVerb objects to the collection.
DesignerVerb* verbs[] = { new DesignerVerb(S"Example designer
 verb", new EventHandler(this, ExampleEvent)), new
DesignerVerb(S"Example designer verb", new EventHandler
 (this, ExampleEvent)) };
collection->AddRange( verbs );

// Adds a collection of DesignerVerb objects to the collection.
DesignerVerbCollection* verbsCollection = new DesignerVerbCollection();
verbsCollection->Add( new DesignerVerb(S"Example designer verb",
 new EventHandler(this, ExampleEvent)) );
verbsCollection->Add( new DesignerVerb(S"Example designer verb",
 new EventHandler(this, ExampleEvent)) );
collection->AddRange( verbsCollection );
```

DesignerVerbCollection.AddRange Method (DesignerVerb[])

Adds the specified set of designer verbs to the collection.

[Visual Basic]

```
Overloads Public Sub AddRange( _
   ByVal value() As DesignerVerb _
)
```

[C#]

```
public void AddRange(
   DesignerVerb[] value
);
```

[C++]

```
public: void AddRange(
   DesignerVerb* value[]
);
```

[JScript]

```
public function AddRange(
   value : DesignerVerb[]
);
```

Parameters

value

An array of **DesignerVerb** objects to add to the collection.

Example

[Visual Basic]

```
' Adds an array of DesignerVerb objects to the collection.
Dim verbs As DesignerVerb() = {New DesignerVerb("Example
 designer verb", New EventHandler(AddressOf Me.ExampleEvent)),
 New DesignerVerb("Example designer verb", New EventHandler
 (AddressOf Me.ExampleEvent))}
collection.AddRange(verbs)

' Adds a collection of DesignerVerb objects to the collection.
Dim verbsCollection As New DesignerVerbCollection()
verbsCollection.Add(New DesignerVerb("Example designer verb",
New EventHandler(AddressOf Me.ExampleEvent)))
verbsCollection.Add(New DesignerVerb("Example designer verb",
New EventHandler(AddressOf Me.ExampleEvent)))
collection.AddRange(verbsCollection)
```

[C#]

```
// Adds an array of DesignerVerb objects to the collection.
DesignerVerb[] verbs = { new DesignerVerb("Example designer
 verb", new EventHandler(this.ExampleEvent)), new DesignerVerb
 ("Example designer verb", new EventHandler(this.ExampleEvent)) };
collection.AddRange( verbs );

// Adds a collection of DesignerVerb objects to the collection.
DesignerVerbCollection verbsCollection = new DesignerVerbCollection();
verbsCollection.Add( new DesignerVerb("Example designer verb",
 new EventHandler(this.ExampleEvent)) );
verbsCollection.Add( new DesignerVerb("Example designer verb",
 new EventHandler(this.ExampleEvent)) );
collection.AddRange( verbsCollection );
```

[C++]

```
// Adds an array of DesignerVerb objects to the collection.
DesignerVerb* verbs[] = { new DesignerVerb(S"Example designer
 verb", new EventHandler(this, ExampleEvent)), new
DesignerVerb(S"Example designer verb", new EventHandler(this,
ExampleEvent)) };
collection->AddRange( verbs );

// Adds a collection of DesignerVerb objects to the collection.
DesignerVerbCollection* verbsCollection = new DesignerVerbCollection();
verbsCollection->Add( new DesignerVerb(S"Example designer verb",
new EventHandler(this, ExampleEvent)) );
verbsCollection->Add( new DesignerVerb(S"Example designer verb",
new EventHandler(this, ExampleEvent)) );
collection->AddRange( verbsCollection );
```

Requirements

Platforms: Windows 98, Windows NT 4.0, Windows Millennium Edition, Windows 2000, Windows XP Home Edition, Windows XP Professional, Windows Server 2003 family

DesignerVerbCollection.AddRange Method (DesignerVerbCollection)

Adds the specified collection of designer verbs to the collection.

```
[Visual Basic]
Overloads Public Sub AddRange( _
   ByVal value As DesignerVerbCollection _
)
[C#]
public void AddRange(
   DesignerVerbCollection value
);
[C++]
public: void AddRange(
   DesignerVerbCollection* value
);
[JScript]
public function AddRange(
   value : DesignerVerbCollection
);
```

Parameters

value

A **DesignerVerbCollection** to add to the collection.

Example

See related example in the **System.ComponentModel.Design.DesignerVerbCollection** class topic.

Requirements

Platforms: Windows 98, Windows NT 4.0, Windows Millennium Edition, Windows 2000, Windows XP Home Edition, Windows XP Professional, Windows Server 2003 family

DesignerVerbCollection.Contains Method

Gets a value indicating whether the specified **DesignerVerb** exists in the collection.

```
[Visual Basic]
Public Function Contains( _
   ByVal value As DesignerVerb _
) As Boolean
[C#]
public bool Contains(
   DesignerVerb value
);
[C++]
public: bool Contains(
   DesignerVerb* value
);
[JScript]
public function Contains(
   value : DesignerVerb
) : Boolean;
```

Parameters

value

The **DesignerVerb** to search for in the collection.

Return Value

true if the specified object exists in the collection; otherwise, **false**.

Example

See related example in the **System.ComponentModel.Design.DesignerVerbCollection** class topic.

Requirements

Platforms: Windows 98, Windows NT 4.0, Windows Millennium Edition, Windows 2000, Windows XP Home Edition, Windows XP Professional, Windows Server 2003 family

DesignerVerbCollection.CopyTo Method

Copies the collection members to the specified **DesignerVerb** array beginning at the specified destination index.

```
[Visual Basic]
Public Sub CopyTo( _
   ByVal array() As DesignerVerb, _
   ByVal index As Integer _
)
[C#]
public void CopyTo(
   DesignerVerb[] array,
   int index
);
[C++]
public: void CopyTo(
   DesignerVerb* array[],
   int index
);
[JScript]
public function CopyTo(
   array : DesignerVerb[],
   index : int
);
```

Parameters

array

The array to copy collection members to.

index

The destination index to begin copying to.

Example

See related example in the **System.ComponentModel.Design.DesignerVerbCollection** class topic.

Requirements

Platforms: Windows 98, Windows NT 4.0, Windows Millennium Edition, Windows 2000, Windows XP Home Edition, Windows XP Professional, Windows Server 2003 family

DesignerVerbCollection.IndexOf Method

Gets the index of the specified **DesignerVerb**.

```
[Visual Basic]
Public Function IndexOf( _
   ByVal value As DesignerVerb _
) As Integer
[C#]
public int IndexOf(
   DesignerVerb value
);
[C++]
public: int IndexOf(
   DesignerVerb* value
);
[JScript]
public function IndexOf(
   value : DesignerVerb
) : int;
```

Parameters

value
The **DesignerVerb** whose index to get in the collection.

Return Value

The index of the specified object if it is found in the list; otherwise, -1.

Example

See related example in the **System.ComponentModel.Design.DesignerVerbCollection** class topic.

Requirements

Platforms: Windows 98, Windows NT 4.0, Windows Millennium Edition, Windows 2000, Windows XP Home Edition, Windows XP Professional, Windows Server 2003 family

DesignerVerbCollection.Insert Method

Inserts the specified **DesignerVerb** at the specified index.

```
[Visual Basic]
Public Sub Insert( _
   ByVal index As Integer, _
   ByVal value As DesignerVerb _
)
[C#]
public void Insert(
   int index,
   DesignerVerb value
);
[C++]
public: void Insert(
   int index,
   DesignerVerb* value
);
[JScript]
public function Insert(
   index : int,
   value : DesignerVerb
);
```

Parameters

index
The index in the collection at which to insert the verb.

value
The **DesignerVerb** to insert in the collection.

Example

See related example in the **System.ComponentModel.Design.DesignerVerbCollection** class topic.

Requirements

Platforms: Windows 98, Windows NT 4.0, Windows Millennium Edition, Windows 2000, Windows XP Home Edition, Windows XP Professional, Windows Server 2003 family

DesignerVerbCollection.OnClear Method

Raises the **Clear** event.

```
[Visual Basic]
Overrides Protected Sub OnClear()
[C#]
protected override void OnClear();
[C++]
protected: void OnClear();
[JScript]
protected override function OnClear();
```

Remarks

Inheritors can override this method to add behavior for the **Clear** event.

Requirements

Platforms: Windows 98, Windows NT 4.0, Windows Millennium Edition, Windows 2000, Windows XP Home Edition, Windows XP Professional, Windows Server 2003 family

DesignerVerbCollection.OnInsert Method

Raises the **Insert** event.

```
[Visual Basic]
Overrides Protected Sub OnInsert( _
   ByVal index As Integer, _
   ByVal value As Object _
)
[C#]
protected override void OnInsert(
   int index,
   object value
);
[C++]
protected: void OnInsert(
   int index,
   Object* value
);
[JScript]
protected override function OnInsert(
   index : int,
   value : Object
);
```

Parameters

index

The index at which to insert an item.

value

The object to insert.

Remarks

Inheritors can override this method to add behavior for the **Insert** event.

Requirements

Platforms: Windows 98, Windows NT 4.0, Windows Millennium Edition, Windows 2000, Windows XP Home Edition, Windows XP Professional, Windows Server 2003 family

DesignerVerbCollection.OnRemove Method

Raises the **Remove** event.

[Visual Basic]
```
Overrides Protected Sub OnRemove( _
   ByVal index As Integer, _
   ByVal value As Object _
)
```
[C#]
```
protected override void OnRemove(
   int index,
   object value
);
```
[C++]
```
protected: void OnRemove(
   int index,
   Object* value
);
```
[JScript]
```
protected override function OnRemove(
   index : int,
   value : Object
);
```

Parameters

index

The index at which to remove the item.

value

The object to remove.

Remarks

Inheritors can override this method to add behavior for the **Remove** event.

Requirements

Platforms: Windows 98, Windows NT 4.0, Windows Millennium Edition, Windows 2000, Windows XP Home Edition, Windows XP Professional, Windows Server 2003 family

DesignerVerbCollection.OnSet Method

Raises the **Set** event.

[Visual Basic]
```
Overrides Protected Sub OnSet( _
   ByVal index As Integer, _
   ByVal oldValue As Object, _
   ByVal newValue As Object _
)
```
[C#]
```
protected override void OnSet(
   int index,
   object oldValue,
   object newValue
);
```
[C++]
```
protected: void OnSet(
   int index,
   Object* oldValue,
   Object* newValue
);
```
[JScript]
```
protected override function OnSet(
   index : int,
   oldValue : Object,
   newValue : Object
);
```

Parameters

index

The index at which to set the item.

oldValue

The old object.

newValue

The new object.

Remarks

Inheritors can override this method to add behavior for the **Set** event.

Requirements

Platforms: Windows 98, Windows NT 4.0, Windows Millennium Edition, Windows 2000, Windows XP Home Edition, Windows XP Professional, Windows Server 2003 family

DesignerVerbCollection.OnValidate Method

Raises the **Validate** event.

[Visual Basic]
```
Overrides Protected Sub OnValidate( _
   ByVal value As Object _
)
```
[C#]
```
protected override void OnValidate(
   object value
);
```
[C++]
```
protected: void OnValidate(
   Object* value
);
```

```
[JScript]
protected override function OnValidate(
   value : Object
);
```

Parameters

value

The object to validate.

Remarks

Inheritors can override this method to add behavior for the **Validate** event.

Requirements

Platforms: Windows 98, Windows NT 4.0, Windows Millennium Edition, Windows 2000, Windows XP Home Edition, Windows XP Professional, Windows Server 2003 family

DesignerVerbCollection.Remove Method

Removes the specified **DesignerVerb** from the collection.

```
[Visual Basic]
Public Sub Remove( _
   ByVal value As DesignerVerb _
)
[C#]
public void Remove(
   DesignerVerb value
);
[C++]
public: void Remove(
   DesignerVerb* value
);
[JScript]
public function Remove(
   value : DesignerVerb
);
```

Parameters

value

The **DesignerVerb** to remove from the collection.

Example

See related example in the **System.ComponentModel.Design.DesignerVerbCollection** class topic.

Requirements

Platforms: Windows 98, Windows NT 4.0, Windows Millennium Edition, Windows 2000, Windows XP Home Edition, Windows XP Professional, Windows Server 2003 family

DesigntimeLicenseContext Class

Represents a design-time license context that can support a license provider at design time.

System.Object
  System.ComponentModel.LicenseContext
    System.ComponentModel.Design.DesigntimeLicenseContext

[Visual Basic]
```
Public Class DesigntimeLicenseContext
   Inherits LicenseContext
```
[C#]
```
public class DesigntimeLicenseContext : LicenseContext
```
[C++]
```
public __gc class DesigntimeLicenseContext : public LicenseContext
```
[JScript]
```
public class DesigntimeLicenseContext extends LicenseContext
```

Thread Safety

Any public static (**Shared** in Visual Basic) members of this type are safe for multithreaded operations. Any instance members are not guaranteed to be thread safe.

Remarks

This class provides methods for managing license keys of the associated context and a property for representing the licensing mode of the associated context.

Requirements

Namespace: System.ComponentModel.Design

Platforms: Windows 98, Windows NT 4.0, Windows Millennium Edition, Windows 2000, Windows XP Home Edition, Windows XP Professional, Windows Server 2003 family

Assembly: System (in System.dll)

DesigntimeLicenseContext Constructor

Initializes a new instance of the **DesigntimeLicenseContext** class.

[Visual Basic]
```
Public Sub New()
```
[C#]
```
public DesigntimeLicenseContext();
```
[C++]
```
public: DesigntimeLicenseContext();
```
[JScript]
```
public function DesigntimeLicenseContext();
```

Remarks

The default constructor initializes any fields to their default values.

Requirements

Platforms: Windows 98, Windows NT 4.0, Windows Millennium Edition, Windows 2000, Windows XP Home Edition, Windows XP Professional, Windows Server 2003 family

DesigntimeLicenseContext.UsageMode Property

Gets the license usage mode.

[Visual Basic]
```
Overrides Public ReadOnly Property UsageMode As LicenseUsageMode
```
[C#]
```
public override LicenseUsageMode UsageMode {get;}
```
[C++]
```
public: __property LicenseUsageMode get_UsageMode();
```
[JScript]
```
public override function get UsageMode() : LicenseUsageMode;
```

Property Value

A **LicenseUsageMode** indicating the licensing mode for the context.

Requirements

Platforms: Windows 98, Windows NT 4.0, Windows Millennium Edition, Windows 2000, Windows XP Home Edition, Windows XP Professional, Windows Server 2003 family

DesigntimeLicenseContext.GetSavedLicense-Key Method

Gets a saved license key.

[Visual Basic]
```
Overrides Public Function GetSavedLicenseKey( _
   ByVal type As Type, _
   ByVal resourceAssembly As Assembly _
) As String
```
[C#]
```
public override string GetSavedLicenseKey(
   Type type,
   Assembly resourceAssembly
);
```
[C++]
```
public: String* GetSavedLicenseKey(
   Type* type,
   Assembly* resourceAssembly
);
```
[JScript]
```
public override function GetSavedLicenseKey(
   type : Type,
   resourceAssembly : Assembly
) : String;
```

Parameters

type
  The type of the license key.

resourceAssembly
  The assembly to get the key from.

Return Value

The saved license key that matches the specified type.

Requirements

Platforms: Windows 98, Windows NT 4.0, Windows Millennium Edition, Windows 2000, Windows XP Home Edition, Windows XP Professional, Windows Server 2003 family

DesigntimeLicenseContext.SetSavedLicenseKey Method

Sets a saved license key.

[Visual Basic]
```
Overrides Public Sub SetSavedLicenseKey( _
   ByVal type As Type, _
   ByVal key As String _
)
```
[C#]
```
public override void SetSavedLicenseKey(
   Type type,
   string key
);
```
[C++]
```
public: void SetSavedLicenseKey(
   Type* type,
   String* key
);
```
[JScript]
```
public override function SetSavedLicenseKey(
   type : Type,
   key : String
);
```

Parameters

type
    The type of the license key.

key
    The license key.

Remarks

This method sets the specified license key to this license context.

Requirements

Platforms: Windows 98, Windows NT 4.0, Windows Millennium Edition, Windows 2000, Windows XP Home Edition, Windows XP Professional, Windows Server 2003 family

DesigntimeLicenseContext-Serializer Class

Provides support for design-time license context serialization.

System.Object
System.ComponentModel.Design.DesigntimeLicenseContext-Serializer

[Visual Basic]
```
Public Class DesigntimeLicenseContextSerializer
```
[C#]
```
public class DesigntimeLicenseContextSerializer
```
[C++]
```
public __gc class DesigntimeLicenseContextSerializer
```
[JScript]
```
public class DesigntimeLicenseContextSerializer
```

Thread Safety

Any public static (**Shared** in Visual Basic) members of this type are safe for multithreaded operations. Any instance members are not guaranteed to be thread safe.

Remarks

This class provides a serialization method that can serialize a specified design-time license context.

Requirements

Namespace: System.ComponentModel.Design

Platforms: Windows 98, Windows NT 4.0, Windows Millennium Edition, Windows 2000, Windows XP Home Edition, Windows XP Professional, Windows Server 2003 family

Assembly: System (in System.dll)

DesigntimeLicenseContextSerializer.Serialize Method

Serializes the licenses within the specified design-time license context using the specified key and output stream.

[Visual Basic]
```
Public Shared Sub Serialize( _
   ByVal o As Stream, _
   ByVal cryptoKey As String, _
   ByVal context As DesigntimeLicenseContext _
)
```
[C#]
```
public static void Serialize(
   Stream o,
   string cryptoKey,
   DesigntimeLicenseContext context
);
```
[C++]
```
public: static void Serialize(
   Stream* o,
   String* cryptoKey,
   DesigntimeLicenseContext* context
);
```
[JScript]
```
public static function Serialize(
   o : Stream,
   cryptoKey : String,
   context : DesigntimeLicenseContext
);
```

Parameters

o
    The stream to output to.

cryptoKey
    The key to use for encryption.

context
    A **DesigntimeLicenseContext** indicating the license context.

Requirements

Platforms: Windows 98, Windows NT 4.0, Windows Millennium Edition, Windows 2000, Windows XP Home Edition, Windows XP Professional, Windows Server 2003 family

DisplayMode Enumeration

Defines identifiers that indicate the display modes used by **ByteViewer**.

[Visual Basic]
```
<Serializable>
Public Enum DisplayMode
```
[C#]
```
[Serializable]
public enum DisplayMode
```
[C++]
```
[Serializable]
__value public enum DisplayMode
```
[JScript]
```
public
   Serializable
enum DisplayMode
```

Remarks

The **DisplayMode** identifiers are used to indicate the display mode used to display each byte sequence.

Members

Member name	Description
Ansi	An ANSI format display.
Auto	A display mode that automatically selects a display mode. In this mode, the bytes are examined to determine if they are hexadecimal or printable. If the bytes are in hexadecimal format, the **Hexdump** mode is selected. If the characters match a printable character set, a test is run to automatically select either the **Ansi** or **Unicode** display mode.
Hexdump	A hexadecimal format display.
Unicode	A Unicode format display.

Requirements

Namespace: System.ComponentModel.Design

Platforms: Windows 98, Windows NT 4.0, Windows Millennium Edition, Windows 2000, Windows XP Home Edition, Windows XP Professional, Windows Server 2003 family

Assembly: System.Design (in System.Design.dll)

HelpContextType Enumeration

Defines identifiers that indicate information about the context in which a request for Help information originated.

[Visual Basic]
```
<Serializable>
Public Enum HelpContextType
```
[C#]
```
[Serializable]
public enum HelpContextType
```
[C++]
```
[Serializable]
__value public enum HelpContextType
```
[JScript]
```
public
   Serializable
enum HelpContextType
```

Remarks

HelpContextType defines identifiers that are used by the Help system to determine the context in which a Help request was initiated.

Members

Member name	Description
Ambient	A general context.
Selection	A selection.
ToolWindowSelection	A tool window selection.
Window	A window.

Requirements

Namespace: System.ComponentModel.Design

Platforms: Windows 98, Windows NT 4.0, Windows Millennium Edition, Windows 2000, Windows XP Home Edition, Windows XP Professional, Windows Server 2003 family

Assembly: System (in System.dll)

HelpKeywordType Enumeration

Defines identifiers that indicate the type of a Help keyword.

[Visual Basic]
```
<Serializable>
Public Enum HelpKeywordType
```
[C#]
```
[Serializable]
public enum HelpKeywordType
```
[C++]
```
[Serializable]
__value public enum HelpKeywordType
```
[JScript]
```
public
   Serializable
enum HelpKeywordType
```

Remarks

HelpKeywordType defines identifiers that indicate the type of a Help keyword to the Help system. Any or all of the keyword type identifiers can be specified for a single keyword. The type of a Help keyword is sometimes used when the Help system is determining the Help topics to display for a Help request.

Members

Member name	Description
F1Keyword	A keyword that F1 was pressed to request help about.
FilterKeyword	A filter keyword.
GeneralKeyword	A general keyword.

Requirements

Namespace: System.ComponentModel.Design

Platforms: Windows 98, Windows NT 4.0, Windows Millennium Edition, Windows 2000, Windows XP Home Edition, Windows XP Professional, Windows Server 2003 family

Assembly: System (in System.dll)

IComponentChangeService Interface

Provides an interface to add and remove the event handlers for events that add, change, remove or rename components, and provides methods to raise a **ComponentChanged** or **ComponentChanging** event.

[Visual Basic]
```
<ComVisible(True)>
Public Interface IComponentChangeService
```
[C#]
```
[ComVisible(true)]
public interface IComponentChangeService
```
[C++]
```
[ComVisible(true)]
public __gc __interface IComponentChangeService
```
[JScript]
```
public
   ComVisible(true)
interface IComponentChangeService
```

Remarks

IComponentChangeService provides an interface that can be used to indicate the methods that handle the following events:

- **ComponentAdded**, raised when a component is added.
- **ComponentAdding**, raised when a component is about to be added.
- **ComponentChanged**, raised when a component is changed.
- **ComponentChanging**, raised when a component is about to be changed.
- **ComponentRemoved**, raised when a component is removed.
- **ComponentRemoving**, raised when a component is about to be removed.
- **ComponentRename**, raised when a component is renamed.

Typically, the design environment raises these component add, change, remove, or rename events. Designers should call the methods of this interface when using **DesignerTransaction** objects to provide undo and redo functionality for design-time actions that affect components. More information is available in the documentation for **DesignerTransaction**. Generally, only the root designer handles these change notifications.

This service also provides methods that raise a component changed event or component changing event. A **PropertyDescriptor** or a component can indicate that a component has changed or is changing with the **OnComponentChanged** and **OnComponentChanging** methods, respectively.

Example

[Visual Basic, C#, C++] This following example demonstrates how to use the **IComponentChangeService** interface to receive notifications about the addition of, removal of, and changes to components in design mode.

[Visual Basic]
```
Imports System
Imports System.Data
Imports System.Drawing
Imports System.Collections
Imports System.ComponentModel
Imports System.ComponentModel.Design
Imports System.Windows.Forms

' This sample illustrates how to use the ↵
IComponentChangeService interface
'    to handle component change events.  The ComponentClass ↵
control attaches
'    event handlers when it is sited in a document, and ↵
displays a message
'    when notification that a component has been added, ↵
removed, or changed
'    is received from the IComponentChangeService.

'    To run this sample, add the ComponentClass control to a Form and
'    add, remove, or change components to see the behavior of the
'    component change event handlers.

Namespace IComponentChangeServiceExample
   _
   Public Class ComponentClass
      Inherits System.Windows.Forms.UserControl
      Private components As System.ComponentModel.Container = Nothing
      Private listBox1 As System.Windows.Forms.ListBox
      Private m_changeService As IComponentChangeService

      Public Sub New()
         InitializeComponent()
      End Sub

      Private Sub InitializeComponent()
         Me.listBox1 = New System.Windows.Forms.ListBox()
         Me.SuspendLayout()

         ' listBox1.
         Me.listBox1.Location = New System.Drawing.Point(24, 16)
         Me.listBox1.Name = "listBox1"
         Me.listBox1.Size = New System.Drawing.Size(576, 277)
         Me.listBox1.TabIndex = 0

         ' ComponentClass.
         Me.Controls.AddRange(New ↵
System.Windows.Forms.Control() {Me.listBox1})
         Me.Name = "ComponentClass"
         Me.Size = New System.Drawing.Size(624, 320)

         Me.ResumeLayout(False)
      End Sub

      ' This override allows the control to register event ↵
handlers for IComponentChangeService events
      ' at the time the control is sited, which happens ↵
only in design mode.
      Public Overrides Property Site() As ISite
         Get
            Return MyBase.Site
         End Get
         Set(ByVal Value As ISite)
            ' Clear any component change event handlers.
            ClearChangeNotifications()

            ' Set the new Site value.
            MyBase.Site = Value

            m_changeService = ↵
CType(GetService(GetType(IComponentChangeService)), ↵
IComponentChangeService)

            ' Register event handlers for component change events.
            RegisterChangeNotifications()
         End Set
      End Property

      Private Sub ClearChangeNotifications()
         ' The m_changeService value is null when not in ↵
design mode,
```

```
            ' as the IComponentChangeService is only available
 at design time.
            m_changeService =
CType(GetService(GetType(IComponentChangeService)),
IComponentChangeService)

            ' Clear our the component change events to prepare
for re-siting.
            If Not (m_changeService Is Nothing) Then
                RemoveHandler m_changeService.ComponentChanged,
AddressOf OnComponentChanged
                RemoveHandler m_changeService.ComponentChanging,
AddressOf OnComponentChanging
                RemoveHandler m_changeService.ComponentAdded,
 AddressOf OnComponentAdded
                RemoveHandler m_changeService.ComponentAdding,
AddressOf OnComponentAdding
                RemoveHandler m_changeService.ComponentRemoved,
AddressOf OnComponentRemoved
                RemoveHandler m_changeService.ComponentRemoving,
AddressOf OnComponentRemoving
                RemoveHandler m_changeService.ComponentRename,
AddressOf OnComponentRename
            End If
        End Sub

        Private Sub RegisterChangeNotifications()
            ' Register the event handlers for the IComponentChangeService
events
            If Not (m_changeService Is Nothing) Then
                AddHandler m_changeService.ComponentChanged,
 AddressOf OnComponentChanged
                AddHandler m_changeService.ComponentChanging,
 AddressOf OnComponentChanging
                AddHandler m_changeService.ComponentAdded,
AddressOf OnComponentAdded
                AddHandler m_changeService.ComponentAdding,
AddressOf OnComponentAdding
                AddHandler m_changeService.ComponentRemoved,
AddressOf OnComponentRemoved
                AddHandler m_changeService.ComponentRemoving,
 AddressOf OnComponentRemoving
                AddHandler m_changeService.ComponentRename,
AddressOf OnComponentRename
            End If
        End Sub

        ' This method handles the OnComponentChanged event to
 display a notification.
        Private Sub OnComponentChanged(ByVal sender As Object,
 ByVal ce As ComponentChangedEventArgs)
            If Not (ce.Component Is Nothing) And Not
(CType(ce.Component, IComponent).Site Is Nothing) And Not
(ce.Member Is Nothing) Then
                OnUserChange(("The " + ce.Member.Name + " member
 of the " + CType(ce.Component, IComponent).Site.Name + "
 component has been changed."))
            End If
        End Sub

        ' This method handles the OnComponentChanging event to
 display a notification.
        Private Sub OnComponentChanging(ByVal sender As Object,
 ByVal ce As ComponentChangingEventArgs)
            If Not (ce.Component Is Nothing) And Not
 (CType(ce.Component, IComponent).Site Is Nothing) And Not
 (ce.Member Is Nothing) Then
                OnUserChange(("The " + ce.Member.Name + " member
 of the " + CType(ce.Component, IComponent).Site.Name + "
component is being changed."))
            End If
        End Sub

        ' This method handles the OnComponentAdded event to
 display a notification.
        Private Sub OnComponentAdded(ByVal sender As Object,
ByVal ce As ComponentEventArgs)
            OnUserChange(("A component, " +
ce.Component.Site.Name + ", has been added."))
        End Sub

        ' This method handles the OnComponentAdding event to
display a notification.
        Private Sub OnComponentAdding(ByVal sender As Object,
 ByVal ce As ComponentEventArgs)
            OnUserChange(("A component of type " +
 (CType(ce.Component, Component)).GetType().FullName + "
is being added."))
        End Sub

        ' This method handles the OnComponentRemoved event to
display a notification.
        Private Sub OnComponentRemoved(ByVal sender As Object,
ByVal ce As ComponentEventArgs)
            OnUserChange(("A component, " +
ce.Component.Site.Name + ", has been removed."))
        End Sub

        ' This method handles the OnComponentRemoving event to
display a notification.
        Private Sub OnComponentRemoving(ByVal sender As Object,
 ByVal ce As ComponentEventArgs)
            OnUserChange(("A component, " +
 ce.Component.Site.Name + ", is being removed."))
        End Sub

        ' This method handles the OnComponentRename event to
display a notification.
        Private Sub OnComponentRename(ByVal sender As Object,
ByVal ce As ComponentRenameEventArgs)
            OnUserChange(("A component, " + ce.OldName + ",
was renamed to " + ce.NewName + "."))
        End Sub

        ' This method adds a specified notification message
to the control's listbox.
        Private Sub OnUserChange(ByVal [text] As String)
            listBox1.Items.Add([text])
        End Sub

        ' Clean up any resources being used.
        Protected Overloads Sub Dispose(ByVal disposing As Boolean)
            If disposing Then
                ClearChangeNotifications()

                If Not (components Is Nothing) Then
                    components.Dispose()
                End If
            End If
            MyBase.Dispose(disposing)
        End Sub

    End Class
End Namespace
```

[C#]

```
using System;
using System.Data;
using System.Drawing;
using System.Collections;
using System.ComponentModel;
using System.ComponentModel.Design;
using System.Windows.Forms;

/* This sample illustrates how to use the
IComponentChangeService interface
    to handle component change events.  The
ComponentClass control attaches
    event handlers when it is sited in a document,
and displays a message
```

```
    when notification that a component has been added, ↵
 removed, or changed
    is received from the IComponentChangeService.

    To run this sample, add the ComponentClass control to a Form and
    add, remove, or change components to see the behavior of the
    component change event handlers. */

namespace IComponentChangeServiceExample
{
    public class ComponentClass : System.Windows.Forms.UserControl
    {
        private System.ComponentModel.Container components = null;
    private System.Windows.Forms.ListBox listBox1;
    private IComponentChangeService m_changeService;

    public ComponentClass()
    {
        InitializeComponent();
    }

    private void InitializeComponent()
    {
          this.listBox1 = new System.Windows.Forms.ListBox();
        this.SuspendLayout();

         // listBox1.
        this.listBox1.Location = new System.Drawing.Point(24, 16);
        this.listBox1.Name = "listBox1";
        this.listBox1.Size = new System.Drawing.Size(576, 277);
        this.listBox1.TabIndex = 0;

        // ComponentClass.
        this.Controls.AddRange(new ↵
System.Windows.Forms.Control[] {this.listBox1});
        this.Name = "ComponentClass";
        this.Size = new System.Drawing.Size(624, 320);

            this.ResumeLayout(false);
    }

    // This override allows the control to register event ↵
handlers for IComponentChangeService events
    // at the time the control is sited, which happens only ↵
 in design mode.
    public override ISite Site
    {
        get
        {
        return base.Site;
        }
        set
        {
        // Clear any component change event handlers.
        ClearChangeNotifications();

        // Set the new Site value.
        base.Site = value;

        m_changeService = ↵
 (IComponentChangeService)GetService(typeof(IComponentChangeService));

        // Register event handlers for component change events.
        RegisterChangeNotifications();
        }
    }

    private void ClearChangeNotifications()
    {
        // The m_changeService value is null when not in design mode,
        // as the IComponentChangeService is only available ↵
 at design time.
        m_changeService = ↵
(IComponentChangeService)GetService(typeof(IComponentChangeService));
```

```
         // Clear our the component change events to ↵
  prepare for re-siting.
        if (m_changeService != null)
        {
         m_changeService.ComponentChanged -= new ↵
ComponentChangedEventHandler(OnComponentChanged);
        m_changeService.ComponentChanging -= new ↵
ComponentChangingEventHandler(OnComponentChanging);
        m_changeService.ComponentAdded -= new ↵
ComponentEventHandler(OnComponentAdded);
        m_changeService.ComponentAdding -= new ↵
ComponentEventHandler(OnComponentAdding);
        m_changeService.ComponentRemoved -= new ↵
ComponentEventHandler(OnComponentRemoved);
        m_changeService.ComponentRemoving -= new ↵
ComponentEventHandler(OnComponentRemoving);
        m_changeService.ComponentRename -= new ↵
ComponentRenameEventHandler(OnComponentRename);
        }
    }

    private void RegisterChangeNotifications()
    {
        // Register the event handlers for the ↵
IComponentChangeService events
        if (m_changeService != null)
        {
        m_changeService.ComponentChanged += new ↵
vComponentChangedEventHandler(OnComponentChanged);
        m_changeService.ComponentChanging += new ↵
ComponentChangingEventHandler(OnComponentChanging);
        m_changeService.ComponentAdded += new ↵
ComponentEventHandler(OnComponentAdded);
        m_changeService.ComponentAdding += new ↵
ComponentEventHandler(OnComponentAdding);
        m_changeService.ComponentRemoved += new ↵
ComponentEventHandler(OnComponentRemoved);
        m_changeService.ComponentRemoving += new ↵
ComponentEventHandler(OnComponentRemoving);
        m_changeService.ComponentRename += new ↵
ComponentRenameEventHandler(OnComponentRename);
        }
    }

    /* This method handles the OnComponentChanged event to ↵
display a notification. */
    private void OnComponentChanged(object sender, ↵
ComponentChangedEventArgs ce)
    {
         if( ce.Component != null && ((IComponent) ↵
ce.Component).Site != null && ce.Member != null )
        OnUserChange("The " + ce.Member.Name + " member of the ↵
 " + ((IComponent)ce.Component).Site.Name + " component has ↵
 been changed.");
    }

    /* This method handles the OnComponentChanging event to ↵
 display a notification. */
    private void OnComponentChanging(object sender, ↵
ComponentChangingEventArgs ce)
    {
        if( ce.Component != null && ↵
 ((IComponent)ce.Component).Site != null && ce.Member != null )
        OnUserChange("The " + ce.Member.Name + " member of the ↵
 " + ((IComponent)ce.Component).Site.Name + " component is ↵
 being changed.");
    }

    /* This method handles the OnComponentAdded event to ↵
 display a notification. */
    private void OnComponentAdded(object sender, ComponentEventArgs ce)
    {
        OnUserChange("A component, " + ce.Component.Site.Name + ↵
 ", has been added.");
    }
```

```
    /* This method handles the OnComponentAdding event to ↲
display a notification. */
    private void OnComponentAdding(object sender, ↲
ComponentEventArgs ce)
    {
        OnUserChange("A component of type " + ↲
ce.Component.GetType().FullName + " is being added.");
    }

    /* This method handles the OnComponentRemoved event ↲
to display a notification. */
    private void OnComponentRemoved(object sender, ↲
ComponentEventArgs ce)
    {
        OnUserChange("A component, " + ce.Component.Site.Name ↲
 + ", has been removed.");
    }

    /* This method handles the OnComponentRemoving event to ↲
 display a notification. */
    private void OnComponentRemoving(object sender, ↲
ComponentEventArgs ce)
    {
        OnUserChange("A component, " + ↲
ce.Component.Site.Name + ", is being removed.");
    }

    /* This method handles the OnComponentRename event to ↲
display a notification. */
    private void OnComponentRename(object sender, ↲
ComponentRenameEventArgs ce)
    {
        OnUserChange("A component, " + ce.OldName + ", ↲
was renamed to " + ce.NewName +".");
    }

    // This method adds a specified notification message to ↲
 the control's listbox.
    private void OnUserChange(string text)
    {
        listBox1.Items.Add(text);
    }

    // Clean up any resources being used.
    protected override void Dispose( bool disposing )
    {
        if( disposing )
        {
        ClearChangeNotifications();

        if(components != null)
        {
            components.Dispose();
        }
        }
        base.Dispose( disposing );
    }
    }
}
```

[C++]

```
#using <mscorlib.dll>
#using <system.dll>
#using <system.windows.forms.dll>
#using <system.drawing.dll>

using namespace System;
using namespace System::Drawing;
using namespace System::Collections;
using namespace System::ComponentModel;
using namespace System::ComponentModel::Design;
using namespace System::Windows::Forms;

/* This sample illustrates how to use the ↲
IComponentChangeService interface
    to handle component change events.  The ComponentClass ↲
control attaches
    event handlers when it is sited in a document, and ↲
displays a message
    when notification that a component has been added, ↲
removed, or changed
    is received from the IComponentChangeService.

    To run this sample, add the ComponentClass control to a Form and
    add, remove, or change components to see the behavior of the
    component change event handlers. */

namespace IComponentChangeServiceExample
{
    public __gc class ComponentClass : public UserControl {
    private:

        System::ComponentModel::Container* components;
        ListBox* listBox1;
        IComponentChangeService* m_changeService;

        void InitializeComponent()
        {
            this->listBox1 = new ListBox();
            this->SuspendLayout();

            // listBox1.
            this->listBox1->Location = System::Drawing::Point(24, 16);
            this->listBox1->Name = S"listBox1";
            this->listBox1->Size = System::Drawing::Size(576, 277);
            this->listBox1->TabIndex = 0;

            // ComponentClass.
            Control* myArray[] = {listBox1};
            this->Controls->AddRange( myArray );
            this->Name = S"ComponentClass";
            this->Size = System::Drawing::Size(624, 320);

            this->ResumeLayout(false);
        }

        void ClearChangeNotifications()
        {
            // The m_changeService value is 0 when not in design mode,
            // as the IComponentChangeService is only available ↲
 at design time.
            m_changeService = ↲
dynamic_cast<IComponentChangeService*>(GetService ↲
 (__typeof(IComponentChangeService)));

            // Clear our the component change events to ↲
prepare for re-siting.
            if (m_changeService != 0)
            {
                m_changeService->ComponentChanged -= new ↲
ComponentChangedEventHandler(this, OnComponentChanged);
                m_changeService->ComponentChanging -= new ↲
ComponentChangingEventHandler(this, OnComponentChanging);
                m_changeService->ComponentAdded -= new ↲
ComponentEventHandler(this, OnComponentAdded);
                m_changeService->ComponentAdding -= new ↲
ComponentEventHandler(this, OnComponentAdding);
                m_changeService->ComponentRemoved -= new ↲
ComponentEventHandler(this, OnComponentRemoved);
                m_changeService->ComponentRemoving -= new ↲
ComponentEventHandler(this, OnComponentRemoving);
                m_changeService->ComponentRename -= new ↲
ComponentRenameEventHandler(this, OnComponentRename);
            }
        }

        void RegisterChangeNotifications()
        {
            // Register the event handlers for the ↲
IComponentChangeService events
            if (m_changeService != 0)
            {
                m_changeService->ComponentChanged += new ↲
ComponentChangedEventHandler(this, OnComponentChanged);
```

```
            m_changeService->ComponentChanging += new ↵
ComponentChangingEventHandler(this, OnComponentChanging);
            m_changeService->ComponentAdded += new ↵
ComponentEventHandler(this, OnComponentAdded);
            m_changeService->ComponentAdding += new ↵
ComponentEventHandler(this, OnComponentAdding);
            m_changeService->ComponentRemoved += new ↵
ComponentEventHandler(this, OnComponentRemoved);
            m_changeService->ComponentRemoving += new ↵
ComponentEventHandler(this, OnComponentRemoving);
            m_changeService->ComponentRename += new ↵
ComponentRenameEventHandler(this, OnComponentRename);
        }
    }

    /* This method handles the OnComponentChanged event to ↵
 display a notification. */
    void OnComponentChanged(Object* sender, ↵
ComponentChangedEventArgs* ce)
    {
        if( ce->Component != 0 && static_cast<IComponent*> ↵
 (ce->Component)->Site != 0 && ce->Member != 0 )
            OnUserChange(String::Concat(S"The ", ce->Member-> ↵
Name, S" member of the ", static_cast<IComponent*> ↵
 (ce->Component)->Site->Name, S" component has been changed." ));
    }

    /* This method handles the OnComponentChanging event ↵
to display a notification. */
    void OnComponentChanging(Object* sender, ↵
ComponentChangingEventArgs* ce)
    {
        if( ce->Component != 0 && static_cast<IComponent*> ↵
 (ce->Component)->Site != 0 && ce->Member != 0 )
            OnUserChange(String::Concat(S"The ", ce->Member-> ↵
Name, S" member of the ", static_cast<IComponent*>(ce-> ↵
Component)->Site->Name, S" component is being changed."));
    }

    /* This method handles the OnComponentAdded event to ↵
 display a notification. */
    void OnComponentAdded(Object* sender, ComponentEventArgs* ce)
    {
        OnUserChange(String::Concat(S"A component, ", ce- ↵
>Component->Site->Name, S", has been added."));
    }

    /* This method handles the OnComponentAdding event to ↵
 display a notification. */
    void OnComponentAdding(Object* sender, ComponentEventArgs* ce)
    {
        OnUserChange(String::Concat(S"A component of type ", ↵
 ce->Component->GetType()->FullName, S" is being added."));
    }

    /* This method handles the OnComponentRemoved event to ↵
 display a notification. */
    void OnComponentRemoved(Object* sender, ComponentEventArgs* ce)
    {
        OnUserChange(String::Concat(S"A component, ", ce- ↵
>Component->Site->Name, S", has been removed."));
    }

    /* This method handles the OnComponentRemoving event to ↵
display a notification. */
    void OnComponentRemoving(Object* sender, ↵
ComponentEventArgs* ce)
    {
        OnUserChange(String::Concat(S"A component, ", ce- ↵
>Component->Site->Name, S", is being removed."));
    }

    /* This method handles the OnComponentRename event to ↵
display a notification. */
    void OnComponentRename(Object* sender, ↵
ComponentRenameEventArgs* ce)
    {
        OnUserChange(String::Concat(S"A component, ", ↵
ce->OldName, S", was renamed to ", ce->NewName, S"."));
    }

    // This method adds a specified notification message ↵
 to the control's listbox.
    void OnUserChange(String* text)
    {
        listBox1->Items->Add(text);
    }

public:

    ComponentClass()
    {
        InitializeComponent();
    }

    // This override allows the control to register ↵
 event handlers for IComponentChangeService events
    // at the time the control is sited, which happens ↵
 only in design mode.
    __property ISite* get_Site()
    {
        return UserControl::get_Site();
    }

    __property void set_Site(ISite* value)
    {
        // Clear any component change event handlers.
        ClearChangeNotifications();

        // Set the new Site value.
        UserControl::set_Site( value );

        m_changeService = ↵
static_cast<IComponentChangeService*>(GetService ↵
 (__typeof(IComponentChangeService)));

        // Register event handlers for component change events.
        RegisterChangeNotifications();
    }

protected:

    // Clean up any resources being used.
    void Dispose( bool disposing )
    {
        if( disposing )
        {
            ClearChangeNotifications();

            if(components != 0)
            {
                components->Dispose();
            }

            UserControl::Dispose( disposing );
        }
    }
};
}
```

Requirements

Namespace: System.ComponentModel.Design

Platforms: Windows 98, Windows NT 4.0, Windows Millennium Edition, Windows 2000, Windows XP Home Edition, Windows XP Professional, Windows Server 2003 family

Assembly: System (in System.dll)

IComponentChangeService.OnComponentChanged Method

Announces to the component change service that a particular component has changed.

```
[Visual Basic]
Sub OnComponentChanged( _
   ByVal component As Object, _
   ByVal member As MemberDescriptor, _
   ByVal oldValue As Object, _
   ByVal newValue As Object _
)
[C#]
void OnComponentChanged(
   object component,
   MemberDescriptor member,
   object oldValue,
   object newValue
);
[C++]
void OnComponentChanged(
   Object* component,
   MemberDescriptor* member,
   Object* oldValue,
   Object* newValue
);
[JScript]
function OnComponentChanged(
   component : Object,
   member : MemberDescriptor,
   oldValue : Object,
   newValue : Object
);
```

Parameters

component
: The component that has changed.

member
: The member that has changed. This is a null reference (**Nothing** in Visual Basic) if this change is not related to a single member.

oldValue
: The old value of the member. This is valid only if the member is not a null reference (**Nothing** in Visual Basic).

newValue
: The new value of the member. This is valid only if the member is not a null reference (**Nothing** in Visual Basic).

Remarks

This method raises the **ComponentChanged** event.

Most designers that ship with the .NET Framework SDK, as well as the Visual Studio .NET design-time environment, typically raise this event for you when a component in a project is changed, so most of the time you do not need to explicitly call this method. The appropriate **IComponentChangeService** events are automatically raised when a **PropertyDescriptor** is used to change a property value or components are added or removed from the **IDesignerHost** container.

Before calling **OnComponentChanged**, first call **OnComponentChanging** to indicate that a component is about to change, and make the change. Then call **OnComponentChanged** to raise the **ComponentChanged** event.

Notes to Implementers: This event allows the implementer to do any post-processing that is needed after a property change. For example, a designer typically updates the source code that sets the property with the new value.

Requirements

Platforms: Windows 98, Windows NT 4.0, Windows Millennium Edition, Windows 2000, Windows XP Home Edition, Windows XP Professional, Windows Server 2003 family

IComponentChangeService.OnComponentChanging Method

Announces to the component change service that a particular component is changing.

```
[Visual Basic]
Sub OnComponentChanging( _
   ByVal component As Object, _
   ByVal member As MemberDescriptor _
)
[C#]
void OnComponentChanging(
   object component,
   MemberDescriptor member
);
[C++]
void OnComponentChanging(
   Object* component,
   MemberDescriptor* member
);
[JScript]
function OnComponentChanging(
   component : Object,
   member : MemberDescriptor
);
```

Parameters

component
: The component that is about to change.

member
: The member that is changing. This is a null reference (**Nothing** in Visual Basic) if this change is not related to a single member.

Remarks

This method raises the **ComponentChanging** event.

Most designers included with the .NET Framework SDK, as well as the Visual Studio .NET design-time environment, typically raise this event automatically, so most of the time, you do not need to explicitly call this method. The appropriate **IComponentChangeService** events are automatically raised when a **PropertyDescriptor** is used to change a property value or components are added or removed from the **IDesignerHost** container.

Notes to Implementers: This method throws an exception if the property cannot be changed. This is not intended to validate the values of a particular property. Instead, it is intended to provide a global method of preventing a component from changing. For example, if a designer file is checked into source code control, this event's handler would typically throw an exception if the user refused to check out the file.

Requirements

Platforms: Windows 98, Windows NT 4.0, Windows Millennium Edition, Windows 2000, Windows XP Home Edition, Windows XP Professional, Windows Server 2003 family

IComponentChangeService.ComponentAdded Event

Occurs when a component has been added.

[Visual Basic]
```
Event ComponentAdded As ComponentEventHandler
```
[C#]
```
event ComponentEventHandler ComponentAdded;
```
[C++]
```
__event ComponentEventHandler* ComponentAdded;
```

[JScript] In JScript, you can handle the events defined by a class, but you cannot define your own.

Event Data

The event handler receives an argument of type **ComponentEventArgs** containing data related to this event. The following **ComponentEventArgs** property provides information specific to this event.

Property	Description
Component	Gets the component associated with the event.

Remarks

This event occurs during load and when new components are created by the user, after the component has been sited.

Requirements

Platforms: Windows 98, Windows NT 4.0, Windows Millennium Edition, Windows 2000, Windows XP Home Edition, Windows XP Professional, Windows Server 2003 family

IComponentChangeService.ComponentAdding Event

Occurs when a component is in the process of being added.

[Visual Basic]
```
Event ComponentAdding As ComponentEventHandler
```
[C#]
```
event ComponentEventHandler ComponentAdding;
```
[C++]
```
__event ComponentEventHandler* ComponentAdding;
```

[JScript] In JScript, you can handle the events defined by a class, but you cannot define your own.

Event Data

The event handler receives an argument of type **ComponentEventArgs** containing data related to this event. The following **ComponentEventArgs** property provides information specific to this event.

Property	Description
Component	Gets the component associated with the event.

Remarks

This event occurs during load and when the user creates a new component. You can cancel the process of adding a component by throwing an exception here.

Requirements

Platforms: Windows 98, Windows NT 4.0, Windows Millennium Edition, Windows 2000, Windows XP Home Edition, Windows XP Professional, Windows Server 2003 family

IComponentChangeService.ComponentChanged Event

Occurs when a component has been changed.

[Visual Basic]
```
Event ComponentChanged As ComponentChangedEventHandler
```
[C#]
```
event ComponentChangedEventHandler ComponentChanged;
```
[C++]
```
__event ComponentChangedEventHandler* ComponentChanged;
```

[JScript] In JScript, you can handle the events defined by a class, but you cannot define your own.

Event Data

The event handler receives an argument of type **ComponentChangedEventArgs** containing data related to this event. The following **ComponentChangedEventArgs** properties provide information specific to this event.

Property	Description
Component	Gets the component that was modified.
Member	Gets the member that has been changed.
NewValue	Gets the new value of the changed member.
OldValue	Gets the old value of the changed member.

Remarks

This event occurs when any component on the form changes. This event will not occur during form load and unload, because changes are expected at this time.

Tip A **DesignerTransaction** can raise multiple **ComponentChanged** events. Some **ComponentChanged** event handlers can interfere with with expected sequences of events, such as if your code alters the values of properties while a transaction is occurring. A **ComponentChanged** event handler can also impair performance if it draws after each change while a **DesignerTransaction** is in progress. In order to allow a **DesignerTransaction** in process to complete without interruption or interference by your **ComponentChanged** event handler, you can test the state of the **InTransaction** property, and defer handling the change events until the completion of the transaction by adding a **DesignerTransactionCloseEventHandler** which will raise your **ComponentChanged** event handler and remove itself upon completion of the transaction.

Requirements

Platforms: Windows 98, Windows NT 4.0, Windows Millennium Edition, Windows 2000, Windows XP Home Edition, Windows XP Professional, Windows Server 2003 family

IComponentChangeService.ComponentChanging Event

Occurs when a component is in the process of being changed.

[Visual Basic]
```
Event ComponentChanging As ComponentChangingEventHandler
```
[C#]
```
event ComponentChangingEventHandler ComponentChanging;
```
[C++]
```
__event ComponentChangingEventHandler* ComponentChanging;
```

[JScript] In JScript, you can handle the events defined by a class, but you cannot define your own.

Event Data

The event handler receives an argument of type **ComponentChangingEventArgs** containing data related to this event. The following **ComponentChangingEventArgs** properties provide information specific to this event.

Property	Description
Component	Gets the component that is about to be changed or the component that is the parent container of the member that is about to be changed.
Member	Gets the member that is about to be changed.

Remarks

This event occurs before the component is actually changed, and gives the designer a chance to abort the change or perform any pre-change processing. This event does not occur during form load and unload, because changes are expected at this time.

Requirements

Platforms: Windows 98, Windows NT 4.0, Windows Millennium Edition, Windows 2000, Windows XP Home Edition, Windows XP Professional, Windows Server 2003 family

IComponentChangeService.ComponentRemoved Event

Occurs when a component has been removed.

[Visual Basic]
```
Event ComponentRemoved As ComponentEventHandler
```
[C#]
```
event ComponentEventHandler ComponentRemoved;
```
[C++]
```
__event ComponentEventHandler* ComponentRemoved;
```

[JScript] In JScript, you can handle the events defined by a class, but you cannot define your own.

Event Data

The event handler receives an argument of type **ComponentEventArgs** containing data related to this event. The following **ComponentEventArgs** property provides information specific to this event.

Property	Description
Component	Gets the component associated with the event.

Remarks

This event occurs during unload and when a component is deleted by the user. The event occurs before the site has been removed from the component.

Requirements

Platforms: Windows 98, Windows NT 4.0, Windows Millennium Edition, Windows 2000, Windows XP Home Edition, Windows XP Professional, Windows Server 2003 family

IComponentChangeService.ComponentRemoving Event

Occurs when a component is in the process of being removed.

[Visual Basic]
```
Event ComponentRemoving As ComponentEventHandler
```
[C#]
```
event ComponentEventHandler ComponentRemoving;
```
[C++]
```
__event ComponentEventHandler* ComponentRemoving;
```

[JScript] In JScript, you can handle the events defined by a class, but you cannot define your own.

Event Data

The event handler receives an argument of type **ComponentEventArgs** containing data related to this event. The following **ComponentEventArgs** property provides information specific to this event.

Property	Description
Component	Gets the component associated with the event.

Remarks

This event occurs during unload and when the user deletes a component. You can cancel the process of removing a component by throwing an exception here.

Requirements

Platforms: Windows 98, Windows NT 4.0, Windows Millennium Edition, Windows 2000, Windows XP Home Edition, Windows XP Professional, Windows Server 2003 family

IComponentChangeService.ComponentRename Event

Occurs when a component is renamed.

[Visual Basic]
```
Event ComponentRename As ComponentRenameEventHandler
```
[C#]
```
event ComponentRenameEventHandler ComponentRename;
```
[C++]
```
__event ComponentRenameEventHandler* ComponentRename;
```

[JScript] In JScript, you can handle the events defined by a class, but you cannot define your own.

Event Data

The event handler receives an argument of type **ComponentRenameEventArgs** containing data related to this event. The following **ComponentRenameEventArgs** properties provide information specific to this event.

Property	Description
Component	Gets the component that is being renamed.
NewName	Gets the name of the component after the rename event.
OldName	Gets the name of the component before the rename event.

Remarks

This event occurs after the **ComponentChanged** event when a component has been renamed.

Requirements

Platforms: Windows 98, Windows NT 4.0, Windows Millennium Edition, Windows 2000, Windows XP Home Edition, Windows XP Professional, Windows Server 2003 family

IDesigner Interface

Provides the basic framework for building a custom designer.

System.IDisposable
 System.ComponentModel.Design.IDesigner

[Visual Basic]
```
<ComVisible(True)>
Public Interface IDesigner
   Inherits IDisposable
```
[C#]
```
[ComVisible(true)]
public interface IDesigner : IDisposable
```
[C++]
```
[ComVisible(true)]
public __gc __interface IDesigner : public IDisposable
```
[JScript]
```
public
   ComVisible(true)
interface IDesigner implements IDisposable
```

Classes that Implement IDesigner

Class	Description
ComponentDesigner	Base designer class for extending the design mode behavior of a component.

Remarks

The **IDesigner** interface provides an interface through which you can implement basic services for a designer. A designer can modify the behavior of a component at design time, and may provide its own services and behavior. A designer is only active at design-time, and must be associated with a type of component using a **Designer-Attribute** in order to be loaded when a component of the associated type is created at design time.

The **IDesigner** interface provides methods and properties that you can implement in order to provide custom behavior at design time.

Implement the **Initialize** method of a designer to perform actions when a component is created. This can be useful if a component should have a special configuration at design-time, or if its configuration should change depending on conditions that the designer can determine.

A designer can provide menu commands on the shortcut menu that is displayed when a user right-clicks a component or control in the design-time environment. You can implement the **Verbs** property to define a get accessor that returns a **DesignerVerbCollection** containing the **DesignerVerb** objects for generating menu commands.

A designer for a component that appears in the component tray can perform a default action when the component is double-clicked. Implement the **DoDefaultAction** method to specify the behavior to perform when the component is double-clicked.

A designer can also use the available design-time services to perform a variety of tasks, including surveying the current design-time environment for components and their properties, reading and setting the values of properties of components, managing the toolbox, managing selected components, or displaying a user interface that can be used to configure values or to apply futher processing.

To implement a designer for a control that can be sited on a form, you can inherit from the **ControlDesigner** class. Controls whose associated designer does not derive from **ControlDesigner** are displayed in the component tray. The **ComponentDesigner** and **ControlDesigner** classes implement the **IDesigner** interface and provide additional design-time support that may be of use to authors of designers. For more information, see the reference documentation for these classes.

For an overview of creating design components, please see **Enhancing Design-Time Support**.

Example

[Visual Basic, C#] This example demonstrates an **IDesigner** implementation that stores a local reference to its component, performs a default action when the component is double-clicked, and provides a designer verb menu command.

[Visual Basic]
```
Imports System
Imports System.Collections
Imports System.ComponentModel
Imports System.ComponentModel.Design
Imports System.Drawing
Imports System.Data
Imports System.Windows.Forms

' A DesignerAttribute associates the example IDesigner with an ↵
example control.
<DesignerAttribute(GetType(ExampleIDesigner))> _
Public Class TestControl
    Inherits System.Windows.Forms.UserControl

    Public Sub New()
    End Sub
End Class

Public Class ExampleIDesigner
    Implements System.ComponentModel.Design.IDesigner

    ' Local reference to the designer's component.
    Private component_ As IComponent

    ' Public accessor to the designer's component.
    Public ReadOnly Property Component() As ↵
System.ComponentModel.IComponent Implements IDesigner.Component
        Get
            Return component_
        End Get
    End Property

    Public Sub New()
    End Sub

    Public Sub Initialize(ByVal component As ↵
System.ComponentModel.IComponent) Implements IDesigner.Initialize
        ' This method is called after a designer for a ↵
 component is created,
        ' and stores a reference to the designer's component.
        Me.component_ = component
    End Sub

    ' This method peforms the 'default' action for the ↵
 designer. The default action
    ' for a basic IDesigner implementation is invoked ↵
when the designer's component
    ' is double-clicked. By default, a component associated ↵
with a basic IDesigner
    ' implementation is displayed in the design-mode component tray.
    Public Sub DoDefaultAction() Implements IDesigner.DoDefaultAction
        ' Shows a message box indicating that the default ↵
action for the designer was invoked.
        MessageBox.Show("The DoDefaultAction method of an ↵
IDesigner implementation was invoked.", "Information")
    End Sub

    ' Returns a collection of designer verb menu items to show in the
    ' shortcut menu for the designer's component.
```

```
    Public ReadOnly Property Verbs() As ↵
System.ComponentModel.Design.DesignerVerbCollection Implements ↵
IDesigner.Verbs
        Get
            Dim verbs_ As New DesignerVerbCollection()
            Dim dv1 As New DesignerVerb("Display Component Name", ↵
 New EventHandler(AddressOf Me.ShowComponentName))
            verbs_.Add(dv1)
            Return verbs_
        End Get
    End Property

    ' Event handler for displaying a message box showing the ↵
 designer's component's name.
    Private Sub ShowComponentName(ByVal sender As Object, ByVal ↵
e As EventArgs)
        If Not (Me.Component Is Nothing) Then
            MessageBox.Show(Me.Component.Site.Name, "Designer ↵
Component's Name")
        End If
    End Sub

    ' Provides an opportunity to release resources before ↵
object destruction.
    Public Sub Dispose() Implements IDesigner.Dispose
    End Sub

End Class
```

[C#]

```
using System;
using System.Collections;
using System.ComponentModel;
using System.ComponentModel.Design;
using System.Drawing;
using System.Data;
using System.Windows.Forms;

namespace IDesignerExample
{
    // A DesignerAttribute associates the example IDesigner ↵
with an example control.
    [DesignerAttribute(typeof(ExampleIDesigner))]
    public class TestControl : System.Windows.Forms.UserControl
    {
        public TestControl()
        {
        }
    }

    public class ExampleIDesigner : ↵
System.ComponentModel.Design.IDesigner
    {
        // Local reference to the designer's component.
        private IComponent component;
        // Public accessor to the designer's component.
        public System.ComponentModel.IComponent Component
        {
            get
            {
                return component;
            }
        }

        public ExampleIDesigner()
        {
        }

        public void Initialize(System.ComponentModel.IComponent ↵
component)
        {
            // This method is called after a designer for a ↵
component is created,
            // and stores a reference to the designer's component.
            this.component = component;
        }

        // This method peforms the 'default' action for the ↵
designer. The default action
        // for a basic IDesigner implementation is invoked when ↵
 the designer's component
        // is double-clicked. By default, a component associated ↵
with a basic IDesigner
        // implementation is displayed in the design-mode ↵
component tray.
        public void DoDefaultAction()
        {
            // Shows a message box indicating that the default ↵
action for the designer was invoked.
            MessageBox.Show("The DoDefaultAction method of an ↵
IDesigner implementation was invoked.", "Information");
        }

        // Returns a collection of designer verb menu items to ↵
 show in the
        // shortcut menu for the designer's component.
        public ↵
 System.ComponentModel.Design.DesignerVerbCollection Verbs
        {
            get
            {
                DesignerVerbCollection verbs = new ↵
DesignerVerbCollection();
                DesignerVerb dv1 = new DesignerVerb ↵
 ("Display Component Name", new EventHandler(this.ShowComponentName));
                verbs.Add( dv1 );
                return verbs;
            }
        }

        // Event handler for displaying a message box showing ↵
 the designer's component's name.
        private void ShowComponentName(object sender, EventArgs e)
        {
            if( this.Component != null )
                MessageBox.Show( this.Component.Site.Name, ↵
"Designer Component's Name" );
        }

        // Provides an opportunity to release resources before ↵
 object destruction.
        public void Dispose()
        {
        }
    }
}
```

Requirements

Namespace: System.ComponentModel.Design

Platforms: Windows 98, Windows NT 4.0, Windows Millennium Edition, Windows 2000, Windows XP Home Edition, Windows XP Professional, Windows Server 2003 family

Assembly: System (in System.dll)

IDesigner.Component Property

Gets or sets the base component that this designer is designing.

[Visual Basic]

```
ReadOnly Property Component As IComponent
```

[C#]

```
IComponent Component {get;}
```

[C++]

```
__property IComponent* get_Component();
```

[JScript]

```
function get Component() : IComponent;
```

Property Value

An **IComponent** indicating the base component that this designer is designing.

Requirements

Platforms: Windows 98, Windows NT 4.0, Windows Millennium Edition, Windows 2000, Windows XP Home Edition, Windows XP Professional, Windows Server 2003 family

IDesigner.Verbs Property

Gets or sets the design-time verbs supported by the designer.

```
[Visual Basic]
ReadOnly Property Verbs As DesignerVerbCollection
[C#]
DesignerVerbCollection Verbs {get;}
[C++]
__property DesignerVerbCollection* get_Verbs();
[JScript]
function get Verbs() : DesignerVerbCollection;
```

Property Value

An array of **DesignerVerb** objects supported by the designer, or a null reference (**Nothing** in Visual Basic) if the component has no verbs.

Remarks

Returns the design time verbs supported by the component associated with the designer. The verbs returned by this method are typically displayed by the design-time environment in a right-click menu. When a user selects one of the verbs, the event handler of the corresponding **DesignerVerb** is invoked.

> **Note** A design-time environment typically provides a **Properties...** entry on a component's right-click menu. To avoid duplicate titles for menu entries, no verb with a title of "Properties..." should be included in a **DesignerVerbCollection**.

Requirements

Platforms: Windows 98, Windows NT 4.0, Windows Millennium Edition, Windows 2000, Windows XP Home Edition, Windows XP Professional, Windows Server 2003 family

IDesigner.DoDefaultAction Method

Performs the default action for this designer.

```
[Visual Basic]
Sub DoDefaultAction()
[C#]
void DoDefaultAction();
[C++]
void DoDefaultAction();
[JScript]
function DoDefaultAction();
```

Remarks

This method is called when a user double-clicks the representation of a component in the component tray.

Requirements

Platforms: Windows 98, Windows NT 4.0, Windows Millennium Edition, Windows 2000, Windows XP Home Edition, Windows XP Professional, Windows Server 2003 family

IDesigner.Initialize Method

Initializes the designer with the specified component.

```
[Visual Basic]
Sub Initialize( _
   ByVal component As IComponent _
)
[C#]
void Initialize(
   IComponent component
);
[C++]
void Initialize(
   IComponent* component
);
[JScript]
function Initialize(
   component : IComponent
);
```

Parameters

component
The component to associate with this designer.

Requirements

Platforms: Windows 98, Windows NT 4.0, Windows Millennium Edition, Windows 2000, Windows XP Home Edition, Windows XP Professional, Windows Server 2003 family

IDesignerEventService Interface

Provides event notifications when root designers are added and removed, when a selected compnent changes, and when the current root designer changes.

[Visual Basic]
```
Public Interface IDesignerEventService
```
[C#]
```
public interface IDesignerEventService
```
[C++]
```
public __gc __interface IDesignerEventService
```
[JScript]
```
public interface IDesignerEventService
```

Remarks

IDesignerEventService provides notification when a new root designer is created, changed, or disposed. A root designer provides design time support for the base component of a document in designer view. The **SelectionChanged** event provides notification when the current component selection has changed.

Example

See related example in the **System.ComponentModel.IDesign.IDesigner** class topic.

Requirements

Namespace: System.ComponentModel.Design

Platforms: Windows 98, Windows NT 4.0, Windows Millennium Edition, Windows 2000, Windows XP Home Edition, Windows XP Professional, Windows Server 2003 family

Assembly: System (in System.dll)

IDesignerEventService.ActiveDesigner Property

Gets the root designer for the currently active document.

[Visual Basic]
```
ReadOnly Property ActiveDesigner As IDesignerHost
```
[C#]
```
IDesignerHost ActiveDesigner {get;}
```
[C++]
```
__property IDesignerHost* get_ActiveDesigner();
```
[JScript]
```
function get ActiveDesigner() : IDesignerHost;
```

Property Value

The currently active document, or a null reference (**Nothing** in Visual Basic) if there is no active document.

Requirements

Platforms: Windows 98, Windows NT 4.0, Windows Millennium Edition, Windows 2000, Windows XP Home Edition, Windows XP Professional, Windows Server 2003 family

IDesignerEventService.Designers Property

Gets a collection of root designers for design documents that are currently active in the development environment.

[Visual Basic]
```
ReadOnly Property Designers As DesignerCollection
```
[C#]
```
DesignerCollection Designers {get;}
```
[C++]
```
__property DesignerCollection* get_Designers();
```
[JScript]
```
function get Designers() : DesignerCollection;
```

Property Value

A **DesignerCollection** containing the root designers that have been created and not yet disposed.

Requirements

Platforms: Windows 98, Windows NT 4.0, Windows Millennium Edition, Windows 2000, Windows XP Home Edition, Windows XP Professional, Windows Server 2003 family

IDesignerEventService.ActiveDesignerChanged Event

Occurs when the current root designer changes.

[Visual Basic]
```
Event ActiveDesignerChanged As ActiveDesignerEventHandler
```
[C#]
```
event ActiveDesignerEventHandler ActiveDesignerChanged;
```
[C++]
```
__event ActiveDesignerEventHandler* ActiveDesignerChanged;
```

[JScript] In JScript, you can handle the events defined by a class, but you cannot define your own.

Event Data

The event handler receives an argument of type **ActiveDesignerEventArgs** containing data related to this event. The following **ActiveDesignerEventArgs** properties provide information specific to this event.

Property	Description
NewDesigner	Gets the document that is gaining activation.
OldDesigner	Gets the document that is losing activation.

Remarks

This event can result from the user opening or setting focus to a new document, or by closing a document.

Requirements

Platforms: Windows 98, Windows NT 4.0, Windows Millennium Edition, Windows 2000, Windows XP Home Edition, Windows XP Professional, Windows Server 2003 family

IDesignerEventService.DesignerCreated Event

Occurs when a root designer is created.

[Visual Basic]
```
Event DesignerCreated As DesignerEventHandler
```
[C#]
```
event DesignerEventHandler DesignerCreated;
```
[C++]
```
__event DesignerEventHandler* DesignerCreated;
```

[JScript] In JScript, you can handle the events defined by a class, but you cannot define your own.

Event Data

The event handler receives an argument of type **DesignerEventArgs** containing data related to this event. The following **DesignerEventArgs** property provides information specific to this event.

Property	Description
Designer	Gets the host of the document.

Remarks

This event is raised when a new document has been loaded and is ready for user input.

Requirements

Platforms: Windows 98, Windows NT 4.0, Windows Millennium Edition, Windows 2000, Windows XP Home Edition, Windows XP Professional, Windows Server 2003 family

IDesignerEventService.DesignerDisposed Event

Occurs when a root designer for a document is disposed.

[Visual Basic]
```
Event DesignerDisposed As DesignerEventHandler
```
[C#]
```
event DesignerEventHandler DesignerDisposed;
```
[C++]
```
__event DesignerEventHandler* DesignerDisposed;
```

[JScript] In JScript, you can handle the events defined by a class, but you cannot define your own.

Event Data

The event handler receives an argument of type **DesignerEventArgs** containing data related to this event. The following **DesignerEventArgs** property provides information specific to this event.

Property	Description
Designer	Gets the host of the document.

Remarks

This event is raised when a document is about to be disposed, but before the document actually starts to dispose itself.

Requirements

Platforms: Windows 98, Windows NT 4.0, Windows Millennium Edition, Windows 2000, Windows XP Home Edition, Windows XP Professional, Windows Server 2003 family

IDesignerEventService.SelectionChanged Event

Occurs when the current design-view selection changes.

[Visual Basic]
```
Event SelectionChanged As EventHandler
```
[C#]
```
event EventHandler SelectionChanged;
```
[C++]
```
__event EventHandler* SelectionChanged;
```

[JScript] In JScript, you can handle the events defined by a class, but you cannot define your own.

Event Data

The event handler receives an argument of type **EventArgs**.

Remarks

This selection changed event can result from the user changing the selection in the currently active document, or from the user switching to a new document.

Requirements

Platforms: Windows 98, Windows NT 4.0, Windows Millennium Edition, Windows 2000, Windows XP Home Edition, Windows XP Professional, Windows Server 2003 family

IDesignerFilter Interface

Provides an interface that enables a designer to access and filter the dictionaries of a **TypeDescriptor** that stores the property, attribute, and event descriptors that a component designer can expose to the design-time environment.

```
[Visual Basic]
Public Interface IDesignerFilter
[C#]
public interface IDesignerFilter
[C++]
public __gc __interface IDesignerFilter
[JScript]
public interface IDesignerFilter
```

Classes that Implement IDesignerFilter

Class	Description
ComponentDesigner	Base designer class for extending the design mode behavior of a component.

Remarks

IDesignerFilter enables a designer to filter the set of property, attribute, and event descriptors that its associated component exposes through a **TypeDescriptor**. The methods of this interface whose names begin with **Pre** are called immediately before the methods whose names begin with **Post**.

If you want to add attribute, event, or property descriptors, use a **PreFilterAttributes**, **PreFilterEvents**, or **PreFilterProperties** method.

If you want to change or remove attribute, event, or property descriptors, use a **PostFilterAttributes**, **PostFilterEvents**, or **PostFilterProperties** method.

Example

See related example in the **System.ComponentModel.IDesign.IDesigner** class topic.

Requirements

Namespace: System.ComponentModel.Design

Platforms: Windows 98, Windows NT 4.0, Windows Millennium Edition, Windows 2000, Windows XP Home Edition, Windows XP Professional, Windows Server 2003 family

Assembly: System (in System.dll)

IDesignerFilter.PostFilterAttributes Method

When overridden in a derived class, allows a designer to change or remove items from the set of attributes that it exposes through a **TypeDescriptor**.

```
[Visual Basic]
Sub PostFilterAttributes( _
   ByVal attributes As IDictionary _
)
[C#]
void PostFilterAttributes(
   IDictionary attributes
);
[C++]
void PostFilterAttributes(
   IDictionary* attributes
);
[JScript]
function PostFilterAttributes(
   attributes : IDictionary
);
```

Parameters

attributes

The **Attribute** objects for the class of the component. The keys in the dictionary of attributes are the **TypeID** values of the attributes.

Remarks

This method provides a way to change or remove items within the dictionary of attributes that the associated component of the designer implementing this interface exposes through a **TypeDescriptor**.

The keys in the dictionary of attributes are the type IDs of the attributes. The objects are of type **Attribute**. This method is called immediately after **PreFilterAttributes**.

The type ID of an attribute can be any object. By default, **Attribute** returns its **Type** as the value of its **TypeID** property. You can check the **TypeID** of an attribute in the dictionary for equivalence with a known **TypeID** for an attribute to identify it, or use **System.Reflection** to identify the attribute object itself.

When an attribute that has the same **TypeID** as an existing or inherited attribute is added to a component, the new attribute replaces the old attribute. For many attributes, a new attribute of the same type will replace any previous attribute of the type. However, some types of attributes return a **TypeID** that distinguishes the attribute selectively. For example, in order to provide different types of simultaneously active designers for a type, such as an **IRootDesigner** and an **IDesigner**, the **DesignerAttribute** class returns a **TypeID** that uniquely identifies both the attribute and the base designer type. The **DesignerAttribute** constructor allows you to specify the base designer type of the designer in addition to its specific type, and **DesignerAttribute** returns a **TypeID** that reflects this. Therefore when you add a new **DesignerAttribute** with a base designer type of the same type as the base designer type of an existing **DesignerAttribute**, the old attribute is replaced with the new attribute.

Notes to Implementers: You can directly filter the dictionary that is accessible through the *attributes* parameter, or you can leave it unchanged. If you are overriding this method, call the base implementation after you perform your own filtering.

Requirements

Platforms: Windows 98, Windows NT 4.0, Windows Millennium Edition, Windows 2000, Windows XP Home Edition, Windows XP Professional, Windows Server 2003 family

IDesignerFilter.PostFilterEvents Method

When overridden in a derived class, allows a designer to change or remove items from the set of events that it exposes through a **TypeDescriptor**.

```
[Visual Basic]
Sub PostFilterEvents( _
   ByVal events As IDictionary _
)
```

[C#]
```
void PostFilterEvents(
   IDictionary events
);
```
[C++]
```
void PostFilterEvents(
   IDictionary* events
);
```
[JScript]
```
function PostFilterEvents(
   events : IDictionary
);
```

Parameters

events

The **EventDescriptor** objects that represent the events of the class of the component. The keys in the dictionary of events are event names.

Remarks

This method provides a way to change or remove items within the dictionary of events that are exposed through a **TypeDescriptor**.

The keys in the dictionary of events are the names of the events. The objects are of type **EventDescriptor**. This method is called immediately after **PreFilterEvents**.

Notes to Implementers: You can directly filter the dictionary that is accessible through the *events* parameter, or you can leave it unchanged. If you are overriding this method, call the base implementation after you perform your own filtering.

Requirements

Platforms: Windows 98, Windows NT 4.0, Windows Millennium Edition, Windows 2000, Windows XP Home Edition, Windows XP Professional, Windows Server 2003 family

IDesignerFilter.PostFilterProperties Method

When overridden in a derived class, allows a designer to change or remove items from the set of properties that it exposes through a **TypeDescriptor**.

[Visual Basic]
```
Sub PostFilterProperties( _
   ByVal properties As IDictionary _
)
```
[C#]
```
void PostFilterProperties(
   IDictionary properties
);
```
[C++]
```
void PostFilterProperties(
   IDictionary* properties
);
```
[JScript]
```
function PostFilterProperties(
   properties : IDictionary
);
```

Parameters

properties

The **PropertyDescriptor** objects that represent the properties of the class of the component. The keys in the dictionary of properties are property names.

Remarks

This method provides a way to change or remove items within the dictionary of properties that are exposed through a **TypeDescriptor**.

The keys in the dictionary of properties are the names of the properties. The objects are of type **PropertyDescriptor**. This method is called immediately after **PreFilterProperties**.

Notes to Implementers: You can directly filter the dictionary that is accessible through the *properties* parameter, or you can leave it unchanged. If you are overriding this method, call the base implementation after you perform your own filtering.

Requirements

Platforms: Windows 98, Windows NT 4.0, Windows Millennium Edition, Windows 2000, Windows XP Home Edition, Windows XP Professional, Windows Server 2003 family

IDesignerFilter.PreFilterAttributes Method

When overridden in a derived class, allows a designer to add items to the set of attributes that it exposes through a **TypeDescriptor**.

[Visual Basic]
```
Sub PreFilterAttributes( _
   ByVal attributes As IDictionary _
)
```
[C#]
```
void PreFilterAttributes(
   IDictionary attributes
);
```
[C++]
```
void PreFilterAttributes(
   IDictionary* attributes
);
```
[JScript]
```
function PreFilterAttributes(
   attributes : IDictionary
);
```

Parameters

attributes

The **Attribute** objects for the class of the component. The keys in the dictionary of attributes are the **TypeID** values of the attributes.

Remarks

This method provides a way to add items to the dictionary of attributes that the associated component of the designer implementing this interface exposes through a **TypeDescriptor**.

The keys in the dictionary of attributes are the type IDs of the attributes. The objects are of type **Attribute**. This method is called immediately after **PostFilterAttributes**.

The type ID of an attribute can be any object. By default, **Attribute** returns its **Type** as the value of its **TypeID** property. You can check the **TypeID** of an attribute in the dictionary for equivalence with a known **TypeID** for an attribute to identify it, or use **System.Reflection** to identify the attribute object itself.

When an attribute that has the same **TypeID** as an existing or inherited attribute is added to a component, the new attribute replaces the old attribute. For many attributes, a new attribute of the same type will replace any previous attribute of the type. However, some types of attributes return a **TypeID** that distinguishes the attribute selectively. For example, in order to provide different types of simultaneously active designers for a type, such as an **IRootDesigner** and an **IDesigner**, the **DesignerAttribute** class returns a **TypeID** that uniquely identifies both the attribute and the base designer type. The **DesignerAttribute** constructor allows you to specify the base designer type of the designer in addition to its specific type, and **DesignerAttribute** returns a **TypeID** that reflects this. Therefore when you add a new **DesignerAttribute** with a base designer type of the same type as the base designer type of an existing **DesignerAttribute**, the old attribute is replaced with the new attribute.

Notes to Implementers: You can directly filter the dictionary that is accessible through the *attributes* parameter, or you can leave it unchanged. If you are overriding this method, call the base implementation after you perform your own filtering.

Requirements

Platforms: Windows 98, Windows NT 4.0,
Windows Millennium Edition, Windows 2000,
Windows XP Home Edition, Windows XP Professional,
Windows Server 2003 family

IDesignerFilter.PreFilterEvents Method

When overridden in a derived class, allows a designer to add items to the set of events that it exposes through a **TypeDescriptor**.

```
[Visual Basic]
Sub PreFilterEvents( _
   ByVal events As IDictionary _
)
[C#]
void PreFilterEvents(
   IDictionary events
);
[C++]
void PreFilterEvents(
   IDictionary* events
);
[JScript]
function PreFilterEvents(
   events : IDictionary
);
```

Parameters

events

The **EventDescriptor** objects that represent the events of the class of the component. The keys in the dictionary of events are event names.

Remarks

This method provides a way to add items to the dictionary of events that a designer exposes through a **TypeDescriptor**.

The keys in the dictionary of events are the names of the events. The objects are of type **EventDescriptor**. This method is called immediately before **PostFilterEvents**.

Notes to Implementers: You can directly modify the dictionary that is accessible through the *events* parameter, or you can leave it unchanged. If you are overriding this method, call the base implementation before you perform your own filtering.

Requirements

Platforms: Windows 98, Windows NT 4.0,
Windows Millennium Edition, Windows 2000,
Windows XP Home Edition, Windows XP Professional,
Windows Server 2003 family

IDesignerFilter.PreFilterProperties Method

When overridden in a derived class, allows a designer to add items to the set of properties that it exposes through a **TypeDescriptor**.

```
[Visual Basic]
Sub PreFilterProperties( _
   ByVal properties As IDictionary _
)
[C#]
void PreFilterProperties(
   IDictionary properties
);
[C++]
void PreFilterProperties(
   IDictionary* properties
);
[JScript]
function PreFilterProperties(
   properties : IDictionary
);
```

Parameters

properties

The **PropertyDescriptor** objects that represent the properties of the class of the component. The keys in the dictionary of properties are property names.

Remarks

This method provides a way to add items to the dictionary of properties that a designer exposes through a **TypeDescriptor**.

The keys in the dictionary of properties are the names of the properties. The objects are of type **PropertyDescriptor**. This method is called immediately before **PostFilterProperties**.

Notes to Implementers: You can directly modify the dictionary that is accessible through the *properties* parameter, or you can leave it unchanged. If you are overriding this method, call the base implementation before you perform your own filtering.

Requirements

Platforms: Windows 98, Windows NT 4.0,
Windows Millennium Edition, Windows 2000,
Windows XP Home Edition, Windows XP Professional,
Windows Server 2003 family

IDesignerHost Interface

Provides an interface for managing designer transactions and components.

[Visual Basic]
```
<ComVisible(True)>
Public Interface IDesignerHost
   Inherits IServiceContainer, IServiceProvider
```
[C#]
```
[ComVisible(true)]
public interface IDesignerHost : IServiceContainer,
   IServiceProvider
```
[C++]
```
[ComVisible(true)]
public __gc __interface IDesignerHost : public IServiceContainer,
   IServiceProvider
```
[JScript]
```
public
   ComVisible(true)
interface IDesignerHost implements IServiceContainer,
   IServiceProvider
```

Remarks

IDesignerHost is an interface that works with the .NET Framework forms designer architecture to provide support for designer transaction and component management.

The .NET Framework does not provide an implementation of this interface. The interface is implemented by development tools that support designers.

Notes to Callers: To obtain an implementation of **IDesignerHost** from a development environment, call **GetService** while your component is active in design mode, passing the type of **IDesigner-Host** to request an **IDesignerHost** service interface.

IDesignerHost provides the following members related to designer state:

- The **Loading** property indicates whether a designer or document is being loaded.
- The **Activated** event occurs when a designer is activated before display.
- The **Deactivated** event occurs when a designer is deactivated.
- The **LoadComplete** event occurs after a document is loaded.
- The **Activate** method activates the designer.

IDesignerHost provides the following members related to managing components:

- The **Container** property indicates the container for the designer host.
- The **RootComponent** property indicates the base class for the root component.
- The **RootComponentClassName** property indicates the name of the class of the root component.
- The **CreateComponent** method creates the specified type of component.
- The **DestroyComponent** method destroys the specified component.
- The **GetDesigner** method gets the designer associated with a specified component.
- The **GetType** method gets an instance of the type with the specified name.

IDesignerHost provides the following members related to managing transactions:

- The **InTransaction** property indicates whether the designer is in a transaction.
- The **TransactionDescription** property indicates the current transaction description.
- The **TransactionClosed** event occurs when a transaction has been completed.
- The **TransactionClosing** event occurs when a transaction is about to be completed.
- The **TransactionOpened** event occurs when a transaction has begun.
- The **TransactionOpening** event occurs when a transaction is about to begin.
- The **CreateTransaction** method creates and returns a new transaction.

Example

See related example in the **System.ComponentModel.IDesign.IDesigner** class topic.

Requirements

Namespace: System.ComponentModel.Design

Platforms: Windows 98, Windows NT 4.0, Windows Millennium Edition, Windows 2000, Windows XP Home Edition, Windows XP Professional, Windows Server 2003 family

Assembly: System (in System.dll)

IDesignerHost.Container Property

Gets the container for this designer host.

[Visual Basic]
```
ReadOnly Property Container As IContainer
```
[C#]
```
IContainer Container {get;}
```
[C++]
```
__property IContainer* get_Container();
```
[JScript]
```
function get Container() : IContainer;
```

Property Value

The **IContainer** for this host.

Remarks

This **IContainer** contains the components of the current design mode document. You can list or access any of the components of the current design mode document through the **Components** member of this **IContainer**.

Requirements

Platforms: Windows 98, Windows NT 4.0, Windows Millennium Edition, Windows 2000, Windows XP Home Edition, Windows XP Professional, Windows Server 2003 family

IDesignerHost.InTransaction Property

Gets a value indicating whether the designer host is currently in a transaction.

[Visual Basic]
```
ReadOnly Property InTransaction As Boolean
```
[C#]
```
bool InTransaction {get;}
```
[C++]
```
__property bool get_InTransaction();
```
[JScript]
```
function get InTransaction() : Boolean;
```

Property Value

true if a transaction is in progress; otherwise, **false**.

Requirements

Platforms: Windows 98, Windows NT 4.0, Windows Millennium Edition, Windows 2000, Windows XP Home Edition, Windows XP Professional, Windows Server 2003 family

IDesignerHost.Loading Property

Gets a value indicating whether the designer host is currently loading the document.

[Visual Basic]
```
ReadOnly Property Loading As Boolean
```
[C#]
```
bool Loading {get;}
```
[C++]
```
__property bool get_Loading();
```
[JScript]
```
function get Loading() : Boolean;
```

Property Value

true if the designer host is currently loading the document; otherwise, **false**.

Requirements

Platforms: Windows 98, Windows NT 4.0, Windows Millennium Edition, Windows 2000, Windows XP Home Edition, Windows XP Professional, Windows Server 2003 family

IDesignerHost.RootComponent Property

Gets the instance of the base class used as the root component for the current design.

[Visual Basic]
```
ReadOnly Property RootComponent As IComponent
```
[C#]
```
IComponent RootComponent {get;}
```
[C++]
```
__property IComponent* get_RootComponent();
```
[JScript]
```
function get RootComponent() : IComponent;
```

Property Value

The instance of the root component class.

Remarks

This base class is typically a **Form** or **UserControl** instance; it defines the class for which the user's derived class extends.

Requirements

Platforms: Windows 98, Windows NT 4.0, Windows Millennium Edition, Windows 2000, Windows XP Home Edition, Windows XP Professional, Windows Server 2003 family

IDesignerHost.RootComponentClassName Property

Gets the fully qualified name of the class being designed.

[Visual Basic]
```
ReadOnly Property RootComponentClassName As String
```
[C#]
```
string RootComponentClassName {get;}
```
[C++]
```
__property String* get_RootComponentClassName();
```
[JScript]
```
function get RootComponentClassName() : String;
```

Property Value

The fully qualified name of the base component class.

Requirements

Platforms: Windows 98, Windows NT 4.0, Windows Millennium Edition, Windows 2000, Windows XP Home Edition, Windows XP Professional, Windows Server 2003 family

IDesignerHost.TransactionDescription Property

Gets the description of the current transaction.

[Visual Basic]
```
ReadOnly Property TransactionDescription As String
```
[C#]
```
string TransactionDescription {get;}
```
[C++]
```
__property String* get_TransactionDescription();
```
[JScript]
```
function get TransactionDescription() : String;
```

Property Value

A description of the current transaction.

Remarks

The description is the last description specified with **CreateTransaction**.

Requirements

Platforms: Windows 98, Windows NT 4.0, Windows Millennium Edition, Windows 2000, Windows XP Home Edition, Windows XP Professional, Windows Server 2003 family

IDesignerHost.Activate Method

Activates the designer that this host is hosting.

```
[Visual Basic]
Sub Activate()
[C#]
void Activate();
[C++]
void Activate();
[JScript]
function Activate();
```

Remarks

Designers should be activated before they display their user interface.

Requirements

Platforms: Windows 98, Windows NT 4.0, Windows Millennium Edition, Windows 2000, Windows XP Home Edition, Windows XP Professional, Windows Server 2003 family

IDesignerHost.CreateComponent Method

Creates a component of the specified type and adds it to the design document.

Overload List

Creates a component of the specified type and adds it to the design document.

[Visual Basic] **Overloads Function CreateComponent(Type) As IComponent**

[C#] **IComponent CreateComponent(Type);**

[C++] **IComponent* CreateComponent(Type*);**

[JScript] **function CreateComponent(Type) : IComponent;**

Creates a component of the specified type and name, and adds it to the design document.

[Visual Basic] **Overloads Function CreateComponent(Type, String) As IComponent**

[C#] **IComponent CreateComponent(Type, string);**

[C++] **IComponent* CreateComponent(Type*, String*);**

[JScript] **function CreateComponent(Type, String) : IComponent;**

IDesignerHost.CreateComponent Method (Type)

Creates a component of the specified type and adds it to the design document.

```
[Visual Basic]
Function CreateComponent( _
   ByVal componentClass As Type _
) As IComponent
[C#]
IComponent CreateComponent(
   Type componentClass
);
[C++]
IComponent* CreateComponent(
   Type* componentClass
);
[JScript]
function CreateComponent(
   componentClass : Type
) : IComponent;
```

Parameters

componentClass

The type of the component to create.

Return Value

The newly created component.

Remarks

If the type cannot be resolved into an object that implements **IComponent**, an exception is thrown.

This method does not specify a name for the component. The method creates the component and adds it to the designer container.

Requirements

Platforms: Windows 98, Windows NT 4.0, Windows Millennium Edition, Windows 2000, Windows XP Home Edition, Windows XP Professional, Windows Server 2003 family

IDesignerHost.CreateComponent Method (Type, String)

Creates a component of the specified type and name, and adds it to the design document.

```
[Visual Basic]
Function CreateComponent( _
   ByVal componentClass As Type, _
   ByVal name As String _
) As IComponent
[C#]
IComponent CreateComponent(
   Type componentClass,
   string name
);
[C++]
IComponent* CreateComponent(
   Type* componentClass,
   String* name
);
[JScript]
function CreateComponent(
   componentClass : Type,
   name : String
) : IComponent;
```

Parameters

componentClass

The type of the component to create.

name

The name for the component.

Return Value

The newly created component.

Remarks

If the type cannot be resolved into an object that implements **IComponent**, an exception is thrown.

This method creates the component and adds it to the designer container.

Requirements

Platforms: Windows 98, Windows NT 4.0, Windows Millennium Edition, Windows 2000, Windows XP Home Edition, Windows XP Professional, Windows Server 2003 family

IDesignerHost.CreateTransaction Method

Creates a **DesignerTransaction** that can encapsulate event sequences to improve performance and enable undo and redo support functionality.

Overload List

Creates a **DesignerTransaction** that can encapsulate event sequences to improve performance and enable undo and redo support functionality.

[Visual Basic] **Overloads Function CreateTransaction() As DesignerTransaction**

[C#] **DesignerTransaction CreateTransaction();**

[C++] **DesignerTransaction* CreateTransaction();**

[JScript] **function CreateTransaction() : DesignerTransaction;**

Creates a **DesignerTransaction** that can encapsulate event sequences to improve performance and enable undo and redo support functionality, using the specified transaction description.

[Visual Basic] **Overloads Function CreateTransaction(String) As DesignerTransaction**

[C#] **DesignerTransaction CreateTransaction(string);**

[C++] **DesignerTransaction* CreateTransaction(String*);**

[JScript] **function CreateTransaction(String) : DesignerTransaction;**

IDesignerHost.CreateTransaction Method ()

Creates a **DesignerTransaction** that can encapsulate event sequences to improve performance and enable undo and redo support functionality.

```
[Visual Basic]
Function CreateTransaction() As DesignerTransaction
[C#]
DesignerTransaction CreateTransaction();
[C++]
DesignerTransaction* CreateTransaction();
[JScript]
function CreateTransaction() : DesignerTransaction;
```

Return Value

A new instance of **DesignerTransaction**. When you complete the steps in your transaction, you should call **Commit** on this object.

Remarks

This method creates a **DesignerTransaction** that can be used to encapsulate a series of operations. Designer transactions can improve performance, reduce flicker caused by multiple updates during a process of operations, and enable most operations to be undone.

Lengthy operations that involve multiple components can raise many events. These events can cause side effects, such as flicker or degraded performance. When operating on multiple components at one time, or setting multiple properties on a single component, you can improve performance by performing these changes within a transaction. Some operations handle the **TransactionOpening** and **TransactionClosed** events and perform work only when a transaction is not in progress. For more information on using transactions, see the documentation for **DesignerTransaction**.

Requirements

Platforms: Windows 98, Windows NT 4.0, Windows Millennium Edition, Windows 2000, Windows XP Home Edition, Windows XP Professional, Windows Server 2003 family

IDesignerHost.CreateTransaction Method (String)

Creates a **DesignerTransaction** that can encapsulate event sequences to improve performance and enable undo and redo support functionality, using the specified transaction description.

```
[Visual Basic]
Function CreateTransaction( _
   ByVal description As String _
) As DesignerTransaction
[C#]
DesignerTransaction CreateTransaction(
   string description
);
[C++]
DesignerTransaction* CreateTransaction(
   String* description
);
[JScript]
function CreateTransaction(
   description : String
) : DesignerTransaction;
```

Parameters

description

A title or description for the newly created transaction.

Return Value

A new **DesignerTransaction**. When you have completed the steps in your transaction, you should call **Commit** on this object.

Remarks

This method creates a **DesignerTransaction** that can be used to encapsulate a series of operations. Designer transactions can improve performance, reduce flicker caused by multiple updates during a process of operations, and enable most operations to be undone.

Lengthy operations that involve multiple components can raise many events. These events can cause side effects, such as flicker or degraded performance. When operating on multiple components at one time, or setting multiple properties on a single component, you can improve performance by performing these changes within a transaction. Some operations handle the **TransactionOpening** and **TransactionClosed** events and perform work only when a transaction is not in progress. For more information on using transactions, see the documentation for **DesignerTransaction**.

Requirements

Platforms: Windows 98, Windows NT 4.0, Windows Millennium Edition, Windows 2000, Windows XP Home Edition, Windows XP Professional, Windows Server 2003 family

IDesignerHost.DestroyComponent Method

Destroys the specified component and removes it from the designer container.

```
[Visual Basic]
Sub DestroyComponent( _
   ByVal component As IComponent _
)
[C#]
void DestroyComponent(
   IComponent component
);
[C++]
void DestroyComponent(
   IComponent* component
);
[JScript]
function DestroyComponent(
   component : IComponent
);
```

Parameters

component
The component to destroy.

Requirements

Platforms: Windows 98, Windows NT 4.0,
Windows Millennium Edition, Windows 2000,
Windows XP Home Edition, Windows XP Professional,
Windows Server 2003 family

IDesignerHost.GetDesigner Method

Gets the designer instance that contains the specified component.

```
[Visual Basic]
Function GetDesigner( _
   ByVal component As IComponent _
) As IDesigner
[C#]
IDesigner GetDesigner(
   IComponent component
);
[C++]
IDesigner* GetDesigner(
   IComponent* component
);
[JScript]
function GetDesigner(
   component : IComponent
) : IDesigner;
```

Parameters

component
The **IComponent** to retrieve the designer for.

Return Value

An **IDesigner**, or a null reference (**Nothing** in Visual Basic) if there is no designer for the specified component.

Requirements

Platforms: Windows 98, Windows NT 4.0,
Windows Millennium Edition, Windows 2000,
Windows XP Home Edition, Windows XP Professional,
Windows Server 2003 family

IDesignerHost.GetType Method

Gets an instance of the specified, fully qualified type name.

```
[Visual Basic]
Function GetType( _
   ByVal typeName As String _
) As Type
[C#]
Type GetType(
   string typeName
);
[C++]
Type* GetType(
   String* typeName
);
[JScript]
function GetType(
   typeName : String
) : Type;
```

Parameters

typeName
The name of the type to load.

Return Value

The type object for the specified type name, or a null reference (**Nothing** in Visual Basic) if the type cannot be found.

Requirements

Platforms: Windows 98, Windows NT 4.0,
Windows Millennium Edition, Windows 2000,
Windows XP Home Edition, Windows XP Professional,
Windows Server 2003 family

IDesignerHost.Activated Event

Occurs when this designer is activated.

```
[Visual Basic]
Event Activated As EventHandler
[C#]
event EventHandler Activated;
[C++]
__event EventHandler* Activated;
```

[JScript] In JScript, you can handle the events defined by a class, but you cannot define your own.

Event Data

The event handler receives an argument of type **EventArgs**.

Remarks

A designer is activated before it is displayed.

Requirements

Platforms: Windows 98, Windows NT 4.0,
Windows Millennium Edition, Windows 2000,
Windows XP Home Edition, Windows XP Professional,
Windows Server 2003 family

IDesignerHost.Deactivated Event

Occurs when this designer is deactivated.

[Visual Basic]
```
Event Deactivated As EventHandler
```
[C#]
```
event EventHandler Deactivated;
```
[C++]
```
__event EventHandler* Deactivated;
```

[JScript] In JScript, you can handle the events defined by a class, but you cannot define your own.

Event Data

The event handler receives an argument of type **EventArgs**.

Remarks

A designer is deactivated just before it is no longer displayed.

Requirements

Platforms: Windows 98, Windows NT 4.0, Windows Millennium Edition, Windows 2000, Windows XP Home Edition, Windows XP Professional, Windows Server 2003 family

IDesignerHost.LoadComplete Event

Occurs when this designer completes loading its document.

[Visual Basic]
```
Event LoadComplete As EventHandler
```
[C#]
```
event EventHandler LoadComplete;
```
[C++]
```
__event EventHandler* LoadComplete;
```

[JScript] In JScript, you can handle the events defined by a class, but you cannot define your own.

Event Data

The event handler receives an argument of type **EventArgs**.

Remarks

This event occurs after a designer completes loading its document.

Requirements

Platforms: Windows 98, Windows NT 4.0, Windows Millennium Edition, Windows 2000, Windows XP Home Edition, Windows XP Professional, Windows Server 2003 family

IDesignerHost.TransactionClosed Event

Adds an event handler for the **TransactionClosed** event.

[Visual Basic]
```
Event TransactionClosed As DesignerTransactionCloseEventHandler
```
[C#]
```
event DesignerTransactionCloseEventHandler TransactionClosed;
```
[C++]
```
__event DesignerTransactionCloseEventHandler* TransactionClosed;
```

[JScript] In JScript, you can handle the events defined by a class, but you cannot define your own.

Event Data

The event handler receives an argument of type **DesignerTransactionCloseEventArgs** containing data related to this event. The following **DesignerTransactionCloseEventArgs** property provides information specific to this event.

Property	Description
TransactionCommitted	Indicates whether the designer called **Commit** on the transaction.

Remarks

This event occurs after a transaction is closed.

A transaction can sometimes change multiple values. The transaction methods provide a way to prevent performance and flicker problems by avoiding repetitive processing. These methods defer processing until after the transaction has closed.

Requirements

Platforms: Windows 98, Windows NT 4.0, Windows Millennium Edition, Windows 2000, Windows XP Home Edition, Windows XP Professional, Windows Server 2003 family

IDesignerHost.TransactionClosing Event

Adds an event handler for the **TransactionClosing** event.

[Visual Basic]
```
Event TransactionClosing As DesignerTransactionCloseEventHandler
```
[C#]
```
event DesignerTransactionCloseEventHandler TransactionClosing;
```
[C++]
```
__event DesignerTransactionCloseEventHandler* TransactionClosing;
```

[JScript] In JScript, you can handle the events defined by a class, but you cannot define your own.

Event Data

The event handler receives an argument of type **DesignerTransactionCloseEventArgs** containing data related to this event. The following **DesignerTransactionCloseEventArgs** property provides information specific to this event.

Property	Description
TransactionCommitted	Indicates whether the designer called **Commit** on the transaction.

Remarks

This event occurs just before a transaction is completed.

A transaction can sometimes change multiple values. The transaction methods provide a way to prevent performance and flicker problems by avoiding repetitive processing. These methods defer processing until after the transaction has closed.

Requirements

Platforms: Windows 98, Windows NT 4.0, Windows Millennium Edition, Windows 2000, Windows XP Home Edition, Windows XP Professional, Windows Server 2003 family

IDesignerHost.TransactionOpened Event

Adds an event handler for the **TransactionOpened** event.

[Visual Basic]
```
Event TransactionOpened As EventHandler
```
[C#]
```
event EventHandler TransactionOpened;
```
[C++]
```
__event EventHandler* TransactionOpened;
```

[JScript] In JScript, you can handle the events defined by a class, but you cannot define your own.

Event Data

The event handler receives an argument of type **EventArgs**.

Remarks

This event occurs when a transaction has begun.

A transaction can sometimes change multiple values. The transaction methods provide a way to prevent performance and flicker problems by avoiding repetitive processing. These methods defer processing until after the transaction has closed.

Requirements

Platforms: Windows 98, Windows NT 4.0, Windows Millennium Edition, Windows 2000, Windows XP Home Edition, Windows XP Professional, Windows Server 2003 family

IDesignerHost.TransactionOpening Event

Adds an event handler for the **TransactionOpening** event.

[Visual Basic]
```
Event TransactionOpening As EventHandler
```
[C#]
```
event EventHandler TransactionOpening;
```
[C++]
```
__event EventHandler* TransactionOpening;
```

[JScript] In JScript, you can handle the events defined by a class, but you cannot define your own.

Event Data

The event handler receives an argument of type **EventArgs**.

Remarks

This event occurs when a transaction is about to begin.

This method allows designer host clients to perform operations before other handlers are notified that a transaction has begun. The specified handler is called only when the first call to **CreateTransaction** is made. Subsequent calls do not generate this event until all transaction objects have been disposed.

Requirements

Platforms: Windows 98, Windows NT 4.0, Windows Millennium Edition, Windows 2000, Windows XP Home Edition, Windows XP Professional, Windows Server 2003 family

IDesignerOptionService Interface

Provides access to the designer options located on the **Tools** menu under the **Options** menu item in the Visual Studio .NET environment.

[Visual Basic]
```
Public Interface IDesignerOptionService
```
[C#]
```
public interface IDesignerOptionService
```
[C++]
```
public __gc __interface IDesignerOptionService
```
[JScript]
```
public interface IDesignerOptionService
```

Remarks

IDesignerOptionService provides an interface that can be used to retrieve and update the values of the Windows Form Designer options. The **GetOptionValue** method retrieves the value of the option indicated by the page and value names. The **SetOptionValue** method sets a specified value for an option on the indicated page name matching the indicated value name.

> **Note** The page and value names are always expected in English. Therefore, the following table is provided to help you access the options you want.

The page name is a concatenation of the **Windows Forms Designer** options category name and the page name, which is typically **General**. Therefore, you can usually access the designer options page with the English page name "Windows Forms Designer\General".

The following table indicates the English value names, their data format, and a description of each:

Value Name	Value Format	Description
"GridSize"	Size(x,y)	The size of each grid square.
"GridSize.Width"	integer	The width of each grid square. This nested property is read-only when accessed through the designer option service.
"GridSize.Height"	integer	The height of each grid square. This nested property is read-only when accessed through the designer option service.
"ShowGrid"	Boolean	**true** if the grid should be shown; **false** if the grid should not be shown.
"SnapToGrid"	Boolean	**true** if the positions of the components should be aligned to the grid; **false** if the positions should not necessarily be aligned.

Example

See related example in the **System.ComponentModel.IDesign.IDesigner** class topic.

Requirements

Namespace: System.ComponentModel.Design

Platforms: Windows 98, Windows NT 4.0, Windows Millennium Edition, Windows 2000, Windows XP Home Edition, Windows XP Professional, Windows Server 2003 family

Assembly: System (in System.dll)

IDesignerOptionService.GetOptionValue Method

Gets the value of the specified option.

[Visual Basic]
```
Function GetOptionValue( _
   ByVal pageName As String, _
   ByVal valueName As String _
) As Object
```
[C#]
```
object GetOptionValue(
   string pageName,
   string valueName
);
```
[C++]
```
Object* GetOptionValue(
   String* pageName,
   String* valueName
);
```
[JScript]
```
function GetOptionValue(
   pageName : String,
   valueName : String
) : Object;
```

Parameters

pageName
The name of the page that defines the option.

valueName
The name of the option property.

Return Value

The value of the specified option.

Remarks

For nested pages, the page name should be a backslash-delineated concatenation of the page names up to the main page node. Specifying just the main node name will access the first (the default) page for the node. For example, to access a value on the page **Windows Forms Designer** >> **General**, specify "Windows Forms Designer\General" as the page name.

Requirements

Platforms: Windows 98, Windows NT 4.0, Windows Millennium Edition, Windows 2000, Windows XP Home Edition, Windows XP Professional, Windows Server 2003 family

IDesignerOptionService.SetOptionValue Method

Sets the value of the specified option.

[Visual Basic]
```
Sub SetOptionValue( _
   ByVal pageName As String, _
   ByVal valueName As String, _
   ByVal value As Object _
)
```
[C#]
```
void SetOptionValue(
   string pageName,
   string valueName,
   object value
);
```
[C++]
```
void SetOptionValue(
   String* pageName,
   String* valueName,
   Object* value
);
```
[JScript]
```
function SetOptionValue(
   pageName : String,
   valueName : String,
   value : Object
);
```

Parameters

pageName
: The name of the page that defines the option.

valueName
: The name of the option property.

value
: The new value.

Remarks

For nested pages, the page name should be a backslash-delineated concatenation of the page names up to the main page node. Specifying just the main node name will access the first (the default) page for the node. For example, to access a value on the page **Windows Forms Designer** >> **General**, specify "Windows Forms Designer\General" as the page name.

Requirements

Platforms: Windows 98, Windows NT 4.0,
Windows Millennium Edition, Windows 2000,
Windows XP Home Edition, Windows XP Professional,
Windows Server 2003 family

IDictionaryService Interface

Provides a basic, component site-specific, key-value pair dictionary through a service that a designer can use to store user-defined data.

[Visual Basic]
```
Public Interface IDictionaryService
```
[C#]
```
public interface IDictionaryService
```
[C++]
```
public __gc __interface IDictionaryService
```
[JScript]
```
public interface IDictionaryService
```

Remarks

This service provides a simple interface to set, retrieve, and look up objects with associated keys.

Example

See related example in the **System.ComponentModel.IDesign.IDesigner** class topic.

Requirements

Namespace: System.ComponentModel.Design

Platforms: Windows 98, Windows NT 4.0, Windows Millennium Edition, Windows 2000, Windows XP Home Edition, Windows XP Professional, Windows Server 2003 family

Assembly: System (in System.dll)

IDictionaryService.GetKey Method

Gets the key corresponding to the specified value.

[Visual Basic]
```
Function GetKey( _
   ByVal value As Object _
) As Object
```
[C#]
```
object GetKey(
   object value
);
```
[C++]
```
Object* GetKey(
   Object* value
);
```
[JScript]
```
function GetKey(
   value : Object
) : Object;
```

Parameters

value
The value to look up in the dictionary.

Return Value

The associated key, or a null reference (**Nothing** in Visual Basic) if no key exists.

Requirements

Platforms: Windows 98, Windows NT 4.0, Windows Millennium Edition, Windows 2000, Windows XP Home Edition, Windows XP Professional, Windows Server 2003 family

IDictionaryService.GetValue Method

Gets the value corresponding to the specified key.

[Visual Basic]
```
Function GetValue( _
   ByVal key As Object _
) As Object
```
[C#]
```
object GetValue(
   object key
);
```
[C++]
```
Object* GetValue(
   Object* key
);
```
[JScript]
```
function GetValue(
   key : Object
) : Object;
```

Parameters

key
The key to look up the value for.

Return Value

The associated value, or a null reference (**Nothing** in Visual Basic) if no value exists.

Requirements

Platforms: Windows 98, Windows NT 4.0, Windows Millennium Edition, Windows 2000, Windows XP Home Edition, Windows XP Professional, Windows Server 2003 family

IDictionaryService.SetValue Method

Sets the specified key-value pair.

[Visual Basic]
```
Sub SetValue( _
   ByVal key As Object, _
   ByVal value As Object _
)
```
[C#]
```
void SetValue(
   object key,
   object value
);
```
[C++]
```
void SetValue(
   Object* key,
   Object* value
);
```
[JScript]
```
function SetValue(
   key : Object,
   value : Object
);
```

Parameters

key

An object to use as the key to associate the value with.

value

The value to store.

Requirements

Platforms: Windows 98, Windows NT 4.0, Windows Millennium Edition, Windows 2000, Windows XP Home Edition, Windows XP Professional, Windows Server 2003 family

IEventBindingService Interface

Provides a service for registering event handlers for component events.

[Visual Basic]
```
<ComVisible(True)>
Public Interface IEventBindingService
```
[C#]
```
[ComVisible(true)]
public interface IEventBindingService
```
[C++]
```
[ComVisible(true)]
public __gc __interface IEventBindingService
```
[JScript]
```
public
   ComVisible(true)
interface IEventBindingService
```

Remarks

The event binding service provides a way to link an event handler with a component event from designer code.

To link an event handler with a component event using the **IEventBindingService**, you must first obtain an **EventDescriptor** for the event of the component you intend to link. The **IEventBindingService** provides methods that can convert an **EventDescriptor** to a **PropertyDescriptor** which you can use to configure the event with an event handler method name.

The **TypeDescriptor** object provides a **GetEvents** method that you can use to obtain an **EventDescriptorCollection** containing **EventDescriptor** objects for each event of a component. The **GetventProperty** and **GetEventProperties** methods of the **IEventBindingService** return a **PropertyDescriptor** for each **EventDescriptor** passed to either method. Each **PropertyDescriptor** returned from **GetEventProperty** or **GetEventProperties** has a property type of string. You can set this string to a value that indicates the name of the event handling method to link the event with using the **SetValue** method of the **PropertyDescriptor**.

Example

See related example in the **System.ComponentModel.IDesign.IDesigner** class topic.

Requirements

Namespace: System.ComponentModel.Design

Platforms: Windows 98, Windows NT 4.0, Windows Millennium Edition, Windows 2000, Windows XP Home Edition, Windows XP Professional, Windows Server 2003 family

Assembly: System (in System.dll)

IEventBindingService.CreateUniqueMethodName Method

Creates a unique name for an event-handler method for the specified component and event.

[Visual Basic]
```
Function CreateUniqueMethodName( _
   ByVal component As IComponent, _
   ByVal e As EventDescriptor _
) As String
```
[C#]
```
string CreateUniqueMethodName(
   IComponent component,
   EventDescriptor e
);
```
[C++]
```
String* CreateUniqueMethodName(
   IComponent* component,
   EventDescriptor* e
);
```
[JScript]
```
function CreateUniqueMethodName(
   component : IComponent,
   e : EventDescriptor
) : String;
```

Parameters

component

The component instance the event is connected to.

e

The event to create a name for.

Return Value

The recommended name for the event-handler method for this event.

Remarks

This method returns a name that is unique from any other method name in the user's source code.

Requirements

Platforms: Windows 98, Windows NT 4.0, Windows Millennium Edition, Windows 2000, Windows XP Home Edition, Windows XP Professional, Windows Server 2003 family

IEventBindingService.GetCompatibleMethods Method

Gets a collection of event-handler methods that have a method signature compatible with the specified event.

[Visual Basic]
```
Function GetCompatibleMethods( _
   ByVal e As EventDescriptor _
) As ICollection
```
[C#]
```
ICollection GetCompatibleMethods(
   EventDescriptor e
);
```
[C++]
```
ICollection* GetCompatibleMethods(
   EventDescriptor* e
);
```
[JScript]
```
function GetCompatibleMethods(
   e : EventDescriptor
) : ICollection;
```

Parameters

e

The event to get the compatible event-handler methods for.

Return Value

A collection of strings.

Remarks

Each string in the collection is the name of a method that has a method signature compatible with the specified event.

Requirements

Platforms: Windows 98, Windows NT 4.0, Windows Millennium Edition, Windows 2000, Windows XP Home Edition, Windows XP Professional, Windows Server 2003 family

IEventBindingService.GetEvent Method

Gets an **EventDescriptor** for the event that the specified property descriptor represents, if it represents an event.

```
[Visual Basic]
Function GetEvent( _
   ByVal property As PropertyDescriptor _
) As EventDescriptor
[C#]
EventDescriptor GetEvent(
   PropertyDescriptor property
);
[C++]
EventDescriptor* GetEvent(
   PropertyDescriptor* property
);
[JScript]
function GetEvent(
   property : PropertyDescriptor
) : EventDescriptor;
```

Parameters

property

The property that represents an event.

Return Value

An **EventDescriptor** for the event that the property represents, or a null reference (**Nothing** in Visual Basic) if the property does not represent an event.

Requirements

Platforms: Windows 98, Windows NT 4.0, Windows Millennium Edition, Windows 2000, Windows XP Home Edition, Windows XP Professional, Windows Server 2003 family

IEventBindingService.GetEventProperties Method

Converts a set of event descriptors to a set of property descriptors.

```
[Visual Basic]
Function GetEventProperties( _
   ByVal events As EventDescriptorCollection _
) As PropertyDescriptorCollection
[C#]
PropertyDescriptorCollection GetEventProperties(
   EventDescriptorCollection events
);
[C++]
PropertyDescriptorCollection* GetEventProperties(
   EventDescriptorCollection* events
);
[JScript]
function GetEventProperties(
   events : EventDescriptorCollection
) : PropertyDescriptorCollection;
```

Parameters

events

The events to convert to properties.

Return Value

An array of **PropertyDescriptor** objects that describe the event set.

Remarks

Each returned **PropertyDescriptor** has a **PropertyType** of string.

Requirements

Platforms: Windows 98, Windows NT 4.0, Windows Millennium Edition, Windows 2000, Windows XP Home Edition, Windows XP Professional, Windows Server 2003 family

IEventBindingService.GetEventProperty Method

Converts a single event descriptor to a property descriptor.

```
[Visual Basic]
Function GetEventProperty( _
   ByVal e As EventDescriptor _
) As PropertyDescriptor
[C#]
PropertyDescriptor GetEventProperty(
   EventDescriptor e
);
[C++]
PropertyDescriptor* GetEventProperty(
   EventDescriptor* e
);
[JScript]
function GetEventProperty(
   e : EventDescriptor
) : PropertyDescriptor;
```

Parameters

e

The event to convert.

Return Value

A **PropertyDescriptor** that describes the event.

Remarks

The returned **PropertyDescriptor** has a **PropertyType** of string.

Requirements

Platforms: Windows 98, Windows NT 4.0, Windows Millennium Edition, Windows 2000, Windows XP Home Edition, Windows XP Professional, Windows Server 2003 family

IEventBindingService.ShowCode Method

Displays the user code for the designer.

Overload List

Displays the user code for the designer.

[Visual Basic] **Overloads Function ShowCode() As Boolean**

[C#] **bool ShowCode();**

[C++] **bool ShowCode();**

[JScript] **function ShowCode() : Boolean;**

Displays the user code for the designer at the specified line.

[Visual Basic] **Overloads Function ShowCode(Integer) As Boolean**

[C#] **bool ShowCode(int);**

[C++] **bool ShowCode(int);**

[JScript] **function ShowCode(int) : Boolean;**

Displays the user code for the specified event.

[Visual Basic] **Overloads Function ShowCode(IComponent, EventDescriptor) As Boolean**

[C#] **bool ShowCode(IComponent, EventDescriptor);**

[C++] **bool ShowCode(IComponent*, EventDescriptor*);**

[JScript] **function ShowCode(IComponent, EventDescriptor) : Boolean;**

IEventBindingService.ShowCode Method ()

Displays the user code for the designer.

```
[Visual Basic]
Function ShowCode() As Boolean
[C#]
bool ShowCode();
[C++]
bool ShowCode();
[JScript]
function ShowCode() : Boolean;
```

Return Value

true if the code is displayed; otherwise, **false**.

Remarks

This method displays the code editor.

Requirements

Platforms: Windows 98, Windows NT 4.0, Windows Millennium Edition, Windows 2000, Windows XP Home Edition, Windows XP Professional, Windows Server 2003 family

IEventBindingService.ShowCode Method (Int32)

Displays the user code for the designer at the specified line.

```
[Visual Basic]
Function ShowCode( _
   ByVal lineNumber As Integer _
) As Boolean
[C#]
bool ShowCode(
   int lineNumber
);
[C++]
bool ShowCode(
   int lineNumber
);
[JScript]
function ShowCode(
   lineNumber : int
) : Boolean;
```

Parameters

lineNumber

The line number to place the caret on.

Return Value

true if the code is displayed; otherwise, **false**.

Remarks

This method displays the code editor and positions the cursor on the specified line.

Requirements

Platforms: Windows 98, Windows NT 4.0, Windows Millennium Edition, Windows 2000, Windows XP Home Edition, Windows XP Professional, Windows Server 2003 family

IEventBindingService.ShowCode Method (IComponent, EventDescriptor)

Displays the user code for the specified event.

```
[Visual Basic]
Function ShowCode( _
   ByVal component As IComponent, _
   ByVal e As EventDescriptor _
) As Boolean
[C#]
bool ShowCode(
   IComponent component,
   EventDescriptor e
);
[C++]
bool ShowCode(
   IComponent* component,
   EventDescriptor* e
);
[JScript]
function ShowCode(
   component : IComponent,
   e : EventDescriptor
) : Boolean;
```

Parameters

component

The component that the event is connected to.

e

The event to display.

Return Value

true if the code is displayed; otherwise, **false**.

Remarks

This method displays the code editor and positions the cursor on the line that the specified event is declared on.

Requirements

Platforms: Windows 98, Windows NT 4.0, Windows Millennium Edition, Windows 2000, Windows XP Home Edition, Windows XP Professional, Windows Server 2003 family

IExtenderListService Interface

Provides an interface that can list extender providers.

[Visual Basic]
```
Public Interface IExtenderListService
```
[C#]
```
public interface IExtenderListService
```
[C++]
```
public __gc __interface IExtenderListService
```
[JScript]
```
public interface IExtenderListService
```

Remarks

A site can implement this service if it wants to provide a list of extender providers. By default, the list of extenders is generated by querying each component in the container that implements **IExtenderProvider** for the extenders each provides. By implementing this interface on a component site, a container can override the list of providers.

Example

[Visual Basic, C#, C++] The following example demonstrates using the **IExtenderListService** to obtain the set of currently active extender providers.

[Visual Basic]
```
Imports System
Imports System.Collections
Imports System.ComponentModel
Imports System.ComponentModel.Design
Imports System.Drawing
Imports System.Data
Imports System.Windows.Forms

' This control lists any active extender providers.
Public Class ExtenderListServiceControl
   Inherits System.Windows.Forms.UserControl
   Private extenderListService As IExtenderListService
   Private extenderNames() As String

   Public Sub New()
      extenderNames = New String(-1) {}
      Me.Width = 600
    End Sub

    ' Queries the IExtenderListService when the control is sited
    ' in design mode.
    Public Overrides Property Site() As System.ComponentModel.ISite
        Get
            Return MyBase.Site
        End Get
        Set(ByVal Value As System.ComponentModel.ISite)
            MyBase.Site = Value
            If Me.DesignMode Then
                extenderListService = ↵
CType(Me.GetService(GetType(IExtenderListService)), ↵
IExtenderListService)
                If Not (extenderListService Is Nothing) Then
                    Dim extenders As IExtenderProvider() = ↵
extenderListService.GetExtenderProviders()
                    extenderNames = New String(extenders.Length) {}
                    Dim i As Integer
                    For i = 0 To extenders.Length - 1
                        Dim types As Type() = ↵
Type.GetTypeArray(extenders)
                        extenderNames(i) = "ExtenderProvider ↵
#" + i.ToString() + ":  " + types(i).FullName
                    Next i
                End If
            Else
                extenderListService = Nothing
                extenderNames = New String(-1) {}
            End If
        End Set
    End Property

    ' Draws a list of any active extender providers
    Protected Overrides Sub OnPaint(ByVal e As ↵
System.Windows.Forms.PaintEventArgs)
        If extenderNames.Length = 0 Then
            e.Graphics.DrawString("No active extender providers", ↵
 New Font("Arial", 9), New SolidBrush(Color.Black), 10, 10)
        Else
            e.Graphics.DrawString("List of types of active ↵
extender providers", New Font("Arial", 9), New SolidBrush ↵
 (Color.Black), 10, 10)
        End If
        Dim i As Integer
        For i = 0 To extenderNames.Length - 1
            e.Graphics.DrawString(extenderNames(i), New Font ↵
 ("Arial", 8), New SolidBrush(Color.Black), 10, 25 + i * 10)
        Next i
    End Sub

End Class
```

[C#]
```
using System;
using System.Collections;
using System.ComponentModel;
using System.ComponentModel.Design;
using System.Drawing;
using System.Data;
using System.Windows.Forms;

namespace ExtenderListServiceExample
{
    // This control lists any active extender providers.
    public class ExtenderListServiceControl : ↵
System.Windows.Forms.UserControl
    {
        private IExtenderListService extenderListService;
        private string[] extenderNames;

        public ExtenderListServiceControl()
        {
            extenderNames = new string[0];
            this.Width = 600;
        }

        // Queries the IExtenderListService when the control is sited
        // in design mode.
        public override System.ComponentModel.ISite Site
        {
            get
            {
                return base.Site;
            }
            set
            {
                base.Site = value;
                if( this.DesignMode )
                {
                    extenderListService = ↵
 (IExtenderListService)this.GetService(typeof(IExtenderListService));
                    if( extenderListService != null )
                    {
                        IExtenderProvider[] extenders = ↵
extenderListService.GetExtenderProviders();
                        extenderNames = new string[extenders.Length];
                        for( int i=0; i<extenders.Length; i++ )
                            extenderNames[i] = "ExtenderProvider ↵
#"+i.ToString()+":  "+extenders[i].GetType().FullName;
                    }
                }
```

```
            else
            {
                extenderListService = null;
                extenderNames = new string[0];
            }
        }
    }

    // Draws a list of any active extender providers
    protected override void
OnPaint(System.Windows.Forms.PaintEventArgs e)
    {
        if( extenderNames.Length == 0 )
            e.Graphics.DrawString("No active extender                ↵
providers", new Font("Arial", 9), new SolidBrush(Color.Black), 10, 10);
        else
            e.Graphics.DrawString("List of types of active          ↵
extender providers", new Font("Arial", 9), new SolidBrush          ↵
 (Color.Black), 10, 10);
        for(int i=0; i<extenderNames.Length; i++)
            e.Graphics.DrawString(extenderNames[i], new             ↵
Font("Arial", 8), new SolidBrush(Color.Black), 10, 25+(i*10));
    }
  }
}
```

[C++]

```
#using <mscorlib.dll>
#using <system.dll>
#using <system.drawing.dll>
#using <system.windows.forms.dll>

using namespace System;
using namespace System::Drawing;
using namespace System::ComponentModel;
using namespace System::ComponentModel::Design;
using namespace System::Windows::Forms;

namespace ExtenderListServiceExample
{
    // This control lists any active extender providers.
    public __gc class ExtenderListServiceControl : public UserControl {
    private:

        IExtenderListService* extenderListService;
        String* extenderNames[];

    public:

        ExtenderListServiceControl()
        {
            this->Width = 600;
        }

        // Queries the IExtenderListService when the control is sited
        // in design mode.
        __property ISite* get_Site()
        {
            return UserControl::get_Site();
        }

        __property void set_Site(ISite* value)
        {
            UserControl::set_Site( value );
            if( this->DesignMode )
            {
                extenderListService =                               ↵
dynamic_cast<IExtenderListService*>(this-                           ↵
>GetService(__typeof(IExtenderListService)));
                if( extenderListService != 0 )
                {
                    IExtenderProvider* extenders[] =                ↵
extenderListService->GetExtenderProviders();
                    extenderNames = new String*[extenders->Length];
                    for( int i=0; i<extenders->Length; i++ )
                        extenderNames[i] = String::Concat(          ↵
S"ExtenderProvider #", i.ToString(), S":  ", extenders[i]->         ↵
GetType()->FullName );
                }
            }
            else
            {
                extenderListService = 0;
            }
        }

    protected:

        // Draws a list of any active extender providers
        void OnPaint(PaintEventArgs* e)
        {
            if( extenderNames->Length == 0 )
                e->Graphics->DrawString(S"No active extender        ↵
providers", new System::Drawing::Font(S"Arial", 9), new             ↵
SolidBrush(Color::Black), 10, 10);
            else
                e->Graphics->DrawString(S"List of types of          ↵
active extender providers", new System::Drawing::Font(S"Arial",     ↵
 9), new SolidBrush(Color::Black), 10, 10);
            for(int i=0; i<extenderNames->Length; i++)
                e->Graphics->DrawString(extenderNames[i], new       ↵
System::Drawing::Font(S"Arial", 8), new SolidBrush                  ↵
 (Color::Black), 10, 25+(i*10));
        }
    };
}
```

Requirements

Namespace: System.ComponentModel.Design

Platforms: Windows 98, Windows NT 4.0, Windows Millennium Edition, Windows 2000, Windows XP Home Edition, Windows XP Professional, Windows Server 2003 family

Assembly: System (in System.dll)

IExtenderListService.GetExtenderProviders Method

Gets the set of extender providers for the component.

[Visual Basic]
```
Function GetExtenderProviders() As IExtenderProvider()
```
[C#]
```
IExtenderProvider[] GetExtenderProviders();
```
[C++]
```
IExtenderProvider* GetExtenderProviders() [];
```
[JScript]
```
function GetExtenderProviders() : IExtenderProvider[];
```

Return Value

An array of type **IExtenderProvider** that lists the active extender providers. If there are no providers, an empty array is returned.

Requirements

Platforms: Windows 98, Windows NT 4.0, Windows Millennium Edition, Windows 2000, Windows XP Home Edition, Windows XP Professional, Windows Server 2003 family

IExtenderProviderService Interface

Provides an interface for adding and removing extender providers at design time.

[Visual Basic]
```
Public Interface IExtenderProviderService
```
[C#]
```
public interface IExtenderProviderService
```
[C++]
```
public __gc __interface IExtenderProviderService
```
[JScript]
```
public interface IExtenderProviderService
```

Remarks

Typically, only components that have been added to a container offer extender providers. The **IExtenderProviderService** allows you to extend this capability to objects that are not in the container.

Example

See related example in the **System.ComponentModel.Design.IExtenderListService** class topic.

Requirements

Namespace: System.ComponentModel.Design

Platforms: Windows 98, Windows NT 4.0, Windows Millennium Edition, Windows 2000, Windows XP Home Edition, Windows XP Professional, Windows Server 2003 family

Assembly: System (in System.dll)

IExtenderProviderService.AddExtenderProvider Method

Adds the specified extender provider.

[Visual Basic]
```
Sub AddExtenderProvider( _
   ByVal provider As IExtenderProvider _
)
```
[C#]
```
void AddExtenderProvider(
   IExtenderProvider provider
);
```
[C++]
```
void AddExtenderProvider(
   IExtenderProvider* provider
);
```
[JScript]
```
function AddExtenderProvider(
   provider : IExtenderProvider
);
```

Parameters

provider

The extender provider to add.

Remarks

This interface allows objects besides components to add extender providers to the design time set of extender providers. All properties that are displayed from these extender providers are marked as design time only.

Requirements

Platforms: Windows 98, Windows NT 4.0, Windows Millennium Edition, Windows 2000, Windows XP Home Edition, Windows XP Professional, Windows Server 2003 family

IExtenderProviderService.RemoveExtender-Provider Method

Removes the specified extender provider.

[Visual Basic]
```
Sub RemoveExtenderProvider( _
   ByVal provider As IExtenderProvider _
)
```
[C#]
```
void RemoveExtenderProvider(
   IExtenderProvider provider
);
```
[C++]
```
void RemoveExtenderProvider(
   IExtenderProvider* provider
);
```
[JScript]
```
function RemoveExtenderProvider(
   provider : IExtenderProvider
);
```

Parameters

provider

The extender provider to remove.

Remarks

This interface allows objects besides components to add extender providers to the design-time set of extender providers. All properties that are displayed from these extender providers are marked as design time only.

Requirements

Platforms: Windows 98, Windows NT 4.0, Windows Millennium Edition, Windows 2000, Windows XP Home Edition, Windows XP Professional, Windows Server 2003 family

IHelpService Interface

Provides methods for showing Help topics and adding and removing Help keywords at design time.

[Visual Basic]
```
Public Interface IHelpService
```
[C#]
```
public interface IHelpService
```
[C++]
```
public __gc __interface IHelpService
```
[JScript]
```
public interface IHelpService
```

Remarks

The design-time environment provides a Help system that attempts to locate relevant Help topics to display when a user presses F1. The Help system maintains a set of current context keywords that are used to identify relevant topics if Help is requested. By default, keywords are associated with selected class objects and properties of objects in the design time environment. The default keyword for a component or property is its fully qualified class or property name. Specific keywords are also associated with certain modes, such as when multiple objects are selected. If a custom Help collection is integrated with the design-time environment by configuring it for an external help provider, a documentation provider can associate a topic for a specific component class or property with a keyword consisting of the item's fully qualified type or member name.

The **IHelpService** can be used to invoke the help service with a specified keyword using the **ShowHelpFromKeyword** method, or to invoke a help topic from a specified URL using the **ShowHelpFromUrl** method.

The **IHelpService** can also be used to add or remove Help keywords at design time. Selecting a component or property at design time sets a default context keyword consisting of the fully qualified type or member name of the selection, and removes the keywords for any previously selected and no longer selected components or properties.

Because the Help system does not automatically remove custom Help keywords, you must explicitly remove a custom keyword when it no longer applies. You can monitor the events defined by the **ISelectionService** interface to determine when a component selection changes. Based on those events, you can add a Help context attribute for a component when it is selected and then remove the Help context attribute when the selection no longer includes the component.

Example

[Visual Basic, C#] The following example demonstrates a designer that uses the **IHelpService** to add and remove Help context attributes for the included control. To use this sample, compile it to a class library and add an instance of the control to a **Form**. In designer view, selecting the component and pressing F1 attempts to look up relevant Help topics based on the current Help context keyword or keywords. Right-click the component and the shortcut menu displays commands, including two custom **DesignerVerb** commands named **Add IHelpService Help Keyword** and **Remove IHelpService Help Keyword**. These commands can be used to add or remove a Help context keyword of the value "IHelpService", which attempts to raise the **IHelpService** topic when F1 is pressed.

[Visual Basic]
```
Imports System
Imports System.ComponentModel
Imports System.ComponentModel.Design
Imports System.Drawing
Imports System.IO
Imports System.Windows.Forms
Imports System.Windows.Forms.Design

Namespace IHelpServiceSample

    Public Class HelpDesigner
        Inherits System.Windows.Forms.Design.ControlDesigner

        Public Sub New()
        End Sub 'New

        Public Overrides ReadOnly Property Verbs() As ↵
System.ComponentModel.Design.DesignerVerbCollection
            Get
                Return New DesignerVerbCollection ↵
 (New DesignerVerb() {New DesignerVerb("Add IHelpService ↵
Help Keyword", AddressOf Me.addKeyword), New DesignerVerb ↵
 ("Remove IHelpService Help Keyword", AddressOf Me.removeKeyword)})
            End Get
        End Property

        Private Sub addKeyword(ByVal sender As Object, ByVal ↵
 e As EventArgs)
            Dim hs As IHelpService = ↵
CType(Me.Control.Site.GetService(GetType(IHelpService)), IHelpService)
            hs.AddContextAttribute("keyword", "IHelpService", ↵
HelpKeywordType.F1Keyword)
        End Sub 'addKeyword

        Private Sub removeKeyword(ByVal sender As Object, ByVal ↵
 e As EventArgs)
            Dim hs As IHelpService = ↵
CType(Me.Control.Site.GetService(GetType(IHelpService)), IHelpService)
            hs.RemoveContextAttribute("keyword", "IHelpService")
        End Sub 'removeKeyword
    End Class 'HelpDesigner

    <Designer(GetType(HelpDesigner))> _
    Public Class HelpTestControl
        Inherits System.Windows.Forms.UserControl

        Public Sub New()
            Me.Size = New Size(320, 100)
            Me.BackColor = Color.White
        End Sub 'New

        Protected Overrides Sub OnPaint(ByVal e As ↵
System.Windows.Forms.PaintEventArgs)
            Dim brush = New SolidBrush(Color.Blue)
            e.Graphics.DrawString("IHelpService Example ↵
 Designer Control", New Font(FontFamily.GenericMonospace, 10), ↵
 brush, 5, 5)
            e.Graphics.DrawString("Right-click this component ↵
 for", New Font(FontFamily.GenericMonospace, 8), brush, 5, 25)
            e.Graphics.DrawString("add/remove Help context ↵
keyword commands.", New Font(FontFamily.GenericMonospace, 8), ↵
 brush, 5, 35)
            e.Graphics.DrawString("Press F1 while this ↵
component is", New Font(FontFamily.GenericMonospace, 8), brush, 5, 55)
            e.Graphics.DrawString("selected to raise Help ↵
topics for", New Font(FontFamily.GenericMonospace, 8), brush, 5, 65)
            e.Graphics.DrawString("the current keyword or ↵
 keywords", New Font(FontFamily.GenericMonospace, 8), brush, 5, 75)
        End Sub 'OnPaint
    End Class 'HelpTestControl
End Namespace 'IHelpServiceSample
```

```
[C#]
using System;
using System.ComponentModel;
using System.ComponentModel.Design;
using System.Drawing;
using System.IO;
using System.Windows.Forms;
using System.Windows.Forms.Design;

namespace IHelpServiceSample
{
    public class HelpDesigner :
System.Windows.Forms.Design.ControlDesigner
    {
        public HelpDesigner()
        {
        }

        public override
System.ComponentModel.Design.DesignerVerbCollection Verbs
        {
            get
            {
                return new DesignerVerbCollection( new DesignerVerb[] {
                        new DesignerVerb("Add IHelpService Help
Keyword", new EventHandler(this.addKeyword)),
                        new DesignerVerb("Remove IHelpService
 Help Keyword", new EventHandler(this.removeKeyword))
                } );
            }
        }

        private void addKeyword(object sender, EventArgs e)
        {
            IHelpService hs = (IHelpService)
this.Control.Site.GetService(typeof(IHelpService));
            hs.AddContextAttribute("keyword", "IHelpService",
HelpKeywordType.F1Keyword)
        }

        private void removeKeyword(object sender, EventArgs e)
        {
            IHelpService hs = (IHelpService)
this.Control.Site.GetService(typeof(IHelpService));
            hs.RemoveContextAttribute("keyword", "IHelpService");
        }
    }

    [Designer(typeof(HelpDesigner))]
    public class HelpTestControl : System.Windows.Forms.UserControl
    {
        public HelpTestControl()
        {
            this.Size = new Size(320, 100);
            this.BackColor = Color.White;
        }

        protected override void
 OnPaint(System.Windows.Forms.PaintEventArgs e)
        {
            Brush brush = new SolidBrush(Color.Blue);
            e.Graphics.DrawString("IHelpService Example Designer
Control", new Font( FontFamily.GenericMonospace, 10 ), brush, 5, 5);
            e.Graphics.DrawString("Right-click this component
for", new Font( FontFamily.GenericMonospace, 8 ), brush, 5, 25);
            e.Graphics.DrawString("add/remove Help context
keyword commands.", new Font( FontFamily.GenericMonospace, 8 ),
 brush, 5, 35);
            e.Graphics.DrawString("Press F1 while this
component is", new Font( FontFamily.GenericMonospace, 8 ),
 brush, 5, 55);
            e.Graphics.DrawString("selected to raise Help
 topics for", new Font( FontFamily.GenericMonospace, 8 ),
brush, 5, 65);
            e.Graphics.DrawString("the current keyword or
keywords", new Font( FontFamily.GenericMonospace, 8 ),
brush, 5, 75);
        }
    }
}
```

Requirements

Namespace: System.ComponentModel.Design

Platforms: Windows 98, Windows NT 4.0, Windows Millennium Edition, Windows 2000, Windows XP Home Edition, Windows XP Professional, Windows Server 2003 family

Assembly: System (in System.dll)

IHelpService.AddContextAttribute Method

Adds a context attribute to the document.

```
[Visual Basic]
Sub AddContextAttribute( _
   ByVal name As String, _
   ByVal value As String, _
   ByVal keywordType As HelpKeywordType _
)
[C#]
void AddContextAttribute(
   string name,
   string value,
   HelpKeywordType keywordType
);
[C++]
void AddContextAttribute(
   String* name,
   String* value,
   HelpKeywordType keywordType
);
[JScript]
function AddContextAttribute(
   name : String,
   value : String,
   keywordType : HelpKeywordType
);
```

Parameters

name
: The name of the attribute to add.

value
: The value of the attribute.

keywordType
: The type of the keyword, from the enumeration **HelpKeywordType**.

Remarks

Context attributes are used to provide context-sensitive Help to users. The designer host automatically adds context attributes from available Help attributes on certain components and properties. This method allows you to further customize the context-sensitive Help.

Requirements

Platforms: Windows 98, Windows NT 4.0, Windows Millennium Edition, Windows 2000, Windows XP Home Edition, Windows XP Professional, Windows Server 2003 family

IHelpService.ClearContextAttributes Method

Removes all existing context attributes from the document.

```
[Visual Basic]
Sub ClearContextAttributes()
[C#]
void ClearContextAttributes();
[C++]
void ClearContextAttributes();
[JScript]
function ClearContextAttributes();
```

Requirements

Platforms: Windows 98, Windows NT 4.0, Windows Millennium Edition, Windows 2000, Windows XP Home Edition, Windows XP Professional, Windows Server 2003 family

IHelpService.CreateLocalContext Method

Creates a local **IHelpService** to manage subcontexts.

```
[Visual Basic]
Function CreateLocalContext( _
   ByVal contextType As HelpContextType _
) As IHelpService
[C#]
IHelpService CreateLocalContext(
   HelpContextType contextType
);
[C++]
IHelpService* CreateLocalContext(
   HelpContextType contextType
);
[JScript]
function CreateLocalContext(
   contextType : HelpContextType
) : IHelpService;
```

Parameters

contextType
The priority type of the subcontext to add.

Return Value

The newly created **IHelpService**.

Requirements

Platforms: Windows 98, Windows NT 4.0, Windows Millennium Edition, Windows 2000, Windows XP Home Edition, Windows XP Professional, Windows Server 2003 family

IHelpService.RemoveContextAttribute Method

Removes a previously added context attribute.

```
[Visual Basic]
Sub RemoveContextAttribute( _
   ByVal name As String, _
   ByVal value As String _
)
[C#]
void RemoveContextAttribute(
   string name,
   string value
);
[C++]
void RemoveContextAttribute(
   String* name,
   String* value
);
[JScript]
function RemoveContextAttribute(
   name : String,
   value : String
);
```

Parameters

name
The name of the attribute to remove.

value
The value of the attribute to remove.

Requirements

Platforms: Windows 98, Windows NT 4.0, Windows Millennium Edition, Windows 2000, Windows XP Home Edition, Windows XP Professional, Windows Server 2003 family

IHelpService.RemoveLocalContext Method

Removes a context created with **CreateLocalContext**.

```
[Visual Basic]
Sub RemoveLocalContext( _
   ByVal localContext As IHelpService _
)
[C#]
void RemoveLocalContext(
   IHelpService localContext
);
[C++]
void RemoveLocalContext(
   IHelpService* localContext
);
[JScript]
function RemoveLocalContext(
   localContext : IHelpService
);
```

Parameters

localContext
The local context **IHelpService** to remove.

Requirements

Platforms: Windows 98, Windows NT 4.0, Windows Millennium Edition, Windows 2000, Windows XP Home Edition, Windows XP Professional, Windows Server 2003 family

IHelpService.ShowHelpFromKeyword Method

Shows the Help topic that corresponds to the specified keyword.

[Visual Basic]
```
Sub ShowHelpFromKeyword( _
   ByVal helpKeyword As String _
)
```
[C#]
```
void ShowHelpFromKeyword(
   string helpKeyword
);
```
[C++]
```
void ShowHelpFromKeyword(
   String* helpKeyword
);
```
[JScript]
```
function ShowHelpFromKeyword(
   helpKeyword : String
);
```

Parameters

helpKeyword
The keyword of the Help topic to display.

Remarks

The Visual Studio .NET integrated development environment's Help system displays the topic.

Requirements

Platforms: Windows 98, Windows NT 4.0, Windows Millennium Edition, Windows 2000, Windows XP Home Edition, Windows XP Professional, Windows Server 2003 family

IHelpService.ShowHelpFromUrl Method

Shows the Help topic that corresponds to the specified URL.

[Visual Basic]
```
Sub ShowHelpFromUrl( _
   ByVal helpUrl As String _
)
```
[C#]
```
void ShowHelpFromUrl(
   string helpUrl
);
```
[C++]
```
void ShowHelpFromUrl(
   String* helpUrl
);
```
[JScript]
```
function ShowHelpFromUrl(
   helpUrl : String
);
```

Parameters

helpUrl
The URL of the Help topic to display.

Remarks

The Visual Studio .NET integrated development environment's Help system displays the topic.

Requirements

Platforms: Windows 98, Windows NT 4.0, Windows Millennium Edition, Windows 2000, Windows XP Home Edition, Windows XP Professional, Windows Server 2003 family

IInheritanceService Interface

This type supports the .NET Framework infrastructure and is not intended to be used directly from your code.

[Visual Basic]
```
Public Interface IInheritanceService
```
[C#]
```
public interface IInheritanceService
```
[C++]
```
public __gc __interface IInheritanceService
```
[JScript]
```
public interface IInheritanceService
```

IInheritanceService.AddInheritedComponents Method

This member supports the .NET Framework infrastructure and is not intended to be used directly from your code.

[Visual Basic]
```
Sub AddInheritedComponents( _
   ByVal component As IComponent, _
   ByVal container As IContainer _
)
```
[C#]
```
void AddInheritedComponents(
   IComponent component,
   IContainer container
);
```
[C++]
```
void AddInheritedComponents(
   IComponent* component,
   IContainer* container
);
```
[JScript]
```
function AddInheritedComponents(
   component : IComponent,
   container : IContainer
);
```

IInheritanceService.GetInheritanceAttribute Method

This member supports the .NET Framework infrastructure and is not intended to be used directly from your code.

[Visual Basic]
```
Function GetInheritanceAttribute( _
   ByVal component As IComponent _
) As InheritanceAttribute
```
[C#]
```
InheritanceAttribute GetInheritanceAttribute(
   IComponent component
);
```
[C++]
```
InheritanceAttribute* GetInheritanceAttribute(
   IComponent* component
);
```
[JScript]
```
function GetInheritanceAttribute(
   component : IComponent
) : InheritanceAttribute;
```

IMenuCommandService Interface

Provides methods to manage the global designer verbs and menu commands available in design mode, and to show some types of context menus.

[Visual Basic]
```
<ComVisible(True)>
Public Interface IMenuCommandService
```
[C#]
```
[ComVisible(true)]
public interface IMenuCommandService
```
[C++]
```
[ComVisible(true)]
public __gc __interface IMenuCommandService
```
[JScript]
```
public
   ComVisible(true)
interface IMenuCommandService
```

Remarks

This interface provides methods to:

- Find, invoke, add and remove global designer verb commands.
- Find, invoke, add and remove standard menu commands.
- Alter the event handlers associated with standard menu commands.
- Display a context menu of standard commands that is associated with a menu **CommandID**.

Designer verbs represent custom-defined commands that are listed on the shortcut menu in design mode. A designer verb can provide a specified text label. Each designer verb is automatically assigned a unique **CommandID**. A designer can provide designer verbs through its **Verbs** property, but these are only available when the designer's component is currently selected. Global designer verbs are designer verb commands that can be accessed from a design-mode shortcut menu regardless of the selected component. This interface allows you to manage the set of global designer verbs that are available in design mode.

You can add a global designer verb using the **AddVerb** method, and you can remove a global designer verb using the **RemoveVerb** method. You can invoke a designer verb using the **GlobalInvoke** method if you know the **CommandID** of the verb. The **Verbs** property of this interface contains the current set of designer verb commands to display in a shortcut menu. This set of designer verb commands consists of all global designer verbs and any designer verbs offered by the designer of any currently selected component. This set of verbs is updated each time a component with a designer offering designer verb commands is selected or deselected.

Menu commands are limited to the set of predefined standard commands. Most of the predefined standard commands are defined in the **StandardCommands** and **MenuCommands** enumerations. You can add, remove, and invoke menu commands, and search for menu commands that have been added to a menu using methods of this interface.

You can add a standard menu command using the **AddCommand** method, and remove a standard menu command using the **RemoveCommand** method. You can attach an event handler to a predefined standard menu command by following the procedure detailed in the documentation for the **AddCommand** method. You can retrieve a menu command by **CommandID** if it has been added to a menu using the **FindCommand** method. You can invoke a menu command or designer verb command by **CommandID** using the **GlobalInvoke** method.

Note An attempt to add a menu command with an already existing **CommandID** will throw an **InvalidOperationException**. When adding a menu command, be sure to check that it is not already on a menu using the **FindCommand** method, or use exception handling wisely.

Note A menu command can be added to a menu, and have its **Visible** or **Enabled** properties set to **false**. If you cannot visually locate a menu command that has been added on a menu, one of these properties may have been set to **false**.

You can show certain standard shortcut menus containing menu commands at a specified location using the **ShowContextMenu** method. The documentation for this method contains a table listing the command IDs that specify the valid menus to show.

Example

[Visual Basic, C#, C++] This example demonstrates using the **IMenuCommandService** to add a **MenuCommand**.

[Visual Basic]
```
' This example illustrates how to add a command of type StandardCommand to a
'   service of type IMenuCommandService.  It defines a class that is a designer
'   to a component, called CDesigner.  Then it creates a MenuCommand object using
'   one of the commands in the StandardCommands class.  Finally, it sets several
'   of the properties in the MenuCommand object and adds the MenuCommand object
'   to the MenuCommandService object.

Public Class CDesigner
   Inherits System.ComponentModel.Design.ComponentDesigner

   Public Overrides Sub Initialize(ByVal comp As IComponent)
      MyBase.Initialize(comp)

      Dim mcs As IMenuCommandService = CType(comp.Site.GetService(GetType(IMenuCommandService)), IMenuCommandService)
      Dim mc As New MenuCommand(New EventHandler(AddressOf OnReplace), StandardCommands.Group)
      mc.Enabled = True
      mc.Visible = True
      mc.Supported = True
      mcs.AddCommand(mc)
      System.Windows.Forms.MessageBox.Show("Initialize() has been invoked.")
   End Sub 'Initialize

   Private Sub OnReplace(ByVal sender As Object, ByVal e As EventArgs)
      System.Windows.Forms.MessageBox.Show("Replace() has been invoked.")
   End Sub 'OnReplace
End Class 'CDesigner
```

[C#]
```
/* This example illustrates how to add a command of type StandardCommand to a
    service of type IMenuCommandService.  It defines a class that is a designer
    to a component, called CDesigner.  Then it creates a MenuCommand object using
```

```
    one of the commands in the StandardCommands class.             ↵
Finally, it sets several
    of the properties in the MenuCommand object and adds           ↵
the MenuCommand object
    to the MenuCommandService object.
*/

public class CDesigner : System.ComponentModel.Design.ComponentDesigner
{
    public override void Initialize(IComponent comp)
    {
        base.Initialize(comp);

        IMenuCommandService mcs = (IMenuCommandService)comp.Site.
                    GetService(typeof(IMenuCommandService));
        MenuCommand mc = new MenuCommand(new                       ↵
EventHandler(OnReplace),StandardCommands.Group);
        mc.Enabled = true;
        mc.Visible = true;
        mc.Supported = true;
        mcs.AddCommand(mc);
        System.Windows.Forms.MessageBox.Show("Initialize()         ↵
 has been invoked.");
    }

    private void OnReplace(object sender, EventArgs e)
    {
        System.Windows.Forms.MessageBox.Show("Replace()            ↵
 has been invoked.");
    }
} // End Class Component1
```

[C++]

```
/* This example illustrates how to add a command of type          ↵
StandardCommand to a
    service of type IMenuCommandService.  It defines a            ↵
class that is a designer
    to a component, called CDesigner.  Then it creates a          ↵
MenuCommand object using
    one of the commands in the StandardCommands class.            ↵
 Finally, it sets several
    of the properties in the MenuCommand object and adds          ↵
the MenuCommand object
    to the MenuCommandService object.
*/

public __gc class CDesigner : public ComponentDesigner {
public:

    void Initialize(IComponent* comp)
    {
        ComponentDesigner::Initialize(comp);

        IMenuCommandService* mcs =
            static_cast<IMenuCommandService*>(comp->Site-         ↵
>GetService(__typeof(IMenuCommandService)));
        MenuCommand* mc = new MenuCommand(new EventHandler        ↵
 (this, OnReplace), StandardCommands::Group);
        mc->Enabled = true;
        mc->Visible = true;
        mc->Supported = true;
        mcs->AddCommand(mc);
        System::Windows::Forms::MessageBox::Show(S"Initialize()   ↵
 has been invoked.");
    }

private:

    void OnReplace(Object* sender, EventArgs* e)
    {
        System::Windows::Forms::MessageBox::Show(S"Replace()      ↵
has been invoked.");
    }
}; // End Class CDesigner
```

Requirements

Namespace: System.ComponentModel.Design

Platforms: Windows 98, Windows NT 4.0, Windows Millennium Edition, Windows 2000, Windows XP Home Edition, Windows XP Professional, Windows Server 2003 family

Assembly: System (in System.dll)

IMenuCommandService.Verbs Property

Gets or sets an array of the designer verbs that are currently available.

[Visual Basic]
```
ReadOnly Property Verbs As DesignerVerbCollection
```
[C#]
```
DesignerVerbCollection Verbs {get;}
```
[C++]
```
__property DesignerVerbCollection* get_Verbs();
```
[JScript]
```
function get Verbs() : DesignerVerbCollection;
```

Property Value

An array of type **DesignerVerb** that indicates the designer verbs that are currently available.

Remarks

The set of currently available designer verbs consists of all global designer verbs, which are added by the **AddVerb** method on this interface, and individual designer verbs, which are offered by the **Verbs** property of individual designers. If the name of a global verb conflicts with the name of a designer verb, the designer-provided designer verb takes precedence.

Requirements

Platforms: Windows 98, Windows NT 4.0, Windows Millennium Edition, Windows 2000, Windows XP Home Edition, Windows XP Professional, Windows Server 2003 family

IMenuCommandService.AddCommand Method

Adds the specified standard menu command to the menu.

[Visual Basic]
```
Sub AddCommand( _
   ByVal command As MenuCommand _
)
```
[C#]
```
void AddCommand(
   MenuCommand command
);
```
[C++]
```
void AddCommand(
   MenuCommand* command
);
```
[JScript]
```
function AddCommand(
   command : MenuCommand
);
```

Parameters

command

The **MenuCommand** to add.

Exceptions

Exception Type	Condition
InvalidOperation-Exception	When the **CommandID** of the specified **MenuCommand** is already present on a menu.

Remarks

The **MenuCommands** and **StandardCommands** enumerations contain **CommandID** identifiers for predefined standarard commands and menu commands that are already associated with a location on a particular menu.

> **Note** An attempt to add a menu command with an already existing **CommandID** will throw an **InvalidOperation-Exception**. When adding a menu command, be sure to check that it is not already on a menu using the **FindCommand** method, or use exception handling wisely.

You can attach an event handler to a predefined menu command with the following procedure:

1. If the menu command to link with an event handler has been added to a menu, or is located with the **FindCommand** method, consider whether you wish to restore this menu command later, and whether you want to invoke the current event handler from your new event handler. If your code might restore the menu command or chain the invocation of event handlers, be sure to store a reference to the menu command somewhere.
2. Ensure that any previously existing menu command with the same **CommandID** has been removed from the menu using the **RemoveCommand** method.
3. Create a new **MenuCommand** and specify your event handler in the constructor, along with a **CommandID** representing the command to add. Each standard menu command is associated with a predefined menu location where it is added to. The supported command IDs are defined in the **StandardCommands** and **MenuCommands** enumerations.
4. If you want to invoke any preexisting event handler for the menu command, call the **Invoke** method of the menu command you have replaced on the menu from the event handler that handles the invoke event of your menu command.
5. If you are interested in restoring the event handler of a preexisting menu command that you have replaced, add the stored, preexisting menu command after you remove the replacement menu command you created. You may want to add this behavior to the **Dispose** method for your type.

Requirements

Platforms: Windows 98, Windows NT 4.0, Windows Millennium Edition, Windows 2000, Windows XP Home Edition, Windows XP Professional, Windows Server 2003 family

IMenuCommandService.AddVerb Method

Adds the specified designer verb to the set of global designer verbs.

```
[Visual Basic]
Sub AddVerb( _
   ByVal verb As DesignerVerb _
)
[C#]
void AddVerb(
   DesignerVerb verb
);
[C++]
void AddVerb(
   DesignerVerb* verb
);
[JScript]
function AddVerb(
   verb : DesignerVerb
);
```

Parameters

verb

The **DesignerVerb** to add.

Remarks

Designers of components that provide designer verbs should use the **Verbs** property of their designer rather than calling this method. This method adds a global designer verb that can be accessed from the right-click shortcut menu in design mode regardless of the currently selected component.

Requirements

Platforms: Windows 98, Windows NT 4.0, Windows Millennium Edition, Windows 2000, Windows XP Home Edition, Windows XP Professional, Windows Server 2003 family

IMenuCommandService.FindCommand Method

Searches for the specified command ID and returns the menu command associated with it.

```
[Visual Basic]
Function FindCommand( _
   ByVal commandID As CommandID _
) As MenuCommand
[C#]
MenuCommand FindCommand(
   CommandID commandID
);
[C++]
MenuCommand* FindCommand(
   CommandID* commandID
);
[JScript]
function FindCommand(
   commandID : CommandID
) : MenuCommand;
```

Parameters

commandID

The **CommandID** to search for.

Return Value

The **MenuCommand** associated with the command ID, or a null reference (**Nothing** in Visual Basic) if no command is found.

Requirements

Platforms: Windows 98, Windows NT 4.0, Windows Millennium Edition, Windows 2000, Windows XP Home Edition, Windows XP Professional, Windows Server 2003 family

IMenuCommandService.GlobalInvoke Method

Invokes a menu or designer verb command matching the specified command ID.

```
[Visual Basic]
Function GlobalInvoke( _
   ByVal commandID As CommandID _
) As Boolean
[C#]
bool GlobalInvoke(
   CommandID commandID
);
[C++]
bool GlobalInvoke(
   CommandID* commandID
);
[JScript]
function GlobalInvoke(
   commandID : CommandID
) : Boolean;
```

Parameters

commandID

The **CommandID** of the command to search for and execute.

Return Value

true if the command was found and invoked successfully; otherwise, **false**.

Remarks

This method searches for a menu command or designer verb with a **CommandID** matching the specified **CommandID**. This method first searches within the designer verbs collection consisting of global and active designer-provided verbs before continuing the search, if necessary, through the global environment command service. If a matching menu command or designer verb is located, the command is invoked.

Requirements

Platforms: Windows 98, Windows NT 4.0, Windows Millennium Edition, Windows 2000, Windows XP Home Edition, Windows XP Professional, Windows Server 2003 family

IMenuCommandService.RemoveCommand Method

Removes the specified standard menu command from the menu.

```
[Visual Basic]
Sub RemoveCommand( _
   ByVal command As MenuCommand _
)
[C#]
void RemoveCommand(
   MenuCommand command
);
[C++]
void RemoveCommand(
   MenuCommand* command
);
[JScript]
function RemoveCommand(
   command : MenuCommand
);
```

Parameters

command

The **MenuCommand** to remove.

Remarks

This method removes the specified **MenuCommand** if it is found. This method does not raise an exception or return a value if the specified **MenuCommand** is not found. Use the **FindCommand** method to determine whether a **MenuCommand** matching a specified **CommandID** is located on a menu.

Requirements

Platforms: Windows 98, Windows NT 4.0, Windows Millennium Edition, Windows 2000, Windows XP Home Edition, Windows XP Professional, Windows Server 2003 family

IMenuCommandService.RemoveVerb Method

Removes the specified designer verb from the collection of global designer verbs.

```
[Visual Basic]
Sub RemoveVerb( _
   ByVal verb As DesignerVerb _
)
[C#]
void RemoveVerb(
   DesignerVerb verb
);
[C++]
void RemoveVerb(
   DesignerVerb* verb
);
[JScript]
function RemoveVerb(
   verb : DesignerVerb
);
```

Parameters

verb

The **DesignerVerb** to remove.

Remarks

This method removes the specified global designer verb if it is within the global designer verbs collection. You can add a designer verb to the global designer verbs collection using the **AddVerb** method.

Requirements

Platforms: Windows 98, Windows NT 4.0, Windows Millennium Edition, Windows 2000, Windows XP Home Edition, Windows XP Professional, Windows Server 2003 family

IMenuCommandService.ShowContextMenu Method

Shows the specified shortcut menu at the specified location.

[Visual Basic]
```
Sub ShowContextMenu( _
   ByVal menuID As CommandID, _
   ByVal x As Integer, _
   ByVal y As Integer _
)
```
[C#]
```
void ShowContextMenu(
   CommandID menuID,
   int x,
   int y
);
```
[C++]
```
void ShowContextMenu(
   CommandID* menuID,
   int x,
   int y
);
```
[JScript]
```
function ShowContextMenu(
   menuID : CommandID,
   x : int,
   y : int
);
```

Parameters

menuID
The **CommandID** for the shortcut menu to show.

x
The x-coordinate at which to display the menu, in screen coordinates.

y
The y-coordinate at which to display the menu, in screen coordinates.

Remarks

The **ShowContextMenu** method can display any of the following Visual Studio .NET shortcut menus containing menu commands at a specifed point:

Menu	CommandID
The context menu displayed for a container	**ContainerMenu**
The context menu displayed for the component tray	**ComponentTrayMenu**
The context menu displayed for a selection	**SelectionMenu**
The context menu displayed for a tray selection	**TraySelectionMenu**

This method can also display other registered context menus.

Requirements

Platforms: Windows 98, Windows NT 4.0, Windows Millennium Edition, Windows 2000, Windows XP Home Edition, Windows XP Professional, Windows Server 2003 family

InheritanceService Class

This type supports the .NET Framework infrastructure and is not intended to be used directly from your code.

```
[Visual Basic]
Public Class InheritanceService
   Implements IDisposable
[C#]
public class InheritanceService : IDisposable
[C++]
public __gc class InheritanceService : public IDisposable
[JScript]
public class InheritanceService implements IDisposable
```

InheritanceService Constructor

This member supports the .NET Framework infrastructure and is not intended to be used directly from your code.

```
[Visual Basic]
Public Sub New()
[C#]
public InheritanceService();
[C++]
public: InheritanceService();
[JScript]
public function InheritanceService();
```

InheritanceService.AddInheritedComponents Method

This member supports the .NET Framework infrastructure and is not intended to be used directly from your code.

Overload List

This member supports the .NET Framework infrastructure and is not intended to be used directly from your code.

[Visual Basic] **Overloads Public Overridable Sub AddInheritedComponents(IComponent, IContainer) Implements IInheritanceService.AddInheritedComponents**

[C#] **public virtual void AddInherited-Components(IComponent, IContainer);**

[C++] **public: virtual void AddInherited-Components(IComponent*, IContainer*);**

[JScript] **public function AddInherited-Components(IComponent, IContainer);**

This member supports the .NET Framework infrastructure and is not intended to be used directly from your code.

[Visual Basic] **Overloads Protected Overridable Sub AddInheritedComponents(Type, IComponent, IContainer)**

[C#] **protected virtual void AddInheritedComponents(Type, IComponent, IContainer);**

[C++] **protected: virtual void AddInherited-Components(Type*, IComponent*, IContainer*);**

[JScript] **protected function AddInheritedComponents(Type, IComponent, IContainer);**

InheritanceService.AddInheritedComponents Method (IComponent, IContainer)

This member supports the .NET Framework infrastructure and is not intended to be used directly from your code.

```
[Visual Basic]
Overloads Public Overridable Sub AddInheritedComponents( _
   ByVal component As IComponent, _
   ByVal container As IContainer _
) Implements IInheritanceService.AddInheritedComponents
[C#]
public virtual void AddInheritedComponents(
   IComponent component,
   IContainer container
);
[C++]
public: virtual void AddInheritedComponents(
   IComponent* component,
   IContainer* container
);
[JScript]
public function AddInheritedComponents(
   component : IComponent,
   container : IContainer
);
```

InheritanceService.AddInheritedComponents Method (Type, IComponent, IContainer)

This member supports the .NET Framework infrastructure and is not intended to be used directly from your code.

```
[Visual Basic]
Overloads Protected Overridable Sub AddInheritedComponents( _
   ByVal type As Type, _
   ByVal component As IComponent, _
   ByVal container As IContainer _
)
[C#]
protected virtual void AddInheritedComponents(
   Type type,
   IComponent component,
   IContainer container
);
[C++]
protected: virtual void AddInheritedComponents(
   Type* type,
   IComponent* component,
   IContainer* container
);
[JScript]
protected function AddInheritedComponents(
   type : Type,
   component : IComponent,
   container : IContainer
);
```

InheritanceService.Dispose Method

This member supports the .NET Framework infrastructure and is not intended to be used directly from your code.

[Visual Basic]
```
Public Overridable Sub Dispose() Implements IDisposable.Dispose
```
[C#]
```
public virtual void Dispose();
```
[C++]
```
public: virtual void Dispose();
```
[JScript]
```
public function Dispose();
```

InheritanceService.GetInheritanceAttribute Method

This member supports the .NET Framework infrastructure and is not intended to be used directly from your code.

[Visual Basic]
```
Public Overridable Function GetInheritanceAttribute( _
   ByVal component As IComponent _
) As InheritanceAttribute Implements
IInheritanceService.GetInheritanceAttribute
```
[C#]
```
public virtual InheritanceAttribute GetInheritanceAttribute(
   IComponent component
);
```
[C++]
```
public: virtual InheritanceAttribute* GetInheritanceAttribute(
   IComponent* component
);
```
[JScript]
```
public function GetInheritanceAttribute(
   component : IComponent
) : InheritanceAttribute;
```

InheritanceService.IgnoreInheritedMember Method

This member supports the .NET Framework infrastructure and is not intended to be used directly from your code.

[Visual Basic]
```
Protected Overridable Function IgnoreInheritedMember( _
   ByVal member As MemberInfo, _
   ByVal component As IComponent _
) As Boolean
```
[C#]
```
protected virtual bool IgnoreInheritedMember(
   MemberInfo member,
   IComponent component
);
```
[C++]
```
protected: virtual bool IgnoreInheritedMember(
   MemberInfo* member,
   IComponent* component
);
```
[JScript]
```
protected function IgnoreInheritedMember(
   member : MemberInfo,
   component : IComponent
) : Boolean;
```

IReferenceService Interface

Provides an interface for obtaining references to objects within a project by name or type, obtaining the name of a specified object, and for locating the parent of a specified object within a designer project.

[Visual Basic]
```
Public Interface IReferenceService
```
[C#]
```
public interface IReferenceService
```
[C++]
```
public __gc __interface IReferenceService
```
[JScript]
```
public interface IReferenceService
```

Remarks

The **IReferenceService** interface provides the following methods:

- The **GetReference** method returns the component with the specified name, or a null reference (**Nothing** in Visual Basic) if no component with the specified name was found.
- The **GetName** method returns the name associated with the specified component.
- The **GetComponent** method returns the parent container of the specified component.
- The **GetReferences** method returns an array of references to all project components, or all project components of an optionally specified type.

Example

[Visual Basic, C#] The following example control uses the **GetReferences** method of the **IReferenceService** interface to obtain a list of components in the current design mode project of the type of the currently selected component.

[Visual Basic]
```
Imports System
Imports System.Collections
Imports System.ComponentModel
Imports System.ComponentModel.Design
Imports System.Drawing
Imports System.Data
Imports System.Windows.Forms

Namespace IReferenceServiceExample

    ' This control displays the name and type of the primary selection
    ' component in design mode, if there is one,
    ' and uses the IReferenceService interface to display the names of
    ' any components of the type of the primary selected component.
    ' This control uses the IComponentChangeService to monitor for
    ' selection changed events.
    Public Class IReferenceServiceControl
        Inherits System.Windows.Forms.UserControl
        ' Indicates the name of the type of the selected                ↵
component, or "None selected."
        Private selected_typename As String
        ' Indicates the name of the base type of the selected           ↵
component, or "None selected."
        Private selected_basetypename As String
        ' Indicates the name of the selected component.
        Private selected_componentname As String
        ' Contains the names of components of the type of the selected
        ' component in design mode.
        Private typeComponents() As String
        ' Contains the names of components of the base type of          ↵
the selected component in design mode.
        Private basetypeComponents() As String
        ' Reference to the IComponentChangeService for the              ↵
current component.
        Private selectionService As ISelectionService

        Public Sub New()
            ' Initializes the control properties.
            Me.BackColor = Color.White
            Me.SetStyle(ControlStyles.ResizeRedraw, True)
            Me.Name = "IReferenceServiceControl"
            Me.Size = New System.Drawing.Size(500, 250)
            ' Initializes the data properties.
            typeComponents = New String(0) {}
            basetypeComponents = New String(0) {}
            selected_typename = "None selected."
            selected_basetypename = "None selected."
            selected_componentname = "None selected."
            selectionService = Nothing
        End Sub

        ' Registers and unregisters design-mode services when
        ' the component is sited and unsited.
        Public Overrides Property Site() As System.ComponentModel.ISite
            Get
                ' Returns the site for the control.
                Return MyBase.Site
            End Get
            Set(ByVal Value As System.ComponentModel.ISite)
                ' The site is set to null when a component is cut or
                ' removed from a design-mode site.

                ' If an event handler has already been linked with
                ' an ISelectionService, remove the handler.
                If Not (selectionService Is Nothing) Then
                    RemoveHandler                                       ↵
selectionService.SelectionChanged, AddressOf Me.OnSelectionChanged
                End If

                ' Sites the control.
                MyBase.Site = Value

                ' Obtains an ISelectionService interface to register
                ' the selection changed event handler with.
                selectionService =                                      ↵
CType(Me.GetService(GetType(ISelectionService)), ISelectionService)
                If Not (selectionService Is Nothing) Then
                    AddHandler                                          ↵
selectionService.SelectionChanged, AddressOf Me.OnSelectionChanged
                    ' Updates the display for the current               ↵
selection, if any.
                    DisplayComponentsOfSelectedComponentType()
                End If
            End Set
        End Property

        ' Updates the display according to the primary                  ↵
selected component,
        ' if any, and the names of design-mode components that the
        ' IReferenceService returns references for when queried for
        ' references to components of the primary selected component's
        ' type and base type.
        Private Sub DisplayComponentsOfSelectedComponentType()
            ' If a component is selected...
            If Not (selectionService.PrimarySelection Is Nothing) Then
                ' Sets the selected type name and selected              ↵
 component name
                ' to the type and name of the primary                   ↵
selected component.
                selected_typename =                                     ↵
selectionService.PrimarySelection.GetType().FullName
                selected_basetypename =                                 ↵
selectionService.PrimarySelection.GetType().BaseType.FullName
                selected_componentname =                                ↵
CType(selectionService.PrimarySelection, IComponent).Site.Name
```

```
            ' Obtain an IReferenceService and obtain references to
            ' each component in the design-mode project.
            ' of the selected component's type and base type.
            Dim rs As IReferenceService =                          ↵
CType(Me.GetService(GetType(IReferenceService)), IReferenceService)
            If Not (rs Is Nothing) Then
                ' Get references to design-mode components of the
                ' primary selected component's type.
                Dim comps As Object() =                            ↵
CType(rs.GetReferences                                             ↵
 (selectionService.PrimarySelection.GetType()), Object())
                typeComponents = New String(comps.Length) {}
                Dim i As Integer
                For i = 0 To comps.Length - 1
                    typeComponents(i) = CType(comps(i),            ↵
IComponent).Site.Name
                Next i
                ' Get references to design-mode components         ↵
with a base type
                ' of the primary selected component's base type.
                comps =                                            ↵
CType(rs.GetReferences                                             ↵
 (selectionService.PrimarySelection.GetType().BaseType), Object())
                basetypeComponents = New String(comps.Length) {}
                For i = 0 To comps.Length - 1
                    basetypeComponents(i) = CType(comps(i),        ↵
IComponent).Site.Name
                Next i
            End If
        Else
            selected_typename = "None selected."
            selected_basetypename = "None selected."
            selected_componentname = "None selected."
            typeComponents = New String(0) {}
            basetypeComponents = New String(0) {}
        End If
        Me.Refresh()
    End Sub 'DisplayComponentsOfSelectedComponentType

    Private Sub OnSelectionChanged(ByVal sender As Object,         ↵
ByVal e As EventArgs)
        DisplayComponentsOfSelectedComponentType()
    End Sub 'OnSelectionChanged

    Protected Overrides Sub OnPaint(ByVal e As                     ↵
System.Windows.Forms.PaintEventArgs)
        e.Graphics.DrawString("IReferenceService Example           ↵
Control", New Font(FontFamily.GenericMonospace, 9), New            ↵
SolidBrush(Color.Blue), 5, 5)

        e.Graphics.DrawString("Primary Selected Component          ↵
from IComponentChangeService:", New Font                           ↵
 (FontFamily.GenericMonospace, 8), New SolidBrush(Color.Red), 5, 20)
        e.Graphics.DrawString("Name:      " +                      ↵
selected_componentname, New Font(FontFamily.GenericMonospace,      ↵
 8), New SolidBrush(Color.Black), 10, 32)
        e.Graphics.DrawString("Type:      " +                      ↵
selected_typename, New Font(FontFamily.GenericMonospace, 8),       ↵
New SolidBrush(Color.Black), 10, 44)
        e.Graphics.DrawString("Base Type: " +                      ↵
selected_basetypename, New Font(FontFamily.GenericMonospace, 8),   ↵
 New SolidBrush(Color.Black), 10, 56)
        e.Graphics.DrawLine(New Pen(New SolidBrush                 ↵
 (Color.Black), 1), 5, 77, Me.Width - 10, 77)

        e.Graphics.DrawString("Components of Type from             ↵
IReferenceService:", New Font(FontFamily.GenericMonospace, 8),     ↵
 New SolidBrush(Color.Red), 5, 85)
        If selected_typename <> "None selected." Then
            Dim i As Integer
            For i = 0 To typeComponents.Length - 1
                e.Graphics.DrawString(typeComponents(i), New       ↵
Font(FontFamily.GenericMonospace, 8), New SolidBrush               ↵
 (Color.Black), 20, 97 + i * 12)
            Next i
        End If
        e.Graphics.DrawString("Components of Base Type from        ↵
IReferenceService:", New Font(FontFamily.GenericMonospace, 8),     ↵
New SolidBrush(Color.Red), 5, 109 + typeComponents.Length * 12)
        If selected_typename <> "None selected." Then
            Dim i As Integer
            For i = 0 To basetypeComponents.Length - 1
                e.Graphics.DrawString(basetypeComponents(i),       ↵
 New Font(FontFamily.GenericMonospace, 8), New SolidBrush          ↵
 (Color.Black), 20, 121 + typeComponents.Length * 12 + i * 12)
            Next i
        End If
    End Sub 'OnPaint

End Class 'IReferenceServiceControl
End Namespace 'IReferenceServiceExample
```

[C#]

```
using System;
using System.Collections;
using System.ComponentModel;
using System.ComponentModel.Design;
using System.Drawing;
using System.Data;
using System.Windows.Forms;

namespace IReferenceServiceExample
{
    // This control displays the name and type of the primary selection
    // component in design mode, if there is one,
    // and uses the IReferenceService interface to display the names of
    // any components of the type of the primary selected component.
    // This control uses the IComponentChangeService to monitor for
    // selection changed events.
    public class IReferenceServiceControl :                        ↵
System.Windows.Forms.UserControl
    {
        // Indicates the name of the type of the selected          ↵
component, or "None selected.".
        private string selected_typename;
        // Indicates the name of the base type of the              ↵
selected component, or "None selected."
        private string selected_basetypename;
        // Indicates the name of the selected component.
        private string selected_componentname;
        // Contains the names of components of the type of         ↵
the selected
        // component in design mode.
        private string[] typeComponents;
        // Contains the names of components of the base type       ↵
 of the selected component in design mode.
        private string[] basetypeComponents;
        // Reference to the IComponentChangeService for the        ↵
 current component.
        private ISelectionService selectionService;

        public IReferenceServiceControl()
        {
            // Initializes the control properties.
            this.BackColor = Color.White;
            this.SetStyle(ControlStyles.ResizeRedraw, true);
            this.Name = "IReferenceServiceControl";
            this.Size = new System.Drawing.Size(500, 250);
            // Initializes the data properties.
            typeComponents = new string[0];
            basetypeComponents = new string[0];
            selected_typename = "None selected.";
            selected_basetypename = "None selected.";
            selected_componentname = "None selected.";
            selectionService = null;
        }

        // Registers and unregisters design-mode services when
        // the component is sited and unsited.
        public override System.ComponentModel.ISite Site
```

```
            {
                get
                {
                    // Returns the site for the control.
                    return base.Site;
                }
                set
                {
                    // The site is set to null when a component         ↵
is cut or
                    // removed from a design-mode site.

                    // If an event handler has already been linked with
                    // an ISelectionService, remove the handler.
                    if(selectionService != null)
                        selectionService.SelectionChanged -= new        ↵
EventHandler(this.OnSelectionChanged);

                    // Sites the control.
                    base.Site = value;

                    // Obtains an ISelectionService interface           ↵
to register
                    // the selection changed event handler with.
                    selectionService =                                  ↵
 (ISelectionService)this.GetService(typeof(ISelectionService));
                    if( selectionService!= null )
                    {
                        selectionService.SelectionChanged +=            ↵
 new EventHandler(this.OnSelectionChanged);
                        // Updates the display for the                  ↵
 current selection, if any.
                        DisplayComponentsOfSelectedComponentType();
                    }
                }
            }

            // Updates the display according to the primary             ↵
 selected component,
            // if any, and the names of design-mode components that the
            // IReferenceService returns references for when           ↵
queried for
            // references to components of the primary selected        ↵
component's
            // type and base type.
            private void DisplayComponentsOfSelectedComponentType()
            {
                // If a component is selected...
                if( selectionService.PrimarySelection != null )
                {
                    // Sets the selected type name and selected         ↵
component name to the type and name of the primary selected component.
                    selected_typename =                                 ↵
selectionService.PrimarySelection.GetType().FullName;
                    selected_basetypename =                             ↵
selectionService.PrimarySelection.GetType().BaseType.FullName;
                    selected_componentname =                            ↵
 ((IComponent)selectionService.PrimarySelection).Site.Name;

                    // Obtain an IReferenceService and obtain           ↵
references to
                    // each component in the design-mode project
                    // of the selected component's type and base type.
                    IReferenceService rs =                              ↵
 (IReferenceService)this.GetService(typeof(IReferenceService));
                    if( rs != null )
                    {
                        // Get references to design-mode                ↵
components of the
                        // primary selected component's type.
                        object[] comps =                                ↵
 (object[])rs.GetReferences(                                            ↵
selectionService.PrimarySelection.GetType() );
                        typeComponents = new string[comps.Length];
                        for(int i=0; i<comps.Length; i++)
                            typeComponents[i] =                         ↵
 ((IComponent)comps[i]).Site.Name;

                        // Get references to design-mode                ↵
 components with a base type
                        // of the primary selected component's          ↵
base type.
                        comps = (object[])rs.GetReferences(             ↵
selectionService.PrimarySelection.GetType().BaseType );
                        basetypeComponents = new string[comps.Length];
                        for(int i=0; i<comps.Length; i++)
                            basetypeComponents[i] =                     ↵
 ((IComponent)comps[i]).Site.Name;
                    }
                }
                else
                {
                    selected_typename = "None selected.";
                    selected_basetypename = "None selected.";
                    selected_componentname = "None selected.";
                    typeComponents = new string[0];
                    basetypeComponents = new string[0];
                }
                this.Refresh();
            }

            private void OnSelectionChanged(object sender, EventArgs e)
            {
                DisplayComponentsOfSelectedComponentType();
            }

            protected override void
OnPaint(System.Windows.Forms.PaintEventArgs e)
            {
                e.Graphics.DrawString("IReferenceService                ↵
Example Control", new Font(FontFamily.GenericMonospace, 9),             ↵
 new SolidBrush(Color.Blue), 5, 5);

                e.Graphics.DrawString("Primary Selected                 ↵
Component from IComponentChangeService:", new                           ↵
Font(FontFamily.GenericMonospace, 8), new SolidBrush                    ↵
 (Color.Red), 5, 20);
                e.Graphics.DrawString("Name:                            ↵
"+selected_componentname, new Font(FontFamily.GenericMonospace,         ↵
 8), new SolidBrush(Color.Black), 10, 32);
                e.Graphics.DrawString("Type:                            ↵
"+selected_typename, new Font(FontFamily.GenericMonospace, 8),          ↵
new SolidBrush(Color.Black), 10, 44);
                e.Graphics.DrawString("Base Type:                       ↵
"+selected_basetypename, new Font(FontFamily.GenericMonospace,          ↵
 8), new SolidBrush(Color.Black), 10, 56);
                e.Graphics.DrawLine(new Pen(new                         ↵
SolidBrush(Color.Black), 1), 5, 77, this.Width-5, 77);

                e.Graphics.DrawString("Components of Type               ↵
from IReferenceService:", new Font                                      ↵
 (FontFamily.GenericMonospace, 8), new SolidBrush(Color.Red),           ↵
 5, 85);
                if( selected_typename != "None selected." )
                    for(int i=0; i<typeComponents.Length; i++)
                        e.Graphics.DrawString                           ↵
 (typeComponents[i], new Font(FontFamily.GenericMonospace, 8),          ↵
new SolidBrush(Color.Black), 20, 97+(i*12));

                e.Graphics.DrawString("Components of Base Type          ↵
from IReferenceService:", new Font(FontFamily.GenericMonospace,         ↵
 8), new SolidBrush(Color.Red), 5, 109+(typeComponents.Length*12));
                if( selected_typename != "None selected." )
                    for(int i=0; i<basetypeComponents.Length; i++)
                        e.Graphics.DrawString                           ↵
 (basetypeComponents[i], new Font(FontFamily.GenericMonospace,          ↵
 8), new SolidBrush(Color.Black), 20,
121+(typeComponents.Length*12)+(i*12));
            }
        }
}
```

Requirements

Namespace: System.ComponentModel.Design

Platforms: Windows 98, Windows NT 4.0, Windows Millennium Edition, Windows 2000, Windows XP Home Edition, Windows XP Professional, Windows Server 2003 family

Assembly: System (in System.dll)

IReferenceService.GetComponent Method

Gets the component that contains the specified component.

```
[Visual Basic]
Function GetComponent( _
   ByVal reference As Object _
) As IComponent
[C#]
IComponent GetComponent(
   object reference
);
[C++]
IComponent* GetComponent(
   Object* reference
);
[JScript]
function GetComponent(
   reference : Object
) : IComponent;
```

Parameters

reference
: The object to retrieve the parent component for.

Return Value

The base **IComponent** that contains the specified object, or a null reference (**Nothing** in Visual Basic) if no parent component exists.

Requirements

Platforms: Windows 98, Windows NT 4.0, Windows Millennium Edition, Windows 2000, Windows XP Home Edition, Windows XP Professional, Windows Server 2003 family

IReferenceService.GetName Method

Gets the name of the specified component.

```
[Visual Basic]
Function GetName( _
   ByVal reference As Object _
) As String
[C#]
string GetName(
   object reference
);
[C++]
String* GetName(
   Object* reference
);
[JScript]
function GetName(
   reference : Object
) : String;
```

Parameters

reference
: The object to return the name of.

Return Value

The name of the object referenced, or a null reference (**Nothing** in Visual Basic) if the object reference is not valid.

Remarks

The name of each component sited in a design time project is set in the **Name** property of the **ISite** where the component is sited.

Requirements

Platforms: Windows 98, Windows NT 4.0, Windows Millennium Edition, Windows 2000, Windows XP Home Edition, Windows XP Professional, Windows Server 2003 family

IReferenceService.GetReference Method

Gets a reference to the component whose name matches the specified name.

```
[Visual Basic]
Function GetReference( _
   ByVal name As String _
) As Object
[C#]
object GetReference(
   string name
);
[C++]
Object* GetReference(
   String* name
);
[JScript]
function GetReference(
   name : String
) : Object;
```

Parameters

name
: The name of the component to return a reference to.

Return Value

An object the specified name refers to, or a null reference (**Nothing** in Visual Basic) if no reference is found.

Requirements

Platforms: Windows 98, Windows NT 4.0, Windows Millennium Edition, Windows 2000, Windows XP Home Edition, Windows XP Professional, Windows Server 2003 family

IReferenceService.GetReferences Method

Gets all available references to project components.

Overload List

Gets all available references to project components.

[Visual Basic] **Overloads Function GetReferences() As Object()**

[C#] **object[] GetReferences();**

[C++] **Object* GetReferences() __gc[];**

[JScript] **function GetReferences() : Object[];**

Gets all available references to components of the specified type.

[Visual Basic] **Overloads Function GetReferences(Type) As Object()**

[C#] **object[] GetReferences(Type);**

[C++] **Object* GetReferences(Type*) __gc[];**

[JScript] **function GetReferences(Type) : Object[];**

IReferenceService.GetReferences Method ()

Gets all available references to project components.

```
[Visual Basic]
Function GetReferences() As Object()
[C#]
object[] GetReferences();
[C++]
Object* GetReferences() __gc[];
[JScript]
function GetReferences() : Object[];
```

Return Value

An array of all objects with references available to the **IReferenceService**.

Requirements

Platforms: Windows 98, Windows NT 4.0, Windows Millennium Edition, Windows 2000, Windows XP Home Edition, Windows XP Professional, Windows Server 2003 family

IReferenceService.GetReferences Method (Type)

Gets all available references to components of the specified type.

```
[Visual Basic]
Function GetReferences( _
   ByVal baseType As Type _
) As Object()
[C#]
object[] GetReferences(
   Type baseType
);
[C++]
Object* GetReferences(
   Type* baseType
) __gc[];
[JScript]
function GetReferences(
   baseType : Type
) : Object[];
```

Parameters

baseType

The type of object to return references to instances of.

Return Value

An array of all available objects of the specified type.

Requirements

Platforms: Windows 98, Windows NT 4.0, Windows Millennium Edition, Windows 2000, Windows XP Home Edition, Windows XP Professional, Windows Server 2003 family

IResourceService Interface

Provides an interface for designers to access resource readers and writers for specific **CultureInfo** resource types.

[Visual Basic]
```
Public Interface IResourceService
```
[C#]
```
public interface IResourceService
```
[C++]
```
public __gc __interface IResourceService
```
[JScript]
```
public interface IResourceService
```

Remarks

A resource writer or resource reader can be used to serialize or deserialze objects or data according to the specified **CultureInfo** resource settings.

Example

[Visual Basic, C#] The following example demonstrates a designer that uses the **IResourceService** to read from and write to resource files in order to configure a property of an associated control.

[Visual Basic]
```
Imports System
Imports System.Collections
Imports System.ComponentModel
Imports System.ComponentModel.Design
Imports System.Drawing
Imports System.Globalization
Imports System.Resources
Imports System.Windows.Forms
Imports System.Windows.Forms.Design

Namespace IResourceServiceExample

    ' Associates the ResourceTestControlDesigner with the
    ' ResourceTestControl class.
    <Designer(GetType(ResourceTestControlDesigner))> _
    Public Class ResourceTestControl
        Inherits System.Windows.Forms.UserControl
        ' Initializes a string array used to store strings that ↵
this control displays.
        Public resource_strings() As String = {"Initial Default ↵
String #1", "Initial Default String #2"}

        Public Sub New()
            Me.BackColor = Color.White
            Me.Size = New Size(408, 160)
        End Sub

        ' Draws the strings contained in the string array.
        Protected Overrides Sub OnPaint(ByVal e As ↵
System.Windows.Forms.PaintEventArgs)
            e.Graphics.DrawString("IResourceService Example ↵
Designer Control", New Font(FontFamily.GenericMonospace, 10), ↵
 New SolidBrush(Color.Blue), 2, 2)
            e.Graphics.DrawString("String list:  (use shortcut ↵
menu in design mode)", New Font(FontFamily.GenericMonospace, 8), ↵
 New SolidBrush(Color.Black), 2, 20)

            Dim i As Integer
            For i = 0 To resource_strings.Length - 1
                e.Graphics.DrawString(resource_strings(i), New ↵
Font(FontFamily.GenericMonospace, 8), New SolidBrush ↵
 (Color.SeaGreen), 2, 38 + (i * 18))
            Next i
        End Sub
    End Class
    _
    ' This designer offers several menu commands for the
    ' shortcut menu for the associated control.
    ' These commands can be used to reset the control's string
    ' list, to generate a default resources file, or to load the string
    ' list for the control from the default resources file.
    Public Class ResourceTestControlDesigner
        Inherits System.Windows.Forms.Design.ControlDesigner

        Public Sub New()
        End Sub

        Public Overrides ReadOnly Property Verbs() As ↵
System.ComponentModel.Design.DesignerVerbCollection
            Get
                ' Creates a collection of designer verb menu commands
                ' that link to event handlers in this designer.
                Return New DesignerVerbCollection(New ↵
DesignerVerb() { _
                        New DesignerVerb("Load Strings From ↵
Default Resources File", AddressOf Me.LoadResources), _
                        New DesignerVerb("Create Default Resources ↵
 File", AddressOf Me.CreateResources), _
                        New DesignerVerb("Clear ResourceTestControl ↵
 String List", AddressOf Me.ClearStrings)})
            End Get
        End Property

        ' Sets the string list for the control to the strings
        ' loaded from a resource file.
        Private Sub LoadResources(ByVal sender As Object, ↵
 ByVal e As EventArgs)
            Dim rs As IResourceService = ↵
CType(Me.Component.Site.GetService(GetType(IResourceService)), ↵
IResourceService)
            If rs Is Nothing Then
                Throw New Exception("Could not obtain ↵
IResourceService.")
            End If
            Dim rr As IResourceReader = ↵
rs.GetResourceReader(CultureInfo.CurrentUICulture)
            If rr Is Nothing Then
                Throw New Exception("Resource file could ↵
 not be obtained. You may need to create one first.")
            End If
            Dim de As IDictionaryEnumerator = rr.GetEnumerator()

            If Me.Control.GetType() Is ↵
GetType(ResourceTestControl) Then
                Dim rtc As ResourceTestControl = ↵
 CType(Me.Control, ResourceTestControl)
                Dim s1, s2, s3 As String
                de.MoveNext()
                s1 = CStr(CType(de.Current, DictionaryEntry).Value)
                de.MoveNext()
                s2 = CStr(CType(de.Current, DictionaryEntry).Value)
                de.MoveNext()
                s3 = CStr(CType(de.Current, DictionaryEntry).Value)
                de.MoveNext()
                rtc.resource_strings = New String() {s1, s2, s3}
                Me.Control.Refresh()
            End If
        End Sub

        ' Creates a default resource file for the current
        ' CultureInfo and adds 3 strings to it.
        Private Sub CreateResources(ByVal sender As Object, ↵
 ByVal e As EventArgs)
            Dim rs As IResourceService = ↵
CType(Me.Component.Site.GetService(GetType(IResourceService)), ↵
IResourceService)
            If rs Is Nothing Then
                Throw New Exception("Could not obtain ↵
IResourceService.")
            End If
            Dim rw As IResourceWriter = ↵
```

```
rs.GetResourceWriter(CultureInfo.CurrentUICulture)
            rw.AddResource("string1", "Persisted resource string #1")
            rw.AddResource("string2", "Persisted resource string #2")
            rw.AddResource("string3", "Persisted resource string #3")
            rw.Generate()
            rw.Close()
        End Sub

        ' Clears the string list of the associated ResourceTestControl.
        Private Sub ClearStrings(ByVal sender As Object, ByVal ↵
 e As EventArgs)
            If Me.Control.GetType() Is GetType ↵
 (ResourceTestControl) Then
                Dim rtc As ResourceTestControl = CType ↵
 (Me.Control, ResourceTestControl)
                rtc.resource_strings = New String() ↵
{"Test String #1", "Test String #2"}
                Me.Control.Refresh()
            End If
        End Sub
    End Class
End Namespace
```

[C#]

```
using System;
using System.Collections;
using System.ComponentModel;
using System.ComponentModel.Design;
using System.Drawing;
using System.Globalization;
using System.Resources;
using System.Windows.Forms;
using System.Windows.Forms.Design;

namespace IResourceServiceExample
{
    // Associates the ResourceTestControlDesigner with the
    // ResourceTestControl class.
    [Designer(typeof(ResourceTestControlDesigner))]
    public class ResourceTestControl : System.Windows.Forms.UserControl
    {
        // Initializes a string array used to store strings that
        // this control displays.
        public string[] resource_strings = new string[] ↵
{ "Initial Default String #1", "Initial Default String #2" };

        public ResourceTestControl()
        {
            this.BackColor = Color.White;
            this.Size = new Size(408, 160);
        }

        // Draws the strings contained in the string array.
        protected override void ↵
OnPaint(System.Windows.Forms.PaintEventArgs e)
        {
            e.Graphics.DrawString("IResourceService Example ↵
 Designer Control", new Font(FontFamily.GenericMonospace, 10), ↵
 new SolidBrush(Color.Blue), 2, 2);
            e.Graphics.DrawString("String list:  (use shortcut ↵
 menu in design mode)", new Font(FontFamily.GenericMonospace, ↵
 8), new SolidBrush(Color.Black), 2, 20);

            for(int i=0; i<resource_strings.Length; i++)
            {
                e.Graphics.DrawString(resource_strings[i], ↵
 new Font(FontFamily.GenericMonospace, 8), new ↵
SolidBrush(Color.SeaGreen), 2, 38+(i*18));
            }
        }
    }

    // This designer offers several menu commands for the
    // shortcut menu for the associated control.
    // These commands can be used to reset the control's string
    // list, to generate a default resources file, or to ↵
load the string
    // list for the control from the default resources file.
    public class ResourceTestControlDesigner : ↵
System.Windows.Forms.Design.ControlDesigner
    {
        public ResourceTestControlDesigner()
        {}

        public override ↵
System.ComponentModel.Design.DesignerVerbCollection Verbs
        {
            get
            {
                // Creates a collection of designer verb menu commands
                // that link to event handlers in this designer.
                return new DesignerVerbCollection( new DesignerVerb[] {
                    new DesignerVerb("Load Strings from Default ↵
Resources File", new EventHandler(this.LoadResources)),
                    new DesignerVerb("Create Default Resources ↵
File", new EventHandler(this.CreateResources)),
                    new DesignerVerb("Clear ResourceTestControl ↵
 String List", new EventHandler(this.ClearStrings)) });
            }
        }

        // Sets the string list for the control to the strings
        // loaded from a resource file.
        private void LoadResources(object sender, EventArgs e)
        {
            IResourceService rs = ↵
 (IResourceService)this.Component.Site.GetService ↵
 (typeof(IResourceService));
            if( rs == null )
                throw new Exception("Could not obtain ↵
IResourceService.");

            IResourceReader rr = ↵
rs.GetResourceReader(CultureInfo.CurrentUICulture);
            if( rr == null )
                throw new Exception("Resource file ↵
could not be obtained. You may need to create one first.");

            IDictionaryEnumerator de = rr.GetEnumerator();

            if(this.Control.GetType() == typeof(ResourceTestControl))
            {
                ResourceTestControl rtc = ↵
 (ResourceTestControl)this.Control;
                string s1, s2, s3;
                de.MoveNext();
                s1 = (string)((DictionaryEntry)de.Current).Value;
                de.MoveNext();
                s2 = (string)((DictionaryEntry)de.Current).Value;
                de.MoveNext();
                s3 = (string)((DictionaryEntry)de.Current).Value;
                de.MoveNext();
                rtc.resource_strings = new string[] {s1, s2, s3};
                this.Control.Refresh();
            }

        }

        // Creates a default resource file for the current
        // CultureInfo and adds 3 strings to it.
        private void CreateResources(object sender, EventArgs e)
        {
            IResourceService rs = ↵
 (IResourceService)this.Component.Site.GetService ↵
 (typeof(IResourceService));
            if( rs == null )
                throw new Exception("Could not obtain ↵
IResourceService.");
```

```
            IResourceWriter rw =                                    ↵
rs.GetResourceWriter(CultureInfo.CurrentUICulture);
            rw.AddResource("string1", "Persisted resource string #1");
            rw.AddResource("string2", "Persisted resource string #2");
            rw.AddResource("string3", "Persisted resource string #3");
            rw.Generate();
            rw.Close();
        }

        // Clears the string list of the associated                 ↵
ResourceTestControl.
        private void ClearStrings(object sender, EventArgs e)
        {
            if(this.Control.GetType() == typeof(ResourceTestControl))
            {
                ResourceTestControl rtc =                           ↵
(ResourceTestControl)this.Control;
                rtc.resource_strings = new string[]                 ↵
{ "Test String #1", "Test String #2" };
                this.Control.Refresh();
            }
        }
    }
}
```

Requirements

Namespace: System.ComponentModel.Design

Platforms: Windows 98, Windows NT 4.0, Windows Millennium Edition, Windows 2000, Windows XP Home Edition, Windows XP Professional, Windows Server 2003 family

Assembly: System (in System.dll)

IResourceService.GetResourceReader Method

Locates the resource reader for the specified culture and returns it.

[Visual Basic]
```
Function GetResourceReader( _
   ByVal info As CultureInfo _
) As IResourceReader
```
[C#]
```
IResourceReader GetResourceReader(
   CultureInfo info
);
```
[C++]
```
IResourceReader* GetResourceReader(
   CultureInfo* info
);
```
[JScript]
```
function GetResourceReader(
   info : CultureInfo
) : IResourceReader;
```

Parameters

info

The **CultureInfo** of the resource for which to retrieve a resource reader.

Return Value

An **IResourceReader** interface that contains the resources for the culture, or a null reference (**Nothing** in Visual Basic) if no resources for the culture exist.

Remarks

If no resources are associated with the designer for the specified culture, this method returns a null reference (**Nothing** in Visual Basic).

Requirements

Platforms: Windows 98, Windows NT 4.0, Windows Millennium Edition, Windows 2000, Windows XP Home Edition, Windows XP Professional, Windows Server 2003 family

IResourceService.GetResourceWriter Method

Locates the resource writer for the specified culture and returns it.

[Visual Basic]
```
Function GetResourceWriter( _
   ByVal info As CultureInfo _
) As IResourceWriter
```
[C#]
```
IResourceWriter GetResourceWriter(
   CultureInfo info
);
```
[C++]
```
IResourceWriter* GetResourceWriter(
   CultureInfo* info
);
```
[JScript]
```
function GetResourceWriter(
   info : CultureInfo
) : IResourceWriter;
```

Parameters

info

The **CultureInfo** of the resource for which to create a resource writer.

Return Value

An **IResourceWriter** interface for the specified culture.

Remarks

This method creates a new resource for the specified culture and destroys an existing resource, if one already exists.

Requirements

Platforms: Windows 98, Windows NT 4.0, Windows Millennium Edition, Windows 2000, Windows XP Home Edition, Windows XP Professional, Windows Server 2003 family

IRootDesigner Interface

Provides support for root-level designer view technologies.

[Visual Basic]
```
<ComVisible(True)>
Public Interface IRootDesigner
   Inherits IDesigner, IDisposable
```
[C#]
```
[ComVisible(true)]
public interface IRootDesigner : IDesigner, IDisposable
```
[C++]
```
[ComVisible(true)]
public __gc __interface IRootDesigner : public IDesigner,
   IDisposable
```
[JScript]
```
public
   ComVisible(true)
interface IRootDesigner implements IDesigner, IDisposable
```

Classes that Implement IRootDesigner

Class	Description
ComponentDocument-Designer	Base designer class for extending the design mode behavior of a root design document that supports nested components.
DocumentDesigner	Base designer class for extending the design mode behavior of, and providing a root-level design mode view for, a **Control** that supports nested controls and should receive scroll messages.

Remarks

A root designer is the designer that is in the top position, or root, of the current design-time document object hierarchy. A root designer must implement the **IRootDesigner** interface. A root designer typically manages the background view in designer view mode, and usually displays the controls within the base container of the current design time project.

Example

[Visual Basic, C#] The following example demonstrates a **IRootDesigner** implementation associated with a sample user control. This **IRootDesigner** implementation displays a control for the background view in designer view by overriding the **GetView** method. To use this example, add the source code to a project and show the RootViewSampleComponent in designer view to display the custom root designer view.

[Visual Basic]
```
Imports System
Imports System.Collections
Imports System.ComponentModel
Imports System.ComponentModel.Design
Imports System.Diagnostics
Imports System.Drawing
Imports System.Windows.Forms
Imports System.Windows.Forms.Design

Namespace SampleRootDesigner

    ' This sample demonstrates how to provide the root designer ↵
 view, or
    ' design mode background view, by overriding ↵
IRootDesigner.GetView().

    ' This sample component inherits from RootDesignedComponent which
    ' uses the SampleRootDesigner.
    Public Class RootViewSampleComponent
        Inherits RootDesignedComponent

        Public Sub New()
        End Sub

    End Class

    ' The following attribute associates the ↵
SampleRootDesigner designer
    ' with the SampleComponent component.
    <Designer(GetType(SampleRootDesigner), GetType(IRootDesigner))> _
    Public Class RootDesignedComponent
        Inherits Component

        Public Sub New()
        End Sub

    End Class

    Public Class SampleRootDesigner
        Inherits ComponentDesigner
        Implements IRootDesigner

        ' Member field of custom type RootDesignerView, a control that
        ' will be shown in the Forms designer view. This member is
        ' cached to reduce processing needed to recreate the
        ' view control on each call to GetView().
        Private m_view As RootDesignerView

        ' This method returns an instance of the view for this root
        ' designer. The "view" is the user interface that is presented
        ' in a document window for the user to manipulate.
        Function GetView(ByVal technology As ViewTechnology) ↵
As Object Implements IRootDesigner.GetView
            If Not technology = ViewTechnology.WindowsForms Then
                Throw New ArgumentException("Not a supported ↵
 view technology", "technology")
            End If
            If m_view Is Nothing Then
                ' Some type of displayable Form or control is ↵
 required for a root designer that overrides
                ' GetView(). In this example, a Control of ↵
type RootDesignerView is used.
                ' Any class that inherits from Control will work.
                m_view = New RootDesignerView(Me)
            End If
            Return m_view
        End Function

        ' IRootDesigner.SupportedTechnologies is a required ↵
 override for an
        ' IRootDesigner. WindowsForms is the view technology ↵
 used by this designer.
        ReadOnly Property SupportedTechnologies() As ↵
ViewTechnology() Implements IRootDesigner.SupportedTechnologies
            Get
                Return New ViewTechnology() ↵
{ViewTechnology.WindowsForms}
            End Get
        End Property

        ' RootDesignerView is a simple control that will be displayed
        ' in the designer window.
        Private Class RootDesignerView
            Inherits Control
            Private m_designer As SampleRootDesigner

            Public Sub New(ByVal designer As SampleRootDesigner)
                m_designer = designer
```

```
            BackColor = Color.Blue
            Font = New Font(Font.FontFamily.Name, 24.0F)
        End Sub

        Protected Overrides Sub OnPaint(ByVal pe As PaintEventArgs)
            MyBase.OnPaint(pe)
            ' Draws the name of the component in large letters.
            Dim rf As New RectangleF(ClientRectangle.X, ↵
ClientRectangle.Y, ClientRectangle.Width, ClientRectangle.Height)
            pe.Graphics.DrawString ↵
 (m_designer.Component.Site.Name, Font, Brushes.Yellow, rf)
        End Sub

    End Class
  End Class

End Namespace
```

[C#]

```
using System;
using System.Collections;
using System.ComponentModel;
using System.ComponentModel.Design;
using System.Diagnostics;
using System.Drawing;
using System.Windows.Forms;
using System.Windows.Forms.Design;

namespace SampleRootDesigner
{
    // This sample demonstrates how to provide the root ↵
 designer view, or
    // design mode background view, by overriding ↵
IRootDesigner.GetView().

    // This sample component inherits from RootDesignedComponent which
    // uses the SampleRootDesigner.
    public class RootViewSampleComponent : RootDesignedComponent
    {
        public RootViewSampleComponent()
        {
        }
    }

    // The following attribute associates the ↵
SampleRootDesigner designer
    // with the SampleComponent component.
    [Designer(typeof(SampleRootDesigner), typeof(IRootDesigner))]
    public class RootDesignedComponent : Component
    {
        public RootDesignedComponent()
        {
        }
    }

    public class SampleRootDesigner : ComponentDesigner, IRootDesigner
    {
        // Member field of custom type RootDesignerView, a control that
        // will be shown in the Forms designer view. This member is
        // cached to reduce processing needed to recreate the
        // view control on each call to GetView().
        private RootDesignerView m_view;

        // This method returns an instance of the view for this root
        // designer. The "view" is the user interface that is presented
        // in a document window for the user to manipulate.
        object IRootDesigner.GetView(ViewTechnology technology)
        {
            if (technology != ViewTechnology.WindowsForms)
            {
                throw new ArgumentException("Not a ↵
 supported view technology", "technology");
            }
            if (m_view == null)
            {
                // Some type of displayable Form or ↵
control is required
                // for a root designer that overrides ↵
 GetView(). In this
                // example, a Control of type ↵
 RootDesignerView is used.
                // Any class that inherits from Control will work.
                m_view = new RootDesignerView(this);
            }
            return m_view;
        }

        // IRootDesigner.SupportedTechnologies is a ↵
required override for an
        // IRootDesigner. WindowsForms is the view technology ↵
 used by this designer.
        ViewTechnology[] IRootDesigner.SupportedTechnologies
        {
            get
            {
                return new ViewTechnology[] ↵
{ViewTechnology.WindowsForms};
            }
        }

        // RootDesignerView is a simple control that will be displayed
        // in the designer window.
        private class RootDesignerView : Control
        {
            private SampleRootDesigner m_designer;

            public RootDesignerView(SampleRootDesigner designer)
            {
                m_designer = designer;
                BackColor = Color.Blue;
                Font = new Font(Font.FontFamily.Name, 24.0f);
            }

            protected override void OnPaint(PaintEventArgs pe)
            {
                base.OnPaint(pe);

                // Draws the name of the component in large letters.
                pe.Graphics.DrawString ↵
 (m_designer.Component.Site.Name, Font, Brushes.Yellow, ↵
ClientRectangle);
            }
        }
    }
}
```

Requirements

Namespace: System.ComponentModel.Design

Platforms: Windows 98, Windows NT 4.0, Windows Millennium Edition, Windows 2000, Windows XP Home Edition, Windows XP Professional, Windows Server 2003 family

Assembly: System (in System.dll)

IRootDesigner.SupportedTechnologies Property

Gets the set of technologies that this designer can support for its display.

[Visual Basic]

```
ReadOnly Property SupportedTechnologies As ViewTechnology ()
```

[C#]

```
ViewTechnology[] SupportedTechnologies {get;}
```

[C++]

```
__property ViewTechnology get_SupportedTechnologies();
```

```
[JScript]
function get SupportedTechnologies() : ViewTechnology[];
```

Property Value

An array of supported **ViewTechnology** objects.

Remarks

The **ViewTechnology** enumeration indicates the supported view technologies.

Requirements

Platforms: Windows 98, Windows NT 4.0,
Windows Millennium Edition, Windows 2000,
Windows XP Home Edition, Windows XP Professional,
Windows Server 2003 family

IRootDesigner.GetView Method

Gets a view object for the specified view technology.

```
[Visual Basic]
Function GetView( _
   ByVal technology As ViewTechnology _
) As Object
[C#]
object GetView(
   ViewTechnology technology
);
[C++]
Object* GetView(
   ViewTechnology technology
);
[JScript]
function GetView(
   technology : ViewTechnology
) : Object;
```

Parameters

technology

A **ViewTechnology** that indicates a particular view technology. This **ViewTechnology** object must be indicated as a value of the **SupportedTechnologies** property. Otherwise, an **ArgumentException** is thrown.

Return Value

An object that represents the view for this designer.

Exceptions

Exception Type	Condition
ArgumentException	The specified view technology is not supported or does not exist.

Remarks

This method returns a view object that can present a user interface to the user. The returned data type is an **Object**, because there can be a variety of different user interface technologies. Development environments typically support more than one technology.

Requirements

Platforms: Windows 98, Windows NT 4.0,
Windows Millennium Edition, Windows 2000,
Windows XP Home Edition, Windows XP Professional,
Windows Server 2003 family

ISelectionService Interface

Provides an interface for a designer to select components.

[Visual Basic]
```
<ComVisible(True)>
Public Interface ISelectionService
```
[C#]
```
[ComVisible(true)]
public interface ISelectionService
```
[C++]
```
[ComVisible(true)]
public __gc __interface ISelectionService
```
[JScript]
```
public
   ComVisible(true)
interface ISelectionService
```

Remarks

When a component is selected, its viewable or editable properties are shown in the Properties window.

Example

[Visual Basic, C#] The following example demonstrates use of the **ISelectionService** to handle the **SelectionChanged** and **SelectionChanging** events.

[Visual Basic]
```
Imports System
Imports System.Drawing
Imports System.Collections
Imports System.ComponentModel
Imports System.ComponentModel.Design
Imports System.Windows.Forms
Imports Microsoft.VisualBasic

'  This sample demonstrates using the ISelectionService
'  interface to receive notification of selection change events.

'  The SelectionComponent control attempts to retrieve an instance
'  of the ISelectionService when it is sited. If it can, it attaches
'  event handlers for events provided by the service that display
'  a message when a component is selected or deselected.
'  To run this sample, add the SelectionComponent control to a Form and
'  then select or deselect components in design mode to see the       ↵
behavior
'  of the component change event handlers.

Namespace ISelectionServiceExample

    Public Class SelectionComponent
        Inherits System.Windows.Forms.UserControl
        Private tbox1 As System.Windows.Forms.TextBox
        Private selectionService As ISelectionService

        Public Sub New()
            ' Initialize control
            Me.SuspendLayout()
            Me.Name = "SelectionComponent"
            Me.Size = New System.Drawing.Size(608, 296)
            Me.tbox1 = New System.Windows.Forms.TextBox()
            Me.tbox1.Location = New System.Drawing.Point(24, 16)
            Me.tbox1.Name = "listBox1"
            Me.tbox1.Multiline = True
            Me.tbox1.Size = New System.Drawing.Size(560, 251)
            Me.tbox1.TabIndex = 0
            Me.Controls.Add(Me.tbox1)
            Me.ResumeLayout()
        End Sub 'New

        Public Overrides Property Site() As ISite
            Get
                Return MyBase.Site
            End Get
            Set(ByVal Value As ISite)
                ' The ISelectionService is available in design mode
                ' only, and only after the component is sited.
                If Not (selectionService Is Nothing) Then
                    ' Because the selection service has been
                    ' previously obtained, the component may be in
                    ' the process of being resited.
                    ' Detatch the previous selection change event
                    ' handlers in case the new selection
                    ' service is a new service instance belonging to
                    ' another design mode service host.
                    RemoveHandler                                    ↵
selectionService.SelectionChanged, AddressOf OnSelectionChanged
                    RemoveHandler                                    ↵
selectionService.SelectionChanging, AddressOf OnSelectionChanging
                End If

                ' Establish the new site for the component.
                MyBase.Site = Value

                If MyBase.Site Is Nothing Then
                    Return
                End If

                ' The selection service is not available outside of
                ' design mode. A call requesting the service
                ' using GetService while not in design mode will
                ' return null.
                selectionService =                                   ↵
Me.Site.GetService(GetType(ISelectionService))

                ' If an instance of the ISelectionService was obtained,
                ' attach event handlers for the selection
                ' changing and selection changed events.
                If Not (selectionService Is Nothing) Then
                    ' Add an event handler for the                   ↵
SelectionChanging and SelectionChanged events.
                    AddHandler                                       ↵
selectionService.SelectionChanging, AddressOf OnSelectionChanging
                    AddHandler                                       ↵
selectionService.SelectionChanged, AddressOf OnSelectionChanged
                End If
            End Set
        End Property

        Private Sub OnSelectionChanged(ByVal sender As               ↵
Object, ByVal args As EventArgs)
            tbox1.AppendText("The selected component was             ↵
 changed.  Selected components:" +                                   ↵
Microsoft.VisualBasic.ControlChars.CrLf + "    " +                   ↵
GetSelectedComponents() + Microsoft.VisualBasic.ControlChars.CrLf)
        End Sub 'OnSelectionChanged

        Private Sub OnSelectionChanging(ByVal sender As              ↵
 Object, ByVal args As EventArgs)
            tbox1.AppendText("The selected component is              ↵
 changing.  Selected components:" +                                  ↵
Microsoft.VisualBasic.ControlChars.CrLf + "    " +                   ↵
GetSelectedComponents() + Microsoft.VisualBasic.ControlChars.CrLf)
        End Sub 'OnSelectionChanging

        Private Function GetSelectedComponents() As String
            Dim selectedString As String = String.Empty
            Dim
components(CType(selectionService.GetSelectedComponents(),           ↵
ICollection).Count - 1) As Object
            CType(selectionService.GetSelectedComponents(),          ↵
ICollection).CopyTo(components, 0)

            Dim i As Integer
            For i = 0 To components.Length - 1
```

```
            If i <> 0 Then
                selectedString += "&& "
            End If
            If CType(selectionService.PrimarySelection,          ↵
 IComponent) Is CType(components(i), IComponent) Then
                selectedString += "PrimarySelection:"
            End If
            selectedString += CType(components(i),               ↵
IComponent).Site.Name + " "
        Next i

        Return selectedString
    End Function 'GetSelectedComponents

    ' Clean up any resources being used.
    Protected Overloads Overrides Sub Dispose(ByVal              ↵
 disposing As Boolean)
        ' Detatch the event handlers for the selection service.
        If Not (selectionService Is Nothing) Then
            RemoveHandler                                        ↵
selectionService.SelectionChanging, AddressOf OnSelectionChanging
            RemoveHandler                                        ↵
selectionService.SelectionChanged, AddressOf OnSelectionChanged
        End If
        MyBase.Dispose(disposing)
    End Sub 'Dispose
  End Class 'SelectionComponent

End Namespace 'ISelectionServiceExample
```

[C#]

```
using System;
using System.Drawing;
using System.Collections;
using System.ComponentModel;
using System.ComponentModel.Design;
using System.Windows.Forms;

/*  This sample demonstrates using the ISelectionService
    interface to receive notification of selection change events.
    The SelectionComponent control attempts to retrieve an instance
    of the ISelectionService when it is sited. If it can, it attaches
    event handlers for events provided by the service that display
    a message when a component is selected or deselected.

    To run this sample, add the SelectionComponent control       ↵
to a Form and
    then select or deselect components in design mode to        ↵
see the behavior
    of the component change event handlers. */

namespace ISelectionServiceExample
{
    public class SelectionComponent : System.Windows.Forms.UserControl
    {
        private System.Windows.Forms.TextBox tbox1;
        private ISelectionService selectionService;

        public SelectionComponent()
        {
            // Initialize control
            this.SuspendLayout();
            this.Name = "SelectionComponent";
            this.Size = new System.Drawing.Size(608, 296);
            this.tbox1 = new System.Windows.Forms.TextBox();
            this.tbox1.Location = new System.Drawing.Point(24, 16);
            this.tbox1.Name = "listBox1";
            this.tbox1.Multiline = true;
            this.tbox1.Size = new System.Drawing.Size(560, 251);
            this.tbox1.TabIndex = 0;
            this.Controls.Add(this.tbox1);
            this.ResumeLayout();
        }

        public override ISite Site
        {
            get
            {
                return base.Site;
            }
            set
            {
                // The ISelectionService is available in design mode
                // only, and only after the component is sited.
                if (selectionService != null)
                {
                    // Because the selection service has been
                    // previously obtained, the component may be in
                    // the process of being resited.
                    // Detatch the previous selection change event
                    // handlers in case the new selection
                    // service is a new service instance belonging to
                    // another design mode service host.
                    selectionService.SelectionChanged -= new     ↵
EventHandler(OnSelectionChanged);
                    selectionService.SelectionChanging -= new    ↵
EventHandler(OnSelectionChanging);
                }

                // Establish the new site for the component.
                base.Site = value;

                if( base.Site == null )
                    return;

                // The selection service is not available outside of
                // design mode. A call requesting the service
                // using GetService while not in design mode will
                // return null.
                selectionService =                               ↵
 (ISelectionService)this.Site.GetService(typeof(ISelectionService));

                // If an instance of the ISelectionService was   ↵
obtained,
                // attach event handlers for the selection
                // changing and selection changed events.
                if (selectionService != null)
                {
                    // Add an event handler for the SelectionChanging
                    // and SelectionChanged events.
                    selectionService.SelectionChanging += new    ↵
EventHandler(OnSelectionChanging);
                    selectionService.SelectionChanged += new     ↵
EventHandler(OnSelectionChanged);
                }
            }
        }

        private void OnSelectionChanged(object sender, EventArgs args)
        {
            tbox1.AppendText("The selected component             ↵
was changed.  Selected components:\r\n    " +                    ↵
GetSelectedComponents() + "\r\n");
        }

        private void OnSelectionChanging(object sender, EventArgs args)
        {
            tbox1.AppendText("The selected component is          ↵
changing. Selected components:\r\n    " + GetSelectedComponents()  ↵
 + "\r\n");
        }

        private string GetSelectedComponents()
        {
            string selectedString = String.Empty;
            object[] components = new                            ↵
object[((ICollection)selectionService.GetSelectedComponents()).Count];
```

```
((ICollection)selectionService.GetSelectedComponents()).CopyTo ↵
(components, 0);

            for(int i=0; i<components.Length; i++)
            {
                if( i != 0 )
                    selectedString += "&& ";
                if( ((IComponent) ↵
selectionService.PrimarySelection) == ((IComponent)components[i]) )
                    selectedString += "PrimarySelection:";
                selectedString += ↵
 ((IComponent)components[i]).Site.Name+" ";
            }
            return selectedString;
        }

        // Clean up any resources being used.
        protected override void Dispose( bool disposing )
        {
            // Detatch the event handlers for the selection service.
            if( selectionService != null )
            {
                selectionService.SelectionChanging -= new ↵
EventHandler(this.OnSelectionChanging);
                selectionService.SelectionChanged -= new ↵
EventHandler(this.OnSelectionChanged);
            }

            base.Dispose( disposing );
        }
    }
}
```

Requirements

Namespace: System.ComponentModel.Design

Platforms: Windows 98, Windows NT 4.0, Windows Millennium Edition, Windows 2000, Windows XP Home Edition, Windows XP Professional, Windows Server 2003 family

Assembly: System (in System.dll)

ISelectionService.PrimarySelection Property

Gets the object that is currently the primary selected object.

[Visual Basic]
```
ReadOnly Property PrimarySelection As Object
```
[C#]
```
object PrimarySelection {get;}
```
[C++]
```
__property Object* get_PrimarySelection();
```
[JScript]
```
function get PrimarySelection() : Object;
```

Property Value

The object that is currently the primary selected object.

Remarks

When multiple components are selected at design time, one of the objects is the primary selected object. Some operations behave differently depending on which selected component is the primary selected object. The primary selected object is typically the last object that was selected, but the primary object of a multiple component selection can be changed to any of the selected components. The primary selected object has a selection border that is distinct in appearance from the other selected objects. The specific type of visual distinction depends on the development environment's implementation of a selection user interface.

Requirements

Platforms: Windows 98, Windows NT 4.0, Windows Millennium Edition, Windows 2000, Windows XP Home Edition, Windows XP Professional, Windows Server 2003 family

ISelectionService.SelectionCount Property

Gets the count of selected objects.

[Visual Basic]
```
ReadOnly Property SelectionCount As Integer
```
[C#]
```
int SelectionCount {get;}
```
[C++]
```
__property int get_SelectionCount();
```
[JScript]
```
function get SelectionCount() : int;
```

Property Value

The number of selected objects.

Requirements

Platforms: Windows 98, Windows NT 4.0, Windows Millennium Edition, Windows 2000, Windows XP Home Edition, Windows XP Professional, Windows Server 2003 family

ISelectionService.GetComponentSelected Method

Gets a value indicating whether the specified component is currently selected.

[Visual Basic]
```
Function GetComponentSelected( _
   ByVal component As Object _
) As Boolean
```
[C#]
```
bool GetComponentSelected(
   object component
);
```
[C++]
```
bool GetComponentSelected(
   Object* component
);
```
[JScript]
```
function GetComponentSelected(
   component : Object
) : Boolean;
```

Parameters

component
: The component to test.

Return Value

true if the component is part of the user's current selection; otherwise, **false**.

Remarks

This method can be used to check whether a specific component is currently selected. This process is generally quicker than getting and parsing the entire list of selected components.

Requirements

Platforms: Windows 98, Windows NT 4.0, Windows Millennium Edition, Windows 2000, Windows XP Home Edition, Windows XP Professional, Windows Server 2003 family

ISelectionService.GetSelectedComponents Method

Gets a collection of components that are currently selected.

```
[Visual Basic]
Function GetSelectedComponents() As ICollection
[C#]
ICollection GetSelectedComponents();
[C++]
ICollection* GetSelectedComponents();
[JScript]
function GetSelectedComponents() : ICollection;
```

Return Value

A collection that represents the current set of components that are selected.

Requirements

Platforms: Windows 98, Windows NT 4.0, Windows Millennium Edition, Windows 2000, Windows XP Home Edition, Windows XP Professional, Windows Server 2003 family

ISelectionService.SetSelectedComponents Method

Selects the specified components.

Overload List

Selects the specified collection of components.

[Visual Basic] **Overloads Sub SetSelected-Components(ICollection)**

[C#] **void SetSelectedComponents(ICollection);**

[C++] **void SetSelectedComponents(ICollection*);**

[JScript] **function SetSelectedComponents(ICollection);**

Selects the components from within the specified collection of components that match the specified selection type.

[Visual Basic] **Overloads Sub SetSelected-Components(ICollection, SelectionTypes)**

[C#] **void SetSelectedComponents(ICollection, SelectionTypes);**

[C++] **void SetSelectedComponents(ICollection*, SelectionTypes);**

[JScript] **function SetSelectedComponents(ICollection, SelectionTypes);**

ISelectionService.SetSelectedComponents Method (ICollection)

Selects the specified collection of components.

```
[Visual Basic]
Sub SetSelectedComponents( _
   ByVal components As ICollection _
)
[C#]
void SetSelectedComponents(
   ICollection components
);
[C++]
void SetSelectedComponents(
   ICollection* components
);
[JScript]
function SetSelectedComponents(
   components : ICollection
);
```

Parameters

components

The collection of components to select.

Remarks

If the array is a null reference (**Nothing** in Visual Basic) or does not contain any components, **SetSelectedComponents** selects the top-level component in the designer.

Requirements

Platforms: Windows 98, Windows NT 4.0, Windows Millennium Edition, Windows 2000, Windows XP Home Edition, Windows XP Professional, Windows Server 2003 family

ISelectionService.SetSelectedComponents Method (ICollection, SelectionTypes)

Selects the components from within the specified collection of components that match the specified selection type.

```
[Visual Basic]
Sub SetSelectedComponents( _
   ByVal components As ICollection, _
   ByVal selectionType As SelectionTypes _
)
[C#]
void SetSelectedComponents(
   ICollection components,
   SelectionTypes selectionType
);
[C++]
void SetSelectedComponents(
   ICollection* components,
   SelectionTypes selectionType
);
[JScript]
function SetSelectedComponents(
   components : ICollection,
   selectionType : SelectionTypes
);
```

Parameters

components

The collection of components to select.

selectionType

A value from the **SelectionTypes** enumeration. The default is **Normal**.

Remarks

If the array is a null reference (**Nothing** in Visual Basic) or does not contain any components, **SetSelectedComponents** selects the top-level component in the designer.

Requirements

Platforms: Windows 98, Windows NT 4.0, Windows Millennium Edition, Windows 2000, Windows XP Home Edition, Windows XP Professional, Windows Server 2003 family

ISelectionService.SelectionChanged Event

Occurs when the current selection changes.

[Visual Basic]
```
Event SelectionChanged As EventHandler
```
[C#]
```
event EventHandler SelectionChanged;
```
[C++]
```
__event EventHandler* SelectionChanged;
```

[JScript] In JScript, you can handle the events defined by a class, but you cannot define your own.

Event Data

The event handler receives an argument of type **EventArgs**.

Remarks

Minimize processing when handling this event, because processing that occurs within this event handler can significantly affect the overall performance of the form designer.

Example

[Visual Basic, C#, C++] The following example illustrates how to use the **SelectionChanged** event.

[Visual Basic]
```
' Add SelectionChanged event handler to event
AddHandler m_selectionService.SelectionChanged, AddressOf OnSelectionChanged

    . . .
      ' This is the OnSelectionChanged handler method.  This method calls
      '   OnUserChange to display a message that indicates the name of the
      '   handler that made the call and the type of the event argument.
      Private Sub OnSelectionChanged(ByVal sender As Object, ByVal args As EventArgs)
          OnUserChange("OnSelectionChanged", args.ToString())
      End Sub 'OnSelectionChanged
```

[C#]
```
// Add SelectionChanged event handler to event
m_selectionService.SelectionChanged += new EventHandler(OnSelectionChanged);

    . . .
        /* This is the OnSelectionChanged handler method.  This method calls
           OnUserChange to display a message that indicates the name of the
           handler that made the call and the type of the event argument. */
        private void OnSelectionChanged(object sender, EventArgs args)
        {
            OnUserChange("OnSelectionChanged", args.ToString());
        }
```

[C++]
```
// Add SelectionChanged event handler to event
m_selectionService->SelectionChanged += new EventHandler(this, OnSelectionChanged);

    . . .
        /* This is the OnSelectionChanged handler method.  This method calls
           OnUserChange to display a message that indicates the name of the
           handler that made the call and the type of the event argument. */
        void OnSelectionChanged(Object* sender, EventArgs* args)
        {
            OnUserChange(S"OnSelectionChanged", args->ToString());
        }
```

Requirements

Platforms: Windows 98, Windows NT 4.0, Windows Millennium Edition, Windows 2000, Windows XP Home Edition, Windows XP Professional, Windows Server 2003 family

ISelectionService.SelectionChanging Event

Occurs when the current selection is about to change.

[Visual Basic]
```
Event SelectionChanging As EventHandler
```
[C#]
```
event EventHandler SelectionChanging;
```
[C++]
```
__event EventHandler* SelectionChanging;
```

[JScript] In JScript, you can handle the events defined by a class, but you cannot define your own.

Event Data

The event handler receives an argument of type **EventArgs**.

Remarks

Minimize processing when handling this event, because processing that occurs within this event handler can significantly affect the overall performance of the form designer.

Example

[Visual Basic, C#, C++] The following example illustrates how to use the **SelectionChanging** event.

[Visual Basic]
```
' Add SelectionChanging event handler to event
AddHandler m_selectionService.SelectionChanging, AddressOf OnSelectionChanging

    . . .
      ' This is the OnSelectionChanging handler method.  This method calls
      '   OnUserChange to display a message that indicates the name of the
      '   handler that made the call and the type of the event argument.
      Private Sub OnSelectionChanging(ByVal sender As Object, ByVal args As EventArgs)
          OnUserChange("OnSelectionChanging", args.ToString())
      End Sub 'OnSelectionChanging
```

[C#]
```
// Add SelectionChanging event handler to event
m_selectionService.SelectionChanging += new                          ↵
EventHandler(OnSelectionChanging);
    . . .
        /* This is the OnSelectionChanging handler method.           ↵
 This method calls
            OnUserChange to display a message that indicates         ↵
the name of the
            handler that made the call and the type of the event     ↵
argument. */
        private void OnSelectionChanging(object sender, EventArgs args)
        {
            OnUserChange("OnSelectionChanging", args.ToString());
        }
```

[C++]
```
// Add SelectionChanging event handler to event
m_selectionService->SelectionChanging += new EventHandler(this,      ↵
OnSelectionChanging);
    . . .
         /* This is the OnSelectionChanging handler method.          ↵
 This method calls
             OnUserChange to display a message that indicates        ↵
 the name of the
             handler that made the call and the type of the          ↵
event argument. */
         void OnSelectionChanging(Object* sender, EventArgs* args)
         {
             OnUserChange(S"OnSelectionChanging", args->ToString());
         }
```

Requirements

Platforms: Windows 98, Windows NT 4.0, Windows Millennium Edition, Windows 2000, Windows XP Home Edition, Windows XP Professional, Windows Server 2003 family

IServiceContainer Interface

Provides a container for services.

System.IServiceProvider
System.ComponentModel.Design.IServiceContainer

[Visual Basic]
```
<ComVisible(True)>
Public Interface IServiceContainer
   Inherits IServiceProvider
```
[C#]
```
[ComVisible(true)]
public interface IServiceContainer : IServiceProvider
```
[C++]
```
[ComVisible(true)]
public __gc __interface IServiceContainer : public
   IServiceProvider
```
[JScript]
```
public
   ComVisible(true)
interface IServiceContainer implements IServiceProvider
```

Classes that Implement IServiceContainer

Class	Description
ServiceContainer	Provides a simple implementation of the **IServiceContainer** interface. This class cannot be inherited.

Remarks

A service container is, by definition, a service provider. In addition to providing services, it also provides a mechanism for adding and removing services. Services are a foundation of the .NET Framework design-time architecture. Services provide design-time objects access to specific features and methods implemented by a service object that provides a service or services.

To obtain a service at design time, call the **GetService** method of a component sited in design mode. Designers and other objects can add or remove services at design time through the **IDesignerHost** interface.

Service containers can be contained by other service containers, forming a tree of service containers. By default, the **IService-Container** interface adds services to the closest service container. When a service is added, it can be added with instructions to promote it. When a service is promoted, it is added to any parent service container, on up until the top of the service container tree is reached. This allows a designer to provide a global service that other objects in the process can use.

Requirements

Namespace: System.ComponentModel.Design

Platforms: Windows 98, Windows NT 4.0, Windows Millennium Edition, Windows 2000, Windows XP Home Edition, Windows XP Professional, Windows Server 2003 family

Assembly: System (in System.dll)

IServiceContainer.AddService Method

Adds the specified service to the service container.

Overload List

Adds the specified service to the service container.

[Visual Basic] **Overloads Sub AddService(Type, Object)**

[C#] **void AddService(Type, object);**

[C++] **void AddService(Type*, Object*);**

[JScript] **function AddService(Type, Object);**

Adds the specified service to the service container.

[Visual Basic] **Overloads Sub AddService(Type, ServiceCreatorCallback)**

[C#] **void AddService(Type, ServiceCreatorCallback);**

[C++] **void AddService(Type*, ServiceCreatorCallback*);**

[JScript] **function AddService(Type, ServiceCreatorCallback);**

Adds the specified service to the service container, and optionally promotes the service to any parent service containers.

[Visual Basic] **Overloads Sub AddService(Type, Object, Boolean)**

[C#] **void AddService(Type, object, bool);**

[C++] **void AddService(Type*, Object*, bool);**

[JScript] **function AddService(Type, Object, Boolean);**

Adds the specified service to the service container, and optionally promotes the service to parent service containers.

[Visual Basic] **Overloads Sub AddService(Type, ServiceCreatorCallback, Boolean)**

[C#] **void AddService(Type, ServiceCreatorCallback, bool);**

[C++] **void AddService(Type*, ServiceCreatorCallback*, bool);**

[JScript] **function AddService(Type, ServiceCreatorCallback, Boolean);**

Example

[Visual Basic, C#, C++] The following example illustrates how to add a service to an **IServiceContainer**.

> [Visual Basic, C#, C++] **Note** This example shows how to use one of the overloaded versions of **AddService**. For other examples that might be available, see the individual overload topics.

[Visual Basic]
```
m_MyServiceContainer.AddService(GetType(Control), New ┘
ServiceCreatorCallback( _
        AddressOf CreateNewControl))
```

[C#]
```
m_MyServiceContainer.AddService(typeof(Control),
    new ServiceCreatorCallback(this.CreateNewControl));
```

[C++]
```
m_MyServiceContainer->AddService(__typeof(Control),
    new ServiceCreatorCallback(this, CreateNewControl));
```

IServiceContainer.AddService Method (Type, Object)

Adds the specified service to the service container.

```
[Visual Basic]
Sub AddService( _
   ByVal serviceType As Type, _
   ByVal serviceInstance As Object _
)
[C#]
void AddService(
   Type serviceType,
   object serviceInstance
);
[C++]
void AddService(
   Type* serviceType,
   Object* serviceInstance
);
[JScript]
function AddService(
   serviceType : Type,
   serviceInstance : Object
);
```

Parameters

serviceType
: The type of service to add.

serviceInstance
: An instance of the service type to add. This object must implement or inherit from the type indicated by the *serviceType* parameter.

Example

[Visual Basic, C#, C++] The following example illustrates how to add a service to an **IServiceContainer**.

```
[Visual Basic]
m_MyServiceContainer.AddService(GetType(Control), sender)
```

```
[C#]
m_MyServiceContainer.AddService(typeof(Control), sender);
```

```
[C++]
m_MyServiceContainer->AddService(__typeof(Control), sender);
```

Requirements

Platforms: Windows 98, Windows NT 4.0, Windows Millennium Edition, Windows 2000, Windows XP Home Edition, Windows XP Professional, Windows Server 2003 family

IServiceContainer.AddService Method (Type, ServiceCreatorCallback)

Adds the specified service to the service container.

```
[Visual Basic]
Sub AddService( _
   ByVal serviceType As Type, _
   ByVal callback As ServiceCreatorCallback _
)
[C#]
void AddService(
   Type serviceType,
   ServiceCreatorCallback callback
);
[C++]
void AddService(
   Type* serviceType,
   ServiceCreatorCallback* callback
);
[JScript]
function AddService(
   serviceType : Type,
   callback : ServiceCreatorCallback
);
```

Parameters

serviceType
: The type of service to add.

callback
: A callback object that is used to create the service. This allows a service to be declared as available, but delays the creation of the object until the service is requested.

Example

[Visual Basic, C#, C++] The following example illustrates how to add a service to an **IServiceContainer**.

```
[Visual Basic]
m_MyServiceContainer.AddService(GetType(Control), New ↵
ServiceCreatorCallback( _
        AddressOf CreateNewControl))
```

```
[C#]
m_MyServiceContainer.AddService(typeof(Control),
    new ServiceCreatorCallback(this.CreateNewControl));
```

```
[C++]
m_MyServiceContainer->AddService(__typeof(Control),
    new ServiceCreatorCallback(this, CreateNewControl));
```

Requirements

Platforms: Windows 98, Windows NT 4.0, Windows Millennium Edition, Windows 2000, Windows XP Home Edition, Windows XP Professional, Windows Server 2003 family

IServiceContainer.AddService Method (Type, Object, Boolean)

Adds the specified service to the service container, and optionally promotes the service to any parent service containers.

```
[Visual Basic]
Sub AddService( _
   ByVal serviceType As Type, _
   ByVal serviceInstance As Object, _
   ByVal promote As Boolean _
)
[C#]
void AddService(
   Type serviceType,
   object serviceInstance,
   bool promote
);
[C++]
void AddService(
   Type* serviceType,
   Object* serviceInstance,
   bool promote
);
```

```
[JScript]
function AddService(
   serviceType : Type,
   serviceInstance : Object,
   promote : Boolean
);
```

Parameters

serviceType
The type of service to add.

serviceInstance
An instance of the service type to add. This object must implement or inherit from the type indicated by the *serviceType* parameter.

promote
true to promote this request to any parent service containers; otherwise, **false**.

Requirements

Platforms: Windows 98, Windows NT 4.0, Windows Millennium Edition, Windows 2000, Windows XP Home Edition, Windows XP Professional, Windows Server 2003 family

IServiceContainer.AddService Method (Type, ServiceCreatorCallback, Boolean)

Adds the specified service to the service container, and optionally promotes the service to parent service containers.

```
[Visual Basic]
Sub AddService( _
   ByVal serviceType As Type, _
   ByVal callback As ServiceCreatorCallback, _
   ByVal promote As Boolean _
)
[C#]
void AddService(
   Type serviceType,
   ServiceCreatorCallback callback,
   bool promote
);
[C++]
void AddService(
   Type* serviceType,
   ServiceCreatorCallback* callback,
   bool promote
);
[JScript]
function AddService(
   serviceType : Type,
   callback : ServiceCreatorCallback,
   promote : Boolean
);
```

Parameters

serviceType
The type of service to add.

callback
A callback object that is used to create the service. This allows a service to be declared as available, but delays the creation of the object until the service is requested.

promote
true to promote this request to any parent service containers; otherwise, **false**.

Requirements

Platforms: Windows 98, Windows NT 4.0, Windows Millennium Edition, Windows 2000, Windows XP Home Edition, Windows XP Professional, Windows Server 2003 family

IServiceContainer.RemoveService Method

Removes the specified service type from the service container.

Overload List

Removes the specified service type from the service container.

[Visual Basic] **Overloads Sub RemoveService(Type)**

[C#] **void RemoveService(Type);**

[C++] **void RemoveService(Type*);**

[JScript] **function RemoveService(Type);**

Removes the specified service type from the service container, and optionally promotes the service to parent service containers.

[Visual Basic] **Overloads Sub RemoveService(Type, Boolean)**

[C#] **void RemoveService(Type, bool);**

[C++] **void RemoveService(Type*, bool);**

[JScript] **function RemoveService(Type, Boolean);**

Example

[Visual Basic, C#, C++] **Note** This example shows how to use one of the overloaded versions of **RemoveService**. For other examples that might be available, see the individual overload topics.

```
[Visual Basic]
m_MyServiceContainer.RemoveService(GetType(Control))

[C#]
m_MyServiceContainer.RemoveService(typeof(Control));

[C++]
m_MyServiceContainer->RemoveService(__typeof(Control));
```

IServiceContainer.RemoveService Method (Type)

Removes the specified service type from the service container.

```
[Visual Basic]
Sub RemoveService( _
   ByVal serviceType As Type _
)
[C#]
void RemoveService(
   Type serviceType
);
[C++]
void RemoveService(
   Type* serviceType
);
[JScript]
function RemoveService(
   serviceType : Type
);
```

Parameters

serviceType
The type of service to remove.

Example

[Visual Basic, C#, C++] The following example illustrates how to remove a service from an **IServiceContainer**.

[Visual Basic]
```
m_MyServiceContainer.RemoveService(GetType(Control))
```

[C#]
```
m_MyServiceContainer.RemoveService(typeof(Control));
```

[C++]
```
m_MyServiceContainer->RemoveService(__typeof(Control));
```

Requirements

Platforms: Windows 98, Windows NT 4.0, Windows Millennium Edition, Windows 2000, Windows XP Home Edition, Windows XP Professional, Windows Server 2003 family

IServiceContainer.RemoveService Method (Type, Boolean)

Removes the specified service type from the service container, and optionally promotes the service to parent service containers.

[Visual Basic]
```
Sub RemoveService( _
   ByVal serviceType As Type, _
   ByVal promote As Boolean _
)
```
[C#]
```
void RemoveService(
   Type serviceType,
   bool promote
);
```
[C++]
```
void RemoveService(
   Type* serviceType,
   bool promote
);
```
[JScript]
```
function RemoveService(
   serviceType : Type,
   promote : Boolean
);
```

Parameters

serviceType
The type of service to remove.

promote
true to promote this request to any parent service containers; otherwise, **false**.

Example

[Visual Basic]
```
m_MyServiceContainer.RemoveService(GetType(Control))
```

[C#]
```
m_MyServiceContainer.RemoveService(typeof(Control));
```

[C++]
```
m_MyServiceContainer->RemoveService(__typeof(Control));
```

Requirements

Platforms: Windows 98, Windows NT 4.0, Windows Millennium Edition, Windows 2000, Windows XP Home Edition, Windows XP Professional, Windows Server 2003 family

ITypeDescriptorFilterService Interface

Provides an interface to modify the set of member descriptors for a component in design mode.

```
[Visual Basic]
Public Interface ITypeDescriptorFilterService
[C#]
public interface ITypeDescriptorFilterService
[C++]
public __gc __interface ITypeDescriptorFilterService
[JScript]
public interface ITypeDescriptorFilterService
```

Classes that Implement ITypeDescriptorFilterService

Class	Description
ComponentDocumentDesigner	Base designer class for extending the design mode behavior of a root design document that supports nested components.

Remarks

ITypeDescriptorFilterService provides an interface that a component can implement to modify the set of descriptors that a component provides through a **TypeDescriptor**. **TypeDescriptor** will query a component's site for the **ITypeDescriptorFilterService** service before providing descriptors representing its properties, attributes, and events.

Notes to Implementers: To filter the member descriptors exposed by a **TypeDescriptor**, implement this interface on a component and override the **FilterAttributes**, **FilterEvents** or **FilterProperties** methods of this class to filter the attributes, events, or properties, respectively.

Requirements

Namespace: System.ComponentModel.Design

Platforms: Windows 98, Windows NT 4.0, Windows Millennium Edition, Windows 2000, Windows XP Home Edition, Windows XP Professional, Windows Server 2003 family

Assembly: System (in System.dll)

ITypeDescriptorFilterService.FilterAttributes Method

Filters the attributes that a component exposes through a **TypeDescriptor**.

```
[Visual Basic]
Function FilterAttributes( _
   ByVal component As IComponent, _
   ByVal attributes As IDictionary _
) As Boolean
[C#]
bool FilterAttributes(
   IComponent component,
   IDictionary attributes
);
[C++]
bool FilterAttributes(
   IComponent* component,
   IDictionary* attributes
);
[JScript]
function FilterAttributes(
   component : IComponent,
   attributes : IDictionary
) : Boolean;
```

Parameters

component

The component to filter the attributes of.

attributes

A dictionary of attributes that can be modified.

Return Value

true if the set of filtered attributes is to be cached; **false** if the filter service must query again.

Remarks

This method is called when a user requests a set of attributes for a component. The attributes are added to the dictionary with the attribute type ID as the keys. Implementers of this service can make changes, add, or remove attributes in the dictionary.

Notes to Implementers: Return **false** only when necessary, because repeated queries to the type descriptor filter service can decrease performance.

Requirements

Platforms: Windows 98, Windows NT 4.0, Windows Millennium Edition, Windows 2000, Windows XP Home Edition, Windows XP Professional, Windows Server 2003 family

ITypeDescriptorFilterService.FilterEvents Method

Filters the events that a component exposes through a **TypeDescriptor**.

```
[Visual Basic]
Function FilterEvents( _
   ByVal component As IComponent, _
   ByVal events As IDictionary _
) As Boolean
[C#]
bool FilterEvents(
   IComponent component,
   IDictionary events
);
[C++]
bool FilterEvents(
   IComponent* component,
   IDictionary* events
);
[JScript]
function FilterEvents(
   component : IComponent,
   events : IDictionary
) : Boolean;
```

Parameters

component

The component to filter events for.

events

A dictionary of events that can be modified.

Return Value

true if the set of filtered events is to be cached; **false** if the filter service must query again.

Remarks

This method is called when a user requests a set of events for a component. The events are added to the dictionary with the event names as the keys. Implementers of this service can make changes, add, or remove events in the dictionary.

Notes to Implementers: Return **false** only when necessary, because repeated queries to the type descriptor filter service can decrease performance.

Requirements

Platforms: Windows 98, Windows NT 4.0, Windows Millennium Edition, Windows 2000, Windows XP Home Edition, Windows XP Professional, Windows Server 2003 family

ITypeDescriptorFilterService.FilterProperties Method

Filters the properties that a component exposes through a **TypeDescriptor**.

[Visual Basic]

```
Function FilterProperties( _
   ByVal component As IComponent, _
   ByVal properties As IDictionary _
) As Boolean
```

[C#]

```
bool FilterProperties(
   IComponent component,
   IDictionary properties
);
```

[C++]

```
bool FilterProperties(
   IComponent* component,
   IDictionary* properties
);
```

[JScript]

```
function FilterProperties(
   component : IComponent,
   properties : IDictionary
) : Boolean;
```

Parameters

component

The component to filter properties for.

properties

A dictionary of properties that can be modified.

Return Value

true if the set of filtered properties is to be cached; **false** if the filter service must query again.

Remarks

This method is called when a user requests a set of properties for a component. The properties are added to the dictionary with the property names as the keys. Implementers of this service can make changes, add, or remove properties in the dictionary.

Notes to Implementers: Return **false** only when necessary, because repeated queries to the type descriptor filter service can decrease performance.

Requirements

Platforms: Windows 98, Windows NT 4.0, Windows Millennium Edition, Windows 2000, Windows XP Home Edition, Windows XP Professional, Windows Server 2003 family

ITypeResolutionService Interface

Provides an interface to retrieve an assembly or type by name.

```
[Visual Basic]
Public Interface ITypeResolutionService
[C#]
public interface ITypeResolutionService
[C++]
public __gc __interface ITypeResolutionService
[JScript]
public interface ITypeResolutionService
```

Remarks

This service is used to load types at design time.

Requirements

Namespace: System.ComponentModel.Design

Platforms: Windows 98, Windows NT 4.0, Windows Millennium Edition, Windows 2000, Windows XP Home Edition, Windows XP Professional, Windows Server 2003 family

Assembly: System (in System.dll)

ITypeResolutionService.GetAssembly Method

Gets the requested assembly.

Overload List

Gets the requested assembly.

[Visual Basic] **Overloads Function GetAssembly(AssemblyName) As Assembly**

[C#] **Assembly GetAssembly(AssemblyName);**

[C++] **Assembly* GetAssembly(AssemblyName*);**

[JScript] **function GetAssembly(AssemblyName) : Assembly;**

Gets the requested assembly.

[Visual Basic] **Overloads Function GetAssembly(AssemblyName, Boolean) As Assembly**

[C#] **Assembly GetAssembly(AssemblyName, bool);**

[C++] **Assembly* GetAssembly(AssemblyName*, bool);**

[JScript] **function GetAssembly(AssemblyName, Boolean) : Assembly;**

ITypeResolutionService.GetAssembly Method (AssemblyName)

Gets the requested assembly.

```
[Visual Basic]
Function GetAssembly( _
   ByVal name As AssemblyName _
) As Assembly
[C#]
Assembly GetAssembly(
   AssemblyName name
);
[C++]
Assembly* GetAssembly(
   AssemblyName* name
);
[JScript]
function GetAssembly(
   name : AssemblyName
) : Assembly;
```

Parameters

name

The name of the assembly to retrieve.

Return Value

An instance of the requested assembly, or a null reference (**Nothing** in Visual Basic) if no assembly can be located.

Requirements

Platforms: Windows 98, Windows NT 4.0, Windows Millennium Edition, Windows 2000, Windows XP Home Edition, Windows XP Professional, Windows Server 2003 family

ITypeResolutionService.GetAssembly Method (AssemblyName, Boolean)

Gets the requested assembly.

```
[Visual Basic]
Function GetAssembly( _
   ByVal name As AssemblyName, _
   ByVal throwOnError As Boolean _
) As Assembly
[C#]
Assembly GetAssembly(
   AssemblyName name,
   bool throwOnError
);
[C++]
Assembly* GetAssembly(
   AssemblyName* name,
   bool throwOnError
);
[JScript]
function GetAssembly(
   name : AssemblyName,
   throwOnError : Boolean
) : Assembly;
```

Parameters

name

The name of the assembly to retrieve.

throwOnError

true if this method should throw an exception if the assembly cannot be located; otherwise, **false**, and this method returns a null reference (**Nothing** in Visual Basic) if the assembly cannot be located.

Return Value

An instance of the requested assembly, or a null reference (**Nothing** in Visual Basic) if no assembly can be located.

Requirements

Platforms: Windows 98, Windows NT 4.0, Windows Millennium Edition, Windows 2000, Windows XP Home Edition, Windows XP Professional, Windows Server 2003 family

ITypeResolutionService.GetPathOfAssembly Method

Gets the path to the file from which the assembly was loaded.

```
[Visual Basic]
Function GetPathOfAssembly( _
   ByVal name As AssemblyName _
) As String
[C#]
string GetPathOfAssembly(
   AssemblyName name
);
[C++]
String* GetPathOfAssembly(
   AssemblyName* name
);
[JScript]
function GetPathOfAssembly(
   name : AssemblyName
) : String;
```

Parameters

name

The name of the assembly.

Return Value

The path to the file from which the assembly was loaded.

Requirements

Platforms: Windows 98, Windows NT 4.0, Windows Millennium Edition, Windows 2000, Windows XP Home Edition, Windows XP Professional, Windows Server 2003 family

ITypeResolutionService.GetType Method

Loads a type with the specified name.

Overload List

Loads a type with the specified name.

[Visual Basic] **Overloads Function GetType(String) As Type**

[C#] **Type GetType(string);**

[C++] **Type* GetType(String*);**

[JScript] **function GetType(String) : Type;**

Loads a type with the specified name.

[Visual Basic] **Overloads Function GetType(String, Boolean) As Type**

[C#] **Type GetType(string, bool);**

[C++] **Type* GetType(String*, bool);**

[JScript] **function GetType(String, Boolean) : Type;**

Loads a type with the specified name.

[Visual Basic] **Overloads Function GetType(String, Boolean, Boolean) As Type**

[C#] **Type GetType(string, bool, bool);**

[C++] **Type* GetType(String*, bool, bool);**

[JScript] **function GetType(String, Boolean, Boolean) : Type;**

ITypeResolutionService.GetType Method (String)

Loads a type with the specified name.

```
[Visual Basic]
Function GetType( _
   ByVal name As String _
) As Type
[C#]
Type GetType(
   string name
);
[C++]
Type* GetType(
   String* name
);
[JScript]
function GetType(
   name : String
) : Type;
```

Parameters

name

The name of the type. If the type name is not a fully qualified name that indicates an assembly, this service will search its internal set of referenced assemblies.

Return Value

An instance of **Type** that corresponds to the specified name, or a null reference (**Nothing** in Visual Basic) if no type can be found.

Requirements

Platforms: Windows 98, Windows NT 4.0, Windows Millennium Edition, Windows 2000, Windows XP Home Edition, Windows XP Professional, Windows Server 2003 family

ITypeResolutionService.GetType Method (String, Boolean)

Loads a type with the specified name.

```
[Visual Basic]
Function GetType( _
   ByVal name As String, _
   ByVal throwOnError As Boolean _
) As Type
[C#]
Type GetType(
   string name,
   bool throwOnError
);
[C++]
Type* GetType(
   String* name,
   bool throwOnError
);
[JScript]
function GetType(
   name : String,
   throwOnError : Boolean
) : Type;
```

Parameters

name

The name of the type. If the type name is not a fully qualified name that indicates an assembly, this service will search its internal set of referenced assemblies.

throwOnError

true if this method should throw an exception if the assembly cannot be located; otherwise, **false**, and this method returns a null reference (**Nothing** in Visual Basic) if the assembly cannot be located.

Return Value

An instance of **Type** that corresponds to the specified name, or a null reference (**Nothing** in Visual Basic) if no type can be found.

Remarks

If the type cannot be loaded and the *throwOnError* parameter is **true**, this will throw an exception.

Requirements

Platforms: Windows 98, Windows NT 4.0, Windows Millennium Edition, Windows 2000, Windows XP Home Edition, Windows XP Professional, Windows Server 2003 family

ITypeResolutionService.GetType Method (String, Boolean, Boolean)

Loads a type with the specified name.

[Visual Basic]
```
Function GetType( _
   ByVal name As String, _
   ByVal throwOnError As Boolean, _
   ByVal ignoreCase As Boolean _
) As Type
```
[C#]
```
Type GetType(
   string name,
   bool throwOnError,
   bool ignoreCase
);
```
[C++]
```
Type* GetType(
   String* name,
   bool throwOnError,
   bool ignoreCase
);
```
[JScript]
```
function GetType(
   name : String,
   throwOnError : Boolean,
   ignoreCase : Boolean
) : Type;
```

Parameters

name

The name of the type. If the type name is not a fully qualified name that indicates an assembly, this service will search its internal set of referenced assemblies.

throwOnError

true if this method should throw an exception if the assembly cannot be located; otherwise, **false**, and this method returns a null reference (**Nothing** in Visual Basic) if the assembly cannot be located.

ignoreCase

true to ignore case when searching for types; otherwise, **false**.

Return Value

An instance of **Type** that corresponds to the specified name, or a null reference (**Nothing** in Visual Basic) if no type can be found.

Remarks

If the type cannot be loaded and the *throwOnError* parameter is **true**, this will throw an exception.

Requirements

Platforms: Windows 98, Windows NT 4.0, Windows Millennium Edition, Windows 2000, Windows XP Home Edition, Windows XP Professional, Windows Server 2003 family

ITypeResolutionService.ReferenceAssembly Method

Adds a reference to the specified assembly.

[Visual Basic]
```
Sub ReferenceAssembly( _
   ByVal name As AssemblyName _
)
```
[C#]
```
void ReferenceAssembly(
   AssemblyName name
);
```
[C++]
```
void ReferenceAssembly(
   AssemblyName* name
);
```
[JScript]
```
function ReferenceAssembly(
   name : AssemblyName
);
```

Parameters

name

An **AssemblyName** that indicates the assembly to reference.

Remarks

Once a reference to an assembly has been added to this service, this service can load types from names that do not specify an assembly.

Requirements

Platforms: Windows 98, Windows NT 4.0, Windows Millennium Edition, Windows 2000, Windows XP Home Edition, Windows XP Professional, Windows Server 2003 family

LocalizationExtenderProvider Class

Provides design-time support for localization features to a root designer.

System.Object
  System.ComponentModel.Design.LocalizationExtender-Provider

[Visual Basic]
```
Public Class LocalizationExtenderProvider
   Implements IExtenderProvider, IDisposable
```
[C#]
```
public class LocalizationExtenderProvider : IExtenderProvider,
   IDisposable
```
[C++]
```
public __gc class LocalizationExtenderProvider : public
   IExtenderProvider, IDisposable
```
[JScript]
```
public class LocalizationExtenderProvider implements
   IExtenderProvider, IDisposable
```

Thread Safety

Any public static (**Shared** in Visual Basic) members of this type are safe for multithreaded operations. Any instance members are not guaranteed to be thread safe.

Remarks

LocalizationExtenderProvider can extend an **IRootDesigner** with a set of properties and methods that provide support for the .NET Framework localization architecture. For more about using resources, see the **Localization** topic.

The localization support architecture enables designers to initialize component properties using resource files that can be swapped at run time to support a variety of languages, culture-specific styles and dynamically configurable features. You can use the methods of this class to enable designers and code generating serializers to load from resources and build initialization code that uses localization features.

The default serializers that ship with Visual Studio .NET are already capable of localizing components and controls, but they only do so if they locate support for the .NET Framework localization architecture. To detect the presence of localization support, the serialization system must locate a public **Boolean** property named "Localizable" on the root designer component. If a serializer finds this property, it searches for a property of type **CultureInfo** named "Language" to determine the current resouce configuration. Default serializers use these properties to determine if it should localize any localizable resources of the component, and if so, what **CultureInfo** format the resource information should be saved in.

Requirements

Namespace: System.ComponentModel.Design

Platforms: Windows 98, Windows NT 4.0, Windows Millennium Edition, Windows 2000, Windows XP Home Edition, Windows XP Professional, Windows Server 2003 family

Assembly: System.Design (in System.Design.dll)

LocalizationExtenderProvider Constructor

Initializes a new instance of the **LocalizationExtenderProvider** class using the specified service provider and base component.

[Visual Basic]
```
Public Sub New( _
   ByVal serviceProvider As ISite, _
   ByVal baseComponent As IComponent _
)
```
[C#]
```
public LocalizationExtenderProvider(
   ISite serviceProvider,
   IComponent baseComponent
);
```
[C++]
```
public: LocalizationExtenderProvider(
   ISite* serviceProvider,
   IComponent* baseComponent
);
```
[JScript]
```
public function LocalizationExtenderProvider(
   serviceProvider : ISite,
   baseComponent : IComponent
);
```

Parameters

serviceProvider
  A service provider for the specified component.

baseComponent
  The base component to localize.

Remarks

By default, a new **LocalizationExtenderProvider** sets the current language to **InvariantCulture**, which is the generic and default language resource setting. This setting causes a designer to generate code that references the generic language resource. You can create other **CultureInfo** objects to represent and identify other localized resource data that a program can use at run time.

Example

[Visual Basic]
```
' Adds a LocalizationExtenderProvider that provides ↵
localization support properties to the specified component.
extender = New LocalizationExtenderProvider ↵
 (Me.component_.Site, Me.component_)
```

[C#]
```
// Adds a LocalizationExtenderProvider that provides ↵
localization support properties to the specified component.
extender = new LocalizationExtenderProvider ↵
 (this.component.Site, this.component);
```

[C++]
```
// Adds a LocalizationExtenderProvider that provides ↵
localization support properties to the specified component.
extender = new LocalizationExtenderProvider(this->component-> ↵
Site, this->component);
```

Requirements

Platforms: Windows 98, Windows NT 4.0, Windows Millennium Edition, Windows 2000, Windows XP Home Edition, Windows XP Professional, Windows Server 2003 family

.NET Framework Security:

- Full trust for the immediate caller. This member cannot be used by partially trusted code.

LocalizationExtenderProvider.CanExtend Method

Indicates whether this object can provide its extender properties to the specified object.

```
[Visual Basic]
Public Overridable Function CanExtend( _
   ByVal o As Object _
) As Boolean Implements IExtenderProvider.CanExtend
[C#]
public virtual bool CanExtend(
   object o
);
[C++]
public: virtual bool CanExtend(
   Object* o
);
[JScript]
public function CanExtend(
   o : Object
) : Boolean;
```

Parameters

o

The object to receive the extender properties.

Return Value

true if this object can provide extender properties to the specified object; otherwise, **false**.

Implements

IExtenderProvider.CanExtend

Requirements

Platforms: Windows 98, Windows NT 4.0, Windows Millennium Edition, Windows 2000, Windows XP Home Edition, Windows XP Professional, Windows Server 2003 family

.NET Framework Security:

- Full trust for the immediate caller. This member cannot be used by partially trusted code.

LocalizationExtenderProvider.Dispose Method

Disposes of the resources (other than memory) used by the **LocalizationExtenderProvider**.

```
[Visual Basic]
Public Overridable Sub Dispose() Implements IDisposable.Dispose
[C#]
public virtual void Dispose();
[C++]
public: virtual void Dispose();
[JScript]
public function Dispose();
```

Implements

IDisposable.Dispose

Remarks

Call **Dispose** when you are finished using the **LocalizationExtenderProvider**. The **Dispose** method leaves the **LocalizationExtenderProvider** in an unusable state. After calling **Dispose**, you must release all references to the **LocalizationExtenderProvider** so the memory it was occupying can be reclaimed by garbage collection.

> **Note** Always call **Dispose** before you release your last reference to the **LocalizationExtenderProvider**. Otherwise, the resources the **LocalizationExtenderProvider** is using will not be freed until garbage collection calls the **LocalizationExtenderProvider** object's destructor.

Requirements

Platforms: Windows 98, Windows NT 4.0, Windows Millennium Edition, Windows 2000, Windows XP Home Edition, Windows XP Professional, Windows Server 2003 family

.NET Framework Security:

- Full trust for the immediate caller. This member cannot be used by partially trusted code.

LocalizationExtenderProvider.GetLanguage Method

Gets the current resource culture for the specified object.

```
[Visual Basic]
Public Function GetLanguage( _
   ByVal o As Object _
) As CultureInfo
[C#]
public CultureInfo GetLanguage(
   object o
);
[C++]
public: CultureInfo* GetLanguage(
   Object* o
);
[JScript]
public function GetLanguage(
   o : Object
) : CultureInfo;
```

Parameters

o

The object to get the current resource culture for.

Return Value

A **CultureInfo** indicating the resource variety.

Remarks

This method returns the current resource culture used to access resource data for the specified object.

Requirements

Platforms: Windows 98, Windows NT 4.0, Windows Millennium Edition, Windows 2000, Windows XP Home Edition, Windows XP Professional, Windows Server 2003 family

.NET Framework Security:

- Full trust for the immediate caller. This member cannot be used by partially trusted code.

LocalizationExtenderProvider.GetLoadLanguage Method

Gets the default resource culture to use when initializing the values of a localized object at design time.

[Visual Basic]
```
Public Function GetLoadLanguage( _
   ByVal o As Object _
) As CultureInfo
```
[C#]
```
public CultureInfo GetLoadLanguage(
   object o
);
```
[C++]
```
public: CultureInfo* GetLoadLanguage(
   Object* o
);
```
[JScript]
```
public function GetLoadLanguage(
   o : Object
) : CultureInfo;
```

Parameters

o

The object to get the resource culture for.

Return Value

A **CultureInfo** indicating the resource culture to use to initialize the values of the specified object.

Requirements

Platforms: Windows 98, Windows NT 4.0, Windows Millennium Edition, Windows 2000, Windows XP Home Edition, Windows XP Professional, Windows Server 2003 family

.NET Framework Security:

- Full trust for the immediate caller. This member cannot be used by partially trusted code.

LocalizationExtenderProvider.GetLocalizable Method

Gets a value indicating whether the specified object supports resource localization.

[Visual Basic]
```
Public Function GetLocalizable( _
   ByVal o As Object _
) As Boolean
```
[C#]
```
public bool GetLocalizable(
   object o
);
```
[C++]
```
public: bool GetLocalizable(
   Object* o
);
```
[JScript]
```
public function GetLocalizable(
   o : Object
) : Boolean;
```

Parameters

o

The object to check for localization support.

Return Value

true if the specified object supports resource localization; otherwise, **false**.

Requirements

Platforms: Windows 98, Windows NT 4.0, Windows Millennium Edition, Windows 2000, Windows XP Home Edition, Windows XP Professional, Windows Server 2003 family

.NET Framework Security:

- Full trust for the immediate caller. This member cannot be used by partially trusted code.

LocalizationExtenderProvider.ResetLanguage Method

Resets the resource culture for the specified object.

[Visual Basic]
```
Public Sub ResetLanguage( _
   ByVal o As Object _
)
```
[C#]
```
public void ResetLanguage(
   object o
);
```
[C++]
```
public: void ResetLanguage(
   Object* o
);
```
[JScript]
```
public function ResetLanguage(
   o : Object
);
```

Parameters

o

The object to reset the resource culture for.

Remarks

If the specified object was initialized with localized resources when the designer loaded, this method sets the resource culture for the specified object to the resource culture used to initialize the values of the specified object when the designer loaded. If the specified object had no previous resource culture setting, the current resource culture is set to **InvariantCulture**.

Requirements

Platforms: Windows 98, Windows NT 4.0, Windows Millennium Edition, Windows 2000, Windows XP Home Edition, Windows XP Professional, Windows Server 2003 family

.NET Framework Security:

- Full trust for the immediate caller. This member cannot be used by partially trusted code.

LocalizationExtenderProvider.SetLanguage Method

Sets the current resource culture for the specified object to the specified resource culture.

```
[Visual Basic]
Public Sub SetLanguage( _
   ByVal o As Object, _
   ByVal language As CultureInfo _
)
[C#]
public void SetLanguage(
   object o,
   CultureInfo language
);
[C++]
public: void SetLanguage(
   Object* o,
   CultureInfo* language
);
[JScript]
public function SetLanguage(
   o : Object,
   language : CultureInfo
);
```

Parameters

o

The base component to set the resource culture for.

language

A **CultureInfo** that indicates the resource culture to use.

Requirements

Platforms: Windows 98, Windows NT 4.0, Windows Millennium Edition, Windows 2000, Windows XP Home Edition, Windows XP Professional, Windows Server 2003 family

.NET Framework Security:

- Full trust for the immediate caller. This member cannot be used by partially trusted code.

LocalizationExtenderProvider.SetLocalizable Method

Sets a value indicating whether the specified object supports localized resources.

```
[Visual Basic]
Public Sub SetLocalizable( _
   ByVal o As Object, _
   ByVal localizable As Boolean _
)
[C#]
public void SetLocalizable(
   object o,
   bool localizable
);
[C++]
public: void SetLocalizable(
   Object* o,
   bool localizable
);
[JScript]
public function SetLocalizable(
   o : Object,
   localizable : Boolean
);
```

Parameters

o

The base component to set as localizable or not localizable.

localizable

true if the object supports resource localization; otherwise, **false**.

Requirements

Platforms: Windows 98, Windows NT 4.0, Windows Millennium Edition, Windows 2000, Windows XP Home Edition, Windows XP Professional, Windows Server 2003 family

.NET Framework Security:

- Full trust for the immediate caller. This member cannot be used by partially trusted code.

LocalizationExtenderProvider.ShouldSerializeLanguage Method

Gets a value indicating whether the specified object must have its localizable values persisted in a resource.

```
[Visual Basic]
Public Function ShouldSerializeLanguage( _
   ByVal o As Object _
) As Boolean
[C#]
public bool ShouldSerializeLanguage(
   object o
);
[C++]
public: bool ShouldSerializeLanguage(
   Object* o
);
[JScript]
public function ShouldSerializeLanguage(
   o : Object
) : Boolean;
```

Parameters

o

The object to get the language support persistence flag for.

Return Value

true if the localizable values should be persisted in resources; otherwise, **false**.

Requirements

Platforms: Windows 98, Windows NT 4.0, Windows Millennium Edition, Windows 2000, Windows XP Home Edition, Windows XP Professional, Windows Server 2003 family

.NET Framework Security:

- Full trust for the immediate caller. This member cannot be used by partially trusted code.

MenuCommand Class

Represents a Windows menu or toolbar command item.

System.Object
  System.ComponentModel.Design.MenuCommand
    System.ComponentModel.Design.DesignerVerb

[Visual Basic]
```
<ComVisible(True)>
Public Class MenuCommand
```
[C#]
```
[ComVisible(true)]
public class MenuCommand
```
[C++]
```
[ComVisible(true)]
public __gc class MenuCommand
```
[JScript]
```
public
   ComVisible(true)
class MenuCommand
```

Thread Safety

Any public static (**Shared** in Visual Basic) members of this type are safe for multithreaded operations. Any instance members are not guaranteed to be thread safe.

Remarks

MenuCommand represents information about a Windows menu or toolbar command. The **IMenuCommandService** interface allows you to add **MenuCommand** objects to the Visual Studio .NET menu.

This class provides the following members:

- An event-handler property to which you can attach an event handler for the command.
- A **CommandID** property that uniquely identifies the command.
- An **Invoke** method that executes the command.
- An **OnCommandChanged** method that can be overridden to handle the event that occurs when a new command is selected.
- Boolean flag states that indicate whether the command is **Checked**, **Enabled**, **Supported**, or **Visible**.
- An **OleStatus** property that indicates the OLE command status code for the command.
- An override for **ToString**.

Example

[Visual Basic, C#, C++] This example creates a **MenuCommand** object, configures its properties, and adds it to a **IMenuCommandService** object.

[Visual Basic]
```
' This example illustrates how to add a command of type ↵
 StandardCommand to a
'   service of type IMenuCommandService.  It defines a class ↵
that is a designer
'   to a component, called CDesigner.  Then it creates a ↵
 MenuCommand object using
'   one of the commands in the StandardCommands class. ↵
Finally, it sets several
'   of the properties in the MenuCommand object and adds ↵
 the MenuCommand object
'   to the MenuCommandService object.

Public Class CDesigner
   Inherits System.ComponentModel.Design.ComponentDesigner
   Public Overrides Sub Initialize(ByVal comp As IComponent)
      MyBase.Initialize(comp)

      Dim mcs As IMenuCommandService = ↵
CType(comp.Site.GetService(GetType(IMenuCommandService)), ↵
IMenuCommandService)
      Dim mc As New MenuCommand(New EventHandler(AddressOf ↵
 OnReplace), StandardCommands.Group)
      mc.Enabled = True
      mc.Visible = True
      mc.Supported = True
      mcs.AddCommand(mc)
      System.Windows.Forms.MessageBox.Show("Initialize() ↵
 has been invoked.")
   End Sub 'Initialize

   Private Sub OnReplace(ByVal sender As Object, ByVal e As EventArgs)
      System.Windows.Forms.MessageBox.Show("Replace() has ↵
 been invoked.")
   End Sub 'OnReplace
End Class 'CDesigner
```

[C#]
```
/* This example illustrates how to add a command of type ↵
StandardCommand to a
    service of type IMenuCommandService.  It defines a class ↵
 that is a designer
    to a component, called CDesigner.  Then it creates a ↵
MenuCommand object using
    one of the commands in the StandardCommands class. ↵
 Finally, it sets several
    of the properties in the MenuCommand object and adds ↵
 the MenuCommand object
    to the MenuCommandService object.
*/

public class CDesigner : System.ComponentModel.Design.ComponentDesigner
{
    public override void Initialize(IComponent comp)
    {
        base.Initialize(comp);

        IMenuCommandService mcs = (IMenuCommandService)comp.Site.
                    GetService(typeof(IMenuCommandService));
        MenuCommand mc = new MenuCommand(new ↵
EventHandler(OnReplace),StandardCommands.Group);
        mc.Enabled = true;
        mc.Visible = true;
        mc.Supported = true;
        mcs.AddCommand(mc);
        System.Windows.Forms.MessageBox.Show("Initialize() ↵
 has been invoked.");
    }

    private void OnReplace(object sender, EventArgs e)
    {
        System.Windows.Forms.MessageBox.Show("Replace() ↵
has been invoked.");
    }
} // End Class Component1
```

[C++]
```
/* This example illustrates how to add a command of type ↵
StandardCommand to a
    service of type IMenuCommandService.  It defines a ↵
class that is a designer
    to a component, called CDesigner.  Then it creates a ↵
 MenuCommand object using
    one of the commands in the StandardCommands class. ↵
 Finally, it sets several
    of the properties in the MenuCommand object and adds ↵
the MenuCommand object
    to the MenuCommandService object.
*/
```

```
public __gc class CDesigner : public ComponentDesigner {
public:

    void Initialize(IComponent* comp)
    {
        ComponentDesigner::Initialize(comp);

        IMenuCommandService* mcs =
            static_cast<IMenuCommandService*>(comp->                ↵
Site->GetService(__typeof(IMenuCommandService)));
        MenuCommand* mc = new MenuCommand(new EventHandler          ↵
 (this, OnReplace), StandardCommands::Group);
        mc->Enabled = true;
        mc->Visible = true;
        mc->Supported = true;
        mcs->AddCommand(mc);
        System::Windows::Forms::MessageBox::Show(S"Initialize()     ↵
 has been invoked.");
    }

private:

    void OnReplace(Object* sender, EventArgs* e)
    {
        System::Windows::Forms::MessageBox::Show(S"Replace()        ↵
 has been invoked.");
    }
}; // End Class CDesigner
```

Requirements

Namespace: System.ComponentModel.Design

Platforms: Windows 98, Windows NT 4.0, Windows Millennium Edition, Windows 2000, Windows XP Home Edition, Windows XP Professional, Windows Server 2003 family

Assembly: System (in System.dll)

MenuCommand Constructor

Initializes a new instance of the **MenuCommand** class.

[Visual Basic]
```
Public Sub New( _
   ByVal handler As EventHandler, _
   ByVal command As CommandID _
)
```
[C#]
```
public MenuCommand(
   EventHandler handler,
   CommandID command
);
```
[C++]
```
public: MenuCommand(
   EventHandler* handler,
   CommandID* command
);
```
[JScript]
```
public function MenuCommand(
   handler : EventHandler,
   command : CommandID
);
```

Parameters

handler

The event to raise when the user selects the menu item or toolbar button.

command

The unique command ID that links this menu command to the environment's menu.

Requirements

Platforms: Windows 98, Windows NT 4.0, Windows Millennium Edition, Windows 2000, Windows XP Home Edition, Windows XP Professional, Windows Server 2003 family

MenuCommand.Checked Property

Gets or sets a value indicating whether this menu item is checked.

[Visual Basic]
```
Public Overridable Property Checked As Boolean
```
[C#]
```
public virtual bool Checked {get; set;}
```
[C++]
```
public: __property virtual bool get_Checked();
public: __property virtual void set_Checked(bool);
```
[JScript]
```
public function get Checked() : Boolean;
public function set Checked(Boolean);
```

Property Value

true if the item is checked; otherwise, **false**.

Requirements

Platforms: Windows 98, Windows NT 4.0, Windows Millennium Edition, Windows 2000, Windows XP Home Edition, Windows XP Professional, Windows Server 2003 family

MenuCommand.CommandID Property

Gets the **CommandID** associated with this menu command.

[Visual Basic]
```
Public Overridable ReadOnly Property CommandID As CommandID
```
[C#]
```
public virtual CommandID CommandID {get;}
```
[C++]
```
public: __property virtual CommandID* get_CommandID();
```
[JScript]
```
public function get CommandID() : CommandID;
```

Property Value

The **CommandID** associated with the menu command.

Requirements

Platforms: Windows 98, Windows NT 4.0, Windows Millennium Edition, Windows 2000, Windows XP Home Edition, Windows XP Professional, Windows Server 2003 family

MenuCommand.Enabled Property

Gets a value indicating whether this menu item is available.

[Visual Basic]
```
Public Overridable Property Enabled As Boolean
```
[C#]
```
public virtual bool Enabled {get; set;}
```

```
[C++]
public: __property virtual bool get_Enabled();
public: __property virtual void set_Enabled(bool);
[JScript]
public function get Enabled() : Boolean;
public function set Enabled(Boolean);
```

Property Value

true if the item is enabled; otherwise, **false**.

Requirements

Platforms: Windows 98, Windows NT 4.0, Windows Millennium Edition, Windows 2000, Windows XP Home Edition, Windows XP Professional, Windows Server 2003 family

MenuCommand.OleStatus Property

Gets the OLE command status code for this menu item.

```
[Visual Basic]
Public Overridable ReadOnly Property OleStatus As Integer
[C#]
public virtual int OleStatus {get;}
[C++]
public: __property virtual int get_OleStatus();
[JScript]
public function get OleStatus() : int;
```

Property Value

An integer containing a mixture of status flags that reflect the state of this menu item.

Requirements

Platforms: Windows 98, Windows NT 4.0, Windows Millennium Edition, Windows 2000, Windows XP Home Edition, Windows XP Professional, Windows Server 2003 family

MenuCommand.Supported Property

Gets or sets a value indicating whether this menu item is supported.

```
[Visual Basic]
Public Overridable Property Supported As Boolean
[C#]
public virtual bool Supported {get; set;}
[C++]
public: __property virtual bool get_Supported();
public: __property virtual void set_Supported(bool);
[JScript]
public function get Supported() : Boolean;
public function set Supported(Boolean);
```

Property Value

true if the item is supported, which is the default; otherwise, **false**.

Requirements

Platforms: Windows 98, Windows NT 4.0, Windows Millennium Edition, Windows 2000, Windows XP Home Edition, Windows XP Professional, Windows Server 2003 family

MenuCommand.Visible Property

Gets or sets a value indicating whether this menu item is visible.

```
[Visual Basic]
Public Overridable Property Visible As Boolean
[C#]
public virtual bool Visible {get; set;}
[C++]
public: __property virtual bool get_Visible();
public: __property virtual void set_Visible(bool);
[JScript]
public function get Visible() : Boolean;
public function set Visible(Boolean);
```

Property Value

true if the item is visible; otherwise, **false**.

Requirements

Platforms: Windows 98, Windows NT 4.0, Windows Millennium Edition, Windows 2000, Windows XP Home Edition, Windows XP Professional, Windows Server 2003 family

MenuCommand.Invoke Method

Invokes the command.

```
[Visual Basic]
Public Overridable Sub Invoke()
[C#]
public virtual void Invoke();
[C++]
public: virtual void Invoke();
[JScript]
public function Invoke();
```

Requirements

Platforms: Windows 98, Windows NT 4.0, Windows Millennium Edition, Windows 2000, Windows XP Home Edition, Windows XP Professional, Windows Server 2003 family

MenuCommand.OnCommandChanged Method

Provides notification and is called in response to a **CommandChanged** event.

```
[Visual Basic]
Protected Overridable Sub OnCommandChanged( _
   ByVal e As EventArgs _
)
[C#]
protected virtual void OnCommandChanged(
   EventArgs e
);
[C++]
protected: virtual void OnCommandChanged(
   EventArgs* e
);
[JScript]
protected function OnCommandChanged(
   e : EventArgs
);
```

Parameters

e

An **EventArgs** that contains the event data.

Remarks

This method provides an opportunity to handle processing or display that occur when the command changes.

Requirements

Platforms: Windows 98, Windows NT 4.0, Windows Millennium Edition, Windows 2000, Windows XP Home Edition, Windows XP Professional, Windows Server 2003 family

MenuCommand.ToString Method

Returns a string representation of this menu command.

[Visual Basic]
```
Overrides Public Function ToString() As String
```
[C#]
```
public override string ToString();
```
[C++]
```
public: String* ToString();
```
[JScript]
```
public override function ToString() : String;
```

Return Value

A string containing the value of the **CommandID** property appended with the names of any flags that are set, separated by "|". These flag properties include **Checked**, **Enabled**, **Supported**, and **Visible**.

Requirements

Platforms: Windows 98, Windows NT 4.0, Windows Millennium Edition, Windows 2000, Windows XP Home Edition, Windows XP Professional, Windows Server 2003 family

MenuCommand.CommandChanged Event

Occurs when the menu command changes.

[Visual Basic]
```
Public Event CommandChanged As EventHandler
```
[C#]
```
public event EventHandler CommandChanged;
```
[C++]
```
public: __event EventHandler* CommandChanged;
```

[JScript] In JScript, you can handle the events defined by a class, but you cannot define your own.

Event Data

The event handler receives an argument of type **EventArgs**.

Remarks

A command can change if it becomes checked or disabled.

Requirements

Platforms: Windows 98, Windows NT 4.0, Windows Millennium Edition, Windows 2000, Windows XP Home Edition, Windows XP Professional, Windows Server 2003 family

ObjectSelectorEditor Class

This type supports the .NET Framework infrastructure and is not intended to be used directly from your code.

```
[Visual Basic]
MustInherit Public Class ObjectSelectorEditor
   Inherits UITypeEditor
[C#]
public abstract class ObjectSelectorEditor : UITypeEditor
[C++]
public __gc __abstract class ObjectSelectorEditor : public
   UITypeEditor
[JScript]
public abstract class ObjectSelectorEditor extends UITypeEditor
```

ObjectSelectorEditor Constructor

This member supports the .NET Framework infrastructure and is not intended to be used directly from your code.

Overload List

This member supports the .NET Framework infrastructure and is not intended to be used directly from your code.

[Visual Basic] **Public Sub New()**

[C#] **public ObjectSelectorEditor();**

[C++] **public: ObjectSelectorEditor();**

[JScript] **public function ObjectSelectorEditor();**

This member supports the .NET Framework infrastructure and is not intended to be used directly from your code.

[Visual Basic] **Public Sub New(Boolean)**

[C#] **public ObjectSelectorEditor(bool);**

[C++] **public: ObjectSelectorEditor(bool);**

[JScript] **public function ObjectSelectorEditor(Boolean);**

ObjectSelectorEditor Constructor ()

This member supports the .NET Framework infrastructure and is not intended to be used directly from your code.

```
[Visual Basic]
Public Sub New()
[C#]
public ObjectSelectorEditor();
[C++]
public: ObjectSelectorEditor();
[JScript]
public function ObjectSelectorEditor();
```

ObjectSelectorEditor Constructor (Boolean)

This member supports the .NET Framework infrastructure and is not intended to be used directly from your code.

```
[Visual Basic]
Public Sub New( _
   ByVal subObjectSelector As Boolean _
)
[C#]
public ObjectSelectorEditor(
   bool subObjectSelector
);
[C++]
public: ObjectSelectorEditor(
   bool subObjectSelector
);
[JScript]
public function ObjectSelectorEditor(
   subObjectSelector : Boolean
);
```

ObjectSelectorEditor.currValue Field

This member supports the .NET Framework infrastructure and is not intended to be used directly from your code.

```
[Visual Basic]
Protected currValue As Object
[C#]
protected object currValue;
[C++]
protected: Object* currValue;
[JScript]
protected var currValue : Object;
```

ObjectSelectorEditor.prevValue Field

This member supports the .NET Framework infrastructure and is not intended to be used directly from your code.

```
[Visual Basic]
Protected prevValue As Object
[C#]
protected object prevValue;
[C++]
protected: Object* prevValue;
[JScript]
protected var prevValue : Object;
```

ObjectSelectorEditor.SubObjectSelector Field

This member supports the .NET Framework infrastructure and is not intended to be used directly from your code.

```
[Visual Basic]
Public SubObjectSelector As Boolean
[C#]
public bool SubObjectSelector;
[C++]
public: bool SubObjectSelector;
[JScript]
public var SubObjectSelector : Boolean;
```

ObjectSelectorEditor.EditValue Method

This member supports the .NET Framework infrastructure and is not intended to be used directly from your code.

Overload List

This member supports the .NET Framework infrastructure and is not intended to be used directly from your code.

[Visual Basic] **Overloads Overrides Public Function EditValue(ITypeDescriptorContext, IServiceProvider, Object) As Object**

[C#] **public override object EditValue(ITypeDescriptorContext, IServiceProvider, object);**

[C++] **public: Object* EditValue(ITypeDescriptorContext*, IServiceProvider*, Object*);**

[JScript] **public override function EditValue(ITypeDescriptorContext, IServiceProvider, Object) : Object;**

This member supports the .NET Framework infrastructure and is not intended to be used directly from your code.

[Visual Basic] **Overloads Public Function EditValue(IServiceProvider, Object) As Object**

[C#] **public object EditValue(IServiceProvider, object);**

[C++] **public: Object* EditValue(IServiceProvider*, Object*);**

[JScript] **public function EditValue(IServiceProvider, Object) : Object;**

ObjectSelectorEditor.EditValue Method (ITypeDescriptorContext, IServiceProvider, Object)

This member supports the .NET Framework infrastructure and is not intended to be used directly from your code.

```
[Visual Basic]
Overrides Overloads Public Function EditValue( _
   ByVal context As ITypeDescriptorContext, _
   ByVal provider As IServiceProvider, _
   ByVal value As Object _
) As Object
[C#]
public override object EditValue(
   ITypeDescriptorContext context,
   IServiceProvider provider,
   object value
);
[C++]
public: Object* EditValue(
   ITypeDescriptorContext* context,
   IServiceProvider* provider,
   Object* value
);
[JScript]
public override function EditValue(
   context : ITypeDescriptorContext,
   provider : IServiceProvider,
   value : Object
) : Object;
```

ObjectSelectorEditor.EqualsToValue Method

This member supports the .NET Framework infrastructure and is not intended to be used directly from your code.

```
[Visual Basic]
Public Function EqualsToValue( _
   ByVal value As Object _
) As Boolean
[C#]
public bool EqualsToValue(
   object value
);
[C++]
public: bool EqualsToValue(
   Object* value
);
[JScript]
public function EqualsToValue(
   value : Object
) : Boolean;
```

ObjectSelectorEditor.FillTreeWithData Method

This member supports the .NET Framework infrastructure and is not intended to be used directly from your code.

```
[Visual Basic]
Protected Overridable Sub FillTreeWithData( _
   ByVal selector As ObjectSelectorEditor.Selector, _
   ByVal context As ITypeDescriptorContext, _
   ByVal provider As IServiceProvider _
)
[C#]
protected virtual void FillTreeWithData(
   ObjectSelectorEditor.Selector selector,
   ITypeDescriptorContext context,
   IServiceProvider provider
);
[C++]
protected: virtual void FillTreeWithData(
   ObjectSelectorEditor.Selector* selector,
   ITypeDescriptorContext* context,
   IServiceProvider* provider
);
[JScript]
protected function FillTreeWithData(
   selector : ObjectSelectorEditor.Selector,
   context : ITypeDescriptorContext,
   provider : IServiceProvider
);
```

ObjectSelectorEditor.GetEditStyle Method

This member supports the .NET Framework infrastructure and is not intended to be used directly from your code.

Overload List

This member supports the .NET Framework infrastructure and is not intended to be used directly from your code.

[Visual Basic] **Overloads Overrides Public Function GetEditStyle(ITypeDescriptorContext) As UITypeEditorEditStyle**

[C#] **public override UITypeEditorEditStyle GetEditStyle(ITypeDescriptorContext);**

[C++] **public: UITypeEditorEditStyle GetEditStyle(ITypeDescriptorContext*);**

[JScript] **public override function GetEditStyle(ITypeDescriptorContext) : UITypeEditorEditStyle;**

This member supports the .NET Framework infrastructure and is not intended to be used directly from your code.

[Visual Basic] **Overloads Public Function GetEditStyle() As UITypeEditorEditStyle**

[C#] **public UITypeEditorEditStyle GetEditStyle();**

[C++] **public: UITypeEditorEditStyle GetEditStyle();**

[JScript] **public function GetEditStyle() : UITypeEditorEditStyle;**

ObjectSelectorEditor.GetEditStyle Method (ITypeDescriptorContext)

This member supports the .NET Framework infrastructure and is not intended to be used directly from your code.

[Visual Basic]
```
Overrides Overloads Public Function GetEditStyle( _
   ByVal context As ITypeDescriptorContext _
) As UITypeEditorEditStyle
```
[C#]
```
public override UITypeEditorEditStyle GetEditStyle(
   ITypeDescriptorContext context
);
```
[C++]
```
public: UITypeEditorEditStyle GetEditStyle(
   ITypeDescriptorContext* context
);
```
[JScript]
```
public override function GetEditStyle(
   context : ITypeDescriptorContext
) : UITypeEditorEditStyle;
```

ObjectSelectorEditor.SetValue Method

This member supports the .NET Framework infrastructure and is not intended to be used directly from your code.

[Visual Basic]
```
Public Overridable Sub SetValue( _
   ByVal value As Object _
)
```
[C#]
```
public virtual void SetValue(
   object value
);
```
[C++]
```
public: virtual void SetValue(
   Object* value
);
```
[JScript]
```
public function SetValue(
   value : Object
);
```

ObjectSelectorEditor.Selector Class

This type supports the .NET Framework infrastructure and is not intended to be used directly from your code.

[Visual Basic]
```
Public Class ObjectSelectorEditor.Selector
   Inherits TreeView
```
[C#]
```
public class ObjectSelectorEditor.Selector : TreeView
```
[C++]
```
public __gc class ObjectSelectorEditor.Selector : public TreeView
```
[JScript]
```
public class ObjectSelectorEditor.Selector extends TreeView
```

ObjectSelectorEditor.Selector Constructor

This member supports the .NET Framework infrastructure and is not intended to be used directly from your code.

[Visual Basic]
```
Public Sub New( _
   ByVal editor As ObjectSelectorEditor _
)
```
[C#]
```
public ObjectSelectorEditor.Selector(
   ObjectSelectorEditor editor
);
```
[C++]
```
public: Selector(
   ObjectSelectorEditor* editor
);
```
[JScript]
```
public function ObjectSelectorEditor.Selector(
   editor : ObjectSelectorEditor
);
```

ObjectSelectorEditor.Selector.clickSeen Field

This member supports the .NET Framework infrastructure and is not intended to be used directly from your code.

[Visual Basic]
```
Public clickSeen As Boolean
```
[C#]
```
public bool clickSeen;
```
[C++]
```
public: bool clickSeen;
```
[JScript]
```
public var clickSeen : Boolean;
```

ObjectSelectorEditor.Selector.AddNode Method

This member supports the .NET Framework infrastructure and is not intended to be used directly from your code.

[Visual Basic]
```
Public Function AddNode( _
   ByVal label As String, _
   ByVal value As Object, _
   ByVal parent As ObjectSelectorEditor.SelectorNode _
) As SelectorNode
```
[C#]
```
public SelectorNode AddNode(
   string label,
   object value,
   ObjectSelectorEditor.SelectorNode parent
);
```
[C++]
```
public: SelectorNode* AddNode(
   String* label,
   Object* value,
   ObjectSelectorEditor.SelectorNode* parent
);
```
[JScript]
```
public function AddNode(
   label : String,
   value : Object,
   parent : ObjectSelectorEditor.SelectorNode
) : SelectorNode;
```

ObjectSelectorEditor.Selector.Clear Method

This member supports the .NET Framework infrastructure and is not intended to be used directly from your code.

[Visual Basic]
```
Public Sub Clear()
```
[C#]
```
public void Clear();
```
[C++]
```
public: void Clear();
```
[JScript]
```
public function Clear();
```

ObjectSelectorEditor.Selector.OnAfterSelect Method

This member supports the .NET Framework infrastructure and is not intended to be used directly from your code.

Overload List

This member supports the .NET Framework infrastructure and is not intended to be used directly from your code.

[Visual Basic] **Overloads Protected Sub OnAfterSelect(Object, TreeViewEventArgs)**

[C#] **protected void OnAfterSelect(object, TreeViewEventArgs);**

[C++] **protected: void OnAfterSelect(Object*, TreeViewEventArgs*);**

[JScript] **protected function OnAfterSelect(Object, TreeViewEventArgs);**

This member supports the .NET Framework infrastructure and is not intended to be used directly from your code.

[Visual Basic] **Overloads Protected Overridable Sub OnAfterSelect(TreeViewEventArgs)**

[C#] **protected virtual void OnAfterSelect(TreeViewEventArgs);**

[C++] **protected: virtual void OnAfterSelect(TreeViewEventArgs*);**

[JScript] **protected function OnAfterSelect(TreeViewEventArgs);**

ObjectSelectorEditor.Selector.OnAfterSelect Method (Object, TreeViewEventArgs)

This member supports the .NET Framework infrastructure and is not intended to be used directly from your code.

```
[Visual Basic]
Overloads Protected Sub OnAfterSelect( _
   ByVal sender As Object, _
   ByVal e As TreeViewEventArgs _
)
[C#]
protected void OnAfterSelect(
   object sender,
   TreeViewEventArgs e
);
[C++]
protected: void OnAfterSelect(
   Object* sender,
   TreeViewEventArgs* e
);
[JScript]
protected function OnAfterSelect(
   sender : Object,
   e : TreeViewEventArgs
);
```

ObjectSelectorEditor.Selector.OnKeyDown Method

This member supports the .NET Framework infrastructure and is not intended to be used directly from your code.

```
[Visual Basic]
Overrides Protected Sub OnKeyDown( _
   ByVal e As KeyEventArgs _
)
[C#]
protected override void OnKeyDown(
   KeyEventArgs e
);
[C++]
protected: void OnKeyDown(
   KeyEventArgs* e
);
[JScript]
protected override function OnKeyDown(
   e : KeyEventArgs
);
```

ObjectSelectorEditor.Selector.OnKeyPress Method

This member supports the .NET Framework infrastructure and is not intended to be used directly from your code.

```
[Visual Basic]
Overrides Protected Sub OnKeyPress( _
   ByVal e As KeyPressEventArgs _
)
[C#]
protected override void OnKeyPress(
   KeyPressEventArgs e
);
[C++]
protected: void OnKeyPress(
   KeyPressEventArgs* e
);
[JScript]
protected override function OnKeyPress(
   e : KeyPressEventArgs
);
```

ObjectSelectorEditor.Selector.SetSelection Method

This member supports the .NET Framework infrastructure and is not intended to be used directly from your code.

```
[Visual Basic]
Public Function SetSelection( _
   ByVal value As Object, _
   ByVal nodes As TreeNodeCollection _
) As Boolean
[C#]
public bool SetSelection(
   object value,
   TreeNodeCollection nodes
);
[C++]
public: bool SetSelection(
   Object* value,
   TreeNodeCollection* nodes
);
[JScript]
public function SetSelection(
   value : Object,
   nodes : TreeNodeCollection
) : Boolean;
```

ObjectSelectorEditor.Selector.Start Method

This member supports the .NET Framework infrastructure and is not intended to be used directly from your code.

```
[Visual Basic]
Public Sub Start( _
   ByVal edSvc As IWindowsFormsEditorService, _
   ByVal value As Object _
)
[C#]
public void Start(
   IWindowsFormsEditorService edSvc,
   object value
);
[C++]
public: void Start(
   IWindowsFormsEditorService* edSvc,
   Object* value
);
[JScript]
public function Start(
   edSvc : IWindowsFormsEditorService,
   value : Object
);
```

ObjectSelectorEditor.Selector.Stop Method

This member supports the .NET Framework infrastructure and is not intended to be used directly from your code.

```
[Visual Basic]
Public Sub Stop()
[C#]
public void Stop();
[C++]
public: void Stop();
[JScript]
public function Stop();
```

ObjectSelectorEditor.Selector.WndProc Method

This member supports the .NET Framework infrastructure and is not intended to be used directly from your code.

```
[Visual Basic]
Overrides Protected Sub WndProc( _
   ByRef m As Message _
)
[C#]
protected override void WndProc(
   ref Message m
);
[C++]
protected: void WndProc(
   Message* m
);
[JScript]
protected override function WndProc(
   m : Message
);
```

ObjectSelectorEditor.SelectorNode Class

This type supports the .NET Framework infrastructure and is not intended to be used directly from your code.

[Visual Basic]
```
Public Class ObjectSelectorEditor.SelectorNode
   Inherits TreeNode
```
[C#]
```
public class ObjectSelectorEditor.SelectorNode : TreeNode
```
[C++]
```
public __gc class ObjectSelectorEditor.SelectorNode : public
   TreeNode
```
[JScript]
```
public class ObjectSelectorEditor.SelectorNode extends TreeNode
```

ObjectSelectorEditor.SelectorNode Constructor

This member supports the .NET Framework infrastructure and is not intended to be used directly from your code.

[Visual Basic]
```
Public Sub New( _
   ByVal label As String, _
   ByVal value As Object _
)
```
[C#]
```
public ObjectSelectorEditor.SelectorNode(
   string label,
   object value
);
```
[C++]
```
public: SelectorNode(
   String* label,
   Object* value
);
```
[JScript]
```
public function ObjectSelectorEditor.SelectorNode(
   label : String,
   value : Object
);
```

ObjectSelectorEditor.SelectorNode.value Field

This member supports the .NET Framework infrastructure and is not intended to be used directly from your code.

[Visual Basic]
```
Public value As Object
```
[C#]
```
public object value;
```
[C++]
```
public: Object* value;
```
[JScript]
```
public var value : Object;
```

SelectionTypes Enumeration

Defines identifiers that indicate the type of a selection.

This enumeration has a **FlagsAttribute** attribute that allows a bitwise combination of its member values.

[Visual Basic]
```
<Flags>
<Serializable>
<ComVisible(True)>
Public Enum SelectionTypes
```
[C#]
```
[Flags]
[Serializable]
[ComVisible(true)]
public enum SelectionTypes
```
[C++]
```
[Flags]
[Serializable]
[ComVisible(true)]
__value public enum SelectionTypes
```
[JScript]
```
public
   Flags
   Serializable
   ComVisible(true)
enum SelectionTypes
```

Remarks

Components of a designer document can be selected using the **SetSelectedComponents** method of the **ISelectionService**. Some types of actions can operate on a selected component or group of selected components. The **ISelectionService** keeps track of the selection type of the current selection. These selection type identifiers indicate whether the selection was completed using a single click, a mouse down or mouse up selection, whether the selection should replace the previous selection, or use the default selection mode.

Use the **SelectionTypes** enumeration to specify the type of a selection when setting a new selection using the **SetSelectedComponents** method.

Members

Member name	Description	Value
Click	A selection that occurs when a user clicks a component. If the newly selected component is already selected, it is promoted to be the primary selected component rather than being deselected.	16
MouseDown	A selection that occurs when the user presses on the mouse button when the mouse pointer is over a component. If the component under the pointer is already selected, it is promoted to become the primary selected component rather than being deselected.	4
MouseUp	A selection that occurs when the user releases the mouse button immediately after a component has been selected. If the newly selected component is already selected, it is promoted to be the primary selected component rather than being deselected.	8
Normal	A regular selection. The selection service responds to the control and shift keys to support adding or removing components to or from the selection.	1
Replace	A selection that occurs when the content of a selection is replaced. The selection service replaces the current selection with the replacement.	2
Valid	Identifies the valid selection types as **Normal**, **Replace**, **MouseDown**, **MouseUp**, or **Click**.	31

Requirements

Namespace: System.ComponentModel.Design

Platforms: Windows 98, Windows NT 4.0, Windows Millennium Edition, Windows 2000, Windows XP Home Edition, Windows XP Professional, Windows Server 2003 family

Assembly: System (in System.dll)

ServiceContainer Class

Provides a simple implementation of the **IServiceContainer** interface. This class cannot be inherited.

System.Object
  System.ComponentModel.Design.ServiceContainer

```
[Visual Basic]
NotInheritable Public Class ServiceContainer
   Implements IServiceContainer, IServiceProvider
[C#]
public sealed class ServiceContainer : IServiceContainer,
   IServiceProvider
[C++]
public __gc __sealed class ServiceContainer : public
   IServiceContainer, IServiceProvider
[JScript]
public class ServiceContainer implements IServiceContainer,
   IServiceProvider
```

Thread Safety

Any public static (**Shared** in Visual Basic) members of this type are safe for multithreaded operations. Any instance members are not guaranteed to be thread safe.

Remarks

The **ServiceContainer** object can be used to store and provide services. **ServiceContainer** implements the **IServiceContainer** interface.

The **ServiceContainer** object can be created using a constructor that adds a parent **IServiceContainer** through which services can be optionally added to or removed from all parent **IServiceContainer** objects, including the immediate parent **IServiceContainer**. To add or remove a service from all **IServiceContainer** implementations that are linked to this **IServiceContainer** through parenting, call the **AddService** or **RemoveService** method overload that accepts a Boolean value indicating whether to promote the service request.

Requirements

Namespace: System.ComponentModel.Design

Platforms: Windows 98, Windows NT 4.0, Windows Millennium Edition, Windows 2000, Windows XP Home Edition, Windows XP Professional, Windows Server 2003 family

Assembly: System (in System.dll)

ServiceContainer Constructor

Initializes a new instance of the **ServiceContainer** class.

Overload List

Initializes a new instance of the **ServiceContainer** class.

[Visual Basic] **Public Sub New()**

[C#] **public ServiceContainer();**

[C++] **public: ServiceContainer();**

[JScript] **public function ServiceContainer();**

Initializes a new instance of the **ServiceContainer** class using the specified parent service provider.

[Visual Basic] **Public Sub New(IServiceProvider)**

[C#] **public ServiceContainer(IServiceProvider);**

[C++] **public: ServiceContainer(IServiceProvider*);**

[JScript] **public function ServiceContainer(IServiceProvider);**

ServiceContainer Constructor ()

Initializes a new instance of the **ServiceContainer** class.

```
[Visual Basic]
Public Sub New()
[C#]
public ServiceContainer();
[C++]
public: ServiceContainer();
[JScript]
public function ServiceContainer();
```

Requirements

Platforms: Windows 98, Windows NT 4.0, Windows Millennium Edition, Windows 2000, Windows XP Home Edition, Windows XP Professional, Windows Server 2003 family

ServiceContainer Constructor (IServiceProvider)

Initializes a new instance of the **ServiceContainer** class using the specified parent service provider.

```
[Visual Basic]
Public Sub New( _
   ByVal parentProvider As IServiceProvider _
)
[C#]
public ServiceContainer(
   IServiceProvider parentProvider
);
[C++]
public: ServiceContainer(
   IServiceProvider* parentProvider
);
[JScript]
public function ServiceContainer(
   parentProvider : IServiceProvider
);
```

Parameters

parentProvider
  A parent service provider.

Remarks

The service container uses this service object provider to retrieve services, if they are not available locally in the container.

Requirements

Platforms: Windows 98, Windows NT 4.0, Windows Millennium Edition, Windows 2000, Windows XP Home Edition, Windows XP Professional, Windows Server 2003 family

ServiceContainer.AddService Method

Adds the specified service to the service container.

Overload List

Adds the specified service to the service container.

[Visual Basic] **Overloads Public Overridable Sub AddService(Type, Object) Implements IServiceContainer.AddService**

[C#] **public virtual void AddService(Type, object);**

[C++] **public: virtual void AddService(Type*, Object*);**

[JScript] **public function AddService(Type, Object);**

Adds the specified service to the service container.

[Visual Basic] **Overloads Public Overridable Sub AddService(Type, ServiceCreatorCallback) Implements IServiceContainer.AddService**

[C#] **public virtual void AddService(Type, ServiceCreatorCallback);**

[C++] **public: virtual void AddService(Type*, ServiceCreatorCallback*);**

[JScript] **public function AddService(Type, ServiceCreatorCallback);**

Adds the specified service to the service container.

[Visual Basic] **Overloads Public Overridable Sub AddService(Type, Object, Boolean) Implements IServiceContainer.AddService**

[C#] **public virtual void AddService(Type, object, bool);**

[C++] **public: virtual void AddService(Type*, Object*, bool);**

[JScript] **public function AddService(Type, Object, Boolean);**

Adds the specified service to the service container.

[Visual Basic] **Overloads Public Overridable Sub AddService(Type, ServiceCreatorCallback, Boolean) Implements IServiceContainer.AddService**

[C#] **public virtual void AddService(Type, ServiceCreatorCallback, bool);**

[C++] **public: virtual void AddService(Type*, ServiceCreatorCallback*, bool);**

[JScript] **public function AddService(Type, ServiceCreatorCallback, Boolean);**

Example

[Visual Basic, C#, C++] The following example illustrates how to add a service to a **ServiceContainer**.

> [Visual Basic, C#, C++] **Note** This example shows how to use one of the overloaded versions of **AddService**. For other examples that might be available, see the individual overload topics.

[Visual Basic]
```
m_MyServiceContainer.AddService(GetType(Control), New ↵
ServiceCreatorCallback( _
        AddressOf CreateNewControl))
```

[C#]
```
m_MyServiceContainer.AddService(typeof(Control),
    new ServiceCreatorCallback(this.CreateNewControl));
```

[C++]
```
m_MyServiceContainer->AddService(__typeof(Control),
    new ServiceCreatorCallback(this, CreateNewControl));
```

ServiceContainer.AddService Method (Type, Object)

Adds the specified service to the service container.

[Visual Basic]
```
Overloads Public Overridable Sub AddService( _
   ByVal serviceType As Type, _
   ByVal serviceInstance As Object _
) Implements IServiceContainer.AddService
```
[C#]
```
public virtual void AddService(
   Type serviceType,
   object serviceInstance
);
```
[C++]
```
public: virtual void AddService(
   Type* serviceType,
   Object* serviceInstance
);
```
[JScript]
```
public function AddService(
   serviceType : Type,
   serviceInstance : Object
);
```

Parameters

serviceType
 The type of service to add.

serviceInstance
 An instance of the service to add. This object must implement or inherit from the type indicated by the *serviceType* parameter.

Implements

IServiceContainer.AddService

Example

[Visual Basic, C#, C++] The following example illustrates how to add a service to a **ServiceContainer**.

[Visual Basic]
```
m_MyServiceContainer.AddService(GetType(Control), sender)
```

[C#]
```
m_MyServiceContainer.AddService(typeof(Control), sender);
```

[C++]
```
m_MyServiceContainer->AddService(__typeof(Control), sender);
```

Requirements

Platforms: Windows 98, Windows NT 4.0, Windows Millennium Edition, Windows 2000, Windows XP Home Edition, Windows XP Professional, Windows Server 2003 family

ServiceContainer.AddService Method (Type, ServiceCreatorCallback)

Adds the specified service to the service container.

[Visual Basic]
```
Overloads Public Overridable Sub AddService( _
   ByVal serviceType As Type, _
   ByVal callback As ServiceCreatorCallback _
) Implements IServiceContainer.AddService
```

[C#]
```
public virtual void AddService(
   Type serviceType,
   ServiceCreatorCallback callback
);
```
[C++]
```
public: virtual void AddService(
   Type* serviceType,
   ServiceCreatorCallback* callback
);
```
[JScript]
```
public function AddService(
   serviceType : Type,
   callback : ServiceCreatorCallback
);
```

Parameters

serviceType
The type of service to add.

callback
A callback object that can create the service. This allows a service to be declared as available, but delays creation of the object until the service is requested.

Implements

IServiceContainer.AddService

Example

[Visual Basic, C#, C++] The following example illustrates how to add a service to a **ServiceContainer**.

[Visual Basic]
```
m_MyServiceContainer.AddService(GetType(Control), New ServiceCreatorCallback( _
        AddressOf CreateNewControl))
```

[C#]
```
m_MyServiceContainer.AddService(typeof(Control),
   new ServiceCreatorCallback(this.CreateNewControl));
```

[C++]
```
m_MyServiceContainer->AddService(__typeof(Control),
   new ServiceCreatorCallback(this, CreateNewControl));
```

Requirements

Platforms: Windows 98, Windows NT 4.0, Windows Millennium Edition, Windows 2000, Windows XP Home Edition, Windows XP Professional, Windows Server 2003 family

ServiceContainer.AddService Method (Type, Object, Boolean)

Adds the specified service to the service container.

[Visual Basic]
```
Overloads Public Overridable Sub AddService( _
   ByVal serviceType As Type, _
   ByVal serviceInstance As Object, _
   ByVal promote As Boolean _
) Implements IServiceContainer.AddService
```
[C#]
```
public virtual void AddService(
   Type serviceType,
   object serviceInstance,
   bool promote
);
```
[C++]
```
public: virtual void AddService(
   Type* serviceType,
   Object* serviceInstance,
   bool promote
);
```
[JScript]
```
public function AddService(
   serviceType : Type,
   serviceInstance : Object,
   promote : Boolean
);
```

Parameters

serviceType
The type of service to add.

serviceInstance
An instance of the service type to add. This object must implement or inherit from the type indicated by the *serviceType* parameter.

promote
true if this service should be added to any parent service containers; otherwise, **false**.

Implements

IServiceContainer.AddService

Requirements

Platforms: Windows 98, Windows NT 4.0, Windows Millennium Edition, Windows 2000, Windows XP Home Edition, Windows XP Professional, Windows Server 2003 family

ServiceContainer.AddService Method (Type, ServiceCreatorCallback, Boolean)

Adds the specified service to the service container.

[Visual Basic]
```
Overloads Public Overridable Sub AddService( _
   ByVal serviceType As Type, _
   ByVal callback As ServiceCreatorCallback, _
   ByVal promote As Boolean _
) Implements IServiceContainer.AddService
```
[C#]
```
public virtual void AddService(
   Type serviceType,
   ServiceCreatorCallback callback,
   bool promote
);
```
[C++]
```
public: virtual void AddService(
   Type* serviceType,
   ServiceCreatorCallback* callback,
   bool promote
);
```

```
[JScript]
public function AddService(
   serviceType : Type,
   callback : ServiceCreatorCallback,
   promote : Boolean
);
```

Parameters

serviceType
The type of service to add.

callback
A callback object that can create the service. This allows a service to be declared as available, but delays creation of the object until the service is requested.

promote
true if this service should be added to any parent service containers; otherwise, **false**.

Implements

IServiceContainer.AddService

Requirements

Platforms: Windows 98, Windows NT 4.0, Windows Millennium Edition, Windows 2000, Windows XP Home Edition, Windows XP Professional, Windows Server 2003 family

ServiceContainer.GetService Method

Gets the requested service.

```
[Visual Basic]
Public Overridable Function GetService( _
   ByVal serviceType As Type _
) As Object Implements IServiceProvider.GetService
[C#]
public virtual object GetService(
   Type serviceType
);
[C++]
public: virtual Object* GetService(
   Type* serviceType
);
[JScript]
public function GetService(
   serviceType : Type
) : Object;
```

Parameters

serviceType
The type of service to retrieve.

Return Value

An instance of the service if it could be found, or a null reference (**Nothing** in Visual Basic) if it could not be found.

Implements

IServiceProvider.GetService

Requirements

Platforms: Windows 98, Windows NT 4.0, Windows Millennium Edition, Windows 2000, Windows XP Home Edition, Windows XP Professional, Windows Server 2003 family

ServiceContainer.RemoveService Method

Removes the specified service type from the service container.

Overload List

Removes the specified service type from the service container.

[Visual Basic] **Overloads Public Overridable Sub RemoveService(Type) Implements IServiceContainer.RemoveService**

[C#] **public virtual void RemoveService(Type);**

[C++] **public: virtual void RemoveService(Type*);**

[JScript] **public function RemoveService(Type);**

Removes the specified service type from the service container.

[Visual Basic] **Overloads Public Overridable Sub RemoveService(Type, Boolean) Implements IServiceContainer.RemoveService**

[C#] **public virtual void RemoveService(Type, bool);**

[C++] **public: virtual void RemoveService(Type*, bool);**

[JScript] **public function RemoveService(Type, Boolean);**

Example

[Visual Basic, C#, C++] The following example illustrates how to remove a service from a **ServiceContainer**.

> [Visual Basic, C#, C++] **Note** This example shows how to use one of the overloaded versions of **RemoveService**. For other examples that might be available, see the individual overload topics.

```
[Visual Basic]
m_MyServiceContainer.RemoveService(GetType(Control))

[C#]
m_MyServiceContainer.RemoveService(typeof(Control));

[C++]
m_MyServiceContainer->RemoveService(__typeof(Control));
```

ServiceContainer.RemoveService Method (Type)

Removes the specified service type from the service container.

```
[Visual Basic]
Overloads Public Overridable Sub RemoveService( _
   ByVal serviceType As Type _
) Implements IServiceContainer.RemoveService
[C#]
public virtual void RemoveService(
   Type serviceType
);
[C++]
public: virtual void RemoveService(
   Type* serviceType
);
[JScript]
public function RemoveService(
   serviceType : Type
);
```

Parameters

serviceType
The type of service to remove.

Implements

IServiceContainer.RemoveService

Example

[Visual Basic, C#, C++] The following example illustrates how to remove a service from a **ServiceContainer**.

[Visual Basic]
```
m_MyServiceContainer.RemoveService(GetType(Control))
```

[C#]
```
m_MyServiceContainer.RemoveService(typeof(Control));
```

[C++]
```
m_MyServiceContainer->RemoveService(__typeof(Control));
```

Requirements

Platforms: Windows 98, Windows NT 4.0, Windows Millennium Edition, Windows 2000, Windows XP Home Edition, Windows XP Professional, Windows Server 2003 family

ServiceContainer.RemoveService Method (Type, Boolean)

Removes the specified service type from the service container.

[Visual Basic]
```
Overloads Public Overridable Sub RemoveService( _
   ByVal serviceType As Type, _
   ByVal promote As Boolean _
) Implements IServiceContainer.RemoveService
```
[C#]
```
public virtual void RemoveService(
   Type serviceType,
   bool promote
);
```
[C++]
```
public: virtual void RemoveService(
   Type* serviceType,
   bool promote
);
```
[JScript]
```
public function RemoveService(
   serviceType : Type,
   promote : Boolean
);
```

Parameters

serviceType
: The type of service to remove.

promote
: **true** if this service should be removed from any parent service containers; otherwise, **false**.

Implements

IServiceContainer.RemoveService

Requirements

Platforms: Windows 98, Windows NT 4.0, Windows Millennium Edition, Windows 2000, Windows XP Home Edition, Windows XP Professional, Windows Server 2003 family

ServiceCreatorCallback Delegate

Provides a callback mechanism that can create an instance of a service on demand.

[Visual Basic]
```
<Serializable>
<ComVisible(True)>
Public Delegate Function Sub ServiceCreatorCallback( _
   ByVal container As IServiceContainer, _
   ByVal serviceType As Type _
) As Object
```
[C#]
```
[Serializable]
[ComVisible(true)]
public delegate object ServiceCreatorCallback(
   IServiceContainer container,
   Type serviceType
);
```
[C++]
```
[Serializable]
[ComVisible(true)]
public __gc __delegate Object* ServiceCreatorCallback(
   IServiceContainer* container,
   Type* serviceType
);
```

[JScript] In JScript, you can use the delegates in the .NET Framework, but you cannot define your own.

Parameters [Visual Basic, C#, C++]

The declaration of your callback method must have the same parameters as the **ServiceCreatorCallback** delegate declaration.

container
: The service container that requested the creation of the service.

serviceType
: The type of service to create.

Remarks

ServiceCreatorCallback provides a mechanism to publish services that you can request to have created when needed, rather than the service being created immediately when the designer loads. You can use a callback function if the service is not essential and may not be used. A service published by using a **ServiceCreatorCallback** does not use as many additional resources if it is not requested and created. To use a callback function to publish your service, pass a **ServiceCreatorCallback** to the **AddService** method of an **IServiceContainer**.

Example

[Visual Basic, C#] The following code example shows how to publish a service using a callback function:

[Visual Basic]
```
' The following code shows how to publish a service using a ↵
callback function.

' Creates a service creator callback.
Dim callback1 As New ServiceCreatorCallback _
(AddressOf myCallBackMethod)

' Adds the service using its type and the service creator.
serviceContainer.AddService(GetType(myService), callback1)
```

[C#]
```
// The following code shows how to publish a service using a ↵
callback function.

// Creates a service creator callback.
ServiceCreatorCallback callback1 =
new ServiceCreatorCallback(myCallBackMethod);

// Adds the service using its type and the service creator callback.
serviceContainer.AddService(typeof(myService), callback1);
```

Requirements

Namespace: System.ComponentModel.Design

Platforms: Windows 98, Windows NT 4.0, Windows Millennium Edition, Windows 2000, Windows XP Home Edition, Windows XP Professional, Windows Server 2003 family

Assembly: System (in System.dll)

StandardCommands Class

Defines identifiers for the standard set of commands that are available to most applications.

System.Object
  System.ComponentModel.Design.StandardCommands
    System.Windows.Forms.Design.MenuCommands

[Visual Basic]
```
Public Class StandardCommands
```
[C#]
```
public class StandardCommands
```
[C++]
```
public __gc class StandardCommands
```
[JScript]
```
public class StandardCommands
```

Thread Safety

Any public static (**Shared** in Visual Basic) members of this type are safe for multithreaded operations. Any instance members are not guaranteed to be thread safe.

Remarks

This class defines **CommandID** identifiers for standard commands that are available to designers.

To add a command from **StandardCommands** to a designer menu, you must call the **AddCommand** of an **IMenuCommandService** object and add a **MenuCommand** that contains a **CommandID** from **StandardCommands**.

Example

[Visual Basic, C#, C++] This example illustrates how to add a member of **StandardCommands** to a **MenuCommand** object and how to add the **MenuCommand** object to a **IMenuCommandService** object.

[Visual Basic]
```
' This example illustrates how to add a command of type
StandardCommand to a
'   service of type IMenuCommandService.  It defines a class
that is a designer
'   to a component, called CDesigner.  Then it creates a
MenuCommand object using
'   one of the commands in the StandardCommands class.
Finally, it sets several
'   of the properties in the MenuCommand object and adds
the MenuCommand object
'   to the MenuCommandService object.

Public Class CDesigner
   Inherits System.ComponentModel.Design.ComponentDesigner

   Public Overrides Sub Initialize(ByVal comp As IComponent)
      MyBase.Initialize(comp)

      Dim mcs As IMenuCommandService =
CType(comp.Site.GetService(GetType(IMenuCommandService)),
IMenuCommandService)
      Dim mc As New MenuCommand(New EventHandler(AddressOf
OnReplace), StandardCommands.Group)
      mc.Enabled = True
      mc.Visible = True
      mc.Supported = True
      mcs.AddCommand(mc)
      System.Windows.Forms.MessageBox.Show("Initialize()
has been invoked.")
   End Sub 'Initialize

   Private Sub OnReplace(ByVal sender As Object, ByVal e As EventArgs)
      System.Windows.Forms.MessageBox.Show("Replace() has been
invoked.")
   End Sub 'OnReplace
End Class 'CDesigner
```

[C#]
```
/* This example illustrates how to add a command of type
StandardCommand to a
    service of type IMenuCommandService.  It defines a class
 that is a designer
    to a component, called CDesigner.  Then it creates a
MenuCommand object using
    one of the commands in the StandardCommands class.
Finally, it sets several
    of the properties in the MenuCommand object and adds
the MenuCommand object
    to the MenuCommandService object.
*/

public class CDesigner : System.ComponentModel.Design.ComponentDesigner
{
    public override void Initialize(IComponent comp)
    {
        base.Initialize(comp);

        IMenuCommandService mcs = (IMenuCommandService)comp.Site.
                    GetService(typeof(IMenuCommandService));
        MenuCommand mc = new MenuCommand(new
EventHandler(OnReplace),StandardCommands.Group);
        mc.Enabled = true;
        mc.Visible = true;
        mc.Supported = true;
        mcs.AddCommand(mc);
        System.Windows.Forms.MessageBox.Show("Initialize()
 has been invoked.");
    }

    private void OnReplace(object sender, EventArgs e)
    {
        System.Windows.Forms.MessageBox.Show("Replace()
has been invoked.");
    }
} // End Class Component1
```

[C++]
```
/* This example illustrates how to add a command of type
StandardCommand to a
    service of type IMenuCommandService.  It defines a class
 that is a designer
    to a component, called CDesigner.  Then it creates a
MenuCommand object using
    one of the commands in the StandardCommands class.
Finally, it sets several
    of the properties in the MenuCommand object and adds the
MenuCommand object
    to the MenuCommandService object.
*/

public __gc class CDesigner : public ComponentDesigner {
public:

    void Initialize(IComponent* comp)
    {
        ComponentDesigner::Initialize(comp);

        IMenuCommandService* mcs =
            static_cast<IMenuCommandService*>(comp->Site-
>GetService(__typeof(IMenuCommandService)));
        MenuCommand* mc = new MenuCommand(new EventHandler
 (this, OnReplace), StandardCommands::Group);
        mc->Enabled = true;
        mc->Visible = true;
        mc->Supported = true;
        mcs->AddCommand(mc);
```

```
        System::Windows::Forms::MessageBox::Show
    (S"Initialize() has been invoked.");
    }

private:

    void OnReplace(Object* sender, EventArgs* e)
    {
        System::Windows::Forms::MessageBox::Show(S"Replace()
has been invoked.");
    }
}; // End Class CDesigner
```

Requirements

Namespace: System.ComponentModel.Design

Platforms: Windows 98, Windows NT 4.0, Windows Millennium Edition, Windows 2000, Windows XP Home Edition, Windows XP Professional, Windows Server 2003 family

Assembly: System (in System.dll)

StandardCommands Constructor

Initializes a new instance of the **StandardCommands** class.

[Visual Basic]
```
Public Sub New()
```
[C#]
```
public StandardCommands();
```
[C++]
```
public: StandardCommands();
```
[JScript]
```
public function StandardCommands();
```

Remarks

The default constructor initializes any fields to their default values.

Requirements

Platforms: Windows 98, Windows NT 4.0, Windows Millennium Edition, Windows 2000, Windows XP Home Edition, Windows XP Professional, Windows Server 2003 family

StandardCommands.AlignBottom Field

Gets the **CommandID** for the **Align -> Bottoms** command. This field is read-only.

[Visual Basic]
```
Public Shared ReadOnly AlignBottom As CommandID
```
[C#]
```
public static readonly CommandID AlignBottom;
```
[C++]
```
public: static CommandID* AlignBottom;
```
[JScript]
```
public static var AlignBottom : CommandID;
```

Requirements

Platforms: Windows 98, Windows NT 4.0, Windows Millennium Edition, Windows 2000, Windows XP Home Edition, Windows XP Professional, Windows Server 2003 family

StandardCommands.AlignHorizontalCenters Field

Gets the **CommandID** for the **Align -> Middles** command. This field is read-only.

[Visual Basic]
```
Public Shared ReadOnly AlignHorizontalCenters As CommandID
```
[C#]
```
public static readonly CommandID AlignHorizontalCenters;
```
[C++]
```
public: static CommandID* AlignHorizontalCenters;
```
[JScript]
```
public static var AlignHorizontalCenters : CommandID;
```

Requirements

Platforms: Windows 98, Windows NT 4.0, Windows Millennium Edition, Windows 2000, Windows XP Home Edition, Windows XP Professional, Windows Server 2003 family

StandardCommands.AlignLeft Field

Gets the **CommandID** for the **Align -> Lefts** command. This field is read-only.

[Visual Basic]
```
Public Shared ReadOnly AlignLeft As CommandID
```
[C#]
```
public static readonly CommandID AlignLeft;
```
[C++]
```
public: static CommandID* AlignLeft;
```
[JScript]
```
public static var AlignLeft : CommandID;
```

Requirements

Platforms: Windows 98, Windows NT 4.0, Windows Millennium Edition, Windows 2000, Windows XP Home Edition, Windows XP Professional, Windows Server 2003 family

StandardCommands.AlignRight Field

Gets the **CommandID** for the **Align -> Rights** command. This field is read-only.

[Visual Basic]
```
Public Shared ReadOnly AlignRight As CommandID
```
[C#]
```
public static readonly CommandID AlignRight;
```
[C++]
```
public: static CommandID* AlignRight;
```
[JScript]
```
public static var AlignRight : CommandID;
```

Requirements

Platforms: Windows 98, Windows NT 4.0, Windows Millennium Edition, Windows 2000, Windows XP Home Edition, Windows XP Professional, Windows Server 2003 family

StandardCommands.AlignToGrid Field

Gets the **CommandID** for the **Align -> toGrid** command. This field is read-only.

[Visual Basic]
```
Public Shared ReadOnly AlignToGrid As CommandID
```
[C#]
```
public static readonly CommandID AlignToGrid;
```
[C++]
```
public: static CommandID* AlignToGrid;
```
[JScript]
```
public static var AlignToGrid : CommandID;
```

Requirements

Platforms: Windows 98, Windows NT 4.0, Windows Millennium Edition, Windows 2000, Windows XP Home Edition, Windows XP Professional, Windows Server 2003 family

StandardCommands.AlignTop Field

Gets the **CommandID** for the **Align -> Tops** command. This field is read-only.

[Visual Basic]
```
Public Shared ReadOnly AlignTop As CommandID
```
[C#]
```
public static readonly CommandID AlignTop;
```
[C++]
```
public: static CommandID* AlignTop;
```
[JScript]
```
public static var AlignTop : CommandID;
```

Requirements

Platforms: Windows 98, Windows NT 4.0, Windows Millennium Edition, Windows 2000, Windows XP Home Edition, Windows XP Professional, Windows Server 2003 family

StandardCommands.AlignVerticalCenters Field

Gets the **CommandID** for the **Align -> Centers** command. This field is read-only.

[Visual Basic]
```
Public Shared ReadOnly AlignVerticalCenters As CommandID
```
[C#]
```
public static readonly CommandID AlignVerticalCenters;
```
[C++]
```
public: static CommandID* AlignVerticalCenters;
```
[JScript]
```
public static var AlignVerticalCenters : CommandID;
```

Requirements

Platforms: Windows 98, Windows NT 4.0, Windows Millennium Edition, Windows 2000, Windows XP Home Edition, Windows XP Professional, Windows Server 2003 family

StandardCommands.ArrangeBottom Field

Gets the **CommandID** for the **ArrangeBottom** command. This field is read-only.

[Visual Basic]
```
Public Shared ReadOnly ArrangeBottom As CommandID
```
[C#]
```
public static readonly CommandID ArrangeBottom;
```
[C++]
```
public: static CommandID* ArrangeBottom;
```
[JScript]
```
public static var ArrangeBottom : CommandID;
```

Requirements

Platforms: Windows 98, Windows NT 4.0, Windows Millennium Edition, Windows 2000, Windows XP Home Edition, Windows XP Professional, Windows Server 2003 family

StandardCommands.ArrangeIcons Field

Gets the **CommandID** for the **ArrangeIcons** command. This field is read-only.

[Visual Basic]
```
Public Shared ReadOnly ArrangeIcons As CommandID
```
[C#]
```
public static readonly CommandID ArrangeIcons;
```
[C++]
```
public: static CommandID* ArrangeIcons;
```
[JScript]
```
public static var ArrangeIcons : CommandID;
```

Requirements

Platforms: Windows 98, Windows NT 4.0, Windows Millennium Edition, Windows 2000, Windows XP Home Edition, Windows XP Professional, Windows Server 2003 family

StandardCommands.ArrangeRight Field

Gets the **CommandID** for the **ArrangeRight** command. This field is read-only.

[Visual Basic]
```
Public Shared ReadOnly ArrangeRight As CommandID
```
[C#]
```
public static readonly CommandID ArrangeRight;
```
[C++]
```
public: static CommandID* ArrangeRight;
```
[JScript]
```
public static var ArrangeRight : CommandID;
```

Requirements

Platforms: Windows 98, Windows NT 4.0, Windows Millennium Edition, Windows 2000, Windows XP Home Edition, Windows XP Professional, Windows Server 2003 family

StandardCommands.BringForward Field

Gets the **CommandID** for the **BringForward** command. This field is read-only.

[Visual Basic]
```
Public Shared ReadOnly BringForward As CommandID
```
[C#]
```
public static readonly CommandID BringForward;
```
[C++]
```
public: static CommandID* BringForward;
```
[JScript]
```
public static var BringForward : CommandID;
```

Requirements

Platforms: Windows 98, Windows NT 4.0, Windows Millennium Edition, Windows 2000, Windows XP Home Edition, Windows XP Professional, Windows Server 2003 family

StandardCommands.BringToFront Field

Gets the **CommandID** for the **BringToFront** command. This field is read-only.

[Visual Basic]
```
Public Shared ReadOnly BringToFront As CommandID
```
[C#]
```
public static readonly CommandID BringToFront;
```
[C++]
```
public: static CommandID* BringToFront;
```
[JScript]
```
public static var BringToFront : CommandID;
```

Requirements

Platforms: Windows 98, Windows NT 4.0, Windows Millennium Edition, Windows 2000, Windows XP Home Edition, Windows XP Professional, Windows Server 2003 family

StandardCommands.CenterHorizontally Field

Gets the **CommandID** for the **CenterHorizontally** command. This field is read-only.

[Visual Basic]
```
Public Shared ReadOnly CenterHorizontally As CommandID
```
[C#]
```
public static readonly CommandID CenterHorizontally;
```
[C++]
```
public: static CommandID* CenterHorizontally;
```
[JScript]
```
public static var CenterHorizontally : CommandID;
```

Requirements

Platforms: Windows 98, Windows NT 4.0, Windows Millennium Edition, Windows 2000, Windows XP Home Edition, Windows XP Professional, Windows Server 2003 family

StandardCommands.CenterVertically Field

Gets the **CommandID** for the **CenterVertically** command. This field is read-only.

[Visual Basic]
```
Public Shared ReadOnly CenterVertically As CommandID
```
[C#]
```
public static readonly CommandID CenterVertically;
```
[C++]
```
public: static CommandID* CenterVertically;
```
[JScript]
```
public static var CenterVertically : CommandID;
```

Requirements

Platforms: Windows 98, Windows NT 4.0, Windows Millennium Edition, Windows 2000, Windows XP Home Edition, Windows XP Professional, Windows Server 2003 family

StandardCommands.Copy Field

Gets the **CommandID** for the **Copy** command. This field is read-only.

[Visual Basic]
```
Public Shared ReadOnly Copy As CommandID
```
[C#]
```
public static readonly CommandID Copy;
```
[C++]
```
public: static CommandID* Copy;
```
[JScript]
```
public static var Copy : CommandID;
```

Requirements

Platforms: Windows 98, Windows NT 4.0, Windows Millennium Edition, Windows 2000, Windows XP Home Edition, Windows XP Professional, Windows Server 2003 family

StandardCommands.Cut Field

Gets the **CommandID** for the **Cut** command. This field is read-only.

[Visual Basic]
```
Public Shared ReadOnly Cut As CommandID
```
[C#]
```
public static readonly CommandID Cut;
```
[C++]
```
public: static CommandID* Cut;
```
[JScript]
```
public static var Cut : CommandID;
```

Requirements

Platforms: Windows 98, Windows NT 4.0, Windows Millennium Edition, Windows 2000, Windows XP Home Edition, Windows XP Professional, Windows Server 2003 family

StandardCommands.Delete Field

Gets the **CommandID** for the **Delete** command. This field is read-only.

[Visual Basic]
```
Public Shared ReadOnly Delete As CommandID
```
[C#]
```
public static readonly CommandID Delete;
```
[C++]
```
public: static CommandID* Delete;
```
[JScript]
```
public static var Delete : CommandID;
```

Requirements

Platforms: Windows 98, Windows NT 4.0, Windows Millennium Edition, Windows 2000, Windows XP Home Edition, Windows XP Professional, Windows Server 2003 family

StandardCommands.F1Help Field

Gets the **CommandID** for the **F1Help** command. This field is read-only.

[Visual Basic]
```
Public Shared ReadOnly F1Help As CommandID
```
[C#]
```
public static readonly CommandID F1Help;
```
[C++]
```
public: static CommandID* F1Help;
```
[JScript]
```
public static var F1Help : CommandID;
```

Requirements

Platforms: Windows 98, Windows NT 4.0, Windows Millennium Edition, Windows 2000, Windows XP Home Edition, Windows XP Professional, Windows Server 2003 family

StandardCommands.Group Field

Gets the **CommandID** for the **Group** command. This field is read-only.

[Visual Basic]
```
Public Shared ReadOnly Group As CommandID
```
[C#]
```
public static readonly CommandID Group;
```
[C++]
```
public: static CommandID* Group;
```
[JScript]
```
public static var Group : CommandID;
```

Requirements

Platforms: Windows 98, Windows NT 4.0, Windows Millennium Edition, Windows 2000, Windows XP Home Edition, Windows XP Professional, Windows Server 2003 family

StandardCommands.HorizSpaceConcatenate Field

Gets the **CommandID** for the **HorizSpaceConcatenate** command. This field is read-only.

[Visual Basic]
```
Public Shared ReadOnly HorizSpaceConcatenate As CommandID
```
[C#]
```
public static readonly CommandID HorizSpaceConcatenate;
```
[C++]
```
public: static CommandID* HorizSpaceConcatenate;
```
[JScript]
```
public static var HorizSpaceConcatenate : CommandID;
```

Requirements

Platforms: Windows 98, Windows NT 4.0, Windows Millennium Edition, Windows 2000, Windows XP Home Edition, Windows XP Professional, Windows Server 2003 family

StandardCommands.HorizSpaceDecrease Field

Gets the **CommandID** for the **HorizSpaceDecrease** command. This field is read-only.

[Visual Basic]
```
Public Shared ReadOnly HorizSpaceDecrease As CommandID
```
[C#]
```
public static readonly CommandID HorizSpaceDecrease;
```
[C++]
```
public: static CommandID* HorizSpaceDecrease;
```
[JScript]
```
public static var HorizSpaceDecrease : CommandID;
```

Requirements

Platforms: Windows 98, Windows NT 4.0, Windows Millennium Edition, Windows 2000, Windows XP Home Edition, Windows XP Professional, Windows Server 2003 family

StandardCommands.HorizSpaceIncrease Field

Gets the **CommandID** for the **HorizSpaceIncrease** command. This field is read-only.

[Visual Basic]
```
Public Shared ReadOnly HorizSpaceIncrease As CommandID
```
[C#]
```
public static readonly CommandID HorizSpaceIncrease;
```
[C++]
```
public: static CommandID* HorizSpaceIncrease;
```
[JScript]
```
public static var HorizSpaceIncrease : CommandID;
```

Requirements

Platforms: Windows 98, Windows NT 4.0, Windows Millennium Edition, Windows 2000, Windows XP Home Edition, Windows XP Professional, Windows Server 2003 family

StandardCommands.HorizSpaceMakeEqual Field

Gets the **CommandID** for the **HorizSpaceMakeEqual** command. This field is read-only.

[Visual Basic]
```
Public Shared ReadOnly HorizSpaceMakeEqual As CommandID
```
[C#]
```
public static readonly CommandID HorizSpaceMakeEqual;
```
[C++]
```
public: static CommandID* HorizSpaceMakeEqual;
```
[JScript]
```
public static var HorizSpaceMakeEqual : CommandID;
```

Requirements

Platforms: Windows 98, Windows NT 4.0, Windows Millennium Edition, Windows 2000, Windows XP Home Edition, Windows XP Professional, Windows Server 2003 family

StandardCommands.LineupIcons Field

Gets the **CommandID** for the **LineupIcons** command. This field is read-only.

[Visual Basic]
```
Public Shared ReadOnly LineupIcons As CommandID
```
[C#]
```
public static readonly CommandID LineupIcons;
```
[C++]
```
public: static CommandID* LineupIcons;
```
[JScript]
```
public static var LineupIcons : CommandID;
```

Requirements

Platforms: Windows 98, Windows NT 4.0, Windows Millennium Edition, Windows 2000, Windows XP Home Edition, Windows XP Professional, Windows Server 2003 family

StandardCommands.LockControls Field

Gets the **CommandID** for the **LockControls** command. This field is read-only.

[Visual Basic]
```
Public Shared ReadOnly LockControls As CommandID
```
[C#]
```
public static readonly CommandID LockControls;
```
[C++]
```
public: static CommandID* LockControls;
```
[JScript]
```
public static var LockControls : CommandID;
```

Requirements

Platforms: Windows 98, Windows NT 4.0, Windows Millennium Edition, Windows 2000, Windows XP Home Edition, Windows XP Professional, Windows Server 2003 family

StandardCommands.MultiLevelRedo Field

Gets the **CommandID** for the **MultiLevelRedo** command. This field is read-only.

[Visual Basic]
```
Public Shared ReadOnly MultiLevelRedo As CommandID
```
[C#]
```
public static readonly CommandID MultiLevelRedo;
```
[C++]
```
public: static CommandID* MultiLevelRedo;
```
[JScript]
```
public static var MultiLevelRedo : CommandID;
```

Requirements

Platforms: Windows 98, Windows NT 4.0, Windows Millennium Edition, Windows 2000, Windows XP Home Edition, Windows XP Professional, Windows Server 2003 family

StandardCommands.MultiLevelUndo Field

Gets the **CommandID** for the **MultiLevelUndo** command. This field is read-only.

[Visual Basic]
```
Public Shared ReadOnly MultiLevelUndo As CommandID
```
[C#]
```
public static readonly CommandID MultiLevelUndo;
```
[C++]
```
public: static CommandID* MultiLevelUndo;
```
[JScript]
```
public static var MultiLevelUndo : CommandID;
```

Requirements

Platforms: Windows 98, Windows NT 4.0, Windows Millennium Edition, Windows 2000, Windows XP Home Edition, Windows XP Professional, Windows Server 2003 family

StandardCommands.Paste Field

Gets the **CommandID** for the **Paste** command. This field is read-only.

[Visual Basic]
```
Public Shared ReadOnly Paste As CommandID
```
[C#]
```
public static readonly CommandID Paste;
```
[C++]
```
public: static CommandID* Paste;
```
[JScript]
```
public static var Paste : CommandID;
```

Requirements

Platforms: Windows 98, Windows NT 4.0, Windows Millennium Edition, Windows 2000, Windows XP Home Edition, Windows XP Professional, Windows Server 2003 family

StandardCommands.Properties Field

Gets the **CommandID** for the **Properties** command. This field is read-only.

[Visual Basic]
```
Public Shared ReadOnly Properties As CommandID
```
[C#]
```
public static readonly CommandID Properties;
```
[C++]
```
public: static CommandID* Properties;
```
[JScript]
```
public static var Properties : CommandID;
```

Requirements

Platforms: Windows 98, Windows NT 4.0, Windows Millennium Edition, Windows 2000, Windows XP Home Edition, Windows XP Professional, Windows Server 2003 family

StandardCommands.PropertiesWindow Field

Gets the **CommandID** for the **PropertiesWindow** command. This field is read-only.

[Visual Basic]
```
Public Shared ReadOnly PropertiesWindow As CommandID
```
[C#]
```
public static readonly CommandID PropertiesWindow;
```
[C++]
```
public: static CommandID* PropertiesWindow;
```
[JScript]
```
public static var PropertiesWindow : CommandID;
```

Requirements

Platforms: Windows 98, Windows NT 4.0, Windows Millennium Edition, Windows 2000, Windows XP Home Edition, Windows XP Professional, Windows Server 2003 family

StandardCommands.Redo Field

Gets the **CommandID** for the **Redo** command. This field is read-only.

[Visual Basic]
```
Public Shared ReadOnly Redo As CommandID
```
[C#]
```
public static readonly CommandID Redo;
```
[C++]
```
public: static CommandID* Redo;
```
[JScript]
```
public static var Redo : CommandID;
```

Requirements

Platforms: Windows 98, Windows NT 4.0, Windows Millennium Edition, Windows 2000, Windows XP Home Edition, Windows XP Professional, Windows Server 2003 family

StandardCommands.Replace Field

Gets the **CommandID** for the **Replace** command. This field is read-only.

[Visual Basic]
```
Public Shared ReadOnly Replace As CommandID
```
[C#]
```
public static readonly CommandID Replace;
```
[C++]
```
public: static CommandID* Replace;
```
[JScript]
```
public static var Replace : CommandID;
```

Requirements

Platforms: Windows 98, Windows NT 4.0, Windows Millennium Edition, Windows 2000, Windows XP Home Edition, Windows XP Professional, Windows Server 2003 family

StandardCommands.SelectAll Field

Gets the **CommandID** for the **SelectAll** command. This field is read-only.

[Visual Basic]
```
Public Shared ReadOnly SelectAll As CommandID
```
[C#]
```
public static readonly CommandID SelectAll;
```
[C++]
```
public: static CommandID* SelectAll;
```
[JScript]
```
public static var SelectAll : CommandID;
```

Requirements

Platforms: Windows 98, Windows NT 4.0, Windows Millennium Edition, Windows 2000, Windows XP Home Edition, Windows XP Professional, Windows Server 2003 family

StandardCommands.SendBackward Field

Gets the **CommandID** for the **SendBackward** command. This field is read-only.

[Visual Basic]
```
Public Shared ReadOnly SendBackward As CommandID
```
[C#]
```
public static readonly CommandID SendBackward;
```
[C++]
```
public: static CommandID* SendBackward;
```
[JScript]
```
public static var SendBackward : CommandID;
```

Requirements

Platforms: Windows 98, Windows NT 4.0, Windows Millennium Edition, Windows 2000, Windows XP Home Edition, Windows XP Professional, Windows Server 2003 family

StandardCommands.SendToBack Field

Gets the **CommandID** for the **SendToBack** command. This field is read-only.

[Visual Basic]
```
Public Shared ReadOnly SendToBack As CommandID
```
[C#]
```
public static readonly CommandID SendToBack;
```
[C++]
```
public: static CommandID* SendToBack;
```
[JScript]
```
public static var SendToBack : CommandID;
```

Requirements

Platforms: Windows 98, Windows NT 4.0, Windows Millennium Edition, Windows 2000, Windows XP Home Edition, Windows XP Professional, Windows Server 2003 family

StandardCommands.ShowGrid Field

Gets the **CommandID** for the **ShowGrid** command. This field is read-only.

[Visual Basic]
```
Public Shared ReadOnly ShowGrid As CommandID
```
[C#]
```
public static readonly CommandID ShowGrid;
```
[C++]
```
public: static CommandID* ShowGrid;
```
[JScript]
```
public static var ShowGrid : CommandID;
```

Requirements

Platforms: Windows 98, Windows NT 4.0, Windows Millennium Edition, Windows 2000, Windows XP Home Edition, Windows XP Professional, Windows Server 2003 family

StandardCommands.ShowLargeIcons Field

Gets the **CommandID** for the **ShowLargeIcons** command. This field is read-only.

[Visual Basic]
```
Public Shared ReadOnly ShowLargeIcons As CommandID
```
[C#]
```
public static readonly CommandID ShowLargeIcons;
```
[C++]
```
public: static CommandID* ShowLargeIcons;
```
[JScript]
```
public static var ShowLargeIcons : CommandID;
```

Requirements

Platforms: Windows 98, Windows NT 4.0, Windows Millennium Edition, Windows 2000, Windows XP Home Edition, Windows XP Professional, Windows Server 2003 family

StandardCommands.SizeToControl Field

Gets the **CommandID** for the **SizeToControl** command. This field is read-only.

[Visual Basic]
```
Public Shared ReadOnly SizeToControl As CommandID
```
[C#]
```
public static readonly CommandID SizeToControl;
```
[C++]
```
public: static CommandID* SizeToControl;
```
[JScript]
```
public static var SizeToControl : CommandID;
```

Requirements

Platforms: Windows 98, Windows NT 4.0, Windows Millennium Edition, Windows 2000, Windows XP Home Edition, Windows XP Professional, Windows Server 2003 family

StandardCommands.SizeToControlHeight Field

Gets the **CommandID** for the **SizeToControlHeight** command. This field is read-only.

[Visual Basic]
```
Public Shared ReadOnly SizeToControlHeight As CommandID
```
[C#]
```
public static readonly CommandID SizeToControlHeight;
```
[C++]
```
public: static CommandID* SizeToControlHeight;
```
[JScript]
```
public static var SizeToControlHeight : CommandID;
```

Requirements

Platforms: Windows 98, Windows NT 4.0, Windows Millennium Edition, Windows 2000, Windows XP Home Edition, Windows XP Professional, Windows Server 2003 family

StandardCommands.SizeToControlWidth Field

Gets the **CommandID** for the **SizeToControlWidth** command. This field is read-only.

[Visual Basic]
```
Public Shared ReadOnly SizeToControlWidth As CommandID
```
[C#]
```
public static readonly CommandID SizeToControlWidth;
```
[C++]
```
public: static CommandID* SizeToControlWidth;
```
[JScript]
```
public static var SizeToControlWidth : CommandID;
```

Requirements

Platforms: Windows 98, Windows NT 4.0, Windows Millennium Edition, Windows 2000, Windows XP Home Edition, Windows XP Professional, Windows Server 2003 family

StandardCommands.SizeToFit Field

Gets the **CommandID** for the **SizeToFit** command. This field is read-only.

[Visual Basic]
```
Public Shared ReadOnly SizeToFit As CommandID
```
[C#]
```
public static readonly CommandID SizeToFit;
```
[C++]
```
public: static CommandID* SizeToFit;
```
[JScript]
```
public static var SizeToFit : CommandID;
```

Requirements

Platforms: Windows 98, Windows NT 4.0, Windows Millennium Edition, Windows 2000, Windows XP Home Edition, Windows XP Professional, Windows Server 2003 family

StandardCommands.SizeToGrid Field

Gets the **CommandID** for the **SizeToGrid** command. This field is read-only.

[Visual Basic]
```
Public Shared ReadOnly SizeToGrid As CommandID
```
[C#]
```
public static readonly CommandID SizeToGrid;
```
[C++]
```
public: static CommandID* SizeToGrid;
```
[JScript]
```
public static var SizeToGrid : CommandID;
```

Requirements

Platforms: Windows 98, Windows NT 4.0, Windows Millennium Edition, Windows 2000, Windows XP Home Edition, Windows XP Professional, Windows Server 2003 family

StandardCommands.SnapToGrid Field

Gets the **CommandID** for the **SnapToGrid** command. This field is read-only.

[Visual Basic]
```
Public Shared ReadOnly SnapToGrid As CommandID
```
[C#]
```
public static readonly CommandID SnapToGrid;
```
[C++]
```
public: static CommandID* SnapToGrid;
```
[JScript]
```
public static var SnapToGrid : CommandID;
```

Requirements

Platforms: Windows 98, Windows NT 4.0, Windows Millennium Edition, Windows 2000, Windows XP Home Edition, Windows XP Professional, Windows Server 2003 family

StandardCommands.TabOrder Field

Gets the **CommandID** for the **TabOrder** command. This field is read-only.

[Visual Basic]
```
Public Shared ReadOnly TabOrder As CommandID
```
[C#]
```
public static readonly CommandID TabOrder;
```
[C++]
```
public: static CommandID* TabOrder;
```
[JScript]
```
public static var TabOrder : CommandID;
```

Requirements

Platforms: Windows 98, Windows NT 4.0, Windows Millennium Edition, Windows 2000, Windows XP Home Edition, Windows XP Professional, Windows Server 2003 family

StandardCommands.Undo Field

Gets the **CommandID** for the **Undo** command. This field is read-only.

[Visual Basic]
```
Public Shared ReadOnly Undo As CommandID
```
[C#]
```
public static readonly CommandID Undo;
```
[C++]
```
public: static CommandID* Undo;
```
[JScript]
```
public static var Undo : CommandID;
```

Requirements

Platforms: Windows 98, Windows NT 4.0, Windows Millennium Edition, Windows 2000, Windows XP Home Edition, Windows XP Professional, Windows Server 2003 family

StandardCommands.Ungroup Field

Gets the **CommandID** for the **Ungroup** command. This field is read-only.

[Visual Basic]
```
Public Shared ReadOnly Ungroup As CommandID
```
[C#]
```
public static readonly CommandID Ungroup;
```
[C++]
```
public: static CommandID* Ungroup;
```
[JScript]
```
public static var Ungroup : CommandID;
```

Requirements

Platforms: Windows 98, Windows NT 4.0, Windows Millennium Edition, Windows 2000, Windows XP Home Edition, Windows XP Professional, Windows Server 2003 family

StandardCommands.VerbFirst Field

Gets the first of a set of verbs. This field is read-only.

[Visual Basic]
```
Public Shared ReadOnly VerbFirst As CommandID
```
[C#]
```
public static readonly CommandID VerbFirst;
```
[C++]
```
public: static CommandID* VerbFirst;
```
[JScript]
```
public static var VerbFirst : CommandID;
```

Remarks

This is a special **CommandID** that identifies the first of a set of designer verbs.

The Visual Studio .NET form designer automatically maps designer verbs to the **Verbs** property on **IDesigner**, so generally you do not need to access this command.

All designer verbs for an object become commands with a **CommandID** within a sequential range of IDs that begins with **VerbFirst** and ends with **VerbLast**.

Requirements

Platforms: Windows 98, Windows NT 4.0, Windows Millennium Edition, Windows 2000, Windows XP Home Edition, Windows XP Professional, Windows Server 2003 family

StandardCommands.VerbLast Field

Gets the last of a set of verbs. This field is read-only.

[Visual Basic]
```
Public Shared ReadOnly VerbLast As CommandID
```
[C#]
```
public static readonly CommandID VerbLast;
```
[C++]
```
public: static CommandID* VerbLast;
```
[JScript]
```
public static var VerbLast : CommandID;
```

Remarks

This is a special **CommandID** that identifies the last of a set of designer verbs.

The Visual Studio .NET form designer automatically maps designer verbs to the **Verbs** property on **IDesigner**, so generally you do not need to access this command.

All designer verbs for an object become commands with a **CommandID** within a sequential range of IDs that begins with **VerbFirst** and ends with **VerbLast**.

Requirements

Platforms: Windows 98, Windows NT 4.0, Windows Millennium Edition, Windows 2000, Windows XP Home Edition, Windows XP Professional, Windows Server 2003 family

StandardCommands.VertSpaceConcatenate Field

Gets the **CommandID** for the **VertSpaceConcatenate** command. This field is read-only.

[Visual Basic]
```
Public Shared ReadOnly VertSpaceConcatenate As CommandID
```
[C#]
```
public static readonly CommandID VertSpaceConcatenate;
```
[C++]
```
public: static CommandID* VertSpaceConcatenate;
```
[JScript]
```
public static var VertSpaceConcatenate : CommandID;
```

Requirements

Platforms: Windows 98, Windows NT 4.0, Windows Millennium Edition, Windows 2000, Windows XP Home Edition, Windows XP Professional, Windows Server 2003 family

StandardCommands.VertSpaceDecrease Field

Gets the **CommandID** for the **VertSpaceDecrease** command. This field is read-only.

[Visual Basic]
```
Public Shared ReadOnly VertSpaceDecrease As CommandID
```
[C#]
```
public static readonly CommandID VertSpaceDecrease;
```
[C++]
```
public: static CommandID* VertSpaceDecrease;
```
[JScript]
```
public static var VertSpaceDecrease : CommandID;
```

Requirements

Platforms: Windows 98, Windows NT 4.0, Windows Millennium Edition, Windows 2000, Windows XP Home Edition, Windows XP Professional, Windows Server 2003 family

StandardCommands.VertSpaceIncrease Field

Gets the **CommandID** for the **VertSpaceIncrease** command. This field is read-only.

[Visual Basic]
```
Public Shared ReadOnly VertSpaceIncrease As CommandID
```
[C#]
```
public static readonly CommandID VertSpaceIncrease;
```
[C++]
```
public: static CommandID* VertSpaceIncrease;
```
[JScript]
```
public static var VertSpaceIncrease : CommandID;
```

Requirements

Platforms: Windows 98, Windows NT 4.0, Windows Millennium Edition, Windows 2000, Windows XP Home Edition, Windows XP Professional, Windows Server 2003 family

StandardCommands.VertSpaceMakeEqual Field

Gets the **CommandID** for the **VertSpaceMakeEqual** command. This field is read-only.

[Visual Basic]
```
Public Shared ReadOnly VertSpaceMakeEqual As CommandID
```
[C#]
```
public static readonly CommandID VertSpaceMakeEqual;
```
[C++]
```
public: static CommandID* VertSpaceMakeEqual;
```
[JScript]
```
public static var VertSpaceMakeEqual : CommandID;
```

Requirements

Platforms: Windows 98, Windows NT 4.0, Windows Millennium Edition, Windows 2000, Windows XP Home Edition, Windows XP Professional, Windows Server 2003 family

StandardCommands.ViewGrid Field

Gets the **CommandID** for the **ViewGrid** command. This field is read-only.

[Visual Basic]
```
Public Shared ReadOnly ViewGrid As CommandID
```
[C#]
```
public static readonly CommandID ViewGrid;
```
[C++]
```
public: static CommandID* ViewGrid;
```
[JScript]
```
public static var ViewGrid : CommandID;
```

Requirements

Platforms: Windows 98, Windows NT 4.0, Windows Millennium Edition, Windows 2000, Windows XP Home Edition, Windows XP Professional, Windows Server 2003 family

StandardToolWindows Class

Defines GUID identifiers that correspond to the standard set of tool windows that are available in the design environment.

System.Object
  System.ComponentModel.Design.StandardToolWindows

[Visual Basic]
```
Public Class StandardToolWindows
```
[C#]
```
public class StandardToolWindows
```
[C++]
```
public __gc class StandardToolWindows
```
[JScript]
```
public class StandardToolWindows
```

Thread Safety

Any public static (**Shared** in Visual Basic) members of this type are safe for multithreaded operations. Any instance members are not guaranteed to be thread safe.

Remarks

These GUIDs can be used to access the standard tool windows that are available to the design-time environment.

Requirements

Namespace: System.ComponentModel.Design

Platforms: Windows 98, Windows NT 4.0, Windows Millennium Edition, Windows 2000, Windows XP Home Edition, Windows XP Professional, Windows Server 2003 family

Assembly: System (in System.dll)

StandardToolWindows Constructor

Initializes a new instance of the **StandardToolWindows** class.

[Visual Basic]
```
Public Sub New()
```
[C#]
```
public StandardToolWindows();
```
[C++]
```
public: StandardToolWindows();
```
[JScript]
```
public function StandardToolWindows();
```

Remarks

The default constructor initializes any fields to their default values.

Requirements

Platforms: Windows 98, Windows NT 4.0, Windows Millennium Edition, Windows 2000, Windows XP Home Edition, Windows XP Professional, Windows Server 2003 family

StandardToolWindows.ObjectBrowser Field

Gets the GUID for the object browser.

[Visual Basic]
```
Public Shared ReadOnly ObjectBrowser As Guid
```
[C#]
```
public static readonly Guid ObjectBrowser;
```
[C++]
```
public: static Guid ObjectBrowser;
```
[JScript]
```
public static var ObjectBrowser : Guid;
```

Requirements

Platforms: Windows 98, Windows NT 4.0, Windows Millennium Edition, Windows 2000, Windows XP Home Edition, Windows XP Professional, Windows Server 2003 family

StandardToolWindows.OutputWindow Field

Gets the GUID for the output window.

[Visual Basic]
```
Public Shared ReadOnly OutputWindow As Guid
```
[C#]
```
public static readonly Guid OutputWindow;
```
[C++]
```
public: static Guid OutputWindow;
```
[JScript]
```
public static var OutputWindow : Guid;
```

Requirements

Platforms: Windows 98, Windows NT 4.0, Windows Millennium Edition, Windows 2000, Windows XP Home Edition, Windows XP Professional, Windows Server 2003 family

StandardToolWindows.ProjectExplorer Field

Gets the GUID for the solution explorer.

[Visual Basic]
```
Public Shared ReadOnly ProjectExplorer As Guid
```
[C#]
```
public static readonly Guid ProjectExplorer;
```
[C++]
```
public: static Guid ProjectExplorer;
```
[JScript]
```
public static var ProjectExplorer : Guid;
```

Requirements

Platforms: Windows 98, Windows NT 4.0, Windows Millennium Edition, Windows 2000, Windows XP Home Edition, Windows XP Professional, Windows Server 2003 family

StandardToolWindows.PropertyBrowser Field

Gets the GUID for the Properties window.

[Visual Basic]
```
Public Shared ReadOnly PropertyBrowser As Guid
```
[C#]
```
public static readonly Guid PropertyBrowser;
```
[C++]
```
public: static Guid PropertyBrowser;
```
[JScript]
```
public static var PropertyBrowser : Guid;
```

Requirements

Platforms: Windows 98, Windows NT 4.0, Windows Millennium Edition, Windows 2000, Windows XP Home Edition, Windows XP Professional, Windows Server 2003 family

StandardToolWindows.RelatedLinks Field

Gets the GUID for the related links frame.

[Visual Basic]
```
Public Shared ReadOnly RelatedLinks As Guid
```
[C#]
```
public static readonly Guid RelatedLinks;
```
[C++]
```
public: static Guid RelatedLinks;
```
[JScript]
```
public static var RelatedLinks : Guid;
```

Requirements

Platforms: Windows 98, Windows NT 4.0, Windows Millennium Edition, Windows 2000, Windows XP Home Edition, Windows XP Professional, Windows Server 2003 family

StandardToolWindows.ServerExplorer Field

Gets the GUID for the server explorer.

[Visual Basic]
```
Public Shared ReadOnly ServerExplorer As Guid
```
[C#]
```
public static readonly Guid ServerExplorer;
```
[C++]
```
public: static Guid ServerExplorer;
```
[JScript]
```
public static var ServerExplorer : Guid;
```

Requirements

Platforms: Windows 98, Windows NT 4.0, Windows Millennium Edition, Windows 2000, Windows XP Home Edition, Windows XP Professional, Windows Server 2003 family

StandardToolWindows.TaskList Field

Gets the GUID for the task list.

[Visual Basic]
```
Public Shared ReadOnly TaskList As Guid
```
[C#]
```
public static readonly Guid TaskList;
```
[C++]
```
public: static Guid TaskList;
```
[JScript]
```
public static var TaskList : Guid;
```

Requirements

Platforms: Windows 98, Windows NT 4.0, Windows Millennium Edition, Windows 2000, Windows XP Home Edition, Windows XP Professional, Windows Server 2003 family

StandardToolWindows.Toolbox Field

Gets the GUID for the toolbox.

[Visual Basic]
```
Public Shared ReadOnly Toolbox As Guid
```
[C#]
```
public static readonly Guid Toolbox;
```
[C++]
```
public: static Guid Toolbox;
```
[JScript]
```
public static var Toolbox : Guid;
```

Requirements

Platforms: Windows 98, Windows NT 4.0, Windows Millennium Edition, Windows 2000, Windows XP Home Edition, Windows XP Professional, Windows Server 2003 family

ViewTechnology Enumeration

Defines identifiers for a set of technologies that designer hosts support.

[Visual Basic]
```
<Serializable>
<ComVisible(True)>
Public Enum ViewTechnology
```
[C#]
```
[Serializable]
[ComVisible(true)]
public enum ViewTechnology
```
[C++]
```
[Serializable]
[ComVisible(true)]
__value public enum ViewTechnology
```
[JScript]
```
public
   Serializable
   ComVisible(true)
enum ViewTechnology
```

Remarks

ViewTechnology defines identifiers that can indicate the mode to use for controlling the display of a designer-hosted document.

Members

Member name	Description
Passthrough	A mode in which the view object is passed directly to the development environment. The view object must implement any interfaces the development environment requires. The Visual Studio .NET development environment supports view objects that are either an ActiveX control, active document, or an object that implements the IVsWindowPane interface that is available through Visual Studio VSI (Visual Studio Integration) program. **Note** The Visual Studio .NET development environment provides support for this view technology. Support for this view technology is not necessarily available in all development environments.
WindowsForms	A mode in which a Windows Forms control object provides the display for the root designer. The designer host fills the development environment document window with this control.

Requirements

Namespace: System.ComponentModel.Design

Platforms: Windows 98, Windows NT 4.0, Windows Millennium Edition, Windows 2000, Windows XP Home Edition, Windows XP Professional, Windows Server 2003 family

Assembly: System (in System.dll)

System.ComponentModel.Design.Serialization Namespace

The **System.ComponentModel.Design.Serialization** namespace provides types that support customization and control of serialization at design time.

The classes in this namespace can be divided into the following categories:

- Serialization attributes that can be used to indicate the serializer to use for a specific type: **DesignerSerializerAttribute**, to indicate the serializer to use for a particular type; and **RootDesignerSerializerAttribute**, to indicate the base serializer to use for the root designer.
- Classes that a designer can implement to customize serialization: **IDesignerLoaderHost**, for loading a designer document from a serialized state; and **IDesignerLoaderService**, for loading a designer document when external components and asynchronous loading are involved.
- Interfaces that a designer can use to manage the serialization process: **IDesignerSerializationManager**, to register or retrieve custom serializers; **IDesignerSerializationProvider**, to make a serializer available to an **IDesignerSerializationManager**; and **IDesignerSerializationService**, which provides methods to invoke serialization and deserialization.
- An interface that can be implemented to customize the loading process of a designer: **DesignerLoader**.
- An interface that can be used to optimize the reloading of a designer: **ICodeDomDesignerReload**.
- Other helper classes: **INameCreationService**, an interface for generating unique names for objects; **ContextStack**, a data structure useful for sharing serialization context information with serializers; and **InstanceDescriptor**, an object that can describe a serializable object.

CodeDomSerializer Class

Serializes an object graph to a series of CodeDOM statements. This class provides an abstract base class for a serializer.

System.Object
  System.ComponentModel.Design.Serialization.CodeDom-Serializer

[Visual Basic]
```
MustInherit Public Class CodeDomSerializer
```
[C#]
```
public abstract class CodeDomSerializer
```
[C++]
```
public __gc __abstract class CodeDomSerializer
```
[JScript]
```
public abstract class CodeDomSerializer
```

Thread Safety

Any public static (**Shared** in Visual Basic) members of this type are safe for multithreaded operations. Any instance members are not guaranteed to be thread safe.

Remarks

You can implement a custom **CodeDomSerializer** to control the generation of component initialization code for a type of component at design time.

To implement a custom **CodeDomSerializer** for a type, you must:

1. Define a class that der0ives from **CodeDomSerializer**.
2. Implement method overrides for serialization or deserialization methods. (See the information below for details.)
3. Associate your custom **CodeDomSerializer** implementation with a type of component using a **DesignerSerializerAttribute**.

To implement a serialization method for generating configuration code for a component:

1. Within a class that derives from **CodeDomSerializer**, override an appropriate serialization or deserialization method of the base class.
2. If you want the default serializer to generate code statements that perform the default component configuration, you must obtain and call the base serializer for the component. To obtain the base serializer for the component, call the **GetSerializer** method of the **IDesignerSerializationManager** passed to your method override. Pass the **GetSerializer** method the type of the component to serialize the configuration of, along with the base type of serializer you are requesting, which is **CodeDomSerializer**. Call the method of the same name you are overriding on the base serializer, using the **IDesignerSerializationManager** and object passed to your method override. If you are implementing the **Serialize** method, the **Serialize** method of the base serializer will return an object. The type of this object depends on the type of base serializer which depends on the type of component you are serializing the values of. If you are implementing the **SerializeEvents**, **SerializeProperties**, or **SerializePropertiesToResources** method, you must create a new **CodeStatementCollection** to contain the generated code statements, and pass it to the method.
3. If you have called a base serializer method, you will have a **CodeStatementCollection** that contains the statements to generate to initialize the component. Otherwise you should create a **CodeStatementCollection**. You can add **CodeStatement** objects representing statements to generate in the component configuration code to this collection.
4. Return the **CodeStatementCollection** that represents the source code to generate to configure the component.

Notes to Inheritors: When you inherit from **CodeDomSerializer**, you must override the following members: **Deserialize** and **Serialize**.

Requirements

Namespace: System.ComponentModel.Design.Serialization

Platforms: Windows 98, Windows NT 4.0, Windows Millennium Edition, Windows 2000, Windows XP Home Edition, Windows XP Professional, Windows Server 2003 family

Assembly: System.Design (in System.Design.dll)

CodeDomSerializer Constructor

Initializes a new instance of the **CodeDomSerializer** class.

```
[Visual Basic]
Protected Sub New()
[C#]
protected CodeDomSerializer();
[C++]
protected: CodeDomSerializer();
[JScript]
protected function CodeDomSerializer();
```

Remarks

This constructor is called by derived class constructors to initialize state in this type.

Requirements

Platforms: Windows 98, Windows NT 4.0, Windows Millennium Edition, Windows 2000, Windows XP Home Edition, Windows XP Professional, Windows Server 2003 family

.NET Framework Security:

- Full trust for the immediate caller. This member cannot be used by partially trusted code.

CodeDomSerializer.Deserialize Method

Deserializes the specified serialized CodeDOM object into an object.

```
[Visual Basic]
Public MustOverride Function Deserialize( _
   ByVal manager As IDesignerSerializationManager, _
   ByVal codeObject As Object _
) As Object
[C#]
public abstract object Deserialize(
   IDesignerSerializationManager manager,
   object codeObject
);
[C++]
public: virtual Object* Deserialize(
   IDesignerSerializationManager* manager,
   Object* codeObject
) = 0;
[JScript]
public abstract function Deserialize(
   manager : IDesignerSerializationManager,
   codeObject : Object
) : Object;
```

Parameters

manager
A serialization manager interface that is used during the deserialization process.

codeObject
A serialized CodeDOM object to deserialize.

Return Value

The deserialized CodeDOM object.

Remarks

This method uses the serialization manager to create objects and resolve data types. The root of the object graph is returned.

Requirements

Platforms: Windows 98, Windows NT 4.0, Windows Millennium Edition, Windows 2000, Windows XP Home Edition, Windows XP Professional, Windows Server 2003 family

.NET Framework Security:

- Full trust for the immediate caller. This member cannot be used by partially trusted code.

CodeDomSerializer.DeserializeExpression Method

Deserializes the specified expression.

```
[Visual Basic]
Protected Function DeserializeExpression( _
   ByVal manager As IDesignerSerializationManager, _
   ByVal name As String, _
   ByVal expression As CodeExpression _
) As Object
[C#]
protected object DeserializeExpression(
   IDesignerSerializationManager manager,
   string name,
   CodeExpression expression
);
[C++]
protected: Object* DeserializeExpression(
   IDesignerSerializationManager* manager,
   String* name,
   CodeExpression* expression
);
[JScript]
protected function DeserializeExpression(
   manager : IDesignerSerializationManager,
   name : String,
   expression : CodeExpression
) : Object;
```

Parameters

manager
A serialization manager interface that is used during the deserialization process.

name
An optional name to give the expression. If the expression results in the creation of an object, the object is given this name for subsequent searches through the serialization manager. If this is a null reference (**Nothing** in Visual Basic), no name will be given.

expression
The CodeDOM expression to deserialize.

Return Value

The deserialized expression.

Remarks

This method deserializes the specified expression by interpreting and deserializing the CodeDOM expression and returning the results.

The specified expression is either another expression or a deserialized object. If the expression cannot be simplified to an object, it is considered another expression. If the expression can be fully simplified, it is considered a deserialized object. For example, if the expression were a **CodeFieldReferenceExpression**, this can be simplified to the value of the field. However, if this were a **CodeMethodReferenceExpression**, this expression cannot be simplified to a deserialized object; so the expression is returned.

Requirements

Platforms: Windows 98, Windows NT 4.0, Windows Millennium Edition, Windows 2000, Windows XP Home Edition, Windows XP Professional, Windows Server 2003 family

.NET Framework Security:

- Full trust for the immediate caller. This member cannot be used by partially trusted code.

CodeDomSerializer.DeserializePropertiesFromResources Method

Deserializes the properties of the specified object that match the specified filter, if a filter was specified.

```
[Visual Basic]
Protected Sub DeserializePropertiesFromResources( _
   ByVal manager As IDesignerSerializationManager, _
   ByVal value As Object, _
   ByVal filter() As Attribute _
)
[C#]
protected void DeserializePropertiesFromResources(
   IDesignerSerializationManager manager,
   object value,
   Attribute[] filter
);
[C++]
protected: void DeserializePropertiesFromResources(
   IDesignerSerializationManager* manager,
   Object* value,
   Attribute* filter[]
);
[JScript]
protected function DeserializePropertiesFromResources(
   manager : IDesignerSerializationManager,
   value : Object,
   filter : Attribute[]
);
```

Parameters

manager
: A serialization manager interface that is used during the deserialization process.

value
: The object to deserialize properties for.

filter
: An optional filter to apply to the properties.

Remarks

This method is useful for deserializing properties that cannot be represented in code, such as design-time properties.

Requirements

Platforms: Windows 98, Windows NT 4.0, Windows Millennium Edition, Windows 2000, Windows XP Home Edition, Windows XP Professional, Windows Server 2003 family

.NET Framework Security:

- Full trust for the immediate caller. This member cannot be used by partially trusted code.

CodeDomSerializer.DeserializeStatement Method

Deserializes the specified statement.

```
[Visual Basic]
Protected Sub DeserializeStatement( _
   ByVal manager As IDesignerSerializationManager, _
   ByVal statement As CodeStatement _
)
[C#]
protected void DeserializeStatement(
   IDesignerSerializationManager manager,
   CodeStatement statement
);
[C++]
protected: void DeserializeStatement(
   IDesignerSerializationManager* manager,
   CodeStatement* statement
);
[JScript]
protected function DeserializeStatement(
   manager : IDesignerSerializationManager,
   statement : CodeStatement
);
```

Parameters

manager
: A serialization manager interface that is used during the deserialization process.

statement
: The CodeDOM statement to deserialize.

Remarks

This method deserializes the statement by interpreting and executing the CodeDOM statement.

Requirements

Platforms: Windows 98, Windows NT 4.0, Windows Millennium Edition, Windows 2000, Windows XP Home Edition, Windows XP Professional, Windows Server 2003 family

.NET Framework Security:

- Full trust for the immediate caller. This member cannot be used by partially trusted code.

CodeDomSerializer.Serialize Method

Serializes the specified object into a CodeDOM object.

[Visual Basic]
```
Public MustOverride Function Serialize( _
   ByVal manager As IDesignerSerializationManager, _
   ByVal value As Object _
) As Object
```
[C#]
```
public abstract object Serialize(
   IDesignerSerializationManager manager,
   object value
);
```
[C++]
```
public: virtual Object* Serialize(
   IDesignerSerializationManager* manager,
   Object* value
) = 0;
```
[JScript]
```
public abstract function Serialize(
   manager : IDesignerSerializationManager,
   value : Object
) : Object;
```

Parameters

manager
The serialization manager to use during serialization.

value
The object to serialize.

Return Value

A CodeDOM object representing the object that has been serialized.

Requirements

Platforms: Windows 98, Windows NT 4.0, Windows Millennium Edition, Windows 2000, Windows XP Home Edition, Windows XP Professional, Windows Server 2003 family

.NET Framework Security:

- Full trust for the immediate caller. This member cannot be used by partially trusted code.

CodeDomSerializer.SerializeEvents Method

Serializes all events of the specified object.

[Visual Basic]
```
Protected Sub SerializeEvents( _
   ByVal manager As IDesignerSerializationManager, _
   ByVal statements As CodeStatementCollection, _
   ByVal value As Object, _
   ByVal filter() As Attribute _
)
```
[C#]
```
protected void SerializeEvents(
   IDesignerSerializationManager manager,
   CodeStatementCollection statements,
   object value,
   Attribute[] filter
);
```
[C++]
```
protected: void SerializeEvents(
   IDesignerSerializationManager* manager,
   CodeStatementCollection* statements,
   Object* value,
   Attribute* filter[]
);
```
[JScript]
```
protected function SerializeEvents(
   manager : IDesignerSerializationManager,
   statements : CodeStatementCollection,
   value : Object,
   filter : Attribute[]
);
```

Parameters

manager
The serialization manager to use during serialization.

statements
A statements collection to which serialized event statements are added.

value
The object whose events are to be serialized.

filter
A member attribute filter to apply to the event search.

Requirements

Platforms: Windows 98, Windows NT 4.0, Windows Millennium Edition, Windows 2000, Windows XP Home Edition, Windows XP Professional, Windows Server 2003 family

.NET Framework Security:

- Full trust for the immediate caller. This member cannot be used by partially trusted code.

CodeDomSerializer.SerializeProperties Method

Serializes all properties for the specified object, using the specified filter.

[Visual Basic]
```
Protected Sub SerializeProperties( _
   ByVal manager As IDesignerSerializationManager, _
   ByVal statements As CodeStatementCollection, _
   ByVal value As Object, _
   ByVal filter() As Attribute _
)
```
[C#]
```
protected void SerializeProperties(
   IDesignerSerializationManager manager,
   CodeStatementCollection statements,
   object value,
   Attribute[] filter
);
```
[C++]
```
protected: void SerializeProperties(
   IDesignerSerializationManager* manager,
   CodeStatementCollection* statements,
   Object* value,
   Attribute* filter[]
);
```

[JScript]
```
protected function SerializeProperties(
   manager : IDesignerSerializationManager,
   statements : CodeStatementCollection,
   value : Object,
   filter : Attribute[]
);
```

Parameters

manager
The serialization manager to use during serialization.

statements
A collection of statements to add the serialized property statements to.

value
The object whose properties are serialized.

filter
A member attribute filter to apply to the property search.

Requirements

Platforms: Windows 98, Windows NT 4.0, Windows Millennium Edition, Windows 2000, Windows XP Home Edition, Windows XP Professional, Windows Server 2003 family

.NET Framework Security:

- Full trust for the immediate caller. This member cannot be used by partially trusted code.

CodeDomSerializer.SerializePropertiesToResources Method

Serializes the specified properties to resources.

[Visual Basic]
```
Protected Sub SerializePropertiesToResources( _
   ByVal manager As IDesignerSerializationManager, _
   ByVal statements As CodeStatementCollection, _
   ByVal value As Object, _
   ByVal filter() As Attribute _
)
```
[C#]
```
protected void SerializePropertiesToResources(
   IDesignerSerializationManager manager,
   CodeStatementCollection statements,
   object value,
   Attribute[] filter
);
```
[C++]
```
protected: void SerializePropertiesToResources(
   IDesignerSerializationManager* manager,
   CodeStatementCollection* statements,
   Object* value,
   Attribute* filter[]
);
```
[JScript]
```
protected function SerializePropertiesToResources(
   manager : IDesignerSerializationManager,
   statements : CodeStatementCollection,
   value : Object,
   filter : Attribute[]
);
```

Parameters

manager
The serialization manager to use during serialization.

statements
A collection of statements to use during serialization. The resource serializer uses this to write resource creation statements, but will not have individual property assign statements because all the properties are serialized to a resource.

value
The object to deserialize properties for.

filter
An optional filter to apply to the properties.

Remarks

This method will inspect all of the properties on the specified object that fits the filter, and check for that property within resource data. This is useful for deserializing properties that cannot be represented in code, such as design time properties.

Requirements

Platforms: Windows 98, Windows NT 4.0, Windows Millennium Edition, Windows 2000, Windows XP Home Edition, Windows XP Professional, Windows Server 2003 family

.NET Framework Security:

- Full trust for the immediate caller. This member cannot be used by partially trusted code.

CodeDomSerializer.SerializeResource Method

Serializes the specified resource value using the specified name.

[Visual Basic]
```
Protected Sub SerializeResource( _
   ByVal manager As IDesignerSerializationManager, _
   ByVal resourceName As String, _
   ByVal value As Object _
)
```
[C#]
```
protected void SerializeResource(
   IDesignerSerializationManager manager,
   string resourceName,
   object value
);
```
[C++]
```
protected: void SerializeResource(
   IDesignerSerializationManager* manager,
   String* resourceName,
   Object* value
);
```
[JScript]
```
protected function SerializeResource(
   manager : IDesignerSerializationManager,
   resourceName : String,
   value : Object
);
```

Parameters

manager
The serialization manager to use during serialization.

resourceName
The name of the resource to serialize.

value
The object to serialize.

Requirements

Platforms: Windows 98, Windows NT 4.0, Windows Millennium Edition, Windows 2000, Windows XP Home Edition, Windows XP Professional, Windows Server 2003 family

.NET Framework Security:

- Full trust for the immediate caller. This member cannot be used by partially trusted code.

CodeDomSerializer.SerializeResourceInvariant Method

Serializes the specified resource value using the specified name.

```
[Visual Basic]
Protected Sub SerializeResourceInvariant( _
   ByVal manager As IDesignerSerializationManager, _
   ByVal resourceName As String, _
   ByVal value As Object _
)
[C#]
protected void SerializeResourceInvariant(
   IDesignerSerializationManager manager,
   string resourceName,
   object value
);
[C++]
protected: void SerializeResourceInvariant(
   IDesignerSerializationManager* manager,
   String* resourceName,
   Object* value
);
[JScript]
protected function SerializeResourceInvariant(
   manager : IDesignerSerializationManager,
   resourceName : String,
   value : Object
);
```

Parameters

manager
The serialization manager to use during serialization.

resourceName
The name of the resource to serialize.

value
The object to serialize.

Requirements

Platforms: Windows 98, Windows NT 4.0, Windows Millennium Edition, Windows 2000, Windows XP Home Edition, Windows XP Professional, Windows Server 2003 family

.NET Framework Security:

- Full trust for the immediate caller. This member cannot be used by partially trusted code.

CodeDomSerializer.SerializeToExpression Method

Serializes the specified value to a CodeDOM expression.

```
[Visual Basic]
Protected Function SerializeToExpression( _
   ByVal manager As IDesignerSerializationManager, _
   ByVal value As Object _
) As CodeExpression
[C#]
protected CodeExpression SerializeToExpression(
   IDesignerSerializationManager manager,
   object value
);
[C++]
protected: CodeExpression* SerializeToExpression(
   IDesignerSerializationManager* manager,
   Object* value
);
[JScript]
protected function SerializeToExpression(
   manager : IDesignerSerializationManager,
   value : Object
) : CodeExpression;
```

Parameters

manager
The serialization manager to use during serialization.

value
The object to serialize.

Return Value

The serialized value. This returns a null reference (**Nothing** in Visual Basic) if there is no serializer for the specified value, or if the serializer for that value did not return a **CodeExpression**.

Requirements

Platforms: Windows 98, Windows NT 4.0, Windows Millennium Edition, Windows 2000, Windows XP Home Edition, Windows XP Professional, Windows Server 2003 family

.NET Framework Security:

- Full trust for the immediate caller. This member cannot be used by partially trusted code.

CodeDomSerializer.SerializeToReference-Expression Method

Serializes the specified value to a CodeDOM expression.

[Visual Basic]
```
Protected Function SerializeToReferenceExpression( _
   ByVal manager As IDesignerSerializationManager, _
   ByVal value As Object _
) As CodeExpression
```
[C#]
```
protected CodeExpression SerializeToReferenceExpression(
   IDesignerSerializationManager manager,
   object value
);
```
[C++]
```
protected: CodeExpression* SerializeToReferenceExpression(
   IDesignerSerializationManager* manager,
   Object* value
);
```
[JScript]
```
protected function SerializeToReferenceExpression(
   manager : IDesignerSerializationManager,
   value : Object
) : CodeExpression;
```

Parameters

manager

The serialization manager to use during serialization.

value

The object to serialize.

Return Value

The serialized value. This returns a null reference (**Nothing** in Visual Basic) if no reference expression can be obtained for the specified value, or the value cannot be serialized.

Remarks

This method is similar to **SerializeToExpression**, except that it stops if it cannot obtain a simple reference expression for the value. Call this method when you expect the resulting expression to be used as a parameter or target of a statement.

Requirements

Platforms: Windows 98, Windows NT 4.0, Windows Millennium Edition, Windows 2000, Windows XP Home Edition, Windows XP Professional, Windows Server 2003 family

.NET Framework Security:

- Full trust for the immediate caller. This member cannot be used by partially trusted code.

CodeDomSerializerException Class

The exception that is thrown when line number information is available for a serialization error.

System.Object
System.Exception
System.SystemException
System.ComponentModel.Design.Serialization.CodeDomSerializerException

```
[Visual Basic]
Public Class CodeDomSerializerException
   Inherits SystemException
[C#]
public class CodeDomSerializerException : SystemException
[C++]
public __gc class CodeDomSerializerException : public
   SystemException
[JScript]
public class CodeDomSerializerException extends SystemException
```

Thread Safety

Any public static (**Shared** in Visual Basic) members of this type are safe for multithreaded operations. Any instance members are not guaranteed to be thread safe.

Remarks

This exception is thrown when the serializer encounters an error. This exception allows the serializer to return information about the location and type of the error.

Example

```
[Visual Basic]
Throw New CodeDomSerializerException("This exception was raised ↵
as an example.", New CodeLinePragma("Example.txt", 20))

[C#]
throw new CodeDomSerializerException("This exception was raised ↵
as an example.", new CodeLinePragma("Example.txt", 20));

[C++]
throw new CodeDomSerializerException(S"This exception was raised ↵
 as an example.", new CodeLinePragma(S"Example.txt", 20));
```

Requirements

Namespace: System.ComponentModel.Design.Serialization

Platforms: Windows 98, Windows NT 4.0, Windows Millennium Edition, Windows 2000, Windows XP Home Edition, Windows XP Professional, Windows Server 2003 family

Assembly: System.Design (in System.Design.dll)

CodeDomSerializerException Constructor

Initializes a new instance of the **CodeDomSerializerException** class.

Overload List

Initializes a new instance of the **CodeDomSerializerException** class using the specified exception and line information.

[Visual Basic] **Public Sub New(Exception, CodeLinePragma)**

[C#] **public CodeDomSerializerException(Exception, CodeLinePragma);**

[C++] **public: CodeDomSerializerException(Exception*, CodeLinePragma*);**

[JScript] **public function CodeDomSerializer-Exception(Exception, CodeLinePragma);**

Initializes a new instance of the **CodeDomSerializerException** class using the specified serialization data and context.

[Visual Basic] **Protected Sub New(SerializationInfo, StreamingContext)**

[C#] **protected CodeDomSerializer-Exception(SerializationInfo, StreamingContext);**

[C++] **protected: CodeDomSerializer-Exception(SerializationInfo*, StreamingContext);**

[JScript] **protected function CodeDomSerializer-Exception(SerializationInfo, StreamingContext);**

Initializes a new instance of the **CodeDomSerializerException** class using the specified message and line information.

[Visual Basic] **Public Sub New(String, CodeLinePragma)**

[C#] **public CodeDomSerializerException(string, CodeLinePragma);**

[C++] **public: CodeDomSerializerException(String*, CodeLinePragma*);**

[JScript] **public function CodeDomSerializer-Exception(String, CodeLinePragma);**

CodeDomSerializerException Constructor (Exception, CodeLinePragma)

Initializes a new instance of the **CodeDomSerializerException** class using the specified exception and line information.

```
[Visual Basic]
Public Sub New( _
   ByVal ex As Exception, _
   ByVal linePragma As CodeLinePragma _
)
[C#]
public CodeDomSerializerException(
   Exception ex,
   CodeLinePragma linePragma
);
[C++]
public: CodeDomSerializerException(
   Exception* ex,
   CodeLinePragma* linePragma
);
```

```
[JScript]
public function CodeDomSerializerException(
   ex : Exception,
   linePragma : CodeLinePragma
);
```

Parameters

ex
The exception to throw.

linePragma
A **CodeLinePragma** that indicates where the exception occurred.

Requirements

Platforms: Windows 98, Windows NT 4.0, Windows Millennium Edition, Windows 2000, Windows XP Home Edition, Windows XP Professional, Windows Server 2003 family

.NET Framework Security:

- Full trust for the immediate caller. This member cannot be used by partially trusted code.

CodeDomSerializerException Constructor (SerializationInfo, StreamingContext)

Initializes a new instance of the **CodeDomSerializerException** class using the specified serialization data and context.

```
[Visual Basic]
Protected Sub New( _
   ByVal info As SerializationInfo, _
   ByVal context As StreamingContext _
)
[C#]
protected CodeDomSerializerException(
   SerializationInfo info,
   StreamingContext context
);
[C++]
protected: CodeDomSerializerException(
   SerializationInfo* info,
   StreamingContext context
);
[JScript]
protected function CodeDomSerializerException(
   info : SerializationInfo,
   context : StreamingContext
);
```

Parameters

info
Stores the data that was being used to serialize or deserialize the object that the **CodeDomSerializer** was serializing or deserializing.

context
Describes the source and destination of the stream that generated the exception, as well as a means for serialization to retain that context and an additional caller-defined context.

Requirements

Platforms: Windows 98, Windows NT 4.0, Windows Millennium Edition, Windows 2000, Windows XP Home Edition, Windows XP Professional, Windows Server 2003 family

.NET Framework Security:

- Full trust for the immediate caller. This member cannot be used by partially trusted code.

CodeDomSerializerException Constructor (String, CodeLinePragma)

Initializes a new instance of the **CodeDomSerializerException** class using the specified message and line information.

```
[Visual Basic]
Public Sub New( _
   ByVal message As String, _
   ByVal linePragma As CodeLinePragma _
)
[C#]
public CodeDomSerializerException(
   string message,
   CodeLinePragma linePragma
);
[C++]
public: CodeDomSerializerException(
   String* message,
   CodeLinePragma* linePragma
);
[JScript]
public function CodeDomSerializerException(
   message : String,
   linePragma : CodeLinePragma
);
```

Parameters

message
A message describing the exception.

linePragma
A **CodeLinePragma** that indicates where the exception occurred.

Requirements

Platforms: Windows 98, Windows NT 4.0, Windows Millennium Edition, Windows 2000, Windows XP Home Edition, Windows XP Professional, Windows Server 2003 family

.NET Framework Security:

- Full trust for the immediate caller. This member cannot be used by partially trusted code.

CodeDomSerializerException.LinePragma Property

Gets or sets the line information for the error associated with this exception.

[Visual Basic]
```
Public ReadOnly Property LinePragma As CodeLinePragma
```
[C#]
```
public CodeLinePragma LinePragma {get;}
```
[C++]
```
public: __property CodeLinePragma* get_LinePragma();
```
[JScript]
```
public function get LinePragma() : CodeLinePragma;
```

Property Value

A **CodeLinePragma** that indicates the line information for the error.

Requirements

Platforms: Windows 98, Windows NT 4.0, Windows Millennium Edition, Windows 2000, Windows XP Home Edition, Windows XP Professional, Windows Server 2003 family

.NET Framework Security:

- Full trust for the immediate caller. This member cannot be used by partially trusted code.

CodeDomSerializerException.GetObjectData Method

This member overrides **Exception.GetObjectData**.

[Visual Basic]
```
Overrides Public Sub GetObjectData( _
   ByVal info As SerializationInfo, _
   ByVal context As StreamingContext _
) Implements ISerializable.GetObjectData
```
[C#]
```
public override void GetObjectData(
   SerializationInfo info,
   StreamingContext context
);
```
[C++]
```
public: void GetObjectData(
   SerializationInfo* info,
   StreamingContext context
);
```
[JScript]
```
public override function GetObjectData(
   info : SerializationInfo,
   context : StreamingContext
);
```

Requirements

Platforms: Windows 98, Windows NT 4.0, Windows Millennium Edition, Windows 2000, Windows XP Home Edition, Windows XP Professional, Windows Server 2003 family

.NET Framework Security:

- Full trust for the immediate caller. This member cannot be used by partially trusted code.

ContextStack Class

Provides a stack object that can be used by a serializer to make information available to nested serializers.

System.Object
System.ComponentModel.Design.Serialization.ContextStack

[Visual Basic]
```
NotInheritable Public Class ContextStack
```
[C#]
```
public sealed class ContextStack
```
[C++]
```
public __gc __sealed class ContextStack
```
[JScript]
```
public class ContextStack
```

Thread Safety

Any public static (**Shared** in Visual Basic) members of this type are safe for multithreaded operations. Any instance members are not guaranteed to be thread safe.

Remarks

Some serializers require information about the context of an object to correctly persist their state. **ContextStack** enables a serializer to set data about the context of an object that is being serialized to a stack where another serializer can access it. The **Context** object is provided by an **IDesignerSerializationManager** to share information of use to some serializers.

A context stack is useful because the process of serializing a design document can be deeply nested, and objects at each level of nesting may require context information to correctly persist the state of the object. A serializer can set a context object to the stack before invoking a nested serializer. Each object set to the stack should be removed by the serializer that set it after a call to a nested serializer returns.

Typically, the objects on the stack contain information about the context of the current object that is being serialized. A parent serializer adds context information to the stack about the next object to be serialized, calls an appropriate serializer, and when the serializer finishes executing on the object, removes the context information from the stack. It is up to the implementation of each serializer to determine what objects get pushed on this stack.

As an example, an object with a property named **Enabled** has a data type of **Boolean**. If a serializer writes this value to a data stream, it might need to include the context or type of property it is writing. The serializer does not have this information, however, because it is only instructed to write the **Boolean** value. To provide this information to the serializer, the parent serializer can push a **PropertyDescriptor** that points to the **Enabled** property on the context stack.

Requirements

Namespace: System.ComponentModel.Design.Serialization

Platforms: Windows 98, Windows NT 4.0, Windows Millennium Edition, Windows 2000, Windows XP Home Edition, Windows XP Professional, Windows Server 2003 family

Assembly: System (in System.dll)

ContextStack Constructor

Initializes a new instance of the **ContextStack** class.

[Visual Basic]
```
Public Sub New()
```
[C#]
```
public ContextStack();
```
[C++]
```
public: ContextStack();
```
[JScript]
```
public function ContextStack();
```

Remarks

The default constructor initializes any fields to their default values.

Requirements

Platforms: Windows 98, Windows NT 4.0, Windows Millennium Edition, Windows 2000, Windows XP Home Edition, Windows XP Professional, Windows Server 2003 family

ContextStack.Current Property

Gets or sets the current object on the stack.

[Visual Basic]
```
Public ReadOnly Property Current As Object
```
[C#]
```
public object Current {get;}
```
[C++]
```
public: __property Object* get_Current();
```
[JScript]
```
public function get Current() : Object;
```

Property Value

The current object on the stack, or a null reference (**Nothing** in Visual Basic) if no objects were pushed.

Remarks

The current object is the object at the top of the stack, or the object last added to the stack.

Requirements

Platforms: Windows 98, Windows NT 4.0, Windows Millennium Edition, Windows 2000, Windows XP Home Edition, Windows XP Professional, Windows Server 2003 family

ContextStack.Item Property

Gets or sets the object on the stack at the specified level.

[C#] In C#, this property is the indexer for the **ContextStack** class.

Overload List

Gets the first object on the stack that inherits from or implements the specified type.

[Visual Basic] **Overloads Public Default ReadOnly Property Item(Type) As Object**

[C#] **public object this[Type] {get;}**

[C++] **public: __property Object* get_Item(Type*);**

[JScript] **ContextStack.Item (Type)**

Gets or sets the object on the stack at the specified level.

[Visual Basic] **Overloads Public Default ReadOnly Property Item(Integer) As Object**

[C#] **public object this[int] {get;}**

[C++] **public: __property Object* get_Item(int);**

[JScript] **ContextStack.Item (int)**

ContextStack.Item Property (Type)

Gets the first object on the stack that inherits from or implements the specified type.

[C#] In C#, this property is the indexer for the **ContextStack** class.

```
[Visual Basic]
Overloads Public Default ReadOnly Property Item( _
   ByVal type As Type _
) As Object
[C#]
public object this[
   Type type
] {get;}
[C++]
public: __property Object* get_Item(
   Type* type
);
[JScript]
returnValue = ContextStackObject.Item(type);
-or-
returnValue = ContextStackObject(type);
```

[JScript] In JScript, you can use the default indexed properties defined by a type, but you cannot explicitly define your own. However, specifying the **expando** attribute on a class automatically provides a default indexed property whose type is **Object** and whose index type is **String**.

Arguments [JScript]

type

A type to retrieve from the context stack.

Parameters [Visual Basic, C#, C++]

type

A type to retrieve from the context stack.

Property Value

The first object on the stack that inherits from or implements the specified type, or a null reference (**Nothing** in Visual Basic) if no object on the stack implements the type.

Remarks

A check is made on each level of the stack, searching for an object that implements or inherits type. If a match is found, it is returned.

Requirements

Platforms: Windows 98, Windows NT 4.0, Windows Millennium Edition, Windows 2000, Windows XP Home Edition, Windows XP Professional, Windows Server 2003 family

ContextStack.Item Property (Int32)

Gets or sets the object on the stack at the specified level.

[C#] In C#, this property is the indexer for the **ContextStack** class.

```
[Visual Basic]
Overloads Public Default ReadOnly Property Item( _
   ByVal level As Integer _
) As Object
[C#]
public object this[
   int level
] {get;}
[C++]
public: __property Object* get_Item(
   int level
);
[JScript]
returnValue = ContextStackObject.Item(level);
-or-
returnValue = ContextStackObject(level);
```

[JScript] In JScript, you can use the default indexed properties defined by a type, but you cannot explicitly define your own. However, specifying the **expando** attribute on a class automatically provides a default indexed property whose type is **Object** and whose index type is **String**.

Arguments [JScript]

level

The level of the object to retrieve on the stack. Level zero is the top of the stack, level one is the next down, and so on. This level must be zero or greater. If level is greater than the number of levels on the stack, it returns a null reference (**Nothing** in Visual Basic).

Parameters [Visual Basic, C#, C++]

level

The level of the object to retrieve on the stack. Level zero is the top of the stack, level one is the next down, and so on. This level must be zero or greater. If level is greater than the number of levels on the stack, it returns a null reference (**Nothing** in Visual Basic).

Property Value

The object on the stack at the specified level, or a null reference (**Nothing** in Visual Basic) if no object exists at that level.

Requirements

Platforms: Windows 98, Windows NT 4.0, Windows Millennium Edition, Windows 2000, Windows XP Home Edition, Windows XP Professional, Windows Server 2003 family

ContextStack.Pop Method

Pops, or removes, the current object off of the stack, returning its value.

[Visual Basic]
```
Public Function Pop() As Object
```
[C#]
```
public object Pop();
```
[C++]
```
public: Object* Pop();
```
[JScript]
```
public function Pop() : Object;
```

Return Value

The object popped off of the stack. This returns a null reference (**Nothing** in Visual Basic) if no objects are on the stack.

Requirements

Platforms: Windows 98, Windows NT 4.0, Windows Millennium Edition, Windows 2000, Windows XP Home Edition, Windows XP Professional, Windows Server 2003 family

ContextStack.Push Method

Pushes, or places, the specified object onto the stack.

[Visual Basic]
```
Public Sub Push( _
   ByVal context As Object _
)
```
[C#]
```
public void Push(
   object context
);
```
[C++]
```
public: void Push(
   Object* context
);
```
[JScript]
```
public function Push(
   context : Object
);
```

Parameters

context
The context object to push onto the stack.

Requirements

Platforms: Windows 98, Windows NT 4.0, Windows Millennium Edition, Windows 2000, Windows XP Home Edition, Windows XP Professional, Windows Server 2003 family

DesignerLoader Class

Provides a basic designer loader interface that can be used to implement a custom designer loader.

System.Object
  System.ComponentModel.Design.Serialization.DesignerLoader

[Visual Basic]
```
MustInherit Public Class DesignerLoader
```
[C#]
```
public abstract class DesignerLoader
```
[C++]
```
public __gc __abstract class DesignerLoader
```
[JScript]
```
public abstract class DesignerLoader
```

Thread Safety

Any public static (**Shared** in Visual Basic) members of this type are safe for multithreaded operations. Any instance members are not guaranteed to be thread safe.

Remarks

DesignerLoader can be implemented to support custom loading of a designer and designer components. A designer loader is also responsible for writing changes to an open document back to the storage the loader used when loading the document after the **Flush** method is called.

By default, the Visual Studio .NET development environment creates its own variety of **DesignerLoader** that can load basic designer projects. To create a custom designer loader, you must inherit from and implement the abstract **DesignerLoader** class. You cannot directly instantiate **DesignerLoader**, as it has no public constructor.

When **BeginLoad** is invoked, the designer loader loads the design document, displays the designer surface using the **IDesignerHost** interface, and calls **EndLoad** on the **IDesignerLoaderHost** interface when done. The **IDesignerLoaderHost** implementation is usually the same class that implements **IDesignerHost**.

Requirements

Namespace: System.ComponentModel.Design.Serialization

Platforms: Windows 98, Windows NT 4.0, Windows Millennium Edition, Windows 2000, Windows XP Home Edition, Windows XP Professional, Windows Server 2003 family

Assembly: System (in System.dll)

DesignerLoader Constructor

Initializes a new instance of the **DesignerLoader** class.

[Visual Basic]
```
Protected Sub New()
```
[C#]
```
protected DesignerLoader();
```
[C++]
```
protected: DesignerLoader();
```
[JScript]
```
protected function DesignerLoader();
```

Remarks

This constructor is called by derived class constructors to initialize state in this type.

Requirements

Platforms: Windows 98, Windows NT 4.0, Windows Millennium Edition, Windows 2000, Windows XP Home Edition, Windows XP Professional, Windows Server 2003 family

DesignerLoader.Loading Property

Gets a value indicating whether the loader is currently loading a document.

[Visual Basic]
```
Public Overridable ReadOnly Property Loading As Boolean
```
[C#]
```
public virtual bool Loading {get;}
```
[C++]
```
public: __property virtual bool get_Loading();
```
[JScript]
```
public function get Loading() : Boolean;
```

Property Value

true if the loader is currently loading a document; otherwise, **false**.

Requirements

Platforms: Windows 98, Windows NT 4.0, Windows Millennium Edition, Windows 2000, Windows XP Home Edition, Windows XP Professional, Windows Server 2003 family

DesignerLoader.BeginLoad Method

Begins loading a designer.

[Visual Basic]
```
Public MustOverride Sub BeginLoad( _
   ByVal host As IDesignerLoaderHost _
)
```
[C#]
```
public abstract void BeginLoad(
   IDesignerLoaderHost host
);
```
[C++]
```
public: virtual void BeginLoad(
   IDesignerLoaderHost* host
) = 0;
```
[JScript]
```
public abstract function BeginLoad(
   host : IDesignerLoaderHost
);
```

Parameters

host
  The loader host through which this loader loads components.

Remarks

The **IDesignerLoaderHost** that is passed to the *host* parameter is typically the same object as the designer host. Through this reference to the loader host, the designer loader can reload the design document and indicate that it has finished loading the design document.

Requirements

Platforms: Windows 98, Windows NT 4.0, Windows Millennium Edition, Windows 2000, Windows XP Home Edition, Windows XP Professional, Windows Server 2003 family

DesignerLoader.Dispose Method

Releases all resources used by the **DesignerLoader**.

[Visual Basic]
```
Public MustOverride Sub Dispose()
```
[C#]
```
public abstract void Dispose();
```
[C++]
```
public: virtual void Dispose() = 0;
```
[JScript]
```
public abstract function Dispose();
```

Remarks

Calling **Dispose** allows the resources used by the **DesignerLoader** to be reallocated for other purposes.

Requirements

Platforms: Windows 98, Windows NT 4.0, Windows Millennium Edition, Windows 2000, Windows XP Home Edition, Windows XP Professional, Windows Server 2003 family

DesignerLoader.Flush Method

Writes cached changes to the location that the designer was loaded from.

[Visual Basic]
```
Public Overridable Sub Flush()
```
[C#]
```
public virtual void Flush();
```
[C++]
```
public: virtual void Flush();
```
[JScript]
```
public function Flush();
```

Remarks

The designer host calls this method periodically to ensure that changes made to the document were saved by the designer loader. This method allows designer loaders to implement an asynchronous write scheme to improve performance. The default implementation of this method does nothing.

Requirements

Platforms: Windows 98, Windows NT 4.0, Windows Millennium Edition, Windows 2000, Windows XP Home Edition, Windows XP Professional, Windows Server 2003 family

DesignerSerializerAttribute Class

Indicates a serializer for the serialization manager to use to serialize the values of the type this attribute is applied to. This class cannot be inherited.

System.Object
  System.Attribute
    System.ComponentModel.Design.Serialization.DesignerSerializerAttribute

[Visual Basic]
```
<AttributeUsage(AttributeTargets.Class Or _
   AttributeTargets.Interface)>
NotInheritable Public Class DesignerSerializerAttribute
   Inherits Attribute
```
[C#]
```
[AttributeUsage(AttributeTargets.Class |
   AttributeTargets.Interface)]
public sealed class DesignerSerializerAttribute : Attribute
```
[C++]
```
[AttributeUsage(AttributeTargets::Class |
   AttributeTargets::Interface)]
public __gc __sealed class DesignerSerializerAttribute : public
   Attribute
```
[JScript]
```
public
   AttributeUsage(AttributeTargets.Class | AttributeTargets.Interface)
class DesignerSerializerAttribute extends Attribute
```

Thread Safety

Any public static (**Shared** in Visual Basic) members of this type are safe for multithreaded operations. Any instance members are not guaranteed to be thread safe.

Remarks

DesignerSerializerAttribute provides a way to indicate to the designer serialization manager that a specific type of serializer should be used when serializing the values of an object. This allows you to specify a serializer that is capable of serializing a custom type, for instance. Place this attribute on a class to indicate the serialization object to use when serializing the class.

Example

[Visual Basic, C#, C++] The following code uses a **DesignerSerializerAttribute** to associate an example serializer with an example component.

[Visual Basic]
```
<DesignerSerializerAttribute(GetType(ExampleSerializer),
GetType(CodeDomSerializer))> _
 Public Class ExampleControl
    Inherits System.Windows.Forms.UserControl
    Public Sub New()
    End Sub
End Class
```

[C#]
```
[DesignerSerializerAttribute(typeof(ExampleSerializer),
typeof(CodeDomSerializer))]
public class ExampleControl : System.Windows.Forms.UserControl
{
    public ExampleControl()
    {
    }
}
```

[C++]
```
[DesignerSerializerAttribute(__typeof(ExampleSerializer),
__typeof(CodeDomSerializer))]
public __gc class ExampleControl : public UserControl {
public:
    ExampleControl()
    {
    }
};
```

Requirements

Namespace: System.ComponentModel.Design.Serialization

Platforms: Windows 98, Windows NT 4.0, Windows Millennium Edition, Windows 2000, Windows XP Home Edition, Windows XP Professional, Windows Server 2003 family

Assembly: System (in System.dll)

DesignerSerializerAttribute Constructor

Initializes a new instance of the **DesignerSerializerAttribute** class.

Overload List

Initializes a new instance of the **DesignerSerializerAttribute** class.

[Visual Basic] **Public Sub New(String, String)**

[C#] **public DesignerSerializerAttribute(string, string);**

[C++] **public: DesignerSerializerAttribute(String*, String*);**

[JScript] **public function DesignerSerializerAttribute(String, String);**

Initializes a new instance of the **DesignerSerializerAttribute** class.

[Visual Basic] **Public Sub New(String, Type)**

[C#] **public DesignerSerializerAttribute(string, Type);**

[C++] **public: DesignerSerializerAttribute(String*, Type*);**

[JScript] **public function DesignerSerializerAttribute(String, Type);**

Initializes a new instance of the **DesignerSerializerAttribute** class.

[Visual Basic] **Public Sub New(Type, Type)**

[C#] **public DesignerSerializerAttribute(Type, Type);**

[C++] **public: DesignerSerializerAttribute(Type*, Type*);**

[JScript] **public function DesignerSerializerAttribute(Type, Type);**

DesignerSerializerAttribute Constructor (String, String)

Initializes a new instance of the **DesignerSerializerAttribute** class.

[Visual Basic]
```
Public Sub New( _
   ByVal serializerTypeName As String, _
   ByVal baseSerializerTypeName As String _
)
```
[C#]
```
public DesignerSerializerAttribute(
   string serializerTypeName,
   string baseSerializerTypeName
);
```

[C++]
```
public: DesignerSerializerAttribute(
   String* serializerTypeName,
   String* baseSerializerTypeName
);
```
[JScript]
```
public function DesignerSerializerAttribute(
   serializerTypeName : String,
   baseSerializerTypeName : String
);
```

Parameters

serializerTypeName
: The fully qualified name of the data type of the serializer.

baseSerializerTypeName
: The fully qualified name of the base data type of the serializer. Multiple serializers can be supplied for a class as long as the serializers have different base types.

Requirements

Platforms: Windows 98, Windows NT 4.0, Windows Millennium Edition, Windows 2000, Windows XP Home Edition, Windows XP Professional, Windows Server 2003 family

DesignerSerializerAttribute Constructor (String, Type)

Initializes a new instance of the **DesignerSerializerAttribute** class.

[Visual Basic]
```
Public Sub New( _
   ByVal serializerTypeName As String, _
   ByVal baseSerializerType As Type _
)
```
[C#]
```
public DesignerSerializerAttribute(
   string serializerTypeName,
   Type baseSerializerType
);
```
[C++]
```
public: DesignerSerializerAttribute(
   String* serializerTypeName,
   Type* baseSerializerType
);
```
[JScript]
```
public function DesignerSerializerAttribute(
   serializerTypeName : String,
   baseSerializerType : Type
);
```

Parameters

serializerTypeName
: The fully qualified name of the data type of the serializer.

baseSerializerType
: The base data type of the serializer. Multiple serializers can be supplied for a class as long as the serializers have different base types.

Requirements

Platforms: Windows 98, Windows NT 4.0, Windows Millennium Edition, Windows 2000, Windows XP Home Edition, Windows XP Professional, Windows Server 2003 family

DesignerSerializerAttribute Constructor (Type, Type)

Initializes a new instance of the **DesignerSerializerAttribute** class.

[Visual Basic]
```
Public Sub New( _
   ByVal serializerType As Type, _
   ByVal baseSerializerType As Type _
)
```
[C#]
```
public DesignerSerializerAttribute(
   Type serializerType,
   Type baseSerializerType
);
```
[C++]
```
public: DesignerSerializerAttribute(
   Type* serializerType,
   Type* baseSerializerType
);
```
[JScript]
```
public function DesignerSerializerAttribute(
   serializerType : Type,
   baseSerializerType : Type
);
```

Parameters

serializerType
: The data type of the serializer.

baseSerializerType
: The base data type of the serializer. Multiple serializers can be supplied for a class as long as the serializers have different base types.

Requirements

Platforms: Windows 98, Windows NT 4.0, Windows Millennium Edition, Windows 2000, Windows XP Home Edition, Windows XP Professional, Windows Server 2003 family

DesignerSerializerAttribute.SerializerBaseTypeName Property

Gets the fully qualified type name of the serializer base type.

[Visual Basic]
```
Public ReadOnly Property SerializerBaseTypeName As String
```
[C#]
```
public string SerializerBaseTypeName {get;}
```
[C++]
```
public: __property String* get_SerializerBaseTypeName();
```
[JScript]
```
public function get SerializerBaseTypeName() : String;
```

Property Value

The fully qualified type name of the serializer base type.

Requirements

Platforms: Windows 98, Windows NT 4.0, Windows Millennium Edition, Windows 2000, Windows XP Home Edition, Windows XP Professional, Windows Server 2003 family

DesignerSerializerAttribute.SerializerTypeName Property

Gets the fully qualified type name of the serializer.

[Visual Basic]
```
Public ReadOnly Property SerializerTypeName As String
```
[C#]
```
public string SerializerTypeName {get;}
```
[C++]
```
public: __property String* get_SerializerTypeName();
```
[JScript]
```
public function get SerializerTypeName() : String;
```

Property Value

The fully qualified type name of the serializer.

Requirements

Platforms: Windows 98, Windows NT 4.0, Windows Millennium Edition, Windows 2000, Windows XP Home Edition, Windows XP Professional, Windows Server 2003 family

DesignerSerializerAttribute.TypeId Property

This member overrides **Attribute.TypeId**.

[Visual Basic]
```
Overrides Public ReadOnly Property TypeId As Object
```
[C#]
```
public override object TypeId {get;}
```
[C++]
```
public: __property Object* get_TypeId();
```
[JScript]
```
public override function get TypeId() : Object;
```

Requirements

Platforms: Windows 98, Windows NT 4.0, Windows Millennium Edition, Windows 2000, Windows XP Home Edition, Windows XP Professional, Windows Server 2003 family

ICodeDomDesignerReload Interface

Provides an interface that can be used to optimize the reloading of a designer.

[Visual Basic]
```
Public Interface ICodeDomDesignerReload
```
[C#]
```
public interface ICodeDomDesignerReload
```
[C++]
```
public __gc __interface ICodeDomDesignerReload
```
[JScript]
```
public interface ICodeDomDesignerReload
```

Remarks

A **CodeDomProvider** can implement this interface to support optimized reloading by the designer. When a designer reparses a file for display, it can use this interface to improve performance.

To support this performance optimization method, the designer can pass a **CodeCompileUnit** that represents the document code to the **ShouldReloadDesigner** method. **ShouldReloadDesigner** returns a value that indicates whether the code has changed and typically, whether your code should reload the designer. Otherwise, it is unnecessary to spend time reloading the designer.

Requirements

Namespace: System.ComponentModel.Design.Serialization

Platforms: Windows 98, Windows NT 4.0, Windows Millennium Edition, Windows 2000, Windows XP Home Edition, Windows XP Professional, Windows Server 2003 family

Assembly: System.Design (in System.Design.dll)

ICodeDomDesignerReload.ShouldReloadDesigner Method

Indicates whether the designer should reload in order to import the specified compile unit correctly.

[Visual Basic]
```
Function ShouldReloadDesigner( _
   ByVal newTree As CodeCompileUnit _
) As Boolean
```
[C#]
```
bool ShouldReloadDesigner(
   CodeCompileUnit newTree
);
```
[C++]
```
bool ShouldReloadDesigner(
   CodeCompileUnit* newTree
);
```
[JScript]
```
function ShouldReloadDesigner(
   newTree : CodeCompileUnit
) : Boolean;
```

Parameters

newTree

A **CodeCompileUnit** containing the designer document code.

Return Value

true if the designer should reload; otherwise, **false**.

Requirements

Platforms: Windows 98, Windows NT 4.0, Windows Millennium Edition, Windows 2000, Windows XP Home Edition, Windows XP Professional, Windows Server 2003 family

.NET Framework Security:

- Full trust for the immediate caller. This member cannot be used by partially trusted code.

IDesignerLoaderHost Interface

Provides an interface that can extend a designer host to support loading from a serialized state.

[Visual Basic]
```
Public Interface IDesignerLoaderHost
   Inherits IDesignerHost, IServiceContainer, IServiceProvider
```
[C#]
```
public interface IDesignerLoaderHost : IDesignerHost,
   IServiceContainer, IServiceProvider
```
[C++]
```
public __gc __interface IDesignerLoaderHost : public IDesignerHost,
   IServiceContainer, IServiceProvider
```
[JScript]
```
public interface IDesignerLoaderHost implements IDesignerHost,
   IServiceContainer, IServiceProvider
```

Remarks

An **IDesignerHost** can implement this interface to enable support for loading by a **DesignerLoader**.

The designer loader informs the designer host that it needs to invoke a load or reload so that the designer host can perform additional tasks at these times.

This class is isolated from **IDesignerHost** to emphasize that the designer loader, not the designer host, must initiate all loading and reloading of the design document.

Requirements

Namespace: System.ComponentModel.Design.Serialization

Platforms: Windows 98, Windows NT 4.0,
Windows Millennium Edition, Windows 2000,
Windows XP Home Edition, Windows XP Professional,
Windows Server 2003 family

Assembly: System (in System.dll)

IDesignerLoaderHost.EndLoad Method

Ends the designer loading operation.

[Visual Basic]
```
Sub EndLoad( _
   ByVal baseClassName As String, _
   ByVal successful As Boolean, _
   ByVal errorCollection As ICollection _
)
```
[C#]
```
void EndLoad(
   string baseClassName,
   bool successful,
   ICollection errorCollection
);
```
[C++]
```
void EndLoad(
   String* baseClassName,
   bool successful,
   ICollection* errorCollection
);
```
[JScript]
```
function EndLoad(
   baseClassName : String,
   successful : Boolean,
   errorCollection : ICollection
);
```

Parameters

baseClassName
The fully qualified name of the base class of the document that this designer is designing.

successful
true if the designer is successfully loaded; otherwise, **false**.

errorCollection
A collection containing the errors encountered during load, if any. If no errors were encountered, pass either an empty collection or a null reference (**Nothing** in Visual Basic).

Remarks

The **DesignerLoader** that loads the design document calls this method to indicate that the load terminated.

If errors are encountered during loading, they must be passed in the *errorCollection* parameter as a collection of exceptions. If they are not exceptions, the designer loader host can call **ToString** on them and pass them as a collection. If the load is successful, then the *errorCollection* parameter must be either a null reference (**Nothing** in Visual Basic) or an empty collection.

Requirements

Platforms: Windows 98, Windows NT 4.0,
Windows Millennium Edition, Windows 2000,
Windows XP Home Edition, Windows XP Professional,
Windows Server 2003 family

IDesignerLoaderHost.Reload Method

Reloads the design document.

[Visual Basic]
```
Sub Reload()
```
[C#]
```
void Reload();
```
[C++]
```
void Reload();
```
[JScript]
```
function Reload();
```

Remarks

The **DesignerLoader** calls this method to reload the design document.

Requirements

Platforms: Windows 98, Windows NT 4.0,
Windows Millennium Edition, Windows 2000,
Windows XP Home Edition, Windows XP Professional,
Windows Server 2003 family

IDesignerLoaderService Interface

Provides an interface that can extend a designer loader to support asynchronous loading of external components.

[Visual Basic]
```
Public Interface IDesignerLoaderService
```
[C#]
```
public interface IDesignerLoaderService
```
[C++]
```
public __gc __interface IDesignerLoaderService
```
[JScript]
```
public interface IDesignerLoaderService
```

Remarks

A **DesignerLoader** can implement this interface to manage designer loading that involves external components. This interface also allows external components to initiate a reload of the design surface by calling **Reload**. A designer loader does not have to implement this interface if it does not require support for asynchronous loading.

Designer loading using a custom implementation of the **IDesignerLoaderService** can occur in a variety of ways. Sometimes external components are involved in the loading process. To facilitate loading with external dependencies, the designer loader service interface provides a mechanism that determines when loading is complete and allows each portion of loading to signal that it has completed. The **IDesignerLoaderService** typically determines when loading is complete by testing a counter that tracks the number of load dependencies remaining. When each portion of the load completes, **DependentLoadComplete** is called, and the service decrements the counter. To set the number of dependent load processes, call **AddLoadDependency** once for each load process that calls **DependentLoadComplete** when its loading is complete. When the final loading is complete, the service calls **EndLoad** on the loader host.

Requirements

Namespace: System.ComponentModel.Design.Serialization

Platforms: Windows 98, Windows NT 4.0, Windows Millennium Edition, Windows 2000, Windows XP Home Edition, Windows XP Professional, Windows Server 2003 family

Assembly: System (in System.dll)

IDesignerLoaderService.AddLoadDependency Method

Registers an external component as part of the load process managed by this interface.

[Visual Basic]
```
Sub AddLoadDependency()
```
[C#]
```
void AddLoadDependency();
```
[C++]
```
void AddLoadDependency();
```
[JScript]
```
function AddLoadDependency();
```

Remarks

Call **AddLoadDependency** once for each external object participating in the load process. **DependentLoadComplete** is called when the work of the load process is done.

Requirements

Platforms: Windows 98, Windows NT 4.0, Windows Millennium Edition, Windows 2000, Windows XP Home Edition, Windows XP Professional, Windows Server 2003 family

IDesignerLoaderService.DependentLoad-Complete Method

Signals that a dependent load has finished.

[Visual Basic]
```
Sub DependentLoadComplete( _
   ByVal successful As Boolean, _
   ByVal errorCollection As ICollection _
)
```
[C#]
```
void DependentLoadComplete(
   bool successful,
   ICollection errorCollection
);
```
[C++]
```
void DependentLoadComplete(
   bool successful,
   ICollection* errorCollection
);
```
[JScript]
```
function DependentLoadComplete(
   successful : Boolean,
   errorCollection : ICollection
);
```

Parameters

successful

true if the load of the designer is successful; **false** if errors prevented the load from finishing.

errorCollection

A collection of errors that occurred during the load, if any. If no errors occurred, pass either an empty collection or a null reference (**Nothing** in Visual Basic).

Remarks

This method is called to signal that a dependent loading operation has completed. Call **DependentLoadComplete** once for every process that was registered by calling **AddLoadDependency**, which has already completed.

If the dependent load succeeds, the caller sets the *successful* parameter to **true** and passes either an empty collection or a null reference (**Nothing** in Visual Basic) to the *errorCollection* parameter. If the dependent load encounters errors, the caller sets the *successful* parameter to **false** and passes a collection of exceptions that indicate the reason or reasons for failure to the *errorCollection* parameter.

Requirements

Platforms: Windows 98, Windows NT 4.0, Windows Millennium Edition, Windows 2000, Windows XP Home Edition, Windows XP Professional, Windows Server 2003 family

IDesignerLoaderService.Reload Method

Reloads the design document.

[Visual Basic]
```
Function Reload() As Boolean
```
[C#]
```
bool Reload();
```
[C++]
```
bool Reload();
```
[JScript]
```
function Reload() : Boolean;
```

Return Value

true if the reload request is accepted, or **false** if the loader does not allow the reload.

Remarks

Any object can call this method to request that the loader reload the design document. If the loader supports reloading and complies with the reload, the designer loader can return **true**. Otherwise, it returns **false**, indicating that the reload will not occur. Callers cannot rely on the reload happening immediately; the designer loader can schedule this for some other time, or it can try to reload at once.

The caller can display a message to the user if the designer cannot be reloaded.

Requirements

Platforms: Windows 98, Windows NT 4.0,
Windows Millennium Edition, Windows 2000,
Windows XP Home Edition, Windows XP Professional,
Windows Server 2003 family

IDesignerSerialization-Manager Interface

Provides an interface that can manage design-time serialization.

System.IServiceProvider
  System.ComponentModel.Design.Serialization.IDesigner-SerializationManager

[Visual Basic]
```
Public Interface IDesignerSerializationManager
   Inherits IServiceProvider
```
[C#]
```
public interface IDesignerSerializationManager : IServiceProvider
```
[C++]
```
public __gc __interface IDesignerSerializationManager : public
   IServiceProvider
```
[JScript]
```
public interface IDesignerSerializationManager implements
   IServiceProvider
```

Remarks

A designer can utilize **IDesignerSerializationManager** to access services useful to managing design-time serialization processes. For example, a class that implements the designer serialization manager can use this interface to create objects, look up types, identify objects, and customize the serialization of particular types.

Example

[Visual Basic, C#] The following example illustrates how to use **IDesignerSerializationManager** to serialize and deserialize Code DOM statements.

[Visual Basic]
```
Imports System
Imports System.CodeDom
Imports System.ComponentModel
Imports System.ComponentModel.Design
Imports System.ComponentModel.Design.Serialization
Imports System.Drawing
Imports System.Windows.Forms
Namespace CodeDomSerializerSample
   Friend Class MyCodeDomSerializer
      Inherits CodeDomSerializer
      Public Overrides Function Deserialize(ByVal manager As
IDesignerSerializationManager, _
                ByVal codeObject As Object) As Object
         ' This is how we associate the component with the serializer.
         Dim baseClassSerializer As CodeDomSerializer =
CType(manager.GetSerializer( _
               GetType(MyComponent).BaseType,
GetType(CodeDomSerializer)), CodeDomSerializer)
         ' This is the simplest case, in which the class just
 calls the base class
         '  to do the work.
         Return baseClassSerializer.Deserialize(manager, codeObject)
      End Function 'Deserialize
      Public Overrides Function Serialize(ByVal manager As
IDesignerSerializationManager, _
                    ByVal value As Object) As Object
         ' Associate the component with the serializer in the
same manner as with
         '  Deserialize
         Dim baseClassSerializer As CodeDomSerializer =
CType(manager.GetSerializer( _
               GetType(MyComponent).BaseType,
GetType(CodeDomSerializer)), CodeDomSerializer)
         Dim codeObject As Object =
baseClassSerializer.Serialize(manager, value)
         ' Anything could be in the codeObject.  This sample
 operates on a
         '  CodeStatementCollection.
         If TypeOf codeObject Is CodeStatementCollection Then
            Dim statements As CodeStatementCollection =
CType(codeObject, CodeStatementCollection)
            ' The code statement collection is valid, so add a comment.
            Dim commentText As String = "This comment was
 added to this object by a custom serializer."
            Dim comment As New CodeCommentStatement(commentText)
            statements.Insert(0, comment)
         End If
         Return codeObject
      End Function 'Serialize
   End Class 'MyCodeDomSerializer
   <DesignerSerializer(GetType(MyCodeDomSerializer),
GetType(CodeDomSerializer))> _
   Public Class MyComponent
      Inherits Component
      Private localProperty As String = "Component Property Value"
      Public Property LocalProp() As String
         Get
            Return localProperty
         End Get
         Set(ByVal Value As String)
            localProperty = Value
         End Set
      End Property
   End Class 'MyComponent
End Namespace
```

[C#]
```
using System;
using System.CodeDom;
using System.ComponentModel;
using System.ComponentModel.Design;
using System.ComponentModel.Design.Serialization;
using System.Drawing;
using System.Windows.Forms;

namespace CodeDomSerializerSample
{
    internal class MyCodeDomSerializer : CodeDomSerializer {
        public override object Deserialize(IDesignerSerializationManager
manager, object codeObject) {
            // This is how we associate the component with the
serializer.
                CodeDomSerializer baseClassSerializer =
 (CodeDomSerializer)manager.
                GetSerializer(typeof(MyComponent).BaseType,
typeof(CodeDomSerializer));
            /* This is the simplest case, in which the class
 just calls the base class
                to do the work. */
            return baseClassSerializer.Deserialize(manager,
codeObject);
        }

        public override object Serialize
 (IDesignerSerializationManager manager, object value) {
            /* Associate the component with the serializer in
the same manner as with
                Deserialize */
            CodeDomSerializer baseClassSerializer =
 (CodeDomSerializer)manager.
                GetSerializer(typeof(MyComponent).BaseType,
typeof(CodeDomSerializer));

            object codeObject = baseClassSerializer.Serialize
 (manager, value);

            /* Anything could be in the codeObject.  This sample
operates on a
                CodeStatementCollection. */
            if (codeObject is CodeStatementCollection) {
```

```
            CodeStatementCollection statements =                 ↵
 (CodeStatementCollection)codeObject;

            // The code statement collection is valid,           ↵
so add a comment.
            string commentText = "This comment was added         ↵
 to this object by a custom serializer.";
            CodeCommentStatement comment = new                   ↵
CodeCommentStatement(commentText);
            statements.Insert(0, comment);
         }
         return codeObject;
      }
   }

   [DesignerSerializer(typeof(MyCodeDomSerializer),              ↵
typeof(CodeDomSerializer))]
   public class MyComponent : Component {
      private string localProperty = "Component Property Value";
      public string LocalProperty {
         get {
            return localProperty;
         }
         set {
            localProperty = value;
         }
      }
   }
}
```

Requirements

Namespace: System.ComponentModel.Design.Serialization

Platforms: Windows 98, Windows NT 4.0, Windows Millennium Edition, Windows 2000, Windows XP Home Edition, Windows XP Professional, Windows Server 2003 family

Assembly: System (in System.dll)

IDesignerSerializationManager.Context Property

Gets a stack-based, user-defined storage area that is useful for communication between serializers.

[Visual Basic]
```
ReadOnly Property Context As ContextStack
```
[C#]
```
ContextStack Context {get;}
```
[C++]
```
__property ContextStack* get_Context();
```
[JScript]
```
function get Context() : ContextStack;
```

Property Value

A **ContextStack** that stores data.

Remarks

This storage area provides communication of object context information to serializers. Context information about objects that are being serialized can be stored and accessed through this **ContextStack**.

Requirements

Platforms: Windows 98, Windows NT 4.0, Windows Millennium Edition, Windows 2000, Windows XP Home Edition, Windows XP Professional, Windows Server 2003 family

IDesignerSerializationManager.Properties Property

Indicates custom properties that can be serializable with available serializers.

[Visual Basic]
```
ReadOnly Property Properties As PropertyDescriptorCollection
```
[C#]
```
PropertyDescriptorCollection Properties {get;}
```
[C++]
```
__property PropertyDescriptorCollection* get_Properties();
```
[JScript]
```
function get Properties() : PropertyDescriptorCollection;
```

Property Value

A **PropertyDescriptorCollection** containing the properties to be serialized.

Remarks

This property can contain an empty collection. A serializer should never assume that such properties exist. A derived class or implementation of **IDesignerSerializationManager** defines the set of properties that are exposed here.

Notes to Implementers: This property can be populated by user code. It may be sufficient to call **GetProperties** of **TypeDescriptor** to populate this collection. The serialization manager must return an empty collection if no custom properties exist.

Requirements

Platforms: Windows 98, Windows NT 4.0, Windows Millennium Edition, Windows 2000, Windows XP Home Edition, Windows XP Professional, Windows Server 2003 family

IDesignerSerializationManager.AddSerializationProvider Method

Adds the specified serialization provider to the serialization manager.

[Visual Basic]
```
Sub AddSerializationProvider( _
   ByVal provider As IDesignerSerializationProvider _
)
```
[C#]
```
void AddSerializationProvider(
   IDesignerSerializationProvider provider
);
```
[C++]
```
void AddSerializationProvider(
   IDesignerSerializationProvider* provider
);
```
[JScript]
```
function AddSerializationProvider(
   provider : IDesignerSerializationProvider
);
```

Parameters

provider
The serialization provider to add.

Remarks

This method adds a custom serialization provider to the serialization manager. Serialization providers can provide custom serializers for a particular type of object or set of types of objects. During serialization, each custom serialization provider is queried to return a serializer for a specific data type, if it can provide one. The serialization manager uses the custom serializer provided by this method before using the default serializer for a particular type.

Requirements

Platforms: Windows 98, Windows NT 4.0, Windows Millennium Edition, Windows 2000, Windows XP Home Edition, Windows XP Professional, Windows Server 2003 family

IDesignerSerializationManager.CreateInstance Method

Creates an instance of the specified type and adds it to a collection of named instances.

[Visual Basic]
```
Function CreateInstance( _
   ByVal type As Type, _
   ByVal arguments As ICollection, _
   ByVal name As String, _
   ByVal addToContainer As Boolean _
) As Object
```
[C#]
```
object CreateInstance(
   Type type,
   ICollection arguments,
   string name,
   bool addToContainer
);
```
[C++]
```
Object* CreateInstance(
   Type* type,
   ICollection* arguments,
   String* name,
   bool addToContainer
);
```
[JScript]
```
function CreateInstance(
   type : Type,
   arguments : ICollection,
   name : String,
   addToContainer : Boolean
) : Object;
```

Parameters

type
: The data type to create.

arguments
: The arguments to pass to the constructor for this type.

name
: The name of the object. This name can be used to access the object later through **GetInstance**. If a null reference (**Nothing** in Visual Basic) is passed, the object is still created but cannot be accessed by name.

addToContainer
: If **true**, this object is added to the design container. The object must implement **IComponent** for this to have any effect.

Return Value

The newly created object instance.

Remarks

Objects that implement **IComponent** are added to the design-time container if the *addToContainer* parameter is **true**.

Requirements

Platforms: Windows 98, Windows NT 4.0, Windows Millennium Edition, Windows 2000, Windows XP Home Edition, Windows XP Professional, Windows Server 2003 family

IDesignerSerializationManager.GetInstance Method

Gets an instance of a created object of the specified name, or a null reference (**Nothing** in Visual Basic) if that object does not exist.

[Visual Basic]
```
Function GetInstance( _
   ByVal name As String _
) As Object
```
[C#]
```
object GetInstance(
   string name
);
```
[C++]
```
Object* GetInstance(
   String* name
);
```
[JScript]
```
function GetInstance(
   name : String
) : Object;
```

Parameters

name
: The name of the object to retrieve.

Return Value

An instance of the object with the given name, or a null reference (**Nothing** in Visual Basic) if no object by that name can be found.

Remarks

The name of the object to retrieve must have been set through a prior call to **CreateInstance**.

Requirements

Platforms: Windows 98, Windows NT 4.0, Windows Millennium Edition, Windows 2000, Windows XP Home Edition, Windows XP Professional, Windows Server 2003 family

IDesignerSerializationManager.GetName Method

Gets the name of the specified object, or a null reference (**Nothing** in Visual Basic) if the object has no name.

[Visual Basic]
```
Function GetName( _
   ByVal value As Object _
) As String
```
[C#]
```
string GetName(
   object value
);
```
[C++]
```
String* GetName(
   Object* value
);
```
[JScript]
```
function GetName(
   value : Object
) : String;
```

Parameters

value
    The object to retrieve the name for.

Return Value

The name of the object, or a null reference (**Nothing** in Visual Basic) if the object is unnamed.

Requirements

Platforms: Windows 98, Windows NT 4.0,
Windows Millennium Edition, Windows 2000,
Windows XP Home Edition, Windows XP Professional,
Windows Server 2003 family

IDesignerSerializationManager.GetSerializer Method

Gets a serializer of the requested type for the specified object type.

[Visual Basic]
```
Function GetSerializer( _
   ByVal objectType As Type, _
   ByVal serializerType As Type _
) As Object
```
[C#]
```
object GetSerializer(
   Type objectType,
   Type serializerType
);
```
[C++]
```
Object* GetSerializer(
   Type* objectType,
   Type* serializerType
);
```
[JScript]
```
function GetSerializer(
   objectType : Type,
   serializerType : Type
) : Object;
```

Parameters

objectType
    The type of the object to get the serializer for.
serializerType
    The type of the serializer to retrieve.

Return Value

An instance of the requested serializer, or a null reference (**Nothing** in Visual Basic) if no appropriate serializer can be located.

Requirements

Platforms: Windows 98, Windows NT 4.0,
Windows Millennium Edition, Windows 2000,
Windows XP Home Edition, Windows XP Professional,
Windows Server 2003 family

IDesignerSerializationManager.GetType Method

Gets a type of the specified name.

[Visual Basic]
```
Function GetType( _
   ByVal typeName As String _
) As Type
```
[C#]
```
Type GetType(
   string typeName
);
```
[C++]
```
Type* GetType(
   String* typeName
);
```
[JScript]
```
function GetType(
   typeName : String
) : Type;
```

Parameters

typeName
    The fully qualified name of the type to load.

Return Value

An instance of the type, or a null reference (**Nothing** in Visual Basic) if the type cannot be loaded.

Requirements

Platforms: Windows 98, Windows NT 4.0,
Windows Millennium Edition, Windows 2000,
Windows XP Home Edition, Windows XP Professional,
Windows Server 2003 family

IDesignerSerializationManager.RemoveSerializationProvider Method

Removes a custom serialization provider from the serialization manager.

[Visual Basic]
```
Sub RemoveSerializationProvider( _
   ByVal provider As IDesignerSerializationProvider _
)
```
[C#]
```
void RemoveSerializationProvider(
   IDesignerSerializationProvider provider
);
```

```
[C++]
void RemoveSerializationProvider(
   IDesignerSerializationProvider* provider
);
[JScript]
function RemoveSerializationProvider(
   provider : IDesignerSerializationProvider
);
```

Parameters

provider
: The provider to remove. This object must have been added using **AddSerializationProvider**.

Requirements

Platforms: Windows 98, Windows NT 4.0, Windows Millennium Edition, Windows 2000, Windows XP Home Edition, Windows XP Professional, Windows Server 2003 family

IDesignerSerializationManager.ReportError Method

Reports an error in serialization.

```
[Visual Basic]
Sub ReportError( _
   ByVal errorInformation As Object _
)
[C#]
void ReportError(
   object errorInformation
);
[C++]
void ReportError(
   Object* errorInformation
);
[JScript]
function ReportError(
   errorInformation : Object
);
```

Parameters

errorInformation
: The error to report. This information object can be of any object type. If it is an exception, the message of the exception is extracted and reported to the user. If it is any other type, **ToString** is called to display the information to the user.

Remarks

If the serialization manager supports logging multiple errors in its implementation of **ReportError**, it can store the error information object for a future report where all the errors encountered can be displayed at once. If this method stores multiple errors, serialization can continue after a call to this method. If this method does not support logging multiple errors, this method should throw an exception, which aborts serialization.

> **Note** The serialization manager should never throw an exception for errors encountered during serialization. It should only throw an exception during deserialization. Otherwise, users become confused because saving the document should never fail.

Requirements

Platforms: Windows 98, Windows NT 4.0, Windows Millennium Edition, Windows 2000, Windows XP Home Edition, Windows XP Professional, Windows Server 2003 family

IDesignerSerializationManager.SetName Method

Sets the name of the specified existing object.

```
[Visual Basic]
Sub SetName( _
   ByVal instance As Object, _
   ByVal name As String _
)
[C#]
void SetName(
   object instance,
   string name
);
[C++]
void SetName(
   Object* instance,
   String* name
);
[JScript]
function SetName(
   instance : Object,
   name : String
);
```

Parameters

instance
: The object instance to name.

name
: The name to give the instance.

Remarks

This method is useful when it is necessary to create and then name an instance of an object without using **CreateInstance**. An exception is thrown if you try to rename an existing object or if you try to give a new object a name that is already taken.

Requirements

Platforms: Windows 98, Windows NT 4.0, Windows Millennium Edition, Windows 2000, Windows XP Home Edition, Windows XP Professional, Windows Server 2003 family

IDesignerSerializationManager.ResolveName Event

Occurs when **GetName** cannot locate the specified name in the serialization manager's name table.

```
[Visual Basic]
Event ResolveName As ResolveNameEventHandler
[C#]
event ResolveNameEventHandler ResolveName;
[C++]
__event ResolveNameEventHandler* ResolveName;
```

[JScript] In JScript, you can handle the events defined by a class, but you cannot define your own.

Event Data

The event handler receives an argument of type **ResolveNameEventArgs** containing data related to this event. The following **ResolveNameEventArgs** properties provide information specific to this event.

Property	Description
Name	Gets the name of the object to resolve.
Value	Gets or sets the object that matches the name.

Remarks

This event provides a way for a serializer to create an object on demand, so that the serializer does not have to order object creation by dependency. The delegate for this event is cleared immediately after serialization or deserialization is complete.

Requirements

Platforms: Windows 98, Windows NT 4.0, Windows Millennium Edition, Windows 2000, Windows XP Home Edition, Windows XP Professional, Windows Server 2003 family

IDesignerSerializationManager.SerializationComplete Event

Occurs when serialization is complete.

[Visual Basic]
```
Event SerializationComplete As EventHandler
```
[C#]
```
event EventHandler SerializationComplete;
```
[C++]
```
__event EventHandler* SerializationComplete;
```

[JScript] In JScript, you can handle the events defined by a class, but you cannot define your own.

Event Data

The event handler receives an argument of type **EventArgs**.

Remarks

This event is raised when serialization or deserialization is complete.

Generally, serialization code is written to emit serialization data and does not typically require state-related checking and processing. If it is necessary to maintain state data throughout serialization, data can be set and accessed by a serializer, which can listen to the **SerializationComplete** event, and clear the data after serialization. Restoring the proper state after serialization can be important because serializers can be reused during serialization, and leftover state data or open streams might not be correct.

For example, if a serializer needs to write to another file, such as a resource file, it is inefficient to design the serializer to close the file when finished. Serializing an object graph usually requires several serializers. The resource file would be opened and closed many times. Instead, the resource file can be closed at the end of serialization by an object that listened to the **SerializationComplete** event.

Requirements

Platforms: Windows 98, Windows NT 4.0, Windows Millennium Edition, Windows 2000, Windows XP Home Edition, Windows XP Professional, Windows Server 2003 family

IDesignerSerialization-Provider Interface

Provides an interface that enables access to a serializer.

```
[Visual Basic]
Public Interface IDesignerSerializationProvider
[C#]
public interface IDesignerSerializationProvider
[C++]
public __gc __interface IDesignerSerializationProvider
[JScript]
public interface IDesignerSerializationProvider
```

Remarks

This interface has only one method, **GetSerializer**, and no properties or events. This interface and this method exist so that the serialization manager and other objects can obtain a serializer for a given object type.

Requirements

Namespace: System.ComponentModel.Design.Serialization

Platforms: Windows 98, Windows NT 4.0, Windows Millennium Edition, Windows 2000, Windows XP Home Edition, Windows XP Professional, Windows Server 2003 family

Assembly: System (in System.dll)

IDesignerSerializationProvider.GetSerializer Method

Gets a serializer using the specified attributes.

```
[Visual Basic]
Function GetSerializer( _
   ByVal manager As IDesignerSerializationManager, _
   ByVal currentSerializer As Object, _
   ByVal objectType As Type, _
   ByVal serializerType As Type _
) As Object
[C#]
object GetSerializer(
   IDesignerSerializationManager manager,
   object currentSerializer,
   Type objectType,
   Type serializerType
);
[C++]
Object* GetSerializer(
   IDesignerSerializationManager* manager,
   Object* currentSerializer,
   Type* objectType,
   Type* serializerType
);
[JScript]
function GetSerializer(
   manager : IDesignerSerializationManager,
   currentSerializer : Object,
   objectType : Type,
   serializerType : Type
) : Object;
```

Parameters

manager
: The serialization manager requesting the serializer.

currentSerializer
: An instance of the current serializer of the specified type. This can be a null reference (**Nothing** in Visual Basic) if no serializer of the specified type exists.

objectType
: The data type of the object to serialize.

serializerType
: The data type of the serializer to create.

Return Value

An instance of a serializer of the type requested, or a null reference (**Nothing** in Visual Basic) if the request cannot be satisfied.

Remarks

The serialization manager calls this method when it is trying to locate a serializer for an object type. If this serialization provider can provide a serializer of the correct type, this provider returns it. Otherwise, it returns a null reference (**Nothing** in Visual Basic).

Requirements

Platforms: Windows 98, Windows NT 4.0, Windows Millennium Edition, Windows 2000, Windows XP Home Edition, Windows XP Professional, Windows Server 2003 family

IDesignerSerializationService Interface

Provides an interface that can invoke serialization and deserialization.

[Visual Basic]
```
Public Interface IDesignerSerializationService
```
[C#]
```
public interface IDesignerSerializationService
```
[C++]
```
public __gc __interface IDesignerSerializationService
```
[JScript]
```
public interface IDesignerSerializationService
```

Remarks

This service provides methods to convert a collection of objects to a serializable object that represents them, and to convert serialization data to the object or objects that it represents.

All components that support a designer must support serialization of each component's type. This occurs when the designer scans the public properties, methods, and events of each type and represents these within a type descriptor.

This interface uses the technique of scanning members to convert a collection of components into a single object that supports run-time serialization. This does not necessarily provide for the serialization of custom types that belong to the class. Many objects require a custom serializer to have their values serialized at run time. To specify a serializer for a custom type, use a **DesignerSerializerAttribute** attribute or implement an **IDesignerSerializationProvider**.

Requirements

Namespace: System.ComponentModel.Design.Serialization

Platforms: Windows 98, Windows NT 4.0, Windows Millennium Edition, Windows 2000, Windows XP Home Edition, Windows XP Professional, Windows Server 2003 family

Assembly: System (in System.dll)

IDesignerSerializationService.Deserialize Method

Deserializes the specified serialization data object and returns a collection of objects represented by that data.

[Visual Basic]
```
Function Deserialize( _
   ByVal serializationData As Object _
) As ICollection
```
[C#]
```
ICollection Deserialize(
   object serializationData
);
```
[C++]
```
ICollection* Deserialize(
   Object* serializationData
);
```
[JScript]
```
function Deserialize(
   serializationData : Object
) : ICollection;
```

Parameters

serializationData

An object consisting of serialized data.

Return Value

An **ICollection** of objects rebuilt from the specified serialization data object.

Requirements

Platforms: Windows 98, Windows NT 4.0, Windows Millennium Edition, Windows 2000, Windows XP Home Edition, Windows XP Professional, Windows Server 2003 family

IDesignerSerializationService.Serialize Method

Serializes the specified collection of objects and stores them in a serialization data object.

[Visual Basic]
```
Function Serialize( _
   ByVal objects As ICollection _
) As Object
```
[C#]
```
object Serialize(
   ICollection objects
);
```
[C++]
```
Object* Serialize(
   ICollection* objects
);
```
[JScript]
```
function Serialize(
   objects : ICollection
) : Object;
```

Parameters

objects

A collection of objects to serialize.

Return Value

An object that contains the serialized state of the specified collection of objects.

Remarks

The returned object fully supports run-time serialization.

The object returned from this method contains live references to objects in the collection. This object can then be passed to any run-time serialization mechanism. The object itself serializes components the same way designers write source for them, by storing their state, property by property.

Requirements

Platforms: Windows 98, Windows NT 4.0, Windows Millennium Edition, Windows 2000, Windows XP Home Edition, Windows XP Professional, Windows Server 2003 family

INameCreationService Interface

Provides a service that can generate unique names for objects.

For a list of all members of this type, see **INameCreationService Members**.

[Visual Basic]
```
Public Interface INameCreationService
```
[C#]
```
public interface INameCreationService
```
[C++]
```
public __gc __interface INameCreationService
```
[JScript]
```
public interface INameCreationService
```

Remarks

A **DesignerLoader** can implement this service to provide a way for a designer to create new, unique names for objects. If this service is not available, the designer uses a default implementation.

Example

[Visual Basic]
```
Imports System
Imports System.ComponentModel.Design
Imports System.ComponentModel.Design.Serialization
Imports System.Globalization
Public Class NameCreationService
    Implements
System.ComponentModel.Design.Serialization.INameCreationService
    Public Sub New()
    End Sub
    ' Creates an identifier for a particular data type that does      ↵
not conflict
    ' with the identifiers of any components in the specified      ↵
collection
    Public Function CreateName(ByVal container As      ↵
System.ComponentModel.IContainer, ByVal dataType As System.Type)      ↵
 As String Implements INameCreationService.CreateName
        ' Create a basic type name string
        Dim baseName As String = dataType.Name
        Dim uniqueID As Integer = 1
        Dim unique As Boolean = False
        ' Continue to increment uniqueID numeral until a unique      ↵
 ID is located.
        While Not unique
            unique = True
            ' Check each component in the container for a matching
            ' base type name and unique ID.
            Dim i As Integer
            For i = 0 To container.Components.Count - 1
                ' Check component name for match with unique ID string.
                If container.Components(i).Site.Name.StartsWith((baseName
+      ↵
uniqueID.ToString())) Then
                    ' If a match is encountered, set flag to recycle
                    ' collection, increment ID numeral, and restart.
                    unique = False
                    uniqueID += 1
                    Exit For
                End If
            Next i
        End While
        Return baseName + uniqueID.ToString()
    End Function
    ' Returns whether the specified name contains
    ' all valid character types.
    Public Function IsValidName(ByVal name As String) As      ↵
 Boolean Implements INameCreationService.IsValidName
        Dim i As Integer
        For i = 0 To name.Length - 1
            Dim ch As Char = name.Chars(i)
            Dim uc As UnicodeCategory = [Char].GetUnicodeCategory(ch)
            Select Case uc
                Case UnicodeCategory.UppercaseLetter,      ↵
UnicodeCategory.LowercaseLetter,      ↵
UnicodeCategory.TitlecaseLetter, UnicodeCategory.DecimalDigitNumber
                Case Else
                    Return False
            End Select
        Next i
        Return True
    End Function
    ' Throws an exception if the specified name does not contain
    ' all valid character types.
    Public Sub ValidateName(ByVal name As String) Implements      ↵
INameCreationService.ValidateName
        Dim i As Integer
        For i = 0 To name.Length - 1
            Dim ch As Char = name.Chars(i)
            Dim uc As UnicodeCategory = [Char].GetUnicodeCategory(ch)
            Select Case uc
                Case UnicodeCategory.UppercaseLetter,      ↵
UnicodeCategory.LowercaseLetter,      ↵
UnicodeCategory.TitlecaseLetter, UnicodeCategory.DecimalDigitNumber
                Case Else
                    Throw New Exception("The name '" + name +      ↵
 "' is not a valid identifier.")
            End Select
        Next i
    End Sub
End Class
```

[C#]
```
using System;
using System.ComponentModel.Design;
using System.ComponentModel.Design.Serialization;
using System.Globalization;
namespace NameCreationServiceExample
{
    public class NameCreationService :      ↵
System.ComponentModel.Design.Serialization.INameCreationService
    {
        public NameCreationService()
        {
        }
        // Creates an identifier for a particular data type      ↵
that does not conflict
        // with the identifiers of any components in the      ↵
specified collection.
        public string CreateName      ↵
 (System.ComponentModel.IContainer container, System.Type dataType)
        {
            // Create a basic type name string.
            string baseName = dataType.Name;
            int uniqueID = 1;
            bool unique = false;
            // Continue to increment uniqueID numeral until a
            // unique ID is located.
            while( !unique )
            {
                unique = true;
                // Check each component in the container for a matching
                // base type name and unique ID.
                for(int i=0; i<container.Components.Count; i++)
                {
                    // Check component name for match with      ↵
unique ID string.
                    if( container.Components[i].Site.Name.StartsWith      ↵
 (baseName+uniqueID.ToString()) )
                    {
                        // If a match is encountered, set      ↵
 flag to recycle
                        // collection, increment ID numeral,      ↵
 and restart.
                        unique = false;
                        uniqueID++;
```

```
                    break;
                }
            }
        }

        return baseName+uniqueID.ToString();
    }
    // Returns whether the specified name contains
    // all valid character types.
    public bool IsValidName(string name)
    {
        for(int i = 0; i < name.Length; i++)
        {
            char ch = name[i];
            UnicodeCategory uc = Char.GetUnicodeCategory(ch);
            switch (uc)
            {
                case UnicodeCategory.UppercaseLetter:
                case UnicodeCategory.LowercaseLetter:
                case UnicodeCategory.TitlecaseLetter:
                case UnicodeCategory.DecimalDigitNumber:
                    break;
                default:
                    return false;
            }
        }
        return true;
    }
    // Throws an exception if the specified name does not contain
    // all valid character types.
    public void ValidateName(string name)
    {
        for(int i = 0; i < name.Length; i++)
        {
            char ch = name[i];
            UnicodeCategory uc = Char.GetUnicodeCategory(ch);
            switch (uc)
            {
                case UnicodeCategory.UppercaseLetter:
                case UnicodeCategory.LowercaseLetter:
                case UnicodeCategory.TitlecaseLetter:
                case UnicodeCategory.DecimalDigitNumber:
                    break;
                default:
                    throw new Exception("The name '"+name+"'     ↵
 is not a valid identifier.");
            }
        }
    }
  }
}
```

Requirements

Namespace: System.ComponentModel.Design.Serialization

Platforms: Windows 98, Windows NT 4.0, Windows Millennium Edition, Windows 2000, Windows XP Home Edition, Windows XP Professional, Windows Server 2003 family

Assembly: System (in System.dll)

INameCreationService.CreateName Method

Creates a new name that is unique to all components in the specified container.

[Visual Basic]
```
Function CreateName( _
   ByVal container As IContainer, _
   ByVal dataType As Type _
) As String
```
[C#]
```
string CreateName(
   IContainer container,
   Type dataType
);
```
[C++]
```
String* CreateName(
   IContainer* container,
   Type* dataType
);
```
[JScript]
```
function CreateName(
   container : IContainer,
   dataType : Type
) : String;
```

Parameters

container

The container where the new object is added.

dataType

The data type of the object that receives the name.

Return Value

A unique name for the data type.

Remarks

This method returns a name for the new object that is unique within the specified container.

Notes to Implementers: This type of service is often implemented to create a unique object name from the name of the data type, often appended with a number that allows the name to be a unique identifier. For example, **ListBox1** for a **ListBox** object.

Example

Requirements

Platforms: Windows 98, Windows NT 4.0, Windows Millennium Edition, Windows 2000, Windows XP Home Edition, Windows XP Professional, Windows Server 2003 family

INameCreationService.IsValidName Method

Gets a value indicating whether the specified name is valid.

[Visual Basic]
```
Function IsValidName( _
   ByVal name As String _
) As Boolean
```
[C#]
```
bool IsValidName(
   string name
);
```
[C++]
```
bool IsValidName(
   String* name
);
```
[JScript]
```
function IsValidName(
   name : String
) : Boolean;
```

Parameters

name

The name to validate.

Return Value

true if the name is valid; otherwise, **false**.

Remarks

An implementation of the **INameCreationService** can have rules that define the parameters for valid names. This method can be implemented to validate a name and enforce those rules.

Example

Requirements

Platforms: Windows 98, Windows NT 4.0, Windows Millennium Edition, Windows 2000, Windows XP Home Edition, Windows XP Professional, Windows Server 2003 family

INameCreationService.ValidateName Method

Gets a value indicating whether the specified name is valid.

```
[Visual Basic]
Sub ValidateName( _
   ByVal name As String _
)
[C#]
void ValidateName(
   string name
);
[C++]
void ValidateName(
   String* name
);
[JScript]
function ValidateName(
   name : String
);
```

Parameters

name

The name to validate.

Remarks

An implementation of the **INameCreationService** can have rules that define the parameters for valid names. This method can be implemented to validate a name and enforce those rules.

This method is similar to **IsValidName**, except that this method throws an exception if the name is invalid. This allows implementers to provide detailed information in the exception message.

Example

Requirements

Platforms: Windows 98, Windows NT 4.0, Windows Millennium Edition, Windows 2000, Windows XP Home Edition, Windows XP Professional, Windows Server 2003 family

InstanceDescriptor Class

Provides information necessary to create an instance of an object. This class cannot be inherited.

System.Object
System.ComponentModel.Design.Serialization.Instance-Descriptor

```
[Visual Basic]
NotInheritable Public Class InstanceDescriptor
[C#]
public sealed class InstanceDescriptor
[C++]
public __gc __sealed class InstanceDescriptor
[JScript]
public class InstanceDescriptor
```

Thread Safety

Any public static (**Shared** in Visual Basic) members of this type are safe for multithreaded operations. Any instance members are not guaranteed to be thread safe.

Remarks

InstanceDescriptor can store information that describes an instance of an object. This information can be used to create an instance of the object.

Some custom serializers use **InstanceDescriptor** to represent serializable objects. Several methods of a **TypeDescriptor** use **InstanceDescriptor** to represent or instantiate objects.

An **InstanceDescriptor** provides the following members:

- A **MemberInfo** property that describes this object.
- An **Arguments** property that consists of the constructor arguments that can be used to instantiate this object.
- A Boolean **IsComplete** property that indicates whether the object is completely represented by the current information.
- An **Invoke** method that can be used to create an instance of the represented object.

Requirements

Namespace: System.ComponentModel.Design.Serialization

Platforms: Windows 98, Windows NT 4.0, Windows Millennium Edition, Windows 2000, Windows XP Home Edition, Windows XP Professional, Windows Server 2003 family

Assembly: System (in System.dll)

InstanceDescriptor Constructor

Initializes a new instance of the **InstanceDescriptor** class.

Overload List

Initializes a new instance of the **InstanceDescriptor** class using the specified member information and arguments.

[Visual Basic] **Public Sub New(MemberInfo, ICollection)**

[C#] **public InstanceDescriptor(MemberInfo, ICollection);**

[C++] **public: InstanceDescriptor(MemberInfo*, ICollection*);**

[JScript] **public function InstanceDescriptor(MemberInfo, ICollection);**

Initializes a new instance of the **InstanceDescriptor** class using the specified member information, arguments, and value indicating whether the specified information completely describes the instance.

[Visual Basic] **Public Sub New(MemberInfo, ICollection, Boolean)**

[C#] **public InstanceDescriptor(MemberInfo, ICollection, bool);**

[C++] **public: InstanceDescriptor(MemberInfo*, ICollection*, bool);**

[JScript] **public function InstanceDescriptor(MemberInfo, ICollection, Boolean);**

InstanceDescriptor Constructor (MemberInfo, ICollection)

Initializes a new instance of the **InstanceDescriptor** class using the specified member information and arguments.

```
[Visual Basic]
Public Sub New( _
   ByVal member As MemberInfo, _
   ByVal arguments As ICollection _
)
[C#]
public InstanceDescriptor(
   MemberInfo member,
   ICollection arguments
);
[C++]
public: InstanceDescriptor(
   MemberInfo* member,
   ICollection* arguments
);
[JScript]
public function InstanceDescriptor(
   member : MemberInfo,
   arguments : ICollection
);
```

Parameters

member
The member information for the descriptor. This can be a **MethodInfo**, **ConstructorInfo**, **FieldInfo**, or **PropertyInfo**. If this is a **MethodInfo**, **FieldInfo**, or **PropertyInfo**, it must represent a static (**Shared** in Visual Basic) member.

arguments
The collection of arguments to pass to the member. This parameter can be a null reference (**Nothing** in Visual Basic) or an empty collection if there are no arguments. The collection can also consist of other instances of **InstanceDescriptor**.

Requirements

Platforms: Windows 98, Windows NT 4.0, Windows Millennium Edition, Windows 2000, Windows XP Home Edition, Windows XP Professional, Windows Server 2003 family

InstanceDescriptor Constructor (MemberInfo, ICollection, Boolean)

Initializes a new instance of the **InstanceDescriptor** class using the specified member information, arguments, and value indicating whether the specified information completely describes the instance.

```
[Visual Basic]
Public Sub New( _
   ByVal member As MemberInfo, _
   ByVal arguments As ICollection, _
   ByVal isComplete As Boolean _
)
[C#]
public InstanceDescriptor(
   MemberInfo member,
   ICollection arguments,
   bool isComplete
);
[C++]
public: InstanceDescriptor(
   MemberInfo* member,
   ICollection* arguments,
   bool isComplete
);
[JScript]
public function InstanceDescriptor(
   member : MemberInfo,
   arguments : ICollection,
   isComplete : Boolean
);
```

Parameters

member

The member information for the descriptor. This can be a **MethodInfo**, **ConstructorInfo**, **FieldInfo**, or **PropertyInfo**. If this is a **MethodInfo**, **FieldInfo**, or **PropertyInfo**, it must represent a static (**Shared** in Visual Basic) member.

arguments

The collection of arguments to pass to the member. This parameter can be a null reference (**Nothing** in Visual Basic) or an empty collection if there are no arguments. The collection can also consist of other instances of **InstanceDescriptor**.

isComplete

true if the specified information completely describes the instance; otherwise, **false**.

Requirements

Platforms: Windows 98, Windows NT 4.0,
Windows Millennium Edition, Windows 2000,
Windows XP Home Edition, Windows XP Professional,
Windows Server 2003 family

InstanceDescriptor.Arguments Property

Gets the collection of arguments that can be used to reconstruct an instance of the object that this instance descriptor represents.

```
[Visual Basic]
Public ReadOnly Property Arguments As ICollection
[C#]
public ICollection Arguments {get;}
[C++]
public: __property ICollection* get_Arguments();
[JScript]
public function get Arguments() : ICollection;
```

Property Value

An **ICollection** of arguments that can be used to create the object.

Requirements

Platforms: Windows 98, Windows NT 4.0,
Windows Millennium Edition, Windows 2000,
Windows XP Home Edition, Windows XP Professional,
Windows Server 2003 family

InstanceDescriptor.IsComplete Property

Gets a value indicating whether the contents of this **InstanceDescriptor** completely identify the instance.

```
[Visual Basic]
Public ReadOnly Property IsComplete As Boolean
[C#]
public bool IsComplete {get;}
[C++]
public: __property bool get_IsComplete();
[JScript]
public function get IsComplete() : Boolean;
```

Property Value

true if the instance is completely described; otherwise, **false**.

Remarks

Typically, an **InstanceDescriptor** completely describes a particular instance. However, some objects are too complex for a single method or constructor to represent. **IsComplete** indicates whether an **InstanceDescriptor** is incomplete, so a user can identify these objects and perform additional processing, if necessary, to further describe their state.

Requirements

Platforms: Windows 98, Windows NT 4.0,
Windows Millennium Edition, Windows 2000,
Windows XP Home Edition, Windows XP Professional,
Windows Server 2003 family

InstanceDescriptor.MemberInfo Property

Gets the member information that describes the instance this descriptor is associated with.

```
[Visual Basic]
Public ReadOnly Property MemberInfo As MemberInfo
[C#]
public MemberInfo MemberInfo {get;}
[C++]
public: __property MemberInfo* get_MemberInfo();
[JScript]
public function get MemberInfo() : MemberInfo;
```

Property Value

A **MemberInfo** that describes the instance that this object is associated with.

Remarks

The value of this property can be a **MethodInfo**, **ConstructorInfo**, **FieldInfo**, or **PropertyInfo**.

Requirements

Platforms: Windows 98, Windows NT 4.0, Windows Millennium Edition, Windows 2000, Windows XP Home Edition, Windows XP Professional, Windows Server 2003 family

InstanceDescriptor.Invoke Method

Invokes this instance descriptor and returns the object the descriptor describes.

[Visual Basic]
```
Public Function Invoke() As Object
```
[C#]
```
public object Invoke();
```
[C++]
```
public: Object* Invoke();
```
[JScript]
```
public function Invoke() : Object;
```

Return Value

The object this instance descriptor describes.

Remarks

This method creates a new instance of the object indicated by the **MemberInfo** property, using the specified arguments to create that particular type of instance.

Requirements

Platforms: Windows 98, Windows NT 4.0, Windows Millennium Edition, Windows 2000, Windows XP Home Edition, Windows XP Professional, Windows Server 2003 family

ResolveNameEventArgs Class

Provides data for the **ResolveName** event.

System.Object
  System.EventArgs
    System.ComponentModel.Design.Serialization.ResolveNameEventArgs

[Visual Basic]
```
Public Class ResolveNameEventArgs
   Inherits EventArgs
```
[C#]
```
public class ResolveNameEventArgs : EventArgs
```
[C++]
```
public __gc class ResolveNameEventArgs : public EventArgs
```
[JScript]
```
public class ResolveNameEventArgs extends EventArgs
```

Thread Safety

Any public static (**Shared** in Visual Basic) members of this type are safe for multithreaded operations. Any instance members are not guaranteed to be thread safe.

Remarks

ResolveNameEventArgs is used by the serialization process to match a name to an object instance.

Example

[Visual Basic, C#, C++] The following example method returns a **ResolveNameEventArgs** that indicates the name of an object that could not be resolved by a serialization process.

[Visual Basic]
```
Public Function CreateResolveNameEventArgs(ByVal value As Object,       ↵
 ByVal name As String) As ResolveNameEventArgs
    Dim e As New ResolveNameEventArgs(name)
    ' The name to resolve                           e.Name
    ' Stores an object matching the name            e.Value
    Return e
End Function
```

[C#]
```
public ResolveNameEventArgs CreateResolveNameEventArgs(object          ↵
value, string name)
{
    ResolveNameEventArgs e = new ResolveNameEventArgs(name);
    // The name to resolve                          e.Name
    // Stores an object matching the name           e.Value
    return e;
}
```

[C++]
```
public:
   ResolveNameEventArgs* CreateResolveNameEventArgs(Object*            ↵
value, String* name) {
      ResolveNameEventArgs* e = new ResolveNameEventArgs(name);
      // The name to resolve                        e.Name
      // Stores an Object matching the name         e.Value
      return e;
   }
```

Requirements

Namespace: System.ComponentModel.Design.Serialization

Platforms: Windows 98, Windows NT 4.0, Windows Millennium Edition, Windows 2000, Windows XP Home Edition, Windows XP Professional, Windows Server 2003 family

Assembly: System (in System.dll)

ResolveNameEventArgs Constructor

Initializes a new instance of the **ResolveNameEventArgs** class.

[Visual Basic]
```
Public Sub New( _
   ByVal name As String _
)
```
[C#]
```
public ResolveNameEventArgs(
   string name
);
```
[C++]
```
public: ResolveNameEventArgs(
   String* name
);
```
[JScript]
```
public function ResolveNameEventArgs(
   name : String
);
```

Parameters

name

The name to resolve.

Requirements

Platforms: Windows 98, Windows NT 4.0, Windows Millennium Edition, Windows 2000, Windows XP Home Edition, Windows XP Professional, Windows Server 2003 family

ResolveNameEventArgs.Name Property

Gets the name of the object to resolve.

[Visual Basic]
```
Public ReadOnly Property Name As String
```
[C#]
```
public string Name {get;}
```
[C++]
```
public: __property String* get_Name();
```
[JScript]
```
public function get Name() : String;
```

Property Value

The name of the object to resolve.

Requirements

Platforms: Windows 98, Windows NT 4.0, Windows Millennium Edition, Windows 2000, Windows XP Home Edition, Windows XP Professional, Windows Server 2003 family

ResolveNameEventArgs.Value Property

Gets or sets the object that matches the name.

[Visual Basic]
```
Public Property Value As Object
```
[C#]
```
public object Value {get; set;}
```
[C++]
```
public: __property Object* get_Value();
public: __property void set_Value(Object*);
```
[JScript]
```
public function get Value() : Object;
public function set Value(Object);
```

Property Value

The object that the name is associated with.

Requirements

Platforms: Windows 98, Windows NT 4.0, Windows Millennium Edition, Windows 2000, Windows XP Home Edition, Windows XP Professional, Windows Server 2003 family

ResolveNameEventHandler Delegate

Represents the method that handles the **ResolveName** event of a serialization manager.

[Visual Basic]
```
<Serializable>
Public Delegate Sub ResolveNameEventHandler( _
   ByVal sender As Object, _
   ByVal e As ResolveNameEventArgs _
)
```
[C#]
```
[Serializable]
public delegate void ResolveNameEventHandler(
   object sender,
   ResolveNameEventArgs e
);
```
[C++]
```
[Serializable]
public __gc __delegate void ResolveNameEventHandler(
   Object* sender,
   ResolveNameEventArgs* e
);
```

[JScript] In JScript, you can use the delegates in the .NET Framework, but you cannot define your own.

Parameters [Visual Basic, C#, C++]

The declaration of your event handler must have the same parameters as the **ResolveNameEventHandler** delegate declaration.

Remarks

This delegate is used by the **IDesignerSerializationManager** to resolve object names during serialization and deserialization.

When you create a **ResolveNameEventHandler** delegate, you identify the method that will handle the event. To associate the event with your event handler, add an instance of the delegate to the event. The event handler is called whenever the event occurs, unless you remove the delegate.

Example

[Visual Basic]
```
Public Sub LinkResolveNameEvent(ByVal serializationManager ↵
 As IDesignerSerializationManager)
    ' Registers an event handler for the resolve name event.
    AddHandler serializationManager.ResolveName, AddressOf ↵
Me.OnResolveName
End Sub
Private Sub OnResolveName(ByVal sender As Object, ByVal e As ↵
ResolveNameEventArgs)
    ' Displays ResolveName event information on the Console.
    Console.WriteLine(("Name of the name to resolve: " + e.Name))
    Console.WriteLine(("ToString output of the object that no ↵
name was resolved for: " + e.Value.ToString()))
End Sub
```

[C#]
```
public void LinkResolveNameEvent(
        IDesignerSerializationManager serializationManager)
{
    // Registers an event handler for the ResolveName event.
    serializationManager.ResolveName +=
        new ResolveNameEventHandler(this.OnResolveName);
}
private void OnResolveName(object sender, ResolveNameEventArgs e)
{
    // Displays ResolveName event information on the console.
    Console.WriteLine("Name of the name to resolve: "+e.Name);
    Console.WriteLine("ToString output of the object that ↵
 no name was resolved for: "+e.Value.ToString());
}
```

[C++]
```
public:
   void LinkResolveNameEvent(IDesignerSerializationManager* ↵
serializationManager) {
      // Registers an event handler for the ResolveName event.
      serializationManager->ResolveName += new ↵
ResolveNameEventHandler(this, OnResolveName);
   }
private:
   void OnResolveName(Object* sender, ResolveNameEventArgs* e) {
      // Displays ResolveName event information on the console.
      Console::WriteLine(S"Name of the name to resolve: {0}", e->Name);
      Console::WriteLine(S"ToString output of the Object that ↵
no name was resolved for: {0}", e->Value);
   }
```

Requirements

Namespace: System.ComponentModel.Design.Serialization

Platforms: Windows 98, Windows NT 4.0, Windows Millennium Edition, Windows 2000, Windows XP Home Edition, Windows XP Professional, Windows Server 2003 family

Assembly: System (in System.dll)

RootDesignerSerializer-Attribute Class

Indicates the base serializer to use for a root designer object. This class cannot be inherited.

System.Object
System.Attribute
System.ComponentModel.Design.Serialization.Root-DesignerSerializerAttribute

[Visual Basic]
```
<AttributeUsage(AttributeTargets.Class Or _
   AttributeTargets.Interface)>
NotInheritable Public Class RootDesignerSerializerAttribute
   Inherits Attribute
```
[C#]
```
[AttributeUsage(AttributeTargets.Class |
   AttributeTargets.Interface)]
public sealed class RootDesignerSerializerAttribute : Attribute
```
[C++]
```
[AttributeUsage(AttributeTargets::Class |
   AttributeTargets::Interface)]
public __gc __sealed class RootDesignerSerializerAttribute :
   public Attribute
```
[JScript]
```
public
   AttributeUsage(AttributeTargets.Class | AttributeTargets.Interface)
class RootDesignerSerializerAttribute extends Attribute
```

Thread Safety

Any public static (**Shared** in Visual Basic) members of this type are safe for multithreaded operations. Any instance members are not guaranteed to be thread safe.

Remarks

RootDesignerSerializerAttribute indicates the serializer to use when the serialization manager serializes the design document, and whether the specified serializer supports automatic reloading of the design document without first completely disposing of the document.

This attribute contains the following significant members:

- **SerializerTypeName** indicates what serialization object to use to serialize the class at design time.
- **SerializerBaseTypeName** indicates the fully qualified name of the serialization object's base type.
- **Reloadable** indicates whether the serializer supports reloading a design document without user interaction to open a new designer view.

Requirements

Namespace: System.ComponentModel.Design.Serialization

Platforms: Windows 98, Windows NT 4.0, Windows Millennium Edition, Windows 2000, Windows XP Home Edition, Windows XP Professional, Windows Server 2003 family

Assembly: System (in System.dll)

RootDesignerSerializerAttribute Constructor

Initializes a new instance of the **RootDesignerSerializerAttribute** class using the specified attributes.

Overload List

Initializes a new instance of the **RootDesignerSerializerAttribute** class using the specified attributes.

[Visual Basic] **Public Sub New(String, String, Boolean)**

[C#] **public RootDesignerSerializerAttribute(string, string, bool);**

[C++] **public: RootDesignerSerializerAttribute(String*, String*, bool);**

[JScript] **public function RootDesignerSerializer-Attribute(String, String, Boolean);**

Initializes a new instance of the **RootDesignerSerializerAttribute** class using the specified attributes.

[Visual Basic] **Public Sub New(String, Type, Boolean)**

[C#] **public RootDesignerSerializerAttribute(string, Type, bool);**

[C++] **public: RootDesignerSerializerAttribute(String*, Type*, bool);**

[JScript] **public function RootDesignerSerializer-Attribute(String, Type, Boolean);**

Initializes a new instance of the **RootDesignerSerializerAttribute** class using the specified attributes.

[Visual Basic] **Public Sub New(Type, Type, Boolean)**

[C#] **public RootDesignerSerializerAttribute(Type, Type, bool);**

[C++] **public: RootDesignerSerializerAttribute(Type*, Type*, bool);**

[JScript] **public function RootDesignerSerializer-Attribute(Type, Type, Boolean);**

RootDesignerSerializerAttribute Constructor (String, String, Boolean)

Initializes a new instance of the **RootDesignerSerializerAttribute** class using the specified attributes.

[Visual Basic]
```
Public Sub New( _
   ByVal serializerTypeName As String, _
   ByVal baseSerializerTypeName As String, _
   ByVal reloadable As Boolean _
)
```
[C#]
```
public RootDesignerSerializerAttribute(
   string serializerTypeName,
   string baseSerializerTypeName,
   bool reloadable
);
```
[C++]
```
public: RootDesignerSerializerAttribute(
   String* serializerTypeName,
   String* baseSerializerTypeName,
   bool reloadable
);
```

```
[JScript]
public function RootDesignerSerializerAttribute(
   serializerTypeName : String,
   baseSerializerTypeName : String,
   reloadable : Boolean
);
```

Parameters

serializerTypeName
: The fully qualified name of the data type of the serializer.

baseSerializerTypeName
: The name of the base type of the serializer. A class can include multiple serializers as they all have different base types.

reloadable
: **true** if this serializer supports dynamic reloading of the document; otherwise, **false**.

Remarks

Creates a new designer serialization attribute.

Requirements

Platforms: Windows 98, Windows NT 4.0, Windows Millennium Edition, Windows 2000, Windows XP Home Edition, Windows XP Professional, Windows Server 2003 family

RootDesignerSerializerAttribute Constructor (String, Type, Boolean)

Initializes a new instance of the **RootDesignerSerializerAttribute** class using the specified attributes.

```
[Visual Basic]
Public Sub New( _
   ByVal serializerTypeName As String, _
   ByVal baseSerializerType As Type, _
   ByVal reloadable As Boolean _
)
[C#]
public RootDesignerSerializerAttribute(
   string serializerTypeName,
   Type baseSerializerType,
   bool reloadable
);
[C++]
public: RootDesignerSerializerAttribute(
   String* serializerTypeName,
   Type* baseSerializerType,
   bool reloadable
);
[JScript]
public function RootDesignerSerializerAttribute(
   serializerTypeName : String,
   baseSerializerType : Type,
   reloadable : Boolean
);
```

Parameters

serializerTypeName
: The fully qualified name of the data type of the serializer.

baseSerializerType
: The name of the base type of the serializer. A class can include multiple serializers, as they all have different base types.

reloadable
: **true** if this serializer supports dynamic reloading of the document; otherwise, **false**.

Remarks

Creates a new designer serialization attribute.

Requirements

Platforms: Windows 98, Windows NT 4.0, Windows Millennium Edition, Windows 2000, Windows XP Home Edition, Windows XP Professional, Windows Server 2003 family

RootDesignerSerializerAttribute Constructor (Type, Type, Boolean)

Initializes a new instance of the **RootDesignerSerializerAttribute** class using the specified attributes.

```
[Visual Basic]
Public Sub New( _
   ByVal serializerType As Type, _
   ByVal baseSerializerType As Type, _
   ByVal reloadable As Boolean _
)
[C#]
public RootDesignerSerializerAttribute(
   Type serializerType,
   Type baseSerializerType,
   bool reloadable
);
[C++]
public: RootDesignerSerializerAttribute(
   Type* serializerType,
   Type* baseSerializerType,
   bool reloadable
);
[JScript]
public function RootDesignerSerializerAttribute(
   serializerType : Type,
   baseSerializerType : Type,
   reloadable : Boolean
);
```

Parameters

serializerType
: The data type of the serializer.

baseSerializerType
: The base type of the serializer. A class can include multiple serializers as they all have different base types.

reloadable
: **true** if this serializer supports dynamic reloading of the document; otherwise, **false**.

Remarks

Creates a new designer serialization attribute.

Requirements

Platforms: Windows 98, Windows NT 4.0, Windows Millennium Edition, Windows 2000, Windows XP Home Edition, Windows XP Professional, Windows Server 2003 family

RootDesignerSerializerAttribute.Reloadable Property

Gets a value indicating whether the root serializer supports reloading of the design document without first disposing the designer host.

```
[Visual Basic]
Public ReadOnly Property Reloadable As Boolean
[C#]
public bool Reloadable {get;}
[C++]
public: __property bool get_Reloadable();
[JScript]
public function get Reloadable() : Boolean;
```

Property Value

true if the root serializer supports reloading; otherwise, **false**.

Remarks

If this property is set to **false**, the design document does not automatically perform a reload on behalf of the user. If this property is set to **false**, it is the user's responsibility to reopen the designer view window for the design document, if an update or reload is desired.

Some serializers require the interaction of external components in the designer loading process in order to rebuild the design document. These serializers sometimes need to create a new designer host each time the design document is loaded. If this is the situation, **Reloadable** will be set to **false**, and the designer host must be recreated by user interaction (launching the designer for the document) after the design document is disposed. The events and services that were connected to the designer host, except through deserialization, do not remain and may need to be set again. If **Reloadable** is **true**, the design document can be reloaded after changes outside the designer are made to the code, without closing the designer window and reopening it.

Requirements

Platforms: Windows 98, Windows NT 4.0, Windows Millennium Edition, Windows 2000, Windows XP Home Edition, Windows XP Professional, Windows Server 2003 family

RootDesignerSerializerAttribute.SerializerBaseTypeName Property

Gets the fully qualified type name of the base type of the serializer.

```
[Visual Basic]
Public ReadOnly Property SerializerBaseTypeName As String
[C#]
public string SerializerBaseTypeName {get;}
[C++]
public: __property String* get_SerializerBaseTypeName();
[JScript]
public function get SerializerBaseTypeName() : String;
```

Property Value

The name of the base type of the serializer.

Requirements

Platforms: Windows 98, Windows NT 4.0, Windows Millennium Edition, Windows 2000, Windows XP Home Edition, Windows XP Professional, Windows Server 2003 family

RootDesignerSerializerAttribute.SerializerTypeName Property

Gets the fully qualified type name of the serializer.

```
[Visual Basic]
Public ReadOnly Property SerializerTypeName As String
[C#]
public string SerializerTypeName {get;}
[C++]
public: __property String* get_SerializerTypeName();
[JScript]
public function get SerializerTypeName() : String;
```

Property Value

The name of the type of the serializer.

Requirements

Platforms: Windows 98, Windows NT 4.0, Windows Millennium Edition, Windows 2000, Windows XP Home Edition, Windows XP Professional, Windows Server 2003 family

RootDesignerSerializerAttribute.TypeId Property

This member overrides **Attribute.TypeId**.

```
[Visual Basic]
Overrides Public ReadOnly Property TypeId As Object
[C#]
public override object TypeId {get;}
[C++]
public: __property Object* get_TypeId();
[JScript]
public override function get TypeId() : Object;
```

Requirements

Platforms: Windows 98, Windows NT 4.0, Windows Millennium Edition, Windows 2000, Windows XP Home Edition, Windows XP Professional, Windows Server 2003 family